SCOTT®

2017
STANDARD POSTAGE STAMP CATALOGUE

ONE HUNDRED AND SEVENTY-THIRD EDITION IN SIX VOLUMES

VOLUME 2

UNITED STATES AND AFFILIATED TERRITORIES
UNITED NATIONS

COUNTRIES OF THE WORLD
C-F

EDITOR	Donna Houseman
MANAGING EDITOR	Charles Snee
EDITOR EMERITUS	James E. Kloetzel
SENIOR EDITOR /NEW ISSUES & VALUING	Martin J. Frankevicz
SENIOR VALUING ANALYST	Steven R. Myers
ADMINISTRATIVE ASSISTANT/CATALOGUE LAYOUT	Eric Wiessinger
PRINTING AND IMAGE COORDINATOR	Stacey Mahan
SENIOR GRAPHIC DESIGNER	Cinda McAlexander
ADVERTISING/SALES – EAST	Stephanie Campana
	David Pistello
ADVERTISING/SALES – MIDWEST	Mike Mandozzi
ADVERTISING/SALES – WEST & FL	Eric Roth
	Victoria Hardy
PRESIDENT	Jeff Greisch

Released May 2016
Includes New Stamp Listings through the March 2016 *Linn's Stamp News Monthly* Catalogue Update

AMOS MEDIA

911 Vandemark Road, Sidney, OH 45365-0828
A division of AMOS MEDIA CO., publishers of *Linn's Stamp News, Linn's Stamp News Monthly, Coin World* and *Coin World Monthly.*

Vol. 2 Number Additions, Deletions & Changes

Number in 2016 Catalogue	Number in 2017 Catalogue
Canadian Provinces-Prince Edward Island	
new	6g
new	6h
7b	deleted
new	9g
Canada	
575b	deleted
922a	deleted
new	926Bh
new	1194Ch
new	1349a
new	1350a
new	1351a
new	1352a
new	1353a
new	1354b
new	1355a
new	1363c
new	1371c
new	1498b
new	1630c
new	2069b
new	2069c
new	2070b
new	2071b
new	2071c
new	J31b
Cayman Islands	
new	MR1b
China, People's Republic of	
new	152a
new	C3a
Comoro Islands	
811a-811c	deleted
811d-811f	811j-811l
Costa Rica	
new	489a
new	491a
new	C924a-c
new	RA117a-c
Crete	
new	2c
new	85a
new	86a
new	88a
new	91a
Croatia	
965	deleted
966-967	969-970
new	965-968
Cuba	
new	78d
new	108c
new	116c
Danzig	
new	12c
new	13a
new	22b
new	26e
new	30h
new	45a
new	84a
new	133b
Danzig	
new	168b
new	168c
new	C3a
new	O8a
Ecuador	
new	RA39Be
Fiji	
1192B	1192Ab
new	1193Ba
new	1197Ba
new	1218b
new	1219C
1220Ba	deleted
new	1223c
new	1249c
new	1249d
new	1249e
new	1249A
new	1249Ab
new	1253a
new	1253b
new	1254f
new	1313A
new	1313Ab
new	1313Ac
new	1314b
new	1314c
new	1314d
Fiume	
103a	103d
new	103a
new	103b
new	103c
new	103e
new	103f
France	
4437b	4437

Table of Contents

See Volume 1 for United States, United Nations and Countries of the World A-B
See Volume 3 through 6 for Countries of the World, G-Z

Volume 3: G-I
Volume 4: J-M
Volume 5: N-Sam
Volume 6: San-Z

Scott Catalogue Mission Statement

The Scott Catalogue Team exists to serve the recreational, educational and commercial hobby needs of stamp collectors and dealers.

We strive to set the industry standard for philatelic information and products by developing and providing goods that help collectors identify, value, organize and present their collections.

Quality customer service is, and will continue to be, our highest priority. We aspire toward achieving total customer satisfaction.

Copyright Notice

Trademark Notice

ISBN 0-89487-508-3

Library of Congress Card No. 2-3301

Acknowledgments

Our appreciation and gratitude go to the following individuals who have assisted us in preparing information included in this year's Scott Catalogues. Some helpers prefer anonymity. These individuals have generously shared their stamp knowledge with others through the medium of the Scott Catalogue.

Those who follow provided information that is in addition to the hundreds of dealer price lists and advertisements and scores of auction catalogues and realizations that were used in producing the catalogue values. It is from those noted here that we have been able to obtain information on items not normally seen in published lists and advertisements. Support from these people goes beyond data leading to catalogue values, for they also are key to editorial changes.

A special acknowledgment to Liane and Sergio Sismondo of The Classic Collector for their assistance and knowledge sharing that have aided in the preparation of this year's Standard and Classic Specialized Catalogues.

Roland Austin
Robert Ausubel (Great Britain Collectors Club)
James K Beck (Latin American Philatelic Society)
Vladimir Berrio-Lemm
John Birkinbine II
Keith & Margie Brown
Josh Buchsbayew (Cherrystone Auctions)
Peter Bylen
Tina & John Carlson (JET Stamps)
Richard A Champagne (Richard A. Champagne, Ltd.)
Henry Chlanda
Frank D. Correl
Christopher Dahle
Charles Deaton
Ubaldo Del Toro
Bob & Rita Dumaine (Sam Houston Duck Co.)
Sister Theresa Durand
Mark Eastzer (Markest Stamp Co.)
Paul G. Eckman
Craig A. Eggleston
George Epstein (Allkor Stamp Co.)
George Eveleth (Spink USA)
Jeffrey M. Forster
Ernest E. Fricks (France & Colonies Philatelic Society)
Michael Fuchs
Frank Geiger (Worldstamps.com)
Allan Grant (Rushstamps, Ltd.)
Daniel E. Grau
Fred F. Gregory
Jan E. Gronwall
Grosvenor Auctions
Chris Harmer (Harmer-Schau Auctions)
Bruce Hecht (Bruce L. Hecht Co.)
Peter Hoffman
Armen Hovsepian (Armenstamp)
Philip J. Hughes
Doug Iams
Eric Jackson
John Jamieson (Saskatoon Stamp and Coin)
N. M. Janoowalla
Peter Jeannopoulos
Stephen Joe (International Stamp Service)
William A. Jones
Sheikh Shafiqul Islam
Allan Katz (Ventura Stamp Co.)
Stanford M. Katz
Lewis Kaufman (The Philatelic Foundation)
Patricia A. Kaufmann (Confederate Stamp Alliance)
William V. Kriebel (Brazil Philatelic Association)
George Krieger
Frederick P. Lawrence
Ken Lawrence
John R. Lewis (The William Henry Stamp Co.)
Ulf Lindahl
Ignacio Llach (Filatelia Llach S.L.)
Marilyn R. Mattke
William K. McDaniel
Gary Morris (Pacific Midwest Co.)
Peter Mosiondz, Jr.
Bruce M. Moyer (Moyer Stamps & Collectibles)
Richard H. Muller
Scott Murphy (Professional Stamp Experts)
Robert P. Odenweller
Nik & Lisa Oquist
Dr. Everett Parker
John Pearson (Pittwater Philatelic Service)
Donald J. Peterson (International Philippine Philatelic Society)
Stanley M. Piller (Stanley M. Piller & Associates)
Virgil Pirvulescu
Todor Drumev Popov
Peter W. W. Powell
Ken Pugh
Siddique Mahmudur Rahman
Ghassan D. Riachi
Mehrdad Sadri (Persiphila)
Theodosios Sampson PhD
Alexander Schauss (Schauss Philatelics)
Jacques C. Schiff, Jr. (Jacques C. Schiff, Jr., Inc.)
Chuck & Joyce Schmidt
Michael Schreiber
Guy Shaw
Jeff Siddiqui
Sergio & Liane Sismondo (The Classic Collector)
Jay Smith
Frank J. Stanley, III
James F. Taff
Peter Thy
Scott R. Trepel (Siegel Auction Galleries)
Dan Undersander (United Postal Stationery Society)
Herbert R. Volin
Philip T. Wall
Giana Wayman
William R. Weiss, Jr. (Weiss Expertizing)
Don White (Dunedin Stamp Centre)
Ralph Yorio
Val Zabijaka (Zabijaka Auctions)
Michal Zika
Steven Zirinsky (Zirinsky Stamps)

AMOS MEDIA

SCOTT 911 VANDEMARK ROAD, SIDNEY, OHIO 45365 937-498-0802

Greetings, Fellow Scott Catalog User:

A total of 5,806 value changes occurred in Canada, 44 of which were sprinkled throughout the provinces. Trends this year are similar to those of last year. The first trend is that the market for classic and high-grade Canada and Provinces stamps remains quite strong. True very fine examples of these early stamps are very elusive, and values remain steady, even though the value of the Canadian dollar has further weakened against the United States dollar.

The second continuing trend is the weak Canadian dollar, valued at only 73¢ in U.S. currency in early 2016. The result is that from Scott 900 to current issues (about 2,000 Scott numbers), almost all stamps, unused and used, have dropped in value somewhat. Last year, the Canadian dollar was valued at 80¢ U.S.

A few modern issues bucked the trend of small decreases in catalog values. One example is No. 2366c, the 2010 Olympics issue souvenir sheet with gold overprint, which jumped to $12 both mint and used, from only $4 in the 2016 Vol. 2. In the Provinces, Newfoundland Scott J3b, the rare perf 9 version of the 3¢ postage due stamp, moved sharply upward to $3,750 unused, from $2,750 last year.

A total of 2,629 value changes were made to Denmark, which received a thorough review for the 2017 Vol. 2. The market for Danish stamps remains strong for the most part. Several increases occurred from 1902 on. Some of the increases are significant. The never-hinged set value for the 1905-17 (Scott 57-64) showing three wavy lines increased from $240 to $310. The 1912 5-krone dark red General Post Office, Copenhagen, stamp (Scott 82) rose from $425 unused to $500 and from $175 used to $200. The never-hinged value went from $1,300 to $1,500.

Classic France received a thorough review this year. An overall weakening of the French market resulted in mostly decreases among the 544 value changes. France No. 1 dropped from $1,800 unused and $250 used to $1,700 unused and $240 used. The values of the 10-centime pale bister on yellow paper (Scott 10) of the President Louis Napoleon issue plummeted, from $39,000 unused to $34,500. The used value fell from $575 used to $500.

Ceylon saw 168 value changes in the classic period, from 1857 to 1941. Most of these changes were increases. The 1859 4-penny rose (Scott 5) jumped from $70,000 unused to $75,000 and from $4,500 used to $5,250.

The 89 value changes in China show substantial decreases. The 1882 1-candareen green of 1882 (Scott 4) dropped from $775 unused and $425 used to $650 unused and $375 used. The 3c brown red (5) slid from $1,350 unused and $400 used to $1,200 unused and $350 used. The 5c orange yellow (6) went from $1,750 used to $1,400. The unused value of $25,000 for No. 6 remained unchanged. Similar declines are found in Republic of China (Taiwan).

People's Republic of China received a line-by-line review up to the ever-popular 8-fen Monkey stamp (Scott 1586) issued in 1980 to celebrate Chinese New Year and the Year of the Monkey. This stamp saw a slight decline in value, going from $1,875 mint, never hinged to $1,800. The value for a used stamp remains at $550. The decline in this stamp is the tip of the iceberg for decreases in values for People's Republic of China stamps. Massive decreases are seen throughout, reflecting a weakening in the Chinese market and substantially lower realizations at auctions.

Christmas Island received a listing-by-listing review. The 757 changes reflect a mostly downward movement throughout. The 1990 World Wildlife Fund sheet of three (Scott 274) falls from $12 both mint, never hinged, and used to $8.25 both ways. The mint and used values for any 41¢ single drop from $4 each to $2.50 each. Similarly the sheet overprinted in purple drops from $20 mint and used to $13.50, and the sheet overprinted in green falls from $35 mint and used to $17.50.

Chile saw 205 changes scattered throughout. The changes are mostly increases. The 1999 170-peso booklet pane of 10, mint, never hinged (Scott 1310a), increases from $9.50 to $10, while the complete booklet jumps from $10 to $11. Scott 1310b, the booklet pane of five for this issue, increases from $5 to $5.50, and the complete booklet goes from $5.50 to $6.

The 94 value changes scattered throughout Costa Rica show mostly increases. The 1988 Summer Olympics, Seoul, stamps show an increase for the pair of the two (Scott 405a), from $50 both mint, never hinged, and used, from the 2016 Vol. 2 value of $4 both ways.

Several decreases also are found among Crete stamps. Scott 1, the 1898 40-para violet, was lowered from $450 unused to $400, and from $250 used to $225. The 2-metallik rose of 1899, issued for the Russian sphere of the administration district of Retymnon, dropped from $350 unused and $300 used to $300 unused and $225 used.

Danzig also received a full line-by-line review for a total of 337 changes. The results were more increases than decreases. The 50-pfennig Danzig Philatelic Exhibition souvenir sheet (Scott 221) rose from $3.25 unused to $4, but the used value of $21 was lowered to $20. The double surcharge variety (Scott C1a) rose from $125 unused to $160.

A thorough vetting of Ecuador resulted in 1,013 changes with few increases from 1940 to 1990.

A review of Finland and Aland resulted in 3,107 and 503 changes, respectively. These changes were less a reflection of the market and more a result of increasing values to reflect the grade of very fine on which Scott catalog values are based.

Editorial enhancements for Canada

On the editorial front for Canada, new listings for imperf and part-perf stamps have been added in Prince Edward Island as Nos. 6g and 6h (imperf. gutter pairs) and 9g (horizontal strip of three, imperf between.

In Canada, many new error listings have been added for various imperf coils, stamps printed on the gummed side (including on the extremely scarce No. J31b), stamps with all color missing (Nos. 926Bh and 1194Ch), and others.

An ongoing Scott project is to include listings for complete booklets. The 2016 Volume 2 included the booklets from 1995 to the present. In the 2017 catalog, these booklet listings have been expanded to include the 1992-1994 booklets, Nos. 1403b to 1536A. Expect further expansions in future years.

Various notes and footnotes have been clarified or expanded to further explain complicated listings, and other notes have been screened carefully to ensure accuracy.

As always, we encourage you to pay special attention to the Number Additions, Deletions & Changes found on page 2A in this volume.

While you settle in with your stamp album and Scott catalog, relax and enjoy the world's greatest hobby.

Donna Houseman

Donna Houseman/Catalogue Editor

Addresses, Telephone Numbers, Web Sites, E-Mail Addresses of General & Specialized Philatelic Societies

Collectors can contact the following groups for information about the philately of the areas within the scope of these societies, or inquire about membership in these groups. Aside from the general societies, we limit this list to groups that specialize in particular fields of philately, particular areas covered by the Scott Standard Postage Stamp Catalogue, and topical groups. Many more specialized philatelic society exist than those listed below. These addresses are updated yearly, and they are, to the best of our knowledge, correct and current. Groups should inform the editors of address changes whenever they occur. The editors also want to hear from other such specialized groups not listed. Unless otherwise noted all website addresses begin with http://

American Philatelic Society
100 Match Factory Place
Bellefonte PA 16823-1367
Ph: (814) 933-3803
www.stamps.org
E-mail: apsinfo@stamps.org

American Stamp Dealers Association, Inc.
P.O. Box 692
Leesport PA 19553
Ph: (800) 369-8207
www.americanstampdealer.com
E-mail: asda@americanstampdealer.com

National Stamp Dealers Association
Robert Klein, President
430 E. Southern Ave.
Tempe AZ 85282-5216
Ph: (800) 875-6635
www.nsdainc.org
E-mail: nsda@nsdainc.org

International Society of Worldwide Stamp Collectors
Joanne Berkowitz, MD
P.O. Box 19006
Sacramento CA 95819
www.iswsc.org
E-mail: executivedirector@iswsc.org

Royal Philatelic Society
41 Devonshire Place
London, W1G 6JY
UNITED KINGDOM
www.rpsl.org.uk
E-mail: secretary@rpsl.org.uk

Royal Philatelic Society of Canada
P.O. Box 929, Station Q
Toronto, ON, M4T 2P1
CANADA
Ph: (888) 285-4143
www.rpsc.org
E-mail: info@rpsc.org

Young Stamp Collectors of America
Janet Houser
100 Match Factory Place
Bellefonte PA 16823-1367
Ph: (814) 933-3820
www.stamps.org/ysca/intro.htm
E-mail: ysca@stamps.org

Philatelic Research Resources

(The Scott editors encourage any additional research organizations to submit data for inclusion in this listing category)

American Philatelic Research Library
Tara Murray
100 Match Factory Place
Bellefonte PA 16823
Ph: (814) 933-3803
www.stamplibrary.org
E-mail: aprl@stamps.org

Institute for Analytical Philately, Inc.
P.O. Box 8035
Holland MI 49422-8035
Ph: (616) 399-9299
www.analyticalphilately.org
E-mail: info@analyticalphilately.org

The Western Philatelic Library
P.O. Box 2219
1500 Partridge Ave.
Sunnyvale CA 94087
Ph: (408) 733-0336
www.fwpf.org

Groups focusing on fields or aspects found in worldwide philately (some might cover U.S. area only)

American Air Mail Society
Stephen Reinhard
P.O. Box 110
Mineola NY 11501
www.americanairmailsociety.org
E-mail: sreinhard1@optonline.net

American First Day Cover Society
Douglas Kelsey
P.O. Box 16277
Tucson AZ 85732-6277
Ph: (520) 321-0880
www.afdcs.org
E-mail: afdcs@afdcs.org

American Revenue Association
Eric Jackson
P.O. Box 728
Leesport PA 19533-0728
Ph: (610) 926-6200
www.revenuer.org
E-mail: eric@revenuer.com

American Topical Association
Vera Felts
P.O. Box 8
Carterville IL 62918-0008
Ph: (618) 985-5100
www.americantopicalassn.org
E-mail: americantopical@msn.com

Christmas Seal & Charity Stamp Society
John Denune
234 E. Broadway
Granville OH 43023
Ph: (740) 587-0276
www.seal-society.org
E-mail: jdenune@roadrunner.com

Errors, Freaks and Oddities Collectors Club
Scott Shaulis
P.O. Box 549
Murrysville PA 15668-0549
Ph: (724) 733-4134
www.efocc.org

First Issues Collectors Club
Kurt Streepy, Secretary
3128 E. Mattatha Drive
Bloomington IN 47401
www.firstissues.org
E-mail: secretary@firstissues.org

International Society of Reply Coupon Collectors
Peter Robin
P.O. Box 353
Bala Cynwyd PA 19004
E-mail: peterrobin@verizon.net

The Joint Stamp Issues Society
Richard Zimmermann
29A Rue Des Eviats
Lalaye F-67220
FRANCE
www.phiparz.net
E-mail: richard.zimmermann@club-internet.fr

National Duck Stamp Collectors Society
Anthony J. Monico
P.O. Box 43
Harleysville PA 19438-0043
www.ndscs.org
E-mail: ndscs@ndscs.org

No Value Identified Club
Albert Sauvanet
Le Clos Royal B, Boulevard des Pas Enchantes
St. Sebastien-sur Loire, 44230
FRANCE
E-mail: alain.vailly@irin.univ nantes.fr

The Perfins Club
Jerry Hejduk
P.O. Box 490450
Leesburg FL 34749-0450
www.perfins.org
Ph: (352) 326-2117
E-mail: flprepers@comcast.net

Postage Due Mail Study Group
John Rawlins
13, Longacre
Chelmsford, CM1 3BJ
UNITED KINGDOM
E-mail: john.rawlins2@ukonline.co.uk.

Post Mark Collectors Club
Bob Milligan
7014 Woodland Oaks
Magnolia TX 77354
Ph: (281) 359-2735
www.postmarks.org
E-mail: bob.milligan@gmail.net

Postal History Society
George McGowan
P.O. Box 482
East Schodack NY 12063-0482
www.postalhistorysociety.org
E-mail: geolotus2003@nycap.rr.com

Precancel Stamp Society
Rick Podwell
P.O. Box 85
Fawn Grove PA 17321
Ph: (717) 817-8807
www.precancels.com
E-mail: psspromosec@comcast.net

United Postal Stationery Society
Stuart Leven
P.O. Box 24764
San Jose CA 95154-4764
www.upss.org
E-mail: poststat@gmail.com

United States Possessions Philatelic Society
Daniel F. Ring
P.O. Box 113
Woodstock IL 60098
www.uspps.net
E-mail: danielfring@hotmail.com

Groups focusing on U.S. area philately as covered in the Standard Catalogue

Canal Zone Study Group
Tom Brougham
737 Neilson St.
Berkeley CA 94707
www.CanalZoneStudyGroup.com
E-mail: czsgsecretary@gmail.com

Carriers and Locals Society
Martin Richardson
P.O. Box 74
Grosse Ile MI 48138
www.pennypost.org
E-mail: martinr362@aol.com

Confederate Stamp Alliance
Patricia A. Kaufmann
10194 N. Old State Road
Lincoln DE 19960
Ph. (302) 422-2656
www.csalliance.org
E-mail: trishkauf@comcast.net

Hawaiian Philatelic Society
Kay H. Hoke
P.O. Box 10115
Honolulu HI 96816-0115
Ph: (808) 521-5721

Plate Number Coil Collectors Club
Gene Trinks
16415 W. Desert Wren Court
Surprise AZ 85374
Ph: (623) 322-4619
www.pnc3.org
E-mail: gctrinks@cox.net

Ryukyu Philatelic Specialist Society
Laura Edmonds, Secy.
P.O. Box 240177
Charlotte NC 28224-0177
Ph: (336) 509-3739
www.ryukyustamps.org
E-mail: secretary@ryukyustamps.org

United Nations Philatelists
Blanton Clement, Jr.
P.O. Box 146
Morrisville PA 19067-0146
www.unpi.com
E-mail: bclemjr@yahoo.com

United States Stamp Society
Executive Secretary
P.O. Box 6634
Katy TX 77491-6631
www.usstamps.org
E-mail: webmaster@usstamps.org

U.S. Cancellation Club
Joe Crosby
E-mail: joecrosby@cox.nat

U.S. Philatelic Classics Society
Rob Lund
2913 Fulton St.
Everett WA 98201-3733
www.uspcs.org
E-mail: membershipchairman@uspcs.org

AMOS MEDIA

SCOTT 911 VANDEMARK ROAD, SIDNEY, OHIO 45365 937-498-0802

Greetings, Fellow Scott Catalog User:

A total of 5,806 value changes occurred in Canada, 44 of which were sprinkled throughout the provinces. Trends this year are similar to those of last year. The first trend is that the market for classic and high-grade Canada and Provinces stamps remains quite strong. True very fine examples of these early stamps are very elusive, and values remain steady, even though the value of the Canadian dollar has further weakened against the United States dollar.

The second continuing trend is the weak Canadian dollar, valued at only 73¢ in U.S. currency in early 2016. The result is that from Scott 900 to current issues (about 2,000 Scott numbers), almost all stamps, unused and used, have dropped in value somewhat. Last year, the Canadian dollar was valued at 80¢ U.S.

A few modern issues bucked the trend of small decreases in catalog values. One example is No. 2366c, the 2010 Olympics issue souvenir sheet with gold overprint, which jumped to $12 both mint and used, from only $4 in the 2016 Vol. 2. In the Provinces, Newfoundland Scott J3b, the rare perf 9 version of the 3¢ postage due stamp, moved sharply upward to $3,750 unused, from $2,750 last year.

A total of 2,629 value changes were made to Denmark, which received a thorough review for the 2017 Vol. 2. The market for Danish stamps remains strong for the most part. Several increases occurred from 1902 on. Some of the increases are significant. The never-hinged set value for the 1905-17 (Scott 57-64) showing three wavy lines increased from $240 to $310. The 1912 5-krone dark red General Post Office, Copenhagen, stamp (Scott 82) rose from $425 unused to $500 and from $175 used to $200. The never-hinged value went from $1,300 to $1,500.

Classic France received a thorough review this year. An overall weakening of the French market resulted in mostly decreases among the 544 value changes. France No. 1 dropped from $1,800 unused and $250 used to $1,700 unused and $240 used. The values of the 10-centime pale bister on yellow paper (Scott 10) of the President Louis Napoleon issue plummeted, from $39,000 unused to $34,500. The used value fell from $575 used to $500.

Ceylon saw 168 value changes in the classic period, from 1857 to 1941. Most of these changes were increases. The 1859 4-penny rose (Scott 5) jumped from $70,000 unused to $75,000 and from $4,500 used to $5,250.

The 89 value changes in China show substantial decreases. The 1882 1-candareen green of 1882 (Scott 4) dropped from $775 unused and $425 used to $650 unused and $375 used. The 3c brown red (5) slid from $1,350 unused and $400 used to $1,200 unused and $350 used. The 5c orange yellow (6) went from $1,750 used to $1,400. The unused value of $25,000 for No. 6 remained unchanged. Similar declines are found in Republic of China (Taiwan).

People's Republic of China received a line-by-line review up to the ever-popular 8-fen Monkey stamp (Scott 1586) issued in 1980 to celebrate Chinese New Year and the Year of the Monkey. This stamp saw a slight decline in value, going from $1,875 mint, never hinged to $1,800. The value for a used stamp remains at $550. The decline in this stamp is the tip of the iceberg for decreases in values for People's Republic of China stamps. Massive decreases are seen throughout, reflecting a weakening in the Chinese market and substantially lower realizations at auctions.

Christmas Island received a listing-by-listing review. The 757 changes reflect a mostly downward movement throughout. The 1990 World Wildlife Fund sheet of three (Scott 274) falls from $12 both mint, never hinged, and used to $8.25 both ways. The mint and used values for any 41¢ single drop from $4 each to $2.50 each. Similarly the sheet overprinted in purple drops from $20 mint and used to $13.50, and the sheet overprinted in green falls from $35 mint and used to $17.50.

Chile saw 205 changes scattered throughout. The changes are mostly increases. The 1999 170-peso booklet pane of 10, mint, never hinged (Scott 1310a), increases from $9.50 to $10, while the complete booklet jumps from $10 to $11. Scott 1310b, the booklet pane of five for this issue, increases from $5 to $5.50, and the complete booklet goes from $5.50 to $6.

The 94 value changes scattered throughout Costa Rica show mostly increases. The 1988 Summer Olympics, Seoul, stamps show an increase for the pair of the two (Scott 405a), from $50 both mint, never hinged, and used, from the 2016 Vol. 2 value of $4 both ways.

Several decreases also are found among Crete stamps. Scott 1, the 1898 40-para violet, was lowered from $450 unused to $400, and from $250 used to $225. The 2-metallik rose of 1899, issued for the Russian sphere of the administration district of Retymnon, dropped from $350 unused and $300 used to $300 unused and $225 used.

Danzig also received a full line-by-line review for a total of 337 changes. The results were more increases than decreases. The 50-pfennig Danzig Philatelic Exhibition souvenir sheet (Scott 221) rose from $3.25 unused to $4, but the used value of $21 was lowered to $20. The double surcharge variety (Scott C1a) rose from $125 unused to $160.

A thorough vetting of Ecuador resulted in 1,013 changes with few increases from 1940 to 1990.

A review of Finland and Aland resulted in 3,107 and 503 changes, respectively. These changes were less a reflection of the market and more a result of increasing values to reflect the grade of very fine on which Scott catalog values are based.

Editorial enhancements for Canada

On the editorial front for Canada, new listings for imperf and part-perf stamps have been added in Prince Edward Island as Nos. 6g and 6h (imperf. gutter pairs) and 9g (horizontal strip of three, imperf between.

In Canada, many new error listings have been added for various imperf coils, stamps printed on the gummed side (including on the extremely scarce No. J31b), stamps with all color missing (Nos. 926Bh and 1194Ch), and others.

An ongoing Scott project is to include listings for complete booklets. The 2016 Volume 2 included the booklets from 1995 to the present. In the 2017 catalog, these booklet listings have been expanded to include the 1992-1994 booklets, Nos. 1403b to 1536A. Expect further expansions in future years.

Various notes and footnotes have been clarified or expanded to further explain complicated listings, and other notes have been screened carefully to ensure accuracy.

As always, we encourage you to pay special attention to the Number Additions, Deletions & Changes found on page 2A in this volume.

While you settle in with your stamp album and Scott catalog, relax and enjoy the world's greatest hobby.

Donna Houseman

Donna Houseman/Catalogue Editor

Addresses, Telephone Numbers, Web Sites, E-Mail Addresses of General & Specialized Philatelic Societies

Collectors can contact the following groups for information about the philately of the areas within the scope of these societies, or inquire about membership in these groups. Aside from the general societies, we limit this list to groups that specialize in particular fields of philately, particular areas covered by the Scott Standard Postage Stamp Catalogue, and topical groups. Many more specialized philatelic society exist than those listed below. These addresses are updated yearly, and they are, to the best of our knowledge, correct and current. Groups should inform the editors of address changes whenever they occur. The editors also want to hear from other such specialized groups not listed. Unless otherwise noted all website addresses begin with http://

American Philatelic Society
100 Match Factory Place
Bellefonte PA 16823-1367
Ph: (814) 933-3803
www.stamps.org
E-mail: apsinfo@stamps.org

American Stamp Dealers Association, Inc.
P.O. Box 692
Leesport PA 19553
Ph: (800) 369-8207
www.americanstampdealer.com
E-mail: asda@americanstampdealer.com

National Stamp Dealers Association
Robert Klein, President
430 E. Southern Ave.
Tempe AZ 85282-5216
Ph: (800) 875-6635
www.nsdainc.org
E-mail: nsda@nsdainc.org

International Society of Worldwide Stamp Collectors
Joanne Berkowitz, MD
P.O. Box 19006
Sacramento CA 95819
www.iswsc.org
E-mail: executivedirector@iswsc.org

Royal Philatelic Society
41 Devonshire Place
London, W1G 6JY
UNITED KINGDOM
www.rpsl.org.uk
E-mail: secretary@rpsl.org.uk

Royal Philatelic Society of Canada
P.O. Box 929, Station Q
Toronto, ON, M4T 2P1
CANADA
Ph: (888) 285-4143
www.rpsc.org
E-mail: info@rpsc.org

Young Stamp Collectors of America
Janet Houser
100 Match Factory Place
Bellefonte PA 16823-1367
Ph: (814) 933-3820
www.stamps.org/ysca/intro.htm
E-mail: ysca@stamps.org

Philatelic Research Resources

(The Scott editors encourage any additional research organizations to submit data for inclusion in this listing category)

American Philatelic Research Library
Tara Murray
100 Match Factory Place
Bellefonte PA 16823
Ph: (814) 933-3803
www.stamplibrary.org
E-mail: aprl@stamps.org

Institute for Analytical Philately, Inc.
P.O. Box 8035
Holland MI 49422-8035
Ph: (616) 399-9299
www.analyticalphilately.org
E-mail: info@analyticalphilately.org

The Western Philatelic Library
P.O. Box 2219
1500 Partridge Ave.
Sunnyvale CA 94087
Ph: (408) 733-0336
www.fwpf.org

Groups focusing on fields or aspects found in worldwide philately (some might cover U.S. area only)

American Air Mail Society
Stephen Reinhard
P.O. Box 110
Mineola NY 11501
www.americanairmailsociety.org
E-mail: sreinhard1@optonline.net

American First Day Cover Society
Douglas Kelsey
P.O. Box 16277
Tucson AZ 85732-6277
Ph: (520) 321-0880
www.afdcs.org
E-mail: afdcs@afdcs.org

American Revenue Association
Eric Jackson
P.O. Box 728
Leesport PA 19533-0728
Ph: (610) 926-6200
www.revenuer.org
E-mail: eric@revenuer.com

American Topical Association
Vera Felts
P.O. Box 8
Carterville IL 62918-0008
Ph: (618) 985-5100
www.americantopicalassn.org
E-mail: americantopical@msn.com

Christmas Seal & Charity Stamp Society
John Denune
234 E. Broadway
Granville OH 43023
Ph: (740) 587-0276
www.seal-society.org
E-mail: jdenune@roadrunner.com

Errors, Freaks and Oddities Collectors Club
Scott Shaulis
P.O. Box 549
Murrysville PA 15668-0549
Ph: (724) 733-4134
www.efocc.org

First Issues Collectors Club
Kurt Streepy, Secretary
3128 E. Mattatha Drive
Bloomington IN 47401
www.firstissues.org
E-mail: secretary@firstissues.org

International Society of Reply Coupon Collectors
Peter Robin
P.O. Box 353
Bala Cynwyd PA 19004
E-mail: peterrobin@verizon.net

The Joint Stamp Issues Society
Richard Zimmermann
29A Rue Des Eviats
Lalaye F-67220
FRANCE
www.phiparz.net
E-mail: richard.zimmermann@club-internet.fr

National Duck Stamp Collectors Society
Anthony J. Monico
P.O. Box 43
Harleysville PA 19438-0043
www.ndscs.org
E-mail: ndscs@ndscs.org

No Value Identified Club
Albert Sauvanet
Le Clos Royal B, Boulevard des Pas Enchantes
St. Sebastien-sur Loire, 44230
FRANCE
E-mail: alain.vailly@irin.univ nantes.fr

The Perfins Club
Jerry Hejduk
P.O. Box 490450
Leesburg FL 34749-0450
www.perfins.org
Ph: (352) 326-2117
E-mail: flprepers@comcast.net

Postage Due Mail Study Group
John Rawlins
13, Longacre
Chelmsford, CM1 3BJ
UNITED KINGDOM
E-mail: john.rawlins2@ukonline.co.uk.

Post Mark Collectors Club
Bob Milligan
7014 Woodland Oaks
Magnolia TX 77354
Ph: (281) 359-2735
www.postmarks.org
E-mail: bob.milligan@gmail.net

Postal History Society
George McGowan
P.O. Box 482
East Schodack NY 12063-0482
www.postalhistorysociety.org
E-mail: geolotus2003@nycap.rr.com

Precancel Stamp Society
Rick Podwell
P.O. Box 85
Fawn Grove PA 17321
Ph: (717) 817-8807
www.precancels.com
E-mail: psspromosec@comcast.net

United Postal Stationery Society
Stuart Leven
P.O. Box 24764
San Jose CA 95154-4764
www.upss.org
E-mail: poststat@gmail.com

United States Possessions Philatelic Society
Daniel F. Ring
P.O. Box 113
Woodstock IL 60098
www.uspps.net
E-mail: danielfring@hotmail.com

Groups focusing on U.S. area philately as covered in the Standard Catalogue

Canal Zone Study Group
Tom Brougham
737 Neilson St.
Berkeley CA 94707
www.CanalZoneStudyGroup.com
E-mail: czsgsecretary@gmail.com

Carriers and Locals Society
Martin Richardson
P.O. Box 74
Grosse Ile MI 48138
www.pennypost.org
E-mail: martinr362@aol.com

Confederate Stamp Alliance
Patricia A. Kaufmann
10194 N. Old State Road
Lincoln DE 19960
Ph. (302) 422-2656
www.csalliance.org
E-mail: trishkauf@comcast.net

Hawaiian Philatelic Society
Kay H. Hoke
P.O. Box 10115
Honolulu HI 96816-0115
Ph: (808) 521-5721

Plate Number Coil Collectors Club
Gene Trinks
16415 W. Desert Wren Court
Surprise AZ 85374
Ph: (623) 322-4619
www.pnc3.org
E-mail: gctrinks@cox.net

Ryukyu Philatelic Specialist Society
Laura Edmonds, Secy.
P.O. Box 240177
Charlotte NC 28224-0177
Ph: (336) 509-3739
www.ryukyustamps.org
E-mail: secretary@ryukyustamps.org

United Nations Philatelists
Blanton Clement, Jr.
P.O. Box 146
Morrisville PA 19067-0146
www.unpi.com
E-mail: bclemjr@yahoo.com

United States Stamp Society
Executive Secretary
P.O. Box 6634
Katy TX 77491-6631
www.usstamps.org
E-mail: webmaster@usstamps.org

U.S. Cancellation Club
Joe Crosby
E-mail: joecrosby@cox.nat

U.S. Philatelic Classics Society
Rob Lund
2913 Fulton St.
Everett WA 98201-3733
www.uspcs.org
E-mail: membershipchairman@uspcs.org

Groups focusing on philately of foreign countries or regions

Aden & Somaliland Study Group
Gary Brown
P.O. Box 106
Briar Hill, Victoria, 3088
AUSTRALIA
E-mail: garyjohn951@optushome.com.au

American Society of Polar Philatelists (Antarctic areas)
Alan Warren
P.O. Box 39
Exton PA 19341-0039
www.polarphilatelists.org

Andorran Philatelic Study Circle
D. Hope
17 Hawthorn Drive
Stalybridge, Cheshire, SK15 1UE
UNITED KINGDOM
apsc.free.fr
E-mail: apsc@free.fr

Australian States Study Circle of The Royal Sydney Philatelic Club
Ben Palmer
GPO 1751
Sydney, N.S.W., 2001
AUSTRALIA
www.philas.org.au/states

Austria Philatelic Society
Ralph Schneider
P.O. Box 23049
Belleville IL 62223
Ph: (618) 277-6152
www.austriaphilatelicsociety.com
E-mail: rschneiderstamps@att.net

American Belgian Philatelic Society
Edward de Bary
11 Wakefield Drive Apt. 2105
Asheville NC 28803

Bechuanalands and Botswana Society
Neville Midwood
69 Porlock Lane
Furzton, Milton Keynes, MK4 1JY
UNITED KINGDOM
www.nevsoft.com
E-mail: bbsoc@nevsoft.com

Bermuda Collectors Society
John Pare
405 Perimeter Road
Mount Horeb WI 53572
www.bermudacollectorssociety.org
E-mail: pare16@mhtc.net

Brazil Philatelic Association
William V. Kriebel
1923 Manning St.
Philadelphia PA 19103-5728
www.brazilphilatelic.org
E-mail: info@brazilphilatelic.org

British Caribbean Philatelic Study Group
Duane Larson
2 Forest Blvd.
Park Forest IL 60466
www.bcpsg.com
E-mail: dlarson283@aol.com

The King George VI Collectors Society (British Commonwealth)
Brian Livingstone
21 York Mansions, Prince of Wales Drive
London, SW11 4DL
UNITED KINGDOM
www.kg6.info
E-mail: livingstone484@btinternet.com

British North America Philatelic Society (Canada & Provinces)
David G. Jones
184 Larkin Drive
Nepean, ON, K2J 1H9
CANADA
www.bnaps.org
E-mail: shibumi.management@gmail.com

British West Indies Study Circle
John Seidl
4324 Granby Way
Marietta GA 30062
Ph: (770) 642-6424
www.bwisc.org
E-mail: john.seidl@gmail.com

Burma Philatelic Study Circle
Michael Whittaker
1, Ecton Leys, Hillside
Rugby, Warwickshire, CV22 5SL
UNITED KINGDOM
www.burmastamps.homecall.co.uk
E-mail: manningham8@mypostoffice.co.uk

Cape and Natal Study Circle
Dr. Guy Dillaway
P.O. Box 181
Weston MA 02493
www.nzsc.demon.co.uk

Ceylon Study Circle
R. W. P. Frost
42 Lonsdale Road, Cannington
Bridgewater, Somerset, TA5 2JS
UNITED KINGDOM
www.ceylonsc.org
E-mail: rodney.frost@tiscali.co.uk

Channel Islands Specialists Society
Moira Edwards
86, Hall Lane, Sandon
Chelmsford, Essex, CM2 7RQ
UNITED KINGDOM
www.ciss1950.org.uk
E-mail: membership@ciss1950.org.uk

China Stamp Society
Paul H. Gault
P.O. Box 20711
Columbus OH 43220
www.chinastampsociety.org
E-mail: secretary@chinastampsociety.org

Colombia/Panama Philatelic Study Group (COPAPHIL)
Thomas P. Myers
P.O. Box 522
Gordonsville VA 22942
www.copaphil.org
E-mail: tpmphil@hotmail.com

Association Filatelic de Costa Rica
Giana Wayman
c/o Interlink 102, P.O. Box 52-6770
Miami FL 33152
E-mail: scotland@racsa.co.cr

Society for Costa Rica Collectors
Dr. Hector R. Mena
P.O. Box 14831
Baton Rouge LA 70808
www.socorico.org
E-mail: hrmena@aol.com

International Cuban Philatelic Society
Ernesto Cuesta
P.O. Box 34434
Bethesda MD 20827
www.cubafil.org
E-mail: ecuesta@philat.com

Cuban Philatelic Society of America ®
P.O. Box 141656
Coral Gables FL 33114-1656
www.cubapsa.com
E-mail: cpsa.usa@gmail.com

Cyprus Study Circle
Colin Dear
10 Marne Close, Wem
Shropshire, SY4 5YE
UNITED KINGDOM
www.cyprusstudycircle.org/index.htm
E-mail: colindear@talktalk.net

Society for Czechoslovak Philately
Tom Cassaboom
P.O. Box 4124
Prescott AZ 86302
www.csphilately.org
E-mail: klfckl@aol.com

Danish West Indies Study Unit of the Scandinavian Collectors Club
Arnold Sorensen
7666 Edgedale Drive
Newburgh IN 47630
Ph: (812) 480-6532
www.scc-online.org
E-mail: valbydwi@hotmail.com

East Africa Study Circle
Michael Vesey-Fitzgerald
Gambles Cottage, 18 Clarence Road
Lyndhurst, SO43 7AL
UNITED KINGDOM
www.easc.org.uk
E-mail: secretary@easc.org.uk

Egypt Study Circle
Mike Murphy
109 Chadwick Road
London, SE15 4PY
UNITED KINGDOM
Trent Ruebush: North American Agent
E-mail: truebrush@usaid.gov
egyptstudycircle.org.uk
E-mail: egyptstudycircle@hotmail.com

Estonian Philatelic Society
Juri Kirsimagi
29 Clifford Ave.
Pelham NY 10803
Ph: (914) 738-3713

Ethiopian Philatelic Society
Ulf Lindahl
21 Westview Place
Riverside CT 06878
Ph: (203) 722-0769
home.comcast.net/~fbheiser/ethiopia5.htm
E-mail: ulindahl@optonline.net

Falkland Islands Philatelic Study Group
Carl J. Faulkner
615 Taconic Trail
Williamstown MA 01267-2745
Ph: (413) 458-4421
www.fipsg.org.uk
E-mail: cfaulkner@taconicwilliamstown.com

Faroe Islands Study Circle
Norman Hudson
40 Queen's Road, Vicar's Cross
Chester, CH3 5HB
UNITED KINGDOM
www.faroeislandssc.org
E-mail: jntropics@hotmail.com

Former French Colonies Specialist Society
COLFRA
BP 628
75367 Paris, Cedex 08
FRANCE
www.colfra.org
E-mail: secretaire@colfra.org

France & Colonies Philatelic Society
Edward Grabowski
111 Prospect St., 4C
Westfield NJ 07090
www.franceandcolps.org
E-mail: edjjg@alum.mit.edu

Germany Philatelic Society
P.O. Box 6547
Chesterfield MO 63006
www.germanyphilatelicusa.org

Plebiscite-Memel-Saar Study Group of the German Philatelic Society
Clayton Wallace
100 Lark Court
Alamo CA 94507
E-mail: claytonwallace@comcast.net

Gibraltar Study Circle
David R. Stirrups
152 The Rowans, Milton
Cambridge, CB24 6YX
UNITED KINGDOM
www.gibraltarstudycircle.wordpress.com
E-mail: beggloops@gmail.com

Great Britain Collectors Club
Steve McGill
10309 Brookhollow Circle
Highlands Ranch CO 80129
www.gbstamps.com/gbcc
E-mail: steve.mcgill@comcast.net

International Society of Guatemala Collectors
Jaime Marckwordt
449 St. Francis Blvd.
Daly City CA 94015-2136
www.guatemalastamps.com
E-mail: membership@guatamalastamps.com

Haiti Philatelic Society
Ubaldo Del Toro
5709 Marble Archway
Alexandria VA 22315
www.haitiphilately.org
E-mail: u007ubi@aol.com

Hong Kong Stamp Society
Ming W. Tsang
P.O. Box 206
Glenside PA 19038
www.hkss.org
E-mail: hkstamps@yahoo.com

Society for Hungarian Philately
Robert Morgan
2201 Roscomare Road
Los Angeles CA 90077-2222
Ph: (617) 645-4045
www.hungarianphilately.org
E-mail: alan@hungarianstamps.com

India Study Circle
John Warren
P.O. Box 7326
Washington DC 20044
Ph: (202) 564-6876
www.indiastudycircle.org
E-mail: warren.john@epa.gov

Indian Ocean Study Circle
E. S. Hutton
29 Patermoster Close
Waltham Abby, Essex, EN9 3JU
UNITED KINGDOM
www.indianoceanstudycircle.com
E-mail:
secretary@indianoceanstudycircle.com

Society of Indo-China Philatelists
Ron Bentley
2600 N. 24th St.
Arlington VA 22207
www.sicp-online.org
E-mail: ron.bentley@verizon.net

Iran Philatelic Study Circle
Mehdi Esmaili
P.O. Box 750096
Forest Hills NY 11375
www.iranphilatelic.org
E-mail: m.esmaili@earthlink.net

Eire Philatelic Association (Ireland)
David J. Brennan
P.O. Box 704
Bernardsville NJ 07924
www.eirephilatelicassoc.org
E-mail: brennan704@aol.com

Society of Israel Philatelists
Edwin Kroft
P.O. Box 507
Northfield OH 44067
www.israelstamps.com
E-mail: israelstamps@gmail.com

Italy and Colonies Study Circle
Richard Harlow
7 Duncombe House, 8 Manor Road
Teddington, TW11 8BE
UNITED KINGDOM
www.icsc.pwp.blueyonder.co.uk
E-mail: harlowr@gmail.com

International Society for Japanese Philately
William Eisenhauer
P.O. Box 230462
Tigard OR 97281
www.isjp.org
E-mail: secretary@isjp.org

Korea Stamp Society
John E. Talmage
P.O. Box 6889
Oak Ridge TN 37831
www.pennfamily.org/KSS-USA
E-mail: jtalmage@usit.net

Latin American Philatelic Society
Jules K. Beck
30½ St. #209
St. Louis Park MN 55426-3551

Liberian Philatelic Society
William Thomas Lockard
P.O. Box 106
Wellston OH 45692
Ph: (740) 384-2020
E-mail: tlockard@zoomnet.net

Liechtenstudy USA (Liechtenstein)
Paul Tremaine
410 SW Ninth St.
Dundee OR 97115
Ph: (503) 538-4500
www.liechtenstudy.org
E-mail: editor@liechtenstudy.org

Lithuania Philatelic Society
John Variakojis
8472 Carlisle Court.
Burr Ridge IL 60527
Ph: (630) 974-6525
www.lithuanianphilately.com/lps
E-mail: variakojis@sbcglobal.net

Luxembourg Collectors Club
Gary B. Little
7319 Beau Road
Sechelt, BC, VON 3A8
CANADA
lcc.luxcentral.com
E-mail: gary@luxcentral.com

Malaya Study Group
David Tett
P.O. Box 34
Wheathampstead, Herts, AL4 8JY
UNITED KINGDOM
www.m-s-g.org.uk
E-mail: davidtett@aol.com

Malta Study Circle
Alec Webster
50 Worcester Road
Sutton, Surrey, SM2 6QB
UNITED KINGDOM
www.maltastudycircle.org.uk
E-mail: alecwebster50@hotmail.com

Mexico-Elmhurst Philatelic Society International
Thurston Bland
50 Regato
Rancho Santa Margarita CA 92688-3003
www.mepsi.org

Asociacion Mexicana de Filatelia
AMEXFIL
Jose Maria Rico, 129, Col. Del Valle
Mexico City DF, 03100
MEXICO
www.amexfil.mx
E-mail: amexfil@gmail.com

Society for Moroccan and Tunisian Philately S.P.L.M.
206, bld. Pereire
75017 Paris
FRANCE
splm-philatelie.org
E-mail: splm206@aol.com

Nepal & Tibet Philatelic Study Group
Roger D. Skinner
1020 Covington Road
Los Altos CA 94024-5003
Ph: (650) 968-4163
www.fuchs-online.com/ntpsc/
E-mail: colinhepper@hotmail.co.uk

American Society for Netherlands Philately
Hans Kremer
50 Rockport Court
Danville CA 94526
Ph: (925) 820-5841
www.asnp1975.com
E-mail: hkremer@usa.net

New Zealand Society of Great Britain
Michael Wilkinson
121 London Road
Sevenoaks, Kent, TN13 1BH
UNITED KINGDOM
www.nzsgb.org.uk
E-mail: mwilkin799@aol.com

Nicaragua Study Group
Erick Rodriguez
11817 SW 11th St.
Miami FL 33184-2501
clubs.yahoo.com/clubs/
nicaraguastudygroup
E-mail: nsgsec@yahoo.com

Society of Australasian Specialists/Oceania
David McNamee
P.O. Box 37
Alamo CA 94507
www.sasoceania.org
E-mail: dmcnamee@aol.com

Orange Free State Study Circle
J. R. Stroud
24 Hooper Close
Burnham-on-sea, Somerset, TA8 1JQ
UNITED KINGDOM
orangefreestatephilately.org.uk
E-mail: richardstroudph@gofast.co.uk

Pacific Islands Study Circle
John Ray
24 Woodvale Ave.
London, SE25 4AE
UNITED KINGDOM
www.pisc.org.uk
E-mail: info@pisc.org.uk

Pakistan Philatelic Study Circle
Jeff Siddiqui
P.O. Box 7002
Lynnwood WA 98046
E-mail: jeffsiddiqui@msn.com

Centro de Filatelistas Independientes de Panama
Vladimir Berrio-Lemm
Apartado 0823-02748
Plaza Concordia Panama
PANAMA
E-mail: panahistoria@gmail.com

Papuan Philatelic Society
Steven Zirinsky
P.O. Box 49, Ansonia Station
New York NY 10023
Ph: (718) 706-0616
www.communigate.co.uk/york/pps
E-mail: szirinsky@cs.com

International Philippine Philatelic Society
Donald J. Peterson
P.O. Box 122
Brunswick MD 21716
Ph: (301) 834-6419
www.theipps.info
E-mail: dpeterson4526@gmail.com

Pitcairn Islands Study Group
Dr. Everett L. Parker
117 Cedar Breeze South
Glenburn ME 04401-1734
Ph: (386) 688-1358
www.pisg.net
E-mail: eparker@hughes.net

Polonus Philatelic Society (Poland)
Daniel Lubelski
P.O. Box 60438
Rossford OH 43460-
Ph: (419) 410-9115
www.polonus.org
E-mail: rvo1937@gmail.com

International Society for Portuguese Philately
Clyde Homen
1491 Bonnie View Road
Hollister CA 95023-5117
www.portugalstamps.com
E-mail: ispp1962@sbcglobal.net

Rhodesian Study Circle
William R. Wallace
P.O. Box 16381
San Francisco CA 94116
www.rhodesianstudycircle.org.uk
E-mail: bwall8rscr@earthlink.net

Rossica Society of Russian Philately
Alexander Kolchinsky
1506 Country Lake Drive
Champaign IL 6821-6428
www.rossica.org
E-mail: alexander.kolchinsky@rossica.org

St. Helena, Ascension & Tristan Da Cunha Philatelic Society
Dr. Everett L. Parker
117 Cedar Breeze South
Glenburn ME 04401-1734
Ph: (386) 754-8524
www.atlanticislands.org
E-mail: eparker@hughes.net

St. Pierre & Miquelon Philatelic Society
James R. (Jim) Taylor
2335 Paliswood Road SW
Calgary, AB, T2V 3P6
CANADA
www.stamps.org/spm

Associated Collectors of El Salvador
Joseph D. Hahn
1015 Old Boalsburg Road Apt G-5
State College PA 16801-6149
www.elsalvadorphilately.org
E-mail: jdhahn2@gmail.com

Fellowship of Samoa Specialists
Donald Mee
23 Leo St.
Christchurch, 8051
NEW ZEALAND
www.samoaexpress.org
E-mail: donanm@xtra.co.nz

Sarawak Specialists' Society
Stephen Schumann
2417 Cabrillo Drive-
Hayward CA 94545
Ph: (510) 785-4794
www.britborneostamps.org.uk
E-mail: sdsch@earthlink.net

Scandinavian Collectors Club
Steve Lund
P.O. Box 16213
St. Paul MN 55116
www.scc-online.org
E-mail: steve88h@aol.com

Slovakia Stamp Society
Jack Benchik
P.O. Box 555
Notre Dame IN 46556

Philatelic Society for Greater Southern Africa
Alan Hanks
34 Seaton Drive
Aurora, ON, L4G 2KI
CANADA
Ph: (905) 727-6993
www.psgsa.thestampweb.com
Email: alan.hanks@sympatico.ca

South Sudan Philatelic Society
William Barclay
134A Spring Hill Road
South Londonerry VT 05155
E-mail: bill.barclay@wfp.org

Spanish Philatelic Society
Robert H. Penn
1108 Walnut Drive
Danielsville PA 18038
Ph: (610) 844-8963
E-mail: roberthpenn43@gmail.com

Sudan Study Group
David Sher
5 Ellis Park Road
Toronto, ON, M6S 2V2
CANADA
www.sudanstamps.org
E-mail: sh3603@hotmail.com

American Helvetia Philatelic Society (Switzerland, Liechtenstein)
Richard T. Hall
P.O. Box 15053
Asheville NC 28813-0053
www.swiss-stamps.org
E-mail: secretary2@swiss-stamps.org

Tannu Tuva Collectors Society
Ken R. Simon
P.O. Box 385
Lake Worth FL 33460-0385
Ph: (561) 588-5954
www.tuva.tk
E-mail: yurttuva@yahoo.com

Society for Thai Philately
H. R. Blakeney
P.O. Box 25644
Oklahoma City OK 73125
E-mail: HRBlakeney@aol.com

Transvaal Study Circle
Chris Board
36 Wakefield Gardens
London, SE19 2NR
UNITED KINGDOM
www.transvaalstamps.org.uk
E-mail: c.board@macace.net

Ottoman and Near East Philatelic Society (Turkey and related areas)
Bob Stuchell
193 Valley Stream Lane
Wayne PA 19087
www.oneps.org
E-mail: rstuchell@msn.com

Ukrainian Philatelic & Numismatic Society
Martin B. Tatuch
5117 8th Road N.
Arlington VA 22205-1201
www.upns.org
E-mail: treasurer@upns.org

Vatican Philatelic Society
Sal Quinonez
1 Aldersgate, Apt. 1002
Riverhead NY 11901-1830
Ph: (516) 727-6426
www.vaticanphilately.org

British Virgin Islands Philatelic Society
Giorgio Migliavacca
P.O. Box 7007
St. Thomas VI 00801-0007
www.islandsun.com/category/collectables/
E-mail: issun@candwbvi.net

West Africa Study Circle
Martin Bratzel
1233 Virginia Ave.
Windsor, ON, N8S 2Z1
CANADA
www.wasc.org.uk/
E-mail: marty_bratzel@yahoo.ca

Western Australia Study Group
Brian Pope
P.O. Box 423
Claremont, Western Australia, 6910
AUSTRALIA
www.wastudygroup.com
E-mail: black5swan@yahoo.com.au

Yugoslavia Study Group of the Croatian Philatelic Society
Michael Lenard
1514 N. Third Ave.
Wausau WI 54401
Ph: (715) 675-2833
E-mail: mjlenard@aol.com

Topical Groups

Americana Unit
Dennis Dengel
17 Peckham Road
Poughkeepsie NY 12603-2018
www.americanaunit.org
E-mail: ddengel@americanaunit.org

Astronomy Study Unit
John W. G. Budd
728 Sugar Camp Way
Brooksville FL 34604
Ph: (352) 345-4799
E-mail: jwgbudd@gmail.com

Bicycle Stamp Club
Steve Andreasen
2000 Alaskan Way, Unit 157
Seattle WA 98121
members.tripod.com/~bicyclestamps
E-mail: steven.w.andreasen@gmail.com

Biology Unit
Alan Hanks
34 Seaton Drive
Aurora, ON, L4G 2K1
CANADA
Ph: (905) 727-6993

Bird Stamp Society
S. A. H. (Tony) Statham
Ashlyns Lodge, Chesham Road,
Berkhamsted, Hertfordshire HP4 2ST
UNITED KINGDOM
www.bird-stamps.org/bss
E-mail: tony.statham@sky.com

Captain Cook Society
Jerry Yucht
8427 Leale Ave.
Stockton CA 95212
www.captaincooksociety.com
E-mail: US@captaincooksociety.com

The CartoPhilatelic Society
Marybeth Sulkowski
2885 Sanford Ave, SW, #32361
Grandville MI 49418-1342
www.mapsonstamps.org
E-mail: secretary@mapsonstamps.org

Casey Jones Railroad Unit
Roy W. Menninger MD
P.O. Box 5511
Topeka KS 66605
Ph: (785) 231-8366
www.uqp.de/cjr/index.htm
E-mail: roymenn85@gmail.com

Cats on Stamps Study Unit
Robert D. Jarvis
2731 Teton Lane
Fairfield CA 94533
www.catsonstamps.org
E-mail: bobmarci@aol.com

Chemistry & Physics on Stamps Study Unit
Dr. Roland Hirsch
20458 Water Point Lane
Germantown MD 20874
www.cpossu.org
E-mail: rfhirsch@cpossu.org

Chess on Stamps Study Unit
Ray C. Alexis
608 Emery St.
Longmont CO 80501
E-mail: chessstuff911459@aol.com

Christmas Philatelic Club
Jim Balog
P.O. Box 774
Geneva OH 44041
www.christmasphilatelicclub.org
E-mail: jpbstamps@windstream.net

Christopher Columbus Philatelic Society
Donald R. Ager
P.O. Box 71
Hillsboro NH 03244-0071
Ph: (603) 464-5379
ccps.maphist.nl/
E-mail: meganddon@tds.net

Collectors of Religion on Stamps
James Bailey
P.O. Box 937
Brownwood TX 76804
www.coros-society.org
E-mail: corosec@directtv.net

Cricket Philatelic Society
A.Melville-Brown, President
11 Weppons, Ravens Road
Shoreham-by-Sea
West Sussex, BN43 5AW
UNITED KINGDOM
www.cricketstamp.net
E-mail: mel.cricket.100@googlemail.com

Dogs on Stamps Study Unit
Morris Raskin
202A Newport Road
Monroe Township NJ 08831
Ph: (609) 655-7411
www.dossu.org
E-mail: mraskin@cellurian.com

Earth's Physical Features Study Group
Fred Klein
515 Magdalena Ave.
Los Altos CA 94024
epfsu.jeffhayward.com

Ebony Society of Philatelic Events and Reflections, Inc. (African-American topicals)
Manuel Gilyard
800 Riverside Drive, Suite 4H
New York NY 10032-7412
www.esperstamps.org
E-mail: gilyardmani@aol.com

Europa Study Unit
Tonny E. Van Loij
3002 S. Xanthia St.
Denver CO 80231-4237
www.europastudyunit.org/
E-mail: tvanloij@gmail.com

Fine & Performing Arts
Deborah L. Washington
6922 S. Jeffery Blvd., #7 - North
Chicago IL 60649
E-mail: brasslady@comcast.net

Fire Service in Philately
John Zaranek
81 Hillpine Road
Cheektowaga NY 14227-2259
Ph: (716) 668-3352
E-mail: jczaranek@roadrunner.com

Gay & Lesbian History on Stamps Club
Joe Petronie
P.O. Box 190842
Dallas TX 75219-0842
www.facebook.com/glhsc
E-mail: glhsc@aol.com

Gems, Minerals & Jewelry Study Unit
Mrs. Gilberte Proteau
138 Lafontaine
Beloeil QC J3G 2G7
CANADA
Ph: (978) 851-8283
E-mail: gilberte.ferland@sympatico.ca

Graphics Philately Association
Mark H. Winnegrad
P.O. Box 380
Bronx NY 10462-0380
www.graphics-stamps.org
E-mail: indybruce1@yahoo.com

Journalists, Authors & Poets on Stamps
Ms. Lee Straayer
P.O. Box 6808
Champaign IL 61826
E-mail: lstraayer@dcbnet.com

Lighthouse Stamp Society
Dalene Thomas
1805 S Balsam St. #106
Lakewood CO 80232
Ph: (303) 986-6620
www.lighthousestampsociety.org
E-mail: dalene@lighthousestampsociety.org

Lions International Stamp Club
John Bargus
108-2777 Barry Road RR 2
Mill Bay, BC, V0R 2P2
CANADA
Ph: (250) 743-5782

Mahatma Gandhi On Stamps Study Circle
Pramod Shivagunde
Pratik Clinic, Akluj
Solapur, Maharashtra, 413101
INDIA
E-mail: drnanda@bom6.vsnl.net.in

Masonic Study Unit
Stanley R. Longenecker
930 Wood St.
Mount Joy PA 17552-1926
Ph: (717) 669-9094
E-mail: natsco@usa.net

Mathematical Study Unit
Monty J. Strauss
4209 88th St.
Lubbock TX 79423-2041
www.mathstamps.org

Medical Subjects Unit
Dr. Frederick C. Skvara
P.O. Box 6228
Bridgewater NJ 08807
E-mail: fcskvara@optonline.net

Military Postal History Society
Ed Dubin
1 S. Wacker Drive, Suite 3500
Chicago IL 60606
www.militaryPHS.org
E-mail: dubine@comcast.net

Mourning Stamps and Covers Club
James Bailey, Jr.
P.O. Box 937
Brownwood TX 76804
E-mail: jamesbailey@wildblue.net

Napoleonic Age Philatelists
Ken Berry
4117 NW 146th St.
Oklahoma City OK 73134-1746
Ph: (405) 748-8646
www.nap-stamps.org
E-mail: krb4117@att.net

Old World Archeological Study Unit
Caroline Scannell
11 Dawn Drive
Smithtown NY 11787-1761
www.owasu.org
E-mail: editor@owasu.org

Petroleum Philatelic Society International
Dr. Chris Coggins
174 Old Bedford Road
Luton, England, LU2 7HW
UNITED KINGDOM
E-mail: WAMTECH@Luton174.fsnet.co.uk

Rotary on Stamps Unit
Gerald L. Fitzsimmons
105 Calla Ricardo
Victoria TX 77904
rotaryonstamps.org
E-mail: glfitz@suddenlink.net

Scouts on Stamps Society International
Lawrence Clay
P.O. Box 6228
Kennewick WA 99336
Ph: (509) 735-3731
www.sossi.org
E-mail: rfrank@sossi.org

Ships on Stamps Unit
Les Smith
302 Conklin Ave.
Penticton, BC, V2A 2T4
CANADA
Ph: (250) 493-7486
www.shipsonstamps.org
E-mail: lessmith440@shaw.ca

Space Unit
Carmine Torrisi
P.O. Box 780241
Maspeth NY 11378
Ph: (917) 620-5687
stargate.1usa.com/stamps/
E-mail: ctorrisi1@nyc.rr.com

Sports Philatelists International
Mark Maestrone
2824 Curie Place
San Diego CA 92122-4110
www.sportstamps.org
Email: president@sportstamps.org

Stamps on Stamps Collectors Club
Alf Jordan
156 W. Elm St.
Yarmouth ME 04096
www.stampsonstamps.org
E-mail: ajordan1@maine.rr.com

Windmill Study Unit
Walter J. Hollien
607 N. Porter St.
Watkins Glenn NY 14891-1345
Ph: (862) 812-0030
E-mail: whollien@earthlink.net

Wine On Stamps Study Unit
David Wolfersberger
768 Chain Ridge Road
St. Louis MO 63122-3259
Ph: (314) 961-5032
www.wine-on-stamps.org
E-mail: dewolf2@swbell.net

Women on Stamps Study Unit
Hugh Gottfried
2232 26th St.
Santa Monica CA 90405-1902
E-mail: hgottfried@adelphia.net

Expertizing Services

The following organizations will, for a fee, provide expert opinions about stamps submitted to them. Collectors should contact these organizations to find out about their fees and requirements before submiting philatelic material to them. The listing of these groups here is not intended as an endorsement by Amos Media Co.

General Expertizing Services

American Philatelic Expertizing Service (a service of the American Philatelic Society)
100 Match Factory Place
Bellefonte PA 16823-1367
Ph: (814) 237-3803
Fax: (814) 237-6128
www.stamps.org
E-mail: ambristo@stamps.org
Areas of Expertise: Worldwide

B. P. A. Expertising, Ltd.
P.O. Box 1141
Guildford, Surrey, GU5 0WR
UNITED KINGDOM
E-mail: sec@bpaexpertising.org
Areas of Expertise: British Commonwealth, Great Britain, Classics of Europe, South America and the Far East

Philatelic Foundation
341 W. 38th St., 5th Floor
New York NY 10018
Ph: (212) 221-6555
Fax: (212) 221-6208
www.philatelicfoundation.org
E-mail: philatelicfoundation@verizon.net
Areas of Expertise: U.S. & Worldwide

Philatelic Stamp Authentication and Grading, Inc.
P.O. Box 41-0880
Melbourne FL 32941-0880
Customer Service: (305) 345-9864
www.psaginc.com
E-mail: info@psaginc.com
Areas of Expertise: U.S., Canal Zone, Hawaii, Philippines, Canada & Provinces

Professional Stamp Experts
P.O. Box 6170
Newport Beach CA 92658
Ph: (877) STAMP-88
Fax: (949) 833-7955
www.collectors.com/pse
E-mail: pseinfo@collectors.com
Areas of Expertise: Stamps and covers of U.S., U.S. Possessions, British Commonwealth

Royal Philatelic Society Expert Committee
41 Devonshire Place
London, W1N 1PE
UNITED KINGDOM
www.rpsl.org.uk/experts.html
E-mail: experts@rpsl.org.uk
Areas of Expertise: Worldwide

Expertizing Services Covering Specific Fields Or Countries

China Stamp Society Expertizing Service
1050 W. Blue Ridge Blvd.
Kansas City MO 64145
Ph: (816) 942-6300
E-mail: hjmesq@aol.com
Areas of Expertise: China

Confederate Stamp Alliance Authentication Service
Gen. Frank Crown, Jr.
P.O. Box 278
Capshaw AL 35742-0396
Ph: (302) 422-2656
Fax: (302) 424-1990
www.csalliance.org
E-mail: csaas@knology.net
Areas of Expertise: Confederate stamps and postal history

Errors, Freaks and Oddities Collectors Club Expertizing Service
138 East Lakemont Drive
Kingsland GA 31548
Ph: (912) 729-1573
Areas of Expertise: U.S. errors, freaks and oddities

Estonian Philatelic Society Expertizing Service
39 Clafford Lane
Melville NY 11747
Ph: (516) 421-2078
E-mail: esto4@aol.com
Areas of Expertise: Estonia

Hawaiian Philatelic Society Expertizing Service
P.O. Box 10115
Honolulu HI 96816-0115
Areas of Expertise: Hawaii

Hong Kong Stamp Society Expertizing Service
P.O. Box 206
Glenside PA 19038
Fax: (215) 576-6850
Areas of Expertise: Hong Kong

International Association of Philatelic Experts United States Associate members:

Paul Buchsbayew
119 W. 57th St.
New York NY 10019
Ph: (212) 977-7734
Fax: (212) 977-8653
Areas of Expertise: Russia, Soviet Union

William T. Crowe
P.O. Box 2090
Danbury CT 06813-2090
E-mail: wtcrowe@aol.com
Areas of Expertise: United States

John Lievsay
(see American Philatelic Expertizing Service and Philatelic Foundation)
Areas of Expertise: France

Robert W. Lyman
P.O. Box 348
Irvington on Hudson NY 10533
Ph and Fax: (914) 591-6937
Areas of Expertise: British North America, New Zealand

Robert Odenweller
P.O. Box 401
Bernardsville NJ 07924-0401
Ph and Fax: (908) 766-5460
Areas of Expertise: New Zealand, Samoa to 1900

Sergio Sismondo
The Regency Tower, Suite 1109
770 James Street
Syracuse NY 13203
Ph: (315) 422-2331
Fax: (315) 422-2956
Areas of Expertise: British East Africa, Cameroons, Cape of Good Hope, Canada, British North America

International Society for Japanese Philately Expertizing Committee
132 North Pine Terrace
Staten Island NY 10312-4052
Ph: (718) 227-5229
Areas of Expertise: Japan and related areas, except WWII Japanese Occupation issues

International Society for Portuguese Philately Expertizing Service
P.O. Box 43146
Philadelphia PA 19129-3146
Ph and Fax: (215) 843-2106
E-mail: s.s.washburne@worldnet.att.net
Areas of Expertise: Portugal and Colonies

Mexico-Elmhurst Philatelic Society International Expert Committee
P.O. Box 1133
West Covina CA 91793
Areas of Expertise: Mexico

Ukrainian Philatelic & Numismatic Society Expertizing Service
30552 Dell Lane
Warren MI 48092-1862
Areas of Expertise: Ukraine, Western Ukraine

V. G. Greene Philatelic Research Foundation
P.O. Box 204, Station Q
Toronto, ON, M4T 2M1
CANADA
Ph: (416) 921-2073
Fax: (416) 921-1282
www.greenefoundation.ca
E-mail: vggfoundation@on.aibn.com
Areas of Expertise: British North America

Information on Catalogue Values, Grade and Condition

Catalogue Value

The Scott Catalogue value is a retail value; that is, an amount you could expect to pay for a stamp in the grade of Very Fine with no faults. Any exceptions to the grade valued will be noted in the text. The general introduction on the following pages and the individual section introductions further explain the type of material that is valued. The value listed for any given stamp is a reference that reflects recent actual dealer selling prices for that item.

Dealer retail price lists, public auction results, published prices in advertising and individual solicitation of retail prices from dealers, collectors and specialty organizations have been used in establishing the values found in this catalogue. Amos Media Co. values stamps, but Amos Media is not a company engaged in the business of buying and selling stamps as a dealer.

Use this catalogue as a guide for buying and selling. The actual price you pay for a stamp may be higher or lower than the catalogue value because of many different factors, including the amount of personal service a dealer offers, or increased or decreased interest in the country or topic represented by a stamp or set. An item may occasionally be offered at a lower price as a "loss leader," or as part of a special sale. You also may obtain an item inexpensively at public auction because of little interest at that time or as part of a large lot.

Stamps that are of a lesser grade than Very Fine, or those with condition problems, generally trade at lower prices than those given in this catalogue. Stamps of exceptional quality in both grade and condition often command higher prices than those listed.

Values for pre-1900 unused issues are for stamps with approximately half or more of their original gum. Stamps with most or all of their original gum may be expected to sell for more, and stamps with less than half of their original gum may be expected to sell for somewhat less than the values listed. On rarer stamps, it may be expected that the original gum will be somewhat more disturbed than it will be on more common issues. Post-1900 unused issues are assumed to have full original gum. From breakpoints in most countries' listings, stamps are valued as never hinged, due to the wide availability of stamps in that condition. These notations are prominently placed in the listings and in the country information preceding the listings. Some countries also feature listings with dual values for hinged and never-hinged stamps.

Grade

A stamp's grade and condition are crucial to its value. The accompanying illustrations show examples of Very Fine stamps from different time periods, along with examples of stamps in Fine to Very Fine and Extremely Fine grades as points of reference. When a stamp seller offers a stamp in any grade from fine to superb without further qualifying statements, that stamp should not only have the centering grade as defined, but it also should be free of faults or other condition problems.

FINE stamps (illustrations not shown) have designs that are quite off center, with the perforations on one or two sides very close to the design but not quite touching it. There is white space between the perforations and the design that is minimal but evident to the unaided eye. Imperforate stamps may have small margins, and earlier issues may show the design just touching one edge of the stamp design. Very early perforated issues normally will have the perforations slightly cutting into the design. Used stamps may have heavier than usual cancellations.

FINE-VERY FINE stamps will be somewhat off center on one side, or slightly off center on two sides. Imperforate stamps will have two margins of at least normal size, and the design will not touch any edge. For perforated stamps, the perfs are well clear of the design, but are still noticeably off center. *However, early issues of a country may be printed in such a way that the design naturally is very close to the edges. In these cases, the perforations may cut into the design very slightly.* Used stamps will not have a cancellation that detracts from the design.

VERY FINE stamps will be just slightly off center on one or two sides, but the design will be well clear of the edge. The stamp will present a nice, balanced appearance. Imperforate stamps will be well centered within normal-sized margins. *However, early issues of many countries may be printed in such a way that the perforations may touch the design on one or more sides. Where this is the case, a boxed note will be found defining the centering and margins of the stamps being valued.* Used stamps will have light or otherwise neat cancellations. This is the grade used to establish Scott Catalogue values.

EXTREMELY FINE stamps are close to being perfectly centered. Imperforate stamps will have even margins that are slightly larger than normal. Even the earliest perforated issues will have perforations clear of the design on all sides.

Amos Media Co. recognizes that there is no formally enforced grading scheme for postage stamps, and that the final price you pay or obtain for a stamp will be determined by individual agreement at the time of transaction.

Condition

Grade addresses only centering and (for used stamps) cancellation. *Condition* refers to factors other than grade that affect a stamp's desirability.

Factors that can increase the value of a stamp include exceptionally wide margins, particularly fresh color, the presence of selvage, and plate or die varieties. Unusual cancels on used stamps (particularly those of the 19th century) can greatly enhance their value as well.

Factors other than faults that decrease the value of a stamp include loss of original gum, regumming, a hinge remnant or foreign object adhering to the gum, natural inclusions, straight edges, and markings or notations applied by collectors or dealers.

Faults include missing pieces, tears, pin or other holes, surface scuffs, thin spots, creases, toning, short or pulled perforations, clipped perforations, oxidation or other forms of color changelings, soiling, stains, and such man-made changes as reperforations or the chemical removal or lightening of a cancellation.

Grading Illustrations

On the following two pages are illustrations of various stamps from countries appearing in this volume. These stamps are arranged by country, and they represent early or important issues that are often found in widely different grades in the marketplace. The editors believe the illustrations will prove useful in showing the margin size and centering that will be seen on the various issues.

In addition to the matters of margin size and centering, collectors are reminded that the very fine stamps valued in the Scott catalogues also will possess fresh color and intact perforations, and they will be free from defects.

Examples shown are computer-manipulated images made from single digitized master illustrations.

Stamp Illustrations Used in the Catalogue

It is important to note that the stamp images used for identification purposes in this catlaogue may not be indicative of the grade of stamp being valued. Refer to the written discussion of grades on this page and to the grading illustrations on the following two pages for grading information.

Fine-Very Fine

SCOTT CATALOGUES VALUE STAMPS IN THIS GRADE

Very Fine

Extremely Fine

Fine-Very Fine

SCOTT CATALOGUES VALUE STAMPS IN THIS GRADE

Very Fine

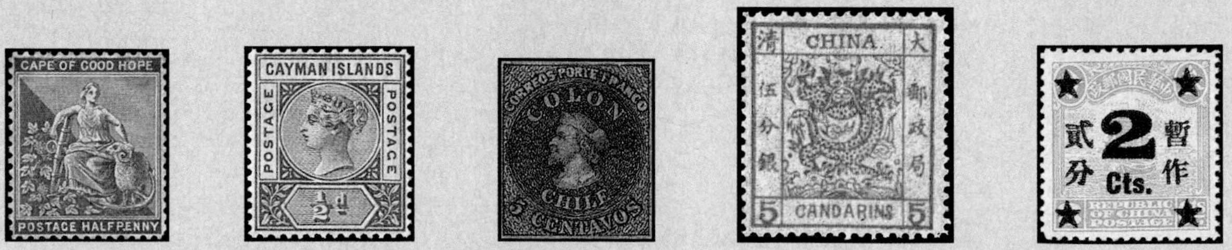

Extremely Fine

Fine-Very Fine

SCOTT CATALOGUES VALUE STAMPS IN THIS GRADE

Very Fine

Extremely Fine

Fine-Very Fine

SCOTT CATALOGUES VALUE STAMPS IN THIS GRADE

Very Fine

Extremely Fine

For purposes of helping to determine the gum condition and value of an unused stamp, Scott presents the following chart which details different gum conditions and indicates how the conditions correlate with the Scott values for unused stamps. Used together, the Illustrated Grading Chart on the previous pages and this Illustrated Gum Chart should allow catalogue users to better understand the grade and gum condition of stamps valued in the Scott catalogues.

Gum Categories:	MINT N.H.	ORIGINAL GUM (O.G.)				NO GUM

	Mint Never Hinged *Free from any disturbance*	**Lightly Hinged** *Faint impression of a removed hinge over a small area*	**Hinge Mark or Remnant** *Prominent hinged spot with part or all of the hinge remaining*	**Large part o.g.** *Approximately half or more of the gum intact*	**Small part o.g.** *Approximately less than half of the gum intact*	**No gum** *Only if issued with gum*
Commonly Used Symbol:	★★	★	★	★	★	(★)
Pre-1900 Issues (Pre-1881 for U.S.)	*Very fine pre-1900 stamps in these categories trade at a premium over Scott value*			Scott Value for "Unused"		Scott "No Gum" listings for selected unused classic stamps
From 1900 to break-points for listings of never-hinged stamps	Scott "Never Hinged" listings for selected unused stamps	Scott Value for "Unused" (Actual value will be affected by the degree of hinging of the full o.g.)				
From breakpoints noted for many countries	Scott Value for "Unused"					

Never Hinged (NH; ★★): A never-hinged stamp will have full original gum that will have no hinge mark or disturbance. The presence of an expertizer's mark does not disqualify a stamp from this designation.

Original Gum (OG; ★): Pre-1900 stamps should have approximately half or more of their original gum. On rarer stamps, it may be expected that the original gum will be somewhat more disturbed than it will be on more common issues. Post-1900 stamps should have full original gum. Original gum will show some disturbance caused by a previous hinge(s) which may be present or entirely removed. The actual value of a post-1900 stamp will be affected by the degree of hinging of the full original gum.

Disturbed Original Gum: Gum showing noticeable effects of humidity, climate or hinging over more than half of the gum. The significance of gum disturbance in valuing a stamp in any of the Original Gum categories depends on the degree of disturbance, the rarity and normal gum condition of the issue and other variables affecting quality.

Regummed (RG; (★)): A regummed stamp is a stamp without gum that has had some type of gum privately applied at a time after it was issued. This normally is done to deceive collectors and/or dealers into thinking that the stamp has original gum and therefore has a higher value. A regummed stamp is considered the same as a stamp with none of its original gum for purposes of grading.

Catalogue Listing Policy

It is the intent of Amos Media Co. to list all postage stamps of the world in the *Scott Standard Postage Stamp Catalogue*. The only strict criteria for listing is that stamps be decreed legal for postage by the issuing country and that the issuing country actually have an operating postal system. Whether the primary intent of issuing a given stamp or set was for sale to postal patrons or to stamp collectors is not part of our listing criteria. Scott's role is to provide basic comprehensive postage stamp information. It is up to each stamp collector to choose which items to include in a collection.

It is Scott's objective to seek reasons why a stamp should be listed, rather than why it should not. Nevertheless, there are certain types of items that will not be listed. These include the following:

1. Unissued items that are not officially distributed or released by the issuing postal authority. If such items are officially issued at a later date by the country, they will be listed. Unissued items consist of those that have been printed and then held from sale for reasons such as change in government, errors found on stamps or something deemed objectionable about a stamp subject or design.

2. Stamps "issued" by non-existent postal entities or fantasy countries, such as Nagaland, Occusi-Ambeno, Staffa, Sedang, Torres Straits and others. Also, stamps "issued" in the names of legitimate, stamp-issuing countries that are not authorized by those countries.

3. Semi-official or unofficial items not required for postage. Examples include items issued by private agencies for their own express services. When such items are required for delivery, or are valid as prepayment of postage, they are listed.

4. Local stamps issued for local use only. Postage stamps issued by governments specifically for "domestic" use, such as Haiti Scott 219-228, or the United States non-denominated stamps, are not considered to be locals, since they are valid for postage throughout the country of origin.

5. Items not valid for postal use. For example, a few countries have issued souvenir sheets that are not valid for postage. This area also includes a number of worldwide charity labels (some denominated) that do not pay postage.

6. Egregiously exploitative issues such as stamps sold for far more than face value, stamps purposefully issued in artificially small quantities or only against advance orders, stamps awarded only to a selected audience such as a philatelic bureau's standing order customers, or stamps sold only in conjunction with other products. All of these kinds of items are usually controlled issues and/or are intended for speculation. These items normally will be included in a footnote.

7. Items distributed by the issuing government only to a limited group, club, philatelic exhibition or a single stamp dealer or other private company. These items normally will be included in a footnote.

8. Stamps not available to collectors. These generally are rare items, all of which are held by public institutions such as museums. The existence of such items often will be cited in footnotes.

The fact that a stamp has been used successfully as postage, even on international mail, is not in itself sufficient proof that it was legitimately issued. Numerous examples of so-called stamps from non-existent countries are known to have been used to post letters that have successfully passed through the international mail system.

There are certain items that are subject to interpretation. When a stamp falls outside our specifications, it may be listed along with a cautionary footnote.

A number of factors are considered in our approach to analyzing how a stamp is listed. The following list of factors is presented to share with you, the catalogue user, the complexity of the listing process.

Additional printings — "Additional printings" of a previously issued stamp may range from an item that is totally different to cases where it is impossible to differentiate from the original. At least a minor number (a small-letter suffix) is assigned if there is a distinct change in stamp shade, noticeably redrawn design, or a significantly different perforation measurement. A major number (numeral or numeral and capital-letter combination) is assigned if the editors feel the "additional printing" is sufficiently different from the original that it constitutes a different issue.

Commemoratives — Where practical, commemoratives with the same theme are placed in a set. For example, the U.S. Civil War Centennial set of 1961-65 and the Constitution Bicentennial series of 1989-90 appear as sets. Countries such as Japan and Korea issue such material on a regular basis, with an announced, or at least predictable, number of stamps known in advance. Occasionally, however, stamp sets that were released over a period of years have been separated. Appropriately placed footnotes will guide you to each set's continuation.

Definitive sets — Blocks of numbers generally have been reserved for definitive sets, based on previous experience with any given country. If a few more stamps were issued in a set than originally expected, they often have been inserted into the original set with a capital-letter suffix, such as U.S. Scott 1059A. If it appears that many more stamps than the originally allotted block will be released before the set is completed, a new block of numbers will be reserved, with the original one being closed off. In some cases, such as the U.S. Transportation and Great Americans series, several blocks of numbers exist. Appropriately placed footnotes will guide you to each set's continuation.

New country — Membership in the Universal Postal Union is not a consideration for listing status or order of placement within the catalogue. The index will tell you in what volume or page number the listings begin.

"No release date" items — The amount of information available for any given stamp issue varies greatly from country to country and even from time to time. Extremely comprehensive information about new stamps is available from some countries well before the stamps are released. By contrast some countries do not provide information about stamps or release dates. Most countries, however, fall between these extremes. A country may provide denominations or subjects of stamps from upcoming issues that are not issued as planned. Sometimes, philatelic agencies, those private firms hired to represent countries, add these later-issued items to sets well after the formal release date. This time period can range from weeks to years. If these items were officially released by the country, they will be added to the appropriate spot in the set. In many cases, the specific release date of a stamp or set of stamps may never be known.

Overprints — The color of an overprint is always noted if it is other than black. Where more than one color of ink has been used on overprints of a single set, the color used is noted. Early overprint and surcharge illustrations were altered to prevent their use by forgers.

Personalized Stamps — Since 1999, the special service of personalizing stamp vignettes, or labels attached to stamps, has been offered to customers by postal administrations of many countries. Sheets of these stamps are sold, singly or in quantity, only through special orders made by mail, in person, or through a sale on a computer website with the postal administrations or their agents for which an extra fee is charged, though some countries offer to collectors at face value personalized stamps having generic images in the vignettes or on the attached labels. It is impossible for any catalogue to know what images have been chosen by customers. Images can be 1) owned or created by the customer, 2) a generic image, or 3) an image pulled from a library of stock images on the stamp creation website. It is also impossible to know the quantity printed for any stamp having a particular image. So from a valuing standpoint, any image is equivalent to any other image for any personalized stamp having the same catalogue number. Illustrations of personalized stamps in the catalogue are not always those of stamps having generic images.

Personalized items are listed with some exceptions. These include:
1. Stamps or sheets that have attached labels that the customer cannot personalize, but which are nonetheless marketed as "personalized," and are sold for far more than the franking value.
2. Stamps or sheets that can be personalized by the customer, but where a portion of the print run must be ceded to the issuing country for sale to other customers.
3. Stamps or sheets that are created exclusively for a particular commercial client, or clients, including stamps that differ from any similar stamp that has been made available to the public.
4. Stamps or sheets that are deliberately conceived by the issuing authority that have been, or are likely to be, created with an excessive number of different face values, sizes, or other features that are changeable.
5. Stamps or sheets that are created by postal administrations using the same system of stamp personalization that has been put in place for use by the public that are printed in limited quantities and sold above face value.
6. Stamps or sheets that are created by licensees not directly affiliated or controlled by a postal administration.

Excluded items may or may not be footnoted.

Se-tenants — Connected stamps of differing features (se-tenants) will be listed in the format most commonly collected. This includes pairs, blocks or larger multiples. Se-tenant units are not always symmetrical. An example is Australia Scott 508, which is a block of seven stamps. If the stamps are primarily collected as a unit, the major number may be assigned to the multiple, with minors going to each component stamp. In cases where continuous-design or other unit se-tenants will receive significant postal use, each stamp is given a major Scott number listing. This includes issues from the United States, Canada, Germany and Great Britain, for example.

Understanding the Listings

On the opposite page is an enlarged "typical" listing from this catalogue. Below are detailed explanations of each of the highlighted parts of the listing.

1 Scott number — Scott catalogue numbers are used to identify specific items when buying, selling or trading stamps. Each listed postage stamp from every country has a unique Scott catalogue number. Therefore, Germany Scott 99, for example, can only refer to a single stamp. Although the Scott catalogue usually lists stamps in chronological order by date of issue, there are exceptions. When a country has issued a set of stamps over a period of time, those stamps within the set are kept together without regard to date of issue. This follows the normal collecting approach of keeping stamps in their natural sets.

When a country issues a set of stamps over a period of time, a group of consecutive catalogue numbers is reserved for the stamps in that set, as issued. If that group of numbers proves to be too few, capital-letter suffixes, such as "A" or "B," may be added to existing numbers to create enough catalogue numbers to cover all items in the set. A capital-letter suffix indicates a major Scott catalogue number listing. Scott generally uses a suffix letter only once. Therefore, a catalogue number listing with a capital-letter suffix will seldom be found with the same letter (lower case) used as a minor-letter listing. If there is a Scott 16A in a set, for example, there will seldom be a Scott 16a. However, a minor-letter "a" listing may be added to a major number containing an "A" suffix (Scott 16Aa, for example).

Suffix letters are cumulative. A minor "b" variety of Scott 16A would be Scott 16Ab, not Scott 16b.

There are times when a reserved block of Scott catalogue numbers is too large for a set, leaving some numbers unused. Such gaps in the numbering sequence also occur when the catalogue editors move an item's listing elsewhere or have removed it entirely from the catalogue. Scott does not attempt to account for every possible number, but rather attempts to assure that each stamp is assigned its own number.

Scott numbers designating regular postage normally are only numerals. Scott numbers for other types of stamps, such as air post, semi-postal, postal tax, postage due, occupation and others have a prefix consisting of one or more capital letters or a combination of numerals and capital letters.

2 Illustration number — Illustration or design-type numbers are used to identify each catalogue illustration. For most sets, the lowest face-value stamp is shown. It then serves as an example of the basic design approach for other stamps not illustrated. Where more than one stamp use the same illustration number, but have differences in design, the design paragraph or the description line clearly indicates the design on each stamp not illustrated. Where there are both vertical and horizontal designs in a set, a single illustration may be used, with the exceptions noted in the design paragraph or description line.

When an illustration is followed by a lower-case letter in parentheses, such as "A2(b)," the trailing letter indicates which overprint or surcharge illustration applies.

Illustrations normally are 70 percent of the original size of the stamp. Oversized stamps, blocks and souvenir sheets are reduced even more. Overprints and surcharges are shown at 100 percent of their original size if shown alone, but are 70 percent of original size if shown on stamps. In some cases, the illustration will be placed above the set, between listings or omitted completely. Overprint and surcharge illustrations are not placed in this catalogue for purposes of expertizing stamps.

3 Paper color — The color of a stamp's paper is noted in italic type when the paper used is not white.

4 Listing styles — There are two principal types of catalogue listings: major and minor.

Major listings are in a larger type style than minor listings. The catalogue number is a numeral that can be found with or without a capital-letter suffix, and with or without a prefix.

Minor listings are in a smaller type style and have a small-letter suffix or (if the listing immediately follows that of the major number) may show only the letter. These listings identify a variety of the major item. Examples include perforation and shade differences, multiples (some souvenir sheets, booklet panes and se-tenant combinations), and singles of multiples.

Examples of major number listings include 16, 28A, B97, C13A, 10N5, and 10N6A. Examples of minor numbers are 16a and C13Ab.

5 Basic information about a stamp or set — Introducing each stamp issue is a small section (usually a line listing) of basic information about a stamp or set. This section normally includes the date of issue, method of printing, perforation, watermark and, sometimes, some additional information of note. *Printing method, perforation and watermark apply to the following sets until a change is noted.* Stamps created by overprinting or surcharging previous issues are assumed to have the same perforation, watermark, printing method and other production characteristics as the original. Dates of issue are as precise as Scott is able to confirm and often reflect the dates on first-day covers, rather than the actual date of release.

6 Denomination — This normally refers to the face value of the stamp; that is, the cost of the unused stamp at the post office at the time of issue. When a denomination is shown in parentheses, it does not appear on the stamp. This includes the non-denominated stamps of the United States, Brazil and Great Britain, for example.

7 Color or other description — This area provides information to solidify identification of a stamp. In many recent cases, a description of the stamp design appears in this space, rather than a listing of colors.

8 Year of issue — In stamp sets that have been released in a period that spans more than a year, the number shown in parentheses is the year that stamp first appeared. Stamps without a date appeared during the first year of the issue. Dates are not always given for minor varieties.

9 Value unused and Value used — The Scott catalogue values are based on stamps that are in a grade of Very Fine unless stated otherwise. Unused values refer to items that have not seen postal, revenue or any other duty for which they were intended. Pre-1900 unused stamps that were issued with gum must have at least most of their original gum. Later issues are assumed to have full original gum. From breakpoints specified in most countries' listings, stamps are valued as never hinged. Stamps issued without gum are noted. Modern issues with PVA or other synthetic adhesives may appear ungummed. Unused self-adhesive stamps are valued as appearing undisturbed on their original backing paper. Values for used self-adhesive stamps are for examples either on piece or off piece. For a more detailed explanation of these values, please see the "Catalogue Value," "Condition" and "Understanding Valuing Notations" sections elsewhere in this introduction.

In some cases, where used stamps are more valuable than unused stamps, the value is for an example with a contemporaneous cancel, rather than a modern cancel or a smudge or other unclear marking. For those stamps that were released for postal and fiscal purposes, the used value represents a postally used stamp. Stamps with revenue cancels generally sell for less.

Stamps separated from a complete se-tenant multiple usually will be worth less than a pro-rated portion of the se-tenant multiple, and stamps lacking the attached labels that are noted in the listings will be worth less than the values shown.

10 Changes in basic set information — Bold type is used to show any changes in the basic data given for a set of stamps. These basic data categories include perforation gauge measurement, paper type, printing method and watermark.

11 Total value of a set — The total value of sets of three or more stamps issued after 1900 are shown. The set line also notes the range of Scott numbers and total number of stamps included in the grouping. The actual value of a set consisting predominantly of stamps having the minimum value of 25 cents may be less than the total value shown. Similarly, the actual value or catalogue value of se-tenant pairs or of blocks consisting of stamps having the minimum value of 25 cents may be less than the catalogue values of the component parts.

A6

King George VI
A7

1938-44		**Engr.**		**Perf. 12½**	
54	A6	½p	green	.25	*2.00*
54A	A6	½p	dk brown ('42)	.25	*2.25*
55	A6	1p	dark brown	2.50	.35
55A	A6	1p	green ('42)	.25	1.75
56	A6	1½p	dark carmine	4.00	*6.00*
56A	A6	1½p	gray ('42)	.25	*5.75*
57	A6	2p	gray	5.00	1.25
57A	A6	2p	dark car ('42)	.25	*2.00*
58	A6	3p	blue	.60	1.00
59	A6	4p	rose lilac	1.60	2.00
60	A6	6p	dark violet	2.00	2.00
61	A6	9p	olive bister	2.00	*4.75*
62	A6	1sh	orange & blk	2.10	*3.25*

Typo.
Perf. 14
Chalky Paper

63	A7	2sh	ultra & dl vio, *bl*	7.00	*17.50*
64	A7	2sh6p	red & blk, *bl*	8.00	*19.50*
65	A7	5sh	red & grn, *yel*	35.00	30.00
a.		5sh	dk red & dp grn, *yel* ('44)	55.00	*140.00*
66	A7	10sh	red & grn, *grn*	35.00	*70.00*

Wmk. 3

67	A7	£1	blk & vio, *red*	30.00	*45.00*
			Nos. 54-67 (18)	136.05	*216.35*
			Set, never hinged	220.00	

1 SCOTT NUMBER

2 ILLUS. NUMBER

3 PAPER COLOR

4 LISTING STYLES — MAJORS, MINORS

5 BASIC INFORMATION ON STAMP OR SET

6 DENOMINATION

7 COLOR OR OTHER DESCRIPTION

8 YEAR OF ISSUE

9 CATALOGUE VALUES — UNUSED, USED

10 CHANGES IN BASIC SET INFORMATION

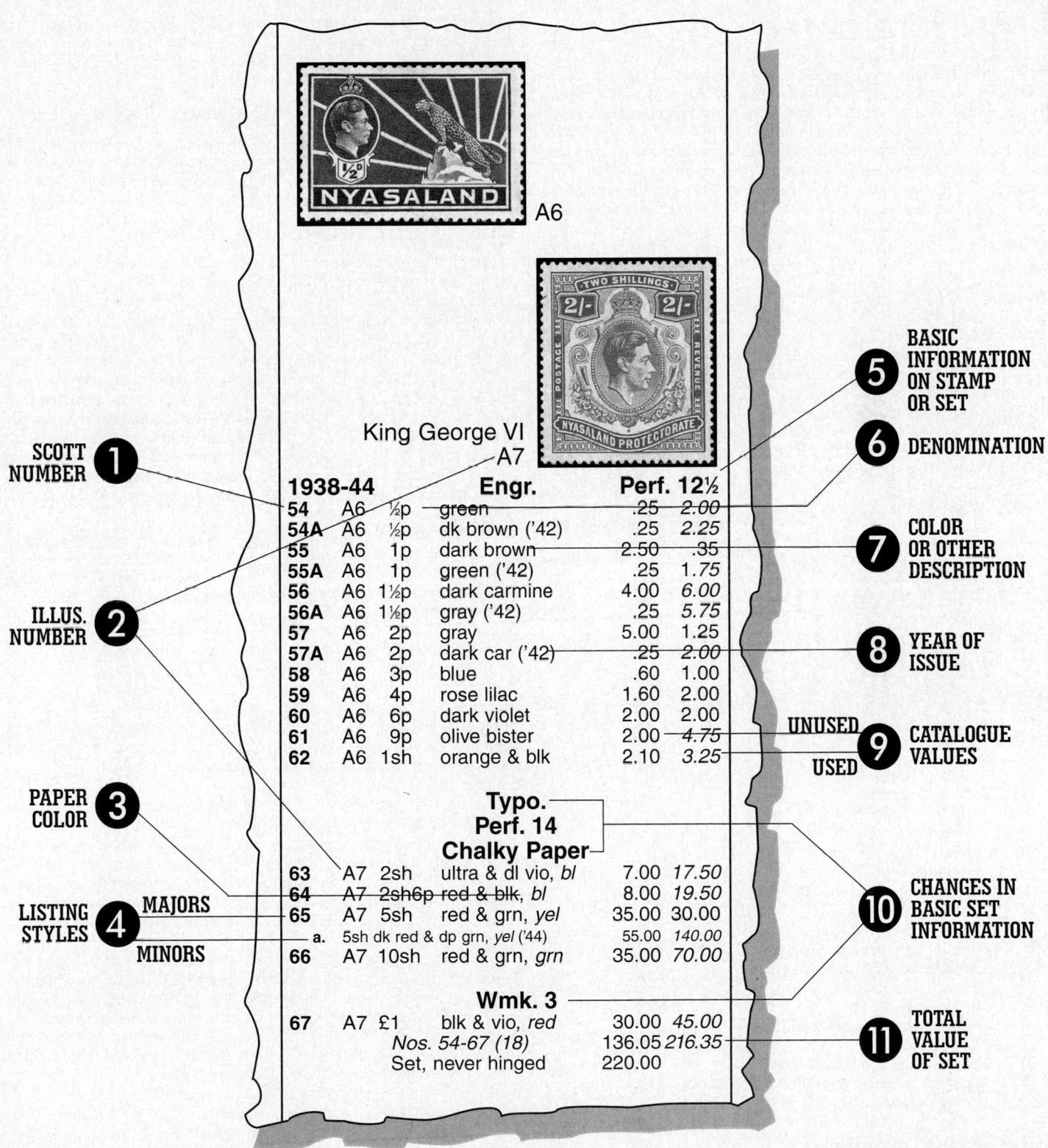

11 TOTAL VALUE OF SET

Special Notices

Classification of stamps

The *Scott Standard Postage Stamp Catalogue* lists stamps by country of issue. The next level of organization is a listing by section on the basis of the function of the stamps. The principal sections cover regular postage, semi-postal, air post, special delivery, registration, postage due and other categories. Except for regular postage, catalogue numbers for all sections include a prefix letter (or number-letter combination) denoting the class to which a given stamp belongs. When some countries issue sets containing stamps from more than one category, the catalogue will at times list all of the stamps in one category (such as air post stamps listed as part of a postage set).

The following is a listing of the most commonly used catalogue prefixes.

Prefix .... Category
C......... Air Post
M........ Military
P......... Newspaper
N......... Occupation - Regular Issues
O .... Official
Q .... Parcel Post
J.......... Postage Due
RA ...... Postal Tax
B......... Semi-Postal
E......... Special Delivery
MR...... War Tax

Other prefixes used by more than one country include the following:
H......... Acknowledgment of Receipt
I.......... Late Fee
CO...... Air Post Official
CQ...... Air Post Parcel Post
RAC.... Air Post Postal Tax
CF ...... Air Post Registration
CB ...... Air Post Semi-Postal
CBO ... Air Post Semi-Postal Official
CE ...... Air Post Special Delivery
EY....... Authorized Delivery
S......... Franchise
G .... Insured Letter
GY...... Marine Insurance
MC ..... Military Air Post
MQ..... Military Parcel Post
NC...... Occupation - Air Post
NO...... Occupation - Official
NJ........ Occupation - Postage Due
NRA.... Occupation - Postal Tax
NB ...... Occupation - Semi-Postal
NE ...... Occupation - Special Delivery
QY...... Parcel Post Authorized Delivery
AR ...... Postal-fiscal
RAJ..... Postal Tax Due
RAB .... Postal Tax Semi-Postal
F......... Registration
EB....... Semi-Postal Special Delivery
EO...... Special Delivery Official
QE...... Special Handling

New issue listings

Updates to this catalogue appear each month in the *Linn's Stamp News* monthly magazine. Included in this update are additions to the listings of countries found in the *Scott Standard Postage Stamp Catalogue* and the *Specialized Catalogue of United States Stamps and Covers*, as well as corrections and updates to current editions of this catalogue.

From time to time there will be changes in the final listings of stamps from the *Linn's Stamp News* magazine to the next edition of the catalogue. This occurs as more information about certain stamps or sets becomes available.

The catalogue update section of the *Linn's Stamp News* magazine is the most timely presentation of this material available. Annual subscriptions to *Linn's Stamp News* are available from Linn's Stamp News, Box 926, Sidney, OH 45365-0926.

Number additions, deletions & changes

A listing of catalogue number additions, deletions and changes from the previous edition of the catalogue appears in each volume. See Catalogue Number Additions, Deletions & Changes in the table of contents for the location of this list.

Understanding valuing notations

The *minimum catalogue value* of an individual stamp or set is 25 cents. This represents a portion of the cost incurred by a dealer when he prepares an individual stamp for resale. As a point of philatelic-economic fact, the lower the value shown for an item in this catalogue, the greater the percentage of that value is attributed to dealer mark up and profit margin. In many cases, such as the 25-cent minimum value, that price does not cover the labor or other costs involved with stocking it as an individual stamp. The sum of minimum values in a set does not properly represent the value of a complete set primarily composed of a number of minimum-value stamps, nor does the sum represent the actual value of a packet made up of minimum-value stamps. Thus a packet of 1,000 different common stamps — each of which has a catalogue value of 25 cents — normally sells for considerably less than 250 dollars!

The *absence of a retail value* for a stamp does not necessarily suggest that a stamp is scarce or rare. A dash in the value column means that the stamp is known in a stated form or variety, but information is either lacking or insufficient for purposes of establishing a usable catalogue value.

Stamp values in *italics* generally refer to items that are difficult to value accurately. For expensive items, such as those priced at $1,000 or higher, a value in italics indicates that the affected item trades very seldom. For inexpensive items, a value in italics represents a warning. One example is a "blocked" issue where the issuing postal administration may have controlled one stamp in a set in an attempt to make the whole set more valuable. Another example is an item that sold at an extreme multiple of face value in the marketplace at the time of its issue.

One type of warning to collectors that appears in the catalogue is illustrated by a stamp that is valued considerably higher in used condition than it is as unused. In this case, collectors are cautioned to be certain the used version has a genuine and contemporaneous cancellation. The type of cancellation on a stamp can be an important factor in determining its sale price. Catalogue values do not apply to fiscal, telegraph or non-contemporaneous postal cancels, unless otherwise noted.

Some countries have released back issues of stamps in canceled-to-order form, sometimes covering as much as a 10-year period. The Scott Catalogue values for used stamps reflect canceled-to-order material when such stamps are found to predominate in the marketplace for the issue involved. Notes frequently appear in the stamp listings to specify which items are valued as canceled-to-order, or if there is a premium for postally used examples.

Many countries sell canceled-to-order stamps at a marked reduction of face value. Countries that sell or have sold canceled-to-order stamps at *full* face value include United Nations, Australia, Netherlands, France and Switzerland. It may be almost impossible to identify such stamps if the gum has been removed, because official government canceling devices are used. Postally used examples of these items on cover, however, are usually worth more than the canceled-to-order stamps with original gum.

Abbreviations

Scott uses a consistent set of abbreviations throughout this catalogue to conserve space, while still providing necessary information.

COLOR ABBREVIATIONS

amb.	amber	crim.	crimson	ol	olive
anil.	aniline	cr	cream	olvn.	olivine
ap	apple	dk	dark	org	orange
aqua	aquamarine	dl	dull	pck	peacock
az	azure	dp	deep	pnksh	pinkish
bis	bister	db	drab	Prus.	Prussian
bl	blue	emer	emerald	pur	purple
bld	blood	gldn.	golden	redsh	reddish
blk	black	grysh	grayish	res	reseda
bril	brilliant	grn	green	ros	rosine
brn	brown	grnsh	greenish	ryl	royal
brnsh	brownish	hel	heliotrope	sal	salmon
brnz.	bronze	hn	henna	saph	sapphire
brt	bright	ind	indigo	scar.	scarlet
brnt.	burnt	int	intense	sep	sepia
car	carmine	lav	lavender	sien.	sienna
cer	cerise	lem	lemon	sil	silver
chlky	chalky	lil	lilac	sl	slate
cham	chamois	lt	light	stl	steel
chnt.	chestnut	mag.	magenta	turq.	turquoise
choc	chocolate	man.	manila	ultra	ultramarine
chr	chrome	mar.	maroon	Ven.	Venetian
cit	citron	mv	mauve	ver	vermilion
cl	claret	multi	multicolored	vio	violet
cob.	cobalt	mlky	milky	yel	yellow
cop.	copper	myr.	myrtle	yelsh	yellowish

When no color is given for an overprint or surcharge, black is the color used. Abbreviations for colors used for overprints and surcharges include: "(B)" or "(Blk)," black; "(Bl)," blue; "(R)," red; and "(G)," green.

Additional abbreviations in this catalogue are shown below:

Adm.	Administration
AFL	American Federation of Labor
Anniv.	Anniversary
APS	American Philatelic Society
Assoc.	Association
ASSR.	Autonomous Soviet Socialist Republic
b.	Born
BEP	Bureau of Engraving and Printing
Bicent.	Bicentennial
Bklt.	Booklet
Brit.	British
btwn.	Between
Bur.	Bureau
c. or ca.	Circa
Cat.	Catalogue
Cent.	Centennial, century, centenary
CIO	Congress of Industrial Organizations
Conf.	Conference
Cong.	Congress
Cpl.	Corporal
CTO	Canceled to order
d.	Died
Dbl.	Double
EDU	Earliest documented use
Engr.	Engraved
Exhib.	Exhibition
Expo.	Exposition
Fed.	Federation
GB	Great Britain
Gen.	General
GPO	General post office
Horiz.	Horizontal
Imperf.	Imperforate
Impt.	Imprint
Intl.	International
Invtd.	Inverted
L	Left
Lieut., lt.	Lieutenant
Litho.	Lithographed
LL	Lower left
LR	Lower right
mm	Millimeter
Ms.	Manuscript
Natl.	National
No.	Number
NY	New York
NYC	New York City
Ovpt.	Overprint
Ovptd.	Overprinted
P	Plate number
Perf.	Perforated, perforation
Phil.	Philatelic
Photo.	Photogravure
PO	Post office
Pr.	Pair
P.R.	Puerto Rico
Prec.	Precancel, precanceled
Pres.	President
PTT	Post, Telephone and Telegraph
R	Right
Rio	Rio de Janeiro
Sgt.	Sergeant
Soc.	Society
Souv.	Souvenir
SSR	Soviet Socialist Republic, see ASSR
St.	Saint, street
Surch.	Surcharge
Typo.	Typographed
UL	Upper left
Unwmkd.	Unwatermarked
UPU	Universal Postal Union
UR	Upper Right
US	United States
USPOD	United States Post Office Department
USSR	Union of Soviet Socialist Republics
Vert.	Vertical
VP	Vice president
Wmk.	Watermark
Wmkd.	Watermarked
WWI	World War I
WWII	World War II

Examination

Amos Media Co. will not comment upon the genuineness, grade or condition of stamps, because of the time and responsibility involved. Rather, there are several expertizing groups that undertake this work for both collectors and dealers. Neither will Amos Media Co. appraise or identify philatelic material. The company cannot take responsibility for unsolicited stamps or covers sent by individuals.

All letters, E-mails, etc. are read attentively, but they are not always answered due to time considerations.

How to order from your dealer

When ordering stamps from a dealer, it is not necessary to write the full description of a stamp as listed in this catalogue. All you need is the name of the country, the Scott catalogue number and whether the desired item is unused or used. For example, "Japan Scott 422 unused" is sufficient to identify the unused stamp of Japan listed as "422 A206 5y brown."

Basic Stamp Information

A stamp collector's knowledge of the combined elements that make a given stamp issue unique determines his or her ability to identify stamps. These elements include paper, watermark, method of separation, printing, design and gum. On the following pages each of these important areas is briefly described.

Paper

Paper is an organic material composed of a compacted weave of cellulose fibers and generally formed into sheets. Paper used to print stamps may be manufactured in sheets, or it may have been part of a large roll (called a web) before being cut to size. The fibers most often used to create paper on which stamps are printed include bark, wood, straw and certain grasses. In many cases, linen or cotton rags have been added for greater strength and durability. Grinding, bleaching, cooking and rinsing these raw fibers reduces them to a slushy pulp, referred to by paper makers as "stuff." Sizing and, sometimes, coloring matter is added to the pulp to make different types of finished paper.

After the stuff is prepared, it is poured onto sieve-like frames that allow the water to run off, while retaining the matted pulp. As fibers fall onto the screen and are held by gravity, they form a natural weave that will later hold the paper together. If the screen has metal bits that are formed into letters or images attached, it leaves slightly thinned areas on the paper. These are called watermarks.

When the stuff is almost dry, it is passed under pressure through smooth or engraved rollers - dandy rolls - or placed between cloth in a press to be flattened and dried.

Wove Laid Granite

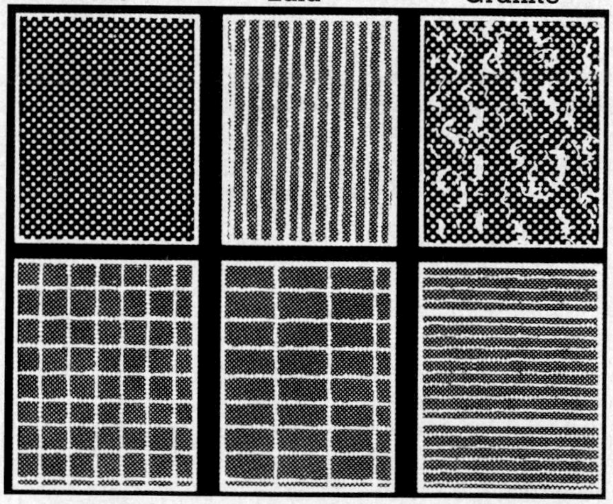

Quadrille Oblong Quadrille Laid Batonne

Stamp paper falls broadly into two types: wove and laid. The nature of the surface of the frame onto which the pulp is first deposited causes the differences in appearance between the two. If the surface is smooth and even, the paper will be of fairly uniform texture throughout. This is known as *wove paper*. Early papermaking machines poured the pulp onto a continuously circulating web of felt, but modern machines feed the pulp onto a cloth-like screen made of closely interwoven fine wires. This paper, when held to a light, will show little dots or points very close together. The proper name for this is "wire wove," but the type is still considered wove. Any U.S. or British stamp printed after 1880 will serve as an example of wire wove paper.

Closely spaced parallel wires, with cross wires at wider intervals, make up the frames used for what is known as *laid paper*. A greater thickness of the pulp will settle between the wires. The paper, when held to a light, will show alternate light and dark lines. The spacing and the thickness of the lines may vary, but on any one sheet of paper they are all alike. See Russia Scott 31-38 for examples of laid paper.

Batonne, from the French word meaning "a staff," is a term used if the lines in the paper are spaced quite far apart, like the printed ruling on a writing tablet. Batonne paper may be either wove or laid. If laid, fine laid lines can be seen between the batons.

Quadrille is the term used when the lines in the paper form little squares. *Oblong quadrille* is the term used when rectangles, rather than squares, are formed. Grid patterns vary from distinct to extremely faint. See Mexico-Guadalajara Scott 35-37 for examples of oblong quadrille paper.

Paper also is classified as thick or thin, hard or soft, and by color. Such colors may include yellowish, greenish, bluish and reddish.

Brief explanations of other types of paper used for printing stamps, as well as examples, follow.

Colored — Colored paper is created by the addition of dye in the paper-making process. Such colors may include shades of yellow, green, blue and red. *Surface-colored papers*, most commonly used for British colonial issues in 1913-14, are created when coloring is added only to the surface during the finishing process. Stamps printed on surface-colored paper have white or uncolored backs, while true colored papers are colored through. See Jamaica Scott 71-73.

Pelure — Pelure paper is a very thin, hard and often brittle paper that is sometimes bluish or grayish in appearance. See Serbia Scott 169-170.

Native — This is a term applied to handmade papers used to produce some of the early stamps of the Indian states. Stamps printed on native paper may be expected to display various natural inclusions that are normal and do not negatively affect value. Japanese paper, originally made of mulberry fibers and rice flour, is part of this group. See Japan Scott 1-18.

Manila — This type of paper is often used to make stamped envelopes and wrappers. It is a coarse-textured stock, usually smooth on one side and rough on the other. A variety of colors of manila paper exist, but the most common range is yellowish-brown.

Silk — Introduced by the British in 1847 as a safeguard against counterfeiting, silk paper contains bits of colored silk thread scattered throughout. The density of these fibers varies greatly and can include as few as one fiber per stamp or hundreds. U.S. revenue Scott R152 is a good example of an easy-to-identify silk paper stamp.

Silk-thread paper has uninterrupted threads of colored silk arranged so that one or more threads run through the stamp or postal stationery. See Great Britain Scott 5-6 and Switzerland Scott 14-19.

Granite — Filled with minute cloth or colored paper fibers of various colors and lengths, granite paper should not be confused with either type of silk paper. Austria Scott 172-175 and a number of Swiss stamps are examples of granite paper.

Chalky — A chalk-like substance coats the surface of chalky paper to discourage the cleaning and reuse of canceled stamps, as well as to provide a smoother, more acceptable printing surface. Because the designs of stamps printed on chalky paper are imprinted on what is often a water-soluble coating, any attempt to remove a cancellation will destroy the stamp. *Do not soak these stamps in any fluid.* To remove a stamp printed on chalky paper from an envelope, wet the paper from underneath the stamp until the gum dissolves enough to release the stamp from the paper. See St. Kitts-Nevis Scott 89-90 for examples of stamps printed on this type of chalky paper.

India — Another name for this paper, originally introduced from China about 1750, is "China Paper." It is a thin, opaque paper often used for plate and die proofs by many countries.

Double — In philately, the term double paper has two distinct meanings. The first is a two-ply paper, usually a combination of a thick and a thin sheet, joined during manufacture. This type was used experimentally as a means to discourage the reuse of stamps.

The design is printed on the thin paper. Any attempt to remove a cancellation would destroy the design. U.S. Scott 158 and other Banknote-era stamps exist on this form of double paper.

The second type of double paper occurs on a rotary press, when the end of one paper roll, or web, is affixed to the next roll to save time feeding the paper through the press. Stamp designs are printed over the joined paper and, if overlooked by inspectors, may get into post office stocks.

Goldbeater's Skin — This type of paper was used for the 1866 issue of Prussia, and was a tough, translucent paper. The design was printed in reverse on the back of the stamp, and the gum applied over the printing. It is impossible to remove stamps printed on this type of paper from the paper to which they are affixed without destroying the design.

Ribbed — Ribbed paper has an uneven, corrugated surface made by passing the paper through ridged rollers. This type exists on some copies of U.S. Scott 156-165.

Various other substances, or substrates, have been used for stamp manufacture, including wood, aluminum, copper, silver and gold foil, plastic, and silk and cotton fabrics.

Watermarks

Watermarks are an integral part of some papers. They are formed in the process of paper manufacture. Watermarks consist of small designs, formed of wire or cut from metal and soldered to the surface of the mold or, sometimes, on the dandy roll. The designs may be in the form of crowns, stars, anchors, letters or other characters or symbols. These pieces of metal - known in the paper-making industry as "bits" - impress a design into the paper. The design sometimes may be seen by holding the stamp to the light. Some are more easily seen with a watermark detector. This important tool is a small black tray into which a stamp is placed face down and dampened with a fast-evaporating watermark detection fluid that brings up the watermark image in the form of dark lines against a lighter background. These dark lines are the thinner areas of the paper known as the watermark. Some watermarks are extremely difficult to locate, due to either a faint impression, watermark location or the color of the stamp. There also are electric watermark detectors that come with plastic filter disks of various colors. The disks neutralize the color of the stamp, permitting the watermark to be seen more easily.

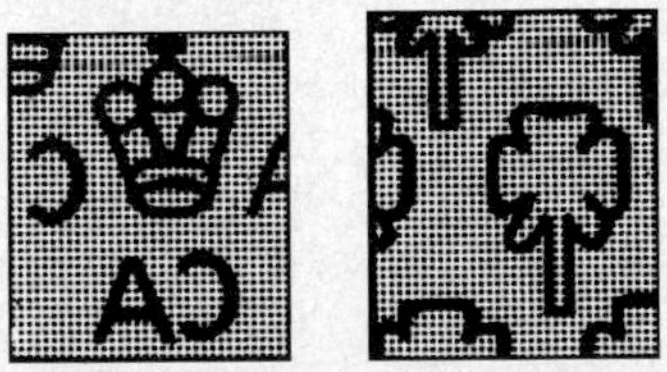

Multiple watermarks of Crown Agents and Burma

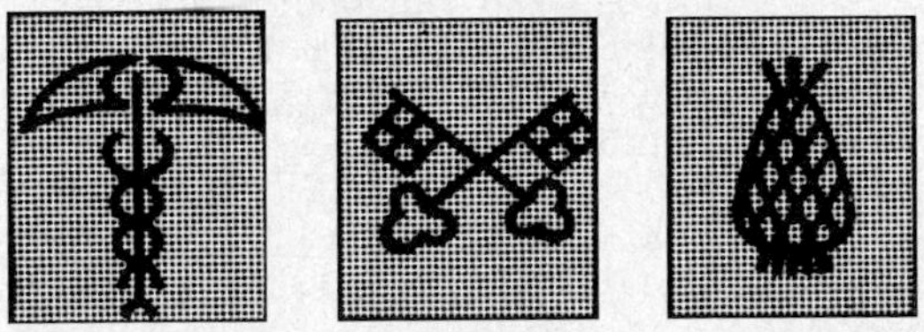

Watermarks of Uruguay, Vatican City and Jamaica

WARNING: Some inks used in the photogravure process dissolve in watermark fluids (Please see the section on Soluble Printing Inks). Also, see "chalky paper."

Watermarks may be found normal, reversed, inverted, reversed and inverted, sideways or diagonal, as seen from the back of the stamp. The relationship of watermark to stamp design depends on the position of the printing plates or how paper is fed through the press. On machine-made paper, watermarks normally are read from right to left. The design is repeated closely throughout the sheet in a "multiple-watermark design." In a "sheet watermark," the design appears only once on the sheet, but extends over many stamps. Individual stamps may carry only a small fraction or none of the watermark.

"Marginal watermarks" occur in the margins of sheets or panes of stamps. They occur on the outside border of paper (ostensibly outside the area where stamps are to be printed). A large row of letters may spell the name of the country or the manufacturer of the paper, or a border of lines may appear. Careless press feeding may cause parts of these letters and/or lines to show on stamps of the outer row of a pane.

Soluble Printing Inks

WARNING: Most stamp colors are permanent; that is, they are not seriously affected by short-term exposure to light or water. Many colors, especially of modern inks, fade from excessive exposure to light. There are stamps printed with inks that dissolve easily in water or in fluids used to detect watermarks. Use of these inks was intentional to prevent the removal of cancellations. Water affects all aniline inks, those on so-called safety paper and some photogravure printings - all such inks are known as fugitive colors. *Removal from paper of such stamps requires care and alternatives to traditional soaking.*

Separation

"Separation" is the general term used to describe methods used to separate stamps. The three standard forms currently in use are perforating, rouletting and die-cutting. These methods are done during the stamp production process, after printing. Sometimes these methods are done on-press or sometimes as a separate step. The earliest issues, such as the 1840 Penny Black of Great Britain (Scott 1), did not have any means provided for separation. It was expected the stamps would be cut apart with scissors or folded and torn. These are examples of imperforate stamps. Many stamps were first issued in imperforate formats and were later issued with perforations. Therefore, care must be observed in buying single imperforate stamps to be certain they were issued imperforate and are not perforated copies that have been altered by having the perforations trimmed away. Stamps issued imperforate usually are valued as singles. However, imperforate varieties of normally perforated stamps should be collected in pairs or larger pieces as indisputable evidence of their imperforate character.

PERFORATION

The chief style of separation of stamps, and the one that is in almost universal use today, is perforating. By this process, paper between the stamps is cut away in a line of holes, usually round, leaving little bridges of paper between the stamps to hold them together. Some types of perforation, such as hyphen-hole perfs, can be confused with roulettes, but a close visual inspection reveals that paper has been removed. The little perforation bridges, which project from the stamp when it is torn from the pane, are called the teeth of the perforation.

As the size of the perforation is sometimes the only way to differentiate between two otherwise identical stamps, it is necessary to be able to accurately measure and describe them. This is done with a perforation gauge, usually a ruler-like device that has dots or graduated lines to show how many perforations may be counted in the space of two centimeters. Two centimeters is the space universally adopted in which to measure perforations.

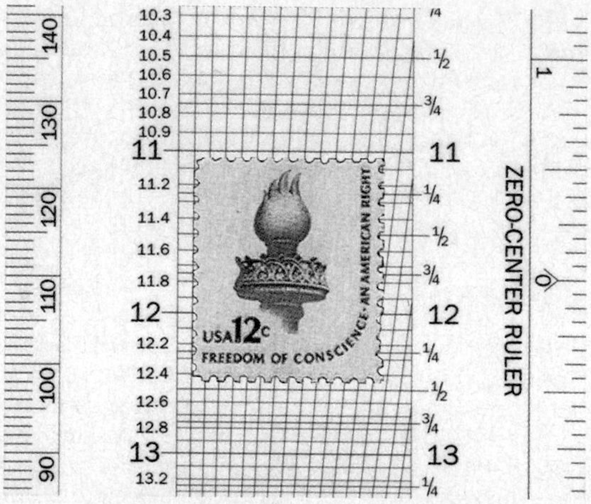

Perforation gauge

To measure a stamp, run it along the gauge until the dots on it fit exactly into the perforations of the stamp. If you are using a graduated-line perforation gauge, simply slide the stamp along the surface until the lines on the gauge perfectly project from the center of the bridges or holes. The number to the side of the line of dots or lines that fit the stamp's perforation is the measurement. For example, an "11" means that 11 perforations fit between two centimeters. The description of the stamp therefore is "perf. 11." If the gauge of the perforations on the top and bottom of a stamp differs from that on the sides, the result is what is known as *compound perforations*. In measuring compound perforations, the gauge at top and bottom is always given first, then the sides. Thus, a stamp that measures 11 at top and bottom and 10½ at the sides is "perf. 11 x 10½." See U.S. Scott 632-642 for examples of compound perforations.

Stamps also are known with perforations different on three or all four sides. Descriptions of such items are clockwise, beginning with the top of the stamp.

A perforation with small holes and teeth close together is a "fine perforation." One with large holes and teeth far apart is a "coarse perforation." Holes that are jagged, rather than clean-cut, are "rough perforations." *Blind perforations* are the slight impressions left by the perforating pins if they fail to puncture the paper. Multiples of stamps showing blind perforations may command a slight premium over normally perforated stamps.

The term *syncopated perfs* describes intentional irregularities in the perforations. The earliest form was used by the Netherlands from 1925-33, where holes were omitted to create distinctive patterns. Beginning in 1992, Great Britain has used an oval perforation to help prevent counterfeiting. Several other countries have started using the oval perfs or other syncopated perf patterns.

A new type of perforation, still primarily used for postal stationery, is known as microperfs. Microperfs are tiny perforations (in some cases hundreds of holes per two centimeters) that allows items to be intentionally separated very easily, while not accidentally breaking apart as easily as standard perforations. These are not currently measured or differentiated by size, as are standard perforations.

perce en arc

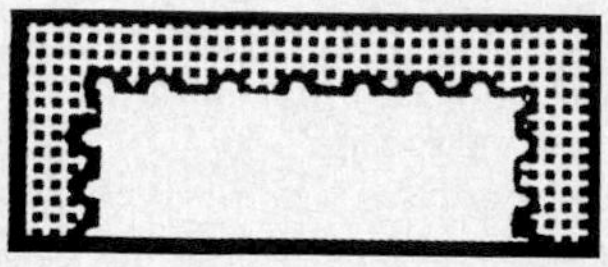

perce en lignes

perce en points

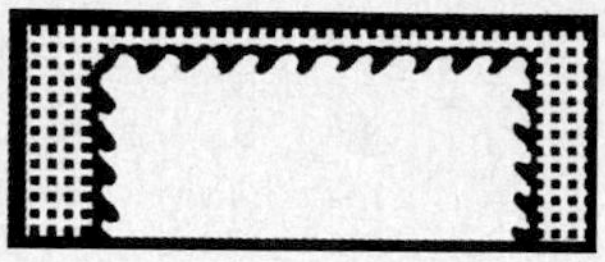

oblique roulette

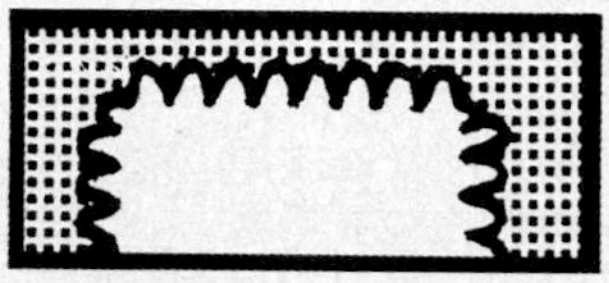

perce en scie

perce serpentin

ROULETTING

In rouletting, the stamp paper is cut partly or wholly through, with no paper removed. In perforating, some paper is removed. Rouletting derives its name from the French roulette, a spur-like wheel. As the wheel is rolled over the paper, each point makes a small cut. The number of cuts made in a two-centimeter space determines the gauge of the roulette, just as the number of perforations in two centimeters determines the gauge of the perforation.

The shape and arrangement of the teeth on the wheels varies. Various roulette types generally carry French names:

Perce en lignes - rouletted in lines. The paper receives short, straight cuts in lines. This is the most common type of rouletting. See Mexico Scott 500.

Perce en points - pin-rouletted or pin-perfed. This differs from a small perforation because no paper is removed, although round, equidistant holes are pricked through the paper. See Mexico Scott 242-256.

Perce en arc and *perce en scie* - pierced in an arc or saw-toothed designs, forming half circles or small triangles. See Hanover (German States) Scott 25-29.

Perce en serpentin - serpentine roulettes. The cuts form a serpentine or wavy line. See Brunswick (German States) Scott 13-18.

Once again, no paper is removed by these processes, leaving the stamps easily separated, but closely attached.

DIE-CUTTING

The third major form of stamp separation is die-cutting. This is a method where a die in the pattern of separation is created that later cuts the stamp paper in a stroke motion. Although some standard stamps bear die-cut perforations, this process is primarily used for self-adhesive postage stamps. Die-cutting can appear in straight lines, such as U.S. Scott 2522, shapes, such as U.S. Scott 1551, or imitating the appearance of perforations, such as New Zealand Scott 935A and 935B.

Printing Processes

ENGRAVING (Intaglio, Line-engraving, Etching)

Master die — The initial operation in the process of line engraving is making the master die. The die is a small, flat block of softened steel upon which the stamp design is recess engraved in reverse.

Master die

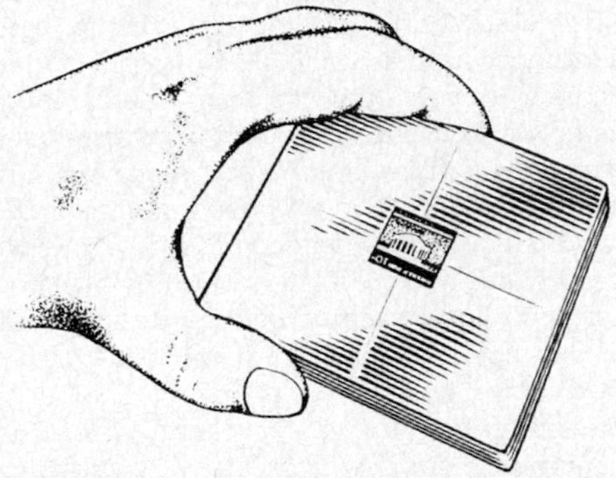

Photographic reduction of the original art is made to the appropriate size. It then serves as a tracing guide for the initial outline of the design. The engraver lightly traces the design on the steel with his graver, then slowly works the design until it is completed. At various points during the engraving process, the engraver hand-inks the die and makes an impression to check his progress. These are known as progressive die proofs. After completion of the engraving, the die is hardened to withstand the stress and pressures of later transfer operations.

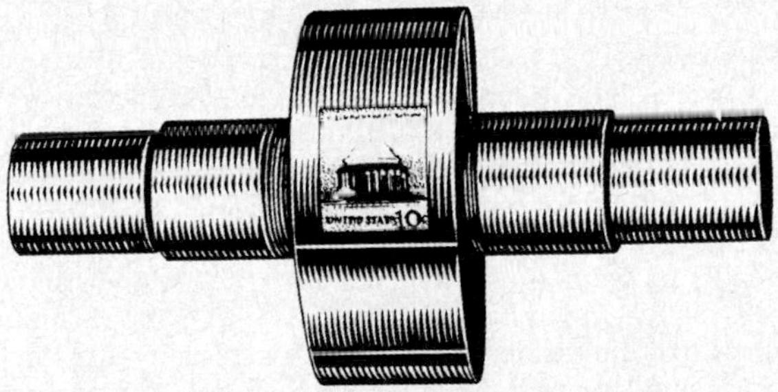

Transfer roll

Transfer roll — Next is production of the transfer roll that, as the name implies, is the medium used to transfer the subject from the master die to the printing plate. A blank roll of soft steel, mounted on a mandrel, is placed under the bearers of the transfer press to allow it to roll freely on its axis. The hardened die is placed on the bed of the press and the face of the transfer roll is applied to the die, under pressure. The bed or the roll is then rocked back and forth under increasing pressure, until the soft steel of the roll is forced into every engraved line of the die. The resulting impression on the roll is known as a "relief" or a "relief transfer." The engraved image is now positive in appearance and stands out from the steel. After the required number of reliefs are "rocked in," the soft steel transfer roll is hardened.

Different flaws may occur during the relief process. A defective relief may occur during the rocking in process because of a minute piece of foreign material lodging on the die, or some other cause. Imperfections in the steel of the transfer roll may result in a breaking away of parts of the design. This is known as a relief break, which will show up on finished stamps as small, unprinted areas. If a damaged relief remains in use, it will transfer a repeating defect to the plate. Deliberate alterations of reliefs sometimes occur. "Altered reliefs" designate these changed conditions.

Plate — The final step in pre-printing production is the making of the printing plate. A flat piece of soft steel replaces the die on the bed of the transfer press. One of the reliefs on the transfer roll is positioned over this soft steel. Position, or layout, dots determine the correct position on the plate. The dots have been lightly marked on the plate in advance. After the correct position of the relief is determined, the design is rocked in by following the same method used in making the transfer roll. The difference is that this time the image is being transferred from the transfer roll, rather than to it. Once the design is entered on the plate, it appears in reverse and is recessed. There are as many transfers entered on the plate as there are subjects printed on the sheet of stamps. It is during this process that double and shifted transfers occur, as well as re-entries. These are the result of improperly entered images that have not been properly burnished out prior to rocking in a new image.

Modern siderography processes, such as those used by the U.S. Bureau of Engraving and Printing, involve an automated form of rocking designs in on preformed cylindrical printing sleeves. The same process also allows for easier removal and re-entry of worn images right on the sleeve.

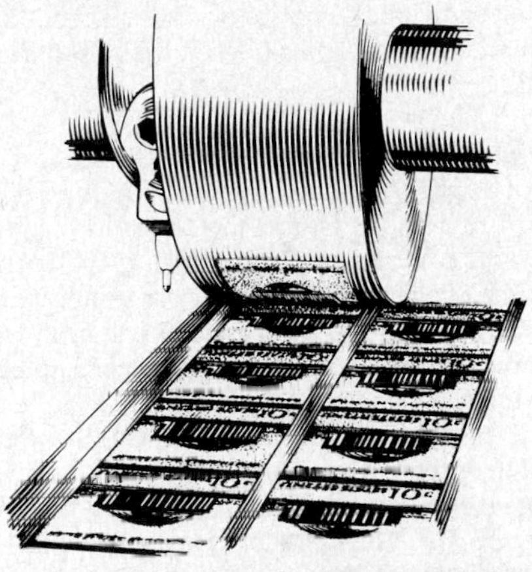

Transferring the design to the plate

Following the entering of the required transfers on the plate, the position dots, layout dots and lines, scratches and other markings generally are burnished out. Added at this time by the siderographer are any required *guide lines, plate numbers* or other *marginal markings.* The plate is then hand-inked and a proof impression is taken. This is known as a plate proof. If the impression is approved, the plate is machined for fitting onto the press, is hardened and sent to the plate vault ready for use.

On press, the plate is inked and the surface is automatically wiped clean, leaving ink only in the recessed lines. Paper is then forced under pressure into the engraved recessed lines, thereby receiving the ink. Thus, the ink lines on engraved stamps are slightly raised, and slight depressions (debossing) occur on the back of the stamp. Prior to the advent of modern high-speed presses and more advanced ink formulations, paper had to be dampened before receiving the ink. This sometimes led to uneven shrinkage by the time the stamps were perforated, resulting in improperly perforated stamps, or misperfs. Newer presses use drier paper, thus both *wet* and *dry printings* exist on some stamps.

Rotary Press — Until 1914, only flat plates were used to print engraved stamps. Rotary press printing was introduced in 1914, and slowly spread. Some countries still use flat-plate printing.

After approval of the plate proof, older *rotary press plates* require additional machining. They are curved to fit the press cylinder. "Gripper slots" are cut into the back of each plate to receive the "grippers," which hold the plate securely on the press. The plate is then hardened. Stamps printed from these bent rotary press plates are longer or wider than the same stamps printed from flat-plate presses. The stretching of the plate during the curving process is what causes this distortion.

Re-entry — To execute a re-entry on a flat plate, the transfer roll is re-applied to the plate, often at some time after its first use on the press. Worn-out designs can be resharpened by carefully burnishing out the original image and re-entering it from the transfer roll. If the original impression has not been sufficiently removed and the transfer roll is not precisely in line with the remaining impression, the resulting double transfer will make the re-entry obvious. If the registration is true, a re-entry may be difficult or impossible to distinguish. Sometimes a stamp printed from a successful re-entry is identified by having a much sharper and clearer impression than its neighbors. With the advent of rotary presses, post-press re-entries were not possible. After a plate was curved for the rotary press, it was impossible to make a re-entry. This is because the plate had already been bent once (with the design distorted).

However, with the introduction of the previously mentioned modern-style siderography machines, entries are made to the preformed cylindrical printing sleeve. Such sleeves are dechromed and softened. This allows individual images to be burnished out and re-entered on the curved sleeve. The sleeve is then rechromed, resulting in longer press life.

Double Transfer — This is a description of the condition of a transfer on a plate that shows evidence of a duplication of all, or a portion of the design. It usually is the result of the changing of the registration between the transfer roll and the plate during the rocking in of the original entry. Double transfers also occur when only a portion of the design has been rocked in and improper positioning is noted. If the worker elected not to burnish out the partial or completed design, a strong double transfer will occur for part or all of the design.

It sometimes is necessary to remove the original transfer from a plate and repeat the process a second time. If the finished re-worked image shows traces of the original impression, attributable to incomplete burnishing, the result is a partial double transfer.

With the modern automatic machines mentioned previously, double transfers are all but impossible to create. Those partially doubled images on stamps printed from such sleeves are more than likely re-entries, rather than true double transfers.

Re-engraved — Alterations to a stamp design are sometimes necessary after some stamps have been printed. In some cases, either the original die or the actual printing plate may have its "temper" drawn (softened), and the design will be re-cut. The resulting impressions from such a re-engraved die or plate may differ slightly from the original issue, and are known as "re-engraved." If the alteration was made to the master die, all future printings will be consistently different from the original. If alterations were made to the printing plate, each altered stamp on the plate will be slightly different from each other, allowing specialists to reconstruct a complete printing plate.

Dropped Transfers — If an impression from the transfer roll has not been properly placed, a dropped transfer may occur. The final stamp image will appear obviously out of line with its neighbors.

Short Transfer — Sometimes a transfer roll is not rocked its entire length when entering a transfer onto a plate. As a result, the finished transfer on the plate fails to show the complete design, and the finished stamp will have an incomplete design printed. This is known as a "short transfer." U.S. Scott No. 8 is a good example of a short transfer.

TYPOGRAPHY (Letterpress, Surface Printing, Flexography, Dry Offset, High Etch)

Although the word "Typography" is obsolete as a term describing a printing method, it was the accepted term throughout the first century of postage stamps. Therefore, appropriate Scott listings in this catalogue refer to typographed stamps. The current term for this form of printing, however, is "letterpress."

As it relates to the production of postage stamps, letterpress printing is the reverse of engraving. Rather than having recessed areas trap the ink and deposit it on paper, only the raised areas of the design are inked. This is comparable to the type of printing seen by inking and using an ordinary rubber stamp. Letterpress includes all printing where the design is above the surface area, whether it is wood, metal or, in some instances, hardened rubber or polymer plastic.

For most letterpress-printed stamps, the engraved master is made in much the same manner as for engraved stamps. In this instance, however, an additional step is needed. The design is transferred to another surface before being transferred to the transfer roll. In this way, the transfer roll has a recessed stamp design, rather than one done in relief. This makes the printing areas on the final plate raised, or relief areas.

For less-detailed stamps of the 19th century, the area on the die not used as a printing surface was cut away, leaving the surface area raised. The original die was then reproduced by stereotyping or electrotyping. The resulting electrotypes were assembled in the required number and format of the desired sheet of stamps. The plate used in printing the stamps was an electroplate of these assembled electrotypes.

Once the final letterpress plates are created, ink is applied to the raised surface and the pressure of the press transfers the ink impression to the paper. In contrast to engraving, the fine lines of letterpress are impressed on the surface of the stamp, leaving a debossed surface. When viewed from the back (as on a typewritten page), the corresponding line work on the stamp will be raised slightly (embossed) above the surface.

PHOTOGRAVURE (Gravure, Rotogravure, Heliogravure)

In this process, the basic principles of photography are applied to a chemically sensitized metal plate, rather than photographic paper. The design is transferred photographically to the plate through a halftone, or dot-matrix screen, breaking the reproduction into tiny dots. The plate is treated chemically and the dots form depressions, called cells, of varying depths and diameters, depending on the degrees of shade in the design. Then, like engraving, ink is applied to the plate and the surface is wiped clean. This leaves ink in the tiny cells that is lifted out and deposited on the paper when it is pressed against the plate.

Gravure is most often used for multicolored stamps, generally using the three primary colors (red, yellow and blue) and black. By varying the dot matrix pattern and density of these colors, virtually any color can be reproduced. A typical full-color gravure stamp will be created from four printing cylinders (one for each color). The original multicolored image will have been photographically separated into its component colors.

Modern gravure printing may use computer-generated dot-matrix screens, and modern plates may be of various types including metal-coated plastic. The catalogue designation of Photogravure (or "Photo") covers any of these older and more modern gravure methods of printing.

For examples of the first photogravure stamps printed (1914), see Bavaria Scott 94-114.

LITHOGRAPHY (Offset Lithography, Stone Lithography, Dilitho, Planography, Collotype)

The principle that oil and water do not mix is the basis for lithography. The stamp design is drawn by hand or transferred from engraving to the surface of a lithographic stone or metal plate in a greasy (oily) substance. This oily substance holds the ink, which will later be transferred to the paper. The stone (or plate) is wet with an acid fluid, causing it to repel the printing ink in all areas not covered by the greasy substance.

Transfer paper is used to transfer the design from the original stone or plate. A series of duplicate transfers are grouped and, in turn, transferred to the final printing plate.

Photolithography — The application of photographic processes to lithography. This process allows greater flexibility of design, related to use of halftone screens combined with line work. Unlike photogravure or engraving, this process can allow large, solid areas to be printed.

Offset — A refinement of the lithographic process. A rubber-covered blanket cylinder takes the impression from the inked lithographic plate. From the "blanket" the impression is *offset* or transferred to the paper. Greater flexibility and speed are the principal reasons offset printing has largely displaced lithography. The term "lithography" covers both processes, and results are almost identical.

EMBOSSED (Relief) Printing

Embossing, not considered one of the four main printing types, is a method in which the design first is sunk into the metal of the die. Printing is done against a yielding platen, such as leather or linoleum. The platen is forced into the depression of the die, thus forming the design on the paper in relief. This process is often used for metallic inks.

Embossing may be done without color (see Sardinia Scott 4-6); with color printed around the embossed area (see Great Britain Scott 5 and most U.S. envelopes); and with color in exact registration with the embossed subject (see Canada Scott 656-657).

HOLOGRAMS

For objects to appear as holograms on stamps, a model exactly the same size as it is to appear on the hologram must be created. Rather than using photographic film to capture the image, holography records an image on a photoresist material. In processing, chemicals eat away at certain exposed areas, leaving a pattern of constructive and destructive interference. When the photoresist is developed, the result is a pattern of uneven ridges that acts as a mold. This mold is then coated with metal, and the resulting form is used to press copies in much the same way phonograph records are produced.

A typical reflective hologram used for stamps consists of a reproduction of the uneven patterns on a plastic film that is applied to a reflective background, usually a silver or gold foil. Light is reflected off the background through the film, making the pattern present on the film visible. Because of the uneven pattern of the film, the viewer will perceive the objects in their proper three-dimensional relationships with appropriate brightness.

The first hologram on a stamp was produced by Austria in 1988 (Scott 1441).

FOIL APPLICATION

A modern technique of applying color to stamps involves the application of metallic foil to the stamp paper. A pattern of foil is applied to the stamp paper by use of a stamping die. The foil usually is flat, but it may be textured. Canada Scott 1735 has three different foil applications in pearl, bronze and gold. The gold foil was textured using a chemical-etch copper embossing die. The printing of this stamp also involved two-color offset lithography plus embossing.

THERMOGRAPHY

In the 1990s stamps began to be enhanced with thermographic printing. In this process, a powdered polymer is applied over a sheet that has just been printed. The powder adheres to ink that lacks drying or hardening agents and does not adhere to areas where the ink has these agents. The excess powder is removed and the sheet is briefly heated to melt the powder. The melted powder solidifies after cooling, producing a raised, shiny effect on the stamps. See Scott New Caledonia C239-C240.

COMBINATION PRINTINGS

Sometimes two or even three printing methods are combined in producing stamps. In these cases, such as Austria Scott 933 or Canada 1735 (described in the preceding paragraph), the multiple-printing technique can be determined by studying the individual characteristics of each printing type. A few stamps, such as Singapore Scott 684-684A, combine as many as three of the four major printing types (lithography, engraving and typography). When this is done it often indicates the incorporation of security devices against counterfeiting.

INK COLORS

Inks or colored papers used in stamp printing often are of mineral origin, although there are numerous examples of organic-based pigments. As a general rule, organic-based pigments are far more subject to varieties and change than those of mineral-based origin.

The appearance of any given color on a stamp may be affected by many aspects, including printing variations, light, color of paper, aging and chemical alterations.

Numerous printing variations may be observed. Heavier pressure or inking will cause a more intense color, while slight interruptions in the ink feed or lighter impressions will cause a lighter appearance. Stamps printed in the same color by water-based and solvent-based inks can differ significantly in appearance. This affects several stamps in the U.S. Prominent Americans series. Hand-mixed ink formulas (primarily from the 19th century) produced under different conditions (humidity and temperature) account for notable color variations in early printings of the same stamp (see U.S. Scott 248-250, 279B, for example). Different sources of pigment can also result in significant differences in color.

Light exposure and aging are closely related in the way they affect stamp color. Both eventually break down the ink and fade colors, so that a carefully kept stamp may differ significantly in color from an identical copy that has been exposed to light. If stamps are exposed to light either intentionally or accidentally, their colors can be faded or completely changed in some cases.

Papers of different quality and consistency used for the same stamp printing may affect color appearance. Most pelure papers, for example, show a richer color when compared with wove or laid papers. See Russia Scott 181a, for an example of this effect.

The very nature of the printing processes can cause a variety of differences in shades or hues of the same stamp. Some of these shades are scarcer than others, and are of particular interest to the advanced collector.

Luminescence

All forms of tagged stamps fall under the general category of luminescence. Within this broad category is fluorescence, dealing with forms of tagging visible under longwave ultraviolet light, and phosphorescence, which deals with tagging visible only under shortwave light. Phosphorescence leaves an afterglow and fluorescence does not. These treated stamps show up in a range of different colors when exposed to UV light. The differing wavelengths of the light activates the tagging material, making it glow in various colors that usually serve different mail processing purposes.

Intentional tagging is a post-World War II phenomenon, brought about by the increased literacy rate and rapidly growing mail volume. It was one of several answers to the problem of the need for more automated mail processes. Early tagged stamps served the purpose of triggering machines to separate different types of mail. A natural outgrowth was to also use the signal to trigger machines that faced all envelopes the same way and canceled them.

Tagged stamps come in many different forms. Some tagged stamps have luminescent shapes or images imprinted on them as a form of security device. Others have blocks (United States), stripes, frames (South Africa and Canada), overall coatings (United States), bars (Great Britain and Canada) and many other types. Some types of tagging are even mixed in with the pigmented printing ink (Australia Scott 366, Netherlands Scott 478 and U.S. Scott 1359 and 2443).

The means of applying taggant to stamps differs as much as the intended purposes for the stamps. The most common form of tagging is a coating applied to the surface of the printed stamp. Since the taggant ink is frequently invisible except under UV light, it does not interfere with the appearance of the stamp. Another common application is the use of phosphored papers. In this case the paper itself either has a coating of taggant applied before the stamp is printed, has taggant applied during the papermaking process (incorporating it into the fibers), or has the taggant mixed into the coating of the paper. The latter method, among others, is currently in use in the United States.

Many countries now use tagging in various forms to either expedite mail handling or to serve as a printing security device against counterfeiting. Following the introduction of tagged stamps for public use in 1959 by Great Britain, other countries have steadily joined the parade. Among those are Germany (1961); Canada and Denmark (1962); United States, Australia, France and Switzerland (1963); Belgium and Japan (1966); Sweden and Norway (1967); Italy (1968); and Russia (1969). Since then, many other countries have begun using forms of tagging, including Brazil, China, Czechoslovakia, Hong Kong, Guatemala, Indonesia, Israel, Lithuania, Luxembourg, Netherlands, Penrhyn Islands, Portugal, St. Vincent, Singapore, South Africa, Spain and Sweden to name a few.

In some cases, including United States, Canada, Great Britain and Switzerland, stamps were released both with and without tagging. Many of these were released during each country's experimental period. Tagged and untagged versions are listed for the aforementioned countries and are noted in some other countries' listings. For at least a few stamps, the experimentally tagged version is worth far more than its untagged counterpart, such as the 1963 experimental tagged version of France Scott 1024.

In some cases, luminescent varieties of stamps were inadvertently created. Several Russian stamps, for example, sport highly fluorescent ink that was not intended as a form of tagging. Older stamps, such as early U.S. postage dues, can be positively identified by the use of UV light, since the organic ink used has become slightly fluorescent over time. Other stamps, such as Austria Scott 70a-82a (varnish bars) and Obock Scott 46-64 (printed quadrille lines), have become fluorescent over time.

Various fluorescent substances have been added to paper to make it appear brighter. These optical brightners, as they are known, greatly affect the appearance of the stamp under UV light. The brightest of these is known as Hi-Brite paper. These paper varieties are beyond the scope of the Scott Catalogue.

Shortwave UV light also is used extensively in expertizing, since each form of paper has its own fluorescent characteristics that are impossible to perfectly match. It is therefore a simple matter to detect filled thins, added perforation teeth and other alterations that involve the addition of paper. UV light also is used to examine stamps that have had cancels chemically removed and for other purposes as well.

Gum

The Illustrated Gum Chart in the first part of this introduction shows and defines various types of gum condition. Because gum condition has an important impact on the value of unused stamps, we recommend studying this chart and the accompanying text carefully.

The gum on the back of a stamp may be shiny, dull, smooth, rough, dark, white, colored or tinted. Most stamp gumming adhesives use gum arabic or dextrine as a base. Certain polymers such as polyvinyl alcohol (PVA) have been used extensively since World War II.

The *Scott Standard Postage Stamp Catalogue* does not list items by types of gum. The *Scott Specialized Catalogue of United States Stamps and Covers* does differentiate among some types of gum for certain issues.

Reprints of stamps may have gum differing from the original issues. In addition, some countries have used different gum formulas for different seasons. These adhesives have different properties that may become more apparent over time.

Many stamps have been issued without gum, and the catalogue will note this fact. See, for example, United States Scott 40-47. Sometimes, gum may have been removed to preserve the stamp. Germany Scott B68, for example, has a highly acidic gum that eventually destroys the stamps. This item is valued in the catalogue with gum removed.

Reprints and Reissues

These are impressions of stamps (usually obsolete) made from the original plates or stones. If they are valid for postage and reproduce obsolete issues (such as U.S. Scott 102-111), the stamps are *reissues.* If they are from current issues, they are designated as *second, third,* etc., *printing*. If designated for a particular purpose, they are called *special printings*.

When special printings are not valid for postage, but are made from original dies and plates by authorized persons, they are *official reprints. Private reprints* are made from the original plates and dies by private hands. An example of a private reprint is that of the 1871-1932 reprints made from the original die of the 1845 New Haven, Conn., postmaster's provisional. *Official reproductions* or imitations are made from new dies and plates by government authorization. Scott will list those reissues that are valid for postage if they differ significantly from the original printing.

The U.S. government made special printings of its first postage stamps in 1875. Produced were official imitations of the first two stamps (listed as Scott 3-4), reprints of the demonetized pre-1861 issues (Scott 40-47) and reissues of the 1861 stamps, the 1869 stamps and the then-current 1875 denominations. Even though the official imitations and the reprints were not valid for postage, Scott lists all of these U.S. special printings.

Most reprints or reissues differ slightly from the original stamp in some characteristic, such as gum, paper, perforation, color or watermark. Sometimes the details are followed so meticulously that only a student of that specific stamp is able to distinguish the reprint or reissue from the original.

Remainders and Canceled to Order

Some countries sell their stock of old stamps when a new issue replaces them. To avoid postal use, the *remainders* usually are canceled with a punch hole, a heavy line or bar, or a more-or-less regular-looking cancellation. The most famous merchant of remainders was Nicholas F. Seebeck. In the 1880s and 1890s, he arranged printing contracts between the Hamilton Bank Note Co., of which he was a director, and several Central and South American countries. The contracts provided that the plates and all remainders of the yearly issues became the property of Hamilton. Seebeck saw to it that ample stock remained. The "Seebecks," both remainders and reprints, were standard packet fillers for decades.

Some countries also issue stamps *canceled-to-order (CTO),* either in sheets with original gum or stuck onto pieces of paper or envelopes and canceled. Such CTO items generally are worth less than postally used stamps. In cases where the CTO material is far more prevalent in the marketplace than postally used examples, the catalogue value relates to the CTO examples, with postally used examples noted as premium items. Most CTOs can be detected by the presence of gum. However, as the CTO practice goes back at least to 1885, the gum inevitably has been soaked off some stamps so they could pass as postally used. The normally applied postmarks usually differ slightly from standard postmarks, and specialists are able to tell the difference. When applied individually to envelopes by philatelically minded persons, CTO material is known as *favor canceled* and generally sells at large discounts.

Cinderellas and Facsimiles

Cinderella is a catch-all term used by stamp collectors to describe phantoms, fantasies, bogus items, municipal issues, exhibition seals, local revenues, transportation stamps, labels, poster stamps and many other types of items. Some cinderella collectors include in their collections local postage issues, telegraph stamps, essays and proofs, forgeries and counterfeits.

A *fantasy* is an adhesive created for a nonexistent stamp-issuing authority. Fantasy items range from imaginary countries (Occusi-Ambeno, Kingdom of Sedang, Principality of Trinidad or Torres Straits), to non-existent locals (Winans City Post), or nonexistent transportation lines (McRobish & Co.'s Acapulco-San Francisco Line).

On the other hand, if the entity exists and could have issued stamps (but did not) or was known to have issued other stamps, the items are considered *bogus* stamps. These would include the Mormon postage stamps of Utah, S. Allan Taylor's Guatemala and Paraguay inventions, the propaganda issues for the South Moluccas and the adhesives of the Page & Keyes local post of Boston.

Phantoms is another term for both fantasy and bogus issues.

Facsimiles are copies or imitations made to represent original stamps, but which do not pretend to be originals. A catalogue illustration is such a facsimile. Illustrations from the Moens catalogue of the last century were occasionally colored and passed off as stamps. Since the beginning of stamp collecting, facsimiles have been made for collectors as space fillers or for reference. They often carry the word "facsimile," "falsch" (German), "sanko" or "mozo" (Japanese), or "faux" (French) overprinted on the face or stamped on the back. Unfortunately, over the years a number of these items have had fake cancels applied over the facsimile notation and have been passed off as genuine.

Forgeries and Counterfeits

Forgeries and counterfeits have been with philately virtually from the beginning of stamp production. Over time, the terminology for the two has been used interchangeably. Although both forgeries and counterfeits are reproductions of stamps, the purposes behind their creation differ considerably.

Among specialists there is an increasing movement to more specifically define such items. Although there is no universally accepted terminology, we feel the following definitions most closely mirror the items and their purposes as they are currently defined.

Forgeries (also often referred to as *Counterfeits*) are reproductions of genuine stamps that have been created to defraud collectors. Such spurious items first appeared on the market around 1860, and most old-time collections contain one or more. Many are crude and easily spotted, but some can deceive experts.

An important supplier of these early philatelic forgeries was the Hamburg printer Gebruder Spiro. Many others with reputations in this craft included S. Allan Taylor, George Hussey, James Chute, George Forune, Benjamin & Sarpy, Julius Goldner, E. Oneglia and L.H. Mercier. Among the noted 20th-century forgers were Francois Fournier, Jean Sperati and the prolific Raoul DeThuin.

Forgeries may be complete replications, or they may be genuine stamps altered to resemble a scarcer (and more valuable) type. Most forgeries, particularly those of rare stamps, are worth only a small fraction of the value of a genuine example, but a few types, created by some of the most notable forgers, such as Sperati, can be worth as much or more than the genuine. Fraudulently produced copies are known of most classic rarities and many medium-priced stamps.

In addition to rare stamps, large numbers of common 19th- and early 20th-century stamps were forged to supply stamps to the early packet trade. Many can still be easily found. Few new philatelic forgeries have appeared in recent decades. Successful imitation of well-engraved work is virtually impossible. It has proven far easier to produce a fake by altering a genuine stamp than to duplicate a stamp completely.

Counterfeit (also often referred to as *Postal Counterfeit* or *Postal Forgery*) is the term generally applied to reproductions of stamps that have been created to defraud the government of revenue. Such items usually are created at the time a stamp is current and, in some cases, are hard to detect. Because most counterfeits are seized when the perpetrator is captured, postal counterfeits, particularly used on cover, are usually worth much more than a genuine example to specialists. The first postal counterfeit was of Spain's 4-cuarto carmine of 1854 (the real one is Scott 25). Apparently, the counterfeiters were not satisfied with their first version, which is now very scarce, and they soon created an engraved counterfeit, which is common. Postal counterfeits quickly followed in Austria, Naples, Sardinia and the Roman States. They have since been created in many other countries as well, including the United States.

An infamous counterfeit to defraud the government is the 1-shilling Great Britain "Stock Exchange" forgery of 1872, used on telegraph forms at the exchange that year. The stamp escaped detection until a stamp dealer noticed it in 1898.

Fakes

Fakes are genuine stamps altered in some way to make them more desirable. One student of this part of stamp collecting has estimated that by the 1950s more than 30,000 varieties of fakes were known. That number has grown greatly since then. The widespread existence of fakes makes it important for stamp collectors to study their philatelic holdings and use relevant literature. Likewise, collectors should buy from reputable dealers who guarantee their stamps and make full and prompt refunds should a purchased item be declared faked or altered by some mutually agreed-upon authority. Because fakes always have some genuine characteristics, it is not always possible to obtain unanimous agreement among experts regarding specific items. These students may change their opinions as philatelic knowledge increases. More than 80 percent of all fakes on the philatelic market today are regummed, reperforated (or perforated for the first time), or bear forged overprints, surcharges or cancellations.

Stamps can be chemically treated to alter or eliminate colors. For example, a pale rose stamp can be re-colored to resemble a blue shade of high market value. In other cases, treated stamps can be made to resemble missing color varieties. Designs may be changed by painting, or a stroke or a dot added or bleached out to turn an ordinary variety into a seemingly scarcer stamp. Part of a stamp can be bleached and reprinted in a different version, achieving an inverted center or frame. Margins can be added or repairs done so deceptively that the stamps move from the "repaired" into the "fake" category.

Fakers have not left the backs of the stamps untouched either. They may create false watermarks, add fake grills or press out genuine grills. A thin India paper proof may be glued onto a thicker backing to create the appearance an issued stamp, or a proof printed on cardboard may be shaved down and perforated to resemble a stamp. Silk threads are impressed into paper and stamps have been split so that a rare paper variety is added to an otherwise inexpensive stamp. The most common treatment to the back of a stamp, however, is regumming.

Some in the business of faking stamps have openly advertised fool-proof application of "original gum" to stamps that lack it, although most publications now ban such ads from their pages. It is believed that very few early stamps have survived without being hinged. The large number of never-hinged examples of such earlier material offered for sale thus suggests the widespread extent of regumming activity. Regumming also may be used to hide repairs or thin spots. Dipping the stamp into watermark fluid, or examining it under longwave ultraviolet light often will reveal these flaws.

Fakers also tamper with separations. Ingenious ways to add margins are known. Perforated wide-margin stamps may be falsely represented as imperforate when trimmed. Reperforating is commonly done to create scarce coil or perforation varieties, and to eliminate the naturally occurring straight-edge stamps found in sheet margin positions of many earlier issues. Custom has made straight-edged stamps less desirable. Fakers have obliged by perforating straight-edged stamps so that many are now uncommon, if not rare.

Another fertile field for the faker is that of overprints, surcharges and cancellations. The forging of rare surcharges or overprints began in the 1880s or 1890s. These forgeries are sometimes difficult to detect, but experts have identified almost all. Occasionally, overprints or cancellations are removed to create non-overprinted stamps or seemingly unused items. This is most commonly done by removing a manuscript cancel to make a stamp resemble an unused example. "SPECIMEN" overprints may be removed by scraping and repainting to create non-overprinted varieties. Fakers use inexpensive revenues or pen-canceled stamps to generate unused stamps for further faking by adding other markings. The quartz lamp or UV lamp and a high-powered magnifying glass help to easily detect removed cancellations.

The bigger problem, however, is the addition of overprints, surcharges or cancellations - many with such precision that they are very difficult to ascertain. Plating of the stamps or the overprint can be an important method of detection.

Fake postmarks may range from many spurious fancy cancellations to a host of markings applied to transatlantic covers, to adding normally appearing postmarks to definitives of some countries with stamps that are valued far higher used than unused. With the increased popularity of cover collecting, and the widespread interest in postal history, a fertile new field for fakers has come about. Some have tried to create entire covers. Others specialize in adding stamps, tied by fake cancellations, to genuine stampless covers, or replacing less expensive or damaged stamps with more valuable ones. Detailed study of postal rates in effect at the time a cover in question was mailed, including the analysis of each handstamp used during the period, ink analysis and similar techniques, usually will unmask the fraud.

Restoration and Repairs

Scott bases its catalogue values on stamps that are free of defects and otherwise meet the standards set forth earlier in this introduction. Most stamp collectors desire to have the finest copy of an item possible. Even within given grading categories there are variances. This leads to a controversial practice that is not defined in any universal manner: stamp *restoration*.

There are broad differences of opinion about what is permissible when it comes to restoration. Carefully applying a soft eraser to a stamp or cover to remove light soiling is one form of restoration, as is washing a stamp in mild soap and water to clean it. These are fairly accepted forms of restoration. More severe forms of restoration include pressing out creases or removing stains caused by tape. To what degree each of these is acceptable is dependent upon the individual situation. Further along the spectrum is the freshening of a stamp's color by removing oxide build-up or the effects of wax paper left next to stamps shipped to the tropics.

At some point in this spectrum the concept of *repair* replaces that of restoration. Repairs include filling thin spots, mending tears by reweaving or adding a missing perforation tooth. Regumming stamps may have been acceptable as a restoration or repair technique many decades ago, but today it is considered a form of fakery.

Restored stamps may or may not sell at a discount, and it is possible that the value of individual restored items may be enhanced over that of their pre-restoration state. Specific situations dictate the resultant value of such an item. Repaired stamps sell at substantial discounts from the value of sound stamps.

Terminology

Booklets — Many countries have issued stamps in small booklets for the convenience of users. This idea continues to become increasingly popular in many countries. Booklets have been issued in many sizes and forms, often with advertising on the covers, the panes of stamps or on the interleaving.

The panes used in booklets may be printed from special plates or made from regular sheets. All panes from booklets issued by the United States and many from those of other countries contain stamps that are straight edged on the sides, but perforated between. Others are distinguished by orientation of watermark or other identifying features. Any stamp-like unit in the pane, either printed or blank, that is not a postage stamp, is considered to be a *label* in the catalogue listings.

Scott lists and values booklet panes. Modern complete booklets also are listed and valued. Individual booklet panes are listed only when they are not fashioned from existing sheet stamps and, therefore, are identifiable from their sheet stamp counterparts.

Panes usually do not have a used value assigned to them because there is little market activity for used booklet panes, even though many exist used and there is some demand for them.

Cancellations — The marks or obliterations put on stamps by postal authorities to show that they have performed service and to prevent their reuse are known as cancellations. If the marking is made with a pen, it is considered a "pen cancel." When the location of the post office appears in the marking, it is a "town cancellation." A "postmark" is technically any postal marking, but in practice the term generally is applied to a town cancellation with a date. When calling attention to a cause or celebration, the marking is known as a "slogan cancellation." Many other types and styles of cancellations exist, such as duplex, numerals, targets, fancy and others. See also "precancels," below.

Coil Stamps — These are stamps that are issued in rolls for use in dispensers, affixing and vending machines. Those coils of the United States, Canada, Sweden and some other countries are perforated horizontally or vertically only, with the outer edges imperforate. Coil stamps of some countries, such as Great Britain and Germany, are perforated on all four sides and may in some cases be distinguished from their sheet stamp counterparts by watermarks, counting numbers on the reverse or other means.

Covers — Entire envelopes, with or without adhesive postage stamps, that have passed through the mail and bear postal or other markings of philatelic interest are known as covers. Before the introduction of envelopes in about 1840, people folded letters and wrote the address on the outside. Some people covered their letters with an extra sheet of paper on the outside for the address, producing the term "cover." Used airletter sheets, stamped envelopes and other items of postal stationery also are considered covers.

Errors — Stamps that have some major, consistent, unintentional deviation from the normal are considered errors. Errors include, but are not limited to, missing or wrong colors, wrong paper, wrong watermarks, inverted centers or frames on multicolor printing, inverted or missing surcharges or overprints, double impressions, missing perforations, unintentionally omitted tagging and others. Factually wrong or misspelled information, if it appears on all examples of a stamp, are not considered errors in the true sense of the word. They are errors of design. Inconsistent or randomly appearing items, such as misperfs or color shifts, are classified as freaks.

Color-Omitted Errors — This term refers to stamps where a missing color is caused by the complete failure of the printing plate to deliver ink to the stamp paper or any other paper. Generally, this is caused by the printing plate not being engaged on the press or the ink station running dry of ink during printing.

Color-Missing Errors — This term refers to stamps where a color or colors were printed somewhere but do not appear on the finished stamp. There are four different classes of color-missing errors, and the catalog indicates with a two-letter code appended to each such listing what caused the color to be missing. These codes are used only for the United States' color-missing error listings.

FO = A *foldover* of the stamp sheet during printing may block ink from appearing on a stamp. Instead, the color will appear on the back of the foldover (where it might fall on the back of the selvage or perhaps on the back of the stamp or another stamp). FO also will be used in the case of foldunders, where the paper may fold underneath the other stamp paper and the color will print on the platen.

EP = A piece of *extraneous paper* falling across the plate or stamp paper will receive the printed ink. When the extraneous paper is removed, an unprinted portion of stamp paper remains and shows partially or totally missing colors.

CM = A misregistration of the printing plates during printing will result in a *color misregistration*, and such a misregistraion may result in a color not appearing on the finished stamp.

PS = *A perforation shift* after printing may remove a color from the finished stamp. Normally, this will occur on a row of stamps at the edge of the stamp pane.

Measurements – When measurements are given in the Scott catalogues for stamp size, grill size or any other reason, the first measurement given is always for the top and bottom dimension, while the second measurement will be for the sides (just as perforation gauges are measured). Thus, a stamp size of 15mm x 21mm will indicate a vertically oriented stamp 15mm wide at top and bottom, and 21mm tall at the sides. The same principle holds for measuring or counting items such as U.S. grills. A grill count of 22x18 points (B grill) indicates that there are 22 grill points across by 18 grill points down.

Overprints and Surcharges — Overprinting involves applying wording or design elements over an already existing stamp. Overprints can be used to alter the place of use (such as "Canal Zone" on U.S. stamps), to adapt them for a special purpose ("Porto" on Denmark's 1913-20 regular issues for use as postage due stamps, Scott J1-J7) or to commemorate a special occasion (United States Scott 647-648).

A *surcharge* is a form of overprint that changes or restates the face value of a stamp or piece of postal stationery.

Surcharges and overprints may be handstamped, typeset or, occasionally, lithographed or engraved. A few hand-written overprints and surcharges are known.

Personalized Stamps — In 1999, Australia issued stamps with se-tenant labels that could be personalized with pictures of the customer's choice. Other countries quickly followed suit, with some offering to print the selected picture on the stamp itself within a frame that was used exclusively for personalized issues. As the picture used on these stamps or labels vary, listings for such stamps are for any picture within the common frame (or any picture on a se-tenant label), be it a "generic" image or one produced especially for a customer, almost invariably at a premium price.

Precancels — Stamps that are canceled before they are placed in the mail are known as precancels. Precanceling usually is done to expedite the handling of large mailings and generally allow the affected mail pieces to skip certain phases of mail handling.

In the United States, precancellations generally identified the point of origin; that is, the city and state. This information appeared across the face of the stamp, usually centered between parallel lines. More recently, bureau precancels retained the parallel lines, but the city and state designations were dropped. Recent coils have a service inscription that is present on the original printing plate. These show the mail service paid for by the stamp. Since these stamps are not intended to receive further cancellations when used as intended, they are considered precancels. Such items often do not have parallel lines as part of the precancellation.

In France, the abbreviation *Affranchts* in a semicircle together with the word *Postes* is the general form of precancel in use. Belgian precancellations usually appear in a box in which the name of the city appears. Netherlands precancels have the name of the city enclosed between concentric circles, sometimes called a "lifesaver." Precancellations of other countries usually follow these patterns, but may be any arrangement of bars, boxes and city names.

Precancels are listed in the Scott catalogues only if the precancel changes the denomination (Belgium Scott 477-478); if the precanceled stamp is different from the non-precanceled version (such as untagged U.S. precancels); or if the stamp exists only precanceled (France Scott 1096-1099, U.S. Scott 2265).

Proofs and Essays — Proofs are impressions taken from an approved die, plate or stone in which the design and color are the same as the stamp issued to the public. Trial color proofs are impressions taken from approved dies, plates or stones in colors that vary from the final version. An essay is the impression of a design that differs in some way from the issued stamp. "Progressive die proofs" generally are considered to be essays.

Provisionals — These are stamps that are issued on short notice and intended for temporary use pending the arrival of regular issues. They usually are issued to meet such contingencies as changes in government or currency, shortage of necessary postage values or military occupation.

During the 1840s, postmasters in certain American cities issued stamps that were valid only at specific post offices. In 1861, postmasters of the Confederate States also issued stamps with limited validity. Both of these examples are known as "postmaster's provisionals."

Se-tenant — This term refers to an unsevered pair, strip or block of stamps that differ in design, denomination or overprint.

Unless the se-tenant item has a continuous design (see U.S. Scott 1451a, 1694a) the stamps do not have to be in the same order as shown in the catalogue (see U.S. Scott 2158a).

Specimens — The Universal Postal Union required member nations to send samples of all stamps they released into service to the International Bureau in Switzerland. Member nations of the UPU received these specimens as samples of what stamps were valid for postage. Many are overprinted, handstamped or initial-perforated "Specimen," "Canceled" or "Muestra." Some are marked with bars across the denominations (China-Taiwan), punched holes (Czechoslovakia) or back inscriptions (Mongolia).

Stamps distributed to government officials or for publicity purposes, and stamps submitted by private security printers for official approval, also may receive such defacements.

The previously described defacement markings prevent postal use, and all such items generally are known as "specimens."

Tete Beche — This term describes a pair of stamps in which one is upside down in relation to the other. Some of these are the result of intentional sheet arrangements, such as Morocco Scott B10-B11. Others occurred when one or more electrotypes accidentally were placed upside down on the plate, such as Colombia Scott 57a. Separation of the tete-beche stamps, of course, destroys the tete beche variety.

Currency Conversion

Country	Dollar	Pound	S Franc	Yen	HK $	Euro	Cdn $	Aus $
Australia	1.3897	2.0506	1.3908	0.0117	0.1793	1.5161	0.9978	—
Canada	1.3927	2.0551	1.3938	0.0117	0.1797	1.5194	—	1.0022
European Union	0.9166	1.3525	0.9173	0.0077	0.1183	—	0.6581	0.6596
Hong Kong	7.7508	11.437	7.7570	0.0651	—	8.4560	5.5653	5.5773
Japan	119.08	175.71	119.18	—	15.364	129.92	85.503	85.688
Switzerland	0.9992	1.4744	—	0.0084	0.1289	1.0901	0.7175	0.7190
United Kingdom	0.6777	—	0.6782	0.0057	0.0874	0.7394	0.4866	0.4877
United States	—	1.4756	1.0008	0.0084	0.1290	1.0910	0.7180	0.7196

Country	Currency	U.S. $ Equiv.
Cambodia	riel	.0002
Cameroun	Community of French Africa (CFA) franc	.0017
Canada	dollar	.7180
Cape Verde	escudo	.0099
Caribbean Netherlands	US dollar	1.0000
Cayman Islands	dollar	1.2195
Central African Republic	CFA franc	.0017
Chad	CFA franc	.0017
Chile	peso	.0014
China (Taiwan)	dollar	.0302
China (People's Republic)	yuan	.1530
Christmas Island	Australian dollar	.7196
Cocos Island	Australian dollar	.7196
Colombia	peso	.0003
Comoro Islands	franc	.0022
Congo Republic	CFA franc	.0017
Cook Islands	New Zealand dollar	.6755
Costa Rica	colon	.0019
Croatia	kuna	.1427
Curacao	guilder	.5587
Cyprus	euro	1.0910
Czech Republic	koruna	.0403
Denmark	krone	.1461
Djibouti	franc	.0056
Dominica	East Caribbean dollar	.3704
Dominican Republic	peso	.0219
Ecuador	US dollar	1.0000
Egypt	pound	.1277
Equatorial Guinea	CFA franc	.0017
Eritrea	nakfa	.0955
Estonia	euro	1.0910
Ethiopia	birr	.0472
Falkland Islands	pound	1.4756
Faroe Islands	krone	.1461
Fiji	dollar	.4703
Finland	euro	1.0910
Aland Islands	euro	1.0910
France	euro	1.0910
French Polynesia	Community of French Pacific (CFP) franc	.0091
French So. & Antarctic Terr.	euro	1.0910

Source: ***xe.com*** *Jan. 4, 2016. Figures reflect values as of Jan. 4, 2016.*

COMMON DESIGN TYPES

Pictured in this section are issues where one illustration has been used for a number of countries in the Catalogue. Not included in this section are overprinted stamps or those issues which are illustrated in each country. Because the location of Never Hinged breakpoints varies from country to country, some of the values in the listings below will be for unused stamps that were previously hinged.

EUROPA

Europa, 1956

The design symbolizing the cooperation among the six countries comprising the Coal and Steel Community is illustrated in each country.

Belgium	*496-497*
France	*805-806*
Germany	*748-749*
Italy	*715-716*
Luxembourg	*318-320*
Netherlands	*368-369*

Nos. 496-497 (2)	9.00	.70
Nos. 805-806 (2)	6.80	1.10
Nos. 748-749 (2)	7.30	1.20
Nos. 715-716 (2)	11.50	1.25
Nos. 318-320 (3)	102.50	56.35
Nos. 368-369 (2)	72.50	1.75
Set total (13) Stamps	209.60	62.35

Europa, 1958

"E" and Dove — CD1

European Postal Union at the service of European Integration.

1958, Sept. 13

Belgium	527-528
France	889-890
Germany	790-791
Italy	750-751
Luxembourg	341-343
Netherlands	375-376
Saar	317-318

Nos. 527-528 (2)	4.25	.60
Nos. 889-890 (2)	1.65	.55
Nos. 790-791 (2)	3.65	.65
Nos. 750-751 (2)	1.85	.60
Nos. 341-343 (3)	2.35	1.15
Nos. 375-376 (2)	2.50	.75
Nos. 317-318 (2)	1.05	2.30
Set total (15) Stamps	17.30	6.60

Europa, 1959

6-Link Enless Chain — CD2

1959, Sept. 19

Belgium	536-537
France	929-930
Germany	805-806
Italy	791-792
Luxembourg	354-355
Netherlands	379-380

Nos. 536-537 (2)	1.55	.60
Nos. 929-930 (2)	1.85	.90
Nos. 805-806 (2)	1.55	.65
Nos. 791-792 (2)	.80	.50
Nos. 354-355 (2)	3.50	1.40
Nos. 379-380 (2)	9.90	1.25
Set total (12) Stamps	19.15	5.30

Europa, 1960

19-Spoke Wheel CD3

First anniversary of the establishment of C.E.P.T. (Conference Europeenne des Administrations des Postes et des Telecommunications.) The spokes symbolize the 19 founding members of the Conference.

1960, Sept.

Belgium	553-554
Denmark	379
Finland	376-377
France	970-971
Germany	818-820
Great Britain	377-378
Greece	688
Iceland	327-328
Ireland	175-176
Italy	809-810
Luxembourg	374-375
Netherlands	385-386
Norway	387
Portugal	866-867
Spain	941-942
Sweden	562-563
Switzerland	400-401
Turkey	1493-1494

Nos. 553-554 (2)	1.25	.55
No. 379 (1)	.55	.50
Nos. 376-377 (2)	1.70	1.80
Nos. 970-971 (2)	.55	.50
Nos. 818-820 (3)	2.25	1.50
Nos. 377-378 (2)	9.00	5.00
No. 688 (1)	5.00	2.00
Nos. 327-328 (2)	1.30	1.30
Nos. 175-176 (2)	75.00	14.00
Nos. 809-810 (2)	.70	.50
Nos. 374-375 (2)	1.00	.80
Nos. 385-386 (2)	3.65	1.50
No. 387 (1)	1.25	1.25
Nos. 866-867 (2)	2.25	1.25
Nos. 941-942 (2)	1.50	.75
Nos. 562-563 (2)	1.05	.55
Nos. 400-401 (2)	1.25	.65
Nos. 1493-1494 (2)	2.10	1.35
Set total (34) Stamps	111.35	35.75

Europa, 1961

19 Doves Flying as One — CD4

The 19 doves represent the 19 members of the Conference of European Postal and Telecommunications Administrations C.E.P.T.

1961-62

Belgium	572-573
Cyprus	201-203
France	1005-1006
Germany	844-845
Great Britain	382-384
Greece	718-719
Iceland	340-341
Italy	845-846
Luxembourg	382-383
Netherlands	387-388
Spain	1010-1011
Switzerland	410-411
Turkey	1518-1520

Nos. 572-573 (2)	.75	.50
Nos. 201-203 (3)	*2.10*	*1.20*
Nos. 1005-1006 (2)	.50	.50
Nos. 844-845 (2)	.60	.75
Nos. 382-384 (3)	.75	.90
Nos. 718-719 (2)	.80	.50
Nos. 340-341 (2)	.90	.90
Nos. 845-846 (2)	.55	.50
Nos. 382-383 (2)	.70	.70
Nos. 387-388 (2)	.55	.50
Nos. 1010-1011 (2)	.70	.55
Nos. 410-411 (2)	1.25	.60
Nos. 1518-1520 (3)	2.45	1.30
Set total (29) Stamps	12.60	9.40

Europa, 1962

Young Tree with 19 Leaves CD5

The 19 leaves represent the 19 original members of C.E.P.T.

1962-63

Belgium	582-583
Cyprus	219-221
France	1045-1046
Germany	852-853
Greece	739-740
Iceland	348-349
Ireland	184-185
Italy	860-861
Luxembourg	386-387
Netherlands	394-395
Norway	414-415
Switzerland	416-417
Turkey	1553-1555

Nos. 582-583 (2)	.65	.65
Nos. 219-221 (3)	*76.25*	*4.40*
Nos. 1045-1046 (2)	.60	.50
Nos. 852-853 (2)	.70	.80
Nos. 739-740 (2)	2.25	1.15
Nos. 348-349 (2)	.85	.85
Nos. 184-185 (2)	2.00	1.50
Nos. 860-861 (2)	1.35	.55
Nos. 386-387 (2)	.85	.70
Nos. 394-395 (2)	1.40	.75
Nos. 414-415 (2)	2.25	2.25
Nos. 416-417 (2)	1.65	1.00
Nos. 1553-1555 (3)	*3.00*	1.55
Set total (28) Stamps	93.80	16.65

Europa, 1963

Stylized Links, Symbolizing Unity — CD6

1963, Sept.

Belgium	598-599
Cyprus	229-231
Finland	419
France	1074-1075
Germany	867-868
Greece	768-769
Iceland	357-358
Ireland	188-189
Italy	880-881
Luxembourg	403-404
Netherlands	416-417
Norway	441-442
Switzerland	429
Turkey	1602-1603

Nos. 598-599 (2)	1.60	.55
Nos. 229-231 (3)	*54.75*	*5.15*
No. 419 (1)	1.25	.55
Nos. 1074-1075 (2)	.60	.50
Nos. 867-868 (2)	.50	.55
Nos. 768-769 (2)	5.25	1.90
Nos. 357-358 (2)	1.50	1.50
Nos. 188-189 (2)	4.75	3.25
Nos. 880-881 (2)	.65	.50
Nos. 403-404 (2)	1.00	.80
Nos. 416-417 (2)	2.25	1.00
Nos. 441-442 (2)	4.75	3.00
No. 429 (1)	.90	.60
Nos. 1602-1603 (2)	1.40	.60
Set total (27) Stamps	81.15	20.45

Europa, 1964

Symbolic Daisy — CD7

5th anniversary of the establishment of C.E.P.T. The 22 petals of the flower symbolize the 22 members of the Conference.

1964, Sept.

Austria	738
Belgium	614-615
Cyprus	244-246
France	1109-1110
Germany	897-898
Greece	801-802
Iceland	367-368
Ireland	196-197
Italy	894-895
Luxembourg	411-412
Monaco	590-591
Netherlands	428-429
Norway	458
Portugal	931-933
Spain	1262-1263
Switzerland	438-439
Turkey	1628-1629

No. 738 (1)	1.20	.80
Nos. 614-615 (2)	1.40	.60
Nos. 244-246 (3)	*35.75*	*3.45*
Nos. 1109-1110 (2)	.50	.50
Nos. 897-898 (2)	.50	.50
Nos. 801-802 (2)	5.00	1.90
Nos. 367-368 (2)	2.00	1.65
Nos. 196-197 (2)	20.00	4.25
Nos. 894-895 (2)	.55	.50
Nos. 411-412 (2)	.90	.55
Nos. 590-591 (2)	2.50	.70
Nos. 428-429 (2)	1.80	.60
No. 458 (1)	4.50	4.50
Nos. 931-933 (3)	*10.00*	*2.00*
Nos. 1262-1263 (2)	1.30	.80
Nos. 438-439 (2)	1.60	.50
Nos. 1628-1629 (2)	2.65	1.35
Set total (34) Stamps	92.15	25.15

Europa, 1965

Leaves and "Fruit" CD8

1965

Belgium	636-637
Cyprus	262-264
Finland	437
France	1131-1132
Germany	934-935
Greece	833-834
Iceland	375-376
Ireland	204-205
Italy	915-916
Luxembourg	432-433
Monaco	616-617
Netherlands	438-439
Norway	475-476
Portugal	958-960
Switzerland	469
Turkey	1665-1666

Nos. 636-637 (2)	.50	.50
Nos. 262-264 (3)	*25.35*	*3.80*
No. 437 (1)	1.25	.55
Nos. 1131-1132 (2)	.75	.80
Nos. 934-935 (2)	.50	.50
Nos. 833-834 (2)	2.25	1.15
Nos. 375-376 (2)	2.50	1.75
Nos. 204-205 (2)	20.00	3.35
Nos. 915-916 (2)	.50	.50
Nos. 432-433 (2)	.80	.60
Nos. 616-617 (2)	3.25	1.65
Nos. 438-439 (2)	.75	.55
Nos. 475-476 (2)	4.00	3.10
Nos. 958-960 (3)	*10.00*	*2.75*
No. 469 (1)	1.15	.25
Nos. 1665-1666 (2)	3.50	2.10
Set total (32) Stamps	77.05	23.90

Europa, 1966

Symbolic Sailboat — CD9

1966, Sept.

Andorra, French	172
Belgium	675-676
Cyprus	275-277
France	1163-1164
Germany	963-964

Greece	862-863
Iceland	384-385
Ireland	216-217
Italy	942-943
Liechtenstein	415
Luxembourg	440-441
Monaco	639-640
Netherlands	441-442
Norway	496-497
Portugal	980-982
Switzerland	477-478
Turkey	1718-1719

No. 172 (1)	3.00	3.00
Nos. 675-676 (2)	.80	.50
Nos. 275-277 (3)	4.75	1.90
Nos. 1163-1164 (2)	.60	.50
Nos. 963-964 (2)	.50	.55
Nos. 862-863 (2)	2.25	1.05
Nos. 384-385 (2)	5.00	3.80
Nos. 216-217 (2)	7.00	2.00
Nos. 942-943 (2)	.50	.50
No. 415 (1)	.40	.35
Nos. 440-441 (2)	.80	.60
Nos. 639-640 (2)	2.00	.65
Nos. 441-442 (2)	1.50	.65
Nos. 496-497 (2)	5.00	3.00
Nos. 980-982 (3)	9.75	2.25
Nos. 477-478 (2)	1.60	.60
Nos. 1718-1719 (2)	3.35	1.75
Set total (34) Stamps	48.80	23.65

Europa, 1967

Cogwheels
CD10

1967

Andorra, French	174-175
Belgium	688-689
Cyprus	297-299
France	1178-1179
Germany	969-970
Greece	891-892
Iceland	389-390
Ireland	232-233
Italy	951-952
Liechtenstein	420
Luxembourg	449-450
Monaco	669-670
Netherlands	444-447
Norway	504-505
Portugal	994-996
Spain	1465-1466
Switzerland	482
Turkey	B120-B121

Nos. 174-175 (2)	10.75	6.25
Nos. 688-689 (2)	1.05	.55
Nos. 297-299 (3)	4.25	1.75
Nos. 1178-1179 (2)	.80	.70
Nos. 969-970 (2)	.55	.55
Nos. 891-892 (2)	3.75	1.00
Nos. 389-390 (2)	3.00	2.00
Nos. 232-233 (2)	6.15	2.30
Nos. 951-952 (2)	.60	.50
No. 420 (1)	.45	.40
Nos. 449-450 (2)	1.00	.70
Nos. 669-670 (2)	2.75	.70
Nos. 444-447 (4)	5.00	1.85
Nos. 504-505 (2)	3.25	2.75
Nos. 994-996 (3)	9.50	1.85
Nos. 1465-1466 (2)	.50	.50
No. 482 (1)	.70	.25
Nos. B120-B121 (2)	3.50	2.75
Set total (38) Stamps	57.55	27.35

Europa, 1968

Golden Key
with
C.E.P.T.
Emblem
CD11

1968

Andorra, French	182-183
Belgium	705-706
Cyprus	314-316
France	1209-1210
Germany	983-984
Greece	916-917
Iceland	395-396
Ireland	242-243
Italy	979-980
Liechtenstein	442
Luxembourg	466-467
Monaco	689-691
Netherlands	452-453
Portugal	1019-1021
San Marino	687
Spain	1526
Switzerland	488
Turkey	1775-1776

Nos. 182-183 (2)	16.50	10.00
Nos. 705-706 (2)	1.25	.50
Nos. 314-316 (3)	2.90	1.75
Nos. 1209-1210 (2)	.90	.55
Nos. 983-984 (2)	.50	.55
Nos. 916-917 (2)	3.75	1.65
Nos. 395-396 (2)	3.00	2.50
Nos. 242-243 (2)	3.75	3.00
Nos. 979-980 (2)	.50	.50
No. 442 (1)	.45	.40
Nos. 466-467 (2)	.80	.70
Nos. 689-691 (3)	5.40	.95
Nos. 452-453 (2)	2.10	.70
Nos. 1019-1021 (3)	9.75	2.10
No. 687 (1)	.55	.35
No. 1526 (1)	.25	.25
No. 488 (1)	.45	.25
Nos. 1775-1776 (2)	5.00	2.00
Set total (35) Stamps	57.80	28.70

Europa, 1969

"EUROPA"
and "CEPT"
CD12

Tenth anniversary of C.E.P.T.

1969

Andorra, French	188-189
Austria	837
Belgium	718-719
Cyprus	326-328
Denmark	458
Finland	483
France	1245-1246
Germany	996-997
Great Britain	585
Greece	947-948
Iceland	406-407
Ireland	270-271
Italy	1000-1001
Liechtenstein	453
Luxembourg	475-476
Monaco	722-724
Netherlands	475-476
Norway	533-534
Portugal	1038-1040
San Marino	701-702
Spain	1567
Sweden	814-816
Switzerland	500-501
Turkey	1799-1800
Vatican	470-472
Yugoslavia	1003-1004

Nos. 188-189 (2)	18.50	12.00
No. 837 (1)	.65	.30
Nos. 718-719 (2)	.75	.50
Nos. 326-328 (3)	3.00	1.35
No. 458 (1)	.75	.75
No. 483 (1)	3.50	.75
Nos. 1245-1246 (2)	.55	.50
Nos. 996-997 (2)	.80	.50
No. 585 (1)	.25	.25
Nos. 947-948 (2)	5.00	1.50
Nos. 406-407 (2)	4.20	2.40
Nos. 270-271 (2)	4.00	2.00
Nos. 1000-1001 (2)	.70	.50
No. 453 (1)	.45	.45
Nos. 475-476 (2)	1.00	.70
Nos. 722-724 (3)	10.50	2.00
Nos. 475-476 (2)	2.60	1.15
Nos. 533-534 (2)	3.75	2.35
Nos. 1038-1040 (3)	17.85	2.40
Nos. 701-702 (2)	.90	.90
No. 1567 (1)	.25	.25
Nos. 814-816 (3)	4.00	2.85
Nos. 500-501 (2)	1.85	.60
Nos. 1799-1800 (2)	3.85	2.25
Nos. 470-472 (3)	.75	.75
Nos. 1003-1004 (2)	4.00	4.00
Set total (51) Stamps	94.40	43.95

Europa, 1970

Interwoven
Threads
CD13

1970

Andorra, French	196-197
Belgium	741-742
Cyprus	340-342
France	1271-1272
Germany	1018-1019
Greece	985, 987
Iceland	420-421
Ireland	279-281
Italy	1013-1014
Liechtenstein	470
Luxembourg	489-490
Monaco	768-770
Netherlands	483-484
Portugal	1060-1062
San Marino	729-730
Spain	1607
Switzerland	515-516
Turkey	1848-1849
Yugoslavia	1024-1025

Nos. 196-197 (2)	20.00	8.50
Nos. 741-742 (2)	1.10	.55
Nos. 340-342 (3)	2.70	1.90
Nos. 1271-1272 (2)	.65	.50
Nos. 1018-1019 (2)	.60	.50
Nos. 985,987 (2)	7.75	2.00
Nos. 420-421 (2)	6.00	4.00
Nos. 279-281 (3)	9.50	3.30
Nos. 1013-1014 (2)	.65	.50
No. 470 (1)	.45	.45
Nos. 489-490 (2)	.80	.80
Nos. 768-770 (3)	6.35	2.10
Nos. 483-484 (2)	2.50	1.15
Nos. 1060-1062 (3)	9.85	2.35
Nos. 729-730 (2)	.90	.55
No. 1607 (1)	.25	.25
Nos. 515-516 (2)	1.85	.60
Nos. 1848-1849 (2)	5.00	2.25
Nos. 1024-1025 (2)	.80	.80
Set total (40) Stamps	77.70	33.05

Europa, 1971

"Fraternity,
Cooperation,
Common
Effort"
CD14

1971

Andorra, French	205-206
Belgium	803-804
Cyprus	365-367
Finland	504
France	1304
Germany	1064-1065
Greece	1029-1030
Iceland	429-430
Ireland	305-306
Italy	1038-1039
Liechtenstein	485
Luxembourg	500-501
Malta	425-427
Monaco	797-799
Netherlands	488-489
Portugal	1094-1096
San Marino	749-750
Spain	1675-1676
Switzerland	531-532
Turkey	1876-1877
Yugoslavia	1052-1053

Nos. 205-206 (2)	20.00	7.75
Nos. 803-804 (2)	1.30	.55
Nos. 365-367 (3)	2.60	1.75
No. 504 (1)	5.00	.75
No. 1304 (1)	.45	.40
Nos. 1064-1065 (2)	.60	.50
Nos. 1029-1030 (2)	4.00	1.80
Nos. 429-430 (2)	5.00	3.75
Nos. 305-306 (2)	5.00	1.50
Nos. 1038-1039 (2)	.65	.50
No. 485 (1)	.45	.45
Nos. 500-501 (2)	1.00	.80
Nos. 425-427 (3)	.80	.80
Nos. 797-799 (3)	15.00	2.80
Nos. 488-489 (2)	2.50	1.15
Nos. 1094-1096 (3)	9.75	1.75
Nos. 749-750 (2)	.65	.55
Nos. 1675-1676 (2)	.75	.55
Nos. 531-532 (2)	1.85	.65
Nos. 1876-1877 (2)	5.60	2.50
Nos. 1052-1053 (2)	.50	.50
Set total (43) Stamps	83.45	31.75

Europa, 1972

Sparkles, Symbolic
of Communications
CD15

1972

Andorra, French	210-211
Andorra, Spanish	62
Belgium	825-826
Cyprus	380-382
Finland	512-513
France	1341
Germany	1089-1090
Greece	1049-1050
Iceland	439-440
Ireland	316-317
Italy	1065-1066
Liechtenstein	504
Luxembourg	512-513
Malta	450-453
Monaco	831-832
Netherlands	494-495
Portugal	1141-1143
San Marino	771-772
Spain	1718
Switzerland	544-545
Turkey	1907-1908
Yugoslavia	1100-1101

Nos. 210-211 (2)	21.00	7.00
No. 62 (1)	45.00	45.00
Nos. 825-826 (2)	.95	.55
Nos. 380-382 (3)	5.95	2.45
Nos. 512-513 (2)	7.00	1.40
No. 1341 (1)	.50	.35
Nos. 1089-1090 (2)	1.30	.50
Nos. 1049-1050 (2)	2.00	1.55
Nos. 439-440 (2)	2.90	2.65
Nos. 316-317 (2)	13.00	4.50
Nos. 1065-1066 (2)	.65	.50
No. 504 (1)	.45	.45
Nos. 512-513 (2)	1.00	.80
Nos. 450-453 (4)	1.05	1.40
Nos. 831-832 (2)	5.00	1.40
Nos. 494-495 (2)	3.25	1.15
Nos. 1141-1143 (3)	9.85	1.50
Nos. 771-772 (2)	.70	.50
No. 1718 (1)	.50	.40
Nos. 544-545 (2)	1.65	.60
Nos. 1907-1908 (2)	7.50	3.00
Nos. 1100-1101 (2)	1.20	1.20
Set total (44) Stamps	132.40	78.85

Europa, 1973

Post Horn
and Arrows
CD16

1973

Andorra, French	219-220
Andorra, Spanish	76
Belgium	839-840
Cyprus	396-398
Finland	526
France	1367
Germany	1114-1115
Greece	1090-1092
Iceland	447-448
Ireland	329-330
Italy	1108-1109
Liechtenstein	528-529
Luxembourg	523-524
Malta	469-471
Monaco	866-867
Netherlands	504-505
Norway	604-605
Portugal	1170-1172
San Marino	802-803
Spain	1753
Switzerland	580-581
Turkey	1935-1936
Yugoslavia	1138-1139

Nos. 219-220 (2)	20.00	11.00
No. 76 (1)	.65	.55
Nos. 839-840 (2)	1.00	.65
Nos. 396-398 (3)	4.25	2.10
No. 526 (1)	1.25	.55
No. 1367 (1)	1.60	.75
Nos. 1114-1115 (2)	.90	.50
Nos. 1090-1092 (3)	2.10	1.40
Nos. 447-448 (2)	7.00	4.05

Nos. 329-330 (2)	5.25	2.00
Nos. 1108-1109 (2)	.65	.50
Nos. 528-529 (2)	.60	.60
Nos. 523-524 (2)	.90	1.00
Nos. 469-471 (3)	.90	1.20
Nos. 866-867 (2)	15.00	2.40
Nos. 504-505 (2)	2.85	1.10
Nos. 604-605 (2)	6.25	2.40
Nos. 1170-1172 (3)	*13.00*	2.15
Nos. 802-803 (2)	*1.00*	.60
No. 1753 (1)	.35	.25
Nos. 580-581 (2)	1.55	.60
Nos. 1935-1936 (2)	10.00	4.50
Nos. 1138-1139 (2)	1.15	1.10
Set total (46) Stamps	98.20	41.95

Europa, 2000

CD17

2000

Albania....................................2621-2622
Andorra, French 522
Andorra, Spanish 262
Armenia....................................610-611
Austria 1814
Azerbaijan.................................698-699
Belarus 350
Belgium..1818
Bosnia & Herzegovina (Moslem) 358
Bosnia & Herzegovina (Serb) 111-112
Croatia....................................428-429
Cyprus..959
Czech Republic 3120
Denmark..1189
Estonia...394
Faroe Islands...................................376
Finland..1129
Aland Islands...................................166
France...2771
Georgia....................................228-229
Germany..................................2086-2087
Gibraltar..................................837-840
Great Britain (Jersey)......................935-936
Great Britain (Isle of Man) 883
Greece...1959
Greenland.......................................363
Hungary..................................3699-3700
Iceland...910
Ireland..................................1230-1231
Italy...2349
Latvia..504
Liechtenstein 1178
Lithuania.......................................668
Luxembourg.....................................1035
Macedonia.......................................187
Malta....................................1011-1012
Moldova...355
Monaco...................................2161-2162
Poland 3519
Portugal.......................................2358
Portugal (Azores) 455
Portugal (Madeira)..............................208
Romania 4370
Russia...6589
San Marino 1480
Slovakia 355
Slovenia..424
Spain 3036
Sweden...2394
Switzerland....................................1074
Turkey...2762
Turkish Rep. of Northern Cyprus....500
Ukraine 379
Vatican City 1152

Nos. 2621-2622 (2)	11.00	11.00
No. 522 (1)	2.00	1.00
No. 262 (1)	1.60	.70
Nos. 610-611 (2)	9.00	9.00
No. 1814 (1)	1.40	1.40
Nos. 698-699 (2)	8.00	8.00
No. 350 (1)	1.75	1.75
No. 1818 (1)	1.40	.60
No. 358 (1)	4.75	4.75
Nos. 111-112 (2)	135.00	135.00
Nos. 428-429 (2)	6.25	6.25
No. 959 (1)	2.10	1.40
No. 3120 (1)	1.00	.40
No. 1189 (1)	3.50	2.25
No. 394 (1)	1.25	1.25
No. 376 (1)	3.00	3.00
No. 1129 (1)	2.00	.60
No. 166 (1)	2.00	1.10
No. 2771 (1)	1.40	.40
No. 228-229 (1)	9.00	9.00
Nos. 2086-2087 (2)	4.15	1.90
Nos. 837-840 (4)	5.50	5.30
Nos. 935-936 (2)	2.40	2.40
No. 883 (1)	1.50	1.50
No. 1959 (1)	3.00	3.00
No. 363 (1)	1.90	1.90
Nos. 3699-3700 (2)	6.50	2.50
No. 910 (1)	2.00	2.00
Nos. 1230-1231 (2)	4.75	4.75
No. 2349 (1)	1.50	.40
No. 504 (1)	5.00	2.40
No. 1178 (1)	2.25	1.75
No. 668 (1)	1.50	1.50
No. 1035 (1)	1.40	1.00
No. 187 (1)	3.25	3.25
Nos. 1011-1012 (2)	4.35	4.35
No. 355 (1)	3.50	3.50
Nos. 2161-2162 (2)	2.80	1.40
No. 3519 (1)	1.10	.50
No. 2358 (1)	1.25	.65
No. 455 (1)	1.25	.50
No. 208 (1)	1.25	.50
No. 4370 (1)	2.50	1.25
No. 6589 (1)	2.00	.85
No. 1480 (1)	1.00	1.00
No. 355 (1)	1.10	.55
No. 424 (1)	3.25	1.60
No. 3036 (1)	.75	.40
No. 2394 (1)	3.00	2.25
No. 1074 (1)	2.10	.75
No. 2762 (1)	2.00	2.00
No. 500 (1)	2.50	2.50
No. 379 (1)	4.50	3.00
No. 1152 (1)	1.25	1.25
Set total (68) Stamps	295.45	263.20

The Gibraltar stamps are similar to the stamp illustrated, but none have the design shown above. All other sets listed above include at least one stamp with the design shown, but some include stamps with entirely different designs. Bulgaria Nos. 4131-4132, Guernsey Nos. 802-803 and Yugoslavia Nos. 2485-2486 are Europa stamps with completely different designs.

PORTUGAL & COLONIES

Vasco da Gama

Fleet Departing CD20

Fleet Arriving at Calicut — CD21

Embarking at Rastello CD22

Muse of History CD23

San Gabriel, da Gama and Camoens CD24

Archangel Gabriel, the Patron Saint CD25

Flagship San Gabriel — CD26

Vasco da Gama — CD27

Fourth centenary of Vasco da Gama's discovery of the route to India.

1898

Azores 93-100
Macao.......................................67-74
Madeira.....................................37-44
Portugal..................................147-154
Port. Africa..................................1-8
Port. Congo.................................75-98
Port. India...............................189-196
St. Thomas & Prince Islands...170-193
Timor.......................................45-52

Nos. 93-100 (8)	122.00	76.25
Nos. 67-74 (8)	136.00	96.75
Nos. 37-44 (8)	44.55	34.00
Nos. 147-154 (8)	169.30	43.45
Nos. 1-8 (8)	23.95	21.70
Nos. 75-98 (24)	34.45	34.45
Nos. 189-196 (8)	20.25	12.95
Nos. 170-193 (24)	37.85	34.30
Nos. 45-52 (8)	21.50	10.45
Set total (104) Stamps	609.85	364.30

Pombal
POSTAL TAX
POSTAL TAX DUES

Marquis de Pombal — CD28

Planning Reconstruction of Lisbon, 1755 — CD29

Pombal Monument, Lisbon — CD30

Sebastiao Jose de Carvalho e Mello, Marquis de Pombal (1699-1782), statesman, rebuilt Lisbon after earthquake of 1755. Tax was for the erection of Pombal monument. Obligatory on all mail on certain days throughout the year. Postal Tax Dues are inscribed "Multa."

1925

Angola RA1-RA3, RAJ1-RAJ3
Azores RA9-RA11, RAJ2-RAJ4
Cape Verde RA1-RA3, RAJ1-RAJ3
Macao.............. RA1-RA3, RAJ1-RAJ3
Madeira............ RA1-RA3, RAJ1-RAJ3
Mozambique..... RA1-RA3, RAJ1-RAJ3
Nyassa............. RA1-RA3, RAJ1-RAJ3
Portugal RA11-RA13, RAJ2-RAJ4
Port. Guinea..... RA1-RA3, RAJ1-RAJ3
Port. India......... RA1-RA3, RAJ1-RAJ3
St. Thomas & Prince
Islands.............. RA1-RA3, RAJ1-RAJ3
Timor RA1-RA3, RAJ1-RAJ3

Nos. RA1-RA3,RAJ1-RAJ3 (6)	7.50	6.00
Nos. RA9-RA11,RAJ2-RAJ4 (6)	6.60	9.30
Nos. RA1-RA3,RAJ1-RAJ3 (6)	6.00	5.40
Nos. RA1-RA3,RAJ1-RAJ3 (6)	19.50	4.20
Nos. RA1-RA3,RAJ1-RAJ3 (6)	4.35	12.45
Nos. RA1-RA3,RAJ1-RAJ3 (6)	2.55	2.70
Nos. RA1-RA3,RAJ1-RAJ3 (6)	52.50	38.25
Nos. RA11-RA13,RAJ2-RAJ4 (6)	5.80	5.20
Nos. RA1-RA3,RAJ1-RAJ3 (6)	3.30	2.70
Nos. RA1-RA3,RAJ1-RAJ3 (6)	3.45	3.45
Nos. RA1-RA3,RAJ1-RAJ3 (6)	3.60	3.60
Nos. RA1-RA3,RAJ1-RAJ3 (6)	2.10	3.90
Set total (72) Stamps	117.25	97.15

Vasco da Gama CD34

Mousinho de Albuquerque CD35

Dam CD36

Prince Henry the Navigator CD37

Affonso de Albuquerque CD38

Plane over Globe CD39

1938-39

Angola 274-291, C1-C9
Cape Verde 234-251, C1-C9
Macao........................289-305, C7-C15
Mozambique...................270-287, C1-C9
Port. Guinea...................233-250. C1-C9
Port. India......................439-453, C1-C8
St. Thomas & Prince
Islands ... 302-319, 323-340, C1-C18
Timor 223-239, C1-C9

Nos. 274-291,C1-C9 (27)	141.35	22.25
Nos. 234-251,C1-C9 (27)	100.00	31.20
Nos. 289-305,C7-C15 (26)	701.70	135.60
Nos. 270-287,C1-C9 (27)	60.95	11.20
Nos. 233-250,C1-C9 (27)	86.05	30.70
Nos. 439-453,C1-C8 (23)	74.75	25.50
Nos. 302-319,323-340,C1-C18 (54)	319.25	190.35
Nos. 223-239,C1-C9 (26)	149.25	73.15
Set total (237) Stamps	1,633.	519.95

Lady of Fatima

Our Lady of the Rosary, Fatima, Portugal — CD40

1948-49

Angola 315-318
Cape Verde 266
Macao..336
Mozambique.................................325-328
Port. Guinea....................................271
Port. India......................................480
St. Thomas & Prince Islands..........351
Timor 254

Nos. 315-318 (4)	88.50	17.90
No. 266 (1)	8.50	4.50
No. 336 (1)	40.00	12.00
Nos. 325-328 (4)	20.00	4.50
No. 271 (1)	3.25	3.00
No. 480 (1)	2.50	2.25
No. 351 (1)	7.25	6.50
No. 254 (1)	3.00	3.00
Set total (14) Stamps	173.00	53.65

A souvenir sheet of 9 stamps was issued in 1951 to mark the extension of the 1950 Holy Year. The sheet contains: Angola No. 316, Cape Verde No. 266, Macao No. 336, Mozambique No. 325, Portuguese Guinea No. 271, Portuguese India Nos. 480, 485, St. Thomas & Prince Islands No. 351, Timor No. 254. The sheet also contains a portrait of Pope Pius XII and is inscribed "Encerramento do

Ano Santo, Fatima 1951." It was sold for 11 escudos.

Holy Year

Church Bells and Dove CD41

Angel Holding Candelabra CD42

Holy Year, 1950.

1950-51

Angola	331-332
Cape Verde	268-269
Macao	339-340
Mozambique	330-331
Port. Guinea	273-274
Port. India	490-491, 496-503
St. Thomas & Prince Islands	353-354
Timor	258-259

Nos. 331-332 (2)	7.60	1.35
Nos. 268-269 (2)	4.75	2.20
Nos. 339-340 (2)	55.00	12.50
Nos. 330-331 (2)	1.75	.85
Nos. 273-274 (2)	3.50	2.60
Nos. 490-491,496-503 (10)	12.80	5.40
Nos. 353-354 (2)	7.50	4.40
Nos. 258-259 (2)	3.75	3.25
Set total (24) Stamps	96.65	32.55

A souvenir sheet of 8 stamps was issued in 1951 to mark the extension of the Holy Year. The sheet contains: Angola No. 331, Cape Verde No. 269, Macao No. 340, Mozambique No. 331, Portuguese Guinea No. 275, Portuguese India No. 490, St. Thomas & Prince Islands No. 354, Timor No. 258, some with colors changed. The sheet contains doves and is inscribed 'Encerramento do Ano Santo, Fatima 1951.' It was sold for 17 escudos.

Holy Year Conclusion

Our Lady of Fatima — CD43

Conclusion of Holy Year. Sheets contain alternate vertical rows of stamps and labels bearing quotation from Pope Pius XII, different for each colony.

1951

Angola	357
Cape Verde	270
Macao	352
Mozambique	356
Port. Guinea	275
Port. India	506
St. Thomas & Prince Islands	355
Timor	270

No. 357 (1)	5.25	1.50
No. 270 (1)	1.50	1.25
No. 352 (1)	37.50	10.00
No. 356 (1)	2.25	1.00
No. 275 (1)	1.00	.65
No. 506 (1)	1.60	1.00
No. 355 (1)	2.50	2.00
No. 270 (1)	2.00	1.75
Set total (8) Stamps	53.60	19.15

Medical Congress

CD44

First National Congress of Tropical Medicine, Lisbon, 1952. Each stamp has a different design.

1952

Angola	358
Cape Verde	287
Macao	364
Mozambique	359
Port. Guinea	276
Port. India	516
St. Thomas & Prince Islands	356
Timor	271

No. 358 (1)	1.25	.45
No. 287 (1)	.70	.50
No. 364 (1)	9.75	4.25
No. 359 (1)	1.10	.55
No. 276 (1)	.45	.35
No. 516 (1)	4.75	2.00
No. 356 (1)	.30	.30
No. 271 (1)	1.00	1.00
Set total (8) Stamps	19.30	9.40

Postage Due Stamps

CD45

1952

Angola	J37-J42
Cape Verde	J31-J36
Macao	J53-J58
Mozambique	J51-J56
Port. Guinea	J40-J45
Port. India	J47-J52
St. Thomas & Prince Islands	J52-J57
Timor	J31-J36

Nos. J37-J42 (6)	4.05	3.15
Nos. J31-J36 (6)	2.80	2.30
Nos. J53-J58 (6)	17.45	6.85
Nos. J51-J56 (6)	1.80	1.55
Nos. J40-J45 (6)	2.55	2.55
Nos. J47-J52 (6)	6.10	6.10
Nos. J52-J57 (6)	4.15	4.15
Nos. J31-J36 (6)	3.50	3.50
Set total (48) Stamps	42.40	30.15

Sao Paulo

Father Manuel da Nobrega and View of Sao Paulo — CD46

Founding of Sao Paulo, Brazil, 400th anniv.

1954

Angola	385
Cape Verde	297
Macao	382
Mozambique	395
Port. Guinea	291
Port. India	530
St. Thomas & Prince Islands	369
Timor	279

No. 385 (1)	.80	.50
No. 297 (1)	.70	.60
No. 382 (1)	14.00	3.00
No. 395 (1)	.40	.30
No. 291 (1)	.35	.25
No. 530 (1)	.80	.40
No. 369 (1)	.80	.60
No. 279 (1)	.85	.70
Set total (8) Stamps	18.70	6.35

Tropical Medicine Congress

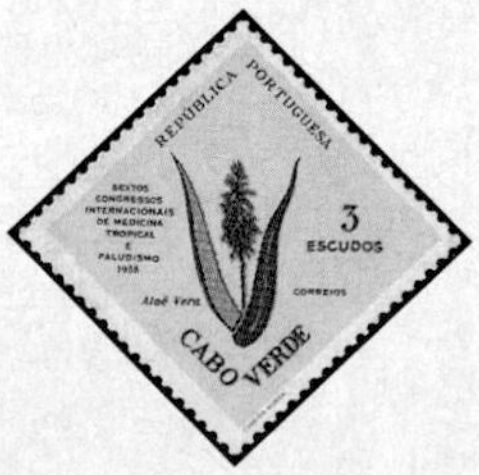

CD47

Sixth International Congress for Tropical Medicine and Malaria, Lisbon, Sept. 1958. Each stamp shows a different plant.

1958

Angola	409
Cape Verde	303
Macao	392
Mozambique	404
Port. Guinea	295
Port. India	569
St. Thomas & Prince Islands	371
Timor	289

No. 409 (1)	3.50	1.10
No. 303 (1)	5.50	2.10
No. 392 (1)	8.00	3.00
No. 404 (1)	4.00	.85
No. 295 (1)	2.75	1.10
No. 569 (1)	1.75	.75
No. 371 (1)	2.75	2.25
No. 289 (1)	3.00	2.75
Set total (8) Stamps	31.25	13.90

Sports

CD48

Each stamp shows a different sport.

1962

Angola	433-438
Cape Verde	320-325
Macao	394-399
Mozambique	424-429
Port. Guinea	299-304
St. Thomas & Prince Islands	374-379
Timor	313-318

Nos. 433-438 (6)	6.50	3.20
Nos. 320-325 (6)	15.25	5.20
Nos. 394-399 (6)	74.00	14.60
Nos. 424-429 (6)	5.00	2.45
Nos. 299-304 (6)	4.95	2.15
Nos. 374-379 (6)	6.75	3.20
Nos. 313-318 (6)	6.40	3.70
Set total (42) Stamps	118.85	34.50

Anti-Malaria

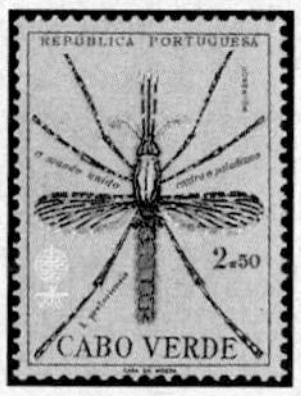

Anopheles Funestus and Malaria Eradication Symbol — CD49

World Health Organization drive to eradicate malaria.

1962

Angola	439
Cape Verde	326
Macao	400
Mozambique	430
Port. Guinea	305
St. Thomas & Prince Islands	380
Timor	319

No. 439 (1)	2.00	.90
No. 326 (1)	1.40	.90
No. 400 (1)	6.50	2.00
No. 430 (1)	1.40	.40
No. 305 (1)	1.25	.45
No. 380 (1)	2.00	1.50
No. 319 (1)	.75	.60
Set total (7) Stamps	15.30	6.75

Airline Anniversary

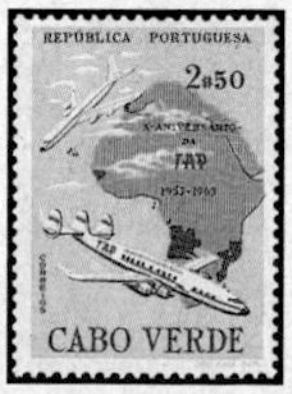

Map of Africa, Super Constellation and Jet Liner — CD50

Tenth anniversary of Transportes Aereos Portugueses (TAP).

1963

Angola	490
Cape Verde	327
Mozambique	434
Port. Guinea	318
St. Thomas & Prince Islands	381

No. 490 (1)	1.25	.50
No. 327 (1)	1.10	.70
No. 434 (1)	.40	.25
No. 318 (1)	.65	.35
No. 381 (1)	.70	.60
Set total (5) Stamps	4.10	2.40

National Overseas Bank

Antonio Teixeira de Sousa — CD51

Centenary of the National Overseas Bank of Portugal.

1964, May 16

Angola	509
Cape Verde	328
Port. Guinea	319
St. Thomas & Prince Islands	382
Timor	320

No. 509 (1)	.90	.30
No. 328 (1)	1.10	.75
No. 319 (1)	.65	.40
No. 382 (1)	.70	.50
No. 320 (1)	.75	.60
Set total (5) Stamps	4.10	2.55

ITU

ITU Emblem and the Archangel Gabriel — CD52

International Communications Union, Cent.

1965, May 17

Angola	511
Cape Verde	329
Macao	402
Mozambique	464
Port. Guinea	320
St. Thomas & Prince Islands	383
Timor	321

No. 511 (1)	1.25	.65
No. 329 (1)	2.10	1.40
No. 402 (1)	5.00	2.00
No. 464 (1)	.40	.25
No. 320 (1)	1.90	.75
No. 383 (1)	1.50	1.00
No. 321 (1)	1.50	.90
Set total (7) Stamps	13.65	6.95

National Revolution

CD53

40th anniv. of the National Revolution. Different buildings on each stamp.

1966, May 28

Angola	525
Cape Verde	338
Macao	403
Mozambique	465
Port. Guinea	329
St. Thomas & Prince Islands	392
Timor	322

No. 525 (1)	.45	.25
No. 338 (1)	.60	.45
No. 403 (1)	5.00	2.00
No. 465 (1)	.50	.30
No. 329 (1)	.55	.35
No. 392 (1)	.75	.50
No. 322 (1)	1.50	.90
Set total (7) Stamps	9.35	4.75

Navy Club

CD54

Centenary of Portugal's Navy Club. Each stamp has a different design.

1967, Jan. 31

Angola	527-528
Cape Verde	339-340
Macao	412-413
Mozambique	478-479
Port. Guinea	330-331
St. Thomas & Prince Islands	393-394
Timor	323-324

Nos. 527-528 (2)	2.25	1.00
Nos. 339-340 (2)	2.00	1.40
Nos. 412-413 (2)	9.50	3.75
Nos. 478-479 (2)	1.20	.65
Nos. 330-331 (2)	1.20	.90
Nos. 393-394 (2)	3.20	1.25
Nos. 323-324 (2)	4.00	2.00
Set total (14) Stamps	23.35	10.95

Admiral Coutinho

CD55

Centenary of the birth of Admiral Carlos Viegas Gago Coutinho (1869-1959), explorer and aviation pioneer. Each stamp has a different design.

1969, Feb. 17

Angola	547
Cape Verde	355
Macao	417
Mozambique	484
Port. Guinea	335
St. Thomas & Prince Islands	397
Timor	335

No. 547 (1)	1.00	.35
No. 355 (1)	.35	.25
No. 417 (1)	3.75	1.50
No. 484 (1)	.25	.25
No. 335 (1)	.35	.25
No. 397 (1)	.50	.35
No. 335 (1)	1.10	.85
Set total (7) Stamps	7.30	3.80

Administration Reform

Luiz Augusto Rebello da Silva — CD56

Centenary of the administration reforms of the overseas territories.

1969, Sept. 25

Angola	549
Cape Verde	357
Macao	419
Mozambique	491
Port. Guinea	337
St. Thomas & Prince Islands	399
Timor	338

No. 549 (1)	.25	.25
No. 357 (1)	.35	.25
No. 419 (1)	5.00	1.00
No. 491 (1)	.25	.25
No. 337 (1)	.25	.25
No. 399 (1)	.45	.45
No. 338 (1)	.40	.25
Set total (7) Stamps	6.95	2.70

Marshal Carmona

CD57

Birth centenary of Marshal Antonio Oscar Carmona de Fragoso (1869-1951), President of Portugal. Each stamp has a different design.

1970, Nov. 15

Angola	563
Cape Verde	359
Macao	422
Mozambique	493
Port. Guinea	340
St. Thomas & Prince Islands	403
Timor	341

No. 563 (1)	.45	.25
No. 359 (1)	.55	.35
No. 422 (1)	2.25	1.25
No. 493 (1)	.40	.25
No. 340 (1)	.35	.25
No. 403 (1)	.75	.45
No. 341 (1)	.25	.25
Set total (7) Stamps	5.00	3.05

Olympic Games

CD59

20th Olympic Games, Munich, Aug. 26-Sept. 11. Each stamp shows a different sport.

1972, June 20

Angola	569
Cape Verde	361
Macao	426
Mozambique	504
Port. Guinea	342
St. Thomas & Prince Islands	408
Timor	343

No. 569 (1)	.65	.25
No. 361 (1)	.65	.30
No. 426 (1)	3.25	1.00
No. 504 (1)	.30	.25
No. 342 (1)	.45	.25
No. 408 (1)	.35	.25
No. 343 (1)	.50	.50
Set total (7) Stamps	6.15	2.80

Lisbon-Rio de Janeiro Flight

CD60

50th anniversary of the Lisbon to Rio de Janeiro flight by Arturo de Sacadura and Coutinho, March 30-June 5, 1922. Each stamp shows a different stage of the flight.

1972, Sept. 20

Angola	570
Cape Verde	362
Macao	427
Mozambique	505
Port. Guinea	343
St. Thomas & Prince Islands	409
Timor	344

No. 570 (1)	.35	.25
No. 362 (1)	1.50	.30
No. 427 (1)	22.50	7.50
No. 505 (1)	.25	.25
No. 343 (1)	.25	.25
No. 409 (1)	.35	.25
No. 344 (1)	.25	.40
Set total (7) Stamps	25.45	9.20

WMO Centenary

WMO Emblem — CD61

Centenary of international meterological cooperation.

1973, Dec. 15

Angola	571
Cape Verde	363
Macao	429
Mozambique	509
Port. Guinea	344
St. Thomas & Prince Islands	410
Timor	345

No. 571 (1)	.45	.25
No. 363 (1)	.65	.30
No. 429 (1)	6.25	1.75
No. 509 (1)	.30	.25
No. 344 (1)	.45	.35
No. 410 (1)	.60	.50
No. 345 (1)	1.75	2.00
Set total (7) Stamps	10.45	5.40

FRENCH COMMUNITY

Upper Volta can be found under Burkina Faso in Vol. 1

Madagascar can be found under Malagasy in Vol. 3

Colonial Exposition

People of French Empire CD70

Women's Heads CD71

France Showing Way to Civilization CD72

"Colonial Commerce" CD73

International Colonial Exposition, Paris.

1931

Cameroun	213-216
Chad	60-63
Dahomey	97-100
Fr. Guiana	152-155
Fr. Guinea	116-119
Fr. India	100-103
Fr. Polynesia	76-79
Fr. Sudan	102-105
Gabon	120-123
Guadeloupe	138-141
Indo-China	140-142
Ivory Coast	92-95
Madagascar	169-172
Martinique	129-132
Mauritania	65-68
Middle Congo	61-64
New Caledonia	176-179
Niger	73-76
Reunion	122-125
St. Pierre & Miquelon	132-135
Senegal	138-141
Somali Coast	135-138
Togo	254-257
Ubangi-Shari	82-85
Upper Volta	66-69
Wallis & Futuna Isls.	85-88

Nos. 213-216 (4)	23.00	18.25
Nos. 60-63 (4)	22.00	22.00
Nos. 97-100 (4)	26.00	26.00
Nos. 152-155 (4)	22.00	22.00
Nos. 116-119 (4)	19.75	19.75
Nos. 100-103 (4)	18.00	*18.00*
Nos. 76-79 (4)	30.00	30.00
Nos. 102-105 (4)	19.00	19.00
Nos. 120-123 (4)	17.50	17.50
Nos. 138-141 (4)	19.00	19.00
Nos. 140-142 (3)	11.50	11.50
Nos. 92-95 (4)	22.50	22.50
Nos. 169-172 (4)	7.90	5.00
Nos. 129-132 (4)	21.00	21.00
Nos. 65-68 (4)	22.00	22.00
Nos. 61-64 (4)	20.50	20.50
Nos. 176-179 (4)	24.00	24.00
Nos. 73-76 (4)	21.50	21.50
Nos. 122-125 (4)	22.00	22.00
Nos. 132-135 (4)	24.00	24.00
Nos. 138-141 (4)	20.00	20.00
Nos. 135-138 (4)	22.00	22.00
Nos. 254-257 (4)	22.00	22.00
Nos. 82-85 (4)	21.00	21.00
Nos. 66-69 (4)	19.00	19.00
Nos. 85-88 (4)	35.00	35.00
Set total (103) Stamps	552.15	544.50

Paris International Exposition Colonial Arts Exposition

"Colonial Resources"
CD74 CD77

Overseas Commerce CD75

Exposition Building and Women CD76

"France and the Empire" CD78

Cultural Treasures of the Colonies CD79

Souvenir sheets contain one imperf. stamp.

1937

Cameroun	217-222A
Dahomey	101-107
Fr. Equatorial Africa	27-32, 73
Fr. Guiana	162-168
Fr. Guinea	120-126
Fr. India	104-110
Fr. Polynesia	117-123
Fr. Sudan	106-112
Guadeloupe	148-154
Indo-China	193-199
Inini	41
Ivory Coast	152-158
Kwangchowan	132
Madagascar	191-197
Martinique	179-185
Mauritania	69-75
New Caledonia	208-214
Niger	73-83
Reunion	167-173
St. Pierre & Miquelon	165-171
Senegal	172-178
Somali Coast	139-145
Togo	258-264
Wallis & Futuna Isls.	89

Nos. 217-222A (7)	18.80	20.30
Nos. 101-107 (7)	23.60	27.60
Nos. 27-32, 73 (7)	28.10	32.10
Nos. 162-168 (7)	22.50	24.50
Nos. 120-126 (7)	24.00	28.00
Nos. 104-110 (7)	21.15	30.50
Nos. 117-123 (7)	58.50	75.00
Nos. 106-112 (7)	23.60	27.60
Nos. 148-154 (7)	19.55	21.05
Nos. 193-199 (7)	17.70	19.70
No. 41 (1)	19.00	22.50
Nos. 152-158 (7)	22.20	26.20
No. 132 (1)	9.25	11.00
Nos. 191-197 (7)	17.55	18.30
Nos. 179-185 (7)	19.95	21.70
Nos. 69-75 (7)	20.50	24.50
Nos. 208-214 (7)	39.00	50.50
Nos. 73-83 (11)	42.70	46.70
Nos. 167-173 (7)	21.70	23.20
Nos. 165-171 (7)	49.60	64.00
Nos. 172-178 (7)	21.00	23.80
Nos. 139-145 (7)	25.60	32.60
Nos. 258-264 (7)	20.40	20.40
No. 89 (1)	28.50	37.50
Set total (154) Stamps	614.45	729.25

Curie

Pierre and Marie Curie CD80

40th anniversary of the discovery of radium. The surtax was for the benefit of the Intl. Union for the Control of Cancer.

1938

Cameroun B1
Cuba B1-B2
Dahomey B2
France B76
Fr. Equatorial Africa B1
Fr. Guiana B3
Fr. Guinea B2
Fr. India B6
Fr. Polynesia B5
Fr. Sudan B1
Guadeloupe B3
Indo-China B14
Ivory Coast B2
Madagascar B2
Martinique B2
Mauritania B3
New Caledonia B4
Niger B1
Reunion B4
St. Pierre & Miquelon B3
Senegal B3
Somali Coast B2
Togo B1

No. B1 (1)	10.00	10.00
Nos. B1-B2 (2)	8.50	2.40
No. B2 (1)	9.50	9.50
No. B76 (1)	21.00	12.50
No. B1 (1)	24.00	24.00
No. B3 (1)	13.50	13.50
No. B2 (1)	8.75	8.75
No. B6 (1)	10.00	10.00
No. B5 (1)	20.00	20.00
No. B1 (1)	12.50	12.50
No. B3 (1)	11.00	10.50
No. B14 (1)	12.00	12.00
No. B2 (1)	11.00	7.50
No. B2 (1)	11.00	11.00
No. B2 (1)	13.00	13.00
No. B3 (1)	7.75	7.75
No. B4 (1)	16.50	17.50
No. B1 (1)	15.00	15.00
No. B4 (1)	14.00	14.00
No. B3 (1)	21.00	22.50
No. B3 (1)	10.50	10.50
No. B2 (1)	7.75	7.75
No. B1 (1)	20.00	20.00
Set total (24) Stamps	308.25	292.15

Caillie

Rene Caillie and Map of Northwestern Africa — CD81

Death centenary of Rene Caillie (1799-1838), French explorer. All three denominations exist with colony name omitted.

1939

Dahomey 108-110
Fr. Guinea 161-163
Fr. Sudan 113-115
Ivory Coast 160-162
Mauritania 109-111
Niger 84-86
Senegal 188-190
Togo 265-267

Nos. 108-110 (3)	1.20	3.60
Nos. 161-163 (3)	1.20	3.20
Nos. 113-115 (3)	1.20	3.20
Nos. 160-162 (3)	1.05	2.55
Nos. 109-111 (3)	1.05	3.80
Nos. 84-86 (3)	1.05	2.35
Nos. 188-190 (3)	1.05	2.90
Nos. 265-267 (3)	1.05	3.30
Set total (24) Stamps	8.85	24.90

New York World's Fair

Natives and New York Skyline CD82

1939

Cameroun 223-224
Dahomey 111-112
Fr. Equatorial Africa 78-79
Fr. Guiana 169-170
Fr. Guinea 164-165
Fr. India 111-112
Fr. Polynesia 124-125
Fr. Sudan 116-117
Guadeloupe 155-156
Indo-China 203-204
Inini 42-43
Ivory Coast 163-164
Kwangchowan 133-134
Madagascar 209-210
Martinique 186-187
Mauritania 112-113
New Caledonia 215-216
Niger 87-88
Reunion 174-175
St. Pierre & Miquelon 205-206
Senegal 191-192
Somali Coast 179-180
Togo 268-269
Wallis & Futuna Isls. 90-91

Nos. 223-224 (2)	2.80	2.40
Nos. 111-112 (2)	1.60	3.20
Nos. 78-79 (2)	1.60	3.20
Nos. 169-170 (2)	2.60	2.60
Nos. 164-165 (2)	1.60	3.20
Nos. 111-112 (2)	3.00	*6.00*
Nos. 124-125 (2)	4.80	4.80
Nos. 116-117 (2)	1.60	3.20
Nos. 155-156 (2)	2.50	2.50
Nos. 203-204 (2)	2.05	2.05
Nos. 42-43 (2)	7.50	9.00
Nos. 163-164 (2)	1.50	3.00
Nos. 133-134 (2)	2.50	2.50
Nos. 209-210 (2)	3.75	3.75
Nos. 186-187 (2)	2.35	2.35
Nos. 112-113 (2)	1.40	2.80
Nos. 215-216 (2)	3.35	3.35
Nos. 87-88 (2)	1.40	2.80
Nos. 174-175 (2)	2.80	2.80
Nos. 205-206 (2)	4.80	6.00
Nos. 191-192 (2)	1.40	2.80
Nos. 179-180 (2)	1.40	2.80
Nos. 268-269 (2)	1.40	2.80
Nos. 90-91 (2)	6.00	6.00
Set total (48) Stamps	65.70	85.90

French Revolution

Storming of the Bastille CD83

French Revolution, 150th anniv. The surtax was for the defense of the colonies.

1939

Cameroun B2-B6
Dahomey B3-B7
Fr. Equatorial Africa B4-B8, CB1
Fr. Guiana B4-B8, CB1
Fr. Guinea B3-B7
Fr. India B7-B11
Fr. Polynesia B6-B10, CB1
Fr. Sudan B2-B6
Guadeloupe B4-B8
Indo-China B15-B19, CB1
Inini B1-B5
Ivory Coast B3-B7
Kwangchowan B1-B5
Madagascar B3-B7, CB1
Martinique B3-B7
Mauritania B4-B8
New Caledonia B5-B9, CB1
Niger B2-B6
Reunion B5-B9, CB1
St. Pierre & Miquelon B4-B8
Senegal B4-B8, CB1
Somali Coast B3-B7
Togo B2-B6
Wallis & Futuna Isls. B1-B5

Nos. B2-B6 (5)	60.00	60.00
Nos. B3-B7 (5)	47.50	47.50
Nos. B4-B8,CB1 (6)	120.00	120.00
Nos. B4-B8,CB1 (6)	79.50	79.50
Nos. B3-B7 (5)	47.50	47.50
Nos. B7-B11 (5)	28.75	*32.50*
Nos. B6-B10,CB1 (6)	122.50	122.50
Nos. B2-B6 (5)	50.00	50.00
Nos. B4-B8 (5)	50.00	50.00
Nos. B15-B19,CB1 (6)	85.00	85.00
Nos. B1-B5 (5)	75.00	87.50
Nos. B3-B7 (5)	43.75	43.75
Nos. B1-B5 (5)	46.25	46.25
Nos. B3-B7,CB1 (6)	65.50	65.50
Nos. B3-B7 (5)	52.50	52.50
Nos. B4-B8 (5)	42.50	42.50
Nos. B5-B9,CB1 (6)	101.50	101.50
Nos. B2-B6 (5)	60.00	60.00
Nos. B5-B9,CB1 (6)	87.50	87.50
Nos. B4-B8 (5)	67.50	72.50
Nos. B4-B8,CB1 (6)	57.00	57.00
Nos. B3-B7 (5)	45.00	45.00
Nos. B2-B6 (5)	42.50	42.50
Nos. B1-B5 (5)	95.00	95.00
Set total (128) Stamps	1,572.	1,594.

Plane over Coastal Area CD85

All five denominations exist with colony name omitted.

1940

Dahomey C1-C5
Fr. Guinea C1-C5
Fr. Sudan C1-C5
Ivory Coast C1-C5
Mauritania C1-C5
Niger C1-C5
Senegal C12-C16
Togo C1-C5

Nos. C1-C5 (5)	4.00	4.00
Nos. C1-C5 (5)	4.00	4.00
Nos. C1-C5 (5)	4.00	4.00
Nos. C1-C5 (5)	3.80	3.80
Nos. C1-C5 (5)	3.50	3.50
Nos. C1-C5 (5)	3.50	3.50
Nos. C12-C16 (5)	3.50	3.50
Nos. C1-C5 (5)	3.15	3.15
Set total (40) Stamps	29.45	29.45

Defense of the Empire

Colonial Infantryman — CD86

1941

Cameroun B13B
Dahomey B13
Fr. Equatorial Africa B8B
Fr. Guiana B10
Fr. Guinea B13
Fr. India B13
Fr. Polynesia B12
Fr. Sudan B12
Guadeloupe B10
Indo-China B19B
Inini B7
Ivory Coast B13
Kwangchowan B7
Madagascar B9
Martinique B9
Mauritania B14
New Caledonia B11
Niger B12
Reunion B11
St. Pierre & Miquelon B8B
Senegal B14
Somali Coast B9
Togo B10B
Wallis & Futuna Isls. B7

No. B13B (1)	1.60
No. B13 (1)	1.20
No. B8B (1)	3.50
No. B10 (1)	1.40
No. B13 (1)	1.40
No. B13 (1)	1.25
No. B12 (1)	3.50
No. B12 (1)	1.40
No. B10 (1)	1.00
No. B19B (1)	1.60
No. B7 (1)	1.75
No. B13 (1)	1.25
No. B7 (1)	.85
No. B9 (1)	1.50
No. B9 (1)	1.40
No. B14 (1)	.95
No. B11 (1)	1.60
No. B12 (1)	1.40
No. B11 (1)	1.60
No. B8B (1)	3.75
No. B14 (1)	1.25
No. B9 (1)	1.60
No. B10B (1)	1.25
No. B7 (1)	2.40
Set total (24) Stamps	40.40

Each of the CD86 stamps listed above is part of a set of three stamps. The designs of the other two stamps in the set vary from country to country. Only the values of the Common Design stamps are listed here.

Colonial Education Fund

CD86a

1942

Cameroun CB3
Dahomey CB4
Fr. Equatorial Africa CB5
Fr. Guiana CB4
Fr. Guinea CB4
Fr. India CB3
Fr. Polynesia CB4
Fr. Sudan CB4
Guadeloupe CB3
Indo-China CB5
Inini CB3
Ivory Coast CB4
Kwangchowan CB4
Malagasy CB5
Martinique CB3
Mauritania CB4
New Caledonia CB4
Niger CB4
Reunion CB4
St. Pierre & Miquelon CB3
Senegal CB5
Somali Coast CB3
Togo CB3
Wallis & Futuna CB3

No. CB3 (1)	1.10	
No. CB4 (1)	.80	5.50
No. CB5 (1)	.80	
No. CB4 (1)	1.10	
No. CB4 (1)	.40	5.50
No. CB3 (1)	.90	
No. CB4 (1)	2.00	
No. CB4 (1)	.40	5.50
No. CB3 (1)	1.10	
No. CB5 (1)	1.10	
No. CB3 (1)	1.25	
No. CB4 (1)	1.00	5.50
No. CB4 (1)	1.00	
No. CB5 (1)	.65	
No. CB3 (1)	1.00	
No. CB4 (1)	.80	
No. CB4 (1)	1.60	
No. CB4 (1)	.35	
No. CB4 (1)	.90	
No. CB3 (1)	5.25	
No. CB5 (1)	.80	6.50
No. CB3 (1)	.70	
No. CB3 (1)	.35	
No. CB3 (1)	2.25	
Set total (24) Stamps	27.60	28.50

Cross of Lorraine & Four-motor Plane CD87

1941-5

Cameroun C1-C7
Fr. Equatorial Africa C17-C23
Fr. Guiana C9-C10
Fr. India C1-C6
Fr. Polynesia C3-C9
Fr. West Africa C1-C3
Guadeloupe C1-C2
Madagascar .... [illegible]

Martinique C1-C2
New Caledonia C7-C13
Reunion C18-C24
St. Pierre & Miquelon C1-C7
Somali Coast C1-C7

Nos. C1-C7 (7)	6.30	6.30
Nos. C17-C23 (7)	10.40	6.35
Nos. C9-C10 (2)	3.80	3.10
Nos. C1-C6 (6)	9.30	*15.00*
Nos. C3-C9 (7)	13.75	10.00
Nos. C1-C3 (3)	9.50	3.90
Nos. C1-C2 (2)	3.75	2.50
Nos. C37-C43 (7)	5.60	3.80
Nos. C1-C2 (2)	3.00	1.60
Nos. C7-C13 (7)	8.35	8.35
Nos. C18-C24 (7)	7.05	5.00
Nos. C1-C7 (7)	11.60	9.40
Nos. C1-C7 (7)	13.95	11.10
Set total (71) Stamps	106.35	86.40

Transport Plane CD88

Caravan and Plane CD89

1942

Dahomey C6-C13
Fr. Guinea C6-C13
Fr. Sudan C6-C13
Ivory Coast C6-C13
Mauritania C6-C13
Niger C6-C13
Senegal C17-C25
Togo C6-C13

Nos. C6-C13 (8)	7.15
Nos. C6-C13 (8)	5.75
Nos. C6-C13 (8)	8.00
Nos. C6-C13 (8)	11.15
Nos. C6-C13 (8)	9.75
Nos. C6-C13 (8)	6.90
Nos. C17-C25 (9)	9.45
Nos. C6-C13 (8)	6.75
Set total (65) Stamps	64.90

Red Cross

Marianne CD90

The surtax was for the French Red Cross and national relief.

1944

Cameroun B28
Fr. Equatorial Africa B38
Fr. Guiana B12
Fr. India B14
Fr. Polynesia B13
Fr. West Africa B1
Guadeloupe B12
Madagascar B15
Martinique B11
New Caledonia B13
Reunion B15
St. Pierre & Miquelon B13
Somali Coast B13
Wallis & Futuna Isls. B9

No. B28 (1)	2.00	1.60
No. B38 (1)	1.60	1.20
No. B12 (1)	1.75	1.25
No. B14 (1)	1.50	1.25
No. B13 (1)	2.00	1.60
No. B1 (1)	6.50	4.75
No. B12 (1)	1.40	1.00
No. B15 (1)	.90	.90
No. B11 (1)	1.20	1.20
No. B13 (1)	1.50	1.50
No. B15 (1)	1.60	1.10
No. B13 (1)	2.75	2.40
No. B13 (1)	1.75	2.00
No. B9 (1)	4.50	3.25
Set total (14) Stamps	30.95	25.00

Eboue

CD91

Felix Eboue, first French colonial administrator to proclaim resistance to Germany after French surrender in World War II.

1945

Cameroun 296-297
Fr. Equatorial Africa 156-157
Fr. Guiana 171-172
Fr. India 210-211
Fr. Polynesia 150-151
Fr. West Africa 15-16
Guadeloupe 187-188
Madagascar 259-260
Martinique 196-197
New Caledonia 274-275
Reunion 238-239
St. Pierre & Miquelon 322-323
Somali Coast 238-239

Nos. 296-297 (2)	2.40	1.95
Nos. 156-157 (2)	2.55	2.00
Nos. 171-172 (2)	2.45	2.00
Nos. 210-211 (2)	2.20	1.95
Nos. 150-151 (2)	3.60	2.85
Nos. 15-16 (2)	2.40	2.40
Nos. 187-188 (2)	2.05	1.60
Nos. 259-260 (2)	1.70	1.45
Nos. 196-197 (2)	2.05	1.55
Nos. 274-275 (2)	3.40	3.00
Nos. 238-239 (2)	2.40	2.00
Nos. 322-323 (2)	4.40	3.45
Nos. 238-239 (2)	2.45	2.10
Set total (26) Stamps	34.05	28.30

Victory

Victory — CD92

European victory of the Allied Nations in World War II.

1946, May 8

Cameroun C8
Fr. Equatorial Africa C24
Fr. Guiana C11
Fr. India C7
Fr. Polynesia C10
Fr. West Africa C4
Guadeloupe C3
Indo-China C19
Madagascar C44
Martinique C3
New Caledonia C14
Reunion C25
St. Pierre & Miquelon C8
Somali Coast C8
Wallis & Futuna Isls. C1

No. C8 (1)	1.60	1.20
No. C24 (1)	1.60	1.25
No. C11 (1)	1.75	1.25
No. C7 (1)	1.00	2.00
No. C10 (1)	2.75	2.00
No. C4 (1)	1.60	1.20
No. C3 (1)	1.25	1.00
No. C19 (1)	1.00	.55
No. C44 (1)	.90	.35
No. C3 (1)	1.30	1.00
No. C14 (1)	2.25	1.25
No. C25 (1)	1.10	.90
No. C8 (1)	2.10	1.75
No. C8 (1)	1.75	1.40
No. C1 (1)	2.50	1.90
Set total (15) Stamps	24.45	19.00

Chad to Rhine

Leclerc's Departure from Chad — CD93

Battle at Cufra Oasis — CD94

Tanks in Action, Mareth — CD95

Normandy Invasion — CD96

Entering Paris — CD97

Liberation of Strasbourg — CD98

"Chad to the Rhine" march, 1942-44, by Gen. Jacques Leclerc's column, later French 2nd Armored Division.

1946, June 6

Cameroun C9-C14
Fr. Equatorial Africa C25-C30
Fr. Guiana C12-C17
Fr. India C8-C13
Fr. Polynesia C11-C16
Fr. West Africa C5-C10
Guadeloupe C4-C9
Indo-China C20-C25
Madagascar C45-C50
Martinique C4-C9
New Caledonia C15-C20
Reunion C26-C31
St. Pierre & Miquelon C9-C14
Somali Coast C9-C14
Wallis & Futuna Isls. C2-C7

Nos. C9-C14 (6)	12.05	9.70
Nos. C25-C30 (6)	14.70	10.80
Nos. C12-C17 (6)	12.65	10.35
Nos. C8-C13 (6)	12.80	*15.00*
Nos. C11-C16 (6)	17.55	13.40
Nos. C5-C10 (6)	16.05	11.95
Nos. C4-C9 (6)	12.00	9.60
Nos. C20-C25 (6)	6.40	6.40
Nos. C45-C50 (6)	10.30	8.40
Nos. C4-C9 (6)	8.85	7.30
Nos. C15-C20 (6)	13.40	11.90
Nos. C26-C31 (6)	10.25	6.55
Nos. C9-C14 (6)	17.30	14.35
Nos. C9-C14 (6)	18.10	12.65
Nos. C2-C7 (6)	13.75	10.45
Set total (90) Stamps	196.15	158.80

UPU

French Colonials, Globe and Plane — CD99

Universal Postal Union, 75th anniv.

1949, July 4

Cameroun C29
Fr. Equatorial Africa C34
Fr. India C17
Fr. Polynesia C20
Fr. West Africa C15
Indo-China C26
Madagascar C55
New Caledonia C24
St. Pierre & Miquelon C18
Somali Coast C18
Togo C18
Wallis & Futuna Isls. C10

No. C29 (1)	8.00	4.75
No. C34 (1)	16.00	12.00
No. C17 (1)	11.50	8.75
No. C20 (1)	20.00	15.00
No. C15 (1)	12.00	8.75
No. C26 (1)	4.75	4.00
No. C55 (1)	4.00	2.75
No. C24 (1)	8.25	5.25
No. C18 (1)	20.00	12.00
No. C18 (1)	14.00	10.50
No. C18 (1)	8.50	7.00
No. C10 (1)	12.50	8.25
Set total (12) Stamps	139.50	99.00

Tropical Medicine

Doctor Treating Infant CD100

The surtax was for charitable work.

1950

Cameroun B29
Fr. Equatorial Africa B39
Fr. India B15
Fr. Polynesia B14
Fr. West Africa B3
Madagascar B17
New Caledonia B14
St. Pierre & Miquelon B14
Somali Coast B14
Togo B11

No. B29 (1)	7.25	5.50
No. B39 (1)	7.25	5.50
No. B15 (1)	6.00	4.00
No. B14 (1)	10.50	8.00
No. B3 (1)	9.50	7.25
No. B17 (1)	5.50	5.50
No. B14 (1)	6.75	5.25
No. B14 (1)	17.00	13.00
No. B14 (1)	7.75	6.25
No. B11 (1)	5.00	3.50
Set total (10) Stamps	82.50	63.75

Military Medal

Medal, Early Marine and Colonial Soldier — CD101

Centenary of the creation of the French Military Medal.

1952

Cameroun 322
Comoro Isls. 39
Fr. Equatorial Africa 186

Fr. India	233
Fr. Polynesia	179
Fr. West Africa	57
Madagascar	286
New Caledonia	295
St. Pierre & Miquelon	345
Somali Coast	267
Togo	327
Wallis & Futuna Isls.	149

No. 322 (1)	7.25	3.25
No. 39 (1)	50.00	40.00
No. 186 (1)	8.00	5.50
No. 233 (1)	5.50	7.00
No. 179 (1)	13.50	10.00
No. 57 (1)	8.75	6.50
No. 286 (1)	3.75	2.50
No. 295 (1)	7.50	6.00
No. 345 (1)	17.00	13.00
No. 267 (1)	9.00	8.00
No. 327 (1)	5.50	4.75
No. 149 (1)	9.50	7.00
Set total (12) Stamps	145.25	113.50

Liberation

Allied Landing, Victory Sign and Cross of Lorraine — CD102

Liberation of France, 10th anniv.

1954, June 6

Cameroun	C32
Comoro Isls.	C4
Fr. Equatorial Africa	C38
Fr. India	C18
Fr. Polynesia	C22
Fr. West Africa	C17
Madagascar	C57
New Caledonia	C25
St. Pierre & Miquelon	C19
Somali Coast	C19
Togo	C19
Wallis & Futuna Isls.	C11

No. C32 (1)	7.25	4.75
No. C4 (1)	35.00	20.00
No. C38 (1)	12.00	8.00
No. C18 (1)	11.00	8.00
No. C22 (1)	10.00	8.00
No. C17 (1)	12.00	5.50
No. C57 (1)	3.25	2.00
No. C25 (1)	8.25	5.00
No. C19 (1)	18.00	12.00
No. C19 (1)	10.50	8.50
No. C19 (1)	7.00	5.50
No. C11 (1)	12.50	8.25
Set total (12) Stamps	146.75	95.50

FIDES

Plowmen CD103

Efforts of FIDES, the Economic and Social Development Fund for Overseas Possessions (Fonds d' Investissement pour le Developpement Economique et Social). Each stamp has a different design.

1956

Cameroun	326-329
Comoro Isls.	43
Fr. Equatorial Africa	189-192
Fr. Polynesia	181
Fr. West Africa	65-72
Madagascar	292-295
New Caledonia	303
St. Pierre & Miquelon	350
Somali Coast	268-269
Togo	331

Nos. 326-329 (4)	6.90	3.20
No. 43 (1)	2.25	1.60
Nos. 189-192 (4)	3.20	1.65
No. 181 (1)	4.00	2.00
Nos. 65-72 (8)	16.00	6.35
Nos. 292-295 (4)	2.25	1.20
No. 303 (1)	1.90	1.10
No. 350 (1)	6.50	3.50
Nos. 268-269 (2)	5.35	3.15
No. 331 (1)	4.25	2.10
Set total (27) Stamps	52.60	25.85

Flower

CD104

Each stamp shows a different flower.

1958-9

Cameroun	333
Comoro Isls.	45
Fr. Equatorial Africa	200-201
Fr. Polynesia	192
Fr. So. & Antarctic Terr.	11
Fr. West Africa	79-83
Madagascar	301-302
New Caledonia	304-305
St. Pierre & Miquelon	357
Somali Coast	270
Togo	348-349
Wallis & Futuna Isls.	152

No. 333 (1)	1.60	.80
No. 45 (1)	5.50	4.50
Nos. 200-201 (2)	3.60	1.60
No. 192 (1)	6.50	4.00
No. 11 (1)	10.00	8.00
Nos. 79-83 (5)	10.45	5.60
Nos. 301-302 (2)	1.50	.55
Nos. 304-305 (2)	9.25	3.00
No. 357 (1)	4.50	2.40
No. 270 (1)	4.25	1.40
Nos. 348-349 (2)	1.10	.50
No. 152 (1)	4.50	2.50
Set total (20) Stamps	62.75	34.85

Human Rights

Sun, Dove and U.N. Emblem CD105

10th anniversary of the signing of the Universal Declaration of Human Rights.

1958

Comoro Isls.	44
Fr. Equatorial Africa	202
Fr. Polynesia	191
Fr. West Africa	85
Madagascar	300
New Caledonia	306
St. Pierre & Miquelon	356
Somali Coast	274
Wallis & Futuna Isls.	153

No. 44 (1)	11.00	11.00
No. 202 (1)	2.40	1.25
No. 191 (1)	13.00	8.75
No. 85 (1)	2.40	2.00
No. 300 (1)	.80	.40
No. 306 (1)	3.00	1.50
No. 356 (1)	3.50	2.50
No. 274 (1)	3.50	2.10
No. 153 (1)	5.75	4.00
Set total (9) Stamps	45.35	33.50

C.C.T.A.

CD106

Commission for Technical Cooperation in Africa south of the Sahara, 10th anniv.

1960

Cameroun	339
Cent. Africa	3
Chad	66
Congo, P.R.	90
Dahomey	138
Gabon	150
Ivory Coast	180
Madagascar	317
Mali	9
Mauritania	117
Niger	104
Upper Volta	89

No. 339 (1)	1.60	.75
No. 3 (1)	1.90	.65
No. 66 (1)	1.90	.50
No. 90 (1)	1.00	1.00
No. 138 (1)	.50	.25
No. 150 (1)	1.40	1.10
No. 180 (1)	1.10	.50
No. 317 (1)	.60	.30
No. 9 (1)	1.40	.50
No. 117 (1)	.75	.40
No. 104 (1)	.85	.45
No. 89 (1)	.45	.40
Set total (12) Stamps	13.45	6.80

Air Afrique, 1961

Modern and Ancient Africa, Map and Planes — CD107

Founding of Air Afrique (African Airlines).

1961-62

Cameroun	C37
Cent. Africa	C5
Chad	C7
Congo, P.R.	C5
Dahomey	C17
Gabon	C5
Ivory Coast	C18
Mauritania	C17
Niger	C22
Senegal	C31
Upper Volta	C4

No. C37 (1)	1.00	.50
No. C5 (1)	1.00	.55
No. C7 (1)	1.00	.25
No. C5 (1)	1.75	.90
No. C17 (1)	.80	.40
No. C5 (1)	11.00	6.00
No. C18 (1)	2.00	1.25
No. C17 (1)	2.50	1.25
No. C22 (1)	1.75	.90
No. C31 (1)	.80	.30
No. C4 (1)	.65	.45
Set total (11) Stamps	24.25	12.75

Anti-Malaria

CD108

World Health Organization drive to eradicate malaria.

1962, Apr. 7

Cameroun	B36
Cent. Africa	B1
Chad	B1
Comoro Isls.	B1
Congo, P.R.	B3
Dahomey	B15
Gabon	B4
Ivory Coast	B15
Madagascar	B19
Mali	B1
Mauritania	B16
Niger	B14
Senegal	B16
Somali Coast	B15
Upper Volta	B1

No. B36 (1)	1.00	.45
No. B1 (1)	1.40	1.40
No. B1 (1)	1.25	.50
No. B1 (1)	4.00	4.00
No. B3 (1)	1.40	1.00
No. B15 (1)	.75	.75
No. B4 (1)	1.00	1.00
No. B15 (1)	1.25	1.25
No. B19 (1)	.90	.50
No. B1 (1)	1.25	.60
No. B16 (1)	.80	.80
No. B14 (1)	.60	.60
No. B16 (1)	1.10	.65
No. B15 (1)	7.00	7.00
No. B1 (1)	.95	.95
Set total (15) Stamps	24.65	21.45

Abidjan Games

CD109

Abidjan Games, Ivory Coast, Dec. 24-31, 1961. Each stamp shows a different sport.

1962

Cent. Africa	19-20, C6
Chad	83-84, C8
Congo, P.R.	103-104, C7
Gabon	163-164, C6
Niger	109-111
Upper Volta	103-105

Nos. 19-20,C6 (3)	3.90	2.60
Nos. 83-84,C8 (3)	6.30	1.55
Nos. 103-104,C7 (3)	3.85	1.80
Nos. 163-164,C6 (3)	5.00	3.00
Nos. 109-111 (3)	2.60	1.10
Nos. 103-105 (3)	3.15	1.80
Set total (18) Stamps	24.80	11.85

African and Malagasy Union

Flag of Union CD110

First anniversary of the Union.

1962, Sept. 8

Cameroun	373
Cent. Africa	21
Chad	85
Congo, P.R.	105
Dahomey	155
Gabon	165
Ivory Coast	198
Madagascar	332
Mauritania	170
Niger	112
Senegal	211
Upper Volta	106

No. 373 (1)	2.00	.75
No. 21 (1)	1.25	.60
No. 85 (1)	1.25	.25
No. 105 (1)	1.50	.50
No. 155 (1)	1.25	.90
No. 165 (1)	1.60	1.25
No. 198 (1)	2.10	.75
No. 332 (1)	.80	.80
No. 170 (1)	.75	.50
No. 112 (1)	.80	.40
No. 211 (1)	.80	.50
No. 106 (1)	1.50	.90
Set total (12) Stamps	15.60	8.10

Telstar

Telstar and Globe Showing Andover and Pleumeur-Bodou — CD111

First television connection of the United States and Europe through the Telstar satellite, July 11-12, 1962.

1962-63

Andorra, French	154
Comoro Isls.	C7
Fr. Polynesia	C29
Fr. So. & Antarctic Terr.	C5
New Caledonia	C33
St. Pierre & Miquelon	C26
Somali Coast	C31
Wallis & Futuna Isls.	C17

No. 154 (1)	2.00	1.60
No. C7 (1)	5.00	3.00
No. C29 (1)	11.50	8.00

No. C5 (1)	29.00	21.00
No. C33 (1)	30.00	18.50
No. C26 (1)	7.25	5.50
No. C31 (1)	1.00	1.00
No. C17 (1)	3.50	3.50
Set total (8) Stamps	89.25	62.10

Freedom From Hunger

World Map and Wheat Emblem CD112

U.N. Food and Agriculture Organization's "Freedom from Hunger" campaign.

1963, Mar. 21

Cameroun	B37-B38
Cent. Africa	B2
Chad	B2
Congo, P.R.	B4
Dahomey	B16
Gabon	B5
Ivory Coast	B16
Madagascar	B21
Mauritania	B17
Niger	B15
Senegal	B17
Upper Volta	B2

Nos. B37-B38 (2)	2.25	.75
No. B2 (1)	1.25	1.25
No. B2 (1)	2.00	.50
No. B4 (1)	1.40	1.00
No. B16 (1)	.80	.80
No. B5 (1)	1.00	1.00
No. B16 (1)	1.50	1.50
No. B21 (1)	.70	.45
No. B17 (1)	.80	.80
No. B15 (1)	.60	.60
No. B17 (1)	.80	.50
No. B2 (1)	.95	.95
Set total (13) Stamps	14.05	10.10

Red Cross Centenary

CD113

Centenary of the International Red Cross.

1963, Sept. 2

Comoro Isls.	55
Fr. Polynesia	205
New Caledonia	328
St. Pierre & Miquelon	367
Somali Coast	297
Wallis & Futuna Isls.	165

No. 55 (1)	9.50	7.00
No. 205 (1)	15.00	12.00
No. 328 (1)	9.00	6.75
No. 367 (1)	12.00	6.75
No. 297 (1)	6.25	6.25
No. 165 (1)	4.00	3.50
Set total (6) Stamps	55.75	42.25

African Postal Union, 1963

UAMPT Emblem, Radio Masts, Plane and Mail CD114

Establishment of the African and Malagasy Posts and Telecommunications Union.

1963, Sept. 8

Cameroun	C47
Cent. Africa	C10
Chad	C9
Congo, P.R.	C13
Dahomey	C19
Gabon	C13
Ivory Coast	C25
Madagascar	C75
Mauritania	C22
Niger	C27
Rwanda	36
Senegal	C32
Upper Volta	C9

No. C47 (1)	2.25	1.00
No. C10 (1)	1.90	.85
No. C9 (1)	2.40	.60
No. C13 (1)	1.40	.75
No. C19 (1)	.75	.25
No. C13 (1)	1.90	.80
No. C25 (1)	2.50	1.50
No. C75 (1)	1.25	.80
No. C22 (1)	1.50	.60
No. C27 (1)	1.25	.60
No. 36 (1)	.90	.55
No. C32 (1)	1.75	.50
No. C9 (1)	1.50	.75
Set total (13) Stamps	21.25	9.55

Air Afrique, 1963

Symbols of Flight — CD115

First anniversary of Air Afrique and inauguration of DC-8 service.

1963, Nov. 19

Cameroun	C48
Chad	C10
Congo, P.R.	C14
Gabon	C18
Ivory Coast	C26
Mauritania	C26
Niger	C35
Senegal	C33

No. C48 (1)	1.25	.40
No. C10 (1)	2.40	.60
No. C14 (1)	1.60	.60
No. C18 (1)	1.40	.65
No. C26 (1)	1.00	.50
No. C26 (1)	.70	.25
No. C35 (1)	.90	.50
No. C33 (1)	2.00	.65
Set total (8) Stamps	11.25	4.15

Europafrica

Europe and Africa Linked — CD116

Signing of an economic agreement between the European Economic Community and the African and Malagasy Union, Yaounde, Cameroun, July 20, 1963.

1963-64

Cameroun	402
Cent. Africa	C12
Chad	C11
Congo, P.R.	C16
Gabon	C19
Ivory Coast	217
Niger	C43
Upper Volta	C11

No. 402 (1)	2.25	.60
No. C12 (1)	2.50	1.75
No. C11 (1)	2.00	.50
No. C16 (1)	1.60	1.00
No. C19 (1)	1.40	.75
No. 217 (1)	1.10	.35
No. C43 (1)	.85	.50
No. C11 (1)	1.50	.80
Set total (8) Stamps	13.20	6.25

Human Rights

Scales of Justice and Globe CD117

15th anniversary of the Universal Declaration of Human Rights.

1963, Dec. 10

Comoro Isls.	56
Fr. Polynesia	206
New Caledonia	329
St. Pierre & Miquelon	368
Somali Coast	300
Wallis & Futuna Isls.	166

No. 56 (1)	9.50	7.50
No. 205 (1)	15.00	12.00
No. 329 (1)	8.00	6.00
No. 368 (1)	6.50	3.50
No. 300 (1)	8.50	8.50
No. 166 (1)	8.00	7.50
Set total (6) Stamps	55.50	45.00

PHILATEC

Stamp Album, Champs Elysees Palace and Horses of Marly CD118

Intl. Philatelic and Postal Techniques Exhibition, Paris, June 5-21, 1964.

1963-64

Comoro Isls.	60
France	1078
Fr. Polynesia	207
New Caledonia	341
St. Pierre & Miquelon	369
Somali Coast	301
Wallis & Futuna Isls.	167

No. 60 (1)	4.50	4.00
No. 1078 (1)	.25	.25
No. 206 (1)	15.00	10.00
No. 341 (1)	8.50	6.75
No. 369 (1)	11.00	8.00
No. 301 (1)	7.75	7.75
No. 167 (1)	3.50	3.50
Set total (7) Stamps	50.50	40.25

Cooperation

CD119

Cooperation between France and the French-speaking countries of Africa and Madagascar.

1964

Cameroun	409-410
Cent. Africa	39
Chad	103
Congo, P.R.	121
Dahomey	193
France	1111
Gabon	175
Ivory Coast	221
Madagascar	360
Mauritania	181
Niger	143
Senegal	236
Togo	495

Nos. 409-410 (2)	2.50	.50
No. 39 (1)	1.00	.55
No. 103 (1)	1.00	.25
No. 121 (1)	.80	.35
No. 193 (1)	.80	.35
No. 1111 (1)	.25	.25
No. 175 (1)	.90	.60
No. 221 (1)	1.10	.35
No. 360 (1)	.60	.25
No. 181 (1)	.60	.35
No. 143 (1)	.80	.40
No. 236 (1)	1.60	.85
No. 495 (1)	.70	.25
Set total (14) Stamps	12.65	5.30

ITU

Telegraph, Syncom Satellite and ITU Emblem CD120

Intl. Telecommunication Union, Cent.

1965, May 17

Comoro Isls.	C14
Fr. Polynesia	C33
Fr. So. & Antarctic Terr.	C8
New Caledonia	C40
New Hebrides	124-125
St. Pierre & Miquelon	C29
Somali Coast	C36
Wallis & Futuna Isls.	C20

No. C14 (1)	20.00	10.00
No. C33 (1)	80.00	52.50
No. C8 (1)	200.00	160.00
No. C40 (1)	12.00	9.00
Nos. 124-125 (2)	40.50	34.00
No. C29 (1)	24.00	11.00
No. C36 (1)	15.00	9.00
No. C20 (1)	21.00	15.00
Set total (9) Stamps	412.50	300.50

French Satellite A-1

Diamant Rocket and Launching Installation — CD121

Launching of France's first satellite, Nov. 26, 1965.

1965-66

Comoro Isls.	C16a
France	1138a
Reunion	359a
Fr. Polynesia	C41a
Fr. So. & Antarctic Terr.	C10a
New Caledonia	C45a
St. Pierre & Miquelon	C31a
Somali Coast	C40a
Wallis & Futuna Isls.	C23a

No. C16a (1)	11.00	11.00
No. 1138a (1)	.65	.65
No. 359a (1)	3.50	3.00
No. C41a (1)	14.00	14.00
No. C10a (1)	29.00	24.00
No. C45a (1)	8.25	7.00
No. C31a (1)	15.00	15.00
No. C40a (1)	7.00	7.00
No. C23a (1)	9.25	9.25
Set total (9) Stamps	97.65	90.90

French Satellite D-1

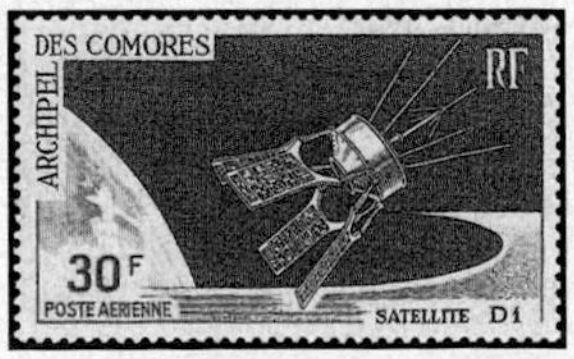

D-1 Satellite in Orbit — CD122

Launching of the D-1 satellite at Hammaguir, Algeria, Feb. 17, 1966.

1966

Comoro Isls.	C17
France	1148

Fr. Polynesia	C42
Fr. So. & Antarctic Terr.	C11
New Caledonia	C46
St. Pierre & Miquelon	C32
Somali Coast	C49
Wallis & Futuna Isls.	C24

No. C17 (1)	4.00	4.00
No. 1148 (1)	.25	.25
No. C42 (1)	7.00	4.75
No. C11 (1)	57.50	40.00
No. C46 (1)	3.00	2.00
No. C32 (1)	10.50	6.50
No. C49 (1)	4.25	2.75
No. C24 (1)	3.50	3.50
Set total (8) Stamps	90.00	63.75

Air Afrique, 1966

Planes and Air Afrique Emblem — CD123

Introduction of DC-8F planes by Air Afrique.

1966

Cameroun	C79
Cent. Africa	C35
Chad	C26
Congo, P.R.	C42
Dahomey	C42
Gabon	C47
Ivory Coast	C32
Mauritania	C57
Niger	C63
Senegal	C47
Togo	C54
Upper Volta	C31

No. C79 (1)	.80	.25
No. C35 (1)	1.00	.40
No. C26 (1)	1.00	.25
No. C42 (1)	1.00	.25
No. C42 (1)	.75	.25
No. C47 (1)	.90	.35
No. C32 (1)	1.00	.60
No. C57 (1)	.80	.30
No. C63 (1)	.65	.35
No. C47 (1)	.80	.30
No. C54 (1)	.80	.25
No. C31 (1)	.75	.50
Set total (12) Stamps	10.25	4.05

African Postal Union, 1967

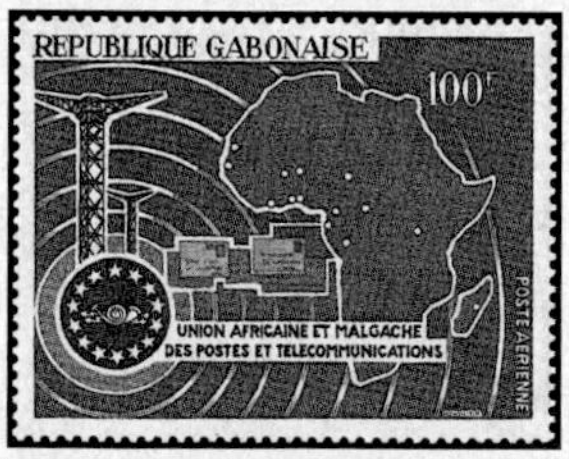

Telecommunications Symbols and Map of Africa — CD124

Fifth anniversary of the establishment of the African and Malagasy Union of Posts and Telecommunications, UAMPT.

1967

Cameroun	C90
Cent. Africa	C46
Chad	C37
Congo, P.R.	C57
Dahomey	C61
Gabon	C58
Ivory Coast	C34
Madagascar	C85
Mauritania	C65
Niger	C75
Rwanda	C1-C3
Senegal	C60
Togo	C81
Upper Volta	C50

No. C90 (1)	2.40	.65
No. C46 (1)	2.25	.85
No. C37 (1)	2.00	.60
No. C57 (1)	1.60	.60
No. C61 (1)	1.75	.95
No. C58 (1)	2.25	.95
No. C34 (1)	3.50	1.50
No. C85 (1)	1.25	.60
No. C65 (1)	1.25	.60
No. C75 (1)	1.40	.60
Nos. C1-C3 (3)	2.30	1.25
No. C60 (1)	1.75	.50
No. C81 (1)	1.90	.30
No. C50 (1)	1.80	.70
Set total (16) Stamps	27.40	10.65

Monetary Union

Gold Token of the Ashantis, 17-18th Centuries — CD125

West African Monetary Union, 5th anniv.

1967, Nov. 4

Dahomey	244
Ivory Coast	259
Mauritania	238
Niger	204
Senegal	294
Togo	623
Upper Volta	181

No. 244 (1)	.65	.65
No. 259 (1)	.85	.40
No. 238 (1)	.45	.25
No. 204 (1)	.45	.25
No. 294 (1)	.60	.25
No. 623 (1)	.60	.25
No. 181 (1)	.70	.35
Set total (7) Stamps	4.30	2.40

WHO Anniversary

Sun, Flowers and WHO Emblem CD126

World Health Organization, 20th anniv.

1968, May 4

Afars & Issas	317
Comoro Isls.	73
Fr. Polynesia	241-242
Fr. So. & Antarctic Terr.	31
New Caledonia	367
St. Pierre & Miquelon	377
Wallis & Futuna Isls.	169

No. 317 (1)	3.00	3.00
No. 73 (1)	2.75	2.00
Nos. 241-242 (2)	22.00	12.75
No. 31 (1)	65.00	45.00
No. 367 (1)	4.50	2.25
No. 377 (1)	12.00	8.00
No. 169 (1)	6.50	4.50
Set total (8) Stamps	115.75	77.50

Human Rights Year

Human Rights Flame — CD127

1968, Aug. 10

Afars & Issas	322-323
Comoro Isls.	76
Fr. Polynesia	243-244
Fr. So. & Antarctic Terr.	32
New Caledonia	369
St. Pierre & Miquelon	382
Wallis & Futuna Isls.	170

Nos. 322-323 (2)	6.50	3.70
No. 76 (1)	3.50	3.50
Nos. 241-242 (2)	22.00	12.75
No. 31 (1)	65.00	45.00
No. 369 (1)	3.00	1.50
No. 382 (1)	10.00	5.50
No. 170 (1)	3.75	3.75
Set total (9) Stamps	113.75	75.70

2nd PHILEXAFRIQUE

CD128

Opening of PHILEXAFRIQUE, Abidjan, Feb. 14. Each stamp shows a local scene and stamp.

1969, Feb. 14

Cameroun	C118
Cent. Africa	C65
Chad	C48
Congo, P.R.	C77
Dahomey	C94
Gabon	C82
Ivory Coast	C38-C40
Madagascar	C92
Mali	C65
Mauritania	C80
Niger	C104
Senegal	C68
Togo	C104
Upper Volta	C62

No. C118 (1)	3.25	1.25
No. C65 (1)	1.90	1.90
No. C48 (1)	2.40	1.00
No. C77 (1)	2.00	1.75
No. C94 (1)	2.25	2.25
No. C82 (1)	2.25	2.25
Nos. C38-C40 (3)	14.50	14.50
No. C92 (1)	1.75	.85
No. C65 (1)	2.00	1.00
No. C80 (1)	1.90	.75
No. C104 (1)	2.75	1.90
No. C68 (1)	2.00	1.40
No. C104 (1)	2.25	.45
No. C62 (1)	4.00	3.75
Set total (16) Stamps	45.20	35.00

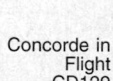

Concorde

Concorde in Flight CD129

First flight of the prototype Concorde supersonic plane at Toulouse, Mar. 1, 1969.

1969

Afars & Issas	C56
Comoro Isls.	C29
France	C42
Fr. Polynesia	C50
Fr. So. & Antarctic Terr.	C18
New Caledonia	C63
St. Pierre & Miquelon	C40
Wallis & Futuna Isls.	C30

No. C56 (1)	25.00	16.00
No. C29 (1)	24.00	16.00
No. C42 (1)	1.00	.35
No. C50 (1)	55.00	35.00
No. C18 (1)	55.00	37.50
No. C63 (1)	35.00	20.00
No. C40 (1)	32.50	12.00
No. C30 (1)	15.00	10.00
Set total (8) Stamps	242.50	146.85

Development Bank

Bank Emblem — CD130

African Development Bank, fifth anniv.

1969

Cameroun	499
Chad	217
Congo, P.R.	181-182
Ivory Coast	281
Mali	127-128
Mauritania	267
Niger	220
Senegal	317-318
Upper Volta	201

No. 499 (1)	.80	.25
No. 217 (1)	.70	.25
Nos. 181-182 (2)	.80	.50
No. 281 (1)	.70	.40
Nos. 127-128 (2)	1.25	.50
No. 267 (1)	.60	.25
No. 220 (1)	.60	.30
Nos. 317-318 (2)	1.55	.50
No. 201 (1)	.70	.30
Set total (12) Stamps	7.70	3.25

ILO

ILO Headquarters, Geneva, and Emblem — CD131

Intl. Labor Organization, 50th anniv.

1969-70

Afars & Issas	337
Comoro Isls.	83
Fr. Polynesia	251-252
Fr. So. & Antarctic Terr.	35
New Caledonia	379
St. Pierre & Miquelon	396
Wallis & Futuna Isls.	172

No. 337 (1)	2.75	2.00
No. 83 (1)	1.25	.75
Nos. 251-252 (2)	24.00	12.50
No. 35 (1)	18.50	11.00
No. 379 (1)	2.25	1.10
No. 396 (1)	10.00	5.50
No. 172 (1)	3.00	2.90
Set total (8) Stamps	61.75	35.75

ASECNA

Map of Africa, Plane and Airport CD132

10th anniversary of the Agency for the Security of Aerial Navigation in Africa and Madagascar (ASECNA, Agence pour la Securite de la Navigation Aerienne en Afrique et a Madagascar).

1969-70

Cameroun	500
Cent. Africa	119
Chad	222
Congo, P.R.	197
Dahomey	269
Gabon	260
Ivory Coast	287
Mali	130
Niger	221
Senegal	321
Upper Volta	204

No. 500 (1)	2.00	.60
No. 119 (1)	2.25	.80
No. 222 (1)	1.00	.25
No. 197 (1)	2.00	.40
No. 269 (1)	.90	.55
No. 260 (1)	1.75	.75
No. 287 (1)	.90	.40
No. 130 (1)	1.00	.40
No. 221 (1)	1.25	.70
No. 321 (1)	1.60	.50
No. 204 (1)	1.75	1.00
Set total (11) Stamps	16.40	6.35

U.P.U. Headquarters

CD133

New Universal Postal Union headquarters, Bern, Switzerland.

1970

Afars & Issas	342
Algeria	443
Cameroun	503-504
Cent. Africa	125
Chad	225
Comoro Isls.	84
Congo, P.R.	216
Fr. Polynesia	261-262
Fr. So. & Antarctic Terr.	36
Gabon	258
Ivory Coast	295
Madagascar	444
Mali	134-135
Mauritania	283
New Caledonia	382
Niger	231-232
St. Pierre & Miquelon	397-398
Senegal	328-329
Tunisia	535
Wallis & Futuna Isls.	173

No. 342 (1)	2.50	1.40
No. 443 (1)	1.10	.40
Nos. 503-504 (2)	2.60	.55
No. 125 (1)	1.90	.70
No. 225 (1)	1.00	.25
No. 84 (1)	5.50	2.00
No. 216 (1)	.80	.25
Nos. 261-262 (2)	20.00	10.00
No. 36 (1)	45.00	29.00
No. 258 (1)	.90	.55
No. 295 (1)	1.10	.50
No. 444 (1)	.55	.25
Nos. 134-135 (2)	1.25	.50
No. 283 (1)	.60	.30
No. 382 (1)	3.00	1.50
Nos. 231-232 (2)	1.20	.60
Nos. 397-398 (2)	34.00	17.50
Nos. 328-329 (2)	1.55	.55
No. 535 (1)	.60	.25
No. 173 (1)	4.00	4.00
Set total (26) Stamps	129.15	71.05

De Gaulle

CD134

First anniversary of the death of Charles de Gaulle, (1890-1970), President of France.

1971-72

Afars & Issas	356-357
Comoro Isls.	104-105
France	1325a
Fr. Polynesia	270-271
Fr. So. & Antarctic Terr.	52-53
New Caledonia	393-394
Reunion	380a
St. Pierre & Miquelon	417-418
Wallis & Futuna Isls.	177-178

Nos. 356-357 (2)	14.50	9.50
Nos. 104-105 (2)	9.00	5.75
No. 1325a (1)	4.50	4.00
Nos. 270-271 (2)	51.50	29.50
Nos. 52-53 (2)	47.00	33.50
Nos. 393-394 (2)	25.00	11.75
No. 380a (1)	9.25	8.00
Nos. 417-418 (2)	57.50	30.00
Nos. 177-178 (2)	24.00	16.25
Set total (16) Stamps	242.25	148.25

African Postal Union, 1971

UAMPT Building, Brazzaville, Congo — CD135

10th anniversary of the establishment of the African and Malagasy Posts and Telecommunications Union, UAMPT. Each stamp has a different native design.

1971, Nov. 13

Cameroun	C177
Cent. Africa	C89
Chad	C94
Congo, P.R.	C136
Dahomey	C146
Gabon	C120
Ivory Coast	C47
Mauritania	C113
Niger	C164
Rwanda	C8
Senegal	C105
Togo	C166
Upper Volta	C97

No. C177 (1)	2.00	.50
No. C89 (1)	2.25	.85
No. C94 (1)	1.50	.50
No. C136 (1)	1.60	.75
No. C146 (1)	1.75	.80
No. C120 (1)	1.75	.70
No. C47 (1)	2.00	1.00
No. C113 (1)	1.20	.65
No. C164 (1)	1.25	.60
No. C8 (1)	2.75	2.25
No. C105 (1)	1.60	.50
No. C166 (1)	1.25	.40
No. C97 (1)	1.50	.70
Set total (13) Stamps	22.40	10.20

West African Monetary Union

African Couple, City, Village and Commemorative Coin — CD136

West African Monetary Union, 10th anniv.

1972, Nov. 2

Dahomey	300
Ivory Coast	331
Mauritania	299
Niger	258
Senegal	374
Togo	825
Upper Volta	280

No. 300 (1)	.65	.25
No. 331 (1)	1.00	.50
No. 299 (1)	.75	.25
No. 258 (1)	.55	.30
No. 374 (1)	.50	.30
No. 825 (1)	.60	.25
No. 280 (1)	.60	.25
Set total (7) Stamps	4.65	2.10

African Postal Union, 1973

Telecommunications Symbols and Map of Africa — CD137

11th anniversary of the African and Malagasy Posts and Telecommunications Union (UAMPT).

1973, Sept. 12

Cameroun	574
Cent. Africa	194
Chad	294
Congo, P.R.	289
Dahomey	311
Gabon	320
Ivory Coast	361
Madagascar	500
Mauritania	304
Niger	287
Rwanda	540
Senegal	393
Togo	849
Upper Volta	297

No. 574 (1)	1.75	.40
No. 194 (1)	1.25	.75
No. 294 (1)	1.75	.40
No. 289 (1)	1.60	.50
No. 311 (1)	1.25	.55
No. 320 (1)	1.40	.75
No. 361 (1)	2.50	1.00
No. 500 (1)	1.00	.35
No. 304 (1)	1.10	.40
No. 287 (1)	.90	.60
No. 540 (1)	3.75	2.00
No. 393 (1)	1.60	.50
No. 849 (1)	1.00	.35
No. 297 (1)	1.25	.70
Set total (14) Stamps	22.10	9.25

Philexafrique II — Essen

CD138

CD139

Designs: Indigenous fauna, local and German stamps. Types CD138-CD139 printed horizontally and vertically se-tenant in sheets of 10 (2x5). Label between horizontal pairs alternately commemoratives Philexafrique II, Libreville, Gabon, June 1978, and 2nd International Stamp Fair, Essen, Germany, Nov. 1-5.

1978-1979

Benin	C286a
Central Africa	C201a
Chad	C239a
Congo Republic	C246a
Djibouti	C122a
Gabon	C216a
Ivory Coast	C65a
Mali	C357a
Mauritania	C186a
Niger	C292a
Rwanda	C13a
Senegal	C141a
Togo	C364a

No. C286a (1)	9.00	8.50
No. C201a (1)	7.50	7.50
No. C239a (1)	8.00	4.00
No. C246a (1)	7.00	7.00
No. C122a (1)	8.50	8.50
No. C216a (1)	6.50	4.00
No. C65a (1)	9.00	9.00
No. C357a (1)	7.50	3.00
No. C186a (1)	4.50	4.00
No. C292a (1)	6.00	5.00
No. C13a (1)	4.00	4.00
No. C147a (1)	10.00	4.00
No. C364a (1)	3.00	1.50
Set total (13) Stamps	90.50	70.00

BRITISH COMMONWEALTH OF NATIONS

The listings follow established trade practices when these issues are offered as units by dealers. The Peace issue, for example, includes only one stamp from the Indian state of Hyderabad. The U.P.U. issue includes the Egypt set. Pairs are included for those varieties issued with bilingual designs se-tenant.

Silver Jubilee

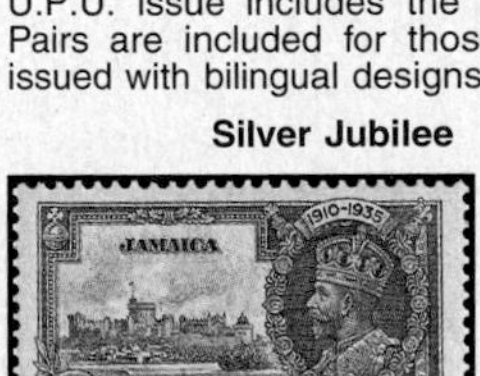

Windsor Castle and King George V CD301

Reign of King George V, 25th anniv.

1935

Antigua	77-80
Ascension	33-36
Bahamas	92-95
Barbados	186-189
Basutoland	11-14
Bechuanaland Protectorate	117-120
Bermuda	100-103
British Guiana	223-226
British Honduras	108-111
Cayman Islands	81-84
Ceylon	260-263
Cyprus	136-139
Dominica	90-93
Falkland Islands	77-80
Fiji	110-113
Gambia	125-128
Gibraltar	100-103
Gilbert & Ellice Islands	33-36
Gold Coast	108-111
Grenada	124-127
Hong Kong	147-150
Jamaica	109-112
Kenya, Uganda, Tanzania	42-45
Leeward Islands	96-99
Malta	184-187
Mauritius	204-207
Montserrat	85-88
Newfoundland	226-229
Nigeria	34-37
Northern Rhodesia	18-21
Nyasaland Protectorate	47-50
St. Helena	111-114
St. Kitts-Nevis	72-75
St. Lucia	91-94
St. Vincent	134-137
Seychelles	118-121
Sierra Leone	166-169
Solomon Islands	60-63
Somaliland Protectorate	77-80
Straits Settlements	213-216
Swaziland	20-23
Trinidad & Tobago	43-46
Turks & Caicos Islands	71-74
Virgin Islands	69-72

The following have different designs but are included in the omnibus set:

Great Britain	226-229
Offices in Morocco (Sp. Curr.)	67-70
Offices in Morocco (Br. Curr.)	226-229
Offices in Morocco (Fr. Curr.)	422-425
Offices in Morocco (Tangier)	508-510
Australia	152-154
Canada	211-216
Cook Islands	98-100
India	142-148
Nauru	31-34
New Guinea	46-47
New Zealand	199-201
Niue	67-69
Papua	114-117
Samoa	163-165
South Africa	68-71
Southern Rhodesia	33-36
South-West Africa	121-124

Nos. 77-80 (4)	22.50	*21.95*
Nos. 33-36 (4)	69.00	*135.00*
Nos. 92-95 (4)	25.00	*43.00*
Nos. 186-189 (4)	30.15	49.30
Nos. 11-14 (4)	12.10	*23.00*
Nos. 117-120 (4)	17.00	*31.25*
Nos. 100-103 (4)	18.00	*58.25*
Nos. 223-226 (4)	18.35	35.50
Nos. 108-111 (4)	15.25	*15.35*
Nos. 81-84 (4)	16.95	17.75
Nos. 260-263 (4)	12.60	23.35
Nos. 136-139 (4)	39.75	*34.40*
Nos. 90-93 (4)	18.85	19.85
Nos. 77-80 (4)	51.00	13.75
Nos. 110-113 (4)	15.25	29.00
Nos. 125-128 (4)	12.65	*29.25*
Nos. 100-103 (4)	32.00	47.50
Nos. 33-36 (4)	34.50	*53.50*
Nos. 108-111 (4)	26.25	*62.85*
Nos. 124-127 (4)	18.60	*45.00*
Nos. 147-150 (4)	76.50	21.00
Nos. 109-112 (4)	22.80	42.00
Nos. 42-45 (4)	9.25	*12.50*
Nos. 96-99 (4)	35.75	49.60
Nos. 184-187 (4)	25.00	34.70
Nos. 204-207 (4)	47.60	58.25
Nos. 85-88 (4)	10.25	*30.25*
Nos. 226-229 (4)	17.50	12.05
Nos. 34-37 (4)	13.25	*59.75*
Nos. 18-21 (4)	16.75	16.25
Nos. 47-50 (4)	39.75	*80.25*
Nos. 111-114 (4)	31.15	*33.25*
Nos. 72-75 (4)	11.55	*18.50*
Nos. 91-94 (4)	16.00	*20.80*
Nos. 134-137 (4)	9.45	*21.25*
Nos. 118-121 (4)	17.50	*31.00*
Nos. 166-169 (4)	21.25	*56.00*
Nos. 60-63 (4)	30.00	38.00
Nos. 77-80 (4)	18.75	*50.75*
Nos. 213-216 (4)	15.00	*25.10*
Nos. 20-23 (4)	6.80	18.25
Nos. 43-46 (4)	12.30	27.75
Nos. 71-74 (4)	9.25	16.25
Nos. 69-72 (4)	22.20	47.50
Nos. 226-229 (4)	7.25	*7.45*

Nos. 67-70 (4)	14.35	26.10
Nos. 226-229 (4)	8.20	28.90
Nos. 422-425 (4)	3.90	2.00
Nos. 508-510 (3)	18.80	23.85
Nos. 152-154 (3)	45.75	60.35
Nos. 211-216 (6)	26.30	13.35
Nos. 98-100 (3)	9.90	14.00
Nos. 142-148 (7)	23.25	11.80
Nos. 31-34 (4)	12.60	13.85
Nos. 46-47 (2)	4.35	1.70
Nos. 199-201 (3)	21.75	31.75
Nos. 67-69 (3)	7.80	22.50
Nos. 114-117 (4)	9.20	17.00
Nos. 163-165 (3)	4.40	5.50
Nos. 68-71 (4)	57.00	155.00
Nos. 33-36 (4)	30.00	45.25
Nos. 121-124 (4)	14.50	36.10
Set total (245) Stamps	1,361.	2,126.

Coronation

Queen Elizabeth and King George VI
CD302

1937

Aden 13-15
Antigua 81-83
Ascension 37-39
Bahamas 97-99
Barbados 190-192
Basutoland....................................15-17
Bechuanaland Protectorate......121-123
Bermuda....................................115-117
British Guiana............................227-229
British Honduras.......................112-114
Cayman Islands...........................97-99
Ceylon 275-277
Cyprus 140-142
Dominica....................................94-96
Falkland Islands 81-83
Fiji....................................114-116
Gambia....................................129-131
Gibraltar....................................104-106
Gilbert & Ellice Islands................37-39
Gold Coast 112-114
Grenada....................................128-130
Hong Kong 151-153
Jamaica 113-115
Kenya, Uganda, Tanzania 60-62
Leeward Islands 100-102
Malta....................................188-190
Mauritius....................................208-210
Montserrat 89-91
Newfoundland...........................230-232
Nigeria 50-52
Northern Rhodesia......................22-24
Nyasaland Protectorate...............51-53
St. Helena 115-117
St. Kitts-Nevis.............................76-78
St. Lucia 107-109
St. Vincent 138-140
Seychelles 122-124
Sierra Leone..............................170-172
Solomon Islands..........................64-66
Somaliland Protectorate..............81-83
Straits Settlements 235-237
Swaziland 24-26
Trinidad & Tobago 47-49
Turks & Caicos Islands 75-77
Virgin Islands.............................73-75

The following have different designs but are included in the omnibus set:

Great Britain 234
Offices in Morocco (Sp. Curr.)..........82
Offices in Morocco (Fr. Curr.)........439
Offices in Morocco (Tangier)..........514
Canada 237
Cook Islands 109-111
Nauru....................................35-38
Newfoundland...........................233-243
New Guinea....................................48-51
New Zealand 223-225
Niue 70-72
Papua 118-121
South Africa....................................74-78
Southern Rhodesia 38-41
South-West Africa 125-132

Nos. 13-15 (3)	3.00	5.75
Nos. 81-83 (3)	2.00	3.75
Nos. 37-39 (3)	2.75	2.75
Nos. 97-99 (3)	1.15	3.05
Nos. 190-192 (3)	1.10	1.95
Nos. 15-17 (3)	1.15	3.00
Nos. 121-123 (3)	.95	3.35
Nos. 115-117 (3)	1.25	5.00
Nos. 227-229 (3)	1.45	3.05
Nos. 112-114 (3)	1.20	2.35
Nos. 97-99 (3)	1.10	2.30
Nos. 275-277 (3)	8.25	10.35
Nos. 140-142 (3)	3.75	6.50
Nos. 94-96 (3)	.85	2.40
Nos. 81-83 (3)	2.90	2.30
Nos. 114-116 (3)	1.35	5.75
Nos. 129-131 (3)	1.00	4.70
Nos. 104-106 (3)	2.60	6.45
Nos. 37-39 (3)	.85	2.00
Nos. 112-114 (3)	3.10	10.00
Nos. 128-130 (3)	1.00	.85
Nos. 151-153 (3)	27.00	12.50
Nos. 113-115 (3)	1.95	1.25
Nos. 60-62 (3)	1.25	2.35
Nos. 100-102 (3)	1.55	4.00
Nos. 188-190 (3)	1.35	1.65
Nos. 208-210 (3)	2.05	3.75
Nos. 89-91 (3)	1.00	3.35
Nos. 230-232 (3)	7.00	2.80
Nos. 50-52 (3)	3.25	8.50
Nos. 22-24 (3)	.95	2.25
Nos. 51-53 (3)	1.05	1.30
Nos. 115-117 (3)	1.45	2.05
Nos. 76-78 (3)	.95	2.05
Nos. 107-109 (3)	1.05	2.05
Nos. 138-140 (3)	.80	4.75
Nos. 122-124 (3)	1.20	1.90
Nos. 170-172 (3)	1.95	5.65
Nos. 64-66 (3)	.90	2.00
Nos. 81-83 (3)	1.10	3.40
Nos. 235-237 (3)	3.25	1.60
Nos. 24-26 (3)	1.05	1.75
Nos. 47-49 (3)	1.00	1.00
Nos. 75-77 (3)	1.30	1.55
Nos. 73-75 (3)	1.20	5.00
No. 234 (1)	.25	.25
No. 82 (1)	.80	.80
No. 439 (1)	.35	.25
No. 514 (1)	.55	.55
No. 237 (1)	.35	.25
Nos. 109-111 (3)	.85	.80
Nos. 35-38 (4)	1.15	5.50
Nos. 233-243 (11)	34.50	30.40
Nos. 48-51 (4)	1.40	7.90
Nos. 223-225 (3)	1.40	2.75
Nos. 70-72 (3)	.80	2.05
Nos. 118-121 (4)	1.60	5.25
Nos. 74-78 (5)	9.25	10.80
Nos. 38-41 (4)	4.00	16.25
Nos. 125-132 (8)	5.50	8.45
Set total (189) Stamps	171.10	258.30

Peace

King George VI and Parliament Buildings, London
CD303

Return to peace at the close of World War II.

1945-46

Aden 28-29
Antigua 96-97
Ascension....................................50-51
Bahamas 130-131
Barbados..............................207-208
Bermuda..............................131-132
British Guiana..........................242-243
British Honduras.......................127-128
Cayman Islands.........................112-113
Ceylon 293-294
Cyprus....................................156-157
Dominica....................................112-113
Falkland Islands 97-98
Falkland Islands Dep.............1L9-1L10
Fiji....................................137-138
Gambia....................................144-145
Gibraltar....................................119-120
Gilbert & Ellice Islands................52-53
Gold Coast 128-129
Grenada....................................143-144
Jamaica 136-137
Kenya, Uganda, Tanzania 90-91
Leeward Islands 116-117
Malta....................................206-207
Mauritius....................................223-224
Montserrat 104-105
Nigeria 71-72
Northern Rhodesia......................46-47
Nyasaland Protectorate...............82-83
Pitcairn Islands..............................9-10
St. Helena 128-129
St. Kitts-Nevis.............................91-92
St. Lucia 127-128
St. Vincent..............................152-153
Seychelles 149-150
Sierra Leone..............................186-187
Solomon Islands..........................80-81
Somaliland Protectorate...........108-109
Trinidad & Tobago 62-63
Turks & Caicos Islands 90-91
Virgin Islands.............................88-89

The following have different designs but are included in the omnibus set:

Great Britain 264-265
Offices in Morocco (Tangier)....523-524
Aden
Kathiri State of Seiyun..............12-13
Qu'aiti State of Shihr and Mukalla .....
....12-13
Australia..............................200-202
Basutoland....................................29-31
Bechuanaland Protectorate......137-139
Burma....................................66-69
Cook Islands 127-130
Hong Kong 174-175
India....................................195-198
Hyderabad 51-53
New Zealand 247-257
Niue 90-93
Pakistan-Bahawalpur.....................O16
Samoa 191-194
South Africa..............................100-102
Southern Rhodesia 67-70
South-West Africa 153-155
Swaziland 38-40
Zanzibar....................................222-223

Nos. 28-29 (2)	.55	2.15
Nos. 96-97 (2)	.50	.80
Nos. 50-51 (2)	.90	1.80
Nos. 130-131 (2)	.50	1.40
Nos. 207-208 (2)	.50	1.10
Nos. 131-132 (2)	.55	.55
Nos. 242-243 (2)	1.05	1.40
Nos. 127-128 (2)	.50	.50
Nos. 112-113 (2)	.60	.80
Nos. 293-294 (2)	.60	2.10
Nos. 156-157 (2)	1.00	.70
Nos. 112-113 (2)	.50	.50
Nos. 97-98 (2)	.90	1.35
Nos. 1L9-1L10 (2)	1.40	1.00
Nos. 137-138 (2)	.50	1.75
Nos. 144-145 (2)	.50	.95
Nos. 119-120 (2)	.75	1.00
Nos. 52-53 (2)	.50	.50
Nos. 128-129 (2)	1.85	3.75
Nos. 143-144 (2)	.50	.95
Nos. 136-137 (2)	.90	12.50
Nos. 90-91 (2)	.65	.65
Nos. 116-117 (2)	.50	1.50
Nos. 206-207 (2)	.65	2.00
Nos. 223-224 (2)	.50	1.05
Nos. 104-105 (2)	.50	.50
Nos. 71-72 (2)	.70	2.75
Nos. 46-47 (2)	1.25	2.00
Nos. 82-83 (2)	.50	.50
Nos. 9-10 (2)	1.40	1.40
Nos. 128-129 (2)	.65	.70
Nos. 91-92 (2)	.50	.50
Nos. 127-128 (2)	.50	.60
Nos. 152-153 (2)	.50	.50
Nos. 149-150 (2)	.55	.50
Nos. 186-187 (2)	.50	.50
Nos. 80-81 (2)	.50	1.30
Nos. 108-109 (2)	.70	.50
Nos. 62-63 (2)	.50	.50
Nos. 90-91 (2)	.50	.50
Nos. 88-89 (2)	.50	.50
Nos. 264-265 (2)	.50	.70
Nos. 523-524 (2)	1.50	3.00
Nos. 12-13 (2)	.50	.90
Nos. 12-13 (2)	.50	1.25
Nos. 200-202 (3)	1.60	3.00
Nos. 29-31 (3)	2.10	2.60
Nos. 137-139 (3)	2.05	4.75
Nos. 66-69 (4)	1.60	1.30
Nos. 127-130 (4)	2.20	2.00
Nos. 174-175 (2)	7.25	3.15
Nos. 195-198 (4)	4.75	3.60
Nos. 51-53 (3)	1.50	1.70
Nos. 247-257 (11)	3.95	3.90
Nos. 90-93 (4)	1.70	2.20
No. O16 (1)	5.50	7.00
Nos. 191-194 (4)	2.05	1.00
Nos. 100-102 (3)	1.20	4.00
Nos. 67-70 (4)	1.40	1.75
Nos. 153-155 (3)	2.55	3.50
Nos. 38-40 (3)	2.40	5.50
Nos. 222-223 (2)	.65	1.00
Set total (151) Stamps	75.55	114.30

Silver Wedding

King George VI and Queen Elizabeth

CD304 CD305

1948-49

Aden 30-31
Kathiri State of Seiyun..............14-15
Qu'aiti State of Shihr and Mukalla .....
....14-15
Antigua 98-99
Ascension....................................52-53
Bahamas 148-149
Barbados..............................210-211
Basutoland....................................39-40
Bechuanaland Protectorate......147-148
Bermuda..............................133-134
British Guiana..........................244-245
British Honduras.......................129-130
Cayman Islands.........................116-117
Cyprus....................................158-159
Dominica....................................114-115
Falkland Islands 99-100
Falkland Islands Dep...........1L11-1L12
Fiji....................................139-140
Gambia....................................146-147
Gibraltar....................................121-122
Gilbert & Ellice Islands................54-55
Gold Coast 142-143
Grenada....................................145-146
Hong Kong 178-179
Jamaica 138-139
Kenya, Uganda, Tanzania 92-93
Leeward Islands 118-119
Malaya
Johore 128-129
Kedah....................................55-56
Kelantan....................................44-45
Malacca....................................1-2
Negri Sembilan 36-37
Pahang....................................44-45
Penang....................................1-2
Perak 99-100
Perlis 1-2
Selangor....................................74-75
Trengganu 47-48
Malta....................................223-224
Mauritius....................................229-230
Montserrat 106-107
Nigeria 73-74
North Borneo.............................238-239
Northern Rhodesia......................48-49
Nyasaland Protectorate...............85-86
Pitcairn Islands..............................11-12
St. Helena 130-131
St. Kitts-Nevis.............................93-94
St. Lucia 129-130
St. Vincent..............................154-155
Sarawak....................................174-175
Seychelles 151-152
Sierra Leone..............................188-189
Singapore 21-22
Solomon Islands..........................82-83
Somaliland Protectorate...........110-111
Swaziland 48-49
Trinidad & Tobago 64-65
Turks & Caicos Islands 92-93
Virgin Islands.............................90-91
Zanzibar....................................224-225

The following have different designs but are included in the omnibus set:

Great Britain 267-268
Offices in Morocco (Sp. Curr.) 93-94
Offices in Morocco (Tangier) 525-526
Bahrain 62-63
Kuwait....................................82-83
Oman....................................25-26
South Africa....................................106
South-West Africa 159

Nos. 30-31 (2)	30.40	42.00
Nos. 14-15 (2)	17.35	12.50
Nos. 14-15 (2)	17.55	14.75
Nos. 98-99 (2)	10.05	13.75
Nos. 52-53 (2)	60.55	57.95
Nos. 148-149 (2)	45.25	40.30
Nos. 210-211 (2)	18.35	13.05
Nos. 39-40 (2)	52.80	55.25
Nos. 147-148 (2)	45.35	50.25
Nos. 133-134 (2)	47.75	55.25
Nos. 244-245 (2)	24.25	28.45
Nos. 129-130 (2)	22.75	53.20
Nos. 116-117 (2)	22.75	28.50
Nos. 158-159 (2)	58.50	78.05
Nos. 114-115 (2)	25.25	32.75
Nos. 99-100 (2)	112.10	83.60
Nos. 1L11-1L12 (2)	4.25	6.00
Nos. 139-140 (2)	18.20	10.75
Nos. 146-147 (2)	22.75	25.25
Nos. 121-122 (2)	66.00	83.00
Nos. 54-55 (2)	16.25	24.25
Nos. 142-143 (2)	35.25	37.75
Nos. 145-146 (2)	25.25	25.25
Nos. 178-179 (2)	363.90	136.60
Nos. 138-139 (2)	20.35	77.75
Nos. 92-93 (2)	52.75	72.75
Nos. 118-119 (2)	7.00	8.25
Nos. 128-129 (2)	29.25	53.25
Nos. 55-56 (2)	35.25	50.25
Nos. 44-45 (2)	35.75	62.75
Nos. 1-2 (2)	35.40	49.75
Nos. 36-37 (2)	28.10	38.20
Nos. 44-45 (2)	28.00	38.05
Nos. 1-2 (2)	40.50	37.80

Nos. 99-100 (2)	27.80	*37.75*
Nos. 1-2 (2)	33.50	*58.00*
Nos. 74-75 (2)	30.25	25.30
Nos. 47-48 (2)	35.25	*62.75*
Nos. 223-224 (2)	40.55	45.25
Nos. 229-230 (2)	17.75	*45.25*
Nos. 106-107 (2)	9.25	*18.25*
Nos. 73-74 (2)	17.85	*22.80*
Nos. 238-239 (2)	35.30	*45.75*
Nos. 48-49 (2)	92.80	90.25
Nos. 85-86 (2)	19.25	*32.75*
Nos. 11-12 (2)	51.75	53.50
Nos. 130-131 (2)	32.80	*42.80*
Nos. 93-94 (2)	11.25	7.25
Nos. 129-130 (2)	22.25	*45.25*
Nos. 154-155 (2)	27.75	*30.25*
Nos. 174-175 (2)	55.40	*60.40*
Nos. 151-152 (2)	16.25	*45.75*
Nos. 188-189 (2)	24.75	*26.25*
Nos. 21-22 (2)	131.25	45.40
Nos. 82-83 (2)	13.40	13.40
Nos. 110-111 (2)	8.40	*8.75*
Nos. 48-49 (2)	40.30	*47.75*
Nos. 64-65 (2)	32.75	*38.25*
Nos. 92-93 (2)	15.25	*20.30*
Nos. 90-91 (2)	18.85	21.35
Nos. 224-225 (2)	29.60	38.00
Nos. 267-268 (2)	40.40	40.25
Nos. 93-94 (2)	20.10	25.35
Nos. 525-526 (2)	23.10	29.25
Nos. 62-63 (2)	38.45	*72.50*
Nos. 82-83 (2)	45.50	45.50
Nos. 25-26 (2)	46.00	*47.50*
No. 106 (1)	.90	1.25
No. 159 (1)	1.25	.35
Set total (136) Stamps	2,582.	2,788.

U.P.U.

Mercury and Symbols of Communications — CD306

Plane, Ship and Hemispheres — CD307

Mercury Scattering Letters over Globe CD308

U.P.U. Monument, Bern CD309

Universal Postal Union, 75th anniversary.

1949

Aden 32-35
Kathiri State of Seiyun 16-19
Qu'aiti State of Shihr and Mukalla 16-19
Antigua 100-103
Ascension 57-60
Bahamas 150-153
Barbados 212-215
Basutoland....................41-44
Bechuanaland Protectorate......149-152
Bermuda....................138-141
British Guiana....................246-249
British Honduras....................137-140
Brunei....................79-82
Cayman Islands....................118-121
Cyprus....................160-163
Dominica....................116-119
Falkland Islands 103-106
Falkland Islands Dep...........1L14-1L17
Fiji....................141-144
Gambia....................148-151
Gibraltar....................123-126
Gilbert & Ellice Islands....................56-59
Gold Coast 144-147
Grenada....................147-150
Hong Kong 180-183
Jamaica 142-145
Kenya, Uganda, Tanzania 94-97
Leeward Islands 126-129
Malaya
Johore 151-154
Kedah....................57-60
Kelantan 46-49
Malacca....................18-21
Negri Sembilan 59-62
Pahang....................46-49
Penang....................23-26
Perak....................101-104
Perlis 3-6
Selangor....................76-79
Trengganu 49-52
Malta....................225-228
Mauritius....................231-234
Montserrat 108-111
New Hebrides, British 62-65
New Hebrides, French 79-82
Nigeria 75-78
North Borneo....................240-243
Northern Rhodesia....................50-53
Nyasaland Protectorate....................87-90
Pitcairn Islands....................13-16
St. Helena 132-135
St. Kitts-Nevis....................95-98
St. Lucia 131-134
St. Vincent....................170-173
Sarawak....................176-179
Seychelles 153-156
Sierra Leone....................190-193
Singapore 23-26
Solomon Islands....................84-87
Somaliland Protectorate..........112-115
Southern Rhodesia 71-72
Swaziland 50-53
Tonga....................87-90
Trinidad & Tobago 66-69
Turks & Caicos Islands 101-104
Virgin Islands....................92-95
Zanzibar....................226-229

The following have different designs but are included in the omnibus set:

Great Britain 276-279
Offices in Morocco (Tangier) 546-549
Australia....................223
Bahrain 68-71
Burma....................116-121
Ceylon 304-306
Egypt 281-283
India....................223-226
Kuwait....................89-92
Oman....................31-34
Pakistan-Bahawalpur 26-29, O25-O28
South Africa....................109-111
South-West Africa 160-162

Nos. 32-35 (4)	5.50	*7.80*
Nos. 16-19 (4)	3.10	*3.60*
Nos. 16-19 (4)	2.75	2.55
Nos. 100-103 (4)	4.15	*6.85*
Nos. 57-60 (4)	12.40	10.00
Nos. 150-153 (4)	5.60	9.55
Nos. 212-215 (4)	4.40	14.15
Nos. 41-44 (4)	4.75	*10.00*
Nos. 149-152 (4)	3.35	*7.25*
Nos. 138-141 (4)	4.75	5.55
Nos. 246-249 (4)	2.65	4.20
Nos. 137-140 (4)	3.35	4.75
Nos. 79-82 (4)	7.75	6.75
Nos. 118-121 (4)	4.00	6.40
Nos. 160-163 (4)	4.60	8.30
Nos. 116-119 (4)	2.30	5.65
Nos. 103-106 (4)	14.90	17.10
Nos. 1L14-1L17 (4)	15.50	14.00
Nos. 141-144 (4)	3.35	14.00
Nos. 148-151 (4)	3.50	7.85
Nos. 123-126 (4)	6.25	9.50
Nos. 56-59 (4)	4.85	*8.75*
Nos. 144-147 (4)	3.05	*6.95*
Nos. 147-150 (4)	2.30	3.55
Nos. 180-183 (4)	74.25	23.60
Nos. 142-145 (4)	2.70	6.00
Nos. 94-97 (4)	2.90	3.40
Nos. 126-129 (4)	3.05	*9.60*
Nos. 151-154 (4)	4.70	8.90
Nos. 57-60 (4)	4.80	12.00
Nos. 46-49 (4)	4.25	12.65
Nos. 18-21 (4)	4.25	*17.30*
Nos. 59-62 (4)	3.50	10.75
Nos. 46-49 (4)	3.00	7.25
Nos. 23-26 (4)	5.10	11.75
Nos. 101-104 (4)	3.65	10.75
Nos. 3-6 (4)	3.95	14.25
Nos. 76-79 (4)	4.90	12.30
Nos. 49-52 (4)	4.95	9.75
Nos. 225-228 (4)	4.50	5.35
Nos. 231-234 (4)	4.35	6.70
Nos. 108-111 (4)	3.40	3.85
Nos. 62-65 (4)	1.60	*4.10*
Nos. 79-82 (4)	24.25	24.25
Nos. 75-78 (4)	2.80	*9.25*
Nos. 240-243 (4)	7.15	6.50
Nos. 50-53 (4)	5.00	*6.50*
Nos. 87-90 (4)	4.05	4.05
Nos. 13-16 (4)	21.25	17.00
Nos. 132-135 (4)	4.85	7.10
Nos. 95-98 (4)	3.35	4.70
Nos. 131-134 (4)	2.55	*3.85*
Nos. 170-173 (4)	2.20	*5.05*
Nos. 176-179 (4)	9.00	11.10
Nos. 153-156 (4)	3.25	4.10
Nos. 190-193 (4)	3.00	5.10
Nos. 23-26 (4)	20.75	14.20
Nos. 84-87 (4)	4.35	4.90
Nos. 112-115 (4)	3.95	8.70
Nos. 71-72 (2)	1.95	*2.25*
Nos. 50-53 (4)	2.80	4.65
Nos. 87-90 (4)	3.25	*5.25*
Nos. 66-69 (4)	3.15	3.15
Nos. 101-104 (4)	3.65	4.00
Nos. 92-95 (4)	2.60	4.60
Nos. 226-229 (4)	5.45	13.50
Nos. 276-279 (4)	1.35	*2.10*
Nos. 546-549 (4)	3.20	*10.15*
No. 223 (1)	.60	.55
Nos. 68-71 (4)	5.00	*16.75*
Nos. 116-121 (6)	7.15	5.30
Nos. 304-306 (3)	3.35	4.25
Nos. 281-283 (3)	5.75	2.70
Nos. 223-226 (4)	35.50	10.50
Nos. 89-92 (4)	6.10	10.25
Nos. 31-34 (4)	5.55	15.75
Nos. 26-29,O25-O28 (8)	2.00	*42.00*
Nos. 109-111 (3)	2.20	3.00
Nos. 160-162 (3)	3.95	6.00
Set total (313) Stamps	499.20	688.35

University

Arms of University College CD310

Alice, Princess of Athlone CD311

1948 opening of University College of the West Indies at Jamaica.

1951

Antigua 104-105
Barbados 228-229
British Guiana....................250-251
British Honduras....................141-142
Dominica....................120-121
Grenada....................164-165
Jamaica 146-147
Leeward Islands 130-131
Montserrat 112-113
St. Kitts-Nevis....................105-106
St. Lucia 149-150
St. Vincent....................174-175
Trinidad & Tobago 70-71
Virgin Islands....................96-97

Nos. 104-105 (2)	1.35	*3.25*
Nos. 228-229 (2)	1.85	1.55
Nos. 250-251 (2)	1.10	*1.25*
Nos. 141-142 (2)	1.40	2.15
Nos. 120-121 (2)	1.40	*1.75*
Nos. 164-165 (2)	1.20	*1.60*
Nos. 146-147 (2)	.95	.85
Nos. 130-131 (2)	1.35	4.00
Nos. 112-113 (2)	.85	*1.50*
Nos. 105-106 (2)	.90	1.50
Nos. 149-150 (2)	1.40	1.50
Nos. 174-175 (2)	1.00	*2.15*
Nos. 70-71 (2)	.75	.75
Nos. 96-97 (2)	1.50	*3.40*
Set total (28) Stamps	17.00	27.20

Coronation

Queen Elizabeth II — CD312

1953

Aden 47
Kathiri State of Seiyun....................28
Qu'aiti State of Shihr and Mukalla 28
Antigua 106
Ascension 61
Bahamas 157
Barbados 234
Basutoland....................45
Bechuanaland Protectorate............153
Bermuda....................142
British Guiana....................252
British Honduras....................143
Cayman Islands....................150
Cyprus....................167
Dominica....................141
Falkland Islands 121
Falkland Islands Dependencies 1L18
Fiji....................145
Gambia 152
Gibraltar....................131
Gilbert & Ellice Islands....................60
Gold Coast 160
Grenada....................170
Hong Kong 184
Jamaica 153
Kenya, Uganda, Tanzania 101
Leeward Islands 132
Malaya
Johore 155
Kedah....................82
Kelantan 71
Malacca....................27
Negri Sembilan 63
Pahang....................71
Penang....................27
Perak....................126
Perlis....................28
Selangor....................101
Trengganu 74
Malta....................241
Mauritius....................250
Montserrat 127
New Hebrides, British 77
Nigeria....................79
North Borneo....................260
Northern Rhodesia....................60
Nyasaland Protectorate....................96
Pitcairn Islands....................19
St. Helena 139
St. Kitts-Nevis....................119
St. Lucia 156
St. Vincent....................185
Sarawak....................196
Seychelles 172
Sierra Leone....................194
Singapore 27
Solomon Islands....................88
Somaliland Protectorate....................127
Swaziland 54
Trinidad & Tobago 84
Tristan da Cunha....................13
Turks & Caicos Islands 118
Virgin Islands....................114

The following have different designs but are included in the omnibus set:

Great Britain 313-316
Offices in Morocco (Tangier) 579-582
Australia....................259-261
Bahrain 92-95
Canada....................330
Ceylon 317
Cook Islands 145-146
Kuwait....................113-116
New Zealand 280-284
Niue 104-105
Oman....................52-55
Samoa 214-215
South Africa....................192
Southern Rhodesia 80
South-West Africa 244-248
Tokelau Islands....................4

No. 47 (1)	1.25	1.25
No. 28 (1)	.40	*1.50*
No. 28 (1)	1.10	.60
No. 106 (1)	.50	*.75*
No. 61 (1)	1.25	2.50
No. 157 (1)	1.25	.75
No. 234 (1)	1.00	.25
No. 45 (1)	.50	*.60*
No. 153 (1)	.75	.35
No. 142 (1)	.85	.40
No. 252 (1)	.45	.25
No. 143 (1)	.55	.40
No. 150 (1)	.40	*1.00*
No. 167 (1)	1.50	1.00
No. 141 (1)	.40	.40
No. 121 (1)	.90	1.50
No. 1L18 (1)	1.50	1.50
No. 145 (1)	1.75	.60
No. 152 (1)	.50	.50
No. 131 (1)	.50	.50
No. 60 (1)	.65	2.25
No. 160 (1)	.95	.25

No. 170 (1)	.30	.25
No. 184 (1)	7.00	.35
No. 153 (1)	1.50	.25
No. 101 (1)	.40	.25
No. 132 (1)	1.00	*2.25*
No. 155 (1)	1.40	.30
No. 82 (1)	2.25	.60
No. 71 (1)	1.60	1.60
No. 27 (1)	1.10	*1.50*
No. 63 (1)	1.40	.65
No. 71 (1)	2.25	.25
No. 27 (1)	1.75	.30
No. 126 (1)	1.60	.25
No. 28 (1)	1.75	*4.00*
No. 101 (1)	1.75	.25
No. 74 (1)	1.50	1.00
No. 241 (1)	.55	.25
No. 250 (1)	1.00	.25
No. 127 (1)	.65	.50
No. 77 (1)	.75	.60
No. 79 (1)	.45	.25
No. 260 (1)	2.00	1.00
No. 60 (1)	.70	.25
No. 96 (1)	.75	.75
No. 19 (1)	2.50	2.50
No. 139 (1)	1.25	1.25
No. 119 (1)	.35	.25
No. 156 (1)	.70	.35
No. 185 (1)	.50	.30
No. 196 (1)	2.00	*2.25*
No. 172 (1)	.80	.80
No. 194 (1)	.40	.40
No. 27 (1)	2.50	.40
No. 88 (1)	1.10	1.10
No. 127 (1)	.40	.25
No. 54 (1)	.30	.25
No. 84 (1)	.25	.25
No. 13 (1)	1.00	1.75
No. 118 (1)	.40	*1.10*
No. 114 (1)	.40	*1.00*
Nos. 313-316 (4)	16.35	8.75
Nos. 579-582 (4)	7.40	5.20
Nos. 259-261 (3)	4.60	3.25
Nos. 92-95 (4)	15.25	12.75
No. 330 (1)	.25	.25
No. 317 (1)	1.50	.25
Nos. 145-146 (2)	2.90	2.90
Nos. 113-116 (4)	16.00	8.50
Nos. 280-284 (5)	5.65	6.85
Nos. 104-105 (2)	1.75	1.75
Nos. 52-55 (4)	15.25	6.50
Nos. 214-215 (2)	2.10	1.00
No. 192 (1)	.30	.25
No. 80 (1)	7.25	7.25
Nos. 244-248 (5)	4.90	3.50
No. 4 (1)	3.75	2.75
Set total (106) Stamps	174.35	122.90

Separate designs for each country for the visit of Queen Elizabeth II and the Duke of Edinburgh.

Royal Visit 1953

1953

Aden	62
Australia	267-269
Bermuda	163
Ceylon	318
Fiji	146
Gibraltar	146
Jamaica	154
Kenya, Uganda, Tanzania	102
Malta	242
New Zealand	286-287

No. 62 (1)	.65	2.00
Nos. 267-269 (3)	2.35	1.90
No. 163 (1)	.50	.25
No. 318 (1)	1.25	.25
No. 146 (1)	.65	.35
No. 146 (1)	.50	.30
No. 154 (1)	.55	.25
No. 102 (1)	.50	.25
No. 242 (1)	.35	.25
Nos. 286-287 (2)	.50	.50
Set total (13) Stamps	7.80	6.30

West Indies Federation

Map of the Caribbean CD313

Federation of the West Indies, April 22, 1958.

1958

Antigua	122-124
Barbados	248-250
Dominica	161-163
Grenada	184-186
Jamaica	175-177
Montserrat	143-145
St. Kitts-Nevis	136-138
St. Lucia	170-172
St. Vincent	198-200
Trinidad & Tobago	86-88

Nos. 122-124 (3)	5.80	3.80
Nos. 248-250 (3)	1.60	*2.90*
Nos. 161-163 (3)	1.95	1.85
Nos. 184-186 (3)	1.50	1.20
Nos. 175-177 (3)	3.10	4.20
Nos. 143-145 (3)	2.35	1.35
Nos. 136-138 (3)	3.00	1.85
Nos. 170-172 (3)	2.05	2.80
Nos. 198-200 (3)	1.50	1.75
Nos. 86-88 (3)	.75	.90
Set total (30) Stamps	23.60	22.60

Freedom from Hunger

Protein Food CD314

U.N. Food and Agricultural Organization's "Freedom from Hunger" campaign.

1963

Aden	65
Antigua	133
Ascension	89
Bahamas	180
Basutoland	83
Bechuanaland Protectorate	194
Bermuda	192
British Guiana	271
British Honduras	179
Brunei	100
Cayman Islands	168
Dominica	181
Falkland Islands	146
Fiji	198
Gambia	172
Gibraltar	161
Gilbert & Ellice Islands	76
Grenada	190
Hong Kong	218
Malta	291
Mauritius	270
Montserrat	150
New Hebrides, British	93
North Borneo	296
Pitcairn Islands	35
St. Helena	173
St. Lucia	179
St. Vincent	201
Sarawak	212
Seychelles	213
Solomon Islands	109
Swaziland	108
Tonga	127
Tristan da Cunha	68
Turks & Caicos Islands	138
Virgin Islands	140
Zanzibar	280

No. 65 (1)	1.75	1.75
No. 133 (1)	.35	.35
No. 89 (1)	1.00	1.00
No. 180 (1)	.65	.65
No. 83 (1)	.50	.25
No. 194 (1)	.50	.50
No. 192 (1)	1.00	.50
No. 271 (1)	.45	.25
No. 179 (1)	.65	.25
No. 100 (1)	3.25	2.25
No. 168 (1)	.50	.30
No. 181 (1)	.30	.30
No. 146 (1)	11.50	3.50
No. 198 (1)	5.25	2.75
No. 172 (1)	.50	.25
No. 161 (1)	4.00	2.25
No. 76 (1)	1.40	.40
No. 190 (1)	.30	.25
No. 218 (1)	57.50	8.75
No. 291 (1)	2.25	2.75
No. 270 (1)	.50	.50
No. 150 (1)	.55	.45
No. 93 (1)	.60	.25
No. 296 (1)	1.90	.75
No. 35 (1)	12.50	5.00
No. 173 (1)	2.25	1.10
No. 179 (1)	.40	.40
No. 201 (1)	.90	.50
No. 212 (1)	1.60	*1.75*
No. 213 (1)	.85	.35
No. 109 (1)	2.00	.85
No. 108 (1)	.50	.50
No. 127 (1)	.70	.35
No. 68 (1)	.90	.40
No. 138 (1)	.50	.50
No. 140 (1)	.50	.50
No. 280 (1)	1.50	.80
Set total (37) Stamps	122.25	44.20

Red Cross Centenary

Red Cross and Elizabeth II CD315

1963

Antigua	134-135
Ascension	90-91
Bahamas	183-184
Basutoland	84-85
Bechuanaland Protectorate	195-196
Bermuda	193-194
British Guiana	272-273
British Honduras	180-181
Cayman Islands	169-170
Dominica	182-183
Falkland Islands	147-148
Fiji	203-204
Gambia	173-174
Gibraltar	162-163
Gilbert & Ellice Islands	77-78
Grenada	191-192
Hong Kong	219-220
Jamaica	203-204
Malta	292-293
Mauritius	271-272
Montserrat	151-152
New Hebrides, British	94-95
Pitcairn Islands	36-37
St. Helena	174-175
St. Kitts-Nevis	143-144
St. Lucia	180-181
St. Vincent	202-203
Seychelles	214-215
Solomon Islands	110-111
South Arabia	1-2
Swaziland	109-110
Tonga	134-135
Tristan da Cunha	69-70
Turks & Caicos Islands	139-140
Virgin Islands	141-142

Nos. 134-135 (2)	1.10	1.50
Nos. 90-91 (2)	8.25	2.70
Nos. 183-184 (2)	2.30	2.55
Nos. 84-85 (2)	1.20	.90
Nos. 195-196 (2)	.95	.85
Nos. 193-194 (2)	2.75	2.55
Nos. 272-273 (2)	1.05	.80
Nos. 180-181 (2)	1.00	2.25
Nos. 169-170 (2)	.95	*2.00*
Nos. 182-183 (2)	.70	*1.05*
Nos. 147-148 (2)	19.75	6.00
Nos. 203-204 (2)	4.00	3.55
Nos. 173-174 (2)	.85	.85
Nos. 162-163 (2)	6.25	5.40
Nos. 77-78 (2)	2.25	*3.25*
Nos. 191-192 (2)	.80	.50
Nos. 219-220 (2)	39.50	8.85
Nos. 203-204 (2)	.75	*1.65*
Nos. 292-293 (2)	3.25	5.00
Nos. 271-272 (2)	.90	.90
Nos. 151-152 (2)	1.00	.80
Nos. 94-95 (2)	1.00	.50
Nos. 36-37 (2)	8.50	6.50
Nos. 174-175 (2)	1.70	2.30
Nos. 143-144 (2)	.90	.90
Nos. 180-181 (2)	1.25	1.25
Nos. 202-203 (2)	.90	.90
Nos. 214-215 (2)	1.10	.90
Nos. 110-111 (2)	1.25	1.15
Nos. 1-2 (2)	1.25	1.25
Nos. 109-110 (2)	1.10	1.10
Nos. 134-135 (2)	1.00	1.25
Nos. 69-70 (2)	1.50	1.00
Nos. 139-140 (2)	.95	1.10
Nos. 141-142 (2)	.80	.80
Set total (70) Stamps	122.75	74.80

Shakespeare

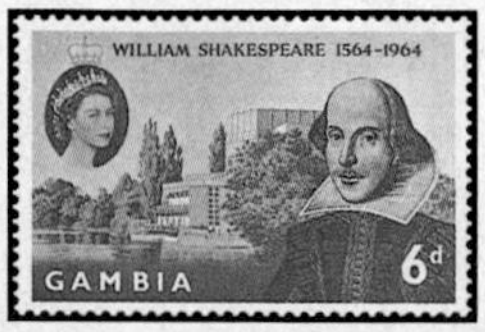

Shakespeare Memorial Theatre, Stratford-on-Avon — CD316

400th anniversary of the birth of William Shakespeare.

1964

Antigua	151
Bahamas	201
Bechuanaland Protectorate	197
Cayman Islands	171
Dominica	184
Falkland Islands	149
Gambia	192
Gibraltar	164
Montserrat	153
St. Lucia	196
Turks & Caicos Islands	141
Virgin Islands	143

No. 151 (1)	.40	.25
No. 201 (1)	.60	.35
No. 197 (1)	.35	.35
No. 171 (1)	.35	.30
No. 184 (1)	.35	.35
No. 149 (1)	1.75	.50
No. 192 (1)	.35	.25
No. 164 (1)	.65	.55
No. 153 (1)	.35	.25
No. 196 (1)	.45	.25
No. 141 (1)	.40	.40
No. 143 (1)	.45	.45
Set total (12) Stamps	6.45	4.25

ITU

ITU Emblem CD317

Intl. Telecommunication Union, cent.

1965

Antigua	153-154
Ascension	92-93
Bahamas	219-220
Barbados	265-266
Basutoland	101-102
Bechuanaland Protectorate	202-203
Bermuda	196-197
British Guiana	293-294
British Honduras	187-188
Brunei	116-117
Cayman Islands	172-173
Dominica	185-186
Falkland Islands	154-155
Fiji	211-212
Gibraltar	167-168
Gilbert & Ellice Islands	87-88
Grenada	205-206
Hong Kong	221-222
Mauritius	291-292
Montserrat	157-158
New Hebrides, British	108-109
Pitcairn Islands	52-53
St. Helena	180-181
St. Kitts-Nevis	163-164
St. Lucia	197-198
St. Vincent	224-225
Seychelles	218-219
Solomon Islands	126-127
Swaziland	115-116
Tristan da Cunha	85-86
Turks & Caicos Islands	142-143
Virgin Islands	159-160

Nos. 153-154 (2)	1.65	1.35
Nos. 92-93 (2)	1.90	1.50
Nos. 219-220 (2)	1.35	1.35
Nos. 265-266 (2)	1.50	1.25
Nos. 101-102 (2)	.85	.65
Nos. 202-203 (2)	1.10	.75
Nos. 196-197 (2)	2.15	*2.25*
Nos. 293-294 (2)	.60	.55
Nos. 187-188 (2)	.85	.85
Nos. 116-117 (2)	1.75	1.75
Nos. 172-173 (2)	1.00	1.00
Nos. 185-186 (2)	.55	.55
Nos. 154-155 (2)	7.75	3.65
Nos. 211-212 (2)	2.70	2.70
Nos. 167-168 (2)	9.00	5.95
Nos. 87-88 (2)	.95	.75
Nos. 205-206 (2)	.50	.50
Nos. 221-222 (2)	32.00	4.55
Nos. 291-292 (2)	1.20	.65
Nos. 157-158 (2)	1.25	1.15
Nos. 108-109 (2)	.65	.50
Nos. 52-53 (2)	10.00	7.55
Nos. 180-181 (2)	.80	.60
Nos. 163-164 (2)	.60	.60
Nos. 197-198 (2)	1.25	1.25
Nos. 224-225 (2)	.80	.90
Nos. 218-219 (2)	.90	.60
Nos. 126-127 (2)	.70	.55
Nos. 115-116 (2)	.75	.75
Nos. 85-86 (2)	1.15	.65
Nos. 142-143 (2)	.90	.90
Nos. 159-160 (2)	.95	.95
Set total (64) Stamps	90.05	49.50

Intl. Cooperation Year

ICY Emblem
CD318

1965

Antigua	155-156
Ascension	94-95
Bahamas	222-223
Basutoland	103-104
Bechuanaland Protectorate	204-205
Bermuda	199-200
British Guiana	295-296
British Honduras	189-190
Brunei	118-119
Cayman Islands	174-175
Dominica	187-188
Falkland Islands	156-157
Fiji	213-214
Gibraltar	169-170
Gilbert & Ellice Islands	104-105
Grenada	207-208
Hong Kong	223-224
Mauritius	293-294
Montserrat	176-177
New Hebrides, British	110-111
New Hebrides, French	126-127
Pitcairn Islands	54-55
St. Helena	182-183
St. Kitts-Nevis	165-166
St. Lucia	199-200
Seychelles	220-221
Solomon Islands	143-144
South Arabia	17-18
Swaziland	117-118
Tristan da Cunha	87-88
Turks & Caicos Islands	144-145
Virgin Islands	161-162

Nos. 155-156 (2)	.60	.50
Nos. 94-95 (2)	1.30	1.50
Nos. 222-223 (2)	.65	1.40
Nos. 103-104 (2)	.75	.85
Nos. 204-205 (2)	.85	1.00
Nos. 199-200 (2)	2.25	1.25
Nos. 295-296 (2)	.65	.60
Nos. 189-190 (2)	.60	.55
Nos. 118-119 (2)	.85	.85
Nos. 174-175 (2)	1.00	.95
Nos. 187-188 (2)	.55	.55
Nos. 156-157 (2)	7.00	1.90
Nos. 213-214 (2)	2.60	2.35
Nos. 169-170 (2)	1.25	*2.75*
Nos. 104-105 (2)	.95	.60
Nos. 207-208 (2)	.50	.50
Nos. 223-224 (2)	26.00	4.10
Nos. 293-294 (2)	.70	.70
Nos. 176-177 (2)	.80	.65
Nos. 110-111 (2)	.50	.50
Nos. 126-127 (2)	12.00	12.00
Nos. 54-55 (2)	9.85	5.25
Nos. 182-183 (2)	.95	.50
Nos. 165-166 (2)	.70	.60
Nos. 199-200 (2)	.55	.55
Nos. 220-221 (2)	.90	.65
Nos. 143-144 (2)	.70	.60
Nos. 17-18 (2)	1.20	.50
Nos. 117-118 (2)	.75	.75
Nos. 87-88 (2)	1.35	.75
Nos. 144-145 (2)	.85	.85
Nos. 161-162 (2)	.80	.80
Set total (64) Stamps	80.95	47.85

Churchill Memorial

Winston Churchill and St. Paul's, London, During Air Attack
CD319

1966

Antigua	157-160
Ascension	96-99
Bahamas	224-227
Barbados	281-284
Basutoland	105-108
Bechuanaland Protectorate	206-209
Bermuda	201-204
British Antarctic Territory	16-19
British Honduras	191-194
Brunei	120-123
Cayman Islands	176-179
Dominica	189-192
Falkland Islands	158-161
Fiji	215-218
Gibraltar	171-174
Gilbert & Ellice Islands	106-109
Grenada	209-212
Hong Kong	225-228
Mauritius	295-298
Montserrat	178-181
New Hebrides, British	112-115
New Hebrides, French	128-131
Pitcairn Islands	56-59
St. Helena	184-187
St. Kitts-Nevis	167-170
St. Lucia	201-204
St. Vincent	241-244
Seychelles	222-225
Solomon Islands	145-148
South Arabia	19-22
Swaziland	119-122
Tristan da Cunha	89-92
Turks & Caicos Islands	146-149
Virgin Islands	163-166

Nos. 157-160 (4)	3.05	2.55
Nos. 96-99 (4)	10.00	7.15
Nos. 224-227 (4)	2.30	*3.20*
Nos. 281-284 (4)	3.00	4.45
Nos. 105-108 (4)	2.80	3.25
Nos. 206-209 (4)	2.50	2.50
Nos. 201-204 (4)	4.00	4.00
Nos. 16-19 (4)	41.35	20.00
Nos. 191-194 (4)	2.55	1.80
Nos. 120-123 (4)	8.00	7.25
Nos. 176-179 (4)	3.40	3.55
Nos. 189-192 (4)	1.15	1.15
Nos. 158-161 (4)	12.75	7.80
Nos. 215-218 (4)	5.15	3.45
Nos. 171-174 (4)	3.05	5.30
Nos. 106-109 (4)	1.75	1.30
Nos. 209-212 (4)	1.10	1.10
Nos. 225-228 (4)	68.00	12.15
Nos. 295-298 (4)	4.05	4.05
Nos. 178-181 (4)	1.60	1.55
Nos. 112-115 (4)	2.30	1.00
Nos. 128-131 (4)	10.25	10.25
Nos. 56-59 (4)	15.00	10.50
Nos. 184-187 (4)	1.85	1.95
Nos. 167-170 (4)	1.70	1.70
Nos. 201-204 (4)	1.50	1.50
Nos. 241-244 (4)	1.50	1.75
Nos. 222-225 (4)	3.20	3.60
Nos. 145-148 (4)	1.75	1.75
Nos. 19-22 (4)	3.80	2.50
Nos. 119-122 (4)	1.70	2.55
Nos. 89-92 (4)	5.95	2.70
Nos. 146-149 (4)	1.60	1.75
Nos. 163-166 (4)	1.90	1.90
Set total (136) Stamps	235.55	142.95

Royal Visit, 1966

Queen Elizabeth II and Prince Philip
CD320

Caribbean visit, Feb. 4 - Mar. 6, 1966.

1966

Antigua	161-162
Bahamas	228-229
Barbados	285-286
British Guiana	299-300
Cayman Islands	180-181
Dominica	193-194
Grenada	213-214
Montserrat	182-183
St. Kitts-Nevis	171-172
St. Lucia	205-206
St. Vincent	245-246
Turks & Caicos Islands	150-151
Virgin Islands	167-168

Nos. 161-162 (2)	3.80	2.60
Nos. 228-229 (2)	3.05	3.05
Nos. 285-286 (2)	3.00	2.00
Nos. 299-300 (2)	3.35	1.60
Nos. 180-181 (2)	3.45	1.80
Nos. 193-194 (2)	3.00	.60
Nos. 213-214 (2)	.90	.50
Nos. 182-183 (2)	1.70	1.00
Nos. 171-172 (2)	.80	.75
Nos. 205-206 (2)	1.50	1.35
Nos. 245-246 (2)	2.75	1.35
Nos. 150-151 (2)	1.20	.70
Nos. 167-168 (2)	2.25	2.25
Set total (26) Stamps	30.75	19.55

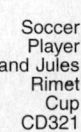

World Cup Soccer

Soccer Player and Jules Rimet Cup
CD321

World Cup Soccer Championship, Wembley, England, July 11-30.

1966

Antigua	163-164
Ascension	100-101
Bahamas	245-246
Bermuda	205-206
Brunei	124-125
Cayman Islands	182-183
Dominica	195-196
Fiji	219-220
Gibraltar	175-176
Gilbert & Ellice Islands	125-126
Grenada	230-231
New Hebrides, British	116-117
New Hebrides, French	132-133
Pitcairn Islands	60-61
St. Helena	188-189
St. Kitts-Nevis	173-174
St. Lucia	207-208
Seychelles	226-227
Solomon Islands	167-168
South Arabia	23-24
Tristan da Cunha	93-94

Nos. 163-164 (2)	.85	.50
Nos. 100-101 (2)	2.50	1.80
Nos. 245-246 (2)	.65	.65
Nos. 205-206 (2)	1.75	1.75
Nos. 124-125 (2)	1.40	1.00
Nos. 182-183 (2)	.75	.75
Nos. 195-196 (2)	1.20	.75
Nos. 219-220 (2)	2.00	1.20
Nos. 175-176 (2)	1.85	1.75
Nos. 125-126 (2)	.80	.60
Nos. 230-231 (2)	.65	*.95*
Nos. 116-117 (2)	1.00	1.00
Nos. 132-133 (2)	7.00	7.00
Nos. 60-61 (2)	8.00	4.75
Nos. 188-189 (2)	1.25	.60
Nos. 173-174 (2)	.85	.80
Nos. 207-208 (2)	1.15	.90
Nos. 226-227 (2)	.85	.85
Nos. 167-168 (2)	.70	.70
Nos. 23-24 (2)	1.90	.55
Nos. 93-94 (2)	1.25	.80
Set total (42) Stamps	38.35	29.65

WHO Headquarters

World Health Organization Headquarters, Geneva — CD322

1966

Antigua	165-166
Ascension	102-103
Bahamas	247-248
Brunei	126-127
Cayman Islands	184-185
Dominica	197-198
Fiji	224-225
Gibraltar	180-181
Gilbert & Ellice Islands	127-128
Grenada	232-233
Hong Kong	229-230
Montserrat	184-185
New Hebrides, British	118-119
New Hebrides, French	134-135
Pitcairn Islands	62-63
St. Helena	190-191
St. Kitts-Nevis	177-178
St. Lucia	209-210
St. Vincent	247-248
Seychelles	228-229
Solomon Islands	169-170
South Arabia	25-26
Tristan da Cunha	99-100

Nos. 165-166 (2)	1.05	.55
Nos. 102-103 (2)	6.60	3.50
Nos. 247-248 (2)	.80	.80
Nos. 126-127 (2)	1.35	1.00
Nos. 184-185 (2)	2.25	1.40
Nos. 197-198 (2)	.75	.75
Nos. 224-225 (2)	5.10	3.90
Nos. 180-181 (2)	6.50	4.50
Nos. 127-128 (2)	.80	.70
Nos. 232-233 (2)	.80	.50
Nos. 229-230 (2)	14.25	2.30
Nos. 184-185 (2)	1.00	1.00
Nos. 118-119 (2)	.75	.50
Nos. 134-135 (2)	8.75	8.75
Nos. 62-63 (2)	10.00	6.50
Nos. 190-191 (2)	3.50	1.50
Nos. 177-178 (2)	.65	.65
Nos. 209-210 (2)	.80	.80
Nos. 247-248 (2)	1.15	1.05
Nos. 228-229 (2)	1.25	.75
Nos. 169-170 (2)	.80	.80
Nos. 25-26 (2)	2.10	.70
Nos. 99-100 (2)	1.90	1.25
Set total (46) Stamps	72.90	44.15

UNESCO Anniversary

"Education" — CD323

"Science" (Wheat ears & flask enclosing globe). "Culture" (lyre & columns). 20th anniversary of the UNESCO.

1966-67

Antigua	183-185
Ascension	108-110
Bahamas	249-251
Barbados	287-289
Bermuda	207-209
Brunei	128-130
Cayman Islands	186-188
Dominica	199-201
Gibraltar	183-185
Gilbert & Ellice Islands	129-131
Grenada	234-236
Hong Kong	231-233
Mauritius	299-301
Montserrat	186-188
New Hebrides, British	120-122
New Hebrides, French	136-138
Pitcairn Islands	64-66
St. Helena	192-194
St. Kitts-Nevis	179-181
St. Lucia	211-213
St. Vincent	249-251
Seychelles	230-232
Solomon Islands	171-173
South Arabia	27-29
Swaziland	123-125
Tristan da Cunha	101-103
Turks & Caicos Islands	155-157
Virgin Islands	176-178

Nos. 183-185 (3)	1.90	*2.50*
Nos. 108-110 (3)	11.00	6.15
Nos. 249-251 (3)	2.35	2.35
Nos. 287-289 (3)	2.50	2.15
Nos. 207-209 (3)	4.30	3.90
Nos. 128-130 (3)	5.00	*7.40*
Nos. 186-188 (3)	2.50	1.70
Nos. 199-201 (3)	1.60	.75
Nos. 183-185 (3)	6.50	3.25
Nos. 129-131 (3)	2.50	1.65
Nos. 234-236 (3)	1.10	1.20
Nos. 231-233 (3)	89.00	20.00
Nos. 299-301 (3)	2.10	1.50
Nos. 186-188 (3)	2.40	2.40
Nos. 120-122 (3)	1.90	1.90
Nos. 136-138 (3)	7.75	7.75
Nos. 64-66 (3)	9.35	6.35
Nos. 192-194 (3)	5.25	3.65
Nos. 179-181 (3)	.90	.90
Nos. 211-213 (3)	1.15	1.15
Nos. 249-251 (3)	2.30	1.35
Nos. 230-232 (3)	2.40	2.40
Nos. 171-173 (3)	2.00	1.50
Nos. 27-29 (3)	5.90	3.05
Nos. 123-125 (3)	1.45	1.45
Nos. 101-103 (3)	2.00	1.40
Nos. 155-157 (3)	1.05	1.05
Nos. 176-178 (3)	1.30	1.30
Set total (84) Stamps	179.45	92.10

Silver Wedding, 1972

Queen Elizabeth II and Prince Philip — CD324

Designs: borders differ for each country.

1972

Anguilla	161-162
Antigua	295-296
Ascension	164-165
Bahamas	344-345
Bermuda	296-297
British Antarctic Territory	43-44
British Honduras	306-307
British Indian Ocean Territory	48-49

Brunei....................186-187
Cayman Islands....................304-305
Dominica....................352-353
Falkland Islands....................223-224
Fiji....................328-329
Gibraltar....................292-293
Gilbert & Ellice Islands....................206-207
Grenada....................466-467
Hong Kong....................271-272
Montserrat....................286-287
New Hebrides, British....................169-170
Pitcairn Islands....................127-128
St. Helena....................271-272
St. Kitts-Nevis....................257-258
St. Lucia....................328-329
St.Vincent....................344-345
Seychelles....................309-310
Solomon Islands....................248-249
South Georgia....................35-36
Tristan da Cunha....................178-179
Turks & Caicos Islands....................257-258
Virgin Islands....................241-242

Nos. 161-162 (2)	1.30	*1.50*
Nos. 295-296 (2)	.50	.50
Nos. 164-165 (2)	.80	.80
Nos. 344-345 (2)	.60	.60
Nos. 296-297 (2)	.50	.50
Nos. 43-44 (2)	7.75	6.10
Nos. 306-307 (2)	.90	.90
Nos. 48-49 (2)	2.30	1.00
Nos. 186-187 (2)	.65	.85
Nos. 304-305 (2)	.75	.75
Nos. 352-353 (2)	.65	.65
Nos. 223-224 (2)	1.10	1.10
Nos. 328-329 (2)	1.00	1.00
Nos. 292-293 (2)	.50	.50
Nos. 206-207 (2)	.50	.50
Nos. 466-467 (2)	.70	.70
Nos. 271-272 (2)	2.10	1.75
Nos. 286-287 (2)	.55	.55
Nos. 169-170 (2)	.50	.50
Nos. 127-128 (2)	1.15	.80
Nos. 271-272 (2)	.70	1.20
Nos. 257-258 (2)	.65	.50
Nos. 328-329 (2)	.75	.75
Nos. 344-345 (2)	.55	.55
Nos. 309-310 (2)	.95	.95
Nos. 248-249 (2)	.60	.60
Nos. 35-36 (2)	1.40	1.40
Nos. 178-179 (2)	.70	.70
Nos. 257-258 (2)	.50	.50
Nos. 241-242 (2)	.50	.50
Set total (60) Stamps	32.10	29.20

Princess Anne's Wedding

Princess Anne and Mark Phillips — CD325

Wedding of Princess Anne and Mark Phillips, Nov. 14, 1973.

1973

Anguilla....................179-180
Ascension....................177-178
Belize....................325-326
Bermuda....................302-303
British Antarctic Territory....................60-61
Cayman Islands....................320-321
Falkland Islands....................225-226
Gibraltar....................305-306
Gilbert & Ellice Islands....................216-217
Hong Kong....................289-290
Montserrat....................300-301
Pitcairn Islands....................135-136
St. Helena....................277-278
St. Kitts-Nevis....................274-275
St. Lucia....................349-350
St. Vincent....................358-359
St. Vincent Grenadines....................1-2
Seychelles....................311-312
Solomon Islands....................259-260
South Georgia....................37-38
Tristan da Cunha....................189-190
Turks & Caicos Islands....................286-287
Virgin Islands....................260-261

Nos. 179-180 (2)	.55	.55
Nos. 177-178 (2)	.65	.65
Nos. 325-326 (2)	.50	.50
Nos. 302-303 (2)	.50	.50
Nos. 60-61 (2)	1.10	1.10
Nos. 320-321 (2)	.55	.55
Nos. 225-226 (2)	.75	.75
Nos. 305-306 (2)	.55	.55
Nos. 216-217 (2)	.50	.50
Nos. 289-290 (2)	3.25	2.25
Nos. 300-301 (2)	.65	.65
Nos. 135-136 (2)	.90	.60
Nos. 277-278 (2)	.50	.50
Nos. 274-275 (2)	.50	.50
Nos. 349-350 (2)	.50	.50
Nos. 358-359 (2)	.50	.50
Nos. 1-2 (2)	.65	.65
Nos. 311-312 (2)	.70	.70
Nos. 259-260 (2)	.70	.70
Nos. 37-38 (2)	.75	.75
Nos. 189-190 (2)	.50	.50
Nos. 286-287 (2)	.50	.50
Nos. 260-261 (2)	.50	.50
Set total (46) Stamps	16.75	15.45

Elizabeth II Coronation Anniv.

CD326

CD327

CD328

Designs: Royal and local beasts in heraldic form and simulated stonework. Portrait of Elizabeth II by Peter Grugeon. 25th anniversary of coronation of Queen Elizabeth II.

1978

Ascension....................229
Barbados....................474
Belize....................397
British Antarctic Territory....................71
Cayman Islands....................404
Christmas Island....................87
Falkland Islands....................275
Fiji....................384
Gambia....................380
Gilbert Islands....................312
Mauritius....................464
New Hebrides, British....................258
St. Helena....................317
St. Kitts-Nevis....................354
Samoa....................472
Solomon Islands....................368
South Georgia....................51
Swaziland....................302
Tristan da Cunha....................238
Virgin Islands....................337

No. 229 (1)	2.25	2.25
No. 474 (1)	1.35	1.35
No. 397 (1)	1.75	1.75
No. 71 (1)	6.00	6.00
No. 404 (1)	2.00	2.50
No. 87 (1)	3.50	*4.00*
No. 275 (1)	4.00	4.00
No. 384 (1)	2.75	2.75
No. 380 (1)	1.50	1.50
No. 312 (1)	1.25	1.25
No. 464 (1)	2.75	2.75
No. 258 (1)	1.75	1.75
No. 317 (1)	1.75	1.75
No. 354 (1)	1.00	1.00
No. 472 (1)	2.00	2.00
No. 368 (1)	3.00	3.00
No. 51 (1)	3.00	3.00
No. 302 (1)	1.75	1.75
No. 238 (1)	1.50	1.50
No. 337 (1)	2.25	2.25
Set total (20) Stamps	47.10	48.10

Queen Mother Elizabeth's 80th Birthday

CD330

Designs: Photographs of Queen Mother Elizabeth. Falkland Islands issued in sheets of 50; others in sheets of 9.

1980

Ascension....................261
Bermuda....................401
Cayman Islands....................443
Falkland Islands....................305
Gambia....................412
Gibraltar....................393
Hong Kong....................364
Pitcairn Islands....................193
St. Helena....................341
Samoa....................532
Solomon Islands....................426
Tristan da Cunha....................277

No. 261 (1)	.50	.50
No. 401 (1)	.45	.45
No. 443 (1)	.45	.45
No. 305 (1)	.40	.40
No. 412 (1)	.40	.50
No. 393 (1)	.35	.35
No. 364 (1)	1.10	1.00
No. 193 (1)	.70	.70
No. 341 (1)	.50	.50
No. 532 (1)	.55	.55
No. 426 (1)	.50	.50
No. 277 (1)	.45	.45
Set total (12) Stamps	6.35	6.35

Royal Wedding, 1981

Prince Charles and Lady Diana — CD331

CD331a

Wedding of Charles, Prince of Wales, and Lady Diana Spencer, St. Paul's Cathedral, London, July 29, 1981.

1981

Antigua....................623-627
Ascension....................294-296
Barbados....................547-549
Barbuda....................497-501
Bermuda....................412-414
Brunei....................268-270
Cayman Islands....................471-473
Dominica....................701-705
Falkland Islands....................324-326
Falkland Islands Dep....................1L59-1L61
Fiji....................442-444
Gambia....................426-428
Ghana....................759-764
Grenada....................1051-1055
Grenada Grenadines....................440-443
Hong Kong....................373-375
Jamaica....................500-503
Lesotho....................335-337
Maldive Islands....................906-909
Mauritius....................520-522
Norfolk Island....................280-282
Pitcairn Islands....................206-208
St. Helena....................353-355
St. Lucia....................543-549
Samoa....................558-560
Sierra Leone....................509-518
Solomon Islands....................450-452
Swaziland....................382-384
Tristan da Cunha....................294-296
Turks & Caicos Islands....................486-489
Caicos Island....................8-11
Uganda....................314-317
Vanuatu....................308-310
Virgin Islands....................406-408

Nos. 623-627 (5)	7.55	2.55
Nos. 294-296 (3)	1.10	1.10
Nos. 547-549 (3)	.90	.90
Nos. 497-501 (5)	10.95	10.95
Nos. 412-414 (3)	2.00	2.00
Nos. 268-270 (3)	2.15	*4.50*
Nos. 471-473 (3)	1.35	1.35
Nos. 701-705 (5)	8.35	2.35
Nos. 324-326 (3)	1.65	1.70
Nos. 1L59-1L61 (3)	1.45	1.45
Nos. 442-444 (3)	1.70	1.70
Nos. 426-428 (3)	.80	.80
Nos. 759-764 (9)	5.00	5.00
Nos. 1051-1055 (5)	9.85	1.85
Nos. 440-443 (4)	2.35	2.35
Nos. 373-375 (3)	3.30	3.10
Nos. 500-503 (4)	1.50	1.25
Nos. 335-337 (3)	1.10	1.10
Nos. 906-909 (4)	1.70	1.80
Nos. 520-522 (3)	2.75	2.75
Nos. 280-282 (3)	1.35	1.35
Nos. 206-208 (3)	1.35	1.35
Nos. 353-355 (3)	.85	.85
Nos. 543-549 (5)	8.50	8.50
Nos. 558-560 (3)	.85	.85
Nos. 509-518 (10)	15.50	15.50
Nos. 450-452 (3)	1.05	1.05
Nos. 382-384 (3)	1.30	1.25
Nos. 294-296 (3)	.90	.90
Nos. 486-489 (4)	2.20	2.20
Nos. 8-11 (4)	6.25	6.25
Nos. 314-317 (4)	3.30	3.00
Nos. 308-310 (3)	1.15	1.15
Nos. 406-408 (3)	1.30	1.30
Set total (131) Stamps	113.35	96.05

Princess Diana

CD332

CD333

Designs: Photographs and portrait of Princess Diana, wedding or honeymoon photographs, royal residences, arms of issuing country. Portrait photograph by Clive Friend. Souvenir sheet margins show family tree, various people related to the princess. 21st birthday of Princess Diana of Wales, July 1.

1982

Antigua....................663-666
Ascension....................313-316
Bahamas....................510-513
Barbados....................585-588
Barbuda....................544-547
British Antarctic Territory....................92-95
Cayman Islands....................486-489
Dominica....................773-776
Falkland Islands....................348-351
Falkland Islands Dep....................1L72-1L75
Fiji....................470-473
Gambia....................447-450
Grenada....................1101A-1105
Grenada Grenadines....................485-491
Lesotho....................372-375
Maldive Islands....................952-955
Mauritius....................548-551
Pitcairn Islands....................213-216
St. Helena....................372-375
St. Lucia....................591-594
Sierra Leone....................531-534
Solomon Islands....................471-474
Swaziland....................406-409
Tristan da Cunha....................310-313
Turks and Caicos Islands....................531-534
Virgin Islands....................430-433

Nos. 663-666 (4)	9.70	9.70
Nos. 313-316 (4)	3.95	3.95
Nos. 510-513 (4)	6.00	3.85
Nos. 585-588 (4)	3.40	3.25
Nos. 544-547 (4)	9.75	7.70
Nos. 92-95 (4)	5.30	3.45
Nos. 486-489 (4)	*5.40*	*2.70*
Nos. 773-776 (4)	7.05	7.05
Nos. 348-351 (4)	3.10	3.10
Nos. 1L72-1L75 (4)	2.50	2.60
Nos. 470-473 (4)	4.50	4.50
Nos. 447-450 (4)	2.85	2.85
Nos. 1101A-1105 (7)	16.05	15.55
Nos. 485-491 (7)	17.65	17.65
Nos. 372-375 (4)	4.00	4.00
Nos. 952-955 (4)	7.25	7.25
Nos. 548-551 (4)	5.50	5.50
Nos. 213-216 (4)	3.40	3.40
Nos. 372-375 (4)	2.95	2.95
Nos. 591-594 (4)	9.90	9.90
Nos. 531-534 (4)	7.60	7.60
Nos. 471-474 (4)	2.90	2.90
Nos. 406-409 (4)	3.85	2.25
Nos. 310-313 (4)	3.65	1.45
Nos. 486-489 (4)	2.20	2.20
Nos. 430-433 (4)	3.55	3.55
Set total (110) Stamps	153.95	140.85

250th anniv. of first edition of Lloyd's List (shipping news publication) & of Lloyd's marine insurance.

CD335

Designs: First page of early edition of the list; historical ships, modern transportation or harbor scenes.

1984

Ascension	351-354
Bahamas	555-558
Barbados	627-630
Cayes of Belize	10-13
Cayman Islands	522-526
Falkland Islands	404-407
Fiji	509-512
Gambia	519-522
Mauritius	587-590
Nauru	280-283
St. Helena	412-415
Samoa	624-627
Seychelles	538-541
Solomon Islands	521-524
Vanuatu	368-371
Virgin Islands	466-469

Nos. 351-354 (4)	3.30	2.55
Nos. 555-558 (4)	4.55	2.95
Nos. 627-630 (4)	6.10	5.15
Nos. 10-13 (4)	3.05	3.05
Nos. 522-526 (5)	9.30	8.45
Nos. 404-407 (4)	3.65	4.00
Nos. 509-512 (4)	6.15	6.15
Nos. 519-522 (4)	4.20	4.30
Nos. 587-590 (4)	8.95	8.95
Nos. 280-283 (4)	2.40	2.35
Nos. 412-415 (4)	2.40	2.40
Nos. 624-627 (4)	2.75	2.55
Nos. 538-541 (4)	5.25	5.25
Nos. 521-524 (4)	4.65	3.95
Nos. 368-371 (4)	2.40	2.40
Nos. 466-469 (4)	5.00	5.00
Set total (65) Stamps	74.10	69.45

Queen Mother 85th Birthday

CD336

Designs: Photographs tracing the life of the Queen Mother, Elizabeth. The high value in each set pictures the same photograph taken of the Queen Mother holding the infant Prince Henry.

1985

Ascension	372-376
Bahamas	580-584
Barbados	660-664
Bermuda	469-473
Falkland Islands	420-424
Falkland Islands Dep.	1L92-1L96
Fiji	531-535
Hong Kong	447-450
Jamaica	599-603
Mauritius	604-608
Norfolk Island	364-368
Pitcairn Islands	253-257
St. Helena	428-432
Samoa	649-653
Seychelles	567-571
Zil Elwannyen Sesel	101-105
Solomon Islands	543-547
Swaziland	476-480
Tristan da Cunha	372-376
Vanuatu	392-396

Nos. 372-376 (5)	5.35	5.35
Nos. 580-584 (5)	7.95	6.45
Nos. 660-664 (5)	8.00	6.70
Nos. 469-473 (5)	9.90	9.90
Nos. 420-424 (5)	8.25	7.60
Nos. 1L92-1L96 (5)	8.25	8.25
Nos. 531-535 (5)	7.05	7.05
Nos. 447-450 (4)	10.25	8.50
Nos. 599-603 (5)	7.50	8.00
Nos. 604-608 (5)	11.80	11.80
Nos. 364-368 (5)	5.05	5.05
Nos. 253-257 (5)	6.00	6.15
Nos. 428-432 (5)	5.25	5.25
Nos. 649-653 (5)	8.65	7.80
Nos. 567-571 (5)	8.70	8.70
Nos. 101-105 (5)	7.15	7.15
Nos. 543-547 (5)	4.45	4.45
Nos. 476-480 (5)	8.00	7.50
Nos. 372-376 (5)	5.40	5.40
Nos. 392-396 (5)	5.25	5.25
Set total (99) Stamps	148.20	142.30

Queen Elizabeth II, 60th Birthday

CD337

1986, April 21

Ascension	389-393
Bahamas	592-596
Barbados	675-679
Bermuda	499-503
Cayman Islands	555-559
Falkland Islands	441-445
Fiji	544-548
Hong Kong	465-469
Jamaica	620-624
Kiribati	470-474
Mauritius	629-633
Papua New Guinea	640-644
Pitcairn Islands	270-274
St. Helena	451-455
Samoa	670-674
Seychelles	592-596
Zil Elwannyen Sesel	114-118
Solomon Islands	562-566
South Georgia	101-105
Swaziland	490-494
Tristan da Cunha	388-392
Vanuatu	414-418
Zambia	343-347

Nos. 389-393 (5)	2.80	2.80
Nos. 592-596 (5)	2.75	*3.70*
Nos. 675-679 (5)	3.35	3.20
Nos. 499-503 (5)	4.90	4.90
Nos. 555-559 (5)	4.55	4.45
Nos. 441-445 (5)	3.95	*4.95*
Nos. 544-548 (5)	4.05	4.05
Nos. 465-469 (5)	9.60	6.85
Nos. 620-624 (5)	2.95	3.05
Nos. 470-474 (5)	2.10	2.10
Nos. 629-633 (5)	3.70	3.70
Nos. 640-644 (5)	4.50	4.50
Nos. 270-274 (5)	3.85	3.85
Nos. 451-455 (5)	3.05	3.05
Nos. 670-674 (5)	2.90	2.90
Nos. 592-596 (5)	2.70	2.70
Nos. 114-118 (5)	2.25	2.25
Nos. 562-566 (5)	2.50	2.50
Nos. 101-105 (5)	3.55	3.55
Nos. 490-494 (5)	2.30	2.30
Nos. 388-392 (5)	3.00	3.00
Nos. 414-418 (5)	3.10	3.10
Nos. 343-347 (5)	1.75	1.75
Set total (115) Stamps	80.15	79.20

Royal Wedding

Marriage of Prince Andrew and Sarah Ferguson CD338

1986, July 23

Ascension	399-400
Bahamas	602-603
Barbados	687-688
Cayman Islands	560-561
Jamaica	629-630
Pitcairn Islands	275-276
St. Helena	460-461
St. Kitts	181-182
Seychelles	602-603
Zil Elwannyen Sesel	119-120
Solomon Islands	567-568
Tristan da Cunha	397-398
Zambia	348-349

Nos. 399-400 (2)	1.60	1.60
Nos. 602-603 (2)	2.75	2.75
Nos. 687-688 (2)	2.25	1.25
Nos. 560-561 (2)	1.50	*2.15*
Nos. 629-630 (2)	1.75	1.75
Nos. 275-276 (2)	2.75	2.75
Nos. 460-461 (2)	1.05	1.05
Nos. 181-182 (2)	1.50	1.50
Nos. 602-603 (2)	2.50	2.50
Nos. 119-120 (2)	2.30	2.30
Nos. 567-568 (2)	1.00	1.00
Nos. 397-398 (2)	1.40	1.40
Nos. 348-349 (2)	1.10	1.30
Set total (26) Stamps	23.45	23.30

Queen Elizabeth II, 60th Birthday

Queen Elizabeth II & Prince Philip, 1947 Wedding Portrait — CD339

Designs: Photographs tracing the life of Queen Elizabeth II.

1986

Anguilla	674-677
Antigua	925-928
Barbuda	783-786
Dominica	950-953
Gambia	611-614
Grenada	1371-1374
Grenada Grenadines	749-752
Lesotho	531-534
Maldive Islands	1172-1175
Sierra Leone	760-763
Uganda	495-498

Nos. 674-677 (4)	8.00	8.00
Nos. 925-928 (4)	6.75	6.75
Nos. 783-786 (4)	25.60	25.60
Nos. 950-953 (4)	7.25	7.25
Nos. 611-614 (4)	8.25	7.90
Nos. 1371-1374 (4)	6.80	6.80
Nos. 749-752 (4)	6.75	6.75
Nos. 531-534 (4)	5.50	5.50
Nos. 1172-1175 (4)	7.00	7.00
Nos. 760-763 (4)	6.30	6.30
Nos. 495-498 (4)	8.50	8.50
Set total (44) Stamps	96.70	96.35

Royal Wedding, 1986

CD340

Designs: Photographs of Prince Andrew and Sarah Ferguson during courtship, engagement and marriage.

1986

Antigua	939-942
Barbuda	809-812
Dominica	970-973
Gambia	635-638
Grenada	1385-1388
Grenada Grenadines	758-761
Lesotho	545-548
Maldive Islands	1181-1184
Sierra Leone	769-772
Uganda	510-513

Nos. 939-942 (4)	8.25	8.25
Nos. 809-812 (4)	15.90	15.80
Nos. 970-973 (4)	7.25	7.25
Nos. 635-638 (4)	8.55	8.55
Nos. 1385-1388 (4)	8.30	8.30
Nos. 758-761 (4)	9.00	9.00
Nos. 545-548 (4)	7.95	7.95
Nos. 1181-1184 (4)	10.20	10.20
Nos. 769-772 (4)	5.55	5.55
Nos. 510-513 (4)	9.50	10.25
Set total (40) Stamps	90.45	91.10

Lloyds of London, 300th Anniv.

CD341

Designs: 17th century aspects of Lloyds, representations of each country's individual connections with Lloyds and publicized disasters insured by the organization.

1986

Ascension	454-457
Bahamas	655-658
Barbados	731-734
Bermuda	541-544
Falkland Islands	481-484
Liberia	1101-1104
Malawi	534-537
Nevis	571-574
St. Helena	501-504
St. Lucia	923-926
Seychelles	649-652
Zil Elwannyen Sesel	146-149
Solomon Islands	627-630
South Georgia	131-134
Trinidad & Tobago	484-487
Tristan da Cunha	439-442
Vanuatu	485-488

Nos. 454-457 (4)	5.00	5.00
Nos. 655-658 (4)	8.90	4.95
Nos. 731-734 (4)	12.50	8.35
Nos. 541-544 (4)	8.25	5.60
Nos. 481-484 (4)	6.30	4.55
Nos. 1101-1104 (4)	5.25	5.25
Nos. 534-537 (4)	11.00	7.85
Nos. 571-574 (4)	8.35	8.35
Nos. 501-504 (4)	8.70	7.15
Nos. 923-926 (4)	9.40	9.40
Nos. 649-652 (4)	13.10	13.10
Nos. 146-149 (4)	11.25	11.25
Nos. 627-630 (4)	7.90	4.45
Nos. 131-134 (4)	6.30	3.70
Nos. 484-487 (4)	11.85	8.50
Nos. 439-442 (4)	7.60	7.60
Nos. 485-488 (4)	5.90	5.90
Set total (68) Stamps	147.55	120.95

Moon Landing, 20th Anniv.

CD342

Designs: Equipment, crew photographs, spacecraft, official emblems and report profiles created for the Apollo Missions. Two stamps in each set are square in format rather than like the stamp shown; see individual country listings for more information.

1989

Ascension	468-472
Bahamas	674-678
Belize	916-920
Kiribati	517-521
Liberia	1125-1129
Nevis	586-590
St. Kitts	248-252
Samoa	760-764
Seychelles	676-680
Zil Elwannyen Sesel	154-158
Solomon Islands	643-647
Vanuatu	507-511

Nos. 468-472 (5)	9.40	8.60
Nos. 674-678 (5)	23.00	19.70
Nos. 916-920 (5)	27.40	23.50
Nos. 517-521 (5)	12.50	12.50
Nos. 1125-1129 (5)	10.65	10.65
Nos. 586-590 (5)	7.50	7.50
Nos. 248-252 (5)	8.00	8.00
Nos. 760-764 (5)	9.60	9.05
Nos. 676-680 (5)	16.65	16.65
Nos. 154-158 (5)	26.85	26.85

Nos. 643-647 (5)	12.75	11.60
Nos. 507-511 (5)	9.90	9.90
Set total (60) Stamps	174.20	164.50

Queen Mother, 90th Birthday

CD343

CD344

Designs: Portraits of Queen Elizabeth, the Queen Mother. See individual country listings for more information.

1990

Ascension	491-492
Bahamas	698-699
Barbados	782-783
British Antarctic Territory	170-171
British Indian Ocean Territory	106-107
Cayman Islands	622-623
Falkland Islands	524-525
Kenya	527-528
Kiribati	555-556
Liberia	1145-1146
Pitcairn Islands	336-337
St. Helena	532-533
St. Lucia	969-970
Seychelles	710-711
Zil Elwannyen Sesel	171-172
Solomon Islands	671-672
South Georgia	143-144
Swaziland	565-566
Tristan da Cunha	480-481

Nos. 491-492 (2)	4.75	5.65
Nos. 698-699 (2)	5.65	5.65
Nos. 782-783 (2)	4.00	3.70
Nos. 170-171 (2)	6.75	6.75
Nos. 106-107 (2)	20.75	21.25
Nos. 622-623 (2)	5.10	*6.75*
Nos. 524-525 (2)	5.25	5.25
Nos. 527-528 (2)	7.00	7.00
Nos. 555-556 (2)	5.60	5.60
Nos. 1145-1146 (2)	4.25	4.25
Nos. 336-337 (2)	5.25	5.25
Nos. 532-533 (2)	5.25	5.25
Nos. 969-970 (2)	5.25	5.25
Nos. 710-711 (2)	6.60	6.60
Nos. 171-172 (2)	8.25	8.25
Nos. 671-672 (2)	6.50	*6.40*
Nos. 143-144 (2)	5.75	5.75
Nos. 565-566 (2)	4.35	4.35
Nos. 480-481 (2)	5.60	5.60
Set total (38) Stamps	121.90	124.55

Queen Elizabeth II, 65th Birthday, and Prince Philip, 70th Birthday

CD345

CD346

Designs: Portraits of Queen Elizabeth II and Prince Philip differ for each country. Printed in sheets of 10 + 5 labels (3 different) between. Stamps alternate, producing 5 different triptychs.

1991

Ascension	506a
Bahamas	731a
Belize	970a
Bermuda	618a
Kiribati	572a
Mauritius	734a
Pitcairn Islands	349a
St. Helena	555a
St. Kitts	319a
Samoa	791a
Seychelles	724a
Zil Elwannyen Sesel	178a
Solomon Islands	689a
South Georgia	150a
Swaziland	587a
Vanuatu	541a

No. 506a (1)	3.50	3.75
No. 731a (1)	4.00	4.00
No. 970a (1)	3.75	3.75
No. 618a (1)	4.00	4.00
No. 572a (1)	4.00	4.00
No. 734a (1)	3.75	3.75
No. 349a (1)	3.50	3.50
No. 555a (1)	2.75	2.75
No. 319a (1)	3.00	3.00
No. 791a (1)	4.25	4.25
No. 724a (1)	5.00	5.00
No. 178a (1)	6.50	6.50
No. 689a (1)	4.50	4.50
No. 150a (1)	7.00	7.00
No. 587a (1)	4.25	4.25
No. 541a (1)	2.50	2.50
Set total (16) Stamps	66.25	66.50

Royal Family Birthday, Anniversary

CD347

Queen Elizabeth II, 65th birthday, Charles and Diana, 10th wedding anniversary: Various photographs of Queen Elizabeth II, Prince Philip, Prince Charles, Princess Diana and their sons William and Henry.

1991

Antigua	1446-1455
Barbuda	1229-1238
Dominica	1328-1337
Gambia	1080-1089
Grenada	2006-2015
Grenada Grenadines	1331-1340
Guyana	2440-2451
Lesotho	871-875
Maldive Islands	1533-1542
Nevis	666-675
St. Vincent	1485-1494
St. Vincent Grenadines	769-778
Sierra Leone	1387-1396
Turks & Caicos Islands	913-922
Uganda	918-927

Nos. 1446-1455 (10)	21.95	20.30
Nos. 1229-1238 (10)	146.25	139.90
Nos. 1328-1337 (10)	30.20	30.20
Nos. 1080-1089 (10)	24.65	24.40
Nos. 2006-2015 (10)	25.45	22.10
Nos. 1331-1340 (10)	23.85	23.35
Nos. 2440-2451 (12)	21.40	21.15
Nos. 871-875 (5)	13.55	13.55
Nos. 1533-1542 (10)	29.60	29.60
Nos. 666-675 (10)	25.65	25.65
Nos. 1485-1494 (10)	26.75	25.90
Nos. 769-778 (10)	27.10	27.10
Nos. 1387-1396 (10)	26.55	26.55
Nos. 913-922 (10)	31.65	30.00
Nos. 918-927 (10)	26.60	26.60
Set total (147) Stamps	501.20	486.35

Queen Elizabeth II's Accession to the Throne, 40th Anniv.

CD348

CD349

Various photographs of Queen Elizabeth II with local Scenes.

1992 - CD348

Antigua	1513-1518
Barbuda	1306-1311
Dominica	1414-1419
Gambia	1172-1177
Grenada	2047-2052
Grenada Grenadines	1368-1373
Lesotho	881-885
Maldive Islands	1637-1642
Nevis	702-707
St. Vincent	1582-1587
St. Vincent Grenadines	829-834
Sierra Leone	1482-1487
Turks and Caicos Islands	978-987
Uganda	990-995
Virgin Islands	742-746

Nos. 1513-1518 (6)	16.00	14.10
Nos. 1306-1311 (6)	144.50	98.75
Nos. 1414-1419 (6)	12.50	12.50
Nos. 1172-1177 (6)	16.60	16.35
Nos. 2047-2052 (6)	15.95	15.95
Nos. 1368-1373 (6)	17.00	15.35
Nos. 881-885 (5)	11.90	11.90
Nos. 1637-1642 (6)	17.55	17.55
Nos. 702-707 (6)	13.80	13.80
Nos. 1582-1587 (6)	14.40	14.40
Nos. 829-834 (6)	20.55	20.55
Nos. 1482-1487 (6)	22.50	22.50
Nos. 913-922 (10)	31.65	30.00
Nos. 990-995 (6)	19.50	19.50
Nos. 742-746 (5)	15.50	15.50
Set total (92) Stamps	389.90	338.70

1992 - CD349

Ascension	*531-535*
Bahamas	*744-748*
Bermuda	*623-627*
British Indian Ocean Territory	*119-123*
Cayman Islands	*648-652*
Falkland Islands	*549-553*
Gibraltar	*605-609*
Hong Kong	*619-623*
Kenya	*563-567*
Kiribati	*582-586*
Pitcairn Islands	*362-366*
St. Helena	*570-574*
St. Kitts	*332-336*
Samoa	*805-809*
Seychelles	*734-738*
Zil Elwannyen Sesel	*183-187*
Solomon Islands	*708-712*
South Georgia	*157-161*
Tristan da Cunha	*508-512*
Vanuatu	*555-559*
Zambia	*561-565*

Nos. 531-535 (5)	6.35	6.35
Nos. 744-748 (5)	6.90	4.70
Nos. 623-627 (5)	8.20	7.30
Nos. 119-123 (5)	24.75	*21.00*
Nos. 648-652 (5)	7.60	7.10
Nos. 549-553 (5)	6.80	8.20
Nos. 605-609 (5)	5.15	*5.50*
Nos. 619-623 (5)	5.65	2.65
Nos. 563-567 (5)	9.10	9.10
Nos. 582-586 (5)	3.85	3.85
Nos. 362-366 (5)	6.55	6.55
Nos. 570-574 (5)	5.70	5.70
Nos. 332-336 (5)	6.60	5.50
Nos. 805-809 (5)	8.10	6.15
Nos. 734-738 (5)	10.80	10.80
Nos. 183-187 (5)	9.40	9.40
Nos. 708-712 (5)	7.95	7.30
Nos. 157-161 (5)	5.85	5.75
Nos. 508-512 (5)	8.75	8.30
Nos. 555-559 (5)	3.65	3.65
Nos. 561-565 (5)	5.60	5.60
Set total (105) Stamps	163.30	150.45

Royal Air Force, 75th Anniversary

CD350

1993

Ascension	557-561
Bahamas	771-775
Barbados	842-846
Belize	1003-1008
Bermuda	648-651
British Indian Ocean Territory	136-140
Falkland Is.	573-577
Fiji	687-691
Montserrat	830-834
St. Kitts	351-355

Nos. 557-561 (5)	16.70	14.85
Nos. 771-775 (5)	26.00	22.20
Nos. 842-846 (5)	13.65	12.35
Nos. 1003-1008 (6)	19.40	18.70
Nos. 648-651 (4)	10.50	9.95
Nos. 136-140 (5)	17.50	17.50
Nos. 573-577 (5)	11.25	11.25
Nos. 687-691 (5)	18.95	18.95
Nos. 830-834 (5)	14.35	14.35
Nos. 351-355 (5)	24.45	23.95
Set total (50) Stamps	172.75	164.05

Royal Air Force, 80th Anniv.

Design CD350 Re-inscribed

1998

Ascension	697-701
Bahamas	907-911
British Indian Ocean Terr	198-202
Cayman Islands	754-758
Fiji	814-818
Gibraltar	755-759
Samoa	957-961
Turks & Caicos Islands	1258-1265
Tuvalu	763-767
Virgin Islands	879-883

Nos. 697-701 (5)	17.35	17.35
Nos. 907-911 (5)	14.25	13.55
Nos. 136-140 (5)	17.50	17.50
Nos. 754-758 (5)	15.75	15.75
Nos. 814-818 (5)	15.50	15.50
Nos. 755-759 (5)	9.70	9.70
Nos. 957-961 (5)	16.70	15.90
Nos. 1258-1265 (2)	32.00	32.00
Nos. 763-767 (5)	9.75	9.75
Nos. 879-883 (5)	17.00	17.00
Set total (47) Stamps	165.50	164.00

End of World War II, 50th Anniv.

CD351

CD352

1995

Ascension	613-617
Bahamas	824-828
Barbados	891-895
Belize	1047-1050
British Indian Ocean Territory	163-167
Cayman Islands	704-708
Falkland Islands	634-638
Fiji	720-724
Kiribati	662-668
Liberia	1175-1179
Mauritius	803-805
St. Helena	646-654
St. Kitts	389-393
St. Lucia	1018-1022
Samoa	890-894
Solomon Islands	799-803
South Georgia	198-200
Tristan da Cunha	562-566

Nos. 613-617 (5)	21.50	21.50
Nos. 824-828 (5)	22.00	18.70
Nos. 891-895 (5)	14.20	11.90
Nos. 1047-1050 (4)	7.45	6.75
Nos. 163-167 (5)	16.25	16.25
Nos. 704-708 (5)	18.15	14.45
Nos. 634-638 (5)	17.90	17.40
Nos. 720-724 (5)	21.35	21.35
Nos. 662-668 (7)	16.30	16.30
Nos. 1175-1179 (5)	19.60	19.60
Nos. 803-805 (3)	7.50	7.50

Nos. 646-654 (9)	26.10	26.10
Nos. 389-393 (5)	13.60	13.60
Nos. 1018-1022 (5)	14.25	11.15
Nos. 890-894 (5)	14.25	13.50
Nos. 799-803 (5)	17.50	17.50
Nos. 198-200 (3)	14.00	14.00
Nos. 562-566 (5)	20.10	20.10
Set total (91) Stamps	302.00	287.65

UN, 50th Anniv.

CD353

1995

Bahamas	839-842
Barbados	901-904
Belize	1055-1058
Jamaica	847-851
Liberia	1187-1190
Mauritius	813-816
Pitcairn Islands	436-439
St. Kitts	398-401
St. Lucia	1023-1026
Samoa	900-903
Tristan da Cunha	568-571
Virgin Islands	807-810

Nos. 839-842 (4)	8.00	7.05
Nos. 901-904 (4)	7.00	5.75
Nos. 1055-1058 (4)	5.70	5.60
Nos. 847-851 (5)	6.30	5.85
Nos. 1187-1190 (4)	15.00	15.00
Nos. 813-816 (4)	3.90	3.90
Nos. 436-439 (4)	11.25	11.25
Nos. 398-401 (4)	6.15	6.15
Nos. 1023-1026 (4)	7.50	7.25
Nos. 900-903 (4)	9.35	8.20
Nos. 568-571 (4)	13.50	13.50
Nos. 807-810 (4)	9.45	9.45
Set total (49) Stamps	103.10	98.95

Queen Elizabeth, 70th Birthday

CD354

1996

Ascension	632-635
British Antarctic Territory	240-243
British Indian Ocean Territory	176-180
Falkland Islands	653-657
Pitcairn Islands	446-449
St. Helena	672-676
Samoa	912-916
Tokelau	223-227
Tristan da Cunha	576-579
Virgin Islands	824-828

Nos. 632-635 (4)	5.90	5.90
Nos. 240-243 (4)	10.50	8.90
Nos. 176-180 (5)	11.50	11.50
Nos. 653-657 (5)	14.35	11.90
Nos. 446-449 (4)	10.50	10.50
Nos. 672-676 (5)	12.70	12.70
Nos. 912-916 (5)	11.50	11.50
Nos. 223-227 (5)	11.35	11.35
Nos. 576-579 (4)	8.35	8.35
Nos. 824-828 (5)	11.80	11.80
Set total (46) Stamps	108.45	104.40

Diana, Princess of Wales (1961-97)

CD355

1998

Ascension	696
Bahamas	901A-902
Barbados	950
Belize	1091
Bermuda	753
Botswana	659-663
British Antarctic Territory	258
British Indian Ocean Terr.	197
Cayman Islands	752A-753
Falkland Islands	694
Fiji	819-820
Gibraltar	754
Kiribati	719A-720
Namibia	909
Niue	706
Norfolk Island	644-645
Papua New Guinea	937
Pitcairn Islands	487
St. Helena	711
St. Kitts	437A-438
Samoa	955A-956
Seycelles	802
Solomon Islands	866-867
South Georgia	220
Tokelau	252B-253
Tonga	980
Niuafo'ou	201
Tristan da Cunha	618
Tuvalu	762
Vanuatu	718A-719
Virgin Islands	878

No. 696 (1)	5.50	5.50
Nos. 901A-902 (2)	5.30	5.30
No. 950 (1)	5.00	5.00
No. 1091 (1)	5.50	5.50
No. 753 (1)	5.50	5.50
Nos. 659-663 (5)	10.25	10.10
No. 258 (1)	6.25	6.25
No. 197 (1)	6.50	6.50
Nos. 752A-753 (3)	7.75	7.75
No. 694 (1)	4.75	4.75
Nos. 819-820 (2)	6.00	6.00
No. 754 (1)	4.75	4.75
Nos. 719A-720 (2)	4.85	4.85
No. 909 (1)	1.90	1.90
No. 706 (1)	5.50	5.50
Nos. 644-645 (2)	5.25	5.25
No. 937 (1)	6.50	6.50
No. 487 (1)	5.25	5.25
No. 711 (1)	4.25	4.25
Nos. 437A-438 (2)	5.15	5.15
Nos. 955A-956 (2)	7.00	7.00
No. 802 (1)	6.25	6.25
Nos. 866-867 (2)	6.90	6.90
No. 220 (1)	5.25	5.25
Nos. 252B-253 (2)	6.75	6.75
No. 980 (1)	5.75	5.75
No. 201 (1)	7.75	7.75
No. 618 (1)	5.00	5.00
No. 762 (1)	4.00	4.00
Nos. 718A-719 (2)	8.00	8.00
No. 878 (1)	5.50	5.50
Set total (46) Stamps	179.85	179.70

Wedding of Prince Edward and Sophie Rhys-Jones

CD356

1999

Ascension	729-730
Cayman Islands	775-776
Falkland Islands	729-730
Pitcairn Islands	505-506
St. Helena	733-734
Samoa	971-972
Tristan da Cunha	636-637
Virgin Islands	908-909

Nos. 729-730 (2)	5.90	5.90
Nos. 775-776 (2)	5.50	5.50
Nos. 729-730 (2)	15.00	15.00
Nos. 505-506 (2)	9.00	9.00
Nos. 733-734 (2)	5.00	5.00
Nos. 971-972 (2)	5.00	5.00
Nos. 636-637 (2)	7.50	7.50
Nos. 908-909 (2)	8.30	8.30
Set total (16) Stamps	61.20	61.20

1st Manned Moon Landing, 30th Anniv.

CD357

1999

Ascension	731-735
Bahamas	942-946
Barbados	967-971
Bermuda	778
Cayman Islands	777-781
Fiji	853-857
Jamaica	889-893
Kirbati	746-750
Nauru	465-469
St. Kitts	460-464
Samoa	973-977
Solomon Islands	875-879
Tuvalu	800-804
Virgin Islands	910-914

Nos. 731-735 (5)	13.90	13.90
Nos. 942-946 (5)	14.10	14.10
Nos. 967-971 (5)	8.65	7.75
No. 778 (1)	8.00	8.00
Nos. 777-781 (5)	10.30	10.30
Nos. 853-857 (5)	10.40	10.40
Nos. 889-893 (5)	10.20	10.00
Nos. 746-750 (5)	8.85	8.85
Nos. 465-469 (5)	8.90	10.15
Nos. 460-464 (5)	12.00	12.00
Nos. 973-977 (5)	13.45	13.30
Nos. 875-879 (5)	10.00	9.85
Nos. 800-804 (5)	7.45	7.45
Nos. 910-914 (5)	15.00	15.00
Set total (66) Stamps	151.20	151.05

Queen Mother's Century

CD358

1999

Ascension	736-740
Bahamas	951-955
Cayman Islands	782-786
Falkland Islands	734-738
Fiji	858-862
Norfolk Island	688-692
St. Helena	740-744
Samoa	978-982
Solomon Islands	880-884
South Georgia	231-235
Tristan da Cunha	638-642
Tuvalu	805-809

Nos. 736-740 (5)	17.00	17.00
Nos. 951-955 (5)	14.00	12.90
Nos. 782-786 (5)	9.15	9.15
Nos. 734-738 (5)	30.75	27.75
Nos. 858-862 (5)	15.00	15.00
Nos. 688-692 (5)	10.30	10.30
Nos. 740-744 (5)	16.15	16.15
Nos. 978-982 (5)	13.25	13.25
Nos. 880-884 (5)	10.00	9.45
Nos. 231-235 (5)	30.25	29.75
Nos. 638-642 (5)	18.00	18.00
Nos. 805-809 (5)	8.65	8.65
Set total (60) Stamps	192.50	187.35

Prince William, 18th Birthday

CD359

2000

Ascension	755-759
Cayman Islands	797-801
Falkland Islands	762-766
Fiji	889-893
South Georgia	257-261
Tristan da Cunha	664-668
Virgin Islands	925-929

Nos. 755-759 (5)	17.75	17.75
Nos. 797-801 (5)	13.05	12.75
Nos. 762-766 (5)	27.15	23.75
Nos. 889-893 (5)	14.00	14.00
Nos. 257-261 (5)	29.00	29.00
Nos. 664-668 (5)	21.50	21.50
Nos. 925-929 (5)	14.75	14.75
Set total (35) Stamps	137.20	133.50

Reign of Queen Elizabeth II, 50th Anniv.

CD360

2002

Ascension	790-794
Bahamas	1033-1037
Barbados	1019-1023
Belize	1152-1156
Bermuda	822-826
British Antarctic Territory	307-311
British Indian Ocean Territory	239-243
Cayman Islands	844-848
Falkland Islands	804-808
Gibraltar	896-900
Jamaica	952-956
Nauru	491-495
Norfolk Island	758-762
Papua New Guinea	1019-1023
Pitcairn Islands	552
St. Helena	788-792
St. Lucia	1146-1150
Solomon Islands	931-935
South Georgia	274-278
Swaziland	706-710
Tokelau	302-306
Tonga	1059
Niuafo'ou	239
Tristan da Cunha	706-710
Virgin Islands	967-971

Nos. 790-794 (5)	16.25	16.25
Nos. 1033-1037 (5)	15.75	15.75
Nos. 1019-1023 (5)	13.15	13.15
Nos. 1152-1156 (5)	15.50	15.15
Nos. 822-826 (5)	18.50	18.50
Nos. 307-311 (5)	25.00	25.00
Nos. 239-243 (5)	22.00	22.00
Nos. 844-848 (5)	14.25	14.25
Nos. 804-808 (5)	23.50	22.50
Nos. 896-900 (5)	6.65	6.65
Nos. 952-956 (5)	18.25	18.25
Nos. 491-495 (5)	18.75	18.75
Nos. 758-762 (5)	19.50	19.50
Nos. 1019-1023 (5)	14.50	14.50
No. 552 (1)	11.50	11.50
Nos. 788-792 (5)	19.75	19.75
Nos. 1146-1150 (5)	12.25	12.25
Nos. 931-935 (5)	16.00	16.00
Nos. 274-278 (5)	28.50	28.50
Nos. 706-710 (5)	12.75	12.75
Nos. 302-306 (5)	17.00	17.00
No. 1059 (1)	8.00	8.00
No. 239 (1)	7.00	7.00
Nos. 706-710 (5)	18.50	18.50
Nos. 967-971 (5)	19.00	19.00
Set total (113) Stamps	411.80	410.45

Queen Mother Elizabeth (1900-2002)

CD361

2002

Ascension	799-801
Bahamas	1044-1046
Bermuda	834-836
British Antarctic Territory	312-314

British Indian Ocean Territory 245-247
Cayman Islands.......................857-861
Falkland Islands 812-816
Nauru......................................499-501
Pitcairn Islands........................561-565
St. Helena 808-812
St. Lucia 1155-1159
Seychelles 830
Solomon Islands......................945-947
South Georgia 281-285
Tokelau 312-314
Tristan da Cunha.....................715-717
Virgin Islands..........................979-983

Nos. 799-801 (3)	9.75	9.75
Nos. 1044-1046 (3)	9.35	9.35
Nos. 834-836 (3)	12.50	12.50
Nos. 312-314 (3)	19.25	19.25
Nos. 245-247 (3)	19.50	19.50
Nos. 857-861 (5)	15.00	15.00
Nos. 812-816 (5)	31.50	31.50
Nos. 499-501 (3)	16.00	16.00
Nos. 561-565 (5)	18.50	18.50
Nos. 808-812 (5)	12.00	12.00
Nos. 1155-1159 (5)	13.00	13.00
No. 830 (1)	6.50	6.50
Nos. 945-947 (3)	11.00	11.00
Nos. 281-285 (5)	20.00	20.00
Nos. 312-314 (3)	14.25	13.75
Nos. 715-717 (3)	16.25	16.25
Nos. 979-983 (5)	26.50	26.50
Set total (63) Stamps	270.85	270.35

Head of Queen Elizabeth II

CD362

2003

Ascension.......................................822
Bermuda...865
British Antarctic Territory.................322
British Indian Ocean Territory.........261
Cayman Islands..............................878
Falkland Islands 828
St. Helena 820
South Georgia 294
Tristan da Cunha............................731
Virgin Islands...............................1003

No. 822 (1)	13.50	13.50
No. 865 (1)	55.00	55.00
No. 322 (1)	10.00	10.00
No. 261 (1)	12.50	12.50
No. 878 (1)	17.00	17.00
No. 828 (1)	10.00	10.00
No. 820 (1)	9.00	9.00
No. 294 (1)	9.00	9.00
No. 731 (1)	10.00	10.00
No. 1003 (1)	10.00	10.00
Set total (10) Stamps	156.00	156.00

Coronation of Queen Elizabeth II, 50th Anniv.

CD363

2003

Ascension 823-825
Bahamas 1073-1075
Bermuda.................................866-868
British Antarctic Territory..........323-325
British Indian Ocean Territory 262-264
Cayman Islands.......................879-881
Jamaica 970-972
Kiribati 825-827
Pitcairn Islands........................577-581
St. Helena 821-823
St. Lucia 1171-1173
Tokelau 320-322
Tristan da Cunha.....................732-734
Virgin Islands.......................1004-1006

Nos. 823-825 (3)	13.50	13.50
Nos. 1073-1075 (3)	13.00	13.00
Nos. 866-868 (3)	14.25	14.25
Nos. 323-325 (3)	26.00	26.00
Nos. 262-264 (3)	31.00	31.00
Nos. 879-881 (3)	20.25	20.25
Nos. 970-972 (3)	11.75	11.75
Nos. 825-827 (3)	13.50	13.50
Nos. 577-581 (5)	18.50	18.50
Nos. 821-823 (3)	7.25	7.25
Nos. 1171-1173 (3)	8.75	8.75
Nos. 320-322 (3)	20.00	20.00
Nos. 732-734 (3)	16.75	16.75
Nos. 1004-1006 (3)	25.00	25.00
Set total (44) Stamps	239.50	239.50

Prince William, 21st Birthday

CD364

2003

Ascension.......................................826
British Indian Ocean Territory.........265
Cayman Islands.......................882-884
Falkland Islands 829
South Georgia 295
Tokelau 323
Tristan da Cunha............................735
Virgin Islands.......................1007-1009

No. 826 (1)	7.50	7.50
No. 265 (1)	9.00	9.00
Nos. 882-884 (3)	7.65	7.65
No. 829 (1)	14.50	14.50
No. 295 (1)	9.00	9.00
No. 323 (1)	7.25	7.25
No. 735 (1)	6.00	6.00
Nos. 1007-1009 (3)	10.00	10.00
Set total (12) Stamps	70.90	70.90

FREIMARKE
70 KREUZER

SOMALIA ITALIANA
RR. POSTE COLONIALI ITALIANE
POSTA AEREA
II^a MOSTRA INTERNAZIONALE D'ARTE COLONIALE NAPOLI A.XII. 1934
CENT. 25

24
Cn
30
cents.

EMPIRE
FRANÇAIS
5
F
TIMBRE
POSTE

REPUB. FRANC.
1 FR. POSTES 1 FR.

POSTA
POSTA
POSTA
GR 10
Napoli

CEYLON
100 Rs
100 Rs
POSTAGE
REVENUE
ONE HUNDRED RUPEES

CHARGÉ
Capestang

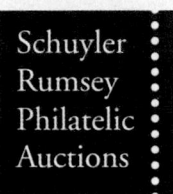

British Commonwealth of Nations

Dominions, Colonies, Territories, Offices and Independent Members

Comprising stamps of the British Commonwealth and associated nations.

A strict observance of technicalities would bar some or all of the stamps listed under Burma, Ireland, Kuwait, Nepal, New Republic, Orange Free State, Samoa, South Africa, South-West Africa, Stellaland, Sudan, Swaziland, the two Transvaal Republics and others but these are included for the convenience of collectors.

1. Great Britain

Great Britain: Including England, Scotland, Wales and Northern Ireland.

2. The Dominions, Present and Past

AUSTRALIA

The Commonwealth of Australia was proclaimed on January 1, 1901. It consists of six former colonies as follows:

New South Wales
Victoria
Queensland
Tasmania
South Australia
Western Australia

The following islands and territories are, or have been, administered by Australia: Australian Antarctic Territory, Christmas Island, Cocos (Keeling) Islands, Nauru, New Guinea, Norfolk Island, Papua.

CANADA

The Dominion of Canada was created by the British North America Act in 1867. The following provinces were former sepa- rate colonies and issued postage stamps:

British Columbia and Vancouver Island
Newfoundland
New Brunswick
Nova Scotia
Prince Edward Island

FIJI

The colony of Fiji became an independent nation with dominion status on Oct. 10, 1970.

GHANA

This state came into existence Mar. 6, 1957, with dominion status. It consists of the former colony of the Gold Coast and the Trusteeship Territory of Togoland. Ghana became a republic July 1, 1960.

INDIA

The Republic of India was inaugurated on January 26, 1950. It succeeded the Dominion of India which was proclaimed August 15, 1947, when the former Empire of India was divided into Pakistan and the Union of India. The Republic is composed of about 40 predominantly Hindu states of three classes: governor's provinces, chief commissioner's provinces and princely states. India also has various territories, such as the Andaman and Nicobar Islands.

The old Empire of India was a federation of British India and the native states. The more important princely states were autonomous. Of the more than 700 Indian states, these 43 are familiar names to philatelists because of their postage stamps.

CONVENTION STATES

Chamba
Faridkot
Gwalior
Jhind
Nabha
Patiala

FEUDATORY STATES

Alwar
Bahawalpur
Bamra
Barwani
Bhopal
Bhor
Bijawar
Bundi
Bussahir
Charkhari
Cochin
Dhar
Dungarpur
Duttia
Faridkot (1879-85)
Hyderabad
Idar
Indore
Jaipur
Jammu
Jammu and Kashmir
Jasdan
Jhalawar
Jhind (1875-76)
Kashmir
Kishangarh
Kotah
Las Bela
Morvi
Nandgaon
Nowanuggur
Orchha
Poonch
Rajasthan
Rajpeepla
Sirmur
Soruth
Tonk
Travancore
Wadhwan

NEW ZEALAND

Became a dominion on September 26, 1907. The following islands and territories are, or have been, administered by New Zealand:

Aitutaki
Cook Islands (Rarotonga)
Niue
Penrhyn
Ross Dependency
Samoa (Western Samoa)
Tokelau Islands

PAKISTAN

The Republic of Pakistan was proclaimed March 23, 1956. It succeeded the Dominion which was proclaimed August 15, 1947. It is made up of all or part of several Moslem provinces and various districts of the former Empire of India, including Bahawalpur and Las Bela. Pakistan withdrew from the Commonwealth in 1972.

SOUTH AFRICA

Under the terms of the South African Act (1909) the self-governing colonies of Cape of Good Hope, Natal, Orange River Colony and Transvaal united on May 31, 1910, to form the Union of South Africa. It became an independent republic May 3, 1961.

Under the terms of the Treaty of Versailles, South-West Africa, formerly German South-West Africa, was mandated to the Union of South Africa.

SRI LANKA (CEYLON)

The Dominion of Ceylon was proclaimed February 4, 1948. The island had been a Crown Colony from 1802 until then. On May 22, 1972, Ceylon became the Republic of Sri Lanka.

3. Colonies, Past and Present; Controlled Territory and Independent Members of the Commonwealth

Aden
Aitutaki
Anguilla
Antigua
Ascension
Bahamas
Bahrain
Bangladesh
Barbados
Barbuda
Basutoland
Batum
Bechuanaland
Bechuanaland Prot.
Belize
Bermuda
Botswana
British Antarctic Territory
British Central Africa
British Columbia and Vancouver Island
British East Africa
British Guiana

British Honduras
British Indian Ocean Territory
British New Guinea
British Solomon Islands
British Somaliland
Brunei
Burma
Bushire
Cameroons
Cape of Good Hope
Cayman Islands
Christmas Island
Cocos (Keeling) Islands
Cook Islands
Crete,
British Administration
Cyprus
Dominica
East Africa & Uganda
Protectorates
Egypt
Falkland Islands
Fiji
Gambia
German East Africa
Gibraltar
Gilbert Islands
Gilbert & Ellice Islands
Gold Coast
Grenada
Griqualand West
Guernsey
Guyana
Heligoland
Hong Kong
Indian Native States
(see India)
Ionian Islands
Jamaica
Jersey
Kenya
Kenya, Uganda & Tanzania
Kuwait
Labuan
Lagos
Leeward Islands
Lesotho
Madagascar
Malawi
Malaya
Federated Malay States
Johore
Kedah
Kelantan
Malacca
Negri Sembilan
Pahang
Penang
Perak
Perlis
Selangor
Singapore
Sungei Ujong
Trengganu
Malaysia
Maldive Islands
Malta
Man, Isle of
Mauritius
Mesopotamia
Montserrat
Muscat
Namibia
Natal
Nauru
Nevis
New Britain
New Brunswick
Newfoundland
New Guinea
New Hebrides
New Republic
New South Wales
Niger Coast Protectorate
Nigeria
Niue
Norfolk Island
North Borneo
Northern Nigeria
Northern Rhodesia
North West Pacific Islands
Nova Scotia
Nyasaland Protectorate
Oman
Orange River Colony
Palestine
Papua New Guinea
Penrhyn Island
Pitcairn Islands
Prince Edward Island
Queensland
Rhodesia
Rhodesia & Nyasaland
Ross Dependency
Sabah
St. Christopher
St. Helena
St. Kitts
St. Kitts-Nevis-Anguilla
St. Lucia
St. Vincent
Samoa
Sarawak
Seychelles
Sierra Leone
Solomon Islands
Somaliland Protectorate
South Arabia
South Australia
South Georgia
Southern Nigeria
Southern Rhodesia
South-West Africa
Stellaland
Straits Settlements
Sudan
Swaziland
Tanganyika
Tanzania
Tasmania
Tobago
Togo
Tokelau Islands
Tonga
Transvaal
Trinidad
Trinidad and Tobago
Tristan da Cunha
Trucial States
Turks and Caicos
Turks Islands
Tuvalu
Uganda
United Arab Emirates
Victoria
Virgin Islands
Western Australia
Zambia
Zanzibar
Zululand

POST OFFICES IN FOREIGN COUNTRIES

Africa
East Africa Forces
Middle East Forces
Bangkok
China
Morocco
Turkish Empire

Colonies, Former Colonies, Offices, Territories Controlled by Parent States

Belgium
Belgian Congo
Ruanda-Urundi

Denmark
Danish West Indies
Faroe Islands
Greenland
Iceland

Finland
Aland Islands

France
COLONIES PAST AND PRESENT, CONTROLLED TERRITORIES
Afars & Issas, Territory of
Alaouites
Alexandretta
Algeria
Alsace & Lorraine
Anjouan
Annam & Tonkin
Benin
Cambodia (Khmer)
Cameroun
Castellorizo
Chad
Cilicia
Cochin China
Comoro Islands
Dahomey
Diego Suarez
Djibouti (Somali Coast)
Fezzan
French Congo
French Equatorial Africa
French Guiana
French Guinea
French India
French Morocco
French Polynesia (Oceania)
French Southern & Antarctic Territories
French Sudan
French West Africa
Gabon
Germany
Ghadames
Grand Comoro
Guadeloupe
Indo-China
Inini
Ivory Coast
Laos
Latakia
Lebanon
Madagascar
Martinique
Mauritania
Mayotte
Memel
Middle Congo
Moheli
New Caledonia
New Hebrides
Niger Territory
Nossi-Be
Obock
Reunion
Rouad, Ile
Ste.-Marie de Madagascar
St. Pierre & Miquelon
Senegal
Senegambia & Niger
Somali Coast
Syria
Tahiti
Togo
Tunisia
Ubangi-Shari
Upper Senegal & Niger
Upper Volta
Viet Nam
Wallis & Futuna Islands

POST OFFICES IN FOREIGN COUNTRIES
China
Crete
Egypt
Turkish Empire
Zanzibar

Germany
EARLY STATES
Baden
Bavaria
Bergedorf
Bremen
Brunswick
Hamburg
Hanover
Lubeck
Mecklenburg-Schwerin
Mecklenburg-Strelitz
Oldenburg
Prussia
Saxony
Schleswig-Holstein
Wurttemberg

FORMER COLONIES
Cameroun (Kamerun)
Caroline Islands
German East Africa
German New Guinea
German South-West Africa
Kiauchau
Mariana Islands
Marshall Islands
Samoa
Togo

Italy
EARLY STATES
Modena
Parma
Romagna
Roman States
Sardinia
Tuscany
Two Sicilies
  Naples
  Neapolitan Provinces
  Sicily

FORMER COLONIES, CONTROLLED TERRITORIES, OCCUPATION AREAS
Aegean Islands
  Calimno (Calino)
  Caso
  Cos (Coo)
  Karki (Carchi)
  Leros (Lero)
  Lipso
  Nisiros (Nisiro)
  Patmos (Patmo)
  Piscopi
  Rodi (Rhodes)
  Scarpanto
  Simi
  Stampalia
Castellorizo
Corfu
Cyrenaica
Eritrea
Ethiopia (Abyssinia)
Fiume
Ionian Islands
  Cephalonia
  Ithaca
  Paxos
Italian East Africa
Libya
Oltre Giuba
Saseno
Somalia (Italian Somaliland)
Tripolitania

POST OFFICES IN FOREIGN COUNTRIES
"ESTERO"*
Austria
China
  Peking
  Tientsin
Crete
Tripoli
Turkish Empire
  Constantinople
  Durazzo
  Janina
Jerusalem
Salonika
Scutari
Smyrna
Valona

*Stamps overprinted "ESTERO" were used in various parts of the world.

Netherlands
Aruba
Caribbean Netherlands
Curacao
Netherlands Antilles (Curacao)
Netherlands Indies
Netherlands New Guinea
St. Martin
Surinam (Dutch Guiana)

Portugal
COLONIES PAST AND PRESENT, CONTROLLED TERRITORIES
Angola
Angra
Azores
Cape Verde
Funchal
Horta
Inhambane
Kionga
Lourenco Marques
Macao
Madeira
Mozambique
Mozambique Co.
Nyassa
Ponta Delgada
Portuguese Africa
Portuguese Congo
Portuguese Guinea
Portuguese India
Quelimane
St. Thomas & Prince Islands
Tete
Timor
Zambezia

Russia
ALLIED TERRITORIES AND REPUBLICS, OCCUPATION AREAS
Armenia
Aunus (Olonets)
Azerbaijan
Batum
Estonia
Far Eastern Republic
Georgia
Karelia
Latvia
Lithuania
North Ingermanland
Ostland
Russian Turkestan
Siberia
South Russia
Tannu Tuva
Transcaucasian Fed. Republics
Ukraine
Wenden (Livonia)
Western Ukraine

Spain
COLONIES PAST AND PRESENT, CONTROLLED TERRITORIES
Aguera, La
Cape Juby
Cuba
Elobey, Annobon & Corisco
Fernando Po
Ifni
Mariana Islands
Philippines
Puerto Rico
Rio de Oro
Rio Muni
Spanish Guinea
Spanish Morocco
Spanish Sahara
Spanish West Africa

POST OFFICES IN FOREIGN COUNTRIES
Morocco
Tangier
Tetuan

Dies of British Colonial Stamps

DIE A:

1. The lines in the groundwork vary in thickness and are not uniformly straight.

2. The seventh and eighth lines from the top, in the groundwork, converge where they meet the head.

3. There is a small dash in the upper part of the second jewel in the band of the crown.

4. The vertical color line in front of the throat stops at the sixth line of shading on the neck.

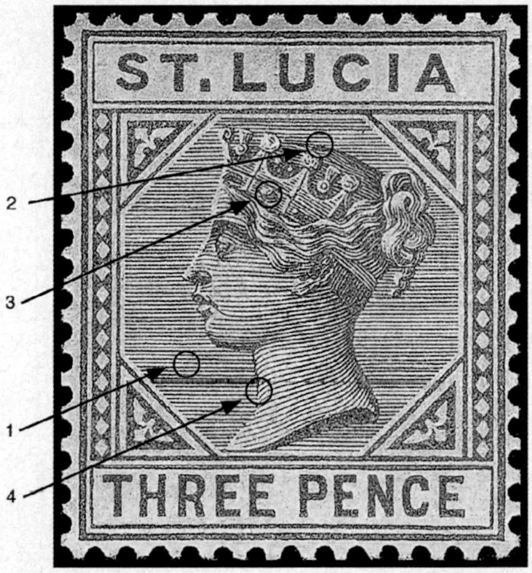

DIE B:

1. The lines in the groundwork are all thin and straight.

2. All the lines of the background are parallel.

3. There is no dash in the upper part of the second jewel in the band of the crown.

4. The vertical color line in front of the throat stops at the eighth line of shading on the neck.

DIE I:

1. The base of the crown is well below the level of the inner white line around the vignette.

2. The labels inscribed "POSTAGE" and "REVENUE" are cut square at the top.

3. There is a white "bud" on the outer side of the main stem of the curved ornaments in each lower corner.

4. The second (thick) line below the country name has the ends next to the crown cut diagonally.

DIE Ia.	DIE Ib.
1 as die II.	1 and 3 as die II.
2 and 3 as die I.	2 as die I.

DIE II:

1. The base of the crown is aligned with the underside of the white line around the vignette.

2. The labels curve inward at the top inner corners.

3. The "bud" has been removed from the outer curve of the ornaments in each corner.

4. The second line below the country name has the ends next to the crown cut vertically.

British Colonial and Crown Agents Watermarks

Watermarks 1 to 4, 314, 373, 384 and 406, common to many British territories, are illustrated here to avoid duplication.

The letters "CC" of Wmk. 1 identify the paper as having been made for the use of the Crown Colonies, while the letters "CA" of the others stand for "Crown Agents." Both Wmks. 1 and 2 were used on stamps printed by De La Rue & Co.

Wmk. 3 was adopted in 1904; Wmk. 4 in 1921; Wmk. 314 in 1957; Wmk. 373 in 1974; Wmk. 384 in 1985; Wmk 406 in 2008.

In Wmk. 4a, a non-matching crown of the general St. Edwards type (bulging on both sides at top) was substituted for one of the Wmk. 4 crowns which fell off the dandy roll. The non-matching crown occurs in 1950-52 printings in a horizontal row of crowns on certain regular stamps of Johore and Seychelles, and on various postage due stamps of Barbados, Basutoland, British Guiana, Gold Coast, Grenada, Northern Rhodesia, St. Lucia, Swaziland and Trinidad and Tobago. A variation of Wmk. 4a, with the non-matching crown in a horizontal row of crown-CA-crown, occurs on regular stamps of Bahamas, St. Kitts-Nevis and Singapore.

Wmk. 314 was intentionally used sideways, starting in 1966. When a stamp was issued with Wmk. 314 both upright and sideways, the sideways varieties usually are listed also – with minor numbers. In many of the later issues, Wmk. 314 is slightly visible.

Wmk. 373 is usually only faintly visible.

Wmk. 1
Crown and C C

Wmk. 2
Crown and C A

Wmk. 3
Multiple Crown and C A

Wmk. 4
Multiple Crown and Script C A

Wmk. 4a

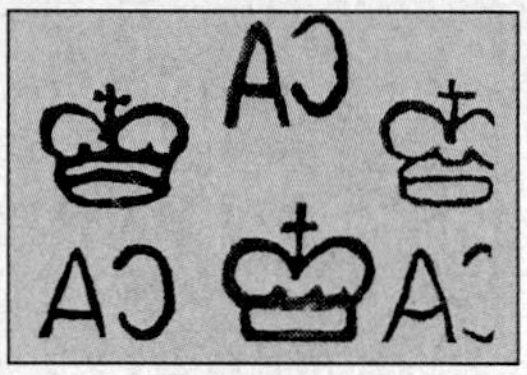
Wmk. 314
St. Edward's Crown and C A Multiple

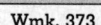

Wmk. 373

Wmk. 384

Wmk. 406

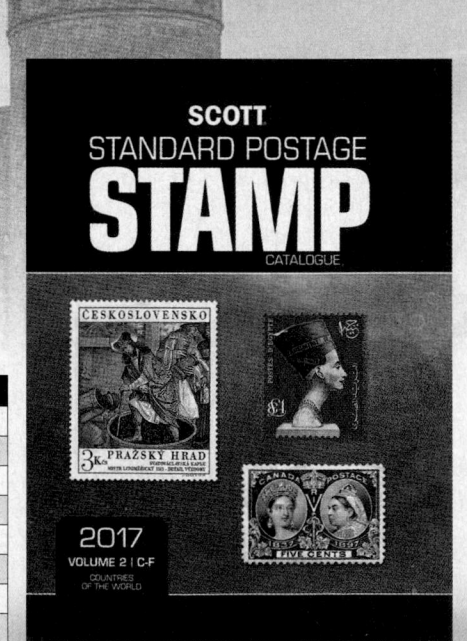

CAMBODIA

kam-ˈbō-dē-ə

(Kampuchea)

(Khmer Republic)

LOCATION — Southern Indo-China
GOVT. — Republic
AREA — 69,898 sq. mi.
POP. — 11,626,520 (1999 est.)
CAPITAL — Phnom Penh

Before 1951, Cambodia used stamps of Indo-China. In October, 1970, the Kingdom of Cambodia became the Khmer Republic.

From 1978 to 1980 money was abolished.

100 Cents = 1 Piaster
100 Cents = 1 Riel (1955)

Imperforates
Most Cambodia stamps exist imperforate in issued and trial colors, and also in small presentation sheets in issued colors.

Catalogue values for all unused stamps in this country are for Never Hinged items.

Apsaras — A1

King Norodom Sihanouk — A3

Enthronement Hall — A2

1951-52 Unwmk. Engr. *Perf. 13*

1	A1	10c dk blue green	.90	*3.00*
2	A1	20c cl & org brn	.60	*1.25*
3	A1	30c pur & indigo	.60	.50
4	A1	40c ultra & brt bl grn	.80	.80
5	A2	50c dk grn & dk ol grn	.70	.70
6	A3	80c bl blk & dk bl grn	1.50	*2.50*
7	A2	1pi indigo & purple	1.40	1.00
8	A3	1.10pi dp car & brt red	1.75	*2.50*
9	A3	1.50pi blk brn & red brn ('51)	1.75	1.25
10	A1	1.50pi dp car & cerise	1.75	1.75
11	A2	1.50pi indigo & dp ultra	1.75	1.25
12	A3	1.90pi indigo & dp ultra	3.50	*5.75*
13	A2	2pi dp car & org brn	2.50	1.00
14	A3	3pi dp car & org brn	3.75	2.00
15	A1	5pi indigo & purple	12.00	6.50
a.		Souvenir sheet of 1	50.00	
16	A2	10pi purple & indigo	14.00	11.00
a.		Souvenir sheet of 1	50.00	
17	A3	15pi dk pur & purple	32.50	22.50
a.		Souvenir sheet of 1	50.00	
		Nos. 1-17 (17)	81.75	65.25

Nos. 15a, 16a, 17a sold in a booklet. Value, $300.

Stamps with completely white gum and no toning sell for a premium.

For surcharges see Nos. B1-B4.

Phnom Daun Penh — A4

East Gate, Angkor Thom — A5

Arms of Cambodia — A6

Methods of Mail Transport — A7

1954-55 Unwmk. *Perf. 13*

18	A4	10c rose carmine	1.25	*1.75*
a.		Souvenir sheet of 5 ('55)	40.00	40.00
19	A4	20c dark green	1.50	.45
20	A4	30c indigo	1.40	*2.10*
21	A4	40c dark purple	1.60	.70
22	A4	50c dk violet brn	1.50	.30
23	A5	70c chocolate	2.00	*3.00*
a.		Souvenir sheet of 5 ('55)	40.00	40.00
24	A5	1pi red violet	2.00	1.60
25	A5	1.50pi red	2.00	.50
26	A6	2pi rose red	2.00	.40
a.		Souvenir sheet of 5 ('55)	40.00	40.00
27	A6	2.50pi green	2.00	.55
28	A7	2.50pi blue green	2.00	.50
a.		Souvenir sheet of 5 ('55)	40.00	40.00
29	A6	3pi ultra	2.10	1.50
30	A7	4pi black brown	3.00	2.75
31	A6	4.50pi purple	2.75	2.75
32	A7	5pi rose red	3.50	1.60
33	A6	6pi chocolate	3.00	2.25
34	A7	10pi purple	3.75	2.50
35	A7	15pi deep blue	4.50	4.50
36	A5	20pi ultra	10.00	4.75
37	A5	30pi blue green	16.00	7.50
		Nos. 18-37 (20)	67.85	41.95
		Nos. 18a//28a, Set of 4	160.00	

The 4 souvenir sheets each contain 5 stamps: No. 18a (10c, 20c, 30c, 40c, 50c); #23a (70c, 1pi, 1.50pi, 20pi, 30pi); No. 26a (2pi, 2.50pi green, 3pi, 4.50pi, 6pi); No. 28a (2.50pi blue green, 4pi, 5pi. 10pi, 15pi). Size of No. 18a, 26a and 28a: 120x120mm. Size of No. 23a: 160x92mm. Values are for very fine, unblemished sheets. Examples with toning and/or gum bends sell for less.

For overprints see Nos. 99-100.

King Norodom Suramarit — A8

King Norodom Suramarit and Queen Kossamak Nearirat Serey Vathana A9

Portraits: 50c (No. 39), 2.50r, 4r, 6r, 15r, Queen Kossamak Nearirat Serey Vathana.

Perf. 14x13(A8), 13(A9)

1955, Nov. 24 Engr. Unwmk.

38	A8	50c violet	.40	.40
39	A8	50c indigo	.40	.40
40	A8	1r car lake	.50	.45
41	A9	1.50r dk brown	.80	.50
42	A9	2r black & indigo	.70	.45
43	A8	2r dp ultra	.80	.60
44	A8	2.50r dk vio brn	1.10	.60
45	A9	3r brn org & car	1.00	.60
46	A8	4r dark green	1.40	.90
47	A9	5r blk & dk grn	1.50	1.10
48	A8	6r deep plum	1.75	1.10
49	A8	7r dark brown	2.00	1.10
50	A9	10r brn car & vio	2.50	1.25
51	A8	15r purple	3.00	2.00
52	A8	20r deep green	4.75	2.75
		Nos. 38-52 (15)	22.60	14.20

Coronation of King Norodom Suramarit and Queen Kossamak Nearirat Serey Vathana.

See Nos. 74-75. For surcharge see No. 122.

King Norodom Suramarit — A10

Portrait: 3r, 5r, 50r, Queen Kossamak Nearirat Serey Vathana.

1956, Mar. 8 *Perf. 13*

53	A10	2r dark red	2.25	2.00
54	A10	3r dark blue	3.00	2.75
55	A10	5r yellow green	4.25	3.75
56	A10	10r dark green	8.50	7.50
57	A10	30r dark violet	20.00	18.00
58	A10	50r rose lilac	40.00	37.50
		Nos. 53-58 (6)	78.00	71.50

Coronation of King Norodom Suramarit and Queen Kossamak Nearirat Serey Vathana.

Prince Sihanouk, Globe and Flags — A11

1957, Mar. 1

59	A11	2r green, ultra & car	1.50	1.10
60	A11	4.50r ultra	1.50	1.10
61	A11	8.50r carmine	1.50	1.10
		Nos. 59-61 (3)	4.50	3.30

Admission to the UN, 1st anniv. (in 1956).

Type of Semi-Postal Stamps, 1957

1957, May 12 Unwmk. *Perf. 13*

62	SP1	1.50r vermilion	1.00	1.00
63	SP1	6.50r bluish violet	1.25	1.25
64	SP1	8r dark green	1.50	1.50
		Nos. 62-64 (3)	3.75	3.75

2500th anniv. of the birth of Buddha.

King Ang Duong A12

1958, Mar. 4

65	A12	1.50r purple & brown	.60	.60
66	A12	5r olive gray & olive	.80	.80
67	A12	10r claret & dull brn	1.50	1.50
a.		Souvenir sheet of 3, #65-67	6.00	5.50
		Nos. 65-67 (3)	2.90	2.90

King Ang Duong (1795-1860).

No. 67a sold for 25r.

King Norodom I — A13

1958-59 Engr. *Perf. 12½x13*

68	A13	2r ultra & olive	.70	.50
69	A13	6r orange & sl grn	1.00	.70
70	A13	15r green & ol gray	2.00	1.40
a.		Souv. sheet of 3, #68-70 ('59)	6.00	5.50
		Nos. 68-70 (3)	3.70	2.60

King Norodom I (1835-1904).

No. 70a sold for 32r.

Issued: Nos. 68-70, 11/3/58; No. 70a, 1/31/59.

For surcharge see No. 184.

Children of the World — A14

1959, Dec. 9 Unwmk. *Perf. 13*

71	A14	20c rose violet	.30	.30
72	A14	50c blue	.55	.55
73	A14	80c rose carmine	1.10	1.10
		Nos. 71-73 (3)	1.95	1.95

Issued to promote friendship among the children of the world.

For surcharges see Nos. 115, B8-B10.

Nos. 49 and 52 with Black Border

1960 *Perf. 14x13*

74	A8	7r dk brown & blk	4.50	4.50
75	A8	20r dp green & blk	4.50	4.50

Death of King Norodom Suramarit.

Port of Sihanoukville, Prince Sihanouk and Serpent Naga — A15

20r (double size)

1960, Apr. *Perf. 13x12½*

76	A15	2r carmine & sepia	.65	.65
a.		Cambodian 20r	3.00	3.00
77	A15	5r ultra & dp brown	.65	.65
a.		Cambodian 20r	3.25	3.25
78	A15	20r lilac & dk blue	2.40	2.40
		Nos. 76-78 (3)	3.70	3.70

Opening of the port of Sihanoukville. By error the denomination in Cambodian on the 2r and 5r was engraved as 20r; it was corrected later.

Ceremonial Plow — A16

1960 *Perf. 12*

79	A16	1r magenta	.65	.65
80	A16	2r brown	.90	.90
81	A16	3r bluish green	1.25	1.25
		Nos. 79-81 (3)	2.80	2.80

Feast of the Sacred Furrow.

Fight Against Illiteracy A17

Water Conservation, Dam at Chhouksar — A18

Dove, Factory and Books A19

Buddhist Ceremony A20

Works of Sangkum: 6r, Workman and house. 10r, Woman in rice field.

1960, Sept. 1 Engr. *Perf. 13*

82 A17 2r dk grn, brn & dk bl .65 .40
a. Souvenir sheet of 3 8.00 8.00
83 A18 3r brown & green .80 .40
a. Souvenir sheet of 3 8.00 8.00
84 A19 4r rose car, vio & grn .80 .55
85 A17 6r brown, org & grn .90 .70
86 A17 10r ultra, grn & bis 2.25 1.40
87 A20 25r dk car, red & mag 4.50 2.75
Nos. 82-87 (6) 9.90 6.20

No. 82a contains one each of Nos. 82, 85 and 87, and sold for 42r. No. 83a contains one each of Nos. 83, 84 and 86, and sold for 23r. Nos. 82a-83a were issued Dec. 5, 1960.

Cambodian Flag and Dove — A21

1960, Dec. 24 Engr. *Perf. 13*
Flag in Ultramarine and Red

88 A21 1.50r brown & green .40 .25
89 A21 5r orange red .60 .35
90 A21 7r green & ultra 1.25 1.00
a. Souvenir sheet of 3, #88-90 15.00 15.00
b. Souv. sheet of 3 (colors changed) 11.00 11.00
Nos. 88-90 (3) 2.25 1.60

Peace propaganda. No. 90a sold for 16r. No. 90b contains one of each denomination with colors changed to: 1.50r orange red, 5r green & ultramarine, 7r brown & green and sold for 20r.

Frangipani — A22

1961, July 1 Unwmk. *Perf. 13*

91 A22 2r shown .65 .65
92 A22 5r Oleander 1.10 1.10
93 A22 10r Amaryllis 2.75 2.75
a. Souvenir sheet of 3, #91-93 8.00 8.00
Nos. 91-93 (3) 4.50 4.50

No. 93a sold for 20r.

Krishna in Chariot, Khmer Frieze — A23

1961-63 Typo. *Perf. 14x13½*

94 A23 1r lilac .40 .25
94A A23 2r blue ('63) 3.25 1.60
95 A23 3r emerald .90 .40
96 A23 6r orange .90 .40
a. Souvenir sheet of 3 7.50 7.50
Nos. 94-96 (4) 5.45 2.65

Issued to honor Cambodian armed forces. No. 94A issued in coils. No. 96a contains one each of Nos. 94, 95, 96. Sold for 12r.

Independence Monument — A24

1961, Nov. 9 Engr. *Perf. 13x12½*

97 A24 2r green .50 .50
98 A24 4r gray brown .50 .50
a. Souvenir sheet of 2, #97-98 5.00 5.00
Nos. 97-98,C15-C17 (5) 9.40 7.05

10th anniv. of Independence.
For surcharge see No. 116.

Nos. 27 and 31 Overprinted in Red

1961, Nov. 11 *Perf. 13*

99 A6 2.50pi green 1.10 .65
100 A6 4.50pi purple 1.75 1.00

Sixth World Conference of Buddhism.

Highway (American Aid) — A25

Foreign Aid: 2r, Power station (Czech aid). 4r, Textile factory (Chinese aid). 5r, Hospital (Russian aid). 6r, Airport (French aid).

1961, Dec. Engr. *Perf. 13*

101 A25 2r org & rose car .45 .30
102 A25 3r brl, grn & org brn .45 .30
103 A25 4r dl bl, org brn & mag .45 .40
104 A25 5r dl grn & lil rose .65 .40
105 A25 6r dk bl & org brn 1.25 .55
a. Souvenir sheet of 5, #101-105 7.00 7.00
Nos. 101-105 (5) 3.25 1.95

Malaria Eradication Emblem — A26

1962, Apr. 7 Unwmk. *Perf. 13*

106 A26 2r magenta & brown .50 .40
107 A26 4r green & dk brown .50 .40
108 A26 6r violet & olive bister .75 .45
Nos. 106-108 (3) 1.75 1.25

WHO drive to eradicate malaria.
For surcharges see Nos. B11-B12.

Fruits A27

1962, June 4 Engr.

109 A27 2r Cardamom .60 .45
110 A27 4r Sugar apple 1.10 .75
111 A27 6r Mangosteens 1.10 .75
a. Souvenir sheet of 3, #109-111 5.00 5.00
Nos. 109-111 (3) 2.80 1.95

Nos. 111a sold for 15r.

Pineapples — A28

1962 Unwmk. *Perf. 13*

112 A28 2r shown .90 .50
113 A28 5r Sugar cane 1.40 .75
114 A28 9r Sugar palms 1.75 .70
Nos. 112-114 (3) 4.05 1.95

No. 73 Surcharged

1962, Nov. 9 *Perf. 13*

115 A14 50c on 80c rose car .70 .40

No. 97 Srchd. in Red and Ovptd. in Black

1962

116 A24 3r on 2r green 1.00 .40

Dedication of Independence Monument. See No. C18.

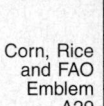

Corn, Rice and FAO Emblem A29

1963, Mar. 21 Engr. *Perf. 13*

117 A29 3r multicolored .70 .55
118 A29 6r org red, vio bl & ocher .70 .55

FAO "Freedom from Hunger" campaign.

Preah Vihear, Ancient Temple — A30

1963, June 15 *Perf. 12½x13*

119 A30 3r claret, brown & sl grn .50 .40
120 A30 6r org, sl grn & grnsh blk .90 .65
121 A30 15r blue, choc & green 1.40 1.10
Nos. 119-121 (3) 2.80 2.15

Return by Thailand of Preah Vihear on the Mekong River.
For overprint see No. 176.

No. 44 Surcharged

1963 Engr. *Perf. 14x13*

122 A8 3r on 2½r dk violet brn .90 .55

Tonsay Lake — A31

7r, Popokvil Falls. 20r, Beach, horiz.

Perf. 12x12½, 12½x12
1963, Aug. 1 Photo.

123 A31 3r multicolored .50 .50
124 A31 7r multicolored .80 .70
125 A31 20r multicolored 2.50 1.10
Nos. 123-125 (3) 3.80 2.30

UNESCO Emblem, Scales and Globe A32

1963, Dec. 10 Engr. *Perf. 13*

126 A32 1r vio bl, rose cl & grn .50 .50
127 A32 3r yel grn, vio bl & rose cl .90 .90
128 A32 12r rose cl, yel grn & vio bl 1.60 1.60
Nos. 126-128 (3) 3.00 3.00

15th anniversary of the Universal Declaration of Human Rights.
For surcharge see No. 183.

Kouprey A33

1964, Mar. 3 Unwmk. *Perf. 13*

129 A33 50c grn, dk brn & org brn .95 .55
130 A33 3r org, brn, dk brn & grn 1.40 .70
131 A33 6r blue, dk brn & grn 2.10 1.40
Nos. 129-131 (3) 4.45 2.65

Black-billed Magpie — A34

1964, May 2 Engr. *Perf. 13*

132 A34 3r shown 1.40 .65
133 A34 6r Kingfisher 2.10 1.00
134 A34 12r Gray heron 3.75 2.00
Nos. 132-134 (3) 7.25 3.65

For overprint & surcharge see Nos. 303, B16.

Emblem of Royal Cambodian Airline A35

1964 Unwmk. Perf. 13x12½

135 A35 1.50r rose car & purple .40 .25
136 A35 3r ver & dk blue .55 .40
137 A35 7.50r ultra & car 1.25 .60
Nos. 135-137 (3) 2.20 1.25

8th anniv. of the Royal Cambodian Airline.

Prince Norodom Sihanouk — A36

1964 Engr. Perf. 12½x13

138 A36 2r purple .55 .40
139 A36 3r red brown .80 .50
140 A36 10r dark blue 1.60 .90
Nos. 138-140 (3) 2.95 1.80

10th anniv. of the Sangkum (political party).
For overprints see Nos. 144-145.

A set of three stamps, imperf, showing clasped hands, was prepared for International Cooperation Year but were never issued. Value, $200.

Woman Weaver A37

Khmer Handicrafts: 3r, Metal worker. 5r, Basket maker.

1965, Feb. 1 Perf. 13x12½

141 A37 1r multicolored .40 .40
142 A37 3r red lil, red brn & gray ol .65 .40
143 A37 5r green, dk brn & car 1.10 .85
Nos. 141-143 (3) 2.15 1.65

Nos. 139-140 Overprinted in Black or Red

1965, Mar. 1 Perf. 12½x13

144 A36 3r red brown .70 .40
145 A36 10r dark blue (R) 1.00 .55

Conference of the people of Indo-China.

ITU Emblem, Old and New Communication Equipment — A38

1965, May 17 Engr. Perf. 13

146 A38 3r green & olive bister .40 .30
147 A38 4r red & blue .70 .40
148 A38 10r violet & rose lilac 1.00 .70
Nos. 146-148 (3) 2.10 1.40

Centenary of the ITU.

Cotton Plant — A39

3r, Peanut plant. 7.50r, Coconut palm.

1965, Aug. 2 Perf. 12½x13

149 A39 1.50r orange, sl grn & pur .55 .40
150 A39 3r blue, yel, grn & brn .90 .60
151 A39 7.50r orange brn & sl grn 1.50 1.00
Nos. 149-151 (3) 2.95 2.00

Preah Ko Temple, Rolouoh — A40

Temples at Angkor: 5r, Baksei Chamkrong, Rolouoh. 7r, Banteay Srei (Citadel of Women). 9r, Angkor Wat. 12r, Bayon, Angkor Thom.

1966, Feb. 1 Engr. Perf. 13

152 A40 3r gray ol, sal & dl grn 1.25 .80
153 A40 5r lil, dk grn & redsh brn 1.50 .85
154 A40 7r dk grn, redsh brn & bis 2.00 1.60
155 A40 9r vio bl, pur & dk grn 2.75 2.10
156 A40 12r dk grn, rose car & ver 3.25 2.75
Nos. 152-156 (5) 10.75 8.10

For overprints see Nos. 172-175, 177.

WHO Headquarters, Geneva — A41

1966, July 1 Photo. Perf. 12½x13
WHO Emblem in Blue and Yellow

157 A41 2r black & pale rose .40 .25
158 A41 3r black & yel grn .50 .40
159 A41 5r black & lt bl .80 .55
Nos. 157-159 (3) 1.70 1.20

Inauguration of WHO Headquarters, Geneva.

Tree Planting — A42

1966, July 22 Engr. Perf. 12½x13

160 A42 1r brn, dull brn & brt grn .30 .25
161 A42 3r org, dull brn & brt grn .55 .30
162 A42 7r gray, dull brn & brt grn .85 .40
Nos. 160-162 (3) 1.70 .95

Issued for Arbor Day.

UNESCO Emblem — A43

1966 Photo. Perf. 13

163 A43 3r multicolored .50 .40
164 A43 7r multicolored .75 .55

20th anniv. of UNESCO.

Wrestlers and Games' Emblem A44

GANEFO Games (Games Emblem and): 3r, Stadium, Phnom Penh. 7r, Swordsmen. 10r, Indian club swingers. Bas-reliefs from Angkor Wat.

1966, Nov. 25 Engr. Perf. 13

165 A44 3r violet blue .40 .25
166 A44 4r green .45 .30
167 A44 7r dk car rose .70 .50
168 A44 10r dark brown 1.10 .65
Nos. 165-168 (4) 2.65 1.70

Indian Wild Boar A45

Perf. 13x12½, 12½x13

1967, Feb. 20 Engr.

169 A45 3r shown 1.25 .40
170 A45 5r Muntjac, vert. 1.60 .65
171 A45 7r Elephant 2.25 .95
Nos. 169-171 (3) 5.10 2.00

Nos. 152-153, 155-156 and 121 Overprinted in Red

1967, Apr. 27 Engr. Perf. 13

172 A40 3r multicolored .85 .75
173 A40 5r multicolored .90 .75
174 A40 9r multicolored 1.40 1.25
175 A40 12r multicolored 1.75 1.50
176 A30 15r multicolored 2.10 1.75
Nos. 172-176 (5) 7.00 6.00

International Tourist Year, 1967.

No. 154 Overprinted in Red

1967, Apr. 27

177 A40 7r multicolored 1.50 .60

Banteay Srei Temple at Angkor, millennium.

Royal Ballet Dancer — A46

Various Dancers

1967, June Engr. Perf. 13

178 A46 1r orange .50 .40
179 A46 3r Prus blue .90 .60
180 A46 5r ultra 1.40 .55
181 A46 7r carmine rose 2.00 .80
182 A46 10r multicolored 2.50 1.00
Nos. 178-182 (5) 7.30 3.35

Cambodian Royal Ballet.

Nos. 128 and 70 Srchd. in Red

1967, Sept. 8 Engr.

183 A32 6r on 12r multi .90 .40
184 A13 7r on 15r grn & olive gray 1.25 .60

Intl. Literacy Day, Sept. 8. The surcharge on No. 184 is adapted to fit the shape of the stamp.

Symbolic Water Cycle — A47

1967, Nov. 1 Typo. Perf. 13x14

185 A47 1r black, bl & org .30 .25
186 A47 6r lilac, lt bl & org .60 .30
187 A47 10r dk blue, emer & org .90 .50
Nos. 185-187 (3) 1.80 1.05

Hydrological Decade (UNESCO), 1965-74.

Royal University, Kompong Cham A48

6r, Engineering School, Phnom Penh. 9r, University Center, Sangkum Reastr Niyum.

1968, Mar. 1 Engr. Perf. 13

188 A48 4r violet bl & multi .50 .40
189 A48 6r slate & multi .65 .40
190 A48 9r Prus blue & multi .90 .55
Nos. 188-190 (3) 2.05 1.35

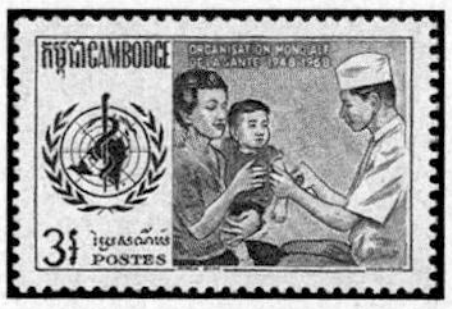

Vaccination and WHO Emblem A49

WHO, 20th Anniv.: 7r, Malaria control and WHO emblem (man spraying DDT).

1968, July 8 Engr. Perf. 13

191 A49 3r ultramarine .60 .40
192 A49 7r deep blue .90 .55

Stadium, Mexico City — A50

1968, Oct. 12 Engr. Perf. 13

193 A50 1r shown .65 .55
194 A50 2r Wrestling .75 .55
195 A50 3r Bicycling .85 .55
196 A50 5r Boxing, vert. 1.00 .55
197 A50 7.50r Torch bearer, vert. 1.40 .75
Nos. 193-197 (5) 4.65 2.95

19th Olympic Games, Mexico City, 12/12-27.

Red Cross Team
A51

1968, Nov. 1 **Engr.** ***Perf. 13***
198 A51 3r Prus bl, grn & red 1.50 .50

Issued to honor the Cambodian Red Cross.

Prince Norodom Sihanouk
A52

8r, Soldiers wading through swamp.

1968, Nov. 9
199 A52 7r emer, ultra & pur .50 .40
200 A52 8r bl, grn & dp brn .75 .55

15th anniversary of independence.

Human Rights Flame and Prince Sihanouk
A53

1968, Dec. 10 **Engr.** ***Perf. 13***
201 A53 3r blue .45 .25
202 A53 5r bright plum .80 .35
203 A53 7r multicolored 1.10 .55
Nos. 201-203 (3) 2.35 1.15

International Human Rights Year.

ILO Emblem
A54

1969, May 1 **Engr.** ***Perf. 13***
204 A54 3r ultra .50 .25
205 A54 6r dp carmine .70 .40
206 A54 9r blue green 1.00 .55
Nos. 204-206 (3) 2.20 1.20

ILO, 50th anniversary.

Globe, Red Cross, Crescent, Lion and Sun Emblems
A55

1969, May 8
207 A55 1r blue, red & yel .40 .25
208 A55 3r sl grn, red & vio brn .65 .40
209 A55 10r brt lil, red & brn 1.40 .60
Nos. 207-209 (3) 2.45 1.25

50th anniv. of the League of Red Cross Societies.

Papilio Oeacus
A56

Butterflies: 4r, Papilio agamenon. 8r, Danaus plexippus.

1969, Oct. 10 **Engr.** ***Perf. 13***
210 A56 3r lilac, blk & yel 3.25 1.00
211 A56 4r ver, blk & grn 4.25 2.00
212 A56 8r yel grn, dk brn & org 6.00 3.00
Nos. 210-212 (3) 13.50 6.00

Map of Cambodia and Diesel Engine
A57

Various railroad stations and trains.

1969, Nov. 27 **Engr.** ***Perf. 13***
213 A57 3r multicolored 1.00 .75
214 A57 6r slate grn & lt brn 2.00 1.50
215 A57 8r black 3.25 2.25
216 A57 9r dk green & blue 3.75 2.40
Nos. 213-216 (4) 10.00 6.90

Issued to publicize the new rail link between Phnom Penh and Sihanoukville.

Fish — A58

1970, Jan. 29 **Photo.** ***Perf. 13***
217 A58 3r Tripletail 1.75 .90
218 A58 7r Sleeper goby 4.00 1.50
219 A58 9r Snakehead 5.75 2.00
Nos. 217-219 (3) 11.50 4.40

Wat Maniratanaram — A59

Monasteries: 2r, Wat Tepthidaram, vert. 6r, Wat Patumavati. 8r, Wat Unnalom.

1970, Apr. 29 **Photo.** ***Perf. 13***
220 A59 2r multicolored .35 .40
221 A59 3r multicolored .40 .40
222 A59 6r multicolored .85 .40
223 A59 8r multicolored 1.60 .55
Nos. 220-223 (4) 3.20 1.75

UPU Headquarters and Monument, Bern — A60

1970, May 20
224 A60 1r green & multi .35 .25
225 A60 3r scarlet & multi .50 .30
226 A60 4r dp blue & multi .65 .30
227 A60 10r brown & multi 1.00 .60
Nos. 224-227 (4) 2.50 1.45

New UPU Headquarters in Bern.

Open Book and Satellite Earth Receiving Station — A61

1970, May 17 **Photo.** ***Perf. 13***
228 A61 3r dk vio bl & multi .30 .25
229 A61 4r sl grn & multi .40 .25
230 A61 9r brn ol & multi .85 .35
Nos. 228-230 (3) 1.55 .85

World Telecommunications Day.

Nelumbium Speciosum
A62

Flowers: 4r, Eichhornia crassipes. 13r, Nymphea lotus.

1970, Aug. 17 **Photo.** ***Perf. 13***
231 A62 3r multicolored .70 .30
a. Cambodian and Arabic 3's transposed 37.50 37.50
232 A62 4r multicolored 1.40 .45
233 A62 13r multicolored 3.00 .70
Nos. 231-233 (3) 5.10 1.45

Elephant God, Bas relief at Banteay Srei — A63

1970, Sept. 21 **Engr.** ***Perf. 13***
234 A63 3r lil rose & dp grn .35 .25
235 A63 4r bl grn, grn & lil rose .55 .25
236 A63 7r bl grn, dk brn & grn .85 .40
Nos. 234-236 (3) 1.75 .90

Issued for World Meteorological Day.

Khmer Republic

Globe, Rocket, Dove and UN Emblem
A64

1970, Nov. 9 **Photo.** ***Perf. 12½x12***
237 A64 3r black & multi .30 .25
238 A64 5r brown red & multi .45 .25
239 A64 10r dp violet & multi .90 .50
Nos. 237-239 (3) 1.65 1.00

25th anniversary of the United Nations.

Education Year Emblem
A65

1970, Nov. 9 **Engr.** ***Perf. 13x12½***
240 A65 1r blue .25 .25
241 A65 3r brt rose lilac .35 .25
242 A65 8r blue green .75 .45
Nos. 240-242 (3) 1.35 .95

Issued for International Education Year.

Chuon-Nath — A66

1971, Jan. 27 **Photo.** ***Perf. 13***
243 A66 3r ol grn & multi .35 .25
244 A66 8r purple & multi .75 .35
245 A66 9r violet & multi 1.00 .55
Nos. 243-245 (3) 2.10 1.15

In memory of Chuon-Nath (1883-1969), Cambodian language expert.
For surcharge see No. 322.

Soldiers in Battle
A67

1971, Mar. 18 **Photo.** ***Perf. 13***
246 A67 1r gray & multi .45 .25
247 A67 3r bister & multi .70 .40
248 A67 10r blue & multi 1.75 .75
Nos. 246-248 (3) 2.90 1.40

National territorial defense.
For overprint see No. 321.

UN Emblem, Men of Four Races
A68

1971, Mar. 21
249 A68 3r blue & multi .65 .25
250 A68 7r green & multi 1.25 .40
251 A68 8r brt rose & multi 2.00 .55
Nos. 249-251 (3) 3.90 1.20

Intl. year against racial discrimination.

General Post Office, Phnom Penh — A69

1971, Apr. 19
252 A69 3r blue & multi .35 .25
253 A69 9r lilac rose & multi .65 .35
254 A69 10r black & multi 1.05 .40
Nos. 252-254 (3) 2.05 1.00

Symbolic Globe and Waves
A70

Design: 7r, 8r, ITU emblem and waves.

1971, May 17 **Photo.** ***Perf. 13***
255 A70 3r green, blk & bl .25 .25
256 A70 4r yellow & multi .40 .25
257 A70 7r lilac, blk & red .50 .25
258 A70 8r sal pink, blk & red .60 .30
Nos. 255-258 (4) 1.75 1.05

3rd World Telecommunications Day.

Erythrina Indica
A71

Wild Flowers: 3r, Bauhinia variegata. 6r, Butea frondosa. 10r, Lagerstroemia floribunda, vert.

1971, July 5 ***Perf. 13x12½, 12½x13***
259 A71 2r lt ultra & multi .55 .45
260 A71 3r yel grn & multi .65 .55
261 A71 6r blue & multi 1.40 1.10
262 A71 10r brown & multi 1.75 1.40
Nos. 259-262 (4) 4.35 3.50

Khmer Coat of Arms — A72

Flag and Square of the Republic — A73

1971, Oct. 9 Engr. *Perf. 13*

263	A72	3r brt grn & bis	.25	.25
264	A73	3r purple & multi	.30	.25
265	A73	4r dp claret & multi	.40	.25
266	A72	8r orange & bis	.50	.25
267	A72	10r lt brn & bis	.80	.30
a.		Souv. sheet of 3, #263, 266-267	3.00	3.00
268	A73	10r slate grn & multi	.80	.35
a.		Souv. sheet of 3, #264-265, 268	3.00	3.00
		Nos. 263-268 (6)	3.05	1.65

Republic, 1st anniv.
No. 267a sold for 25r, No. 268a for 20r.
For overprints and surcharges see Nos. 301-302, B13-B14.

UNICEF Emblem — A74

1971, Dec. 11

269	A74	3r black brown	.35	.25
270	A74	5r ultra	.50	.25
271	A74	9r dk pur & brn red	1.00	.45
		Nos. 269-271 (3)	1.85	.95

25th anniv. of UNICEF.
This set and others exist with overprint "RPK," both with and without frame. Status has not been determined.

Book Year Emblem A75

1972, Feb. 7

272	A75	3r blue, grn & vio	.40	.25
273	A75	8r violet, grn & bl	.60	.30
274	A75	9r emerald & multi	1.00	.50
a.		Souvenir sheet of 3, #272-274	3.00	3.00
		Nos. 272-274 (3)	2.00	1.05

Intl. Book Year. No. 274a sold for 23r.

Lion of St. Mark A76

Designs: 5r, Waves engulfing St. Mark's Basilica. 10r, Bridge of Sighs, vert.

1972, Feb. 7 Engr. *Perf. 13*

275	A76	3r lil rose & org brn	.50	.25
276	A76	5r yel grn & org brn	1.00	.40
277	A76	10r org brn, bl & yel grn	1.25	.50
a.		Souvenir sheet of 3, #275-277	3.00	3.00
		Nos. 275-277 (3)	2.75	1.15

UNESCO campaign to save Venice. No. 277a sold for 23r.

UN Emblem A77

1972, Mar. 28

278	A77	3r deep carmine	.50	.25
279	A77	6r deep blue	.75	.35
280	A77	9r deep orange	.90	.50
a.		Souvenir sheet of 3, #278-280	3.00	3.00
		Nos. 278-280 (3)	2.15	1.10

25th anniv. UN Economic Commission for Asia and the Far East (ECAFE). No. 280a sold for 23r.

Dancing Apsarases — A78

1972, May 5 Engr. *Perf. 13*

281	A78	1r golden brn	.25	.25
282	A78	3r violet	.35	.25
283	A78	7r rose claret	.45	.30
284	A78	8r olive brn	.60	.30
285	A78	9r blue grn	.70	.30
286	A78	10r ultra	1.10	.30
287	A78	12r purple	1.40	.30
288	A78	14r Prus blue	1.75	.45
		Nos. 281-288 (8)	6.60	2.45

"UIT" A79

1972, May 17 Litho.

289	A79	3r blk, yel & grnsh bl	.40	.25
290	A79	9r blk, dp lil rose & bl grn	.75	.30
291	A79	14r blk, brn & bl grn	1.10	.45
		Nos. 289-291 (3)	2.25	1.00

4th World Telecommunications Day.

"Human Environment" — A80

1972, June 5 Engr.

292	A80	3r org, plum & grn	.50	.25
293	A80	12r brt grn & plum	.75	.30
294	A80	15r plum & brt grn	1.25	.50
a.		Souvenir sheet of 3, #292-294	3.00	3.00
		Nos. 292-294 (3)	2.50	1.05

UN Conf. on Human Environment, Stockholm, June 5-16. No. 294a sold for 35r.
For overprints and surcharges see Nos. 304-305, B15, B17.

Javan Rhinoceros A81

1972, Aug. 1 Engr. *Perf. 13*

295	A81	3r shown	.60	.25
296	A81	4r Serow	.70	.25
297	A81	6r Malayan sambar	1.40	.30
298	A81	7r Banteng	2.00	.30
299	A81	8r Water buffalo	2.50	.50
300	A81	10r Gaur	3.25	.60
		Nos. 295-300 (6)	10.45	2.20

Nos. 263, 267, 134, 293, 294 Overprinted in Red

1972, Sept. 9 Engr. *Perf. 13*

301	A72	3r brt grn & bister	.75	.30
302	A72	10r orange & bister	1.50	.65
303	A34	12r multicolored	1.50	.80
304	A80	12r brt grn & plum	1.60	.80
305	A80	15r plum & brt grn	2.10	1.00
		Nos. 301-305 (5)	7.45	3.55

20th Olympic Games, Munich, 8/26-9/11.

Raising Khmer Flag — A82

1972, Oct. 9 Photo. *Perf. 12½x13*

306	A82	3r multicolored	.25	.25
307	A82	5r brt rose & multi	.40	.30
308	A82	9r yel grn & multi	.90	.50
		Nos. 306-308 (3)	1.55	1.05

2nd anniversary of the establishment of the Khmer Republic.
For surcharge see No. 323.

Stupa and Crest — A83

1973, May 12 Engr. *Perf. 13*

309	A83	3r ocher & multi	.45	.25
310	A83	12r yel grn & multi	.45	.25
311	A83	14r blue & multi	.75	.50
a.		Souvenir sheet of 3, #309-311	3.25	3.25
		Nos. 309-311 (3)	1.65	1.00

New Constitution. No. 311a sold for 34r.

Apsaras — A84

Sculptures from Angkor Wat: 8r, 10r, Devata, diff.

1973, July 23 Engr. *Perf. 13*

312	A84	3r brown black	.50	.25
313	A84	8r Prus green	.65	.30
314	A84	10r olive bister	1.60	.50
a.		Souvenir sheet of 3, #312-314	3.00	3.00
		Nos. 312-314 (3)	2.75	1.05

No. 314a sold for 25r.

INTERPOL Emblem — A85

1973, Oct. 2 Engr. *Perf. 13*

315	A85	3r green & multi	.45	.25
316	A85	7r red brn & multi	.55	.30
317	A85	10r olive & multi	.75	.45
a.		Souvenir sheet of 3, #315-317	4.50	4.50
		Nos. 315-317 (3)	1.75	1.00

50th anniv. of the Intl. Criminal Police Org. No. 317a sold for 30r.

Marshal Lon Nol — A86

1973, Oct. 9

318	A86	3r lt grn, blk & brn	.40	.25
319	A86	8r brown, ol & blk	.60	.30
320	A86	14r black & brn	1.00	.40
a.		Souvenir sheet of 3	5.00	5.00
		Nos. 318-320 (3)	2.00	.95

Marshal Lon Nol, 1st pres. of the Republic. No. 320a contains stamps similar to Nos. 318-320 in changed colors. Sold for 50r.

Nos. 248, 243 and 307 Srchd. & Ovptd. in Red or Silver

1974 Photo. *Perf. 13, 12½x13*

321	A67	10r multi (R)	*4.00*	1.00
322	A66	50r on 3r multi	*9.00*	2.50
323	A82	100r on 5r multi	*17.50*	6.50
		Nos. 321-323 (3)	*30.50*	10.00

4th anniversary of the Republic.

Copernicus and "Nerva" — A87

Copernicus, various spacecraft and events.

1974, Sept. 10 Litho. *Perf. 13*

324	A87	1r shown	.35	.30
325	A87	5r Mariner II	.45	.30
326	A87	10r Apollo	.75	.40
327	A87	25r Telstar	1.75	.75
328	A87	50r Space walk	3.00	1.50
329	A87	100r Moon landing	6.50	3.50
330	A87	150r Separation of spaceship and module	9.00	5.00
		Nos. 324-330 (7)	21.80	11.75
		Nos. 324-330,C46-C47 (9)	45.80	26.75

500th anniversary of the birth of Nicolaus Copernicus (1473-1543), Polish astronomer.

Carrier Pigeon and UPU Emblem — A88

Design: 60r, Sailing ship and UPU emblem.

1974, Nov. 2

331	A88	10r multicolored	*1.00*	*1.00*
332	A88	60r multicolored	*3.00*	*3.00*
		Nos. 331-332,C50 (3)	*14.00*	*14.00*

Cent. of UPU. Souvenir sheets of one exist, both imperf. and simulated perfs for Nos. 331 and 332.

A set of 8 stamps picturing musical instruments, overprinted and surcharged for use by the Khmer Republic just before the fall of the government in Apr. 1975, exists. Value, $1,100. Value for same set without surcharge, $500.

A89

1976 Summer Olympic Games, Montreal — A90

1r, 18th cent. swordsmen. 5r, Modern fencers. 10r, Ancient Olympic runner. 25r, Modern runner. 50r, Ancient rowers. 100r, Modern kayakers. 150r, Ancient horseman. 200r, Modern equestrian competitor. 250r, Buildings, Olympic flame.

1975, Jan. 2 Litho. *Perf. 13½*

333-341 A89 Set of 9 11.00

Litho. & Embossed

342 A90 1200r gold & multi *22.00*

Souvenir Sheets

343 A89 200r silver & multi *8.50*
344 A89 250r silver & multi *8.50*

Nos. 337-344 are airmail.

A number has been reserved for another souvenir sheet released with this set.

A91

1974 World Cup Soccer Championships — A92

Soccer players and arms of: 1r, Hamburg. 5r, Gelsenkirchen. 10r, Dortmund. 25r, Stuttgart. 50r, Dusseldorf. 100r, Hannover. 150r, Frankfurt. 200r, Munich. 250r, Berlin.

Litho. (#346-354, 356-357)
Litho. & Embossed (#355, 358)

1975, Feb. 13

346-354 A91 Set of 9 12.00
355 A92 1200r gold & multi *20.00*

Souvenir Sheets

356 A91 200r gold & multi *6.00*
357 A91 250r gold & multi *6.00*
358 A92 1200r gold & multi *16.00*

Nos. 350-358 are airmail. Nos. 346-354 exist in imperforate souvenir sheets.

UPU, Cent. — A93

Designs: 15r, Letter carrier, pack mule. 20r, Biplane. 70r, Post coach. 160r, Biplane, Concorde. 180r, Steam-powered wagon. 235r, Postrider, tail of mailplane. 500r, Railway mail car. 1000r, Airship. 2000r, Caravel.

1975, Apr. 12

359-367 A93 Set of 9 9.00
366a Souvenir sheet of 1 *4.50*
367a Souvenir sheet of 1 *4.50*

Nos. 365-367 are airmail. Nos. 366a and 367a exist imperf. Values, each $25.

People's Republic of Kampuchea

Soldiers — A94

Designs, horiz.: 20c, People, flag. 50c, Fishermen. 1r, Soldiers passing flag.

1980, Apr. 10 Litho. *Perf. 11*

368-371 A94 Set of 4 *47.50 47.50*

Soviet Union, 60th Anniv. — A95

Designs: 50c, Globe, Kremlin. 1r, Buildings, map of USSR.

1982, Dec. 30 *Perf. 12x12½*

372-373 A95 Set of 2 1.60 .55

People's Republic of Kampuchea, 4th Anniv. — A96

Designs: 50c, Natl. arms, vert. 1r, shown. 3r, Map, stylized figures, vert. 6r, Temple, vert.

1983, Jan. 7 Litho. *Perf. 13*

374-376 A96 Set of 3 4.75 1.25

Souvenir Sheet

377 A96 6r multicolored 6.00 2.25

1984 Summer Olympic Games, Los Angeles A97

Designs: 20c, Runner with torch. 50c, Javelin. 80c, Pole vault. 1r, Discus. 1.50r, Relay race. 2r, Swimming. 3r, Basketball.

20c-1r, 3r are vert.

1983, Jan. 20 Litho. *Perf. 13*

378-384 A97 Set of 7 7.00 1.50

Souvenir Sheet

385 A97 6r Soccer 5.25 3.00

No. 385 contains one 32x40mm stamp.

Butterflies — A98

20c, Salatura genutia. 50c, Euploea althaea. 80c, Byasa polyeuctes. 1r, Stichophthalma howqua. 1.50r, Kallima inachus. 2r, Precis orithya. 3r, Catopsilia pomona.

20c, 50c, 1.50r, 2r, 3r are vert.

1983, Feb. 18 Litho. *Perf. 13*

386-392 A98 Set of 7 10.00 2.00

Khmer Culture A99

Designs: 20c, Ruins, Srah Srang. 50c, Temple, Bakong. 80c, Ta Son. 1r, North Gate, Angkor Thom. 1.50r, Two winged figures. 2r, Apsara, Angkor. 3r, Statue of Banteai Srei.

80c-3r are vert.

1983, Mar. 15

393-399 A99 Set of 7 7.00 1.75

Folk Dances A100

Various dances. Denominations 50c, 1r, 3r.

1983, Apr. 17 Litho. *Perf. 13*

400-402 A100 Set of 3 4.00 1.25

Souvenir Sheet

403 A100 6r Native, "buffalo" 6.50 1.40

No. 403 contains one 32x40mm stamp.

Raphael (1483-1520) — A101

Parnassus (details): No. 404, 20c, Dante, Ennius, Homer. No. 406, 80c, Horace, Ovid, others. No. 409, 2r, The Muses. No. 410, 3r, Alcaeus, Petrarch, others.

School at Athens (details): No. 407, 1r, Euclid, disciples. No. 408, 1.50r, Telange, Pythagoras.

Details from: No. 405, 50c, Mass of Bolsena). 6r, Angels from Dispute of the Holy Sacrament, horiz.

1983, May 10 Litho. *Perf. 12½x13*

404-410 A101 Set of 7 6.50 2.25

Souvenir Sheet

Perf. 13

411 A101 6r multicolored 7.25 2.50

No. 411 contains one 40x32mm stamp.

1st Hot Air Balloon Ascension, Bicent. A102

Designs: 20c, Montgolfier. 30c, Ville d'Orleans. 50c, Hydrogen balloon. 1r, Blanchard & Jeffries, 1785. 1.50r, Ascension in Arctic. 2r, Stratosphere balloon. 3r, Balloon race. 6r, Balloons over town.

1983, June 3 *Perf. 12½*

412-418 A102 Set of 7 6.50 2.00

Souvenir Sheet

Perf. 13

419 A102 6r multicolored 7.25 1.50

Reptiles — A103

Designs: 20c, Iguana. 30c, Cobra. 80c, Trionyx turtle. 1r, Chameleon. 1.50r, Boa constrictor. 2r, Crocodile. 3r, Turtle.

30c, 1r, 1.50r are vert.

1983, June 28

420-426 A103 Set of 7 8.00 2.50

Birds A104

Designs: 20c, Lorikeet. 50c, Swallow. 80c, Eagle. 1r, Vulture. 1.50r, Turtle dove. 2r, Magpie. 3r, Hornbill.

20c-50c, 2r-3r are vert.

1983, Sept. 20

427-433 A104 Set of 7 10.50 2.50

Flowers — A105

20c, Sunflower. 50c, Caprifoliacae. 80c, Bougainvillea. 1r, Renonculacae. 1.50r, Nyctaginaceae. 2r, Cockscomb. 3r, Roses.

1983, Oct. 18 *Perf. 13*

434-440 A105 Set of 7 7.50 1.75

1984 Winter Olympic Games, Sarajevo — A106

Designs: 1r, Luge. 2r, Biathlon. 4r, Ski jumping. 5r, Two-man bobsled. 7r, Hockey.

1983, Nov. 10 *Perf. 12½*
441-445 A106 Set of 5 15.00 2.75

Souvenir Sheet

446 A106 6r Cross-country skiing 6.50 1.75

No. 446 contains one 40x32mm stamp.

Fish A107

20c, 1.50r, 2r, 3r, Various Cyprinidae. 50c, Trout. 80c, Catfish. 1r, Moray eel.

1983, Nov. 16 *Perf. 13*
447-453 A107 Set of 7 8.00 2.00

Festival of Rebirth — A108

50c, Factory. 1r, Bull, tractor. 3r, Bridge, ship, train. 6r, Radio antenna. 50c, 3r, 6r vert.

Perf. 12½x13, 13x12½

1983, Dec. 2 **Litho.**
454-456 A108 Set of 3 3.50 1.00

Souvenir Sheet

457 A108 6r multicolored 6.50 1.50

No. 457 contains one 32x40mm stamp.

People's Republic of Kampuchea, 5th Anniv. — A109

Designs: 50c, Red Cross. 1r, Soldiers. 3r, People celebrating. 6r, Man carrying water.

1984, Jan. 7 **Litho.** *Perf. 13*
458-460 A109 Set of 3 3.75 1.25

Souvenir Sheet

461 A109 6r multicolored 6.50 1.50

No. 461 contains one 32x40mm stamp.
For surcharges see Nos. 775-776.

1984 Winter Olympics, Sarajevo A110

Designs: 20c, Speed skating. 50c, Hockey. 80c, Slalom skiing. 1r, Ski jumping. 1.50r, Biathlon. 2r, Cross-country skiing. 3r, Pairs figure skating. 6r, Women's figure skating.

1984, Jan. 6 **Litho.** *Perf. 13*
462-468 A110 Set of 7 7.25 2.00

Souvenir Sheet

469 A110 6r multicolored 5.50 1.40

No. 469 contains one 32x40mm stamp.

Birds — A111

Designs: 10c, Bubulcus ibis. 40c, Lanius schach. 80c, Psittacula himalayana. 1r, Chloropsis aurifrons. 1.20r, Clamator coromandus. 2r, Motacilla cinerea. 2.50r, Dendronanthus indicus.

1984, Feb. 2
470-476 A111 Set of 7 15.00 3.00

Intl. Peace in Southeast Asia Forum — A112

Background color: 50c, Green. 1r, Blue. 3r, Violet.

1984, Feb. 25 *Perf. 13x12½*
477-479 A112 Set of 3 3.75 1.00

Space Exploration — A113

Designs: 10c, Luna 1. 40c, Luna 2. 80c, Luna 3. 1r, Soyuz 6. 1.20r, Soyuz 7. 2r, Soyuz 8. 2.50r, Book, rocket, S.P. Koralev. 6r, Salyut space station.
1r-2.50r are vert.

1984, Mar. 8 *Perf. 12½*
480-486 A113 Set of 7 6.50 2.00

Souvenir Sheet

487 A113 6r multicolored 6.50 1.75

No. 487 contains one 40x32mm stamp.

1984 Summer Olympic Games, Los Angeles A114

Designs: 20c, Discus. 50c, Long jump. 80c, Hurdles. 1r, Relay race. 1.50r, Pole vault. 2r, Javelin. 3r, High jump. 6r, Sprint race.

1984, Apr. 20 *Perf. 13*
488-494 A114 Set of 7 7.50 2.00

Souvenir Sheet

495 A114 6r multicolored 6.50 2.00

No. 495 contains one 32x40mm stamp.

Souvenir Sheet

ESPAÑA '84, Madrid — A115

1984, Apr. 24 *Perf. 12½*
496 A115 5r 1933 Hispano-Suiza K6 6.50 2.25

Wild Animals A116

Designs: 10c, Canis latrans. 40c, Canis dingo. 80c, Lycaon pictus. 1r, Canis aureus. 1.20r, Vulpes vulpes. 2r, Chrysocyon brachyurus, vert. 2.50r, Canis lupus.

1984, May 5 *Perf. 13*
497-503 A116 Set of 7 9.50 1.60

Locomotives — A117

Designs: 10c, BB-1002, France, 1966. 40c, BB-1052, France, 1966. 80c, Franco-Belgian, 1945. 1r, #231-505, Franco-Belgian, 1929. 1.20r, #803, Germany, 1968. 2r, BDE-405, France, 1957. 2.50r, DS-01, France, 1979.

1984, June 15 **Litho.** *Perf. 12½*
504-510 A117 Set of 7 8.75 1.75

Flowers A118

Designs: 10c, Magnolia. 40c, Plumeria. 80c, Himenoballis. 1r, Peltophorum roxburghii. 1.20r, Couroupita guianensis. 2r, Lagerstroemia. 2.50r, Thevetia perubiana.

1984, July 10 **Litho.** *Perf. 13*
511-517 A118 Set of 7 11.00 2.00

Classic Automobiles — A119

Designs: 20c, Mercedes-Benz. 50c, Bugatti. 80c, Alfa Romeo. 1r, Franklin. 1.50r, Hispano-Suiza. 2r, Rolls Royce. 3r, Tatra. 6r, Mercedes Benz, diff.

1984, Sept. 15 *Perf. 13x12½*
518-524 A119 Set of 7 9.50 2.00

Souvenir Sheet

Perf. 12½

525 A119 6r multicolored 7.25 1.50

No. 525 contains one 40x32mm stamp.

Musical Instruments — A120

Designs: 10c, Sra Lai. 40c, Skor drum. 80c, Skor thom. 1r, Thro khmer. 1.20r, Raneat ek. 2r, Raneat kong. 2.50r, Thro khe.
10c, 80c are vert.

1984, Oct. 10 *Perf. 13*
526-532 A120 Set of 7 7.50 1.75

Wild Animals A121

Designs: 10c, Gazelle. 40c, Capreolus capreolus. 80c, Lepus. 1r, Cervus elaphus. 1.20r, Elephas maximus. 2r, Genet. 2.50r, Bibos sauveli.
10c-40c, 1r-1.20r are vert.

1984, Nov. 11 *Perf. 13*
533-539 A121 Set of 7 7.50 1.75

Correggio (1489-1534) — A122

Details from paintings: 20c, Rest on Flight into Egypt. 50c, Martyrdom of the Four Saints. 80c, Mystic Marriage of St. Catherine with Saints Francis and Dominic. 1r, Madonna & Child with Saints John the Baptist, Geminian, Peter Martyr and George. 1.50r, Mystic Marriage of St. Catherine. 2r, The Deposition. 2.50r, The Deposition, diff. 6r, Virgin Crowned by Christ.

1984, Dec. 10 *Perf. 12½x13*
540-546 A122 Set of 7 5.00 1.00

Souvenir Sheet

Perf. 12½

547 A122 6r multicolored 6.00 1.00

No. 547 contains one 40x32mm stamp.

Natl. Festival — A123

50c, Oxcart. 1r, Horse-drawn cart. 3r, Elephants. 6r, Oxcart with passengers, vert.

1985, Jan. 5 *Perf. 12½x12*
548-550 A123 Set of 3 4.50 1.00

Souvenir Sheet

Perf. 12½

551 A123 6r multicolored 6.50 1.00

No. 551 contains one 32x40mm stamp.

1986 World Cup Soccer Championships, Mexico — A124

Various soccer players; 20c, vert. 50c, vert. 80c, vert. 1r. 1.50r. 2r, vert. 3r, vert.

1985, Feb. 4 *Perf. 13*
552-558 A124 Set of 7 5.25 1.25

Souvenir Sheet

559 A124 6r multicolored 6.00 1.00

No. 559 contains one 40x32mm stamp.

Motorcycles — A125

20c, 1939 Eska-Mofa. 50c, 1939 Wanderer. 80c, 1929 Premier. 1r, 1939 Ardie. 1.50r, 1932 Jawa. 2r, 1983 Simson. 3r, 1984 CZ-125.

1985, Mar. 8 Litho. *Perf. 13*
560-566 A125 Set of 7 5.50 1.75

Souvenir Sheet

567 A125 6r 1984 MBA 6.50 1.50

No. 567 contains one 40x32mm stamp.

Mushrooms — A126

Designs: 20c, Gymnopilus spectabilis. 50c, Coprinus micaceus. 80c, Amanita panterina. 1r, Hebelona crustuliniforme. 1.50r, Amanita muscaria. 2r, Coprinus comatus. 3r, Amanita caesarea.

Nos. 569-574 are vert.

1985, Apr. 4 *Perf. 13*
568-574 A126 Set of 7 8.50 1.40

Soviet Space Achievements — A127

Designs: 20c, Sputnik. 50c, Yuri Gagarin, rocket. 80c, Valentina Tereshkova, Vostok 6. 1r, Cosmonaut walking in space. 1.50r, Soyuz 4 docked with Soyuz 5. 2r, Lunar rover. 3r, Apollo-Soyuz mission. 6r, Soyuz capsule.

1985, Apr. 12 *Perf. 13*
575-581 A127 Set of 7 5.25 1.25

Souvenir Sheet

582 A127 6r multicolored 6.00 1.00

No. 582 contains one 40x32mm stamp.

Traditional Dances — A128

Designs: 50c, Four dancers. 1r, Three dancers. 3r, One dancer, vert.

1985, Apr. 13 Litho. *Perf. 12½*
583-585 A128 Set of 3 3.50 1.25

End of World War II, 40th Anniv. A129

Designs: 50c, Soldiers celebrating. 1r, Victory parade, Moscow. 3r, Tank battle.

1985, May 9 Litho. *Perf. 12x12½*
586-588 A129 Set of 3 4.25 1.50

Cats — A130

Various cats: 20c, 50c, 80c, 1r, 1.50r, 2r, 3r.

1985, May 16 Litho. *Perf. 12x12½*
589-595 A130 Set of 7 6.25 1.50

Flowers — A131

20c, Lilium Black Dragon. 50c, Iris delavayi. 80c, Crocus aureus. 1r, Cyclamen persicum, wild form. 1.50r, Primula malacoides. 2r, Viola tricolor. 3r, Crocus purpureus.

1985, June 5 Litho. *Perf. 13*
596-602 A131 Set of 7 6.00 1.25

Intl. Music Year — A132

Paintings: 20c, Mezzetin, by Watteau. 50c, St. Cecilia and the Angel, by Saraceni. 80c, Still Life with Violin, Flute and Guitar, by Oudry, horiz. 1r, Three Musicians, by F. Leger. 1.50r, Opera Orchestra, by Degas. 2r, St. Cecilia, by Schedoni. 3r, Young Harlequin with Violin, by Caillard. 6r, The Fifer, by Manet.

1985, June 13 *Perf. 13*
603-609 A132 Set of 7 4.75 1.25

Souvenir Sheet

610 A132 6r multicolored 4.75 1.25

No. 610 contains one 32x40mm stamp.

Lenin (1870-1924) A133

1r, Portrait. 3r, Lenin standing, map of Soviet Union.

1985, June 20 Litho. *Perf. 13*
611-612 A133 Set of 2 3.50 1.00

ARGENTINA '85 — A134

Birds: 20c, Xanthopsar flavus. 50c, Sicalis flaveola. 80c, Thraupis bonariensis. 1r, Amblyramphus holosericeus. 1.50r, Chiloroceryle amazona. 2r, Ramphastos toco. 3r, Turdus rufiventris.

20c-80c, 1.50r-2r are vert.

1985, July 5 Litho. *Perf. 12½*
613-619 A134 Set of 7 8.75 2.00

Ships A135

Designs: 10c, River boat, 1942. 40c, River boat, 1948. 80c, Tugboat, Japan, 1913. 1r, Dredge. 1.20r, Tugboat, US. 2r, Freighter. 2.50r, Tanker, Panama.

1985, Aug. 8
620-626 A135 Set of 7 4.75 1.40

ITALIA 85 — A136

Paintings: 20c, The Flood, by Michelangelo. 50c, Virgin & St. Margaret, by Il Parmigianino (Filippo Mazzola). 80c, Martyrdom of St. Peter Martyr, by Domenichino. 1r, Spring, by Botticelli. 1.50r, Sacrifice of Abraham, by Veronese. 2r, Meeting of St. Joachim and St. Anne, by Giotto. 3r, Bacchus, by Caravaggio.

6r, Early train.

1985, Oct. 25
627-633 A136 Set of 7 6.00 1.10

Souvenir Sheet

634 A136 6r multicolored 4.50 1.25

No. 634 contains one 32x40mm stamp.

Son Ngoc Minh — A137

1985, Dec. 2 Litho. *Perf. 12x12½*
635-637 A137 Set of 3, 50c, 1r, 3r 2.50 1.25

Fish A138

20c, Barbus tetrazona. 50c, Ophiocephalus micropeltes. 80c, Carassius auratus. 1r, Trichogaster leeri. 1.50r, Puntius hexazona. 2r, Betta splendens. 3r, Datnioides microlepis.

1985, Dec. 28 Litho. *Perf. 13*
638-644 A138 Set of 7 6.50 1.50

1986 World Cup Soccer Championships, Mexico — A139

Various soccer players: 20c, 50c, 80c, 1r, 1.50r, 2r, 3r.

1986, Jan. 29
645-651 A139 Set of 7 4.75 1.25

Souvenir Sheet

652 A139 6r multicolored 6.00 1.00

No. 652 contains one 32x40mm stamp.

Horses A140

Designs: 20c, Cob. 50c, Arabian. 80c, Australian pony. 1r, Appaloosa. 1.50r, Quarter horse. 2r, Vladimir heavy draft. 3r, Andalusian.

1986, Feb. 15
653-659 A140 Set of 7 5.50 1.50

27th Soviet Communist Party Congress A141

Designs: 50c, Space capsules. 1r, Lenin. 5r, Statue, rocket lift-off.

1986, Feb. 25 *Perf. 12x12½*
660-662 A141 Set of 3 4.25 1.25

Prehistoric Animals — A142

Designs: 20c, Edaphosaurus, horiz. 50c, Sauroctonus, horiz. 80c, Mastodonsaurus, horiz. 1r, Rhamphorhynchus. 1.50r, Brachiosaurus. 2r, Tarbosaurus. 3r, Indricotherium.

1986, Mar. 20 *Perf. 12½*
663-669 A142 Set of 7 11.00 3.00

Manned Space Flight, 25th Anniv. — A143

10c, Luna 16. 40c, Luna 3. 80c, Vostok. 1r, Alexei Leonov walking in space. 1.20r, Apollo-Soyuz mission. 2r, Soyuz capsule docking with Salyut station. 2.50r, Yuri Gagarin.

1986, Apr. 12 *Perf. 12½*
670-676 A143 Set of 7 5.25 1.50

Khmer Culture — A144

20c, Temple. 50c, Head of Buddha. 80c, Temple entrance. 1r, 1.50r, 2r, 3r, Various fans.

1986, Apr. 12 *Perf. 13*
677-683 A144 Set of 7 4.00 1.60

Mercedes-Benz Automobiles — A145

20c, 1885 3-wheel. 50c, 1935 sedan. 80c, 1907 open touring car. 1r, 1920 convertible. 1.50r, 1932 cabriolet. 2r, 1938 2-door. 3r, 1985 sedan.

1986, May 14 *Perf. 13x12½*
684-690 A145 Set of 7 5.25 1.50

Butterflies A146

Designs: 20c, Danaus genutia. 50c, Graphium amtiphates. 80c, Papilio demoleus. 1r, Danaus sita. 1.50r, Idea blanchardi. 2r, Papilio polytes. 3r, Dabasa payeni.

1986, June 19 *Perf. 13*
691-697 A146 Set of 7 5.50 1.75

Ships A147

20c, English cog. 50c, Cog. 80c, Nile barge. 1r, Galley. 1.50r, Viking long ship. 2r, Two-masted lateen-rigged ship. 3r, Cog, diff.

1986, July 7 *Perf. 13*
698-704 A147 Set of 7 4.75 1.50

Halley's Comet — A148

Designs: 10c, Solar system, Copernicus, Galileo, Brahe. 20c, Comet above Adoration of the Magi in painting by Giotto. 50c, Comet, observatory. 80c, Edmond Halley. 1.20r, Giotto probe. 1.50r, Vega probe. 2r, Computer-enhanced images of comet. 6r, Vega probe, diff.

1986, July 21 **Litho.** *Perf. 12x12½*
705-711 A148 Set of 7 3.75 1.40

Souvenir Sheet

Perf. 13

712 A148 6r multicolored 4.75 1.25

No. 712 contains one 32x40mm stamp.

STOCKHOLMIA 86 — A149

Chess masters: 20c, Ruy Lopez. 50c, Francois Philador. 80c, Adolph Anderssen. 1r, Wilhelm Steinetz. 1.50r, Emanuel Lasker. 2r, José Capablanca. 3r, Alexander Alekhine. 6r, Chess pieces.

1986, Aug. 28 **Litho.** *Perf. 12½*
713-719 A149 Set of 7 6.00 1.40

Souvenir Sheet

Perf. 13

720 A149 6r multicolored 7.25 1.40

No. 720 contains one 40x32mm stamp.

Cactus — A150

20c, Parodia maasii. 50c, Rebutia marsoneri. 80c, Melocactus evae. 1r, Gymnocalycium valnicekianum. 1.50r, Discocactus silichromus. 2r, Neochilenia simulans. 3r, Weingartia chiqichuquensis.

1986, Sept. 25 *Perf. 13*
721-727 A150 Set of 7 5.50 1.40

Fruit — A151

Designs: 10c, Bananas. 40c, Papayas. 80c, Mangos. 1r, Breadfruit. 1.20r, Litchi. 2r, Pineapple. 2.50r, Grapefruit, horiz.

1986, Oct. 4 *Perf. 12½*
728-734 A151 Set of 7 4.00 1.50

Aircraft — A152

20c, Concorde. 50c, DC-10. 80c, 747. 1r, IL-62. 1.50r, IL-86. 2r, AN-124. 3r, A-300.

1986, Nov. 21
735-741 A152 Set of 7 4.75 1.60

Silverware — A153

Designs: 50c, Elephant, containers. 1r, Covered bowl. 3r, Serving dish.

1986, Dec. 2 *Perf. 13*
742-744 A153 Set of 3 3.75 1.40

World Wildlife Fund A154

Designs: No. 745, 20c, Kouprey. No. 746, 20c, Gaur. 80c, Banteng. 1.50r, Buffalo.

1986, Dec. 30 **Litho.** *Perf. 13*
745-748 A154 Set of 4 *14.00* 4.00

Tou Samouth A155

Denominations and background colors: 50c, green. 1r, blue, 3r, yellow.

1987, Jan. 7 **Litho.** *Perf. 13*
749-751 A155 Set of 3 2.75 1.00

1988 Winter Olympic Games, Calgary — A156

Designs: 20c, Biathlon. 50c, Women's figure skating. 80c, Speed skating. 1r, Hockey. 1.50r, Luge. 2r, Two-man bobsled. 3r, Cross-country skiing. 6r, Slalom skiing.

1987, Jan. 14 *Perf. 13x12½*
752-758 A156 Set of 7 4.75 1.25

Souvenir Sheet

Perf. 12½

759 A156 6r multicolored 4.75 1.10

No. 759 contains one 40x32mm stamp.

1988 Summer Olympic Games, Seoul — A157

Designs: 20c, Weight lifting, vert. 50c, Archery. 80c, Fencing. 1r, Gymnastics, vert. 1.50r, Discus. 2r, Javelin, vert. 3r, Hurdles. 6r, Wrestling.

1987, Feb. 2 *Perf. 12½x13, 13x12½*
760-766 A157 Set of 7 4.75 1.25

Souvenir Sheet

Perf. 13

767 A157 6r multicolored 4.75 1.25

No. 767 contains one 40x32mm stamp.

Dogs A158

Designs: 20c, shown. 50c, Greyhound. 80c, Great Dane. 1r, Doberman pinscher. 1.50r, Samoyed. 2r, Borzoi. 3r, Collie.

1987, Mar. 3 *Perf. 13*
768-774 A158 Set of 7 8.00 1.50

Nos. 458, 463 Surcharged

1987, Mar. **Litho.** *Perf. 13*
775 A110 35r on 50c #463 5.00
776 A109 50r on 50c #458 5.00

Soviet Spacecraft A159

Designs: 20c, Sputnik. 50c, Weather satellite. 80c, Proton. 1r, Vostok 1. 1.50r, Electron-2. 2r, Kosmos. 3r, Luna 2. 6r, Electron-4.

1987, Apr. 12 **Litho.** ***Perf. 13***
777-783 A159 Set of 7 4.75 1.60

Souvenir Sheet

784 A159 6r multicolored 4.75 1.25

No. 784 contains one 40x32mm stamp.

Silverware — A159a

Designs: 50c, Long-necked pot, vert. 1r, Box. 1.50r, Tea set. 3r, Sword.

1987, Apr. 13 ***Perf. 13***
785-788 A159a Set of 4 3.50 1.00

CAPEX 87 — A160

Birds: 20c, Merops nubicus. 50c, Upupa epops. 80c, Balearica pavonina. 1r, Tyto alba. 1.50r, Halcyon leucocephala. 2r, Pycnonotus jocosus. 3r, Ardea purpurea. 6r, Terpsiphone paradisi.

50c-1.50r, 3r are vert.

1987, May 5 ***Perf. 13***
789-795 A160 Set of 7 5.25 1.25

Souvenir Sheet

796 A160 6r multicolored 5.25 1.25

No. 796 contains one 32x40mm stamp.

Early Aircraft Designs A161

Designs by: 20c, Horatio F. Phillips, 1893. 50c, John Stringfellow, 1848. 80c, Thomas Moy, 1875. 1r, Leonardo da Vinci, 1490. 1.50r, Sir George Cayley, 1840. 2r, Sir Hiram Maxim, 1894. 3r, William S. Henson, 1842. 6r, Da Vinci, diff.

1987, Aug. 7 ***Perf. 13***
797-803 A161 Set of 7 5.25 1.40

Souvenir Sheet

Perf. 12½

804 A161 6r multicolored 4.75 1.00

No. 804 contains one 32x40mm stamp.

Reptiles A162

Designs: 20c, Testudo gigantea. 50c, Uromastix acanthinuros. 80c, Cyclura macleayi. 1r, Phrynosoma coronatum. 1.50r, Sauromalus obesus. 2r, Ophisaurus apodus. 3r, Thamnophis sirtalis.

1987, Sept. 9 ***Perf. 13***
805-811 A162 Set of 7 4.75 1.75

HAFNIA 87 — A163

Helicopters: 20c, Kamov KA-15. 50c, Kamov KA-18. 80c, Westland Lynx WG-13. 1r, Sud Aviation Gazelle. 1.50r, Sud Aviation Puma. 2r, Boeing CH-47 Chinook. 3r, Boeing UTTAS. 6r, Fairey Rotodyne.

1987, Oct. 16 ***Perf. 12½x12***
812-818 A163 Set of 7 4.75 1.40

Souvenir Sheet

Perf. 13

819 A163 6r multicolored 4.75 1.25

No. 819 contains one 40x32mm stamp.

Russian October Revolution, 70th Anniv. — A164

1987 **Litho.** ***Perf. 12x12¼***
820 A164 2r Soldiers, horse 1.25 .30
821 A164 3r Soldiers 1.75 .50
822 A164 5r Lenin, aides 3.50 .80

Two additional stamps were issued in this set. The editors would like to examine them.

Fire Trucks A165

1987, Nov. 24 **Litho.** ***Perf. 13***
823-829 A165 20c, 50c, 80c, 1r, 1.50r, 2r, 3r, set of 7 5.50 2.00

Telecommunications — A166

50c, Dish antenna, vert. 1r, Broadcast center, vert. 3r, Dish antenna, broadcast center.

Perf. 13x12½, 12x12½, 12½x12

1987, Dec. 2
830-832 A166 Set of 3 3.00 1.10

No. 830 is 29x40mm. No. 831 is 28x44mm. No. 832 printed with se-tenant label.

1988 Winter Olympic Games, Calgary A167

Designs: 20c, Speed skating. 50c, Hockey. 80c, Downhill skiing. 1r, Ski jumping. 1.50r, Biathlon. 2r, Pairs figure skating. 3r, Cross-country skiing. 6r, Four-man bobsled.

1988, Jan. 7 ***Perf. 12½***
833-839 A167 Set of 7 4.75 1.00

Souvenir Sheet

Perf. 13

840 A167 6r multicolored 3.25 1.10

No. 840 contains one 32x40mm stamp.

Water Projects A168

Designs: 50c, Canal. 1r, Dam under construction. 3r, Dam, bridge.

1988, Jan. 7 **Litho.** ***Perf. 13***
841-843 A168 Set of 3 3.00 1.25

1988 Summer Olympic Games, Seoul — A169

Designs: 20c, Balance beam, vert. 50c, Uneven bars. 80c, Rhythmic gymnastics ribbon, vert. 1r, Rhythmic gymnastics hoop, vert. 1.50r, Rhythmic gymnastics clubs, vert. 2r, Rhythmic gymnastics ball. 3r, Floor exercise.

Perf. 12½x13, 13x12½

1988, Feb. 2 **Litho.**
844-850 A169 Set of 7 4.50 1.50

Souvenir Sheet

Perf. 12½

851 A169 6r Rhythmic gymnastics, diff. 4.75 1.50

No. 851 contains one 32x40mm stamp.

JUVALUX 88 A170

Various cats. Denominations: 20c, 50c, 80c, 1r, 1.50r, 2r, 3r. Nos. 853-854, 856-858 are vert.

1988, Mar. 15 ***Perf. 12½***
852-858 A170 Set of 7 5.25 1.25

Souvenir Sheet

Perf. 13

859 A170 6r multicolored 6.00 1.25

No. 859 contains one 40x32mm stamp.

ESSEN 88 — A171

Ships: 20c, Passenger liner. 50c, Passenger liner, diff. 80c, Research ship. 1r, Communications ship. 1.50r, Tanker. 2r, Hydrofoil. 3r, Hovercraft.

1988, Apr. 14 **Litho.** ***Perf. 12½***
860-866 A171 Set of 7 6.50 1.50

Souvenir Sheet

Perf. 13

867 A171 6r Hydrofoil 5.25 1.10

Satellites — A172

Various satellites. Denominations: 20c, 50c, 80c, 1r, 1.50r, 2r, 3r. Nos. 868-870 are vert.

1988, Apr. 24 ***Perf. 12½x13, 13x12½***
868-874 A172 Set of 7 4.25 1.50

Souvenir Sheet

Perf. 13

875 A172 6r multicolored 4.75 1.25

No. 875 contains one 40x32mm stamp.

FINLANDIA 88 — A173

Fish: 20c, Xiphophorus helleri. 50c, Hemigrammus ocellifer. 80c, Macropodus opercularis. 1r, Carassius auratus. 1.50r, Hyphessobrycon inesi. 2r, Corynopoma riisei. 3r, Mollienisia latipinna.

6r, Pterophyllum scalare.

1988, Jun 10 **Litho.** ***Perf. 13x12½***
876-882 A173 Set of 7 6.50 1.50

Souvenir Sheet

Perf. 12½

883 A173 6r multicolored 5.50 1.25

No. 883 contains one 32x40mm stamp.

Shells — A174

Designs: 20c, Helicostyla florida. 50c, Helicostyla marinduquensis. 80c, Helicostyla fulgens. 1r, Helicostyla woodiana. 1.50r, Chloraea sirena. 2r, Helicostyla mirabilis. 3r, Helicostyla limansauensis.

1988, Aug. 5 **Litho.** ***Perf. 13x12½***
884-890 A174 Set of 7 5.25 1.50

Insects — A175

Designs: 20c, Coccinellidae. 50c, Zonabride geminata. 80c, Carabus auronitens. 1r, Apis mellifera. 1.50r, Praying mantis. 2r, Odonata. 3r, Malachius aeneus.

1988, Sept. 6 *Perf. 13x12½*
891-897 A175 Set of 7 6.50 1.40

Orchids
A176

Designs: 20c, Cattleya aclandiae. 50c, Odontoglossum Royal Sovereign. 80c, Cattleya labiata. 1r, Ophrys apifera. 1.50r, Laelia anceps. 2r, Laelia pumila. 3r, Stanhopea tigrina, horiz.

1988, Oct. 10 *Perf. 12½x13, 13x12½*
898-904 A176 Set of 7 4.75 1.25

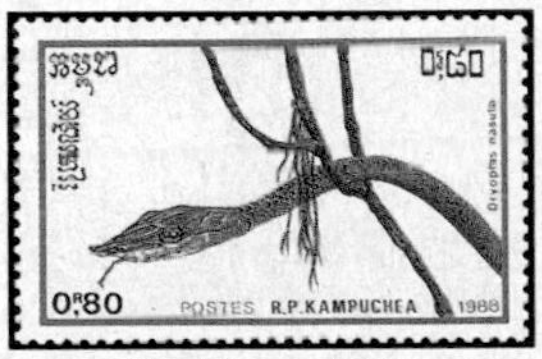

Reptiles — A177

Designs: 20c, Naja haje, vert. 50c, Iguana iguana, vert. 80c, Dryophis nasuta. 1r, Terrapene carolina. 1.50r, Cyclura macleayi. 2r, Bothrops bicolor. 3r, Naja naja, with hood spread, vert.

1988, Nov. 7 *Perf. 12x12½, 12½x12*
905-911 A177 Set of 7 6.50 1.75

Dance of the Peacock
A178

50c, 3 dancers, vert. 1r, shown. 3r, 2 dancers.

1988, Dec. 2 *Perf. 13*
912-914 A178 Set of 3 3.50 1.25

For surcharges see Nos. 1195-1196.

Bridges — A179

1989 *Perf. 13x12½*
915-917 A179 50c, 1r, 3r, set of 3 3.25 1.40

Decade of Progress — A180

3r, Telecommunications station. 12r, Central Electrical Plant No. 4. 30r, Cement plant, vert.

1989
918-920 A180 Set of 3 2.75 1.50

1990 World Cup Soccer Championships, Italy — A181

Various soccer players. Denominations: 2r, 3r, 5r, 10r, 15r, 20r, 35r.

1989 *Perf. 12½x13*
921-927 A181 Set of 7 6.50 1.50

Souvenir Sheet

Perf. 13

928 A181 45r multicolored 4.75 1.00

No. 928 contains one 32x40mm stamp.

Trains
A182

Various locomotives. Denominations: 2r, 3r, 5r, 10r, 15r, 20r, 35r.

1989 *Perf. 13*
929-935 A182 Set of 7 6.75 1.50

Souvenir Sheet

Perf. 12½

936 A182 45r multicolored 6.00 1.00

No. 936 contains one 40x32mm stamp.

A183

1989 *Perf. 13*
937 A183 12r red & black 1.25 .55

Cuban Revolution, 30th anniv.

A184

Birds: 20c, Ara macao. 80c, Kakatoe galerita. 3r, Psittacula krameri. 6r, Ara ararauna. 10r, Poicephalus robustus. 15r, Amazona aestiva. 25r, Pionus senilis, horiz.
45r, Cyanoramphus novaezelandiae.

1989
938-944 A184 Set of 7 6.75 1.25

Souvenir Sheet

Perf. 12½

945 A184 45r multicolored 5.50 1.00

No. 945 contains one 40x32mm stamp.

1992 Winter Olympic Games, Albertville
A185

2r, Slalom skiing. 3r, Biathlon. 5r, Cross-country skiing. 10r, Ski jumping. 15r, Speed skating. 20r, Hockey. 35r, Bobsled. 45r, Pairs figure skating.

1989, Mar. 30 *Perf. 13*
946-952 A185 Set of 7 4.75 1.50

Souvenir Sheet

Perf. 12½

953 A185 45r multicolored 3.00 1.00

No. 953 contains one 32x40mm stamp.

Water Lilies
A186

20c, Nymphaea capensis (pink). 80c, Nymphaea capensis (purple). 3r, Nymphaea lotus. 6r, Nymphaea Dir. Geo. T. Moore. 10r, Nymphaea Sunrise. 15r, Nymphaea Escarboncie. 25r, Nymphaea Cladstoniana. 45r, Nymphaea Paul Hariot.

1989 *Perf. 12½x13*
954-960 A186 Set of 7 4.50 1.25

Souvenir Sheet

Perf. 12½

961 A186 45r multicolored 4.75 1.00

No. 961 contains one 32x40mm stamp.

1992 Summer Olympic Games, Barcelona — A187

Designs: 2r, Wrestling. 3r, Pommel horse, vert. 5r, Shot put. 10r, Running, vert. 15r, Fencing. 20r, Canoeing, vert. 35r, Steeplechase, vert. 45r, Weight lifting, vert.

1989 *Perf. 13*
962-968 A187 Set of 7 5.50 1.50

Souvenir Sheet

Perf. 12½

969 A187 45r multicolored 4.75 1.50

No. 969 contains one 32x40mm stamp.

Mushrooms
A188

Designs: 20c, Xerocomus subtomentosus. 80c, Inocybe patouillardii. 3r, Armillaria mellea. 6r, Agaricus campestris. 10r, Paxillus involutus. 15r, Coprinus comatus. 25r, Lepiota procera.

1989 *Perf. 12½x13*
970-976 A188 Set of 7 5.25 1.10

Horses — A189

Designs: 2r, Shire. 3r, Brabant. 5r, Bolounais. 10r, Breton. 15r, Vladimir heavy draft. 20r, Italian heavy draft. 35r, Freiberger. 45r, Horse-drawn cart.

1989 *Perf. 12½*
977-983 A189 Set of 7 5.50 1.50

Souvenir Sheet

984 A189 45r multicolored 4.75 1.10

Nos. 977-983 printed with se-tenant label. No. 984 contains one 40x32mm stamp.

Angkor Wat — A190

Denominations: 35r, 50r, 80r, 100r.

1989, May 15 **Litho.** *Perf. 13¼*
985-988 A190 Set of 4 *175.00 175.00*

Cambodia

PHILEXFRANCE 89 — A191

Mail coaches: 2r, 17th cent. 3r, Paris-Lyon, 1720. 5r, 1793. 10r, 1805. 15r, Royal Mail. 20r, 1843. 35r, Paris-Lille, 1837, vert. 45r, 1815, vert.

1989 **Litho.** *Perf. 13*
989-995 A191 Set of 7 5.75 1.50

Souvenir Sheet

Perf. 12½

996 A191 45r multicolored 3.25 1.50

No. 996 contains one 23x40mm stamp.

BRASILIANA 89 — A192

Butterflies: 2r, Papilio zagreus. 3r, Morpho catenarius. 5r, Morpho aega. 10r, Callithea sapphira. 15r, Catagramma sorana. 20r, Pierella nereis. 35r, Papilio brasiliensis. 45r, Thacia marsyas, horiz.

1989 ***Perf. 13***
997-1003 A192 Set of 7 7.00 1.50

Souvenir Sheet

1004 A192 45r multicolored 5.50 1.50

No. 1004 contains one 40x32mm stamp.

Khmer Boats A193

Various pirogues. Denominations: 3r, 12r, 30r.

1989, Dec. 2 **Litho.** ***Perf. 12½***
1005-1007 A193 Set of 3 3.00 1.25

Natl. Organizations — A194

3r, Youth, vert. 12r, Labor. 30r, Natl. Front.

1990, Jan. 7 **Litho.** ***Perf. 13***
1008-1010 A194 Set of 3 3.50 1.25

1990 World Cup Soccer Championships, Italy — A195

Various soccer players. Denominations: 2r, 3r, 5r, 10r, 15r, 20r, 35r.

1990, Jan. 5 **Litho.** ***Perf. 13***
1011-1017 A195 Set of 7 5.50 1.50

Souvenir Sheet

1018 A195 45r multicolored 4.00 1.00

No. 1018 contains one 32x40mm stamp.
For surcharges see Nos. 1072-1076A.

STAMPWORLD LONDON 90 — A196

Various mail coaches. Denominations: 2r, 3r, 5r, 10r, 15r, 20r, 35r.
45r, Single horse van for rural deliveries.

1990 ***Perf. 12½x12***
1019-1025 A196 Set of 7 5.50 1.25

Souvenir Sheet

Perf. 13

1026 A196 45r multicolored 4.75 1.00

Nos. 1019-1025 are printed with se-tenant label. No. 1026 contains one 40x32mm stamp.

Rice — A197

Designs: 3r, Woman, rice. 12r, People hauling rice, horiz. 30r, Women threshing rice.

1990, June 19 **Litho.** ***Perf. 13***
1027-1029 A197 Set of 3 3.50 1.25

1992 Winter Olympic Games, Albertville A198

2r, 4-man bobsled. 3r, Speed skating. 5r, Pairs figure skating. 10r, Hockey. 15r, Biathlon. 20r, Luge. 35r, Ski jumping. 45r, Hockey goalie.

1990 **Litho.** ***Perf. 13***
1030-1036 A198 Set of 7 5.50 1.50

Souvenir Sheet

1037 A198 45r multicolored 4.50 1.00

No. 1037 contains one 32x40mm stamp.

1992 Summer Olympic Games, Barcelona A199

Designs: 2r, Shooting. 3r, Shot put. 5r, Weight lifting. 10r, Boxing. 15r, Pole vault. 20r, Basketball. 35r, Fencing. 45r, Rhythmic gymnastics.

1990
1038-1044 A199 Set of 7 5.50 1.50

Souvenir Sheet

1045 A199 45r multicolored 4.00 1.00

No. 1045 contains one 32x40mm stamp.

Khmer Culture A200

Designs: 3r, Facade, Bantey Srei. 12r, Relief. 30r, Ruins, Banon.

Perf. 12½, 12½x13 (#1048)

1990, Dec. 2 **Litho.**
1046-1048 A200 Set of 3 3.75 1.25

No. 1048 is 36x21mm.

Dogs A201

20c, Poodle. 80c, Shetland. 3r, Samoyed. 6r, Springer spaniel. 10r, Fox terrier. 15r, Afghan. 25r, Dalmatian. 45r, Bernese.

1990 **Litho.** ***Perf. 13***
1049-1055 A201 Set of 7 5.50 1.25

Souvenir Sheet

1056 A201 45r multicolored 4.25 1.00

No. 1056 contains one 40x32mm stamp.

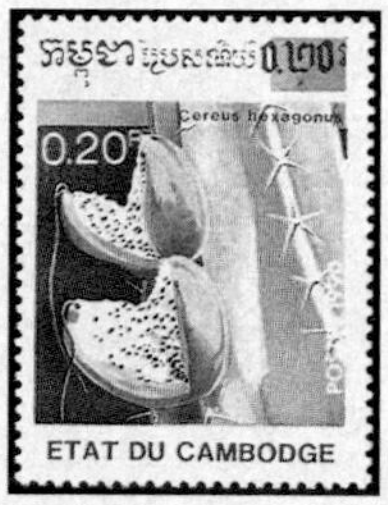

Cacti — A202

Designs: 20c, Cereus hexagonus. 80c, Arthrocereus rondonianus. 3r, Matucana multicolor. 6r, Hildewintera aureispina. 10r, Opuntia retrosa. 15r, Erdisia tenuicula. 25r, Mamillaria yaquensis.

1990
1057-1063 A202 Set of 7 5.00 1.50

NEW ZEALAND 90 — A203

Butterflies: 2r, Zizina oxleyi. 3r, Cupha prosope. 5r, Heteronympha merope. 10r, Dodonidia helmsi. 15r, Argirophenga antipodum. 20r, Tysonotis danis. 35r, Pyrameis gonnarilla. 45r, Pyrameis itea.

1990 ***Perf. 13***
1064-1070 A203 Set of 7 8.00 1.50

Souvenir Sheet

Perf. 12½

1071 A203 45r multicolored 5.50 1.25

No. 1071 contains one 40x32mm stamp.

Nos. 1012-1017 Surcharged in Red

1990 **Litho.** ***Perf. 13***
1072 A195 200r on 3r #1012
1073 A195 300r on 5r #1013
1074 A195 500r on 10r #1014
1075 A195 800r on 15r #1015
1076 A195 1000r on 20r #1016
1076A A195 2000r on 35r #1017

Intl. Literacy Year — A204

Denominations: 3r, 12r, 30r.

1990 **Litho.** ***Perf. 13***
1077-1079 A204 Set of 3 5.25 1.50

Ships A205

Designs: 20c, English, 1200. 80c, Spanish galleon, 16th cent. 3r, Dutch ship, 1627. 6r, La Couronne, 1638. 10r, L'Astrolabe, 1826. 15r, French packet, Louisiana, 1864. 25r, Clipper ship, 1900, vert. 45r, Merchant ship, 1800.

1990 **Litho.** ***Perf. 13***
1080-1086 A205 Set of 7 6.50 1.50

Souvenir Sheet

Perf. 12½

1087 A205 45r multicolored 4.50 1.00

No. 1087 contains one 32x40mm stamp.

Natl. Building Campaign — A206

3r, Railroad. 12r, Cargo ship, Kampong Som. 30r, Fishing boats, Kampong Som.

1990 **Litho.** ***Perf. 13***
1088-1090 A206 Set of 3 5.50 1.25

PARIS 90 — A207

Chess pieces and: 2r, Sacré Coeur. 3r, Equestrian statue. 5r, Winged Victory of Samothrace. 10r, Chateau, Azay le Rideau. 15r, Sculpture, "The Dance." 20r, Eiffel Tower. 35r, Arc de Triomphe.
45r, Chess pieces, horiz.

1990, Nov. 15 **Litho.** ***Perf. 13***
1091-1097 A207 Set of 7 6.50 2.00

Souvenir Sheet

1098 A207 45r multicolored 5.50 1.50

No. 1098 contains one 40x32mm stamp.

Space Day — A208

Designs: 2r, Vostok. 3r, Soyuz. 5r, Artificial satellite. 10r, Luna 10. 15r, Mars 1. 20r, Venera 3. 35r, Mir. 45r, Energia, Buran.

1990 **Litho.** ***Perf. 13***
1099-1105 A208 Set of 7 5.50 1.50

Souvenir Sheet

1106 A208 45r multicolored 4.00 1.00

No. 1106 contains one 32x40mm stamp.
For surcharges see Nos. 1145-1151.

Discovery of America, 500th Anniv. (in 1992) — A209

Designs: 2r, Columbus. 3r, Queen Isabella's jewelry chest. 5r, Queen Isabella. 10r, Santa Maria. 15r, Juan de la Cosa. 20r, Columbus Monument. 35r, Pyramid, Yucatan.
45r, Columbus, diff.

1990, Oct. 12 Litho. *Perf. 13*
1107-1113 A209 Set of 7 7.50 2.00

Souvenir Sheet

1114 A209 45r multicolored 4.75 1.25

No. 1114 contains one 32x40mm stamp.

Natl. Festival A210

Designs: 100r, Tire production. 300r, Rural infirmary. 500r, Fisherman, vert.

Perf. 12½, 13 (#1117)

1991, Jan. 7 Litho.
1115-1117 A210 Set of 3 5.00 1.75

No. 1117 is 28x40mm.

1994 World Cup Soccer Championships, US — A211

Various soccer players. Denominations: 5r, 25r, 70r, 100r, 200r, 400r, 1000r.

1991, Feb. 15 Litho. *Perf. 13*
1118-1124 A211 Set of 7 6.25 1.75

Souvenir Sheet

1125 A211 900r multicolored 3.50 1.10

No. 1125 contains one 32x40mm stamp.

1992 Winter Olympic Games, Albertville A212

Designs: 5r, Speed skating. 25r, Slalom skiing. 70r, Hockey. 100r, Bobsled. 200r, Freestyle skiing. 400r, Pairs figure skating. 1000r, Downhill skiing.
900r, Ski jumping.

1991, Mar. 30 Litho. *Perf. 12½*
1126-1132 A212 Set of 7 6.50 2.00

Souvenir Sheet

Perf. 13

1133 A212 900r multicolored 3.75 1.00

No. 1133 contains one 32x40mm stamp.

Khmer Culture A213

Statues: 100r, Garuda, 10th cent. 300r, Torso of Vishnu reclining, 11th cent. 500r, Reclining Nandin, 7th cent.

1991, Apr. 13 Litho. *Perf. 12½*
1134-1136 A213 Set of 3 3.50 2.00

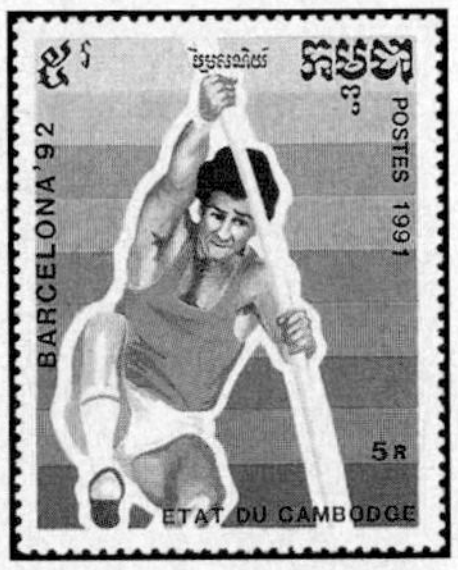

1992 Summer Olympic Games, Barcelona A214

Designs: 5r, Pole vault. 25r, Table tennis. 70r, Women's running. 100r, Wrestling. 200r, Women's gymnastics. 400r, Tennis. 1000r, Boxing.
900r, Balance beam.

1991, Apr. 25 Litho. *Perf. 12½x13*
1137-1143 A214 Set of 7 5.75 1.50

Souvenir Sheet

Perf. 13

1144 A214 900r multicolored 4.00 1.00

No. 1144 contains one 32x40mm stamp.

Nos. 1099-1105 Surcharged in Red

1991 Litho. *Perf. 13*

1145	A208	100r on 2r #1099	—	
1146	A208	150r on 3r #1100	*75.00*	
1147	A208	200r on 5r #1101	*75.00*	
1148	A208	300r on 10r #1102	*75.00*	
1149	A208	500r on 15r #1103	*75.00*	
1150	A208	1500r on 20r #1104	—	—
1151	A208	2000r on 35r #1105	*75.00*	

Aircraft — A215

Designs: 5r, DC-10-30. 25r, MD-11. 70r, IL-96-300. 100r, A-310. 200r, YAK-42. 400r, TU-154. 1000r, DC-9

1991, June 15 Litho. *Perf. 13x12½*
1152-1158 A215 Set of 7 6.00 1.75

ESPAMER 91 — A216

Pre-Columbian pottery: 5r, Catamarca. 25r, Catamarca, vert. 70r, Tucuman, vert. 100r, Santiago del Estero. 200r, Santiago del Estero, diff. 400r, Tucuman, diff., vert. 1000r, Catamarca, diff.
900r, Catamarca, diff.

1991, July 10 *Perf. 13*
1159-1165 A216 Set of 7 6.50 2.00

Souvenir Sheet

Perf. 12½

1166 A216 900r multicolored 4.50 1.25

No. 1166 contains one 40x32mm stamp.

Discovery of America, 500th Anniv. (in 1992) — A217

Designs: 5r, Pinta, vert. 25r, Niña, vert. 70r, Santa Maria, vert. 100r, Landing of Columbus. 200r, Encountering new cultures. 400r, First European settlement in Americas. 1000r, Native village.
900r, Columbus.

1991, Oct. 12 *Perf. 12½x13, 13x12½*
1167-1173 A217 Set of 7 7.00 2.00

Souvenir Sheet

Perf. 12½

1174 A217 900r multicolored 4.00 1.10

No. 1174 contains one 40x32mm stamp.

PHILANIPPON 91 — A218

Butterflies: 5r, Neptis pryeri. 25r, Papilio xuthus. 70r, Cyrestis thyodamas. 100r, Argynnis anadiomene. 200r, Lethe marginalis. 400r, Artopoetes pryeri. 1000r, Danaus chrysippus.
900r, Ochlodes subhyalina.

1991, Nov. 16 *Perf. 13*
1175-1181 A218 Set of 7 8.50 2.00

Souvenir Sheet

Perf. 12½

1182 A218 900r multicolored 7.00 1.25

No. 1182 contains one 40x32mm stamp.

Natl. Building Campaign A219

Designs: 100r, Fishing port. 300r, Preparing palm sugar, vert. 500r, Harvesting peppers.

1991, Dec. 2 Litho. *Perf. 12½*
1183-1185 A219 Set of 3 4.75 2.40

Natl. Festival — A220

Traditional costumes: 150r, Chakdomuk. 350r, Longvek. 1000r, Angkor.

1992, Jan. 7 *Perf. 13*
1186-1188 A220 Set of 3 4.50 1.25

1992 Summer Olympic Games, Barcelona A221

5r, Wrestling. 15r, Soccer. 80r, Weight lifting. 400r, Archery. 1500r, Balance beam.
1000r, Equestrian.

1992, Jan. Litho. *Perf. 13*
1189-1193 A221 Set of 5 4.50 1.25

Souvenir Sheet

Perf. 12½

1194 A221 1000r multicolored 4.25 1.00

No. 1194 contains one 32x40mm stamp.

Nos. 913-914 Surcharged in Red

1992, Jan. Litho. *Perf. 13*
1195 A178 200r on 3r #914
1196 A178 300r on 1r #913

Fish A222

Designs: 5r, Hyphessobrycon innesi. 15r, Betta splendens. 80r, Nematobrycon palmen. 400r, Colisa lalia. 1500r, Hoplosternum thoracatum.
1000r, Pterophyllum scalare.

1992, Feb. 8 Litho. *Perf. 12½*
1197-1201 A222 Set of 5 5.25 1.50

Souvenir Sheet

1202 A222 1000r multicolored 4.00 1.00

No. 1202 contains one 40x32mm stamp.

1994 World Cup Soccer Championships, US — A223

Various soccer plays. Denominations: 5r, 15r, 80r, 400r, 1500r. Nos. 1203, 1205-1207 are vert.

1992, Mar. 6 Litho. *Perf. 12½*
1203-1207 A223 Set of 5 4.50 1.50

Souvenir Sheet

1208 A223 1000r multicolored 3.25 1.00

No. 1208 contains one 40x32mm stamp.

Khmer Culture — A224

19th cent. structures: 150r, Monument. 350r, Stupa. 1000r, Library of Mandapa.

1992, Apr. 13 Litho. *Perf. 12½*
1209-1211 A224 Set of 3 5.50 3.25

Leonardo da Vinci (1452-1519) — A225

Designs: 5r, Automobile. 15r, Container ship. 80r, Helicopter. 400r, Scuba gear. 1500r, Parachute, vert.
1000r, Portrait.

1992, Apr. 15 Litho. *Perf. 12x12½*
1212-1216 A225 Set of 5 7.00 1.50

Souvenir Sheet
Perf. 13

1217 A225 1000r multicolored 4.75 1.00

Nos. 1212-1216 each printed with se-tenant labels showing Da Vinci's conceptions of the items shown on the stamps. No. 1217 contains one 32x40mm stamp.

EXPO 92, Seville A226

Inventors, builders: 5r, De la Cierva, autogyro. 15r, Edison, electric light bulb. 80r, Morse, telegraph. 400r, Monturiol, submarine. No. 1222, 1500r, Bell, telephone.
No. 1223, 1500r, Fulton, steamship.

1992, Apr. 23 *Perf. 12½*
1218-1222 A226 Set of 5 4.75 1.25

Souvenir Sheet
Perf. 13

1223 A226 1000r pink & black 3.50 1.00

No. 1223 contains one 32x40mm stamp.

1992 Summer Olympic Games, Barcelona — A227

Designs: 5r, Weight lifting. 15r, Boxing. 80r, Basketball. 400r, Sprints. 1500r, Water polo.
1000r, Women's gymnastics.

1992, May 15 *Perf. 13*
1224-1228 A227 Set of 5 7.50 1.50

Souvenir Sheet
Perf. 12½

1229 A227 1000r multicolored 4.75 1.25

No. 1229 contains one 40x32mm stamp.

Environmental Protection — A228

Designs: 5r, Women filling water jars. 15r, Pagoda. 80r, Palm trees. 400r, Boy riding water buffalo. 1500r, Lake, swimmers.
1000r, Angkor Wat.

1992, June 16 Litho. *Perf. 12½*
1230-1234 A228 Set of 5 6.75 1.75

Souvenir Sheet
Perf. 13

1235 A228 1000r multicolored 5.00 1.25

No. 1235 contains one 42x32mm stamp.

GENOA 92 — A229

Explorers, ship: 5r, Bougainville, Boudeuse. 15r, Cook, Endeavour. 80r, Darwin, Beagle. 400r, Cousteau, Calypso. 1500r, Heyerdahl, Kon Tiki.
1000r, Columbus.

1992, Aug. 1 Litho. *Perf. 12x12½*
1236-1240 A229 Set of 5 5.50 1.50

Souvenir Sheet
Perf. 12½

1241 A229 1000r multicolored 4.75 1.00

No. 1241 contains one 32x40mm stamp.

Mushrooms A230

Designs: 5r, Albatrellus confluens. 15r, Boletus calopus. 80r, Stropharia aeruginosa. 400r, Telamonia armillata. 1500r, Cortinarius traganus.

1992, Sept. 25 *Perf. 13*
1242-1246 A230 Set of 5 5.50 1.50

Seaplanes — A231

Designs: 5r, Bellanca Pacemaker, 1930. 15r, Canadair CL-215, 1965. 80r, G-21A Goose, 1937. 400r, Sealand SA-6, 1947. 1500r, Short S-23, 1936.
1000r, G-44 Widgeon, 1940.

1992, Oct. 16 *Perf. 12½x12*
1247-1251 A231 Set of 5 4.50 1.25

Souvenir Sheet
Perf. 13

1252 A231 1000r multicolored 3.50 1.00

No. 1252 contains one 32x40mm stamp.

Natl. Development A232

Designs: 150r, Dish antenna. 350r, Dish antenna, flags. 1000r, Hotel Cambodiana.

1992, Dec. 2 Litho. *Perf. 12½*
1253-1255 A232 Set of 3 5.50 1.25

Natl. Festival A233

Designs: 50r, Sociological Institute. 450r, Motel Cambodiana. 1000r, Theater.

1993, Jan. 7 Litho. *Perf. 12½*
1256-1258 A233 Set of 3 5.50 1.25

Dolphin, Bathyscaph — A234

Fauna, machine: 150r, shown. 200r, Falcon, jet fighter. 250r, Beaver, dam. 500r, Bat, satellite. 900r, Hummingbird, helicopter.

1993, Feb. 5 Litho. *Perf. 13*
Without Gum
1259-1263 A234 Set of 5 4.75 1.25

Flowers — A235

Designs: 150r, Datura suaveolens. 200r, Convolvulus tricolor. 250r, Hippeastrum hybrid. 500r, Camellia hybrid. 900r, Lilium speciosum.
1000r, Datura suaveolens, camellia, lilium speciosum.

1993, Mar. 15 *Perf. 13*
Without Gum
1264-1268 A235 Set of 5 6.25 1.25

Souvenir Sheet
Perf. 12½

1269 A235 1000r multicolored 3.75 1.00

No. 1269 contains one 40x32mm stamp.

Khmer Culture A236

Designs: 50r, Statue of a Nandin. 450r, Temple Vihear. 1000r, Man with offerings.

1993, Apr. 13 Litho. *Perf. 12½*
1270-1272 A236 Set of 3 5.50 2.75

Wildlife — A237

150r, Cynocephalus volans. 200r, Petuarista petuarista. 250r, Ptychozoon homalocephalum. 500r, Rhacophorus nigropalmatus. 900r, Draco volans.

1993, May 4 Litho. *Perf. 12½x12*
Without Gum
1273-1277 A237 Set of 5 5.00 1.50

BRASILIANA 93 — A238

Butterflies: 250r, Symbrenthia hypselis. 350r, Sithon nedymond. 600r, Geitoneura minyas. 800r, Argyreus hyperbius. 1000r, Argyrophenga antipodum.
1500r, Pararge schakra.

1993, June 15 *Perf. 12½x12*
Without Gum
1278-1282 A238 Set of 5 8.50 1.50

Souvenir Sheet
Perf. 12½

1283 A238 1500r multicolored 5.75 1.25

No. 1283 contains one 40x32mm stamp.

UN Transitional Authority in Cambodia (UNTAC) Pacification Program A239

150r, Cambodian soldiers approaching UN base. 200r, Cambodians entering camp. 250r, Cambodians surrendering weapons to UN. 500r, Vocational training. 900r, Cambodians re-entering society.
1000r, Returning to homes and family.

1993, Aug. 4 Litho. *Perf. 12½*
1284-1288 A239 Set of 5 5.75 1.50

Souvenir Sheet
Perf. 13

1289 A239 1000r blue & black 4.50 1.25

No. 1289 contains one 32x40mm stamp.

Ships A240

150r, Venetian caravel. 200r, Phoenician galley. 250r, Egyptian merchantman. 500r, Genoese merchantman. 900r, English merchantman.

1993, Aug. 27 Litho. *Perf. 13*
Without Gum
1290-1294 A240 Set of 5 4.75 1.25

Alberto Santos-Dumont (1873-1932) — A241

Designs: 150r, Portrait, Balloon, Eiffel Tower, vert. 200r, 14-bis, 1906. 250r, Demoiselle. 500r, EMB-201A. 900r, EMB-111.

1993, Sept. 10 *Perf. 13*
Without Gum
1295-1299 A241 Set of 5 4.75 1.25

1994 World Cup Soccer Championships, US — A242

Various soccer plays. Denominations: 250r, 350r, 600r, 800r, 1000r, vert.

1993, Sept. 23 Litho. *Perf. 12½*
1300-1304 A242 Set of 5 6.00 1.75
Souvenir Sheet
1305 A242 1500r multicolored 5.00 1.50

No. 1305 contains one 40x32mm stamp.

BANGKOK 93 — A243

Ducks: 250r, Anas penelope. 350r, Anas formosa. 600r, Aix galericulata. 800r, Aix sponsa. 1000r, Histrionicus histrionicus.
1500r, Head of Air galericulata.

1993, Oct. 1 Litho. *Perf. 13*
Without Gum
1306-1310 A243 Set of 5 6.00 1.75
Souvenir Sheet
1311 A243 1500r multicolored 4.00 1.10

No. 1311 contains one 40x32mm stamp.

Vertical Take-Off Aircraft — A244

Designs: 150r, First helicopter model, France, 1784, vert. 200r, Steam helicopter model, 1863, vert. 250r, New York-Atlanta-Miami autogyro flight, 1927. 500r, Sikorsky helicopter, 1943. 900r, French VTOL jet.
1000r, Juan de la Cierva's autogyro C-4, 1923.

Perf. 12x12½, 12½x12
1993, Nov. 6 Without Gum
1312-1316 A244 Set of 5 4.75 1.25
Souvenir Sheet
Perf. 12½
1317 A244 1000r multicolored 3.50 1.00

No. 1317 contains one 40x32mm stamp.

Insects — A245

Designs: 50r, Cnaphalocrosis medinalis. 450r, Cicadelle brune. 500r, Scirpophaga incertulas. No. 1321, 1000r, Diopsis macrophthlalma.
No. 1322, Leptocorisa oratorius.

1993, Dec. 2 *Perf. 13*
1318-1321 A245 Set of 4 5.00 1.25
Souvenir Sheet
Perf. 12½
1322 A245 1000r multicolored 4.00 1.00

Issued without gum.
No. 1322 contains one 32x40mm stamp.

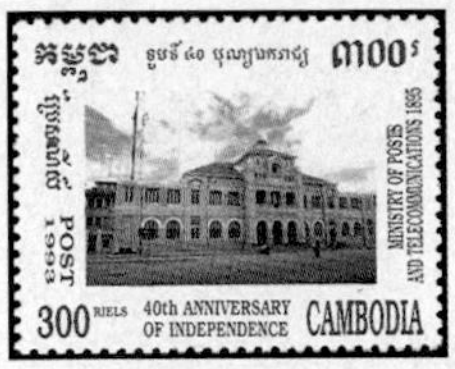

Independence, 40th Anniv. — A246

Designs: 300r, Ministry of Posts and Telecommunications. 500r, Independence Monument, 1953, vert. 700r, Natl. flag.

1993 Litho. *Perf. 12½*
1323-1325 A246 Set of 3 5.25 2.00

Hummel Figurines A247

Designs: 50r, Boy riding pony. 100r, Girl with baby carriage. 150r, Girl bathing doll. 200r, Girl holding doll. 250r, Boys playing. 300r, Girls pulling boy in cart. 350r, Girls playing ring-around-the-rosie. 600r, Boys with stick and drum.

1993 Litho. *Perf. 12½*
1326-1333 A247 Set of 8 6.25 1.75

1994 Winter Olympic Games, Lillehammer — A248

150r, Women's figure skating, vert. 250r, Two-man luge. 400r, Downhill skiing. 700r, Biathlon. 1000r, Speed skating, vert.
1500r, Curling, vert.

1994, Jan. 23 *Perf. 13*
1334-1338 A248 Set of 5 6.00 1.50
Souvenir Sheet
1339 A248 1500r multicolored 4.00 1.25

No. 1339 contains one 32x40mm stamp.

Classic Automobiles — A249

Designs: 150r, 1924 Opel. 200r, 1901 Mercedes. 250r, 1927 Model T Ford. 500r, 1907 Rolls Royce. 900r, 1908 Hutton.
1000r, 1931 Duesenberg.

1994, Feb. 20 *Perf. 13*
1340-1344 A249 Set of 5 5.25 1.50
Souvenir Sheet
1345 A249 1000r multicolored 4.25 1.00

No. 1345 contains one 32x40mm stamp.

1996 Summer Olympic Games, Atlanta — A250

Designs: 150r, Women's gymnastics. 200r, Soccer. 250r, Javelin. 300r, Canoeing. 600r, Running. 1000r, Diving, horiz.
1500r, Equestrian.

1994, Mar. 20 *Perf. 13*
1346-1351 A250 Set of 6 5.50 1.50
Souvenir Sheet
1352 A250 1500r multicolored 4.75 1.25

No. 1352 contains one 32x40mm stamp.

Khmer Statues — A251

Designs: 300r, Siva and Uma. 500r, Vishnu. 700r, King Jayavarman VII.

1994, Apr. 13
1353-1355 A251 Set of 3 5.50 2.75

Intl. Olympic Committee, Cent. — A252

Designs: 100r, Olympic Flag. 300r, Flag, Torch. 600r, Flag, Baron de Coubertin.

1994, Apr. 23 *Perf. 12½*
1356-1358 A252 Set of 3 3.25 1.40

Prehistoric Animals — A253

150r, Mesonyx. 250r, Doedicurus. 400r, Mylodon. 700r, Uintatherium. 1000r, Hyrachyus.

1994, May 10 *Perf. 12½*
1359-1363 A253 Set of 5 6.50 2.00

1994 World Cup Soccer Championships, U.S. — A254

Various soccer plays. Denominations: 150r, 250r, 400r, 700r, 1000r.

1994, June 17 *Perf. 12½*
1364-1368 A254 Set of 5 6.25 1.50
Souvenir Sheet
1369 A254 1500r multicolored 4.50 1.25

No. 1369 contains one 32x40mm stamp.

Statues A255

Designs: 300r, shown. 500r, Soldiers in combat, vert. 700r, Lions, vert.

1994 *Perf. 13*
1370-1372 A255 Set of 3 4.50 2.75

Beetles A256

Designs: 150r, Chlorophanus viridis. 200r, Chrysochroa fulgidissima. 250r, Lytta vesicatoria. 500r, Purpuricenus kaehleri. 900r, Dynastes hercules.
1000r, Timarcha tenebricosa.

1994, July 7 *Perf. 12½*
1373-1377 A256 Set of 5 6.50 1.50
Souvenir Sheet
1378 A256 1000r multicolored 4.00 1.00

No. 1378 contains one 40x32mm stamp.

Submarines — A257

Designs: 150r, Halley's diving bell, 1690, vert. 200r, Gimnote, 1886. 250r, Peral, 1888. 500r, Nuclear-powered Nautilus, 1954. 900r, Bathyscaphe Trieste, 1953.
1000r, Ictineo, 1885.

1994, Aug. 12 *Perf. 13*
1379-1383 A257 Set of 5 5.75 1.50
Souvenir Sheet
Perf. 12½
1384 A257 1000r multicolored 3.75 1.00

No. 1384 contains one 40x32mm stamp.

Chess Champions — A258

Designs: 150r, Francois-André Philador, 1795. 200r, Louis de la Bourdonnais, 1821. 250r, Adolph Anderssen, 1851. 500r, Paul Morphy, 1858. 900r, Wilhelm Steinitz, 1866.
1000r, Emanuel Lasker, 1894.

1994, Sept. 20 *Perf. 13*
1385-1389 A258 Set of 5 5.50 1.50
Souvenir Sheet
1390 A258 1000r multicolored 3.50 1.00

No. 1390 contains one 32x40mm stamp.

Aircraft A259

Designs: 150r, Sikorsky S-42 flying boat. 200r, Vought-Sikorsky VS-300A helicopter. 250r, Sikorsky S-37 biplane. 500r, Sikorsky S-35 biplane. 900r, Sikorsky S-43 amphibian.
1000r, 1st 4-engine bomber, Ilya Mourometz.

1994, Oct. 6 *Perf. 13*

1391-1395 A259 Set of 5 5.25 1.50

Souvenir Sheet

Perf. 12½

1396 A259 1000r multicolored 3.75 1.00

No. 1396 contains one 40x32mm stamp.

Birds A260

Designs: 150r, Remiz pendulinus, vert. 250r, Panurus biarmicus. 400r, Emberiza rustica. 700r, Emberiza schoeniclus. 1000r, Regulus regulus.
1500r, Pitta angolensis.

1994, Nov. 20 *Perf. 12½*

1397-1401 A260 Set of 5 6.50 1.50

Souvenir Sheet

Perf. 13

1402 A260 1500r multicolored 4.25 1.40

No. 1402 contains one 32x40mm stamp.

Independence Festival — A261

Designs: 300r, Postal Service float. 500r, Soldiers marching. 700r, Army unit marching.

1994, Dec. 9 *Perf. 13*

1403-1405 A261 Set of 3 5.00 1.75

Natl. Development — A262

Designs: 300r, Chruoi Changwar Bridge. 500r, Olympic Commercial Center. 700r, Sakamony Chedei Temple.

1994, Dec. 10

1406-1408 A262 Set of 3 5.00 1.50

Prehistoric Animals — A263

100r, Psittacosaurus. 200r, Protoceratops. 300r, Montanoceraptors. 400r, Centrosaurus. 700r, Styracosaurus. 800r, Triceratops.

1995, Jan. 10

1409-1414 A263 Set of 6 7.00 1.50

Butterflies A264

100r, Anthocharis cardamines. 200r, Iphiclides podalirius. 300r, Mesoacidalia aglaja. 600r, Vanessa atalanta. 800r, Inachis io.

1995, Feb. 12

1415-1419 A264 Set of 5 7.50 1.50

1996 Summer Olympic Games, Atlanta A265

Designs: 100r, Swimming. 200r, Rhythmic gymnastics. 400r, Basketball. 800r, Soccer. 1000r, Cycling. 1500r, Running.
200r-1500r are vert.

1995, Mar. 9

1420-1424 A265 Set of 5 6.25 1.50

Souvenir Sheet

1425 A265 1500r multicolored 4.00 1.00

No. 1425 contains one 32x40mm stamp.

Mushrooms A266

Designs: 100r, Amanita phalloides. 200r, Cantharellus cibarius. 300r, Armillaria mellea. 600r, Agaricus campestris. 800r, Amanita muscaria.

1995, Mar. 23

1426-1430 A266 Set of 5 5.75 1.50

Statues — A267

Designs: 300r, Kneeling ascetic. 500r, Parasurama. 700r, Siva.

1995, Apr. 13 *Perf. 12½*

1431-1433 A267 Set of 3 4.50 1.40

Protected Wildlife — A268

Designs: 300r, Bos gaurus. 500r, Bos sauveli, vert. 700r, Grus antigone, vert.

1995, May 5 *Perf. 13*

1434-1436 A268 Set of 3 4.50 1.25

Parrots — A269

Designs: 100r, Lorus lory. 200r, Polytelis alexandrae. 400r, Eclectus voratus. 800r, Ara macao. 1000r, Melopsittacus undulatus.
1500r, Amazona ochrocephala.

1995, May 23 *Perf. 13*

1437-1441 A269 Set of 5 7.00 1.50

Souvenir Sheet

Perf. 12½

1442 A269 1500r multicolored 5.50 1.50

No. 1442 contains one 32x40mm stamp.

Tourism A270

Public gardens: 300r, Sculpture of Garuda. 500r, Fountain. 700r, Sculpture of mythological figures.

1995, July 15 *Perf. 12½*

1443-1445 A270 Set of 3 4.00 1.50

Locomotives — A271

100r, Richard Trevithick's steam locomotive, 1804. 200r, George Stephenson's Rocket, 1830. 300r, Stephenson's Locomotion, 1825. 600r, Lafayette, 1837. 800r, Best Friend of Charleston, 1830.
1000r, Stephenson, vert.

1995, Aug. 17

1446-1450 A271 Set of 5 5.25 1.50

Souvenir Sheet

1451 A271 1000r multicolored 3.50 1.25

No. 1451 contains one 32x40mm stamp.

World War II Aircraft A272

100r, Bristol Blenheim II, vert. 200r, North American B-25. 300r, Avro Anson. 600r, Avro Manchester. 800r, Consolidated B-24.
1000r, Boeing B-17E.

Perf. 12x12½, 12½x12

1995, Sept. 15

1452-1456 A272 Set of 5 5.50 1.50

Souvenir Sheet

Perf. 12½

1457 A272 1000r multicolored 3.75 1.00

No. 1457 contains one 32x40mm stamp.

FAO, 50th Anniv. A273

Designs: 300r, Separating rice plants. 500r, Transplanting rice. 700r, Model rice farm.

1995, Oct. 24 *Perf. 13*

1458-1460 A273 Set of 3 3.50 1.00

UN, 50th Anniv. A274

Designs: 300r, Bridge. 500r, People on bridge. 700r, Central spans of bridge.

1995, Oct. 24 *Perf. 12½*

1461-1463 A274 Set of 3 4.00 1.50

Queen Monineath A275

700r, shown. 800r, King Norodom Sihanouk.

1995, Nov. 9 *Perf. 12½x13*

1464-1465 A275 Set of 2 4.75 1.50

Fish A276

100r, Heniochus acuminatus. 200r, Chelmon rostratus. 400r, Amphiprion percula. 800r, Paracanthurus hepatus. 1000r, Holocanthus ciliaris.
1500r, Coris angulata, vert.

1995, Nov. 19 *Perf. 12½*

1466-1470 A276 Set of 5 6.25 1.50

Souvenir Sheet

1471 A276 1500r multicolored 5.00 1.00

Main Post Office, Cent. A277

Denominations: 300r, 500r, 700r.

1995, Dec. 2 *Perf. 12½*

1472-1474 A277 Set of 3 6.00 1.40

Admission to UN, 40th Anniv. — A278

300r, Independence Monument. 400r, Angkor Wat. 800r, Natl. flag, vert.

Perf. 12½x13, 13x12½

1995, Dec. 14 **Litho.**

1475-1477 A278 Set of 3 5.50 1.25

1996 Summer Olympic Games, Atlanta — A279

Designs: 100r, Tennis. 200r, Volleyball. 300r, Soccer. No. 1480A, 500r, Running. 900r, Baseball. 1000r, Basketball.
1500r, Windsurfing.

1996, Jan. 10 **Litho.** ***Perf. 12½x13***

1478-1482 A279 Set of 6 6.00 1.50

Souvenir Sheet

Perf. 12½

1483 A279 1500r multicolored 3.50 1.00

No. 1483 contains one 32x40mm stamp.

A280

50r, Kep State Chalet. 100r, Power station. 200r, Wheelchair. 500r, Wheelchair basketball. 800r, Making crutches, vert. 1000r, Kep beach. 1500r, Serpent Island.

1996, Jan. 30 ***Perf. 12½***

1484	A280	50r multi	.25	.25
1485	A280	100r multi	.25	.25
1486	A280	200r multi	.30	.25
1487	A280	500r multi	.60	.25
1488	A280	800r multi	1.00	.25
1489	A280	1000r multi	1.40	.35
1490	A280	1500r multi	2.00	.45
		Nos. 1484-1490 (7)	5.80	2.05

Wild Cats A281

100r, Felis libyca, vert. 200r, Felis silvestris. 300r, Felis caracal. 500r, Felis geoffroyi. 900r, Felis nigripes. 1000r, Felis planiceps.

1996, Feb. 8 ***Perf. 13***

1491-1496 A281 Set of 6 6.25 2.00

1998 World Cup Soccer Championships, France — A282

Various soccer players. Denominations: 100r, 200r, 300r, 500r, 900r, 1000r. No. 1502 is horiz.

1996, Mar. 15 ***Perf. 13***

1497-1502 A282 Set of 6 6.00 1.50

Souvenir Sheet

1503 A282 1500r multicolored 4.25 1.00

No. 1503 contains one 32x40mm stamp.

Khmer Culture — A283

100r, Tusmukh. 500r, Ream Iso. 900r, Isei.

1996, Apr. 13 **Litho.** ***Perf. 12½x13***

1504-1506 A283 Set of 3 3.75 1.50

Locomotives — A284

100r, Pacific Type. 200r, Unidentified, 1902. 300r, Unidentified, 1930. 500r, Unidentified, 1914. 900r, LMS #6202, 1930. 1000r, Snake, 1864.
1500r, Canadian Pacific.

1996, Apr. 20

1507-1512 A284 Set of 6 5.00 1.50

Souvenir Sheet

1513 A284 1500r multicolored 3.60 1.00

No. 1513 contains one 40x32mm stamp. CAPEX 96 (No. 1513).

Birds A285

Designs: 100r, Kittacinela malabarica, vert. 200r, Leiothrix lutea. 300r, Parus varius, vert. 500r, Oriolus chinensis. 900r, Cettia diphone. 1000r, Cyanoptila cyanomelana, vert.

1996, May 7

1514-1519 A285 Set of 6 5.25 1.50

Olymphilex '96 — A286

Designs: 100r, Rhythmic gymnastics. 200r, Judo. 300r, High jump. 500r, Wrestling. 900r, Weight lifting. 1000r, Soccer.
1500r, Diving.

1996, June 14 **Litho.** ***Perf. 13x12½***

1520-1525 A286 Set of 6 4.50 1.25

Souvenir Sheet

Perf. 12½

1526 A286 1500r multicolored 3.00 1.00

No. 1526 contains one 32x40mm stamp.

Early Aircraft — A287

100r, Douglas M-2, 1926. 200r, Pitcairn PA-5 Mailwing, 1928. 300r, Boeing 40 B, 1928. 500r, Potez 25, 1925. 900r, Stearman C-3MB, 1927. 1000r, De Havilland DH4, 1918.
1500r, Standard JR-1B, 1918.

1996, July 5 ***Perf. 12½x12***

1527-1532 A287 Set of 6 4.75 1.50

Souvenir Sheet

Perf. 13

1533 A287 1500r multicolored 3.25 1.00

No. 1533 contains one 40x32mm stamp.

Historic Sites — A288

50r, 100r, 200r, Diff. Apsaras, Tonle Batl. No. 1537, Statue, Angkor Wat. No. 1538, Statue of a Goddess. 500r, Carved wall, Tonle Bati. No. 1540, 1000r, No. 1543, Various structures, Tonle Bati. No. 1541, No. 1544, 1700r, 2500r, 3000r, Various views of Angkor Wat.

Nos. 1539, 1543, 1545-1547 are horiz.

1996-97 **Litho.** ***Perf. 12½***

1534	A288	50r black & yel org	.25	.25
1535	A288	100r black & blue	.25	.25
1536	A288	200r black & tan	.40	.25
1537	A288	300r blk & light bl	.30	.25
1538	A288	300r black & red	.30	.25
1539	A288	500r blk & bright bl	.80	.25
1540	A288	800r black & yel grn	1.00	.25
1541	A288	800r black & yel grn	.60	.25
1542	A288	1000r black & green	1.10	.40
1543	A288	1500r black & bister	1.40	.50
1544	A288	1500r black & brown	1.40	.25
1545	A288	1700r black & org brn	1.50	.30
1546	A288	2500r black & blue	2.00	.40
1547	A288	3000r black & dk grn	3.50	.60
		Nos. 1534-1547 (14)	14.80	4.35

Issued: 50r, 100r, 200r, 500r, No. 1540, 1000r, No. 1543, 7/30/96; others, 3/26/97.

See Nos. 1686-1692, 1846-1852.

Dinosaurs — A289

No. 1548: a, 50r, Coelophysis. b, 100r, Euparkeria. c, 150r, Plateosaurus. d, 200r, Herrerasaurus.
No. 1549: a, 250r, Dilophosaurus. b, 300r, Tuojiangosaurus. c, 350r, Camarasaurs. d, 400r, Ceratosaurus.
No. 1550: a, 500r, Spinosaurus. b, 700r, Ouranosaurus. c, 800r, Avimimus. d, 1200r, Deinonychus.

1996, Aug. 8 **Litho.** ***Perf. 13***

1548	A289	Sheet of 4, #a.-d.	1.00	.25
1549	A289	Sheet of 4, #a.-d.	2.75	.60
1550	A289	Sheet of 4, #a.-d.	6.75	1.50

Chess Champions A290

100r, José Raul Capablanca. 200r, Alexander Alekhine. 300r, Vassily Smyslov. 500r, Mikhail Tal. 900r, Bobby Fischer. 1000r, Anatoly Karpov.
1500r, Garry Kasparov.

1996, Sept. 10 ***Perf. 13***

1551-1556 A290 Set of 6 5.50 1.50

Souvenir Sheet

Perf. 12½

1557 A290 1500r multicolored 3.50 1.00

No. 1557 contains one 32x40mm stamp.

Wild Animals A291

Designs: 100r, Ursus arctos. 200r, Panthera leo. 300r, Tapirus indicus. 500r, Camelus ferus. 900r, Capra ibex. 1000r, Zalophus californianus.

1996, Oct. 3 ***Perf. 13x12½***

1558-1563 A291 Set of 6 4.75 1.25

Dogs — A292

Designs: 200r, Collie. 300r, Labrador retriever. 500r, Doberman pinscher. 900r, German shepherd. 1000r, Boxer.

1996, Nov. 8 ***Perf. 12½x13***

1564-1568 A292 Set of 5 4.75 1.25

Independence — A293

100, 500, 900r, Various water treatment plants.

1996, Nov. 9 ***Perf. 13***

1569-1571 A293 Set of 3 3.75 1.50

Ships A294

Designs: 200r, Chinese junk. 300r, Galley. 500r, Roman galley. 900r, Clipper ship, 19th cent. 1000r, Paddle steamer Sirius, 1838.
1500r, Great Eastern, 1858.

1996, Dec. 15 *Perf. 12½x13*
1572-1576 A294 Set of 5 4.75 1.25

Souvenir Sheet

Perf. 12½

1577 A294 1500r multicolored 3.25 1.00

No. 1577 contains one 40x32mm stamp.

Cambodia's Admission to UPU, 45th Anniv. — A295

Denominations: 200r, 400r, 900r.

1996, Dec. 21 *Perf. 12½*
1578-1580 A295 Set of 3 3.75 1.50

New Year 1997 (Year of the Ox) — A296

Paintings of oxen, attributed to Han Huang 723-87): a, Facing left. b, Looking right. c, Brown & white spotted. d, Facing left, head down.

1996, Dec. 28 *Perf. 13x12½*
1581 A296 500r Strip of 4, #a.-d. + label 3.00 .90

UN Intl. Day of Volunteers — A297

Designs: 100r, Phnom Kaun Sat Dam. 900r, Chrey Krem Dam. 1500r, Angkrung Canal.

1996, Dec. 30
1582-1584 A297 Set of 3 4.00 1.50

Greenpeace, 25th Anniv. — A298

Helicopter: 200r, Hovering over cargo. 300r, Hovering over ship. 500r, On helipad. 900r, Lifting cargo.
1000r, Close-up of helicopter.

1996, Dec. 30 *Perf. 12½x13*
1585-1588 A298 Set of 4 6.00 1.75

Souvenir Sheet

Perf. 12½

1589 A298 1000r multicolored 5.50 1.00

No. 1589 contains one 32x40mm stamp.

1998 World Cup Soccer Championships, France — A299

Various soccer plays. Denominations: 100r, 200r, 300r, 500r, 900r, 1000r.

1997, Jan. 6 **Litho.** *Perf. 12½x13*
1590-1595 A299 Set of 6 5.25 1.50

Souvenir Sheet

Perf. 13

1596 A299 2000r multicolored 3.25 1.00

No. 1596 contains one 40x32mm stamp.

Elephas Maximus — A300

World Wilflife Fund: a, 300r, Two walking. b, 500r, Three standing. c, 900r, Two fighting. d, 1000r, Adult, calf.

1997, Feb. 12 *Perf. 12½x12*
1597 A300 Strip of 4, #a.-d. 8.00 3.00

Birds — A301

600r, Bombycilla garrulus. 900r, Lanius excubitor. 1000r, Passer montanus. 2000r, Phoenicurus phoenicurus. 2500r, Emberiza schoeniclus. 3000r, Emberiza hortulana.

1997, Feb. 20 *Perf. 13x12½*
1598-1603 A301 Set of 6 13.50 4.50

Express mail service.

Fire Fighting Vehicles A302

Designs: 200r, English, 1731. 500r, Putnam, 1863. 900r, Merryweather, 1894. 1000r, Shand Mason Co., 1901. 1500r, Maxim Motor Co., Ford, 1949. 4000r, Merryweather, 1950.
5400r, Mack Truck Co., 1953.

1997, Mar. 11 *Perf. 12½x13*
1604-1609 A302 Set of 6 7.00 1.50

Souvenir Sheet

Perf. 13

1610 A302 5400r multicolored 4.75 1.10

No. 1610 contains one 40x32mm stamp.

Ducks A303

Designs: 200r, Polystieta stelleri. 500r, Alopochen aegyptiacus. 900r, Anas americana. 1000r, Anas falcata. 1500r, Melanitta perspicillata. 4000r, Anas discors.
5400r, Anas formosa, vert.

1997, Apr. 7 *Perf. 12½x13*
1611-1616 A303 Set of 6 5.00 1.50

Souvenir Sheet

Perf. 12½

1617 A303 5400r multicolored 3.75 1.10

No. 1617 contains one 32x40mm stamp.

Heinrich Von Stephan (1831-1897), Founder of UPU — A304

Denominations: 500r, 1500r, 2000r.

1997, Apr. 8 *Perf. 12½x13*
1618-1620 A304 Set of 3 3.50 1.00

Khmer Culture — A305

Various views of Bantea Srei Temple. Denominations: 500r, 1500r, 2000r.

1997, Apr. 13 *Perf. 13x12½*
1621-1623 A305 Set of 3 3.75 1.00

Cats — A306

Designs: 200r, Birman. 500r, Exotic short-hair. 900r, Persian. 1000r, Turkish. 1500r, American short-hair. 4000r, Scottish fold.
5400r, Sphinx.

1997, May 8 *Perf. 13x12½*
1624-1629 A306 Set of 6 9.00 1.75

Souvenir Sheet

Perf. 13

1630 A306 5400r multicolored 4.00 1.10

No. 1630 contains one 32x40mm stamp.

Trains A307

200r, 4-4-2T, #488. 500r, Frederick Smith 4-6-0. 900r, 0-8-0, #3131. 1000r, Transport #1, London #L44, 0-4-4. 1500r, 0-6-2, #1711. 4000r, 4-6-2, #60523.
5400r, North Yorkshire Moor (K1), 2-6-0, #2005.

1997, Jun 9 *Perf. 12½x12*
1631-1636 A307 Set of 6 5.50 1.50

Souvenir Sheet

Perf. 13

1637 A307 5400r multicolored 3.75 1.00

No. 1637 contains one 40x32mm stamp.

Dogs A308

Designs: 200r, Shar-pei. 500r, Tchin-tchin. 900r, Pekinese. 1000r, Chow-chow, vert. 1500r, Pug, vert. 4000r, Akita, vert.
5400r, Tufted Chinese, vert.

1997, July 4 *Perf. 12½x13, 13x12½*
1638-1643 A308 Set of 6 4.75 1.50

Souvenir Sheet

Perf. 12½

1644 A308 5400r multicolored 3.50 1.25

No. 1644 contains one 32x40mm stamp.

ASEAN, 30th Anniv. A309

Designs: 500r, Dunalom Wat. 1500r, Royal Palace. 2000r, Natl. Museum.

1997, Aug. 5 *Perf. 12½x13*
1645-1647 A309 Set of 3 4.00 1.00

Ships A310

Designs: 200r, Caravelle, 15th cent. 500r, Spanish galleon, 16th cent. 900r, Galleon "Great Harry," 16th cent. 1000r, Galleon "Le Couronne," 17th cent. 1500r, Cargo ship, 18th cent. 4000r, Clipper ship, 19th cent.
5400r, HMS Victory.

1997, Sept. 10 *Perf. 12½x12*
1648-1653 A310 Set of 6 5.50 1.50

Souvenir Sheet

Perf. 13

1654 A310 5400r multicolored 4.25 1.10

No. 1654 contains one 40x32mm stamp.

A311

Nos. 1655-1658, Various public gardens. Nos. 1659-1661, Various dams. No. 1657 is vert.

1997, Sept. 30 *Perf. 12½*

1655	A311	300r black & yel grn	.30	.25
1656	A311	300r black & red	.30	.25
1657	A311	800r black & citron	.65	.25
1658	A311	1500r black & org brn	1.25	.30
1659	A311	1700r blk & red brn	1.40	.35
1660	A311	2500r blk & grn bl	1.60	.50
1661	A311	3000r black & blue	2.00	.65
		Nos. 1655-1661 (7)	7.50	2.55

Mushrooms A312

Designs: 200r, Boletus satanas. 500r, Amanita regalis. 900r, Morchella semilibera. 1000r, Gomphus clavatus. 1500r, Hygrophorus hypothejus. 4000r, Albatrellus confluens.
5400r, Boletus chrysenteron.

1997, Oct. 5 *Perf. 12½x13*
1662-1667 A312 Set of 6 6.00 1.50

Souvenir Sheet

Perf. 12½

1668 A312 5400r multicolored 4.00 1.10

No. 1668 contains one 32x40mm stamp.

Fish
A313

200r, Betta imbellis. 500r, Colisa fasciata. 900r, Puntius conchonius. 1000r, Macropodus concolor. 1500r, Epalzeorhynchos frenatus. 4000r, Capoeta tetrazona.
5400r, Rasbora heteromorpha.

1997, Nov. 8 ***Perf. 12½x13***

1669-1674 A313 Set of 6 5.25 1.50

Souvenir Sheet

Perf. 13

1675 A313 5400r multicolored 3.50 1.00

No. 1675 contains one 40x32mm stamp.

Independence, 44th Anniv. — A314

Post Offices: 1000r, Kampot. 3000r, Prey Veng.

1997, Nov. 9 ***Perf. 13***

1676-1677 A314 Set of 2 3.25 1.00

Orchids — A315

200r, Orchis milicaris. 500r, Orchiaceras bivonae. 900r, Orchiaceras spuria. 1000r, Gymnadenia conopsea. 1500r, Serapias neglecta. 4000r, Pseudorhiza bruniana.
5400r, Dactylodenia wintonii.

1997, Dec. 12 ***Perf. 13***

1678-1683 A315 Set of 6 9.00 1.75

Souvenir Sheet

1684 A315 5400r multicolored 6.75 1.10

No. 1684 contains one 32x40mm stamp.

Princess Diana (1961-97)
A316

Designs: a, 100r, In dark blue jacket. b, 200r, In black dress. c, 300r, Holding hand to throat. d, 500r, Wearing face shield. e, 1000r, Watching mine clearing operation. f, 1500r, With Elizabeth Dole. g, 2000r, Holding land mine. h, 2500r, With members of Mother Teresa's Order.

1997, Dec. 30 ***Perf. 12x12½***

1685 A316 Sheet of 8, #a.-h. + label 7.00 1.75

Historic Sites Type of 1996-97

Temples: 300r, Prasat Suorprat. 500r, Preah Kumlung, horiz. 1200r, Prasat Bapuon, horiz. 1500r, Palilai. 1700r, Prasat Prerup, horiz. 2000r, Prasat Preah Khan, horiz. 3000r, Prasat Bayon.

1998 **Litho.** ***Perf. 12½***

1686 A288	300r black & orange	.25	.25
1687 A288	500r black & pink	.30	.25
1688 A288	1200r black & buff	.70	.25
1689 A288	1500r black & buff	.90	.30
1690 A288	1700r black & blue	1.00	.35
1691 A288	2000r black & green	1.25	.45
1692 A288	3000r black & violet	1.75	.65
	Nos. 1686-1692 (7)	6.15	2.50

New Year 1998 (Year of the Tiger)
A317

Various pictures of panthera tigris: 200r, vert., 500r, vert., 900r, vert., 1000r, 1500r, 4000r.
5400r, Tiger, vert.

1998 ***Perf. 13***

1693-1698 A317 Set of 6 5.00 1.50

Souvenir Sheet

Perf. 12½

1699 A317 5400r multicolored 4.25 1.00

No. 1699 contains one 32x40mm stamp.

1998 World Cup Soccer Championships, France — A318

Designs showing portion of soccer player at left, various plays at right, stadium: 200r, 500r, 900r, 1000r, 1500r, 4000r.
5400r, Two players kicking ball.

1998 ***Perf. 13***

1700-1705 A318 Set of 6 4.50 1.50

Souvenir Sheet

1706 A318 5400r multicolored 3.25 1.00

No. 1706 contains one 40x32mm stamp.

Domestic Cats
A319

Designs: 200r, Scottish fold. 500r, Ragdoll. 900r, Welsh. 1000r, Devon rex. 1500r, American curl. 4000r, Sphinx.
5400r, Japanese bobtail.

1998

1707-1712 A319 Set of 6 4.50 1.50

Souvenir Sheet

1713 A319 5400r multi 3.50 1.00

No. 1713 contains one 40x32mm stamp.

Italia '98, Intl. Philatelic Exhibition
A320

Paintings: 200r, Baptism of Christ from triptych, Jean de Trompes, by Gerard David. 500r, The Virgin of Martin van Niuwenhoven, by Hans Memling. 900r, Baptism of Christ, by Hendrich Goltzius. 1000r, Christ Carrying the Cross, by Luis de Morales. 1500r, Angel in the Desert, by Dirk Bouts. 4000r, The Virgin, by Petrus Christus.
5400r, The Immaculate Conception, by Bartolomé Esteban Murillo.

1998 **Litho.** ***Perf. 12½x13***

1714-1719 A320 Set of 6 5.50 1.50

Souvenir Sheet

Perf. 12½

1720 A320 5400r multicolored 4.00 1.00

No. 1720 contains one 40x32mm stamp.

Butterflies — A321

200r, Phyciodes tharos. 500r, Pararge mergera. 900r, Danaus plexippus. 1000r, Parnassius apollo. 1500r, Papilio machaon. 4000r, Eumenis semele.
5400r, Morpho rhetenor.

1998 ***Perf. 12½***

1721-1726 A321 Set of 6 5.50 1.50

Souvenir Sheet

1727 A321 5400r multicolored 5.00 1.00

No. 1727 contains one 40x32mm stamp.

Mail Boxes — A322

Designs: 1000r, 1997. 3000r, 1951.

1998 **Litho.** ***Perf. 13***

1728-1729 A322 Set of 2 2.75 1.00

Trains — A323

No. 1730a, 200r, Oakland, Antioch & Eastern. No. 1730b, 500r, New York, Westchester & Boston. No. 1731a, 900r, Spokane & Inland. No. 1731b, 1000r, International Railway. No. 1732a, 1500r, British columbia Electric Railway. No. 1732b, 4000r, Southern Pacific.
5400r, Storage battery locomotive.

1998, Mar. 2 **Litho.** ***Perf. 12½***

Pairs, #a.-b.

1730-1732 A323 Set of 3 5.75 1.50

Souvenir Sheet

1733 A323 5400r multicolored 4.00 1.25

Dogs — A324

200r, Rottweiler. 500r, Beauceron. 900r, Boxer. 1000r, Siberian husky. 1500r, Welsh corgi (Pembroke). 4000r, Basset hound.
5400r, Schnauzer.

1998, Mar. 30 **Litho.** ***Perf. 12¼***

1734-1739 A324 Set of 6 4.75 1.50

Souvenir Sheet

Perf. 12½

1740 A324 5400r multicolored 3.25 1.00

Insects
A325

200r, Lucanus cervus. 500r, Carabus auronitens. 900r, Rosalia alpina. 1000r, Geotrupes. 1500r, Megasoma elephas. 4000r, Chalcosoma.
5400r, Leptura rubra.

1998, Apr. 10 **Litho.** ***Perf. 12½***

1741-1746 A325 Set of 6 5.00 1.50

Souvenir Sheet

1747 A325 5400r multicolored 4.25 1.25

Khmer Culture
A326

Designs: 500r, Prasat Prerup. 1500r, Prasat Bayon. 2000r, Angkor Wat.

1998, Apr. 13 **Litho.** ***Perf. 12¾***

1748-1750 A326 Set of 3 3.75 1.10

Historic Ships
A327

200r, Cutter. 500r, Steamship "Britannia." 900r, Viking ship. 1000r, Steamship "Great Britain." 1500r, Coaster. 4000r, Frigate.
5400r, Tartan.

1998, May 7 **Litho.** ***Perf. 12¾***

1751-1756 A327 Set of 6 5.75 1.50

Souvenir Sheet

Perf. 13

1757 A327 5400r multicolored 3.50 1.00

No. 1757 contains one 40x32mm stamp.

Flowers — A328

200r, Petasites japonica. 500r, Gentiana triflora. 900r, Doronicum cordatum. 1000r, Scabiosa japonica. 1500r, Magnolia sieboldii. 4000r, Erythronium japonica.
5400r, Callistephus chinensis.

1998 **Litho.** ***Perf. 12¾***

1758-1763 A328 Set of 6 4.75 1.50

Souvenir Sheet

Perf. 13

1764 A328 5400r multicolored 3.25 1.00

No. 1764 contains one 32x40mm stamp.

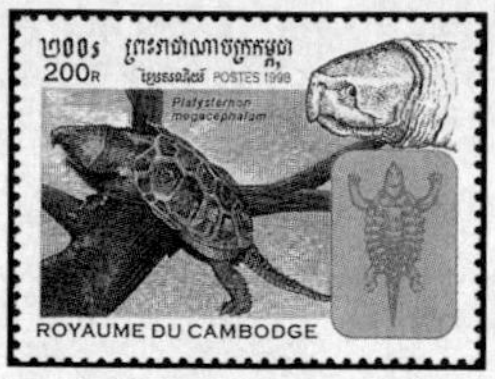

Turtles
A329

200r, Platysternon megacephalum. 500r, Chelonia mydas. 900r, Trionyx spiniferus. 1000r, Eretmochelys imbricata. 1500r, Megalochelys gigantea. 4000r, Dermochelys coriacea.
5400r, Chelus fimbriatus.

1998, Nov. 8 Litho. *Perf. 12¾*
1765-1770 A329 Set of 6 5.00 1.50

Souvenir Sheet
Perf. 13x13¼
1771 A329 5400r multi 4.75 1.00

No. 1771 contains one 40x32mm stamp.

Independence, 45th Anniv. — A330

Various dancers: 500r, 1500r, 2000r.

1998, Nov. 9 Litho. *Perf. 12½x12¼*
1772-1774 A330 Set of 3 2.75 1.00

Gemstones
A331

Designs: 200r, Aquamarine. 500r, Cat's eye. 900r, Malachite. 1000r, Emerald. 1500r, Turquoise. 4000r, Ruby.
5400r, Diamond, horiz.

1998, Dec. 28 Litho. *Perf. 12¾*
1775-1780 A331 Set of 6 4.75 1.50

Souvenir Sheet
Perf. 13
1781 A331 5400r multi 3.75 1.00

No. 1781 contains one 40x32mm stamp.

Wild Cats
A332

Designs: 200r, Acinonyx juabatus. 500r, Panthera uncia. 900r, Felis pardalis. 1000r, Panthera pardus. 1500r, Felis serval. 4000r, Panthera onca.
5400r, Panthera tigris.

1998 Litho. *Perf. 12½x12¼*
1782-1787 A332 Set of 6 5.00 1.50

Souvenir Sheet
Perf. 13
1788 A332 5400r multi 4.00 1.00

No. 1788 contains one 32x40mm stamp.

New Year 1999 (Year of the Rabbit)
A333

Various rabbits: 200r, 500r, 900r, 1000r, 1500r, 4000r. 4000r is vert.

1999, Jan. 5 Litho. *Perf. 12¾*
1790-1795 A333 Set of 6 6.75 1.50

Souvenir Sheet
Perf. 13
1796 A333 5400r Rabbit, diff. 5.00 1.00

No. 1796 contains one 40x32mm stamp.

Trains — A334

Designs: 200r, Stourbridge Lion. 500r, Atlantic. 900r, 035. 100r, Iron Duke. 1500r, 4-6-0. 4000r, 4-4-2.

Perf. 12½x12¼
1999, Nov. 20 Litho.
1797-1802 A334 Set of 6 5.75 1.50

Souvenir Sheet
Perf. 12½
1803 A334 5400r Firefly 3.75 1.00

No. 1803 contains one 40x32mm stamp.

Dogs
A335

Designs: 200r, Shiba inu, vert. 500r, Shih tzu. 900r, Tibetan spaniel. 1000r, Ainu, vert. 1500r, Lhasa apso. 4000r, Tibetan terrier.

Perf. 12¼x12½ (200, 1000r), 12¾
1999, Feb. 3 Litho.
1804-1809 A335 Set of 6 5.75 1.50

Souvenir Sheet
Perf. 12½
1810 A335 5400r Tosa inu, vert. 3.50 1.00

Size of Nos. 1804, 1807: 48x30mm. No. 1810 contains one 32x40mm stamp.

Antique Automobiles — A336

Designs: 200r, 1881 La Rapide. 500r, 1895 Duryea. 900r, 1898 Barbarou. 1000r, 1898 Panhard. 1500r, 1901 Mercedes-Benz. 4000r, 1915 Ford.
5400r, 1875 Siegfried Marcus.

1999, Mar. 5 Litho. *Perf. 13x12¾*
1811-1816 A336 Set of 6 4.75 1.50

Souvenir Sheet
Perf. 13
1817 A336 5400r multi 3.75 1.00

No. 1817 contains one 40x32mm stamp.

Cats — A337

Designs: 200r, Ragdoll. 500r, Russian blue. 900r, Bombay. 1000r, Snowshoe. 1500r, Oriental. 4000r, Somali.

1999, Mar. 30 Litho. *Perf. 13*
1818-1823 A337 Set of 6 5.75 1.50

Souvenir Sheet
1824 A337 5400r Egyptian mau 3.50 1.00

No. 1824 contains one 32x40mm stamp.

Butterflies
A338

Designs: 200r, Araschnia levana. 500r, Vanessa cardui, horiz. 900r, Clossiana euphrosyne. 1000r, Coenonympha hero. 1500r, Parnassius apollo, horiz. 4000r, Plebejus argus.
5400r, Palaeochrysophanus hippothoe.

1999, Apr. 25 *Perf. 12¾*
1825-1830 A338 Set of 6 6.75 1.50

Souvenir Sheet
Perf. 12½
1831 A338 5400r multi 4.75 1.00

No. 1831 contains one 32x40mm stamp.

Dinosaurs — A339

Designs: 200r, Saurornitholestes. 500r, Prenocephalus. 900r, Wuerhosaurus. 1000r, Muttaburrasaurus. 1500r, Shantungosaurus. 4000r, Microceratops.
5400r, Daspletosaurus.

1999, May 10 Litho. *Perf. 12¾*
1832-1837 A339 Set of 6 4.75 1.50

Souvenir Sheet
Perf. 13
1838 A339 5400r multi 3.25 1.00

No. 1838 contains one 40x32mm stamp.

Molluscs
A340

Designs: 200r, Flabellina affinis. 500r, Octopus macropus. 900r, Helix hortensis. 1000r, Lima hians. 1500r, Arion empiricorum. 4000r, Anodonta cygnaea.
5400r, Eledone aldrovandii.

1999, May 31 Litho. *Perf. 12¾*
1839-1844 A340 Set of 6 4.75 1.50

Souvenir Sheet
Perf. 12½
1845 A340 5400r multi 3.50 1.00

No. 1845 contains one 32x40mm stamp.

Historic Sites Type of 1996-97

Designs: 100r, Prasat Neak Poan, horiz. 300r, Statue, Prasat Neak Poan, horiz. 500r, Prasat Banteay Srey. 1400r, Prasat Banteay Samré, horiz. 1600r, Prasat Banteay Srey, horiz. 1800r, Bas-relief, Angkor Wat. 1900r, Prasat Takeo, horiz.

1999 Litho. *Perf. 12½*
Vignette Colors

1846	A288	100r blue	.30	.25
1847	A288	300r red	.30	.25
1848	A288	500r olive green	.40	.25
1849	A288	1400r bright green	1.00	.30
1850	A288	1600r pink	1.10	.30
1851	A288	1800r violet	1.25	.35
1852	A288	1900r brown	1.50	.45
		Nos. 1846-1852 (7)	5.85	2.15

Khmer Culture
A341

Designs: 500r, Dragon Bridge. 1500r, Temple with 100 columns, Kratie. 2000r, Krapum Chhouk stupa, Kratie.

1999, Apr. 13 *Perf. 13*
1853-1855 A341 Set of 3 3.00 .85

UPU, 125th Anniv.
A342

1999 Litho. *Perf. 12½x12¼*
1856 A342 1600r multi 1.50 .85

Independence — A343

People and: 500r, Map. 1500r, Ship, airplane, dove, public works. 2000r, Buildings.

1999, Nov. 9 *Perf. 12½*
1857-1859 A343 Set of 3 2.75 1.00

Snakes
A344

Designs: 200r, Aspidelaps lubricus. 500r, Epicrates cenchria. 900r, Eunectes notaeus. 1000r, Diadophus punctatus. 1500r, Micrurus fulvius. 4000r, Telescopus semiannulatus.
5400r, Chondropython viridis.

1999, Dec. 6 *Perf. 12¾*
1860-1865 A344 Set of 6 5.75 1.50

Souvenir Sheet
Perf. 13
1866 A344 5400r multi 3.25 1.00

No. 1866 contains one 39x31mm stamp.

Birds of Prey A345

Designs: 200r, Harpia harpyja. 500r, Terthopius ecaudatus, vert. 900r, Neophron pernopterus, vert. 1000r, Falco peregrinus, vert. 1500r, Buteo jamaicensis, vert. 4000r, Haliaetus leucocephalus.
5400r, Milvus milvus.

1999, Oct. 5 Litho. *Perf. 12¾*
1867-1872 A345 Set of 6 5.75 1.50

Souvenir Sheet
Perf. 12½
1873 A345 5400r multi 3.50 1.00
No. 1873 contains one 31x39mm stamp.

Philex France 99 — A346

Still life paintings by: 200r, Henri Fantin-Latour. 500r, Paul Cézanne. 900r, André Derain. 1000r, Henri Matisse. 1500r, Othon Friesz. 4000r, Matisse, diff.
5400r, Cézanne, diff.

1999, June 10 Litho. *Perf. 12½*
1874-1879 A346 Set of 6 7.50 1.50

Souvenir Sheet
Perf. 13
1880 A346 5400r multi 5.25 1.00

Souvenir Sheet

China 1999 World Philatleic Exhibition — A347

Pagodas: a, 200r, Tongzhou. b, 500r, Tianing Temple. c, 900r, Summer Palace. d, 900r, Temple of the Clouds. e, 1000r, Bei Hai. f, 1000r, Perfumed Hill. g, 1500r, Yunju. h, 4000r, Miaoying Temple.

Perf. 12¼x12½
1999, Aug. 12 Litho.
1881 A347 Sheet of 8, #a-h, + label 6.75 2.00

Orchids A348

Designs: 200r, Cymbidium insigne. 500r, Papillonanthe teres. 900r, Panisea uniflora. 1000r, Euanthe sanderiana. 1500r, Dendrobium trigonopus. 4000r, Vanda coerulea.
5400r, Paphiopedilum callosum.

1999, Aug. 5 Litho. *Perf. 12¾*
1889-1894 A348 Set of 6 5.75 1.50

Souvenir Sheet
Perf. 12½
1895 A348 5400r multi 5.00 1.25
No. 1895 contains one 32x40mm stamp.

Birds A349

Designs: 200r, Pyrrhula pyrrhula. 500r, Coccothraustes coccothraustes. 900r, Carduelis chloris. 1000r, Dendroica petechia. 1500r, Lanius excubitor. 4000r, Parus caeruleus.
5400r, Erithacus rubecula.

1999, Sept. 5 Litho. *Perf. 12¾*
1896-1901 A349 Set of 6 5.50 1.50

Souvenir Sheet
Perf. 13
1902 A349 5400r multi 5.00 1.25
No. 1902 contains one 40x32mm stamp.

Fish A350

Designs: 200r, Capoeta tetrazona. 500r, Epalzeorhynchus frenatus. 900r, Rasbora kalochroma. 1000r, Etroplus maculatus. 1500r, Betta imbellis. 4000r, Colisa sota.
5400r, Tetraodon biocellatus.

Perf. 12½x12¼
1999, Sept. 20 Litho.
1903-1908 A350 Set of 6 6.00 1.50

Souvenir Sheet
Perf. 13
1909 A350 5400r multi 4.50 1.00
No. 1909 contains one 40x32mm stamp.

Wildlife — A351

Designs: 200r, Ailuropada melanoleuca. 500r, Bos mutus. 900r, Hydropotes inermis. 1000r, Neomys fodiens, horiz. 1500r, Lutra lutra, horiz. 4000r, Panthera tigris, horiz.
5400r, Elaphurus davidianus, vert.

1999, Nov. 20 Litho. *Perf. 12¾*
1910-1915 A351 Set of 6 5.50 1.50

Souvenir Sheet
Perf. 12½
1916 A351 5400r multi 4.25 1.00
No. 1916 contains one 32x40mm stamp.

Bangkok 2000 Stamp Exhibition — A352

Turtle-shaped objects and turtles: 200r, Cuora amboinensis, vert. 500r, Cuora flavomarginata, vert. 900r, Geoemyda spengleri. 1000r, Manouria impressa. 1500r, Chinemys reevesi. 4000r, Heosemys spinosa.
4500r, Hieremys annandalei.

2000, Feb. 27 *Perf. 12¾*
1917-1922 A352 Set of 6 7.00 1.50

Souvenir Sheet
Perf. 13
1923 A352 4500r multi 5.00 1.00
No. 1923 contains one 40x32mm stamp.

Dinosaurs — A353

Designs: 200r, Iguanodon. 500r, Euoplocephalus. 900r, Dilophosaurus. 1000r, Diplodocus. 1500r, Stegoceras. 4000r, Stegosaurus.
4500r, Brachiosaurus, vert.

2000, Jan. 30 Litho. *Perf. 12½x12¼*
1924-1929 A353 Set of 6 4.50 1.50

Souvenir Sheet
Perf. 12½
1930 A353 4500r multi 3.00 1.00
No. 1930 contains one 32x40mm stamp.

Beetles A354

Designs: 200r, Calosoma sycophanta. 500r, Oryctes nasicornis. 900r, Diochrysa fastuosa. 1000r, Blaps gigas. 1500r, Cincindela campestris. 4000r, Cissistes cephalotes.
4500r, Scarabeus aegyptiorum.

2000, Feb. 5 Litho. *Perf. 12¾*
1931-1936 A354 Set of 6 6.00 1.50

Souvenir Sheet
Perf. 13
1937 A354 4500r multi 2.75 1.00
No. 1937 contains one 40x32mm stamp.

New Year 2000 (Year of the Dragon) — A355

Various dragons. Denominations: 200r, 500r, 900r, 1000r, 1500r, 4000r.

2000, Jan. 20 Litho. *Perf. 12¼x12½*
1938-1943 A355 Set of 6 7.00 1.50

Souvenir Sheet
Perf. 13
1944 A355 4500r multi 3.25 1.00
No. 1944 contains one 32x40mm stamp.

Bettas — A356

Designs: 200r, Unimaculata, Pugnax. 500r, Macrostoma, Taeniata. 900r, Foerschi, Imbellis. 1000r, Tessyae, Picta. 1500r, Edithae, Belica. 4000r, Smaragdina.
4500r, Splendens.

2000, Apr. 10 Litho. *Perf. 12½x12¼*
1945-1950 A356 Set of 6 5.00 1.50

Souvenir Sheet
Perf. 13
1951 A356 4500r multi 3.75 1.00
No. 1951 contains one 40x32mm stamp.

Mushrooms A357

Designs: 200r, Amanita muscaria. 500r, Amanita pantherina. 900r, Clitocybe oleana. 1000r, Lactarius scrobiculatus. 1500r, Scleroderma vulgare. 4000r, Amanita verna.
4500r, Amanita phalloides.

2000, Mar. 20 Litho. *Perf. 12¾*
1952-1957 A357 Set of 6 5.00 1.50

Souvenir Sheet
Perf. 13
1958 A357 4500r multi 3.00 1.00
No. 1958 contains one 32x40mm stamp.

Khmer Culture — A358

Designs: 500r, Srei Snam. 1500r, Srei Snam, diff. 2000r, Srei Krub Lakhna,

2000, Apr. 13 Litho. *Perf. 13*
1959-1961 A358 Set of 3 3.00 1.10

Growing Rice — A359

Designs: 100r, Transporting seedlings. 300r, Harrowing. 500r, Threshing. 1400r, Winnowing. 1600r, Transplanting. 1900r, Plowing. 2200r, Harvesting.

2000, Mar. 1 *Perf. 12¼x12½*
Vignette Color

1962	A359	100r	brt yel grn	.25	.25
1963	A359	300r	brt blue	.30	.25
1964	A359	500r	brt pink	.40	.25
1965	A359	1400r	brn orange	1.10	.25
1966	A359	1600r	dull blue	1.25	.30
1967	A359	1900r	bister brn	1.50	.35
1968	A359	2200r	red	1.75	.40
	Nos. 1962-1968 (7)			6.55	2.05

Locomotives — A360

Designs: 200r, Jules Petiet. 500r, Longue Chaudiere. 900r, Les Grand Chocolats. 1000r, Glehn du Bousquet. 1500r, Le Pendule Français. 4000r, TGV 001.
4500r, Le Shuttle.

2000, Mar. 5 Litho. *Perf. 12½x12¼*
1969-1974 A360 Set of 6 6.75 1.50

Souvenir Sheet
Perf. 13

1975 A360 4500r multi 3.25 1.00

WIPA 2000 Philatelic Exhibition, Vienna (No. 1975). No. 1975 contains one 80x32mm stamp.

Birds A361

Designs: 200r, Diomedea irrorata. 500r, Charadrius alexandrinus, vert. 900r, Sula nebouxii. 1000r, Sterna hirundo. 1500r, Larus argentatus, vert. 4000r, Chlidonia hybrida.
4500r, Sula bassana.

2000, May 8 *Perf. 12¾*
1976-1981 A361 Set of 6 5.00 1.50

Souvenir Sheet
Perf. 13

1982 A361 4500r multi 3.25 1.00

No. 1982 contains one 40x32mm stamp.

Orchids — A362

Designs: 200r, Cypripedium macranthum. 500r, Vandopsis gigantea. 900r, Calypso bulbosa. 1000r, Vanda luzonica. 1500r, Paphiopedilum villosum. 4000r, Vanda merrillii.
4500r, Paphiopedilum victoria.

2000, May 30 *Perf. 12¾*
1983-1988 A362 Set of 6 6.00 1.50

Souvenir Sheet
Perf. 13

1989 A362 4500r multi 4.00 1.00

No. 1989 contains one 32x40mm stamp.

Children's Stories — A363

Designs: 200r, The Courageous Little Tailor, vert. 500r, Tom Thumb, vert. 900r, Thumbelina, vert. 1000r, Pinocchio. 1500r, The Crayfish. 4000r, Peter Pan.
4500r, The Pied Piper, vert.

2000, Nov. 20 Litho. *Perf. 12¾*
1990-1995 A363 Set of 6 5.25 5.25

Souvenir Sheet
Perf. 12½

1996 A363 4500r multi 2.75 3.00

No. 1996 contains one 32x40mm stamp.

Water Festival and Tourism A364

Designs: 500r, Men rowing canoe. 1500r, Men at canoe prow. 2000r, Temples, elephant, woman.

2000, June 1 Litho. *Perf. 13*
1997-1999 A364 Set of 3 4.25 2.75

Fire Trucks A365

Designs: 200r, Metz DLK 23-6. 500r, Iveco-Magirus SLF24/100. 900r, Metz SLF 7000 WS. 1000r, Iveco-Magirus TLF 24/50. 1500r, Saval-Kronenburg RFF 11000. 4000r, Metz TLF 24/50.
4500r, Metz TLF 16/25.

2000, July 30 *Perf. 12¾*
2000-2005 A365 Set of 6 5.25 5.25

Souvenir Sheet
Perf. 13

2006 A365 4500r multi 3.50 3.50

No. 2006 contains one 40x32mm stamp.

Independence, 47th Anniv. — A366

Flag, temple and: 500r, Flowers. 1500r, Dove. 2000r, People carrying torch.

2000, Oct. 9 *Perf. 12¾*
2007-2009 A366 Set of 3 4.25 2.75

Antique Automobiles — A367

Designs: 200r, 1912 Rover 12C. 500r, 1907, Austin 30CV. 900r, 1909 Rolls-Royce Silver Ghost. 1000r, 1929 Graham Paige Phaeton DC. 1500r, 1937 Austin 12. 4000r, 1957 Mercedes-Benz 300SL.
4500r, 1936 MG.

2000, Sept. 30 *Perf. 12¾*
2010-2015 A367 Set of 6 5.00 2.50

Souvenir Sheet
Perf. 13

2016 A367 4500r multi 3.50 2.00

España 2000 Intl. Philatelic Exhibition (No. 2016). No. 2016 contains one 40x32mm stamp.

Dachshunds — A368

Designs: 200r, Smooth-haired dachshund. 500r, Wire-haired dachshund. 900r, Long-haired dachshund. 1000r, Two dachshunds. 1500r, Dachshund with pups. 4000r, Dachshunds resting.
4500r, Wire-haired dachshund, vert.

2000, Aug. 30 *Perf. 13*
2017-2022 A368 Set of 6 5.75 2.50

Souvenir Sheet
Perf. 12½

2023 A368 4500r multi 2.75 2.00

No. 2023 contains one 32x40mm stamp.

Cats and Art A369

Cat or cats and: 200r, Korean silk painting, 18th cent. 500r, Portuguese tile, 18th cent. 900r, Japanese ceramic cat. 1000r, Egyptian metallic cat. 1500r, Scandinavian engraving. 4000r, Japanese painting.
4500r, Cat on hind legs.

2000, Oct. 5 *Perf. 12½x12¼*
2024-2029 A369 Set of 6 5.75 2.50

Souvenir Sheet
Perf. 13x13¼

2030 A369 4500r multi 3.00 1.50

No. 2030 contains one 40x32mm stamp.

Birds A370

Designs: 200r, Creatophora cinerea. 500r, Sturnus vulgaris. 900r, Leiothrix lutea. 1000r, Rupicola rupicola. 1500r, Prunella collaris. 4000r, Panurus biarnicus.
4500r, Muscicapula pallipes, vert.

2000, Dec. 10 *Perf. 13*
2031-2036 A370 Set of 6 6.00 3.50

Souvenir Sheet

2037 A370 4500r multi 3.75 2.00

No. 2037 contains one 32x40mm stamp.

Sports — A371

Designs: 200r, Weight lifting. 500r, Rhythmic gymnastics. 900r, Baseball. 1000r, Women's tennis. 1500r, Basketball. 4000r, Women's high jump.

Perf. 12¾, 12½ (#2044)
2000, June 30 Litho.
2038-2043 A371 Set of 6 5.75 2.75

Souvenir Sheet

2044 A371 4500r Runners 2.75 1.75

No. 2044 contains one 32x40mm stamp.

New Year 2001 (Year of the Snake) — A372

Various stylized snakes with background colors of: 200r, Beige. 500r, Dull bister. 900r, Light blue. 1000r, Greenish blue. 1500r, Dull green. 4000r, Blue.
5400r, Blue, horiz.

2001, Jan. 15 Litho. *Perf. 12¼x12½*
2045-2050 A372 Set of 6 6.00 3.50

Souvenir Sheet
Perf. 13x13¼

2051 A372 5400r multi 4.50 2.75

No. 2051 contains one 40x32mm stamp.

Millennium — A373

Designs: 200r, Johannes Gutenberg, printers. 500r, Michael Faraday, electric motor. 900r, Samuel F. B. Morse, telegraph. 1000r, Alexander Graham Bell, telephone. 1500r, Enrico Fermi, nuclear energy. 4000r, Edward Roberts, computer.
No. 2058: a, Christopher Columbus, ships. b, Neil Armstrong, lunar module.

2001, Jan. 5 Litho. *Perf. 12¾*
2052-2057 A373 Set of 6 7.00 4.00

Souvenir Sheet
Perf. 12½

2058 A373 5400r Sheet of 2, #a-b + label 8.00 8.00

No. 2058 contains two 40x32mm stamps.

Fire and Rescue Equipment A374

Designs: 200r, 1910 Sandou ladder wagon. 500r, 1899 Gallo cart. 900r, Merryweather pumper, 1950s. 1000r, 1940 Merryweather ambulance. 1500r, 1972 Man-Metz pumper. 4000r, Roman Diesel pumper, 1970s.
5400r, 1898 Metropolitan steam pumper.

2001, Feb. 5 *Perf. 12¾*
2059-2064 A374 Set of 6 7.00 4.00

Souvenir Sheet
Perf. 13x13¼

2065 A374 5400r multi 4.00 4.00

No. 2065 contains one 40x32mm stamp.

Mushrooms — A375

Designs: 200r, Lycoperdon perlatum. 500r, Trametes versicolor. 900r, Hipholoma sublateritium. 1000r, Amanita muscaria. 1500r, Lycoperdon umbrinum. 4000r, Cortinarius orellanus.
5400r Amanita phalloides, vert.

2001, Feb. 25 *Perf. 12¾*

2066-2071 A375 Set of 6 7.00 4.00

Souvenir Sheet

Perf. 12½

2072 A375 5400r multi 4.00 4.00

No. 2072 contains one 32x40mm stamp.

Belgica 2001 Intl. Stamp Exhibition, Brussels — A376

Butterflies: 200r, Nymphalis polychloros. 500r, Cethosia hypsea. 900r, Papilio palinurus. 1000r, Apatura ilia. 1500r, Parthenos sylvia. 4000r, Morpho grandensis.
5400r, Heliconius melpomene.

2001, Apr. 5 *Perf. 12¾*

2073-2078 A376 Set of 6 7.00 4.00

Souvenir Sheet

Perf. 13x13¼

2079 A376 5400r multi 4.00 2.50

Film Personalities A377

Designs: 200r, Gary Cooper. 500r, Marlene Dietrich. 900r, Walt Disney. 1000r, Clark Gable. 1500r, Jeanette MacDonald. 4000r, Melvyn Douglas.
No. 2086: a, Rudolph Valentino. b, Marilyn Monroe.

2001, Apr. 25 **Litho.** *Perf. 12¾*

2080	A377	200r multi	.25	.25
2081	A377	500r multi	.50	.30
2082	A377	900r multi	.70	.40
2083	A377	1000r multi	.90	.50
2084	A377	1500r multi	1.25	.75
2085	A377	4000r multi	3.25	1.75
		Nos. 2080-2085 (6)	6.85	3.95

Souvenir Sheet

Perf. 13

2086 A377 5400r Sheet of 2, #a-b 9.00 6.00

Natl. Culture Day A378

Sculptures: 500r, Angkor. 1500r, Bayon. 2000r, Bayon, diff.

2001, Apr. 3 **Litho.** *Perf. 12¾*

2087-2089 A378 Set of 3 3.50 2.00

Temples — A379

Designs: 200r, Preah Vihear. 300r, Thonmanom. 600r, Tasom. 1000r, Kravan. 1500r, Takeo. 1700r, Mebon. 2200r, Banteay Kdei.

2001, Mar. 15 *Perf. 12¼x12½*

2090-2096 A379 Set of 7 6.00 3.50

Automobiles — A380

Designs: 200r, 1972 TVR Series M. 500r, 1958 Ferrari 410. 900r, 1995 Peugeot 405. 1000r, 1953 Fiat 8VZ. 1500r, 1997 Citroen Xsara. 4000r, 1997 Renault Espace.
5400r, 1963 Ferrari 250 GT SWB.

2001, June 5 **Litho.** *Perf. 12¾*

2097-2102 A380 Set of 6 7.00 4.00

Souvenir Sheet

Perf. 13x13¼

2103 A380 5400r multi 3.50 2.50

No. 2103 contains one 40x32mm stamp.

Tourism A381

Designs: 600r, Sourire de Bayon. 1500r, Bayon. 2000r, Bayon, diff.

2001, June 5 *Perf. 12¾*

2104-2106 A381 Set of 3 3.25 2.50

Philanippon '01 — A382

Locomotives: 200r, 4-6-0. 500r, 4-6-4. 900r, 4-4-0. 1000r, 4-6-4, diff. 1500r, 4-6-2. 4000r, 4-8-2.
5400r, Undescribed locomotive.

2001, July 5 *Perf. 12½x12¼*

2107-2112 A382 Set of 6 7.50 6.00

Souvenir Sheet

Perf. 13x13¼

2113 A382 5400r multi 5.50 4.50

No. 2113 contains one 40x32mm stamp.

Penguins A383

Designs: 200r, Aptenodytes forsteri. 500r, Spheniscus demersus. 900r, Spheniscus humboldti. 1000r, Eudypes cristatus. 1500r, Aptenodytes patagonica. 4000r, Pygoscelis antarctica.
5400r, Pygoscelis papua.

2001, Aug. 5 *Perf. 12¾*

2114-2119 A383 Set of 6 8.25 5.50

Souvenir Sheet

Perf. 13x13¼

2120 A383 5400r multi 6.00 5.00

No. 2120 contains one 40x32mm stamp.

Cats A384

Designs: 200r, Singapura. 500r, Cymric. 900r, Exotic shorthair. 1000r, Ragdoll. 1500r, Manx. 4000r, Somali.
5400r, Egyptian Mau.

2001, Aug. 25 *Perf. 12½x12¼*

2121-2126 A384 Set of 6 8.25 6.00

Souvenir Sheet

Perf. 13x13¼

2127 A384 5400r multi 5.75 4.75

No. 2127 contains one 40x32mm stamp.

Kites A385

Designs: 300r, Khleng Chak. 500r, Khleng Kanton. 1000r, Khleng Phnong. 1500r, Khleng Kaun Morn. 3000r, Khleng Me Ambao.

2001, Sept. 7 *Perf. 12¾*

2128-2132 A385 Set of 5 6.50 5.50

Cacti — A386

Designs: 200r, Parodia cintiensis. 500r, Astrophytum astenas. 900r, Parodia faustiana. 1000r, Coryphantha sulcolanata. 1500r, Neochilenia hankena. 4000r, Mammilaria boolii.
5400r, Mammilaria swinglei.

2001, Sept. 15 *Perf. 12¾*

2133-2138 A386 Set of 6 8.25 6.00

Souvenir Sheet

Perf. 12½

2139 A386 5400r multi 6.25 5.00

No. 2139 contains one 32x40mm stamp.

Khmer Culture A387

Designs: 500r, Fish Dance. 1500r, Red Fish Ballet. 2000r, Apsara Ballet.

2001, Oct. 9 *Perf. 12¾*

2140-2142 A387 Set of 3 4.25 3.50

Wolves and Foxes A388

Designs: 200r, Canis lupus occidentalis. 500r, Canis lupus tundrorum, vert. 900r, Vulpes fulvas. 1000r, Canis latrans. 1500r, Vulpes zerda, vert. 4000r, Alopex lagopus.
5400r, Canis lupus signatus, vert.

2001, Oct. 15 *Perf. 12¾*

2143-2148 A388 Set of 6 8.25 6.00

Souvenir Sheet

Perf. 12½

2149 A388 5400r multi 3.50 3.00

No. 2103 contains one 32x40mm stamp.

Human Evolution — A389

Designs: 100r, Australopithecus anamensis. 200r, Australopithecus afarensis. 300r, Australopithecus africanus. No. 2153, 500r, Australopithecus rudolfensis. No. 2154, 500r, Australopithecus boisei. 1000r, Homo habilis. 1500r, Homo erectus. 4000r, Homo sapiens neanderthalensis.
5400r, Homo sapiens sapiens.

2001, Oct. 25 *Perf. 13*

2150-2157 A389 Set of 8 9.50 6.00

Souvenir Sheet

2158 A389 5400r multi 6.50 5.00

No. 2158 contains one 40x32mm stamp.

King Norodom Sihanouk, 80th Birthday (in 2002) A389a

Various photos: 100r, 200r, 300r, 400r, 500r, 600r, 700r, 800r, 900r, 1000r, 1500r, 2000r, 3000r.

2001, Oct. 31 **Litho.** *Perf. 13*

2158A-2158M A389a Set of 13 *15.00 15.00*

Chess A390

Designs: 200r, Rook. 500r, Pawn. 900r, King. 1000r, Bishop. 1500r, Queen. 4000r, Knight.
5400r, Pieces of Oriental chess-like game.

2001, Dec. 25 *Perf. 12¾*

2159-2164 A390 Set of 6 6.00 6.00

Souvenir Sheet

Perf. 13

2165 A390 5400r multi 5.00 4.00

No. 2165 contains one 40x32mm stamp.

Italian Soccer A391

Designs: 200r, 1934 World Cup championship team. 500r, 1938 World Cup championship team. 900r, 1968 European Cup championship team. 1000r, 1982 World Cup championship team. 1500r, 2002 World Cup team. 4000r, Italian soccer federation emblem.

2001 *Perf. 12¾*

2166-2171 A391 Set of 6 7.00 7.00

ASEAN Post, 10th Anniv A392

Temples: 500r, Prasat Preah Vihear. 1000r, Prasat Preah Ko. 1500r, Prasat Banteay Srei. 2500r, Prasat Bayon. 3500r, Prasat Angkor Wat.

2002, July 9 *Perf. 13*

2172-2176 A392 Set of 5 11.00 10.00

Sugar Palm — A393

Designs: 300r, Tree. 500r, Female flower. 700r, Male flower. 1500r, Fruit.

2003, June 20 **Litho.**

2177-2180 A393 Set of 4 7.50 7.00

Japanese Grant Aid — A394

Designs: 100r, Drawing of Bridge No. 26, Highway 6A. 200r, Bridge No. 26, Highway 6A. 400r, Chroy Changvar Bridge. 800r, Kizuna Bridge. 3500r, Monument, vert.

2003, Apr. 25

2181-2185 A394 Set of 5 7.50 6.00

Cambodian Red Cross — A395

Designs: 100r, Ox cart. 200r, Woman carrying rice bag, vert. 300r, Queen with Red Cross volunteers. 400r, Queen and women. 500r, Queen and elderly people. 700r, Queen and women, diff. 800r, Queen and Prime Minister's wife giving items to people. 1000r, Like 800r, diff. 1900r, Like 800r, diff., vert. 2100r, Like 800r, diff., vert. 4000r, Queen and Prime Minister's wife with baby.

2003, May 8

2186-2196 A395 Set of 11 12.00 12.00

Cambodia/People's Republic of China Diplomatic Relations, 50th Anniv. — A396

No. 2197: a, Angkor Wat. b, Great Wall of China.

2003, July 19 *Perf. 12¼x12*

2197 A396 2000r Horiz. pair, #a-b 5.00 4.00

Association of South East Asian Nations, 36th Anniv. — A397

Designs: 400r, Conference emblem. 500r, Apsara dancer. 600r, Apsara dancer, diff. 1600r, Apsara dancers. 1900r, Temonorom dancers.

2003, Aug. 8 *Perf. 13*

2198-2202 A397 Set of 5 8.00 6.50

King Norodom Sihanouk — A398

Designs: 200r, Pointing at map. 400r, Meeting rural Cambodians, vert. 500r, Sitting in forest, vert. 800r, Pointing in forest, vert. 1000r, Saluting, vert. 2000r, Saluting, with flag and Independence Monument, vert. 5000r, With handicapped people.

2003, Nov. 9

2203-2209 A398 Set of 7 10.00 7.00

Khmer Culture A399

Sculptures: 100r, Bayon. 200r, Banteay Srei. 400r, Banteay Srei, diff. 800r, Bayon, vert. 3500r, Banteay Srei, vert.

2000r, Unattributed sculpture, vert.

2004, Apr. 3

2210-2214 A399 Set of 5 5.00 4.00

Souvenir Sheet

2215 A399 2000r multi 3.25 2.00

Rural Areas A400

Designs: 600r, Mill. 900r, House, field and cattle. 2000r, House and trees.

2000r, Ox cart and driver.

2004, Apr. 13

2216-2218 A400 Set of 3 6.00 4.00

Souvenir Sheet

2219 A400 2000r multi 3.00 2.25

Tepmonorum Dancers — A401

Dancers with: 400r, Yellow costumes. 1000r, Blue costumes. 2100r, Blue and yellow costumes.

2100r, Blue and yellow costumes, diff.

2004, May 5

2220-2222 A401 Set of 3 5.00 4.00

Souvenir Sheet

2223 A401 2000r multi 3.00 2.50

Flowers — A402

Designs: 600r, Cassia fistula. 700r, Butea monosperma. 900r, Couroupita quianensis. 1000r, Delonix regia, horiz. 1800r, Lagerstroemia floribunda.

2000r, Lagerstroemia floribunda, horiz.

2004, Aug. 25 **Litho.** *Perf. 13*

2224-2228 A402 Set of 5 5.50 4.00

Souvenir Sheet

2229 A402 2000r multi 3.25 1.75

Tourism — A403

Designs: 200r, Prasat Preah Khan. 500r, Prasat Preup. 600r, PrasatBanteay Samre. 1600r, Prasat Bayon. 1900r, Angkor Wat.

2000r, Prasat Bayon, vert.

2004, Sept. 27 **Litho.** *Perf. 13*

2230-2234 A403 Set of 5 5.00 3.50

Souvenir Sheet

2235 A403 2000r multi 3.25 2.00

Coronation of King Norodom Shiamoni A404

Various photos: 100r, 400r, 500r, 600r, 700r, 900r, 2100r, 2200r, 4000r. 700r-4000r are horiz.

2004, Oct. 29

2236-2244 A404 Set of 9 8.00 8.00

Ancient Fishing Tools A405

Various scoops and baskets: 100r, 200r, 800r, 1700r, 2200r. 1700r and 2200r are vert.

2000r, Child with basket, vert.

2004, Dec. 5

2245-2249 A405 Set of 5 5.50 4.00

Souvenir Sheet

2250 A405 2000r multi 4.25 2.50

Cambodian Red Cross, 50th Anniv. — A406

Designs: 400r, Emblem. 700r, Volunteers, horiz. 800r, Volunteers, diff., horiz. 1900r, Volunteers, diff., horiz. 2100r, Volunteers, diff. horiz. 2200r, Royalty on dais, horiz.

2005, Feb. 18

2251-2256 A406 Set of 6 7.25 7.25

Apsaras Dance — A407

Dancer with background color of: 800r, Pink. 900r, Light blue. 1400r, Green. 1600r, Rose. 2000r, Blue.

4000r, Brown.

2005, Apr. 12

2257-2261 A407 Set of 5 6.50 5.00

Souvenir Sheet

2262 A407 4000r multi 4.25 3.00

Khmer Culture A408

Designs: 500r, Banteay Kdei. 700r, Elephant Terrace. 1000r, Thommanon. 2000r, Ta Prohm. 2500r, Angkor Wat.

4000r, Ta Reach, vert.

2005, May 16

2263-2267 A408 Set of 5 6.25 5.00

Souvenir Sheet

2268 A408 4000r multi 4.25 3.00

Flowers — A409

Nymphaea lotus in: 100r, Purple. 500r, White. 1200r, Blue. 2000r, Yellow. 2500r, Red.

4000r, Red flowers in canoe, horiz.

2005, July 25 **Litho.** *Perf. 13*

2269-2273 A409 Set of 5 6.00 4.50

Souvenir Sheet

2274 A409 4000r multi 4.25 3.00

Fish A410

Designs: 700r, Pangasionodon gigas. 800r, Catlocarpio siamensis. 1000r, Mekongina erythrospila. 1900r, Probarbus labeaminor, vert. 2200r, Wallago leeri, vert.
4000r, Scleropages formosus.

2005, Sept. 5 *Perf. 13*
2275-2279 A410 Set of 5 6.25 5.50

Souvenir Sheet

2280 A410 4000r multi 4.25 3.75

Coronation of King Norodom Sihamoni, 1st Anniv. — A411

Frame colors: 500r, Green. 1500r, Blue. 2200r, Red.

2005, Oct. 29 **Litho.** *Perf. 13*
2281-2283 A411 Set of 3 3.25 3.25

Miniature Sheet

Birds — A412

No. 2284: a, 200r, Great egret. b, 400r, Great-billed heron. c, 1000r, Painted stork. d, 1200r, Spot-billed pelican. e, 1800r, Sarus crane, horiz. f, 3500r, Greater adjutant, horiz.

2005, Dec. 5
2284 A412 Sheet of 6, #a-f 8.00 8.00

Khmer Culture A413

Women at work: 100r, Scooping dyes. 800r, Washing clothes. 1500r, Weaving. 2200r, Spinning thread. 3500r, Weaving, diff.
5400r, Weaving, diff.

2006, Jan. 26
2285-2289 A413 Set of 5 6.75 6.00

Souvenir Sheet

2290 A413 5400r multi 4.00 3.00

Marine Mammals — A414

Designs: 500r, Sousa chinensis. 900r, Neophocaena phocaenoides. 1400r, Dolphinus capensis tropicalis. 2100r, Stenella longirostris roseinventris. 3500r, Tursiops aduncus.
5400r, Neophocaena phocaenoides and boat.

2006, Mar. 9
2291-2295 A414 Set of 5 7.50 6.50

Souvenir Sheet

2296 A414 5400r multi 4.00 3.00

Reamker Legend — A415

Designs: 1000r, Jup Leak and Ream Leak. 1400r, Preah Ream, vert. 1600r, Neang Seda, vert. 1900r, Krong Reap, vert. 2100r, Hanuman, vert.
5400r, Two characters in water.

2006, Apr. 13
2297-2301 A415 Set of 5 6.50 5.50

Souvenir Sheet

2302 A415 5400r multi 4.25 3.25

Elephants — A416

Designs: 400r, Adult and juvenile elephant. 700r, Elephants in water. 1600r, Elephant, vert. 2200r, Elephant facing right. 3500r, Elephant facing left.
5400r, Elephants in water, diff.

2006, June 15 **Litho.** *Perf. 13*
2303-2307 A416 Set of 5 7.00 5.50

Souvenir Sheet

2308 A416 5400r multi 4.25 3.50

Dances — A417

Designs: 600r, Chhai Yaim dance. 1900r, Sacrifice of Buffalo dance. 2200r, Mouth Organ dance. 3500r, Rice Harvest dance.

2006, Aug. 17
2309-2312 A417 Set of 4 6.50 5.50

Birds A418

Designs: 600r, Threskionis melanocephalus. 800r, Plegadis facinellus. 1500r, Houbaropsis bengalensis. 2100r, Pseudibis gigantea. 3500r, Pseudibis davisoni.
5400r, Pseudibis gigantea, vert.

2006, Nov. 8 **Litho.** *Perf. 13*
2313-2317 A418 Set of 5 7.50 6.00

Souvenir Sheet

2318 A418 5400r multi 7.00 5.50

Condom Use Program — A419

Designs: 300r, Man, woman, program emblem. 500r, Man, motorcycle, program emblem. 2200r, Men on boat, flag with program emblem.

2006, Dec. 1 **Litho.** *Perf. 13*
2319-2321 A419 Set of 3 2.25 2.25

World AIDS Day.

Cambodian Red Cross HIV/AIDS Campaign — A420

Campaign leader Bun Rany, wife of Prime Minister Hun Sen and captions: 1500r, Caring. 1900r, Stop discrimination, vert. 2000r, Give hope to families. 2100r, National and Asia-Pacific Leadership Forum Champion. 2200r, National and Asia-Pacific Leadership Forum Champion, diff.

2007 **Litho.** *Perf. 13*
2322-2326 A420 Set of 5 6.50 6.50

Sculpture A421

Flags of Viet Nam and Cambodia A422

2007, June 24

2327	A421	500r shown		.45	.45
2328	A421	800r Sculpture, diff.		.65	.65
2329	A421	1000r Sculpture, diff.		.75	.75
2330	A421	1500r Sculpture, diff.		1.25	1.25
2331	A422	1900r shown		1.50	1.50
		Nos. 2327-2331 (5)		4.60	4.60

Diplomatic relations between Cambodia and Viet Nam, 40th anniv.

Handicap International, 25th Anniv. — A423

Denominations: 1000r, 1500r.

2007, July 25
2332-2333 A423 Set of 2 2.00 2.00

Dancers — A424

Architecture — A425

Various dancers with denominations of: 800r, 900r, 1400r, 1600r, 2000r.

No. 2339: a, Secretariat Building, Bandar Seri Begawan, Brunei. b, National Museum of Cambodia. c, Fatahillah Museum, Jakarta, Indonesia. d, Typical house, Laos. e, Malayan Railway Headquarters Building, Kuala Lumpur, Malaysia. f, Yangon Post Office, Myanmar (Burma). g, Malacañang Palace, Philippines. h, National Museum of Singapore. i, Vimanmek Mansion, Bangkok, Thailand. j, Presidential Palace, Hanoi, Viet Nam.

2007, Aug. 8
2334-2338 A424 Set of 5 5.00 5.00
2339 A425 1000r Sheet of 10, #a-j 10.00 10.00

Association of South East Asian Nations (ASEAN), 40th anniv. See Brunei No. 607, Burma No. 370, Indonesia Nos. 2120-2121, Laos Nos. 1717-1718, Malaysia No. 1170, Philippines Nos. 3103-3105, Singapore No. 1265, Thailand No. 2315, and Viet Nam Nos. 3302-3311.

Friendship Between Cambodia and People's Republic of China, 50th Anniv. — A427

No. 2346: a, Tian An Men Rostrum, flag of People's Republic of China. b, Royal Palace, flag of Cambodia.

2008, July 25 **Litho.** *Perf. 12*
2346 A427 2000r Horiz. pair, #a-b 2.00 2.00

A430

Pottery Making — A431

Various women making pottery: 100r, 700r, 1900r, 2000r, 2200r.
6000r, Oxcart with pottery.

2008, Dec. 5 Litho. *Perf. 13*
2359-2363 A430 Set of 5 3.50 3.50

Souvenir Sheet
Perf. 13¾x13½

2364 A431 6000r multi 3.00 3.00

Ancient Agricultural Tools — A434

Designs: 300r, Plow. 1200r, Harrow. 1700r, Spiked roller. 1800r, Water wheel. 2800r, Cart.
6000r, Farmer operating water wheel, vert.

2010, Mar. 30 Litho. *Perf. 13*
2377-2381 A434 Set of 5 3.75 3.75

Souvenir Sheet
Perf. 13¾x13½

2382 A434 6000r multi 3.00 3.00

Environmental Protection A435

Designs: 200r, Filled trash can, face on Earth. 800r, Watering can pouring water on Earth, cars in flood. 1400r, Tree inside split Earth. 1700r, Buildings in hourglass. 3000r, Tree in hands.
6000r, Cars in flood, palm trees.

2010, May 25 Litho. *Perf. 13*
2383-2387 A435 Set of 5 3.50 3.50

Souvenir Sheet
Perf. 13¾x13½

2388 A435 6000r multi 3.00 3.00

Diplomatic Relations Between Cambodia and the United States, 60th Anniv. — A436

2010, July 11 Litho. *Perf. 13*
2389 A436 2800r multi 1.40 1.40

Campaign Against AIDS — A437

Red AIDS ribbon and: 1000r, Wrapped and unwrapped condoms, condom with face. 1500r, Man, woman and child. 2800r, Men and woman at night club. 4000r, Two birds.

2011, June 29 Litho. *Perf. 13*
2390-2393 A437 Set of 4 4.75 4.75

First day cancels show a June 5 date, but the stamps were not sold until June 29.

Fish A438

Designs: 500r, Barbonymus schwanenfeldii. 1500r, Hypsibarbus lagleri. 2800r, Puntioplites falcifer. 3000r, Osteochilus melanopleurus. 3500r, Hampala macrolepidota.
6000r, Fish, fishermen and nets.

2011, Aug. 8 Litho. *Perf. 13*
2394-2398 A438 Set of 5 5.75 5.75

Souvenir Sheet
Perf. 13½x13¾

2399 A438 6000r multi 3.00 3.00

SEMI-POSTAL STAMPS

Nos. 8, 12, 14 and 15 Surcharged in Black

1952, Oct. 20 Unwmk. *Perf. 13*
B1 A3 1.10pi + 40c 4.25 *8.00*
B2 A3 1.90pi + 60c 4.25 *8.00*
B3 A3 3pi + 1pi 4.25 *8.00*
B4 A1 5pi + 2pi 4.25 *8.00*
Nos. B1-B4 (4) 17.00 *32.00*

For students assistance.

Preah Stupa — SP1

1957, Mar. 15 Engr. *Perf. 13*
B5 SP1 1.50r + 50c ind, ol & red 2.00 2.00
B6 SP1 6.50r + 1.50r red lil, ol & red 3.00 3.00
B7 SP1 8r + 2r bl, ol & red 5.00 5.00
Nos. B5-B7 (3) 10.00 10.00

Birth of Buddha, 1500th anniv. See #62-64.

Regular Issue, 1959, with Red Typographed Surcharge

1959, Dec. 9
B8 A14 20c + 20c rose vio .50 .50
B9 A14 50c + 30c blue .80 .80
B10 A14 80c + 50c rose car 1.75 1.75
Nos. B8-B10 (3) 3.05 3.05

The surtax was for the Red Cross.

Nos. 107-108 Surcharged and Overprinted in Red

1963, Oct. 1 Unwmk. *Perf. 13*
B11 A26 4r + 40c grn & dk brn 1.00 1.00
B12 A26 6r + 60c vio & ol bis 1.50 1.50

Centenary of International Red Cross.

Nos. 263, 267, 293-294, 134 Surcharged in Red

1972, Nov. 15 Engr. *Perf. 13*
B13 A72 3r + 2r multi .40 .40
B14 A72 10r + 6r multi .80 .80
B15 A80 12r + 7r multi .90 .90
B16 A34 12r + 7r multi .90 .90
B17 A80 15r + 8r multi 1.60 1.60
Nos. B13-B17 (5) 4.60 4.60

Surtax was for war victims. Surcharge arranged differently on Nos. B15-B17.

AIR POST STAMPS

Kinnari — AP1

Unwmk.

1953, Apr. 16 Engr. *Perf. 13*
C1 AP1 50c deep green 2.00 1.00
a. Souv. sheet of 4, #C1, C3, C5, C9 80.00 80.00
C2 AP1 3pi red brown 2.00 1.25
a. Souv. sheet of 3, #C2, C4, C8 80.00 80.00
C3 AP1 3.30pi rose violet 3.00 2.00
C4 AP1 4pi dk brn & dp bl 2.00 2.00
C5 AP1 5.10pi brn, red & org 3.75 3.00
C6 AP1 6.50pi dk brn & lil rose 3.75 3.25
a. Souv. sheet of 2, #C6-C7 80.00 80.00
C7 AP1 9pi lil rose & dp grn 4.50 5.00
C8 AP1 11.50pi multi 9.00 7.00
C9 AP1 30pi dk brn, bl grn & org 17.50 12.00
Nos. C1-C9 (9) 47.50 36.50

No. C1a sold for 50pi, No. C2a for 25pi, No. C6a for 20pi.
Souvenir sheets with completely white gum, no toning and no gum bends sell for a premium.

AP2

1957, Dec. 11
C10 AP2 50c maroon .40 .25
C11 AP2 1r emerald .70 .25
C12 AP2 4r ultra 2.25 .75
C13 AP2 50r carmine rose 8.75 4.00
C14 AP2 100r grn, bl & car 16.00 6.00
a. Souv. sheet of 5, #C10-C14 32.50 32.50
Nos. C10-C14 (5) 28.10 11.25

No. C14a sold for 160r.
See note after No. C9.

Independence Type of 1961

1961, Nov. 9 *Perf. 13x12½*
C15 A24 7r multicolored .90 .80
C16 A24 30r grn, car & ultra 3.00 2.25
C17 A24 50r ind, grn & ol 4.50 3.00
a. Souv. sheet of 3, #C15-C17 9.00 9.00
Nos. C15-C17 (3) 7.55 7.55

No. C15 Srchd. in Red and Ovptd. in Black

1962, Nov. 9
C18 A24 12r on 7r multi 2.25 1.25

Dedication of Independence Monument.

Hanuman, Monkey God — AP3

1964, Sept. 1 Engr. *Perf. 13*
C19 AP3 5r multicolored 1.10 .55
C20 AP3 10r ol bis, lil rose & grn 1.60 .65
C21 AP3 20r vio, bl & ol bis 2.50 1.40
C22 AP3 40r bl, ol bis & dk bl 6.00 2.25
C23 AP3 80r multicolored 10.00 6.00
Nos. C19-C23 (5) 21.20 10.85

Nos. C19-C22 Surcharged in Red

1964, Oct.
C24 AP3 3r on 5r multi .90 .55
C25 AP3 6r on 10r multi 1.40 .85
C26 AP3 9r on 20r multi 1.75 1.10
C27 AP3 12r on 40r multi 3.50 2.00
Nos. C24-C27 (4) 7.55 4.50

18th Olympic Games, Tokyo, Oct. 10-25.

1972 Summer Olympic Games, Munich — AP4

Designs: No. C28, shown. No. C29, Munich churches, Olympic emblem, vert.

Litho. & Embossed

1972, Sept. 28 *Perf. 13½*

C28	AP4 900r gold & multi		*40.00*	*40.00*
C29	AP4 900r gold & multi		*40.00*	*40.00*
a.	Souvenir sheet of 2, #C28-C29		*87.50*	

No. C29a exists imperf. Value, $90.

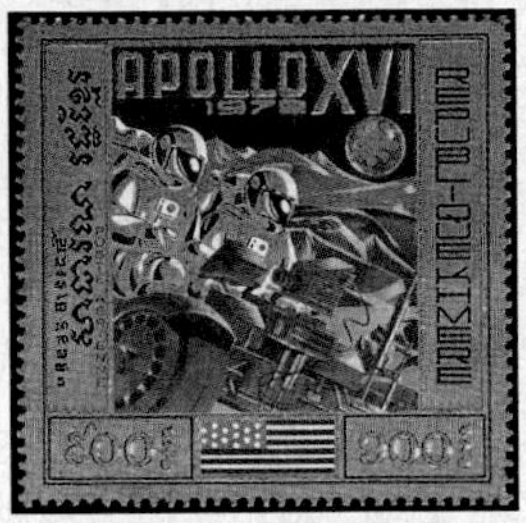

Apollo 16 AP5

Designs: No. C30, Astronauts in Lunar Rover. No. C31, Astronaut walking on moon.

1972, Sept. 28

C30	AP5 900r gold & multi	*42.50*	*42.50*
C31	AP5 900r gold & multi	*42.50*	*42.50*
a.	Souvenir sheet of 2, #C30-C31	*80.00*	

No. C31a exists imperf. Value, $120.

Pres. Nixon's Visit to the People's Republic of China — AP6

Nixon, Mao Zedong: No. C32, Large portraits (shown). No. C33, Small portraits.

1972, Sept. 28 *Perf. 12½*

C32	AP6 900r gold & multi	*80.00*	*80.00*
C33	AP6 900r gold & multi	*80.00*	*80.00*

Garuda, 12th Century, Angkor Thom — AP7

1973, Jan. 18 **Engr.** *Perf. 13*

C34	AP7	3r carmine	.35	.25
C35	AP7	30r violet blue	2.00	1.00
C36	AP7	50r dull purple	3.75	2.00
C37	AP7	100r dull green	5.25	3.00
		Nos. C34-C37 (4)	11.35	6.25

1972 Summer Olympic Games, Munich AP8

Gold medalists: No. C38, Heide Rosendahl. No. C39, Mark Spitz.

Litho. & Embossed

1973, May 18 *Perf. 13½*

C38	AP8 900r gold & multi	*35.00*	*35.00*
C39	AP8 900r gold & multi	*35.00*	*35.00*
a.	Souvenir sheet, #C38-C39	*70.00*	

No. C39a exists imperf. Value $100.

Nos. C38-C39 Overprinted

1973, Nov. 19

C40	AP8 900r on C38	*40.00*	*40.00*
C41	AP8 900r on C39	*40.00*	*40.00*
a.	Souvenir sheet, #C40-C41	*80.00*	

No. C41a exists imperf. Value, $160.

1974 World Cup Soccer Championships, Munich — AP9

Designs: No. C42, Trophy, players. No. C43, Trophy, players, vert.

1973, Nov. 19 **Litho. & Embossed**

C42	AP9 900r gold & multi	*35.00*	*35.00*
C43	AP9 900r gold & multi	*35.00*	*35.00*
a.	Souvenir sheet, #C42-C43	*70.00*	

No. C43a exists imperf. Value, $100.

John F. Kennedy, Apollo 11 — AP10

No. C44, shown. No. C45, Kennedy, Apollo 17.

1974, Feb. 18

C44	AP10 1100r gold & multi	*95.00*	*95.00*
C45	AP10 1100r gold & multi	*95.00*	*95.00*
a.	Souv. sheet of 2, #C44-C45	*200.00*	

Nos. C44-C45a exist imperf. Values slightly higher.

Copernicus Type of 1974 and

Copernicus, Sun — AP11

200r, Copernicus and Skylab III. 250r, Copernicus, Concorde and solar eclipse. No. C48, shown. No. C49, Moon, Skylab, hand holding symbol of sun.

1974, Sept. 10 **Litho.** *Perf. 13*

C46	A87	200r multi	9.00	5.00
C47	A87	250r multi	15.00	10.00

Litho. & Engraved

Perf. 13½

C48	AP11 1200r gold & multi	*27.50*	*27.50*

Souvenir Sheet of 1

C49	AP11 1200r gold & multi	*27.50*	*27.50*

Nos. C46-C47 exist in perf or imperf souvenir sheets of 1. Values, each $20. C48-C49 exist imperf. Values, each $50.

UPU Type of 1974 and

AP12

700r, Rocket, globe and UPU emblem. No. C51, UPU Headquarters. No. C52, US #1434-1435.

1974, Nov. 2 **Litho.** *Perf. 13*

C50	A88	700r gold & multi	*10.00*	*10.00*

Litho. & Embossed

Perf. 13½

C51	AP12 1200r gold & multi	*20.00*	*20.00*

Souvenir Sheet

C52	AP12 1200r gold & multi	*30.00*

Nos. C50-C51 exist in souvenir sheets of one. Nos. C51-C52 exist imperf.

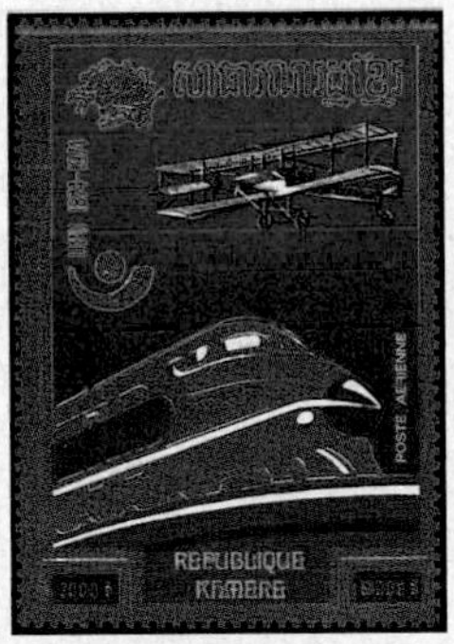

UPU, Cent. (in 1974) AP13

UPU emblem and: No. C53, Biplane, train. No. C54, Satellite, sailboat.

Litho. & Embossed

1975, Apr. 12 *Perf. 13¼*

C53	AP13 2000r gold & multi	*13.50*	—

Souvenir Sheet

C54	AP13 2000r gold & multi	*40.00*	—

No. C53 exists in a souvenir sheet of 1.

Post Aerienne at Right — AP14

Denominations: 5r, 10r, 15r, 25r.

1984, Feb. 1 **Litho.** *Perf. 12x12½*

C55-C58	AP14	Set of 4	45.00	8.50

Post Aerienne at Left — AP15

Denominations: 5r, 10r, 15r, 25r.

1986, Mar. 4 **Litho.** *Perf. 12x12½*

C59-C62	AP15	Set of 4	40.00	8.00

POSTAGE DUE STAMPS

D1

1957 **Unwmk.** **Typo.** *Perf. 13½*

Denomination in Black

J1	D1	10c ver & pale blue	.30	.30
J2	D1	50c ver & pale blue	.55	.55
J3	D1	1r ver & pale blue	.85	.85
J4	D1	3r ver & pale blue	1.25	1.25
J5	D1	5r ver & pale blue	1.90	1.90
		Nos. J1-J5 (5)	4.85	4.85

Frieze, Angkor Wat — D2

1974, Feb. 18 **Engr.** *Perf. 12½x13*

J6	D2	2r ocher	.30	.30
J7	D2	6r green	.45	.45
J8	D2	8r deep carmine	.70	.70
J9	D2	10r violet blue	1.10	1.10
		Nos. J6-J9 (4)	2.55	2.55

CAMEROONS

ˌka-mə-ˈrüns

LOCATION — West coast of Africa, north of equator
GOVT. — British Trust Territory
AREA — 34,081 sq. mi.
POP. — 868,637 (estimated)
CAPITAL — Buea

Prior to World War I, Cameroons (Kamerun) was a German Protectorate. It was occupied during the War by Great Britain and France and in 1922 was mandated to these countries by the League of Nations. Stamps of Nigeria were used in the British part until 1960. The northern section of the British Cameroons became part of the independent state of Nigeria in 1960, and the southern section became a United Kingdom Trust Territory. After a referendum, this U.K.T.T. joined the independent State of Cameroun to form the Federal Republic of Cameroun, Oct. 1, 1961.

Stamps of the German Protectorate, the French Mandate, the independent state and the Cameroun Federal Republic are listed under Cameroun.

Catalogue values for unused stamps in this country are for Never Hinged items.

United Kingdom Trust Territory

Stamps and Type of Nigeria, 1953, Ovptd. in Red

Perf. 13½, 14

1960, Oct. 1 Wmk. 4 Engr.

Size: 35½x22½mm

66	A17	½p red org & black	.25	*1.75*
67	A17	1p ol gray & black	.25	*.70*
68	A17	1½p blue green	.25	.25
69	A17	2p gray (II)	.65	*2.00*
70	A17	3p purple & black	.25	.25
71	A17	4p ultra & black	.25	*2.25*
72	A18	6p blk & org brn, perf. 14	.50	.25
a.		Perf. 13x13½ ('61)	.40	*2.25*
73	A17	1sh brown vio & blk	.35	.25

Size: 40½x24½mm

74	A17	2sh6p green & black	2.00	1.00
75	A17	5sh ver & black	2.75	*3.00*
76	A17	10sh red brn & blk	3.75	*7.00*

Size: 42x31½mm

77	A17	£1 violet & black	20.00	*27.50*
		Nos. 66-77 (12)	31.25	*46.20*

Nos. 66-77 were withdrawn in Northern Cameroons on May 31, 1961, when that territory joined Nigeria and in Southern Cameroons Sept. 30, 1961, when that territory joined the Cameroun Federal Republic.

CAMEROUN

ˌka-mə-ˈrün

(Kamerun)

LOCATION — On the west coast of Africa, north of the equator
GOVT. — Republic
AREA — 183,520 sq. mi.
POP. — 15,456,092 (1999 est.)
CAPITAL — Yaounde

Before World War I, Cameroun (Kamerun) was a German Protectorate. It was occupied during the war by Great Britain and France and in 1922 was mandated to these countries by the League of Nations. The French-mandated part became the independent State of Cameroun on January 1, 1960.

The Southern Cameroons, a United Kingdom Trust Territory, joined this state to form the Federal Republic of Cameroun on October 1, 1961. The name was changed to United Republic of Cameroon on May 20, 1972.

Stamps of Southern Cameroons are listed under Cameroons.

100 Pfennig = 1 Mark
12 Pence = 1 Shilling
100 Centimes = 1 Franc

Catalogue values for unused stamps in this country are for Never Hinged items, beginning with Scott 296 in the regular postage section, Scott B29 in the semi-postal section, Scott C8 in the air-post section, Scott J24 in the postage due section, and Scott M1 in the military stamp section.

Watermark

Wmk. 125 — Lozenges

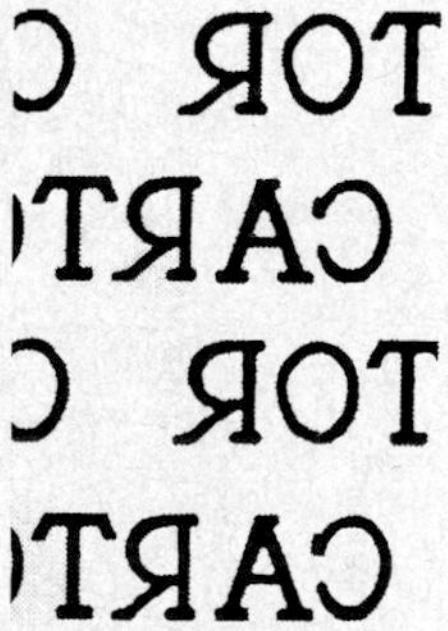

Wmk. 385

Issued under German Dominion

Stamps of Germany Overprinted in Black

1897 Unwmk. *Perf. 13½x14½*

1	A9	3pf yel brn	11.00	*16.00*
a.		3pf red brown	45.00	*130.00*
b.		3pf dark brown	16.00	*37.50*
c.		3pf olive brown	8.75	*37.50*
2	A9	5pf green	5.25	*8.00*
3	A10	10pf carmine	5.25	*5.00*
4	A10	20pf ultra	4.00	*8.00*
a.		Diagonal half used as 10pf on cover		*18,750.*
5	A10	25pf orange	20.00	*37.50*
6	A10	50pf red brn	16.00	*29.00*
		Nos. 1-6 (6)	61.50	*103.50*

A3

Kaiser's Yacht "Hohenzollern" — A4

1900 Unwmk. Typo. *Perf. 14*

7	A3	3pf brown	1.25	*1.45*
8	A3	5pf green	13.50	1.20
9	A3	10pf carmine	40.00	1.25
10	A3	20pf ultra	25.00	2.20
a.		Vertical half used as 10pf on cover (Longii, '11)		6,750.
11	A3	25pf org & blk, *yel*	1.35	*5.00*
12	A3	30pf org & blk, *sal*	1.75	*4.00*
13	A3	40pf lake & blk	1.75	*4.00*
14	A3	50pf pur & blk, *sal*	2.00	*6.00*
15	A3	80pf lake & blk, *rose*	2.75	*11.00*

Engr. *Perf. 14½x14*

16	A4	1m carmine	67.50	*67.50*
17	A4	2m blue	5.00	*65.00*
18	A4	3m blk vio	5.00	*105.00*
19	A4	5m slate & car	140.00	*440.00*
		Nos. 7-19 (13)	306.85	*713.60*

1905-18 Wmk. 125 Typo.

20	A3	3pf brown ('18)	.70	
21	A3	5pf green	.70	*1.60*
a.		Bklt. pane of 6	15.00	
b.		Bklt. pane of 6, 2 #21 + 4 #22	62.50	
c.		Booklet pane of 5 + label	375.00	
22	A3	10pf carmine ('06)	2.25	*1.50*
a.		Bklt pane of 6	17.50	
b.		Booklet pane of 5 + label	*500.00*	
23	A3	20pf ultra ('14)	3.00	*125.00*
24	A4	1m carmine ('15)	11.00	
25	A4	5m slate & car ('13)	40.00	*4,250.*
		Nos. 20-25 (6)	68.35	

The 3pf and 1m were not placed in use.

Nos. 21a, 22a were made from sheet stamps.

Issued under British Occupation

Stamps of German Cameroun Surcharged

No. 53

No. 62

Wmk. Lozenges (125) (#54-56, 65); Unwmk. (Other Values)

1915 *Perf. 14, 14½*

Blue Surcharge

53	A3	½p on 3pf brn	15.00	*60.00*
54	A3	½p on 5pf grn	7.75	*11.00*
a.		Double surcharge		*1,100.*
b.		Black surcharge	—	—
55	A3	1p on 10pf car	1.45	*10.00*
a.		"1" with thin serifs	15.00	*75.00*
b.		Double surcharge	475.00	
c.		Black surcharge	18.00	*65.00*
d.		As "c," "1" with thin serifs	300.00	

Black Surcharge

56	A3	2p on 20pf ultra	4.00	*24.00*
57	A3	2½p on 25pf org & blk, *yel*	18.50	*60.00*
a.		Double surcharge	*15,000.*	
58	A3	3p on 30pf org & blk, *sal*	14.00	*65.00*
59	A3	4p on 40pf lake & blk	14.00	*65.00*
60	A3	6p on 50pf pur & blk, *sal*	14.00	*65.00*
61	A3	8p on 80pf lake & blk, *rose*	14.00	*65.00*
62	A4	1sh on 1m car	220.00	*1,000.*
a.		"S" inverted	1,100.	*4,000.*
63	A4	2sh on 2m bl	250.00	*1,050.*
a.		"S" inverted	1,100.	*4,000.*
64	A4	3sh on 3m blk vio	250.00	*1,050.*
a.		"S" inverted	1,100.	*4,400.*
b.		Double surcharge	*16,500.*	
65	A4	5sh on 5m sl & car	300.00	*1,100.*
a.		"S" inverted	1,425.	*4,750.*
		Nos. 53-65 (13)	1,122.	*4,625.*

The letters "C. E. F." are the initials of "Cameroons Expeditionary Force."

Numerous overprint varieties exist for Nos. 53-65.

Counterfeits exist of Nos. 54a, 54b.

See Cameroons for Nos. 66-77.

Issued under French Occupation

Gabon Nos. 37, 49-52, 54, 57-58, 60, 62-64, 66, 69-70 Overprinted

1915 Unwmk. *Perf. 13½x14*

Inscribed "Congo Français"

101	A10	10c red & car	32.50	24.00

Inscribed "Afrique Equatoriale"

102	A10	1c choc & org	110.00	47.50
103	A10	2c blk & choc	200.00	150.00
104	A10	4c vio & dp bl	200.00	150.00
105	A10	5c ol gray & grn	40.00	24.00
105A	A10	10c red & car	*21,500.*	*24,000.*
106	A10	20c ol brn & dk vio	210.00	210.00
107	A11	25c dp bl & choc	60.00	47.50
108	A11	30c gray blk & red	200.00	200.00
109	A11	35c dk vio & grn	67.50	45.00
a.		Double overprint	1,900.	
110	A11	40c choc & ultra	200.00	200.00
111	A11	45c car & vio	225.00	225.00
112	A11	50c bl grn & gray	225.00	225.00
113	A11	75c org & choc	275.00	225.00
114	A12	1fr dk brn & bis	260.00	225.00
115	A12	2fr car & brn	300.00	260.00
		Nos. 101-105,106-115 (15)	2,605.	2,258.

The overprint is vertical, reading up, on Nos. 101-106, 114-115, and horizontal on Nos. 107-113.

Stamps of Middle Congo, Issue of 1907, Overprinted

1916 Unwmk.

116	A1	1c ol gray & brn	110.00	110.00
117	A1	2c violet & brn	110.00	110.00
118	A1	4c blue & brown	120.00	120.00
119	A1	5c dk green & blue	32.50	32.50
120	A2	35c violet brn & bl	110.00	75.00
121	A2	45c violet & red	87.50	75.00

The overprint is vert., reading down, on Nos. 120-121.

Same Overprint On Stamps of French Congo, 1900

Wmk. Branch of Thistle (122)

122	A4	15c dull vio & ol grn	120.00	120.00
a.		Inverted overprint	200.00	180.00

Wmk. Branch of Rose Tree (123)

123	A5	20c yellow grn & org	140.00	92.50
124	A5	30c car rose & org	110.00	87.50
125	A5	40c org brn & brt grn	105.00	80.00
126	A5	50c gray vio & lil	110.00	87.50
127	A5	75c red vio & org	110.00	85.00

Wmk. Branch of Olive (124)

128	A6	1fr gray lilac & ol	125.00	120.00
129	A6	2fr carmine & brn	160.00	120.00
		Nos. 116-129 (14)	1,550.	1,315.

The overprint is horiz. on No. 122. The overprint is vert., reading down or up, on Nos. 123-129. Values are for the cheaper variety. See the *Scott Classic Specialized Catalogue of Stamps & Covers* for detailed listings.

Values are for stamps centered in the grade of fine.

Counterfeits exist of Nos. 101-129.

Stamps of Middle Congo, Issue of 1907 Overprinted

1916-17 Unwmk.

130	A1	1c ol gray & brn	.40	.40
131	A1	2c violet & brn	.50	.50
132	A1	4c blue & brn	.75	.75

133	A1	5c	dk green & bl	.50	.40
134	A1	10c	carmine & bl	1.10	.80
135	A1	15c	brn vio & rose ('17)	2.00	.80
136	A1	20c	brown & bl	.80	.80
137	A2	25c	blue & grn	.80	.80
a.			Triple overprint	550.00	*700.00*
138	A2	30c	scarlet & grn	1.25	.80
a.			Double overprint	400.00	*575.00*
139	A2	35c	vio brn & bl	.80	.80
140	A2	40c	dull grn & brn	2.40	1.60
141	A2	45c	violet & red	2.40	1.60
142	A2	50c	blue grn & red	2.40	1.60
143	A2	75c	brown & blue	2.40	1.60
144	A3	1fr	dp grn & vio	2.00	1.60
145	A3	2fr	vio & gray grn	8.00	6.75
146	A3	5fr	blue & rose	13.50	11.00
			Nos. 130-146 (17)	42.00	32.60

Nos. 130-146 exist on ordinary paper and, with the exception of No. 135, on chalk surfaced paper. Nos. 137-146 are known with inverted 'S' in 'Francaise' and without period after 'Francaise.' See the *Scott Classic Specialized Catalogue of Stamps & Covers* for detailed listings.

On Nos. 137-146 there is 7mm between "Cameroun" and "Occupation."

Provisional French Mandate

Types of Middle Congo, 1907, Overprinted

1921

147	A1	1c	ol grn & org	.35	.30
148	A1	2c	brown & rose	.35	.30
149	A1	4c	gray & lt grn	.55	.55
150	A1	5c	dl red & org	.55	.55
a.			Double overprint	1,200.	
151	A1	10c	bl grn & lt grn	1.25	.90
152	A1	15c	blue & org	.55	.55
153	A1	20c	red brn & ol	.80	.80
154	A2	25c	slate & org	1.20	.80
155	A2	30c	rose & ver	1.25	.80
156	A2	35c	gray & ultra	.80	.80
157	A2	40c	ol grn & org	1.25	.80
158	A2	45c	brown & rose	.80	.80
159	A2	50c	blue & ultra	1.25	.80
160	A2	75c	red brn & lt grn	1.25	.80
161	A3	1fr	slate & org	2.40	2.40
162	A3	2fr	ol grn & rose	6.50	5.50
163	A3	5fr	dull red & gray	9.50	8.00
			Nos. 147-163 (17)	30.60	25.45

The 1c, 2c, 4c, 15c, 20c, 25c and 50c exist with overprint omitted. For listings, see the *Scott Specialized Catalogue of Stamps & Covers.*

Nos. 152, 162, 163, 158, 160 Surcharged with New Value and Bars

1924-25

164	A1	25c	on 15c bl & org ('25)	1.25	1.25
165	A3	25c	on 2fr ol grn & rose	1.25	1.60
166	A3	25c	on 5fr red & gray	1.25	1.60
a.			Pair, one without new value and bars		
167	A2	65c	on 45c brn & rose ('25)	2.00	2.00
168	A2	85c	on 75c red brn & lt grn ('25)	2.40	2.40
			Nos. 164-168 (5)	8.15	8.85

French Mandate

Herder and Cattle Crossing Sanaga River — A5

Tapping Rubber Tree — A6

Rope Suspension Bridge A7

1925-38 Typo. *Perf. 14x13½*

170	A5	1c	ol grn & brn vio, *lav*	.25	.25
171	A5	2c	rose & grn, *grnsh*	.25	.25
172	A5	4c	blue & blk	.25	.25
173	A5	5c	org & red vio, *lav*	.25	.25
174	A5	10c	red brn & org, *yel*	.45	.40
175	A5	15c	sl grn & grn	.45	.40
176	A5	15c	lilac & red ('27)	1.00	.80

Perf. 13½x14

177	A6	20c	ol brn & red brn	.70	.40
178	A6	20c	green ('26)	.65	.50
179	A6	20c	brn red & ol brn ('27)	.65	.65
180	A6	25c	lt green & blk	.95	.50
181	A6	30c	bluish grn & ver	.50	.30
182	A6	30c	dk grn & grn ('27)	.90	.65
183	A6	35c	brown & black	1.10	.50
184	A6	35c	dl grn & grn ('38)	1.90	1.20
185	A6	40c	orange & vio	2.00	1.20
186	A6	45c	dp rose & cer	.80	.50
187	A6	45c	vio & org brn ('27)	2.25	1.60
188	A6	50c	lt green & cer	.80	.30
189	A6	55c	ultra & car ('38)	1.60	1.60
190	A6	60c	red vio & blk	.80	.55
191	A6	60c	brown red ('26)	.95	.55
192	A6	65c	indigo & brn	1.20	1.20
193	A6	75c	indigo & dp bl	.80	.80
194	A6	75c	org brn & red vio ('27)	1.40	1.10
195	A6	80c	carmine & brn ('38)	1.40	1.20
196	A6	85c	dp rose & bl	1.60	1.20
197	A6	90c	brn red & cer ('27)	2.75	1.20

Perf. 14x13½

198	A7	1fr	indigo & brn	1.20	1.20
199	A7	1fr	dull bl ('26)	.80	.55
200	A7	1fr	ol brn & red vio ('27)	1.10	.80
201	A7	1fr	grn & dk brn ('29)	2.40	1.20
202	A7	1.10fr	rose red & dk brn ('28)	4.75	*6.50*
203	A7	1.25fr	gray & dp bl ('33)	4.75	3.50
204	A7	1.50fr	dull bl ('27)	1.20	.80
205	A7	1.75fr	brn & org ('33)	1.60	1.20
206	A7	1.75fr	dk bl & lt bl ('38)	2.40	1.60
207	A7	2fr	dl grn & brn org	2.00	1.20
208	A7	3fr	ol brn & red vio ('27)	8.00	2.75
209	A7	5fr	brn & blk, *bluish*	3.50	2.00
a.			Cliché of 2fr in plate of 5fr	1,450.	
b.			As "a," in pair with #209	1,700.	
210	A7	10fr	org & vio ('27)	14.50	7.25
211	A7	20fr	rose & ol grn ('27)	21.00	15.00
			Nos. 170-211 (42)	97.80	65.85

Shades exist for several values.

For overprints and surcharge see Nos. 212, 264, 276, 278, 279, B7-B9, B21.

No. 199 Surcharged with New Value and Bars in Red

1926

212	A7	1.25fr	on 1fr dull blue	1.20	.80

Common Design Types pictured following the introduction.

Colonial Exposition Issue

Common Design Types

Name of Country in Black

1931 Engr. *Perf. 12½*

213	CD70	40c	deep green	5.50	4.00
214	CD71	50c	violet	5.50	4.75
215	CD72	90c	red orange	5.50	4.75
216	CD73	1.50fr	dull blue	6.50	4.75
			Nos. 213-216 (4)	23.00	18.25

Paris International Exposition Issue

Common Design Types

1937 *Perf. 13*

217	CD74	20c	deep violet	1.75	1.75
218	CD75	30c	dark green	1.75	1.75
219	CD76	40c	carmine rose	1.75	1.75
220	CD77	50c	dark brown	1.75	1.75
221	CD78	90c	red	1.90	1.90
222	CD79	1.50fr	ultramarine	1.90	1.90
			Nos. 217-222 (6)	10.80	10.80

French Colonial Art Exhibition

Common Design Type

Souvenir Sheet

1937 *Imperf.*

222A	CD77	3fr	org red & blk	8.00	*9.50*

New York World's Fair Issue

Common Design Type

1939 *Perf. 12½x12*

223	CD82	1.25fr	carmine lake	1.40	1.20
224	CD82	2.25fr	ultra	1.40	1.20

For overprints and surcharges see Nos. 280-281, B14-B17, B23, B25.

Mandara Woman — A19

Falls on M'bam River near Banyo — A20

Elephants A21

Man in Yaré — A22

1939-40 Engr. *Perf. 13*

225	A19	2c	black brn	.25	.25
226	A19	3c	magenta ('40)	.25	.25
227	A19	4c	deep ultra	.25	.25
228	A19	5c	red brown	.25	.25
229	A19	10c	dp bl grn	.25	.25
230	A19	15c	rose red	.30	.30
231	A19	20c	plum	.30	.30
232	A20	25c	black brn	.65	.65
233	A20	30c	dk red	.80	.70
234	A20	40c	ultra ('40)	.80	.80
235	A20	45c	slate green ('40)	2.60	2.25
236	A20	50c	brown car	.90	.70
237	A20	60c	pck blue ('40)	.75	.65
238	A20	70c	plum ('40)	3.25	2.90
239	A21	80c	Prus blue	2.60	2.10
240	A21	90c	Prus blue	.95	.75
241	A21	1fr	car rose	1.90	.95
242	A21	1fr	choc ('40)	1.40	.80
243	A21	1.25fr	car rose	4.00	3.25
244	A21	1.40fr	org red ('40)	1.25	.95
245	A21	1.50fr	chocolate	1.20	.95
246	A21	1.60fr	black brn ('40)	2.50	2.25
247	A21	1.75fr	dk blue	1.40	.95
248	A21	2fr	dk green	.90	.90
249	A21	2.25fr	dk blue	1.40	.90
250	A21	2.50fr	brt red vio ('40)	1.20	1.00
251	A21	3fr	dk violet	1.40	.80
252	A22	5fr	black brn	1.40	.95
253	A22	10fr	brt red vio	2.00	1.60
254	A22	20fr	dk green	4.00	3.25
			Nos. 225-254 (30)	41.10	32.85

For overprints and surcharges see Nos. 255-263, 265-275, 277, 278A, 279A, B10-B13, B22, B24.

Stamps of 1925-40 Overprinted in Black or Orange

1940 *Perf. 14x13½, 13½x14, 13*

255	A19	2c	blk brn (O)	1.60	1.60
256	A19	3c	magenta	2.40	2.40
257	A19	4c	dp ultra (O)	1.60	1.60
258	A19	5c	red brn	5.50	5.50
259	A19	10c	dp bl grn (O)	1.60	1.60
260	A19	15c	rose red	2.40	2.40
260A	A19	20c	plum (O)	13.50	13.50
261	A20	25c	blk brn	1.60	1.60
b.			Inverted overprint	260.00	260.00
261A	A20	30c	dk red	14.50	14.50
262	A20	40c	ultra	5.50	5.50
263	A20	45c	slate green	4.00	4.00
264	A6	50c	lt grn & cer	2.40	1.60
a.			Inverted overprint	225.00	
265	A20	60c	pck bl	6.50	6.50
266	A20	70c	plum	3.25	3.25
267	A21	80c	Prus bl (O)	5.50	5.50
268	A21	90c	Prus bl (O)	1.60	1.60
269	A21	1.25fr	car rose	1.60	1.60
270	A21	1.40fr	org red	4.75	4.75
271	A21	1.50fr	chocolate	1.60	1.60
272	A21	1.60fr	blk brn (O)	3.25	3.25
273	A21	1.75fr	dk bl (O)	2.40	2.40
274	A21	2.25fr	dk bl (O)	1.60	1.60
275	A21	2.50fr	brt red vio	1.60	1.60
276	A7	5fr	brn & blk, *bluish*	24.00	24.00
277	A22	5fr	black brn	24.00	16.00
278	A7	10fr	org & vio	32.50	32.50
278A	A22	10fr	brt red vio	65.00	45.00
279	A7	20fr	rose & ol grn	55.00	55.00
279A	A22	20fr	dk green	190.00	190.00

Same Overprint on Stamps of 1939

Perf. 12½x12

280	CD82	1.25fr	car lake	12.00	12.00
281	CD82	2.25fr	ultra	12.00	12.00
			Nos. 255-281 (31)	504.75	475.95

Issued to note Cameroun's affiliation with General de Gaulle's "Free France" movement. Numerous overprint varieties exist.

Cattle Fording Sanaga River and Marshal Petain A22a

1941 Engr. *Perf. 12½x12*

281A	A22a	1fr	green	.40	
281B	A22a	2.50fr	dark blue	.40	
			Set, never hinged	1.60	

Nos. 281A-281B were issued by the Vichy government in France, but were not placed on sale in Cameroun.

For surcharges, see Nos. B25A-B25B.

Lorraine Cross and Joan of Arc Shield — A23

1941 Photo. *Perf. 14x14½*

282	A23	5c	brown	.25	.25
283	A23	10c	dk blue	.25	.25
284	A23	25c	emerald	.25	.25
285	A23	30c	dp orange	.25	.25
286	A23	40c	dk slate green	.25	.25
287	A23	80c	red brown	.50	.25
288	A23	1fr	dp red lilac	.50	.50
289	A23	1.50fr	brt red	.50	.50
290	A23	2fr	gray black	.75	.50
291	A23	2.50fr	brt ultra	.80	.50
292	A23	4fr	dull violet	.90	.75
293	A23	5fr	bister	.95	.90
294	A23	10fr	dp brown	.95	.90
295	A23	20fr	dp green	1.90	1.40
			Nos. 282-295 (14)	9.00	7.45

For surcharges see Nos. 297A-303.

Catalogue values for unused stamps in this section, from this point to the end of the section, are for Never Hinged items.

Eboue Issue

Common Design Type

1945 Unwmk. Engr. *Perf. 13*

296	CD91	2fr	black	.80	.55
297	CD91	25fr	Prus green	1.60	1.40

Nos. 282, 284, 291 Surcharged with New Values and Bars in Red, Carmine or Black

1946 *Perf. 14x14½*

297A	A23	50c	on 5c (R)	.65	.50
298	A23	60c	on 5c (R)	.75	.55
a.			Inverted surcharge	200.00	
299	A23	70c	on 5c (R)	1.00	.75
300	A23	1.20fr	on 5c (C)	1.00	.75
301	A23	2.40fr	on 25c	.95	.75

302	A23	3fr on 25c	1.40	1.00
302A	A23	4.50fr on 25c	1.90	1.40
303	A23	15fr on 2.50fr (C)	2.00	1.50
		Nos. 297A-303 (8)	9.65	7.20

Zebu and Herder A25

Tikar Women — A26

Porters Carrying Bananas — A27

Bowman A28

Lamido Horsemen A29

Farmer — A30

1946 Engr. *Perf. 12½x12, 12x12½*

304	A25	10c blue grn	.50	.30
305	A25	30c brown org	.50	.30
306	A25	40c brt ultra	.50	.30
307	A26	50c olive brn	.50	.30
308	A26	60c dp plum	.65	.30
309	A26	80c chnt brn	.80	.50
310	A27	1fr org red	.50	.25
311	A27	1.20fr dp green	.90	.50
312	A27	1.50fr dk car	2.25	1.40
313	A28	2fr black	.50	.25
314	A28	3fr dk carmine	.65	.30
314A	A28	3.60fr red brn	1.60	1.10
315	A28	4fr dp blue	.90	.40
316	A29	5fr brown car	1.00	.65
317	A29	6fr ultra	1.00	.55
318	A29	10fr slate green	1.75	.50
319	A30	15fr grnsh blue	2.40	.90
320	A30	20fr dk green	3.25	.90
321	A30	25fr black	3.25	1.40
		Nos. 304-321 (19)	23.40	11.10

Shades exist for most values.
For surcharges see Nos. 343-344, 346.

Imperforates
Most Cameroun stamps from 1952 onward exist imperforate in issued and trial colors, and also in small presentation sheets in issued colors.

Military Medal Issue
Common Design Type
Engraved and Typographed

1952 Unwmk. *Perf. 13*

322	CD101	15fr multicolored	7.25	3.25

Porters Carrying Bananas — A32

Picking Coffee Beans — A33

1954 Engr.

323	A32	8fr red vio, org brn & vio bl	1.20	.80
324	A32	15fr brn red, yel & blk brn	1.60	.80
325	A33	40fr blk brn, org brn & lil rose	2.00	.80
		Nos. 323-325 (3)	4.80	2.40

FIDES Issue
Common Design Type

Designs: 5fr, Plowmen. 15fr, Wouri bridge. 20fr, Technical instruction. 25fr, Mobile medical station.

1956 Unwmk. *Perf. 13*

326	CD103	5fr org brn & dk brn	1.20	.50
327	CD103	15fr aqua, slate & blk	1.60	.80
328	CD103	20fr grnsh bl & dp ultra	1.60	.80
329	CD103	25fr dp ultra	2.50	1.10
		Nos. 326-329 (4)	6.90	3.20

For surcharges see Nos. 345, 347.

Coffee Issue

Coffee A35

1956 Engr. *Perf. 13*

330	A35	15fr car & brt red	1.60	.80

For surcharge see No. 348.

Autonomous Government

Flag and Woman Holding Child A36

1958

331	A36	20fr multicolored	1.60	.80

Anniv. of the installation of the 1st autonomous government of Cameroun.

Men Looking to the Sun — A37

1958

332	A37	20fr sepia & brn red	1.60	.80

10th anniv. of the signing of the Universal Declaration of Human Rights.

Flower Issue
Common Design Type

Design: 20fr, Randia malleifera.

1959 Photo. *Perf. 12½x12*

333	CD104	20fr dp grn, yel & rose	1.60	.80

Loading Bananas A38

Harvesting Bananas — A39

1959 Engr. *Perf. 13*

334	A38	20fr dk grn & org	1.20	.40
335	A39	25fr maroon & slate grn	1.60	.80

For surcharge see No. 349.

Independent State

Map and Flag of Cameroun — A40

Prime Minister Ahmadou Ahidjo — A41

1960 Unwmk. Engr. *Perf. 13*

336	A40	20fr multicolored	.80	.25
337	A41	25fr blk, grn & pale lem	.85	.25

Declaration of independence, Jan. 1, 1960.
For surcharge see No. 350.

Uprooted Oak Emblem A42

1960

338	A42	30fr red brn, ultra & yel grn	1.10	.45

World Refugee Year, 7/1/59-6/30/60.
For surcharge see No. 351.

C.C.T.A. Issue
Common Design Type

1960

339	CD106	50fr dull claret & slate	1.60	.75

UN Headquarters, NYC, and Flag — A43

1961, May 20 *Perf. 13*
Flag in Green, Red and Yellow

340	A43	15fr grn, dk bl & brn	.60	.30
341	A43	25fr dk blue & grn	.75	.30
342	A43	85fr red, dk bl & vio brn	2.40	1.20
		Nos. 340-342 (3)	3.75	1.80

Cameroun's admission to the UN, Sept. 20, 1960.

Federal Republic

Stamps of 1946-60 Surcharged in Red or Black

Type I

Type II

Two types of 2sh6p:
I — Large figures. "2/6" measures 8x3¾mm.
II — Small figures. "2/6" measures 6x2½mm.

Perf. 12x12½, 13

1961, Oct. 1 Engr.

343	A27	½p on 1fr (#310)	.35	.25
344	A28	1p on 2fr (#313)	.45	.30
345	CD103	1½p on 5fr (#326)	.55	.35
346	A29	2p on 10fr (#318)	1.00	.45
347	CD103	3p on 15fr (#327)	1.40	.60
348	A35	4p on 15fr (Bk) (#330)	1.10	.70
349	A38	6p on 20fr (#334)	2.40	1.00
350	A41	1sh on 25fr (#337)	2.75	1.50
351	A42	2sh6p on 30fr (#338) (I)	5.00	5.00
a.		Type II	21.00	21.00
		Nos. 343-351 (9)	15.00	10.15

Issued for use in the former United Kingdom Trust Territory of Southern Cameroons.
The "Republique Federale" overprint is in one line on Nos. 345, 347-349, in two vertical lines on No. 350. See Nos. C38-C40.

President Ahidjo and Prime Minister Foncha A45

Unwmk.

1962, Jan. 1 Engr. *Perf. 13*

352	A45	20fr vio & choc	8.00	7.00
353	A45	25fr dk grn & brn	14.00	11.00
354	A45	60fr car & dl grn	40.00	32.50
		Nos. 352-354 (3)	62.00	50.50

Surcharged for Use in Southern Cameroons

355	A45	3p on 20fr	175.00	160.00
356	A45	6p on 25fr	175.00	160.00
357	A45	2sh6p on 60fr	175.00	160.00
		Nos. 355-357 (3)	525.00	480.00

Reunification of the former French and British Sections of Cameroun. It is reported that Nos. 352-357 were withdrawn after a few days and destroyed.

Mustache Monkey
A46

Designs: 1fr, 4fr, Elephant, Ntem Falls. 1.50fr, 3fr, Buffon's kob, Dschang. 2fr, 5fr, Hippopotamus. 6fr, 15fr, Mustache monkey. 8fr, 30fr, Manatee, Lake Ossa. 10fr, 25fr, Buffalo, Batouri. 20fr, 40fr, Giraffes, Waza Reservation, vert.

1962 Unwmk. Engr. *Perf. 12*

358 A46 50c brn, brt grn & bl .25 .25
359 A46 1fr gray brn, bl grn & org .25 .25
360 A46 1.50fr brn, lt grn & sl grn .25 .25
361 A46 2fr dk gray, grnsh bl & grn .25 .25
362 A46 3fr brn, org & lil rose .25 .25
363 A46 4fr brn, yel grn & bl grn .25 .25
364 A46 5fr gray brn, grn & sal .25 .25
365 A46 6fr brn, yel & bl .45 .25
366 A46 8fr dk bl, red & grn .90 .50
367 A46 10fr ol blk, org & brt bl .75 .25
368 A46 15fr brn, Prus bl & bl 1.00 .40
369 A46 20fr brn & gray 1.25 .40
370 A46 25fr red brn, grn & yel 3.25 1.00
371 A46 30fr blk, org & bl 4.50 1.10
372 A46 40fr dp cl, yel grn & blk 7.50 1.50
Nos. 358-372 (15) 21.35 7.15

See Nos. 396-397.

African and Malagasy Union Issue
Common Design Type

1962, Sept. 8 Photo. *Perf. 12½x12*
373 CD110 30fr multicolored 2.00 .75

Village and Map of Cameroun
A48

Designs: 20fr, 25fr, Sun rising over city. 50fr, Hands holding scroll.

1962, Oct. 1 Engr. *Perf. 13*
374 A48 9fr pur, olive & dk brn .40 .25
375 A48 18fr grn, org brn & dk bl .50 .25
376 A48 20fr lil rose, ol bis & Ind .50 .25
377 A48 25fr bl, red org & sep .60 .25
378 A48 50fr dk red, sepia & bl 1.75 .50
Nos. 374-378 (5) 3.75 1.50

1st anniv. of the reunification of Cameroun.

"School under the Trees" — A49

1962, Nov. 5 Photo. *Perf. 12x12½*
379 A49 20fr ver, emerald & yel 1.00 .35

Literacy and popular education campaign.

Telstar and Globe
A50

1963, Feb. 9 Engr. *Perf. 13*
Size: 36x22mm
380 A50 1fr dk bl, olive & pur .25 .25
381 A50 2fr dk bl, claret & grn .25 .25
382 A50 3fr dk grn, ol & dp cl .25 .25
383 A50 25fr grn, dp cl & brt bl .75 .40
Nos. 380-383,C45 (5) 4.00 1.80

1st TV connection of the US and Europe through the Telstar satellite, July 11-12, 1962.

High Frequency Transmission Station, Mt. Bankolo — A51

Design: 20fr, Station and wiring plan.

1963, May 18 Photo. *Perf. 12x12½*
384 A51 15fr multicolored .45 .25
385 A51 20fr multicolored .60 .25
Nos. 384-385,C46 (3) 3.55 1.15

Issued to publicize the high frequency telegraph connection Douala-Yaounde.

"Yaoundé-Regional Center of Textbook Production" — A52

1963, Aug. 10 Unwmk. *Perf. 12½*
386 A52 20fr emer, blk & red .45 .25
387 A52 25fr org, blk & red .55 .25
388 A52 100fr gold, blk & red 2.10 .60
Nos. 386-388 (3) 3.10 1.10

UNESCO regional center for the production of school books at Yaounde.

Pres. Ahmadou Ahidjo and Flag — A53

Design: 18fr, Flag and map of Cameroun.

1963, Oct. 1 *Perf. 12x12½*
Flag in Green, Red and Yellow
389 A53 9fr grn, bl & dk brn .45 .25
390 A53 18fr grn, bl & lil .65 .25
391 A53 20fr grn, blk & yel grn .70 .25
Nos. 389-391 (3) 1.80 .75

Second anniversary of reunification.

Scales, Globe, UNESCO Emblem
A54

1963, Dec. 10 Photo. *Perf. 12½x12*
392 A54 9fr ultra, blk & sal .40 .25
393 A54 18fr brt yel grn, blk & rose red .50 .25
394 A54 25fr rose red, blk & brt yel grn .70 .25
395 A54 75fr yel, blk & ultra 2.00 .50
Nos. 392-395 (4) 3.60 1.25

Universal Declaration of Human Rights, 15th anniv.

Animal Type of 1962

Design: 10fr, 25fr, Lion, Waza National Park, North Cameroun.

1964, June 20 Engr. *Perf. 13*
396 A46 10fr red brn, bis & grn 1.25 .40
397 A46 25fr green & bister 3.00 1.25

Soccer Game in Stadium
A55

18fr, Pile of sports equipment. 30fr, Stadium (outside), flags and map of Africa.

1964, July 11 Engr. *Perf. 13*
398 A55 10fr grn, bl & red brn .50 .25
399 A55 18fr car, grn & vio .60 .35
400 A55 30fr blk, dk bl & org brn 1.00 .50
Nos. 398-400 (3) 2.10 1.10

Tropics Cup Games, Yaounde, July 11-19.

Europafrica Issue
Common Design Type and

Palace of Justice, Yaounde — A56

40fr, Emblems of Science, Agriculture, Industry and Education and two sunbursts.

1964, July 20 Photo. *Perf. 12x13*
401 A56 15fr multicolored 1.25 .25
402 CD116 40fr multicolored 2.25 60

1st anniv. of the economic agreement between the European Economic Community and the African and Malgache Union.

Hurdling and Olympic Flame — A57

Design: 10fr, Runners, vert.

1964, Oct. 10 Engr. *Perf. 13*
403 A57 9fr red, yel grn & blk 1.50 .40
404 A57 10fr red, vio & ol gray 2.25 .40
Nos. 403-404,C49 (3) 11.25 2.80

18th Olympic Games, Tokyo, Oct. 10-25.

Bamileke Dance Dress — A58

Ntem Falls, Ebolowa Region — A59

Designs: 18fr, Dance mask, Bamenda region. 25fr, Fulani horseman, North Cameroun, horiz.

1964 Unwmk. *Perf. 13*
405 A58 9fr red, yel grn & bl .55 .25
406 A58 18fr bl, red & brn .70 .25
407 A59 20fr dk car, grn & ol .90 .25
408 A58 25fr dk brn, org & car 1.40 .25
Nos. 405-408,C50 (5) 4.55 1.35

Cooperation Issue
Common Design Type

1964, Nov. 7 Engr.
409 CD119 18fr dk bl, yel grn & dk brn 1.00 .25
410 CD119 30fr red brn, bl grn & dk brn 1.50 .25

Memorial Stone — A60

1965, Jan. 1 Engr. *Perf. 13*
411 A60 12fr bl, indigo & grn 1.00 .25

Diesel Train
A61

Typo. *Perf. 14x13*
412 A61 20fr rose car, yel & grn 2.50 .25

Laying of the 1st rail of the Mbanga-Kumba Railroad, Mar. 28, 1964.

Red Cross Station and Ambulance
A62

50fr, Red Cross nurse and infant, vert.

1965, May 8 Engr. *Perf. 13*
413 A62 25fr car, slate grn & ocher .95 .25
414 A62 50fr gray, red & red brn 2.25 .30

Issued for the Cameroun Red Cross.

Coins Inserted in Map of Cameroun, and Bankbook — A63

Savings Bank Building — A64

Design: 20fr, Bankbook and coins inserted in cacao pod-shaped bank, vert.

1965, June 10 Size: 22x37mm
415 A63 9fr grn, red & org .45 .25

Size: 48x27mm, 27x48mm
416 A64 15fr choc, ultra & grn .55 .25
417 A63 20fr ocher, brt grn & brn .65 .25
Nos. 415-417 (3) 1.65 .75

Federal Postal Savings Banks.

Soccer Players and Africa Cup — A65

Unwmk.

1965, June 26 Engr. *Perf. 13*

418 A65 9fr car, brn & yel .55 .25
419 A65 20fr car, slate bl & yel 1.40 .25

Cameroun Oryx Club, winner of the club champions' Africa Cup, February 1965.

Symbolic Map of Europe and Africa — A66

40fr, Delegates around conference table.

1965, July 20 Photo. *Perf. 12x12½*

420 A66 5fr car, blk & lilac .30 .25
421 A66 40fr brn, buff, grn & ultra 1.50 .35

2nd, anniv. of the economic agreement between the European Economic Community and the African and Malgache Union.

UPU Monument, Bern A67

1965, July 26 Engr. *Perf. 13*

422 A67 30fr black & red .80 .25

Cameroun's admission to the UPU, 5th anniv.

ICY Emblem — A68

1965, Sept. 11 Unwmk. *Perf. 13*

423 A68 10fr dk bl & car rose .45 .25

Issued for the International Cooperation Year, 1964-65. See No. C57.

Pres. Ahidjo and Government House — A69

Design: 9fr, 20fr, Pres. Ahidjo and Government House, vert.

Perf. 12x12½, 12½x12

1965, Oct. 1 Photo. Unwmk.

424 A69 9fr multicolored .25 .25
425 A69 18fr multicolored .55 .25
426 A69 20fr multicolored .65 .25
427 A69 25fr multicolored .80 .25
Nos. 424-427 (4) 2.25 1.00

Reelection of Pres. Ahmadou Ahidjo.

National Tourist Office, Yaoundé A70

Designs: 9fr, Pouss Musgum houses. 18fr, Great Calao's dance (North Cameroun). 20fr, Gate of Sultan's Palace, Foumban, vert.

1965 Engr. *Perf. 13*

428 A70 9fr brn, rose red & grn .45 .25
429 A70 18fr brt bl, brn & grn .65 .25
430 A70 20fr bl, brn & choc 1.00 .25
431 A70 25fr mar, emer & gray .90 .25
Nos. 428-431 (4) 3.00 1.00

See No. C58.

Mountain Hotel, Buea — A71

Designs: 20fr, Hotel of the Deputies, Yaoundé. 35fr, Dschang Health Center.

1966

432 A71 9fr sl grn, rose cl & brn .35 .25
433 A71 20fr brt bl, sl grn & blk .45 .25
434 A71 35fr brn, sl grn & car .80 .30
Nos. 432-434,C63-C69 (10) 15.10 4.90

Bas-relief, Foumban A72

Designs: 18fr, Ekoi mask, vert. 20fr, Mother and child, carving, Bamiléké, vert. 25fr, Ceremonial stool, Bamoun.

1966, Apr. 15 Unwmk.

435 A72 9fr red & blk .60 .25
436 A72 18fr brt grn, org brn & choc .75 .25
437 A72 20fr brt bl, red brn & pur 1.15 .25
438 A72 25fr pur & dk brn 1.25 .25
Nos. 435-438 (4) 3.75 1.00

Intl. Negro Arts Festival, Dakar, Senegal, 4/1-24.

New WHO Headquarters, Geneva — A73

1966, May 3 Photo. *Perf. 12½x13*

439 A73 50fr ultra, red brn & yel 1.25 .50

ITU Headquarters, Geneva — A74

1966, May 3 Photo. *Perf. 12½x13*

440 A74 50fr ultra & yellow 1.25 .50

Phaeomeria Magnifica — A75

Flowers: 18fr, Hibiscus (rose of China). 20fr, Mountain rose.

1966, May 20 *Perf. 12x12½*

Flowers in Natural Colors

Size: 22x36mm

441 A75 9fr red brown .55 .25
442 A75 18fr green .70 .25
443 A75 20fr dark green .70 .25
Nos. 441-443,C70-C72 (6) 7.55 1.50

See No. 469.

"6" and Men Dancing around UN Emblem — A76

Design: 50fr, UN General Assembly, horiz.

1966, Sept. 20 Engr. *Perf. 13*

444 A76 50fr ultra, grn & vio brn .90 .25
445 A76 100fr red brn, grn & ultra 2.00 .50

6th anniv. of Cameroun's admission to the UN.

Prime Minister's Residence, Buea — A77

Designs (Prime Minister's Residences): 18fr, at Yaoundé, front view. 20fr, at Yaoundé, side view. 25fr, at Buea, front view.

1966, Oct. 1 Photo.

446 A77 9fr multicolored .45 .25
447 A77 18fr multicolored .65 .25
448 A77 20fr multicolored .60 .35
449 A77 25fr multicolored .80 .35
Nos. 446-449 (4) 2.50 1.20

5th anniversary of re-unification.

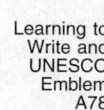

Learning to Write and UNESCO Emblem A78

No. 451, Children's heads & UNICEF emblem.

1966, Nov. 24 Engr. *Perf. 13*

450 A78 50fr red lil, bl & brn 1.40 .30
451 A78 50fr red lil, blk & brt bl 1.40 .30

20th anniv. of UNESCO, 20th anniv. of UNICEF.

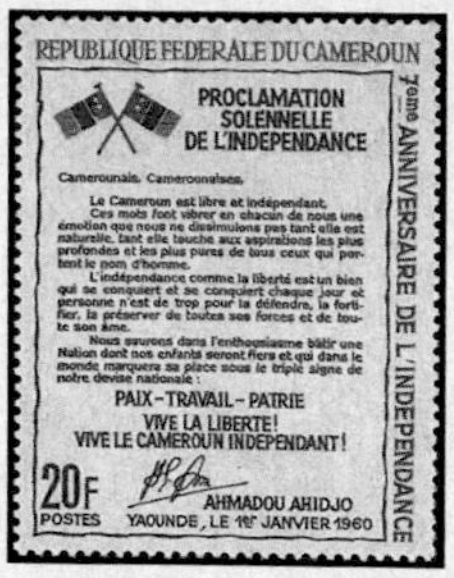

Independence Proclamation — A79

1967, Jan. 1 Engr. *Perf. 13*

452 A79 20fr grn, red & yel 2.25 .60

7th anniversary of independence.

Map of Africa and Madagascar, Railroad Tracks and Symbols — A80

25fr, Map of Africa and Madagascar and train.

1967, Feb. 21 Photo. *Perf. 13*

453 A80 20fr multicolored 3.50 1.50
454 A80 25fr multicolored 5.00 2.00

5th Conf. of African and Madagascan Railroad Technicians.

Lions Emblem and Forest — A81

Design: 100fr, Lions emblem and palms.

1967, Mar. 3

455 A81 50fr multicolored .90 .35
456 A81 100fr multicolored 2.10 .65

Lions International, 50th anniversary.

Jet and I.C.A.O. Emblem — A82

Dove and I.A.E.A. Emblem A83

Perf. 13x12½, 12½x13

1967, Mar. 15 Photo.

457 A82 50fr ultra, lt bl, brn & gold 1.40 .35
458 A83 50fr ultra & emer 1.40 .35

UN agencies: No. 457, the ICAO; No. 458, the Intl. Atomic Energy Agency.

Rotary International Emblem — A84

1967, Apr. 17 Photo. *Perf. 12½*

459 A84 25fr crim, vio bl & gold 1.25 .25

10th anniversary of the Douala, Cameroun, branch of Rotary International.

Grapefruit — A85

1967, May 10 Photo. *Perf. 12x12½*

460 A85 1fr shown .25 .25
461 A85 2fr Papaya .25 .25
462 A85 3fr Custard apple .25 .25
463 A85 4fr Breadfruit .25 .25
464 A85 5fr Coconut .35 .25
465 A85 6fr Mango .45 .25
466 A85 8fr Avacado .90 .25
467 A85 10fr Pineapple 1.40 .25
468 A85 30fr Bananas 3.50 .25
Nos. 460-468 (9) 7.60 2.25

For surcharges see Nos. 550, 593.

Bird of Paradise Flower — A86

1967, June 22 Photo. *Perf. 12x12½*
Size: 22x36mm

469 A86 15fr lt blue & multi .90 .25

Sanaga Falls and ITY Emblem — A87

1967, Aug. 14 Photo. *Perf. 13x12½*

470 A87 30fr multicolored .85 .25

Issued for International Tourist Year 1967.

Art of Cameroun: Coconut Harvest A88

Carved Bas-relief: 20fr, Lion hunt. 30fr, Women carrying baskets. 100fr, Carved chest.

1967, Sept. 22 *Perf. 12½x13*

471 A88 10fr brn, bl & car .35 .25
472 A88 20fr brn, yel & grn .55 .25
473 A88 30fr emer, brn & car .90 .25
474 A88 100fr red org, brn & emer 2.25 .40
Nos. 471-474 (4) 4.05 1.15

Coat of Arms A89

1968, Jan. 1 Litho. *Perf. 12½x13*

475 A89 30fr gold & multi 1.00 .25

Spiny Lobster A90

Designs (Fish and Crustaceans): 10fr, River crayfish. 15fr, Nile mouth-breeder. 20fr, Sole. 25fr, Common pike. 30fr, Crab. 40fr, Spadefish, vert. 50fr, Shrimp, vert. 55fr, African snakehead. 60fr, Threadfin.

1968, July 25 Engr. *Perf. 13*

476 A90 5fr brn, vio bl & dl grn .30 .25
477 A90 10fr ultra, brn ol & slate .30 .25
478 A90 15fr sal, red lil & sepia .85 .25
479 A90 20fr red brn, dp bl & sep 1.00 .25
480 A90 25fr lt brn, emer & slate 1.10 .25
481 A90 30fr mag, dk bl & dk brn 1.50 .25
482 A90 40fr slate bl & org 2.25 .25
483 A90 50fr emer, gray & rose car 3.00 .25
484 A90 55fr lt brn, Prus bl & dk brn 4.50 .25
485 A90 60fr brn, bl grn & indigo 6.75 .35
Nos. 476-485 (10) 21.55 2.60

Tanker, Refinery and Map of Area Served — A91

1968, July 30 Photo. *Perf. 12½*

486 A91 30fr multicolored 1.60 .25

Port Gentil (Gabon) Refinery opening, 6/12/68.

Human Rights Flame A92

1968, Sept. 14 Photo. *Perf. 12½x13*

487 A92 15fr blue & salmon .65 .25

Intl. Human Rights Year. See No. C110.

Pres. Ahmadou Ahidjo A93

1969, Apr. 10 Photo. *Perf. 12½x12*

488 A93 30fr carmine & multi .80 .25

Chocolate Vat — A94

Designs: 30fr, Chocolate factory. 50fr, Candy making, vert.

1969, Apr. 24 Engr. *Perf. 13*

489 A94 15fr red brn, ind & choc .50 .25
490 A94 30fr grn, blk & red brn .80 .25
491 A94 50fr brown & multi 1.10 .25
Nos. 489-491 (3) 2.40 .75

Cameroun chocolate industry.

Fertility Symbol, Abbia — A95

Art and Folklore from Abbia: 10fr, Two toucans, horiz. 15fr, Forest symbol. 30fr, Vulture attacking monkey, horiz. 70fr, Oliphant player.

1969, May 30 Engr. *Perf. 13*

492 A95 5fr ultra, Prus bl & brt rose lil .25 .25
493 A95 10fr bl, ol gray & org .35 .25
494 A95 15fr ultra, dk red & blk .50 .25
495 A95 30fr brt bl, lem & grn .90 .25
496 A95 70fr brt bl, dk grn & ver 1.90 .50
Nos. 492-496 (5) 3.90 1.50

Diesel Train on Bridge — A96

Design: 30fr, Kumba Railroad station, horiz.

Perf. 12½x13, 13x12½

1969, July 11 Photo.

497 A96 30fr blue & multi 1.25 .30
498 A96 50fr black & multi 3.25 .60

Opening of Mbanga-Kumba Railroad.

Development Bank Issue
Common Design Type

1969, Sept. 10 Engr. *Perf. 13*

499 CD130 30fr vio bl, grn & ocher .80 .25

African Development Bank, 5th anniv.

ASECNA Issue
Common Design Type

1969, Dec. 12 Engr. *Perf. 13*

500 CD132 100fr slate green 2.00 .60

Red Sage — A99

Design: 30fr, Passionflower.

1970, Mar. 24 Photo. *Perf. 12x12½*
Size: 22x36½mm

501 A99 15fr yel grn & multi .45 .25
502 A99 30fr multicolored 1.00 .25
Nos. 501-502,C140-C141 (4) 5.60 1.75

UPU Headquarters Issue
Common Design Type

1970, May 20 Engr. *Perf. 13*

503 CD133 30fr blue, pur & grn 1.00 .25
504 CD133 50fr gray, red & bl 1.60 .30

Brewery A100

Design: 30fr, Cellar with barrels.

1970, July 9 Engr. *Perf. 13*

505 A100 15fr brn, gray & dk grn .50 .25
506 A100 30fr bl grn, dk brn & brn red 1.00 .30

Cameroun brewing industry.

Ozila Dancers — A101

Design: 50fr, Ozila dancer and drummer.

1970, Oct. 19 Engr. *Perf. 13*

507 A101 30fr multicolored 1.00 .35
508 A101 50fr red & multi 1.25 .75

Cameroun Doll — A102

Designs: 15fr, Doll in short skirt. 30fr, Doll with basket on back.

1970, Nov. 2

509 A102 10fr car & multi .60 .25
510 A102 15fr dk grn & multi .70 .25
511 A102 30fr brn red & multi 1.90 .30
Nos. 509-511 (3) 3.20 .80

Cogwheels and Grain A103

1970, Feb. 9 Photo. *Perf. 13*

512 A103 30fr multicolored .85 .25

Europafrica Economic Conference.

Federal University, Yaoundé
A104

1971, Jan. 19 **Engr.**

513 A104 50fr multicolored 1.00 .25

Inauguration of Federal University at Yaoundé.

Presidents Ahidjo and Pompidou, Flags of Cameroun and France — A105

1971, Feb. 9 **Photo.** ***Perf. 13***

514 A105 30fr multicolored 1.50 .35

Visit of Georges Pompidou, Pres. of France.

Young People, Globe, Map of Cameroun
A106

1971, Feb. 11

515 A106 30fr blue & multi .90 .30

Fifth National Youth Festival, Feb. 11.

Gerbera Hybrida — A107

Designs: 40fr, Opuntia polyantha (cactus). 50fr, Hemerocallis hybrida (lily).

1971, Mar. 14 **Photo.**

516 A107 20fr multicolored .60 .25
517 A107 40fr green & multi 1.50 .25
518 A107 50fr blue & multi 2.10 .25
Nos. 516-518 (3) 4.20 .75

Men of Four Races — A108

Design: 30fr, Hands and globe.

1971, Mar. 21 ***Perf. 13x12½***

519 A108 20fr green & multi .55 .25
520 A108 30fr ultra & multi .75 .25

Intl. year against racial discrimination.

Crowned Cranes at Waza Camp
A109

20fr, Canoe on Sanaga River. 30fr, Sanaga River.

1971, Apr. 9. **Engr.** ***Perf. 13***

521 A109 10fr red, grn & blk 1.50 .25
522 A109 20fr dk grn, brn & red 1.00 .25
523 A109 30fr red, dk grn & brt bl 1.50 .25
Nos. 521-523 (3) 4.00 .75

International Court, The Hague — A110

1971, June 14 **Engr.** ***Perf. 13***

524 A110 50fr ultra, org brn & sl grn 1.25 .35

25th anniversary of the International Court in The Hague, Netherlands.

Liana Bridge — A111

Local Market
A112

1971, Aug. 16 **Photo.** ***Perf. 13***

525 A111 40fr multicolored 1.60 .25
526 A112 45fr multicolored 1.60 .25

Bamoun Horseman
A113

African Art: 15fr, Animal fetish statuette.

1971, Sept. 18

527 A113 10fr brown & yellow .50 .50
528 A113 15fr dp brn & org yel .50 .50

Communications Satellite and Globe — A114

1971, Oct. 14 ***Perf. 13x12½***

529 A114 40fr Prus bl, sl grn & org .80 .25

Pan-African telecommunications system.

UNICEF Emblem
A115

50fr, UNICEF emblem and grain, vert.

1971, Dec. 11 **Engr.** ***Perf. 13***

530 A115 40fr sl grn, bl grn & plum .95 .25
531 A115 50fr dp bl, dk red & lt grn 1.25 .25

25th anniv. of UNICEF.

Houses from South-Central Region — A116

Design: 15fr, Adamaua round houses.

1972, Jan. 15 **Photo.** ***Perf. 13***

532 A116 10fr dk blue & multi .25 .25
533 A116 15fr black & multi .55 .25

Giraffe — A117

Designs: 5fr, Home industries. 10fr, Smith, horiz. 15fr, Women carrying burdens.

Perf. 13x13½, 13½x13

1972, Feb. 18 **Litho.**

534 A117 2fr multicolored .30 .25
535 A117 5fr black, org & red .30 .25
536 A117 10fr multicolored .30 .25
537 A117 15fr multicolored .30 .25
Nos. 534-537 (4) 1.20 1.00

Youth Day 1972.

Soccer Players and Field — A118

Designs: 20fr, African Soccer Cup, vert. 45fr, Team captains shaking hands, vert.

1972, Feb. 22 ***Perf. 13½***

538 A118 20fr gray & multi .55 .25
539 A118 40fr gray & multi .95 .25
540 A118 45fr yellow & multi 1.50 .25
Nos. 538-540 (3) 3.00 .75

African Soccer Cup, Yaoundé, 2/23-3/5.

Government Building, Yaoundé, and Laurel — A119

1972, Apr. 6 **Photo.** ***Perf. 12½x12***

541 A119 40fr multicolored .80 .25

110th session of Inter-Parliamentary Council, Yaoundé, Apr. 1972.

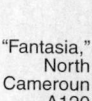

"Fantasia," North Cameroun
A120

Bororo Woman — A121

40fr, Boat on Wouri River & Mt. Cameroun.

1972, Apr. 24 ***Perf. 13x12½, 12½x13***

542 A120 15fr dk vio & multi .35 .25
543 A121 20fr multicolored .45 .25
544 A120 40fr multicolored 1.50 .25
Nos. 542-544 (3) 2.30 .75

Chemical Apparatus
A122

1972, May 15 **Engr.** ***Perf. 13***

545 A122 40fr lilac, red & green .80 .25

President Ahmadou Ahidjo Prize.

United Republic

Solanum Macranthum
A123

Design: 45fr, Wax plant.

1972, July 20 **Photo.** ***Perf. 13***

546 A123 40fr multicolored .95 .25
547 A123 45fr yellow & multi 1.25 .25

Charaxes Ameliae
A124

Design: 45fr, Papilio tynderaeus.

1972, Aug. 20 **Photo.** ***Perf. 13***

548 A124 40fr bl, dk bl & gold 4.00 .40
549 A124 45fr lt grn, blk & gold 5.50 .60

No. 468 Surcharged

1972, Aug. 30 **Photo.** ***Perf. 12x12½***

550 A85 40fr on 30fr multicolored 1.00 .25

Resurrection Lily — A125

Flowers: 45fr, Candlestick cassia. 50fr, Amaryllis.

1972, Sept. 16 *Perf. 13*

551 A125 40fr lt green & multi	1.00	.25
552 A125 45fr multicolored	1.25	.25
553 A125 50fr lt blue & multi	1.50	.35
Nos. 551-553 (3)	3.75	.85

Great Blue Touraco — A126

Design: 45fr, Red-faced lovebirds, horiz.

Perf. 12½x13, 13x12½

1972, Nov. 20 **Litho.**

554 A126 10fr yellow & multi	1.75	.25
555 A126 45fr yellow & multi	3.75	.25

Cotton (North) — A127

10fr, Cacao (south central). 15fr, Logging (southeast & southern coast). 20fr, Coffee (west). 45fr, Tea (northwest & southwest).

1973, Mar. 26 **Photo.** *Perf. 12½x13*

556 A127 5fr black & multi	.25	.25
557 A127 10fr black & multi	.25	.25
558 A127 15fr black & multi	.75	.25
559 A127 20fr black & multi	1.50	.25
560 A127 45fr black & multi	2.50	.40
Nos. 556-560 (5)	5.25	1.40

Third 5-Year Plan.
For surcharge see No. 568.

Flag and Map of Cameroun, Pres. Ahidjo and No. 331 — A128

Design: 20fr, Proclamation of independence, Pres. Ahidjo and No. 336.

1973, May 20 **Engr.** *Perf. 13*

561 A128 10fr ultra & multi	.65	.25
562 A128 20fr multicolored	1.00	.25
Nos. 561-562,C200-C201 (4)	3.45	1.15

United Republic of Cameroun, 1st anniv.

Bamoun Mask — A129

Designs: Various Bamoun masks.

1973, July 10 **Engr.** *Perf. 13*

563 A129 5fr green, brn & blk	.25	.25
564 A129 10fr lilac, brn & blk	.25	.25
565 A129 45fr red, brn & blk	.75	.25
566 A129 100fr ultra, brn & blk	2.00	.40
Nos. 563-566 (4)	3.25	1.15

Dr. Hansen — A130

1973, July 25 **Engr.** *Perf. 13*

567 A130 45fr multicolored	2.00	.25

Centenary of the discovery by Dr. Armauer G. Hansen of the Hansen bacillus, the cause of leprosy.

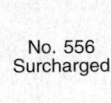

No. 556 Surcharged

1973, Aug. 16 **Photo.** *Perf. 12½x13*

568 A127 100fr on 5fr	1.75	.40

African solidarity in drought emergency.

Dancers, South West Africa — A131

Designs: Southwest African dances.

1973, Aug. 17 *Perf. 13*

569 A131 10fr multicolored	.25	.25
570 A131 25fr multicolored	.55	.25
571 A131 45fr multicolored	1.10	.25
Nos. 569-571 (3)	1.90	.75

WMO Emblem — A132

1973, Sept. 1 **Engr.** *Perf. 13*

572 A132 45fr green & ultra	1.60	.25

Cent. of intl. meteorological cooperation.

Garoua Party Headquarters — A133

1973, Sept. 1 **Photo.**

573 A133 40fr multicolored	.80	.25

7th anniv. of Cameroun National Union.

African Postal Union Issue, 1973
Common Design Type

1973, Sept. 12 **Engr.**

574 CD137 100fr brt bl, bl & sl grn	1.75	.40

Avocados — A135

1973, Sept. 20

575 A135 10fr shown	.70	.25
576 A135 20fr Mangos	.80	.25
577 A135 45fr Plums	2.00	.25
578 A135 50fr Custard apple	2.50	.25
Nos. 575-578 (4)	6.00	1.00

Kirdi Village A136

45fr, Mabas village. 50fr, Fishing village.

1973, Oct. 25 **Engr.** *Perf. 13*

579 A136 15fr black, bis & grn	.25	.25
580 A136 45fr magenta, brn & org	.90	.25
581 A136 50fr green, blk & org	1.25	.25
Nos. 579-581 (3)	2.40	.75

Handshake on Map of Africa — A137

1974, May 15 **Engr.** *Perf. 12½x13*

582 A137 40fr carmine & multi	.55	.25
583 A137 45fr indigo & multi	.70	.25

Organization for African Unity, 10th anniv.

Spinning Mill — A138

1974, May 25 **Engr.** *Perf. 13x12½*

584 A138 45fr multicolored	.80	.25

CICAM Industrial Complex.

Carved Panel from Bilinga A139

Cameroun Art (Carvings): 40fr, Detail from Bubinga chair. 45fr, Detail Acajou Ngollon panel.

1974, May 30

585 A139 10fr brt grn & ocher	.25	.25
586 A139 40fr red & brown	.80	.25
587 A139 45fr blue & rose brn	1.10	.25
Nos. 585-587 (3)	2.15	.75

Zebu — A140

1974, June 1 *Perf. 13½*

588 A140 40fr multicolored	1.40	.25

North Cameroun cattle raising. See No. C210.

Laying Rail Section A141

Designs: 5fr, Map showing line Yaoundé to Ngaoundéré, vert. 40fr, Welding rail joint, vert. 100fr, Train on Djerem River Bridge.

Perf. 12½x13, 13x12½

1974, June 10 **Engr.**

589 A141 5fr multicolored	.65	.25
590 A141 20fr multicolored	1.25	.30
591 A141 40fr multicolored	2.00	.60
592 A141 100fr multicolored	3.25	.90
Nos. 589-592 (4)	7.15	2.05

Opening of Yaoundé-Ngaoundéré railroad line.
For surcharge see No. 596.

No. 466 Surcharged

1974, June 1 **Photo.** *Perf. 12x12½*

593 A85 40fr on 8fr multi	.80	.25

UPU Emblem, Hands Holding Letters A142

1974, Oct. 8 **Engr.** *Perf. 13*

594 A142 40fr multicolored	.90	.25
Nos. 594,C218-C219 (3)	5.90	1.75

Cent. of the UPU.

Presidents and Flags of Cameroun, CAR, Congo, Gabon and Meeting Center — A143

1974, Dec. 8 **Photo.** ***Perf. 13***
595 A143 40fr gold & multi 1.50 .25

10th anniversary of Central African Customs and Economic Union (Union Douanière et Economique de l'Afrique Centrale, UDEAC). See No. C223.

No. 589 Surcharged in Violet Blue

1974, Dec. 10 **Engr.** ***Perf. 12½x13***
596 A141 100fr on 5fr multi 2.50 .85

Virgin of Autun, 15th Century Sculpture A144

Christmas: 45fr, Virgin and Child, by Luis de Morales (c. 1509-1586).

1974, Dec. 20 **Photo.** ***Perf. 13***
597 A144 40fr gold & multi .95 .25
598 A144 45fr gold & multi 1.25 .25

Tropical Plants — A145

5fr, Cockscomb. 40fr, Costus spectabilis. 45fr, Mussaenda erythrophylla.

1975, Mar. 10 **Photo.** ***Perf. 13***
599 A145 5fr multicolored .30 .25
600 A145 40fr multicolored 1.50 .25
601 A145 45fr multicolored 1.90 .35
Nos. 599-601 (3) 3.70 .85

Fishing by Night — A146

1975, Apr. 1 **Engr.** ***Perf. 13***
602 A146 40fr shown 1.75 .40
603 A146 45fr Fishing by day 1.75 .40

Afo Akom Statue and Chief's Stool — A147

1975, Apr. 1 **Photo.**
604 A147 40fr multicolored .65 .25
605 A147 45fr multicolored .85 .25
606 A147 200fr multicolored 2.50 .75
Nos. 604-606 (3) 4.00 1.25

Tree Fungus — A148

1975, Apr. 14
607 A148 15fr shown *125.00* 2.00
608 A148 40fr Chrysalis *85.00* 1.00

Ministry of Posts and Telecommunications — A149

1975, July 21 **Engr.** ***Perf. 13***
609 A149 40fr brn, grn & Prus bl .65 .25
610 A149 45fr Prus bl, brn & grn .90 .25

Presbyterian Church, Elat — A150

Designs: No. 612, Foumban Mosque. 45fr, Catholic Church, Ngaoundere.

1975, Aug. 20 **Engr.** ***Perf. 13***
611 A150 40fr multicolored .45 .25
612 A150 40fr multicolored .45 .25
613 A150 45fr multicolored .65 .25
Nos. 611-613 (3) 1.55 .75

Plowing A151

Design: No. 615, Corn harvest, vert.

Perf. 13x12½, 12½x13

1975, Dec. 15 **Photo.**
614 A151 40fr deep grn & multi .70 .25
615 A151 40fr deep grn & multi .70 .25

Green revolution.

Zamengoe Satellite Monitoring Station — A152

1976, May 20 **Litho.** ***Perf. 13***
616 A152 40fr shown .50 .25
617 A152 100fr Radar, vert. 1.25 .40

Porcelain Rose — A153

Design: 50fr, Flower of North Cameroun.

1976, July 20 **Litho.** ***Perf. 12½***
618 A153 40fr multicolored 1.00 .25
619 A153 50fr multicolored 1.40 .35

Leopard Dance — A154

1976, Sept. 15 **Litho.** ***Perf. 12***
620 A154 40fr gray & multi .80 .25
Nos. 620,C233-C234 (3) 2.55 .85

Telephone Exchange A155

1976, Oct. 5 ***Perf. 13***
621 A155 50fr multicolored .80 .25

Centenary of first telephone call by Alexander Graham Bell, Mar. 10, 1876.

Young Men Building House — A156

Design: 45fr, Young women working in field.

1976, Oct. 10 **Litho.** ***Perf. 12***
622 A156 40fr multicolored .35 .25
623 A156 45fr multicolored .60 .25

10th National Youth Day.

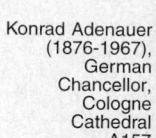

Konrad Adenauer (1876-1967), German Chancellor, Cologne Cathedral A157

1976, Oct. 20
624 A157 100fr multicolored .95 .40

Party Headquarters, Douala — A158

No. 626, Party Headquarters, Yaoundé.

1976, Dec. 28 **Litho.** ***Perf. 12***
625 A158 50fr orange & multi .45 .25
626 A158 50fr blue & multi .45 .25

10th anniv. of the Cameroun National Union.

Bamoun Copper Pipe — A159

1977, Feb. 4 **Litho.** ***Perf. 12½***
627 A159 50fr multicolored .70 .25

2nd World Black and African Festival, Lagos, Nigeria, 1/15-2/12. See No. C239.

Ostrich — A160

1977, Mar. 20 **Litho.** ***Perf. 12***
628 A160 30fr shown 2.50 .40
629 A160 50fr Crowned cranes 3.00 .75

Cameroun No. 609 and Switzerland No. 3L1 — A161

1977, June 5 **Litho.** ***Perf. 12***
630 A161 50fr multicolored 1.00 .30
Nos. 630,C252-C253 (3) 4.35 1.25

Jufilex Philatelic Exhibition, Bern, Switzerland. See Nos. C252-C253.

Winter Olympics 1976, set of five, 40, 50fr, airmail 140, 200, 350fr, and airmail souv. sheet, 500fr, issued Aug. 10, 1977. Nos. 7701-7706. Value, set $7.50, souvenir sheet $5.

Apollo-Soyuz — A163

Designs: 40fr, Astronaut Thomas P. Stafford, Apollo lifting off. 60fr, Cosmonaut Alexei Leonov, Soyuz lifting off.

1977, Aug. 10 Litho. *Perf. 14x13½*
633 A163 40fr multicolored .45 .25
634 A163 60fr multicolored .70 .50
Nos. 633-634,C256-C258 (5) 7.55 2.60

No. 617 Overprinted in French and English

1977, Aug. 22 Litho. *Perf. 13*
635 A152 100fr multicolored .90 .40

Palestinian fighters and their families.

Chairman Mao and Great Wall A164

1977, Sept. 9 Engr. *Perf. 13*
636 A164 100fr olive & brown 4.25 .55

Mao Tse-tung (1893-1976), Chinese communist leader, first death anniversary.

Nativity, by Albrecht Altdorfer A165

50fr, Madonna of the Grand Duke, by Raphael.

1977, Dec. 15 Litho. *Perf. 12½x12*
637 A165 30fr multicolored .55 .25
638 A165 50fr multicolored 1.10 .25
Nos. 637-638,C264-C265 (4) 7.65 2.50

Christmas 1977.

Gazelle and Rotary Emblem — A166

1978, Feb. 11 Litho. *Perf. 12*
639 A166 50fr orange & multi .70 .25

Rotary Club of Yaounde, 20th anniversary.

Pres. Ahidjo, Flag and Map of Cameroun A167

1978, Apr. 3 Litho. *Perf. 12½*
640 A167 50fr multicolored .90 .25

New flag of Cameroun. See No. C266.

Cardioglossa Escalerae — A168

Design: 60fr, Cardioglossa elegans.

1978, Apr. 5
641 A168 50fr multicolored 1.75 .25
642 A168 60fr multicolored 3.00 .25
Nos. 641-642,C267 (3) 8.50 1.25

Jules Verne and "From Earth to Moon" — A169

1978, Oct. 10 Litho. *Perf. 12*
643 A169 250fr multicolored 2.25 1.40

Jules Verne (1828-1905), science fiction writer, birth sesquicentennial. See No. C276.

Hypolimnas Salmacis Drury — A170

Butterflies: 25fr, Euxanthe trajanus ward. 30fr, Euphaedra cyparissa cramer.

1978, Oct. 15
644 A170 20fr multicolored 2.00 .60
645 A170 25fr multicolored 2.25 .60
646 A170 30fr multicolored 3.75 .60
Nos. 644-646 (3) 8.00 1.80

Men Planting Seedlings — A171

1978, Oct. 30 *Perf. 12½*
647 A171 10fr multicolored .25 .25
648 A171 15fr multicolored .35 .25

Green barrier against the desert.

Carved Bamun Drum — A172

60fr, String instrument (Gueguerou), horiz.

1978, Nov. 20 Litho. *Perf. 12½*
649 A172 50fr multicolored .45 .25
650 A172 60fr multicolored .90 .25
Nos. 649-650,C277 (3) 2.60 .90

Pres. Ahidjo, Giscard D'Estaing, Flags of Cameroun and France — A173

1979, Feb. 8 Photo. *Perf. 13*
651 A173 60fr multicolored 1.50 .60

Visit of Pres. Valery Giscard D'Estaing of France to Cameroun.

Human Rights Emblem, Globe, Scroll and African — A174

1979, Feb. 11 Litho. *Perf. 12x12½*
652 A174 5fr multicolored .25 .25

Universal Declaration of Human Rights, 30th anniversary (in 1978). See No. C278. See No. 803.

Boy and Girl Greeting Sun — A175

1979, Aug. 15 Litho. *Perf. 12*
653 A175 50fr multicolored .80 .25

International Year of the Child.

Protected Animals A176

Nos. 655, 658 vert.

1979, Sept. 20 *Perf. 12½*
654 A176 50fr Rhinoceros 1.40 .30
655 A176 60fr Giraffe 1.90 .40
656 A176 60fr Gorilla 1.90 .40
657 A176 100fr Leopard 2.90 .60
658 A176 100fr Elephant 2.90 .60
Nos. 654-658 (5) 11.00 2.30

Eugene Jamot, Map of Cameroun, Tsetse Fly — A177

1979, Nov. 5 Engr. *Perf. 13*
659 A177 50fr multicolored 3.00 .40

Eugene Jamot (1879-1937), discoverer of sleeping sickness cure.

Annunciation, by Fra Filippo Lippi — A178

Paintings; 50fr, Rest During the Flight to Egypt, c. 1620. No. 622, Flight into Egypt, by Jan Joest, No. 663, Nativity, by Joest. 100fr, Nativity, by Botticelli.

1979, Dec. 6 Litho. *Perf. 12½x12*
660 A178 10fr multicolored .25 .25
661 A178 50fr multicolored .60 .25
662 A178 60fr multicolored .75 .30
663 A178 60fr multicolored .75 .30
a. Pair, #662-663 1.50 1.50
664 A178 100fr multicolored 1.50 .40
Nos. 660-664 (5) 3.85 1.50

Christmas 1979.

Piper Capense A179

Medicinal Plants: 60fr, Bracken fern.

1979, Dec. 15 Litho. *Perf. 12½*
665 A179 50fr multicolored 1.25 .30
666 A179 60fr multicolored 1.50 .40

Pres. Ahidjo, Cameroun Map, Arms and No. 331 A180

1980, Feb. 12 Litho. *Perf. 12½*
667 A180 50fr multicolored .65 .25

Independence, 20th anniversary.

Congress Building, Bafoussam
A181

1980, Feb. 12

668 A181 50fr multicolored .65 .25

Cameroun National Union, 3rd Ordinary Congress, Bafoussam, Feb. 12-17.

Rotary Emblem, Map of Cameroun
A182

Rotary Intl., 75th Anniv.: No. 670, Anniv. emblem.

1980, Mar. 15 **Litho.** ***Perf. 12½***

669	A182 200fr multicolored	2.00	.80
670	A182 200fr multicolored	2.00	.80
a.	Souvenir sheet of 2, #669-670	5.25	4.00

Voacanga Medicinal Beans
A183

60fr, Voacanga tree, vert. 100fr, Voacanga flower, vert.

1980, Dec. 3 **Litho.** ***Perf. 12½***

671	A183 50fr shown	1.00	.25
672	A183 60fr multicolored	1.25	.25
673	A183 100fr multicolored	1.75	.40
	Nos. 671-673 (3)	4.00	.90

Violet Mellowstone
A184

1980, Dec. 5

674	A184 50fr shown	.70	.25
675	A184 60fr Patula	1.00	.25
676	A184 100fr Cashmere bouquet	1.60	.40
	Nos. 674-676 (3)	3.30	.90

Occupation of Mecca by Mohammed, 1350th Anniversary — A185

1980, Dec. 9

677 A185 50fr multicolored 1.00 .30

African Slender-snouted Crocodile (Endangered Species) — A186

1980, Dec. 24

678	A186 200fr shown	3.25	.80
679	A186 300fr Buffon's antelope, vert.	4.00	1.20

See Nos. 888-889.

Bororo Girls and Roumsiki Peaks — A187

1980, Dec. 29

680	A187 50fr shown	.55	.25
681	A187 60fr Dschang tourist center	.55	.25

Banana Tree
A188

1981, Feb. 5

682	A188 50fr shown	.65	.30
683	A188 60fr Cattle, vert.	.80	.40

Girl on Crutches — A189

1981, Feb. 20 **Litho.** ***Perf. 12½***

684	A189 60fr shown	.55	.25
685	A189 150fr Boy in motorized wheelchair	1.25	.65

International Year of the Disabled.

Air Terminal, Douala Airport — A190

1981, Apr. 4 **Litho.** ***Perf. 12½***

686	A190 100fr shown	1.00	.55
687	A190 200fr Boeing 747	2.00	1.10
688	A190 300fr Douala Intl. Airport	3.00	1.60
	Nos. 686-688 (3)	6.00	3.25

Cameroun Airlines, 10th anniv.

Pres. Ahidjo Presenting Trophy to Canon Soccer Team — A191

1981, Apr. 20

689	A191 60fr shown	.90	.40
690	A191 60fr Union team captain	.90	.40

1979 African Soccer Cup champions.

Scaly Anteater
A192

Designs: Endangered species.

1981, July 20 **Litho.** ***Perf. 12½***

691	A192 50fr Moutourou	1.50	.25
692	A192 50fr Tortoise	1.50	.25
693	A192 100fr shown	3.25	.40
	Nos. 691-693 (3)	6.25	.90

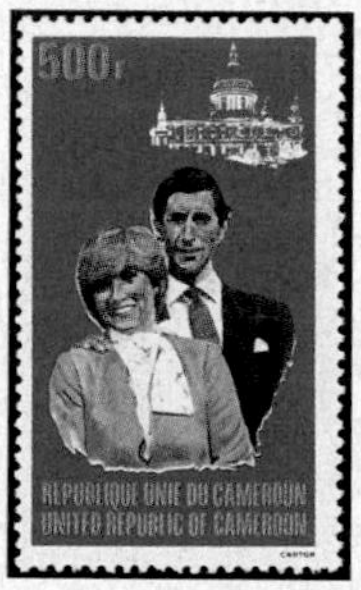

Prince Charles and Lady Diana, St. Paul's Cathedral
A193

1981, July 29 **Litho.** ***Perf. 12½***

694	A193 500fr shown	4.50	2.00
695	A193 500fr Couple, royal coach	4.50	2.00
a.	Souvenir sheet of 2, #694-695	10.00	4.00

Royal wedding.

Bafoussam-Bamenda Highway — A194

1981, Sept. 10 **Litho.** ***Perf. 12½***

696 A194 50fr multicolored .55 .25

Freighter Cam Iroko (Cameroun Shipping Line)
A195

1981, Sept. 25

697 A195 60fr multicolored 1.00 .40

20th Anniv. of Reunification — A196

1981, Oct. 10 ***Perf. 12½x13***

698 A196 50fr multicolored .70 .25

Medicinal Plants — A197

1981, Dec. 31 **Litho.** ***Perf. 12½***

699	A197 60fr Voacanga thouarsii	1.10	.30
700	A197 70fr Cassia alata	1.40	.40

Easter 1982 — A198

Paintings: 100fr, Christ in the Garden of Olives, by Delacroix. 200fr, Descent from the Cross, by Giotto. 250fr, Pieta in the Countryside, by Bellini.

1982, Apr. 10 **Litho.** ***Perf. 13***

701	A198 100fr multicolored	.90	.35
702	A198 200fr multicolored	1.75	.65
703	A198 250fr multicolored	2.25	.90
	Nos. 701-703 (3)	4.90	1.90

PHILEXFRANCE '82 Stamp Exhibition, Paris, June 11-21 — A199

1982, Apr. 25 ***Perf. 12***

704 A199 90fr multicolored 1.90 .40

Snakeskin Handbag — A200

1982, Apr. 30 ***Perf. 12½***

705	A200 60fr shown	.70	.25
706	A200 70fr Clay water jug	.80	.35

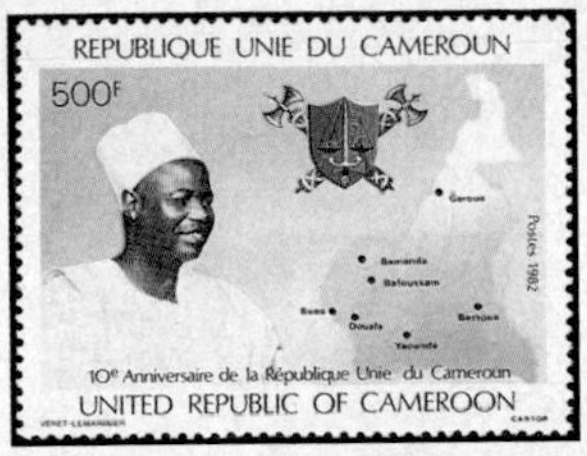

10th Anniv. of Republic — A201

1982, May 20 *Perf. 13*
707 A201 500fr multicolored 4.50 2.00

Town Hall, Douala — A202

1982, June 15 Litho. *Perf. 12½*
708 A202 40fr shown .45 .25
709 A202 60fr Yaounde .65 .25

See Nos. 730-731, 757-758, 790-791, 867.

1982 World Cup — A203

1982, July 10 *Perf. 13*
710 A203 100fr Natl. team 1.40 .40
711 A203 200fr Semi-finalists 2.75 .75
712 A203 300fr Players, vert. 4.50 1.25
713 A203 400fr Natl. team 2nd lineup 5.75 1.60
a. Souvenir sheet of 2, #713 14.50 3.50
Nos. 710-713 (4) 14.40 4.00

Partridge — A204

1982 *Perf. 12½x13*
714 A204 10fr shown 2.50 .40
715 A204 15fr Turtle dove 3.00 .85
716 A204 20fr Swallow 5.50 1.10
717 A204 200fr Bongo antelope 3.00 .80
718 A204 300fr Black colobus 4.00 1.25
Nos. 714-718 (5) 18.00 4.40

Issued: 200fr, 300fr, July 20; others Aug. 10.
See No. 804.

Scouting Year A205

1982, Sept. 30 Litho. *Perf. 13x12½*
719 A205 200fr Campfire 2.50 .80
720 A205 400fr Baden-Powell 4.50 1.60

25th Anniv. of the Presbyterian Church in Cameroun — A206

1982, Oct. 30 *Perf. 13x12½, 12½x13*
721 A206 45fr Buea Chapel .55 .25
722 A206 60fr Nyasoso Chapel, vert. .65 .25

ITU Plenipotentiaries Conference, Nairobi, Sept. — A207

1982, Oct. 5 Litho. *Perf. 12½x13*
723 A207 70fr multicolored .70 .25

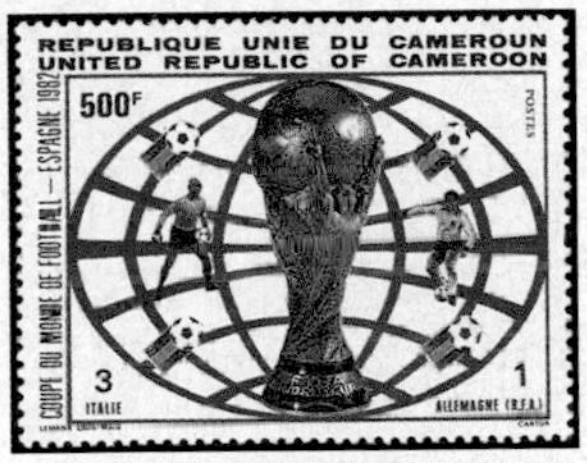

Italy's Victory in 1982 World Cup — A208

1982, Nov. *Perf. 13*
724 A208 500fr multicolored 5.50 2.00
725 A208 1000fr multicolored 10.50 4.00

30th Anniv. of Customs Cooperation Council — A209

1983, Jan. 10 *Perf. 12½x13*
726 A209 250fr Emblem 2.25 .80
727 A209 250fr Headquarters, Brussels 2.25 .80

2nd Yaoundé Medical Conference — A210

1983, Jan. 23 Litho. *Perf. 13*
728 A210 60fr grn & multi .70 .25
729 A210 70fr brn & multi .90 .25

City Hall Type of 1982

1983, Feb. 25 Litho. *Perf. 12½*
730 A202 60fr Bafoussam .60 .25
731 A202 70fr Garoua .70 .30

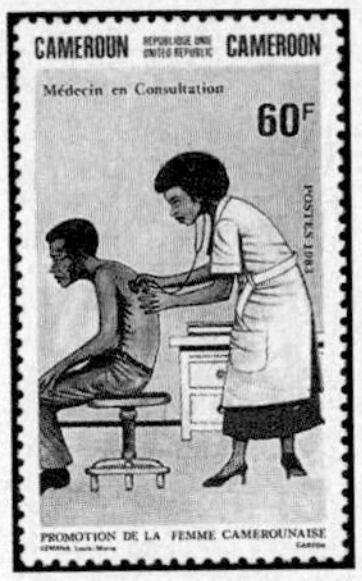

Homage to Women — A211

1983, Apr. 25 Litho. *Perf. 12½*
733 A211 60fr Nurse .75 .25
734 A211 70fr Lawyer .75 .25

11th Anniv. of Independence — A212

Flag and Pres. Paul Biya.

1983, May 18 Litho. *Perf. 13*
735 A212 60fr dk grn & multi .55 .25
736 A212 70fr dk bl & multi .70 .30

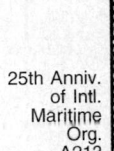

25th Anniv. of Intl. Maritime Org. A213

1983, May 23 *Perf. 13x12½*
737 A213 500fr multicolored 5.50 1.50

Eagle — A214

1983, June 15 Litho. *Perf. 12½x13*
738 A214 25fr shown 1.50 .40
739 A214 30fr Sparrowhawk 2.50 .75
740 A214 50fr Purple heron 4.50 1.00
Nos. 738-740 (3) 8.50 2.15

See Nos. 798-800, 873, 882, 886.

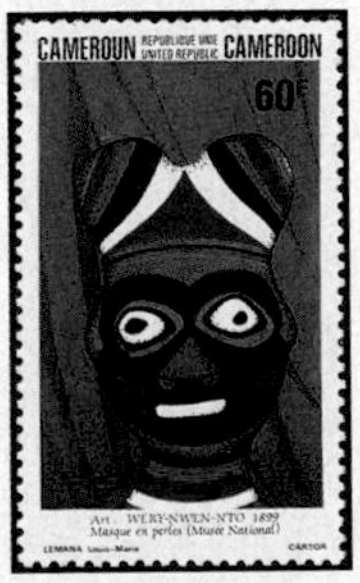

A215

60fr, Pearl mask, by Wery-Nwen-Nto, 1899. 70fr, Basket with lid.

1983, July 25 Litho. *Perf. 12*
741 A215 60fr multicolored .70 .25
742 A215 70fr multicolored .90 .30

A216

90fr, Mobile Post Office, horiz. 150fr, Telegraph Operator. 250fr, Tom-tom.

1983, Aug. 20 Litho. *Perf. 12*
743 A216 90fr multicolored .90 .25
744 A216 150fr multicolored 1.40 .35
745 A216 250fr multicolored 2.75 .55
Nos. 743-745 (3) 5.05 1.15

World Communications Year.

Endangered Species — A217

1983, Sept. 22 *Perf. 12*
746 A217 200fr Civet Cat 2.75 .50
747 A217 200fr Gorilla, vert 2.75 .50
748 A217 350fr Cobaya, vert 4.50 1.25
Nos. 746-748 (3) 10.00 2.25

See No. 887.

Lake Tizon — A218

1983, Nov. 25 Litho. *Perf. 13*
749 A218 60fr shown .55 .25
750 A218 70fr Mt. Cameroon .70 .25

Human Rights Declaration, 35th Anniv — A219

1983, Dec. 20 Litho. *Perf. 12½x13*
751 A219 60fr multicolored .55 .25
752 A219 70fr multicolored .70 .25

Christmas 1983 — A220

60fr, Christmas tree. 200fr, Stained glass window, Yaoundé Cathedral. No. 755, Rest during Flight into Egypt, by Philipp Otto Runge. No. 756, Angel of the Annunciation. 60fr, 200fr, No. 756 vert.

1983, Dec. 20 Litho. *Perf. 12½*
753 A220 60fr multicolored .45 .25
754 A220 200fr multicolored 1.75 .50
755 A220 500fr multicolored 4.50 1.25

756 A220 500fr multicolored 4.50 1.25
a. Souvenir sheet of 3, #754-756 12.50 12.50
Nos. 753-756 (4) 11.20 3.25

City Hall Type of 1982

1984, Apr. 20 Litho. *Perf. 12½*
757 A202 60fr Bamenda .55 .25
758 A202 70fr Mbalmayo .70 .25

Catholic Church, Zoetele — A221

1984, July 25 Litho. *Perf. 13*
759 A221 60fr shown .55 .25
760 A221 70fr Protestant Church, Yaounde .70 .25

Endangered Species — A222

1984, Aug. 15
761 A222 250fr Wild pig 3.50 .75
762 A222 250fr Deer 3.50 .75

1984, Oct. 10 Litho. *Perf. 13½*
763 A222 60fr Nightingale 4.50 1.00
764 A222 60fr Vultures 4.50 1.00

See No. 883.

Bamenda Farming Fair — A223

1984, Dec. 10 Litho. *Perf. 13*
765 A223 60fr Corn .60 .25
766 A223 70fr Cattle .90 .25
767 A223 300fr Potatoes 3.50 .90
Nos. 765-767 (3) 5.00 1.40

International Civil Aviation Organization, 40th Anniv. — A224

No. 768, Icarus. No. 769, ICAO emblem, vert. No. 770, Boeing 747. No. 771, Solar Princess painting.

1984, Dec. 20 Litho. *Perf. 12½*
768 A224 200fr multi 1.75 .60
769 A224 200fr multi 1.75 .60
770 A224 300fr multi 2.75 .90
771 A224 300fr multi 3.25 .90
Nos. 768-771 (4) 9.50 3.00

Olymphilex '85, Lausanne — A225

150fr, Wrestlers, exhibition emblem.

Wmk. 385

1985, Apr. 5 Photo. *Perf. 13*
772 A225 150fr multicolored 1.50 .40

Domestic Musical Instruments A226

1985, Apr. 23 *Perf. 13½*
773 A226 60fr Balafons (xylophone) .65 .25
774 A226 70fr Guitar .80 .25
775 A226 100fr Flute 1.10 .30
Nos. 773-775 (3) 2.55 .80

INTELSAT Org., 20th Anniv. — A227

1985, May 8 *Perf. 13*
776 A227 125fr Intelsat V 1.60 .35
777 A227 200fr Intelcam, Yaounde 2.10 .60

New York Headquarters — A228

1985, May 30
778 A228 250fr multicolored 2.40 1.10
779 A228 500fr multicolored 4.50 2.25

UN, 40th anniv.

Pres. Mitterand, Biya — A229

1985, June 20
780 A229 60fr multicolored 2.25 .25
781 A229 70fr multicolored 2.50 .25

Visit of Pres. Mitterand of France.

UNICEF A230

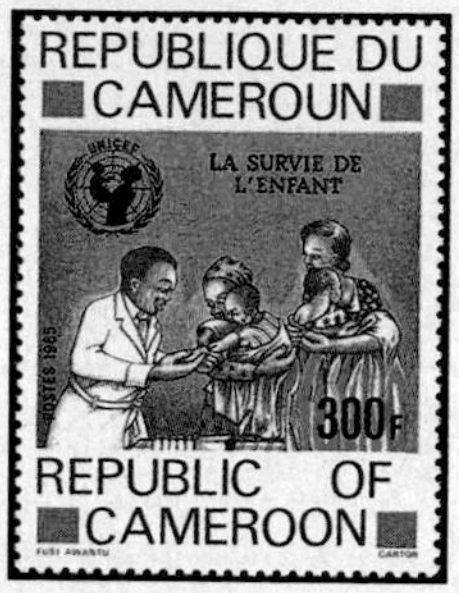

UN Infant Survival Campaign A231

1985, July 15
782 A230 60fr multicolored .55 .25
783 A231 300fr multicolored 2.75 1.00

Visit of Pope John Paul II, Aug. 10-14 — A232

60fr, Pope, papal arms. 70fr, Pope, crosier. 200fr, Pres. Biya, John Paul II.

1985, Aug. 9 *Perf. 13x12½*
784 A232 60fr multi 1.10 .40
785 A232 70fr multi 1.25 .55

Size: 55x38mm

786 A232 200fr multi 4.00 2.25
a. Souv. sheet of 3, #784-786 8.00 8.00
Nos. 784-786 (3) 6.35 3.20

Landscapes — A233

60fr, Lake Barumbi, Kumba. 70fr, Bonando Pygmy Village, Doume. 150fr, Cameroun River.

1985, July 25 Litho. *Perf. 12½*
787 A233 60fr multicolored .70 .25
788 A233 70fr multicolored .70 .25
789 A233 150fr multicolored 1.40 .40
Nos. 787-789 (3) 2.80 .90

City Hall Type of 1982

1985, July 30
790 A202 60fr Ngaoundere .55 .25
791 A202 60fr D'Ebolowa .55 .25

Wildlife — A234

1985, Aug. 20 *Perf. 13½*
792 A234 125fr Porcupine 1.50 .40
793 A234 200fr Squirrel 2.50 .60
794 A234 350fr Hedgehog 4.00 1.10
Nos. 792-794 (3) 8.00 2.10

Wood Sculptures A235

1985, Sept. 15
795 A235 60fr Mask .65 .25
796 A235 70fr Mask, diff. .90 .25
797 A235 100fr Wood bas-relief, horiz. 1.25 .30
Nos. 795-797 (3) 2.80 .80

Bird Type of 1983 Redrawn

1985, Nov. 10
798 A214 140fr Toucans 2.25 .50
799 A214 150fr Rooster 2.25 .55
800 A214 200fr Red-throated bee-eater 3.25 .70
Nos. 798-800 (3) 7.75 1.75

Nos. 798-800 inscribed "Republic of Cameroon".

See No. 873. For surcharge see No. 871.

American Peace Corps in Cameroun, 25th Anniv. — A237

1986, Jan. 1 Litho. *Perf. 12½*
801 A237 70fr multicolored .70 .25
802 A237 100fr multicolored 1.00 .30

Stamps of 1979-1982 Redrawn

1986, Mar. *Perf. 13, 13½*
803 A174 5fr multicolored .35 .35
804 A204 10fr multicolored .35 .35

Nos. 803-804 inscribed "Republic of Cameroon" instead of "United Republic of Cameroon."

Easter — A238

Paintings: 210fr, Head of the Virgin, by Pierre-Paul Prud'Hon (1758-1823). 350fr, The Stoning of St. Steven, by Van Scorel (1495-1562).

1986, Apr. 15 *Perf. 13½*
805 A238 210fr multicolored 1.75 .60
806 A238 350fr multicolored 3.00 1.00

Insects — A239

1986, Apr. 20

807 A239 70fr Honeybee 1.75 .40
808 A239 70fr Dragonfly 1.75 .40
809 A239 100fr Grasshopper 2.50 .65
Nos. 807-809 (3) 6.00 1.45

Nos. 808-809 horiz.

Flags, Conference Center — A240

1986, Apr. 25 Litho. *Perf. 13*

810 A240 100fr Map, vert. 1.00 .30
811 A240 175fr shown 2.00 .60

Conference of Ministers of the Economic Commission for Africa, Apr. 9-29.

Statues — A241

70fr, Bronze earth mother. 100fr, Wood funerary figure. 130fr, Wood equestrian figure.

1986, July 5 Litho. *Perf. 13½*

812 A241 70fr multicolored .85 .25
813 A241 100fr multicolored .95 .30
814 A241 130fr multicolored 1.60 .40
Nos. 812-814 (3) 3.40 .95

Queen Elizabeth II, 60th Birthday — A242

1986, July 15 Litho. *Perf. 13*

815 A242 100fr Elizabeth 1.00 .40
816 A242 175fr Elizabeth, Pres. Biya 1.40 .60
817 A242 210fr Elizabeth, diff. 2.00 .75
Nos. 815-817 (3) 4.40 1.75

Natl. Democratic Party, 1st Anniv. — A243

No. 818, Party headquarters, Bamenda. No. 819, Pres. Biya, vert. No. 820, Presidential address, vert.

1986, July 25 *Perf. 12½*

818 A243 70fr multicolored .70 .25
819 A243 70fr multicolored .70 .25
820 A243 100fr multicolored 1.00 .35
Nos. 818-820 (3) 2.40 .85

Kwem Mask Dancers of the Northeast — A244

1986, Aug. 1 *Perf. 13½*

821 A244 100fr multicolored 1.00 .35
822 A244 130fr multicolored 1.25 .45

Endangered Species — A245

1986, Aug. 20

823 300fr Varanus niloticus 3.50 1.00
824 300fr Panthera pardus 3.50 1.00

For surcharge see No. 872.

A246

Intl. Peace Year: 175fr, 200fr, Desmond Tutu, South Africa, Nobel Peace Prize winner. 250fr, UN and IPY emblems.

1986, Sept. 7 Litho. *Perf. 13½*

825 A246 175fr multicolored 1.75 1.10
826 A246 200fr multicolored 2.00 1.25
827 A246 250fr multicolored 2.50 1.50
Nos. 825-827 (3) 6.25 3.85

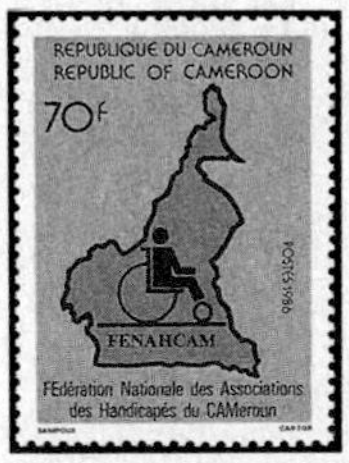

A247

1986, Oct. 30 Litho. *Perf. 13½*

828 A247 70fr multicolored .65 .25

Natl. Fed. of Associations for the Handicapped.

A248

70fr, Family under umbrella. 100fr, Child immunization.

1986, Nov. 9

829 A248 70fr multicolored .90 .25
830 A248 100fr multicolored 1.10 .35

African Vaccination Year.

A249

1986, Dec. 20 Litho. *Perf. 13½*

831 A249 70fr Afforestation map .90 .25
832 A249 100fr Hands, seedling 1.10 .35

Arbor Day.

Agricultural Development — A250

No. 833, ONCPB seminar. No. 834, Coconut farming, Dibombari. No. 835, Pineapple farm.

1986, Dec. 24

833 A250 70fr multicolored .75 .40
834 A250 70fr multicolored .75 .40
835 A250 200fr multicolored 2.00 1.10
Nos. 833-835 (3) 3.50 1.90

Insects Destructive to Agriculture A251

70fr, Antestiopsis lineaticollis intricata. 100fr, Distantiella theobroma.

1987, Sept. 25 Litho. *Perf. 13½*

836 A251 70fr multicolored 1.50 .50
837 A251 100fr multicolored 2.00 .70

4th African Games, Nairobi — A252

1987, Oct. 1 *Perf. 12½*

838 A252 100fr Shot put .90 .70
839 A252 140fr Pole vault 1.25 1.00

Maroua Agricultural Show — A253

1988, Jan. 6

840 A253 70fr Millet field .90 .50
841 A253 100fr Cotton 1.10 .70
842 A253 150fr Cattle 1.60 1.10
Nos. 840-842 (3) 3.60 2.30

World Wildlife Fund — A254

Baboons, Papio leucophaeus: 30fr, Adult. 40fr, Adult grooming young. 70fr, Baboon on branch. 100fr, Adult carrying young.

1988, Apr. 25 Litho. *Perf. 13*

843 A254 30fr multicolored 1.75 .75
844 A254 40fr multicolored 2.25 .75
845 A254 70fr multicolored 3.50 1.25
846 A254 100fr multicolored 6.00 1.75
Nos. 843-846 (4) 13.50 4.50

Interparliamentary Union, Cent. — A255

1989 Litho. *Perf. 13½*

847 A255 50fr Natl. Assembly .60 .30

World Cup Soccer Championships, Italy — A256

1990, Oct. 27 Litho. *Perf. 11½*

Granite Paper

848 A256 200fr shown 1.75 1.00
849 A256 250fr Players, diff. 2.25 1.25
850 A256 250fr Goalkeeper, flags 2.25 1.25
851 A256 300fr Team 3.00 1.50
a. Souv. sheet of 4, #848-851 9.00 6.50
Nos. 848-851 (4) 9.25 5.00

Roger Milla, World Cup Soccer Player A257

1990, July 4 Litho. *Perf. 11½*

Granite Paper

852 A257 500fr multicolored 6.50 3.50
a. Souv. sheet of 1 9.00 6.00

Agriculture A258

70fr, Treating cacao plants. 100fr, Sheep.

1990, Dec. 1 Litho. *Perf. 13½*

853 A258 70fr multicolored 1.25 .55
854 A258 100fr multicolored 1.75 .80
a. Sheet of 2, #853-854, perf. 12½ 8.00 8.00

For surcharges see Nos. 894-895.

UN Development Program, 40th Anniv. — A259

1990, Dec. 31 Litho. *Perf. 13½*
855 A259 50fr multicolored .60 .40

Intl. Literacy Year A260

1990, Dec. 31
856 A260 200fr bl, blk, & lt bl 2.00 .75

Independence, 30th Anniv. — A261

1991, Jan. 1 *Perf. 13*
857 A261 150fr shown 1.75 1.25
858 A261 1000fr Flag, Palace, #336 9.00 8.00
a. Souv. sheet. of 2, #857-858 12.50 12.50

Fight Against AIDS A262

1991, Jan. 15
859 A262 15fr Hearts, map, vert. .25 .25
860 A262 25fr shown .35 .25

See Nos. 884-885.

Birds A263

Designs: Nos. 861, 864, Pie grieche, vert. Nos. 862, 863, Picathartes chauve.

1991, May 3 Litho. *Perf. 13½*
861 A263 70fr grn & multi .75 .35
862 A263 70fr bl & multi .75 .40
863 A263 300fr blk & multi 3.25 2.00
864 A263 350fr blk & multi 3.50 2.25
a. Souv. sheet of 2, #863-864 9.00 5.50
Nos. 861-864 (4) 8.25 5.00

Wild Animals A264

1991, May 8 *Perf. 13½*
865 A264 125fr Elephant 1.60 1.00
866 A264 250fr Water buffalo 3.00 2.00
a. Souvenir sheet of 2, #865-866, perf. 12½ 9.00 3.50

City Hall Type of 1982 Redrawn

1991 *Perf. 13*
867 A202 40fr multicolored .60 .25

No. 867 inscribed "Republic of Cameroon" instead of "United Republic of Cameroon."

Cameroun Catholic Church, Cent. (in 1990) A265

1991, Dec. 8 Litho. *Perf. 13½*
868 A265 125fr Mvolye church 1.25 .75
a. Booklet pane of 4 — —
Complete booklet, #868a —
869 A265 250fr Akono church 2.25 1.75
a. Souvenir sheet of 2, #868-869 perf. 12½x13 4.00 3.00
b. Booklet pane of 4 — —
Complete booklet, #869a —

Issued: Nos. 868a, 869b, 1993.

Intl. Savings Banks Institute, 7th Meeting of the African Group A266

1991, Dec. 9
870 A266 250fr multicolored 2.40 1.60
a. Souv. sheet of 1, perf. 12½x13 3.00 2.00

No. 799 Surcharged

No. 824 Surcharged

1992 *Perf. 13½*
871 A214 20fr on 150fr #799 1.75 .25
872 A245 70fr on 300fr #824 5.75 .55

Bird Type of 1983

1992 Litho. *Perf. 13½*
873 A214 125fr like #800 1.50 .95

Dated 1985.

Cameroun Soccer League A267

125fr, Mbappe Mbappe Samuel (1936-85), soccer player, vert. 250fr, Linafoote League emblem, vert. 400fr, Linafoote emblem, diff. 500fr, Stadium.

1992, Aug. *Perf. 11½*
874 A267 125fr multicolored 1.25 .75
875 A267 250fr multicolored 2.40 1.75
876 A267 400fr multicolored 3.50 2.75
877 A267 500fr multicolored 5.50 3.50
Nos. 874-877 (4) 12.65 8.75

See Nos. 896-896B.

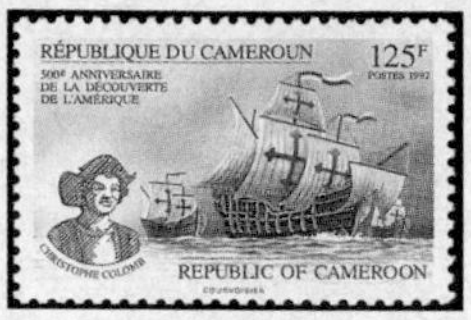

Discovery of America, 500th Anniv. A268

Columbus and: 125fr, Fleet of ships. 250fr, Landing in New World. 400fr, Meeting with natives. 500fr, Map, ships.

1992, Aug.
878 A268 125fr multicolored 1.40 .75
879 A268 250fr multicolored 2.10 1.75
880 A268 400fr multicolored 3.50 2.75
881 A268 500fr multicolored 5.00 3.50
Nos. 878-881 (4) 12.00 8.75

Types of 1983-84 Redrawn

1992 Litho. *Perf. 13½*
882 A214 200fr like #739 2.25 1.40
a. Booklet pane of 5
Complete booklet, #882a
883 A222 350fr like #763 3.75 2.50

Nos. 882-883 inscribed "Republic of Cameroon".

AIDS Type of 1991

1993 Litho. *Perf. 13½*
884 A262 100fr like #859 1.10 .70
885 A262 175fr like #860 1.90 1.25

Types of 1983 Redrawn

886 A214 370fr like #738 3.50 2.50
Perf. 13
887 A217 410fr like #746 4.50 2.90

Nos. 886-887 inscribed "Republic of Cameroon".

Wild Animal Type of 1980 Redrawn

1993 Litho. *Serpentine Die Cut 9½*
Booklet Stamps
Self-Adhesive
888 A186 125fr Crocodile 1.40 .65
a. Booklet pane of 4 5.75
889 A186 250fr Buffon's antelope, vert. 2.75 1.25
a. Booklet pane of 4 11.50

Nos. 888-889 inscribed "Republic of Cameroon".
By their nature, Nos. 888a, 889a are complete booklets. The peelable backing serves as a booklet cover.

1994 World Cup Soccer Championships, US — A270

Designs: 125fr, Pres. Paul Biya holding soccer ball, lion. 250fr, Logo, lion, player, map. 450fr, Players, globe, World Cup, flag. 500fr, US eagle, Cameroun lion, soccer ball.

1994, Mar. 28 Litho. *Perf. 13*
890 A270 125fr multicolored .75 .40
891 A270 250fr multicolored 1.50 .75
892 A270 450fr multicolored 2.75 1.50
893 A270 500fr multicolored 3.00 1.75
a. Min. sheet of 4, #890-893 80.00 60.00
Nos. 890-893 (4) 8.00 4.40

Nos. 853-854 Srchd. in Gold and Black

1993 Litho. *Perf. 13½*
894 A258 125fr on 70fr #853 — —
895 A258 125fr on 100fr #854 — —
a. With gold obliterator, new denomination in black omitted — —

Cameroun Soccer League Type of 1992

1992-93 Litho. *Perf. 11½*
896 A267 10fr like #876 — —
896A A267 25fr like #875 — —
896B A267 50fr like #874 — —

Nos. 896-896A dated 1993.
Issued: 50fr, 8/1/92; others, 1993.

Psittacus Erithacus — A271

1995 Litho. *Perf. 11½*
Granite Paper
897 A271 125fr multicolored 3.00 1.00

Visit of Pope John Paul II A272

1995, Sept. 14 *Perf. 12½*
898 A272 55fr shown .35 .25
a. Souvenir sheet of 1 — —
899 A272 125fr Pope, open text, cross .95 .50
a. Souvenir sheet of 1 — —

UN, 50th Anniv. A273

1995, Oct. 24 *Perf. 11½*
900 A273 200fr shown 1.25 .60
901 A273 250fr "50," people 1.50 .80

Conf. of Heads of State & Govt., Yaounde A274

Perf. 12½, 14¾x14 (200fr, 250fr)
1996-97 Litho.
902 A274 125fr blue & multi *1.00* *.50*
c. A274 125fr Perf. 14¾x14 — —
902A A274 200fr lt grn & multi ('97) *1.50* *.75*
902B A274 250fr yel & multi ('97) *2.00* *1.00*
903 A274 410fr pink & multi, vert. *3.00* *2.00*

No. 902c is dated "1997."

World Records Set at 1996 Summer Olympic Games, Atlanta A275

125fr, Baily, M. Johnson. 250fr, Harrison, Galfione, Perec, vert.

1996 *Perf. 11½*
904 A275 125fr multi — 1.00
905 A275 250fr multi — 1.50

Universal Declaration of Human Rights, 50th Anniv. — A279

1998 **Litho.** ***Perf. 14x14¾***
918 A279 370fr multicolored — 2.00

1998 World Cup Soccer Championships, France — A280

Design: 125fr, Flag of Cameroun, World Cup trophy, vert.

1998 **Litho.** ***Perf. 13***
922 A280 125fr multicolored — 2.00
923 A280 250fr multicolored — 2.50

Shrike A281

1998 **Litho.** ***Perf. 13x13½***
926 A281 125fr multicolored — 3.00

Economic and Monetary Community of Central Africa Week — A281a

Design: 125fr, Flags surrounding map of Africa. 225fr, Flags above map of Africa.

1999 **Litho.** ***Perf. 14½***
927 A281a 125fr multi — —
928 A281a 225fr multi — —

Flora & Fauna — A282

2000 **Litho.** ***Perf. 14x14½***
929 A282 100fr Pineapple — 2.00
930 A282 125fr Pineapple — 2.00
930A A282 150fr Coffee beans — —
930B A282 175fr Crowned crane — —
931 A282 200fr Baboon — 2.00
932 A282 250fr Coffee beans — 2.00
934 A282 410fr Crowned crane — 2.00

Dated 1998.

Peace, Work, Country A283

Map and Scenes — A284

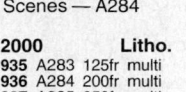

Airplane and Wildlife — A285

2000 **Litho.** ***Perf. 11¾***
935 A283 125fr multi — 2.00
936 A284 200fr multi — 2.00
937 A285 250fr multi — 2.00

Palais des Congrés, Yaounde A286

Perf. 11¾x11½
2001, Mar. 26 **Litho.**
938 A286 125fr multi — —

Cooperation between Cameroun and People's Republic of China, 30th anniv.

Campaign Against AIDS — A287

Design: 125fr, Woman vaccinating child, Chantal Biya Foundation emblem. 250fr, Chantal Biya Foundation emblem, globe, ribbon, woman with fetus.

2001 **Litho.** ***Perf. 13¼x13***
939 A287 125fr multi — —
941 A287 250fr multi — —
a. Souvenir sheet, #939, 941 150.00 —
Nos. 939-941 (2) 40.00

2002 World Cup Soccer Championships, Japan and Korea — A287a

Indomitable Lions Soccer Team, 20th Anniv. of Success A288

2002, June 20 **Litho.** ***Perf. 13¾***
943 A287a 125fr multi — —
Perf. 13x13¼
944 A288 250fr multi — —
Nos. 943-944 (2) 100.00

Souvenir Sheet

945 Sheet of 2, #943, 945a 100.00 —
a. As #944, 40x44mm, perf. 13½

71st Interpol General Assembly, Yaounde — A289

2002 **Litho.** ***Perf. 13¼x13***
946 A289 125fr multi 4.00 —
a. Souvenir sheet of 1 8.00 8.00

Cooperation Between Cameroun and Japan — A290

2005 **Litho.** ***Perf. 13***
948 A290 100fr multi 2.00 1.00
949 A290 125fr multi 2.00 —
950 A290 200fr multi — —
951 A290 250fr multi — —
952 A290 370fr multi 2.75 1.50
953 A290 410fr multi 3.00 2.00
954 A290 500fr multi 3.50 —
955 A290 1000fr multi 6.50 —

Nos. 948-951, 954-955 exist with "2005" year date.

Cameroun postal officials have declared as illegal a stamp inscribed "Republic of Cameroon" dated "2005" marking the 70th birthday of Elvis Presley.

Postal Savings Bank — A291

2006 **Litho.** ***Perf. 15x14***
956 A291 500fr multi — —

No. 956 was issued in 1997 as a stamp to pay fees for opening an account with the Postal Savings Bank. It was made available for postal use in 2006.

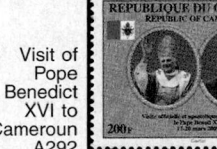

Visit of Pope Benedict XVI to Cameroun A292

Flags of Vatican City and Cameroun, Pope Benedict XVI, Pres. Paul Biya and background color of: 200fr, Yellow. 250fr, Bright pink.

2009 **Litho.** ***Perf. 13x13¼***
957-958 A292 Set of 2 6.00 —

New Challenges for Africa Conference, Yaounde — A293

Colors: 125fr, Black & gray. 250fr, Multicolored.

2010 **Litho.** ***Perf. 13½***
959-960 A293 Set of 2 5.00 —

Reunification and Independence, 50th Anniv. — A294

Designs: 125fr, Cameroun flag shown rotated 90 degrees clockwise. 200fr, 50th anniversary emblem. 250fr, Arms of Cameroun. 500fr, Pres. Paul Biya in black. 1000fr, Pres. Biya in color.

2010
961-964 A294 Set of 4 40.00 —
964a Horiz. strip of 4, #961-964 — —
964b Booklet pane of 8, 2 each #961-964 — —
Complete booklet, #964b —

Souvenir Sheet

965 A294 1000fr multi 20.00 —

No. 965 sold for 1500fr.

Diplomatic Relations Between Cameroun and People's Republic of China, 25th Anniv. A295

Designs: 125fr, Workers digging trenches for optical fibers. 200fr, Gynecological, Obstetrics and Pediatric Hospital, Yaounde. 250fr, Multi-purpose Sports Complex, Yaounde. 500fr, Cameroun Pres. Paul Biya and Chinese Pres. Hu Jintao shaking hands.

2011, Mar. 26 ***Perf. 12***
966-969 A295 Set of 4 20.00 —
968a Souvenir sheet of 3, #966-968 15.00 —

See Nos. 975-976.

First Douala-Paris Camair-Co Flight — A296

Litho. & Embossed
2011, Mar. 28 ***Perf. 13x13¼***
Denomination Color
970 A296 250fr green — —
971 A296 500fr white — —
a. Souvenir sheet of 2, #970-971 — —

Discovery of AIDS and HIV, 30th Anniv. A297

Designs: 100fr, Emblem of Cameroun National Committee for the Campaign Against AIDS. 250fr, AIDS ribbon, map of Africa. 500fr, Chantal Biya, First Lady of Cameroun and founder of Synergies Africaines charity.

2011, June 3 **Litho.**
972-974 A297 Set of 3 — —

Diplomatic Relations Type of 2011
Souvenir Sheets

Design as before.

2011, Sept. 14 **Litho.** ***Perf. 12***
975 A295 500fr multi — —

Litho. With Three-Dimensional Plastic Affixed
Without Gum

976 A295 500fr multi — —

No. 975 contains one 60x40mm stamp. No. 976 contains one 76x50mm stamp.

SEMI-POSTAL STAMPS

Curie Issue
Common Design Type

1938 Unwmk. *Perf. 13*
B1 CD80 1.75fr + 50c brt ultra 10.00 10.00

French Revolution Issue
Common Design Type

Photogravure; Name and Value Typographed in Black

1939
B2 CD83 45c + 25c green 11.50 11.50
B3 CD83 70c + 30c brown 11.50 11.50
B4 CD83 90c + 35c red org 11.50 11.50
B5 CD83 1.25fr + 1fr rose pink 11.50 11.50
B6 CD83 2.25fr + 2fr blue 14.00 14.00
Nos. B2-B6 (5) 60.00 60.00

Stamps of 1925-33 Srchd. in Black

1940 *Perf. 14x13½*
B7 A7 1.25fr + 2fr gray & dp bl 32.50 24.00
B8 A7 1.75fr + 3fr brn & org 32.50 24.00
B9 A7 2fr + 5fr dl grn & brn org 32.50 24.00
Nos. B7-B9 (3) 97.50 72.00

The surtax was used for war relief work.

Regular Stamps of 1939 Surcharged in Black

1940 *Perf. 13*
B10 A20 25c + 5fr blk brn 130.00 110.00
B11 A20 45c + 5fr slate grn 130.00 110.00
B12 A20 60c + 5fr peacock bl 130.00 120.00
B13 A20 70c + 5fr plum 130.00 120.00
Nos. B10-B13 (4) 520.00 460.00

The surtax was used to purchase Spitfire planes for the Free French army.

Common Design Type and

Military Doctor SP2

Cameroun Militiaman — SP4

1941 Photo. *Perf. 13½*
B13A SP2 1fr + 1fr red 1.60
B13B CD86 1.50fr + 3fr maroon 1.60
B13C SP4 2.50fr + 1fr dk bl 1.60
Nos. B13A-B13C (3) 4.80

Nos. B13A-B13C were issued by the Vichy government in France, but were not placed on sale in Cameroun.

Nos. 223-224 Surcharged in Black or Blue

1941 *Perf. 12½x12*
B14 CD82 1.25fr + 10fr car lake 120.00 120.00
B15 CD82 2.25fr + 10fr ultra 120.00 120.00

Nos. 223-224 Surcharged in Black or Blue

1941
B16 CD82 1.25fr + 10fr car lake (Bl) 40.00 40.00
B17 CD82 2.25fr + 10fr ultra (Bk) 40.00 40.00

The surtax was used to purchase ambulances for the Free French army.

Regular Stamps of 1933-39 Surcharged in Black

1943 *Perf. 14x13½, 13, 12½x12*
B21 A7 1.25fr + 100 gray & dp bl 27.50 27.50
B22 A21 1.25fr + 100fr car rose 27.50 27.50
B23 CD82 1.25fr + 100fr car lake 27.50 27.50
B24 A21 1.50fr + 100fr choc 27.50 27.50
B25 CD82 2.25fr + 100fr ultra 27.50 27.50
Nos. B21-B25 (5) 137.50 137.50

Nos. 281A-281B Surcharged in Black or Red

1944 Engr. *Perf. 12½x12*
B25A 50c + 1.50fr on 2.50fr deep blue (R) .40
B25B + 2.50fr on 1fr green .40

Colonial Development Fund.

Nos. B25A-B25B were issued by the Vichy government in France, but were not placed on sale in Cameroun.

Red Cross Issue
Common Design Type

1944 Photo. *Perf. 14½x14*
B28 CD90 5fr + 20fr rose 2.00 1.60

The surtax was for the French Red Cross and national relief.

Catalogue values for unused stamps in this section, from this point to the end of the section, are for Never Hinged items.

Tropical Medicine Issue
Common Design Type

1950 Engr. *Perf. 13*
B29 CD100 10fr + 2fr dk bl grn & dk grn 7.25 5.50

The surtax was for charitable work.

Independent State

Map and Flag — SP7

Unwmk.
1961, Mar. 25 Engr. *Perf. 13*
B30 SP7 20fr + 5fr grn, car & yel 1.10 1.00
B31 SP7 25fr + 10fr multi 1.40 1.25
B32 SP7 30fr + 15fr car, yel & grn 2.00 1.75
Nos. B30-B32 (3) 4.50 4.00

The surtax was for the Red Cross.

Federal Republic

Map of Cameroun, Lions Emblem and Physician Helping Leper SP8

1962, Jan. 28
B33 SP8 20fr + 5fr multi .70 .40
B34 SP8 25fr + 10fr multi .90 .50
B35 SP8 50fr + 15fr multi 1.75 .85
Nos. B33-B35 (3) 3.35 1.75

Issued for leprosy relief work.

Anti-Malaria Issue
Common Design Type

1962, Apr. 7 *Perf. 12½x12*
B36 CD108 25fr + 5fr rose lilac 1.00 .45

WHO drive to eradicate malaria.

Freedom from Hunger Issue
Common Design Type

1963, Mar. 21 Engr. *Perf. 13*
B37 CD112 18fr + 5fr multi 1.00 .35
B38 CD112 25fr + 5fr multi 1.25 .40

Antelopes — SP9

Designs: 125fr+10fr, Ourebia ourebi. 250fr+20fr, Kobus defassa.

1991, Apr. 30 Litho. *Perf. 13½x13*
B39 SP9 125fr + 10fr multi 2.00 1.10
B40 SP9 250fr + 20fr multi 3.00 2.25
a. Souvenir sheet of 2, #B39-B40, perf. 12½ 8.00 8.00

AIR POST STAMPS

Common Design Type

1942 Unwmk. Photo. *Perf. 14½x14*
C1 CD87 1fr dk orange .30 .30
C2 CD87 1.50fr brt red .30 .30
C3 CD87 5fr brown red .65 .65
C4 CD87 10fr black .80 .80
C5 CD87 25fr ultra 1.10 1.10
C6 CD87 50fr dk green 1.40 1.40
C7 CD87 100fr plum 1.75 1.75
Nos. C1-C7 (7) 6.30 6.30

Types AP9 and AP10 without "RF" and

Plane Over Coast AP3

1943-44 Photo. *Perf. 13, 13½*
C7A AP9 25c brown red .25
C7B AP9 50c green .25
C7C AP9 1fr brt violet .30
C7D AP10 5fr red brown .55
C7E AP10 10fr black .65
C7F AP10 12fr orange .70
C7G AP10 20fr crimson .95
C7H AP10 50fr blue 1.10
C7I AP3 100fr lilac brown 1.25
Nos. C7A-C7I (9) 6.00

Nos. C7A to C7I were issued by the Vichy Government in France, but were not placed on sale in Cameroun.

For Types AP9 and AP10 inscribed RF, see Nos. C15-C24.

Catalogue values for unused stamps in this section, from this point to the end of the section, are for Never Hinged items.

Victory Issue
Common Design Type

1946, May 8 Engr. *Perf. 12½*
C8 CD92 8fr dk violet brn 1.60 1.20

European victory of the Allied Nations in WWII.

Chad to Rhine Issue
Common Design Types

1946, June 6
C9 CD93 5fr dk blue grn 1.60 1.25
C10 CD94 10fr dk rose vio 1.60 1.25
C11 CD95 15fr red 2.00 1.60
C12 CD96 20fr brt blue 2.00 1.60
C13 CD97 25fr orange red 2.10 1.75
C14 CD98 50fr gray 2.75 2.25
Nos. C9-C14 (6) 12.05 9.70

Plane and Map — AP9

Seaplane Alighting AP10

Plane and Freighters AP11

1946 Photo. *Perf. 13, 13½*
C15 AP9 25c brown red .40 .25
C16 AP9 50c green .40 .25
C17 AP9 1fr brt violet .50 .30
C18 AP10 2fr olive grn .65 .50
C19 AP10 3fr chocolate .65 .50
C20 AP10 4fr deep ultra .65 .50
C21 AP10 6fr blue grn .65 .50
C22 AP10 7fr brt violet 1.10 .80
C23 AP10 12fr orange 5.50 3.50
C24 AP10 20fr crimson 1.90 1.40
C25 AP11 50fr dk ultra 2.75 1.90
Nos. C15-C25 (11) 15.15 10.40

Nos. C15 to C25 were issued in 1941 in France by the Vichy Government, but were not sold in Cameroun until 1946.

See Nos. C7A-C7H for stamps without "RF."

Birds over Mountains — AP12

Cavalry and Plane — AP13

Warrior, Dance Mask and Nose of Plane — AP14

Perf. 12½

1947, Feb. 10 Unwmk. Engr.

C26 AP12 50fr dk green 3.25 1.20
C27 AP13 100fr brn red 4.75 1.20
C28 AP14 200fr black 7.25 2.40
Nos. C26-C28 (3) 15.25 4.80

UPU Issue

Common Design Type

1949, July *Perf. 13*

C29 CD99 25fr multicolored 8.00 4.75

Rhumsiki Peak — AP16

1953, Feb. 16

C30 AP16 500fr grnsh blk, dk vio & vio bl 26.00 4.00

For surcharge see No. C40.

Edéa Dam and Sacred Ibis — AP17

1953, Nov. 18

C31 AP17 15fr choc, brn lake & ultra 5.50 1.60

Dedication of Edea Dam on the Sanaga River.

Liberation Issue

Common Design Type

1954, June 6

C32 CD102 15fr dk grnsh bl & bl grn 7.25 4.75

Dr. Eugene Jamot, Research Laboratory and Tsetse Flies — AP19

1954, Nov. 29

C33 AP19 15fr dk grn, ind & dk brn 4.75 2.75

75th anniv. of the birth of Dr. Eugene Jamot.

Logging — AP20

100fr, Giraffes. 200fr, Port of Douala.

1955, Jan. 24

C34 AP20 50fr ol grn, brn & vio brn 4.00 .80
C35 AP20 100fr grnsh bl, brn & dk brn 8.00 1.60
C36 AP20 200fr dk grn, choc & dp ultra 10.50 2.40
Nos. C34-C36 (3) 22.50 4.80

For surcharges see Nos. C38-C39.

Federal Republic

Air Afrique Issue

Common Design Type

Unwmk.

1962, Feb. 17 Engr. *Perf. 13*

C37 CD107 25fr mar, pur & lt grn 1.00 .50

Nos. C35-C36 and C30 Surcharged in Red

Type I

Two types of 5sh:
I — "5/-" measures 6½x4mm.
II — "5/" measures 3¾x3mm, No dash after diagonal line.

Three types of 10sh:
I — "10/-" measures 9x3¾mm.
II — "10/-" measures 7x2½-3mm.
III — "1" of "10/" vertically in line with last "E" of "FEDERALE".

Two types of £1:
I — "REPUBLIQUE / FEDERALE" 17¼mm wide.
II — "REPUBLIQUE / FEDERALE" 22mm wide.

1961, Oct. 1 Engr. *Perf. 13*

C38 AP20 5sh on 100fr (I) 10.00 6.00
a. Type II 32.50 18.00
C39 AP20 10sh on 200fr (I) 22.00 13.00
a. Type II 77.50 42.50
b. Type III 32.50 30.00
C40 AP16 £1 on 500fr (I) 35.00 22.00
a. Type II 60.00 35.00
Nos. C38-C40 (3) 67.00 41.00

Issued for use in the former United Kingdom Trust Territory of Southern Cameroons.

Kapsikis Mokolo — AP21

Designs: 50fr, Cocotieres Hotel, Douala. 100fr, Cymothoe sangaris butterflies. 200fr, Ostriches, Waza Reservation.

1962, June 15

C41 AP21 50fr sl grn, bl & dl red .90 .25
C42 AP21 100fr multicolored 5.75 .60
C43 AP21 200fr dk grn, blk & bis 8.00 1.40
C44 AP21 500fr vio brn, bl & ocher 9.00 2.25
Nos. C41-C44 (4) 23.65 4.50

Telstar Type of Regular Issue

1963, Feb. 9 Size: 48x27mm

C45 A50 100fr dk grn & red brn 2.50 .65

Edéa Relay Station — AP22

1963, May 18 Photo. *Perf. 12x12½*

C46 AP22 100fr multicolored 2.50 .65

Issued to publicize the high frequency telegraph connection Douala-Yaoundé.

African Postal Union Issue

Common Design Type

1963, Sept. 8 Unwmk. *Perf. 12½*

C47 CD114 85fr ultra, ocher & red 2.25 1.00

Air Afrique Issue, 1963

Common Design Type

1963, Nov. 19 *Perf. 13x12*

C48 CD115 50fr pink, gray, blk & grn 1.25 .40

Olympic Games Type of 1964

300fr, Greco-Roman wrestlers (ancient).

1964, Oct. 10 Engr. *Perf. 13*

C49 A57 300fr red, dk brn & dl grn 7.50 2.00
a. Sheet of 3, #403-404, C49 13.50 4.25

Kribi Port — AP25

1964, Oct. 26 Unwmk. *Perf. 13*

C50 AP25 50fr red brn, ultra & grn 1.00 .35

Black Rhinoceros — AP26

1964, Dec. 15 Engr. *Perf. 13*

C51 AP26 250fr brn red, grn & dk brn 10.00 3.00

Pres. John F. Kennedy — AP27

1964, Dec. 8 Photo. *Perf. 12½*

C52 AP27 100fr grn, yel grn & brn 2.50 1.10
a. Souvenir sheet of 4 10.00 4.50

Pres. John F. Kennedy (1917-63).

Abraham Lincoln — AP28

1965, Apr. 20 Unwmk. *Perf. 13*

C53 AP28 100fr multicolored 2.50 .80

Abraham Lincoln, death centenary.

Syncom Satellite and ITU Emblem — AP29

1965, May 17 Engr.

C54 AP29 70fr red, dk bl, & blk 1.60 .60

Cent. of the ITU.

Sir Winston Spencer Churchill, Statesman and World War II Leader — AP30

Designs: 12fr, Churchill giving V sign. 18fr, Churchill, battleship and oak leaves with acorns.

Perf. 13x12½

1965, May 28 Photo. Unwmk.

C55 12fr multicolored 1.00 .50
C56 18fr multicolored 1.00 .50
a. AP40 Strip of 2, #C55-C56 + label 2.75 1.40

ICY Type of Regular Issue

1965, Sept. 11 Engr. *Perf. 13*

C57 A68 100fr dk red & dk bl 2.25 .70

Racing Boat, Sanaga River, Edéa — AP31

1965, Oct. 27 Unwmk. *Perf. 13*

C58 AP31 50fr brn, dk grn & sl 2.25 .35

Edward H. White Floating in Space and Gemini IV — AP32

Designs: 50fr, Vostok 6. 200fr, Gemini V and REP (rendezvous evaluation pod). 500fr, Gemini VI & VII rendezvous.

1966, Mar. 30 Engr. *Perf. 13*

C59 AP32 50fr car rose & dk sl grn .90 .35
C60 AP32 100fr red lil & vio bl 2.10 .65
C61 AP32 200fr ultra & dk pur 3.75 1.40
C62 AP32 500fr brt bl & indigo 9.00 3.00
Nos. C59-C62 (4) 15.75 5.40

Man's conquest of space.

Hotel Type of Regular Issue

18fr, Mountain Hotel, Buea. 25fr, Hotel Akwa Palace, Douala. 50fr, Terminus Hotel, Yaoundé. 60fr, Imperial Hotel, Yaoundé. 85fr, Independence Hotel, Yaoundé. 100fr, Hunting Lodge, Mora, vert. 150fr, Boukarous (round huts), Waza Camp.

1966

C63 A71 18fr sl grn, brt bl & blk .45 .25
C64 A71 25fr car, ultra & sl .65 .25
C65 A71 50fr choc, grn & ocher 2.50 .90
C66 A71 60fr choc, grn & brt bl 1.50 .50
C67 A71 85fr dk car rose, dl bl & grn 1.90 .60
C68 A71 100fr brn, grn & sl 2.75 .70
C69 A71 150fr brn, dl bl & ocher 3.75 .90
Nos. C63-C69 (7) 13.50 4.05

Issued: Nos. C63-C64, 4/6; Nos. C65-C69, 6/4.

Flower Type of Regular Issue

Flowers: 25fr, Hibiscus mutabilis. 50fr, Delonix regia. 100fr, Bougainvillea.

1966, May 20 Photo. *Perf. 12½*
Flowers in Natural Colors
Size: 26x45mm

C70 A75 25fr slate green .75 .25
C71 A75 50fr brt grnsh bl 1.60 .25
C72 A75 100fr gold 3.25 .25
Nos. C70-C72 (3) 5.60 .65

Military Police — AP33

25fr, "Army," soldier, tanks & parachutes. 60fr, "Navy," & "Vigilante." 100fr, "Air Force," plane.

1966, June 21 Engr. *Perf. 13*

C73 AP33 20fr vio bl, org brn & dl pur .55 .25
C74 AP33 25fr dk grn, dl pur & brn .55 .25
C75 AP33 60fr bl grn, bl & ind 1.60 .30
C76 AP33 100fr brn, Prus bl & car rose 2.75 .65
Nos. C73-C76 (4) 5.45 1.45

Issued to honor Cameroun's armed forces.

Wembley Stadium, London — AP34

1966, July 20

C77 AP34 50fr shown 1.40 .25
C78 AP34 200fr Soccer 4.75 1.10

8th World Cup Soccer Championship, Wembley, England, July 11-30.

Air Afrique Issue, 1966
Common Design Type

1966, Aug. 31 Photo. *Perf. 13*

C79 CD123 25fr red lil, blk & gray .80 .25

Yaoundé Cathedral — AP35

18fr, Buea Cathedral. 30fr, Orthodox Church, Yaoundé. 60fr, Mosque, Garoua.

1966, Dec. 19 Engr. *Perf. 13*

C80 AP35 18fr choc, bl & grn .45 .25
C81 AP35 25fr brn, grn & brt vio .55 .25
C82 AP35 30fr lil, grn & dl red .70 .25
C83 AP35 60fr mar, brt grn & grn 1.40 .35
Nos. C80-C83 (4) 3.10 1.10

Pioneer A and Moon — AP36

1967, Apr. 30 Engr. *Perf. 13*

C84 AP36 25fr shown .50 .25
C85 AP36 50fr Ranger 6 .90 .35
C86 AP36 100fr Luna 9 2.25 .65
C87 AP36 250fr Luna 10 4.75 2.00
Nos. C84-C87 (4) 8.40 3.25

"Conquest of the Moon."

Flower Type of Regular Issue

1967, June 22 Photo. *Perf. 12½*
Size: 26x46mm

C88 A86 200fr Thevetia Peruviana 4.50 .90
C89 A86 250fr Amaryllis 5.50 1.10

African Postal Union Issue, 1967
Common Design Type

1967, Sept. 9 Engr. *Perf. 13*

C90 CD124 100fr red brn, Prus bl & brt lil 2.40 .65

Skis, Ice Skates, Olympic Flame and Emblem — AP38

1967, Oct. 11 Engr. *Perf. 13*

C91 AP38 30fr ultra & sepia 1.60 .25

Issued to publicize the 10th Winter Olympic Games, Grenoble, Feb. 6-8, 1968.

Cameroun Exhibit, EXPO '67 — AP39

100fr, Bangwa house poles carved with ancestor figures. 200fr, Canadian Pavilions.

1967, Oct. 18

C92 AP39 50fr mag, ol & mar 1.00 .25
C93 AP39 100fr dk grn, mar & dk brn 3.25 .70
C94 AP39 200fr brn, lil rose & sl grn 4.25 1.25
Nos. C92-C94 (3) 8.50 2.20

EXPO '67, International Exhibition, Montreal, Apr. 28-Oct. 27, 1967.

See note after No. C116 regarding 1969 moon overprint.

Konrad Adenauer (1876-1967), Chancellor of West Germany (1949-63) and Cologne Cathedral AP40

70fr, Adenauer and Chancellery, Bonn.

1967, Dec. 1 Photo. *Perf. 12½*

C95 AP40 30fr multi .90 .25
C96 AP40 70fr multi 1.50 .40
a. Pair, #C95-C96 + label 3.50 2.50

Pres. Ahidjo, King Faisal and View of Mecca — AP41

60fr, Pres. Ahidjo, Pope Paul VI & view of Rome.

1968, Feb. 18 Photo. *Perf. 12½*

C97 AP41 30fr multi .90 .25
C98 AP41 60fr multi 2.10 .30

Issued to commemorate President Ahidjo's Pilgrimage to Mecca and visit to Rome.

Earth on Television Transmitted by Explorer VI — AP42

30fr, Molniya spacecraft. 40fr, Earth on television screen transmitted by Molniya.

1968, Apr. 20 Engr. *Perf. 13*

C99 AP42 20fr multi .55 .25
C100 AP42 30fr multi .80 .25
C101 AP42 40fr multi 1.10 .25
Nos. C99-C101 (3) 2.45 .75

Telecommunication by satellite.

Forge — AP43

No. C103, Tea harvest. No. C104, Trans-Cameroun railroad (diesel train emerging from tunnel). 40fr, Rubber harvest. 60fr, Douala Harbor, horiz.

1968, June 5 Engr. *Perf. 13*

C102 AP43 20fr red brn, dk grn & ind .60 .25
C103 AP43 30fr dk brn, grn & ultra 1.10 .35
C104 AP43 30fr ind, sl grn & bis brn 7.50 2.50
C105 AP43 40fr ol bis, dk grn & bl grn 1.10 .35
C106 AP43 60fr ultra, dk brn & sl 3.00 1.00
Nos. C102-C106 (5) 13.30 4.45

Second Economic Development Five-Year Plan.

Boxing — AP44

50fr, Long jump. 60fr, Athlete on rings.

1968, Aug. 19 Engr. *Perf. 13*

C107 AP44 30fr brt grn, dk grn & choc .65 .25
C108 AP44 50fr brt grn, brn red & choc 1.25 .30
C109 AP44 60fr brt grn, ultra & choc 1.50 .35
a. Min. sheet of 3, #C107-C109 4.00 4.00
Nos. C107-C109 (3) 3.40 .90

19th Olympic Games, Mexico City, 10/12-27.

Human Rights Type of Regular Issue

1968, Sept. 14 Photo. *Perf. 12½x13*

C110 A92 30fr grn & brt pink .80 .25

Martin Luther King, Jr. — AP45

Portraits: No. C112, Mahatma Gandhi and map of India. 40fr, John F. Kennedy. 60fr, Robert F. Kennedy. No. C115, Rev. Martin Luther King, Jr. No. C116, Mahatma Gandhi.

1968, Dec. 5 Photo. *Perf. 12½*

C111 AP45 30fr bl & blk .60 .25
C112 AP45 30fr multi .60 .25
C113 AP45 40fr pink & blk 1.00 .50
C114 AP45 60fr bluish lil & blk 1.25 .50
C115 AP45 70fr yel grn & blk 1.40 .60
a. Souvenir sheet of 4, #C112-C115 8.00 8.00
C116 AP45 70fr multi 1.40 .60
Nos. C111-C116 (6) 6.25 2.70

Issued to honor exponents of non-violence. The 2 King stamps (Nos. C111 and C115), the 2 Gandhi stamps (Nos. C112 and C116) and the 2 Kennedy stamps (Nos. C113-C114) are each printed as triptychs with a descriptive label between.

In 1969 Nos. C111-C116 and C94 were overprinted in carmine capitals: "Premier Homme / sur la Lune / 20 Juillet 1969" and "First Man / Landing on Moon / 20 July 1969". Two types of overprints were used: Type I - English and French text 25mm apart; Type II - English and French text close together. Values: on No. C94, $50; on Nos. C111-C116, $325; on No. C115a (2 different souvenir sheets, with both overprint types on different stamps), each $300.

PHILEXAFRIQUE Issue

The Letter, by Armand Cambon AP46

1968, Dec. 10
C117 AP46 100fr multi 3.25 1.25

PHILEXAFRIQUE, Philatelic Exhibition in Abidjan, Feb. 14-23, 1969. Printed with alternating light green label.

2nd PHILEXAFRIQUE Issue
Common Design Type

Design: Cameroun #199 and Wouri Bridge.

1969, Feb. 14 Engr. *Perf. 13*
C118 CD128 50fr multi 3.25 1.25

Caladlum Bicolor — AP47

Flowers: 50fr, Aristolochia elegans. 100fr, Gloriosa simplex.

1969, May 14 Photo. *Perf. 12½*
C119 AP47 30fr lil & multi .75 .25
C120 AP47 50fr grn & multi 1.50 .40
C121 AP47 100fr brn & multi 3.50 1.00
Nos. C119-C121 (3) 5.75 1.65

3rd Intl. Flower Show, Paris, Apr. 23-Oct. 5.

Douala Post Office — AP48

50fr, Buèa P.O. 100fr, Bafoussam P.O.

1969, June 19 Engr. *Perf. 13*
C122 AP48 30fr grn, vio bl & brn .55 .25
C123 AP48 50fr sl, emer & red brn .90 .25
C124 AP48 100fr dk brn, brt grn & brn 1.75 .50
Nos. C122-C124 (3) 3.20 1.00

Coronation of Napoleon I, by Jacques Louis David — AP49

Napoleon Crossing Saint Bernard, after J. L. David — AP50

1969, July 4 Photo. *Perf. 12x12½*
C125 AP49 30fr vio bl & multi 1.00 .40

Die-cut Perf. 10
Embossed on Gold Foil
C126 AP50 1000fr gold 45.00 45.00

Bicentenary of birth of Napoleon I.

William E. B. Du Bois (1868-1963), American Writer — AP51

15fr, Dr. Price Mars, Haiti (1876-1969). No. C128, Aimé Cesaire, Martinique (1913-). No. C130, Langston Hughes, US (1902-67). No. C131, Marcus Garvey, Jamaica (1887-1940). 100fr, René Maran, Martinique (1887-1960).

1969, Sept. 25 Photo. *Perf. 12½*
C127 AP51 15fr lt bl & blk .45 .25
C128 AP51 30fr lem & blk .55 .25
C129 AP51 30fr rose brn & blk .55 .25
C130 AP51 50fr gray & blk .80 .25
C131 AP51 50fr emer & blk .80 .25
C132 AP51 100fr yel & blk 2.00 .60
a. Min. sheet of 6, #C127-C132 6.75 4.50
Nos. C127-C132 (6) 5.15 1.85

Issued to honor Negro writers.

ILO Emblem — AP52

1969, Oct. 29 Photo. *Perf. 13*
C133 AP52 30fr blk, bl grn & gray .80 .25
C134 AP52 50fr blk, dp lil rose & gray 1.40 .35

50th anniv. of the ILO.

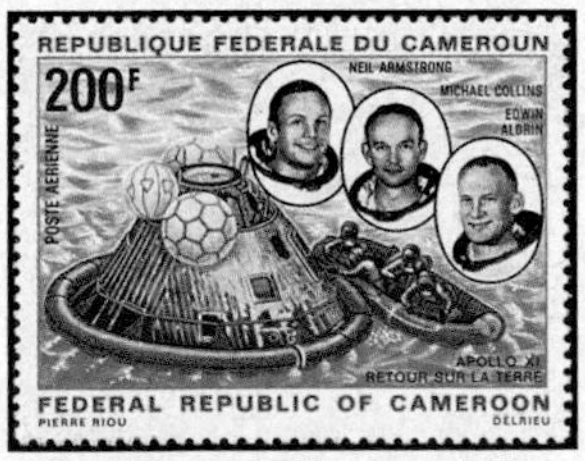

Armstrong, Collins and Aldrin Splashdown in the Pacific — AP53

Design: 500fr, Landing module and Neil A. Armstrong's first step on moon.

1969, Nov. 29 Photo. *Perf. 12½*
C135 AP53 200fr multi 5.00 1.25
C136 AP53 500fr multi 12.00 3.00

See note after Algeria No. 427.

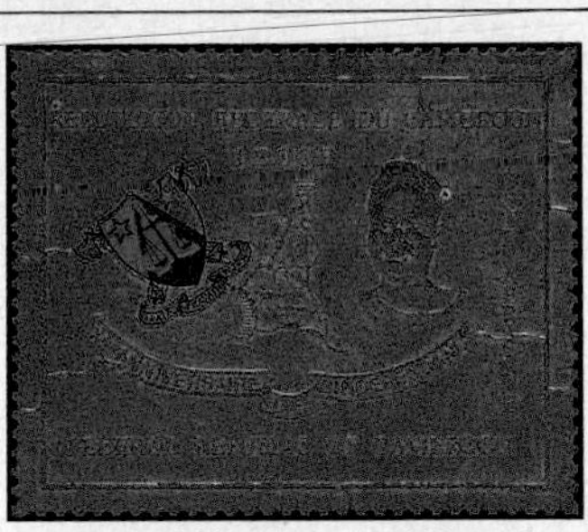
Pres. Ahidjo, Arms and Map of Cameroun — AP54

Embossed on Gold Foil
1970, Jan. 1 *Die-cut Perf. 10*
C137 AP54 1000fr gold & multi 26.00 25.00

10th anniversary of independence.

Hotel Mont Fébé, Yaoundé — AP55

1970, Jan. 15 Engr. *Perf. 13*
C138 AP55 30fr lt brn, sl grn & gray .80 .25

Lenin — AP56

1970, Jan. 25 Photo. *Perf. 12½*
C139 AP56 50fr org & blk 2.00 .55

Plant Type of Regular Issue

Designs: 50fr, Cleome speciosa (caper). 100fr, Mussaenda erythrophylla (madder).

1970, Mar. 24 Photo. *Perf. 12½*
Size: 26x46mm
C140 A99 50fr blk & multi 1.40 .35
C141 A99 100fr multi 2.75 .90

Map of Africa and Lions Emblem Pinpointing Yaoundé — AP57

1970, May 2 Photo. *Perf. 12½*
C142 AP57 100fr multi 2.25 .75

13th Lions International Congress of District 13, Yaoundé, May 2, 1970.

UN Emblem and Doves — AP58

Design: 50fr, UN emblem and dove, vert.

1970, June 26 Engr. *Perf. 13*
C143 AP58 30fr brn & org 1.00 .25
C144 AP58 50fr Prus bl & sl bl 1.25 .40

25th anniversary of the United Nations.

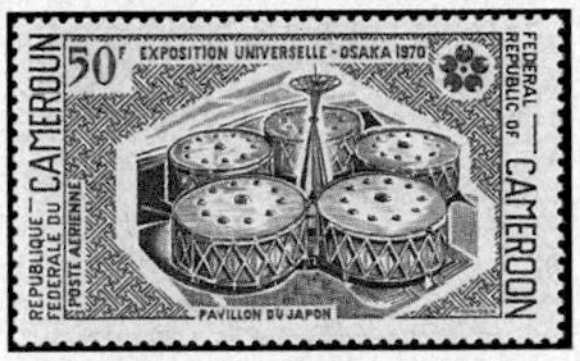

Japanese Pavilion and EXPO Emblem — AP59

Designs (EXPO Emblem and): 100fr, Map of Japan, vert. 150fr, Australian pavilion.

1970, Aug. 1 Engr. *Perf. 13*
C145 AP59 50fr ind, lt grn & ver .90 .30
C146 AP59 100fr bl, lt grn & red 2.00 .55
C147 AP59 150fr choc, bl & gray 3.25 .65
Nos. C145-C147 (3) 6.15 1.50

EXPO '70 International Exhibition, Osaka, Japan, Mar. 15-Sept. 13.

Charles de Gaulle — AP60

Design: 200fr, de Gaulle in unifrom.

1970, Aug. 27
C148 100fr grn, vio bl & ol brn 2.25 .80
C149 200fr ol brn, vio bl & grn 4.50 1.40
a. AP60 Pair, #C148-C149 + label 8.00 8.00

Rallying of the Free French, 30th anniv.
For overprints see Nos. C159-C160.

Pelé and Team — AP61

Designs: 50fr, Aztec Stadium, Mexico City, horiz. 100fr, Mexican soccer team, horiz.

1970, Oct. 14 Photo. *Perf. 12½*
C150 AP61 50fr multi .90 .30
C151 AP61 100fr multi 2.00 .65
C152 AP61 200fr multi 3.50 1.00
Nos. C150-C152 (3) 6.40 1.95

9th World Soccer Championships for the Jules Rimet Cup, Mexico City, May 30-June 21, and the final victory of Brazil over Italy.

Ludwig van Beethoven (1770-1827), Composer AP62

1970, Nov. 23 Engr. *Perf. 13*
C153 AP62 250fr multi 5.75 1.75

Christ at Emmaus, by Rembrandt — AP63

150fr, The Anatomy Lesson, by Rembrandt.

1970, Dec. 5 Photo. *Perf. 12x12½*

C154	AP63	70fr grn & multi	1.40	.35
C155	AP63	150fr multi	2.75	.75

Charles Dickens — AP64

Designs: 50fr, Scenes from David Copperfield. 100fr, Dickens holding quill.

1970, Dec. 22 *Perf. 13*

C156	AP64	40fr blk & rose	.95	.25
C157	AP64	50fr bis & multi	1.00	.30
C158	AP64	100fr rose & multi	2.00	.65
a.		Strip of 3, #C156-C158	5.00	2.00

Charles Dickens (1812-1870), English novelist.

De Gaulle Type of 1970 Overprinted

1971, Jan. 15 Engr. *Perf. 13*

C159	100fr vio bl, emer & brn red	2.75	.75
C160	200fr brn red, emer & vio bl	5.00	1.25
a.	AP60 Pair, #C159-C160 + label	8.00	8.00

In memory of Gen. Charles de Gaulle (1890-1970), President of France.

Timber Storage, Douala — AP65

Industrialization: 70fr, ALUCAM aluminum plant, Edea, vert. 100fr, Mbakaou Dam.

1971, Feb. 14 Engr. *Perf. 13*

C161	AP65	40fr dk red, bl grn & ol brn	.55	.25
C162	AP65	70fr ol brn, sl grn & brt bl	1.10	.30
C163	AP65	100fr Prus bl, yel grn & red brn	1.75	.40
		Nos. C161-C163 (3)	3.40	.95

Relay Race — AP66

50fr, Torch bearer, vert. 100fr, Discus.

1971, Apr. 24 Engr. *Perf. 13*

C164	AP66	30fr dk brn, ver & ind	.65	.25
C165	AP66	50fr blk, bl & choc	.80	.25
C166	AP66	100fr multi	1.75	.40
		Nos. C164-C166 (3)	3.20	.90

75th anniv. of revival of Olympic Games.

Fishing Trawler — AP67

Designs: 40fr, Local fishermen, Northern Cameroun. 70fr, Fishing harbor, Douala. 150fr, Shrimp boats, Douala.

1971, May 14 Engr. *Perf. 13*

C167	AP67	30fr lt brn, bl & grn	.70	.30
C168	AP67	40fr sl grn, bl & dk brn	.90	.30
C169	AP67	70fr dk brn, bl & red org	2.00	.40
C170	AP67	150fr multi	4.25	1.00
		Nos. C167-C170 (4)	7.85	2.00

Cameroun fishing industry.

Cameroun No. 123 and War Memorial, Yaoundé — AP68

Designs (Cameroun Stamps): 25fr, No. C33 and Jamot memorial. 40fr, No. 431 and government buildings, Yaoundé. 50fr, No. 19 and Imperial German postal emblem. 100fr, No. 101 and World War II memorial.

1971, Aug. 1 Engr. *Perf. 13*

C171	AP68	20fr grn, ocher & dk brn	.45	.25
C172	AP68	25fr dk brn, vio bl & sl grn	.65	.25
C173	AP68	40fr grn, mar & sl	.80	.25
C174	AP68	50fr dk brn, blk & ver	1.25	.25
C175	AP68	100fr mar, sl grn & org	1.75	.50
		Nos. C171-C175 (5)	4.90	1.50

PHILATECAM 1971 Philatelic Exhibition.

Cameroun Flag, Pres. Ahidjo and Reunification Highway — AP69

Typographed, Silk Screen, Embossed

1971, Oct. 1 *Perf. 12½*

C176	AP69	250fr gold & multi	6.00	4.50

PHILATECAM Philatelic Exhibition, Yaoundé-Douala.

African Postal Union Issue, 1971
Common Design Type

1971, Nov. 13 Photo. *Perf. 13x13½*

C177	CD135	100fr bl & multi	2.00	.50

Annunciation, by Fra Angelico — AP71

Christmmas (Paintings): 45fr, Virgin and Child, by Andrea del Sarto. 150fr, Christ Child with Lamb, detail from Holy Family, by Raphael, vert.

1971, Dec. 19 *Perf. 13x13½, 13½x13*

C178	AP71	40fr multi	.55	.25
C179	AP71	45fr multi	.70	.25
C180	AP71	150fr multi	3.25	.75
		Nos. C178-C180 (3)	4.50	1.25

Cameroun Airlines Emblem AP72

1972, Feb. 2 Photo. *Perf. 12½x12*

C181	AP72	50fr lt bl & multi	.80	.25

Inauguration of Cameroun Airlines.

Doge's Palace, by Ippolito Caffi AP73

100fr, 200fr, Details from "Regatta on the Grand Canal," by School of Canaletto.

1972, Mar. 19 Photo. *Perf. 13*

C182	AP73	40fr gold & multi	.70	.25
C183	AP73	100fr gold & multi	1.75	.40
C184	AP73	200fr gold & multi	4.00	.80
		Nos. C182-C184 (3)	6.45	1.45

UNESCO campaign to save Venice.

Cosmonauts Patsayev, Dobrovolsky and Volkov — AP74

1972, May 1 Photo. *Perf. 13x13½*

C185	AP74	50fr multi	1.00	.30

Salute-Soyuz 11 space mission, and in memory of the Russian cosmonauts Victor I. Patsayev, Georgi T. Dobrovolsky and Vladislav N. Volkov, who died during Soyuz 11 space mission, June 6-30, 1971.

UN Headquarters, Chinese Flag and Gate of Heavenly Peace — AP75

1972, May 19 *Perf. 13*

C186	AP75	50fr blk, scar & gold	3.25	.35

Admission of People's Republic of China to UN.

United Republic

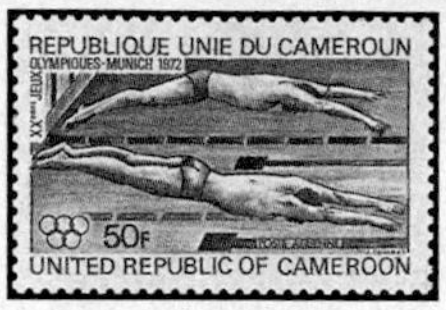

Olympic Rings, Swimming AP76

Designs (Olympic Rings and): No. C188, Boxing, vert. 200fr, Equestrian.

1972, Aug. 1 Engr. *Perf. 13*

C187	AP76	50fr lake & slate grn	.90	.25
C188	AP76	50fr choc & slate	.90	.25
C189	AP76	200fr cl, gray & dk brn	3.50	1.00
a.		Min. sheet of 3	5.75	5.75
		Nos. C187-C189 (3)	5.30	1.50

20th Olympic Games, Munich, Aug. 26-Sept. 11. No. C189a contains stamps similar to Nos. C187-C189, but in changed colors. The 50fr (swimming) is Prussian blue, violet & brown; the 50c (boxing) lilac, Prussian blue & brown; the 200fr, Prussian blue & brown.

Nos. C187-C189 Overprinted in Red or Black

a

b

c

1972, Oct. 23 Engr. *Perf. 13*

C190	AP76(a)	50fr (R)	.90	.25
C191	AP76(b)	50fr	.90	.25
C192	AP76(c)	200fr	3.50	1.00
		Nos. C190-C192 (3)	5.30	1.50

Gold Medal Winners in 20th Olympic Games: Mark Spitz, US, swimming (No. C190); Dieter Kottysch, West Germany, light middleweight boxing (No. C191); Richard Meade, Great Britain, 3-day equestrian (No. C192).

Madonna with Angels, by Cimabue AP77

Christmas: 140fr, Madonna of the Rose Arbor, by Stefan Lochner.

1972, Dec. 21 Photo. *Perf. 13*

C193	AP77	45fr gold & multi	1.00	.25
C194	AP77	140fr gold & multi	2.75	1.00

St. Teresa, the Little Flower — AP78

100fr, Lisieux Cathedral and St. Teresa.

1973, Jan. 2 Engr.

C195	AP78	45fr vio bl, pur & mar	.70	.25
C196	AP78	100fr mag, ultra & brn	1.75	.40

Centenary of the birth of St. Teresa of Lisieux (1873-1897), Carmelite nun.

African Unity Hall, Addis Ababa and Emperor Haile Selassie — AP79

1973, Mar. 14 Photo. *Perf. 13*

C197	AP79	45fr yellow & multi	1.00	.25

80th birthday of Emperor Haile Selassie of Ethiopia.

Corn, Grain, Healthy and Starving People — AP80

1973, Apr. 10 Typo. *Perf. 13*

C198	AP80	45fr multi	.80	.25

World Food Program, 10th anniversary.

Hearts and Blood Vessels — AP81

1973, May 5 Engr.

C199	AP81	50fr dk car rose & dk vio bl	1.00	.25

"Your Heart is Your Health" and for the 25th anniv. of the WHO.

Type of Regular Issue

Designs: 45fr, Map of Cameroun, Pres. Ahidjo and No. C176. 70fr, National colors and commemorative inscriptions.

1973, May 20 Engr. *Perf. 13*

C200	A128	45fr grn & multi	.80	.25
C201	A128	70fr red & multi	1.00	.40

Scout Emblem and Flags — AP82

1973, July 31 Typo. *Perf. 13*

C202	AP82	40fr multi	1.00	.25
C203	AP82	45fr multi	1.25	.35
C204	AP82	100fr multi	3.25	.60
		Nos. C202-C204 (3)	5.50	1.20

Cameroun's admission to the World Scout Conference, Mar. 26, 1971.

African Weeks Issue

Head and City Hall, Brussels — AP83

1973, Sept. 17 Engr. *Perf. 13*

C205	AP83	40fr dp brn & rose claret	.80	.25

African Weeks, Brussels, Sept. 15-30.

Map of Africa with Cameroun — AP84

1973, Sept. 29 Engr. *Perf. 13*

C206	AP84	40fr blk, red & grn	.80	.25

Help for handicapped children.

Zamengoe Radar Station AP85

1973, Dec. 8 Engr. *Perf. 13*

C207	AP85	100fr bl, lt brn & grn	1.50	.45

Chancellor Rolin Madonna, by Van Eyck AP86

Christmas: 140fr, Nativity, by Federigo Barocci.

1973, Dec. 11 Photo. *Perf. 13*

C208	AP86	45fr gold & multi	1.00	.30
C209	AP86	140fr gold & multi	2.75	1.00

Zebu Type of 1974

1974, June 1 Litho. *Perf. 13*

C210	A140	45fr Zebu herd	1.40	.35

Churchill and Union Jack AP87

1974, July 10 Engr. *Perf. 13*

C211	AP87	100fr blk, bl & red	1.60	.45

Winston Churchill (1874-1965).

Soccer, Arms of Frankfurt, Dortmund, Gelsenkirchen and Stuttgart — AP88

100fr, Soccer & arms of Berlin, Hamburg, Hanover & Düsseldorf. 200fr, Soccer cup & game.

1974, Aug. 5 Photo. *Perf. 13*

C212	AP88	45fr gray, sl & org	.70	.25
C213	AP88	100fr gray, sl & org	1.25	.40
C214	AP88	200fr org, slate & bl	2.75	1.00
a.		Strip of 3, Nos. C212-C214	5.00	5.00

World Cup Soccer Championship, Munich, June 13-July 7.

Nos. C212-C214 Overprinted in Dark Blue

1974, Sept. 16 Photo. *Perf. 13*

C215	AP88	45fr multi	.65	.25
C216	AP88	100fr multi	1.25	.40
C217	AP88	200fr multi	2.40	1.00
a.		Strip of 3, Nos. C215-C217	5.00	5.00

World Cup Soccer Championship, 1974, victory of German Federal Republic.

UPU Type of 1974

100fr, Cameroun #503. 200fr, Cameroun #C29.

1974, Oct. 8 Engr. *Perf. 13*

C218	A142	100fr blue & multi	1.75	.50
C219	A142	200fr red & multi	3.25	1.00

Copernicus and Planets Circling Sun — AP89

1974, Oct. 15 Engr. *Perf. 13*

C220	AP89	250fr multi	3.50	1.25

500th anniversary of the birth of Nicolaus Copernicus (1473-1543), Polish astronomer.

21st Chess Olympiad, Nice, France, June 6-30 — AP90

1974, Nov. 3 Photo. *Perf. 13x12½*

C221	AP90	100fr Chess pieces	5.25	1.00

Mask and ARPHILA Emblem — AP91

1974, Nov. 30 Engr. *Perf. 13*

C222	AP91	50fr choc & magenta	.80	.25

ARPHILA 75, Paris, June 6-16, 1975.

Presidents and Flags of Cameroun, CAR, Gabon and Congo — AP92

1974, Dec. 8 Photo.

C223	AP92	100fr gold & multi	2.25	.45

See note after No. 595.

Man Landing on Moon — AP93

1974, Dec. 15 Engr.

C224	AP93	200fr brn, bl & car	3.25	1.00

5th anniv. of man's 1st landing on the moon.

Charles de Gaulle and Félix Eboué — AP94

1975, Feb. 24 Typo. *Perf. 13*

C225	AP94	45fr multi	1.50	.35
C226	AP94	200fr multi	5.00	1.50

Felix A. Eboué (1884-1944), Governor of Chad, first colonial governor to join Free French in WWII, 30th death anniversary.

Marquis de Lafayette AP95

American Bicentennial: 140fr, Washington and soldiers. 500fr, Franklin and Independence Hall.

1975, Oct. 20 Engr. *Perf. 13*

C227 AP95 100fr vio bl & multi 2.25 .60
C228 AP95 140fr brn & multi 2.40 .65
C229 AP95 500fr grn & multi 7.25 2.00
Nos. C227-C229 (3) 11.90 3.25

The Burning Bush, by Nicolas Froment AP96

Painting: 500fr, Adoration of the Kings, by Gentile da Fabriano, horiz.

1975, Dec. 25 Photo. *Perf. 13*

C230 AP96 50fr gold & multi .90 .30
C231 AP96 500fr gold & multi 7.25 3.00

Christmas 1975.

Concorde and Route: Paris-Dakar-Rio de Janeiro — AP97

1976, July 20 Litho. *Perf. 13*

C232 AP97 500fr lt bl & multi 6.50 1.60
a. Souvenir sheet of 1 9.00 9.00

1st commercial flight of supersonic jet Concorde from Paris to Rio de Janeiro, Jan. 21. No. C232a sold for 600fr.
For overprint see No. C263.

Dance Type of 1976

50fr, Dancers & drummer. 100fr, Woman dancer.

1976, Sept. 15 Litho. *Perf. 12*

C233 A154 50fr gray & multi .65 .25
C234 A154 100fr gray & multi 1.10 .35

Virgin and Child, by Giovanni Bellini — AP98

Paintings: 30fr, Adoration of the Shepherds, by Le Brun. 60fr, Adoration of the Kings, by Rubens. 500fr, The Newborn, by Georges de la Tour.

1976, Dec. 15 Litho. *Perf. 12½*

C235 AP98 30fr gold & multi .70 .25
C236 AP98 60fr gold & multi .90 .25
C237 AP98 70fr gold & multi 1.25 .35
C238 AP98 500fr gold & multi 9.00 3.00
a. Souv. sheet of 4, #C235-C238 12.50 12.00
Nos. C235-C238 (4) 11.85 3.85

Christmas 1976.

Festival Type of 1977

Traditional Chief on his throne, sculpture.

1977, Feb. 4 Litho. *Perf. 12½*

C239 A159 60fr multi 1.10 .25

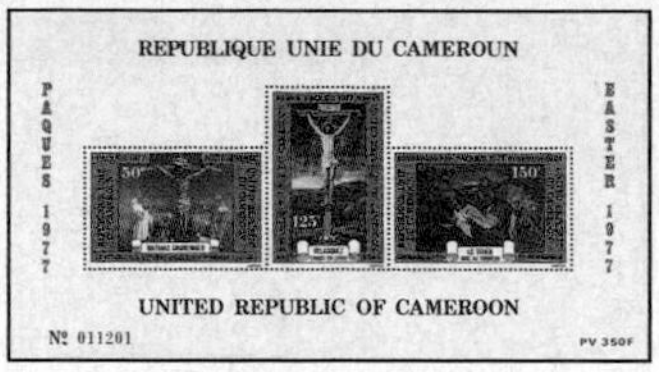

Easter — AP99

75fr, Crucifixion, by Matthias Grunewald. 125fr, Christ on the Cross, by Velazquez, vert. 150fr, The Deposition, by Titian.

1977, Apr. 2 Litho. *Perf. 12½*

C240 50fr gold & multi .90 .25
C241 125fr gold & multi 1.75 .45
C242 150fr gold & multi 2.50 .65
a. AP99 Souv. sheet of 3, #C240-C242, perf. 12 6.75 1.75
Nos. C240-C242 (3) 5.15 1.35

No. C242a sold for 350fr.

Lions Emblem, Map of Africa — AP100

1977, Apr. 29 Litho. *Perf. 12½*

C243 AP100 250fr multi 3.00 1.00

Lions Club of Douala, 19th Cong., 4/29-30.

Rotary Emblem AP101

1977, May 18

C244 AP101 60fr multi .70 .25

Rotary Club of Douala, 20th anniversary.

Antoine de Saint-Exupéry AP102

Charles Lindbergh and Spirit of St. Louis — AP103

Designs: 50fr, Jean Mermoz and his plane. 80fr, Maryse Bastié and her plane. 100fr, Sikorsky S-43. 300fr, Concorde.

1977, May 20 Engr. *Perf. 13*

C245 AP103 50fr org & bl .90 .25
C246 AP102 60fr mag & org .95 .25
C247 AP103 80fr mag & bl 1.25 .30
a. Souv. sheet, #C245-C247 3.25 3.25
C248 AP103 100fr grn & yel 1.50 .40
C249 AP103 300fr multi 5.50 1.25
C250 AP103 500fr multi 8.00 2.50
a. Souv. sheet, #C248-C250 14.50 14.50
Nos. C245-C250 (6) 18.10 4.95

Aviation pioneers and events. No. C247a sold for 200fr. No. C250a sold for 1000fr.
For overprint see No. C262.

Sassenage Castle, Grenoble — AP104

1977, May 21 Litho. *Perf. 12½*

C251 AP104 70fr multi 1.60 1.00

10th anniv. of Intl. French Language Council.

Jufilex Type of 1977

Designs: 70fr, Switzerland (Zurich) No. 1L1 and Cameroun No. 16. 100fr, Switzerland (Geneva) No. 2L1 and Cameroun No. 254.

1977, June 5 Litho. *Perf. 12*

C252 A161 70fr multi 1.25 .35
C253 A161 100fr multi 2.10 .60

Apollo-Soyuz Type

100fr, Astronaut Vance Brand, Apollo in orbit. 250fr, Apollo and Soyuz docking. 350fr, Cosmonaut Valery Kubasov, Soyuz in orbit. 500fr, Astronaut Donald Slayton, handshake.

1977, Aug. 10 Litho. *Perf. 14x13½*

C256 A163 100fr multicolored .90 .25
C257 A163 250fr multicolored 2.25 .60
C258 A163 350fr multicolored 3.25 1.00
Nos. C256-C258 (3) 6.40 5.85

Souvenir Sheet

C259 A163 500fr multicolored 5.00 5.00

Diseased Knee, WHO Emblem AP105

1977, Oct. 15 Engr. *Perf. 13*

C260 AP105 70fr multi .70 .25

World Rheumatism Year.

Nos. C249 and C232 Overprinted in Red

Engraved, Lithographed

1977, Nov. 22 *Perf. 13*

C262 AP103 300fr multi 3.25 1.25
C263 AP97 500fr multi 5.00 2.00

Concorde, 1st commercial flight Paris to NY.

Christmas Type of 1977

Paintings: 60fr, Virgin and Child with 4 Saints, by Bellini, horiz. 400fr, Adoration of the Shepherds, by George de la Tour, horiz.

1977, Dec. 15 Litho. *Perf. 12x12½*

C264 A165 60fr multi 1.00 .25
C265 A165 400fr multi 5.00 1.75

Flag Type of 1978

60fr, New flag, Pres. Ahidjo and spear.

1978, Apr. 3 Litho. *Perf. 12½*

C266 A167 60fr multi .55 .25

Frog Type of 1978

Design: 100fr, Cardioglossa trifasciata.

1978, Apr. 5

C267 A168 100fr multi 3.75 .75

L'Arlesienne, by Van Gogh — AP106

No. C269, Burial of Christ, by Albrecht Dürer.

1978, May 15 Litho. *Perf. 12½*

C268 AP106 200fr multi 4.25 1.10
C269 AP106 200fr multi 5.75 1.10

Leprosy Distribution on World Map, Raoul Follereau — AP107

1978, June 6 Litho. *Perf. 12*

C270 AP107 100fr multi 1.10 .55

25th World Leprosy Day.

Capt. Cook and Siege of Quebec — AP108

Design: 250fr, Capt. Cook, Adventure and Resolution, map of voyages.

1978, July 26 Engr. *Perf. 13*

C271 AP108 100fr multi 2.10 .55
C272 AP108 250fr multi 5.00 1.40

Capt. James Cook (1728-1779), explorer.

Argentine Soccer Team, Coat of Arms and Rimet Cup — AP109

200fr, Two soccer players, vert. 1000fr, Soccer ball illuminating world map, vert.

1978, Sept. 1 Litho. *Perf. 13*

C273	AP109	100fr multi	1.00	.55
C274	AP109	200fr multi	1.75	1.10
C275	AP109	1000fr multi	10.00	5.50
		Nos. C273-C275 (3)	12.75	7.15

11th World Cup Soccer Championship, Argentina, June 1-25.

Jules Verne Type of 1978

Design: 400fr, Jules Verne and "20,000 Leagues Under the Sea," horiz.

1978, Oct. 10 Litho. *Perf. 12*

C276 A169 400fr multi 4.00 2.00

Musical Instrument Type of 1978

Design: 100fr, Man playing Mvet zither.

1978, Nov. 20 Litho. *Perf. 12½*

C277 A172 100fr multi 1.25 .40

Human Rights Type of 1979

1979, Feb. 11 Litho. *Perf. 12x12½*

C278 A174 500fr multi 5.50 2.50

Lions Emblem, Map of District 403 — AP110

1979, Apr. 26 Litho. *Perf. 12½*

C279 AP110 60fr multi .70 .25

21st Congress of Lions Club of Yaoundé.

Penny Black, Hill, Cameroun No. 9 — AP111

1979, Oct. 10 Engr. *Perf. 13*

C280 AP111 100fr multi 1.00 .40

Sir Rowland Hill (1795-1879), originator of penny postage.

"TELECOM 79" — AP112

1979, Sept. 26 Litho. *Perf. 13x12½*

C281 AP112 100fr multi 1.10 .40

3rd World Telecommunications Exhibition, Geneva, Sept. 20-26.

Pope Paul VI — AP113

1979, Oct. 23 Engr. *Perf. 12½x13*

C282	AP113	100fr shown	2.25	.50
C283	AP113	100fr John Paul I	2.25	.50
C284	AP113	100fr John Paul II	2.25	.50
		Nos. C282-C284 (3)	6.75	1.50

"Double Eagle" over French Coastline AP114

Design: No. C286, Balloonists and balloon.

1979, Dec. 15 Litho. *Perf. 12½*

C285	AP114	500fr multi	5.00	2.25
C286	AP114	500fr multi	5.00	2.25

First Transatlantic balloon crossing.

100-Meter Race — AP115

Designs: 150fr, Figure skating pairs. 200fr, Javelin. 300fr, Wrestling.

1980, Dec. 18 Litho. *Perf. 12½*

C287	AP115	100fr yel brn & brn	.90	.50
C288	AP115	150fr bl & brn	1.25	.70
C289	AP115	200fr grn & brn	1.75	1.00
C290	AP115	300fr red & brn	2.50	1.40
		Nos. C287-C290 (4)	6.40	3.60

22nd Summer Olympic Games, Moscow, July 19-Aug. 3; 13th Winter Olympic Games, Lake Placid, Feb. 12-24 (150fr).

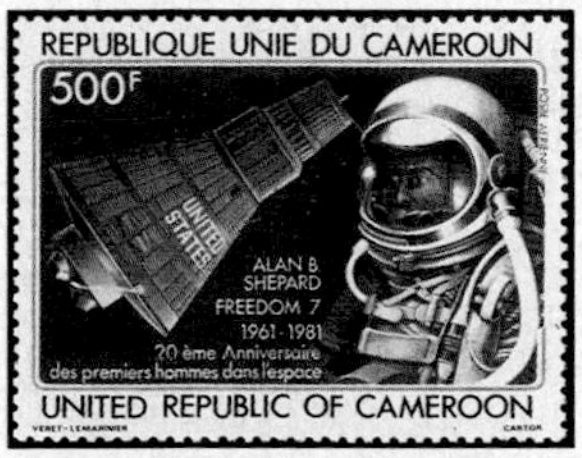

Alan Shepard and Freedom 7 — AP116

No. C292, Yuri Gagarin, Vostok I.

1981, Sept. 15 Litho. *Perf. 12½*

C291	AP116	500fr shown	5.00	2.25
C292	AP116	500fr multi	5.00	2.25

Manned space flight, 20th anniv.

4th African Scouting Conference, Abidjan, June — AP117

100fr, Emblem, salute, badge. 500fr, Scout saluting.

1981, Oct. 5

C293	AP117	100fr multi	.70	.40
C294	AP117	500fr multi	4.50	2.00

Guernica (detail), by Pablo Picasso (1881-1973) — AP118

No. C296, Landscape, by Paul Cezanne (1839-1906).

1981, Nov. 10 Litho. *Perf. 12½*

C295	AP118	500fr multi	6.00	2.00
C296	AP118	500fr multi	6.00	2.00

Christmas 1981 — AP119

Designs: 50fr, Virgin and Child, by Froment, vert. 60f, San Zeno Altarpiece, by Mantegna, vert. 400fr, Flight into Egypt, by Giotto.

1981, Dec. 1 Litho. *Perf. 12½*

C297	AP119	50fr multi	.45	.25
C298	AP119	60fr multi	.65	.30
C299	AP119	400fr multi	3.50	2.00
a.		Souv. sheet of 3, #C297-C299, perf. 13x13½	9.00	9.00
		Nos. C297-C299 (3)	4.60	2.55

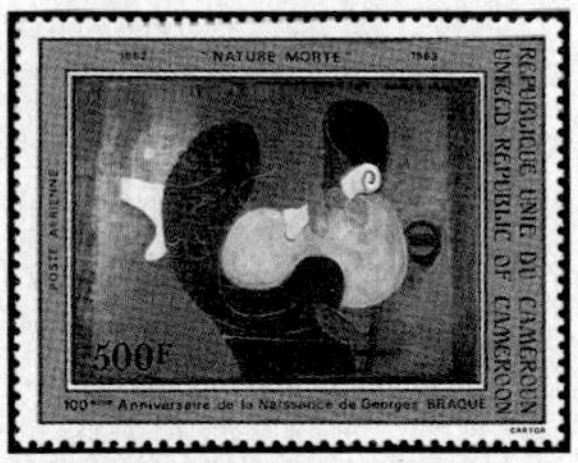

Still Life, by Georges Braque (1882-1963) — AP120

Paintings: No. C301, Olympia, by Edouard Manet (1832-1883).

1982, Dec. 5 Litho. *Perf. 13*

C300	AP120	500fr multi	5.00	2.00
C301	AP120	500fr multi	5.00	2.00

Pres. John F. Kennedy (1917-63) AP121

1983, Mar. 15 Litho. *Perf. 13*

C302 AP121 500fr multi 4.50 2.00

Lions District 403 (Douala), 2nd Convention, May — AP122

1983, May 5 Litho. *Perf. 12½*

C303	AP122	70fr multi	.55	.30
C304	AP122	150fr multi	1.25	.65

Jeanne of Aragon by Raphael AP123

No. C306, Massacre of Scio by Delacroix.

1983, Oct. 15 Litho. *Perf. 13*

C305	AP123	500fr multi	5.00	1.00
C306	AP123	500fr multi	5.00	1.00

Easter 1984 — AP124

200fr, Pieta, by G. Hernandez. 500fr, Martyrdom of St. John the Evangelist, by C. Le Brun.

1984, Mar. 30 Litho. *Perf. 13*

C307	AP124	200fr multi	1.75	.50
C308	AP124	500fr multi	4.50	1.40
a.		Souv. sheet of 2, #C307-C308	7.25	7.25

1984 Summer Olympics AP125

1984, Apr. 30 *Perf. 12½*

C309	AP125	100fr High jump	.90	.25
C310	AP125	150fr Volleyball	1.25	.35
C311	AP125	250fr Handball	2.25	.55
C312	AP125	500fr Bicycling	4.50	1.10
		Nos. C309-C312 (4)	8.90	2.25

See Nos. C321-C324.

European Soccer Championship, June 12-27 — AP126

1984, June 5 Litho. *Perf. 12½*

C313	AP126	250fr	Player in red shorts	2.25	.65
C314	AP126	250fr	Yellow shorts	2.25	.65
C315	AP126	500fr	Players	4.50	1.25
a.			Souvenir sheet of 3	10.00	10.00
			Nos. C313-C315 (3)	9.00	2.55

No. C315a contains Nos. C313-C315 in changed panel colors.

Presidential Oath — AP127

1984 Litho. *Perf. 13*

C316	AP127	60fr	French inscription	.55	.25
a.			English inscription	.55	.25
C317	AP127	70fr	French inscription	.55	.25
a.			English inscription	.55	.25
C318	AP127	200fr	French inscription	1.75	.40
a.			English inscription	1.75	.40
			Nos. C316-C318 (3)	2.85	.90

Issue dates: French, Sept. 15; English, Nov.

Paintings — AP128

No. C319, Diana in the Bath, by Watteau (1684-1721). No. C320, Portrait of Diderot (1713-1784).

1984, Sept. 20 Litho. *Perf. 13*

C319	AP128	500fr	Watteau	5.00	1.00
C320	AP128	500fr	Diderot, vert.	5.00	1.00

Nos. C309-C312 in Changed Colors with Added Inscriptions

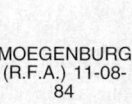

MOEGENBURG (R.F.A.) 11-08-84

U.S.A. 11-08-84

YOUGOSLAVIE 9-08-84

GORSKI (U.S.A.) 3-08-84

1984, Sept. 25 Litho. *Perf. 12½*

C321	AP125	100fr	multi	.90	.25
C322	AP125	150fr	multi	1.25	.30
C323	AP125	250fr	multi	2.25	.50
C324	AP125	500fr	multi	4.50	1.00
			Nos. C321-C324 (4)	8.90	2.05

Moon Landing, 15th Anniv. — AP129

No. C325, Neil Armstrong. No. C326, Apollo 12 launching.

1984, Nov. 15 Litho. *Perf. 12½*

C325	AP129	500fr	multi	4.50	1.50
C326	AP129	500fr	multi	4.50	1.50

Louis Pasteur (1822-1895), Chemist, Microbiologist — AP130

No. C328, Mourning Woman (detail), Mausoleum of Henri Claude d'Harcourt, by sculptor Jean Baptiste Pigalle (1714-1785).

1985, Oct. 10 Litho. *Perf. 13*

C327	AP130	500fr	multi	6.00	1.75
C328	AP130	500fr	multi	6.00	1.75

Christmas AP131

250fr, Children's gifts. 300fr, Akono Church. 400fr, Holy Family & drummer boy. 500fr, The Virgin with the Blue Diadem, by Raphael.

1985, Dec. 20 Litho. *Perf. 13*

C329	AP131	250fr	multi	2.25	.90
C330	AP131	300fr	multi	2.50	1.10
C331	AP131	400fr	multi	3.25	1.50
C332	AP131	500fr	multi	5.00	2.00
			Nos. C329-C332 (4)	13.00	5.50

1986 World Cup Soccer Championships, Mexico — AP132

250fr, Argentina, winner. 300fr, Stadium. 400fr, Mexican team.

1986 *Perf. 13½*

C333	AP132	250fr	multi	2.75	1.40
C334	AP132	300fr	multi	2.75	1.60
C335	AP132	400fr	multi	3.50	2.25
			Nos. C333-C335 (3)	9.00	5.25

Issued: 300fr, 400fr, 5/15; 250fr, 7/26.

Famous Men — AP133

No. C336, Pierre Curie (1859-1906), chemist, atom, and elements. No. C337, Jean Mermoz (1901-1936), aviator, and aircraft.

1986, Sept. 10 Litho. *Perf. 12½*

C336	AP133	500fr	multi	6.25	2.00
C337	AP133	500fr	multi	6.25	2.00

AIR POST SEMI-POSTAL STAMPS

Doctor Examining Child — SPAP1

Unwmk.

1942, June 22 Engr. *Perf. 13*

CB1	SPAP1	1.50fr + 50c green	1.00	
CB2	SPAP1	2fr + 6fr brn & red brn	1.00	

Native children's welfare fund.

Nos. CB1-CB2 were issued by the Vichy government in France, but were not placed on sale in Cameroun.

Colonial Education Fund

Common Design Type

1942, June 22

CB3	CD86a	1.20fr + 1.80fr blue & red	1.10	

No. CB3 was issued by the Vichy government in France, but was not placed on sale in Cameroun.

POSTAGE DUE STAMPS

Man Felling Tree — D1

Perf. 14x13½

1925-27 Unwmk. Typo.

J1	D1	2c	lt bl & blk	.30	.50
J2	D1	4c	ol bis & red vio	.30	.50
J3	D1	5c	vio & blk	.65	.80
J4	D1	10c	red & blk	.65	.80
J5	D1	15c	gray & blk	.75	.95
J6	D1	20c	olive grn & blk	.75	.95
J7	D1	25c	yel & blk	1.40	1.60
J8	D1	30c	blue & org	1.60	1.90
J9	D1	50c	brn & blk	2.00	2.40
J10	D1	60c	bl grn & rose red	2.00	2.40
J11	D1	1fr	dl red & grn, *grnsh*	2.40	3.25
J12	D1	2fr	red & vio ('27)	4.75	5.50
J13	D1	3fr	org brn & ultra ('27)	7.25	8.00
			Nos. J1-J13 (13)	24.80	29.55

Shades occur for several values.

Carved Figures — D2

1939 Engr. *Perf. 14x13*

J14	D2	5c	brt red vio	.25	.80
J15	D2	10c	Prus blue	.75	.90
J16	D2	15c	car rose	.25	.40
J17	D2	20c	blk brn	.25	.40
J18	D2	30c	ultra	.50	.65
J19	D2	50c	dk grn	.50	.65
J20	D2	60c	brn vio	.85	1.00
J21	D2	1fr	dk vio	1.10	1.20
J22	D2	2fr	org red	1.60	1.60
J23	D2	3fr	dark blue	2.25	2.40
			Nos. J14-J23 (10)	8.30	10.00

1944 Type D2 without "RF"

J23A	D2	10c	Prussian blue	.80

No. J23A was issued by the Vichy government in France, but was not placed on sale in Cameroun.

Catalogue values for unused stamps in this section, from this point to the end of the section, are for Never Hinged items.

D3

1947 Unwmk. *Perf. 13*

J24	D3	10c	dark red	.40	.30
J25	D3	30c	dp org	.40	.30
J26	D3	50c	grnsh blk	.40	.30
J27	D3	1fr	dark car	.50	.40
J28	D3	2fr	dp yel grn	.65	.55
J29	D3	3fr	dp red lil	.65	.55
J30	D3	4fr	dp ultra	.90	.70
J31	D3	5fr	red brn	1.00	.90
J32	D3	10fr	peacock bl	1.90	1.60
J33	D3	20fr	sepia	2.75	2.25
			Nos. J24-J33 (10)	9.55	7.85

Federal Republic

Hibiscus
D4

Flowers: No. J35, Erythrina. No. J36, Plumeria lutea. No. J37, Ipomoea. No. J38, Hoodia gordonii. No. J39, Crinum. No. J40, Ochna. No. J41, Gloriosa. No. J42, Costus spectabilis. No. J43, Bougainvillea spectabilis. No. J44, Delonix regia. No. J45, Haemanthus. No. J46, Ophthalmophyllum. No. J47, Titanopsis. No. J48, Amorphophallus. No. J49, Zingiberacee.

Unwmk.

1963, Apr. 10 Engr. *Perf. 11*

J34	D4	50c car, bl, grn & yel	.25	.25
J35	D4	50c car, bl, grn & yel	.25	.25
a.		Pair, #J34-J35	.55	.45
J36	D4	1fr mag, grn & yel	.25	.25
J37	D4	1fr mag, grn & yel	.25	.25
a.		Pair, #J36-J37	.55	.45
J38	D4	1.50fr dk grn, lil & yel	.25	.25
J39	D4	1.50fr dk grn, lil & yel	.25	.25
a.		Pair, #J38-J39	.55	.45
J40	D4	2fr org ver, yel & grn	.25	.25
J41	D4	2fr org ver, yel & grn	.25	.25
a.		Pair, #J40-J41	.55	.45
J42	D4	5fr mag, grn & yel	.25	.25
J43	D4	5fr mag, grn & yel	.25	.25
a.		Pair, #J42-J43	.55	.45
J44	D4	10fr crim, grn & yel	.50	.25
J45	D4	10fr crim, grn & yel	.50	.25
a.		Pair, #J44-J45	1.20	.45
J46	D4	20fr grn, yel & lil	1.10	.45
J47	D4	20fr grn, yel & lil	1.10	.45
a.		Pair, #J46-J47	2.40	1.00
J48	D4	40fr lilac & yel	2.00	.80
J49	D4	40fr lilac & yel	2.00	.80
a.		Pair, #J48-J49	4.25	1.75
		Nos. J34-J49 (16)	9.70	5.50

The pairs are se-tenant at the base.

MILITARY STAMPS

Catalogue values for unused stamps in this section are for Never Hinged items.

M1

Unwmk.

1963, July 1 Typo. *Perf. 13*

M1	M1	rose claret	3.00	3.00

Type of 1963 Inscribed
"REPUBLIC UNIE DU CAMEROUN / UNITED REPUBLIC OF CAMEROUN"

1976? Litho. *Perf. 13x13½*

M2 M1 rose claret

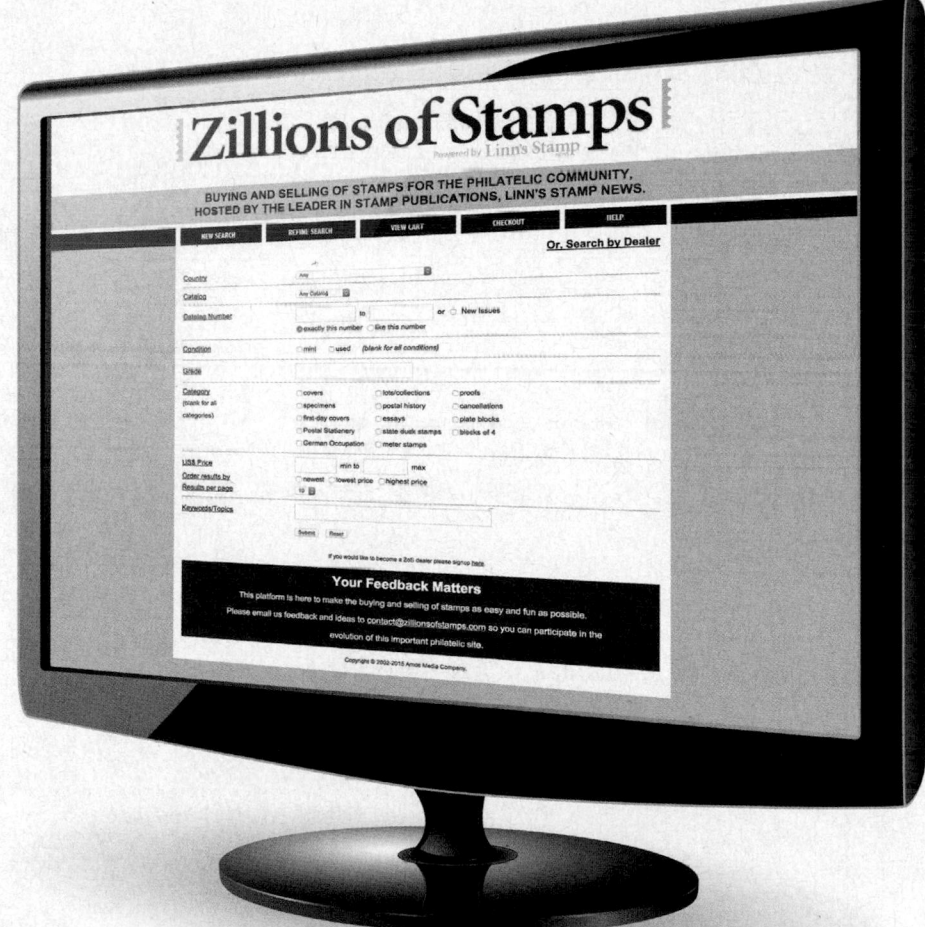

CANADIAN PROVINCES

BRITISH COLUMBIA & VANCOUVER IS.

'bri-tish kə-'ləm-bē-ə

and van-'kü-vər 'ī-lənd

LOCATION — On the northwest coast of North America
GOVT. — British Colony
AREA — 355,900 sq. mi.
POP. — 694,300

In 1871 the colony became a part of the Canadian Confederation and the postage stamps of Canada have since been used.

12 Pence = 1 Shilling
20 Shillings = 1 Pound
100 Cents = 1 Dollar (1865)

Values for unused stamps are for examples with original gum as defined in the catalogue introduction. Very fine examples of Nos. 2 and 5-18 will have perforations touching the design on at least one side due to the narrow spacing of the stamps on the plates. Stamps with perfs clear of the design on all four sides are extremely scarce and will command much higher prices.

Queen Victoria — A1

1860 Unwmk. Typo. *Imperf.*

1	A1	2½p dull rose	*30,000.*	

No. 1 was not placed in use and may be a proof or reprint. Most examples are without gum. Value without gum, $20,000.

Perf. 14

2	A1	2½p dull rose	*1,000.*	250.

VANCOUVER ISLAND

A2

A3

1865 Wmk. 1 *Imperf.*

3	A2	5c rose	*75,000.*	*11,000.*
		No gum	*40,000.*	
4	A3	10c blue	4,500.	1,250.

Perf. 14

5	A2	5c rose	500.	300.
6	A3	10c blue	475.	300.

BRITISH COLUMBIA

Seal of British Columbia — A4

1865, Nov. 1

7	A4	3p blue	160.00	125.00

Type A4 of 1865 Surcharged in Various Colors

1867-69 *Perf. 14*

8	2c on 3p brown (Bk)	175.00	160.00
9	5c on 3p brt red (Bk) ('69)	300.00	250.00
10	10c on 3p lilac rose (Bl)	1,900.	
11	25c on 3p orange (V) ('69)	400.00	350.00
12	50c on 3p violet (R)	900.00	*1,150.*
13	$1 on 3p green (G)	2,000.	

Nos. 10 and 13 were not placed in use.

1869 *Perf. 12½*

14	5c on 3p brt red (Bk)	2,250.	1,400.
15	10c on 3p lilac rose (Bl)	1,300.	1,100.
16	25c on 3p orange (V)	1,100.	900.00
17	50c on 3p violet (R)	1,600.	1,100.
18	$1 on 3p green (G)	2,500.	2,000.

NEW BRUNSWICK

'nü 'brənz-ˌwik

LOCATION — Eastern Canada, bordering on the Bay of Fundy and the Gulf of St. Lawrence.
GOVT. — British Province
AREA — 27,985 sq. mi.
POP. — 285,594 (1871)
CAPITAL — Fredericton

At one time a part of Nova Scotia, New Brunswick became a separate province in 1784. Upon joining the Canadian Confederation in 1867 its postage stamps were superseded by those of Canada.

12 Pence = 1 Shilling
100 Cents = 1 Dollar (1860)

Crown of Great Britain and Heraldic Flowers of the United Kingdom A1

1851 Unwmk. Engr. *Imperf.*
Blue Paper

1	A1	3p red	5,500.	575.
a.		3p dark red	5,750.	625.
b.		Half used as 1½p on cover		*4,750.*
2	A1	6p olive yellow	7,000.	1,250.
a.		6p orange yellow	7,000.	1,250.
b.		Half used as 3p on cover		*3,500.*
c.		Quarter used as 1½p on cover		*30,000.*
d.		6p mustard yellow	10,500.	1,500.
3	A1	1sh brt red violet	32,500.	7,000.
a.		Half used as 6p on cover		*22,500.*
b.		Quarter used as 3p on cover		*22,500.*
4	A1	1sh dull violet	40,000.	8,000.
a.		Half used as 6p on cover		*22,500.*
b.		Quarter used as 3p on cover		*22,500.*

The reprints are on stout white paper. The 3p is printed in orange and the 6p and 1sh in violet black. Value about $275 per set of 3.

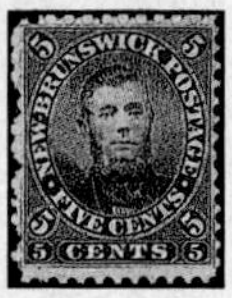

Charles Connell — A2

1860 *Perf. 12*

5	A2	5c brown	*15,000.*	

No. 5 was prepared for use but not issued.

Most examples of No. 5 have creases or other faults. Value of an average example is about half that shown here.

Locomotive A3

Victoria A4

A5

A6

Steam and Sailing Ship — A7

Edward VII as Prince of Wales — A8

1860-63 White Paper *Perf. 12*

6	A3	1c red lilac	42.50	37.50
a.		1c brown violet	100.00	70.00
b.		Horiz. pair, imperf. vert.	700.00	
7	A4	2c orange ('63)	19.00	16.00
a.		Vertical pair, imperf. horiz.	750.00	
8	A5	5c yellow green	27.50	22.50
a.		5c blue green	30.00	22.50
b.		5c olive green	175.00	37.50
9	A6	10c vermilion	55.00	47.50
a.		Half used as 5c on cover		800.00
b.		Double impression	*350.00*	175.00
10	A7	12½c blue	100.00	75.00
11	A8	17c black	55.00	*65.00*
		Nos. 6-11 (6)	299.00	263.50
		Set, never hinged	640.00	

NEWFOUNDLAND

'nü-fən d-lənd

LOCATION — Island in the Atlantic Ocean off the coast of Canada, and Labrador, a part of the mainland
GOVT. — British Dominion
AREA — 42,734 sq. mi.
POP. — 321,177 (1945)
CAPITAL — St. John's

Newfoundland was a self-governing Dominion of the British Empire from 1855 to 1933, when it became a Crown Colony. In 1949 it united with Canada.

12 Pence = 1 Shilling
100 Cents = 1 Dollar (1866)

Values for unused stamps are for examples with original gum as defined in the catalogue introduction. However, very fine examples of Nos. 2-7, 9, 11, 12, 13 and 15 without gum are often traded at values very close to those for examples with original gum.

Watermark

Wmk. 224 Coat of Arms

As the watermark 224 does not show on every stamp in the sheet, pairs are found one with and one without watermark. This applies to all stamps with watermark 224.

Crown of Great Britain and Heraldic Flowers of the United Kingdom — A1

Rose, Thistle and Shamrock — A3

A2

A4

A5

A6

A7

A8

1857 Unwmk. Engr. *Imperf.*
Thick Porous Wove Paper with Mesh

1	A1	1p brn vio	125.00	*200.00*
a.		Half used as ½p on cover		*15,000.*
2	A2	2p scar ver	*17,500.*	7,000.
a.		Vert. half used as 1p on cover		*19,000.*
3	A3	3p green	575.00	500.00
4	A4	4p scar ver	*12,000.*	4,250.
a.		Half used as 2p on cover		*20,000.*
5	A1	5p brn vio	325.00	*425.00*
6	A5	6p scar ver	*25,000.*	5,000.
7	A6	6½p scar ver	5,000.	*4,000.*
8	A7	8p scar ver	400.00	*475.00*
a.		Half used as 4p on cover		5,750.
9	A8	1sh scar ver	*45,000.*	10,000.
a.		Half used as 6p on cover		*20,000.*

1860
Thin to Thick Wove Paper, No Mesh

11	A2	2p orange	475.00	475.00
11A	A3	3p green	85.00	*100.00*
12	A4	4p orange	3,750.	1,350.
b.		Half used as 2p on cover		*15,000.*
12A	A1	5p vio brown	85.00	*150.00*
13	A5	6p orange	5,250.	1,000.
15	A8	1sh orange	*35,000.*	12,000.
b.		Half used as 6p on cover		*17,500.*

A 6½p orange exists as a souvenir item.

A 1sh exists in orange on horizontally or vertically laid paper. Most authorities consider these to be proofs. Value, $10,500.

1861-62

15A	A1	1p	vio brown	175.00	*250.00*
16	A1	1p	reddish brown	*12,500.*	
17	A2	2p	rose	175.00	*175.00*
18	A4	4p	rose	37.50	*70.00*
a.			Half used as 2p on cover		—
19	A1	5p	reddish brown	75.00	*77.50*
20	A5	6p	rose	22.50	*62.50*
a.			Half used as 3p on cover		*10,000.*
21	A6	6½p	rose	85.00	*275.00*
22	A7	8p	rose	85.00	*300.00*
23	A8	1sh	rose	42.50	*250.00*
a.			Half used as 6p on cover		*20,000.*

Some sheets of Nos. 11-23 are known with the papermaker's watermark "STACEY WISE 1858" in large capitals. Values unused and used about 25% more than values shown, except about 50% more for unused Nos. 12 and 13, and 75% more for unused No. 16.

No. 16 was prepared but not issued.

False cancellations are found on Nos. 1, 3, 5, 8, 11, 11A, 12A and 17-23.

Forgeries exist of most or all of Nos. 1-23.

Codfish — A9

Harp Seal — A10

Prince Albert — A11

Victoria — A12

Fishing Ship — A13

Victoria — A14

1865-94 ***Perf. 12***

White Paper(#24, 27, 28)

Thin Yellowish Paper (#25-26, 29-31)

24	A9	2c	green	110.00	30.00
a.			Thin yellowish paper	140.00	50.00
b.			Half used as 1c on cover		*4,000.*
25	A10	5c	brown	600.00	375.00
a.			Half used as 2c on cover		*5,250.*
26	A10	5c	black ('68)	400.00	175.00
27	A11	10c	black	375.00	60.00
a.			Thin yellowish paper	425.00	115.00
b.			Half used as 5c on cover		*4,250.*
28	A12	12c	pale red brn	85.00	47.50
a.			Thin yellowish paper	600.00	190.00
b.			Half used as 6c on cover		*3,250.*
29	A12	12c	brn, *white* ('94)	70.00	55.00
30	A13	13c	orange	250.00	115.00
31	A14	24c	blue, thin transluscent paper	75.00	35.00
a.			Thicker white paper ('70)	375.00	300.00

See Nos. 38, 40.

Edward VII as Prince of Wales — A15

Queen Victoria — A16

1868-94

32	A15	1c	violet	75.00	60.00
32A	A15	1c	brn lil (re-engr. '71)	115.00	75.00
33	A16	3c	ver ('70)	400.00	190.00
34	A16	3c	blue ('73)	375.00	75.00
35	A16	6c	dull rose ('70)	35.00	17.50
36	A16	6c	car lake ('94)	50.00	22.50
			Nos. 32-36 (6)	1,050.	440.00

In the re-engraved 1c the top of the letters "N" and "F" are about ½mm from the ribbon with "ONE CENT." In No. 32 they are fully 1mm away. There are many small differences in the engraving.

1876-79 ***Rouletted***

37	A15	1c	brn lilac ('77)	160.00	52.50
38	A9	2c	green ('79)	200.00	52.50
39	A16	3c	blue ('77)	425.00	15.00
40	A10	5c	blue	275.00	15.00
			Nos. 37-40 (4)	1,060.	135.00

A17

A19

A18

A20

1880-96 ***Perf. 12***

41	A17	1c	violet brown	60.00	11.50
42	A17	1c	gray brown	60.00	11.50
43	A17	1c	brown ('96)	140.00	70.00
44	A17	1c	deep green ('87)	27.50	4.25
45	A17	1c	green ('97)	27.50	4.25
46	A19	2c	yellow green	75.00	14.00
47	A19	2c	green ('96)	120.00	27.50
48	A19	2c	red org ('87)	40.00	9.50
a.			Imperf., pair	325.00	
49	A18	3c	blue	70.00	7.00
51	A18	3c	umber brn ('87)	65.00	4.75
52	A18	3c	vio brown ('96)	130.00	90.00
53	A20	5c	pale blue	375.00	14.00
54	A20	5c	dark blue ('87)	200.00	10.00
55	A20	5c	bright bl ('94)	70.00	6.50
			Nos. 41-55 (14)	1,460.	284.75

Newfoundland Dog — A21

Schooner — A22

1887-96

56	A21	½c	rose red	12.50	7.25
57	A21	½c	org red ('96)	85.00	45.00
58	A21	½c	black ('94)	15.00	7.25
59	A22	10c	black	140.00	67.50
			Nos. 56-59 (4)	252.50	127.00
			Set, never hinged	462.50	

Queen Victoria — A23

1890

60	A23 3c slate		35.00	1.60
a.	3c gray lilac		35.00	1.60
b.	3c brown lilac		55.00	1.60
c.	3c lilac		35.00	1.60
d.	3c slate violet		75.00	3.00
e.	Vert. pair, imperf. horiz.		750.00	

For surcharges see Nos. 75-77.

Victoria — A24

Cabot (John?) — A25

Cape Bonavista A26

Caribou Hunting A27

Mining — A28

Logging — A29

Fishing — A30

Cabot's Ship "Matthew" A31

Willow Ptarmigan A32

Seals — A33

Salmon Fishing — A34

Colony Seal — A35

Iceberg off St. John's — A36

Henry VII — A37

1897, June 24

61	A24	1c deep green		1.75	1.75
62	A25	2c carmine lake		2.25	1.40
63	A26	3c ultramarine		4.25	1.40
64	A27	4c olive green		5.75	2.75
65	A28	5c violet		12.00	2.75
66	A29	6c red brown		6.00	3.25
67	A30	8c red orange		25.00	15.00
68	A31	10c black brown		25.00	7.50
69	A32	12c dark blue		30.00	15.00
70	A33	15c scarlet		22.50	13.00
71	A34	24c gray violet		30.00	12.00
72	A35	30c slate		65.00	55.00
73	A36	35c red		120.00	60.00
74	A37	60c black		18.00	11.50
		Nos. 61-74 (14)		367.50	202.30
		Set, never hinged		733.00	

400th anniv. of John Cabot's discovery of Newfoundland; 60th year of Victoria's reign. The ship on the 10c was previously used by the American Bank Note Co. as the "Flagship of Columbus" on US No. 232. The portrait on the 2c, intended to be of John Cabot, is said to be a Holbein painting of his son, Sebastian.

For surcharges and overprints see Nos. 127-130, C2-C4.

No. 60a Surcharged with Bars and

No. 75

No. 76

No. 77

1897, Oct.

75	A23 1c on 3c gray lil		90.00	50.00
a.	Dbl. surch., one diagonal		*2,000.*	
b.	Vert. pair, "ONE CENT" and lower bar omitted on bottom stamp		*4,250.*	
76	A23 1c on 3c gray lil		300.00	225.00
77	A23 1c on 3c gray lil		875.00	700.00
	Nos. 75-77 (3)		1,265.	975.00
	Set, never hinged		2,680.	

Most examples of Nos. 75-77 are poorly centered. Fine examples sell for about 60% of the values given. No. 75b is valued in the grade of fine.

Trial surcharges of Nos. 75-77 exist with red surcharge and with double surcharge, one in red and one in black, but these were not issued.

Edward VIII as a Child — A38

Victoria — A39

Edward VII as Prince of Wales — A40

Queen Alexandra as Princess of Wales — A41

Queen Mary as Duchess of York — A42

George V as Duke of York — A43

1897-1901 Engr.

78	A38	½c olive green		4.50	2.75
79	A39	1c carmine rose		5.50	5.00
80	A39	1c yel grn ('98)		5.50	.35
b.		Vert. pair, imperf. horiz.		450.00	
81	A40	2c orange		7.00	4.25
82	A40	2c ver ('98)		12.50	.75
b.		Pair, imperf. between		575.00	
83	A41	3c orange ('98)		32.50	.75
a.		Vert. pair, imperf. horiz.		500.00	
84	A42	4c violet ('01)		42.50	4.50
85	A43	5c blue ('99)		42.50	3.00
		Nos. 78-85 (8)		152.50	21.35
		Set, never hinged		305.00	

No. 80b is valued in the grade of fine.

Imperf., Pairs

78a	A38	½c	600.00	*800.00*
81a	A40	2c		*425.00*
82a	A40	2c	350.00	*950.00*
83b	A41	3c	425.00	
84a	A42	4c	700.00	

No. 82a used is valued on cover. Three such covers are recorded.

Imperf., Pairs

Newfoundland imperforates virtually always are proofs on stamp paper or "postmaster's perquisites." Most part-perforate varieties also are "postmaster's perquisites." These items were not regularly issued, but rather were sold or given to favored persons.

Map of Newfoundland — A44

1908, Sept.

86	A44 2c rose carmine	55.00	3.50
	Never hinged	110.00	

Guy Issue

James I — A45

Arms of the London and Bristol Co. — A46

John Guy A47

Guy's Ship, the "Endeavour" A48

View of Cupids — A49

Lord Bacon — A50

View of Mosquito — A51

Logging Camp — A52

Paper Mills — A53

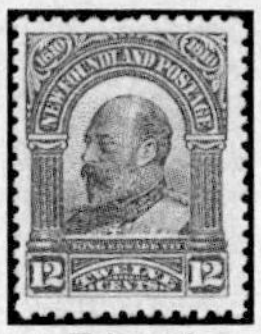
Edward VII — A54

George V — A55

Type I

Type II

SIX CENT TYPES
I — "Z" of "COLONIZATION" reversed.
II — "Z" of normal.

1910, Aug. 15 Litho. *Perf. 12*

87	A45	1c deep green, perf. 12x11	2.25	1.10
a.		Perf. 12	4.75	1.90
b.		Perf. 12x14	7.50	2.25
c.		Horiz. pair, imperf. btwn.	400.00	—
d.		Vert. pair, imperf. btwn.	475.00	
h.		Perf. 12x12x12x11		—
88	A46	2c carmine	11.00	1.15
a.		Perf. 12x14	8.50	.85
b.		As "a," horiz. pair, imperf. between	900.00	
c.		Perf. 12x11 ½	750.00	350.00
89	A47	3c brown olive	25.00	14.00
90	A48	4c dull violet	25.00	14.00
91	A49	5c ultramarine, perf. 14x12	22.50	4.50
a.		Perf. 12	27.50	7.50
92	A50	6c claret, type I	90.00	70.00
92A	A50	6c claret, type II	50.00	37.50
b.		Imperf., pair	450.00	
93	A51	8c pale brown	75.00	55.00
94	A52	9c olive green	75.00	55.00
95	A53	10c vio black	75.00	55.00
96	A54	12c lilac brown	75.00	55.00
a.		Imperf., pair	375.00	
97	A55	15c gray black	80.00	65.00
		Nos. 87-97 (12)	605.75	427.25
		Set, never hinged	1,212.	

Tercentenary of the Colonization of Newfoundland.

On No. 87 printing flaws such as "NFW" and "JANES" exist.

1911 Engr. *Perf. 14*

98	A50	6c brown vio	35.00	22.50
b.		Horiz. pair, imperf. btwn.	*1,100.*	
99	A51	8c bister brn	75.00	67.50
b.		Horiz. pair, imperf. btwn.	*1,200.*	
100	A52	9c olive grn	75.00	60.00
b.		Horiz. pair, imperf. btwn.	*1,200.*	
101	A53	10c violet blk	95.00	95.00
b.		Horiz. pair, imperf. btwn.	*1,200.*	
102	A54	12c red brown	75.00	75.00
b.		Horiz. pair, imperf. btwn.	—	
103	A55	15c slate grn	75.00	75.00
b.		Horiz. pair, imperf. btwn.	*1,200.*	
		Nos. 98-103 (6)	430.00	*395.00*
		Set, never hinged	759.50	

Nos. 100 and 103 are known with papermaker's watermark "E. TOWGOOD FINE." Values, unused or used: No. 100, $800; No. 103, $1,000.

Imperf., Pairs

98a	A50	6c	325.00
99a	A51	8c	325.00
100a	A52	9c	325.00
101a	A53	10c	325.00
102a	A54	12c	325.00
103a	A55	15c	325.00

Nos. 98a-103a were made with and without gum. Values the same.

Royal Family Issue

Queen Mary — A56

George V — A57

Prince of Wales (Edward VIII) — A58

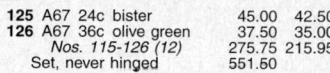

Prince Albert (George VI) — A59

Princess Mary — A60

Prince Henry — A61

Prince George A62

Prince John A63

Queen Alexandra A64

Duke of Connaught A65

Seal of Colony — A66

1911, June 19 *Perf. 13½x14, 14*

104	A56	1c yellow grn	3.00	.25
105	A57	2c carmine	2.75	1.00
106	A58	3c red brown	35.00	19.00
107	A59	4c violet	35.00	13.50
108	A60	5c ultra	20.00	1.90
109	A61	6c black	32.50	22.50
110	A62	8c blue (paper colored through)	85.00	65.00
a.		8c peacock blue	95.00	70.00
111	A63	9c bl violet	35.00	20.00
112	A64	10c dark green	50.00	37.50
113	A65	12c plum	42.50	37.50
114	A66	15c magenta	35.00	*37.50*
		Nos. 104-114 (11)	375.75	255.65
		Set, never hinged	749.00	

Coronation of King George V.

Imperf., Pairs
Without Gum

104a	A56	1c	325.00
105a	A57	2c	325.00
108a	A60	5c	325.00
113a	A65	12c	425.00
114a	A66	15c	140.00

Trail of the Caribou Issue

Caribou
A67 A68

1919, Jan. 2 *Perf. 14*

115	A67	1c green	2.75	.35
116	A68	2c scarlet	3.00	.50
117	A67	3c red brown	3.50	.30
118	A67	4c violet	5.00	1.40
119	A68	5c ultramarine	9.00	1.40
120	A67	6c gray	22.50	22.50
121	A68	8c magenta	22.50	19.00
122	A67	10c dark green	17.50	5.50
123	A68	12c orange	65.00	45.00
124	A67	15c dark blue	42.50	42.50
125	A67	24c bister	45.00	42.50
126	A67	36c olive green	37.50	35.00
		Nos. 115-126 (12)	275.75	215.95
		Set, never hinged	551.50	

Services of the Newfoundland contingent in WWI.

Each denomination of type A67 is inscribed with the name of a different action in which Newfoundland troops took part.

For overprint and surcharge see Nos. C1, C5.

Imperf., Pairs
Without Gum

115a	A67	1c	275.00
116a	A68	2c	275.00
117a	A67	3c red brown	275.00
118a	A67	4c	275.00
119a	A68	5c	275.00
120a	A67	6c	275.00
121a	A68	8c	275.00
122a	A67	10c	275.00
123a	A68	12c	275.00
124a	A67	15c	275.00
125a	A67	24c	275.00
126a	A67	36c	275.00

No. 72 Surcharged in Black

1920 *Perf. 12*

127	A35	2c on 30c slate	5.75	5.50
		Never hinged	8.75	
a.		Inverted surcharge	1,100.	

No. 127 with red surcharge is an unissued color trial. 25 examples are known. Value, $1,000.

Also known reading "TWO / 2 / CENTS," with surcharge in red. 50 stamps were so surcharged, including examples with double surcharge. Value, $2,000.

Nos. 70 and 73 Surcharged in Black

THREE CENTS
Type I — Bars 10½mm apart.
Type II — Bars 13½mm apart.

128	A33	3c on 15c scar (I)	230.00	250.00
		Never hinged	350.00	
a.		Inverted surcharge	*3,000.*	
129	A33	3c on 15c scar (II)	19.00	11.00
		Never hinged	35.00	
130	A36	3c on 35c red	11.50	9.50
		Never hinged	20.00	
a.		Lower bar omitted	150.00	135.00

All examples of the former No. 130c ("THREE" omitted) examined show part of the tops or bottoms of the letters. It is probable that no examples with "THREE" completely omitted exist.

Twin Hills, Tor's Cove — A70

South West Arm, Trinity — A71

War Memorial, St. John's — A72

Humber River A73

Coast of Trinity — A74

Upper Steadies, Humber River — A75

Quidi Vidi, near St. John's — A76

Caribou Crossing Lake — A77

Humber River Canyon A78

Shell Bird Island A79

Mt. Moriah, Bay of Islands A80

Humber River near Little Rapids A81

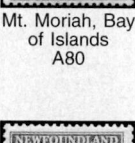

Placentia, from Mt. Pleasant A82

Topsail Falls near St. John's A83

1923-24 **Engr.** *Perf. 14, 13½x14*

131	A70	1c gray green	1.90	.30
a.		Booklet pane of 8	500.00	
132	A71	2c carmine	1.90	.30
a.		Booklet pane of 8	300.00	
133	A72	3c brown	2.50	.30
134	A73	4c brn violet	2.75	1.80
135	A74	5c ultramarine	7.00	2.25
136	A75	6c gray black	6.00	6.00
137	A76	8c dull violet	4.50	4.50
138	A77	9c slate green	40.00	27.50
139	A78	10c dark violet	4.25	2.50
140	A79	11c olive green	7.00	7.00
141	A80	12c lake	7.50	7.50
142	A81	15c deep blue	9.50	8.00
143	A82	20c red brn ('24)	13.00	7.50
144	A83	24c blk brn ('24)	75.00	50.00
		Nos. 131-144 (14)	182.80	125.45
		Set, never hinged	327.00	

For surcharge see No. 160.

Imperf., Pairs

131b	A70	1c	200.00
132b	A71	2c	200.00
133a	A72	3c	300.00
134a	A73	4c	250.00
135a	A74	5c	250.00
136a	A75	6c	250.00
137a	A76	8c	250.00
138a	A77	9c	250.00
139a	A78	10c	250.00
140a	A79	11c	250.00
141a	A80	12c	250.00
142a	A81	15c	160.00

Nos. 133a-139a, 141a-142a are without gum. Others are either with or without gum; values about the same.

Map of Newfoundland A84

Steamship "Caribou" A85

Queen Mary, George V — A86

Prince of Wales — A87

Express Train — A88

Newfoundland Hotel, St. John's — A89

Heart's Content — A90

Cabot Tower, St. John's — A91

War Memorial, St. John's — A92

GPO, St. John's — A93

First Nonstop Transatlantic Flight, 1919 — A94

Colonial Building, St. John's — A95

Grand Falls, Labrador — A96

Perf. 14, 13½x13, 13x13½
1928, Jan. 3

145	A84	1c deep green	1.85	.75
146	A85	2c deep carmine	2.50	.70
a.		Imperf., pair	300.00	
147	A86	3c brown	2.75	.50
148	A87	4c lilac rose	3.50	1.80
149	A88	5c slate green	10.00	4.25
150	A89	6c ultramarine	5.75	5.00
151	A90	8c lt red brown	7.25	4.50
152	A91	9c myrtle green	7.00	7.00
153	A92	10c dark violet	9.00	4.25
154	A93	12c brn carmine	5.50	5.00
155	A91	14c red brown	10.50	7.00
156	A94	15c dark blue	9.25	7.00
157	A95	20c gray black	12.50	6.50
158	A93	28c gray green	35.00	27.50
159	A96	30c olive brown	17.50	7.50
		Nos. 145-159 (15)	139.85	89.25
		Set, never hinged	280.25	

See Nos. 163-182.

No. 136 Surcharged in Red or Black

Type I — 5mm between "CENTS" and bar.
Type II — 3mm between "CENTS" and bar.

1929 *Perf. 14x13½*

160 A75 3c on 6c gray black (II) (R) 4.25 4.25
Never hinged 6.75
a. Inverted surcharge (II) 1,000.

The stamps with black surcharge, type I and II, were 1st or trial printings, and were not issued. There were 50 examples of each. Value, each $1,750.

Types of 1928 Issue Re-engraved

1c — On No. 145 the lines of the engraving are thinner and the impression is clearer than on No. 163. On the former "C. BAULD" is above "C. NORMAN." On the latter these words are transposed.

2c — On the 1928 stamp the "D" of "NEWFOUNDLAND" is 1mm from the scroll at the right; the flag at the stern is lower than the top of the boat davit. On the 1929 stamp the "D" is ½mm from the scroll and the flag rises above the davits.

3c — On the 1928 stamp the pearls at the top of the crown, the jewels of the tiara and the pillars flanking the portraits are all unshaded. On the reengraved stamp there are small curved lines inside the pearls, the jewels of the tiara are in solid color, and the pillars have vertical shading lines. On the 1928 stamps the tablets with "THREE" and "CENTS" have a background of crossed lines (vertical and horizontal). On the 1929 stamp the background is of horizontal lines only.

4c — On the 1928 stamp the figures "4" have shading of horizontal and diagonal crossed lines. There are six circles at each side of the portrait.

On the 1929 stamp the "4s" have shading of horizontal lines only. There are five roses at each side of the portrait.

5c — The crossbars of the telegraph pole touch the frame at the left on the 1929 stamp but just clear it on the 1928 stamp. In the 1928 issue the foliate ornaments beside and below the figures "5" end in small scrolls and a small spur. These spurs are omitted on the 1929 stamp.

6c — On the re-engraved stamp the columns at right and left of the picture have heavy wavy outlines on the inner sides. There is no period after "JOHNS." The numerals in the lower corners are 1½mm wide instead of 1¼mm.

8c — The impression of the 1928 stamp is clear, that of 1931 is slightly blurred. The 1928 stamp has three horizontal lines above "EIGHT CENTS" and four berries on the laurel branch at the right side. On the 1931 stamp there are two horizontal lines and three berries.

10c — On the re-engraved stamp there is no period after "ST. JOHN'S." The letters of "TEN CENTS" are slightly larger and the numerals "10" slightly smaller than in 1928. Inside the "0" of "10" at the right there are two vertical lines instead of three. The clouds are fainter in 1929 and the cross upheld by the figure on the monument is more distinct. On the 1928 stamp the torch at the left side terminates in a single tongue of flame. On the 1929-30 stamp it terminates in two tongues.

15c — On the 1928 stamp the "N" of "NEWFOUNDLAND" is 1½mm from the left frame, the "L" of "LEAVING" is under the first "A" of "AIRPLANE" and the apostrophe in "JOHN'S" breaks the first line above it.

On the 1929 stamp the "N" of "NEWFOUNDLAND" is 1mm from the left frame, the "L" of "LEAVING" is below the "T" of "FIRST" and the apostrophe in "JOHN'S" does not touch the line above it.

20c — On the 1928 stamp the points of the "W" of "NEWFOUNDLAND" are truncated. The "O" is wide and nearly round. The columns that form the sides of the frame have a shading of evenly spaced horizontal lines at their inner sides.

On the 1929-31 stamp the points of the "W" form sharp angles. The "O" is narrow and has a small opening. Many lines have been added to the shading on the inner sides of the columns, making it almost solid.

30c — 1928 stamp. Size: 19¼x24½mm. At the outer side of the right column there are three strong and two faint vertical lines. Faint period after "FALLS."

1931 stamp. Size: 19x25mm. At the outer side of the right column there are two strong vertical lines and a fragment of the lower end of a faint one. Clear period after "FALLS." A great many of the small lines of the design have been deepened making the whole stamp appear darker.

1929-31 **Unwmk.** *Perf. 13½ to 14*

163 A84 1c green 2.25 .65
a. Double impression *325.00*
b. Vert. pair, imperf. btwn. 210.00
164 A85 2c deep carmine 2.25 .70
165 A86 3c dp red brown 2.50 .70
166 A87 4c magenta 3.75 1.25
167 A88 5c slate green 7.50 2.50
168 A89 6c ultramarine 10.00 9.00
169 A92 10c dark violet 8.75 2.25
170 A94 15c deep blue ('30) 50.00 37.50
171 A95 20c gray blk ('31) 75.00 27.50
Nos. 163-171 (9) 162.00 82.05
Set, never hinged 324.50

Imperf., Pairs

163c A84 1c 120.00
164a A85 2c pale carmine, *cream* 145.00
b. 2c dark carmine 145.00
165a A86 3c 145.00
166a A87 4c 145.00

No. 164b is without gum, others with gum.

Types of 1928 Issue Re-engraved

1931 **Wmk. 224** *Perf. 13½x14*

172 A84 1c green, perf. 13½ 2.25 1.30
a. Horiz. pair, imperf. btwn. 425.00
173 A85 2c red 7.00 1.30
174 A86 3c red brown 3.50 1.30
175 A87 4c rose 4.25 2.75
176 A88 5c grnsh gray 12.50 7.00
177 A89 6c ultramarine 17.50 17.50
178 A90 8c lt red brn 22.50 17.50
179 A92 10c dk violet 15.00 9.00
180 A94 15c deep blue 45.00 27.50
181 A95 20c gray black 55.00 17.50
182 A96 30c olive brown 45.00 25.00
Nos. 172-182 (11) 229.50 127.65
Set, never hinged 459.00

Codfish — A97

George V — A98

Queen Mary — A99

Prince of Wales — A100

Caribou A101

Princess Elizabeth A102

Salmon Leaping Falls — A103

Newfoundland Dog — A104

Harp Seal Pup — A105

Cape Race — A106

Sealing Fleet — A107

Fishing Fleet Leaving for "The Banks" — A108

Type I

Type II

FIVE CENT
Die I — Antlers even, or equal in height.
Die II — Antler under "T" higher.

1932-37 **Engr.** *Perf. 13½, 14*

183 A97 1c green 2.75 .50
a. Booklet pane of 4, perf. 13 75.00
c. Vert. pair, imperf. btwn. 200.00
184 A97 1c gray black .60 .25
a. Bklt. pane of 4, perf. 13½ 57.50
b. Booklet pane of 4, perf. 14 72.50
185 A98 2c rose 2.25 .35
a. Booklet pane of 4, perf. 13½ 35.00
b. Booklet pane of 4, perf. 13 47.50
186 A98 2c green 1.10 .25
a. Bklt. pane of 4, perf. 13½ 25.00
b. Booklet pane of 4, perf. 14 35.00
d. Horiz. pair, imperf. btwn. 160.00
187 A99 3c orange brn 1.10 .35
a. Bklt. pane of 4, perf. 13½ 55.00
b. Booklet pane of 4, perf. 14 67.50
c. Booklet pane of 4, perf. 13 75.00
e. Vert. pair, imperf. btwn. 300.00
188 A100 4c deep violet 7.00 2.00
189 A100 4c rose lake .75 .50
b. Vert. pair, imperf. btwn. 120.00
c. Horiz. pair, imperf. btwn. 120.00
190 A101 5c vio brn, perf. 13½ (Die I) 9.50 2.00
191 A101 5c dp vio, perf. 13½ (Die II) 1.10 .40
a. 5c dp vio, perf. 13½ (Die I) 14.00 1.25
c. Horiz. pair, imperf. btwn. (I) 240.00
g. Horiz. pair, imperf. btwn. (II) 240.00
192 A102 6c dull blue 11.00 11.00
193 A103 10c olive black 1.40 .85
194 A104 14c int black 3.25 2.75
195 A105 15c magenta 2.50 2.25
196 A106 20c gray green 2.50 1.00
197 A107 25c gray 2.75 2.00
b. Horiz. pair, imperf. btwn. 450.00
c. Vert. pair, imperf. btwn. 450.00
198 A108 30c ultra 32.50 24.00
b. Vert. pair, imperf. btwn. 1,000.
199 A108 48c red brn ('37) 11.00 5.25
Nos. 183-199 (17) 93.05 55.70
Set, never hinged 134.55

Two dies were used for 2c green, one for 2c rose.

See Nos. 253-266.

Imperf., Pairs

183b A97 1c 240.00
184c A97 1c 47.50
185c A98 2c 250.00
186c A98 2c 47.50
187d A99 3c 95.00
189a A100 4c 60.00
190a A101 5c 200.00
191b A101 5c (II) 75.00
191d A101 5c (I) 100.00
192a A102 6c 175.00
193a A103 10c 110.00
194a A103 14c 130.00
195a A103 15c 130.00
196a A106 20c 225.00
197a A107 25c 225.00
198a A108 30c 750.00
199a A108 48c 120.00

All with gum. Nos. 186c, 187d, 192a, 193a and 196a also made without gum; values about 10% less.

Queen Elizabeth when Duchess of York — A109

Corner Brook Paper Mills — A110

Loading Iron Ore at Bell Island — A111

1932

208 A109 7c red brown 1.40 1.25
a. Imperf., pair 160.00
b. Horiz. pair, imperf. between 600.00
209 A110 8c orange red 1.40 1.10
a. Imperf., pair 140.00
210 A111 24c light blue 2.75 2.75
a. Imperf., pair 200.00
b. Double impression 1,500.
Nos. 208-210 (3) 5.55 5.10
Set, never hinged 7.75

No. 208a was made both with and without gum. Values about the same.

See Nos. 259, 264.

No. C9 Overprinted Bars and

1933, Feb. 9 **Wmk. 224** *Perf. 14*

211 AP6 15c brown 11.00 9.50
Never hinged 17.00
a. Vert. pair, one without overprint 7,500.
b. Overprint reading up 4,750.

"L. & S." stands for "Land and Sea."

Sir Humphrey Gilbert Issue

Sir Humphrey Gilbert — A112

Compton Castle, Home of the Gilbert Family — A113

Gilbert Coat of Arms — A114

Eton College — A115

Token from Queen Elizabeth I — A116

Sir Humphrey Receiving Royal Patents for Colonization A117

Sir Humphrey's Ships Leaving Plymouth, 1583 — A118

The Ships Arriving at St. John's — A119

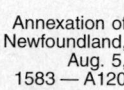

Annexation of Newfoundland, Aug. 5, 1583 — A120

Coat of Arms of England A121

Sir Humphrey on the Deck of the "Squirrel" A122

Capt. John Mason's Map of Newfoundland, 1626 — A123

Queen Elizabeth I A124

Gilbert Statue at Truro A125

Wmk. 224

1933, Aug. 3 Engr. *Perf. 13½*

212	A112	1c gray black	1.10	.75
213	A113	2c green	1.10	.75
b.		Double impression	*600.00*	
214	A114	3c yellow brn	2.00	.75
215	A115	4c carmine	1.90	.75
216	A116	5c dull violet	2.75	1.10
217	A117	7c blue	19.00	12.50
218	A118	8c orange red	7.50	7.00
219	A119	9c ultramarine	8.00	7.50
220	A120	10c red brown	8.00	6.25
221	A121	14c black	16.00	15.00
222	A122	15c claret	15.00	15.00
223	A123	20c deep green	13.00	10.00
224	A124	24c vio brown	22.50	22.50
225	A125	32c gray	22.50	22.50
		Nos. 212-225 (14)	140.35	122.35
		Set, never hinged	204.70	

350th anniv. of annexation of Newfoundland to England, Aug. 5, 1583, by authority of Letters Patent issued by Queen Elizabeth I to Sir Humphrey Gilbert.

Imperf., Pairs

212a	A112	1c	45.00
213a	A113	2c	45.00
214a	A114	3c	375.00
215a	A115	4c	50.00
216a	A116	5c	375.00
219a	A119	9c	500.00
220a	A120	10c	500.00
221a	A120	14c	400.00
222a	A120	15c	240.00
224a	A124	24c	225.00

No. 212a was made both with and without gum. Value of pair without gum about 10% less.

Common Design Types pictured following the introduction.

Silver Jubilee Issue

Common Design Type

1935, May 6 Wmk. 4 *Perf. 11x12*

226	CD301	4c bright rose	2.25	.70
227	CD301	5c violet	2.25	.85
228	CD301	7c dark blue	4.00	3.50
229	CD301	24c olive green	9.00	7.00
		Nos. 226-229 (4)	17.50	12.05
		Set, never hinged	25.35	

Coronation Issue

Common Design Type

1937, May 12 *Perf. 11x11½*

230	CD302	2c deep green	1.75	.70
231	CD302	4c carmine rose	1.75	.70
232	CD302	5c dark violet	3.50	1.40
		Nos. 230-232 (3)	7.00	2.80
		Set, never hinged	9.80	

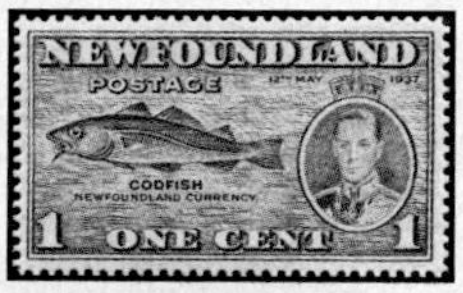

Codfish A126

Map of Newfoundland — A127

Caribou A128

Corner Brook Paper Mills A129

Salmon A130

Newfoundland Dog — A131

Harp Seal Pup A132

Cape Race A133

Loading Iron Ore at Bell Island A134

Sealing Fleet A135

Fishing Fleet Leaving for "The Banks" A136

Type I

Type II

Two types of the 3c
Type I — Fine impression; no lines on bridge of nose.
Type II — Coarse impression; lines on bridge of nose.

Perf. 13½, 14 (#234-235)

1937, May 12 Wmk. 224

233	A126	1c gray black	.50	.30
234	A127	3c org brn, die I	2.50	1.10
a.		Die II	1.75	1.10
b.		Vert. pair, imperf. btwn. (I)	700.00	
c.		Vert. pair, imperf. btwn. (II)	700.00	
d.		Horiz. pair, imperf. btwn. (I)	575.00	
e.		Horiz. pair, imperf. btwn. (II)	575.00	
f.		Imperf., pair	240.00	
i.		Horiz. pair, imperf. vert., never hinged	*1,600.*	
235	A128	7c blue	2.50	2.50
236	A129	8c orange red	2.50	2.50
a.		Imperf., pair	280.00	
b.		Vert. pair, imperf. between	1,250.	
c.		Horiz. pair, imperf. vert.	*2,000.*	
237	A130	10c olive gray	4.25	4.25
a.		Double impression	280.00	
238	A131	14c black	4.00	3.50
a.		Imperf., pair	400.00	
239	A132	15c rose lake	3.50	3.50
a.		Vert. pair, imperf. between	1,000.	
240	A133	20c green	2.75	2.25
a.		Vert. pair, imperf. between	1,250.	
241	A134	24c turq blue	3.50	3.25
a.		Vert. pair, imperf. between	2,000.	
242	A135	25c gray	3.50	3.25
a.		Imperf., pair	275.00	
243	A136	48c dark violet	5.00	4.00
a.		Vert. pair, imperf. between	2,000.	
b.		Imperf., pair	275.00	
		Nos. 233-243 (11)	34.50	30.40
		Set, never hinged	49.05	

Imperfs are with gum. No. 243b also made without gum; value the same.

Princess Elizabeth — A139

Designs: 2c, King George VI. 3c, Queen Elizabeth. 7c, Queen Mother Mary.

1938, May 12 *Perf. 13½*

245	A139	2c green	1.75	.25
246	A139	3c dark carmine	1.75	.25
247	A139	4c light blue	2.40	.25
248	A139	7c dark ultra	1.60	1.10
		Nos. 245-248 (4)	7.50	1.85
		Set, never hinged	9.50	

See Nos. 254-256, 258, 269.

Imperf., Pairs

245a	A139	2c	120.00
246a	A139	3c	120.00
247a	A139	4c	120.00
248a	A139	7c	120.00
		Set, never hinged	700.00

George VI and Queen Elizabeth A141

1939, June 17 Unwmk.

249	A141	5c violet blue	1.25	1.10
		Never hinged	1.75	

Visit of King George and Queen Elizabeth.

No. 249 Surcharged in Brown or Red

1939, Nov. 20

250	A141	2c on 5c vio blue (Br)	1.40	1.00
251	A141	4c on 5c vio blue (R)	1.10	1.00
		Set, never hinged	3.30	

There are many varieties of broken letters and figures in the settings of the surcharges.

Sir Wilfred Grenfell and "Strathcona II" — A142

1941, Dec. 1 *Perf. 12*

252	A142	5c dull blue	.40	.30
		Never hinged	.50	

Grenfell Mission, 50th anniv.

Types of 1931-38

1941-44 Wmk. 224 *Perf. 12½*

253	A97	1c dark gray	.35	.25
a.		Imperf., pair	150.00	
254	A139	2c deep green	.35	.25
255	A139	3c rose carmine	.50	.25
a.		Imperf., pair	275.00	
256	A139	4c blue	.70	.30
257	A101	5c violet (Die I)	1.00	.25
a.		Imperf., pair	175.00	
b.		Horiz. pair, imperf. vert.	475.00	
c.		Double impression	400.00	
258	A139	7c vio blue ('42)	1.20	1.00
259	A110	8c red	1.40	.65
260	A103	10c brownish blk	1.40	.60
261	A104	14c black	2.10	1.75
a.		Imperf., pair	240.00	
o.		Vert. pair, imperf. horiz.	350.00	
262	A105	15c pale rose vio	2.00	1.40
263	A106	20c green	2.00	1.10
264	A111	24c deep blue	2.25	2.00
265	A107	25c slate	2.25	2.00
266	A108	48c red brown ('44)	3.25	1.75
		Nos. 253-266 (14)	20.75	13.55
		Set, never hinged	26.60	

Nos. 254 and 255 are re-engraved.

Memorial University College A143

1943, Jan. 2 Unwmk. *Perf. 12*

267	A143	30c carmine	1.40	1.00
		Never hinged	1.85	

No. 267 Surcharged in Black

1946, Mar. 23

268	A143	2c on 30c carmine	.30	.30
		Never hinged	.40	

Princess Elizabeth — A144

Wmk. 224

1947, Apr. 21 Engr. *Perf. 12½*

269	A144	4c light blue	.30	.25
		Never hinged	.40	
a.		Imperf., pair	240.00	
b.		Horiz. pair, imperf. vert.	325.00	

Princess Elizabeth's 21st birthday.

Deck of the Matthew A145

1947, June 24

270 A145 5c rose violet .30 .25
Never hinged .40
a. Horiz. pair, imperf. between 1,200.
b. Imperf., pair 240.00

Cabot's arrival off Cape Bonavista, 450th anniv.

AIR POST STAMPS

No. 117 Overprinted in Black

1919, Apr. 12 Unwmk. *Perf. 14*

C1 A67 3c red brown *27,500. 16,000.*
Never hinged *37,500.*

No. 70 Surcharged in Black

1919, June 9 *Perf. 12*

C2 A33 $1 on 15c scarlet 225.00 225.00
Never hinged 375.00
a. Without comma after "Post" 240.00 *275.00*
b. As "a," without period after "1919" 450.00 450.00

No. 73 Overprinted in Black

1921, Nov. 7

C3 A36 35c red, 2½mm between "AIR" and "MAIL" 145.00 *180.00*
a. Inverted overprint 6,000.
b. With period after "1921" 160.00 *200.00*
c. As "b," inverted overprint 6,500.

No. C3 was printed in sheets of twenty-five, containing varieties of wide and narrow space between "AIR" and "MAIL," date shifted to right, and with and without period after date.

No. 74 Overprinted in Red

1927, May 21

C4 A37 60c black *45,000. 20,000.*
Never hinged *60,000.*

No. 126 Surcharged in Black

1930, Sept. 25 *Perf. 14*

C5 A67 50c on 36c ol grn *9,000. 9,000.*
Never hinged *14,000.*

Dog Sled and Airplane — AP6

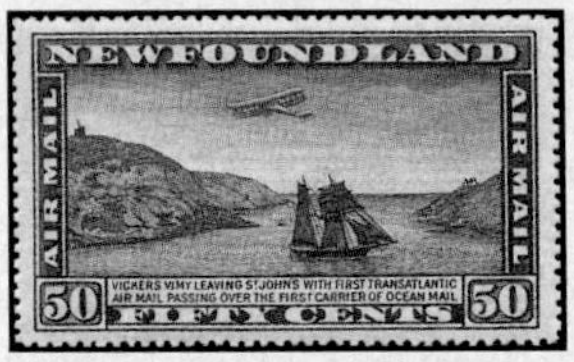

First Transatlantic Mail Airplane and Packet Ship — AP7

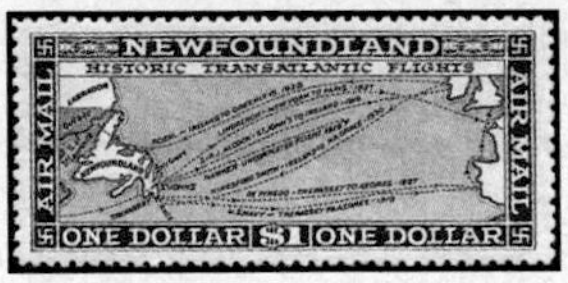

Routes of Historic Transatlantic Flights — AP8

1931, Jan. 2 Engr. Unwmk.

C6 AP6 15c brown 11.00 7.50
a. Horiz. pair, imperf. between 950.00
b. Vert. pair, imperf. between 950.00
c. Imperf., pair 625.00
C7 AP7 50c green 35.00 25.00
a. Horiz. pair, imperf. between 1,350. 825.00
b. Vert. pair, imperf. between 1,350.
c. Imperf., pair 725.00
C8 AP8 $1 blue 70.00 55.00
a. Horiz. pair, imperf. between 1,000.
b. Vert. pair, imperf. between 1,000.
c. Imperf., pair 725.00
Nos. C6-C8 (3) 116.00 87.50
Set, never hinged 195.00

1931 Wmk. 224

C9 AP6 15c brown 11.00 7.50
a. Horiz. pair, imperf. between 950.00
b. Vert. pair, imperf. between 1,100.
c. Imperf., pair 600.00
C10 AP7 50c green 40.00 35.00
a. Horiz. pair, imperf. between 950.00
b. Vert. pair, imperf. between 950.00
c. Horiz. pair, Imperf. vert. 950.00
C11 AP8 $1 blue 100.00 90.00
a. Vert. pair, imperf. between 1,000.
c. Horiz. pair, imperf. between 1,000.
d. Vert. pair, imperf. horiz. 1,000.
e. Imperf., pair 600.00
Nos. C9-C11 (3) 151.00 132.50
Set, never hinged 263.50

As the watermark 224 does not show on every stamp in the sheet, pairs are found one with and one without watermark.

For overprint and surcharge see Nos. 211, C12.

No. C11 Surcharged in Red

1932, May 19

C12 AP8 $1.50 on $1 blue 275.00 275.00
Never hinged 425.00
a. Inverted surcharge *18,500.*
Never hinged *32,500.*

A stamp of this design was produced in the US in 1932 by a private company under contract with Newfoundland authorities. The government canceled the contract and the stamp was not valid for prepayment of postage. Value, $35.

"Put to Flight" — AP9

"Land of Heart's Delight" AP10

"Spotting the Herd" AP11

"News from Home" AP12

"Labrador, The Land of Gold" AP13

Perf. 11½ (10, 60c), 14 (5, 30, 75c)

1933, June 9 Engr.

C13 AP9 5c lt brown 11.00 11.00
b. Horiz. pair, imperf. between *1,150.*
c. Vert. pair, imperf. between *1,150.*
C14 AP10 10c yellow 19.00 17.50
C15 AP11 30c blue 30.00 30.00
C16 AP12 60c green 65.00 57.50
C17 AP13 75c bister 60.00 57.50
b. Horiz. pair, imperf. between *2,500.*
c. Vert. pair, imperf. between *2,500.*
Nos. C13-C17 (5) 185.00 173.50
Set, never hinged 262.50

Beware of clever forgeries of Nos. C13b, C13c, C17b and C17c. Certificates of authenticity are highly recommended.

Imperf., Pairs

C13a	AP9	5c	275.00
C14a	AP10	10c	200.00
C15a	AP11	30c	725.00
C16a	AP12	60c	725.00
C17a	AP13	75c	725.00
Set, never hinged			3,150.

No. C17 Surcharged in Black

1933, July 24 *Perf. 14*

C18 AP13 $4.50 on 75c bister 325.00 350.00
Never hinged 500.00
a. Inverted surcharge *100,000.*
Never hinged *130,000.*

Return flight from Chicago to Rome of the squadron of Italian seaplanes under the command of Gen. Italo Balbo.

No. C18a was not regularly issued.

The $4.50 on No. C14, 10c yellow, is a proof. Value, $62,500.

View of St. John's AP14

1943, June 1 Unwmk. *Perf. 12*

C19 AP14 7c bright ultra .35 .30
Never hinged .45

POSTAGE DUE STAMPS

D1

Perf. 10-10½, Compound

1939-49 Litho. Unwmk.

J1 D1 1c yellow green, perf. 11 ('49) 4.25 *5.50*
a. Perf. 10-10½ 7.00 5.50
J2 D1 2c vermilion 7.00 5.50
a. Perf. 11x9 ('46) 7.00 5.50
J3 D1 3c ultramarine 7.00 5.50
a. Perf. 11x9 ('49) 7.50 7.50
b. Perf. 9 *3,750.*
J4 D1 4c yel org, perf. 11x9 ('49) 9.50 9.50
a. Perf 10-10½ 15.00 15.00
J5 D1 5c pale brown 15.00 4.25
J6 D1 10c dark violet 7.00 6.50
Nos. J1-J6 (6) 49.75 36.75
Set, never hinged 80.50

1949 Wmk. 224 *Perf. 11*

J7 D1 10c dark violet 11.00 *15.00*
Never hinged 19.00
a. Vert. pair, imperf. between *850.00*

For used examples of Nos. J1-J7 with dated cancels from 1939-49, triple the values shown.

NOVA SCOTIA

ˌnō-və-ˈskō-shə

LOCATION — Eastern coast of Canada between the Gulf of St. Lawrence and the Atlantic Ocean
GOVT. — British Crown Colony
AREA — 21,428 sq. mi.
POP. — 386,500 (1871)
CAPITAL — Halifax

Nova Scotia joined the Canadian Confederation in 1867 and is now a province of the Dominion. Postage stamps of Canada are used.

12 Pence = 1 Shilling
100 Cents = 1 Dollar (1860)

Values for unused stamps are for examples with original gum as defined in the catalogue introduction except for Nos. 4-7, which are rarely found with any remaining original gum.

Queen Victoria — A1

Crown of Great Britain and Heraldic Flowers of the Empire — A2

Blue Paper

1851-57 Unwmk. Engr. *Imperf.*

1 A1 1p red brown ('53) 2,500. 525.
a. Half used as ½p on cover —
2 A2 3p bright blue 1,750. 250.
a. Half used as 1½p on cover *3,750.*
b. 3p pale blue ('57) 1,750. 275.
c. As "b," half used as 1½p on cover *3,750.*
3 A2 3p dark blue 2,250. 300.
a. Half used as 1½p on cover *4,500.*
4 A2 6p yellow green 5,000. 850.
a. Half used as 3p on cover *4,500.*
5 A2 6p dark green ('57) 11,000. 2,250.
a. Half used as 3p on cover *5,000.*
b. Quarter used as 1½p on cover *47,500.*
6 A2 1sh reddish pur ('57) 25,000. 5,250.
a. Half used as 6p on cover *32,500.*
b. 1sh deep purple *27,500.* 6,000.
7 A2 1sh dull violet 24,000. 6,500.
a. Half used as 6p on cover *47,500.*
b. Quarter used as 3p on cover *60,000.*

Reprints are on thin hard white paper. 1p in brown, 3p in blue, 6p dark green. 1sh violet black. Value about $300 per set.

No. 6 was reproduced by the collotype process in a souvenir sheet distributed at the London International Stamp Exhibition 1950.

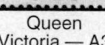

Queen Victoria — A3

A5

A6

White or Yellowish Paper

1860-63 *Perf. 12*

8 A3 1c black 15.00 7.50
a. White paper 15.00 7.50
b. Half used as ½c on cover *5,750.*
c. Horiz. pair, imperf. vert. 325.00
9 A3 2c lilac 15.00 12.50
a. Yellowish paper 15.00 12.50
b. Half used as 1c on cover *3,250.*
10 A3 5c blue 425.00 12.00
a. Yellowish paper 425.00 12.00
b. Half used as 2½c on cover *5,000.*
11 A5 8½c green 15.00 *22.00*
a. White paper 15.00 *20.00*
12 A5 10c vermilion 15.00 12.00
a. Yellowish paper 15.00 12.00
b. Half used as 5c on cover *1,200.*
13 A6 12½c black 42.50 37.50
a. White paper 42.50 37.50
Nos. 8-13 (6) 527.50 103.50
Set, never hinged 1,460.

The stamps of Nova Scotia were replaced by those of Canada.

PRINCE EDWARD ISLAND

ˈprin(t)s ˈed-wərd ˈī-lənd

LOCATION — In the Gulf of St. Lawrence, opposite the provinces of New Brunswick and Nova Scotia
GOVT. — British Crown Colony
AREA — 2,184 sq. mi.
POP. — 92,000 (estimated)
CAPITAL — Charlottetown

Originally annexed to Nova Scotia, Prince Edward Island was a separate colony from 1769 to 1873, when it became a part of the Canadian Confederation. Postage stamps of Canada are now used.

12 Pence = 1 Shilling
100 Cents = 1 Dollar (1872)

A1

A2

Queen Victoria — A3

1861, Jan. 1 Unwmk. Typo. *Perf. 9*

1 A1 2p dull rose 1,100. 325.
a. 2p deep rose 1,350. 350.
b. Rouletted *22,500.*
c. Horiz. pair, imperf. between *6,500.*
d. Diagonal half used as 1p on cover *1,900.*
2 A2 3p blue 2,250. 750.
a. Diagonal half used as 1½p on cover *2,250.*
b. Double impression 4,500.

No. 2b is valued with very small faults.

3 A3 6p yellow green 2,750. 1,200.

A4

A5

White or Yellowish Paper

1862-65 *Perf. 11½-12*

4 A4 1p yellow orange 37.50 35.00
a. 1p brown orange, perf. 11 45.00 35.00
b. Imperf., pair 200.00
c. Half used as ½p on cover *2,000.*
5 A1 2p rose 8.50 7.50
a. Yellowish paper 14.00 7.50
b. Imperf., pair 100.00
c. Horiz. pair, imperf. vert. 275.00
d. Vert. pair, imperf. horiz. 375.00
e. Diagonal half used as 1p on cover *1,900.*
f. "TWC" for "TWO" 75.00 30.00
6 A2 3p blue 16.00 *15.00*
a. Yellowish paper 32.50 15.00
b. Imperf., pair 150.00
c. Vert. pair, imperf. horiz. 400.00
d. Horiz. pair, imperf. vert. 400.00
e. Diagonal half used as 1½p on cover 250.00
g. Imperf. pair with gutter btwn. 950.00
h. Imperf. tete-beche pair with gutter btwn. *1,250.*
7 A3 6p yellow green 125.00 95.00
a. 6p blue green 125.00 95.00
c. Diagonal half used as 3p on cover *3,000.*
8 A5 9p violet 95.00 80.00
a. Imperf., pair 400.00
b. Horiz. pair, imperf. vert. 450.00
c. Diagonal half used as 4½p on cover *2,250.*
Nos. 4-8 (5) 282.00 232.50
Set, never hinged 457.50

Some specialists question the existence of No. 7b. The editors would like to see authenticated evidence of the existence of this item.

Queen Victoria
A6 A7

1868

9 A6 4p black 9.50 19.00
a. Yellowish paper 15.00 22.50
b. Horiz. pair, imperf. vert. 190.00
c. Diagonal half used as 2p on cover *2,250.*
d. Imperf., pair 140.00
e. Horiz. pair, imperf. between 160.00
g. Horiz. strip of 3, imperf. btwn. *1,100.*

1870, June 1 Engr. *Perf. 12*

10 A7 4½p brown 100.00 75.00

A8

A9

A10

A11

A12

A13

1872, Jan. 1 Typo. *Perf. 12, 12½*

11 A8 1c brown orange 7.00 *7.50*
a. Imperf., pair 240.00
12 A9 2c ultra 27.50 *42.50*
a. Imperf., pair 450.00
b. Diagonal half used as 1c on cover —
13 A10 3c rose 27.50 22.50
a. Imperf., pair 425.00
b. Diagonal half used as 1½c on cover —
c. Horiz. or vert. pair, imperf. between 275.00
14 A11 4c green 11.50 *16.00*
a. Imperf., pair 425.00
b. Diagonal half used as 2c on cover 2,000.
15 A12 6c black 8.00 *13.00*
a. Horiz. pair, imperf. btwn. 250.00
b. Half used as 3c on cover *900.00*
16 A13 12c violet 7.75 *30.00*
a. Imperf., pair 425.00
b. Half used as 6c on cover —
Nos. 11-16 (6) 89.25 *131.50*
Set, never hinged 134.00

CANADA

ˈka-nə-də

LOCATION — Northern part of North American continent, except for Alaska
GOVT. — Self-governing dominion in the British Commonwealth of Nations
AREA — 3,851,809 sq. mi.
POP. — 28,846,761 (1996)
CAPITAL — Ottawa

Included in the dominion are British Columbia, Vancouver Island, Prince Edward Island, Nova Scotia, New Brunswick and Newfoundland, all of which formerly issued stamps.

12 Pence = 1 Shilling
100 Cents = 1 Dollar (1859)

Catalogue values for unused stamps in this country are for Never Hinged items, beginning with Scott 268 in the regular postage section, Scott B1 in the semi-postal section, Scott C9 in the air post section, Scott CE3 in the air post special delivery section, Scott CO1 in the air post official section, Scott E11 in the special delivery section, Scott EO1 in the special delivery official section, Scott J15 in the postage due section, and Scott O1 in the official section.

Values for unused stamps of Nos. 1-33 are for examples with partial original gum. Stamps without gum often trade at prices very close to those of stamps with partial gum. Examples with full original gum and lightly hinged are extremely scarce and generally sell for substantially more than the values listed.

Very fine examples of the perforated issues between Nos. 11-20 will have perforations touching the design or frameline on at least one side due to the narrow spacing of the stamps on the plates. Stamps with perfs clear of the designs on all four sides are extremely scarce and will command much higher prices.

Province of Canada

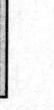

Beaver — A1

Prince Albert — A2

Queen Victoria — A3

1851 Unwmk. Engr. *Imperf.*

Laid Paper

1 A1 3p red *40,000.* 1,000.
2 A2 6p slate violet *40,000.* 1,650.
a. Diagonal half used as 3p on cover *32,500.*
3 A3 12p black *175,000. 135,000.*

On some stamps the laid lines of Nos. 1-3 are practically invisible.

1852-57 Wove Paper

4 A1 3p red 1,500. 225.
a. 3p brown red ('53) 1,700. 250.
b. Diagonal half used as 1½p on cover *32,500.*
c. Ribbed paper 4,500. 575.
d. Thin paper 1,600. 225.
5 A2 6p slate gray ('55) 30,000. 1,200.
a. 6p brownish gray 40,000. 1,750.
b. 6p greenish gray 30,000. 1,200.

c.	Diagonal half used as 3p on cover			*17,500.*
d.	Thick hard paper (gray vio) ('57)		30,000.	3,000.

Re-entries of the 3p are numerous. The main re-entry is distinguishable most easily by the line through "EE" and "PEN".

Most authorities believe the 12p black does not exist on wove paper.

Jacques Cartier — A4

1855

7	A4	10p blue	12,000.	1,750.
a.		Thick paper	13,000.	2,250.

Queen Victoria
A5 A6

1857

8	A5	½p rose	1,100.	700.
a.		Horizontally ribbed paper	10,000.	2,500.
b.		Vertically ribbed paper	10,000.	3,750.
9	A6	7½p green	10,000.	3,500.

Very Thick Soft Wove Paper

10	A2	6p reddish pur	32,500.	7,500.
a.		Half used as 3p on cover		*25,000.*

1858-59 Wove Paper *Perf. 12*

11	A5	½p rose	3,500.	1,900.
12	A1	3p red	17,500.	1,350.
13	A2	6p brown vio ('59)	22,500.	7,500.
a.		6p gray violet	22,500.	7,500.
b.		Diagonal half used as 3p on cover		*17,500.*

Nos. 11-13 values are for examples with perfs touching the design.

A7

A8

A9

A10

A11

A12

1859

14	A7	1c rose	425.00	90.00
a.		Imperf., pair	5,500.	
b.		1c deep rose	575.00	140.00
15	A8	5c ver	575.00	37.50
		On cover		47.50
a.		Imperf., pair	15,000.	—
b.		Diagonal half used as 2½c on cover		*6,000.*
c.		5c brick red	625.00	42.50
16	A9	10c black brn, perf. 11¾	20,000.	6,500.
a.		Half used as 5c on cover		*9,000.*
17	A9	10c red lilac	1,500.	150.00
a.		10c violet	2,000.	160.00
b.		10c brown	1,500.	140.00
c.		Imperf., pair	11,000.	
d.		Diagonal half used as 5c on cover		*5,500.*
e.		10c deep red purple	3,250.	1,100.
18	A10	12½c yel green	900.00	130.00
a.		12½c blue green	1,100.	125.00
b.		Imperf., pair	5,750.	
19	A11	17c blue	1,250.	200.00
a.		17c slate blue	1,300.	225.00
b.		Imperf., pair	5,250.	

Values for Nos. 14-19 are for examples with perfs touching the design.

No. 15b was used with a 10c for a 12½c rate.

No. 16 should be accompanied by a certificate of authenticity issued by a recognized expertizing authority. Less expensive dark brown shades of the 10c often are offered as the rare black brown.

Imperfs. are without gum.

Re-entries of the 5c are numerous. Many of them are slight and have only small premium value. The major re-entry has many lines of the design double, especially the outlines of the ovals and frame at left. Value, used, about $800.

1864

20	A12	2c rose	800.00	300.00
a.		2c deep claret rose	850.00	350.00
b.		Imperf., pair	3,500.	

Imperfs. are without gum.

Values are for examples with perfs touching the design.

Dominion of Canada

Queen Victoria
A13 A14

A15

A16

A17

A18

A19

A20

1868-76 *Perf. 12, 11½x12 (5c)*

21	A13	½c black	110.00	80.00
a.		Perf. 11½x12 ('73)	150.00	90.00
b.		Watermarked	*22,500.*	*11,000.*
c.		Thin paper	150.00	80.00
22	A14	1c brn red	800.00	160.00
a.		Watermarked	*3,250.*	500.00
b.		Thin paper	950.00	140.00
23	A14	1c yell org	1,750.	225.00
a.		1c deep orange	2,500.	260.00
24	A15	2c green	900.00	100.00
a.		Watermarked	3,250.	425.00
b.		Thin paper	950.00	110.00
c.		Diagonal half used as 1c on cover		*4,000.*
25	A16	3c red	2,250.	40.00
a.		Watermarked	5,250.	475.00
b.		Thin paper	2,500.	55.00
26	A17	5c ol grn ('75)	2,000.	225.00
a.		Perf. 12	*8,000.*	1,000.
b.		Imperf., pair	*32,500.*	
27	A18	6c dk brn	2,250.	140.00
a.		6c yellow brown	2,000.	125.00
b.		Watermarked	*24,000.*	*2,500.*
c.		Thin paper	2,100.	160.00
d.		Diagonal half used as 3c on cover		*3,000.*
e.		Vert. half used as 3c on cover		—
f.		6c black brown, thin paper (Mar. '68, 1st printing)	3,250.	250.00
28	A19	12½c blue	1,250.	125.00
a.		Watermarked	*7,000.*	425.00
b.		Thin paper	1,200.	150.00
c.		Horiz. pair, imperf. vert.		—
d.		Vert. pair, imperf. horiz.		*16,000.*
29	A20	15c gray vio	100.00	65.00
a.		Perf. 11½x12 ('74)	1,750.	425.00
b.		15c red lilac	1,000.	125.00
c.		Watermarked	*12,500.*	1,250.
d.		Imperf., pair	1,200.	
e.		Thin paper	800.00	150.00
30	A20	15c gray	110.00	65.00
a.		Perf. 11½x12 ('73)	1,050.	400.00
b.		15c blue gray ('75)	135.00	75.00
c.		Very thick paper (dp vio)	*5,250.*	1,600.
d.		Script wmk., Perf. 11½x12, ('76)	*25,000.*	*9,000.*
e.		15c deep blue	1,850.	425.00

The watermark on Nos. 21b, 22a, 24a, 25a, 27b, 28a and 29c consists of double-lined letters reading: "E. & G. BOTHWELL CLUTHA MILLS." The script watermark on No. 30d reads in full: "Alexr. Pirie & Sons." Values for all these watermarked stamps are for fine examples. Very fine examples are rare, seldom traded, and generally command premiums of about 100% over the values listed.

No. 21b unused and used, and No. 26a unused are valued in the grade of fine. No. 26b is a unique pair.

The existence of No. 28c has been questioned.

1868 *Laid Paper*

31	A14	1c brown red	*40,000.*	*9,000.*
32	A15	2c green		*250,000.*
33	A16	3c bright red	*25,000.*	2,250.

Only three examples of No. 32 are recorded, none being very fine.

Montreal and Ottawa Printings

A21

A22

A23

A24

A25

A26

A27

1870-89 Wove Paper *Perf. 12*

34	A21	½c black ('82)	22.50	10.00
a.		Imperf., pair	650.00	
b.		Horiz. pair, imperf. between	1,000.	
35	A22	1c yellow	50.00	1.25
a.		1c orange ('70)	300.00	11.00
b.		Imperf., pair	475.00	
c.		Diagonal half used as ½c on circular		4,500.
36	A23	2c green ('72)	85.00	2.50
a.		Imperf., pair	725.00	
b.		Diagonal half used as 1c on cover		2,100.
c.		Vertical half used as 1c on cover		2,100.
d.		2c blue green ('89)	110.00	5.00
f.		Double impression	*6,000.*	—
37	A24	3c org red ('73)	175.00	1.50
a.		3c rose ('71)	625.00	17.50
b.		3c copper red ('70)	1,750.	65.00
c.		3c dull red ('72)	175.00	3.25

38 A25 5c sl green ('76) 1,000. 27.50
39 A26 6c yel brn ('72) 800.00 27.50
a. Diagonal half used as 3c on cover 4,500.
c. Imperf., pair 3,500.
40 A27 10c dull rose lil ('77) 1,600. 90.00
a. 10c magenta ('80) 1,600. 90.00
b. 10c deep lilac rose 1,600. 90.00

No. 34a was made with and without gum; values the same.

Examples of Nos. 36b and 36c postmarked "Halifax" are a private speculation.

No. 39c is unique and in the form of a strip of three.

1870 ***Perf. 12½***

37d A24 3c copper red (Ottawa) 11,000. 1,500.

1873-79 ***Perf. 11½x12***

35d A22 1c orange 500.00 20.00
36e A23 2c green 750.00 25.00
37e A24 3c red 450.00 12.50
38a A25 5c slate green 1,250. 52.50
39b A26 6c yellow brown 1,000. 65.00
40c A27 10c dull rose lilac 1,700. 260.00

The gum on Nos. 35d-40c is always dull and usually blotchy or streaky. It is distinct from the earlier clear, smooth gum and from the bright shiny gums of the later periods.

Nos. 38 and 40 were printed at Montreal. Printings of Nos. 34 to 37, and 39 were made at Ottawa or Montreal and can be separated only by differences in paper and gum.

Ottawa Printing

A28

A29

1888-97 ***Perf. 12***

41 A24 3c brt vermilion 65.00 .80
a. 3c rose carmine 525.00 15.00
42 A25 5c gray 230.00 5.25
43 A26 6c red brown 240.00 12.50
a. 6c chocolate ('90) 400.00 32.50
44 A28 8c viol blk ('93) 260.00 6.50
a. 8c blue gray 425.00 8.50
b. 8c slate 300.00 6.50
c. 8c gray 300.00 6.50
45 A27 10c brn red ('97) 725.00 65.00
a. 10c dull rose 625.00 55.00
b. 10c pink 725.00 65.00
46 A29 20c ver ('93) 425.00 125.00
47 A29 50c dp blue ('93) 425.00 85.00

Stamps of the 1870-93 issues are found on paper varying from very thin to thick, also occasionally on paper showing a distinctly ribbed surface.

The gum on Nos. 41-47 appears bright and shiny, often with a yellowish tint.

Imperf., Pairs

41b A24 3c 500.
42a A25 5c 750.
43b A26 6c 625.
44d A28 8c 850.
45c A27 10c 625.
46a A29 20c 1,500.
47a A29 50c 1,500.

Nos. 41b-45c made with and without gum. Without gum sell for the same as the unused hinged price.

Imperforates and Part-Perforates

From 1859 through 1943 (Nos. 14a/262a), imperforate stamps were printed. The earliest imperforates through perhaps 1917 most likely were from imprimatur sheets (i.e. the first sheets from the approved plates, normally kept in government files) or proof sheets on stamp paper that once were in the post office archives. The imperforates from approximately 1927 to 1943 (often made both with and without gum) were specially created and traded for classic stamps needed for the post office museum, given as gifts to governmental or other dignitaries, or sold or given to favored persons.

The only imperforates from this entire period that were issued to the public were Nos. 90A and 136-138.

Similarly, almost all stamps that are known part-perforate (i.e., horizontal pairs imperforate vertically and vertical pairs imperforate horizontally) were specially made for trading purposes or as presentation items to be given to favored persons. These part-perforates are not listed here, but they are listed in *Scott Classic Specialized Catalogue of Stamps & Covers.* Part-perforate error stamps that are believed to have been actually issued to the public are listed in this catalogue.

See the similar imperforates in the air post, Nos. CE1a and CE2a, special delivery, No. F2c (but not No. F1c which was an issued error), postage dues, and Nos. MR4b and MR4c.

Jubilee Issue

Queen Victoria, "1837" and "1897" — A30

1897, June 19 **Unwmk.** ***Perf. 12***

50 A30 ½c black 110.00 110.00
Never hinged 275.00
51 A30 1c orange 30.00 8.00
Never hinged 75.00
52 A30 2c green 37.50 15.00
Never hinged 92.50
53 A30 3c bright rose 30.00 2.50
Never hinged 75.00
54 A30 5c deep blue 70.00 45.00
Never hinged 180.00
55 A30 6c yell brn 230.00 175.00
Never hinged 575.00
56 A30 8c dark violet 130.00 65.00
Never hinged 325.00
57 A30 10c brown violet 160.00 120.00
Never hinged 400.00
58 A30 15c steel blue 275.00 190.00
Never hinged 675.00
59 A30 20c vermilion 275.00 190.00
Never hinged 650.00
60 A30 50c ultra 375.00 190.00
Never hinged 775.00
61 A30 $1 lake 1,000. 700.00
Never hinged 2,900.
62 A30 $2 dk purple 1,400. 600.00
Never hinged 4,000.
63 A30 $3 yel bister 1,400. 1,100.
Never hinged 4,000.
64 A30 $4 purple 1,400. 1,100.
Never hinged 4,000.
65 A30 $5 olive green 1,500. 1,100.
Never hinged 4,250.
Nos. 50-60 (11) 1,722. 1,110.
Set, never hinged 4,097.

60th year of Queen Victoria's reign.

Roller and smudged cancels on Nos. 61-65 sell for less.

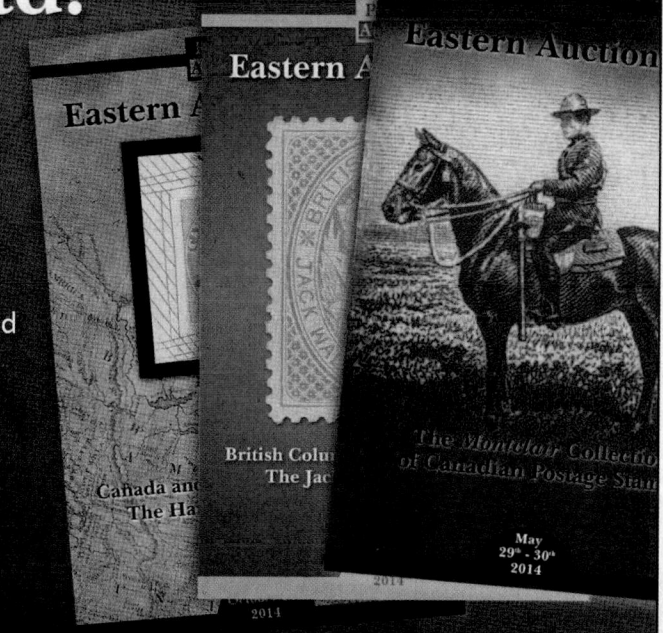

A31

1897-98

66	A31	½c black	15.00	8.50
		Never hinged	37.50	
67	A31	1c blue green	45.00	2.00
		Never hinged	115.00	
68	A31	2c purple	50.00	2.25
		Never hinged	125.00	
69	A31	3c carmine ('98)	80.00	2.00
		Never hinged	200.00	
70	A31	5c dk bl, *bluish*	150.00	10.00
		Never hinged	375.00	
71	A31	6c brown	140.00	45.00
		Never hinged	350.00	
72	A31	8c orange	325.00	21.00
		Never hinged	800.00	
73	A31	10c brn vio ('98)	600.00	100.00
		Never hinged	1,500.	
		Nos. 66-73 (8)	1,405.	190.75
		Set, never hinged	3,503.	

For surcharge see No. 87.

Imperf., Pairs

66a	A31	½c	500.
		Never hinged	950.
67a	A31	1c	400.
		Never hinged	750.
68a	A31	2c	500.
		Never hinged	950.
69a	A31	3c	800.
		Never hinged	1,450.
70a	A31	5c	500.
		Never hinged	750.
71a	A31	6c	800.
		Never hinged	1,450.
72a	A31	8c	600.
		Never hinged	1,100.
73a	A31	10c	600.
		Never hinged	1,100.

Nos. 66a, 67a, 68a and 70a made with and without gum. Specialists can distinguish printings made with and without gum by shade and paper quality. Without gum sell for about 95% of the unused hinged price.

A32

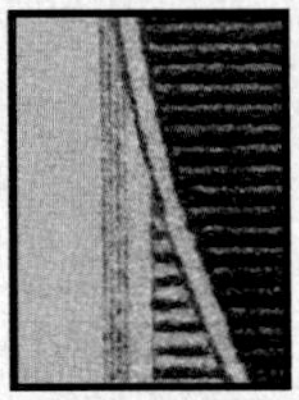

Type I

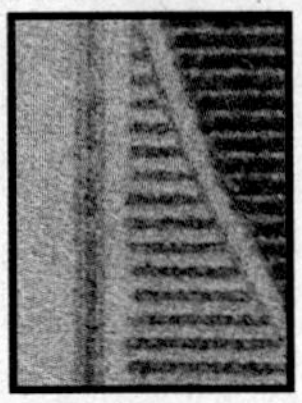

Type II

TWO CENTS:
Type I — Frame of four very thin lines.
Type II — Frame of a thick line between two thin ones.

1898-1902

74	A32	½c black	12.50	2.75
		Never hinged	25.00	
75	A32	1c gray green	40.00	.75
		Never hinged	80.00	
76	A32	2c purple (I)	40.00	.75
		Never hinged	80.00	
a.		Thick paper ('99)	175.00	12.00
		Never hinged	350.00	
77	A32	2c car (I) ('99)	55.00	.75
		Never hinged	110.00	
a.		2c carmine (II) ('99)	70.00	.60
		Never hinged	140.00	
b.		Booklet pane of 6 (II) ('00)	1,600.	—
		Never hinged	3,000.	
78	A32	3c carmine	90.00	1.10
		Never hinged	180.00	
79	A32	5c blue, *bluish* ('99)	220.00	3.00
		Never hinged	440.00	
80	A32	6c brown	200.00	57.50
		Never hinged	400.00	
81	A32	7c ol yel ('02)	150.00	22.50
		Never hinged	300.00	
82	A32	8c orange	375.00	27.50
		Never hinged	750.00	
83	A32	10c brown vio	425.00	30.00
		Never hinged	850.00	
84	A32	20c ol grn ('00)	650.00	110.00
		Never hinged	1,300.	
		Nos. 74-84 (11)	2,257.	256.60
		Set, never hinged	4,515.	

For surcharges see Nos. 88-88C.

Imperf., Pairs

74a	A32	½c	475.
		Never hinged	775.
75a	A32	1c	1,250.
		Never hinged	2,250.
77c	A32	2c (I)	475.
		Never hinged	775.
77d	A32	2c (II)	*1,250.*
e.		As No. 77b, imperf., 2 panes tete beche ('00)	*15,000.*
79a	A32	5c	1,200.
		Never hinged	1,900.
80a	A32	6c	1,200.
		Never hinged	1,900.
81a	A32	7c	600.
82a	A32	8c	1,200.
		Never hinged	1,900.
83a	A32	10c	1,200.
		Never hinged	1,900.
84a	A32	20c	5,500.

Nos. 77d, 77e, 81a and 84a were made only without gum. No. 80a was made only with gum. Others either with or without gum and of these those without gum sell for about ⅔ of the values shown for unused hinged. Specialists can distinguish printings made with and without gum by shade and paper quality.

Imperial Penny Postage Issue

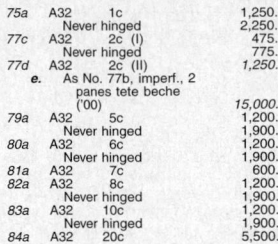

Map of British Empire on Mercator Projection A33

No. 86

1898, Dec. 7 **Engr. & Typo.**

85	A33	2c black, lav & car	45.00	9.00
		Never hinged	100.00	
a.		Imperf., pair	550.00	
86	A33	2c black, bl & car	45.00	9.00
		Never hinged	100.00	
a.		Imperf., pair	550.00	

Imperfs. are without gum.

Nos. 69 and 78 Surcharged in

1899, July

87	A31	2c on 3c carmine	17.50	7.50
		Never hinged	45.00	
88	A32	2c on 3c carmine	32.50	6.00
		Never hinged	82.50	

No. 78 Surcharged in Blue or Violet

A32a A32b

1899, Jan. 5

88B	A32a	1(c) on ⅓ of 3c, on cover (Bl)		*7,750.*
88C	A32b	2(c) on ⅔ of 3c, on cover (V)		*7,250.*

Nos. 88B-88C were prepared and used at Port Hood, Nova Scotia, without official authorization.

Nos. 88B-88C must be accompanied by certificates from recognized expertizing organizations.

King Edward VII — A34

Type I

Type II

1903-08 **Engr.**

89	A34	1c green	45.00	.40
		Never hinged	115.00	
90	A34	2c carmine, type II	55.00	.40
		Never hinged	135.00	
b.		Booklet pane of 6	1,600.	*1,250.*
		Never hinged	*2,750.*	
e.		2c carmine, type I	160.00	2.00
		Never hinged	400.00	
f.		Vert. pair, imperf. btwn and at either top or bottom	*5,000.*	
91	A34	5c blue, *blue*	250.00	5.75
		Never hinged	625.00	
92	A34	7c olive bister	260.00	6.25
		Never hinged	650.00	
93	A34	10c brown lilac	425.00	15.00
		Never hinged	1,050.	
94	A34	20c ol grn ('04)	800.00	50.00
		Never hinged	2,000.	
95	A34	50c purple ('08)	950.00	175.00
		Never hinged	2,350.	
		Nos. 89-95 (7)	2,785.	252.80
		Set, never hinged	6,925.	

Values for Nos. 94 and 95 used are for examples with contemporaneous circular datestamps. Stamps with heavy cancellations or parcel cancellations sell for much less.

Issued: 1c-10c, 7/1/03; 20c, 9/27/04; 50c, 11/19/08.

Imperf., Type II

90A	A34	2c carmine	50.00	50.00
		Never hinged	100.00	

No. 90A is the only imperforate Canada stamp besides Nos. 136-138 regularly issued to the public. 100,000 were issued.

Imperf., Pairs, Without Gum

89a	A34	1c	725.00
90c	A34	2c Type I	850.00
d.		As No. 90c, imperf, 2 panes tete beche	*17,500.*
91a	A34	5c	1,200.
92a	A34	7c	800.
93a	A34	10c	1,200.

Quebec Tercentenary Issue

Prince and Princess of Wales, 1908 — A35

Jacques Cartier and Samuel de Champlain A36

Queen Alexandra and King Edward A37

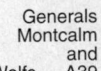

Champlain's Home in Quebec A38

Generals Montcalm and Wolfe — A39

View of Quebec in 1700 — A40

Champlain's Departure for the West — A41

Arrival of Cartier at Quebec A42

1908, July 16 ***Perf. 12***

96	A35	½c black brown	8.00	5.00
		Never hinged	19.00	
97	A36	1c blue green	30.00	6.00
		Never hinged	75.00	
98	A37	2c carmine	40.00	3.00
		Never hinged	100.00	
99	A38	5c dark blue	85.00	70.00
		Never hinged	210.00	
100	A39	7c olive green	160.00	100.00
		Never hinged	400.00	
101	A40	10c dark violet	200.00	125.00
		Never hinged	500.00	
102	A41	15c red orange	225.00	160.00
		Never hinged	550.00	
103	A42	20c yellow brown	250.00	225.00
		Never hinged	625.00	
		Nos. 96-103 (8)	998.00	694.00
		Set, never hinged	2,479.	

Imperf., Pairs

96a	A35	½c	750.
		Never hinged	1,300.
97a	A36	1c	750.
		Never hinged	1,300.
98a	A37	2c	750.
		Never hinged	1,300.
99a	A38	5c	750.
		Never hinged	1,300.
100a	A39	7c	750.
		Never hinged	1,300.
101a	A40	10c	750.
		Never hinged	1,300.
102a	A41	15c	750.
		Never hinged	1,300.
103a	A42	20c	750.
		Never hinged	1,300.

100 pairs of imperfs made, 50 with gum and 50 without. Due to demand, pairs without gum generally sell for 90-95% of the unused hinged price.

King George V — A43

Type I

Type II

Two types of 1c.
Type I — The "N" of "ONE" is separated from the oval above it.
Type II — The "N" of "ONE" almost touches the oval above it.

Type I

Type II

Two types of 3c carmine.
Type I — The "R" of "THREE" is separated from the oval above it. The bottom line of the vignette does not touch the heavy diagonal stroke at right.
Type II — The "R" of "THREE" almost touches the oval above it. The bottom horizontal line of the vignette touches the heavy diagonal stroke at right.

Note that the values for Nos. 104-122 are for sheet stamps with perforations on four sides. Single stamps from booklet panes Nos. 104a, 105a, 105b, 106a, 106d, 107b, 107c, 108a and 109a all have natural straight edges on one or two sides, and (except for No. 107d singles) they are worth much less than the listed sheet stamps.

1911-25

104	A43 1c green	25.00	.25
	Never hinged	60.00	
a.	Booklet pane of 6	35.00	*35.00*
	Never hinged	70.00	
105	A43 1c org yell (I) ('22)	25.00	.25
	Never hinged	60.00	
a.	Booklet pane of 4 + 2 labels	55.00	*55.00*
	Never hinged	110.00	
b.	Booklet pane of 6	62.50	*62.50*
	Never hinged	125.00	
d.	1c org yellow (II)	20.00	.25
	Never hinged	50.00	
106	A43 2c carmine	25.00	.25
	Never hinged	60.00	
a.	Booklet pane of 6	40.00	40.00
	Never hinged	80.00	
b.	2c pink	150.00	18.00
	Never hinged	350.00	
c.	2c rose carmine	25.00	.25
	Never hinged	60.00	
d.	As "c," booklet pane of 6	160.00	160.00
	Never hinged	320.00	
107	A43 2c yel grn ('22)	27.50	.25
	Never hinged	65.00	
a.	Thin paper ('24)	20.00	2.50
	Never hinged	50.00	
b.	Booklet pane of 4 + 2 labels ('22)	70.00	*80.00*
	Never hinged	140.00	
c.	Booklet pane of 6 ('22)	350.00	*325.00*
	Never hinged	625.00	
108	A43 3c brown ('18)	25.00	.40
	Never hinged	60.00	
a.	Booklet pane of 4 + 2 labels	90.00	*95.00*
	Never hinged	180.00	
109	A43 3c car (I) ('23)	17.50	.25
	Never hinged	42.50	
a.	Booklet pane of 4 + 2 labels	70.00	*75.00*
	Never hinged	140.00	
c.	Die II ('24)	50.00	.25
	Never hinged	125.00	
110	A43 4c ol bis ('22)	47.50	4.50
	Never hinged	120.00	
111	A43 5c dark blue ('12)	175.00	1.75
	Never hinged	450.00	
112	A43 5c violet ('22)	40.00	1.00
	Never hinged	100.00	
a.	Thin paper ('24)	35.00	7.50
	Never hinged	87.50	
113	A43 7c yel ocher ('12)	75.00	3.50
	Never hinged	180.00	
114	A43 7c red brn ('24)	22.50	10.00
	Never hinged	55.00	
115	A43 8c blue ('25)	37.50	10.00
	Never hinged	92.50	
116	A43 10c plum ('12)	275.00	4.00
	Never hinged	675.00	
117	A43 10c blue ('22)	47.50	2.00
	Never hinged	115.00	
118	A43 10c bis brn ('25)	40.00	2.00
	Never hinged	95.00	
119	A43 20c ol grn ('25)	100.00	1.75
	Never hinged	250.00	
120	A43 50c blk brn ('25)	80.00	3.75
	Never hinged	200.00	
a.	50c black ('12)	300.00	12.00
	Never hinged	725.00	
122	A43 $1 orange ('23)	95.00	10.00
	Never hinged	240.00	
	Nos. 104-122 (18)	1,180.	55.90
	Set, never hinged	2,920.	

For type A43 perforated 12x8 see No. 184.
For surcharges see Nos. 139-140.
Issued: Nos. 104, 106, 12/22/11; No. 105, 6/7/22; No. 108, 8/6/18; No. 109, 12/18/23; 4c, 7/7/22; No. 111, 1/17/12; No. 112, 2/2/22; Nos. 113, 116, 1/12/12; No. 114, 12/12/24; 8c, 9/1/25; No. 117, 2/20/22; No. 118, 8/1/25; 20c, 1/23/12; 50c, 1/26/12; $1, 7/22/23.

Imperf., Panes

105c	As No. 105b, imperf, 2 panes tete beche	*15,000.*
107d	As No. 107c, imperf, 2 panes tete beche	*15,000.*
109b	As No. 109a, imperf, 2 panes tete beche	*15,000.*

Imperf., Pairs

110a	A43 4c	2,250.
	Never hinged	4,000.
112b	A43 5c	2,250.
	Never hinged	4,000.
114a	A43 7c	2,250.
	Never hinged	4,000.
115a	A43 8c	2,250.
	Never hinged	4,000.
118a	A43 10c	2,250.
	Never hinged	4,000.
119a	A43 20c	2,250.
	Never hinged	4,000.
120b	A43 50c	3,000.
	Never hinged	6,000.
122a	A43 $1	2,250.
	Never hinged	4,000.

Nos. 105c and 109b made without gum, others with gum. About half of the No. 120b pairs have creases; value thus $500.

Coll Stamps

1913 ***Perf. 8 Horizontally***

123	A43 1c dark green	110.00	65.00
	Never hinged	275.00	
124	A43 2c carmine	120.00	65.00
	Never hinged	300.00	

1912-24 ***Perf. 8 Vertically***

125	A43 1c green	25.00	2.00
	Never hinged	50.00	
126	A43 1c org yell (II) ('23)	12.00	7.50
	Never hinged	24.00	
a.	As #126, block of 4 (II)	65.00	50.00
	Never hinged	100.00	
b.	1c org yellow (I)	30.00	11.00
	Never hinged	60.00	
c.	As "b," block of 4 (I)	700.00	
	Never hinged	1,200.	
127	A43 2c carmine	40.00	2.00
	Never hinged	80.00	
128	A43 2c green ('22)	25.00	1.10
	Never hinged	50.00	
a.	Block of 4	65.00	60.00
	Never hinged	100.00	
129	A43 3c brown ('18)	30.00	1.30
	Never hinged	60.00	
130	A43 3c carmine (I) ('24)	75.00	9.00
	Never hinged	150.00	
a.	Block of 4 (I)	1,050.	750.00
	Never hinged	1,650.	
b.	Die II	100.00	10.00
	Never hinged	200.00	
	Nos. 125-130 (6)	207.00	22.90
	Set, never hinged	386.50	

Nos. 126a and 128a were issued to the public. Nos. 126c and 130a were issued "by favor" as were the various other imperf and part-perfs of this era.
Beware of fakes of No. 130a made from No. 138.

1915-24 ***Perf. 12 Horizontally***

131	A43 1c dark green	7.50	6.50
	Never hinged	15.00	
132	A43 2c carmine	40.00	10.00
	Never hinged	80.00	
133	A43 2c yell grn ('24)	85.00	75.00
	Never hinged	170.00	
134	A43 3c brown ('21)	12.50	6.50
	Never hinged	25.00	
	Nos. 131-134 (4)	145.00	98.00
	Set, never hinged	290.00	

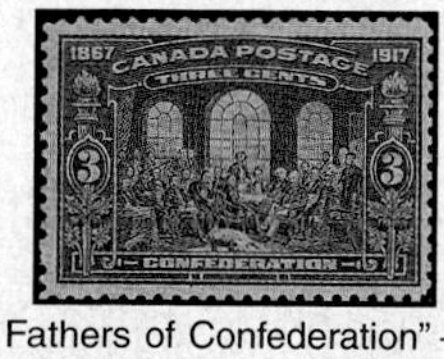
"The Fathers of Confederation" — A44

1917, Sept. 15 ***Perf. 12***

135	A44 3c brown	47.50	2.25
	Never hinged	120.00	
a.	Imperf., pair	600.00	

50th anniv. of the Canadian Confederation.
Imperfs. are without gum.

1924 ***Imperf.***

136	A43 1c orange yellow (I)	35.00	35.00
	Never hinged	65.00	
	Pair	87.50	87.50
	Never hinged	160.00	
137	A43 2c green	35.00	35.00
	Never hinged	65.00	
	Pair	87.50	87.50
	Never hinged	160.00	
138	A43 3c carmine (I)	17.50	17.50
	Never hinged	32.50	
	Pair	42.50	42.50
	Never hinged	77.50	
	Nos. 136-138 (3)	87.50	87.50
	Set, never hinged	162.50	

No. 109 Surcharged

a

b

1926 ***Perf. 12***

139	A43(a) 2c on 3c carmine (I)	55.00	55.00
	Never hinged	90.00	
a.	Pair, one without surcharge	725.00	
	Never hinged	1,150.	
b.	Double surcharge	275.00	
	Never hinged	425.00	
c.	Die II	850.00	
	Never hinged	1,500.	
140	A43(b) 2c on 3c carmine	27.50	30.00
	Never hinged	47.50	
a.	Double surcharge	250.00	*225.00*
	Never hinged	390.00	
b.	Triple surcharge	250.00	*250.00*
	Never hinged	390.00	
c.	Double surch., one invtd.	400.00	
	Never hinged	600.00	

Sir John A. Macdonald A45

Sir Wilfrid Laurier A48

"The Fathers of Confederation" — A46

Parliament Building at Ottawa A47

Map of Canada A49

1927, June 29

141	A45 1c orange	3.00	1.30
	Never hinged	5.50	
142	A46 2c green	2.00	.25
	Never hinged	3.75	
143	A47 3c brown carmine	8.75	6.50
	Never hinged	16.00	
144	A48 5c violet	4.25	3.50
	Never hinged	8.00	
145	A49 12c dark blue	25.00	6.50
	Never hinged	45.00	
	Nos. 141-145 (5)	43.00	18.05
	Set, never hinged	78.25	

60th year of the Canadian Confederation.
Nos. 141-145 exist partly perforated.

Imperf., Pairs

141a	A45 1c	125.00
	Never hinged	180.00
142a	A46 2c	125.00
	Never hinged	180.00
143a	A47 3c	125.00
	Never hinged	180.00
144a	A48 5c	125.00
	Never hinged	180.00
145a	A49 12c	125.00
	Never hinged	180.00

Thomas d'Arcy McGee — A50

Laurier and Macdonald A51

Robert Baldwin and Sir Louis Hypolyte Lafontaine A52

1927, June 29

146	A50	5c violet	4.00	3.00
		Never hinged	7.25	
147	A51	12c green	10.00	5.50
		Never hinged	18.00	
148	A52	20c brown carmine	27.50	6.50
		Never hinged	50.00	
		Nos. 146-148 (3)	41.50	15.00
		Set, never hinged	75.25	

Nos. 146-148 were to have been issued in July, 1926, as a commemorative series, but were withheld and issued June 29, 1927.

Imperf., Pairs

146a	A50	5c	125.00
		Never hinged	180.00
147a	A51	12c	125.00
		Never hinged	180.00
148a	A52	20c	125.00
		Never hinged	180.00

King George V — A53

Mt. Hurd from Bell-Smith's Painting "The Ice-crowned Monarch of the Rockies" A54

Quebec Bridge A55

Harvesting Wheat A56

Schooner "Bluenose" A57

Parliament Building A58

1928-29

149	A53	1c orange	3.50	.40
		Never hinged	6.50	
a.		Booklet pane of 6	27.50	25.00
		Never hinged	40.00	
150	A53	2c green	1.90	.25
		Never hinged	3.50	
a.		Booklet pane of 6	27.50	25.00
		Never hinged	40.00	
151	A53	3c dk carmine	27.50	12.50
		Never hinged	50.00	
152	A53	4c bister ('29)	25.00	6.00
		Never hinged	45.00	
153	A53	5c dp violet	16.00	3.00
		Never hinged	30.00	
a.		Booklet pane of 6	200.00	140.00
		Never hinged	280.00	
154	A53	8c blue	18.00	9.00
		Never hinged	32.50	
155	A54	10c green	22.50	2.50
		Never hinged	42.50	
156	A55	12c gray ('29)	45.00	9.00
		Never hinged	85.00	
157	A56	20c dk car ('29)	65.00	12.00
		Never hinged	120.00	
158	A57	50c dk blue ('29)	225.00	65.00
		Never hinged	450.00	
159	A58	$1 ol grn ('29)	300.00	80.00
		Never hinged	600.00	
		Nos. 149-159 (11)	749.40	199.65
		Set, never hinged	1,465.	

Imperf., Panes

149c	As No. 149a, imperf, 2 panes tete beche	1,000.
	Never hinged	1,450.
150c	As No. 150a, imperf, 2 panes tete beche	1,000.
	Never hinged	1,450.
153c	As No. 153a, imperf, 2 panes tete beche	1,000.
	Never hinged	1,450.

Imperf., Pairs

149b	A53	1c	100.00
		Never hinged	140.00
150b	A53	2c	100.00
		Never hinged	140.00
151a	A53	3c	120.00
		Never hinged	170.00
152a	A53	4c	120.00
		Never hinged	170.00
153b	A53	5c	100.00
		Never hinged	140.00
154a	A53	8c	120.00
		Never hinged	170.00
155a	A54	10c	200.00
		Never hinged	280.00
156a	A55	12c	200.00
		Never hinged	280.00
157a	A56	20c	200.00
		Never hinged	280.00
158a	A57	50c	800.00
		Never hinged	1,150.
159a	A58	$1	725.00
		Never hinged	1,050.

Coil Stamps

1929 ***Perf. 8 Vertically***

160	A53	1c orange	40.00	22.50
		Never hinged	75.00	
		Precanceled		22.50
161	A53	2c green	40.00	3.50
		Never hinged	75.00	

King George V A59

Library of Parliament A60

The Citadel at Quebec A61

Harvesting Wheat A62

Museum at Grand Pré and Monument to Evangeline A63

Mt. Edith Cavell A64

Type I

Type II

Two types of 1c.

Type I — Three thick and one thin colored lines between "P" at right and ornament above it.

Type II — Four thick colored lines. Curved line in ball of ornament at right is longer than in die I.

Type I

Type II

Two types of 2c.

Type I — The top of the letter "P" encloses a tiny dot of color.

Type II — The top of the "P" encloses a larger spot of color than in die I. The "P" appears almost like a "D."

1930-31 ***Perf. 11***

162	A59	1c orange	1.25	.70
		Never hinged	2.50	
163	A59	1c dp grn (II)	2.00	.25
		Never hinged	4.00	
a.		Booklet pane of 4 + 2 labels (II)	120.00	100.00
		Never hinged	180.00	
b.		Die I	2.00	.25
		Never hinged	4.00	
c.		Booklet pane of 6 (I)	22.50	20.00
		Never hinged	35.00	
164	A59	2c dull green (I)	1.75	.25
		Never hinged	3.50	
a.		Booklet pane of 6	32.50	32.50
		Never hinged	47.50	
165	A59	2c deep red (I)	1.75	.30
		Never hinged	3.50	
a.		Die II	2.10	.25
		Never hinged	4.20	
b.		Booklet pane of 6 (I)	25.00	22.50
		Never hinged	37.50	
166	A59	2c dk brn (II) ('31)	2.00	.25
		Never hinged	4.00	
a.		Booklet pane of 4 + 2 labels (II)	130.00	130.00
		Never hinged	200.00	
b.		Die I	5.00	4.00
		Never hinged	10.00	
c.		Booklet pane of 6 (I)	57.50	57.50
		Never hinged	87.50	
167	A59	3c deep red ('31)	3.25	.25
		Never hinged	6.50	
a.		Booklet pane of 4 + 2 labels	40.00	40.00
		Never hinged	60.00	
168	A59	4c yel bister	15.00	7.50
		Never hinged	30.00	
169	A59	5c dull violet	7.25	5.00
		Never hinged	14.50	

170	A59	5c dull blue	8.50	1.25
		Never hinged	17.00	
171	A59	8c dark blue	27.50	13.50
		Never hinged	55.00	
172	A59	8c red orange	8.50	5.50
		Never hinged	17.00	
173	A60	10c olive green	11.00	1.30
		Never hinged	22.00	
174	A61	12c gray black	30.00	6.50
		Never hinged	60.00	
175	A62	20c brown red	50.00	1.40
		Never hinged	100.00	
176	A63	50c dull blue	175.00	14.00
		Never hinged	350.00	
177	A64	$1 dk ol green	175.00	27.50
		Never hinged	350.00	
		Nos. 162-177 (16)	519.75	85.45
		Set, never hinged	1,037.	

No. 169 rotary printing is distinguished unused from No. 169a flat plate printing by the former having gum ridges about 5mm apart.

See No. 201. For surcharge see No. 191. For overprint see No. 203.

Imperf., Pairs

163d	A59	1c (II)	1,600.
		Never hinged	2,500.
173a	A60	10c	1,600.
		Never hinged	2,500.
174a	A61	12c	900.
		Never hinged	1,350.
175a	A62	20c	900.
		Never hinged	1,350.
176a	A63	50c	1,000.
		Never hinged	1,550.
177a	A64	$1	1,000.
		Never hinged	1,550.

Coil Stamps

1930-31 ***Perf. 8½ Vertically***

178	A59	1c orange	15.00	10.00
		Never hinged	30.00	
179	A59	1c deep green	9.00	5.75
		Never hinged	18.00	
180	A59	2c dull green	6.00	3.00
		Never hinged	12.00	
181	A59	2c deep red	25.00	2.50
		Never hinged	50.00	
182	A59	2c dark brown ('31)	14.00	.75
		Never hinged	28.00	
183	A59	3c deep red ('31)	18.00	.75
		Never hinged	36.00	
		Nos. 178-183 (6)	87.00	22.75
		Set, never hinged	174.00	

George V Type of 1912-25

1931, June 24 ***Perf. 12x8***

184	A43	3c carmine	8.00	4.50
		Never hinged	20.00	

Sir Georges Etienne Cartier — A65

1931, Sept. 30 ***Perf. 11***

190	A65	10c dark green	14.00	.25
		Never hinged	30.00	
a.		Imperf., pair	500.00	
		Never hinged	750.00	

Nos. 165, 165a Surcharged

1932, June 21

191	A59	3c on 2c dp red (II)	1.40	.25
		Never hinged	2.25	
a.		Die I	3.00	1.90
		Never hinged	5.00	

King George V — A66

Edward, Prince of Wales — A67

Allegory of British Empire A68

1932, July 12

192	A66	3c deep red	1.25	.25
		Never hinged	2.50	
193	A67	5c dull blue	7.00	3.00
		Never hinged	14.00	
194	A68	13c deep green	10.00	7.00
		Never hinged	20.00	
		Nos. 192-194 (3)	18.25	10.25
		Set, never hinged	36.50	

Imperial Economic Conference, Ottawa.

Type of 1930 and

King George V — A69

Type I

Type II

Two types of 3c.

Type I — Upper left tip of "3" level with horizontal line to its left.

Type II — Raised "3"; upper left tip of "3" is above horizontal line.

1932, Dec. 1

195	A69	1c dk green	1.25	.25
		Never hinged	2.50	
a.		Booklet pane of 4 + 2 labels ('33)	90.00	85.00
		Never hinged	135.00	
b.		Booklet pane of 6 ('33)	47.50	47.50
		Never hinged	72.50	
196	A69	2c black brown	1.40	.25
		Never hinged	2.80	
a.		Booklet pane of 4 + 2 labels ('33)	120.00	110.00
		Never hinged	180.00	
b.		Booklet pane of 6 ('33)	90.00	70.00
		Never hinged	135.00	
197	A69	3c deep red (I)	1.40	.25
		Never hinged	2.80	
c.		Die II	1.50	.25
		Never hinged	3.00	
d.		Booklet pane of 4 + 2 labels, die II ('33)	42.50	37.50
		Never hinged	85.00	
198	A69	4c ocher	50.00	7.00
		Never hinged	100.00	
199	A69	5c dark blue	11.50	.50
		Never hinged	23.00	
a.		Horiz. pair, imperf. vert.	1,600.	
		Never hinged	2,250.	
200	A69	8c red orange	45.00	3.50
		Never hinged	90.00	
201	A61	13c dull violet	42.50	3.50
		Never hinged	85.00	
		Nos. 195-201 (7)	153.05	15.25
		Set, never hinged	306.10	

Type A66 has at the foot of the stamp "OTTAWA-CONFERENCE 1932". This inscription does not appear on the stamps of type A69.

Imperf., Pairs

195c	A69	1c	240.00
		Never hinged	360.00
196c	A69	2c	240.00
		Never hinged	360.00
197b	A69	3c (I)	240.00
		Never hinged	360.00
197e	A69	3c (II)	*2,000.*
198a	A69	4c	240.00
		Never hinged	360.00
199b	A69	5c	240.00
		Never hinged	360.00
200a	A69	8c	240.00
		Never hinged	360.00
201a	A69	13c	800.00
		Never hinged	1,200.

No. 197e exists as one unused block of 4.

Government Buildings, Ottawa — A70

1933, May 18 *Perf. 11*

202 A70 5c dark blue 10.00 3.75
Never hinged 18.50
a. Imperf., pair 625.00
Never hinged 950.00

Meeting of the Executive Committee of the UPU at Ottawa, May and June, 1933.

No. 175 Overprinted in Blue

1933, July 24

203 A62 20c brown red 45.00 14.00
Never hinged 80.00
a. Imperf., pair 625.00
Never hinged 950.00

World's Grain Exhibition and Conference at Regina.

Steamship Royal William — A71

1933, Aug. 17

204 A71 5c dark blue 11.00 3.75
Never hinged 20.00
a. Imperf., pair 700.00
Never hinged 1,100.

Centenary of the linking by steam of the Dominion, then a colony, with Great Britain, the mother country. The Royal William's 1833 voyage was the first Trans-Atlantic passage under steam all the way.

George V Type of 1932 Coil Stamps

1933 *Perf. 8½ Vertically*

205 A69 1c dark green 15.00 3.00
Never hinged 26.00
206 A69 2c black brown 20.00 1.10
Never hinged 35.00
207 A69 3c deep red 20.00 .40
Never hinged 35.00
Nos. 205-207 (3) 55.00 4.50
Set, never hinged 96.00

Cartier's Arrival at Quebec — A72

1934, July 1 *Perf. 11*

208 A72 3c blue 4.50 1.40
Never hinged 9.00
a. Imperf., pair 625.00
Never hinged 950.00

Landing of Jacques Cartier, 400th anniv.

Group from Loyalists Monument, Hamilton, Ontario A73

1934, July 1

209 A73 10c olive green 28.00 7.50
Never hinged 52.50
a. Imperf., pair 1,400.
Never hinged 2,100.

Emigration of the United Empire Loyalists from the US to Canada, 150th anniv.

Seal of New Brunswick — A74

1934, Aug. 16

210 A74 2c red brown 2.75 2.25
Never hinged 5.00
a. Imperf., pair 650.00
Never hinged 1,000.

150th anniv. of the founding of the Province of New Brunswick.

Princess Elizabeth A75

Duke of York A76

King George V and Queen Mary — A77

Prince of Wales — A78

Windsor Castle A79

Royal Yacht Britannia A80

1935, May 4 *Perf. 12*

211 A75 1c green .75 .35
Never hinged 1.10
212 A76 2c brown .80 .25
Never hinged 1.15
213 A77 3c carmine 2.00 .25
Never hinged 3.25
214 A78 5c blue 4.25 3.00
Never hinged 7.00
215 A79 10c green 8.50 3.00
Never hinged 13.50
216 A80 13c dark blue 10.00 6.50
Never hinged 16.00
Nos. 211-216 (6) 26.30 13.35
Set, never hinged 42.00

25th anniv. of the accession to the throne of George V.

Imperf., Pairs

211a A75 1c 275.00
Never hinged 425.00
212a A76 2c 275.00
Never hinged 425.00
213a A77 3c 275.00
Never hinged 425.00
214a A78 5c 275.00
Never hinged 425.00
215a A79 10c 275.00
Never hinged 425.00
216b A80 13c 275.00
Never hinged 425.00

King George V — A81

Royal Canadian Mounted Police — A82

Confederation Conference at Charlottetown, 1864 — A83

Niagara Falls — A84

Parliament Buildings, Victoria, B.C. — A85

Champlain Monument, Quebec A86

1935, June 1 *Perf. 12*

217 A81 1c green .35 .25
Never hinged .50
a. Bklt. pane of 4 + 2 labels 70.00 70.00
Never hinged 105.00
b. Booklet pane of 6 55.00 55.00
Never hinged 82.50
218 A81 2c brown .35 .25
Never hinged .50
a. Bklt. pane of 4 + 2 labels 70.00 70.00
Never hinged 105.00
b. Booklet pane of 6 55.00 55.00
Never hinged 82.50
219 A81 3c dk carmine .75 .25
Never hinged 1.10
a. Bklt. pane of 4 + 2 labels 40.00 40.00
Never hinged 60.00
c. Printed on gummed side 600.00
220 A81 4c yelwsh org 2.50 .55
Never hinged 3.75
221 A81 5c blue 3.25 .35
Never hinged 5.00
a. Horiz. pair, imperf. vert. 225.00
Never hinged 340.00
222 A81 8c dp orange 2.75 2.25
Never hinged 4.25
223 A82 10c car rose 9.00 .25
Never hinged 14.00
224 A83 13c violet 9.00 .75
Never hinged 14.00
225 A84 20c olive green 18.00 .75
Never hinged 27.50
226 A85 50c dull violet 27.50 6.00
Never hinged 40.00
227 A86 $1 deep blue 60.00 11.00
Never hinged 90.00
Nos. 217-227 (11) 133.45 22.65
Set, never hinged 200.60

No. 219c is valued in the grade of fine. Very fine examples are rare and sell for much more.

Imperf., Pairs

217c A81 1c 150.00
Never hinged 220.00
218c A81 2c 150.00
Never hinged 220.00
219b A81 3c 150.00
Never hinged 220.00
220a A81 4c 150.00
Never hinged 220.00
221b A81 5c 150.00
Never hinged 220.00
222a A81 8c 150.00
Never hinged 220.00
223a A82 10c 225.00
Never hinged 340.00
224a A83 13c 225.00
Never hinged 340.00
225a A84 20c 225.00
Never hinged 340.00
226a A85 50c 225.00
Never hinged 340.00
227a A86 $1 300.00
Never hinged 450.00

Coil Stamps

1935 *Perf. 8 Vertically*

228 A81 1c green 15.00 3.25
Never hinged 22.50
229 A81 2c brown 19.00 1.00
Never hinged 28.50
230 A81 3c dark carmine 16.00 .60
Never hinged 24.00
Nos. 228-230 (3) 50.00 4.85
Set, never hinged 75.00

George VI — A87

1937 *Perf. 12*

231 A87 1c green .30 .25
Never hinged .45
a. Booklet pane of 4 + 2 labels 20.00 *25.00*
Never hinged 30.00
b. Booklet pane of 6 7.50 *20.00*
Never hinged 11.50
232 A87 2c brown .70 .25
Never hinged 1.05
a. Booklet pane of 4 + 2 labels 20.00 *22.50*
Never hinged 30.00
b. Booklet pane of 6 12.00 *15.00*
Never hinged 18.00
233 A87 3c carmine .70 .25
Never hinged 1.05
a. Booklet pane of 4 + 2 labels 7.00 *14.00*
Never hinged 10.50
234 A87 4c yellow 2.75 .25
Never hinged 4.00
235 A87 5c blue 3.50 .25
Never hinged 5.00
236 A87 8c orange 2.75 .45
Never hinged 4.00
Nos. 231-236 (6) 10.70 1.70
Set, never hinged 15.55

Imperf., Pairs

231c A87 1c 300.00
Never hinged 450.00
232c A87 2c 300.00
Never hinged 450.00

233b A87 3c 300.00
Never hinged 450.00
234a A87 4c 300.00
Never hinged 450.00
235a A87 5c 300.00
Never hinged 450.00
236a A87 8c 300.00
Never hinged 450.00

George VI and Queen Elizabeth A88

1937, May 10

237 A88 3c carmine .35 .25
Never hinged .40
a. Imperf., pair 625.00
Never hinged 950.00

Coronation of King George VI and Queen Elizabeth.

George VI Types of 1937 Coil Stamps

1937 ***Perf. 8 Vertically***

238 A87 1c green 3.00 1.10
Never hinged 4.50
239 A87 2c brown 5.50 .40
Never hinged 8.25
240 A87 3c carmine 9.00 .25
Never hinged 13.50
Nos. 238-240 (3) 17.50 1.75
Set, never hinged 26.25

Memorial Chamber, Parliament Building, Ottawa — A89

Entrance to Halifax Harbor A90

Fort Garry Gate, Winnipeg A91

Vancouver Harbor A92

Chateau de Ramezay, Montreal A93

1938 ***Perf. 12***

241 A89 10c dk carmine 9.00 .25
Never hinged 13.50
a. 10c carmine rose 9.00 .25
Never hinged 13.50
242 A90 13c deep blue 12.00 .60
Never hinged 18.00
243 A91 20c red brown 16.00 .45
Never hinged 24.00
244 A92 50c green 37.50 6.00
Never hinged 55.00
245 A93 $1 dull violet 80.00 7.75
Never hinged 120.00
a. Vert. pair, imperf., horiz. *4,750.*
Never hinged *6,750.*
Nos. 241-245 (5) 154.50 15.05
Set, never hinged 230.50

Imperf., Pairs

241b A89 10c dark carmine 500.00
Never hinged 750.00
241c A89 10c carmine rose 500.00
Never hinged 750.00
242a A90 13c 500.00
Never hinged 750.00
243a A91 20c 500.00
Never hinged 750.00
244a A92 50c 500.00
Never hinged 750.00
245b A93 $1 700.00
Never hinged 1,050.

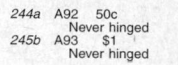

Princess Elizabeth and Princess Margaret Rose — A94

War Memorial, Ottawa — A95

King George VI and Queen Elizabeth A96

Unwmk.

1939, May 15 **Engr.** ***Perf. 12***

246 A94 1c green & black .35 .25
Never hinged .40
247 A95 2c brown & black .35 .25
Never hinged .40
248 A96 3c dk car & black .35 .25
Never hinged .40
Nos. 246-248 (3) 1.05 .75
Set, never hinged 1.20

Visit of George VI and Queen Elizabeth to Canada and the US.

Imperf., Pairs

246a A94 1c 550.00
Never hinged 800.00
247a A95 2c 550.00
Never hinged 800.00
248a A96 3c 550.00
Never hinged 800.00

A97

A98

King George VI — A99

Grain Elevators A100

Farm Scene A101

Parliament Buildings — A102

"Ram" Tank — A103

Corvette A104

Munitions Factory A105

Destroyer A106

1942-43 **Engr.** ***Perf. 12***

249 A97 1c green .35 .25
Never hinged .45
a. Booklet pane of 4 + 2 labels 3.50 *3.75*
Never hinged 5.25
b. Booklet pane of 6 5.00 *5.50*
Never hinged 7.50
c. Booklet pane of 3 ('43) 2.50 *5.00*
Never hinged 3.75
250 A98 2c brown .40 .25
Never hinged .60
a. Booklet pane of 4 + 2 labels ('43) 7.00 *8.00*
Never hinged 10.50
b. Booklet pane of 6 10.50 *11.50*
Never hinged 16.00
d. Vert. strip of 3, imperf. horiz. *5,500.*
251 A99 3c dk carmine .60 .25
Never hinged .90
a. Booklet pane of 4 + 2 labels 4.25 *5.25*
Never hinged 6.50
252 A99 3c rose violet ('43) .50 .25
Never hinged .70
a. Booklet pane of 4 + 2 labels 3.25 4.50
Never hinged 5.00
b. Booklet pane of 3 3.25 *4.50*
Never hinged 4.75
c. Booklet pane of 6 ('47) 3.75 *4.00*
Never hinged 5.50
253 A100 4c greenish black 1.25 .60
Never hinged 1.90
254 A98 4c dk car ('43) .70 .25
Never hinged 1.00
a. Booklet pane of 6 5.25 *10.00*
Never hinged 8.00
b. Booklet pane of 3 3.25 *4.50*
Never hinged 4.75
255 A97 5c deep blue 1.20 .25
Never hinged 1.80
256 A101 8c red brown 1.60 .50
Never hinged 2.40
257 A102 10c brown 4.75 .25
Never hinged 7.00
258 A103 13c dull green 5.00 3.60
Never hinged 7.50
259 A103 14c dull grn ('43) 7.50 .35
Never hinged 11.25
260 A104 20c chocolate 9.00 .25
Never hinged 13.50
261 A105 50c violet 30.00 1.75
Never hinged 45.00
262 A106 $1 deep blue 65.00 7.50
Never hinged 100.00
Nos. 249-262 (14) 127.85 16.30
Set, never hinged 194.00

Canada's contribution to the war effort of the Allied Nations.

No. 250d totally imperf horiz. is unique and is valued in the grade of fine. Beware of strips with blind perfs; these sell for much less.

For overprints see Nos. O1-O4.

Imperf., Pairs

249d	A97	1c	300.00
		Never hinged	450.00
250c	A98	2c	300.00
		Never hinged	450.00
251b	A99	3c	300.00
		Never hinged	450.00
252d	A99	3c	300.00
		Never hinged	450.00
253a	A100	4c	300.00
		Never hinged	450.00
254c	A98	4c	300.00
		Never hinged	450.00
255a	A97	5c	300.00
		Never hinged	450.00
256a	A100	8c	300.00
		Never hinged	450.00
257a	A102	10c	450.00
		Never hinged	675.00
258a	A103	13c	450.00
		Never hinged	675.00
259a	A103	14c	450.00
		Never hinged	675.00
260a	A104	20c	450.00
		Never hinged	675.00
261a	A105	50c	450.00
		Never hinged	675.00
262a	A106	$1	600.00
		Never hinged	900.00

Types of 1942
Coil Stamps

1942-43 ***Perf. 8 Vertically***

263 A97 1c green ('43)	1.50	.55
Never hinged	2.25	
264 A98 2c brown	2.25	1.10
Never hinged	3.40	
265 A99 3c dark carmine	2.25	1.10
Never hinged	3.40	
266 A99 3c rose violet ('43)	4.00	.40
Never hinged	6.00	
267 A98 4c dk carmine ('43)	6.00	.30
Never hinged	9.00	
Nos. 263-267 (5)	16.00	3.45
Set, never hinged	24.05	

See Nos. 278-281.

Catalogue values for unused stamps in this section, from this point to the end of the section, are for Never Hinged items.

Farm Scene, Ontario A107

Great Bear Lake, Mackenzie A108

Hydroelectric Station, Saint Maurice River A109

Combine A110

Logging, British Columbia A111

Train Ferry, Prince Edward Island A112

1946, Sept. 16 **Engr.** ***Perf. 12***

268 A107 8c red brown	2.00	.70
269 A108 10c olive	2.75	.25
270 A109 14c black brown	4.25	.25
271 A110 20c slate black	5.00	.25
272 A111 50c dk blue green	20.00	1.75
273 A112 $1 red violet	45.00	3.00
Nos. 268-273 (6)	79.00	6.20

For overprints see Nos. O6-O10, O21-O23, O25.

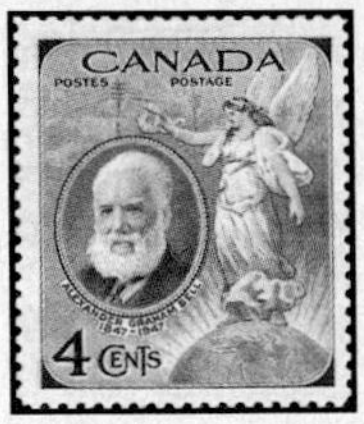

Alexander Graham Bell — A113

1947, Mar. 3

274 A113 4c deep blue	.25	.25

Birth centenary of Alexander Graham Bell.

Citizen of Canada — A114

1947, July 1

275 A114 4c deep blue	.25	.25

Issued on the 80th anniv. of the Canadian Confederation, to mark the advent of Canadian Citizenship.

Princess Elizabeth — A115

1948, Feb. 16

276 A115 4c deep blue	.25	.25

Marriage of Princess Elizabeth to Lieut. Philip Mountbatten, R. N., on Nov. 20, 1947.

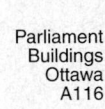

Parliament Buildings Ottawa A116

1948, Oct. 1

277 A116 4c gray	.25	.25

Centenary of Responsible Government.

George VI Types of 1942
Coil Stamps

1948 ***Perf. 9½ Vertically***

278 A97 1c green	7.00	2.00
279 A98 2c brown	22.50	8.50
280 A99 3c rose violet	15.00	2.00
281 A98 4c dark carmine	22.50	2.25
Nos. 278-281 (4)	67.00	14.75

John Cabot's Ship "Matthew" A117

1949, Apr. 1 **Engr.** ***Perf. 12***

282 A117 4c deep green	.25	.25

Entry of Newfoundland into confederation with Canada.

"Founding of Halifax, 1749" A118

1949, June 21 **Unwmk.**

283 A118 4c purple	.25	.25

200th anniv. of the founding of Halifax, Nova Scotia.

A119

A120

A121

A122

A123

1949, Nov. 15

284 A119 1c green	.25	.25
a. Booklet pane of 3 ('50)	.75	*2.00*
285 A120 2c sepia	.30	.25
286 A121 3c rose violet	.35	.25
a. Booklet pane of 3 ('50)	2.50	*6.50*
b. Booklet pane of 4 + 2 labels ('50)	3.25	*3.75*
287 A122 4c dk carmine	.60	.25
a. Booklet pane of 3 ('50)	12.50	12.50
b. Booklet pane of 6 ('50)	18.00	18.00
288 A123 5c deep blue	1.25	.65
Nos. 284-288 (5)	2.75	1.65

Stamps from booklet panes of 3 are imperf. on 2 or 3 sides.

"POSTES POSTAGE" Omitted

1950, Jan. 19

289 A119 1c green	.25	.25
290 A120 2c sepia	.35	.25
291 A121 3c rose violet	.35	.25
292 A122 4c dark carmine	.40	.25
293 A123 5c deep blue	1.50	1.00
Nos. 289-293 (5)	2.85	2.00

See Nos. 295-300, 305-306, 309-310. For overprints see Nos. O12-O20.

Oil Wells, Alberta A124

1950, Mar. 1 **Engr.** ***Perf. 12***

294 A124 50c dull green	8.50	1.30

Development of oil wells in Canada. For overprints see Nos. O11, O24.

Types of 1949
"POSTES POSTAGE" Omitted
Coil Stamps

1950 ***Perf. 9½ Vertically***

295 A119 1c green	.75	.30
296 A121 3c rose violet	1.10	.55

With "POSTES POSTAGE"
Perf. 9½ Vertically

297 A119 1c green	.45	.25
298 A120 2c sepia	3.50	1.30
299 A121 3c rose violet	2.25	.25
300 A122 4c dark carmine	19.00	.75
Nos. 297-300 (4)	25.20	2.55

See note after No. 288.

Indians Drying Skins on Stretchers A125

1950, Oct. 2 ***Perf. 12***

301 A125 10c black brown	.90	.25

Canada's fur resources. For overprint see No. O26.

Fishing A126

1951, Feb. 1 **Unwmk.**

302 A126 $1 bright ultra	42.50	10.00

Canada's fish resources. For overprint see No. O27.

Sir Robert Laird Borden A127

William L. Mackenzie King A128

1951, June 25 ***Perf. 12***

303 A127 3c turquoise green	.25	.25
304 A128 4c rose pink	.30	.25

George VI Types of 1949

1951 ***Perf. 12***

305 A120 2c olive green	.25	.25
306 A122 4c orange vermilion	.35	.25
a. Booklet pane of 3	5.25	2.75
b. Booklet pane of 6	5.00	5.00

For overprints see Nos. O28-O29.

Coil Stamps
Perf. 9½ Vertically

309 A120 2c olive green	1.40	.60
310 A122 4c orange vermilion	3.00	.70

Trains of 1851 and 1951 — A129

"Threepenny Beaver" of 1851 — A130

Designs: 5c, Steamships City of Toronto and Prince George. 7c, Stagecoach and Plane.

1951, Sept. 24 **Unwmk.** ***Perf. 12***

311 A129 4c dark gray	.60	.25
312 A129 5c purple	1.80	1.25
313 A129 7c deep blue	1.10	.30
314 A130 15c bright red	1.20	.30
Nos. 311-314 (4)	4.70	2.10

Centenary of British North American postal administration.

Princess Elizabeth and Duke of Edinburgh A131

1951, Oct. 26 **Engr.**

315 A131 4c violet	.25	.25

Visit of Princess Elizabeth, Duchess of Edinburgh and the Duke of Edinburgh to Canada and the US.

Symbols of Newsprint Paper Production A132

1952, Apr. 1 **Unwmk.** ***Perf. 12***

316 A132 20c gray 1.65 .25

Canada's paper production. For overprint see No. O30.

Red Cross on Sun — A133

1952, July 26 **Engr. and Litho.**

317 A133 4c blue & red .25 .25

18th Intl. Red Cross Conf., Toronto, July 1952.

Sir John J. C. Abbott A134

Alexander Mackenzie A135

1952, Nov. 3 **Engr.**

318 A134 3c rose lilac .25 .25
319 A135 4c orange vermilion .25 .25

Canada Goose A136

1952, Nov. 3

320 A136 7c blue .40 .25

For overprint see No. O31.

Pacific Coast Indian House and Totem Pole — A137

1953, Feb. 2

321 A137 $1 gray 5.75 .90

For overprint see No. O32.

Natl. Wildlife Week — A138

1953, Apr. 1

322 A138 2c Polar bear .25 .25
323 A138 3c Moose .25 .25
324 A138 4c Bighorn sheep .25 .25
Nos. 322-324 (3) .75 .75

Elizabeth II — A139

1953, May 1

325 A139 1c violet brown .25 .25
a. Booklet pane of 3 1.40 1.40
326 A139 2c green .25 .25
327 A139 3c carmine rose .25 .25
a. Booklet pane of 3 1.90 1.40
b. Booklet pane of 4 + 2 labels 1.30 *1.75*
328 A139 4c violet .25 .25
a. Booklet pane of 3 1.90 1.75
b. Booklet pane of 6 1.40 1.40
329 A139 5c ultramarine .35 .25
Nos. 325-329 (5) 1.35 1.25

Stamps from booklet panes of 3 are imperf. on 2 or 3 sides.

See Nos. 331-333. For overprints see Nos. O33-O37.

Coronation Issue

Queen Elizabeth II — A140

1953, June 1

330 A140 4c violet .25 .25

Coil Stamps

1953 ***Perf. 9½ Vertically***

331 A139 2c green 1.40 .90
332 A139 3c carmine rose 1.40 .90
333 A139 4c violet 3.25 1.40
Nos. 331-333 (3) 6.05 3.20

See note after No. 329.
Issued: 2c, 7/30; 3c, 7/27; 4c, 9/3.

Bobbin, Cloth and Spinning Wheel A141

1953, Nov. 2 ***Perf. 12***

334 A141 50c light green 2.75 .25

For overprint see No. O38.

Walrus A142

Beaver A143

1954, Apr. 1

335 A142 4c gray .30 .25
336 A143 5c ultramarine .35 .25
a. Booklet pane of 5 + label 1.75 1.40

National Wildlife Week, 1954.

Elizabeth II A144

Gannet A145

1954-61

337 A144 1c violet brn .25 .25
a. Booklet pane of 5 + label ('56) 1.10 1.10
338 A144 2c green .25 .25
a. Pane of 25 ('61) 3.75 3.75
339 A144 3c carmine rose .25 .25
a. Horiz. pair, imperf. vert. *1,400.*
340 A144 4c violet .25 .25
a. Booklet pane of 5 + label ('56) 1.40 1.40
b. Booklet pane of 6 ('55) 3.00 3.00
341 A144 5c bright blue .25 .25
a. Booklet pane of 5 + label 1.10 1.10
b. Pane of 20 (5 x 4) ('61) 6.50 6.50
c. Horiz. pair, imperf. vert. *6,000.*
342 A144 6c orange .50 .25
343 A145 15c gray 1.50 .25
Nos. 337-343 (7) 3.25 1.75

Panes of 20 and 25 are imperf. on 4 sides.
Issued: 5c, 15c, 4/1; others, 6/10.
For overprints see Nos. O40-O44.

Luminescence

The overprinting of regular stamps with vertical luminescent bands began experimentally in 1962 when Nos. 337p-341p were released at Winnipeg. The bands are of varying number, position and chemical content.

Tagged varieties of stamps which were issued both untagged and with luminescent overprint are listed with suffix letter "p".

1962, Jan. 13 **Tagged**

337p A144 1c violet brown 1.30 .95
338p A144 2c green 1.30 .95
339p A144 3c carmine rose 1.30 .95
340p A144 4c violet 3.75 3.25
341p A144 5c bright blue 4.00 2.25
Nos. 337p-341p (5) 11.65 8.35

Coil Stamps

1954 ***Perf. 9½ Vertically***

345 A144 2c green .55 .25
347 A144 4c violet 1.50 .25
348 A144 5c bright blue 2.25 .25
Nos. 345-348 (3) 4.30 .75

Issued: 2c, 9/9; 3c, 8/23; 4c, 7/6.

Sir John Sparrow David Thompson A146

Sir Mackenzie Bowell A147

1954, Nov. 1 ***Perf. 12***

349 A146 4c violet .35 .25
350 A147 5c bright blue .35 .25

Eskimo and Kayak A148

1955, Feb. 21

351 A148 10c violet brown .40 .25

For overprint see No. O39.

Musk Ox — A149

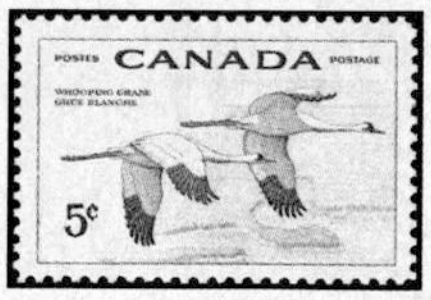
Whooping Cranes A150

1955, Apr. 4

352 A149 4c purple .35 .25
353 A150 5c blue .40 .25

National Wildlife Week, April 10-16.

Torch, Dove and Maple Leaves — A151

1955, June 1 **Unwmk.**

354 A151 5c light blue .40 .25

ICAO, 10th anniversary.

Pioneer Settlers A152

1955, June 30 ***Perf. 12***

355 A152 5c ultramarine .45 .25

50th anniv. of the founding of the provinces of Alberta and Saskatchewan.

Globe and Scout Emblem A153

1955, Aug. 20 **Engr.**

356 A153 5c green & org brown .40 .25

8th Boy Scout World Jamboree, Niagara-on-the-Lake, Ont.

Richard Bedford Bennett
A154

Sir Charles Tupper
A155

1955, Nov. 8

357	A154	4c violet	.35	.25
358	A155	5c ultramarine	.35	.25

Ice Hockey Players
A156

1956, Jan. 23

359	A156	5c ultramarine	.35	.25

Issued to publicize Canada's most popular winter sport.

Caribou
A157

Mountain Goat
A158

1956, Apr. 12

360	A157	4c deep violet	.40	.25
361	A158	5c ultramarine	.40	.25

National Wildlife Week, 1956.

"Paper Industry"
A159

"Chemical Industry" — A160

1956, June 7 **Engr.**

362	A159	20c green	1.40	.25
363	A160	25c red	1.50	.25

For overprint see No. O45.

House on Fire — A161

1956, Oct. 9 **Unwmk.** ***Perf. 12***

364	A161	5c gray & red	.35	.25

Issued to emphasize the needless waste caused by preventable fires.

Canada's Outdoor Recreation Facilities
A162

1957, Mar. 7

365	A162	5c Fishing	.40	.25
366	A162	5c Swimming	.40	.25
367	A162	5c Hunter and dog	.40	.25
368	A162	5c Skiing	.40	.25
a.		Block of 4, #365-368	1.60	1.10

All four designs are printed alternating in sheet of 50, with various combinations possible.

Loon — A163

1957, Apr. 10 ***Perf. 12***

369	A163	5c black	.35	.25

David Thompson and Map of Western Canada
A164

1957, June 5 **Unwmk.**

370	A164	5c ultramarine	.35	.25

David Thompson (1770-1857), explorer and geographer.

Parliament Building, Ottawa — A165

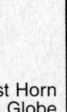

Post Horn and Globe
A166

1957, Aug. 14 ***Perf. 12***

371	A165	5c dark blue	.35	.25
372	A166	15c dark blue	2.25	2.00

UPU, 14th Congress, Ottawa, Aug. 1957.

Miner With Pneumatic Drill — A167

1957, Sept. 5

373	A167	5c black	.30	.25

Canada's mining industry; 6th Commonwealth Mining and Metallurgical Congress, Vancouver, Sept. 8-Oct. 8.

Elizabeth II and Prince Philip — A168

1957, Oct. 10 **Unwmk.**

374	A168	5c black	.30	.25

Visit of Queen Elizabeth II and Prince Philip to Canada, Oct. 12-16.

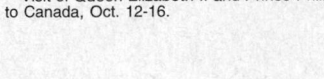

Newspapers and Symbols of Industry
A169

1958, Jan. 22 **Engr.**

375	A169	5c black	.35	.25

Canadian press; the importance of a free press.

Microscope and Globe — A170

1958, Mar. 5 ***Perf. 12***

376	A170	5c blue	.35	.25

Intl. Geophysical Year, 1957-1958.

Miner Panning Gold — A171

1958, May 8

377	A171	5c bluish green	.35	.25

Province of British Columbia, cent.

La Verendrye
A172

1958, June 4

378	A172	5c bright ultra	.35	.25

Pierre Gaultier de Varenne, Sieur de la Verendrye, 18th century French explorer of Western Canada.

Champlain and View of Quebec
A173

1958, June 26

379	A173	5c dk green & bis brn	.35	.25

Founding of Quebec, 350th anniv.

Nurse — A174

1958, July 30 **Engr.**

380	A174	5c rose lilac	.35	.25

Importance of health, both to the individual and to the nation.

Kerosene Lamp and Refinery — A175

1958, Sept. 10 ***Perf. 12***

381	A175	5c olive & red	.35	.25

Centennial of Canada's oil industry.

Speaker's Chair and Mace
A176

1958, Oct. 2

382	A176	5c slate blue	.35	.25

Bicentennial of the meeting of the first House of Representatives in Canada, Halifax, Oct. 2, 1758.

"Silver Dart" and Delta Wing Planes
A177

1959, Feb. 23

383	A177	5c blue & black	.35	.25

50th anniv. of the 1st airplane flight in Canada near Baddeck, N. S., with J. A. D. McCurdy as pilot.

Globe and Dove — A178

1959, Apr. 2

384	A178	5c violet blue	.35	.25

NATO, 10th anniversary.

Woman Tending Tree — A179

1959, May 13

385	A179	5c apple green & blk	.35	.25

Associated Country Women of the World.

Elizabeth II — A180

1959, June 18

386	A180	5c dark carmine	.35	.25

Visit of Queen Elizabeth and Prince Philip to Canada, June 18-Aug. 1.

Great Lakes, Maple Leaf and Eagle Emblems
A181

1959, June 26 **Engr.**

387	A181	5c red & blue	.35	.25
a.		Center inverted	*9,500.*	*7,500.*

Opening of the St. Lawrence Seaway, June 26, 1959.

See United States No. 1131.

British Lion, Fleur-de-Lis and Maple Leaves A182

1959, Sept. 10 *Perf. 12*

388 A182 5c crim rose & dk green .35 .25

Bicentenary of the Battle of the Plains of Abraham.

Girl Guide Emblem — A183

1960, Apr. 20 **Unwmk.**

389 A183 5c brown org & ultra .35 .25

Canadian Girl Guides Assoc., 50th anniv.

Dollard des Ormeaux and Battle Scene — A184

1960, May 19

390 A184 5c ultra & bis brown .35 .25

Battle of the Long Sault, 300th anniv.

Compass Rose, Earth Mover and Surveyor — A185

1961, Feb. 8 **Engr.**

391 A185 5c green & vermilion .35 .25

Development of Canada's Northland.

Emily Pauline Johnson — A186

1961, Mar. 10

392 A186 5c green & red .35 .25

Emily Pauline Johnson (1861-1913), Mohawk princess and poet.

Arthur Meighen — A187

1961, Apr. 19

393 A187 5c ultramarine .35 .25

Arthur Meighen, Prime Minister of Canada, (1920-21, 1926).

Power Plant and Men Holding Blueprint A188

1961, June 28 **Unwmk.**

394 A188 5c lt red brn & blue .35 .25

10th anniv. of the Colombo Plan, initiated to assist underdeveloped countries by providing trained manpower and resources.

Natural Resources and Hands Holding Cogwheel — A189

1961, Oct. 12 **Engr.**

395 A189 5c brown & blue grn .35 .25

Canada's "Resources for Tomorrow Program" and to publicize the close link between industry and the country's renewable natural resources.

Young Adults and Education Symbols — A190

1962, Feb. 28

396 A190 5c black & lt red brn .35 .25

Issued to stimulate public awareness of the importance of education.

Scottish Settler and Lord Selkirk A191

1962, May 3

397 A191 5c lt green & vio brn .35 .25

150th anniv. of the Red River Settlement in Western Canada (Prairie Provinces).

Jean Talon Presenting Gifts to Young Farm Couple — A192

1962, June 13 **Unwmk.**

398 A192 5c dark blue .35 .25

Jean Talon, administrator of New France (Canada), 1665-1668.

British Columbia Legislative Building and Stamp of 1860 — A193

1962, Aug. 22 **Engr.**

399 A193 5c black & rose .35 .25

Centenary of Victoria as incorporated city.

Arms of the Provinces A194

1962, Aug. 31

400 A194 5c brown orange & black .35 .25

Official opening of the Trans-Canada Highway, Rogers Pass, Glacier National Park, Sept. 4.

Queen Elizabeth II and Wheat — A195

Designs (Symbol in upper left corner): 1c, Mineral crystals. 2c, Tree. 3c, Fish. 4c, Electric high tension tower.

1962-63 **Engr.** *Perf. 12*

401	A195 1c dp brn ('63)	.25	.25
a.	Booklet pane of 5 + label ('63)	3.00	3.00
402	A195 2c green ('63)	.25	.25
a.	Pane of 25 ('63)	7.50	7.50
403	A195 3c purple ('63)	.25	.25
404	A195 4c carmine ('63)	.25	.25
a.	Booklet pane of 5 + label ('63)	3.00	3.00
b.	Pane of 25 ('63)	11.00	11.00
405	A195 5c violet blue	.25	.25
a.	Booklet pane of 5 + label ('63)	3.00	3.00
b.	Pane of 20 ('63)	13.00	13.00
c.	Imperf., pair (#405b)	*3,750.*	
d.	Vert. pair, imperf. horiz.	*4,000.*	*575.00*
	Nos. 401-405 (5)	1.25	1.25

Nos. 402a, 404b, and 405b are imperf. on four sides.

Used examples of No. 405d are canceled "Gonor, MB." Beware of examples with traces of blind perfs; a certificate of authenticity is recommended.

Issued: 5c, 10/3; 1c, 4c, 2/4/63; 2c, 3c, 5/2/63.

For overprints see Nos. O46-O49.

1963 **Tagged**

401p	A195	1c deep brown	.25	.25
402p	A195	2c green	.25	.25
403p	A195	3c purple	.25	.25
404p	A195	4c carmine	.75	.50
405p	A195	5c violet blue	.45	.25
q.		Pane of 20	42.50	42.50
		Nos. 401p-405p (5)	1.95	1.50

See note after No. 343.

Coil Stamps

1962-63 *Perf. 9½ Horiz.*

406	A195 2c green	4.75	2.25
407	A195 3c purple	3.50	1.75
408	A195 4c carmine	4.75	2.25
a.	Pair, imperf between	*3,000.*	
409	A195 5c violet blue	4.75	1.00
	Nos. 406-409 (4)	17.75	7.25

No. 408a is valued in the grade of fine. Beware of dangerous fakes; a certificate of authenticity is necessary.

Issued: 5c, 10/3; 4c, 2/4/63; 2c, 3c, 5/2/63.

Sir Casimir Stanislaus Gzowski (1813-98), Engineer, Soldier and Educator — A196

1963, Mar. 5 **Unwmk.** *Perf. 12*

410 A196 5c rose lilac .30 .25

Export Crate and Mercator Map — A197

1963, June 14
411 A197 $1 rose carmine 9.00 2.25

Sir Martin Frobisher (1535-1594), Explorer and Discoverer of Frobisher Bay — A198

1963, Aug. 21
412 A198 5c ultramarine .30 .25

Postrider and First Land Mail Routes A199

1963, Sept. 25
413 A199 5c green & red brn .30 .25

Bicentennial of the 1st regular postal service between Quebec, Three Rivers & Montreal.

Jet at Ottawa Airport — A200

Canada Geese — A201

1963-64
414 A200 7c blue ('64) .50 .40
415 A201 15c deep ultra 1.80 .25

See No. 436. For surcharge see No. 430.

"Peace on Earth" — A202

1964, Apr. 8 **Engr. & Litho.**
416 A202 5c grnsh blue, Prus bl & ocher .30 .25

Issued to promote world peace.

Three-Maple-Leaf Emblem (Canadian Unity) — A203

White Trillium and Arms of Ontario A204

No. 419, White garden lily and arms of Quebec. No. 420, Mayflower (trailing arbutus) and arms of Nova Scotia. No. 421, Purple violet and arms of New Brunswick. No. 422, Prairie crocus and arms of Manitoba. No. 423, Dogwood and arms of British Columbia. No. 424, Lady's slipper and arms of Prince Edward Island. No. 425, Prairie lily and arms of Saskatchewan. No. 426, Wild rose and arms of Alberta. No. 427, Pitcher plant and arms of Newfoundland. No. 428, Fireweed and arms of Yukon. No. 429, Mountain avens and arms of Northwest Territories. No. 429A, Maple leaf and arms of Canada.

1964-66 **Engr. & Litho.** ***Perf. 12***
417 A203 5c lt blue & dk car .25 .25
418 A204 5c red brn, buff & green .25 .25
419 A204 5c grn, yel & org .25 .25
420 A204 5c blue, pink & grn .25 .25
421 A204 5c car, green & vio .25 .25
422 A204 5c red brn, lil & dl grn .25 .25
423 A204 5c lilac, grn & bis .25 .25
424 A204 5c vio, grn & dp rose .25 .25
425 A204 5c sepia, org & grn .25 .25
426 A204 5c dl grn, yel & car .25 .25
427 A204 5c black, grn & car .25 .25
428 A204 5c dk bl, rose & grn .25 .25
429 A204 5c ol, yel & green .25 .25
429A A204 5c dk blue & dp red .25 .25
Nos. 417-429A (14) 3.50 3.50

Issued: No. 417, 5/14/64; Nos. 418-419, 6/30/64; Nos. 420-421, 2/3/65; Nos. 422-423, 4/28/65; No. 424, 7/21/65; Nos. 425-426, 1/19/66; No. 427, 2/23/66; Nos. 428-429, 3/23/66; No. 429A, 6/30/66.

No. 414 Surcharged

1964, July 15 **Engr.**
430 A200 8c on 7c blue .45 .25
a. Pair, one without surcharge 11,500.
b. Surcharge on reverse, inverted 3,750.

Nos. 430a and 430b are each unique.

Fathers of Confederation Memorial, Charlottetown — A205

1964, July 29
431 A205 5c black .30 .25

Centenary of the Charlottetown, P.E.I., Conference, Sept. 1-9, 1864, which led to the creation of the Canadian nation in 1867.

Maple Leaf and Hand Holding Quill Pen — A206

1964, Sept. 9
432 A206 5c dark brown & rose .25 .25

Centenary of the Quebec Conference, Oct. 10-27, 1864, which led to the creation of the Canadian nation.

Elizabeth II — A207

1964, Oct. 5
433 A207 5c claret .25 .25

Queen Elizabeth's visit, Oct. 6-13.

Family and Star of Bethlehem — A208

1964, Oct. 14 ***Perf. 12***
434 A208 3c red .25 .25
a. Pane of 25 7.50 7.50
p. Tagged .65 .35
q. As "a," tagged 11.00 11.00
435 A208 5c blue .25 .25
p. Tagged 1.10 .35

Panes of 25 are imperf. on four sides.

Jet Type of 1964

1964, Nov. 18 **Unwmk.**
436 A200 8c blue .40 .25

Maple Leaf and ICY Emblem A209

1965, Mar. 3
437 A209 5c slate green .25 .25

International Cooperation Year.

Sir Wilfred Grenfell at Wheel of Hospital Ship Strathcona II A210

1965, June 9
438 A210 5c Prussian blue .25 .25

Sir Wilfred Grenfell, author, medical missionary and founder of the Grenfell Mission, birth cent.

Canada's Maple Leaf Flag, 1965 A211

1965, June 30
439 A211 5c blue & red .25 .25

Winston Churchill — A212

1965, Aug. 12 **Litho.** ***Perf. 12***
440 A212 5c brown .25 .25

Sir Winston Spencer Churchill (1874-1965).

Peace Tower, Ottawa — A213

1965, Sept. 8 **Engr.**
441 A213 5c slate green .25 .25

Meeting of the Inter-Parliamentary Union, Ottawa, Sept. 8-17.

Parliament and Ottawa River A214

1965, Sept. 8
442 A214 5c brown .25 .25

Centenary of the final selection of Ottawa as national capital.

Gifts of the Wise Men — A215

1965, Oct. 13
443 A215 3c olive .25 .25
a. Pane of 25 6.25 6.25
p. Tagged .25 .25
q. As "a," tagged 8.50 8.50
444 A215 5c violet blue .25 .25
p. Tagged .35 .25

Christmas. Panes of 25 are imperf. on four sides.

Alouette II Orbiting Globe — A216

1966, Jan. 5
445 A216 5c dark violet blue .25 .25

Launching (in California) of the Canadian satellite Alouette II, Nov. 28, 1965, as part of the Canadian-American program of space research.

La Salle, Map of 17th Century Canada, Ship, Canoe, Spyglass and Compass — A217

1966, Apr. 13
446 A217 5c blue green .25 .25

Tercentenary of the arrival in Canada of Rene Robert Cavelier, Sieur de La Salle (1643-1687).

Traffic Signs — A218

1966, May 2
447 A218 5c black, blue & yel .25 .25

Issued to publicize traffic safety.

House of Commons, Thames River and Canadian Delegates A219

1966, May 26
448 A219 5c brown .25 .25

Centenary of the London Conf., Dec. 4, 1866, which resulted in the British North America Act.

Atomic Reactor, Heavy Water Atom Symbol and Microscope A220

1966, July 27
449 A220 5c deep ultra .25 .25

Peaceful uses of atomic power. The design shows a stylized view of the Douglas Point Nuclear Power Station, Lake Huron, Ontario.

Parliamentary Library, Ottawa — A221

1966, Sept. 8

450	A221	5c plum	.25	.25

12th General Conf. of the Commonwealth Parliamentary Assoc., Ottawa, Sept. 8-Oct. 5.

Praying Hands, by Albrecht Dürer — A222

1966, Oct. 12

451	A222	3c carmine rose	.25	.25
a.		Pane of 25	3.75	3.75
p.		Tagged	.25	.25
q.		As "a," tagged	5.00	5.00
452	A222	5c orange	.25	.25
p.		Tagged	.45	.25

Christmas. Panes of 25 are imperf. on four sides.

Canadian Flag over Globe and Centennial Emblem — A223

1967, Jan. 11

453	A223	5c blue & red	.25	.25
p.		Tagged	.40	.30

Canada's centenary as a nation.

Northern Lights and Dog Team — A224

"Alaska Highway" by A. Y. Jackson A225

Two Types of 6c Black

Type I

Type II

Designs: 2c, Totem pole (Pacific Area). 3c, Combine and oil rig (Prairie Region). 4c, Ship in lock (Central Canada). 5c, Lobster traps and boat (Atlantic Provinces). 6c, Transportation means. 10c, "The Jack Pine" by Tom Thomson. 15c, "Bylot Island" by Lawren Harris. 20c, "The Ferry, Quebec" by James Wilson Morrice. 25c, "The Solemn Land" by J. E. H. MacDonald. 50c, "Summer's Stores" by John Ensor (grain elevators). $1, Oilfield near Edmonton, by H. G. Glyde.

1967-72 Engr. *Perf. 12*

454	A224	1c brown	.25	.25
a.		Booklet pane of 5 + label	.45	.35
b.		Bklt. pane, 1 #454d, 4 #459 + label, perf. 10 ('68)	3.00	2.50
c.		Bklt. pane, 5 #454d + 5 #457d, perf. 10 ('68)	1.40	1.40
d.		Perf. 10 ('68)	.25	.25
e.		Perf. 12½x12 ('71)	.25	.25
f.		Printed on gummed side	*1,000.*	
455	A224	2c green	.25	.25
a.		Bklt. pane, 4 #455, 4 #456 with gutter btwn. ('70)	1.45	1.45
456	A224	3c dull purple	.25	.25
a.		Perf. 12½x12 ('71)	.75	.30
457	A224	4c car rose	.25	.25
a.		Booklet pane of 5 + label	1.25	1.25
b.		Pane of 25 (5x5)	25.00	20.00
c.		Booklet pane of 25 + 2 labels, perf. 10 ('68)	7.50	7.00
d.		Perf. 10	.50	.25
458	A224	5c blue	.25	.25
a.		Booklet pane of 5 + label	5.25	5.25
b.		Pane of 20	30.00	27.50
c.		Bklt. pane of 20, perf. 10 ('68)	7.50	7.50
d.		Perf. 10	.60	.25
459	A224	6c org, perf. 10	.25	.25
a.		Bklt. pane of 25 + 2 labels, perf. 10 ('68)	7.50	7.50
b.		Perf. 12½x12 ('69)	.25	.25
460	A224	6c black (I), perf. 12½x12	.25	.25
a.		Bklt. pane of 25 + 2 labels (I), perf. 10 ('70)	11.00	7.50
b.		As "a," perf. 12½x12	15.00	13.00
c.		Type II, perf. 12½x12	.25	.25
d.		As "c," booklet pane of 4	3.50	3.25
e.		As "d," perf. 10 ('70)	10.00	6.00
f.		Type II, perf. 12 ('72)	.35	.25
g.		Type I, perf. 10	1.50	.30
h.		Type II, perf. 10	2.00	.65
i.		As "f," printed on gummed side	18.00	
461	A225	8c violet brown	.25	.25
462	A225	10c olive green	.25	.25
463	A225	15c dull purple	.45	.25
464	A225	20c dark blue	.55	.25
465	A225	25c slate green	1.50	.25
465A	A225	50c brown org	3.75	.25
465B	A225	$1 carmine rose	6.00	.75
		Nos. 454-465B (14)	14.50	4.00

Nos. 454d, 454e, 456a, 457d, 458d, 460c, 460g and 460h are from booklet panes.

Issued: No. 459, 11/1/68; No. 460, 1/7/70; others, 2/8/67.

See Nos. 543-544, 549-550.

Tagged

454p	A224	1c brown	.25	.25
ep.		Perf. 12½x12 ('71)	.25	.25
455p	A224	2c green	.25	.25
456p	A224	3c dull purple	.25	.25
457p	A224	4c car rose	.60	.25
458p	A224	5c blue	.60	.25
bp.		Pane of 20	55.00	47.50
459p	A224	6c org, perf. 10	.70	.25
bp.		Perf. 12½x12 ('69)	.75	.30
460p	A224	6c black (I), perf. 12½x12	.35	.25
cp.		Type II ('70)	.45	.50
fp.		As "cp," perf. 12 ('72)	.25	.25
462p	A225	10c olive green	.90	.35
463p	A225	15c dull purple	.90	.35
464p	A225	20c dark blue	1.50	.55
465p	A225	25c slate green	7.00	2.25
		Nos. 454p-465p (11)	13.30	5.25

Nos. 454ep and 460cp are from booklet panes Nos. 544q-544s.

Issued: 1c-5c, 2/8/67; No. 459p, 11/1/68; No. 460p, 1/7/70; others, 12/9/69.

See note after No. 343.

Coil Stamps

1967-70 *Perf. 9½ Horiz.*

466	A224	3c dull purple	3.75	.85
467	A224	4c carmine rose	1.10	.50
468	A224	5c blue	2.25	.65

Perf. 10 Horiz.

468A	A224	6c orange	.45	.25
c.		Imperf., pair	275.00	
468B	A224	6c black, die II	.35	.25
d.		Imperf., pair	2,500.	
		Nos. 466-468B (5)	7.90	2.50

Horizontal pairs or blocks of Nos. 468A and 468B may be found with a fine vertical score line between the stamps. These sell for little more than vertical pairs or strips.

Issued: No. 468A, 1/69; No. 468B, 8/70; others, 2/8/67.

EXPO '67 Emblem and Canadian Pavilion A226

1967, Apr. 28 Engr. *Perf. 12*

469	A226	5c blue & red	.25	.25

EXPO '67, Intl. Exhib., Montreal, Apr. 28-Oct. 27.

Symbolic Woman and Ballot — A227

1967, May 24 Litho.

470	A227	5c black & rose lilac	.25	.25

50th anniversary of woman suffrage.

Elizabeth II — A228

1967, June 30 Engr.

471	A228	5c deep org & purple	.25	.25

Centennial Year visit of Queen Elizabeth II and the Duke of Edinburgh.

Runner A229

1967, July 19

472	A229	5c red	.25	.25

Pan-American Games, Winnipeg, Manitoba, July 22-Aug. 7.

Globe and Flash A230

1967, Aug. 31

473	A230	5c deep ultra	.25	.25

50th anniv. of the Canadian Press, news gathering and distributing service.

Georges Philias Vanier A231

1967, Sept. 15 Engr. & Litho.

474	A231	5c black	.25	.25

Georges Philias Vanier (1888-1967), Governor General of Canada, 1959-1967.

Toronto in 1967 and Citizens of 1867 — A232

1967, Sept. 28

475	A232	5c sl grn & sal pink	.25	.25

Centenary of Toronto as capital of Ontario.

Singing Children and Peace Tower, Ottawa — A233

1967, Oct. 11

476	A233	3c carmine	.25	.25
a.		Pane of 25	3.25	3.25
p.		Tagged	.25	.25
q.		As "a" tagged	4.50	4.50
477	A233	5c green	.25	.25
p.		Tagged	.30	.25

Christmas. Panes of 25 are imperf. on four sides.

Gray Jays — A234

1968, Feb. 15 Litho.

478	A234	5c green, blk & red	.45	.25

Weather Map and Composite of Instruments A235

1968, Mar. 13 *Perf. 11*

479	A235	5c dk & lt blue, yel & red	.25	.25

200th anniv. of Canada's first long-term fixed point weather observations at Fort Prince of Wales, Churchill, by William Wales and Joseph Dymond.

Male Narwhal A236

1968, Apr. 10

480	A236	5c multicolored	.25	.25

Weighing Rain Gauge, World Map and Maple Leaf
A237

1968, May 8

481 A237 5c multicolored .25 .25

Intl. Hydrological Decade, 1965-74.

The Nonsuch
A238

Photo. & Engr.

1968, June 5 ***Perf. 10***

482 A238 5c dk blue & multi .25 .25

300th anniv. of the voyage of the Nonsuch which opened the way to Canada's West through the fur trade.

Contemporary and Indian Lacrosse Players — A239

1968, July 3

483 A239 5c yel, black & red .25 .25

George Brown, "Globe" Front Page and Legislature, Prince Edward Island
A240

1968, Aug. 21

484 A240 5c multicolored .25 .25

George Brown (1818-1880), founder of Toronto "Globe" and political leader.

Henri Bourassa and Newspaper Page — A241

Litho. & Engr.

1968, Sept. 4 ***Perf. 12***

485 A241 5c ver, buff & black .25 .25

Henri Bourassa (1868-1952), jounalist and statesman.

Canadian Memorial, Near Vimy, France — A242

1968, Oct. 15 **Engr.**

486 A242 15c slate 2.00 1.25

50th anniv. of the Armistice which ended WWI. The stamp shows "The Defenders and the Breaking of the Sword," a detail from the memorial designed by W. S. Allward.

John McCrae and "Flanders Fields"
A243

1968, Oct. 15 **Litho. & Engr.**

487 A243 5c multicolored .25 .25

50th death anniv. of Lt. Col. John McCrae (1872-1918), author of "In Flanders Fields."

Eskimo Family, Carving — A244

Eskimo soapstone carving: 6c, Mother and infant, by Munamee of Cape Dorset.

1968, Nov. **Photo.**

488	A244 5c brt blue & black	.25	.25
a.	Booklet pane of 10	3.00	3.00
p.	Tagged	.25	.25
q.	As "a," tagged	3.75	3.75
489	A244 6c dp bister & black	.25	.25
p.	Tagged	.25	.25

Christmas. Issued: 5c, Nov. 1; 6c, Nov. 15.

Curling
A245

Photo. & Engr.

1969, Jan. 15 ***Perf. 10***

490 A245 6c black, brt blue & car .25 .25

Vincent Massey — A246

Litho. & Engr.

1969, Feb. 20 ***Perf. 12***

491 A246 6c yel olive & dk brn .25 .25

Vincent Massey (1887-1967), 1st Canadian-born Gov. General of Canada, 1952-59.

Return from the Harvest Field, by Aurele de Foy Suzor-Cote
A247

1969, Mar. 14 **Photo.**

492 A247 50c multicolored 3.50 2.50

Aurele de Foy Suzor-Cote (1869-1937), painter.

Globe and Tools of Various Trades
A248

1969, May 21 **Engr.** ***Perf. 12x12½***

493 A248 6c dk olive green .25 .25

50th anniv. of the ILO.

Vickers Vimy, 1919, and Map of the Atlantic
A249

1969, June 13 **Photo. and Engr.**

494 A249 15c red brn, yel grn & lt ultra 1.75 1.50

50th anniv. of the first non-stop Atlantic flight from Newfoundland to Ireland of Capt. John Alcock and Lt. Arthur Whitten Brown.

Sir William Osler — A250

1969, June 23 ***Perf. 12½x12***

495 A250 6c dk blue & lt red brn .25 .25

Osler (1849-1919), physician, professor of physiology and pathology in Canada, US and England.

Ipswich Sparrow
A251

Birds: 6c, White-throated sparrows, vert. 25c, Hermit thrush.

1969, July 23 **Litho.** ***Perf. 12***

496	A251 6c multicolored	.35	.25
497	A251 10c ultra & multi	.70	.40
498	A251 25c black & multi	1.75	1.50
	Nos. 496-498 (3)	2.80	2.15

Map of Prince Edward Island
A252

Photo. & Engr.

1969, Aug. 15 ***Perf. 12x12½***

499 A252 6c ultra, org brn & black .25 .25

Bicentenary of Charlottetown as capital of Prince Edward Island.

Flags of Summer and Winter Canada Games — A253

Litho. & Engr.

1969, Aug. 15 ***Perf. 12***

500 A253 6c ultra, brt green & red .25 .25

1st Canada Summer Games, Halifax and Dartmouth, N.S., Aug. 16-24.

Sir Isaac Brock and Memorial Queenston Heights — A254

1969, Sept. 12

501 A254 6c yel brn, brn & pale sal .25 .25

Major General Sir Isaac Brock (1769-1812), administrator of Upper Canada and leader in the war of 1812.

Children of Various Races — A255

1969, Oct. 8 **Litho.**

502	A255 5c blue & multi	.25	.25
a.	Booklet pane of 10	3.00	3.00
p.	Tagged	.25	.25
q.	As "a" tagged	3.75	3.75
503	A255 6c red & multi	.25	.25
a.	Black (inscriptions & frame line) omitted	1,750.	1,500.
p.	Tagged	.25	.25

Christmas.

Stephen Leacock, Comedy Mask and Mariposa View
A256

Photo. & Engr.

1969, Nov. 12 ***Perf. 12x12½***

504 A256 6c multicolored .25 .25

Stephen Butler Leacock (1869-1944), humorist, historian and economist.

Manitoba, Crossroads of Canada
A257

1970, Jan. 27 **Litho.** ***Perf. 12***

505	A257 6c violet blue & multi	.25	.25
p.	Tagged	.30	.25

Centenary of the province of Manitoba.

Enchanted Owl, by Kenojuak — A258

1970, Jan. 27 **Engr.**

506 A258 6c dark red & black .25 .25

Centenary of Nortwest Territories.

Microscopic View of Inside of Leaf
A259

1970, Feb. 18 **Photo. & Engr.**

507 A259 6c green, lt org & blue .25 .25

Canada's participation in the Intl. Biological Program, 1967-1972.

Emblems of EXPO '67 and '70 — A260

EXPO '70 Emblem and Dogwood, British Columbia A261

Designs: No. 510, EXPO '70 emblem and white garden lily, Quebec. No. 511, EXPO '70 emblem and white trillium, Ontario.

1970, Mar. 18 **Litho.**

508	A260 25c red emblem	2.00	2.00
p.	Tagged	2.50	2.50
509	A261 25c violet emblem	2.00	2.00
p.	Tagged	2.50	2.50
510	A261 25c green emblem	2.00	2.00
p.	Tagged	2.50	2.50
511	A261 25c blue emblem	2.00	2.00
p.	Tagged	2.50	2.50
a.	Block of 4, #508-511	8.00	8.00
b.	As "a," tagged	10.00	10.00
	Nos. 508-511 (4)	8.00	8.00

EXPO '70 Intl. Exhibition, Osaka, Japan, Mar. 15-Sept. 13. Nos. 508-511 printed se-tenant in panes of 50 (5x10), with various combinations possible.

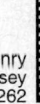

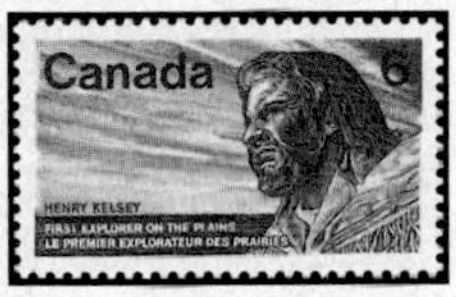

Henry Kelsey A262

Photo. & Engr.

1970, Apr. 15 ***Perf. 12x12½***

512	A262 6c multicolored	.25	.25

300th birth anniv. of Henry Kelsey, explorer of Canada's western plains.

"A Divided World, with Energy Focused on Unification..." — A263

1970, May 13 **Litho.** ***Perf. 11***

513	A263 10c blue	.70	.55
p.	Tagged	.85	.85
514	A263 15c lilac & dk red	1.10	.70
p.	Tagged	1.50	1.50

25th anniversary of the United Nations.

Louis Riel — A264

1970, June 19 **Photo.** ***Perf. 12½x12***

515	A264 6c red & brt blue	.25	.25

Louis Riel (1844-1885), Metis leader who became president of the Council of Assiniboin in 1870.

Mackenzie Rock, Dean Channel — A265

1970, June 25 **Engr.** ***Perf. 12***

516	A265 6c brown	.25	.25

Sir Alexander Mackenzie (1764-1820), Scottish explorer who in 1793 completed the first crossing of the North American continent north of Mexico.

Sir Oliver Mowat and Parliament, Ottawa A266

Photo. & Engr.

1970, Aug. 12 ***Perf. 12x12½***

517	A266 6c red & black	.25	.25

Sir Oliver Mowat (1820-1903), government leader and a Father of Confederation.

Isle of Spruce, by Arthur Lismer A267

1970, Sept. 18 **Litho.** ***Perf. 11***

518	A267 6c multicolored	.25	.25

50th anniv. of "The Group of Seven," Canadian landscape artists.

Santa Claus — A268

Christ Child — A269

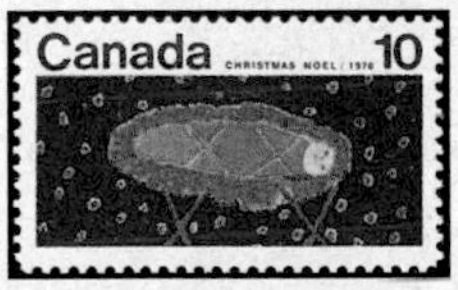

Child in the Manger and Star-studded Sky — A270

Christmas, Designs by Canadian School Children: No. 519, 527 Santa Claus. No. 520, Horse-drawn Sleigh. No. 521, Nativity. No. 522, Children Skiing. No. 523, Snowmen and Christmas Tree. No. 524, 529 Christ Child. No. 525, Christmas Tree and Children. No. 526, Toy Store. . No. 528, Church. No. 530, Snowmobile and Trees.

1970, Oct. 7 **Litho.** ***Perf. 12***

519	A268	5c multicolored	.30	.25
520	A268	5c multicolored	.30	.25
521	A268	5c multicolored	.30	.25
522	A268	5c multicolored	.30	.25
523	A268	5c multicolored	.30	.25
a.		Strip of 5, #519-523	2.75	2.25
b.		As "a," triple impression of black	*550.00*	
524	A269	6c multicolored	.35	.25
525	A269	6c multicolored	.35	.25
526	A269	6c multicolored	.35	.25
527	A269	6c multicolored	.35	.25
528	A269	6c multicolored	.35	.25
a.		Strip of 5, #524-528	3.00	2.50
529	A270	10c multicolored	.40	.35
530	A270	15c multicolored	.90	.90
		Nos. 519-530 (12)	4.55	3.75

Tagged

519p	A268	5c multicolored	.35	.25
520p	A268	5c multicolored	.35	.25
521p	A268	5c multicolored	.35	.25
522p	A268	5c multicolored	.35	.25
523p	A268	5c multicolored	.35	.25
ap.		Strip of 5, #519p-523p	3.25	2.75
524p	A269	6c multicolored	.40	.25
525p	A269	6c multicolored	.40	.25
526p	A269	6c multicolored	.40	.25
527p	A269	6c multicolored	.40	.25
528p	A269	6c multicolored	.40	.25
ap.		Strip of 5, #524p-528p	4.50	3.00
529p	A270	10c multicolored	.50	.50
530p	A270	15c multicolored	1.10	1.10
		Nos. 519p-530p (12)	5.35	4.10

Christmas.

The sheets of 100 of both 5c and 6c contain all 5 designs, generally alternating, and arranged to permit vertical and horizontal pairs of each design in the two center vertical and horizontal rows. The center block of 4 is entirely of No. 522 (5c) and 525 (6c). The sheet may also be broken to provide 20 strips of 5, each stamp of different design.

Sir Donald Alexander Smith — A271

1970, Nov. 4

531	A271 6c dk grn, yel & black	.25	.25

Smith (1820-1914), railroad builder and Canadian High Commissioner, 1896-1914.

Big Raven, by Emily Carr — A272

1971, Feb. 12

532	A272 6c multicolored	.25	.25

Emily Carr (1871-1945), painter and writer.

Laboratory Equipment Used for Insulin Discovery — A273

1971, Mar. 3 ***Perf. 11***

533	A273 6c multicolored	.25	.25

Discovery of insulin by Dr. Frederick G. Banting and Dr. Charles H. Best, 50th anniversary.

A274

1971, Mar. 24

534	A274 6c red, org & black	.25	.25

Sir Ernest Rutherford (1871-1937), physicist, developer of theory of spontaneous disintegration of the atom.

Spring, Winged Maple Seed — A275

1971

535	A275 6c shown	.30	.25
a.	Imperf., pair	*850.00*	750.00
536	A275 6c Summer	.30	.25
537	A275 7c Autumn	.30	.25
538	A275 7c Winter	.30	.25
	Nos. 535-538 (4)	1.20	1.00

Issue dates: No. 535, Apr. 14; No. 536, June 16; No. 537, Sept. 3; No. 538, Nov. 19.

Louis Joseph Papineau — A276

Litho. & Engr.

1971, May 7 ***Perf. 12½x12***

539	A276 6c multicolored	.25	.25

Louis Joseph Papineau (1786-1871), member of Legislative Assembly and leader of French Canadian Patriote party.

Map of Copper Mine River Basin A277

1971, May 7 ***Perf. 12x12½***

540	A277 6c buff, red & brown	.25	.25

Bicentenary of Samuel Hearne's expedition to the Copper Mine River.

Maple Leaves A278

1971, June 1

541	A278 15c blk, red org & yel	1.70	1.10
p.	Tagged	2.40	2.25

Inauguration of new transmitters for Radio Canada International.

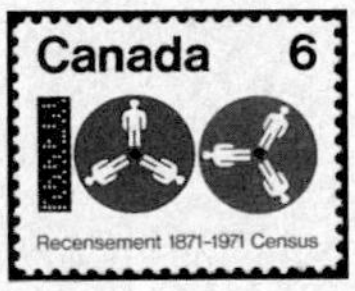

Computer Tape and Reels — A279

1971, June 1

542	A279 6c black, ultra & red	.25	.25

Centenary of measured progress through census.

Migrating Phosphor

Canada's "Ottawa/General" tagging of engraved stamps printed March-October, 1972, used a phosphor which migrates onto or through other stamps, booklet covers and album pages. It fluoresces yellow under ultraviolet light.

This bleeding, contaminating "OP4" phosphor can be somewhat contained in mounts or envelopes of acetate, glassine or polyethylene, but it may leak or penetrate.

The migrating phosphor is found on all examples of Nos. 560p-561p, and on some of Nos. 544p, 544q, 544r, 544s, 562p-565p and 594-598.

Transportation Means — A280

Design: 8c, Library of Parliament.

1971-72 Engr. *Perf. 12½x12*

543 A280 7c slate green .35 .25
- a. Booklet pane of 5 + label (#454e, #456a + 3#543) 7.50 4.50
- b. Booklet pane of 20 (4 #454e, 4 #456a, 12 #543) 8.00 6.50
- p. Tagged .60 .25

544 A280 8c slate .25 .25
- a. Booklet pane of 6 (3 #454e, 1 #460c, 2 #544) 3.50 1.75
- b. Booklet pane of 18 (6 #454e, 1 #460c, 11 #544) 5.25 3.00
- c. Booklet pane of 10 (4 #454e, 1 #460c, 5 #544 ('72) 2.25 2.25
- p. Tagged .30 .25
- q. As "a," tagged 1.75 1.75
- r. As "b," tagged 3.25 3.25
- s. As "c," tagged 2.00 2.00

Coil Stamps

1971 *Perf. 10 Horiz.*

549 A280 7c slate green .40 .25
- a. Imperf, pair 1,050.

550 A280 8c slate .30 .25
- a. Imperf, pair 600.00
- p. Tagged .25 .25
- q. As "p," imperf, pair 1,000.

See note below No. 468B.
Issued: 7c, 6/30/71; 8c, 12/30/71.

Abstract "BC" A282

1971, July 20 Litho. *Perf. 12*

552 A282 7c multicolored .25 .25

Centenary of British Columbia's entry into Canadian Confederation.

Indian Encampment on Lake Huron, by Kane — A283

1971, Aug. 11 *Perf. 12½*

553 A283 7c multicolored .40 .25

Paul Kane (1810-1871), painter.

Snowflake — A284

1971, Oct. 6 Engr. *Perf. 12*

Size: 24x30mm

554 A284 6c dark blue .25 .25
- p. Tagged .25 .25
- a. All color omitted (from foldover) *2,000.*
- b. Printed on gummed side (from foldover) *1,200.*

555 A284 7c bright green .25 .25
- p. Tagged .30 .25

Litho. and Engr.

Size: 30x30mm

556 A284 10c dp car & silver .35 .30
- p. Tagged .45 .30

557 A284 15c lt ultra, dp car & silver .70 .65
- p. Tagged .90 .75

Nos. 554-557 (4) 1.55 1.45

Christmas.

Pierre Laporte — A285

1971, Oct. 20 *Perf. 12½x12*

558 A285 7c black .25 .25

Pierre Laporte (1921-1970), Minister of Labor, kidnapped and killed.

Figure Skating — A286

1972, Mar. 1 Litho. *Perf. 12*

559 A286 8c deep red lilac .25 .25

World Figure Skating Championships, Calgary, Alberta, Mar. 6-12.

"Your Heart is your Health" A287

1972, Apr. 7 Engr. *Perf. 12x12½*

560 A287 8c red .30 .25
- p. Tagged .55 .35

World Health Day, Apr. 7.

Frontenac, by Philippe Hébert and Fort Saint Louis, Quebec A288

1972, May 17 Photo. and Engr.

561 A288 8c red brown & multi .25 .25
- p. Tagged .75 .75

Tercentenary of the appointment of Louis de Buade, Count of Frontenac and Palluau (1622-1698), as Governor of New France.

Indians of Canada

Buffalo Chase, by George Catlin A289

Thunderbird, Assiniboin Pattern — A290

In Nos. 562-581, the first two and last two stamps of each annual set are printed checkerwise in same sheet of 50.

1972 Litho. *Perf. 12x12½*

562 A289 8c shown .40 .25
- p. Tagged .55 .30

563 A289 8c Plains Indian artifacts .40 .25
- p. Tagged .55 .30
- a. Pair, #562-563 .80 .50
- b. As "a," tagged 1.10 .75

Perf. 12½x12

Photo. & Engr.

564 A290 8c shown .40 .25
- p. Tagged .55 .30

565 A290 8c Ceremonial sun dance costume .40 .25
- p. Tagged .55 .30
- a. Pair, #564-565 .80 .50
- b. As "a," tagged 1.10 .75

Plains Indians of Canada.
Issued: Nos. 562-563, 7/6; Nos. 564-565, 10/4.

Tagged (Nos. 566-581)

1973 Litho. *Perf. 12x12½*

566 A289 8c Algonkian artifacts .40 .25
567 A289 8c "Micmac Indians" .40 .25
- a. Pair, #566-567 .80 .50

Perf. 12½x12

Photo. & Engr.

568 A290 8c Thunderbird and belt .35 .25
569 A290 8c Algonkian man and woman .35 .25
- a. Pair, #568-569 .70 .50

Algonkian-speaking Indians of Canada (Malecite, Micmac, Montagnais, Algonquin and Ojibwa).
Issued: Nos. 566-567, 2/21; Nos. 568-569, 11/28.

1974 Litho. *Perf. 12x12½*

570 A289 8c Nootka Sound, house, inside .30 .25
571 A289 8c Artifacts .30 .25
- a. Pair, #570-571 .60 .50

Perf. 12½x12

Photo. & Engr.

572 A290 8c Chief wearing Chilkat blanket .30 .25
573 A290 8c Thunderbird from Kwakiutl house .30 .25
- a. Pair, #572-573 .60 .50

Pacific Coast Indians of Canada (Haida, Salish, Tsimshian, Chilkat and Kwakiutl).
Issued: Nos. 570-571, 1/16; Nos. 572-573, 2/22.

1975, Apr. 4 Litho. *Perf. 13½*

574 A289 8c Montagnais-Naskapi artifacts .25 .25
575 A289 8c Dance of the Kutcha-Kutchin .25 .25
- a. Pair, #574-575 .50 .50

Perf. 12½

576 A290 8c Kutchin ceremonial costume .25 .25

Litho. and Embossed

577 A290 8c Ojibwa thunderbird and Naskapi pattern .25 .25
- a. Pair, #576-577 .50 .50

Subarctic Indians.

1976, Sept. 17 Litho. *Perf. 13½*

578 A289 10c Cornhusk mask, artifacts .25 .25
579 A289 10c Iroquoian Encampment, by George Heriot .25 .25
- a. Pair, #578-579 .50 .50

Perf. 12½

Litho. & Embossed

580 A290 10c Iroquoian thunderbird .25 .25

Litho.

581 A290 10c Iroquoian man, woman .25 .25
- a. Pair, #580-581 .50 .50

Nos. 562-581 (20) 6.30 5.00

Iroquois (Mohawk, Cayuga, Seneca, Oneida, Onondaga and Tuscarora).

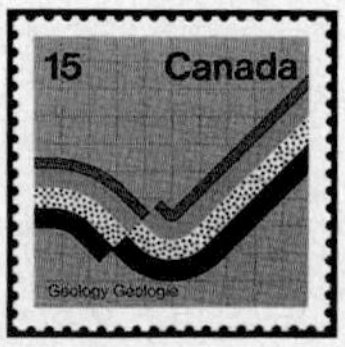

Geological Fault — A291

No. 583, Bird's eye view of town. No. 584, Aerial map photography. No. 585, Contour lines.

1972, Aug. 2 *Perf. 12*

582 A291 15c shown 1.50 1.10
- p. Tagged 2.00 1.50

583 A291 15c multicolored 1.50 1.10
- p. Tagged 2.00 1.50

584 A291 15c multicolored 1.50 1.10
- p. Tagged 2.00 1.50

585 A291 15c multicolored 1.50 1.10
- p. Tagged 2.00 1.50
- a. Block of 4, #582-585 6.00 5.50
- b. As "a," tagged 8.00 *11.00*

Nos. 582-585 (4) 6.00 4.40

Earth sciences: 24th Intl. Geological Cong. (No. 582); 22nd Intl. Geographical Cong. (No. 583); 12th Cong. of Intl. Soc. of Photogrammetry (No. 584); 6th Cong. of Intl. Cartographic Assoc. (No. 585).

Sir John A. Macdonald A292

Elizabeth II A292a

Forest, Central Canada — A293

Vancouver, B.C. — A294

Designs: 2c, Sir Wilfrid Laurier. 3c, Sir Robert L. Borden. 4c, William Lyon Mackenzie King. 5c Richard Bedford Bennett. 6c, Lester B. Pearson. 7c, Louis St. Laurent. 15c, Mountain sheep, Western Canada. 20c, Grain fields, Prairie. 25c, Polar bears, North. 50c, Seashore. $2, Quebec.

1972-76 Engr. *Perf. 12x12½*

Tagged

586 A292 1c orange ('73) .25 .25
- a. Booklet pane, 3 #586, 1 #591, 2 #593 ('74) 1.25 1.10
- b. Bklt. pane, 6 #586, 1 #591, 11 #593 ('75) 1.50 1.50
- c. Bklt. pane, 2 #586, 4 #587, 4 #593Ac ('76) 1.25 1.10
- d. Printed on gummed side 900.00

587 A292 2c green ('73) .25 .25
588 A292 3c brown ('73) .25 .25
589 A292 4c black ('73) .25 .25
590 A292 5c lilac ('73) .25 .25
591 A292 6c dk red ('73) .25 .25
- a. Printed on gummed side 180.00

592 A292 7c dk brn ('74) .25 .25
593 A292a 8c ultra ('73) .25 .25
- b. Perf. 13x13½ ('76) .75 .25

Perf. 13x13½

593A A292a 10c dk car ('76) .25 .25
- c. Perf. 12x12½ .35 .25

Perf. 12½x12

Photo. & Engr.

594 A293 10c multicolored .30 .25
595 A293 15c multicolored .50 .25
596 A293 20c multicolored .50 .25
597 A293 25c multicolored .55 .25
598 A293 50c multicolored 1.20 .25
599 A294 $1 multi ('73) 2.50 .50

Perf. 11

Litho. & Engraved

600 A294 $1 multicolored 6.00 1.60
601 A294 $2 multicolored 4.50 2.25

Nos. 586-601 (17) 18.30 7.85

No. 599 has engraved shading added in some areas.

Plates 1 and 2 of the scenic 10c differ in impression and colors. Plate 1 has distinct crosshatching of "Canada" background. On plate 2, released in 1974, this area appears solidly inked.

A 1976 printing of the 15c shows the blue trees on the hillside as solid color, while the 1972 printing shows clear detail on the trees.

A 1974 printing of the 50c has darker shading and a deeper tone for the dark blue areas of the photogravure impression.

Nos. 600 and 601 are untagged.

1976-77 Photo. & Engr. *Perf. 13½*

594a A293 10c multicolored .30 .25
595a A293 15c multicolored .45 .25
596a A293 20c multicolored .60 .25
597a A293 25c multicolored .65 .25
598a A293 50c multicolored 1.75 .25
599a A294 $1 multi ('77) 2.50 .30

Nos. 594a-599a (6) 6.25 1.55

Coil Stamps

1974-76 Engr. *Perf. 10 Vert.*

604 A292a 8c ultramarine .25 .25
a. Imperf., horiz. pair 150.00
605 A292a 10c dk carmine ('76) .30 .25
a. Imperf., horiz. pair 160.00

See note below No. 468B. No. 604 also exists in vertical multiples without score line.

Candles — A295

Candles and Fruit A296

Christmas: 8c, Like 6c. 15c, Candles, 15th century prayer book, boxes and brass vase.

1972, Nov. 1 Litho. *Perf. 12½x12*

606 A295 6c red & multi .25 .25
p. Tagged .30 .25
607 A295 8c vio blue & multi .25 .25
p. Tagged .35 .25

Perf. 11

608 A296 10c green & multi .45 .35
p. Tagged .65 .55
609 A296 15c yel bister & multi .70 .70
p. Tagged 1.25 1.20
Nos. 606-609 (4) 1.65 1.55

"The Blacksmith's Shop," by Krieghoff — A297

1972, Nov. 29 *Perf. 12½*

610 A297 8c multicolored .30 .25
p. Tagged .35 .25

Cornelius Krieghoff (1815-1872), painter.

Tagged
From No. 611 onward, all stamps are tagged unless otherwise noted.

Monsignor de Laval — A298

1973, Jan. 31 *Perf. 11*

611 A298 8c silver, ultra & gold .25 .25

Francois-Xavier de Montmorency-Laval de Montigny (1623-1708), 1st Bishop of Quebec and founder of many educational institutions; one of the builders of New France.

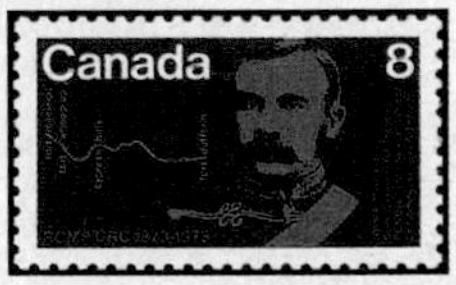

Commissioner G. A. French and Map of 1874 Trek — A299

10c, Spectrograph. 15c, R.C.M.P. Musical Ride.

1973, Mar. 9

612 A299 8c dk brn, org & red .25 .25
613 A299 10c dk blue & multi .35 .30
614 A299 15c yel grn & multi .75 .50
a. Imperf., pair 375.00
Nos. 612-614 (3) 1.35 1.05

Royal Canadian Mounted Police, cent.
Imperfs of No. 614 with a double impression and examples with 15c printed on 10c are from printer's waste.

Jeanne Mance A300

1973, Apr. 18

615 A300 8c multicolored .25 .25
a. Printed on gummed side *750.00*

Jeanne Mance (1606-1673), first secular nurse in North America and founder of first hospital, the Hôtel-Dieu in Montreal settlement.

Joseph Howe — A301

1973, May 16

616 A301 8c gold & black .25 .25

Joseph Howe (1804-1873), journalist, poet and Lieutenant-Governor of Nova Scotia.

Mist Fantasy, by James MacDonald A302

1973, June 8 *Perf. 12½*

617 A302 15c multicolored .60 .50

Centenary of the birth of James E. H. MacDonald (1873-1932), painter.

Oaks on Shore A303

Photo. & Engr.

1973, June 22 *Perf. 12x12½*

618 A303 8c orange & red brn .25 .25

Centenary of Prince Edward Island's entry into Confederation.

Scottish Settlers and "Hector" A304

1973, July 20

619 A304 8c multicolored .25 .25

Bicentenary of arrival of Scottish settlers at Pictou, N.S.

Queen Elizabeth II — A305

1973, Aug. 2 Photo. and Engr.

620 A305 8c silver & multi .25 .25
621 A305 15c gold & multi .70 .60

Visit to Ottawa of Elizabeth II and the Duke of Edinburgh, July 31-Aug. 4, and meeting of Commonwealth Heads of Government, Ottawa, Aug. 2-10.

Nellie McClung — A306

1973, Aug. 29 Litho. *Perf. 10½x11*

622 A306 8c multicolored .25 .25

Nellie McClung (1873-1951), leader of women's suffrage movement, social reformer and writer.

Montreal Olympic Games — A307

1973, Sept. 20 *Perf. 12x12½*
Size: 26x44mm

623 A307 8c silver & multi .25 .25
624 A307 15c gold & multi .60 .50

21st Olympic Games, Montreal, 1976.
See Nos. B1-B3.

Ice Skate — A308

Santa Claus — A309

1973, Nov. 7 *Perf. 12½x12*

625 A308 6c shown .25 .25
a. Double impression of black 110.00
626 A308 8c Dove .25 .25

Perf. 10½

627 A309 10c shown .30 .30
628 A309 15c Shepherd and star .60 .60
Nos. 625-628 (4) 1.40 1.40

Christmas.

Children Diving from Dock — A310

1974, Mar. 22 Engr. *Perf. 12*

629 A310 8c shown .40 .25
630 A310 8c Joggers .40 .25
631 A310 8c Bicycling family .40 .25
632 A310 8c Hikers .40 .25
a. Block of 4, #629-632 1.60 1.00

"Keep Fit." 21st Summer Olympic Games, Montreal, 1976. When stamps are observed at an angle the Montreal Olympic Games' emblem can be seen.

Main St. and Portage Ave., Winnipeg, 1872 — A311

Litho. & Engr.

1974, May 3 *Perf. 12x12½*

633 A311 8c multicolored .25 .25

Winnipeg's Incorporation as a city, cent.

Postmaster A312

1974, June 11 Litho. *Perf. 13½x13*

634 A312 8c shown .35 .30
635 A312 8c Mail collector and truck .35 .30
636 A312 8c Mail handler .35 .30
637 A312 8c Mail sorters .35 .30
638 A312 8c Mailman .35 .30
639 A312 8c Rural mail delivery .35 .30
a. Block of 6, #634-639 2.25 2.25

Centenary of letter carrier delivery service. Printed in sheets of 50 (5x10).

Agricultural Education A313

1974, July 12 *Perf. 12½x12*

640 A313 8c multicolored .25 .25

Ontario Agricultural College centenary.

Pedestal, Gallows Frame and Contempra Telephones A314

1974, July 26 *Perf. 12½*

641 A314 8c multicolored .25 .25
a. Imperf., pair *1,500.*

Centenary of the idea for the telephone by Alexander Graham Bell while visiting Brantford, Canada.

Bicycle Wheel and Cycling Emblem A315

Photo. & Engr.

1974, Aug. 7 *Perf. 12x12½*

642 A315 8c black, red & silver .25 .25

World Cycling Championships, Montreal, Aug. 14-25.

Mennonite Settlers A316

1974, Aug. 28 Litho. *Perf. 12x12½*

643 A316 8c multicolored .25 .25

Centenary of arrival of Mennonite settlers in Manitoba.

Snowshoeing A317

1974, Sept. 23 Engr. *Perf. 13½*

644 A317 8c shown .35 .25
645 A317 8c Skiing .35 .25
646 A317 8c Skating .35 .25
647 A317 8c Curling .35 .25
a. Block of 4, #644-647 1.40 1.40
b. Block or strip of 4, printed on gummed side *3,000.*

"Keep Fit." 1976 Winter Olympic Games. When the stamps are observed at an angle the Montreal Olympic Games' emblem can be seen.

Warning: No. 647b must show each design; blocks exist that contain 2 No. 645 but no example of No. 647. Value thus, $1,500.

Mercury with Winged Horses, UPU Emblem A318

Photo. & Engr.

1974, Oct. 9 *Perf. 12x12½*

648 A318 8c violet, red & blue .25 .25
649 A318 15c violet, red & blue .90 .75

Centenary of Universal Postal Union.

Nativity, by Jean Paul Lemieux A319

Skaters at Hull, by Henri Masson — A320

Christmas (Paintings): 10c, The Ice Cone, Montmorency Falls, by Robert C. Todd. 15c, Village in the Laurentian Mountains, by Clarence A. Gagnon.

1974, Nov. 1 Litho. *Perf. 13½*

650 A319 6c multicolored .25 .25
651 A320 8c multicolored .25 .25
652 A319 10c multicolored .35 .30
653 A319 15c multicolored .60 .55
Nos. 650-653 (4) 1.45 1.35

Marconi and St. John's, Newfoundland, from Signal Hill — A321

1974, Nov. 15 *Perf. 13*

654 A321 8c multicolored .25 .25

Guglielmo Marconi (1874-1937), Italian electrical engineer and inventor.

Merritt and Welland Canal A322

Litho. & Engr.

1974, Nov. 29 *Perf. 13x13½*

655 A322 8c multicolored .25 .25

Sesquicentennial of the start of construction of the Welland Canal between Lakes Ontario and Erie, a project conceived and supervised by William Hamilton Merritt (1793-1862). Portrait by Robert Whale.

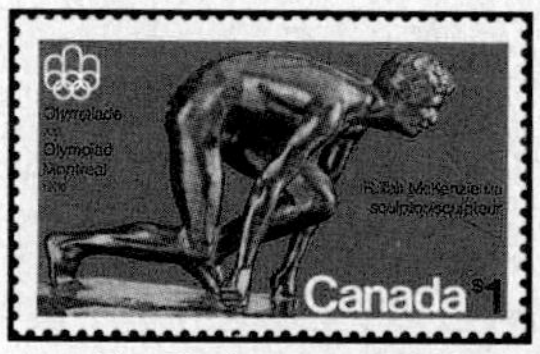

The Sprinter — A323

The Plunger — A324

Designs: Sculptures by Robert Tait McKenzie, M.D. (1867-1938), and Montreal Olympic Games' emblem.

Perf. 12½x12, 12x12½

1975, Mar. 14 Litho.; Embossed

656 A323 $1 multicolored 2.25 2.25
657 A324 $2 multicolored 4.50 4.50

21st Olympic Games, Montreal, July 17-Aug. 1, 1976.

A325

No. 658, Anne of Green Gables. No. 659, Maria Chapdelaine.

1975, May 15 Litho. *Perf. 13*

658 8c blue & multi .25 .25
659 8c brown & multi .25 .25
a. A325 Pair, #658-659 .50 .50

Birth centenary of Lucy Maud Montgomery (1874-1942), writer and author of "Anne of Green Gables"; Louis Hémon (1880-1913), writer and author of "Maria Chapdelaine." Nos. 658-659 printed checkerwise.

Marguerite Bourgeoys A327

Alphonse Desjardins A328

1975, May 30 Litho. *Perf. 12½x12*

660 A327 8c red & multi .25 .25
661 A328 8c red & multi .25 .25

Marguerite Bourgeoys (1620-1700), founder of the Congrégation de Notre-Dame, Montreal, first girls' school in New France; Alphonse Desjardins (1854-1920), journalist, founder of first credit union in North America.

A329

No. 662, Samuel Dwight Chown (1853-1933), Methodist minister, leader of temperance movement, founder of United Church. No. 663, Dr. John Cook (1805-92), 1st Moderator of the United Presbyterian Church in Canada.

Nos. 662-663 printed checkerwise.

Photo. & Engr.

1975, May 30 *Perf. 12x12½*

662 8c dk brown, yel & buff .25 .25
663 8c dk brown, yel & buff .25 .25
a. A329 Pair, #662-663 .50 .50

Pole Vaulting — A331

Hurdling — A332

Design: 25c, Marathon running and Montreal Olympic Games' emblem.

1975, June 11 Litho. *Perf. 12x12½*

664 A331 20c dk blue & multi .60 .45
665 A331 25c maroon & multi .75 .50
666 A332 50c green & multi 1.50 1.00
Nos. 664-666 (3) 2.85 1.95

21st Olympic Games, Montreal, July 17-Aug. 1, 1976.

"Untamed" (Wild Horse Race) A333

1975, July 3

667 A333 8c gray & multi .25 .25

Centenary of the founding of Calgary.

Female Symbol — A334

Photo. & Engr.

1975, July 14 *Perf. 13*

668 A334 8c dp yel, gray & black .25 .25

International Women's Year.

"Justice," by Walter S. Allward — A335

1975, Sept. 2 Litho. *Perf. 12½*

669 A335 8c multicolored .25 .25

Supreme Court of Canada, centenary.

"Wm. D. Lawrence" A336

Photo. & Engr.

1975, Sept. 24 *Perf. 13*

670 A336 8c shown .35 .30
671 A336 8c "Beaver" .35 .30
672 A336 8c "Neptune" .35 .30
673 A336 8c "Quadra" .35 .30
a. Block of 4, #670-673 1.40 1.40

Coastal ships.

Santa Claus — A337

Child — A338

Trees — A339

Designs by Canadian School Children: "What Christmas Means to Me."

1975, Oct. 22 Litho. *Perf. 13½*

No.	Type	Description	Unused	Used
674	A337	6c shown	.25	.25
675	A337	6c Skater	.25	.25
a.		Pair, #674-675	.50	.50
676	A338	8c shown	.25	.25
677	A338	8c Family and Christmas tree	.25	.25
a.		Pair, #676-677	.50	.50
b.		Double impression of black	100.00	
c.		As "a," triple impression of black	300.00	
678	A338	10c Gift box	.25	.25
679	A339	15c shown	.45	.45
		Nos. 674-679 (6)	1.70	1.70

Christmas. Stamps of same denomination printed checkerwise.

Legion Emblem and Bugle A340

Photo. & Engr.

1975, Nov. 10 *Perf. 13*

No.	Type	Description	Unused	Used
680	A340	8c gray & multi	.25	.25

Royal Canadian Legion, 50th anniversary.

Olympic Torch Ignited by Satellite in Canada A341

Montreal Olympic Games' Emblem and: 20c, Canadian athletes carrying Olympic flag. 25c, Women athletes receiving Olympic medals.

1976, June 18 Litho. *Perf. 13*

No.	Type	Description	Unused	Used
681	A341	8c black & multi	.25	.25
682	A341	20c black & multi	.70	.55
683	A341	25c black & multi	.90	.60
		Nos. 681-683 (3)	1.85	1.40

1976 Olympic Games ceremonies.

Communication Arts — A342

25c, Handicraft tools. 50c, Performing arts.

1976, Feb. 6 Photo. *Perf. 12x12½*

No.	Type	Description	Unused	Used
684	A342	20c gray & multi	1.25	.60
685	A342	25c ocher & multi	1.50	.75
686	A342	50c blue & multi	2.50	1.25
		Nos. 684-686 (3)	5.25	2.60

Olympic Fine Arts and Cultural Program.

High-rise Tower, Notre Dame Church, Montreal, and Games' Emblem — A343

Design: $2, Olympic Stadium, Velodrome, flags and emblem.

Photo. & Engr.

1976, Mar. 12 *Perf. 13*

No.	Type	Description	Unused	Used
687	A343	$1 silver & multi	3.25	2.25
688	A343	$2 gold & multi	5.25	4.50

Nos. 681-688 were issued in commemoration of, or in connection with the 21st Olympic Games, Montreal, July 17-Aug. 1. Nos. 687-688 were issued in panes of 8.

Snowflake, Winter Olympics' Emblem — A344

Photo. and Embossed

1976, Feb. 6 *Perf. 12½*

No.	Type	Description	Unused	Used
689	A344	20c multicolored	.90	.65

12th Winter Olympic Games, Innsbruck, Austria, Feb. 4-15.

Flower Growing from City — A345

1976, May 12 Litho. *Perf. 12x12½*

No.	Type	Description	Unused	Used
690	A345	20c multicolored	.60	.45

Habitat, UN Conference on Human Settlements, Vancouver, May 31-June 11.

Franklin and Map of North America, 1776 A346

Litho. & Engr.

1976, June 1 *Perf. 13*

No.	Type	Description	Unused	Used
691	A346	10c multicolored	.35	.25

American Bicentennial; Benjamin Franklin (1706-1790), deputy postmaster general for the colonies (1753-1774).

See US No. 1690.

Royal Military College, Kingston, Ont., Cent. — A347

No. 692, Color Parade, Memorial Arch. No. 693, Wing Parade, Mackenzie Building.

1976, June 1 Litho. *Perf. 12*

No.	Type	Description	Unused	Used
692		8c red & multi	.25	.25
693		8c red & multi	.25	.25
a.	A347	Pair, #692-693	.50	.50
b.		As "a," imperf.	*2,000.*	
c.		Block of 4, imperf. horiz.	*650.00*	
d.		As "a," double impression	*3,500.*	

A few used singles exist of Nos. 692-693 with double impression. Very rare.

Archer in Wheelchair A349

1976, Aug. 3 *Perf. 12x12½*

No.	Type	Description	Unused	Used
694	A349	20c green & multi	.60	.50

Olympiad for the Physically Disabled (25th Stoke Mandeville Games), Toronto, Aug. 3-11.

A350

No. 695, The Cremation of Sam McGee. No. 696, The Outlander.

1976, Aug. 17 *Perf. 13½*

No.	Type	Description	Unused	Used
695		8c multicolored	.25	.25
696		8c multicolored	.25	.25
a.	A350	Pair, #695-696	.50	.50

Robert W. Service (1874-1958), author of poem "The Cremation of Sam McGee"; Germaine Guevremont, author of "Le Survenant" (The Outlander).

Nativity, St. Michael's, Toronto — A352

Stained-glass windows: 10c, Nativity, St. Jude, London, Ontario. 20c, Nativity, by Yvonne Williams.

1976, Nov. 3 *Perf. 13½*

No.	Type	Description	Unused	Used
697	A352	8c multicolored	.25	.25
698	A352	10c multicolored	.25	.25
699	A352	20c multicolored	.40	.40
		Nos. 697-699 (3)	.90	.90

Christmas.

Inland Vessels A353

Litho. & Engr.

1976, Nov. 19 *Perf. 12*

No.	Type	Description	Unused	Used
700	A353	10c Northcote	.35	.30
701	A353	10c Passport	.35	.30
a.		Double impression of purple	275.00	
702	A353	10c Chicora	.35	.30
a.		Double impression of blue	275.00	
703	A353	10c Athabasca	.35	.30
a.		Block of 4, #700-703	1.40	1.25

Elizabeth II A354

Litho. and Typo.

1977, Feb. 4 *Perf. 12½x12*

No.	Type	Description	Unused	Used
704	A354	25c silver & multi	.70	.50
a.		Silver omitted	*1,100.*	

25th anniv. of the reign of Elizabeth II.

Authentication strongly recommended for No. 704a. Fakes exist.

Bottle Gentian A355

Elizabeth II A356

Parliament, Ottawa A357

Trembling Aspen A358

Main Street, Prairie Town — A359

Fundy National Park — A359a

Designs: 2c, Western columbine. 3c, Canada lily. 4c, Hepatica. 5c, Shooting star. 10c, Franklin's lady's-slipper. No. 712, Jewelweed. No. 715, Parliament, Ottawa. No. 716, Queen Elizabeth II. 20c, Douglas fir. 25c, Maple. 30c, Red oak. 35c, White pine. 60c, Street scene, Ontario City. 75c, Old houses, eastern City Street. 80c, Street leading to the sea, Eastern Maritime Provinces. $2 Kluane National Park.

Litho. & Engr.

1977-82 *Perf. 12x12½*

No.	Type	Description	Unused	Used
705	A355	1c multicolored	.25	.25
a.		Printed on gummed side, precanceled	1,100.	
707	A355	2c multicolored	.25	.25
a.		Printed on gummed side	950.00	
708	A355	3c multicolored	.25	.25
709	A355	4c multicolored	.25	.25
a.		Printed on gummed side	300.00	
710	A355	5c multicolored	.25	.25
711	A355	10c multicolored	.25	.25
a.		Perf. 13x13½ ('78)	.25	.25

Photo. & Engr.

Perf. 13x13½

No.	Type	Description	Unused	Used
712	A355	12c multi ('78)	.30	.25
713	A356	12c blue & multi	.25	.25
a.		Perf. 12x12½	.30	.25

Engraved

Perf. 13x13½

No.	Type	Description	Unused	Used
714	A357	12c blue	.25	.25
a.		Printed on gummed side	300.00	
715	A357	14c red ('78)	.25	.25
a.		Printed on gummed side	37.50	
b.		All color omitted	400.00	

Photo. & Engr.

Perf. 13x13½

No.	Type	Description	Unused	Used
716	A356	14c red & blk ('78)	.25	.25
a.		Perf. 12x12½	.25	.25
b.		As "a," booklet pane of 25 + 2 labels ('78)	5.50	6.00
c.		Red omitted	*1,150.*	

Perf. 13½

No.	Type	Description	Unused	Used
717	A358	15c multi	.45	.25
718	A358	20c multi	.35	.25
a.		Black (denomination) omitted	*750.00*	
719	A358	25c multi	.50	.25
720	A358	30c multi ('78)	.60	.25
721	A358	35c multi ('79)	.60	.25
723	A359	50c multi ('78)	1.10	.25
723A	A359	50c multi, litho. & engr. ('78)	.90	.25
b.		Dark brown (engr., all inscriptions, etc.) omitted	*2,000.*	
c.		Magenta (litho.) and dark brown (engr.) missing (from foldover)	*15,000.*	
723C	A359	60c multi, litho. ('82)	1.25	.25
724	A359	75c multi ('78)	1.30	.30
725	A359	80c multi ('78)	1.50	.35

Lithographed and Engraved

No.	Type	Description	Unused	Used
726	A359a	$1 multi ('79)	1.50	.55
a.		Untagged	2.50	.70
b.		As "a," blk inscriptions omitted	550.00	550.00

727 A359a $2 multi ('79) 3.60 1.40
a. Silver inscriptions omitted 325.00
b. Double impression of silver inscriptions *750.00*
Nos. 705-727 (23) 16.45 7.35

On No. 715b, a strong embossed impression from the plate, without color, is evident.

On No. 723A license plate on yellow car reads "1978."

No. 723Ac is unique.

Certificate of authenticity recommended for No. 727b. "Kiss prints" also exist that are not true double impressions.

See Nos. 781-806, 934-937, 1084.

Coil Stamps

1977-78 Engr. *Perf. 10 Vert.*
729 A357 12c blue .25 .25
a. Imperf., pair 150.00
730 A357 14c red ('78) .30 .25
a. Imperf., pair 170.00

See note below No. 468B.

Eastern Cougar A360

1977, Mar. 30 Litho. *Perf. 12½*
732 A360 12c multicolored .25 .25

Wildlife protection.

April in Algonquin Park, by Thomson — A361

No. 734, Autumn Birches, by Tom Thomson.

1977, May 26 *Perf. 12*
733 A361 12c black & multi .25 .25
734 A361 12c ocher & multi .25 .25
a. Pair, #733-734 .50 .50

Tom Thomson (1877-1917), landscape painter, birth centenary. Nos. 733-734 printed checkerwise.

Names of Governors General and Standard A362

1977, June 30 *Perf. 12½*
735 A362 12c vio blue & multi .25 .25

Honoring Canadian-born Governors General: Vincent Massey, Georges Philias Vanier, Daniel Roland Michener and Jules Léger.

Order of Canada A363

Litho. & Embossed

1977, June 30
736 A363 12c multicolored .25 .25

Order of Canada, 10th anniversary.

Peace Bridge, Canadian, US and UN Flags A364

1977, Aug. 4 Litho.
737 A364 12c blue & multi .25 .25

50th anniversary of the Peace Bridge, connecting Fort Erie, Ontario, with Buffalo, N.Y.

Joseph E. Bernier, CGS Arctic A365

Sandford Fleming, Railroad Bridge A366

1977, Sept. 16 Engr. *Perf. 13*
738 A365 12c dark blue .25 .25
739 A366 12c brown .25 .25
a. Pair, #738-739 .50 .50

Joseph-Elzéar Bernier (1852-1934), explorer; Sandford Fleming (1827-1915), mapped route for Intercolonial Railway and designed Canada's first stamp.

Nos. 738-739 printed checkerwise.

Peace Tower, Parliament, Ottawa A367

1977, Sept. 19 Litho. *Perf. 12½*
740 A367 25c multicolored .75 .65

23rd Commonwealth Parliamentary Conference, Ottawa, Sept. 19-25.

Hunters Following Star — A368

Christmas: 12c, Angelic choir in northern light. 25c, Christ Child in Ring of Glory blessing chiefs from afar. Illustrations for Canada's first Christmas carol, written by Father Brébeuf, 1649.

1977, Oct. 26 *Perf. 13½*
741 A368 10c multicolored .25 .25
a. Horiz. pair, imperf between *1,050.*
b. Printed on gummed side 650.00
c. Imperf., pair *1,150.*
742 A368 12c multicolored .25 .25
a. Left margin block of 4, left vert. pair imperf, right pair part perf *1,900.*
b. Double impression of purple, blue, green; quadruple impression of black (inscriptions) 650.00
743 A368 25c multicolored .45 .35
Nos. 741-743 (3) .95 .85

Pinky A369

Designs: Canadian sailing ships.

Litho. and Engr.

1977, Nov. 18 *Perf. 12x12½*
744 A369 12c shown .25 .25
745 A369 12c Tern schooner .25 .25
746 A369 12c 5-masted schooner .25 .25
747 A369 12c Mackinaw boat .25 .25
a. Block of 4, #744-747 1.00 1.00
b. As "a," #745, 747 imperf; #744, 746 part perf *3,500.*

See Nos. 776-779.

Seal Hunter, Soapstone Sculpture A370

Disguised Caribou Hunter, Print — A371

Inuit Art: No. 749, Spear fishing. No. 751, Walrus hunt. Nos. 749-751 are after stonecut prints.

1977, Nov. 18 Litho.
748 A370 12c multicolored .25 .25
749 A371 12c multicolored .25 .25
a. Pair, #748-749 .50 .50
b. As "a," gray (inscriptions) omitted on No. 749 *2,250.*
750 A371 12c multicolored .25 .25
751 A371 12c multicolored .25 .25
a. Pair, #750-751 .50 .50
Nos. 748-751 (4) 1.00 1.00

Inuit hunting. Nos. 748-749 and Nos. 750-751 printed se-tenant checkerwise.

Peregrine Falcon A372

1978, Jan. 18
752 A372 12c multicolored .25 .25

Endangered wildlife.

Canada No. 3, 1851 — A373

1978 Photo. & Engr. *Perf. 13½*
753 A373 12c shown .25 .25
754 A373 14c No. 7 .25 .25
755 A373 30c No. 8 .55 .30
756 A373 $1.25 No. 2 2.00 1.00
a. Souvenir sheet of 3 3.25 3.25
Nos. 753-756 (4) 3.05 1.80

CAPEX '78, Canadian Intl. Phil. Exhib., Toronto, June 9-18 (cent. of Canada's admission to UPU).

No. 756a contains one each of Nos. 754-756 ($1.25 untagged). Value of No. 756 untagged, $2.75.

Issue dates: 12c, Jan. 18; others, June 10.

Games' Emblem A374

Design: 30c, Badminton.

1978, Mar. 31 Litho. *Perf. 12½*
757 A374 14c silver & multi .25 .25
758 A374 30c silver & multi .55 .45

Stadium A375

No. 760, Running. No. 761, Alberta Legislature building, Edmonton. No. 762, Lawn bowling.

1978, Aug. 3
759 A375 14c silver & multi .30 .25
760 A375 14c silver & multi .30 .25
a. Pair, #759-760 .60 .50
761 A375 30c silver & multi .55 .50
762 A375 30c silver & multi .55 .50
a. Pair, #761-762 1.10 1.00
Nos. 759-762 (4) 1.70 1.50

Nos. 757-762 commemorate 11th Commonwealth Games, Edmonton, Aug. 3-12.

Nos. 760a, 762a printed checkerwise.

A376

No. 763, Capt. Cook, by Nathaniel Dance. No. 764, Nootka Sound, by John Webber.

1978, Apr. 26 *Perf. 13*
763 14c multicolored .25 .25
764 14c multicolored .25 .25
a. A376 Pair, #763-764 .60 .50

Capt. James Cook (1728-1779), explorer of Canada's East and West Coasts and bicentenary of his anchorage near Anchorage, June 1, 1778. Nos. 763-764 printed checkerwise.

Silver Mine, Cobalt Lake A378

Stripmining, Athabasca Tar Sands A379

1978, May 19 *Perf. 12½*
765 A378 14c multicolored .25 .25
766 A379 14c multicolored .25 .25
a. Pair, #765-766 .50 .50
b. As "a," No. 766 with double impression of brown (inscriptions) 600.00

Development of national resources. Nos. 765-766 printed checkerwise.

Prince's Gate A380

1978, Aug. 16
767 A380 14c multicolored .25 .25

Canadian National Exhibition, centenary.

Mère d'Youville and Miracle of Food — A381

1978, Sept. 21 *Perf. 13x13½*
768 A381 14c multicolored .25 .25

Marguerite d'Youville (1701-1771), founder of the Gray Nuns, beatified 1959.

Woman Walking, by Pitseolak A382

Migration, Soapstone by Joe Talurinili A383

Works by Eskimo Artists: No. 771, Plane over village, stonecut and stencil print by Pudlo. No. 772, Dogteam and sled, ivory sculpture by Abraham Kingmeatook.

1978, Sept. 27 *Perf. 13½*

769	A382	14c multicolored	.25	.25
770	A383	14c multicolored	.25	.25
a.		Pair, #769-770	.50	.50
771	A382	14c multicolored	.25	.25
772	A383	14c multicolored	.25	.25
a.		Pair, #771-772	.50	.50
		Nos. 769-772 (4)	1.00	1.00

Travels of the Inuit. Printed checkerwise.

Madonna of the Flowering Pea, Cologne School — A384

Renaissance Paintings in National Gallery of Canada: 14c, Virgin and Child, by Hans Memling. 30c, Virgin and Child, by Jacopo Di Cione.

1978, Oct. 20 *Perf. 12½*

773	A384	12c multicolored	.25	.25
774	A384	14c multicolored	.25	.25
a.		Black omitted	1,000.	
775	A384	30c multicolored	.55	.25
		Nos. 773-775 (3)	1.05	.75

Christmas.

Sailing Ships Type of 1977

No. 776, "Chief Justice Robinson," 1842. No. 777, "St. Roch," 1928. No. 778, "Northern Light," 1928. No. 779, "Labrador," 1954.

Litho. & Engr.

1978, Nov. 15 *Perf. 13*

776	A369	14c multicolored	.30	.25
777	A369	14c multicolored	.30	.25
778	A369	14c multicolored	.30	.25
779	A369	14c multicolored	.30	.25
a.		Block of 4, #776-779	1.25	1.10

Ice vessels.

Quebec Carnival — A386

1979, Feb. 1 **Litho.** *Perf. 13½*

780	A386	14c multicolored	.25	.25

Flower, Queen & Parliament Types

1c, Bottle gentian. 2c, Western columbine. 3c, Canada lily. 4c, Hepatica. 5c, Shooting star. 10c, Franklin's lady's-slipper. 15c, Canada violet. No. 789, Elizabeth II. No. 790, Parliament, Ottawa.

Photo. & Engr., Engr. (#790)

1977-83 *Perf. 13x13½*

781	A355	1c multi ('79)	.25	.25
a.		Perf. 12x12½ ('77)	.25	.25
b.		Bklt. pane, 2 #781a, 4 #713a	1.00	1.00
782	A355	2c multi ('79)	.25	.25
a.		Bklt. pane, 4 #782b, 3 #716a + label	1.00	1.00
b.		Perf. 12x12½ ('78)	.25	.25
783	A355	3c multi ('79)	.25	.25
784	A355	4c multi ('79)	.25	.25
785	A355	5c multi ('79)	.25	.25
786	A355	10c multi ('79)	.25	.25
787	A355	15c multi ('79)	.30	.25
789	A356	17c green & blk ('79)	.30	.25
a.		Perf. 12x12½	.35	.25
b.		Bklt. pane of 25 #789a + 2 labels	6.50	*7.50*
c.		Horiz. pair, imperf. btwn. and at left and bottom	*1,800.*	
d.		Black inscriptions omitted	*950.00*	
790	A357	17c slate green ('79)	.25	.25
a.		Printed on gummed side	37.50	
791	A356	30c multi ('82)	.45	.25
a.		Black (engr.) omitted	*2,250.*	
792	A356	32c multi ('83)	.50	.25
		Nos. 781-792 (11)	3.30	2.75

Nos. 781a, 782b, 789a are from booklet panes. No. 782b has one straight edge, others one or two.

Beware of examples purported to be No. 791a that actually have tiny amounts of black present. Only two examples have been confirmed with 100% omission. Certification strongly recommended.

No. 789d also shows the horiz. perfs. shifted.

Parliament Type of 1977
Booklet Stamps

1979, Mar. 28 **Engr.** *Perf. 12x12½*

797	A357	1c slate blue	.40	.25
a.		Bklt. pane, 1 #797, 3 #800, 2 #789a	1.40	
800	A357	5c violet brown	.30	.25

No. 797 has one straight edge, No. 800 has one or two.

Coil Stamps

1979, Mar. 8 *Perf. 10 Vert.*

806	A357	17c slate green	.25	.25
a.		Imperf., pair	150.00	

Endangered Wildlife A392

1979, Apr. 10 **Litho.** *Perf. 12½*

813	A392	17c Soft-shelled turtle	.30	.25
814	A392	35c Bowhead whale	.75	.40

Ribbon Around Woman's Finger — A393

No. 816, String around man's finger.

1979, Apr. 10

815	A393	17c multicolored	.25	.25
816	A393	17c multicolored	.25	.25
a.		Pair, #815-816	.50	.50
b.		As "a," double impression of black	110.00	
c.		As "a," triple impression of black	225.00	
d.		As "a," double impression of red	110.00	

Use postal code. Printed checkerwise.

Fruits of the Earth, by F. P. Grove A394

The Golden Vessel, by Emile Nelligan A395

1979, May 3 *Perf. 13x13½*

817	A394	17c multicolored	.25	.25
a.		Double impression of brown	375.00	
818	A395	17c multicolored	.25	.25
a.		Double impression of blue	375.00	
b.		Pair, #817-818	.50	.55
c.		As "b," left margin block of 4, left vert. pair imperf, right pair part perf	*2,000.*	*2,000.*

Frederick Philip Grove (1879-1948), teacher and writer; Emile Nelligan (1879-1941), French-Canadian poet. Nos. 817-818 printed checkerwise.

Warning: horizontal pairs exist of No. 818a that appear to be imperforate. These actually are pairs made from No. 818c with normal perforations trimmed off the right edge.

A396

1979, May 11 *Perf. 13½*

819		17c De Salaberry	.25	.25
820		17c John By	.25	.25
a.	A396	Pair, #819-820	.50	.50

Charles-Michel d'Irumberry de Salaberry (1778-1829), and John By (1779-1836), Canadian colonels. Printed checkerwise.

Flag of Ontario A398

Designs: Provincial and Territorial flags.

1979, June 15 *Perf. 13½*

821	A398	17c shown	.30	.25
822	A398	17c Quebec	.30	.25
823	A398	17c Nova Scotia	.30	.25
824	A398	17c New Brunswick	.30	.25
825	A398	17c Manitoba	.30	.25
826	A398	17c British Columbia	.30	.25
827	A398	17c Prince Edward Island	.30	.25
828	A398	17c Saskatchewan	.30	.25
829	A398	17c Alberta	.30	.25
830	A398	17c Newfoundland	.30	.25
831	A398	17c Northwest Territories	.30	.25
832	A398	17c Yukon Territory	.30	.25
a.		Pane of 12, #821-832	4.00	3.75

White Water Kayak Race A399

1979, July 3 *Perf. 12½*

833	A399	17c multicolored	.30	.25

Canoe-Kayak (Slalom and Wild Water) World Championships, Jonquière and Desbiens, Quebec, June 30-July 8.

Women's Field Hockey A400

1979, Aug. 16

834	A400	17c multicolored	.30	.25

Women's Field Hockey Championship, Vancouver, B.C., Aug. 16-30.

Summer Tent, Print by Kiakshuk A401

Eskimos Building Igloo, by Abraham of Povungnituk A402

Works by Eskimo Artists: No. 837, The Dance, print by Kalvak of Holman Island. No. 838, Two soapstone figures from Repulse Bay, by Madeleine Isserkut and Jean Mapsalak.

1979, Sept. 13 *Perf. 13½*

835	A401	17c multicolored	.25	.25
836	A402	17c multicolored	.25	.25
a.		Pair, #835-836	.50	.50
837	A401	17c multicolored	.25	.25
838	A402	17c multicolored	.25	.25
a.		Pair, #837-838	.50	.50
		Nos. 835-838 (4)	1.00	1.00

Inuit shelters and community. Printed checkerwise.

Painted Wooden Train A403

Antique Toys: 17c, Horse, pull toy. 35c, Knitted doll, vert.

1979, Oct. 17 *Perf. 13*

839	A403	15c multicolored	.25	.25
840	A403	17c multicolored	.30	.25
841	A403	35c multicolored	.60	.30
a.		Gold (and tagging) omitted	*1,100.*	*700.00*
		Nos. 839-841 (3)	1.15	.80

Christmas.

Girl Watering Tree of Life — A404

1979, Oct. 24

842	A404	17c multicolored	.25	.25

International Year of the Child.

Curtiss HS-2L A405

1979, Nov. 15 *Perf. 12½*

843	A405	17c shown	.30	.25
844	A405	17c Canadair CL-215	.30	.25
a.		Pair, #843-844	.65	.55
845	A405	35c Vickers Vedette	.65	.50
846	A405	35c Consolidated Canso	.65	.50
a.		Pair, #845-846	1.30	1.25
		Nos. 843-846 (4)	1.90	1.50

Map of Canada Showing Arctic Islands A406

1980, Jan. 23 *Perf. 13½*

847	A406	17c multicolored	.25	.25

Acquisition of the Arctic Islands, centenary.

Downhill Skiing A407

1980, Jan. 23

848	A407	35c multicolored	.65	.45

13th Winter Olympic Games, Lake Placid, NY, Feb. 12-24.

Meeting of the School Trustees, by Robert Harris
A408

Royal Canadian Academy of Arts Centenary: No. 850, Inspiration, bronze sculpture, by Louis-Philippe Hebert (1850-1917). No. 851, Parliament Buildings, by Thomas Fuller (1822-1919). No. 852, Sunrise on the Saguenay, by Lucius O'Brien (1832-99).

1980, Mar. 6

849	A408 17c multicolored	.30	.25
850	A408 17c multicolored	.30	.25
a.	Pair, #849-850	.60	.55
851	A408 35c multicolored	.65	.50
852	A408 35c multicolored	.65	.50
a.	Pair, #851-852	1.30	1.25
	Nos. 849-852 (4)	1.90	1.50

Printed checkerwise.

Atlantic Whitefish
A409

Endangered wildlife. No. 854, Greater prairie chicken.

1980, May 6 *Perf. 12½*

853	A409 17c multicolored	.35	.25
854	A409 17c multicolored	.35	.25

Garden — A410

1980, May 29 *Perf. 13½*

855	A410 17c multicolored	.25	.25

Intl. Flower Show, Montreal, May 17-Sept. 1.

Helping Hands — A411

Litho. & Embossed

1980, May 29 *Perf. 12½*

856	A411 17c ultra & gold	.25	.25

14th World Congress of Rehabilitation International, Winnipeg, June 22-27.

"O Canada" Opening Bars
A412

Composers Lavallee, Routhier, Weir
A413

1980, June 6 **Litho.**

857	A412 17c multicolored	.25	.25
858	A413 17c multicolored	.25	.25
a.	Pair, #857-858	.50	.50

"O Canada" centenary. Printed checkerwise in sheets of 16.

John George Diefenbaker (1895-1979), Prime Minister, 1956-63 — A414

1980, June 20 **Engr.** *Perf. 13½*

859	A414 17c dark blue	.25	.25

Emma Albani (1847-1930), Soprano — A415

No. 861, Healey Willan (1880-1968), organist, composer. Printed checkerwise.

1980, July 4 **Litho.**

860	A415 17c multicolored	.25	.25
861	A415 17c multicolored	.25	.25
a.	Pair, #860-861	.50	.50

Ned Hanlan (1855-1908), Oarsman
A416

1980, July 4

862	A416 17c multicolored	.25	.25

Wheat Fields, Saskatchewan
A417

No. 864, Strip mining and town, Alberta.

1980, Aug. 27

863	A417 17c multicolored	.25	.25
864	A417 17c multicolored	.25	.25

75th anniversary of Saskatchewan's and Alberta's creation as Provinces.

Uraninite Molecular Structure
A418

1980, Sept. 3

865	A418 35c multicolored	.65	.50
a.	Printed on gummed side	900.00	

Discovery of uranium in Canada, 80th anniversary.

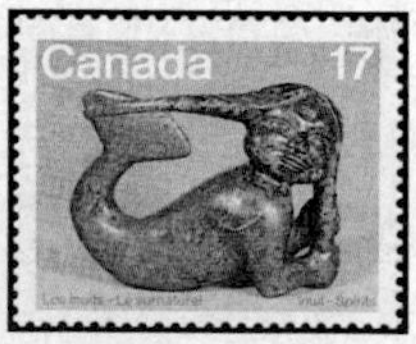

Sedna, by Ashoona Kiawak
A419

Return of the Sun, Print by Kenojouak
A420

Works by Eskimo Artists: No. 868, Bird Spirit, by Doris Hagiolok. No. 869, Shaman, print by Simon Tookoome.

1980, Sept. 25

866	A419 17c multicolored	.25	.25
867	A420 17c multicolored	.25	.25
a.	Pair, #866-867	.50	.50
868	A419 35c multicolored	.55	.55
869	A420 35c multicolored	.55	.55
a.	Pair, #868-869	1.10	1.10
b.	As No. 869, double impression of gray	675.00	
	Nos. 866-869 (4)	1.60	1.60

Inuit spirits. Printed checkerwise.

Christmas Morning, by Frank Charles Hennessey — A421

Christmas (Greeting Cards, 1931): 17c, Sleigh Ride, by Joseph Sydney Hallam. 35c, McGill Cab Stand, by Kathleen Morris.

1980, Oct. 22 *Perf. 12½x12*

870	A421 15c multicolored	.25	.25
871	A421 17c multicolored	.25	.25
872	A421 35c multicolored	.55	.45
	Nos. 870-872 (3)	1.05	.95

Avro Canada CF-100, 1950
A422

Military Aircraft: No. 874, Avro Lancaster, 1941. No. 875, Curtiss JN-4 Canuck. No. 876, Hawker Hurricane, 1935.

1980, Nov. 10 *Perf. 13x13½*

873	A422 17c multicolored	.30	.25
874	A422 17c multicolored	.30	.25
a.	Pair, #873-874	.60	.55
875	A422 35c multicolored	.65	.55
876	A422 35c multicolored	.65	.55
a.	Pair, #875-876	1.30	1.25
	Nos. 873-876 (4)	1.90	1.60

Printed checkerwise.

Emmanuel-Persillier Lachapelle, Caduceus — A423

1980, Dec. 5 *Perf. 13½*

877	A423 17c multicolored	.25	.25

Lachapelle (1845-1918), physician, founded Notre Dame Hospital, Montreal, 1880.

Mandora, 18th Century
A424

1981, Jan. 19 *Perf. 12½*

878	A424 17c multicolored	.25	.25

"The Look of Music" rare musical instrument exhibition, Vancouver, Nov. 2, 1980-Apr. 5, 1981.

No. 878 exists printed on gummed side with gold color and tagging omitted, from printer's waste.

Emily Stowe (1831-1903) and Toronto General Hospital — A425

Designs: No. 880, Louise McKinney, (1868-1931) Alberta legislative building. No. 881, Idola Saint-Jean, (1875-1945) Quebec legislative building. No. 882, Henrietta Edwards, (1849-1931) clubwomen.

1981, Mar. 4 *Perf. 13x13½*

879	A425 17c multicolored	.35	.25
880	A425 17c multicolored	.35	.25
881	A425 17c multicolored	.35	.25
882	A425 17c multicolored	.35	.25
a.	Block of 4, #879-882	1.40	1.25

Vancouver Island Marmot, by Michael Dumas
A426

Endangered Wildlife: 35c, Wood bison, by Robert Bateman.

1981, Apr. 6

883	A426 17c multicolored	.30	.25
884	A426 35c multicolored	.70	.60

Kateri Tekakwitha ("Lily of the Mohawks"), by Emile Brunet — A427

Brunet Sculpture: No. 886, Marie de L'Incarnation.

1981, Apr. 24 *Perf. 12½*

885	A427 17c brown & pale grn	.25	.25
886	A427 17c lt blue & ultra	.25	.25
a.	Pair, #885-886	.50	.50

Beatification of Kateri Tekakwitha (1656-1680), first North American Indian saint, and Marie De L'Incarnation (1599-1672), founder of Ursuline Order.

At Baie Saint-Paul, by Marc-Aurele Fortin (1888-1970) — A428

Paintings: No. 888, Self-portrait, by Frederick H. Varley (1881-1969). 35c, Untitled No. 6, by Paul-Emile Borduas (1905-60).

1981, May 22

887	A428 17c multi	.25	.25
888	A428 17c multi, vert.	.25	.25
a.	Imperf, pair	1,500.	

Photo.

Perf. 13

889	A428 35c multi, vert.	.60	.60
	Nos. 887-889 (3)	1.10	1.10

Map of Canada Showing Provincial Boundaries, 1867 — A429

1981, June 30 Litho. *Perf. 13½*

890 A429 17c shown .30 .25
891 A429 17c 1873 .30 .25
892 A429 17c 1905 .30 .25
893 A429 17c 1949 .30 .25
a. Strip of 4, #890-893 1.20 1.20

Canada Day.

Frere Marie-Victorin (1885-1944) Botanist — A430

Botanists: No. 895, John Macoun (1831-1920).

1981, July 22 *Perf. 12½*

894 A430 17c multicolored .25 .25
895 A430 17c multicolored .25 .25
a. Pair, #894-895 .50 .50

Montreal Rose — A431

1981, July 22 *Perf. 13½*

896 A431 17c multicolored .25 .25

A432

1981, July 31 Photo. & Engr.

897 A432 17c multicolored .25 .25

Niagara-on-the-Lake (1st capital of Upper Canada).

A433

1981, Aug. 14 Litho.

898 A433 17c multicolored .25 .25

Acadian Congress centenary.

A434

1981, Sept. 8

899 A434 17c multicolored .25 .25

Aaron Mosher (1881-1959), Labor Congress founder.

A435

1981, Nov. 16 Litho.

900 A435 15c 1781 .25 .25
901 A435 15c 1881 .25 .25
902 A435 15c 1981 .25 .25
Nos. 900-902 (3) .75 .75

Christmas; bicentenary of 1st illuminated Christmas tree in Canada.

Canadair CL-41 Tutor A436

No. 904, de Havilland Tiger Moth. No. 905, Avro Canada C-102. No. 906, de Havilland Canada Dash-7.

1981, Nov. 24 *Perf. 12½*

903 A436 17c shown .30 .25
904 A436 17c multicolored .30 .25
a. Pair, #903-904 .60 .55
905 A436 35c multicolored .60 .55
906 A436 35c multicolored .60 .55
a. Pair, #905-906 1.20 1.10
Nos. 903-906 (4) 1.80 1.60

A437

1981, Dec. 29 Engr. *Perf. 13x13½*

907 A437 (30c) red .90 .25
a. Printed on gummed side *750.00*

Coil Stamp

Perf. 10 Vert.

908 A437 (30c) red .75 .25
a. Imperf., pair *375.00 225.00*

See Nos. 923-924, 940, 943-946, 950-951.

CANADA '82 Intl. Philatelic Youth Exhibition, Toronto, May 20-24 — A438

1982 Litho. *Perf. 13½*

909 A438 30c No. 1 .50 .25
910 A438 30c No. 102 .50 .25
911 A438 35c No. 223 .60 .50
912 A438 35c No. 155 .60 .50
913 A438 60c No. 158 1.20 .75
a. Souvenir sheet of 5, #909-913 3.75 3.75
b. As No. 913, triple impression of reddish brown *1,400.*
Nos. 909-913 (5) 3.40 2.25

Issued: Nos. 909, 911, 3/11; others, 5/20.

Jules Leger (1913-1980), 26th Governor General — A439

1982, Apr. 2

914 A439 30c multicolored .45 .25

Terry Fox (1958-1981), Marathon of Hope — A440

1982, Apr. 13 *Perf. 12½*

915 A440 30c multicolored .45 .25

1982 Constitution — A441

1982, Apr. 16 *Perf. 12x12½*

916 A441 30c multicolored .45 .25

Types of 1979-81 and

18th-19th Cent. Artifacts A442

Parliament (Library) A443

Parliament (West Block) — A444

Parliament (East Block) — A445

Elizabeth II — A446

Designs: 1c, Duck decoy. 2c, Fishing spear. 3c, Stable lantern. 5c, Bucket. 10c, Weathercock. 20c, Ice skates. 37c, Wooden plow. 39c, Settle-bed. 48c, Cradle. 50c, Sleigh. 64c, Wood stove. 68c, Spinning wheel. $1, Glacier National Park. $1.50, Waterton Lakes National Park. $2, Moraine Lake, Banff National Park. $5, Point Pelee National Park.

1982-87 Litho. *Perf. 14x13½*

917 A442 1c multicolored .25 .25
a. Perf. 13x13½ ('85) .25 .25
918 A442 2c multicolored .25 .25
a. Perf. 13x13½ ('84) .25 .25
b. Bottom margin block of 4, bottom pair imperf, top pair part perf *2,100.*
c. As "a," printed on gummed side 60.00
919 A442 3c multicolored .25 .25
a. Perf. 13x13½ ('85) .25 .25
920 A442 5c multicolored .25 .25
a. Perf. 13x13½ ('84) .25 .25
921 A442 10c multicolored .25 .25
a. Perf. 13x13½ ('85) .25 .25
922 A442 20c multicolored .30 .25

The previously listed No. 922 variety with "brown omitted" has been determined to be a normal No. 922 with a color shade or a color changeling.

Photo. & Engr.

Perf. 13x13½

923 A437 30c lt blue, bl, & red .50 .25
a. Bklt. pane of 20, perf. 12x12½ 10.00
b. Perf. 12x12½ 1.40 .45
924 A437 32c beige, red & brn .50 .25
a. Bklt. pane of 25, perf. 12x12½ 12.50 *13.50*
b. Perf. 12x12½ 1.00 .70
c. As #924, beige (and tagging) omitted 1,000.

Litho.

Perf. 13½x13

925 A443 34c multicolored .55 .25
a. Booklet pane of 25 13.75
b. Perf. 13½x14 ('86) .75 .25
c. Bklt. pane of 25, perf. 13½x14 14.00 *16.50*

Photo. & Engr.

Perf. 13x13½

926 A446 34c lt bl & int bl .55 .25
926A A446 36c plum 3.00 2.25

Perf. 13½x13

926B A443 36c multicolored .55 .25
c. Booklet pane of 10 #926Be 5.50
d. Booklet pane of 25 #926Be 17.50
e. Perf. 13½x14 ('87) .70 .25
f. Left margin block of 4, left vert. pair imperf, right pair part perf *1,500.*
g. Imperf., horiz. pair 600.00
h. All color missing *1,500.*

No. 926Bh was caused by an extraneous piece of paper overlaying the pane during printing. Two such panes are recorded, one with two color-missing stamps and the other with 16 color-missing stamps. All adjoining stamps have some to most color missing, and if the panes are broken, the color-missing variety must be left se-tenant with a partially printed stamp.

Litho. *Perf. 12x12½*

Size A442: 26x20mm

927 A442 37c multi .55 .25
928 A442 39c multi .60 .25
929 A442 48c multi .75 .30
930 A442 50c multi .75 .25
932 A442 64c multi .95 .35
933 A442 68c multi 1.10 .36

Litho. & Engr.

Perf. 13½

934 A359a $1 multi 1.50 .60
a. Blue inscriptions omitted *900.00*
b. Imperf., pair *3,000.*
935 A359a $1.50 multi 3.25 .55
a. Black omitted *2,250.*
936 A359a $2 multi 3.25 1.10
a. Bluish green inscriptions omitted *1,100.*
937 A359a $5 multi 9.00 2.00
Nos. 917-937 (22) 28.90 10.90

Issued: 1c-20c, 10/19; 30c, 5/11; $1.50, 6/18; $5, 1/10/83; 32c, 2/10/83; 37c, 48c, 64c, 4/8/83; $1, 8/15/84; No. 925, $2, 6/21/85; No. 926, 7/12/85; 39c, 50c, 68c, 8/1/85; No. 926B, 3/30/87; No. 926A, 10/1/87.

For former No. 931, see new No. 723C.

Booklet Stamps

Perf. 12x12½ (A437), 12½x12

Engr.

938 A445 1c sage green ('87) .25 .25
939 A444 2c myrtle grn ('85) .25 .25
a. 2c slate green ('89) .25 .25
940 A437 5c deep claret .25 .25
941 A445 5c dp brown ('85) .25 .25
942 A444 6c henna brn ('87) .25 .25
943 A437 8c dk blue ('83) .50 .25
944 A437 10c dark green .45 .25
945 A437 30c red .75 .30
a. Bklt. pane of 4 + 2 labels (2 #940, 944, 945) 1.20 *1.40*
946 A437 32c brown ('83) .60 .25
b. Bklt. pane of 4 + 2 labels (2 #940, 943, 946) 1.10 *1.30*
947 A443 34c dp slate bl ('85) 1.15 .70
a. Bklt. pane of 6 (3 #939, 2 #941, #947) 1.70 *1.25*
948 A443 36c dark lil rose ('87) 1.35 .70
a. Bklt. pane of 5 + label (2 #938, 2 #942, #948) 2.25 *1.40*

Issued: No. 940, 10c, 30c, 3/1; 8c, 32c, 2/15/83; No. 941, 30c, 6/21/85; 1c, 6c, 36c, 3/30/87.

Coil Stamps

Engr. *Perf. 10 Vert.*

950 A437 30c red .90 .25
a. Imperf., pair 325.00
951 A437 32c brown ('83) .75 .25
a. Imperf., pair 160.00

Perf. 10 Horiz.

952 A443 34c dull red brn ('85) .75 .25
a. Imperf., pair 150.00
953 A443 36c dark red ('87) .75 .25
a. Imperf., pair 275.00

Issued: 30c, 5/11; 32c, 2/10/83; 34c, 8/1/85; 36c, 5/19/87.

See Nos. 1080-1083, 1186-1188, 1194-1194A.

Centenary of Salvation Army in Canada A457

1982, June 25 **Litho.** ***Perf. 13***
954 A457 30c multicolored .50 .25

Canada Day A458

Paintings: No. 955, The Highway near Kluana Lake, by A.Y. Jackson. No. 956, Montreal Street Scene, by Adrien Hebert. No. 957, Breakwater, by Christopher Pratt. No. 958, Along Great Slave Lake, by Rene Richard. No. 959, Tea Hill, by Molly Lamb. No. 960, Family and Rainstorm, by Alex Colville. No. 961, Brown Shadows, by Dorothy Knowles. No. 962, The Red Brick House, by David Milne. No. 963, Campus Gates, by Bruno Bobak. No. 964, Prairie Town—Early Morning, by Illingworth Kerr. No. 965, Totems at Ninstints, by Joe Plaskett. No. 966, Doc Snider's House, by Lionel LeMoine FitzGerald.

1982, June 30 ***Perf. 12½x12***
955 A458 30c multicolored .65 .65
956 A458 30c multicolored .65 .65
957 A458 30c multicolored .65 .65
958 A458 30c multicolored .65 .65
959 A458 30c multicolored .65 .65
960 A458 30c multicolored .65 .65
961 A458 30c multicolored .65 .65
962 A458 30c multicolored .65 .65
963 A458 30c multicolored .65 .65
964 A458 30c multicolored .65 .65
965 A458 30c multicolored .65 .65
966 A458 30c multicolored .65 .65
a. Min. pane of 12, #955-966 8.00 8.00

Regina Centenary A459

1982, Aug. 3 ***Perf. 13½x13***
967 A459 30c multicolored .50 .25

Centenary of Royal Canadian Henley Regatta, St. Catharines, Aug. 4-8 — A460

1982, Aug. 4
968 A460 30c multicolored .50 .25

Fairchild FC-2W1 A461

No. 970, De Havilland Canada Beaver. No. 971, Noorduyn Norseman. No. 972, Fokker Super Universal.

1982, Oct. 5 **Litho.** ***Perf. 12½***
969 A461 30c shown .75 .25
970 A461 30c multicolored .75 .25
a. Pair, #969-970 1.50 1.10
971 A461 60c multicolored 1.10 .75
972 A461 60c multicolored 1.10 .75
a. Pair, #971-972 2.20 1.75
Nos. 969-972 (4) 3.70 2.00

Christmas A462

Designs: Creche figures.

1982, Nov. 3 ***Perf. 13½***
973 A462 30c Holy Family .45 .25
a. All colors except black omitted *11,000.*
b. Printed on gummed side, black omitted *11,000.*
974 A462 35c Shepherds .55 .45
975 A462 60c Three Kings .90 .75
Nos. 973-975 (3) 1.90 1.45

Nos. 973a and 973b are each unique and were caused by a paper foldover.

World Communications Year — A463

1983, Mar. 10 **Litho.** ***Perf. 12x12½***
976 A463 32c multicolored .50 .25
a. Double impression of central multicolored globe 750.00

Commonwealth Day — A464

1983, Mar. 14
977 A464 $2 multicolored 9.00 3.75

Scene from Angeline de Montbrun, by Laure Conan (1845-1924), Painted by Rene Milot — A465

Design: No. 979, Sea Gulls, by Edwin John Pratt (1882-1966), woodcut by Claire Pratt.

1983, Apr. 22 **Litho.** ***Perf. 13½***
978 A465 32c multicolored .50 .25
979 A465 32c multicolored .50 .25
a. Pair, #978-979 1.00 .90
b. As "a," all color missing *4,000.*

No. 979b resulted from an extraneous piece of paper receiving the colors. After removal, the issued pane shows two horizontal pairs without color plus six other stamps with only partial color.

St. John Ambulance Centenary A466

1983, June 3 ***Perf. 13½***
980 A466 32c Emblem .50 .25

World University Games, Edmonton, July 1-11 — A467

1983, June 28 ***Perf. 13½***
981 A467 32c multicolored .50 .25
a. Printed on gummed side 900.00
982 A467 64c multicolored 1.10 .75

Canada Day — A468

No. 983, Fort Henry, Ontario. No. 984, Fort William, Ontario. No. 985, Fort Rodd Hill, British Columbia. No. 986, Fort Wellington, Ontario. No. 987, Fort Prince of Wales, Manitoba. No. 988, Halifax Citadel, Nova Scotia. No. 989, Fort Chambly, Quebec. No. 990, Fort No. 1, Point Levis, Quebec. No. 991, Fort at Coteau-du-Lac, Quebec. No. 992, Fort Beausejour, New Brunswick. Sizes: Nos. 983, 988: 44x22mm; Nos. 984-985, 989-990, 36x22mm; Nos. 986-987, 991-992, 28x22mm.

Booklet Stamps

1983, June 30 ***Perf. 12½x13***
983 A468 32c multicolored .75 .75
984 A468 32c multicolored .75 .75
985 A468 32c multicolored .75 .75
986 A468 32c multicolored .75 .75
987 A468 32c multicolored .75 .75
988 A468 32c multicolored .75 .75
989 A468 32c multicolored .75 .75
990 A468 32c multicolored .75 .75
991 A468 32c multicolored .75 .75
992 A468 32c multicolored .75 .75
a. Booklet pane of 10, #983-992 7.50 7.50

Scouting Year — A469

1983, July 6 ***Perf. 13½***
993 A469 32c multicolored .55 .25

Church Council Emblem — A470

1983, July 22 **Litho.**
994 A470 32c tan & green .50 .25

6th World Council of Churches Assembly, Vancouver, July 24-Aug. 10.

Humphrey Gilbert — A471

1983, Aug. 3 **Litho.**
995 A471 32c multicolored .50 .25

400th anniv. of discovery of Newfoundland by Sir Humphrey Gilbert (1537-1583).

Centenary of Discovery of Nickel, Sudbury, Ontario A472

Litho. & Typo.

1983, Aug. 12 ***Perf. 13***
996 A472 32c multicolored .60 .25
a. Silver (and tagging) omitted *675.00*

Beware of forgeries of No. 996a. A certificate of authenticity is mandatory.

Josiah Henson (1789-1883), Preacher — A473

1983, Sept. 16 **Litho.** ***Perf. 13x13½***
997 A473 32c multicolored .50 .25

Antoine Labelle (1833-1891), Deputy Minister for Settlement A474

1983, Sept. 16 ***Perf. 13½***
998 A474 32c multicolored .50 .25

Locomotives — A475

No. 999, Toronto 4-4-0, 1853. No. 1000, Dorchester 0-4-0, 1836. No. 1001, Samson 0-6-0, 1838. No. 1002, Adam Brown 4-4-0, 1860.

1983, Oct. 3 ***Perf. 12½x13***
999 A475 32c multicolored .50 .25
1000 A475 32c multicolored .50 .25
a. Pair, #999-1000 1.00 .90
1001 A475 37c multicolored .65 .60
1002 A475 64c multicolored 1.10 .90
Nos. 999-1002 (4) 2.75 2.00

Dalhousie Law School Centenary A476

1983, Oct. 28 ***Perf. 13***
1003 A476 32c Arms .50 .25

Christmas A477

32c, Urban church. 37c, Family going to church. 64c, Rural church.

1983, Nov. 3 ***Perf. 13½***
1004 A477 32c multicolored .50 .25
1005 A477 37c multicolored .55 .45
1006 A477 64c multicolored .95 .75
Nos. 1004-1006 (3) 2.00 1.45

Army Regiments, Centenaries A478

19th Cent. Uniforms: No. 1007, Royal Canadian Regiment, British Columbia Regiment. No. 1008, Royal Winnipeg Rifles, Royal Canadian Dragoons.

1983, Nov. 10 *Perf. 13½x13*

1007 A478 32c shown .50 .25
1008 A478 32c multicolored .50 .25
a. Pair, #1007-1008 1.00 .90

Yellowknife, 50th Anniv. — A479

1984, Mar. 15 *Perf. 13½*

1009 A479 32c Gold mine .50 .25

50th Anniv. of Montreal Symphony Orchestra A480

1984, Mar. 24 *Perf. 12½*

1010 A480 32c multicolored .50 .25

450th Anniv. of Cartier's Landing in Quebec A481

1984, Apr. 20 **Photo. & Engr.**

1011 A481 32c multicolored .50 .25

See France No. 1923.

Voyage of Tall Ships, Saint-Malo, France, to Quebec City — A482

1984, May 18 **Litho.** *Perf. 12x12½*

1012 A482 32c multicolored .50 .25

450th anniv. of Cartier's landing in Quebec.

Canadian Red Cross Society, 75th Anniv. — A483

32c, Meritorious Service Medal.

1984, May 28 *Perf. 13*

1013 A483 32c multicolored .50 .25

New Brunswick, Bicentenary A484

1984, June 18 **Photo. & Engr.**

1014 A484 32c Galleys .50 .25

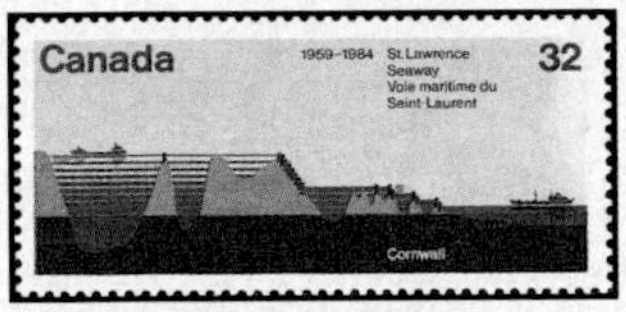

St. Lawrence Seaway, 25th Anniv. — A485

32c, Seaway, Lake Superior.

1984, June 26 **Litho.**

1015 A485 32c multicolored .50 .25

Canada Day A486

Provincial Landscapes by Jean Paul Lemieux (b. 1904): No. 1016, New Brunswick. No. 1017, British Columbia. No. 1018, Yukon Territory. No. 1019, Quebec. No. 1020, Manitoba. No. 1021, Alberta. No. 1022, Prince Edward Island. No. 1023, Saskatchewan. No. 1024, Nova Scotia, vert. No. 1025, Northwest Territories. No. 1026, Newfoundland. No. 1027, Ontario, vert.

1984, June 29

1016 A486 32c multicolored .55 .40
1017 A486 32c multicolored .55 .40
1018 A486 32c multicolored .55 .40
1019 A486 32c multicolored .55 .40
1020 A486 32c multicolored .55 .40
1021 A486 32c multicolored .55 .40
1022 A486 32c multicolored .55 .40
1023 A486 32c multicolored .55 .40
1024 A486 32c multicolored .55 .40
1025 A486 32c multicolored .55 .40
1026 A486 32c multicolored .55 .40
1027 A486 32c multicolored .55 .40
a. Min. pane of 12, #1016-1027 6.75 6.25

Nos. 1018 and 1025 incorrectly inscribed. No. 1018 shows Northwest Territories landscape; No. 1025, Yukon Territory church.

Loyalists, British Flag (1606-1801) — A487

1984, July 3

1028 A487 32c multicolored .50 .25

United Empire Loyalists, American colonists who remained loyal to British throne and emigrated to Canada during American Revolution.

Roman Catholic Church in Newfoundland A488

32c, St. John's Basilica.

1984, Aug. 17 *Perf. 13½*

1029 A488 32c multicolored .50 .25

Papal Visit A489

1984, Aug. 31 *Perf. 12½*

1030 A489 32c multicolored .50 .25
1031 A489 64c multicolored 1.10 .65

Lighthouses — A490

No. 1032, Louisbourg, 1734. No. 1033, Fisgard, 1860. No. 1034, Ile Verte, 1809. No. 1035, Gibraltar Point, 1808.

1984, Sept. 21

1032 A490 32c multicolored .55 .25
1033 A490 32c multicolored .55 .25
1034 A490 32c multicolored .55 .25
1035 A490 32c multicolored .55 .25
a. Block of 4, #1032-1035 2.20 1.20

Steam Locomotives — A491

No. 1036, Scotia. No. 1037, Countess of Dufferin. No. 1038, Grand Trunk Class E3. No. 1039, Canadian Pacific D10a.

1984, Oct. 25 *Perf. 12½x13*

1036 A491 32c multicolored .50 .25
1037 A491 32c multicolored .50 .25
a. Pair, #1036-1037 1.00 .90
1038 A491 37c multicolored .75 .65
1039 A491 64c multicolored 1.30 .90
a. Souvenir sheet 3.00 3.00
Nos. 1036-1039 (4) 3.05 2.05

No. 1039a contains Nos. 1036-1039 in changed colors.

See Nos. 1071-1074, 1118-1121.

Christmas A492

Paintings: 32c, The Annunciation, by Jean Dallaire. 37c, The Three Kings, by Simone Mary Bouchard. 64c, Snow in Bethlehem, by David Milne.

1984, Nov. 2 *Perf. 13*

1040 A492 32c multicolored .50 .25
1041 A492 37c multicolored .55 .55
1042 A492 64c multicolored .95 .75
Nos. 1040-1042 (3) 2.00 1.55

Royal Canadian Air Force — A493

1984, Nov. 9 *Perf. 12x12½*

1043 A493 32c Pilots .50 .25

Cent. of La Presse — A494

32c, Treffle Berthiaume.

1984, Nov. 16 *Perf. 13x13½*

1044 A494 32c multicolored .50 .25

Heart, Arrow, Jeans A495

1985, Feb. 8 *Perf. 12½*

1045 A495 32c multicolored .50 .25

International Youth Year.

Canadians in Space — A496

1985, Mar. 15 *Perf. 13½*

1046 A496 32c Astronaut .55 .25

Therese Casgrain (1896-1981), Suffragist A497

Emily Murphy (1868-1933), Writer A498

1985, Apr. 17

1047 A497 32c multicolored .50 .25
1048 A498 32c multicolored .50 .25
a. Pair, #1047-1048 1.00 .90

Gabriel Dumont (1837-1906), Metis Leader — A499

1985, May 6 *Perf. 13*

1049 A499 32c multicolored .50 .25

Centenary of the Northwest Rebellion.

Canada Day — A500

No. 1050, Lower Ft. Garry, Manitoba. No. 1051, Ft. Anne, Nova Scotia. No. 1052, Ft. York, Ontario. No. 1053, Castle Hill, Newfoundland. No. 1054, Ft. Whoop Up, Alberta. No. 1055, Ft. Erie, Ontario. No. 1056, Ft. Walsh, Saskatchewan. No. 1057, Ft. Lennox,

Quebec. No. 1058, York Redoubt, Nova Scotia. No. 1059, Ft. Frederick, Ontario.

Sizes: Nos. 1050, 1055: 48x26mm. Nos. 1051-1052, 1056-1057: 40x26mm. Nos. 1053-1054, 1058-1059, 32x26mm.

Booklet Stamps

1985, June 28 ***Perf. 12½x13***

1050	A500	34c multicolored	.95	.65
1051	A500	34c multicolored	.95	.65
1052	A500	34c multicolored	.95	.65
1053	A500	34c multicolored	.95	.65
1054	A500	34c multicolored	.95	.65
1055	A500	34c multicolored	.95	.65
1056	A500	34c multicolored	.95	.65
1057	A500	34c multicolored	.95	.65
1058	A500	34c multicolored	.95	.65
1059	A500	34c multicolored	.95	.65
a.		Bklt. pane of 10, #1050-1059	9.50	*12.50*

Intl. Pharmaceutical Federation Congress — A501

Design: Louis Hebert (1575-1627), 1st French Apothecary in North America.

1985, Aug. 30 ***Perf. 12½***

1060	A501	34c multicolored	.50	.25

Interparliamentary Union '85, Ottawa — A502

1985, Sept. 3 ***Perf. 13½***

1061	A502	34c multicolored	.50	.25

Guide, Brownie Saluting — A503

1985, Sept. 12 **Photo.** ***Perf. 13½x13***

1062	A503	34c multicolored	.50	.25

Natl. Girl Guides movement, cent.

Lighthouses A504

1985, Oct. 3 **Litho.** ***Perf. 13½***

1063	A504	34c Sisters Islets	.75	.25
1064	A504	34c Pelee Passage	.75	.25
1065	A504	34c Haut-fond Prince	.75	.25
1066	A504	34c Rose Blanche	.75	.25
a.		Block of 4, #1063-1066	3.00	2.50
b.		Souv. sheet of 4, #1063-1066	4.50	4.50

Santa Claus Parade A505

Paintings by Barbara Carroll: 34c, Santa Claus. 39c, Horse-drawn coach. 68c, Christmas tree. No. 1070, 32c, Polar float.

1985, Oct. 23

1067	A505	34c multicolored	.50	.25
1068	A505	39c multicolored	.60	.55
1069	A505	68c multicolored	1.25	.90

Perf. 13½ on 3 Sides

1070	A505	32c multicolored	1.10	.50
a.		Booklet pane of 10	11.00	10.00
		Nos. 1067-1070 (4)	3.45	2.20

No. 1070 printed in booklets only.

Locomotives Type of 1984

No. 1071, Grand Trunk K2. No. 1072, Canadian Pacific P2a. No. 1073, Canadian Northern O10a. No. 1074, Canadian Govt. Railways H4D.

1985, Nov. 7 ***Perf. 12½x13***

1071	A491	34c multicolored	.75	.25
1072	A491	34c multicolored	.75	.25
a.		Pair, #1071-1072	1.50	1.10
1073	A491	39c multicolored	.60	.70
1074	A491	68c multicolored	1.30	1.00
		Nos. 1071-1074 (4)	3.40	2.20

1910 Gunner's Mate, World War II Officer, 1985 Woman Recruit — A507

1985, Nov. 8 ***Perf. 13½x13***

1075	A507	34c multicolored	.50	.25

Royal Canadian Navy, 75th anniv.

Old Holton House, Sherbrooke Street, Montreal, by James Wilson Morrice (1865-1924) A508

1985, Nov. 15 ***Perf. 13½***

1076	A508	34c multicolored	.50	.25

Montreal Museum of Fine Arts, 120th anniv.

Southwestern Alberta, Computer Design Map — A509

1986, Feb. 13 **Litho.** ***Perf. 12½x13***

1077	A509	34c multicolored	.50	.25

1988 Winter Olympics, Calgary, Alberta, Feb. 13-28.

EXPO '86, Vancouver, May 2-Oct. 13 — A510

1986, Mar. 7 **Photo. & Engr.**

1078	A510	34c Canada Pavilion	.50	.25
1079	A510	39c Communications	.65	.55

Artifacts Type of 1982

Designs: 25c Butter stamp. 42c, Linen chest. 55c, Iron kettle. 72c, Hand-drawn cart.

1987, May 6 **Litho.** ***Perf. 14x13½***

1080	A442	25c multicolored	.55	.30

Size: 20x26mm

Perf. 12x12½

1081	A442	42c multicolored	1.10	.25
1082	A442	55c multicolored	1.40	.30
1083	A442	72c multicolored	1.70	.35
a.		Imperf., pair	900.00	
		Nos. 1080-1083 (4)	4.75	1.20

Park Type of 1979

Design: La Mauricie National Park.

Litho. & Engr.

1986, Mar. 14 ***Perf. 13½***

1084	A359a	$5 multi	9.00	2.00
a.		Dark blue inscriptions omitted	*2,600.*	*1,500.*

No. 1084a is valued in the grade of fine as all known examples are centered thus.

Philippe Aubert de Gaspe (1786-1871), Novelist A511

Molly Brant (1736-1796), Iroquois Leader and Loyalist A512

1986, Apr. 14 **Litho.** ***Perf. 12½***

1090	A511	34c multicolored	.50	.25

Perf. 13½

1091	A512	34c multicolored	.50	.25

EXPO '86 — A513

34c, Expo Center, Vancouver. 68c, Transportation, horiz.

Photo. & Engr.

1986, Apr. 28 ***Perf. 13x13½***

1092	A513	34c multicolored	.50	.25
1093	A513	68c multicolored	1.10	.70

Canadian Forces Postal Service, 75th Anniv. A514

1986, May 9 **Litho.** ***Perf. 13½***

1094	A514	34c multicolored	.50	.25

Indigenous Birds — A515

1986, May 22

1095	A515	34c Great blue heron	.70	.30
1096	A515	34c Snow goose	.70	.30
1097	A515	34c Great horned owl	.70	.30
1098	A515	34c Spruce grouse	.70	.30
a.		Block of 4, #1095-1098	2.80	2.50

19th Intl. Ornithological Congress, Ottawa, June 22-29.

Canada Day — A516

Invention blueprints: No. 1099, Rotary snowplow, 1869. No. 1100, Canadarm, 1986. No. 1101, Anti-gravity flight suit, 1938. No. 1102, Variable pitch propeller, 1923.

1986, June 27

1099	A516	34c multicolored	.75	.25
1100	A516	34c multicolored	.75	.25
1101	A516	34c multicolored	.75	.25
1102	A516	34c multicolored	.75	.25
a.		Block of 4, #1099-1102	3.00	2.50

Canadian Broadcasting Corp., 50th Anniv. — A517

1986, July 23 ***Perf. 12½***

1103	A517	34c Emblem, map	.50	.25

Exploration of Canada A518

No. 1104, Siberian Indians discover and inhabit America, 10,000 B.C. No. 1105, Viking settlement, A.D. 1000. No. 1106, John Cabot lands, 1498. No. 1107, Henry Hudson pioneers Hudson Strait and Bay, 1610.

1986, Aug. 29 ***Perf. 12½x13***

1104	A518	34c multicolored	.55	.30
1105	A518	34c multicolored	.55	.30
1106	A518	34c multicolored	.55	.30
1107	A518	34c multicolored	.55	.30
a.		Block of 4, #1104-1107	2.20	2.00
b.		Souv. sheet of 4, #1104-1107	3.00	2.50

No. 1107b issued Oct. 1 for CAPEX '87.

See Nos. 1126-1129, 1199-1202, 1233-1236.

Peacemakers of the Frontier, 1870s — A519

Designs: No. 1108, Crowfoot (1830-1890), Blackfoot Indian chief. No. 1109, James F. Macleod (1836-1894), asst. commissioner of Northwest Mounted Police.

1986, Sept. 5 ***Perf. 13x13½***

1108	A519	34c scar, gray & ind	.50	.25
1109	A519	34c ind, gray & scar	.50	.25
a.		Pair, #1108-1109	1.00	.90

Intl. Peace Year — A520

Litho. & Embossed

1986, Sept. 16 ***Perf. 13½***

1110	A520	34c multicolored	.50	.25

1988 Calgary Winter Olympics — A521

1986, Oct. 15 *Perf. 13½x13*

1111 A521 34c Ice hockey .50 .25
1112 A521 34c Biathlon .50 .25
a. Pair, #1111-1112 1.00 .90

See Nos. 1130-1131, 1152-1153, 1195-1198.

Christmas Angels — A522

1986, Oct. 29 *Perf. 12½*

1113 A522 34c multicolored .50 .25
1114 A522 39c multicolored .65 .55
1115 A522 68c multicolored 1.10 .80

Booklet Stamps

Size: 72x26mm

Perf. 13½ Horiz.

1116 A522 29c multicolored 1.50 1.10
a. Booklet pane of 10 15.00 14.00
b. Perf. 12½ horiz. 6.00 2.25
c. Bklt. pane of 10, #1116b 60.00 52.50
Nos. 1113-1116 (4) 3.75 2.70

No. 1116 has bar code at left, for use on covers with printed postal code matrix.

John Molson (1763-1836), Entrepreneur — A523

1986, Nov. 4

1117 A523 34c multicolored .50 .25

Locomotives Type of 1984

Locomotives, 1925-1945.

1986, Nov. 21 *Perf. 12½x13*

1118 A491 34c CN V1a .75 .30
1119 A491 34c CP T1a .75 .30
a. Pair, #1118-1119 1.50 1.10
1120 A491 39c CN U2a .90 .75
1121 A491 68c CP H1c 1.30 1.10
Nos. 1118-1121 (4) 3.70 2.45

CAPEX '87 — A524

34c, 1st Toronto P.O. 36c, Nelson-Miramichi P.O. 42c, Saint Ours P.O. 72c, Battleford P.O.

1987 **Litho. & Engr.** *Perf. 13x13½*

1122 A524 34c multicolored .50 .25
1123 A524 36c multicolored .55 .25
1124 A524 42c multicolored .75 .65
1125 A524 72c multicolored 1.30 1.10
Nos. 1122-1125 (4) 3.10 2.25

Souvenir Sheet

Yellow Green Inscription

1125A Sheet of 4 3.50 3.50
b. A524 36c like #1122 .65 .65
c. A524 36c like #1123 .65 .65
d. A524 42c like #1124 .80 .80
e. A524 72c like #1125 1.20 1.20

Issue dates: 34c, Feb. 16; others, June 12.

Exploration Type of 1986

Pioneers of New France: No. 1126, Etienne Brule (c. 1592-1633), 1st European to see the Great Lakes. No. 1127, Pierre Esprit Radisson (c. 1636-1710) & Medard Chouart des Groseilliers 1625-98), British expedition to Hudson Bay, 1668. No. 1128, Louis Jolliet (1645-1700) & Fr. Jacques Marquette (1637-75) discovering the Mississippi River, 1673. No. 1129, Recollet wilderness mission, 1615.

1987, Mar. 13 **Litho.** *Perf. 12½x13*

1126 A518 34c multicolored .55 .30
1127 A518 34c multicolored .55 .30
1128 A518 34c multicolored .55 .30
1129 A518 34c multicolored .55 .30
a. Block of 4, #1126-1129 2.20 2.00

Olympics Type of 1986

1987, Apr. 3 *Perf. 13½x13*

1130 A521 36c Speed skating .55 .25
1131 A521 42c Bobsledding .75 .65

Volunteers Week — A525

1987, Apr. 13 *Perf. 12½x13*

1132 A525 36c multicolored .55 .25

Law Day — A526

1987, Apr. 15 *Perf. 14x13½*

1133 A526 36c Coat of arms .55 .25
a. Imperf, pair *1,500.*

Canadian Charter of Rights and Freedoms, 5th anniv.

Engineering Institute of Canada, Cent. — A527

1987, May 19 *Perf. 12½x13*

1134 A527 36c multicolored .55 .25

Canada Day — A528

Inventors & communications innovations: No. 1135, Reginald Aubrey Fessenden (1866-1932), AM radio, 1900. No. 1136, Charles Fenerty, newsprint, 1838. No. 1137, Georges-Edouard Desbarats and William Leggo, halftone engraving, 1869. No. 1138, Frederick Newton Gisborne, No. America's 1st undersea cable, 1852, New Brunswick-Prince Edward Island.

1987, June 25 *Perf. 13½*

1135 A528 36c multicolored .60 .30
1136 A528 36c multicolored .60 .30
1137 A528 36c multicolored .60 .30
1138 A528 36c multicolored .60 .30
a. Block of 4, #1135-1138 2.40 2.20

Steamships A529

No. 1139, Segwun, 1887. No. 1140, Princess Marguerite, 1948.

1987, July 20 *Perf. 13½x13*

1139 A529 36c multicolored .55 .30

51x22mm

1140 A529 36c multicolored .55 .30
a. Pair, #1139-1140 1.10 1.00

Shipwrecks A530

No. 1141, Hamilton & Scourge, 1813. No. 1142, San Juan, 1565. No. 1143, Breadalbane, 1853. No. 1144, Ericsson, 1892.

1987, Aug. 7

1141 A530 36c multicolored .55 .30
1142 A530 36c multicolored .55 .30
1143 A530 36c multicolored .55 .30
1144 A530 36c multicolored .55 .30
a. Block of 4, #1141-1144 2.20 2.00

Air Canada, 50th Anniv. — A531

1987, Sept. 1 *Perf. 13½*

1145 A531 36c multicolored .55 .25

2nd Intl. Francophone Summit, Quebec, 9/2-4 — A532

1987, Sept. 2 *Perf. 13x12½*

1146 A532 36c multicolored .55 .25

9th Commonwealth Meeting, Vancouver, Oct. 13-17 — A533

1987, Oct. 13

1147 A533 36c multicolored .55 .25

Christmas A534

36c, Poinsettia. 42c, Holly wreath. 72c, Mistletoe, Christmas tree. 31c, Gifts, Christmas tree.

1987, Nov. 2 **Litho.** *Perf. 13½*

1148 A534 36c multicolored .55 .25
1149 A534 42c multicolored .75 .65
1150 A534 72c multicolored 1.20 .90

Size: 39x25mm

1151 A534 31c multicolored .75 .75
a. Booklet pane of 10 7.50 *10.00*
b. Imperf. btwn., pair, from miscut bklt. pane *2,600.*
Nos. 1148-1151 (4) 3.25 2.55

No. 1151 has bar code at left, for use on covers with printed postal code matrix. Issued in booklets only.

Olympics Type of 1986

1987, Nov. 13 *Perf. 13½x13*

1152 A521 36c Cross-country skiing .55 .25
1153 A521 36c Ski jumping .55 .25
a. Pair, #1152-1153 1.10 .90

75th Grey Cup, Vancouver, Nov. 29 — A535

1987, Nov. 20 *Perf. 12½*

1154 A535 36c multicolored .55 .25

Types of 1982 and

Queen Elizabeth II A536

Mammals A538

Parliament (Center Block) A537 A539

Architecture — A540

Flag and Clouds A541

Flag A542

Natl. Flag, Deciduous Forest A543

Flag and Mountains A544

Designs: No. 1155, Flying squirrel. 2c, Prickly porcupine. 3c, Muskrat. No. 1158, Varying hare. No. 1159, Red fox. 10c, Skunk. 25c, Beaver. 43c, Lynx. 44c, Walrus. 45c, Pronghorn. 46c, Wolverine. 57c, Killer whale. 59c, Musk-ox. 61c, Timber wolf. 63c, Harbor porpoise. 74c, Wapiti. 76c, Grizzly bear. 78c, Beluga whale. 80c, Peary caribou. $1, Runnymede Library, Toronto. $2, McAdam Railway Station, New Brunswick. $5, Bonsecours Market, Montreal. No. 1192, Flag and field. No. 1193, Flag and seacoast.

Sizes Vary on A536, A538

1987-91 Litho. *Perf. 13x13½*

1155 A538 1c multicolored .25 .25
a. Perf. 13x12½ 4.00 .85
b. Imperf, pair 750.00
1156 A538 2c multicolored .25 .25
a. Imperf, pair 750.00
1157 A538 3c multicolored .25 .25
a. Imperf, pair 900.00
1158 A538 5c multicolored .25 .25
a. Imperf, pair 1,500.
1159 A538 6c multicolored .25 .25
a. Horiz. pair, imperf 2,250.
1160 A538 10c multicolored .25 .25
a. Perf. 13x12½ 6.00 .40
b. Imperf., pair 750.00
1161 A538 25c multicolored .40 .25

Perf. 13½x13

1162 A536 37c multicolored .75 .25
1163 A537 37c multicolored .75 .25
a. Bklt. pane of 10, #1163c 7.50 7.50
b. Bklt. pane of 25, #1163c 19.00 17.50
c. Perf. 13½x14 1.40 .40

Perf. 13x12½

1164 A536 38c multicolored .75 .25
a. Perf. 13x13½ .75 .35
b. As "a," bklt. pane of 10 + 2 labels 7.50 7.00
c. Vert. block of 10, middle pair imperf, 2nd and 4th pairs part perf 1,050.
d. As "a," horiz. pair, imperf btwn. 900.00
e. Bottom margin horiz. pair, imperf —

Perf. 13x13½ on 3 or 4 Sides

1165 A539 38c multicolored .75 .25
a. Bklt. pane of 10 + 2 labels 7.50 7.50
b. Bklt. pane of 25 + 2 labels 19.00 19.00
c. Printed on gummed side 90.00
d. Double impression of all litho colors except black 225.00

Perf. 13½x13

1166 A541 39c multicolored .75 .25
a. Bklt. pane of 10 + 2 labels 7.50
b. Bklt. pane of 25 + 2 labels 19.00
c. Perf. 12½x13 18.00 .75
d. Imperf, pair 575.00

Perf. 13x13½

1167 A536 39c multicolored .75 .25
a. Bklt. pane of 10 + 2 labels 7.50 7.50
b. Perf. 13 15.00 .85
c. Imperf, pair 525.00
d. Horiz. pair, imperf btwn. 375.00
1168 A536 40c multicolored .75 .25
a. Bklt. pane of 10 + 2 labels 7.50 7.00

Perf. 13½x13

1169 A544 40c multicolored .75 .25
a. Bklt. pane of 25 + 2 labels 25.00
b. Bklt. pane of 10 + 2 labels 7.50

Perf. 12x12½

1170 A538 43c multicolored 1.10 .40

Perf. 14½x14

1171 A538 44c multicolored 1.40 .25
a. Perf. 12½x13 2.75 1.75
b. As "a," bklt. pane of 5 + label 12.50 11.50
c. Perf. 13½x13 450.00 450.00
1172 A538 45c multicolored .90 .25
b. As "f," bklt. pane of 5 + label 13.00 14.00
d. Perf. 13 20.00 1.20
f. Perf. 12½x13 2.60 .50
h. Imperf., pair 900.00

Perf. 13

1172A A538 46c multicolored .90 .25
c. Perf. 12½x13 1.25 .50
e. As "c," bklt. pane of 5 + label 6.25 5.50
g. Perf. 14½x14 5.25 .40

Perf. 12x12½

1173 A538 57c multicolored 1.10 .35

Perf. 14½x14

1174 A538 59c multicolored 1.20 .30
a. Perf. 13 10.00 2.50
1175 A538 61c multicolored 1.20 .35
a. Perf. 13 80.00 6.50
1176 A538 63c multicolored 3.00 .40
a. Perf. 13 6.50 3.00

Perf. 12x12½

1177 A538 74c multicolored 1.90 .75

Perf. 14½x14

1178 A538 76c multicolored 1.90 .75
a. Perf. 12½x13 3.00 2.50
b. As "a," bklt. pane of 5 + label 15.00 15.00
c. Perf. 13 37.50 14.00
1179 A538 78c multicolored 2.20 .75
a. As "c," bklt. pane of 5 15.00 15.00
b. Perf. 13 35.00 6.00
c. Perf. 12½x13 3.50 2.00
d. Imperf, pair 950.00

Perf. 13

1180 A538 80c multicolored 1.80 .75
a. Perf. 12½x13 3.00 1.10
b. As "a," bklt. pane of 5 + label 15.00 15.00
c. Perf. 14½x14 5.50 2.25
d. Imperf, pair 1,100.

Perf. 13½

Litho. & Engr.

1181 A540 $1 multicolored 1.50 .55
a. Engr. inscriptions inverted 13,000.
b. Imperf, pair 1,500.
1182 A540 $2 multicolored 3.75 1.00
a. Imperf., pair 900.00
b. Vert. strip of 5, stamps 3 and 4 imperf vert., horiz. imperf btwn. stamps 2 and 3, and btwn. stamps 3 and 4 1,500.
1183 A540 $5 multicolored 8.00 2.25
a. Vert. strip of 5, top stamp imperf on 3 sides, stamp 4 imperf at top and sides 2,600.
Nos. 1155-1183 (30) 39.75 13.10

A later printing of No. 1182 has more intense and clearly defined green shading on the roofline and the deep orange background extends closer to the roofline.

Imperfs exist of Nos. 1155-1157 and 1160, from printer's waste.

Issued: 1c, 2c, 3c, 5c, 6c, 10c, 25c, 10/3/88; 37c, 12/30/87; 38c, 12/29/88; 43c, 57c, 74c, 1/18/88; 44c, 59c, 76c, 1/18/89; $1, $2, 5/5/89; No. 1166, 12/28/89; 45c, 61c, 78c, No. 1167, 1/12/90; $5, 5/28/90; 40c, 46c, 63c, 80c, 12/28/90.

Booklet Stamps

Perf. 13½x14 on 3 Sides

Litho.

1184 A542 1c multicolored .25 .25
a. Perf. 12½x13 11.00 11.00
1185 A542 5c multicolored .25 .25
a. Perf. 12½x13 7.50 7.50

Perf. 12½x12 on 2 or 3 sides

Engr.

1186 A445 6c dark purple .70 .30
1187 A443 37c dark blue .90 .70
a. Bklt. pane of 4 + 2 labels (#938, 2 #942, #1187) 1.40 1.40
1188 A443 38c dark blue .90 .40
a. Bklt. pane of 5 (3 #939a, #1186, #1188) 1.40 1.40

Perf. 13½x14 on 3 Sides

Litho.

1189 A542 39c multicolored .90 .40
a. Bklt. pane of 4 (#1184, 2 #1185, #1189) 1.65 .65
b. Perf. 12½x13 12.00 12.00
c. Bklt. pane of 4 (#1184a, 2 #1185a, 1189b) 37.50 37.50
1190 A542 40c multicolored 1.50 .55
a. Bklt. pane of 4 (2 #1184, #1185, #1190) 2.40 1.20
b. As "a," imperf 1,500.

Nos. 1190a, 1190c sold for 50c.

Issued: No. 1187, 2/3/88; No. 1188, 1/18/89; No. 1186, 1989; Nos. 1184-1185, 1189, 1/12/90; No. 1190, 12/28/90.

Self-Adhesives

Die Cut

Booklet Stamps

1191 A543 38c multicolored 1.50 .75
a. Booklet of 12 18.00
b. Blue omitted 1,900.
c. Yellow omitted 900.00
1192 A543 39c multicolored 1.40 .75
a. Booklet of 12 17.00
1193 A543 40c multicolored 1.40 .75
a. Booklet of 12 17.00

Issued: 38c, 6/30/89; 39c, 2/8/90; 40c, 1/11/91.

Issued on peelable paper backing serving as booklet cover. Nos. 1191a, 1192a sold for $5, No. 1193a for $5.25.

Coil Stamps

Perf. 10 Horiz.

Engr.

1194 A443 37c dark blue .75 .25
d. Imperf., pair 170.00
1194A A443 38c dark green 1.10 .25
e. Imperf., pair 375.00
1194B A542 39c violet .75 .25
f. Imperf., pair 150.00
1194C A542 40c blue gray .75 .25
g. Imperf., pair 275.00
h. All color omitted (tagged) 400.00

Issued: 37c, 2/22/88; 38c, 2/1/89; 39c, 2/8/90; 40c, 12/28/90.

No. 1194Ch must be collected in a pair with normal or misperfed stamp or (more often) in a strip of four with a pair of normal (or misperfed) stamps and a pair of the color-omitted stamps.

See Nos. 1356-1362, 1375-1376, 1388, 1394-1396, 1682-1683, 1687, 1695, 1698.

Olympics Type of 1986

1988, Feb. 12 Litho. *Perf. 12x12½*

1195 A521 37c Alpine skiing .60 .25
1196 A521 37c Curling .60 .25
a. Pair, #1195-1196 1.20 .90
1197 A521 43c Figure skating .65 .65
1198 A521 74c Luge 1.20 .90
Nos. 1195-1198 (4) 3.05 2.05

Exploration Type of 1986

18th Cent. explorers of the western territories: No. 1199, Anthony Henday, who traveled the Prairies in 1754 from the Hayes River to Red Deer, Alberta. No. 1200, George Vancouver (1757-1798), who circumnavigated Vancouver Is. and explored the Pacific Coast, 1792-94. No. 1201, Simon Fraser (1776-1862), fur trader who discovered and navigated the Fraser River. No. 1202, John Palliser (1807-1887), geographer who determined the topographical boundary between Canada and the US from Lake Superior to the Pacific Coast.

1988, Mar. 17 Litho. *Perf. 12½x13*

1199 A518 37c multicolored .55 .35
1200 A518 37c multicolored .55 .35
1201 A518 37c multicolored .55 .35
1202 A518 37c multicolored .55 .35
a. Block of 4, #1199-1202 2.20 2.00

The Young Reader, by Ozias Leduc A546

Photo. & Engr. with Foil Application

1988, May 20 *Perf. 13x13½*

1203 A546 50c multicolored 1.10 .90

Masterpieces of Canadian art. Printed in sheets of 16.

See Nos. 1241, 1271, 1310, 1419, 1466, 1516, 1545, 1602, 1635, 1754, 1800, 1863, 1916, 1945.

Wildlife and Habitat Conservation A547

1988, June 1 Litho. *Perf. 13x13½*

1204 A547 37c Duck landing .55 .35
1205 A547 37c Moose at water hole .55 .35
a. Pair, #1204-1205 1.10 .90

Grey Owl, born Archibald Belaney, (b. 1888), conservationist; Ducks Unlimited Canada, 50th anniv.

Science and Technology — A548

Inventions: No. 1206, Kerosene, invented by Abraham Gesner (1797-1864), patented in 1854. No. 1207, Marquis wheat, developed in 1908 by Charles Saunders. No. 1208, Electron microscope, developed in 1938 at the University of Toronto by James Hillier and Albert Prebus under the supervision of Eli Burton. No. 1209, Cobalt cancer therapy, introduced by Dr. Harold Johns and Atomic Energy of Canada, Ltd., in 1951.

1988, June 17 *Perf. 12½x13*

1206 A548 37c multicolored .55 .30
1207 A548 37c multicolored .55 .30
1208 A548 37c multicolored .55 .30
1209 A548 37c multicolored .55 .30
a. Block of 4, #1206-1209 2.20 2.00

Intl. Entomology Congress, Vancouver A549

No. 1210, Short-tailed swallowtail. No. 1211, Northern blue. No. 1212, Macoun's Arctic. No. 1213, Canadian tiger swallowtail.

1988, July 4 *Perf. 12*

1210 A549 37c multicolored .55 .35
1211 A549 37c multicolored .55 .35
1212 A549 37c multicolored .55 .35
1213 A549 37c multicolored .55 .35
a. Block of 4, #1210-1213 2.20 1.80

St. John's, Newfoundland, Cent. of Incorporation — A550

37c, Harbor entrance, skyline.

1988, July 22 *Perf. 13½x13*

1214 A550 37c multicolored .55 .25

Canadian 4-H Council, 75th Anniv. A551

37c, Motto, farm, young scientists.

1988, Aug. 5

1215 A551 37c multicolored .55 .25

Les Forges Du St. Maurice (1738-1883), Canada's 1st Industrial Complex — A552

Litho. & Engr.

1988, Aug. 19 *Perf. 13½*

1216 A552 37c multicolored .55 .25

Canadian Kennel Club, Cent. A553

No. 1217, Tahltan bear dog. No. 1218, Nova Scotia duck-tolling retriever. No. 1219, Canadian Eskimo dog. No. 1220, Newfoundland.

1988, Aug. 26 *Perf. 12½x12*

1217 A553 37c multicolored .90 .40
1218 A553 37c multicolored .90 .40
1219 A553 37c multicolored .90 .40
1220 A553 37c multicolored .90 .40
a. Block of 4, #1217-1220 3.60 2.75

A554

1988, Sept. 14 Litho. *Perf. 13½x13*
1221 A554 37c multicolored .55 .25

Sesquicentennial of the 1st baseball game played in Canada, June 4, 1838 at Beachville, Upper Canada.

A555

Christmas (Icons of the Eastern Church): 32c, Nativity. 37c, Conception. 43c, Virgin and Child. 74c, Virgin and Child, diff.

1988, Oct. 27 *Perf. 13½*
1222 A555 37c multicolored .60 .25
1223 A555 43c multicolored .75 .65
1224 A555 74c multicolored 1.50 .90

Booklet Stamp
Size: 35½x21mm
Perf. 12½x13½

1225 A555 32c multicolored .90 .75
a. Booklet pane of 10 9.00 9.00
Nos. 1222-1225 (4) 3.75 2.55

Millennium of Christianity in the Ukraine. No. 1225 has bar code at left; for use on covers with printed postal code matrix.

Inglis and Anglican Church A556

1988, Nov. 1 *Perf. 12½x12*
1226 A556 37c multicolored .55 .25

Charles Inglis (1734-1816), Canada's 1st Anglican bishop and founder of the Kings-Edgehill School, Nova Scotia, and the University of King's College at Halifax, bicent.

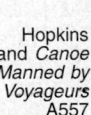

Hopkins and *Canoe Manned by Voyageurs* A557

1988, Nov. 18 *Perf. 13½x13*
1227 A557 37c multicolored .55 .25

Frances Ann Hopkins (1838-1918), painter.

The Bluenose and Capt. Walters — A558

1988, Nov. 18 *Perf. 13½*
1228 A558 37c multicolored .60 .25

Angus Walters (1882-1968), mariner.

Small Craft A559

1989, Feb. 1 *Perf. 13½x13*
1229 A559 38c Chipewyan canoe .55 .35
1230 A559 38c Haida canoe .55 .35
1231 A559 38c Inuit kayak .55 .35
1232 A559 38c Micmac canoe .55 .35
a. Block of 4, #1229-1232 2.20 2.00

See Nos. 1266-1269, 1317-1320.

Exploration Type of 1986

Explorers of the North: No. 1233, Matonabbee (c. 1737-1782), Indian guide who led 1st overland European expedition to the Arctic Ocean. No. 1234, Relics of expedition led by Sir John Franklin (1786-1847) that proved the existence of the Northwest Passage. No. 1235, Relics of the discovery of the Alberta fossil bed by geologist Joseph Burr Tyrrell (1858-1957). No. 1236, Vilhjalmur Stefansson (1879-1962), American ethnologist who discovered the last uncharted islands in the Arctic Archipelago.

1989, Mar. 22 *Perf. 12½x13*
1233 A518 38c multicolored .55 .35
1234 A518 38c multicolored .55 .35
1235 A518 38c multicolored .55 .35
1236 A518 38c multicolored .55 .35
a. Block of 4, #1233-1236 2.20 2.00

Photography in Canada, Sesquicentennial — A560

Photographers and their work: No. 1237, William Notman (1826-1891). No. 1238, W. Hanson Boorne (1859-1945). No. 1239, Alexander Henderson (1831-1913). No. 1240, Jules-Ernest Livernois (1851-1933).

1989, June 23 *Perf. 12½x12*
1237 A560 38c multicolored .55 .35
1238 A560 38c multicolored .55 .35
1239 A560 38c multicolored .55 .35
1240 A560 38c multicolored .55 .35
a. Block of 4, #1237-1240 2.20 2.00

Art Type of 1988

Ceremonial Frontlet (headpiece) Worn by Tsimshian Indian Chiefs, Early 20th Cent.

Litho. with Foil Application
1989, June 29 *Perf. 12½x13*
1241 A546 50c multicolored 1.10 .90

Masterpieces of Canadian Art and opening of the Museum of Civilization.

Poets — A562

No. 1243, Louis Frechette (1839-1908). No. 1244, Archibald Lampman (1861-1899).

1989, July 7 Litho. *Perf. 13½*
1243 A562 38c multicolored .55 .35
1244 A562 38c multicolored .55 .35
a. Pair, #1243-1244 1.10 .90

Mushrooms A563

No. 1245, Clavulinopsis fusiformis. No. 1246, Boletus mirabilis. No. 1247, Cantharellus cinnabarinus. No. 1248, Morchella esculenta.

1989, Aug. 4
1245 A563 38c multicolored .55 .35
1246 A563 38c multicolored .55 .35
1247 A563 38c multicolored .55 .35
1248 A563 38c multicolored .55 .35
a. Block of 4, #1245-1248 2.20 2.00

Infantry Regiments, 75th Annivs. A564

No. 1249, Princess Patricia's Canadian Light Infantry. No. 1250, Royal 22nd Regiment.

Litho. & Engr.
1989, Sept. 8 *Perf. 13*
1249 A564 38c multicolored .75 .40
1250 A564 38c multicolored .75 .40
a. Pair, #1249-1250 1.50 1.25

Intl. Trade A565

1989, Oct. 2 Litho. *Perf. 13½x13*
1251 A565 38c multicolored .55 .25

Performing Arts — A566

1989, Oct. 4 *Perf. 13x13½*
1252 A566 38c Dancers .55 .35
1253 A566 38c Musicians .55 .35
1254 A566 38c Camera, director .55 .35
1255 A566 38c Youth and adult entertainers .55 .35
a. Block of 4, #1252-1255 2.20 1.80

Royal Winnipeg Ballet 50th anniv. (No. 1252), Vancouver Opera 30th anniv. (No. 1253), Natl. Film Board 50th anniv. (No. 1254), and Confederation Center of the Arts, Charlottetown, P.E.I., 25th anniv. (No. 1255).

A566a

A567

Winter landscapes: 33c, *Champ-de-Mars, Winter,* 1892, by William Brymner (1855-1925). 38c, *Bend in the Gosselin River, Arthabaska,* c. 1906, by Marc-Aurele de Foy Suzor-Cote (1869-1937). 44c, *Snow II,* 1915, by Lawren S. Harris (1885-1970). 76c, *Ste. Agnes,* c. 1925-30, by Albert H. Robinson (1881-1956). Nos. 1256-1258 vert.

1989, Oct. 26
Size of 44c, 76c: 25x31mm
1256 A566a 38c multi .55 .25
a. Bklt. pane of 10, #1256b 45.00 45.00
b. Perf. 13x12½ 4.50 4.50

Perf. 13½
1257 A566a 44c multi .75 .60
a. Booklet pane of 5 + label 15.00 15.00
1258 A566a 76c multi 1.30 .90
a. Booklet pane of 5 + label 27.50 27.50

Booklet Stamp
Size: 35x21mm
Perf. 12½x13½

1259 A567 33c shown 1.50 1.50
a. Booklet pane of 10 15.00
b. Horiz. pair, imperf btwn. *2,250.*
c. As "a," imperf. vert. between *11,000.*
Nos. 1256-1259 (4) 4.10 3.25

Christmas. No. 1259 has bar code at left; for use on covers with printed postal code matrix. Booklet panes separate easily.

Declaration of War, 1939 — A568

Political and military actions taken by Canada at the outbreak of World War II: No. 1261, Army mobilization. No. 1262, Navy convoy system. No. 1263, Commonwealth Air Training Plan.

1989, Nov. 10 *Perf. 13½*
1260 A568 38c shown .75 .55
1261 A568 38c multicolored .75 .55
1262 A568 38c multicolored .75 .55
1263 A568 38c multicolored .75 .55
a. Block of 4, #1260-1263 3.00 2.50

See Nos. 1298-1301, 1345-1348, 1448-1451, 1503-1506, 1537-1544.

Norman Bethune (1890-1939), Surgeon — A569

Litho. & Engr.
1990, Mar. 2 *Perf. 13x13½*
1264 A569 39c In Canada .90 .40
1265 A569 39c In China .90 .40
a. Pair, #1264-1265 1.80 1.10

See People's Republic of China Nos. 2263-2264.

Small Craft Type of 1989
1990, Mar. 15 Litho. *Perf. 13½x13*
1266 A559 39c Dory .70 .35
1267 A559 39c Pointer .70 .35
1268 A559 39c York boat .70 .35
1269 A559 39c North canoe .70 .35
a. Block of 4, #1266-1269 2.80 2.40

Multicultural Heritage of Canada A570

Litho. & Engr.
1990, Apr. 5 *Perf. 13*
1270 A570 39c multicolored .60 .25
a. Black (inscriptions) omitted *1,200.*

Art Type of 1988

Painting: *The West Wind,* by Tom Thomson.

Litho. with Foil Application
1990, May 3 *Perf. 12½x13*
1271 A546 50c multicolored 1.10 .90

Masterpieces of Canadian Art.

Mail Trucks
A571 A572

1990, May 3 Litho. *Perf. 13½*

Booklet Stamps

1272 A571 39c multicolored .75 .55
1273 A572 39c multicolored .75 .55
a. Bklt. pane of 8+printed margin (4 each #1272-1273) 6.00 6.00
b. Bklt. pane of 9+3 labels, printed margin (5 #1272, 4 #1273) 11.50 11.50

Dolls
A573

1990, June 8 *Perf. 12½x12*

1274 A573 39c Native .65 .35
1275 A573 39c Settlers .65 .35
1276 A573 39c 4 Commercial .65 .35
1277 A573 39c 5 Commercial .65 .35
a. Block of 4, #1274-1277 2.60 2.40

Natl. Flag, 25th Anniv. — A574

1990, June 29 *Perf. 13x12½*

1278 A574 39c Flag, fireworks .60 .25
a. Silver (inscriptions) omitted *2,000.*

Printed in sheets of 16.

Prehistoric Life
A575

Litho. & Engr.

1990, July 12 *Perf. 13x13½*

1279 A575 39c Trilobite .65 .35
1280 A575 39c Sea scorpion .65 .35
1281 A575 39c Fossil algae .65 .35
1282 A575 39c Soft invertebrate .65 .35
a. Block of 4, #1279-1282 2.60 2.20

See Nos. 1306-1309.

Canadian Forests
A576

1990, Aug. 7 Litho. *Perf. 12½x13*

1283 A576 39c Acadian .65 .30
a. Pane of 4 9.00 7.50
1284 A576 39c Great Lakes-St. Lawrence .65 .30
a. Pane of 4 9.00 7.50
1285 A576 39c Coast .65 .30
a. Pane of 4 9.00 7.50
1286 A576 39c Boreal .65 .30
a. Block of 4, #1283-1286 2.60 2.20
b. Pane of 4 9.00 7.50

Panes of four sold for $1 each through Petro-Canada gas stations, and for full face value through the philatelic bureau. Issue date: Sept. 7.

Weather Observations in Canada, 150th Anniv. — A577

1990, Sept. 5 *Perf. 12½x13½*

1287 A577 39c multicolored .60 .25

The left and right margin singles of No. 1287 differ slightly in design from stamps from columns 2-4, due to the nature of the continuous cloud design across the pane.

Intl. Literacy Year — A578

1990, Sept. 7 *Perf. 13½x13*

1288 A578 39c multicolored .60 .25

Legendary Creatures
A579

1990, Oct. 1 *Perf. 12½x13½*

1289 A579 39c Sasquatch .75 .75
1290 A579 39c Kraken .75 .75
1291 A579 39c Werewolf .75 .75
1292 A579 39c Ogopogo .75 .75
a. Block of 4, #1289-1292 3.00 3.00
b. As "a," imperf. *1,750.*

Perf. 12½x12

1289a A579 39c 11.00 3.75
1290a A579 39c 11.00 3.75
1291a A579 39c 11.00 3.75
1292c A579 39c 11.00 3.75
d. Block of 4, #1289a-1292c 45.00 32.50

Agnes Campbell Macphail (1890-1954), First Woman Member of Parliament — A580

1990, Oct. 9 *Perf. 13x13½*

1293 A580 39c multicolored .60 .25

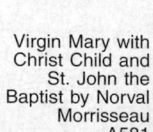

Virgin Mary with Christ Child and St. John the Baptist by Norval Morrisseau
A581

Rebirth by Jackson Beardy
A582

Indian Art: 45c, Sculpture of Mother and Child by an Inuit artist. 78c, Children of the Raven by Bill Reid.

1990, Oct. 25 *Perf. 13½*

1294 A581 39c multicolored .75 .25
a. Booklet pane of 10 7.50 *9.00*
1295 A581 45c multicolored .75 .65
a. Bklt. pane of 5 + label 3.75 4.00
1296 A581 78c multicolored 1.50 1.10
a. Bklt. pane of 5 + label 7.50 6.50

Booklet Stamp

Perf. 12½x13 on 2 or 3 Sides

1297 A582 34c multicolored .85 .30
a. Booklet pane of 10 8.50 *10.00*
Nos. 1294-1297 (4) 3.85 2.30

Christmas. No. 1297 has bar code at left; for use on covers with printed postal code matrix.

World War II Type of 1989

1990, Nov. 9 *Perf. 12½x12*

1298 A568 39c Home front .75 .60
1299 A568 39c Communal war efforts .75 .60
1300 A568 39c Food production .75 .60
1301 A568 39c Science and war .75 .60
a. Block of 4, #1298-1301 3.00 3.00

A583

Physicians: No. 1302, Jennie Trout (1841-1921), first licensed Canadian woman physician. No. 1303, Wilder Penfield (1891-1976), neurosurgeon. No. 1304, Sir Frederick Banting (1891-1941), discoverer of insulin. No. 1305, Harold Griffith (1894-1985), anesthesiologist.

1991, Mar. 15 *Perf. 13½*

1302 A583 40c multicolored .65 .35
1303 A583 40c multicolored .65 .35
1304 A583 40c multicolored .65 .35
1305 A583 40c multicolored .65 .35
a. Block of 4, #1302-1305 2.60 2.20

Prehistoric Life Type of 1990

1991, Apr. 5 *Perf. 12½x13½*

1306 A575 40c Microfossils .65 .35
1307 A575 40c Early tree .65 .35
1308 A575 40c Early fish .65 .35
1309 A575 40c Land reptile .65 .35
a. Block of 4, #1306-1309 2.60 2.20

Art Type of 1988

Forest, British Columbia by Emily Carr.

Litho. with Foil Application

1991, May 7 *Perf. 12½x13*

1310 A546 50c multicolored 1.10 .90

Masterpieces of Canadian Art.

A584

Public Gardens: No. 1311, Butchart Gardens, Victoria, B.C. No. 1312, Intl. Peace Garden, Boissevain, Manitoba. No. 1313, Royal Botanical Gardens, Hamilton, Ontario. No. 1314, Montreal Botanical Gardens. No. 1315, Halifax Public Gardens, Nova Scotia.

Booklet Stamps

1991, May 22 Litho. *Perf. 13x12½*

1311 A584 40c multicolored .75 .40
1312 A584 40c multicolored .75 .40
1313 A584 40c multicolored .75 .40
1314 A584 40c multicolored .75 .40
1315 A584 40c multicolored .75 .40
a. Strip of 5, #1311-1315 3.75 2.75
b. Bklt. pane, 2 each #1311-1315 7.50 7.00

Canada Day — A585

1991, June 28 *Perf. 13½x13*

1316 A585 40c multicolored .75 .25

Small Craft Type of 1989

1991, July 18

1317 A559 40c Verchere rowboat .65 .35
1318 A559 40c Touring kayak .65 .35
1319 A559 40c Sailing dinghy .65 .35
1320 A559 40c Cedar strip canoe .65 .35
a. Block of 4, #1317-1320 2.60 2.25

Canadian Rivers — A586

No. 1321, South Nahanni. No. 1322, Athabasca. No. 1323, Boundary Waters-Voyageur Waterway. No. 1324, Jacques Cartier. No. 1325, Main.

Booklet Stamps

1991, Aug. 20 *Perf. 13x12½*

1321 A586 40c multicolored .75 .40
1322 A586 40c multicolored .75 .40
1323 A586 40c multicolored .75 .40
1324 A586 40c multicolored .75 .40
1325 A586 40c multicolored .75 .40
a. Strip of 5, #1321-1325 3.75 3.25
b. Bklt. pane, 2 each #1321-1325 7.50 6.75

See Nos. 1408-1412, 1485-1489, 1511-1515.

Arrival of Ukrainians, Cent. — A587

Paintings by William Kurelek.

1991, Aug. 29 *Perf. 13½x13*

1326 A587 40c Leaving homeland .65 .35
1327 A587 40c Winter in Canada .65 .35
1328 A587 40c Clearing land .65 .35
1329 A587 40c Growing wheat .65 .35
a. Block of 4, #1326-1329 2.60 2.20

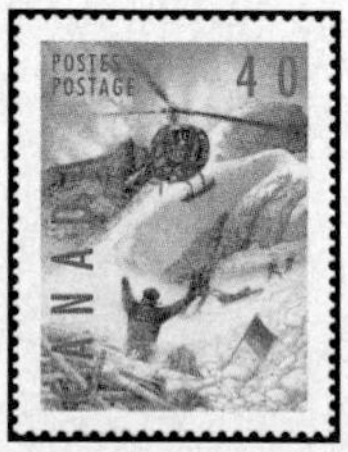

Dangerous Public Service Occupations
A588

1991, Sept. 23 *Perf. 13½*

1330 A588 40c Ski Patrol 1.10 .35
1331 A588 40c Police 1.10 .35
1332 A588 40c Fire fighters 1.10 .35
1333 A588 40c Search & Rescue 1.10 .35
a. Block of 4, #1330-1333 4.40 2.60

Folktales A589

1991, Oct. 1 Litho. *Perf. 13½x12½*

1334 A589 40c Witched Canoe .75 .30
1335 A589 40c Orphan Boy .75 .30
1336 A589 40c Chinook Wind .75 .30
1337 A589 40c Buried Treasure .75 .30
a. Block of 4, #1334-1337 3.00 2.50

Queen's University, Kingston, Ont., Sesqui. — A590

1991, Oct. 16

1338 A590 40c multicolored .75 .55
a. Bklt. pane of 10 + 2 labels 7.50 6.00

A591

Santa Claus A592

1991, Oct. 23 *Perf. 13½*

1339 A591 40c At fireplace .75 .25
a. Booklet pane of 10 7.50 6.00
1340 A591 46c With white horse, tree .75 .50
a. Bklt. pane of 5 + label 3.75 3.00
1341 A591 80c Sinterklaas, girl 1.30 .90
a. Bklt. pane of 5 + label 6.50 6.00

Booklet Stamp

Perf. 12½x13 on 2 or 3 Sides

1342 A592 35c With punchbowl .75 .25
a. Booklet pane of 10 7.50 4.50
Nos. 1339-1342 (4) 3.55 1.90

Christmas. No. 1342 has bar code at left; for use on covers with printed postal code matrix.

Basketball, Cent. — A593

1991, Oct. 25 *Perf. 13x13½*

1343 A593 40c multicolored .75 .25

Souvenir Sheet

1344 Pane of 3 5.00 5.00
a. A593 40c like #1343 1.10 1.10
b. A593 46c Player shooting, diff. 1.50 1.50
c. A593 80c Player dribbling 2.20 2.20

No. 1344a has 3-line inscription.

World War II Type of 1989

No. 1345, Women's Armed Forces. No. 1346, War industry. No. 1347, Cadets and veterans. No. 1348, Defense of Hong Kong.

1991, Nov. 8 *Perf. 13½*

1345 A568 40c multicolored .75 .55
1346 A568 40c multicolored .75 .55
1347 A568 40c multicolored .75 .55
1348 A568 40c multicolored .75 .55
a. Block or strip of 4, #1345-1348 3.00 2.50

Types of 1987-91 and

Edible Berries — A594

Flag and Hills — A595

Flag and Prairie A596

Flag and Building A597

Trees — A598

Designs: 1c, Blueberry. 2c, Wild strawberry. 3c, Black crowberry. 5c, Rose hip. 6c, Black raspberry. 10c, Kinnikinnick. 25c, Saskatoon berry. 48c, McIntosh apple. 49c, Delicious apple. 50¢, Snow apple. 52c, Gravenstein apple. 65c, Black walnut. 67c, Beaked hazelnut. 69c, Shagbark hickory. 71c, American chestnut. 84c, Stanley plum. 86c, Bartlett pear. 88c, Westcot apricot. 90c, Elberta peach. $1, Court House, Yorkton, Saskatchewan. $2, Provincial Normal School, Truro, Nova Scotia. $5, Carnegie Public Library, Victoria, British Columbia. No. 1388, Flag and mountains. No. 1389, Flag and estuary shore.

1991-98 Litho. *Perf. 13x13½*

1349 A594 1c multicolored .25 .25
a. Imperf., pair *650.00*
1350 A594 2c multicolored .25 .25
a. Imperf., pair *650.00*
1351 A594 3c multicolored .25 .25
a. Imperf., pair *650.00*
1352 A594 5c multicolored .25 .25
a. Imperf., pair *650.00*
1353 A594 6c multicolored .25 .25
a. Imperf., pair *650.00*
1354 A594 10c multicolored .25 .25
a. Horiz. pair, imperf at sides and bottom *1,100.*
b. Imperf., pair *650.00*
1355 A594 25c multicolored .75 .25
a. Imperf., pair *650.00*

Perf. 13½x13

1356 A595 42c multicolored .80 .25
a. Booklet pane of 10 7.50 5.75
b. Bklt. pane of 50 + 2 labels 90.00 75.00
c. Bklt. pane of 25 + 2 labels 17.50 12.50
d. Vert. pair, imperf between *900.00*

Perf. 13x13½

1357 A536 42c multicolored .75 .25
a. Booklet pane of 10 7.50 6.00
1358 A536 43c multicolored .90 .25
a. Booklet pane of 10 9.00 8.50
b. Imperf., pair 900.00

Perf. 13½x13

1359 A596 43c multicolored .90 .25
a. Booklet pane of 10 9.00 7.00
b. Bklt. pane of 25 + 2 labels 22.50 17.50
c. Perf. 14½ 1.10 .25
d. As "c," bklt. pane of 10 9.00 7.50
e. As "c," bklt. pane of 25 + 2 labels 25.00 25.00
f. Vert. pair, imperf between (from #1359e) 750.00
g. Imperf., pair 750.00

Perf. 13x13½

1360 A536 45c multicolored .75 .25
a. Booklet pane of 10 7.50 6.00
Complete booklet, #1360a 7.50

Perf. 14½

1361 A597 45c multicolored .75 .25
a. Booklet pane of 10 7.50 7.00
Complete booklet, #1361a 7.50
b. Bklt. pane of 25 + 2 labels 27.50 22.50
Complete booklet, #1361b 27.50
c. Perf. 13½x13 .75 .25
d. As "c," bklt. pane of 10 7.50 6.75
Complete booklet, #1361d 7.50
e. As "c," bklt. pane of 25 + 2 labels 19.00
Complete booklet, #1361e 19.00

Perf. 13x13½

Size: 16x20mm

1362 A597 45c multicolored .65 .25
a. Booklet pane of 10 6.50 *8.25*
Complete booklet, #1362a 6.50
b. Booklet pane of 30 22.50 22.50
Complete booklet, #1362b 22.50
c. Imperf, pair *500.00*

No. 1361 is 17x21mm.

Perf. 13

1363 A598 48c multicolored 1.00 .25
a. Perf. 14½x14 on 3 sides 1.50 .40
b. As "a," bklt. pane of 5 + label 7.50 5.75
c. Imperf., pair *850.00*
1364 A598 49c multicolored .90 .25
a. Perf. 14½x14 2.60 .35
b. As "a," bklt. pane of 5 + 1 label 13.00 6.00
c. Booklet pane of 5 + label 12.00 9.50
1365 A598 50c multicolored .90 .30
a. Booklet pane of 5 + label 6.50 5.00
b. Perf. 14½x14 2.25 .45
c. As "b," bklt. pane of 5 + label 13.00 11.50
1366 A598 52c multicolored 1.50 .40
a. Booklet pane of 5 + label 7.50 6.00
Complete booklet, #1366a 8.00
b. Perf. 14½x14 2.25 .55
c. As "b," bklt. pane of 5 + label 11.50 10.00
Complete booklet, #1366c 12.00
1367 A598 65c multicolored 1.10 .40
a. Imperf., pair *1,000.*
1368 A598 67c multicolored 1.10 .40
a. Imperf., pair *1,500.*
1369 A598 69c multicolored 1.10 .35
1370 A598 71c multicolored 1.10 .35
a. Perf. 14½x14 70.00 7.50
1371 A598 84c multicolored 1.50 .40
a. Perf. 14½x14 on 3 sides 2.25 .60
b. As "a," bklt. pane of 5 + label 11.50 9.00
c. Imperf., pair *1,350.*
1372 A598 86c multicolored 1.80 .55
a. Perf. 14½x14 3.00 1.50
b. As "a," bklt. pane of 5 + 1 label 15.00 12.50
c. Booklet pane of 5 + label 17.00 15.00
1373 A598 88c multicolored 1.50 .50
a. Booklet pane of 5 + label 11.00 7.50
b. Perf. 14½x14 4.00 2.25
c. As "b," bklt. pane of 5 + label 20.00 15.00
1374 A598 90c multicolored 1.80 .45
a. Booklet pane of 5 + label 10.00 8.00
Complete booklet, #1374a 10.50
b. Perf. 14½x14 3.75 1.50
c. As "b," bklt. pane of 5+label 19.00 13.00
Complete booklet, #1374c 20.00

Size: 48x40mm

Litho. & Engr.

Perf. 14½x14

1375 A540 $1 multicolored 1.80 .55
a. Dk bl (inscriptions) omitted *1,250.*
b. Perf 13½x13 1.80 .55
c. As "b," dk bl (inscriptions) omitted *1,350.*
1376 A540 $2 multicolored 3.75 1.00
a. Dk grn (inscriptions) omitted *1,000.*
b. Engr. inscriptions inverted *8,750.*
c. Perf. 13½x13 3.75 1.10
d. As "c," dk grn (inscriptions) omitted *1,500.*

Perf. 13½x13

1378 A540 $5 multicolored 7.50 2.20
Nos. 1349-1378 (29) 36.10 11.85

Self-Adhesive

Die Cut

Imperf

Booklet Stamps

1388 A543 42c multicolored 1.10 .75
a. Booklet of 12 13.50
1389 A543 43c multicolored 1.10 .75
a. Booklet pane of 12 13.50

Nos. 1388a, 1389a issued on peelable paper backing serving as booklet cover and sold for $5.25.

Coil Stamps

Perf. 10 Horiz.

Engr.

1394 A542 42c red .75 .25
a. Imperf., pair 170.00
1395 A542 43c olive green .75 .25
a. Imperf., pair 150.00
1396 A542 45c blue green .75 .25
a. Imperf., pair 150.00
Nos. 1394-1396 (3) 2.25 .75

Nos. 1349-1363 are known imperf from printer's waste. Items exist imperf in wrong colors and with wrong denominations. These may be essays or printer's waste.

Issued: 1c-25c, 8/5/92; Nos. 1356-1357, 1394, 48c, 65c, 84c, 12/27/91; No. 1388, 1/28/92; Nos. 1358-1359, 1364, 1368, 1372, 1395, 12/30/92; No. 1389, 2/15/93; Nos. 1359c-1359e, 1/18/94; Nos. 1364c, 1372c, 1/7/94; 50c, 69c, 88c, 2/25/94; $1, $2, 2/21/94; NOs. 1375b, 1376c, 2/20/95; Nos. 1365c, 1373c, 3/27/95; Nos. 1360-1361, 1396, 52c, 71c, 90c, 7/31/95; $5, 2/29/96; No. 1362, 2/2/98.

1992 Winter Olympics, Albertville A601

Booklet Stamps

1992, Feb. 7 Litho. *Perf. 12½x13*

1399 A601 42c Ski jumping .75 .40
1400 A601 42c Pairs figure skating .75 .40
1401 A601 42c Hockey .75 .40
1402 A601 42c Bobsledding .75 .40
1403 A601 42c Alpine skiing .75 .40
a. Strip of 5, #1399-1403 3.75 3.00
b. Bklt. pane, 2 each #1399-1403 7.50 7.50
Complete booklet, #1403b 8.50

See Nos. 1414-1418.

City of Montreal, 350th Anniv. — A602

Designs: No. 1404, City of Montreal, modern times. No. 1405, Early settlement of Montreal (Ville-Marie). 48c, Jacques Cartier's chart of Canada, snowshoe, ship's mast. 84c, World map, nocturnal and Aztec calendar stone.

1992, Mar. 25 *Perf. 13½*

1404 A602 42c multicolored .60 .30
1405 A602 42c multicolored .60 .30
a. Pair, #1404-1405 1.20 .75
1406 A602 48c multicolored .75 .70
1407 A602 84c multicolored 1.30 .90
a. Souvenir sheet of 4, #1404-1407 4.00 4.00
Nos. 1404-1407 (4) 3.25 2.20

Discovery of America, 500th anniv. (No. 1407).

Nos. 1404-1405 printed checkerwise. No. 1407a with engraved signatures in margin was produced in limited quantities for World Philatelic Youth Exhibition catalogue which sold for $12.

Canadian Rivers Type of 1991

Booklet Stamps

1992, Apr. 22 *Perf. 12½*

1408 A586 42c Margaree .75 .40
1409 A586 42c West (Eliot) .75 .40
1410 A586 42c Ottawa .75 .40
1411 A586 42c Niagara .75 .40
1412 A586 42c South Saskatchewan .75 .40
a. Strip of 5, #1408-1412 3.75 3.25
b. Bklt. pane, 2 each #1408-1412 7.50
Complete booklet, #1412b 8.50

Nos. 1408-1412 are horiz.

Alaska Highway, 50th Anniv. — A603

1992, May 15 *Perf. 13½*

1413 A603 42c multicolored .65 .25

1992 Olympic Games Type

1992, June 15 *Perf. 12½x13*

1414 A601 42c Gymnastics .75 .40
1415 A601 42c Running .75 .40
1416 A601 42c Diving .75 .40
1417 A601 42c Cycling .75 .40
1418 A601 42c Swimming .75 .40
a. Strip of 5, #1414-1418 3.75 3.75
b. Bklt. pane, 2 each #1414-1418 7.50 7.50
Complete booklet, #1418b 8.50

1992 Summer Olympics, Barcelona.

Stamps in bottom row of No. 1418b are in different sequence than those in No. 1418a.

Art Type of 1988

Painting: Red Nasturtiums, by David Milne.

Litho. with Foil Application

1992, June 29

1419	A546 50c multicolored	.90	.75

Masterpieces in Canadian Art.

Miniature Sheet

Canada Day A604

No. 1420, Nova Scotia. No. 1421, Ontario. No. 1422, Prince Edward Island. No. 1423, New Brunswick. No. 1424, Quebec. No. 1425, Saskatchewan. No. 1426, Manitoba. No. 1427, Northwest Territories. No. 1428, Alberta. No. 1429, British Columbia. No. 1430, Yukon. No. 1431, Newfoundland.

1992, June 29

1420	A604 42c multicolored	1.50	1.50
1421	A604 42c multicolored	1.50	1.50
1422	A604 42c multicolored	1.50	1.50
1423	A604 42c multicolored	1.50	1.50
1424	A604 42c multicolored	1.50	1.50
1425	A604 42c multicolored	1.50	1.50
1426	A604 42c multicolored	1.50	1.50
1427	A604 42c multicolored	1.50	1.50
1428	A604 42c multicolored	1.50	1.50
1429	A604 42c multicolored	1.50	1.50
1430	A604 42c multicolored	1.50	1.50
1431	A604 42c multicolored	1.50	1.50
a.	Pane of 12, #1420-1431 + 13 labels	18.00	18.00

Canadian Folklore — A605

Legendary heroes: No. 1432, Jerry Potts, guide, interpreter. No. 1433, Captain William Jackman, rescuer. No. 1434, Laura Secord, patriot. No. 1435, Jos Monferrand, lumberjack.

1992, Sept. 8 *Perf. 12½*

1432	A605 42c multicolored	.75	.35
1433	A605 42c multicolored	.75	.35
1434	A605 42c multicolored	.75	.35
1435	A605 42c multicolored	.75	.35
a.	Block of 4, #1432-1435	3.00	2.50

Minerals A606

1992, Sept. 21

1436	A606 42c Copper	.90	.40
1437	A606 42c Sodalite	.90	.40
1438	A606 42c Gold	.90	.40
1439	A606 42c Galena	.90	.40
1440	A606 42c Grossular	.90	.40
a.	Strip of 5, #1436-1440	4.50	4.50
b.	Bklt. pane, 2 each #1436-1440	9.00	9.00
	Complete booklet, #1440b	8.50	

Canada in Space A607

No. 1441, Anik E2 satellite. No. 1442, Earth, space shuttle.

1992, Oct. 1 *Perf. 13*

1441	A607 42c multicolored	.75	.80
a.	Silver omitted	*2,750.*	*2,000.*

Size: 32x26mm

1442	A607 42c multicolored	1.10	1.10
a.	Pair, #1441-1442	1.80	*1.80*
b.	As "a," hologram omitted on #1442	*1,500.*	*1,400.*

No. 1442 has a holographic image. Soaking in water may affect the hologram.

Natl. Hockey League, 75th Anniv. A608

Designs: No. 1443, Skates, stick, puck, photograph from the early years (1917-1942). No. 1444, Photograph, team emblems from the six-team years (1942-1967). No. 1445, Goalie's mask, gloves, photograph from the expansion years (1967-1992).

Booklet Stamps

1992, Oct. 9 *Perf. 13x12½*

1443	A608 42c multicolored	.75	.25
a.	Bklt. pane of 8 + 4 labels	6.00	5.00
1444	A608 42c multicolored	.75	.25
a.	Bklt. pane of 8 + 4 labels	6.00	5.00
1445	A608 42c multicolored	.75	.25
a.	Bklt. pane of 9 + 3 labels	6.75	5.75
	Complete booklet, #1443a, 1444a, 1445a	21.00	
	Nos. 1443-1445 (3)	2.25	.75

A609

No. 1446, Order of Canada, 25th anniv. No. 1447, Daniel Roland Michener (1900-1991), Governor General.

1992, Oct. 21 *Perf. 12½*

1446	42c multicolored	.65	.25
1447	42c multicolored	.65	.30
a.	A609 Pair, #1446-1447	1.30	1.10

Nos. 1446-1447 printed in panes of 25 containing 16 No. 1446 and 9 No. 1447.

World War II Type of 1989

1992, Nov. 10 *Perf. 13½*

1448	A568 42c War reporting	.75	.45
1449	A568 42c Newfoundland air bases	.75	.45
1450	A568 42c Raid on Dieppe	.75	.45
1451	A568 42c U-boats offshore	.75	.45
a.	Block or strip of 4, #1448-1451	3.00	2.50

A611

Santa Claus A612

1992, Nov. 13 *Perf. 12½*

1452	A611 42c Jouluvana	.65	.25
a.	Perf. 13½	.90	.25
b.	As "a," booklet pane of 10	9.00	5.00
	Complete booklet, #1452b	10.00	

Perf. 13½

1453	A611 48c La Befana	1.10	.75
a.	Booklet pane of 5 + label	5.50	4.75
	Complete booklet, #1453a	6.00	
1454	A611 84c Weihnachtsmann	1.50	.75
a.	Booklet pane of 5 + label	7.50	6.00
	Complete booklet, #1454a	8.50	

Booklet Stamp

Perf. 12½x13

1455	A612 37c Santa Claus	.75	.75
a.	Booklet pane of 10	7.50	
	Complete booklet, #1455a	8.50	
	Nos. 1452-1455 (4)	4.00	2.50

Christmas. No. 1455 has bar code at left; for use on covers with printed postal code matrix.

A613

Canadian Women: No. 1456, Adelaide Sophia Hoodless (1857-1910), founder of Victorian Order of Nurses. No. 1457, Marie-Josephine Gerin-Lajoie (1890-1971), founder of Notre-Dame du Bon Conseil Institute. No. 1458, Pitseolak Ashoona (c. 1904-83), Inuit graphic artist. No. 1459, Helen Alice Kinnear (1894-1970), first woman appointed King's Counsel and first federally appointed woman judge.

1993, Mar. 8 *Perf. 12½*

1456	A613 43c multicolored	.65	.30
1457	A613 43c multicolored	.65	.30
1458	A613 43c multicolored	.65	.30
1459	A613 43c multicolored	.65	.30
a.	Block or strip of 4, #1456-1459	2.60	2.25

Natl. Council of Women of Canada (NCWC), and Natl. office of YWCA, cent.

Stanley Cup, Cent. — A614

1993, Apr. 16 *Perf. 13½*

1460	A614 43c multicolored	.75	.25

Handcrafted Textiles — A615

No. 1461, Coverlet, New Brunswick. No. 1462, Pieced quilt, Ontario. No. 1463, Doukhobor bedcover, Saskatchewan. No. 1464, Kwakwaka'wakw ceremonial robe, British Columbia. No. 1465, Boutonne coverlet, Quebec.

Booklet Stamps

Perf. 13x12½ on 3 Sides

1993, Apr. 30

1461	A615 43c multicolored	.75	.40
1462	A615 43c multicolored	.75	.40
1463	A615 43c multicolored	.75	.40
1464	A615 43c multicolored	.75	.40
1465	A615 43c multicolored	.75	.40
a.	Strip of 5, #1461-1465	3.75	3.00
b.	Bklt. pane, 2 ea #1461-1465	7.50	
	Complete booklet, #1465b	8.50	

Stamps in bottom row of No. 1465b are in different sequence than those in No. 1465a.

Art Type of 1988

Painting: Drawing for The Owl, by Kenojuak Ashevak.

Litho. with Foil Application

1993, May 17 *Perf. 12½x13½*

1466	A546 86c multicolored	1.50	1.10

Intl. Year of Indigenous People.

Historic Canadian Pacific Railway Hotels A616

No. 1467, Empress, Victoria, B.C. No. 1468, Banff Springs, Banff, Alberta. No. 1469, Royal York, Toronto, Ont. No. 1470, Chateau Frontenac, Quebec. No. 1471, Algonquin, St. Andrews, N.B.

Booklet Stamps

1993, June 14 *Perf. 13½ on 3 Sides*

1467	A616 43c multicolored	.90	.60
1468	A616 43c multicolored	.90	.65
1469	A616 43c multicolored	.90	.60
1470	A616 43c multicolored	.90	.60
1471	A616 43c multicolored	.90	.60
a.	Strip of 5, #1467-1471	4.50	3.50
b.	Booklet pane, 2 #1471a	9.00	
	Complete booklet, #1471b	10.00	

Opening of Chateau Frontenac, cent.

Miniature Sheet

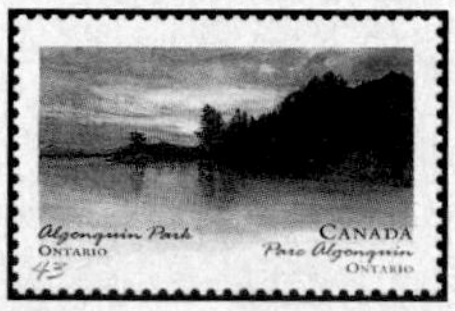

Canada Day A617

Provincial and Territorial Parks: No. 1472, Algonquin, Ontario. No. 1473, De la Gaspesie, Quebec. No. 1474, Cedar Dunes, Prince Edward Island. No. 1475, Cape St. Mary's Seabird Ecological Reserve, Newfoundland. No. 1476, Mount Robson, British Columbia. No. 1477, Writing-On-Stone, Alberta. No. 1478, Spruce Woods, Manitoba. No. 1479, Herschel Island, Yukon. No. 1480, Cypress Hills, Saskatchewan. No. 1481, The Rocks, New Brunswick, No. 1482, Blomidon, Nova Scotia. No. 1483, Katannilik, Northwest Territories.

1993, June 30 *Perf. 13*

1472	A617 43c multicolored	1.00	1.00
1473	A617 43c multicolored	1.00	1.00
1474	A617 43c multicolored	1.00	1.00
1475	A617 43c multicolored	1.00	1.00
1476	A617 43c multicolored	1.00	1.00
1477	A617 43c multicolored	1.00	1.00
1478	A617 43c multicolored	1.00	1.00
1479	A617 43c multicolored	1.00	1.00
1480	A617 43c multicolored	1.00	1.00
1481	A617 43c multicolored	1.00	1.00
1482	A617 43c multicolored	1.00	1.00
1483	A617 43c multicolored	1.00	1.00
a.	Pane of 12, #1472-1483	12.00	12.00

Algonquin Park, centennial.

City of Toronto, Bicent. — A618

1993, Aug. 6 *Perf. 13½x13*

1484	A618 43c multicolored	.75	.25

Canadian Rivers Type of 1991
Booklet Stamps

1993, Aug. 10 *Perf. 13x12½*

1485	A586 43c Fraser	.75	.40
1486	A586 43c Yukon	.75	.40
1487	A586 43c Red	.75	.40
1488	A586 43c St. Lawrence	.75	.40
1489	A586 43c St. John	.75	.40
a.	Strip of 5, #1485-1489	3.75	3.50
b.	Bklt. pane, 2 each #1485-1489	7.50	
	Complete booklet, #1489b	8.50	
c.	As "a," imperf	*3,000.*	

Miniature Sheet

Historic Automobiles — A619

a, 1867 H.S. Taylor Steam Buggy. b, 1908 Russell Model L Touring Car. c, 1914 Ford Model T Open Touring Car. d, 1950 Studebaker Champion Deluxe Starlight Coupe. e, 1928 McLaughlin-Buick Model 28-496 Special Car. f, 1923-24 Gray-Dort 25-SM Luxury Sedan.

1993, Aug. 23 *Perf. 12½x13*

1490 A619 Pane of 6 7.50 7.50
a.-b. 43c any single, 35x22mm .75 .75
c.-d. 49c any single, 43x22mm .90 .90
e.-f. 86c any single, 51x22mm 1.50 1.40

See Nos. 1527, 1552, 1604-1605.

Folk Songs A620

Designs: No. 1491, The Alberta Homesteader, Alberta. No. 1492, Les Raftmans, Quebec. No. 1493, I'se the B'y That Builds the Boat, Newfoundland. No. 1494, Onkwa:ri tenhanonniahkwe, Kanien'kehaka (Mohawk).

1993, Sept. 7 *Perf. 12½*

1491 A620 43c multicolored .65 .30
1492 A620 43c multicolored .65 .30
1493 A620 43c multicolored .65 .30
1494 A620 43c multicolored .65 .30
a. Block of 4, #1491-1494 2.60 2.20

Dinosaurs — A621

1993, Oct. 1 *Perf. 13½*

1495 A621 43c Massospondylus .65 .30
1496 A621 43c Styracosaurus .65 .30
1497 A621 43c Albertosaurus .65 .30
1498 A621 43c Platecarpus .65 .30
a. Block or strip of 4, #1495-1498 2.60 2.20
b. As "a," imperf. *2,750.*

See Nos. 1529-1532.

A622

Santa Claus A623

1993, Nov. 4

1499 A622 43c Swiety Mikolaj .65 .25
a. Booklet pane of 10 6.50 5.00
Complete booklet, #1499a 7.50
b. Horiz. pair, imperf between *1,200.*
1500 A622 49c Ded Moroz .75 .45
a. Booklet pane of 5 + label 3.75 3.25
Complete booklet, #1500a 4.75
1501 A622 86c Father Christmas, Australia 1.50 .55
a. Booklet pane of 5 + label 7.50 6.50
Complete booklet, #1501a 8.50

Booklet Stamp

Perf. 13

1502 A623 38c Santa Claus .75 .60
a. Booklet pane of 10 7.50 7.00
Complete booklet, #1502a 8.50
Nos. 1499-1502 (4) 3.65 1.85

Christmas. No. 1502 has bar code at left; for use on covers with printed postal code matrix.

World War II Type of 1989

1993, Nov. 8 *Perf. 13½*

1503 A568 43c Aid to Allies .75 .45
1504 A568 43c Bomber forces .75 .45
1505 A568 43c Battle of the Atlantic .75 .45
1506 A568 43c Italian campaign .75 .45
a. Block or strip of 4, #1503-1506 3.00 2.50

Greetings — A624

Design: No. 1508, "Canada" at right.

1994, Jan. 28 *Die Cut*

Self-Adhesive

1507 A624 43c multicolored .90 .70
1508 A624 43c multicolored .90 .70
a. Bklt. pane of 10, 5 each #1507-1508 9.00

No. 1508a also contains 35 self-adhesive greetings labels in seven designs that complete the design when placed in the central circle of Nos. 1507-1508.

See Nos. 1568-1569, 1600-1601.

Jeanne Sauve (1922-93), Governor General — A625

1994, Mar. 8 *Perf. 12½x13*

1509 A625 43c + label, multi .75 .30
a. Block or horiz. strip of 4 + 4 labels 3.00 2.25

No. 1509 issued se-tenant with label in sheets of 20 + 20 labels in four designs. In alternating rows, labels appear on left or right side of stamp.

T. Eaton Company, 125th Anniv. — A626

1994, Mar. 17 *Perf. 13½x13*

1510 A626 43c multicolored .75 .30
a. Booklet pane of 10 + 2 labels 7.50 6.25
Complete booklet, #1510a 8.50

Canadian Rivers Type of 1991

Booklet Stamps

1994, Apr. 22 *Perf. 13½*

1511 A586 43c Saguenay .90 .45
1512 A586 43c French .90 .45
1513 A586 43c Mackenzie .90 .45
1514 A586 43c Churchill .90 .45
1515 A586 43c Columbia .90 .45
a. Strip of 5, #1511-1515 4.50 3.50
b. Bklt. pane, 2 ea #1511-1515 9.00 9.00
Complete booklet, #1515b 10.00

Art Type of 1988

Vera, by Frederick H. Varley (1881-1969).

Litho. with Foil Application

1994, May 6 *Perf. 14x14½*

1516 A546 88c multicolored 1.50 1.10

XV Commonwealth Games, Victoria, BC — A627

1994 **Litho.** *Perf. 14*

1517 A627 43c Lawn bowls .75 .25
1518 A627 43c Lacrosse .75 .25
a. Pair, #1517-1518 1.50 1.10
1519 A627 43c Wheelchair marathon .75 .25
1520 A627 43c High jump .75 .25
a. Pair, #1519-1520 1.50 1.10
1521 A627 50c Diving .90 .75
a. Gold ("CANADA 50") omitted *1,600.*
1522 A627 88c Cycling 1.50 .90
a. Gold ("CANADA 88") omitted *2,000.*
Nos. 1517-1522 (6) 5.40 2.65

Certificates of authenticity recommended for Nos. 1521a and 1522a.

Issued: Nos. 1517-1518, 5/20; Nos. 1519-1522, 8/5.

Souvenir Sheet

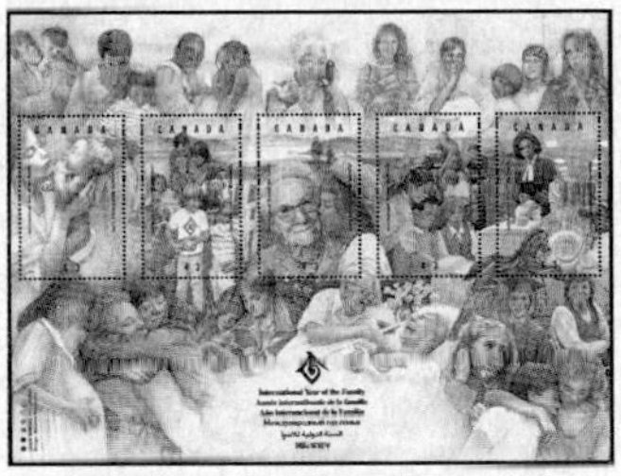

Intl. Year of the Family — A628

Designs: a, Mother and infant. b, Adults, children playing. c, Elderly woman, child. d, Adults, children in class. e, Judge, health care worker, child.

1994, June 2

1523 A628 Pane of 5 3.75 3.75
a.-e. 43c any single .75 .75

Canada Day — A629

Maple trees: a, Big leaf. b, Sugar. c, Silver. d, Striped. e, Norway. f, Manitoba. g, Black. h, Douglas. i, Mountain. j, Vine. k, Hedge. l, Red.

1994, June 30 *Perf. 13x13½*

1524 A629 Pane of 12 9.00 9.00
a.-l. 43c any single .75 .75

Billy Bishop (1894-1956), Fighter Ace — A630

Design: No. 1526, Mary Travers, "La Bolduc" (1894-1941), folk singer.

1994, Aug. 12 *Perf. 13*

1525 A630 43c multicolored .65 .30
1526 A630 43c multicolored .65 .30
a. Pair, #1525-1526 1.30 .90

Historic Vehicles Type of 1993

Miniature Sheet

Designs: a, 1942 Ford F60L-AMB military ambulance. b, 1925 REO Speed Wagon Police Wagon. c, 1927 Sicard Snow Remover/Snowblower. d, 1936 Bickle Chieftain Fire Engine. e, 1894 Ottawa Car Company Streetcar. f, 1950 Motor Coach Industries Courier 50 Skyview bus.

1994, Aug. 19 *Perf. 12½x13*

1527 Pane of 6 6.75 6.75
a.-b. A619 43c any single .75 .75
c.-d. A619 50c any single .90 .90
e.-f. A619 88c any single 1.70 1.60

ICAO, 50th Anniv. A632

1994, Sept. 16 *Perf. 13*

1528 A632 43c multicolored 1.10 .25

Dinosaur Type of 1993

Prehistoric animals: No. 1529, Coryphodon. No. 1530, Megacerops. No. 1531, Short-faced bear. No. 1532, Woolly mammoth.

1994, Sept. 26

1529 A621 43c multicolored .65 .30
1530 A621 43c multicolored .65 .30
1531 A621 43c multicolored .65 .30
1532 A621 43c multicolored .65 .30
a. Block or strip of 4, #1529-1532 2.60 2.20

Family Singing Carols A633

Soloist A634

1994, Nov. 3 *Perf. 13½*

1533 A633 43c multicolored .65 .25
a. Booklet pane of 10 6.50 6.50
Complete booklet, #1533a 7.00
1534 A633 50c Choir, vert. .75 .55
a. Booklet pane of 5 + label 5.00 4.00
Complete booklet, #1534a 5.50
1535 A633 88c Caroling, vert. 1.50 .90
a. Booklet pane of 5 + label 7.50 7.00
Complete booklet, #1535a 8.00

Booklet Stamp

Perf. 13

1536 A634 38c multicolored .75 .55
a. Booklet pane of 10 7.50 6.00
Complete booklet, #1536a 8.00
Nos. 1533-1536 (4) 3.65 2.25

Christmas. No. 1536 has bar code at left; for use on covers with printed postal code matrix.

Examples exist of 52c and 90c denominations with the same designs as Nos. 1534 (52c) and 1535 (90c). These were prepared in advance in anticipation of a rate increase that was not approved. Virtually all were destroyed, but a small quantity are known in private hands. None were regularly issued or sold at post offices. Values: 52c, $150; 90c, $475.

World War II Type of 1989

No. 1537, D-Day beachhead. No. 1538, Artillery-Normandy. No. 1539, Tactical Air Forces. No. 1540, Walcheren and the Scheldt.

1994, Nov. 7 *Perf. 13½*

1537 A568 43c multicolored .90 .35
1538 A568 43c multicolored .90 .35
1539 A568 43c multicolored .90 .35
1540 A568 43c multicolored .90 .35
a. Block or strip of 4, #1537-1540 3.60 2.20

World War II Type of 1989

No. 1541, Veterans return home. No. 1542, Freeing the POW. No. 1543, Liberation of civilians. No. 1544, Crossing the Rhine.

1995, Mar. 20

1541 A568 43c multicolored .90 .35
1542 A568 43c multicolored .90 .35
1543 A568 43c multicolored .90 .35
1544 A568 43c multicolored .90 .35
a. Block or strip of 4, #1541-1544 3.60 3.00

Art Type of 1988

Painting: Floraison, by Alfred Pellan (1906-88).

Litho. with Foil Application

1995, Apr. 21 *Perf. 13*

1545	A546 88c multicolored	1.70	1.10
a.	Gold foil omitted	*1,600.*	

Flag Over Lake — A635

1995, May 1 Litho. *Perf. 13½x13*

1546	A635 (43c) multicolored	.90	.25

No. 1546 was valued at the first class domestic letter rate on day of issue.

Fortress of Louisbourg, 275th Anniv. — A636

No. 1547, Louisbourg Harbor, ships near Dauphin Gate. No. 1548, Walls, streets, buildings of Louisbourg. No. 1549, Museum behind King's Bastion. No. 1550, Drawing of King's Garden, Convent, Hospital and barracks. No. 1551, Partially eroded fortifications.

1995, May 5 *Perf. 12½x13*

1547	A636 (43c) 48x32mm	.75	.40
1548	A636 (43c) 32x32mm	.75	.40
1549	A636 (43c) 40x32mm	.75	.40
1550	A636 (43c) 56x32mm	.75	.40
1551	A636 (43c) 48x32mm	.75	.40
a.	Strip of 5, #1547-1551	3.75	3.25
b.	Booklet pane, 2 #1551a	7.50	6.75
	Complete booklet, #1551b	7.75	

Nos. 1547-1551 were valued at the first class domestic letter rate on day of issue. No. 1551a is a continuous design.

Historic Vehicles Type of 1993

Miniature Sheet

Farm, frontier vehicles: a, 1950 Cockshutt "30" farm tractor. b, 1970 Bombardier Ski-Doo Olympique 335 snowmobile. c, 1948 Bombardier B-12 CS multi-passenger snowmobile. d, 1924 Gotfredson model 20 farm truck. e, 1962 Robin-Nodwell RN 110 tracked carrier. f, 1942 Massey-Harris No. 21 self-propelled combine.

1995, May 26

1552	Pane of 6	7.00	7.00
a.-b.	A619 43c any single, 35x22mm	.75	.75
c.-d.	A619 50c any single, 43x22mm	.95	.95
e.-f.	A619 88c any single, 43x22mm	1.80	1.80

Golf in Canada A637

Designs: No. 1553, Banff Springs Golf Club. No. 1554, Riverside Country Club. No. 1555, Glen Abbey Golf Club. No. 1556, Victoria Golf Club. No. 1557, Royal Montreal Golf Club.

Booklet Stamps

Perf. 13½x13 on 3 Sides

1995, June 6

1553	A637 43c multicolored	.90	.40
1554	A637 43c multicolored	.90	.40
1555	A637 43c multicolored	.90	.40
1556	A637 43c multicolored	.90	.40
1557	A637 43c multicolored	.90	.40
a.	Strip of 5, #1553-1557	4.50	3.75
b.	Booklet pane, 2 #1557a	9.00	8.00
	Complete booklet, #1557b	9.50	

Nat. Golf Week. Canadian Amateur Golf Championship, cent. Royal Canadian Golf Assoc., cent.

Lunenburg Academy, Cent. — A638

1995, June 29 *Perf. 13*

1558	A638 43c multicolored	.65	.25

Souvenir Sheets

Group of Seven — A639

Painting, original members: No. 1559a, October Gold, by Franklin Carmichael. b, From the North Shore, Lake Superior, by Lawren Harris. c, Evening, Les Eboulements, Quebec, by A.Y. Jackson.

No. 1560a, Serenity, Lake of the Woods, by Frank H. Johnston. b, A September Gale, Georgian Bay, by Arthur Lismer. c, Falls, Montreal River, by J.E.H. MacDonald. d, Open Window, by Frederick Horsman Varley.

Painting, new members: No. 1561a, Mill Houses, by Alfred J. Casson. b, Pembina Valley, by Lionel LeMoine FitzGerald. c, The Lumberjack, by Edwin Headley Holgate.

1995, June 29

1559	A639 Pane of 3	2.75	2.75
a.-c.	43c any single	.90	.90
1560	A639 Pane of 4	3.60	3.60
a.-d.	43c any single	.90	.90
1561	A639 Pane of 3	2.75	2.75
a.-c.	43c any single	.90	.90

Manitoba's Entry Into Confederation, 125th Anniv. — A640

1995, July 14 *Perf. 13½x13*

1562	A640 43c multicolored	.65	.30

Migratory Wildlife — A641

1995, Aug. 15 *Perf. 13x12½*

1563	A641 45c Monarch butterfly	.75	.25
1564	A641 45c Belted kingfisher	.75	.40
1565	A641 45c Northern pintail	.75	.25
1566	A641 45c Hoary bat	.75	.25
a.	Block or strip of 4, #1563-1566	3.00	2.50

No. 1564 with Revised Inscription

1995, Sept. 26

1567	A641 45c like #1564	.90	.75
a.	Block or strip of 4, #1563, 1565-1567	3.60	3.60

No. 1564 inscribed "aune," No. 1567 "Faune." See Mexico No. 1924.

Greetings Type of 1994

Designs: No. 1568, "Canada" at left. No. 1569, "Canada" at right.

Self-Adhesive

Size: 46x22mm

1995, Sept. 1 *Die Cut*

1568	A624 45c green & multi	.90	.75
1569	A624 45c green & multi	.90	.75
a.	Bklt. pane, 5 ea #1568-1569	9.00	

By its nature, No. 1569a is a complete booklet. The peelable backing serves as a booklet cover.

No. 1569a also contains 15 self-adhesive greetings labels in four designs that complete the design when placed in the central circle of Nos. 1568-1569.

No. 1569a exists with special cover and labels commemorating the Canadian Memorial Chiropractic College, Toronto, 50th anniv.

Bridges A642

No. 1570, Quebec Bridge, Quebec. No. 1571, Highway 403-401-410 interchange, Ontario. No. 1572, Hartland Covered Wooden Bridge, New Brunswick. No. 1573, Alex Fraser Bridge, British Columbia.

1995, Sept. 1 *Perf. 12½x13*

1570	A642 45c multicolored	.75	.30
1571	A642 45c multicolored	.75	.30
1572	A642 45c multicolored	.75	.30
1573	A642 45c multicolored	.75	.30
a.	Block or strip of 4, #1570-1573	3.00	2.50

Canadian Arctic A643

No. 1574, Polar bear, caribou. No. 1575, Arctic poppy, cargo canoe. No. 1576, Inuk man, igloo, sled dogs. No. 1577, Dog-sled team, ski plane. No. 1578, Children.

Booklet Stamps

1995, Sept. 15 *Perf. 13x12½*

1574	A643 45c multicolored	.75	.30
1575	A643 45c multicolored	.75	.30
1576	A643 45c multicolored	.75	.30
1577	A643 45c multicolored	.75	.30
1578	A643 45c multicolored	.75	.30
a.	Strip of 5, #1574-1578	3.75	3.25
b.	Bklt. pane, 2 #1578a	7.50	7.50
	Complete booklet, #1578b	8.00	

Stamps in bottom row of No. 1578b are in different sequence.

Comic Book Characters A644

Booklet Stamps

1995, Oct. 2 *Perf. 13x12½*

1579	A644 45c Superman	1.10	.40
1580	A644 45c Johnny Canuck	1.10	.40
1581	A644 45c Nelvana	1.10	.40
1582	A644 45c Captain Canuck	1.10	.40
1583	A644 45c Fleur de Lys	1.10	.40
a.	Strip of 5, #1579-1583	5.50	5.00
b.	Booklet pane, 2 #1583a	11.00	11.00
	Complete booklet, #1583b	11.50	

Stamps in the bottom row of No. 1583b are in different sequence.

UN, 50th Anniv. A645

1995, Oct. 24 *Perf. 13½*

1584	A645 45c blue & multi	1.20	.25

No. 1584 printed in panes of 10 with top label equal to 10 stamps. Label shows details of Canadian participation in UN activities. UN emblem on No. 1584 is stamped in blue foil.

Capital Sculptures, by Emile Brunet (1893-1977), Sainte-Anne-de-Deaupre Basilica — A646

Holly A647

1995, Nov. 2

1585	A646 45c The Nativity	.65	.25
a.	Booklet pane of 10	6.50	5.50
	Complete booklet, #1585a	7.00	
1586	A646 52c The Annunciation	.75	.50
a.	Booklet pane of 5 + label	3.75	3.75
	Complete booklet, #1586a	4.00	
1587	A646 90c Flight to Egypt	1.30	.60
a.	Booklet pane of 5 + label	6.50	6.00
	Complete booklet, #1587a	7.00	

Booklet Stamp

Perf. 12½x13

1588	A647 40c multicolored	.75	.75
a.	Booklet pane of 10	7.50	*10.00*
	Complete booklet, #1588a	7.75	
	Nos. 1585-1588 (4)	3.45	2.10

Christmas. No. 1588 has bar code at left; for use on covers with printed postal code matrix.

La Francophonie's Agency for Cultural and Technical Cooperation, 25th Anniv. — A648

1995, Nov. 6 *Perf. 13x13½*

1589	A648 45c multicolored	.65	.25

End of the Holocaust, 50th Anniv. — A649

1995, Nov. 9 *Perf. 12½x13*

1590	A649 45c multicolored	.65	.25

Birds A650

No. 1591, American kestrel. No. 1592, Atlantic puffin. No. 1593, Pileated woodpecker. No. 1594, Ruby-throated hummingbird.

1996, Jan. 9 ***Perf. 13½***

1591	A650	45c multicolored	.75	.30
1592	A650	45c multicolored	.75	.30
1593	A650	45c multicolored	.75	.30
1594	A650	45c multicolored	.75	.30
a.		Strip of 4, Nos. 1591-1594	3.00	2.75

Issued in panes of 12 stamps, printed checkerwise, and in uncut sheets of 5 panes.

See Nos. 1631-1634, 1710-1713, 1770-1777, 1839-1846, 1886-1893.

High Technology Industries — A651

Designs: No. 1595, Ocean technology. No. 1596, Aerospace technology. No. 1597, Information technology. No. 1598, Biotechnology.

Booklet Stamps

1996, Feb. 15 ***Perf. 13½ on 3 Sides***

1595	A651	45c multicolored	.90	.35
1596	A651	45c multicolored	.90	.35
1597	A651	45c multicolored	.90	.35
1598	A651	45c multicolored	.90	.35
a.		Booklet pane of 12, 3 each Nos. 1595-1598	11.00	7.50
		Complete booklet, No. 1598a	11.50	
		Nos. 1595-1598 (4)	3.60	1.40

Greetings Type of 1994

"Canada": No. 1600, at L. No. 1601, at R.

Self-Adhesive

Size: 51x25mm

1996, Jan. 15 ***Die Cut***

1600	A624	45c green & multi	1.50	1.20
1601	A624	45c green & multi	1.50	1.20
a.		Booklet pane, 5 ea #1600-1601	15.00	
b.		As "a," die cutting omitted	*3,500.*	

By its nature No. 1601a is a complete booklet. The peelable backing serves as a booklet cover.

No. 1601a also contains 35 self-adhesive greetings labels in seven designs that complete the design when placed in the central circle of Nos. 1600-1601.

Art Type of 1988

Sculpture: The Spirit of Haida Gwaii, by Bill Reid.

Litho. with Foil Application

1996, Apr. 30 ***Perf. 12½x13***

1602	A546	90c multicolored	1.50	1.00

AIDS Awareness — A652

1996, May 8 **Litho.** ***Perf. 13½***

1603	A652	45c multicolored	.65	.25

Historic Vehicles Type of 1993

No. 1604: a, 1899 Still Motor Co. Ltd. Electric Van. b. 1914 Waterous Engine Works Road Roller. c, 1938 International D-35 Delivery Truck. d, 1936 Champion Road Grader. e, 1947 White Model WA 122 Tractor Trailer. f, 1975 Hayes HDX 45-115 Logging Truck.

No. 1605: a, like #1490a. b, like #1490b. c, like 1527a. d, like #1527b. e, like #1552b. f, like #1604a. g, like #1604b, h, like #1552a. i, like #1604c. j, like 1604d. k, like #1527e. l, like #1527f. m, like #1604e. n, like #1604f. o, like #1490c. p, like #1490d. q, like #1527d. r, like #1490e. s, like #1490f. t, like #1527c. u, like #1552c. v, like #1552d. w, like #1552e. x, like #1552f. y, 1975 Bricklin SV-1 Sports car.

1996 ***Perf. 12½x13***

1604	A619	Pane of 6	6.50	6.50
a.-b.		45c any single	.80	.80
c.-d.		52c any single	.90	.90
e.-f.		90c any single	1.50	1.50
1605	A619	Pane of 25	9.00	9.00
a.-j.		5c any single	.25	.25
k.-n.		10c any single	.30	.30
o.-x.		20c any single	.45	.45
y.		45c multicolored	1.00	1.00

Nos. 1604e-1604f, 1605k-1605n, 1605y are 51x22mm. Nos. 1605o-1605x are 43x21mm.

Yukon Gold Rush, Cent. — A653

Designs: a, "Skookum" Jim Mason's discovery on Rabbit (Bonanza) Creek, 1896. b, Miners trekking to gold fields, boats on Lake Laberge. c, Supr. Sam Steele, North West Mounted Police, Alaska-Yukon border. d, Dawson, boom town, city of entertainment. e, Klondike gold fields.

1996, June 13 ***Perf. 13½***

1606	A653	Strip of 5	5.50	4.75
a.-e.		45c any single	1.10	.60

CAPEX '96. No. 1606 was issued in panes of 10 stamps.

Canada Day — A654

Self-Adhesive

1996, June 28 ***Die Cut***

1607	A654	45c multicolored	.75	.25
a.		Pane of 12	9.00	4.00

Canadian Olympic Gold Medalists A655

No. 1608, Ethel Catherwood, high jump, 1928. No. 1609, Etienne Desmarteau, 56 lb. weight throw, 1904. No. 1610, Fanny Rosenfeld, 100m, 400m relay, 1928. No. 1611, Gerald Ouellette, smallbore rifle, prone, 1956. No. 1612, Percy Williams, 100m, 200m, 1928.

Booklet Stamps

Litho. & Typo.

1996, July 8 ***Perf. 13x12½***

1608	A655	45c multicolored	1.00	.60
1609	A655	45c multicolored	1.00	.60
1610	A655	45c multicolored	1.00	.60
1611	A655	45c multicolored	1.00	.60
1612	A655	45c multicolored	1.00	.60
a.		Strip of 5, #1608-1612	5.00	4.00
b.		Booklet pane, 2 #1612a	10.00	
		Complete booklet, #1612b	10.50	

British Columbia's Entry Into Confederation, 125th Anniv. — A656

1996, July 19

1613	A656	45c multicolored	.65	.25

A657

1996, Aug. 19 **Litho.** ***Perf. 12½x12***

1614	A657	45c Canadian Heraldry	.65	.25

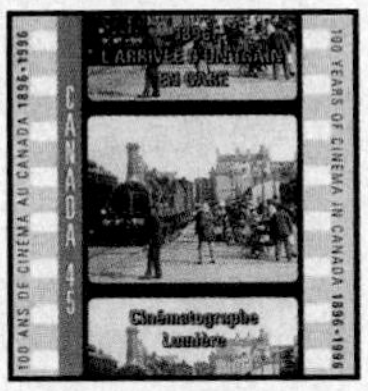

Motion Pictures, Cent. — A658

Film strips from motion pictures: No. 1615a, L'arrivée d'un train en gare, Lumière cinematography, 1896. b, Back to God's Country, Nell & Ernest Shipman, 1919. c, Hen Hop, Norman McLaren, 1942. d, Pour la suite du monde, Pierre Perrault, Michel Brault, 1963. e, Goin' Down the Road, Don Shebib, 1970.

No. 1616a, Mon oncle Antoine, Claude Jutra, 1971. b, The Apprenticeship of Duddy Kravitz, Ted Kotcheff, 1974. c, Les Ordres, Michel Brault, 1974. d, Les Bons Débarras, Francis Mankiewiez, 1980. e, The Grey Fox, Philip Borsos, 1982.

Self-Adhesive

1996, Aug. 22 ***Die Cut***

1615		Pane of 5	3.25	3.25
a.-e.		A658 45c Any single	.65	.65
1616		Pane of 5	3.25	3.25
a.-e.		A658 45c Any single	.65	.65

Edouard Montpetit (1881-1954), Educator A659

1996, Sept. 26 ***Perf. 12½***

1617	A659	45c multicolored	.65	.25

Winnie the Pooh A660

Designs: No. 1618, Winnie, Lt. Colebourne, 1914. No. 1619, Winnie, Christopher Robin, 1925. No. 1620, Milne and Shepard's Winnie the Pooh, 1926. No. 1621, Winnie the Pooh at Walt Disney World, 1996.

1996, Oct. 1 ***Perf. 12½x13***

1618	A660	45c multicolored	.75	.40
1619	A660	45c multicolored	.75	.40
1620	A660	45c multicolored	.75	.40
1621	A660	45c multicolored	.75	.40
a.		Block of 4, #1618-1621	3.00	2.50
b.		Souv. sheet of 4, #1618-1621	7.50	7.50
c.		Booklet pane of 16, 4 each #1618-1621	12.00	12.00
		Complete booklet, #1621c	12.50	

No. 1621c was issued with the halves of the booklet pane printed tete-beche. The booklet pane of 16 was used as a cover for a souvenir story booklet.

Walt Disney World, 25th anniv.

Authors — A661

No. 1622, Margaret Laurence (1926-87). No. 1623, Donald G. Creighton (1902-79). No. 1624, Gabrielle Roy (1909-83). No. 1625, Felix-Antoine Savard (1896-1982). No. 1626, Thomas C. Haliburton (1796-1865).

Booklet Stamps

Perf. 13½x13 on 3 Sides

1996, Oct. 10 **Litho. & Engr.**

1622	A661	45c multicolored	1.10	.40
1623	A661	45c multicolored	1.10	.40
1624	A661	45c multicolored	1.10	.40
1625	A661	45c multicolored	1.10	.40
1626	A661	45c multicolored	1.10	.40
a.		Strip of 5, #1622-1626	5.50	5.00
b.		Booklet pane, 2 #1626a	11.00	12.00
		Complete booklet, #1626b	11.50	

A662

Christmas: 45c, Children on snowshoes, sled. 52c, Santa Claus skiing. 90c, Children skating.

Perf. 13½ (#1627, 1629a), 12¾x12¼ (#1628, 1629), 13½x13 (#1627a, 1628a)

1996, Nov. 1 **Litho.**

1627	A662	45c multicolored	.65	.25
a.		Booklet pane of 10	6.50	6.50
		Complete booklet, #1627a	7.00	
1628	A662	52c multicolored	.80	.25
a.		Booklet pane of 5 + label	4.00	4.50
		Complete booklet, #1628a	4.25	
1629	A662	90c multicolored	1.30	.50
a.		Booklet pane of 5 + label	6.50	7.00
		Complete booklet, #1629a	7.00	

UNICEF, 50th anniv.

New Year 1997 (Year of the Ox) — A663

1997, Jan. 7 ***Perf. 13x12½***

1630	A663	45c multicolored	.90	.25
a.		Souvenir sheet of 2	2.60	2.60
b.		As No. 1630, gold omitted	*4,000.*	
c.		As "a," gold omitted	*9,000.*	

No. 1630a is fan shaped.

No. 1630a with Hong Kong 97 overprint was sold as a limited edition only at the show. Value $7.50.

Bird Type of 1996

No. 1631, Mountain bluebird. No. 1632, Western grebe. No. 1633, Northern gannet. No. 1634, Scarlet tanager.

1997, Jan. 10 ***Perf. 12½x13***

1631	A650	45c multicolored	.75	.25
1632	A650	45c multicolored	.75	.25
1633	A650	45c multicolored	.75	.25
1634	A650	45c multicolored	.75	.25
a.		Block or strip of 4, #1631-1634	3.00	2.50

Nos. 1631-1634 were issued in panes of 20, 5 each, printed checkerwise to contain 4 complete blocks or 5 strips.

Art Type of 1988

Painting: York Boat on Lake Winnipeg, by Walter J. Phillips.

Litho. with Foil Application

1997, Feb. 17

1635	A546	90c gold & multi	1.80	1.10

Canadian Tire, 75th Anniv. A664

1997, Mar. 3 **Litho.** ***Perf. 13x13½***

1636	A664	45c multicolored	.75	.25

Father Charles-Emile Gadbois (1906-81), Musicologist
A665

1997, Mar. 20 *Perf. 13½x13*
1637 A665 45c multicolored .75 .25

Québec en Fleurs 97, Intl. Horticultural Exhibition
A666

Booklet Stamps

Perf. 13x12½ on 3 Sides

1997, Apr. 4
1638 A666 45c Blue poppy .75 .25
a. Booklet pane of 12 9.00 10.00
Complete booklet, #1638a 9.50

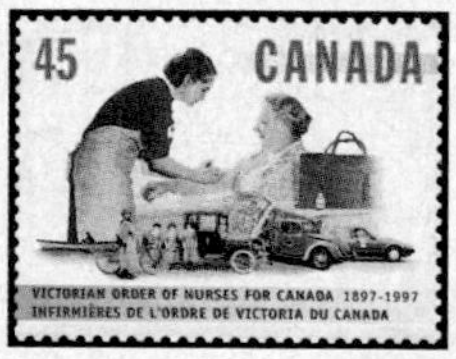

Victorian Order of Nurses for Canada, Cent.
A667

1997, May 12 *Perf. 12½x13*
1639 A667 45c multicolored .75 .25

Law Society of Upper Canada, Bicent. — A668

1997, May 23 *Perf. 13½x13*
1640 A668 45c multicolored .75 .25

Salt Water Fish
A669

No. 1641, Great white shark. No. 1642, Pacific halibut. No. 1643, Atlantic sturgeon. No. 1644, Bluefin tuna.

1997, May 30 *Perf. 12½x13*
1641 A669 45c multicolored .65 .25
1642 A669 45c multicolored .65 .25
1643 A669 45c multicolored .65 .25
1644 A669 45c multicolored .65 .25
a. Block or strip of 4, #1641-1644 2.60 2.20

Opening of the Confederation Bridge — A670

1997, May 31
1645 A670 45c Lighthouse, bridge .65 .25
1646 A670 45c Bridge, bird .65 .25
a. Pair, #1645-1646 + label 1.30 1.10

Gilles Villeneuve (1950-82), Formula One Race Car Driver — A671

45c, Villeneuve winning race in Ferrari T-4. 90c, Close-up, racing in Number 12 Ferrari T-3.

1997, June 12
1647 A671 45c multicolored .75 .25
1648 A671 90c multicolored 1.50 .90
a. Pair, #1647-1648 2.25 2.25
b. Pane of 4 #1648a 9.00 9.00

John Cabot's Voyage to Canada, 500th Anniv.
A672

1997, June 24
1649 A672 45c multicolored .75 .25

See Italy No. 2162.

Scenic Canadian Highways — A673

Designs: No. 1650, Sea to Sky Highway, British Columbia. No. 1651, The Cabot Trail, Nova Scotia. No. 1652, The Wine Route, starting in Ontario. No. 1653, The Big Muddy, Saskatchewan.

1997, June 30
1650 A673 45c multicolored .65 .40
1651 A673 45c multicolored .65 .40
1652 A673 45c multicolored .65 .40
1653 A673 45c multicolored .65 .40
a. Block or strip of 4, #1650-1653 2.60 2.20

See Nos. 1739-1742, 1780-1783.

Canadian Industrial Design — A674

1997, July 23
1654 A674 45c multicolored .65 .25

No. 1654 was issued with se-tenant label in panes of 24 + 24 labels. The 12 different labels each appear twice in different colors. In alternating rows, labels appear on left or right side of stamp.

Association of Canadian Industrial Designers, 50th anniv. and 20th Intl. Congress of Intl. Council of Societies of Industrial Design.

Highland Games, Maxville, Ontario — A675

1997, Aug. 1
1655 A675 45c multicolored .65 .25

Knights of Columbus in Canada, Cent. — A676

1997, Aug. 5 *Perf. 13*
1656 A676 45c multicolored .65 .25

28th World Congress of Postal, Telegraph and Telephone Intl. Labor Union, Montreal
A677

1997, Aug. 18
1657 A677 45c multicolored .65 .25

Asia Pacific Year
A678

1997, Aug. 25 *Perf. 13½*
1658 A678 45c multicolored .65 .25

Canada-USSR Ice Hockey "Series of the Century," 25th Anniv. — A679

Designs: No. 1659, Canadian players, Paul Henderson, Yvan Cournoyer (No. 12), after scoring winning goal in final game. No. 1660, Canadian team members celebrating victory.

Booklet Stamps

1997, Sept. 20 *Perf. 14x13*
1659 A679 45c multicolored .75 .30
1660 A679 45c multicolored .75 .30
a. Bklt. pane, 5 ea #1659-1660 7.50 8.00
Complete booklet, #1660a 8.00

Famous Politicians
A680

No. 1661, Martha Black (1866-1957). No. 1662, Lionel Chevrier (1903-87). No. 1663, Judy LaMarsh (1924-80). No. 1664, Réal Caouette (1917-76).

1997, Sept. 26 *Perf. 13½x13*
1661 A680 45c multicolored .65 .35
1662 A680 45c multicolored .65 .35
1663 A680 45c multicolored .65 .35
a. Double impression of "Canada 45" 55.00
b. Quadruple impression of "Canada 45" 300.00
1664 A680 45c multicolored .65 .35
a. Quintuple impression of "Canada 45" 375.00
b. Block or strip of 4, #1661-1664 2.60 2.00

Supernatural — A681

1997, Oct. 1 *Perf. 13x12½*
1665 A681 45c Vampire .65 .35
1666 A681 45c Werewolf .65 .35
1667 A681 45c Ghost .65 .35
1668 A681 45c Goblin .65 .35
a. Block of 4, #1665-1668 2.60 2.20

Christmas — A682

Stained glass windows: 45c, "Our Lady of the Rosary," Holy Rosary Cathedral, Vancouver. 52c, "Nativity Scene," United Church, Leith, Ontario. 90c, Madonna and Child, St. Stephen's Ukrainian Byzantine Rite Roman Catholic Church, Calgary.

1997, Nov. 3 *Perf. 12½x13*
1669 A682 45c multicolored .70 .25
a. Booklet pane of 10 7.00 7.00
Complete booklet, #1669a 7.50
1670 A682 52c multicolored .80 .35
a. Booklet pane of 5 4.00 4.00
Complete booklet, #1670a 4.25
1671 A682 90c multicolored 1.40 .55
a. Booklet pane of 5 7.00 7.00
Complete booklet, #1671a 7.50
Nos. 1669-1671 (3) 2.90 1.15

75th Royal Agriculture Winter Fair, Toronto
A683

1997, Nov. 6
1672 A683 45c multicolored .65 .25

Types of 1987-98 and

Traditional Handiwork
A684

Maple Leaf
A685

Loon
A686

Moose — A687

Flag and Inukshuk — A688

Designs: 1c, Bookbinding. 2c, Ironwork. 3c, Glass blowing. 4c, Oyster farmer. 5c, Weaving. 9c, Quilting. 10c, Artistic woodworking. 25c, Leatherwork. Nos. 1682, 1698, Flag over icebergs. No. 1688, White-tailed deer. No. 1689, Atlantic walrus. No. 1690, Polar bear. No. 1691, Peregrine falcon. No. 1692, Sable Island horses. $8, Grizzly bear.

1997-2005 Litho. *Perf. 13¼*

1673	A684	1c multicolored	.25	.25
a.		Gray (In numeral "1") omitted	300.00	
1674	A684	2c multicolored	.25	.25
1675	A684	3c multicolored	.25	.25
1676	A684	4c multicolored	.25	.25
a.		Imperf., pair	950.00	
1677	A684	5c multicolored	.25	.25
1678	A684	9c multicolored	.25	.25
1679	A684	10c multicolored	.25	.25
a.		Imperf, single	—	
b.		Block of 4, top two stamps imperf (cut between)	750.00	
1680	A684	25c multicolored	.40	.25

Perf. 13¼x13

1681	A536	46c multicolored	.70	.25

Perf. 13x13¼

1682	A541	46c multicolored	.75	.25
a.		Booklet pane of 10	7.50	*11.00*
		Complete booklet, #1682a	8.00	

Perf. 13¼x13

1683	A536	47c multicolored	.70	.25
a.		Imperf, pair	*650.00*	

Perf. 13x13¼

1684	A685	55c multicolored	.90	.25
a.		Booklet pane of 5 + label	4.50	3.75
		Complete booklet, #1684a	4.75	
1685	A685	73c multicolored	1.10	.40
1686	A685	95c multicolored	1.70	.50
a.		Booklet pane of 5 + label	8.50	8.00
		Complete booklet, #1686a	9.00	

Litho. & Engr.

Perf. 13¼x13

1687	A686	$1 multicolored	1.50	.55

Perf. 12½x13

1688	A686	$1 multicolored	1.50	.55
1689	A686	$1 multicolored	1.50	.55
a.		Pair, #1688-1689	3.00	2.50
b.		Souvenir sheet, 2 each #1688-1689	7.50	7.50

Perf. 13¼x13

1690	A686	$2 multicolored	3.00	1.00

Perf. 12½x13

1691	A686	$2 multicolored	3.25	1.00
1692	A686	$2 multicolored	3.25	1.00
a.		Pair, #1691-1692	6.50	4.75
b.		Souvenir sheet, 2 each #1691-1692	14.00	14.00

Size 63x48mm

1693	A687	$5 multicolored	7.50	2.00
a.		Engraved colors (Moose, etc.) omitted	*5,500.*	
1694	A687	$8 multicolored	12.00	4.50
		Nos. 1673-1694 (22)	41.50	15.05

Coil Stamp

Engr.

Perf. 10 Horiz.

1695	A542	46c red	.75	.25
a.		Imperf, pair	170.00	

Photo.

Booklet Stamp

Self-Adhesive

Die Cut

1696	A685	45c multicolored	1.30	*2.00*
a.		Booklet pane of 18	25.00	

Typo. & Embossed

Die Cut Perf. 13

Coil Stamp

1697	A685	45c multicolored	1.10	.75

Litho.

Booklet Stamps

Die Cut

1698	A541	46c multicolored	.90	.25
a.		Booklet pane of 30	27.00	
b.		Imperf, pair	*300.00*	

Photo.

1699	A685	46c multicolored	2.75	2.75
a.		Booklet pane of 18	50.00	

Litho.

1700	A688	47c multicolored	.75	.25
a.		Booklet of 10	7.50	
b.		Booklet of 30	22.50	
c.		All colors omitted	225.00	
d.		As "a," all colors omitted	2,250.	
e.		As "a," die cutting omitted	1,900.	

Nos. 1696a, 1698a-1699a are complete booklets. The peelable backing serves as a booklet cover.

Issued: Nos. 1681, 1682, 1684-1686, 1695, 1698-1700, 12/28/98; No. 1693, 12/19/03; No. 1694, 10/15; No. 1696, 4/14/98. No. 1697, 9/30/98; Nos. 1687, 1690, 10/27/98; Nos. 1673-1680, 4/29/99; No. 1683, 12/28/00; Nos. 1688-1689, 10/20/05; Nos. 1691-1692, 12/19/05.

No. 1697 does not have the "POSTAGE / POSTES" and copyright inscriptions found in No. 1696. The gold on No. 1697 is embossed and brighter than that on No. 1696.

On Nos. 1700c and 1700d, the booklet cover on the reverse side is properly printed.

See Nos. 1928-1930.

New Year 1998 (Year of the Tiger) A690

1998, Jan. 8 Litho. *Perf. 13x12½*

1708	A690	45c multicolored	.75	.25
a.		Souvenir sheet of 2	1.60	1.40

No. 1708a overprinted exists. Value $3.

Provincial Leaders — A691

Designs: a, John P. Robarts (1917-82), Ontario. b, Jean Lesage (1912-80), Quebec. c, John B. McNair (1889-1968), New Brunswick. d, Tommy Douglas (1904-86), Saskatchewan. e, Joseph R. Smallwood (1900-91), Newfoundland. f, Angus L. MacDonald (1890-1954), Nova Scotia. g, W.A.C. Bennett (1900-79), British Columbia. h, Ernest C. Manning (1908-95), Alberta. i, John Bracken (1883-1969), Manitoba. j, J. Walter Jones (1878-1954), Prince Edward Island.

1998, Feb. 18 *Perf. 13½*

1709	A691	Sheet of 10	11.00	9.00
a.-j.		45c any single	1.10	.75

Bird Type of 1996

No. 1710, Hairy woodpecker. No. 1711, Great crested flycatcher. No. 1712, Eastern screech owl. No. 1713, Gray-crowned rosy-finch.

1998, Mar. 13 *Perf. 13x13½*

1710	A650	45c multicolored	.75	.30
1711	A650	45c multicolored	.75	.30
1712	A650	45c multicolored	.75	.30
1713	A650	45c multicolored	.75	.30
a.		Block or strip of 4, #1710-1713	3.00	2.25

Nos. 1710-1713 were issued in panes of 20, 5 each, printed checkerwise to contain 4 complete blocks or 5 strips.

Fly Fishing in Canada — A693

Lure, type of fish: No. 1715, Coquihalla orange, steelhead trout. No. 1716, Steelhead bee, steelhead trout. No. 1717, Dark Montreal, brook trout. No. 1718, Lady Amherst, Atlantic salmon. No. 1719, Coho blue, coho salmon. No. 1720, Cosseboom special, Atlantic salmon.

1998, Apr. 16 *Perf. 12½x13*

1715	A693	45c multicolored	.90	.45
1716	A693	45c multicolored	.90	.45
1717	A693	45c multicolored	.90	.45
1718	A693	45c multicolored	.90	.45
1719	A693	45c multicolored	.90	.45
1720	A693	45c multicolored	.90	.45
a.		Vertical strip of 6, #1715-1720	5.50	4.50
b.		Bklt. pane, 2 ea #1715-1720	11.00	
		Complete booklet, #1720a	11.50	

Canadian Institute of Mining, Metallurgy and Petroleum, Cent. — A694

1998, May 4 *Perf. 12½*

1721	A694	45c multicolored	.75	.25

Imperial Penny Post, Cent. A695

St. Edward's Crown, #86, Sir William Mulock.

1998, May 29 *Perf. 12½x13*

1722	A695	45c multicolored	.75	.25

No. 1722 was issued in panes of 14 + 1 label.

Sumo Wrestling Tournament, Vancouver — A696

Rising sun, mapleleaf and: No. 1723, Two wrestlers. No. 1724, Sumo champion performing bow twirling ceremony.

1998, June 5 Litho. & Embossed

1723	A696	45c multicolored	.75	.25
1724	A696	45c multicolored	.75	.25
a.		Horiz. or Vert. Pair, #1723-1724 + 4 labels	1.50	1.50
b.		Souvenir sheet, #1723-1724	3.75	3.75

Nos. 1723-1724 were printed checkerwise in panes of 20, 10 each + 40 labels.

Canals of Canada — A697

No. 1725, St. Peters Canal, Nova Scotia. No. 1726, St. Ours Canal, Quebec. No. 1727, Port Carling Lock, Ontario. No. 1728, Locks, Rideau Canal, Ontario. No. 1729, Peterborough lift lock, Trent-Severn Waterway, Ontario. No. 1730, Chambly Canal, Quebec. No. 1731, Lachine Canal, Quebec. No. 1732, Ice skating on Rideau Canal, Ottawa. No. 1733, Boat on Big Chute Marine Railway, Trent-Severn Waterway. No. 1734, Sault Ste. Marie Canal, Ontario.

Booklet Stamps

1998, June 17 Litho. *Perf. 12½*

1725	A697	45c multicolored	1.10	.75
1726	A697	45c multicolored	1.10	.75
1727	A697	45c multicolored	1.10	.75
1728	A697	45c multicolored	1.10	.75
1729	A697	45c multicolored	1.10	.75
1730	A697	45c multicolored	1.10	.75
1731	A697	45c multicolored	1.10	.75
1732	A697	45c multicolored	1.10	.75
1733	A697	45c multicolored	1.10	.75
1734	A697	45c multicolored	1.10	.75
a.		Bklt. pane, #1725-1734 + 10 labels	14.00	
		Complete booklet, #1734a	15.00	

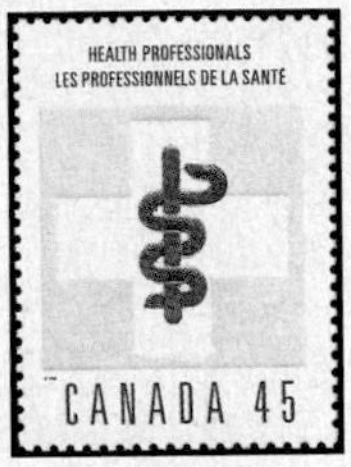

Health Professionals A698

Litho. & Embossed with Foil Application

1998, June 25

1735	A698	45c multicolored	.65	.25

Royal Canadian Mounted Police, 125th Anniv. — A699

No. 1736, Male mountie, native, horse. No. 1737, Female mountie, helicopter, cityscape.

1998, July 3 *Perf. 12½x13*

1736	A699	45c multicolored	.65	.25
1737	A699	45c multicolored	.65	.25
a.		Pair, #1736-1737 + 2 labels	1.30	1.10
b.		Souvenir sheet, #1736-1737 + 1 label	1.50	1.50
c.		As "b," with signature	3.00	3.00
d.		As "b," with Portugal 98 emblem	4.50	4.50
e.		As "b," with Italia 98 emblem	4.50	4.50
f.		As "d," gold embossed emblem omitted	*750.00*	

Nos. 1737c-1737e have added inscriptions in gold. Issued: No. 1737c, 7/3; No. 1737d, 9/4; No. 1737e, 10/23.

William James Roué (1879-1970), Naval Architect — A700

Litho. & Engr.

1998, July 24 *Perf. 13*

1738	A700	45c multicolored	.75	.25

Scenic Highway Type of 1997

Designs: No. 1739, Dempster Highway, Yukon. No. 1740, Dinosaur Trail, Alberta. No. 1741, River Valley Scenic Drive, New Brunswick. No. 1742, Blue Heron Route, Prince Edward Island.

1998, July 28 Litho. *Perf. 12½x13*

1739	A673	45c multicolored	.65	.35
1740	A673	45c multicolored	.65	.35
1741	A673	45c multicolored	.65	.35
1742	A673	45c multicolored	.65	.35
a.		Block or strip of 4, #1739-1742	2.60	2.30

Publication of "Refus Global" by The Automatistes, 50th Anniv. — A701

Painting, artist: No. 1743, "Peinture," Jean-Paul Riopelle. No. 1744, "La dernière campagne de Napoléon," Fernand Leduc. No. 1745, "Jet fuligineux sur noir torturé," Jean-Paul Mousseau. No. 1746, "Le fond du garde-robe," Pierre Gauvreau. No. 1747, "Joie lacustre," Paul-Emile Borduas. No. 1748, "Syndicat des gens de mer," Marcelle Ferron. No. 1749, "Le tumulte á la machoire crispée," Marcel Barbeau.

Self-Adhesive Booklet Stamps

1998, Aug. 7 *Die Cut*

1743 A701 45c multicolored 1.10 1.10
1744 A701 45c multicolored 1.10 1.10
1745 A701 45c multicolored 1.10 1.10
1746 A701 45c multicolored 1.10 1.10
1747 A701 45c multicolored 1.10 1.10
1748 A701 45c multicolored 1.10 1.10
1749 A701 45c multicolored 1.10 1.10
a. Booklet pane, #1743-1749 7.75

No. 1746 is 34x48mm. No. 1749a is a complete booklet. The peelable paper backing serves as a booklet cover.

Legendary Canadians A702

No. 1750, Napoléon-Alexandre Comeau (1848-1923), outdoorsman, "King of the North Shore." No. 1751, Phyllis Munday (1894-1990), mountaineer, community service worker. No. 1752, Bill Mason (1929-88), film maker, canoe enthusiast. No. 1753, Harry "Red" Foster (1905-1985), founder of Canadian Special Olympics, sports enthusiast.

1998, Aug. 15 *Perf. 13½*

1750 A702 45c multicolored .65 .25
1751 A702 45c multicolored .65 .25
1752 A702 45c multicolored .65 .25
1753 A702 45c multicolored .65 .25
a. Block or strip of 4, #1750-1753 2.60 2.20

Art Type of 1988

Painting: The Farmer's Family (detail), by Bruno Bobak.

Litho. with Foil Application

1998, Sept. 8 *Perf. 12½x13*

1754 A546 90c gold & multi 1.50 .90

Housing in Canada A703

a, Native peoples. b, Settler. c, Regional. d, Heritage preservation. e, Multiple unit. f, Prefabricated. g, Veterans. h, Planned community. i, Innovative.

1998, Sept. 23 **Litho.**

1755 Pane of 9 10.00 10.00
a.-i. A703 45c Any single 1.10 1.10

University of Ottawa, 150th Anniv. — A704

1998, Sept. 25 *Perf. 13*

1756 A704 45c multicolored .65 .25

The Circus — A705

Various circus clowns and: No. 1757, Elephant, bear performing tricks. No. 1758, Woman standing on horse, aerial act. No. 1759, Lion tamer. No. 1760, Contortionists, acrobats.

Booklet Stamps

1998, Oct. 1 *Perf. 13 on 3 Sides*

1757 A705 45c multicolored .65 .30
1758 A705 45c multicolored .65 .30
1759 A705 45c multicolored .65 .30
1760 A705 45c multicolored .65 .30
a. Bklt. pane, 3 ea #1757-1760 6.50 6.50
Complete booklet, #1760a 7.00
b. Souvenir sheet, #1757-1760 4.50 3.75

Stamps in No. 1760b are perforated on all four sides.

John Peters Humphrey (1905-95), Author of Universal Declaration of Human Rights A706

1998, Oct. 7 *Perf. 13*

1761 A706 45c multicolored .65 .25

Canadian Naval Reserve, 75th Anniv. — A707

1998, Nov. 4 *Perf. 12½x13*

1762 A707 45c HMCS Sackville .75 .25
1763 A707 45c HMCS Shawinigan .75 .25
a. Pair, #1762-1763 1.50 1.40

Christmas — A708

Sculpted wooden angels: 45c, "Angel of Last Judgment" blowing trumpet. 52c, "Adoring Angel" raising hand. 90c, "Adoring Angel, Kneeling," by Thomas Baillairgé.

1998, Nov. 6 *Perf. 13*

1764 A708 45c multicolored .75 .25
a. Booklet pane of 10 32.50 32.50
Complete booklet, #1764a 35.00
b. Perf 13x13½ 350.00 16.00
c. As "b," booklet pane of 10 15.00 13.50
Complete booklet, #1764c 16.00

The values for No. 1764b are for singles perfed on all four sides from sheet format. These are extremely scarce. Single stamps from booklet pane No. 1764c have a straight edge on one side. Value, booklet single, unused $1.50, used $.30.

Perf. 13x13½

1765 A708 52c multicolored .80 .40
a. Booklet pane of 5 + label 22.50 22.50
Complete booklet, #1765a 23.50
b. Perf 13 1.10 .60
c. As "b," booklet pane of 5 + label 5.50 5.00
Complete booklet, #1765c 6.00

1766 A708 90c multicolored 1.50 .75
a. Booklet pane of 5 + label 37.50 37.50
Complete booklet, #1766a 40.00
b. Perf 13 1.50 .75
c. As "b," booklet pane of 5 + label 7.50 6.75
Complete booklet, #1766c 8.00
Nos. 1764-1766 (3) 3.05 1.40

New Year 1999 (Year of the Rabbit) A709

1999, Jan. 8 *Perf. 13½*

1767 A709 46c multicolored .75 .25
a. Red and tagging omitted *800.00*

Souvenir Sheet

Perf. 12½x13

1768 A709 95c Pane of 1 2.25 2.00
a. Single stamp 1.50 1.25
b. Red and tagging omitted *950.00*

No. 1768 with China 99 overprint was sold only at the show. Value same as unoverprinted pane. Also known with red and tagging omitted. Value $1,750.

Le Theatre du Rideau Vert, 50th Anniv. — A710

1999, Feb. 17 *Perf. 13x12½*

1769 A710 46c multicolored .70 .25

Bird Type of 1996

Designs: No. 1770, Northern goshawk. No. 1771, Red-winged blackbird. No. 1772, American goldfinch. No. 1773, Sandhill crane.

1999, Feb. 24 *Perf. 12½x13*

1770 A650 46c multicolored .70 .30
1771 A650 46c multicolored .70 .30
1772 A650 46c multicolored .70 .30
1773 A650 46c multicolored .70 .30
a. Block or strip of 4, #1770-1773 2.80 1.50

Booklet Stamps Self-Adhesive

Die Cut Perf. 11½

1774 A650 46c like #1770 .90 .35
1775 A650 46c like #1771 .90 .35
1776 A650 46c like #1772 .90 .35
1777 A650 46c like #1773 .90 .35
a. Booklet pane, 2 each #1774-1775, 1 each #1776-1777 5.50
b. Booklet pane, 2 each #1776-1777, 1 each #1774-1775 5.50
Complete booklet, #1777a, #1777b 11.00

Nos. 1770-1773 were issued in panes of 20, 5 each, printed checkerwise to contain 4 complete blocks or strips.

The peelable paper backing of Nos. 1777a, 1777b serves as the booklet cover.

Univ. of British Columbia's Museum of Anthropology, 50th Anniv. — A711

1999, Mar. 9 *Perf. 13½*

1778 A711 46c multicolored .70 .25

Sailing Ship Marco Polo — A712

1999, Mar. 19 *Perf. 13x12½*

1779 A712 46c multicolored .70 .25
a. Pane of 2, #1779b, Australia #1631 perf. 13½ 2.75 2.75
b. Perf 13 (from No. 1779a) 1.80 1.80

Australia '99 World Stamp Expo. See Australia No. 1631a.

Scenic Highway Type of 1997

No. 1780, Gaspé Peninsula, Highway 132, Quebec. No. 1781, Yellowhead Highway (PTH 16), Manitoba. No. 1782, Dempster Highway 8, Northwest Territories. No. 1783, Discovery Trail, Route 230N, Newfoundland.

1999, Mar. 31 *Perf. 12½x13*

1780 A673 46c multicolored .70 .35
1781 A673 46c multicolored .70 .35
1782 A673 46c multicolored .70 .35
1783 A673 46c multicolored .70 .35
a. Block or strip of 4, #1780-1783 2.80 2.50

Creation of the Nunavut Territory — A713

1999, Apr. 1

1784 A713 46c multicolored .70 .25

Intl. Year of Older Persons — A714

1999, Apr. 12 *Perf. 13½*

1785 A714 46c multicolored .70 .25

A715

1999, Apr. 19 *Perf. 13*

1786 A715 46c multicolored 1.80 .40

Baisakhi, Religious Holiday of Sikh Canadians, 300th Anniv.

A716

Paintings (Canadian Orchids): No. 1787, Arethusa bulbosa, by Poon-Kuen Chow. No. 1788, Amerorchis rotundifolia, by Yakman Lai. No. 1789, Platanthera psycodes, by Lai. No. 1790, Cypripedium pubescens, by Chow.

Booklet Stamps

1999, Apr. 27 *Perf. 13x12½*

1787 A716 46c multicolored .90 .30
1788 A716 46c multicolored .90 .30
1789 A716 46c multicolored .90 .30
1790 A716 46c multicolored .90 .30
a. Bklt. pane, 3 ea #1787-1790 11.00
Complete booklet, #1790a 11.50
b. Souvenir sheet, #1787-1790 3.75 3.75

China '99 World Philatelic Exhibition, Beijing. Designs of some stamps contained in No. 1790a extend into selvage of booklet pane.
Issued: No. 1790b, 8/21/99.

Horses
A717

No. 1791, Northern Dancer, thoroughbred race horse. No. 1792, Kingsway Skoal, bucking horse. No. 1793, Big Ben, show horse. No. 1794, Armbro Flight, harness race horse.

1999, June 2 *Perf. 13x13½*

1791 A717 46c multicolored .90 .40
1792 A717 46c multicolored .90 .40
1793 A717 46c multicolored .90 .40
1794 A717 46c multicolored .90 .40
a. Block or strip of 4, #1791-1794 3.60 3.00

Booklet Stamps
Self-Adhesive
Serpentine Die Cut 11½

1795 A717 46c like #1791 1.10 .30
1796 A717 46c like #1792 1.10 .30
1797 A717 46c like #1793 1.10 .30
1798 A717 46c like #1794 1.10 .30
a. Block of 4, #1795-1798 4.40
b. Complete booklet, 3 each #1795-1798 13.25

Nos. 1791-1794 were issued in panes of 16, 4 each, printed checkerwise to contain 4 complete blocks or strips.

Quebec Bar Assoc., 150th Anniv. — A718

1999, June 3 *Perf. 13½*

1799 A718 46c multicolored .70 .25

Art Type of 1988

Coq Licorne, by Jean Dallaire (1916-65).

Litho. with Foil Application

1999, July 3 *Perf. 12½x13¼*

1800 A546 95c multicolored 1.50 1.10
a. Silver omitted *1,250.*

1999 Pan American Games, Winnipeg A719

Designs: No. 1801, Track & field. No. 1802, Cycling, weight lifting, gymnastics. No. 1803, Swimming, sailboarding, kayaking. No. 1804, Soccer, tennis, medal winners.

1999, July 12 **Litho.** *Perf. 13¼*

1801 A719 46c multicolored .70 .35
1802 A719 46c multicolored .70 .35
1803 A719 46c multicolored .70 .35
1804 A719 46c multicolored .70 .35
a. Block of 4, #1801-1804 2.80 2.50

Issued in panes of 16 stamps.

23rd World Rowing Championships, St. Catharines, Ont. — A720

1999, Aug. 22 *Perf. 12½x13*

1805 A720 46c multicolored .70 .25

UPU, 125th Anniv. — A721

1999, Aug. 26

1806 A721 46c multicolored .70 .25

Airplanes — A722

No. 1807: a, Fokker DR-1, CT-114 Tutors. b, Tutors, H101 Salto sailplane. c, De Havilland DH100 Vampire MKIII. d, Stearman A-75.
No. 1808: a, De Havilland Mosquito FBVI. b, Sopwith F1 Camel. c, De Havilland Canada DHC-3 Otter. d, De Havilland Canada CC-108 Caribou. e, Canadair CL-28 Argus MK 2. f, North American F-86 Sabre 6. g, McDonnell Douglas CF-18 Hornet. h, Sopwith SF-1 Dolphin. i, Armstrong Whitworth Siskin IIIA. j, Canadian Vickers (Northrop) Delta II. k, Sikorsky CH-124A Sea King helicopter. l, Vickers-Armstrong Wellington MKII. m, Avro Anson MKI. n, Canadair (Lockheed) CF-104G Starfighter. o, Burgess-Dunne seaplane. p, Avro 504K.

1999, Sept. 4

1807 A722 Pane of 4 4.40 4.40
a.-d. 46c any single 1.10 .90
1808 A722 Pane of 16 18.00 18.00
a.-p. 46c any single 1.00 1.00

Canadian Intl. Air Show, 50th anniv. (No. 1807). Royal Canadian Air Force, 75th anniv. (No. 1808). Nos. 1808a-1808p are each 56x28mm.

NATO, 50th Anniv. — A723

1999, Sept. 21

1809 A723 46c multicolored .75 .25

Frontier College, 100th Anniv. A724

1999, Sept. 24 *Perf. 13x13½*

1810 A724 46c multicolored .70 .25

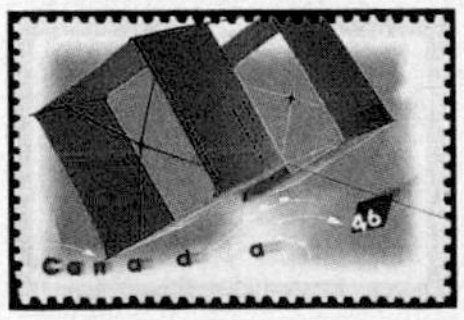

Kites A725

Designs: a, Master Control, sport kite by Lam Hoac (triagular). b, Indian Garden Flying Carpet, edo kite by Skye Morrison (trapezoidal). c, Gibson Girl, manufactured box kite (rectangular). d, Dragon centipede kite by Zhang tian Wei (oval).

Die cut in various patterns

1999, Oct. 1 **Self-Adhesive**

1811 Complete booklet, 2 each #a.-d. 8.00
a.-d. A725 46c any single 1.00 .35

A726

A727

Millennium A728

Self-Adhesive (46c)

1999, Oct. 12 **Holography** *Die Cut*

1812 A726 46c silver 1.00 .40
Pane of 4 4.75 4.75

Litho.
Perf. 13¼

1813 A727 55c multicolored 1.00 .80
Pane of 4 4.75 4.75

Engr.
Perf. 12¾

1814 A728 95c brown 1.70 1.50
Pane of 4 7.00 7.00
Nos. 1812-1814 (3) 3.70 2.70

Nos. 1812-1814 each exist in souvenir sheets of 1 with decorative border.

Christmas — A729

1999, Nov. 4 **Litho.** *Perf. 13¼*

1815 A729 46c Angel, drum .70 .25
a. Booklet pane of 10 7.00 *8.00*
Complete booklet 7.50
b. Horiz. pair, imperf. btwn. 1,100.
1816 A729 55c Angel, toys .80 .35
a. Booklet pane of 5 + label 4.00 *6.00*
Complete booklet 4.50
1817 A729 95c Angel, candle 1.50 .75
a. Booklet pane of 5 + label 8.00 *10.00*
Complete booklet 8.50
b. Horiz. pair, imperf. btwn. *1,200.*
Nos. 1815-1817 (3) 3.00 1.35

Souvenir Sheets

Millennium — A730

No. 1818 — Media Technologies: a, IMAX movies. b, Softimage animation software. c, Ted Rogers, Sr. (1900-39) and radio tube. d, Invention of radio facsimile device for transmission of photographs for publishing by Sir William Stephenson (1896-1989).
No. 1819 — Canadian Entertainment: a, Calgary Stampede. b, Performers from Cirque du Soleil. c, Hockey Night in Canada. d, La Soiree du Hockey.
No. 1820 — Entertainers: a, Portia White (1911-68), singer. b, Glenn Gould (1932-82), pianist. c, Guy Lombardo (1902-77), band leader. d, Félix Leclerc (1914-88), singer, guitarist.
No. 1821 — Fostering Canadian Talent: a, Royal Canadian Academy of Arts (men viewing painting). b, Canada Council (sky, musical staff, "A"). c, National Film Board of Canada. d, Canadian Broadcasting Corporation.
No. 1822 — Medical Innovators: a, Sir Frederick Banting (1891-1941), co-discoverer of insulin, syringe and dog. b, Dr. Armand Frappier (1904-91), microbiologist, holding flask. c, Dr. Hans Selye (1907-82), endocrinologist, and molecular diagram. d, Maude Abbott (1869-1940), pathologist, and roses.
No. 1823 — Social Progress: a, Nun, doctor, hospital. b, Statue of woman holding decree. c, Alphonse Desjardins (1854-1920) and wife Dorimène (1858-1932), credit union founders, and credit union emblem. d, Father Moses Coady (1882-1959), educator of adults.
No. 1824 — Charity: a, Canadian International Development Agency (hands and tools). b, Dr. Lucille Teasdale (1929-96), hospital administrator in Uganda. c, Marathon of Hope inspired by Terry Fox (1958-81). d, Meals on Wheels program.
No. 1825 — Humanitarians and Peacekeepers: a, Raoul Dandurand (1861-1942), b, Pauline Vanier (1898-1991), Red Cross volunteer, and Elizabeth Smellie (1884-1968), head of various nursing services. c, Lester B. Pearson (1897-1972), prime minister, and Nobel Peace Prize winner, and dove. d, Amputee and shadow (Ottawa Convention on Land Mines).
No. 1826 — Canada's First People: a, Chief Pontiac (c. 1720-69). b, Tom Longboat (1887-1949), marathon runner. c, Inuit sculpture of shaman. d, Medicine man.
No. 1827 — Canada's Cultural Fabric: a, Norse boat, L'Anse aux Meadows. b, Immigrants on Halifax's Pier 21. c, Neptune Theater, Halifax (head of Neptune). d, Stratford Festival (actor and theater).
No. 1828 — Literary Legends: a, W. O. Mitchell (1914-98), novelist, and prairie scene. b, Gratien Gélinas (1909-99), actor and playwright, and stars. c, Le Cercle du Livre de France book club. d, Harlequin paperback books.
No. 1829 — Great Thinkers: a, Marshall McLuhan (1911-80), philosopher, and television set. b, Northrop Frye (1912-91), literary critic, and word "code." c, Roger Lemelin (1919-92), novelist, and cast of "The Plouffe Family" TV series. d, Hilda Marion Neatby (1904-75), historian, and farm scene.
No. 1830 — A Tradition of Generosity: a, Hart Massey (1823-96), Hart House, University of Toronto. b, Dorothy (1899-1965) and Izaak Killam (1885-1955), philantropists, and molecular model. c, Eric Lafferty Harvie (1892-1975), philantropist, and mountain scene. d, Macdonald Stewart Foundation.
No. 1831 — Engineering and Technological Marvels: a, Map of Rogers Pass, locomotive, tunnel diggers. b, Manic Dams. c, Canadian satellites, Remote Manipulator Arm. d, CN Tower.
No. 1832 — Fathers of Invention: a, George Klein (1904-92), gearwheels. b, Abraham Gesner (1797-1864), beaker of kerosene and lamp. c, Alexander Graham Bell (1847-1922), passenger-carrying kite, hydrofoil. d, Joseph-Armand Bombardier (1907-64), snowmobile.
No. 1833 — Food: a, Sir Charles Saunders (1867-1937), Marquis wheat. b, Pablum. c, Dr. Archibald Gowanlock Huntsman (1883-1973), marketer of frozen fish. d, Products of McCain Foods, Ltd., tractor.

No. 1834 — Enterprising Giants: a, Hudson's Bay Company (Colonist, Indian, canoe). b, Bell Canada Enterprises (earth, satellite, string of binary digits). c, Vachon Co. snack cakes. d, George Weston Limited (Baked goods, eggs).

1999-2000 Litho. *Perf. 13¼*

1818	A730	Pane of 4	6.50	6.50
a.-d.		46c any single	1.60	1.25
1819	A730	Pane of 4	6.50	6.50
a.-d.		46c any single	1.60	1.25
1820	A730	Pane of 4	6.50	6.50
a.-d.		46c any single	1.60	1.25
1821	A730	Pane of 4	6.50	6.50
a.-d.		46c any single	1.60	1.25
1822	A730	Pane of 4	6.50	6.50
a.-d.		46c any single	1.60	1.25
1823	A730	Pane of 4	6.50	6.50
a.-d.		46c any single	1.60	1.25
1824	A730	Pane of 4	6.50	6.50
a.-d.		46c any single	1.60	1.25
1825	A730	Pane of 4	6.50	6.50
a.-d.		46c any single	1.60	1.25
1826	A730	Pane of 4	6.50	6.50
a.-d.		46c any single	1.60	1.25
1827	A730	Pane of 4	6.50	6.50
a.-d.		46c any single	1.60	1.25
1828	A730	Pane of 4	6.50	6.50
a.-d.		46c any single	1.60	1.25
1829	A730	Pane of 4	6.50	6.50
a.-d.		46c any single	1.60	1.25
1830	A730	Pane of 4	6.50	6.50
a.-d.		46c any single	1.60	1.25
1831	A730	Pane of 4	6.50	6.50
a.-d.		46c any single	1.60	1.25
1832	A730	Pane of 4	6.50	6.50
a.-d.		46c any single	1.60	1.25
1833	A730	Pane of 4	6.50	6.50
a.-d.		46c any single	1.60	1.25
1834	A730	Pane of 4	6.50	6.50
a.-d.		46c any single	1.60	1.25
		Nos. 1818-1834 (17)	110.50	110.50

Issued: Nos. 1818-1821, 12/17; Nos. 1822-1825, 1/17/00; Nos. 1826-1830, 2/17/00; Nos. 1831-1834, 3/17/00.

Stamps similar to these were printed in a hardcover book produced by Canada Post Sept. 15, 1999 that sold for $59.99. Stamps from souvenir panes show a distinct upward turn of the tails of the nines in the small 1999 date at upper left. The tails of the nines on stamps from the book are flat.

Millennium — A731

2000, Jan. 1 *Perf. 13x12½*

1835 A731 46c multicolored .75 .25

New Year 2000 (Year of the Dragon) — A732

Litho. & Embossed

2000, Jan. 5 *Perf. 12½x12¾*

1836	A732	46c multicolored	.75	.25
a.		Red and tagging omitted	1,100.	

Souvenir Sheet

Perf. 13¾x13¼

1837	A732	95c multicolored	1.70	1.70
a.		Orange and tagging omitted	*1,500.*	

No. 1837 has rounded corners and contains one 56x29mm stamp.

50th National Hockey League All-Star Game A733

Famous NHL players: a, Wayne Gretzky (Oilers jersey No. 99). b, Gordie Howe (Red Wings jersey No. 9). c, Maurice Richard (red, white and blue Canadiens jersey No. 9). d, Doug Harvey (Canadiens jersey No. 2). e, Bobby Orr (Bruins jersey No. 4). f, Jacques Plante (Canadiens jersey No. 1).

2000, Feb. 5 Litho. *Perf. 12¾*

1838		Pane of 6	4.50	4.50
a.-f.	A733	46c any single	.75	.60

Bird Type of 1996

Designs: Nos. 1839, 1843, Canada warbler. Nos. 1840, 1844, Osprey. Nos. 1841, 1845, Pacific loon. Nos. 1842, 1846, Blue jay.

2000, Mar. 1 Litho. *Perf. 12½x13¼*

1839	A650	46c multi	.90	.30
1840	A650	46c multi	.90	.30
1841	A650	46c multi	.90	.30
1842	A650	46c multi	.90	.30
a.		Block or strip of 4	3.60	2.50

Booklet Stamps

Self-Adhesive

Die Cut 11½x11¼

1843	A650	46c multi	.90	.30
1844	A650	46c multi	.90	.30
1845	A650	46c multi	.90	.30
1846	A650	46c multi	.90	.30
a.		Booklet pane, 2 each #1843-1844, 1 each #1845-1846	5.50	
b.		Booklet pane, 2 each #1845-1846, 1 each #1843-1844	5.50	
		Complete bklt., #1846a, 1846b	11.00	

Nos. 1839-1842 were issued in panes of 20, 5 each printed checkerwise to contain 4 complete blocks or strips.

Supreme Court, 125th Anniv. A734

2000, Apr. 10 *Perf. 12½x13¼*

1847 A734 46c multi .75 .25

Ritual of the Calling of an Engineer, 75th Anniv. — A735

2000, Apr. 25

1848	A735	46c multi	.75	.25
a.		Tete-beche pair	1.50	1.10
b.		Silver ("CANADA 46") omitted	*2,250.*	

Decorated Rural Mailboxes — A736

Mailboxes with: No. 1849, Ship, fish, house designs. No. 1850, Flower, cow and church designs. No. 1851, Tractor design. No. 1852, Goose head, house designs.

Booklet Stamps

Perf. 12½x13¼ on 3 sides

2000, Apr. 28

1849	A736	46c multi	.90	.40
1850	A736	46c multi	.90	.40
1851	A736	46c multi	.90	.40
1852	A736	46c multi	.90	.40
a.		Block of 4, #1849-1852	3.60	2.75
b.		Bklt. pane, 3 ea #1849-1852	11.00	
		Complete booklet, #1852a	11.50	

Picture Frame A737

Self-Adhesive

Serpentine Die Cut 11½

2000, Apr. 28

1853	A737	46c multi	.90	.60
a.		Booklet pane of 5 + 5 different labels	4.50	
		Complete booklet, #1853a	5.00	
b.		Pane of 25 + stickers	*75.00*	

No. 1853b sold for $24.95 each for one or two panes, and $22.95 for three to ten panes. Twenty-five self-adhesive, die cut address labels and reproductions of a photo sent in by the customer are on the reverse of No. 1853b. These panes were not available at post offices or through the philatelic bureau, but special orders from the printer, Ashton-Potter. The front cover of the booklet containing No. 1853a served as the order blank for No. 1853b.

See Nos. 1872, 1882.

A738

A739

A740

A741

A742

A743

A744

A745

A746

Fresh Waters — A747

Self-Adhesive

Serpentine Die Cut 2½ Horiz.

2000, Feb. 23

1854		Complete booklet, #a.-e.	7.50	
a.	A738	55c multi	1.50	.90
b.	A739	55c multi	1.50	.90
c.	A740	55c multi	1.50	.90
d.	A741	55c multi	1.50	.90
e.	A742	55c multi	1.50	.90
1855		Complete booklet, #a.-e.	9.50	
a.	A743	95c multi	1.90	1.50
b.	A744	95c multi	1.90	1.50
c.	A745	95c multi	1.90	1.50
d.	A746	95c multi	1.90	1.50
e.	A747	95c multi	1.90	1.50

Queen Mother (b. 1900) A748

2000, May 23 *Perf. 13x13¼*

1856	A748	95c multi	1.50	.90
a.		Imperf., pair	*750.00*	

Boys and Girls Clubs of Canada, Cent. — A749

2000, June 1 *Perf. 13*

1857 A749 46c multi .70 .25

World Session of Seventh Day Adventist Church, Toronto A750

2000, June 29 *Perf. 13½x13¼*

1858 A750 46c multi .90 .25

Stampin' the Future Children's Stamp Design Contest Winners A751

Designs: No. 1859, Rainbow, space vehicle, astronauts, flag, by Rosalie Anne Nardelli. No. 1860, Three children in space vehicle, three children on ground, by Sarah Lutgen. No. 1861, Children and map of Canada, by Christine Weera. No. 1862, Two astronauts in space vehicle, planets, by Andrew Wright.

2000, July 1 *Perf. 13¼*

1859	A751	46c multi	.70	.35
1860	A751	46c multi	.70	.35
1861	A751	46c multi	.70	.35
1862	A751	46c multi	.70	.35
a.		Block or strip, #1859-1862	2.80	2.25
b.		Souvenir sheet, #1859-1862	4.50	3.00

Art Type of 1988

The Artist at Niagara, by Cornelius Krieghoff.

Litho. with Foil Application

2000, July 7 *Perf. 12½x13¼*

1863 A546 95c multi 1.40 .90

Tall Ships in Halifax Harbor — A752

Various ships: No. 1864, Denomination at L. No. 1865, Denomination at R.

Self-Adhesive
Booklet Stamps

Serpentine Die Cut 4¾x5

2000, July 19 **Litho.**

1864 A752 46c multi .90 .40
1865 A752 46c multi .90 .40
a. Pair, #1864-1865 1.80
b. Booklet, 5 #1864a 9.00

Dept. of Labor, Cent. — A753

2000, Sept. 1 *Perf. 12½x13¼*

1866 A753 46c multi .70 .25

Petro-Canada, 25th Anniv. — A754

Self-Adhesive
Booklet Stamp

2000, Sept. 13 *Die Cut*

1867 A754 46c multi .90 .40
a. Booklet pane of 12 11.00
Booklet, #1867a 11.50
b. Die cutting inverted (2 points jut at T, L) 7.50 7.50

No. 1867a is the cover of an informational booket about Petro-Canada. No. 1867b was issued in collector packs.

Cetaceans — A755

No. 1868, Monodon monoceros. No. 1869, Balaenoptera musculus. No. 1870, Balaena mysticetus. No. 1871, Delphinapterus leucas.

2000, Oct. 2 *Perf. 12½x13*

1868 A755 46c multi .75 .30
1869 A755 46c multi .75 .30
1870 A755 46c multi .75 .30
1871 A755 46c multi .75 .30
a. Block of 4, #1868-1871 3.00 2.25

Christmas A756

Self-Adhesive
Booklet Stamp

Serpentine Die Cut 11¾

2000, Oct. 5

1872 A756 46c multi .90 .80
a. Booklet pane of 5 + 5 labels 4.50
Booklet, #1872a 5.00
b. Pane of 25 + stickers 75.00

See No. 1882f.

Christmas A757

Designs: 46c, Adoration of the shepherds. 55c, Creche. 95c Flight into Egypt.

2000, Nov. 3 *Perf. 13¼*

1873 A757 46c multi .70 .25
a. Booklet pane of 10 7.00 *8.50*
Booklet, #1873a 7.50
1874 A757 55c multi .80 .35
a. Booklet pane of 6 5.00 *6.00*
Booklet, #1874a 5.50
1875 A757 95c multi 1.40 .65
a. Booklet pane of 6 8.50 *9.50*
Booklet, #1875a 9.00
Nos. 1873-1875 (3) 2.90 1.25

Regiments A758

No. 1876, Lord Strathcona's Horse Regiment. No. 1877, Les Voltigeurs de Quebec.

2000, Nov. 11 *Perf. 13¼x13*

1876 A758 46c multi .70 .30
1877 A758 46c multi .70 .30
a. Pair, #1876-1877 1.40 .90

Maple Leaves A759

Animals A760

Designs: 60c, Red fox. 75c, Gray wolf. $1.05, White-tailed deer.

Coil Stamps

Serpentine Die Cut 8½ Horiz.

2000, Dec. 28 **Self-Adhesive**

1878 A759 47c multi .70 .25
a. Blue inscriptions omitted *625.00*
1879 A760 60c multi 1.00 .35
a. Booklet pane of 6 10.00
1880 A760 75c multi 1.10 .45
1881 A760 $1.05 multi 1.60 .75
a. Booklet pane of 6 11.00
Nos. 1878-1881 (4) 4.40 1.80

Nos. 1879a and 1881a are complete booklets. See No. 1927.

Frame Type of 2000

No. 1882: a, Silver. b, Like #1853. c, Mahogany. d, Love (roses). e, Christmas.

Booklet Stamps

Serpentine Die Cut 11¾

2000, Dec. 28 **Self-Adhesive**

1882 Bklt. pane of 5+5 labels 4.50
a.-e. A737 47c Any single .90 .90
Booklet, #1882 5.00
f. Pane of 25 + stickers 75.00

No. 1882f was available only by special order.

New Year 2001 (Year of the Snake) A761

Litho. & Embossed

2001, Jan. 5 *Perf. 13¼*

1883 A761 47c green & multi .75 .25
a. Gold omitted 1,400.

Souvenir Sheet

1884 A761 $1.05 brown & multi 2.25 2.25

National Hockey League Stars A762

No. 1885: a, Jean Beliveau (Montreal Canadiens jersey No. 4). b, Terry Sawchuk (goalie in Detroit Red Wings uniform). c, Eddie Shore (Boston Bruins jersey No. 2). d, Denis Potvin (Islanders jersey No. 5). e, Bobby Hull (Chicago Black Hawks jersey No. 9). f, Syl Apps, Sr. (Toronto Maple Leafs jersey).

Perf. 12½x13 on 3 sides

2001, Jan. 18 **Litho.**

1885 Sheet of 6 + 3 labels 4.50 4.50
a.-f. A762 47c Any single .75 .45
g. Strip of 3 (#1885a, 1885c, 1885e), blue circle and text omitted *8,000.*

Bird Type of 1996

Designs: Nos. 1886, 1890, Golden eagle. Nos. 1887, 1891, Arctic tern. Nos. 1888, 1892, Rock ptarmigan. Nos. 1889, 1893, Lapland longspur.

2001, Feb. 1 *Perf. 12½x13*

1886 A650 47c multi .75 .30
1887 A650 47c multi .75 .30
1888 A650 47c multi .75 .30
1889 A650 47c multi .75 .30
a. Block or strip of 4, #1886-1889 3.00 2.25

Booklet Stamps
Self-Adhesive

Die Cut Perf 11½x11¼

1890 A650 47c multi .90 .35
1891 A650 47c multi .90 .35
1892 A650 47c multi .90 .35
1893 A650 47c multi .90 .35
a. Booklet pane, 2 each #1890-1891, 1 each #1892-1893 5.50
b. Booklet pane, 2 each #1892-1893, 1 each #1890-1891 5.50
Booklet, #1893a, 1893b 11.00

Nos. 1886-1889 were issued in panes of 20, 5 each printed checkerwise to contain 4 complete blocks or strips.

Games of La Francophonie, Ottawa and Hull — A763

2001, Feb. 28 *Perf. 13¼*

1894 A763 47c High jumper .70 .25
1895 A763 47c Dancer .70 .25
a. Horiz. pair, #1894-1895 1.40 .90

World Figure Skating Championships, Vancouver — A764

Designs: No. 1896, Pairs. No. 1897, Ice dancing. No. 1898, Men's singles. No. 1899, Women's singles.

2001, Mar. 19 *Perf. 13x12½*

1896 A764 47c shown .70 .30
1897 A764 47c multi .70 .30
1898 A764 47c multi .70 .30
1899 A764 47c multi .70 .30
a. Block of 4, #1896-1899 2.80 2.25

First Canadian Postage Stamps, 150th Anniv. — A765

Litho. & Engr.

2001, Apr. 6 *Perf. 13*

1900 A765 47c multi .75 .25

Toronto Blue Jays Baseball Team, 25th Anniv. A766

Self-Adhesive

2001, Apr. 9 **Litho.** *Die Cut*

1901 A766 47c multi .90 .25
a. Booklet pane of 8 7.25

No. 1901a is a complete booklet.

Summit of the Americas, Quebec — A767

2001, Apr. 20 *Perf. 13¼x13*

1902 A767 47c multi .75 .25

Tourist Attractions — A768

No. 1903: a, Butchart Gardens, British Columbia. b, Apple Blossom Festival, Nova Scotia. c, White Pass and Yukon Route. d, Sugar bushes, Quebec. e, Niagara-on-the-Lake, Ontario.

No. 1904: a, The Forks, Manitoba. b, Barkerville, British Columbia. c, Canadian Tulip Festival, Ontario. d, Auyuittuq National Park, Nunavut. e, Signal Hill National Historic Site, Newfoundland.

Self-Adhesive

2001, May 11 ***Die Cut Perf. 11x11¼***

1903	Booklet of 5	4.50	
a.-e.	A768 60c Any single	.90	.75
1904	Booklet of 5	8.50	
a.-e.	A768 $1.05 Any single	1.70	1.10

See Nos. 1952-1953, 1989-1990, 2019-2023.

Armenian Church, 1,700th Anniv. — A769

2001, May 16 ***Perf. 13x12½***

1905 A769 47c multi .70 .25

Royal Military College of Canada, 125th Anniv. — A770

2001, June 1 ***Perf. 12½x13***

1906 A770 47c multi .70 .25

Eighth Intl. Amateur Athletic Federation World Championships, Edmonton A771

2001, June 25 ***Perf. 12¾x12½***

1907	A771 47c Pole vault	.70	.25
1908	A771 47c Runner	.70	.25
a.	Pair, #1907-1908	1.40	.90

Pierre Elliott Trudeau (1919-2000), Prime Minister — A772

2001, July 1 ***Perf. 13x12½***

1909	A772 47c multi	.70	.25
a.	Souvenir sheet of 4	3.00	3.00

Roses — A773

Designs: Nos. 1910a, 1911, Morden Centennial. Nos. 1910b, 1912, Agnes. Nos. 1910c, 1913, Champlain. Nos. 1910d, 1914, Canadian White Star.

Souvenir Sheet

2001, Aug. 1 ***Perf. 12½x13***

1910	Pane of 4	4.40	4.40
a.-d.	A773 47c Any single	1.10	1.10

Booklet Stamps

Die Cut

1911	A773 47c multi	.75	.30
1912	A773 47c multi	.75	.30
1913	A773 47c multi	.75	.30
1914	A773 47c multi	.75	.30
a.	Booklet pane, #1911-1914	3.00	
	Booklet, 3 #1914a	9.00	

Phila Nippon '01, Japan (No. 1910). Die cutting on Nos. 1911-1914 has "thorn" at the center of each side, pointing outward at top and left and toward the design at bottom and right.

Great Peace of Montreal, 300th Anniv. — A774

2001, Aug. 3 ***Perf. 12½x13***

1915 A774 47c multi .70 .25

Art Type of 1988

Design: The Space Between Columns #21 (Italian), by Jack Shadbolt.

Litho. with Foil Application

2001, Aug. 24 ***Perf. 13x13¼***

1916 A546 $1.05 multi 1.70 .90

Shriners — A775

2001, Sept. 19 Litho. ***Perf. 13¼x13***

1917 A775 47c multi .70 .25

Frame Type of 2000 Inscribed "Domestic Lettermail / Poste-lettres du régime intérieur"

No. 1918: a, Like #1882a. b, Like #1882b. c, Baby toys and flowers. d, Like #1882d. e, Like #1882e.

Serpentine Die Cut 11¾

2001, Sept. 21 **Self-Adhesive**

1918	Bklt. pane of 5 + 5 labels	5.00	
a.-e.	A737 (47c) Any single	1.00	1.00
	Booklet, #1918	5.50	
f.	Pane of 25 + stickers	75.00	
g.	Pane of 10 + stickers	60.00	

Nos. 1918f and 1918g were available only by special order.

Theater Anniversaries — A776

Designs: No. 1919, Théatre du Nouveau Monde, Montreal, 50th anniv. No. 1920, Grand Theater, London, Ont., cent.

2001, Sept. 28 ***Perf. 12½x12¾***

1919	A776 47c multi	.75	.25
1920	A776 47c multi	.75	.25
a.	Horiz. pair, #1919-1920	1.50	.90

Hot Air Balloons A777

Background colors: a, Green. b, Blue violet. c, Red violet. d, Olive.

Self-Adhesive

2001, Oct. 1 ***Die Cut***

1921	Booklet, 2 each #a-d	7.25	
a.-d.	A777 47c Any single	.90	.40

Christmas A778

Illuminated trees and: 47c, Horse-drawn sleigh. 60c, Skaters. $1.05, Children making snowman.

2001, Nov. 1 ***Perf. 12½x13¼***

1922	A778 47c multi	.75	.25
a.	Booklet pane of 10	7.50	7.50
	Booklet, #1922a	8.00	
1923	A778 60c multi	.90	.40
a.	Booklet pane of 6	5.50	5.50
	Booklet, #1923a	6.00	
1924	A778 $1.05 multi	1.65	.60
a.	Booklet pane of 6	10.00	10.00
	Booklet, #1924a	10.50	

YMCA in Canada, 150th Anniv. — A779

2001, Nov. 8 ***Perf. 13¼***

1925 A779 47c multi .75 .25

Royal Canadian Legion, 75th Anniv. — A780

2001, Nov. 11 ***Perf. 12½x13***

1926 A780 47c multi .75 .25

Maple Leaves Type of 2000, Traditional Handiwork Type of 1999 and

Flag and Canada Post Headquarters, Ottawa — A781

Designs: 65c, Jewelry making, horiz. 77c, Basket weaving, horiz. $1.25, Sculpture, horiz.

Self-Adhesive

Coil Stamps

Serpentine Die Cut 8½ Horiz.

2002, Jan. 2

1927	A759 48c multi	.75	.25
1928	A684 65c multi	1.00	.30
a.	Booklet of 6	6.00	
1929	A684 77c multi	1.10	.40
1930	A684 $1.25 multi	1.80	.65
a.	Booklet of 6	11.00	

Booklet Stamp

Serpentine Die Cut 8½

1931	A781 48c multi	.75	.25
a.	Booklet of 10	7.50	
b.	Booklet of 30	22.50	
c.	Blue omitted	375.00	
	Nos. 1927-1931 (5)	5.40	1.85

By separating the booklet along the columns of rouletting, No. 1931b could be broken up into three separately obtainable examples of No. 1931a. See No. 1991.

Reign of Queen Elizabeth II, 50th Anniv. A782

2002, Jan. 2 ***Perf. 13¼x12½***

1932	A782 48c multi	.70	.25
a.	Imperf, pair	*1,200.*	
b.	Gold omitted		1,300.

New Year 2002 (Year of the Horse) — A783

Horse and: 48c, Bamboo leaves. $1.25, Peach blossoms.

Litho. & Embossed With Foil Application

2002, Jan. 3 ***Perf. 13¼***

1933	A783 48c multi	.75	.25
a.	Foil (horse) omitted	*1,200.*	

Souvenir Sheet

1934 A783 $1.25 multi 2.25 2.25

National Hockey League Stars A784

No. 1935: a, Tim Horton (Toronto Maple Leafs jersey No. 7). b, Guy Lafleur (Montreal Canadiens jersey No. 10). c, Howie Morenz (Canadiens jersey, with brown gloves). d, Glenn Hall (Chicago Black Hawks jersey No. 1). e, Red Kelly (Maple Leafs jersey No. 4). f, Phil Esposito (Boston Bruins jersey no. 7).

Perf. 12½x13 on 3 Sides

2002, Jan. 12

1935	Pane of 6 + 3 labels	5.00	5.00
a.-f.	A784 48c Any single	.80	.60

2002 Winter Olympics, Salt Lake City — A785

Designs: No. 1936, Short track speed skating. No. 1937, Curling. No. 1938, Freestyle aerial skiing. No. 1939, Women's hockey.

2002, Jan. 25 ***Perf. 13¼x13***

1936	A785 48c multi	.75	.35
1937	A785 48c multi	.75	.35
1938	A785 48c multi	.75	.35
1939	A785 48c multi	.75	.35
a.	Block or strip of 4, #1936-1939	3.00	2.50

Appointment of First Canadian Governor General, 50th Anniv.
A786

2002, Feb. 1 ***Perf. 13¼x12½***

1940 A786 48c multi .75 .25

Universities — A787

Design: No. 1941, University of Manitoba, 125th anniv. No. 1942, Laval University, 150th anniv. No. 1943, University of Trinity College, 150th anniv. No. 1944, Saint Mary's University, Halifax, 200th anniv.

2002 Booklet Stamp ***Perf. 13½***

1941 A787 48c multi .75 .25
a. Booklet pane of 8 6.00 6.00
Booklet, #1941a 6.50
1942 A787 48c multi .75 .25
a. Booklet pane of 8 6.00 6.00
Booklet, #1942a 6.50
1943 A787 48c multi .75 .25
a. Booklet pane of 8 6.00 6.00
Booklet, #1943a 6.50
1944 A787 48c multi .75 .25
a. Booklet pane of 8 6.00 6.00
Booklet, #1944a 6.50
Nos. 1941-1944 (4) 3.00 1.00

Issued: No. 1941, 2/28. No. 1942, 4/4. No. 1943, 4/30. No. 1944, 5/27.

Art Type of 1988

Design: Church and Horse, by Alex Colville.

Litho. with Foil Application

2002, Mar. 22 ***Perf. 12½x13***

1945 A546 $1.25 multi 1.80 1.10
a. Foil only (all other colors and tagging omitted) *1,500.*
b. Imperf, pair *1,350.*

Tulips — A788

Tulip varieties: a, City of Vancouver. b, Monte Carlo. c, Ottawa. d, The Bishop.
No. 1947: a, Like #1946a. b, Like #1946b. c, Like #1946c. d, Like #1946d.

Self-Adhesive

2002, May 3 Litho. ***Die Cut***

1946 Booklet pane of 4 3.00
a.-d. A788 48c Any single .75 .30
Booklet, 2 #1946 6.00

Souvenir Sheet

Perf. 13x12½

1947 Pane of 4 3.25 3.25
a.-d. A788 48c Any single .80 .80

Issued: No. 1946, 5/3; No. 1947, 8/30.

Dendronepthea Gigantea and Dendronepthea Corals — A789

Tubastrea and Echinogorgia Corals — A790

North Atlantic Pink Tree, Pacific Orange Cup and North Pacific Horn Corals
A791

North Atlantic Giant Orange Tree and Black Corals
A792

2002, May 19 ***Perf. 12½x13***

1948 A789 48c multi .70 .30
1949 A790 48c multi .70 .30
1950 A791 48c multi .70 .30
1951 A792 48c multi .70 .30
a. Block of 4, #1948-1951 2.80 2.00
b. Souvenir sheet, #1948-1951, perf. 13¼x13 3.75 3.75

See Hong Kong Nos. 979-982.

Tourist Attractions Type of 2001

No. 1952: a, Yukon Quest, Yukon Territory. b, Icefields Parkway, Alberta. c, Agawa Canyon, Ontario. d, Old Port of Montreal, Quebec. e, Kings Landing, New Brunswick.
No. 1953: a, Northern Lights, Northwest Territories. b, Stanley Park, Vancouver, British Columbia. c, Head-Smashed-In Buffalo Jump, Alberta. d, Saguenay Fjord, Quebec. e, Peggy's Cove, Nova Scotia.

Self-Adhesive

2002, June 1 ***Die Cut Perf. 11x11¼***

1952 Booklet of 5 5.50
a.-e. A768 65c Any single 1.10 .75
1953 Booklet of 5 10.00
a.-e. A768 $1.25 Any single 2.00 1.10

Sculpture — A793

Designs: No. 1954, Embacle, by Charles Daudelin. No. 1955, Lumberjacks, by Leo Mol.

2002, June 10 ***Perf. 13¼***

1954 A793 48c multi .75 .25
1955 A793 48c multi .75 .25
a. Horiz. or vert. pair, #1954-1955 1.50 .90

Canadian Postmasters and Assistants Association, Cent. — A794

2002, July 5 ***Perf. 13¼x12½***

1956 A794 48c multi .75 .25

Printed in panes of 16 stamps + 12 labels.

17th World Youth Day, Toronto — A795

Self-Adhesive
Booklet Stamp

2002, July 23 ***Die Cut***

1957 A795 48c multi .75 .30
a. Booklet of 8 6.00

Public Services International World Congress, Ottawa — A796

2002, Sept. 4 ***Perf. 12½x13***

1958 A796 48c multi .75 .25

Public Pensions, 75th Anniv. — A797

2002, Sept. 10 ***Perf. 13¼***

1959 A797 48c multi .75 .25

Souvenir Sheet

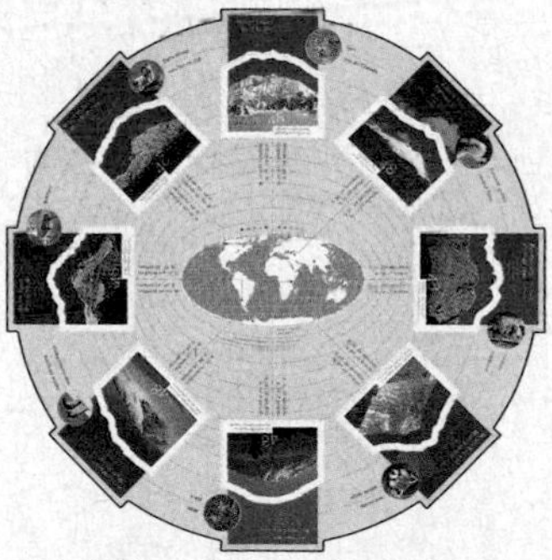

Intl. Year of Mountains — A798

No. 1960: a, Mt. Logan, Canada. b, Mt. Elbrus, Russia. c, Puncak Jaya, Indonesia. d, Mt. Everest, Nepal and China. e, Mt. Kilimanjaro, Tanzania. f, Vinson Massif, Antarctica. g, Mt. Aconcagua, Argentina. h, Mt. McKinley, Alaska.

Self-Adhesive

2002, Oct. 1 ***Die Cut***

1960 A798 Pane of 8 + 8 labels 7.25
a.-h. 48c Any single .90 *1.10*

World Teachers' Day — A799

2002, Oct. 4 ***Perf. 12½x13***

1961 A799 48c multi .75 .25

Toronto Stock Exchange, 150th Anniv. — A800

2002, Oct. 24

1962 A800 48c multi .75 .25

Communication Technology Centenaries — A801

Part of map of North America and: No. 1963, Sir Sandford Fleming (1827-1915), cable-laying ship. No. 1964, Guglielmo Marconi (1874-1937), radio and transmission towers.

2002, Oct. 31 ***Perf. 13x12½***

1963 48c multi .75 .25
1964 48c multi .75 .25
a. A801 Horiz. pair, #1963-1964 1.50 1.10

Cent. of first telegraph message sent over transpacific cable (No. 1963); first transatlantic radio message (No. 1964).

Christmas
A802

Art by aboriginals: 48c, Genesis, by Daphne Odjig. 65c, Winter Travel, by Cecil Youngfox. $1.25, Mary and Child, sculpture by Irene Katak Angutitaq.

2002, Nov. 4 ***Perf. 12½x13***

1965 A802 48c multi .75 .25
a. Booklet pane of 10 7.50 7.50
Booklet, #1965a 8.00
1966 A802 65c multi 1.00 .40
a. Booklet pane of 6 6.00 6.00
Booklet, #1966a 6.50
1967 A802 $1.25 multi 2.00 .75
a. Booklet pane of 6 12.00 12.00
Booklet, #1967a 12.50
Nos. 1965-1967 (3) 3.75 1.40

Quebec Symphony Orchestra, Cent.
A803

2002, Nov. 7

1968 A803 48c multi .80 .30

New Year 2003 (Year of the Ram) — A804

Litho. & Embossed with Foil Application

2003, Jan. 3 *Perf. 13*

1969 A804 48c shown .75 .25
a. Gold omitted 400.00
b. Imperf, pair 2,000.

Souvenir Sheet

Perf. 13¼

1970 A804 $1.25 Ram, diff. 2.50 2.50

No. 1970 contains one 33x58mm stamp. Slits replace perforations on the vertical sides of the stamps between the point of the acute angle made with the curving perforations and the point perpendicular to where the perforations on the opposite side form the obtuse angle with the curving perforations.

National Hockey League Stars A805

Designs: Nos. 1971a, 1972a, Frank Mahovlich (orange panel). Nos. 1971b, 1972b, Raymond Bourque (lilac panel). Nos. 1971c, 1972c, Serge Savard (blue panel). Nos. 1971d, 1972d, Stan Mikita (red violet panel). Nos. 1971e, 1972e, Mike Bossy (bright pink panel). Nos. 1971f, 1972f, Bill Durnan (green panel).

Perf. 12½x13¼ on 3 Sides

2003, Jan. 18

1971 Pane of 6 + 3 labels 14.00 —
a.-f. A805 48c Any single 2.25 1.50

Self-Adhseive

Die Cut

1972 Pane of 6 65.00 —
a.-f. A805 48c Any single 7.00 1.50

Universities A806

Design: No. 1973, Bishop's University, Lennoxville, Quebec, 150th anniv. No. 1974, University of Western Ontario, London, Ont., 125th anniv. No. 1975, St. Francis Xavier University, Antigonish, N. S., 150th Anniv. No. 1976, Macdonald Institute, Guelph, Ont., cent. No. 1977, University of Montreal, 125th anniv.

Booklet Stamps

2003 *Perf. 13¼x13½*

1973 A806 48c multi .75 .25
a. Booklet pane of 8 6.00 6.00
Booklet, #1973a 6.50
1974 A806 48c multi .75 .25
a. Booklet pane of 8 6.00 6.00
Booklet, #1974a 6.50
1975 A806 48c multi .75 .25
a. Booklet pane of 8 6.00 6.00
Complete booklet, #1975a 6.50
1976 A806 48c multi .75 .25
a. Booklet pane of 8 6.00 6.00
Complete booklet, #1976a 6.50
1977 A806 48c multi .75 .25
a. Booklet pane of 8 6.00 6.00
Complete booklet, #1977a 6.50

Issued: No. 1973, 1/28. No. 1975, 4/4. No. 1976, 6/20. No. 1977, 9/4. No. 1974, 3/19.

See Nos. 2033-2034, 2089, 2172, 2209-2210.

Bird Paintings by John James Audubon — A807

Designs: No. 1979, Leach's storm petrel. No. 1980, Brant. No. 1981, Great cormorant. No. 1982, Common murre. 65c, Gyrfalcon, vert.

2003, Feb. 21 *Perf. 13¼x12½*

1979 A807 48c multi .75 .35
1980 A807 48c multi .75 .35
1981 A807 48c multi .75 .35
1982 A807 48c multi .75 .35
a. Block of 4, #1979-1982 3.00 2.25

Booklet Stamp

Self-Adhesive

Die Cut

1983 A807 65c multi 1.10 .75
a. Booklet pane of 6 6.75
Nos. 1979-1983 (5) 4.10 2.15

Canadian Rangers — A808

2003, Mar. 3 *Perf. 12½x13¼*

1984 A808 48c multi .75 .25

American Hellenic Educational Progressive Association In Canada, 75th Anniv. — A809

2003, Mar. 25

1985 A809 48c multi .75 .25

Volunteer Firefighters A810

2003, May 30 *Perf. 13¼*

1986 A810 48c multi .75 .25

Coronation of Queen Elizabeth II, 50th Anniv. A811

2003, June 2 *Perf. 13x12½*

1987 A811 48c multi .75 .25

Quebec City, Seal of Sovereign Council of New France, Signature of Pedro da Silva — A812

2003, June 6 *Perf. 13*

1988 A812 48c multi .75 .25

Pedro da Silva, first courier in New France, 50th anniv. of Portuguese immigration to Canada.

Tourist Attractions Type of 2001

No. 1989: a, Wilberforce Falls, Nunavut. b, Inside Passage, B. C. c, Royal Canadian Mounted Police Depot Division, Regina, Sask. d, Casa Loma, Toronto, Ont. e, Gatineau Park, Que.

No. 1990: a, Dragon boat races, Vancouver, B. C. b, Polar bear watching, Man. c, Niagara Falls, Ont. d, Magdalen Islands, Que. e, Charlottestown, P. E. I.

Self-Adhesive

2003, June 12 *Die Cut Perf. 11¼*

1989 Booklet of 5 5.50
a.-e. A768 65c Any single 1.10 .75
1990 Booklet of 5 10.00
a.-e. A768 $1.25 Any single 2.00 1.10

"Vancouver 2010" Added in Red

Self-Adhesive Booklet Stamp

Serpentine Die Cut 8½

2003, July 11 **Litho.**

1991 A781 48c multi 1.50 1.20
a. Booklet of 10 15.00
b. Booklet of 30 45.00
e. Die cutting omitted, pair 800.00

Selection of Vancouver as site of 2010 Winter Olympics. By separating the booklet along the columns of rouletting, No. 1991b could be broken up into three separately obtainable examples of No. 1991a.

Canada-Alaska Cruise Scenes — A813

Mountains and: No. 1991C, Totem pole. No. 1991D, Whale's tail.

Self-Adhesive

2003, July 19 *Die Cut*

1991C A813 ($1.25) multi 7.50 7.50
1991D A813 ($1.25) multi 7.50 7.50
e. Horiz. pair, #19901C-1991D 15.00

Nos. 1991C-1991D were printed in panes of 10 containing five of each stamp. The blank spaces in each stamp and the three stamp-like vignettes at the left of the pane that lack die cutting and "Postage Paid / Port Payé" inscription could be personalized on cruise ships. Personalized panes sold for $19.95 in US currency, while unpersonalized panes sold for $12.50. Value, unpersonalized complete pane $85.

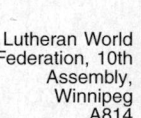

Lutheran World Federation, 10th Assembly, Winnipeg A814

2003, July 21 *Perf. 12½x13*

1992 A814 48c multi .75 .25

Korean War Armistice Agreement, 50th Anniv. — A815

2003, July 25 *Perf. 12¾*

1993 A815 48c multi .75 .25

Authors A816

Designs: No. 1994, Anne Hébert (1916-2000). No. 1995, Hector de Saint-Denys Garneau (1912-43). No. 1996, Morley Callaghan (1903-90). No. 1997, Susanna Moodie (1803-85), and Catharine Parr Traill (1802-99).

Booklet Stamps

2003, Sept. 8 *Perf. 13¼x12½*

1994 A816 48c multi .75 .35
1995 A816 48c multi .75 .35
1996 A816 48c multi .75 .35
1997 A816 48c multi .75 .35
a. Block of 4, #1994-1997 3.00 2.25
b. Booklet pane, 2 #1997a 6.00 —
Complete booklet, #1997b 6.50

2003 Road Cycling World Championships, Hamilton, Ont. — A817

Booklet Stamp

2003, Sept. 10 *Perf. 12½x13*

1998 A817 48c multi .75 .55
a. Booklet pane of 8 6.00 —
Complete booklet, #1998a 6.50

Canadian Astronauts A818

No. 1999: a, Marc Garneau. b, Roberta Bondar. c, Steve MacLean. d, Chris Hadfield. e, Robert Thirsk. f, Bjarni Tryggvason. g, Dave Williams. h, Julie Payette.

Self-Adhesive

Litho. With Foil Application

2003, Oct. 1 *Die Cut*

1999 Pane of 8 8.00
a.-h. A818 48c Any single .90 .90

Trees of Canada and Thailand — A819

Designs: No. 2000, Acer saccharum leaves (Canada). No. 2001, Cassia fistula (Thailand).

2003, Oct. 4 **Litho.** *Perf. 12¾x12½*

2000 A819 48c multi .75 .25
2001 A819 48c multi .75 .25
a. Pair, #2000-2001 1.50 1.10
b. Souvenir sheet, #2000-2001 7.50 4.00
c. As "a," imperf 950.00
d. As "b," imperf 1,350.

Bangkok 2003 Intl. Philatelic Exhibition (No. 2001b).

See Thailand No. 2090.

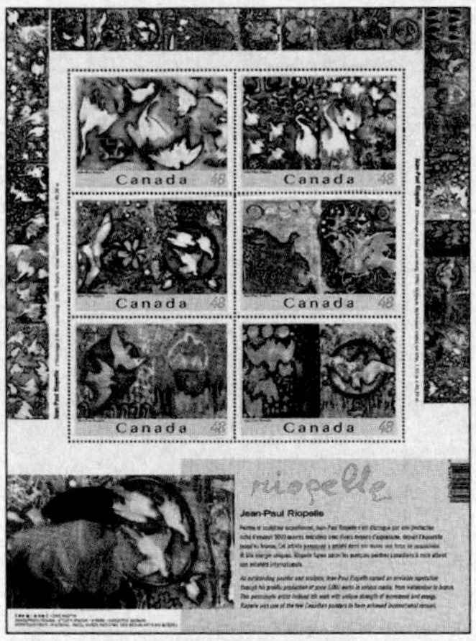

L'Hommage à Rosa Luxemburg, by Jean-Paul Riopelle — A820

Painting details — No. 2002; a, Red and blue dots between birds at LR. b, Bird with yellow beak at center. c, Three birds in circle at R. d, Sun at UR. e, Birds with purple outlines at L. f, Bird with red outline in circle at R. $1.25, Pink bird in red circle at R.

2003, Oct. 7 ***Perf. 12½x13***

2002 A820 Pane of 6 7.50 7.50
a.-f. 48c Any single 1.25 1.25

Souvenir Sheet
Perf. 12¾

2003 A820 $1.25 multi 3.00 3.00

Christmas A821

Gift boxes and: 48c, Ice skates. 65c, Teddy bear. $1.25, Toy duck.

Self-Adhesive
Booklet Stamps

2003, Nov. 4 ***Die Cut***

2004 A821 48c multi .75 .25
a. Booklet pane of 6 4.50
Complete booklet, 2 #2004a 9.00
b. Pair, die cutting omitted 375.00
2005 A821 65c multi 1.00 .60
a. Booklet pane of 6 6.00
b. As "a," die cutting omitted 1,500.
c. Die cutting omitted, pair *450.00*
2006 A821 $1.25 multi 2.00 1.00
a. Booklet pane of 6 12.00
b. Die cutting omitted, pair 450.00
Nos. 2004-2006 (3) 3.75 1.85

Maple Leaf and Samara A822

Maple Leaf on Twig A823

Flag Over Edmonton, Alberta A824

Queen Elizabeth II A825

Coil Stamps
Serpentine Die Cut 8½ Horiz.

2003, Dec. 19 **Self-Adhesive**

2008 A822 49c multi .75 .25
a. Die cutting omitted, pair 150.00

Serpentine Die Cut 8½ Vert.

2009 A823 80c red & multi 1.20 .40
2010 A823 $1.40 grn & multi 3.00 .55

Booklet Stamps
Die Cut

2011 A824 49c multi .75 .25
a. Booklet pane of 10 7.50
b. Die cutting omitted, pair 150.00
c. As "a," die cutting omitted *750.00*
2012 A825 49c multi .75 .25
a. Booklet pane of 10 7.50
2013 A823 80c red & multi 1.50 .40
a. Booklet pane of 6 9.00
2014 A823 $1.40 grn & multi 2.25 .75
a. Booklet pane of 6 13.50
Nos. 2008-2014 (7) 10.20 2.85

See Nos. 2053-2055, 2075.

New Year 2004 (Year of the Monkey) — A826

Scenes from Chinese story *Journey to the West*: 49c, Monkey King. $1.40, Monkey King, Xuan Zang, Sandy, Pigsy and horse.

Litho. & Embossed with Foil Application

2004, Jan. 8 ***Perf. 13x12½***

2015 A826 49c multi .75 .25

Souvenir Sheet

2016 A826 $1.40 multi 3.00 3.00
a. As No. 2016, with 2004 Hong Kong Stamp Expo ovpt. in margin 3.75 3.75

No. 2016 has rouletted tab at right showing bar code.

National Hockey League Stars A827

Designs: Nos. 2017a, 2018a, Larry Robinson (blue background). Nos. 2017b, 2018b, Marcel Dionne (orange background). Nos. 2017c, 2018c, Ted Lindsay (red background). Nos. 2017d, 2018d, Johnny Bower (green background). Nos. 2017e, 2018e, Brad Park (brown background). Nos. 2017f, 2018f, Milt Schmidt (purple background).

Perf. 12½x13¼ on 3 Sides

2004, Jan. 24 **Litho.**

2017 Pane of 6 + 3 labels 6.50 6.50
a.-f. A827 49c Any single .80 .60

Self-Adhesive
Die Cut

2018 Pane of 6 6.50
a.-f. A827 49c Any single .80 .55

Tourist Attractions Type of 2001

Design: No. 2019, Quebec Winter Carnival; No. 2020, St. Joseph's Oratory, Montreal, Quebec; No. 2021, International Jazz Festival, Montreal. No. 2022, Traversée Internationale du Lac St. Jean Swimming Marathon, Quebec; No. 2023, Canadian National Exhibition, Toronto.

Self-Adhesive
Booklet Stamp

2004, Jan. 29 ***Die Cut***

2019 A768 49c multi .85 .35
a. Booklet of 6 5.50
2020 A768 49c multi .85 .35
a. Booklet of 6 5.50
2021 A768 49c multi .85 .35
a. Booklet of 6 5.50
2022 A768 49c multi .85 .35
a. Booklet of 6 5.50
2023 A768 49c multi .85 .35
a. Booklet of 6 5.50

Issued: No. 2019, 1/29; No. 2020, 4/2; No. 2021, 6/1; No. 2022, 6/18; No. 2023, 7/19.

Governor General Ramon John Hnatyshyn (1934-2002) — A828

2004, Mar. 16 ***Perf. 12½x13***

2024 A828 49c multi .75 .25

Royal Canadian Army Cadets, 125th Anniv. A829

Self-Adhesive
Booklet Stamp

2004, Mar. 26 ***Die Cut***

2025 A829 49c multi .75 .30
a. Booklet pane of 4 3.00
Complete booklet, 2 #2025a 6.00

The Fram, Ship of Otto Sverdrup (1854-1930), Arctic Explorer — A830

Litho. & Engr.

2004, Mar. 26 ***Perf. 13¼***

2026 A830 49c multi .75 .25

Souvenir Sheet

2027 A830 $1.40 multi + 2 labels 3.00 3.00

See Greenland No. 426, Norway Nos. 1398-1399.

Urban Transit and Light Rail Systems — A831

Train cars, station names and system emblems of: No. 2028, Toronto Transit Commission. No. 2029, TransLink SkyTrain, Vancouver. No. 2030, Société de Transport de Montreal. No. 2031, Calgary Transit Light Rail.

2004, Mar. 30 **Litho.** ***Perf. 12½x13***

2028 A831 49c multi .75 .30
2029 A831 49c multi .75 .30
2030 A831 49c multi .75 .30
2031 A831 49c multi .75 .30
a. Vert. strip of 4, #2028-2031 3.00 2.50

Home Hardware, 40th Anniv. — A832

Self-Adhesive
Booklet Stamp

2004, Apr. 19 ***Die Cut Perf. 11***

2032 A832 49c multi .75 .30
a. Booklet pane of 10 + label 7.50
Complete booklet, #2032a 8.00

No. 2032a is the inside front cover of the complete booklet. Fifteen self-adhesive seals are on the inside back cover of the complete booklet.

Universities Type of 2003

Designs: No. 2033, Sherbrooke University, Sherbrooke, Quebec, 50th anniv. No. 2034, University of Prince Edward Island, Charlottetown, bicent.

Booklet Stamps

2004 ***Perf. 13¼x13½***

2033 A806 49c multi .75 .30
a. Booklet pane of 8 6.00 6.00
Complete booklet, #2033a 6.50
2034 A806 49c multi .75 .30
a. Booklet pane of 8 6.00 6.00
Complete booklet, #2034a 6.50

Issued: No. 2033, 5/4; No. 2034, 5/8.

Montreal Children's Hospital, Cent. — A833

Self-Adhesive
Booklet Stamp

2004, May 6 ***Die Cut Perf. 9½x10¾***

2035 A833 49c multi .75 .30
a. Booklet pane of 4 3.00
Complete booklet, 2 #2035a 6.00

Bird Paintings by John James Audubon A834

Designs: No. 2036, Ruby-crowned kinglet. No. 2037, White-winged crossbill. No. 2038, Bohemian waxwing. No. 2039, Boreal chickadee. 80c, Lincoln's sparrow.

2004, May 14 ***Perf. 12½x13***

2036 A834 49c multi .75 .35
2037 A834 49c multi .75 .35
2038 A834 49c multi .75 .35
2039 A834 49c multi .75 .35
a. Block of 4, #2036-2039 3.00 2.50

Self-Adhesive
Booklet Stamp
Die Cut

2040 A834 80c multi 1.20 .75
a. Booklet pane of 6 7.25
Nos. 2036-2040 (5) 4.20 2.15

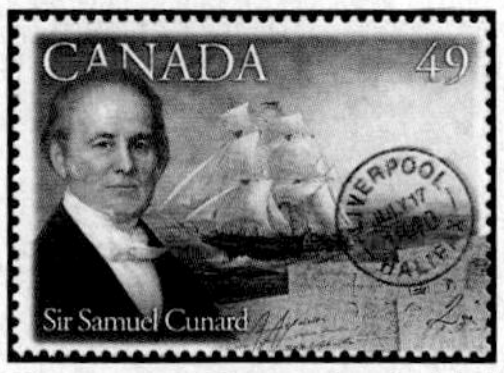

Pioneers of Transatlantic Mail Service — A835

Designs: No. 2041, Sir Samuel Cunard (1787-1865). No. 2042, Sir Hugh Allan (1810-82).

Self-Adhesive

2004, May 28 ***Perf. 13¼x12½***

2041 A835 49c multi .75 .30
2042 A835 49c multi .75 .30
a. Horiz. pair, #2041-2042 1.50 1.10

D-Day, 60th Anniv. A836

2004, June 6 *Perf. 13x12½*
2043 A836 49c multi .75 .30

Pierre Dugua de Mons, Leader of First French Settlement in Acadia, and Ship A837

2004, June 26 **Litho. & Engr.**
2044 A837 49c multi .75 .30

See France No. 3032.

Butterfly and Flower A838

Children on Beach A839

Rose A840

Dog A841

Self-Adhesive
Booklet Stamps

Serpentine Die Cut 11¾

2004, June **Litho.**
2045 A838 (49c) multi 22.50 *13.00*
a. Booklet pane of 2 45.00
Complete booklet, #2045a + phonecard in greeting card 50.00
2046 A839 (49c) multi 9.00 *13.00*
a. Booklet pane of 2 18.00
Complete booklet, #2046a + phonecard in greeting card 22.00
2047 A840 (49c) multi 9.00 *13.00*
a. Booklet pane of 2 18.00
Complete booklet, #2047a + phonecard in greeting card 22.00
2048 A841 (49c) multi 9.00 *13.00*
a. Booklet pane of 2 18.00
Complete booklet, #2048a + phonecard in greeting card 22.00
Nos. 2045-2048 (4) 49.50 52.00

Nos. 2045-2048, have a frame like No. 1918a, and are similarly inscribed "Domestic Lettermail" and "Poste-lettres du régime intérieur," but Nos. 2045-2048 have the vignettes printed on the stamps, while any vignettes found on No. 1918a are affixed stickers. Nos. 2045a-2048a are affixed to the insides of greeting cards that contain detachable phonecards valid for 15 minutes calling time on any touchtone phone in Canada or the United States. The stamps were available only in the greeting card, which sold for $5.99 along with a blank envelope for sending the greeting card.

2004 Summer Olympics, Athens — A842

Olympic rings and: No. 2049, Spyros Louis, 1896 Marathon gold medalist, diagram of track, "Athens" in Greek, and stylized runner. No. 2050, Soccer net inscribed "Canada," girls playing soccer.

2004, July 28 *Perf. 12½x13¼*
2049 A842 49c multi .75 .30
2050 A842 49c multi .75 .30
a. Horiz. pair, #2049-2050 1.50 1.10

Canadian Open Golf Championship, Cent. — A843

Crowd, trophy and golfer: No. 2051, Finishing swing. No. 2052, Ready to putt.

Self-Adhesive

Litho. & Embossed With Foil Application

2004, Aug. 12 ***Serpentine Die Cut***
2051 A843 49c multi .75 .30
2052 A843 49c multi .75 .30

Nos. 2051-2052 were issued in a sheet containing four of each stamp.

Maple Leaf Types of 2003
Self-Adhesive Coil Stamps

2004, Aug. 18 **Litho.** ***Die Cut***
2053 A822 49c multi .75 .25
a. Die cutting omitted, pair 180.00

Serpentine Die Cut 8¼ Horiz.

2054 A823 80c red & multi 2.00 .50
2055 A823 $1.40 grn & multi 3.75 .90
a. Die cutting omitted, pair —
Nos. 2053-2055 (3) 6.50 1.65

Die cut gauges on Nos. 2054-2055 vary widely within the roll, from 8¼-8¾. Gauge 8¼ is the most common.

Montreal Heart Institute, 50th Anniv. — A844

Self-Adhesive
Booklet Stamp

2004, Sept. 15 ***Die Cut Perf. 13½***
2056 A844 49c multi .75 .30
a. Booklet pane of 4 3.00
Complete booklet, 2 #2056 6.00

Pets A845

Self-Adhesive
Booklet Stamps

2004, Oct. 1 ***Die Cut***
2057 A845 49c Fish .80 .35
2058 A845 49c Cats .80 .35
2059 A845 49c Rabbit .80 .35
2060 A845 49c Dog .80 .35
a. Booklet pane, #2057-2060 3.25
Complete booklet, 2 #2060a 6.50

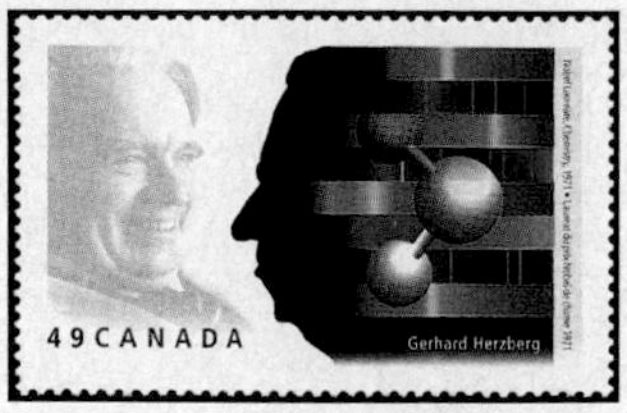

Nobel Laureates in Chemistry — A846

Designs: No. 2061, Gerhard Herzberg, 1971 laureate, and molecular structures. No. 2062, Michael Smith, 1993 laureate, and DNA double helix.

2004, Oct. 4 *Perf. 12½x13*
2061 A846 49c multi .75 .30
2062 A846 49c multi .75 .30
a. Pair, #2061-2062 1.50 1.10

Ribbon Frame A847

Picture Album Frame A848

Serpentine Die Cut 12¾x13

2004, Oct. 8 **Self-Adhesive**
2063 A847 (49c) multi 1.50 1.25
2064 A848 (49c) multi 1.50 1.25

Nos. 2063 and 2064 were each printed in panes of 21 that sold for $9.80. These panes were split by a row of rouletting in the center, with 20 stamps on one side and one on the other side. Panes of 21 with vignettes that could be personalized by the customer were available for $24.95. Panes of 40 stamps with personalized vignettes were also available for $39.95.

Victoria Cross, 150th Anniv. — A849

Designs: No. 2065, Victoria Cross. No. 2066, Design for Canadian Victoria Cross, approved with Queen Elizabeth II's signature.

Litho. & Embossed

2004, Oct. 21 *Perf. 13x12½*
2065 A849 49c multi .75 .30

Litho.

2066 A849 49c multi .75 .30
a. Pair, #2065-2066 1.50 1.20

Paintings by Jean Paul Lemieux — A850

Designs: 49c, Self-portrait. 80c, A June Wedding, horiz. (53x35mm). $1.40, Summer, horiz. (64x31mm).

2004, Oct. 22 *Perf. 13x13¼*
2067 A850 49c multi .75 .30
a. Perf. 13 1.50 1.50

Souvenir Sheet
Perf. 13

2068 Sheet, #2067a, 2068a, 2068b 4.00 4.00
a. A850 80c multi 1.50 1.50
b. A850 $1.40 multi 2.20 2.20

Christmas — A851

Santa Claus and: 49c, Sleigh. 80c, Automobile. $1.40, Train.

Booklet Stamps

Serpentine Die Cut 7¼ Horiz.

2004, Nov. 2 **Self-Adhesive**
2069 A851 49c multi .75 .25
a. Booklet pane of 6 4.50
Complete booklet, 2 #2069a 9.00
b. Printed on gummed side 11.00
c. As "a," printed on gummed side 150.00
2070 A851 80c multi 1.20 .45
a. Booklet pane of 6 7.25
b. Printed on gummed side —
2071 A851 $1.40 multi 2.10 .75
a. Booklet pane of 6 12.50
b. Printed on gummed side 45.00
c. As "a," printed on gummed side *750.00*

Queen Type of 2003 and

Red Calla Lilies A852

Flag and Saskatoon, Saskatchewan A853

Flag and Durrell, Newfoundland A854

Flag and Shannon Falls, British Columbia A855

Flag and Mont-Saint-Hilaire, Quebec — A856

Flag and Toronto — A857

Designs: 85c, Yellow calla lily. $1.45, Dutch iris.

Coil Stamps

Serpentine Die Cut 6½-8¾ Horiz.

2004-05 Self-Adhesive

2072 A852 50c multi .75 .25
a. Serpentine die cut 6¾ horiz. ('05) .75 .25
b. Die cutting omitted, pair 75.00
2073 A852 85c multi 1.25 .25
a. Serpentine die cut 6¾ horiz. ('05) 1.50 .25
2074 A852 $1.45 multi 2.25 .60
a. Serpentine die cut 6¾ horiz. ('05) 5.50 2.20

The die cutting gauge on Nos. 2072-2074a will vary between stamps on a roll and between stamps on one roll and other rolls.

Issued: Nos. 2072, 2073, 2074, 12/20/04. Nos. 2072a, 2073a, 2074a, 2/2005. Die cuttings on these issues are variable.

Booklet Stamps

Die Cut

2075 A825 50c multi .75 .25
a. Booklet pane of 10 7.50
2076 A853 50c multi .75 .25
2077 A854 50c multi .75 .25
2078 A855 50c multi .75 .25
2079 A856 50c multi .75 .25
2080 A857 50c multi .75 .25
a. Booklet pane, 2 each #2076-2080 7.50
2081 A852 85c multi 1.65 .40
a. Booklet pane of 6 10.00
b. As "a," black inscriptions omitted *5,000.*
2082 A852 $1.45 multi 2.20 .60
a. Booklet pane of 6 13.25
Nos. 2072-2082 (11) 12.60 3.60

New Year 2005 (Year of the Cock) — A858

Rooster with: 50c, Red tail feathers. $1.45, Gold tail feathers.

Litho. & Embossed with Foil Application

2005, Jan. 7 *Perf. 13¼*

2083 A858 50c multi .75 .30
a. Red omitted *1,400.*

Souvenir Sheet

Perf. 12½x13

2084 A858 $1.45 multi 2.25 2.25
a. With dates, Canadian and Chinese flags added in sheet margin 3.00 3.00

Canada — People's Republic of China diplomatic relations, 35th anniv. (No. 2084a). No. 2084 contains one 40x40mm stamp.

National Hockey League Stars A859

Designs: Nos. 2085a, 2086a, Henri Richard (blue background). Nos. 2085b, 2086b, Grant Fuhr (orange background). Nos. 2085c, 2086c, Allan Stanley (red background). Nos. 2085d, 2086d, Pierre Pilote (green background). Nos. 2085e, 2086e, Bryan Trottier (purple background). Nos. 2085f, 2086f, John Bucyk (yellow background).

Perf. 12½x13¼ on 3 Sides

2005, Jan. 29 Litho.

2085 Pane of 6 + 3 labels 4.75 4.75
a.-f. A859 50c Any single .80 .55

Self-Adhesive

Die Cut

2086 Pane of 6 4.75
a.-f. A859 50c Any single .80 .55

Fishing Flies — A860

Designs: Nos. 2087a, 2088a, Alevin. Nos. 2087b, 2088b, Jock Scott. Nos. 2087c, 2088d, P. E. I. Fly. Nos. 2087d, 2088c, Mickey Finn.

2005, Feb. 4 *Perf. 12½x13¼*

2087 A860 Pane of 4 7.25 5.50
a.-d. 50c Any single 1.80 1.10

Self-Adhesive

Serpentine Die Cut 10 Syncopated

2088 A860 Booklet pane of 4 3.60
a.-d. 50c Any single .90 .35
Complete booklet, 2 #2088 7.25

Universities Type of 2003

Design: Nova Scotia Agricultural College, cent.

Booklet Stamp

Die Cut Perf. 12¾x13¼

2005, Feb. 14 Self-Adhesive

2089 A806 50c multi .75 .30
a. Booklet pane of 4 3.00
Complete booklet, 2 #2089a 6.00

Expo 2005, Aichi, Japan — A861

2005, Mar. 4 *Perf. 13½*

2090 A861 50c multi .75 .30

Daffodils A862

Designs: Nos. 2091a, 2092, Yellow daffodils, green and yellow background. Nos. 2091b, 2093, White daffodils, red orange and yellow background.

Souvenir Sheet

2005, Mar. 10 *Perf. 13x13¼*

2091 Pane of 2 2.20 2.20
a.-b. A862 50c Either single 1.10 .75

Booklet Stamps

Self-Adhesive

Die Cut Perf. 10

2092 A862 50c multi .80 .30
2093 A862 50c multi .80 .30
a. Booklet pane, 5 each #2092-2093 + 10 stickers 8.00

Pacific Explore 2005 World Stamp Expo, Sydney, Australia (No. 2091).

TD Bank Financial Group, 150th Anniv. — A863

Self-Adhesive

Booklet Stamp

2005, Mar. 18 *Die Cut Perf. 11¼*

2094 A863 50c multi .75 .35
a. Booklet pane of 10 7.50
Complete booklet, #2094a 10.00

The booklet pane of 10 is the inside front cover of the booklet. Fifteen stickers are on inside back cover.

Bird Paintings by John James Audubon — A864

Designs: No. 2095, Horned lark. No. 2096, Piping plover. No. 2097, Stilt sandpiper. No. 2098, Willow ptarmigan. 85c, Double-crested cormorant.

2005, Mar. 23 *Perf. 12½x13¼*

2095 A864 50c multi .75 .40
2096 A864 50c multi .75 .40
2097 A864 50c multi .75 .40
2098 A864 50c multi .75 .40
a. Block of 4, #2095-2098 3.00 2.50

Booklet Stamp

Self-Adhesive

Size: 48x39mm

Die Cut

2099 A864 85c multi 1.10 .45
a. Booklet pane of 6 6.50

Bridges — A865

Designs: No. 2100, Jacques Cartier Bridge, Quebec. No. 2101, Souris Swinging Bridge, Manitoba. No. 2102, Angus L. Macdonald Bridge, Nova Scotia. No. 2103, Canso Causeway, Nova Scotia.

Self-Adhesive

2005, Apr. 2 *Perf. 12½x13*

2100 A865 50c multi .75 .45
2101 A865 50c multi .75 .45
2102 A865 50c multi .75 .45
2103 A865 50c multi .75 .45
a. Block or strip of 4, #2100-2103 3.00 2.75
b. As "a," imperf. 1,500.

Maclean's Magazine, Cent. A866

2005, Apr. 12

2104 A866 50c multi .75 .30

Biosphere Reserves in Canada and Ireland — A867

Designs: No. 2105, Saskatoon berries, Waterton Lakes National Park, Canada. No. 2106, Deer, Killarney National Park, Ireland.

2005, Apr. 22

2105 A867 50c multi .75 .30
2106 A867 50c multi .75 .30
a. Pair, #2105-2106 1.50 1.10
b. Souvenir sheet, #2105-2106 2.25 2.25

See Ireland Nos. 1611-1612.

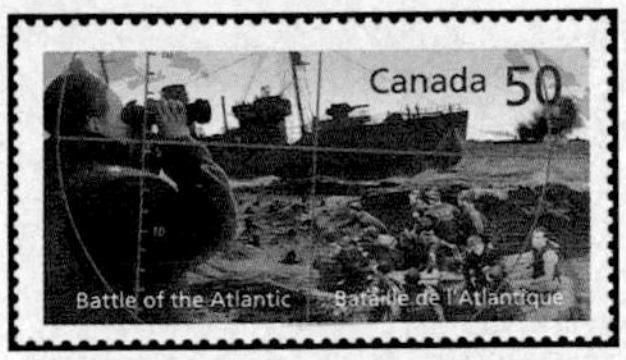

Battle of the Atlantic, World War II — A868

2005, Apr. 29

2107 A868 50c multi .75 .30

Opening of Canadian War Museum, Ottawa — A869

Booklet Stamp

Serpentine Die Cut 8x8½ Syncopated

2005, May 6 Self-Adhesive

2108 A869 50c multi .75 .30
a. Booklet pane of 4 3.00
Complete booklet, 2 #2108a 6.00

Paintings by Homer Watson (1855-1936) — A870

Designs: 50c, Down In the Laurentides. 85c, The Flood Gate (54x40mm)

2005, May 27 *Perf. 13¼x13*

2109 A870 50c multi .75 .30
a. Perf. 13½x13 1.50 1.50

Souvenir Sheet

Perf. 13½x13

2110 Pane of 2, Nos. 2109a, 2110a 4.50 4.50
a. A870 85c multi 3.00 3.00

Miniature Sheet

Search and Rescue — A871

No. 2111: a, Rescuer and dog at plane crash. b, Rescuers at shipwreck. c, Helicopter, airplane and rescuers. d, Mountainside rescuers.

2005, June 13 *Perf. 13x13¼*

2111 A871 Pane of 8, 2 each #a-d 6.00 6.00
a.-d. 50c Any single .75 .55

No. 2111 contains two horizontal strips, one of which is inverted, so that a tete-beche pair of No. 2111c and two tete-beche pairs containing Nos. 2111b and 2111d can be created.

Ellen Fairclough (1905-2004), First Female Cabinet Minister — A872

2005, June 21 *Perf. 13x12½*
2112 A872 50c multi .75 .30

Diver A873

Swimmer A874

2005, July 5 *Perf. 13¼*
2113 A873 50c multi .75 .45
2114 A874 50c multi .75 .45
a. Horiz. pair, #2113-2114 1.50 .90

9th FINA World Championships, Montreal. In No. 2114a, the denomination for one stamp is on the opposite side of the pair from that of the other stamp.

Founding of Port-Royal, Nova Scotia, 400th Anniv. A875

Litho. & Engr.

2005, July 16 *Perf. 13x12½*
2115 A875 50c multi .75 .30

Province of Alberta, Cent. — A876

Self-Adhesive

2005, July 21 Litho. *Perf. 12½x13*
2116 A876 50c multi .75 .30

Printed in panes of 8 with each stamp having a different design on the backing.

Province of Saskatchewan, Cent. — A877

2005, Aug. 2 *Perf. 13x12½*
2117 A877 50c multi .75 .30

Oscar Peterson, Pianist, 80th Birthday — A878

2005, Aug. 15
2118 A878 50c multi .75 .30
a. Souvenir sheet of 4 3.00 3.00

No. 176 and Acadian Flag A879

2005, Aug. 15
2119 A879 50c multi .75 .30

Acadian Deportation, 250th anniv.

Children Playing and Leg Braces — A880

2005, Sept. 2 *Perf. 12½x13*
2120 A880 50c multi .75 .30

Mass polio vaccinations in Canada, 50th anniv.

Youth Sports — A881

No. 2121: a, Wall climbing. b, Skateboarding. c, Mountain biking. d, Snowboarding.

Self-Adhesive

2005, Oct. 1 *Die Cut*
2121 Complete booklet, 2 each #a-d 6.00
a.-d. A881 50c Any single .75 .40

Wild Cats — A882

Designs: No. 2122, Puma concolor. No. 2123, Panthera pardus orientalis.

Perf. 13½x13¼ Syncopated

2005, Oct. 13
2122 50c multi .75 .40
2123 50c multi .75 .40
a. A882 Horiz. pair, #2122-2123 1.50 .90
b. Souvenir sheet, #2123a 1.80 1.80

Diplomatic relations with People's Republic of China, 35th anniv. (No. 2123b). The perforation column between the two stamps, which gauges perf. 13½, has a maple leaf shaped syncopation.

See People's Republic of China Nos. 3458-3459.

Snowman — A883

Self-Adhesive

Litho. with Hologram Applied

Serpentine Die Cut 8¼ Horiz.

2005, Nov. 2 Booklet Stamp
2124 A883 50c multi .75 .30
a. Booklet pane of 6 4.50
Complete booklet, 2 #2124a 9.00

A884

A885

Creche Figures, St. Joseph's Oratory, Montreal — A886

Self-Adhesive

Serpentine Die Cut 6¾ Horiz.

2005, Nov. 2 Booklet Stamps
2125 A884 50c multi .75 .30
a. Booklet pane of 6 4.50
Complete booklet, 2 #2125a 9.00

Serpentine Die Cut 6½ Horiz.

2126 A885 85c multi 1.25 .60
a. Booklet pane of 6 7.50

Serpentine Die Cut 6¾ Horiz.

2127 A886 $1.45 multi 2.20 1.10
a. Booklet pane of 6 13.00

Flowers — A887

Designs: 51c, Red bergamot. 89c, Yellow lady's slipper. $1.05, Pink fairy slipper. $1.49, Himalayan blue poppy.

Coil Stamps

Serpentine Die Cut 7 to 9¼ Horiz.

2005, Dec. 19 Self-Adhesive
2128 A887 51c multi .75 .25
2129 A887 89c multi 1.30 .45
2130 A887 $1.05 multi 1.50 .60
2131 A887 $1.49 multi 2.20 .90

Booklet Stamps

Die Cut

2132 A887 89c multi 1.50 .40
a. Booklet pane of 6 9.00
2133 A887 $1.05 multi 1.80 .65
a. Booklet pane of 6 11.00
2134 A887 $1.49 multi 2.20 1.00
a. Booklet pane of 6 13.00
Nos. 2128-2134 (7) 11.25 4.25

Flag and Houses, New Glasgow, Prince Edward Island A888

Flag and Bridge, Bouctouche, New Brunswick A889

Flag and Windmills, Pincher Creek, Alberta A890

Flag and Lower Fort Garry, Manitoba A891

Flag and Dogsled, Yukon Territory — A892

Self-Adhesive

Booklet Stamps

2005, Dec. 19 *Die Cut*
2135 A888 51c multi .75 .25
2136 A889 51c multi .75 .25
2137 A890 51c multi .75 .25
2138 A891 51c multi .75 .25
2139 A892 51c multi .75 .25
a. Booklet pane, 2 each #2135-2139 7.50
b. As "a," die cutting omitted *1,500.*
Nos. 2135-2139 (5) 3.75 1.25

New Year 2006 (Year of the Dog) — A893

Litho. & Embossed With Foil Application

2006, Jan. 6 *Perf. 13¼*
2140 A893 51c shown .75 .30

Souvenir Sheet

2141 A893 $1.49 Dog and pup 2.20 2.20

Queen Elizabeth II, 80th Birthday A894

Self-Adhesive

Booklet Stamp

Serpentine Die Cut 10

2006, Jan. 12 Litho.
2142 A894 51c multi .75 .30
a. Booklet pane of 10 7.50
b. Die cutting omitted, pair 250.00

See No. 2150.

2006 Winter Olympics, Turin, Italy A895

Designs: No. 2143, Team pursuit speed skating. No. 2144, Skeleton.

2006, Feb. 3 *Perf. 12½x13*
2143 A895 51c multi .75 .30
2144 A895 51c multi .75 .30
a. Horiz. pair, #2143-2144 1.50 .90

Gardens — A896

No. 2145: a, Shade garden and black-throated blue warbler. b, Flower garden and American painted lady butterfly. c, Water garden and green darner dragonfly. d, Rock garden and blue-spotted salamander.

Self-Adhesive

2006, Mar. 8 ***Serpentine Die Cut 10***

2145 Complete booklet, 2 each #a-d 6.00
a.-d. A896 51c Any single .75 .45

Party Balloons A897

Booklet Stamp

Serpentine Die Cut 6¾ Horiz.

2006, Apr. 3 **Self-Adhesive**

2146 A897 51c multi .75 .30
a. Booklet pane of 6 6.00

Paintings by Dorothy Knowles — A898

Designs: 51c, The Field of Rapeseed. 89c, North Saskatchewan River, vert. (42x51mm).

2006, Apr. 7 ***Perf. 13¼x12½***

2147 A898 51c multi .75 .30
a. Perf. 12¾x12½ 1.50 1.50

Souvenir Sheet

Perf. 13

2148 Pane, Nos. 2147a, 2148a 3.75 3.75
a. A898 89c multi 2.20 2.20

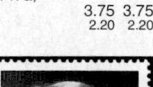

Canadian Labor Congress, 50th Anniv. — A899

2006, Apr. 20 ***Perf. 13½x13¼***

2149 A899 51c multi .75 .30

Queen Elizabeth II, 80th Birthday Type of 2006

Souvenir Sheet

2006, Apr. 21 ***Perf. 12½x13***

2150 Pane of 2, No. 2150a 4.50 4.50
a. A894 149c multi, 36x28mm 2.25 2.25

McClelland & Stewart Publishing House, Cent. — A900

Self-Adhesive

Booklet Stamp

2006, Apr. 26 ***Die Cut Perf. 11¼x11***

2151 A900 51c slate grn & sil .75 .30
a. Booklet pane of 4 + 4 stickers 3.00
Complete booklet, 2 #2151a 6.00

Northwest Coast Transformation Mask and Northwest Coast Exhibit — A901

Booklet Stamp

Serpentine Die Cut 8 Horiz. Syncopated

2006, May 11 **Self-Adhesive**

2152 A901 89c multi 1.30 .80
a. Booklet pane of 4 3.25
Complete booklet, 2 #2152a 7.00
b. Die cutting omitted, pair *750.00*

Canadian Museum of Civilization, 150th anniv.

Canadians in Hollywood A903

Actors and actresses: Nos. 2153a, 2154a, John Candy (1950-94). Nos. 2153b, 2154c, Fay Wray (1907-2004). Nos. 2153c, 2154d, Lorne Greene (1915-87). Nos. 2153d, 2154b, Mary Pickford (1893-1979).

2006, May 26 ***Perf. 13x12½***

2153 Souvenir sheet of 4 4.50 4.50
a.-d. A903 51c Any single 1.10 1.10

Self-Adhesive

Serpentine Die Cut 9¾x10

2154 Booklet pane of 4 + 4 stickers 3.00
a.-d. A903 51c Any single .75 .45
Complete booklet, 2 #2154 6.00

Complete booklets were issued with four different covers depicting the featured actors or actresses.

See Nos. 2279-2280.

A904

Exploration of Eastern Coast by Samuel de Champlain, 400th Anniv. — A905

Litho. & Engr.

2006, May 28 ***Perf. 13x12½***

2155 A904 51c multi .75 .30

Souvenir Sheet

Perf. 11

2156 A905 Pane of 2 #2156a, 2 US #4074a 7.50 7.00
a. A904 51c multi 1.45 1.10

Washington 2006 World Philatelic Exhibition (No. 2156). No. 2156, sold only by Canada Post for $2, has bar code in pane margin at lower left. United States No. 4074, sold only by the United States Postal Service, lacks this bar code.

Vancouver Aquarium, 50th Anniv. — A906

Self-Adhesive

Booklet Stamp

Serpentine Die Cut 9½

2006, June 15 **Litho.**

2157 A906 51c multi .75 .30
a. Booklet pane of 5 3.75
Complete booklet, 2 #2157a 7.50

Canadian Forces Snowbirds Aerobatics Team — A907

Designs: No. 2158, Pilot in cockpit, two airplanes. No. 2159, Three airplanes.

2006, June 28 ***Perf. 12½x13¼***

2158 A907 51c multi .75 .30
2159 A907 51c multi .75 .30
a. Horiz. pair, #2158-2159 1.50 1.10
b. Souvenir sheet, #2159a 2.20 2.20

James White, Dividers and Map of Canada — A908

2006, June 30 ***Perf. 13¼x12½***

2160 A908 51c multi .75 .30

Atlas of Canada, cent. Printed in panes of 16 + 4 labels.

World Lacrosse Championships, London, Ontario — A909

Booklet Stamp

Serpentine Die Cut 11¾ Horiz.

2006, July 6 **Self-Adhesive**

2161 A909 51c multi .75 .30
a. Booklet pane of 8 6.00

Alpine Club of Canada, Cent. — A910

Self-Adhesive

Booklet Stamp

2006, July 19 ***Die Cut Perf. 12½x13***

2162 A910 51c multi .75 .30
a. Booklet pane of 8 6.00

Ducks and Duck Decoys A911

Designs: No. 2163, Barrow's goldeneyes. No. 2164, Mallards. No. 2165, American black ducks. No. 2166, Redbreasted mergansers.

2006, Aug. 3 ***Perf. 13¼x12½***

2163 A911 51c blue & multi .75 .45
2164 A911 51c yel & multi .75 .45
2165 A911 51c red & multi .75 .45
2166 A911 51c grn & multi .75 .45
a. Block of 4, #2163-2166 3.00 2.20
b. Souvenir sheet, #2163-2166 3.75 3.75

Society of Graphic Designers of Canada, 50th Anniv. — A912

2006, Aug. 16 ***Perf. 12½x13***

2167 A912 51c multi .75 .30

Canadian Wines A913

Canadian Cheeses A914

Designs: No. 2168, Three glasses of wine. No. 2169, Wine taster, barrels. No. 2170, Various cheeses. No. 2171, Woman with tray of cheeses and fruit.

Self-Adhesive

Booklet Stamps

2006, Aug. 23 ***Die Cut***

2168 A913 51c multi .75 .45
2169 A913 51c multi .75 .45
2170 A914 51c multi .75 .45
2171 A914 51c multi .75 .45
a. Booklet pane, 2 each #2168-2171 6.00
Nos. 2168-2171 (4) 3.00 1.80

Universities Type of 2003

Design: Macdonald College, Sainte-Anne-de-Bellevue, Quebec, cent.

Booklet Stamp

Die Cut Perf. 12¾x13¼

2006, Sept. 26 **Self-Adhesive**

2172 A806 51c multi .75 .30
a. Booklet pane of 4 3.00
Complete booklet, 2 #2172a 6.00

Endangered Animals — A915

Designs: Nos. 2173a, 2174, Newfoundland marten. Nos. 2173b, 2175, Blotched tiger salamander. Nos. 2173c, 2176, Blue racer snake. Nos. 2173d, 2177, Swift fox.

2006, Sept. 29 *Perf. 13¼*

2173 Pane of 4 + 4 labels 4.50 4.00
a.-d. A915 51c Any single 1.10 .90

Booklet Stamps
Self-Adhesive
Size: 47x24mm

Die Cut

2174 A915 51c multi .75 .45
2175 A915 51c multi .75 .45
2176 A915 51c multi .75 .45
2177 A915 51c multi .75 .45
a. Block of 4, #2174-2177 3.00
b. Booklet pane, 2, #2177a 6.00

See Nos. 2229-2233, 2285-2289.

Opera Singers — A916

Designs: No. 2178, Maureen Forrester. No. 2179, Raoul Jobin (1906-74). No. 2180, Léopold Simoneau (1916-2006) and Pierrette Alarie. No. 2181, Jon Vickers. No. 2182, Edward Johnson (1878-1959).

2006, Oct. 17 *Perf. 13½x13*

2178 A916 51c multi .75 .45
2179 A916 51c multi .75 .45
2180 A916 51c multi .75 .45
2181 A916 51c multi .75 .45
2182 A916 51c multi .75 .45
a. Vert. strip of 5, #2178-2182 3.75 3.75

Madonna and Child, by Antoine-Sébastien Falardeau
A917

Christmas Card Art
A918

Designs: No. 2184, Snowman, by Yvonne McKague Housser. 89c, Winter Joys, by J. E. Sampson. $1.49, Contemplation, by Edwin Holgate.

Self-Adhesive
Booklet Stamp

2006, Nov. 1 *Die Cut*

2183 A917 51c multi .75 .25
a. Booklet pane of 12 9.00

Serpentine Die Cut 13¼ Horiz.

2184 A918 51c multi .75 .25
a. Booklet pane of 12 9.00
2185 A918 89c multi 1.30 .55
a. Booklet pane of 6 8.00
2186 A918 $1.49 multi 2.20 .90
a. Booklet pane of 6 13.25
Nos. 2183-2186 (4) 5.00 1.95

Spotted Coralroot
A919

Queen Elizabeth II
A920

Flag and Sirmilik Natl. Park, Nunavut
A921

Flag and Cliff Near Chemainus, British Columbia
A922

Flag and Polar Bears Near Churchill, Manitoba
A923

Flag and Bras d'Or Lake, Nova Scotia
A924

Flag and Tuktut Nogait Natl. Park, Northwest Territories — A925

Self-Adhesive
Coil Stamp

Serpentine Die Cut 7½-9 Horiz.

2006, Nov. 16 **Litho.**

2187 A919 P multi 1.25 .25

Booklet Stamps

Die Cut

2188 A920 P multi 1.25 .25
a. Booklet pane of 10 12.50
2189 A921 P multi 1.25 .25
2190 A922 P multi 1.25 .25
2191 A923 P multi 1.25 .25
2192 A924 P multi 1.25 .25
2193 A925 P multi 1.25 .25
a. Booklet pane, 2 each #2189-2193 12.50
b. Booklet pane, 6 each #2189-2193 37.50
Nos. 2187-2193 (7) 8.75 1.75

Nos. 2187-2193 each sold for 51c on day of issue. On Nos. 2188a, 2193a and 2193b, adjacent stamps that are on both sides of the booklet fold have rouletting rather than die cutting between them. No. 2193b is sold folded into thirds. Each of the thirds has selvage surrounding the ten stamps on it, unlike No. 2193a.

See No. 2194a.

Spotted Coralroot Type of 2006 and

Flat-leaved Bladderwort — A926

Designs: $1.10, Marsh skullcap. $1.55, Little larkspur.

2006, Dec. 19 *Perf. 13¼x13*

2194 Souvenir sheet of 4 7.50 7.50
a. A919 P multi 1.25 .75
b. A926 93c multi 1.50 1.10
c. A926 $1.10 multi 1.65 1.25
d. A926 $1.55 multi 2.20 2.20

Self-Adhesive
Coil Stamps

Serpentine Die Cut 7½-9 Horiz.

2195 A926 93c multi 1.35 .40
2196 A926 $1.10 multi 1.65 .60
2197 A926 $1.55 multi 2.25 .60

Booklet Stamps

Die Cut

2198 A926 93c multi 1.50 .60
a. Booklet pane of 6 9.00
2199 A926 $1.10 multi 1.75 .75
a. Booklet pane of 6 10.50
2200 A926 $1.55 multi 2.50 1.10
a. Booklet pane of 6 15.00
Nos. 2195-2200 (6) 11.00 4.05

No. 2194a sold for 51c on day of issue.
See Nos. 2243, 2245-2247, 2254-2256.

New Year 2007 (Year of the Pig) A927

Pig facing: 52c, Left. $1.55, Right.

Litho. & Embossed with Foil Application

2007, Jan. 5 *Perf. 13½x13*

2201 A927 52c red & multi .75 .30
a. Gold foil omitted 75.00

Souvenir Sheet

2202 A927 $1.55 grn & multi 2.50 2.50

Confetti and Streamers A928

Self-Adhesive
Booklet Stamp

Serpentine Die Cut 6¾ Horiz.

2007, Jan. 15 **Litho.**

2203 A928 52c multi .75 .30
a. Booklet pane of 6 4.50

International Polar Year — A929

Designs: No. 2204, Somateria spectabilis. No. 2205, Crossota millsaeare.

Perf. 13½ Syncopated

2007, Feb. 12

2204 A929 52c multi .75 .30
2205 A929 52c multi .75 .30
a. Horiz. pair, #2204-2205 1.50 .90
b. Souvenir sheet, #2205a 2.20 2.20

Lilacs — A930

Color of lilacs: Nos. 2206a, 2207, White. Nos. 2206b, 2208, Purple.

Souvenir Sheet

2007, Mar. 1 *Perf. 12¾*

2206 A930 Pane of 2 2.20 2.20
a.-b. 52c Either single 1.10 .75

Booklet Stamps
Self-Adhesive

Die Cut

2207 A930 52c multi .75 .30
2208 A930 52c multi .75 .30
a. Booklet pane of 10, 5 each #2207-2208 7.50

Universities Type of 2003

Design: No. 2209, HEC Montreal, cent. No. 2210, University of Saskatchewan, cent.

Self-Adhesive
Booklet Stamp

2007 *Die Cut Perf. 12¾x13¼*

2209 A806 52c multi .75 .30
a. Booklet pane of 4 2.00
Complete booklet, 2 #2209a 6.00
2210 A806 52c multi .75 .30
a. Booklet pane of 4 3.00
Complete booklet, 2 #2210a 6.00

Issued: No. 2209, 3/12. No. 2210, 4/3.

Art by Mary Pratt — A931

Designs: 52c, Jelly Shelf. $1.55 Iceberg in the North Atlantic (58x36mm).

2007, Mar. 15 *Perf. 13x12½*

2211 A931 52c multi .75 .30

Souvenir Sheet

2212 Pane, #2211, 2212a 3.50 3.50
a. A931 $1.55 multi 2.20 2.20

Selection of Ottawa as National Capital, 150th Anniv. — A932

Litho., Litho & Embossed with Foil Application (#2213b)

2007, May 3 *Perf. 13¼*

2213 Pane of 2, #2213a, 2213b 3.50 3.50
a. A932 52c multi 1.10 1.10
b. A932 $1.55 multi 2.20 2.20

Booklet Stamp
Self-Adhesive

Serpentine Die Cut 7¼ Horiz.

2214 A932 52c multi .85 .30
a. Booklet pane of 4 3.50
Complete booklet, 2 #2214a 7.00

Royal Architectural Institute of Canada, Cent. — A933

Buildings: No. 2215, University of Lethbridge, by Arthur Erickson. No. 2216, St. Mary's Church, by Douglas Cardinal. No. 2217, Ontario Science Centre, by Raymond Moriyama. No. 2218, National Gallery of Canada, by Moshe Safdie.

2007, May 9 **Litho.** *Perf. 13*

2215 A933 52c multi + label .75 .45
2216 A933 52c multi + label .75 .45
2217 A933 52c multi + label .75 .45
2218 A933 52c multi + label .75 .45
a. Vert. strip of 4, #2215-2218, + 4 labels 3.00 2.20

Nos. 2215-2218 were printed in panes containing two of each stamp. Labels flank the stamps, with labels on the left showing drawings of the buildings and the labels on the right showing the architect.

Capt. George Vancouver (1757-98), Explorer — A934

Litho. & Embossed

2007, June 22 *Perf. 13x12½*

2219 A934 $1.55 multi 2.20 1.00
a. Souvenir sheet of 1, perf. 13 2.20 2.20

FIFA Under-20 World Soccer Championships, Canada — A935

2007, June 26 Litho. *Perf. 12½x13*

2220 A935 52c multi .75 .30
a. Imperf., pair *950.00*

Popular Singers — A936

Designs: Nos. 2221a, 2222a, Gordon Lightfoot. Nos. 2221b, 2222b, Joni Mitchell. Nos. 2221c, 2222c, Anne Murray. Nos. 2221d, 2222d, Paul Anka.

2007, June 29 *Perf. 12½x13*

2221 A936 Pane of 4 3.00 3.00
a.-d. 52c Any single .75 .75

Self-Adhesive

Serpentine Die Cut 13½

2222 A936 Booklet pane of 4 3.00
a.-d. 52c Any single .75 .40
Complete booklet, 2 #2222 6.00

Complete booklets were issued with four different covers depicting the featured singers.

National Parks — A937

Designs: No. 2223, Terra Nova National Park, Newfoundland, 50th anniv. No. 2224, Jasper National Park, Alberta, cent.

Self-Adhesive

Booklet Stamps

2007 *Serpentine Die Cut 13½*

2223 A937 52c multi .75 .30
a. Booklet pane of 5 3.75
Complete booklet, 2 #2223a 7.50
2224 A937 52c multi .75 .30
a. Booklet pane of 5 3.75
Complete booklet, 2 #2224a 7.50
b. Gutter pane, 5 each #2223-2224 11.00

Issued: No. 2223, 7/6; No. 2224, 7/20.

Scouting, Cent. A938

Self-Adhesive

Booklet Stamp

2007, July 25

2225 A938 52c multi .75 .30
a. Booklet pane of 4 + 4 labels 3.00
Complete booklet, 2 #2225a 6.00

Henri Membertou, Grand Chief of Mi'kmaq Tribe — A939

2007, June 26 Engr. *Perf. 13x12½*

2226 A939 52c multi .75 .30

Law Society of Saskatchewan, Cent. — A940

2007, Sept. 13 Litho. *Perf. 13*

2227 A940 52c multi 1.50 .75

Printed in panes of 8 + 8 labels.

Law Society of Alberta, Cent. A941

2007, Sept. 13 *Perf. 12½x13*

2228 A941 52c multi .75 .30

Endangered Animals Type of 2006

Designs: Nos. 2229a, 2230, North Atlantic right whale. Nos. 2229b, 2231, Northern cricket frog. Nos. 2229c, 2232, White sturgeon. Nos. 2229d, 2233, Leatherback turtle.

2007, Oct. 1 *Perf. 13¼*

2229 Pane of 4 + 4 labels 3.00 3.00
a.-d. A915 52c Any single .75 .75

Booklet Stamps

Self-Adhesive

Size: 47x24mm

Die Cut

2230 A915 52c multi .80 .30
2231 A915 52c multi .80 .30
2232 A915 52c multi .80 .30
2233 A915 52c multi .80 .30
a. Block of 4, #2230-2233 3.20
b. Booklet pane, 2 #2233a 6.50

Beneficial Insects — A942

Designs: 1c, Convergent lady beetle (Hippodamia convergens). 3c, Golden-eyed lacewing (Chrysopa oculata). 5c, Northern bumblebee (Bombus polaris). 10c, Canada darner (Aeshna canadensis). 25c, Cecropia moth (Hyalophora cecropia).

No. 2235

No. 2235a

2007, Oct. 12 *Perf. 13¼x13*

2234 A942 1c multi .25 .25
2235 A942 3c multi .25 .25
a. "Canada" shifted to right, touching "Oculata" (pos. 11-14) .40 .25
b. Dated "2012," with added microprinting and small design features (#2409b) .25 .25
2236 A942 5c multi .25 .25
2237 A942 10c multi .25 .25
2238 A942 25c multi .40 .25
a. Souvenir sheet, #2234-2238 1.10 1.00
Nos. 2234-2238 (5) 1.40 1.25

No. 2235a occurs four times on each pane of 50. Panes printed in 2010 correct the errors. See Nos. 2328, 2406-2410, 2708.

Issued: No. 2235b, 10/16/12.

Christmas

A943 A944

Designs: No. 2239, Reindeer and snowflakes. No. 2240, Holy Family. 93c, Angel over town. $1.55, Dove.

Booklet Stamps

Litho. With Hologram Affixed

Serpentine Die Cut 8¼ Horiz.

2007, Nov. 1 Self-Adhesive

2239 A943 (52c) multi 1.25 .25
a. Booklet pane of 6 7.50
Complete booklet, 2 #2239a 15.00
b. Die cutting omitted, pair *500.00*

Litho.

Serpentine Die Cut 13½

2240 A944 (52c) multi 1.25 .25
a. Booklet pane of 6 7.50
Complete booklet, 2 #2240a 15.00
2241 A944 93c multi 1.30 .40
a. Booklet pane of 6 8.00
2242 A944 $1.55 multi 2.20 .60
a. Booklet pane of 6 13.25
b. Die cutting omitted, pair *575.00*
Nos. 2239-2242 (4) 6.00 1.50

Flowers Type of 2006 and

Odontioda Island Red Orchid — A945

Queen Elizabeth II — A946

Flag and Sambro Island Lighthouse, Nova Scotia A947

Flag and Point Clark Lighthouse, Ontario A948

Flag and Cap-des-Rosiers Lighthouse, Quebec — A949

Flag and Warren Landing Lighthouse, Manitoba A950

Flag and Pachena Point Lighthouse, British Columbia A951

Flag and Pachena Point Lighthouse, British Columbia — A951a

Designs: 96c, Potinara Janet Elizabeth "Fire Dancer" orchid. $1.15, Laeliocattleya Memoria Evelyn Light orchid. $1.60, Masdevallia Kaleidoscope "Conni" orchid.

2007, Dec. 27 Litho. *Perf. 13¼x13*

2243 Pane of 4 6.75 6.75
a. A945 P multi 1.25 .85
b. A926 96c multi 1.50 1.20
c. A926 $1.15 multi 1.65 1.30
d. A926 $1.60 multi 2.20 1.80

Self-Adhesive

Coil Stamps

Serpentine Die Cut 8-9½ Horiz.

2244 A945 P multi 1.25 .25

Serpentine Die Cut 9.2 Horiz.

2244A A945 P multi 1.45 1.45

Serpentine Die Cut 8-9½

2245 A926 96c multi 1.25 .30
2246 A926 $1.15 multi 1.80 .45
2247 A926 $1.60 multi 2.50 .60
Nos. 2244-2247 (5) 8.25 3.05

Die cutting is irregular across the stamp (saw tooth tips) on Nos. 2244 and 2245-2247 compared to being consistent across the stamp (rounded tips) on No. 2244A. On No. 2244, stamps are vertically contiguous on the backing paper, while on No. 2244A the stamps are separated on horizontal backing paper that is taller than the stamp.

Booklet Stamps

2248 A946 P multi 1.25 .25
a. Booklet pane of 10 12.50
2249 A947 P multi 1.25 .25
2250 A948 P multi 1.25 .25
2251 A949 P multi 1.25 .25
2252 A950 P multi 1.25 .25
2253 A951 P multi 1.25 .25
a. Booklet pane of 10, 2 each #2249-2253 12.50

Serpentine Die Cut 13¼

2253B A951a P multi 1.25 .25
c. Booklet pane of 10, 2 each #2249-2252, 2253B 12.50
d. Booklet pane of 30, 6 each #2249-2252, 2253B 37.50

Die Cut

2254 A926 96c multi 1.50 .25
a. Booklet pane of 6 9.00
2255 A926 $1.15 multi 1.80 .40
a. Booklet pane of 6 11.00
2256 A926 $1.60 multi 2.40 .60
a. Booklet pane of 6 14.50
Nos. 2248-2256 (10) 14.45 3.00

Nos. 2243a, 2244, 2248-2253 each sold for 52c on day of issue.

No. 2244A issued 2/21/08.

No. 2253B issued 5/1/08. No. 2253Bd was separated into thirds by two rows of rouletting. The separated thirds of this booklet have the same contents as No. 2253Bc, but have different selvage markings.

New Year 2008 (Year of the Rat) — A952

Designs: 52c, Rat with umbrella. $1.60, Rat with fan.

Litho. & Embossed With Foil Application

2008, Jan. 8 *Perf. 13*

2257 A952 52c multi .75 .30

Souvenir Sheet

2258 A952 $1.60 multi 3.00 3.00

No. 2257 printed in panes of 25 + 20 labels.

Fireworks A953

Self-Adhesive

Booklet Stamp

Serpentine Die Cut 13½ Horiz.

2008, Jan. 15 **Litho.**

2259 A953 P multi 1.25 .30
- *a.* Booklet pane of 6 7.50

No. 2259 sold for 52c on day of issue.

Peonies A954

Peony color: Nos. 2260a, 2261, Pink. Nos. 2260b, 2262, Red.

2008, Mar. 3 **Litho.** *Perf. 13¼*

2260 Pane of 2 2.20 2.20
- *a.-b.* A954 52c Either single 1.10 .75

Booklet Stamps

Self-Adhesive

Serpentine Die Cut 13¼

2261 A954 52c multi .75 .30

2262 A954 52c multi .75 .30
- *a.* Pair, #2261-2262 1.50
- *b.* Booklet pane, 5 each #2261-2262, + 10 stickers 7.50
- *c.* Die cutting omitted, pair *375.00*

The country name and denomination are closer to the flowers on Nos. 2261-2262 than on Nos. 2260a-2260b.

Universities A955

Designs: No. 2263, University of Alberta, cent. No. 2264, University of British Columbia, cent.

Self-Adhesive

Serpentine Die Cut 13¼

2008, Mar. 7 **Booklet Stamps**

2263 A955 52c multi .75 .25
- *a.* Booklet pane of 8 6.00
- *b.* Die cutting omitted, pair *325.00*

2264 A955 52c multi .75 .25
- *a.* Booklet pane of 8 6.00
- *b.* Gutter pane, 4 each #2263-2264 11.00

2008 Intl. Ice Hockey Federation Championships, Halifax and Quebec — A956

Self-Adhesive

Serpentine Die Cut 13½

2008, Apr. 3 **Booklet Stamp**

2265 A956 52c multi .75 .25
- *a.* Booklet pane of 10 7.50
- *b.* Die cutting omitted, pair *300.00*

No. 2265a was printed with two different booklet covers.

Guide Dog A957

Self-Adhesive

Booklet Stamp

Serpentine Die Cut 13½x13

2008, Apr. 21 **Litho. & Embossed**

2266 A957 52c multi .75 .25
- *a.* Booklet pane of 10 7.50

Montreal Association for the Blind, cent.

Oil and Gas Anniversaries — A958

Designs: No. 2267, Welder welding Trans-Canada Pipeline. No. 2268, James M. Williams, Charles Tripp, Oil Springs, Ontario oil field.

Self-Adhesive

Booklet Stamps

Serpentine Die Cut 13¼

2008, May 2 **Litho.**

2267 A958 52c multi .75 .25
- *a.* Die cutting omitted, pair 750.00

2268 A958 52c multi .75 .25
- *a.* Die cutting omitted, pair 750.00
- *b.* Booklet pane of 10, 5 each #2267-2268 7.50

Trans-Canada Pipeline, 50th anniv., First commercial oil well in Canada, 150th anniv.

Quebec City, 400th Anniv. A959

Litho. & Engr.

2008, May 16 *Perf. 13x12½*

2269 A959 52c multi .75 .30

See France No. 3437. A souvenir sheet containing No. 2269 and France No. 3437 sold for $4.99.

Photographic Portraits by Yousuf Karsh (1908-2008) A960

Designs: 52c, Self-portrait, 1952. 96c, Audrey Hepburn, 1956. $1.60, Sir Winston Churchill, 1941.

2008, May 21 **Litho.** *Perf. 13x12½*

2270 A960 52c multi .75 .30

Souvenir Sheet

2271 Pane of 3, #2270, 2271a, 2271b 4.00 4.00
- *a.* A960 96c multi 1.50 1.10
- *b.* A960 $1.60 multi 2.40 2.20

Booklet Stamps

Self-Adhesive

2272 A960 96c multi 1.50 .60
- *a.* Booklet pane of 4 6.00
- Complete booklet, 2 #2272a 12.00

2273 A960 $1.60 multi 2.40 .90
- *a.* Booklet pane of 4 9.50
- Complete booklet, 2 #2273a 19.00
- *b.* Gutter pane, #2272a, 2273a 15.00

No. 2270 printed in panes of 16 + 4 labels.

1908 Fifty-cent Coin — A961

Litho. & Embossed

2008, June 4 *Perf. 13x13¼*

2274 A961 52c multi .75 .30

Royal Canadian Mint, cent. Printed in panes of 16 + 4 labels.

Canadian Nurses Association, Cent. — A962

Self-Adhesive

Booklet Stamp

Serpentine Die Cut 13¼

2008, June 16 **Litho.**

2275 A962 52c multi .75 .25
- *a.* Booklet pane of 10 7.50

Publication of *Anne of Green Gables*, by Lucy Maud Montgomery, Cent. — A963

Designs: Nos. 2276a, 2277, Anne holding buttercups. Nos. 2276b, 2278, Green Gables House.

Perf. 13½ Syncopated

2008, June 20

Souvenir Sheet

2276 A963 Pane of 2 2.40 2.40
- *a.-b.* 52c Either single 1.20 .75

Booklet Stamps

Self-Adhesive

Serpentine Die Cut 13¼x13

2277 A963 52c multi .75 .30

2278 A963 52c multi .75 .30
- *a.* Booklet pane of 10, 5 each #2277-2278 + 10 stickers 7.50
- *b.* Die cutting omitted, pair (#2277-2278) *375.00*

See Japan No. 3028.

Canadians in Hollywood Type of 2006

Actors and actresses: Nos. 2279a, 2280c, Norma Shearer (1902?-83). Nos. 2279b, 2280b, Chief Dan George (1899-1981). Nos. 2279c, 2280a, Marie Dressler (1868-1934). Nos. 2279d, 2280d, Raymond Burr (1917-93).

2008, June 30 *Perf. 13x12½*

2279 Souvenir sheet of 4 4.40 4.40
- *a.-d.* A903 52c Any single 1.10 .90

Self-Adhesive

Serpentine Die Cut 13½x13¼

2280 Booklet pane of 4 + 4 stickers 3.00
- *a.-d.* A903 52c Any single .75 .30
- Complete booklet, 2 #2280 6.00

Complete booklets were issued with four different covers depicting the featured actors or actresses. The order of the stamps and labels in the booklet pane differed in the four booklets.

2008 Summer Olympics, Beijing — A964

Self-Adhesive

Serpentine Die Cut 13½

2008, July 18 **Booklet Stamp**

2281 A964 52c multi .75 .30
- *a.* Booklet pane of 10 7.50
- *b.* Die cutting omitted, strip of 3 900.00

Lifesaving Society, Cent. A965

Self-Adhesive

Serpentine Die Cut 13¼x12¾

2008, July 25 **Booklet Stamp**

2282 A965 52c multi .75 .25
- *a.* Booklet pane of 10 7.50

British Columbia, 150th Anniv. — A966

Self-Adhesive

2008, Aug. 1 *Perf. 12½x13*

2283 A966 52c multi .75 .30

R. Samuel McLaughlin (1871-1972), Automobile Manufacturer, and Buick Automobile — A967

2008, Sept. 8 *Perf. 12½x13*

2284 A967 52c multi .75 .30

Endangered Animals Type of 2006

Designs: Nos. 2285a, 2286, Prothonotary warbler. Nos. 2285b, 2287, Taylor's checker-spot butterfly. Nos. 2285c, 2288, Roseate tern. Nos. 2285d, 2289, Burrowing owl.

2008, Oct. 1 *Perf. 13¼*

2285 Pane of 4 + 4 labels 3.00 3.00
- *a.-d.* A915 52c Any single .75 .75

Booklet Stamps

Self-Adhesive

Size: 48x24mm

Die Cut

2286 A915 52c multi .75 .30

2287 A915 52c multi .75 .30

2288 A915 52c multi .75 .30

2289 A915 52c multi .75 .30
- *a.* Block of 4, #2286-2289 3.00
- *b.* Booklet pane, 2 #2289a 6.00

12th Francophone Summit, Quebec — A968

2008, Oct. 15 *Perf. 12½x13¼*

2290 A968 52c multi .75 .30

A969

Christmas — A970

Child: Nos. 2291a, 2293, Making snow angel. Nos. 2291b, 2294, Skiing. Nos. 2291c, 2295, Tobogganing.

Souvenir Sheet

2008, Nov. 3 ***Perf. 13½***

2291 Pane of 3 5.25 5.25
a. A969 P multi 1.25 .90
b. A969 96c multi 1.50 1.50
c. A969 $1.60 multi 2.40 2.40

Booklet Stamps

Self-Adhesive

Serpentine Die Cut 13¼

2292 A970 P multi 1.25 .25
a. Booklet pane of 6 7.50
Complete booklet, 2 #2292a 15.00
b. Die cutting omitted, pair 600.00

Serpentine Die Cut 13¾

2293 A969 P multi 1.25 .25
a. Booklet pane of 6 7.50
Complete booklet, 2 #2293a 15.00
2294 A969 96c multi 1.50 .60
a. Booklet pane of 6 9.00
2295 A969 $1.60 multi 2.40 .90
a. Booklet pane of 6 14.50
b. Gutter pane, #2294a, 2295a 24.00
Nos. 2292-2295 (4) 6.40 2.00

Nos. 2291a, 2292 and 2293 each sold for 52c on day of issue.

See No. 2343a.

A971

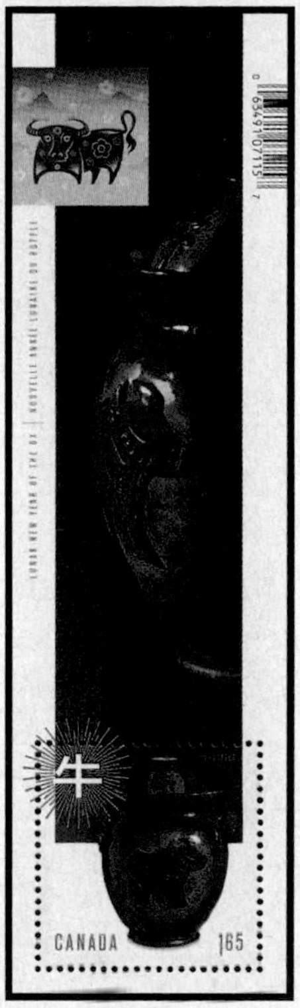

New Year 2009 (Year of the Ox) A972

Litho. & Embossed With Foil Application

2009, Jan. 8 ***Perf. 12½***

2296 A971 P multi 1.25 .25

Souvenir Sheet

2297 A972 $1.65 multi 2.40 2.40
a. With China 2009 emblem overprinted in gold in pane margin 3.25 3.25

No. 2296 sold for 54c on day of issue.

Queen Elizabeth II — A973

Self-Adhesive

Booklet Stamp

Serpentine Die Cut 13½x13¼

2009, Jan. 12 **Litho.**

2298 A973 P multi 1.25 .25
a. Booklet pane of 10 12.50

No. 2298 sold for 54c on day of issue.

Sports of the Winter Olympics and Paralympics
A974 A975

Designs: Nos. 2299a, 2303, Curling. Nos. 2299b, 2302, Bobsledding. Nos. 2299c, 2304, Snowboarding. Nos. 2299d, 2300, Freestyle skiing. Nos. 2299e, 2301, Ice-sled hockey.

2009, Jan. 12 ***Perf. 13¼x13***

2299 Pane of 5 6.25 3.75
a.-d. A974 P Any single 1.25 .90
e. A975 P multi 1.25 .90
f. As No. 2299, with "Vancouver / 2010" overprinted in sheet margin in silver 17.50 17.50

Booklet Stamps

Self-Adhesive

Serpentine Die Cut 13¼x13½

2300 A974 P multi 1.25 .25
2301 A975 P multi 1.25 .25
2302 A974 P multi 1.25 .25
2303 A974 P multi 1.25 .25
2304 A974 P multi 1.25 .25
a. Booklet pane of 10, 2 each #2300-2304 12.50
b. Booklet pane of 30, 6 each #2300-2304 37.50

On day of issue, Nos. 2299a-2299e, 2300-2304 each sold for 54c.

No. 2299f was originally sold with a set of coins in 2009. It was made available in 2010 in a set of 3 sheets, Nos. 2299f, 2305f, and 2366c that sold for $8.73.

2010 Vancouver Winter Olympics Emblem A976

2010 Vancouver Winter Paralympics Emblem A977

Miga, Winter Olympics Mascot — A978

Sumi, Paralympics Mascot — A979

Quatchi, Winter Olympics Mascot — A980

2009 ***Perf. 13¼x13***

2305 Pane of 5 9.00 9.00
a. A976 P multi 1.25 .90
b. A977 P multi 1.25 .90
c. A978 98c multi 1.50 1.50
d. A979 $1.18 multi 1.75 1.75
e. A980 $1.65 multi 2.40 2.40
f. As No. 2305, with "Vancouver / 2010" overprinted in sheet margin in bronze 18.00 18.00

Self-Adhesive

Coil Stamps

Serpentine Die Cut 9¼ (Rounded Tips)

2306 A976 P multi 1.40 1.40
2307 A977 P multi 1.40 1.40

Serpentine Die Cut 7¾-9½ (Sawtooth Tips)

2307A A976 P multi 1.25 .25
2307B A977 P multi 1.25 .25
c. Vert. pair, #2307A-2307B 2.50
2308 A978 98c multi 1.50 .30
2309 A979 $1.18 multi 1.80 .45
2310 A980 $1.65 multi 2.40 .60

Booklet Stamps

Serpentine Die Cut 9¼ (Rounded Tips)

2311 A978 98c multi 1.40 .25
a. Booklet pane of 6 8.50
2312 A979 $1.18 multi 1.80 .40
a. Booklet pane of 6 11.00
2313 A980 $1.65 multi 2.40 .55
a. Booklet pane of 6 14.50
Nos. 2306-2313 (10) 16.60 5.85

Issued: Nos. 2305, 2309, 2312, 2/12; Nos. 2306-2308, 2310-2311, 2313, 1/12. On day of issue, Nos. 2305a, 2305b, 2306-2307B each sold for 54c. Rolls of Nos. 2306 and 2307 have horizontal pairs of the same stamp that do not abut each other. Stamps from rolls containing Nos. 2307A and 2307B have pairs of different stamps that abut each other vertically.

No. 2305f was originally sold with a set of coins in 2009. It was made available in 2010 in a set of 3 sheets, Nos. 2299f, 2305f, and 2366c that sold for $8.73.

Celebration A981

Self-Adhesive

Serpentine Die Cut 13½ Horiz.

2009, Feb. 2 **Booklet Stamp**

2314 A981 P multi 1.25 .30
a. Booklet pane of 6 7.50

No. 2314 sold for 54c on day of issue.

Rosemary Brown (1930-2003) — A982

Abraham Doras Shadd (1801-82) A983

2009, Feb. 2 ***Perf. 13x12½***

2315 A982 54c multi .75 .30
2316 A983 54c multi .75 .30
a. Pair, #2315-2316 1.50 .40

Black History Month. Brown and Shadd were the first black woman and man elected to public office in Canada.

First Airplane Flight in Canada, Cent. — A984

Self-Adhesive

2009, Feb. 23 ***Perf. 12½x13***

2317 A984 P multi 1.25 .30

No. 2317 sold for 54c on day of issue.

Rhododendrons — A985

Color of rhododendrons: Nos. 2318a, 2319, White and pink. Nos. 2318b, 2320, Pink.

2009, Mar. 13 ***Perf. 13¼***

2318 A985 Pane of 2 2.20 2.20
a.-b. 54c Either single 1.10 .75

Booklet Stamps

Self-Adhesive

Serpentine Die Cut 13½x12¾

2319 A985 54c multi .75 .30
2320 A985 54c multi .75 .30
a. Booklet pane of 10, 5 each #2319-2320 7.50
b. Die cutting omitted, pair 550.00

Paintings by Jack Bush (1909-77) A986

Designs: 54c, Striped Column. $1.65, Chopsticks, horiz. (57x23mm).

2009, Mar. 20 ***Perf. 13x13¼***

2321 A986 54c multi .75 .30
a. Perf. 12½x13¼ 1.10 1.10

Souvenir Sheet

Perf. 12½x13¼

2322 Pane, #2321a, 2322a 3.75 3.75
a. A986 $1.65 multi 2.20 2.20

Souvenir Sheet

Intl. Year of Astronomy — A987

Designs: Nos. 2323a, 2324, Dominion Astrophysical Observatory, Saanich, British Columbia, and Horsehead Nebula. Nos. 2323b, 2325, Canada-France-Hawaii Telescope, Hawaii, and Eagle Nebula.

2009, Apr. 2 ***Perf. 13¼x13***
2323 A987 Pane of 2 2.20 2.20
a.-b. 54c Either single 1.10 .75
c. As #2323, with buff background behind product code 3.75 3.75

Booklet Stamps
Size: 24x34mm
Self-Adhesive
Serpentine Die Cut 13½

2324 A987 54c multi .75 .30
2325 A987 54c multi .75 .30
a. Booklet pane, 5 each #2324-2325 7.50

The product code on No. 2323 is "063491072031," and on No. 2323c, "063491072024." The background behind the product code on No. 2323 is white. No. 2323c also has a fluorescent overprint in the margin, not found on No. 2323. Nos. 2323a and 2323b are 27x36mm.

Preservation of Polar Regions and Glaciers — A988

2009, Apr. 9 ***Perf. 13x12¾***
2326 A988 54c Polar bear .75 .30
2327 A988 54c Arctic tern .75 .30
a. Pair, #2326-2327 1.50 .90
b. Souvenir sheet, #2326-2327 1.80 1.80

Beneficial Insects Type of 2007

Design: Danaus plexippus caterpillar.

2009, Apr. 22 ***Perf. 13¼x13***
2328 A942 2c multi .25 .25

Horses A989

Designs: No. 2329, Canadian horse. No. 2330, Newfoundland pony.

Self-Adhesive
Serpentine Die Cut 13¼

2009, May 15 **Booklet Stamps**
2329 A989 54c multi .90 .30
2330 A989 54c multi .90 .30
a. Booklet pane of 10, 5 each #2329-2330 9.00

Department of Foreign Affairs and International Trade, Cent. A990

2009, June 1 ***Perf. 13¼x13***
2331 A990 54c multi .80 .30

Boundary Waters Treaty, Cent. A991

2009, June 12 ***Perf. 13¼***
2332 A991 54c multi .80 .30

Popular Singers — A992

Designs: Nos. 2333a, 2334d, Robert Charlebois. Nos. 2333b, 2334c, Edith Butler. Nos. 2333c, 2334b, Stompin' Tom Connors. Nos. 2333d, 2334a, Bryan Adams.

2009, July 2 ***Perf. 12½x13***
2333 A992 Pane of 4 3.20 3.20
a.-d. 54c Any single .80 .80

Self-Adhesive
Serpentine Die Cut 13½

2334 A992 Booklet pane of 4 3.20
a.-d. 54c Any single .80 .40
Complete booklet, 2 #2334 6.50

Complete booklets were issued with four different covers depicting the featured singers. The order of the stamps is different in each booklet.

Roadside Attractions — A993

Designs: Nos. 2335a, 2336a, Mr. PG, Prince George, British Columbia. Nos. 2335b, 2336b, Sign Post Forest, Watson Lake, Yukon Territory. Nos. 2335c, 2336c, Inukshuk, Hay River, Northwest Territories. Nos. 2335d, 2336d, Pysanka, Vegreville, Alberta.

2009, July 6 ***Perf. 13***
2335 A993 Pane of 4 3.20 3.20
a.-d. 54c Any single .80 .80

Self-Adhesive
Serpentine Die Cut 13½

2336 A993 Booklet pane of 4 3.20
a.-d. 54c Any single .80 .40
Complete booklet, 2 #2336 6.50

Captain Robert Abram Bartlett (1875-1946), Arctic Explorer — A994

2009, July 10 ***Perf. 13***
2337 A994 54c multi .80 .30

Sports Invented By Canadians — A995

No. 2338: a, Five-pin bowling. b, Ringette. c, Lacrosse. d, Basketball.

Serpentine Die Cut 13¼

2009, Aug. 10
2338 Booklet pane of 4 3.20
a.-d. A995 54c Any single .80 .40
Complete booklet, 2 #2338 6.50

Montreal Canadiens Hockey Jersey — A996

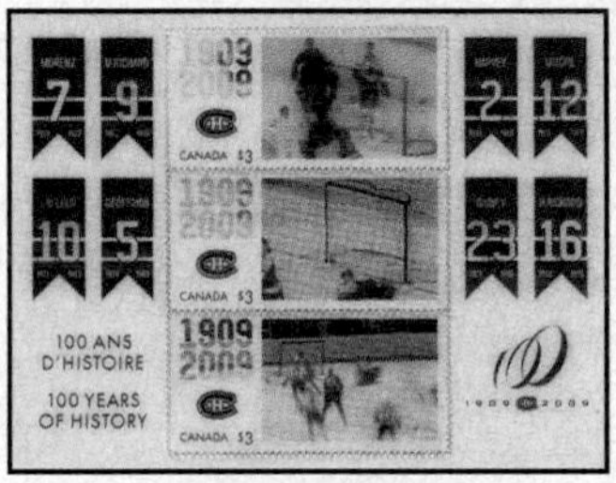

500-Goal Scorers of the Montreal Canadiens — A997

No. 2340 — 500th goal of: a, Maurice Richard. b, Jean Béliveau. c, Guy Lafleur.

Self-Adhesive
Serpentine Die Cut 13½x13¼

2009, Oct. 17 **Booklet Stamp**
2339 A996 P multi 1.25 .30
a. Booklet pane of 10 12.50

Souvenir Sheet
Litho. With Three-Dimensional Plastic Affixed
Serpentine Die Cut 13x13¼
Self-Adhesive

2340 A997 Pane of 3 14.00 14.00
a.-c. $3 Any single 4.50 4.50
d. Die cutting omitted, pane of 3 *1,800.*

Montreal Canadiens hockey team, cent. No. 2339 sold for 54c on day of issue.

Soaking of No. 2340 may cause the stamps to separate into layers. Soaking of used examples also may cause the cancellations to dissolve.

National War Memorial, Ottawa, and Poppy — A998

2009, Oct. 19 **Litho.** ***Perf. 12½***
2341 A998 P multi 1.25 .55
a. Souvenir sheet of 2 2.50 1.10

Booklet Stamp
Self-Adhesive
Serpentine Die Cut 13¼

2342 A998 P multi 1.25 .25
a. Booklet pane of 10 12.50

End of World War I, 91st anniv. On day of issue, Nos. 2341-2342 each sold for 54c. No. 2341 was issued only in the souvenir sheet of 2.

Christmas Type of 2008 and

Christmas
A999 A1000

Designs: Nos. 2343b, 2345, Madonna and child. 98c, Magus. $1.65, Shepherd and lamb.

2009, Nov. 2 ***Perf. 13x12½***
2343 Pane of 4 + 6 labels 7.25 7.25
a. A970 P multi 1.25 .90
b. A999 P multi 1.25 .90
c. A999 98c multi 1.50 1.50
d. A999 $1.65 multi 2.40 2.40

Booklet Stamps
Self-Adhesive
Litho. With Hologram Affixed
Serpentine Die Cut 8¼ Horiz.

2344 A1000 P multi 1.25 .25
a. Booklet pane of 6 7.50
Complete booklet, 2 #2344a 15.00

Litho.
Serpentine Die Cut 13½

2345 A999 P multi 1.25 .25
a. Booklet pane of 6 7.50
Complete booklet, 2 #2345 15.00
2346 A999 98c multi 1.50 .60
a. Booklet pane of 6 9.00
2347 A999 $1.65 multi 2.30 .90
a. Booklet pane of 6 14.00
b. Booklet pane of 12, 6 each #2346-2347 28.00
Nos. 2344-2347 (4) 6.30 2.00

On day of issue, Nos. 2343a, 2343b, 2344, and 2345 each sold for 54c. No. 2347b is Nos. 2346a and 2347a unseparated but with horizontal slits cut in margin between the panes.

New Year 2010 (Year of the Tiger) — A1001

Designs: P, Seal impression of tiger in circle. $1.70, Sculpted tiger seal.

Litho. & Embossed With Foil Application

2010, Jan. 8 ***Perf. 12½***
2348 A1001 P multi 1.25 .25

Souvenir Sheet

2349 A1001 $1.70 multi 2.40 2.40

No. 2348 sold for 57c on day of issue.

Flag Over Watson's Mill, Manotick, Ont. A1002

Flag Over Keremeos Grist Mill, Keremeos, B.C. A1003

Flag Over Old Stone Mill Natl. Historic Site, Delta, Ont. — A1004

Flag Over Riordon Grist Mill, Caraquet, N. B. — A1005

Flag Over Cornell Mill, Stanbridge East, Que. — A1006

2010, Jan. 11 Litho. *Perf. 13x13¼*

2350 Souvenir sheet of 5 6.50 5.00
- *a.* A1002 P multi 1.25 .80
- *b.* A1003 P multi 1.25 .80
- *c.* A1004 P multi 1.25 .80
- *d.* A1005 P multi 1.25 .80
- *e.* A1006 P multi 1.25 .80

Booklet Stamps

Self-Adhesive

Serpentine Die Cut 13¼

2351 A1002 P multi 1.25 .25
2352 A1003 P multi 1.25 .25
2353 A1004 P multi 1.25 .25
2354 A1005 P multi 1.25 .25
2355 A1006 P multi 1.25 .25
- *a.* Booklet pane of 10, 2 each #2351-2355 12.50
- *b.* Booklet pane of 30, 6 each #2351-2355 37.50

Nos. 2351-2355 (5) 6.25 1.25

On day of issue, Nos. 2350a-2350e and 2351-2355 each sold for 57c.

Striped Coralroot Orchid — A1007

Giant Helleborine Orchid — A1008

Rose Pogonia Orchid — A1009

Grass Pink Orchid — A1010

2010, Jan. 11 *Perf. 13¼x13*

2356 Souvenir sheet of 4 6.75 6.75
- *a.* A1007 P multi 1.25 .90
- *b.* A1008 $1 multi 1.50 1.10
- *c.* A1009 $1.22 multi 1.65 1.30
- *d.* A1010 $1.70 multi 2.20 1.80

Coil Stamps

Self-Adhesive

Serpentine Die Cut 8 to 9½ (Saw-tooth Tips)

2357 A1007 P multi 1.25 .25
2358 A1008 $1 multi 1.35 .30
2359 A1009 $1.22 multi 1.80 .40
2360 A1010 $1.70 multi 2.50 .60

Horiz. pairs, imperf. between, of No. 2357 are from uncut press panels of 100. Value unused, $4.

Serpentine Die Cut 9¼ (Rounded Tips)

2361 A1007 P multi 1.40 1.40

Nos. 2357-2361 (5) 8.30 2.95

Booklet Stamps

2362 A1008 $1 multi 1.50 .30
- *a.* Booklet pane of 6 9.00

2363 A1009 $1.22 multi 1.80 .45
- *a.* Booklet pane of 6 11.00

2364 A1010 $1.70 multi 2.40 .60
- *a.* Booklet pane of 6 14.50

Nos. 2362-2364 (3) 5.70 1.35

On day of issue, Nos. 2356a and 2357 each sold for 57c. No. 2357 was printed in vertical rolls with stamps that are adjacent. No. 2361 was printed in horizontal rolls with stamps that are separated.

Queen Elizabeth II — A1011

Self-Adhesive

Serpentine Die Cut 13¼

2010, Jan. 11 Booklet Stamp

2365 A1011 P multi 1.25 .25
- *a.* Booklet pane of 10 12.50

No. 2365 sold for 57c on day of issue.

Venues of the 2010 Winter Olympics — A1012

Designs: Nos. 2366a, 2367, Whistler, B.C. Nos. 2366b, 2368, Vancouver.

2010, Jan. 12 *Perf. 13½x13¼*

2366 A1012 Souvenir sheet of 2 2.20 2.20
- *a.-b.* 57c Either single 1.00 .75
- *c.* As No. 2366, with "Vancouver / 2010" overprinted in sheet margin in gold 12.00 12.00

Booklet Stamps

Self-Adhesive

Serpentine Die Cut 13¼

2367 A1012 57c multi .85 .30
2368 A1012 57c multi .85 .30
- *a.* Booklet pane of 10, 5 each #2367-2368, + 10 stickers 8.50

No. 2366c was sold in a package of 3 sheets that also contained Nos. 2299f and 2305f.

William Hall (1827-1904), First Black Recipient of Victoria Cross — A1013

2010, Feb. 1 *Perf. 12¾x12½*

2369 A1013 57c multi .85 .30

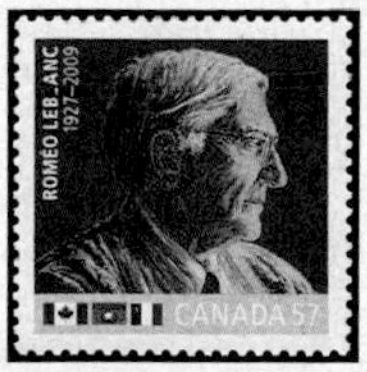

Roméo LeBlanc (1927-2009), Governor-General — A1014

2010, Feb. 8 *Perf. 12½*

2370 A1014 57c multi .85 .30

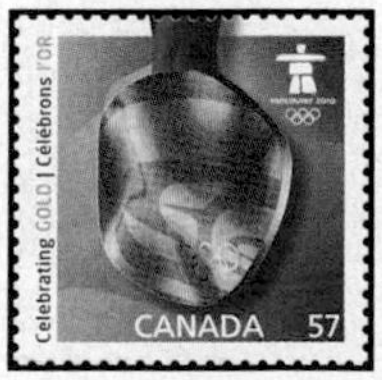

Gold Medal From Vancouver Winter Olympics A1015

2010, Feb. 15 *Perf. 12½*

2371 Sheet of 2 #2371a 2.20 2.20
- *a.* A1015 57c Single stamp 1.10 .75

First day cancels have a Feb. 14 date, which was the date on which the first gold medal was awarded to a Canadian athlete on home soil, but which also was a Sunday. Post offices in Vancouver had the stamp available for sale on Feb. 15.

Booklet Stamp

Self-Adhesive

Serpentine Die Cut 13½

2372 A1015 57c multi .85 .30
- *a.* Booklet pane of 10 8.50

Awarding of first gold medal to a Canadian on home soil.

Spirit of the Winter Olympics — A1016

Winter Olympic athletes and: Nos. 2373a, 2374, Woman with painted face at left. Nos. 2373b, 2375, Woman with painted face at right.

2010, Feb. 22 *Perf. 13*

2373 A1016 Souvenir sheet of 2 2.20 2.20
- *a.-b.* 57c Either single 1.10 .75

Booklet Stamps

Self-Adhesive

Serpentine Die Cut 13¼

2374 A1016 57c multi .85 .30
2375 A1016 57c multi .85 .30
- *a.* Booklet pane of 10, 5 each #2374-2375 8.50

African Violet Hybrids — A1017

Flower colors: Nos. 2376a, 2377, Red (Descelles' Avalanche). Nos. 2376b, 2378, Purple (Picasso).

2010, Mar. 3 Litho. *Perf. 13*

2376 A1017 Souvenir sheet of 2 2.50 2.25
- *a.-b.* P Either single 1.25 .75

Booklet Stamps

Self-Adhesive

Serpentine Die Cut 13½

2377 A1017 P multi 1.25 .30
2378 A1017 P multi 1.25 .30
- *a.* Booklet pane of 10, 5 each #2377-2378 12.50

On day of issue, Nos. 2376a, 2376b, 2377 and 2378 each sold for 57c.

Friendship Between Canada and Israel, 60th Anniv. A1018

Booklet Stamp

Self-Adhesive

Serpentine Die Cut 13¼

2010, Apr. 14 Litho.

2379 A1018 $1.70 multi 2.50 .90
- *a.* Booklet pane of 3 + label 7.50
- Complete booklet, 2 #2379a 15.00

See Israel No. 1812.

Indian Kings — A1019

Portraits by John Verelst of: No. 2380, Tee Yee Neen Ho Ga Row. No. 2381, Sa Ga Yeath Qua Pieth Tow. No. 2382, Ho Nee Yeath Taw No Row. No. 2383, Etow Oh Koam.

2010, Apr. 19 Litho. *Perf. 12½*

2380 A1019 57c multi .85 .40
2381 A1019 57c multi .85 .40
2382 A1019 57c multi .85 .40
2383 A1019 57c multi .85 .40
- *a.* Block or strip of 4, #2380-2383 3.20 2.20
- *b.* Souvenir sheet of 4, #2380-2383 3.75 3.75
- *c.* As "b," with London 2010 emblem on sheet margin 5.50 5.50

Nos. 2380-2383 (4) 3.40 1.60

Meeting of the four Indian Kings and Queen Anne in London, 300th anniv.

Canadian Navy, Cent. — A1020

Designs: Nos. 2384a, 2385, Male sailor, HMCS Niobe. Nos. 2384b, 2386, Female sailor, HMCS Halifax.

2010, May 4 Litho. *Perf. 12½*

2384 A1020 Sheet of 2 2.20 2.20
- *a.-b.* 57c Either single 1.10 .75

Booklet Stamps

Self-Adhesive

Serpentine Die Cut 13¼x13½

2385 A1020 57c multi .85 .30
2386 A1020 57c multi .85
- *a.* Booklet pane of 10, 5 each #2385-2386 8.50

Sea Mammals — A1021

Designs: No. 2387a, Harbor porpoise. No. 2387b, Sea otter.

Perf. 13x12¼x13x13 Syncopated (#2387a), 13x13x13x12¼ Syncopated (#2387b)

2010, May 13 Litho. & Engr.

2387 A1021 Sheet of 2 2.20 2.20
- *a.-b.* 57c Either single 1.10 .75
- *c.* As "a," perf. 13x12¾ syncopated 1.10 .35
- *d.* As "b," perf. 13x12¾ syncopated 1.10 .35
- *e.* Booklet pane of 8, 4 each #2387c-2387d 8.75 8.75
- Complete booklet, #2387e 9.00

Nos. 2387a and 2387b have syncopation on left and right side, with the syncopation between the stamps in the shape of a maple leaf. Nos. 2387c and 2387d have syncopation on one side only, with the syncopation between pairs of stamps in the shape of conjoined ovals.

See Sweden No. 2638.

Canadian Geographic's Wildlife Photography of the Year — A1022

Designs: Nos. 2388a, 2393, Ardia herodias, by Martin Cooper. Nos. 2388b, 2392, Vulpes vulpes, by Ben Boulter. Nos. 2388c, 2391, Tettigoniidae, by Julie Bazinet. Nos. 2388d, 2390, Tachycineta bicolor, by Mark Bradley. Nos. 2388e, 2389, Selasphorus rufus, by Wing Yan Tam.

2010, May 22 Litho. *Perf. 12½x13*

2388 A1022 Sheet of 5 4.25 4.25
a.-e. 57c Any single .85 .75

Booklet Stamps

Self-Adhesive

Serpentine Die Cut 13¼

2389 A1022 57c multi .85 .30
2390 A1022 57c multi .85 .30
2391 A1022 57c multi .85 .30
2392 A1022 57c multi .85 .30
2393 A1022 57c multi .85 .30
a. Booklet pane of 10, 2 each #2389-2393 8.50
Nos. 2389-2393 (5) 4.25 1.50

Rotary International in Canada, Cent. A1023

Self-Adhesive

Booklet Stamp

Serpentine Die Cut 13½x12¾

2010, June 18 Litho.

2394 A1023 57c multi .85 .30
a. Booklet pane of 8 6.75

Paintings by Prudence Heward (1896-1947) A1024

Designs: 57c, Rollande. $1.70, At the Theatre, horiz. (42x40mm).

2010, July 2 *Perf. 13¼x13*

2395 A1024 57c multi .85 .30

Souvenir Sheet

2396 Sheet of 2, #2395, 2396a 3.00 3.00
a. A1024 $1.70 multi 2.20 2.20

Roadside Attractions — A1025

Designs: Nos. 2397a, 2398, Coffee Pot, Davidson, Saskatchewan. Nos. 2397b, 2399, Happy Rock, Gladstone, Manitoba. Nos. 2397c, 2400, Wawa Goose, Wawa, Ontario. Nos. 2397d, 2401, Puffin, Longue-Pointe-de-Mingan, Quebec.

2010, July 5 *Perf. 13*

2397 A1025 Sheet of 4 5.00 3.50
a.-d. P Any single 1.25 .90

Booklet Stamps

Self-Adhesive

Serpentine Die Cut 13½

2398 A1025 P multi 1.25 .35
2399 A1025 P multi 1.25 .35
2400 A1025 P multi 1.25 .35
2401 A1025 P multi 1.25 .35
a. Booklet pane of 4, #2398-2401 5.00
Complete booklet, 2 #2401a 10.00

On day of issue, Nos. 2397a-2397d, 2398-2401 each sold for 57c.

Girl Guides, Cent. — A1026

Self-Adhesive

Serpentine Die Cut 13¾

2010, July 8 Booklet Stamp

2402 A1026 P multi 1.25 .25
a. Booklet pane of 10 12.50

No. 2402 sold for 57c on day of issue.

Founding of Cupids, Newfoundland Settlement, 400th Anniv. — A1027

2010, Aug. 17 *Perf. 12½*

2403 A1027 57c multi .85 .30

Year of British Home Children A1028

2010, Sept. 1

2404 A1028 57c multi .85 .30

Blue Whale — A1029

Litho., Engr. & Silk-screened

2010, Oct. 4 *Perf. 12½x13*

2405 A1029 $10 multi 15.00 5.50

Printed in sheets of 2.

Beneficial Insects Type of 2007

Designs: 4c, Paper wasp (Polistes fuscatus). 6c, Assassin bug (Zelus luridus). 7c, Large milkweed bug (Oncopeltus fasciatus). 8c, Margined leatherwing (Chauliognathus marginatus). 9c, Dogbane beetle (Chrysochus auratus).

2010, Oct. 19 Litho. *Perf. 13¼x13*

2406 A942 4c multi .25 .25
a. With added microprinting and small design features (#2409b) .25 .25
2407 A942 6c multi .25 .25
2408 A942 7c multi .25 .25
2409 A942 8c multi .25 .25
a. With added microprinting and small design features (#2409b) .25 .25
b. Souvenir sheet of 3, #2235b, 2406a, 2409a .25 .25
2410 A942 9c multi .25 .25
a. Souvenir sheet, #2406-2410 2.20 .40
Nos. 2406-2410 (5) 1.25 1.25

Issued: Nos. 2406a, 2409a, 2409b, 10/16/12.

Christmas Ornaments A1030

Madonna and Child, Sculpture by Antonio Caruso — A1031

Designs: Nos. 2411a, 2413, Three red ornaments, greenish blue background. $1, Two blue ornaments, purple background. $1.70, Three red ornaments, dull blue background.

2010, Nov. 1 Litho. *Perf. 12½*

2411 Souvenir sheet of 3 5.25 4.75
a. A1030 P multi 1.25 .90
b. A1030 $1 multi 1.50 1.50
c. A1030 $1.70 multi 2.50 2.50

Booklet Stamps

Self-Adhesive

Serpentine Die Cut 13¼

2412 A1031 P multi 1.25 .25
a. Booklet pane of 6 7.50
Complete booklet, 2 #2412a 15.00

Serpentine Die Cut 13½

2413 A1030 P multi 1.25 .25
a. Booklet pane of 6 7.50
Complete booklet, 2 #2413a 15.00
2414 A1030 $1 multi 1.50 .60
a. Booklet pane of 6 9.00
2415 A1030 $1.70 multi 2.50 .90
a. Booklet pane of 6 15.00
b. Gutter pane, #2414a, 2415a 26.00
Nos. 2412-2415 (4) 6.50 2.00

Nos. 2411a, 2412 and 2413 each sold for 57c on day of issue.

New Year 2011 (Year of the Rabbit) A1032

Design: $1.75, Two rabbits in circle.

Litho. & Embossed With Foil Application

2011, Jan. 7 *Perf. 12½*

2416 A1032 P shown 1.25 .25

Souvenir Sheet

2417 A1032 $1.75 multi 2.50 2.50

No. 2416 sold for 59c on day of issue.

Canadian Flag on Soldier's Uniform A1033

Canadian Flag on Hot-air Balloon A1034

Canadian Flag on Search and Rescue Team's Uniform A1035

Canadian Flag on Canadarm A1036

Canadian Flag on Backpack — A1037

2011, Jan. 17 Litho. *Perf. 13x13¼*

2418 Sheet of 5 6.25 4.75
a. A1033 P multi 1.25 .90
b. A1034 P multi 1.25 .90
c. A1035 P multi 1.25 .90
d. A1036 P multi 1.25 .90
e. A1037 P multi 1.25 .90

Booklet Stamps

Self-Adhesive

Serpentine Die Cut 13¼

2419 A1033 P multi 1.25 .25
2420 A1034 P multi 1.25 .25
2421 A1035 P multi 1.25 .25
2422 A1036 P multi 1.25 .25
2423 A1037 P multi 1.25 .25
a. Booklet pane of 10, 2 each #2419-2423 12.50
b. Booklet pane of 30, 6 each #2419-2423 37.50
Nos. 2419-2423 (5) 6.25 3.00

On day of issue, Nos. 2418a-2418e, 2419-2423 each sold for 59c.

Juvenile Wildlife — A1038

Designs: P, Arctic hare leverets. $1.03, Red fox kit in hollow log. $1.25, Canada goslings. $1.75, Polar bear cub.

2011, Jan. 17 *Perf. 13¼x13*

2424 Sheet of 4 8.00 8.00
a. A1038 P multi 1.25 .90
b. A1038 $1.03 multi 1.50 1.10
c. A1038 $1.25 multi 1.75 1.30
d. A1038 $1.75 multi 2.50 1.80

Coil Stamps

Self-Adhesive

Serpentine Die Cut 9¼ Horiz.

2425 A1038 P multi 1.40 1.40

Serpentine Die Cut 8¼ Horiz.

2426 A1038 P multi 1.25 .25
2427 A1038 $1.03 multi 1.35 .30

Horiz. pairs, imperf. between, of No. 2426 are from uncut press panels of 100. Value unused, $3.25.

Serpentine Die Cut 8½ Horiz.

2428 A1038 $1.25 multi 1.80 .45

Serpentine Die Cut 8¼ Horiz.

2429 A1038 $1.75 multi 2.50 .60

Booklet Stamps

Serpentine Die Cut 9¼ Horiz.

2430 A1038 $1.03 multi 1.50 .30
a. Booklet pane of 6 9.00
2431 A1038 $1.25 multi 1.80 .45
a. Booklet pane of 6 11.00
2432 A1038 $1.75 multi 2.40 .60
a. Booklet pane of 6 14.50
Nos. 2425-2432 (8) 18.70 9.40

On day of issue, Nos. 2424a, 2425 and 2426 each sold for 59c. On rolls of No. 2425, stamps do not touch each other and pairs are horizontal. On rolls of No. 2426, stamps touch each other and pairs are vertical.

See Nos. 2504-2512, 2602-2610, 2692, 2692A, 2709-2717.

Black History Month — A1039

Order of Canada recipients: No. 2433, Carrie Best (1903-2001), journalist. No. 2434, Ferguson Jenkins, baseball player.

Self-Adhesive

Serpentine Die Cut 13½x13¾

2011, Feb. 1 Booklet Stamps

2433 A1039 59c multi	.85	.30
a. Booklet pane of 10	8.50	
2434 A1039 59c multi	.85	.30
a. Booklet pane of 10	8.50	

Gift Box — A1040

Self-Adhesive

Serpentine Die Cut 13½ Horiz.

2011, Feb. 7 Booklet Stamp

2435 A1040 P multi	1.25	.25
a. Booklet pane of 6	7.50	

No. 2435 sold for 59c on day of issue.

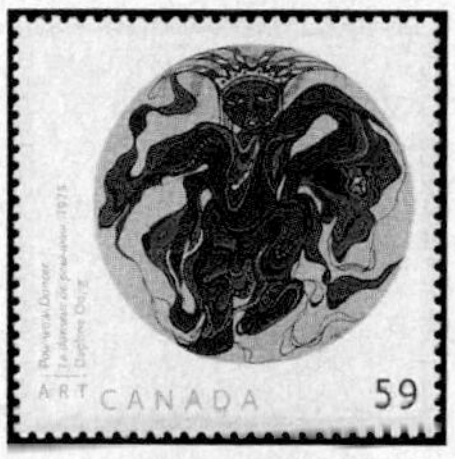

Paintings of Daphne Odjig A1041

Paintings: 59c, Pow-wow Dancer. $1.03, Pow-wow (32x39mm). $1.75, Spiritual Renewal (56x39mm).

2011, Feb. 21 *Perf. 12½*

2436 A1041 59c multi	.85	.30

Souvenir Sheet

2437 Sheet of 3, #2436, 2437a-2437b	4.00	4.00
a. A1041 $1.03 multi	1.50	1.50
b. A1041 $1.75 multi	2.50	2.50

Booklet Stamps

Self-Adhesive

Serpentine Die Cut 13½x13¼

2438 A1041 $1.03 multi	1.50	.60
a. Booklet pane of 6	9.00	
2439 A1041 $1.75 multi	2.50	.90
a. Booklet pane of 6	15.00	

Sunflower

A1042 A1043

Sunflower varieties: Nos. 2440a, 2441, 2443, Prado Red. Nos. 2440b, 2442, 2444, Sunbright (yellow flower).

2011, Mar. 3 Litho. *Perf. 13¼*

Souvenir Sheet

2440 Sheet of 2	2.50	2.00
a.-b. A1042 P Either single	1.25	.90

Coil Stamps

Self-Adhesive

Serpentine Die Cut 8¼ Horiz.

2441 A1043 P multi	1.25	.35
2442 A1043 P multi	1.25	.35
a. Vert. pair, #2441-2442	2.50	

Booklet Stamps

Serpentine Die Cut 13½

2443 A1042 P multi	1.25	.30
2444 A1042 P multi	1.25	.30
a. Booklet pane of 10, 5 each #2443-2444	12.50	

On day of issue, Nos. 2440a-2440b, 2441-2444 each sold for 59c.

Signs of the Zodiac A1044

No. 2445: a, Aries. b, Taurus. c, Gemini. d, Cancer. No. 2446: a, Leo. b, Virgo. c, Libra. d, Scorpio. No. 2447: a, Sagittarius. b, Capricorn. c, Aquarius. d, Pisces.

No. 2448: a, Aries. b, Taurus. c, Gemini. d, Cancer. e, Leo. f, Virgo. g, Libra. h, Scorpio. i, Sagittarius. j, Capricorn. k, Aquarius. l, Pisces.

No. 2449, Aries. No. 2450, Taurus. No. 2451, Gemini. No. 2452, Cancer. No. 2453, Leo. No. 2454, Virgo. No. 2455, Libra. No. 2456, Scorpio. No. 2457, Sagittarius. No. 2458, Capricorn. No. 2459, Aquarius. No. 2460, Pisces.

2011-13 Litho. *Perf. 12½*

2445 Sheet of 4	5.00	3.75
a.-d. A1044 P Any single	1.25	.90
2446 Sheet of 4	5.00	3.75
a.-d. A1044 P Any single	1.25	.90
2447 Sheet of 4	5.00	3.75
a.-d. A1044 P Any single	1.25	.90

Perf. 12½x13

2448 Sheet of 12	15.00	11.00
a.-l A1044 P Any single	1.25	.90

Booklet Stamps

Self-Adhesive

Serpentine Die Cut 13½

2449 A1044 P multi	1.25	.30
a. Booklet pane of 10	12.50	
2450 A1044 P multi	1.25	.30
a. Booklet pane of 10	12.50	
b. Gutter pane of 12, 6 each #2449-2450	15.00	
2451 A1044 P multi	1.25	.30
a. Booklet pane of 10	12.50	
2452 A1044 P multi	1.25	.30
a. Booklet pane of 10	12.50	
b. Gutter pane of 12, 6 each #2451-2452	15.00	
2453 A1044 P multi	1.25	.30
a. Booklet pane of 10	12.50	
2454 A1044 P multi	1.25	.30
a. Booklet pane of 10	12.50	
2455 A1044 P multi	1.25	.30
a. Booklet pane of 10	12.50	
2456 A1044 P multi	1.25	.30
a. Booklet pane of 10	12.50	
b. Gutter pane of 24, 6 each #2453-2456	30.00	
2457 A1044 P multi	1.25	.30
a. Booklet pane of 10	12.50	
2458 A1044 P multi	1.25	.30
a. Booklet pane of 10	12.50	
2459 A1044 P multi	1.25	.30
a. Booklet pane of 10	12.50	
2460 A1044 P multi	1.25	.30
a. Booklet pane of 10	12.50	
b. Gutter pane of 24, 6 each #2457-2460	30.00	
Nos. 2449-2460 (12)	15.00	3.60

Issued: No. 2449, 3/21; Nos. 2450, 2450b, 4/21; No. 2451, 5/20; Nos. 2445, 2452, 2452b, 6/22, Nos. 2446, 2453-2456, 2456b, 7/23/12. Nos. 2447-2448, 2457-2460, 2460b, 2/20/13. Nos. 2445a-2445d, 2449-2452 each sold for 59c on day of issue. Nos. 2446a-2446d, 2453-2456 each sold for 61c on day of issue. Nos. 2447a-2447d, 2448a-2448l, 2457-2460 each sold for 63c on day of issue.

Intl. Year of Forests — A1045

Designs: Nos. 2461a, 2462, Tree. Nos. 2461b, 2463, Mushrooms and plants on forest floor.

2011, Apr. 21 Litho. *Perf. 13½x13*

2461 A1045 Sheet of 2	2.50	2.25
a.-b. P Either single	1.25	.90

Booklet Stamps

Self-Adhesive

Serpentine Die Cut 13x13¼

2462 A1045 P multi	1.25	.30
2463 A1045 P multi	1.25	.30
a. Booklet pane of 8, 4 each #2462-2463	10.00	

On day of issue, Nos. 2461a-2461b, 2462-2463 each sold for 59c.

Wedding of Prince William and Catherine Middleton — A1046

Couple with Prince William at: P, Right. $1.75, Left.

2011, Apr. 29 *Perf. 12¾x13¼*

2464 A1046 P multi	1.25	.30
2465 A1046 $1.75 multi	2.50	1.10
a. Horiz. pair, #2464-2465	3.75	1.50
b. Souvenir sheet, #2464-2465	4.00	4.00
c. As "b," with arms of Prince William overprinted in sheet margin in gold	4.50	4.50

Booklet Stamps

Self-Adhesive

Serpentine Die Cut 13¼

2466 A1046 P multi	1.25	.30
a. Booklet pane of 10	12.50	
2467 A1046 $1.75 multi	2.50	1.10
a. Booklet pane of 10	25.00	
b. Gutter pane, 6 #2466, 4 #2467	55.00	

On day of issue, Nos. 2464 and 2468 each sold for 59c.

Methods of Mail Delivery — A1047

Designs: No. 2468, Ponchon. No. 2469, Dog sled.

2011, May 13 *Perf. 12½*

2468 59c multi	.85	.30
2469 59c multi	.85	.30
a. A1047 Horiz. pair, #2468-2469	1.70	.75

Parks Canada, Cent. — A1048

Self-Adhesive

Serpentine Die Cut 13½

2011, May 19 Booklet Stamp

2470 A1048 59c multi	.85	.30
a. Booklet pane of 10	8.50	

Details of Art Deco Structures — A1049

Designs: Nos. 2471a, 2472, Burrard Bridge, Vancouver. Nos. 2471b, 2473, Cormier House, Montreal. Nos. 2471c, 2474, R. C. Harris Water Treatment Plant, Toronto. Nos. 2471d, 2475, Supreme Court of Canada, Ottawa. Nos. 2471e, 2476, Dominion Building, Regina, Saskatchewan.

2011, June 9 Litho. *Perf. 13x12½*

2471 A1049 Sheet of 5 + 5 labels	6.25	4.25
a.-e. P Any single	1.25	.90

Booklet Stamps

Self-Adhesive

Serpentine Die Cut 13¼x13½

2472 A1049 P multi	1.25	.30
2473 A1049 P multi	1.25	.30
2474 A1049 P multi	1.25	.30
2475 A1049 P multi	1.25	.30
2476 A1049 P multi	1.25	.30
a. Booklet pane of 10, 2 each #2472-2476	12.50	
Nos. 2472-2476 (5)	6.25	1.50

On day of issue, Nos. 2471a-2471e, 2472-2476 each sold for 59c.

Duke and Duchess of Cambridge on Their Wedding Day — A1050

2011, June 22 *Perf. 12¾x13¼*

2477 Sheet of 2 #2477a	2.50	1.90
a. A1050 P multi	1.25	.90
b. Sheet similar to #2477, with Royal Tour emblem overprinted in gold in sheet margin	2.50	1.90

Booklet Stamp

Self-Adhesive

Serpentine Die Cut 13¼

2478 A1050 P multi	1.25	.30
a. Booklet pane of 10	12.50	

On day of issue, Nos. 2477a and 2478 each sold for 59c. Margin of No. 2477 depicts Westminster Abbey, and that of No. 2477b depicts the Canadian Parliament.

Popular Singers A1051

Designs: Nos. 2479, 2483c, Ginette Reno. Nos. 2480, 2483a, Bruce Cockburn. Nos. 2481, 2483d, Robbie Robertson. Nos. 2482, 2483b, Kate and Anna McGarrigle.

2011 ***Perf. 12½***

2479 A1051 P multi 1.50 1.50
 a. Perf. 12½x13 1.30 .90
2480 A1051 P multi 1.50 1.50
 a. Perf. 12½x13 1.30 .90
2481 A1051 P multi 1.50 1.50
 a. Perf. 12½x13 1.30 .90
2482 A1051 P multi 1.50 1.50
 a. Perf. 12½x13 1.30 .90
 b. Souvenir sheet of 4, #2479a-2482a 5.25 3.50
 Nos. 2479-2482 (4) 6.00 6.00

Self-Adhesive

Serpentine Die Cut 13½

2483 Booklet pane of 4 5.00
 a.-d. A1051 P Any single 1.25 .40
 Complete booklet, 2 #2483 10.00

Issued: Nos. 2479-2482, 7/30; Nos. 2479a-2482a, 2482b, 2483, 6/30. On day of issue, Nos. 2479a2482, 2479a-2482a and 2483a-2483d each sold for 59c.

Complete booklets were issued with four different covers depicting the featured singers. The order of the stamps is different in each booklet.

Roadside Attractions — A1052

Designs: Nos. 2484a, 2485a, World's Largest Lobster, Shediac, New Brunswick. Nos. 2484b, 2485b, Wild Blueberry, Oxford, Nova Scotia. Nos. 2484c, 2485c, Big Potato, O'Leary, Prince Edward Island. Nos. 2484d, 2485d, Giant Squid, Glover's Harbour, Newfoundland.

2011, July 7 ***Perf. 12¾***

2484 A1052 Sheet of 4 5.00 3.50
 a.-d. P Any single 1.25 .90

Self-Adhesive

Serpentine Die Cut13½

2485 A1052 Booklet pane of 4 5.00
 a.-d. P Any single 1.25 .35
 Complete booklet, 2 #2485 10.00

Third Consecutive Victory of Intl. Harmsworth Trophy by Miss Supertest III Hydroplane — A1053

Designs: P, Miss Supertest III. $1.75, Miss Supertest III, diff.

2011, Aug. 8 Litho. ***Perf. 13¼***

2486 A1053 Sheet of 2 4.25 4.00
 a. P multi 1.25 .90
 b. $1.75 multi 2.85 2.60

Booklet Stamp
Self-Adhesive

Serpentine Die Cut 13¼ Horiz.

2487 A1053 P multi 1.25 .30
 a. Booklet pane of 10 12.50

Nos. 2486a and 2487 each sold for 59c on day of issue.

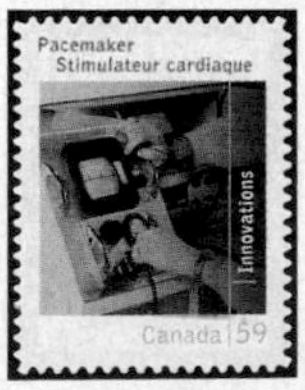

Canadian Inventions — A1054

No. 2488: a, Pacemaker, developed by Dr. John Hopps. b, BlackBerry, developed by Research in Motion. c, Electric oven, developed by Thomas Ahearn. d, Electric wheelchair, developed by George J. Klein.

Serpentine Die Cut 13¼

2011, Aug. 17 Self-Adhesive

2488 Booklet pane of 4 3.50
 a.-d. A1054 59c Any single .85 .40
 Complete booklet, 2 #2488 7.00

Dr. John Charles Polanyi, Winner of 1986 Nobel Prize for Chemistry A1055

Self-Adhesive
Booklet Stamp

Serpentine Die Cut 13½

2011, Oct. 3 Litho.

2489 A1055 P multi 1.25 .30
 a. Booklet pane of 10 12.50

Intl. Year of Chemistry. No. 2489 sold for 59c on day of issue.

Christmas
A1056 A1057

Stained-glass windows, Cathedral of Saint Mary of the Immaculate Conception, Kingston, Ontario: Nos. 2490a, 2492, Angel. $1.03, Nativity. $1.75, Epiphany.

2011, Nov. 1 Litho. ***Perf. 13x12½***

2490 Sheet of 3 5.25 4.75
 a. A1056 P multi 1.25 .90
 b. A1056 $1.03 multi 1.50 1.50
 c. A1056 $1.75 multi 2.50 2.50

Booklet Stamps
Self-Adhesive
Litho. With Hologram Affixed

Serpentine Die Cut 8¼ Horiz.

2491 A1057 P multi 1.25 .25
 a. Booklet pane of 6 7.50
 Complete booklet, 2 #2491a 15.00

Litho.

Serpentine Die Cut 13¼

2492 A1056 P multi 1.25 .25
 a. Booklet pane of 6 7.50
 Complete booklet, 2 #2492a 15.00
2493 A1056 $1.03 multi 1.50 .60
 a. Booklet pane of 6 9.00
2494 A1056 $1.75 multi 2.50 .90
 a. Booklet pane of 6 15.00
 b. Gutter pane, #2493a, 2494a 25.00
 Nos. 2491-2494 (4) 6.50 2.00

On day of issue, Nos. 2490a, 2491 and 2492 each sold for 59c.

New Year 2012 (Year of the Dragon) A1058

Design: $1.80, Dragon's head.

Litho. & Embossed With Foil Application

2012, Jan. 10 ***Perf. 12½***

2495 A1058 P shown 1.25 .25

Souvenir Sheet

2496 A1058 $1.80 multi 2.50 2.50
 a. Souvenir sheet of 2, #2417, 2496 5.00 5.00

Booklet Stamp
Self-Adhesive
Litho.

Serpentine Die Cut 13½

2497 A1058 $1.80 multi 2.50 .90
 a. Booklet pane of 6 15.00

No. 2495 sold for 61c on day of issue.

Flag on Coast Guard Ship A1059

Flag in Van Window A1060

Olympic Athlete Carrying Flag A1061

Flag on Bobsled A1062

Inuit Child Waving Flag — A1063

2012, Jan. 16 Litho. ***Perf. 13x13¼***

2498 Souvenir sheet of 5 6.25 4.75
 a. A1059 P multi 1.25 .90
 b. A1060 P multi 1.25 .90
 c. A1061 P multi 1.25 .90
 d. A1062 P multi 1.25 .90
 e. A1063 P multi 1.25 .90

Booklet Stamps
Self-Adhesive

Serpentine Die Cut 13¼

2499 A1059 P multi 1.25 .25
 a. With "Canada" visible on reverse of stamp 7.25 .35
2500 A1060 P multi 1.25 .25
 a. With "Canada" visible on reverse of stamp 2.25 .35
2501 A1061 P multi 1.25 .25
 a. With "Canada" visible on reverse of stamp 2.25 .35
2502 A1062 P multi 1.25 .25
 a. Microprinting with corrected spelling "Lueders" 1.50 .25
 b. As "a," with "Canada" visible on reverse of stamp 2.25 .35
2503 A1063 P multi 1.25 .25
 a. Booklet pane of 10, 2 each #2499-2503 12.50
 b. Booklet pane of 30, 6 each #2499-2503 37.50
 c. Booklet pane of 10, 2 each #2499-2502, 2502a, 2503 18.00
 d. With "Canada" visible on reverse of stamp 2.25 .35
 e. Booklet pane of 10, 2 each #2499a, 2500a, 2501a, 2502b, 2503d 22.50
 Nos. 2499-2503 (5) 6.25 1.25

On day of issue, Nos. 2498a-2498e, 2499-2503 each sold for 61c. The printing on the backing paper on No. 2503a differs from that on the backing paper of any of the component thirds of No. 2503b.

Issued: Nos. 2502a, 2503c, 9/28/12; Nos. 2499a, 2500a, 2501a, 2502b, 2503d, 2013. Nos. 2498d and 2502 have incorrect spelling in microprinting of "Leuders."

Juvenile Wildlife Type of 2011

Designs: P, Three raccoon kits. $1.05, Two caribou calves. $1.29, Adult loon and two chicks. $1.80, Moose calves.

2012, Jan. 16 ***Perf. 13¼x13***

2504 Souvenir sheet of 4 7.00 5.75
 a. A1038 P multi 1.25 .90
 b. A1038 $1.05 multi 1.50 1.10
 c. A1038 $1.29 multi 1.80 1.30
 d. A1038 $1.80 multi 2.50 1.80

Self-Adhesive
Coil Stamps

Serpentine Die Cut 9¼ Horiz.

2505 A1038 P multi 1.40 1.40

Serpentine Die Cut 8¼ Horiz.

2506 A1038 P multi 1.25 .25
2507 A1038 $1.05 multi 1.50 .30
2508 A1038 $1.29 multi 1.80 .45
2509 A1038 $1.80 multi 2.50 .55
 Nos. 2505-2509 (5) 8.45 2.95

Booklet Stamps

Serpentine Die Cut 9¼ Horiz.

2510 A1038 $1.05 multi 1.50 .30
 a. Booklet pane of 6 9.00
2511 A1038 $1.29 multi 1.80 .45
 a. Booklet pane of 6 11.00
2512 A1038 $1.80 multi 2.50 .60
 a. Booklet pane of 6 15.00
 Nos. 2510-2512 (3) 5.80 1.35

On day of issue, Nos. 2504a, 2505 and 2506 each sold for 61c. On rolls of No. 2505, stamps do not touch each other and pairs are horizontal. On rolls of No. 2506, stamps touch each other and pairs are vertical.

A1064

Reign of Queen Elizabeth II, 60th Anniv. A1065

Designs: No. 2513, Crown, Canada #330. No. 2514, Map of Canada, Canada #471. No. 2515, Document, pen, Canada #704. No. 2516, Jubilee bouquet, Canada #1168. No. 2517, Tiara details, Canada #1932. Nos. 2518, 2519, Queen Elizabeth II wearing robe and tiara.

2012 Litho. ***Perf. 13¼***

2513 A1064 P multi 1.25 .75
2514 A1064 P multi 1.25 .75
2515 A1064 P multi 1.25 .75
2516 A1064 P multi 1.25 .75
2517 A1064 P multi 1.25 .75

Perf. 13¼x12½

2518 A1065 P multi 1.25 .75

Booklet Stamp
Self-Adhesive

2519 A1065 P multi 1.25 .30
 a. Booklet pane of 10 12.50

Issued: Nos. 2513, 2519, 1/16; No. 2514, 2/6; No. 2515, 3/6; No. 2516, 4/10; No. 2517, 5/7; No. 2518, 6/1. On day of issue, Nos. 2513-2519 each sold for 61c. Nos. 2513-2518 each were printed in sheets of 4.

Black History Month A1066

Designs: No. 2520, John Ware (c. 1845-1905), cattle driver and rancher. No. 2521, Viola Desmond (1914-65), civil rights activist.

Self-Adhesive
Booklet Stamps

Serpentine Die Cut 13½

2012, Feb. 1 Litho.

2520 A1066 P multi 1.25 .30
 a. Booklet pane of 10 12.50

2521 A1066 P multi 1.25 .30
a. Booklet pane of 10 12.50
b. Gutter pane of 12, 6 each #2520-2521 15.00

On day of issue, Nos. 2520-2521 each sold for 61c.

Sculptures by Joe Fafard — A1067

Designs: P, Smoothly She Shifted. $1.05, Dear Vincent, vert. (32x40mm). $1.80, Capillery, horiz. (64x32mm).

2012, Feb. 23 *Perf. 12½*

2522 A1067 P multi 1.25 .30

Souvenir Sheet

2523 Sheet of 3, #2522, 2523a, 2523b 5.25 4.50
a. A1067 $1.05 multi 1.50 1.70
b. A1067 $1.80 multi 2.50 2.90

Booklet Stamps
Self-Adhesive

Serpentine Die Cut 13½

2524 A1067 $1.05 multi 1.50 .60
a. Booklet pane of 6 9.00

Serpentine Die Cut 13¼

2525 A1067 $1.80 multi 2.50 .90
a. Booklet pane of 6 15.00
b. Gutter pane of 6, 3 each #2524-2525 15.00

No. 2522 sold for 61c on day of issue.

A1068

Daylilies — A1069

Color of daylily: Nos. 2526a, 2527, 2529, Orange. Nos. 2526b, 2528, 2530, Purple.

2012, Mar. 1 *Perf. 13¼*

Souvenir Sheet

2526 Sheet of 2 2.50 1.80
a.-b. A1068 P Either single 1.25 .90

Coil Stamps
Self-Adhesive

Serpentine Die Cut 8¼ Horiz.

2527 A1069 P multi 1.25 .30
2528 A1069 P multi 1.25 .30
a. Vert. pair, #2527-2528 2.50

Booklet Stamps

Serpentine Die Cut 13½

2529 A1068 P multi 1.25 .30
2530 A1068 P multi 1.25 .30
a. Booklet pane of 10, 5 each #2529-2530 12.50

On day of issue, Nos. 2526a, 2526b, 2527-2530 each sold for 61c.

A1070

Sinking of the Titanic, Cent. — A1071

Flag of the White Star Line and: Nos. 2531, 2536, Bow of Titanic, map showing Halifax, Nova Scotia. Nos. 2532, 2537, Bow of Titanic, map showing Southampton, England. No. 2533, Propellers of Titanic, three men. No. 2534, Propellers of Titanic, six men.

$1.80, Titanic, map of North Atlantic, flag of the White Star Line.

2012, Apr. 5 **Litho.** *Perf. 12½*

2531 A1070 P multi 1.25 .45
2532 A1070 P multi 1.25 .45
2533 A1070 P multi 1.25 .45
2534 A1070 P multi 1.25 .45
a. Block of 4, #2531-2534 5.00 2.25
Nos. 2531-2534 (4) 5.00 1.80

Souvenir Sheet

Perf. 13

2535 A1071 $1.80 multi 2.50 2.50

Booklet Stamps
Self-Adhesive

Serpentine Die Cut 13½

2536 A1070 P multi 1.25 .30
2537 A1070 P multi 1.25 .30
a. Booklet pane of 10, 5 each #2536-2537 12.50
2538 A1071 $1.80 multi 2.50 1.50
a. Booklet pane of 6 15.00
Nos. 2536-2538 (3) 5.00 2.10

On day of issue, Nos. 2531-2534, 2536-2537 each sold for 61c.

Thomas Douglas, 5th Earl of Selkirk (1771-1820), Founder of Red River Settlement, and Settlers — A1072

2012, May 3 **Litho.** *Perf. 13¼*

2539 A1072 P multi 1.25 .30

Red River Settlement, bicent. No. 2539 sold for 61c on day of issue.

Reign Of Queen Elizabeth II, 60th Anniv. A1073

2012, May 7 **Engr.** *Perf. 11½*

2540 A1073 $2 purple 3.00 1.50
a. Souvenir sheet of 1 3.75 3.75

Franklin the Turtle, Children's Book Character by Paulette Bourgeois — A1074

Designs: Nos. 2541a, 2542, Franklin, bear and teddy bear. Nos. 2541b, 2543, Franklin helping young turtle to read book. Nos. 2541c, 2544, Franklin and snail. Nos. 2541d, 2545, Franklin watching bear feed fish in bowl.

2012, May 11 *Perf. 13x12½*

2541 Miniature sheet of 4 5.00 4.50
a.-d. A1074 P Any single 1.25 .90

Booklet Stamps
Self-Adhesive

Serpentine Die Cut 13¼

2542 A1074 P multi 1.25 .35
2543 A1074 P multi 1.25 .35
2544 A1074 P multi 1.25 .35
2545 A1074 P multi 1.25 .35
a. Booklet pane of 12, 3 each #2542-2545 15.00
Nos. 2542-2545 (4) 5.00 1.40

Nos. 2541a-2541d, 2542-2545 each sold for 61c on day of issue.

Calgary Stampede, Cent. — A1075

Designs: P, Saddle on rodeo horse. $1.05, Commemorative belt buckle.

2012, May 17 *Perf. 13x13¼*

2546 Souvenir sheet of 2 3.00 2.50
a. A1075 P multi 1.25 .90
b. A1075 $1.05 multi 1.80 1.60

Booklet Stamps
Self-Adhesive

Serpentine Die Cut 13¼x13

2547 A1075 P multi 1.25 .30
a. Booklet pane of 10 12.50
2548 A1075 $1.05 multi 1.50 .60
a. Booklet pane of 10 15.00
b. Gutter pane of 10, 6 #2547, 4 #2548 15.00

Nos. 2546a and 2547 each sold for 61c on day of issue.

Order of Canada Recipients A1076

Designs: Nos. 2549a, 2550, Louise Arbour, president of International Crisis Group. Nos. 2549b, 2551, Rick Hansen, founder of Rick Hansen Foundation (spinal cord injury research). Nos. 2549c, 2552, Sheila Watt-Cloutier, Inuit rights activist. Nos. 2549d, 2553, Michael J. Fox, actor, founder of Michael J. Fox Foundation for Parkinson's Research.

2012, May 22 **Litho.** *Perf. 12½*

2549 Miniature sheet of 4 5.00 4.50
a.-d. A1076 P Any single 1.25 .90

Booklet Stamps
Self-Adhesive

Serpentine Die Cut 13½

2550 A1076 P multi 1.25 .30
a. Booklet pane of 10 12.50
2551 A1076 P multi 1.25 .30
a. Booklet pane of 10 12.50
2552 A1076 P multi 1.25 .30
a. Booklet pane of 10 12.50
2553 A1076 P multi 1.25 .30
a. Booklet pane of 10 12.50
Nos. 2550-2553 (4) 5.00 1.20

On day of issue Nos. 2549a-2549d, 2550-2553 each sold for 61c.

War of 1812, Bicent. — A1077

Designs: No. 2554, Sir Isaac Brock (1769-1812), British Major General. No. 2555, Tecumseh (1768-1813), leader of Indian confederacy.

2012, June 15 *Perf. 13¼x12½*

2554 P multi 1.25 .30
2555 P multi 1.25 .30
a. A1077 Horiz. pair, #2554-2555 2.50 .90

On day of issue, Nos. 2554-2555 each sold for 61c. See Guernsey No. 1172.

2012 Summer Olympics, London A1078

Self-Adhesive
Booklet Stamp

2012, June 27 ***Serpentine Die Cut 8***

2556 A1078 P multi 1.25 .35
a. Booklet pane of 10 12.50

No. 2556 sold for 61c on day of issue.

Tommy Douglas (1904-86), Politician A1079

2012, June 29 *Perf. 12½*

2557 A1079 P multi 1.25 .30

Passage of Saskatchewan's Medical Care Insurance Act, 50th anniv. (start of socialized medicine in Canada). No. 2557 sold for 61c on day of issue.

Canadian Football League Team Emblems — A1080

Designs: Nos. 2558a, 2559, British Columbia Lions. Nos. 2558b, 2560, Edmonton Eskimos. Nos. 2558c, 2561, Calgary Stampeders. Nos. 2558d, 2562, Saskatchewan Roughriders. Nos. 2558e, 2563, Winnipeg Blue Bombers. Nos. 2558f, 2564, Hamilton Tiger-Cats. Nos. 2558g, 2565, Toronto Argonauts. Nos. 2558h, 2566, Montreal Alouettes.

2012, June 29 *Perf. 13¼x13*

2558 A1080 Sheet of 8 10.00 8.00
a.-h. P Any single 1.25 .90

Coil Stamps
Self-Adhesive

Serpentine Die Cut 8¼ Horiz.

2559 A1080 P multi 1.25 .30
2560 A1080 P multi 1.25 .30
2561 A1080 P multi 1.25 .30
2562 A1080 P multi 1.25 .30
2563 A1080 P multi 1.25 .30
2564 A1080 P multi 1.25 .30
2565 A1080 P multi 1.25 .30
2566 A1080 P multi 1.25 .30
Nos. 2559-2566 (8) 10.00 2.40

On day of issue, Nos. 2558a-2558h, 2559-2566 each sold for 61c. See No. 2754.

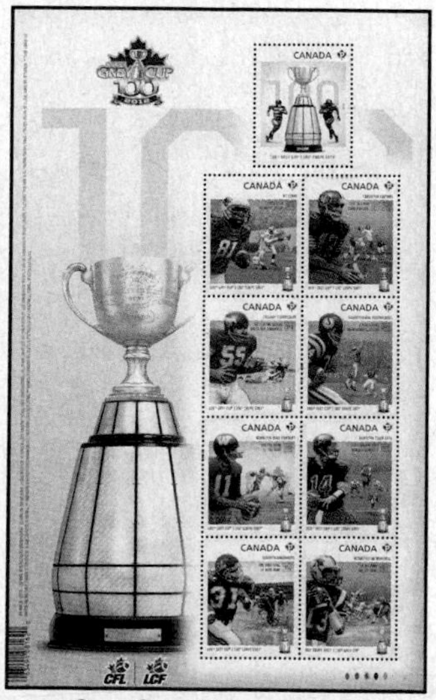

Grey Cup, Cent. — A1081

Grey Cup and: Nos. 2567a, 2568, Two football players, "100." Nos. 2567b, 2569, British Columbia Lions player Geroy Simon, kicker and holder in 1994 game. Nos. 2567c, 2570, Edmonton Eskimos player Tom Wilkinson, quarterback ready to throw pass. Nos. 2567d,

2571, Calgary Stampeders player "Thumper" Wayne Harris, running back and tacklers from 1948 game. Nos. 2567e, 2572, Saskatchewan Roughriders player George Reed, players celebrating in 1989 game. Nos. 2567f, 2573, Winnipeg Blue Bombers player Ken Pipen, players in fog in 1962 game. Nos. 2567g, 2574, Hamilton Tiger-Cats player Danny Mcmanus, player catching ball in 1972 game. Nos. 2567h, 2575, Toronto Argonauts player Michael "Pinball" Clemons, players on muddy field in 1950 game. Nos. 2567i, 2576, Montreal Alouettes player Anthony Calvillo, players at line of scrimmage in 1977 game.

Litho. & Embossed

2012, Aug. 16 *Perf. 12½*

2567 A1081 Sheet of 9 11.25 8.00
a.-i. P Any single 1.25 .85

Litho.

Booklet Stamps
Self-Adhesive

Serpentine Die Cut 13¼

2568 A1081 P multi 1.25 .30
a. Booklet pane of 10 12.50
2569 A1081 P multi 1.25 .30
a. Booklet pane of 10 12.50
2570 A1081 P multi 1.25 .30
a. Booklet pane of 10 12.50
2571 A1081 P multi 1.25 .30
a. Booklet pane of 10 12.50
2572 A1081 P multi 1.25 .30
a. Booklet pane of 10 12.50
2573 A1081 P multi 1.25 .30
a. Booklet pane of 10 12.50
2574 A1081 P multi 1.25 .30
a. Booklet pane of 10 12.50
2575 A1081 P multi 1.25 .30
a. Booklet pane of 10 12.50
2576 A1081 P multi 1.25 .30
a. Booklet pane of 10 12.50
Nos. 2568-2576 (9) 11.25 2.70

Nos. 2567a-2567i, 2568-2576 each sold for 61c on day of issue. For overprint, see No. 2598.

Military Regiments, 150th Anniv.
A1082

Uniforms of: Nos. 2577a, 2578, Black Watch (Royal Highland) Regiment of Canada. Nos. 2577b, 2579, Royal Hamilton Light Infantry (Wentworth Regiment). Nos. 2577c, 2580, Royal Regiment of Canada

2012, Oct. 11 **Litho.** *Perf. 13x13½*

2577 Souvenir sheet of 3 3.75 3.00
a.-c. A1082 P Any single 1.25 .90

Booklet Stamps
Self-Adhesive

Serpentine Die Cut 13¼x13

2578 A1082 P multi 1.25 .35
a. Booklet pane of 10 12.50
2579 A1082 P multi 1.25 .35
a. Booklet pane of 10 12.50
2580 A1082 P multi 1.25 .35
a. Booklet pane of 10 12.50
Nos. 2578-2580 (3) 3.75 1.05

On day of issue, Nos. 2577a-2577c, 2578-2580 each sold for 61c.

Gingerbread Cookies
A1083

Stained Glass Window From St. Mary's of the Immaculate Conception Cathedral, Kingsoton, Ontario
A1084

Ribbons on Christmas cookies shaped as: P, Man and woman. $1.05, Five-pointed star. $1.80, Snowflake.

Souvenir Sheet

2012, Oct. 15 *Perf. 13¾x13¼*

2581 Sheet of 3 5.50 4.50
a. A1083 P multi 1.25 .90
b. A1083 $1.05 multi 1.50 1.50
c. A1083 $1.80 multi 2.60 2.60

Booklet Stamps
Self-Adhesive

Serpentine Die Cut 13¼

2582 A1084 P multi 1.25 .25
a. Booklet pane of 12 15.00

Serpentine Die Cut 13¼x13

2583 A1083 P multi 1.25 .25
a. Booklet pane of 12 12.50
2584 A1083 $1.05 multi 1.50 .60
a. Booklet pane of 6 9.00
2585 A1083 $1.80 multi 2.90 1.00
a. Booklet pane of 6 17.50
Nos. 2582-2585 (4) 6.90 2.10

Christmas. On day of issue, Nos. 2581a, 2582 and 2583 each sold for 61c.

Dots — A1085

Frame — A1086

Hearts
A1087

Creatures
A1088

Butterflies
A1089

Maple Leaves
A1090

Flowers
A1091

Snowflakes
A1092

Wedding Bells — A1093

Doves and Flowers — A1094

Balloons, Stars, Party Hat — A1095

Holly — A1096

Serpentine Die Cut 13¼

2012, Nov. **Self-Adhesive** **Litho.**

2586 A1085 P gray 2.25 2.25
a. Personalized version, any denomination or orientation — —
2587 A1086 P gray 2.25 2.25
a. Personalized version, any denomination or orientation — —
2588 A1087 P gray & red 2.25 2.25
a. Personalized version, any denomination or orientation — —
2589 A1088 P multi 2.25 2.25
a. Personalized version, any denomination or orientation — —
2590 A1089 P multi 2.25 2.25
a. Personalized version, any denomination or orientation — —
2591 A1090 P multi 2.25 2.25
a. Personalized version, any denomination or orientation — —
2592 A1091 P multi 2.25 2.25
a. Personalized version, any denomination or orientation — —
2593 A1092 P multi 2.25 2.25
a. Personalized version, any denomination or orientation — —
2594 A1093 P gray & black 2.25 2.25
a. Personalized version, any denomination or orientation — —
2595 A1094 P gray 2.25 2.25
a. Personalized version, any denomination or orientation — —
2596 A1095 P multi 2.25 2.25
a. Personalized version, any denomination or orientation — —
2597 A1096 P multi 2.25 2.25
a. Personalized version, any denomination or orientation — —
Nos. 2586-2597 (12) 27.00 27.00

Nos. 2586-2597 had a franking value on the day of issue of 61c, and were sold together in a package of single stamps that sold for $7.32. Each vertically-oriented stamp in the package had a gray image area. Horizontally-oriented stamps were not made available in these packages. First day covers of Nos. 2586-2597 are dated 11/5.

Nos. 2586a-2597a have personalized photographs in the image area, and were available with vertical or horizontal orientations and in various denominations. On Nov. 16-24 personalized stamps were offered for sale on iPad and iPhone apps at the P rate (with a franking value of 61c), $1.05, $1.29 and $1.80. It is not known if any personalized stamps of the $1.05, $1.29 and $1.80 denominations were created for customers through these apps during this brief period. On Nov. 24 stamps at the P rate (with a franking value of 61c), $1.10, $1.34 and $1.85 were offered to customers through the Picture Postage page of the Canada Post website, as well as through the apps. Additional stamps with different denominations may be offered for sale later. A $1.29 stamp featuring the image of a Turtle was made available on Nov. 1. It was only available affixed to packages containing a box of Nestle's Turtles candy. A box of candy and affixed stamp sold at post offices for $4.99, and the package could only be sent to Canadian addresses.

Except for the stamp with the turtle's image, the stamps of the various denominations were each made available in sheets of 26, sheets of 50 and booklet panes of 12 (a minimum of three booklet panes needed to be ordered). The selling prices of the personalized sheets and booklets were substantially higher than the face value of the stamps within them.

Vertically oriented stamps have the denomination in the lower right corner of the stamp, with the "C" of "Canada" at the upper left of the stamp, as shown in the illustrations. Horizontally oriented stamps have the denomination in the lower right corner of the stamp, with the "C" of "Canada" at the lower left corner. The dots, frame, hearts, creatures and butterflies images on horizontally-oriented stamps differ from those shown on the vertically-oriented stamps.

No. 2568 Overprinted in Dark Blue, Light Blue, Black and Silver

Booklet Stamp

Serpentine Die Cut 13¼

2012, Nov. 28 **Litho.**

Self-Adhesive

2598 A1081 P multi 1.25 .30
a. Booklet pane of 10 12.50

Grey Cup victory of Toronto Argonauts. No. 2598 sold for 61c on day of issue.

New Year 2013 (Year of the Snake) — A1097

Design: $1.85, Snake's head.

Litho. & Embossed

2013, Jan. 8 *Perf. 12½*

2599 A1097 P shown 1.25 .30

Souvenir Sheet

Litho. & Embossed With Foil Application

2600 A1097 $1.85 multi 2.75 2.75
a. Souvenir sheet of 2, #2496, 2600 5.25 4.75

Booklet Stamp
Self-Adhesive

Litho.

Serpentine Die Cut 13½

2601 A1097 $1.85 multi 2.90 1.20
a. Booklet pane of 6 17.50

No. 2599 sold for 63c on day of issue. See No. 2700a.

Juvenile Wildlife Type of 2011

Designs: P, Four woodchuck pups. $1.10, Porcupette. $1.34, Fawn. $1.85, Bear cub.

2013, Jan. 14 *Perf. 13¼x13*

2602 Souvenir sheet of 4 7.25 6.25
a. A1038 P multi 1.25 .90
b. A1038 $1.10 multi 1.50 1.10
c. A1038 $1.34 multi 1.80 1.30
d. A1038 $1.85 multi 2.50 1.80

Self-Adhesive
Coil Stamps

Serpentine Die Cut 9¼ Horiz.

2603 A1038 P multi 1.50 1.50

Serpentine Die Cut 8¼ Horiz.

2604 A1038 P multi 1.25 .25
2605 A1038 $1.10 multi 1.50 .30
2606 A1038 $1.34 multi 1.80 .40
2607 A1038 $1.85 multi 2.50 .55

Booklet Stamps

Serpentine Die Cut 9¼ Horiz.

2608 A1038 $1.10 multi 1.60 .30
a. Booklet pane of 6 9.50
2609 A1038 $1.34 multi 2.00 .45
a. Booklet pane of 6 12.00
2610 A1038 $1.85 multi 2.75 .60
a. Booklet pane of 6 16.50
Nos. 2603-2610 (8) 14.90 4.35

On day of issue, Nos. 2602a, 2603 and 2604 each sold for 63c. On rolls of No. 2603, stamps do not touch each other and pairs are horizontal. On rolls of No. 2604, stamps touch each other and pairs are vertical.

See No. 2692.

Flag Design on Chairs
A1098

Flag on Hay Roll
A1099

Flag Design on Spinnaker A1100

Flag in Flower Bed A1101

Flag Design on Hut — A1102

2013, Jan. 14 Litho. *Perf. 13x13¼*

2611 Souvenir sheet of 5 6.25 4.50
a. A1098 P multi 1.25 .90
b. A1099 P multi 1.25 .90
c. A1100 P multi 1.25 .90
d. A1101 P multi 1.25 .90
e. A1102 P multi 1.25 .90

Booklet Stamps
Self-Adhesive
Serpentine Die Cut 13¼

2612 A1098 P multi 1.25 .25
a. With "Canada" visible on reverse of stamp 1.25 .25
2613 A1099 P multi 1.25 .25
a. With "Canada" visible on reverse of stamp 1.25 .25
2614 A1100 P multi 1.25 .25
a. With "Canada" visible on reverse of stamp 1.25 .25
2615 A1101 P multi 1.25 .25
a. With "Canada" visible on reverse of stamp 1.25 .25
2616 A1102 P multi 1.25 .25
a. With "Canada" visible on reverse of stamp 1.25 .25
b. Booklet pane of 10, 2 each #2612-2616 12.50
c. Booklet pane of 10, 2 each #2612a-2616a 12.50
d. Booklet pane of 30, 6 each #2612-2616 37.50
e. Booklet pane of 30, 6 each #2612a-2616a 37.50
Nos. 2612-2616 (5) 6.25 1.25

On day of issue, Nos. 2611a-2611e, 2612-2616, 2612a-2616a each sold for 63c. The printing on the backing paper on Nos. 2616b and 2616c differs from that on the backing paper of any of the component thirds of Nos. 2616d and 2616e.

See Nos. 2693-2697.

Queen Elizabeth II — A1103

Booklet Stamp
Serpentine Die Cut 13¼
2013, Jan. 14 Self-Adhesive

2617 A1103 P multi 1.25 .25
a. Booklet pane of 10 12.50
b. As #2617, with "Canada" visible on reverse of stamp 1.25 .25
c. Booklet pane of 10 #2617b 12.50

No. 2617 sold for 63c on day of issue. Issued: Nos. 2617b, 2617c, 6/1.

See No. 2698.

Raoul Wallenberg (1912-47), Swedish Diplomat Who Rescued Jews During World War II — A1104

Booklet Stamp
Serpentine Die Cut 13¼
2013, Jan. 17 Self-Adhesive

2618 A1104 185c multi 2.75 1.10
a. Booklet pane of 6 16.50

Oliver Jones, Jazz Musician — A1105

Joe Fortes (1863-1922), First Official Lifeguard of Vancouver — A1106

Booklet Stamps
Serpentine Die Cut 13¼
2013, Feb. 1 Self-Adhesive

2619 A1105 P multi 1.25 .30
a. Booklet pane of 10 12.50
2620 A1106 P multi 1.25 .30
a. Booklet pane of 10 12.50

On day of issue, Nos. 2619-2620 each sold for 63c.

Magnolias
A1107 A1108

Magnolia varieties: Nos. 2621a, 2622, 2624, Yellow Bird (yellow flower). Nos. 2621b, 2623, 2625, Eskimo (lilac and white flower).

2013, Mar. 4 Litho. *Perf. 13¼*
Souvenir Sheet

2621 Sheet of 2 2.50 2.00
a.-b. A1107 P Either single 1.25 .90

Coil Stamps
Self-Adhesive
Serpentine Die Cut 8¼ Horiz.

2622 A1108 P multi 1.25 .30
2623 A1108 P multi 1.25 .30
a. Vert. pair, #2622-2623 2.50

Booklet Stamps
Serpentine Die Cut 13½

2624 A1107 P multi 1.25 .30
2625 A1107 P multi 1.25 .30
a. Booklet pane of 10, 5 each #2624-2625 12.50

On day of issue, Nos. 2621a-2621b, 2622-2625 each sold for 63c.

Photography — A1109

Designs: Nos. 2626a, 2629, Louis-Joseph Papineau, by Thomas Coffin Doane, 1852. Nos. 2626b, 2630, The Kitchen Sink, by Margaret Watkins, 1919. Nos. 2626c, 2632, Kootuck-tuck, by Geraldine Moodie, 1903-05. Nos. 2627a, 2628, Hot Properties #1, by Jim Breukelman, 1987, horiz. Nos. 2627b, 2631, Andor Pasztor, by Gabor Szilasi, 1978, horiz. $1.10, Basement Camera Shop circa 1937, by Rodney Graham, 2011, horiz. $1.85, Yousuf Karsh, by Arnaud Maggs, 1981, horiz.

2013, Mar. 22 *Perf. 13¼*

2626 A1109 Sheet of 3 3.75 3.25
a.-c. P Any single 1.25 .90
2627 A1109 Sheet of 4 7.00 6.25
a.-b. P Any single 1.25 .90
c. $1.10 multi 1.60 1.50
d. $1.85 multi 2.75 2.50

Booklet Stamps
Self-Adhesive
Serpentine Die Cut 13½

2628 A1109 P multi 1.25 .30
2629 A1109 P multi 1.25 .30
2630 A1109 P multi 1.25 .30
2631 A1109 P multi 1.25 .30
2632 A1109 P multi 1.25 .30
a. Booklet pane of 10, 2 each #2628-2632 12.50
2633 A1109 $1.10 multi 1.60 .75
a. Booklet pane of 6 9.50
2634 A1109 $1.85 multi 2.75 1.10
a. Booklet pane of 6 16.50
Nos. 2628-2634 (7) 10.60 3.35

On day of issue, Nos. 2626a-2626c, 2627a, 2627b, 2628-2632 each sold for 63c.

See Nos. 2756-2764, 2814-2822.

The Prince of Wales' Own Regiment, 150th Anniv. A1110

Serpentine Die Cut 13¼x13
2013, Apr. 9 Self-Adhesive
Booklet Stamp

2635 A1110 P multi 1.25 .35
a. Booklet pane of 10 12.50

No. 2635 sold for 63c on day of issue.

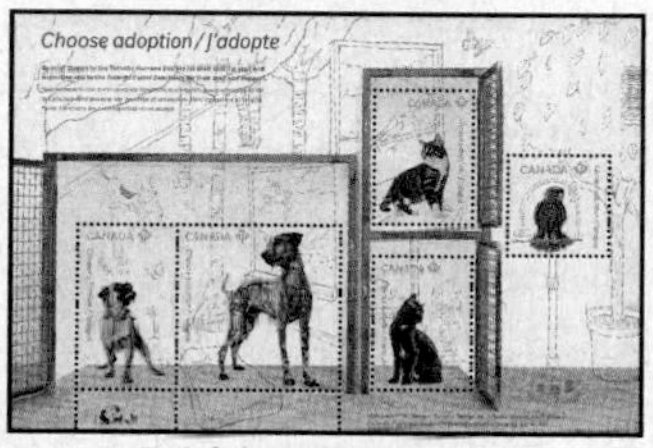

Pet Adoption — A1111

Designs: Nos. 2636a, 2637, Cat with bird on branch in background (24x32mm). Nos. 2636b, 2638, Parrot on perch (24x24mm). Nos. 2636c, 2639, Dog with squirrel, butterfly, flower and ball in background (24x40mm). Nos. 2636d, 2640, Dog with fireplace, dog bed and bone in background (40x40mm). Nos. 2636e, 2641, Cat with cat toys in background (24x32mm).

Perf. 12½ (#2636a, 2636e), 13¼ (#2636b), 12½x13¼
2013, Apr. 22

2636 A1111 Sheet of 5 6.25 5.00
a.-e. P Any single 1.25 .90

Booklet Stamps
Self-Adhesive
Serpentine Die Cut 13x13¼

2637 A1111 P multi 1.25 .30

Serpentine Die Cut 13

2638 A1111 P multi 1.25 .30

Serpentine Die Cut 13½

2639 A1111 P multi 1.25 .30
2640 A1111 P multi 1.25 .30

Serpentine Die Cut 13x13¼

2641 A1111 P multi 1.25 .30
a. Booklet pane of 10, 2 each #2637-2641 12.50
Nos. 2637-2641 (5) 6.25 1.50

On day of issue, Nos. 2636a-2636e, 2637-2641 each sold for 63c.

Chinatown Gates — A1112

Gates in: Nos. 2642a, 2643a, Toronto. Nos. 2642b, 2643b, Montreal. Nos. 2642c, 2643c, Winnipeg. Nos. 2642d, 2643e, Edmonton. Nos. 2642e, 2643d, Vancouver. Nos. 2642f, 2643f, Ottawa. Nos. 2642g, 2643g, Mississauga, Ontario. Nos. 2642h, 2643h, Victoria.

Litho. With Foil Application
2013, May 1 *Perf. 12½*

2642 A1112 Miniature sheet of 8 + central label 10.00 7.50
a.-h. P Any single 1.25 .90

An imperf. pane of 8 exists of No. 2642. Sold only in a "Gates of Chinatown Collection," along with a normal No. 2642 and two coins, for $88.88. Value of imperf. pane, $140.

Litho.
Booklet Stamps
Self-Adhesive
Serpentine Die Cut 13½

2643 A1112 Booklet pane of 8 10.00
a.-h. P Any single 1.25 .30

On day of issue Nos. 2642a-2642h, 2643a-2643h each sold for 63c. Label on No. 2642 has a die cut square opening in center.

Coronation of Queen Elizabeth II, 60th Anniv. — A1113

Serpentine Die Cut 13¼
2013, May 8 Litho.
Booklet Stamp
Self-Adhesive

2644 A1113 P multi 1.25 .30
a. Booklet pane of 10 12.50

No. 2644 sold for 63c on day of issue.

Big Brothers Big Sisters of Canada, Cent. — A1114

Serpentine Die Cut 13x13½
2013, May 14 Litho.
Booklet Stamp
Self-Adhesive

2645 A1114 P multi 1.25 .30
a. Booklet pane of 10 12.50

No. 2645 sold for 63c on day of issue.

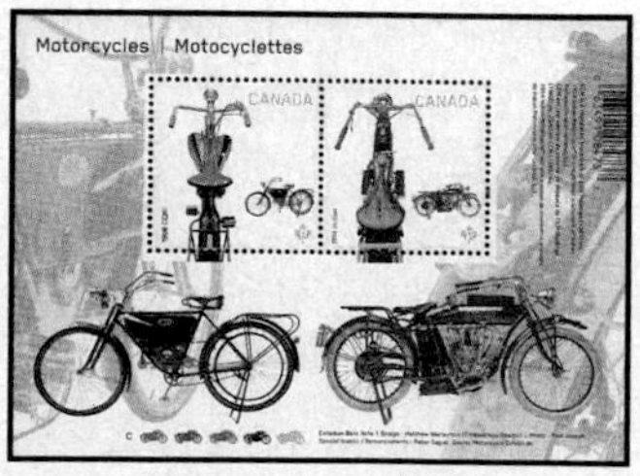

Motorcycles — A1115

Designs: Nos. 2646a, 2647, 1908 CCM. Nos. 2646b, 2648, 1914 Indian.

2013, June 5 *Perf. 12½x13*
Souvenir Sheet

2646 A1115 Sheet of 2 2.50 1.80
a.-b. P Either single 1.25 .90

Booklet Stamps
Self-Adhesive
Serpentine Die Cut 13¼

2647 A1115 P multi 1.25 .30
2648 A1115 P multi 1.25 .30
a. Booklet pane of 10, 5 each #2647-2648 12.50

On day of issue, Nos. 2646a-2646b, 2647-2648 each sold for 63c.

Quebec Harbor Scene and Benjamin Franklin (1706-90), British North America Deputy Postmaster
A1116

Booklet Stamp

Serpentine Die Cut 13½

2013, June 10 Self-Adhesive

2649 A1116 P multi 1.25 .30
a. Booklet pane of 10 12.50

Mail packet service from Montreal to New York, 250th anniv. No. 2649 sold for 63c on day of issue.

War of 1812 — A1117

Heroic figures of War of 1812: No. 2650, Lieutenant Colonel Charles de Salaberry (1778-1829). No. 2651, Laura Secord (1775-1868).

2013, June 20 ***Perf. 13x12½***

2650 P multi 1.25 .30
2651 P multi 1.25 .30
a. A1117 Horiz. pair, #2650-2651 2.50 .90

On day of issue, Nos. 2650-2651 each sold for 63c.

Children's Literature — A1118

Characters from series of *Stella* books, by Marie-Louise Gay: Nos. 2652a, 2653, Stella hanging by legs from tree. Nos. 2652b, 2654, Stella, brother Sam, and dog, Fred.

2013, July 5 ***Perf. 12½***

Souvenir Sheet

2652 A1118 Sheet of 2 2.50 2.25
a.-b. P Either single 1.25 .90

Booklet Stamps
Self-Adhesive

Serpentine Die Cut 13¼

2653 A1118 P multi 1.25 .30
2654 A1118 P multi 1.25 .30
a. Booklet pane of 10, 5 each #2653-2654 12.50

On day of issue, Nos. 2652a-2652b, 2653-2654 each sold for 63c.

Canadian Bands — A1119

Designs: Nos. 2655a, 2656, The Tragically Hip (36x28mm). Nos. 2655b, 2657, Rush (28x28mm). Nos. 2655c, 2658, Beau Dommage (36x28mm). Nos. 2655d, 2659, The Guess Who (28x28mm).

2013, July 19 ***Perf. 12½***

Souvenir Sheet

2655 A1119 Sheet of 4 5.00 4.25
a.-d. P Any single 1.25 .90

Booklet Stamps
Self-Adhesive

Serpentine Die Cut 13½

2656 A1119 P multi 1.25 .30
a. Booklet pane of 10 12.50
2657 A1119 P multi 1.25 .30
a. Booklet pane of 10 12.50
2658 A1119 P multi 1.25 .30
a. Booklet pane of 10 12.50
2659 A1119 P multi 1.25 .30
a. Booklet pane of 10 12.50
Nos. 2656-2659 (4) 5.00 1.20

On day of issue, Nos. 2655a-2655d, 2656-2659 each sold for 63c.

Robertson Davies (1913-95), Writer — A1120

Booklet Stamp

Serpentine Die Cut 13¼

2013, Aug. 28 Self-Adhesive

2660 A1120 63c multi .90 .35
a. Booklet pane of 10 9.00

Pucks With Emblems of Canadian National Hockey League Teams — A1121

Pucks with emblem of: Nos. 2661a, 2662, Vancouver Canucks. Nos. 2661b, 2663, Edmonton Oilers. Nos. 2661c, 2664, Toronto Maple Leafs. Nos. 2661d, 2665, Montreal Canadiens. Nos. 2661e, 2666, Calgary Flames. Nos. 2661f, 2667, Winnipeg Jets. Nos. 2661g, 2668, Ottawa Senators.

2013, Sept. 3 Litho. ***Perf. 13¼x13***

2661 A1121 Sheet of 7 7.00 6.50
a.-g. 63c Any single 1.00 .80

Coil Stamps
Self-Adhesive

Serpentine Die Cut 8¼ Horiz.

2662 A1121 63c multi .90 .30
2663 A1121 63c multi .90 .30
2664 A1121 63c multi .90 .30
2665 A1121 63c multi .90 .30
2666 A1121 63c multi .90 .30
2667 A1121 63c multi .90 .30
2668 A1121 63c multi .90 .30
Nos. 2662-2668 (7) 6.30 2.10

Player and Fans Wearing Home and Away Uniforms of Canadian National Hockey League Teams
A1122

Uniforms of: Nos. 2669a, 2670, Vancouver Canucks. Nos. 2669b, 2671, Montreal Canadiens. Nos. 2669c, 2672, Edmonton Oilers. Nos. 2669d, 2673, Ottawa Senators. Nos. 2669e, 2674, Calgary Flames. Nos. 2669f, 2675, Winnipeg Jets. Nos. 2669g, 2676, Toronto Maple Leafs.

Serpentine Die Cut 13¼x13½

2013, Sept. 3 Litho. & Embossed

2669 Sheet of 7 + 2 labels 7.00 6.50
a.-g. A1122 63c Any single 1.00 .80

Litho.

Booklet Stamps
Self-Adhesive

2670 A1122 63c multi .90 .30
a. Booklet pane of 10 9.00
2671 A1122 63c multi .90 .30
a. Booklet pane of 10 9.00
2672 A1122 63c multi .90 .30
a. Booklet pane of 10 9.00
2673 A1122 63c multi .90 .30
a. Booklet pane of 10 9.00
2674 A1122 63c multi .90 .30
a. Booklet pane of 10 9.00
2675 A1122 63c multi .90 .30
a. Booklet pane of 10 9.00
2676 A1122 63c multi .90 .30
a. Booklet pane of 10 9.00
Nos. 2670-2676 (7) 6.30 2.10

A1123

A1124

A1125

A1126

A1127

Superman Comics, 75th Anniv. — A1128

2013, Sept. 10 ***Perf. 12½***

2677 Sheet of 5 6.25 5.50
a. A1123 P multi 1.25 .90
b. A1124 P multi 1.25 .90
c. A1125 P multi 1.25 .90
d. A1126 P multi 1.25 .90
e. A1127 P multi 1.25 .90

Coil Stamp
Self-Adhesive

Die Cut Perf. 13½

2678 A1128 P multi 1.25 .40

Booklet Stamps

Serpentine Die Cut 13½x13¼

2679 A1123 P multi 1.25 .30
2680 A1124 P multi 1.25 .30
2681 A1125 P multi 1.25 .30
2682 A1126 P multi 1.25 .30
2683 A1127 P multi 1.25 .30
a. Booklet pane of 10, 2 each #2679-2683 12.50
Nos. 2678-2683 (6) 7.50 1.90

Nos. 2677a-2677e, 2678-2683 each sold for 63c on day of issue.

Hastings and Prince Edward Regiment, 150th Anniv.
A1129

Serpentine Die Cut 13¼x13

2013, Oct. 18 Litho.

Booklet Stamp
Self-Adhesive

2684 A1129 P multi 1.25 .30
a. Booklet pane of 10 12.50

No. 2684 sold for 63c on day of issue.

Birth of Prince George of Cambridge
A1130

2013, Oct. 22 Litho. ***Perf. 12½***

2685 Sheet of 2 #2685a 2.50 1.80
a. A1130 P Single stamp 1.25 .90

Booklet Stamp
Self-Adhesive

Serpentine Die Cut 13½

2686 A1130 P multi 1.25 .30
a. Booklet pane of 10 12.50

On day of issue, Nos. 2685a and 2686 each sold for 63c.

Christmas
A1131 A1132

Designs: Nos. 2687a, 2689, Cross-stitched horn. $1.10, Cross-stitched reindeer. $1.85, Cross-stitched Christmas tree. No. 2688, St. Anne with the Christ Child, by Georges de La Tour.

2013, Oct. 22 Litho. ***Perf. 13½x13¼***

2687 Sheet of 3 5.25 5.25
a. A1131 63c multi .90 .90
b. A1131 $1.10 multi 1.60 1.50
c. A1131 $1.85 multi 2.75 2.60

Booklet Stamps
Self-Adhesive

Serpentine Die Cut 13½

2688 A1132 63c multi .90 .25
a. Booklet pane of 12 11.00

Serpentine Die Cut 13¼x13

2689 A1131 63c multi .90 .25
a. Booklet pane of 12 11.00
2690 A1131 $1.10 multi 1.50 .60
a. Booklet pane of 6 9.00
2691 A1131 $1.85 multi 2.75 .90
a. Booklet pane of 6 16.50
Nos. 2688-2691 (4) 6.05 2.00

Juvenile Wildlife Type of 2011

Design: 63c, Four woodchuck pups.

Serpentine Die Cut 9¼ Horiz.

2013, Dec. 11 Litho.

Coil Stamps
Self-Adhesive

2692 A1038 63c multi .90 .25
b. Without repeating "Canada" underprint on reverse 75.00 8.00

Serpentine Die Cut 8¼ Horiz.

2692A A1038 63c multi 1.10 1.10

Coils containing No. 2692A are adjacent in vertical strips. Coils containing No. 2692 are in horizontal strips with stamps separated.

Flag Types of 2013
Serpentine Die Cut 13¼
2013, Dec. 11 Litho.
Booklet Stamps
Self-Adhesive

2693 A1098 63c multi .90 .25
2694 A1099 63c multi .90 .25
2695 A1100 63c multi .90 .25
2696 A1101 63c multi .90 .25
2697 A1102 63c multi .90 .25
a. Booklet pane of 10, 2 each #2693-2697 9.00
Nos. 2693-2697 (5) 4.50 1.25

Queen Elizabeth II Type of 2013
Serpentine Die Cut 13¼
2013, Dec. 11 Litho.
Booklet Stamp
Self-Adhesive

2698 A1103 63c multi .90 .25
a. Booklet pane of 10 9.00

New Year 2014 (Year of the Horse) — A1133

Design: $1.85, Horse, diff.

Litho. & Embossed
2014, Jan. 13 ***Perf. 12½***

2699 A1133 63c multi .90 .30

Litho. & Embossed With Foil Application
Souvenir Sheet

2700 A1133 $1.85 multi 2.75 2.75
a. Souvenir sheet of 2, #2600, 2700 5.50 5.50

Litho. With Foil Application
Booklet Stamp
Self-Adhesive
Serpentine Die Cut 13½

2701 A1133 $1.85 multi 2.75 2.40
a. Booklet pane of 6 16.50

African-Canadian Neighborhoods — A1134

Residents and buildings of: No. 2702, Africville, neighborhood of Halifax, Nova Scotia. No. 2703, Hogan's Alley, neighborhood of Vancouver, British Columbia.

Serpentine Die Cut 13¼
2014, Jan. 30 Litho.
Booklet Stamps
Self-Adhesive

2702 A1134 63c multi .90 .35
a. Booklet pane of 10 9.00
2703 A1134 63c multi .90 .35
a. Booklet pane of 10 9.00

Female Athletes — A1135

Designs: Nos. 2704a, 2705, Barbara Ann Scott (1928-2012), figure skater. Nos. 2704b, 2706, Sandra Schmirler (1963-2000), curler. Nos. 2704c, 2707, Sarah Burke (1982-2012), freestyle skier.

2014, Feb. 3 Litho. ***Perf. 13***
Souvenir Sheet

2704 Sheet of 3 2.75 2.75
a.-c. A1135 63c Any single .90 .90

Booklet Stamps
Self-Adhesive
Serpentine Die Cut 13¼

2705 A1135 63c multi .90 .30
a. Booklet pane of 10 9.00
2706 A1135 63c multi .90 .30
a. Booklet pane of 10 9.00
2707 A1135 63c multi .90 .30
a. Booklet pane of 10 9.00
Nos. 2705-2707 (3) 2.70 .90

Beneficial Insects Type of 2007

Design: 22c, Monarch butterfly.

2014, Mar. 31 Litho. ***Perf. 13¼x13***

2708 A942 22c multi .30 .25

Juvenile Wildlife Type of 2011

Designs: P, Beaver kits. $1, Burrowing owl chicks. $1.20, Mountain goat kid. $1.80, Puffin chicks. $2.50, Newborn wapiti.

2014, Mar. 31 Litho. ***Perf. 13¼x13***

2709 Souvenir sheet of 5 11.00 10.00
a. A1038 P multi 1.25 .90
b. A1038 $1 multi 1.50 1.50
c. A1038 $1.20 multi 1.75 1.60
d. A1038 $1.80 multi 2.60 2.50
e. A1038 $2.50 multi 3.75 3.75

Coil Stamps
Self-Adhesive
Die Cut Perf. 13½

2710 A1038 $1 multi 1.50 .25

Serpentine Die Cut 9¼ Horiz.

2710A A1038 P multi 1.40 1.40

Serpentine Die Cut 8¼ Horiz.

2711 A1038 P multi 1.25 .25
2712 A1038 $1.20 multi 1.75 .30
2713 A1038 $1.80 multi 2.60 .60
2714 A1038 $2.50 multi 3.75 .90
Nos. 2710-2714 (5) 10.85 2.30

Booklet Stamps
Serpentine Die Cut 9¼ Horiz.

2715 A1038 $1.20 multi 1.75 .30
a. Booklet pane of 6 10.50
2716 A1038 $1.80 multi 2.60 .60
a. Booklet pane of 6 15.50
2717 A1038 $2.50 multi 3.75 .90
a. Booklet pane of 6 22.50
Nos. 2715-2717 (3) 8.10 1.80

On day of issue, Nos. 2709a, 2710A, 2711 each sold for 85c. On rolls of No. 2710A, stamps do not touch each other and pairs are horizontal. On rolls of No. 2711, stamps touch each other and pairs are vertical.

Gros Morne National Park, Newfoundland and Labrador A1136

Joggins Fossil Cliffs, Nova Scotia A1137

Canadian Rocky Mountain Parks, Alberta and British Columbia A1138

Nahinni National Park, Northwest Territories A1139

Miguasha National Park, Quebec — A1140

2014, Mar. 31 Litho. ***Perf. 13¼x13***

2718 Souvenir sheet of 5 6.25 5.75
a. A1136 P multi 1.25 .90
b. A1137 P multi 1.25 .90
c. A1138 P multi 1.25 .90
d. A1139 P multi 1.25 .90
e. A1140 P multi 1.25 .90

Booklet Stamps
Self-Adhesive
Serpentine Die Cut 13¼

2719 A1136 P multi 1.25 .25
2720 A1139 P multi 1.25 .25
2721 A1137 P multi 1.25 .25
2722 A1140 P multi 1.25 .25
2723 A1138 P multi 1.25 .25
a. Booklet pane of 10, 2 each #2719-2723 12.50
b. Booklet pane of 30, 6 each #2719-2723 37.50
Nos. 2719-2723 (5) 6.25 1.25

UNESCO World Heritage Sites. On day of issue, Nos. 2718a-2718f, 2719-2723 each sold for 85c.

Shiva Natajara Sculpture, Mummified Cat and Bison — A1141

Hadrasaur Skeleton and Luohan Chinese Sculpture A1142

2014, Apr. 14 Litho. ***Perf. 12½***

2724 Souvenir sheet of 2 2.50 2.50
a. A1141 P multi 1.25 .90
b. A1142 P multi 1.25 .90

Booklet Stamps
Self-Adhesive
Serpentine Die Cut 13½x13¼

2725 A1141 P multi 1.25 .30
2726 A1142 P multi 1.25 .30
a. Booklet pane of 10, 5 each #2725-2726 12.50

Royal Ontario Museum, cent. On day of issue, Nos. 2724a-2724b, 2725-2726 each sold for 85c.

Roses
A1143 A1144

Rose varieties: Nos. 2727a, 2729, 2730, Konrad Henkel (red) rose. Nos. 2727b, 2728, 2731, Maid of Honor (white) rose.

2014, Apr. 23 Litho. ***Perf. 13***
Souvenir Sheet

2727 Sheet of 2 2.50 2.50
a.-b. A1143 P Either single 1.25 .90

Coil Stamps
Self-Adhesive
Serpentine Die Cut 8¼ Horiz.

2728 A1144 P multi 1.25 .30
2729 A1144 P multi 1.25 .30
a. Vert. pair, #2728-2729 2.50

Booklet Stamps
Serpentine Die Cut 13¼

2730 A1143 P multi 1.25 .30
2731 A1143 P multi 1.25 .30
a. Booklet pane of 10, 5 each #2730-2731 12.50
Nos. 2728-2731 (4) 5.00 1.20

On day of issue, Nos. 2727a-2727b, 2728-2731 each sold for 85c.

Komagata Maru Incident, Cent. — A1145

Serpentine Die Cut 13x12¾
2014, May 1 Litho.
Booklet Stamp
Self-Adhesive

2732 A1145 $2.50 multi 3.75 1.50
a. Booklet pane of 6 22.50

National Film Board, 75th Anniv. — A1146

Scenes from Canadian films: Nos. 2733a, 2734, *Flamenco at 5:15*, 1983. Nos. 2733b, 2735, *The Railrodder*, 1965. Nos. 2733c, 2736, *Mon Oncle Antoine*, 1971. Nos. 2733d, 2737, *Log Driver's Waltz*, 1979. Nos. 2733e, 2738, *Neighbours*, 1952.

2014, May 2 Litho. ***Perf. 13¼x12½***

2733 A1146 Sheet of 5 + label 6.25 6.00
a.-e. P Any single 1.25 .90

Booklet Stamps
Self-Adhesive
Serpentine Die Cut 13¼

2734 A1146 P multi 1.25 .30
2735 A1146 P multi 1.25 .30
2736 A1146 P multi 1.25 .30
2737 A1146 P multi 1.25 .30
2738 A1146 P multi 1.25 .30
a. Booklet pane of 10, 2 each #2734-2738 12.50
Nos. 2734-2738 (5) 6.25 1.50

On day of issue, Nos. 2733a-2733e and 2734-2738 each sold for 85c.

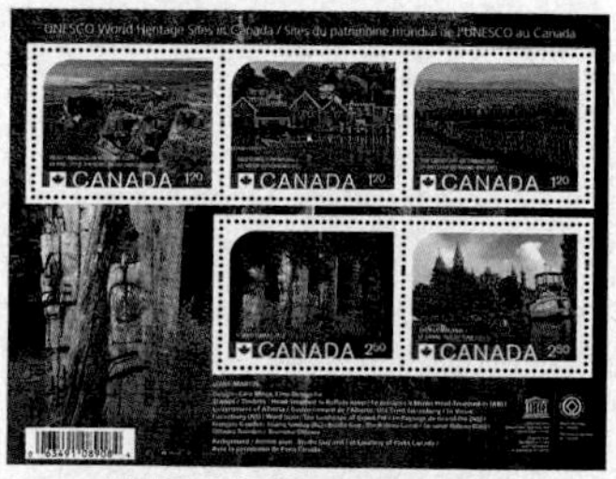
UNESCO World Heritage Sites — A1147

Designs: Nos. 2739a, 2741, Head-Smashed-In Buffalo Jump, Alberta. Nos. 2739b, 2740, Old Town Lunenburg, Nova Scotia. Nos. 2739c, 2742, Landscape of Grand Pré, Nova Scotia. Nos. 2739d, 2743, SGang Gwaay, British Columbia. Nos. 2739e, 2744, Rideau Canal, Ontario.

2014, May 16 Litho. ***Perf. 12½***
Miniature Sheet

2739 A1147 Sheet of 5 12.75 11.00
a.-c. $1.20 Any single 1.75 1.50
d.-e. $2.50 Either single 3.75 2.20

Booklet Stamps
Self-Adhesive
Serpentine Die Cut 13¼x13½

2740 A1147 $1.20 multi 1.75 1.10
2741 A1147 $1.20 multi 1.75 1.10
2742 A1147 $1.20 multi 1.75 1.10
a. Booklet pane of 6, 2 each #2740-2742 10.50

2743 A1147 $2.50 multi 3.75 2.20
2744 A1147 $2.50 multi 3.75 2.20
a. Booklet pane of 6, 3 each #2743-2744 22.50
Nos. 2740-2744 (5) 12.75 7.70

Sinking of the RMS Empress of Ireland, Cent. — A1148

Designs: P, Empress of Ireland facing right. $2.50, Empress of Ireland facing left, horiz.

2014, May 29 Litho. *Perf. 12½*
2745 A1148 P multi 1.25 .45

Souvenir Sheet
Perf. 12¾
2746 A1148 $2.50 multi 3.75 3.25

Booklet Stamp
Self-Adhesive
Serpentine Die Cut 13½
2747 A1148 P multi 1.25 .30
a. Booklet pane of 10 12.50

On day of issue, Nos. 2745 and 2747 each sold for 85c. No. 2745 was printed in sheets of 16 + 4 labels. No. 2746 contains one 80x32mm stamp.

Haunted Canada A1149

Designs: Nos. 2748a, 2749, Ghost bride, Banff Springs, Alberta. Nos. 2748b, 2751, Ghost train, St. Louis, Saskatchewan. Nos. 2748c, 2753, Apparitions of Fort George, Ontario. Nos. 2748d, 2752, Count of Frontenac Apparition, Château Frontenac Hotel, Quebec. Nos. 2748e, 2750, Phantom ship off Nova Scotia and Prince Edward Island.

2014, June 13 Litho. *Perf. 12½*
2748 Sheet of 5 6.25 5.75
a.-e. A1149 P Any single 1.25 .90

Booklet Stamps
Self-Adhesive
Serpentine Die Cut 13¼
2749 A1149 P multi 1.25 .30
2750 A1149 P multi 1.25 .30
2751 A1149 P multi 1.25 .30
2752 A1149 P multi 1.25 .30
2753 A1149 P multi 1.25 .30
a. Booklet pane of 10, 2 each #2749-2753 12.50
Nos. 2749-2753 (5) 6.25 1.50

On day of issue, Nos. 2748a-2748e, 2749-2753 each sold for 85c.

Canadian Football League Team Emblems Type of 2012 and

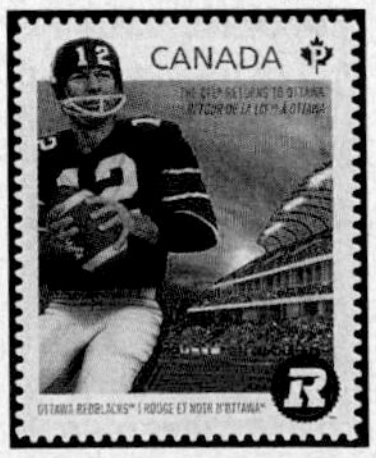

Russ Jackson in Ottawa Rough Riders Uniform, TD Place Stadium, Ottawa Redblacks Emblem A1150

Design: No. 2754, Ottawa Redblacks emblem.

Serpentine Die Cut 8¼ Horiz.
2014, June 19 Litho.

Coil Stamp
Self-Adhesive
2754 A1080 P multi 1.25 .30

Booklet Stamp
2755 A1150 P multi 1.25 .30
a. Booklet pane of 10 12.50

On day of issue, Nos. 2754 and 2755 each sold for 85c.

Photography Type of 2013

Designs: Nos. 2756a, 2762, Unidentified Chinese Man, by C. D. Hoy, c. 1912. Nos. 2756b, 2759, St. Joseph's Convent School, by Michel Lambeth, 1960. Nos. 2756c, 2763, Sitting Bull and Buffalo Bill, Montreal, by William Notman, 1885. Nos. 2757a, 2761, Untitled, by Lynne Cohen, 1970, horiz. Nos. 2757b, 2760, La Ville de Québec en Hiver (Quebec City in Winter), by Louis-Prudent Vallée, 1894, horiz. Nos. 2757c, 2758, Bogner's Grocery, by Fred Herzog, 1960, horiz. Nos. 2757d, 2764, Railcuts: #1, by Edward Burtynsky, 1985, horiz.

2014, July 7 Litho. *Perf. 13¼*
2756 Sheet of 3 4.25 3.50
a.-b. A1109 P Either single 1.25 .90
c. A1109 $1.20 multi 1.75 1.50
2757 Sheet of 4 7.50 7.50
a.-c. A1109 P Any single 1.25 .90
d. A1109 $2.50 multi 3.75 3.75

Booklet Stamps
Self-Adhesive
Serpentine Die Cut 13¼
2758 A1109 P multi 1.25 .30
2759 A1109 P multi 1.25 .30
2760 A1109 P multi 1.25 .30
2761 A1109 P multi 1.25 .30
2762 A1109 P multi 1.25 .30
a. Booklet pane of 10, 2 each #2758-2762 12.50
2763 A1109 $1.20 multi 1.75 .65
a. Booklet pane of 6 10.50
2764 A1109 $2.50 multi 3.75 1.10
a. Booklet pane of 6 22.50
Nos. 2758-2764 (7) 11.75 3.25

On day of issue, Nos. 2756a-2756b, 2757a-2757c, 2758-2762 each sold for 85c.

Hank Snow (1914-99), Country Music Recording Artist A1151

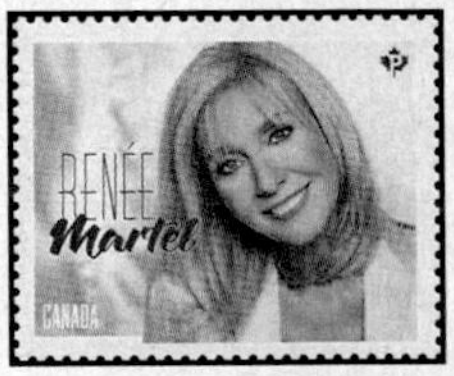

Renée Martel, Country Music Recording Artist A1152

Shania Twain, Country Music Recording Artist A1153

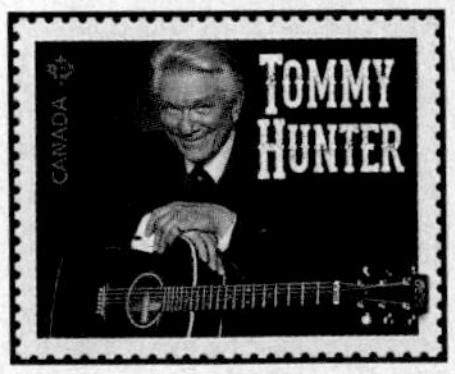

Tommy Hunter, Country Music Recording Artist A1154

K. D. Lang, Country Music Recording Artist A1155

2014, July 31 Litho. *Perf. 12½*
2765 Sheet of 5 6.25 5.75
a. A1151 P multi 1.25 .90
b. A1152 P multi 1.25 .90
c. A1153 P multi 1.25 .90
d. A1154 P multi 1.25 .90
e. A1155 P multi 1.25 .90

Booklet Stamps
Self-Adhesive
Serpentine Die Cut 13¼
2766 A1151 P multi 1.25 .30
a. Booklet pane of 10 12.50
2767 A1152 P multi 1.25 .30
a. Booklet pane of 10 12.50
2768 A1153 P multi 1.25 .30
a. Booklet pane of 10 12.50
2769 A1154 P multi 1.25 .30
a. Booklet pane of 10 12.50
2770 A1155 P multi 1.25 .30
a. Booklet pane of 10 12.50
Nos. 2766-2770 (5) 6.25 1.50

On day of issue, Nos. 2765a-2765e, 2766-2770 each sold for 85c.

Canadian Museum for Human Rights, Winnipeg A1156

Serpentine Die Cut 13¼
2014, Aug. 20 Litho.

Booklet Stamp
Self-Adhesive
2771 A1156 P multi 1.25 .30
a. Booklet pane of 10 12.50

No. 2771 sold for 85c on day of issue.

Comedians — A1157

Designs: Nos. 2772a, 2773, Mike Myers. Nos. 2772b, 2774, Martin Short. Nos. 2772c, 2775, Catherine O'Hara. Nos. 2772d, 2776, Olivier Guimond (1914-71). Nos. 2772e, 2777, Jim Carrey.

2014, Aug. 29 Litho. *Perf. 12½x13*
2772 Sheet of 5 + label 6.25 5.75
a.-e. A1157 P Any single 1.25 .90

Booklet Stamps
Self-Adhesive
Serpentine Die Cut 13¼
2773 A1157 P multi 1.25 .30
a. Booklet pane of 10, #2774-2777, 6#2773 12.50
2774 A1157 P multi 1.25 .30
a. Booklet pane of 10, #2773, 2775-2777, 6#2774 12.50
2775 A1157 P multi 1.25 .30
a. Booklet pane of 10, #2773-2774, 2776-2777, 6#2775 12.50
2776 A1157 P multi 1.25 .30
a. Booklet pane of 10, #2773-2775, 2777, 6#2776 12.50
2777 A1157 P multi 1.25 .30
a. Booklet pane of 10, #2773-2776, 6#2777 12.50
Nos. 2773-2777 (5) 6.25 1.50

On day of issue, Nos. 2772a-2772e, 2773-2777 each sold for 85c.

Zamboni With Canadian National Hockey League Team Emblems — A1158

Zamboni with emblem of: Nos. 2778a, 2779, Winnipeg Jets. Nos. 2778b, 2780, Ottawa Senators. Nos. 2778c, 2781, Toronto Maple Leafs. Nos. 2778d, 2782, Montreal Canadiens. Nos. 2778e, 2783, Vancouver Canucks. Nos. 2778f, 2784, Calgary Flames. Nos. 2778g, 2785, Edmonton Oilers.

2014, Oct. 3 Litho. *Perf. 13¼x13*
Miniature Sheet
2778 Sheet of 7 8.75 8.25
a.-g. A1158 P Any single 1.25 .90

Coil Stamps
Self-Adhesive
Serpentine Die Cut 8¼ Horiz.
2779 A1158 P multi 1.25 .30
2780 A1158 P multi 1.25 .30
2781 A1158 P multi 1.25 .30
2782 A1158 P multi 1.25 .30
2783 A1158 P multi 1.25 .30
2784 A1158 P multi 1.25 .30
2785 A1158 P multi 1.25 .30
Nos. 2779-2785 (7) 8.75 2.10

On day of issue, Nos. 2778a-2778g, 2779-2785 each sold for 85c.

Defensemen in National Hockey League Hall of Fame — A1159

Designs: Nos. 2786a, 2787a, 2788, Tim Horton (1930-74). Nos. 2786b, 2787b, 2789, Doug Harvey. Nos. 2786c, 2787c, 2790, Bobby Orr. Nos. 2786d, 2787d, 2791, Harry Howell. Nos. 2786e, 2787e, 2792, Pierre Pilote. Nos. 2786f, 2787f, 2793, Red Kelly.

Litho., Sheet Margin Litho. & Embossed With Foil Application
2014, Oct. 3 *Perf. 12½x13*
Miniature Sheet
2786 Sheet of 6 7.50 6.50
a.-f. A1159 P Any single 1.25 .90

Litho.
Booklet Stamps
Self-Adhesive
Serpentine Die Cut 13¼x13½
2787 Booklet pane of 6 7.50
a.-f. A1159 P Any single 1.25 .30

Souvenir Sheets
Serpentine Die Cut 13½x13¼
2788 A1159 $2.50 multi 3.75 1.80
2789 A1159 $2.50 multi 3.75 1.80
2790 A1159 $2.50 multi 3.75 1.80
2791 A1159 $2.50 multi 3.75 1.80
2792 A1159 $2.50 multi 3.75 1.80
2793 A1159 $2.50 multi 3.75 1.80
Nos. 2788-2793 (6) 22.50 10.80

Nos. 2786a-2786f, 2787a-2787f each sold for 85c on day of issue. Nos. 2788-2793 each contain one 52x78mm stamp. Nos, 2788-2793 were sold together in a sealed opaque plastic package. One of every 50 packages contained a souvenir sheet that was autographed by one of the 5 living players depicted.

"Wait for Me Daddy," Photograph by Claude P. Dettloff — A1160

2014, Oct. 4 Litho. *Perf. 13½x13¼*
2794 A1160 P multi 1.25 .45

Booklet Stamp
Self-Adhesive
Serpentine Die Cut 13¼x13½
2795 A1160 P multi 1.25 .30
a. Booklet pane of 10 12.50

Dedication of statue depicting photograph in New Westminster, British Columbia. Nos. 2794 and 2795 each sold for 85c on day of issue. No. 2794 was printed in sheets of 5.

Santa Claus A1161

The Virgin and Child with St. John the Baptist, by Abraham Janssens van Nuyssen A1162

Santa Claus: P, Writing letter. $1.20, Carrying sack. $2.50, With dove.

2014, Oct. 23 Litho. *Perf. 13½x13¼*
Souvenir Sheet
2796 Sheet of 3 6.75 5.25
a. A1161 P multi 1.25 .90
b. A1161 $1.20 multi 1.75 1.50
c. A1161 $2.50 multi 3.75 2.60

Booklet Stamps
Self-Adhesive

Serpentine Die Cut 13½

2797	A1162	P multi	1.25	.25
a.		Booklet pane of 12	15.00	

Serpentine Die Cut 13¼x13

2798	A1161	P multi	1.25	.25
a.		Booklet pane of 12	15.00	
2799	A1161	$1.20 multi	1.75	.60
a.		Booklet pane of 6	10.50	
2800	A1161	$2.50 multi	3.75	.90
a.		Booklet pane of 6	27.00	
		Nos. 2797-2800 (4)	8.00	2.00

Christmas. Nos. 2796a, 2797 and 2798 each sold for 85c on day of issue.

New Year 2015 (Year of the Ram) — A1163

Design: $2.50, Ram facing left.

Litho. & Embossed With Foil Application

2015, Jan. 8 *Perf. 12½*

2801	A1163	P multi	1.25	.35

Souvenir Sheet

2802	A1163	$2.50 multi	3.75	3.50
a.		Souvenir sheet of 2, #2700, 2802	6.50	5.75

Litho. With Foil Application

Booklet Stamp
Self-Adhesive

Serpentine Die Cut 13½

2803	A1163	$2.50 multi	3.75	1.65
a.		Booklet pane of 6	22.50	

No. 2801 sold for 85c on day of issue.

Sir John A. Macdonald (1815-91), First Prime Minister of Canada A1164

Serpentine Die Cut 13¼

2015, Jan. 11 **Litho.**

Self-Adhesive
Booklet Stamp

2804	A1164	P multi	1.25	.30
a.		Booklet pane of 10	12.50	

No. 2804 sold for 85c on day of issue.

Nelson Mandela (1918-2013), President of South Africa — A1165

2015, Jan. 30 **Litho.** *Perf. 12½x13*

Souvenir Sheet

2805	A1165	$2.50 multi	3.75	3.25

Booklet Stamp
Self-Adhesive
Size: 33x33mm

Serpentine Die Cut 13¼

2806	A1165	P multi	1.25	.30
a.		Booklet pane of 10	12.50	

No. 2806 sold for 85c on day of issue.

A1166

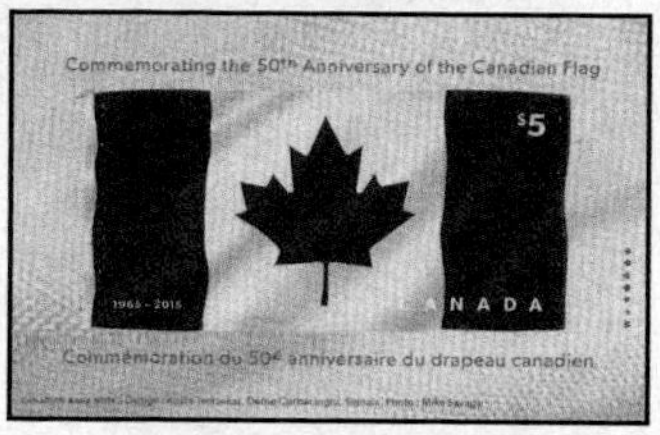

Canadian Flag, 50th Anniv. — A1167

Serpentine Die Cut 13¼x13½

2015, Feb. 15 **Litho.**

Booklet Stamp
Self-Adhesive

2807	A1166	P multi	1.25	.30
a.		Booklet pane of 10	12.50	

Souvenir Sheet
On Rayon Fabric

Serpentine Die Cut 9½

2808	A1167	$5 multi	7.50	3.50

No. 2807 sold for 85c on day of issue.

Pansies
A1168 A1169

Designs: Nos. 2809a, 2810, 2812, Delta Premium Pure Light Blue pansy (blue and yellow flower). No. 2809b, 2811, 2813, Midnight Glow pansy (purple and yellow flower).

2015, Mar. 2 **Litho.** *Perf. 13x13¼*

Souvenir Sheet

2809		Sheet of 2	2.50	2.50
a.-b.	A1168	P Either single	1.25	.90

Coil Stamps
Self-Adhesive

Serpentine Die Cut 8¼ Horiz.

2810	A1169	P multi	1.25	.30
2811	A1169	P multi	1.25	.30
a.		Vert. pair, #2810-2811	2.50	

Booklet Stamps

Serpentine Die Cut 13½

2812	A1168	P multi	1.25	.30
2813	A1168	P multi	1.25	.30
a.		Booklet pane of 10, 5 each #2812-2813	12.50	

On day of issue Nos. 2809a-2809b, 2810-2813 each sold for 85c.

Photography Type of 2013

Designs: Nos. 2814a, 2820, Shoeshine Stand, by Nina Raginsky, 1974. Nos. 2814b, 2817, Southan Sisters, Montreal, by Harold Mortimer-Lamb, c. 1915-19, horiz. Nos. 2814c, 2822, La Voie Lactée, by Geneviève Cadieux, 1992, horiz. Nos. 2815a, 2816, Angels, Saint-Jean-Baptiste Day, by Sam Tata, 1962, horiz. Nos. 2815b, 2819, Isaac's First Swim, Lambton County, Ontario, Canada, by Larry Towell, 1996, horiz. Nos. 2815c, 2818, Friends and Family and Trips. In Front of Simpsons, by Conrad Poirer, 1936, horiz. Nos. 2815d, 2821, Alex Colville on the Tantramar Marshes, by Geoffrey James, c. 1970, horiz.

2015, Apr. 8 **Litho.** *Perf. 12¾*

2814	A1109	Sheet of 3	6.25	6.00
a.-b.		P Either single	1.25	.90
c.		$2.50 multi	3.75	3.75
2815	A1109	Sheet of 4	5.50	5.00
a.-c.		P Any single	1.25	.90
d.		$1.20 multi	1.75	1.50

Booklet Stamps
Self-Adhesive

Serpentine Die Cut 13¼

2816	A1109	P multi	1.25	.30
2817	A1109	P multi	1.25	.30
2818	A1109	P multi	1.25	.30
2819	A1109	P multi	1.25	.30
2820	A1109	P multi	1.25	.30
a.		Booklet pane of 10, 2 each #2816-2820	12.50	
2821	A1109	$1.20 multi	1.75	.65
a.		Booklet pane of 6	10.50	
2822	A1109	$2.50 multi	3.75	1.50
a.		Booklet pane of 6	22.50	
		Nos. 2816-2822 (7)	11.75	3.65

On day of issue, Nos. 2814a-2814b, 2815a-2815c, 2816-2820 each sold for 85c.

Dinosaurs A1170

Designs: Nos. 2823a, 2827, Euplocephalus tutus (33x28mm). Nos. 2823b, 2826, Chasmosaurus belli (28x28mm). Nos. 2823c, 2824, Tyrannosaurus rex. Nos. 2823d, 2828, Ornithomimus edmontonicus. Nos. 2823e, 2825, Tylosaurus pembinensis.

Litho. & Embossed With Foil Application

Serpentine Die Cut 13¼

2015, Apr. 3 **Self-Adhesive**

2823		Sheet of 5	6.25	5.75
a.-e.	A1170	P Any single	1.25	.90

Booklet Stamps

Litho. With Foil Application

2824	A1170	P multi	1.25	.30
2825	A1170	P multi	1.25	.30
2826	A1170	P multi	1.25	.30
2827	A1170	P multi	1.25	.30
2828	A1170	P multi	1.25	.30
a.		Booklet pane of 10, 2 each #2824-2828	12.50	

On day of issue, Nos. 2823a-2823e, 2824-2828 each sold for 85c.

Love Your Pet A1171

Designs: Nos. 2829a, 2830, Cat in head cone sniffing flowers. Nos. 2829b, 2831, Dog chasing snowball. Nos. 2829c, 2832, Veterinarian examining cat. Nos. 2829d, 2834, Dog drinking water from bowl. Nos. 2829e, 2833, Cat on leash wearing identification tags.

2015, May 2 **Litho.** *Perf. 13*

2829		Sheet of 5	6.25	5.75
a.-e.	A1171	P Any single	1.25	.90

Booklet Stamps
Self-Adhesive

Serpentine Die Cut 13¼

2830	A1171	P multi	1.25	.30
2831	A1171	P multi	1.25	.30
2832	A1171	P multi	1.25	.30
2833	A1171	P multi	1.25	.30
2834	A1171	P multi	1.25	.30
a.		Booklet pane of 10, 2 each #2830-2834	12.50	
		Nos. 2830-2834 (5)	6.25	1.50

On day of issue, Nos. 2829a-2829e, 2830-2834 each sold for 85c.

In Flanders Fields, Poem by John McCrae, Cent. A1172

2015, May 3 **Litho.** *Perf. 12½*

2835	A1172	P multi	1.25	.45

Booklet Stamp
Self-Adhesive

Serpentine Die Cut 13¼x13½

2836	A1172	P multi	1.25	.30
a.		Booklet pane of 10	12.50	

On day of issue, Nos. 2835-2836 each sold for 85c. No. 2835 was printed in sheets of 5.

2015 Women's World Cup Soccer Championships, Canada — A1173

Serpentine Die Cut 13¼x13½

2015, May 6 **Litho.**

Booklet Stamp
Self-Adhesive

2837	A1173	P multi	1.25	.30
a.		Booklet pane of 10	12.50	

No. 2837 sold for 85c on day of issue.

Weather Phenomena — A1174

Designs: Nos. 2838a, 2839, Lightning. Nos. 2838b, 2842, Double rainbow. Nos. 2838c, 2843, Sun dog over Iqaluit, Nunavut. Nos. 2838d, 2841, Fog near Cape Spear Lighthouse. Nos. 2838e, 2840, Hoar frost on tree.

Perf. 12½x13¼

2015, June 18 **Litho.**

2838	A1174	Sheet of 5 + label	6.25	5.75
a.-e.		P Any single	1.25	.90

Booklet Stamps
Self-Adhesive

Serpentine Die Cut 13¼

2839	A1174	P multi	1.25	.30
2840	A1174	P multi	1.25	.30
2841	A1174	P multi	1.25	.30
2842	A1174	P multi	1.25	.30
2843	A1174	P multi	1.25	.30
a.		Booklet pane of 10, 2 each #2839-2843	12.50	

Nos. 2838a-2838e, 2839-2843 each sold for 85c on day of issue.

Hoodoos, Alberta A1175

Wood Buffalo National Park, Alberta and Northwest Territories A1176

Red Bay Basque Whaling Station, Newfoundland and Labrador — A1177

Waterton Glacier International Peace Park, Alberta and Montana — A1178

Kluane National Park, Yukon, Wrangell-St. Elias and Glacier Bay National Parks, Alaska, Tatshenshini-Alsek Park, British Columbia — A1179

2015, July 3 Litho. *Perf. 12½*

2844	Sheet of 5	*42.50*	*42.50*
a.	A1175 $1.20 multi	*30.00*	*15.00*
b.	A1176 $1.20 multi	1.80	.90
c.	A1177 $1.20 multi	1.80	.90
d.	A1178 $2.50 multi	3.75	1.90
e.	A1179 $2.50 multi	3.75	1.90

Booklet Stamps
Self-Adhesive

Serpentine Die Cut 13¼

2845	A1175 $1.20 multi	*15.00*	*7.50*
2846	A1177 $1.20 multi	1.80	.90
2847	A1176 $1.20 multi	1.80	.90
a.	Booklet pane of 6, 2 each #2845-2847	*37.50*	
2848	A1178 $2.50 multi	3.75	1.90
2849	A1179 $2.50 multi	3.75	1.90
a.	Booklet pane of 6, 3 each #2848-2849	22.50	

UNESCO World Heritage Sites. Nos. 2844 and 2847a were withdrawn from sale on July 6 after it was discovered that illustration A1175 shows hoodoos not located in Dinosaur Provincial Park in Alberta. See Nos. 2857-2858.

Alice Munro, 2013 Nobel Literature Laureate — A1180

Serpentine Die Cut 13¾

2015, July 10 Litho.

Booklet Stamp
Self-Adhesive

2850	A1180 P multi	1.25	.30
a.	Booklet pane of 10	12.50	

No. 2850 sold for 85c on day of issue.

HMS Erebus Trapped in Ice — A1181

Map of Northern Canadian Islands — A1182

Wreckage and Diagram of HMS Erebus — A1183

Litho & Embossed, Litho (A1183)

2015, Aug. 6 *Perf. 12½*

2851	A1181 P multi	1.40	.70
2852	A1182 P multi	1.40	.70
a.	Horiz. pair, #2851-2852	2.80	1.40

Souvenir Sheet

Perf. 13¼

2853	A1183 $2.50 multi	3.75	1.90

Booklet Stamps
Self-Adhesive

Serpentine Die Cut 13½x13¼

2854	A1181 P multi	1.40	.70
2855	A1182 P multi	1.40	.70
a.	Booklet pane of 10, 5 each #2854-2855	14.00	

Serpentine Die Cut 13¼x13¾

2856	A1183 $2.50 multi	3.75	1.90
a.	Booklet pane of 6	22.50	
	Nos. 2854-2856 (3)	6.55	3.30

Discovery of wreckage of HMS Erebus, 1st anniv. Nos. 2851-2852, 2854-2855 each sold for 85c on day of issue.

Dinosaur Provincial Park, Alberta A1184

2015, Aug. 21 Litho. *Perf. 12½*

2857	Sheet of 5, #2844b-2844e, 2857a	14.00	14.00
a.	A1184 $1.20 multi	1.90	.95

Booklet Stamp
Self-Adhesive

2858	A1184 $1.20 multi	1.90	.95
a.	Booklet pane of 6, 2 each #2846, 2847, 2858	11.50	

UNESCO World Heritage Sites. Nos. 2857a and 2858 show correct images of landscapes in Dinosaur Provincial Park.

Queen Elizabeth II, Longest-Reigning British Monarch — A1185

Serpentine Die Cut 13¼

2015, Sept. 9 Litho.

Booklet Stamp
Self-Adhesive

2859	A1185 P multi	1.40	.70
a.	Booklet pane of 10	14.00	

No. 2859 sold for 85c on day of issue.

Haunted Canada — A1186

Designs: Nos. 2860a, 2861, Brakeman ghost, Vancouver, British Columbia. Nos. 2860b, 2864, Red River Trail Oxcart, Winnipeg, Manitoba. Nos. 2860c, 2863, Gray Lady of the Citadel, Halifax, Nova Scotia. Nos. 2860d, 2862, Ghost of Marie-Josephte Corriveau, Lévis, Quebec. Nos. 2860e, 2865, Ghost of Caribou Hotel, Carcross, Yukon.

Litho. With Holographic Foil

2015, Sept. 14 *Perf. 12½x13*

2860	A1186 Sheet of 5	7.00	7.00
a.-e.	P Any single	1.40	.70

Booklet Stamps
Self-Adhesive

Serpentine Die Cut 13¼

2861	A1186 P multi	1.40	.70
2862	A1186 P multi	1.40	.70
2863	A1186 P multi	1.40	.70
2864	A1186 P multi	1.40	.70
2865	A1186 P multi	1.40	.70
a.	Booklet pane of 10, 2 each #2861-2865	14.00	
	Nos. 2861-2865 (5)	7.00	3.50

On day of issue, Nos. 2860a-2860e, 2861-2865 each sold for 85c.

A1187

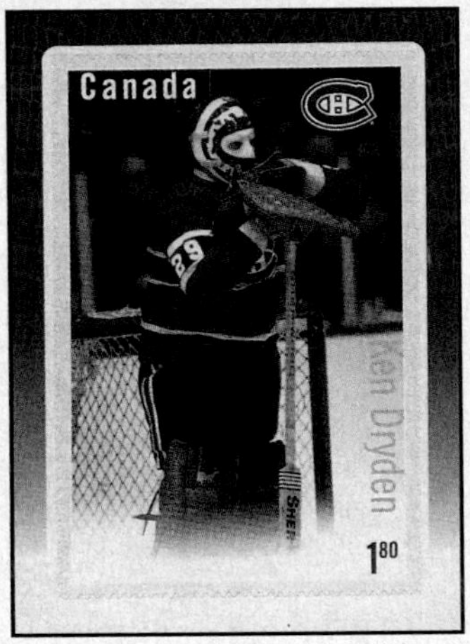

Hockey Goaltenders — A1188

Designs: Nos. 2866a, 2867, 2873, Ken Dryden. Nos. 2866b, 2868, 2874, Tony Esposito. Nos. 2866c, 2869, 2875, Johnny Bower. Nos. 2866d, 2870, 2876, Gump Worsley (1929-2007). Nos. 2866e, 2871, 2877, Bernie Parent. Nos. 2866f, 2872, 2878, Martin Brodeur.

Litho., Sheet Margin Litho. & Embossed With Foil Application

2015, Oct. 2 *Perf. 12½*

2866	Sheet of 6 + 3 labels	8.50	8.50
a.-f.	A1187 P Any single	1.40	.70

Booklet Stamps
Self-Adhesive

Serpentine Die Cut 13¼x13½

2867	A1187 P multi	1.40	.70
2868	A1187 P multi	1.40	.70
2869	A1187 P multi	1.40	.70
2870	A1187 P multi	1.40	.70
2871	A1187 P multi	1.40	.70
2872	A1187 P multi	1.40	.70
a.	Booklet pane of 6, #2867-2872	8.50	
	Nos. 2867-2872 (6)	8.40	4.20

Souvenir Sheets

Serpentine Die Cut 13½x13¼

2873	A1188 $1.80 multi	2.75	1.40
2874	A1188 $1.80 multi	2.75	1.40
2875	A1188 $1.80 multi	2.75	1.40
2876	A1188 $1.80 multi	2.75	1.40
2877	A1188 $1.80 multi	2.75	1.40
2878	A1188 $1.80 multi	2.75	1.40
	Nos. 2873-2878 (6)	16.50	8.40

Nos. 2866a-2866f, 2867-2872 each sold for 85c on day of issue. Nos. 2873-2878 each contain one 52x78mm stamp. Nos. 2873-2878 were sold together in a sealed opaque plastic package. One of every 40 packages contained a souvenir sheet signed by Esposito, Bower, Parent or Brodeur.

A1189

Christmas — A1190

Designs: Nos. 2879a, 2881, Moose. Nos. 2879b, 2882, Beaver. Nos. 2879c, 2883, Polar bear. No. 2880, Adoration of the Magi, by Adriaen Isenbrandt.

2015, Nov. 2 Litho. *Perf. 13¾x13¼*

2879	Sheet of 3	7.50	7.50
a.	A1189 P multi	1.40	.70
b.	A1189 $1.20 multi	1.90	.95
c.	A1189 $2.50 multi	4.00	2.00

Booklet Stamps
Self-Adhesive

Serpentine Die Cut 13¼x13½

2880	A1190 P multi	1.40	.70
a.	Booklet pane of 12	17.00	

Serpentine Die Cut 13¼x13

2881	A1189 P multi	1.40	.70
a.	Booklet pane of 12	17.00	
2882	A1189 $1.20 multi	1.90	.95
a.	Booklet pane of 6	11.50	
2883	A1189 $2.50 multi	4.00	2.00
a.	Booklet pane of 6	24.00	
	Nos. 2880-2883 (4)	8.70	4.35

Nos. 2879a, 2880 and 2881 each sold for 85c on day of issue.

New Year 2016 (Year of the Monkey) A1191

Design: $2.50, Monkey's head.

Litho. & Embossed With Foil Application

2016 *Perf. 13¼*

2884	A1191 P multi	1.25	.60

Souvenir Sheet

2885	A1191 $2.50 multi	3.75	3.75

Litho.

Booklet Stamps
Self-Adhesive

Serpentine Die Cut 13½

2886	A1191 P multi	1.25	.60
a.	Booklet pane of 10	12.50	
2887	A1191 $2.50 multi	3.75	1.90
a.	Booklet pane of 6	22.50	

Issued: Nos. 2884, 2886, 1/11; Nos. 2885, 2887, 2/1. Nos. 2884 and 2886 each sold for 85c on day of issue.

Queen Elizabeth II — A1192

Serpentine Die Cut 13½x13¾

2016, Jan. 11 Litho.

Booklet Stamp
Self-Adhesive

2888	A1192 P multi	1.25	.60
a.	Booklet pane of 10	12.50	

No. 2888 sold for 85c on day of issue.

Landscape of Grand Pré, Nova Scotia A1193

Rideau Canal, Ontario A1194

SGang Gwaay, British Columbia — A1195

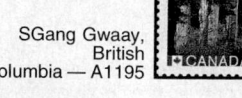

Head-Smashed-In Buffalo Jump, Alberta — A1196

Old Town Lunenburg, Nova Scotia — A1197

2016, Jan. 11 Litho. *Perf. 13¼x13*

Souvenir Sheet

2889	Sheet of 5	6.25	6.25
a.	A1193 P multi	1.25	.60
b.	A1194 P multi	1.25	.60
c.	A1195 P multi	1.25	.60
d.	A1196 P multi	1.25	.60
e.	A1197 P multi	1.25	.60

Booklet Stamps

Self-Adhesive

Serpentine Die Cut 13¾x13½

2890	A1193 P multi	1.25	.60
2891	A1195 P multi	1.25	.60
2892	A1197 P multi	1.25	.60
2893	A1194 P multi	1.25	.60
2894	A1196 P multi	1.25	.60
a.	Booklet pane of 10, 2 each #2890-2894	12.50	
b.	Booklet pane of 30, 6 each #2890-2894	37.50	

UNESCO World Heritage Sites. On day of issue, Nos. 2889a-2889e, 2890-2894 each sold for 85c.

SEMI-POSTAL STAMPS

Catalogue values for unused stamps in this section are for Never Hinged items.

Olympic Type of 1973

Size: 20x36mm

1974, Apr. 17 Litho. *Perf. 12½*

B1	A307	8c + 2c multi	.40	.40
B2	A307	10c + 5c multi	.60	.60
B3	A307	15c + 5c multi	.75	.75
		Nos. B1-B3 (3)	1.75	1.75

SP1

1975, Feb. 5 *Perf. 13*

B4	SP1	8c + 2c Swimming	.40	.40
B5	SP1	10c + 5c Rowing	.60	.60
B6	SP1	15c + 5c Sailing	.75	.75
		Nos. B4-B6 (3)	1.75	1.75

SP2

1975, Aug. 6

B7	SP2	8c + 2c Fencing	.40	.40
B8	SP2	10c + 5c Boxing	.60	.60
B9	SP2	15c + 5c Judo	.75	.75
		Nos. B7-B9 (3)	1.75	1.75

1976, Jan. 7

B10	SP2	8c + 2c Basketball	.40	.40
B11	SP2	10c + 5c Vaulting	.60	.60
B12	SP2	20c + 5c Soccer	.90	.90
		Nos. B10-B12 (3)	1.90	1.90

21st Olympic Games, Montreal, July 17-Aug. 1. The surtax was for the Canadian Olympic Committee.

Literacy — SP3

1996, Sept. 9 Litho. *Perf. 13x12½*

B13	SP3 45c +5c multi	1.00	.60
a.	Booklet pane of 10	10.00	
	Complete booklet	11.50	

No. B13 has die cut opening in center to represent missing puzzle piece.

Surcharge donated to ABC CANADA literacy organization.

Mental Health — SP4

Self-Adhesive

Booklet Stamp

Serpentine Die Cut 13¼

2008, Oct. 6 Litho.

B14	SP4 P +10c multi	1.40	.45
a.	Booklet pane of 10	14.00	

No. B14 had a franking value of 52c on day of issue. Surtax for Canada Post Foundation for Mental Health.

Mental Health — SP5

Self-Adhesive

Booklet Stamp

Serpentine Die Cut 13¼

2009, Sept. 14 Litho.

B15	SP5 P +10c multi	1.40	.45
a.	Booklet pane of 10	14.00	

No. B15 had a franking value of 54c on day of issue. Surtax for Canada Post Foundation for Mental Health.

Mental Health — SP6

Self-Adhesive

Booklet Stamp

Serpentine Die Cut 13¼

2010, Sept. 7 Litho.

B16	SP6 P + 10c multi	1.35	.45
a.	Booklet pane of 10	13.50	

No. B16 had a franking value of 57c on day of issue. Surtax for Canada Post Foundation for Mental Health.

Mental Health — SP7

2011, Sept. 6 Litho. *Perf. 12¾x13¼*

B17	Souvenir sheet of 2 #B17a	2.75	1.80
a.	SP7 P+10c multi	1.35	.75

Booklet Stamp

Self-Adhesive

Serpentine Die Cut 13¼

B18	SP7 P+10c multi	1.35	.45
a.	Booklet pane of 10	13.50	

Nos. B17a and B18 each had a franking value of 59c on day of issue. Surtax was for Canada Post Foundation for Mental Health.

Hands and Heart — SP8

Self-Adhesive

Serpentine Die Cut13x13¼

2012, Sept. 17 Litho.

Booklet Stamp

B19	SP8 P +10c multi	1.35	.45
a.	Booklet pane of 10	13.50	

No. B19 had a franking value of 61c on day of issue. Surtax for Canada Post Community Foundation.

Floating Abroad, Children's Art by Ezra Peters — SP9

Serpentine Die Cut 13x12½

2013, Sept. 30 Booklet Stamp

Self-Adhesive

B20	SP9 63c+10c multi	.95	.45
a.	Booklet pane of 10	9.50	

Surtax for Canada Post Community Foundation.

Children in Paper Sailboat SP10

Serpentine Die Cut 13½

2014, Sept. 29 Litho.

Booklet Stamp

Self-Adhesive

B21	SP10 P+10c multi	1.35	.45
a.	Booklet pane of 10	13.50	

No. B21 had a franking value of 85c. Surtax for Canada Post Community Foundation.

Children Reading Story Under Tented Bedsheet — SP11

Serpentine Die Cut 13x12½

2015, Sept. 28 Litho.

Booklet Stamp

Self-Adhesive

B22	SP11 P+10c multi	1.50	1.50
a.	Booklet pane of 10	15.00	

No. B22 had a franking value of 85c on day of issue. Surtax for Canada Post Community Foundation.

AIR POST STAMPS

Allegory of Flight — AP1

Unwmk.

1928, Sept. 21 Engr. *Perf. 12*

C1	AP1 5c brown olive	15.00	5.50
	Never hinged	27.50	
a.	Imperf., pair	275.00	
	Never hinged	375.00	

No. C1 is known imperforate horizontally and imperforate vertically.

For surcharge see No. C3.

For information on imperforate and part-perforate varieties, see note following No. 47a.

Allegory-Air Mail Circles Globe AP2

1930, Dec. 4 *Perf. 11*

C2	AP2 5c olive brown	70.00	24.00
	Never hinged	120.00	

For surcharge see No. C4.

No. C1 Surcharged

1932, Feb. 22 *Perf. 12*

C3	AP1 6c on 5c brown olive	11.00	4.00
	Never hinged	20.00	
a.	Inverted surcharge	225.00	
	Never hinged	325.00	
b.	Double surcharge	650.00	
	Never hinged	925.00	
c.	Triple surcharge	400.00	
	Never hinged	550.00	
d.	Pair, one without surcharge	950.00	
	Never hinged	1,350.	

Counterfeit surcharges exist.

No. C3b is valued in the grade of fine.

No. C2 Surcharged in Dark Blue

1932, July 12 *Perf. 11*

C4 AP2 6c on 5c olive brown 40.00 14.00
Never hinged 70.00

Daedalus
AP3

1935, June 1 *Perf. 12*

C5 AP3 6c red brown 4.25 1.25
Never hinged 6.00
a. Horiz. pair, imperf. vert. *7,500.*
b. Imperf., pair 600.00
Never hinged 900.00

No. C5a is unique and is the result of a pre-perforating paper foldover.

Mackenzie River Steamer and Seaplane
AP4

1938, June 15

C6 AP4 6c blue 3.75 .40
Never hinged 5.25
a. Imperf., pair 650.00
Never hinged 1,000.

Planes and Student Flyers
AP5

1942-43

C7 AP5 6c deep blue 6.50 1.30
Never hinged 7.50
a. Imperf., pair 650.00
Never hinged 1,000.
C8 AP5 7c deep blue ('43) 1.10 .25
Never hinged 1.60
a. Imperf., pair 650.00
Never hinged 1,000.

Canada's contribution to the war effort of the Allied Nations.

Catalogue values for unused stamps in this section, from this point to the end of the section, are for Never Hinged items.

Canada Geese in Flight — AP6

1946, Sept. 16

C9 AP6 7c deep blue 1.10 .25
a. Booklet pane of 4 4.00 3.50

For overprints see Nos. CO1, CO2.

AIR POST SPECIAL DELIVERY STAMPS

Trans-Canada Airplane and Aerial View of a City — APSD1

1942-43 Unwmk. Engr. *Perf. 12*

CE1 APSD1 16c bright ultra 2.50 2.00
Never hinged 3.50
a. Imperf., pair 650.00
Never hinged 1,025.
CE2 APSD1 17c brt ultra ('43) 3.25 3.00
Never hinged 4.75
a. Imperf., pair 650.00
Never hinged 1,025.

Canada's contribution to the war effort of the Allied Nations.

Catalogue values for unused stamps in this section, from this point to the end of the section, are for Never Hinged items.

DC-4 Transatlantic Mail Plane Over Quebec — APSD2

1946, Sept. 16

CE3 APSD2 17c bright ultra 7.50 4.75

Circumflex accent on second "E" of "EXPRES."

1946, Dec. 3 **Corrected Die**

CE4 APSD2 17c bright ultra 7.50 6.00

Grave accent on the 2nd "E" of "EXPRES."

AIR POST OFFICIAL STAMPS

Catalogue values for unused stamps in this section are for Never Hinged items.

No. C9 Overprinted in Black

1949 Unwmk. *Perf. 12*

CO1 AP6 7c deep blue 12.00 4.75
a. No period after "S" 110.00 60.00

Same Overprinted

1950

CO2 AP6 7c deep blue 17.50 13.50

SPECIAL DELIVERY STAMPS

SD1

Unwmk.

1898, June 28 Engr. *Perf. 12*

E1 SD1 10c blue green 125.00 11.00
Never hinged 350.00

SD2

1922, Aug. 21

E2 SD2 20c carmine 100.00 9.00
Never hinged 220.00

Five Stages of Mail Transportation
SD3

1927, June 29

E3 SD3 20c orange 35.00 22.50
Never hinged 70.00
a. Imperf., pair 225.00
Never hinged 400.00

No. E3 forms part of the Confederation Commemorative issue. It is known imperforate vertically and imperforate horizontally.

SD4

1930, Sept. 2 *Perf. 11*

E4 SD4 20c henna brown 65.00 17.50
Never hinged 125.00

SD5

1932, Dec. 24

E5 SD5 20c henna brown 60.00 17.50
Never hinged 115.00
a. Imperf., pair 650.00
Never hinged 950.00

Allegory of Progress — SD6

1935, June 1 *Perf. 12*

E6 SD6 20c dark carmine 12.00 7.50
Never hinged 20.00
a. Imperf., pair 650.00
Never hinged 950.00

Arms of Canada — SD7

1938-39

E7 SD7 10c dk green (4/1/39) 9.50 3.50
Never hinged 15.50
a. Imperf., pair 725.00
Never hinged 1,250.
E8 SD7 20c dark carmine (6/15/38) 30.00 25.00
Never hinged 50.00
a. Imperf., pair 650.00
Never hinged 1,050.

No. E8 Surcharged in Black

1939, Mar. 1

E9 SD7 10c on 20c dk car 8.00 6.50
Never hinged 12.00

Coat of Arms and Flags
SD8

1942, July 1

E10 SD8 10c green 3.50 2.00
Never hinged 5.00
a. Imperf., pair 650.00
Never hinged 950.00

Canada's contribution to the war effort of the Allied Nations.

Catalogue values for unused stamps in this section, from this point to the end of the section, are for Never Hinged items.

Arms of Canada — SD9

1946, Sept. 16

E11 SD9 10c green 4.50 1.25

The laurel and olive branches symbolize Victory and Peace.
For overprints see Nos. EO1, EO2.

SPECIAL DELIVERY OFFICIAL STAMPS

Catalogue values for unused stamps in this section are for Never Hinged items.

No. E11 Overprinted in Black

1950 Unwmk. *Perf. 12*

EO1 SD9 10c green 17.50 12.50

Same Overprinted

EO2 SD9 10c green 25.00 17.50

REGISTRATION STAMPS

R1

1875-88 Unwmk. Engr. *Perf. 12*

F1	R1 2c orange	115.00	6.00
	Never hinged	250.00	
a.	2c vermilion	170.00	15.00
	Never hinged	375.00	
b.	2c rose carmine	340.00	110.00
	Never hinged	725.00	
c.	As "a," imperf., pair		*3,000.*
d.	Perf. 12x11½	575.00	110.00
	Never hinged	1,200.	
F2	R1 5c dark green	150.00	6.00
	Never hinged	300.00	
a.	5c blue green ('88)	160.00	6.00
	Never hinged	325.00	
b.	5c yellow green	240.00	7.50
	Never hinged	475.00	
c.	Imperf., pair	1,200.	
	Never hinged	*2,250.*	
d.	Perf. 12x11½	1,750.	280.00
	Never hinged	*3,350.*	
F3	R1 8c dull blue ('76)	600.00	350.00
	Never hinged	1,500.	
	Nos. F1-F3 (3)	865.00	362.00

The used No. F1c is unique (fine centering).

POSTAGE DUE STAMPS

D1

1906-28 Unwmk. Engr. *Perf. 12*

J1	D1 1c violet	25.00	4.75
	Never hinged	40.00	
a.	Thin paper ('24)	45.00	7.50
	Never hinged	80.00	
b.	Imperf., pair	400.00	
J2	D1 2c violet	25.00	1.00
	Never hinged	40.00	
a.	Thin paper ('24)	45.00	11.00
	Never hinged	80.00	
b.	Imperf., pair	400.00	
J3	D1 4c violet ('28)	65.00	22.50
	Never hinged	110.00	
J4	D1 5c violet	25.00	2.00
	Never hinged	40.00	
a.	As "c," thin paper	20.00	7.50
	Never hinged	35.00	
b.	Imperf., pair	400.00	
c.	5c reddish violet ('28)	25.00	2.00
	Never hinged	40.00	
J5	D1 10c violet ('28)	85.00	14.00
	Never hinged	160.00	
	Nos. J1-J5 (5)	225.00	44.25
	Set, never hinged	390.00	

In 1924 there was a printing of Nos. J1, J2 and J4 on thin semi-transparent paper. Imperf pairs are without gum.

D2

1930-32 *Perf. 11*

J6	D2 1c dark violet	12.50	4.25
	Never hinged	22.50	
J7	D2 2c dark violet	7.00	1.10
	Never hinged	12.50	
J8	D2 4c dark violet	17.50	5.50
	Never hinged	30.00	
J9	D2 5c dark violet	25.00	6.50
	Never hinged	42.50	
J10	D2 10c dark violet ('32)	110.00	10.00
	Never hinged	200.00	
a.	Vert. pair, imperf. horiz.	1,750.	—
	Never hinged	2,750.	
	Nos. J6-J10 (5)	172.00	27.35
	Set, never hinged	312.50	

No. J10a is valued in the grade of fine.

D3

1933-34

J11	D3 1c dark violet ('34)	15.00	6.50
	Never hinged	27.50	
a.	Imperf., pair	400.00	
	Never hinged	575.00	
J12	D3 2c dark violet	9.00	1.25
	Never hinged	16.50	
J13	D3 4c dark violet	15.00	8.00
	Never hinged	27.50	
J14	D3 10c dark violet	35.00	7.25
	Never hinged	57.50	
	Nos. J11-J14 (4)	74.00	23.00
	Set, never hinged	115.50	

Catalogue values for unused stamps in this section, from this point to the end of the section, are for Never Hinged items.

D4

1935-65 *Perf. 12*

J15	D4 1c dark violet	.30	.25
a.	Imperf., pair	200.00	
J16	D4 2c dark violet	.30	.25
a.	Imperf., pair	200.00	
J16B	D4 3c dark vio ('65)	2.00	1.50
J17	D4 4c dark violet	.35	.25
a.	Imperf., pair	200.00	
J18	D4 5c dark vio ('48)	.40	.35
J19	D4 6c dark vio ('57)	2.25	1.75
J20	D4 10c dark violet	.40	.25
a.	Imperf., pair	200.00	
	Nos. J15-J20 (7)	6.00	4.60

D5

Size: 20x17mm

1967, Feb. 8 Litho. *Perf. 12*

J21	D5 1c carmine rose	.25	.25
J22	D5 2c carmine rose	.25	.25
J23	D5 3c carmine rose	.25	.25
J24	D5 4c carmine rose	.30	.25
J25	D5 5c carmine rose	1.50	1.50
J26	D5 6c carmine rose	.30	.25
J27	D5 10c carmine rose	.40	.30
	Nos. J21-J27 (7)	3.25	3.05

Size: 20x15¾mm

1969-78 *Perf. 12*

J28	D5 1c car rose ('70)	.45	.30
a.	Perf. 12½x12 ('77)	.25	.25
J29	D5 2c car rose ('72)	.25	.25
J30	D5 3c car rose ('74)	.25	.25
J31	D5 4c carmine rose	.40	.30
a.	Perf. 12½x12 ('77)	.25	.25
b.	Printed on gummed side	*1,400.*	
J32	D5 5c car rose, perf. 12½x12 ('77)	.25	.25
a.	Perf. 12	16.00	12.50
J33	D5 6c car rose ('72)	.25	.25
J34	D5 8c carmine rose	.25	.25
a.	Perf. 12½x12 ('78)	.40	.30
J35	D5 10c carmine rose	.55	.25
a.	Perf. 12½x12 ('77)	.25	.25
J36	D5 12c carmine rose	.75	.60
a.	Perf. 12½x12 ('77)	1.50	.70
J37	D5 16c carmine rose ('74)	.40	.25

Perf. 12½x12

J38	D5 20c carmine rose ('77)	.55	.40
J39	D5 24c carmine rose ('77)	.65	.40
J40	D5 50c carmine rose ('77)	1.00	.75
	Nos. J28-J40 (13)	6.00	4.50

WAR TAX STAMPS

WT1

Unwmk.

1915, Mar. 25 Engr. *Perf. 12*

MR1	WT1 1c green	25.00	.40
	Never hinged	60.00	
MR2	WT1 2c carmine	25.00	.40
	Never hinged	60.00	

In 1915 postage stamps of 5, 20 and 50 cents were overprinted "WAR TAX" in two lines. These stamps were intended for fiscal use, the war tax on postal matter being 1 cent. A few of these stamps were used to pay postage.

WT2

Type I

Type II

TWO TYPES:

Type I — There is a colored line between two white lines below the large letter "T."

Type II — The right half of the colored line is replaced by two short diagonal lines and five small dots.

1916

MR3	WT2 2c + 1c car (I)	40.00	.25
	Never hinged	100.00	
a.	2c + 1c carmine (II)	275.00	4.50
	Never hinged	625.00	
b.	2c + 1c rose red (I)	50.00	.40
	Never hinged	120.00	
MR4	WT2 2c + 1c brn (II)	25.00	.25
	Never hinged	62.50	
a.	2c + 1c brown (I)	700.00	10.00
	Never hinged	1,300.	
b.	Imperf., pair (I)	175.00	
c.	Imperf., pair (II)	2,250.	

Nos. MR4b and MR4c were made without gum.

Perf. 12x8

MR5	WT2 2c + 1c car (I)	65.00	30.00
	Never hinged	140.00	

Coil Stamps

Perf. 8 Vertically

MR6	WT2 2c + 1c car (I)	150.00	10.00
	Never hinged	350.00	
MR7	WT2 2c + 1c brn (II)	45.00	2.25
	Never hinged	100.00	
a.	2c + 1c brown (I)	200.00	7.50
	Never hinged	500.00	

OVERPRINTED OFFICIAL STAMPS

Catalogue values for unused stamps in this section are for Never Hinged items.

With Perforated Initials O H M S

On March 28, 1939 the Treasury Board ruled that on and after June 30, 1939 all stamps used by government departments throughout the country should be perforated O H M S (On His Majesty's Service) and that "the Post Office Department is to make arrangements required to provide that all stamps sold to Government Departments are perforated with the letters O H M S." The sale of such perforated stamps was discontinued in 1948.

For listings see the *Scott Classic Specialized Catalogue.*

Nos. 249, 250, 252 and 254 Overprinted in Black

1949-50 Unwmk. *Perf. 12*

O1	A97 1c green	2.25	1.75
a.	No period after "S"	150.00	75.00
O2	A98 2c brown	10.00	7.50
a.	No period after "S"	150.00	75.00
O3	A99 3c rose violet	2.25	1.25
O4	A98 4c dark carmine	3.00	.75

Nos. 269 to 273 Overprinted in Black

O6	A108 10c olive	3.50	.60
a.	No period after "S"	85.00	60.00
O7	A109 14c black brown	6.50	2.25
a.	No period after "S"	125.00	80.00
O8	A110 20c slate black	17.50	3.25
a.	No period after "S"	150.00	80.00
O9	A111 50c dk blue grn	200.00	110.00
a.	No period after "S"	1,000.	600.00
O10	A112 $1 red violet	70.00	35.00
a.	No period after "S"	*3,500.*	*1,750.*
	Nos. O1-O4,O6-O10 (9)	315.00	162.35

It is recommended that a certificate of authenticity be acquired for No. O10a.

Same Overprint on No. 294

1950

O11	A124 50c dull green	40.00	15.00

Nos. 284 to 288 Overprinted in Black

1950

O12	A119 1c green	.40	.35
O13	A120 2c sepia	1.10	.80
O14	A121 3c rose violet	1.10	.50
O15	A122 4c dark carmine	1.10	.25
b.	No period after "S"	250.00	175.00
O15A	A123 5c deep blue	2.25	1.50
c.	No period after "S"	80.00	60.00
	Nos. O12-O15A (5)	5.95	3.40

Stamps of 1946-50 Overprinted in Black

a

b

c

1950

O16	A119(a) 1c grn (#284)	.50	.25
O17	A120(a) 2c sep (#285)	1.30	.90
O18	A121(a) 3c rose vio (#286)	1.30	.25
O19	A122(a) 4c dk car (#287)	1.30	.25
O20	A123(a) 5c dp bl (#288)	1.60	.90
O21	A108(b) 10c olive	4.25	.50
O22	A109(b) 14c black brn	8.50	2.00
O23	A110(b) 20c slate blk	14.00	1.00
O24	A124(b) 50c dull green	10.00	5.50
O25	A112(b) $1 red violet	100.00	85.00
	Nos. O16-O25 (10)	142.75	96.55

Nos. 301-302 Overprinted Type "b"

1950-51

O26	A125 10c black brown	1.30	.25
a.	Pair, one without "G"	775.00	650.00
O27	A126 $1 brt ultra ('51)	100.00	90.00

It is recommended that a certificate of authenticity be acquired for No. O26a.

Nos. 305-306 Overprinted Type "a"

1951-52 Unwmk. *Perf. 12*

O28	A120 2c olive green	.60	.25
O29	A122 4c orange ver ('52)	.95	.25

No. 316 Overprinted Type "b"

1952

O30 A132 20c gray 2.25 .25

Nos. 320-321 Overprinted Type "b"

1952-53

O31 A136 7c blue 4.00 1.25
O32 A137 $1 gray ('53) 12.00 7.50

Same Overprints on #325-329, 334

1953-61

O33 A139(a) 1c violet brown .35 .25
O34 A139(a) 2c green .35 .25
O35 A139(a) 3c carmine rose .35 .25
O36 A139(a) 4c violet .45 .25
O37 A139(a) 5c ultramarine .45 .25
O38 A141(b) 50c light green 5.00 1.20
a. Overprinted type "c" ('61) 5.00 2.00
Nos. O33-O38 (6) 6.95 2.45

No. 351 Overprinted Type "b"

1955-62

O39 A148 10c violet brown .90 .25
a. Overprinted type "c" ('62) 1.90 1.25

#337-338, 340-341 Ovptd. Type "a"

1955-56

O40 A144 1c vio brown ('56) .35 .30
O41 A144 2c green ('56) .35 .25
O43 A144 4c violet ('56) 1.00 .25
O44 A144 5c bright blue .60 .25
Nos. O40-O44 (4) 2.30 1.05

No. 362 Overprinted Type "b"

1956-62

O45 A159 20c green 1.75 .25
a. Overprinted type "c" ('62) 7.00 .50

#401-402, 404-405 Ovptd. Type "a"

1963, May 15 Engr. *Perf. 12*

O46 A195 1c deep brown .75 .70
a. Double overprint 750.00
O47 A195 2c green .75 .70
a. Pair, one without "G" 1,000.
O48 A195 4c carmine .80 .70
O49 A195 5c violet blue .50 .50
Nos. O46-O49 (4) 2.80 2.60

CAPE JUBY

'kāp 'jü-bē

LOCATION — Northwest coast of Africa in Spanish Sahara
GOVT. — Spanish administration
AREA — 12,700 sq. mi.
POP. — 9,836
CAPITAL — Villa Bens (Cape Juby)

By agreement with France, Spain's Sahara possessions were extended to include Cape Juby and in 1916 Spanish troops occupied the territory. It was attached for administrative purposes to Spanish Sahara.

100 Centimos = 1 Peseta

Stamps of Rio de Oro, 1914 Surcharged in Violet, Red, Green or Blue

1916 Unwmk. *Perf. 13*

1 A6 5c on 4p rose (V) 240.00 19.00
a. Inverted surcharge 250.00 30.00
d. Double surcharge 325.00 50.00
2 A6 10c on 10p dl vio (R) 50.00 19.00
a. Inverted surcharge 55.00 30.00
d. Double surcharge 75.00 50.00
2E A6 10c on 10p dl vio (V) 125.00 72.50
f. Double surcharge (R, V) 150.00 90.00
2G A6 10c on 10p dl vio (B) 125.00 72.50
3 A6 15c on 50c dk brn (G) 52.50 30.00
a. Inverted surcharge 57.50 30.00
4 A6 15c on 50c dk brn (R) 50.00 19.00
a. Inverted surcharge 55.00 30.00
5 A6 40c on 1p red vio (G) 87.50 35.00
a. Inverted surcharge 75.00 37.50
6 A6 40c on 1p red vio (R) 85.00 26.00
a. Inverted surcharge 75.00 42.50
Nos. 1-6 (8) 815.00 293.00
Set, never hinged 1,300.

Very fine examples of Nos. 1-6 will be somewhat off center. Well centered examples are uncommon and will sell for more.

Stamps of Spain, 1876-1917, Overprinted in Red or Black

1919 *Imperf.*

7 A21 ¼c bl grn (R) .30 .30

Perf. 13x12½, 14

8 A46 2c dk brn (Bk) .30 .30
a. Double overprint 40.00 *50.00*
b. Double overprint (Bk + R) 100.00 52.50
9 A46 5c grn (R) .75 .60
a. Double overprint 40.00 *50.00*
b. Inverted overprint 30.00 *47.50*
10 A46 10c car (Bk) 1.00 .70
a. Double overprint (Bk + R) 100.00 52.50
b. Double overprint (R) 40.00 *50.00*
11 A46 15c ocher (Bk) 3.50 3.00
b. Double overprint 40.00 *50.00*
c. Red control # 6.50 3.75
d. As "c," inverted overprint 13.00
12 A46 20c ol grn (R) 22.00 16.00
13 A46 25c dp bl (R) 3.25 3.00
a. Double overprint 40.00 *50.00*
14 A46 30c bl grn (R) 3.25 3.00
15 A46 40c rose (Bk) 3.50 3.25
16 A46 50c sl bl (R) 4.00 3.50
17 A46 1p lake (Bk) 11.00 8.75
18 A46 4p dp vio (R) 45.00 34.00
19 A46 10p org (Bk) 60.00 45.00
Nos. 7-19 (13) 157.85 121.40
Set, never hinged 300.00

Nos. 8-19 have blue control number on back. For imperfs, see the *Scott Classic Catalogue.*

Same on Stamps of Spain, 1920-21

1922 *Imperf.*

20 A47 1c blue green (R) 25.00 14.00
Never hinged 45.00

Engr. *Perf. 13x12½*

Blue Control Number on Back

23 A46 20c violet 145.00 42.50

A 2c and a 15c exist, values $400 and $10, respectively, for unused, hinged examples, $600 and $15 for never hinged. Overprint on 2c privately applied.

Same on Stamps of Spain, 1922-23

1925 *Perf. 13½x13*

25 A49 5c red vio 5.25 3.50
26 A49 10c bl grn 13.00 3.50
28 A49 20c violet 27.50 10.00
Nos. 25-28 (3) 45.75 17.00
Set, never hinged 72.50

Exists on Spain No. 331, 2c olive green. Value $425 unused hinged and $650 never hinged. Overprint was privately applied.

Seville-Barcelona Exposition Issue

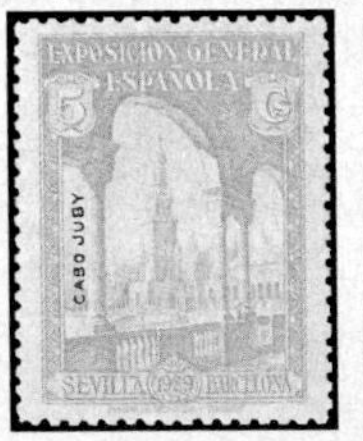

Stamps of Spain, 1929, Overprinted in Red or Blue

1929 *Perf. 11*

29 A52 5c rose lake (Bl) .45 .45
30 A53 10c green (R) .45 .45
31 A50 15c Prus bl (R) .45 .45
32 A51 20c pur (R) .45 .45
33 A50 25c brt rose (Bl) .45 .45
34 A52 30c blk brn (Bl) .45 .45
35 A53 40c dk bl (R) .45 .45
36 A51 50c dp org (Bl) .60 .60
37 A52 1p bl blk (R) 21.00 21.00
38 A53 4p dp rose (Bl) 27.50 27.50
39 A53 10p brn (Bl) 27.50 27.50
Nos. 29-39 (11) 79.75 79.75
Set, never hinged 150.00

Stamps of Spanish Morocco, 1928-33, Overprinted in Black or Red

1934 *Perf. 14*

40 A7 1c brt rose (Bk) .55 .55
41 A2 2c dk vio (R) 5.00 5.00
42 A2 5c dp bl (R) 5.75 5.75
43 A2 10c dk grn (Bk) 14.00 11.50
43A A10 10c dk grn (R) 3.50 3.50
44 A2 15c org brn (Bk) 32.50 29.00
45 A7 20c sl grn (R) 13.00 10.00
46 A3 25c cop red (Bk) 6.00 5.50
47 A10 30c red brn (Bk) 11.00 10.00
48 A13 40c dp bl (R) 40.00 37.50
49 A13 50c red org (Bk) 80.00 70.00
50 A4 1p yel grn (Bk) 57.50 57.50
51 A5 2.50p red vio (Bk) 120.00 115.00
52 A6 4p ultra (R) 160.00 145.00

No. 43A and 1c, 20c, 30c, 40c, 50c, with control numbers.

Same Overprint in Black on Stamp of Spanish Morocco, 1932

53 A2 1c car rose ("Ct") 2.40 2.40
Nos. 40-53 (15) 551.20 508.20
Set, never hinged 900.00

Stamps of Spanish Morocco, 1933-35, Overprinted in Black, Blue or Red

1935-36

54 A8 2c grn (R) 1.25 1.00
55 A9 5c mag (Bk) 3.75 3.50
55A A10 10c dk grn (R) ('36) 22.50 21.00
56 A11 15c yel (Bl) 8.75 8.25
57 A12 25c crim (Bk) 130.00 100.00
58 A8 1p sl blk (R) 14.50 13.50
59 A9 2.50p brn (Bl) 65.00 52.50
60 A11 4p yel grn (R) 115.00 90.00
61 A12 5p blk (R) 90.00 70.00
Nos. 54-61 (9) 450.75 359.75
Set, never hinged 850.00

Same Overprint in Black or Red on Stamps of Spanish Morocco, 1935

1935 *Perf. 13½*

62 A14 25c vio (R) 4.00 4.00
63 A15 30c crim (Bk) 4.00 4.00
64 A14 40c org (Bk) 5.75 5.25
65 A15 50c brt bl (R) 15.00 11.00
66 A14 60c dk bl grn (R) 17.50 14.00
67 A15 2p brn lake (Bk) 95.00 75.00

Same Overprint on Stamps of Spanish Morocco, 1933

Perf. 13½, 14

68 A7 1c brt rose (Bk) .30 .30

Perf. 14

69 A7 20c slate grn (R) 6.75 6.75
Nos. 62-69 (8) 148.30 120.30
Set, never hinged 200.00

Same Overprint on Stamps of Spanish Morocco, 1937

1937 *Perf. 13½*

70 A21 1c dk bl (Bk) .50 .50
71 A21 2c org brn (Bk) .50 .50
72 A21 5c cer (Bk) .50 .50
73 A21 10c emer (Bk) .50 .50
74 A21 15c brt bl (Bk) .50 .50
75 A21 20c red brn (Bk) .50 .50
76 A21 25c mag (Bk) .50 .50
77 A21 30c red org (Bk) .50 .50
78 A21 40c org (Bk) 1.60 1.60
79 A21 50c ultra (R) 1.60 1.60
80 A21 60c yel grn (Bk) 1.60 1.60
81 A21 1p bl vio (Bk) 1.60 1.60
82 A21 2p Prus bl (Bk) 87.50 87.50
83 A21 2.50p gray blk (R) 87.50 87.50
84 A21 4p dk brn (Bk) 87.50 87.50
85 A22 10p vio blk (R) 87.50 87.50
Nos. 70-85 (16) 360.40 360.40
Set, never hinged 550.00

1st Year of the Revolution.

Same Overprint in Black on Types of Spanish Morocco, 1939

Designs: 5c, Spanish quarter. 10c, Moroccan quarter. 15c, Street scene, Larache. 20c, Tetuan.

1939 Photo. *Perf. 13½*

86 A25 5c vermilion .50 .50
87 A25 10c deep green .50 .50
88 A25 15c brown lake .50 .50
89 A25 20c bright blue .50 .50
Nos. 86-89 (4) 2.00 2.00
Set, never hinged 4.00

Same Overprint in Black or Red on Stamps of Spanish Morocco, 1940

1940 *Perf. 11½x11*

90 A26 1c dk brn (Bk) .25 .25
91 A27 2c ol grn (R) .25 .25
92 A28 5c dk bl (R) .25 .25
93 A29 10c dk red lil (Bk) .25 .25
94 A30 15c dk grn (R) .25 .25
95 A31 20c pur (R) .30 .30
96 A32 25c blk brn (R) .30 .30
97 A33 30c brt grn (Bk) .35 .35
98 A34 40c slate grn (R) .85 .75
99 A35 45c org ver (Bk) .85 .75
100 A36 50c brn org (Bk) .90 .90
101 A37 70c saph (R) 2.40 2.25
102 A38 1p ind & brn (Bk) 5.00 5.00
103 A39 2.50p choc & dk grn (Bk) 14.00 12.50
104 A40 5p dk cer & sep (Bk) 14.00 13.00
105 A41 10p dk ol grn & brn org (Bk) 40.00 35.00
Nos. 90-105 (16) 80.20 72.35
Set, never hinged 150.00

Imperfs exist. Value, set $300.

Stamps of Spanish Morocco, 1944, Overprinted in Black or Red

1944, Oct. 2 Unwmk. *Perf. 12½*

106 A47 1c choc & lt bl .25 .25
107 A48 2c slate grn & lt grn .25 .25
108 A49 5c choc & grnsh blk (R) .25 .25
109 A50 10c brt ultra & red org .25 .25
110 A51 15c sl grn & lt grn .25 .25
111 A52 20c dp cl & blk (R) .25 .25
112 A53 25c lt bl & choc .25 .25
113 A47 30c yel grn & brt ultra (R) .25 .25
114 A48 40c choc & red vio .25 .25
115 A49 50c brt ultra, & red brn .25 .25
116 A50 75c yel grn & brt ultra (R) 1.25 1.25
117 A51 1p brt ultra & choc 1.40 1.40
118 A52 2.50p blk & brt ultra (R) 3.25 3.25
119 A53 10p sal & gray blk (R) 25.00 25.00
Nos. 106-119 (14) 33.40 33.40
Set, never hinged 75.00

Same Overprint on Stamps of Spanish Morocco, 1946

1946, Mar. *Perf. 10½x10*

120 A54 1c pur & brn .25 .25
121 A55 2c dk Prus grn & vio blk (R) .25 .25
122 A54 10c dp org vio bl .25 .25
123 A55 15c dk bl & bl grn .25 .25
124 A54 25c yel grn & ultra .25 .25
125 A56 40c dk bl & brn (R) .30 .30
126 A55 45c blk & rose .45 .45
127 A57 1p dk Prus grn & dp bl 1.60 1.60
128 A58 2.50p dp org & grnsh gray (R) 4.75 4.75
129 A59 10p dk bl & gray (R) 13.50 13.50
Nos. 120-129 (10) 21.85 21.85
Set, never hinged 45.00

Same Overprint in Carmine, Black or Brown on Stamps of Spanish Morocco, 1948

1948, Jan. 1 *Perf. 10, 10x10½*

130 A64 2c pur & brn .40 *1.00*
131 A65 5c dp claret & vio .25 .25
132 A66 15c brt ultra & bl grn (Bk) .25 .25
133 A67 25c blk & Prus grn .25 .25
134 A65 35c brt ultra & gray blk .25 .25
135 A68 50c red & vio (Br) .25 .25
136 A66 70c dk gray grn & ultra (Bk) .25 .25
137 A67 90c cer & dk gray grn (Bk) .30 .30
138 A68 1p brt ultra & vio (Br) .45 .45
139 A64 2.50p vio brn & sl grn 1.60 1.60
140 A69 10p blk & dp ultra 3.00 3.00
Nos. 130-140 (11) 7.25 7.85
Set, never hinged 12.00

SEMI-POSTAL STAMPS

Types of Semi-Postal Stamps of Spain, 1926, Overprinted

1926 Unwmk. *Perf. 12½, 13*

B1	SP1	1c orange	11.50	11.50
B2	SP2	2c rose	11.50	11.50
B3	SP3	5c blk brn	3.00	3.00
B4	SP4	10c dk grn	1.60	1.60
B5	SP1	15c dk vio	1.10	1.10
B6	SP4	20c vio brn	1.10	1.10
B7	SP5	25c dp car	1.10	1.10
B8	SP1	30c ol grn	1.10	1.10
B9	SP3	40c ultra	.45	.45
B10	SP2	50c red brn	.45	.45
B11	SP4	1p vermilion	.45	.45
B12	SP3	4p bister	2.00	2.00
B13	SP5	10p lt vio	3.00	3.00
		Nos. B1-B13 (13)	38.35	38.35
		Set, never hinged	75.00	

Nos. B12-B13 surcharged "Alfonso XIII" and new value are listed as Spain Nos. B68-B69. See Spain No. B6a.

AIR POST STAMPS

Spanish Morocco, Nos. C1 to C10 Overprinted "CABO JUBY" as on #54-61

1938, June 1 Unwmk. *Perf. 13½*

C1	AP1	5c brown	.25	.25
C2	AP1	10c brt grn	.25	.25
C3	AP1	25c crimson	.25	.25
C4	AP1	40c light blue	2.10	2.10
C5	AP2	50c brt mag	.25	.25
C6	AP2	75c dk bl	.25	.25
C7	AP1	1p sepia	.25	.25
C8	AP1	1.50p dp vio	1.90	1.90
C9	AP1	2p dp red brn	2.75	2.75
C10	AP1	3p brn blk	7.25	7.25
		Nos. C1-C10 (10)	15.50	15.50
		Set, never hinged	45.00	

Moroccan Views — AP3

Designs: 5c, Ketama landscape. 10c, Mosque, Tangier. 15c, Velez. 90c, Sanjurjo. 5p, Strait of Gibraltar

1942, Apr. 1 Photo. *Perf. 12½*

C11	AP3	5c deep blue	.25	.25
C12	AP3	10c org brn	.25	.25
C13	AP3	15c grnsh blk	.25	.25
C14	AP3	90c dk rose	.50	.50
C15	AP3	5p black	1.75	1.75
		Nos. C11-C15 (5)	3.00	3.00
		Set, never hinged	4.00	

SPECIAL DELIVERY STAMPS

Special Delivery Stamp of Spain Ovptd. "CABO JUBY" as on #7-28

1919 Unwmk. *Perf. 14*

E1	SD1	20c red (Bk)	3.25	3.25
b.		Double overprint	27.50	13.00

Spanish Morocco #E4 Overprinted "CABO JUBY" as on #40-52 in Red

1934

E2	SD2	20c black	10.00	10.00

Spanish Morocco No. E5 Overprinted "CABO JUBY" as on Nos. 54-61

1935

E3	SD3	20c vermilion	3.50	3.50

Same Ovpt. on Spanish Morocco #E6

1937 *Perf. 13½*

E4	SD4	20c bright carmine	1.10	1.10

1st Year of the Revolution.

Same Ovpt. on Spanish Morocco #E8

1940 *Perf. 11½x11*

E5	SD5	25c scarlet	.65	.65

SEMI-POSTAL SPECIAL DELIVERY STAMP

Type of Semi-Postal Special Delivery Stamp of Spain, 1926, Overprinted "CABO-JUBY" as on Nos. B1-B13

1926 Unwmk. *Perf. 12½, 13*

EB1	SPSD1	20c ultra & black	3.50	3.50

CAPE OF GOOD HOPE

'kāp əv 'gud 'hōp

LOCATION — In the extreme southern part of South Africa
GOVT. — Former British Colony
AREA — 276,995 sq mi. (1911)
POP. — 2,564,965 (1911)
CAPITAL — Cape Town

Cape of Good Hope joined with Natal, the Transvaal and the Orange River Colony in 1910, forming the Union of South Africa.

12 Pence = 1 Shilling

Watermarks

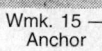

Wmk. 15 — Anchor

Wmk. 16 — Anchor

"Hope" Seated A1

Printed by Perkins, Bacon & Co. Wmk. 15

1853, Sept. 1 Engr. *Imperf.*

1	A1	1p brick red, bluish paper	3,500.	400.00
a.		1p pale brick red, deeply blued paper	*4,500.*	450.00
b.		1p deep brick red, deeply blued paper	*10,500.*	475.00
2	A1	4p deep blue, lightly blued paper	1,750.	170.00
a.		4p deep blue, deeply blued paper	3,500.	375.00
b.		4p blue, bluish paper	3,250.	200.00

Counterfeits exist.

1855-58 White Paper

3	A1	1p rose ('57)	750.00	325.00
a.		1p dull red	1,100.	425.00
b.		1p brick red	6,000.	1,050.
4	A1	4p blue	700.00	85.00
a.		Half used as 2p on cover		*42,000.*
b.		4p deep blue	900.00	90.00
e.		4p bright blue	900.00	90.00
5	A1	6p pale lilac ('58)	1,200.	300.00
a.		6p rose lilac	2,500.	400.00
b.		6p grayish lilac on bluish paper	5,000.	540.00
c.		6p slate purple on bluish paper	4,150.	1,200.
d.		Half used as 3p on cover		—
6	A1	1sh yellow grn ('58)	*4,000.*	300.00
a.		1sh dark green	450.00	*600.00*
b.		Half used as 6p on cover		—

Nos. 3-6 are known rouletted unofficially. Counterfeits exist.

No. 4 was reproduced by the collotype process in an unwatermarked souvenir sheet distributed at the London Intl. Stamp Exhib. 1950.

A2

Printed by Saul Solomon & Co.

1861 Laid Paper Unwmk. Typo.

7	A2	1p vermilion	*17,000.*	2,750.
a.		1p carmine	*42,500.*	4,000.
b.		1p red	*50,000.*	5,000.
c.		1p milky blue (error)	*200,000.*	*32,500.*
d.		1p pale blue (error)		*36,000.*
9	A2	4p milky blue	*40,000.*	3,000.
a.		4p pale blue	*42,000.*	3,250.
b.		4p blue	*45,000.*	3,500.
c.		4p dark blue	*120,000.*	5,750.
d.		As #9, right corner retouched		7,750.
e.		As #9a, right corner retouched		7,750.
f.		4p vermilion (error)	*200,000.*	*65,000.*
g.		4p carmine (error)		*112,500.*

Nos. 7 and 9 are usually called Wood Blocks. The plates were made locally and composed of clichés mounted on wood. The errors were caused by a cliché of each value being mounted in the plate of the other value.

In 1883 plate proofs of both values on white paper, usually called "reprints," were made. The 1p is in dull orange red; the 4p in dark blue. These are known canceled, as a few were misused as stamps. The proofs do not include the errors.

Counterfeits exist.

Printed by De La Rue & Co.

1863-64 Wmk. 15 Engr.

12	A1	1p dark carmine	300.00	*325.00*
a.		1p reddish brown	650.00	350.00
b.		1p brownish red	650.00	350.00
13	A1	4p dark blue	275.00	120.00
a.		4p slate blue	2,500.	600.00
14	A1	6p purple	400.00	*500.00*
15	A1	1sh emerald	600.00	*650.00*
a.		1sh pale emerald	1,400.	—

Nos. 12-15 can be distinguished from Nos. 3-6 not only by colors but because Nos. 12-15 often appear in a granular ink or with the background lightly printed in whole or part.

No. 12a, Wmk. 1, is believed to be a proof. Value, $29,000.

Counterfeits exist.

"Hope" and Symbols of Colony — A3

Frame Line Around Stamp

1864-77 Typo. Wmk. 1 *Perf. 14*

16	A3	1p rose ('65)	130.00	42.50
17	A3	4p blue ('65)	190.00	4.50
a.		4p pale blue	190.00	4.50
b.		4p dull ultramarine	350.00	65.00
c.		4p deep blue ('72)	275.00	4.50
18	A3	6p bright vio ('77)	200.00	1.75
a.		6p dull violet	375.00	8.25
b.		6p pale lilac	225.00	28.00
19	A3	1sh yellow green	225.00	4.75
a.		1sh blue green	250.00	6.00
		Nos. 16-19 (4)	745.00	53.50

Imperf. stamps are believed to be proofs.

For surcharges see Nos. 20-21, N3.

For types A3 and A6 with manuscript surcharge of 1d or overprints "G. W." or "G," see Griqualand West listings.

Stamps of 1864 Surcharged in Red or Black

a

b

1868-74 Red Surcharge

20	A3(a)	4p on 6p	550.00	19.00
a.		"Peuce" for "Pence"	2,500.	900.00
b.		"Fonr" for "Four"		850.00
21	A3(b)	1p on 6p ('74)	800.00	140.00
a.		"E" of "PENNY" omitted		1,800.

Space between words and bars varies from 12½-16mm on No. 20, and 16½-18mm on No. 21.

1876 Black Surcharge

22	A3 (b)	1p on 1sh green	140.00	80.00

"Hope" and Symbols of Colony — A6

Without Frame Line Around Stamp

1871-81 *Perf. 14*

23	A6	½p gray black ('75)	37.50	16.00
24	A6	1p rose ('72)	55.00	1.25
25	A6	3p lilac rose ('80)	375.00	42.50
26	A6	3p claret ('81)	190.00	4.50
27	A6	4p blue ('76)	190.00	.90
a.		4p ultramarine	350.00	60.00
28	A6	5sh orange	650.00	25.00
		Nos. 23-28 (6)	1,497.	90.15

For surcharges see Nos. 29-32, 39, 55.

No. 27 Surcharged in Red

1879

29 A6 3p on 4p blue 180.00 3.00
- *a.* "THE.EE" 3,500. 350.00
- *b.* "PENCB" 4,000. 275.00
- *c.* Double surcharge *13,000.* *4,500.*
- *d.* As "a," double surcharge — —

Type of 1871 Surcharged in Black

1880

30 A6 3p on 4p lilac rose 130.00 3.25

No. 25 Surcharged in Black

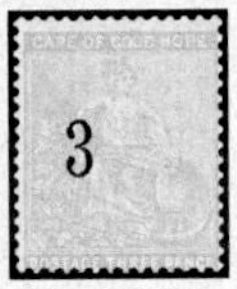

e

f

31 A6(e) 3p on 3p lilac rose 400.00 12.00
- *a.* Inverted surcharge 13,000. 1,600.

32 A6(f) 3p on 3p lilac rose 130.00 2.25
- *a.* Inverted surcharge 1,600. 47.50

1882-83 Wmk. 2

33 A6 ½p gray black 47.50 3.25
34 A6 1p rose 90.00 2.50
35 A6 2p bister 150.00 1.75
36 A6 3p claret 13.00 1.75
37 A3 6p bright violet 160.00 1.00
38 A6 5sh orange ('83) 950.00 300.00

For overprint see Rhodesia No. 49.

Nos. 26 and 36 Surcharged in Black

1882 Wmk. 1

39 A6 ½p on 3p claret 7,000. 180.00
- *a.* Hyphen omitted *4,000.*

Wmk. 2

40 A6 ½p on 3p claret 60.00 8.00
- *a.* "ENNY" 2,500. 825.00
- *b.* "PENN" 2,000. *800.00*
- *c.* Hyphen omitted 900.00 425.00

1884-98 Wmk. 16

41 A6 ½p gray black ('86) 12.00 .25
42 A6 ½p yel green ('96) 1.80 .60
43 A6 1p rose ('85) 15.00 .25
44 A6 2p bister 15.00 .25
45 A6 2p choc brown ('97) 4.00 3.50
46 A6 3p red violet ('98) 25.00 1.20
47 A6 4p blue ('90) 26.00 1.50
48 A6 4p pale ol grn ('97) 12.00 4.25
49 A3 6p violet 16.00 .50
50 A3 1sh dull bluish grn ('89) 180.00 1.25
51 A6 1sh blue grn ('94) 110.00 8.50
52 A6 1sh yel buff ('96) 19.00 3.25
53 A6 5sh orange ('87) 175.00 9.50
54 A6 5sh brown org ('96) 140.00 5.00
Nos. 41-54 (14) 750.80 39.80

For surcharges see Nos. 58, 162, 165-166. For overprints see Rhodesia Nos. 43, 45-48.

Type of 1871 Surcharged in Black

1891, Mar.

55 A6 2½p on 3p deep magenta 8.00 .25
- *a.* "1" of "½" has straight serif 95.00 37.50

Hope Seated — A13

1892-96

56 A13 2½p sage green 26.00 .25
57 A13 2½p ultra ('96) 13.00 .25

For surcharge see No. N4. For overprint see Orange River Colony No. 55.

No. 44 Surcharged in Black

1893, Mar.

58 A6 1p on 2p bister 6.00 .60
- *a.* Double surcharge 600.00
- *b.* No period after "PENNY" 100.00 25.00

Hope Standing — A15

1893-1902

59 A15 ½p green ('98) 11.00 .25
60 A15 1p carmine 4.00 .25
61 A15 3p red violet ('02) 8.00 3.50
Nos. 59-61 (3) 23.00 4.00

For surcharges see Nos. 163-164, N2. For overprints see Orange River Colony Nos. 54, 56, Rhodesia No. 44, Transvaal Nos. 236-236A.

Table Mountain and Bay; Coat of Arms — A16

1900, Jan.

62 A16 1p carmine rose 8.50 .25

King Edward VII — A17

Various frames.

1902-04 Wmk. 16

63 A17 ½p emerald 3.50 .25
64 A17 1p car rose 3.00 .25
65 A17 2p brown ('04) 24.00 .95
66 A17 2½p ultra ('04) 5.00 *13.00*
67 A17 3p red violet ('03) 17.00 1.40
68 A17 4p ol green ('03) 20.00 .80
69 A17 6p violet ('03) 30.00 .60
70 A17 1sh bister 20.00 1.25
71 A17 5sh brown org ('03) 175.00 27.50
Nos. 63-71 (9) 297.50 46.00

Imperf. stamps are proofs.

Cape of Good Hope stamps were replaced by those of Union of South Africa.

ISSUED IN MAFEKING

Excellent forgeries of Nos. 162-179 are known.

Stamps of Cape of Good Hope Surcharged

1900, Mar. 24

162 A6 1p on ½p grn 325.00 85.00
163 A15 1p on ½p grn 375.00 125.00
164 A15 3p on 1p rose 325.00 65.00
165 A6 6p on 3p red vio 45,000. 350.00
166 A6 1sh on 4p pale ol green 8,000. 425.00

Stamps of Bechuanaland Protectorate Surcharged

1900 Wmk. 30

167 A54 1p on ½p ver 325.00 85.00
- *a.* Inverted surcharge — 8,000.
- *b.* Vert. pair, surcharge tête bêche *40,000.*

168 A40 3p on 1p lilac 1,000. 130.00
- *a.* Double surcharge *37,500.*

169 A56 6p on 2p grn & car 3,000. 120.00

170 A58 6p on 3p vio, *yel* 7,500. 425.00
- *a.* Inverted surcharge *42,500.*
- *b.* Double surcharge — —

The lettering of "Mafeking Besieged" shows varying breaks in various letters, and may have either a period or no punctuation after "Mafeking."

On Stamps of Bechuanaland Wmk. 29

171 A1 6p on 3p violet & black 550.00 95.00

Wmk. 30

172 A59 1sh on 4p brn & grn 1,650. 110.00
- *a.* Double surch., one inverted — *30,000.*
- *b.* Triple surcharge — *30,000.*
- *c.* Inverted surcharge — —
- *d.* Double surcharge — *30,000.*

Stamps of Bechuanaland Protectorate Surcharged

173 A40 3p on 1p lilac 1,100. 100.00
- *a.* Double surcharge — *11,000.*

174 A56 6p on 2p grn & car 1,600. 100.00
175 A62 1sh on 6p vio, *rose* 7,500. 130.00

On Stamps of Bechuanaland

176 A62 1sh on 6p vio, *rose* 45,000. 900.00
177 A65 2sh on 1sh green 15,000. 650.00

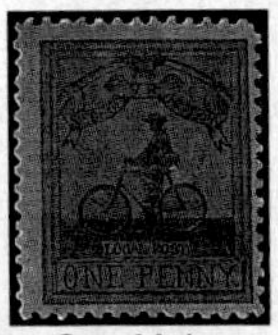

Sgt. Major Goodyear M1

Gen. Robert S. S. Baden-Powell M2

Wmk. OCEANA FINE Photographic Print

1900, Apr. *Perf. 12*

Laid Paper

178 M1 1p blue, *blue* 1,300. 475.00
- On cover *11,000.*
- *a.* Imperf, pair 27,000.

179 M2 3p blue, *blue,* 18½mm wide 1,900. 525.00
- On cover 8,250.
- *a.* Horiz. pair, imperf. between — *110,000.*
- *b.* Double impression — *28,000.*
- *c.* Reversed design *110,000.* *72,500.*

180 M2 3p blue, *blue,* 21mm wide 13,000. 1,650.
- On cover *15,000.*
- *a.* 3p deep blue 15,000. 1,500.
- On cover *16,500.*

The color of the paper varies from pale to deep blue.

OCEANA FINE is a sheet watermark and does not appear on every stamp.

Imperfs of No. 178 are proofs.

There is one used pair of No. 179a privately owned. A single used, partially imperf. example of No. 179 exists. Value, *$37,000.* There are four used examples of No. 179b reported. There are 2 unused and 6 used examples of No. 179c privately owned.

Issued: No. 179, Apr. 6; Nos. 178 and 180, Apr. 10.

ISSUED IN VRYBURG

Under Boer Occupation

Cape of Good Hope Stamps of 1884-96 Surcharged

Two Types of Surcharge:

Type I — Surcharge 10mm high. Space between lines 5½mm.

Type II — Surcharge 12mm high. Space between lines 7½mm.

1899, Nov. Wmk. 16 *Perf. 14*

N1 A6 ½p on ½p emer (I) 240. 95.
- *a.* Type II 2,000. 825.

N2 A15 1p on 1p rose (I) 275. 120.
- *a.* Double surcharge — —
- *b.* Type II 2,250. 950.

N3 A3 2p on 6p vio (II) 2,500. 600.

N4 A13 2½p on 2½p ultra (I) 2,000. 500.
- *a.* Type II *12,000.* *5,000.*

"Z.A.R." stands for Zuid Afrikaansche Republiek (South African Republic).

The italic "Z" variety (Nos. N1b-N4b) occurs in one position in the setting of 60.

Under British Occupation

Transvaal Stamps of 1895-96 Handstamped

1900 Unwmk. *Perf. 12½*

N5 A13 ½p green — *3,500.*
N6 A13 1p rose & grn *14,000.* *6,000.*
N7 A13 2p brown & grn — *47,500.*
N8 A13 2½p ultra & grn — *47,500.*

No. N5 exists used with double handstamp. Nos. N5 and N6 exist inverted (overprint reading down).

CAPE VERDE

'kāp 'vərd

LOCATION — A group of 10 islands and five islets in the Atlantic Ocean, about 500 miles due west of Senegal.
GOVT. — Republic
AREA — 1,557 sq. mi.
POP. — 405,748 (1999 est.)
CAPITAL — Praia

The Portuguese territory of Cape Verde became independent on July 5, 1975.

1000 Reis = 1 Milreis
100 Centavos = 1 Escudo (1913)

Catalogue values for unused stamps in this country are for Never Hinged items, beginning with Scott 268 in the regular postage section, Scott J31 in the postage due section, and Scott RA6 in the postal tax section.

Crown of Portugal — A1

1877 Unwmk. Typo. *Perf. 12½*

1 A1 5r black 5.00 2.00
2 A1 10r yellow 60.00 11.00
3 A1 20r bister 3.00 1.40
4 A1 25r rose 2.50 1.40
5 A1 40r blue 82.50 50.00
b. Cliche of Mozambique in Cape Verde plate, in pair with #5 2,200. 1,400.
6 A1 50r green 165.00 72.50
7 A1 100r lilac 8.25 3.50
8 A1 200r orange 5.00 3.75
9 A1 300r brown 6.00 5.25
Nos. 1-9 (9) 337.25 150.80

For expanded treatment of Nos. 1-9, see the *Scott Classic Catalogue.*

1881-85 *Perf. 12½*

10 A1 10r green 2.75 2.10
11 A1 20r carmine ('85) 5.50 3.75
12 A1 25r violet ('85) 4.00 3.00
13 A1 40r yellow buff 2.40 1.75
a. Imperf. 40.00
b. Cliche of Mozambique in Cape Verde plate, in pair with #13 110.00 110.00
c. As "b," imperf. —
14 A1 50r blue 6.75 4.25
Nos. 10-14 (5) 21.40 14.85

Reprints of the 1877-85 issues are on smooth white chalky paper, ungummed, and on thin white paper with shiny white gum. They are perf 13½.

For expanded treatment of nos. 10-14, see the *Scott Classic Catalogue.*

King Luiz — A2

1886 Embossed *Perf. 12½, 13½*
Chalk-Surfaced Paper

15 A2 5r black 4.50 3.00
16 A2 10r green 6.75 3.00
17 A2 20r carmine 9.00 5.25
18 A2 25r violet 10.00 5.50
19 A2 40r chocolate 10.00 3.50
20 A2 50r blue 10.00 3.50
21 A2 100r yel brown 10.00 4.50
22 A2 200r gray lilac 20.00 10.50
23 A2 300r orange 24.00 4.25
Nos. 15-23 (9) 104.25 43.00

The 25r, 50r and 100r have been reprinted in aniline colors with clean-cut Perf. 13½.

For expanded treatment of nos. 15-19, see the *Scott Classic Catalogue.*

For surcharges see Nos. 59-67, 184-187.

King Carlos — A3

1894-95 Typo. *Perf. 11½, 12½, 13½*

24 A3 5r orange 2.00 1.25
25 A3 10r redsh violet 2.00 1.25
26 A3 15r chocolate 5.00 2.60
a. Perf. 12½ 150.00 120.00
27 A3 20r lavender 4.00 2.60
28 A3 25r dp green 4.00 2.25
a. Perf. 12½ 4.00 3.25
29 A3 50r lt blue 4.00 2.25
a. Perf. 13 1/2 14.00 4.50
30 A3 75r carmine ('95) 11.50 5.75
a. Perf. 13½ 55.00 42.00
31 A3 80r yel grn ('95) 12.00 6.50
a. Perf. 13½ 45.00 35.00
32 A3 100r brn, *buff* ('95) 10.00 5.25
a. Perf. 12½ 100.00 55.00
33 A3 150r car, *rose* ('95) 50.00 27.00
a. Perf. 12½ 400.00 300.00
b. Perf. 11½ 70.00 45.00
34 A3 200r dk blue, *lt blue* ('95) 50.00 27.00
a. Perf. 12½ 150.00 120.00
35 A3 300r dk blue, *sal* ('95) 60.00 17.00
Nos. 24-35 (12) 214.50 100.70

For surcharges see Nos. 68-78, 137, 189-193, 201-205.

King Carlos — A4

1898-1903 *Perf. 11½*
Name and Value in Black except 500r

36 A4 2½r gray .40 .30
37 A4 5r orange .50 .30
38 A4 10r lt green .55 .30
39 A4 15r brown 5.50 2.00
40 A4 15r gray green ('03) 1.90 1.25
41 A4 20r gray violet 1.60 1.00
42 A4 25r sea green 3.50 1.25
a. Perf 12½ 300.00 180.00
43 A4 25r carmine ('03) 1.00 .40
44 A4 50r dark blue 3.50 1.50
45 A4 50r brown ('03) 3.75 2.40
46 A4 65r slate blue ('03) 60.00 30.00
47 A4 75r rose 10.00 3.50
48 A4 75r lilac ('03) 3.50 2.25
49 A4 80r violet 8.50 3.50
50 A4 100r dk blue, *blue* 3.50 2.00
51 A4 115r org brn, *pink* ('03) 15.00 13.50
52 A4 130r brown, *straw* ('03) 15.00 13.50
53 A4 150r brown, *straw* 10.00 6.75
54 A4 200r red vio, *pnksh* 4.00 3.00
55 A4 300r dk blue, *rose* 10.00 5.00
56 A4 400r dull blue, *straw* ('03) 16.00 10.50
57 A4 500r blk & red, *blue* ('01) 15.00 5.00
58 A4 700r violet, *yelsh* ('01) 30.00 17.50
Nos. 36-58 (23) 222.70 126.70

For overprints and suecharges see Nos. 80-99, 139, 200.

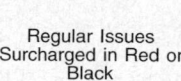

Regular Issues Surcharged in Red or Black

Two spacing types of surcharge. See note above Angola No. 61.

On Issue of 1886

1902, Dec. 1 *Perf. 12½, 13½*

59 A2 65r on 5r black (R) 7.00 3.75
60 A2 65r on 200r gray lilac 7.00 3.75
61 A2 65r on 300r orange 7.00 3.75
62 A2 115r on 10r green 7.00 3.75
63 A2 115r on 20r rose 7.00 3.75
a. Perf 13½ 60.00 35.00
64 A2 130r on 50r blue 7.00 3.75
65 A2 130r on 100r brown 7.00 3.75
66 A2 400r on 25r violet 5.00 2.60
67 A2 400r on 40r choc 9.00 3.75
a. Perf 13½ 50.00 35.00

On Issue of 1894
Perf. 11½, 12½, 13½

68 A3 65r on 10r red violet 7.00 3.75
69 A3 65r on 20r lavender 7.00 3.75
70 A3 65r on 100r brown, *buff* 8.50 5.25
a. Perf 12½ 26.00 24.00
71 A3 115r on 5r orange 5.00 3.00
a. Inverted surcharge 60.00 60.00
72 A3 115r on 25r blue grn 4.00 2.10
a. Perf 11½ 55.00 55.00
73 A3 115r on 150r car, *rose* 9.00 6.50
a. Perf 13½ 55.00 25.00
74 A3 130r on 75r car 5.00 3.00
a. Perf 13½ *250.00 200.00*
75 A3 130r on 80r yel grn 4.00 2.00
76 A3 130r on 200r dk blue, *blue* 4.00 2.60
77 A3 400r on 50r lt blue 9.00 3.00
a. Inverted surcharge 65.00 55.00
b. Perf 13½ *300.00 300.00*
78 A3 400r on 300r dk blue, *sal* 4.00 1.75

On Newspaper Stamp of 1893

79 N1 400r on 2½r brown 1.60 1.50
a. Inverted surcharge 30.00
b. Perf 12½ *225.00 200.00*
Nos. 59-79 (21) 131.10 70.80

Reprints of Nos. 59, 66, 67, and 77 have shiny white gum and clean-cut perforation 13½.

For overprint and surcharge see Nos. 137, 205-206.

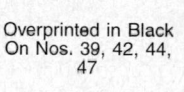

Overprinted in Black On Nos. 39, 42, 44, 47

1902-03 *Perf. 11½*

80 A4 15r brown 2.00 1.25
81 A4 25r sea green 2.00 1.25
82 A4 50r blue ('03) 2.00 1.25
83 A4 75r rose ('03) 3.75 2.75
a. Inverted overprint 42.50 42.50
Nos. 80-83 (4) 9.75 6.50

For overprint see No. 139.

No. 46 Surcharged in Black

1905, July 1

84 A4 50r on 65r slate blue 5.00 3.00

Stamps of 1898-1903 Overprinted in Carmine or Green

1911, Aug. 20

85 A4 2½r gray .25 .25
86 A4 5r orange .25 .25
87 A4 10r lt green 1.00 .80
88 A4 15r gray green .90 .45
89 A4 20r gray violet 1.50 .80
90 A4 25r carmine (G) .90 .45
91 A4 50r brown 8.50 6.00
92 A4 75r red lilac 1.40 .80
93 A4 100r dk blue, *blue* 1.40 .80
94 A4 115r org brn, *pink* 1.40 .80
95 A4 130r brown, *straw* 1.40 .80
96 A4 200r red vio, *pnksh* 6.50 4.00
97 A4 400r dull bl, *straw* 3.50 1.25
98 A4 500r blk & red, *bl* 3.50 1.25
99 A4 700r violet, *straw* 3.50 1.40
Nos. 85-99 (15) 35.90 20.10

King Manuel II — A5

Overprinted in Carmine or Green

1912 *Perf. 11½x12*

100 A5 2½r violet .25 .25
101 A5 5r black .25 .25
102 A5 10r gray grn .45 .40
103 A5 20r carmine (G) 2.40 1.40
104 A5 25r vio brown .45 .25
105 A5 50r dk blue 5.00 3.50
106 A5 75r bister brn 1.10 1.00
107 A5 100r brown, *lt grn* 1.10 1.00
108 A5 200r dk green, *sal* 1.75 1.10
109 A5 300r black, *azure* 1.75 1.10

Perf. 14½x15

110 A5 400r black & blue 3.75 3.00
111 A5 500r ol grn & vio brn 3.75 3.00
Nos. 100-111 (12) 22.00 16.25

Common Design Types pictured following the introduction.

Vasco da Gama Issue of Various Portuguese Colonies

Common Design Types CD20-CD27 Surcharged

On Stamps of Macao

1913, Feb. 13 *Perf. 12½ to 16*

112 ¼c on ½a blue grn 2.00 .85
113 ½c on 1a red 2.00 .85
114 1c on 2a red violet 2.00 .85
115 2½c on 4a yel grn 2.00 .85
116 5c on 8a dk blue 7.00 6.00
117 7½c on 12a vio brn 5.75 2.40
118 10c on 16a bister brn 2.25 1.60
119 15c on 24a bister 5.75 3.50
Nos. 112-119 (8) 28.75 16.90

On Stamps of Portuguese Africa
Perf. 14 to 15

120 ¼c on 2½r bl grn 1.40 .60
121 ½c on 5r red 1.40 .60
122 1c on 10r red vio 1.40 .60
123 2½c on 25r yel grn 1.40 .60
124 5c on 50r dk blue 2.00 1.50
125 7½c on 75r vio brn 3.75 3.00
126 10c on 100r bis brn 2.00 1.90
127 15c on 150r bister 2.50 2.50
Nos. 120-127 (8) 15.85 11.30

On Stamps of Timor

128 ¼c on ½a bl grn 1.40 .85
129 ½c on 1a red 1.40 .85
130 1c on 2a red vio 1.40 .85
131 2½c on 4a yel grn 1.40 .85
132 5c on 8a dk blue 7.00 5.50
133 7½c On 12a vio brn 5.50 3.00
134 10c on 16a bis brn 2.25 1.90
135 15c on 24a bister 4.50 2.40
Nos. 128-135 (8) 24.85 16.20
Nos. 112-135 (24) 69.45 44.40

For surcharges see Nos. 197-198.

No. 75 Overprinted in Red

1913 *Perf. 11½, 12½, 13½*

137 A3 130r on 80r yel grn 5.00 3.75

Nos. 73 and 76 overprinted but not issued. Values, $20, $25.

Same Overprint on No. 83 in Green

1914 *Perf. 12*

139 A4 75r rose 5.50 3.75
a. "PROVISORIO" double (G and R) 80.00 57.50

Ceres — A6

1914 Typo. *Perf. 15x14*
Name and Value in Black
Chalky Paper

144 A6 ¼c olive brn .75 .55
145 A6 ½c black .45 .30
146 A6 1c blue grn 5.25 4.75
147 A6 1½c lilac brown .75 .55
148 A6 2c carmine 1.25 .70

149	A6	2½c lt violet	.60	.50
150	A6	5c deep blue	1.00	.80
151	A6	7½c yel brn	1.25	.70
152	A6	8c slate	1.25	.75
153	A6	10c orange brn	2.00	.90
154	A6	15c brn rose ('22)	8.50	5.00
155	A6	20c yel grn	2.00	.90
156	A6	30c brown, *grn*	4.00	3.00
157	A6	40c brown, *pink*	4.00	3.00
158	A6	50c orange, *sal*	4.00	3.00
159	A6	1e green, *blue*	3.00	3.00
		Nos. 144-159 (16)	40.05	28.40

1916

Enamel-Surfaced Paper

160	A6	¼c olive brn	.45	.30
161	A6	5c deep blue	.75	.45

Ordinary Paper

162	A6	¼c olive brn	.25	.25
163	A6	½c black	.25	.25
164	A6	1c blue grn	.85	.75
165	A6	1c yel grn ('22)	.25	.25
166	A6	1½c lilac brown	.25	.25
167	A6	2c carmine	.25	.25
168	A6	2½c lt violet	.25	.25
169	A6	3c org ('22)	.30	.25
170	A6	4c rose ('22)	.25	*.25*
171	A6	12c blue grn ('22)	.35	.25
172	A6	15c plum	.90	.75
		Nos. 162-172 (11)	4.15	3.75

1920-26 ***Perf. 12x11½***

173	A6	¼c olive brn	.25	.25
174	A6	½c black	.25	.25
175	A6	1c yel grn ('22)	.25	.25
176	A6	1½c lilac brown	.25	.25
177	A6	2c carmine	.25	.25
178	A6	2c gray ('26)	.25	.25
179	A6	2½c lt violet	.25	.25
180	A6	3c org ('22)	2.40	2.25
181	A6	4c rose ('22)	.35	*.50*
182	A6	4½c gray ('22)	.25	*.50*
183	A6	5c brt blue ('22)	.25	.25
183A	A6	6c lilac ('22)	.25	.50
183B	A6	7c ultra ('22)	.25	*.50*
183C	A6	7½c yel brn	.25	*.50*
183D	A6	8c slate	.40	.30
183E	A6	10c orange brn	.25	.25
183F	A6	12c blue grn ('22)	.35	.25
183G	A6	15c plum	.30	.30
183H	A6	20c yel grn	.25	.25
183I	A6	24c ultra ('26)	1.50	1.40
183J	A6	25c choc ('26)	1.50	1.40
183K	A6	30c gray grn ('22)	.75	.25
183L	A6	40c turq blue ('22)	1.75	.25
183M	A6	50c violet ('26)	1.75	.30
183N	A6	60c dk blue ('22)	1.75	.45
183O	A6	60c rose ('26)	1.75	.45
183P	A6	80c brt rose ('22)	2.00	1.10
		Nos. 173-183P (27)	20.05	13.70

For surcharge see No. 214.

Glazed Paper

183Q	A6	1e rose ('22)	7.00	2.25
183R	A6	1e dp blue ('26)	9.00	1.50
183S	A6	2e dk violet ('22)	10.00	4.00
183T	A6	5e buff ('26)	45.00	12.00
183U	A6	10e pink ('26)	150.00	60.00
183V	A6	20e pale turq ('26)	200.00	80.00
		Nos. 183Q-183V (6)	421.00	159.75

Provisional Issue of 1902 Overprinted in Carmine

1915 ***Perf. 11½, 12½, 13½***

184	A2	115r on 10r green (11½)	2.50	2.00
a.		Perf. 13½	*100.00*	*100.00*
185	A2	115r on 20r rose (12½)	2.75	1.75
a.		Perf. 13½	30.00	30.00
186	A2	130r on 50r blue (12½)	2.50	1.25
187	A2	130r on 100r brown (12½)	1.60	1.00
188	A3	115r on 5r orange (11½)	1.40	.75
a.		Inverted overprint	45.00	
189	A3	115r on 25r blue grn (12½)	2.50	1.75
a.		Perf. 11½	*70.00*	*70.00*
190	A3	115r on 150r car, *rose* (11½)	1.00	.75
191	A3	130r on 75r carmine (12½)	2.50	1.00
192	A3	130r on 80r yel grn (11½)	2.50	1.00
a.		Inverted overprint	50.00	
193	A3	130r on 200r bl, *bl* (13½)	2.00	1.00
a.		Perf. 12½	*90.00*	*80.00*
		Nos. 184-193 (10)	21.25	12.25

War Tax Stamps of Portuguese Africa Srchd.

1921, Feb. 3 ***Perf. 15x14***

194	WT1	¼c on 1c green	.60	.40
195	WT1	½c on 1c green	.70	.50
a.		"1/2" instead of "½" as shown	17.50	15.00
196	WT1	1c green	.65	.50

Perf. 12x11½

194B	WT1	¼c on 1c green	1.20	1.00
195B	WT1	½c on 1c green	1.20	1.00
a.		"1/2" instead of "½" as shown	25.00	19.00
196B	WT1	1c green	1.10	.95

Nos. 194B-196B also exist on enameled paper. The values are the same.

Nos. 127 and 126 Surcharged

Perf. 14 to 15

197	CD27	2c on 15c on 150r	2.25	1.50
198	CD26	4c on 10c on 100r	2.75	2.60
a.		On No. 118 (error)	300.00	175.00

The 4c surcharge also exists on No. 134. Value, $500.

No. 50 Surcharged

Perf. 12

200	A4	6c on 100r dk bl, *bl*	2.75	2.10
a.		No accent on "U" of surcharge	17.50	15.00
		Nos. 194-200 (6)	9.70	7.60

No. 200 has an accent on the "U" of the surcharge.

Stamps of 1913-15 Surcharged

1922, Apr. ***Perf. 11½, 12½, 13½***

On No. 137

201	A3	4c on 130r on 80r	1.25	1.25

On Nos. 191-193

202	A3	4c on 130r on 75r	1.60	1.60
203	A3	4c on 130r on 80r	1.25	1.25
204	A3	4c on 130r on 200r	1.00	.80
a.		Perf. 12½	15.00	15.00
		Nos. 201-204 (4)	5.10	4.90

Surcharge of Nos. 201-204 with smaller $ occurs once in sheet of 28. Value eight times normal.

Nos. 78-79 Surcharged

1925 ***Perf. 13½, 11½***

205	A3	40c on 400r on 300r	1.00	.80
206	N1	40c on 400r on 2½r	1.00	.75

No. 176 Surcharged

1931, Nov. ***Perf. 12x11½***

214	A6	70c on 80c brt rose	3.75	2.50

Ceres — A7

1934, May 1 **Wmk. 232**

215	A7	1c bister	.25	*.25*
216	A7	5c olive brown	.25	.25
217	A7	10c violet	.25	.25
218	A7	15c black	.25	.25
219	A7	20c gray	.25	.25
220	A7	30c dk green	.25	.25
221	A7	40c red org	.25	.25
222	A7	45c brt blue	2.00	.85
223	A7	50c brown	.90	.55
224	A7	60c olive grn	.90	.55
225	A7	70c brown org	.90	.55
226	A7	80c emerald	.90	.55
227	A7	85c deep rose	4.00	2.60
228	A7	1e maroon	2.75	.50
229	A7	1.40e dk blue	3.75	3.00
230	A7	2e dk violet	4.50	2.60
231	A7	5e apple green	21.00	5.00
232	A7	10e olive bister	32.50	18.00
233	A7	20e orange	60.00	24.00
		Nos. 215-233 (19)	135.85	60.50

For surcharge see No. 256.

Vasco da Gama Issue

Common Design Types

1938 **Unwmk.** ***Perf. 13½x13***

Name and Value in Black

234	CD34	1c gray green	.25	.25
235	CD34	5c orange brn	.25	.25
236	CD34	10c dk carmine	.25	.25
237	CD34	15c dk vio brn	1.00	.85
238	CD34	20c slate	.50	.25
239	CD35	30c rose vio	.50	.25
240	CD35	35c brt green	.50	.25
241	CD35	40c brown	.50	.25
242	CD35	50c brt red vio	.50	.25
243	CD36	60c gray blk	.50	.25
244	CD36	70c brown vio	.50	.25
245	CD36	80c orange	.45	.25
246	CD36	1e red	.60	.25
247	CD37	1.75e blue	1.90	.70
248	CD37	2e dk blue grn	3.50	2.00
249	CD37	5e ol grn	8.00	2.00
250	CD38	10e blue vio	13.00	2.60
251	CD38	20e red brown	37.50	5.00
		Nos. 234-251 (18)	70.20	16.15

For surcharges see Nos. 255, 271-276, 288-292.

Outline Map of Africa — A8

1939, June 23 **Litho.** ***Perf. 11½x12***

252	A8	80c vio, *pale rose*	5.00	3.50
253	A8	1.75e blue, *pale bl*	40.00	30.00
254	A8	20e brown, *buff*	85.00	26.00
		Nos. 252-254 (3)	130.00	59.50

Visit of the President of Portugal in 1939.

Nos. 239 and 221 Surcharged with New Value and Bars in Black

1948 **Unwmk.** ***Perf. 13½x13***

255	CD35	10c on 30c rose violet	2.00	*1.25*

Perf. 12x11½

Wmk. 232

256	A7	25c on 40c red orange	2.00	*1.25*

Machado Pt., Sao Vicente — A9

Brava Creek, Sao Nicoláo — A10

Designs: 10c, Ribeira Grande. 1e, Harbor, Sao Vicente. 1.75e, Mindelo, distant view. 2e, Joao de Evora Beach. 5e, Mindelo. 10e, Volcano, Fire Island. 20e, Mt. Paul.

Perf. 14½

1948, Oct. 1 **Litho.** **Unwmk.**

257	A9	5c vio brn & bis	.35	.30
258	A9	10c ol grn & pale grn	.35	.30
259	A10	50c mag & lil rose	.65	.30
260	A10	1e brn vio & rose lil	2.00	1.25
261	A10	1.75e ultra & grnsh bl	3.00	2.25
262	A10	2e dk brn & buff	6.00	2.00
263	A10	5e ol grn & yel	12.00	5.00
264	A10	10e red & cream	22.50	16.00
265	A10	20e dk vio & bis	50.00	32.00
		Nos. 257-265 (9)	96.85	59.40

Lady of Fatima Issue

Common Design Type

1948, Dec.

266	CD40	50c dark blue	8.50	4.50

UPU Symbols — A10a

1949, Oct. ***Perf. 14***

267	A10a	1e red vio & pink	7.00	3.00

UPU, 75th anniversary.

Catalogue values for unused stamps in this section, from this point to the end of the section, are for Never Hinged items.

Holy Year Issue

Common Design Types

1950, May ***Perf. 13x13½***

268	CD41	1e orange brown	1.00	.45
269	CD42	2e slate	3.75	1.75

Holy Year Conclusion Issue

Common Design Type

1951, Oct. **Unwmk.** ***Perf. 14***

270	CD43	2e purple & lilac + label	1.50	1.25

Stamps without labels sell for less.

Nos. 240, 244-245, 247, 250 Surcharged with New Value and Bars

Perf. 13½x13

1951, May 21 **Unwmk.**

271	CD35	10c on 35c	.70	.55
272	CD36	20c on 70c	.90	.65
273	CD36	40c on 70c	1.10	.65
274	CD36	50c on 80c	1.10	.65
275	CD37	1e on 1.75e	1.25	.65
276	CD38	2e on 10e	5.75	2.00
a.		1e on 10e	200.00	125.00
		Nos. 271-276 (6)	10.80	5.15

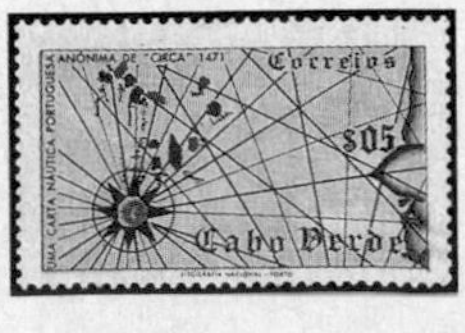

Map of Cape Verde Islands, 1502 — A11

Vicente Dias and Gonçalo de Cintra
A12

Portraits: 30c, Diogo Alfonso and Alvaro Fernandes. 50c, Lançarote and Soeiro da Costa. 1e, Diogo Gomes and Antonio da Nola. 2e, Prince Fernando and Prince Henry the Navigator. 3e, Antao Gonçalves and Dinis Dias. 5e, Alfonso Goncalves Baldaia and Joao Fernandes. 10e, Dinis Eanes da Gra and Alvaro de Freitas. 20e, Map of Cape Verde Islands, 1502.

1952, Feb. 24 *Perf. 14*

277	A11	5c multicolored		.25	.25
278	A12	10c multicolored		.25	.25
279	A12	30c multicolored		.25	.25
280	A12	50c multicolored		.25	.25
281	A12	1e multicolored		.25	.25
282	A12	2e multicolored		1.50	.25
283	A12	3e multicolored		11.50	1.50
284	A12	5e multicolored		4.00	.70
285	A12	10e multicolored		8.00	1.75
286	A11	20e multicolored		14.00	2.40
		Nos. 277-286 (10)		40.25	7.85

Medical Congress Issue
Common Design Type

Design: Hypodermic Injection.

1952, June *Perf. 13½*

287	CD44	20c ol grn & dk brn	.70	.50

No. 247 Surcharged with New Values and "X" in Black

1952, Jan. 25 *Perf. 13½x13*

288	CD37	10c on 1.75e	2.00	1.10
289	CD37	20c on 1.75e	2.00	1.10
290	CD37	50c on 1.75e	8.00	5.00
291	CD37	1e on 1.75e	1.00	.25
292	CD37	1.50e on 1.75e	1.00	.25
		Nos. 288-292 (5)	14.00	7.70

Facade of Jeronymos Convent
A13

Perf. 13½

1953, Jan. **Unwmk.** **Litho.**

293	A13	10c brown & pale olive	.25	.25
294	A13	50c purple & fawn	.90	.40
295	A13	1e dark green & fawn	2.10	1.10
		Nos. 293-295 (3)	3.25	1.75

Exhibition of Sacred Missionary Art held at Lisbon in 1951.

Stamp of Portugal and Arms of Colonies — A13a

1953 **Photo.**

296	A13a	50c multicolored	1.75	1.10

Centenary of Portuguese stamps.

Sao Paulo Issue
Common Design Type

1954 **Litho.** *Perf. 13½*

297	CD46	1e green, cream & gray	.70	.60

Belem Tower, Lisbon, and Colonial Arms — A14

1955, May 15 **Litho.** *Perf. 13½*

298	A14	1e multicolored	.50	.25
299	A14	1.60e buff & multi	.75	.60

Visit of Pres. Francisco H. C. Lopes.

Arms of Praia — A15

1958, June 14 *Perf. 12x11½*

300	A15	1e multicolored	.65	.45
301	A15	2.50e pink & multi	1.10	.90

Centenary of city of Praia.

Fair Emblem, Globe and Arms — A15a

1958 *Perf. 12x11½*

302	A15a	2e multicolored	.90	.40

World's Fair, Brussels, Apr. 17-Oct. 19.

Tropical Medicine Congress Issue
Common Design Type

1958, Sept. 5 *Perf. 13½*

303	CD47	3e Aloe vera	5.50	2.10

Prince Henry — A16

1960, June 25 **Litho.** *Perf. 13½*

304	A16	2e multicolored	.50	.25

500th anniv. of the death of Prince Henry the Navigator.

Antonio da Nola — A17

Design: 2.50e, Diogo Gomes.

1960, Oct. **Unwmk.** *Perf. 14½*

305	A17	1e multicolored	.75	.45
306	A17	2.50e multicolored	2.50	1.00

Discovery of Cape Verde, 500th anniv.

School Children
A18

1960

307	A18	2.50e multicolored	1.25	.65

10th anniv. of the Commission for Technical Cooperation in Africa South of the Sahara (C.C.T.A.).

Arms of Praia — A19

Arms of various cities & towns of Cape Verde.

1961, July **Litho.** *Perf. 13½*

308	A19	5c shown	.25	.25
309	A19	15c Nova Sintra	.25	.25
310	A19	20c Ribeira Brava	.25	.25
311	A19	30c Assomada	.25	.25
312	A19	1e Maio	.65	.25
313	A19	2e Mindelo	.65	.25
314	A19	2.50e Santa Maria	1.00	.25
315	A19	3e Pombas	2.00	.50
316	A19	5e Sal-Rei	2.00	.50
317	A19	7.50e Tarrafal	3.00	.90
318	A19	15e Maria Pia	5.00	.90
319	A19	30e San Felipe	9.00	2.50
		Nos. 308-319 (12)	24.30	7.05

Sports Issue
Common Design Type

Sports: 50c, Javelin. 1e, Discus. 1.50e, Cricket. 2.50e, Boxing. 4.50e, Hurdling. 12.50e, Golf.

1962, Jan. 18 *Perf. 13½*

320	CD48	50c lt brown	.25	.25
321	CD48	1e lt green	.75	.25
322	CD48	1.50e lt blue grn	10.00	2.00
323	CD48	2.50e pale vio bl	.75	.35
324	CD48	4.50e orange	1.10	.75
325	CD48	12.50e beige	2.40	1.60
		Nos. 320-325 (6)	15.25	5.20

Anti-Malaria Issue
Common Design Type

Design: Anopheles pretoriensis.

1962 **Litho.** *Perf. 13½*

326	CD49	2.50e multicolored	1.40	.90

Airline Anniversary Issue
Common Design Type

1963, Oct. **Unwmk.** *Perf. 14½*

327	CD50	2.50e gray & multi	1.10	.70

National Overseas Bank Issue
Common Design Type

Design: 1.50e, Jose da Silva Mendes Leal.

1964, May 16 *Perf. 13½*

328	CD51	1.50e multicolored	1.10	.75

ITU Issue
Common Design Type

1965, May 17 **Litho.** *Perf. 14½*

329	CD52	2.50e buff & multi	2.10	1.40

Militia Drummer, 1806 — A20

Designs: 1e, Soldier, Militia, 1806. 1.50e, Grenadier officer, 1833. 2.50e, Grenadier, 1833. 3e, Cavalry officer, 1834. 4e, Grenadier, 1835. 5e, Artillery officer, 1848. 10e, Drum major, infantry, 1856.

1965, Dec. 1 **Litho.** *Perf. 14½*

330	A20	50c multicolored	.25	.25
331	A20	1e multicolored	.45	.25
332	A20	1.50e multicolored	.45	.40
333	A20	2.50e multicolored	1.25	.35
334	A20	3e multicolored	2.50	.55
335	A20	4e multicolored	1.10	.55
336	A20	5e multicolored	1.25	.55
337	A20	10e multicolored	2.75	1.75
		Nos. 330-337 (8)	10.00	4.65

National Revolution Issue
Common Design Type

1e, Dr. Adriano Moreira School & Health Center.

1966, May 28 **Litho.** *Perf. 12*

338	CD53	1e multicolored	.60	.45

Navy Club Issue
Common Design Type

Designs: 1e, Capt. Fontoura da Costa and gunboat Mandovy. 1.50e, Capt. Carvalho Araujo and minesweeper Augusto Castilho.

1967, Jan. 31 **Litho.** *Perf. 13*

339	CD54	1e multicolored	.75	.50
340	CD54	1.50e multicolored	1.25	.90

Virgin Mary Statue — A21

1967, May 13 **Litho.** *Perf. 12½x13*

341	A21	1e multicolored	.35	.25

50th anniv. of the apparition of the Virgin Mary to 3 shepherd children at Fatima.

Pres. Rodrigues Thomaz — A22

1968, Feb. 9 **Litho.** *Perf. 13½*

342	A22	1e multicolored	.35	.25

Issued to commemorate the 1968 visit of Pres. Americo de Deus Rodrigues Thomaz.

Cabral Issue

Pedro Alvares Cabral — A23

1e, Cantino's world map, 1502, horiz.

1968, Apr. 22 **Litho.** *Perf. 14*

343	A23	1e multicolored	.85	.70
344	A23	1.50e multicolored	1.40	.75

See note after Angola No. 545.
For overprint see No. 365.

Sao Vicente Harbor — A24

Physic Nut — A25

Designs: 1.50e, Peanut plant. 2.50e, Castor-oil plant. 3.50e, Yams. 4e, Date palm. 4.50e, Guavas. 5e, Tamarind. 10e, Bitter cassava. 30e, Woman carrying fruit baskets.

1968, Oct. 15 **Litho.** *Perf. 14*

345	A24	50c multicolored	.25	.25
346	A25	1e multicolored	.50	.25
347	A25	1.50e multicolored	.50	.25
348	A25	2.50e multicolored	.50	.25
349	A25	3.50e multicolored	.50	.25
350	A25	4e multicolored	.50	.25
351	A25	4.50e multicolored	1.00	.25
352	A25	5 multicolored	2.00	.30
353	A25	10e multicolored	2.00	.60
354	A25	30e multicolored	4.00	2.50
		Nos. 345-354 (10)	11.75	5.15

For overprint see No. 372.

Admiral Coutinho Issue
Common Design Type

Adm. Coutinho & map showing route of 1st flight from Lisbon to Rio de Janeiro.

1969, Feb. 17 Litho. *Perf. 14*
355 CD55 30c multi, vert. .35 .25

For surcharge see No. 388.

Vasco da Gama Issue

Vasco da Gama — A26

1969, Aug. 29 Litho. *Perf. 14*
356 A26 1.50e multicolored .35 .25

Vasco da Gama (1469-1524), navigator.

Administration Reform Issue
Common Design Type

1969, Sept. 25 Litho. *Perf. 14*
357 CD56 2e multicolored .35 .25

King Manuel I Issue

King Manuel I — A27

1969, Dec. 1 Litho. *Perf. 14*
358 A27 3e multicolored .55 .35

500th anniv. of the birth of King Manuel I.

Marshal Carmona Issue
Common Design Type

Design: 2.50e, Antonio Oscar Carmona in marshal's uniform.

1970, Nov. 15 Litho. *Perf. 14*
359 CD57 2.50e multi .55 .35
Nos. 359 (1) .55 .35

Galleons on Sanaga River — A28

1972, May 25 Litho. *Perf. 13*
360 A28 5e lilac rose & multi 1.00 .30

4th centenary of the publication of The Lusiads by Luiz Camoens.

Olympic Games Issue
Common Design Type

4e, Basketball & boxing, Olympic emblem.

1972, June 20 *Perf. 14x13½*
361 CD59 4e multicolored .65 .30

For surcharge see No. 371.

Lisbon-Rio de Janeiro Flight Issue
Common Design Type

Design: "Lusitania" landing at San Vicente.

1972, Sept. 20 Litho. *Perf. 13½*
362 CD60 3.50e multi 1.50 .30

WMO Centenary Issue
Common Design Type

1973, Dec. 15 Litho. *Perf. 13*
363 CD61 2.50e ultra & multi .65 .30

For overprint see No. 387.

Mindelo Desalination Plant — A29

1974 Litho. *Perf. 13½*
364 A29 4e multicolored 1.25 .85

Opening of the Mindelo desalination plant. For surcharge see No. 371A.

Republic

No. 343 Overprinted

1975, Dec. 19 Litho. *Perf. 14*
365 A23 1e multicolored .35 .25

Proclamation of Independence.

Amilcar Cabral, Flag and Crowd — A30

1976, Jan. 20
366 A30 5e multicolored .55 .25

3rd anniv. of the assassination of Amilcar Cabral (1924-73), revolutionary leader.

Rising Sun, Coat of Arms, Liberated People — A31

1976, July 5 Litho. *Perf. 14*

367	A31	50c multicolored	.25	.25
368	A31	3e multicolored	.90	.25
369	A31	15e multicolored	2.00	.35
370	A31	50e multicolored	6.25	1.25
a.		Miniature sheet, #367-370	*12.00*	*12.00*
		Nos. 367-370 (4)	9.40	2.10

First anniversary of independence.

Nos. 351, 361, 364 Overprinted

1976 Litho. *Perf. 14*

371	CD59	4e multi	*1,150.*	—
371A	A29	4e multi	*50.00*	*27.50*
372	A25	4.50e multi	4.25	2.25

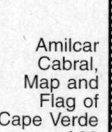

Amilcar Cabral, Map and Flag of Cape Verde A32

1976, Sept. 19 *Perf. 14*
373 A32 1e multicolored .45 .25

Party of Intl. Action (PAICC), 20th anniv.

Electronic Tree and ITU Emblem — A33

1977, May 17 Litho. *Perf. 13½x13*
374 A33 5.50e multi .45 .25

World Telecommunications Day.

Ashtray — A34

Carved Coconut Shells: 30c, Bell on stand. 50c, Lamp with Adam and Eve. 1e, Hollow shell with Nativity. 1.50e, Desk lamp. 5e, Jar. 10e, Jar with hinged cover. 20e, Tobacco jar with palms. 30e, Stringed instrument.

1977, July 5 Litho. *Perf. 14*

375	A34	20c lilac & multi	.25	.25
376	A34	30c rose & multi	.25	.25
377	A34	50c salmon & multi	.25	.25
378	A34	1e lt green & multi	.35	.25
379	A34	1.50e orange yel & multi	.35	.25
380	A34	5e gray & multi	.75	.35
381	A34	10e lt blue & multi	1.25	.55
382	A34	20e yellow & multi	2.00	1.25
383	A34	30e rose lilac & multi	3.25	1.40
		Nos. 375-383 (9)	8.70	4.80

Cape Verde No. 1 and Coat of Arms — A35

1977, Sept. 12 Litho. *Perf. 13½*
384 A35 4e blue & multi .40 .25
385 A35 8e lilac & multi .80 .35

Centenary of Cape Verde stamps.

Congress Emblem — A36

1977, Nov. 15 *Perf. 14*
386 A36 3.50e multi .60 .25

African Party of Independence of Guinea-Bissau and Cape Verde (PAIGC), 3rd cong., Nov. 15-20.

No. 363 Overprinted

1978, May 1 *Perf. 12*
387 CD61 2.50e ultra & multi .60 .25

No. 355 Surcharged

1978, May 1 *Perf. 14*
388 CD55 3e on 30c multi 2.25 .35

Antenna and ITU Emblem — A37

1978, May 17 Litho. *Perf. 14*
389 A37 3.50e silver & multi .55 .25

10th World Telecommunications Day.

Freighter Cabo Verde — A38

1978, June 25 Litho. *Perf. 14*
391 A38 1e multicolored .70 .25

First ship of Cape Verde merchant marine.

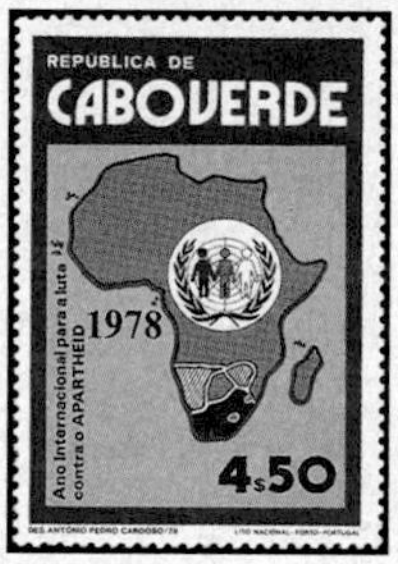

Map of Africa and Equality Emblem — A39

1978, June 21
392 A39 4.50e multicolored .55 .25

Anti-Apartheid Year.

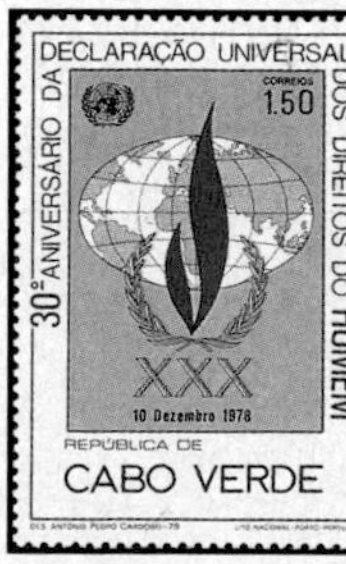

Human Rights Emblem — A40

1978, Dec. 10 Litho. *Perf. 14*
393 A40 1.50e multicolored .35 .25
394 A40 2e multicolored .55 .35

Universal Declaration of Human Rights, 30th anniversary.

Children and Balloons, IYC Emblem — A41

IYC Emblem and Child's Drawing: 3.50e, Children and flowers.

1979, June 1 **Litho.** ***Perf. 14***

395	A41	1.50e multi	.65	.25
396	A41	3.50e multi	1.10	.35

International Year of the Child.

Pindjiguiti Massacre Monument — A42

1979, Aug. 3 ***Perf. 13***

397	A42	4.50e multi	3.00	.25

Massacre of Pindjiguiti, 20th anniversary.

Natl. Youth Week — A42a

1979, Sept. 1 **Litho.** ***Perf. 14***

397A	A42a	3.50e Poster	1.10	.25

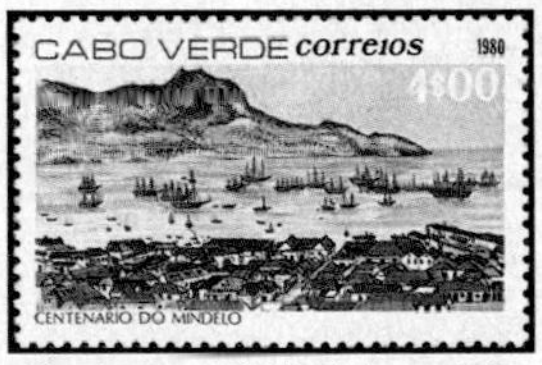

Centenary of Mindelo — A43

1980, Apr. 23 **Litho.** ***Perf. 12½***

398	A43	4e multicolored	.70	.25

Flag of Cape Verde — A44

Stylized Bird, "V" — A45

1980 **Litho.** ***Perf. 12½***

399	A44	4e multicolored	1.25	.25
400	A45	4e multicolored	.45	.25
401	A45	7e multicolored	.80	.35
402	A45	11e multicolored	1.10	.45
		Nos. 399-402 (4)	3.60	1.30

5th anniversary of independence. Issued: No. 399, June 1; others July 5.

A45a

1980, May 13

402A	A45a	3.50e multi	.55	.25
402B	A45a	4.50e multi	.70	.25

1980 Natl. census.

A46

1980, June 6

403	A46	1e Running	.25	.25
404	A46	2.50e Boxing	.25	.25
405	A46	3e Basketball	.35	.25
406	A46	4e Volleyball	.50	.30
407	A46	20e Swimming	1.40	.90
408	A46	50e Tennis	4.00	1.75
		Nos. 403-408 (6)	6.75	3.70

Souvenir Sheet

Perf. 13

409	A46	30e Soccer, horiz.	*18.00*	*18.00*

22nd Summer Olympic Games, Moscow, July 19-Aug. 3.

Thunnus Alalunga A47

4.50e, Trachurus trachurus. 8e, Muraena helena. 10e, Corvina nigra. 12e, Katsuwonus pelamis. 50e, Prionace glauca.

1980, Nov. 11 **Litho.** ***Perf. 13***

410	A47	50c shown	.25	.25
411	A47	4.50e multicolored	.50	.25
412	A47	8e multicolored	.90	.25
413	A47	10e multicolored	1.50	.35
414	A47	12e multicolored	2.00	.60
415	A47	50e multicolored	5.00	1.90
		Nos. 410-415 (6)	10.15	3.60

Lochnera Rosea — A48

4.50e, Poinciana regia-bojer. 8e, Mirabilis jalapa. 10e, Nerium oleander. 12e, Bougainvillia litoralis. 30e, Hibiscus.

1980, Dec. 29

416	A48	50c shown	.25	.25
417	A48	4.50e multicolored	.30	.25
418	A48	8e multicolored	.75	.35
419	A48	10e multicolored	.95	.45
420	A48	12e multicolored	1.10	.55
421	A48	30e multicolored	2.60	1.50
		Nos. 416-421 (6)	5.95	3.35

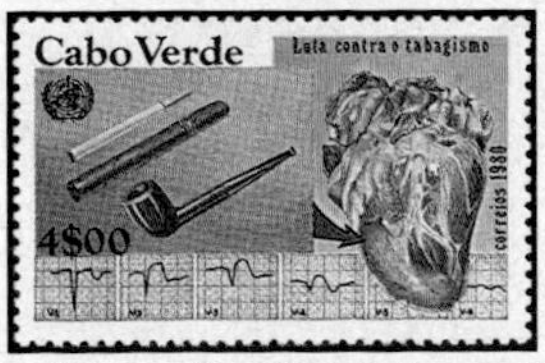

WHO Anti-smoking Campaign — A48a

1980, Sept. 19 ***Perf. 12½***

421A	A48a	4e multicolored	.50	.25
421B	A48a	7e multicolored	1.10	.35

Arca Verde A49

1980, Nov. 30 **Litho.** ***Perf. 12½x12***

422	A49	3e shown	.30	.25
423	A49	5.50e Ilha do Maio	.50	.25
424	A49	7.50e Ilha de Komo	.95	.55
425	A49	9e Boa Vista	1.25	.75
426	A49	12e Santo Antao	1.40	.55
427	A49	30e Santiago	3.25	1.40
		Nos. 422-427 (6)	7.65	3.75

Hand-woven Bag, Map — A49a

Various hand-woven articles. 10e, vert.

1978, May 21 **Litho.** ***Perf. 14***

427A	A49a	50c multi	.25	.25
427B	A49a	1.50e multi	.25	.25
427C	A49a	2e multi	.55	.25
427D	A49a	3e multi	.55	.30
427E	A49a	10e multi	1.40	.70
		Nos. 427A-427E (5)	3.00	1.75

Desert Erosion Prevention Campaign — A50

1981, Mar. 30 **Litho.** ***Perf. 13***

428	A50	4.50e multi	.60	.25
429	A50	10.50e multi	1.25	.50

6th Anniv. of Constitution A51

1981, Apr. 15

430	A51	4.50e multicolored	.60	.25

Souvenir Sheet

Austria No. B336 — A52

1981, May 18

431	A52	50e multicolored	6.50	6.50

WIPA '81 Philatelic Exhibition, Vienna, Austria, May 22-31.

Antenna — A53

1981, Aug. 25 **Litho.** ***Perf. 12½***

432	A53	4.50e shown	.65	.25
433	A53	8e Dish antenna	.95	.40
434	A53	20e Dish antenna, diff.	2.00	.95
		Nos. 432-434 (3)	3.60	1.60

Intl. Year of the Disabled A54

1981, Dec. 25 **Litho.** ***Perf. 12½***

435	A54	4.50e multicolored	.65	.35

Purple Gallinule A55

1981, Dec. 30

436	A55	1e Egret, vert.	.60	.25
437	A55	4.50e Barn owl, vert.	1.25	.40
438	A55	8e Passerine, vert.	2.75	.55
439	A55	10e shown	3.00	.65
440	A55	12e Guinea fowl	3.75	.75
		Nos. 436-440 (5)	11.35	2.60

Souvenir Sheet

Perf. 13

441	A55	50e Razo Isld. lark	9.50	9.50

No. 441 contains 31x39mm one stamp.

CILSS Congress, Praia, Jan. 17 — A56

1982, Jan. 17 ***Perf. 13x12½***

442	A56	11.50e multicolored	1.40	.65

Amilcar Cabral Soccer Championship — A57

Designs: Soccer players and flags.

1982, Feb. 10 **Litho.** ***Perf. 12½***

443	A57	4.50e multicolored	.55	.25
444	A57	7.50e multicolored	.85	.40
445	A57	11.50e multicolored	1.40	.70
		Nos. 443-445 (3)	2.80	1.35

1982 World Cup — A58

Designs: Soccer players and ball.

1982, Apr. 25

446	A58	1.50e multi	.25	.25
447	A58	4.50e multi	.50	.25
448	A58	8e multi	.85	.35
449	A58	10.50e multi	1.00	.45
450	A58	12e multi	1.25	.55
451	A58	20e multi	2.25	.90
		Nos. 446-451 (6)	6.10	2.75

Souvenir Sheet

452	A58	50e multi	6.25	6.25

First Anniv. of Women's Organization — A59

1982, Apr. 15 Litho. *Perf. 12½x12*

453	A59	4.50e Marching	.55	.25
454	A59	8e Farming	1.10	.40
455	A59	12e Child care	1.60	.70
		Nos. 453-455 (3)	3.25	1.35

Estaleiros Navais Port, St. Vincent A59a

1982, July 5 Litho. *Perf. 13x12½*

455A	A59a	10.50e multi	1.75	.60

Natl. independence, 7th anniv.

Return of Barque Morrissey-Ernestina — A60

1982, July 5 Litho. *Perf. 13*

456	A60	12e multi	1.75	.80

Butterflies — A61

2e, Hypolimnas misippus. 4.50e, Melanitis lede. 8e, Catopsilia florella. 10.50e, Colias electo. 11.50e, Danaus chrysippus. 12e, Papilio demodecus.

1982, July 27 Litho.

457	A61	2e multicolored	.35	.25
458	A61	4.50e multicolored	.70	.25
459	A61	8e multicolored	1.10	.25
460	A61	10.50e multicolored	1.50	.40
461	A61	11.50e multicolored	1.60	.60
462	A61	12e multicolored	2.75	.70
		Nos. 457-462 (6)	8.00	2.45

Francisco Xavier da Cruz (1905-1958), Composer — A62

14e, Eugenio Tavares (1867-1930), poet.

1983, Feb. 20 Litho. *Perf. 13*

463	A62	7e multicolored	.45	.30
464	A62	14e multicolored	1.90	.80

World Communications Year — A63

1983, Oct. 10 Litho.

465	A63	13e multicolored	1.60	.80

Local Seashells — A64

1983, Nov. 30 *Perf. 13½*

466	A64	50c Conus ateralbus	.25	.25
467	A64	1e Conus decoratus	.25	.25
468	A64	3e Conus salreiensis	.35	.25
469	A64	10e Conus verdensis	1.50	.55
470	A64	50e Conus cuneolus	5.00	2.75
		Nos. 466-470 (5)	7.35	4.05

40th Anniv. of Intl. Civil Aviation Org. A65

Airplanes: 50c, Ogma-Auster D5/160, 1966. 2e, De Havilland DH-104 Dove, 1945. 10e, Hawker Siddeley 748-200, 1972. 13e, De Havilland Dragon Rapide, 1945. 20e, De Havilland Twin Otter, 1977. 50e, Britten-Norman Islander, 1971.

1984, Feb. 15 Litho.

471	A65	50c multicolored	.25	.25
472	A65	2e multicolored	.30	.25
473	A65	10e multicolored	1.10	.50
474	A65	13e multicolored	1.25	.85
475	A65	20e multicolored	1.90	1.25
476	A65	50e multicolored	4.50	2.50
		Nos. 471-476 (6)	9.30	5.60

Amilcar Cabral — A66

1983, Jan. 17 Litho. *Perf. 14½*

477	A66	7e multi	1.00	.50
478	A66	10.50e multi	1.50	.90
a.		Souvenir sheet of 2, #477-478	30.00	30.00

Amilcar Cabral Symposium, Jan. 17-20. No. 478a sold for 30e.

Cross Over Islands — A67

1983, Dec. 10 Photo. *Perf. 14½*

479	A67	7e multicolored	1.10	.50

Christianity in Cape Verde, 450th anniv.

Natl. Solidarity Campaign A68

1984, Sept. 12 *Perf. 13½*

480	A68	6.50e multicolored	1.10	.25
481	A68	13.50e multicolored	2.10	.85

2nd Conference of Natl. Women's Orgs., Mar. 23-27 — A69

1985, Mar. 27 Litho. *Perf. 13½*

482	A69	8e multicolored	1.10	.55

Miniature Sheet

483	A69	30e multicolored	100.00	100.00

Natl. Independence, 10th Anniv. — A70

1985, July 5 Litho. *Perf. 14*

484	A70	8c multicolored	1.25	.55
485	A70	12e multicolored	1.90	.80

Intl. Youth Year — A71

1985, Sept. 12 Litho. *Perf. 14*

486	A71	12e multicolored	2.50	.90

Vapor, by Hundertwasser A72

Photogravure and Engraved

1986, Apr. 25 *Perf. 14*

Black Surcharge

487	A72	30e on 10e multi	22.50	4.00

Souvenir Sheets

Background Color

488		Sheet of 4	150.00	
a.	A72	50e yellow & multi	17.50	17.50
489		Sheet of 4	150.00	
a.	A72	50e red & multi	17.50	17.50
490		Sheet of 4	150.00	
a.	A72	50e green & multi	17.50	17.50

No. 487 exists without surcharge. Value $40.

World Wildlife Fund — A73

8e, Mabuya vaillanti. 10e, Tarentola gigas brancoensis. 15e, Tarentola gigas gigas. 30e, Hemidactylus bouvieri.

No. 495a, Mabuya vaillanti. No. 495b, Hemidactylus bouvieri.

Perf. 13½x14½

1986, June 15 Litho.

491	A73	8e multicolored	6.50	2.50
492	A73	10e multicolored	8.00	3.25
493	A73	15e multicolored	12.00	4.00
494	A73	30e multicolored	24.00	5.00
		Nos. 491-494 (4)	50.50	14.75

Souvenir Sheet

495		Sheet of 2	30.00	22.50
a.	A73	50e multi	14.00	10.00
b.	A73	50e multi	14.00	10.00

No. 495 printed with center label picturing progress union emblem. Nos. 495a-495b printed without WWF emblem.

World Food Day — A74

1986, June 20 *Perf. 14*

496	A74	8e Cauldron	.50	.25
497	A74	12e Mortar & pestle	.80	.35
498	A74	15e Quern stone	1.40	.50
		Nos. 496-498 (3)	2.70	1.10

Intl. Peace Year — A75

1986, Dec. 24 Litho. *Perf. 14*

499	A75	12e multicolored	.60	.25
500	A75	30e multicolored	2.10	1.40

Natl. Child Survival Campaign A76

1987, Mar. 27 Litho. *Perf. 14*

501	A76	8e multicolored	.45	.25
502	A76	10e multicolored	.55	.25
503	A76	12e multicolored	.65	.35
504	A76	16e multicolored	.95	.50
505	A76	100e multicolored	4.50	2.75
		Nos. 501-505 (5)	7.10	4.10

Tourism A77

1987, May 17

506	A77	1e Bay, Mindelo	.25	.25
507	A77	2.50e Hill country	.25	.25
508	A77	5e Mountain peak	.25	.25
509	A77	8e Monument	.45	.25
510	A77	10e Mountain peaks	1.00	.30
511	A77	12e Beached boats	1.00	.40
512	A77	100e Harbor	5.25	3.00
		Nos. 506-512 (7)	8.45	4.70

For surcharge see No. 710.

Ships — A78

1987, Aug. 3 *Perf. 13½x14½*

513	A78	12e Carvalho, 1937	.75	.25
514	A78	16e Nauta, 1943	1.25	.25
515	A78	50e Maria Sony, 1911	3.75	1.25
		Nos. 513-515 (3)	5.75	1.75

Souvenir Sheet

516		Sheet of 2	9.00	9.00
a.	A78	60e Madalan, 1928	4.00	4.00

Crop Protection A80

50c, Identification of insect plague. 2e, Use of insecticides. 9e, Import of parasites. 13e, Import of predators. 16e, Locust. 19e, Estimation of crop loss.
50e, Agricultural Research Institute.

1988, May 9 **Litho.** *Perf. 13½*

518	A80	50c multicolored	.25	.25
519	A80	2e multicolored	.25	.25
520	A80	9e multicolored	.50	.25
521	A80	13e multicolored	.60	.25
522	A80	16e multicolored	1.00	.40
523	A80	19e multicolored	1.25	.60
		Nos. 518-523 (6)	3.85	2.00

Souvenir Sheet

524	A80	50e multicolored	5.00	5.00

Maps — A81

1e, Dutch, 17th cent. 2.50e, Belgian, 18th cent. 4.50e, French, 18th cent. 9.50e, English, 18th cent. 19.50e, English, 19th cent. 20e, French, 18th cent., vert.

1988, July 5 **Litho.** *Perf. 14*

525	A81	1e multicolored	.25	.25
526	A81	2.50e multicolored	.25	.25
527	A81	4.50e multicolored	.30	.25
528	A81	9.50e multicolored	.60	.25
529	A81	19.50e multicolored	1.25	.55
530	A81	20e multicolored	1.40	.65
		Nos. 525-530 (6)	4.05	2.20

Churches A82

5e, St. Amaro Abade, Tarrafal, Santiago Is. 8e, Our Lady of the Light, Maio Is. 10e, Nazarene, Praia, Santiago Is. 12e, Our Lady of Rosa'rio, Sao Nicolau Is. 15e, Nazarene, Mindelo, Sao Vicente Is. 20e, Our Lady of Grace, Praia, Santiago Is.

1988, Aug. 15 *Perf. 13½x14½*

531	A82	5e multicolored	.25	.25
532	A82	8e multicolored	.45	.25
533	A82	10e multicolored	.55	.25
534	A82	12e multicolored	.60	.25
535	A82	15e multicolored	.85	.35
536	A82	20e multicolored	1.25	.45
		Nos. 531-536 (6)	3.95	1.80

Water Conservation — A83

1988, Sept. 26 **Litho.** *Perf. 14*

537	A83	12e multicolored	.75	.35

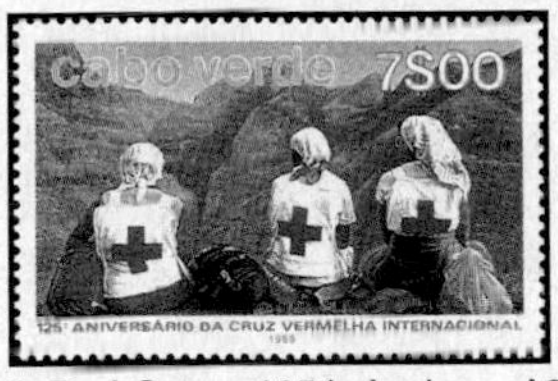

Intl. Red Cross, 125th Anniv. — A84

1988, Oct. 20

538	A84	7e multi	.45	.25

3rd Communist Party (PAICV) Congress — A85

Portrait of Pres. Pereira, PAICV secretary-general, and: 7e, S. Jorginho Vocational Training Center. 10.50e, UN Secretary-General Perez de Cuellar. 30e, 100e, Star and text.

Perf. 14½x13½

1988, Nov. 25 **Litho.**

539	A85	7e multi	.40	.25
540	A85	10.50e multi	.60	.25
541	A85	30e multi	1.75	.75
		Nos. 539-541 (3)	2.75	1.25

Souvenir Sheet

542	A85	100e multi	6.25	6.25

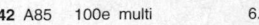

1988 Summer Olympics, Seoul — A86

1988, Dec. 26

543	A86	12e shown	.60	.25
544	A86	15e Tennis	.90	.35
545	A86	20e Soccer	1.25	.50
546	A86	30e Boxing	1.75	.90
		Nos. 543-546 (4)	4.50	2.00

Souvenir Sheet

547	A86	50e Long jump	4.00	4.00

Roberto Duarte Silva (1837-89), Chemist — A86a

1989, May 2 **Litho.** *Perf. 14¼x14*

547A	A86a	12.50e multi	.45	.25

2nd JAAC-CV Congress, Sept. 7-12 — A87

1989, Apr. 7 **Litho.** *Perf. 14*

548	A87	30e Hot air balloon	1.10	.75

Liberty Guiding the People — A88

Relief, Arc de Triomphe — A89

1989, July 7 **Litho.** *Perf. 14*

549	A88	20e multicolored	.85	.45
550	A88	24e multicolored	1.10	.55
551	A88	25e multicolored	1.25	.65
		Nos. 549-551 (3)	3.20	1.65

Souvenir Sheet

Perf. 14½x13½

552	A89	100e multicolored	5.50	5.50

French revolution, bicent.

Interparliamentary Union, Cent. — A90

1989, Sept. 18 **Litho.** *Perf. 14*

553	A90	2e shown	.25	.25
554	A90	4e Dove	.25	.25
555	A90	13e Natl. Assembly Bldg.	.45	.25
		Nos. 553-555 (3)	.95	.75

Traditional Ceramics A91

1989, Nov. 13 **Litho.** *Perf. 13½*

Panel Colors

556	A91	13e lilac	.50	.25
557	A91	20e red, vert.	.70	.40
558	A91	24e brown	.90	.50
559	A91	25e orange, vert.	1.00	.55
		Nos. 556-559 (4)	3.10	1.70

Outdoor Toys — A92

1989, Dec. 23

560	A92	1e Yellow truck	.25	.25
561	A92	6e Car	.25	.25
562	A92	8e White truck	.35	.25
563	A92	11.50e Trucks	.45	.25
564	A92	18e Scooter	.75	.45
565	A92	100e Boat	4.00	2.25
		Nos. 560-565 (6)	6.05	3.70

Visit of Pope John Paul II — A93

1990, Jan. 25

566	A93	13e blue & multi	.40	.25
567	A93	20e purple & multi	.75	.40

Souvenir Sheet

568	A93	200e multi, diff.	8.00	8.00

Turtles A94

50c, Chelonia mydas. 1e, Dermochelys coriacea. 5e, Lepidochelys olivacea. 10e, Caretta caretta. 42e, Eretmochelys imbricata.

1990, May 17 **Litho.** *Perf. 13½*

569	A94	50c multicolored	.30	.25
570	A94	1e multicolored	.30	.25
571	A94	5e multicolored	.50	.25
572	A94	10e multicolored	.70	.25
573	A94	42e multicolored	3.00	.90
		Nos. 569-573 (5)	4.80	1.90

Women's Congress A95

1990, Aug. 13

574	A95	9e multicolored	.35	.25

A96

Various drawings of soccer players in action.

1990, Aug. 7

575	A96	4e multicolored	.25	.25
576	A96	7.50e multicolored	.25	.25
577	A96	8e multicolored	.25	.25
578	A96	100e multicolored	3.50	2.10
		Nos. 575-578 (4)	4.25	2.85

Souvenir Sheet

579	A96	100e multi, diff.	4.50	4.50

World Cup Soccer Championships, Italy.
For surcharges see Nos. 711-712.

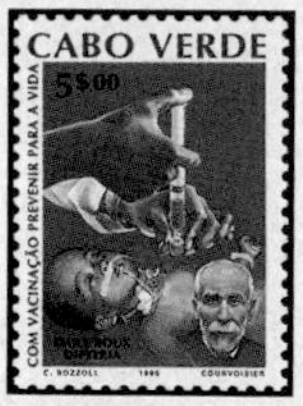

A97

Vaccinations: 5e, Emile Roux (1853-1933), diphtheria. 13e, Robert Koch (1843-1910), tuberculosis. 20e, Gaston Ramon (1886-1963), tetanus. 24e, Jonas Salk (1914-95), polio.

Granite Paper

1990, Oct. 15 *Perf. 11½*

580 A97 5e multicolored	.35	.25
581 A97 13e multicolored	1.00	.25
582 A97 20e multicolored	1.40	.40
583 A97 24e multicolored	1.75	.50
Nos. 580-583 (4)	4.50	1.40

Intl. Literacy Year — A98

Designs: 3e, Adult literacy class. 15e, Teacher holding flash card, children. 19e, Teacher, student at blackboard.

1990, Sept. 28 **Granite Paper**

584 A98 2e shown	.25	.25
585 A98 3e multicolored	.25	.25
586 A98 15e multicolored	.50	.25
587 A98 19e multicolored	.75	.30
Nos. 584-587 (4)	1.75	1.05

Traditional Fairy Tales A99

2.50e, Man catching mermaid. 12e, Woman, snake. 25e, Man, eggs, woman.

1990, Dec. 20 **Litho.** *Perf. 12½*

588 A99 50c shown	.25	.25
589 A99 2.50e multicolored	.25	.25
590 A99 12e multicolored	.50	.45
591 A99 25e multicolored	1.00	.40
Nos. 588-591 (4)	2.00	1.35

Fight Against AIDS A100

1991, Feb. 20 **Litho.** *Perf. 14*

Granite Paper

592 A100 13e multicolored	.75	.30
593 A100 24e multi, diff.	1.25	.75

Fishing — A101

24e, Man removing hook from fish. 25e, Fishing boats. 50e, Two men long-line fishing.

1991, Apr. 23 **Litho.** *Perf. 11½*

594 A101 10e multicolored	.35	.25
595 A101 24e multicolored	1.10	.60
596 A101 25e multicolored	1.25	.65
597 A101 50e multicolored	2.40	1.50
Nos. 594-597 (4)	5.10	3.00

Medicinal Plants — A102

10e, Lavandula rotundifolia. 15e, Micromeria forbesii. 21e, Sarcostemma daltonii. 24e, Periploca chevalieri. 30e, Echium hypertropicum. 35e, Erysimum caboverdeanum.

1991, July 5 **Litho.** *Perf. 11½*

598 A102 10e multicolored	.30	.25
599 A102 15e multicolored	.55	.25
600 A102 21e multicolored	1.00	.30
601 A102 24e multicolored	1.25	.35
602 A102 30e multicolored	2.00	.45
603 A102 35e multicolored	3.00	.55
Nos. 598-603 (6)	8.10	2.15

Landmarks in Old Ribeira Grande on Santiago Island A103

12.50e, Church of Our Lady of the Rosary, 1495. 15e, Ruins of the Cathedral, 1556. 20e, Fortress of San Felipe, 1587. 30e, Ruins of the Convent of St. Francis, 1642. 100e, Pillory, 1520, vert.

1991, June 25 **Litho.** *Perf. 11½*

604 A103 12.50e multicolored	.45	.25
605 A103 15e multicolored	.55	.25
606 A103 20e multicolored	.75	.45
607 A103 30e multicolored	1.10	.75
Nos. 604-607 (4)	2.85	1.70

Souvenir Sheet

608 A103 100e multicolored	4.00	4.00

Musical Instruments — A104

1991, Oct. 9 **Litho.** *Perf. 11½*

609 A104 10e 6-string guitar	.35	.25
610 A104 20e Violin	.85	.55
611 A104 29e 5-string guitar	1.40	.65
612 A104 47e Cimba	2.00	1.25
Nos. 609-612 (4)	4.60	2.70

Souvenir Sheet

613 A104 60e Accordion, horiz.	3.00	3.00

Christmas A105

1991, Dec. 20 **Litho.** *Perf. 11½*

614 A105 31e Nativity scene	1.10	.50
615 A105 50e Nativity scene, diff.	1.75	.90

Discovery of America, 500th Anniv. A106

1992, Mar. 31 **Litho.** *Perf. 11½*

616 A106 40e shown	2.00	1.10
617 A106 40e Columbus on ship	2.00	1.10
a. Pair, #616-617	4.50	4.50

Souvenir Sheet

618 A106 Sheet of 2	8.00	8.00

Stamps in No. 618 are smaller, without white border and "Luis Duran" and "Courvoisier" inscriptions. No. 618 was printed in continuous design and sold for 150e.

Souvenir Sheet

Granada '92 — A107

1992, Apr.24 *Perf. 11½*

619 A107 50e multicolored	8.00	8.00

No. 619 sold for 150e.

Tropical Fruits A108

16e, Syzygium jambos. 25e, Mangifera indica. 31e, Anacardium occidentale. 32e, Persea americana.

1992, Feb. 29 *Perf. 12x11½*

620 A108 16e multicolored	.65	.30
621 A108 25e multicolored	1.10	.50
622 A108 31e multicolored	1.40	.65
623 A108 32e multicolored	1.60	.75
Nos. 620-623 (4)	4.75	2.20

1992 Summer Olympics, Barcelona A109

16e, Women's javelin. 20e, Weight lifting. 32e, Women's pole vault. 40e, Women's shot put.

100e, Women's gymnastics.

1992, June 30 **Litho.** *Perf. 13½*

624 A109 16e multicolored	.60	.25
625 A109 20e multicolored	.75	.30
626 A109 32e multicolored	1.40	.65
627 A109 40e multicolored	1.60	.85
Nos. 624-627 (4)	4.35	2.05

Souvenir Sheet

628 A109 100e multicolored	4.25	4.25

Sugar Cane Production — A110

Designs: 19e, Oxen, sugar cane. 20e, Oxen yoked to press. 37e, Man placing cane inside press. 38e, Refining process.

1992, Nov. **Litho.** *Perf. 11*

629 A110 19e multicolored	.65	.30
630 A110 20e multicolored	.65	.30
631 A110 37e multicolored	1.25	.60
632 A110 38e multicolored	1.40	.60
Nos. 629-632 (4)	3.95	1.80

Domestic Animals A111

1992, Nov. *Perf. 13½*

633 A111 16e Cat	.65	.40
634 A111 31e Chickens	1.10	.80
635 A111 32e Dog, vert.	1.25	.90
636 A111 50e Horse	2.00	1.25
Nos. 633-636 (4)	5.00	3.35

Corals A112

1993, Apr. 29 **Litho.** *Perf. 11½*

637 A112 5e Tubastrea aurea	.25	.25
638 A112 31e Corallium rubrum	1.25	.80
639 A112 37e Porites porites	1.50	1.00
640 A112 50e Millepora alcicornis	2.00	1.25
Nos. 637-640 (4)	5.00	3.30

Treaty of Tordesillas, 500th Anniv. (in 1994) — A113

Designs: No. 641, King Ferdinand, Queen Isabella of Spain, Pope Alexander VI. No. 642, Pope Julius II, King John II of Portugal. No. 643, Astrolabe, treaty signing. No. 644, Compass rose, map.

1993, Aug. 1 **Litho.** *Perf. 12x11½*

641 37e multicolored	1.50	.65
642 37e multicolored	1.50	.65
a. A113 Pair, #641-642	3.50	3.25
643 38e multicolored	1.50	.65
644 38e multicolored	1.50	.65
a. A113 Pair, #643-644	3.50	3.25
Nos. 641-644 (4)	6.00	2.60

Souvenir Sheet

Santiago Island, 1806 — A114

1993, July 30 *Perf. 13½*

645 A114 100e multicolored	5.00	5.00

Brasiliana '93.

Lobsters — A115

2e, Palinurus charlestoni. 10e, Panulirus echinatus. 17e, Panulirus regius. 38e, Scyllarides latus.

100e, Panulirus regius, diff.

1993, Sept. 29 **Litho.** *Perf. 11½*

646 A115 2e multicolored	.35	.25
647 A115 10e multicolored	.70	.25
648 A115 17e multicolored	1.25	.50
649 A115 38e multicolored	2.75	1.00
Nos. 646-649 (4)	5.05	2.00

Souvenir Sheet

650 A115 100e multicolored	6.50	6.50

No. 650 contains one 51x36mm stamp.

Birds
A116

10e, Calonectris edwardsii. 30e, Sula leucogaster. 40e, Fregata magnificens. 41e, Phaeton aethereus.

1993, Oct. 29 Litho. *Perf. 12x11½*

651 A116 10e multicolored .75 .25
652 A116 30e multicolored 3.00 .85
653 A116 40e multicolored 4.00 1.10
a. Souvenir sheet of 1 12.00 11.00
654 A116 41e multicolored 4.00 1.10
Nos. 651-654 (4) 11.75 3.30

Hong Kong '94 (No. 653a).
No. 653a sold for 150e.

Flowers
A117

1993, Dec. 16 Litho. *Perf. 12x11½*

655 A117 5e Rosa alexandra .25 .25
656 A117 30e Strelitzia reginae 1.10 .80
657 A117 37e Dianthus barbatus 1.50 1.00
a. Souvenir sheet of 1 7.50 7.50
658 A117 50e Dahlia 1.90 1.25
Nos. 655-658 (4) 4.75 3.30

Singapore '95 (No. 657a). Issued 9/1/95.
No. 657a sold for 150e.

1994 World Cup Soccer Championships, US — A118

Players, US flag, and: 1e, Giant's Stadium, New Jersey. 20e, Rose Bowl Stadium, Pasadena. 37e, Foxboro Stadium, Boston. 38e, Silverdome, Pontiac. 100e, RFK Stadium, Washington DC.

1994, May 31 Litho. *Perf. 11½*

659 A118 1e multicolored .25 .25
660 A118 20e multicolored .85 .50
661 A118 37e multicolored 1.50 1.00
662 A118 38e multicolored 1.60 1.10
Nos. 659-662 (4) 4.20 2.85

Souvenir Sheet

663 A118 100e multicolored 5.50 5.50

Prince Henry the Navigator (1394-1460) — A119

1994, Mar. 4 Litho. *Perf. 12*

664 A119 37e multicolored 3.00 1.00

See Brazil No. 2463, Macao No. 719, Portugal No. 1987.

Sharks
A120

21e, Eugomphodus taurus. 27e, Carcharhinus limbatus. 37e, Rhiniodon typus. 38e, Etmopterus spinax.

1994, June 27 Litho. *Perf. 12x11½*

665 A120 21e multicolored 1.00 .60
666 A120 27e multicolored 1.25 .75
667 A120 37e multicolored 1.75 1.25
668 A120 38e multicolored 2.00 1.40
Nos. 665-668 (4) 6.00 4.00

Bananas
A121

1994, Aug. 16 Litho. *Perf. 11½*

669 A121 12e Prata, vert. .50 .25
670 A121 16e Pao .75 .40
671 A121 30e Ana roberta, vert. 1.50 .85
672 A121 40e Roxa, vert. 2.00 1.10
Nos. 669-672 (4) 4.75 2.60

Souvenir Sheet

673 A121 100e Prata, diff., vert. 9.00 9.00

PHILAKOREA '94, SINGPEX '94 (No. 673).
No. 673 sold for 150e.

Lighthouses — A122

1994, Oct. 17 *Perf. 12*

674 A122 2e Fontes Pereira de Melo .25 .25
675 A122 37e Morro Negro 1.75 1.00
676 A122 38e Amelia, vert. 1.75 1.10
677 A122 50e Maria Pia, vert. 2.25 1.40
Nos. 674-677 (4) 6.00 3.75

Wilhelm Roentgen (1845-1923), Discovery of the X-Ray, Cent. — A123

1995, Mar. 31 Litho. *Perf. 12*

678 A123 20e yellow & multi .80 .50
679 A123 37e blue & multi 1.50 1.00
a. Souvenir sheet of 2, #678-679 4.50 4.50

No. 679a sold for 100e.

A124

FAO, 50th Anniv. — A125

1995, May 17 Litho. *Perf. 12*

680 A124 37e multicolored 1.50 .90
681 A125 38e multicolored 1.50 .90

Dogs
A126

Dog, scene depicting story of dogs: 1e, Fox terrier, Two foxhounds and fox terrier, by John Emms. 10e, Cavalier King Charles, Shooting over Dogs, by Richard Ansdell. 40e, Rough collie, German shepherd. 50e, Braco, Hounds at Full Cry, by Thomas Blinks.

1995, June 16 Litho. *Perf. 12x11½*

682 A126 1e multicolored .25 .25
683 A126 10e multicolored .55 .25
684 A126 40e multicolored 2.25 1.25
685 A126 50e multicolored 2.75 1.10
Nos. 682-685 (4) 5.80 2.85

Independence, 20th Anniv. — A127

1995, July 20 Litho. *Perf. 12*

686 A127 37e multicolored 1.90 1.25

Traditional Festival
A128

Designs: 2e, Horse race. 10e, Horseman leading parade. 37e, People singing, playing drums. 40e, Playing game on horseback.

1995, Oct. 9 *Perf. 12x11½*

687 A128 2e multicolored .25 .25
688 A128 10e multicolored .45 .25
689 A128 37e multicolored 1.50 .85
690 A128 40e multicolored 1.75 1.00
Nos. 687-690 (4) 3.95 2.35

Children's Stories
A130

Designs: 10e, The cicadas making music, ants. 25e, Cicada being exposed to light. 38e, Cicada with guitar, ants working. 45e, Ants at table making fun of cicada.

1995, Dec. 15 Litho. *Perf. 11½*

692 A130 10e multicolored .40 .55
693 A130 25e multicolored .85 .85
694 A130 38e multicolored 1.40 1.10
695 A130 45e multicolored 1.60 1.00
Nos. 692-695 (4) 4.25 3.50

Endangered Plants — A131

20e, Sonchus daltonii. 37e, Echium vulcanorum. 38e, Nauplius smithii. 50e, Campanula jacobaea.

1996, Apr. 24 Litho. *Perf. 11½*

696 A131 20e multicolored .65 .40
697 A131 37e multicolored 1.20 .75
698 A131 38e multicolored 1.20 .75
699 A131 50e multicolored 1.60 1.10
Nos. 696-699 (4) 4.65 3.00

1996 Summer Olympic Games, Atlanta
A132

1996, June 30 Litho. *Perf. 11½*

700 A132 1e Tennis .25 .25
701 A132 37e Gymnastics 1.10 .75
702 A132 100e Athletics 3.25 2.10
Nos. 700-702 (3) 4.60 3.10

UNICEF, 50th Anniv. — A133

1996, Aug. 1 Litho. *Perf. 12*

703 A133 20e Young girl .90 .40
704 A133 40e Mother, child 1.75 .85

Water Sports — A134

Designs: 2.50e, Fishing. 10e, Windsurfing. 22e, Jet skiing. No. 708, Surfing, horiz. No. 709, Diver's hand, pufferfish, horiz.

1996, Oct. 9 Litho. *Perf. 12*

705 A134 2.50e multicolored .25 .25
706 A134 10e multicolored .35 .25
707 A134 22e multicolored .70 .45
708 A134 100e multicolored 3.25 2.10
Nos. 705-708 (4) 4.55 3.05

Souvenir Sheet

709 A134 100e multicolored 4.50 4.50

No. 709 contains one 80x61mm stamp.

Nos. 507, 575-576 Surcharged

a

b

1997 Litho. *Perf. 14*

710 A77(a) 3e on 2.50e #507 .25 .25

Perf. 13½

711 A96(b) 37e on 4e #575 2.00 .75
712 A96(a) 38e on 7.50e #576 2.00 .75
Nos. 710-712 (3) 4.25 1.75

Natl. Symbols
A135

1997 *Perf. 12*

713 A135 25e Arms .80 .50
714 A135 37e Anthem 1.10 .75
715 A135 50e Flag 1.60 1.00
Nos. 713-715 (3) 3.50 2.25

World Wildlife Fund — A136

Pristis pectinata: a, On seabed. b, Swimming, school of small fish. c, Swimming along seabed, small fish. d, Two near seabed.

1997 **Litho.** ***Perf. 11½***
716 A136 15e Strip of 4, #a.-d. 10.00 10.00

Legends of the Sea — A137

a, Fish, dolphins. b, Merman, mermaid. c, Fish swimming through portal, moray eel.

1997 **Litho.** ***Perf. 11½***
717 A137 45e Strip of 3, #a.-c. 5.00 5.00

Fish A138

Designs: 13e, Thunnus albacares. 21e, Thunnus obesus. 41e, Euthynnus alletteratus. 45e, Katsuwonus pelamis.

1997 **Litho.** ***Perf. 12***

718	A138	13e multicolored	.35	.30
719	A138	21e multicolored	.65	.60
720	A138	41e multicolored	1.40	1.25
721	A138	45e multicolored	1.60	1.50
		Nos. 718-721 (4)	4.00	3.65

1998 World Cup Soccer Championships, France — A139

Designs: 30e, Soccer ball in net, vert. 45e, Soccer player, ball, vert. 50e, Globe, ball, World Cup trophy, fans in stadium.

1998 **Litho.** ***Perf. 12x11½, 11½x12***

722	A139	10e shown	.30	.25
723	A139	30e multicolored	.80	.80
724	A139	45e multicolored	1.25	1.25
725	A139	50e multicolored	1.50	1.40
		Nos. 722-725 (4)	3.85	3.70

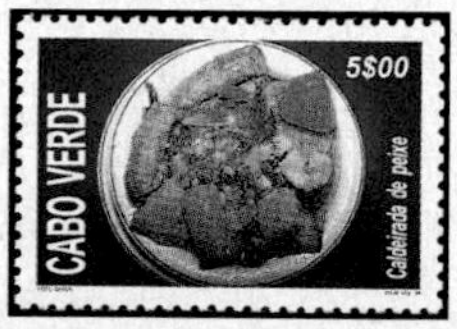

Traditional Cuisine A140

5e, Boiled fish. 25e, Xerém com friginato. 35e, Cachupa. 40e, Molho de Saint-Nicholas.

1998 **Litho.** ***Perf. 12x11½***

726	A140	5e multicolored	.25	.25
727	A140	25e multicolored	.65	.65
728	A140	35e multicolored	1.00	1.00
729	A140	40e multicolored	1.10	1.10
		Nos. 726-729 (4)	3.00	3.00

Early Exploration — A141

a, Quotation from Lusiadas, two men looking at maps. b, Man with sword, man & woman. c, Compass, map, sailing ship, buildings on cliff.

1998 ***Perf. 11½***
730 A141 50e Strip of 3, #a.-c. 6.00 6.00

Women's Traditional Costumes — A142

1998 **Litho.** ***Perf. 12***

731	A142	10e Brava	.25	.25
732	A142	18e Fogo	.50	.50
733	A142	30e Boa Vista	.80	.80
734	A142	50e Santiago	1.40	1.40
		Nos. 731-734 (4)	2.95	2.95

Butterflies and Moths A143

Designs: 5e, Byblia ilithyia. 10e, Aganais speciosa. 20e, Utetheisia pulchella. 30e, Vanessa cardui. 50e, Trichoplusia ni. 100e, Grammodes congenita.

1999, Mar. 16 **Litho.** ***Perf. 11¾***

735	A143	5e multi	.25	.25
736	A143	10e multi	.25	.25
737	A143	20e multi	.50	.50
738	A143	30e multi	.80	.80
a.		Souvenir sheet, #737-738	4.00	4.00
739	A143	50e multi	1.25	1.25
740	A143	100e multi	2.60	2.60
		Nos. 735-740 (6)	5.65	5.65

No. 738a sold for 100e.

First Concorde Flight, 30th Anniv. A144

Concorde: 30e, In flight. 50e, On ground.

1999, June 14 **Litho.** ***Perf. 12***
741-742 A144 Set of 2 2.75 2.75

Famous People — A145

Design: 30e, Alain Gerbault (1893-1941), sailor, boats at dock. 50e, Roberto Duarte Silva (1837-89), chemist, Eiffel Tower.

1999, July 2 **Litho.** ***Perf. 14½***

743	A145	30e multi	2.00	2.00
744	A145	50e multi	3.25	3.25
a.		Souvenir sheet, #743-744	6.50	6.50

Philex France 99 (No. 744a).

A146

UPU, 125th Anniv. A147

1999, Sept. 15 ***Perf. 12x11¾***

745	A146	30e shown	20.00	20.00
746	A147	50e shown	20.00	20.00

With Country Name Added

No. 747

No. 748

747	A146	30e multi	.65	.65
748	A147	50e multi	1.10	1.10
		Nos. 745-748 (4)	41.75	41.75

Dance A148

Designs: 10e, Colá Sanjon, vert. 30e, Contradança, vert. 50e, Desfile de tabanca. 100e, Batuque.

Perf. 11¾x12, 12x11¾
1999, Nov. 5 **Litho.**
749-752 A148 Set of 4 5.00 5.00

Millennium — A149

Designs: 40e, Globe, hourglass and open antique book inscribed "2000," vert. 50e, "2000 Milenio."

2000, Jan. 31 **Litho.** ***Perf. 11¾x11½***
753-754 A149 Set of 2 2.50 2.50

SOS Children's Villages A150

Emblem and child: 50e, Seated, vert. 100e, With arms outstretched.

Perf. 11¾x12, 12x11¾
2000, Apr. 28 **Litho.**
755-756 A150 Set of 2 4.00 4.00

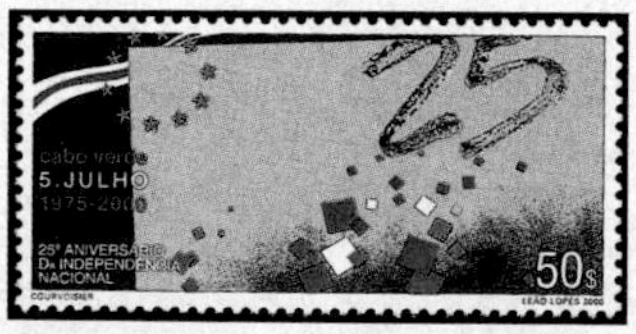

Independence, 25th Anniv. — A151

2000, July 5 ***Perf. 11¾***
757 A151 50e multi 2.00 1.25

2000 Summer Olympics, Sydney A152

Designs: 10e, Women's gymnastics. 40e, Taekwondo. 50e, Women's hurdles.

2000, Sept. 15 **Litho.** ***Perf. 11¾***

758-760	A152	Set of 3	2.60	2.60
760a		Souvenir sheet of 3, #758-760	2.75	2.75

Dragoeiro Tree — A153

2000, Oct. 9 **Litho.** ***Perf. 11¾x11½***

761	A153	5e green	.25	.25
762	A153	40e red	1.00	1.00
763	A153	60e brown	1.60	1.60

Sao Nicolau Seminary and School — A154

No. 764: a, Seminarians and students (denomination at LR, 27x26mm). b, Seminarians and students (denomination at LL, 29x26mm). c, José Alves Feijo, Dr. Julio Dias and Canon António Bouças (56x26mm).

2000, Dec. 15 **Litho.** ***Perf. 14½***
764 A154 60e Horiz. strip of 3, #a-c 5.00 5.00

Fish A155

Designs: 10e, Diplodus sargus lineatus. 22e, Diplodus prayensis. 28e, Lithognathus mormyrus. 48e, Diplodus fasciatus. 60e, Diplodus puntazzo.

2001, Apr. 24 ***Perf. 12x11¾***
765-769 A155 Set of 5 5.00 5.00

Spiders A156

Designs: 13e, Thomisus onustus. 16e, Scytodes velutina. 40e, Hersiliola simoni. 100e, Loxosceles rufescens.

2001, May 28
770-773 A156 Set of 4 5.00 5.00

Trees — A156a

Designs: 50e, Acacia albida. 60e, Ficus sycomorus.

2001, June 9 **Litho.** ***Perf. 11¾x11½***
773A-773B A156a Set of 2 2.75 2.75

Souvenir Sheet

Belgica 2001 Intl. Stamp Exhibition, Brussels — A157

Perf. 11¾x11½
2001, June 9 **Photo.**
774 A157 100e multi 2.75 2.75

Medicinal Plants — A157a

Designs: 20e, Artimisia gorgonum. 27e, Globularia amygdalifolia. 47.50e, Sidereoxylon marginata, horiz. 50e, Umbilicus schmidtii, horiz. 60e, Verbascum cystolithicum. 100e, Limonium lobinii.

Perf. 11¾x12, 12x11¾

2001, Sept. 27 **Litho.**
774A-774F A157a Set of 6 8.00 8.00

Year of Dialogue Among Civilizations — A158

2001, Oct. 9 **Litho.** ***Perf. 11¾x12***
775 A158 60e multi 1.60 1.60

António Aurélio Gonçalves (1901-84), Writer — A159

2001, Dec. 20 ***Perf. 12¼***
776 A159 100e multi 2.75 2.75

Medicinal Plants A160

Designs: 10e, Euphorbia tuckeyna. 50e, Limonium sunding, vert. 60e, Aeonium gorgoneum, vert. 100e, Polycarpaea gayi, vert.

Perf. 12x11¾, 11¾x12

2002, Apr. 26 **Litho.**
777-780 A160 Set of 4 5.75 5.75

2002 World Cup Soccer Championships, Japan and Korea — A161

Designs: 60e, Player heading ball towards goal. 100e, Player kicking ball towards goal.

2002, July 22 ***Perf. 12x11¾***
781-782 A161 Set of 2 4.00 4.00

Caretta Caretta A162

Designs: 10e, Pair mating. 20e, Female laying eggs, vert. 30e, Eggs hatching. 60e, Hatchlings heading for sea, vert. No. 787, 100e, Turtle swimming underwater.
No. 788, 100e, Turtle on beach.

2002, Sept. 9 ***Perf. 12x11¾, 11¾x12***
783-787 A162 Set of 5 6.50 6.50

Souvenir Sheet

788 A162 100e multi 3.00 3.00

No. 788 contains one 80x60mm stamp.

Basketry A163

Baskets and basket weavers from: 20e, Sao Nicolau Island. 33e, Santo Antao Island. 60e, Santiago Island, 100e, Boa Vista Island.

2002, Oct. 29 ***Perf. 12x11¾***
789-792 A163 Set of 4 6.50 6.50

Composers and Poets A164

Designs: 12e, Katcháss (1951-88), composer. 20e, Jorge Monteiro (1913-98), composer. 32e, Luis Rendall (1898-1986), composer. 47.50e, Jorge Barbosa (1902-71), poet. 60e, Januário Leite (1865-1930), poet. 100e, José Lopes (1872-1962), poet.

2003, Feb. 24
793-798 A164 Set of 6 7.50 7.50

Birds — A165

Designs: 10e, Ardea bournei. 27e, Ardea cinerea. 42e, Bubulcus ibis. 60e, Egretta garzeta.

2003, July 9 ***Perf. 14x13¾***
799-802 A165 Set of 4 4.00 4.00

Cesaria Evora, Singer A166

Designs: 60e, Evora at left. 100e, Evora at right.
200e, Feet of Evora.

2003, May 26 ***Perf. 13¾x14***
803-804 A166 Set of 2 4.50 4.50

Souvenir Sheet

Perf. 12¼x12

805 A166 200e multi + label 6.00 6.00

No. 805 contains one 50x38mm stamp.

Scouting in Cape Verde A167

Emblem and scout of: 60e, Scouts Association of Cape Verde. 100e, Cape Verde Scouts Corps.

2003, Oct. 24 **Litho.** ***Perf. 13¾x14***
806-807 A167 Set of 2 4.50 4.50

Whales A168

Designs: 10e, Balaenoptera musculus. 20e, Physeter macrocephalus. 50e, Megaptera novaeangliae. 60e, Globicephala macrorhynchus.

2003, Nov. 25 ***Perf. 12***
808-811 A168 Set of 4 12.00 12.00

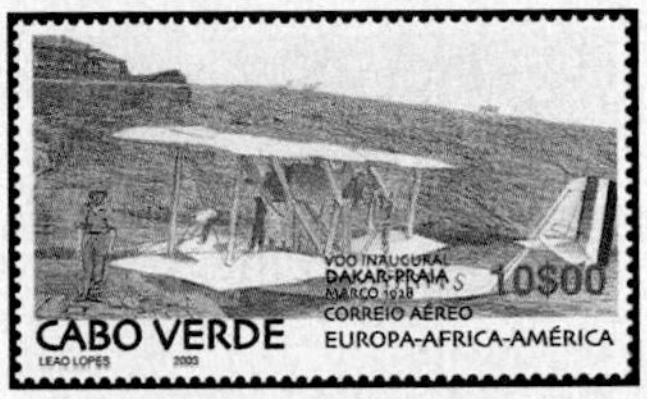

First Dakar — Praia Seaplane Flight of Europe — Africa — South America Airmail Service, 75th Anniv. — A169

Seaplane and: 10e, Crew. 42e, Pilot Paulin Paris, map of South America — Africa route. 60e, Map of entire route.
100e, Like 10e.

2003, Dec. 11 ***Perf. 14***
812-814 A169 Set of 3 3.25 3.25

Souvenir Sheet

815 A169 100e multi 3.00 3.00

Election of Pope John Paul II, 25th Anniv. — A170

Pope John Paul II and: 30e, Girl. 60e, Boats, horiz.
100e, Censer and crucifix.

2003, Dec. 29 ***Perf. 14x13¾, 13¾x14***
816-817 A170 Set of 2 2.40 2.40

Souvenir Sheet

818 A170 100e multi 3.00 3.00

Trees — A171

Designs: 20e, Khaya senegalensis. 27e, Acacia nilotica. 60e, Ceiba pentandra. 100e, Phoenix atlantica.

2004, Jan. 25 ***Perf. 14x13¾***
819-822 A171 Set of 4 5.50 5.50

Windmill — A172

Colors: 20e, Blue. 60e, Red. 100e, Green.

2004, June 3 ***Perf. 13¼x13***
823-825 A172 Set of 3 4.75 4.75

2004 Summer Olympics, Athens — A173

Designs: 10e, Taekwondo. 60e, Rhythmic gymnastics. 100e, Boxing, horiz.

Perf. 13¼x13, 13x13¼

2004, Aug. 13 **Litho.**
826-828 A173 Set of 3 4.75 4.75

Lighthouses A174

Designs: 10e, Ponta do Barril Lighthouse, Sao Nicolau Island. 30e, Ponta Jalunga Lighthouse, Brava Island. 40e, D. Luis Lighthouse, Passaros Islands, horiz. 50e, Ponta Preta Lighthouse, Santiago Island, horiz.

2004, Sept. 7
829-832 A174 Set of 4 4.00 4.00

Houses on Fogo Island A175

Various houses: 20e, 40e, 50e, 60e.

2004, Oct. 9 ***Perf. 13x13¼***
833-836 A175 Set of 4 4.75 4.75

Telephones — A176

Old telephones and: 10e, Switchboard. 40e, Operator. 60e, Telephone directory. 100e, Truck and telephone poles.

2004, Nov. 12
837-840 A176 Set of 4 5.50 5.50

Oral Stories and Legends A177

Designs: 10e, Stória Stória. 20e, Era um Vez! 30e, Sapatinha Ribera Baxu. 60e, Quem ki Sabi Mas, Conta Midjor!, vert.

Perf. 13x13¼, 13¼x13

2005, Feb. 21 **Litho.**
841-844 A177 Set of 4 3.50 3.50

Amilcar Cabral (1924-73), Revolutionary Leader — A178

2005, June 30 Litho. ***Perf. 13¼x13***
845 A178 60e multicolored 1.60 1.60

Independence, 30th anniv.

Shells A179

Designs: 30e, Conus evorai. 40e, Harpa doris. 50e, Strombus lotus. 60e, Phyllonotus duplex.

2005, July 18 ***Perf. 13x13¼***
846-849 A179 Set of 4 6.00 6.00

Birds — A180

Designs: 19e, Passer iagoensis. 42e, Estrilda astrild. 44e, Passer domesticus. 55e, Acrocephalus brevipennis.

2005, Aug. 8 ***Perf. 13¼x13***
850-853 A180 Set of 4 4.25 4.25

World Summit on the Information Society, Tunis A181

2005, Nov. 16 Litho. ***Perf. 13x13¼***
854 A181 60e multi 1.60 1.60

Artifacts of the Slave Trade A182

Designs: 5e, Pipe. 10e, Telescope. 30e, Cannon. 60e, Nautical instrument. 100e, Shackles.

2006, Jan. 31
855-858 A182 Set of 4 3.00 3.00

Souvenir Sheet

859 A182 100e multi 3.00 3.00

No. 859 contains one 80x60mm stamp.

Whaling A183

Designs: 10e, Ship and map. 20e, Whalers in ship and longboat chasing whales off shore. 40e, Ship, longboat and whale. 60e, Crew on whaling ship.

2006, May 18 Litho. ***Perf. 13¼x13½***
Granite Paper
860-863 A183 Set of 4 — —

2006 World Cup Soccer Championships, Germany — A184

Designs: 30e, Emblem and soccer players. 40e, Emblem, vert. 60e, World Cup trophy and soccer players.

Perf. 13x13¼, 13¼x13
2006, Oct. 18 Litho.
Granite Paper
864-866 A184 Set of 3 — —

Ribeira Grande and the International Slave Route — A185

Designs: 24e, Ship and buildings. 36e, Ship, slaves, map of Africa, North America and South America. 50e, Ship, slaves, map of Europe, North America, South America and Africa. 60e, Ship, small boat and buildings.

2006, Oct. 30 Litho. ***Perf. 13x13¼***
Granite Paper
867-870 A185 Set of 4 — —

An additional stamp was issued in this set. The editors would like to examine any example of it.

Community of Portuguese-Speaking Nations, 10th Anniv. — A186

2006, Nov. 2
872 A186 60e multi *2.40 2.40*

Sir Francis Drake (c. 1540-96), Explorer — A187

Drake and: 5e, Sextant. 16e, Ship, map of Cape Verde, compass wheel, horiz. 44e, Ships, horiz. 60e, Old map of Atlantic Ocean, horiz.

2006, Nov. 27 ***Perf. 13¼x13***
Granite Paper (5e, 16e, 60e)

873	A187	5e multi	—	—
874	A187	16e multi	—	—
875	A187	44e multi	—	—
876	A187	60e multi	—	—

Aeronautics — A188

Designs: 10e, Map of Rome-Rio de Janeiro flight via Ilha do Sal, airplane and hangar on Ilha do Sal. 20e, Seaplane, map of Portugal-Brazil flight, monument. 40e, Zeppelin in flight over town. 50e, Ferdinand von Zeppelin, Zeppelins in flight. 60e, Graf Zeppelin in flight, Cape Verde newspaper article.

2006, Dec. 15 Litho. ***Perf. 13x13¼***
Granite Paper
877-881 A188 Set of 5 — —

Writers — A189

Designs: No. 882, 60e, Manuel Lopes (1907-2005). No. 883, 60e, Baltasar Lopes da Silva (Osvaldo Alcantara) (1907-89).

2007 ***Perf. 13¼***
882-883 A189 Set of 2 *4.75 4.75*

Pico do Fogo Volcano A190

Various depictions of erupting volcano: 10e, 50e, 55e, 60e. 50e and 55e are vert.

2007 ***Perf. 13x13¼, 13¼x13***
884-887 A190 Set of 4 *7.00 7.00*

Luis de Cadamosto (1432-88), Discoverer of Cape Verde Islands — A191

Designs: 16e, Cadamosto and ship. 44e, Ship and compass rose. 60e, Cadamosto. 100e, Cadamosto, ship and astrolabe.

2007 ***Perf. 13¼x13***

888	A191	16e multi	—	—
889	A191	44e multi	—	—
890	A191	60e multi	—	—
891	A191	100e multi	—	—

Whaling A192

Designs: 20e, Whale, map of Cape Verde and world showing whale reproduction sites. 30e, Crew on whaling ship stripping whale. 40e, Whale and ship near shore. 60e, Whale breaching near ship.

2007, June 14 Litho. ***Perf. 13x13¼***
Granite Paper
892-895 A192 Set of 4 — —

Aviation A193

Designs: 10e, Airplane, map of South America, Cape Verde, and Africa. 50e, Concorde. 60e, Airplane, map of Africa and Asia. 100e, Airplane over airport.

2007 ***Perf. 13x13¼***
896-899 A193 Set of 4 6.00 6.00

Local Cuisine A194

Designs: 10e, Cozido (stew). 20e, Cuscus com mel (couscous with honey), vert. 60e, Trotxida. 100e, Xerem (cornmeal puree).

2008 ***Perf. 13x13¼, 13¼x13***
900-903 A194 Set of 4 *9.75 9.75*

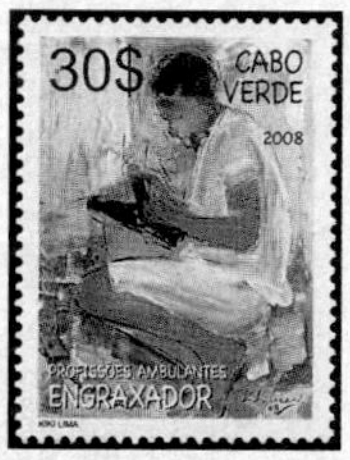

Occupations A195

Designs: 30e, Engraxador (shoe polisher). 40e, Vendedeira de pao (bread seller). 50e, Vendedeira de leite (milk seller), horiz. 100e, Vendedeira de peixe (fish seller).

2008 ***Perf. 13¼x13, 13x13¼***
904-907 A195 Set of 4 *10.50 10.50*

Souvenir Sheet

Praia, 150th Anniv. — A196

2008 ***Perf. 13¼x13***
908 A196 200e multi 9.75 9.75

Peace Corps in Cape Verde, 20th Anniv. — A197

2008
909 A197 60e multi *3.00 3.00*

Birds of Prey — A198

Designs: 5e, Buteo bannermani. 20e, Falco tinnunculus. 40e, Pandion haliaetus. 60e, Falco peregrinus madeus.

2008
910-913 A198 Set of 4 4.75 4.75

Louis Braille (1809-52), Educator of the Blind A199

Designs: No. 914, 60e, Hands reading Braille text. No. 915, 60e, Blind man with cane. No. 916, 60e, Blind children. No. 917, 60e, Blind man with seeing-eye dog, vert.

2009 ***Perf. 13x13¼, 13¼x13***
Granite Paper
914-917 A199 Set of 4 7.50 7.50

Charles Darwin (1809-82), Naturalist — A200

No. 918 — Map of Darwin's voyages and: a, Darwin, skulls. b, Skull, ship, Darwin's legs. c, Darwin and octopus.

2009 ***Perf. 13½x13¼***
918 Horiz. strip of 3 8.25 8.25
a.-c. A200 60e Any single 2.75 2.75

Red Cross, 150th Anniv. A201

2009 **Litho.** ***Perf. 13x13¼***
Granite Paper
919 A201 100e multi 2.75 2.75

Flora and Fauna A202

Designs: 5e, Chioninia delalandii. 10e, Tornabenea annua. 20e, Tarentola darwini. 30e, Satureja forbesii, vert. 40e, Campylnatus glaber glaber, vert. 60e, Chioninia vailanti.

2009 ***Perf. 13x13¼, 13¼x13***
Granite Paper
920-925 A202 Set of 6 4.50 4.50

Souvenir Sheet

Serra Malagueta Protected Areas — A203

No. 926 — Various views of Serra Malagueta: a, 50e. b, 100e.

2009 **Granite Paper** ***Perf. 13¼***
926 A203 Sheet of 2, #a-b 4.25 4.25

Discovery of Cape Verde Islands, 550th Anniv. — A204

No. 927: a, Two ships. b, Map of Cape Verde and Africa, compass rose, birds, "14." c, Ship, rowboat, map of Africa and Asia, compass rose, "60."

2010 **Granite Paper** ***Perf. 13½x13¼***
927 A204 Horiz. strip of 3 4.50 4.50
a.-c. 60e Any single 1.50 1.50

Monte Gordo Protected Areas — A205

Flora and birds of Monte Gordo Protected Areas: 5e, Diplotaxis gracilis. 20e, Theresia. 30e, Verbascum capitis-viridis. 40e, Coturnix coturnix, horiz. 50e, Corvus ruficollis, horiz. 60e, Columba livia, horiz.
100e, Monte Gordo, horiz.

2010 ***Perf. 13¼x13, 13x13¼***
928-933 A205 Set of 6 5.25 5.25

Souvenir Sheet

934 A205 100e multi 2.50 2.50

2010 World Cup Soccer Championships, South Africa — A206

Designs: 40e, Mascot, silhouettes of players. 50e, Emblem, players, vert. 60e, Mascot, players. 100e, World Cup, silhouettes of players.

2010 ***Perf. 13x13¼, 13¼x13***
935-938 A206 Set of 4 6.25 6.25

Independence, 35th Anniv. — A207

2010, July 5 **Litho.** ***Perf. 13¼***
939 A207 100e multi *4.75 4.75*

Campaigns Against Chronic Diseases A208

Campaign against: 10e, Alcoholism. 20e, Alcoholism, diff. 30e, Diabetes. 40e, Diabetes, diff. 50e, Tuberculosis. 60e, Tuberculosis, diff.

2010, Aug. 12 ***Perf. 13x13¼***
940-945 A208 Set of 6 *10.00 10.00*

Assoc. of Postal and Telecommunications Operators of Portuguese-Speaking Countries and Territories, 20th Anniv. — A209

2010
946 A209 100e multi *4.75 4.75*

Rebellions — A210

Rebellions at: 40e, Mindelo, 1934. 50e, Paul, 1894. 60e, Rubon Manel, 1910.

2010 ***Perf. 13½***
947-949 A210 Set of 3 *7.25 7.25*

Heart Health A211

Designs: 20e, Hearts, electrocardiogram waves, mother lifting child. 40e, Heart and stethoscope. 60e, Family, hearts, electrocardiogram waves. 100e, Heart and arteries.

2011 ***Perf. 13x13¼***
950-953 A211 Set of 4 6.25 6.25

Nudibranchs — A212

Designs: 5e, Flabelina arveleoi. 10e, Flabelina bulbosa. 20e, Aplysia dactylomela. 40e, Pleurobranchus garciagomezis. 60e, Hypselodoris sp., vert.

2011 ***Perf. 13x13¼, 13¼x13***
954-958 A212 Set of 5 3.75 3.75

Flora and Fauna of Cha das Caldeiras Protected Area — A213

Designs: 5e, Halcion leucocephala. 10e, Verbascum cystolithicum. 20e, Acrocephalus brevipennis. 40e, Echium vulcanorum. 60e, Pterodroma feae. 100e, Erisimum caboverdeanum.
150e, Halcion leucocephala, Acrocephalus brevipennis, horiz.

2011 ***Perf. 13¼x13***
959-964 A213 Set of 6 6.75 6.75

Souvenir Sheet
Perf. 13x13¼

965 A213 150e multi 4.25 4.25

Baltazar Lopes da Silva (1907-89), Writer A214

2012 ***Perf. 13x13¼***
966 A214 100e multi 2.75 2.75

Old Household Objects — A215

Designs: No. 967, 60e, Oil burner (Fogao a petróleo). No. 968, 60e, Oil lamp (Conddeeiro a petróleo). No. 969, 60e, Washbasin (Lavatório). No. 970, 60e, Iron (Ferro de engomar a carvao), horiz.

2012 ***Perf. 13¼x13, 13x13¼***
967-970 A215 Set of 4 6.75 6.75

Emigration A216

Designs: 30e, Compass rose, man on boat waving to family on dock. 50e, Man writing on envelope. 60e, Agricultural worker, hand picking cacao pod. 100e, Man wheeling suitcase, world map, horiz.

2012 ***Perf. 13¼x13, 13x13¼***
971-974 A216 Set of 4 6.75 6.75

Composers and Musicians — A217

Designs: 10e, Ano Nobu (1933-2004), composer. 20e, Ildo Lobo (1953-2004), singer. 30e, Renato Cardoso (1951-89), composer. 40e, Manuel d'Novas (1938-2009), composer. 50e, Codé di Dona (1940-2010), composer. 60e, Orlando Pantera (1967-2001), composer.

2012 **Litho.** ***Perf. 13¼***
975-980 A217 Set of 6 6.00 6.00

Cape Verde National Soccer Team A218

Designs: 40e, Team emblem. 60e, Team jersey, vert.
100e, Like 40e.

2012 *Perf. 13x13¼, 13¼x13*
981-982 A218 Set of 2 2.75 2.75

Souvenir Sheet

983 A218 100e multi 2.75 2.75

Flora and Fauna of Santo Antao Proctected Area — A219

Designs: 10e, Buteo bannermani. 20e, Pterodroma feae. 30e, Sideroxylon marginata. 40e, Carex antolensis, horiz. 50e, Tarentola caboverdiana caboverdiana, horiz. 60e, Papaver gorgoneum, horiz.
100e, Birds in flight over Coza Natural Park, horiz.

2012 *Perf. 13¼x13, 13x13¼*
984-989 A219 Set of 6 6.00 6.00

Souvenir Sheet

990 A219 100e multi 2.75 2.75

Brasiliana 2013 Intl. Philatelic Exhibition, Rio de Janeiro A220

Brasiliana 2013 emblem, Brazil Nos. 1, 2 and 3, and: 60e, Map of Brazil and circle indicating location of Cape Verde. 150e, Cape Verde #1, map of Cape Verde, label without denomination similar to 60e.

2013 **Litho.** *Perf. 13½*
991 A220 60e multi 1.50 1.50

Size: 145x81mm

Imperf

992 A220 150e multi + label 4.00 4.00

African Union, 50th Anniv. — A221

2013 **Litho.** *Perf. 13½*
993 A221 60e multi 1.50 1.50

Father Custódio Ferreira de Campos and Church A222

2013, Oct. 9 **Litho.** *Perf. 13x13¼*
994 A222 60e multi 1.50 1.50

Carnaval — A223

Carnaval participants and animators: No. 995, 60e, Capote (1916-85). No. 996, 60e, Artur Boxe (1910-2004). No. 997, 60e, Negro Sarafe (1924-92).

2014, Feb. 28 **Litho.** *Perf. 13½*
995-997 A223 Set of 3 4.50 4.50

Portuguese Language, 800th Anniv. A224

2014, May 5 **Litho.** *Perf. 12x12½*
998 A224 60e multi 1.50 1.50

A225

Intl. Children's Day A226

2014, June 1 **Litho.** *Perf. 13x13½*
999 A225 60e multi 1.50 1.50
1000 A226 60e multi 1.50 1.50

A227

A228

Corn Processing A229

2014, Oct. 9 **Litho.** *Perf. 13x13½*
1001 A227 60e multi 1.40 1.40
1002 A228 60e multi 1.40 1.40
1003 A229 60e multi 1.40 1.40
Nos. 1001-1003 (3) 4.20 4.20

Intl. Association of Portuguese-Speaking Countries, 25th Anniv. — A230

2015, Apr. 27 **Litho.** *Perf. 13¼x13*
1004 A230 60e multi 1.25 1.25

AIR POST STAMPS

Common Design Type
Name and Value in Black

Perf. 13½x13

1938, July 26 **Unwmk.**
C1 CD39 10c red orange .60 .50
C2 CD39 20c purple .60 .50
C3 CD39 50c orange .60 .50
C4 CD39 1e ultra .60 .50
C5 CD39 2e lilac brown 1.40 .80
C6 CD39 3e dk green 1.75 1.40
C7 CD39 5e red brown 5.50 2.10
C8 CD39 9e rose carmine 9.00 3.75
C9 CD39 10e magenta 9.75 5.00
Nos. C1-C9 (9) 29.80 15.05
Set, never hinged 50.00

No. C7 exists with overprint "Exposicao Internacional de Nova York, 1939-1940" and Trylon and Perisphere.

POSTAGE DUE STAMPS

D1

1904 **Unwmk.** **Typo.** *Perf. 12*
J1 D1 5r yellow grn .40 *.25*
J2 D1 10r slate .40 *.25*
J3 D1 20r yellow brn .50 *.40*
J4 D1 30r red orange 1.25 *.40*
J5 D1 50r gray brown .50 *.35*
J6 D1 60r red brown 9.25 4.25
J7 D1 100r lilac 1.75 1.25
J8 D1 130r dull blue 1.90 1.25
J9 D1 200r carmine 1.60 1.60
J10 D1 500r dull violet 5.00 *3.00*
Nos. J1-J10 (10) 22.55 *13.00*

Overprinted in Carmine or Green

1911
J11 D1 5r yellow grn .30 .25
J12 D1 10r slate .30 .25
J13 D1 20r yellow brn .35 .25
J14 D1 30r orange .35 .25
J15 D1 50r gray brown .65 .40
J16 D1 60r red brown .65 .40
J17 D1 100r lilac .65 .40
J18 D1 130r dull blue .75 .65
J19 D1 200r carmine (G) 2.00 1.50
J20 D1 500r dull violet 2.50 1.75
Nos. J11-J20 (10) 8.50 6.10

D2

1921 *Perf. 11½*
J21 D2 ½c yellow grn .30 .25
J22 D2 1c slate .30 .25
J23 D2 2c red brown .30 .25
J24 D2 3c orange .30 .25
J25 D2 5c gray brown .30 .25
J26 D2 6c lt brown .30 .25
J27 D2 10c red violet .30 .25
J28 D2 13c dull blue .55 *.40*
J29 D2 20c carmine .60 *.50*
J30 D2 50c gray 1.75 *1.10*
Nos. J21-J30 (10) 5.00 *3.75*

Catalogue values for unused stamps in this section, from this point to the end of the section, are for Never Hinged items.

Common Design Type
Photogravure and Typographed

1952 **Unwmk.** *Perf. 14*

Numeral in Red, Frame Multicolored

J31 CD45 10c chocolate .30 .25
J32 CD45 30c black brown .30 .25
J33 CD45 50c dark blue .30 .25
J34 CD45 1e dark blue .40 .25
J35 CD45 2e red brown .40 .30
J36 CD45 5e olive green 1.10 1.00
Nos. J31-J36 (6) 2.80 2.30

NEWSPAPER STAMP

N1

1893 **Typo.** **Unwmk.** *Perf. 11½*
P1 N1 2½r brown 1.50 .60
a. Perf. 12½ 3.00 1.50
b. Perf. 13½ 6.50 3.00

For surcharges see Nos. 79, 206.

POSTAL TAX STAMPS

Pombal Issue
Common Design Types

1925 **Unwmk.** **Engr.** *Perf. 12½*
RA1 CD28 15c dull vio & blk 1.25 1.10
RA2 CD29 15c dull vio & blk 1.25 1.10
RA3 CD30 15c dull vio & blk 1.25 1.10
Nos. RA1-RA3 (3) 3.75 3.30

St. Isabel — PT1

1948 **Litho.** *Perf. 11*
RA4 PT1 50c dark green 3.75 2.40
RA5 PT1 1e henna brown 7.50 3.00

Catalogue values for unused stamps in this section, from this point to the end of the section, are for Never Hinged items.

No. RA5 Surcharged with New Value and Bars

1959
RA6 PT1 50c on 1e henna brown 1.40 1.10

Perf. 14

RA7 PT1 50c carmine rose 2.10 1.00
RA8 PT1 1e blue 2.10 1.00

St. Isabel Type Redrawn

1967-73 **Litho.** *Perf. 14*
RA9 PT1 30c (blue panel) .50 .50
RA9A PT1 30c (orange panel) .50 .50
RA10 PT1 50c (lilac rose panel) .85 .85
RA11 PT1 50c (red panel) ('72) *.50* *.50*
RA12 PT1 1e (brn panel) 1.00 1.00
RA13 PT1 1e (red lilac panel) ('72) *1.00* *1.00*
Nos. RA9-RA13 (6) *4.35* *4.35*

Nos. RA9-RA13 are inscribed "ASSISTENCIA" in large letters in bottom panel and "PORTUGAL" and "CABO VERDE" in small letters in upper left corner.

Revenue Stamps Surcharged in Green, Blue or Black — PT2

Black "CABO VERDE" & Value
Pale Green Burelage

1967-72 Typo. *Perf. 12*

RA14	PT2 50c on 1c org (Bl) ('71)	1.40	.90
a.	Black surcharge ('68?)	*20.00*	*14.50*
RA15	PT2 50c on 2c org (Bk) ('69)	*25.00*	*14.50*
c.	Inverted surcharge	*50.00*	*35.00*
RA16	PT2 50c on 3c org (G) ('72)	1.10	.60
RA17	PT2 50c on 5c org (G) ('72)	1.10	.60
RA18	PT2 50c on 10c org (G) ('71)	1.25	1.00
RA19	PT2 1e on 1c org (Bk)	2.75	2.10
RA20	PT2 1e on 2c org (G) ('71)	2.00	1.75
a.	Blue surcharge ('71)	3.00	1.10
b.	Black surcharge	4.00	2.10
	Nos. RA14-RA20 (7)	*34.60*	*21.45*

POSTAL TAX DUE STAMPS

Pombal Issue
Common Design Types

1925 Unwmk. *Perf. 12½*

RAJ1	CD28 30c dull vio & blk	.75	.70
RAJ2	CD29 30c dull vio & blk	.75	.70
RAJ3	CD30 30c dull vio & blk	.75	.70
	Nos. RAJ1-RAJ3 (3)	2.25	2.10

CARIBBEAN NETHERLANDS

ˈkar-ē-bbe-ə-n ˈne-t͟hər-lənˌdˌz

LOCATION — The islands of Bonaire (north of Venezuela), Saint Eustatius and Saba (south of Anguilla)
AREA — 125 sq. mi.
POP. — 18,012 (2010)
CAPITAL — Kralendijk, Bonaire; Oranjestad, Saint Eustatius; The Bottom, Saba

On Oct. 10, 2010, Caribbean Netherlands, formerly part of Netherlands Antilles, became special municipalities within the Kingdom of the Netherlands.

100 Cents = 1 Gulden
100 Cents = 1 Dollar (2011)

Catalogue values for all unused stamps in this country are for Never Hinged items.

Map of Islands and West Indies, Arms, Queen Beatrix
A1

Perf. 13¾
2010, Oct. 10 Litho. Unwmk.
1 A1 111c multicolored 1.50 1.50

New Constitutional Status — A2

Designs: 63c, Triangle with flags of Bonaire, Saint Eustatius and Saba, Acropora palmata. 81c, Three Glassy sweepers with elements of flags of Bonaire, Saint Eustatius and Saba. 93c, Two Yellowcheek wrasses with elements of Bonaire flag. 96c, Parrotfish with elements of Saint Eustatius flag. 159c, Blue tang surgeonfish with elements of Saba flag.

2011, June 1 *Perf. 13¼x13*
2-6 A2 Set of 5 10.00 10.00

Greetings — A3

Inscriptions: 33c, Thinking of you. 63c, Always in my prayers. 93c, Celebrate another year. 159c, Love U so much. 226c, For you my cup of tea.

2011, July 11 *Perf. 13x13¼*
7-11 A3 Set of 5 8.50 8.50

Corals — A4

Designs: 45c, Scolymia wellsi. 63c, Diodogorgia nodulifera, vert. 159c, Eusmilia fastigiata. 226c, Acropora palmata, vert.

Perf. 13¼x13, 13x13¼
2011, Sept. 11
12-15 A4 Set of 4 8.00 7.00

Visit of Queen Beatrix — A5

Queen Beatrix: 81c, Without hat. 159c, Wearing hat.
250c, Queen Beatrix in coach, horiz.

2011, Nov. 4 *Perf. 14*
16-17 A5 Set of 2 5.00 5.00

Souvenir Sheet

18 A5 250c multi 5.00 5.00

Holiday Light Decorations A6

Designs: 63c, Snowflakes. 81c, Reindeer. 93c, Flowers. 159c, Bells.

2011, Nov. 11 *Perf. 13½x12¾*
19-22 A6 Set of 4 8.00 8.00

Sailboats A7

Designs: 66c, Catamaran. 99c, Optimist. 101c, Sunfish. 168c, Laser, vert.

Perf. 13½x12¾, 12¾x13½
2012, Feb. 1
23-26 A7 Set of 4 8.75 8.75

Parrots — A8

Designs: 100c, Ara chloropterus. 150c, Aratinga pertinax. 200c, Amazona ochrocephala ochrocephala. 250c, Anodorhynchus hyacinthinus.

2012, June 1 *Perf. 12¾x13½*
27-30 A8 Set of 4 14.00 14.00

Rafflesia Flower — A9

Mandala — A10

2012, June 18 *Perf. 13½x12¾*
31 A9 10c multicolored .25 .25

Souvenir Sheet
Perf.

32 A10 200c multicolored 4.00 4.00

Indoensia 2012 World Stamp Exhibition, Jakarta.

Miniature Sheet

Dutch Queens and Heraldry — A11

No. 33: a, Queen Emma. b, Queen Wilhelmina. c, Queen Juliana. d, Queen Beatrix. e, Royal arms.

Litho. & Embossed
2012, Sept. 3 *Perf. 12¾x13½*
33 A11 300c Sheet of 5, #a-e 30.00 30.00

Arms and Christmas Ornaments A12

Designs: 66c, Arms of Saba, ornament in shape of Saba, ornament with Saba flag elements. 99c, Arms of St. Eustatius, ornament in shape of St. Eustatius, ornament with St. Eustatius flag elements. 101c, Arms of Bonaire, ornament in shape of Bonaire, ornament with Bonaire flag elements. 168c, Arms of Netherlands, ornaments with flag elements of Saba, St. Eustatius and Bonaire.

2012, Nov. 1 Litho. *Perf. 13¼x13*
34-37 A12 Set of 4 8.75 8.75

Emblem and Flamingo A13

No. 38 — Inscribed: a, Bonaire. b, Saba. c, St. Eustatius. d, Bonaire. e, Saba. f, St. Eustatius.

2014, Oct. 10 Litho. *Rouletted 6½*

38	Horiz. strip of 6	11.50	11.50
a.-c.	A13 88c Any single	1.75	1.75
d.-f.	A13 99c Any single	2.00	2.00

Miniature Sheets

Flamingos — A14

Pelicans — A15

Hummingbirds — A16

Various birds, as shown.

Perf. 13¼x13½
2014, Nov. 10 Litho.

Inscribed "Bonaire"

39 A14 99c Sheet of 5, #a-e 10.00 10.00

Inscribed "Saba"

40 A15 99c Sheet of 5, #a-e 10.00 10.00

Inscribed "St. Eustatius"

41 A16 99c Sheet of 5, #a-e 10.00 10.00
Nos. 39-41 (3) 30.00 30.00

Personalized Stamp — A17

Serpentine Die Cut 14¼
2014, Nov. 10 Litho.
Self-Adhesive

42 A17 99c multi + label 2.00 2.00

No. 42 was printed in sheets of 10 + 10 labels. The label shown is a generic label. Two other generic labels, depicting scenes of Saba and St. Eustatius were created. Labels could also be personalized. Sheets containing personalized labels sold for $15.

Miniature Sheet

Flag and King Willem-Alexander — A18

Flag of Bonaire (No. 43), Saba (No. 44) or St. Eustatius (No. 45) with King Willem-Alexander in: a, 99c, Sepia. b, 99c, Full color. c, $1.36, Sepia. d, $1.36, Full color. e, $1.98, Sepia, f, $1.98, Full color. g, $2.82, Sepia, h, $2.82, Full color. i, $4.40, Sepia. j, $4.40, Full color.

2015, Apr. 30 Litho. *Perf. 14x13½*

Inscribed "Bonaire"

43	A18	Sheet of 10, #a-j	46.50	46.50

Inscribed "Saba"

44	A18	Sheet of 10, #a-j	46.50	46.50

Inscribed "St. Eustatius"

45	A18	Sheet of 10, #a-j	46.50	46.50
		Nos. 43-45 (3)	139.50	139.50

SEMI-POSTAL STAMPS

Intl. Year of Cooperatives SP1

2012, Oct. 9 Litho. *Perf. 13½x12¾*

B1	SP1	99c+45c multi	3.00	3.00

CAROLINE ISLANDS

ˈkar-ə-ˌlīn ˈī-ləndz

LOCATION — A group of about 549 small islands in the West Pacific Ocean, north of the Equator.
GOVT. — German colony
AREA — 550 sq. mi.
POP. — 40,000 (approx. 1915)

100 Pfennig = 1 Mark

Watermark

Wmk. 125 — Lozenges

Stamps of Germany 1889-90 Overprinted in Black

#1-6

#1a-6a

Overprinted at 56 degree Angle

1900 Unwmk. *Perf. 13½x14½*

1	A9	3pf dk brown	13.00	*14.00*
2	A9	5pf green	18.00	*18.00*
3	A10	10pf carmine	19.00	*19.00*
4	A10	20pf ultra	24.00	*30.00*
5	A10	25pf orange	55.00	*65.00*
6	A10	50pf red brown	55.00	*65.00*
		Nos. 1-6 (6)	184.00	*211.00*

1899

Overprinted at 48 degree Angle

1a	A9	3pf light brown	625.00	*750.00*
2a	A9	5pf green	650.00	650.00
3a	A10	10pf carmine	65.00	*150.00*
4a	A10	20pf ultra	65.00	*150.00*
5a	A10	25pf orange	1,650.	*3,100.*
6a	A10	50pf red brown	900.00	*1,600.*

A3

Kaiser's Yacht "Hohenzollern" — A4

1901, Jan. Typo. *Perf. 14*

7	A3	3pf brown	1.10	*1.75*
8	A3	5pf green	1.10	*2.10*
9	A3	10pf carmine	1.10	*5.00*
	a.	Half used as 5pf on cover, back-stamped in Jaluit ('05)		*120.00*
10	A3	20pf ultra	1.25	*9.00*
	a.	Half used as 10pf on cover ('10)		*8,500.*
11	A3	25pf org & blk, *yel*	1.60	*14.50*
12	A3	30pf org & blk, *sal*	1.60	*14.50*
13	A3	40pf lake & blk	1.60	*16.50*
14	A3	50pf pur & blk, *sal*	2.00	*22.50*
15	A3	80pf lake & blk, *rose*	3.00	*25.00*

Engr. *Perf. 14½x14*

16	A4	1m carmine	4.50	*62.50*
17	A4	2m blue	7.25	*87.50*
18	A4	3m black violet	10.00	*150.00*
19	A4	5m slate & carmine	160.00	550.00
		Nos. 7-19 (13)	196.10	960.85

No. 9a is known as the "typhoon provisional" the stock of 5pf stamps having been destroyed during a typhoon. Covers (cards) without backstamp, value about $72.50.

Forged cancellations are found on #7-19.

No. 7 Handstamp Surcharged

1910, July 12

20	A3	5pf on 3pf brown	*5,500.*
	a.	Inverted surcharge	*7,750.*
	b.	Double surcharge	*11,000.*

Values are for stamps tied to cover. Stamps on piece sell for about 40% less.

1915-19 Wmk. 125 Typo.

21	A3	3pf brown ('19)	.90
22	A3	5pf green	12.50

Engr.

23	A4	5m slate & carmine	35.00
		Nos. 21-23 (3)	48.40

Nos. 21-23 were not placed in use.

CASTELLORIZO

ˌkäs-tə-ˈlor-ə-ˌzō

(Castelrosso)

LOCATION — A Mediterranean island in the Dodecanese group lying close to the coast of Asia Minor and about 60 miles east of Rhodes.
GOVT. — Former Italian Colony
AREA — 4 sq. mi.
POP. — 2,238 (1936)

Formerly a Turkish possession, Castellorizo was occupied by the French in 1915 and ceded to Italy after World War I. In 1945 it became part of Greece.

25 Centimes = 1 Piaster
100 Centimes = 1 Franc

Used values in italics are for postally used copies. Stamps with CTO cancels sell for about the same as hinged, unused stamps.

Issued under French Occupation

Stamps of French Offices in Turkey Overprinted

1920 Unwmk. *Perf. 14x13½*

1	A2	1c gray	45.00	*65.00*
a.		Inverted overprint	175.00	*250.00*
b.		Double overprint	175.00	*350.00*
2	A2	2c vio brn	50.00	*70.00*
a.		Double overprint	225.00	*300.00*
3	A2	3c red org	45.00	*65.00*
a.		Inverted overprint	175.00	*250.00*
4	A2	5c green	75.00	*90.00*
a.		Inverted overprint	225.00	*300.00*
5	A3	10c rose	90.00	*125.00*
6	A3	15c pale red	115.00	*150.00*
a.		Inverted overprint	450.00	*625.00*
7	A3	20c brn vio	125.00	*150.00*
8	A5	1pi on 25c blue	115.00	125.00
a.		Pair, one without overprint	750.00	800.00
9	A3	30c lilac	125.00	*150.00*

Overprint Reading Down

10	A4	40c red & pale bl (down)	200.00	*250.00*
a.		Inverted ovpt (reading up)	850.00	900.00
11	A6	2pi on 50c bis brn & lav (down)	225.00	*275.00*
a.		Inverted ovpt (reading up)	900.00	1,000.
b.		Double overprint	1,250.	1,300.
12	A6	4pi on 1fr cl & ol grn (down)	275.00	*350.00*
a.		Double overprint	1,300.	1,350.
b.		Inverted ovpt (reading up)	1,050.	1,100.
13	A6	20pi on 5fr dk bl & buff	625.00	*800.00*
a.		Double overprint	1,850.	*2,000.*
		Nos. 1-13 (13)	2,110.	2,665.
		Set, never hinged	4,500.	

No. 1-9 were overprinted in blocks of 25. Position 4 had "CASTELLIORIZO" inverted and Positions 8 and 18 had "CASTELLORISO." The later variety also occurred in the setting of the form for Nos. 10-13.

"B. N. F." are the initials of "Base Navale Francaise".

Overprinted in Black or Red

1920

On Stamps of French Offices in Turkey

14	A2	1c gray	32.50	*40.00*
15	A2	2c vio brn	37.50	*50.00*
16	A2	3c red org	67.50	*80.00*
17	A2	5c green (R)	32.50	*37.50*
19	A3	10c rose	40.00	*47.50*
20	A3	15c pale red	70.00	*80.00*
21	A3	20c brn vio	105.00	*110.00*
22	A5	1pi on 25c bl (R)	67.50	*70.00*
23	A3	30c lilac (R)	77.50	*85.00*
24	A4	40c red & pale bl	72.50	*75.00*
25	A6	2pi on 50c bis brn & lav	72.50	*80.00*
26	A6	4pi on 1fr claret & ol grn	115.00	*140.00*
28	A6	20pi on 5fr dk bl & buff	375.00	450.00
		Nos. 14-28 (13)	1,165.	1,345.

On Nos. 25, 26 and 28 the two lines of the overprint are set wider apart than on the lower values.

"O.N.F." are the initials of "Occupation Navale Francaise."

"Casetllorizo" and "astellorizo" varieties are known on Nos. 14-23.

Overprint on 5c in black and on 8pi on 2fr (#37) were prepared but not issued. Values: 5c, $1,300; 8pi on 2fr, $1,450.

On Stamps of France

30	A22	10c red	50.00	*60.00*
a.		Inverted overprint	200.00	*250.00*
31	A22	25c blue (R)	50.00	*60.00*
a.		Inverted overprint	200.00	*250.00*

This overprint exists on 8 other 1900-1907 denominations of France (5c, 15c, 20c, 30c, 40c, 50c, 1fr, 5fr). These are believed not to have been issued or postally used. Values: 5c, $775; 15c, $775; 20c, $825; 30c, $1,250; 40c, $1,250; 50c, $1,250; 1fr, $1,350; 5fr, $12,500.

Stamps of France, 1900-1907, Handstamped in Black or Violet

1920

33	A22	5c green	175.00	*200.00*
a.		Overprint inverted (reading up)	1,300.	
b.		Double overprint		1,000.
34	A22	10c red	175.00	*200.00*
35	A22	20c vio brn	175.00	*200.00*
a.		Overprint inverted (reading up)	*1,500.*	
b.		Double overprint		*1,000.*
36	A22	25c blue	175.00	*200.00*
37	A18	50c bis brn & lav	1,000.	*1,200.*
a.		Double overprint	*1,700.*	
38	A18	1fr cl & ol grn (V)	1,000.	1,200.
		Nos. 33-38 (6)	2,700.	3,200.
		Set, never hinged	5,400.	

Nos. 1-38 are considered speculative.

Forgeries of overprints on Nos. 1-38 exist. They abound of Nos. 33-38.

French Offices in Turkey Nos. 25//38 were hand-stamped "Occupation Francaise Castellorizo" locally by the officers in charge of the French Navy postal facilities but were not issued. Values: 5c, 10c, 15c, 20c, 1pi on 25c, each $1,050; 40c, 2pi on 50c, each $2,000; 4pi on 1fr, $2,350; 20pl on 5fr, $9,250.

Issued under Italian Dominion

100 Centesimi = 1 Lira

Italian Stamps of 1906-20 Overprinted

1922, July 22 Wmk. 140 *Perf. 14*

51	A48	5c green	5.00	*30.00*
52	A48	10c claret	3.50	*30.00*
53	A48	15c slate	3.50	*30.00*
54	A50	20c brn org	3.50	*30.00*
a.		Double overprint	500.00	
b.		Vertical pair, one without overprint	2,250.	
55	A49	25c blue	3.50	*30.00*
56	A49	40c brown	48.00	35.00
57	A49	50c violet	50.00	37.50
58	A49	60c carmine	50.00	57.50
a.		Diagonal overprint		800.00
59	A49	85c chocolate	5.50	*65.00*
		Nos. 51-59 (9)	172.50	*345.00*
		Set, never hinged	450.00	

Map of Castellorizo; Flag of Italy — A1

1923, Jan.

60	A1	5c gray green	6.00	*40.00*
61	A1	10c dull rose	6.00	*40.00*
62	A1	25c dull blue	6.00	*40.00*
63	A1	50c gray lilac	6.00	*40.00*
64	A1	1 l brown	6.00	*40.00*
		Nos. 60-64 (5)	30.00	*200.00*
		Set, never hinged	65.00	

Italian Stamps of 1901-20 Overprinted

1924, March

65	A48	5c green	2.50	*30.00*
66	A48	10c claret	2.50	*30.00*
67	A48	15c slate	2.50	*40.00*
68	A50	20c brn orange	2.50	*40.00*
a.		Double overprint	150.00	
69	A49	25c blue	2.50	*30.00*
70	A49	40c brown	2.50	*30.00*
71	A49	50c violet	2.50	*40.00*
72	A49	60c carmine	2.50	*50.00*
a.		Double overprint	450.00	
73	A49	85c red brown	2.50	*60.00*
74	A46	1 l brn & green	2.50	*60.00*
		Nos. 65-74 (10)	25.00	*410.00*
		Set, never hinged	55.00	

Ferrucci Issue

Italian Stamps of 1930, Ovptd. in Red or Blue

1930, Oct. 20 Wmk. Crowns (140)

75	A102	20c violet	10.00	10.00
76	A103	25c dark green	10.00	*25.00*
77	A103	50c black	10.00	10.00
78	A103	1.25 l deep blue	10.00	*25.00*
79	A104	5 l + 2 l dp car (Bl)	10.00	*77.50*
		Nos. 75-79 (5)	50.00	*147.50*
		Set, never hinged	150.00	

Garibaldi Issue

Types of Italian Stamps of 1932, Overprinted like Nos. 75-79 in Red or Blue

1932, Aug. 28

80	A138	10c brown	20.00	*25.00*
81	A138	20c red brn (Bl)	20.00	*25.00*
82	A138	25c dp grn	20.00	*25.00*
83	A138	30c bluish slate	20.00	*25.00*
84	A138	50c red vio (Bl)	20.00	*25.00*
85	A141	75c cop red (Bl)	20.00	*25.00*
86	A141	1.25 l dull blue	20.00	*25.00*
87	A141	1.75 l + 25c brn	20.00	*25.00*
88	A144	2.55 l + 50c org (Bl)	20.00	*25.00*
89	A145	5 l + 1 l dl vio	20.00	*25.00*
		Nos. 80-89 (10)	200.00	*250.00*
		Set, never hinged	400.00	

CAYMAN ISLANDS

kā-ˈman ˈī-ləndz

LOCATION — Three islands in the Caribbean Sea, about 200 miles northwest of Jamaica
GOVT. — British Crown Colony, formerly a dependency of Jamaica
AREA — 100 sq. mi.
POP. — 39,335 (1999 est.)
CAPITAL — George Town, located on Grand Cayman

12 Pence = 1 Shilling
20 Shilling = 1 Pound
100 Cents = 1 Dollar (1969)

Catalogue values for unused stamps in this country are for Never Hinged items, beginning with Scott 112.

Victoria — A1

1900 Typo. Wmk. 2 *Perf. 14*

1	A1	½p pale green	15.00	*22.50*
2	A1	1p carmine rose	16.00	4.25

Edward VII — A2

1901-03

3	A2	½p green ('02)	5.50	*30.00*
4	A2	1p car rose ('03)	12.00	*12.00*
5	A2	2½p ultramarine	12.00	*19.00*
6	A2	6p chocolate	35.00	*70.00*
7	A2	1sh brown orange	72.50	*125.00*
		Nos. 3-7 (5)	137.00	*256.00*

1905 Wmk. 3

8	A2	½p green	12.00	*16.00*
9	A2	1p carmine rose	22.00	*20.00*
10	A2	2½p ultramarine	12.00	5.50
11	A2	6p chocolate	19.00	*45.00*
12	A2	1sh brown orange	37.50	*55.00*
		Nos. 8-12 (5)	102.50	*141.50*

For surcharge see No. 17.

1907, Mar. 13

13	A2	4p brown & blue	40.00	*67.50*
14	A2	6p ol green & rose	45.00	*80.00*
15	A2	1sh violet & green	65.00	*95.00*
16	A2	5sh ver & green	225.00	*350.00*
		Nos. 13-16 (4)	375.00	*592.50*

Numerals of 4p, 1sh and 5sh of type A2 are in color on colorless tablet.

For surcharges see Nos. 18-20.

Nos. 9, 16, 13 Handstamped

No. 17

No. 18

No. 19

No. 20

1907-08

17	A2	½p on 1p	60.00	*92.50*
18	A2	½p on 5sh	325.00	*525.00*
a.		Inverted surcharge	*100,000.*	
b.		Double surcharge	*12,750.*	*12,750.*
c.		Double surcharge, one inverted		
d.		Pair, one without surcharge	*100,000.*	
19	A2	1p on 5sh	350.00	*525.00*
a.		Double surcharge	*22,500.*	*20,000.*
b.		Inverted surcharge	*150,000.*	
20	A2	2½p on 4p ('08)	2,000.	*3,750.*
a.		Double surcharge	*60,000.*	*30,000.*

No. 19b is unique. It exists on the upper left stamp in an upper left corner margin plate no. 1 block of four that is lightly hinged in the top margin only.

The 1p on 4p is a revenue stamp not authorized for postal use, although postally used examples exist. Value for unused is about $300.

A3

1907-09 *Perf. 14*

21	A3	½p green	4.75	*5.50*
22	A3	1p carmine rose	2.10	1.10
23	A3	2½p ultramarine	6.50	3.00

Chalky Paper

24	A3	3p violet, *yellow*	4.50	*9.75*
25	A3	4p blk & red, *yel*	67.50	*100.00*
26	A3	6p purple & br pur	25.00	*52.50*
27	A3	1sh black, *grn*	11.00	*32.50*
28	A3	5sh grn & red, *yel*	60.00	*90.00*
		Nos. 21-28 (8)	181.35	*294.35*

Issued: ½p, 1p, 12/27/07; 2½p, 3p, 4p, 5sh, 3/30/08; 6d, 10/2/08; 1sh, 4/5/09.

Forged cancellations are found on No. 28.

1908, Mar. 30 **Wmk. 2**

29	A3	1sh black, *green*	85.00	*125.00*
30	A3	10sh grn & red, *grn*	225.00	*400.00*

Numerals of 3p, 4p, 1sh and 5sh of type A3 are in color on plain tablet.

Forged cancellations are found on No. 30.

A4

1908 **Wmk. 3** **Ordinary Paper**

31	A4	¼p brown	6.00	1.00

King George V — A5

1912-20

32	A5	¼p brown ('13)	1.25	.50
33	A5	½p green	3.25	*6.00*
34	A5	1p carmine ('13)	4.00	3.00
35	A5	2p gray	1.25	*12.50*
36	A5	2½p ultra ('14)	8.50	*13.50*

Chalky Paper

37	A5	3p vio, *yel* ('13)	3.00	*22.50*
38	A5	4p blk & red, *yel* ('13)	1.25	*12.50*
39	A5	6p vio & red vio ('13)	4.50	*9.00*
40	A5	1sh blk, *grn* ('13)	4.25	*32.50*
41	A5	2sh vio & ultra, *bl*	14.50	*65.00*
42	A5	3sh green & vio	22.50	*77.50*
43	A5	5sh grn & red, *yel* ('14)	90.00	*190.00*
44	A5	10sh grn & red, *bl grn,* olive back ('18)	125.00	*250.00*
a.		10sh green & red, *grn* ('14)	150.00	*250.00*
		Nos. 32-44 (13)	283.25	*694.50*

The first printings of the 3p, 1sh and 10sh have a white back.

For surcharges, see Nos. MR1-MR7.

1913, Nov. 19

Surface-colored Paper

45	A5	3p violet, *yel*	4.25	*9.50*
46	A5	1sh black, *green*	4.25	*4.25*
47	A5	10sh grn & red, *grn*	130.00	*190.00*
		Nos. 45-47 (3)	138.50	*203.75*

Numeral of ¼p, 2p, 3p, 4p, 1sh, 2sh, 3sh and 5sh of type A5 are in color on plain tablet.

King George V — A6

1921-26 **Wmk. 4** ***Perf. 14***

50	A6	¼p yel brown	.60	*1.75*
51	A6	½p gray green	.60	.35
52	A6	1p rose red	1.75	*1.00*
53	A6	1½p orange brn	2.10	.35
54	A6	2p gray	2.10	*4.75*
55	A6	2½p ultramarine ('22)	.60	*.60*
56	A6	3p violet, *yel*	3.25	*4.75*
57	A6	4½p olive grn	4.00	*3.75*
58	A6	6p claret	6.50	*37.50*
59	A6	1sh black, *grn* ('25)	11.50	*37.50*
60	A6	2sh violet, *blue*	17.00	*30.00*
61	A6	3sh violet	27.50	19.00
62	A6	5sh green, *yel*	29.00	*55.00*
63	A6	10sh car, *green*	72.50	*100.00*
		Nos. 50-63 (14)	179.00	*296.30*

Issued: 1½p, 4/4/21; ¼p, ½p, 1p, 2p, 2½p, 6p, 2sh, 3sh, 4/1/22; 3p, 4½p, 6/29/23; 5sh, 2/15/25; 1sh, 5/15/25; 10sh, 9/5/26.

1921-22 **Wmk. 3**

64	A6	3p violet, *org*	1.75	*9.50*
65	A6	4p red, *yel*	1.25	*5.00*
66	A6	1sh black, *green*	2.25	*11.50*
67	A6	5sh green, *yel*	19.00	*85.00*
68	A6	10sh car, *green*	75.00	*125.00*
		Nos. 64-68 (5)	99.25	*236.00*

Issued: 4p, 4/1/22; others, 4/4/21.

King William IV, King George V
A7

Perf. 12½

1932, Dec. 5 **Wmk. 4** **Engr.**

69	A7	¼p brown	1.90	1.40
70	A7	½p green	3.25	*11.00*
71	A7	1p carmine	3.25	*15.00*
72	A7	1½p orange	3.25	3.75
73	A7	2p gray	3.25	*4.75*
74	A7	2½p ultramarine	3.25	2.00
75	A7	3p olive green	8.00	*6.75*
76	A7	6p red violet	13.00	*30.00*
77	A7	1sh brn & black	20.00	*42.50*
78	A7	2sh ultra & blk	55.00	*100.00*
79	A7	5sh green & blk	100.00	*160.00*
80	A7	10sh car & black	350.00	*475.00*
		Nos. 69-80 (12)	564.15	*852.15*
		Set, never hinged	1,250.	

Centenary of the formation of the Cayman Islands Assembly.

Common Design Types pictured following the introduction.

Silver Jubilee Issue

Common Design Type

1935, May 6 ***Perf. 13½x14***

81	CD301	½p green & black	.35	*1.50*
82	CD301	2½p blue & brown	4.00	*1.50*
83	CD301	6p ol grn & lt bl	1.60	*4.75*
84	CD301	1sh brt vio & ind	11.00	10.00
		Nos. 81-84 (4)	16.95	17.75
		Set, never hinged	24.00	

King George V
A8

Catboat
A9

Red-footed Boobies
A10

Conches and Coconut Palms — A11

Hawksbill Turtles
A12

1935-36 ***Perf. 12½***

85	A8	¼p brown & blk	.60	*1.25*
86	A9	½p yel grn & ultra	1.25	*1.25*
87	A10	1p car & ultra	5.00	3.00
88	A11	1½p org & black	1.75	*2.40*
89	A9	2p brown vio & ultra	4.50	1.50
90	A12	2½p dp blue & blk	4.00	1.60
91	A8	3p ol grn & blk	3.00	*3.75*
92	A10	6p red vio & blk	10.50	6.00
93	A9	1sh org & ultra	7.25	*9.25*
94	A10	2sh black & ultra	55.00	50.00
95	A12	5sh green & blk	65.00	70.00
96	A11	10sh car & black	125.00	*140.00*
		Nos. 85-96 (12)	282.85	290.00
		Set, never hinged	525.00	

Issued: No. 86, 2½p, 6p, 1sh, 1/1/36; others, 5/1/35.

Coronation Issue

Common Design Type

1937, May 13 ***Perf. 11x11½***

97	CD302	½p deep green	.25	*1.50*
98	CD302	1p dark carmine	.30	.25
99	CD302	2½p deep ultra	.55	.55
		Nos. 97-99 (3)	1.10	2.30
		Set, never hinged	2.25	

Beach View, Grand Cayman
A13

Dolphin — A14

Map of the Islands
A15

Hawksbill Turtles — A16

Cayman Schooner
A17

Perf. 12½; 11½x13 or 13x11½ (A14, #111); 14 (#104, 107)

1938-43 **Engr.**

100	A13	¼p red orange	.55	*.75*
a.		Perf. 13½x12½ ('43)	.25	*.85*
101	A14	½p yel green	.85	*.75*
a.		Perf. 14 ('43)	1.50	*1.75*
102	A15	1p carmine	.25	*1.00*
103	A13	1½p black	.25	.25
104	A16	2p dp violet ('43)	.50	.35
a.		Perf. 11½x13	3.00	.40
105	A17	2½p ultra	.40	.25
106	A15	3p orange	.40	.25
107	A16	6p dk ol grn ('43)	2.50	2.50
a.		Perf. 11½x13	7.25	5.25
108	A14	1sh reddish brown	5.00	2.00
a.		Perf. 14 ('43)	4.00	2.50
109	A13	2sh green	22.50	18.00
110	A17	5sh deep rose	24.50	19.00
111	A16	10sh dark brown	22.50	12.00
a.		Perf. 14 ('43)	20.00	12.00
		Nos. 100-111 (12)	80.20	57.10
		Set, never hinged	125.00	

See Nos. 114-115.

Catalogue values for unused stamps in this section, from this point to the end of the section, are for Never Hinged items.

Peace Issue

Common Design Type

1946, Aug. 26 **Wmk. 4** ***Perf. 13½***

112	CD303	1½p black	.30	.40
113	CD303	3p orange	.30	.40

Types of 1938

1947, Aug. 25 ***Perf. 12½***

114	A17	2½p orange	3.50	.65
115	A15	3p ultramarine	3.50	.45

Silver Wedding Issue

Common Design Types

1948, Nov. 29 **Photo.** ***Perf. 14x14½***

116	CD304	½p dark green	.25	1.00

Perf. 11½x11

Engr.; Name Typo.

117	CD305	10sh blue violet	22.50	27.50

UPU Issue

Common Design Types

Engr.; Name Typo. on #119, 120

1949, Oct. 10 ***Perf. 13½, 11x11½***

118	CD306	2½p orange	.40	*1.00*
119	CD307	3p indigo	1.90	*2.50*
120	CD308	6p olive	.85	*2.50*
121	CD309	1sh red brown	.85	.40
		Nos. 118-121 (4)	4.00	6.40

Catboat
A18

Designs: ½p, Coconut grove. 1p, Green turtle. 1½p, Thatch rope industry. 2p, Caymanian seamen. 2½p, Map. 3p, Parrot fish. 6p, Bluff, Cayman Brac. 9p, George Town harbor. 1sh, Turtle "crawl". 2sh, Cayman schooner. 5sh, Boat-building. 10sh, Government offices.

Perf. 11½x11

1950, Oct. 2 **Wmk. 4** **Engr.**

122	A18	¼p rose red & blue	.25	*.80*
123	A18	½p bl grn & red violet	.25	*1.75*
124	A18	1p dp blue & olive	.75	*1.00*
125	A18	1½p choc & bl grn	.45	*1.00*
126	A18	2p rose car & vio	1.75	*2.00*
127	A18	2½p sepia & aqua	1.75	.85
128	A18	3p bl & blue grn	2.10	2.00
129	A18	6p dp bl & org brn	2.50	1.75
130	A18	9p dk grn & rose red	12.00	2.50
131	A18	1sh red org & brn	4.50	3.75
132	A18	2sh red vio & vio	13.00	*14.50*
133	A18	5sh vio & olive	22.50	9.50
134	A18	10sh rose red & blk	27.50	20.00
		Nos. 122-134 (13)	89.30	61.40

Types of 1950 with Portrait of Queen Elizabeth II and

Lighthouse, South Sound — A20

Elizabeth II and Turtles — A21

Perf. 11½x11, 11x11½

1953-59 **Engr.**

135	A18	¼p rose red & bl	1.40	.80
136	A18	½p bl grn & red vio	1.10	.75
137	A18	1p dp bl & olive	1.00	.70
138	A18	1½p choc & bl grn	.75	.35
139	A18	2p rose car & vio	3.50	1.40
140	A18	2½p black & aqua	4.25	1.25
141	A18	3p blue & bl grn	5.25	1.00
142	A20	4p dp blue & black	2.50	.70
143	A18	6p dp bl & red brn	2.10	.30
144	A18	9p dk green & rose red	8.50	.40
145	A18	1sh red org & brn	4.75	.40
146	A18	2sh red vio & vio	16.00	11.50
147	A18	5sh violet & olive	17.50	10.00
148	A18	10sh rose red & blk	19.00	11.50
149	A21	£1 bright blue	37.50	16.00
		Nos. 135-149 (15)	125.10	57.05

Issued: 4p, 3/2; 2p, 2½p, 9p, 6/2/54; ½p, 1p, 1½p, 6p, 7/7/54; ¼p, 3p, 1sh-10sh, 2/21/55; £1, 1/6/59.

Coronation Issue

Common Design Type

1953, June 2 ***Perf. 13½x13***

150	CD312	1p brt green & black	.40	*1.00*

Arms of Cayman Islands A22

Perf. 12

1959, July 4 Wmk. 4 Photo.

151 A22 2½p dull blue & blk .65 1.25
152 A22 1sh red orange & blk .70 .50

Granting of a new constitution.

Cayman Parrot — A23

Catboat A24

1½p, Orchid. 2p, Map of Islands. 2½p, Fisherman casting net. 3p, West Bay Beach. 4p, Green turtle. 6p, Cayman schooner. 9p, Angler with kingfish. 1sh, Iguana. 1sh3p, Swimming pool, Cayman Brac. 1sh9p, Girl and sailboat. 5sh, Fort George. 10sh, Coat of Arms. £1, Queen Elizabeth II.

Perf. 11x11½, 11½x11

1962, Nov. 28 Wmk. 314 Engr.

153 A23 ¼p rose red & ember 1.10 *1.50*
154 A24 1p olive & black .95 .40
155 A24 1½p purple & yel 4.75 1.25
156 A24 2p sepia & blue 1.20 .50
157 A24 2½p green & vio .95 *1.50*
158 A24 3p car & blue .45 .40
159 A24 4p pur & green 1.50 .95
160 A24 6p sepia & green 3.50 .55
161 A23 9p pur & vio bl 2.50 .85
162 A24 1sh rose & sepia .95 .25
163 A24 1sh3p brn org & lt grn 4.00 3.50
164 A24 1sh9p vio & bl grn 16.50 2.25
165 A24 5sh grn & dl pur 13.00 9.50
166 A23 10sh blue & olive 22.50 13.00
167 A23 £1 blk & car rose 22.50 *24.00*
Revenue cancel .80
Nos. 153-167 (15) 96.35 60.40

Freedom from Hunger Issue
Common Design Type

1963, June 4 Photo. *Perf. 14x14½*

168 CD314 1sh9p car rose .50 .30

Red Cross Centenary Issue
Common Design Type

Wmk. 314

1963, Sept. 2 Litho. *Perf. 13*

169 CD315 1p black & red .25 .25
170 CD315 1sh9p ultra & red .70 *1.75*

Shakespeare Issue
Common Design Type

1964, Apr. 23 Photo. *Perf. 14x14½*

171 CD316 6p deep lilac rose .35 .30

ITU Issue
Common Design Type

1965, May 17 Litho. Wmk. 314

172 CD317 1p ultra & red lil .25 .25
173 CD317 1sh3p rose lil & grn .75 .75

Intl. Cooperation Year Issue
Common Design Type

1965, Oct. 25 Wmk. 314 *Perf. 14½*

174 CD318 1p blue grn & claret .30 .25
175 CD318 1sh lt vio & green .70 .70

Churchill Memorial Issue
Common Design Type

1966, Jan. 24 Photo. *Perf. 14*

Design in Black, Gold and Carmine Rose

176 CD319 ¼p bright blue .25 1.50
177 CD319 1p green .50 .50
178 CD319 1sh brown .90 .65
179 CD319 1sh9p violet 1.75 .90
Nos. 176-179 (4) 3.40 3.55

Royal Visit Issue
Common Design Type

1966, Feb. 4 Litho. *Perf. 11x12*

180 CD320 1p violet blue .70 .30
181 CD320 1sh9p dk car rose 2.75 1.50

World Cup Soccer Issue
Common Design Type

1966, July 1 Litho. *Perf. 14*

182 CD321 1½p multicolored .25 .25
183 CD321 1sh9p multicolored .50 .50

WHO Headquarters Issue
Common Design Type

1966, Sept. 20 Litho. *Perf. 14*

184 CD322 2p multicolored .65 .30
185 CD322 1sh3p multicolored 1.60 1.10

UNESCO Anniversary Issue
Common Design Type

1966, Dec. 1 Litho. *Perf. 14*

186 CD323 1p "Education" .25 .25
187 CD323 1sh9p "Science" .75 .35
188 CD323 5sh "Culture" 1.50 1.10
Nos. 186-188 (3) 2.50 1.70

Telephone and Map of Caymans — A25

Perf. 14½x14

1966, Dec. 5 Litho. Wmk. 314

189 A25 4p multicolored .25 .25
190 A25 9p multicolored .30 .30

Linking of the Cayman telephone system with the intl. system.

BAC 1-11 Jet Liner over Schooner — A26

1966, Dec. 17

191 A26 1sh blue, ol & black .35 .35
192 A26 1sh9p ultra, grn & sepia .60 .60

Opening of the Grand Cayman Airport jet service.

Water Skiing and ITY Emblem A27

ITY Emblem and: 6p, Skin diving. 1sh, Sport fishing. 1sh9p, Sailing.

Perf. 14½x14

1967, Dec. 1 Photo. Wmk. 314

193 A27 4p multi & gold .35 .25
a. Gold omitted 250.00 225.00
194 A27 6p multi & gold .35 .25
195 A27 1sh multi & gold .35 .35
196 A27 1sh9p multi & gold .50 *.75*
Nos. 193-196 (4) 1.55 1.60

International Tourist Year.

Human Rights Flame and Freed Slaves A28

1968, June 3 Photo. Wmk. 314

197 A28 3p slate bl, grn & gold .25 .25
198 A28 9p lt brn, grn & gold .25 .25
199 A28 5sh ultra, grn & gold .70 .70
Nos. 197-199 (3) 1.20 1.20

International Human Rights Year.

Long Jump A29

1sh3p, High jump. 2sh, Pole vault, vert.

1968, Oct. 1 Litho. *Perf. 13½*

200 A29 1sh multicolored .25 .25
201 A29 1sh3p multicolored .25 .25
202 A29 2sh yellow & multi .30 .30
Nos. 200-202 (3) .80 .80

19th Olympic Games, Mexico City, 10/12-27.

Adoration of Shepherds, by Carel Fabritius — A30

Christmas: 1p, 8p, 2sh, Adoration of the Shepherds, by Rembrandt.

Perf. 14x14½

1968, Nov. 18 Photo. Wmk. 314

203 A30 ¼p brown & multi .25 .25
a. Gold omitted 250.00
204 A30 1p violet & multi .25 .25
205 A30 6p multicolored .25 .25
206 A30 8p car & multi .25 .25
207 A30 1sh3p multicolored .30 .25
208 A30 2sh gray & multi .30 .30
Nos. 203-208 (6) 1.60 1.60

1969, Jan. 8 Unwmk.

209 A30 ¼p red lilac & multi .75 .35

Grand Cayman Thrush A31

1p, Brahman cattle. 2p, Blowholes on coast. 2½p, Map of Grand Cayman. 3p, Town scene in George Town. 4p, Royal poinciana. 6p, Map of Cayman Brac and Little Cayman. 8p, Motor vessels at berth. 1sh, Basket making. 1sh3p, Beach scene. 1sh6p, Rope making. 2sh, Barracudas. 4sh, Government House. 10sh, Coat of arms. £1, Queen Elizabeth II.

Unwmk.

1969, June 5 Litho. *Perf. 14*

210 A31 ¼p multi .25 *.90*
211 A31 1p multi .25 .25
212 A31 2p multi .25 .25
213 A31 2½p multi .25 .25
214 A31 3p multi .25 .25
215 A31 4p multi .25 .25
216 A31 6p multi .25 .25
217 A31 8p multi .25 .25
218 A31 1sh multi .25 .25
219 A31 1sh3p multi .30 *1.90*
220 A31 1sh6p multi .35 *1.90*
221 A31 2sh multi 1.25 *1.40*
222 A31 4sh multi .60 *1.40*
223 A31 10sh multi, vert. 1.25 *2.50*
224 A31 £1 multi, vert. 3.00 3.50
Nos. 210-224 (15) 9.00 *15.50*

See Nos. 262-276. For surcharges see Nos. 227-241.

1969, Aug. 11 Wmk. 314 Sideways

225 A31 ¼p multicolored .70 .70

Type of 1969 Surcharged

1969, Sept. 8 Wmk. 314 *Perf. 14*

227 A31 ¼c on ¼p multi .25 *.85*
228 A31 1c on 1p multi .25 .25
229 A31 2c on 2p multi .25 .25
230 A31 3c on 4p multi .25 .25
231 A31 4c on 2½p multi .25 .25
232 A31 5c on 6p multi .25 .25
233 A31 7c on 8p multi .25 .25
234 A31 8c on 3p multi .25 .25
235 A31 10c on 1s multi .35 .25
236 A31 12c on 1sh3p multi .45 *1.90*
237 A31 15c on 1sh6p multi .55 *1.25*
238 A31 20c on 2sh multi 2.00 *2.10*
239 A31 40c on 4sh multi .55 *1.25*
240 A31 $1 on 10sh multi 1.45 *3.75*
241 A31 $2 on £1 multi 2.25 *4.50*
Nos. 227-241 (15) 9.60 17.60

The surcharge is arranged differently on various denominations.

Madonna and Child, by Alvise Vivarini — A32

Christmas: 1c, 7c, 20c, The Adoration of the Kings, by Jan Gossaert.

1969, Nov. 4 Photo. *Perf. 14*

242 A32 ¼c blue & multi .25 .25
243 A32 ¼c emer & multi .25 .25
244 A32 ¼c red org & multi .25 .25
245 A32 ¼c brt pink & multi .25 .25
246 A32 1c vio blue & multi .25 .25
247 A32 5c red org & multi .25 .25
248 A32 7c dk green & multi .25 .25
249 A32 12c emer & multi .25 .25
250 A32 20c multicolored .25 .25
Nos. 242-250 (9) 2.25 2.25

"Noli me Tangere," by Titian — A33

1970, Mar. 23 Litho. Unwmk.

251 A33 ¼c dull grn & multi .25 .25
252 A33 ¼c dk car & multi .25 .25
253 A33 ¼c violet & multi .25 .25
254 A33 ¼c bister & multi .25 .25
255 A33 10c vio blue & multi .25 .25
256 A33 12c red brn & multi .25 .25
257 A33 40c brn vio & multi .60 .60
Nos. 251-257 (7) 2.10 2.10

Easter.

Barnaby from "Barnaby Rudge" by Dickens (1812-70), English Novelist — A34

Characters from Charles Dickens: 12c, Sairey Gamp, from "Martin Chuzzlewit." 20c, Mr. Micawber and David, from "David Copperfield." 40c, The Marchioness from "The Old Curiosity Shop."

1970, June 17 Photo. *Perf. 14½x14*

258	A34	1c ol green, yel & blk	.25	.25
259	A34	12c red brn, brick red & black	.25	.25
260	A34	20c dk ol bister, gold & black	.35	.35
261	A34	40c dp ultra, lt bl & blk	.60	.60
		Nos. 258-261 (4)	1.45	1.45

Type of Regular Issue 1969 Values in Cents and Dollars

Designs: ¼c, Grand Cayman thrush. 1c, Brahman cattle. 2c, Blowholes on coast. 3c, Royal poinciana. 4c, Map of Grand Cayman. 5c, Map of Cayman Brac and Little Cayman. 7c, Motor vessels at berth. 8c, Town scene in George Town. 10c, Basket making. 12c, Beach scene. 15c, Rope making. 20c, Barracudas. 40c, Government House. $1, Coat of arms, vert. $2, Queen Elizabeth II, vert.

Wmk. 314

1970, Sept. 8 Litho. *Perf. 14*

262	A31	¼c multicolored	.60	.30
263	A31	1c multicolored	.25	.25
264	A31	2c multicolored	.25	.25
265	A31	3c multicolored	.25	.25
266	A31	4c multicolored	.25	.25
267	A31	5c multicolored	.45	.25
268	A31	7c multicolored	.40	.25
269	A31	8c multicolored	.40	.25
270	A31	10c multicolored	.40	.25
271	A31	12c multicolored	1.00	*1.10*
272	A31	15c multicolored	1.10	*3.50*
273	A31	20c multicolored	2.50	1.75
274	A31	40c multicolored	.85	.85
275	A31	$1 multicolored	1.10	*5.75*
276	A31	$2 multicolored	1.75	*5.75*
		Nos. 262-276 (15)	11.55	21.00

The Three Wise Men A35

Christmas: 1c, 10c, 20c, Nativity and globe.

1970, Oct. 8 Litho. *Perf. 14*

277	A35	¼c brt grn & yel grn	.25	.25
278	A35	1c bl grn, yel grn & blk	.25	.25
279	A35	5c dp claret & org	.25	.25
280	A35	10c red org, yel & blk	.25	.25
281	A35	12c ultra & lt grnsh bl	.25	.25
282	A35	20c grn, yel grn & blk	.25	.25
		Nos. 277-282 (6)	1.50	1.50

Grand Cayman Terrapin A36

Cayman Islands Turtles: 7c, Green turtle. 12c, Hawksbill turtle. 20c, Turtle farm.

1971, Jan. 28 *Perf. 14x14½*

283	A36	5c multicolored	.70	.40
284	A36	7c multicolored	.85	.40
285	A36	12c multicolored	1.75	.50
286	A36	20c multicolored	3.00	2.00
		Nos. 283-286 (4)	6.30	3.30

Dendrophylax Fawcetii — A37

Wild Orchids of West Indies: 2c, Schomburgkia thomsoniana. 10c, Vanilla claviculata. 40c, Oncidium variegatum.

1971, Apr. 7 Wmk. 314 *Perf. 14*

287	A37	¼c brown & multi	.35	*1.60*
288	A37	2c ol green & multi	1.00	*1.25*
289	A37	10c gray bl & multi	3.50	.75
290	A37	40c lt violet & multi	5.00	4.00
		Nos. 287-290 (4)	9.85	*7.60*

Adoration of the Kings, 15th Century — A38

Christmas: 1c, 15c, Nativity (detail), Paris, 14th cent. 5c, 20c, Adoration of the Kings (detail), Burgundian, 15th cent.

1971, Sept. 27 *Perf. 14*

291	A38	¼c gold & multi	.25	.25
292	A38	1c gold & multi	.25	.25
293	A38	5c gold & multi	.25	.25
294	A38	12c gold & multi	.25	.25
295	A38	15c gold & multi	.30	.30
296	A38	20c gold & multi	.40	.40
a.		Souvenir sheet of 6, #291-296	4.75	4.75
		Nos. 291-296 (6)	1.70	1.70

Underwater Cable, Turtle and Telephone — A39

1972, Jan. 10

297	A39	2c multicolored	.25	.25
298	A39	10c multicolored	.25	.25
299	A39	40c multicolored	.75	.75
		Nos. 297-299 (3)	1.25	1.25

Coaxial cable for world communications.

Courthouse — A40

Designs: 15c, 40c, Legislative Assembly Building, George Town.

1972, Aug. 15 *Perf. 13½x14*

300	A40	5c dp car & multi	.25	.25
301	A40	15c lilac rose & multi	.25	.25
302	A40	25c dull grn & multi	.25	.25
303	A40	40c dk blue & multi	.40	.40
a.		Souvenir sheet of 4, #300-303	1.10	1.10
		Nos. 300-303 (4)	1.15	1.15

New Cayman Islands government buildings.

Silver Wedding Issue, 1972

Common Design Type

Design: Queen Elizabeth II, Prince Philip, hawksbill turtle and conch.

1972, Nov. 20 Photo. *Perf. 14x14½*

304	CD324	12c vio black & multi	.25	.25
305	CD324	30c olive & multi	.50	.50

$1 Note and 1c Coin A41

6c, $5 note and 5c coin. 15c, $10 note and 10c coin. 25c, $25 note and 25c coin.

1973, Jan. 15

306	A41	3c emerald & multi	.25	.25
307	A41	6c yellow & multi	.30	.60
308	A41	15c lilac & multi	.65	.50
309	A41	25c orange & multi	1.25	.90
a.		Souvenir sheet of 4, #306-309	4.00	4.00
		Nos. 306-309 (4)	2.45	2.25

First Cayman Islands coinage and bank notes, May 1, 1972.

Last Supper A42

Stained Glass Windows: 10c, Christ Carrying Cross, vert. 12c, Resurrection, vert. 30c, Crucifixion.

Perf. 14½x14, 14x14½

1973, Apr. 11 Litho.

310	A42	10c pink & multi	.25	.25
311	A42	12c yel green & multi	.25	.25
312	A42	20c lt blue & multi	.30	.30
313	A42	30c yellow & multi	.40	.40
a.		Souvenir sheet of 4	1.45	1.45
		Nos. 310-313 (4)	1.20	1.20

Easter. No. 313a contains 4 stamps similar to Nos. 310-313 with simulated perforations.

Nativity — A43

Christmas: 5c, 12c, 25c, Adoration of the Magi, from Breviary of Queen Isabella. 9c, 15c, Like 3c, Nativity from Sforza Book of Hours.

1973, Oct. 2 *Perf. 14½*

314	A43	3c dull green & multi	.25	.25
315	A43	5c dull pur & multi	.25	.25
316	A43	9c sepia & multi	.25	.25
317	A43	12c dk blue & multi	.25	.25
318	A43	15c dp rose & multi	.25	.25
319	A43	25c black & multi	.40	.40
		Nos. 314-319 (6)	1.65	1.65

Princess Anne's Wedding Issue

Common Design Type

1973, Nov. 14 Wmk. 314 *Perf. 14*

320	CD325	10c brt green & multi	.25	.25
321	CD325	30c lilac & multi	.30	.30

White-winged Dove — A44

10c, Vitelline warblers. 12c, Greater Antillean grackles. 20c, West Indian red-bellied woodpecker. 30c, Stripe-headed tanagers. 50c, Yucatan vireos.

1974, Jan. 2 Litho. *Perf. 14x14½*

322	A44	3c shown	2.75	.40
323	A44	10c multicolored	3.50	.40
324	A44	12c multicolored	3.50	.40
325	A44	20c multicolored	5.75	1.00
326	A44	30c multicolored	7.25	2.25
327	A44	50c multicolored	9.75	6.25
		Nos. 322-327 (6)	32.50	10.70

See Nos. 354-359.

One-room Schoolhouse — A45

Designs: 20c, New comprehensive school. 30c, Creative Arts Center, Mona, Jamaica.

1974, May 1 *Perf. 14*

328	A45	12c multicolored	.25	.25
329	A45	20c multicolored	.25	.25
330	A45	30c multicolored	.30	.30
		Nos. 328-330 (3)	.80	.80

25th anniv. of the University College of the West Indies.

Hermit Crab and Pirate Gold (#346) A46

Coat of Arms (#344) — A47

Elizabeth II (#348) — A48

Designs: 3c, Pirate, treasure chest and lion's paw. 4c, Spotted scorpionfish and crown. 5c, Flint-lock pistol and brain coral. 6c, Blackbeard on Grand Cayman and green turtle. 8c, 9c, Jeweled pomander and porkfish. 10c, Spiny lobster and gold coins. 12c, Jeweled sword, dagger and sea fan. 15c, Cabrit's murex and jeweled necklace. 20c, Queen conch, pistol and gold cup. 25c, Hogfish and pirate chest. 40c, Gold chalice and sea whip.

Wmk. 314 Upright, Sideways (#331-332, 336, 344-345)

1974-75 Litho. *Perf. 14*

Size: 41x26.5mm

331	A46	1c multi ('75)	4.25	1.75
a.		Wmk. upright	3.75	1.25
332	A46	3c multicolored	4.25	1.75
a.		Wmk. upright	3.75	.70
333	A46	4c multicolored	.70	*.95*
334	A46	5c multicolored	3.50	1.00
335	A46	6c multicolored	.50	*2.75*
336	A46	8c multicolored	3.00	*9.50*
337	A46	9c multicolored	5.00	*12.50*
338	A46	10c multicolored	5.50	1.10
339	A46	12c multicolored	.50	*2.25*
340	A46	15c multicolored	.55	*1.75*
341	A46	20c multicolored	5.00	4.00
342	A46	25c multicolored	.60	*.85*
343	A46	40c multicolored	5.00	1.50
344	A47	$1 multicolored	3.25	*3.50*
345	A48	$2 multicolored	9.50	*10.00*
		Nos. 331-345 (15)	51.10	*55.15*

Issued: No. 332, 11/12; 8c, 12/16; No. 331, 9/29; others, 8/1.

1976-77 Wmk. 373

332b	A46	3c multicolored	1.00	*4.50*
333a	A46	4c multi ('77)	1.50	*5.00*
334a	A46	5c multi ('77)	7.50	7.50
336b	A46	8c multicolored	8.50	6.25
338b	A46	10c multicolored	3.75	*5.00*
341b	A46	20c multicolored	4.25	3.50
344a	A47	$1 multi ('77)	7.50	*11.00*
345b	A48	$2 multicolored	8.50	9.25
		Nos. 332b-345b (8)	42.50	*52.00*

Issued: 3c, 8c, 10c, 20c, $2, 9/3; 4c, 5c, $1, 10/19.

Design Smaller
Size: 39.5x25mm
Wmk. 373 (Sideways on 1c-40c)

1978-80

346	A46	1c multicolored	1.25	*1.75*
346A	A46	3c multicolored	1.00	.75
346B	A46	5c multi ('79)	2.75	*3.00*
347	A46	10c multicolored	2.00	1.00
347A	A46	20c multicolored	4.00	1.75
347B	A46	40c multi ('79)	15.00	22.50
347C	A47	$1 multi ('80)	22.50	7.00
348	A48	$2 multi ('80)	6.50	*25.00*
		Nos. 346-348 (8)	55.00	*62.75*

Issued: 1c, 3c, 3/16; 10c, 20c, 5/25; 5c, 12/11; $2, 4/3; $1, 7/30.

Sea Captain and Ship — A49

1974, Oct. 7 Wmk. 314 *Perf. 14*

349	A49	8c shown	.25	.25
350	A49	12c Thatch weaver	.25	.25
351	A49	20c Farmer	.55	.50
a.		Miniature sheet of 3, #349-351	2.00	*2.50*
		Nos. 349-351 (3)	1.05	1.00

Arms of Cinque Ports and Lord Warden's Flag — A50

Churchill Coat of Arms — A51

1974, Nov. 30

352	A50	12c multicolored	.25	.25
353	A51	50c multicolored	.70	.70
a.		Souvenir sheet of 2, #352-353	1.10	*1.25*

Sir Winston Churchill (1874-1965).

Bird Type of 1974

3c, Yellow-shafted flicker. 10c, West Indian tree duck. 12c, Yellow warblers. 20c, White-bellied dove. 30c, Magnificent frigate bird. 50c, Cayman amazon.

Wmk. 314

1975, Jan. 1 Litho. *Perf. 14*

354	A44	3c multicolored	.70	.45
355	A44	10c multicolored	1.25	.45
356	A44	12c multicolored	1.60	.70
357	A44	20c multicolored	2.50	2.50
358	A44	30c multicolored	3.75	*4.25*
359	A44	50c multicolored	4.60	*11.50*
a.		Wmk. 362 (Lesotho)	650.00	
		Nos. 354-359 (6)	14.30	*19.85*

Ivory Crosier with Crucifixion — A52

Design: 35c, Crucifixion, ivory and gilt. Designs show heads of 14th century French pastoral staffs.

Wmk. 314

1975, Mar. 24 Litho. *Perf. 14*

360	A52	15c plum & multi	.25	.25
361	A52	35c gray & multi	.65	.65
a.		Souvenir sheet of 2, #360-361	1.10	1.10

Easter. No. 361a exists imperf.
See Nos. 366-367.

Israel Hands A53

Designs: Pirates and various scenes.

1975, July 25 Wmk. 314

362	A53	10c shown	.50	.25
363	A53	12c John Fenn	.50	.25
364	A53	20c Thomas Anstis	.85	.50
365	A53	30c Edward Low	1.10	*1.50*
		Nos. 362-365 (4)	2.95	2.50

Easter Type of 1975

Designs after ivory carved pastoral staffs showing Virgin and Child with angels, French, 14th century.

Wmk. 373

1975, Oct. 31 Litho. *Perf. 14*

366	A52	12c dk green & multi	.25	.25
367	A52	50c multicolored	.70	.70
a.		Souvenir sheet of 2, #366-367	1.50	*1.90*

Christmas.

Registered Letter with Nos. 1-2; Cayman Brac Government House and Sub Post Office — A54

Cayman Islands 1st postage stamps, 75th anniv.: 20c, Cayman Islands #1 and cancelation used 1890-94; 30c, #2, 20; 50c, #1-2.

1976, Mar. 12 Litho. *Perf. 13½x14*

368	A54	10c lt blue & multi	.25	.25
369	A54	20c pink & multi	.25	.25
370	A54	30c multicolored	.40	.40
371	A54	50c yellow & multi	.60	.60
a.		Souvenir sheet of 4, #368-371	4.00	4.00
		Nos. 368-371 (4)	1.50	1.50

Seals of Georgia, Delaware and New Hampshire — A55

15c, Seals of SC, NJ, MD. 20c, Seals of VA, RI, MA. 25c, Seals of NY, CT, NC. 30c, Seal of PA, Liberty Bell and Great Seal of the US.

Wmk. 373

1976, May 29 Litho. *Perf. 14*

372	A55	10c olive & multi	.35	.25
373	A55	15c blue & multi	.45	.25
374	A55	20c multicolored	.60	.30
375	A55	25c blue grn & multi	.90	.60
376	A55	30c red brn & multi	1.10	.85
a.		Souvenir sheet of 5 + label	6.25	6.25
		Nos. 372-376 (5)	3.40	2.25

American Bicentennial. Nos. 372-376 printed in sheets of 5. No. 376a contains one each of Nos. 372-376 and corner label inscribed "USA 200."

French Class 470 Racing Dinghies — A56

Design: 50c, One racing dinghy.

1976, Aug. 16 Litho. *Perf. 14*

377	A56	20c multicolored	.60	.45
378	A56	50c multicolored	1.10	1.10

21st Olympic Games, Montreal, Canada, July 17-Aug. 1.

Queen Elizabeth II — A57

8c, Prince Charles, 1973 visit. 50c, Preparation for anointing ceremony, horiz.

Perf. 14x13½, 13½x14

1977, Feb. 7 Litho. Wmk. 373

379	A57	8c multicolored	.25	.25
380	A57	30c multicolored	.25	.25
381	A57	50c multicolored	.25	.25
		Nos. 379-381 (3)	.75	.75

25th anniv. of the reign of Elizabeth II.

Scuba Diving A58

10c, Divers examining underwater wreck. 20c, Fairy basslets (fish). 25c, Sergeant majors (fish).

1977, July 25 *Perf. 13½*

382	A58	5c multicolored	.25	.25
383	A58	10c multicolored	.25	.25
384	A58	20c multicolored	.45	.45
385	A58	25c multicolored	.60	.60
a.		Souvenir sheet of 4	3.00	3.00
		Nos. 382-385 (4)	1.55	1.55

Tourist publicity. No. 385a contains one each of Nos. 382-385, perf. 14½.

Composia Fidelissima — A59

Butterflies: 8c, Heliconius charitonius. 10c, Danaus gilippus. 15c, Agraulis vanillae. 20c, Junonia evarete. 30c, Anartia jatrophae.

1977, Dec. 2 Wmk. 373 *Perf. 14x13*

386	A59	5c multicolored	1.10	.25
387	A59	8c multicolored	1.25	.30
388	A59	10c multicolored	1.35	.35
389	A59	15c multicolored	1.60	.55
390	A59	20c multicolored	1.75	.60
391	A59	30c multicolored	2.00	1.10
		Nos. 386-391 (6)	9.05	3.15

Cruise Ship "Southward" A60

Designs: 5c, "Renaissance." 30c, New harbor, vert. 50c, "Daphne," vert.

1978, Jan. 23 Litho. *Perf. 14*

392	A60	3c multicolored	.45	.25
393	A60	5c multicolored	.45	.25
394	A60	30c multicolored	1.25	.50
395	A60	50c multicolored	1.50	.75
		Nos. 392-395 (4)	3.65	1.75

New harbor and cruise ships.

Crucifixion, by Dürer — A61

Etchings by Dürer: 15c, Christ at Emmaus. 20c, Entry into Jerusalem. 30c, Christ washing Peter's feet.

1978, Mar. 20 Litho. *Perf. 12*

396	A61	10c multicolored	.30	.25
397	A61	15c multicolored	.45	.30
398	A61	20c multicolored	.55	.40
399	A61	30c multicolored	.65	.55
a.		Souvenir sheet of 4, #396-399	6.50	6.50
		Nos. 396-399 (4)	1.95	1.50

Easter; Albrecht Dürer (1471-1528). Nos. 396-399 issued in sheets of 6.

Explorers, Singing Game — A62

10c, Girls' Brigade presenting flag. 20c, Guides studying Bible, playing guitar, tennis and volleyball. 50c, Guides setting table.

1978, Apr. 25 Litho. *Perf. 14*

400	A62	3c multicolored	.25	.25
401	A62	10c multicolored	.35	.35
402	A62	20c multicolored	.60	.60
403	A62	50c multicolored	1.25	1.25
		Nos. 400-403 (4)	2.45	2.45

3rd Intl. Council Meeting of Girls' Brigade.

Elizabeth II Coronation Anniversary Issue

Common Design Types
Souvenir Sheet

1978, June 2 Unwmk. *Perf. 15*

404		Sheet of 6	2.00	*2.50*
a.		CD326 30c Yale of Beaufort	.30	.30
b.		CD327 30c Elizabeth II	.30	.30
c.		CD328 30c Screech owl	.30	.30

No. 404 contains 2 se-tenant strips of Nos. 404a-404c, separated by horizontal gutter with commemorative and descriptive inscriptions.

A63

A63a

A63: 1c, Trumpetfish. 3c, Nassau grouper. 5c, French angelfish. 10c, Schoolmaster snappers. 20c, Banded butterflyfish. 50c, Black-bar soldierfish.

A63a: 3c, Four-eyed butterflyfish. 5c, Grey angel fish. 10c, Squirrelfish. 15c, Parrotfish. 20c, Spanish hogfish. 30c, Queen angelfish.

1978-79 Wmk. 373 Litho. *Perf. 14*

405	A63	1c multicolored	.25	.25
406	A63	3c multicolored	.35	.25
407	A63a	3c multicolored	.30	.25
408	A63a	5c multicolored	.35	.25
409	A63	5c multicolored	.30	.25
412	A63a	10c multicolored	.55	.25
413	A63	10c multicolored	.55	.25
414	A63a	15c multicolored	.65	.35
415	A63a	20c multicolored	.85	.45

416 A63 20c multicolored 1.05 .45
417 A63a 30c multicolored 1.75 .70
418 A63 50c multicolored 2.75 1.10
Nos. 405-418 (12) 9.70 4.80

Issued: design A63, 4/20/79; design A63a, 8/28/78.

Lockheed Lodestar — A64

Aircraft: 5c, Consolidated PBY. 10c, Vickers Viking. 15c, BAC1-11. 20c, Piper Cheyenne, HS 125 and Bell 47. 30c, BAC1-11.

1979, Feb. 5 *Perf. 14½*

420 A64 3c multicolored .40 .25
421 A64 5c multicolored .40 .25
422 A64 10c multicolored .45 .25
423 A64 15c multicolored .75 .40
424 A64 20c multicolored .95 .45
425 A64 30c multicolored 1.10 .55
Nos. 420-425 (6) 4.05 2.15

Opening of Owen Roberts Airport, 25th anniv.

Rowland Hill and No. 2 — A65

Sir Rowland Hill (1795-1879), originator of penny postage, and: 10c, Great Britain #132. 20c, Cayman Islands #149. 50c,Cayman Islands #20.

Perf. 13½x14½

1979, Aug. 15 **Litho.**

426 A65 5c multicolored .25 .25
427 A65 10c multicolored .25 .25
428 A65 20c multicolored .60 .60
Nos. 426-428 (3) 1.10 1.10

Souvenir Sheet

429 A65 50c multicolored 1.50 1.50

Flight into Egypt A66

Christmas: 20c, Shepherds, Star of Bethlehem. 30c, Nativity. 40c, Three Kings, Star of Bethlehem.

1979, Nov. 20 **Litho.** *Perf. 13½*

430 A66 10c multicolored .25 .25
431 A66 20c multicolored .25 .25
432 A66 30c multicolored .40 .25
433 A66 40c multicolored .70 .30
Nos. 430-433 (4) 1.60 1.05

Bonaventure House, Rotary Emblem — A67

30c, Paul P. Harris, vert. 50c, Anniversary emblem, vert.

Perf. 14x13½, 13½x14

1980, Feb. 14 **Litho.** **Wmk. 373**

434 A67 20c shown .30 .25
435 A67 30c multicolored .50 .25
436 A67 50c multicolored .80 .50
Nos. 434-436 (3) 1.60 1.00

Rotary International, 75th anniversary.

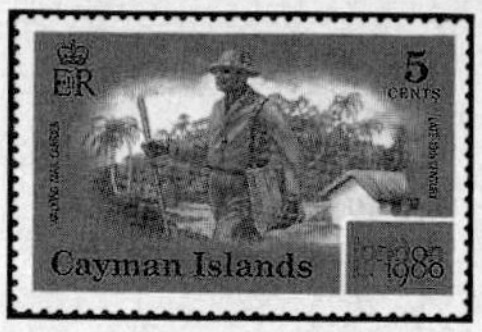

Mailman, London 1980 Emblem A68

1980, May 6 **Litho.** *Perf. 14*

437 A68 5c shown .25 .25
438 A68 10c Cat boat .25 .25
439 A68 15c Mounted mailman .25 .25
440 A68 30c Mail wagon .40 .35
441 A68 40c Mailman on bicycle .50 .45
442 A68 $1 Mail truck 1.00 .90
Nos. 437-442 (6) 2.65 2.45

London '80 Intl. Stamp Exhib., May 6-14.

Queen Mother Elizabeth Birthday Issue

Common Design Type

1980, Aug. 4 **Litho.** *Perf. 14*

443 CD330 20c multicolored .45 .45

Spondylus Americanus A69

1980, Aug. 12 *Perf. 14½x14*

444 A69 5c shown .80 .25
445 A69 10c Murex brevifrons .80 .30
446 A69 30c Cymatium femorale 1.60 .65
447 A69 50c Vasum muricatum 1.75 1.25
Nos. 444-447 (4) 4.95 2.45

See Nos. 502-505, 518-521.

Lantana — A70

1980, Oct. 21 **Litho.** *Perf. 14*

448 A70 5c shown .25 .25
449 A70 15c Bauhinia .30 .25
450 A70 30c Hibiscus .55 .30
451 A70 $1 Milk and wine lily 1.45 1.40
Nos. 448-451 (4) 2.55 2.20

See Nos. 478-481.

Juvenile Tarpon and Fire Sponges — A71

5c, Mangrove root oysters. 10c, Mangrove crab. 15c, Lizard, crescent spot butterfly. 20c, Tricolored heron. 30c, Red mangrove flower. 40c, Red mangrove seeds. 50c, Waterhouse's leaf-nosed bat. $1, Black-crowned night heron. $2, Cayman Islands arms. $4, Queen Elizabeth II.

1980, Dec. 9 **Litho.** *Perf. 13½x13*

Without Imprint

452 A71 3c shown 1.10 *2.25*
453 A71 5c multicolored 1.25 *1.10*
d. Wmk. 384 8.00 8.00
e. Wmk. 384, perf. 14 6.75 7.00
454 A71 10c multicolored .65 *1.10*
d. Wmk. 384, perf. 14 10.00 9.75
455 A71 15c multicolored 1.10 *2.25*
456 A71 20c multicolored 1.50 *2.75*
457 A71 30c multicolored .90 *1.40*
458 A71 40c multicolored .95 *1.25*
459 A71 50c multicolored 1.50 *1.75*
460 A71 $1 multicolored 6.00 *5.50*
461 A71 $2 multicolored 2.25 *3.75*
462 A71 $4 multicolored 4.25 4.25
Nos. 452-462 (11) 21.45 *27.35*

Nos. 453d, 453e and 454d inscribed "1986" below design. Issued: No. 453d, 4/86; Nos. 453e, 454fa, 6/86.

1982, June 14 **Inscribed "1982"**

452a A71 3c shown 5.00 *4.00*
453a A71 5c multicolored 1.25 *.90*
454a A71 10c multicolored 1.25 *.90*
455a A71 15c multicolored 4.50 *2.00*
456a A71 20c multicolored 2.50 *2.25*
457a A71 30c multicolored 1.50 *1.50*
458a A71 40c multicolored 1.50 *1.50*
459a A71 50c multicolored 2.00 *2.00*
460a A71 $1 multicolored 6.00 *5.00*
461a A71 $2 multicolored 4.00 *4.00*
462a A71 $4 multicolored 9.00 9.00
Nos. 452a-462a (11) 38.50 33.05

Issued: No. 453a, 4/86; No. 454a, 6/86.

1984 **Inscribed "1984"**

453b A71 5c multicolored 2.50 *2.50*

Issued: No. 453b, 6/86.

1985 **Inscribed "1985"**

453c A71 5c multicolored 1.25 *1.25*
454c A71 10c multicolored 1.25 *1.25*
455c A71 15c multicolored 4.50 *4.50*
456c A71 20c multicolored 2.50 *2.50*
457c A71 30c multicolored 1.50 *1.50*
458c A71 40c multicolored 1.50 *1.50*
459c A71 50c multicolored 2.00 *2.00*
460c A71 $1 multicolored 6.00 *5.00*
461c A71 $2 multicolored 5.00 *5.00*
Nos. 453c-461c (9) 25.50 *24.50*

Bread and Wine — A72

1981, Mar. 17 **Wmk. 373** *Perf. 14*

463 A72 3c shown .25 .25
464 A72 10c Crown of thorns .25 .25
465 A72 20c Crucifix .25 .25
466 A72 $1 Christ .60 *1.10*
Nos. 463-466 (4) 1.35 1.85

Easter.

Wood Slave A73

1981, June 16 **Litho.** *Perf. 13½*

467 A73 20c shown .40 .40
468 A73 30c Cayman iguana .60 .60
469 A73 40c Lion lizard .80 .80
470 A73 50c Freshwater turtle .95 .95
Nos. 467-470 (4) 2.75 2.75

Royal Wedding Issue

Common Design Type

1981, July 22 **Litho.** *Perf. 14*

471 CD331 20c Bouquet .25 .25
472 CD331 30c Charles .30 .30
473 CD331 $1 Couple .80 .80
Nos. 471-473 (3) 1.35 1.35

Intl. Year of the Disabled A74

5c, Scuba divers. 15c, Old School for Handicapped. 20c, New School for Handicapped. $1, Beach scene.

1981, Sept. 29 **Litho.** *Perf. 14*

474 A74 5c multicolored .25 .25
475 A74 15c multicolored .25 .25
476 A74 20c multicolored .35 .35
477 A74 $1 multicolored 1.40 1.40
Nos. 474-477 (4) 2.25 2.25

Flower Type of 1980

1981, Oct. 20 **Litho.** *Perf. 14*

478 A70 3c Bougainvillea .25 .25
479 A70 10c Morning glory .25 .25
480 A70 20c Wild amaryllis .55 .55
481 A70 $1 Cordia 2.25 2.25
Nos. 478-481 (4) 3.30 3.30

TB Bacillus Centenary — A75

1982, Mar. 24 **Litho.** *Perf. 14½*

482 A75 15c Koch, horizontal microscope .30 .30
483 A75 30c Koch, vert. .65 .65
484 A75 40c Microscope, vert. .80 .80
485 A75 50c Koch, diff., vert. 1.10 1.10
Nos. 482-485 (4) 2.85 2.85

Princess Diana Issue

Common Design Type

1982, July 1 **Litho.** *Perf. 13*

486 CD333 20c Arms *.50 .40*
487 CD333 30c Diana *.90 .55*
488 CD333 40c Wedding *1.00 .75*
489 CD333 50c Portrait *3.00 1.00*
Nos. 486-489 (4) *5.40 2.70*

Scouting Year A76

1982, Aug. 24 **Wmk. 373** *Perf. 14*

490 A76 3c Pitching tent .30 .25
491 A76 20c Cooking .65 .65
492 A76 30c Troop 1.10 1.10
493 A76 50c Boating skills 1.50 1.50
Nos. 490-493 (4) 3.55 3.50

Christmas 1982 — A77

Virgin and Child Paintings by Raphael.

1982, Oct. 26 *Perf. 14½*

494 A77 3c multicolored .25 .25
495 A77 10c multicolored .30 .30
496 A77 20c multicolored .60 .60
497 A77 30c multicolored .85 .85
Nos. 494-497 (4) 2.00 2.00

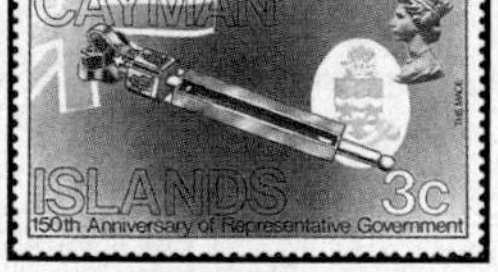

Representative Govt. Sesquicentennial — A78

3c, Mace. 10c, Old Courthouse. 20c, Commonwealth Parliamentary Assoc. arms. 30c, Legislative Assembley building.

1982, Nov. 9 **Litho.** **Wmk. 373**

498 A78 3c multicolored .25 .25
499 A78 10c multicolored .25 .25
500 A78 20c multicolored .40 .40
501 A78 30c multicolored .60 .60
Nos. 498-501 (4) 1.50 1.50

Shell Type of 1980

1983, Jan. 11 **Litho.** *Perf. 13½*

502 A69 5c Natica canrena .25 .25
503 A69 10c Cassis tuberosa .40 .40
504 A69 20c Strombus gallus .85 .85
505 A69 $1 Cypraecassis testiculus 3.50 3.50
Nos. 502-505 (4) 5.00 5.00

Visit of Queen Elizabeth II and Prince Philip A79

20c, Legislative Building, Cayman Brac. 30c, Leg. Bldg., Grand Cayman. 50c, Prince Philip. $1, Queen Elizabeth II.

1983, Feb. 15 Litho. *Perf. 14*

506 A79 20c multicolored .50 .50
507 A79 30c multicolored .85 .75
508 A79 50c multicolored 1.50 1.25
509 A79 $1 multicolored 2.50 2.50
a. Souvenir sheet of 4, #506-509 6.50 6.50
Nos. 506-509 (4) 5.35 5.00

A80

1983, Mar. 14

510 A80 3c Globe .30 .25
511 A80 15c Flags .65 .60
512 A80 20c Fisherman .70 .70
513 A80 40c Elizabeth II 1.10 .95
Nos. 510-513 (4) 2.75 2.50

Commonwealth Day.

Manned Flight Bicentenary and Mosquito Research and Control Unit — A81

Airplanes: 3c, MRCU Cessna. 10c, Consolidated Catalina PBY. 20c, Boeing 727. 40c, Hawker Siddeley HS-748.

1983, Oct. 10 Litho. *Perf. 14½*

514 A81 3c multicolored .95 .70
515 A81 10c multicolored 1.10 .70
516 A81 20c multicolored 1.90 1.90
517 A81 40c multicolored 2.50 3.75
Nos. 514-517 (4) 6.45 7.05

Shell Type of 1980

1984, Jan. 18 *Perf. 14x14½*

518 A69 3c Natica floridana 1.25 .40
519 A69 10c Conus austini 1.60 .40
520 A69 30c Colubrania obscura 4.50 4.50
521 A69 50c Turbo cailletii 4.75 4.75
Nos. 518-521 (4) 12.10 10.05

Lloyd's List Issue
Common Design Type

1984, May 16 Litho. *Perf. 14*

522 CD335 5c Cruise ship .65 .25
523 CD335 10c The Old Harbor .75 .30
524 CD335 25c Ridgefield 1.40 1.40
525 CD335 50c Goldfield 3.00 3.00
Nos. 522-525 (4) 5.80 4.95

Souvenir Sheet

526 CD335 $1 Goldfield, diff. 3.50 3.50

No. 525 Overprinted

1984, June 18

527 CD335 50c multicolored 2.00 2.00

Local Birds — A82

Perf. 14x14½

1984, Aug. 15 Litho. Wmk. 373

528 A82 5c Snowy egret 1.25 .65
529 A82 10c Bananaquit 1.25 .65
530 A82 35c Kingfisher 4.00 2.50
531 A82 $1 Brown booby 7.50 9.50
Nos. 528-531 (4) 14.00 13.30

Christmas — A83

Nos. 532a-532d, evening beach scenes. Nos. 533a-533d, daytime boating and beach scenes.

1984, Oct. 17 Litho. *Perf. 14*

532 A83 Strip of 4 5.00 5.00
a.-d. 5c Any single 1.25 1.25
533 A83 Strip of 4 6.00 5.00
a.-d. 25c Any single 1.50 1.25

Souvenir Sheet

534 A83 $1 Bonfire, diff. 6.75 6.75

No. 534 contains one stamp 29x48mm.

Orchids — A84

5c, Schomburgkia thomsoniana var. 10c, Schomburgkia thomsoniana. 25c, Encyclia plicata. 50c, Dendrophylax fawcetti.

1985, Mar. 13 Litho. *Perf. 14x13½*

535 A84 5c multicolored 1.50 .55
536 A84 10c multicolored 1.50 .55
537 A84 25c multicolored 3.75 1.25
538 A84 50c multicolored 4.75 3.50
Nos. 535-538 (4) 11.50 5.85

Shipwrecks A85

Unspecified shipwrecks found in Cayman waters.

1985, May 22 *Perf. 14*

539 A85 5c multicolored 1.25 .55
540 A85 25c multicolored 4.00 1.50
541 A85 35c multicolored 4.25 2.75
542 A85 40c multicolored 4.50 3.75
Nos. 539-542 (4) 14.00 8.55

Intl. Youth Year — A86

5c, Natl. Athletic Assoc. track competition. 15c, High school students studying in Grand Cayman Campus Library. 25c, Amateur League Competition Football. 50c, Natl. Netball Assoc. competition.

1985, Aug. 14 *Perf. 14½*

543 A86 5c multicolored .25 .25
544 A86 15c multicolored .45 .40
545 A86 25c multicolored .95 .85
546 A86 50c multicolored 1.90 1.90
Nos. 543-546 (4) 3.55 3.40

Telecommunications, 50th Anniv. — A87

Designs: 5c, Morse Code transmitter, 1935. 10c, Hand-cranked telephone, 1935. 25c, Tropospheric scatter dish, 1966. 50c, Earth dish receiver, 1979.

1985, Oct. 25 *Perf. 14*

547 A87 5c multicolored .55 .55
548 A87 10c multicolored .60 .60
549 A87 25c multicolored 1.75 1.10
550 A87 50c multicolored 2.75 3.50
Nos. 547-550 (4) 5.65 5.75

Birds A88

10c, Magnificent frigatebird. 25c, West Indian whistling duck. 35c, La Sagra's flycatcher. 40c, Yellow-faced grassquit.

1986, Mar. 20 Litho. Wmk. 384

551 A88 10c multicolored 2.25 1.00
552 A88 25c multicolored 3.00 1.60
553 A88 35c multicolored 3.50 3.50
554 A88 40c multicolored 4.00 4.00
Nos. 551-554 (4) 12.75 10.10

Nos. 552-553 vert.

Queen Elizabeth II 60th Birthday
Common Design Type

Designs: 5c, As bridesmaid at wedding of Lady Mary Cambridge, 1931. 10c, Royal visit to Norway, 1955. 25c, Inspecting West Indian troop, royal tour, 1985. 50c, Gulf tour, 1979. $1, Visiting Crown Agents' offices, 1983.

1986, Apr. 21 *Perf. 14x14½*

555 CD337 5c scar, blk & sil .25 .25
556 CD337 10c ultra, blk & sil .25 .25
557 CD337 25c grn & multi 1.75 .95
558 CD337 50c vio & multi .90 1.10
559 CD337 $1 rose vio & multi 1.40 1.90
Nos. 555-559 (5) 4.55 4.45

Royal Wedding Issue, 1986
Common Design Type

Designs: 5c, Informal portrait. 50c, Andrew in uniform, helicopter.

Perf. 14½x14

1986, July 23 Litho. Wmk. 384

560 CD338 5c multicolored .30 .25
561 CD338 50c multicolored 1.20 1.90

Marine Life — A89

5c, Rhynchocinetes rigeus. 10c, Nemaster rubiginosa. 15c, Calcinus tibicen. 20c, Rhodactis sanctithomae. 25c, Spirobranchus gigantea. 35c, Diodon holacanthus. 50c, Pseudocorynactis aribbeorum. 60c, Astrophyton muricatum. 75c, Cyphoma gibbosum. $1, Conolylactis gigantea. $2, Malacoctenus boehlkei. $4, Lima scabra.

Perf. 13½x13

1986, Sept. 15 Wmk. 373

Inscribed "1986"

562 A89 5c multicolored .80 .65
563 A89 10c multicolored .80 .65
c. Wmk. 384, inscribed "1990" 2.75 3.00
564 A89 15c multicolored .70 .75
565 A89 20c multicolored .70 .95
566 A89 25c multicolored .45 3.00
567 A89 35c multicolored .70 3.25
568 A89 50c multicolored .80 5.00
569 A89 60c multicolored 3.50 9.50
570 A89 75c multicolored 9.50 12.00
571 A89 $1 multicolored 2.25 3.25
572 A89 $2 multicolored 5.00 5.25
573 A89 $4 multicolored 10.00 8.25
Nos. 562-573 (12) 35.20 52.50

1987 Inscribed "1987"

562a A89 5c multicolored .80 1.60
563a A89 10c multicolored .80 1.25
564a A89 15c multicolored .70 1.50
565a A89 20c multicolored .70 2.00
571a A89 $1 multicolored 2.25 6.50
572a A89 $2 multicolored 5.00 10.50
573a A89 $4 multicolored 10.00 17.50
Nos. 562a-573a (7) 20.25 40.85

1990 Inscribed "1990"

562b A89 5c multicolored 2.75 5.00
563b A89 10c multicolored 2.75 4.00
564b A89 15c multicolored 2.50 5.00
565b A89 20c multicolored 2.50 7.00
566b A89 25c multicolored 1.50 10.00
567b A89 35c multicolored —
568b A89 50c multicolored —
571b A89 $1 multicolored 8.00 10.00
572b A89 $2 multicolored 17.50 17.50
Nos. 562b-572b (7) 37.50 58.50

Tourism A90

Perf. 13x13½

1987, Jan. 26 Wmk. 384

574 A90 10c Golfing 2.50 1.00
575 A90 15c Sailing 2.60 1.00
576 A90 25c Snorkeling 2.60 1.50
577 A90 35c Parasailing 2.60 2.00
578 A90 $1 Fishing 5.75 9.75
Nos. 574-578 (5) 16.05 15.25

Fruit — A91

1987, May 20 *Perf. 14½*

579 A91 5c Akee 1.00 1.00
580 A91 25c Breadfruit 2.25 .75
581 A91 35c Papaya 2.25 1.00
582 A91 $1 Soursop 6.00 7.50
Nos. 579-582 (4) 11.50 10.25

Lizards — A92

1987, Aug. 26 Litho. *Perf. 14*

583 A92 10c Lion lizard 2.00 1.00
584 A92 50c Iguana 5.25 4.50
585 A92 $1 Anole 6.25 8.75
Nos. 583-585 (3) 13.50 14.25

Flowers — A93

1987, Nov. 18 *Perf. 14½x14*

586 A93 5c Poinsettia 1.25 .55
587 A93 25c Periwinkle 3.00 .90
588 A93 35c Yellow allamanda 3.00 1.25
589 A93 75c Blood lily 5.25 6.00
Nos. 586-589 (4) 12.50 8.70

Butterflies A94

Designs: 5c, Hemiargus ammon erembis and Strymon martialis. 25c, Phocides pigmalion batabano. 50c, Anaea troglodyta cubana. $1, Papilio andraemon andraemon.

1988, Mar. 29 Wmk. 384 *Perf. 14*

590 A94 5c multicolored 1.60 .65
591 A94 25c multicolored 3.50 1.40
592 A94 50c multicolored 5.25 5.25
593 A94 $1 multicolored 6.75 6.75
Nos. 590-593 (4) 17.10 14.05

Herons — A95

1988, Jan. 26 Litho. *Perf. 14*

594 A95 5c Butorides striatus 2.40 .65
595 A95 25c Egretta tricolor 4.50 .90
596 A95 50c Nycticorax violaceus 5.50 5.25
597 A95 $1 Egretta caerulea 6.00 5.50
Nos. 594-597 (4) 18.40 12.30

1988 Summer Olympics, Seoul — A96

10c, Cycling. 50c, Natl. team, passenger jet. $1, Yachting.
No. 601, Tennis.

1988, Sept. 21 *Perf. 14½*

598 A96 10c multicolored 2.25 .65
599 A96 50c multicolored 3.75 2.75
600 A96 $1 multicolored 4.00 4.00
Nos. 598-600 (3) 10.00 7.40

Souvenir Sheet

Wmk. 373

601 A96 $1 multicolored 6.25 6.25

No. 601 commemorates the 75th anniv. of the Intl. Tennis Federation.

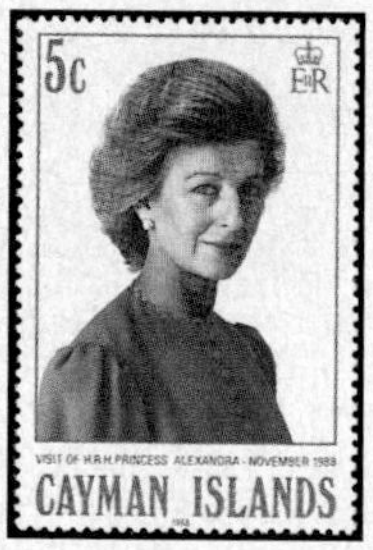

Visit of Princess Alexandra A97

1988, Nov. 1 Wmk. 373 *Perf. 15*

602 A97 5c Portrait 2.75 1.25
603 A97 $1 Seated in garden 9.75 7.50

Cayman Islands P.O., Cent. — A98

Designs: 5c, P.O., Georgetown, 1889, and Jamaica #24, canceled. 25c, S.S. Orinoco and Cayman Isls. #1. 35c, Grand Cayman G.P.O. and #442. $1, Cayman Airways mail plane and #191.

1989, Apr. 12 Wmk. 384 *Perf. 14½*

604 A98 5c multicolored 1.25 1.25
605 A98 25c multicolored 2.75 1.50
606 A98 35c multicolored 3.00 1.75
607 A98 $1 multicolored 11.00 11.00
Nos. 604-607 (4) 18.00 15.50

A99

Mutiny on the Bounty: a, Capt. Bligh. b, HMS Providence, two crewmen. c, HMS Assistant, transplanted breadfruit. d, Moving breadfruit on land, in longboat. e, Midshipman among casks and crates.

1989, May 24 *Perf. 14*

608 Strip of 5 32.50 32.50
a.-e. A99 50c any single 6.50 6.50

A100

5c, Panton House. 10c, Town Hall. 25c, Old Courts House. 35c, Elmslie Memorial Church. $1, Post office.

Perf. 14½x14

1989, Oct. 18 Litho. Wmk. 373

609 A100 5c multicolored 1.00 1.00
610 A100 10c multicolored 1.00 1.00
611 A100 25c multicolored 2.25 .90
612 A100 35c multicolored 2.25 1.25
613 A100 $1 multicolored 5.50 5.75
Nos. 609-613 (5) 12.00 9.90

Natl. Trust emblem & architecture, George Town.

Island Surveys A101

Maps or survey ships: 5c, Navigational instruments and George Gauld's map of 1773. 25c, Instruments and map created by surveyors aboard HMS *Vidal,* 1956. 50c, *Mutine,* 1914. $1, HMS *Vidal.*

1989, Nov. 15

614 A101 5c multicolored 1.75 1.40
615 A101 25c multicolored 4.50 1.75
616 A101 50c multicolored 7.00 5.25
617 A101 $1 multicolored 11.00 11.00
Nos. 614-617 (4) 24.25 19.40

Angelfish A102

1990, Apr. 25 Wmk. 384 *Perf. 14*

618 A102 10c French 2.10 .65
619 A102 25c Gray 3.75 1.40
620 A102 50c Queen 5.50 5.50
621 A102 $1 Rock beauty 9.00 9.00
Nos. 618-621 (4) 20.35 16.55

Queen Mother, 90th Birthday

Common Design Types

50c, King, Queen Elizabeth, 1948. $1, King, Queen with Churchill, 1940.

1990, Aug. 4 Wmk. 384 *Perf. 14x15*

622 CD343 50c multicolored 1.60 *2.50*

Perf. 14½

623 CD344 $1 multicolored 3.50 *4.25*

Butterflies A103

1990, Oct. 24 *Perf. 14½x14*

624 A103 5c Soldier 1.35 1.25
625 A103 25c Pygmy blue 3.00 2.40
626 A103 35c Cayman crescent spot 3.75 2.75
627 A103 $1 Gulf fritillary 8.75 10.50
Nos. 624-627 (4) 16.85 16.90

Expo '90, International Garden and Greenery Exposition, Osaka, Japan.

Hurricane Awareness — A104

Designs: 5c, Goes weather satellite. 30c, Meteorologist tracks storm. 40c, Hurricane damage. $1, Lockheed WP-3D Orion flying in hurricane's eye.

1991, Aug. 8 *Perf. 14*

628 A104 5c multicolored 1.40 1.40
629 A104 30c multicolored 3.25 1.75
630 A104 40c multicolored 3.50 2.10
631 A104 $1 multicolored 8.50 8.50
Nos. 628-631 (4) 16.65 13.75

Christmas A105

Local flowers and Christmas scenes: 5c, Angel's trumpet, angels with trumpets. 30c, Golden trumpet, Mary on donkey led by Joseph. 40c, Christmas flower, Adoration of the Magi. 60c, Tree of life, nativity scene.

1991, Nov. 6 Wmk. 373

632 A105 5c multicolored 1.00 1.00
633 A105 30c multicolored 3.00 .85
634 A105 40c multicolored 3.25 1.40
635 A105 60c multicolored 3.75 *5.00*
Nos. 632-635 (4) 11.00 *8.25*

Island Scenes A106

5c, Coconut tree, vert. 15c, Beach scene. 20c, Poincianas in bloom. 30c, Blowholes. 40c, Police band. 50c, Downtown scene, vert. 60c, The Bluff, Cayman Brac. 80c, Coat of arms, vert. 90c, View of Hell. $1, Sportfishing. $2, Harbor scene, vert. $8, Queen Elizabeth II, vert.

Perf. 12½x13, 13x12½

1991, Dec. 11 Litho. Wmk. 373

636 A106 5c multicolored .75 .55
a. Inscribed "1994" 1.00 .75
637 A106 15c multicolored 1.60 .55
638 A106 20c multicolored .85 .70
639 A106 30c multicolored 2.25 .90
640 A106 40c multicolored 3.75 2.25
641 A106 50c multicolored 3.00 2.25
642 A106 60c multicolored 2.50 3.50
643 A106 80c multicolored 2.25 3.75
644 A106 90c multicolored 2.25 3.75
645 A106 $1 multicolored 4.50 3.75
646 A106 $2 multicolored 9.50 9.00
647 A106 $8 multicolored 22.50 25.00
Nos. 636-647 (12) 55.70 55.95

Queen Elizabeth II's Accession to the Throne, 40th Anniv.

Common Design Type

Wmk. 373, 384 (40c)

1992, Feb. 6 Litho. *Perf. 14*

648 CD349 5c multicolored .45 .45
649 CD349 20c multicolored 1.40 .50
650 CD349 30c multicolored 1.50 .75
651 CD349 40c multicolored 1.50 1.40
652 CD349 $1 multicolored 2.75 *4.00*
Nos. 648-652 (5) 7.60 7.10

1992 Summer Olympics, Barcelona A107

1992, Aug. 5 Wmk. 373

653 A107 15c Cyclist 2.00 .55
654 A107 40c Two cyclists 3.50 1.50
655 A107 60c Feet, pedals 4.00 4.00
656 A107 $1 Two cyclists, diff. 5.00 5.00
Nos. 653-656 (4) 14.50 11.05

Island Heritage — A108

5c, Lady with donkey. 30c, Making fish nets. 40c, Maypole dancing. 60c, Basket making. $1, Cooking on caboose.

1992, Oct. 21

657 A108 5c multicolored .70 .70
658 A108 30c multicolored 1.75 1.00
659 A108 40c multicolored 3.00 1.60
660 A108 60c multicolored 3.50 *3.50*
661 A108 $1 multicolored 4.25 *4.25*
Nos. 657-661 (5) 13.20 *11.05*

Rays A109

5c, Yellow stingray. 30c, Southern stingray. 40c, Spotted eagle ray. $1, Manta ray.

Perf. 13½x14

1993, June 16 Litho. Wmk. 373

662 A109 5c multicolored .95 .85
663 A109 30c multicolored 2.40 1.60
664 A109 40c multicolored 2.75 1.90
665 A109 $1 multicolored 6.25 6.25
Nos. 662-665 (4) 12.35 10.60

A110

Tourism: No. 666a, Turtle, sailboats. b, Diver, coral, boats. c, Golf. d, Beach, tennis. e, Pirates, sailing ship.
No. 667: a, Cruise ship, boat, sailboat. b, City street scene. c, Submarines. d, Cyclist, scooters. e, Jet planes.

Perf. 14x13½

1993, Sept. 30 Litho. Wmk. 373

666 A110 15c Strip of 5, #a.-e. 11.50 11.50
667 A110 30c Strip of 5, #a.-e. 12.50 12.50
f. Booklet pane of 10, #666-667 32.50

A111

Various views of Grand Cayman Parrot.

1993, Oct. 29 *Perf. 14*

668 A111	5c green & multi	1.25	1.25
669 A111	5c red & multi	1.25	1.25
670 A111	30c yellow & multi	3.00	3.00
671 A111	30c blue & multi	3.00	3.00
	Nos. 668-671 (4)	8.50	8.50

Christmas A112

Christmas scenes, orchids: 5c, Manger, Ionopsis utricularioides. 40c, Shepherd, lamb, Encyclia cochleata. 60c, Magi, Vanilla pompona. $1, Virgin in prayer, Oncidium caymanense.

Perf. 13½x14

1993, Dec. 6 **Litho.** **Wmk. 384**

672 A112	5c multicolored	1.40	.75
673 A112	40c multicolored	3.75	1.00
674 A112	60c multicolored	4.75	4.75
675 A112	$1 multicolored	6.25	6.25
	Nos. 672-675 (4)	16.15	12.75

Souvenir Sheet

Reef Life — A113

Designs: a, Holocanthus ciliaris. b, Bodianus pulchellus, anisotremus virginicus. c, Holocanthus tricolor, gramma loreto. d, Pomacanthus paru, chaeton striatus.

Perf. 14½x13

1994, Feb. 18 **Litho.** **Wmk. 373**

676 A113	60c Sheet of 4, #a.-d.	13.50	13.50

Hong Kong '94.

Royal Visit — A114

Designs: 5c, Cayman Islands, United Kingdom flags. 15c, Royal yacht Britannia. 30c, Queen Elizabeth II. $2, Queen, Prince Philip.

1994, Feb. 22 *Perf. 14½*

677 A114	5c multicolored	2.00	.95
678 A114	15c multicolored	3.75	1.60
679 A114	30c multicolored	3.75	1.75
680 A114	$2 multicolored	10.50	10.50
	Nos. 677-680 (4)	20.00	14.80

West Indian Whistling Duck A115

5c, One standing. 15c, Landing in water. 20c, Four ducks, various activities. 80c, One raising wings. $1, Adult, chick.

Wmk. 373

1994, Apr. 21 **Litho.** *Perf. 14*

681 A115	5c multi, vert.	1.75	.90
682 A115	15c multi	2.50	.95
683 A115	20c multi	2.50	1.00
684 A115	80c multi, vert.	5.50	6.00
685 A115	$1 multi, vert.	6.25	6.50
a.	Souvenir sheet of 1	13.00	13.00
	Nos. 681-685 (5)	18.50	*15.35*

No. 685a has a continuous design and contains Cayman Islands Natl. Trust emblem.

Butterflies A116

No. 686: a, Fulvous hairstreak. b, Atala butterfly.
No. 687: a, Barred sulphur. b, Dorantes skipper.

Wmk. 373

1994, Aug. 16 **Litho.** *Perf. 13½*

686 A116	10c Pair, #a.-b.	2.75	*3.00*
687 A116	$1 Pair, #a.-b.	13.00	13.00

Wreck of the Ten Sail, Bicent. — A117

Perf. 13½x14

1994, Oct. 12 **Litho.** **Wmk. 373**

688 A117	10c shown	.75	.75
689 A117	10c multicolored	.75	.75
690 A117	15c multicolored	1.25	.60
691 A117	20c multicolored	1.50	.70
692 A117	$2 multicolored	7.75	7.75
	Nos. 688-692 (5)	12.00	10.55

Sea Turtles A118

Wmk. 384

1995, Feb. 28 **Litho.** *Perf. 14*

693 A118	10c Green	.75	.45
694 A118	20c Kemp's ridley	1.10	.55
695 A118	25c Hawksbill	1.25	.65
696 A118	30c Leatherback	1.45	.75
697 A118	$1.30 Loggerhead	5.25	5.25
698 A118	$2 Pacific ridley	6.50	6.50
a.	Souvenir sheet, #693-698	16.50	16.50
	Nos. 693-698 (6)	16.30	14.15

1995 CARIFTA & IAAF Games A119

1995, Apr. 15 **Litho.** *Perf. 14*

699 A119	10c Running	1.00	.55
700 A119	20c Pole vault	1.50	1.10
701 A119	30c Javelin	2.10	1.25
702 A119	$1.30 Sailing	7.25	7.25
	Nos. 699-702 (4)	11.85	10.15

Souvenir Sheet

703 A119	$2 Medal winners	11.00	11.00

End of World War II, 50th Anniv.

Common Design Type

10c, Two soldiers, Cayman Home Guard. 25c, Freighter Comayagua torpedoed off Caymans, 5/14/42. 40c, Type IXc U-Boat U-125. $1, Navy airship L-3 used for U-boat patrol. $1.30, Reverse of War Medal 1939-45.

Wmk. 373

1995, May 8 **Litho.** *Perf. 13½*

704 CD351	10c multicolored	1.40	.55
705 CD351	25c multicolored	2.75	.90
706 CD351	40c multicolored	3.25	2.25
707 CD351	$1 multicolored	5.75	5.75
	Nos. 704-707 (4)	13.15	*9.45*

Souvenir Sheet

Perf. 14

708 CD352	$1.30 multicolored	5.00	5.00

Souvenir Sheet

Queen Mother, 95th Birthday — A120

1995, Aug. 25 *Perf. 14½*

709 A120	$4 multicolored	12.00	12.00

Singapore '95.

A121

Animals of the Nativity.

1995, Nov. 1 *Perf. 14*

710 A121	10c Ox	.90	.30
711 A121	20c Sheep, lamb	1.40	.50
712 A121	30c Donkey	2.25	.60
713 A121	$2 Camels	8.50	10.50
a.	Souvenir sheet of 4, #710-713	14.00	14.00
	Nos. 710-713 (4)	13.05	11.90

A122

Wild fruit.

Wmk. 384

1996, Mar. 21 **Litho.** *Perf. 14*

714 A122	10c Sea grape	.60	.50
715 A122	25c Guava	1.25	.70
716 A122	40c West Indian cherry	2.00	1.25
717 A122	$1 Tamarind	4.00	5.25
	Nos. 714-717 (4)	7.85	7.70

Modern Olympic Games, Cent. — A123

Perf. 14x13½

1996, June 19 **Litho.** **Wmk. 384**

718 A123	10c Sailing	.65	.45
719 A123	20c Sailboarding	1.25	.55
720 A123	30c Sailing, diff.	1.60	.80
721 A123	$2 Running	6.50	6.50
	Nos. 718-721 (4)	10.00	8.30

Symbols of National Identity — A124

Designs: 10c, Guitar, music, natl. song. 20c, Boeing 737. 25c, Queen Elizabeth II opening Legislative Assembly. 30c, Seven Mile Beach. 40c, Scuba diver, stingrays. 60c, School children, Cayman Turtle Farm. 80c, Cayman parrot, natl. bird. 90c, Silver thatch palm, natl. tree. $1, Natl. flag. $2, Wild banana orchid, natl. flower. $4, Natl. arms. $6, Natl. currency.

Wmk. 373

1996, Sept. 26 **Litho.** *Perf. 14*

Inscribed "1996"

722 A124	10c multicolored	.50	.45
	Complete booklet, 10 #722	5.25	
a.	Inscribed "1997"	.50	.45
723 A124	20c multicolored	1.10	.85
724 A124	25c multicolored	1.25	.80
725 A124	30c multicolored	1.25	.80
	Complete booklet, 10 #725	13.00	
726 A124	40c multicolored	1.60	1.25
	Complete booklet, 10 #726	17.00	
727 A124	60c multicolored	2.25	1.60
728 A124	80c multicolored	3.75	3.00
a.	Souvenir sheet of 1	4.25	4.25
729 A124	90c multicolored	2.50	3.00
730 A124	$1 multicolored	4.00	3.25
731 A124	$2 multicolored	7.25	7.00
732 A124	$4 multicolored	13.00	16.00
733 A124	$6 multicolored	17.00	20.00
	Nos. 722-733 (12)	55.45	58.00

No. 728a for Hong Kong '97. Issued 2/3/97.

1999, Feb. 5 **Wmk. 373 Sideways**

723a A124	20c multicolored	1.10	.85
725a A124	30c multicolored	1.25	.80
727a A124	60c multicolored	2.25	1.60
	Nos. 723a-727a (3)	4.60	3.25

Christmas A125

Designs: 10c, Christmas time on North Church Street. 25c, Santa "Gone Fishing." 30c, "Claus Encounters." $2, "Caymanian Christmas."

Wmk. 373

1996, Nov. 12 **Litho.** *Perf. 14*

734 A125	10c multicolored	.65	.35
735 A125	25c multicolored	1.60	.90
736 A125	30c multicolored	2.00	1.25
737 A125	$2 multicolored	4.50	4.50
	Nos. 734-737 (4)	8.75	7.00

Queen Elizabeth II and Prince Philip, 50th Wedding Anniv. — A126

No. 738, Queen. No. 739, Royal Guard. No. 740, Young Prince riding horse. No. 741, Queen in blue, Prince in military attire in open carriage. No. 742 Prince holding horse's reins. No. 743, Queen looking at horses.
$1, Queen, Prince in open carriage.

Perf. 14x13½

1997, July 10 Litho. Wmk. 373

738 A126 10c multicolored 1.25 1.25
739 A126 10c multicolored 1.25 1.25
a. Pair, #738-739 2.50 2.50
740 A126 30c multicolored 2.00 2.00
741 A126 30c multicolored 2.00 2.00
a. Pair, #740-741 4.00 4.00
742 A126 40c multicolored 2.40 2.40
743 A126 40c multicolored 2.40 2.40
a. Pair, #742-743 5.00 5.00
Nos. 738-743 (6) 11.30 11.30

Souvenir Sheet

744 A126 $1 multicolored 7.25 7.25

Telecommunications — A127

Designs: 10c, Children using the Internet. 25c, Cable and wireless ship. 30c, Children wearing numbers of new area code, "345." 60c, Cable and wireless satellite communications.

Perf. 14x14½

1997, Oct. 10 Litho. Wmk. 384

745 A127 10c multicolored .45 .30
746 A127 25c multicolored 1.25 .80
747 A127 30c multicolored 1.40 .95
748 A127 60c multicolored 2.25 2.25
Nos. 745-748 (4) 5.35 4.30

Christmas A128

Santa Claus: 10c, Relaxing in hammock, Little Cayman. 30c, With children on bluff, Cayman Brac. 40c, Playing golf. $1, Diving with stingrays.

Wmk. 373

1997, Dec. 3 Litho. *Perf. 13*

749 A128 10c multicolored .35 .25
750 A128 30c multicolored .80 .45
751 A128 40c multicolored 1.75 .80
752 A128 $1 multicolored 3.00 *3.50*
Nos. 749-752 (4) 5.90 5.00

Diana, Princess of Wales (1961-97)

Common Design Type

Portraits: a, 10c. b, 20c. c, 40c. d, $1.

Perf. 14½x14

1998 Litho. Wmk. 373

752A CD355 10c Like #753a .75 .75
752B CD355 20c Like #753b 1.50 1.50

Sheet of 4

753 CD355 #a.-d. 5.50 5.50

No. 753 sold for $1.70 + 30c, with surtax from international sales being donated to the Princess Diana Memorial Fund and surtax from national sales being donated to designated local charity.

Royal Air Force, 80th Anniv.

Common Design Type of 1993 Re-Inscribed

Designs: 10c, Hawker Horsley. 20c, Fairey Hendon. 25c, Hawker Siddeley Gnat. 30c, Hawker Siddeley Dominie.
No. 758: a, 40c, Airco DH-9. b, 60c, Spad 13 Scout. c, 80c, Airspeed Oxford. d, $1, Martin Baltimore.

Wmk. 373

1998, Apr. 1 Litho. *Perf. 14*

754 CD350 10c multicolored 1.00 1.00
755 CD350 20c multicolored 1.25 1.25
756 CD350 25c multicolored 1.60 1.60
757 CD350 30c multicolored 1.90 1.90
Nos. 754-757 (4) 5.75 5.75

Souvenir Sheet

758 CD350 Sheet of 4, #a.-d. 10.00 10.00

Birds — A129

Designs: 10c, West Indian whistling duck. 20c, Magnificent frigatebird. 60c, Red footed booby. $1, Grand Cayman parrot.

1998 Litho. Wmk. 373 *Perf. 13½*

759 A129 10c multicolored 1.10 .60
760 A129 20c multicolored 2.00 .60
761 A129 60c multicolored 3.50 3.50
762 A129 $1 multicolored 4.25 4.25
Nos. 759-762 (4) 10.85 8.95

Christmas A130

Santa at various island locations: 10c, At Blowholes. 30c, Diving on wreck of MV Capt. Keith Tibbetts. 40c, Visiting Pedro Castle. 60c, Arriving at Little Cayman.

1998 *Perf. 14x14½*

763 A130 10c multicolored .40 .40
764 A130 30c multicolored 1.10 .85
765 A130 40c multicolored 1.50 1.10
766 A130 60c multicolored 3.00 3.00
Nos. 763-766 (4) 6.00 5.35

Easter A131

Artworks by Miss Lassie (Gladwyn Bush): 10c, "They Rolled the Stone Away." 20c, "Ascension," vert. 30c, "The World Praying for Peace." 40c, "Calvary," vert.

Wmk. 373

1999, Mar. 26 Litho. *Perf. 13*

767 A131 10c multicolored .50 .50
768 A131 20c multicolored .90 .90
769 A131 30c multicolored 1.40 1.40
770 A131 40c multicolored 1.50 1.50
Nos. 767-770 (4) 4.30 4.30

Vision 2008 A132

Children's drawings: 10c, "Cayman House." 30c, "Coral Reef." 40c, "Fisherman on North Sound." $2, "Three Fish and A Turtle."

1999, June *Perf. 13½*

771 A132 10c multicolored .30 .30
772 A132 30c multicolored 1.10 1.10
773 A132 40c multicolored 1.25 1.25
774 A132 $2 multicolored 6.50 6.50
Nos. 771-774 (4) 9.15 9.15

Wedding of Prince Edward and Sophie Rhys-Jones

Common Design Type

Perf. 13¾x14

1999, June 16 Litho. Wmk. 384

775 CD356 10c Separate portraits .50 .50
776 CD356 $2 Couple 5.00 5.00

1st Manned Moon Landing, 30th Anniv.

Common Design Type

Designs: 10c, Coast Guard during launch. 25c, 3rd stage fires and puts rocket in orbit. 30c, Aldrin descends to lunar surface. 60c, Lander module sent back to moon.
$1.50, Looking at earth from moon.

1999, July 20 *Perf. 14x13¾*

777 CD357 10c multicolored .45 .45
778 CD357 25c multicolored 1.10 1.10
779 CD357 30c multicolored 1.25 1.25
780 CD357 60c multicolored 2.50 2.50
Nos. 777-780 (4) 5.30 5.30

Souvenir Sheet

Perf. 14

781 CD357 $1.50 multicolored 5.00 5.00

No. 781 contains one circular stamp 40mm in diameter.

Queen Mother's Century

Common Design Type

Queen Mother: 10c, Looking at London's defenses, 1940. 20c, At Clarence House, 94th birthday. 30c, With Princes Charles and William. 40c, Reviewing the Chelsea Pensioners, 1986.
$1.50, At her wedding.

Wmk. 384

1999, Aug. 18 Litho. *Perf. 13¼*

782 CD358 10c multicolored .45 .45
783 CD358 20c multicolored .80 .80
784 CD358 30c multicolored 1.40 1.40
785 CD358 40c multicolored 1.75 1.75
Nos. 782-785 (4) 4.40 4.40

Souvenir Sheet

786 CD358 $1.50 multicolored 4.75 4.75

Christmas — A133

Wmk. 373

1999, Nov. 17 Litho. *Perf. 13¼*

787 A133 10c #242, vert. .40 .35
788 A133 30c #532d, vert. 1.10 .90
789 A133 40c #749, vert. 1.50 1.25
790 A133 $1 #431 3.00 3.00
a. Souv. sheet, #787-790, perf. 12 6.00 6.00
Nos. 787-790 (4) 6.00 5.50

British Monarchs — A134

No. 792: a, Henry VIII. b, Mary I. c, Charles II. d, Anne. e, George IV. f, George V.

Wmk. 373

2000, Feb. 29 Litho. *Perf. 14*

791 A134 10c Henry VII .70 .70

Sheet of 6

792 A134 40c #a.-f. 10.00 10.00

The Stamp Show 2000, London.

Sesame Street — A135

Designs: 10c, Ernie. 30c, Big Bird.
No. 795: a, Grover. b, Zoe. c, Oscar the Grouch. d, The Count. e, Like 30c. f, Cookie Monster. g, Like 10c. h, Bert. i, Elmo in pond.
No. 796, Elmo collecting stamps.

Perf. 14½x14¾

2000, Mar. 15 Litho. Wmk. 373

793 A135 10c multi .40 .40
794 A135 30c multi 1.10 1.10
795 A135 20c Sheet of 9, #a-i 6.25 6.25

Souvenir Sheet

796 A135 20c multi 1.90 1.90

Prince William, 18th Birthday

Common Design Type

10c, In checked shirt and in sweater and checked shirt. 20c, In white shirt and black bow tie. 30c, In blue casual shirt, vert. 40c, As child, with beret, vert. $1, As infant.

Perf. 14¼x13¾, 13¾x14¼

2000, June 21 Litho. Wmk. 373

Stamps With White Border

797 CD359 10c multi .50 .40
798 CD359 20c multi 1.00 .95
799 CD359 30c multi 1.40 1.25
800 CD359 40c multi 1.90 1.90
Nos. 797-800 (4) 4.80 4.50

Souvenir Sheet

Stamps Without White Border

Perf. 14¼

801 Sheet of 5 8.25 8.25
a. CD359 10c multi .35 .35
b. CD359 20c multi .75 .75
c. CD359 30c multi 1.00 1.00
d. CD359 40c multi 1.40 1.40
e. CD359 $1 multi 4.00 4.00

Marine Life A136

10c, Green turtle. 20c, Queen angelfish. 30c, Parrotfish. $1, Green moray eel.

Wmk. 384

2000, Aug. 25 Litho. *Perf. 14*

802-805 A136 Set of 4 7.25 7.25

National Drug Council A137

Various children's drawings. Denominations, 10c, 15c, 30c, $2.

2000, Aug. 25

806-809 A137 Set of 4 11.00 11.00

Christmas A138

10c, Backing sand. 30c, Christmas dinner. 40c, Yard dance. 60c, Conch shell border.

Perf. 14½x14¼

2000, Nov. 14 Wmk. 373

810-813 A138 Set of 4 8.50 8.50

UN Women's Human Rights Campaign — A139

Wmk. 373

2001, Mar. 8 Litho. *Perf. 14*

814 A139 10c multi .90 .90

Cayman Brac A140

Designs: 15c, Red mangrove. 20c, Peter's Cave, vert. 25c, Bight Road stairway, vert. 30c, Westerly Pond. 40c, Aerial view. 60c, Marshes.

2001, Apr. 21

815-820 A140 Set of 6 9.50 9.50

Non-profit Organizations — A141

Designs: Nos. 821, 826a, 15c, National Council of Voluntary Organizations. Nos. 822, 826b, 20c, Cayman Humane Society. Nos. 823, 826c, 25c, Red Cross/Red Crescent. Nos. 824, 826d, 30c, Cayman Islands Cancer Society, vert. Nos. 825, 826e, 40c, Lions Club of Tropical Gardens, vert.

Wmk. 373

2001, Aug. 15 Litho. *Perf. 14*

Stamps With White Margins

821-825 A141 Set of 5 11.00 11.00

Souvenir Sheet

Stamps With Pink Margins

826 A141 Sheet of 5, #a-e 11.00 11.00

No. 826 sold for $1.80, 50c of which went to the various organizations honored.

Transportation — A142

Designs: No. 827, Walking home. No. 828, Boy on donkey. 20c, Bananas by canoe. 25c, Horse and buggy. 30c, Catboats. 40c, Schooner. 60c, Police bicycle, vert. 80c, Lady drivers. 90c, Launcing Cimboco, vert. $1, Seaplane. $4, Freighter. $10, Boeing 767.

Perf. 14¼x14½, 14½x14¼

2001, Sept. 29 Litho. Wmk. 373

827	A142	15c multi	.40	.40
828	A142	15c multi	.40	.40
829	A142	20c multi	.55	.55
830	A142	25c multi	.70	.70
831	A142	30c multi	.80	.80
832	A142	40c multi	1.10	1.10
833	A142	60c multi	1.60	1.60
834	A142	80c multi	2.25	2.25
835	A142	90c multi	2.50	2.50
836	A142	$1 multi	2.75	2.75
837	A142	$4 multi	11.00	11.00
838	A142	$10 multi	26.00	26.00
		Nos. 827-838 (12)	50.05	50.05

Christmas A143

Santa Claus: 15c, With children on dock. 30c, On eagle ray. 40c, In catboat. 60c, Parasailing.

Perf. 14¼x14½

2001, Nov. 21 Litho. Wmk. 373

839-842 A143 Set of 4 7.50 7.50

In Remembrance of Sept. 11, 2001 Terrorist Attacks — A144

Perf. 14x14¾

2002, Jan. 22 Litho. Wmk. 373

843 A144 $1 multi 4.25 4.25

Reign Of Queen Elizabeth II, 50th Anniv. Issue

Common Design Type

Designs: Nos. 844, 848a, 15c, Princess Elizabeth as child. Nos. 845, 848b, 20c, In 1976. Nos. 846, 848c, 30c, With Princess Margaret, 1942. Nos. 847, 848d, 80c, In 1996. No. 848e, $1, 1955 portrait by Annigoni (38x50mm).

Perf. 14¼x14½, 13¾ (#848e)

2002, Feb. 6 Litho. Wmk. 373

With Gold Frames

844	CD360	15c multicolored	.45	.45
845	CD360	20c multicolored	.65	.65
846	CD360	30c multicolored	.90	.90
847	CD360	80c multicolored	2.25	2.25
		Nos. 844-847 (4)	4.25	4.25

Souvenir Sheet

Without Gold Frames

848 CD360 Sheet of 5, #a-e 10.00 10.00

Peanuts Comic Strip Characters A145

Designs: 15c, Snoopy painting Woodstock at Cayman Brac Bluff. 20c, Charlie Brown and Sally at Hell Post Office. 25c, Peppermint Patty and Marcie at Little Cayman beach. 30c, Snoopy and Boeing 737-200. 40c, Linus and Snoopy at Point of Sand. 60c, Charlie Brown at Links Golf Course.

Wmk. 373

2002, Mar. 9 Litho. *Perf. 14*

849-854 A145 Set of 6 8.50 8.50

854a Souvenir sheet, #849-854 8.50 8.50

2002 World Cup Soccer Championships, Japan and Korea — A146

Denominations: 30c, 40c.

2002, Apr. 30 *Perf. 13¾*

855-856 A146 Set of 2 4.25 4.25

Queen Mother Elizabeth (1900-2002)

Common Design Type

Designs: 15c, Wearing hat (sepia photograph). 30c, Wearing dark blue hat. Nos. 859, 861a, 40c, Wearing hat (black and white photograph). Nos. 860, 861b, $1, Wearing tiara.

Perf. 13¾x14¼, 14¼ (#859-860)

2002, Aug. 5 Litho. Wmk. 373

With Purple Frames

857	CD361	15c multicolored	.65	.65
858	CD361	30c multicolored	1.25	1.25
859	CD361	40c multicolored	1.60	1.60
860	CD361	$1 multicolored	4.00	4.00
		Nos. 857-860 (4)	7.50	7.50

Souvenir Sheet

Without Purple Frames

Perf. 14½x14¼

861 CD361 Sheet of 2, #a-b 7.50 7.50

Christmas A147

Designs: 15c, Hail Mary. 20c, Journey to Bethlehem. 30c, Her firstborn Son. 40c, I bring good tidings. 60c Star in the east.

Wmk. 373

2002, Oct. 18 Litho. *Perf. 14*

Stamps + labels

862-866 A147 Set of 5 5.50 5.50

866a Souvenir sheet of 5, #862-866 + 5 labels 6.50 6.50

Aviation in the Cayman Islands, 50th Anniv. A148

Designs: 15c, PBY Catalina Flying Boat. 20c, First landing at Grand Cayman Airport, 1952. 25c, Cayman Brac Airways AC 50. 30c, Cayman Airways B-737. 40c, Concorde at original airport, 1984. $1.30, Island Air DHC6.

2002, Nov. 8

867-872 A148 Set of 6 12.50 12.50

Children's Games A149

Designs: 15c, Rope skipping. 20c, Maypole dancing. 25c, Gig. 30c, Hopscotch. $1, Marbles.

Wmk. 373

2003, May 27 Litho. *Perf. 13¾*

873-877 A149 Set of 5 8.00 8.00

Head of Queen Elizabeth II

Common Design Type

Wmk. 373

2003, June 2 Litho. *Perf. 13¾*

878 CD362 $4 multi 17.00 17.00

Coronation of Queen Elizabeth II, 50th Anniv.

Common Design Type

Designs: Nos. 879, 15c, 881a, 20c, Queen wearing crown. Nos. 880, $2, 881b, $4, Queen holding symbols of office.

Perf. 14¼x14½

2003, June 2 Litho. Wmk. 373

Vignettes Framed, Red Background

879	CD363	15c multicolored	.50	.50
880	CD363	$2 multicolored	6.75	6.75

Souvenir Sheet

Vignettes Without Frame, Purple Panel

881 CD363 Sheet of 2, #a-b 13.00 13.00

Prince William, 21st Birthday

Common Design Type

Color photographs: 15c, William with backpack at right. 40c, William in suit and tie at left.

No. 884: a, William with hand on chin at right. b, William with white bow tie at left.

Wmk. 373

2003, June 21 Litho. *Perf. 14¼*

882	CD364	15c multi	.50	.50
883	CD364	40c multi	1.40	1.40
884		Horiz. pair	5.75	5.75
a.	CD364	80c multi	2.50	2.50
b.	CD364	$1 multi	3.25	3.25
		Nos. 882-884 (3)	7.65	7.65

Discovery of the Cayman Islands, 500th Anniv. A150

Designs: 15c, Turtle hatchlings. No. 886, 20c, Old waterfront. No. 887, 20c, Turtle and ship of Christopher Columbus. 25c, Nassau grouper. 30c, Cayman Brac schooner "Kirk-B." 40c, George Town harbor. 60c, Musical instruments. 80c, Smokewood tree. 90c, Little Cayman Baptist Church. $1, Thatch rope. $1.30, Children's dance troupe. $2, Parliament in session.

Wmk. 373

2003, July 24 Litho. *Perf. 13¾*

885-896 A150 Set of 12 29.00 29.00

896a Souvenir sheet, #885-896 29.00 29.00

Holiday Greetings A151

Various Christmas decorations and inscriptions of: 15c, Merry Christmas. 20c, Celebrate With Family. 30c, Happy New Year. 40c, Happy Holidays. 60c, Seasons Greetings.

Wmk. 373

2003, Nov. 4 Litho. *Perf. 13¼*

897-901 A151 Set of 5 8.00 8.00

Worldwide Fund for Nature (WWF) A152

Short-finned pilot whale: 15c, Adult and calf. 20c, Pod of four whales. 30c, Two whales at surface. 40c, One adult.

2003, Nov. 26 *Perf. 14*

902-905 A152 Set of 4 7.00 7.00

905a Sheet, 4 each #902-905 30.00 30.00

Shipping Registry, Cent. — A153

Ships: 15c, Lady Slater. 20c, Seanostrum. 30c, Kirk Pride. $1, Boadicea.

Perf. 14x14¾

2004, Jan. 29 Litho. Wmk. 373

906-909 A153 Set of 4 9.50 9.50

Easter — A154

Designs: 15c, Jesus Carrying His Cross. 30c, The Ascension.

2004, Mar. 16 *Perf. 14¾x14*

910-911 A154 Set of 2 3.25 3.25

2004 Summer Olympics, Athens — A155

Designs: 15c, Swimmer. 40c, Runner. 60c, Long jumper. 80c, Swimmers.

Perf. 13½x13¼

2004, Aug. 23 Litho. Wmk. 373

912-915 A155 Set of 4 6.50 6.50

Blue Iguana A156

Designs: 15c, Adult on rocks. 20c, Eggs. 25c, Four juveniles. 30c, Juvenile on finger. 40c, Adult with open mouth. 90c, Eye.

No. 922: a, 60c, On rock facing right. b, 80c, On rock facing left.

2004, Oct. 26 Litho. *Perf. 13¾*

916-921 A156 Set of 6 8.50 8.50

Souvenir Sheet

922 A156 Sheet of 2, #a-b 7.00 7.00

No. 922 sold for $1.90.

Battle of Trafalgar, Bicent. — A157

Designs: 15c, HMS Victory. 20c, HMS Tonnant tangles into the bow of the Algesiras. 25c, Flint cannon lock and linstock. No. 926, 60c, Royal Navy boatswain's mate. $1, Adm. Horatio Nelson, vert. No. 928, $2, HMS Orion in action against the Intrepide.

No. 929, vert.: a, 60c, French gunship Pluton. b, $2, HMS Tonnant.

Wmk. 373, Unwmkd. (15c)

2005, June 8 Litho. *Perf. 13¼*

923-928 A157 Set of 6 12.00 12.00

Souvenir Sheet

929 A157 Sheet of 2, #a-b 7.00 7.00

No. 923 has particles of wood from the HMS Victory embedded in the areas covered by a thermographic process that produces a raised, shiny effect.

Rotary International, Cent. — A158

Designs: 15c, Centennial emblem. 30c, PolioPlus emblem.

2005, June 30 Wmk. 373 *Perf. 13¾*

930-931 A158 Set of 2 2.50 2.50

Orchids A159

Designs: 15c, Myrmecophila albopurpurea. 20c, Prosthechea boothiana. 30c, Tolumnia calochila, vert. 40c, Encyclia phoenicia. 80c, Prosthechea cochleata, vert. $1.50, Encyclia kingsii.

2005, July 28 *Perf. 14*

932-936 A159 Set of 5 7.25 7.25

Souvenir Sheet

937 A159 $1.50 multi 6.00 6.00

Pope John Paul II (1920-2005) A160

2005, Aug. 18

938 A160 30c multi 1.75 1.75

A161

Butterflies A162

Designs: 15c, Queen. 20c, Mexican fritillary. 25c, Malachite. 30c, Cayman crescent spot. 40c, Cloudless sulphur. 90c, Swallowtail.

Wmk. 373

2005, Sept. 21 Litho. *Perf. 14*

939	A161 15c multi	.60	.60
940	A161 20c multi	.75	.75
941	A161 25c multi	.85	.85
942	A161 30c multi	1.10	1.10
943	A161 40c multi	1.60	1.60
944	A161 90c multi	3.25	3.25
	Nos. 939-944 (6)	8.15	8.15

Booklet Stamps

Self-Adhesive

Unwmk.

Serpentine Die Cut 9½x9

945	A162 15c multi	.60	.60
a.	Booklet pane of 10	6.00	
946	A162 20c multi	.70	.70
a.	Booklet pane of 6	4.20	
947	A162 30c multi	1.00	1.00
a.	Booklet pane of 10	10.00	
	Nos. 945-947 (3)	2.30	2.30

Christmas A163

Designs: 15c, Angels. 30c, Magi, horiz. 40c, Holy Family. 60c, Shepherds, horiz.

Perf. 14x14¾, 14¾x14

2005, Oct. 26 Wmk. 373

948-951 A163 Set of 4 5.50 5.50

951a Souvenir sheet, #948-951, perf. 14¾ 5.50 5.50

Trees and Blossoms — A164

Designs: 15c, Wash wood. 20c, Red mangrove. 30c, Ironwood. 60c, West Indian cedar. $2, Spanish elm.

Wmk. 373

2006, Feb. 23 Litho. *Perf. 13¼*

Stamp + Label

952-956 A164 Set of 5 12.00 12.00

Queen Elizabeth II, 80th Birthday A165

Designs: 15c, As child. 40c, Wearing uniform and cap. $1, Wearing tiara. $2, Wearing sunglasses.

No. 961: a, 40c, Like #958. b, $1, Like #959.

2006, Apr. 21 *Perf. 14*

With White Frames

957-960 A165 Set of 4 12.00 12.00

Souvenir Sheet

Without White Frames

961 A165 Sheet of 2, #a-b 12.00 12.00

A166

Marine Life — A167

Designs: Nos. 962, 967a, 968, Hawksbill turtle. Nos. 963, 967b, 969, Gray angelfish. Nos. 964, 967c, 970, Queen angelfish. Nos. 965, 967c, 971, Diamond blenny. Nos. 966, 967e, Juvenile spotted drum,vert. Nos. 964 and 967c are vert.

Wmk. 373

2006, July 18 Litho. *Perf. 14*

With White Margins

962	A166 25c multi	1.00	1.00
963	A166 25c multi	1.00	1.00
964	A166 60c multi	2.50	2.50
965	A166 75c multi	3.25	3.25
966	A166 $1 multi	4.25	4.25
	Nos. 962-966 (5)	12.00	12.00

Souvenir Sheet

Without White Margin

967 A166 Sheet of 5, #a-e 12.00 12.00

Booklet Stamps

Self-Adhesive

Serpentine Die Cut 9½x9

Unwmk.

968	A167 25c multi	.70	.70
a.	Booklet pane of 10	7.00	
969	A167 25c multi	.70	.70
a.	Booklet pane of 10	7.00	
970	A167 60c multi	1.75	1.75
a.	Booklet pane of 10	17.50	
971	A167 75c multi	2.00	2.00
a.	Booklet pane of 10	20.00	
	Nos. 968-971 (4)	5.15	5.15

Birds A168

Designs: 25c, Bananaquit. 50c, Vitelline warbler. 75c, Grand Cayman parrot. 80c, Caribbean dove. $1, Caribbean elaenia. $1.50, West Indian woodpecker. $1.60, Thick-billed vireo. $2, Northern flicker. $4, Cuban bullfinch. $5, Western spindalis. $10, Loggerhead kingbird. $20, Red-legged thrush.

Perf. 13½x13¾

2006, Oct. 9 Litho. Wmk. 373

972	A168	25c multi	.60	.60
973	A168	50c multi	1.25	1.25
974	A168	75c multi	1.90	1.90
975	A168	80c multi	2.00	2.00
976	A168	$1 multi	2.50	2.50
977	A168	$1.50 multi	3.75	3.75
978	A168	$1.60 multi	4.00	4.00
979	A168	$2 multi	5.00	5.00
980	A168	$4 multi	9.75	9.75
981	A168	$5 multi	12.00	12.00
982	A168	$10 multi	24.00	24.00
983	A168	$20 multi	50.00	50.00
	Nos. 972-983 (12)		116.75	116.75

Booklet Stamps

Self-Adhesive

Unwmk.

Serpentine Die Cut 10x9½

Size:29x24mm

983A	A168	25c multi	.60	.60
d.	Booklet pane of 10		6.00	
983B	A168	75c multi	1.90	1.90
e.	Booklet pane of 10		19.00	
983C	A168	80c multi	2.00	2.00
f.	Booklet pane of 10		20.00	
	Nos. 983A-983C (3)		4.50	4.50

Christmas A169

Designs: 25c, "Faith," Magi. 75c, "Hope," Prophet with scroll. 80c, "Joy," angel. $1, "Love," Madonna and Child.

Perf. 12½x13¼

2006, Oct. 26 Litho. Wmk. 373

984-987 A169 Set of 4 12.50 12.50

Island Scenes A170

Designs: 20c, Brac Reed dock. 25c, Waterfront buildings, Hog Sty Bay. 30c, East End blowholes, vert. 40c, Man in hammock, vert. 75c, Poinciana blooms. $1, Driftwood on Little Cayman.

Wmk. 373

2007, June 26 **Litho.** ***Perf. 13¾***
988-993 A170 Set of 6 10.50 10.50

Scouting, Cent. A171

Designs: 25c, Wolf Cubs and leaders, hands lashing rope. 75c, Cub Scouts and leaders, hands with trumpet. 80c, Scouts camping, hand with compass. $1, Scout Drill Team, poppies.
No. 998, vert.: a, 50c, Scouts marching. b, $1.50, Lord Robert Baden-Powell and dog.

2007, July 9
994-997 A171 Set of 4 9.00 9.00

Souvenir Sheet

998 A171 Sheet of 2, #a-b 5.50 5.50

Wedding of Queen Elizabeth II and Prince Philip, 60th Anniv. — A172

Designs: 50c, Couple and wedding coach. 75c, Elizabeth wearing bridal veil. 80c, Princess Elizabeth, Philip, Queen Mother Elizabeth, King George VI, Princess Margaret. $1, Wedding procession, Westminster Abbey.
$2, Couple.

Wmk. 373

2007, Sept. 12 **Litho.** ***Perf. 13¾***
999-1002 A172 Set of 4 10.50 10.50

Souvenir Sheet

Perf. 14

1003 A172 $2 multi 6.50 6.50

No. 1003 contains one 42x57mm stamp.

Christmas A173

Stained-glass windows from local churches: 25c, Nativity, Wesleyan Holiness Church. 50c, Jesus Praying, Elmslie Memorial Church. 75c, Jesus Calling First Disciples, St. George's Anglican Church. 80c, Dove, East End Adventist Church. $1, Orb, First Baptist Church of Grand Cayman. $1.50, Shepherd, Frank Sound Church of God.

2007, Oct. 22 ***Perf. 15x14***
1004-1009 A173 Set of 6 15.00 15.00

A174

Greetings A175

Nos. 1010-1015: a, Hello. b, Good Luck. c, Congratulations. d, You're Invited. e, Best Wishes. f, Love.
No. 1016, Hello. No. 1017, Congratulations. No. 1018, You're Invited. No. 1019, Love.

Wmk. 373

2008, Feb. 5 **Litho.** ***Perf. 14¼***

1010 A174 20c Sheet of 6, #a-f	3.00	3.00
1011 A174 25c Sheet of 6, #a-f	3.75	3.75
1012 A174 50c Sheet of 6, #a-f	7.50	7.50
1013 A174 75c Sheet of 6, #a-f	11.00	11.00
1014 A174 80c Sheet of 6, #a-f	12.00	12.00
1015 A174 $1 Sheet of 6, #a-f	15.00	15.00
Nos. 1010-1015 (6)	52.25	52.25

Booklet Stamps
Self-Adhesive

Serpentine Die Cut 9½x9

Unwmk.

1016 A175 20c multi	.60	.60
a. Booklet pane of 10	6.00	
1017 A175 25c multi	.70	.70
a. Booklet pane of 10	7.00	
1018 A175 25c multi	.60	.60
a. Booklet pane of 10	7.00	
1019 A175 25c multi	.70	.70
a. Booklet pane of 10	7.00	
Nos. 1016-1019 (4)	2.60	2.60

Darwin Initiative A176

Fauna: 20c, Land crab. 25c, Needlecase. 75c, Little Cayman green anole, vert. 80c, Cayman Brac ground boa. $1, White-shouldered bat.
$2, Caribbean reef squid, vert.

Wmk. 373

2008, July 9 **Litho.** ***Perf. 14***
1020-1024 A176 Set of 5 11.00 11.00

Souvenir Sheet

1025 A176 $2 multi 6.50 6.50

2008 Olympic Games, Beijing A177

Designs: 20c, Lanterns, swimming. 25c, Fish, swimming. 50c, Bamboo, running. 75c, Dragon, hurdles.

Wmk. 373

2008, Aug. 8 **Litho.** ***Perf. 13¼***
1026-1029 A177 Set of 4 6.75 6.75

Water Authority, 25th Anniv. A178

Children's art: 25c, Stop Water Pollution. 75c, Water droplets. $2, Splash of Life.

Wmk. 373

2008, Oct. 16 **Litho.** ***Perf. 13¼***
1030-1032 A178 Set of 3 11.50 11.50

Christmas A179

Santa Claus and: 25c, Ship. 75c, Horse-drawn carriage. 80c, Helicopter. $1, Race car.

2008, Nov. 12 ***Perf. 13¾***
1033-1036 A179 Set of 4 11.00 11.00

A180

No. 1037: a, Silver thatch plant. b, People making rope strands. c, Man cobbing rope. d, Thatch products. e, Traditional home.

Wmk. 406

2009, Jan. 28 **Litho.** ***Perf. 13¾***

1037 A180 Horiz. strip of 5	5.00	5.00
a.-e. 25c Any single	1.00	1.00
Complete booklet, 2 #1037	10.00	

Island Scenes A181

Designs: 20c, Hammock, palm trees, boat. 25c, House. 75c, Hammock under shelter at beach, palm trees, vert. 80c, Three cruise liners. $1, Direction signs near bus depot, vert. $1.50, Limestone pinnacles, Hell.
$2, Iguana.

2009, Apr. 9 ***Perf. 12½***
1038-1043 A181 Set of 6 12.50 12.50

Souvenir Sheet

Perf. 13

1044 A181 $2 multi 5.75 5.75

Space Exploration A182

Designs: 20c, Mars Rover, 2004. 25c, Space Shuttle STS-71 launch, 1995. 75c, Hubble Space Telescope. $1, Apollo 11 launch, 1969. $1.50, International Space Station.
$2, Lunar Rover on Moon, painting by Capt. Alan Bean, vert.

Wmk. 406

2009, July 20 **Litho.** ***Perf. 13¼***
1045-1049 A182 Set of 5 9.00 9.00

Souvenir Sheet

Perf. 13x13¼

1050 A182 $2 multi 5.00 5.00

No. 1050 contains one 40x60mm stamp. Nos. 1045-1049 each were printed in sheets of 6.

Equality Through Democracy A183

Designs: No. 1051, 25c, Hands holding pens signing voting rolls. No. 1052, 25c, George Town Town Hall. 50c, Woman casting ballot.

Wmk. 406

2009, Sept. 23 **Litho.** ***Perf. 13¾***

1051-1053 A183 Set of 3	2.75	2.75
1053a Sheet of 3, #1051-1053	2.75	2.75

Woman suffrage and Cayman Islands constitution, 50th anniv.

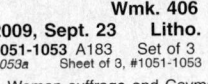

Christmas — A184

Images of Christmas stamps of 1997: 25c, Cayman Islands #749. 75c, Cayman Islands #750. 80c, Cayman Islands #751. $1, Cayman Islands #752.

Wmk. 406

2009, Oct. 22 **Litho.** ***Perf. 14***
1054-1057 A184 Set of 4 7.00 7.00

Shells A185

Designs: 20c, Hawk-wing conch. 25c, Ornate scallop. 60c, Chestnut turban. 75c Beautiful mitre. 80c, Four-toothed nerite. $1.60, White-spotted marginella.
$3, Queen conch.

Wmk. 406

2010, June 30 **Litho.** ***Perf. 13¼***
1058-1063 A185 Set of 6 12.00 12.00

Souvenir Sheet

1064 A185 $3 multi 8.50 8.75

Shells — A186

Designs: 25c, Ornate scallop. 75c, Beautiful mitre.

Serpentine Die Cut 9½x9

2010, June 30 **Unwmk.**

Booklet Stamps
Self-Adhesive

1065 A186 25c multi	.90	.90
a. Booklet pane of 10	9.00	
1066 A186 75c multi	2.10	2.10
a. Booklet pane of 10	21.00	

Girld Guides, Cent. A187

Girl Guides: 20c Uniforms. 25c, Camping. 50c, Parade. 80c, Badges.

Wmk. 406

2010, Dec. 17 **Litho.** ***Perf. 12½***
1067-1070 A187 Set of 4 4.75 4.75

Wedding of Prince William and Catherine Middleton — A188

Designs: 25c, Couple kissing. 75c, Couple in carriage waving, horiz. 80c, Couple holding hands. $2, Couple and father of the bride, horiz.

2011, Aug. 4 ***Perf. 14***

1071-1074 A188 Set of 4 9.50 9.50

Catboats A189

Designs: No. 1075, 20c, Men in catboats catching turtles. Nos. 1076, 1081, 25c, Men building catboat. No. 1077, 25c, Catboat sailing around Cayman Brac's Bluff. No. 1078, 50c, Catboats racing regatta style. No. 1079, $1.60, Catboats unloading cargo. No. 1080, $2, Women sewing catboat sail.

2011, Aug. 31 **Wmk. 406** ***Perf. 14***

1075-1080 A189 Set of 6 11.50 11.50

Booklet Stamp
Self-Adhesive
Size:30x25mm
Serpentine Die Cut 9½x9
Unwmk.

1081 A189 25c multi .60 .60
a. Booklet pane of 10 6.00

Christmas A190

Designs: 25c, Frontispiece for 1611 edition of the King James Bible. 75c, King James I. 80c, William Tyndale, Bible tanslator. $1, Printers printing the King James Bible. $1.60, Translators in the Jerusalem Chamber.

2011, Nov. 8 **Wmk. 406** ***Perf. 12½***

1082-1086 A190 Set of 5 10.50 10.50

King James Bible, 400th anniv.

Famous Cayman Islanders A191

Designs: 20c, Almerian Labertha McLaughlin Tomlinson (1882-1974), midwife. 25c, Captain Rayal Brazley Bodden (1885-1976), shipwright and builder. 75c, Irskie Leila Yates (1899-1996), maternity nurse. $1.50, Major Joseph Rodriguez Watler (1890-1965), police inspector.

Perf. 13¼x13¾

2011, Nov. 11 **Wmk. 406**

1087 A191 20c multi .50 .50
a. Booklet pane of 6 3.00 —
Complete booklet, #1087a 3.00
1088 A191 25c multi .60 .60
a. Booklet pane of 6 3.75 —
Complete booklet, #1088a 3.75
1089 A191 75c multi 1.75 1.75
a. Booklet pane of 6 10.50 —
Complete booklet, #1089a 10.50
1090 A191 $1.50 multi 3.50 3.50
a. Booklet pane of 6 21.00 —
Complete booklet, #1090a 21.00
Nos. 1087-1090 (4) 6.35 6.35

A192

Reign of Queen Elizabeth II, 60th Anniv. — A193

Various photographs of Queen Elizabeth II: 25c, 80c, $1, $1.50.

2012, June 12 **Wmk. 406** ***Perf. 14***

1091-1094 A192 Set of 4 8.25 8.25

Booklet Stamp
Self-Adhesive
Serpentine Die Cut 9½x9
Unwmk.

1095 A193 25c multi .60 .60
a. Booklet pane of 10 6.00

2012 Summer Olympics, London A194

Designs: 25c, Runner. 50c, Hurdler. 75c, Swimmer. 80c, Two runners. $1.60, Swimmer, diff.

Wmk. 406

2012, Aug. 2 **Litho.** ***Perf. 13¼***

1096-1100 A194 Set of 5 9.50 9.50

A195

A195a

Emergency Services: 20c, Patrol boats. 25c, Ambulance service. 75c, Fire department. $1.50, 911 public safety communications. $2, Police helicopter.

2012, Aug. 30 **Wmk. 406** ***Perf. 14***

1101-1105 A195 Set of 5 12.00 12.00
1101a Dated "2013" .50 .50

Booklet Stamps
Self-Adhesive
Unwmk.
Serpentine Die Cut 9½x9

1105A A195a 25c multi .65 .65
c. Booklet pane of 10 6.50
1105B A195a 75c multi 1.90 1.90
d. Booklet pane of 10 19.00

A196

A197

Marine Life: 25c, Stoplight parrotfish. 50c, Green sea turtle. 75c, Common sea fan, Yellow tube sponge. 80c, Upside-down jellyfish. $1, Juvenile yellowtail damselfish. $1.50, Spotted trunkfish. $1.60, Caribbean spiny lobster. $2, Giant barrel sponge. $4, Caribbean reef shark. $5, Great barracuda. $10, Southern stingray.$20, West Indian spider crab.

2012, Oct. 9 **Wmk. 406** ***Perf. 14***

1106 A196 25c multi .60 .60
1107 A196 50c multi 1.25 1.25
1108 A196 75c multi 1.90 1.90
1109 A196 80c multi 2.00 2.00
1110 A196 $1 multi 2.50 2.50
a. Souvenir sheet of 4 10.00 10.00
1111 A196 $1.50 multi 3.75 3.75
1112 A196 $1.60 multi 4.00 4.00
1113 A196 $2 multi 5.00 5.00
1114 A196 $4 multi 9.75 9.75
1115 A196 $5 multi 12.50 12.50
1116 A196 $10 multi 25.00 25.00
1117 A196 $20 multi 50.00 50.00
Nos. 1106-1117 (12) 118.25 118.25

Booklet Stamps
Self-Adhesive
Die Cut Perf. 14x15¼
Unwmk.

1118 A197 25c multi .60 .60
a. Booklet pane of 10 6.00
1119 A197 75c multi 1.90 1.90
a. Booklet pane of 10 19.00
1120 A197 80c multi 2.00 2.00
a. Booklet pane of 10 20.00
Nos. 1118-1120 (3) 4.50 4.50

Christmas A198

Paintings by Gladwyn K. Bush: 25c, Mary and Jesus. 75c, His Name is Jesus. 80c, Every Knee Shall Bow. $1, Nativity.

2012, Dec. 6 **Wmk. 406** ***Perf. 14***
Stamps + Label

1121-1124 A198 Set of 4 7.00 7.00

A199

Shipwrecks and Anchors — A200

Shipwreck: 20c, Mathusalem. Nos. 1126, 1130, 25c, Inga. No. 1127, 25c, Topsy. $1.50, Tofa. $2, Glamis.

Wmk. 406

2013, Aug. 2 **Litho.** ***Perf. 14***

1125-1129 A199 Set of 5 10.50 10.50

Booklet Stamp
Self-Adhesive
Die Cut Perf. 14x15¼
Unwmk.

1130 A200 25c multi .60 .60
a. Booklet pane of 10 6.00

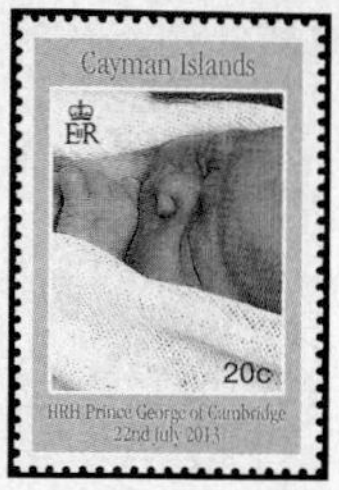

Birth of Prince George of Cambridge A201

Designs: 20c, Prince George. 25c, Duchess of Cambridge holding Prince George. 80c, Duke of Cambridge holding Prince George. $2, Duke and Duchess of Cambridge, Prince George.

Wmk. 406

2013, Oct. 31 **Litho.** ***Perf. 12½***

1131-1134 A201 Set of 4 7.75 7.75

Christmas A202

Santa Claus and: 25c, Old Government House. 75c, Old Homestead. 80c, Bodden Town Mission House. $1, Old District Administration Building.

Wmk. 406

2013, Nov. 5 **Litho.** ***Perf. 13***

1135-1138 A202 Set of 4 6.75 6.75

Houses on Little Cayman and Cayman Brac A203

Designs: 20c, Captain Theo's Villa, Little Cayman. 25c, Carter's House, Cayman Brac. 75c, Captain Charlie's House, Cayman Brac. $1, Foster's House, Cayman Brac.

Wmk. 406

2014, June 10 **Litho.** ***Perf. 13***

1139-1142 A203 Set of 4 5.50 5.50

A204

20th Commonwealth Games, Glasgow, Scotland — A205

Scottish flag and: 20c, Cycling. 25c, Swimming. 55c, Boxing. 80c, Squash. $1, Shooting. $1.60, Gymnastics. $2, Javelin.

Perf. 13¼x13

2014, Oct. 3 **Litho.** **Wmk. 406**

1143-1149 A204 Set of 7 16.00 16.00

Booklet Stamp
Self-Adhesive
Serpentine Die Cut 13¾x14
Unwmk.

1150 A205 25c multi .60 .60
a. Booklet pane of 10 6.00

A206

Christmas A207

Christmas ornaments, poinsettia and: Nos. 1151, 1154, 25c, Little Cayman Baptist Church. Nos. 1152, 1155, 25c, South Sound United Church. Nos. 1153, 1156, 25c, Stake Bay Baptist Church.

Wmk. 406

2014, Nov. 15 Litho. *Perf. 13¾*

1151-1153	A206	Set of 3	1.90	1.90

Booklet Stamps Self-Adhesive

Die Cut Perf. 14x15¼

Unwmk.

1154-1156	A207	Set of 3	1.90	1.90
1156a		Booklet pane of 12, 4 each #1154-1156	7.75	

Famous Cayman Islanders Type of 2011

Designs: 25c, Timothy E. McField (1928-95), educator. 50c, Annie Huldah Bodden (1908-89), politician. 80c, Ormond L. Panton (1920-92), politician. $1, Captain Keith P. Tibbetts, Sr. (1916-96), politician.

Perf. 13¼x13¾

2015, May 20 Litho. Wmk. 406

1157	A191 25c multi		.60	.60
	a.	Booklet pane of 6	3.75	—
		Complete booklet, #1157a	3.75	
1158	A191 50c multi		1.25	1.25
	a.	Booklet pane of 6	7.50	—
		Complete booklet, #1158a	7.50	
1159	A191 80c multi		2.00	2.00
	a.	Booklet pane of 6	12.00	—
		Complete booklet, #1159a	12.00	
1160	A191 $1 multi		2.50	2.50
	a.	Booklet pane of 6	15.00	—
		Complete booklet, #1160a	15.00	
	Nos. 1157-1160 (4)		6.35	6.35

WAR TAX STAMPS

No. 36 Surcharged

a

b

1917, Feb. 26 Wmk. 3 *Perf. 14*

MR1	A5(a) 1½p on 2½p		16.00	*17.00*
	a.	Fraction bar omitted	225.00	*250.00*
	b.	Period missing after "STAMP"	900.00	
MR2	A5(b) 1½p on 2½p		2.10	*7.25*
	a.	Fraction bar omitted	85.00	*150.00*

On No. 1 the distance between "WAR STAMP" and "1½" varies.

Surcharged

1917, Sept. 4

MR3	A5 1½p on 2½p ultra	850.00	*2,500.*

Surcharged

1917, Sept. 4

MR4	A5 1½p on 2½p ultra	.30	*.65*

No. 33 Overprinted

1919, Feb. 4

MR5	A5 ½p green	.70	*3.00*

The "brownish paper" variety comes from the interleaving used for shipment from England.

Type of 1912-16 Surcharged

1919, Feb. 4

MR6	A5 1½p on 2½p orange	1.25	*2.50*

No. 35 Surcharged

1920, Mar. 10

MR7	A5 1½p on 2p gray	4.00	*8.50*

The "rose-tinted paper" variety comes from the interleaving used for shipment from England.
A surcharge in red was not issued.

CENTRAL AFRICAN REPUBLIC

'sen-trəl 'a-fri-kən ri-'pə-blik

LOCATION — Western Africa, north of equator
GOVT. — Republic
AREA — 241,243 sq. mi.
POP. — 3,444,951 (1999 est.)
CAPITAL — Bangui

The former French colony of Ubangi-Shari, a unit in French Equatorial Africa, proclaimed itself the Central African Republic Dec. 1, 1958. It became the Central African Empire Dec. 4, 1976. It became the Central African Republic again in 1979.

100 Centimes = 1 Franc

Catalogue values for all unused stamps in this country are for Never Hinged items.

Watermark

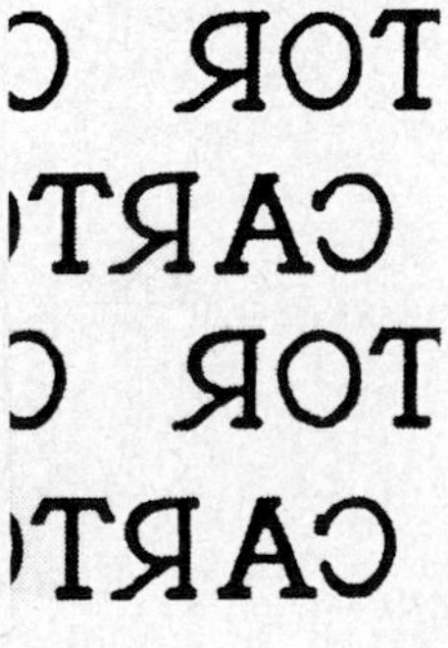

Wmk. 385

Premier Barthélemy Boganda and Flag — A1

Design: 25fr, Boganda and flag, horiz.

Unwmk.

1959, Dec. 1 Engr. *Perf. 13*

1	A1 15fr multi	.40	.25
2	A1 25fr multi	.60	.25

1st anniv. of the Republic and honoring Premier Barthélemy Boganda (1910-59).
For overprints & surcharge see Nos. 12, 59, M1-M2.

Imperforates
Many stamps of Central African Republic exist imperforate in issued and trial colors, and also in small presentation sheets in issued colors.

Common Design Types pictured following the introduction.

C.C.T.A. Issue
Common Design Type

1960, May 21 Unwmk. *Perf. 13*

3	CD106 50fr lt grn & dk bl	1.90	.65

Dactyloceras Widenmanni — A2

Designs: Various butterflies.

1960-61

4	A2	50c bl grn & dk red	.25	.25
5	A2	1fr multi	.25	.25
6	A2	2fr dk grn & brn	.25	.25
7	A2	3fr yel grn & dk red	.30	.25
8	A2	5fr multi	.35	.25
9	A2	10fr multi	.85	.35
10	A2	20fr multi	2.00	.50
11	A2	85fr multi	8.00	1.60
		Nos. 4-11 (8)	12.25	3.70

Issued: 50c-3fr, 6/10/61; others, 9/3/60.

No. 2 Overprinted

1960, Dec. 1

12	A1 25fr multi	1.60	1.60

National Holiday, Dec. 1, 1960.

Louis Pasteur and Pasteur Institute, Bangui A3

1961, Feb. 25 Unwmk. *Perf. 13*

13	A3 20fr multi	1.25	.80

Opening of Pasteur Institute at Bangui.

Flag, Map, and UN Emblem A4

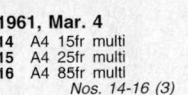

1961, Mar. 4 Engr.

14	A4 15fr multi	.50	.30
15	A4 25fr multi	.50	.30
16	A4 85fr multi	1.75	1.00
	Nos. 14-16 (3)	2.75	1.60

Admission to the UN.

No. 15 Overprinted in Green

1961, Dec. 1

17	A4 25fr multi	2.25	2.25

National Holiday, Dec. 1.

No. 16 Srchd. in Red Brown

1962, Mar. 25

18	A4 50fr on 85fr multi	1.90	1.90

Conf. of the African and Malgache Union at Bangui, Mar. 25-27.

Abidjan Games Issue
Common Design Type

1962, July 21 Photo. *Perf. 12½x12*

19	CD109 20fr Hurdling	.45	.30
20	CD109 50fr Bicycling	1.20	.80
	Nos. 19-20,C6 (3)	3.90	2.60

African-Malgache Union Issue
Common Design Type

1962, Sept. 8 Unwmk.

21	CD110 30fr multi	1.25	.60

African and Malgache Union, 1st anniv.

Pres. David Dacko — A5

1962 *Perf. 12*

22	A5 20fr multi	.40	.25
23	A5 25fr multi	.60	.25

For surcharge see No. 60.

Soldiers with Flag — A6

1963, Aug. 13 Photo.

24	A6 20fr blk & multi	.75	.35

National Army, third anniversary.

Waves Around Globe A6a

Design: 100fr, Orbit patterns around globe.

1963, Sept. 19 Unwmk. *Perf. 12½*

25 A6a 25fr plum & grn .75 .55
26 A6a 100fr org, bl & grn 1.90 1.50

Issued to publicize space communications.

Young Pioneers A7

1963, Oct. 14 Engr. *Perf. 12½*

27 A7 50fr grnsh bl, vio bl & brn .90 .50

Issued to honor Young Pioneers.

Boali Falls — A8

1963, Oct. 28 *Perf. 13*

28 A8 30fr bl, grn & red brn .90 .45

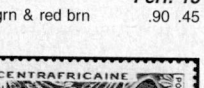

Colotis Evippe A9

Designs: Various butterflies.

1963, Nov. 18 Photo. *Perf. 12½x13*

29 A9 1fr multi .25 .25
30 A9 3fr multi .75 .25
31 A9 4fr multi .85 .30
32 A9 60fr multi 6.00 3.00
Nos. 29-32 (4) 7.85 3.80

For surcharge see No. 58.

UNESCO Emblem, Scales and Tree — A9a

1963, Dec. 10 *Perf. 13*

33 A9a 25fr grn, ol & red brn 1.00 .55

15th anniversary of the Universal Declaration of Human Rights.

Leaves and IQSY Emblem A10

1964, Apr. 20 Engr. *Perf. 13*

34 A10 25fr org, Prus grn & bis 1.25 .75

International Quiet Sun Year, 1964-65.

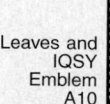

Child — A11

Designs: Heads of Children.

1964, Aug. 13 Unwmk. *Perf. 13*

35 A11 20fr multi .35 .25
36 A11 25fr multi .40 .30
37 A11 40fr multi .55 .45
38 A11 50fr multi .70 .45
a. Miniature sheet of 4, #35-38 3.00 3.00
Nos. 35-38 (4) 2.00 1.45

Cooperation Issue

Common Design Type

1964, Nov. 7 Engr.

39 CD119 25fr grn, mag & dk brn 1.00 .55

"All Men Are Men" — A12

1964, Dec. 1 Litho. *Perf. 13x12½*

40 A12 25fr multi 1.00 .45

Issued to publicize National Unity.

Putting Yoke on Oxen A13

Designs: 50fr, Ox pulling harrow. 85fr, Team of oxen in field. 100fr, Hay wagon.

1965, Apr. 28 Engr. *Perf. 13*

41 A13 25fr sl grn, sep & rose .60 .30
42 A13 50fr sl grn, lt bl & brn 1.00 .45
43 A13 85fr bl, grn & red brn 1.40 .70
44 A13 100fr multi 1.90 .90
Nos. 41-44 (4) 4.90 2.35

For surcharges see Nos. 63-64.

Telegraph Receiver by Pouget-Maisonneuve — A14

ITU cent.: 30fr, Chappe telegraph, vert. 50fr, Doignon regulator, vert. 85fr, Pouillet telegraph transcriber.

1965, May 17 Unwmk.

45 A14 25fr red, grn & ultra .60 .40
46 A14 30fr lake & grn .65 .40
47 A14 50fr car & vio 1.00 .60
48 A14 85fr red lil & slate 1.90 1.00
Nos. 45-48 (4) 4.15 2.40

"Health" A15

25fr, "Clothes;" shuttle, cloth & women. 60fr, "Teaching;" student & school. 85fr, "Food;" mother feeding child, tractor in wheat field.

1965, June 10 Engr. *Perf. 13*

49 A15 25fr ultra, brt grn & brn .50 .30
50 A15 50fr ultra, brn & grn .90 .45
51 A15 60fr grn, ultra & brn 1.00 .60
52 A15 85fr multi 1.40 .70
Nos. 49-52 (4) 3.80 2.05

Issued to publicize the slogans and aims of "M.E.S.A.N." (Mouvement d'Évolution Sociale de l'Afrique Noire). See No. C30.

Caterpillars and Moth on Coffee Branch — A16

Designs: 3fr, Hawk moth and caterpillar on coffee leaves, horiz. 30fr, Platyedra moth and larvae on cotton plant.

1965, Aug. 25 Engr. *Perf. 13*

53 A16 2fr dk pur, dp org & sl grn .40 .25
54 A16 3fr blk, sl grn & red 1.00 .25
55 A16 30fr red lil, red & sl grn 6.50 .90
Nos. 53-55 (3) 7.90 1.40

Issued to publicize plant protection.

Boy Scout, Tents and Animals A17

Design: 25fr, Campfire and Scout emblem.

1965, Sept. 27 Unwmk. *Perf. 13*

56 A17 25fr red org, bl & red lil 1.00 .25
57 A17 50fr brn & Prus bl 1.25 .60

Issued to honor the Boy Scouts.

Nos. 30, 1 and 22 Surcharged in Black or Brown

Engraved; Photogravure

Perf. 13, 12, 12½x13

1965, Aug. 26 Unwmk.

58 A9 2fr on 3fr multi 5.75 5.75
59 A1 5fr on 15fr multi 4.50 4.50
60 A5 10fr on 20fr multi (Br) 6.25 6.25
Nos. 58-60 (3) 16.50 16.50

The surcharges are adjusted to shape of stamps.

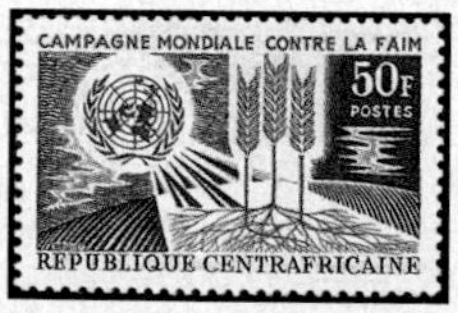

UN Emblem and Wheat A18

1965, Oct. 16 Engr. *Perf. 13*

61 A18 50fr ocher, sl grn & brt bl 1.25 .70

FAO "Freedom from Hunger Campaign."

Diamond Cutter A19

1966, Mar. 14 Engr. *Perf. 13*

62 A19 25fr car rose, dk pur & brn 1.40 .45

Nos. 43-44 Surcharged

1966, Feb.

63 A13 5fr on 85fr multi .40 .40
64 A13 10fr on 100fr multi .65 .65

Issue dates: 5fr, Feb. 17; 10fr, Feb. 15.

Statue of Mbaka Woman Porter — A20

1966, Apr. 9 Photo. *Perf. 13x12½*

65 A20 25fr multi 1.00 .45

Intl. Negro Arts Festival, Dakar, Senegal, Apr. 1-24.

WHO Headquarters, Geneva — A21

1966, May 3 Photo. Unwmk.

66 A21 25fr pur, bl & yel 1.00 .45

Inauguration of the WHO Headquarters, Geneva.

Eulophia Cucullata — A22

Orchids: 5fr, Lissochilus horsfalii. 10fr, Tridactyle bicaudata. 15fr, Polystachya. 20fr, Eulophia alta. 25fr, Microcelia macrorrhynchium.

1966, May 16 Photo. *Perf. 12x12½*

Orchids in Natural Colors

67 A22 2fr dk red .30 .25
68 A22 5fr brn org & vio .75 .25
69 A22 10fr bl grn & blk .90 .40
70 A22 15fr lt grn & dk brn 1.40 .65
71 A22 20fr dk grn 2.00 .70
72 A22 25fr lt ultra & brn 3.00 .80
Nos. 67-72 (6) 8.35 3.05

For surcharge see No. 78.

Congo Forest Mouse A23

Rodents: 10fr, One-stripe mouse. 20fr, Dollman's tree mouse, vert.

1966, Sept. 15 Photo. *Perf. 12½x12*

73 A23 5fr yel & multi .65 .30
74 A23 10fr tan & multi 1.25 .45
75 A23 20fr lt grn & multi 2.10 .80
Nos. 73-75 (3) 4.00 1.55

UNESCO Emblem — A24

1966, Dec. 5 Photo. *Perf. 13*

76 A24 30fr multi .80 .40

20th anniv. of UNESCO.

Pres. Jean Bedel Bokassa — A25

1967, Jan. 1 *Perf. 12x12½*

77 A25 30fr yel grn, blk & bis brn .75 .35

No. 72 Surcharged In Black

1967, May 8 Photo. *Perf. 12x12½*

78 A22 10fr on 25fr multi .80 .30

See No. C43.

Central Market, Bangui A26

1967, Aug. 8 Photo. *Perf. 12½x13*

79 A26 30fr multi 1.00 .40

Safari Hotel, Bangui A27

1967, Sept. 26 Photo. *Perf. 12½x13*

80 A27 30fr multi 1.00 .40

Leucocoprinus Africanus — A28

Various Mushrooms

1967, Oct. 3 Photo. *Perf. 13*

81 A28 5fr dk brn, ol & ocher *10.00 .80*
82 A28 10fr dk brn, ultra & yel *15.00 1.25*
83 A28 15fr dk brn, sl grn & yel *17.50 1.40*
84 A28 30fr multi *50.00 4.00*
85 A28 50fr multi *75.00 6.00*
Nos. 81-85 (5) 167.50 13.45

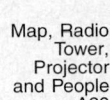

Map, Radio Tower, Projector and People A29

1967, Oct. 31 Engr.

86 A29 30fr emer, ocher & indigo 1.00 .45

Radiovision service.

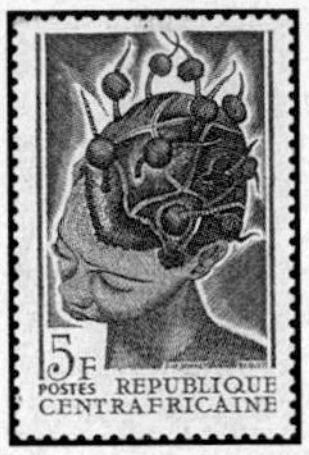

African Hair Style — A30

Various African Hair Styles.

1967, Nov. 7 Engr. *Perf. 13*

87 A30 5fr ultra, dk brn & bis brn .30 .25
88 A30 10fr car, dk brn & bis brn .50 .25
89 A30 15fr dp grn, dk brn & bis brn .75 .40
90 A30 20fr org, dk brn & bis brn .75 .50
91 A30 30fr red lil, dk brn & bis brn 1.40 .65
Nos. 87-91 (5) 3.70 2.05

Nurse Vaccinating Children A31

1967, Nov. 14

92 A31 30fr dk red brn & brt grn .90 .50

Vaccination campaign, 1967-70.

Douglas DC-3 A32

1967, Nov. 24

93 A32 1fr shown .35 .25
94 A32 2fr Beechcraft Baron .35 .25
95 A32 5fr Douglas DC-4 .35 .25
Nos. 93-95,C47-C49 (6) 23.05 7.55

Pierced Stone, Kwe Tribe — A33

Designs: 30fr, Primitive dwelling at Toulou, horiz. 100fr, Megaliths, Bouar. 130fr, Rock painting (people), Toulou, horiz.

1967, Dec. 26 Engr. *Perf. 13*

96 A33 30fr crim, ind & mar .85 .45
97 A33 50fr ol brn, ocher & dk grn 1.60 .90
98 A33 100fr dk brn, brt bl & brn 3.00 1.20
99 A33 130fr dk red, brn & dk grn 3.25 1.20
Nos. 96-99 (4) 8.70 3.75

6th Pan-African Prehistoric Cong., Dakar.

Tanker, Refinery and Map of Area Served — A33a

1968, July 30 Photo. *Perf. 12½*

100 A33a 30fr multi 1.00 .30

Issued to commemorate the opening of the Port Gentil (Gabon) Refinery, June 12, 1968.

Bulldozer Clearing Land — A34

Designs: 10fr, Baoule cattle. 20fr, 15,000-spindle spinning machine. No. 104, Automatic Diederichs looms. No. 105, Bulldozer.

1968, Oct. 1 Engr. *Perf. 13*

101 A34 5fr blk, grn & dk brn .40 .25
102 A34 10fr blk, pale grn & bis brn .55 .30
103 A34 20fr grn, red brn & yel .90 .30
104 A34 30fr brn, ol & ultra 1.40 .55
105 A34 30fr ind, red brn & sl grn 1.40 .55
Nos. 101-105 (5) 4.65 1.95

Issued to publicize "Operation Bokassa."

Bangui Mosque A35

1968, Oct. 14

106 A35 30fr grn, bl & ocher .85 .40

Hunting Knife of Baya and Boufl Tribes A36

20fr, Hunting knife of Nzakara tribe. 30fr, Crossbow of Babinga & Babenzele (pygmy) tribes.

1968, Nov. 19 Engr. *Perf. 13*

107 A36 10fr lem, Prus bl & ultra .50 .25
108 A36 20fr ultra, dk ol & sl grn .70 .30
109 A36 30fr sl grn, ultra & brn org 1.25 .40
Nos. 107-109 (3) 2.45 .95

"Ville de Bangui," 1958 — A37

River Boats: 30fr, "J. B. Gouandjia," 1968. 50fr, "Lamblin," 1944.

1968, Dec. 10 Engr. *Perf. 13*

Size: 36x22mm

110 A37 10fr mag, brt grn & vio bl .65 .40
111 A37 30fr bl, grn & brn 1.25 .45
112 A37 50fr brn, sl & ol grn 2.00 .55
Nos. 110-112,C62-C63 (5) 9.40 3.65

Woman Javelin Thrower — A38

1969, Mar. 18 Photo. *Perf. 13x12½*

113 A38 5fr shown .30 .25
114 A38 10fr Women runners .30 .25
115 A38 15fr Soccer .50 .25
Nos. 113-115,C71-C72 (5) 4.45 1.65

BIT and ILO Emblems and Worker A39

1969, May 20 Photo. *Perf. 12½x13*

116 A39 30fr dp bl, grn & ol brn 1.00 .40
117 A39 50fr dp car, grn & ol brn 1.50 .55

50th anniv. of the ILO.

Pres. Bokassa — A40

1969, Dec. 1 Litho. *Perf. 13x13½*

118 A40 30fr vermilion & multi .65 .30

ASECNA Issue

Common Design Type

1969, Dec. 12 Engr. *Perf. 13*

119 CD132 100fr dp bl 2.25 .80

Garayah — A41

Musical Instuments: 15fr, Ngombi (harp) horiz. 30fr, Xylophone, horiz. 50fr, Ndala (lute) horiz. 130fr, Gatta and babyon (drums).

1970, Jan. 6 Engr. *Perf. 13*

120 A41 10fr yel grn, dk grn & ocher .60 .25
121 A41 15fr bl grn, ocher & dk brn .60 .25
122 A41 30fr mar, ocher & dk brn 1.00 .45
123 A41 50fr rose car & ind 1.50 .55
124 A41 130fr brt bl, brn & ol 4.75 .95
Nos. 120-124 (5) 8.45 2.45

UPU Headquarters Issue

Common Design Type

1970, May 20 Engr. *Perf. 13*

125 CD133 100fr ultra, ver & red brn 1.90 .70

Loading Platform and Flour Storage Bins A42

50fr, Flour milling machinery. 100fr, View of mill.

1970, Feb. 24 Litho. *Perf. 14*

126 A42 25fr sl & multi	11.00	.70
127 A42 50fr lil & multi	26.50	1.50
128 A42 100fr red & multi	37.50	2.50
Nos. 126-128 (3)	75.00	4.70

Inauguration of SICPAD (Société Industrielle Centrafricaine des Produits Alimentaires et Dérivés), a part of Operation Bokassa, 2/22/68.

Pres. Bokassa — A43

1970, Aug. 13 Litho. *Perf. 14*

129 A43 30fr multi	9.00	5.00
130 A43 40fr multi	10.00	5.00

Cheese Factory, Sarki — A44

Silk Worm — A45

10fr, M'Bali Ranch. 20fr, Zebu, vert.

Perf. 13x13½, 13½x13

1970, Sept. 15

131 A44 5fr red & multi	.55	.30
132 A44 10fr red & multi	6.50	4.25
133 A44 20fr red & multi	1.40	.55
134 A45 40fr red & multi	3.00	.95
Nos. 131-134,C83 (5)	15.95	7.15

Issued to publicize Operation Bokassa, a national development plan.

Nos. 131-134 exist perf 10. See No. C83.

Gnathonemus Monteiri — A46

River Fish: 20fr, Mormyrus proboscirostris. 30fr, Marcusenius wilverthi. 40fr, Gnathonemus elephas. 50fr, Gnathonemus curvirostris.

1971, Apr. 6 Photo. *Perf. 12½*

135 A46 10fr multi	.40	.25
136 A46 20fr multi	.75	.30
137 A46 30fr multi	1.10	.60
138 A46 40fr multi	2.50	.70
139 A46 50fr multi	2.75	1.10
Nos. 135-139 (5)	7.50	2.95

Berberati Cathedral A47

1971, July 20 Litho. *Perf. 13½*

140 A47 5fr grn & multi	.65	.25

New Roman Catholic Cathedral at Berberati.

Charles de Gaulle — A48

1971, Aug. 20 *Perf. 13½x13*

141 A48 100fr brt bl & multi	3.50	2.00

In memory of Gen. Charles de Gaulle (1890-1970), president of France.

Gray Galago — A49

Designs: 40fr, Elegant galago. 100fr, Calabar potto, horiz. 150fr, Bosman's potto, horiz. 200fr, Oustalet's colobo, horiz.

1971, Oct. 25 Photo. *Perf. 13*

142 A49 30fr pink & multi	.70	.45
143 A49 40fr lt bl & multi	.90	.55
144 A49 100fr multi	2.75	1.10
145 A49 150fr multi	4.75	1.75
146 A49 200fr multi	5.75	2.25
Nos. 142-146 (5)	14.85	6.10

Alan B. Shepard — A50

No. 148, Yuri Gagarin. No. 149, Edwin E. Aldrin, Jr. No. 150, Alexei Leonov. No. 151, Neil A. Armstrong on moon. No. 152, Lunokhod I on moon.

1971, Nov. 19 Litho. *Perf. 14*

147 A50 40fr vio & multi	.50	.30
148 A50 40fr vio & multi	.50	.30
149 A50 100fr multi	1.25	.45
150 A50 100fr multi	1.25	.45
151 A50 200fr red & multi	2.50	1.10
152 A50 200fr red & multi	2.50	1.10
Nos. 147-152 (6)	8.50	3.70

Space achievements of US and Russia.

"Operation Bokassa" and Pres. Bokassa A51

1971, Dec. 1 Photo. *Perf. 13*

153 A51 40fr red & multi	.80	.40

12th anniversary of independence.

Racial Equality Emblem A52

1971, Dec. 6 Litho.

154 A52 50fr multi	.90	.45

Intl. Year Against Racial Discrimination.

Bokassa School Emblem and Cadets — A53

1972, Jan. 1 Photo.

155 A53 30fr gold & multi	.90	.45

J. B. Bokassa Military School.

Book Year Emblem — A54

1972, Mar. 11 Photo. *Perf. 12½x13*

156 A54 100fr red brn, gold & org	3.00	1.00

International Book Year 1972.

"Your Heart is your Health" A55

1972, Apr. 7 Photo. *Perf. 13x12½*

157 A55 100fr yel, blk & car	1.75	.85

World Health Day.

Red Cross Workers in Village — A56

1972, May 8 *Perf. 13*

158 A56 150fr multi	3.00	1.40

25th World Red Cross Day.

Globe A57

1972, May 17 Litho.

159 A57 50fr yel, blk & dp org	.90	.55

4th World Telecommunications Day.

Pres. and Mrs. Bokassa and Family — A58

1972, May 28 *Perf. 14*

160 A58 30fr yel & multi	.65	.35

Mother's Day. Mothers' gold medal awarded to Catherine Bokassa.

Pres. Bokassa Planting Cotton, Map of Africa — A59

1972, June 5 Photo. *Perf. 13*

161 A59 40fr yel & multi	.90	.45

Operation Bokassa, a natl. development plan.

Postal Checking and Savings Center A60

1972, June 21

162 A60 30fr yel org & multi	.65	.40

Irrigated Rice Fields — A61

"Le Pacifique" Apartment House A62

25fr, Plowing rice field. No. 166, Swimming pool, Hotel St. Sylvestre. No. 167, Entrance, Hotel St. Sylvestre. No. 168, J. B. Bokassa University.

1972 **Litho.** ***Perf. 13x13½***
163 A61 5fr multi 1.25 .25
164 A61 25fr multi 2.10 .30

Engr. ***Perf. 13***
165 A62 30fr multi .40 .25
166 A62 30fr multi .50 .30
167 A62 40fr multi .60 .40
168 A62 40fr multi .65 .40
Nos. 163-168 (6) 5.50 1.90

Operation Bokassa. Issued: 5fr, 25fr, 11/10; No. 165, 6/27; Nos. 166-167, 12/9; No. 168, 8/26.

Bull Chasing Woman on Clock Face — A63

Scenes Painted on Clock Faces: 10fr, Men & open cooking fire. 20fr, Fishermen. 30fr, Palms, monkeys & giraffe. 40fr, Warriors.

1972, July 31 **Photo.** ***Perf. 12½***
169 A63 5fr dk red & multi .30 .30
170 A63 10fr brt bl & multi .30 .30
171 A63 20fr grn & multi .60 .30
172 A63 30fr yel & multi .85 .45
173 A63 40fr vio & multi 1.25 .60
Nos. 169-173 (5) 3.30 1.95

HORCEN Central African clock and watch factory.

Protestant Youth Center — A64

10fr, Postal runner carrying mail in cleft stick.

1972, Aug. 12 ***Perf. 13***
174 A64 10fr multi, vert. .30 .30
175 A64 20fr multi .50 .30
Nos. 174-175,C95-C98 (6) 8.35 5.10

Centraphilex 1972, Central African Philatelic Exhibition, Bangui.

Mail Truck A65

1972, Oct. 23 **Photo.** ***Perf. 13***
176 A65 100fr ocher & multi 1.90 .70

Universal Postal Union Day.

Mother Teaching Child to Write — A66

Central African Mothers: 10fr, Caring for infant. 15fr, Combing child's hair. 20fr, Teaching to read. 180fr, Nursing. 190fr, Teaching to walk.

1972, Dec. 27 ***Perf. 13½x13***
177 A66 5fr multi .25 .25
178 A66 10fr lil & multi .30 .25
179 A66 15fr dl org & multi .30 .25
180 A66 20fr yel grn & multi .50 .25
181 A66 180fr multi 2.75 1.25
182 A66 190fr pink & multi 2.75 1.25
Nos. 177-182 (6) 6.85 3.50

Farmer Carrying Sheaf — A67

1973, May 30 **Photo.** ***Perf. 13***
183 A67 50fr vio bl & multi .90 .45

10th anniv. of the World Food Program.

Garcinia Punctata A68

African Flora: 20fr, Bertiera racemosa. 30fr, Corynanthe pachyceras. 40fr, Combretodendron africanum. 50fr, Xylopla Villosa, vert.

1973, June 8
184 A68 10fr pale bl & multi .50 .25
185 A68 20fr multi .85 .30
186 A68 30fr lt gray & multi 1.00 .45
187 A68 40fr multi 1.60 .60
188 A68 50fr multi 2.00 .80
Nos. 184-188 (5) 5.95 2.40

For surcharge see No. 193.

Pygmy Chameleon A69

1973, June 26 **Photo.** ***Perf. 13***
189 A69 15fr multi 1.50 .40

Caterpillar — A70

Designs: Various caterpillars.

1973, Aug. 6 **Photo.** ***Perf. 13***
190 A70 3fr multi 1.25 .30
191 A70 5fr multi 2.00 .40
192 A70 25fr multi 4.00 .60
Nos. 190-192 (3) 7.25 1.30

For surcharge see No. 259.

No. 184 Srchd. and Ovptd. in Red

1973, Aug. 16
193 A68 100fr on 10fr multi 1.75 1.00

African solidarity in drought emergency.

African Postal Union Issue
Common Design Type

1973, Sept. 12 **Engr.** ***Perf. 13***
194 CD137 100fr dk brn, red org & ol 1.25 .75

Pres. Bokassa and CAR Flag — A71

1973, Nov. 30 **Photo.** ***Perf. 12½***
195 A71 1fr brn & multi .25 .25
196 A71 2fr pur & multi .25 .25
197 A71 3fr vio bl & multi .25 .25
198 A71 5fr ocher & multi .25 .25
199 A71 10fr multi .40 .25
200 A71 15fr org & multi .40 .25
201 A71 20fr multi .50 .25
202 A71 30fr dk grn & multi .50 .30
203 A71 40fr dk brn & multi .65 .40
Nos. 195-203,C117-C118 (11) 5.60 3.55

INTERPOL Emblem A72

1973, Dec. 20 ***Perf. 13x12½***
204 A72 50fr yellow & multi 1.40 .60

Intl. Criminal Police Organization, 50th anniv.

Catherine Bokassa Center A73

40fr, Ambulance in front of Catherine Bokassa Center.

1974, Jan. 24 **Engr.** ***Perf. 13***
205 A73 30fr multi .40 .25
206 A73 40fr multi .55 .30

Catherine Bokassa Center for Mothers and Children.

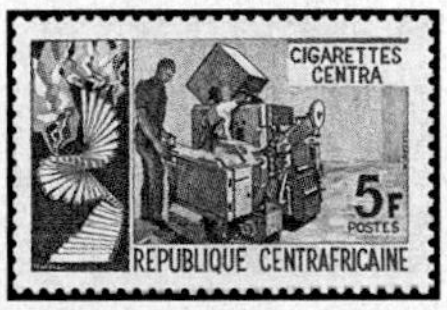

Cigarette-making Machine — A74

10fr, Cigarette in ashtray, & factory. 30fr, Hand lighting cigarette, & Administration Building.

1974, Jan. 29
207 A74 5fr slate grn & multi .25 .25
208 A74 10fr slate grn & multi .40 .25
209 A74 30fr slate grn & multi .50 .25
Nos. 207-209 (3) 1.15 .75

Publicity for Centra cigarettes.

"Communications" A75

1974, June 8 **Photo.** ***Perf. 12½x13***
210 A75 100fr multi 1.75 .85

World Telecommunications Day.
For surcharge see No. 280.

People and WPY Emblem A76

1974, June 20 **Engr.** ***Perf. 13***
211 A76 100fr red, slate grn & brn 1.25 .65

World Population Year.
For surcharge see No. 281.

Mother, Child, WHO Emblem — A77

1974, July 10
212 A77 100fr multi 1.75 .70

26th anniv. of WHO.
For surcharge see No. 282.

Hoeing — A78

Veterans' activities: 10fr, Battle scene ("yesterday"). 15fr, Pastoral scene ("today"). 20fr, Rice planting. 25fr, Storehouse. 40fr, Veterans Headquarters. Borders show tanks and tractors.

1974, Nov. 15 **Litho.** ***Perf. 13***
213 A78 10fr multi .25 .25
214 A78 15fr multi .30 .25
215 A78 20fr multi .30 .25
216 A78 25fr multi .40 .25
217 A78 30fr multi .40 .25
218 A78 40fr multi .60 .25
Nos. 213-218 (6) 2.25 1.50

For surcharges see Nos. 260, 265, 267.

Presidents and Flags of Cameroun, CAR, Congo, Gabon and Meeting Center — A79

1974, Dec. 8 **Photo.** ***Perf. 13***
219 A79 40fr gold & multi .65 .40

See No. C126 and note after Cameroun No. 595.
For surcharge see No. 272.

House in OCAM City — A80

Scenes in housing development, OCAM City.

1975, Feb. 1 **Photo.** ***Perf. 13***
220 A80 30fr multi .40 .25
221 A80 40fr multi .50 .30
222 A80 50fr multi .60 .30
223 A80 100fr multi 1.00 .55
Nos. 220-223 (4) 2.50 1.40

For surcharges see Nos. 269, 273.

1975, Feb. 22

Cottage scenes in J. B. Bokassa "pilot village."

224 A80 25fr multi .30 .25
225 A80 30fr multi .40 .25
226 A80 40fr multi .50 .30
Nos. 224-226 (3) 1.20 .80

For surcharges see Nos. 268, 270, 274.

Foreign Ministry A81

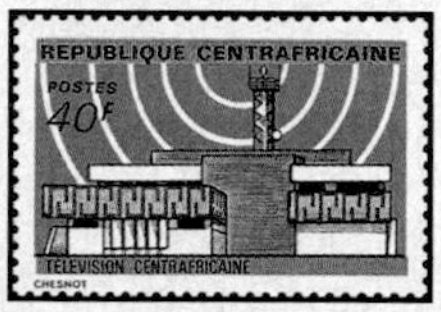

Television Station A82

1975, Feb. 28 ***Perf. 13x12½***
227 A81 40fr multi .65 .40

Perf. 13
228 A82 40fr multi .65 .40

Public buildings, Bangui.
For surcharges see Nos. 275-276.

Bokassa's Saber — A83

Design: 40fr, Bokassa's baton.

1975, Feb. 22 **Photo.** ***Perf. 13***
229 A83 30fr dp bl & multi .55 .30
230 A83 40fr vio bl & multi .55 .30

Jean Bedel Bokassa, President for Life and Marshal of the Republic. See Nos. C127-C128. For surcharge see No. 286.

Traffic Signs A84

1975, Mar. 20
231 A84 5fr Do Not Enter .25 .25
232 A84 10fr Stop .25 .25
233 A84 20fr No parking .30 .25
234 A84 30fr School .50 .25
235 A84 40fr Intersection .75 .30
Nos. 231-235 (5) 2.05 1.30

For surcharges see Nos. 261, 277.

Buffon's Kob — A85

1975, June 24 **Photo.** ***Perf. 13***
236 A85 10fr shown .45 .25
237 A85 15fr Wart hog 1.10 .35
238 A85 20fr Waterbuck 1.50 .25
239 A85 30fr Lion 1.50 .40
Nos. 236-239 (4) 4.55 1.25

For surcharges see Nos. 262-263, 266, 271.

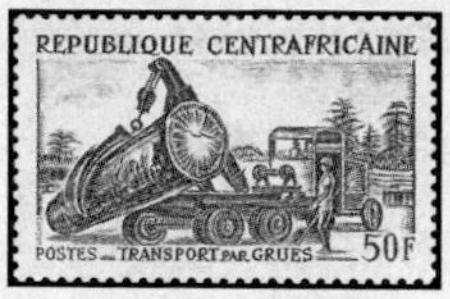

Crane Lifting Log onto Truck A86

Designs: 10fr, Forest, vert. 15fr, Tree felling, vert. 100fr, Log pile. 150fr, Logs transported by raft. 200fr, Lumberyard.

1975, Nov. 28 **Engr.** ***Perf. 13***
240 A86 10fr multi .25 .25
241 A86 15fr multi .30 .25
242 A86 50fr multi .55 .25
243 A86 100fr multi 1.50 .55
244 A86 150fr multi 1.75 1.00
245 A86 200fr multi 2.25 1.10
Nos. 240-245 (6) 6.60 3.40

Promotion of Central African wood.
For surcharges see Nos. 264, 279.

Women's Heads and Various Occupations — A87

1975, Dec. 10 **Photo.**
246 A87 40fr multi .50 .25
247 A87 100fr multi 1.40 .55

International Women's Year 1975.

Alexander Graham Bell — A88

1976, Mar. 25 **Litho.** ***Perf. 12½x13***
248 A88 100fr yel & blk 2.25 1.00

Centenary of first telephone call by Alexander Graham Bell, Mar. 10, 1876.
For surcharge see No. 283.

Satellite and ITU Emblem — A89

No. 250, UPU emblem, various forms of mail transport.

1976 **Engr.** ***Perf. 13***
249 A89 100fr vio bl, claret & grn 1.90 1.00
250 A89 100fr car, grn & ocher 1.60 .80

World Telecommunications Day (No. 249); Universal Postal Union Day (No. 250).
For surcharges see Nos. 284-285.

Soyuz on Launching Pad — A90

Design: 50fr, Apollo rocket.

1976, June 14 **Litho.** ***Perf. 14x13½***
251 A90 40fr multi .55 .25
252 A90 50fr multi .80 .25
Nos. 251-252,C135-C137 (5) 6.45 2.25

Apollo Soyuz space test project, Russo-American cooperation, launched July 15, link-up July 17, 1975.
For surcharges see Nos. 287, 290, C161, C168, C173, C177.

Drurya Antimachus — A91

Butterfly: 40fr, Argema mittrei, vert.

1976, Sept. 20 **Litho.** ***Perf. 12½***
253 A91 30fr ocher & multi 7.00 1.00
254 A91 40fr ultra & multi 9.00 1.00
Nos. 253-254,C145-C146 (4) 43.00 5.50

For surcharge see No. 278.

Slalom, Piero Gros — A92

60fr, Karl Schnabel and Toni Innauer.

1976, Sept. 23 ***Perf. 13½***
255 A92 40fr multi .65 .25
256 A92 60fr multi 1.00 .30
Nos. 255-256,C147-C149 (5) 8.05 2.45

12th Winter Olympic Games winners, Innsbruck.
For surcharges see Nos. 288, 291, C164, C170, C174, C178.

Viking Components A93

Design: 60fr, Viking take-off.

1976, Dec.
257 A93 40fr multi .65 .25
258 A93 60fr multi 1.00 .30
Nos. 257-258,C151-C153 (5) 8.05 2.40

Viking Mars project.
For surcharges and overprints see Nos. 289, 292, 391-392, C165, C171, C175, C179.

Central African Empire

Stamps of 1973-76 Overprinted in Black, Green, Violet Blue, Silver, Carmine, Brown or Red

Nos. 259, 278, 283

Nos. 260, 265, 267, 269, 273, 276, 279

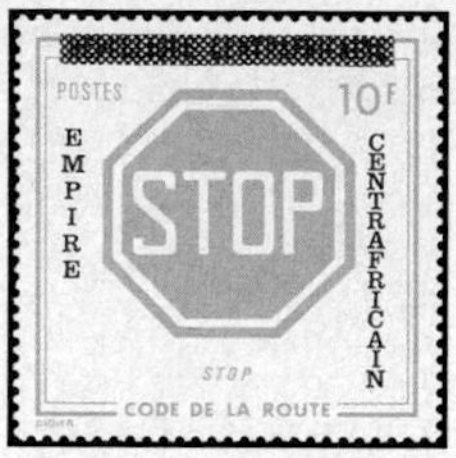

Nos. 261, 277

Nos. 262-263, 266, 271

Nos. 264, 282

Nos. 268, 270, 274, 280, 284-285

Nos. 272, 275

No. 281

Printing and Perforations as Before
1977, Mar.

259	A70	3fr	(#190; B)	.50	.45
260	A78	10fr	(#213;B)	.35	.35
261	A84	10fr	(#232;VB)	.35	.35
262	A85	10fr	(#236;C)	.50	.50
263	A85	15fr	(#237;C)	.85	.85
264	A86	15fr	(#241;B)	.35	.35
265	A78	20fr	(#215;B)	.50	.50
266	A85	20fr	(#238;C)	.50	.50
267	A78	25fr	(#216;B)	.40	.40
268	A80	25fr	(#224;B)	.40	.40
269	A80	30fr	(#220;VB)	.50	.50
270	A80	30fr	(#225;B)	.50	.50
271	A85	30fr	(#239;C)	.60	.60
272	A79	40fr	(#219;B)	.50	.50
273	A80	40fr	(#221;VB)	.50	.50
274	A80	40fr	(#226;B)	.50	.50
275	A81	40fr	(#227;B & S)	.70	.70
276	A82	40fr	(#228;B)	.75	.75
277	A84	40fr	(#235;VB)	.75	.75
278	A91	40fr	(#254;B)	1.00	1.00
279	A86	50fr	(#242;Br)	1.00	1.00
280	A75	100fr	(#210;B)	1.90	1.90
281	A76	100fr	(#211;B)	1.90	1.90
282	A77	100fr	(#212;G)	2.25	2.25
283	A88	100fr	(#248;R)	1.90	1.90

284 A89 100fr (#249;B) 2.25 2.25
285 A89 100fr (#250;B) 2.50 2.50
Nos. 259-285 (27) 24.70 24.65

Stamps of 1975-76 Overprinted in Black on Silver Panel

1977, Apr. 1
286 A83 40fr multi (#230) .90 .90
287 A90 40fr multi (#251) .70 .70
288 A92 40fr multi (#255) .70 .70
289 A93 40fr multi (#257) .70 .70
290 A90 50fr multi (#252) 1.00 1.00
291 A92 60fr multi (#256) .90 .90
292 A93 60fr multi (#258) .90 .90
Nos. 286-292 (7) 5.80 5.80

Pierre and Marie Curie — A94

Design: 60fr, Wilhelm C. Roentgen.

1977, Apr. 1 Litho. *Perf. 13½*
293 A94 40fr multi 1.00 .30
294 A94 60fr multi 1.00 .40
Nos. 293-294,C180-C182 (5) 14.25 2.75

Nobel Prize winners.

Italy No. C42 and Faustine Temple, Rome — A95

60fr, Russia #C12 & St. Basil's Cathedral, Moscow.

1977, Apr. 11 Litho. *Perf. 11*
295 A95 40fr multi 1.00 .25
296 A95 60fr multi 1.10 .40
Nos. 295-296,C184-C186 (5) 9.75 2.55

75th anniversary of the Zeppelin.

Lindbergh over Paris — A96

Designs: 60fr, Santos Dumont and "14 bis." 100fr, Bleriot and monoplane. 200fr, Roald Amundsen and "N24." 300fr, Concorde. 500fr, Lindbergh and Spirit of St. Louis.

1977, Sept. 30 Litho. *Perf. 13½*
297 A96 50fr multi .65 .25
298 A96 60fr multi 1.00 .25
299 A96 100fr multi 1.75 .40
300 A96 200fr multi 2.50 .55
301 A96 300fr multi 5.00 1.25
Nos. 297-301 (5) 10.90 2.70

Souvenir Sheet

302 A96 500fr multi 6.00 2.00

History of aviation, famous fliers.

Shot on Goal A97

Designs: 60fr, Heading ball in net. 100fr, Backfield defense. 200fr, Argentina '78 poster. 300fr, Mario Zagalo and stadium. 500fr, Ferenc Puskas.

1977, Nov. 18 Litho. *Perf. 13½*
303 A97 50fr multi .50 .25
304 A97 60fr multi .65 .25
305 A97 100fr multi 1.25 .30
306 A97 200fr multi 2.10 .55
307 A97 300fr multi 3.50 .90
Nos. 303-307 (5) 8.00 2.25

Souvenir Sheet

308 A97 500fr multi 5.50 1.75

World Soccer Championships, Argentina, June 1-25, 1978.
For overprints see Nos. 370-375.

Emperor Bokassa I, Central African Flag — A98

1977, Dec. 4 Litho. *Perf. 13½*
309 A98 40fr multi .40 .25
310 A98 60fr multi .55 .25
311 A98 100fr multi 1.00 .45
312 A98 150fr multi 1.40 .60
Nos. 309-312,C188-C189 (6) 8.00 3.60

Coronation of Emperor Bokassa I, Dec. 4.

Lilium — A99

1977 Litho. *Perf. 13½x14*
313 A99 5fr shown .55 .30
314 A99 10fr Hibiscus 1.10 .55

For overprints see Nos. 408-409.

Electronic Tree, ITU Emblem — A100

1977
315 A100 100fr blk, org & brn 3.00 2.00

World Telecommunications Day.

Bible and People A101

1977 Litho. *Perf. 14x13½*
316 A101 40fr multi 8.00 1.25

Bible Week.

People and Rotary Emblem A102

1977
317 A102 60fr multi 4.50 2.00

Rotary Club of Bangui, 20th anniversary.

Holy Family, by Rubens A103

Rubens Paintings: 150fr, Marie de Medicis. 200fr, Son of artist. 300fr, Neptune. 500fr, Marie de Medicis, diff.

1978, Jan. 26
318 A103 60fr multi .60 .25
319 A103 150fr multi 1.50 .40
320 A103 200fr multi 2.40 .60
321 A103 300fr multi 3.50 .80
Nos. 318-321 (4) 8.00 2.05

Souvenir Sheet

322 A103 500fr gold & multi 6.00 2.00

Peter Paul Rubens (1577-1640).

Rhinoceros — A104

Endangered Animals and Wildlife Fund Emblem: 50fr, Slender-nosed crocodile. 60fr, Leopard, vert. 100fr, Giraffe, vert. 200fr, Elephant. 300fr, Gorilla, vert.

1978, Feb. 21 Litho. *Perf. 13½*
323 A104 40fr multi *1.75* .30
324 A104 50fr multi *2.50* .35
325 A104 60fr multi *2.75* .55
326 A104 100fr multi *4.75* .90
327 A104 200fr multi *12.00* 1.25
328 A104 300fr multi *14.00* 2.00
Nos. 323-328 (6) *37.75* 5.35

Bokassa Sports Palace A105

Design: 60fr, Sports Palace, side view.

1978 *Perf. 14*
329 A105 40fr multi .50 .25
330 A105 60fr multi .65 .40

Automatic Telephone Exchange, Bangui A106

1978
331 A106 40fr multi .50 .25
332 A106 60fr multi .65 .40

Diligence and Satellite — A107

Designs (UPU Emblem and): 50fr, Steam locomotive and communications via satellite. 60fr, Paddle-wheel steamer and ship-to-shore communication via satellite. 80fr, Old mail truck and satellite.

1978, May 17 *Perf. 13½*
333 A107 40fr multi .25 .25
334 A107 50fr multi 3.00 1.25
335 A107 60fr multi .30 .25
336 A107 80fr multi .40 .25
Nos. 333-336,C191-C192 (6) 6.15 2.55

Posts and telecommunications, cent. of progress.

Mask — A108

Designs: 30fr, Mask. 60fr, Women dancers, horiz. 100fr, Men dancers, horiz.

Perf. 13½x14, 14x13½
1978, July 11 Litho.
337 A108 20fr blk & yel .75 .30
338 A108 30fr blk & brt bl .75 .30
339 A108 60fr blk & multi 1.90 .60
340 A108 100fr blk & multi 3.25 .95
Nos. 337-340 (4) 6.65 2.15

Black-African World Arts Festival, Lagos.
For overprints see Nos. 411-412.

Capt. Cook on "Endeavour" A109

60fr, Resolution off Hawaii. 200fr, Hawaiians welcoming Capt. Cook. 350fr, Masked rowers in Hawaiian boat.

1978, Aug. 30 *Perf. 14½*
341 A109 60fr multi, horiz. .75 .25
342 A109 80fr multi 1.25 .25
343 A109 200fr multi, horiz. 2.50 .70
344 A109 350fr multi, horiz. 4.50 1.25
Nos. 341-344 (4) 9.00 2.45

Capt. James Cook (1728-1779), explorer.

Dürer, Self-portrait A110

Dürer Paintings: 80fr, The Four Apostles. 200fr, Virgin and Child. 350fr, Emperor Maximilian I.

1978, Oct. 24 Litho. *Perf. 13½*

345	A110	60fr multi	.65	.25
346	A110	80fr multi	1.10	.25
347	A110	200fr multi	2.50	.85
348	A110	350fr multi	4.75	1.40
		Nos. 345-348 (4)	9.00	2.75

Albrecht Dürer (1471-1528), German painter.

Tutankhamen's Gold Mask — A111

Treasures of Tutankhamen: 60fr, King and Queen, gold back panel of throne. 80fr, Gilt folding chair. 100fr, King wearing crowns of Upper and Lower Egypt, painted wood sculpture. 120fr, Lion's head. 150fr, Tutankhamen, wood stature. 180fr, Gold throne. 250fr, Gold miniature coffin.

1978, Nov. 22

349	A111	40fr multi	.60	.30
350	A111	60fr multi	.70	.40
351	A111	80fr multi	1.10	.55
352	A111	100fr multi	1.25	.55
353	A111	120fr multi	1.75	.60
354	A111	150fr multi	2.00	.70
355	A111	180fr multi	2.50	.85
356	A111	250fr multi	3.00	1.10
		Nos. 349-356 (8)	12.90	5.05

Tutankhamen, c. 1358 B.C., King of Egypt.

Lenin at Smolny Institute — A112

Soviet Union, 60th anniv.: 60fr, 200fr, 300fr, Various Lenin portraits. 100fr, Ulyanov family, horiz. 150fr, Lenin, Cruiser "Aurora" and flag, horiz. 500fr, "Aurora" and star.

1978, Nov. *Perf. 14*

357	A112	40fr multi	.50	.30
358	A112	60fr multi	.60	.40
359	A112	100fr blk & gold	1.00	.45
360	A112	150fr blk, gold & red	1.90	.70
361	A112	200fr multi	3.00	1.00
362	A112	300fr multi	4.00	1.40
		Nos. 357-362 (6)	11.00	4.25

Souvenir Sheet

363	A112	500fr multi	6.00	4.00

Catherine Bokassa A113

Design: 60fr, Emperor Bokassa.

1978, Dec. 4 Litho. *Perf. 13*

364	A113	40fr multi	.65	.25
365	A113	60fr multi	.90	.30

1st anniv. of coronation. See No. C202.

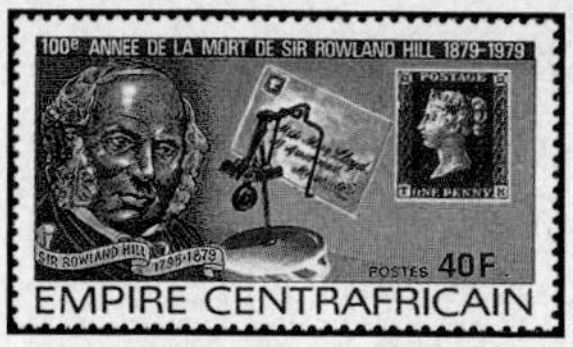

Rowland Hill, Letter Scale and G.B. No. 1 — A114

Rowland Hill and: 50fr, US #1, mailman on bicycle. 60fr, Austria #P4, 19th cent. mailman. 80fr, Switzerland #2L1, postilion and mailcoach.

1978, Dec. 9 Litho. *Perf. 13½*

366	A114	40fr multi	.65	.30
367	A114	50fr multi	.65	.30
368	A114	60fr multi	.90	.40
369	A114	80fr multi	1.00	.50
		Nos. 366-369,C203-C204 (6)	8.95	3.55

Sir Rowland Hill (1795-1879), originator of penny postage.

Nos. 303-307 Overprinted in Silver

1978, Dec. 27

370	A97	50fr multi	.55	.25
371	A97	60fr multi	.65	.30
372	A97	100fr multi	1.00	.55
373	A97	200fr multi	2.25	1.00
374	A97	300fr multi	3.25	1.40
		Nos. 370-374 (5)	7.70	3.50

Souvenir Sheet
No. 308 Overprinted in Silver

375	A97	500fr multi	5.00	5.00

Argentina's victory in World Cup Soccer Championship 1978.

Children Painting and Dutch Portrait — A115

UNICEF, Eagle Emblems and: 50fr, Eskimo children skiing, ski jump. 60fr, Children with toy racing car, Carl Benz with early car model. 80fr, Children launching rocket, Mariner 5.

1979, Mar. 6 Litho. *Perf. 13½*

376	A115	40fr multi	.65	.25
377	A115	50fr multi	.75	.25
378	A115	60fr multi	.90	.25
379	A115	80fr multi	1.25	.30
		Nos. 376-379,C206-C207 (6)	7.70	2.10

International Year of the Child.

High Jump, Moscow '80 Emblem and "M" — A116

Designs (Moscow '80 Emblem, Various Sports and): 50fr, Bicycling and "O." 60fr, Weight lifting and "C." 80fr, Judo and "K."

1979, Mar. 16 Litho. *Perf. 13*

380	A116	40fr multi	.55	.25
381	A116	50fr multi	.65	.25
382	A116	60fr multi	.75	.25
383	A116	80fr multi	1.10	.30
		Nos. 380-383,C209-C210 (6)	6.25	2.05

22nd Olympic Games, Moscow, July 19-Aug. 3, 1980. Background letters on Nos. 380-383, C209-C210 spell "Mockba." A 1500fr gold embossed stamp showing emblems and Discobolus exists.

Memorial, Bangui, Butterfly, Hibiscus — A117

Design: 150fr, Canoe, truck and letters.

1979, June 8 Litho. *Perf. 12x12½*

384	A117	60fr multi	3.00	1.25
385	A117	150fr multi	5.50	2.50

Philexafrique II, Libreville, Gabon, June 8-17. Nos. 384, 385 each printed in sheets of 10 with 5 labels showing exhibition emblem.

Schoolgirl A118

1979, July 25 Litho. *Perf. 12½x12*

386	A118	70fr multi	.95	.40

Intl. Bureau of Education, Geneva, 50th anniv.

Chicken A119

1979, Aug. *Perf. 13*

387	A119	10fr shown	1.90	1.10
388	A119	20fr Bull	1.90	1.10
389	A119	40fr Sheep	4.00	2.10
		Nos. 387-389,C211 (4)	13.55	6.30

National Husbandry Assoc.

Souvenir Sheet

Virgin and Child, by Dürer — A120

1979, Aug. *Perf. 13½*

390	A120	500fr lt grn & dl red	5.50	1.60

Albrecht Dürer (1471-1528), German engraver and printer.

Central African Republic

Nos. 257-258 Overprinted

1979, Nov. 11 Litho. *Perf. 13½*

391	A93	40fr multi	.65	.30
392	A93	60fr multi	.75	.40
		Nos. 391-392,C212-C214 (5)	7.05	3.35

Apollo 11 moon landing, 10th anniversary.

Girl and Rose A121

30fr, Butterfly and girl, vert. 60fr, Hansel and Gretel, vert. 200fr, The Little Match Girl. 250fr, Mermaid, vert.

1979, Dec. 15

393	A121	30fr multicolored	.30	.25
394	A121	40fr shown	.50	.25
395	A121	60fr multicolored	.55	.25
396	A121	200fr multicolored	2.25	.70
397	A121	250fr multicolored	2.75	.80
		Nos. 393-397 (5)	6.35	2.25

International Year of the Child.

Locomotive, U.S. Type A27, Hill — A122

Locomotives, Hill and Stamps: 100fr, France #1. 150fr, Germany type A11. 250fr, Great Britain #32. 500fr, CAR #2.

1979, Dec. 20

398	A122	60fr multi	.55	.25
399	A122	100fr multi	1.10	.30
400	A122	150fr multi	1.75	.45
401	A122	250fr multi	3.00	.95
		Nos. 398-401 (4)	6.40	1.95

Souvenir Sheet

402	A122	500fr multi	5.75	2.00

Sir Rowland Hill (1795-1879), originator of penny postage.

Basketball, Moscow '80 Emblem — A123

Pre-Olympic Year: Men's or women's basketball.

1979, Dec. 28 Litho. *Perf. 14½*

403	A123	50fr multi	.50	.25
404	A123	125fr multi	1.10	.35
405	A123	200fr multi	1.90	.55
406	A123	300fr multi	3.25	.80
407	A123	500fr multi	5.00	1.40
		Nos. 403-407 (5)	11.75	3.35

For overprints see Nos. 425-429.

Nos. 313-314 Overprinted in Black on Silver Panel

and

Balambo Chair A124

and

Nos. 337-338 Overprinted in Black on Silver Panel

Perf. 13½x14, 14x13½

1980, Mar. 20 Litho.

408	A99	5fr multi	.35	.30
409	A99	10fr multi	.35	.30
410	A124	20fr multi	.25	.25
411	A108	20fr multi	.25	.25
412	A108	30fr multi	.40	.25
		Nos. 408-412 (5)	1.60	1.35

Apollo-Soyuz — A125

1980, Apr. 8 *Perf. 13½*

413	A125	40fr Viking Satellite	.55	.25
414	A125	50fr Apollo-Soyuz	.65	.25
415	A125	60fr Voyager	.75	.25
416	A125	100fr European Space Agency emblem, flags	1.25	.30
		Nos. 413-416,C221-C222 (6)	6.70	2.00

Walking, Olympic Medal, Moscow '80 Emblem — A126

1980, July 25 Litho. *Perf. 13½*

417	A126	30fr shown	.50	.25
418	A126	40fr Relay race	.55	.25
419	A126	70fr Running	.75	.25
420	A126	80fr High jump	.90	.25
		Nos. 417-420,C231-C232 (6)	5.30	1.65

For overprints see Nos. 462-465, C248-C250.

Fruit — A126a

1980, Aug. 1 Litho. *Perf. 13½*

420A	A126a	40fr multicolored		
420B	A126a	70fr green & multi	—	—

Agricultural Development A127

40fr, Telecommunications. 70fr, Engineering. 100fr, Civil engineering.

1980, Nov. 4 Litho. *Perf. 13½*

421	A127	30fr shown	.30	.25
422	A127	40fr multicolored	.50	.25
423	A127	70fr multicolored	.90	.25
424	A127	100fr multicolored	1.10	.40
		Nos. 421-424,C234-C235 (6)	6.20	2.25

Europe-Africa cooperation.

Nos. 403-407 Overprinted in Black

1980, Nov. 12 *Perf. 14½*

425	A123	50fr multi	.55	.25
426	A123	125fr multi	1.10	.40
427	A123	200fr multi	1.90	.55
428	A123	300fr multi	3.60	.90
429	A123	500fr multi	5.00	1.60
		Nos. 425-429 (5)	12.15	3.70

Virgin and Child, by Raphael — A128

Christmas: Paintings by Raphael.

1980, Dec. 20 *Perf. 12½*

430	A128	60fr multi	.65	.25
431	A128	150fr multi	1.60	.60
432	A128	250fr multi	3.00	1.10
		Nos. 430-432 (3)	5.25	1.95

African Postal Union, 5th Anniversary A129

1980, Dec. 24 Photo. *Perf. 13½*

433	A129	70fr multi	.85	.45

Peruvian Soccer Team, Soccer Cup — A130

1981, Jan. 13 Litho. *Perf. 13½*

434	A130	10fr shown	.25	.25
435	A130	15fr Scotland	.25	.25
436	A130	20fr Mexico	.30	.25
437	A130	25fr Sweden	.30	.25
438	A130	30fr Austria	.40	.25
439	A130	40fr Poland	.50	.25
440	A130	50fr France	.55	.25
441	A130	60fr Italy	.65	.25
442	A130	70fr Germany	.75	.25
443	A130	80fr Brazil	.90	.25
		Nos. 434-443,C237-C238 (12)	7.60	3.30

ESPANA '82 World Cup Soccer Championship.

13th World Telecommunications Day — A131

1981, May 17 Litho. *Perf. 12½*

444	A131	150fr multi	1.40	.70

Apollo 15 Crew on Moon — A132

Space Exploration: Columbia space shuttle.

1981, June 10 Litho. *Perf. 14*

445	A132	100fr multi	.90	.30
446	A132	150fr multi	1.50	.40
447	A132	200fr multi	2.10	.60
448	A132	300fr multi	3.50	1.00
		Nos. 445-448 (4)	8.00	2.30

Souvenir Sheet

449	A132	500fr multi	5.00	1.60

Family of Acrobats with Monkey, by Picasso A133

Picasso Birth Cent.: 50fr, The Balcony. 80fr, The Artist's Son as Pierrot. 100fr, The Three Dancers.

1981, June 30 *Perf. 13½*

450	A133	40fr multi	.50	.25
451	A133	50fr multi	.65	.25
452	A133	80fr multi	1.10	.25
453	A133	100fr multi	1.40	.40
		Nos. 450-453,C245-C246 (6)	8.40	2.20

First Anniv. of Zimbabwe's Independence — A134

1981, July 9 Litho. *Perf. 12½*

454	A134	100fr multi	1.10	.45
455	A134	150fr multi	1.50	.55
456	A134	200fr multi	2.25	.70
		Nos. 454-456 (3)	4.85	1.70

Prince Charles and Lady Diana — A135

1981, July, 24 *Perf. 14*

457	A135	75fr Charles	.50	.25
458	A135	100fr Diana	.70	.25
459	A135	150fr St. Paul's Cathedral	1.20	.40
460	A135	175fr shown	1.50	.40
		Nos. 457-460 (4)	3.90	1.30

Souvenir Sheet

461	A135	500fr Couple	5.00	1.40

Royal Wedding.
For overprints see Nos. 529-533.

Nos. 417-420 Overprinted in Gold

1981	Litho.	*Perf. 13½*	
462 A126 30fr multi		.35	.25
463 A126 40fr multi		.50	.25
464 A126 70fr multi		.85	.30
465 A126 80fr multi		.85	.40
Nos. 462-465,C248-C249 (6)		4.95	1.85

Prince Charles and Lady Diana — A136

50fr, Crowned Prince of Wales. 80fr, Diana. 100fr, Naval training.

1981, Aug. 20	Litho.	*Perf. 13½*	
466 A136 40fr shown		.50	.25
467 A136 50fr multicolored		.50	.25
468 A136 80fr multicolored		.85	.30
469 A136 100fr multicolored		1.10	.40
Nos. 466-469,C251-C252 (6)		6.65	2.15

Royal wedding.

1906 Renault — A137

40fr, Mercedes-Benz, 1937. 50fr, Matra-Ford, 1969. 110fr, Tazio Nuvolari, 1927. 150fr, Jackie Stewart, 1965.
450fr, Finish line, 1914.

1981, Sept. 22	Litho.	*Perf. 12½*	
470 A137 20fr shown		.30	.25
471 A137 40fr multicolored		.65	.25
472 A137 50fr multicolored		.75	.25
473 A137 110fr multicolored		1.50	.40
474 A137 150fr multicolored		2.25	.55
Nos. 470-474 (5)		5.45	1.70

Souvenir Sheet

Perf. 10

475 A137 450fr multicolored	6.00	6.00

Grand Prix of France, 75th anniv.

World Food Day A138

1981, Oct. 16		
476 A138 90fr multi	.95	.30
477 A138 110fr multi	1.10	.40

Navigators and their Ships — A139

1981, Sept. 4	Litho.	*Perf. 13½*	
478 A139 40fr C.V. Rietschoten		.50	.30
479 A139 50fr M. Pajot		.55	.45
480 A139 60fr K. Jaworski		.75	.55
481 A139 80fr M. Birch		1.00	.60
Nos. 478-481,C254-C255 (6)		6.30	4.00

Downfall of Empire A140

5fr, Bayonet through crown. 25fr, Victory holding map. 90fr, Toppled Bokassa statue.

1981, Oct. 6		
482 A140 5fr multicolored	.25	.25
483 A140 10fr like #482	.25	.25
484 A140 25fr multicolored	.30	.25
485 A140 60fr like #484	.75	.25
486 A140 90fr multicolored	1.10	.40
487 A140 500fr like #486	4.75	2.00
Nos. 482-487 (6)	7.40	3.40

Komba — A141

1981, Nov. 17		
488 A141 50fr shown	.65	.25
489 A141 90fr Dodoro, horiz.	1.25	.30
490 A141 140fr Kaya, horiz.	2.10	.40
Nos. 488-490 (3)	4.00	.95

Central African States Bank A142

1981, Dec. 12	Litho.	*Perf. 12½x13*	
491 A142 90fr multi		1.00	.30
492 A142 110fr multi		1.10	.40

Christmas 1981 — A143

Virgin and Child Paintings: 50fr, Fra Angelico, 1430. 60fr, Cosimo Tura, 1484. 90fr, Bramantino. 110fr, Memling.

1981, Dec. 24		
493 A143 50fr multicolored	1.00	.30
494 A143 60fr multicolored	1.10	.40
495 A143 90fr multicolored	1.75	.45
496 A143 110fr multicolored	2.25	.70
Nos. 493-496,C260-C261 (6)	13.10	3.00

Scouting Year — A144

100fr, Hiking. 150fr, Scouts, horiz. 200fr, Leaning against railing. 300fr, Salute, flag, vert.
500fr, Scout, Baden-Powell, vert.

1982, Jan. 13	*Perf. 12½*	
497 A144 100fr multicolored	1.25	.40
498 A144 150fr multicolored	1.90	.55
499 A144 200fr multicolored	2.75	.80
500 A144 300fr multicolored	3.75	1.25
Nos. 497-500 (4)	9.65	3.00

Souvenir Sheet

Perf. 13

501 A144 500fr multicolored	6.25	1.60

Elephant A145

1982, Jan. 22	*Perf. 13½*	
502 A145 60fr shown	.90	.25
503 A145 90fr Giraffes	1.10	.30
504 A145 100fr Addaxes	1.25	.30
505 A145 110fr Okapi	1.50	.45
Nos. 502-505,C263-C264 (6)	13.50	3.35

Norman Rockwell Illustrations A146

30fr, Grandfather snowman. 60fr, Croquet players. 110fr, Women talking. 150fr, Searching.

1982, Feb. 17	*Perf. 13½x14*	
506 A146 30fr multicolored	.30	.25
507 A146 60fr multicolored	.75	.30
508 A146 110fr multicolored	1.25	.40
509 A146 150fr multicolored	1.75	.55
Nos. 506-509 (4)	4.05	1.50

AT 16 Dirigible A147

10fr, Beyer-Garrat locomotive. 20fr, Bugatti 24 "Royale," 1924. 110fr, Vickers "Valentia," 1928.

1982, Feb. 27	Litho.	*Perf. 13½*	
510 A147 5fr shown		.25	.25
511 A147 10fr multicolored		.25	.25
512 A147 20fr multicolored		.30	.25
513 A147 110fr multicolored		1.40	.40
Nos. 510-513,C266-C267 (6)		11.45	3.20

Bellvue Garden, by Edouard Manet — A148

Anniversaries: 400fr, Goethe, vert. Nos. 519-520, Princess Diana, 21st birthday, July 1, vert. 300fr, George Washington, vert.

1982, Apr. 6	Litho.	*Perf. 13*	
517 A148 200fr multi		3.25	1.00
517A A148 300fr multi		3.00	1.00
518 A148 400fr multi		4.00	1.25
519 A148 500fr multi		5.00	2.00
Nos. 517-519 (4)		15.25	5.25

Souvenir Sheet

520 A148 500fr multi	5.50	1.40

23rd Olympic Games, Los Angeles, 1984 — A149

1982, July 24	Litho.	*Perf. 13½*	
521 A149 5fr Soccer		.25	.25
522 A149 10fr Boxing		.25	.25
523 A149 20fr Running		.30	.25
524 A149 110fr Long jump		1.00	.30
Nos. 521-524,C269-C270 (6)		9.80	3.25

21st Birthday of Princess Diana — A150

Portraits.

1982, July 20	Litho.	*Perf. 13½*	
525 A150 5fr multi		.25	.25
526 A150 10fr multi		.25	.25
527 A150 20fr multi		.30	.25
528 A150 110fr multi		1.00	.30
Nos. 525-528,C272-C273 (6)		10.55	3.25

Nos. 457-461 Overprinted in Blue

1982, Aug. 20	*Perf. 14*	
529 A135 75fr multi	.55	.25
530 A135 110fr multi	.75	.40
531 A135 150fr multi	1.40	.55
532 A135 175fr multi	2.25	.80
Nos. 529-532 (4)	4.95	2.00

Souvenir Sheet

533 A135 500fr multi	5.50	3.75

Birth of Prince William of Wales, June 21.

2nd UN Conference on Peaceful Uses of Outer Space, Vienna, Aug. 9-21 — A151

Various satellites and space scenes.

1982, Aug. 15	Litho.	*Perf. 13½*	
534 A151 5fr multi		.25	.25
535 A151 10fr multi		.25	.25
536 A151 20fr multi		.30	.25
537 A151 110fr multi		1.00	.30
Nos. 534-537,C277-C278 (6)		9.80	3.25

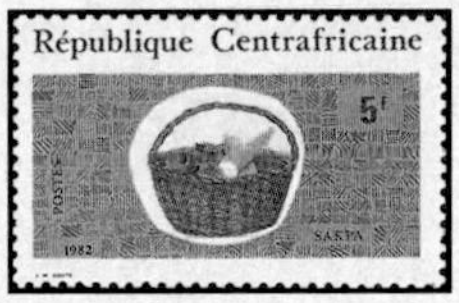

Sakpa Basket
A152

Baskets and bowls: 25fr, Ngbenda gourd, vert. 120fr, Ta ti ngou jugs. 175fr, Kangu bowls. 300fr, Kolongo bowls, vert.

1982, Sept. 2 ***Perf. 13***

538	A152	5fr shown	.25	.25
539	A152	10fr like 5fr	.25	.25
540	A152	25fr multicolored	.30	.25
541	A152	60fr like 25fr	.75	.25
542	A152	120fr multicolored	1.60	.40
543	A152	175fr multicolored	1.75	.60
544	A152	300fr multicolored	3.50	1.25
		Nos. 538-544 (7)	8.40	3.25

For surcharges see Nos. 792A-792B.

1982 World Cup Soccer Championships, Spain — A152a

Various soccer plays.

1982, Sept. Litho. ***Perf. 13½x13***

Overprinted in Silver or Gold

545	A152a	60fr Italy, 1st, 2nd	.90	.25
546	A152a	150fr Poland, 3rd	1.75	.55
547	A152a	300fr France, 4th	3.50	1.25
		Nos. 545-547 (3)	6.15	2.05

Souvenir Sheet

548	A152a	500fr Italy, 1st (G)	5.75	1.40

Not issued without overprint.

13th World UPU Day — A153

1982, Oct. 9

549	A153	60fr multi	.60	.25
550	A153	120fr multi	1.40	.45

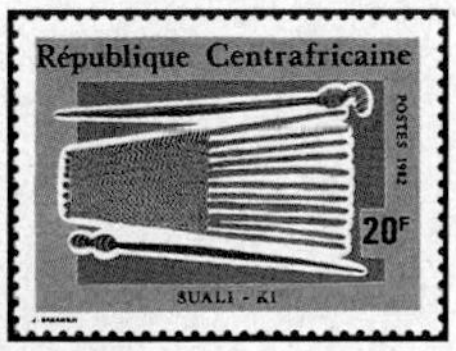

Comb and Hairpins
A154

1982, Oct. 20 ***Perf. 13x12½***

551	A154	20fr multi	.25	.25
552	A154	30fr multi	.40	.25
553	A154	60fr multi	.75	.30
554	A154	80fr multi	1.10	.40
555	A154	120fr multi	1.50	.45
		Nos. 551-555 (5)	4.00	1.65

Artist Pierre Ndarata and No.69
A155

1982, Oct. ***Perf. 13***

556	A155	40fr Jean Tubind at easel, vert.	.25	.25
557	A155	70fr shown	.45	.25
558	A155	90fr like 70fr	.55	.25
559	A155	140fr like 40fr	1.00	.35
		Nos. 556-559 (4)	2.25	1.10

TB Bacillus Centenary
A156

1982, Nov. 30 ***Perf. 13½x13***

560	A156	100fr vio & blk	1.40	.30
561	A156	120fr red org & blk	1.60	.45
562	A156	175fr bl & blk	2.25	.80
		Nos. 560-562 (3)	5.25	1.55

10th Anniv. of UN Conference on Human Environment
A157

1982, Dec. 8

563	A157	120fr multi	1.40	.40
564	A157	150fr multi	1.50	.55
565	A157	300fr multi	3.00	1.00
		Nos. 563-565 (3)	5.90	1.95

Granary
A158

1982, Dec. 15 ***Perf. 13***

566	A158	60fr multi	.65	.25
567	A158	80fr multi	1.00	.40
568	A158	120fr multi	1.40	.60
569	A158	200fr multi	2.40	1.20
		Nos. 566-569 (4)	5.45	2.45

A159

1982, Dec.

570	A159	100fr multi	1.00	.40
571	A159	120fr multi	1.40	.45

ITU Plenipotentiaries Conf., Nairobi, Sept.

A160

5fr, Modes of communication. 120fr, Map, jet.

1983, Jan. 31 Litho. ***Perf. 13½x13***

572	A160	5fr multicolored	.25	.25
573	A160	60fr like 5fr	.75	.30
574	A160	120fr multicolored	1.40	.40
575	A160	175fr like 120fr	1.75	.55
		Nos. 572-575 (4)	4.15	1.50

UN Decade for African Transportation and Communication, 1978-88.

Chess Champions — A161

Men and Chess Pieces: 5fr, Steinitz, first world champion, 1886. 10fr, Aaron Niemzovitch, castle. 20fr, Alexander Alekhine, knights. 110fr, Botvinnik. 300fr, Boris Spassky, glass pieces. 500fr, Bobby Fischer, king, knight. 600fr, Korchnoi, Karpov, pawn. No. 582A, Bobby Fischer. No. 582B, Reti, Larsen, Petrossian, and Mecking, horiz.

1983, Jan. 15

576	A161	5fr multi	.25	.25
577	A161	10fr multi	.25	.25
578	A161	20fr multi	.35	.25
579	A161	110fr multi	1.40	.25
580	A161	300fr multi	3.75	.75
581	A161	500fr multi	5.50	1.40
		Nos. 576-581 (6)	11.50	3.15

Souvenir Sheet

582	A161	600fr multi	7.00	2.00

Litho. & Embossed

Perf. 13½

Size: 35x60mm

582A	A161	1500fr gold & multi	42.50	3.50

Souvenir Sheet

582B	A161	1500fr gold & multi	10.00	10.00

No. 582 contains one 56x33mm stamp, No. 582B one 35x60mm stamp. 300fr, 500fr, 600fr, Nos. 582A and 582B are airmail.

Marshal Tito (1892-1980)
A162

20fr, George Washington.

1983, Jan. 22

583	A162	20fr multicolored	.25	.25
a.		Souvenir sheet	5.50	—
584	A162	110fr shown	1.25	.30
a.		Souvenir sheet	5.50	—

1982 World Cup Soccer Championships, Spain — A162a

Trophy, flags, scores, players: 5fr, Hamilton, Pezzey. 10fr, Borovski, Boniek. 20fr, Littbarski, Zamora. 110fr, Zico, Passarella. 300fr, Rossi, Smolarek. 500fr, Rummenigge, Giresse. 600fr, Rossi, Rummenigge. No. 584I, Platini. No. 584J, Rossi.

1983, Feb. 8 Litho. ***Perf. 13½***

584B	A162a	5fr multi	.25	.25
584C	A162a	10fr multi	.25	.25
584D	A162a	20fr multi	.40	.25
584E	A162a	110fr multi	1.50	.30
584F	A162a	300fr multi	3.25	.70
584G	A162a	500fr multi	5.50	1.40
		Nos. 584B-584G (6)	11.15	3.15

Souvenir Sheet

584H	A162a	600fr multi	5.50	4.25

Litho. & Embossed

584I	A162a	1500fr gold & multi	35.00	6.50

Souvenir Sheet

584J	A162a	1500fr gold & multi	10.00	10.00

Nos. 584F-584J are airmail.

Easter 1983
A163

Rembrandt Paintings: 100fr, Entombment. 300fr, Crucifixion. 400fr, Descent from the Cross.

1983, Apr. 16

585	A163	100fr multicolored	1.00	.40
586	A163	300fr multicolored	3.00	1.25
587	A163	400fr multicolored	4.00	1.75
		Nos. 585-587 (3)	8.00	3.40

Vintage Cars and their Makers
A164

A164a

Designs: 10fr, Emile Levassor, Rene Panhard, 1895 car. 20fr, Henry Ford, 1896 car. 30fr, Louis Renault, 1899 car. 80fr, Ettore Bugatti, type 37, 1925. 400fr, Enzo Ferrari, 815 sport, 1940. 500fr, Ferdinand Porsche, 356 coupe, 1951. 600fr, Karl Benz, velocipede, 1886. No. 594A, F.H. Royce and C.S. Rolls, 1911 Rolls-Royce Silver Ghost. No. 594B, G. Daimler, 1900 Mercedes 35CV.

1983, June 3 Litho. ***Perf. 13½***

588	A164	10fr multi	.25	.25
589	A164	20fr multi	.25	.25
590	A164	30fr multi	.30	.25
591	A164	80fr multi	1.00	.30
592	A164	400fr multi	4.50	1.10
593	A164	500fr multi	5.50	1.40
		Nos. 588-593 (6)	11.80	3.55

Souvenir Sheet

594	A164	600fr multi	5.75	1.60

Litho. & Embossed

594A	A164a	1500fr gold & multi	25.00	4.00

Souvenir Sheet

594B	A164a	1500fr gold & multi	10.00	6.00

Nos. 592-594B are airmail.

25th Anniv. of Intl. Maritime Org. — A165

1983, July 8 Litho. ***Perf. 12½x13***

595	A165	40fr multi	.50	.25
596	A165	100fr multi	1.00	.40

World Communications Year — A166

1983, July 22

597	A166	50fr multi	.50	.25
598	A166	130fr multi	1.40	.45

Pre-Olympics, Los Angeles A167

1984 Summer Olympics, Los Angeles A167a

5fr, Gymnast. 40fr, Javelin throwing. 60fr, Pole vault. 120fr, Fencing. 200fr, Cycling. 300fr, Sailing.

600fr, Handball. No. 605A, 1500fr, Shot put. No. 605B, 1500fr, Dressage, horiz.

1983, Aug. 3 Litho. *Perf. 13*

599	A167	5fr multi	.25	.25
600	A167	40fr multi	.40	.25
601	A167	60fr multi	.65	.25
602	A167	120fr multi	1.40	.30
603	A167	200fr multi	2.25	.40
604	A167	300fr multi	3.25	.80
		Nos. 599-604 (6)	8.20	2.25

Souvenir Sheet

605	A167	600fr multi	5.00	1.60

Litho. & Embossed

Perf. 13½

605A	A167a	1500fr multi	35.00	3.50

Souvenir Sheet

605B	A167a	1500fr multi	10.00	10.00

Nos. 603-605B are airmail.

Namibia Day — A168

1983, Sept. 16 Litho. *Perf. 13*

606	A168	100fr multi	1.10	.40
607	A168	200fr multi	1.90	.80

Manned Flight Bicentenary — A169

A169a

Designs: 50fr, J. Montgolfier and his balloon, 1783. 100fr, J.P. Blanchard, English Channel crossing, 1785. 200fr, L.-J. Gay-Lussac, 4000-meter balloon ascent, 1804. 300fr, Giffard and his dirigible, 1852. 400fr, Santos Dumont, dirigible, Eiffel Tower. 500fr, A. Laquot, captive observation balloon, 1914. 600fr, J.A. Charles, first gas balloon; G. Tissandier, dirigible, 1883. No. 614, Marquis d'Arlandes and Jean Francois Pilatre de Rozier, Montgolfier balloon. No. 614B, Ferdinand von Zeppelin, Graf Zeppelin, horiz.

1983, Sept. 30 Litho. *Perf. 13½*

608	A169	50fr multi	.50	.25
609	A169	100fr multi	1.10	.40
610	A169	200fr multi	2.50	.80
611	A169	300fr multi	3.25	1.10
612	A169	400fr multi	4.25	1.50
613	A169	500fr multi	5.75	1.90
		Nos. 608-613 (6)	17.35	5.95

Souvenir Sheet

614	A169	600fr multi	5.50	1.40

Litho. & Embossed

614A	A169a	1500fr gold & multi	37.50	4.00

Souvenir Sheet

614B	A169a	1500fr gold & multi	10.00	10.00

Nos. 612-614B are airmail.

Black Rhinoceros and World Wildlife Emblem — A170

Various black rhinoceroses.

1983, Nov. 14

615	A170	10fr multi	1.25	.50
616	A170	40fr multi	1.50	.75
617	A170	70fr multi	2.25	1.00
618	A170	180fr multi	6.75	2.00
		Nos. 615-618 (4)	11.75	4.25

Nos. 615-618 were issued in support of the World Wildlife Fund.

See Nos. C291A-C293.

UPU Day, World Communications Year — A171

1983, Nov. 2 Litho. *Perf. 13*

619	A171	205fr multi	2.00	.90

2nd Anniv. of the Natl. Military Committee A172

Gen. Andre Kolingba, head of state.

1983, Sept. 1 *Perf. 12½*

620	A172	65fr sil & multi	.55	.25
621	A172	130fr gold & multi	1.40	.45

Earth Satellite Receiving Station, Bangui M'Poko — A173

1983 *Perf. 13*

622	A173	130fr multi	1.40	.55

Natl. Day of the Handicapped and the Elderly — A174

1983, Dec. 20 Engr. *Perf. 13x12½*

623	A174	65fr vio & org	.55	.30
624	A174	130fr ultra & org	1.10	.45
625	A174	205fr dk grn & org	1.75	.80
		Nos. 623-625 (3)	3.40	1.55

Fishing Resources A175

1983, Dec. 31 Litho. *Perf. 12½*

626	A175	25fr Breeding tank	.25	.25
627	A175	65fr Net fishing	1.10	.25
628	A175	100fr Dam fishing	1.25	.40
629	A175	130fr Still life with fish	2.50	.70
630	A175	205fr Basket trap	2.75	.70
		Nos. 626-630 (5)	7.85	2.30

Wildlife Protection — A176

1984, Jan. 25 *Perf. 13*

631	A176	30fr Forest fire	3.50	.40
632	A176	130fr Hunters	5.00	1.10

CC-1500 Locomotive — A177

110fr, CC-1500 locomotive. 240fr, PLM series 210, 1868. 350fr, 231-726 locomotive, 1937. 440fr, Pacific S3/6, 1908. 500fr, Henschel 151 series 45, 1937.

1984, July 16 Litho. *Perf. 12½*

633	A177	110fr multicolored	1.40	.30
634	A177	240fr multicolored	3.00	.85
635	A177	350fr multicolored	4.25	1.10
636	A177	440fr multicolored	5.75	1.25
637	A177	500fr multicolored	6.75	1.60
		Nos. 633-637 (5)	21.15	5.10

For overprints see Nos. 702, 704.

Packet Ship Pericles — A177a

120fr, Three-master Pereire. 250fr, Admella. 400fr, Royal William. 500fr, Great Britain.

1984, July 23 Litho. *Perf. 12½*

638	A177a	65fr shown	.90	.30
639	A177a	120fr multicolored	1.40	.55
640	A177a	250fr multicolored	3.00	1.10
641	A177a	400fr multicolored	5.50	1.90
642	A177a	500fr multicolored	6.25	2.40
		Nos. 638-642 (5)	17.05	6.25

For overprints see Nos. 701, 703.

J. W. Goethe, Scene from Faust A178

Designs: 100fr, Henri Dunant, Red Cross Founder, Battle of Solferino, 125th anniv. 200fr, Alfred Nobel, Nobel Foundation headquarters. 300fr, Lord Baden-Powell, World Scouting Jamboree, Alberta, 1983. 400fr, John F. Kennedy, first man on the Moon, 1969. 500fr, 600fr, wedding of Prince and Princess of Wales.

1984, Feb. 25 Litho. *Perf. 13½*

643	A178	50fr multi	.55	.25
644	A178	100fr multi	1.10	.40
645	A178	200fr multi	2.50	.55
646	A178	300fr multi	3.25	1.10
647	A178	400fr multi	4.50	1.10
648	A178	500fr multi	5.50	1.10
		Nos. 643-648 (6)	17.40	4.50

Souvenir Sheet

649	A178	600fr multi	5.00	1.40

Nos. 647-649 are airmail.

Old Masters A179

Paintings: 50fr, Madonna and Child, by Raphael. 100fr, Madonna with Pear, by Durer. 200fr, Aldobrandini Madonna, by Raphael. 300fr, Madonna with Carnation, by Durer. 400fr, Virgin and Child, by Correggio. 500fr, La Bohemienne, by Modigliani. 600fr, Madonna and Child on the Throne, by Raphael.

1984, Mar. 30 Litho. *Perf. 13½*

650	A179	50fr multi	.60	.25
651	A179	100fr multi	1.10	.25
652	A179	200fr multi	2.50	.45
653	A179	300fr multi	3.50	.85

654 A179 400fr multi 4.75 1.90
655 A179 500fr multi 5.75 2.50
Nos. 650-655 (6) 18.20 6.20

Miniature Sheet

656 A179 600fr multi 5.50 1.40

No. 656 contains 1 stamp, size 30x59mm.
Nos. 654-656 are airmail.

Space — A180

20fr, Galileo, Ariane rocket. 70fr, Piccard, X-15, balloon. 150fr, Oberth, satellite. 205fr, Einstein, satellites. 300fr, Curie, Viking vehicle. 500fr, Merbold, Spacelab.
600fr, Armstrong, Apollo 11, horiz.

1984, Aug. 6 Litho. ***Perf. 13½***

657 A180 20fr multicolored .30 .25
658 A180 70fr multicolored .75 .25
659 A180 150fr multicolored 1.50 .45
660 A180 205fr multicolored 2.25 .55
661 A180 300fr multicolored 3.50 .80
662 A180 500fr multicolored 5.00 1.00
Nos. 657-662 (6) 13.30 3.30

Miniature Sheet

663 A180 600fr multicolored 5.00 1.50

No. 663 contains 1 stamp, size: 42x66mm.
300fr, 500fr and 600fr are airmail.

Forestry Resources A181

1984, Oct. 9 Litho. ***Perf. 13x12½***

664 A181 70fr Forest 1.00 .30
665 A181 130fr Logging 2.00 .55

UNICEF — A182

1984, Oct. 27 Litho. ***Perf. 13x12½***

666 A182 10fr Weighing child .25 .25
667 A182 30fr Vaccinating child .50 .30
668 A182 65fr Giving liquids .60 .40
669 A182 100fr Balancing diet 1.25 .55
Nos. 666-669 (4) 2.60 1.50

Fishing Traps A183

1984, Nov. 6 Litho. ***Perf. 13***

670 A183 50fr Bangui-Kette .85 .30
671 A183 80fr Mbres 1.10 .55
672 A183 150fr Bangui-Kette 2.50 .90
Nos. 670-672 (3) 4.45 1.75

Mushrooms A184

5fr, Leptoporus lignosus. 10fr, Phlebopus sudanicus. 40fr, Termitomyces letestui. 130fr, Lepiota esculenta. 300fr, Termitomyces aurantiacus. 500fr, Termitomyces robustus.
600fr, Tricholoma- lobayensis.

1984, Nov. 15 Litho. ***Perf. 13½***

673 A184 5fr multicolored .25 .25
674 A184 10fr multicolored .25 .25
675 A184 40fr multicolored .75 .30
676 A184 130fr multicolored 2.25 .30
677 A184 300fr multicolored 3.50 .80
678 A184 500fr multicolored 6.25 1.25
Nos. 673-678 (6) 13.25 3.15

Souvenir Sheet

679 A184 600fr multicolored 6.50 2.00

Nos. 677-679 are airmail.

1984 Winter Olympics, Sarajevo A184a

Gold medalists, communications satellite and events: 30fr, Gaetan Boucher, Canada, 1000 and 1500-meter speed skating. 90fr, W. Hoppe, R. Wetzig, D. Schauerhammer and A. Kirchner, German Democratic Republic, 4-man bobsled. 140fr, Paoletta Magoni, Italy, women's slalom. 200fr, Jayne Torvill and Christopher Dean, Great Britain, ice dancing. 400fr, Matti Nykaenen, Finland, 90-meter ski jumping. 500fr, USSR, ice hockey. 600fr, Bill Johnson, US, men's downhill.

1984, Nov. 30 Litho. ***Perf. 13½***

679A A184a 30fr multi .30 .25
679B A184a 90fr multi 1.00 .30
679C A184a 140fr multi 1.50 .40
679D A184a 200fr multi 2.25 .55
679E A184a 400fr multi 4.00 1.00
679F A184a 500fr multi 5.25 1.25
Nos. 679A-679F (6) 14.30 3.75

Souvenir Sheet

679G A184a 600fr multi 5.50 1.60

Nos. 679E-679G are airmail.

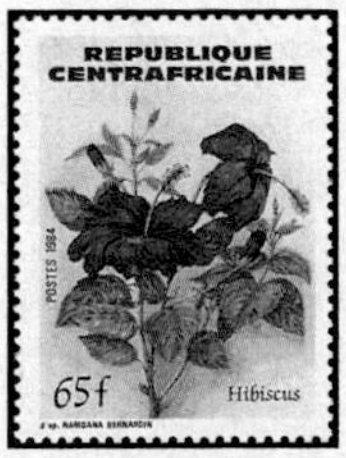

Flowers — A185

65fr, Hibiscus. 130fr, Canna Indica. 205fr, Eichlornia Crassipes.

1984, Nov. 22 Litho. ***Perf. 13½***

680 A185 65fr multicolored 1.10 .40
681 A185 130fr multicolored 1.90 .50
682 A185 205fr multicolored 3.00 1.00
Nos. 680-682 (3) 6.00 1.90

Economic Campaign — A186

25fr, Cotton planting. 40fr, Selling cotton crop. 130fr, Cotton market.

1984, Dec. 3 Litho. ***Perf. 13½***

683 A186 25fr multicolored .40 .25
684 A186 40fr multicolored .65 .40
685 A186 130fr multicolored 1.70 .55
Nos. 683-685 (3) 2.75 1.20

World Food Day A187

1984, Dec. 10 Litho. ***Perf. 13½***

686 A187 205fr Picking corn 2.50 .90

OLYMPHILEX '85 — A188

Publicity posters from previous Games and host city landmarks: 5fr, Stockholm, 1912. 10fr, Paris, 1924. 20fr, London, 1948. 100fr, Tokyo, 1964. 400fr, Mexico. 500fr, Munich, 1972.
600fr, Athens, 1896, Baron Pierre de Coubertin.

1985, Mar 18 Litho. ***Perf. 13½***

687 A188 5fr multicolored .25 .25
688 A188 10fr multicolored .25 .25
689 A188 20fr multicolored .30 .25
690 A188 100fr multicolored 5.25 1.00
691 A188 400fr multicolored 2.25 .45
692 A188 500fr multicolored 2.75 .55
Nos. 687-692 (6) 11.05 2.75

Souvenir Sheet

693 A188 600fr multicolored 5.50 1.50

Nos. 691-693 are airmail. No. 693 contains one 60x30mm stamp.

Anniversaries and Events — A189

Famous men: 50fr, Abraham Lincoln, American Civil War soldiers. 90fr, Auguste Piccard (1884-1962), inventor, bathyscaphe Trieste. 120fr, Gottlieb Daimler (1834-1900), 1938 Mercedes Type 540. 200fr, Louis Bleriot (1872-1936), inventor, plane. 350fr, Anatoly Karpov, world chess champion. 400fr, Jean Henri Dunant (1828-1910), Red Cross founder, worker caring for wounded soldier.

1984, Dec. 22 Litho. ***Perf. 13½***

694 A189 50fr multi .55 .25
695 A189 90fr multi 1.00 .30
696 A189 120fr multi 1.60 .40
697 A189 200fr multi 2.50 .55
698 A189 350fr multi 3.75 .80
698A A189 400fr multi 3.75 .90
Nos. 694-698A (6) 13.15 3.20

Nos. 698-698A are airmail.

Souvenir Sheet

Queen Mother, 85th Birthday — A189a

1984 Litho. ***Perf. 13½***

698B A189a 600fr multi 5.50 1.60

Bangui Rotary Club and Water — A190

1984, Dec. 29

699 A190 130fr multi 1.90 .45
700 A190 205fr multi 2.75 .80

Nos. 635//641, C302A Overprinted with Exhibitions in Red

1985, Mar. 13 Litho. ***Perf. 12½***

701 A177 250fr Argentina '85, Buenos Aires (#640) 2.75 1.25
702 A177a 350fr Tsukuba Expo '85 (#635) 3.50 1.60
703 A177 400fr Italia '85, Rome (#641) 5.00 2.25
704 A177a 440fr Mophila '85, Hamburg (#636) 5.50 2.40
Nos. 701-704 (4) 16.75 7.50

Souvenir Sheet

Perf. 13½x13

705 AP89 500fr Olymphilex '85, Lausanne 5.50 5.50

500fr airmail.

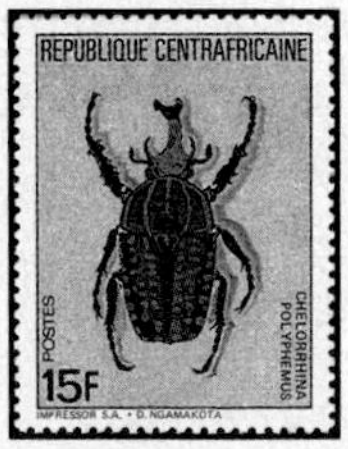

Beetles — A191

15fr, Chelorrhina polyphemus. 20fr, Fornasinius russus. 25fr, Goliathus giganteus. 65fr, Goliathus meleagris.

1985, Mar. Litho. ***Perf. 13½***

706 A191 15fr multicolored *.25 .25*
707 A191 20fr multicolored *.45 .25*
708 A191 25fr multicolored *.65 .25*
709 A191 65fr multicolored *1.50 .30*
Nos. 706-709 (4) *2.85 1.05*

Audubon Birth Bicentenary — A192

Illustrations of North American bird species by John Audubon: 40fr, Cyanocitta cristata. 80fr, Caprimulgus carolinensis. 130fr, Campephilus principales. 250fr, Calocitta formosa. 300fr, Coccizus minor, horiz. 500fr, Hirundo rustica, horiz.
600fr, Dryocopus pileatus, horiz.

1985, Mar. 25 Litho. *Perf. 13½*

710	A192	40fr multicolored	.90	.25
711	A192	80fr multicolored	1.25	.25
712	A192	130fr multicolored	2.40	.25
713	A192	250fr multicolored	3.25	.55
714	A192	300fr multicolored	3.50	.60
715	A192	500fr multicolored	5.75	1.10
		Nos. 710-715 (6)	17.05	3.00

Souvenir Sheet

716	A192	600fr multicolored	7.75	2.50

Nos. 714-716 are airmail.

Intl. Youth Year A193

Famous children's book authors and scenes from their best-known novels: 100fr, The Jungle Book, 1894, by Kipling, vert. 200fr, Les Cavaliers, 1967, by Joseph Kessel (1898-1979). 300fr, Twenty-Thousand Leagues Under the Sea, 1873, by Verne. 400fr, The Adventures of Tom Sawyer, 1876, by Twain.

1985, Apr. Litho. *Perf. 13*

718	A193	100fr multi	1.40	.45
719	A193	200fr multi	2.50	.85
720	A193	300fr multi	3.00	1.25
721	A193	400fr multi	4.50	2.10
		Nos. 718-721 (4)	11.40	4.65

Philexafrica '85, Lome — A194

No. 722, UPU emblem, Postmen unloading parcel post van. No. 723, Exhibition emblem, scout troop.

1985, May 15 *Perf. 13x12½*

722	A194	200fr multi	2.50	.90
723	A194	200fr multi	2.50	.90
a.		Pair, #722-723 + label	5.25	4.50

Rabies Vaccine Cent., Louis Pasteur (1822-95), Chemist, Microbiologist — A195

Anniversaries and events: 200fr, Battle of Solferino, founding of the Red Cross, 125th Anniv., founder Jean-Henri Dunant (1828-1910), horiz. 300fr, Girl Guides, 75th anniv. 450fr, Elizabeth, the Queen Mother, 85th birthday. 500fr, Statue of Liberty, cent.

1985, June *Perf. 13*

724	A195	150fr multi	2.50	.50
725	A195	200fr multi	3.00	.60
726	A195	300fr multi	2.50	.90
727	A195	450fr multi	4.50	1.50
728	A195	500fr multi	5.50	1.75
		Nos. 724-728 (5)	18.00	5.25

1986 World Cup Soccer Championships, Mexico — A196

Famous soccer players and match scenes: 5fr, Pele. 10fr, Tony Schumacher. 20fr, Paolo Rossi. 350fr, Kevin Keegan. 400fr, Michel Platini. 500fr, Karl Heinz Rummenigge.
600fr, Diego Armando Maradona.

1985, July 24 Litho. *Perf. 13½*

730	A196	5fr multicolored	.25	.25
731	A196	10fr multicolored	.25	.25
732	A196	20fr multicolored	.25	.25
733	A196	350fr multicolored	3.50	.90
734	A196	400fr multicolored	4.00	.90
735	A196	500fr multicolored	5.00	1.10
		Nos. 730-735 (6)	13.25	3.65

Souvenir Sheet

736	A196	600fr multicolored	5.00	1.40

Nos. 734-736 are airmail.

Kotto Waterfalls A197

1985, July 27 Litho. *Perf. 13½*

737	A197	65fr multi	1.00	.30
738	A197	90fr multi	1.10	.40
739	A197	130fr multi	1.75	.60
		Nos. 737-739 (3)	3.85	1.30

State Visit of Pope John Paul II — A198

Portraits.

1985, Aug. 14

740	A198	65fr multi	1.25	.40
741	A198	130fr multi	2.50	.80

Natl. Economic Development Campaign — A199

Designs: 5fr, Troops plowing. 60fr, Soldier preparing field for planting, vert. 130fr, Planting cotton seeds, vert.

1985, Sept. 1 *Perf. 13*

742	A199	5fr multi	.25	.25
743	A199	60fr multi	.75	.30
744	A199	130fr multi	1.50	.45
		Nos. 742-744 (3)	2.50	1.00

Queen Mother, 85th Birthday — A200

100fr, Age 4, with brother. 200fr, Duchess of York, 1923. 300fr, Reviewing Irish Guards, 1928. 350fr, Family portrait, 1936. 400fr, George VI coronation, 1937. 500fr, Wedding anniv., 1948.
600fr, Christening Prince Charles, 1948.

1985, Sept. 16 Litho. *Perf. 13½*

745	A200	100fr multicolored	.90	.25
746	A200	200fr multicolored	2.10	.35
747	A200	300fr multicolored	3.25	.70
748	A200	350fr multicolored	3.50	.75
749	A200	400fr multicolored	4.25	.90
750	A200	500fr multicolored	5.50	1.00
		Nos. 745-750 (6)	19.50	3.95

Souvenir Sheet

751	A200	600fr multicolored	4.50	1.40

Nos. 749-751 are airmail.

Dr. Rene Labusquiere (1919-1977), Promoter of Preventive Medicine — A201

1985, Sept. 22 Litho. *Perf. 13½*

752	A201	10fr multi	.25	.25
753	A201	45fr multi	.50	.25
754	A201	110fr multi	.75	.45
		Nos. 752-754 (3)	1.50	.95

Natl. Postal Service — A202

15fr, Loading mail van. 60fr, Bangui P.O., van. 150fr, Hdqtrs, Bangui, and vans.

1985, Oct. 9 *Perf. 12½*

755	A202	15fr multicolored	.25	.25
756	A202	60fr multicolored	.65	.25
757	A202	150fr multicolored	1.60	.80
		Nos. 755-757 (3)	2.50	1.30

Space Research — A203

Designs: 40fr, Yuri Gagarin, Soviet cosmonaut, and Sergei Korolev, rocket engineer. 110fr, Nicolaus Copernicus, Cassini probe. 240fr, Galileo, Viking orbiter. 300fr, Theodor von Karman (1881-1963), American aeronautical engineer, and space shuttle recovering Palapa B satellite. 450fr, Percival Lowell (1855-1916), American astronomer, and Viking probe. 500fr, Dr. U. Merbold and orbiting space station project Colombo. 600fr, Apollo 11 Project, first step on Moon by Neil Armstrong.

1985, Oct. 31 Litho. *Perf. 13½*

758	A203	40fr multi	.25	.25
759	A203	110fr multi	1.00	.30
760	A203	240fr multi	2.75	.55
761	A203	300fr multi	3.50	.80
762	A203	450fr multi	5.50	1.00
763	A203	500fr multi	6.00	1.10
		Nos. 758-763 (6)	19.00	4.00

Souvenir Sheet

Imperf

764	A203	600fr multi	5.00	1.40

Nos. 762-764 are airmail.

Solar Energy Apparatus, Damara A204

1985, Nov. 4 Litho. *Perf. 13½*

765	A204	65fr multi	.65	.30
766	A204	130fr multi	1.40	.55

Girl Guides Nature Study — A205

1985, Nov. 16 *Perf. 13*

767	A205	250fr shown	4.50	1.75
768	A205	250fr Quaka Sugar Refinery	4.50	1.75
a.		Pair, #767-768 + label	13.00	6.50

PHILEXAFRICA '85, Lome, Togo, 11/16-24.

State Visit of Pres. Mitterand of France, Dec. 12-13 — A206

1985-86 Litho. *Perf. 13x12½*

769	A206	65fr multi	.75	.25
770	A206	130fr multi	1.50	.55
770A	A206	160fr multi ('86)	2.10	.80
		Nos. 769-770A (3)	4.35	1.60

Issued: Nos. 769-770, Dec. 12.

UN 40th Anniv., Central Africa Admission, 25th Anniv. — A207

1985, Dec. 18 *Perf. 13½*

771 A207 140fr multi 1.40 .55

Intl. Youth Year A208

Designs: 40fr, David, by Andrea del Verrocchio; Madonna with the Carnation, 1470, by Leonardo da Vinci. 80fr, Johann Sebastian Bach. 100fr, St. John at Patmos, 1619, by Velazquez. 250fr, The Erl King score, by Franz Schubert. 400fr, Portrait of Vicente Osorio de Moscoso, by Goya. 500fr, The Young Mozart Playing in Paris, 1764. 600fr, Woman in a Plumed Hat, 1901, by Picasso.

1985, Dec. 28

772 A208 40fr multi .40 .25
773 A208 80fr multi .90 .25
774 A208 100fr multi 1.25 .25
775 A208 250fr multi 2.50 .55
776 A208 400fr multi 4.50 .90
777 A208 500fr multi 5.00 1.10
Nos. 772-777 (6) 14.55 3.30

Souvenir Sheet

778 A208 600fr multi 5.25 1.40

Nos. 776-778 are airmail.

Halley's Comet A209

100fr, Edmond Halley, British astronomer. 200fr, Sir Isaac Newton's telescope & comet sighting. 300fr, Halley & Newton observing comet. 350fr, US probe. 400fr, Soviet probe plotting comet's perihelion. 500fr, Isodensity photograph of comet. 600fr, Comet, Earth, Sun & probe.

1985, Dec. 31

779 A209 100fr multi .90 .30
780 A209 200fr multi 2.00 .45
781 A209 300fr multi 3.00 .90
782 A209 350fr multi 3.50 1.10
783 A209 400fr multi 4.25 1.00
784 A209 500fr multi 5.25 1.25
Nos. 779-784 (6) 18.90 5.00

Souvenir Sheet

785 A209 600fr multi 6.00 1.75

Nos. 783-785 are airmail.

Christopher Columbus — A210

Various events leading to the discovery of America and beyond: 90fr, Plotting course. 110fr, Receiving blessing. 240fr, Fleet in port. 300fr, Trade with natives. 400fr, Storm at sea. 500fr, Fleet at sea.
600fr, Portrait.

1986

786 A210 90fr multicolored 1.00 .30
787 A210 110fr multicolored 1.40 .45
788 A210 240fr multicolored 2.75 .60
789 A210 300fr multicolored 3.50 .90
790 A210 400fr multicolored 4.75 1.00
791 A210 500fr multicolored 5.50 2.40
Nos. 786-791 (6) 18.90 5.65

Souvenir Sheet

792 A210 600fr multicolored 6.50 1.75

Nos. 790-792 are airmail.

Nos. 543-544 Surcharged

No. 792A, Kangu bowls. No. 792B, Kolongo bowls.

1986, Apr. 1 **Litho.** *Perf. 13*

792A A152 30fr on 175fr
792B A152 65fr on 300fr

Hairstyles A211

1986, May 21 **Litho.** *Perf. 12½*

793 A211 20fr multi .45 .25
794 A211 30fr multi .55 .25
795 A211 65fr multi .80 .40
796 A211 160fr multi 2.75 .70
Nos. 793-796 (4) 4.55 1.60

France - Central Africa Week — A212

1986, May 26

797 A212 40fr Communications, horiz. .50 .25
798 A212 60fr Youth, horiz. .65 .30
799 A212 100fr Basket maker 1.40 .45
800 A212 130fr Bicycling 2.00 .60
Nos. 797-800 (4) 4.55 1.60

Centrapalm Palm Oil — A213

25fr, 65fr, Refinery, Bossongo, and palm tree. 120fr, 160fr, Refinery and palm tree.

1986, Aug. 12 **Litho.** *Perf. 13½*

801 A213 25fr multi .30 .25
802 A213 65fr multi .75 .40
803 A213 120fr multi, vert. 1.40 .80
804 A213 160fr multi, vert. 1.90 .60
Nos. 801-804 (4) 4.35 2.05

Dogs and Cats A214

10fr, Pointer. 20fr, Egyptian mau. 200fr, Newfoundland. 300fr, Borzoi. 400fr, Persian red.
500fr, Spaniel, Burmese-Malayan.

1986, Sept. 9

805 A214 10fr multicolored .25 .25
806 A214 20fr multicolored .50 .25
807 A214 200fr multicolored 3.00 .55
808 A214 300fr multicolored 3.75 .60
809 A214 400fr multicolored 5.50 .85
Nos. 805-809 (5) 13.00 2.50

Souvenir Sheet

810 A214 500fr multicolored 7.00 1.75

Nos. 808-810 are airmail.

African Coffee Producers Organization, 25th Anniv. — A215

1986, Sept. 25 **Litho.** *Perf. 13*

811 A215 160fr multi 1.60 .55

1986 World Cup Soccer Championships, Mexico — A216

Satellites, final scores, World Cup and athletes: 30fr, Muller, Socrates. 110fr, Scifo, Ceulemans. 160fr, Stopyra, Platini. 350fr, Brehme, Schumacher. 450fr, Maradona. 500fr, Schumacher, Burruchaga.

1986, Nov. 12 *Perf. 13½*

812 A216 30fr multi .30 .25
813 A216 110fr multi 1.00 .25
814 A216 160fr multi 1.40 .30
815 A216 350fr multi 3.25 .80
816 A216 450fr multi 4.50 1.10
Nos. 812-816 (5) 10.45 2.70

Souvenir Sheet

817 A216 500fr multi 5.50 1.40

Nos. 816-817 are airmail.

US Anniversaries and Events A217

15fr, Judith Resnik. 25fr, Frederic Auguste Bartholdi. 70fr, Elvis Presley. 300fr, Ronald McNair. 450fr, Christa McAuliffe. 500fr, Challenger Astronauts: McAuliffe, Scobee, Smith, Resnik, Onizuka, McNair, Jarvis.

1986, Nov. 19

818 A217 15fr multi .25 .25
819 A217 25fr multi .40 .25
820 A217 70fr multi 1.90 .25
821 A217 300fr multi 3.00 .60
822 A217 450fr multi 4.50 1.10
Nos. 818-822 (5) 10.05 2.45

Souvenir Sheet

823 A217 500fr multi 6.25 1.50

US space shuttle Challenger explosion; Statue of Liberty, cent. Nos. 822-823 are airmail.

For surcharges & overprint see Nos. 851-851B.

Flora and Fauna A218

25fr, Allamanda neriifolia. 65fr, Taurotragus eurycerus. 160fr, Plumieria acuminata. 300fr, Acinonyx jubatus. 400fr, Eulophia erthoplata. 500fr, Leopard.
600fr, Derby's eland, eulophia cucullata.

1986, May 30 **Litho.** *Perf. 13½*

824 A218 25fr multicolored .25 .25
825 A218 65fr multicolored .90 .25
826 A218 160fr multicolored 2.10 .30
827 A218 300fr multicolored 4.50 .80
828 A218 400fr multicolored 4.75 .90
829 A218 500fr multicolored 6.50 1.10
Nos. 824-829 (6) 19.00 3.60

Souvenir Sheet

830 A218 600fr multicolored 5.75 1.75

Nos. 824, 826, 828 vert. Nos. 828-830 are airmail. No. 830 contains one 51x30mm stamp.

Intl. Peace Year — A219

1986, Nov. 29

831 A219 160fr multi 2.00 .75

Air Africa, 25th Anniv. — A220

1986, Dec. 15

832 A220 200fr multi 1.90 .80

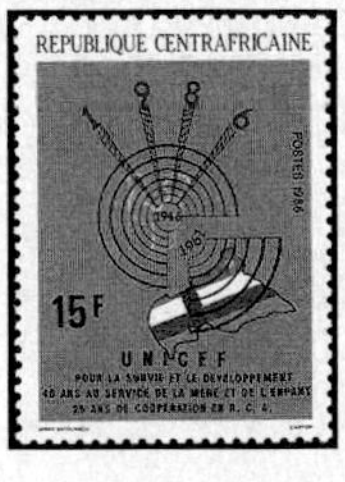

UNICEF, 40th Anniv. — A221

130fr, Child immunization. 160fr, Youth, food, map.

1986, Dec. 24

833 A221 15fr shown .25 .25
834 A221 130fr multicolored 1.50 .55
835 A221 160fr multicolored 1.75 .70
Nos. 833-835 (3) 3.50 1.50

German Railways Sesquicentenary — A222

Inventors and locomotives: 40fr, Alfred de Glehn, Prussian Railways DH2 Green Elephant. 70fr, Rudolf Diesel, S3/6 No. 1829 Rheingold. 160fr, Carl Golsdorf, Trans-Europe Express train Type 103. 300fr, Wilhelm Schmidt, Beyer Garratt locomotive. 400fr, Monsieur Du Bousquet, Series 3500 compound locomotive. 500fr, Werner von Siemens, 1980s electric locomotive.

1986, Dec. 31

836 A222 40fr multi .55 .25
837 A222 70fr multi 1.00 .25
838 A222 160fr multi 2.25 .40
839 A222 300fr multi 3.75 .60
840 A222 400fr multi 4.50 1.10
Nos. 836-840 (5) 12.05 2.60

Souvenir Sheet

841 A222 500fr multi 5.00 1.40

Nos. 840-841 are airmail. No. 841 contains one 42x36mm stamp.

Agriculture Radio Project A223

265fr, Satellite communication.

1986, Dec. 27 Litho. *Perf. 13½*

842 A223 170fr shown 2.25 .90
843 A223 265fr multicolored 3.25 1.40

Pan-African Telecommunications Union congress, Dec. 7, 1986.

No. 842 exists in souvenir sheet of one.

Space A224

Scientists and inventions: 25fr, Sir William Herschel (1738-1822), British astronomer, and Mariner Mark II. 65fr, Wernher von Braun (1912-1977), American engineer, and Mars rover. 160fr, Rudolf Hanel, Mariner Mark II and Titan. 300fr, Patrick Baudry, Hermes shuttle and Eureka platform. 400fr, U. Keller, Halley's Comet and Giotto probe. 500fr, Wubbo Ockels, Ulf Merbold and Columbus European Space Station. 600fr, Wilhelm Obers (1758-1840) and Mariner Mark II surveying asteroids. No. 850 horiz.

1987, Jan. 27

844 A224 25fr multi .35 .25
845 A224 65fr multi .75 .25
846 A224 160fr multi 1.75 .30
847 A224 300fr multi 3.00 .75
848 A224 400fr multi 3.25 .90
849 A224 500fr multi 4.00 1.25
Nos. 844-849 (6) 13.10 3.70

Souvenir Sheet

850 A224 600fr multi 6.25 1.75

Nos. 848-850 are airmail.

No. 820 Surcharged

1987, Feb. 20 Litho. *Perf. 13½*

851 A217 485fr on 70fr Elvis Presley 7.75 2.00

Nos. 820 and 851 Overprinted in Black

1987, Feb. 20 Litho. *Perf. 13½*

851A A217 70fr multi 1.40 .40
851B A217 485fr on 70fr multi 6.50 2.00

Overprint in red exists.

1992 Barcelona Olympics A225

Athletes and landmarks or sights: 30fr, Soccer player, Lady with Umbrella fountain. 150fr, Judo, Barcelona Cathedral. 265fr, Cyclist, Church of the Holy Family, by Gaudi. 350fr, Gymnast, Tomb of Columbus. 495fr, Runner, human tower. 500fr, Swimmer, Statue of Columbus.

1987, June 4

852 A225 30fr multi .40 .25
853 A225 150fr multi 1.40 .45
854 A225 265fr multi 2.50 .80
855 A225 350fr multi 3.50 1.00
856 A225 495fr multi 5.50 1.40
Nos. 852-856 (5) 13.30 3.90

Souvenir Sheet

857 A225 500fr multi 4.50 1.40

Nos. 855-857 are airmail.

A226

1988 Winter Olympics, Calgary — A227

20fr, Two-man luge. 140fr, Cross-country skiing. 250fr, Women's figure skating. 300fr, Hockey. 400fr, Men's slalom.

500fr, Downhill skiing.

1987, June 26

858 A226 20fr multicolored .30 .25
859 A226 140fr multicolored 1.40 .45
860 A226 250fr multicolored 2.25 .80
861 A226 300fr multicolored 3.00 .90
862 A226 400fr multicolored 3.75 1.10
Nos. 858-862 (5) 10.70 3.50

Souvenir Sheet

863 A227 500fr multicolored 4.50 1.40

Nos. 861-863 are airmail.

Intl. Peace Year — A228

1987, July 20

864 A228 50fr dull ultra, sepia & blk .50 .25
865 A228 160fr lt ol grn, sep & blk 1.40 .60

Intl. Decade of Drinkable Water — A228a

Designs: 5fr, Woman at village pump; 10fr, Two women at village pump; 200fr, Three women at village pump.

1987, Sept. 22 Litho. *Perf. 13½*

865A A228a 5fr multi 32.50 —
865B A228a 10fr multi 32.50 —
865C A228a 200fr multi 37.50 —
Nos. 865A-865C (3) 102.50

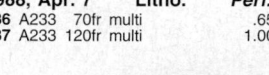

Butterflies A229

1987, Oct. 5 Litho. *Perf. 13½*

866 A229 100fr Charaxes candiope 2.00 .85
867 A229 120fr Graphium leonidas 2.75 .90
868 A229 130fr Charaxes brutus 3.00 .90
869 A229 160fr Salamis aetiops 3.25 1.10
Nos. 866-869 (4) 11.00 3.75

Pygmy Soccer Team from Nola — A230

1987, Nov. 30 Litho. *Perf. 13*

870 A230 90fr multi 1.50 .75
871 A230 160fr multi 2.25 1.25

Integration of the pygmy people into Central African society.

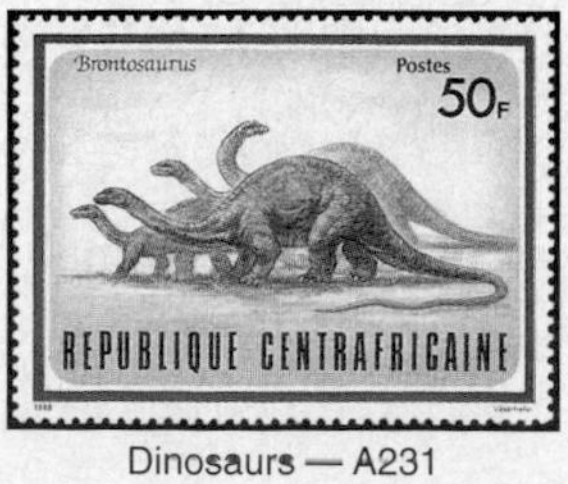

Dinosaurs — A231

Perf. 14x13½, 13½x14

1988, Mar. 19 Litho.

872 A231 50fr Brontosaurus .45 .25
873 A231 65fr Triceratops .80 .25
874 A231 100fr Ankylosaurus 1.10 .40
875 A231 160fr Stegosaurus 1.90 .60
876 A231 200fr Tyrannosaurus rex 2.00 .80
877 A231 240fr Corythosaurus 3.00 .90
878 A231 300fr Allosaurus 3.50 1.25
879 A231 350fr Brachiosaurus 4.25 1.50
Nos. 872-879 (8) 17.00 5.95

Nos. 876-879 vert.

Anniversaries and Events A232

Designs: 40fr, Pres. James Madison and "We the People..." from the US Constitution. 160fr, Elizabeth II and Duke of Edinburgh. 200fr, Steffi Graf, tennis champion. 300fr, Garri Kasparov of Russia, 1985 world chess champion. 400fr, Boris Becker, 1985-86 Wimbledon champion. 500fr, Christoph Willibald Gluck (1714-87), composer. Nos. 880-884 vert.

1988, Feb. 15 *Perf. 13½*

880 A232 40fr multi .40 .25
881 A232 160fr multi 1.50 .25
882 A232 200fr multi 1.90 .45
883 A232 300fr multi 3.00 .80
884 A232 400fr multi 3.50 1.25
Nos. 880-884 (5) 10.30 3.00

Souvenir Sheet

885 A232 500fr multi 6.25 1.75

US Constitution bicentennial (40fr); 40th wedding anniv. of Elizabeth II and Prince Philip (160fr). Nos. 883-885 are airmail.

World Health Organization, 40th Anniv. — A233

1988, Apr. 7 Litho. *Perf. 13½*

886 A233 70fr multi .65 .40
887 A233 120fr multi 1.00 .55

Scout Ornithological Activities A234

Scouts and: 25fr, *Merops nubicus*. 170fr, *Euplectes hordeacea*. 300fr, *Ceryle rudis*. 400fr, *Estrilda bengala*. 450fr, *Kaupifalco monogrammicus*. 500fr, *Lamprotornis splendidus*.

1988, July 1 Litho. *Perf. 13½*

888 A234 25fr multi .25 .25
889 A234 170fr multi 1.50 .70
890 A234 300fr multi 3.00 2.00
891 A234 400fr multi 4.25 2.00
892 A234 450fr multi 5.00 2.40
Nos. 888-892 (5) 14.00 7.35

Souvenir Sheet

893 A234 500fr multi 6.25 1.75

Nos. 891-893 are airmail.

For surcharges see Nos. 921-924.

1988 Summer Olympics, Seoul A235

1988, Sept. 30

894 A235 150fr Running, vert. 1.25 .25
895 A235 300fr Judo, vert. 2.75 .70
896 A235 400fr Soccer, vert. 3.00 1.00
897 A235 450fr Tennis, vert. 3.50 1.10
Nos. 894-897 (4) 10.50 3.05

Souvenir Sheet

898 A235 500fr Boxing 5.00 1.50

Nos. 896-898 are airmail.

1988 Winter Olympics, Calgary — A236

170fr, Cross-country skiing. 350fr, Ice hockey. 400fr, Downhill skiing. 460fr, Freestyle.

1988, Sept. 30 Litho. *Perf. 13½*

899 A236 170fr multicolored 1.40 .30
900 A236 350fr multicolored 2.25 .60
901 A236 400fr multicolored 3.00 .90
902 A236 450fr multicolored 3.25 1.00
Nos. 899-902 (4) 9.90 2.80

Souvenir Sheet

903 A236 500fr shown 5.50 1.50

Nos. 899-902 vert. Nos. 901-903 are airmail.

Natl. Arbor Day — A237

50fr, Students planting trees. 130fr, Forest (before and after).

1988, July 16 Litho. *Perf. 13½*

904 A237 50fr multicolored .50 .25
905 A237 100fr like 50fr 1.00 .55
906 A237 130fr multicolored 1.40 .60
Nos. 904-906 (3) 2.90 1.40

L'Amitie Hospital, 1st Anniv. A238

1988, Nov. 30

907 A238 5fr shown .25 .25
908 A238 60fr Aerial view .65 .40
909 A238 160fr Front gate 1.40 .80
Nos. 907-909 (3) 2.30 1.45

Proclamation of Central African Republic, 30th Anniv. A238a

Design: 65fr, 160fr, Dove, map, flag, people. 240fr, Government buildings, horiz.

1988 (?) Litho. *Perf. 13½*

909A A238a 65fr multi 52.50 —
909B A238b 160fr multi 52.50 —
909C A238a 240fr multi 52.50 —

A239

Olympic Medalists, Seoul, 1988: 150fr, Kristine Otto, DDR, swimming. 240fr, Matt Biondi, US, swimming. 300fr, Florence Griffith-Joyner, US, running. 450fr, Pierre Durand, France, equestrian. 600fr, Carl Lewis, US, running.

1989, Apr. 1

910 A239 150fr multi 2.25 .55
911 A239 240fr multi 3.50 .80
912 A239 300fr multi 4.50 1.10
913 A239 450fr multi 7.50 1.75
a. Souv. sheet of 4, #910-913 17.50
Nos. 910-913 (4) 17.75 4.20

Souvenir Sheet

914 A239 600fr multi 5.75 2.00

Nos. 913-914 airmail. No. 914 contains one 37x43mm stamp.

A240

Transportation Innovations, Inventors: 20fr, Hebmuller and 1953 Volkswagen Beetle. 205fr, Werner von Siemens (1816-1892) and 1879 Locomotive B. 300fr, Dennis Conner, skipper of *Stars and Stripes*, winner of the 1988 America's Cup. 400fr, Andre Citroen (1878-1935) and 1955 Citroen-15 SIX. 450fr, Marc Seguin (1786-1875) and 1895 Decauville-Mallet 020-020. 750fr, Frederick S. Duesenberg (1876-1932), brother August, US flag and 1929 J Phaeton.

1989, Apr. 10 Litho. *Perf. 13½*

915 A240 20fr multi .25 .25
916 A240 205fr multi 1.90 .55
917 A240 300fr multi 2.50 .60
918 A240 400fr multi 3.50 1.10
919 A240 450fr multi 4.50 1.25
Nos. 915-919 (5) 12.65 3.75

Souvenir Sheet

920 A240 750fr multi 6.25 1.50

Nos. 919-920 airmail. No. 920 contains one 43x37mm stamp.

Nos. 915-919 exist in souvenir sheets of 1.

Nos. 889-892 Surcharged in Black or Silver

1988, Oct. 7 Litho. *Perf. 13½*

921 A234 30fr on 170fr (B) .40 .25
922 A234 70fr on 300fr 1.10 .55
923 A234 160fr on 400fr 1.90 .85
924 A234 200fr on 450fr 2.50 1.10
Nos. 921-924 (4) 5.90 2.75

Nos. 923-924 are airmail.

PHILEXFRANCE '89, French Revolution Bicent. — A241

Designs: 200fr, Allegory in Honor of Liberty. 300fr, Declaration of Human Rights and Citizenship. 500fr, The Bastille, horiz.

1989, July 7 Litho. *Perf. 13*

925 A241 200fr multi 1.90 .80
926 A241 300fr multi 4.00 1.25
a. Pair, #925-926 + label 6.50 6.50

Souvenir Sheet

927 A241 500fr multi 6.25 3.75

Souvenir Sheet

Statue of Liberty — A242

Designs: a, Crown and torch observatories lit at night. b, Working on statue's coiffure. c, Face and scaffolding. d, Workman sanding copper sheeting around the crown observatory. e, Re-opening ceremony, 1986. f, Crown observatory at night.

Wmk. 385

1989, July Litho. *Perf. 13*

928 A242 Sheet of 6 11.00 11.00
a.-c. 150fr any single 1.60 .60
d.-f. 200fr any single 1.75 1.00

Statue of Liberty cent. (in 1986). Photograph of the statue is reversed.

M. Champagnat (1789-1840), Founder of the Marist Order — A243

15fr, Madonna and child, map. 50fr, Cross, Earth.

1989 Litho. Unwmk. *Perf. 13½*

929 A243 15fr multicolored .25 .25
930 A243 50fr multicolored .45 .25
931 A243 160fr shown 1.75 1.25
Nos. 929-931 (3) 2.45 1.75

Nos. 929-930 vert.

Harvest Feast, Bambari A244

1989, Oct. 15

932 A244 100fr Produce 1.25 .60
933 A244 160fr Ox plow 1.75 .80

World Food Day A245

60fr, Domestic animals. 240fr, Arresting ivory poachers.

1989, Oct. 16

934 A245 60fr multicolored .55 .30
935 A245 240fr multicolored 2.25 1.00

French Revolution, Bicent. — A246

Battle scenes and leaders: 160fr, Brig.-Gen. Francois-Christophe Kellermann (1735-1820), Battle of Valmy, Sept. 22, 1792. 200fr, Minister of War Charles-Francois du Perier Dumouriez (1739-1823), Battle of Jemappes, Nov. 7, 1792. 500fr, Gen. Jean-Charles Pichegru (1761-1804), capture of the Dutch fleet, Jan. 22, 1795. 600fr, Gen. Louis-Lazare Hoche (1768-97), Battle of Quiberon Bay, July 21, 1795. 1000fr, Napoleon at the Battle of Rivoli Veronese, Jan. 15, 1797. 1500fr, General Jean-Baptiste Jourdan.

1989, Dec. 5 Litho. *Perf. 13½*

936 A246 160fr multicolored 1.40 .40
937 A246 200fr multicolored 1.75 .55
938 A246 500fr multicolored 5.50 1.10
939 A246 600fr multicolored 5.00 1.00
a. Souvenir sheet of 4, #936-939 15.00 15.00
Nos. 936-939 (4) 13.65 3.05

Souvenir Sheet

940 A246 1000fr multicolored 10.00 3.00

Litho. & Embossed

940A A246 1500fr gold & multi — —

PHILEXFRANCE '89. Nos. 938-940A are airmail.

No. 936 is incorrectly inscribed "Francois-Etienne." Jemappes is incorrectly spelled on No. 937. No. 940 is incorrectly inscribed "January 14."

1990 World Cup Soccer Championships, Italy — A247

Various athletes and Italian landmarks: 20fr, Bell tower, Palermo Cathedral. 120fr, Trinity of the Mount, Rome. 160fr, St. Francis Church apse, Bologna. 200fr, Palace, Florence. 1000fr, Milan Cathedral.

1989, Dec. 23

941 A247 20fr multicolored .25 .25
942 A247 120fr multicolored 1.25 .40
943 A247 160fr multicolored 1.40 .40
944 A247 200fr multicolored 1.60 .55
Nos. 941-944 (4) 4.50 1.60

Souvenir Sheet

945 A247 1000fr multicolored 9.25 2.00

Nos. 942 and 945 are airmail.

Save the Forests A247a

1989 Litho. *Perf. 13½*

945A A247a 160fr multicolored 2.00 .75

Town of Bangui, Cent. A247b

Designs: 100fr, Governor's Palace, 1906. 160fr, Outpost. 200fr, A. Dolisie, founder of Bangui, vert. 1000fr, Signing of peace treaty between Michel Dolisie and Chief Gbembo, 1889, vert.

1989 Litho. *Perf. 13½*

945B	A247b	100fr multi	1.25	.40
945C	A247b	160fr multi	1.75	1.00
945D	A247b	200fr multi	2.50	.95
945E	A247b	1000fr multi	10.50	4.25
		Nos. 945B-945E (4)	16.00	6.60

Championship Team from Central Africa, 1987 — A248

1990, Feb. 23 Litho. *Perf. 13½*

946	A248	160fr Flag, players, trophy	1.60	.75
947	A248	240fr shown	2.25	1.00
948	A248	500fr like 160fr	5.50	2.25
		Nos. 946-948 (3)	9.35	4.00

African Basketball Championships. Dated 1988. Nos. 946 and 948 vert.

A249

1990, Feb. 23 Litho. *Perf. 13½*

949	A249	100fr multicolored	1.00	.40
950	A249	130fr multicolored	1.10	.55

Central Africa, winner of the 1987 African Basketball Cup Championships, Tunis. Dated 1989.

A250

1992 Winter Olympics, Albertville: 10fr, Speed skating. 60fr, Cross-country skiing. 500fr, Slalom. 750fr, Figure skating.
1000fr, Downhill skiing. No. 955A, Slalom skier. No. 955B, Pairs figure skating.

1990, Mar. 12 Litho. *Perf. 13½*

951	A250	10fr multi	.25	.25
952	A250	60fr multi	.55	.25
953	A250	500fr multi	4.50	1.00
954	A250	750fr multi	6.25	1.40
		Nos. 951-954 (4)	11.55	2.90

Souvenir Sheet

955	A250	1000fr multi	8.75	2.00

Litho. & Embossed

955A	A250	1500fr gold & multi	12.00	3.50

Souvenir Sheet

955B	A250	1500fr gold & multi	30.00	30.00

Nos. 953-955B are airmail. No. 955 contains one 36x42mm stamp. Nos. 951-954 exist in souvenir sheets of one.

Scout, *Euphaera eusemoides* — A251

Boy scouts and butterflies: 65fr, *Cymothoe beckeri*. 160fr, *Pseudacraea clarki*. 250fr, *Charaxes castor*.300fr, *Euphaedra gausape*. 500fr, *Graphium ridleyanus*. 1000fr, *Euphaedra edwardsi*. No. 962A, Antanartia delius. No. 962B, Spotted flycatcher. No. 962C, Cymothoe sangaris.

1990, Mar. 26

956	A251	25fr multicolored	.30	.25
957	A251	65fr multicolored	.65	.35
958	A251	160fr multicolored	1.60	.45
959	A251	250fr multicolored	2.75	.75
960	A251	300fr multicolored	3.00	.90
961	A251	500fr multicolored	5.25	1.25
		Nos. 956-961 (6)	13.55	3.95

Souvenir Sheet

962	A251	1000fr multicolored	11.00	2.25

Litho. & Embossed

Perf. 12½

962A	A251	1500fr gold & multi	15.00	5.00

Perf. 13½

962B	A251	1500fr gold & multi	45.00	4.00

Souvenir Sheet

962C	A251	1500fr gold & multi	12.00	12.00

Nos. 962A-962C are airmail. No. 962A exists in a souvenir sheet of 1.

1992 Summer Olympics, Barcelona A252

1990, Apr. 1 Litho. *Perf. 13½*

963	A252	10fr Javelin	.25	.25
964	A252	40fr Runner	.40	.25
965	A252	130fr Tennis	1.25	.45
966	A252	240fr Hurdles	2.50	.55
967	A252	400fr Yachting	4.00	1.00
968	A252	500fr Soccer	5.25	1.25
		Nos. 963-968 (6)	13.65	3.75

Souvenir Sheet

969	A252	1000fr Boxing	10.00	2.25

Nos. 963-965 vert. Nos. 967-969 are airmail.

Pres. Gorbachev, Pres. Bush — A253

Pres. Gorbachev, Pope John Paul II — A254

1990, July 27 Litho. *Perf. 13½*

970	A253	120fr multicolored	1.00	.30
971	A254	200fr multicolored	2.00	.45

Pope John Paul II-Gorbachev meeting Dec. 2, 1989. Bush-Gorbachev Summit Meeting Dec. 3, 1989. Nos. 970-971 exist in souvenir sheets of 1. Value, each $20.

Great Britain No. 1, Sir Rowland Hill (1795-1879) — A255

1990, July 27

972	A255	130fr multicolored	1.40	.30

No. 972 exists in a souvenir sheet of 1.

Events and Anniversaries — A256

Designs: 160fr, Galileo Probe to Jupiter. 240fr, Neil Armstrong, 1st man on moon. 250fr, Concorde, rapid-transit train, Rotary Intl. emblem.

1990, July 27 Litho. *Perf. 13½*

973	A256	160fr multicolored	1.50	.40
974	A256	240fr multicolored	2.40	.50
975	A256	250fr multicolored	2.75	.75
		Nos. 973-975 (3)	6.65	1.65

Wildlife Protection A258

100fr, Declining elephant population, vert.

1991, Jan. 25 Litho. *Perf. 13½*

976	A258	15fr gold & multi	.75	.25
977	A258	60fr multicolored	2.40	.40
978	A258	100fr multicolored	3.25	.55
		Nos. 976-978 (3)	6.40	1.20

Eutropius A259

Design: 240fr, Distichodus.

1991, Jan. 26

979	A259	50fr multicolored	1.25	.25
980	A259	160fr gold & multi	2.75	.75
981	A259	240fr multicolored	3.50	.50
		Nos. 979-981 (3)	7.50	1.50

Fight Against AIDS A260

Design: 120fr, Class speaker, vert.

1991, Jan. 24

982	A260	5fr gold & multi	.90	.25
983	A260	70fr multicolored	2.75	.55
984	A260	120fr multicolored	3.50	.80
		Nos. 982-984 (3)	7.15	1.60

Central African Diamonds A260a

Designs: 65fr, Woman polishing diamond, 160fr, Map, diamond.

1991, Feb. 14 Litho. *Perf. 11½*

Granite Paper

984A	A260a	65fr multicolored	—	
984B	A260a	160fr multicolored	—	

Assumption of Power by Pres. Andre Kolingba, 10th Anniv. (in 1991) — A261

1992, Sept. 1 Litho. *Perf. 13x13½*

985	A261	160fr multicolored	3.00	.60

Anniversaries and Events — A262

Designs: 80fr, Maybach Zeppelin, zeppelin airship, Count Ferdinand Zeppelin. 140fr, Child being comforted, Jean-Henri Dunant. 160fr, Benetton-Ford B 192, Michael Schumacher. 350fr, Konrad Adenauer signing Constitution of German Republic. 500fr, Pope John Paul II, mother and child, map. 600fr, Wolfgang Amadeus Mozart. 1000fr, Columbus at La Rabida, sailing ship, and building in Seville, Spain.

1992, Sept. 22 Litho. *Perf. 13½*

986	A262	80fr multicolored	1.00	.25
987	A262	140fr multicolored	1.60	.50
988	A262	160fr multicolored	2.00	.75
989	A262	350fr multicolored	4.50	1.10
990	A262	500fr multicolored	6.25	1.40
991	A262	600fr multicolored	8.25	1.50
		Nos. 986-991 (6)	23.60	5.50

Souvenir Sheet

992	A262	1000fr multicolored	10.00	2.00

Count Zeppelin, 75th anniv. of death (No. 986). Jean-Henri Dunant, first recipient of Nobel Peace Prize, 90th anniv. (in 1991) (No. 987). Grand Prix of Monaco (No. 988). Brandenburg Gate, bicent (No. 989). Visit of Pope John Paul II to Africa (No. 990). Wolfgang Amadeus Mozart, bicent. of death (in 1991) (No. 991). Discovery of America, 500th anniv. and Expo '92, Seville (No. 992).

Nos. 990-992 are airmail. Nos. 986-991 exist in souvenir sheets of 1.

For overprint see No. 1073.

A264

Elvis Presley (1935-1977) — A264a

Portrait of Presley, song or movie: 200fr, Heartbreak Hotel, 1956. 300fr, Love Me Tender, 1957. 400fr, Jailhouse Rock, 1957. 600fr, Harem Scarum, 1965.
1000fr, With guitar, at microphone.
No. 1001A, Holding microphone. No. 1001B, Playing guitar.

1993, July 12 Litho. *Perf. 13½*

997	A264	200fr multi	2.40	.25
998	A264	300fr multi	3.50	.50
999	A264	400fr multi	4.25	.60
1000	A264	600fr multi	6.00	1.00
		Nos. 997-1000 (4)	16.15	2.35

Souvenir Sheet

1001	A264	1000fr multi	9.50	2.40

Litho. & Embossed

1001A	A264a	1500fr gold & multi	20.00	7.50

Souvenir Sheet

1001B	A264a	1500fr gold & multi	13.00	8.00

Nos. 1000-1001B are airmail. Nos. 997-1000, 1001A exist imperf. and in souvenir sheets of one. Nos. 1001, 1001B exist imperf.

A265

Wedding of Japan's Crown Prince Naruhito and Masako Owada — A265a

Designs: 50fr, Princess Masako, parents. 65fr, Crown Prince Naruhito, parents. 160fr, Princess Masako, Harvard University 450fr, Crown Prince Naruhito, Oxford University. 750fr, Crown Prince, Princess.

1993, July 12 Litho. *Perf. 13½*

1002	A265	50fr multi	.40	.25
1003	A265	65fr multi	.65	.25
1004	A265	160fr multi	1.75	.25
1005	A265	450fr multi	4.50	1.00
		Nos. 1002-1005 (4)	7.30	1.75

Souvenir Sheet

1006	A265	750fr multi	7.75	3.00

Litho. & Embossed

1006A	A265a	1500fr gold & multi	26.00	4.00

Nos. 1005-1006A are airmail. Nos. 1002-1005, 1006A exist imperf. and in souvenir sheets of one. No. 1006 exists imperf.

A266

1994 World Cup Soccer Championships, US — A266a

Designs show winning team, scenes from: 40fr, Amsterdam, 1928; Montevideo, 1930. 50fr, Rome, 1934; Paris, 1938. 60fr, Rio, 1950; Berne, 1954. 80fr, Stockholm, 1958; Santiago, 1962. 160fr, London, 1966; Mexico City, 1970. 200fr, Munich, 1974; Buenos Aires, 1978. 400fr, Madrid, 1982; Mexico City, 1986. 500fr, Rome, 1990; emblem for US competition, 1994.
1000fr, 1990 German team; 1994 US team.
No. 1015A, Pele, Brazil. No. 1015B, Gerd Muller, Germany.

1993, Oct. 9 Litho. *Perf. 13½*

1007	A266	40fr multi	.40	.25
1008	A266	50fr multi	.40	.25
1009	A266	60fr multi	.50	.25
1010	A266	80fr multi	.65	.25
1011	A266	160fr multi	1.40	.40
1012	A266	200fr multi	1.90	.70
1013	A266	400fr multi	3.50	.70
1014	A266	500fr multi	5.00	1.00
		Nos. 1007-1014 (8)	13.75	3.80

Souvenir Sheet

1015	A266	1000fr multi	10.00	2.75

Litho. & Embossed

1015A	A266a	1500fr gold & multi	26.00	

Souvenir Sheet

1015B	A266a	1500fr gold & multi	13.50	

No. 1015 contains one 60x30mm stamp. No. 1007-1014 exist in souvenir sheets of one.
Nos. 1015A-1015B are airmail.

Miniature Sheets

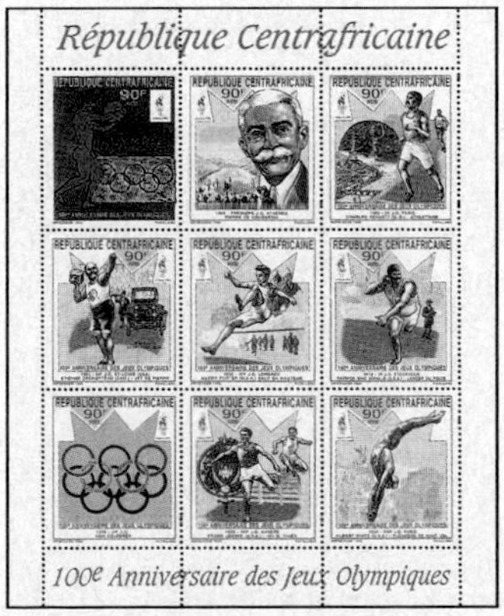

Modern Olympic Games, Cent. (in 1996) — A267

No. 1016: a, Ancient olympian. b, Baron de Coubertin, 1896. c, Charles Bennett, 1900. d, Etienne Desmarteau, 1904. e, Harry Porter, 1908. f, Patrick MacDonald, 1912. g, No games, 1916. h, Frank Loomis, 1920. i, Albert White, 1924.
No. 1017: a, El Ouafi, 1928. b, Eddie Tolan, 1932. c, Jesse Owens, 1936. d, No games, 1940. e, No games, 1944. f, Tapio Rautavaara, 1948. g, Jean Boiteux, 1952. h, Petrus Kasterman, 1956. i, Sante Gaiardoni, 1960.

No. 1018: a, Anton Geesink, 1964. b, Bob Beamon, 1968. c, Mark Spitz, 1972. d, Nadia Comaneci, 1976. e, Aleksandre Dityatin, 1980. f, J.F. Lamour, 1984. g, Pierre Durand, 1988. h, Michael Jordan, 1992. i, Soccer player, 1996.

1993 Litho. *Perf. 13½*

1016	A267	90fr Sheet of 9, #a.-i.	7.50	3.25
1017	A267	100fr Sheet of 9, #a.-i.	9.00	3.75
1018	A267	160fr Sheet of 9, #a.-i.	15.00	5.75

Miniature Sheet

Dinosaurs — A268

Designs: No. 1019a, 25fr, Saltoposuchus. b, 25fr, Rhamphorhynchus. c, 25fr, Dimorphodon. d, 25fr, Archaeopteryx. e, 30fr, Compsognathus longipes. f, 30fr, Cryptocleidus oxonlensis. g, 30fr, Stegosaurus. h, 30fr, Cetiosaurus. i, 50fr, Brontosaurus. j, 50fr, Corythosaurus casuarius. k, 50fr, Styracosaurus. l, 50fr, Gorgosaurus. m, 500fr, Scolosaurus. n, 500fr, Trachodon. o, 500fr, Struthiomimus. p, 500fr, Tarbosaurus.
No. 1020, Tylosaur.

1993, Dec. 3

1019	A268	Sheet of 16, #a.-p.	26.00	26.00

Souvenir Sheet

1020	A268	1000fr multicolored	10.50	2.75

No. 1020 is airmail and contains one 51x60mm stamp.

Biodiversity A269

Various fauna surrounding: 100fr, Man planting tree. 130fr, Man with local fauna, vert.

1993, Oct. 20 Litho. *Perf. 13½*

1021	A269	100fr multicolored	3.50	.75
1022	A269	130fr multicolored	5.00	1.00

M'Bali Dam — A270

200fr, Women, men with fish.

1993, Jan. 14 Litho. *Perf. 13*

1023	A270	160fr shown	1.60	.30
1024	A270	200fr multi	2.25	.40

Cooperation Council, 40th Anniv. — A271

1993, Jan. 26

1025	A271	240fr multicolored	2.50	.50

Intl. Conference on Nutrition, Rome — A272

1993, Apr. 1

1026	A272	90fr shown	.75	.45
1027	A272	140fr Fresh foods	1.40	.75

University of Bangui A273

1993, Apr. 8

1028	A273	100fr multicolored	1.00	.45

Dated 1992.

Environmental Development A274

Designs: 160fr, Woman with vegetables, fruit. 240fr, Woman cooking food.

1993, Oct. 27 Litho. *Perf. 13½*

1029	A274	160fr multicolored	1.75	.80
1030	A274	240fr multicolored	2.50	.95

Miniature Sheets

1994 Winter Olympics, Lillehammer — A275

Past Winter Olympic champions: 1031a, Th. Haug, Nordic combined skiing, Chamonix, 1924. b, J. Heaton, 1-man sled, St. Moritz, 1928. c, B. Ruud, ski jumping, Lake Placid, 1932. d, I. Ballangrud, speed skating, Garmisch-Partenkirchen, 1936. e, G. Fraser, women's slalom skiing, St. Moritz, 1948. f, German 4-man bobsled, Oslo, 1952. g, USSR hockey team, Cortina D'Ampezzo, 1956. h, J. Vuarnet, downhill skiing, Squaw Valley, 1960.

No. 1032a, M. Goitschel, giant slalom, Innsbruck, 1964. b, Jean-Claude Killy, slalom skiing, Grenoble, 1968. c, U. Wehling, Nordic combined, Sapporo, 1972. d, Rodnina & Zaitsev, pairs figure skating, Innsbruck, 1976. e, E. Heiden, speed skating, Lake Placid, 1980. f, K. Witt, figure skating, Sarajevo, 1984. g, J. Mueller, luge, Calgary, 1988. h, E. Grospiron, freestyle skiing, Albertville, 1992. i, Speed skiing, Lillehammer, 1994.

1994, Jan. 14 Litho. *Perf. 13½*

1031 A275 100fr Sheet of 8, #a.-h. + label 9.00 9.00
1032 A275 200fr Sheet of 9, #a.-i. 15.00 15.00

1994 Winter Olympics, Lillehammer — A276

Design: 1500fr, Women figure skaters.

1994 Litho. & Embossed *Perf. 13½*

1033 A276 1500fr gold & multi 15.00

No. 1033 is airmail & exists in a souvenir sheet of 1. Value $24.

Flowers, Vegetables, Fruit, & Mushrooms A277

Flowers: No. 1034a, 25fr, Ansellia africana. b, 60fr, Polystachia bella. c, 90fr, Aerangis rhodosticta. d, 500fr, Angraecum eburneum.
Vegetables: No. 1035a, 30r, Yams. b, 65fr, Manioc. c, 100fr, Corn. d, 400fr, Sweet potato.
Fruits: No. 1036a, 40fr, Orange. b, 70fr, Banana. c, 160fr, Mango. d, 300fr, Coffee.
Mushrooms: No. 1037a, 50fr, Termitomyces schimperi. b, 80fr, Sympodia arborescens. c, 200fr, Phlebopus sudanicus. d, 600fr, Leucocoprinus africanus.

1994, Jan. 21 Litho. *Perf. 13½*

1034 A277 Strip of 4, #a.-d. 5.50 2.50
1035 A277 Strip of 4, #a.-d. 5.00 2.25
1036 A277 Strip of 4, #a.-d. 4.50 2.00
1037 A277 Strip of 4, #a.-d. 8.75 3.75
e. Sheet of 16, #1034-1037 26.00 12.00

Catholic Church in Africa, Cent. — A278

Designs: 130fr, Monsignor Augouard, founder of mission, St. Paul of the Rapids. 160fr, Monsignor Grandin, Abbe Boganda, first sacred ordainment, 1938. 240fr, Father Louis Godart, House of Charity, Bangui.

1994, June 2 Litho. *Perf. 13½*

1038 A278 130fr multicolored .65 .45
1039 A278 160fr multicolored .80 .45
1040 A278 240fr multicolored 1.40 .60
Nos. 1038-1040 (3) 2.85 1.50

Relics from Early Civilizations, Landmarks — A279

Designs: 10fr, Cabin-shaped cinerary urn, Rome. 25fr, Face of the secret denunciation, Venice, vert. 30fr, Statue of the Tetrarchs, Venice, vert. 50fr, Little cube-shaped building, Palermo, vert. 65fr, Frieze, The Alhambra, Granada, vert. 90fr, Grand Chateau, Bellinzona. 100fr, Museum D'Orsay, Paris, vert. 130fr, Granary, Galicia. 140fr, Mural, by Diego Rivera, Mexico, vert. 160fr, Guacamaya mask, Mexico, vert. 200fr, Ivory mask, Western Africa, vert. 240fr, La Sagrada Familia, Barcelona, vert. 260fr, Casbah of Amerhidil. 300fr, Gold aureus of Sulla, Rome, 82 BC. 400fr, Chimborazo volcano.

1994, June 2 *Perf. 13*

1041-1055 A279 Set of 15 12.00 4.50

D-Day, 50th Anniv. — A280

Pegasus Bridge, June 6: No. 1056a, British troops crossing bridge, piper. b, Glider, British and German soldiers. c, German soldiers.
Operation COBRA, July 24: a, Tank, monument, soldiers. b, Bombers, soldiers, gun barrel. c, Tank, soldiers up close.

1994, Oct. 25 Litho. *Perf. 13½*

1056 A280 600fr Strip of 3, #a.-c. 10.00 3.75
1057 A280 600fr Strip of 3, #a.-c. 10.00 3.75

Nos. 1056b, 1057b are 30x46mm. Nos. 1056-1057 are continuous designs. See No. C359.

Anniversaries & Events — A281

No. 1058, 600fr — Characters from "Star Wars:" a, Han Solo, Chewbaca. b, Darth Vader, Princess Leia, Luke Skywalker, R2D2, C3PO. c, Obi Wan Kenobi.
No. 1059 — First manned moon landing, 25th anniv.: a, 400fr, Buzz Aldrin. b, 500fr, Neil Armstrong, Apollo 11 liftoff. c, 600fr, Michael Collins.
No. 1060: a, 400fr, Theodor von Karman. b, 500fr, Apollo 11 command module, Wernher von Braun. c, 600fr, Hermes Rocket, Hermann Oberth.

1994, Oct. 25 Litho. *Perf. 13½*

1058 A281 Strip of 3, #a.-c. 8.00 3.50
1059 A281 Strip of 3, #a.-c. 7.50 3.00
1060 A281 Strip of 3, #a.-c. 7.50 3.00

Motion Pictures, cent. (No. 1058).
Nos. 1058b, 1059b, 1060b are 60x51mm. Nos. 1058-1060 are continuous design and exist in a souvenir sheet of 1.

Natl. Assembly A282

1994, Dec. 8

1061 A282 65fr blue & multi .35 .25
1062 A282 430fr yel brn & multi 1.90 .90

Antoine de Saint-Exupery (1900-44), Aviator, Author — A283

1994, Dec 16

1063 A283 80fr Airplane .50 .30
1064 A283 235fr Portrait, vert. 1.00 .50

Inauguration of Pres. Ange-Felix Patasse, 1st Anniv. — A284

1994, Oct. 22

1065 A284 65fr blue & multi .40 .25
1066 A284 300fr yellow & multi 1.60 .60
1067 A284 385fr green & multi 2.00 .75
Nos. 1065-1067 (3) 4.00 1.60

A285

Intl. Olympic Committee, Cent. — A286

1994, Oct. 25

1068 A285 60fr bl grn & multi .35 .25
1069 A285 405fr yel grn & multi 1.75 .80

Souvenir Sheet

1070 A286 675fr Pierre de Coubertin 3.00 1.40

No. 1070 is airmail.

Nos. 1031-1032 Ovptd. with Medalist & Country Name in Gold

Overprints on No. 1031: No. 1071a, "F.B. LUNDBERG / NORVEGE." b, "G. HACKL / ALLEMAGNE." c, "B. DAEHLIE / NORVEGE." d, "J.O. KOSS / NORVEGE." e, "V. SCHNEIDER / SUISSE." f, "MEDAILLE D'OR / ALLEMAGNE." g, "MEDAILLE D'OR / SUEDE." h, "T. MOE / U.S.A."
Overprints on No. 1032: No. 1072a, "M. WASMEIER / ALLEMAGNE." b, "T. STANGASSINGER / AUTRICHE." c, "MEDAILLE D'OR / PAR EQUIPES / JAPON." d, "Y. GORDEYEVA / S. GRINKOV / RUSSIE." e, "D. JANSEN / U.S.A." f, "O. BAYUL / UKRAINE." g, "G. HACKL / ALLEMAGNE." h, "J.-L. BRASSARO / CANADA." i, "K. SEIZINGER / ALLEMAGNE."

1994

1071 A275 100fr Sheet of 8, #a.-h. + label 6.50 3.00
1072 A275 200fr Sheet of 9, #a.-i. 15.00 7.00

No. 988 Overprinted in Silver

1994, Dec. 28 Litho. *Perf. 13½*

1073 A262 160fr multicolored 10.00 4.50

No. 1073 also exists in souvenir sheet of 1.

1995 Boy Scout Jamboree, Holland — A287

Scout with mushrooms or butterflies: 300fr, Armillariela mellea. 385fr, Charaxes pleione. 405fr, Charaxes candiope. 430fr, Charaxes pollux. 500fr, Volvaria esculenta. 1000fr, Cortinarius.
2000fr, Euphaedra medon.

1995, May 24

1074-1079 A287 Set of 6 15.00 7.00
1077a Sheet, #1075-1077 10.00 2.75
1079a Sheet, #1074, #1078-1079 14.50 4.00

Souvenir Sheet

1080 A287 2000fr multicolored 18.00 4.25

Nos. 1074-1079 exist in souvenir sheets of 1. No. 1080 is airmail and contains one 39x57mm stamp.

1994 World Cup Soccer Championships, US — A288

Stadium: 300fr, Citrus Bowl, Orlando. 385fr, RFK Stadium, Washington, DC. 405fr, Soldier Field, Chicago. 430fr, Cotton Bowl, Dallas. 500fr, Giants Stadium, East Rutherford, NJ. 1000fr, Foxboro Stadium, Foxboro, MA.
2000fr, Rose Bowl, vert.

1995, July 14 Litho. *Perf. 13½*

1081-1086 A288 Set of 6 14.00 6.50

Souvenir Sheet

1087 A288 2000fr multicolored 12.50 5.75

No. 1087 is airmail.

African Development Bank, 30th Anniv. — A289

1995, June 29

1088 A289 70fr multicolored .35 .25
1089 A289 200fr multicolored 1.00 .45

Nos. 1088-1089 also exist in souvenir sheet of 1.

Fish A290

Designs, 25fr, 300fr, Auchenoglanis. 30fr, 50fr, Chrisicntys.

1995, June 22

1090-1093 A290 Set of 4 2.75 .90

Entertainers A291

Designs: 300fr, Freddie Mercury (Queen). 385fr, Jimi Hendrix. 430fr, Marilyn Monroe. 500fr, Michael Jackson. 600fr, Jerry Garcia (Grateful Dead). 800fr, Elvis Presley.

1500fr, Charlton Heston in "Planet of the Apes." 2000fr, Marilyn Monroe, diff.

1995, July 21

1094-1099 A291 Set of 6 15.00 6.50

Souvenir Sheets

1099B A291 1500fr multicolored 8.25 3.25
1100 A291 2000fr multicolored 10.50 4.25

Nos. 1094-1099 exist in souvenir sheets of 1. No. 1100 is airmail. No. 1099B contains one 51x60mm airmail stamp.

Volleyball, Cent. — A292

1995, Oct. 3 Litho. *Perf. 13½*

1101 A292 300fr multicolored 1.50 .65

No. 1101 exists in a souvenir sheet of 1. Value $10.

Sports Figures A293

400fr, Andre Agassi, tennis. 500fr, Boris Becker, tennis. 700fr, Ayrton Senna (1960-94) race car driver. 800fr, Michael Schumacher, F-1 world driving champion.

2000fr, Michael Schumacher, diff.

1996, June 20 Litho. *Perf. 13½*

1102-1105 A293 Set of 4 12.00 5.50

Souvenir Sheet

1106 A293 2000fr multicolored 10.00 4.50

No. 1102-1105 exist in souvenir sheets of 1. Value $30.

1996 Summer Olympic Games, Atlanta A294

Olympic athletes, sites in Atlanta: 170fr, Atlanta-Fulton County Stadium. 300fr, Martin Luther King Memorial. 350fr, Alexander H. Stephens Monument. 600fr, High Museum of Art.

2000fr, Pierre de Coubertin, runner.

1996, June 20

1107-1110 A294 Set of 4 7.50 3.25

Souvenir Sheet

1110A A294 2000fr multicolored 9.50 4.00

No. 1110A contains one 42x51mm stamp.

UN, 50th Anniv. (in 1995) A295

1996, July 15 *Perf. 14*

1111 A295 5fr "50," emblem, vert. .25 .25
1112 A295 430fr shown 2.25 .90

Nos. 1111-1112 each exist in souvenir sheets of 1. Value, set of two sheets $2.75.

1996 Summer Olympic Games, Atlanta A296

1900 Summer Olympics, Paris: 235fr, Alvin Kraenzlein, vert. 300fr, Paris Stadium. 385fr, Irving Baxter. 430fr, British soccer team.

Past Olympic medalists: No. 1117a, Miruts Yifter, 5,000-meters, 1980. b, Germany, team dressage, 1976. c, Bruce Jenner, decathlon, 1976. d, Mark Gorski, 1000-meter match sprint, 1984. e, Randy Williams, long jump, 1972. f, Shinodu Sekine, judo, 1972. g, Kiyomi Kato, wrestling, 1972. h, Mitsuo Tsukahama, gymnastics, 1976. i, Hartwig Steenken, Germany, 1972.

Each 1000fr: No. 1118, Betty Cuthbert, 100-meters, 1956. No. 1119, Gerhard Stock, javelin, 1936.

1996, July 19

1113-1116 A296 Set of 4 6.00 2.75
1117 A296 200fr Sheet of 9, #a.-i. 8.00 3.50

Souvenir Sheets

1118-1119 A296 Set of 2 8.75 4.00

Olymphilex '96 (Nos. 1113-1116, 1118-1119).

Francophonie, 25th Anniv. (in 1995) — A297

300fr, "25 ANS" surrounded by "1970-1995."

1996, July 22

1120 A297 235fr multicolored 1.00 .50
1121 A297 300fr multicolored 1.50 .60

Nos. 1120-1121 each exist in souvenir sheets of 1. Value, set of two sheets $7.50.

FAO, 50th Anniv. (in 1995) A298

Designs: 10fr, Fish being lifted in net, vert. 385fr, Boy drinking water.

1996

1122 A298 10fr multicolored .25 .25
1123 A298 385fr multicolored 2.00 .75

Nos. 1122-1123 each exist in souvenir sheets of 1. Value, set of two sheets $2.75.

Queen Elizabeth II, 70th Birthday — A299

a, Formal portrait. b, In blue suit. c, In red hat.

1000fr, Balmoral Castle.

1996, July 24 *Perf. 13½x14*

1124 A299 300fr Strip of 3, #a.-c. 3.75 1.75

Souvenir Sheet

1125 A299 1000fr multicolored 4.50 2.00

Nos. 1124 was issued in sheets of 9 stamps.

Pets — A300

1996 Litho. *Perf. 13½*

1126 A300 250fr Dog 1.25 .60
1127 A300 600fr Cat 3.00 1.40

Nos. 1126-1127 exist in souvenir sheets of 1.

1998 World Cup Soccer Championships, France — A301

Winning country, year, player: No. 1128a, Uruguay 1930, Pedro Cea (Argentina), Italy 1934. b, Italy 1938, Piola (Italy), Uruguay 1950. c, Germany 1954, Brazil 1958, Walter, (Germany). d, Amarildo, (Brazil), Brazil 1962, England 1966.

No. 1129: a, Brazil 1970, Pele (Brazil), Germany 1974. b, Kempes (Argentina), Argentina 1978, Italy 1982. c, Argentina 1986, Mattaus (Germany), Germany 1990. d, Platini (France), Brazil 1994.

1996 Litho. *Perf. 13½*

1128 A301 375fr Sheet of 4, #a.-d. 7.25 3.25
1129 A301 425fr Sheet of 4, #a.-d. 8.25 3.75

Dinosaur Eggs — A302

Denomination at: a, LR. b, LL.

1996, Apr. 28

1130 A302 140fr Pair, #a.-b. 2.10 .65
c. Souv. Sheet, #1130a-1130b 3.00 .65

CHINA '96 (No. 1130c).

Scouting A303

Raptors, butterflies, mushrooms: 175fr, Buzzard. 200fr, H. misippus. 300fr, Lepiota aspera. 350fr, Raptor with feathers ruffled. 450fr, Amanita caesarea. 500fr, Morpho portis-nymphalidae.

1996 Litho. *Perf. 13½*

1131-1136 A303 Set of 6 10.00 4.50

Nos. 1132-1133, 1135-1136 exist in souvenir sheets of 1.

Horses — A304

No. 1137, 235fr: a, Appaloosa. b, Arabian. c, Quarter horse. d, Belgian. e, Pure blood English. f, Mustang. g, Haflinger. h, Welsh pony.

No. 1138, 235fr: a, Pinto. b, Palomino. c, Welara. d, Morgan. e, Standard American. f, Norwegian fjord. g, Shetland. h, Shire.

1000fr, Saddlebred.

1996, Nov. 20 *Perf. 14*

Sheets of 8, #a-h

1137-1138 A304 235fr Set of 2 16.00 7.50

Souvenir Sheet

1139 A304 1000fr multicolored 4.50 2.25

Great Nebula, Andromeda — A305

Designs: b, Halley's Comet. c, Jupiter. d, Saturn. e, Moon. f, Mars.

1996, Nov. 22

1140 A305 300fr Sheet of 6, #a.-f. 8.00 3.50

Wildlife — A306

Flowers: a, Bomax costatum. b, Clappertonia ficifolia. c, Canarina abyssinica. d, Kigelia africana. e, Adenium obesum. f, Oncoba spinosa. g, Orinum ornatum. h, Gloriosa simplex. i, Strophanthus gratus.
Bird: 1500fr, Sagittarius serpentarius.

1997, Feb. 6 Litho. *Perf. 14*
1141 A306 205fr Sheet of 9, #a.-i. 8.25 3.75

Souvenir Sheet

1142 A306 1500fr multicolored 8.25 3.00

Intl. Express Mail Service A307

300fr, Globe, international express mail routes. 405fr, Emblem of hand holding letter.

1996 Litho. *Perf. 13½*
1143 A307 300fr multicolored 1.40 .65
1144 A307 405fr multicolored 1.90 .90

No. 1144 exists in a souvenir sheet of 1.

Human Rights Advocates — A308

Designs: a, Dalai Lama. b, Martin Luther King. c, John F. Kennedy. d, Nelson Mandela. e, Mother Teresa. f, Mahatma Gandhi.

1996
1145 A308 175fr Sheet of 6, #a.-f. + 2 labels 5.00 2.25

Red Cross and Red Crescent Societies — A309

Designs: a, Doctor with patient. b, Man sifting grain. c, Using stethoscope on patient. d, Wounded man. e, Bandaging patient. f, Aiding infant.

1996
1146 A309 250fr Sheet of 6, #a.-f. + 2 labels 7.25 3.25

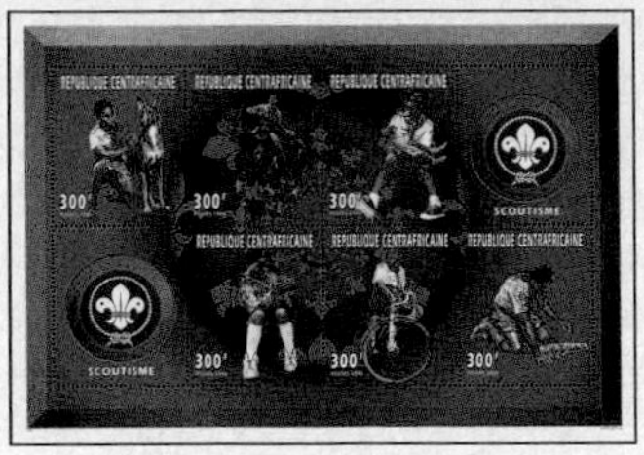

Boy Scouts — A310

Boy scout: a, With dog. b, Riding horse. c, Holding cat. d, Holding butterfly. e, On bicycle. f, Playing game.
Butterfly: 2000fr, Saturnidae, horiz.

1996 Litho. *Perf. 13½*
1147 A310 300fr Sheet of 6, #a.-f. + 2 labels 9.00 4.00

Souvenir Sheet

1148 A310 2000fr multicolored 10.00 4.50

No. 1148 contains one 42x36mm stamp.

Lions Intl., Rotary Intl. — A311

Designs: a, Child drinking from cup. b, Child carrying sack. c, Girl holding sheaves of grain. d, Man breaking bread. e, Woman cooking over fire. f, Boy, corn stalk.

1996
1149 A311 500fr Sheet of 6, #a.-f. + 2 labels 14.00 6.50

Flora and Fauna A312

15fr, Cucumis sativus, vert. 20fr, Phyllochistis citrella. 40fr, Cetonia aurata. 65fr, Nomadacris septemfasciata. 100fr, Crocodilus vulgaris. 140fr, Athyrium filix, vert. 405fr, Rhopalo ceres.

1996
1150-1156 A312 Set of 7 5.00 1.75

Nos. 1151, 1156 exist in sourvenir sheets of 1.

UN, UNICEF, 50th Anniv. — A313

Designs: a, Futuristic space vehicle. b, MIR space station. c, US space shuttle, space station. d, Woman carrying food. e, Child receiving vaccination. f, Baby being weighed.

1996
1157 A313 350fr Sheet of 6, #a.-f. + 2 labels 10.00 4.50

Elizabeth Taylor, Actress — A314

Princess Diana — A315

Various portraits.

1997, Apr. 10 Litho. *Perf. 14*
1158 A314 300fr Sheet of 6, #a.-f. 8.00 3.50
1159 A315 300fr Sheet of 6, #a.-f. 8.00 3.50

Souvenir Sheets

1160 A314 1500fr multicolored 6.50 3.00
1161 A315 1500fr multicolored 6.50 3.00

For overprints see Nos. 1181-1182.

UNESCO, 50th Anniv. A316

No. 1162, 235fr: a, Fortress ruins, Ethiopia. b, Victoria Falls, Zambia. c, River during dry season, Zimbabwe. d, Nature Reserve, Niger. e, Pelican, Natl. Park, Mauritania. f, Native huts in village, Niokolo-Kobo Natl. Park, Senegal. g, M'Zab Valley, Algeria. h, Mosque, Morocco.
No. 1163, 235fr: a, c, Ruins of Roman Amphitheater, France. b, Split, Croatia. d, e, Quedlinberg, Germany. f, h, Tower of London, England. g, Olympic Natl. Park, US.
No. 1164, 235fr: a, Horyu-Ji, Japan. b, Waterfalls, Amazon River, Los Katios Natl. Park, Colombia. c, Abu Mena Church, Egypt. d, Boat on river, Fortress of Suomenlinna, Finland. e, Venice, Italy. f, Mural, Potala Palace, Lhasa, Tibet, China. g, Cathedral, town of Olinda, Brazil. h, Monastery, Mystras, Greece.
No. 1165, 1000fr, Jiuzhaigou Valley, China. No. 1166, 1000fr, Interior, Pilgrimage Church of Wies, Germany. No. 1167, 1000fr Ruins of Fountains Abbey, Studley Park, England.

1997, Apr. 30 *Perf. 13½x14*

Sheets of 8, #a-h + Label

1162-1164 A316 Set of 3 25.00 12.00

Souvenir Sheets

1165-1167 A316 Set of 3 13.00 6.00

UNICEF, 50th Anniv. — A317

No. 1168: a, 200fr, UN headquarters building. b, 250fr, Baby. c, 500fr, Danny Kaye seated inside vehicle.
1500fr, Child.

1997, Apr. 30 *Perf. 14*
1168 A317 Sheet of 3, #a.-c. 4.00 1.90

Souvenir Sheet

1169 A317 1500fr multicolored 6.50 3.00

US Pres. Bill Clinton and His Cat, "Socks" — A318

Designs: a, b, c, e, g, h, i, Socks in various poses. d, f, Clinton, Socks.

1996
1170 A318 200fr Sheet of 9, #a.-i. 9.00 3.75

Conquest of Space — A319

Events in 1977: No. 1171: a, Voyager 1, US. b, Space Shuttle Enterprise, US. c, Meteosat 1, US. d, Salyut 6 Space Station, USSR.
Events in 1982: No. 1172: a, Salyut 7 Space Station, USSR. b, Landsat 4 Satellite, US. c, Venera 13, USSR. d, IRAS Infrared Telescope, US.
Events of 1967: No. 1173: a, Cosmos 186 & 188. b, Molniya satellite. c, Surveyor 3. d, Mariner 5.
Events in 1972: No. 1174: a, Copernicus probe, US. b, Pioneer 10, US. c, Apollo 16, US. d, Apollo 17, John F. Kennedy.
Events of 1962: No. 1175: a, Mariner 2, US. b, OSO 1, US. c, John Glenn. d, Mars 1, USSR.
Events of 1957: No. 1176: a, Vostok 1, Yuri Gagarin, USSR. b, Sputnik 2, USSR. c, Sputnik 1, USSR. d, Bell X15, US.
2000fr, Voyager, Pioneer 10, Apollo 11, US.

1997 *Perf. 13½*
1171 A319 250fr Sheet of 4, #a.-d. 5.00 2.00
1172 A319 350fr Sheet of 4, #a.-d. 6.50 3.00
1173 A319 450fr Sheet of 4, #a.-d. 9.00 3.75
1174 A319 500fr Sheet of 4, #a.-d. 10.00 4.00
1175 A319 600fr Sheet of 4, #a.-d. 11.00 5.00
1176 A319 800fr Sheet of 4, #a.-d. 14.50 6.50

Souvenir Sheet

1177 A319 2000fr multicolored 10.00 4.00

No. 1177 contains one 60x30mm stamp.
No. 1173 exists imperf.

Marilyn Monroe (1926-62) — A320

Various portraits.

1997

1178 A320 375fr Sheet of 9, #a.-i. 16.00 6.50

John F. Kennedy (1917-63) — A321

Various portraits.

1997

1179 A321 300fr Sheet of 9, #a.-i. 13.00 5.00

Bruce Lee (1940-73), Actor — A322

Various portraits.

1997 **Litho.** ***Perf. 13½***

1180 A322 200fr Sheet of 9, #a.-i. 9.00 3.25

Nos. 1159, 1161 Ovptd. "In Memoriam"

1997 ***Perf. 14***

1181 A315 300fr Sheet of 6, #a.-f. 9.00 3.50

Souvenir Sheet

1182 A315 1500fr multicolored 7.50 3.00

Nos. 1181-1182 each contain "Diana, Princess of Wales (1961-1997) IN MEMORIAM" in sheet margin and on each stamp in No. 1181.

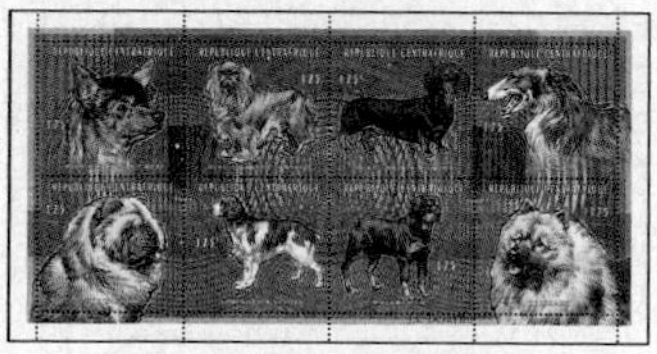

Dogs & Cats — A323

Dogs: No. 1183: a, Chinese crested. b, King Charles spaniel. c, Dachshund. d, Borzoi. e, Chow chow. f, Welsh springer. g, Rottweiler. h, Keeshond.

Cats: No. 1184: a, Birman. b, Black and white Persian. c, Siamese kitten. d, Red and black. e, American curl. f, Cornish rex. g, Silver shaded. h, White-footed cat.

1500fr, Pekingese. 2000fr, Somali.

1997 **Litho.** ***Perf. 13½***

1183 A323 175fr Sheet of 8, #a.-h. 6.50 2.50

1184 A323 250fr Sheet of 8, #a.-h. 9.00 3.75

Souvenir Sheets

1185 A323 1500fr multicolored 7.50 2.75

1186 A323 2000fr multicolored 10.00 3.75

Nos. 1185-1186 each contain one 42x51mm stamp.

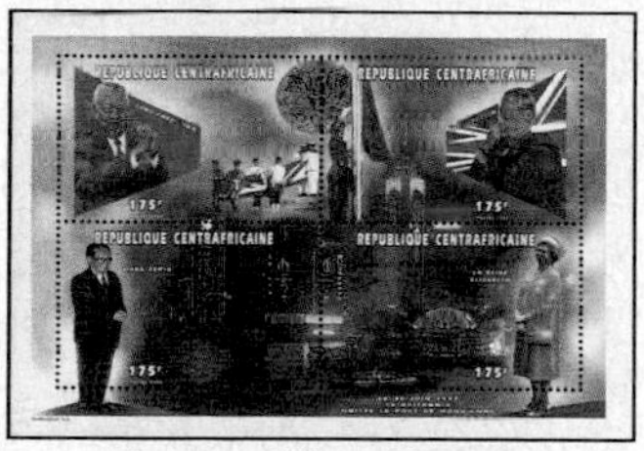

Return of Hong Kong to China — A324

No. 1187: a, Tung Chee-Hwa, taking down British flag. b, Raising Chinese flag, Chris Patten, British flag. c, Jiang Zemin, skyline at night. d, City lights, Queen Elizabeth II.

600fr, Tung Chee-Hwa.

1997

1187 A324 175fr Sheet of 4, #a.-d. 3.25 1.50

Souvenir Sheet

1188 A324 600fr multicolored 3.25 1.25

No. 1188 contains one 38x42mm stamp.

Paintings by Hiroshige (1797-1858) A325

No. 1189: a, Minami-Shinagawa and Samezu Coast. b, Plum Garden, Kamata. c, The Kawaguchi Ferry and Zenkoji Temple. d, Armor-Hanging Pine, Hakkeizaka. e, Robe-Hanging Pine, Senzoku Pond. f, Benten Shrine, Inokashira Pond.

No. 1190: a, A Little Brown Owl on a Pine Branch with a Crescent Moon Behind. b, Sparrows and Camellia in snow. c, Three Wild Geese Flying Downward across the Moon. d, A Blue Bird on a Yellow-flowered Hibiscus. e, Five Swallows in flight.

No. 1191: a, Sparrows and Wild Rose. b, Peonies. c, Morning Glory and Cricket. d, Blossoming Plum Tree. e, Kingfisher above a Yellow-flowered Water Plant.

No. 1192, 1500fr, Haneda Ferry and Benten Shrine. No. 1193, 1500fr, A Bird Clinging to a Tendril of Wisteria. No. 1194, 1500fr, Butterfly and Peony.

1998, Feb. 20 **Litho.** ***Perf. 14***

1189 A325 300fr Sheet of 6, #a.-f. 9.00 3.00

1190 A325 430fr Sheet of 5, #a.-e. 11.00 3.75

1191 A325 500fr Sheet of 5, #a.-e. 9.25 4.25

Souvenir Sheets

1192-1194 A325 Set of 3 18.00 7.50

Nos. 1190-1191 each contain five 26x72mm stamps. Nos. 1192-1194 each contain one 26x72mm stamp.

Chinese Lunar New Year A326

Animals representing lunar year: a, Rat. b, Ox. c, Tiger. d, Hare. e, Dragon. f, Snake. g, Horse. h, Sheep. i, Monkey. j, Rooster. k, Dog. l, Boar.

1000fr, Tiger, diff.

1998 **Litho. & Typo.** ***Perf. 14***

1195 A326 150fr Sheet of 12, #a.-l. 8.00 3.75

Souvenir Sheet

1196 A326 1000fr gold & multi 3.75 1.75

Intl. Scouting, 90th Anniv. — A327

Insects: No. 1196A: b, Apis mellifica. c, Lucanus cervus. d, Oryctes nasicornis. e, Pseudacraea boisduvalii. f, Helictopleurus quadripunctatus, euchroea spininasuta. g, Bombus terrestris. h, Charaxes smaragdalis. i, Euchroea coelestis, mantis religiosa.

Wildlife — No. 1197: a, Coracias caudata, Otocyon megalotis. b, Gnu. c, Milvus aegyptus, pelecanus onocrotalus. d, Panthera leo. e, Loxondonta africana. f, Buffalo. g, Hippopotamus amphibius. h, Acinonyx jubatus.

Raptors — No. 1198: a, Buteo rufinus. b, Circus aeruginosus. c, Aquila verreauxii. d, Circaetus gallicus. e, Terathopius ecaudatus. f, Haliaeetus vocifer. g, Milvus milvus. h, Accipiter badius.

1997(?) **Litho.** ***Perf. 13***

1196A A327 200fr Sheet of 8, #b.-i. 7.00 3.00

1197 A327 300fr Sheet of 8, #a.-h. 10.00 4.50

1198 A327 350fr Sheet of 8, #a.-h. 13.00 5.25

1998 World Cup Soccer Championships, France — A328

Player, country, vert: No. 1199, 300fr, Moore, England. No. 1200, 300fr, Rahn, Germany. No. 1201, 300fr, Paulao, Angola. No. 1202, 300fr, Shearer, England.

No. 1203: a, Seaman, England. b, Schillaci, Italy. c, Romario, Brazil. d, McCoist, Scotland. e, Makanaky, Angola. f, Moore, England. g, Muller, Germany. h, Schmeichel, Denmark.

No. 1204, 1500fr, Moore, England, diff. No. 1205, 1500fr, Pele, Brazil.

1998, June 2 ***Perf. 13½x14, 14x13½***

1199-1202 A328 Set of 4 4.50 2.00

1203 A328 205fr Sheet of 8, #a-h, + label 7.00 7.00

Souvenir Sheets

1204-1205 A328 Set of 2 12.00 12.00

Diana, Princess of Wales (1961-97) — A329

Various portraits.

1998 ***Perf. 13½***

1206 A329 200fr Sheet of 9, #a.-i. 8.00 3.50

1207 A329 250fr Sheet of 9, #a.-i. 10.00 4.50

Diana, Princess of Wales (1961-97) — A330

Diana wearing gowns in one of four seasons: No. 1208, White gown, spring. No. 1209, Blue gown, summer. No. 1210, Bridal gown, fall. No. 1211, High-collared white gown, winter.

1998 **Litho.** ***Perf. 13½***

Souvenir Sheets

1208 A330 1500fr multicolored 7.50 2.50

1209 A330 1500fr multicolored 7.50 2.50

1210 A330 2000fr multicolored 9.00 3.50

1211 A330 2000fr multicolored 9.00 3.50

Nos. 1208-1211 each contain one 50x60mm stamp.

Jacqueline Kennedy Onassis (1929-94) A331

Various portraits.

1997 **Litho.** ***Perf. 13½***

1212 A331 250fr Sheet of 9, #a.-i. 10.50 4.25

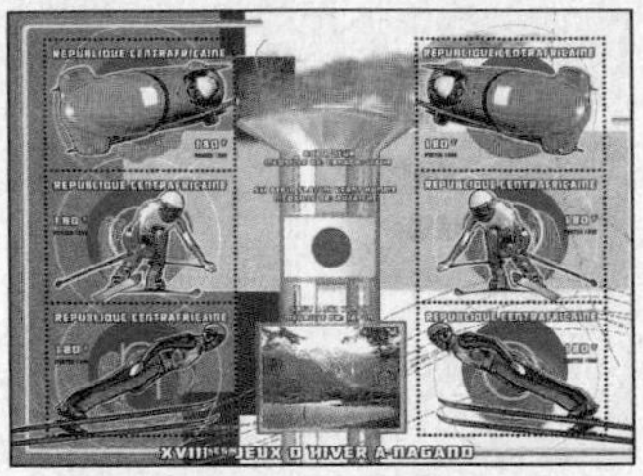

1998 Winter Olympic Games, Nagano — A332

Mirror images of vignette with different backgrounds, denomination at — No. 1213: a, Bobsled, LR. b, Slalom skier, CL. c, Ski jumper, CL. d, Bobsled, LL. e, Slalom skier, CR. f, Ski jumper, CR.

No. 1214: a, Ice hockey, LR. b, Cross-country skier, CR. c, Speed skater, LR. d, Ice hockey, LL. e, Cross-country skier, CL. f, Speed skater, LL.

No. 1215: a, Snow boarding, UR. b, Downhill skier, CR. c, Pairs figure skating, CR. d, Snow boarding, UL. e, Downhill skier, CL. f, Pairs figure skating, CL.

No. 1216, Cross-country, freestyle skiers.

1998

1213 A332 180fr Sheet of 6, #a.-f. 4.00 1.75
1214 A332 300fr Sheet of 6, #a.-f. 7.00 3.00
1215 A332 350fr Sheet of 6, #a.-f. 8.25 3.75

Souvenir Sheet

1216 A332 2000fr multicolored 9.25 3.50

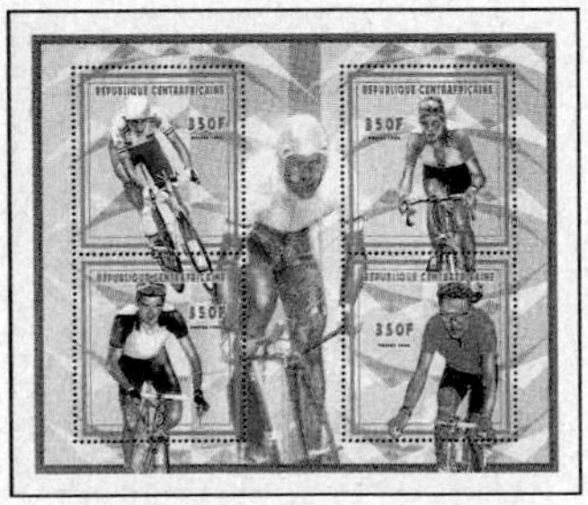

Sports — A333

No. 1217 — Cyclists: a, Woman wearing helmet. b, Woman in pink, white & black outfit. c, Man in black & white outfit. d, Man in yellow & black outfit.

No. 1218 — Female tennis players: a, Holding racket above head. b, Wearing black head band. c, Wearing white head band. d, Wearing dreadlocks.

No. 1219 — Male tennis players: a, Holding racket with his right hand. b, In blue shirt, shorts. c, Holding racket behind head. d, Wearing cap backwards.

No. 1220 — Golfers: a, Completing swing. b, Hitting ball in sand trap. c, In orange knickers, argyle socks. d, Lining up putt.

1998 Litho. *Perf. 13½*

1217 A333 350fr Sheet of 4, #a.-d. 6.50 3.00
1218 A333 375fr Sheet of 4, #a.-d. 7.50 3.50
1219 A333 450fr Sheet of 4, #a.-d. 8.50 3.50
1220 A333 500fr Sheet of 4, #a.-d. 9.00 3.50

Mickey Mouse, 70th Birthday A334

Scenes from various Disney films drawn by Floyd Gottfredson.

No. 1221: a, 10/78. b, 11/78. c, 3/79. d, 7/79. e, 9/79.

No. 1222: a, 10/79. b, 2/80. c, 4/80. d, 6/80. e, 7/80.

No. 1223: a, 11/80. b, 3/81. c, 6/81. d, 9/81. e, 3/82.

No. 1224: a, 5/82. b, 7/82. c, 10/82. d, 3/83. e, 5/83.

No. 1225, 1500fr, Mickey with camera, flashlight. No. 1226, 1500fr, Mickey with pearl in box. No. 1227, 2000fr, Mickey and magic lamp. No. 1228, 2000fr, Floyd Gottfredson.

Perf. 13½x14, 14x13½

1999, Feb. 10 Litho.

1221 A334 280fr Sheet of 5, #a.-e., + label 7.00 3.00
1222 A334 365fr Sheet of 5, #a.-e., + label 9.00 3.50
1223 A334 390fr Sheet of 5, #a.-e., + label 10.00 4.00
1224 A334 440fr Sheet of 5, #a.-e., + label 11.00 4.00

Souvenir Sheets

1225-1226 A334 1500fr Set of 2 15.00 5.00
1227-1228 A334 2000fr Set of 2 20.00 6.50

Birds of Africa — A335

Designs: No. 1229, 500fr, Pandion haliaetus. No. 1230, 500fr,Chaetops frenatus. No. 1231, 500fr, Tachymarptis melba. No. 1232, 500fr, Ceratogymna bucinator. No. 1233, 500fr, Laniarius atrococcineus. No. 1234, 500fr, Coturnix coturnix.

No. 1235: a, Lamprotornis superbus. b, Agapornis personatus. c, Coracias spatulata. d, Euplectes jacksoni. e, Nectarinia violacea. f, Emberiza schoeniclus. g, Pica pica. h, Tauraco erythrolophus. i, Sitta europaea.

No. 1236: a, Merops apiaster. b, Coracias garrulus. c, Cuculus canorus. d, Hirundo rustica. e, Motacilla flava. f, Ardea cinerea. g, Falco tinnunculus. h, Tyto alba. i, Charadrius hiaticula.

1500fr, Eremophila alpestris. 2000fr, Delichon urbica.

1999, Mar. 10 Litho. *Perf. 14*

1229-1234 A335 Set of 6 11.00 5.00
1235 A335 280fr Sheet of 9, #a.-i. 9.25 4.25
1236 A335 490fr Sheet of 9, #a.-i. 16.00 7.50

Souvenir Sheets

1237 A335 1500fr multicolored 5.50 2.50
1238 A335 2000fr multicolored 7.50 3.50

World Wildlife Fund — A336

Balaeniceps rex: a, Eating fish. b, Up close. c, Standing. d, One in flight, one up close.

1999

1239 A336 200fr Strip of 4, #a.-d. 5.00 4.00

No. 1239 was issued in sheets of 16 stamps.

Trains A337

No. 1240: a, 40fr, 2-4-0 Steam locomotive. b, 50fr, German Mallat. c, 60fr, Shunting locomotive. d, 260fr, Rhodesian 14A 2-6-2+2-6-2 Garrat. e, 280fr, Steam train. f, 390fr, Engine No. 7, 0-6-0 Baldwin, 1920. g, 440fr, Amtrak passenger train. h, 460fr, German TEE diesel. i, 490fr, "Sir Nigel Gresley."

No. 1241: a, 40fr, Steam train. b, 50fr, 4-4-0, LNWR, 1897. c, 60fr, 2-4-0 locomotive, Midland. d, 260fr, Class XC. e, 280fr, 2-6-0T Sernada and Aveiro, 1910. f, 390fr, East Daggafontein Mines train, Great Britain. g, 440fr, Union Pacific. h, 460fr, Engine No. 6, Baldwin. i, 490fr, 4-4-2 aerodynamic train, Belgium, 1939.

No. 1242, 2000fr, Fairlie, Snake and Auckland, New Zealand, 1874. No. 1243, 2000fr, Steam train arriving at the London-Brighton Depot.

1999, Mar. 11 Sheets of 9

1240-1241 A337 Set of 2 25.00 10.00

Souvenir Sheets

1242-1243 A337 Set of 2 18.00 6.50

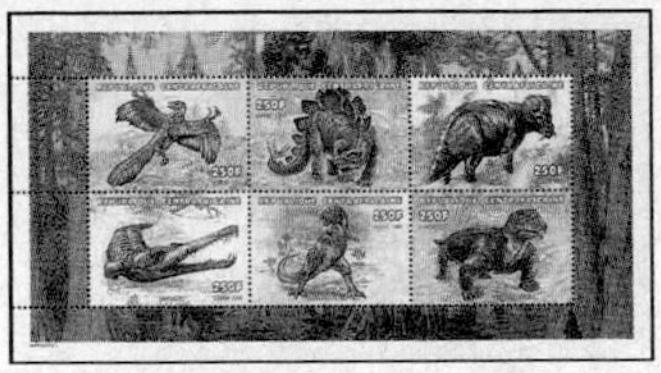

Prehistoric Animals — A338

No. 1244: a, Archaeopteryx. b, Stegosaurus. c, Placerias. d, Rutiodon. e, Tyrannosaurus rex. f, Lystrosaurus.

No. 1245: a, Spinosaurus. b, Cynognathus. c, Kuehneosaurus. d, Compsognathus. e, Triceratops. f, Euoplocephalus.

2000fr, Desmatosuchus.

1998 Litho. *Perf. 13½*

1244 A338 250fr Sheet of 6, #a.-f. 7.50 2.75
1245 A338 300fr Sheet of 6, #a.-f. 8.50 3.25

Souvenir Sheet

1246 A338 2000fr multicolored 9.00 3.75

No. 1246 contains one 51x36mm stamp.

Transportation — A339

No. 1247 — Antique automobiles: a, 1899 Fiat. b, First Chevrolet. c, Serpolet steam carriage. d, 130HP Fiat.

No. 1248 — Cyclists: a, Swiss rider. b, US rider. c, Miguel Indurain (riding to right). d, Jan. Ullrich (riding to left).

No. 1249 — Sports cars: a, Porsche Boxster. b, Corvette. c, Jaguar S-type. d, Maserati 3200 GT.

No. 1250 — High-speed trains: a, TGV Atlantique. b, Shin Kansen. c, ETR X-500. d, Advanced passenger train.

No. 1251 — Trains: a, Cornish Riviera Express. b, Lancashire and Yorkshire Railway. c, Type 230. d, Pacific Mallard.

No. 1252 — Fire trucks: a, 1916 Seagrave. b, 1927 Ahrens-Fox Model JS-2. c, 1992 Diesel. d, 1958 Mack Bulldog, Type B-95.

No. 1253 — Space flight of John Glenn: a, Portrait in business suit. b, In Project Mercury spacesuit. c, In shuttle launch suit, 1998. d, Orbiting earth, Space Shuttle.

No. 1254 — Supersonic airplanes: a, Boeing 2707. b, Transatmospheric prototype. c, Tupolev 144. d, Project of European Supersonic ESRP.

1998

1247 A339 300fr Sheet of 4, #a.-d. 6.00 3.00
1248 A339 350fr Sheet of 4, #a.-d. 6.50 2.50
1249 A339 400fr Sheet of 4, #a.-d. 8.00 3.00
1250 A339 450fr Sheet of 4, #a.-d. 9.00 3.50
1251 A339 500fr Sheet of 4, #a.-d. 9.00 3.75
1252 A339 600fr Sheet of 4, #a.-d. 11.00 4.50
1253 A339 800fr Sheet of 4, #a.-d. 15.00 6.00
1254 A339 1000fr Sheet of 4, #a.-d. 20.00 7.50

Scouting — A340

No. 1255 — Scouts with flowers: a, Vanilla planifolia. b, Flamboyant. c, Angraecum sesquipedale.

No. 1256 — Scouts with butterflies or bird: a, Hesperie a bande. b, Philepitte souimanga. c, Dryope.

No. 1257 — Scouts with dogs, cats, and their young: a, Basenji. b, Egyptian mau cat. c, White dog.

No. 1258 — Scouts with minerals: a, Tourmaline. b, Jasper. c, Madgascar corundum.

No. 1259 — Scouts administrering Red Cross aid: a, Girl Scout wiping child's tears. b, Scout bandaging child. c, Scout kneeling to help child.

No. 1260 — Scouts in leisure activities: a, Playing table tennis. b, Playing chess. c, Riding horse.

1998 Litho. *Perf. 13½*

1255 A340 400fr Sheet of 3, #a.-c. 6.00 2.25
1256 A340 475fr Sheet of 3, #a.-c. 7.00 2.50
1257 A340 500fr Sheet of 3, #a.-c. 8.00 2.75
1258 A340 600fr Sheet of 3, #a.-c. 9.00 3.25
1259 A340 700fr Sheet of 3, #a.-c. 10.00 3.75
1260 A340 800fr Sheet of 3, #a.-c. 10.00 4.50

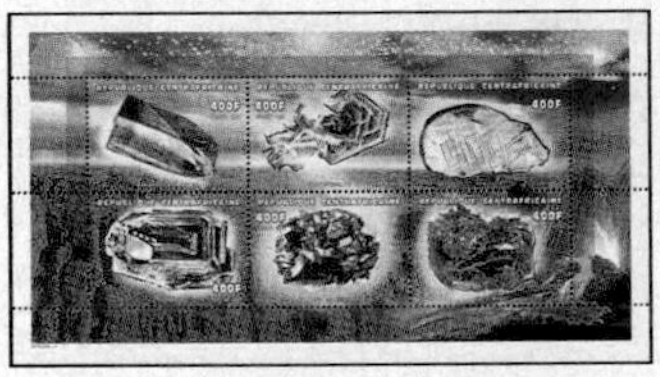

Minerals — A341

No. 1261: a, Hematite (red). b, Challophyllite. c, Fer natif. d, Sylvanite. e. Hematite (specularite). f, Spodumene.

No. 1262: a, Amber. b, Opal. c, Struvite. d, Rhodochrosite. e, Polybasite. f, Silver.

1998 Litho. *Perf. 13½*

1261 A341 400fr Sheet of 6, #a.-f. 12.00 4.50
1262 A341 600fr Sheet of 6, #a.-f. 17.00 6.75

A number has been reserved for a souvenir sheet to go with this set.

Mushrooms A342

40fr, Jelly babies. 50fr, Herald of winter. 65fr, Dentate elf cup. 280fr, Pink wax cap. 345fr, Tripe fungus. 465fr, Funnel tooth. 485fr, Common white saddle. 600fr, False morel.

No. 1272: a, Parrot wax cap. b, Orange naval cap. c, Amethyst deceiver. d, Plums and custard. e, Blue legs. f, Tawny funnel cap. g, Goblet. h, Spindle-shank. i, Buttery tough shank.

No. 1273: a, Fetid mummy cap. b, Stainer. c, Lilac bonnet. d, Firm-fleshed brittle gill. e, Fly agaric. f, Arched bonnet. g, King bolete. h, Orange birch bolete. i, Dog stinkhorn.

1500fr, Hedgehog puffball. 2000fr, Striated earth star.

1999, June 11 Litho. *Perf. 14*

1264-1271 A342 Set of 8 9.50 4.25
1272 A342 390fr Sheet of 9, #a.-i. 15.00 6.50

1273 A342 440fr Sheet of 9, #a.-i. 20.00 6.75

Souvenir Sheets

1274 A342 1500fr multicolored 9.00 4.00
1275 A342 2000fr multicolored 11.00 5.00

Birds — A343

No. 1276: a, Psittacula himalayama. b, Anodorhynchus hyacinthinus. c, Trichoglossus haematodus. d, Xipholena punicea. e, Chloebia gouldiae. f, Ramphastos tucanus.

No. 1277: a, Falco sparverius. b, Polyborus plancus. c, Terathopius ecaudatus. d, Tyto alba. e, Glaucidium passerinum. f, Speotyto cunicularia.

1999 **Litho.** ***Perf. 13½***

1276 A343 350fr Sheet of 6, #a.-f. 12.00 4.00
1277 A343 500fr Sheet of 6, #a.-f. 17.50 5.25

Dogs, Cats, & Horses A344

Designs: 60fr, Doberman, vert. 280fr, Domestic cat, vert. No. 1280, 390fr, Korat, vert. No. 1281, 390fr, Hanoverian, vert. 440fr, Ardennais. 490fr, Lhasa apso.

Dogs — No. 1284: a, Alaskan malamute. b, Musterlander. c, German shepherd. d, Borzoi. e, Afghan hound. f, Irish terrier. g, Komondor. h, Finnish spitz.

Cats — No. 1285: a, American bobtail. b, American curl. c, Singapura. d, Burmese. e, Tortoise shell. f, Scottish fold. g, British shorthair blue. h, Turkish van.

Horses — No. 1286: a, Shire. b, Clydesdale. c, Arabian. d, Soviet work horse. e, Finnish work horse. f, Percheron. g, Draco. h, North Swedish.

No. 1287, 2000fr, Beagle. No. 1288, 2000fr, Havana. No. 1289, 2000fr, Hanoverian.

1999, July 9 **Litho.** ***Perf. 14***

1278-1283 A344 Set of 6 12.00 5.00
1284 A344 465fr Sheet of 8, #a.-h. 20.00 9.00
1285 A344 485fr Sheet of 8, #a.-h. 20.00 8.00
1286 A344 515fr Sheet of 8, #a.-h. 20.00 9.00

Souvenir Sheets

1287-1289 A344 Set of 3 30.00 10.50

Nos. 1287-1289 each contain one 44x56mm stamp.

Butterflies A345

Designs: 40fr, Heliconius melpomene. 65fr, Large oak blue. 280fr, Danaus chrysippus. 345fr, Aricia agestis. 485fr, Danis danis. 600fr, Plebejus argus.

No. 1296: a, Delias mysis. b, Ornithoptera priamus. c, Phoebis philea. d, Heliconius doris. e, Thecla coronata f, Lycaena dispar. g, Bematistes aganise. h, Pereute leucodrosime.

No. 1297: a, Colotis danae. b, Eueides isabella. c, Papilio cresphontes. d, Mimacraea marshalli. e, Parathyma nefte. f, Appias nero. g, Uraneis ucubis. h, Eurema brigitta.

No. 1298: a, Heliconius melpomene, diff. b, Mylothris chloris. c, Catopsilia florella. d, Hebomoia glaucippe. e, Palla ussheri. f, Papilio glaucus. g, Colias erytheme. h, Euploea corus.

No. 1299, 1500fr, Unnamed. No. 1300, 1500fr, Papilio, glaucus, vert.

1999, Dec. **Litho.** ***Perf. 14***

1290-1295 A345 Set of 6 9.00 3.25
1296 A345 280fr Sheet of 8, #a.-h. 12.50 5.00
1297 A345 390fr Sheet of 8, #a.-h. 16.00 6.00
1298 A345 465fr Sheet of 8, #a.-h. 19.00 6.50

Souvenir Sheets

1299-1300 A345 Set of 2 15.00 6.00

Trains A346

Designs: No. 1301, 280fr, Le Capitole, France. No. 1302, 390fr, Montreaux-Bern Line, Switzerland. No. 1303, 485fr, Zugspitzbahn, Switzerland. No. 1304, 485fr, Rhatische Bahn, Swizerland.

No. 1305: a, Schwebebahn, Germany. b, Reichsbahn Class 44, Germany. c, Rembrandt, Germany. d, Trans-Europe Express, Germany. e, Inter-city, Germany. f, Steam locomotive, Germany.

No. 1306: a, ETR300, Italy. b, Mistral, France. c, ER200, Russia. d, Pendoline, Italy. e, Class 1100, Netherlands. f, Rheingold Express, Germany.

No. 1307, 1500fr, TGV, France. No. 1308, 1500fr, Austrian train.

2000, Jan. 25

1301-1304 A346 Set of 4 8.50 3.00
1305 A346 280fr Sheet of 6, #a.-f. 9.00 3.00
1306 A346 390fr Sheet of 6, #a.-f. 12.00 4.25

Souvenir Sheets

1307-1308 A346 Set of 2 17.50 5.00

Flowers — A347

No. 1309: a, Orchid, b, Water crinum. c, Flame lily. d, Narcissus poeticus. e, Belladonna lily. f, Table Mountain orchid. g, Upland cotton. h, Narcissus jonquilla.

No. 1310: a, Moore's crinum. b, Cyrtanthus brachyscyphus. c, Namaqualand daisy. d, "Narcissus poeticus," diff. e, Painted homeria. f, Helen O'Connor. g, Pink oxalis. h, Pink oxalis and pink arum.

No. 1311: a, Yellow wild iris. b, White arum lily (mountains in background). c, Blue tulip. d, Osteospermum. e, Table Mountain orchid, diff. f, White arum lily (with stems and leaves). g, Daisy. h, Meadow saffron.

No. 1312, 1500fr, Amaryllis belladonna, horiz. No. 1313, 1500fr, African tulip tree, horiz. No. 1314, 1500fr, Bird of paradise, horiz.

2000, Feb. 24

1309 A347 280fr Sheet of 8, #a.-h. 12.00 3.50
1310 A347 390fr Sheet of 8, #a.-h. 16.00 4.75
1311 A347 515fr Sheet of 8, #a.-h. 20.00 6.00

Souvenir Sheets

1312-1314 A347 Set of 3 22.50 8.00

Inscription on No. 1310d is incorrect.

Birds A348

Designs: 100fr, Dendrocygna bicolor, vert. 150fr, Tockis flavirostris, vert. 200fr, Treron calva. 300fr, Ardeola ralloides. 450fr, Passer melanus, vert. 750fr, Sturnus vulgaris, vert.

No. 1321, vert.: a, Trachyphonus vaillantii. b, Polyhierax semitorquatus. c, Tockus nasutus. d, Estrilda astrild. e, Merops persicus. f, Amandava subflava. g, Guttera pucherani. h, Oriolus oriolus. i, Bycanistes brevis.

No. 1322: a, Butoides striatus. b, Limnocorax flavirostra. c, Terathopius ecaudatus. d, Mycteria ibis. e, Actophilornis africanus. f, Poicephalus rueppellii. g, Alopochen aegyptiacus. h, Morus capensis. i, Sagittarius serpentarius.

No. 1323: a, Gyps africanus. b, Tyto alba. c, Pelecanus onocrotalus. d, Ephippiorhynchus senegalensis. e, Ardea goliath. f, Sylvia communis. g, Buteo rufofuscus. h, Parus caeruleus. i, Dromas ardeola.

No. 1324, 2000fr, Buphagus africanus. No. 1325, 2000fr, Haliaeetus vocifer. No. 1326, 2000fr, Erythropgia coryphaeus, vert.

2000, Feb. 25

1315-1320 A348 Set of 6 8.50 3.00
1321 A348 390fr Sheet of 9, #a.-i. 16.00 5.25
1322 A348 440fr Sheet of 9, #a.-i. 18.00 6.00
1323 A348 485fr Sheet of 9, #a.-i. 18.00 6.50

Souvenir Sheets

1324-1326 A348 Set of 3 27.50 10.00

Aviation A349

Designs: 280fr, Spirit of St. Louis. 345fr, Hindenburg. 465fr, Flight at Kitty Hawk. 485fr, AH-1 Cobra.

No. 1331: a, Fokker triplane. b, Spad XIII. c, Blériot XI. d, Nieuport 12. e, Sopwith Camel. f, 1920s US Mail plane. g, Otto Lilienthal's hang glider. h, Hydrogen-filled balloon of J. A. C. Charles.

No. 1332: a, Mitchell-B25. b, P-38E Lightning. c, Vought F-4U Corsair. d, Mitsubishi Zero. e, B-17 Flying Fortress. f, P-51 Mustang. g, Flying Tiger plane. h, Messerschmitt Bf-109.

No. 1333: a, X-1. b, B-52C. c, Boeing 707. d, F-16C. e, Sabre jet. f, MiG-15. g, F-4 Phantom. h, F-117A Stealth.

No. 1334, 1500fr, Concorde. No. 1335, 1500fr, Space shuttle "Enterprise."

2000, Feb. 28

1327-1330 A349 Set of 4 7.50 2.40
1331 A349 345fr Sheet of 8, #a.-h. 13.00 4.25
1332 A349 390fr Sheet of 8, #a.-h. 14.50 4.75
1333 A349 515fr Sheet of 8, #a.-h. 19.00 6.25

Souvenir Sheets

1334-1335 A349 1500fr Set of 2 13.00 5.00

Chess Players — A350

No. 1336, 280fr: a, Otto IV of Brandenburg. b, Mme. de Verzu and Chevalier de Bourgogne. c, Chess Players by Estienne Porcher. d, Fresco by F. Pella.

No. 1337, 300fr: a, Two Nobles. b, Depiction from book of Jean Wauquelin. c, Girolamo de Cremona. d, Ashtapada.

No. 1338, 390fr: a, Ulysses and Palamedes. b, Christian cavalier and Muslim. c, Two Moorish women. d, Burzurgmikhr and Kannuja.

No. 1339, 465fr: a, Two men, 18th Cent. b, Napoleon and Cornwallis. c, Adolf Anderssen and Wilhelm Steinitz. d, Queen Victoria.

No. 1340, 485fr: a, Two women. b, Chess on an enlarged board. c, Xerxes. d, King Evil-Merodach.

No. 1341, 515fr: a, King Henry VIII of England. b, Queen Elizabeth I of England. c, King Charles I of England. d, Russian czarevitch.

1999 **Litho.** ***Perf. 13½***

Sheets of 4, #a-d

1336-1341 A350 Set of 6 45.00 18.00

Cosmonauts and Astronauts — A351

No. 1342, 485fr: a, Vladimir Soloviev. b, Georgi Beregovoy. c, Alexei Leonov. d, Pavel Popovich. e, Yuri Gagarin. f, Valentina Tereshkova. g, Helena Kondakova. h, Gherman Titov. i, Alexander Volkov.

No. 1343, 515fr: a, Neil Armstrong. b, Edwin Aldrin. c, Michael Collins. d, Alan Bean. e, James Lovell. f, Alan Shepard. g, David Scott. h, John Young. i, Eugene Cernan.

2000fr, Armstrong and Gagarin, horiz.

1999 **Sheets of 9, #a-i**

1342-1343 A351 Set of 2 35.00 14.00

Souvenir Sheet

1344 A351 2000fr multi 9.00 3.25

No. 1344 contains one 60x51mm stamp.

Millennium — A352

2000, Mar. 31 ***Perf. 14***

1345 A352 515fr multicolored 2.50 1.00

Issued in sheets of six.

2000 Summer Olympics, Sydney — A353

No. 1346, 300fr: a, Individual dressage. b, Rhythmic gymnastics. c, Women's 100-meter hurdles. d, Cycling.

No. 1347, 485fr: a, Tennis. b, Diving. c, Soccer. d, Pole vault.

No. 1348, 750fr: a, Long jump. b, Judo. c, Basketball. d, Show jumping.

No. 1349, 800fr: a, Boxing. b, Table tennis. c, Women's 200-meter sprint. d, Individual three-day equestrian event.

2000 ***Perf. 13½***

Sheets of 4, #a-d

1346-1349 A353 Set of 4 40.00 15.00

2002 Winter Olympics, Salt Lake City — A354

No. 1350, 280fr: a, Freestyle skiing. b, Cross-country skiing. c, Bobsled. d, Men's slalom.

No. 1351, 390fr: a, Luge. b, Women's ski relay. c, Downhill skiing. d, Short track skating.

No. 1352, 465fr: a, Women's figure skating. b, Hockey. c, Ski jumping. d, Biathlon.

No. 1353, 515fr, a, Pairs figure skating. b, Women's giant slalom. c, Speed skating. d, Nordic combined.

2000 **Sheets of 4, #a-d**

1350-1353 A354 Set of 4 30.00 12.00

UPU, 125th Anniv. — A355

UPU emblem and various men: 280fr, 300fr, 390fr, 465fr, 485fr, 515fr, 750fr, 800fr.

2000, Sept. 8 **Litho.** ***Perf. 13¼***

1354-1361 A355 Set of 8 18.00 6.50

Millennium — A356

No. 1362: a, Roald Amundsen, first polar exploration by dirigible, 1926. b, Vladimir Zworykin, inventor of television camera, 1928. c, Sir Alexander Fleming, discoverer of penicillin, 1928.

No. 1363: a, Henri Dunant, 1901 Nobel Peace prize winner. b, Wilbur and Orville Wright, first airplane, 1903. c, Enrico Caruso, opera singer.

No. 1364: a, Theodore Roosevelt, opening of Panama Canal, 1914. b, Albert Einstein, theory of general relativity, 1916. c, Battle of Verdun, 1916.

No. 1365: a, Auguste Piccard, flight to stratosphere in balloon, 1931. b, Robert Goddard, rocketry pioneer, 1935. c, Ferdinand von Zeppelin and Graf Zeppelin, 1928-37.

No. 1366: a, Felix Eboue, governor of Chad, 1940. b, Mahatma Gandhi, independence of India, 1947. c, Marilyn Monroe (1926-62), actress.

No. 1367: a, Juan Manuel Fangio, race car driver. b, James Dean (1931-55), actor. c, Sputnik 1, 1957.

No. 1368: a, Charles De Gaulle (1890-1970), French general and political leader. b, Yuri Gagarin (1934-68), Soviet Cosmonaut. c, Neil Armstrong (1930-), American Astronaut.

No. 1369: a, Apollo-Soyuz. b, Elvis Presley (1935-77), American entertainer. b, Muhammad Ali (1942-), American boxer.

No. 1370: a, John Young, Space Shuttle, 1981. b, Mikhail Gorbachev, fall of the Berlin Wall, 1989. c, Dalai Lama, 1989 Nobel Peace prize winner.

No. 1371: a, Nelson Mandela, 1993 Nobel Peace prize winner. b, Galileo probe reaches Jupiter, 1995. c, Mars Pathfinder, 1998.

2000, Sept. 28 ***Perf. 13¼***

1362 A356 100fr Sheet of 3, #a-c 1.50 .75
1363 A356 280fr Sheet of 3, #a-c 4.00 1.50
1364 A356 300fr Sheet of 3, #a-c 4.50 2.25
1365 A356 390fr Sheet of 3, #a-c 6.00 2.25
1366 A356 465fr Sheet of 3, #a-c 7.50 3.00
1367 A356 485fr Sheet of 3, #a-c 7.50 3.00
1368 A356 515fr Sheet of 3, #a-c 7.50 3.00
1369 A356 750fr Sheet of 3, #a-c 9.00 4.50
1370 A356 800fr Sheet of 3, #a-c 12.00 4.50
1371 A356 1000fr Sheet of 3, #a-c 15.00 6.50
Nos. 1362-1371 (10) 74.50 31.25

Flora, Dinosaurs and Mushrooms — A357

No. 1372 — Buttlerflies: a, Cymothoe lurida. b, Charaxes lasti. c, Charaxes lactetinctus. d, Charaxes opinatus. e, Charaxes subornatus. f, Coelides hanno.

No. 1373 — Butterflies: a, Charaxes cithaeron. b, Charaxes anticlea. c, Bebearia plistonax. d, Charaxes jahlusa. e, Charaxes acraeoides. f, Bebearia oxione.

No. 1374 — Dinosaurs: a, Compsognathus. b, Kritosaurus. c, Nodosaurus. d, Tuojiangosaurus. e, Homalocephalus. f, Tsintaosaurus.

No. 1375 — Birds: a, Veuve royale. b, Travailleur cardinal. c, Gonolek a ventre rouge. d, Touraco de Schalow. e, Touraco Pauline. f, Souimanga orange.

No. 1376 — Dinosaurs: a, Monoclonius. b, Dryosaurus. c, Anatosaurus. d, Styracosaurus. e, Pinacosaurus. f, Kentrosaurus.

No. 1377 — Birds: a, Bateleur de savanes. b, Corbeau a nuque blanche. c, Corvinelle pie. d, Cordon-bleu violace. e, Fauvette passerinette. f, Crombec a face rousse.

No. 1378 — Mushrooms: a, Lentinus sajorcaju. b, Lentinus velutinus. c, Pleurotus luteoalbus. d, Pluteus congolensis. e, Lentinus crinitus. f, Leucoagaricus ferruginosus.

No. 1379 — Mushrooms: a, Lentinus squarrosulus. b, Phlebopus colossus. c, Lentinus tuberregium. d, Phlebopus sudanicus. e, Phlebopus silvaticus. f, Volvariella congolensis.

No. 1380 — Dogs: a, Briard. b, Pyrenees shepherd. c, Chow chow. d, Cocker spaniel. e, Puli. f, Yorkshire terrier.

No. 1381 — Cats: a, American wirehair. b, California spangled cat. c, Chinchilla. d, Exotic shorthair. e, Selkirk Rex. f, Oriental.

No. 1382 — Dogs: a, Greenland dog. b, Alaskan malamute. c, Samoyed. d, Siberian husky.

2001, May 28 **Litho.** ***Perf. 13¼***

1372 A357 280fr Sheet of 6, #a-f 7.25 3.00
1373 A357 300fr Sheet of 6, #a-f 7.75 3.00
1374 A357 300fr Sheet of 6, #a-f 7.75 3.00
1375 A357 350fr Sheet of 6, #a-f 9.50 3.50
1376 A357 390fr Sheet of 6, #a-f 9.50 4.00
1377 A357 390fr Sheet of 6, #a-f 9.50 4.00
1378 A357 390fr Sheet of 6, #a-f 9.50 4.00
1379 A357 465fr Sheet of 6, #a-f 11.50 4.50
1380 A357 465fr Sheet of 6, #a-f 11.00 4.50
1381 A357 485fr Sheet of 6, #a-f 12.00 4.50
1382 A357 600fr Sheet of 4, #a-d 10.00 4.00
Nos. 1372-1382 (11) 105.25 42.00

Fauna and Fish A358

Designs: 280fr, Salamandra salamandra. No. 1384, 300fr, Epiplatys annualatus. No. 1385, 350fr, Pseudotropheus zebra. 400fr, Trichechus senegalensis. 450fr, Pelomedusa subrufa. 500fr, Xenomystus nigri.

No. 1389, vert.: a, Damaliscus dorcas. b, Manis temmincki. c, Hyaena brunnea. d, Lycaon pictus. e, Diceros bicornis. f, Osteolaemis tetraspis. g, Cercocebus torquatus. h, Bunologus monticularis. i, Myosciurus pumilia.

No. 1390: a, Plotosus lineatus. b, Protopterus dolloi. c, Calamoichthys calabaricus. d, Malapterurus electricus. e, Discoglossus pictus. f, Dugong dugon.

No. 1391, 1500fr, Julidochromis ornatus, vert. No. 1392, 1500fr, Hippopotamus amphibius, vert. No. 1393, 1500fr, Afropavo congensis, vert.

Perf. 13¼x13½, 13½x13¼

2001, July 12

1383-1388 A358 Set of 6 10.00 3.00
1389 A358 300fr Sheet of 9, #a-i 12.50 3.50
1390 A358 350fr Sheet of 6, #a-f 9.50 2.75

Souvenir Sheets

1391-1393 A358 Set of 3 21.00 7.50

Reptiles and Amphibians — A359

No. 1394, 350fr: a, Boa arc-en-ciel. b, Crapaud marine. c, Basilic vert. d, Grenouille taureau. e, Tortue happante. f, Pseudoeurycea leprosa.

No. 1395, 350fr: a, Trionix epinelix. b, Iguane rhinoceros. c, Boa constrictor. d, Boa canin. e, Tortue d'etang. f, Dermophis mexicanus.

No. 1396, 1500fr, Serpent des arbres. No. 1397, 1500fr, Grenouille poison.

2001, July 12 ***Perf. 13¼x13½***

Sheets of 6, #a-f

1394-1395 A359 Set of 2 20.00 5.50

Souvenir Sheets

1396-1397 A359 Set of 2 14.00 6.00

Butterflies — A360

No. 1398, 350fr, vert.: a, Papilio garamus. b, Eunica orphise. c, Parides lysander. d, Julia dryas iulia. e, Adelpha mythra. f, Thecla coronata.

No. 1399, 350fr, vert.: a, Battus polydamas. b, Mesene phareus. c, Anartia jatrophae. d, Siproeta epaphus. e, Uraneis ucubis. f, Pereute leucodrosime.

No. 1400, 1500fr, Prepona meander. No. 1401, 1500fr, Morpho peleides. No. 1402, 1500fr, Pieris rapae. No. 1403, 1500fr, Helconius melpomene.

2001, July 12 ***Perf. 13½x13¼***

Sheets of 6, #a-f

1398-1399 A360 Set of 2 20.00 6.00

Souvenir Sheets

1400-1403 A360 Set of 4 27.50 10.00

Nos. 1398-1399 each contain six 28x42mm stamps.

A361

Birds — A362

Designs: 50fr, Macareux moine. 75fr, Harfang des neiges, vert. 100fr, Manchots, vert. 150fr, Fou à pieds bleus, vert.

No. 1408, 325fr: a, Perruche soleil. b, Toucan de cuviée. c, Colibri. d, Ara hyacinthe. e, Pione à tete bleue. f, Perruche flavéolée. g, Pelican. h, Flamant rose. i, Toucan toco.

No. 1409, 325fr: a, Touraco à gros bec. b, Martin-chaseur à poitrine bleue. c, Faucon lanier. d, Inséparable masqué. e, Loriquet à tete bleue. f, Perroquet jaco. g, Perenoptere d'Egypte. h, Grue grise couronnée. i, Marabou.

No. 1410, 350fr, vert.: a, Colibri caraibe. b, Jaseur des cèdres. c, Colibri d'abeille. d, Bruant indigo. e, Tourterelle pleureuse. f, Talève pourprée.

No. 1411, 350fr: a, Gros-bec bleu. b, Fauvette à gorge orangée. c, Pic flamboyant. d, Passerin nonpareil. e, Fauvette à capuchon. f, Bananaquit.

No. 1412, 1500fr, Cygne, vert. No. 1413, 1500fr, Pygargue à tete blanche, vert.

No. 1414, 1500fr, shown. No. 1415, 1500fr, Balbuzard, vert.

Perf. 13¼x13½, 13½x13¼

2001, July 19

1404-1407 A361 Set of 4 3.75 1.50

Sheets of 9, #a-i

1408-1409 A361 Set of 2 26.50 8.25

Sheets of 6, #a-f

Perf. 13¼x13, 13x13¼

1410-1411 A362 Set of 2 20.00 6.00

Souvenir Sheets

Perf. 13½x13¼

1412-1413 A361 Set of 2 14.00 5.00

Perf. 13¼

1414-1415 A362 Set of 2 14.00 5.00

No. 1410 contains six 30x40mm stamps; No. 1411 contains six 40x30mm stamps.

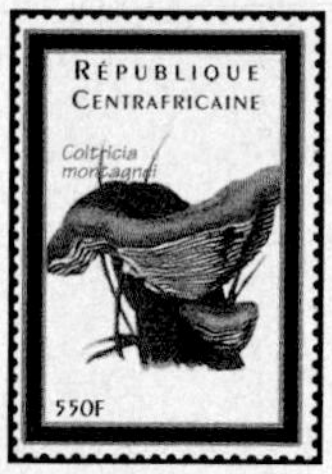

Mushrooms A363

Designs: 550fr, Coltricia montagnei. 600fr, Inocybe fuscodisca. 650fr, Hydnum imbricatum. 700fr, Hygrophorus miniatus.
No. 1420: a, Coprinus picaceus. b, Crinipellis zonata. c, Naematoloma fasciculare. d, Cortinarius caerulescens. e, Amanita muscaria. f, Cortinarius obtusus. g, Entoloma serrulatum. h, Strobilomyces floccopus.
1500fr, Sarcosphaera crassa, horiz.

Perf. 13½x13¼, 13¼x13½

2001, July 26

1416-1419 A363 Set of 4 12.00 3.50
1420 A363 350fr Sheet of 8, #a-h 13.00 4.00

Souvenir Sheet

1421 A363 1500fr multi 7.00 2.50

Prehistoric Animals — A364

Designs: 50fr, Anatasaurus. 100fr, Apatosaurus. 150fr, Allosaurus. 200fr, Velociraptor.
No. 1426, 240fr: a, Rhamphorhynchus. b, Pteranodon. c, Tyrannosaurus rex. d, Deinonychus antirrhopus. e, Parasaurolophus. f, Corythosaurus. g, Patagosaurus. h, Triceratops. i, Brachylophosaurus. j, Europlocephalus. k, Dimetrodon. l, Leptoceratops.
No. 1427, 240fr: a, Perosaur. b, Albertosaurus. c, Dryptosaurus. d, Archaeopteryx. e, Ouranosaurus. f, Myahuera. g, Camptosaurus. h, Ichthyosaurus. i, Geosaurus. j, Trilobita. k, Plesiosaurus. l, Lewisiceras.
No. 1428, 1500fr, Herrerasaurus. No. 1429, 1500fr, Stegosaurus.

2001, July 31 *Perf. 12½*

1422-1425 A364 Set of 4 2.50 .70

Sheets of 12, #a-l, + 8 labels

1426-1427 A364 Set of 2 27.50 8.25

Souvenir Sheets

1428-1429 A364 Set of 2 14.00 4.25

Dinosaurs A365

Designs: 250fr, Apatosaurus. 300fr, Baryonyx. 325fr, Albertosaurus. 375fr, Dimetrodon.
No. 1434, 350fr: a, Triceratops. b, Ornithocherius. c, Brachiosaurus. d, Utahraptor. e, Tyrannosaurus rex. f, Stegosaurus.
No. 1435, 350fr: a, Diplodicus. b, Pachycephalosaurus. c, Archaeopteryx. d, Pteranodon. e, Herrerasaurus. f, Struthiomimus.
No. 1436, 1500fr, Rhamphorhynchus. No. 1437, 1500fr, Proleratops and Deinonychus.

2001, July 31 *Perf. 13¼x13½*

1430-1433 A365 Set of 4 6.00 1.75

Sheets of 6, #a-f

1434-1435 A365 Set of 2 20.00 6.00

Souvenir Sheets

1436-1437 A365 Set of 2 12.00 5.00

Belgica 2001 Intl. Stamp Exhibition, Brussels (Nos. 1434-1437).

2001 Catastrophes — A366

No. 1438: a, Jan. 26 earthquake, India. b, Sept. 11 terrorist attacks, US. c, Dec. 26 fires, Australia. d, Hurricane Michelle, Cuba, Oct. 27. e, July 4 tornado, Canada. f, July 24 eruption of Mt. Etna, Italy.

2002, July 23 *Perf. 13¼*

1438 A366 390fr Sheet of 6, #a-f 9.00 4.00

Each stamp in sheet exists in a souvenir sheet of 1.

Painters and Paintings — A367

No. 1439, 390fr: a, Claude Monet. b, Woman with an Umbrella, by Monet. c, Argenteuil, by Edouard Manet. d, Manet. e, Joseph Mallord William Turner. f, Mornings Amongst the Conniston Falls, Cumberland, by Turner.
No. 1440, 390fr: a, Girl with a Mandolin, by Pablo Picasso. b, Picasso. c, Georges Braque. d, The Musician, by Braque. e, Woman in Blue, by Fernand Leger. f, Leger.

2002, July 23 **Sheets of 6, #a-f**

1439-1440 A367 Set of 2 17.00 7.00

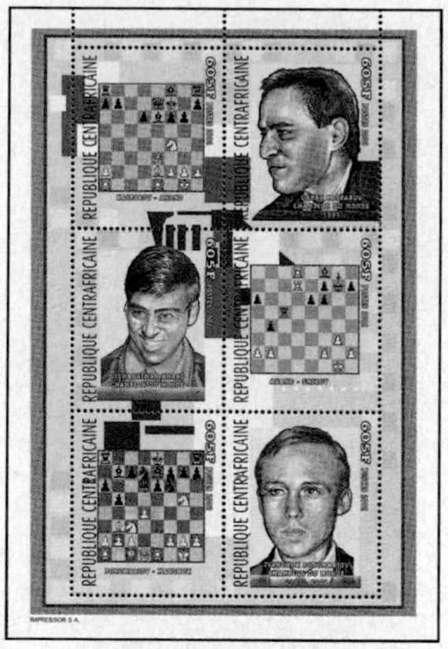

Chess — A368

No. 1441: a, Board from match between Garry Kasparov and Viswantathan Anand. b, Kasparov. c, Anand. d, Board from match between Anand and Shirov. e, Board from match between Ruslan Ponomariov and Vassily Ivanchuk. f, Ponomariov.

2002, July 23

1441 A368 605fr Sheet of 6, #a-f 13.00 5.50

Each horizontal pair in the sheet exists in a souvenir sheet of 2 stamps.

Cosmonauts — A369

No. 1442: a, Yuri Gagarin, Vostok 1. b, Pavel Vinogradov, Mir 24. c, Valentina Tereshkova, Vostok 6. d, Valeri Kubasov, Apollo-Soyuz. e, Alexei Leonov, Voskhod 2. f, Sergei Treschev, Intl. Space Station.

2002, July 23

1442 A369 605fr Sheet of 6, #a-f 13.00 5.50

Zeppelin NT and Concorde — A370

No. 1443: a, Zeppelin NT over Friedrichshafen, Germany. b, Concorde over Rio de Janeiro. c, Concorde over Alaska. d, Zeppelin NT over Lake Constance. e, Zeppelin NT over Orly Airport, Paris. f, Concorde over New York.

2002, July 23

1443 A370 665fr Sheet of 6, #a-f 15.00 6.00

Each stamp in sheet exists in a souvenir sheet of 1.

Famous People — A371

No. 1444: a, Paul Harris, founder of Rotary International. b, Princess Diana, Intl. Red Cross Ambassador against land mines. c, Pope John Paul II. d, Sir Alexander Fleming. e, Mother Teresa. f, Melvin Jones, founder of Lions Club International.

2002, July 23

1444 A371 665fr Sheet of 6, #a-f 15.00 6.00

Each stamp in sheet exists in a souvenir sheet of 1.

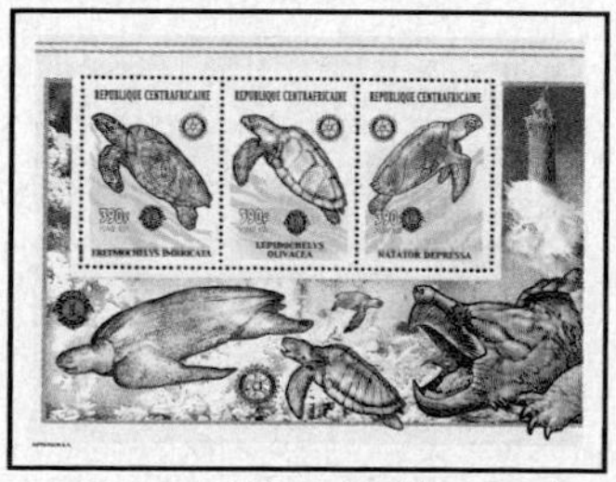

Rotary and Lions Emblems and Animals — A372

No. 1445, 390fr — Turtles: a, Eretmochelys imbricata. b, Lepidochelys olivacea. c, Natator depressa.

No. 1446, 600fr — Dinosaurs: a, Sauropelta. b, Chasmosaurus. c, Herrerasaurus.

2002, Dec. 23 Sheets of 3, #a-c

1445-1446 A372 Set of 2 11.00 4.75

Scouts — A373

No. 1447, 605fr — Orchids: a, Dactylorhiza markusii. b, Cephalanthera rubra. c, Neotinea maculata.

No. 1448, 665fr — Mushrooms: a, Agaricus ostreatus. b, Russula virescens. c, Lactarius deliciosus.

No. 1449, 815fr — Dinosaurs: a, Brachiosaurus. b, Sarcosuchus. c, Gigantosaurus carolinii.

No. 1450, 840fr — Minerals: a, Guilleminite. b, Torbernite. c, Bornite.

Nos. 1451-1452A (each 3000fr), Scout playing: Nos. 1451, 1451A, Chess. Nos. 1452, 1452A, Table tennis.

2002, Dec. 23 Sheets of 3, #a-c

1447-1450 A373 Set of 4 32.50 14.00

A373a

Litho. & Embossed

Perf. 13½

1451	A373a	gold & multi	9.50	9.50
1451A	A373a	sil & multi	9.50	9.50
1452	A373a	gold & multi	9.50	9.50
1452A	A373a	sil & multi	9.50	9.50
	Nos. 1451-1452A (4)		38.00	38.00

Each stamp in each sheet and Nos. 4151-4152A exists in a souvenir sheet of 1.

Famous People A374

Designs: No. 1453, 485fr, Christopher Columbus (1450-1506), explorer. No. 1454, 485fr, Admiral Horatio Nelson (1758-1805). No. 1455, 605fr, Jacques Cartier (1491-1557), explorer. No. 1456, 605fr, Vladimir Yourkevitch (1885-1964), naval designer. No. 1457, 665fr, Columbus, diff. No. 1458, 665fr, Sir Francis Drake (1540-96), explorer. No. 1459, 815fr, Jean-François Champollion (1790-1832), Egyptologist. No. 1460, 815fr, Queen Mother Elizabeth of England (1900-2002). No. 1461, 840fr, Marilyn Monroe (1926-62), actress. No. 1462, 840fr, Elvis Presley (1935-77), singer. No. 1463, 1000fr, Pres. John F. Kennedy (1917-63). No. 1464, 1000fr, French President Charles de Gaulle (1890-1970).

2003, May 15 Litho. *Perf. 13½*

1453-1464 A374 Set of 12 40.00 16.00

Dated 2002. Each stamp also exists in souvenir sheet of 1.

2004 Summer Olympics, Athens A375

Designs: 390fr, Boxing. 485fr, Basketball. 605fr, Equestrian. 655fr, Tennis. 815fr, Table tennis.

2004, Mar. 3 Litho. *Perf. 13½*

1465-1469 A375 Set of 5 14.00 5.75

Dated 2003. Each stamp also exists in souvenir sheet of 1.

2006 World Cup Soccer Championships, Germany — A376

Various soccer players and stadia: 160fr, 390fr, 485fr, 605fr, 815fr.

2004, Mar. 3 Litho. *Perf. 13½*

1470-1474 A376 Set of 5 9.25 9.25

1474a Horiz. strip of 5, #1470-1474 9.25 9.25

Each stamp also exists in a souvenir sheet of 1.

2004 Summer Olympics, Athens — A376a

Designs: Nos. 1475, 1476, Table tennis. Nos. 1477, 1478, Tennis.

Litho. & Embossed

2004, Mar. 3 *Perf. 13½*

1475	A376a	3000fr gold & multi	11.00	11.00
1476	A376a	3000fr sil & multi	11.00	11.00
1477	A376a	3000fr gold & multi	11.00	11.00
1478	A376a	3000fr sil & multi	11.00	11.00
	Nos. 1475-1478 (4)		44.00	44.00

Europa Stamps, 50th Anniv. (in 2006) — A377

Top stamp: 5fr, Netherlands #387. 20fr, Italy #810. 100fr, San Marino #1065. 150fr, Greece #718. 300fr, Italy #1039. 390fr, Italy #916. 465fr, Liechtenstein #368. 485fr, Germany #996. 515fr, Spain #941. 750fr, Finland #419. 800fr, Italy #979. 1500fr, Belgium #840.

2005, Apr. 10 Litho. *Perf. 13½*

1479-1490 A377 Set of 12 22.00 22.00

Gen. François Bozizé, President of Central Africa — A378

2005 ? Litho. *Perf. 13¼*

Frame Color

1493	A378	15fr purple	—
1498	A378	100fr blue	—
1501	A378	300fr red	—
1504	A378	515fr bister	—

Nos. 1498, 1501 and 1504 are dated 2004. No. 1493 is dated 2006. Ten additional stamps were issued in this set. The editors would like to examine any examples.

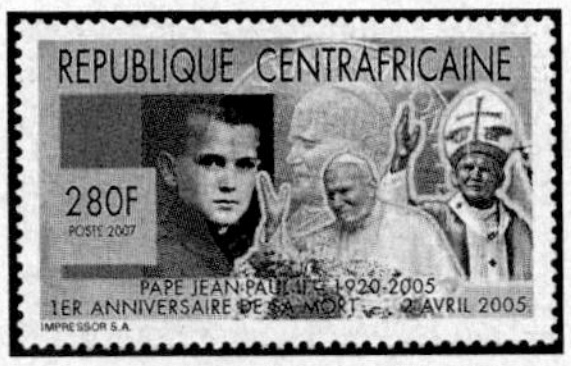

Pope John Paul II (1920-2005) — A379

Various portraits of Pope John Paul II: 280fr, 1000fr.

2007, Aug. 24 Litho. *Perf. 13¼*

1505-1506 A379 Set of 2 5.50 2.75

Each stamp also exists in a souvenir sheet of 1.

2008 Summer Olympics, Beijing — A380

Designs: 300fr, Chinese female athlete, swimmer. 390fr, Chinese soccer players, stadium. 1000fr, Chinese table tennis players, building.

2007, Apr. 24

1507-1509 A380 Set of 3 7.00 3.50

Each stamp also exists in a souvenir sheet of 1.

Princess Diana (1961-97) — A381

Princess Diana with: No. 1510, 390fr, Mother Teresa. No. 1511, 390fr, Pope John Paul II.

2007, Aug. 24 Litho. *Perf. 13¼*

1510-1511 A381 Set of 2 3.25 3.25

Nos. 1510 and 1511 each exist in souvenir sheets of 1.

Worldwide Fund For Nature (WWF) — A382

Civettictis civetta: 390fr, Standing in grass. 485fr, Adult and juvenile at den. 515fr, Head. 750fr, On branch.

2007, Aug. 24

1512-1515 A382 Set of 4 9.00 9.00

Nos. 1512-1515 exist with printer's inscription at lower left in a souvenir sheet of 4.

A386

No. 1522, 650fr — Rhinoceroses: a, Two rhinocersoses facing left. b, Head of rhinoceros facing right, rhinoceros walking left. c, Two rhinoceroses, one facing right, one facing forward. d, Three rhinoceroses.

No. 1523, 650fr — Gorillas: a, Gorilla beringei, adult and juvenile at left, large gorilla at right. b, Gorilla beringei, gorilla in foliage at left, large gorilla at right. c, Gorilla gorilla, large gorilla at left. d, Gorilla beringei, adult and juvenile at left, large gorilla showing teeth at right.

No. 1524, 650fr — Bats: a, Two Rousettus lanosus. b, Three Rousettus lanosus. c, Two Megaloglossus woermanni. d, Two Hipposideros abae.

No. 1525, 650fr — Lions: a, Male and female. b, Two females in tree. c, Three cubs, two playing, one front paws on rock. d, Head of male, cub chewing on stick.

No. 1526, 650fr — Wild cats: a, Felis margarita. b, Pardofelis temminckii. c, Felis silvestris lybica. d, Caracal aurata.

No. 1527, 650fr — Dogs: a, Dogues de Bordeaux. b, Irish terriers. c, Basenjis. d, Boerboels.

No. 1528, 650fr — Elephants: a, Two Loxondonta africana, grass in foreground. b, Two Loxodonta cyclotis, grass in foreground. c, Two Loxodonta africana, elephant with raised trunk at left. d, Loxodonta cyclotis, elephant eating at right..

No. 1529, 650fr — Horses: a, Horse leaping in background. b, Horse running left in background. c, Light brown horses. d, White horse at left, brown horse in background.

No. 1530, 650fr — Dolphins: a, Sousa teuszii, Tursiops truncatus. b,Two Tursiops truncatus, Latin name at LR. c, Two Sousa teuszii. d, Two Tursiops truncatus, latin name at LL.

No. 1531, 650fr — Whales: a, Balaenoptera acutorostrata, Latin name at LL. b, Eubalaena australis. c, Balaenoptera acutorostrata, Latin name at center left. d, Megaptera novaeangliae.

No. 1532, 650fr — Birds of prey: a, Aquila rapax rapax. b, Terathopius ecaudatus. c, Buteo augur. d, Haliaeetus vocifer.

No. 1533, 650fr — Parrots: a, Poicephalus senegalus, Latin name in white. b, Poicephalus rueppellii. c, Psittacus erithacus. d, Poicephalus senegalus, Latin name in black.

No. 1534, 650fr — Peacocks (Afropavo congensis) with Latin name at: a, UR, denomination at LL. b, LL, denomination at top center. c, UR, denomination at right center. d, LR, denomination at UL.

No. 1535, 650fr — Kingfishers: a, Ceryle rudis, Latin name at top. b, Merops apiaster. c, Megaceryle maxima. d, Ceryle rudis, Latin name at right.

No. 1536, 650fr — Owls: a, Asio madagascariensis. b, Asio capensis. c, Bubo africanus. d, Asio flammeus.

No. 1537, 650fr — Owls: a, Scotopelia peli. b, Strix aluco yamadae. c, Scotopelia peli, Strix aluco aluco. d, Strix aluco aluco, denomination at LL.

No. 1538, 650fr — Bees: a, Apis mellifera scutellata and Jean-Henri Fabre (1823-1915), entomologist. b, Apis mellifera monticola and Charles Valentine Riley (1843-95), entomologist. c, Apis mellifera scutellata and Pierre André Latreille (1762-1833), zoologist. d, Apis mellifera scutellata and Léon Provancher (1820-92), naturalist.

No. 1539, 650fr — Beetles: a, Chrysocarabus auronitens, Cleridae. b, Cortodera humeralis, Goliathus goliathus. c, Cleridae. d, Ips typographus, Stictoleptura tripartita.

No. 1540, 650fr — Butterflies: a, Papilio demodocus. b, Phalanta phalantha, Latin name at top center. c, Tarucus thespis. d, Phalanta phalantha, Latin name at left center.

No. 1541, 650fr — Butterflies: a, Tarucus theophrastus, Melanitis leda. b, Catopsilia florella. c, Colotis danae. d, Junonia hierta.

No. 1542, 650fr — Fish: a, Sphyraena barracuda. b, Balistes vetula. c, Pomacanthus imperator. d, Naso elegans.

No. 1543, 650fr — Marine life (Homarus gammarus) and: a, Ostreidae. b, Pecten maximus. c, Tripneustes ventricosus. d, Sepia officinalis.

No. 1544, 650fr — Cacti: a, Opuntia ficus-indica, denomination at UR. b, Opuntia ficus-indica, denomination at LR. c, Brachycereus nesioticus, Rhipsalis baccifera. d, Euphorbia lactea.

No. 1545, 650fr — Orchids: a, Spathoglottis kimballiana and Pierre Marie Auguste Broussonet (1761-1807), naturalist. b, Spathoglottis plicata and Jean-Baptiste de Lamarck (1744-1829), naturalist. c, Eurychone galeandrae and Antoine Gouan (1733-1821), naturalist. d, Eulophia alta and Joseph Pitton de Tournefort (1656-1708), botanist.

No. 1546, 650fr — Minerals: a, Hématite and rutile. b, Limonite, denomination at LL. c, Limonite, denomination at LR. d, Gold.

No. 1547, 650fr — Worldwide Fund for Nature stamps of other countries: a, Botswana #915. b, Niue #730. c, Sierra Leone #588. d, British Antarctic Territory #192.

No. 1548, 2400fr, Two rhinoceroses, diff. No. 1549, 2400fr, Gorilla gorilla and Dian Fossey (1932-85), primatologist. No. 1550, 2400fr, Epomops franqueti. No. 1551, 2400fr, Two male lions. No. 1552, 2400fr, Profelis aurata. No. 1553, 2400fr, Azawakhs. No. 1554, 2400fr, Two elephants, diff. No. 1555, 2400fr, Horse and man. No. 1556, 2400fr, Cephalorhynchus heavisidii. No. 1557, 2400fr, Caperea marginata, Balaenoptera acutorostrata. No. 1558, 2400fr, Aquila nipalensis, Aquila rapax. No. 1559, 2400fr, Poicephalus senegalus, Poicephalus gulielmi. No. 1560, 2400fr, Two Afropavo congensis, diff. No. 1561, 2400fr, Megaceryle maxima, diff. No. 1562, 2400fr, Asio capensis, diff. No. 1563, 2400fr, Strix butleri, Scotopelia peli. No. 1564, 2400fr, Apis mellifera scutellata and Fabre, diff. No. 1565, 2400fr, Phchyntoeus, Goliathus goliathus. No. 1566, 2400fr, Belenols aurota and boy with butterfly net. No. 1567, 2400fr, Leptotes pirithous, Eurema hecabe. No. 1568, 2400fr, Ctenochaetus hawaiiensis. No. 1569, 2400fr, Homarus, Venerupis decussata. No. 1570, 2400fr, Opuntia ficus-indica and bat. No. 1571, 2400fr, Eulophia alta and Jean Jules Linden (1817-98), botanist. No. 1572, 2400fr, Quartz and boy. No. 1573, 2400fr, Slovenia #247c.

2011, Dec. 20 Litho. *Perf. 13¼*

Sheets of 4, #a-d

1522-1547 A386 Set of 26 275.00 275.00

Souvenir Sheets

1548-1573 A386 Set of 26 250.00 250.00

A387

No. 1574, 1000fr — Wedding of Prince William and Catherine Middleton: a, Couple. b, Couple and archbishop. c, Couple, vert.

No. 1575, 1000fr — Princess Diana (1961-97): a, Visiting child in Japanese hospital, 1995. b, Visiting child at Mother Teresa Hospice, 1995. c, Holding Camila Fiocco at Northwick Park Hospital, 1997, vert.

No. 1576, 1000fr — Mohandas K. Gandhi (1869-1948), Indian nationalist: a, Leading march, 1931. b, Addressing crowd in Calcutta, 1919. c, With Sarojini Naidu in Salt March, 1930, vert.

No. 1577, 1000fr — Pope John Paul II (1920-2005), papal arms and: a, African animals. b, Map of Africa. c, Tree, vert.

No. 1578, 1000fr — Yuri Gagarin (1934-68), first man in space, and: a, MiG-15. b, His children, monument to Gagarin in Moscow. c, Vostok 1 lifting off, vert.

No. 1579, 1000fr — Marilyn Monroe (1926-62), actress: a, With camera and flag in background. b, With flag stripes in background. c, With mouth open, vert.

No. 1580, 1000fr — Brigitte Bardot, actress, and scene from: a, Viva Maria!, 1965. b, Don Juan, 1973. c, Shalako, 1968, vert.

No. 1581, 1000fr — Romy Schneider (1938-82), actress, and scene from: a, Max and the Junkmen, 1971. b, 10:30 P.M. Summer, 1966. c, Otley, 1968, vert.

No. 1582, 1000fr — Elvis Presley (1935-77), playing guitar, and: a, Denomination at UL. b, Wife, Priscilla, and daughter, Lisa Marie. c, White star in background, vert.

No. 1583, 1000fr — Composers: a, Felix Mendelssohn (1809-47). b, Johann Sebastian Bach (1685-1750). c, Johannes Brahms (1833-97), vert.

No. 1584, 1000fr — Presidents of France: a, Charles de Gaulle (1890-1970). b, Jacques Chirac and Nicolas Sarkozy. c, Georges Pompidou (1911-74), vert.

No. 1585, 1000fr — Nobel Prize winners: a, Ada Yonath, 2009 Chemistry laureate, and ribosome. b, Andre Geim, 2010 Physics laureate, and graphene lattice. c, Elizabeth Blackburn, 2009 Physiology or Medicine laureate, and telomerase, vert.

No. 1586, 1000fr — Impressionist painters and their paintings: a, View of Pontoise: Quai du Pothuis, by Camille Pissarro (1830-1903). b, Flood at Port Marly, by Alfred Sisley (1839-99). c, The Absinthe Drinker, by Edgar Degas (1834-1917), vert.

No. 1587, 1000fr — Entomologists: a, Andrey Avinoff (1884-1949), and Daphnis nerii. b, Eleanor Anne Ormerod (1828-1901), and Junonia orithya. c, Jean-Henri Fabre (1823-1915), and Graphium agamemnon, vert.

No. 1588, 1000fr — Mycologists: a, William Murrill (1869-1957), and Cantharellus aurantiacus. b, Fred Jay Seaver (1877-1970), and Stropharia viridula. c, Arthur Henry Reginald Buller (1874-1944), and Amanita mappa, vert.

No. 1589, 1000fr — Mineralogists: a, Florence Bascom (1862-1945), and kyanite. b, Otto Wilhelm Herrmann von Abich (1806-86), and abichite. c, Auguste Michel-Lévy (1844-1911), and calcaires, vert.

No. 1590, 1000fr — Sports of 2012 Summer Olympics, London: a, Taekwondo. b, Boxing. c, Archery, vert.

No. 1591, 1000fr — Table tennis players: a, Timo Boll. b, Wang Liqin. c, Liu Shiwen, vert.

No. 1592, 1000fr — World chess champions: a, Paul Morphy (1837-84). b, Mikhail Botvinnik (1911-95). c, Alexander Alekhine (1892-1946), vert.

No. 1593, 1000fr — Scouts: a, Five Boy Scouts. b, Boy Scout bugler, Boy Scout with pigeons. c, Boy Scouts adjusting tent, Olave Baden-Powell (1889-1977), vert.

No. 1594, 1000fr — Survivors of the sinking of the Titanic: a, Eva Hart (1905-96). b, Dorothy Gibson (1889-1946). c, Ruth Elizabeth Becker (1899-1990), vert.

No. 1595, 1000fr — New Year 2012 (Year of the Dragon): a, Dragon, denomination at UL. b, Dragon, denomination at UR. c, Dragon, vert.

No. 1596, 1000fr — Indonesia 2012 Intl. Philatelic Exhibition emblem and: a, Rinjani Volcano, Panthera tigris sumatrae. b, Ijen volcanic crater, Pongo abelii, vert. c, Krakatoa Volcano, Elephas maximus borneensis, vert.

No. 1597, 2700fr, Prince William and Catherine Middleton, diff. No. 1598, 2700fr, Princess Diana with child at Hindu temple, London. No. 1599, 2700fr, Gandhi and young girl. No. 1600, 2700fr, Pope John Paul II kissing ground at Bangui Airport. No. 1601, 2700fr, Gagarin and Vostok 1 lifting off, diff. No. 1602, 2700fr, Monroe, diff. No. 1603, 2700fr, Bardot, diff. No. 1604, 2700fr, Schneider, scene from Adorable Sinner, 1959. No. 1605, 2700fr, Presley, diff. No. 1606, 2700fr, Wolfgang Amadeus Mozart (1756-91), composer. No. 1607, 2700fr, French President Nicolas Sarkozy, U.S. President Barack Obama. No. 1608, 2700fr, Robert G. Edwards, 2010 Physiology and Medicine Nobel laureate and in-vitro fertilization. No. 1609, 2700fr, Impression, Soleil Levant, by Clause Monet (1840-1926). No. 1610, 2700fr, Evelyn Cheesman (1881-1969), entomologist, and Phalacrognathus muelleri. No. 1611, 2700fr, Elsie Maud Wakefield (1886-1972), mycologist, and Lactaria vellerea. No. 1612, 2700fr, Ignacy Domeyko (1802-89), mineralogist, and domeykite. No. 1613, 2700fr, Dressage. No. 1614, 2700fr, Table tennis player Ding Ning. No. 1615, 2700fr, World chess champion Anatoly Karpov. No. 1616, 2700fr, Boy Scouts and Lord Robert Baden-Powell (1857-1941). No. 1617, 2700fr, Lolo and Edmond Navratil, survivors of sinking of the Titanic. No. 1618, 2700fr, Dragon, diff. No. 1619, 2700fr, Indonesia 2012 Intl. Philatelic Exhibition emblem and Varanus komodoensis, vert.

2011, Dec. 27 Litho. *Perf. 13¼*

Sheets of 3, #a-c

1574-1596 A387 Set of 23 275.00 275.00

Souvenir Sheets

1597-1619 A387 Set of 23 250.00 250.00

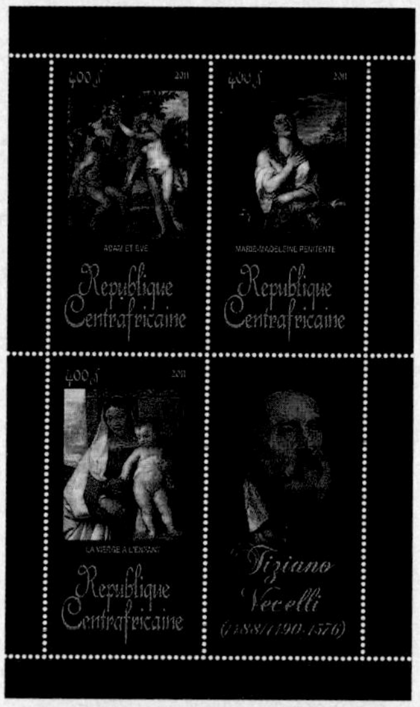

A388

A389

Art — A390

No. 1620, 400fr — Inscriptions: a, Adam et Eve. b, Marie-Madeleine Pénitente. c, La Vierge à L'Enfant.

No. 1621, 400fr — Inscriptions: a, Venus en Devant le Miroir. b, La Flore. c, Le Suicide de Lucrèce.

No. 1622, 400fr — Inscriptions: a, Noli Me Tangere. b, Mater Dolorosa. c, Marei avec L'Enfant et des Saintes.

No. 1623, 400fr, horiz. — Inscriptions: a, La Venus d'Urbino (woman in background). b, La Venus d'Urbino (no woman in background). c, Danaé avec Nourrice.

No. 1624, 3200fr, Like #1620a. No. 1625, 3200fr, Like #1620b. No. 1626, 3200fr, Like #1620c. No. 1627, 3200fr, Like #1621a. No. 1628, 3200fr, Like #1621b. No. 1629, 3200fr, Like #1621c. No. 1630, 3200fr, Like #1622a. No. 1631, 3200fr, Like #1622b. No. 1632, 3200fr, Like #1622c, horiz. No. 1633, 3200fr, Like #1623a (image flipped). No. 1634, 3200fr, Like #1623b. No. 1635, 3200fr, Like #1623c.

No. 1636, 4000fr, Venus et Adonis.

No. 1637, 400fr — Inscriptions: a, La Toilette de Venus. b, Hercuse et Omfala. c, Marquise de Pompadour.

No. 1638, 400fr — Inscriptions: a, Venus Consoler Amour. b, Jeune Femme avec un Bouquet de Roses. c, Venus Fin Cupidon.

No. 1639, 400fr — Inscriptions: a, Portrait d'une Femme. b, Putti avec des Oiseaux. c, Diana au Bain.

No. 1640, 400fr, horiz. — Inscriptions: a, Portrait de Marie-Louise O'Murphy. b, L'Odalisque. c, Léda et la Cygne.

No. 1641, 3200fr, Like #1637a. No. 1642, 3200fr, Like #1637b. No. 1643, 3200fr, Like #1637c. No. 1644, 3200fr, Like #1638a. No. 1645, 3200fr, Like #1638b. No. 1646, 3200fr, Like #1638c. No. 1647, 3200fr, Like #1639a. No. 1648, 3200fr, Like #1639b. No. 1649, 3200fr, Like #1639c, horiz. No. 1650, 3200fr, Like #1640a. No. 1651, 3200fr, Like #1640b. No. 1652, 3200fr, Like #1640c.

No. 1653, 4000fr, Renaud et Armide.

No. 1654, 400fr — Inscriptions: a, Portrait de Victor Jaquemont. b, Déjeuner sur l'Herbe de l'Etude. c, Peupliers le Long du Fleuve Epte.

No. 1655, 400fr — Inscriptions: a, Camille avec un Petit Chien. b, Camille Monet en Costume Japonais. c, Femme à l'Ombrelle.

No. 1656, 400fr — Inscriptions: a, Femme à l'Ombrelle Tournée vers la Droite. b, Poly, Pêcheur de Belle-Ile. c, Le Déjeuner.

No. 1657, 400fr, horiz. — Inscriptions: a, Le Pont sur la Seine. b, Le Pont, D'Amsterdam. c, Chambres du Parlement, Coucher de Soleil.

No. 1658, 3200fr, Like #1654a. No. 1659, 3200fr, Like #1654b. No. 1660, 3200fr, Like #1654c. No. 1661, 3200fr, Like #1655a. No. 1662, 3200fr, Like #1655b. No. 1663, 3200fr, Like #1655c. No. 1664, 3200fr, Like #1656a. No. 1665, 3200fr, Like #1656b. No. 1666, 3200fr, Like #1656c. No. 1667, 3200fr, Like #1657a. No. 1668, 3200fr, Like #1657b. No. 1669, 3200fr, Like #1657c.

No. 1670, 4000fr, Camille Monet et un Enfant dans le Jardin de l'Artiste à Argenteuil.

No. 1671, 400fr — Inscriptions: a, Sainte-Anne avec la Vierge et l'Enfant. b, Portrait d'une Jeune Femme Vénitienne. c, Christ comme l'Homme des Douleurs. d, Portrait de Maximilien I. e, Portrait d'Elsbeth Tucher. f, Portrait de Oswolt Krel.

No. 1672, 400fr — Inscriptions: a, Madone et l'Enfant. b, Adam et Eve. c, Lamentations sur le Christ Mort. d, Vierge et l'Enfant avant d'une Arcade. e, Le Vol à Destination de l'Egypte Résineux. f, Jérôme Pénitent.

No. 1673, 3200fr, Like #1671a. No. 1674, 3200fr, Like #1671b. No. 1675, 3200fr, Like #1671c. No. 1676, 3200fr, Like #1671d. No. 1677, 3200fr, Like #1671e. No. 1678, 3200fr, Like #1671f. No. 1679, 3200fr, Like #1672a. No. 1680, 3200fr, Like #1672b. No. 1681, 3200fr, Like #1672c. No. 1682, 3200fr, Like #1672d. No. 1683, 3200fr, Like #1672e. No. 1684, 3200fr, Like #1672f.

No. 1685, 4000fr, Bacchanales avec Silene.

No. 1686, 400fr — Inscriptions: a, David (statue). b, La Pietà (statue). c, Jugement Dernier Christ Juge. d, Le Prophète Zacharie. e, Le Prophète Jérémie. f, La Sibylle de Cumes.

No. 1687, 400fr — Inscriptions: a, Le Prophète Joel. b, Le Prophète Jessaja. c, Le Prophète Ezéchiel. d, La Sibylle d'Erythrée. e, La Sibylle de Delphes. f, La Sibylle de Libye.

No. 1688, 3200fr, Like #1686a. No. 1689, 3200fr, Like #1686b. No. 1690, 3200fr, Like #1686c. No. 1691, 3200fr, Like #1686d. No. 1692, 3200fr, Like #1686e. No. 1693, 3200fr, Like #1686f. No. 1694, 3200fr, Like #1687a. No. 1695, 3200fr, Like #1687b. No. 1696, 3200fr, Like #1687c. No. 1697, 3200fr, Like #1687d. No. 1698, 3200fr, Like #1687e. No. 1699, 3200fr, Like #1687f.

No. 1700, 4000fr, La Chapelle Sixtine.

No. 1701, 400fr — Inscriptions: a, Le Christ Bénissant. b, La Vierge Colonna. c, Saint-George aux Prises avec les Dragons. d, Madone du Chardonneret. e, La Vierge Garvagh. f, La Madone Sixtine.

No. 1702, 400fr — Inscriptions: a, Saint-Michel. b, Le Portrait d'une Jeune Femme. c, Sainte-Catherine d'Alexandrie. d, Madonna del Baldacchio. e, La Sainte Famille avec les Saints Elizabeth et John. f, La Vierge de la Maison d'Orléans.

No. 1703, 3200fr, Like #1701a. No. 1704, 3200fr, Like #1701b. No. 1705, 3200fr, Like #1701c. No. 1706, 3200fr, Like #1701d. No. 1707, 3200fr, Like #1701e. No. 1708, 3200fr, Like #1701f. No. 1709, 3200fr, Like #1702a. No. 1710, 3200fr, Like #1702b. No. 1711, 3200fr, Like #1702c. No. 1712, 3200fr, Like #1702d. No. 1713, 3200fr, Like #1702e. No. 1714, 3200fr, Like #1702f.

No. 1715, 4000fr, La Dispute du Saint Sacrement.

No. 1716, 400fr — Inscriptions: a, Alexandre et de Roxane. b, Viol des Filles de Leucippe. c, Le Débarquement de Marie de Médicis à Marseille. d, Bethsabée à la Fontaine. e, Persée Libératrice Andromède. f, Diane et ses Nymphes Surpris par les Faunes.

No. 1717, 400fr — Inscriptions: a, L'Union de la Terre et de l'Eau. b, Bacchus. c, Vénus à un Miroir. d, Les Trois Grâces. e, Isabelle, Gouverneur des Pays Bas. f, Erection de la Croix.

No. 1718, 3200fr, Like #1716a. No. 1719, 3200fr, Like #1716b. No. 1720, 3200fr, Like #1716c. No. 1721, 3200fr, Like #1716d. No. 1722, 3200fr, Like #1716e. No. 1723, 3200fr, Like #1716f. No. 1724, 3200fr, Like #1717a. No. 1725, 3200fr, Like #1717b. No. 1726, 3200fr, Like #1717c. No. 1727, 3200fr, Like #1717d. No. 1728, 3200fr, Like #1717e. No. 1729, 3200fr, Like #1717f.

No. 1730, 4000fr, Ixion.

No. 1731, 400fr — Inscriptions: a, Philadelphie et Elisabeth Cary. b, Marchesa Durazzo. c, Saint-Pierre. d, Susanna & Aînés. e, Saint Jean le Baptiste dans le Desert. f, St. Rosalie Intercédant pour les Pestiférés de Palerme.

No. 1732, 400fr — Inscriptions: a, Charles Ier de Chasse. b, Golgotha. c, Silène Ivre. d, L'Homme en Armure avec Foulard Rouge. e, Portrait de Famille. f, Tête d'une Jeune Femme.

No. 1733, 3200fr, Like #1731a. No. 1734, 3200fr, Like #1731b. No. 1735, 3200fr, Like #1731c. No. 1736, 3200fr, Like #1731d. No. 1737, 3200fr, Like #1731e. No. 1738, 3200fr, Like #1731f. No. 1739, 3200fr, Like #1732a. No. 1740, 3200fr, Like #1732b. No. 1741, 3200fr, Like #1732c. No. 1742, 3200fr, Like #1732d. No. 1743, 3200fr, Like #1732e. No. 1744, 3200fr, Like #1732f.

No. 1745, 4000fr, Déploration du Christ.

No. 1746, 400fr — Inscriptions: a, Saskia en Flore. b, Artemis. c, Une Jeune Femme qui Tente sur Boucles d'Oreilles. d, David et Jonathan. e, La Sainte Famille (Jesus in cradle). f, La Sainte Famille (Mary holding Jesus).

No. 1747, 400fr — Inscriptions: a, Abraham le Sacrifice. b, Balaam Ass. c, Tobie Accusant Anna de Voler le Kid. d, La Fête de la Musique. e, Christ dans la Tempête sur le Lac de Galilée. f, Enlèvement de Ganymède.

No. 1748, 3200fr, Like #1746a. No. 1749, 3200fr, Like #1746b. No. 1750, 3200fr, Like #1746c. No. 1751, 3200fr, Like #1746d. No. 1752, 3200fr, Like #1746e. No. 1753, 3200fr, Like #1746f. No. 1754, 3200fr, Like #1747a. No. 1755, 3200fr, Like #1747b. No. 1756, 3200fr, Like #1747c. No. 1757, 3200fr, Like #1747d. No. 1758, 3200fr, Like #1747e. No. 1759, 3200fr, Like #1747f.

No. 1760, 4000fr, La Scène de l'Enfant Prodigue dans la Taverne.

No. 1761, 400fr — Inscriptions: a, Baigneuse Arrangeant ses Cheveux. b, Femme Endormie. c, Baigneuse aux Cheveux Longs. d, La Promenade. e, Une Femme Jouant de la Guitare. f, Femme Arranger ses Cheveux.

No. 1762, 400fr — Inscriptions: a, Femme de Baignade. b, Jeanne Samary. c, Junge Badende. d, La Loge. e, Gabrielle à la Rose. f, Deux Soeurs sur la Terrasse.

No. 1763, 3200fr, Like #1761a. No. 1764, 3200fr, Like #1761b. No. 1765, 3200fr, Like #1761c. No. 1766, 3200fr, Like #1761d. No. 1767, 3200fr, Like #1761e. No. 1768, 3200fr, Like #1761f. No. 1769, 3200fr, Like #1762a. No. 1770, 3200fr, Like #1762b. No. 1771, 3200fr, Like #1762c. No. 1772, 3200fr, Like #1762d. No. 1773, 3200fr, Like #1762e. No. 1774, 3200fr, Like #1762f.

No. 1775, 4000fr, Oarsmen at Chatou.

No. 1776, 400fr — Inscriptions: a, Après le Bain (woman kneeling, striped floral wallpaper in background). b, Les Buveurs d'Absinthe. c, Après le Bain (woman standing with leg lifted). d, La Ballerine. e, Après le Bain (woman kneeling, plain background). f, Petit-Déjeuner Après un Bain.

No. 1777, 400fr — Inscriptions: a, Danseuse Assise. b, Inclinaison Dancer. c, Mademoiselle Malo. d, Femme se Coiffant Devant un Miroir. e, Musiciens de l'Orchestre. f, Six Amis de l'Artiste.

No. 1778, 3200fr, Like #1776a. No. 1779, 3200fr, Like #1776b. No. 1780, 3200fr, Like #1776c. No. 1781, 3200fr, Like #1776d. No. 1782, 3200fr, Like #1776e. No. 1783, 3200fr, Like #1776f. No. 1784, 3200fr, Like #1777a. No. 1785, 3200fr, Like #1777b. No. 1786, 3200fr, Like #1777c. No. 1787, 3200fr, Like #1777d. No. 1788, 3200fr, Like #1777e. No. 1789, 3200fr, Like #1777f.

No. 1790, 4000fr, Filles Spartiates Difficile Garçons.

Illustrations on Nos. 1776a-1776f, 1777a-1777f are flipped in comparison to Nos. 1778-1789.

No. 1791, 400fr — Inscriptions: a, Ange. b, Chef de une Vielle Femme dans un Bonnet Blanc. c, Portrait de Camille Roulin. d, Joseph Etienne Roulin. e, Chef de une Vielle Femme dans un Bonnet Blanc (woman with hand touching her face). f, Le Zouave Assis.

No. 1792, 400fr — Inscriptions: a, Vase avec Douze Tournesols. b, Irisews (Irises). c, Portrait du Père Tanguy. d, Chef de une Paysanne avec un Bonnet de Dentelles Verdatre. e, Van Gogh Chair. f, Berceuse.

No. 1793, 3200fr, Like #1791a. No. 1794, 3200fr, Like #1791b. No. 1795, 3200fr, Like #1791c. No. 1796, 3200fr, Like #1791d. No. 1797, 3200fr, Like #1791e. No. 1798, 3200fr, Like #1791f. No. 1799, 3200fr, Like #1792a. No. 1800, 3200fr, Like #1792b. No. 1801, 3200fr, Like #1792c. No. 1802, 3200fr, Like #1792d. No. 1803, 3200fr, Like #1792e. No. 1804, 3200fr, Like #1792f.

No. 1805, 4000fr, Village de Rue et Escalier avec Chiffres.

No. 1806, 400fr — Inscriptions: a, Nu Assis (blue area at LL). b, Jeanne Hebuterne (head). c, Portrait de Madame Kisling. d, Nu Assise sur un Canapé. e, Portrait de Chaim Soutner. f, Portrait de Celso Lagar.

No. 1807, 400fr — Inscriptions: a, Femme nue. b, Jeanne Hebuterne (seated). c, Nu Assis (seated, dark blue background). d, Nu Assis (seated, blue green background). e, Madame Pompadour. f, Jeune Fille Assise.

No. 1808, 3200fr, Like #1806a. No. 1809, 3200fr, Like #1806b. No. 1810, 3200fr, Like #1806c. No. 1811, 3200fr, Like #1806d. No. 1812, 3200fr, Like #1806e. No. 1813, 3200fr, Like #1806f. No. 1814, 3200fr, Like #1807a. No. 1815, 3200fr, Like #1807b. No. 1816, 3200fr, Like #1807c. No. 1817, 3200fr, Like #1807d. No. 1818, 3200fr, Like #1807e. No. 1819, 3200fr, Like #1807f.

No. 1820, 4000fr, Nu Couché.

No. 1821, 400fr — Inscriptions: a, A. S. Pouchkine. b, Bateau à Voile. c, Mer (Etude). d, Tapez Leandrovoy Tour à Constantinople. e, Navire dans la Mer Orageuse. f, Acropole d'Athènes. g, Portrait de l'Epouse de l'Artiste.

No. 1822, 400fr, horiz. — Inscriptions: a, Brigue "Mercury" Attaque par Deux Navires Turcs. b, L'Arrivée de Flotille Colomb. c, La Bataille dans la Manche Chios. d, Examen de la Flotte de la Mer Noire en 1849. e, Bataille Navale Russo-Turque de Sinop. f, La Bataille de Navarin. g, Bataille près de Sinop.

No. 1823, 400fr, horiz. — Inscriptions: a, Paysage Italien. b, Napoléon. c, La Flotte de la Mer Noire à Feodosiya. d, Vue de Saint-Pétersbourg. e, Vue de Kertch. f, Pêcheurs sur Littoral. g, Pouchkine.

No. 1824, 400fr, horiz — Inscriptions: a, Un Naufrage près du Mont Athos. b, La Tempête. c, Tempête sur la Mer. d, Sur l'île de Crète. e, La Neuvième Vague. f, Signal de la Tempête. g, Le Bulow

No. 1825, 4000fr, Tempête.

2011, Dec. 29 Litho. *Perf. 13¾*

Works of Titian (Tiziano Vecelli)
Sheets of 3, #a-c, + label

1620-1623 A388 Set of 4 19.50 19.50

Souvenir Sheets
Perf. 13x13¼, 13¼x13

1624-1635 A389 Set of 12 155.00 155.00
1636 A390 4000fr multi 16.00 16.00

Works of François Boucher
Sheets of 3, #a-c, + label
Perf. 13¾

1637-1640 A388 Set of 4 19.50 19.50

Souvenir Sheets
Perf. 13x13¼, 13¼x13

1641-1652 A389 Set of 12 155.00 155.00
1653 A390 4000fr multi 16.00 16.00

Works of Claude Monet
Sheets of 3, #a-c, + label
Perf. 13¾

1654-1657 A388 Set of 4 19.50 19.50

Souvenir Sheets
Perf. 13x13¼, 13¼x13

1658-1669 A389 Set of 12 155.00 155.00
1670 A390 4000fr multi 16.00 16.00

Works of Albrecht Dürer
Sheets of 6, #a-f, + 2 labels
Perf. 13¾

1671-1672 A388 Set of 2 19.50 19.50

Souvenir Sheets
Perf. 13x13¼

1673-1684 A389 Set of 12 155.00 155.00
1685 A390 4000fr multi 16.00 16.00

Works of Michelangelo
Sheets of 6, #a-f, + 2 labels
Perf. 13¾

1686-1687 A388 Set of 2 19.50 19.50

Souvenir Sheets
Perf. 13x13¼

1688-1699 A389 Set of 12 155.00 155.00
1700 A390 4000fr multi 16.00 16.00

Works of Raphael (Raffaello Sanzio)
Sheets of 6, #a-f, + 2 labels
Perf. 13¾

1701-1702 A388 Set of 2 19.50 19.50

Souvenir Sheets
Perf. 13x13¼

1703-1714 A389 Set of 12 155.00 155.00
1715 A390 4000fr multi 16.00 16.00

Works of Peter Paul Rubens
Sheets of 6, #a-f, + 2 labels
Perf. 13¾

1716-1717 A388 Set of 2 19.50 19.50

Souvenir Sheets
Perf. 13x13¼

1718-1729 A389 Set of 12 155.00 155.00
1730 A390 4000fr multi 16.00 16.00

Works of Anthony van Dyck
Sheets of 6, #a-f, + 2 labels
Perf. 13¾

1731-1732 A388 Set of 2 19.50 19.50

Souvenir Sheets
Perf. 13x13¼

1733-1744 A389 Set of 12 155.00 155.00
1745 A390 4000fr multi 16.00 16.00

Works of Rembrandt van Rijn
Sheets of 6, #a-f, + 2 labels
Perf. 13¾

1746-1747 A388 Set of 2 19.50 19.50

Souvenir Sheets
Perf. 13x13¼

1748-1759 A389 Set of 12 155.00 155.00
1760 A390 4000fr multi 16.00 16.00

Works of Pierre-Auguste Renoir
Sheets of 6, #a-f, + 2 labels
Perf. 13¾

1761-1762 A388 Set of 2 19.50 19.50

Souvenir Sheets
Perf. 13x13¼

1763-1774 A389 Set of 12 155.00 155.00
1775 A390 4000fr multi 16.00 16.00

Works of Edgar Degas
Sheets of 6, #a-f, + 2 labels
Perf. 13¾

1776-1777 A388 Set of 2 19.50 19.50

Souvenir Sheets
Perf. 13x13¼

1778-1789 A389 Set of 12 155.00 155.00
1790 A390 4000fr multi 16.00 16.00

Works of Vincent van Gogh
Sheets of 6, #a-f, + 2 labels
Perf. 13¾

1791-1792 A388 Set of 2 19.50 19.50

Souvenir Sheets
Perf. 13x13¼

1793-1804 A389 Set of 12 155.00 155.00
1805 A390 4000fr multi 16.00 16.00

Works of Amedeo Modigliani
Sheets of 6, #a-f, + 2 labels
Perf. 13¾

1806-1807 A388 Set of 2 19.50 19.50

Souvenir Sheets
Perf. 13x13¼

1808-1819 A389 Set of 12 155.00 155.00
1820 A390 4000fr multi 16.00 16.00

Works of Ivan Aivazovsky
Sheets of 7, #a-g, + label
Perf. 13¾

1821-1824 A388 Set of 4 45.00 45.00

Souvenir Sheets
Perf. 13x13¼

1825 A390 4000fr multi 16.00 16.00

SEMI-POSTAL STAMPS

Anti-Malaria Issue
Common Design Type
Perf. 12½x12

1962, Apr. 7 Engr. Unwmk.

B1 CD108 25fr + 5fr slate 1.40 1.40

WHO drive to eradicate malaria.

Freedom from Hunger Issue
Common Design Type

1963, Mar. 21 *Perf. 13*

B2 CD112 25fr + 5fr multi 1.25 1.25

Guinea Fowl and Partridge SP1

Designs: 10fr+5fr, Yellow-backed duiker and snail. 20fr+5fr, Elephant, tortoise and hippopotamus playing tug-of-war. 30fr+10fr, Cuckoo and tortoise. 50fr+20fr, Patas monkey and leopard.

1971, Feb. 9 Photo. *Perf. 12½x12*

B3	SP1	5fr + 5fr multi	4.50	2.00
B4	SP1	10fr + 5fr multi	5.75	2.50
B5	SP1	20fr + 5fr multi	7.50	2.75
B6	SP1	30fr + 10fr multi	10.00	7.00
B7	SP1	50fr + 20fr multi	16.00	12.00
		Nos. B3-B7 (5)	43.75	26.25

Lengué Dancer — SP2

Dancers: 40fr+10fr, Le Lengué. 100fr+40fr, Teke. 140fr+40fr, Englabolo.

1971 Litho. *Perf. 13*

B8	SP2	20fr + 5fr multi	.65	.25
B9	SP2	40fr + 10fr multi	1.10	.40
B10	SP2	100fr + 40fr multi	2.50	1.25
B11	SP2	140fr + 40fr multi	3.25	1.50
		Nos. B8-B11 (4)	7.50	3.40

AIR POST STAMPS

Abyssinian Roller — AP1

Birds: 200fr, Gold Coast touraco. 500fr, African fish eagle.

Unwmk.

1960, Sept. 3 Engr. *Perf. 13*

C1	AP1	100fr vio bl, org brn & emer	2.50	.70
C2	AP1	200fr multi	4.75	2.00
C3	AP1	500fr Prus bl, emer & red brn	14.75	4.75
		Nos. C1-C3 (3)	22.00	7.45

French Equatorial Africa No. C37 Surcharged in Red

1960, Dec. 15 *Perf. 13*

C4 AP8 250fr on 500fr grnsh blk, blk & slate 9.00 8.25

17th Olympic Games, Rome, 8/25-9/11.

Air Afrique Issue
Common Design Type

1962, Feb. 17 Unwmk. *Perf. 13*

C5 CD107 50fr vio, lt grn & red brn 1.00 .55

Founding of Air Afrique airline.

Pole Vault — AP1a

1962, July 21 Photo. *Perf. 12x12½*

C6 AP1a 100fr grn, yel, brn & blk 2.25 1.50

Abidjan games.

Red-faced Lovebirds — AP2

1962-63 Engr. *Perf. 13*

C7 AP2 50fr Great blue touraco 2.25 .55
C8 AP2 250fr shown ('63) 7.00 2.50

Issued: 50fr, Nov. 15; 250fr, Mar. 11, 1963.

Runner with Torch and Palm Branch — AP3

1962, Dec. 24

C9 AP3 100fr gray grn, brn & car 2.25 1.25

Tropics Cup Games, Bangui, Dec. 24-31.

African Postal Union Issue
Common Design Type

1963, Sept. 8 Photo. *Perf. 12½*

C10 CD114 85fr emer, ocher & red 1.90 .85

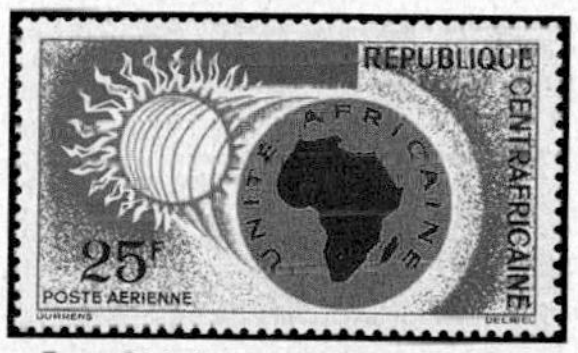

Sun Shining on Africa — AP4

1963, Nov. 9 *Perf. 13x12*

C11 AP4 25fr bl, yel & vio bl .75 .40

Issued for African unity.

Europafrica Issue
Common Design Type

1963, Nov. 30 *Perf. 12x13*

C12 CD116 50fr ultra, yel & dk brn 2.50 1.75

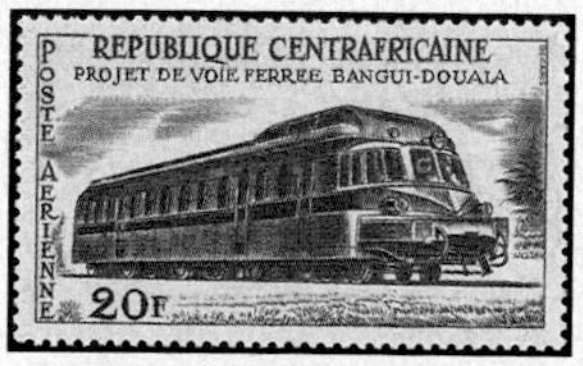

Diesel Engine — AP5

Various Locomotives; 25fr, 50fr, vertical.

1963, Dec. 1 Engr. *Perf. 13*

C13 AP5 20fr brn, cl & dk grn .70 .70
C14 AP5 25fr brn, bl & choc .80 .80
C15 AP5 50r brn, red lil & vio 2.75 2.75
C16 AP5 100fr brn, grn & dl red brn 3.75 3.75
a. Min. sheet of 4, #C13-C16 12.00 12.00
Nos. C13-C16 (4) 8.00 8.00

Bangui-Douala railroad project.

Bangui Cathedral — AP6

1964, Jan. 21 Unwmk. *Perf. 13*

C17 AP6 100fr yel grn, org brn & bl 1.90 1.00

Radar Tracking Station and WMO Emblem — AP7

1964, Mar. 23 Engr. *Perf. 13*

C18 AP7 50fr org brn, bl & pur 1.25 1.25

World Meteorological Day.

Map and Presidents of Chad, Congo, Gabon and Central African Republic AP8

1964, June 23 Photo. *Perf. 12½*

C19 AP8 100fr multi 2.00 .80

5th anniversary of the Conference of Chiefs of State of Equatorial Africa.

Javelin Throwers — AP9

Designs: 50fr, Basketball game. 100fr, Four runners. 250fr, Swimmers, one in water.

1964, June 23 Engr. *Perf. 13*

C20 AP9 25fr grn, dk brn & lt vio bl .55 .30
C21 AP9 50fr blk, car & grn 1.10 .45
C22 AP9 100fr grn, vio bl & dk brn 2.50 .95
C23 AP9 250fr grn, blk & car 6.75 2.50
a. Min. sheet of 4, #C20-C23 18.00 18.00
Nos. C20-C23 (4) 10.90 4.20

18th Olympic Games, Tokyo, 10/10-25/64.

John F. Kennedy — AP10

1964, July 4 Photo. *Perf. 12½*

C24 AP10 100fr lil, brn & blk 2.50 1.50
a. Min. sheet of 4 10.00 10.00

Industrial Symbols, Maps of Africa and Europe — AP11

1964, Dec. 19 Unwmk. *Perf. 13x12*

C25 AP11 50fr yel, org & grn 1.50 .85

See note after Cameroun No. 402.

International Cooperation Year Emblem — AP12

1965, Jan. 2 *Perf. 13*

C26 AP12 100fr red brn, yel & bl 1.75 .75

International Cooperation Year.

Nimbus Weather Satellite — AP13

1965, Mar. 23 Engr. *Perf. 13*

C27 AP13 100fr org brn, ultra & blk 1.90 .80

Fifth World Meteorological Day.

Lincoln and Statue of Liberty — AP14

1965, Apr. 15 Photo. *Perf. 13*

C28 AP14 100fr bluish grn, ind & bis 1.75 .75

Centenary of death of Abraham Lincoln.

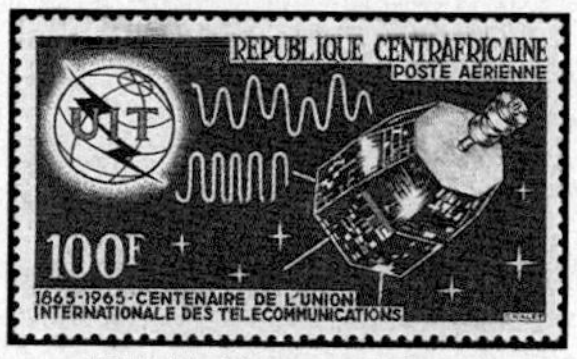

ITU Emblem and Relay Satellite — AP15

1965, May 17 Engr. *Perf. 13*

C29 AP15 100fr dk grn vio bl & brn 1.90 1.10

Centenary of the ITU.

"Housing," New Home in Village — AP16

1965, June 10 Unwmk.

C30 AP16 100fr ultra, brn & sl grn 1.10 .65

See note after No. 52.

Europafrica Issue

Tractor, Cotton Picker, Cotton, Sun and Emblem — AP17

1965, Nov. 7 Photo. *Perf. 12x13*

C31 AP17 50fr multl .90 .65

See note after Chad No. C11.

Mercury by Antoine Coysevox AP18

1965, Dec. 5 Engr. *Perf. 13*

C32 AP18 100fr red brn, bl & blk 2.75 1.10

5th anniv. of Central African Republic's admission to the UPU.

Father Holding Sick Child — AP19

Design: 100fr, Mother and child.

1965, Dec. 12

C33 AP19 50fr dk bl, car & blk 1.25 .45
C34 AP19 100fr red brn, red & brt grn 2.75 1.10

Issued to honor the Red Cross.

Air Afrique Issue
Common Design Type

1966, Aug. 31 Photo. *Perf. 13*

C35 CD123 25fr bl, blk & lem 1.00 .40

For surcharge see No. C43.

Surveyor Spacecraft on Moon — AP20

Designs: No. C37, Luna 9 on Moon and Earth. 200fr, Rocket take-off, Jules Verne's "From the Earth to the Moon."

1966, Oct. 24 Photo. *Perf. 12x12½*

C36 AP20 130fr multi 1.60 .95
C37 AP20 130fr multi 1.60 .95
C38 AP20 200fr multi 3.00 1.75
a. Souv. sheet of 3, #C36-C38 9.00 9.00
Nos. C36-C38 (3) 6.20 3.65

Conquest of the Moon.
For surcharges see Nos. C58, C61.

Eugene A. Cernan, Gemini 9 and Agena Rocket — AP21

No. C40, Pavel R. Popovich and rocket.

1966, Nov. 14 Photo. *Perf. 13*

C39 AP21 50fr multi 1.10 .50
C40 AP21 50fr multi 1.10 .50

American and Russian astronauts.

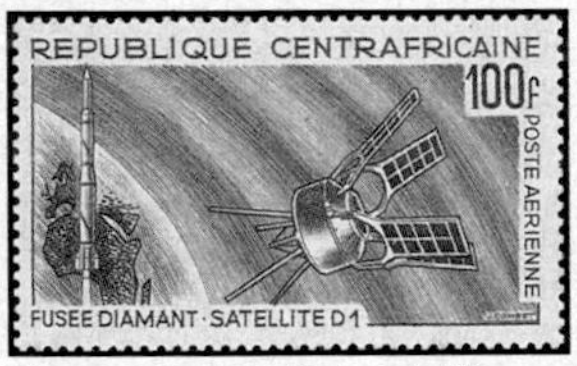

Diamant Rocket, D-1 Satellite and Globe with Map of Africa — AP22

1966, Nov. 14 Engr.

C41 AP22 100fr brt rose lil & brn 1.75 .85

Issued to commemorate the launching of France's first satellite, Nov. 26, 1965, and the launching of the D-1 satellite, Feb. 17, 1966.

Exchange of Agricultural and Industrial Products between Africa and Europe — AP23

1966, Dec. 5 Photo. *Perf. 12x13*

C42 AP23 50fr multi 1.25 .85

See note after Gabon No. C46.

No. C35 Surcharged

1967, May 8 *Perf. 13*

C43 CD123 5fr on 25fr multi .55 .30

The surcharge obliterates the "2" of the original 25fr denomination.

DC-8F Over M'Poko Airport, Bangui — AP24

1967, July 3 Engr. *Perf. 13*

C44 AP24 100fr sl, dk grn & brn 2.50 1.00

View of EXPO '67, Montreal — AP25

1967, July 17

C45 AP25 100fr vio bl, dk red brn & dk grn 2.25 .80

International Exposition. EXPO '67, Montreal, Apr. 28-Oct. 27.

African Postal Union Issue, 1967

Common Design Type

1967, Sept. 9 Engr. *Perf. 13*

C46 CD124 100fr brt grn, dk car rose & plum 2.25 .85
Nos. C46 (1) 2.25 .85

Potez 25 TOE — AP26

1967, Nov. 24 Engr. *Perf. 13*

C47 AP26 100fr shown 2.50 .80
C48 AP26 200fr Junkers 52 5.50 1.75
C49 AP26 500fr Caravelle 11R 14.00 4.25
Nos. C47-C49 (3) 22.00 6.80

For surcharges see Nos. C59-C60.

Presidents Boganda and Bokassa — AP27

1967, Dec. 1 Photo. *Perf. 12½*

C50 AP27 130fr org, red, lt bl & blk 2.00 1.00

9th anniversary of the republic.

Pres. Jean Bedel Bokassa AP28

1968, Jan. 1 *Perf. 12½x12*

C51 AP28 30fr multi .80 .40

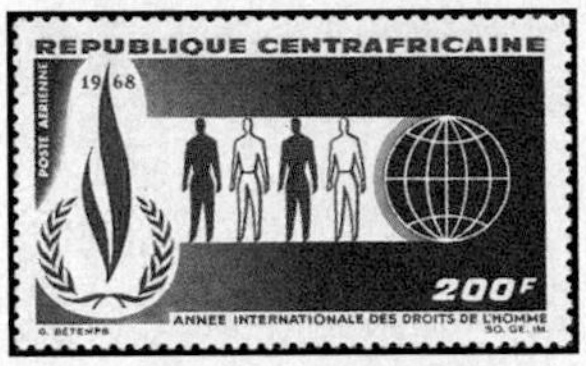

Human Rights Flame, Men and Globe — AP29

1968, Mar. 26 Photo. *Perf. 13*

C52 AP29 200fr brt grn, vio & ver 3.50 1.40

International Human Rights Year.

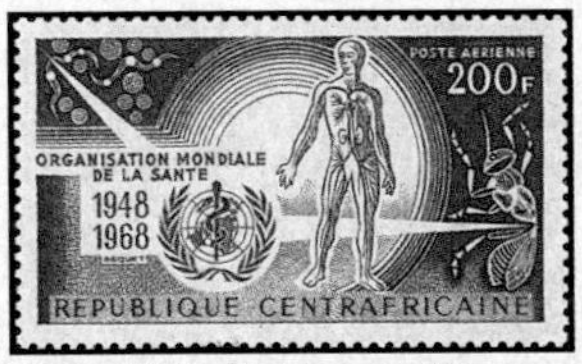

Man, WHO Emblem and Tsetse Fly — AP30

1968, Apr. 8 Engr.

C53 AP30 200fr multi 4.00 2.00

20th anniv. of WHO.

Javelin Thrower — AP31

1968, Apr. 16 Engr. *Perf. 13*

C54 AP31 200fr shown 4.50 3.00
C55 AP31 200fr Downhill skier 4.50 3.00

The 1968 Olympic Games.

Space Probe Landing on Venus — AP32

1968, Apr. 23

C56 AP32 100fr ultra, dk & brt grn 1.75 .95

Venus exploration by Venera 4, 10/18/67.

Marie Curie and "Cancer Destroyed" — AP33

1968, Apr. 30

C57 AP33 100fr vio, brt bl & brn 2.75 1.10

Marie Curie (1867-1934), scientist.

Nos. C36-C37 and C47-C48 Surcharged with New Value

Photogravure; Engraved

1968, Sept. 16 *Perf. 12x12½, 13*

C58 AP20 5fr on 130fr multi .25 .25
C59 AP26 10fr on 100fr multi .30 .25
C60 AP26 20fr on 200fr multi .50 .30
C61 AP20 50fr on 130fr multi 1.10 .55
Nos. C58-C61 (4) 2.15 1.35

On No. C58 the old denomination has been obliterated with "XIX," on No. C61 the obliteration is a rectangular bar. On Nos. C59-C60 the last zero of the old denomination has been obliterated with a black square.

River Boat Type of Regular Issue

Craft: 100fr, "Pie X," Bangui, 1894. 130fr, "Ballay," Bangui, 1891.

1968, Dec. 10 Engr. *Perf. 13*

Size: 48x27mm

C62 A37 100fr bl, dk brn & ol 2.50 1.00
C63 A37 130fr brt pink, sl grn & slate 3.00 1.25

PHILEXAFRIQUE Issue

Mme. de Sévigné, French School, 17th Century AP34

1968, Dec. 17 Photo. *Perf. 12½*

C64 AP34 100fr brn & multi 3.00 2.25

Issued to publicize PHILEXAFRIQUE, Philatelic Exhibition in Abidjan, Feb. 14-23. Printed with alternating brown label.

2nd PHILEXAFRIQUE Issue

Common Design Type

Design: 50fr, Ubangi-Shari No. J16, cotton field and Pres. Bokassa.

1969, Feb. 14 Engr. *Perf. 13*

C65 CD128 50fr bis brn, blk & dk grn 1.90 1.90

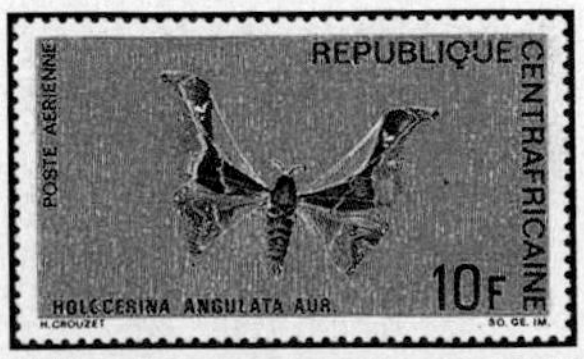

Holocerina Angulata Aur. — AP35

Butterflies and Moths: 20fr, Nudaurelia dione fabr. 30fr, Eustera troglophylla hamp., vert. 50fr, Aurivillius aratus west. 100fr, Epiphora albida druce.

1969, Feb. 25 Photo.

C66 AP35 10fr yel & multi 1.10 .35
C67 AP35 20fr vio & multi 1.60 .55
C68 AP35 30fr multi 3.75 1.00
C69 AP35 50fr multi 5.25 2.25
C70 AP35 100fr multi 9.00 3.25
Nos. C66-C70 (5) 20.70 7.40

Boxing — AP36

1969, Mar. 18 Photo. *Perf. 13*

C71 AP36 50fr shown 1.10 .30
C72 AP36 100fr Basketball 2.25 .60

Apollo 8 over Moonscape — AP37

1969, May 27 Photo. *Perf. 13*

C73 AP37 200fr dp bl, gray & yel 3.50 1.75

US Apollo 8 mission, the 1st men in orbit around the moon, Dec. 21-27, 1968.
For overprint see No. C81.

Market Cross, Nuremberg, and Toys — AP38

1969, June 3

C74 AP38 100fr blk, brt rose lil & emer 2.25 .95

Intl. Toy Fair in Nuremberg, Germany.

Napoleon as First Consul, by Anne-Louis Girodet-Trioson — AP39

Designs: 130fr, Napoleon meeting Emperor Francis II, by Antoine Jean Gros, horiz. 200fr, The Wedding of Napoleon and Marie-Louise, by Georges Rouget, horiz.

1969, Nov. 4 Photo. *Perf. 12½*

C75 AP39 100fr multi 2.25 1.25
C76 AP39 130fr brn & multi 3.25 1.50
C77 AP39 200fr multi 5.50 2.75
Nos. C75-C77 (3) 11.00 5.50

Napoleon Bonaparte (1769-1821).

Pres. Bokassa, Map of Africa and Flag — AP40

1970, Jan. 1 *Die-cut; Perf. 10½*
Embossed on Gold Foil

C78 AP40 2000fr gold 40.00 40.00

Franklin Delano Roosevelt — AP41

1970 Litho. *Perf. 13½x14*

C79 AP41 100fr shown 2.00 1.00
C80 AP41 100fr Lenin 3.00 1.25

Roosevelt, 25th death anniv., Lenin, birth cent.
Issue dates: No. C79, Apr. 29; No. C80. Apr. 22.

No. C73 Overprinted in Red

1970, June 1 Photo. *Perf. 13*

C81 AP37 200fr multi 15.00 9.00

Moon landing mission of Apollo 12, 11/14-24/69.

AP42

1970, Sept. 15 Litho. *Perf. 10*

C82 AP42 Pair + label 4.50 3.00
a. 100fr Dancer 1.90 .55
b. 100fr Still life 1.90 .55

Knokphila 70, 6th Intl. Phil. Exhib. at Knokke, Belgium, July 4-10. Imperf. between stamps and label.

Sericulture Type of Regular Issue

1970, Sept. 15 *Perf. 10*

C83 A45 140fr multi 4.50 1.10

C.A.R. Flag, EXPO Emblem and Pavilion AP43

1970, Dec. 18 Litho. *Perf. 13½x13*

C84 AP43 200fr red & multi 3.50 1.50

Intl. Exposition EXPO '70, Osaka, Japan.

Soccer — AP44

1970, Dec. 8 *Perf. 13x13½*

C85 AP44 200fr multi 3.50 1.50

World Soccer Championships, Mexico, May 30-June 21, 1970.

Dove — AP45

1970, Dec. 31

C86 AP45 200fr bl, yel & blk 3.50 1.50

25th anniversary of the United Nations.

Presidents Mobutu, Bokassa, and Tombalbaye — AP46

1971, Jan. 10

C87 AP46 140fr multi 3.00 1.00

Return of Central African Republic to the United States of Central Africa which also includes Congo Democratic Republic and Chad.

Satellite over Globe — AP47

1971, May 17 Photo. *Perf. 12½*

C88 AP47 100fr multi 2.25 .85

3rd World Telecommunications Day.

African Postal Union Issue, 1971
Common Design Type

Design: 100fr, Carved head and UAMPT building, Brazzaville, Congo.

1971, Nov. 13 Photo. *Perf. 13x13½*

C89 CD135 100fr bl & multi 2.25 .85

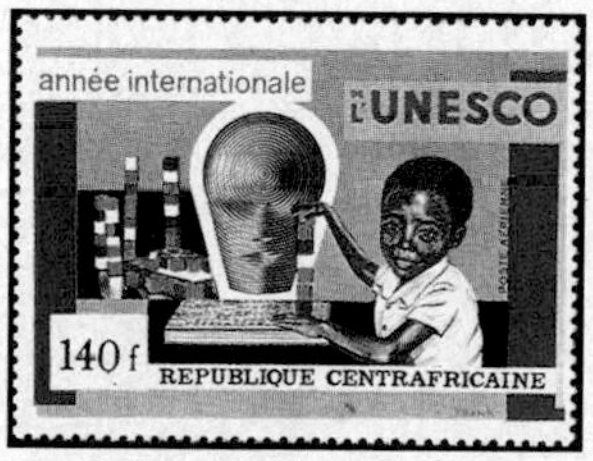

Child and Education Year Emblem — AP48

1971, Nov. 11 Litho. *Perf. 13x13½*

C90 AP48 140fr multi 2.25 .80

25th anniv. of UNESCO.

Fight Against Cancer — AP49

1971, Nov. 20 Photo. *Perf. 12½*

C91 AP49 100fr grn & multi 2.75 1.10

Gamal Abdel Nasser — AP50

1972, Jan. 15

C92 AP50 100fr dk red, blk & bister 2.50 .85

In memory of Gamal Abdel Nasser (1918-1970), president of Egypt.

Olympic Rings and Boxing — AP51

No. C94, Track and Olympic rings, vert.

1972, May 26 Engr. *Perf. 13*

C93 AP51 100fr brn org & sepia 1.75 .80
C94 AP51 100fr green & violet 1.75 1.10
a. Miniature sheet of 2 5.00 5.00

20th Olympic Games, Munich, Aug. 26-Sept. 10. No. C94a contains 2 stamps similar to Nos. C93-C94, but in changed colors. The boxing stamp is red lilac and green, the track stamp ocher and red lilac.
For overprints see Nos. C100-C101.

Tiling's Mail Rocket, 1931, and Mailman — AP52

Designs: 50fr, DC-3 and mailman riding camel, vert. 150fr, Sirio satellite and rocket, vert. 200fr, Intelsat 4 and rocket.

1972, Aug. 12

C95 AP52 40fr bl, org & indigo .65 .45
C96 AP52 50fr bl, brn & org .90 .55
C97 AP52 150fr brn, org & gray 2.50 1.25
C98 AP52 200fr brn, bl & org 3.50 2.25
a. Souv. sheet of 4, #C95-C98 9.25 9.25
Nos. C95-C98 (4) 7.55 4.50

Centraphilex 1972, Central African Philatelic Exhibition, Bangui.

Europafrica Issue

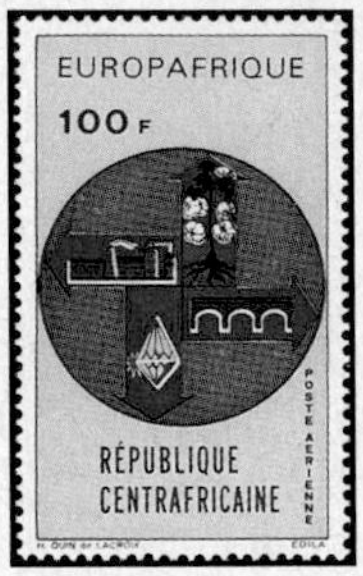

Arrows with Symbols of Agriculture and Industry — AP53

1972, Nov. 17 **Litho.** ***Perf. 13***

C99 AP53 100fr multi 1.75 .80

Nos. C93-C94, C94a Overprinted

(a)

(b)

1972, Nov. 24 **Engr.**

C100 AP51 (a) 100fr 1.75 .95
C101 AP51 (b) 100fr 1.75 .95
a. Miniature sheet of 2 3.75 3.75

Gold Medal Winners in 20th Olympic Games: Viatscheslav Lemechev, USSR, middleweight boxing; Randy Williams, US, broad jump.

Lunar Rover and Module — AP54

1972, Dec. 18 **Engr.** ***Perf. 13***

C102 AP54 100fr slate grn, bl & gray 1.75 .80

Apollo 16 US moon mission, 4/15-27/72.

Virgin and Child, by Francesco Pesellino AP55

Christmas: 150fr, Adoration of the Child with St. John the Baptist and St. Romuald, by Fra Filippo Lippi.

1972, Dec. 25 **Photo.**

C103 AP55 100fr gold & multi 1.60 .85
C104 AP55 150fr gold & multi 2.75 1.25

Parthenon, Athens, Spyridon Louis, Marathon, 1896 — AP56

Olympic Rings and: 40fr, Arc de Triomphe, Paris, H. Barrelet, single scull, 1900. 50fr, Old Courthouse and Western Arch, St. Louis, Myer Prinstein, triple jump, 1904. 100fr, Tower, London, Henry Taylor, swimming, 1908. 150fr, City Hall, Stockholm, Greco-Roman wrestling, 1912.

1972, Dec. 28 **Engr.**

C105 AP56 30fr brt grn, mag & brn .40 .25
C106 AP56 40fr vio bl, emer & brn .50 .25
C107 AP56 50fr car rose, vio bl & Prus bl .55 .40
C108 AP56 100fr sl, red lil & brn 1.10 .45
C109 AP56 150fr red lil, blk & Prus bl 1.75 1.10
Nos. C105-C109 (5) 4.30 2.45

Olympic Games 1896-1912.

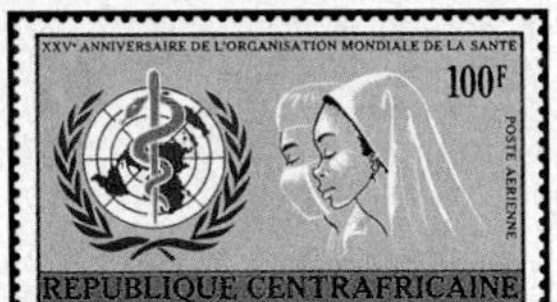

WHO Emblem, Surgeon and Nurse — AP57

1973, Apr. 7 **Photo.** ***Perf. 13***

C110 AP57 100fr multi 1.50 .75

WHO, 25th anniv.

AP58

1973, May 17 **Litho.** ***Perf. 12½***

C111 AP58 200fr World map, arrows, waves 2.50 1.00

5th International Telecommunications Day.

AP58a

Head and City Hall, Brussels.

1973, Sept. 17 **Engr.** ***Perf. 13***

C112 AP58a 100fr pur, ocher & brn 1.40 .70

African Weeks, Brussels, Sept. 15-30, 1973.

Europafrica Issue

Map of Central African Republic with Industry and Agriculture, Young Man — AP59

1973, Sept. 28 **Engr.** ***Perf. 13***

C113 AP59 100fr sepia, grn & org 1.75 .80

Carrier Pigeon with Letter and UPU Emblem — AP60

1973, Oct. 9 **Photo.**

C114 AP60 200fr multi 2.50 1.10

Universal Postal Union Day.

WMO Emblem, Weather Map — AP61

1973, Oct. 20 **Engr.** ***Perf. 13***

C115 AP61 150fr brt ultra & sl grn 2.75 1.00

Cent. of intl. meteorological cooperation.

Copernicus, Heliocentric System — AP62

1973, Nov. 2 **Photo.**

C116 AP62 100fr gold & multi 3.00 1.75

Copernicus (1473-1543), Polish astronomer.

Pres. Bokassa AP63

Pres. Bokassa — AP64

1973, Nov. 30 **Photo.** ***Perf. 12½***

C117 AP63 50fr multi .75 .40
C118 AP64 100fr multi 1.40 .70

Rocket Launch and Apollo 17 Badge — AP65

65fr, Capsule over moonscape, horiz. 100fr, Moon landing, horiz. 150fr, Astronauts on moon. 200fr, Splashdown with parachutes and badge.

1973, Dec. 15 **Engr.** ***Perf. 13***

C119 AP65 50fr ver, gray grn & brn .55 .30
C120 AP65 65fr dk brn, brn red & sl grn .75 .40
C121 AP65 100fr ver, slate & choc 1.25 .60
C122 AP65 150fr brn, ol & sl grn 1.90 .80
C123 AP65 200fr red, bl & sl grn 2.25 1.10
Nos. C119-C123 (5) 6.70 3.20

Apollo 17 US moon mission, 12/7-19/72.

St. Teresa — AP66

1973, Dec. 25

C124 AP66 500fr vio bl & grnsh bl 6.75 3.50

St. Teresa of the Infant Jesus, the Little Flower (1873-1897), Carmelite nun.

UPU Emblem, Letter — AP67

1974, Oct. 9 **Engr.** ***Perf. 13***

C125 AP67 500fr multi 7.50 4.00

Centenary of Universal Postal Union.
For surcharge see No. C159.

Presidents and Flags of Cameroun, CAR, Gabon and Congo — AP68

1974, Dec. 8 **Photo.** ***Perf. 13***

C126 AP68 100fr gold & multi 1.40 .80

See note after Cameroun No. 595.
For surcharge see No. C155.

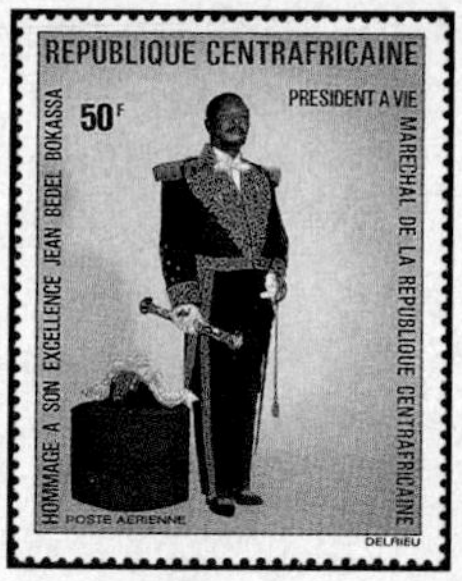

Marshal Bokassa AP69

100fr, Bokassa in Marshal's uniform with cape.

1975, Feb. 22 Photo. *Perf. 13*

C127 AP69	50fr tan & multi	.65	.40
C128 AP69	100fr tan & multi	1.40	.45

Jean Bedel Bokassa, President for Life and Marshal of the Republic.

Monument to Franco-CAR Cooperation AP73

Presidents and Flags of France and CAR AP74

1976, Mar. 5

C133 AP73	100fr multi	1.40	.80
C134 AP74	200fr multi	2.50	1.25

Official visit of Pres. Valery Giscard d'Estaing to Central African Republic, 3/5-8.
For surcharge see No. C157.

Mask, Map of Africa, Arphila Emblem — AP70

1975, Aug. 25 Engr. *Perf. 13*

C129 AP70	100fr brt bl, red brn & red	1.40	.60

ARPHILA 75 International Philatelic Exhibition, Paris, June 6-16.
For surcharge see No. C156.

Albert Schweitzer and Dugout, Lambarene AP71

1975, Sept. 30 Engr. *Perf. 13*

C130 AP71	200fr blk, ultra & ol	5.00	2.00

Dr. Albert Schweitzer (1875-1965), medical missionary and musician.
For surcharge see No. C158.

Pres. Bokassa's Houseboat, Bow — AP72

40fr, Pres. Bokassa's houseboat, stern.

1976, Feb. 22 Litho. *Perf. 13*

C131 AP72	30fr multi	.65	.30
C132 AP72	40fr multi	.85	.45

Apollo Soyuz Type, 1976

Designs: 100fr, Soyuz space ship. 200fr, Apollo space ship. 300fr, Astronauts and cosmonauts in cabin. 500fr, Apollo and Soyuz after link-up.

1976, June 14 Litho. *Perf. 14x13½*

C135 A90	100fr multi	.90	.25
C136 A90	200fr multi	1.60	.55
C137 A90	300fr multi	2.60	.95
	Nos. C135-C137 (3)	6.45	1.75

Souvenir Sheet

C138 A90	500fr multi	5.00	1.75

For surcharges see Nos. C161, C168, C173, C177.

French Hussar AP75

Uniforms: 125fr, Scottish "Black Watch." 150fr, German dragoon. 200fr, British grenadier. 250fr, American ranger. 450fr, American dragoon.

1976, July 4 *Perf. 13½*

C139 AP75	100fr multi	.90	.30
C140 AP75	125fr multi	1.00	.45
C141 AP75	150fr multi	1.25	.45
C142 AP75	200fr multi	1.90	.55
C143 AP75	250fr multi	2.50	.95
	Nos. C139-C143 (5)	7.55	2.70

Souvenir Sheet

C144 AP75	450fr multi	7.50	2.00

American Bicentennial.
For surcharges see Nos. C162, C166-C167, C169, C172, C176.

Acherontia Atropos — AP76

100fr, Papilio nireus & niocha marnois.

1976, Sept. 20 Litho. *Perf. 12½*

C145 AP76	50fr multi	9.00	1.50
C146 AP76	100fr multi	18.00	2.00

For surcharges see Nos. C160, C163.

Olympic Winners Type, 1976

Designs: 100fr, Women's figure skating, Dorothy Hamill, vert. 200fr, Ice skating, Alexander Gorshkov and Ludmilla Pakhomova. 300fr, Men's figure skating, John Curry, vert. 500fr, Downhill skiing, Rosi Mittermaier, vert.

1976, Sept. 23 Litho. *Perf. 13½*

C147 A92	100fr multi	.75	.30
C148 A92	200fr multi	2.40	.60
C149 A92	300fr multi	3.25	1.00
	Nos. C147-C149 (3)	6.40	1.90

Souvenir Sheet

C150 A92	500fr multi	6.00	1.75

For surcharges see Nos. C164, C170, C174, C178.

Viking Mars Type, 1976

Designs: 100fr, Phases of Mars landing. 200fr, Viking descending on Mars, horiz. 300fr, Viking probe. 500fr, Viking flight to Mars, horiz.

1976, Dec.

C151 A93	100fr multi	1.00	.30
C152 A93	200fr multi	2.40	.60
C153 A93	300fr multi	3.00	.95
	Nos. C151-C153 (3)	6.40	1.85

Souvenir Sheet

C154 A93	500fr multi	5.50	1.75

For surcharges and overprints see Nos. C165, C171, C175, C179, C212-C215.

Central African Empire

Stamps of 1973-76 Overprinted in Black, Violet Blue or Gold

Printing and Perforations as Before

1977, Mar.

C155 AP68	100fr	(#C126;B)	1.10	1.10
C156 AP70	100fr	(#C129;VB)	1.10	1.10
C157 AP73	100fr	(#C133;G)	1.10	1.10
C158 AP71	200fr	(#C130;B)	3.25	1.50
C159 AP67	500fr	(#C125;B)	10.00	10.00
	Nos. C155-C159 (5)		16.55	14.80

No bar on No. C159.

Stamps of 1976 Overprinted in Black on Silver Panel

1977, Apr. 1

C160 AP76	50fr	(#C145)	.55	.55
C161 A90	100fr	(#C135)	1.10	1.10
C162 AP75	100fr	(#C139)	1.10	1.10
C163 AP76	100fr	(#C146)	1.10	1.10
C164 A92	100fr	(#C147)	1.10	1.10
C165 A93	100fr	(#C151)	1.10	1.10
C166 AP75	125fr	(#C140)	1.40	1.40
C167 AP75	150fr	(#C141)	1.60	1.60
C168 A90	200fr	(#C136)	2.75	2.75
C169 AP75	200fr	(#C142)	2.50	2.50
C170 A92	200fr	(#C148)	2.25	2.25
C171 A93	200fr	(#C152)	2.25	2.25
C172 AP75	250fr	(#C143)	2.75	2.75
C173 A90	300fr	(#C137)	3.50	3.50
C174 A92	300fr	(#C149)	3.50	3.50
C175 A93	300fr	(#C153)	3.50	3.50
	Nos. C160-C175 (16)		32.05	32.05

Souvenir Sheets

C176 AP75	450fr	(#C144)	5.50	5.50
C177 A90	500fr	(#C138)	8.00	8.00
C178 A92	500fr	(#C150)	5.50	5.50
C179 A93	500fr	(#C154)	5.50	5.50

Overprint on type AP75 is in upper and lower case letters.

Nobel Prize Type, 1977

Designs: 100fr, Rudyard Kipling. 200fr, Ernest Hemingway. 300fr, Luigi Pirandello. 500fr, Rabindranath Tagore.

1977, Apr. 1 Litho. *Perf. 13½*

C180 A94	100fr multi	2.00	.40
C181 A94	200fr multi	4.00	.70
C182 A94	300fr multi	6.25	.95
	Nos. C180-C182 (3)	12.25	2.05

Souvenir Sheet

C183 A94	500fr multi	6.00	1.75

Zeppelin Type of 1977

100fr, Germany #C42 and North Pole. 200fr, Germany #C44 and Science and Industry Building, Chicago. 300fr, Germany #C35 and Brandenburg Gate, Berlin. 500fr, US #C14 and US Capitol.

1977, Apr. 11 Litho. *Perf. 11*

C184 A95	100fr multi	1.40	.30
C185 A95	200fr multi	2.75	.60
C186 A95	300fr multi	3.50	1.00
	Nos. C184-C186 (3)	7.65	1.90

Souvenir Sheet

C187 A95	500fr multi	5.50	2.00

75th anniversary of Zeppelin.

Bokassa Type of 1977

1977, Dec. 4 Litho. *Perf. 13½*

C188 A98	200fr multi	1.90	.80
C189 A98	300fr multi	2.75	1.25
a.	Souvenir sheet, 500fr	6.00	2.50

Coronation of Emperor Bokassa I, Dec. 4. No. C189a contains a horizontal stamp in similar design. A 2500fr gold embossed horizontal stamp in similar design exists. Value $25.

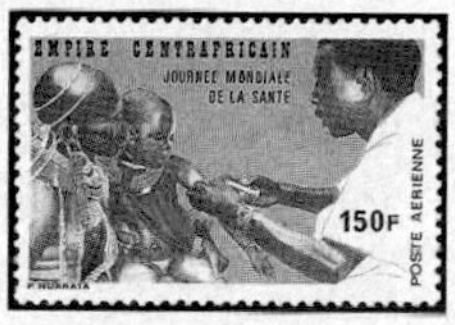

Vaccination AP77

1977 Litho. *Perf. 14x13½*

C190 AP77	150fr multi	4.00	1.25

World Health Day.

Communications Type of 1978

Designs: 100fr, Balloon and spaceships docking in space. 200fr, Hydrofoil and Concorde. 500fr, Tom-tom and Zeppelin. No. C193A, Early postman and rider, UPU emblem, Concorde. No. C193B, Mail coach, dove, satellites.

1978, May 17 Litho. *Perf. 13½*

C191 A107	100fr multi	1.10	.25
C192 A107	200fr multi	1.10	.30

Souvenir Sheet

C193 A107	500fr multi	5.75	2.25

Cent. of progress of posts and telecommunications. No. C193 contains one 53x35mm stamp.

1978, Mar. 21 Litho. & Embossed

Size: 57x39mm

C193A A107	1500fr gold & multi	55.00	4.00

Souvenir Sheet

C193B A107	1500fr gold & multi	15.00	4.75

Nos. C193A-C193B exist imperf. No. C193A exists in a souvenir sheet of one. No. C193B contains one 57x39mm stamp.

Clement Ader and his Plane — AP78

Designs: 50fr, Wilbur and Orville Wright and plane. 60fr, John W. Alcock, Arthur W. Brown and plane. 100fr, Alan Cobham and plane. 150fr, Claude Dornier and hydroplane. 500fr, Wilbur and Orville Wright and plane.

1978, Sept. 19 *Perf. 14*

C194 AP78 40fr multi .55 .25
C195 AP78 50fr multi .55 .25
C196 AP78 60fr multi .65 .25
C197 AP78 100fr multi 1.25 .40
C198 AP78 150fr multi 1.90 .60
Nos. C194-C198 (5) 4.90 1.75

Souvenir Sheet

C199 AP78 500fr multi 6.00 1.75

History of aviation.

Philexafrique II-Essen Issue
Common Design Types

No. C200, Crocodile, #C3. No. C201, Birds, Mecklenburg-Schwerin #1.

1978, Nov. 1 Litho. *Perf. 12½*

C200 CD138 100fr multi 1.90 1.10
C201 CD139 100fr multi 1.90 1.10
a. Pair, #C200-C201 + label 7.50 7.50

Bokassa Type of 1978

150fr, Catherine & Jean Bedel Bokassa.

1978, Dec. 4 Litho. *Perf. 13*

C202 A113 150fr multi, horiz. 1.90 .70

First anniv. of coronation. A 1000fr gold embossed souvenir sheet showing Emperor Bokassa exists. Value $9.

Rowland Hill Type of 1978

Designs (Rowland Hill and): 100fr, Mailman and Tuscany No. 23. 200fr, Balloon and France No. 1. 500fr, Central Africa Nos. 1-2.

1978, Dec. 27

C203 A114 100fr multi 4.00 1.40
C204 A114 200fr multi 1.75 .65

Souvenir Sheet

C205 A114 500fr multi 5.50 1.75

Sir Rowland Hill (1795-1879), originator of penny postage. No. C205 contains one 37½x39mm stamp. 1500fr gold embossed stamp and souvenir sheet exist.

IYC Type of 1979

Designs (UNICEF, Eagle Emblems and): 100fr, Chinese girl flying kites and German Do-X flying boat, 1929. 200fr, Boys playing leapfrog, hurdler and Olympic emblem. 500fr, Child with abacus and Albert Einstein with his equation.

1979, Mar. 6 *Perf. 13½*

C206 A115 100fr multi 1.40 .40
C207 A115 200fr multi 2.75 .65

Souvenir Sheet

C208 A115 500fr multi 5.50 1.75

International Year of the Child. No. C208 contains one 56x33mm stamp. 1500fr gold embossed stamp and souvenir sheet exist.

Olympic Type of 1979

Moscow '80 Emblem, various sports and: 100fr, Hurdles & "B." 200fr, Broad jump & "A." 500fr, Pole vault, horiz.

1979, Mar. 16 Litho. *Perf. 13*

C209 A116 100fr multi 1.10 .35
C210 A116 200fr multi 2.10 .65

Souvenir Sheet

C210A A116 500fr multi — —

22nd Olympic Games, Moscow, July 19-Aug. 3, 1980. No. C210A cpmtaoms pme 57x39mm stamp. A 1500fr gold embossed souvenir sheet exists showing diver, runner and javelin.

National Husbandry Association Type

1979, Aug. Litho. *Perf. 13*

C211 A119 60fr Horse 5.75 2.00

Central African Republic

Nos. C151-C154 Overprinted in Black or Silver

1979, Oct. Litho. *Perf. 14x13½*

C212 A93 100fr multi 1.00 .55
C213 A93 200fr multi 1.90 .85
C214 A93 300fr multi 2.75 1.25
Nos. C212-C214 (3) 5.65 2.65

Souvenir Sheet

C215 A93 500fr multi (S) 5.50 5.50

Apollo 11 moon landing, 10th anniversary.

Ski Jump, Lake Placid '80 Emblem — AP79

1979, Nov. 11 Litho. *Perf. 13½*

C216 AP79 60fr shown .65 .25
C217 AP79 100fr Downhill skiing 1.10 .40
C218 AP79 200fr Hockey 2.25 .85
C219 AP79 300fr Slalom 3.25 1.25
Nos. C216-C219 (4) 7.25 2.75

Souvenir Sheet

C220 AP79 500fr Bobsledding 5.50 1.75

13th Winter Olympics Games, Lake Placid, NY, Feb. 12-24, 1980.
For overprints see Nos. C224-C228.

Space Type of 1980

150fr, Early satellites. 200fr, Space shuttle. 500fr, Apollo 11, Armstrong. No. C223A, Armstrong, Apollo 11. No. C223B, Space shuttle, horiz.

1980, Apr. 8 Litho. *Perf. 13½*

C221 A125 150fr multi 1.60 .40
C222 A125 200fr multi 1.90 .55

Souvenir Sheet

C223 A125 500fr multi 5.50 1.40

Litho. & Embossed
Size: 51x57mm

C223A A125 1500fr multi 50.00 3.00

Souvenir Sheet

C223B A125 1500fr multi 10.00

C223A-C223B exist imperf. No. C223A exists in a souvenir sheet of one. Value $40. No. C223B contains one 57x51mm stamp.

Nos. C216-C220 Overprinted

a

b

c

d

e

1980, May 12 Litho. *Perf. 13½*

C224 AP79 (a) 60fr multi .50 .25
C225 AP79 (b) 100fr multi .75 .40
C226 AP79 (c) 200fr multi 1.90 .85
C227 AP79 (d) 300fr multi 2.75 1.25
Nos. C224-C227 (4) 5.90 2.75

Souvenir Sheet

C228 AP79 (e) 500fr multi 5.00 5.00

World Telecommunications Day — AP80

1980, June 26 Litho. *Perf. 12½*

C229 AP80 100fr multi 1.10 .55
C230 AP80 150fr multi, vert. 1.40 .80

Olympic Type of 1980

100fr, Boxing. 150fr, Hurdles.
250fr, Long jump. No. C233A, Relay race, diff. No. C233B, Basketball, vert.

1980, July 25 Litho. *Perf. 13½*

C231 A126 100fr multi 1.00 .25
C232 A126 150fr multi 1.60 .40

Souvenir Sheet

C233 A126 250fr multi 3.00 .65

Litho. & Embossed

C233A A126 1500fr multi 35.00 4.00

Souvenir Sheet

C233B A126 1500fr multi 11.00 4.75

22nd Summer Olympic Games, Moscow, July 19-Aug. 3. No. C233 contains one 39x36mm stamp.
For overprints see Nos. C248-C250B.

Europe-Africa Type of 1980

150fr, Meteorology. 200fr, Aviation.
500fr, Concorde jet. No. C236A, Boy Scouts. No. C236B, Concorde.

1980, Nov. 4 Litho. *Perf. 13½*

C234 A127 150fr multi 1.50 .50
C235 A127 200fr multi 1.90 .60

Souvenir Sheet

C236 A127 500fr multi 5.50 1.60

No. C236 contains one 41½x29mm stamp.

Litho. & Embossed
Size: 42x39mm

C236A A127 1500fr multi 15.00 4.00

Souvenir Sheet

C236B A127 1500fr multi 12.00 4.75

Nos. C236A-C236B exist imperf. No. C236B contains one 42x39mm stamp.
No. C236A exists in a souvenir sheet of one. Value $30.

Soccer Type of 1981

100fr, Netherlands. 200fr, Spain.
500fr, Argentina. No. C239A, Players, trophy. No. C239B, Players, trophy, diff.

1981, Jan. 13 Litho. *Perf. 13½*

C237 A130 100fr multi 1.00 .25
C238 A130 200fr multi 1.75 .55

Souvenir Sheet

C239 A130 500fr multi 6.25 1.75

Litho. & Embossed
Size: 57x39mm

C239A A130 1500fr multi 24.00 5.50

Souvenir Sheet

C239B A130 1500fr multi 10.00 4.00

No. C239A exists with tabs for either Philexafrique II or Essen 78.
Nos. C239A-C239B exist imperf. No. C239A exists in a souvenir sheet of one. Value $38. No. C239B contains one 36x60mm stamp.

Jacob Wrestling with the Angel, by Rembrandt AP81

Rembrandt Paintings: 90fr, Christ during the Storm. 150fr, Jeremiah Mourning the Destruction of Jerusalem. 250fr, Tobit Accusing Anne of Theft of a Goat. 500fr, Belshazzar's Feast, horiz.

1981, Feb. 20 *Perf. 12½*

C240 AP81 60fr multi .55 .25
C241 AP81 90fr multi 1.00 .25
C242 AP81 150fr multi 1.75 .65
C243 AP81 250fr multi 3.00 .75
Nos. C240-C243 (4) 6.30 1.90

Souvenir Sheet

C244 AP81 500fr multi 6.00 1.75

Picasso Type of 1981

Paintings: 150fr, Woman in Mirror with Self-portrait. 200fr, Woman Sleeping, The Dream. 500fr, Portrait of Maia (the Artist's Daughter). No. C247A, Two Women and Glasses, Picasso. No. C247B, Woman with Handbag, statue of standing woman, vert.

1981, June 30 Litho. *Perf. 13½*

C245 A133 150fr multi 2.25 .45
C246 A133 200fr multi 2.50 .60

Souvenir Sheet

C247 A133 500fr multi 5.75 1.40

No. C247 contains one 42x46mm stamp.

Litho. & Embossed
Size: 57x39mm

C247A A133 1500fr gold & multi 17.50 6.00

Souvenir Sheet

C247B A133 1500fr gold & multi 12.00

Nos. C247A-C247B exist imperf. No. C247A exists in a souvenir sheet of one. Value $30. No. C247B contains one 39x58mm stamp.

Nos. C231-C233B Overprinted in Gold

1981 Litho. *Perf. 13½*

C248 A126 100fr multi 1.00 .25
C249 A126 150fr multi 1.40 .40

Souvenir Sheet

C250 A126 250fr multi 3.00 .65

Litho. & Embossed

C250A A126 1500fr on #C233A 14.00

Souvenir Sheet

C250B A126 1500fr on #C233B 15.00

No. C250A exists in a souvenir sheet of 1. Value $35.

Royal Wedding Type of 1981

150fr, Prince of Wales arms. 200fr, Palace. 500fr, St. Paul's Cathedral. No. C253A, Diana, Charles. No. C253B, Charles, Diana, ship.

1981, Aug. 20 Litho. *Perf. 13½*

C251 A136 150fr multi 1.60 .40
C252 A136 200fr multi 2.10 .55

Souvenir Sheet

C253 A136 500fr multi 4.75 1.40

No. C253 contains one 60x32mm stamp.

Litho. & Embossed
Size: 51x42mm

C253A A136 1500fr multi 15.00 4.00

Souvenir Sheet

C253B A136 1500fr multi 12.00

Nos. C253A-C253B exist imperf. No. C253A exists in a souvenir sheet of one. Value $21. No. C253B contains one 51x42mm stamp.

Navigator Type of 1981

100fr, O. Kersauson. 200fr, Chichester. 500fr, A. Colas. No. C256A, Riguidel. No. C256B, Tabarly.

1981, Sept. 4 Litho. *Perf. 13½*

C254 A139 100fr multi 1.10 .70
C255 A139 200fr multi 2.40 1.40

Souvenir Sheet

C256 A139 500fr multi 6.50 1.40

Litho. & Embossed
Size: 51x42mm

C256A A139 1500fr multi 16.00 4.50

Souvenir Sheet

C256B A139 1500fr multi 13.00

Nos. C256A-C256B exist imperf. No. C256A exists in a souvenir sheet of one. Value $40. No. C256B contains one 51x42mm stamp.

Lizard AP82

1981, Oct. 30 *Perf. 12½x13*

C257 AP82 30fr shown 1.00 .25
C258 AP82 60fr Snake 1.25 .30
C259 AP82 110fr Crocodile 2.50 .45
Nos. C257-C259 (3) 4.75 1.00

Christmas Type of 1981

140fr, Correggio. 200fr, Gentileschi, 1610. 500fr, Holy Family, by Cranach. No. C262A, Hans Memling, c. 1470. No. C262B, Fra Angelico, 1438.

1981, Dec. 24 *Perf. 13½*

C260 A143 140fr multi 2.50 .45
C261 A143 200fr multi 4.50 .70

Souvenir Sheet

C262 A143 500fr multi 6.75 1.75

No. C262 contains one 41x50mm stamp.

Litho. & Embossed
Size: 30x60mm

C262A A143 1500fr multi 15.00 4.50

Souvenir Sheet

C262B A143 1500fr multi 11.00

Nos. C262A-C262B exist imperf. No. C262A exists in a souvenir sheet of one. Value $25. No. C262B contains one 30x60mm stamp.

Animal Type of 1982

300fr, Mandrill. 500fr, Lion. 600fr, Nile crocodiles. No. C265A, Leopard, Rotary emblem. No. C265B, Emblem, eagle, horiz.

1982, Jan. 22 Litho. *Perf. 13½*

C263 A145 300fr multi 3.25 .65
C264 A145 500fr multi 5.50 1.40

Souvenir Sheet

C265 A145 600fr multi 6.75 1.60

No. C265 contains one 47x38mm stamp.

Litho. & Embossed
Size: 51x57mm

C265A A145 1500fr multi 15.00 4.00

Souvenir Sheet

C265B A145 1500fr multi 13.00

Nos. C265A-C265B exist imperf. No. C265A exists in a souvenir sheet of one. Value $42.50. No. C265B contains one 57x51mm stamp.

Transportation Type of 1982 and

AP82a

Designs: 300fr, Savannah cargo ship. 500fr, Columbia space shuttle. 600fr, Spirit of Locomotion emblem. No. C268A, Space shuttle launch, horiz. No. C268B, Shuttle, space telescope.

1982, Feb. 27 Litho. *Perf. 13½*

C266 A147 300fr multi 3.75 .65
C267 A147 500fr multi 5.50 1.40

Souvenir Sheet

C268 A147 600fr multi 5.50 1.60

Litho. & Embossed

C268A AP82a 1500fr gold & multi 15.00 4.50

Souvenir Sheet

C268B AP82a 1500fr gold & multi 11.50

No. C268 contains one 39x43mm stamp. No. C268B contains one 51x42mm stamp.

No. C268A exists in a souvenir sheet of 1. Value $50.

Olympic Type of 1982

1982, July 24 Litho. *Perf. 13½*

C269 A149 300fr Diving 3.00 .80
C270 A149 500fr Equestrian 5.00 1.40

Souvenir Sheet

C271 A149 600fr Basketball 5.50 1.60

No. C271 contains one 38x56mm stamp.

Diana Type of 1982

1982, July 20 Litho. *Perf. 13½*

C272 A150 300fr multi 3.25 .80
C273 A150 500fr multi 5.50 1.40

Souvenir Sheet

C274 A150 600fr multi 5.75 1.60

No. C274 contains one 56x32mm stamp.

Christmas 1982 AP83

Raphael Paintings: 150fr, Beautiful Gardener. 500fr, Holy Family.

1982, Dec. *Perf. 13*

C275 AP83 150fr multi 2.00 .50
C276 AP83 500fr multi 5.50 1.40

Space Type of 1982

Designs: Various satellites and space scenes. No. C279A, European communications satellite, controller. No. C279B, Viking on Mars, vert.

1982, Aug. 15 Litho. *Perf. 13½*

C277 A151 300fr multi 3.00 .80
C278 A151 500fr multi 5.00 1.40

Souvenir Sheet

C279 A151 600fr multi 5.00 1.60

Litho. & Embossed
Size: 60x36mm

C279A A151 1500fr gold & multi 15.00 4.50

Souvenir Sheet

C279B A151 1500fr gold & multi 12.00

Nos. C279A-C279B exist imperf. No. C279A exists in a souvenir sheet of one. Value $55. No. C279B contains one 36x60mm stamp.

Birth of Prince William of Wales, June 21, 1982 — AP84

500fr, Diana, William.
600fr, Family. No. C281A, Diana, William, Charles. No. 281B, Diana, William, vert.

1983, Jan. 22

C280 AP84 500fr multi 5.50 1.40

Souvenir Sheet

C281 AP84 600fr multi 5.50 4.00

Litho. & Embossed

C281A AP84 1500fr gold & multi 15.00 3.50

Souvenir Sheet

C281B AP84 1500fr gold & multi 10.00

No. C281A exists in a souvenir sheet of 1. Value $40.

Manned Flight Bicentenary AP85

65fr, Robert's & Hullin's balloon. 130fr, John Wise's, 1859. 350fr, Mail balloon, 1870. 400fr, Dirigible Underberg.
500fr, Montgolfiere, 1783.

1983, Apr.

C282 AP85 65fr multicolored 1.00 .25
C283 AP85 130fr multicolored 1.50 .35
C284 AP85 350fr multicolored 3.25 .90
C285 AP85 400fr multicolored 4.25 1.10
Nos. C282-C285 (4) 10.00 2.60

Souvenir Sheet

C286 AP85 500fr multicolored 5.75 1.40

Pre-Olympics — AP86

Various equestrian events.

1983, July Litho. *Perf. 13*

C287 AP86 100fr multi 1.00 .40
C288 AP86 200fr multi 2.10 .60
C289 AP86 300fr multi 2.75 .80
C290 AP86 400fr multi 3.50 1.10
Nos. C287-C290 (4) 9.35 2.90

Souvenir Sheet

C291 AP86 500fr multi 5.75 1.40

Animal Type of 1983

Endangered Animals, Rotary Emblem: 400fr, Black rhinoceros, parrot, zebra, scouts. 500fr, Lions, parrot, antelope, elephant, flag, Rotary Int'l emblem. 600fr, Leopard.

1983, Nov. 14 Litho. *Perf. 13½*

C291A A170 400fr multicolored 10.00 3.00
C292 A170 500fr multicolored 12.00 3.50

Souvenir Sheet

C293 A170 600fr multicolored 16.00 4.00

15th World Scout Jamboree, Alberta (400fr). No. C293 contains one 47x32mm stamp.

Christmas 1983 AP88

Paintings: 130fr, Annunciation, by da Vinci. 205fr, Virgin of the Rocks, by da Vinci. 350fr, Adoration of the Shepherds, by Rubens. 500fr, Virgin and Child with Donor, by Rubens.

1984, Jan. 3 Litho. *Perf. 13*

C294 AP88 130fr multi 1.25 .35
C295 AP88 205fr multi 2.00 .50
C296 AP88 350fr multi 3.50 1.00
C297 AP88 500fr multi 5.00 1.25
Nos. C294-C297 (4) 11.75 3.10

1984 Summer Olympics — AP89

Various gymnastic and rhythmic gymnastic events. 65fr, 100fr, 205fr, 350fr vert.
500fr, Rhythmic formation.

1984, Mar. 13 Litho. *Perf. 13*

C298 AP89 65fr multi .55 .25
C299 AP89 100fr multi 1.10 .25
C300 AP89 130fr multi 1.40 .30
C301 AP89 205fr multi 2.25 .60
C302 AP89 350fr multi 4.00 1.00
Nos. C298-C302 (5) 9.30 2.40

Souvenir Sheet
Perf. 13½x13

C302A AP89 500fr multi 5.00 1.25

For overprint see No. 705.

Summer Olympics Winners AP90

60fr, 400 meter relay. 140fr, 400 meter hurdles. 300fr, 5000 meter race. 440fr, Decathlon. 550fr, 800 meter race, horiz.

1985, Jan. 7 Litho. *Perf. 14*

C303 AP90 60fr multicolored .55 .25
C304 AP90 140fr multicolored 1.75 .40
C305 AP90 300fr multicolored 3.50 .80
C306 AP90 440fr multicolored 4.50 1.00
Nos. C303-C306 (4) 10.30 2.45

Souvenir Sheet

C307 AP90 500fr multicolored 5.00 4.50

Christmas 1984 — AP91

Paintings by Titian: 130fr, Virgin and Infant Jesus. 350fr, Virgin with Rabbit. 400fr, Virgin and Child.

1985, Jan. 17 Litho. *Perf. 13*

C308 AP91 130fr multi 1.25 .55
C309 AP91 350fr multi 2.75 1.10
C310 AP91 400fr multi 3.75 1.25
Nos. C308-C310 (3) 7.75 2.90

Audubon Bicentenary — AP92

60fr, Otus asio. 110fr, Coccizus minor, vert. 200fr, Zenaidura macroura, vert. 500fr, Aix sponsa.

1985, Jan. 25 Litho. *Perf. 13*

C311 AP92 60fr multicolored .80 .25
C312 AP92 110fr multicolored 1.25 .45
C313 AP92 200fr multicolored 2.10 1.00
C314 AP92 500fr multicolored 5.25 2.50
Nos. C311-C314 (4) 9.40 4.20

Christmas 1985
AP93

Religious paintings: 100fr, Virgin with Angels, by the Master of Burgo de Osma. 200fr, Nativity, by Louis Le Nain (1593-1648). 400fr, Virgin and Child with Dove, by Piero de Cosimo (1462-1521).

1985, Dec. 24 Litho. *Perf. 13*

C315 AP93 100fr multi 1.10 .40
C316 AP93 200fr multi 2.50 .85
C317 AP93 400fr multi 4.75 1.90
Nos. C315-C317 (3) 8.35 3.15

Halley's Comet — AP94

110fr, Edmond Halley. 130fr, Giotto probe. 200fr, Comet, planet. 300fr, Vega probe. 400fr, Space shuttle.

1986, Mar. 8

C318 AP94 110fr multicolored 1.00 .25
C319 AP94 130fr multicolored 1.40 .25
C320 AP94 200fr multicolored 2.25 .50
C321 AP94 300fr multicolored 3.00 .75
C322 AP94 400fr multicolored 4.50 1.00
Nos. C318-C322 (5) 12.15 2.75

Christmas
AP95

Painting details: 250fr, Nativity, by Giotto. 440fr, Adoration of the Magi, by Botticelli, vert. 500fr, Nativity, by Giotto, diff.

1986, Dec. 24 Litho. *Perf. 13½*

C323 AP95 250fr multi 2.50 1.10
C324 AP95 440fr multi 4.25 1.75
C325 AP95 500fr multi 5.25 2.10
Nos. C323-C325 (3) 12.00 4.95

Tennis at the 1988 Olympics — AP96

Various plays.

1986, Dec. 31 *Perf. 12½*

C326 AP96 150fr multi 1.60 .60
C327 AP96 250fr multi, vert. 3.00 .70
C328 AP96 440fr multi, vert. 3.75 1.25
C329 AP96 600fr multi 6.25 1.40
Nos. C326-C329 (4) 14.60 3.95

1988 Summer Olympics, Seoul — AP97

100fr, Triple jump, vert. 200fr, High jump. 300fr, Long jump. 400fr, Pole vault, vert. 500fr, High jump, diff.

1987, June 15 Litho. *Perf. 13*

C330 AP97 100fr multicolored .90 .40
C331 AP97 200fr multicolored 1.75 .80
C332 AP97 300fr multicolored 2.60 1.10
C333 AP97 400fr multicolored 3.50 1.60
Nos. C330-C333 (4) 8.75 3.90

Souvenir Sheet

C334 AP97 500fr multicolored 4.50 3.25

1988 Summer Olympics, Seoul — AP98

Stamps on stamps and gymnasts: 90fr, No. C94, balance beam, vert. 200fr, No. C21, balance beam, diff. 300fr, No. C22, pommel horse. 400fr, No. C23, parallel bars. 500fr, No. C93, rings.

1988, July 26 Litho. *Perf. 13*

C335 AP98 90fr multi .90 .30
C336 AP98 200fr multi 2.00 .50
C337 AP98 300fr multi 3.00 .90
C338 AP98 400fr multi 4.00 1.40
Nos. C335-C338 (4) 9.90 3.10

Souvenir Sheet

C339 AP98 500fr multi 5.00 2.75

1st Moon Landing, 20th Anniv.
AP99

1989, Aug. 4 Litho. *Perf. 13*

C340 AP99 40fr Apollo 11 .35 .25
C341 AP99 80fr Apollo 15 .75 .30
C342 AP99 130fr Apollo 16 1.50 .55
C343 AP99 1000fr Apollo 17 10.00 2.75
Nos. C340-C343 (4) 12.60 3.85

World Cup Soccer Championships, Italy — AP100

1990, July 7 Litho. *Perf. 13*

C344 AP100 5fr multicolored .25 .25
C345 AP100 30fr multi, diff. .30 .25
C346 AP100 500fr multi, diff. 5.00 1.00
C347 AP100 1000fr multi, diff. 9.25 1.60
Nos. C344-C347 (4) 14.80 3.10

Charles de Gaulle (1890-1979) — AP101

1990, July 27 *Perf. 13½*

C348 AP101 500fr multicolored 3.75 .90

No. C348 exists in a souvenir sheet of 1.
For overprint see No. C360.

Don Mattingly, Baseball Player — AP102

Saturn V Rocket, Apollo 11 Astronauts — AP103

Charles de Gaulle, Birth Cent.
AP104

No. C352, De Gaulle and Cross of Lorraine.

1990, July 27 Litho. *Perf. 13½*

C349 AP102 300fr multicolored 2.50 .80

Souvenir Sheet

C350 AP103 1000fr multicolored 8.25 1.75

Litho. & Embossed

C351 AP104 1500fr gold & multi 15.00 5.00

Souvenir Sheet

C352 AP104 1500fr gold & multi 11.00

No. C351 exists in souvenir sheet of 1. Value $14. This souvenir sheet also exists imperf. and with an overprint in the sheet margin.
For overprints see Nos. C355-C356.

Visit of Pope John Paul II to Africa
AP105

Pope John Paul II and: No. C353, Mother Theresa, portrait. No. C354, Papal arms, globe.

1993 Litho. & Embossed *Perf. 13½*

C353 AP105 1500fr gold & multi 15.00 5.00

Souvenir Sheet

C354 AP105 1500fr gold & multi 20.00

No. C353 exists in a souvenir sheet of 1. Value $20.

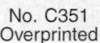

No. C351 Overprinted

Litho. & Embossed

1994, June 6 *Perf. 13½*

C355	AP104	1500fr gold & multi	12.00	9.00

No. C352 Ovptd. in Silver in Sheet Margin

Souvenir Sheet

C356	AP104	1500fr gold & multi	12.00	9.00

Overprint on No. C356 contains map, soldiers and "50 eme ANNIVERSAIRE DU /DEBARQUEMENT."

No. C355 exists in souvenir sheet of 1. Value $12.

Souvenir Sheets

Japanese Exploration of Antarctica — AP106

No. C357, Nobu Shirase. No. C358, Schooner Kainman Maru, horiz.

1994, Oct. 25

C357	AP106	1200fr multi	5.00	4.75
C358	AP106	1200fr multi	5.00	4.75

D-Day, 50th Anniv. (in 1994) — AP107

Designs: a, Gliders over Pegasus Bridge, Sword beach. b, Fighter planes over Juno, Gold and Omaha beaches. c, Planes over Utah beach, St. Mere Eglise.

Litho. & Embossed

1995, Oct. 25 *Perf. 13½*

C359	AP107	1000fr Strip of 3, #a.-c.	13.00	13.00

No. C359b is 60x45mm.

Souvenir Sheet

No. C348 Overprinted

1995, Oct. 10 **Litho.** *Perf. 13½*

C360	AP101	500fr multicolored	11.50	11.50

AIR POST SEMI-POSTAL STAMPS

Isis of Kalabsha SPAP1

Unwmk.

1964, Mar. 7 **Engr.** *Perf. 13*

CB1	SPAP1	25fr + 10fr multi	1.40	1.40
CB2	SPAP1	50fr + 10fr multi	2.25	2.25
CB3	SPAP1	100fr + 10fr multi	3.50	3.50
		Nos. CB1-CB3 (3)	7.15	7.15

UNESCO world campaign to save historic monuments in Nubia.

African Infants and Globe — SPAP2

1971, Dec. 11 **Litho.** *Perf. 13x13½*

CB4	SPAP2	140fr + 50fr multi	3.25	1.75

25th anniv. of UNICEF, and Children's Day.

POSTAGE DUE STAMPS

Sternotomis Virescens — D1

Beetles: No. J2, Sternotomis gama. No. J3, Augosoma centaurus. No. J4, Phosphorus virescens, ceroplesis carabarica. No. J5, Cetoine scaraboidae. No. J6, Ceroplesis S.P. No. J7, Macrorhina S.P. No. J8, Cetoine scaraboidae. No. J9, Phryneta leprosa. No. J10, Taurina longiceps. No. J11, Monohamus griseoplagiatus. No. J12, Jambonus trifasciatus.

Unwmk.

1962, Oct. 15 **Engr.** *Perf. 11*

J1	D1	50c grn & dp org	.25	.25
J2	D1	50c grn & dp org	.25	.25
a.		Pair, #J1-J2	.45	
J3	D1	1fr blk, brn & lt grn	.30	.30
J4	D1	1fr blk, brn & lt grn	.30	.30
a.		Pair, #J3-J4	.75	
J5	D1	2fr blk, org & yel grn	.40	.40
J6	D1	2fr blk & red org	.40	.40
a.		Pair, #J5-J6	.85	
J7	D1	5fr brn, org & grn	.55	.55
J8	D1	5fr brn, org, grn & red	.55	.55
a.		Pair, #J7-J8	1.25	
J9	D1	10fr blk, grn & brn	1.00	1.00
J10	D1	10fr blk, brn & grn	1.00	1.00
a.		Pair, #J9-J10	2.25	
J11	D1	25fr blk, bl grn & brn	3.00	2.40
J12	D1	25fr blk, brn & bl grn	3.00	2.40
a.		Pair, #J11-J12	6.50	
		Nos. J1-J12 (12)	11.00	9.80

Pairs se-tenant at the base.

Giant Anteater — D2

1985, Jan. 25 **Litho.** *Perf. 12½*

J13	D2	5fr multi	.50	.50
J14	D2	20fr multi	.90	.90
J15	D2	30fr multi	1.10	1.10
		Nos. J13-J15 (3)	2.50	2.50

MILITARY STAMPS

No. 1 Overprinted

Unwmk.

1962, Jan. 1 **Engr.** *Perf. 13*

M1	A1	bl, car, grn & yel	15.00	—

No. 1 Overprinted

1963

M2	A1	bl, car, grn & yel	16.00	—

OFFICIAL STAMPS

Coat of Arms — O1

Imprint: "d'après G. RICHER SO.GE.IM."

Perf. 13x12½

1965-69 **Litho.** **Unwmk.**

Arms in Original Colors

O1	O1	1fr blk & brn org	.25	.25
O2	O1	2fr blk & violet	.25	.25
O3	O1	5fr blk & gray	.25	.25
O4	O1	10fr blk & green	.25	.25
O5	O1	20fr blk & red brn	.55	.25
O6	O1	30fr blk & emer ('69)	1.10	.55
O7	O1	50fr blk & dk bl	1.25	.70
O8	O1	100fr blk & bister	2.75	1.10
O9	O1	130fr blk & ver ('69)	4.25	2.25
O10	O1	200fr blk & claret	6.25	2.75
		Nos. O1-O10 (10)	17.15	8.60

Redrawn

Imprint: "d'après G. RICHER DELRIEU"

1971 **Photo.** *Perf. 12x12½*

Arms in Original Colors

O11	O1	5fr blk & gray	.25	.25
O12	O1	30fr blk & emer	.50	.25
O13	O1	40fr blk & dp claret	.65	.30
O14	O1	100fr blk & bister	1.50	.55
O15	O1	140fr blk & lt bl	2.75	.85
O16	O1	200fr blk & claret	3.25	1.40
		Nos. O11-O16 (6)	8.90	3.60

Empire

Nos. O11, O13-O16 Overprinted in Black

1977 **Litho.** *Perf. 12x12½*

O17	O1	5fr multi	.35	.25
O18	O1	40fr multi	.50	.30
O19	O1	100fr multi	1.40	.45
O20	O1	140fr multi	1.75	.70
O21	O1	200fr multi	2.75	1.00
		Nos. O17-O21 (5)	6.75	2.70

Type of 1965 Inscribed: "EMPIRE CENTRAFRICAIN"

1978, July **Litho.** *Perf. 12½*

O22	O1	1fr multi	.25	.25
O23	O1	2fr multi	.25	.25
O24	O1	5fr multi	.25	.25
O25	O1	10fr multi	.25	.25
O26	O1	15fr multi	.25	.25
O27	O1	20fr multi	.25	.25
O28	O1	30fr multi	.30	.25
O29	O1	40fr multi	.40	.25
O30	O1	50fr multi	.55	.30
O31	O1	60fr multi	.75	.40
O32	O1	100fr multi	1.00	.55
O33	O1	130fr multi	1.60	.95
O34	O1	140fr multi	1.75	.95
O35	O1	200fr multi	3.50	1.25
		Nos. O22-O35 (14)	11.35	6.40

CENTRAL LITHUANIA

'sen-trəl ˌli-thə-'wā-nē-ə

LOCATION — North of Poland and east of Lithuania
CAPITAL — Vilnius

At one time Central Lithuania was a grand duchy of Lithuania but at the end of the 18th Century it fell under Russian rule. After World War I, Lithuania regained her sovereignty but certain areas were occupied by Poland. During the Russo-Polish war this territory was seized by Lithuania whose claim was promptly recognized by the Soviet Government. Under the leadership of the Polish General Zeligowski the territory was recaptured and it was during this occupation the stamps of Central Lithuania came into being. Subsequently the territory became a part of Poland.

100 Fennigi = 1 Markka

Coat of Arms — A1

Perf. 11½, Imperf.

1920-21 Typo. Unwmk.

1	A1	25f red		.40	*.55*
2	A1	25f dark grn ('21)		.40	*.55*
3	A1	1m blue		.40	*.55*
4	A1	1m dark brn ('21)		.40	*.55*
5	A1	2m violet		.40	*.55*
6	A1	2m orange ('21)		.40	*.55*
		Nos. 1-6 (6)		2.40	*3.30*

For surcharges see Nos. B1-B5.

Lithuanian Stamps of 1919 Surcharged in Blue or Black

Perf. 11½x12, 12½x11½, 14

1920, Nov. 23 Wmk. 145

13	A5	2m on 15sk lil	47.50	*55.00*
a.		Inverted surcharge	*200.00*	*900.00*
14	A5	4m on 10sk red	47.50	*52.50*
a.		Inverted surcharge	*150.00*	
15	A5	4m on 20sk dl bl (Bk)	47.50	*52.50*
a.		Inverted surcharge	*150.00*	
16	A5	4m on 30sk buff	47.50	*52.50*
a.		Inverted surcharge	*150.00*	
17	A6	6m on 50sk lt grn	47.50	*52.50*
a.		4m on 50sk (error)	*200.00*	
b.		10m on 50sk (error)	*200.00*	
c.		Surcharge inverted		—
18	A6	6m on 60sk vio & red	47.50	*52.50*
a.		4m on 60sk (error)	*200.00*	
b.		10m on 60sk (error)	*200.00*	
19	A6	6m on 75sk bis & red	47.50	*52.50*
a.		4m on 75sk (error)	*200.00*	
b.		10m on 75sk (error)	*200.00*	
20	A8	10m on 1auk gray & red	95.00	110.00
a.		Inverted surcharge	*210.00*	
21	A8	10m on 3auk lt brn & red	*1,400.*	*1,800.*
22	A8	10m on 5auk bl grn & red	*1,400.*	*1,800.*
		Nos. 13-20 (8)	427.50	*480.00*
		Nos. 13-22 (10)	*3,227.*	*4,080.*

The overprint on Nos. 17-19 is down-reading, i.e., the top of the overprint is at the right of the original design, the bottom at the left. The inverted overprint on No. 17c is up-reading.

Reprints of Nos. 17a, 17b, 18a, 18b, 19a, 19b. Value, each $45.

Counterfeits of Nos. 21-22 exist.

Lithuanian Girl — A2

Warrior — A3

Holy Gate of Vilnius — A4

Tower and Cathedral, Vilnius — A5

Rector's Insignia — A6

Gen. Lucien Zeligowski — A7

Perf. 11½, Imperf.

1920 Litho. Unwmk.

23	A2	25f gray	.25	*.75*
24	A3	1m orange	.25	*.75*
25	A4	2m claret	.50	*1.00*
26	A5	4m gray grn & buff	.75	*1.50*
27	A6	6m rose & gray	2.50	*3.25*
28	A7	10m brown & yellow	3.50	*4.75*
		Nos. 23-28 (6)	7.75	*12.00*

For surcharges see Nos. B13-B14, B17-B19.

St. Anne's Church, Vilnius — A8

St. Stanislas Cathedral, Vilnius — A9

White Eagle, White Knight Vytis — A10

Queen Hedwig and King Ladislas II Jagello — A11

Coat of Arms of Vilnius — A12

Poczobut Astronomical Observatory A13

Union of Lithuania and Poland — A14

Tadeusz Kosciuszko and Adam Mickiewicz A15

1921 ***Perf. 14, Imperf.***

35	A8	1m dk gray & yel	.75	*1.25*
36	A9	2m rose & green	.75	*1.25*
37	A10	3m dark green	.75	*1.25*
38	A11	4m brown & buff	.75	*1.25*
39	A12	5m red brown	.75	*1.25*
40	A13	6m slate & buff	.75	*1.50*
41	A14	10m red vio & buff	1.00	*2.50*
42	A15	20m blk brn & buff	1.00	*2.50*
		Nos. 35-42 (8)	6.50	*12.75*

Set, perf. 13½, $150.

Peasant Girl Sowing — A16

White Eagle and Vytis — A17

Great Theater at Vilnius — A18

Allegory: Peace and Industry — A19

Gen. Zeligowski Entering Vilnius — A20

Gen. Zeligowski — A21

1921-22 ***Perf. 11½, Imperf.***

53	A16	10m brown ('22)	3.25	*6.25*
54	A17	25m red & yel ('22)	3.50	*8.00*
55	A18	50m dk blue ('22)	5.00	*12.00*
56	A19	75m violet ('22)	6.00	*22.50*
57	A20	100m bl & bister	2.50	*5.25*
58	A21	150m ol grn & brn	3.50	*6.75*
		Nos. 53-58 (6)	23.75	*60.75*

Opening of the Natl. Parliament, Nos. 53-56; anniv. of the entry of General Zeligowski into Vilnius, Nos. 57-58.

SEMI-POSTAL STAMPS

Nos. 1-6 Surcharged in Black or Red

1921 Unwmk. ***Perf. 11½, Imperf.***

B1	A1	25f + 2m red (Bk)	1.25	*2.25*
B2	A1	25f + 2m dk green	1.25	*2.25*
B3	A1	1m + 2m blue	1.50	*2.25*
B4	A1	1m + 2m dk brown	1.50	*2.25*
B5	A1	2m + 2m violet	1.50	*2.25*
B6	A1	2m + 2m orange	1.50	*2.25*
		Nos. B1-B6 (6)	8.50	*13.50*

The surcharge means "For Silesia 2 marks." The stamps were intended to provide a fund to assist the plebiscite in Upper Silesia.

Nos. 25, 26 Surcharged

a

b

Perf. 11½, Imperf.

B13	A4 (a)	2m + 1(m) claret	1.00	*2.00*
B14	A5 (b)	4m + 1m gray green & buff	1.00	*2.00*

Nos. 25-26, 28 with inset

Perf. 11½, Imperf.

B17	A4	2m + 1m claret	.65	*1.25*
B18	A5	4m + 1m gray green & buff	.65	*1.25*
B19	A7	10m + 2m brn & yel	.90	*1.25*
		Nos. B13-B19 (5)	4.20	*7.75*

POSTAGE DUE STAMPS

University, Vilnius D1

Castle Hill, Vilnius D2

Castle Ruins, Troki — D3

Holy Gate, Vilnius — D4

St. Stanislas Cathedral D5

St. Anne's Church, Vilnius D6

1920-21 Unwmk. ***Perf. 11½, Imperf.***

J1	D1	50f red violet	.40	*1.25*
J2	D2	1m green	.40	*1.25*
J3	D3	2m red violet	.50	*1.25*
J4	D4	3m red violet	.85	*1.60*
J5	D5	5m red violet	1.00	*2.50*
J6	D6	20m scarlet	2.00	*3.25*
		Nos. J1-J6 (6)	5.15	*11.10*

CEYLON

si-'lăn

LOCATION — An island in the Indian Ocean separated from India by the Gulf of Manaar
GOVT. — Independent republic within the British Commonwealth
AREA — 25,332 sq. mi.
POP. — 12,670,000 (est. 1971)
CAPITAL — Colombo

Ceylon changed its name to Republic of Sri Lanka on May 22, 1972.

12 Pence = 1 Shilling
100 Cents = 1 Rupee (1872)

Values for unused stamps are for examples with original gum as defined in the catalogue introduction except for Nos. 2, 5, 8-9 which seldom have any remaining trace of their original gum. Many unused stamps of Ceylon, especially between Nos. 59 and 274, have toned gum or tropical stains. Values quoted are for stamps with fresh gum. Toned stamps have lower values, and common stamps with toned gum are worth very little.

Very fine examples of Nos. 1-15 will be cut square, will have small margins, but will show an intact design. Inferior examples with the design partly cut away will sell for much less, and examples with large margins will command higher prices. Very fine examples of Nos. 17-58b will have perforations just cutting into the design on one or more sides due to the narrow spacing of the stamps on the plates and to imperfect perforating methods. Stamps with perfs clear on all four sides are extremely scarce and will command substantially higher prices.

Catalogue values for unused stamps in this country are for Never Hinged items, beginning with Scott 290 in the regular postage section and Scott B1 in the semi-postal section.

Watermarks

Wmk. 1a — 22½mm high, Oval Letters

Wmk. 1b — 21mm high, Round Letters

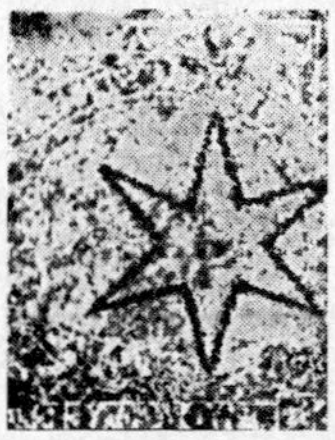
Wmk. 6 — Large Star

Wmk. 290 — Lotus and "Sri" Multiple

Queen Victoria
A1 A2

1857 Engr. Wmk. 6 *Imperf.*
Blued Paper

1	A1	1p blue	—	240.
2	A1	6p plum	*12,500.*	525.

1857-59 White Paper

3	A1	1p dp turq	1,150.	47.50
4	A1	2p deep grn	210.00	75.00
a.		2p yellow green	575.00	105.00
5	A2	4p dl rose ('59)	*75,000.*	5,250.
6	A1	5p org brown	1,750.	175.00
6A	A1	6p plum	*2,850.*	170.00
7	A1	6p brown	*10,500.*	575.00
8	A2	8p brown ('59)	*30,000.*	1,750.
9	A2	9p lil brn ('59)	*62,500.*	1,050.
10	A1	10p vermilion	950.00	350.00
11	A1	1sh violet	5,750.	225.00
12	A2	1sh9p green ('59)	950.00	925.00
a.		1sh9p yellow green	5,500.	3,500.
13	A2	2sh blue ('59)	6,750.	1,400.

Stamps of type A2 frequently have repaired corners.

Nos. 3-4 exist unofficially rouletted. See the *Scott Classic Specialized Catalogue of Stamps & Covers* for listings.

Beware of Nos. 17-57 trimmed to resemble Nos. 3-13. Values are for stamps with clear margins on all sides.

No. 5 was reproduced by the collotype process in a souvenir sheet distributed at the London International Stamp Exhibition 1950. The paper is unwatermarked.

A3

1857-58 Typo. Unwmk.

14	A3	½p lilac ('58)	200.	*250.*
15	A3	½p lilac, *bluish*	4,250.	650.

Values are for stamps without cracking of the surface, and examples showing cracking should be discounted.

Clean-Cut Perf. 14 to 15½

1861 Wmk. 6 Engr.

17	A1	1p blue	210.00	18.00
18	A1	2p yel grn	275.00	27.50
b.		Vert. pair, imperf between		—
19	A2	4p dull rose	2,300.	350.00
20	A1	5p org brown	125.00	10.00
20A	A1	6p brown	3,200.	190.00
b.		6p bister brown	2,250.	290.00
21	A2	8p brown	2,600.	575.00
22	A2	9p lilac brown	16,000.	275.00
23	A1	1sh violet	145.00	17.50
24	A2	2sh blue	4,750.	875.00

Rough Perf. 14 to 15½

25	A1	1p blue	170.00	12.50
b.		Blued paper	850.00	27.50
26	A1	2p yel green	475.00	92.50
27	A2	4p rose red	600.00	130.00
28	A1	6p olive brown	1,250.	120.00
a.		6p deep brown	1,350.	130.00
b.		6p bister brown	2,300.	200.00
29	A2	8p brown	1,775.	675.00
30	A2	8p yel brown	1,800.	425.00
31	A2	9p olive brown	875.00	85.00
32	A2	9p deep brown	160.00	120.00
33	A1	10p vermilion	325.00	30.00
a.		Imperf. vert., pair		—
34	A1	1sh violet	300.00	17.50
35	A2	1sh9p green	825.00	
36	A2	2sh blue	800.00	160.00

The 1sh9p green was never placed in use.

1863 *Perf. 12½*

37	A1	10p vermilion	340.00	22.50

1864 Typo. Unwmk.

38	A3	½p lilac	260.00	210.00

See note following No. 15.

1862 Engr. *Perf. 13*

39	A1	1p blue	180.00	7.00
40	A1	5p car brown	1,850.	175.00
41	A1	6p deep brown	210.00	30.00
42	A2	9p brown	1,400.	120.00
43	A1	1sh grayish violet	2,100.	95.00

Parts of the papermaker's sheet watermark, "T. H. SAUNDERS 1862," may be found on some examples of Nos. 39-43.

Perf. 12

44	A1	1p blue	1,900.	150.00
a.		Horiz. pair, imperf. btwn.		*18,000.*

Two Types of Watermark Crown and CC (1)

1863-67 Typo. Wmk. 1a *Perf. 12½*

45	A3	½p lilac	80.00	50.00
a.		½p reddish lilac	90.00	65.00

Engr.

46	A1	1p blue	180.00	9.00
a.		1p dark blue	180.00	9.00
c.		Perf. 11½	3,650.	350.00
47	A1	2p gray green	100.00	15.00
48	A1	2p emerald	190.00	120.00
48A	A1	2p yel green	*10,000.*	475.00
48B	A1	2p bottle green		*4,250.*
49	A1	2p olive	325.00	275.00
50	A2	4p rose	550.00	130.00
a.		4p carmine rose	900.00	275.00
51	A1	5p car brown	325.00	110.00
52	A1	5p olive green	1,700.	350.00
e.		5p deep sage green	2,100.	425.00
53	A1	6p choc brown	250.00	7.50
a.		Perf. 13	2,850.	260.00
b.		6p black brown	300.00	11.50
c.		As "b," double impression		*4,500.*
d.		6p reddish brown	350.00	14.00
54	A2	8p red brown	150.00	80.00
55	A2	9p brown	360.00	52.50
c.		Perf. 13	6,750.	1,100.
56	A1	10p vermilion	5,000.	70.00
a.		10p orange	7,500.	500.00
58	A2	2sh blue	375.00	45.00

The ½p, 1p blue, 2p olive, 4p and 5p green exist imperf.

Wmk. 1b

46d	A1	1p blue	325.00	17.50
e.		1p dark blue	275.00	16.00
49d	A1	2p orange yellow	135.00	8.00
e.		2p olive yellow	175.00	14.00
f.		2p olive green	175.00	30.00
50b	A2	4p rose	325.00	65.00
c.		4p carmine rose	125.00	40.00
52b	A1	5p myrtle green	160.00	25.00
c.		5p olive green	150.00	27.50
d.		5p bronze green	60.00	*60.00*
53e	A1	6p chocolate brown	140.00	11.00
f.		6p brown	190.00	9.00
54a	A2	8p red brown	140.00	80.00
55a	A2	9p dark brown	70.00	7.00
b.		9p bister brown	975.00	40.00
56b	A1	10p orange	150.00	17.00
c.		10p orange red	90.00	18.00
d.		10p vermilion	*5,500.*	170.00
57	A1	1sh purple	150.00	12.00
a.		1sh reddish lilac	325.00	32.50
58a	A2	2sh deep blue	160.00	17.50
b.		2sh indigo	300.00	22.50

The 1p blue and 6p brown exist imperf.
For overprints see Nos. O2, O4-O7.

A4

A5

1866 Typo. Wmk. 1 *Perf. 12½*

59	A5	3p rose	300.00	105.00
a.		Imperf., pair	*1,000.*	

For overprint see No. O3.

1868 *Perf. 14*

61	A4	1p blue	30.00	12.00
62	A5	3p rose	95.00	52.50

For overprint see No. O1.

A6

A7

A8

A9

A10

A11

A12

A13

A14

A15

1872-80 *Perf. 14*

63	A6	2c brown	32.50	4.50
64	A7	4c gray	50.00	1.75
65	A7	4c lil rose ('80)	75.00	1.60
66	A8	8c orange	55.00	7.25
a.		8c orange yellow	45.00	8.00
67	A9	16c violet	150.00	3.00
68	A10	24c green	90.00	2.25
69	A11	32c slate bl ('77)	190.00	16.00
70	A12	36c blue	210.00	30.00
71	A13	48c rose	110.00	9.50
72	A14	64c red brn ('77)	325.00	77.50
73	A15	96c olive gray	300.00	30.00
		Nos. 63-73 (11)	1,587.	183.35

For surcharges see Nos. 83-84, 94A-110, 112-114. For types surcharged see Nos. 124-129.

1872 *Perf. 12½*

74	A6	2c brown	*4,750.*	275.00
75	A7	4c gray	*3,250.*	350.00

A16

1879 *Perf. 14x12½*

77	A6	2c brown	450.00	75.00
78	A7	4c gray	2,600.	40.00
79	A8	8c orange	500.00	57.50

Perf. 12½x14

82	A16	2r50c claret	825.00	440.00

The 32c and 64c are known perf. 14x12½, but were not regularly issued.

No. 82, perf. 12½, was not regularly issued.

See Nos. 142, 158. For surcharges see Nos. 111, 115, 130. For types surcharged see Nos. 160-161.

Nos. 68, 72 Surcharged

1882 *Perf. 14*

83 A10 16c on 24c green 42.50 10.00
a. Inverted surcharge —
84 A14 20c on 64c red brn 14.50 10.00
a. Double surcharge 1,850.

1883-99 **Wmk. 2**

85 A6 2c pale brown 75.00 3.50
86 A6 2c green ('84) 3.25 .25
a. Perf. 12 7,000.
87 A6 2c org brn ('99) 5.00 .40
88 A7 4c lilac rose 6.50 .50
89 A7 4c rose ('84) 7.75 *13.50*
a. Perf. 12 7,250.
90 A7 4c brt rose ('98) 13.00 *15.00*
91 A7 4c yellow ('99) 4.25 4.00
92 A8 8c orange 8.00 *14.00*
93 A9 16c violet 2,100. 180.00
94 A10 24c purple brown 1,750.
b. Perf. 12 *7,750.*

Nos. 86a, 89a, 94 and 94b were never placed in use. A 48c brown, perf. 12, was prepared but not issued.

For surcharges and overprints see Nos.116-123, 143-151D, 155-156, O8-O9.

Issues of 1872-82 Surcharged

a

b

c

d

1885 **Wmk. 1** *Perf. 14*

94A A9 (a) 5c on 16c *3,250.*
95 A10 (a) 5c on 24c *6,750.* 115.00
96 A11 (a) 5c on 32c 72.50 20.00
a. Inverted surcharge 3,000.
97 A12 (a) 5c on 36c 325.00 13.50
a. Inverted surcharge *2,850.*
98 A13 (a) 5c on 48c 2,550. 75.00
99 A14 (a) 5c on 64c 145.00 14.00
a. Double surcharge 3,750.
100 A15 (a) 5c on 96c 575.00 75.00
101 A9 (b) 10c on 16c *12,500.* 3,250.
102 A10 (b) 10c on 24c 525.00 145.00
103 A12 (b) 10c on 36c 500.00 290.00
104 A14 (b) 10c on 64c 475.00 275.00
105 A10 (b) 20c on 24c 80.00 30.00
106 A11 (c) 20c on 32c 95.00 80.00
107 A11 (c) 25c on 32c 27.50 8.25
108 A13 (c) 28c on 48c 45.00 11.50
a. Double surcharge 3,250.
109 A12 (b) 30c on 36c 16.00 12.50
a. Inverted surcharge 350.00 160.00
110 A15 (b) 56c on 96c 37.50 27.50

Perf. 12½

111 A16 (d) 1r12c on 2r50c 750.00 115.00

Perf. 14x12½

112 A11 (a) 5c on 32c 900.00 57.50
113 A14 (a) 5c on 64c 975.00 57.50
114 A14 (b) 10c on 64c 100.00 *175.00*
a. Vert. pair, imperf. btwn. 6,750.

Perf. 12½x14

115 A16 (d) 1r12c on 2r50c 115.00 55.00

Perf. 14

Wmk. 2

117 A7 (a) 5c on 4c rose 27.50 6.00
a. Inverted surcharge *350.00*
118 A8 (a) 5c on 8c org 100.00 12.00
a. Inverted surcharge *4,400.*
b. Double surcharge *4,000.*
119 A9 (a) 5c on 16c vio 190.00 18.00
a. Inverted surcharge *260.00*
120 A10 (a) 5c on 24c pur brn — 600.00
121 A9 (b) 10c on 16c vio 13,500. 1,800.
122 A10 (b) 10c on 24c pur brn 18.50 11.50
123 A9 (b) 15c on 16c vio 15.50 11.50

A 5c on 4c lilac rose and a 5c on 24c green are known to exist and are considered to be a forgeries.

Types of 1872-80 Surcharged

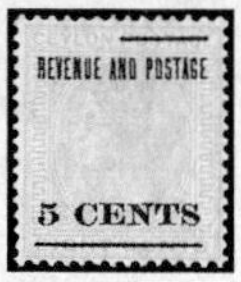

e

f

g

1885-87

124 A 8 (e) 5c on 8c lilac 27.50 1.60
125 A10 (f) 10c on 24c pur brn 14.50 9.00
126 A 9 (f) 15c on 16c org 62.50 15.50
127 A11 (f) 28c on 32c sl bl 30.00 2.75
128 A12 (f) 30c on 36c ol grn 30.00 16.00
129 A15 (f) 56c on 96c ol gray 55.00 18.00

Wmk. 1 Sideways

130 A16 (g) 1r12c on 2r50c cl 62.50 *145.00*
Nos. 124-130 (7) *282.00* *207.85*

A23

Type I

Type II

FIVE CENTS

Type I — Thin lines in background. Hair and curl clear.

Type II — Thicker lines in background. Heavier shading under chin.

1886 **Wmk. 2**

131 A23 5c lilac, type I 4.00 .25
a. Type II 4.00 .25

For overprint see No. O12.

A24

1886-1900

132 A24 3c org brn & green ('93) 7.00 .50
133 A24 3c green ('00) 5.00 .60
134 A24 6c rose & blk ('99) 3.25 .50
135 A24 12c ol grn & car ('00) 5.50 *9.00*
136 A24 15c olive green 9.00 2.40
137 A24 15c ultra ('00) 8.00 1.50
138 A24 25c brown 5.75 2.00
a. 25c brown, value in ol yel 155.00 90.00
139 A24 28c slate 25.00 1.50
140 A24 30c vio & org brown ('93) 4.75 3.50
141 A24 75c blk & org brown ('00) 9.50 9.50
Nos. 132-141 (10) 82.75 *31.00*

Numeral tablet of 3c, 12c and 75c has lined background with colorless value and "c."

For surcharges & overprints see Nos. 152-154, 157, 159, O10-O11, O13-O17.

1887 **Wmk. 1**

142 A16 1r12c claret 32.50 30.00

For overprint see No. O18.

Issue of 1883-84 Surcharged

1888-90 **Wmk. 2**

143 A7 2c on 4c lilac rose 1.60 .95
a. Inverted surcharge 25.00 24.00
b. Double surcharge, one invtd. 400.00
144 A7 2c on 4c rose 2.75 .35
a. Inverted surcharge 20.00 *21.00*
b. Double surcharge 400.00

Surcharged

145 A7 2c on 4c lilac rose 1.10 .30
a. Inverted surcharge 42.50 *42.50*
b. Double surcharge 100.00 110.00
c. Double surcharge, one invtd. 85.00 85.00
146 A7 2c on 4c rose 8.00 .25
a. Double surcharge, one invtd. 105.00 *125.00*
b. Double surcharge 110.00 *125.00*
c. Inverted surcharge 425.00

Surcharged

147 A7 2c on 4c lilac rose 82.50 35.00
a. Inverted surcharge 175.00 47.50
b. Double surcharge, one inverted 210.00
148 A7 2c on 4c rose 4.00 1.00
a. Inverted surcharge 19.00 10.00
b. Double surcharge, one inverted 9.50 *15.00*
c. Double surcharge 210.00 175.00

Surcharged

149 A7 2c on 4c lilac rose 67.50 30.00
a. Inverted surcharge 200.00 32.50
150 A7 2c on 4c rose 3.00 1.25
a. Inverted surcharge 19.00 8.50
b. Double surcharge 160.00 150.00
c. Double surcharge, one inverted 19.00 11.00

Surcharged

151 A7 2c on 4c rose 13.50 1.20
a. Inverted surcharge 24.00 7.50
b. Double surcharge 135.00 135.00
c. Double surch., one invtd. 27.50 13.50
i. "S" of "Cents" inverted 525.00 350.00
151D A7 2c on 4c lilac rose 67.50 37.50
e. Inverted surcharge 95.00 42.50
f. Double surcharge 450.00
g. Double surch., one invtd. 150.00 150.00
h. "S" of "Cents" inverted 750.00

Counterfeit errors of surcharges of Nos. 143 to 151D are prevalent.

No. 136 Surcharged

1890

152 A24 5c on 15c ol green 4.00 2.75
a. "Flve" instead of "Five" 140.00 100.00
b. "REVENUE" omitted 225.00 200.00
c. Inverted surcharge 65.00 *75.00*
d. Double surcharge 125.00 *145.00*
e. As "a," inverted surcharge — 1,800.
f. Inverted "s" in "Cents" 130.00 *120.00*
g. As "f," inverted surcharge 2,200.
h. As "b," invtd. "s" in "Cents" 1,800.

Nos. 138-139 Surcharged

1891

153 A24 15c on 25c brown 20.00 20.00
154 A24 15c on 28c slate 21.00 10.00

Nos. 88, 89 and 139 Surcharged

1892

155 A7 3c on 4c lilac rose 1.10 *3.50*
156 A7 3c on 4c rose 7.25 *11.00*
a. Double surcharge, one invtd.
157 A24 3c on 28c slate 6.25 5.75
a. Double surcharge 180.00
Nos. 155-157 (3) 14.60 *20.25*

Type of 1879

1898

158 A16 2r50c violet, *red* 42.50 *65.00*

No. 136 Surcharged in Black

1899

159 A24 6c on 15c olive green 1.35 *.85*

Surcharged Type "g" in Black

1899 **Wmk. 1**

160 A16 1r50c on 2r50c gray 24.00 *55.00*
161 A16 2r25c on 2r50c yel 50.00 *95.00*

A35

1900 **Wmk. 1**

162 A35 1r50c car rose 35.00 *55.00*
163 A35 2r25c dull blue 37.50 *55.00*

Nos. 166-292 exist in many different shades, representing different printings for each stamp.

King Edward VII

A36 A37

A38

A39

A40

1903-05 **Wmk. 2**

166 A36 2c org brown 2.40 .25
167 A37 3c green 2.40 1.20
168 A37 4c yel & blue 2.40 *6.00*
169 A38 5c dull lilac 2.75 .70

170 A39 6c car rose 11.00 1.75
171 A37 12c ol grn & car 5.50 *11.50*
172 A40 15c ultra 6.75 3.50
173 A40 25c bister 5.00 *12.00*
174 A40 30c vio & green 3.50 *4.25*
175 A37 75c bl & org ('05) 3.50 *24.00*
176 A40 1r50c gray ('04) 67.50 60.00
177 A40 2r25c brn & grn ('04) 95.00 60.00
Nos. 166-177 (12) 207.70 185.15
Set, never hinged 400.00

For overprints see Nos. O19-O24.

1904-10 **Wmk. 3**

178 A36 2c orange brown 2.00 .25
a. 2c orange 1.60 .60
179 A37 3c green 1.75 .25
180 A37 4c yel & blue 3.00 1.75
181 A38 5c dull lilac 3.50 1.50
a. Booklet pane of 12
b. 5c dull lilac, "chalky paper" 7.50 .75
182 A39 6c car rose 4.75 .25
183 A40 10c ol grn & vio ('10) 2.50 3.50
184 A37 12c ol grn & car 1.75 *2.00*
185 A40 15c ultra 3.75 .70
186 A40 25c bister ('05) 6.25 4.00
187 A40 25c slate ('10) 2.75 3.00
188 A40 30c vio & grn ('05) 2.75 *3.25*
189 A40 50c brown ('10) 4.25 *7.75*
190 A37 75c bl & org ('05) 5.50 *8.25*
191 A40 1r vio, *yel* ('10) 8.50 *13.00*
192 A40 1r50c gray ('05) 32.50 12.00
193 A40 2r scar, *yel* ('10) 16.00 *30.00*
194 A40 2r25c brn & grn 26.00 *32.50*
195 A40 5r blk, *grn* ('10) 45.00 *100.00*
196 A40 10r blk, *red* ('10) 130.00 *275.00*
Nos. 178-196 (19) 302.50 *498.95*
Set, never hinged 600.00

A41

A42

1908

197 A41 5c deep red violet 6.00 .25
a. Booklet pane of 12
198 A42 6c carmine rose 2.00 .25

1911, July 5

199 A40 3c green 1.10 .85

A44

King George V — A45

Type I

Type II

3 AND 6 CENTS
Type I — Small "c" after value, 2¼mm wide and 2mm high.
Type II — Large "c" after value, 2½mm wide and 2¼mm high.
1, 5 AND 9 CENTS are Type II, other denominations Type I.

For description of dies I and II see "Dies of British Colonial Stamps" in the Table of Contents.

1912-25 **Die I** **Wmk. 3**

200 A44 1c dp brn (Die Ib) ('20) 1.20 .25
201 A44 2c brown org .45 .25
202 A44 3c dp grn (Die Ia, type II) 5.25 .50
a. 3c deep green, die I, type I 6.75 2.40
203 A44 5c red violet 1.20 .70
a. 5c purple 12.00 3.00
204 A44 6c car (Die Ib, type II) 1.75 1.60
a. 6c carmine, die I, type I 20.00 1.25
b. As "a," bklt. pane of 6
205 A44 10c olive green 3.50 2.00
206 A44 15c ultra 3.00 1.50

Chalky Paper

207 A44 25c yel & ultra 2.10 2.10
208 A44 30c green & vio 4.75 3.75
209 A44 50c black & scar 1.75 *2.10*
210 A44 1r violet, *yel* 5.25 4.25
211 A44 2r blk & red, *yel* 3.75 *15.00*
212 A44 5r blk, *green* 20.00 *40.00*
a. 5r black, *bl grn*, olive back 25.00 *45.00*
b. 5r blk, *emer* (Die II) ('20) 52.50 *120.00*
213 A44 10r vio & blk, *red* 85.00 *105.00*
a. Die II ('20) 95.00 *165.00*
214 A44 20r blk & red, *bl* 165.00 *175.00*
215 A45 50r dull violet 550.00
216 A45 100r gray black 2,200.
217 A45 500r gray green *8,000.*
218 A45 1000r vio, *red* ('25) *30,000.*
Nos. 200-214 (15) 303.95 *354.00*
Set, never hinged 600.00

Although Nos. 217 and 218 were theoretically available for postage it is not probable that they were ever used for other than fiscal purposes.
The 1r through 100r with revenue cancellations sell for minimal prices.
For surcharge & overprints see Nos. 223, MR1-MR3.

Die I
1913-14 **Surface-colored Paper**

220 A44 1r violet, *yellow* 5.00 *5.75*
221 A44 2r black & red, *yel* 3.25 *15.00*
222 A44 5r black, *green* 26.00 *37.50*
Nos. 220-222 (3) 34.25 *58.25*

No. 203 Surcharged

1918

223 A44 1c on 5c red violet 3.00 *3.50*
a. 1c on 5c purple .25 .30

For overprint see No. MR4.

Die I
1921-33 **Wmk. 4** **Ordinary Paper**

225 A44 1c dp brn (Die Ib) ('27) 1.20 .40
226 A44 2c brn org (Die II) .85 .30
227 A44 3c green (Die Ia, type II) 4.75 .90
228 A44 3c slate (Die Ia, type II) ('22) .90 .25
229 A44 5c red vio (Die I) .70 .25
230 A44 6c carmine (Die Ib, type II) 2.60 .90
231 A44 6c vio (Die Ib, type II) ('22) 2.00 .25
232 A44 9c red, *yel* (Die II) ('26) 2.40 .35
233 A44 10c olive green 1.60 .45
a. Die II 2.10 .70
234 A44 12c scarlet, Die II 1.20 *6.00*
a. Die I ('25) 10.00 *12.50*
235 A44 15c ultramarine 3.75 *16.50*
236 A44 15c green, *yel*, Die II 4.25 1.20
a. Die I ('22) 4.75 *6.00*
237 A44 20c ultra, Die II ('24) 4.25 .50
a. Die I ('22) 6.00 *7.25*
238 A44 25c yel & blue 2.40 2.25
a. Die II 4.50 1.50

For surcharges see Nos. 248-249.

Chalky Paper

239 A44 30c green & violet 1.90 *4.75*
a. Die II 5.75 1.50
240 A44 50c blk & scar (Die II) 1.90 .95
a. Die I 65.00 *100.00*
241 A44 1r vio, *yel*, Die II 24.00 *32.50*
a. Die I 15.00 *40.00*
242 A44 2r blk & red, *yel* (Die II) 8.50 *12.00*
243 A44 5r blk, *emer*, (Die II) 50.00 *85.00*
244 A44 20r blk & red, *bl*, (Die II) 260.00 *350.00*
245 A45 50r dull vio 625.00 *1,050.*
246 A45 100r gray black 2,750.
247 A45 100r ultra & dl vio ('27) 2,500.
Nos. 225-244 (20) 379.15 515.70
Set, never hinged 625.00

Nos. 228, 231 Surcharged

1926

248 A44 2c on 3c slate 2.40 1.20
a. Double surcharge 85.00
b. Bar omitted 90.00 *100.00*
249 A44 5c on 6c violet .65 .45
a. Double surcharge

A46

1927-29 **Chalky Paper** **Wmk. 4**

254 A46 1r red vio & dl vio ('28) 3.00 1.50
255 A46 2r car & green ('29) 4.50 3.25
256 A46 5r brn vio & grn ('28) 16.00 *24.00*
257 A46 10r org & green 52.50 *115.00*
258 A46 20r ultra & dl vio 190.00 *340.00*
Nos. 254-258 (5) 266.00 *483.75*
Set, never hinged 450.00

Common Design Types pictured following the introduction.

Silver Jubilee Issue
Common Design Type

1935, May 6 **Engr.** ***Perf. 13½x14***

260 CD301 6c gray blk & ultra .80 .35
261 CD301 9c indigo & green .80 3.25
262 CD301 20c blue & brown 5.00 3.25
263 CD301 50c brt vio & ind 6.00 16.50
Nos. 260-263 (4) 12.60 23.35
Set, never hinged 22.50

Tapping Rubber Tree — A47

Colombo Harbor — A49

Adam's Peak — A48

Picking Tea — A50

Coconut Palms — A53

Rice Terraces A51

River Scene A52

Temple of the Tooth, Kandy A54

Ancient Reservoir A55

Wild Elephants A56

View of Trincomalee A57

Perf. 11x11½, 11½x11; 11½x13, 13x11½ (A47, A48, A53); 14 (A56)

1935-36 **Wmk. 4**

264 A47 2c car rose & blk .45 *.55*
a. Perf. 14 12.00 .55
265 A48 3c olive & black .50 *.55*
a. Perf. 14 35.00 *.40*
266 A49 6c blue & black .45 .40
267 A50 9c org red & ol grn 1.50 .90
268 A51 10c dk vio & blk 1.75 *3.25*
269 A52 15c grn & org brn 1.50 .70
270 A53 20c ultra & black 2.50 *3.50*
271 A54 25c choc & dk ultra 2.00 1.75
272 A55 30c green & lake 3.00 *3.75*
273 A56 50c dk vio & blk 15.00 2.50
274 A57 1r brown & vio 35.00 24.00
Nos. 264-274 (11) 63.65 41.85
Set, never hinged 200.00

Issued: 2c, 15c, 25c, 5/1/35; 10c, 6/1/35; 1r, 7/1/35; 30c, 8/1/35; 3c, 10/1/35; 6c, 9c, 20c, 50c, 1/1/36.

Coronation Issue
Common Design Type

1937, May 12 ***Perf. 11x11½***

275 CD302 6c dark carmine .75 1.10
a. Booklet pane of 10 20.00
276 CD302 9c deep green 3.00 *4.75*
a. Booklet pane of 10 300.00
277 CD302 20c deep ultra 4.50 *4.50*
Nos. 275-277 (3) 8.25 10.35
Set, never hinged 16.00

Types of 1935 with "Postage & Revenue Removed" and Picturing George VI and

Sigiriya (Lion Rock) — A61

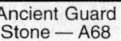

Ancient Guard Stone — A68

George VI — A69

Perf. 11x11½, 11½x11; 12 (#286)

1938-52 **Engr.** **Wmk. 4**

278 A47 2c car rose & blk ('44) .45 *1.25*
a. Perf. 13½x13 ('38) 100.00 2.00
b. Perf. 13½ ('38) 2.00 .25
c. Perf. 12 ('49) 1.25 *4.50*
d. Perf. 11½x13 ('38) 10.00 2.75
279 A48 3c dk grn & blk ('42) .50 .25
a. Perf. 13x13½ ('38) 225.00 12.50
b. Perf. 14 ('41) 100.00 1.10
c. Perf. 13½ ('38) 3.50 .25
d. Perf. 12 ('46) .70 *.95*
e. Perf. 13x11½ 8.00 2.50
280 A49 6c blue & black .25 .25
281 A61 10c blue & black 1.75 .25
282 A52 15c red brn & grn 1.25 .25
283 A50 20c dull bl & blk 2.25 .25
284 A54 25c choc & dk ultra 3.25 .30
285 A55 30c dk grn & rose car 8.00 3.75

286 A56 50c dk vio & blk ('46) 2.75 .25
- *a.* Perf. 14 ('42) 90.00 29.00
- *b.* Perf. 13x11½ ('38) 140.00 52.50
- *c.* Perf. 13x13½ ('38) 300.00 3.00
- *d.* Perf. 13½ ('38) 15.00 .55
- *e.* Perf. 11½x11 ('42) 4.00 4.25

287 A57 1r dk brn & bl vio 10.50 1.60
288 A68 2r dark car & blk 9.25 4.00

Perf. 14

Typo.

289 A69 5r brn vio & grn 27.50 13.50
289A A69 10r yel org & dl grn ('52) 50.00 50.00
Nos. 278-289A (13) 117.70 75.90
Set, never hinged 360.00

No. 289A differs from type A69 in having "REVENUE" inscribed vertically at either side of the frame. This revenue 10r was valid for postage Dec. 1, 1952-Mar. 14, 1954.

See Nos. 292, 295. For surcharges see Nos. 290-291.

Catalogue values for unused stamps in this section, from this point to the end of the section, are for Never Hinged items.

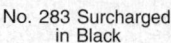

No. 283 Surcharged in Black

1940, Nov. 5 ***Perf. 11x11½***
290 A50 3c on 20c dull bl & blk 5.00 *6.00*

No. 280 Surcharged

1941, May 10
291 A49 3c on 6c blue & black .65 *3.00*

Coconut Palms — A70

1943-47 Wmk. 4 Engr. ***Perf. 12***
292 A70 5c red org & ol grn ('47) 1.75 .35
- *a.* Perf. 13½ ('43) .35 .25

Peace Issue

Common Design Type

1946, Dec. 10 ***Perf. 13½x14***
293 CD303 6c deep blue .30 *.35*
294 CD303 15c brown .30 *1.75*

Guard Stone Type of 1938

1947, Mar. 15 ***Perf. 11x11½***
295 A68 2r violet & black 2.40 *2.75*

Parliament Building, Colombo — A71

Adam's Peak A72

Dagoba at Anuradhapura A74

Temple of the Tooth, Kandy A73

1947, Nov. 25 ***Perf. 11x12, 12x11***
296 A71 6c deep ultra & black .25 .25
297 A72 10c car, orange & black .25 *.40*
298 A73 15c red vio & grnsh blk .25 *.80*
299 A74 25c brt green & bister .25 *1.75*
Nos. 296-299 (4) 1.00 3.20

New constitution of 1947.

National Flag A75

D. S. Senanayake A76

Engr., Flag Typo. (A75); Engr. (A76)
Perf. 12½x12, 12x12½, 13x12½

1949 **Wmk. 4**
300 A75 4c org brn, car & yel .25 .25
301 A76 5c dark green & brn .25 .25

Wmk. 290

302 A75 15c red org, car & yel 1.00 .40
303 A76 25c dp blue & brown .25 1.00
Nos. 300-303 (4) 1.75 1.90

Size of No. 302: 28x22¼mm.
1st anniv. of Ceylon's independence.
Issued: Nos. 300-301, Feb. 4; Nos. 302-303, Apr. 5.

A77

A78

Design: 15c, Lion Rock and UPU symbols.

Wmk. 290

1949, Oct. 10 Engr. ***Perf. 12***
304 A77 5c dk green & brown .85 .25
305 A77 15c dark car & black 1.25 *2.75*
306 A78 25c ultra & black 1.25 1.25
Nos. 304-306 (3) 3.35 4.25

75th anniv. of the UPU.

Kandyan Dancer A79

Kiri Vehera, Polonnaruwa A80

Vesak Orchid — A81

Sigiriya — A82

Ratmalana, Plane — A83

Vatadage Ruins at Madirigiriya A84

1950, Feb. 4 ***Perf. 12x12½***
307 A79 4c bright red & choc .25 .25
308 A80 5c green .25 .25
309 A81 15c pur & blue green 2.75 .50
310 A82 30c carmine & yel .40 *.70*

Perf. 11x11½, 11½x11

311 A83 75c red org & blue 8.50 .25
312 A84 1r red brn & dp blue 2.50 .45
Nos. 307-312 (6) 14.65 2.40

See Nos. 340-345.

Coconut Palms — A85

Star Orchid — A86

1951-52 Unwmk. Photo. ***Perf. 11½***
313 A85 10c gray & dark green 1.25 .75
314 A86 35c dk grn & rose brn ('52) 1.50 1.50
- *a.* Corrected inscription ('54) 6.00 .70

On No. 314a a dot has been added above the third character in the second line of the Tamil inscription.

Issue dates: 10c, Aug. 1; 35c, Feb. 1.

See No. 351.

Mace and Symbols of Industry A87

Perf. 12½x14

1952, Feb. 23 **Wmk. 290**
315 A87 5c green .25 .30
316 A87 15c brt ultramarine .40 .60

Colombo Plan Exhibition, February 1952.

Coronation Issue

Queen Elizabeth II — A88

1953, June 2 Engr. ***Perf. 12x12½***
317 A88 5c green 1.50 .25

Royal Procession A89

1954, Apr. 10 ***Perf. 13x12½***
318 A89 10c deep blue 1.25 .25

Visit of Queen Elizabeth II and the Duke of Edinburgh, 1954.

Sambar in Ruhuna National Park — A90

Rubber Trees — A91

Designs: 3c, Ancient guard stone. 6c and 10r, Harvesting rice. 25c, Sigiriya fresco. 50c, Outrigger fishing canoe. 85c, Tea Picker. 2r, Gal Oya dam. 5r, Bas-relief, "The Lovers."

1954 Unwmk. Photo. ***Perf. 11½***

Size: 21x25½mm

319 A90 2c green & brown .25 *1.25*
320 A90 3c violet & black .25 *1.00*
321 A90 6c yel grn & blk brn .25 *.30*
322 A90 25c vio bl, bl & brn orange .25 .25

Size: 25½x21mm

323 A91 40c black brown 5.50 1.25
324 A91 50c indigo .45 .25

Size: 23x32½mm, 32½x23mm

325 A90 85c dk grn & gray 1.50 .40
326 A91 2r blue & blk brn 9.25 1.40
327 A90 5r dp org & blk brn 8.00 1.50
328 A90 10r brown 60.00 20.00
Nos. 319-328 (10) 85.70 27.60

See Nos. 346-356.

Issued: 25c, 50c, 5r, 10r, 3/15; others, 5/15.

Nos. 327-328 with revenue cancellations sell for minimal prices.

King Coconuts — A92

1954, Dec. 1
329 A92 10c brown & orange .30 .25

See No. 349.

Symbols of Agriculture A93

Perf. 14x14½

1955, Dec. 10 **Wmk. 290**
330 A93 10c orange & brown .30 .25

Royal Agricultural and Food Exhibition.

House of Representatives — A94

1956, Mar. 26 Unwmk. *Perf. 11½*
Granite Paper

331 A94 10c deep green .25 .25

25th anniv. of Prime Minister Sir John Kotelawala's entry into the Ceylon Legislature.

Arrival of Vijaya in Ceylon — A95

Dharmachakra Encircling Globe — A96

1956, May 23 Granite Paper

332 A95 3c dull vio gray & seph .25 .25
333 A96 15c ultramarine .25 .25

Birth of Buddha, 2500th anniv. See Nos. B1-B2.

Methods of Transportation — A97

35c, 85c, Ceylon's 1st stamp & coat of arms.

1957, Apr. 1 Photo. *Perf. 12½x13*

334 A97 4c blue green & ver .80 .50
335 A97 10c blue & vermilion .80 .25

Perf. 11½
Granite Paper

336 A97 35c blue, yel & brown .40 *.55*
337 A97 85c dull grn, yel & brn .85 *1.60*
Nos. 334-337 (4) 2.85 2.90

Ceylon's 1st postage stamps, cent.

Nos. B1-B2 Overprinted with Black Bars and Squares

1958, Jan. 15 Unwmk.
Granite Paper

338 SP1 4c dp blue & lt yel .25 .25
a. Inverted overprint 15.00 *22.50*
b. Double overprint 22.50 *29.00*
339 SP1 10c dk gray, yel & brt pink .25 .25
a. Inverted overprint 15.00 *17.00*

The overprint obliterates the surtax and inscription at right.

Types of 1950-54 Redrawn

Perf. 12x12½

1958-59 Engr. Wmk. 290

340 A79 4c brt red & chocolate .25 .25
341 A80 5c green .25 *1.60*
342 A81 15c purple & blue grn 3.50 1.10
343 A82 30c car & yel ('59) .25 *1.50*

Perf. 11½x11

344 A83 75c red org & bl ('59) 9.50 3.25

Perf. 11x11½

345 A84 1r red brn & dp blue .65 .25
Nos. 340-345 (6) 14.40 7.95

Issued: 4c, 5/14; 5c, 15c, 1r, 10/1; 30c, 75c, 5/1.

For surcharge see No. 368.

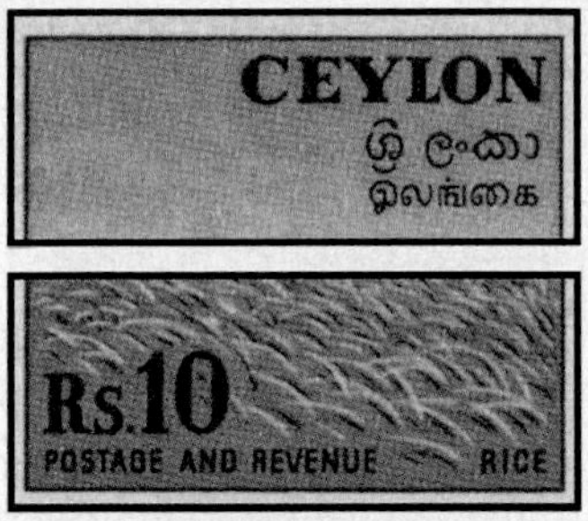

No. 328

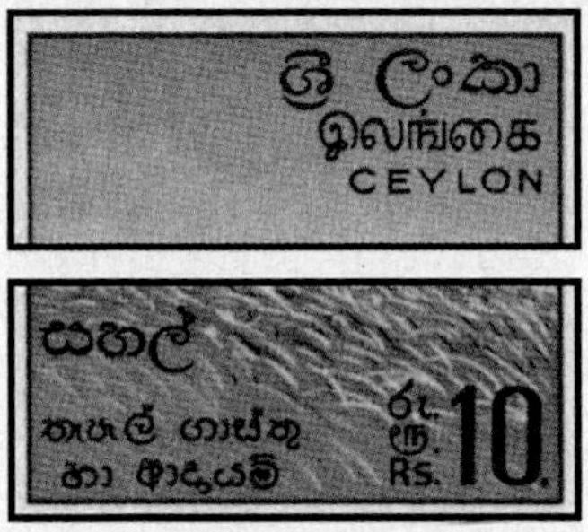

No. 356

1958-59 Unwmk. Photo. *Perf. 11½*
Granite Paper

346 A90 2c green & brown .25 .50
347 A90 3c violet & black .25 .70
348 A90 6c yel grn & blk brn .25 .65
349 A92 10c brown & orange .25 .25
350 A90 25c vio bl, bl & brn orange .25 .25
351 A86 35c dk grn & rose brn 7.75 .40
352 A91 50c indigo .25 .25
353 A90 85c dark green & gray 4.50 8.50
354 A91 2r blue & blk brn 2.00 .30
355 A90 5r dp org & blk brn 10.00 .40
356 A90 10r brown 12.00 1.40
Nos. 346-356 (11) 37.75 13.60

Designs and sizes of Nos. 340-356 remain as before, but wording has been changed to be predominantly Singhalese. "Ceylon" appears in small letters only in English and Tamil.

Nos. 355-356 with revenue cancellations sell for minimal prices.

Issue dates: 35c, 50c, July 15; 10c, Oct. 1; 85c, May 1, 1959; others, May 14, 1958.

For surcharges, see Sri Lanka Nos. 1572, 1577.

Hands Reaching for UN Symbol A98

Perf. 13x12½

1958, Dec. 10 Photo. Unwmk.

357 A98 10c red brown & red .25 .25
358 A98 85c Prus green & red .30 .30

10th anniv. of the signing of the Universal Declaration of Human Rights.

Pirivena Universities and Founders A99

1959, Dec. 31

359 A99 10c brt ultra & dp org .30 .30

Institution of Pirivena Universities; founders Hikkaduwe Sri Sumangala Nayaka Thero and Ratmalane Sri Dharmaloka Nayake Thero.

Uprooted Oak Emblem — A100

1960, Apr. 7 Photo. *Perf. 11½*
Granite Paper

360 A100 4c chocolate & gold .25 *.85*
361 A100 25c vio blue & gold .25 .25

World Refugee Year, 7/1/59-6/30/60.

Prime Minister Bandaranaike A101

Type I

Type II

Two types:
I — Gray hair at temple.
II — Dark hair at temple (redrawn).

1961, Jan. 8 Granite Paper

362 A101 10c vio bl & gray bl (I) .40 .60
a. Type II .90 .25

Solomon West Ridgeway Dias Bandaranaike, assassinated Sept. 26, 1959.

Badge of Singhalese Scouts — A102

1962, Feb. 26 Unwmk. *Perf. 11½*
Granite Paper

363 A102 35c dark blue & ocher .35 .25

Boy Scouts of Ceylon, 50th anniv.

Malaria Eradication Emblem — A103

Perf. 14½x14

1962, Apr. 7 Photo. Wmk. 290

364 A103 25c lt sep, red org & brn .40 .40

WHO drive to eradicate malaria.

Monoplane 1938, and De Havilland Comet IV — A104

1963, Feb. 28 Unwmk. *Perf. 11½*
Granite Paper

365 A104 50c lt grnsh blue & blk .60 .60

25th anniv. of Ceylonese airmail service.

Stylized Vase and Wheat Emblem A105

1963, Mar. 21 Granite Paper

366 A105 5c blue & orange ver .75 *2.50*
367 A105 25c olive & brown 3.00 .50

FAO "Freedom from Hunger" campaign.

No. 340 Surcharged

Perf. 12x12½

1963, June 1 Engr. Wmk. 290

368 A79 2c on 4c brt red & choc .40 .40
a. Inverted surcharge 20.00
b. Double surcharge 40.00

Rural Life — A106

1963, July 5 Photo. *Perf. 14x14½*

369 A106 60c dull red & black 2.00 .75

50th anniv. of the Cooperative Movement.

Landscape and Elephant A107

1963, Dec. 2 Wmk. 290

370 A107 5c blue & black .65 .45

National Conservation Week.

S.W.R.D. Bandaranaike A108

Perf. 11½

1963, Sept. 26 Unwmk. Engr.
Granite Paper

371 A108 10c blue .30 .30

Redrawn
Granite Paper

1964, July 1 Photo.

372 A108 10c grnsh gray & bl vio .30 .30

Frame redrawn on No. 372; inscription in bottom panel replaced by ornament.

For surcharge see No. 389.

Anagarika Dharmapala — A109

1964, Sept. 16 Unwmk. *Perf. 11½*
Granite Paper

373 A109 25c gray brn & dull yel .30 .30

Anagarika Dharmapala, Buddhist missionary, birth cent.

Ceylon Jungle Fowl — A110

Tea Picker — A112

Vatadage Ruins at Madirigiriya A111

Designs: 5c, Hill myna. 15c, Blue peafowl. 75c, Asiatic black-headed oriole. 5r, Girls, working in rice field. 10r, Map of Ceylon on scroll, showing agricultural development stations.

Wmk. 290, Unwmkd. (20c)
1964-69 Photo. *Perf. 14, 11½ (20c)*

374 A110 5c brt bl, blk, yel & grn 2.00 1.40
375 A110 15c yel, grn, blk, brt bl & rose 3.75 .30
376 A111 20c dk red brn, *buff* .25 .25
377 A110 60c yel & multi 4.50 1.10
  a. Blue omitted 50.00
  b. Red omitted 50.00
378 A110 75c ol, blk, org & brn 3.00 .75
  a. Souvenir sheet of 4 10.00 14.00
  b. As "a," overprinted 10.00
379 A112 1r brown & grn 1.00 .25
  c. Brown omitted *750.00*
379A A111 5r multicolored 9.50 9.50
379B A112 10r brown & multi 22.50 3.50
  Nos. 374-379B (8) 46.50 17.05

No. 378a contains four imperf. stamps with simulated perforations similar to Nos. 374-375 and 377-378.

No. 378b is overprinted "First National Stamp Exhibition 1967" in two lines of black capitals.

No. 376 is on granite paper.

Issued: 20c, 1r, 10/1; 5c, 15c, 60c, 75c, 2/5/66; 5r, 8/15/69; 10r, 10/1/69.

See No. 325.

Exhibition Buildings, Cogwheels — A113

"Industrial Exhibition" in Singhalese and English

1964, Dec. 1 Unwmk. *Perf. 11*

380 A113 5c multicolored .25 *.75*

"Industrial Exhibition" in Singhalese and Tamil

381 A113 5c multicolored .25 *.75*
  a. Pair, #380-381 .35 *2.50*

1965 Industrial Exhibition.

Railroad Trains, 1864-1964 A114

"Railway Centenary" in Singhalese and English

Wmk. 290
1964, Dec. 21 Photo. *Perf. 14*

382 A114 60c lil rose, bl & yel grn 3.25 .55

"Railway Centenary" in Singhalese and Tamil

383 A114 60c lil rose, bl & yel grn 3.25 .55
  a. Vertical pair, #382-383 7.75 7.75

Centenary of Ceylonese railroads.

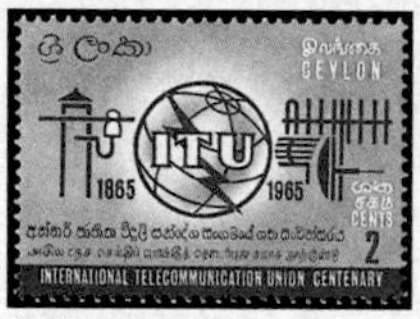

ITU Emblem, Old and New Communication Equipment — A115

1965, May 17 *Perf. 14*

384 A115 2c ultra & red 1.60 1.40
385 A115 30c brown & red 4.50 .55

ITU, centenary.

ICY Emblem A116

1965, June 26 Unwmk. *Perf. 11½*
Granite Paper

386 A116 3c rose car & dk bl 1.50 1.25
387 A116 50c gold, rose car & blk 4.00 .60

International Cooperation Year.

Municipal Council Building A117

1965, Oct. 29 Photo. *Perf. 11½*
Granite Paper

388 A117 25c gray & green .30 .30

Centenary of Colombo Municipal Council.

No. 372 Surcharged

1965, Dec. 18 Photo. *Perf. 11½*

389 A108 5c on 10c .30 1.25

D. S. Senanayake — A118

1966, Mar. 22 Unwmk. *Perf. 11½*
Granite Paper

390 A118 10c bright green .85 .25

D. S. Senanayake, first prime minister of Ceylon, 14th death anniv. See No. 418.

View and Arms of Kandy — A119

Perf. 14x13½
1966, June 15 Photo. Wmk. 290

391 A119 25c multicolored .30 .30

Centenary of Kandy Municipal Council.

Opening of WHO Headquarters, Geneva A120

Unwmk.
1966, Oct. 8 Litho. *Perf. 14*

392 A120 4c multicolored 2.50 3.00
393 A120 1r multicolored 8.00 1.60

Rice, Map of Ceylon, FAO Emblem — A121

Design: 30c, Rice and globe.

1966, Oct. 25 Photo. *Perf. 11½*
Granite Paper

394 A121 6c dk green, org & brn .25 *.75*
395 A121 30c brt blue, org & brn .50 .25

Intl. Rice Year under sponsorship of the FAO.

UNESCO Emblem A122

1966, Nov. 3 Litho. *Perf. 12*

396 A122 3c tan & multi 4.00 4.00
397 A122 50c brt green & multi 7.75 1.00

20th anniv. of UNESCO.
For surcharge, see Sri Lanka No. 1578.

Map of Ceylon and UNESCO Emblem — A123

1966, Dec. 1 Unwmk. *Perf. 14*

398 A123 2c yel brn, yel & blue .35 *1.00*
399 A123 2r multicolored 1.50 *2.25*

Intl. Hydrological Decade (UNESCO), 1965-74.

Worshippers at Buddhist Shrine A124

Designs: 20c, Muhintale Rock. 35c, Sacred Bo Tree. 60c, Adam's Peak.

1967, Jan. 2 Photo. *Perf. 12*

400 A124 5c multicolored .25 *.60*
401 A124 20c multicolored .25 .25
402 A124 35c multicolored .25 .25
403 A124 60c multicolored .25 .25
  Nos. 400-403 (4) 1.00 1.35

1st anniv. of the Poya Holiday System, Buddhist holiday replacing Sunday.
For surcharge, see Sri Lanka No. 1573.

Dutch Ramparts, Clock Tower and Arms of Galle A125

1967, Jan. 5 Litho. *Perf. 14x13½*

404 A125 25c dk green & multi .80 .25

Centenary of Galle Municipal Council.

Tea Research A126

40c, Tea tasting (cup & loose tea). 50c, Tea picking. 1r, Tea export (crate & freighter).

1967, Aug. 1 Unwmk. *Perf. 13½*

405 A126 4c multicolored .60 .60
406 A126 40c multicolored 1.75 1.60
407 A126 50c multicolored 1.75 .40
408 A126 1r multicolored 1.75 .25
  Nos. 405-408 (4) 5.85 2.85

Centenary of the Ceylonese tea industry.

Elephant and ITY Emblem A127

1967, Aug. 15 Litho.

409 A127 45c multicolored 3.00 .85

Intl. Tourist Year.

Girl Guide, Jubilee Emblem and Flag — A128

1967, Sept. 19 *Perf. 12x12½*

410 A128 3c green & multi .60 .25
411 A128 25c org yel & multi .90 .25

Ceylon Girl Guide Assoc., 50th anniv.

Henry S. Olcott and Buddhist Flag A129

Perf. 13½
1967, Dec. 12 Unwmk. Litho.

412 A129 15c multicolored .40 .25

Colonel Henry S. Olcott (1832-1907), an American who reorganized the Buddhist hierarchy and school system in Ceylon and was the first president of the Theosophical Society.

Independence Memorial, Colombo A130

Design: 1r, Flag of Ceylon and mace.

1968, Feb. 4 Wmk. 290 *Perf. 14*

413 A130 5c multicolored .25 .55
414 A130 1r multicolored .60 .25

20th anniversary of independence.

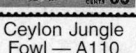

D. B. Jayatilaka — A131

1968, Feb. 14 **Photo.**

415	A131	25c brown	.30	.30

Sir Don Baron Jayatilaka (1868-1944), Buddhist leader and scholar.

Hygiene Institute, Kalutara A132

Perf. 11½x12

1968, Apr. 4 **Litho.** **Wmk. 290**

416	A132	50c multicolored	.30	.30

WHO, 20th anniversary.

Jet over Colombo Terminal A133

1968, Aug. 5 ***Perf. 13½***

417	A133	60c org brn, dk bl & org	.75	.25

Opening of Colombo Airport.

D. S. Senanayake — A134

1968, Sept. 23 **Photo.** ***Perf. 14***

418	A134	10c deep green	.25	.25

See No. 390.

Open Koran A135

1968, Oct. 14 **Photo.** ***Perf. 14***

419	A135	25c org brn, blk, blue & emerald	.30	.30

1,400th anniversary of the Koran.

Human Rights Flame A136

Perf. 12½x13½

1968, Dec. 10 **Unwmk.**

420	A136	2c multicolored	.25	.30
421	A136	20c multicolored	.25	.25
422	A136	40c multicolored	.25	.25
423	A136	2r multicolored	.90	*4.00*
		Nos. 420-423 (4)	1.65	4.80

International Human Rights Year.

Ceylon Buddhist Headquarters, Colombo — A137

1968, Dec. 19 **Litho.** ***Perf. 13½***

424	A137	5c multicolored	.40	*.60*

All-Ceylon Buddhist Cong., 50th anniv.

A multicolored 50c showing the Sri Padmaya (Sacred Footprint) on Adam's Peak was prepared but the issuance order was countermanded on Dec. 18. Some were sold in ignorance of the withdrawal order. Value $65.

E. W. Perera — A138

Wmk. 290

1969, Feb. 17 **Photo.** ***Perf. 14***

425	A138	60c brown	.30	.50

E. W. Perera, member of Legislative Council.

"Strength in Saving" — A139

1969, Mar. 20

426	A139	3c blue, yel & black	.30	.40

National Savings Movement, 25th anniv.

A140

4c, Seat of Enlightenment under Bodhi Tree. 6c, Buduresmala (disk symbolic of six-fold Buddha rays).

Wmk. 290

1969, Apr. 10 **Litho.** ***Perf. 15***

427	A140	4c orange & multi	.25	.50
428	A140	6c gold & multi	.25	.50
429	A140	35c scarlet & multi	.25	.25
		Nos. 427-429 (3)	.75	1.25

Vesak Day, which commemorates the birth, enlightenment and death of Buddha.

For surcharges see Nos. 463, 466.

A141

1969, Apr. 29 **Photo.** ***Perf. 14x14½***

430	A141	15c org yel & multi	.30	.30

Alexander Ekanayake Goonesingha (1891-1967), trade unionist, political leader and diplomat.

ILO, 50th Anniv. A142

1969, May 4 ***Perf. 14½x14***

431	A142	5c grnsh bl & black	.25	.25
432	A142	25c car rose & black	.25	.25

Convocation Hall, University of Ceylon A143

Elephant Lamp (Ath Pana) — A144

35c, "Lamp of Education," globe & flags. 50c, Uranium atom diagram. 60c, Symbols of science education. 1r, Aerial view of Sigiriya rock fortress.

Inscribed: "SIYAWASA"

Unwmk.

1969, Aug. 1 **Litho.** ***Perf. 14***

433	A143	4c yellow & multi	.25	*.80*
434	A144	6c multicolored	.40	*1.50*
435	A143	35c multicolored	.25	.25
436	A144	50c red & multi	.25	.25
437	A143	60c blue & multi	.30	.25
438	A144	1r yel & multi	.40	.25
		Nos. 433-438 (6)	1.85	3.30

Centenary of public education and archaeological research.

For surcharges see Nos. 464-467.

Wild Water Buffalo A145

15c, Slender loris. 50c, Axis deer. 1r, Leopard.

Perf. 14x13½

1970, May 11 **Litho.** **Unwmk.**

439	A145	5c lt blue & multi	1.25	*1.40*
440	A145	15c buff & multi	2.00	1.00
441	A145	50c salmon & multi	1.50	1.40
442	A145	1r gray & multi	1.50	*1.90*
		Nos. 439-442 (4)	6.25	5.70

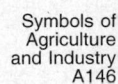

Symbols of Agriculture and Industry A146

1970, June 17

443	A146	60c multicolored	.30	.30

Asian Productivity Year.

Inauguration of UPU Headquarters, Bern — A147

1970, Aug. 14 **Litho.** **Unwmk.**

444	A147	50c org, black & blue	.50	.25
445	A147	1.10r red, black & blue	4.50	.60

Caduceus and Oil Lamp — A148

1970, Sept. 1 ***Perf. 13½x14***

446	A148	5c multicolored	1.00	*1.40*
447	A148	45c gray & multi	1.00	*1.10*

Centenary of the Ceylon Medical School.

Victory March and S.W.R.D. Bandaranaike A149

1970, Sept. 25 ***Perf. 14***

448	A149	10c red & multi	.25	.25

For surcharge see No. 465.

UN Emblem and Dove — A150

1970, Oct. 24 **Photo.** ***Perf. 12½x14***

449	A150	2r dp orange & multi	3.00	*3.50*

25th anniversary of the United Nations.

Keppetipola Dissawe — A151

1970, Nov. 26 **Litho.** ***Perf. 14x14½***

450	A151	25c multicolored	.30	.25

The 152nd anniversary of the execution of Keppetipola Dissawe, leader of the Great Rebellion of 1817-18.

Ola Leaf Manuscript and Education Year Emblem — A152

1970, Dec. 21 **Photo.** ***Perf. 13***

451	A152	15c brown & multi	2.75	1.75

International Education Year.

Charles Henry de Soysa — A153

1971, Mar. 3 **Litho.** ***Perf. 14x13½***

452	A153	20c orange & multi	.40	.50

de Soysa (1836-90), philanthropist who founded hospitals and schools.

Edward Henry Pedris — A154

1971, July 8 Litho. *Perf. 14x14½*

453	A154	25c blue & multi	.40	.40

Edward Henry Pedris (1888-1925), patriot.

A 5c stamp for the 10th Conf. of World Fellowship of Buddhists, Ceylon, May 9-13, was supposedly not issued without "1972" overprint. See Sri Lanka No. 471.

Lenin (1870-1924) — A156

1971, Aug. 31 *Perf. 14½*

455	A156	40c dp car & multi	.55	.55

Cumaratunga Munidasa — A157

Poets and Philosophers: No. 457, Ananda Coomaraswamy (1887-1947). No. 458, Rev. S. Mahinda Thero (1905-51). No. 459, Ananda Rajakaruna (1885-1957). No. 460, Arumuga Navalar (1822-78).

1971, Oct. 29 *Perf. 14*

456	A157	5c brown	.25	.25
457	A157	5c slate	.25	.25
458	A157	5c deep orange	.25	.25
459	A157	5c dp vio blue	.25	.25
460	A157	5c brown red	.25	.25
		Nos. 456-460 (5)	1.25	1.25

CARE Package A158

1971, Dec. 28 *Perf. 14x13*

461	A158	50c purple, blue & pink	.55	.35

25th anniv. of CARE, a US-Canadian Co-operative for American Relief Everywhere.

Map of Ceylon, Colombo Plan Emblem A159

1971, Dec. 28 Litho. *Perf. 14x14½*

462	A159	20c multicolored	.40	.40

20th anniversary of the Colombo Plan.

Issues of 1969-70 Surcharged

a

b

c

d

e

Wmk. 290, Unwmkd.

1971, Dec. 5 *Perf. 15, 14*

463	A140 (a)	5c on 4c (#427)	6.00	2.50
464	A143 (b)	5c on 4c (#433)	.25	1.90
465	A149 (c)	15c on 10c (#448)	.25	.50
466	A140 (d)	25c on 6c (#428)	.65	.95
467	A144 (e)	25c on 6c (#434)	.65	*3.25*
		Nos. 463-467 (5)	7.80	9.10

Nos. 463-466 exist with surcharge inverted.

WHO Emblem and Heart — A160

1972, May 2 Unwmk. *Perf. 13x13½*

468	A160	25c multicolored	3.00	.90

"Your heart is your health," World Health Day.

UN Emblem, Map Showing Asian Highway A161

1972, May 2 *Perf. 13x12½*

469	A161	85c lt blue & multi	5.25	3.25

Economic Commission for Asia and the Far East (ECAFE), 25th anniversary.

SEMI-POSTAL STAMPS

> **Catalogue values for unused stamps in this section are for Never Hinged items.**

Lamp and Dharmachakra SP1

Design: 10c+5c, Hand of Peace.

Perf. 11½

1956, May 10 Unwmk. Photo.

Granite Paper

B1	SP1	4c + 2c dp bl & lt yel	.35	*.75*
B2	SP1	10c + 5c dk gray, yel & brt pink	.50	*1.00*

2500th anniv. of the birth of Buddha. The surtax went to the Buddha Jayanti Fund. For overprints, see Nos. 338-339.

WAR TAX STAMPS

Nos. 201, 202, 202a and 203 Overprinted

Die I

1918 Wmk. 3 *Perf. 14*

MR1	A44	2c brown orange	.25	*.45*
a.		Double overprint	35.00	47.50
b.		Inverted overprint	65.00	*75.00*
MR2	A44	3c dp grn (Die Ia, type II)	3.00	.45
a.		3c dp green (Die I, type I)	.25	*.60*
b.		Double overprint (Die I)	95.00	*110.00*
MR3	A44	5c red violet	4.00	3.50
a.		Double overprint	60.00	*70.00*
b.		Inverted overprint	120.00	
c.		5c purple	.60	.35

No. 223 Overprinted in Black

MR4	A44	1c on 5c red violet	2.75	*.30*
a.		Double overprint	210.00	
b.		1c on No. 223a	.60	.45
		Nos. MR1-MR4 (4)	10.00	4.70

OFFICIAL STAMPS

Regular Issues Overprinted

Black Overprint

1869 Wmk. 1 *Perf. 12½, 14*

O1	A4	1p blue	77.50
O2	A1	2p yellow	77.50
O3	A5	3p rose	155.00
O4	A2	8p red brown	77.50
O5	A1	1sh gray lilac	175.00

Red Overprint

O6	A1	6p brown	77.50
O7	A2	2sh blue	125.00
a.		Imperf.	*1,150.*
		Nos. O1-O7 (7)	765.00

Nos. O1-O7 were never placed in use.

The overprint measures 15mm on Nos. O1, O3.

Regular Issues Overprinted in Black or Red

1895-1900 Wmk. 2 *Perf. 14*

O8	A6	2c green	16.50	.75
O9	A6	2c org brn ('00)	10.50	.65
O10	A24	3c org brn & grn	11.00	2.50
O11	A24	3c green ('00)	12.50	4.50
O12	A23	5c lilac	5.25	.30
O13	A24	15c olive green	20.00	.55
O14	A24	15c ultra ('00)	25.00	.65
O15	A24	25c brown	13.50	3.00
O16	A24	30c vio & org brn	13.50	.65
O17	A24	75c blk & org brn (R) ('99)	8.50	*8.50*

Wmk. 1

O18	A16	1r12c claret	100.00	62.50
		Nos. O8-O18 (11)	236.25	84.55

1903-04 Wmk. 2

O19	A36	2c orange brown	20.00	1.75
O20	A37	3c green	13.50	2.40
O21	A38	5c dull lilac	28.00	1.60
O22	A40	15c ultramarine	40.00	3.25
O23	A40	25c bister	35.00	22.50
O24	A40	30c violet & green	20.00	2.25
		Nos. O19-O24 (6)	156.50	33.75

CHAD

'chad

(Tchad)

LOCATION — Central Africa, south of Libya
GOVT. — Republic
AREA — 495,572 sq. mi.
POP. — 7,557,436 (1999 est.)
CAPITAL — N'Djamena

A former dependency of Ubangi-Shari, Chad became a separate French colony in 1920. In 1934, the colonies of Chad, Gabon, Middle Congo and Ubangi-Shari were grouped in a single administrative unit known as French Equatorial Africa, with the capital at Brazzaville. The Republic of Chad was proclaimed November 28, 1958.

100 Centimes = 1 Franc

> **Catalogue values for unused stamps in this country are for Never Hinged items, beginning with Scott 64 in the regular postage section, Scott B1 in the semi-postal section, Scott C1 in the air post section, Scott CB1 in the air post semi-postal section, Scott J23 in the postage due section, Scott M1 in the military stamp section, and Scott O1 in the officials section.**

See French Equatorial Africa No. 190 for stamp inscribed "Tchad."

Types of Middle Congo, 1907-17, Overprinted

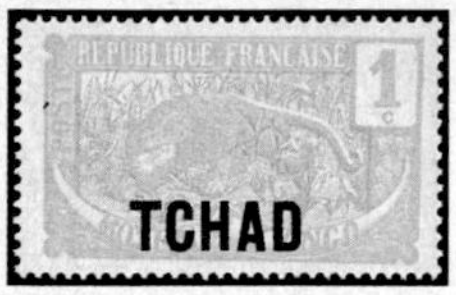

Perf. 14x13½, 13½x14

1922 Unwmk.

1	A1	1c red & violet	.40	.55
a.		Overprint omitted	225.00	
2	A1	2c ol brn & salmon	.40	.80
a.		Overprint omitted	260.00	
3	A1	4c ind & vio	1.20	1.60
4	A1	5c choc & grn	1.25	1.60
5	A1	10c dp grn & gray grn	2.40	2.75
6	A1	15c vio & red	2.50	2.75
7	A1	20c grn & vio	4.00	4.75
8	A2	25c ol brn & brn	12.00	12.00
9	A2	30c rose & pale rose	2.40	2.00
10	A2	35c dl bl & dl rose	3.25	3.25
11	A2	40c choc & grn	4.00	4.00
12	A2	45c vio & grn	3.25	3.25
13	A2	50c dk bl & pale bl	3.25	4.00
14	A2	60c on 75c vio, *pnksh*	4.00	4.75
a.		"TCHAD" omitted	300.00	
b.		"60" omitted	300.00	
15	A1	75c red & violet	4.00	4.00
16	A3	1fr indigo & salmon	12.00	16.00
17	A3	2fr indigo & violet	24.00	24.00
18	A3	5fr ind & olive brn	24.00	24.00
		Nos. 1-18 (18)	108.30	116.05

See Nos. 26a, 32a, 38a, 55a.

Stamps of 1922 Overprinted in Various Colors

Nos. 19-28

Nos. 29-50

1924-33

19 A1 1c red & vio .40 .80
a. "TCHAD" omitted 225.00 *250.00*
b. Double overprint 300.00
c. Violet omitted 300.00
20 A1 2c ol brn & sal .40 *.50*
a. "TCHAD" omitted 225.00
b. Double overprint 240.00
21 A1 4c ind & vio .40 *.50*
a. "TCHAD" omitted 950.00
22 A1 5c choc & grn (Bl) 1.60 *2.00*
a. "TCHAD" omitted 200.00 225.00
23 A1 5c choc & grn .80 *.70*
a. "TCHAD" omitted 225.00
24 A1 10c dp grn & gray grn (Bl) 1.60 1.40
25 A1 10c dp grn & gray grn 1.60 1.40
26 A1 10c red org & blk ('25) .60 .80
a. "Afrique Equatoriale Francaise" omitted 225.00 250.00
b. "TCHAD" omitted 240.00 260.00
27 A1 15c vio & red .80 .85
28 A1 20c grn & vio .80 .80
a. "TCHAD" omitted 225.00
b. "Afrique Equatoriale Francaise" doubled 340.00
29 A2 25c ol brn & brn .80 .85
a. "Afrique Equatoriale Francaise" doubled 160.00
30 A2 30c rose & pale rose .80 1.10
31 A2 30c gray & bl (R) ('25) .40 .80
32 A2 30c dk grn & grn ('27) 1.20 1.60
a. "Afrique Equatoriale Francaise" omitted 340.00
33 A2 35c indigo & dl rose .80 .85
34 A2 40c choc & grn 1.25 1.60
a. Double overprint (R + Bk) 275.00
35 A2 45c vio & grn 1.20 1.40
a. Double overprint (R + Bk) 275.00
36 A2 50c dk bl & pale bl (R) 2.40 1.90
a. Inverted overprint 160.00
37 A2 50c grn & vio ('25) 2.40 2.00
38 A2 65c org brn & bl ('28) 2.40 2.40
a. "Afrique Equatoriale Francaise" omitted 260.00
39 A2 75c red & vio (Bl) 2.00 1.90
40 A2 75c dp bl & lt bl (R) ('25) .80 1.20
a. "TCHAD" omitted 260.00
41 A2 75c rose & dk brn ('28) 3.25 3.25
42 A2 90c brn red & pink ('30) 8.00 12.00
43 A3 1fr ind & salmon 2.40 2.50
44 A3 1.10fr dl grn & bl ('28) 4.00 4.00
45 A3 1.25fr org brn & lt bl ('33) 8.00 9.50
46 A3 1.50fr ultra & bl ('30) 8.00 12.00
47 A3 1.75fr ol brn & vio ('33) 40.00 45.00
48 A3 2fr ind & vio 3.25 3.50
a. Double impression of frame 550.00
49 A3 3fr red vio ('30) 12.00 16.00
50 A3 5fr ind & ol brn 4.00 4.75
Nos. 19-50 (32) 118.35 139.85

See No. 58a.

Types of 1922 Overprinted like Nos. 29-50 and Surcharged with New Values

1924-27

51 A2 60c on 75c dk vio, *pnksh* .80 1.20
a. "60" omitted 200.00
52 A3 65c on 1fr brn & ol grn ('25) 2.50 2.00
53 A3 85c on 1fr brn & ol grn ('25) 2.50 2.00
54 A2 90c on 75c brn red & rose red ('27) 2.50 2.00
55 A3 1.25fr on 1fr dk bl & ultra (R) ('26) 1.25 .80
a. "Afrique Equatoriale Francaise" omitted 175.00
56 A3 1.50fr on 1fr ultra & bl ('27) 2.50 2.00
57 A3 3fr on 5fr org brn & dl red ('27) 6.50 6.00
58 A3 10fr on 5fr ol grn & cer ('27) 16.00 14.50
a. "10fr" omitted 400.00 400.00
59 A3 20fr on 5fr vio & ver ('27) 20.00 21.00
Nos. 51-59 (9) 54.55 51.50

Common Design Types pictured following the introduction.

Colonial Exposition Issue
Common Design Types

1931 **Engr.** ***Perf. 12½***

Name of Country in Black

60 CD70 40c deep green 5.50 5.50
61 CD71 50c violet 5.50 5.50
62 CD72 90c red orange 5.50 5.50
63 CD73 1.50fr dull blue 5.50 5.50
Nos. 60-63 (4) 22.00 22.00

Catalogue values for unused stamps in this section, from this point to the end of the section, are for Never Hinged items.

Republic

"Birth of the Republic" A1

"Solidarity of the Community" A2

1959 **Unwmk.** **Engr.** ***Perf. 13***

64 A1 15fr ultra, grn & maroon .80 .25
65 A2 25fr dk grn & dp claret 1.00 .25

1st anniv. of the proclamation of the Republic.

Imperforates
Most Chad stamps from 1959 onward exist imperforate in issued and trial colors, and also in small presentation sheets in issued colors.

C.C.T.A. Issue
Common Design Type

1960

66 CD106 50fr rose lil & dk pur 1.90 .50

Flag and Map of Chad and UN Emblem — A3

Unwmk.

1961, Jan. 11 **Engr.** ***Perf. 13***

Flag in blue, yellow and carmine

67 A3 15fr brn & dk bl .60 .25
68 A3 25fr org brn & dk bl .90 .25
69 A3 85fr slate grn & dk bl 2.50 .40
Nos. 67-69 (3) 4.00 .90

Admission of Chad to United Nations.

Chari Bridge and Hippopotamus — A4

Abtouyoua Mountain and Ox — A5

Designs: 50c, Biltine and dorcas gazelle. 1fr, Logone and elephant. 2fr, Batha and lion. 3fr, Salamat and buffalo. 4fr, Ouaddai and Kudu. 15fr, Bessada and giant eland. 20fr, Tibesti mountains and mouflon. 25fr, Rocherg and antelope. 30fr, Kanem and cheetah. 60fr, Borkou and oryx. 85fr, Gorge of Archet and addax.

Perf. 13½x14, 14x13½

1961-62 **Typo.**

70 A5 50c yel grn & dk grn ('62) .25 .25
71 A5 1fr bl grn & dk bl grn ('62) .25 .25
72 A5 2fr dk red brn & blk ('62) .25 .25
73 A5 3fr ocher & dl grn ('62) .25 .25
74 A5 4fr dk crim & blk ('62) .25 .25
75 A4 5fr yellow & blk .25 .25
76 A5 10fr pink & blk .35 .25
77 A5 15fr lilac & blk ('62) .70 .25
78 A5 20fr red & blk .85 .25
79 A5 25fr blue & blk ('62) .90 .25
80 A5 30fr ultra & blk ('62) 1.00 .25
81 A5 60fr yel & ol grn ('62) 2.25 .25
82 A5 85fr org & blk 2.75 .25
Nos. 70-82 (13) 10.30 3.25

First anniversary of Independence.
For overprint see No. M1.

Abidjan Games Issue
Common Design Type

1962, July 21 **Photo.** ***Perf. 12½x12***

83 CD109 20fr Relay race .80 .25
84 CD109 50fr High jump 2.00 .30
Nos. 83-84,C8 (3) 6.80 1.55

African-Malgache Union Issue
Common Design Type

1962, Sept. 8 **Unwmk.**

85 CD110 30fr dk bl, bluish grn, red & gold 1.25 .25

Pres. Ngarta Tombalbaye — A7

1963, Apr. 22 ***Perf. 12x12½***

86 A7 20fr multi .65 .25
87 A7 85fr multi 1.75 .30

For surcharge, see No. 125.

Space Communciations Issue

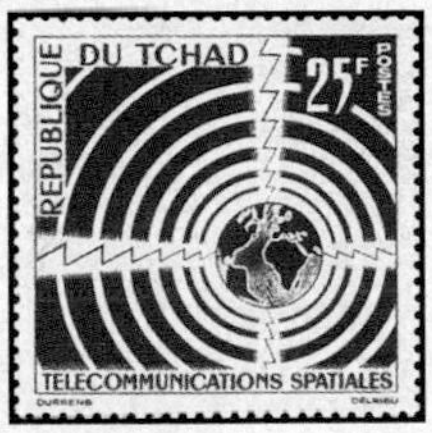

Waves Around Globe — A8

Design: 100fr, Orbit patterns around globe.

Perf. 12½

1963, Sept. 19 **Unwmk.** **Photo.**

88 A8 25fr grn & pur 1.00 .25
89 A8 100fr pink & ultra 3.00 .60

Ancestral Mask — A9

Excavated Sao Art: 5fr, Clay weight. 25fr, Ancestral clay statuette. 60fr, Gazelle, bronze. 80fr, Bronze pectoral.

1963, Dec. 2 **Engr.** ***Perf. 13***

90 A9 5fr brt grn & red brn .25 .25
91 A9 15fr gray, dl cl & red .45 .25
92 A9 25fr dk bl & org brn 1.10 .25
93 A9 60fr org brn & slate grn 2.75 .35
94 A9 80fr org red & olive 3.00 .40
Nos. 90-94 (5) 7.55 1.50

UNESCO Emblem, Scales and Tree — A10

1963, Dec. 10

95 A10 25fr green & maroon 1.00 .25

15th anniv. of the Universal Declaration of Human Rights.

Potter A11

Perf. 12½

1964, Feb. 5 **Unwmk.** **Engr.**

96 A11 10fr shown .35 .25
97 A11 30fr Boatmaker .90 .25
98 A11 50fr Weaver 1.50 .25
99 A11 85fr Smiths 2.25 .35
Nos. 96-99 (4) 5.00 1.10

Barograph and WMO Emblem A12

1964, Mar. 23 ***Perf. 13***

100 A12 50fr red lil, pur & ultra 1.40 .25

Fourth World Meteorological Day.

Cotton A13

1964, Apr. 6 **Photo.** ***Perf. 12½x13***

101 A13 20fr shown 1.75 .35
102 A13 25fr Royal poinciana 2.00 .40

Co-operation Issue
Common Design Type

1964, Nov. 7 **Engr.** ***Perf. 13***

103 CD119 25fr ver, dk bl & dk brn 1.00 .25

National Guard and Map of Chad A14

Design: 25fr, Infantry, flag and map, vert.

Perf. 12½x13, 13x12½

1964, Dec. 11 **Photo.**
104 A14 20fr multi .85 .25
105 A14 25fr lt bl & multi 1.00 .25

Issued to honor the army of Chad.

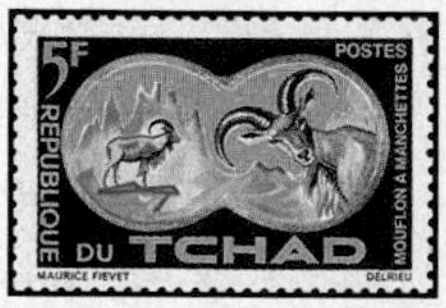

Aoudad or Barbary Sheep A15

10fr, Addax. 20fr, Oryx. 25fr, Derby's eland, vert. 30fr, Giraffe, buffalo & lion, Zakouma Park, vert. 85fr, Great kudu at water hole, vert.

Perf. 12½x12, 12x12½

1965, Jan. 11 **Unwmk.**
106 A15 5fr dk brn, ultra & yel .50 .25
107 A15 10fr ultra, org & blk .75 .25
108 A15 20fr multi 1.50 .25
109 A15 25fr multi 1.75 .25
110 A15 30fr multi 2.50 .40
111 A15 85fr multi 5.00 .75
Nos. 106-111 (6) 12.00 2.15

Olsen Perforator A16

Designs: 60fr, Mildé telephone, vert. 100fr, Distributor of Baudot telegraph.

1965, May 17 **Engr.** ***Perf. 13***
112 A16 30fr multi .75 .25
113 A16 60fr multi 1.25 .45
114 A16 100fr multi 2.00 .60
Nos. 112-114 (3) 4.00 1.30

Cent. of the ITU.

Motorized Police A17

Perf. 12½x12

1965, June 22 **Photo.** **Unwmk.**
115 A17 25fr ol, dk grn, gold & brn 1.00 .25

Issued to honor the national police.

Drum and stool — A18

Musical Instruments from National Museum: 2fr, Guitar. 3fr, Shoulder drums, vert. 15fr, Viol. 60fr, Harp, vert.

1965, Oct. 26 **Engr.** ***Perf. 13***
Size: 22x36mm, 36x22mm
116 A18 1fr car, emer & brn .25 .25
117 A18 2fr red, brt lil & brn .25 .25
118 A18 3fr red & sepia .25 .25
119 A18 15fr red, ocher & sl grn .75 .25
120 A18 60fr maroon & slate grn 1.75 .60
Nos. 116-120,C23 (6) 6.00 2.60

See No. C23.

Head and Bowl — A19

Sao Art: 20fr, Head. 60fr, Head with crown. 80fr, Circlet with human head. From excavations at Bouta Kebira and Gawi.

1966, Apr. 1 **Engr.** ***Perf. 13***
121 A19 15fr ol, choc & ultra .40 .25
122 A19 20fr dk red, brn & bl grn .75 .25
123 A19 60fr brt bl, choc & ver 1.75 .50
124 A19 80fr brn org, grn & pur 2.50 .60
Nos. 121-124 (4) 5.40 1.60

Issued to publicize the International Negro Arts Festival, Dakar, Senegal, Apr. 1-24.

No. 86 Surcharged in Orange

1966, Apr. 15 **Photo.** ***Perf. 12x12½***
125 A7 25fr on 20fr multi 1.00 .30

WHO Headquarters, Geneva — A20

1966, May 3
126 A20 25fr car, lt ultra & yel .90 .25
127 A20 32fr emer, ultra & yel 1.00 .25

New WHO Headquarters, Geneva.

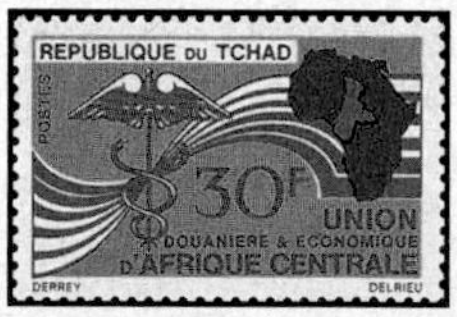

Staff of Mercury and Map of Africa A21

1966, May 24 ***Perf. 12½x12***
128 A21 30fr multi 1.00 .25

Central African Customs and Economic Union (Union Douaniere et Economique de l'Afrique Centrale, UDEAC).

Soccer Player — A22

Design: 60fr, Soccer player facing left.

1966, July 12 **Engr.** ***Perf. 13***
129 A22 30fr grn, bl grn & mar 1.00 .25
130 A22 60fr dk bl, gray & car 2.00 .40

8th World Cup Soccer Championship, Wembley, England, July 11-30.

Young Men, Flag and Emblem A23

1966, Aug. 11 **Photo.** ***Perf. 12½x13***
131 A23 25fr dk bl & multi 1.00 .25

Chad Youth Movement.

Greek Columns and UNESCO Emblem — A24

1966, Aug. 23 **Engr.** ***Perf. 13***
132 A24 32fr sl bl, vio & car rose 1.00 .25

20th anniv. of UNESCO.

Reconstructed Skull of Chadanthropus — A25

1966, Sept. 20 **Engr.** ***Perf. 13***
133 A25 30fr gray, red & ocher 2.00 .50

Yves Coppens' discovery of Lake Chad man.

Stone Axe — A26

Prehistoric Tools: 30fr, Flint arrow head. 85fr, Bone harpoon. 100fr, Sandstone millstone with grinder.

1966, Dec. 11 **Engr.** ***Perf. 13***
134 A26 25fr dp bl, red & dk brn .70 .25
135 A26 30fr brn, dp bl & blk .80 .25
136 A26 85fr dk red, brt bl & brn 2.50 .50
137 A26 100fr Prus grn, dk brn & bis brn 2.75 .65
a. Miniature sheet of 4, #134-137 15.00 8.00
Nos. 134-137 (4) 6.75 1.65

Map of Chad and Various Sports — A27

1967, Apr. 10 **Photo.** ***Perf. 12x12½***
138 A27 25fr multi 1.00 .30

Issued for Sports Day, Apr. 10, 1967.

Colotis Protomedia A28

Various Butterflies.

1967, May 23 **Photo.** ***Perf. 12½x12***
139 A28 5fr blue & multi 2.00 .30
140 A28 10fr emerald & multi 4.25 .75
141 A28 20fr orange & multi 8.50 1.50
142 A28 130fr red & multi 17.50 2.50
Nos. 139-142 (4) 32.25 5.05

WHO Headquarters, Brazzaville — A29

1967, Sept. 23 **Photo.** ***Perf. 12½x13***
143 A29 30fr vio bl & multi 1.00 .25

Opening of the Regional Office of the WHO, Brazzaville.

Jamboree Emblem and Boy Scouts A30

32fr, Jamboree emblem and Boy Scout.

1967, Oct. 17 **Photo.** ***Perf. 12½x13***
144 A30 25fr multi .90 .25
145 A30 32fr multi 1.00 .25

12th Boy Scout World Jamboree, Farragut State Park, Idaho, Aug. 1-9.

Great Mills of Chad A31

30fr, Lake reclamation project, grain fields.

1967, Nov. 14 **Engr.** ***Perf. 13***
146 A31 25fr brt bl, ind & sep .90 .25
147 A31 30fr ultra, emer & ol brn 1.00 .25

Economic development of Chad.

Woman and Harp Player A32

Rock Paintings: 30fr, Giraffes. 50fr, Camel rider hunting ostrich.

1967, Dec. 19 **Engr.** ***Perf. 13***
Size: 36x22mm
148 A32 15fr bl, sal & mar 2.00 .25
149 A32 30fr grnsh bl, sal & mar 4.00 .40
150 A32 50fr emer, sal & mar 5.50 .55
Nos. 148-150,C38-C39 (5) 28.50 3.65

Balloud expedition in the Ennedi Mountains. See Nos. 163-166.

Rotary Emblem — A33

1968, Jan. 9 **Photo.** ***Perf. 13x12½***
151 A33 50fr multi 2.00 .50

Rotary Club of Chad, 10th anniversary.

Map of Chad, WHO Emblem, Well, Physicians, Mother and Child — A34

1968, Apr. 6 ***Perf. 13x12½***

152 A34 25fr multi .90 .25
153 A34 32fr multi 1.10 .25

20th anniv. of WHO.

"Water" Aiding Agriculture and Industry A35

1968, Apr. 23 **Engr.** ***Perf. 13***

154 A35 50fr grnsh bl, brn & brt grn 1.10 .25

Hydrological Decade (UNESCO), 1965-74.

National Administration School — A36

1968, Aug. 20 **Engr.** ***Perf. 13***

155 A36 25fr slate, brn red & rose vio 1.00 .25

Boy Learning to Write A37

1968, Sept. 10

156 A37 60fr dk bl, dk brn & blk 2.00 .50

Issued for National Literacy Day.

Cotton Harvest A38

Loom, Fort Archambault Factory — A39

1968, Sept. 24 **Engr.** ***Perf. 13***

157 A38 25fr Prus bl, choc & dk grn .90 .25
158 A39 30fr brt grn, ol & ultra 1.00 .25

Issued to publicize the cotton industry.

Tiger Moth — A40

Moths: 30fr, Owlet. 50fr, Saturnid (Gynanisa maja). 100fr, Saturnid (Epiphora bauhiniae).

1968, Oct. 1 **Photo.**

159 A40 25fr multi 5.25 .60
160 A40 30fr multi 6.25 .75
161 A40 50fr multi 9.50 .85
162 A40 100fr multi 11.00 1.50
Nos. 159-162 (4) 32.00 3.70

Rock Paintings Type of 1967

Rock Paintings: 2fr, Archers. 10fr, Costumes (4 women, 1 man). 20fr, Funeral vigil. 25fr, Dispute.

1968, Nov. 19 **Engr.** ***Perf. 13***

Size: 36x22mm

163 A32 2fr scar, salmon & brn .65 .25
164 A32 10fr pur, salmon & dk red 1.60 .25
165 A32 20fr grn, salmon & mar 3.25 .50
166 A32 25fr bl, salmon & maroon 3.50 .60
Nos. 163-166 (4) 9.00 1.60

Man and Human Rights Flame — A41

1968, Dec. 10 **Engr.** ***Perf. 13***

167 A41 32fr grn, brt bl & red 1.00 .25

International Human Rights Year.

St. Paul — A42

Apostles: 1fr, St. Peter. 2fr, St. Thomas. 5fr, St. John the Evangelist. 10fr, St. Bartholomew. 20fr, St. Matthew. 25fr, St. James the Less. 30fr, St. Andrew. 40fr, St. Jude. 50fr, St. James the Greater. 85fr, St. Philip. 100fr, St. Simon.

1969, May 6 **Litho.** ***Perf. 12½x13***

168 A42 50c multi .25 .25
169 A42 1fr multi .25 .25
170 A42 2fr multi .25 .25
171 A42 5fr multi .25 .25
172 A42 10fr multi .25 .25
173 A42 20fr multi .30 .25
174 A42 25fr multi .40 .25
175 A42 30fr multi .50 .25
176 A42 40fr multi .60 .25
177 A42 50fr multi .70 .25
178 A42 85fr multi 1.10 .40
179 A42 100fr multi 1.25 .40
a. Sheet of 12, #168-179 6.00 1.75

Jubilee Year of the Catholic Church in Chad.

Tractors and Trucks — A43

1969, June 19 **Engr.** ***Perf. 13***

180 A43 32fr grn, red brn & ind .75 .25

50th anniv. of the ILO.

Deborah Meyer, US, 200 Meter Freestyle A44

Woman with Flowers, by Veneto — A45

Winners of 1968 Olympic Games: No. 182, Roland Matthes, East Germany, 100m backstroke. No. 183, Klaus DiBiasi, Italy, springboard diving. No. 184, Bruno Cipolla, Primo Baran and Renzo Sambo, Italy, pair with coxswain. No. 185, Annemarie Zimmermann and Rosewitha Esser, West Germany, women's kayak tandem. No. 186, Sailing, G.B. No. 187, Pierre Trentin, France, 1000 meter bicycling. No. 188, Pier Franco Vianelli, Italy, 196k bicycle road race. No. 189, Daniel Morelon and Pierre Trentin, France, tandem.

No. 190, Daniel R. Rebillard, France, 4000m pursuit (bicycle). No. 191, Ingrid Becker, West Germany, pentathlon. No. 192, Jean J. Guyon, France, equestrian. No. 193, Olympic dressage team, West Germany. No. 194, Bernd Klinger, West Germany, small bore rifle. No. 195, Manfred Wolke, East Germany, welterweight. No. 196, Randy Matson, US, shot put. No. 197, Colette Besson, France, 400m run. No. 198, Mohammed Gammoudi, Tunisia, 5,000m run. No. 199, Tommie Smith, US, 200m run.

No. 200, David Hemery, G.B., 200m hurdles. No. 201, Willie Davenport, US, 110m hurdles. No. 202, Bob Beamon, US, long jump. No. 203, Sawao Kato, Japan, all around gymnastics. No. 204, Dick Fosbury, US, high jump.

Paintings: No. 206, Holy Family, by Murillo, horiz. No. 207, Adoration of the Magi, by Rubens. No. 208, Portrait of an African Woman, by Bezombes. No. 209, Three Black Men, by Rubens. No. 210, Mother and Child, by Gauguin.

1969, June 30 **Litho.** ***Perf. 12½x13***

181-204 A44 1fr set of 24 8.00 8.00

Perf. 12½x13, 13x12½

205-210 A45 1fr set of 6 1.90 1.90

Issued to stress the brotherhood of mankind.

For overprints see Nos. 244A-244F, 245A-245X.

Cochlospermum Tinctorium — A46

Flowers: 4fr, Parkia biglobosa. 10fr, Pancratium trianthum. 15fr, Morning glory.

1969, July 8 **Photo.** ***Perf. 12½x13***

211 A46 1fr pink, yel & blk .60 .25
212 A46 4fr dk grn, yel & red .90 .25
213 A46 10fr dk grn, yel & gray 1.10 .25
214 A46 15fr vio bl & multi 1.90 .25
Nos. 211-214 (4) 4.50 1.00

Meat Freezer, Farcha A47

30fr, Cattle at Farcha slaughterhouse.

1969, Aug. 19 **Engr.** ***Perf. 13***

215 A47 25fr sl grn, ocher & red brn .60 .25
216 A47 30fr red brn, sl grn & gray .75 .25

Economic development in Chad.

Development Bank Issue

Common Design Type

1969, Sept. 10

217 CD130 30fr dl red, grn & ocher .70 .25

Tilapia Nilotica A48

Fish: 3fr, Citharinus latus. 5fr, Tetraodon fahaka strigosus. 20fr, Hydrocyon forskali.

1969, Nov. 25 **Engr.** ***Perf. 13***

218 A48 2fr choc, grn & gray .55 .25
219 A48 3fr gray, red & bl 1.10 .25
220 A48 5fr ocher, blk & yel 1.75 .25
221 A48 20fr blk, red & grn 4.75 .60
Nos. 218-221 (4) 8.15 1.35

ASECNA Issue

Common Design Type

1969, Dec. 12 **Engr.** ***Perf. 13***

222 CD132 30fr orange 1.00 .25

Pres. François Tombalbaye A49

1970, Jan. 11 **Litho.** ***Perf. 14***

223 A49 25fr multi 1.00 .25

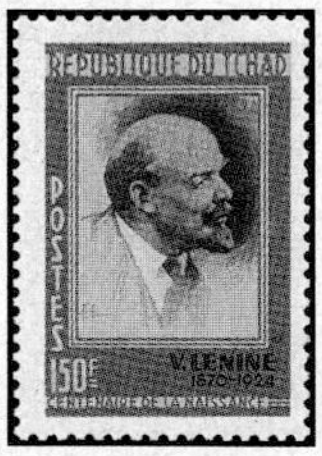

Lenin — A50

1970, Apr. 22 **Photo.** ***Perf. 11½***

224 A50 150fr gold, blk & buff 3.25 1.10

Lenin (1870-1924), Russian communist leader.

UPU Headquarters Issue

Common Design Type

1970, May 20 **Engr.** ***Perf. 13***

225 CD133 30fr dk red, pur & brn 1.00 .25

During the 1970-73 period three different agents had entered into contracts to produce stamps with various officials of the Chad government, apparently including Pres. Tombalbaye.

In June 1973, Tombalbaye declared that some of the stamps produced by these agents were not recognized by the Chad government but might be put on sale at a later date, and that other stamps produced and shipped to Chad were refused by the government.

In July 1973, the Chad government announced that the stamps that were not recognized would be put on sale by the end of the year. We have no evidence that this actually happened.

Apollo Program A50a

Designs: 15fr, Apollo 11 in Lunar orbit. 25fr, Apollo 12 astronaut deploying lunar research equipment. 40fr, Astronaunt, lunar module on moon. 50fr, Astronauts Conrad and Bean in life raft after splashdown, horiz.

1970, June 12 Litho. ***Perf. 12x12½***

225A A50a Strip of 3, #b-d 6.00 —

Souvenir Sheet

Perf. 13½x13

225E A50a 50fr multicolored 10.00 —

No. 225E contains one 66x44mm stamp. 15fr, 25fr are airmail.

Expo '70, Japan — A50b

Japanese prints of women: 50c, by Kiyonaga. 1fr, by Utamaro. 2fr, from Heian period.

1970, June 12 Litho. ***Perf. 12x12½***

225F A50b Strip of 3, #a-c 13.50 —

For overprint see No. 239C.

Adult Education Class and UN Emblem — A52

1970, June 16 Litho. ***Perf. 14***

226 A52 100fr blue & multi 2.00 .60

International Education Year.

Bull's Head, Symbols of Weather and Agriculture — A53

1970, July 22 Engr. ***Perf. 13***

227 A53 50fr org, gray & grn 1.00 .25

Issued for World Meteorological Day.

1970 World Cup Soccer Championships, Mexico City — A53a

Designs: 1fr, Three players, Italian flag. 4fr, Franz Beckenbauer, German flag. Nos. 227C, 227E, English players receiving World Cup trophy, 1966. No. 227D, Three players, Brazilian flag. No. 227F, Four players, "1970."

1970-71 Litho. ***Perf. 12***

227A A53a 1fr multicolored
227B A53a 4fr multicolored
227C A53a 5fr multicolored
227D A53a 5fr multicolored
Nos. 227A-227D (4) 3.75 —

Embossed

Die Cut Perf 13

227E A53a 5fr gold 17.50 —

Souvenir Sheet

Litho.

Perf. 13½x13

227F A53a 15fr multicolored 6.25 —

No. 227F contains one 66x44mm stamp. Nos. 227D, 227F are airmail.

Issued: Nos. 227A-227D, 227F, 7/2; No. 227E, 11/1/71.

For overprints see Nos. 267A-267E.

Christmas A53b

Virgin and Child by: 3fr, Solario. 25fr, Durer. 32fr, Fouquet.

1970, Aug. 19 Litho. ***Perf. 12x12½***

227G A53b 3fr multicolored
227H A53b 25fr multicolored
227I A53b 32fr multicolored
Nos. 227G-227I (3) 13.50 —

No. 227I is airmail.

Ahmed Mangue, Minister of Education — A54

1970, Sept. 15 Litho. & Engr.

228 A54 100fr gold, car & blk 2.00 .50

1972 Summer Olympics, Munich — A54a

Designs: No. 228A, 3fr, Horses pulling chariot. 8fr, Men running. 10fr, No. 228C, Woman hurdling. No. 228B, 20fr, Equestrian. 35fr, Woman diving. No. 228D, Woman diver in tuck position.

1970 Litho. ***Perf. 12½x12***

228A A54a Strip of 3, #a-c 4.00 —

Perf. 12x12½

228B A54a Pair, #a-b + label 4.00 —

Embossed

Die Cut Perf 13

228C A54a 10fr gold 17.50 —

Souvenir Sheet

Litho.

Perf. 13½x13

228D A54a 40fr multicolored 10.00 —

10fr, 35fr, Nos. 228C-228D are airmail. No. 228D contains one 66x43mm stamp.

Issued: Nos. 228A-228B, 228D, Sept; No. 228C, 10/14.

For overprints see Nos. 239D-239F.

Tanner A55

Designs: 2fr, Cloth dyer, vert. 3fr, Camel turning oil press. 4fr, Water carrier, vert.. 5fr, Copper worker.

1970, Oct. 10 Engr. ***Perf. 13***

229 A55 1fr ol brn, bl & brn .25 .25
229A A55 2fr dk brn, ol & ind .25 .25
229B A55 3fr pur, ol brn & rose car .40 .25
229C A55 4fr choc, lem & bl grn .50 .25
229D A55 5fr red, choc & sl grn .50 .25
Nos. 229-229D (5) 1.90 1.25

UN Emblem, Grain and Dove — A56

1970, Oct. 24 Photo. ***Perf. 12x12½***

230 A56 32fr dk bl & multi 1.00 .25

25th anniversary of United Nations.

OCAM Headquarters, Map of Africa, Stars — A57

1971, Jan. 23 Photo. ***Perf. 12½x12***

231 A57 30fr dk grn & multi 1.00 .25

OCAM (Organisation Commune Africaine, Malgache et Mauricienne) Summit Conference, N'djamena, Jan. 22-30.

Space Exploration — A57a

10fr, Apollo 11. 35fr, Soviet space station. 40fr, John F. Kennedy, Apollo spacecraft, vert.

1971, Feb. 16 Litho. ***Perf. 13x13½***

231A A57a 8fr shown .60 —
231B A57a 10fr multi .90 —
231C A57a 35fr multi 6.25 —
Nos. 231A-231C (3) 7.75

Embossed

Die Cut Perf 13

231D A57a 8fr gold, like #231A 8.25 —
f. Sheet of 1, Imperf.

Souvenir Sheet

Perf. 13½x13

231E A57a 40fr multi 10.00 —

Nos. 231C, 231E are airmail. No. 231Df contains one 73x45mm stamp with same size design as No. 231D. No. 231E contains one 33x50mm stamp.

Nos. 231D, 231Df probably were not available in Chad.

1972 Winter Olympics, Sapporo A57b

Paintings by Kiyonaga: 50c, Cherry Trees in Bloom, Tokyo. 1fr, Snowy Morning. 2fr, Sake Party.

1971 Litho. ***Perf. 12x12½***

231G A57b 50c multicolored .80
231H A57b 1fr multicolored 1.40
231I A57b 2fr multicolored 2.25
Nos. 231G-231I (3) 4.45

Embossed

Die Cut Perf 13

231J A57b 2fr gold, like #231I 17.50
k. Sheet of 1, Imperf. 35.00

Issued: Nos. 231G-231I, 2/16; Nos. 231J-231Jk, 11/1. No. 231Jk contains one 43x54mm stamp with same size design as No. 231I.

For overprints see Nos. 246A-246C.

Nos. 231J-231Jk probably were not available in Chad.

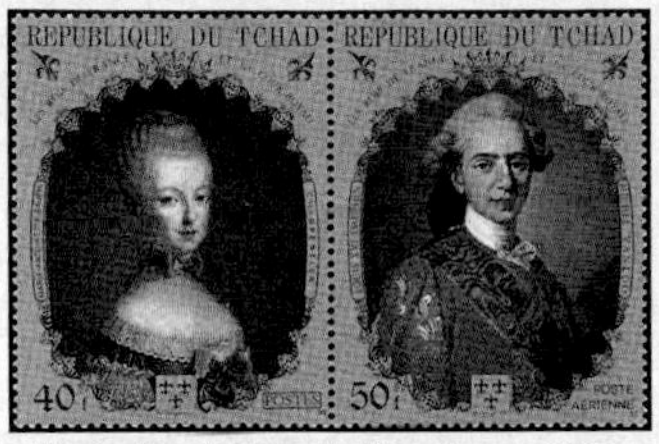

Portraits of French Royalty — A57c

Designs: No. 232A, 25fr, The Dauphin (Louis XVII), by J.M. Vien the Younger. 32fr, Marie Antoinette, by E. Vigee-Lebrun. 60fr, Louis XVI, by J.S. Duplessis.

No. 232B, 25fr, Comtesse du Barry, by E. Vigee-Lebrun. 40fr, Louis XV, by M.Q. Delatour.

No. 232C, 40fr, Marie Antoinette, by Charpentier. 50fr, Louis XVI (Dauphin), by Michel Van Loo.

No. 232D, 35fr, Madame de Pompadour (detail), by Delatour. 70fr, Louis XV by Delatour.

No. 232E, 30fr, Madame de Pompadour (entire), by Delatour. 60fr, Marie Leszczynska, by Jean Marc Nattier. 80fr, Louis XV, by Van Loo.

No. 232F, 40fr, Duc D'Orleans as Regent, by 19th cent. French school. 200fr, Louis XIV, by H. Rigaud.

No. 232G, 100fr, Madame de Montespan, by Henry Gascard. 100fr, Madame de Maintenon, by Pierre Mignard.

No. 232H, 50fr, Colbert, by Claude Lefebvre. 200fr, Louis XIV, by J. Garnier.

No. 232J, 50fr, Marie Therese, by Mignard. 200fr, Louis XIV, by Marot.

No. 232K, 50fr, Marie de la Valliere, by English school. 200fr, Louis XIV, by French school.

No. 232L, 100fr, Giulio Cardinal Mazarin, by Mignard. 100fr, Anne of Austria, by Rubens.

No. 232M, 50fr, Vicomte de Turenne, by Champaigne. 200fr, Louis XIV as a Boy, by Mignard.

No. 232N, 100fr, Marquis de Cinq-Mars, by M. le Nain. 150fr, Cardinal Richelieu, by Champaigne.

No. 232P, 150fr, Anne of Austria, by Rubens. 250fr, Louis XIII (detail), by Simon Vouet.

No. 232Q, 150fr, Marriage of Marie de Medicis (looking right), by Rubens. 150fr, Mirror image.

No. 232R, 150fr, Duke of Sully, by Quesnel. 150fr, Mirror image.

No. 232S, 150fr, Henry IV, by Rubens. 150fr, Marie de Medicis, by Rubens.

No. 232T, 200fr, Gabrielle d'Estrees, by unknown artist. 250fr, Henry IV, by French school, c. 1595.

No. 232U, 150fr, Jeanne d'Albret, by Francois Clouet. 200fr, Marie de Medicis as a Girl, by Angelo Bronzino.

No. 232V, 200fr, Henry III, by Clouet. 250fr, Ambroise Pare, by 16th century French school.

No. 232W, 150fr, Catherine de Medicis, by Clouet. 250fr, Henry II, by Clouet.

No. 233A, 200fr, Elizabeth of Austria, by Clouet. 250fr, Charles IX, by Clouet.

No. 233B, 200fr, Mary Stuart, by 16th cent. Scottish school. 300fr, Diane of Poitiers, by Fontainbleu school.

No. 233C, 200fr, Elizabeth of Valois, by Alonso S. Coello. 250fr, Francis, Duke of Alencon, by Clouet.

No. 233D, 150fr, Marguerite d'Angouleme, by Clouet. 300fr, Francis I, by Clouet.

No. 233E, 200fr, Francis I, by Titian. 300fr, Francis I as Dauphin, by Corneille of Lyon.

No. 233F, 100fr, Anne of Austria, by Coello. 250fr, Louis XIII, by Champaigne.

No. 233G, 200fr, Marie de Medicis, by Rubens. 200fr, Marie de Medicis, Louis XIII, by Rubens.

No. 233H, 150fr, The Exchange of Princess Elizabeth of France and Princess Anne of Austria on the Andaye River, by Rubens. 250fr, Louis XIII of France and Navarre, by Vouet.

No. 233J, 250fr, Marie de Medicis, by Rubens. 250fr, Henry IV, by Rubens.

No. 233K, Louis XV and the Dauphin at Battle of Fontenoy. No. 233L, The Grand Dauphin and his Family, by Mignard. No. 233M, Madame de Montespan, horiz. No. 233N, Madame de la Valliere and her Children. No. 233P, The Birth of Louis XIII at Fontainebleau, by Rubens. No. 233Q, Reconciliation of the Queen and Louis XIII, by Rubens. No. 233R, Henry IV Entrusting Regency to Marie de Medici, by Rubens. No. 233S, The Majority of Louis XIII, by Rubens. No. 233T, The Apotheosis of Henry IV and the Proclamation of Regency, by Rubens. No. 233U, Felicity of the Regency, by Rubens.

Small numbers appear at the lower right on Nos. 232A-233J. To ease identication, these numbers are shown in parentheses after each listing.

1971-73 Litho. *Perf. 12½x13*

232A	A57c	Strip of 3, #aa-ac (58-60)	3.00
232B	A57c	Pair, #aa-ab (53-54)	2.00
232C	A57c	Pair, #aa-ab (56-57)	2.00
232D	A57c	Pair, #aa-ab (51-52)	2.00
232E	A57c	Strip of 3, #aa-ac (48-50)	4.00
232F	A57c	Pair, #aa-ab (45, 47)	4.00
232G	A57c	Pair, #aa-ab (44, 45B)	3.00
232H	A57c	Pair, #aa-ab (42-43)	4.00
232J	A57c	Pair, #aa-ab (40-41)	4.00
232K	A57c	Pair, #aa-ab (38-39)	4.00
232L	A57c	Pair, #aa-ab (36-37)	2.50
232M	A57c	Pair, #aa-ab (34-35)	4.00
232N	A57c	Pair, #aa-ab (32-33)	4.00
232P	A57c	Pair, #aa-ab (30-31)	6.00
232Q	A57c	Pair, #aa-ab (22-23)	4.00
232R	A57c	Pair, #aa-ab (22A-22B)	4.50
232S	A57c	Pair, #aa-ab (26, 27A)	4.50
232T	A57c	Pair, #aa-ab (18-19)	7.50
232U	A57c	Pair, #aa-ab (16-17)	5.50
232V	A57c	Pair, #aa-ab (16-16A)	7.50
232W	A57c	Pair, #aa-ab (14-15)	6.50
233A	A57c	Pair, #aa-ab (13-13A)	7.50
233B	A57c	Pair, #aa-ab (11-12)	8.00
233C	A57c	Pair, #aa-ab (10, 11A)	6.50
233D	A57c	Pair, #aa-ab (8-9)	7.50
233E	A57c	Pair, #aa-ab (7, 8A)	8.00
233F	A57c	Pair, #aa-ab (29, 32B)	6.00
233G	A57c	Pair, #aa-ab (24-25)	6.00
233H	A57c	Pair, #aa-ab (27-28)	6.00
233J	A57c	Pair, #aa-ab (20-21)	7.50
		Nos. 232A-233J (30)	151.50

Souvenir Sheets

Perf. 13x13½, 13½x13, 13½

233K	A57c	75fr multi	6.50
233L	A57c	100fr multi	6.00
233M	A57c	200fr multi	6.00
233N	A57c	300fr multi	6.00
233P	A57c	350fr multi	12.00
233Q	A57c	400fr multi	16.00
233R	A57c	400fr multi	10.00
233S	A57c	400fr multi	10.00
233T	A57c	400fr multi	6.00
233U	A57c	500fr multi	13.50
		Nos. 233K-233U (10)	92.00

Nos. 232A 60fr, 232B 40fr, 232C 50fr, 232D 70fr, 232E 80fr, 232F 200fr, 232G, 232H 200fr, 232J 200fr, 232K, 232L, 232M 200fr, 232N-233U are airmail.

Issued: 1971 — No. 232A, 2/24; No. 232B, 3/30; No. 232C, 3/4; Nos. 232D, 233K, 3/15; No. 232E, 4/12; Nos. 232F, 233L, 4/26; No. 232G, 8/10; No. 232H, 9/6; No. 232J, 9/23; No. 232K, 10/6; No. 232L, 10/26; No. 232M, 11/16; No. 232N, 11/20.

1972 — Nos. 232P, 233P, Jan.; Nos. 232Q, 233M-233N, Feb.; Nos. 233Q-233R, May; Nos. 232R, 233S, 6/15; Nos. 232S, 233T, 6/26; No. 232T, 8/8; No. 232U, 8/17; No. 232V, 8/30; Nos. 232W, 233U, 12/11; No. 233A, 12/18; No. 233B, 12/28.

1973 — Nos. 233C-233J.

Nos. 233K-233L, 233T-233U each contain one 37x62mm stamp. Nos. 233N, 233P each contain one 32x50mm stamp. No. 233M contains one 45x65mm stamp. Nos. 233Q-233R, 233U each contain one 65x45mm stamp.

Nos. 232Q-232V, 233G, 233J, 233R-233U and possibly 232P, 232W-233F, 233H probably were not available in Chad.

Symbolic Tree — A58

1971, Mar. 21 Engr. *Perf. 13*

236 A58 40fr bl grn, dk red & grn 1.00 .25

Intl. year against racial discrimination.

Paintings of Flowers A58a

Designs: 1fr, The Three Graces (detail), by Rubens. 4fr, Imperial Bouquet, by Van Os. 5fr, Bouquet, by Jan Brueghel.

1971, Apr. 28 Litho. *Perf. 12x12½*

236A A58a Strip of 3, #a-c 5.50 —

For overprint see No. 278A.

Summer Olympic Games — A58b

15fr, Swimming. 20fr, Women's relay races. 25fr, Swimming, medals. 50fr, Running.

Perf. 12x12½, 12½x12

1971, Apr. 28 Litho.

236B	A58b 15fr multi, vert.	1.75	—
236C	A58b 20fr multi, vert.	2.75	—
236D	A58b 25fr multi	3.50	—
	Nos. 236B-236D (3)	8.00	

Embossed

Perf. 13

236E A58b 25fr gold, like No. 236D 17.50

Souvenir Sheet

Litho.

Die Cut Perf 13

236F A58b 50fr multicolored 10.00

Nos. 236D-236F are airmail. No. 236F contains one 62x36mm stamp.

Issued: Nos. 236B-236D, 236F, 4/28; No. 236E, 11/1.

For overprints see Nos. 251A-251D.

No. 236E probably was not available in Chad.

Map of Africa, Radar Antenna A59

Map of Africa and: 40fr, Communications tower. 50fr, Communications satellite.

1971, May 17 Engr. *Perf. 13*

237 A59	5fr ultra, org & dk red	.25	.25
238 A59	40fr pur, emer & brn	.75	.25
239 A59	50fr dk red, blk & brn	1.00	.25
	Nos. 237-239 (3)	2.00	.75

3rd World Telecommunications Day.

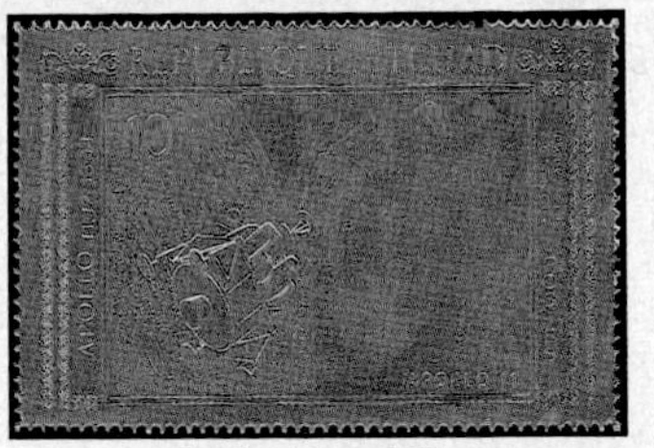

Apollo 11 — A59a

1971, July 5 Embossed *Perf. 13*

239A A59a 10fr gold 22.50

b. Sheet of 1, Imperf. 40.00

No. 239Ab contains one 73x45mm stamp with same size design as No. 239A.

Nos. 239A-239Ab probably were not available in Chad.

No. 225F Overprinted in Gold

1971, July 17 Litho. *Perf. 12x12½*

239C A50b Strip of 3, #a-c 6.00

1972 Winter Olympics, Sapporo.

Nos. 228A-228B, 228D Ovptd. with "MUNICH 72" and Olympic Rings in Gold

Perf. 12½x12, 12x12½

1971, Nov. 1 Litho.

239D A54a Strip of 3, #a-c 10.00
239E A54a Pair, #a-b + label 6.00

Souvenir Sheet

Perf. 13½x13

239F A54a 40fr on #228D 20.00

UNICEF Emblem and Children — A60

1971, Dec. 11 Engr. *Perf. 13*

240 A60 50fr Prus bl, emer & brt pink 2.00 .25

25th anniv. of UNICEF.

Gorane Nangara Dancers A61

Dancers: 15fr, Girls' initiation dance, Yondo. 30fr, Women of M'Boum, vert. 40fr, Men of Sara Kaba, vert.

1971, Dec. 18 Litho. *Perf. 13*

241 A61	10fr blk & multi	.75	.25
242 A61	15fr brn org & multi	1.10	.25
243 A61	30fr bl & multi	1.50	.25
244 A61	40fr yel grn & multi	1.90	.25
	Nos. 241-244 (4)	5.25	1.00

Nos. 205-210 Ovptd. in Gold

1971 Litho. ***Perf. 12½x13, 13x12½***
244A-244F A45 1fr on #205-210 4.50

Nos. 244A-244F probably were not available in Chad.

Presidents Pompidou and Tombalbaye, Map with Paris and Fort Lamy — A62

1972, Jan. 25 Photo. ***Perf. 13***
245 A62 40fr blue & multi 1.75 .25

Visit of Pres. Georges Pompidou of France, Jan. 1972.

Nos. 181-204 Ovptd. in Gold

1972, Feb. 7 Litho. ***Perf. 12½x13***
245A-245X A44 1fr on #181-204 20.00

Nos. 245A-245X probably were not available in Chad.

Nos. 231G-231I Ovptd. in Gold

a

b

1972, Feb. Litho. ***Perf. 12x12½***
246A A57b 50c Pair, #d.-e. 1.50
246B A57b 1fr Pair, #f.-g. 2.25
246C A57b 2fr Pair, #h.-i. 2.75

Nos. 246A-246C probably were not available in Chad.

President Tombalbaye — A63

1972, Apr. 13 Litho. ***Perf. 13***
247 A63 30fr multi .40 .25
247A A63 40fr multi .60 .25
Nos. 247-247A,C112-C113 (4) 3.00 1.15

Downhill Skiing — A64

75fr, Women's figure skating. 150fr, Luge.

1972, Apr. 13 ***Perf. 13½***
248 A64 25fr multi .30 .25
249 A64 75fr multi .75 .25
250 A64 150fr multi 1.50 .45
Nos. 248-250,C114-C115 (5) 6.45 2.00

11th Winter Olympic Games, Sapporo, Japan.

Heart — A65

1972, Apr. 25 Engr. ***Perf. 13***
251 A65 100fr purple, bl & car 1.75 .25

"Your heart is your health," World Health Month.

Nos. 236B-236D, 236F Ovptd. in Gold

1972 Litho. ***Perf. 12x12½, 12½x12***
251A A58b 15fr multicolored 3.25
251B A58b 20fr multicolored 5.00
251C A58b 25fr multicolored 7.75
Nos. 251A-251C (3) 16.00

Souvenir Sheet

Die Cut Perf 13

251D A58b 50fr multicolored 47.50

Nos. 251C-251D are airmail.

Gorrizia Dubiosa — A66

Insects and Spiders: 2fr, Spider (argiope sector). 3fr, Silk spider (nephila senegalense). 4fr, Beetle (oryctes boas). 5fr, Dragonfly (hemistigma albipunctata).

1972, May 6 **Photo.**
252 A66 1fr green & multi 1.40 .25
253 A66 2fr blue & multi 2.25 .25
254 A66 3fr car rose & multi 2.50 .30
255 A66 4fr yellow grn & multi 4.50 .40
256 A66 5fr dp green & multi 5.00 .60
Nos. 252-256 (5) 15.65 1.80

Trains — A66a

10fr, Orient Express. 40fr, Osaka Express. 50fr, St. Germain. 150fr, Blue train. 200fr, Trans-Europe Express.
300fr, Rogers "Madison," 1855.

1972 Litho. ***Perf. 12***
256A A66a 10fr multi 1.00
256B A66a 40fr multi 2.25
256C A66a 50fr multi 2.50
256D A66a 150fr multi 5.00
256E A66a 200fr multi 9.25
Nos. 256A-256E (5) 20.00

Souvenir Sheet

256F A66a 300fr multi 14.00

No. 256F contains one 60x40mm stamp. See note before No. 225A.

Scout Greeting — A67

70fr, Mountain climbing. 80fr, Canoeing.

1972, May 15 **Photo.**
257 A67 30fr multi .75 .25
258 A67 70fr multi 1.40 .25
259 A67 80fr multi 1.75 .25
Nos. 257-259,C118-C119 (5) 8.55 1.65

Scout Jamboree.

Hurdles, Motion and Olympic Emblems A68

Motion and Olympic Emblems and: 130fr, Gymnast on rings. 150fr, Swimming. 300fr, Bicycling.

1972, June 9 Litho. ***Perf. 13½***
260 A68 50fr blk & multi .75 .25
261 A68 130fr blk & multi 1.90 .25
262 A68 150fr blk & multi 2.25 .30
Nos. 260-262 (3) 4.90 .80

Souvenir Sheet

263 A68 300fr blk & multi 5.00 2.00

20th Olympic Games, Munich, Aug. 26-Sept. 10.

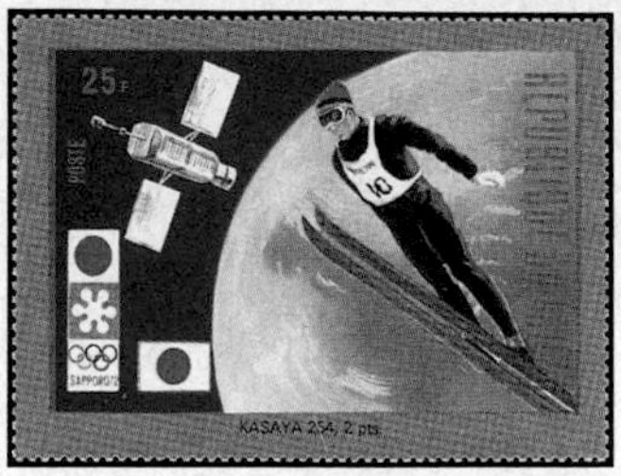

Ski Jump, Kasaya, Japan — A69

Designs: 75fr, Cross-country skiing, P. Tyldum, Sweden. 100fr, Figure-skating, pairs, L. Rodnina and A. Ulanov, USSR. 130fr, Men's speed skating, A. Schenk, Netherlands.

1972, June 15 ***Perf. 14½***
264 A69 25fr gold & multi .40 .25
265 A69 75fr gold & multi 1.00 .25
266 A69 100fr gold & multi 1.50 .40
267 A69 130fr gold & multi 1.90 .50
Nos. 264-267,C130-C131 (6) 11.55 3.15

11th Winter Olympic Games, gold-medal winners. Nos. 264-267 exist se-tenant with label showing earth satellite.

Nos. 227A-227D, 227F Ovptd. in Gold

1972 Litho. ***Perf. 12***
267A A53a 1fr multicolored .95
267B A53a 4fr multicolored 1.20
267C A53a 5fr multicolored 1.90
267D A53a 5fr multicolored 1.90
Nos. 267A-267D (4) 5.95

Souvenir Sheet

Perf. 13½x13

267E A53a 15fr multicolored 9.00

Nos. 267D-267E are airmail.
Nos. 267A-267E probably were not available in Chad.

TV Tower and Weight-lifting — A70

Designs (TV Tower, Munich and): 40fr, Woman sprinter. 60fr, Soccer goalkeeper.

1972, Aug. 15 Litho. ***Perf. 14½***
268 A70 20fr gold & multi .65 .25
269 A70 40fr gold & multi .80 .25
270 A70 60fr gold & multi 1.40 .25
Nos. 268-270,C135-C137 (6) 10.70 2.65

20th Summer Olympic Games, Munich. Nos. 268-270 exist se-tenant with label showing arms of Munich.

Domestic Animals A71

1972, Aug. 29 **Engr.** ***Perf. 13***

271 A71 25fr Dromedary 1.75 .25
272 A71 30fr Horse 2.25 .25
273 A71 40fr Dog 3.25 .30
274 A71 45fr Goat 3.75 .40
Nos. 271-274 (4) 11.00 1.20

For surcharge see No. 293.

Tobacco Cultivation A72

1972, Oct. 24 **Engr.** ***Perf. 13***

275 A72 40fr shown .75 .25
276 A72 50fr Plowing 1.25 .25

Massa Warrior — A73

Design: 20fr, Moundang warrior.

1972, Nov. 15 **Photo.** ***Perf. 14x13***

277 A73 15fr orange & multi .75 .25
278 A73 20fr yellow & multi 1.00 .25

No. 236A Overprinted in Gold

1972 **Litho.** ***Perf. 12x12½***

278A A58a Strip of 3, #a-c 5.50

No. 278A probably was not available in Chad.

King Faisal and Pres. Tombalbaye — A74

1972, Nov. 17 **Litho.** ***Perf. 13***

279 A74 100fr gold & multi 2.50 .75

Visit of King Faisal of Saudi Arabia. See No. C143.

Gen. Gowon and Pres. Tombalbaye — A75

1972, Dec. 7

280 A75 70fr multi 1.00 .25

Visit of Gen. Yakubu Gowon of Nigeria.

Olympic Emblem and 100-meter Sprint, Valeri Borzov, USSR — A76

Designs (Olympic Emblem and): 20fr, Shotput, Komar, Poland. 40fr, Hammer throw, Bondartchuk, USSR. 60fr, Discus, Danek, Czechoslovakia.

1972, Dec. 22 ***Perf. 11***

281 A76 10fr multi .55 .25
282 A76 20fr multi .55 .25
283 A76 40fr multi .70 .25
284 A76 60fr multi 1.10 .30
Nos. 281-284,C148-C149 (6) 10.15 2.40

20th Summer Olympic Games, winners.

Olympic Emblem and Fencing, Woyda, Poland — A77

Olympic Emblem and: 30fr, 3-day equestrian event, Richard Meade, Gt. Britain. 50fr, Two-man sculls, Brietzke-Mager, East Germany.

1972, Dec. 22

285 A77 20fr gold & multi .65 .25
286 A77 30fr gold & multi .65 .25
287 A77 50fr gold & multi 1.00 .25
Nos. 285-287,C151-C152 (5) 10.55 2.50

20th Summer Olympic Games, winners.

1972 Summer Olympics Gold Medalists — A77a

20fr, Teofilo Stevenson, boxing, Cuba. 25fr, Yugoslavia, team handball. 30fr, M. Peters, pentathlon, Great Britain. 40fr, basketball, USSR. No. 287E, W. Ruska, judo, Netherlands. No. 287F, Women's gynmastics, Ludmila Tourischeva, USSR. 75fr, Men's volleyball, Japan. No. 287H, A. Scalzone, shooting, Italy. No. 287I, Soccer, Poland. 130fr, J. Williams, archery, US. No. 287K, A. Nakayama, men's rings, Japan. No. 287L, Field hockey, West Germany. 200fr, Vassily Alexeiev, weight lifting, USSR. 250fr, D. Morelon, cycling, France.

1972, Dec. 22 **Litho.** ***Perf. 11½***

287A A77a 20fr multicolored
287B A77a 25fr multicolored
287C A77a 30fr multicolored
287D A77a 40fr multicolored
287E A77a 50fr multicolored
287F A77a 50fr multicolored
287G A77a 75fr multicolored
287H A77a 100fr multicolored
287I A77a 100fr multicolored
287J A77a 130fr multicolored
287K A77a 150fr multicolored
287L A77a 150fr multicolored
Nos. 287A-287L (12) 19.00

Souvenir Sheets

Perf. 15

287M A77a 200fr multicolored 13.50
287N A77a 250fr multicolored 13.50

Nos. 287G-287N are airmail.

Soviet Flag and Shield — A78

1972, Dec. 30 **Litho.** ***Perf. 12***

288 A78 150fr red & multi 1.90 .40

50th anniversary of the Soviet Union.

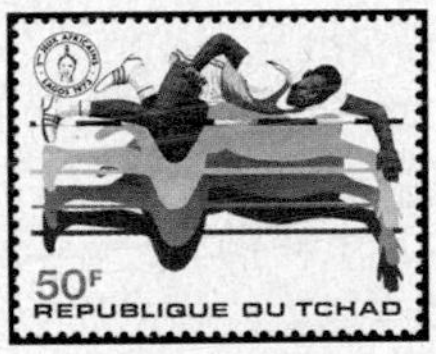

High Jump — A79

Designs (Games Emblem and): 125fr, Running. 200fr, Shot put. 250fr, Discus.

1973, Jan. 17 **Litho.** ***Perf. 13½x13***

289 A79 50fr vio bl & multi .75 .25
290 A79 125fr olive & multi 1.60 .40
291 A79 200fr lilac & multi 3.00 .65
Nos. 289-291 (3) 5.35 1.30

Souvenir Sheet

292 A79 250fr brn & multi 3.75 2.25

2nd African Games, Lagos, Nigeria, 1/7-18.

Paintings with Musical Instruments — A79a

Details from Paintings: 30fr, Madeleine Playing her Lute, by unknown artist. 70fr, A Concert, by Lorenzo Costa. 100fr, Bass and Sheet Music, by Jean-Baptiste Oudry, horiz. 125fr, St. Cecilia and Angel, by Carlo Saraceni. 150fr, Woman Listening to Violinist, by Gabriel Metsu. 300fr, Still Life with Musical Instruments, by Pieter Claesz, horiz.

1973, Apr. **Litho.** ***Perf. 11½***

292A A79a 30fr multicolored
292B A79a 70fr multicolored
292C A79a 100fr multicolored
292D A79a 125fr multicolored
292E A79a 150fr multicolored
Nos. 292A-292E (5) 13.50

Souvenir Sheet

Perf. 15

292F A79a 300fr multicolored 13.50

Nos. 292D-292F are airmail.

No. 271 Srchd. and Ovptd. in Red

1973, Aug. 16 **Engr.** ***Perf. 13***

293 A71 100fr on 25fr multi 2.25 .50

African solidarity in drought emergency.

African Postal Union Issue

Common Design Type

1973, Sept. 17 **Engr.** ***Perf. 13***

294 CD137 100fr multicolored 1.75 .40

Easter A79b

Details from paintings: 40fr, Christ on the Cross, by Lucas Cranach. 60fr, Supper in Emmaus, by Titian, horiz. 120fr, The Crucifixion, by Durer. 150fr, The Tribute, by Titian. 250fr, The Pieta, by Botticelli. 400fr, Entombment of Christ, by Gaspard Isenmann, horiz.

1973 **Litho.** ***Perf. 11½***

294A A79b 40fr multicolored
294B A79b 60fr multicolored
294C A79b 120fr multicolored
294D A79b 150fr multicolored
294E A79b 250fr multicolored
Nos. 294A-294E (5) 13.50

Souvenir Sheet

Perf. 15

294F A79b 400fr multicolored 13.50

Nos. 294A, 294D-294F are airmail.

Animals A79c

1973 **Litho.** ***Perf. 13½***

294G A79c 20fr Sheep
294H A79c 30fr Camels
294J A79c 100fr Cats
294K A79c 130fr Dogs
294L A79c 150fr Horses
Nos. 294G-294L (5) 13.50

Nos. 294J-294L are airmail.
See note before No. 225A.

Christmas — A79d

30fr, The Virgin & Infant Surrounded by Saints, by Lorenzo Lotto. 40fr, Madonna and Child with St. Peter and a Martyred Saint, by Paolo Veronese (not Tintoretto), vert. 55fr, Nativity Scene, by Martin Schongauer, vert. 60fr, Nativity Scene, by Federico Barocci, vert. 250fr, Adoration of the Magi, by Stephan Lochner, vert. 400fr, Epiphany, by Hans Memling.

1973 Litho. *Perf. 11½*

294M	A79d	30fr multicolored	
294N	A79d	40fr multicolored	
294P	A79d	55fr multicolored	
294Q	A79d	60fr multicolored	
294R	A79d	250fr multicolored	
		Nos. 294M-294R (5)	13.50

Souvenir Sheet

Perf. 15

294S	A79d	400fr multicolored	13.50

Nos. 294Q-294S are airmail.
See note before No. 225A.

Insects — A80

No. 295, Dinothrombium Tinctorium. No. 296, Bupreste sternocera. No. 297, Diptere hyperechia. No. 298, Chrysis. No. 299, Longicorn beetle. No. 300, Spider.

1974, Sept. 3 Photo. *Perf. 13*

295	A80	25fr multicolored	1.50	.25
296	A80	30fr multicolored	2.25	.25
297	A80	40fr multicolored	2.75	.25
298	A80	50fr multicolored	3.25	.35
299	A80	100fr multicolored	4.75	.65
300	A80	130fr multicolored	7.50	.95
		Nos. 295-300 (6)	22.00	2.70

Rotary Emblem — A81

1975, Apr. 11 Typo. *Perf. 13*

301	A81	50fr multi	1.00	.25

Rotary International, 70th anniversary.

Craterostigma Plantagineum — A82

Flowers: 10fr, Tapinanthus globiferus. 15fr, Commelina forskalaei, vert. 20fr, Adenium obesum. 25fr, Yellow hibiscus. 30fr, Red hibiscus. 40fr, Kigelia africana.

1975, Sept. 25 Photo. *Perf. 13*

302	A82	5fr org & multi	.40	.25
303	A82	10fr gray bl & multi	.60	.25
304	A82	15fr yel grn & multi	.75	.25
305	A82	20fr lt brn & multi	1.00	.25
306	A82	25fr lil & multi	1.75	.25
307	A82	30fr bis & multi	1.90	.35
308	A82	40fr ultra & multi	3.00	.50
		Nos. 302-308 (7)	9.40	2.10

A. G. Bell, Satellite and Waves — A83

1976, June 10 Litho. *Perf. 12½*

309	A83	100fr bl, brn & ocher	1.40	.40
310	A83	125fr lt grn, brn & ocher	1.90	.60

Centenary of first telephone call by Alexander Graham Bell, Mar. 10, 1876.

Ice Hockey, USSR — A84

90fr, Ski jump, Karl Schnabl, Austria.

1976, June 21 *Perf. 14*

311	A84	60fr multi	.75	.25
312	A84	90fr multi	1.25	.25
		Nos. 311-312,C178-C179 (4)	8.25	2.10

12th Winter Olympic Games, winners. See No. C180.

High Hurdles A85

1976, July 12 Litho. *Perf. 13½*

313	A85	45fr multi	.70	.25
		Nos. 313,C187-C189 (4)	8.70	1.70

21st Summer Olympic Games, Montreal, Canada.
See No. C190.

Mars Landing and Viking Rocket A86

Mars Landing and: 90fr, Viking trajectory, Earth to Mars.

1976, July 23 *Perf. 14*

314	A86	45fr multi	.50	.25
315	A86	90fr multi	1.00	.25
		Nos. 314-315,C191-C193 (5)	7.35	2.10

Viking Mars project.

For overprints see Nos. 379-380.

Robert Koch, Medicine — A87

Design: 90fr, Anatole France, literature.

1976, Dec. 15

316	A87	45fr multi	.75	.25
317	A87	90fr multi	1.50	.25
		Nos. 316-317,C196-C198 (5)	9.75	2.05

Nobel Prize winners.

Map and Flag of Chad, Clasped Hands A88

120fr, Map of Chad, people & occupations.

1976, Sept. 15 Litho. *Perf. 12½x13*

318	A88	30fr multi	.60	.25
319	A88	60fr orange & multi	1.10	.30
320	A88	120fr brown & multi	2.25	.50
		Nos. 318-320 (3)	3.95	1.05

National reconciliation.

Freed Political Prisoners — A89

Designs: 60fr, Parade of cadets.

1976, Sept. 25 Litho. *Perf. 12½*

321	A89	30fr blue & multi	.30	.25
322	A89	60fr black & multi	.75	.25
323	A89	120fr red & multi	1.40	.25
		Nos. 321-323 (3)	2.45	.75

Revolution of Apr. 13, 1975, 1st anniv.

Decorated Calabashes — A90

Designs: Various pyrographed calabashes.

1976, Nov. Litho. *Perf. 12½x13*

324	A90	30fr multi	.40	.25
325	A90	60fr multi	.90	.25
326	A90	120fr multi	1.75	.25
		Nos. 324-326 (3)	3.05	.75

Germany No. C57 and Friedrichshafen, Germany — A91

1977, Mar. 30 *Perf. 14*

327	A91	100fr multi	1.40	.25
		Nos. 327,C206-C209 (5)	11.55	2.10

75th anniversary of the Zeppelin.

Elizabeth II in Coronation Regalia and Clergy — A92

Design: 450fr, Elizabeth II and Prince Philip.

1977, June 15 Litho. *Perf. 14x13½*

328	A92	250fr multi	3.25	.75

Souvenir Sheet

329	A92	450fr multi	5.75	2.50

25th anniv. of the reign of Elizabeth II.
Nos. 328-329 exist imperf. For overprints see Nos. 347-348.

Simon Bolivar A93

Famous Personalities: 175fr, Joseph J. Roberts. No. 332, Queen Wilhelmina of Netherlands. No. 333, Charles de Gaulle. 325fr, King Baudouin and Queen Fabiola of Belgium.

1977, June 15 *Perf. 13½x14*

330	A93	150fr multi	1.50	.30
331	A93	175fr multi	2.25	.45
332	A93	200fr multi	3.00	.65
333	A93	200fr multi	3.00	.75
334	A93	325fr multi	4.00	1.00
		Nos. 330-334 (5)	13.75	3.15

Post and Telecommunications Emblem — A94

Map of Chad and Waves — A95

Society Emblem — A96

1977, Aug. 15		**Litho.**		***Perf. 13***
335 A94	30fr yel & blk		.50	.25
		Perf. 12½		
336 A95	60fr multi		.75	.25
		Perf. 13½x13		
337 A96	120fr multi		1.60	.50
	Nos. 335-337 (3)		2.85	1.00

Telecommunications (30fr); Natl. Telecommunications School, 10th anniv. (60fr); Intl. Telecommunication Soc. of Chad (120fr).

WHO Emblem and Man (Back Pain) — A97

World Rheumatism Year (WHO Emblem and): 60fr, Woman's head (neck pain), horiz. 120fr, Leg (knee pain).

	Perf. 12½x13, 13x12½		
1977, Nov. 10			**Engr.**
338 A97	30fr multi	.50	.25
339 A97	60fr multi	1.00	.25
340 A97	120fr multi	1.40	.40
	Nos. 338-340 (3)	2.90	.90

World Cup Emblems and Saving a Goal — A98

Designs (Argentina '78, World Cup Emblems and): 60fr, Heading the ball. 100fr, Referee whistling a goal. 200fr, World Cup poster. 300fr, Pelé. 500fr, Helmut Schoen and Munich stadium.

1977, Nov. 25		**Litho.**		***Perf. 13½***
341 A98	40fr multi		.50	.25
342 A98	60fr multi		.75	.25
343 A98	100fr multi		1.10	.25
344 A98	200fr multi		2.50	.50
345 A98	300fr multi		3.75	.75
	Nos. 341-345 (5)		8.60	2.00

Souvenir Sheet

346 A98	500fr multi	5.75	3.00

World Cup Soccer Championship, Argentina '78.

For overprints see Nos. 359-364.

Nos. 328-329 Overprinted in Silver

1978, Sept. 13			***Perf. 14x13½***
347 A92	250fr multi	3.00	1.00

Souvenir Sheet

348 A92	450fr multi	5.50	4.50

25th anniv. of coronation of Elizabeth II.

Abraham and Melchisedek, by Rubens — A99

Rubens Paintings: 120fr, Helene Fourment, vert. 200fr, David and the Elders of Israel. 300fr, Anne of Austria, vert. 500fr, Marie de Medicis, vert.

1978, Nov. 23		**Litho.**		***Perf. 13½***
349 A99	60fr multi		.75	.25
350 A99	120fr multi		1.75	.35
351 A99	200fr multi		3.00	.75
352 A99	300fr multi		4.50	1.25
	Nos. 349-352 (4)		10.00	2.60

Souvenir Sheet

353 A99	500fr multi	6.75	3.00

Peter Paul Rubens (1577-1640).

Dürer Portrait A100

Dürer Paintings: 150fr, Jacob Muffel. 250fr, Young Woman. 350fr, Oswolt Krel.

1978, Nov. 23			
354 A100	60fr multi	.60	.25
355 A100	150fr multi	1.75	.50
356 A100	250fr multi	3.00	.80
357 A100	350fr multi	4.50	1.25
	Nos. 354-357 (4)	9.85	2.80

Head, Village and Fly — A101

1978, Nov. 28			***Perf. 13***
358 A101	60f multi	.75	.25

National Health Day.

Nos. 341-346 Overprinted in Silver

a

b

c

d

e

f

1978, Dec. 30		**Litho.**		***Perf. 13½***
359 A98(a)	40fr multi		.50	.25
360 A98(b)	60fr multi		.75	.25
361 A98(c)	100fr multi		1.40	.40
362 A98(d)	200fr multi		2.50	.75
363 A98(e)	300fr multi		3.50	1.25
	Nos. 359-363 (5)		8.65	2.90

Souvenir Sheet

364 A98(f)	500fr multi	5.75	5.00

World Soccer Championship winners.

UPU Emblems, Camel Caravan, Satellites — A102

Design: 150fr, Obus woman and houses, Massa Territory, hibiscus.

1979, June 8		**Litho.**		***Perf. 12x12½***
365 A102	60fr multi		3.00	.25
366 A102	150fr multi		5.00	.40

Philexafrique II, Libreville, Gabon, June 8-17. Nos. 365, 366 each printed in sheets of 10 with 5 labels showing exhibition emblem.

Wildlife Fund Emblem and Gazelle — A103

Protected Animals.

1979, Sept. 15		**Litho.**		***Perf. 14½***
367 A103	40fr shown		2.00	.30
368 A103	50fr Addax		2.25	.50
369 A103	60fr Oryx antelope		2.75	.75
370 A103	100fr Cheetah		4.25	1.40
371 A103	150fr Zebra		5.75	1.90
372 A103	300fr Rhinoceros		11.50	3.00
	Nos. 367-372 (6)		28.50	7.85

Souvenir Sheet

Holy Family, by Dürer — A104

1979, Sept. 1			***Perf. 13½***
373 A104	500fr brown & dull red	6.75	2.50

Boy and Handpainted Doors — A105

IYC Emblem and: 75fr, Oriental girl. 100fr, Caucasian girl, doves. 150fr, African boys. 250fr, Pencil and outlines of child's hands.

1979, Sept. 19		**Litho.**		***Perf. 13½***
374 A105	65fr multi		.60	.25
375 A105	75fr multi		.75	.25
376 A105	100fr multi		1.00	.25
377 A105	150fr multi		1.50	.40
	Nos. 374-377 (4)		3.85	1.15

Souvenir Sheet

378 A105	250fr multi	3.00	1.50

Nos. 314-315 Overprinted

1979, Nov. 26		**Litho.**		***Perf. 13½x14***
379 A86	45fr multi		.60	.25
380 A86	90fr multi		1.00	.30
	Nos. 379-380,C240-C242 (5)		7.45	2.55

Apollo 11 moon landing, 10th anniversary.

Ski Jump, Lake Placid '80 Emblem — A106

Lake Placid '80 Emblem and: 20fr, Slalom, vert. 40fr, Biathlon, vert. 150fr, Women's slalom, vert. 350fr, Cross-country skiing. 500fr, Downhill skiing.

1979, Dec. 18 *Perf. 14½*

381	A106	20fr multi	.30	.25
382	A106	40fr multi	.65	.25
383	A106	60fr multi	.80	.25
384	A106	150fr multi	1.75	.50
385	A106	350fr multi	3.00	1.40
386	A106	500fr multi	4.50	1.90
		Nos. 381-386 (6)	11.00	4.55

13th Winter Olympic Games, Lake Placid, NY, Feb. 12-24, 1980.

Jet over Map of Africa A107

1980, Feb. 20 **Litho.** *Perf. 12½*

387	A107	15fr yellow & multi	.25	.25
388	A107	30fr blue & multi	.40	.25
389	A107	60fr red & multi	.60	.25
		Nos. 387-389 (3)	1.25	.75

ASECNA (Air Safety Board), 20th anniv.

A set of four stamps (50fr, 80fr, 100fr air post, 200fr air post) commemorating cooperation between Chad and Libya were prepared for use in 1981 but not issued. Value, $300.

1982 World Cup Soccer Championships, Spain — A108

1982 **Litho.** *Perf. 13½*

390	A108	30fr Hungary	.30	.25
391	A108	40fr Italy	.40	.25
392	A108	50fr Algeria	.50	.25
393	A108	60fr Argentina	.60	.25
		Nos. 390-393,C258-C259 (6)	5.80	1.75

21st Birthday of Princess Diana A109

1982, July 2 **Litho.** *Perf. 13½*

395	A109	30fr 1961	.30	.25
396	A109	40fr 1965	.40	.25
397	A109	50fr 1967	.50	.25
398	A109	60fr 1975	.60	.25
		Nos. 395-398,C260-C261 (6)	5.80	2.20

For overprints see Nos. 413-419B.

A110

1984 Summer Olympics, Los Angeles — A110a

No. 405A, Runner. No. 405B, Long jumper, vert.

1982, Aug. 2 **Litho.** *Perf. 13½*

399	A110	30fr Gymnast	.30	.25
400	A110	40fr Equestrian	.40	.25
401	A110	50fr Judo	.50	.25
402	A110	60fr High jump	.60	.25
403	A110	80fr Hurdles	1.00	.25
404	A110	300fr Woman gymnast	3.00	.95
		Nos. 399-404 (6)	5.80	2.20

Souvenir Sheet

405	A110	500fr Relay race	5.50	1.50

For surcharge see No. C302.

1982, July 31 **Litho. & Embossed**

405A	A110a	1500fr gold & multi	16.00	

Souvenir Sheet

405B	A110a	1500fr gold & multi	12.00	

No. 405 contains one 56x39mm stamp. Nos. 403-405B airmail.

No. 405A exists in a souvenir sheet of 1. Value $47.50.

Scouting Year — A111

Boy Scouts, 75th Anniv. A111a

Scouts from various countries. No. 412A, Lord Robert Baden-Powell. No. 412B, Scouts at campsite, Baden-Powell, horiz.

1982, July 15

406	A111	30fr West Germany	.30	.25
407	A111	40fr Upper Volta	.40	.25
408	A111	50fr Mali	.50	.25
409	A111	60fr Scotland	.60	.25
410	A111	80fr Kuwait	1.00	.25
411	A111	300fr Chad	3.00	.95
		Nos. 406-411 (6)	5.80	2.20

Souvenir Sheet

412	A111	500fr Chad, diff.	5.50	2.00

Litho. & Embossed

412A	A111a	1500fr gold & multi	17.00	

Souvenir Sheet

412B	A111a	1500fr gold & multi	17.00	

No. 412 contains one 53x35mm stamp. Nos. 410-412B airmail.

No. 412A exists in a souvenir sheet of 1. Value $40.

For overprints see Nos. 466-472B.

Nos. 395-398, C260-C262B Overprinted "21 JUIN 1982 / WILLIAM ARTHUR PHILIP LOUIS/ PRINCE DE GALLES"

1982, Oct. 4 **Litho.** *Perf. 13½*

413	A109	30fr multi	.30	.25
414	A109	40fr multi	.40	.25
415	A109	50fr multi	.50	.25
416	A109	60fr multi	.60	.25
417	A109	80fr multi	1.00	.25
418	A109	300fr multi	3.00	.95
		Nos. 413-418 (6)	5.80	2.20

Souvenir Sheet

419	A109	500fr multi	5.50	1.60

Litho. & Embossed

419A	AP71b	1500fr on #C262A	16.00	

Souvenir Sheet

419B	AP71b	1500fr on #C262B	13.50	

Birth of Prince William of Wales, June 21. Nos. 417-419B airmail.

No. 419A exists in a souvenir sheet of 1. Value $42.50.

A112

1982 World Cup Soccer Championships, Spain — A112a

Various players and flags. No. 426A, Dino Zoff, Italy, holding World Cup trophy. No. 426B, Paolo Rossi, Italy, two players, trophy, horiz.

1982, Nov. 30

420	A112	30fr multi	.30	.25
421	A112	40fr multi	.40	.25
422	A112	50fr multi	.50	.25
423	A112	60fr multi	.60	.25
424	A112	80fr multi	1.00	.25
425	A112	300fr multi	3.00	.95
		Nos. 420-425 (6)	5.80	2.20

Souvenir Sheet

426	A112	500fr multi	5.50	2.00

Litho. & Embossed

426A	A112a	1500fr gold & multi	16.00	

Souvenir Sheet

426B	A112a	1500fr gold & multi	16.00	

No. 426 contains one 56x32mm stamp. Nos. 424-426B airmail.

No. 426A exists in a souvenir sheet of 1. Value $42.50.

For surcharge see No. C306.

A113

Chess Champions — A113a

30fr, Philidor. 40fr, Paul Morphy. 50fr, Howard Staunton. 60fr, Capablanca. 80fr, Boris Spassky. 300fr, Anatoly Karpov.

500fr, Victor Korchnoi. No. 433A, Bobby Fischer. No. 433B, William Steinitz.

1982, Dec. 24

427	A113	30fr multi	1.00	.25
428	A113	40fr multi	1.10	.25
429	A113	50fr multi	1.25	.25
430	A113	60fr multi	1.40	.25
431	A113	80fr multi	2.10	.25
432	A113	300fr multi	3.75	.75
		Nos. 427-432 (6)	10.60	2.00

Souvenir Sheet

433	A113	500fr multi	9.00	3.00

Litho. & Embossed

433A	A113a	1500fr gold & multi	17.50	

Souvenir Sheet

433B	A113a	1500fr gold & multi	12.00	

No. 433 contains one 53x35mm stamp. Nos. 431-433B airmail.

No. 433A exists in a souvenir sheet of 1. Value $50.

For overprints see Nos. 459-465.

2nd UN Conference on Peaceful Uses of Outer Space, Vienna, Aug. 9-21 — A114

A114a

Inventors and Satellites: 30fr, K.E. Tsiolkovsky, Soyuz. 40fr, R.H. Goddard, space telescope design. 50fr, Korolev, ultraviolet telescope. 60fr, von Braun, Columbia space shuttle. 80fr, Esnault Pelterie, Ariana rocket. 300fr, H. Oberth, orbital space station. 500fr, Pres. Kennedy, Apollo 11 badge, lunar rover. No. 440A, Sir Bernard Lovell, Viking I & II. No. 440B, Sir Isaac Newton, satellite TDF 1.

1983, Feb. 1 **Litho.** *Perf. 13½*

434	A114	30fr multi	.30	.25
435	A114	40fr multi	.40	.25
436	A114	50fr multi	.50	.25
437	A114	60fr multi	.60	.25
438	A114	80fr multi	1.00	.25
439	A114	300fr multi	3.00	.95
		Nos. 434-439 (6)	5.80	2.20

Souvenir Sheet

440	A114	500fr multi	5.50	2.50

Litho. & Embossed

440A	A114a	1500fr gold & multi	16.00	

Souvenir Sheet

440B	A114a	1500fr gold & multi	12.00	

No. 440 contains one 42x50mm stamp.
Nos. 438-440B airmail.
No. 440A exists in a souvenir sheet of 1. Value $50.

Bobsledding — A115

Woman Figure Skater A115a

40fr, Speed skating. 50fr, Cross-country skiing. 60fr, Hockey. 80fr, Ski jumping. 300fr, Downhill skiing.
500fr, Figure skating. No. 447B, Slalom skier, horiz.

1983, Apr. 25 Litho. *Perf. 13½*

441	A115	30fr shown	.30	.25
442	A115	40fr multi	.40	.25
443	A115	50fr multi	.50	.25
444	A115	60fr multi	.60	.25
445	A115	80fr multi	1.00	.30
446	A115	300fr multi	3.00	1.10
		Nos. 441-446 (6)	5.80	2.40

Souvenir Sheet

447	A115	500fr multi	5.50	1.60

Litho. & Embossed

447A	A115a	1500fr gold & multi	16.00	

Souvenir Sheet

447B	A115a	1500fr gold & multi	12.00	

14th Winter Olympic Games, Sarajevo, Yugoslavia, Feb. 8-19, 1984.
Nos. 445-447B airmail.
No. 447A exists in a souvenir sheet of 1. Value $45.
For surcharge see No. C298.

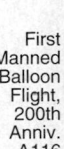

First Manned Balloon Flight, 200th Anniv. A116

Designs: 25fr, Hot air balloon, Montgolfier Brothers. 45fr, Captive balloon, Pilatre De Rozier. 50fr, First parachute descent, Jacques Garnerin. 60fr, Chelsea balloon, J.P. Blanchard.

1983, May 30 Litho. *Perf. 13½*

448	A116	25fr multi	.30	.25
449	A116	45fr multi	.40	.25
450	A116	50fr multi	.50	.25
451	A116	60fr multi	.60	.25
		Nos. 448-451,C268-C269 (6)	5.80	1.65

Automobiles — A116a

Automobiles and their builders: 25fr, 1927 Mercedes Type S, Gottlieb Daimler and Karl Benz. 45fr, 1913 Torpedo Martini Type GC 32-2, 6L, Friedrich Martini. 50fr, 1926 Chrysler "70," Walter P. Chrysler. 60fr, 1929 Alfa Romeo 6C 1750 Grand Sport, Nicola Romeo. 80fr, 1934 Phantom II Continental, Stewart Rolls and Henry Royce. 250fr, 1948 Talbot Lago, Lord Shrewsbury and Talbot.

1983, July 15 Litho. *Perf. 13½*

451A	A116a	25fr multicolored		
451B	A116a	45fr multicolored		
451C	A116a	50fr multicolored		
451D	A116a	60fr multicolored		
451E	A116a	80fr multicolored		
451F	A116a	250fr multicolored		
		Nos. 451A-451F (6)	6.75	1.60

Nos. 451E-451F are airmail.

1984 Summer Olympics, Los Angeles A117

A117a

1983, Nov. 15 Litho. *Perf. 13½*

452	A117	25fr Kayak	.30	.25
453	A117	45fr Long jump	.60	.25
454	A117	50fr Boxing	.70	.25
455	A117	60fr Discus	.75	.25
456	A117	80fr Running	1.00	.25
457	A117	350fr Equestrian	3.50	.75
		Nos. 452-457 (6)	6.85	2.00

Souvenir Sheet

458	A117	500fr Gymnastics	5.50	2.50

Litho. & Embossed

458A	A117a	1500fr Hurdles	16.00	

Souvenir Sheet

458B	A117a	1500fr Equestrian, vert.	12.00	

Nos. 456-458B are airmail.
No. 458A exists in a souvenir sheet of 1. Value $47.50.

Pres. Hissein Habre — A117b

Designs: Nos. 458D, 458H, Sources of food. Nos. 458E, 458I, Dove of peace, different tribal groups, country map.

1983, Dec. 26 Litho. *Perf. 13½*

458C	A117b	50fr multicolored	.60	.25
458D	A117b	50fr multicolored	.60	.25
458E	A117b	50fr multicolored	.60	.25
458F	A117b	60fr multicolored	.70	.25
458G	A117b	80fr multicolored	.90	.25
458H	A117b	80fr multicolored	.90	.25
458I	A117b	80fr multicolored	.90	.25
458J	A117b	100fr multicolored	1.10	.35

See Nos. C276-C279.

Nos. 427-433 Overprinted: "60e ANNIVERSAIRE FEDERATION / MONDIALE D'ECHECS 1924-1984"

1983, Dec. 27 Litho. *Perf. 13½*

459	A113	30fr multi	.90	.25
460	A113	40fr multi	1.10	.25
461	A113	50fr multi	1.40	.25
462	A113	60fr multi	1.75	.25
463	A113	80fr multi	2.25	.30
464	A113	300fr multi	4.50	.75
		Nos. 459-464 (6)	11.90	2.05

Souvenir Sheet

465	A113	500fr multi	4.50	2.50

World Chess Fedn., 60th anniv.

Nos. 406-412B Ovptd. with Emblem for the 15th World Scout Jamboree, Alberta, Canada, 1983

1983, Dec. 27 Litho. *Perf. 13½*

466	A111	30fr multi	.30	.25
467	A111	40fr multi	.40	.25
468	A111	50fr multi	.50	.25
469	A111	60fr multi	.60	.25
470	A111	80fr multi	.70	.25
471	A111	300fr multi	3.00	.50
		Nos. 466-471 (6)	5.50	1.75

Souvenir Sheet

472	A111	500fr multi	6.00	2.50

Litho. & Embossed

472A	A111a	1500fr on #412A	16.00	

Souvenir Sheet

472B	A111a	1500fr on #412B	12.00	

Locomotive "Lady," 1879 — A118

200fr, Sailboat, Lake Chad. 300fr, Graf Zeppelin. 350fr, Renault desert transport, 1930. 400fr, Bloch 120 monoplane. 500fr, Air Africa DC-8.
600fr, Intelsat V satellite.

1984, Mar. 15

473	A118	50fr shown	.60	.25
474	A118	200fr multicolored	2.40	.60
475	A118	300fr multicolored	3.25	.90
476	A118	350fr multicolored	4.00	1.10
477	A118	400fr multicolored	4.25	1.25
478	A118	500fr multicolored	5.50	1.50
		Nos. 473-478 (6)	20.00	5.60

Souvenir Sheet

479	A118	600fr multicolored	5.75	5.00

Nos. 477-479 airmail. For surcharge see No. 579.

Liberation, 2nd Anniv. — A119

1984, June 6 *Perf. 12½*

480	A119	50fr multi	.60	.25

Pres. Hissein Habre — A120

1984, June 18 *Perf. 12½x13*

481	A120	125fr multi	1.50	.40

Anniversaries and Events — A121

Designs: 50fr, Pres. Habre, civil war martyrs. 200fr, Paul Harris, Rotary Intl. headquarters, Illinois. 300fr, Alfred Nobel, will establishing fund for Prizes. 350fr, Raphael, detail from Virgin with Child and St. John the Baptist. 400fr, Rembrandt, detail from The Holy Family. 500fr, J.W. Goethe, scene from Faust. 600fr, Rubens, detail from Helene Fourment and Her Two Children.

1984, Jan. 16 Litho. *Perf. 13½*

482	A121	50fr multi	.50	.25
483	A121	200fr multi	1.90	.30
484	A121	300fr multi	3.00	.45
485	A121	350fr multi	3.75	.55
486	A121	400fr multi	4.60	.60
487	A121	500fr multi	5.75	.70
		Nos. 482-487 (6)	19.40	2.85

Souvenir Sheet

488	A121	600fr multi	6.75	2.50

Nos. 486-488 are airmail.

Homage to Our Martyred Dead — A122

1984, Feb. 22 Litho. *Perf. 13½*

500	A122	50fr multi	.50	.25
501	A122	80fr multi	.75	.25
502	A122	120fr multi	1.10	.25
503	A122	200fr multi	1.90	.40
504	A122	250fr multi	2.50	.50
		Nos. 500-504 (5)	6.75	1.65

Nos. 503-504 airmail. For surcharge see Nos. 228A-228B, 228D Ovptd. with "MUNICH 72" and Olympic Rings in GoldC303.

World Communications Year — A123

1984, Feb. 29 Litho. *Perf. 13½*

505	A123	50fr sil & multi	.50	.25
506	A123	60fr sil & multi	.60	.25
507	A123	70fr sil & multi	.75	.25
508	A123	125fr sil & multi	1.10	.25
509	A123	250fr sil & multi	2.50	.50
		Nos. 505-509 (5)	5.45	1.50

Nos. 508-509 airmail. For surcharge see Nos. 228A-228B, 228D Ovptd. with "MUNICH 72" and Olympic Rings in GoldC304.

Anniversaries and Events — A123a

50fr, Durer, detail from Madonna of the Rosary. 200fr, Henri Dunant, Red Cross founder, Battle of Solferino. 300fr, Early telephone, Goonhilly Downs Satellite Station, Britain. 350fr, J.F. Kennedy, Neil Armstrong's 1st step on Moon, 1969. 400fr, Europe-Africa Satellite infrared photograph. 500fr, Prince Charles & Lady Diana. 600fr, Wedding photograph of Prince Charles & Lady Diana.

1984

510	A123a	50fr multi	.50	.25
511	A123a	200fr multi	2.10	.30
512	A123a	300fr multi	3.00	.45
513	A123a	350fr multi	3.50	.50
514	A123a	400fr multi	3.75	.55
515	A123a	500fr multi	5.00	.80
		Nos. 510-515 (6)	17.85	2.85

Souvenir Sheet

516	A121	600fr multicolored	5.25	

A souvenir sheet of 6 containing Nos. 510-515 exists. Nos. 514-516 are airmail.
For surcharge see No. 578.

Development of Communications — A123b

Ships and locomotives: 90fr, Indiaman, East India Co. 100fr, Nord 701, 1885. 125fr, Vera Cruz. 150fr, Columbia, 1888. 200fr, Carlisle Castle. 250fr, Rete Mediterranea, 1900. 300fr, Britannia. 350fr, Mav 114.

1984, Aug. 1 Litho. *Perf. 12½*

517	A123b	90fr multi	1.10	.25
518	A123b	100fr multi	1.10	.25
519	A123b	125fr multi	1.75	.25
520	A123b	150fr multi	1.75	.25
521	A123b	200fr multi	2.50	.25
522	A123b	250fr multi	3.00	.30
523	A123b	300fr multi	3.25	.35
524	A123b	350fr multi	3.75	.50
		Nos. 517-524 (8)	18.20	2.40

Christmas — A124

1984, Dec. 28 Litho. *Perf. 13*

525	A124	50fr lt bl & org brn	.50	.25
526	A124	60fr ver & org brn	.60	.25
527	A124	80fr emer & org brn	.75	.25
528	A124	85fr rose lil & org brn	.75	.25
529	A124	100fr org yel & org brn	1.00	.30
530	A124	135fr dp bl vio & org brn	1.25	.40
		Nos. 525-530 (6)	4.85	1.70

European Music Year — A125

Instruments.

1985, Apr. 30 Litho. *Perf. 12x12½*

531	A125	20fr Guitar	.25	.25
532	A125	25fr Harp	.30	.25
533	A125	30fr Xylophone	.40	.25
534	A125	50fr Shoulder drum	.50	.25
535	A125	70fr like #534	.70	.25
536	A125	80fr like #532	.75	.30
537	A125	100fr like #531	1.00	.40
538	A125	250fr like #533	2.50	.80
		Nos. 531-538 (8)	6.40	2.75

Mushrooms A126

25fr, Chlorophyllum molybdites. 30fr, Tulostoma volvulatum. 50fr, Lentinus tuber-regium. 80fr, Podaxis pistillaris.

1985, May 15 Litho. *Perf. 12½*

539	A126	25fr multi	.60	.25
540	A126	30fr multi	.70	.25
541	A126	50fr multi	1.00	.25
542	A126	70fr like #541	1.40	.25
543	A126	80fr multi	1.60	.25
544	A126	100fr like #539	2.50	.35
		Nos. 539-544 (6)	7.80	1.60

Anniversaries and Events — A127

25fr, Abraham Lincoln. 45fr, Henri Dunant, Geneva birthplace and red cross. 50fr, Gottlieb Daimler, 1887 Motor Carriage. 60fr, Louis Bleriot, Bleriot XI monoplane, 1909. 80fr, Paul Harris, Chicago site of Rotary Intl. founding. 350fr, Auguste Piccard, bathyscaphe Trieste, 1953.
600fr, Anatoly Karpov, 1981 world chess champion. 1500fr, Paul Harris on Medal.

1985, May 25 Litho. *Perf. 13½*

545	A127	25fr multi	.30	.25
546	A127	45fr multi	.60	.25
547	A127	50fr multi	.75	.25
548	A127	60fr multi	1.00	.25
549	A127	80fr multi	1.10	.35
550	A127	350fr multi	4.00	1.25
		Nos. 545-550 (6)	7.75	2.60

Souvenir Sheets

551	A127	600fr multi	6.75	5.00

Litho. & Embossed

551A	A127	1500fr multi	14.50	

No. 551A contains one 130x90mm stamp. Nos. 548-551A are airmail.
Souvenir sheets of 1 exist for Nos. 545-551.

Intl. Youth Year — A128

70fr, Development levels. 200fr, Globe, horiz.

1985, May 30 Litho. *Perf. 13*

552	A128	70fr multi	.70	.25
553	A128	200fr multi	1.75	.50

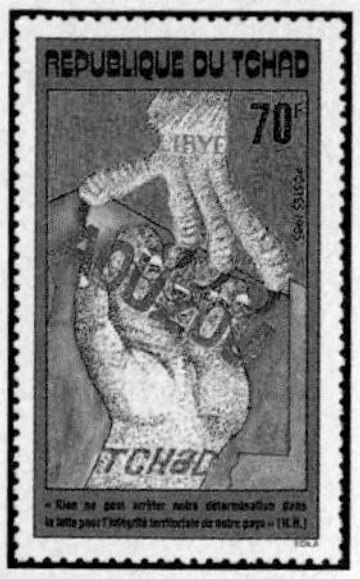

A129

3rd Anniv. of the Republic A130

Perf. 13, 12½x13

1985, June 7 Litho.

554	A129	70fr Hand, claw	.70	.25
555	A129	70fr Hands, map	.70	.25
556	A130	70fr Pres. Hissein Habre	.70	.25
557	A129	110fr like #554	1.10	.40
558	A129	110fr like #555	1.25	.40
559	A130	110fr like #556	1.25	.40
		Nos. 554-559 (6)	5.70	1.95

Audubon Birth Bicent. — A131

1985, July 20 Engr. *Perf. 13*

560	A131	70fr Stork	1.10	.30
561	A131	110fr Ostrich	1.60	.40
562	A131	150fr Marabou	2.25	.65
563	A131	200fr Snake eagle	3.00	.90
		Nos. 560-563 (4)	7.95	2.25

Souvenir Sheet

564	A131	500fr like 200fr	6.75	5.00

Mammals A132

1985, Aug. 25

565	A132	50fr Waterbuck	.75	.25
566	A132	70fr Kudus, horiz.	1.00	.40
567	A132	250fr Shaggy mouflon	3.25	1.25
		Nos. 565-567 (3)	5.00	1.90

Souvenir Sheet

568	A132	500fr White rhinoceros	5.75	5.00

UN, 40th Anniv. — A133

1985, Nov. 24

569	A133	200fr brt bl, red & brn	2.25	.75

Chad Admission to UN, 25th Anniv. — A134

1985, Nov. 24

570	A134	300fr red, brt bl & yel	3.25	1.00

President's Visit to the Nation's Interior A135

1986, June 7 Litho. *Perf. 12½x13*

571	A135	100fr multi	1.10	.25
572	A135	170fr multi	2.25	.35
573	A135	200fr multi	2.50	.45
		Nos. 571-573 (3)	5.85	1.05

Lions Club Intl. — A135a

100fr, Sick child. 170fr, Three children, horiz. 200fr, Eye exam, horiz.

1987 Litho. *Perf. 14*

573A	A135a	30fr Like #573C	50.00	—
573C	A135a	100fr multi		
573E	A135a	170fr multi		
573F	A135a	200fr multi		

There are two additional stamps in this set. The editors would like to examine them.

World Wildlife Fund — A136

Various mouflons, *Ammotragus lervia.*

1988, Nov. 10 Litho. *Perf. 13*

574	A136	25fr shown	2.50	.50
575	A136	45fr Adult, young	3.25	.75
576	A136	70fr Two adults, diff.	4.25	1.25
577	A136	100fr Adults, young	6.00	1.75
		Nos. 574-577 (4)	16.00	4.25

Nos. 475, 512 and 570 Surcharged

Methods and Perfs. As Before

1989

578	A123a	170fr on 300fr #512	
578A	A134	230fr on 300fr #570	
579	A118	240fr on 300fr #475	

Liberation — A137

1989 *Perf. 11½x12*

580	A137	20fr multi	.50	.30
581	A137	25fr multi	.60	.30
582	A137	40fr multi	1.00	.50
583	A137	100fr multi	1.50	.75
584	A137	170fr multi	2.50	1.25
		Nos. 580-584 (5)	6.10	3.10

World Post Day — A137a

1989, Oct. 9 Photo. *Perf. 12*

Granite Paper

584A	A137a	100fr grn bl & multi	
584B	A137a	120fr red & multi	
584C	A137a	170fr purple & multi	
584D	A137a	250fr olive & multi	
		Nos. 584A-584D (4)	160.00

Visit of Pope John Paul II — A138

Cathedral in Chad and: 20fr, 100fr, Pope holding crosier. 80fr, 170fr, Pope, diff.

1989, Dec. 20 Litho. *Perf. 13*

585	A138	20fr multicolored	.35	.25
586	A138	80fr multicolored	1.10	.40
587	A138	100fr multicolored	1.40	.50
588	A138	170fr multicolored	2.25	1.10
		Nos. 585-588 (4)	5.10	2.25

Traditional Hair Styles — A139

1989, Oct. 9 Photo. *Perf. 12*

Granite Paper

589	A139	100fr apple grn & multi	
590	A139	120fr purple & multi	
591	A139	170fr pink & multi	
592	A139	250fr org yel & multi	
		Nos. 589-592 (4)	160.00

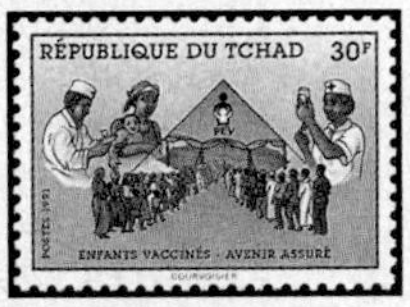

Vaccinations A140

1991, Dec. 1 Photo. *Perf. 11½*

Granite Paper

593	A140	30fr brown & multi	.30	.25
594	A140	100fr green & multi	1.00	.45
595	A140	170fr vio & multi	1.60	.75
596	A140	180fr blue & multi	1.75	.80
597	A140	200fr red & multi	1.90	.90
		Nos. 593-597 (5)	6.55	3.15

Liberty and Democracy Day — A141

1991, Dec. 1 **Litho.**

598	A141	10fr green & multi	.25	.25
599	A141	20fr lilac & multi	.25	.25
600	A141	40fr yellow & multi	.40	.25
601	A141	70fr blue & multi	.65	.30
602	A141	130fr tan & multi	1.25	.75
603	A141	200fr pink & multi	1.90	1.00
		Nos. 598-603 (6)	4.70	2.80

Fight Against Insect Pests — A141a

1992, Sept. 1 Photo. *Perf. 12*

603A	A141a	25fr multi	30.00	15.00
603B	A141a	45fr multi	30.00	15.00
603C	A141a	100fr multi	30.00	15.00
603D	A141a	150fr multi	30.00	15.00
603E	A141a	170fr multi	30.00	15.00
		Nos. 603A-603E (5)	150.00	75.00

A142

1992, Nov. 15 Litho. *Perf. 11½*

604	A142	20fr bright yel & multi	.25	.25
605	A142	45fr golden yel & multi	.40	.25
606	A142	85fr pink & multi	.75	.35
607	A142	170fr blue & multi	1.50	.70
608	A142	300fr gray & multi	3.00	1.40
		Nos. 604-608 (5)	5.90	2.95

Doctors Without Borders, 20th anniv.

Campaign Against Illiteracy A143

1992, Nov. 30

609	A143	25fr yel grn & multi	.25	.25
610	A143	40fr golden yel & multi	.40	.25
611	A143	70fr pink & multi	.60	.30
612	A143	100fr lilac & multi	.75	.40
613	A143	180fr blue & multi	1.60	.60
614	A143	200fr gray & multi	1.75	.70
		Nos. 609-614 (6)	5.35	2.50

Intl. Conference on Nutrition, Rome — A144

1992, Dec. 15

615	A144	10fr yellow & multi	.25	.25
616	A144	60fr pink & multi	1.00	.25
617	A144	120fr yel grn & multi	1.75	.40
618	A144	500fr blue & multi	4.50	1.60
		Nos. 615-618 (4)	7.50	2.50

Palace of the People A145

1993, Apr. 15 Litho. *Perf. 11½*

619	A145	80fr multi	40.00	5.00
620	A145	100fr multi	40.00	5.00
621	A145	130fr multi	40.00	5.00
622	A145	400fr multi	40.00	5.00
		Nos. 619-622 (4)	160.00	20.00

Natl. Conference — A146

1993, Dec. 1 Litho. *Perf. 11¾*

Granite paper

623	A146	55fr multi	.80	.35
624	A146	70fr multi	1.00	.45
625	A146	110fr multi	1.40	.80
626	A146	125fr multi	1.75	.90
		Nos. 623-626 (4)	4.95	2.50

OAU, 30th Anniv. — A147

1993, Dec. 4 Litho. *Perf. 11½x11¾*

627	A147	15fr multi	.25	.25
628	A147	30fr multi	.30	.25
629	A147	110fr multi	1.10	.80
630	A147	190fr multi	2.00	1.50
		Nos. 627-630 (4)	3.65	2.80

Victor Schoelcher (1804-93), Abolitionist A148

Perf. 11¾x11½

1993, Dec. 26 **Litho.**

631	A148	55fr multi	.40	.40
632	A148	105fr multi	1.10	.75
633	A148	125fr multi	1.40	1.10
634	A148	300fr multi	2.75	2.00

Tourism A149

Perf. 11¾x11½

1993, Dec. 27 **Litho.**

635	A149	15fr multi	40.00	20.00
636	A149	95fr multi	40.00	20.00
637	A149	100fr multi	40.00	20.00
638	A149	190fr multi	—	—

Bank of Central African States A150

1994 Litho. *Perf. 11½*

639	A150	20fr multicolored	.25	.25
640	A150	30fr pink & multi	.40	.25
641	A150	105fr blue & multi	.90	.30
642	A150	190fr lilac & multi	1.60	.90
		Nos. 639-642 (4)	3.15	1.70

Huts for Storing Grain A151

Designs: 75fr, Arabe, kim. 150fr, Sara, moundang. 300fr, Boulala, kotoko. 450fr, Ouaddai, kenga.

1995, Oct. 15 Litho. *Perf. 14*

643	A151	75fr multicolored	.50	.25
644	A151	150fr multicolored	.90	.30
645	A151	300fr multicolored	1.50	.75
646	A151	450fr multicolored	2.50	1.00
		Nos. 643-646 (4)	5.40	2.30

Souvenir Sheet

Chinese Post, Cent. — A151a

1996 Litho. *Perf. 13¼*

646A	A151a	270fr multi	2.25	2.00

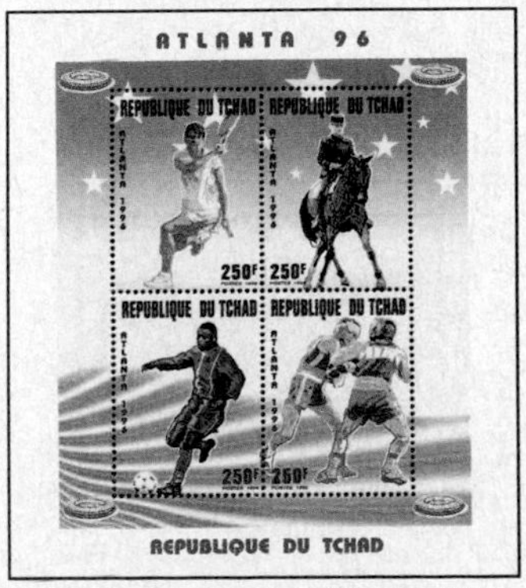

1996 Olympic Games, Atlanta A151b

No. 646B: e, Tennis. f, Equestrian. g, Soccer. h, Boxing.
No. 646C: i, Judo. j, Running. k, Cycling. l, Table tennis.
1500fr, Hurdler.

1996 Litho. Perf. 13¼

646B A151b 250fr Sheet of 4, #e-h 4.00 4.00
646C A151b 300fr Sheet of 4, #i-l 5.00 5.00

Souvenir Sheet

646D A151b 1500fr multi 6.25 6.25

No. 646D contains one 39x57mm stamp.

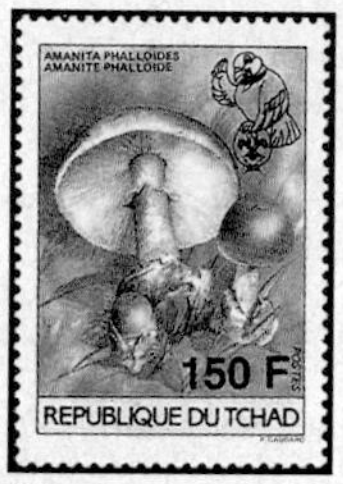

1995 Boy Scout Jamboree, Holland — A152

Mushrooms: 150fr, Amanita phalloides. 170fr, Phallus impudicus. 200fr, Lyloperdon perlatum. 350fr, Hydne commun. 450fr, Agaricus bisporus. 800fr, Cortinarius orellanus.
1500fr, Pleurotus ostreatus.

1996, Apr. 15 Litho. Perf. 13½

647-652 A152 Set of 6 9.25 4.75
a. Souvenir sheet, #647-652 9.25 4.75

Souvenir Sheet

653 A152 1500fr multicolored 6.50 5.00

Nos. 647-652 exist in souvenir sheets of 1.

Butterflies, Mushrooms and Minerals A152a

No. 653A: g, Papilio zalmoxis. h, Anacridium melanorhodon. i, Otidea leporina. j, Haliaetus vocifer.
No. 653B: k, Amanita phalloides, Papilio dardanus. l, Papilio antimachus, Cortinarius praestans. m, Phallus impudicus, Chrysidia croesus. n, Papilio dardanus, Lycoperon perlatum.
No. 653C: o, Charaxes brutus. p, Epiphora albida. q, Euchloron megaera. r, Salamis duprei.
No. 653D: s, Disthene. t, Olivine. u, Sphene. v, Hemimorphite.
No. 653E, Argema mittrei. No. 653F, Zoisite.

1996 Litho. Perf. 13¼

653A A152a 350fr Sheet of 4, #g-j 7.00 6.00
653B A152a 400fr Sheet of 4, #k-n 8.00 7.00
653C A152a 650fr Sheet of 4, #o-r 12.00 10.00
653D A152a 800fr Sheet of 4, #s-v 15.00 12.00
Nos. 653A-653D (4) 42.00 35.00

Souvenir Sheets

653E A152a 2000fr multi 8.50 8.50
653F A152a 2000fr multi 8.50 8.50

A number has been reserved for an additional sheet in this set. Nos. 653E-653F each contain one 42x36mm stamp.

Greenpeace, 25th Anniv. — A153

No. 654: a, 170fr, Green coral, school of small fish. b, 200fr, Yellow & orange coral. c, 300fr, Red orange coral. d, 350fr, White coral.
1500fr, Diver, coral, vert.

1996, July 16

654 A153 Block of 4, #a.-d. 5.00 5.00

Souvenir Sheet

655 A153 1500fr multicolored 9.50 9.50

Entertainers A154

Designs: No. 656, 170fr, Bob Marley. No. 657, 170fr, Marilyn Monroe. No. 658, 200fr, Elvis Presley. No. 659, 200fr, Monroe. No. 660, 300fr, Monroe. No. 661, 350fr, Stevie Wonder. No. 662, 350fr, Presley. No. 663, 400fr, John Lennon. No. 664, 500fr, Presley. No. 665, 600fr, Lennon. No. 666, 700fr, Madonna. No. 667, 800fr, Presley. No. 668, 1000fr, Monroe.
No. 669, 1500fr, Tina Turner. No. 670, 1500fr, Clint Eastwood. No. 670A, 1500fr, Presley.

1996, May 15

656-668 A154 Set of 13 29.00 22.50
665a Sheet of 2, #663, 665 4.50 2.25
667a Sheet of 4, #658, 662, 664, 667 8.00 3.75
668a Sheet of 4, #657, 659-660, 668 7.00 3.50

Souvenir Sheets

669-670A A154 Set of 3 20.00 10.00

Nos. 656-668 exist in souvenir sheets of 1. No. 670A contains one 51x90mm stamp.
See No. 674.

A155

No. 671: a, Pres. Bill Clinton. b, Elvis Presley in white jumpsuit.
No. 672: a, Pres. Richard Nixon. b, Presley in white shirt, black jacket.

1996, Dec. 17 Litho. Perf. 13½

671 A155 1500fr Sheet of 2, #a.-b. 16.00 16.00
672 A155 1500fr Sheet of 2, #a.-b. 16.00 16.00

Giant Panda — A156

No. 673: a, Holding branch, left claw out. b, Holding branch. c, Lying on back. d, Holding branch in mouth.

1996, Oct. 15

673 A156 100fr Sheet of 4, #a.-d. 2.00 2.00

Entertainers Type of 1996

1996 Litho. Perf. 13½

674 A154 500fr Jerry Garcia 2.50 1.75

No. 674 exists in a souvenir sheet of 1.

1998 World Cup Soccer Championships, France — A157

1998 World Cup Soccer Championships, France — A157a

Unidentified players, stadium: No. 675, 150fr, The Beaujoire, Nantes. No. 676, 200fr, Lescure Park, Bordeaux. No. 676A, 300fr, Municipal Stadium, Toulouse. No. 676B, 600fr, Felix Bollaert, Lens.
No. 677A: b, Player in white shirt. c, Player in red shirt.

1996, Dec. 17

675-676B A157 Set of 4 6.00 4.50

Souvenir Sheet

677 A157a 1500fr George Weah 7.50 5.00
677A A157a 3000fr Sheet of 2, #b-c 13.00 11.00

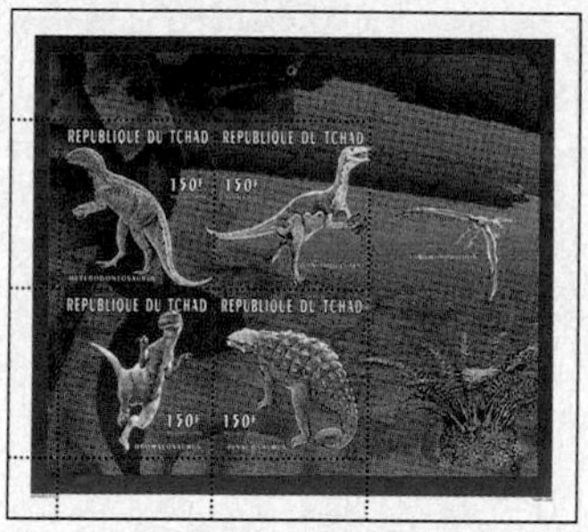

Dinosaurs, Dog & Cats, Butterflies & Insects — A158

No. 678 — Dinosaurs: a, Heterodontosaurus. b, Ornitholestes. c, Dromaeosaurus. d, Pinacosaurus.
No. 679 — Dinosaurs: a, Corythosaurus. b, Ankylosaurides. c, Ornithomimus. d, Styracosaurus.
No. 680 — Dogs & cats: a, Artois. b, Bengal. c, Persian. d, Vendeen.
No. 681 — Butterflies & insects: a, Euphaedra zaddachi. b, Pseudacraea dolomena. c, Cicindela barbara. d, Goliath.

1996, Oct. 15

678 A158 150fr Sheet of 4, #a.-d. 3.00 3.00
679 A158 200fr Sheet of 4, #a.-d. 3.75 3.75
680 A158 250fr Sheet of 4, #a.-d. 5.00 5.00
681 A158 300fr Sheet of 4, #a.-d. 6.00 4.00

Ovptd. in Gold in Sheet Margin

1997 Litho. Perf. 13½

678e Sheet of 4 3.00 3.00
679e Sheet of 4 3.75 3.75
680e Sheet of 4 5.00 5.00

Gold overprints on Nos. 678e-680e contain two-line inscription in Chinese and Hong Kong '97 exhibition emblem.

UNICEF, UN, 50th Anniv., Lions Intl. — A159

No. 682 — UNICEF, 50th anniv.: a, 150fr, Girl, boy turtles. b, 400fr, Feeding small child.
No. 683 — UN, 50th anniv.: a, 170fr, Huygens probe, starving child. b, 500fr, Man with plant, Marsnet probe.
No. 684 — Lions Intl.: a, 200fr, Man carrying sack of grain. b, 800fr, Men examining plants, native man stirring kettle over fire.

1996, Oct. 15 Litho. Perf. 13½

682 A159 Pair, #a.-b. + label 3.00 2.00
683 A159 Pair, #a.-b. + label 3.50 2.50
684 A159 Pair, #a.-b. + label 5.50 3.50

Nos. 682-684 exist as souvenir sheets with colored margins. Value, each $13.

1996 European Soccer Championships — A160

No. 685: a, Oliver Bierhoff holding trophy. b, Two players. c, Two players, referee. d, Queen Elizabeth II, player holding trophy.

1996, Dec. 17

685 A160 350fr Sheet of 4, #a.-d. 6.75 5.00

Michael Schumacher, 1995 World Driving Champion — A161

No. 686: a, Ferrari Formula-1 race car. b, Schumacher close-up. c, Schumacher in Benetton uniform. d, Benetton Formula-1 race car.
No. 687, Schumacher with arms raised. No. 687A, Winner of 1996 Italian Grand Prix.

1997, June 16

686 A161 700fr Sheet of 4, #a.-d. 13.50 10.00

Souvenir Sheets

687 A161 2000fr multicolored 10.00 7.50
687A A161 2000fr multicolored 10.00 7.50

No. 687 contains one 36x51mm stamp.

1998 Winter Olympic Games, Nagano, Japan A162

Designs: 100fr, Women's figure skating. 170fr, Hockey. 350fr, Downhill skiing. 750fr, Speed skating.
1500fr, Slalom skiing.

1996, Dec. 17

688-691 A162 Set of 4 6.75 5.00

Souvenir Sheet

692 A162 1500fr multicolored 7.50 5.00

World Wildlife Fund — A163

No. 693 — Struthio camelus rothschildi: a, Female. b. Male. c, Chicks. d, Male, female up close.

1996, Dec. 17 Litho. *Perf. 13½*

693 A163 200fr Block of 4, #a.-d. 17.00 17.00

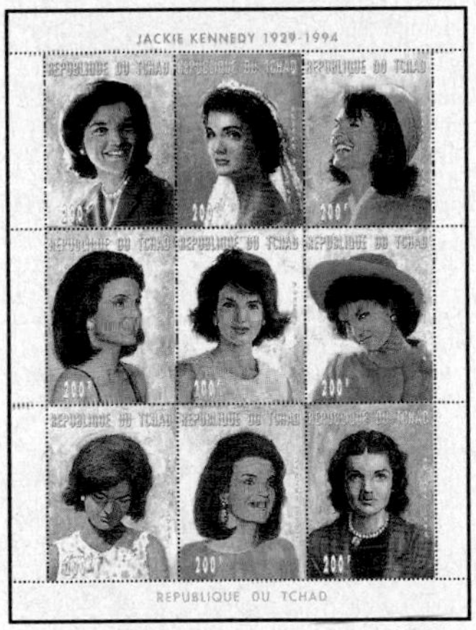

Jacqueline Kennedy Onassis (1929-94) — A164

Various portraits.

1996, Dec. 17

694 A164 200fr Sheet of 9, #a.-i. 9.50 7.00

Intl. Red Cross, Rotary Intl., Scouts — A165

No. 695 — Intl. Red Cross: a, 100fr, Woman, airplane. b, 350fr, Man, train.

No. 696 — Rotary Intl.: a, 300fr, Boy, water coming through pipes. b, 700fr, Native boy and man, volunteers.

No. 697 — Scouts: a, 250fr, Boy scout holding book, hyena. b, 1000fr, Garry Kasparov, chess player, scout.

1996, Oct. 15 Litho. *Perf. 13½*

695 A165 Pair, #a.-b. + label 2.50 1.75
696 A165 Pair, #a.-b. + label 5.50 3.50
697 A165 Pair, #a.-b. + label 6.50 4.50

Nos. 695-697 exist in souvenir sheets with colored margins. Value, each $13.

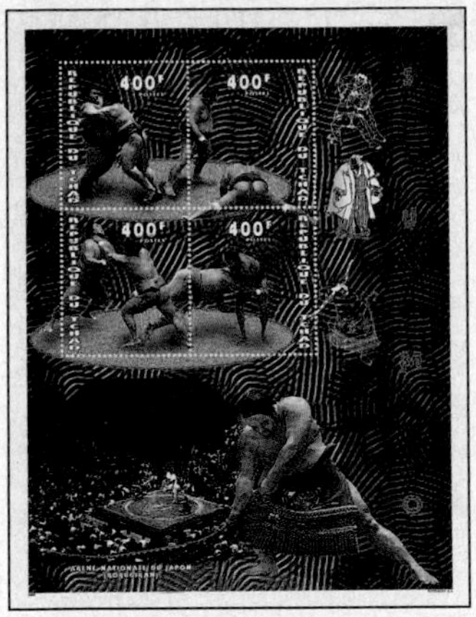

Japanese Sumo Wrestling — A166

Various wrestlers in ring.

1996, Dec. 17 Litho. *Perf. 13½*

698 A166 400fr Sheet of 4, #a.-d. 8.00 6.00

China '96 — A168

Various paintings showing mountains and trees.

1996

704 A168 100fr Sheet of 9, #a.-i. 4.50 3.50

Marilyn Monroe — A168a

Various portraits.

1997 Litho. *Perf. 13¼*

704J A168a 500fr Sheet of 9, #k-s 16.00 16.00

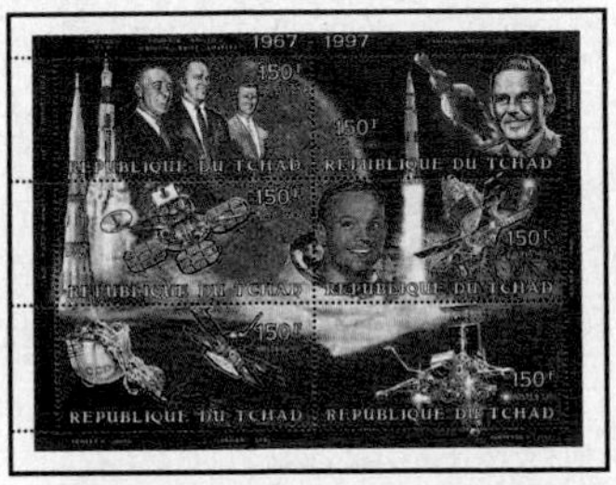

History of Space Travel — A169

No. 705: a, Lunar N1 rocket, USSR, Saturn 1, US, Apollo 1 crew, Grissom, White, Chaffee. b, Launch of Soyuz, USSR, V.M. Komarov. c, US Lunar Orbiter 4. d, Neil Armstrong, US, Molniya 1, USSR. e, Venera 4, USSR, Mariner, US. f, Surveyor 3, US.

No. 706: a, Ariane 1, Landsat 4, US. b, Spacelab & space shuttle, NASA, ESA, Thomas Mattingly, US. c, L-Sat Telecom Satelite, ESA. d, J.L. Chretien, Soviet Salyut 7, US Space Shuttle. e, Venera 13, USSR. f, Intelsat 6, US.

No. 707: a, John Glenn, Atlas rocket, Mercury capsule. b, Mariner 2, US. c, Scott Carpenter, US. d, Telstar, Tiros 6, US. e, Vostok capsule, USSR, Bell X15 airplane, US. f, Mars 1, USSR.

No. 708: a, "Sounds of Earth" record, Voyager 1 & 2, US. b, Himawari 1, MU-3H, Japan, Atlas Centaur, US. c, Soviet Salyut 6, Proton rocket, Galileo (1564-1642). d, Meteosat, SMS Geos, Atlas EF, US. e, Boeing 747, space shuttle, US. f, ISEE, US.

No. 709: a, Saturn 5, US, OAO 3 Copernicus. b, Pioneer 10, US. c, Luna 20, USSR, John F. Kennedy. d, Landsat 1, US. e, Apollo 16, US astronauts Mattingly, Duke, Young. f, Lunar Rover, US Apollo 17 astronauts Schmitt, Evans, Cernan.

No. 710: a, RD 107 rocket, USSR, Vanguard rocket, US, Vanguard I, US. b, Aerobee, Goddard rockets, Robert H. Goddard. c, Laika, 1st dog in space, USSR. d, Theodor von Karman, V2A, Gird 09 rockets, USSR. e, Sputnik 1, USSR, Korolev airplane. f, Sanger, Bell X1 airplanes, US, Eugene Sanger.

No. 711, US Astronauts, Neil Armstrong, Michael Collins, Edwin E. Aldrin, Jr., USSR animals in space, Laika, Felix the cat.

Illustration reduced.

1997 Litho. *Perf. 13½*

705 A169 150fr Sheet of 6, #a.-f. 4.00 4.00
706 A169 250fr Sheet of 6, #a.-f. 6.00 6.00
707 A169 300fr Sheet of 6, #a.-f. 7.50 7.50
708 A169 450fr Sheet of 6, #a.-f. 9.00 9.00
709 A169 475fr Sheet of 6, #a.-f. 11.50 11.00
710 A169 800fr Sheet of 6, #a.-f. 18.00 18.00

Souvenir Sheet

711 A169 2000fr multicolored 8.25 8.25

No. 711 contains one 80x85mm stamp.

Elvis Presley — A169a

Various portraits.

1997 Litho. *Perf. 13¼*

711A A169a 300fr Sheet of 9, #b-j 12.00 12.00

Jacqueline Kennedy Onassis (1929-94) — A170

Various portraits.

1997, July 15 Litho. *Perf. 13½*

712 A170 150fr Sheet of 9, #a.-i. 5.75 2.75

Pres. John F. Kennedy — A170a

No. 712J: k, Standing, looking right. l, With family. m, Looking left. n, With statue of George Washington. o, Seated, with Great Seal of the United States. p, Facing forward, with stars and arrows. q, In chair. r, With statue of Lincoln. s, Behind podium, with flag and Capitol.

1997 Litho. *Perf. 13¼*

712J A170a 250fr Sheet of 9, #k-s 9.00 9.00

Diana, Princess of Wales (1961-97) — A171

Various portraits.

1997

713 A171 300fr Sheet of 9, #a.-i. 11.00 11.00

714 A171 450fr Sheet of 9, #a.-i. 16.00 16.00

Souvenir Sheet

715 A171 2000fr multicolored 8.25 7.50

No. 715 contains one 42x60mm stamp.

Deng Xiaoping and Bruce Lee — A171a

No. 715A — Deng and: c, Child. d, Chinese flag. e, Dancer. f, Boats in water. g, Farmers. h, Cityscape.

No. 715B — Lee and movie titles: i, Opera-tion Dragon. j, La Fureur du Dragon. k, La Fureur de Vaincre. l, La Flute Silencieuse. m, Le Jeu de la Mort. n, Le Retour du Dragon.

1000fr, Deng and stars.

1997 **Litho.** ***Perf. 13¼***

715A A171a 75fr Sheet of 6, #c-h 1.75 1.75
715B A171a 125fr Sheet of 6, #i-n 3.00 3.00

Souvenir Sheet

715O A171a 1000fr multi — —

No. 715O contains one 36x41mm stamp.

Mahatma Gandhi (1869-1948), Mother Teresa (1910-97) — A172

No. 716: a, Gandhi seated, dendrobium speciosum. b, Mother Teresa with Indian peo-ple. c, Bulbophyllum umbellatum, Gandhi with 2 women.

1998, Feb. 5 **Litho.** ***Perf. 13½***

716 A172 150fr Sheet of 3, #a.-c. 1.90 1.90

Famous Men — A173

Designs: 300fr, Nelson Mandela, Pres. of South Africa, diamond. 450fr, Albert Einstein (1879-1955), physicist, satellite. 800fr, Robert Barany (1876-1936), physician, Felix the space cat.

2000fr, Alfred Nobel (1833-96).

1998, Feb. 5

717-719 A173 Set of 3 7.00 5.50

Souvenir Sheet

720 A173 2000fr multicolored 8.25 7.50

Nos. 717-719 exist in souvenir sheets of 1. No. 720 contains one 41x60mm stamp.

See Nos. 729-734.

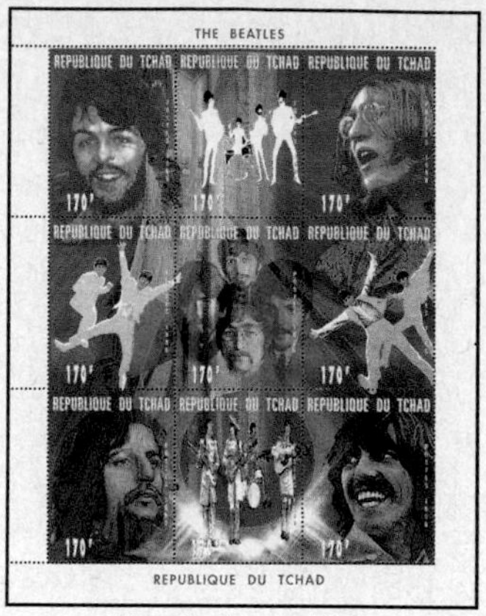

The Beatles — A174

No. 721: a-i, Various portraits of John Lennon.

No. 722 — The Beatles: a, Paul McCartney. b, Silhouettes. c, John Lennon. d, George Har-rison, Lennon. e, Four faces. f, McCartney, Ringo Starr. g, Starr. h, Four in Sgt. Pepper's costumes. i, Harrison.

No. 723 — Life of John Lennon: a, Yoko Ono. b, With McCartney. c, In profile. d, Wear-ing suit. e, Wearing white shirt, tie. f, With mother. g, Wearing dark glasses. h, With guru. i, In white suit.

No. 724: Various portraits of Lennon, McCartney, Harrison, Starr.

No. 724J, Beatles in suits and ties. No. 724K, Beatles in Sgt. Pepper uniforms.

1996 **Litho.** ***Perf. 13½***

721 A174 100fr Sheet of 9, #a-f 3.50 3.50
722 A174 170fr Sheet of 9, #a.-i. 7.00 7.00
723 A174 200fr Sheet of 9, #a.-i. 6.75 6.75
724 A174 300fr Sheet of 9, #a.-i. 14.00 14.00

Souvenir Sheets

724J A174 1500fr multi 7.50 6.00
724K A174 1500fr multi 7.50 6.00

Antelopes — A175

Designs: a, 170fr, Damaliscus dorcas. b, 350fr, Oryx gazella. c, 500fr, Addax nasomaculatus. d, 600fr, Aepyceros melampus.

1996, Dec. 17

725 A175 Block of 4, #a.-d. 7.00 7.00

Nos. 725a-725d exist in souvenir sheets of 1.

No. 725 Overprinted in Gold

1996

726 A175 Block of 4, #a.-d. 7.00 7.00

Nos. 726a-726d exist in souvenir sheets of 1.

Marilyn Monroe (1926-1962) — A176

Various portraits.

1996

727 A176 250fr Sheet of 9, #a.-i. 10.50 9.00

Souvenir Sheet

728 A176 1500fr multicolored 6.00 6.00

No. 728 contains one 51x90mm stamp.

Famous People Type of 1997

Nobel Prize winners: 100fr, Mother Teresa (1910-97), humanitarian. 150fr, Martin Luther King, Jr. (1929-68), civil rights leader. 475fr, Otto Hahn (1879-1968), chemist, nuclear pow-ered ship. 500fr, Ivan Pavlov (1849-1936), physiologist, Russian space dog, Laika. 600fr, Johannes van der Waals (1837-1923), physi-cist. 1000fr, Sir Edward Appleton (1892-1965), physicist, Concorde jet.

1998, Feb. 5

729-734 A173 Set of 6 14.50 10.00

Nos. 729-734 exist in souvenir sheets of 1.

Scouting A177

Wild animals: No. 735: a, Hyena. b, Mongoose.

No. 736: a, Wildcat. b, Addax nasomaculatus.

No. 737: a, Fennec. b, Hyena, diff.

1998, Feb. 6

735 A177 150fr Pair, #a.-b. 2.00 2.00
736 A177 550fr Pair, #a.-b. 5.75 5.75
737 A177 600fr Pair, #a.-b. 7.00 7.00

Cats and Dogs — A178

No. 738: a, Maine coon. b. Singapore.

No. 739: a, Siberian husky. b, Malamute.

No. 740: a, Spitz. b, Eskimo.

No. 741: a, Siamese. b, Common cat.

No. 742, 1500fr, Abyssinian. No. 743, 1500fr, Samoyed.

1998, Feb. 6

738 A178 300fr Pair, #a.-b. 2.75 2.75
739 A178 450fr Pair, #a.-b. 3.00 3.00
740 A178 475fr Pair, #a.-b. 3.75 3.75
741 A178 500fr Pair, #a.-b. 4.00 4.00

Souvenir Sheets

742-743 A178 Set of 2 12.50 12.50

Nos. 742-743 each contain one 42x60mm stamp.

Airplanes, Ships, & Trains — A179

No. 743A — Early aircraft: b, Latecoere 28, France. c, D'Equeuilly, France. d, Liore et Oli-vier Leo-213, France. e, Louis Bleriot mono-plane. f, Graf Zeppelin LZ 127. g, Caproni CA 133, Italy.

No. 744 — Airplanes: a, Sikorsky VS-44A. b, Short S25/V Sandringham 4. c, Bristol 167 Brabazon 1. d, Savoia S13 Bis. e, Curtiss CR-3. f, Curtiss R3C-2.

No. 745 — Ships: a, Normandy, 1935. b, Persia, 1856. c, Queen Elizabeth II, 1968. d, Christian Radich, 1937. e, Amerigo Vespucci, 1933. f, Tovarich, 1933.

No. 745G — Classic sports cars: h, 1963-65 Porsche 356 SC. i, 1961-66 AC Cobra. j, 1960-61 Maserati Tipo 63 Birdcage. k, 1962-63 Austin Healey 3000 MK11. l, 1959-62 Fer-rari 250 GT Berlinetta SWB. m, 1958 Aston Martin DB4.

No. 746 — Trains: a, BRB cog steam train. b, AE 4/7 10969. c, Crocodile of Saint-Gothard BE 6/8 111. d, RAE 2/4 1001. e, Steam train, Spain. f, RE 6/6 11612 express.

No. 746G — High speed trains: h, ETR 470, Italy. i, TGV Metro, France. j, Hikari, Japan. k, TGV 001 turbotrain, France. l, Eurostar 3203/3204 Metro train, France, Germany, Great Britain. m, 990 ICE train, Germany.

1500fr, Steam locomotive, C5/6 2978. 2000fr, TGV, France.

1998, Feb. 4

743A A179 150fr Sheet of 6, #b.-g. 4.00 4.00
744 A179 200fr Sheet of 6, #a.-f. 5.00 5.00
745 A179 250fr Sheet of 6, #a.-f. 6.25 6.25
745G A179 300fr Sheet of 6, #h.-m. 7.50 7.50
746 A179 350fr Sheet of 6, #a.-f. 9.00 9.00
746G A179 400fr Sheet of 6, #h.-m. 10.00 11.00

Souvenir Sheets

747 A179 1500fr multicolored 6.25 6.25
748 A179 2000fr multicolored 8.25 8.25

Nos. 747-748 contain one 36x42mm stamp.

Swiss rail service, 150th anniv. (Nos. 746-747).

Issued: No. 745G, 2/6.

See No. 758.

Diana, Princess of Wales (1961-97) A180

Various portraits.

2000fr, Portrait wearing high lace collar.

1997 **Litho.** ***Perf. 13½***

749 A180 250fr Sheet of 9, #a.-i. 9.00 9.00

Souvenir Sheet

749J A180 2000fr multicolored 8.50 7.50

Literacy Campaign A181

1997, June 16

750	A181 150fr olive & multi	.80	.80
751	A181 300fr buff & multi	1.75	1.60
752	A181 475fr salmon & multi	2.50	2.50
	Nos. 750-752 (3)	5.05	4.90

Kellou Dahalob — A182

1998, Apr. 8

753	A182 50fr pink & multi	.30	.30
754	A182 100fr blue & multi	.40	.40
755	A182 150fr green & multi	.65	.65
756	A182 300fr lilac & multi	1.10	1.10
757	A182 400fr yellow & multi	1.50	1.50
	Nos. 753-757 (5)	3.95	3.95

Transportation Type of 1997

No. 758 — Modern aircraft: a, SAT, France, Germany. b, BAC/Aerospatiale Concorde. c, X001, Japan. d, Bell X-2, US. e, Douglas X-3, US. f, Aerospatiale STS 2000, France.

1998, Feb. 4 Litho. *Perf. 13½*

758	A179 475fr Sheet of 6, #a.-f.	12.00	12.00

Women — A183

Women: 50fr, 100fr, 150fr, Using grindstone. 300fr, 450fr, 500fr, Kneeling.

1997, June 16

759	A183 50fr vio & multi, vert.	.30	.30
760	A183 100fr grn & multi, vert.	.40	.40
761	A183 150fr yel & multi, vert.	.55	.55
762	A183 300fr vio & multi	1.10	1.10
763	A183 450fr grn & multi	1.75	1.75
764	A183 500fr yel & multi	1.90	1.90
	Nos. 759-764 (6)	6.00	6.00

Protect the Ozone Layer — A184

1998 Litho. *Perf. 13½*

765	A184 150fr blue & multi	.60	.60
766	A184 300fr green & multi	1.25	1.25
767	A184 475fr pink & multi	1.90	1.60
768	A184 500fr blue green & multi	1.90	1.90
	Nos. 765-768 (4)	5.65	5.35

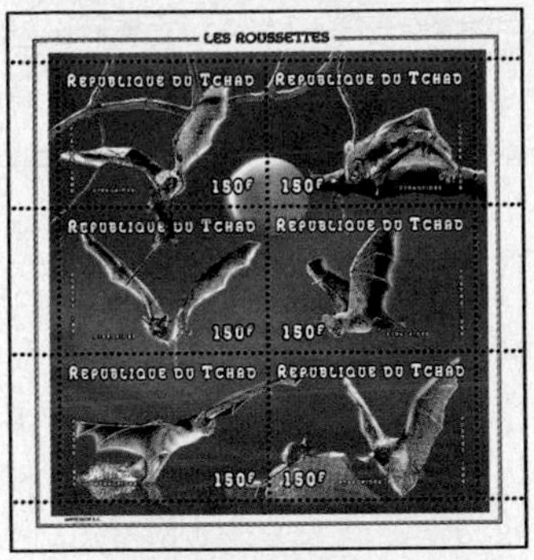

Fauna — A185

No. 769 — Bats: a, Holding mouse, tree branch. b, Drinking. c, One in flight, bottom of mouse. d, One flying left. e, One flying right. f, Mouse on rock, bat landing.

No. 769G — Horses: h, Gray Arabian. i, Brown Arabian. j, Przewalski's. k, Australian brumbies. l, Camargue. m, Zebras.

No. 769N — Sea mammals: o-t, Various portraits of Trichechus senegalensis.

No. 770 — Gorillas & chimpanzees: a, Chimpanzee scratching head. b, Gorilla walking on all fours. c, Gorilla seated. d, Chimpanzee swinging from branch. e, Chimpanzee using stick. f, Two gorillas.

No. 771 — Raptors: a, Terathopius ecaudatus. b, Buteo buteo. c, Sagittarius serpentarius. d, Polemaetus belligosus. e, Circaetus allicus. f, Aquila chrysaetos.

No. 771G — Reptiles: h, Crocodylus niloticus. i, Drendroaspis angusticeps. j, Bitis nasicornis. k, Chamaeleo johnstoni. l, Naja nigricolis. m, Meroles cuneirostris.

No. 771N — Mushrooms: o, Coprinus atramentarius. p, Romaria botrytis. q, Aleuria aurantia. r, Amanita muscaria. s, Macrolepiota rhacodes. t, Helvella crispa.

No. 771U — Mushrooms: v, Morchella vulgaris. w, Tuber aestiuum. x, Tuber melanosporum. y, Mitrophora hybrida. z, Morchella conica. aa, Choeromyces meandriformis.

No. 772 — Butterflies: a, Charaxes jasius. b, Hamanumidia daedalus. c, Charaxes bohemani. d, Hallimoides rumia, denomination LL. e, Hallimoides rumia, denomination LR. f, Pseudacraea bolsduuali.

1500fr, Ooelogyne ovalis, palla ussheri. 2000fr, Baleniceps, Neurophyllum clauatum.

1998, June 20

769	A185	150fr Sheet of 6, #a.-f.	5.00	5.00
769G	A185	250fr Sheet of 6, #h.-m.	5.50	5.50
769N	A185	300fr Sheet of 6, #o.-t.	6.50	6.50
770	A185	300fr Sheet of 6, #a.-f.	8.00	8.00
771	A185	350fr Sheet of 6, #a.-f.	10.00	10.00
771G	A185	450fr Sheet of 6, #h.-m.	12.00	12.00
771N	A185	475fr Sheet of 6, #o.-t.	10.50	10.50
771U	A185	500fr Sheet of 6, #v.-aa.	12.00	12.00
772	A185	600fr Sheet of 6, #a.-f.	16.00	8.00

Souvenir Sheets

773	A185	1500fr multicolored	6.50	6.50
773A	A185	2000fr multicolored	7.50	7.50

Nos. 773-773A contain one 51x42mm stamp.

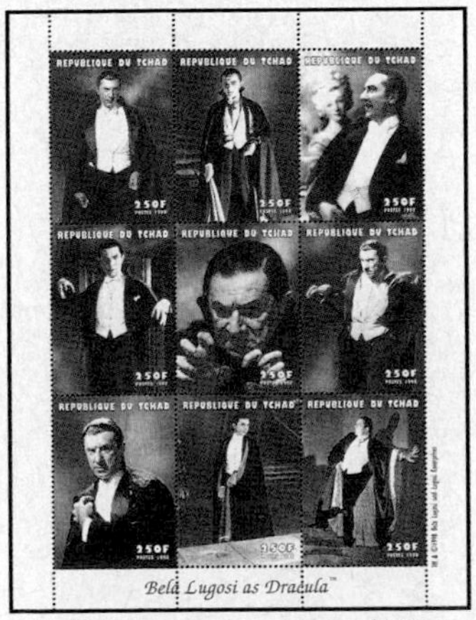

Bela Lugosi as Dracula — A185a

Lugosi in various poses.

1998, Dec. 11 Litho. *Perf. 13½*

773B	A185a	250fr Sheet of 9, #d.-l.	8.50	8.50

Souvenir Sheet

773C	A185a	1500fr multi, horiz.	5.75	5.75

Diana, Princess of Wales — A186

No. 774 — Various portraits: a, 200fr. b, 250fr. c, 300fr. d, 400fr. e, 475fr. f, 500fr. g, 800fr. h, 900fr. i, 1000fr.

1999, Jan. 10 Litho. *Perf. 12½*

774	A186	Sheet of 9, #a.-i.	18.00	18.00

Birds — A187

Designs: 75fr, Ibis ibis. 150fr, Ephippiorhynchus senegalensis. 200fr, Phoenicopterus ruber. 300fr, Leptoptilus crumeniferus. 400fr, Scopus umbretta. 475fr, Platalea alba.

1000fr, Balaeniceps rex.

1999, Jan. 15 Litho. *Perf. 12¾*

775-780	A187	Set of 6	5.75	5.75

Souvenir Sheet

781	A187	1000fr multicolored	3.50	3.50

No. 781 contains one 32x40mm stamp.

Fire Trucks A188

Designs: 50fr, 1840 model. 150fr, 1920 Fiat. 200fr, 1915 Mack. 300fr, 1930 Renault. 400fr, Pegaso M 1090. 500fr, 1960 Jet Fire Power.

700fr, 1720 King George III Fire Company.

1998, Dec. 30

782-787	A188	Set of 6	5.75	5.75

Souvenir Sheet

788	A188	700fr multicolored	2.50	2.50

No. 788 contains one 35x28mm stamp.

Minerals — A188a

No. 788A: a, Opal. b, Cyanite. c, Chalcopyrite. d, Apatite. e, Celestite. f, Scorodite.

No. 788B: a, Agate. b, Wulfenite. c, Barytine. d, Tanzanite. e, Amazonite. f, Malachite.

1998 Litho. *Perf. 13½*

788A	A188a	475fr Sheet of 6, #a.-f.	11.00	11.00
788B	A188a	500f Sheet of 6, #a.-f.	11.50	11.50

Dinosaurs — A188b

No. 788C: a, Dilophosaurus. b, Argentinosaurus. c, Kritosaurus. d, Scutellosaurus. e, Ornithomimosaurus. f, Bactrosaurus.

No. 788D: a, Coelophysis. b, Kannemeyeria. c, Apatosaurus. d, Scipionyx. e, Lystrosaurus. f, Kentrosaurus.

No. 788E, Giganotosaurus, vert.

1998, Nov. 12 Litho. *Perf. 13¼*

Sheets of 6

788C	A188b	400fr #a.-f.	9.25	9.25
788D	A188b	450fr #a.-f.	10.50	10.50

Souvenir Sheet

788E	A188b	2000fr multi	7.50	7.50

US Pres. Ronald Reagan — A189

No. 789: a, Family portrait as young boy. b, In front of family home. c, In football uniform, as radio announcer. d, Riding horse. e, Up close portrait. f, With Nancy, greeting Pope John Paul II. g, Making speech at podium. h, Being sworn in as president. I, At desk in Oval Office.

2000fr, At desk, White House.

1999, Feb. 2 Litho. *Perf. 13½*

789 A189 450fr Sheet of 9, #a.-i. 16.00 18.00

Souvenir Sheet

790 A189 2000fr multicolored 8.00 8.00

American Railroads — A190

No. 791 — Train, railroad pioneer: a, "Alco" Santa Fe, 1945, Cyrus Holliday. b, Rio Grande, 1961, J.F. Stevens. c, Amtrak, 1976, Thomas Dehone Judah. d, 250 Gobernador, 1884, Mark Hopkins. e, Meeting of Central Pacific and Union Pacific at Promontory Point, 1869, Leland Stanford, Thomas Durant. f, Great Northern W1, 1947, Jim Hill. g, Union Pacific Railroad, 1951, G.M. Dodge. h, Pennsylvania GG1, 1934, S.M. Vauclain. i, 151 Santa Fe U.P, 1917, S. Barstow Strong.

1998, Dec. 11

791 A190 200fr Sheet of 9, #a.-i. 7.00 7.00

Fossils and Cave Paintings — A191

No. 792: a, Harlania enigmatica. b, Spirophyton. c, Fossils, dunes of Djourab. d, Chain of people, oxen, Bardai. e, Man of Gonoa. f, Oxen, Kozen, Borkou.

1998, Dec. 11

792 A191 150fr Sheet of 6, #a.-f. 4.00 4.00

Frank Sinatra — A191a

No. 792G — Sinatra with: h, Blonde actress. i, Green jacket. j, Ava Gardner. k, Striped suit. l, Actor. m, Gun. n, Dark green hat. o, Oscar statuette. p, Military cap.

1998, Dec. 30 Litho. *Perf. 13½*

792G A191a 300fr Sheet of 9, #h.-p. 11.00 11.00

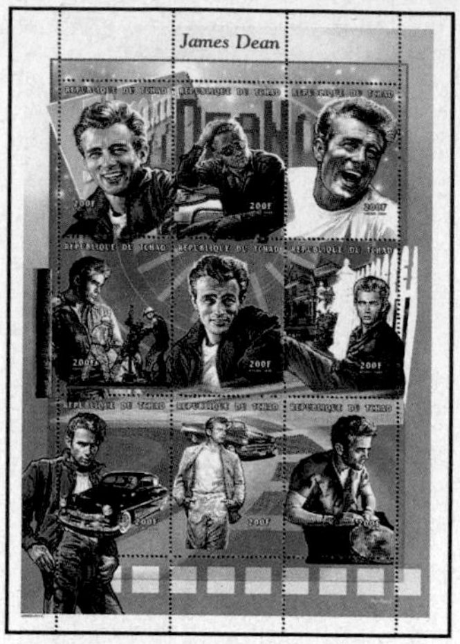

James Dean (1931-55), Actor — A192

Various portraits.

1999, Feb. 2

793 A192 200fr Sheet of 9, #a.-i. 7.00 7.00

Pope John Paul II — A193

Various portraits.

1999, Feb. 2

794 A193 300fr Sheet of 9, #a.-i. 10.50 10.50

Souvenir Sheet

795 A193 1500fr multicolored 6.00 5.50

No. 795 contains one 58x51mm stamp.

John Glenn's Return to Space — A194

Various portraits.

1999, Feb. 11 Litho. *Perf. 13½*

796 A194 500fr Sheet of 9, #a.-i. 17.50 17.50

Souvenir Sheet

797 A194 2000fr multicolored 8.00 8.00

No. 797 contains one 57x51mm stamp.

Kofi Annan, UN Secretary-General — A195

Various portraits.

1998, Dec. 11

798 A195 150fr Sheet of 9, #a.-i. 5.25 5.25

Chess — A196

No. 798J: k, Paul Morphy. l, Chess board, Morphy-Anderssen, 1858. m, Adolf Anderssen. n, Emanuel Lasker. o, Chess board, Lasker-Capablanca, 1914. p, José Raul Capablanca. q, David Bronstein. r, Chess board, Bronstein-Botvinnik, 1951. s, Mikhail Botvinnik.

a, Bobby Fischer. b, Chess board, Fischer-Tal, 1961. c, Mikhail Tal. d, Boris Spassky. e, Chess board, Spassky-Petrosian, 1969. f, Tigran Petrosian. g, Garry Kasparov. h, Chess board, Kasparov-Karpov, 1960. i, Anatoly Karpov.

No. 800, Margrave Othon IV of Brandenburg.

No. 800A, King Louis XVI playing chess, horiz.

1999, Feb. 20

798J A196 375fr Sheet of 9, #k.-s. 13.00 13.00

799 A196 500fr Sheet of 9, #a.-i. 17.50 17.50

Souvenir Sheets

800 A196 2000fr multi 7.75 7.75

800A A196 2000fr multi 7.75 7.75

Dated 1998. No. 800 contains one 58x51mm stamp. No. 800A contains one 58x51mm stamp. Sheets of 3 stamps, containing Nos. 798Jk-798Jm, 798Jn-798Jp, 798Jq-798Js, 799a-799c, 799d-799f, or 799g-799i exist.

Souvenir Sheets

France, 1998 World Cup Champions — A197

No. 801: a, Bikente Lizarazu. b, Christian Karembeu. c, Frank Leboeuf. d, Emmanuel Petit.

No. 802: a, Fabien Barthez. b, Marcel Desailly. c, Didier Deschamps. d, Christophe Dugarry.

No. 803: Youri Djorkaeff. b, Aime Jacquet. c, Lilian Thuram. d, Zinedine Zidane.

2000fr, Deschamps holding World Cup.

1999, Feb. 20 Litho. *Perf. 13½*

801 A197 300fr Sheet of 4, #a.-d. 4.50 4.50

802 A197 400fr Sheet of 4, #a.-d. 6.25 6.25

803 A197 500fr Sheet of 4, #a.-d. 8.00 8.00

Perf. 13¼

804 A197 2000fr multicolored 8.00 8.00

No. 804 contains one 57x51mm stamp.

Hokusai Paintings A198

Designs: a, Voyagers Crossing the Oi River. b, Bird. c, On Totomi Mountain. d, Evening at Ueno. e, Higashimachi-matsuri-yatai-tenjou. f, Evening shower at Yoshiwara. g, Woman with Umbrella. h, Cascade. i, Courtesan.

1999, Sept. 10 Litho. *Perf. 13½*

805 A198 475fr Sheet of 9, #a.-i. 17.50 17.50

Japex '99.

Millennium — A199

No. 806 — Highlights of 1000-1899: a, Commercial routes in West Africa. b, Crusades. c, Notre Dame Cathedral. d, Ming dynasty tombs. e, Discovery of America. f, Albrecht Dürer. g, Sir Isaac Newton. h, American Independence. i, Napoleon.

No. 807 — 1900-24: a, Return of Halley's Comet. b, Lord Baden-Powell founds Scouting movement. c, Sinking of the Titanic. d, 1st film in Technicolor. e, Marconi sends 1st message across Atlantic, birth of radio. f, Harry Houdini. g, Capablanca-Lasker chess matches. h,

Pierre & Marie Curie win Nobel Prize. i, Theft of the Mona Lisa.

No. 808 — 1925-49: a, Birth of Marilyn Monroe. b, Discovery of Pluto. c, Laurel and Hardy. d, Independence of India. e, Alexander Fleming discovers penicillin. f, Introduction of Volkswagen Beetle & Vespa motor scooter. g, Opening of film "Dracula." h, World War II. i, Discovery of Lascaux cave drawings.

No. 809 — 1950-74: a, 1st flight of the Concorde, 7 original astronauts. b, Death of Buddy Holly. c, 1st Super Bowl. d, Death of Eva Peron. e, Art by Andy Warhol. f, The Beatles. g, Cultural Revolution in China. h, Assassination of Pres. John F. Kennedy. i, Cuban Revolution.

No. 810 — 1975-99: a, Death of Princess Diana. b, Death of Enzo Ferrari. c, Akira. d, Argentina, 1986 World Cup Soccer champions. e, B. Lara breaks cricket records. f, France, 1998 World Cup Soccer champions. g, Explosion of the Space Shuttle Challenger. h, Pope John Paul II meets Lech Walesa. i, Deaths of Frank Sinatra, Freddie Mercury.

1999, Sept. 10

806 A199 150fr Sheet of 9, #a.-i. 5.25 5.25
807 A199 300fr Sheet of 9, #a.-i. 10.00 10.00
808 A199 450fr Sheet of 9, #a.-i. 15.00 15.00
809 A199 475fr Sheet of 9, #a.-i. 16.00 16.00
810 A199 500fr Sheet of 9, #a.-i. 16.00 16.00
Nos. 806-810 (5) 62.25 62.25

Souvenir Sheet

PhilexFrance '99 — A200

1999, Sept. 10

811 A200 1500fr multi 6.00 6.00

I Love Lucy — A201

No. 812: a, Lucy leaning against tree, Ricky. b, Lucy, Ricky kissing. c, Lucy pointing gun. d, Ricky falling to ground. e, Lucy in apartment. f, Ricky holding animal. g, Ricky drinking from canteen. h, Lucy, Ricky talking. i, Lucy behind bush.

No. 813, Lucy in grape vat. No. 814, Lucy, Ricky in bed.

1999, Feb. 20 Litho. *Perf. 13¼*

812 A201 450fr Sheet of 9, #a.-i. 18.00 18.00

Souvenir Sheets

813 A201 1500fr multi 7.00 7.00
814 A201 2000fr multi 9.00 9.00

Dated 1998.

See Nos. 865-867.

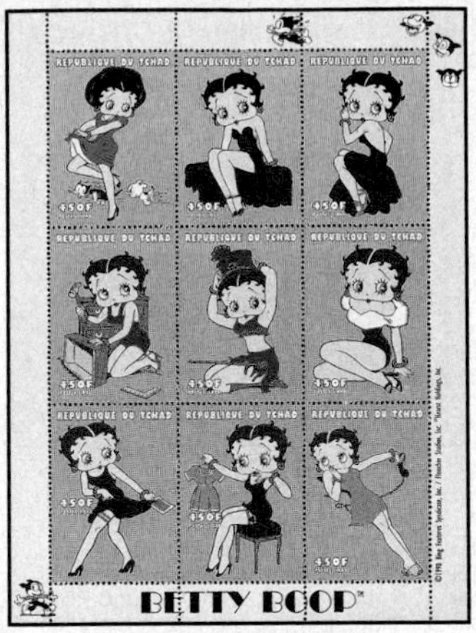

Betty Boop — A202

No. 815: a, With cat and dog. b, In flowered dress. c, Looking back over shoulder. d, With hammer, dresser. e, As majorette. f, In red dress with fur collar. g, Holding paper. h, Holding blue dress. i, Holding telephone.

No. 816, With feathered hat. No. 817, In leopard-spotted blouse.

1999, Feb. 20 Litho. *Perf. 13¼*

815 A202 450fr Sheet of 9, #a.-i. 18.00 18.00

Souvenir Sheets

816 A202 1500fr multi 7.00 7.00
817 A202 2000fr multi 9.00 9.00

Dated 1998.

See Nos. 856-858.

Antique Automobiles — A203

150fr, 1900 F.N. 300fr, 1906 Bianchi. 400fr, 1906 Renault. 500fr, 1919 Pierce-Arrow. 700fr, 1919 Citroen 5CV. 900fr, 1928 Ford.
1000fr, 1898 Renault.

1999 Litho. *Perf. 13x12¾*

818-823 A203 Set of 6 14.00 14.00

Souvenir Sheet

Perf. 13x13¼

824 A203 1000fr multi 5.00 5.00

No. 824 contains one 40x31mm stamp.

Locomotives — A204

Designs: 150fr, 0-4-4-0. 300fr, Red 0-4-0. 400fr, Green 0-6-0. 500fr, Brown 0-4-0. 700fr, Blue 0-4-0. 900fr, Blue 0-6-0.
1000fr, Electric locomotive.

1999 *Perf. 12¾*

825-830 A204 Set of 6 14.00 14.00

Souvenir Sheet

Perf. 13x13¼

831 A204 1000fr multi 5.00 5.00

No. 831 contains one 36x28mm stamp.

Wonders of Forgotten Cultures — A205

Designs: 50fr, Easter Island. 150fr, Stonehenge. 300fr, Jericho. 400fr, Machu Picchu. 500fr, Valley of Statues. 700fr, Chichén Itzá. 900fr, Persepolis.

1999 *Perf. 12¾*

832-838 A205 Set of 7 15.00 15.00

Chad postal officials have declared the following items to be "not authorized:"

Set of six stamps of various denominations: New Year 2000 (Year of the Dragon)

Sheet of nine stamps of various denominations: Orchids

Sheet of nine 150fr stamps: Spanish Impressionist paintings

Sheet of nine 300fr stamps: Millennium (Composers), Van Gogh paintings

Sheet of nine 450fr stamps: Millennium (Marilyn Monroe), French Impressionist paintings

Sheet of nine 475fr stamps: Impressionist paintings

Sheet of nine 500fr stamps: Renoir nudes, Elvis Presley, Olympics

Souvenir sheets of one: Millennium (three 300fr, two 450fr, one 475fr, three 500fr, one 1500fr), New Year 2000 (1000fr), Palace of Versailles (1500fr, 2000fr), Hiroshige paintings (1500fr, 2000fr).

Minerals A206

Designs: 150fr, Wulfenite. 200fr, Argentite. 400fr, Siderite. 500fr, Dolomite and quartz. 700fr, Azurite. 900fr, Spinel and calcite.
1000fr, Cassiterite.

2000, Jan. 15 Litho. *Perf. 12¾*

839-844 A206 Set of 6 14.00 14.00

Souvenir Sheet

845 A206 1000fr multi 5.00 5.00

Dated 1999.

Dogs — A206a

Designs: 150fr, Caucasian Mountain dog (Berger caucasique). 300fr, Belgian shepherd (Berger Belgue). 400fr, Spanish mastiff (Mâtin Espagne). 500fr, Kuvasz. 700fr, Beauceron. 900fr, Rough collie.

2000, Jan. 15 Litho. *Perf. 13*

845A A206a 150fr multi —
845B A206a 300fr multi —
845C A206a 400fr multi —
845D A206a 500fr multi —
845E A206a 700fr multi —
845F A206a 900fr multi —

Dated 1999.

Elvis Presley — A207

No. 846: a, Playing guitar, wearing red jacket. b, Holding microphone and guitar, wearing red jacket. c, Holding guitar, wearing gold jacket. d, Playing guitar wearing black leather jacket. e, Playing guitar, wearing black jacket. f, Playing guitar, wearing blue jacket. g, Holding microphone, wearing blue shirt. h, Singing, wearing brown jacket. i, Holding microphone, wearing striped yellow jacket.

2000, Mar. 10 *Perf. 13¼*

846 A207 300fr Sheet of 9, #a-i 12.00 12.00

Dated 1999.

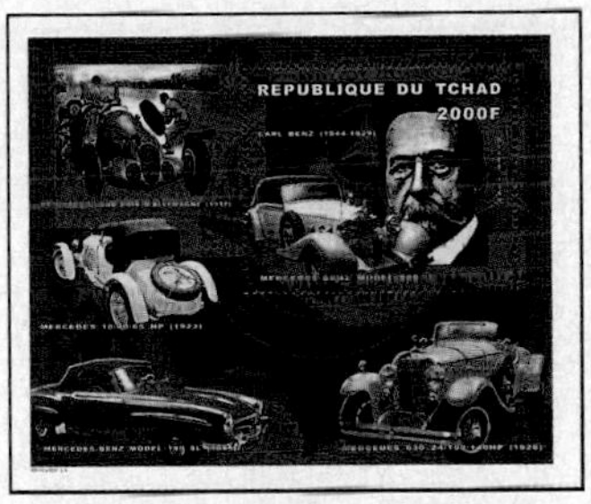

Carl Benz and Mercedes-Benz Automobiles — A208

No. 847: a, 1934 W-25. b, 1934 500 K. c, 1964 230 SL. d, 1935 150. e, 1954 300 SL. f, 1971 280 SE.
2000fr, 1934 500 K, diff.

2000, Mar. 10

847 A208 250fr Sheet of 6, #a-f 7.00 7.00

Souvenir Sheet

848 A208 2000fr multi 9.00 9.00

No. 847 contains six 30x30mm stamps. Dated 1999.

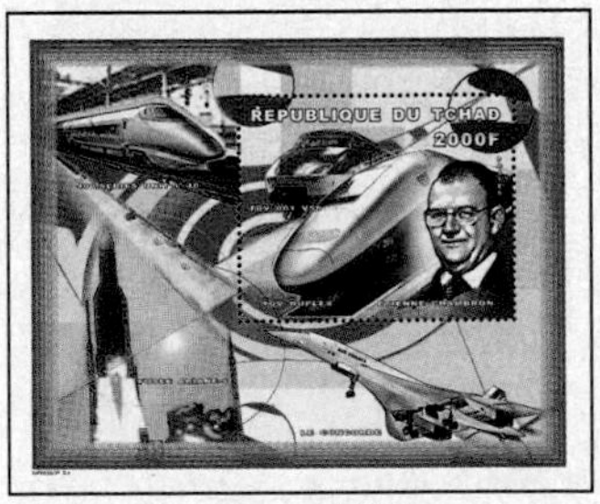

Trains — A209

No. 849: a, FES 3228, European Union flag. b, TGV Duplex, French flag. c, 500 Series Unit W1, Japanese flag. d, AVE Class 100, Spanish flag. e, ICE3, German flag. f, ETR 500, Italian flag.
2000fr, TGC 001 V56, TGV Duplex, Etienne Chambron.

2000, Mar. 10
849 A209 600fr Sheet of 6, #a-f 11.50 11.50

Souvenir Sheet

850 A209 2000fr multi 6.50 6.50

No. 849 contains six 30x30mm stamps. Dated 1999.

French Rulers — A210

No. 851, 150fr: a, Charlemagne. b, King Charles VIII. c, King Francis I. d, King Henry II. e, Catherine de Medici. f, King Henry III.
No. 852, 200fr: a, King Louis XII. b, King Louis XIII. c, King Louis XIV. d, King Louis XV. e, King Louis XVI. f, King Louis XVIII.
No. 853, 300fr — Napoleon Bonaparte: a, Standing, wearing red cape. b, On horseback, wearing red cape. c, On horseback, with soldier at right. d, On horseback, with crowd at right. e, Standing with other people. f, On white horse, leading battle.

2000, Mar. 10 **Sheets of 6, #a-f**
851-853 A210 Set of 3 17.50 17.50

Dated 1999.

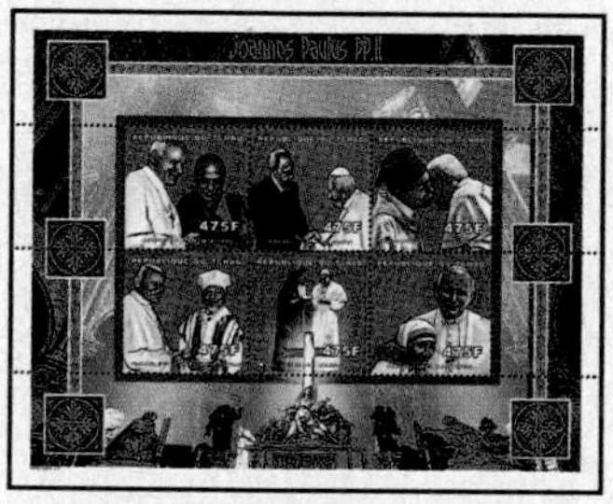
Pope John Paul II — A211

No. 854 — Pope John Paul II and: a, Dalai Lama. b, Fidel Castro. c, King Hassan II of Morocco. d, Grand Rabbi Elio Toaff. e, Patriarch Bartholomew I. f, Mother Teresa.

2000, Mar. 10
854 A211 475fr Sheet of 6, #a-f 13.00 13.00

Dated 1999.

Space — A212

No. 855: a, Sputnik, dog Laika. b, Yuri Gagarin, Vostok 1. c, Konstantin Feoktistov, Vladimir Komarov, Boris Yegorov, Voskhod 1. d, Luna 1, chimpanzee Ham. e, Neil Armstrong, Michael Collins, Edwin Aldrin, Apollo 11. f, Aldrin, splashdown of capsule.

2000, Mar. 10
855 A212 500fr Sheet of 6, #a-f 13.00 13.00

Dated 1999.

Betty Boop Type of 1999

No. 856: a, Wearing red and violet striped leotard, kicking leg up. b, As cheerleader. c, At football field, holding pennant. d, At ice cream shop. e, Wearing yellow and green striped leotard. f, Wearing baseball cap and orange shorts. g, Wearing baseball cap and checked shirt. h, Seated, drinking beverage. i, Wearing cut-off shorts.
No. 857, 1500fr, Riding bicycle. No. 858, 2000fr, Wearing glasses, elbow and knee pads.

2000, Mar. 30
856 A202 250fr Sheet of 9, #a-i 10.00 10.00

Souvenir Sheets

857-858 A202 Set of 2 16.00 16.00

The Three Stooges — A213

No. 859, 250fr, horiz.: a, Larry, in surgeon's gown, and Curly. b, Curly, Moe, Larry around barrel. c, Moe, Larry and Curly on horse. d, Larry attacking man. e, Moe getting hair pulled. f, Moe with mallet. g, Curly, Moe and Larry in western outfits, outdoors. h, Larry, Curly and Moe in white doctor's jackets. i, Man looking at Moe.
No. 860, 300fr, horiz.: a, Larry grabbing Moe's chin. b, Moe and Larry holding scrolls. c, Moe, yellow background. d, Larry, blue background. e, Moe, Shemp and Larry. f, Shemp, blue background. g, Shemp, yellow background. h, Shemp pointing bellows at Larry. i, Moe and Larry in white.
No. 861, 1500fr, Moe in surgeon's gown. No. 862, 1500fr, Moe wearing hat. No. 863, 2000fr, Curly, Moe and Larry in western outfits, outdoors. No. 864, 2000fr, Larry with violin.

2000 **Sheets of 9, #a-i**
859-860 A213 Set of 2 22.50 22.50

Souvenir Sheets

861-864 A213 Set of 4 32.50 32.50

Issued: Nos. 859, 861, 863, 3/30; Nos. 860, 862, 864, 5/29.

I Love Lucy Type of 1999

No. 865: a, Lucy dancing, man in background. b, Lucy dancing, with knees bent and arms extended. c, Lucy in doorway. d, Lucy dancing behind sofa. e, Lucy kicking out leg. f, Lucy being caught by two men. g, Lucy with one arm extended. h, Lucy being sprayed with seltzer water. i, Lucy with leg on dance rail.
No. 866, 1500fr, Lucy looking at clock, horiz. No. 867, 2000fr, Lucy with clown costume and arms extended.

2000, May 29
865 A201 225fr Sheet of 9, #a-i 9.00 9.00

Souvenir Sheets

866-867 A201 Set of 2 16.00 16.00

N'Djamena, Cent. — A213a

Background colors: 150fr, Blue. 300fr, Red. 475fr, Green.

2000, May 29 **Litho.** ***Perf. 13¼***
867A-867C A213a Set of 3 — —

Chadian Political History — A214

No. 868, 150fr: a, Louis Léon César Faidherbe. b, François Joseph Lamy. c, Henri Eugène Gouraud. d, Gustav Nachtigal. e, Head of Rabah on spike. f, Fernand Foureau.
No. 869, 300fr: a, Pierre Savorgnan de Brazza. b, Philippe Marie de Hautecloque Leclerc. c, Emile Gentil. d, Gabriel Lisette. e, Charles de Gaulle. f, Felix Eboué.

2000, May 29 ***Perf. 13½***
Sheets of 6, #a-f
868-869 A214 Set of 2 18.00 18.00

Wildlife, Map of Chad, Scouting Emblem — A215

No. 870, 150fr — Giraffa camelopardalis: a, Pair, one with head lowered. b, Pair, both with heads extended. c, Pair near forest. d, Trio.
No. 871, 200fr: a, Pair of Gazella granti in field. b, Gazella cuiveri. c, Gazella dorcas. d, Pair of Gazella granti at waterhole.
No. 872, 250fr — Addax nasomaculatus: a, View of head. b, Lying in grass. c, Standing. d, Grazing.
No. 873, 300fr — Ammotragus lervia: a, Pair. b, View of head. c, Standing on mountain ledge. d, Standing, with purple mountain in background
No. 874, 375fr — Diceros bicornis: a, View of head. b, Facing right, line of dark green foliage in background. c, Facing left. d, Facing right, with trees in background.
No. 875, 400fr — Panthera pardus: a, On tree branch. b, Lying in grass. c, Standing. d, View of head.
No. 876, 450fr: a, Head of Theropithecus gelada. b, Cercopithecus aethiops. c, Papio anubis. d, Adult and juvenile Thereopithecus gelada.
No. 877, 450fr — Hippopotamus amphibius: a, Pair laying in mud. b, With open mouth. c, Standing. d, Herd.
No. 878, 475fr — Oryx dammah: a, Facing right, green foliage in background. b, View of head. c, Pair. d, Grazing, mountain in background.
No. 879, 500fr — Panthera leo: a, Male on female. b, Females at waterhole. c, Female and cub. d, Female and male.
No. 880, 600fr — Loxodonta africana: a, With tree at right. b, Facing right. c, View of head. d, With tree and mountain in background.
No. 881, 750fr — Syncerus caffer: a, Juvenile, adult grazing. b, Adult in field. c, Pair lying on ground. d, With grass in mouth.
No. 882, 1000fr, Pair of Diceros bicornis. No. 883, 1000fr, Pair of Hippopotamus amphibius fighting. No. 884, 1500fr, Panthera leo with kill.
Illustration reduced.

2000, Aug. 1 ***Perf. 13¼***
Horiz. Strips of 4, #a-d
870-881 A215 Set of 12 90.00 90.00

Souvenir Sheets

882-884 A215 Set of 3 16.00 16.00

Nos. 882-884 each contain one 36x51mm stamp.

Miniature Sheet

Baseball Player — A216

2000, Oct. 11 **Litho. & Embossed**
885 A216 3000fr gold & multi 10.00 10.00

Exists with silver background.

High-five of Teenagers — A217

No. 886: a, Moon Hee-jun and Lee Jae-won. b, Jang Woo-hyuk and ear of Tony An. c, Tony an and Kang Ta. d, Jang Woo-hyuk. e, Entire group. f, Kang Ta. g, Moon Hee-jun. h, Lee Jae-won. i, Tony An.

2000 **Litho.**
886 A217 150fr Sheet of 9, #a-i 4.50 4.50

Sports and Chess — A218

No. 887, 30fr — Dogs involved in sport activities: a, Sled dogs. b, Dog racing. c, Hunting dogs. d, Dogs and skier.
No. 888, 70fr — Various sports: a, Petanque. b, Rugby. c, Archery. d, Jai alai.
No. 889, 250fr — 2000 Summer Olympics, Sydney: a, Fencing. b, Judo. c, Tennis. d, Boxing.
No. 890, 300fr — 2000 Summer Olympics, Sydney: a, Cycling. b, Basketball. c, Beach volleyball. d, Baseball.
No. 891, 400fr — Soccer players: a, Zinedine Zidane. b, Lilian Thuram. c, Yuri Djorkaeff. d, Nicolas Anelka
No. 892, 475fr — 2000 Summer Olympics, Sydney: a, Table tennis. b, Equestrian. c, Swimming. d, Kayaking.
No. 893, 500fr — Golf: a, Man with white pants swinging club. b, Golfer analyzing putt. c, Man with black pants swinging club. d, Woman golfer.
No. 894, 750fr — Formula I race drivers: a, Michael Schumacher. b, Mikka Hakkinen. c, Ralf Schumacher. d, David Coulthard.

No. 895, 1000fr — Chess: a, Knight with shield. b, Knight on donkey. c, Knight with attendant. d, Horses and wheeled castle.
2000fr, Venus Williams.

2001, Jan. 31 *Perf. 13¼*

Sheets of 4, #a-d

887-895 A218 Set of 9 85.00 85.00

Souvenir Sheet

896 A218 2000fr multi 9.00 9.00

2000 Summer Olympics, Sydney (No. 896). No. 896 contains one 36x51mm stamp.

Trains — A219

No. 897, 200fr: a, Mallard, 1935. b, P8 Prussian, 1908. c, F2A, 1936. b, 240 P, 1940.
No. 898, 300fr: a, NSB No. 3641. b, New Zealand Railways Sereis EW. c, Series 277, Renfe. d, Series DF4 Vent d'Est IV Co-Co.
No. 899, 400fr: a, SNCF Series 9100 2-D-2, 1950. b, SNCF Series 72000 C-C, 1967. c, CC 21000, 1969. d, VL-80, 1963.
No. 900, 475fr: a, GNER Eurostar. b, Electric EMU ETR 500. c, DER OBB 1016 001. d, GNER train.
No. 901, 500fr: a, OL-49, 1951. b, Pacific Series 16E, 1935. c, Andaluces 030, 1877. d, Franco-Crosti Gr, 743, 1937.
No. 902, 500fr: a, JR West 8-car unit E4. b, TGV KTX. c, 300 Series unit J3. d, E3 Series unit R6.
No. 903, 600fr: a, 2D2 PO, 1926. b, Metropolitan BB Vickers, 1920. c, DB ET 491, 1935. d, Series D, 1925.
No. 904, 600fr: a, Electric EMU 490. b, Acela, 2001. c, CFF-FFS Electric EMU RABe 500. d, ICE-T Bavereihe 41.
No. 905, 750fr: a, Single Driver, 1870. b, Great Western Railway Castle, 1923. c, Schools Class, 1930. d, 230 Besa, 1905.
No. 906, 750fr: a, TGV Thalys. b, TGV Duplex. c, TGV La Poste. d, TGV Atlantique.
1500fr, SAR Series 26 2-D-2. 2000fr, TGV Sud-est.

2001, June 22 **Litho.**

Sheets of 4, #a-d

897-906 A219 Set of 10 90.00 90.00

Souvenir Sheets

907-908 A219 Set of 2 16.00 16.00

Nos. 907-908 each contain one 51x36mm stamp.

British Royalty — A220

No. 909, 300fr — Queen Mother: a, With King George VI. b, With young daughter. c, With Prince Charles. d, Waving. e, Wearing tiara and yellow dress. f, Wearing pink dress and hat. g, Wearing green dress and hat. h, Holding flowers. i, With dogs.
No. 910, 300fr — Prince William wearing: a, Black suit with lapel handkerchief. b, Suit with red and blue vest. c, Suit with gold vest. d, Sweater, looking right. e, Black suit and dark blue tie. f, Sweater, facing forward. g, Blue shirt with button. h, Dark blue shirt without button. i, Light blue suit.

2001, July 22 *Perf. 13¼*

Sheets of 9, #a-i

909-910 A220 Set of 2 24.00 24.00

No. 910 contains nine 36x51mm stamps.

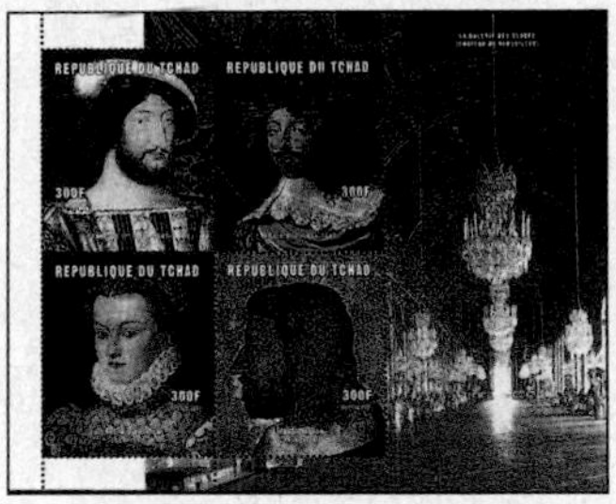

French Rulers — A221

No. 911, 300fr: a, King Francis I. b, King Louis XIII. c, Elizabeth of Austria, consort of King Charles IX. d, King John II the Good.
No. 912, 375fr: a, King Louis XIV. b, King Francis I, diff. c, King Louis XVI. d, King Louis XVIII.
No. 913, 475fr: a, King Louis XV as child. b, King Louis XV as adult. c, Queen Marie Antoinette. d, King Charles VII.
No. 914, 500fr — Napoleon Bonaparte wearing: a, White tunic. b, Black jacket. c, Emperor's robes. d, Red tunic.

2001, July 22 **Sheets of 4, #a-d**

911-914 A221 Set of 4 30.00 30.00

Stamps of Nos. 911-913 exist in souvenir sheets of 1. Value, set $70.

Pope John Paul II — A222

No. 915, 800fr: a, Standing in room, looking left. b, Waving, c, Holding flowers. d, With blue sky background.
No. 916, 1000fr: a, Wearing red hat. b, Wearing miter, waving. c, Bending to kiss ground. d, Wearing miter, holding crucifix.
4000fr, Wearing zucchetto.

2001 **Litho.** *Perf. 13¼*

Sheets of 4, #a-d

915-916 A222 Set of 2 32.50 32.50

Miniature Sheet

Litho. & Embossed

917 A222 4000fr gold & multi 22.50 22.50

Issued: Nos. 915-916, 7/22; No. 917, 7/23. No. 917 contains one 60x90mm stamp and exists with a silver background. Stamps of Nos. 915-916 exist in souvenir sheets of 1. Value, set $60.

Famous Men — A223

Designs: 200fr, Charles Darwin (1809-82), naturalist. 250fr, Christopher Columbus (1451-1506), explorer. 300fr, Jacques-Yves Cousteau (1910-97), marine scientist. 350fr, Albert Schweitzer (1875-1965), missionary. 400fr, Juan Manuel Fangio (1911-95), race car driver. 450fr, Nicolaus Copernicus (1473-1543), astronomer. 500fr, Robert Stephenson (1803-59), engineer. 550fr, Etienne Chambron, high speed rail pioneer. 600fr, Garry Kasparov, chess player. 750fr, Lord Robert Baden-Powell (1857-1941), founder of scouting. 800fr, Neil Armstrong, astronaut. 1000fr, Sir Alexander Fleming (1881-1955), bacteriologist.

2001, Oct. 30 **Litho.**

918-929 A223 Set of 12 29.00 29.00

Nos. 918-929 exist in souvenir sheets of 1. Value, set $115.

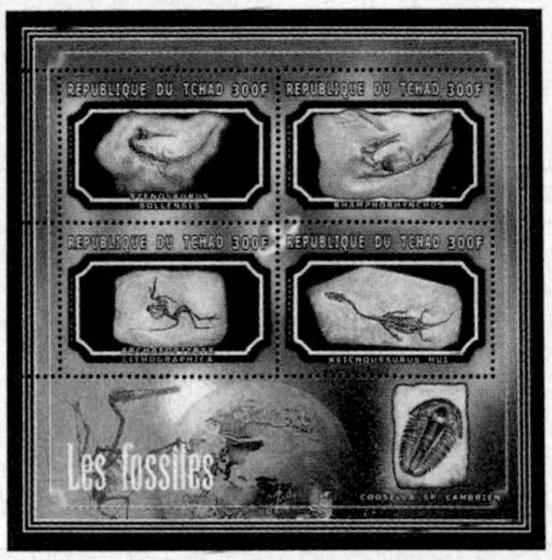

Fossils, Dinosaurs, Meteorites and Minerals — A224

No. 930, 300fr — Fossils: a, Stenosaurus bollensis. b, Rhamphorhynchus. c, Archaeopteryx lithographica. d, Keichousaurus hui.
No. 931, 375fr — Dinosaurs: a, Mesadactylus. b, Pteranodon. c, Tropeognathus. d, Quetzalcoatlus.
No. 932, 400fr — Meteorites found in; a, India. b, Nigeria. c, US. d, Australia.
No. 933, 500fr — Dinosaurs: a, Deinonychus. b, Seismosaurus. c, Pleurocoelus, Acrocanthosaur. d, Styracosaurus.
No. 934, 500fr — Minerals: a, Fluorite. b, Pyrite. c, Wulfenite. d, Merovingian scoria.
No. 935, 550fr — Meteorites found in: a, Antarctica. b, Libya. c, USSR. d, China.
No. 936, 600fr — Minerals: a, Magnetite. b, Kunzite. c, Apophyllite, Stilbite. d, Fluorite, diff.
No. 937, 750fr — Minerals: a, Quartz. b, Merovingian scoria, diff. c, Epidote. d, Amethyst, agate.
3000fr, Tyrannosaurus rex, vert.

2001, Dec. 27 **Litho.**

Sheets of 4, #a-d

930-937 A224 Set of 8 77.50 77.50

Miniature Sheet

Litho. & Embossed

938 A224 3000fr gold & multi 17.00 17.00

No. 938 contains one 60x90mm stamp and exists with silver background.

French Kings — A225

Designs: No. 939, 3000fr, Louis IX. No. 940, 3000fr, Francis I. No. 941, 3000fr, Henry IV. No. 942, 3000fr, Louis XIII. No. 943, 3000fr, Louis XV.

2002, Apr. 10 **Litho. & Embossed**

Gold & Multicolored

939-943 A225 Set of 5 50.00 50.00

Nos. 939-943 exist with silver background.

Egyptian Treasures A225a

Designs: No. 943A, 3000fr, Painted wooden box. No. 943B, 3000fr, Nekhbet vulture. No. 943C, 3000fr, Oushebti of Tutankhamen, vert. No. 943D, 3000fr, Pair of royal scepters, vert. No. 943E, 3000fr, Diadem, vert. No. 943F, 3000fr, Gold-plated throne, vert. No. 943G, 3000fr, Cynocephalic pectoral, vert. No. 943H, 3000fr, Coffin of Tutankhamen, vert. No. 943I, 3000fr, Statue of Ka, vert. No. 943J, 3000fr, Duck earring, vert. No. 943K, 3000fr, Lion-shaped vase, vert. No. 943L, 3000fr, Canopic dais and chapel, vert.

Embossed on Gold Paper

2002, Apr. 10 *Perf. 13¼*

943A-943L A225a Set of 12 140.00 140.00

Artists and Their Paintings — A226

On Nos. 944-957, painting titles (in French) and artist's birth and death dates are in margins adjacent to each stamp. On Nos. 958-962 painting titles are not shown, but artist's name is in sheet margin
No. 944, 150fr: a, Berthe Morisot (1841-95). b, Cache-cache. c, Le Berceau. d, Au bal. e, Jeune femme se poudrant. f, Paule Gobillard peignant.
No. 945, 200fr: a, Marc Chagall (1887-1985). b, Nature morte. c, Le violoniste vert. d, La maison bleue. e, Mariage. f, Le soldat ivre.
No. 946, 250fr: a, Camille Pissarro (1830-1903). b, Les chataigniers a Osny. c, Le verger. d, Le repos des glaneuses. e, Jeune paysanne prenant son cafe. f, Le bergére.
No. 947, 300fr: a, Alfred Sisley (1839-99). b, Le pont de Villeneuve la Garenne. c, Allee de jardin a Louveciennes. d, Meule de foin bord du Loing. e, Moret sur Loing. f, Moulin a Moret.
No. 948, 325fr: a, Paul Delvaux (1897-1994). b, La voix publique. c, Nocturnes. d, Baignade des Nymphes. e, Pygmalion. f, Jeunes femmes revant.
No. 949, 350fr: a, Edouard Manet (1832-83). b, Le Déjeuner sur l'herbe. c, Olympia. d, Le fifre. e, La serveuse de bocks. f, Le balcon.
No. 950, 375fr: a, Vincent van Gogh (1853-90). b, Champ de blé avec cypres. c, Rue a Auvers. d, La sieste. e, Chambre jaune a Arles. f, Rue de village.
No. 951, 400fr: a, Salvador Dali (1904-89). b, Cannibalisme en automne. c, Corpus Hypercubicus. d, Le sommeil. e, Le tentation de St. Antoine. f, Meditation sur harpe.
No. 952, 425fr: a, Paul Cézanne (1839-1906). b, Les baigneurs. c, Les grandes baigneuses (light blue background). d, Les grandes baigneuses, diff. (dark blue background). e, Les baigneueses. f, Les baigneurs au repos.
No. 953, 450fr: a, Pablo Picasso (1881-1973). b, Les demoiselles d'Avignon. c, Femme a l'eventail. d, La danse. e, La vie. f, La mere et son fils.
No. 954, 475fr: a, Amadeo Modigliani (1884-1920). b, Nu souche sur un divan. c, Nu debout. d, Cariatide debout. e, Nu allongé. f, Nu assis de dos.
No. 955, 500fr: a, Auguste Renoir (1841-1919). b, Diane chasseresse. c, Nu allongé. d, Baigneuses. e, Baigneuse assise. f, Nymphe au printemps.
No. 956, 550fr: a, Edgar Degas (1834-1917). b, Femme se coiffant. c, Aprés le bain (view of front of seated woman). d, Femme se peignant. e, Aprés le bain (view of back of woman). f, Aprés le bain (woman dressing).
No. 957, 600fr: a, Henri Matisse (1869-1954). b, Le nu bleu. c, Le genou levé. d, Nu assis sur un fauteuil. e, Odalisques. f, Nu allongé.
No. 958, 1500fr, Gustave Caillebotte. No. 959, 1500fr, Picasso, diff. No. 960, 1500fr, Auguste Renoir, diff. No. 961, 2000fr, Pablo Picasso, diff. No. 962, 2000fr, Van Gogh, diff.

2002, Apr. 10 *Perf. 12¾x13¼*

Sheets of 6, #a-f

944-957 A226 Set of 14 140.00 140.00

Souvenir Sheets

Perf. 13¼x12¾

958-962 A226 Set of 5 27.50 27.50

Nos. 944a-955a and 957a exist in souvenir sheets of 1 that are perf. 13¼x12¾. Value, set $92.50.

Miniature Sheet

Zeppelin NT — A227

No. 963: a, 475fr, Over Lake Constance. b, 500fr, Over Frankfurt. c, 600fr, Over Nürburgring, Germany. d, 750fr, At 2001 Salon du Bourget.

2002, Oct. 30 *Perf. 13¼*

963 A227 Sheet of 4, #a-d 11.00 11.00

Nos. 963a-963d exist in souvenir sheets of 1. Value, set $45.

Fauna and Mushrooms — A228

No. 964, 150fr: a, Hemichromis lifalili. b, Trichechus senegalensis. c, Synodontis nigriventris. d, Gnathonemus petersii. e, Ctenopoma ansorgii. f, Pseudocrenilabrus multicolor.

No. 965, 300fr, vert.: a, Nectarina venusta. b, Lamprotornis splendidus. c, Poicephalus meyeri. d, Halcyon leucocephala. e, Quelea quelea. f, Merops pusillus.

No. 966, 350fr, vert.: a, Terathopius ecaudatus. b, Gymnogyps californianus. c, Buteo jamaicensis. d, Lophaetus occipitalis. e, Aquila rapax. f, Melierax metabates.

No. 967, 375fr, vert.: a, Elanus caeruleus. b, Harpia harpyja. c, Gyps rueppellii. d, Milvus migrans. e, Torgos tracheliotus. f, Aquila chrysaetos.

No. 968, 550fr: a, Kallimoides rumia. b, Zophopetes dysmephila. c, Megalopalpus zymna. d, Coeliades forestan. e, Catopsilia florella. f, Anaphaesis aurota.

No. 969, 600fr: a, Amanita muscaria. b, Amanita rubescens. c, Cortinarius orellanus. d, Hygrophorus hypothejus. e, Leccinum piceinum. f, Strobilomyces strobilaceus.

2003, June 2 **Litho.**

Sheets of 6, #a-f

964-969 A228 Set of 6 55.00 55.00

Stamps of Nos. 965-969 exist in a set of twelve souvenir sheets of two, with each souvenir sheet of two containing adjacent stamps found in the sheet of six. Value, set $160.

Chad - Taiwan Cooperation — A229

Flags and: 50fr, Grain. 100fr, Surgeon's hands, Red Cross. 150fr, Bridge. 300fr, Handshake, maps.

2003, Dec. 1

970-973 A229 Set of 4 2.50 2.50

973a Booklet pane, 2 each #970-973 5.00 —

Complete booklet, #973a 5.00

973b Souvenir sheet, #970-973 2.50 2.50

AIDS Prevention A230

Red ribbon and: 50fr, People under umbrella. 100fr, Man and woman. 150fr, Doctor. 300fr, "Prudence, Abstinence, Fidelité."

2004, July 7 **Litho.** *Perf. 13x12¾*

974-977 A230 Set of 4 2.50 2.50

Opening of Petroleum Refinery, 1st Anniv. A231

Pres. Idriss Deby opening pipeline and: 150fr, Storage tank. 350fr, Storage tanks. 400fr, Refinery. 500fr, Tower, vert.

2004, Oct. 10 *Perf. 12¾x13, 13x12¾*

978-981 A231 Set of 4 6.50 6.50

Women's Hairstyles A232

Designs: 150fr, Figuerier. 350fr, Sakkindjala. 550fr, Kileskou. 575fr, Dabbou.

2005, Mar. 8 *Perf. 13*

982-985 A232 Set of 4 8.00 8.00

Toumai Skull A233

Color of skull: 25fr, Purple. 50fr, Green. 100fr, Gray. 150fr, Red. 1500fr, Gray.

2005, July 19 **Litho.** *Perf. 12¾x13*

986-989 A233 Set of 4 1.40 1.40

Souvenir Sheet

990 A233 1500fr multi 5.75 5.75

Campaign Against Trypanosomiasis, 10th Anniv. — A234

Tsetse fly and: 150fr, Trypanosomiasis protozoa, eradication campaign emblem. 300fr, Eradication campaign emblem, map of Africa. 350fr, Pan-African Postal Union emblem, eradication campaign emblem, map of Africa. 550fr, Trypanosomiasis protozoa, maps of Chad and Africa.

2010 *Perf. 12¾*

991-994 A234 Set of 4 5.50 5.50

Independence, 50th Anniv. — A235

Emblem with denomination color of: 150fr, Red. 300fr, White. 350fr, Yellow. 550fr, Blue.

2010

995-998 A235 Set of 4 5.50 5.50

A236

Designs: No. 999, 150fr, Cyphotilapia frontosa, Lysmata amboinensis. No. 1000, 150fr, Cyrtocara moorii, Potamonautes maculata. No. 1001, 150fr, Placidochromis milomo, Sesarma mederi. No. 1002, 150fr, Tropheus brichardi, Atyopsis gabonensis. No. 1003, 200fr, Phocidae, Swakopmund Lighthouse, Namibia. No. 1004, 200fr, Odobenus rosmarus, Nosy Iranja Lighthouse, Madagascar. No. 1005, 200fr, Lobodon carcinophaga, Pelican Point Lighthouse, Namibia. No. 1006, 200fr, Odobenus rosmarus, Katsepy Lighthouse, Madagascar. No. 1007, 300fr, Morus capensis, Pointe-Noire Lighthouse, Congo. No. 1008, 300fr, Phalacrocorax capensis, Slangkop Point Lighthouse, South Africa. No. 1009, 300fr, Fregata magnificens, Cap Agulhas Lighthouse, South Africa. No. 1010, 300fr, Phalacrocorax melanoleucos, Ngombe Lighthouse, Gabon. No. 1011, 300fr, Strombus gibberulus albus, Grand Bassam Lighthouse, Ivory Coast. No. 1012, 300fr, Argonauta cornuta, Cap Blanc Lighthouse, Mauritania. No. 1013, 300fr, Calpurnus verrucosus, Conakry Lighthouse, Guinea. No. 1014, 300fr, Haliotis queketti, Cap Miné Lighthouse, Madagascar. No. 1015, 350fr, Galeocerdo cuvier, Cherchell Lighthouse, Algeria. No. 1016, 350fr, Isurus paucus, l'ilot d'Arzew Lighthouse, Algeria. No. 1017, 350fr, Sphyrna mokarran, Amirauté Lighthouse, Algeria. No. 1018, 350fr, Carcharodon carcharias, Cap Ivi Lighthouse, Algeria. No. 1019, 500fr, Amanita jacksonii, Eugaster spinulosa. No. 1020, 500fr, Amanita caesarea, Zographus regalis. No. 1021, 500fr, Armillaria gallica, Megaponera foetens. No. 1022, 500fr, Sarcoscypha coccinea, Mylabris sp. No. 1023, 600fr, Cystodermella cinnabarina, Schistocerca gregaria. No. 1024, 600fr, Marasmius rotula, Palpopleura lucia. No. 1025, 600fr, Periphragmoides lysurus, Myrmeleontidae. No. 1026, 600fr, Boletus edulis, Trithemis kirbyi. No. 1027, 750fr, Fluorine. No. 1028, 750fr, Malachite. No. 1029, 750fr, Pyrite. No. 1030, 750fr, Vanadinite.

2012, Sept. 4 **Litho.** *Perf. 13¼*

999-1030 A236 Set of 32 50.00 50.00

Nos. 999-1030 each exist in souvenir sheets of 1.

SEMI-POSTAL STAMPS

Catalogue values for unused stamps in this section are for Never Hinged items.

Anti-Malaria Issue

Common Design Type

Perf. 12½x12

1962, Apr. 7 **Engr.** **Unwmk.**

B1 CD108 25fr + 5fr orange 1.25 .50

Freedom from Hunger Issue

Common Design Type

1963, Mar. 21 *Perf. 13*

B2 CD112 25fr + 5fr dk grn, dk bl & brn 2.00 .50

Red Cross, Mother and Children — SP1

1974, Oct. 2 **Photo.** *Perf. 12½x13*

B3 SP1 30fr + 10fr multi 1.00 .40

Red Cross of Chad, first anniversary.

AIR POST STAMPS

Catalogue values for unused stamps in this section are for Never Hinged items.

Olympic Games Issue

French Equatorial Africa No. C37 Surcharged in Red

Unwmk.

1960, Dec. 15 **Engr.** *Perf. 13*

C1 AP8 250fr on 500fr grnsh blk, blk & slate 12.00 7.50

17th Olympic Games, Rome, Aug. 25-Sept. 11. Surcharge 46mm wide.

Red Bishops — AP1

Birds in pairs: 100fr, Scarlet-chested sunbird. 200fr, African paradise flycatcher. 250fr, Malachite kingfisher. 500fr, Nubian carmine bee-eater.

1961-63 **Unwmk.** **Engr.** *Perf. 13*

C2	AP1	50fr dk grn, mag & blk	1.25	.35
C3	AP1	100fr multi	3.75	1.25
C4	AP1	200fr multi	6.50	1.90
C5	AP1	250fr dk bl, grn & dp org ('63)	10.00	3.00
C6	AP1	500fr multi	22.50	9.50
		Nos. C2-C6 (5)	44.00	16.00

Air Afrique Issue

Common Design Type

1962, Feb. 17 **Unwmk.** *Perf. 13*

C7 CD107 25fr lt bl, org brn & blk 1.00 .25

Abidjan Games Issue

Discus Thrower — AP2

1962, July 21 Photo. *Perf. 12x12½*
C8 AP2 100fr brn, lt grn & blk 3.50 1.00

African Postal Union Issue
Common Design Type

1963, Sept. 8 Unwmk. *Perf. 12½*
C9 CD114 85fr dk bl, ocher & red 2.40 .60

Air Afrique Issue, 1963
Common Design Type

1963, Nov. 19 *Perf. 13x12*
C10 CD115 50fr multi 2.40 .60

Europafrica Issue
Common Design Type

1963, Nov. 30 Photo. *Perf. 12x13*
C11 CD116 50fr dp grn, yel & dk brn 2.00 .50

Mail Truck and Broussard Plane — AP4

Unwmk.
1963, Dec. 16 Engr. *Perf. 13*
C12 AP4 100fr sl grn, ultra & red brn 4.00 .90

Chiefs of State Issue

Map and Presidents of Chad, Congo, Gabon and Central African Republic AP4a

1964, June 23 Photo. *Perf. 12½*
C13 AP4a 100fr multi 2.40 .60

See note after Central African Republic No. C19.

Europafrica Issue

Globe and Emblems of Industry and Agriculture — AP5

1964, July 20 *Perf. 13x12*
C14 AP5 50fr brn, pur & dp org 2.00 .40

See note after Cameroun No. 402.

Soccer — AP6

Designs: 50fr, Javelin throw, vert. 100fr, High jump, vert. 200fr, Runners.

1964, Aug. 12 Engr. *Perf. 13*
C15 AP6 25fr yel grn, sl grn & org brn 1.00 .30
C16 AP6 50fr org brn, ind & brt bl 2.00 .60
C17 AP6 100fr blk, red & brt grn 3.50 1.00
C18 AP6 200fr bis, blk & car 6.00 2.00
a. Min. sheet of 4, #C15-C18 18.00 6.50
Nos. C15-C18 (4) 12.50 3.90

18th Olympic Games, Tokyo, 10/10-25/64.

Communications Symbols — AP7

1964, Nov. 2 Litho. *Perf. 12½x13*
C19 AP7 25fr lil, dk brn & lt red brn 1.00 .25

Pan-African and Malagasy Posts and Telecommunications Cong., Cairo, Oct. 24-Nov. 6.

President John F. Kennedy (1917-63) — AP8

1964, Nov. 3 Photo. *Perf. 12½*
C20 AP8 100fr multi 3.00 1.00
a. Souvenir sheet of 4 12.00 6.00

ICY Emblem — AP9

1965, July 5 Photo. *Perf. 13*
C21 AP9 100fr multi 2.00 .60

International Cooperation Year, 1965.

Abraham Lincoln — AP10

1965, Sept. 7 Unwmk. *Perf. 13*
C22 AP10 100fr multi 3.00 .75

Centenary of death of Abraham Lincoln.

Musical Instrument Type

Design: 100fr, Xylophone (marimba).

1965, Oct. 26 Engr. *Perf. 13*
Size: 48x27mm
C23 A18 100fr ocher, brt bl & vio bl 2.75 1.00

Sir Winston Spencer Churchill (1874-1965) AP11

1965, Nov. 23 Engr. *Perf. 13*
C24 AP11 50fr dk grn & blk 2.00 .50

Dr. Albert Schweitzer and Outstretched Hands — AP12

1966, Feb. 15 Photo. *Perf. 12½*
C25 AP12 100fr multi 2.75 .80

Dr. Albert Schweitzer (1875-1965), medical missionary, theologian and musician.

Air Afrique Issue, 1966
Common Design Type

1966, Aug. 31 Photo. *Perf. 13*
C26 CD123 30fr yel grn, blk & gray 1.00 .25

White-throated Bee-eater — AP13

Birds: 50fr, Blue-eared glossy starling. 200fr, African pygmy kingfisher. 250fr, Red-throated bee-eater. 500fr, Little green bee-eater.

1966-67 Photo. *Perf. 13x12½*
C27 AP13 50fr gold & multi 1.50 .40
C28 AP13 100fr bluish gray & multi 3.50 1.00
C29 AP13 200fr grnsh gray & multi 6.75 1.75
C30 AP13 250fr pale bl & multi 7.50 1.75
C31 AP13 500fr pale sal & multi 14.00 3.25
Nos. C27-C31 (5) 33.25 8.15

Issued: 100fr, 200fr, 500fr, 8/18/66; others, 3/21/67.

For surcharges see Nos. C67-C69.

Congress Hall — AP14

1967, Jan. 5 Photo. *Perf. 12½*
C32 AP14 25fr multi 1.00 .25

Opening of the new Congress Hall.

Breguet 19 Biplane — AP15

Planes: 30fr, Latécoère 631 hydroplane. 50fr, Douglas DC-3. 100fr, Piper Cherokee 6.

1967, Aug. 1 Engr. *Perf. 13*
C33 AP15 25fr sky bl, sl grn & lt brn .75 .25
C34 AP15 30fr sky bl, indigo & grn 1.00 .30
C35 AP15 50fr sky bl, ol bis & sl grn 1.75 .60
C36 AP15 100fr dk bl, sl grn & dk red 3.50 .90
Nos. C33-C36 (4) 7.00 2.05

First anniversary of Air Chad.

African Postal Union Issue, 1967
Common Design Type

1967, Sept. 9 Engr. *Perf. 13*
C37 CD124 100fr ol, brt pink & red brn 2.00 .60

Rock Painting Type of Regular Issue

1967, Dec. 19 Engr. *Perf. 13*
Size: 48x27mm
C38 A32 100fr Masked dancers 8.00 .95
C39 A32 125fr Rabbit hunt 9.00 1.50

Downhill Skiing — AP16

1968, Feb. 5 Engr. *Perf. 13*
C40 AP16 30fr shown 1.25 .30
C41 AP16 100fr Ski jump, vert. 3.25 .90

10th Winter Olympic Games, Grenoble, France, Feb. 6-18.

Konrad Adenauer (1876-1967), Chancellor of West Germany (1949-63) AP17

1968, Mar. 19 Photo. *Perf. 12½*
C42 AP17 52fr grn, dk brn & lt lil 2.00 .50
a. Souvenir sheet of 4 6.00 3.00

The Snake Charmer, by Henri Rousseau — AP18

Design: 130fr, "War" by Henri Rousseau.

1968, May 14 Photo. *Perf. 13½*
Size: 41x41mm
C43 AP18 100fr ultra & multi 3.50 1.00

Size: 48x35mm

Perf. 12½

C44 AP18 130fr brn & multi 5.50 1.50

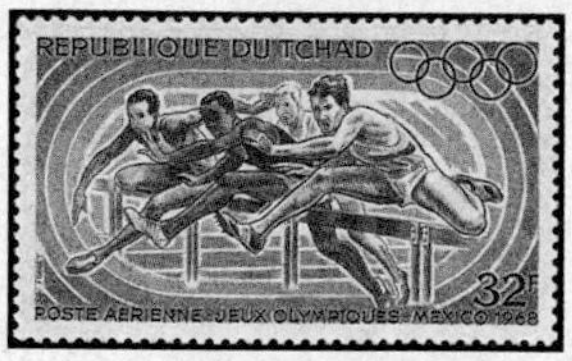

Hurdlers — AP19

1968, Oct. 16 Engr. *Perf. 13*

C45 AP19 32fr shown 1.20 .40
C46 AP19 80fr Relay race 2.75 .80

19th Olympic Games, Mexico City, 10/12-27.

PHILEXAFRIQUE Issue

The Actor Wolf (Bernard), by Jacques L. David AP20

1969, Jan. 15 Photo. *Perf. 12½*

C47 AP20 100fr multi 3.75 1.75

PHILEXAFRIQUE, Philatelic Exhib. in Abidjan, Feb. 14-23. Printed with alternating label. Value is for stamp with label attached.

2nd PHILEXAFRIQUE Issue

Common Design Type

50fr, Chad #J12 and Moundang Dancers.

1969, Feb. 14 Engr. *Perf. 13*

C48 CD128 50fr red, brt bl, brn & grn 2.40 1.00

Gustav Nachtigal and Tibesti Gorge, 1869 — AP21

No. C50, Heinrich Barth & Lake Chad, 1851.

1969, Feb. 17

C49 AP21 100fr vio bl, dk brn & brn 2.40 .60
C50 AP21 100fr grn, pur & bl 2.40 .60

German explorers Gustav Nachtigal (1834-85) and Heinrich Barth (1821-65), and state visit of the Pres. of West Germany Heinrich Lubke.

Apollo 8, Earth and Moon — AP22

1969, Apr. 10 Photo. *Perf. 13*

C51 AP22 100fr multi 3.00 .75

US Apollo 8 mission, the 1st men in orbit around the moon, Dec. 21-27, 1968.

Mahatma Gandhi — AP23

No. C53, John F. Kennedy. No. C54, Dr. Martin Luther King, Jr. No. C55, Robert F. Kennedy.

1969, May 20 Photo. *Perf. 12½*

C52 AP23 50fr blk & lt grn 1.25 .40
C53 AP23 50fr blk & tan 1.25 .40
C54 AP23 50fr blk & pink 1.25 .40
C55 AP23 50fr blk & lt vio bl 1.25 .40
a. Souvenir sheet of 4, #C52-C55 6.00 6.00
Nos. C52-C55 (4) 5.00 1.60

Issued to honor exponents of non-violence.

Presidents Tombalbaye and Mobutu, Map and Flags of Chad and Congo — AP24

Embossed on Gold Foil

1969 *Die-cut Perf. 13½*

C56 AP24 1000fr gold, dk bl & red 27.50 27.50

1st anniv. of the establishment of the Union of Central African States, comprising Chad, Congo Democratic Republic and Central African Republic.

Napoleon Visiting Hospital, by Alexandre Veron-Bellecourt — AP25

Paintings: 85fr, Battle of Wagram, by Horace Vernet. 130fr, Battle of Austerlitz, by Francois Pascal Gerard.

1969, July 23 Photo. *Perf. 12x12½*

C57 AP25 30fr multi 1.20 .40
C58 AP25 85fr multi 2.50 .75
C59 AP25 130fr multi 4.50 1.25
Nos. C57-C59 (3) 8.20 2.40

Bicentenary of birth of Napoleon I.

Apollo 11 Issue

Astronaut on Moon — AP26

Embossed on Gold Foil

1969, Oct. 17 *Die-cut Perf. 13½*

C60 AP26 1000fr gold 27.50 27.50

See note after Algeria No. 427.

Village Life, by Goto Narcisse — AP27

No. 62, Women at the Market, by Iba N'Diaye. No. 63, Woman with Flowers, by Iba N'Diaye, vert.

1970 Photo. *Perf. 12x12½, 12½x12*

C61 AP27 100fr multi 3.25 .75
C62 AP27 250fr grn & multi 5.00 1.00
C63 AP27 250fr brn & multi 5.00 1.00
Nos. C61-C63 (3) 13.25 2.75

Issued: 100fr, Mar. 17; Nos. C62-C63, Aug. 28.

Napoleon — AP27a

Designs: Nos. C63A, C63E, Napoleon II, Duke of Reichstadt, vert.

No. C63B: g, 10fr, Crossing the Grand St. Bernard, by David. h, 25fr, Emperor Napoleon, by Gerard. i, 32fr, Marriage of Napoleon and Marie Louise, by Rouget.

40fr, Napoleon after return from Elba, vert.

Perf. 12x12½, 12½x12

1970-71 Litho.

C63A AP27a 10fr multicolored 4.00 —
C63B AP27a Strip of 3, #g.-i. 14.00 —

Embossed

Perf. 13

C63C AP27a 10fr gold 20.00 —
f. Sheet of 1, Imperf. 37.50 —

Souvenir Sheets

Litho.

Perf. 13x13½

C63D AP27a 40fr multicolored 10.00 —

Embossed

Imperf

C63E AP27a 10fr gold, like #C63A 37.50 —

No. C63A is printed se-tenant with label. No. C63D contains one 43x67mm stamp. No. C63Cf contains one 53x42mm stamp with same size design as No. C63Bg. No. C63E contains one 43x104mm stamp with same size design as No. C63A.

No. C63E probably was not available in Chad.

Issued: No. C63B, 6/12; Nos. C63A, C63D-C63E, 4/1971; No. C63C, 11/1/71.

EXPO Emblem and Osaka Print — AP28

EXPO Emblem and: 100fr, Tower of the Sun. 125fr, Osaka print, diff.

1970, June 30 Engr. *Perf. 13*

C64 AP28 50fr bl, red brn & sl grn .70 .25
C65 AP28 100fr red, yel grn & Prus bl 1.40 .40
C66 AP28 125fr blk, dk red & bis 1.90 .60
Nos. C64-C66 (3) 4.00 1.25

Issued to publicize EXPO '70 International Exhibition, Osaka, Japan, Mar. 15-Sept. 13.

1968 Summer Olympics, 1970 World Cup Soccer Championships, Mexico AP28a

1970, July 1 Litho. *Perf. 12½x12*

C66A AP28a 5fr Flags, soccer players 1.50

Souvenir Sheet

Perf. 13½x13

C66C AP28a 15fr Olympic torch, soccer player 6.50

No. C66A printed in sheets of 2 + 2 labels.
No. C66C contains one 66x43mm stamp.
For overprints see Nos. C88A-C88B.

Nos. C28-C30 Surcharged and Overprinted in Carmine

a

b

c

1970, July 9 Photo. *Perf. 13x12½*

C67 AP13 (a) 50fr on 100fr 1.90 .25
C68 AP13 (b) 100fr on 200fr 3.25 .45
C69 AP13 (c) 125fr on 250fr 4.75 .55
Nos. C67-C69 (3) 9.90 1.25

Space missions of Apollo 11, 12 and 13.

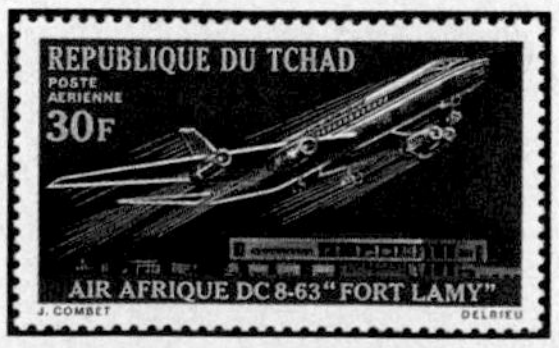

DC-8 "Fort Lamy" over Airport — AP29

1970, Aug. 5 *Perf. 12½*

C70 AP29 30fr dk sl grn & multi 1.20 .30

Souvenir Sheet

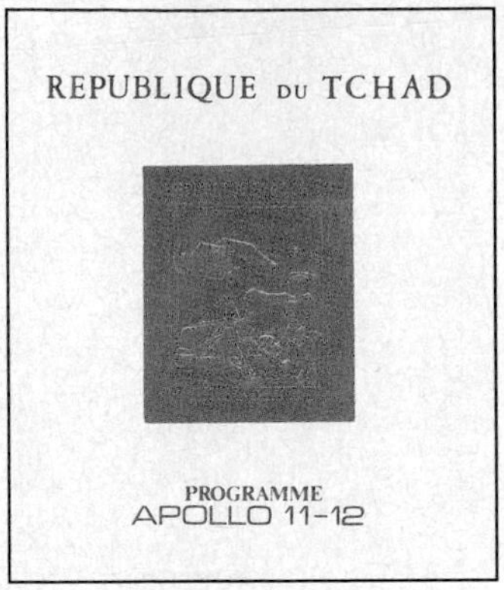

Apollo 12 — AP29a

1970, Sept. Embossed *Perf. 12¾*

C70A	AP29a 25fr gold	18.00	

No. C70A exists imperf. Value, $35.
No. C70A probably was not available in Chad.

The Visitation, Venetian School, 15th Century AP30

Paintings, Venetian School: 25fr, Nativity, 15th century. 30fr, Virgin and Child, c. 1350.

1970, Dec. 15 Photo. *Perf. 12½x12*

C71	AP30 20fr gold & multi	.75	.25
C72	AP30 25fr gold & multi	1.10	.25
C73	AP30 30fr gold & multi	1.25	.25
	Nos. C71-C73 (3)	3.10	.75

Christmas 1970. See Nos. C144-C147.

Post Office Mauritius and Emblem AP31

1971, Jan. 23 Engr. *Perf. 13*

C74	AP31 10fr shown	.25	.25
C75	AP31 20fr Tuscany #23	.40	.25
C76	AP31 30fr France #8	.60	.25
C77	AP31 60fr US #2	1.10	.30
C78	AP31 80fr Japan #8	1.50	.60
C79	AP31 100fr Saxony #1	1.90	.75
a.	Souvenir sheet of 6, #C74-C79	8.00	5.00
	Nos. C74-C79 (6)	5.75	2.40

Publicity for PHILEXOCAM, philatelic exhibition, Fort Lamy, Jan. 23-30.

Gamal Abdel Nasser — AP32

1971, Feb. 16 Photo. *Perf. 12½*

C80	AP32 75fr multi	2.00	.50

In memory of Gamal Abdel Nasser (1918-1970), President of Egypt.

Presidents Mobutu, Bokassa and Tombalbaye — AP33

1971, Apr. 28 Photo. *Perf. 13*

C81	AP33 100fr multi	2.00	.60

Return of Central African Republic to the United States of Central Africa which also includes Congo Democratic Republic and Chad.

Map of Africa, Communications Network and Symbols — AP34

1971, May 17 Engr. *Perf. 13*

C82	AP34 125fr ultra, sl grn & brn red	3.00	.75

Pan-African telecommunications system.

Boys Around Campfire, Torii AP35

1971, Aug. 24 Photo. *Perf. 12½*

C83	AP35 250fr multi	1.50	.40

13th Boy Scout World Jamboree, Asagiri Plain, Japan, Aug. 2-10.

White Egret — AP36

1971, Sept. 28 Photo. *Perf. 13x12½*

C84	AP36 1000fr blk, dk bl & ocher	75.00	12.50

Greek Marathon Runners — AP37

45fr, Ancient Olympic Stadium. 75fr, Greek wrestlers. 130fr, Olympic Stadium, Athens, 1896.

1971, Oct. 5 *Perf. 12½*

C85	AP37 40fr multi	.75	.25
C86	AP37 45fr multi	1.00	.25
C87	AP37 75fr multi	1.75	.40
C88	AP37 130fr multi	2.00	.75
	Nos. C85-C88 (4)	5.50	1.65

75th anniv. of modern Olympic Games.

Nos. C66A, C66C Ovptd. in Gold

1971 Litho. *Perf. 12½x12*

C88A	AP28a 5fr multi	2.50	

Souvenir Sheet

Perf. 13½x13

C88B	AP28a 15fr multi	5.50	

Overprint on No. C88B is 36mm long.

Duke Ellington — AP38

50fr, Sidney Bechet. 100fr, Louis Armstrong.

1971, Oct. 20 Litho. *Perf. 13*

C89	AP38 50fr multi	2.00	.50
C90	AP38 75fr lt bl & multi	3.00	.70
C91	AP38 100fr multi	5.00	.85
	Nos. C89-C91 (3)	10.00	2.05

Famous American jazz musicians.

Charles de Gaulle — AP39

Design: No. C93, Félix Eboué.

Lithographed and Embossed

1971, Nov. 9 *Perf. 12½*

C92	AP39 200fr grn, yel grn & gold	8.00	4.00
C93	AP39 200fr bl, lt bl & gold	8.00	4.00
a.	Souv. sheet, #C92-C93 + label	20.00	20.00

Charles de Gaulle (1890-1970), pres. of France.

African Postal Union Issue, 1971

Common Design Type

Design: 100fr, Sao antelope head and UAMPT building, Brazzaville, Congo.

1971, Nov. 13 Photo. *Perf. 13x13½*

C94	CD135 100fr bl & multi	1.50	.50

Apollo 15 Rocket AP40

80fr, Apollo 15 capsule, horiz. 150fr, Lunar module on Moon, horiz. 250fr, Astronaut making tests. 300fr, Moon-buggy. No. C100, Successful splashdown, horiz. No. C101, Apollo 15 insignia.

1972, Jan. 5 Litho. *Perf. 13½*

C95	AP40 40fr multi	.50	.25
C96	AP40 80fr multi	.90	.25
C97	AP40 150fr multi	1.50	.30
C98	AP40 250fr multi	2.50	.45
C99	AP40 300fr multi	3.00	.60
C100	AP40 500fr multi	5.50	1.40
	Nos. C95-C100 (6)	13.90	3.25

Souvenir Sheet

C101	AP40 500fr multi	8.00	2.50

Apollo 15 moon landing.

Soyuz 11 Link-up — AP41

Designs: 30fr, Soyuz 11 on launching pad, vert. 50fr, No. C108, Cosmonauts in uniform. 200fr, V. I. Patsayev. No. C106, V. N. Volkov. 400fr, G. L. Dobrovolsky. No. C109, Three cosmonauts.

1972, Jan. 5 *Perf. 13½x13*

C102	AP41 30fr multi	.25	.25
C103	AP41 50fr multi	.45	.25
C104	AP41 100fr multi	.80	.25
C105	AP41 200fr multi	2.00	.50
C106	AP41 300fr multi	3.25	.75
C107	AP41 400fr multi	4.25	1.10
	Nos. C102-C107 (6)	11.00	3.10

Souvenir Sheets

C108	AP41 300fr multi	3.50	1.25
C109	AP41 400fr multi	4.00	1.50

Soyuz 11 link-up project.

Bobsledding — AP42

Design: 100fr, Slalom.

1972, Feb. 24 Engr. *Perf. 13*

C110	AP42 50fr Prus bl & rose red	1.00	.30
C111	AP42 100fr red lil & slate grn	1.90	.50

11th Winter Olympic Games, Sapporo, Japan, Feb. 3-13.

Pres. Tombalbaye Type, 1972

1972, Apr. 13 Litho. *Perf. 13*

C112	A63 70fr multi	.90	.30
C113	A63 80fr multi	1.10	.35

11th Winter Olympic Type, 1972

130fr, Speed skating. No. C115, Ice hockey. No. C116, Ski jumping. 250fr, 4-man bobsled.

1972, Apr. 13 *Perf. 13½*

C114	A64 130fr multi	1.40	.45
C115	A64 200fr multi	2.50	.60

Souvenir Sheets

C116	A64 200fr multi	3.50	1.25
C117	A64 250fr multi	4.50	1.50

Scout Jamboree Type, 1972

Designs: 100fr, Cooking preparation. 120fr, Lord Baden Powell. 250fr, Hiking.

1972, May 15

C118	A67 100fr multi	2.25	.40
C119	A67 120fr multi	2.40	.50

Souvenir Sheet

C120	A67 250fr multi	8.50	1.75

Zebras — AP43

African wild animals: 30fr, Mandrills. 100fr, African elephants. 130fr, Gazelles. 150fr, Hippopotamuses. 200fr, Lion cub.

1972, May 15 Litho. *Perf. 13*

C121 AP43 20fr multi .35 .25
C122 AP43 30fr multi .50 .25
C123 AP43 100fr multi 1.40 .35
C124 AP43 130fr multi 2.25 .50
C125 AP43 150fr multi 3.50 .75
Nos. C121-C125 (5) 8.00 2.10

Souvenir Sheet

C126 AP43 200fr multi 35.00 25.00

View of Venice, by Caffi — AP44

Paintings by Ippolito Caffi: 40fr, Sailing ship and Doge's Palace, vert. 140fr, Grand Canal, vert.

1972, May 23 Photo.

C127 AP44 40fr gold & multi 1.10 .25
C128 AP44 45fr gold & multi 1.90 .25
C129 AP44 140fr gold & multi 3.50 .60
Nos. C127-C129 (3) 6.50 1.10

UNESCO campaign to save Venice.

11th Winter Olympic Winners Type, 1972

Designs: 150fr, Slalom, B. Cochran, US. 200fr, Women's figure skating, B. Schuba, Austria. 250fr, Ice hockey, USSR. 300fr, 2-man bobsled. W. Zimmerer and P. Utzschneider, West Germany.

1972, June 15 *Perf. 14½*

C130 A69 150fr gold & multi 3.00 .75
C131 A69 200fr gold & multi 3.75 1.00

Souvenir Sheets

C132 A69 250fr gold & multi 3.25 2.75
C133 A69 300fr gold & multi 3.75 3.00

Nos. C130-C131 exist se-tenant with label showing earth satellite.

Daudet, "Tartarin de Tarascon," Book Year Emblem — AP45

1972, July 22 Engr. *Perf. 13*

C134 AP45 100fr dk red, lil & dk brn 2.00 .60

Intl. Book Year, 1972, and to honor Alphonse Daudet (1840-1897), French writer.

20th Summer Olympics Type, 1972

Designs (TV Tower, Munich and): 100fr, Gymnast. 120fr, Pole vault. 150fr, Fencing. 250fr, Hammer throw. 300fr, Boxing.

1972, Aug. 15 *Perf. 14½*

C135 A70 100fr gold & multi 2.10 .50
C136 A70 120fr gold & multi 2.50 .60
C137 A70 150fr gold & multi 3.25 .80
Nos. C135-C137 (3) 7.85 1.90

Souvenir Sheets

C138 A70 250fr gold & multi 3.50 2.75
C139 A70 300fr gold & multi 4.00 3.00

Nos. C135-C137 exist se-tenant with label showing arms of Munich.

Lunokhod on Moon — AP46

Russian moon missions: 100fr, Luna 16 on moon and rocket in flight, vert.

1972, Sept. 19 *Perf. 13*

C140 AP46 100fr dk bl, pur & bis 1.90 .50
C141 AP46 150fr slate, brn & lil 2.50 .75

Farcha Laboratory, Cattle, Scientist — AP47

1972, Nov. 11 Photo. *Perf. 13*

C142 AP47 75fr yellow & multi 1.40 .30

20th anniversary of the Farcha Laboratory for veterinary research.

King Faisal and Holy Kaaba, Mecca — AP48

1972, Nov. 17

C143 AP48 75fr multi 1.40 .40

Visit of King Faisal of Saudi Arabia.

Christmas Type of 1970

Christmas: 40fr, Virgin and Child, by Giovanni Bellini. 75fr, Virgin and Child, by Dall'Occhio. 80fr, Nativity, by Fra Angelico, horiz. 95fr, Adoration of the Kings, by Il Perugino.

1972, Dec. 15 Photo. *Perf. 13*

C144 AP30 40fr gold & multi .25 .25
C145 AP30 75fr gold & multi 1.75 .30
C146 AP30 80fr gold & multi 2.00 .40
C147 AP30 95fr gold & multi 2.00 .50
Nos. C144-C147 (4) 6.00 1.45

Summer Olympic Winners Type, 1972

Olympic Emblems and: 150fr, Pole vault, Nordwig, East Germany. 250fr, Hurdles, Milburn, US. 300fr, Javelin, Wolfermann, West Germany.

1972, Dec. 22 *Perf. 11*

C148 A76 150fr multi 3.00 .60
C149 A76 250fr multi 4.25 .75

Souvenir Sheet

C150 A76 300fr multi 15.00 3.00

Summer Olympic Winners Type, 1972

Olympic Emblem and: 150fr, Dressage, Mancinelli, Italy. No. C152, Finn class sailing, Serge Maury, France. No. C153, Swimming, Mark Spitz.

1972, Dec. 22 Litho. *Perf. 11*

C151 A77 150fr gold & multi 3.25 .75
C152 A77 250fr gold & multi 5.00 1.00

Souvenir Sheet

C153 A77 250fr multi 15.00 3.00

Copernicus and Solar System — AP49

1973, Mar. 31 Engr. *Perf. 13*

C154 AP49 250fr gray, mag & brn 5.25 1.25

500th anniversary of the birth of Nicolaus Copernicus (1473-1543), Polish astronomer.

Horses — AP49a

Details from paintings: 20fr, A Horse Frightened by Lightning, by Theordore Gericault. 60fr, The White Horse, by Paul Potter. 100fr, Mares and Foals, by George Stubbs. 150fr, Horse Head, by Theordore Gericault, vert. 500fr, The Carriage, by Vernet.

1973 Litho. *Perf. 11½*

C154A AP49a 20fr multi
C154B AP49a 60fr multi
C154C AP49a 100fr multi
C154D AP49a 150fr multi
Nos. C154A-C154D (4) 14.00

Souvenir Sheet

Perf. 15

C154E AP49a 500fr multi 15.00

See note before No. 225A.

Airplanes — AP49b

5fr, Fokker F VII/3M. 25fr, DH 89A Rapide. 70fr, Viscount. 150fr, Boeing 747. 200fr, Concorde.
350fr, Concorde, diff.

1973 Litho. *Perf. 12*

C154F AP49b 5fr multi
C154G AP49b 25fr multi
C154H AP49b 70fr multi
C154J AP49b 150fr multi
C154K AP49b 200fr multi
Nos. C154F-C154K (5) 14.00

Souvenir Sheet

Perf. 12

C154L AP49b 350fr multi 14.00

Nos. C154L contains one 60x40mm stamp.
See note before No. 225A.

Skylab over Africa — AP50

1974, Aug. 6 Engr. *Perf. 13*

C155 AP50 100fr shown 1.50 .25
C156 AP50 150fr Skylab 2.50 .60

Exploits of Skylab, US manned space station.

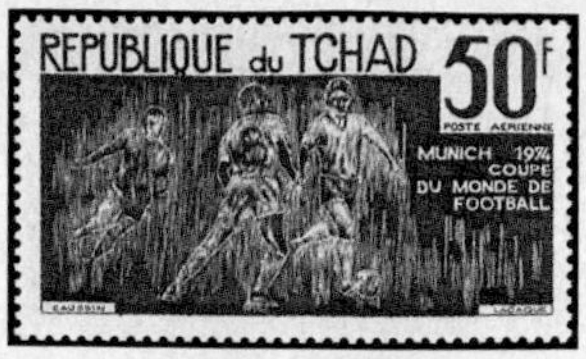

Soccer — AP51

125fr, 150fr, Soccer players; 125fr, vert.

1974, Oct. 22 Engr. *Perf. 13*

C157 AP51 50fr dl red & choc .75 .25
C158 AP51 125fr red & dp grn 1.75 .50
C159 AP51 150fr grn & rose red 2.50 .75
Nos. C157-C159 (3) 5.00 1.50

World Cup Soccer Championship, Munich, June 13-July 7.

Family and WPY Emblem — AP52

1974, Nov. 11

C160 AP52 250fr multi 4.00 1.25

World Population Year.

Mail Delivery by Canoe — AP53

UPU Cent.: 40fr, Diesel train. 100fr, Jet. 150fr, Spacecraft.

1974, Dec. 20 Engr. *Perf. 13*

C161 AP53 30fr car & multi .60 .25
C162 AP53 40fr ultra & blk 1.00 .25
C163 AP53 100fr brn, ultra & blk 1.90 .40
C164 AP53 150fr grn, lil & ol 2.40 .55
Nos. C161-C164 (4) 5.90 1.45

Women of Different Races, IWY Emblem — AP54

1975, June 25 Photo. *Perf. 13*

C165 AP54 250fr bl & multi 4.50 1.25

International Women's Year 1975.

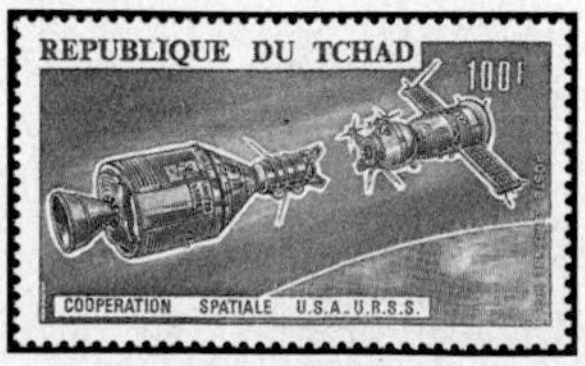

Apollo and Soyuz Before Link-up — AP55

130fr, Apollo and Soyuz after link-up.

1975, July 15 Engr. *Perf. 13*

C166 AP55 100fr ultra, choc & grn 1.50 .40
C167 AP55 130fr vio bl, brn & grn 2.00 .50

Apollo Soyuz space test project (Russo-American space cooperation), launching 7/15; link-up 7/17.

For overprints see Nos. C171-C172.

Soccer Player, View of Montreal — AP56

Olympic Rings, Montreal Skyline: 100fr, Discus thrower. 125fr, Runner.

1975, Oct. 14 Engr. *Perf. 13*

C168 AP56 75fr car & slate grn 1.00 .25
C169 AP56 100fr car, choc & bl grn 1.40 .40
C170 AP56 125fr brn, bl & car 1.90 .75
Nos. C168-C170 (3) 4.30 1.40

Pre-Olympic Year 1975.

Nos. C166-C167 Overprinted: "JONCTION / 17 JUILLET 1975"

1975, Nov. 4 Engr. *Perf. 13*

C171 AP55 100fr multi 1.75 .25
C172 AP55 130fr multi 2.10 .35

Apollo-Soyuz link-up in space, July 17.

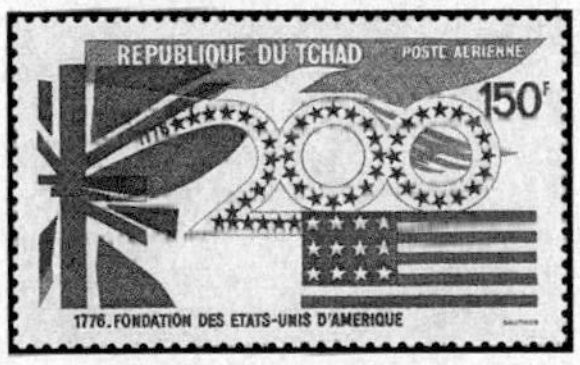

Stylized British and American Flags, "200" — AP57

1975, Dec. 5 Engr. *Perf. 13*

C173 AP57 150fr vio bl, car & ol bls 2.25 .75

American Bicentennial.

Adoration of the Shepherds, by Murillo — AP58

Christmas (Paintings): 75fr, Adoration of the Shepherds, by Georges de La Tour. 80fr, Virgin and Child with Bible, by Rogier van der Weyden, vert. 100fr, Holy Family, by Raphael, vert.

1975, Dec. 15 Litho. *Perf. 13x12½*

C174 AP58 40fr yel & multi .75 .25
C175 AP58 75fr yel & multi 1.25 .35
C176 AP58 80fr yel & multi 1.75 .40
C177 AP58 100fr yel & multi 2.75 .75
Nos. C174-C177 (4) 6.50 1.75

12th Winter Olympic Winners Type, 1976

250fr, 4-man bobsled, West Germany. 300fr, Speed skating, J. E. Storholt, Norway. 500fr, Downhill skiing, F. Klammer, Austria.

1976, June 21 *Perf. 14*

C178 A84 250fr multi 2.75 .60
C179 A84 300fr multi 3.50 1.00

Souvenir Sheet

C180 A84 500fr multi 6.00 3.00

Paul Revere's Ride and Portrait by Copley — AP59

American Bicentennial: 125fr, Washington crossing Delaware. 150fr, Lafayette offering his services to America. 200fr, Rochambeau at Yorktown with Washington. 250fr, Franklin presenting Declaration of Independence. 400fr, Count de Grasse's victory at Cape Charles.

1976, July 4 Litho. *Perf. 14*

C181 AP59 100fr multi 1.10 .30
C182 AP59 125fr multi 1.25 .35
C183 AP59 150fr multi 1.90 .40
C184 AP59 200fr multi 2.25 .50
C185 AP59 250fr multi 3.00 .55
Nos. C181-C185 (5) 9.50 2.10

Souvenir Sheet

C186 AP59 400fr multi 6.00 3.00

Summer Olympics Type, 1976

1976, July 12 *Perf. 13½*

C187 A85 100fr Boxing 1.50 .30
C188 A85 200fr Pole vault 2.50 .50
C189 A85 300fr Shot put 4.00 .65
Nos. C187-C189 (3) 8.00 1.45

Souvenir Sheet

C190 A85 500fr Sprint 6.00 3.00

Viking Mars Project Type, 1976

Mars Lander and: 100fr, Viking landing on Mars. 200fr, Capsule over Mars. 250fr, Lander over Mars. 450fr, Lander and probe.

1976, July 23 Litho. *Perf. 14*

C191 A86 100fr multi 1.10 .30
C192 A86 200fr multi 2.25 .55
C193 A86 250fr multi 2.50 .75
Nos. C191-C193 (3) 5.85 1.60

Souvenir Sheet

C194 A86 450fr multi 7.50 3.00

For overprints see Nos. C240-C243.

Concorde — AP60

1976, Oct. 15 Litho. *Perf. 12½*

C195 AP60 250fr bl, blk & ver 6.00 1.75

First commercial flight of supersonic jet Concorde, Jan. 21.

Nobel Prize Type, 1976

100fr, Albert Einstein, physics. 200fr, Dag Hammarskjold, peace. 300fr, Shinichiro Tomanaga, physics. 500fr, Alexander Fleming, medicine.

1976, Dec. 15 *Perf. 14*

C196 A87 100fr multi 1.50 .30
C197 A87 200fr multi 2.50 .55
C198 A87 300fr multi 3.50 .70
Nos. C196-C198 (3) 7.50 1.55

Souvenir Sheet

C199 A87 500fr multi 8.00 3.50

Adoration of the Shepherds, by Gerard van Honthorst — AP61

Christmas (Paintings): 30fr, Nativity, by Albrecht Altdorfer, vert. 60fr, Nativity, by Hans Holbein, vert. 150fr, Adoration of the Kings, by Gerard David.

1976, Dec. 22 Litho. *Perf. 12½*

C200 AP61 30fr gold & multi .50 .25
C201 AP61 60fr gold & multi .75 .25
C202 AP61 120fr gold & blk 1.50 .50
C203 AP61 150fr gold & blk 2.25 .75
Nos. C200-C203 (4) 5.00 1.75

Lesdiguières Bridge, by Jongkind — AP62

Design: 120fr, Sailing Ship and Boats, by Johan Barthold Jongkind (1819-1891).

1976, Dec. 27 Photo. *Perf. 13*

C204 AP62 100fr multi 1.75 .55
C205 AP62 120fr multi 2.25 .60

Centenary of impressionism.

Zeppelin Type of 1977

125fr, Germany #C40, North Pole. 150fr, Germany #C45, Chicago department store. 175fr, Germany #C38 and scenes of NYC and London. 200fr, 500fr, US #C15, NYC.

1977, Mar. 30 *Perf. 11*

C206 A91 125fr multi 1.90 .35
C207 A91 150fr multi 2.25 .40
C208 A91 175fr multi 2.75 .50
C209 A91 200fr multi 3.25 .60
Nos. C206-C209 (4) 10.15 1.85

Souvenir Sheet

C210 A91 500fr multi 8.00 3.00

Sassenage Castle, Grenoble — AP63

1977, May 21 Litho. *Perf. 12½*

C211 AP63 100fr multi 1.00 .30

Intl. French Language Council, 10th Anniv.

Lafayette and Ships — AP64

American Bicentennial: 120fr, Abraham Lincoln, eagle and flags, vert. 150fr, James Madison and family.

1977, July 30 Engr. *Perf. 13*

C212 AP64 100fr multi 1.40 .35
C213 AP64 120fr multi 1.75 .40
C214 AP64 150fr multi 2.25 .50
Nos. C212-C214 (3) 5.40 1.25

Lindbergh and Spirit of St. Louis — AP65

100fr, Concorde. 150fr, 200fr, 300fr, Various Lindbergh portraits & Spirit of St. Louis.

1977, Sept. 27

C215 AP65 100fr multi 1.25 .30
C216 AP65 120fr multi 1.25 .40
C217 AP65 150fr multi 1.40 .55
C218 AP65 200fr multi 2.25 .65
C219 AP65 300fr multi 3.00 .90
Nos. C215-C219 (5) 9.15 2.80

Charles A. Lindbergh's solo transatlantic flight from NY to Paris, 50th anniv., and 1st supersonic transatlantic flight of Concorde.

For overprint see No. C227.

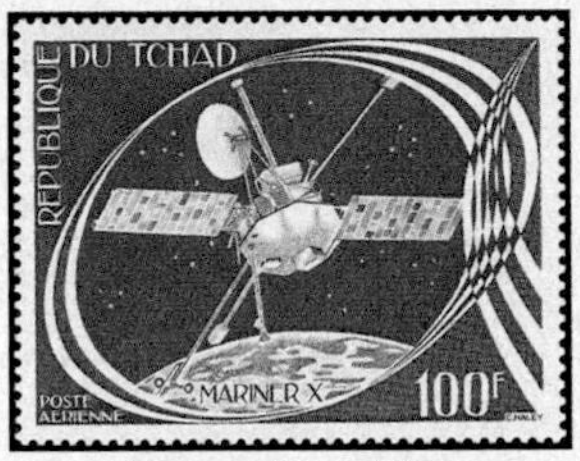

Mariner 10 — AP66

Spacecraft: 200fr, Lunokhod on moon, Luna 21. 300fr, Viking on Mars.

1977, Oct. 10 Engr. *Perf. 13*

C220 AP66 100fr multi 1.25 .40
C221 AP66 200fr multi 2.00 .70
C222 AP66 300fr multi 2.75 .90
Nos. C220-C222 (3) 6.00 2.00

Running — AP67

1977, Oct. 24 Engr. *Perf. 13*

C223 AP67 30fr shown .40 .25
C224 AP67 60fr Volleyball .85 .25
C225 AP67 120fr Soccer 1.50 .45
C226 AP67 125fr Basketball 1.25 .50
Nos. C223-C226 (4) 4.00 1.45

No. C215 Overprinted: "PARIS NEW-YORK / 22.11.77"

1977, Nov. 22

C227 AP65 100fr multi 3.25 .25

Concorde, 1st commercial flight Paris-NYC.

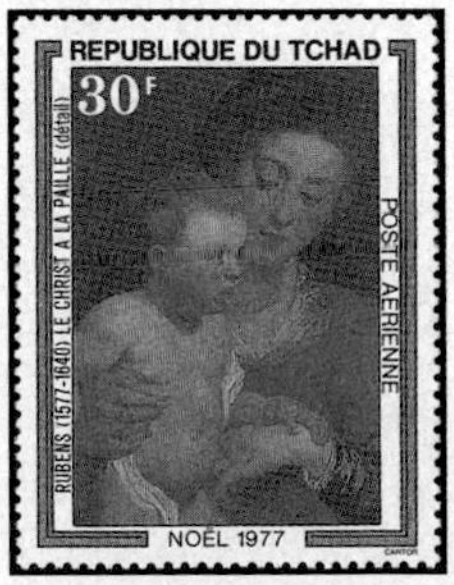

Virgin and Child, by Rubens AP68

Rubens Paintings: 60fr, Virgin and Child and Two Donors. 100fr, Adoration of the Shepherds. 125fr, Adoration of the Kings.

1977, Dec. 20 Litho. *Perf. 12½x12*

C228 AP68 30fr multi .75 .25
C229 AP68 60fr multi 1.10 .30
C230 AP68 100fr multi 1.50 .40
C231 AP68 125fr multi 1.90 .60
Nos. C228-C231 (4) 5.25 1.55

Christmas 1977.

Antoine de Saint-Exupéry — AP69

50fr, Wilbur & Orville Wright & Flyer. 80fr, Hugo Junkers & his plane. 100fr, Gen. Italo Balbo & his plane. 120fr, Concorde. 500fr, Wilbur & Orville Wright & Flyer.

1978, Oct. 25 Litho. *Perf. 13½*

C232	AP69	40fr multi	.60	.25
C233	AP69	50fr multi	.75	.25
C234	AP69	80fr multi	1.10	.30
C235	AP69	100fr multi	1.50	.40
C236	AP69	120fr multi	1.75	.50
		Nos. C232-C236 (5)	5.70	1.70

Souvenir Sheet

C237	AP69	500fr multi	6.75	2.00

History of aviation and 75th anniversary of 1st powered flight.

Philexafrique II-Essen Issue

Common Design Types

No. C238, Rhinoceros & Chad #C6. No. C239, Kingfisher & Mecklenburg-Strelitz #1.

1978, Nov. 1 *Perf. 12½*

C238	CD138	100fr multi	3.00	1.00
C239	CD139	100fr multi	3.00	1.00
a.		Pair, #C238-C239 + label	8.00	4.00

Nos. C191-C194 Overprinted "ALUNISSAGE/APOLLO XI/ JUILLET 1969"

1979, Nov. 26 Litho. *Perf. 13½x14*

C240	A86	100fr multi	1.10	.35
C241	A86	200fr multi	2.25	.65
C242	A86	250fr multi	2.50	1.00
		Nos. C240-C242 (3)	5.85	2.00

Souvenir Sheet

C243	A86	450fr multi	5.50	4.50

Apollo 11 moon landing, 10th anniversary.

Hurdles, Moscow '80 Emblem — AP70

Emblem and: 30fr, Field hockey. 250fr, Swimming. 350fr, Running. 500fr, Yachting.

1979, Nov. 30 *Perf. 13½*

C244	AP70	15fr multi	.25	.25
C245	AP70	30fr multi	.30	.25
C246	AP70	250fr multi	1.90	.60
C247	AP70	350fr multi	3.00	1.10
		Nos. C244-C247 (4)	5.45	2.20

Souvenir Sheet

C248	AP70	500fr multi	5.75	3.00

Pre-Olympic Year.

For overprints see Nos. C254-C255.

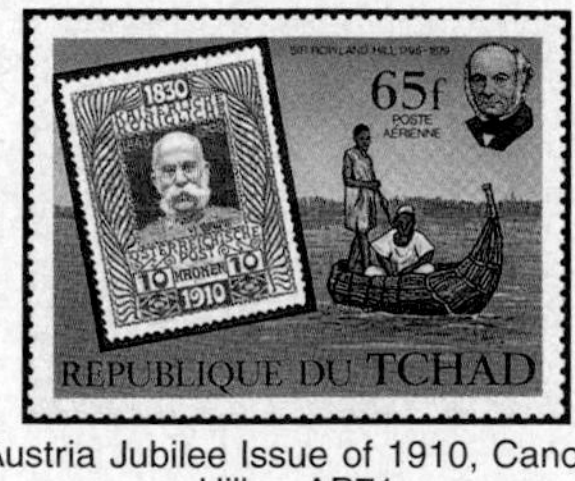

Austria Jubilee Issue of 1910, Canoe, Hill — AP71

Hill, Stamps & Vessels: 100fr, US design A97, dhow. 200fr, France #21, Sidewheeler. 300fr, Holstein #16, ocean liner. 500fr, Chad #J13, ocean liner.

1979, Dec. 3 *Perf. 14x13½*

C249	AP71	65fr multi	.60	.25
C250	AP71	100fr multi	1.40	.25
C251	AP71	200fr multi	2.25	.45
C252	AP71	300fr multi	2.75	.70
		Nos. C249-C252 (4)	7.00	1.65

Souvenir Sheet

C253	AP71	500fr multi	5.75	3.00

Sir Rowland Hill (1795-1879), originator of penny postage.

For overprints see Nos. C256-C257.

Nos. C244-C245, C249-C250 Overprinted: "POSTES 1981" in Red or Overprinted and Surcharged Silver on Red

Perf. 13½, 14x13½

1981, Nov. 15 Litho.

C254	AP70	30fr on 15fr multi	1.25	.40
C255	AP70	30fr multi	1.25	.40
C256	AP71	60fr on 65fr multi	2.25	.70
C257	AP71	60fr on 100fr multi	2.25	.70
		Nos. C254-C257 (4)	7.00	2.20

Soccer Type of 1982 and

1982 World Cup Soccer Championships, Spain — AP71a

80fr, Brazil. 300fr, W. Germany.

No. C259C, Soccer players, ball, & trophy, vert.

1982 Litho. *Perf. 13½*

C258	A108	80fr multi	1.00	.25
C259	A108	300fr multi	3.00	.50

Souvenir Sheet

C259A	A108	500fr like 300fr	6.00	2.00

Litho. & Embossed

C259B	AP71a	1500fr shown	16.00	

Souvenir Sheet

C259C	AP71a	1500fr gold & multi	14.00	

No. C259A contains one 42x51mm stamp.

No. C259B exists in a souvenir sheet of 1. Value $42.50.

For surcharge see No. C305.

Diana Type of 1982 and

Princess Diana, 21st Birthday — AP71b

Design: No. C262A, Portrait, horiz.

1982, July 2 Litho. *Perf. 13½*

C260	A109	80fr 1977	1.00	.25
C261	A109	300fr 1980	3.00	.95

Souvenir Sheet

C262	A109	500fr 1981	5.50	2.00

Litho. & Embossed

C262A	AP71b	1500fr gold & multi	16.00	

Souvenir Sheet

C262B	AP71b	1500fr gold & multi	16.00	

No. C262A exists in a souvenir sheet of 1. Value $42.50.

For overprints see Nos. 419A-419B.

Manned Flight Bicentenary AP72

Balloons: 100fr, Charles' & Roberts', 1783. 200fr, J.P. Blanchard, Berlin, 1788. 300fr, Charles Green, London, 1837. 400fr, Modern blimp. 500fr, Montgolfiere, 1783.

1983, Apr. Litho. *Perf. 13*

C263	AP72	100fr multi, vert.	1.25	.25
C264	AP72	200fr multi, vert.	2.50	.40
C265	AP72	300fr multi	3.50	.60
C266	AP72	400fr multi	4.75	.75
		Nos. C263-C266 (4)	12.00	2.00

Souvenir Sheet

C267	AP72	500fr multi, vert.	5.75	2.50

Balloon Type and

First Balloon Ascension, Bicent. — AP72a

80fr, Steam Powered Airship, H. Giffard. 250fr, Graf Zeppelin; Airship L-1, 1st flight. 300fr, 1st Balloon Flight, Montgolfier & Rozier. No. C270A, Airship Hindenburg, Count Ferdinand von Zeppelin. No. C270B, Jean-Francois Pilatre de Rozier & Marquis d'Arlandes, 1st balloon ascension.

1983, May 30 Litho. *Perf. 13½*

C268	A116	80fr multi	1.00	.25
C269	A116	250fr multi	3.00	.40

Souvenir Sheet

C270	A116	300fr multi	3.75	2.50

Litho. & Embossed

Perf. 13½

C270A	AP72a	1500fr gold & multi	16.00	

Souvenir Sheet

C270B	AP72a	1500fr gold & multi	12.00	

No. C270A exists in a souvenir sheet of 1. Value $25.

For surcharge see No. C299.

1984 Summer Olympics — AP73

Various kayak scenes.

1984, Mar. 1 Litho. *Perf. 13*

C271	AP73	100fr multi	1.00	.25
C272	AP73	200fr multi	2.00	.25
C273	AP73	300fr multi	3.00	.50
C274	AP73	400fr multi	4.00	.60
		Nos. C271-C274 (4)	10.00	1.60

Souvenir Sheet

C275	AP73	500fr multi	5.00	3.50

Natl. Goals AP73a

Nos. C276, C278, Peace & reconciliation. Nos. C277, C279, Self-sufficiency in food production.

1983, Dec. 26 Litho. *Perf. 13½*

C276	AP73a	150fr multi	1.50	.40
C277	AP73a	150fr multi	1.50	.40
C278	AP73a	200fr multi	2.25	.55
C279	AP73a	200fr multi	2.25	.55
		Nos. C276-C279 (4)	7.50	1.90

For surcharges see Nos. C300-C301.

Souvenir Sheet

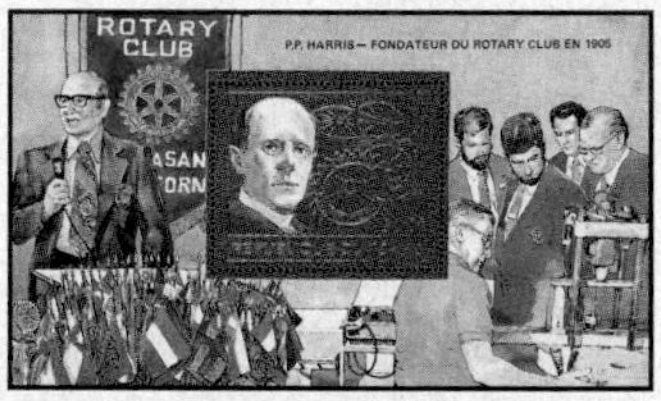

Paul P. Harris (1868-1947), Founder of Rotary Intl. — AP73b

Litho. & Embossed

1984, Jan. 16 *Perf. 13½*

C279B	AP73b	1500fr gold & multi	12.00	

IYY, PHILEXAFRICA '85 — AP74

No. C280, Boy scout, tree. No. C281, Air Chad Fokker 27.

1985, May 2 Litho. *Perf. 13*

C280	AP74	200fr multicolored	3.00	1.50
C281	AP74	200fr multicolored	3.00	1.50
a.		Pair, #C280-C281 + label	6.75	5.00

IYY, PHILEXAFRICA Type of 1985

No. C283, Girl, Scout ceremony. No. C284, Communications and transportation.

1985, Nov. 1 Litho. *Perf. 13x12½*

C283	AP74	250fr multicolored	3.00	1.50
C284	AP74	250fr multicolored	3.00	1.50
a.		Pair, #C283-C284 + label	6.75	5.00

ASCENA Airlines, 25th Anniv. — AP75

1985, Aug. 25 *Perf. 12½*

C285	AP75	70fr bl & multi	.60	.25
C286	AP75	110fr org & multi	1.00	.25
C287	AP75	250fr yel & multi	2.25	.80
		Nos. C285-C287 (3)	3.85	1.30

Victor Hugo (1802-1885), French Novelist — AP76

Scene from Les Miserables.

1985, Nov. 24 Engr. *Perf. 13*

C288	AP76	70fr org brn, chlky bl & dp brn	.75	.25
C289	AP76	110fr lake, dk brn & dk grn	1.00	.30
C290	AP76	250fr brt org, blk & dk red	2.50	.80
C291	AP76	300fr dk red, cl & sl bl	2.75	.90
		Nos. C288-C291 (4)	7.00	2.25

Adoration of the Magi — AP77

1985, Dec. 22 Litho. *Perf. 13½*

C292	250fr multicolored	2.25	.60

Christmas 1985.

1988 Summer Olympics, Seoul — AP78

100fr, 400-Meter hurdles, vert. 170fr, 5000-Meter race. 200fr, Long jump. 600fr, Triple jump, vert.
750fr, 10,000-Meter race, vert.

1988, June 1 Litho. *Perf. 13*

C293	AP78	100fr multi	1.10	.30
C294	AP78	170fr multi	1.75	.55
C295	AP78	200fr multi	2.25	.65
C296	AP78	600fr multi	5.75	2.00
		Nos. C293-C296 (4)	10.85	3.50

Souvenir Sheet

C297	AP78	750fr multi	8.00	6.00

Stamps of 1982-84 Surcharged

1989 *Perfs. as Before*

C298	A115	100 on 300fr #446
C299	A116	100 on 250fr #C269
C300	AP73a	100 on 200fr #C278
C301	AP73a	100 on 200fr #C279
C302	A110	170 on 300fr #404
C303	A122	170 on 200fr #503
C304	A123	170 on 250fr #509
C305	A108	170 on 300fr #C259
C306	A112	240 on 300fr #425

AIR POST SEMI-POSTAL STAMPS

Catalogue values for unused stamps in this section are for Never Hinged items.

Ramses II Battling the Hittites (from Abu Simbel) — SPAP1

Unwmk.

1964, Mar. 9 Engr. *Perf. 13*

CB1	SPAP1	10fr + 5fr multi	.75	.25
CB2	SPAP1	25fr + 5fr multi	1.40	.40
CB3	SPAP1	50fr + 5fr multi	2.75	.75
		Nos. CB1-CB3 (3)	4.90	1.40

UNESCO world campaign to save historic monuments in Nubia.

Lions Emblem SPAP2

1967, July 5 Photo. *Perf. 13*

CB4	SPAP2	50fr + 10fr multi	2.00	.25

50th anniv. of Lions Intl. and to publicize the Lions work for the blind.

POSTAGE DUE STAMPS

Postage Due Stamps of France Overprinted

1928 Unwmk. *Perf. 14x13½*

J1	D2	5c light blue	.80	1.20
J2	D2	10c gray brown	.80	1.20
J3	D2	20c olive green	.80	1.20
J4	D2	25c bright rose	1.20	1.60
J5	D2	30c light red	1.20	1.60
J6	D2	45c blue green	1.60	2.00
J7	D2	50c brown violet	2.40	2.40
J8	D2	60c yellow brown	2.40	2.40
J9	D2	1fr red brown	2.40	2.75
J10	D2	2fr orange red	5.50	6.00
J11	D2	3fr bright violet	4.75	5.50
		Nos. J1-J11 (11)	23.85	27.85

Huts — D3

Canoe — D4

1930 Typo. *Perf. 14x13½, 13½x14*

J12	D3	5c dp bl & olive	.40	.80
J13	D3	10c dk red & brn	.40	.80
J14	D3	20c grn & brn	1.20	1.60
J15	D3	25c lt bl & brn	1.20	2.40
J16	D3	30c bis brn & Prus bl	1.60	2.00
J17	D3	45c Prus bl & olive	2.40	2.75
J18	D3	50c red vio & brn	2.40	4.00
J19	D3	60c gray lil & bl blk	3.25	4.75
J20	D4	1fr bis brn & bl blk	3.25	4.75
J21	D4	2fr vio & brn	8.00	8.00
J22	D4	3fr dp red & brn	35.00	40.00
		Nos. J12-J22 (11)	59.10	71.85

In 1934 stamps of Chad were superseded by those of French Equatorial Africa.

Catalogue values for unused stamps in this section, from this point to the end of the section, are for Never Hinged items.

Republic

Rhinoceros — D5

Tibesti Pictographs: #J24, Kudu. #J25, 2 antelopes. #J26, 3 antelopes. #J27, Ostrich. #J28, Horned bull. #J29, Bull. #J30, Wild swine. #J31, Elephant. #J32, Rhinoceros. #J33, Warrior with spear and shield. #J34, Masked archer.

Unwmk.

1962, Apr. 20 Engr. *Perf. 13*

J23	D5	50c olive bister	.30	.25
J24	D5	50c brown red	.30	.25
a.		Pair, #J23-J24	.55	
J25	D5	1fr blue	.40	.25
J26	D5	1fr green	.40	.25
a.		Pair, #J25-J26	.75	
J27	D5	2fr vermilion	.50	.25
J28	D5	2fr maroon	.50	.25
a.		Pair, #J27-J28	1.00	
J29	D5	5fr slate green	.75	.40
J30	D5	5fr violet blue	.75	.40
a.		Pair, #J29-J30	1.50	
J31	D5	10fr brown	1.40	.75
J32	D5	10fr orange brown	1.40	.75
a.		Pair, #J31-J32	2.75	
J33	D5	25fr carmine rose	3.25	1.75
J34	D5	25fr violet	3.25	1.75
a.		Pair, #J33-J34	6.50	
		Nos. J23-J34 (12)	13.20	7.30

Dolls — D6

1969, Sept. 19 Engr. *Perf. 14x13*

J35	D6	1fr Kanem	.25	.25
J36	D6	2fr Kotoko	.25	.25
J37	D6	5fr Leather	.40	.25
J38	D6	10fr Kotoko	.50	.25
J39	D6	25fr Guera	.60	.25
		Nos. J35-J39 (5)	2.00	1.25

MILITARY STAMPS

Catalogue values for unused stamps in this section are for Never Hinged items.

No. 78 Overprinted "F.M."

1965 Typo. *Perf. 14x13½*

M1	A5	20fr red & black	300.00	300.00

Flag Bearer and Map of Chad — M1

1968 Unwmk. Litho. *Perf. 13x12½*

M2	M1	tan & multi	2.00	5.00

1st Regiment Emblem — M2

1972, Jan. 21 Photo. *Perf. 13*

M3	M2	blue & multi	1.00	2.00

OFFICIAL STAMPS

Catalogue values for unused stamps in this section are for Never Hinged items.

Flag and Map of Chad — O1

Perf. 13½x14

1966-71 Typo. Unwmk.

Flag in blue, yellow and carmine

O1	O1	1fr light blue	.25	.25
O2	O1	2fr gray	.25	.25
O3	O1	5fr black	.25	.25
O4	O1	10fr violet blue	.25	.25
O5	O1	25fr orange	.30	.25
O6	O1	30fr bright green	.50	.25
O7	O1	40fr carmine ('71)	.75	.25
O8	O1	50fr red lilac	.75	.25
O9	O1	85fr green	1.10	.30
O10	O1	100fr brown	1.75	.35
O11	O1	200fr red	3.00	.50
		Nos. O1-O11 (11)	9.15	3.15

Flag and Map Type of 1966-71 Redrawn with "N'Djamena" as Capital on Map

Perf. 13½x13¼, 11¾ (100fr)

1993-2000 ? Litho.

Center Flag Stripe in Yellow Frame Color

O13	O1	100fr brown	—	—
O14	O1	200fr red	—	—

Nos. O13 and O14 have a large "F" in denomination, "POSTES" without serifs, and has printer's inscription of "COURVOISIER."

Center Flag Stripe in Orange Frame Color

O17	O1	50fr green	—	—
O18	O1	85fr orange	—	—
O19	O1	100fr red orange	—	—
O20	O1	150fr blue green	—	—
O21	O1	200fr green	—	—
O22	O1	250fr lilac	—	—
O23	O1	300fr blue	—	—
O24	O1	500fr red	—	—
O25	O1	1000fr dark green	—	—

Additional stamps may have been issued in this set. The editors would like to examine any examples. Numbers may change.

CHILE

'chi-lē

LOCATION — Southwest corner of South America
GOVT. — Republic
AREA — 284,520 sq. mi.
POP. — 14,973,843 (1999 est.)
CAPITAL — Santiago

100 Centavos = 1 Peso
1000 Milésimos = 100 Centésimos = 1 Escudo (1960)
100 Centavos = 1 Peso (1975)

Catalogue values for unused stamps in this country are for Never Hinged items, beginning with Scott 257 in the regular postage section, Scott B3 in the semi-postal section, Scott C125 in the airpost section, and Scott CB1 in the airpost semi-postal section.

Issues of the Republic

Unused values for Nos. 1-14 are for stamps without gum. Examples with original gum are very scarce and are worth considerably more.

Pen cancellations are common on the 1862-67 issues. Such stamps sell for much less than the quoted values which are for those with handstamped postal cancellations.

Watermarks

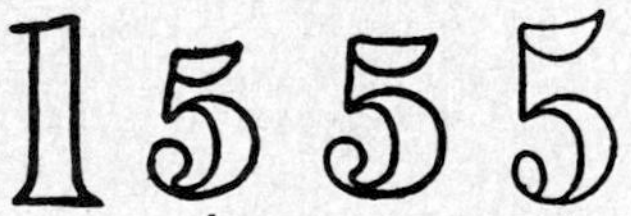

a b c d

e f g

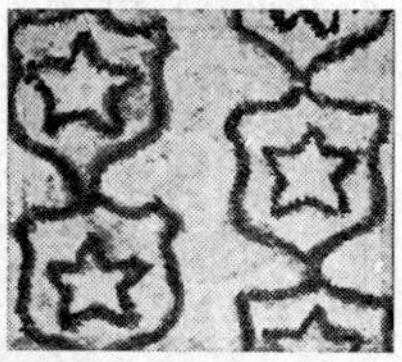

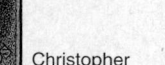

Wmk. 215 — Small Star in Shield, Multiple

Christopher Columbus — A1

London Prints

1853 Wmk. b Engr. *Imperf.*

Blued Paper

1	A1	5c brown red	650.00	150.00
a.		White paper		250.00

Wmk. e

White Paper

2	A1	10c dp brt bl	1,000.	175.00
a.		Blued paper		225.00
b.		Diag. half used as 5c on cover		800.00
c.		Horiz. half used as 5c on cover		800.00
d.		Vert. half used as 5c on cover		800.00

Santiago Prints

Impressions Fine and Clear

1854 Wmk. b and e

White Paper

3	A1	5c pale red brn	600.00	67.50
a.		5c deep red brown	650.00	67.50
b.		5c chestnut	1,000.	200.00
e.		Double impression		275.00
4	A1	5c burnt sienna	1,800.	300.00
a.		5c dull chocolate	3,500.	2,000.
5	A1	10c deep blue	1,200.	275.00
a.		10c slate blue		275.00
b.		10c greenish blue		*475.00*
d.		Diag. half used as 5c on cover		450.00
e.		Horiz. half used as 5c on cover		450.00
f.		Vert. half used as 5c on cover		450.00
6	A1	10c lt dl bl	800.00	150.00
a.		10c pale blue		190.00
b.		Diag. half used as 5c on cover		425.00
c.		Horiz. half used as 5c on cover		425.00
d.		Vert. half used as 5c on cover		425.00

Litho.

7	A1	5c pale brown	*1,200.*	300.00

London Print

1855 Blued Paper Wmk. c Engr.

8	A1	5c brown red	220.00	16.00
		Fiscal cancellation		2.75

Santiago Prints

Impressions Worn and Blurred

1856-62 Wmk. b and e

White Paper

9	A1	5c rose red ('58)	60.00	8.00
		Fiscal cancellation		1.40
a.		5c carmine red ('62)	90.00	20.00
b.		5c orange red ('61)	*225.00*	100.00
c.		5c dull redsh brn ('57)	*250.00*	27.50
f.		Printed on both sides	*450.00*	*250.00*
g.		Double impression	*450.00*	140.00
10	A1	10c sky blue ('57)	160.00	40.00
		Fiscal cancellation		1.40
a.		10c deep blue	*160.00*	40.00
b.		10c light blue ('59)	*160.00*	40.00
c.		10c indigo blue ('60)	*175.00*	50.00
k.		Printed on both sides		*350.00*
n.		As "j," half used as 5c on cover		165.00
o.		Any shade, horiz. half used as 5c on cover		200.00
p.		Any shade, vert. half used as 5c on cover		200.00

London Prints

1862 Wmk. a, f and g

11	A1	1c lemon yellow	67.50	40.00
		Fiscal cancellation		1.50
a.		Double impression, one inverted		*200.00*
12	A1	10c bright blue	40.00	15.00
		Fiscally used		1.50
a.		10c deep blue	32.50	21.00
b.		Blued paper	—	17.50
c.		Wmkd. "20" (error)	*5,000.*	*5,200.*
d.		Diag. half used as 5c on cover		110.00
e.		Horiz. half used as 5c on cover		125.00
f.		Vert. half used as 5c on cover		125.00
13	A1	20c green	160.00	67.50
		Fiscally used		6.75
		Nos. 11-13 (3)	267.50	122.50

No. 11a is only known fiscally used.

Santiago Print

1865 Wmk. d

14	A1	5c rose red	80.00	20.00
		Fiscally used		1.50
a.		5c carmine red	80.00	20.00
b.		Printed on both sides	*375.00*	*200.00*
c.		Laid paper	—	*90.00*
d.		Double impression, entire stamp	*825.00*	*160.00*

The 5c rose red (shades) on unwatermaked paper, either wove or ribbed, and on paper watermarked Chilean arms in the sheet are reprints made about 1870.

No. 13 has been reprinted in the color of issue and in fancy colors, both from the original engraved plate and from lithographic transfers. The reprints are on paper without watermark or with watermark CHILE and Star.

A2

1867 Unwmk. *Perf. 12*

15	A2	1c orange	70.00	15.00
		Pen cancellation		1.25
16	A2	2c black	80.00	30.00
		Pen cancellation		2.00
17	A2	5c red	60.00	2.00
		Pen cancellation		.40
18	A2	10c blue	80.00	6.00
		Pen cancellation		1.25
19	A2	20c green	80.00	8.00
		Pen cancellation		1.60
		Nos. 15-19 (5)	370.00	61.00

Unused values for Nos. 15-19 are for stamps with original gum.

A3

1877 *Rouletted*

20	A3	1c gray	10.00	3.00
		Pen cancellation		.60
21	A3	2c orange	30.00	3.00
		Pen cancellation		.60
22	A3	5c dull lake	24.00	2.00
		Pen cancellation		.40
23	A3	10c blue	18.00	2.75
a.		Diagonal half used as 5c on cover		—
24	A3	20c green	20.00	4.50
		Nos. 20-24 (5)	102.00	15.25

The panel inscribed "CENTAVO" is straight on No. 22.

A4

A5

Columbus — A6

1878-99 *Rouletted*

25	A4	1c green ('81)	1.00	.25
26	A4	2c rose ('81)	1.00	.25
27	A5	5c dull lake ('78)	7.25	.90
28	A5	5c ultra ('83)	1.90	.50
29	A5	10c orange ('85)	2.75	.35
a.		10c yellow	9.00	1.90
30	A5	15c dk grn ('92)	3.00	.55
31	A5	20c gray ('86)	3.00	.55
32	A5	25c org brn ('92)	3.00	.55
33	A5	30c rose car ('99)	7.25	3.75
34	A5	50c lilac ('78)	45.00	27.50
35	A5	50c violet ('85)	3.00	2.00
36	A6	1p dk brn & blk ('92)	19.00	2.75
a.		Imperf. horiz. or vert., pair	75.00	
		Nos. 25-36 (12)	97.15	39.90

For surcharge and overprint see Nos. 50, O16.

Columbus — A7

1894 Re-engraved

37	A7	1c blue green	.90	.25
38	A7	2c carmine lake	.90	.25

In type A4 there is a small colorless ornament at each side of the base of the numeral, above the "E" and "V" of "CENTAVO." In type A7 these ornaments are missing, the figure "1" is broader than in type A4 and the head of the figure "2" is formed by a curved line instead of a ball.

Columbus — A8

Type I

Type II

Type I — There is a heavy shading of short horizontal lines below "Chile" and the adjacent ornaments.

Type II — There is practically no shading below "Chile" and the ornaments.

Type I

1900-01

39	A8	1c yel grn	.80	.25
40	A8	2c brn rose	1.25	.25
41	A8	5c dp bl	6.50	.35
42	A8	10c violet	6.50	.70
43	A8	20c gray	6.50	2.50
44	A8	30c dp org ('01)	6.50	2.50
45	A8	50c red brn	7.50	2.50
		Nos. 39-45 (7)	35.55	9.05

Type II

46	A8	1c yel grn ('01)	.85	.25
47	A8	2c rose ('01)	.85	.30
48	A8	5c dull blue ('01)	5.00	.25
a.		Printed on both sides		—
49	A8	10c vio ('01)	6.00	.85
		Nos. 46-49 (4)	12.70	1.65

For surcharge see No. 57.

No. 33 Surcharged in Black

1900 Black Surcharge

50	A5	5c on 30c rose car	1.25	.35
a.		Inverted surcharge	32.50	24.00
b.		Double surcharge	90.00	60.00
c.		Double surcharge, both invtd.	90.00	60.00
d.		Double surcharge, one invtd.	90.00	60.00

Columbus — A10

1901-02 *Perf. 12*

51	A10	1c green	.50	.30
52	A10	2c carmine	.65	.25
53	A10	5c ultra	1.50	.25
54	A10	10c red & blk	2.25	.35
55	A10	30c vio & blk	6.75	.85
56	A10	50c red org & blk	7.25	2.25
		Nos. 51-56 (6)	18.90	4.25

No. 44 Surcharged in Dark Blue

1903 *Rouletted*

57	A8	10c on 30c orange	1.90	.75
a.		Inverted surcharge	18.00	12.00
b.		Double surcharge	25.00	15.00
c.		Double surch., one inverted	25.00	15.00
d.		Double surch., both invtd.	25.00	15.00
e.		Stamp design printed on both sides		

Telegraph Stamps Surcharged or Overprinted in Black

Pedro de Valdivia — A11

Coat of Arms — A12

A13

Type I

Type II

Type I — Animal at left has neither mane nor tail.
Type II — Animal at left has mane and tail.

1904 *Perf. 12*

58	A11	1c on 20c ultra	.40	.30
a.		Imperf. horiz., pair	40.00	40.00
b.		Inverted surcharge	50.00	50.00
59	A13	2c yel brn, I	.35	.25
a.		Inverted overprint	20.00	20.00
b.		Pair, one without overprint	50.00	50.00
60	A13	5c red, I	.55	.25
a.		Inverted overprint	20.00	20.00
c.		Pair, one without overprint	50.00	50.00
61	A13	10c ol grn, I	1.50	.50
a.		Inverted overprint	50.00	50.00
		Nos. 58-61 (4)	2.80	1.30

Perf. 12½ to 16

62	A13	2c yel, brn, II	5.25	4.50
63	A11	3c on 5c brn red	37.50	32.50
a.		Inverted surcharge		
64	A12	3c on 1p brn, II	.45	.30
a.		Double surcharge	50.00	50.00
65	A13	5c red, II	6.25	5.50
a.		Inverted overprint		
66	A13	10c ol grn, II	14.50	10.00
67	A11	12c on 5c brn red	1.00	.45
a.		No star at left of "Centavos"	3.00	2.50
b.		Inverted surcharge	40.00	40.00
c.		Double surcharge	50.00	50.00
		Nos. 62-67 (6)	64.95	53.25

Counterfeits exist of the overprint and surcharge varieties of Nos. 57-67.
For overprint see No. O12.

A14

A15

Columbus — A16

1905-09 *Perf. 12*

68	A14	1c green	.25	.25
69	A14	2c carmine	.30	.25
70	A14	3c yel brn	.65	.30
71	A14	5c ultra	.70	.25
72	A15	10c gray & blk	1.10	.25
73	A15	12c lake & blk	5.50	2.25
74	A15	15c vio & blk	1.25	.25
75	A15	20c org brn & blk	2.25	.25
76	A15	30c bl grn & blk	3.50	.35
77	A15	50c ultra & blk	3.50	.40
78	A16	1p gold, grn & gray	16.00	11.00
		Nos. 68-78 (11)	35.00	15.80

A 20c dull red and black, type A15, was prepared but not issued. Value $125. "Specimen" examples of Nos. 74, 76-78 exist, punched to prevent postal use.
For surcharges and overprints see Nos. 79-82, O9, O11-O15.

Nos. 73, 78 Surcharged in Blue or Red

a

b

1910

79	A15 (a)	5c on 12c (Bl)	.50	.25
80	A16 (b)	10c on 1p (R)	1.10	.30
81	A16 (b)	20c on 1p (R)	1.60	.60
82	A16 (b)	1p (R)	3.00	1.10
		Nos. 79-82 (4)	6.20	2.25

The 1p is overprinted "ISLAS DE JUAN FERNANDEZ" only. The use of these stamps throughout Chile was authorized.

Independence Centenary Issue

Oath of Independence — A17

Monument to O'Higgins — A26

Adm. Lord Thomas Cochrane — A29

Designs: 2c, Battle of Chacabuco. 3c, Battle of Roble. 5c, Battle of Maipu. 10c, Naval Engagement of "Lautaro" and "Esmeralda." 12c, Capturing the "Maria Isabel." 15c, First Sortie of Liberating Forces. 20c, Abdication of O'Higgins. 25c, Chile's First Congress. 50c, Monument to José M. Carrera. 1p, Monument to San Martin. 2p, Gen. Manuel Blanco Encalada. 5p, Gen. José Ignacio Zenteno.

1910 **Center in Black**

83	A17	1c dk green	.25	.25
a.		Center inverted	7,000.	
84	A17	2c lake	1.10	.75
85	A17	3c red brown	.80	.45
86	A17	5c dp blue	.45	.25
87	A17	10c gray brn	1.20	.30
88	A17	12c vermilion	2.50	1.00
89	A17	15c slate	1.90	.55
90	A17	20c red orange	2.50	.85
91	A17	25c ultra	3.25	2.00
92	A26	30c violet	3.25	1.40
93	A26	50c olive grn	6.75	2.25
94	A26	1p yel org	14.00	5.25
95	A29	2p red	14.00	5.25
96	A29	5p yel grn	37.50	17.50
97	A29	10p dk violet	35.00	16.00
		Nos. 83-97 (15)	124.45	54.05

Columbus A32

De Valdivia A33

Mateo de Toro Zambrano A34

Bernardo O'Higgins A35

Ramón Freire — A36

F. A. Pinto — A37

Joaquín Prieto — A38

Manuel Bulnes — A39

Manuel Montt — A40

José Joaquín Pérez — A41

Federico Errázuriz Zanartu — A42

José de Balmaceda — A43

Designs: 1p, Anibal Pinto, 2p, Domingo Santa María. 10p, Federico Errázuriz Echaurren.

Outer backgrounds consist of horizontal and diagonal lines

1911 **Engr.** *Perf. 12*

98	A32	1c dp green	.25	.25
99	A33	2c scarlet	.25	.25
100	A34	3c sepia	.75	.25
101	A35	5c dk blue	.25	.25
102	A36	10c gray & blk	.75	.25
a.		Center inverted	800.00	600.00
103	A37	12c carmine & blk	1.00	.25
104	A38	15c violet & blk	.90	.25
a.		Center inverted	1,000.	
105	A39	20c org red & blk	1.75	.25
a.		Center inverted	50.00	50.00
106	A40	25c lt blue & blk	2.75	.60
107	A41	30c bis brn & blk	4.00	.30
108	A42	50c myr grn & blk	5.00	.30
109	A43	1p green & blk	9.00	.40
110	A43	2p ver & blk	17.50	1.75
111	A43	5p ol grn & blk	50.00	9.50
112	A43	10p org yel & blk	45.00	8.50
		Nos. 98-112 (15)	139.15	23.35

See Nos. 117, 121, 123, 127-128, 133-141, 143, 155A, 157-161, 165-169,171-172 and designs A47-A55, A57. For overprints see Nos. C6, C6B-C6D, C7-C8, C10-C11, C13-C21, O19-O22, O24-O27, O30-O34, O40.

Columbus A47

Toro Zambrano A48

Freire A49

O'Higgins A50

1912-13 **Engr.** *Perf. 12*

113	A47	2c scarlet	.25	.25
114	A48	4c black brn	.30	.25
115	A49	8c gray	1.00	.25
116	A50	10c blue & blk	1.00	.25
a.		Center inverted	500.00	400.00
b.		Imperf. horiz. or vert., pair	50.00	
117	A37	14c car & blk	1.50	.25
121	A38	40c violet & blk	5.75	.60
123	A40	60c lt blue & blk	14.00	1.75
		Nos. 113-123 (7)	23.80	3.60

See Nos. 125-126, 131, 164, 170, 173. For overprints see Nos. C6E, O18, O23, O28, O29.

Cochrane — A52

1915 **Engr.** *Perf. 13½x14*

124	A52	5c slate blue	.60	.35
a.		Imperf., pair	11.50	

See Nos. 155, 162-163. For overprints see Nos. O17, O37.

1918

125	A49	8c slate	17.50	.80

No. 125 is from a plate made in Chile to resemble No. 115. The top of the head is further from the oval, the spots of color enclosed in the figures "8" are oval instead of round, and there are many small differences in the design.

1921 **Worn Plate**

126	A49	8c gray	20.00	5.00

No. 126 differs from No. 125 in not having diagonal lines in the frame and only a few diagonal lines above the shoulders (due to wear), while No. 125 has diagonal lines in the oval up to the level of the forehead.

Columbus — A53

1915-25 **Typo.** *Perf. 13½ to 14½*

127	A32	1c gray green	.25	.25
128	A33	2c red	.25	.25
129	A53	4c brown ('18)	.25	.25

Frame Litho.; Head Engr.

131	A50	10c bl & blk	1.25	.25
a.		10c dark blue & black	1.25	.25
b.		Imperf., pair	110.00	
c.		Center inverted	325.00	
133	A38	15c vio & blk	.90	.25
134	A39	20c org red & blk	1.40	.25
a.		20c brown orange & blk	1.75	.25
135	A40	25c dl bl & blk	.55	.25
136	A41	30c bis brn & blk	1.75	.25
137	A42	50c dp grn & blk	1.75	.25

Perf. 14

138	A43	1p grn & blk	8.00	.25
139	A43	2p red & blk	9.75	.25
a.		2p vermilion & black	32.50	.60
140	A43	5p ol grn & blk ('20)	24.00	.60
141	A43	10p org & blk ('25)	25.00	1.75
		Nos. 127-141 (13)	75.10	5.10

The frames have crosshatching on the 15c, 20c, 30c, 2p, 5p and 10p. They have no crosshatching on the 10c, 25c, 50c and 1p.
Nos. 131a and 134a are printed from new head plates which give blacker and heavier impressions. No. 131a exists with; (a) frame litho., head engr.; (b) frame typo., head engr.; (c) frame typo., head litho. No. 134a is with frame typo., head engr.
A 4c stamp with portrait of Balmaceda and a 14c with portrait of Manuel de Salas were prepared but not placed in use. Both stamps were sent to the paper mill at Puente Alto for destruction. They were not all destroyed as some were privately preserved and sold.

Columbus — A54

Types of 1915-20 Redrawn

1918-20 *Perf. 13½x14½*

143	A32	1c gray grn ('20)	.30	.25
144	A54	4c brown	.50	.25

No. 143 has all the lines much finer and clearer than No. 127. The white shirt front is also much less shaded.

Manuel Rengifo — A55

1921

145	A55	40c dk vio & blk	2.00	.40

For overprints see Nos. C6A, C9.

Pan-American Congress Building — A56

1923, Apr. 25 **Typo.** *Perf. 14½x14*

146	A56	2c red	.25	.25
147	A56	4c brown	.25	.25

Typo.; Center Engr.

148	A56	10c blue & blk	.25	.25
149	A56	20c orange & blk	.75	.25
150	A56	40c dl vio & blk	1.00	.30
151	A56	1p green & blk	1.25	.50
152	A56	2p red & blk	5.00	.60
153	A56	5p dk grn & blk	17.00	4.50
		Nos. 146-153 (8)	25.75	6.90

Fifth Pan-American Congress.

Adm. Juan José Latorre — A57

Typographed; Head Engraved

1927 *Perf. 13½x14½*

154	A57	80c dk brn & blk	2.00	.60

Types of 1915-25 Issues Inscribed: "Chile Correos"

Perf. 13½x14½

1928-31 **Engr.** **Wmk. 215**

155	A52	5c slate blue	1.40	.25

Frame Typo.; Center Engr.

155A	A38	15c violet & blk	*2,200.*	
156	A55	40c dk vio & blk	.60	.25
157	A42	50c dp grn & blk	2.50	.25

Perf. 14

158	A43	1p green & blk	1.00	.25
159	A43	2p red & blk	5.00	.25
160	A43	5p ol grn & blk	9.75	.45
161	A43	10p orange & blk	9.75	1.90
		Nos. 155,156-161 (7)	30.00	3.60

Paper of Nos. 155-161 varies from thin to thick.

Types of 1915-25 Issues Inscribed: "Correos de Chile"

1928 **Engr.** *Perf. 13½x14½*

162	A52	5c deep blue	.35	.25

1929 **Litho.**

163	A52	5c light green	.50	.25

Frame Litho.; Center Engr.

164	A50	10c blue & blk	2.00	.25
165	A38	15c violet & blk	2.40	.25
166	A39	20c org red & blk	5.75	.25
167	A40	25c blue & blk	.95	.25
168	A41	30c brown & blk	.75	.25
169	A42	50c dp grn & blk	.65	.25
		Nos. 163-169 (7)	13.00	1.75

Redrawn

1929 **Frame Typo.; Center Litho.**

170	A50	10c blue & blk	3.00	.25
171	A38	15c violet & blk	2.75	.25
172	A39	20c org red & blk	4.25	.25
		Nos. 170-172 (3)	10.00	.75

1931 **Unwmk.**

173	A50	10c blue & blk	.70	.25

In the redrawn stamps the lines behind the portraits are heavier and completely fill the ovals. There are strong diagonal lines above the shoulders. On No. 170 the head is larger than on Nos. 164, 173.

A58

Prosperity of Saltpeter Trade
A59 A60

Perf. 13½x14

1930, July 21 **Litho.** **Wmk. 215**

Size: 20x25mm

175	A58	5c yellow grn	.60	.40
176	A58	10c red brown	.60	.30
177	A58	15c violet	.60	.30
178	A59	25c deep gray	1.90	.60
179	A60	70c dark blue	4.50	1.50

Perf. 14

Size: 24½x30mm

180	A60	1p dk gray grn	3.75	.75
		Nos. 175-180 (6)	11.95	3.85

Cent. of the 1st shipment of saltpeter from Chile, July 21, 1830.

Manuel Bulnes — A61

1931 *Perf. 13½, 14*

181	A61	20c dark brown	1.00	.30

For overprints see Nos. O35, O39.

Bernardo O'Higgins — A62

1932

182	A62	10c deep blue	1.50	.45

For overprints see Nos. O36, O38.

Mariano Egana — A63 Joaquin Tocornal — A64

1934 *Perf. 13½x14*

183	A63	30c magenta	.60	.25

Perf. 14

184	A64	1.20p bright blue	1.00	.25

Centenary of the constitution.

José Joaquín Pérez — A65

1934 *Perf. 13½x14*

185	A65	30c bright pink	1.60	.35

Atacama Desert — A66

Designs: 10c, Fishing boats. 20c, Coquito palms. 25c, Sheep. 30c, Mining. 40c, Lonquimay forest. 50c, Colliery at Port Lota. 1p, Shipping at Valparaiso. 1.20p, Puntiagudo volcano. 2p, Diego de Almagro. 5p, Cattle. 10p, Mining saltpeter.

Wmk. 215

1936, Mar. 1 **Litho.** *Perf. 14*

186	A66	5c vermilion	.60	.30
187	A66	10c violet	.30	.25
188	A66	20c magenta	.40	.25
189	A66	25c grnsh blue	3.00	.80
190	A66	30c lt green	.40	.25
191	A66	40c blk, *cream*	3.25	.85
192	A66	50c bl, *bluish*	1.75	.30

Engr.

193	A66	1p dk green	1.75	.50
194	A66	1.20p dp blue	2.00	.70
195	A66	2p dk brown	2.50	.80
196	A66	5p copper red	5.75	2.25
197	A66	10p dk violet	14.00	8.00
		Nos. 186-197 (12)	35.70	15.25

400th anniv. of the discovery of Chile by Diego de Almagro.

Laja Waterfall — A78 Fishing in Chiloé — A84

Designs: 10c, Agriculture. 15c, Boldo tree. 20c, Nitrate Industry. 30c, Mineral spas. 40c, Copper mine. 50c, Mining. 1.80p, Osorno Volcano. 2p, Mercantile marine. 5p, Lake Villarrica. 10p, State railways.

Perf. 13½x14

1938-40 **Litho.** **Wmk. 215**

198	A78	5c brn car ('39)	.25	.25
199	A78	10c sal pink ('39)	.25	.25
200	A78	15c brn org ('40)	.25	.25
201	A78	20c light blue	.25	.25
202	A78	30c brt pink	.25	.25
203	A78	40c lt grn ('39)	.25	.25
204	A78	50c violet	.25	.25

Engr. *Perf. 14*

205	A84	1p orange brn	.25	.25
206	A84	1.80p deep blue	.45	.40
207	A84	2p car lake	.25	.25
208	A84	5p dk slate grn	.35	.25
209	A84	10p rose vio ('40)	.90	.25
		Nos. 198-209 (12)	3.95	3.15

See Nos. 217-227. For surcharge and overprints see Nos. 253, O41-O66, O70-O71.

Map of the Americas — A89

Unwmk.

1940, Sept. 11 **Litho.** *Perf. 14*

210	A89	40c dl grn & yel grn	.35	.25

Pan American Union, 50th anniversary.

Camilo Henríquez — A90

Founding of Santiago A93

Designs: 40c, Pedro de Valdivia. 1.10p, Benjamin Vicuna Mackenna. 3.60p, Diego Barros Arana.

Perf. 14½x14, 14½

1941, Jan. 23 **Engr.** **Wmk. 215**

211	A90	10c carmine lake	.25	.25
212	A90	40c green	.35	.25
213	A90	1.10p red	1.25	.70
214	A93	1.80p blue	1.25	.70
215	A90	3.60p indigo	3.75	2.75
		Nos. 211-215 (5)	6.85	4.65

400th anniversary of Santiago.

Types of 1938

Perf. 13½x14

1942-46 **Unwmk.** **Litho.**

217	A78	10c sal pink ('43)	.25	.25
218	A78	15c brown org ('43)	.25	.25
219	A78	20c lt blue ('43)	.25	.25
220	A78	30c brt pink ('43)	.25	.25
221	A78	40c yellow grn	.80	.25
222	A78	50c violet ('43)	.25	.25

Engr. *Perf. 14*

223	A84	1p brown orange	1.50	.25
225	A84	2p car lake ('43)	.25	.25
226	A84	5p dk sl grn ('43)	.50	.25
227	A84	10p rose violet ('46)	.90	.25
		Nos. 217-227 (10)	5.20	2.50

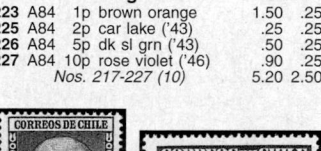

Valentin Letelier — A95 University of Chile — A98

Designs: 40c, Andrés Bello. 90c, Manuel Bulnes. 1.80p, Manuel Montt.

1942, Nov. 1 *Perf. 14x14½, 14 (1p)*

228	A95	30c rose red	.25	.25
229	A95	40c deep green	.25	.25
230	A95	90c rose violet	1.90	1.50
231	A98	1p deep brown	1.10	.90
232	A95	1.80p dark blue	3.50	3.00
		Nos. 228-232 (5)	7.00	5.90

University of Chile cent. See No. C89.

Manuel Bulnes — A100

Map Showing Strait of Magellan — A104

Designs: 30c, Juan Williams Wilson. 40c, Diego Duble Almeida. 1p, José Mardones.

1944, Mar. 2 Litho. *Perf. 14*

233 A100 15c black .25 .25
234 A100 30c deep rose .25 .25
235 A100 40c yellow green .25 .25
236 A100 1p brown carmine .95 .25
237 A104 1.80p ultra 1.40 .95
Nos. 233-237 (5) 3.10 1.95

100th anniversary of the occupation of the Strait of Magellan.

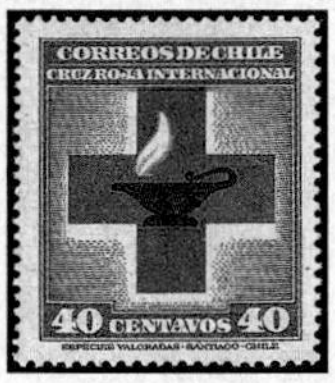

Red Cross and Lamp of Life — A105

Serpent and Cup — A106

1944, Oct. 18 Unwmk.

238 A105 40c green, red & blk .30 .25
239 A106 1.80p ultra & red .90 .45

80th anniv. of the Intl. Red Cross Soc.

Bernardo O'Higgins — A107

"Embrace of Maipú" (O'Higgins Joining San Martin) — A108

Designs: 40c, Abdication of O'Higgins. 1.80p, Battle of Rancagua.

1945 Engr. *Perf. 14 (15c), 14½*
Center in Black

240 A107 15c carmine .30 .25
241 A108 30c brown .30 .25
242 A108 40c deep green .30 .25
243 A108 1.80p dark blue 1.40 .90
Nos. 240-243 (4) 2.30 1.65

Death of Bernardo O'Higgins in 1842, cent.

A111

Proposed Columbus lighthouse.

Wmk. 215
1945, Sept. 10 Litho. *Perf. 14*

244 A111 40c light green .50 .25

Issued in honor of the discovery of America by Columbus and the Memorial Lighthouse to be erected in his memory.

A112

1946 Engr.

245 A112 40c dark green .25 .25
246 A112 1.80p dark blue .25 .25

80th anniv. of the death of Andrés Bello, poet and educator.

Map Showing Chile's Claims of Antarctic Territory A113

1947, May 12 Litho. *Perf. 14½*

247 A113 40c carmine .60 .30
248 A113 2.50p deep blue 1.60 .50

Eusebio Lillo and Ramon Carnicer A114

1947, Sept. 18 Engr.

249 A114 40c dark green .25 .25

Centenary of national anthem.

Miguel de Cervantes Saavedra A115

1947, Oct. 11 Wmk. 215

250 A115 40c dk carmine .25 .25

400th anniv. of the birth of Cervantes, novelist, playwright and poet.

Arturo Prat Chacón and Iquique Naval Battle A116

1948, Dec. 24 *Perf. 14½*

251 A116 40c deep blue .25 .25

Centenary of the birth of Arturo Prat Chacon, Chilean naval hero.

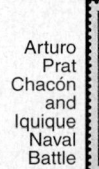

Bernardo O'Higgins — A117

Perf. 13½x14
1948 Wmk. 215 Litho.

252 A117 60c black .25 .25

See No. 262. For surcharges see Nos. 266-267.

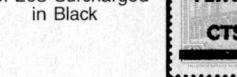

No. 203 Surcharged in Black

1948

253 A78 20c on 40c lt grn .25 .25

Chilean Pigeons — A118

FAUNA: a, Chilean Otter. b, tree. d, American skunk. f, Southern sea lions. g, Sugarcane borer moth. h, Emperor penguins. i, Bat. j, Chinchilla. k, Grant's stag beetle. l, Trevally (fish). m, Chilean slender lizard. o, Crested caracara. q, Red-gartered coot. r, Chilean guemal (deer). s, Spiny rock lobster. u, Tilefish. v, Praying mantis. x, Torrent duck. y, Red conger.

FLORA: b, Araucarian pine (monkey puzzle tree). e, Evening primrose. n, Chilean red bell flower. p, Loxodon (flower). t, Boldo tree. w, Coquito palm trees.

Wmk. 215
1948, Dec. 6 Litho. *Perf. 14*

254 60c Block of 25 60.00 60.00
a.-y. A118 any single 1.00 .80
255 2.60p Block of 25 90.00 90.00
a.-y. A118 any single 1.75 1.25

Issued in panes of 100.

Cent. (in 1944) of the publication of the 1st volume of Claudio Gay's Natural History of Chile. See No. C124.

Catalogue values for unused stamps in this section, from this point to the end of the section, are for Never Hinged items.

Benjamin Vicuna Mackenna — A121

1949, Mar. 22 Engr. *Perf. 13½x14*

257 A121 60c deep blue .30 .25

See No. C126.

Symbols of Arts and Crafts Education — A122

Design: 2.60p, Badge and book.

Unwmk.
1949, Nov. 11 Litho. *Perf. 14*

258 A122 60c lilac rose .25 .25
259 A122 2.60p violet blue .40 .30
Nos. 258-259,C127-C128 (4) 2.90 1.55

Cent. of the foundation of Chile's School of Arts and Crafts.

Heinrich von Stephan — A123

1950, Jan. 6 Engr.

260 A123 60c deep carmine .25 .25
261 A123 2.50p deep blue .70 .50
Nos. 260-261,C129-C130 (4) 2.55 1.60

UPU, 75th anniv.

O'Higgins Type of 1948
1950 Litho. *Perf. 13x14*

262 A117 60c black .25 .25

For surcharge see No. 266.

San Martín — A124

Wmk. 215
1951, Mar. 16 Engr. *Perf. 14*

263 A124 60c deep blue .40 .25

Cent. of the death of Gen. José de San Martin. See No. C165.

Isabella I — A125

1952, Mar. 20

264 A125 60c brt blue .35 .25

500th anniv. of the birth of Queen Isabella I of Spain. See No. C166.

Bernardo O'Higgins — A126

1952 Unwmk. Litho. *Perf. 13½x14*

265 A126 1p dk blue grn .30 .25

See No. 275. For overprints see Nos. O67-O69.

No. 262 Surcharged in Red, Numbers & Letters Thicker

No. 252 Surcharged in Red, Numbers & Letters Thinner

1952, Sept.

266 A117 40c on 60c black .35 .25

Wmk. 215

267 A117 40c on 60c black .35 .25

Mateo de Toro Zambrano — A127

1953, Mar. 13 **Wmk. 215**

268 A127 80c green .25 .25

See No. 285.

Valdivia Arms — A128

Old Fort — A129

3p, Modern Valdivia. 5p, Street in ancient Valdivia.

1953, May ***Perf. 14***

269 A128 1p brt ultra .40 .25
270 A129 2p dull rose vio .40 .25
271 A129 3p blue green .50 .25
272 A129 5p deep brown .50 .25
Nos. 269-272,C167 (5) 4.05 1.45

4th centenary of the founding of Valdivia, capital of Valdivia province.

José Toribio Medina (1852-1930), Historian and Bibliographer A130

1953, June **Engr.** ***Perf. 14½***

273 A130 1p brown .35 .25
274 A130 2.50p deep blue .45 .25

O'Higgins Type of 1952

Perf. 13½x14

1953, Oct. **Wmk. 215** **Litho.**

275 A126 1p dk blue green .35 .25

For overprint see No. O69.

Stamp of 1853 — A131

1953, Oct. 15 **Engr.** ***Perf. 14½***

276 A131 1p brown .50 .25

Centenary of Chile's first postage stamps.
Souvenir sheet including No. 276 is noted below No. C168.

A132

Census chart and map.

1953, Nov. 5 **Litho.** ***Perf. 13½x14***

277 A132 1p blue green .30 .25
278 A132 2.50p violet blue .30 .25
279 A132 3p chocolate .50 .25
280 A132 4p carmine .50 .25
Nos. 277-280 (4) 1.60 1.00

12th general census of population and housing.

Arms of Angol — A133

1954, May 28 **Unwmk.** ***Perf. 14***

281 A133 2p deep carmine .35 .25

400th anniversary of the founding of Angol, capital of Malleco province.

Ignacio Domeyko — A134

1954, Aug. 16 **Engr.** ***Perf. 13½x14***

282 A134 1p greenish blue .35 .25

150th anniversary of the birth of Ignacio Domeyko (1802-89), mineralogist and educator. See No. C171.

Early Steam Locomotive — A135

1954, Sept. 10 **Wmk. 215** ***Perf. 14½***

283 A135 1p red .60 .30

Centenary (in 1951) of the first South American railroad. See No. C172.

Adm. Arturo Prat Chacón — A136

1954 **Unwmk.** **Litho.** ***Perf. 14***

284 A136 2p dk violet blue .35 .25

75th anniv. of the naval Battle of Iquique.

Toro Zambrano Type of 1953

1954, Nov. 6 ***Perf. 13½x14***

285 A127 80c green .30 .25

Arms of Viña del Mar — A137

Design: 2p, Arms of Valparaiso.

1955, Mar. 5 **Wmk. 215** ***Perf. 14***

286 A137 1p violet blue .35 .25
287 A137 2p carmine .35 .25

1st Intl. Phil. Exhib., Valparaiso, Mar. 1955.

Dr. Alejandro del Rio — A138

1955, May 24 ***Perf. 13½x14***

288 A138 2p violet blue .40 .25

14th Pan-American Sanitary Conference.

Christ of the Andes, Emblems of Chile, Argentina A139

1955, Aug. 31 **Unwmk.** ***Perf. 14½***

289 A139 1p violet blue .35 .25

Reciprocal visits of Presidents Juan D. Peron and Carlos Ibanez del Campo. See No. C173.

Manuel Rengifo — A140

5p, Mariano Egana. 50p, Diego Portales.

1955-56 **Unwmk.** ***Perf. 14x14½***

290 A140 3p violet blue .35 .25
291 A140 5p dk car rose .35 .25
292 A140 50p rose lilac ('56) 1.90 .45
Nos. 290-292 (3) 2.60 .95

Joaquin Prieto (1786-1854), soldier and political leader; president, 1831-41. See No. QRA1.

Jose M. Carrera A141

Ramón Freire A142

Portraits: 5p, Manuel Bulnes. 10p, Pres. Francisco A. Pinto. 50p, Manuel Montt.

Perf. 14x14½

1956-58 **Unwmk.** **Litho.**

293 A141 2p purple .30 .25
293A A142 3p lt violet blue .25 .25
294 A141 5p redsh brn (19½x23mm) .30 .25
a. Size 19x22mm .30 .25
295 A142 10p vio (19x22¼mm) .30 .25
a. Perf. 13½x14 (19¼x22½mm) ('58) .55 .25
296 A141 50p rose red .50 .25
Nos. 293-296 (5) 1.65 1.25

Wmk. 215

297 A141 2p dull purple .30 .25
298 A142 3p violet blue .30 .25

No. 294 has yellow gum; No. 294a, white gum.
For overprints see Nos. O72-O76.

Federico Santa Maria — A143

Unwmk.

1957, Jan. 31 **Engr.** ***Perf. 14***

299 A143 5p dk red brown .30 .25

25th anniv. of the Federico Santa Maria Technical University. See Nos. C190-C191.
Souvenir sheet including No. 299 is noted below No. C191.

Gabriela Mistral — A144

1958, Jan. 10

300 A144 10p red brown .45 .25

Issued in honor of Gabriela Mistral, poet and educator. See No. C192.

Arms of Osorno — A145

Design: 50p, Garcia Hdo. de Mendoza.

1958, Mar. 23 **Litho.** ***Perf. 14***

301 A145 10p carmine .25 .25

Engr.

302 A145 50p green .40 .25

400th anniversary of the founding of the city of Osorno, capital of Osorno province.
Souvenir sheet including No. 302 in red brown is noted below No. C193.

Arms of Santiago — A146

1958, Oct. 18 **Unwmk.** ***Perf. 14***

303 A146 10p dark violet .30 .25

Natl. Philatelic Exposition, Santiago, Oct. 18-26.
Souvenir sheet including No. 303 in deep red is noted below No. C194.

Symbolical Savings Bank — A147

1958, Dec. 18

304 A147 10p dark blue .40 .25

Savings Bank for Public Employees, cent.
Souvenir sheet including No. 304 in violet is noted below No. C195.

Modern Map of Antarctica — A148

1958, Aug. 28 **Unwmk.** ***Perf. 14***

305 A148 40p rose carmine .60 .60

IGY, 1957-1958. See No. C214.

Antarctic Map and "La Araucana" A149

Map of Strait of Magellan, 1588 — A150

1958 Litho. *Perf. 14*
310 A149 10p violet blue .75 .25

Engr.
311 A150 200p dull purple 2.75 1.75
Nos. 310-311,C199-C200 (4) 7.75 4.00

For overprint see No. O77.

Valdivia River Bridge — A153

1959, Feb. 9 Engr. *Perf. 14*
319 A153 40p green .45 .25

Cent. of the German School in Valdivia and to publicize the Valdivia Phil. Exhb., 2/9-18.

Souvenir sheet including No. 319 is noted below No. C213.

Strait of Magellan, Map by Pedro Sarmiento de Gamboa, c. 1582 — A154

1959, Aug. 27 Litho.
320 A154 10p dull purple .45 .25

Juan Ladrillero expedition to explore the Strait of Magellan, 1557-58, 400th anniv. See No. C215.

Diego Barros Arana — A155

1959, Aug. 27
321 A155 40p ultra .45 .25

50th anniv. of the death of Diego Barros Arana (1830-1907), historian. See No. C216.

Henri Dunant — A156

1959, Oct. 6 Unwmk. *Perf. 14*
322 A156 20p red & red brn .45 .25

Cent. of the Red Cross idea. See No. C217.

Manuel Bulnes — A157

Francisco A. Pinto — A158

Choshuenco Volcano A159

No. 326, Choshuenco volcano, redrawn. 5c, Manuel Montt. 10c, Maule River Valley. 20c, 1e, Inca Lake.

1960-67 Litho. *Perf. 13x14*
323 A157 5m bluish grn .25 .25
324 A158 1c carmine .25 .25

Perf. 14
Size: 29x25mm
325 A159 2c ultra ('61) .25 .25

Perf. 14x13
Size: 23½x18mm
326 A159 2c ultra ('62) .25 .25

Perf. 13x14
327 A157 5c blue .25 .25

Perf. 14
Size: 29x25mm
328 A159 10c green ('62) .25 .25
329 A159 20c Prus blue ('62) .35 .25
329A A159 1e bluish grn ('67) .65 .25
Nos. 323-329A (8) 2.50 2.00

On No. 325 "Volcan Choshuenco" is at upper left, below "Correos." On No. 326, it is at bottom, above "Centesimos."

For overprint and surcharge see Nos. B7, O79, RA1.

Refugee Family A160

1960, Apr. 7 *Perf. 14½*
330 A160 1c green .30 .25

WRY, July 1, 1959-June 30, 1960. A souvenir sheet is noted below No. C218.

Type of Air Post Issue, 1962, and

Arms of Chile A161

José M. Carrera A162

No. 332, Palace of Justice. 5c, Natl. Memorial. 10c, Manuel de Toro y Zambrano and Martinez de Rozas. 20c, Manuel de Salas and Juan Egana. 50c, Manuel Rodriguez and Juan Mackenna.

Wmk. 215 (#331, 1e); Unwmk.
1960-65 Engr. *Perf. 14½*
331 A161 1c maroon & sepia .25 .25
332 A161 1c brn & claret ('62) .25 .25
333 A162 5c grn & Prus grn ('61) .25 .25
334 AP54 10c brn & vio brn ('64) .40 .25
334A AP54 20c ind & bl grn ('65) .40 .25
335 AP54 50c red brn & mar ('65) .70 .25
336 A162 1e gray ol & brn 1.25 .40
Nos. 331-336,C218A-C220D (14) 6.90 3.80

150th anniv. of the formation of the 1st Natl. Government. A souvenir sheet is noted below No. C220B. See No. C285.

Family — A163

Design: 10c, Various buildings.

Unwmk.
1960, Jan. 18 Litho. *Perf. 14*
337 A163 5c green .25 .25
338 A163 10c brt violet .25 .25

13th population census (No. 337) and 2nd housing census (No. 338).

Chamber of Deputies A164

1961, Aug. 14 Unwmk. *Perf. 14½*
339 A164 2c red brown .65 .25

150th anniv. of the 1st National Congress. See No. C245.

Soccer Players and Globe A165

Design: 5c, Goalkeeper and stadium, vert.

1962, May 30 Engr. *Perf. 14½*
340 A165 2c blue .40 .25
341 A165 5c green .55 .25

World Soccer Championship, Chile, May 30-June 17. Note on souvenir sheet follows No. C247.

Mother and Child — A166

1963, Mar. 21 Litho. *Perf. 14*
342 A166 3c maroon .35 .25

FAO "Freedom from Hunger" campaign. See No. C248.

Centenary Emblem — A167

1963, Aug. 23 Unwmk. *Perf. 14*
343 A167 3c red & gray .35 .25

Cent. of the Intl. Red Cross. See No. C249.

Fireman Carrying Woman — A168

1963, Dec. 20 Unwmk. *Perf. 14*
344 A168 3c violet .45 .25

Centenary of the Santiago Fire Brigade. See No. C250.

Enrique Molina — A169

Design: No. 346, Magr. Carlos Casanueva.

1964, Nov. 14 Litho. *Perf. 14*
345 A169 4c bister brown .35 .25
346 A169 4c rose claret .35 .25
Nos. 345-346,C257-C258 (4) 1.30 1.00

Enrique Molina, founder of the University of Concepcion, and Msgr. Carlos Casanueva, rector of the Catholic University, 1920-53.

Easter Island Statue — A170

Copihue, National Flower — A171

Design: 30c, Robinson Crusoe.

1965-69 Litho. *Perf. 14x14½*
347 A170 6c rose lilac .95 .25
347A A170 10c rose pink ('68) .30 .25

Perf. 14
348 A171 15c yel grn & rose red .75 .25
348A A171 20c yel grn & rose red ('69) .35 .25

Perf. 14x14½
349 A170 30c rose claret .55 .25
Nos. 347-349 (5) 2.90 1.25

For surcharge see No. RA2.

Skier — A172

1965, Aug. 30 *Perf. 14*
350 A172 4c blue green .40 .25

World Skiing Championships, Chile, 1966.

Lorenzo Sazie — A173

1966, Feb. 9 Litho. ***Perf. 14x14½***

351 A173 1e green .95 .25

Cent. of the death of Dr. Lorenzo Sazie, dean of the Faculty of Medicine, University of Santiago.

Capt. Luis Pardo and Ship in Antarctica — A178

1967, Jan. Litho. ***Perf. 14½***

361 A178 20c turquoise blue .45 .25

Rescue of the Shackleton South Pole expedition by Capt. Luis Pardo of Chile, 50th anniv. See No. C271.

José Maria Cardinal Caro — A183

1967, Dec. 4 Engr. ***Perf. 14½***

366 A183 20c deep carmine .75 .35

Cent. of the birth of José Maria Cardinal Caro, the first Chilean cardinal. See No. C279.

Map of Chiloé Province, Sailing Ship and Coastal Vessel A188

1968, Oct. 7 ***Perf. 14½***

371 A188 30c ultra .40 .25

Anniversaries of the founding of five towns in Chiloé Province. See No. C283.

German Riesco, President in 1901-1906 — A174

Portrait: 30c, Jorge Montt (1847-1922), president in 1891-1896.

1966 Unwmk. ***Perf. 13x14***

354 A174 30c violet .30 .25
355 A174 50c dull brown .35 .25

For surcharge see No. 450.

William Wheelwright and S.S. Chile — A175

1966, Aug. 2 ***Perf. 14½***

358 A175 10c ultra & lt bl .35 .25

125th anniv. (in 1965) of the arrival of the paddle steamers "Chile" and "Peru." See No. C268.

Learning to Read — A176

1966, Aug. 13 Litho. ***Perf. 14***

359 A176 10c red brown .35 .25

Literacy campaign.

UN and ICY Emblems A177

1966, Oct. 28 Unwmk. ***Perf. 14½***

360 A177 1e green & brown 1.40 .25

Intl. Cooperation Year, 1965. See No. C269.

Family — A179

1967, Apr. 13 Unwmk. ***Perf. 14***

362 A179 10c magenta & blk .35 .25

8th Intl. Conf. for Family Planning, Santiago, Apr. 1967. See No. C272.

Trees and Mountains A180

1967, June 9 Litho. ***Perf. 14½***

363 A180 10c blue grn & lt bl .35 .25

Reforestation Campaign. See No. C274.

Lions Emblem — A181

1967, July 12 Litho. ***Perf. 14***

364 A181 20c Prus blue & yel .35 .25
Nos. 364,C275-C276 (3) 1.85 .80

50th anniv. of Lions Intl.

Chilean Flag A182

1967, Oct. 20 Unwmk. ***Perf. 14½***

365 A182 80c crimson & ultra .60 .25

Natl, flag, 150th anniv. See No. C277.

San Martin and O'Higgins — A184

1968, Apr. 23 Litho. Unwmk.

367 A184 3e blue .65 .25

Sesquicentennial of the Battles of Chacabuco and Maipu. See No. C280.

Farm Couple — A185

1968, June 18 ***Perf. 14½***

368 A185 20c black, org & grn .40 .25

Agrarian reforms. See No. C281.

Juan I. Molina A186

1968, Aug. 27 Litho. ***Perf. 14½***

369 A186 2e red lilac .60 .25

Issued to honor Juan I. Molina, educator and scientist. See No. C282.

Hand Holding Cogwheel — A187

1968, Sept. ***Perf. 14x14½***

370 A187 30c deep carmine .30 .25

Fourth census of manufacturers.

Automobile Club Emblem A189

1968, Nov. 10 Engr. ***Perf. 14½x14***

372 A189 1e carmine rose .35 .25

40th anniversary of the Automobile Club of Chile. See No. C284.

Francisco Garcia Huidobro A190

Design: 5e, King Philip V of Spain.

1968, Dec. 31 Litho. ***Perf. 14½***

373 A190 2e pale rose & ultra .40 .25
374 A190 5e brown & yel grn .40 .25
Nos. 373-374,C288-C289 (4) 1.40 1.00

225th anniv. of the founding of the State Mint (Casa de Moneda de Chile).

Satellite and Radar Station A191

1969, May 20 Litho. ***Perf. 14½***

375 A191 30c blue .30 .25

Inauguration of ENTEL-Chile, the 1st commercial satellite communications ground station, Longovilo.

See No. C290. For surcharges see Nos. 397, C308.

Red Cross, Crescent and Lion and Sun Emblems A192

1969, Sept. Litho. ***Perf. 14½***

376 A192 2e violet blue & red .40 .25

50th anniversary of the League of Red Cross Societies. See No. C291.

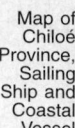

Rapel Hydroelectric Plant — A193

1969, Nov. 18 Litho. ***Perf. 14½***

377 A193 40c green .30 .25

See No. C292. For surcharge see No. B8.

Col. Rodriguez Monument — A194

1969, Nov. 24

378 A194 2e rose claret .40 .25

150th anniversary of the death of Col. Manuel Rodriguez. See No. C293.

EXPO '70 Emblem — A195

1969, Dec. 2 **Litho.** ***Perf. 14***

379 A195 3e blue .55 .25

EXPO '70 Intl. Exhibition, Osaka, Japan, Mar. 15-Sept. 13, 1970. See No. C294.

Open Book A196

1969, Dec. 3 ***Perf. 14½***

380 A196 40c red brown .40 .25

Translation of the Bible into Spanish by Casiodoro de Reina, 400th anniv. See No. C295. For surcharge see No. B10.

Globes and ILO Emblem A197

1969, Dec. 17 ***Perf. 14½***

381 A197 1e green & blk .35 .25

ILO, 50th anniv. See No. C296.

Human Rights Flame A198

1969, Dec. 18

382 A198 4e blue & red .60 .25

Human Rights Year, 1968. See No. C297.

Policarpo Toro and Easter Island A199

1970, Jan. 26 ***Perf. 14½***

383 A199 5e lilac .90 .25

80th anniversary of the acquisition of Easter Island. See No. C298.

Sailing Ship and Arms of Valdivia A200

1970, Feb. 4 **Litho.** ***Perf. 14½***

384 A200 40c dk carmine .60 .25

150th anniv. of the capture of Valdivia during Chile's war of independence by Thomas Cochrane (1775-1860), naval commander. See No. C299.

Paul Harris and Rotary Emblem — A201

1970, Mar. 18 **Litho.** ***Perf. 14***

385 A201 10e violet blue 1.10 .25

Cent. of the birth of Paul Harris (1868-1947), founder of Rotary Intl. See No. C300.

Mahatma Gandhi — A202

1970, Apr. 1 **Litho.** ***Perf. 14½***

386 A202 40c blue green 3.50 .30

Mohandas K. Gandhi (1869-1948), leader in India's fight for independence, birth cent. See No. C301. For surcharge see No. 449.

Santo Domingo Church, Santiago, Chile — A203

Designs: 2e, Casa de Moneda de Chile, horiz. 3e, Pedro de Valdivia. 5e, Bridge, horiz. 10e, Ambrosio O'Higgins.

1970, Apr. 30 **Engr.**

387	A203	2e violet brown	.40	.25
388	A203	3e dark red	.40	.25
389	A203	4e dark blue	.30	.25
390	A203	5e brown	.30	.25
391	A203	10e green	.30	.25
		Nos. 387-391 (5)	1.70	1.25

Exploration and development of Chile by Spanish explorers.

A sheet containing imperf examples of Nos. 388, 390 and 391 exists. It was not valid for postage.

Education Year Emblem — A204

1970, July 17 **Litho.** ***Perf. 14½***

392 A204 2e claret .35 .25

International Education Year. See No. C302.

Virgin and Child — A205

1970, July 28

393 A205 40c green .30 .25

O'Higgins National Shrine at Maipu. See No. C303. For surcharge see No. 454.

Torch and Snake — A206

1970, Aug. 11

394 A206 40c claret & light blue .50 .25

International Cancer Congress, Houston, Texas, May 22-29. See No. C304.

Copper Symbol, Chile Arms — A207

1970, Oct. 21 **Litho.** ***Perf. 14½***

395 A207 40c car & lt red brn .35 .25

Nationalization of the copper industry. See No. C305. For surcharges see Nos. 459, B9.

Dove and World Map A208

1970, Oct. 22

396 A208 3e rose magenta & pur .40 .25

25th anniv. of the UN. See No. C306.

No. 375 Surcharged in Red

1970, Dec. 24 **Litho.** ***Perf. 14½***

397 A191 52c on 30c blue .45 .25

Freighter and Ship's Wheel — A209

1971, Jan. 18 **Litho.** ***Perf. 14***

398 A209 52c deep carmine .35 .25

Natl. Maritime Commission. See No. C307.

Bernardo O'Higgins and Ship A210

1971, Feb. 3 ***Perf. 14½***

399 A210 5e grnsh bl & grn .55 .25

150th anniv. of the expedition to liberate Peru from Spanish rule. See No. C309.

Youth, Girl and UN Emblem A211

1971, Feb. 11 **Litho.** ***Perf. 14½***

400 A211 52c dk blue & brn .35 .25

1st meeting in Latin America of the Executive Council of UNICEF, Santiago, May 20-31, 1969. See No. C310.

Chilean Boy Scout Emblem — A212

1971, Feb. 10 ***Perf. 14***

401 A212 1e green & brn .45 .25

Founding of Chilean Boy Scouts, 60th anniversary. See No. C311.

Satellite and Radar Station A213

1971, May 25 **Litho.** ***Perf. 14½***

402 A213 40c dull green .50 .25

First commercial Chilean satellite communications ground station, Longovilo. See No. C312.

Diver with Harpoon Gun
A214

1971, Sept. 1

403 A214 1.15e lt & dk green 1.10 .25
404 A214 2.35e vio bl & dp vio bl .40 .25

10th World Championship of Underwater Fishing.

Ferdinand Magellan and Sailing Ship — A215

1971, Nov. 3

405 A215 35c lt vio & brn vio .35 .25

450th anniv. of 1st trip through and discovery of the Strait of Magellan, Oct. 21-Nov. 28, 1520.

Dagoberto Godoy and Plane over Andes — A216

1971, Nov. 4

406 A216 1.15e blue & grn .40 .25

First trans-Andean flight, Dec. 12, 1918.

Virgin of San Cristobal — A217

Chilean Flag and Congress Emblem
A218

Congress Emblem and: 4.35e, Church of San Francisco. 9.35e, Central post office, horiz. 18.35e, La Posada (Inn) del Corregidor, horiz.

1971

407 A217 1.15e dk blue .60 .30
408 A218 2.35e ultra & car .60 .30
409 A217 4.35e brown red .60 .30
410 A217 9.35e violet .60 .30
411 A217 18.35e lilac rose 1.25 .30
Nos. 407-411 (5) 3.65 1.50

10th Cong. of the Postal Union of the Americas and Spain, Santiago.

An imperf souvenir sheet containing Nos. 407-411 was not valid for postage. Value $11.

Issued: 2.35e, 4.35e, Nov. 5; 1.15e, Nov. 11; 9.35e, Nov. 18; 18.35e, Nov. 19.

Observation Dome, Cerro el Tololo Observatory — A219

1971, Dec. 18

412 A219 1.95e lt & dk blue .35 .25

Boeing 707 over Easter Island
A220

1971, Dec. 18

413 A220 2.35e dk brn & yel .45 .25

Inauguration of regular flights: Santiago, Easter Island, Tahiti.

Alonso de Ercilla y Zuniga — A221

1972, Mar. 20 Engr. *Perf. 14*

414 A221 1e dark red .40 .25

4th centenary (in 1969) of "La Araucana," by Alonso de Ercilla y Zuniga (1533-1596), Spanish author. See No. C313.

Map of Antarctica and Dog Sled — A222

1972, Mar. 20 Litho. *Perf. 14½x15*

415 A222 1.15e vio bl & blk .65 .30
416 A222 3.50e blue grn & grn 1.10 .30

10th anniversary (in 1971) of the Antarctic Treaty pledging peaceful uses of and scientific cooperation in Antarctica.

For surcharge see No. 630.

"Your Heart is your Health" — A223

1972, Apr. 2 Litho. *Perf. 14½*

417 A223 1.15e black & car .40 .25

World Health Month.

For surcharge see No. 631.

People and Statement by Pres. Allende — A224

Conference Hall and UN Emblem — A225

1972, Apr. 13 Litho. *Perf. 14½*

418 A224 35c dl grn & buff .35 .25
419 A225 1.15e ultra & pur .40 .25
420 A224 4e dk pur & pale rose .60 .35
421 A225 6e orange & vio bl .50 .25
Nos. 418-421 (4) 1.85 1.10

3rd UN Conf. on Trade and Development (UNCTAD III), Santiago, Apr.-May 1972. Design A224 is perf. horiz. in the middle.

Soldier, 1822, Andes, Military College Emblem
A226

1972, June 9

422 A226 1.15e blue & yel .35 .25

Sesquicentennial of Bernardo O'Higgins Military College.

Miner Holding Copper Ingot, Chilean Flag — A227

1972, July 11 Litho. *Perf. 15x14½*

423 A227 1.15e blue & rose red .35 .25
424 A227 5e blue, blk & rose red .45 .25

Nationalization of copper industry.

Sailing Ship — A228

1972, Aug. 4

425 A228 1.15e violet brown .55 .25

Arturo Pratt Naval Training School, sesqui.

Mt. Calan Observatory — A229

1972, Aug. 31 Litho. *Perf. 14½*

426 A229 50c ultra .40 .25

University of Chile Mt. Calan Observatory.

Carrier Pigeon — A230

1972, Oct. 9 Litho. *Perf. 14½*

427 A230 1.15e red lilac & vio .40 .25

Intl. Letter Writing Week, Oct. 9-15.

René Schneider and Army Flag — A231

1972, Oct. 25 *Perf. 14*

428 A231 2.30e multi .40 .30

2nd anniv. of the death of Gen. René Schneider. No. 428 is perforated vertically in the middle.

Book and Young People
A232

1972, Oct. 31 *Perf. 14½*

429 A232 50c black & dp org .40 .25

International Book Year 1972.

Guitar and Earthen Jar
A233

Designs: 2.65e, Fish and produce. 3.50e, Stove, pots and rug, vert.

1972, Nov. 20 Litho. *Perf. 14½*

430 A233 1.15e red & blk .30 .25
431 A233 2.65e ultra & rose lake .40 .25
432 A233 3.50e red & red brn .40 .25
Nos. 430-432 (3) 1.10 .75

Tourism Year of the Americas.

José M. Carrera Before Execution A234

1973, Feb. 1 Litho. *Perf. 14½*
433 A234 2.30e lt ultra .40 .25

Sesquicentennial of the death of José Miguel Carrera (1785-1821), Chilean revolutionist and dictator.

Map of Antarctica, Flag at Base — A235

1973, Feb. 8
434 A235 10e ultra & red .90 .25

Bernardo O'Higgins Antarctic Base, 25th anniv.

Naval Air Service Emblem, Destroyer A236

1973, Mar. 16 Litho. *Perf. 14½*
435 A236 20e brt bl & ocher .45 .25

Chilean Naval Aviation, 50th anniversary.

La Silla Observatory A237

1973, Apr. 25 Litho. *Perf. 14½*
436 A237 2.30e ultra & blk .40 .25

INTERPOL Emblem A238

Designs: 50e, Fingerprint over globe.

1973, Sept. 23 Litho. *Perf. 14½*
437 A238 30e bister & ultra .65 .30
438 A238 50e black & red .85 .30

50th anniversary of International Criminal Police Organization.

Grapes — A239

Chilean wine export: 100e, Globe inscribed "Chile Exporta Vino."

1973, Dec. 10 Litho. *Perf. 14½*
439 A239 20e buff & lilac .45 .25
440 A239 100e blue & claret 1.00 .25

UPU Headquarters, Bern — A240

1974, Apr. 4
441 A240 500e on 45c green .75 .25

UPU cent. No. 441 was not issued without dark green surcharge and overprint.

Bernardo O'Higgins, Armed Forces Emblems — A241

No. 443, Soldiers with mortar. No. 444, Navy anti-aircraft gunners. No. 445, Pilot in cockpit. No. 446, Mounted policeman.

1974, Apr. 11 Litho. *Perf. 14½*
442 A241 30e shown .30 .25
443 A241 30e multicolored .30 .25
444 A241 30e multicolored .30 .25
445 A241 30e multicolored .30 .25
446 A241 30e multicolored .30 .25
Nos. 442-446 (5) 1.50 1.25

Honoring the Armed Forces.

Soccer Ball and Globe — A242

1000e, Soccer ball and stadium, horiz.

1974 Litho. *Perf. 14*
447 A242 500e dk red & org .60 .25
448 A242 1000e bl & indigo 1.25 .30

World Cup Soccer Championship, Munich, June 13-July 7.

A souvenir sheet contains 2 imperf. stamps similar to Nos. 447-448, with blue marginal inscription. Printed on thin card. Size: 90x119mm. Value, $15.

Nos. 386, 355 Surcharged

1974, June Litho. *Perf. 14½*
449 A202 100e on 40c bl grn .35 .25
Perf. 13x14
450 A174 300e on 50c dl brn .40 .25

Traffic Police — A243

1974, June 20 *Perf. 14½*
451 A243 30e red brn & grn .40 .25

Traffic safety.

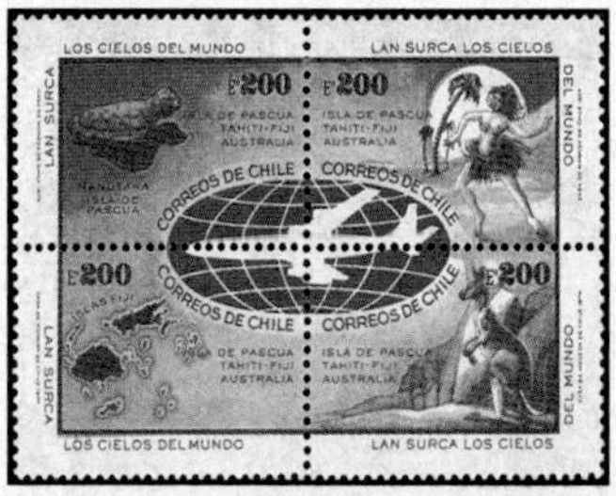

Santiago-Australia Air Service — A244

1974, Sept. 5 Litho. *Perf. 14½x14*
452 A244 Block of 4 4.75 3.00
a. 200e Easter Island turtle .70 .30
b. 200e Polynesian dancer .70 .30
c. 200e Map of Fiji Islands .70 .30
d. 200e Kangaroo .70 .30

Inauguration of air service by LAN (Chile's national airline) from Santiago to Easter Island, Tahiti, Fiji, Australia.

Globe Cut to Show Mantle and Core — A245

1974, Sept. 9 *Perf. 14x14½*
453 A245 500e red brn & org 1.00 .25

International Volcanology Congress, Santiago, Sept. 9-14.

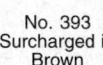

No. 393 Surcharged in Brown

1974, Oct. 24 Litho. *Perf. 14½*
454 A205 100e on 40c green .40 .25

Inauguration of the O'Higgins National Shrine at Maipu, Oct. 24, 1974.

Juan Fernandez Archipelago — A246

1974, Nov. 22 Litho. *Perf. 14½x14*
455 A246 Block of 4 5.00 2.50
a. 200e Robinson Crusoe Island .75 .35
b. 200e Chonta palms .75 .35
c. 200e Mountain goat .75 .35
d. 200e Spiny rock lobster .75 .35

400th anniversary of discovery of Juan Fernandez Archipelago.

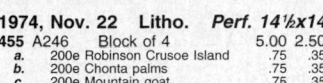

O'Higgins and Bolivar A247

1974, Dec. 9 *Perf. 14½*
456 A247 100e red brn & buff .30 .25

Sesquicentennial of the Battles of Junin and Ayacucho.

F. Vidal Gormaz and Institute Seal — A248

1975, Jan. 22 Litho. *Perf. 14½*
457 A248 100e rose claret & bl .35 .25

Centenary of the Naval Hydrographic Institute; F. Vidal Gormaz was first commandant.

Albert Schweitzer — A249

1975, Apr. 7 Litho. *Perf. 14x14½*
458 A249 500e yel & red brn .70 .25

Dr. Albert Schweitzer (1875-1965), medical missionary, birth centenary.

No. 395 Surcharged in Red

1975, Apr. 7 *Perf. 14½*
459 A207 70e on 40c car & lt red brn .35 .25

Volunteer Lifeboat Service — A250

1975, Apr. 15 Litho. *Perf. 14½x14*
460 A250 Block of 4 6.00 3.75
a. 150e Lighthouse .85 .30
b. 150e Shipwreck .85 .30

c.	150e Lifeboat		.85	.30
d.	150e Sailor reaching for life preserver		.85	.30

Valparaiso Volunteer Lifeboat service, 50th anniversary.

Note: souvenir cards were issued by Chile starting in 1975 for various issues. They were printed on thin card. These are not souvenir sheets.

Frigate Lautaro A251

No. 462, Corvette Baquedano. No. 463, Cruiser Chacabuco. No. 464, Brigantine Goleta Esmeralda.

1975, May 21 **Photo. & Engr.**

461	A251	500e shown	.75	.30
462	A251	500e multi	.75	.30
463	A251	500e multi	.75	.30
464	A251	500e multi	.75	.30
a.		Block of 4, #461-464	7.50	7.50
465	A251	800e like #461	1.00	.35
466	A251	800e like #462	1.00	.35
467	A251	800e like #463	1.00	.35
468	A251	800e like #464	1.00	.35
a.		Block of 4, #465-468	10.00	10.00
469	A251	1000e like #461	1.50	.50
470	A251	1000e like #462	1.50	.50
471	A251	1000e like #463	1.50	.50
472	A251	1000e like #464	1.50	.50
a.		Block of 4, #469-472	12.50	12.50
		Nos. 461-472 (12)	13.00	4.60

Shipwreck of training frigate Lautaro, 30th anniversary. Se-tenant in sheets of 25 (5x5) with 7 Lautaro stamps and 6 each of the others.

Happy Mother, by Alfredo Valenzuela P. — A252

Paintings: No. 474, Young Girl, by Francisco Javier Mandiola. No. 475, Lucia Guzman, by Pedro Lira Rencoret. No. 476, Woman, by Magdalena Mira Mena.

1975, Oct. 13 **Litho.** ***Perf. 14½***

473	A252	50c multicolored	.90	.25
474	A252	50c multicolored	.90	.25
475	A252	50c multicolored	.90	.25
476	A252	50c multicolored	.90	.25
		Nos. 473-476 (4)	3.60	1.00

International Women's Year 1975. Gray inscription on back, printed beneath gum, gives details about painting shown.

Diego Portales, Finance Minister — A253

Inscribed: D. Portales

1975-78 **Litho.** ***Perf. 13½x14½***

477	A253	10c gray grn	.30	.25
478	A253	20c violet ('76)	.30	.25
479	A253	30c orange ('76)	.30	.25
480	A253	50c lt brown	.30	.25
481	A253	1p blue	.30	.25
482	A253	1.50p ocher ('76)	.30	.25
483	A253	2p gray ('77)	.30	.25
483A	A253	2.50p citron ('78)	.30	.25
483B	A253	3.50p pnksh rose ('78)	.35	.25
484	A253	5p rose claret	.35	.25
		Nos. 477-484 (10)	3.10	2.50

See Nos. 635-639. For surcharge see No. 533.

Cochrane and Liberating Squadron, 1820 — A254

No. 486, Capture of Valdivia, 1820. No. 487, Capture of Three-master Esmeralda, 1820. No. 488, Cruiser Cochrane, 1874. No. 489, Destroyer Cochrane, 1962.

1976, Jan. 6 ***Perf. 14½***

485	A254	1p multicolored	.70	.25
486	A254	1p multicolored	.70	.25
487	A254	1p multicolored	.70	.25
488	A254	1p multicolored	.70	.25
489	A254	1p multicolored	.70	.25
a.		Strip of 5, #485-489	4.00	4.00

Lord Thomas Cochrane, first commander of Chilean Navy, birth bicentenary.

Flags of Chile and Bolivia A255

1976, May 25 **Litho.** ***Perf. 14½***

490	A255	1.50p multicolored	1.50	.25

Sesquicentennial of Bolivia's independence.

Lake of the Inca, OAS Emblem A256

1976, June 11

491	A256	1.50p multicolored	1.40	.25

6th General Assembly of the Organization of American States.

George Washington A257

1976, July 3

492	A257	5p multicolored	.80	.25

American Bicentennial.

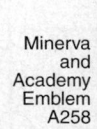

Minerva and Academy Emblem A258

1976, July

493	A258	2.50p multicolored	1.50	.25

Polytechnic Military Academy, 50th anniv.

Araucan Indian — A259

Designs: 2p, Condor with broken chain. 3p, Winged woman, symbolizing rebirth.

1976, Sept. 20 **Litho.** ***Perf. 14½***

494	A259	1p blue & multi	.30	.25
495	A259	2p blue & multi	1.50	.75
496	A259	3p yellow & multi	.60	.25
a.		Strip of 3, #494-496	2.75	2.00

3rd anniversary of the Military Junta.

View, Antarctica — A260

1977, Feb. 10 **Litho.** ***Perf. 14½***

497	A260	2p multicolored	9.00	.50

Visit of President Augusto Pinochet to Antarctica.

School Emblem, Planted Field — A261

1977, Mar. 10 ***Perf. 14½***

498	A261	2p multicolored	1.50	.30

Cent. of advanced agricultural education.

Justice — A262

1977, Mar. 30 **Litho.** ***Perf. 14½***

499	A262	2p brown & slate	1.60	.35

Supreme Court of Justice, sesquicentennial.

Eye with Globe, Caduceus — A263

1977, Mar. 30 **Litho.** ***Perf. 14½***

500	A263	2p multicolored	2.00	.55

11th Pan-American Ophthalmological Cong.

Mounted Policeman A264

Designs: No. 502, Policewoman with children. No. 503, Paine Peaks and Osorno Volcano, crossed rifle emblem. No. 504, Crossed rifle emblem, mounted and motorcycle policemen, helicopter and automobile, horiz.

1977, Apr. 27

501	A264	2p multicolored	.45	.25
502	A264	2p multicolored	.45	.25
503	A264	2p multicolored	.45	.25
504	A264	2p multicolored	.45	.25
		Nos. 501-504 (4)	1.80	1.00

Chilean police organization, 50th anniv.

Intelsat Satellite over Globe — A265

1977, May 17 **Litho.** ***Perf. 14½***

505	A265	2p multi	.90	.35

World Telecommunications Day.

El Mercurio's First Front Page, Press and Ship — A266

1977, July 5 **Litho.** ***Perf. 14½***

506	A266	2p multi	.40	.25

El Mercurio de Valparaiso, first Chilean newspaper, 150th anniversary.

St. Francis, Birds and Cross — A267

1977, July 26 **Litho.** ***Perf. 14½***

507	A267	5p multi	1.75	.30

St. Francis of Assisi, 750th death anniv.

Science and Technology A268

1977, Aug. 26 **Litho.** ***Perf. 14½***

508	A268	4p multi	.55	.25

Young Mother Weaving — A269

No. 510, Handicapped boy in wheelchair & nurse. No. 511, Children dancing in circle. No. 512, Old man & home.

1977, Sept. 13 Litho. *Perf. 14½*

509	A269	5p multi	.60	.25
510	A269	5p multi	.60	.25
511	A269	10p multi, horiz.	1.25	.25
512	A269	10p multi, horiz.	1.25	.25
		Nos. 509-512 (4)	3.70	1.00

4th anniversary of Government Junta and social services of armed forces.

Diego de Almagro — A270

1977, Oct. 31 Engr. *Perf. 14½*

513	A270	5p rose & carmine	.40	.25

Diego de Almagro (1475-1538), leader of Spanish expedition to Chile.

Bell, Letters, Dove and Child A271

1977, Dec. 12 Litho. *Perf. 14½*

514	A271	2.50p multi	.40	.25

Christmas 1977.

Loading Timber A272

1978 Litho. *Perf. 15*

515	A272	10p multi	1.25	.25
516	A272	20p multi	1.75	.35

No. 516 inscribed "CORREOS," ship is flying Chilean flag.

Papal Arms and Globe A273

University — A274

1978 Litho. *Perf. 14½*

521	A273	10p multi	1.00	.30
522	A274	25p multi	2.25	.75

World Peace Day (10p); Catholic University of Valparaiso, 50th anniversary (25p). Issue dates: 10p, July 28; 25p, July 31.

O'Higgins, by Gil de Castro — A275

1978, Aug. 20 Litho. *Perf. 15*

523	A275	10p multi	.90	.30

Bernardo O'Higgins (1778-1842), soldier and statesman.

Chacabuco Victory Monument A276

1978, Sept. 11

524	A276	10p multi	.90	.30

160th anniv. of O'Higgins victory at Chacabuco, and 5th anniv. of military government.

Teacher Writing on Blackboard — A277

1978, Sept. 21

525	A277	15p multi	1.00	.25

10th anniversary and 9th Reunion of Inter-american Council for Education, Science and Culture (C.I.E.C.C.), Sept. 21-29.

First National Fleet, by Thomas Somerscales — A278

Design: 30p, Last Moments of Rancagua Battle, by Pedro Subercaseaux.

1978 Litho. *Perf. 15*

526	A278	20p multi	2.25	.55
527	A278	30p multi	2.75	.90

Bernardo O'Higgins (1778-1842), soldier and statesman.

Issue dates: 20p, Oct. 9; 30p, Oct. 2.

San Martin-O'Higgins Medal, by Rene Thenot, 1942 — A279

1978, Oct. 20

528	A279	7p multi	.50	.25

José de San Martin and Bernardo O'Higgins, 200th birth anniversaries.

Council Emblem — A280

1978, Nov. 27 Litho. *Perf. 14½*

529	A280	50p multi	5.25	2.10

Intl. Council of Military Sports, 30th anniv.

Three Kings — A281

Virgin and Child — A282

1978, Dec. 14 Litho. *Perf. 14½*

530	A281	3p multi	.75	.25
531	A282	11p multi	1.40	.40

Christmas 1978.

Philippi Brothers A283

1978, Dec. 29 Litho. *Perf. 14½x15*

532	A283	3.50p multi	.70	.25

Bernardo E. Philippi (1811-1852) and Rodulfo A. Philippi (1808-1904), scientists and travelers.

No. 477 Surcharged in Bright Green

1979 Litho. *Perf. 13x14*

533	A253	3.50p on 10c gray grn	.30	.25

Flags of Chile and Salvation Army — A284

1979, Mar. 17 Litho. *Perf. 14½*

534	A284	10p multi	1.25	.65

Salvation Army in Chile, 70th anniversary.

Pope Paul VI (1897-1978) — A285

1979, Mar. 30

535	A285	11p multi	1.50	.90

Battle of Maipu Monument — A286

1979, Apr. 17 Litho. *Perf. 14½*

536	A286	8.50p multi	1.40	.50

Bernardo O'Higgins (1778-1842), Liberator of Chile.

Naval Battles A287

1979, May 21 Litho. *Perf. 14½*

537	A287	3.50p Angamos	.80	.30
538	A287	3.50p Iquique	.80	.30
539	A287	3.50p Punta Gruesa	.80	.30
		Nos. 537-539 (3)	2.40	.90

Centenary of victorious naval battles against Peru.

1903 Ambulance and Red Cross — A288

1979, June 29 Litho. *Perf. 14½*

540	A288	25p multi	4.00	1.10

75th anniversary of Chilean Red Cross.

Diego Portales — A289

1979-86 Litho. *Perf. 13½*

542	A289	1.50p ocher	.25	.25
543	A289	2p gray ('81)	.25	.25
544	A289	3.50p red	.30	.25

545 A289 4.50p bl grn ('81) .40 .25
546 A289 5p rose claret .50 .25
547 A289 6p emerald .60 .30
548 A289 7p yellow ('82) .55 .30
549 A289 10p blue ('82) .80 .30
550 A289 12p orange ('86) .35 .25
Nos. 542-550 (9) 4.00 2.40

1.50p, 3.50p, 5p and 6p inscribed "D. Portales."

People and Flag — A290

1979, Aug. 28 Litho. *Perf. 14½*
551 A290 10p multi 1.00 .60

Yugoslavian immigration, centenary.

Coat of Arms and Mt. Castillo A290a

1979, Oct. 12 Litho. *Perf. 14½*
552 A290a 20p multi 2.25 1.00

Coyhaique 50th anniv.

IYC Emblem, Playground — A291

IYC Emblem, Children's Drawings: 11p, Girl and shadow, vert. 12p, Dancing.

1979, Oct. 9 *Perf. 14½*
553 A291 9.50p multi .95 .60
554 A291 11p multi 1.10 .75
555 A291 12p multi 1.60 .85
Nos. 553-555 (3) 3.65 2.20

International Year of the Child.

Telecom 79 A292

1979, Oct. 26 Litho. *Perf. 14½*
556 A292 15p multi 1.50 .75

3rd World Telecommunications Exhibition, Geneva, Sept. 20-26.

Puerto Williams, 25th Anniversary — A293

1979, Nov. 21
557 A293 3.50p multi .60 .25

Adoration of the Kings A294

1979, Dec. 4 Litho. *Perf. 15*
558 A294 3.50p multi .60 .25

Christmas 1979.

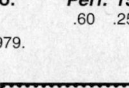

Rafael Sotomayor, Minister of War — A295

Military heroes: No. 560, Erasmo Escala. No. 561, Emilio Sotomayor. No. 562, Eleuterio Ramirez.

1979, Dec. 29 *Perf. 13½*
559 A295 3.50p ocher & brn .50 .25
560 A295 3.50p multi .50 .25
561 A295 3.50p multi .50 .25
562 A295 3.50p multi .50 .25
a. Block of 4, #559-562 2.00 2.00

Bell UH-1 Rescue Helicopter at Tinguiririca Volcano, by S.O. Mococain — A296

Air Force, 50th Anniversary: No. 564, Flying boat Catalina Skua over Antarctic, by E.F. Alvarez. No. 565, F5-E Tiger II over Andes, by M.M. Barria.

1980, Mar. 21 Litho. *Perf. 13½*
563 A296 3.50p shown .50 .25
564 A296 3.50p Jet .50 .25
565 A296 3.50p Sea plane .50 .25
Nos. 563-565 (3) 1.50 .75

The Death of Bueras, by Pedro Leon Carmona — A297

1980, Apr. 14 Litho. *Perf. 13½*
566 A297 12p multi 1.50 .50

Charge of Bueras, Battle of Maipo, 1818.

Rotary International, 75th Anniversary — A298

1980, Apr. 15
567 A298 10p multi 1.25 .45

Gen. Manuel Baquedano, by Pedro Subercaseaux A299

Gen. Pedro Lagos, Battle Scene, by Subercaseaux — A300

Battle of Morro de Arica Centenary (Subercaseaux Paintings): No. 570, Commander Juan J. San Martin, battle scene.

1980, June 7 Litho. *Perf. 13½*
568 A299 3.50p multi .40 .25
569 A300 3.50p multi .40 .25
570 A300 3.50p multi .40 .25
Nos. 568-570 (3) 1.20 .75

Score and Perez's Silhouette — A301

1980, June 27 Litho. *Perf. 13½*
571 A301 6p multi .60 .30

Osman Perez Freire (1880-1930), composer, and fragment from his song "Ay, Ay, Ay."

Mt. Gasherbrum II, Chilean Flag, Ice Pick — A302

1980, July 9
572 A302 15p multi 1.40 .60

Chilean Himalayan expedition, June 1979.

"Charity," Stained-glass Window A303

1980, July 18
573 A303 10p multi 1.50 .35

Daughters of Charity, 125th anniv. in Chile.

Condor, Colors of Chile — A304

1980, Sept. 11 Litho. *Perf. 13½*
574 A304 3.50p multi .40 .25

Plebiscite to vote on new constitution.

Inca Child Mummy — A305

1980, Sept. 14
575 A305 5p shown .60 .25
576 A305 5p Claudio Gay .60 .25
a. Pair, #575-576 + label 1.40 1.25

Natl. Museum of Natural History (founded by Claudio Gay, 1800-73) sesqui.

Pablo Burchard, by Pedro Lira — A306

1980, Sept. 27 Litho. *Perf. 13½*
577 A306 3.50p multi .45 .25

Museum of Fine Art centenary (directed by Burchard, 1932).

Santiago International Fair — A307

1980, Oct. 30
578 A307 3.50p multi .50 .25

Nativity — A308

Christmas 1980: 3.50p, Family, vert.

1980, Nov. 25 Litho. *Perf. 13½*
579 A308 3.50p multi .80 .30
580 A308 10.50p multi 2.00 .55

Infantryman 1879 — A309

Pacific War period uniforms, 1879.

1980, Nov. 27

581	A309	3.50p	shown	.75	.25
582	A309	3.50p	Cavalry officer	.75	.25
583	A309	3.50p	Artillery officer	.75	.25
584	A309	3.50p	Engineer colonel	.75	.25
a.			Block of 4, #581-584	4.00	4.00

See Nos. 606-609.

Congress Emblem — A310

1980, Dec. 1

585	A310	11.50p	multi	2.00	.60

23rd Intl. Cong. of Military Medicine & Pharmacy.

Eradication of Hoof and Mouth Disease A311

1981, Jan. 16 Litho. *Perf. 13½*

586	A311	9.50p	multi	.90	.25

Moai Statues, Easter Island — A312

No. 588, Robinson Crusoe Island. No. 589, Penguins, Antarctic Territory.

1981, Jan. 28 Litho. *Perf. 13½*

587	A312	3.50p	shown	.45	.35
588	A312	3.50p	multi	.80	.35
589	A312	10.50p	multi	3.50	1.00
			Nos. 587-589 (3)	4.75	1.70

National Heroine Javiera Carrera, by O.M. Pizarro, Birth Bicentenary — A313

1981, Mar. 20

590	A313	3.50p	multi	.40	.25

UPU Membership Centenary A314

1981, Apr. 1

591	A314	3.50p	multi	.40	.25

C130 Hercules Air Force Transport Plane Unloading Cargo — A315

1981, Apr. 21

592	A315	3.50p	multi	1.25	.40

Lieutenant Marsh Air Force Base, 1st anniv.

13th World Telecommunications Day — A316

1981, May 17 Litho. *Perf. 13½*

593	A316	3.50p	multi	.45	.25

Arturo Prat Naval Base A317

1981, June 23 Litho. *Perf. 13½*

594	A317	3.50p	multi	1.50	.25

Capt. Jose Luis Araneda A318

1981, June 26

595	A318	3.50p	multi	.45	.25

Battle of Sangrar centenary.

Philatelic Society of Chile, 90th Anniv. A319

1981, July 29 Litho. *Perf. 13½*

596	A319	4.50p	multi	.40	.25

Minister Recabarren and Chief Conuepan Giving Speeches, by Hector Robles Acuna — A320

1981, Aug. 7

597	A320	4.50p	multi	1.00	.25

Temuco city centenary.

Exports A321

1981, Aug. 31 Litho. *Perf. 13½*

598	A321	14p	multi	.90	.35

Presidential Palace — A322

1981, Sept. 11

599	A322	4.50p	multi	.80	.25

Natl. liberation, 8th anniv.

St. Vincent de Paul, 400th Birth Anniv. A323

1981, Sept. 27 Litho. *Perf. 13½*

600	A323	4.50p	multi	.50	.25

Andres Bello, Poet and Sholar, Birth Bicentenary A324

1981, Sept. 29

601	A324	4.50p	Coin	.45	.25
602	A324	9.50p	Bust, books	.75	.30
603	A324	11.50p	Statue, arms	1.10	.40
			Nos. 601-603 (3)	2.30	.95

2nd Congress of South American Uniformed Police A325

1981, Oct. 15

604	A325	4.50p	multi	.55	.25

World Food Day A326

1981, Oct. 16

605	A326	5.50p	multi	.55	.25

Uniform Type of 1980

1879 Parade Uniforms.

1981, Nov. 6 *Perf. 13½*

606	A309	5.50p	Infantry private	.80	.25
607	A309	5.50p	Cadet	.80	.25
608	A309	5.50p	Cavalryman	.80	.25
609	A309	5.50p	Artilleryman	.80	.25
a.			Block of 4, #606-609	4.00	3.00

Intl. Year of the Disabled A327

1981, Nov. 11

610	A327	5.50p	multi	1.10	.30

Christmas 1981 — A328

1981, Nov. 25
611 A328 5.50p Nativity .50 .25
612 A328 11.50p Three Kings 1.00 .40

50th Anniv. of Federico Santa Maria Technical University — A329

1981, Dec 1 Litho. *Perf. 13½*
613 A329 5.50p multi .50 .25

Dario Salas (1881-1941), Educator — A330

1981, Dec. 4
614 A330 5.50p multi .50 .25

FIDA '82, 2nd Natl. Air Force Fair — A331

1982, Mar. 6 Litho. *Perf. 13½*
615 A331 4.50p multi .50 .25

1980 Constitution — A332

4.50p, Cardinal Caro, family. 11p, Diego Portales. 30p, Bernardo O'Higgins.

1982, Mar. 11
616 A332 4.50p multi .50 .25
617 A332 11p multi 1.25 .40
618 A332 30p multi 3.00 .90
Nos. 616-618 (3) 4.75 1.55

Panamerican Institute of Geography and History, 12th General Assembly A333

1982, Mar. 22 Litho. *Perf. 13½*
619 A333 4.50p multi .50 .25

American Air Forces Cooperation System — A334

1982, Apr. 12
620 A334 4.50p multi .45 .25

Pedro Montt — A335

1982, Mar. 27
621 A335 4.50p light vio .50 .25

Fish Exports — A336

1982, May 3 Litho. *Perf. 13½*
622 A336 20p multi 2.25 .75

Scouting Year — A337

No. 623b, Robert Baden-Powell.

1982, May 21 Litho. *Perf. 13*
623 A337 Pair *42.50 32.50*
a.-b. 4.50p, either single *15.00 8.00*

Battle of Concepcion Centenary A338

Chacabuco Regiment officers killed in battle.

1982, June 18 Litho. *Perf. 13½*
624 Block of 4 2.50 2.50
a. A338 4.50p I. Carrera Pinto .50 .25
b. A338 4.50p A. Perez Canto .50 .25
c. A338 4.50p J. Montt Salamanca .50 .25
d. A338 4.50p L. Cruz Martinez .50 .25

UN World Assembly on Aging, July 26-Aug. 6 — A339

1982, Aug. 5
625 A339 4.50p multi .40 .25

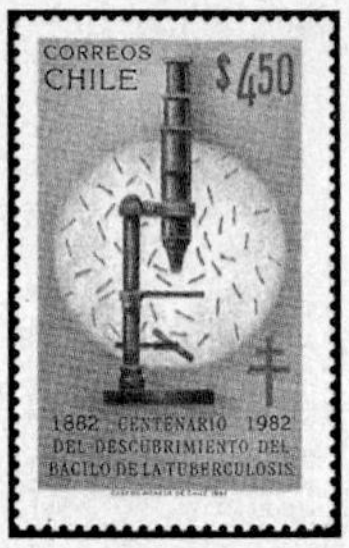

TB Bacillus Centenary A340

1982, Aug. 31
626 A340 4.50p multi .40 .25

9th Anniv. of National Liberation — A341

1982, Sept. 11 Litho. *Perf. 13½*
627 A341 4.50p multi .40 .25

Christmas 1982 — A342

Children's drawings.

1982, Nov. 2
628 A342 10p multi 1.00 .25
629 A342 25p multi, vert. 1.50 .60

Nos. 416 Surcharged in Green

Nos. 417 Surcharged in Black

1982, Nov. *Perf. 14½x15, 14½*
630 A222 1p on 3.50p bl grn & grn (G) .25 .25
631 A223 2p on 1.15p blk & car .25 .25

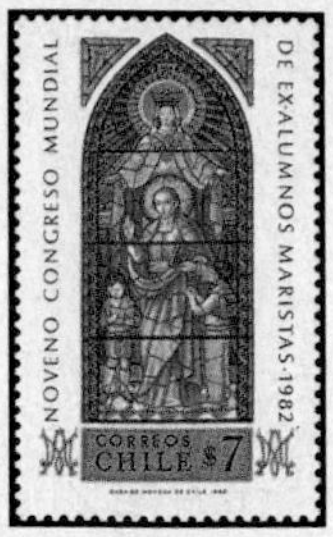

Marist Alumni, 9th World Congress A342a

Virgin Mary & Marcellus Champagnat (founder of Marist Brotherhood), stained glass window, Church of the Sacred Heart of Jesus, Barcelona.

1982, Nov. 11 Litho. *Perf. 13½*
631A A342a 7p multi 1.50 .40

El Sur Newspaper Centenary A342b

7p, Wooden handpress, masthead.

1982, Nov. 15
631B A342b 7p multi .50 .25

110th Anniv. of South American Steamship Co. — A342c

1982, Dec. 20
631C A342c 7p Steamer Copiapo 1.00 .35

60th Anniv. of Radio Club of Chile — A342d

1982, Dec. 29
631D A342d 7p multi .50 .25

First Anniv. of Postal Agreement with Order of Malta — A343

1983, Mar. 30 Litho. *Perf. 13½*
632 25p Arms of Order of Malta 2.00 .40
633 50p Chile 4.00 .80
a. Pair, #632-633 8.00 6.50

D.D. No. 20
This and similar inscriptions indicate that the stamps would be sold at a discount if purchased in large quantities.

D. Portales Type of 1975 Inscribed Diego Portales and

Ramon Barros Luco
A344

Juan Luis Sanfuentes
A344a

1983-88 Litho. *Perf. 13½*

634	A344	1p grnsh bl	.25	.25
635	A253	1p chalky bl	.25	.25
636	A253	1.50p ocher	.25	.25
637	A344	2p dl vio ('84)	.25	.25
638	A253	2p ol gray	.25	.25
639	A253	2.50p lemon	.25	.25
640	A253	5p red lilac	.35	.25
641	A344	5p crim rose	.25	.25
642	A344a	5p red ('84)	.25	.25
643	A344	7p ultra	.30	.25
644	A344a	9p brn ('84)	.25	.25
645	A344a	9p grn ('84)	.25	.25
646	A344	10p black	.25	.25
646A	A344a	10p gray ('84)	.25	.25
647	A344a	15p ultra ('87)	.25	.25
a.		Booklet pane of 10	1.50	
648	A344a	20p yel ('88)	.25	.25
b.		Booklet pane of 10	2.00	

Nos. 644, 647, 648 inscribed "D.S. No. 20."
Issued: No. 640, 8/85.
For surcharge see No. 779.

50th Anniv. of Bureau of Investigation
A345

1983, June 19 Litho. *Perf. 13½*
649 A345 20p multi 1.25 .50

Antonio Cardinal Samore (1905-1983) — A346

1983, June 26
650 A346 30p multi 2.00 .60

Centenary of Cliff Elevators in Valparaiso
A347

1983, Aug. 19 Litho. *Perf. 13½*
651 A347 40p multi 4.00 .45

Pucara de Quitor Settlement Ruins, San Pedro de Atacama — A348

No. 653, Llamas, rock painting, Rio Ibanez, Aisen. No. 654, Duck-shaped jug with human head, Diaguita cultures. No. 655, Puoko Tangata carved stone head, Easter Isld.

1983, Aug. 26

652 A348 7p multi	1.00	.40
653 A348 7p multi	1.00	.40
654 A348 7p multi	1.00	.40
655 A348 7p multi, vert.	.25	.25
Nos. 652-655 (4)	3.25	1.45

10th Anniv. of National Liberation — A349

1983, Sept. 11 Litho. *Perf. 13½*

656 A349 7p Angel with broken chains	.60	.25
657 A349 7p Couple, flag	.60	.25
658 A349 10p Family, torch	.60	.25
659 A349 40p Coat of arms, "10"	2.00	.75
a. Strip of 4, #656-659	5.00	3.50

For surcharges see Nos. 669-670.

Famous Hondurans
A350

No. 660, Francisco Morazan (1792-1842), Advocate of United Central America. No. 661, Jose Cecilio Del Valle (1777-1834), Scholar and Leader of Pan Americanism.

1983, Oct. 3 Litho. *Perf. 13½*

660 A350 7p multi	.40	.25
661 A350 7p multi	.40	.25
a. Pair, #660-661	.80	.80

World Communications Year — A351

1983, Oct. 13 Litho. *Perf. 13½*

662 7p Central P.O.	.85	.25
663 7p Challenger spaceship	.85	.25
a. A351 Pair, #662-663	1.75	1.75

Christmas 1983 — A353

Childrens' Drawings: 10p Chilean Peasant, Hanny Chacon. 30p, Holy Family. Lucrecia Cardenas, vert.

1983, Nov. 14 Litho. *Perf. 13*

664 A353 10p multi	.50	.25
665 A353 30p multi	1.50	.40

Design descriptions printed on back on top of gum.

State Railways Centenary — A354

Train Cars: a, Presidential coach, 1911. b, Service coach, 1910; tender, 1929. c, Locomotive Type 80, 1929.

1984, Jan. 4 Litho. *Perf. 13½*

666 A354 Strip of 3	10.00	8.75
a.-c. 9p, any single	2.40	.45

3rd Intl. Air Fair, Santiago, Mar. 3-11 — A355

1984, Jan. 31 Litho. *Perf. 13½*
667 A355 9p Flags, plane 1.00 .25

20th Anniv. of Nuclear Energy Commission — A356

1984, Apr. 16 Litho. *Perf. 13*
668 A356 9p multi .50 .25

Nos. 656-657 Surcharged in Purple

1984, June 11 Litho. *Perf. 13½*

669 A349 9p on 7p #656	.45	.25
670 A349 9p on 7p #657	.45	.25
a. Pair, #669-670	1.25	.95

Antarctic Colonization — A357

No. 671, Women's expedition. No. 672, Villa las Estrellas Station. No. 673, Scouts, flag, Air Force base.

1984, June 18

671 A357 15p multicolored	.75	.35
672 A357 15p multicolored	.75	.35
673 A357 15p multicolored	.75	.35
a. Strip of 3, #671-673	5.75	5.50

10th Anniv. of Regionalization — A358

Designs: a, Parinacota Church, Tarapaca. b, El Tatio geyser, Antofagasta. c, Copper mining, Atacama. d, Tololo Observatory, Coquimbo. e, Valparaiso Harbor, Valparaiso. f, Ahu Akivi head sculptures, Easter Isld. g, St. Francis Church, Santiago. h, El Hunique House, O'Higgins. i, Colburn Machicura Dam and Hydroelectric Power Station, Maule. j, Sta. Juana de Guadalcazar Fort, Bio-Bio. k, Indian woman, Araucania. l, Guar Isld. Church, Los Lagos. m, Main road, Gen. del Campo. n, Shepherds' Monument, Magellanes and Antarctic. o, Family, Villa las Estrellas Station, Antarctic.

1984, July 11

674 Sheet of 15	15.00	15.00
a.-o. A358 9p multi, any single	.75	.40

Capt. Pedro Sarmiento de Gamboa, Map, 1584 — A359

1984, July 31 Litho. *Perf. 13*
675 A359 100p multi 5.25 1.10

400th anniv. of Spanish presence in Straits of Magellan.

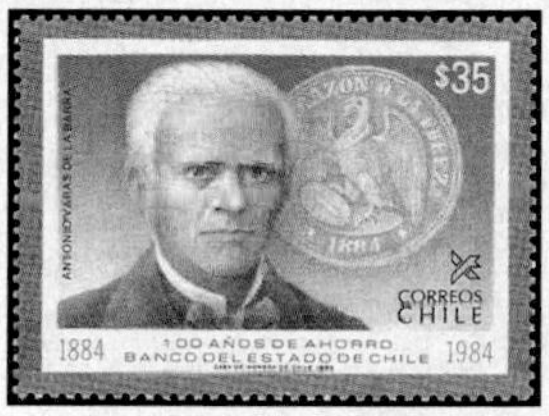

State Bank of Chile Centenary — A360

35p, Founder Antonio Varas de la Barra, coin.

1984, Sept. 6 Litho. *Perf. 13½*
676 A360 35p multi 1.25 .55

11th Anniv. of Liberation — A361

20p, Monument to O'Higgins.

1984, Sept. 11
677 A361 20p multi 1.10 .30

Circus Centenary — A362

1984, Sept. 28 Litho. *Perf. 13½*
678 A362 45p Clown 1.50 .70

Endangered Species, World Wildlife Emblem — A363

1985, July **Litho.** ***Perf. 13½***

679 A363 9p Chinchilla *9.00* 2.50
680 A363 9p Blue whale *9.00* 2.50
681 A363 9p Sea lions *9.00* 2.50
682 A363 9p Chilean huemuls *9.00* 2.50
a. Block of 4, #679-682 *48.00* *25.00*

Christmas 1984 — A364

Children's drawings.

1984, Nov. 20 **Litho.** ***Perf. 13½***

683 A364 9p Shepherds .40 .25
684 A364 40p Bethlehem 1.50 .40

Santiago University Planetarium Opening — A365

1984, Dec. 29

685 A365 10p multi .70 .25

Flora and Fauna — A366

Wildlife: a, Conepatus chinga. b, Leucocoryne purpurea. c, Himantopus himantopus. d, Lutra felina. e, Balbisia peduncularis. f, Psittacus cyanalysias. g, Pudu pudu. h, Fuschia magellanica. i, Diuca diuca. j, Dusicyon griseus. k, Alstroemeria sierrae. l, Glaucidium nanum.

1985, Feb.

686 Block of 12 15.00 10.00
a.-l. A366 10p, Any single .75 .40

American Airforces Cooperation System, 25th Anniv. A367

1985, Mar. 26

687 A367 45p Emblem, flags 2.00 1.10

Chile-Argentina Peace Treaty — A368

1985, May 2 **Litho.** ***Perf. 13½***

688 A368 20p Papal arms, flags 3.00 .60

Fr. Joseph Kentenich (1885-1968), Founder, Intl. Schonstatt Movement of Catholic Laymen A369

40p, Portrait, La Florida Sanctuary, Santiago.

1985, May 19 **Litho.** ***Perf. 13½***

689 A369 40p multi .70 .40

Antarctic Treaty, 25th Anniv. — A370

Resources, research: 15p, Krill, pack ice, map. 20p, Seismological Station, O'Higgins' Base. 35p, Georeception Station, dish receiver.

1985, June 21

690 A370 15p multi .65 .35
691 A370 20p multi .85 .50
692 A370 35p multi 1.50 .75
Nos. 690-692 (3) 3.00 1.60

Canis Fulvipes — A371

Endangered wildlife: b, Phoenicoparrus jamesi. c, Fulica gigantea. d, Lutra provocax.

1985, Aug. 9 **Litho.** ***Perf. 13½***

693 A371 Block of 4 13.00 4.50
a.-d. 20p, any single 1.75 .35

Intl. Youth Year A372

UN, 40th Anniv. A373

1985, Aug. 31

694 A372 15p multi .50 .25
695 A373 15p multi .50 .25
a. Pair, #694-695 1.50 1.50

Gen. Jose Miguel Carrera Verdugo (1785-1821) — A374

1985, Oct. 8 **Litho.** ***Perf. 13½***

696 A374 40p multi 2.25 .55

Farmer and Ox-drawn Hay Cart — A375

Folklore: b, Street photographer, wet plate camera. c, One-man band. d, Basket maker.

1985, Oct.

697 A375 Block of 4 1.25 .90
a.-d. 10p, any single .25 .25

For surcharges see Nos. 770-771.

Christmas 1985 — A376

Winning children's drawings, 7th natl. design contest.

1985, Nov. 4

698 A376 15p Nativity .55 .25
699 A376 100p Father Christmas, vert. 3.75 1.00

Nos. 698-699 inscribed in black on gummed side with child's name, age, school and region.

Holy Family — A376a

1985 **Litho.** ***Perf. 13½***

699A A376a 10p buff & brn .60 .25

For surcharge see No. 768.

16th Armed Forces Conference — A377

20p, Cavalryman, Directorial Escort, 1818. 35p, Officer, Grand Guard, 1813.

1985, Nov. 15 **Litho.** ***Perf. 13½***

700 A377 20p multicolored .75 .25
701 A377 35p multicolored 1.25 .35

Halley's Comet — A378

1985, Nov. 29 **Litho.** ***Perf. 13½***

702 A378 45p multicolored 1.00 .25
a. Souvenir sheet *20.00* 20.00

No. 702a exists imperf. Value $30.

Natl. Solidarity Campaign — A379

1985

703 A379 5p red & blue .50 .50

Campaign for Prevention of Forest Fires — A380

1985, Dec. 27

704 A380 40p Forest .75 .40
705 A380 40p Fire destruction .75 .40
a. Pair, #704-705 2.75 1.50

No. 705a has continuous design.

Dungeness Point Lighthouse, Straits of Magellan — A381

1986, Jan. 26

706 A381 45p shown 1.40 .45
707 A381 45p Evangelistas Lighthouse 1.40 .45
a. Pair, #706-707 4.00 2.50

No. 707a continuous design.

View of Santiago, Mackenna — A382

1986, Jan. 28

708 A382 30p multi .45 .25

Benjamin Vicuna Mackenna (d. 1886), municipal superintendent of Santiago, 1872-1875.

Diego Portales, Natl. Crest, Text — A382a

1986, Feb. **Litho.** ***Perf. 13½***

708A A382a 12p on 3.50p multi .45 .25

No. 708A not issued without surcharge.

1986 World Cup Soccer Championships, Mexico — A383

Host stadiums: 15p, Natl. Stadium, Chile, 1962. 20p, Aztec Stadium, Mexico, 1970. 35p, Maracana Stadium, Brazil, 1950. 50p, Wembley Stadium, Great Britain, 1966.

1986, Feb. 18

709 A383 15p multi .40 .25
710 A383 20p multi .55 .25
711 A383 35p multi .80 .35
712 A383 50p multi 1.25 .50
Nos. 709-712 (4) 3.00 1.35

Environmental Conservation — A384

1986, Feb. 28

713 A384 20p Water .75 .25
714 A384 20p Air .75 .25
715 A384 20p Soil .75 .25
Nos. 713-715 (3) 2.25 .75

Sailing Ship Santiaguillo, Flags — A385

1986, Mar. 20

716 A385 40p multi 1.00 .55

Discovery of Valparaiso Bay, 450th anniv.

A386

1986, Apr. 9

717 A386 45p multi 1.00 .45

Interamerican Development Bank, 25th anniv.

A387

1986, Apr. 30 **Litho.** ***Perf. 13½***

718 A387 15p multi .65 .25

St. Rosa de Lima (1586-1617), sanctuary at Pelequen.

Moai Statues, Easter Is. — A388

60p, Raraku Volcano. 100p, Tongariki Ruins.

1986, May 15

719 A388 60p multi 2.50 .60
a. Souvenir sheet *12.50 12.50*
720 A388 100p multi 5.00 1.00
a. Souvenir sheet *19.00 19.00*

AMERIPEX '86 — A389

1986, May 23

721 A389 100p multi 2.50 1.10

Historic Naval Ships — A390

No. 722, Schooner Ancud, 1843. No. 723, Armed merchantman Aguilar, 1830. No. 724, Corvette Esmeralda, 1856. No. 725, Frigate O'Higgins, 1834.

1986, May 30

722 A390 35p multi 1.25 .60
723 A390 35p multi 1.25 .60
724 A390 35p multi 1.25 .60
725 A390 35p multi 1.25 .60
a. Block of 4, #722-725 7.00 6.50

See Nos. 752-753.

Paintings by Juan Francisco Gonzalez (1853-1933) A391

No. 726, Rush and Chrysanthemums. No. 727, Gate of La Serena.

1986, June 24

726 A391 30p multi 1.00 .35
727 A391 30p multi 1.00 .35
a. Pair, #726-727 2.50 1.75

Exports — A392

Designs: a, Saltpeter. b, Iron. c, Copper. d, Molybdenum.

1986 **Litho.** ***Perf. 13½***

728 A392 Block of 4 1.60 1.25
a.-d. 12p, any single .25 .25

Antarctic Fauna — A393

a, Sterna vittata. b, Phalacrocorax atriceps. c, Aptenodytes forsteri. d, Catharacta lonnberg.

1986, July 16 **Litho.** ***Perf. 13½***

729 Block of 4 9.00 5.50
a.-d. A393 40p, any single 1.75 .70

Writers — A394

No. 730, Pedro de Ona (1570-1643). No. 731, Vicente Huidobro (1893-1948).

1986, Aug. 19

730 A394 20p multi .65 .40
731 A394 20p multi .65 .40
a. Pair, #730-731 1.75 1.00

Has continuous design.

Military Academy, Cent. — A395

No. 732, Major-General, 1878. No. 733, Major, 1950.

1986, Sept. 8 **Litho.** ***Perf. 13½***

732 A395 45p multi .75 .40
733 A395 45p multi .75 .40
a. Pair, #732-733 1.75 1.10

Art A396

No. 734, Diaguita urn, duck jug. No. 735, Mapuche silver ornament, embroidery.

1986, Oct. 17 ***Perf. 13½***

734 A396 30p multi .65 .40
735 A396 30p multi .65 .40
a. Pair, #734-735 2.50 1.60

Christmas — A397

8th Natl. design contest-winning children's drawings.

1986, Nov. 19 **Litho.** ***Perf. 13½***

736 A397 15p multi .65 .25
737 A397 105p multi 2.75 .70

Nos. 736-737 inscribed in black on gummed side with child's name, age, school and region.

Christmas A397a

Design: Shepherds see star, Bethlehem.

1986, Nov. **Litho.** ***Perf. 13½***

737A A397a 12p multi .35 .25

Intl. Peace Year — A398

1986, Nov. 26

738 A398 85p multi 1.50 .60

Natl. Women Volunteers — A399

1986, Dec. 15 **Litho.** ***Perf. 13½***

739 A399 15p multi .70 .25

Crowning of Our Lady of Mt. Carmel, Patron of Chile, by Pius XI, 60th Anniv. — A400

1986, Dec. 19

740 A400 25p multi .70 .25

Andean Railways Kitson-Meyer No. 59, 1907, Designed by Robert Sterling — A401

1987, Jan. 27 Litho. *Perf. 13½*

741 A401 95p multi 3.00 1.25

Arturo Prat Naval Base, Greenwich Island, the Antarctic, 40th Anniv. — A402

No. 742, Storage and power supplies. No. 743, Working and living quarters.

1987, Feb. 6

742 100p multi 4.50 2.00
743 100p multi 4.50 2.00
a. A402 Pair, #742-743 10.00 7.75

State Visit of Pope John Paul II, Apr. 1-6, 1987 — A403

Pope John Paul II and: 20p, Christ the Redeemer statue. 25p, Votive Church, Maipu. 90p, Cross of the Seas, Straits of Magellan. 115p, Virgin of the Hill.

1987 Litho. *Perf. 13½*

744 A403 20p multi .30 .25
745 A403 25p multi .40 .25
746 A403 90p multi 1.40 .60
747 A403 115p multi 1.90 .95
a. Souv. sheet of one 5.25 5.25
747B A403 115p multi 2.00 1.00
Nos. 744-747B (5) 6.00 3.05

No. 747a sold for 250p.
No. 747B differs from No. 747 in that the Statue of the Virgin has a halo and Pope John Paul II is smiling.
Issue date: Nos. 744-747a, Apr. 6.

Los Carabineros (Natl. Guard), 60th Anniv. — A404

No. 748, Cavalry showmanship. No. 749, Air-sea rescue.

1987, Apr. 21

748 A404 50p multi .80 .35
749 A404 50p multi .80 .35
a. Pair, #748-749 2.40 2.00

World Youth Soccer Championships A405

b, Concepcion Stadium, kick play. c, Antofagasta Stadium, dribbling the ball. d, Valparaiso Stadium, heading the ball.

1987, May 28

750 Block of 4 4.50 4.50
a.-d. A405 45p any single 1.10 .60

Souvenir Sheet

751 A405 45p Four players 5.00 5.00

No. 751 sold for 150p.

Naval Ships Type of 1986

No. 752, Battleship Almirante Latorre, 1913. No. 753, Cruiser O'Higgins, 1936.

1987, May 29

752 A390 60p multi 1.00 .60
753 A390 60p multi 1.00 .60
a. Pair, #752-753 3.75 2.25

Diego Portales (1793-1837), Finance Minister — A406

1987, June 16

754 A406 30p multi .50 .25

Public Works Ministry, Cent. — A407

1987, June 26

755 A407 25p multi .55 .30

Infantry School, Cent. — A408

1987, July 9

756 A408 50p Entrance .50 .25
757 A408 100p Soldiers, natl. flag 1.00 .50

Miniature Sheet

Flora and Fauna — A409

Designs: a, Chiasognathus granti. b, Calidris alba. c, Hippocamelus antisensis. d, Jubaea chilensis. e, Colias vauthieri. f, Pandion haliaetus. g, Cephalorhynchus commersonii. h, Austrocedrus chilensis. i, Jasus frontalis. j, Stephanoides fernandensis. k, Vicugna vicugna. l, Thyrsopteris elegans. m, Lithodes antarctica. n, Pteroсnemia pennata. o, Lagidium viscacia. p, Cereus atacamensis.

1987, July 30

758 Sheet of 16 15.00 15.00
a.-p. A409 25p any single .55 .30

Intl. Year of Shelter for the Homeless A410

1987, Aug. 6

759 A410 40p multi .60 .30

Legends and Folk Tales — A411

a, The Guitarist of Quinchamali. b, El Caleuche. c, El Pihuychen. d, La Lola.

1987, July Litho. *Perf. 13½*

760 A411 Block of 4 1.60 1.00
a.-d. 15p any single .25 .25

Nos. 760a-760d exist ovptd. "D.S. No 20." in golden brown on back. Value $2.50.
For surcharges see Nos. 812, 1104.

FISA '87, Santiago — A412

1987, Oct. 16 Litho. *Perf. 13½*

761 A412 20p multi .40 .25

25th Intl. agriculture and exports exhibition.

Rear Admiral Carlos Condell de la Haza (1843-1887), Naval Hero at the Battle of the Pacific — A413

1987, Nov. 7

762 A413 50p multi 1.50 .90

Christmas 1987 — A414

Children's drawings: 30p, Holy Family. 100p, Star Over Bethlehem, horiz.

1987, Nov. 13

763 A414 30p multi .75 .30
764 A414 100p multi 3.00 .95

COBRE '87, Intl. Conf. on Copper — A415

1987, Nov. 23

765 A415 40p Foundry 2.10 .60
a. Souv. sheet of one 2.50 2.50

No. 765 sold for 150p.

Natl. Antarctic Exploration Commission, 25th Anniv. — A415a

1987, Dec. 11 Litho. *Perf. 13½*

765B A415a 45p multi 1.25 .55

Ramon Freire Serrano (1787-1851), Chief of State — A416

1987, Dec. 29 *Perf. 13x13½*

766 A416 20p pale lil & rose claret .40 .30

To Smoke Is To Contaminate — A417

1987, Dec. Litho. *Perf. 13½*

767 A417 15p blue & ver .40 .25

Natl. Commission for the Control of Smoking.

No. 699A Surcharged in Green

1987 Litho. *Perf. 13½*

768 A376a 12p on 10p buff & brn .30 .25

Christmas 1987 — A418

1987, Dec.

769 A418 15p ultra, org yel & blk .30 .25
a. Bklt. pane of 10 4.50

No. 769a exists ovptd. "D.S. No 20." on back.

No. 697 Surcharged in Black and Rose Red

1987, Dec.

770 A375 Block of 4 1.10 .80
a.-d. 12p on 10p, #697a-697d .25 .25
771 A375 Block of 4 1.10 .80
a.-d. 15p on 10p, #697a-697d .25 .25

St. John Bosco (1815-1888), Educator Canonized in 1934 — A419

1988, Jan. 29

772 A419 40p multi .75 .30

20th Music Week, Frutillar — A420

1988, Jan. 27

773 A420 30p multi .75 .25

FIDA '88, 5th Intl. Aviation Fair — A421

1988, Mar. 4 **Litho.** ***Perf. 13½***

774 A421 60p dark blue & blue .90 .60

1988 Summer Olympics, Seoul — A422

Flags of Chile and Korea, events: 50p, Shot put, pole vault, javelin. 100p, Swimming, cycling, running.

1988, Mar. 18 ***Perf. 13½***

775 A422 50p multi 1.25 .60
776 A422 100p multi 2.50 1.00
a. Souv. sheet of 2, #775-776 3.75 3.75

No. 776a sold for 250p.

Natl. Agricultural Soc., 150th Anniv. — A423

1988, Apr. 8

777 A423 45p multi 1.40 .35

Intl. Red Cross and Red Crescent Organizations, 125th Annivs. — A424

1988, May 10

778 A424 150p multi 2.10 .65

No. 645 Surcharged

1988 **Litho.** ***Perf. 13½***

779 A344a 20p on 9p green .25 .25

Easter Island Folk Art — A425

Designs: Nos. 780, 782, Carved wooden head from Kava Kava. Nos. 781, 783, Bird man stone carving from Tangata Manu.

1988, Apr. 1 **Litho.** ***Perf. 13½***

780 A425 20p brick red & blk .30 .25
781 A425 20p brick red & blk .30 .25
a. Bklt. pane, 6 #780, 4 #781 4.00
b. Pair, #780-781 2.40 2.40
782 A425 20p yel & blk .30 .25
783 A425 20p yel & blk .30 .25
a. Bklt. pane, 6 #782, 4 #783 4.00
b. Pair, #782-783 2.40 2.40
Nos. 780-783 (4) 1.20 1.00

Nos. 782-783 inscribed "D.S. No 20."
For surcharges see Nos. 813-816, 955-956.

Merino, Biplane, Jet Passenger Plane and Supersonic Fighter Plane — A426

1988, May 17 **Litho.** ***Perf. 13½***

784 A426 35p multi .90 .25

Commodore Arturo Merino Benitez (b. 1888), aviation pioneer.

Naval Tradition — A427

Designs: No. 785, Training ship *Esmeralda.* No. 786, Capt. Arturo Pratt, a stained-glass window in the Naval Museum, Valparaiso.

1988, May 23

785 50p multi .90 .50
786 50p multi .90 .50
a. A427 Pair, #785-786 2.25 1.75

Pontifical Catholic University of Chile, Santiago, Cent. — A429

1988, June 21

787 A429 40p Papal & university arms .90 .25

Locomotives — A430

No. 788, Esslingen No. 3331. No. 789, North British No. 45.

1988, July 22 **Litho.** ***Perf. 13½***

788 60p multi 1.00 .70
789 60p multi 1.00 .70
a. Souv. sheet, #788-789, imperf 7.00 7.00
b. A430 Pair, #788-789 2.40 2.40

Arica-La Paz Railway, 75th anniv. (No. 788); Antofagasta Bolivia Railway, cent. (No. 789).

Jose Miguel Carrera Natl. Institute, 175th Anniv. — A431

1988, Aug. 10 **Litho.** ***Perf. 13½***

790 A431 45p multi .70 .35

Annexation of Easter Is., Cent. — A432

1988, Sept. 9

791 50p Ship, officer 1.00 .40
792 50p Map, globe 1.00 .40
a. A432 Pair, #791-792 2.50 1.50
793 100p Easter Is. folk dancers 1.50 .75
794 100p Stone ruins 1.50 .75
a. Souv. sheet of 4, #791-794, imperf. 7.00 6.50
b. A432 Pair, #793-794 5.00 3.00
Nos. 791-794 (4) 5.00 2.30

Miniature Sheet

Flowers — A433

Designs: a, Chloraea chrysantha. b, Lapageria rosea. c, Nolana paradoxa. d, Rhodophiala advena. e, Schizanthus hookeri. f, Acacia caven. g, Cordia decandra. h, Leontochir ovallei. i, Alstroemeria pelegrina. j, Copiapoa cinerea. k, Salpiglossis sinuata. l, Leucocoryne coquimbensis. m, Eucryphia glutinosa. n, Calandrinia longiscapa. o, Desfontainia spinosa. p, Sophora macrocarpa.

1988, Aug. 23 **Litho.** ***Perf. 13½***

795 Sheet of 16 20.00 20.00
a.-p. A433 30p any single .85 .40

First Domestic Airmail Route, 1919 — A434

150p, Clodomiro Figueroa Ponce's aircraft.

1988, Oct. 11

796 A434 150p multi 2.25 1.10

Christmas 1988
A435 A436

Children's drawings: 35p, Nativity, by Paulette Thiers, age 8. 100p, Going to church, by Jose M. Lamas, age 9, horiz.

1988, Nov. 17

797 A435 20p rose lake & org yel .45 .25
a. Bklt. pane of 10 6.50
798 A435 20p rose lake & org yel .45 .25
a. Bklt. pane of 10 6.50
799 A436 35p multi .65 .25
800 A436 100p multi 1.10 .40
Nos. 797-800 (4) 2.65 1.15

No. 798 inscribed "D.S. No 20."

Artisans — A437

1988, Oct. 25 **Litho.** ***Perf. 13½***

801 25p Potter .70 .25
802 25p Weaver .70 .25
a. A437 Pair, #801-802 1.60 1.25

No. 802a has continuous design.

Natl. Philatelic Soc., Cent. — A438

1988, Nov. 24

803 A438 40p No. 38, cancellation .60 .25

School Crossing Guards — A439

1988, Oct. 26

804 A439 45p multi .60 .25

A440

Battle scenes and: No. 805, Manuel Bulnes (1799-1866) Commander. No. 806, Cavalryman, Servicemen. No. 807, Roberto Simpson, Commander. No. 808, Seaman, Servicemen.

1989, Jan. 12 **Litho.** ***Perf. 13½***

805 50p multi .85 .40
806 50p multi .85 .40
a. A440 Pair, #805-806 3.00 1.00
807 100p multi 1.60 .85
808 100p multi 1.60 .85
a. A440 Pair, #807-808 3.50 2.10
Nos. 805-808 (4) 4.90 2.50

Battles of 1839: Yungay (50p) and Casma (100p). Nos. 806a, 808a have continuous designs.

Municipal Annivs. A442

Municipal coats of arms and: 30p, San Ambrosio Church. 35p, Craftsman sculpting marble. 45p, Laja Spring and falls.

1989, Jan. 20

809 A442 30p multi .30 .25
810 A442 35p multi .45 .25
811 A442 45p multi .50 .25
Nos. 809-811 (3) 1.25 .75

Founding of Vallenar, 200th anniv. (30p); founding of Combarbala, 200th anniv. (35p); founding of Los Angeles, 250th anniv. (45p).

Nos. 760a-760d and 780-783 Surcharged

a

b

1989, Mar. 20 **Litho.** ***Perf. 13½***

812 Block of 4 1.25 .75
a.-d. A411(a) 25p on 15p #760a-760d, any single .25 .25
813 A425(b) 25p on 20p #780 .25 .25
814 A425(b) 25p on 20p #781 .25 .25
Complete booklet, 6 #813, 4 #814 2.50
815 A425(b) 25p on 20p #782 .25 .25
816 A425(b) 25p on 20p #783 .25 .25
Complete booklet, 6 #815, 4 #816 2.50
Nos. 812-816 (5) 2.25 1.75

Surcharge differs on Nos. 814, 816.

Issued: Nos. 812-814, 3/20. Nos. 815-816, 11/30.

Women Beatified — A443

No. 818, Sr. Teresa de Los Andes. No. 819, Laura Vicuna.

1989, Mar. 21 **Litho.** ***Perf. 13½***

818 A443 40p multicolored .75 .35
819 A443 40p multicolored .75 .35
a. Pair, #818-819 1.75 1.10

No. 819a has continuous design.

EXFINA '89, Santiago — A444

No. 820, Christopher Columbus. No. 821, Galleons.

1989, Mar. 31

820 100p multi 1.75 .80
821 100p multi 1.75 .80
a. A444 Pair, #820-821 4.00 3.25
b. Souvenir sheet of 2, #820-821 7.00 5.25
c. Souvenir sheet of 2, #820-821 10.50 6.25

No. 821a has continuous design. No. 821b margin pictures Columbus's coat of arms and the Order of the Great Admiralty, No. 821c margin Nos. 55, 69, 18, 76, 37, 1, 20 and 98.

CORFO Development Corp., 50th Anniv. — A445

1989, Apr. 4

822 A445 60p Shipping .60 .30
823 A445 60p Lumber .60 .30
824 A445 60p Communication .60 .30
825 A445 60p Coal .60 .30
a. Block of 4, #822-825 3.00 2.50

Gabriela Mistral (1889-1957), Poet — A446

1989, Apr. 7 **Litho.** ***Perf. 13½***

826 A446 30p Poet, steeple .50 .25
827 A446 30p Poet, children .50 .25
828 A446 30p Poet working .50 .25
829 A446 30p Receiving Nobel Prize, 1945 .50 .25
a. Block of 4, #826-829 3.25 2.00

Exports — A447

Nos. 830, 832, Grapes. Nos. 831, 833, Apple.

1989, Apr. 19

830 A447 25p indigo & brt yel grn .45 .25
831 A447 25p ver & brt yel grn .45 .25
a. Bklt. pane, 5 each #830-831 3.50
b. Pair, #830-831 2.00 1.00
832 A447 25p indigo & pale yel org .45 .25
833 A447 25p ver & pale yel org .45 .25
a. Bklt. pane, 5 each #832-833 3.50
b. Pair, #832-833 2.00 1.00
Nos. 830-833 (4) 1.80 1.00

Nos. 832-833 inscribed "D.S. No 20."

See Nos. 861-864, 943-946. For surcharges see Nos. 956B-956C, 1085-1088.

Military Justice Department, 150th Anniv. — A448

1989, Apr. 24 **Litho.** ***Perf. 13½***

834 A448 50p multicolored .60 .25

Monument to the Martyrs of Carabineros de Chile — A449

1989, Apr. 26

835 A449 35p multicolored .50 .25

Surveyor and Penguins — A450

1989, May 29

836 A450 150p multicolored 2.75 1.00

Antarctic Research Institute expeditions, 25th anniv.

Naval Engineers, Cent. — A451

No. 837, Naval school. No. 838, Seamen in boiler room. No. 839, Ship, helicopter, submarine. No. 840, *Aquiles* launch, Asmar-Talcahuano.

1989, May 31

837 A451 45p multicolored .75 .25
838 A451 45p multicolored .75 .25
839 A451 45p multicolored .75 .25
840 A451 45p multicolored .75 .25
a. Block of 4, #837-840 3.50 3.50

Horse-drawn Carriage (Victoria), Vina del Mar — A452

Early transportation: 35p, Launch off Chiloe Is., vert. 40p, Cart, Cautin. 45p, Ferry, Rio Palena. 50p, Car transport, Lake Gral, Carretta. 60p, Incline railroad, Valparaiso. 100p, Cable car (funicular), Santiago.

1989-92 **Litho.** ***Perf. 13½***

841 A452 30p black & orange .55 .25
842 A452 60p black & lemon 1.00 .45
843 A452 60p like No. 842 .85 .25
844 A452 100p black & brt yel grn 1.75 .85

1989-91

845 A452 35p black & brt blue .55 .25
846 A452 40p black & olive .65 .25
847 A452 45p blk & pale blue grn .65 .25
a. Inscribed "1991" .65 .25
848 A452 45p black & lt ol grn .35 .25
849 A452 50p black & scarlet .45 .25
a. Inscribed "1992" .45 .25
Nos. 841-849 (9) 6.80 3.05

Nos. 843, 848 inscribed DS No. 20.

Issued: Nos. 841-842, 844, 4/22/89; No. 848, 2/1/91; No. 843, 1992; others, 8/1989.

For surcharge see No. 1002.

Export Type of 1989

Nos. 861, 863, Grapes. Nos. 862, 864, Apple.

1989, May 22

861 A447 5p dark blue & gray .40 .40
862 A447 5p brt red, dark blue & gray .40 .40
a. Pair, #861-862 .90 .90
863 A447 10p dark blue & gray .40 .40
864 A447 10p brt red, dark blue & gray .40 .40
a. Pair, #863-864 .90 .90

World Stamp Expo '89 — A453

1989, Aug. 25 **Litho.** ***Perf. 13½***

865 A453 250p multicolored 3.50 1.40
a. Souvenir sheet of 1 8.00 8.00

A454

UPAE emblem and pre-Columbian peoples: 30p, Atacamena potter. 150p, Selk'nam-onas bow hunter.

1989, Oct. 12

866 A454 30p multicolored .75 .25
867 A454 150p multicolored 3.00 .95

Drawing by Christina Lopez — A455

1989, Nov. 20 Litho. *Perf. 13½*

868 A455 100p multicolored 1.40 .45

Christmas.

Christmas Ornaments — A456

Nos. 869, 871, Balls. Nos. 870, 872, Bells.

1989

869 A456 25p dull green & org .45 .25
870 A456 25p dull green & org .45 .25
  a. Bklt. pane, 5 each Nos. 869-870 4.50
  b. Pair, #869-870 1.00 .70
871 A456 25p dull green & ver .45 .25
872 A456 25p dull green & ver .45 .25
  a. Bklt. pane, 5 each Nos. 871-872 4.50
  b. Pair, #871-872 1.00 .70
  Nos. 869-872 (4) 1.80 1.00

Nos. 871-872 inscribed "D.S. No 20."

Miniature Sheet

Wildlife, Natl. Parks — A457

Designs: a, Vicuna, Lauca Park. b, Chilean flamingos, Salar de Surire. c, Cactus, La Chimba Reserve. d, Guanaco, Pan de Azucar Park. e, Song bird, Father Jorge Park. f, Terns, Rapa Nui Park. g, Ferret, La Campana Park. h, Duck, Rio Clarillo Park. i, Cypress tree, Rio de Los Cipreses Reserve. j, Black-headed swan, Laguna de Torca Reserve. k, Puma, Laguna del Laja Park. l, Araucaria tree, Villarrica Park. m, Flower, Vicente Perez Rosales Park. n, Lenga tree, Dos Lagunas. o, Sea lion, Laguna San Rafael Park. p, Rhea, Torres del Paine Park.

1990, Jan. 25

873 Sheet of 16 18.00 13.00
  a.-p. A457 35p any single .65 .25

1990 World Cup Soccer Championships, Italy — A458

1990, Feb. 23

874 A458 50p Cleated shoe .60 .25
875 A458 50p Hand .60 .25
876 A458 50p Soccer ball .60 .25
877 A458 50p Athlete .60 .25
  a. Block of 4, #874-877 3.00 2.40

Natl. Air Force A459

Various aircraft: No. 878, Vickers Wibault. No. 879, Curtiss O1E Falcon. No. 880, Pitts S2A. No. 881, Extra 300.

1990, Mar. 16 Litho. *Perf. 13½*

878 A459 40p multicolored .70 .25
879 A459 40p multicolored .70 .25
880 A459 40p multicolored .70 .25
881 A459 40p multicolored .70 .25
  a. Souvenir sheet of 4, #878-881 3.50 2.00
  Nos. 878-881 (4) 2.80 1.00

FIDAE '90.

Discovery of America 500th Anniv. (in 1992) — A460

Maps and 16th cent. men: No. 882, Incan. No. 883, Spanish infantryman.

1990, Apr. 20 Litho. *Perf. 13½*

882 60p multicolored 1.00 .25
883 60p multicolored 1.00 .25
  a. A460 Pair, #882-883 4.00 3.00

Port Cities A462

1990, Apr. 27

884 A462 40p Valparaiso .60 .25
885 A462 40p San Vicente .60 .25
  a. Pair, #884-885 1.60 1.25

Democracy — A463

1990, June 8 Litho. *Perf. 13½*

886 A463 20p Sunrise .25 .25
887 A463 30p Peace dove .55 .25
888 A463 60p Pleasure .90 .40
889 A463 100p Star 1.60 .75
  a. Souvenir sheet of 4, #886-889 6.25 6.25
  Nos. 886-889 (4) 3.30 1.65

Equality — A464

1990, June 8

890 A464 45p multicolored .75 .30
  a. Souvenir sheet 2.50 2.50

No. 890a margin continues the design.

Naval Tradition — A465

No. 891, Transport ship Piloto Pardo. No. 892, Oceanographic research ship Yelcho.

1990, May 30 Litho. *Perf. 13½*

891 A465 50p multicolored .60 .25
892 A465 50p multicolored .60 .25
  a. Pair, #891-892 1.50 1.00

A466

1990, June 12

893 A466 250p Sir Rowland Hill 3.50 1.25
  a. Souvenir sheet of 1 6.00 4.50

Penny Black, 150th anniv.
No. 893a margin continues the design.

A467

1990, June 21

894 A467 150p multicolored 1.75 .75

Organization of American States, cent.

Marine Resources — A468

Designs: a, Scallop. b, Clam. c, Swordfish. d, Crab. e, Fish. f, Baiting, processing.

1990, July 27 Litho. *Perf. 13½*

895 Block of 6 4.00 3.00
  a.-f. A468 40p any single .40 .25

Curimon Convent A469

1990, Aug. 1

896 A469 50p multicolored .60 .25

250th anniversary of San Felipe.

Environmental Protection — A470

1990, Sept. 1 Litho. *Perf. 13½*

897 A470 35p Aerosol propellants .35 .25
898 A470 35p Deforestation .35 .25
899 A470 35p Smokestacks .35 .25
900 A470 35p Oil slick, shore .35 .25
901 A470 35p Forest fire .35 .25
  a. Strip of 5, #897-901 2.75 2.00
  b. Bklt. pane, 2 each #897-901 7.25

Inscribed "D.S. No 20"

902 A470 35p Aerosol propellants .35 .25
903 A470 35p Deforestation .35 .25
904 A470 35p Smokestacks .35 .25
905 A470 35p Oil slick, shore .35 .25
906 A470 35p Forest fire .35 .25
  a. Strip of 5, #902-906 2.75 2.00
  b. Bklt. pane, 2 each #902-906 7.25
  Nos. 897-906 (10) 3.50 2.50

See Nos. 988-997.

Presidents of Chile — A471

No. 912, Salvador Allende. No. 913, Eduardo Frei. No. 914, Jorge Alessandri. No. 915, Gabriel Gonzalez V. No. 916, Juan Antonio Rios. No. 917, Pedro Aguirre Cerda. No. 918, Juan E. Montero. No. 919, Carlos Ibanez. No. 920, Emiliano Figueroa. No. 921, Arturo Alessandri.

1990, Sept. 4

912 A471 35p multicolored .35 .25
913 A471 35p multicolored .35 .25
914 A471 40p multicolored .50 .25
  a. Inscribed "1992" .50 .25
915 A471 45p multicolored .55 .25
916 A471 50p multicolored .65 .35
917 A471 60p multicolored .70 .40
918 A471 70p multicolored .85 .40
  a. Inscribed "1992" .85 .40
919 A471 80p multicolored 1.00 .50
920 A471 90p multicolored 1.10 .55
  a. Inscribed "1992" 1.10 .55
921 A471 100p multicolored 1.25 .65
  a. Inscribed "1992" 1.75 .90
  Nos. 912-921 (10) 7.30 3.85

Rodeos — A472

Designs: a, Rodeo ring. b, Men on horses. c, Man stopping horse. d, Men, horses, bull.

1990, Sept. 24

926 Block of 4 2.75 2.00
  a.-d. A472 45p any single .45 .25

Discovery of America, 500th Anniv. (in 1992) — A473

30p, Phoenicopterus chilensis. 150p, Arctocephalus australis.

1990, Oct. 12 Litho. *Perf. 13½*

927 A473 30p multicolored 1.00 .25
928 A473 150p multicolored 4.00 .85

King and Queen of Spain's Visit — A474

No. 930, Arms of King Juan Carlos I, Chilean Arms.

1990, Oct. 18

929 A474 100p shown 1.25 .60
930 A474 100p Denomination at LR 1.25 .60
  a. Pair, #929-930 3.25 2.25

Malleco Bridge, Cent. — A475

Design: No. 932, Boy waving at train on bridge.

1990, Oct. 26 Litho. *Perf. 13½*

931 A475 60p multicolored 1.25 .55
932 A475 60p multicolored 1.25 .55
a. Pair, #931-932 3.00 2.10

Chilean Antarctic Territorial Claims, 50th Anniv. — A476

Design: No. 934, Penguins, helicopter, camp.

1990, Nov. 6 *Perf. 13½*

933 A476 250p multicolored 2.75 1.40
934 A476 250p multicolored 2.75 1.40
a. Pair, #933-934 8.00 8.00
b. Souvenir sheet of 2, #933-934 12.00 12.00

A477

Christmas — A478

150p, Underwater dwelling.

1990, Nov. 20 Litho. *Perf. 13½*

935 A477 35p lt green & bl grn .45 .25
a. Booklet pane of 10 4.00
936 A477 35p dull org & bl grn .30 .25
a. Booklet pane of 10 4.00
937 A478 35p shown .65 .25
938 A478 150p multi 2.75 1.50
Nos. 935-938 (4) 4.15 2.25

No. 936 inscribed "D.S. No.20."

National Congress — A479

No. 939, Congress chamber. No. 940, Early congressional session.

1990, Dec. 21 Litho. *Perf. 13½*

939 A479 100p multicolored 1.25 .55
940 A479 100p multicolored 1.25 .55
a. Pair, #939-940 2.75 1.75

City of Santiago, 450th Anniv. — A480

1991, Feb. 7

941 A480 100p Colorado House 1.25 .55
942 A480 100p Skyline 1.25 .55
a. Pair, #941-942 4.00 2.50
b. Souvenir sheet of 2, #941-942 5.00 5.00

Exports Type of 1989

Nos. 943, 945, Grapes. Nos. 944, 946, Apple.

1991, Feb. 8 *Perf. 13½ on 3 Sides*

943 A447 45p indigo & brt pink .50 .25
944 A447 45p ver & brt pink .50 .25
a. Bklt. pane, 5 each #943-944 8.25
945 A447 45p indigo & yel .50 .25
946 A447 45p ver & yel .50 .25
a. Bklt. pane, 5 each #945-946 8.25
Nos. 943-946 (4) 2.00 1.00

Nos. 945-946 inscribed "D.S. No.20." For surcharges see Nos. 1085-1088.

Historical Aircraft — A481

Designs: a, Voisin. b, S.E. 5a. c, Morane Saulnier MS 35. d, Consolidated PBY-5A/OA-10 Catalina.

1991, Mar. 21 Litho. *Perf. 13½*

947 A481 150p Block of 4, #a.-d. 7.25 4.50

American Soccer Cup, Chile — A482

1991, Apr. 12 Litho. *Perf. 13½*

948 100p Player, map 1.10 .40
949 100p Ball, goalie 1.10 .40
a. A482 Pair, #948-949 2.25 1.00

Coal Mining A483

Design: No. 951, Miners dumping cart of coal.

1991, Apr. 18

950 A483 200p shown 2.00 .95
951 A483 200p multicolored 2.00 .95
a. Pair, #950-951 4.50 3.00

Cultural Art — A484

1991, Apr. 29

952 90p multicolored 1.00 .50
953 90p multicolored 1.00 .50
a. A484 Pair, #952-953 2.25 1.40

Chilean Scientific Society, Cent. — A485

1991, Apr. 29

954 A485 45p blue grn & blk .50 .25

Nos. 782-783 Surcharged

a

b

1991, Apr. 30

955 A425(a) 45p on 20p, #782 .30 .25
956 A425(b) 45p on 20p, #783 .30 .25
a. Pair, #955-956 1.00 .75

Nos. 832-833 Surcharged

1991, May 6 Litho. *Perf. 13½*

956B A447 45p on 25p, #832 .70 .25
956C A447 45p on 25p, #833 .70 .25
d. Pair, #956B-956C 1.60 1.10

Santiago Cathedral A486

1991, May 9 Litho & Engr.

957 A486 300p red brn, sal & blk 3.75 1.75

World Telecommunications Day — A487

1991, May 17 Litho.

958 A487 90p multicolored 1.25 .30

A488

1991, May 23

959 A488 100p Pope Leo XIII 1.00 .40

Rerum Novarum Encyclical, cent.

A489

Rescue of Shackleton Expedition, 75th anniv.: a, Lt. Luis Pardo, Sir Ernest Shackleton. b, Rescue ship, Yelcho. c, Sailor pointing to survivors. d, Shackleton's ship, Endurance.

1991, May 28 Litho. *Perf. 13½*

960 A489 50p Block of 4, #a.-d. 2.50 1.50
e. Miniature sheet, #960 2.50 2.50

21st General Assembly of Organization of American States, Santiago — A490

1991, June 5

961 A490 70p multicolored .70 .25

New Carabinero School — A491

1991, June 12

962 A491 50p multicolored .60 .25

Natl. Merchant Marine Day — A492

1991, June 26

963 A492 45p black & red .60 .25

11th Pan American Games, Havana — A493

1991, July 23

964 A493 100p Runners, torch, flags .90 .35
965 A493 100p Cycling, running, basketball .90 .35
a. Pair, #964-965 2.25 1.60

Founding of the City of Los Andes, Bicent. — A494

1991, July 29

966 A494 100p multicolored 1.25 .40

Miniature Sheet

Marine Life — A495

Designs: No. 967a, Octopus vulgaris. b, Durvillaea antarctica. c, Paralichthys adspersus. d, Austromegabalanus psittacus. e, Concholepas concholepas. f, Cancer setosus. g, Lessonia nigrescens. h, Loxechinus albus. i, Homalaspis plana. j, Porphyra columbina. k, Oplegnathus insignis. l, Chorus giganteus. m, Rhynchocinetes typus. n, Engraulis ringens. o, Gracilaria spp. p, Pyura chilensis.

1991, Aug. 20 Litho. ***Perf. 13½***

967 Sheet of 16 16.00 7.50
a.-p. A495 50p any single .90 .25

1891 Revolution, Cent. — A496

Jose M. Balmaceda (1840-1891) and: No. 968, Machinery. No. 969, Teacher, students at Valentin Letelier School of Medicine.

1991, Aug. 29

968 A496 100p multicolored 1.00 .45
969 A496 100p multicolored 1.00 .45
a. Pair, #968-969 2.25 1.25

Chilean Art — A497

Paintings: 50p, Woman in Red, by Pedro Reszka. 70p, The Traveler, by Camilo Mori. 200p, Head of Child, by Benito Rebolledo. 300p, Boy Wearing a Fez, by A. Valenzuela Puelma.

1991, Sept. 26

970 A497 50p multicolored .60 .25
971 A497 70p multicolored .60 .30
972 A497 200p multicolored 2.40 .85
973 A497 300p multicolored 3.50 1.25
Nos. 970-973 (4) 7.10 2.65

Antarctic Treaty, 30th Anniv. — A498

1991, Oct. 7 Litho. ***Perf. 13½***

974 A498 80p shown 1.75 .70
975 A498 80p Birds, sea life 1.75 .70
a. Pair, #974-975 4.50 1.60

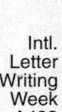

Intl. Letter Writing Week A499

1991, Oct. 9

976 A499 45p shown .45 .25
977 A499 70p Envelope filled with people .70 .30

America Issue — A500

UPAEP emblem, sailing ships and: 150p, Navigator.

1991, Oct. 14

978 A500 50p multicolored .75 .25
979 A500 150p multicolored 2.10 .75

A501

1991, Oct. 21

980 A501 45p blue hat .45 .25
981 A501 45p red hat .45 .25
a. Pair, #980-981 1.50 .75
b. Souvenir sheet of 2, #980-981 2.75 2.75

Pablo Neruda, (1904-1973), Nobel Prize winner for literature, 1971. Nos. 981a has a continuous design.

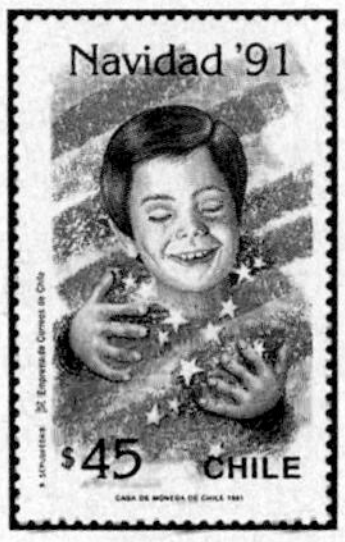

A502

1991, Nov. 4

982 A502 45p Boy with stars .50 .25
983 A502 100p Girl with stars 1.00 .50

Christmas.

Christmas

A503 A504

1991, Nov. 18 Litho. ***Perf. 13½***

984 A503 45p violet & brt pink .45 .25
985 A504 45p violet & brt pink .45 .25
a. Pair, #984-985 1.10 .25
b. Bklt. pane of 5 #985a 7.00
986 A503 45p violet & brt pink .45 .25
987 A504 45p violet & brt pink .45 .25
a. Pair, #986-987 1.10 .25
b. Bklt. pane of 5 #987a 7.00
Nos. 984-987 (4) 1.80 1.00

Nos. 986-987 inscribed "D.S. No. 20."
For surcharges see Nos. 1016-1019.

Environmental Protection Type of 1990

1992, Jan. 28 Litho. ***Perf. 13½***

Lemon & Black

988 A470 60p like #897 .55 .25
989 A470 60p like #898 .55 .25
990 A470 60p like #899 .55 .25
991 A470 60p like #900 .55 .25
992 A470 60p like #901 .55 .25
a. Strip of 5, #988-992 4.00 2.50
b. Bklt. pane, 2 each #988-992 8.00

Inscribed "D.S. No. 20"

Orange & Dark Green

993 A470 60p like #902 .55 .25
994 A470 60p like #903 .55 .25
995 A470 60p like #904 .55 .25
996 A470 60p like #905 .55 .25
997 A470 60p like #906 .55 .25
a. Strip of 5, #993-997 4.00 2.50
b. Bklt. pane, 2 each #993-997 8.00
Nos. 988-997 (10) 5.50 2.50

Wolfgang Amadeus Mozart, Death Bicent. (in 1991) — A505

1992, Jan. 31

998 A505 60p shown .60 .25
999 A505 200p Hands at piano 1.90 .90
a. Sheet of 2, #998-999 4.00 4.00

FIDAE '92, Intl. Air and Space Fair — A506

1992, Mar. 5 Litho. ***Perf. 13½***

1000 A506 60p multicolored .60 .25

16th Population and Housing Census A507

1992, Mar.

1001 A507 60p multicolored .60 .25

No. 847 Surcharged in Red Brown

1992, Mar.

1002 A452 60p on 45p .60 .25

Chilean Cities — A508

Cities' coat of arms and: 80p, Church of San Jose de Maipo. 90p, People making pottery. 100p, Lircunlauta House. 150p, Wine and lumber industries. 250p, Hullquilemu cultural center.

1992, Apr. 10 Litho. ***Perf. 13½***

1003 A508 80p multicolored .65 .25
1004 A508 90p multicolored .75 .25
1005 A508 100p multicolored .95 .35
1006 A508 150p multicolored 1.50 .50
1007 A508 250p multicolored 2.40 .80
Nos. 1003-1007 (5) 6.25 2.15

80p, San Jose de Maipo, 200th anniv. 90p, Melipilla, 250th anniv. 100p, San Fernando, 250th anniv. 150p, Cauquenes, 250th anniv. 250p, Talca, 250th anniv.

Expo '92, Seville A509

1992, Apr. 23

1008 A509 150p Pavilion 1.40 .50
1009 A509 200p Iceberg 2.00 .65
a. Sheet of 2, #1008-1009 *4.50 4.50*

A510

Easter Island — A511

Marine life: No. 1010a, Morula praecipua, Strombus maculatus, Cypraea caputdraconis. b, Codium pocockiae. c, Myripristis tiki. d, Sargassum skottsbergii. e, Pseudolabrus fuentesi. f, Pocillopora danae. g, Panulirus pascuensis. h, Tripneustes gratilla.
No. 1011b, Natives, airplane, petroglyph.

1992, June 9 Litho. ***Perf. 13½***

1010 A510 60p Sheet of 8, #a.-h. 5.00 2.75
1011 A511 200p Pair, #a.-b. 4.00 1.50

Natl. Council of the Disabled — A512

1992, June 23

1012 A512 60p multicolored .60 .25

Military Chiefs of Staff, 50th Anniv. — A513

1992, July 3

1013 A513 60p multicolored .60 .25

Submarine Forces, 75th Anniv. — A514

Coat of arms and: 250p, Officer using periscope, control room.

1992, July 4

1014 A514 150p multicolored 1.60 .50
1015 A514 250p multicolored 2.40 .90

Nos. 984-987 Surcharged

1992, Aug. 11 Litho. *Perf. 13½*

1016	A503 60p on 45p No. 984	.45	.25
1017	A504 60p on 45p No. 985	.45	.25
a.	Pair, #1016-1017	1.90	.90
1018	A503 60p on 45p No. 986	.45	.25
1019	A504 60p on 45p No. 987	.45	.25
a.	Pair, #1018-1019	1.90	.90
	Nos. 1016-1019 (4)	1.80	1.00

Nos. 1018-1019 inscribed "D.S. No. 20."

Emperor Penguins — A515

1992, Sept. 28 Litho. *Perf. 13½*

1020	A515 200p shown	1.00	.75
1021	A515 250p Adults with young	2.40	1.00
a.	Souv. sheet of 2, #1020-1021	6.25	6.25

Central Post Office, Santiago, 1772 — A516

1992, Oct. 9

1022	A516 200p multicolored	1.75	.70

Discovery of America, 500th Anniv. — A517

UPAEP emblem and: 200p, Calendar stone, astrolabe, Columbus. 250p, Church, map of Central and South America, sailing ship.

1992, Oct. 20

1023	A517 200p multicolored	1.75	.65
1024	A517 250p multicolored	2.25	.75

Radio Chile, 75th Anniv. — A518

1992, Oct. 22

1025	A518 250p multicolored	2.00	.80

Bernardo O'Higgins (1778-1842) A519

1992, Oct. 23

1026	A519 60p multicolored	.60	.25

Claudio Arrau, Pianist — A520

1992, Nov. 12 Litho. *Perf. 13½*

1027	A520 150p As child	1.25	.55
1028	A520 200p As adult	1.60	.75
a.	Souv. sheet of 2, #1027-1028	3.50	3.50

Natl. Human Rights Day — A521

1992, Dec. 10

1029	A521 100p multicolored	.80	.40
a.	Souvenir sheet of 1	1.50	1.50

Christmas — A522

Designs: Nos. 1030, 1032, Denomination at LR. Nos. 1031, 1033, Denomination at LL.

1992, Dec. 12 Litho. *Perf. 13½*

1030	A522 60p buff & brown	.45	.25
1031	A522 60p buff & brown	.45	.25
a.	Pair, #1030-1031	1.00	.45
b.	Booklet pane of 5 #1031a	4.50	4.50
1032	A522 60p buff & red	.45	.25
1033	A522 60p buff & red	.45	.25
a.	Pair, #1032-1033	1.00	.45
b.	Booklet pane of 5 #1033a	4.50	
	Nos. 1030-1033 (4)	1.80	1.00

Nos. 1032-1033 inscribed "DS/20."

A523

University of Chile, 150th Anniv.: a, Statue. b, Coat of arms, facade of building.

1992, Nov. 19 Litho. *Perf. 13½*

1034	A523 200p Pair, #a.-b.	3.00	1.25
c.	Souvenir sheet of 1, #1034	4.00	4.00

Nos. 1034a-1034b have a continuous design.

A524

1992, Dec. 12

1035	A524 70p black & yellow	.60	.25

23rd meeting of Latin American Energy Ministers.

Churches of Chiloe — A525

Nos. 1036, 1038, Achao. Nos. 1037, 1039, Castro.

1993, Mar. 1 Litho. *Perf. 13½*

1036	A525 70p black & pink	.70	.55
1037	A525 70p black & pink	.70	.55
a.	Pair #1036-1037	1.50	1.50
b.	Booklet pane of 5 #1037a	7.50	

Inscribed "DS/20"

1038	A525 70p black & yellow	.70	.55
1039	A525 70p black & yellow	.70	.55
a.	Pair, #1038-1039	1.50	1.50
b.	Booklet pane of 5 #1039a	7.50	
	Nos. 1036-1039 (4)	2.80	2.20

See Nos. 1053-1060, 1093-1098.
For surcharges see Nos. 1129-1130.

Arrival of the Jesuits, 400th Anniv. — A526

Canonization of St. Teresa of the Andes, 1993 — A527

200p, St. Ignatius of Loyola. 300p, St. Teresa of the Andes.

1993 Litho. *Perf. 13½*

1040	A526 200p multicolored	1.50	.60
a.	Souvenir sheet of 1	2.50	2.50
1041	A527 300p multicolored	2.50	1.00

Issue dates: 200p, Mar. 15; 300p, Mar. 31.
No. 1040a sold for 250p.

World Festival of Theatre of the Nations — A528

1993, Apr. 22

1042	A528 250p multicolored	2.00	.75

Second Space Conference of the Americas — A529

1993, Apr. 26

1043	A529 150p multicolored	1.50	.75
a.	Souvenir sheet of 1	3.25	3.25

No. 1043a sold for 350p.

Clotario Blest (1899-1990), Syndicalist A530

1993, Apr. 30

1044	A530 70p multicolored	.60	.25

Intl. Labor Day.

Vicente Huidobro, Poet (1893-1948) A531

1993, May 19 Litho. *Perf. 13½*

1045	A531 100p shown	.80	.40
1046	A531 100p Portrait, seated	.80	.40
a.	Pair, #1045-1046	1.75	1.10

Antique Fire Engines — A532

Nos. 1047, 1902 Watterous Engineering Co. Ltd., Canada. Nos. 1048, 1872 Merryweather, England.

1993, June 30 Litho. *Perf. 13½*

1047	A532 100p multicolored	1.10	.40
1048	A532 100p multicolored	1.10	.40
a.	Souv. sheet of 2, #1047-1048	2.50	2.50

No. 1048a sold for 400p.

Aircraft — A533

Designs: No. 1049, Douglas B-26 Invader. No. 1050, Mirage M50 Panther. No. 1051, Sanchez Besa. No. 1052, Bell 47D1 helicopter.

1993, July 13

1049 A533 100p multicolored .65 .35
1050 A533 100p multicolored .65 .35
1051 A533 100p multicolored .65 .35
1052 A533 100p multicolored .65 .35
a. Block of 4, #1049-1052 3.50 3.00

Church Type of 1993

Designs: 10p, Chonchi. 20p, Vilupulli. 30p, Llau-llao. 40p, Dalcahue. 50p, Tenaun. 80p, Quinchao. 90p, Quehui. 100p, Nercon.

1993, July Litho. *Perf. 13½*

1053 A525 10p green & black .25 .25
1054 A525 20p black & brown .25 .25
1055 A525 30p black & vermilion .25 .25
1056 A525 40p black & blue .30 .30
1057 A525 50p black & green blue .35 .35
1058 A525 80p black & buff .55 .55
a. Booklet pane of 10 8.25
b. Inscribed "1994" .60 .60
1059 A525 90p olive & black .60 .60
a. Booklet pane of 10 8.25
Complete booklet, #1059a 8.25
1060 A525 100p gray vio & blk .65 .65
a. Booklet pane of 10 8.25
Nos. 1053-1060 (8) 3.20 3.20

Issued: No. 1058a, 1/1/94; No. 1059a, 1995; No. 1060a, 2/1/96.

See No. 1093 for 80p black and violet.

Natl. Dance, "La Cueca" — A534

1993, Sept. 15 Litho. *Perf. 13½*

1061 A534 70p Cueca chilota .60 .25
1062 A534 70p Cueca central .60 .25
1063 A534 70p Cueca nortina .60 .25
Nos. 1061-1063 (3) 1.80 .75

Paintings — A535

Designs: 80p, Tarde Amanecer, by Mario Carreno, horiz. 90p, Summer, by Gracia Barrios, horiz. 150p, Figura Protegida, by Roser Bru. 200p, Tangueria-Valparaiso, by Nemesio Antunez, horiz.

1993, Sept. 28

1064 A535 80p multicolored .55 .25
1065 A535 90p multicolored .60 .25
1066 A535 150p multicolored 1.00 .40
1067 A535 200p multicolored 1.40 .55
Nos. 1064-1067 (4) 3.55 1.45

Chilean Mint, 250th Anniv. A536

1993, Oct. 7 Litho. & Engr.

1068 A536 250p multicolored 2.40 .95
a. Souvenir sheet of 1 3.50 3.50

A537

1993, Oct. 19 Litho.

1069 A537 80p multicolored .70 .25

Urban transportation system, 25th anniv.

A538

150p, Cyanoliseus patagonus. 200p, Hippocamelus bisulcus.

1993, Oct. 12 Litho. *Perf. 13½*

1070 A538 150p multicolored 1.50 .55
1071 A538 200p multicolored 2.50 .75

America issue.

Chilean Possession of Straits of Magellan, 150th Anniv. — A539

1993, Oct. 21

1072 A539 100p multicolored 3.50 .35

Naval Anniversaries — A540

1993, Oct. 27

1073 A540 80p Sailing ships .75 .30
1074 A540 80p Schooner .75 .30
1075 A540 80p Assault ship .75 .30
1076 A540 80p Patrol boat .75 .30
Nos. 1073-1076 (4) 3.00 1.20

Sailing of first naval squadron (No. 1073), Arturo Prat Naval Academy (No. 1074), Marine Corps (No. 1075), 175th anniversaries. Alejandro Navarette School for Cadets (No. 1076), 125th anniv.

Intl. Year of Indigenous Peoples — A541

1993, Nov. 24

1077 A541 100p multicolored .90 .40

Christmas — A542

1993, Dec. 1 Litho. *Perf. 13½*

1078 A542 70p tan & violet .55 .25
a. Booklet pane of 10 6.00
1079 A542 70p green & blue .65 .25
a. Booklet pane of 10 7.00

No. 1079 inscribed "DS/20."

For surcharge see No. 1131.

Pygoscelis Adelie — A543

1993, Dec. 3

1080 A543 200p Nesting 1.60 .60
1081 A543 250p Adult, chicks 2.00 .80
a. Souv. sheet of 2, #1080-1081, imperf. 4.75 4.75

Chilean Antarctica.

No. 1081a has simulated perfs.

Chilean Cities — A544

1993, Dec. 15

1082 A544 80p Rancagua .70 .25
1083 A544 80p Curico .70 .25
1084 A544 80p Ancud .70 .25
Nos. 1082-1084 (3) 2.10 .75

Rancagua and Curico, 250th anniv. Ancud, 225th anniv.

Nos. 943-946 Surcharged

1993 Litho. *Perf. 13½ on 3 Sides*

1085 A447 60p on 45p, #943 .35 .25
1086 A447 60p on 45p, #944 .35 .25
a. Bklt. pane, 5 each #1085-1086 3.50
1087 A447 60p on 45p, #945 .35 .25
1088 A447 60p on 45p, #946 .35 .25
a. Bklt. pane, 5 each #1087-1088 3.50
Nos. 1085-1088 (4) 1.40 1.00

Nos. 1087-1088 inscribed "D.S. No. 20."

Intl. Year of the Family — A545

1994, Jan. 17 Litho. *Perf. 13½*

1089 A545 100p multicolored .70 .25

Musical Instruments — A546

Designs: a, Violin. b, Cello.

1994, Jan. 27 Litho. *Perf. 13½*

1091 A546 150p Pair, #a.-b. 3.25 3.25

No. 1091 has a continuous design.

Church Type of 1993

Designs: 80p, Quinchao. 90p, Quehui. Nos. 1097, 1098, Nercon.

1994-96 Litho. *Perf. 13½*

1093 A525 80p black & violet .50 .25
1095 A525 90p red & black .50 .25
a. Booklet pane of 10 4.75
Complete booklet, #1095a 4.75
1097 A525 100p yellow & black .55 .30
a. Booklet pane of 10 6.00
Complete booklet, #1097a 6.00
1098 A525 100p gray vio & blk .60 .30
a. Booklet pane of 10 6.50
Complete booklet, #1098a 6.50
Nos. 1093-1098 (4) 2.15 1.10

Issued: 80p, 1/1/94; 90p, 1995; Nos. 1097-1098, 2/1/96.

Nos. 1093, 1095, 1097 inscribed "DS/20."

Souvenir Sheet

Natl. Aviation Museum, 50th Anniv. — A547

Aircraft: a, Sukhoi SU-30 Flanker. b, Vought-Sikorsky OS-2U3 Kingfisher. c, Lockheed F-117A Nighthawk. d, Northrop F-5E Tiger III.

1994, Mar. 17 Litho. *Perf. 13*

1102 A547 300p Sheet of 4, #a.-d. + 2 labels 9.00 5.50

Intl. Air and Space Fair, FIDAE '94.

See No. 1159.

College of Agronomy, 50th Anniv. — A548

1994, Apr. 28 Litho. *Perf. 13*

1103 A548 220p multicolored 1.50 .75

No. 760 Surcharged

1994, May 1 **Litho.** ***Perf. 13½***
1104 Block of 4 2.75 1.50
a.-d. A411 80p on 15p any single .60 .25

Concepcion University, 75th Anniv. — A549

Sections of mural, by Jorge Gonzalez Camarena: No. 1105, Cactus plant, skeletons. No. 1106, Flags, pillars, nude woman, faces. No. 1107, Flags, bodies, woman, soldier in armor. No. 1108, Women's faces, pipelines.

1994, May 14 **Litho.** ***Perf. 13***
1105 A549 250p multicolored 1.75 .75
1106 A549 250p multicolored 1.75 .75
1107 A549 250p multicolored 1.75 .75
1108 A549 250p multicolored 1.75 .75
a. Strip of 4, #1105-1108 + label 7.50 5.00

No. 1108a is a continuous design.

Chilean Antarctic Institute, 30th Anniv. — A550

Designs: No. 1109, Penguins, buildings. No. 1110, Buildings, coastal waters.

1994, May 31 ***Perf. 13***
1109 300p multicolored 2.00 1.10
1110 300p multicolored 2.00 1.10
a. A550 Pair, #1109-1110 4.50 2.50

No. 1110a is a continuous design.

Antique Fire Engines — A551

No. 1111, Merryweather steam pumper, England, 1869. No. 1112, Western lever pumper, US, 1863. No. 1113, Mieusset steam pumper, France, 1905. No. 1114, Merryweather pumper, England, 1903.

1994, July 19 **Litho.** ***Perf. 13***
1111 A551 150p multicolored .90 .50
1112 A551 150p multicolored .90 .50
1113 A551 150p multicolored .90 .50
1114 A551 150p multicolored .90 .50
a. Block of 4, #1111-1114 4.50 3.50

Javiera Carrera Girls' School, Cent. — A552

1994, Aug. 10
1115 A552 200p multicolored 1.25 .60

Arms, Sights from Chilean Cities — A553

Designs: 90p, Porvenir, cent. 100p, Villa Alemana, cent. 150p, Constitucion, bicent. 200p, Linares, bicent. 250p, Copiapo, 250th anniv. 300p, La Serena, 450th anniv.

1994, Aug. 26
1116 A553 90p multicolored .50 .25
1117 A553 100p multicolored .60 .30
1118 A553 150p multicolored .95 .40
1119 A553 200p multicolored 1.40 .55
1120 A553 250p multicolored 1.75 .65
1121 A553 300p multicolored 2.00 .85
Nos. 1116-1121 (6) 7.20 3.00

Butterflies — A554

Designs: a, Vanessa terpsichore. b, Hypsochila wagenknechti. c, Battus polydamas. d, Polythysana apollina. e, Satyridae. f, Tetraphloebia stellygera. g, Eroessa chilensis. h, Phoebis sennae.

1994, June 24 **Litho.** ***Perf. 13***
1122 A554 100p Sheet of 8, #a.-h. 9.00 9.00

20th Intl. Conference on Data Bases — A555

1994, Sept. 21 **Litho.** ***Perf. 13½***
1123 A555 100p multicolored .60 .30

America Issue — A556

Early postal transport vehicles: 80p, Van. 220p, DH-60-G, Gypsy Moth.

1994, Oct. 12
1124 A556 80p multicolored 1.00 .30
1125 A556 220p multicolored 2.00 .70

A557

1994, Oct. 31 **Litho. & Engr.**
1126 A557 300p multicolored 2.00 1.00

Beatification of Father Alberto Hurtado.

A558

1994 **Litho.** ***Perf. 13½***
1127 A558 80p multicolored .60 .25
a. Booklet pane of 10 6.00
Complete booklet, #1127a 6.00

Inscribed "DS/20"

1128 A558 80p multicolored .60 .25
a. Booklet pane of 10 7.00
Complete booklet, #1128a 7.00

Christmas.

Nos. 1036-1037, 1079 Surcharged

Perf. 13½ on 3 Sides

1994, Nov. 4 **Litho.**
1129 A525 80p on 70p #1036 .45 .25
1130 A525 80p on 70p #1037 .45 .25
a. Pair, #1129-1130 .90 .50
b. Booklet pane, 5 #1130a 7.00
Complete booklet, #1130b 7.00
1131 A542 80p on 70p #1079 .45 .25
a. Booklet pane, 10 #1131 7.00
Complete booklet, #1131a 7.00

Size and location of surcharge varies.

Miniature Sheet

Intl. Women's Day — A559

Designs: a, Star, "Women enriching the future." b, Moon, sun, "Women bringing harmony." c, Bird, "Women bringing peace." d, Earth, "Women changing the world."

1995, Mar. 8 **Litho.** ***Perf. 13½***
1132 A559 90p Sheet of 4, #a.-d. 5.00 2.50

Ancud Seminary of Conciliation, 150th Anniv. — A560

1995, Apr. 27
1133 A560 200p multicolored 1.25 .60

Destroyer Admiral Williams A561

1995, Apr. 21
1134 A561 100p multicolored .70 .30

World Conference on Social Development A562

1995, Apr. 25
1135 A562 150p multicolored 1.00 .45

Order of St. Augustine in Chile, 400th Anniv. — A563

Stained glass, Cathedral of Santiago.

1995, Apr. 28
1136 A563 250p multicolored 1.60 .75

Petroglyphs — A564

Designs: a, Ceremonial mask, Buitre, Limari Province. b, Lamas, Taira Sector, El Loa Province. c, Harpooned whale, El Medano, Taltal Province. d, Two masks, Encanto, Ovalle.

1995, June 16 **Litho.** ***Perf. 13½***
1137 A564 150p Block of 4, #a.-d. 7.00 4.00

Miniature Sheet

Motion Pictures, Cent. — A565

Posters: a, Director's chair, camera. b, Charlie Chaplin in "The Kid." c, Lumiere brothers' 1895 Cinematographe. d, "Valparaiso, My Love", with Aldo Francia.

1995, June 21
1138 A565 100p Sheet of 4, #a.-d. 7.00 3.00

City of Parral, Bicent. A566

1995, June 30 **Litho.** ***Perf. 13½***
1139 A566 200p multicolored 1.60 .85

Miniature Sheet

Insects and Cacti — A567

a, Cheloderus childreni. b, Eulychnia acida. c, Chiasognathus grantii. d, Browningia candelaris. e, Copiapoa dealbata. f, Acanthinodera cummingi. g, Neoporteria subgibbosa. h, Semiotus luteipennis.

1995, Aug. 10 Litho. *Perf. 13½*
1140 A567 100p Sheet of 8, #a.-h. 10.00 7.50

2nd World Congress of Police, Santiago — A568

1995, Oct. 2
1141 A568 200p multicolored 1.60 .80

Ministry of Housing and Urban Development, 30th Anniv. — A569

Design: Tower of Babel V, by Mario Toral.

1995, Oct. 5 Litho. *Perf. 13½*
1142 A569 200p multicolored 1.60 .85

Andres Bello (1781-1865), Scholar, Author A570

1995, Oct. 9 Litho. & Engr.
1143 A570 250p dk brn & blk 1.75 .85

Andres Bello Covenant, 25th anniv.

UNESCO, UN, FAO, 50th Anniv. — A571

Designs: a, Hands holding book, UNESCO emblem. b, Hands clasped between two globes, UN emblem. c, Hand holding seedling, FAO emblem.

1995, Oct. 10 Litho. *Perf. 13½*
1144 A571 100p Strip of 3, #a.-c. 2.75 1.40

No. 1144 is a continuous design.

America Issue — A572

Children's drawings of environmental protection: 100p, Family in garden, trees, vert. 250p, Three people working with trees.

1995, Oct. 12 Litho. *Perf. 13½*
1145 A572 100p multicolored 1.00 .45
1146 A572 250p multicolored 2.50 1.10

A573

Chilean Soccer, Cent.: a, Carlos Dittborn. b, Hugo Lepe. c, Eladio Rojas. d, Honorino Landa.

1995, Nov. 13 Litho. *Perf. 13½*
1147 A573 100p Sheet of 4, #a.-d. 3.00 1.40

A574

1995, Oct. 24 Litho. *Perf. 13½*
1148 A574 250p multicolored 1.60 .95

51st World Congress of Cape Horn captains.

Gabriela Mistral (1889-1957), 50th Anniv. of Receiving Nobel Prize for Literature A575

Litho. & Engr.

1995, Nov. 15 *Perf. 13½*
1149 A575 300p blue black & blk 2.00 1.00

Eudyptes Chrysolophus A576

1995, Nov. 22 Litho. *Perf. 13½*
1150 A576 100p shown 1.25 .45
1151 A576 250p Penguins, diff. 2.25 1.10
a. Souv. sheet, #1150-1151 5.00 5.00

No. 1151a sold for 600p.

Chilean Export Assoc., 60th Anniv. — A577

Cargo ship and: a, Kiwi fruit. b, Grapes. c, Peaches. d, Apples.
Jet plane and: e, Various berries.

1995, Dec. 1
1152 A577 100p Strip of 5, #a.-e. 3.50 3.50

Christmas
A578 A579

1995, Nov. 13 Booklet Stamps
1153 A578 90p brt blue & blue .60 .30
1154 A579 90p brt blue & blue .60 .30
a. Bklt. pane, 5 ea #1153-1154 6.50
Complete booklet, #1154a 6.75
1155 A578 90p brt grn & brown .60 .30
1156 A579 90p brt grn & brown .60 .30
a. Bklt. pane, 5 ea #1155-1156 6.50
Complete booklet, #1156a 6.75

Nos. 1155-1156 inscribed "DS/20."

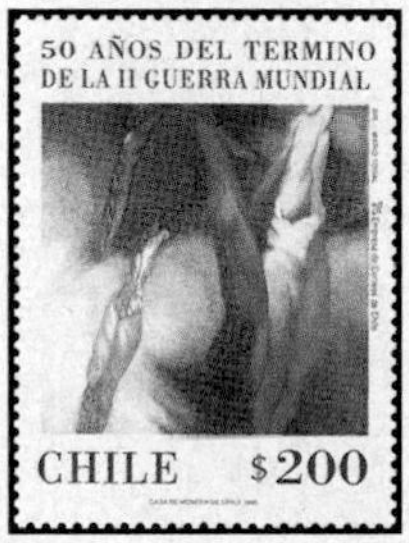

End of World War II, 50th Anniv. A580

1995, Dec. 20 Litho. *Perf. 13½*
1157 A580 200p multicolored 1.50 .75

Petroleum Production in Chile, 50th Anniv. — A581

Designs: a, Off-shore oil derrick, one main tower. b, Refinery, road trees, building. c, Refinery, up close. d, Off-shore oil derrick, four towers.

1995, Dec. 29
1158 A581 100p Block of 4, #a.-d. 3.00 3.00

Aviation Type of 1994

Designs: a, Embraer EMB-145. b, Mirage M5M Elkan. c, DHC-6 Twin Otter Series 300. d, SAAB JAS 39, Gripen.

1996, Mar. 9 Litho. *Perf. 13½*
1159 A547 400p Sheet of 4, #a.-d. 13.00 8.50

Intl. Air and Space Fair, FIDAE '96.

Men's High School, La Serena, 175th Anniv. — A582

1996, Apr. 12
1160 A582 100p multicolored .70 .35

Espamer '96, World Philatelic Exhibition — A583

Designs: No. 1161, Old Train Station, Cordoba. No. 1162, Lope de Vega Theater.

1996, Apr. 25
1161 A583 200p multicolored 1.25 .70
1162 A583 200p multicolored 1.25 .70
a. Pair, #1161-1162 3.00 3.00

Accident Prevention A584

Traffic safety: No. 1163a, Cross street at crosswalk. b, Respect traffic police. c, Obey traffic signals. d, Wait for ride on sidewalk. e, Don't cross street between parked cars. f, Never ride on side of bus. g, Walk beside road facing oncoming traffic. h, Pay attention to where you are walking. i, Don't play on streets. j, Obey traffic rules while riding a bicycle.

Safety in the home: No. 1164a, Extinguish matches after using. b, Be careful with boiling water. c, Curb sharp objects. d, Protect electrical outlets. e, Don't improvise electrical connections. f, Don't play radio or TV too loudly. g, Check all gas connections. h, Don't overload electrical outlets. i, Keep flammable materials away from furnace. j, Keep toys off floor.

Recreational safety: No. 1165a, Swim only in designated areas. b, Keep hands, head inside the car. c, Don't get a sunburn. d, Don't contaminate water with detergents. e, Don't litter. f, Extinguish camp fires. g, Don't bother others when swimming. h, Check car safety features. i, Keep kites away from electrical wires. j, Don't run in swimming pool area.

Safety in the workplace: No. 1166a, Use protective gear. b, Use only safe tools. c, Keep you mind on your work. d, Use proper tools. e, Avoid work accidents. f, Keep stairs free of objects. g, Don't carry objects that obstruct your view. h, Check ladder before using. i, Keep area clean, organized. j, Be aware of protruding nails.

Proper use of drugs and alcohol: No. 1167a, Don't drink and drive. b, Don't drink if you are pregnant. c, Don't encourage friends to drink. d, Alcohol and work don't mix. e, Drinking could destroy your family. f, Drugs can't make you happy. g, Drugs don't make you successful. h, Be happy without drugs. i, For your family say "no" to drugs. j, Drug free, happy and confident.

Safety in schools: No. 1168a, Keep calm in case of fire. b, Don't run along sides of buildings. c, Don't play dangerous jokes. d, Don't sit or stand in high dangerous places. e, Don't run on stairs. f, Don't walk and drink at the same time. g, Don't rock on chairs. h, Don't play with sharp objects. i, Don't open doors abruptly. j, Don't talk to strangers outside the school.

1996, May 2

1163 A584 50p Block of 10, #a.-j. 4.75 2.25
1164 A584 50p Block of 10, #a.-j. 4.75 2.25
1165 A584 50p Block of 10, #a.-j. 4.75 2.25
1166 A584 50p Block of 10, #a.-j. 4.75 2.25
1167 A584 50p Block of 10, #a.-j. 4.75 2.25
1168 A584 50p Block of 10, #a.-j. 4.75 2.25

No. 1 Dry Dock, Talcahuano, Cent. — A585

1996, May 20

1169 A585 200p multicolored 1.40 .70

Sculptures — A586

No. 1170, Mariner's Compass, by Ricardo Mesa, vert. No. 1171, Friendship, by Francisca Cerda, vert. No. 1172, Andes Winds, by Benito Rojo. No. 1173, Memory, by Fernando Undurraga.

1996, June 20 **Litho.** ***Perf. 13½***

1170 A586 150p multicolored 1.75 .90
1171 A586 150p multicolored 1.75 .90
a. Pair, #1170-1171 4.75 4.75
1172 A586 200p multicolored 2.25 .90
1173 A586 200p multicolored 2.25 .90
a. Pair, #1172-1173 6.00 6.00
Nos. 1170-1173 (4) 8.00 3.60

Intl. Day Against Use of Illegal Drugs and Drug Trafficking — A587

1996, June 26

1174 A587 250p multicolored 2.00 1.25

1996 Summer Olympic Games, Atlanta — A588

Designs: a, Boxer's glove. b, Runner's shoe. c, Roller blade. d, Ball.

1996, July 3

1175 A588 450p Block of 4, #a.-d. 13.50 11.00

Order of Mother of God, 50th Anniv. of Presence in Chile — A589

1996, Aug. **Litho.** ***Perf. 13½***

1176 A589 200p multicolored 1.50 .75

Lyceum of San Fernando, 150th Anniv. — A590

1996, Aug. 2

1177 A590 200p multicolored 1.50 .75

4th Intl. Congress of Earth Sciences — A591

Globe showing portions of continents, and: a, Forest fire. b, Smoke stacks creating air pollution. c, Cutting down trees. d, Surveying equipment, desert.

1996, Aug. 5 **Litho.** ***Perf. 13½***

1178 A591 200p Block of 4, #a.-d. 6.75 6.75

Minerals — A592

a, Kroehnkita. b, Lapis lazuli. c, Bornite. d, Azurite.

1996, Aug. 9

1179 A592 150p Block of 4, #a.-d. 5.00 4.25

German Immigration, 150th Anniv. — A593

Designs: 250p, House, lake, mountain. 300p, Monument showing arrival on boat.

1996, Aug. 22

1180 A593 250p multicolored 1.90 .90
1181 A593 300p multicolored 2.10 1.00

Aptenodytes Patagonica A594

1996, Sept. 9 **Litho.** ***Perf. 13½***

1182 A594 250p shown 2.00 1.00
1183 A594 300p Molting 2.10 1.10
a. Souvenir sheet, #1182-1183 5.75 5.75

Castro Fire Dept., Cent. A595

Designs: a, 1937 Italian pumper. b, 1940 Ford fire truck. c, Gorlitz G.A. Fischer manual 4-speed pumper. d, 1907 pumper.

1996, Sept. 14

1184 A595 200p Block of 4, #a.-d. 6.00 6.00

Ecotourism in National Parks — A596

Designs: a, River rafting. b, Horseback riding. c, Snow skiing. d, Hiking around cacti.

1996, Sept. 27

1185 A596 100p Sheet of 4, #a.-d. 3.25 3.25

Juan José Latorre Benavente (1846-1912), Admiral — A597

1996, Oct. 8

1186 A597 200p multicolored 1.50 .75

Historical Costumes — A598

America issue: No. 1187, Two women, child, dog, vert. No. 1188, Two men with horse, vert. 250p, Two men on horseback.

1996, Oct. 23

1187 A598 100p multicolored .95 .50
1188 A598 100p multicolored .95 .50
a. Pair, #1187-1188 2.00 2.00
1189 A598 250p multicolored 1.75 1.10

Church, City of Arica — A599

150p, Fauna, mountains, Parinacota Park.

1996, Nov. 18 **Litho.** ***Perf. 13½***

1190 A599 100p multicolored .65 .35
1191 A599 150p multicolored .85 .45

Christmas — A600

1996, Nov. 25

1192 A600 100p black & multi .70 .30
a. Booklet pane of 10 7.50
Complete booklet, #1192a 8.00
1193 A600 100p orange & multi .70 .30
a. Booklet pane of 10 7.50
Complete booklet, #1193a 8.00

No. 1193 is inscribed DS/20.

Mythology
A601 A602

1997, Feb. 12 **Litho.** ***Perf. 13½***

1194 A601 40p black & blue .25 .25
1195 A602 110p black & green .80 .40
a Booklet pane of 10 8.00
Complete booklet, #1195a 8.50
1196 A602 110p black & orange .80 .40
a. Booklet pane of 10 8.00
Complete booklet, #1196a 8.50

No. 1195 inscribed DS/20.

Sixth Summit of Spanish-Americana Heads of State and Government — A603

Mural, Visual Memory of the Nation, by Mario Toral: No. 1198, Left half. No. 1199, Right half.

1996, Nov. 6

1198 A603 110p multicolored .90 .45
1199 A603 110p multicolored .90 .45
a. Pair, #1198-1199 2.00 .95

No. 1199a is a continuous design.

State Visit of King Carl XVI Gustaf, Queen Silvia of Sweden — A604

Design: Nobel Laureates Pablo Neruda, Gabriela Mistral, Nobel medal.

1996, Dec. 3
1200 A604 300p multicolored 2.25 1.10

UNICEF, 50th Anniv. — A605

1996, Dec. 11
1201 A605 200p multicolored 1.50 .75

Frontier Region, Cent. — A606

No. 1202, Christian Alliance & Missionary Church, cent. No. 1203, Lonquimay municipality, cent.

1997
1202 A606 110p multicolored .80 .40
1203 A606 110p multicolored .90 .45

Issued: No. 1202, 1/19; No. 1203, 1/25.

Arturo Prat Antarctic Naval Base, 50th Anniv. — A607

1997, Feb. 6 Litho. *Perf. 13½*
1204 A607 250p Aerial view, vert. 1.90 .95
1205 A607 300p shown 2.40 1.10

Controller General of the Republic, 70th Anniv. — A608

1997, Mar. 26
1206 A608 110p multicolored 2.00 .40

Opening of Metro Line 5 — A609

1997, Apr. 2
1207 A609 200p multicolored 1.50 .75

Interamerican Masonic Confederation, 50th Anniv. — A610

1200p, Emblems, compass, square, book.

1997, Apr. 8
1208 A610 250p shown 2.00 1.00

Souvenir Sheet

1209 A610 1200p multicolored 9.00 9.00

No. 1209 contains one 48x60mm stamp.

Heinrich von Stephan (1831-97) A611

1997, Apr. 15
1210 A611 250p multicolored 2.00 1.00

World Book and Copyright Day — A612

1997, Apr. 23
1211 A612 110p multicolored .80 .45

Details from "Death to the Invader," by David Alfaro Siqueiros (1896-1974), Muralist — A613

1997, June 26 Litho. *Perf. 13½*
1212 A613 150p shown 1.50 .40
1213 A613 200p Detail, diff. 1.75 .60

Souvenir Sheets

1214 A613 1000p like #1212 6.25 6.25
1215 A613 1000p like #1213 6.25 6.25

Nos. 1214-1215 each contain one 48x36mm stamp.

Providencia, Cent. — A614

1997, July 17
1216 A614 250p multicolored 1.60 .90

A615

1997, Sept. 1
1217 A615 300p multicolored 2.00 1.10

Diplomatic relations between Chile and Japan, cent. See Japan No. 2578.

A616

1997, Oct. 1 Litho. *Perf. 13½*
1218 A616 110p Quality .80 .40

1st Radio Broadcast in Chile, 75th Anniv. — A617

1997 Litho. *Perf. 13½*
1219 A617 110p multicolored .80 .50

Chilean Opera Singers A618

Singer, opera: 120p, Carlo Morelli, "Rigoletto." 200p, Pedro Navia, "La Bohéme." 250p, Renato Zanelli, "Faust." 300p, Rayèn Quitral, "The Magic Flute." 500p, Ramón Vinay, "Othello."

1997, Oct. 15
1220 A618 120p multicolored 1.00 .55
1221 A618 200p multicolored 1.75 .85
1222 A618 250p multicolored 2.25 1.10
1223 A618 300p multicolored 2.50 1.25
1224 A618 500p multicolored 4.25 2.25
Nos. 1220-1224 (5) 11.75 6.00

America Issue — A619

Life of a postman: 110p, Delivering mail on bicycle. 250p, Delivering mail on horseback.

1997, Oct. 12 Litho. *Perf. 13½*
1225 A619 110p multicolored 1.00 .45
1226 A619 250p multicolored 2.50 1.00

Christmas — A620

1997 Litho. *Perf. 13½*
1227 A620 110p multicolored .80 .40
a. Booklet pane of 10 8.00
Complete booklet, #1227a 8.50
1228 A620 110p multicolored .80 .40
a. Booklet pane of 10 8.00
Complete booklet, #1228a 8.50

No. 1228 is inscribed D/S20 and was only issued in booklets.

Chilean Post, 250th Anniv. A621

Designs: 120p, Postman canceling letters. 300p, Man depositing letter into postbox.

1997, Dec. 22
1229 A621 120p multicolored .75 .40
1230 A621 300p multicolored 1.90 .95

Dogs
A622 A623

1998 Litho. *Perf. 13½*
1231 A622 120p Great Dane .60 .25
1232 A623 120p Dalmatian .60 .25
a. Pair, #1231-1232 1.25 1.00
b. Booklet pane, 5 #1232a 7.00
Complete booklet, #1232b 7.00
1233 A622 120p Great Dane .60 .25
1234 A623 120p Dalmatian .60 .25
a. Pair, #1233-1234 1.25 1.00
b. Booklet pane, 5 #1234a 7.00
Complete booklet, #1234b 7.00

Nos. 1233-1234 are inscribed DS/20.

2nd Summit of the Americas, Santiago — A624

1998, Apr. 17 Litho. *Perf. 13½*

1235 A624 150p multicolored .85 .40

Souvenir Sheet

1236 A624 1000p Logo, diff. 10.00 10.00

No. 1236 contains one 26x42mm stamp.

Paintings — A625

350p, "Los Zambos de Calama," by Mauricio Moran. 400p, "Sandia Calada," by Roser Bru.

1998, May 14 Litho. *Perf. 13½*

1237 A625 350p multicolored 2.10 1.25
1238 A625 400p multicolored 2.40 1.50

Capuchin Order in Chile, 150th Anniv. — A626

Designs: 150p, Native village, friar writing in book. 250p, Friar aiding injured man.

1998, May 18

1239 A626 150p multicolored .90 .50
1240 A626 250p multicolored 1.40 .70

1998 World Cup Soccer Championships, France — A627

Players and: 250p, Crowd. 350p, World Cup Trophy. 500p, Map of France. 700p, Chilean flag.
1500p, Player, vert.

1998, May 23

1241 A627 250p multicolored 1.50 .70
1242 A627 350p multicolored 2.00 1.00
1243 A627 500p multicolored 3.00 1.50
1244 A627 700p multicolored 4.25 2.00
Nos. 1241-1244 (4) 10.75 5.20

Souvenir Sheet

1245 A627 1500p multicolored 9.00 9.00

A628

Antarctic Research: 250p, Scientific Committee on Antarctic Research, 25th meeting. 350p, Natl. Administrators of Antarctic Programs, 10th meeting.

1998, July 22

1246 A628 250p Logo, penguin 1.50 .75
1247 A628 350p Penguins, map, logo 2.25 1.10

A629

1998, Apr. 3

1248 A629 120p multicolored .80 .40

Captain Arturo Prat Chacon, 150th birth anniv.

Army Veterinarian Service, Cent. — A630

350p, Veterinarian listening to horse's heartbeat.

1998, Apr. 20

1249 A630 250p multicolored 1.50 .75
1250 A630 350p multicolored 2.25 1.10

Merchant Marine's Director General of Maritime Territory, 150th Anniv. — A631

1998, Aug. 31 Litho. *Perf. 13½*

1251 A631 500p multicolored 3.25 1.40

Intl. Year of the Ocean.

Intl. Year of the Ocean A632

No. 1252, Nautical cartography. No. 1253, Iceberg. 500p, Silhouette of stone head, Easter Island.

1998, Sept. 10

1252 A632 400p multicolored 2.50 1.25
1253 A632 400p multicolored 2.50 1.25
1254 A632 500p multicolored 3.25 1.50
Nos. 1252-1254 (3) 8.25 4.00

Folk Singers and Composers — A633

Designs: 200p, Clara Solovera Cortes (1909-92). 250p, Francisco Flores del Campo (1908-93). 300p, Victor Jara Martinez (1932-73). 350p, Violeta Parra Sandoval (1917-67).

1998, Sept. 14

1255 A633 200p multicolored 1.00 .50
1256 A633 250p multicolored 1.40 .60
1257 A633 300p multicolored 1.50 .70
1258 A633 350p multicolored 1.90 .80
Nos. 1255-1258 (4) 5.80 2.60

World Stamp Day A634

1998, Oct. 9 Litho. *Perf. 13½*

1259 A634 250p multicolored 1.25 .60

Francisco Bilbao (1823-65), Writer A635

Litho. & Engr.

1998, Oct. 29 *Perf. 13½*

1260 A635 250p multicolored 1.75 .85

Chilean Painters — A636

Designs: 300p, Self-portrait, by Augusto Eguiluz (1894-1969), vert. 450p, Landscape, by Agustin Abarca (1882-1953).
1500p, "Two Nudes," by Henriette Petit (1894-1983).

1998, Nov. 3 Litho.

1261 A636 300p multi 1.50 .80
1262 A636 450p multi 2.25 1.10

Souvenir Sheet

1262A A636 1500p multi 8.00 8.00

No. 1262A contains one 36x47mm stamp.

Catholic University of Valparaiso, 70th Anniv. — A637

1998, Nov. 18 Litho. *Perf. 13½*

1263 A637 130p multicolored .70 .35

Prominent Women from the University of Chile — A638

America Issue: 120p, Amanda Labarca, edcuator. 250p, Marta Brunet, writer.

1998, Nov. 19 Litho. *Perf. 13½*

1264 A638 120p multicolored .80 .45
1265 A638 250p multicolored 1.60 .85

1999 World Scout Jamboree, Chile — A639

Scouting emblems and: 120p, Children of two races, stylized tents. 200p, Robert Baden-Powell. 250p, Stylized doves. 300p, Scout, stylized tents. 1000p, Scouts, leaders seated in semi-circle, vert.
3000p, Jamboree emblem over drawing of Jamboree site at Picarquin, emblems of past jamborees, Intl. Scouting Emblem.

1998, Dec. 27

1266 A639 120p multicolored .75 .35
1267 A639 200p multicolored 1.10 .55
1268 A639 250p multicolored 1.40 .70
1269 A639 300p multicolored 1.50 .80
1270 A639 1000p multicolored 5.25 2.75
Nos. 1266-1270 (5) 10.00 5.15

Imperf

Size: 126x104mm

1270A A639 3000p multi 17.00 17.00

Birds — A640

Designs: 10p, Zonotrichia capensis. 20p, Curaeus curaeus.

1998, Nov. 29

1271 A640 10p multicolored .80 .25
a. Inscribed "2000" .80 .25
1272 A640 20p multicolored .80 .25
a. Inscribed "2000" .80 .25

See Nos. 1313-1314, 1356, 1385-1386, 1418-1419.

World Equestrian High Jump Record, 50th Anniv. — A641

Captain Alberto Larraguibel and Huaso.

1999, Feb. 5 Litho. *Perf. 13½*

1273 A641 200p multicolored 1.10 .65

Temuco Fire Dept., Cent. — A642

Designs: 140p, 1900 pumper. 200p, 1929 Ford. 300p, 1955 Ford K tanker. 350p, 1967 Mercedes Benz hook and ladder truck.
1500p, Firefighter rescuing victim, vert.

1999, Feb. 18 Litho. *Perf. 13½*

1274 A642 140p multicolored .65 .30
1275 A642 200p multicolored .95 .40
1276 A642 300p multicolored 1.50 .60
1277 A642 350p multicolored 1.75 .70
Nos. 1274-1277 (4) 4.85 2.00

Souvenir Sheet

1278 A642 1500p multicolored 8.50 8.50

Chilean Chamber of Deputies, 1000th Session — A643

1999, Mar. 3 *Perf. 13½*

1279 A643 140p multicolored .70 .50

Sacred Heart College, 150th Anniv. — A644

1999, Mar. 15

1280 A644 250p multicolored 1.25 .85

Economic Development Corporation (CORFO), 60th Anniv. — A645

Pedro Aguirre Cerda, former president of Chile.

1999, Apr. 29 *Perf. 13½*

1281 A645 140p multicolored .80 .50

Chilean Insurance Assoc., Cent. — A646

1999, May 18 **Litho.** *Perf. 13½*

1282 A646 140p multicolored .65 .50

Chilean Antarctica A647

Designs: 360p, Leptonychotes weddellii. 450p, Pygoscelis antarctica.
1500p, Arctocephalus gazella, penguins.

1999, June 15

1283 A647 360p multicolored 1.75 .90

1284 A647 450p multicolored 3.25 1.25

Souvenir Sheet

1285 A647 1500p multicolored 8.50 8.50

No. 1285 contains one 35x48mm stamp.

Easter Island A648

1999, June 25

1286 A648 360p multicolored 2.00 2.00

Souvenir Sheet

Barcelona Soccer Club, Cent. — A649

1999

1287 A649 1000p multicolored 5.00 5.00

University of Santiago, 150th Anniv. — A650

Designs: 140p, Monument, students in training room, School of Arts and Sciences, 1849. 250p, Technical equipment, building on campus, State Technical University, 1947. 300p, Student looking into microscope, computer, modern building, 1999.

1999, July 6 **Litho.** *Perf. 13½*

1288 A650 140p multicolored .75 .35

1289 A650 250p multicolored 1.25 .60

1290 A650 300p multicolored 1.60 .75

Nos. 1288-1290 (3) 3.60 1.70

Alexander von Humboldt (1769-1859), 200th Anniv. of Scientific Research in Latin America — A651

Face from monument and: 300p, Bust of Humboldt, wildlife, mountains. 360p, Portrait of Humboldt, penguins, sea.

1999, July 16

1291 A651 300p multicolored 1.75 .75

1292 A651 360p multicolored 1.90 .95

China '99, World Philatelic Exhibition, Beijing — A652

Chinese, Chilean flags and: 140p, Pagoda. 450p, Chinese junk.
1500p, Great Wall of China, Gate of Heavenly Peace.

1999, Aug. 10

1293 A652 140p multicolored .75 .35

1294 A652 450p multicolored 2.10 1.10

Souvenir Sheet

1295 A652 1500p multicolored 8.00 5.00

No. 1295 contains one 60x48mm stamp.

City of Quilpue, Cent. — A653

1999, Aug. 20

1296 A653 250p multicolored 1.60 .80

A654

140p, Raúl Cardinal Silva Henriquez (1907-99). 200p, Walking in street clothes, administering sacrament, face of Christ.

1999, Aug. 9

1297 A654 140p shown .80 .40

1298 A654 200p multicolored 1.00 .50

Holy Year 2000.

A655

1999, Sept. 23 **Litho.** *Perf. 13½*

1299 A655 140p multicolored .70 .35

Red Cross blood donation campaign.

2000 World Congress of Authors & Composers, Santiago — A656

1999, Oct. 5

1300 A656 170p multicolored .90 .45

Intl. Year of Older Persons — A657

1999, Oct. 6

1301 A657 250p multicolored 1.25 .60

UPU, 125th Anniv. A658

1999, Oct. 9

1302 A658 300p Red mailbox 2.75 .90

1303 A658 360p Gold mailbox 2.75 1.10

a. Pair, #1302-1303 + label 6.75 5.25

Nos. 1302-1303 printed in sheets of 16 pairs, with label in central column.

America Issue, A New Millennium Without Arms — A659

1999, Oct. 12

1304 A659 140p shown 1.25 .30

1305 A659 320p Broken bomb 1.75 .65

Labor Management, 75th Anniv. — A660

1999, Aug. 23

1306 A660 320p multicolored 1.50 .75

Interamerican Development Bank, 40th Anniv. — A661

1999, Oct. 29 **Litho.** *Perf. 13½*

1307 A661 360p multicolored 1.75 .85

A662

1999, Dec. 1

1308 A662 450p multicolored 2.10 1.10

Holy Year 2000.

A663

1999, Dec. 1

1309 A663 170p multicolored .90 .45

Inscribed "D.S. 20"

1310 A663 170p multicolored .90 .45
a. Booklet pane of 10 10.00
Complete booklet, #1310a 11.00
b. Booklet pane of 5 5.50
Complete booklet, #1310b 6.00

Nos. 1309-1310 each were issued se-tenant with two labels that served as a lottery ticket and stub.

Union Leaders — A664

No. 1311, Luis Emilio Recabarren Serrano (1876-1924), Clotario Leopoldo Blest Riffo (1899-1990). No. 1312, Tucapel Jiménez Alfaro (1921-82), Manuel Bustos Huerta (1943-99).

1999, Dec. 29 Litho. *Perf. 13½*

1311 A664 200p multi .90 .50
1312 A664 200p multi .90 .50
a. Pair, #1311-1312 + label 4.00 3.00

Bird Type of 1998

Designs: 50p, Campephilus magellanicus, vert. 100p, Falco peregrinus cassini, vert.

2000, Feb. *Perf. 13½*

1313 A640 50p multi .25 .25
1314 A640 100p multi .90 .25

Discovery of Juan Fernández, Archipelago, 425th Anniv. — A665

a, Más Afuera (Alejandro Selkirk) Island, Santa Clara Island, tip of Más a Tierra (Robinson Crusoe) Island. b, Más a Tierra Island. c, Dendroseris litoralis. d, Rhaphythamnus venustus. e, Lobster. f, Lobster's antenna, boat. g, Boat, Gavilea insularis. h, Gavilea insularis.

2000, Feb. 29 *Perf. 13¼*

1315 A665 360p Sheet of 8, #a.-h. 16.00 16.00

Condorito, Cartoon Character by Rene Rios Boettiger Pepo — A666

Condorito: 150p, Celebrating millennium. 260p, As soccer player. 480p, As fire fighter. 980p, On horse.
2000p, With people.

2000, Mar. 20 *Perf. 13½*

1316 A666 150p multi .75 .30
1317 A666 260p multi 1.50 .50
1318 A666 480p multi 2.50 .95
1319 A666 980p multi 5.25 2.00
Nos. 1316-1319 (4) 10.00 3.75

Souvenir Sheet

1320 A666 2000p multi 11.00 11.00

Easter Island — A667

Designs: 200p, Dancer, stone weapon. 260p, Stone statue and carvings. 340p, Island native, stone statue. 480p, Female dancer, inscribed tablet, map of island.

2000, Apr. 27 Litho. *Perf. 13¼*

1321 A667 200p multi 1.10 .60
1322 A667 260p multi 1.50 .70
1323 A667 340p multi 2.00 1.00
1324 A667 480p multi 2.75 1.40
Nos. 1321-1324 (4) 7.35 3.70

Town of Carahue, Cent. (in 1998) — A668

Bridge and: No. 1325, Locomotive, pottery. No. 1326, Potatoes.

2000, May 5

1325 220p multi 1.10 .55
1326 220p multi 1.10 .55
a. A668 Pair, #1325-1326 2.50 2.00

El Mercurio Newspaper, Cent. — A669

2000, June 1

1327 A669 370p multi 2.00 1.00

4th Natl. Masonic Convention — A670

2000, June 23

1328 A670 460p multi 2.50 1.25

Medicinal Plants — A671

Designs: 200p, Quillaja saponaria. 360p, Fabiana imbricata.

2000, July 3

1329 A671 200p multi 1.25 .60
1330 A671 360p multi 3.00 1.50

Discovery of Brazil, 500th Anniv. — A672

Designs: 260p, Map of Brazil, butterfly, girl. 1500p, Monkey, parrots, boy.

2000, July 10

1331 A672 260p multi 1.50 .75

Souvenir Sheet

1332 A672 1500p multi 8.50 8.50

No. 1332 contains one 48x36mm stamp.

Folklore A673

Religious festivals: 150p, Dancer in devil costume, La Tirana. 200p, Festival of San Pedro de Atacama. 370p, Candlemas Festival, Copiapo. 460p, Chinese dancers, Andacollo.

2000, July 13

1333 A673 150p multi .80 .40
1334 A673 200p multi 1.10 .55
1335 A673 370p multi 2.00 1.00
1336 A673 460p multi 2.50 1.25
Nos. 1333-1336 (4) 6.40 3.20

Prehistoric Animals — A674

No. 1337: a, Milodon. b, Titanosaurus. c, Plesiosaurus. d, Iguanodon.

2000

1337 A674 150p Block of 4, #a-d 2.75 1.40

José de San Martín (1778-1850) — A675

2000, Aug. 25 Litho. *Perf. 13½*

1338 A675 320p multi 1.60 .80

World Meteorological Organization, 50th Anniv. — A676

2000, Aug. 28

1339 A676 320p multi 1.60 .80

Antarctic Fauna — A677

450p, Sphenis magellanicus, vert. 650p, Megaptera novaeangliae. 940p, Orcinus orca. 2000p, Mirounga leonina, vert.

2000, Sept. 15

1340-1342 A677 Set of 3 25.00 19.00

Souvenir Sheet

1343 A677 2000p multi 25.00 15.00

No. 1343 contains one 36x48mm stamp.

2000 Summer Olympics, Sydney — A678

Sydney Opera House, Olympic flag and: a, 290p, Chilean flag, tennis player, soccer player, sprinter. b, 290p, Australian flag, archer, high jumper, cyclist.

2000, Sept. 20

1344 A678 Pair, #a-b 4.50 2.25

City of Concepcion, 450th Anniv. — A679

Mural by Gregorio De La Fuente: a, Indian holding stick. b, Soldier on white horse. c, Finger pointing upward. d, Seated figure, arms, horse-drawn carriage. e, Horse, statue, train. f, People and rainbow.

2000, Oct. 2

1345 Horiz. strip of 6 10.00 10.00
a.-f. A679 250p Any single 1.50 .75

America Issue, World AIDS Day — A680

Designs: 150p, Heart, clasped hands of adult and child. 220p, Clasped hands.

2000, Oct. 12

1346-1347 A680 Set of 2 3.00 1.50

Penal Reform — A681

Designs: 150p, Flag, court proceedings. 2000p, People, doors of Justice Ministry.

2000, Nov. 16

1348 A681 150p multi .80 .40

Souvenir Sheet

1349 A681 2000p multi 11.50 11.50

Christmas — A682

Designs: a, Star of Bethlehem. b, Santa Claus flying over town. c, Three Magi on camels. d, Star on top of Christmas tree. e, Boy at mailbox. f, Sleeping child. g, Two Magi, cow. h, Baby Jesus, cow. i, Mary, Joseph. j, Girl putting ornaments on tree.

2000, Nov. 20 ***Perf. 13½***

1350 Block of 10 10.00 10.00
a.-j. A682 150p Any single .75 .40

Inscribed "DS/20"

Perf. 13½ on 3 sides

1351 Booklet pane of 10 10.00
a.-j. A682 150p Any single .90 .45
Booklet, #1351 10.00

National Zoo, 75th Anniv. — A683

Various animals and birds, denomination in: a, LL. b, LR. c, UL. d, UR.

2001, Jan. 13 Litho. *Perf. 13½*

1352 A683 160p Block of 4, #a-d 5.50 5.50

San Sebastian Festival, Yumbel — A684

2001, Jan. 18

1353 A684 210p multi 1.50 .75

Father Alberto Hurtado (1901-52) A685

Hurtado and: 160p, Truck. 340p, Children.

2001, Jan. 20

1354-1355 A685 Set of 2 2.50 1.25

Bird Type of 1998

No. 1356, vert.: a, Sephanoides fernandensis. b, Mimus thenca. c, Pteroptochos megapodius. d, Enicognathus leptorhynchus. Size of Nos. 1356a-1356d: 24x29mm.

2001, Jan. 29

1356 A640 160p Block of 4, #a-d 4.50 4.50

Assembly of Governors of Inter-American Development Bank and Investment Corporation — A686

2001, Mar. 16

1357 A686 230p multi 1.10 .55

Souvenir Sheet

Air Force Anniversaries — A687

No. 1358: a, Lockheed C-130 Hercules, map of Antarctica. b, Flugzeugbau Extra-300, acrobatic squadron. c, North American AT-6 Texan. d, Consolidated PBY-5A/OA-10 Catalina, map of Easter Island.

2001, Mar. 29

1358 A687 260p Sheet of 4, #a-d 5.50 5.50

Air Force presence in Antarctica, 50th anniv. (No. 1358a); Halcones acrobatic squadron, 20th anniv. (No. 1358b); Aviation Group No. 1, 75th anniv. (No. 1358c); First flight of Easter Island, 50th anniv. (No. 1358d).

Nationalization of Copper Industry, 30th Anniv. — A688

Design: 2000p, Miner and equipment.

2001, Apr. 26 Litho. *Perf. 13¼*

1359 A688 400p multi 2.25 1.10

Souvenir Sheet

1359A A688 2000p multi 12.50 12.50

Organ Donation — A689

2001, May 3

1360 A689 160p multi 1.10 .45

Easter Island — A690

Designs: No. 1361, Stone carvings, map of island and: a, Compass rose. b, Bird and native. No. 1361C, Artifact and map of island.

2001, June 25

1361 A690 260p Horiz. pair, #a-b 3.25 3.25

Souvenir Sheet

1361C A690 2000p multi 11.50 11.50

Lynchailurus Colocolo — A691

2001

1362 A691 100p multi .60 .30

Endangered species. See Nos. 1394-1395.

Valparaiso Firefighting Corps, 150th Anniv. — A692

Firefighters and: 160p, Manuel Blanco Encalada. 260p, Old pumper, building on fire, modern fire truck. 350p, Flags, building. 490p, Helicopter, rail tank car.
2000p, Helicopter, modern fire truck.

2001, June 28 Litho. *Perf. 13¼*

1363-1366 A692 Set of 4 6.75 3.25

Souvenir Sheet

1367 A692 2000p multi 11.50 11.50

Mushrooms A693

Designs: 300p, Macrolepiota rhacodes. 400p, Laccata ohiensis.

2001, July 25 Litho. *Perf. 13¼*

1368-1369 A693 Set of 2 4.50 2.75

24th Conference of American Armies, Santiago — A694

2001, Aug. 13

1370 A694 350p multi 2.00 .95

Bernardo O'Higgins (1778-1842), Soldier and Statesman — A695

2001, Aug. 17

1371 A695 260p multi 1.50 .70

Chilean Antarctic Research — A696

Designs: 350p, Researcher, Leptonychotes weddellii. 700p, Researchers, Macronectes giganteus. 2000p, Chionis alba.

2001, Aug. 29

1372-1373 A696 Set of 2 5.75 2.75

Souvenir Sheet

1374 A696 2000p multicolored 11.50 11.50

America Issue — UNESCO World Heritage — A697

World Heritage Sites and stamps: 160p, Quinchao Church, #1058. 230p, Tenaun Church, #1057.

2001, Oct. 9 Litho. *Perf. 13¼*

1375-1376 A697 Set of 2 9.00 2.50

Cape Horn A698

2001, Nov. 22

1377 A698 220p multi 1.25 .60

El Indice del Indice, by Roberto Matta (1911-2002) — A699

2001, Nov. 5 Litho. *Perf. 13¼*

1378 A699 300p multi 1.75 .85

Railroads in Chile, 150th Anniv. — A700

No. 1379 (50x29mm): a, Caldera Station, train cars. b, Locomotive and Copiapó Station.
220p, Train on bridge.

2001, Nov. 20

1379 A700 200p Horiz. pair, #a-b 3.00 1.50
1380 A700 220p multi 1.50 .85

Christmas — A701

Designs: a, Heads of three shepherds. b, Shepherd and cow. c, Joseph and Mary. d, Donkey and Magus. e, Cow and two Magi. f, Head of shepherd. g, Two sheep. h, Infant Jesus. i, Shepherd with staff. j, One sheep.

2001, Nov.

1381 A701 160p Block of 10, #a-j 8.00 8.00

Inscribed "DS/20"

1382 A701 160p Block of 10, #a-j 9.00 9.00
k. Booklet pane, #1382 with straight edge at right 10.00 —
Complete booklet, #1382k 10.00

Rotary Intl. Emblem, Map of Chile, Globe, Tropic of Capricorn Monument — A702

2001, Dec. 21
1383 A702 240p multi 1.40 .70

Antofagasta Rotary Club, 75th anniv.

Taxation Department, Cent. — A703

2002, Jan. 14
1384 A703 180p multi .80 .40

Bird Type of 1998

Designs: 10p, Turdus falcklandii. 20p, Sturnella loyca.

2002, Jan. 25
1385 A640 10p multi .55 .25
1386 A640 20p multi .55 .25

City of Valdivia, 450th Anniv. — A704

2002, Feb. 9
1387 A704 260p multi 1.25 .65

Carabinero Force, 75th Anniv. — A705

2002, Apr. 8
1388 A705 250p multi 1.25 .65

Ignacy Domeyko (1802-89), Mineralogist — A706

2002, Apr. 11
1389 A706 290p multi *5.00* .85

See Poland No. 3645.

City of Villarrica, 450th Anniv. — A707

2002, Apr. 26
1390 A707 290p multi 1.50 .75

Town of Calbuco, 400th Anniv. — A708

2002, May 2
1391 A708 230p multi 1.25 .60

Barros Arana Natl. Boarding School — A709

2002, May 20
1392 A709 250p multi 1.25 .65

Abolition of Death Penalty, 1st Anniv. — A710

2002, May 29
1393 A710 240p multi 1.25 .65

Endangered Species Type of 2001

Designs: 10p, Oreailurus jacobita. 20p, Oncifelis geoffrovi.

2002, June 5
1394 A691 10p multi .55 .25
1395 A691 20p multi .55 .25

Easter Island A711

Map of Easter Island and: 250p, Toromiro sophora, moai. 450p, Bird, row of moai statues, native in traditional costume.
2000p, Toromiro sophora and bird.

2002, July 1
1396-1397 A711 Set of 2 3.50 1.75

Souvenir Sheet

1398 A711 2000p multi 10.50 10.50

No. 1398 contains one 47x47mm stamp.

World Heritage Sites — A712

Churches and stamps: 230p, Achao, #1036. 290p, Dalcahue, #1056.

2002, July 27
1399-1400 A712 Set of 2 2.25 1.10

America Issue — Youth, Education, and Literacy — A713

Designs: 230p, Adult students. 450p, Woman reading to child, teacher, boy at computer.

2002, Sept. 9
1401-1402 A713 Set of 2 3.25 1.60

Children's Toys — A714

Designs: 290p, Pinwheel. 380p, Kite, vert.

2002, Sept. 16
1403-1404 A714 Set of 2 3.00 1.50

Observatories — A715

Designs: 450p, Cerro-Tololo. 550p, Paranal. 2000p, Cerro-Tololo, diff.

2002, Sept. 27
1405-1406 A715 Set of 2 4.00 2.00

Souvenir Sheet

1407 A715 2000p multi 8.50 8.50

No. 1407 contains one 47x47mm stamp.

University of Chile Clinical Hospital, 50th Anniv. — A716

2002, Oct. 17
1408 A716 250p multi 1.10 .55

Forestry Education, 50th Anniv. — A717

2002, Oct. 22
1409 A717 250p multi 1.10 .55

12th Convention on International Trade in Endangered Species Conference — A718

Designs: 300p, Phoenicoparrus andinus. 450p, Vicugna vicugna.
2000p, Chinchilla lanigera.

2002, Oct. 29
1410-1411 A718 Set of 2 4.00 2.00

Souvenir Sheet

1412 A718 2000p multi 10.00 10.00

No. 1412 contains one 47x47mm stamp.

Protected Whales — A719

Designs: 250p, Eubalaena australis. 500p, Balaenoptera acutorostrata.
2000p, Physeter macrocephalus.

2002, Nov. 2
1413-1414 A719 Set of 2 3.50 1.50

Souvenir Sheet

1415 A719 2000p multi 10.00 10.00

Violence Against Women Prevention Day — A720

2002, Nov. 22
1416 A720 230p multi 1.00 .50

Town of Puerto Varas, 150th Anniv. A721

2002, Nov. 29
1417 A721 190p multi 1.00 .50

Bird Type of 1998

Designs: 500p, Campephilus magellanicus, vert. 1000p, Falco peregrinus cassini, vert.

2003, Jan. 15 **Litho.** *Perf. 13¼*
1418 A640 500p multi 2.10 .75
1419 A640 1000p multi 4.00 1.75

Puerto Montt, 150th Anniv. A722

2003, Feb. 13
1420 A722 240p multi 1.00 .45

Claudio Arrau (1903-91), Pianist — A723

2003, June 9 **Litho.** ***Perf. 13¼***
1421 A723 200p multi .85 .30

First Chilean Postage Stamps, 150th Anniv. — A724

No. 1422 — Mailbox, building and: a, #1. b, #2.
2000p, Building, #1 and various other stamps.

2003, July 1
1422 A724 300p Horiz. pair, #a-b 2.50 1.25

Souvenir Sheet

1423 A724 2000p multi 8.00 3.00

America Issue — Flora and Fauna — A725

Designs: 240p, Trees, flowers, cactus. 300p, Frog, fox, butterfly, pudu, parrot.

2003, Oct. 12 **Litho.** ***Perf. 13¼***
1424-1425 A725 Set of 2 2.00 1.00

Supreme Court, 180th Anniv. — A726

2003, Nov. 5
1426 A726 200p multi .85 .35

Chilean Red Cross, Cent. A727

2003, Nov. 18
1427 A727 200p black & red .85 .35

Christmas — A728

2003, Nov. 28
1428 A728 190p multi .80 .30

Inscribed "DS-20"

1429 A728 190p multi .80 .30

Powered Flight, Cent. — A729

2003, Dec. 11
1430 A729 200p multi .85 .35

Cristo Redentor Statue, Cent. A730

2004, Apr. 22 **Litho.**
1431 A730 200p multi .85 .30

Seventh World Conference of Grand Masonic Lodges — A731

2004, May 5 ***Perf. 13¼***
1432 A731 190p multi 1.25 .30

Pablo Neruda (1904-73), Poet — A732

2004, June 11
1433 A732 300p multi 1.25 .45

Social Security, 80th Anniv. — A733

2004, Aug. 18
1434 A733 190p multi .80 .30

America Issue — Environmental Protection — A734

Designs: 100p, Burnt forest, logs, field of flowers, puma, flower. 600p, Flower, wildlife, tanker truck, smokestacks.

2004, Sept. 27
1435-1436 A734 Set of 2 2.60 1.50

German Institute, Osorno, 150th Anniv. — A735

2004, Oct. 6
1437 A735 250p multi *18.00 18.00*

Tematica 2004 National Philatelic Exhibition A736

2004, Oct. 19
1438 A736 310p multi 1.40 .55

Naval Telecommunications, Cent. — A737

2004, Nov. 5
1439 A737 400p multi 1.75 .80

Electricity and Fuel Superintendency, Cent. — A738

2004, Dec. 7
1440 A738 240p multi 1.00 .40

Chilean Air Force, 75th Anniv. — A739

2005, Mar. 15 **Litho.** ***Perf. 13¼***
1441 A739 230p multi 1.00 .40

Law No. 20,000 — A740

2005, May 4
1442 A740 220p multi 1.00 .40

Pope John Paul II (1920-2005) — A741

Pope John Paul II and: a, Child, condor, mountain. b, Crucifix, Chilean flag, mountain. c, Church, Chilean flag.

2005, May 13
1443 A741 Horiz. strip of 3 3.25 1.75
a.-c. 230p Any single 1.00 .50

Rotary International, Cent. — A742

2005, June 30 **Litho.** ***Perf. 13¼***
1444 A742 230p multi 1.00 .40

Treasury Building, Bicent. — A743

2005, June 30
1445 A743 230p multi 1.00 .40

Publication of Don Quixote, 400th Anniv. A744

No. 1446: a, Don Quixote on horseback. b, Windmill. c, Windmills. d, Miguel de Cervantes, author.

2005, July 14
1446 Horiz. strip of 4 .50 .50
a.-b. A744 10p Either single .25 .25
c.-d. A744 20p Either single .25 .25

See No. 1462.

El Teniente Copper Mine, Cent. — A745

2005, Aug. 3
1447 A745 390p multi 1.90 .75

Undersecretariat of Aviation, 75th Anniv. — A746

2005, Aug. 19
1448 A746 400p multi 1.75 1.00

Valparaiso Customs House, 150th Anniv. — A747

2005, Sept. 1
1449 A747 390p multi 1.75 .75

Bicentennial Fountain, Santiago — A748

2005, Sept. 5
1450 A748 230p multi 1.00 .45

America Issue — Fight Against Poverty — A749

No. 1451: a, Denomination at right. b, Denomination at left.

2005, Oct. 3 Litho. ***Perf. 13¼***
1451 A749 250p Horiz. pair, #a-b 2.25 .95

Canonization of Father Alberto Hurtado (1901-52) — A750

2005, Oct. 13 Litho. ***Perf. 13¼***
1452 A750 390p multi 1.75 .75

Expo Austral 2005 Philatelic Exhibition, Punta Arenas — A751

2005, Oct. 22
1453 A751 390p multi 1.75 .75

New Civil Matrimony Law — A752

2005, Nov. 18 Litho. ***Perf. 13¼***
1454 A752 260p multi 1.40 .60

German Clinic, Cent. — A753

2005, Nov. 23
1455 A753 230p multi 1.25 .55

Restoration of Central Post Office, Santiago A754

2005, Nov. 30
1456 A754 230p multi 1.25 .55

Political Constitution A755

2005, Dec. 1
1457 A755 230p multi 1.25 .55

Department of Physical Education, Sports and Recreation, Cent. — A756

2006, Mar. 6 Litho. ***Perf. 13¼***
1458 A756 230p multi 1.25 .55

Intl. Women's Day — A757

2006, Mar. 7
1459 A757 390p multi 1.75 .75

Wulff Castle, Cent. — A758

No. 1460 — Castle, arms of Vina del Mar and: a, Birds. b, Windmill.

2006, Mar. 21
1460 Horiz. pair 3.00 1.50
a. A758 230p multi 1.00 .55
b. A758 390p multi 1.75 .85

Tourism — A759

No. 1461: a, Morro de Arica. b, Moais, Easter Island. c, Palafittes, Castro. d, Torres del Paine. e, Penguins, Chilean Antarctic Territory.

2006, May 19
1461 Horiz. strip of 5 6.25 3.00
a.-e. A759 230p Any single 1.10 .55

Don Quixote Type of 2005

No. 1462: a, Building. b, Windmills. c, Windmill, country name at LR. d, Don Quixote and Sancho Panza.

2006, May 31
1462 Horiz. strip of 4 .25 .25
a.-d. A744 10p Any single .25 .25

Catholic University of the North, 50th Anniv. — A760

No. 1463: a, Students using computers, denomination at UR. b, Students, denomination at LL.

2006, June 9
1463 Horiz. pair 2.50 1.25
a.-b. A760 230p Either single 1.10 .55

Citizenship Plaza, Santiago — A761

2006, July 7
1464 A761 390p multi 1.75 .85

World Quality Forum — A762

No. 1465: a, Building. b, Building and flags.

2006, Aug. 29 Litho. ***Perf. 13¼***
1465 A762 230p Horiz. pair, #a-b 2.50 1.25

America Issue, Energy Conservation — A763

No. 1466: a, River and mountains. b, Clouds. c, Oil rigs in water. d, Windmill.

2006, Sept. 29
1466 A763 390p Block of 4, #a-d 7.25 3.50

Adventist University of Chile, Cent. — A764

No. 1467 — University emblem and: a, Building, 1906. b, Family and building, 1922. c, Building, 1960-70. d, Building, 2006.

2006, Oct. 20

1467 Horiz. strip of 4 + central label 4.50 2.25
a.-d. A764 250p Any single 1.10 .55

Antarctic Wildlife — A765

No. 1468 — Chilean and Estonian flags and: a, Balaenoptera acutorostrata. b, Aptenodytes forsteri.

2006, Oct. 25 ***Perf. 13½***

1468 A765 500p Horiz. pair, #a-b 4.50 2.25

See Estonia No. 555.

Anniversaries — A766

No. 1469: a, Colonization of the Straits of Magellan area, 160th anniv. b, Fort Bulnes, 160th anniv.

2006, Dec. 7 ***Perf. 13¼***

1469 A766 250p Horiz. pair, #a-b 2.25 2.10

Gasco, 150th Anniv. — A767

No. 1470: a, San Borja facility. b, Gasco headquarters.

2006, Dec. 14

1470 A767 250p Horiz. pair, #a-b 2.25 1.10

Federico Santa Maria Technical University, 75th Anniv. — A768

2006, Dec. 20

1471 A768 250p multi 1.10 .50

Carabineros, 80th Anniv. — A769

No. 1472: a, Carabineros and mountains. b, Carabineros on horseback.

2007, Apr. 10 **Litho.** ***Perf. 13¼***

1472 A769 250p Pair, #a-b 2.25 1.10

Tourism — A770

No. 1473: a, Valley of the Moon, Antofagasta Region. b, Easter Island, Valparaiso Region. c, Tourism emblem. d, Villarrica-Pucón Volcano, Araucania Region. e, Penguin in Chilean Antarctic.

2007, May 9

1473 Horiz. strip of 5 9.00 4.50
a.-e. A770 390p Any single 1.75 .90

Church Centenaries — A771

No. 1474: a, Parinacota Church. b, San Pedro de Atacama Church.

Litho. With Foil Application

2007, June 29

1474 A771 250p Pair, #a-b 2.25 1.10

Raul Cardinal Silva Henríquez (1907-99) — A772

No. 1475 — Color of portrait and panel: a, Blue violet. b, Red violet. c, Red orange. d, Green.

2007, Aug. 21 **Litho.**

1475 Horiz. strip of 4 + central label 4.50 2.25
a.-d. A772 250p Any single 1.10 .55

A773

A774

A775

Sculptures by Marta Colvin (1907-95) — A776

2007, Aug. 24 ***Perf. 13¼***

1476 Horiz. strip of 4 + central label 4.50 2.25
a. A773 250p multi 1.10 .55
b. A774 250p multi 1.10 .55
c. A775 250p multi 1.10 .55
d. A776 250p multi 1.10 .55

Las Condes, 106th Anniv. — A777

2007, Aug. 28

1477 A777 330p multi 1.50 .75

Museums in Santiago A778

Designs: 10p, Artequin Museum. 20p, National Museum of Fine Arts. 30p, National Museum of Natural History. 50p, Museum of Santiago.

2007, Aug. 31 **Engr.**

1478 A778 10p green .25 .25
1479 A778 20p black .25 .25
1480 A778 30p purple .25 .25
1481 A778 50p red .25 .25
Nos. 1478-1481 (4) 1.00 1.00

Los Rios Region — A779

No. 1482: a, Lake Ranco. b, Huilo Huilo Waterfall. c, Bridge, Valdivia. d, Choshuenco Volcano.

2007, Oct. 2 **Litho.**

1482 Horiz strip of 4 + central label 7.25 3.75
a.-d. A779 390p Any single 1.75 .90

Arica and Parinacota Region — A780

No. 1483: a, Morro de Arica. b, Parinacota Volcano. c, Anzota Caves. d, Vicunas.

2007, Oct. 8

1483 Horiz strip of 4 + central label 4.50 2.25
a.-d. A780 250p Any single 1.10 .55

Chilean Postal Service, 260th Anniv. — A781

No. 1484: a, Half of original General Post Office, Santiago (denomination at UR). b, Half of modern General Post Office, Santiago (denomination at UL). c, Original and modern General Post Offices.

3000p, Statue of postal carrier on bicycle.

Litho. With Foil Application

2007, Oct. 9

1484 A781 390p Horiz. strip of 3, #a-c 5.50 2.75

Souvenir Sheet

1485 A781 3000p multi 13.50 6.75

Comptroller of the Navy, 80th Anniv. — A782

Arms of Chilean Navy and: a, Chilean Navy Building, denomination at UL. b, Naval and Maritime Museum, denomination at UR.

2007, Oct. 11 **Litho.** ***Perf. 13¼***

1486 A782 390p Horiz. pair, #a-b 3.50 1.75

America Issue, Education For All — A783

No. 1487: a, Children at computer. b, Boy watching chemistry experiment. c, Children running. d, Children playing musical instruments. e, Boy pointing to globe.

2007, Nov. 5

1487 Horiz. strip of 5 5.75 2.75
a.-e. A783 250p Any single 1.10 .55

Christmas — A784

No. 1488 — Santa Claus: a, In chimney. b, In automobile. c, Near sleigh. d, In front of fan.

Litho. With Foil Application

2007, Nov. 16

1488 A784 250p Block of 4, #a-d 4.50 2.25

Malleco National Reserve, Cent. — A785

No. 1489: a, Tree, flower. b, Tree, puma. c, Waterfall, flowers. d, Forest, fox.

2007, Nov. 20 **Litho.**

1489 Horiz. strip of 4 + central label 4.50 2.25
a.-d. A785 250p Any single 1.00 .50

La Nación Newspaper, 90th Anniv. — A786

No. 1490 — Newspaper's office building, Chilean flag and: a, Newspapers at end of production line. b, Newspaper pages.

2007, Dec. 7

1490 A786 250p Horiz. pair, #a-b 2.25 1.10

Santa María de Iquique Massacre, Cent. — A787

No. 1491: a, People, ships. b, Man raising shovel. c, School, dead on ground. d, Wagon, people weeping. e, People hugging, woman weeping.

3000p, Family, vert.

2007, Dec. 19

1491 Horiz. strip of 5 5.75 2.75
a.-e. A787 250p Any single 1.10 .55

Souvenir Sheet

1492 A787 3000p multi 15.00 7.00

Miniature Sheet

Easter Island — A788

No. 1493 — Natives in traditional garb and: a, Ahu Koteriku moais overlooking water. b, Motu Nui, Motu Iti and Motu Kaokao Islets. c, Rock painting. d, Petroglyphs. e, Orongo stone houses. f, Ahu Tahai moai. g, Anakena Beach. h, Rano Kau Volcanic Lake.

No. 1494, vert.: a, Native male. b, Native female.

2008, Jan. 18

1493 A788 390p Sheet of 8, #a-h 15.00 7.50

Souvenir Sheet

1494 A788 1500p Sheet of 2, #a-b 15.00 7.50

Miniature Sheet

Intl. Polar Year — A789

No. 1495: a, Antarctic base, penguins. b, Ship and icebergs. c, Helicopter and direction signs. d, Cargo airplane and snow vehicle. e, Man directing small airplane. f, People on snowmobiles.

2008, Jan. 29 *Perf. 13¼*

1495 A789 250p Sheet of 6, #a-f 7.50 3.75

Occupations — A790

No. 1496, 20p: a, Knife grinder. b, Street sweeper.

No. 1497, 30p: a, Photographer. b, Peanut vendor.

No. 1498, 50p: a, Ice cream vendor. b, Shoeshine man.

No. 1499, 100p: a, Laundry worker. b, Organ grinder.

No. 1500, 500p: a, Street musician. b, Newspaper vendor.

2008, Feb. 25 **Pairs, #a-b** **Litho.**

1496-1500 A790 Set of 5 7.50 3.75

Visit to Chile of Italian Pres. Giorgio Napolitano — A791

No. 1501 — Chilean poet Pablo Neruda and: a, His house on Isla Negra, Chile, Chilean flag. b, His house on Isle of Capri, Italy, Italian flag. c, His house on Isla Negra, flags of Chile and Italy. d, Rocks off Capri, flags of Chile and Italy.

2008, Mar. 17

1501 A791 280p Block of 4, #a-d 5.25 2.10

Miniature Sheets

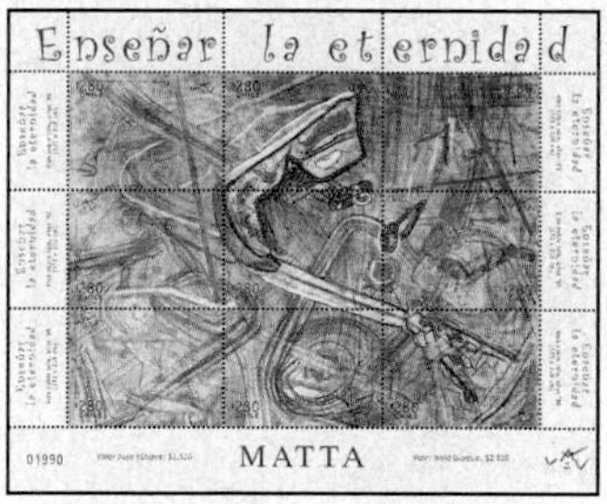

Ensenar la Eternidad, by Roberto Matta — A792

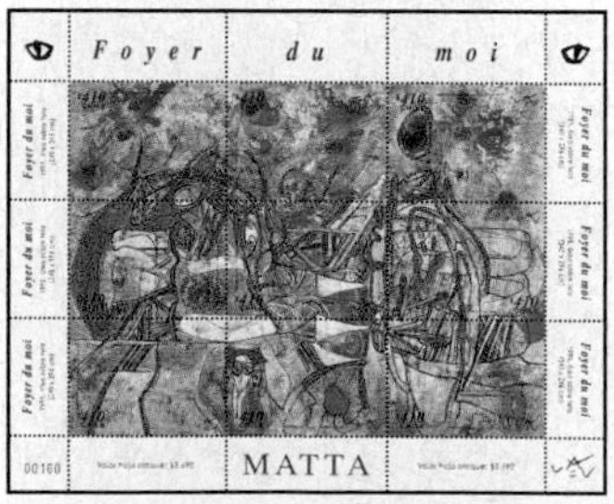

Foyer du Moi, by Matta — A793

Espejo de Cronos, by Matta — A794

Nos. 1502-1504 — Portion of painting: a, Upper left. b, Top center. c, Upper right. d, Left center. e, Center. f, Right center. g, Lower left. h, Bottom center. i, Lower right.

2008, Mar. 25 *Perf. 13¼*

1502 A792 280p Sheet of 9, #a-i 12.00 6.00
1503 A793 410p Sheet of 9, #a-i 17.00 8.50
1504 A794 410p Sheet of 9, #a-i 17.00 8.50
Nos. 1502-1504 (3) 46.00 23.00

Pres. Salvador Allende (1908-73) — A795

2008, June 26 **Litho.** *Perf. 13¼*

1505 A795 410p multi 2.00 1.00

Taltal, 150th Anniv. A796

2008, July 18

1506 A796 280p multi 1.40 .70

Women's Under-20 Soccer World Championships, Chillán — A797

No. 1507 — Quarter of soccer ball and stadium and: a, Cross. b, Group of people. c, Fruits and vegetables. d, Pottery.

2008, July 31

1507 A797 280p Block of 4, #a-d 5.50 2.75

Chilean Accountancy Association, 50th Anniv. — A798

No. 1508 — Emblem and: a, Accountants, building. b, Map of Western hemisphere.

2008, Aug. 14

1508 A798 280p Horiz. pair, #a-b 2.75 1.25

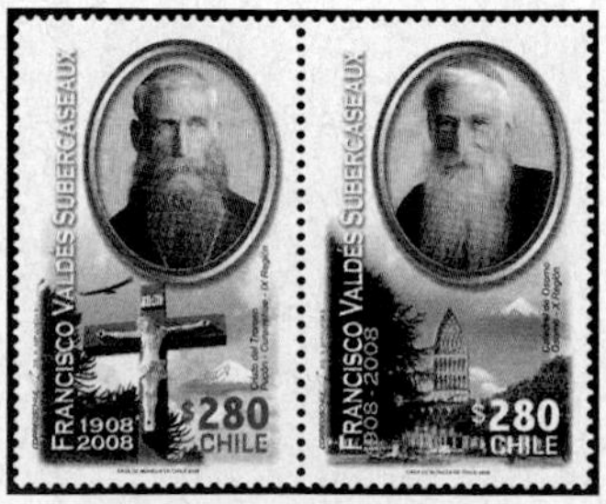

Bishop Francisco Valdés Subercaseaux (1908-82) — A799

No. 1509 — Bishop Valdés Subercaseaux and: a, Christ of Tromen. b, Osorno Cathedral.

2008, Sept. 5 **Litho.** *Perf. 13¼*

1509 A799 280p Horiz. pair, #a-b 2.25 1.10

Miniature Sheet

La Vida Allende la Muerte, by Roberto Matta — A800

No. 1510 — Section of painting: a, Upper left. b, Top center. c, Upper right. d, Left center. e, Center. f, Right center. g, Lower left. h, Bottom center. i, Lower right.

2008, Sept. 15

1510 A800 410p Sheet of 9, #a-i 13.00 6.50

America Issue, National Festivals — A801

Designs; 10p, Cuasimodo. 200p, La Vendimia. 1000p, La Tirana. 2000p, Fiestas Patrias. 5000p, El Rodeo.

2008, Oct. 30

1511	A801	10p multi	.25	.25
1512	A801	200p multi	1.90	.90
1513	A801	1000p multi	4.50	4.50
1514	A801	2000p multi	9.00	9.00
1515	A801	5000p multi	22.50	22.50
		Nos. 1511-1515 (5)	38.15	37.15

Miniature Sheet

Torres del Paine National Park, 50th Anniv. — A802

No. 1516: a, Fox, Torres del Paine. b, Puma, Grey Glacier. c, Condor (at right), Paine Grande. d, Condor (at left), Cuernos del Paine. e, Guanaco, Cuernos del Paine. f, Guemal, Macizo Paine and Cordillera Paine.

2008, Nov. 21

1516 A802 500p Sheet of 6, #a-f 9.00 4.50

Telethon, 30th Anniv. — A803

2008, Nov. 25

1517 A803 280p multi 1.00 .40

Christmas — A804

No. 1518 — Children's art: a, Drawing by Antonia Retamal Figueroa. b, Drawing by Lucas Bastidas Escobar. c, Drawing by Oscar Maya Lazo. d, Drawing of girl, Christmas tree, mountains, Santa Claus. e, Drawing of Christmas tree, cross and handprints.

2008, Nov. 26

1518	Horiz. strip of 5	5.00	2.10
a.-e.	A804 280p Any single	.85	.40

Osorno, 450th Anniv. — A805

2008, Nov. 28

1519	A805 280p multi	1.25	.40

General Carlos Ibáñez del Campo Carabineros School, Cent. — A806

No. 1520: a, Carabineros, old school building (sepia photograph). b, Carabineros, new school building (color photograph).

2008, Dec. 10

1520	A806 310p Horiz. pair, #a-b	2.90	2.00

Expo Antarctica Chile 2009 Philatelic Exhibition, Pres. Eduardo Frei Montalva Antarctic Base — A807

Designs: 470p, Map of Antarctica, Pres. Eduardo Frei Montalva Antarctic Base. 3000p, Villa Las Estrellas, horiz.

2009, Mar. 12

1521	A807 470p multi	2.00	.85

Souvenir Sheet

1522	A807 3000p multi	19.00	19.00

Antarctic Treaty, 50th anniv. No. 1522 contains one 48x30mm stamp.

Preservation of Polar Regions and Glaciers — A808

Nos. 1523, 1524 — Emblem and map of: a, Arctic area. b, Antarctic area. No. 1524 has vert. stamps.

Litho. with Foil Application

2009, Mar. 18 *Perf. 13¼*

1523	A808 470p Vert. pair, #a-b	4.00	2.00

Souvenir Sheet

1524	A808 1500p Sheet of 2, #a-b	19.00	19.00

Miniature Sheets

Independence, Bicent. — A809

No. 1525: a, Chile #92. b, Chile #93. c, Chile #94. d, Chile #95. e, Chile #96. f, Chile #97.

No. 1526, horiz.: a, Chile #83. b, Chile #84. c, Chile #85. d, Chile #86. e, Chile #87. f, Chile #88. g, Chile #89. h, Chile #90. i, Chile #91. j, Bicentennial emblem.

2009, Apr. 20 **Litho.**

1525	A809 310p Sheet of 6, #a-f	6.50	3.25
1526	A809 310p Sheet of 10, #a-j	10.50	5.25

University of Concepción, 90th Anniv. — A810

No. 1527: a, Homage to the Founders, sculpture by Samuel Román. b, Campanile.

2009, May 14

1527	A810 310p Horiz. pair, #a-b	2.25	1.10

Santa María de Los Angeles Diocese, 50th Anniv. — A811

No. 1528: a, Virgin Mary, Jesus and angels. b, Los Angeles Cathedral.

2009, June 10

1528	A811 470p Horiz. pair, #a-b	3.50	1.75

Protected Birds — A812

Designs: 10p, Condor. 20p Tricahue parrot. 50p, Chilean flamingo. 100p, Humboldt penguin. 500p, Black-necked swan.

2009, July 15 **Litho.** *Perf. 13¼*

1529	A812 10p black	.25	.25
1530	A812 20p black	.25	.25
1531	A812 50p black	.25	.25
1532	A812 100p black	.55	.25
1533	A812 500p black	2.25	.95
	Nos. 1529-1533 (5)	3.55	1.95

21st UPAEP Congress, Santiago — A813

2009, Aug. 17 **Litho.** *Perf. 13¼*

1534	A813 500p multi	2.60	.95

Mutual de Seguros Insurance Company, 90th Anniv. — A814

No. 1535: a, Old building, emblem with black gear. b, Modern building, emblem with blue gray gear.

Litho. With Foil Application

2009, Oct. 14 *Perf. 13¼*

1535	A814 310p Horiz. pair, #a-b	2.75	1.40

A815

Winning Art in Bicentennial Stamp Design Contest — A816

No. 1536: a, Flag with mountains and city, by Andrea Barreda, elementary school competition. b, City, by Javiera Monreal Arcil, middle school competition.

No. 1537: a, People in various costumes, by Patricio Díaz Donay, visual arts competition. b, Pepper, by Joshua Arévalo Carreño, university and technical school competition.

2009, Oct. 15 **Litho.** *Perf. 13¼*

1536	A815 310p Pair, #a-b	2.40	1.25
1537	A816 310p Horiz. pair, #a-b	2.40	1.25

America Issue, Traditional Games — A817

Designs: 310p, Spinning top. 470p, Girl flying kite.

2009, Oct. 30

1538-1539	A817 Set of 2	3.50	1.75

Christmas — A818

No. 1540 — Children: a, Painting nativity scene. b, Drawing pictures of Santa Claus. c, Opening presents under Christmas tree. d, Looking out of window.

2009, Nov. 26

1540	A818 310p Block of 4, #a-d	5.00	2.50

Gabriela Mistral (1889-1957), 1945 Nobel Laureate in Literature — A819

No. 1451: a, Mistral at left, mountain at right. b, Church at left, Mistral at right. c, Mistral at left, church at right. d, Mountain at left, Mistral at right.

2009, Dec. 18

1541 A819 500p Block of 4, #a-d 8.00 4.00

Chile Philatelic Society, 120th Anniv. — A820

2009, Dec. 30

1542 A820 500p multi 2.00 1.00

Bicentennial Art by National Art Prize Winners — A821

No. 1543 — Works of art by: a, José Balmes. b, Eugenio Dittborn. c, Guillermo Núñez.

2010, Mar. 3

1543 Horiz. strip of 3 6.75 3.50
a.-c. A821 290p Any single 2.25 1.10

Bicentenary Regatta — A822

No. 1544 — Flags and: a, Ships. b, Map of South America, ship.

2010, Apr. 15 Litho. *Perf. 13¼*

1544 A822 430p Horiz. pair, #a-b 3.75 1.75

Miniature Sheet

Pres. Eduardo Frei Montalva Antarctic Air Base, 40th Anniv. — A823

No. 1545: a, People near cargo airplane. b, Hangar. c, Airplane over base. d, Helicopter. e, Small airplane. f, Penguin, people, base.

2010, May 4

1545 A823 500p Sheet of 6, #a-f 11.50 5.75

Bauer Tower, Vicuña, 105th Anniv. — A824

Designs: 500p, Tower. 3000p, Tower, diff.

2010, May 7

1546 A824 500p multi 1.90 .95

Souvenir Sheet

1547 A824 3000p multi 11.50 5.75

2010 World Cup Soccer Championships, South Africa — A825

No. 1548 — Flags of Chile and South Africa, emblem of Chile Soccer Federation and: a, Soccer ball and players. b, Map of Africa, leopard skin.

2010, June 25

1548 A825 500p Vert. pair, #a-b 5.00 2.00

Inauguration of Mini University of Tokyo Atacama Observatory Telescope, Mt. Chajnantor — A826

2010, July 7 Litho. *Perf. 13¼*

1549 A826 430p multi 1.60 .80

Souvenir Sheet

1550 A826 3000p multi 11.00 5.50

Valparaiso, UNESCO World Heritage Site — A827

No. 1551: a, British Arch. b, Heroes of Iquique Monument.

No. 1552, horiz.: a, Palacio Polanco. b, Palacio Lyon.

No. 1553: a, Polanco Funicular. b, Artillería Funicular.

No. 1554, horiz.: a, Trolley bus with doors closed. b, Trolley bus with front doors open.

2010, July 12 Litho. *Perf. 13¼*

1551 A827 10p Horiz. pair, #a-b .25 .25
1552 A827 20p Horiz. pair, #a-b .25 .25
1553 A827 50p Horiz. pair, #a-b .40 .25
1554 A827 100p Horiz. pair, #a-b .75 .40
Nos. 1551-1554 (4) 1.65 1.15

Independence of Latin America, Bicent. — A828

2010, Sept. 10

1555 A828 430p multi 1.75 .85

La Serena — A829

No. 1556: a, Monumental Lighthouse. b, Plaza de Armas Fountain.

2010, Sept. 15

1556 A829 420p Pair, #a-b 3.50 1.75

Bicentennial Naval Review — A830

No. 1557: a, Steamship from 1910 naval review. b, Ships and sailing vessel with flags hoisted from 1910 naval review. c, Ships from 2010, denomination at UR. d, Ships from 2010, denomination at UL.

2010, Sept. 20

1557 A830 430p Block of 4, #a-d 7.75 4.00

Miniature Sheet

Antofagasta — A831

No. 1558: a, La Portada. b, Fishing terminal. c, Costanera Avenue. d, Historic District. e, Huanchaca Ruins. f, Antofagasta at night.

2010, Sept. 24

1558 A831 500p Sheet of 6, #a-f 12.50 6.25

Arica — A832

No. 1559: a, Fountain, Morro de Arica. b, Fuerza del Sol Carnival.

2010, Sept. 30 Litho. *Perf. 13¼*

1559 A832 420p Horiz. pair, #a-b 3.50 1.75

America Issue, National Symbols — A833

2010, Oct. 12 Litho. *Perf. 13¼*

1560 A833 290p multi 2.60 .60

Third International Culture Forum, Valparaíso A834

2010, Oct. 19

1561 A834 500p multi 2.10 1.10

Irishmen Involved With Chilean Independence — A835

No. 1562: a, Commander General John Mackenna (1771-1814). b, Supreme Director Bernardo O'Higgins (1778-1842).

2010, Oct. 28
1562 A835 500p Horiz. pair, #a-b 4.25 2.10

See Ireland Nos. 1902-1903.

Bicentennial Clock, La Serena University — A836

2010, Oct. 29 **Litho.** ***Perf. 13¼***
1563 A836 420p multi 1.75 .90

Souvenir Sheet

1564 A836 3000p Clock, vert. 12.50 6.25

Chile 2010 Bicentennial Philatelic Exhibition — A837

2010, Nov. 12 **Litho.** ***Perf. 13¼***
1565 A837 290p multi 1.25 .60

Christmas A838

2010, Nov. 26
1566 A838 290p multi 1.25 .60

Miniature Sheet

Chilean Army, Bicent. — A839

No. 1567: a, Cavalry, back of army vehicle. b, Army vehicle, helicopter, tank, rocket launcher. c, Soldiers, flag, truck. d, Soldiers, people awaiting humanitarian aid. e, Soldiers at fort. f, Bulldozer and road grader. g, Soldiers working on railroad track and building. h, Soldiers on pontoon bridge beside damaged bridge.

2010, Dec. 2
1567 A839 500p Sheet of 8, #a-h 21.00 21.00

Purranque, Cent. — A840

2011, Apr. 8
1568 A840 290p multi 1.25 .60

Pres. Eduardo Frei Montalva (1911-82) A841

2011, May 6
1569 A841 290p multi 1.25 .60

Postal Union of the Americas, Spain and Portugal (UPAEP), Cent. — A842

2011, May 20
1570 A842 290p multi 1.25 .60

National Congress, Bicent. — A843

2011, July 3
1571 A843 290p multi 1.25 .60

First Competition of Urban Intervention Ideas — A844

2011, July 29 **Litho.** ***Perf. 13¼***
1572 A844 500p multi 2.25 1.10

Rapa Nui Face Decorations — A845

Various face decorations.

2011, Aug. 5

1573	A845	10p brown		.25	.25
1574	A845	20p lt brown		.25	.25
1575	A845	50p lt brown		.25	.25
1576	A845	100p brown		.45	.25
		Nos. 1573-1576 (4)		1.20	1.00

FAMAE (Weapons Manufacturer for Chilean Armed Forces), Bicent. — A846

2011, Sept. 30
1577 A846 290p multi 1.25 .60

El Tabo, Cent. — A847

No. 1578 — Arms of El Tabo and: a, Nuestra Senora del Rosario Church, El Tabo. b, La Asuncion Church, Las Cruces.

2011, Oct. 7
1578 A847 290p Horiz. pair, #a-b 4.25 2.25

Talca University, 30th Anniv. — A848

No. 1579 — Sculpture and: a, Legal and Social Sciences Building. b, Kinetic Frieze, by Matilde Perez. c, Botanical Garden. d, Curicó Campus Engineering Building.

2011, Oct. 12
1579 A848 290p Block of 4, #a-d 4.75 2.40

Mailbox A849

2011, Oct. 21
1580 A849 290p multi 1.60 .60

America issue.

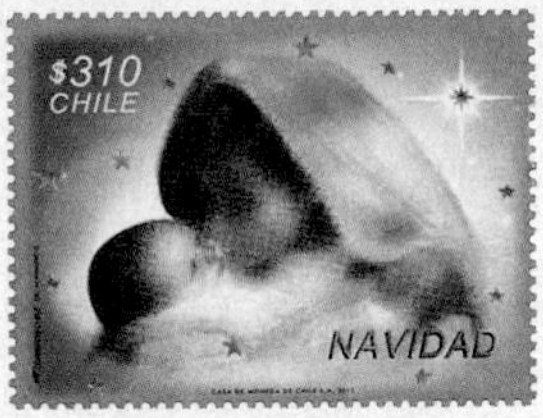

Christmas — A850

2011, Nov. 28
1581 A850 310p multi 1.50 .60

Carabineros, 85th Anniv. — A851

No. 1582 — Anniversary emblem and: a, Male and female carabineros. b, Flag and silhouettes of carabineros.

2012, Apr. 24
1582 A851 310p Horiz. pair, #a-b 2.60 1.40

Diplomatic Relations Between Chile and South Korea, 50th Anniv. — A852

2012, July 23 ***Perf. 13¼***
1583 A852 310p multi 1.40 .70

University of Chile, 170th Anniv. — A853

No. 1584: a, University building. b, Statue of first University rector, Andrés Bello López (1781-1865). c, Valentín Letelier, (1852-1919) rector. d, Amanda Labarca (1886-1975), educator.

2012, Sept. 7
1584 A853 500p Block of 4, #a-d 8.50 4.25

Trauco (Mythological Forest Dweller) A854

2012, Oct. 22
1585 A854 310p multi 1.40 .70

America issue.

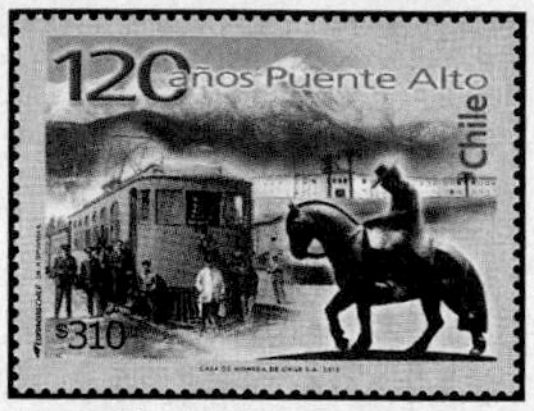

Puente Alto, 120th Anniv. — A855

2012, Nov. 12
1586 A855 310p multi 1.40 .70

Christmas — A856

No. 1587: a, Boy and open mail box. b, Children opening Christmas gifts.

2012, Nov. 30
1587 A856 310p Horiz. pair, #a-b 2.75 1.40

Diplomatic Relations Between Thailand and Chile, 50th Anniv. — A857

2012, Dec. 5
1588 A857 500p multi 2.25 1.10

Pontifical Catholic University of Chile, 125th Anniv. — A858

2013, May 15
1589 A858 500p multi 2.10 1.00

Arica-La Paz Railway, Cent. — A859

No. 1590: a, Steam locomotive. b, Diesel locomotive.

2013, May 29
1590 A859 310p Horiz. pair, #a-b 2.50 1.25

Salvador Allende School of Public Health at University of Chile, 70th Anniv. — A860

No. 1591: a, Dr. Benjamin Viel (1913-98), Dr. Abraham Horwitz (1910-2000), Dr. Hugo Behm (1913-2011). b, Building.

2013, June 7
1591 A860 500p Pair, #a-b 4.60 2.00

Historic Aricraft — A861

No. 1592: a, Voisin biplane, 1910 (airplane used in first flight in Chile). b, Batuco biplane, 1913 (first airplane made in Chile).

No. 1593: a, De Havilland DH-60G "Gipsy Moth," 1929 (airplane used on first airmail route in Chile). b, Junkers R42, 1930 (seaplane flown from Puerto Montt to Straits of Magellan).

No. 1594: a, Blériot XI, 1916 (airplane used in first military flight and first airmail flight in Chile). b, Bristol M1C, 1918 (first airplane to cross the Andes at highest point).

No. 1595: a, Let L-13 "Blanik," 1964 (first glider to cross Andes). b, Bell 47 D-1 "Sioux" helicopter, 1960 (helicopter used in airlift after Valdivia earthquake).

No. 1596: a, PBY-5A Catalina, 1951 (seaplane used in first flight to Easter Island). b, Vought Sikorsky OS2U-3 "Kingfisher," 1947 (seaplane used in first flight from Chile to Antarctica).

2013, Aug. 9 Litho. *Perf. 13¼*

1592	Horiz. pair	.25	.25
a.-b.	A861 10p Either single	.25	.25
1593	Horiz. pair	.25	.25
a.-b.	A861 20p Either single	.25	.25
1594	Horiz. pair	.40	.25
a.-b.	A861 50p Either single	.25	.25
1595	Horiz. pair	.60	.30
a.-b.	A861 70p Either single	.30	.25
1596	Horiz. pair	.80	.40
a.-b.	A861 100p Either single	.40	.25
	Nos. 1592-1596 (5)	2.30	1.45

Annexation of Easter Island, 125th Anniv. — A862

2013, Sept. 27 Litho. *Perf. 13¼*
1597 A862 500p multi 2.00 1.00

National Library, 200th Anniv. — A863

2013, Sept. 30 Litho. *Perf. 13¼*
1598 A863 310p multi 1.25 .60

General José Miguel Carrera National Institute (School for Boys), 200th Anniv. — A864

2013, Sept. 30 Litho. *Perf. 13¼*
1599 A864 430p multi 1.75 .85

Federation of Catholic University Students, 75th Anniv. — A865

2013, Oct. 8 Litho. *Perf. 13¼*
1600 A865 310p multi 1.25 .60

Campaign Against Discrimination A866

2013, Oct. 25 Litho. *Perf. 13¼*
1601 A866 310p multi 1.25 .60

America Issue.

Miniature Sheet

San José Mine Rescue, 3rd Anniv. — A867

No. 1602: a, Fénix 2 rescue capsule. b, Names of 33 rescued miners. c, Note indicating condition and number of miners sent to surface on probe. d, Monument to the rescue of the miners. e, Drilling equipment at surface. f. 33 Chilean flags.

2013, Oct. 30 Litho. *Perf. 13¼*
1602 A867 500p Sheet of 6, #a-f 11.50 5.75

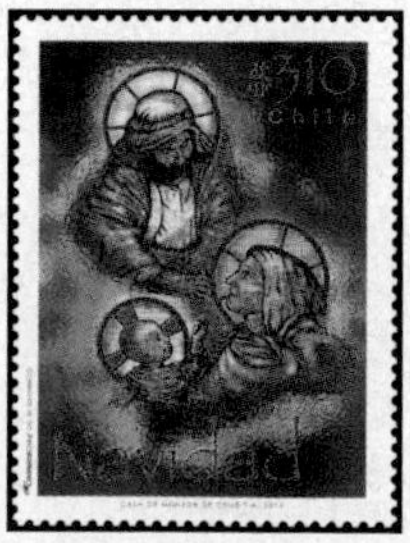

Christmas A868

2013, Nov. 27 Litho. *Perf. 13¼*
1603 A868 310p multi 1.25 .60

Public Education in Chile, Cent. — A869

2013, Dec. 30 Litho. *Perf. 13¼*
1604 A869 310p multi 1.25 .60

Philatelic Society of Chile, 125th Anniv. — A870

2014, Mar. 18 Litho. *Perf. 13¼*
1605 A870 310p multi 5.25 2.50

Los Angeles, 275th Anniv. — A871

No. 1606: a, Statue of Bernardo O'Higgins. b, Liceo de Hombres. c, Laguna Esmeralda. d, Laja Waterfalls.

2014, May 26 Litho. *Perf. 13¼*
1606 A871 310p Block of 4, #a-d 5.50 3.00

Printed in sheets containing four blocks of 4 + 4 labels.

2014 World Cup Soccer Championships, Brazil — A872

2014, June 16 Litho. *Perf. 13¼*
1607 A872 500p multi 1.90 .95

Battle of Rancagua, 200th Anniv. — A873

No. 1608 — Soldiers and: a, Angel holding shield. b, Swordsmen on horseback.

2014, Sept. 30 Litho. *Perf. 13¼*

1608	A873 Horiz pair	2.50	1.25
a.-b.	310p Either single	1.10	.55

Printed in sheets containing 12 pairs and 6 labels.

Exfina 2014 Philatelic Exhibition, Santiago — A874

Designs: 470p, Chile #1. 500p, Chile #2. 1500p, Emblem of Philatelic Society of Chile.

2014, Oct. 14 Litho. *Perf. 13¼*
1609-1610 A874 Set of 2 3.50 1.75

Souvenir Sheet
1611 A874 1500p multi 5.75 4.50

Philatelic Society of Chile, 125th anniv.

America Issue — A875

No. 1612: a, Lautaro (c. 1534-1557), Mapuche leader of resistance to Spanish rule. b. Caupolicán (d. 1558), Mapuche military leader.

2014, Oct. 30 Litho. *Perf. 13¼*
1612 A875 310p Vert. pair, #a-b 2.10 1.10

Christmas A876

2014, Nov. 10 Litho. *Perf. 13¼*
1613 A876 310p multi 1.00 .50

Chinchorro Mummies — A877

No. 1614: a, Mummy of a child with stake point at top of head. b, Mummy with outer coating missing under eye.

2014, Nov. 28 Litho. *Perf. 13¼*
1614 A877 500p Horiz. pair, #a-b 3.25 1.60

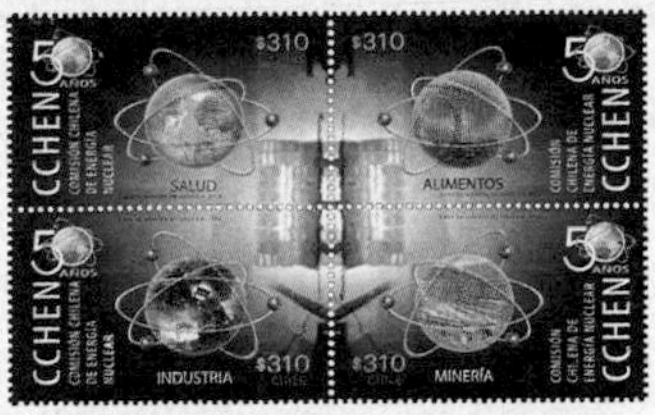

Chilean Nuclear Energy Commission, 50th Anniv. — A878

No. 1615 — Stylized atom with inscription: a, Salud (health). b, Alimentos (food). c, Industria (industry). d, Minería (mining).

2014, Dec. 10 Litho. *Perf. 13¼*
1615 A878 310p Block of 4, #a-d 4.25 2.10

Miniature Sheet

Talcahuano, 250th Anniv. — A879

No. 1616: a, Cacique Talcahueñu, painting by Héctor Robles Acuña. b, R.H. Huáscar. c, David Fuentes Sosa and his Blériot airplane "Talcahuano." d, Alcalde Luis Macera Dellarossa Coliseum. e, Boats in water near Caleta Tumbes. f, Sailboats off Talcahuano.

2014, Dec. 12 Litho. *Perf. 13¼*
1616 A879 500p Sheet of 6, #a-f 10.00 5.00

Hippocamelus Bisulcus — A880

No. 1617 — Huemul: a, Head, with foliage in background. b, Entire animal on hill, head at right. c, Entire animal with head at left. d, Head, Moon in clouds.

2015, Apr. 7 Litho. *Perf. 13¼*
1617 A880 600p Block of 4, #a-d 8.00 4.00

Protection of the huemul.

Miniature Sheet

Chuquicamata, Cent. — A881

No. 1618: a, Pres. Ramón Barros Luco. b, Steam shovel. c, Chuquicamata Mine. d, Chuquicamata Arch. e, Chile Theater. f, El Salvador Church.

2015, June 3 Litho. *Perf. 13¼*
1618 A881 500p Sheet of 6, #a-f 9.50 4.75

2015 Copa América Soccer Championships, Chile — A882

No. 1619 — Map of chile and; a, Soccer ball. b, Mascot and soccer ball.

2015, June 8 Litho. *Perf. 13¼*
1619 A882 500p Horiz. pair, #a-b 3.25 1.60

Josefina Martínez Children's Hospital, 75th Anniv. — A883

2015, July 28 Litho. *Perf. 13¼*
1620 A883 310p multi .95 .45

POSTAL FISCAL STAMPS

Revenue stamps and telegraph stamp authorized for postal use until the end of 1914.

Arms — PF1

1880-91 Engr. Unwmk. *Perf. 12*
AR1 PF1 1c red 1.75 1.50
Revenue cancel .25
AR2 PF1 2c brown 3.50 2.75
Revenue cancel .25
AR3 PF1 5c blue 3.50 1.50
Revenue cancel .25
AR4 PF1 10c green ('91) 5.25 3.50
Revenue cancel .25
AR5 PF1 20c orange ('91) 7.50 6.25
Revenue cancel .25

Printed by the American Banknote Co. Issued: 1c, 2c, 11/27/80; 5c, 7/3/80; 10c, 20c, 4/1/91.

Arms — PF2

1891, Apr. 21
AR6 PF2 2c yellow brown 3.25 2.00
Telegraph cancel .35
AR7 PF2 10c olive green 1.00 2.50
Telegraph cancel .35
AR8 PF2 20c blue 8.50 3.25
Telegraph cancel .35
AR9 PF2 1p brown 1.50 —
Revenue cancel 1.00

Printed by Bradbury, Wilkinson & Co. Nos. AR6-AR9 are telegraph stamps, authorized for postal use.

PF3

1900-13 *Perf. 14*
AR10 PF3 1c vermilion 1.00 .25
Revenue cancel .25
AR11 PF3 2c brown ('13) 1.00 .35
Revenue cancel .25
AR12 PF3 5c blue 2.00 .35
Revenue cancel .25

Printed by Waterlow & Sons, London. Issued: 1c, 10/25/00; 2c, 1/21/13; 5c, 12/6/00.

SEMI-POSTAL STAMPS

S. S. Abtao and Captain Policarpo Toro SP1

S. S. Abtao and Brother Eugenio Eyraud SP2

Perf. 14½x15
1940, Mar. 1 Engr. Unwmk.
B1 SP1 80c + 2.20p dk grn & lake 2.50 2.00
B2 SP2 3.60p + 6.40p lake & dk grn 2.50 2.00
a. Pair, #B1-B2 10.00 8.00
Set, never hinged 8.00

50th anniv. of Chilean ownership of Easter Is. Surtax used for charitable institutions.

Sheets containing 15 of each value, with 9 se-tenant pairs.

Catalogue values for unused stamps in this section, from this point to the end of the section, are for Never Hinged items.

Pedro de Valdivia — SP3

Portraits: 10c+10c, Jose Toribio Medina.

1961, Apr. 29 Photo. *Perf. 13x12½*
B3 SP3 5c + 5c pale brn & sl grn 1.40 .45
B4 SP3 10c + 10c buff & vio blk 1.00 .35

Printed without charge by the Spanish Mint as a gift to Chile. The surtax was to aid the 1960 earthquake victims and to increase teachers' salaries. See Nos. CB1-CB2.

No. 402 Surcharged in Dark Green

1974, Mar. 25 Litho. *Perf. 14½*

B5 A213 27e + 3e on 40c dl grn .50 .25

Cent. of intl. meteorological cooperation.

The 3e surtax of Nos. B5-B10 was for modernization of the postal system.

No. 412 Surcharged in Dark Blue

1974, Apr. 25 Litho. *Perf. 14½*

B6 A219 27e + 3e on 1.95e 1.00 .30

500th anniversary of the birth of Nicolaus Copernicus (1473-1534), Polish astronomer.

No. 329A Surcharged

1974, May 2 Litho. *Perf. 14*

B7 A159 27e + 3e on 1e bluish grn .40 .30

Centenary of the city of Vina del Mar.

No. 377 Surcharged in Blk, Nos. 395, 380 in Red

1974 Litho. *Perf. 14½*

B8 A193 47e + 3e on 40c grn .40 .30
B9 A207 67e + 3e on 40c multi .60 .40
B10 A196 97e + 3e on 40c red brn .40 .30
Nos. B8-B10 (3) 1.40 1.00

Issued: No. B8, 6/7; No. B9, 7/9; No. B10, 6/20.

AIR POST STAMPS

Surcharged in Black

Lithographed; Center Engraved

1927 Unwmk. *Perf. 13½x14*

Black Brown & Blue

C1 40c on 10c 400.00 50.00
C2 80c on 10c 400.00 65.00
C3 1.20p on 10c 400.00 75.00
C4 1.60p on 10c 400.00 75.00
C5 2p on 10c 400.00 75.00
Nos. C1-C5 (5) 2,000. 340.00

Issued for air post service between Santiago and Valparaiso. The stamps picture Bernardo O'Higgins and are not known without surcharge.

Regular Issues of 1915-28 Overprinted or Surcharged in Black, Red or Blue

Inscribed: "Chile Correos"

1928-29 *Perf. 13½x14, 14*

C6 A39 20c brn org & blk (Bk) .50 .30
C6A A55 40c dk vio & blk (R) .50 .30
C6B A43 1p grn & blk (Bl) 1.60 .70
C6C A43 2p red & blk (Bl) 2.60 .40
f. 2p ver & blk (Bl) 120.00 30.00
C6D A43 5p ol grn & blk (Bl) 4.00 1.10
C6E A50 6p on 10c dp bl & blk (R) 65.00 22.50
C7 A43 10p org & blk (Bk) ('29) 16.00 4.50
C8 A43 10p org & blk (Bl) 60.00 35.00
Nos. C6-C8 (8) 150.20 64.80

On Nos. C6B to C6D, C7 and C8 the overprint is larger than on the other stamps of the issue.

Same Overprint or Surcharge on Nos. 155, 156, 158-161

Inscribed: "Chile Correos"

1928-32 Wmk. 215

C9 A55 40c vio & blk (R) .70 .40
C10 A43 1p grn & blk (Bl) 1.90 .60
C11 A43 2p red & blk (Bl) 11.00 2.25
C12 A52 3p on 5c sl bl (R) 65.00 40.00
C13 A43 5p ol grn & blk (Bl) 8.50 2.25
C14 A43 10p org & blk (Bk) 45.00 11.00
Nos. C9-C14 (6) 132.10 56.50

Same Overprint on Nos. 166-169, 172 and 158 in Black or Red

Inscribed: "Correos de Chile"

1928-30

C15 A39 20c (#166) ('29) 1.20 .70
C16 A39 20c (#172) ('30) .50 .25
C17 A40 25c bl & blk (R) .60 .25
C18 A41 30c brn & blk .40 .25
a. Double ovpt., one inverted 250.00 250.00
C19 A42 50c dp grn & blk (R) .50 .25
Nos. C15-C19 (5) 3.20 1.70

Inscribed: "Chile Correos"

1932 *Perf. 13½x14, 14*

C21 A43 1p yel grn & blk (Bk) 2.75 1.50

Condor on Andes — AP1a

Airplane Crossing Andes — AP3

Los Cerrillos Airport — AP2

1931 Litho. *Perf. 13½x14, 14½x14*

C22 AP1a 5c yellow grn .25 .25
C23 AP1a 10c yellow brn .25 .25
C24 AP1a 20c rose .25 .25
C25 AP2 50c dark blue 1.50 .50
C26 AP3 50c black brn .75 .25
C27 AP3 1p purple .60 .25
C28 AP3 2p blue blk .90 .30
a. 2p bluish slate 1.00 .45
C29 AP2 5p lt red 3.00 .30
Nos. C22-C29 (8) 7.50 2.35

For surcharges see Nos. C51-C53.

Airplane over City — AP4

Two Airplanes over Globe — AP9

Designs: 30c, 40c, 50c, Wings over Chile. 60c, Condor. 70c, Airplane and Star of Chile. 80c, Condor and Statue of Canpolican. 3p, 4p, 5p, Seaplane. 6p, 8p, 10p, Airplane. 20p, 30p, Airplane and Southern Cross. 40p, 50p, Airplane and symbols of space.

Perf. 13½x14

1934-39 Engr. Wmk. 215

C30 AP4 10c yel grn ('35) .30 .25
C31 AP4 15c dk grn ('35) .45 .25
C32 AP4 20c dp bl ('36) .25 .25
C33 AP4 30c blk brn ('35) .25 .25
C34 AP4 40c indigo ('38) .25 .25
C35 AP4 50c dk brn ('36) .25 .25
C36 AP4 60c vio blk ('35) .25 .25
C37 AP4 70c blue ('35) .45 .25
C38 AP4 80c ol blk ('35) .25 .25

Perf. 14

C39 AP9 1p slate blk .25 .25
C40 AP9 2p grnsh bl .25 .25
C41 AP9 3p org brn ('35) .30 .25
C42 AP9 4p brn ('35) .30 .25
C43 AP9 5p org red .30 .25
C44 AP9 6p yel brn ('35) .45 .25
a. 6p brown ('39) 2.75 1.90
C45 AP9 8p grn ('35) .40 .25
C46 AP9 10p brn lake .45 .25
C47 AP9 20p olive .45 .25
C48 AP9 30p gray blk .50 .25
C49 AP9 40p gray vio 1.40 .70
C50 AP9 50p brn vio 1.60 .70
Nos. C30-C50 (21) 9.35 6.15

Nos. C30-C50 have been re-issued in slightly different colors, with white gum. The first printings are considerably scarcer.

See Nos. C90-C107B, C148-C154.

Types of 1931 Surcharged in Black or Red

Perf. 13½x14, 14½x14

1940 Wmk. 215

C51 AP1a 80c on 20c lt rose .70 .25
C52 AP2 1.60p on 5p lt red 4.25 1.50
C53 AP3 5.10p on 2p sl bl (R) 3.50 1.75
Nos. C51-C53 (3) 8.45 3.50

The surcharge on No. C52 measures 21½mm.

Plane and Weather Vane — AP14

Plane and Caravel — AP23

Designs (Plane and): 20c, Globe. 30c, Chilean flag. 40c, Star of Chile and Southern Cross. 50c, Mountains. 60c, Tree. 70c, Lakes. 80c, Shore. 90c, Sunrise. 2p, Compass. 3p, Telegraph lines. 4p, Rainbow. 5p, Factory. 10p, Snow-capped mountain.

1941-42 Wmk. 215 Litho. *Perf. 14*

C54 AP14 10c ol gray .25 .25
C55 AP14 20c dp rose .25 .25
C56 AP14 30c blue vio .25 .25
C57 AP14 40c dl red brn .25 .25
C58 AP14 50c red org ('42) .35 .25
C59 AP14 60c dp green .25 .25
C60 AP14 70c rose .30 .25
C61 AP14 80c ultra ('42) 1.50 .45
C62 AP14 90c dk brown .45 .25
C63 AP23 1p brt blue .30 .25
C64 AP23 2p rose lake .80 .30
C65 AP23 3p dk bl grn & yel grn 1.20 .60
C66 AP23 4p bl vio & buff 1.75 1.00
C67 AP23 5p dk org red ('42) 17.00 6.00
C68 AP23 10p gray grn & bl grn 9.50 6.00
Nos. C54-C68 (15) 34.40 16.60

The 1p, dated "1541-1941", commemorates the 400th anniversary of Santiago.

1942-46 Unwmk.

C69 AP14 10c ultra ('43) .25 .25
C70 AP14 10c rose lil ('45) .25 .25
C71 AP14 20c dull grn ('43) .25 .25
C72 AP14 20c cop brn ('45) .25 .25
C73 AP14 30c dull vio ('44) .25 .25
C74 AP14 30c ol blk ('45) .25 .25
C75 AP14 40c red brn ('44) .30 .25
C76 AP14 40c ultra ('45) .25 .25
C77 AP14 50c rose ('43) .25 .25
C78 AP14 50c org red ('45) .25 .25
C79 AP14 60c orange .25 .25
C79B AP14 60c dp grn ('46) .25 .25
C80 AP14 70c rose ('45) .45 .35
C81 AP14 80c slate grn .25 .25
C82 AP14 90c brown ('45) .45 .35
C83 AP23 1p gray grn & lt bl ('43) .25 .25
C84 AP23 2p org red ('43) .45 .25
C85 AP23 3p dk pur & pale org ('43) .45 .25
C86 AP23 4p bl grn & yel grn .45 .35
C87 AP23 5p dk rose car ('43) .35 .25
a. 5p dk car rose ('44) .25 .25
C88 AP23 10p sapphire ('43) .45 .35
Nos. C69-C88 (21) 6.60 5.65

No. C83 is without dates "1541-1941."

See Nos. C109-C123. For surcharges see Nos. C145-C147

Coat of Arms and Plane AP29

1942, Nov. 5 Engr. *Perf. 14½*

C89 AP29 100p car lake 25.00 20.00

University of Chile centenary.

Types of 1934-39

Perf. 13½x14

1944-55 Unwmk. Engr.

C90 AP4 10c yel grn ('55) .25 .25
C92 AP4 20c deep blue .25 .25
C93 AP4 30c black brn .25 .25
C94 AP4 40c indigo .25 .25
C95 AP4 50c dk brn ('47) .25 .25
C96 AP4 60c slate vio .25 .25
C97 AP4 70c blue ('48) .25 .25
C98 AP4 80c olive blk .25 .25

Perf. 14

C99 AP9 1p slate blk .25 .25
C100 AP9 2p grnsh bl .25 .25
C101 AP9 3p org brn ('45) .25 .25
C102 AP9 4p brown .25 .25
C103 AP9 5p org red .35 .25
C104 AP9 6p yel brn ('46) .40 .25
C105 AP9 8p green .40 .25
C106 AP9 10p brn lake 1.10 .25
C107 AP9 20p ol gray ('45) .75 .25
a. Imperf., pair 70.00
C107B AP9 50p rose vio ('50) 17.50 2.50
Nos. C90-C107B (18) 23.50 6.75

Plane and Radio Tower — AP30

1945 Unwmk. Litho. *Perf. 14*

C108 AP30 1.60p brt violet .55 .25

See Nos. C118-C119.

Types of 1941-45

1946-48 Wmk. 215

C109 AP14 10c rose lil ('47) .25 .25
C110 AP14 20c dk red brn ('48) .25 .25
C111 AP14 20c dull grn ('48) 1.50 .30
C112 AP14 30c black ('48) .25 .25
C113 AP14 40c ultra ('48) .25 .25
C114 AP14 60c ol grn ('48) .25 .25
C115 AP14 80c ol blk ('48) .25 .25

C116 AP14 90c choc ('48) .25 .25
C117 AP23 1p gray grn & lt bl ('48) .25 .25
C118 AP30 1.60p brt violet .25 .25
C119 AP30 1.80p brt vio ('48) .25 .25
C119A AP23 2p org red .40 .25
C120 AP23 3p dk pur & pale org ('47) 1.50 .30
C121 AP23 4p bl grn & yel grn ('48) 1.10 .45
C122 AP23 5p rose car ('47) .80 .25
C123 AP23 10p sapphire ('47) 1.00 .25
Nos. C109-C123 (16) 8.80 4.30

No. C117 is without dates "1541-1941."
For surcharges see Nos. C145, C147.

Flora and Fauna Type of 1948

1948

C124 A118 3p Block of 25 80.00 80.00
Never hinged 110.00
a.-y. any single 2.00 1.50

Catalogue values for unused stamps in this section, from this point to the end of the section, are for Never Hinged items.

Air Line Emblem and Planes — AP32

1949 Wmk. 215 Litho. *Perf. 14*

C125 AP32 2p ultra .45 .25

20th anniversary of the establishment of Chile's National Air Line.

Benjamin Vicuna Mackenna — AP33

1949, Mar. 22 Engr. *Perf. 13½x14*

C126 AP33 3p dk car rose .30 .25

Factory, Badge and Book — AP34

Design: 10p, Column and cogwheel.

Unwmk.

1949, Nov. 11 Litho. *Perf. 14*

C127 AP34 5p green .85 .45
C128 AP34 10p red brown 1.40 .55

Centenary of the founding of Chile's School of Arts and Crafts.

Plane and Globe — AP35

1950, Jan. Engr.

C129 AP35 5p green .60 .25
C130 AP35 10p red brown 1.00 .60

75th anniv. of the UPU.

Plane over Snow-capped Mountain AP36

Araucarian Pine and Plane — AP38

Plane and: 40c, Coast and Sunrise. 60c, Over fishing boat. 2p, Chilean flag. 3p, Dock crane. 4p, Above river. 5p, Blast furnace. 10p, Mountain lake. 20p, Cable cars.

Imprint: "Especies Valoradas-Chile"

1950-54 Wmk. 215 Litho. *Perf. 14*

C135 AP36 20c yel brn ('54) .35 .25
C136 AP36 40c purple ('52) .35 .25
C137 AP36 60c lt bl ('53) 1.60 .90
C138 AP38 1p dull green .35 .25
C139 AP38 2p brown red .35 .25
C140 AP38 3p violet bl .35 .25
C141 AP38 4p red org ('54) .35 .25
C142 AP38 5p violet .35 .25
C143 AP38 10p yel grn ('53) .35 .25
C144 AP38 20p red brn ('54) .60 .25
Nos. C135-C144 (10) 5.00 3.15

See Nos. C155-C164, C207-C212.

Nos. C115, C81 and C116 Surcharged with New Value in Carmine or Black

1951-52 Wmk. 215

C145 AP14 40c on 80c ol blk (C) ('52) .25 .25

Unwmk.

C146 AP14 40c on 80c sl grn (C) ('52) 5.50 3.50

Wmk. 215

C147 AP14 1p on 90c choc .25 .25
Nos. C145-C147 (3) 6.00 4.00

Types of 1934-39

1951-53 Unwmk. Engr. *Perf. 14*

C148 AP9 1p deep blue .25 .25
C149 AP9 2p blue .35 .25
C150 AP9 6p bis brn ('52) .45 .25
C151 AP9 30p dk gray ('53) .60 .90
C152 AP9 40p dk pur brn 18.00 2.40
C153 AP9 50p dark purple 25.00 5.00
Nos. C148-C153 (6) 44.65 9.05

Wmk. 215

C154 AP9 50p dk pur ('52) .80 .40

Types of 1950-54
Designs as Before
Imprint: "Especies Valoradas-Chile"

1951-55 Unwmk. Litho. *Perf. 14*

C155 AP36 20c yel brn ('54) .25 .25
C156 AP36 40c purple .25 .25
C157 AP36 60c lt blue ('53) .25 .25
C158 AP38 1p dk bl grn ('55) .25 .25
C159 AP38 2p brown red .25 .25
C160 AP38 3p violet bl .25 .25
C161 AP38 4p red org ('52) .30 .25
C162 AP38 5p violet .30 .25
C163 AP38 10p emerald .30 .25
C164 AP38 20p brown .40 .25
Nos. C155-C164 (10) 2.80 2.50

San Martin Crossing Andes AP40

Wmk. 215

1951, Mar. 16 Engr. *Perf. 14½*

C165 AP40 5p red violet .90 .50

Gen. José de San Martín, death cent.

Isabella Type of Regular Issue, 1952

1952, Mar. 21 *Perf. 14*

C166 A125 10p carmine .70 .40

A souvenir card without franking value was issued for the Hispano-Chilean Philatelic Exhibition at Santiago, Oct. 12, 1969. It contains 2 imperf. stamps similar to Nos. 264 and C166-60c green and 10p rose red. Size: 115x137½mm.

Ancient Fortress AP42

1953, Apr. 28

C167 AP42 10p brown car 2.25 .45

4th centenary of the founding of Valdivia.

Stamp Centenary Type of 1953

1953, Oct. 15 Engr. *Perf. 14½*

C168 A131 100p dp grnsh bl 2.75 1.00

An imperf. souvenir sheet contains one each of Nos. 276 and C168, with inscriptions in black at top and bottom center. Sheet measures 178x229mm. It is stated that this sheet was not valid for postage.

Early Plane and Stylized Modern Version — AP44

Unwmk.

1954, May 26 Engr. *Perf. 14*

C170 AP44 3p deep blue .30 .25

25th anniversary of the founding of Chile's National Air Line.

Domeyko Type of Regular Issue, 1954

1954, Aug. 16 *Perf. 13½x14*

C171 A134 5p orange brown .30 .25

Railroad Type of Regular Issue, 1954

1954, Sept. 10 Wmk. 215 *Perf. 14½*

C172 A135 10p dk purple 1.50 .25

An imperforate souvenir sheet contains one each of Nos. 283 and C172.
Size: 174x232mm. Value, $200.

Presidential Visits Type of 1955

1955, May 24

C173 A139 100p red 1.50 1.25

Jet Plane in Clouds — AP48

Comet Air Liner — AP49

Designs: 2p, Helicopter over bridge. 10p, Oil derricks and plane. 50p, Control tower and plane. 200p, Beechcraft monoplane. 500p, Douglas DC-6.

Perf. 14½x14, 14x13½ (AP49)

1955-56 Engr. Wmk. 215

C174 AP48 1p dp red lil ('56) .25 .25
C175 AP48 2p pale brn ('56) .25 .25
C176 AP48 10p bluish grn ('56) .25 .25
C177 AP48 50p rose ('56) .60 .25
C178 AP49 100p green 1.00 .25
C179 AP49 200p dp ultra 6.50 .90
C180 AP49 500p dk carmine 7.50 .90
Nos. C174-C180 (7) 16.35 3.05

Stamps similar to type AP49, but inscribed in escudo currency, are listed as type AP58.

1956-58 Unwmk.

Designs: 5p, Train and plane. 20p, Jet plane and Easter Island statue.

C183 AP48 5p violet .25 .25
C184 AP48 10p grn ('57) .25 .25
C185 AP48 20p ultra .25 .25
C186 AP48 50p rose ('57) .25 .25
C187 AP49 100p bl grn ('57) .55 .25
a. Lithographed ('60) .55 .25
C188 AP49 200p dp ultra ('57) .65 .25
C189 AP49 500p car ('58) .85 .25
Nos. C183-C189 (7) 3.05 1.75

Symbols of University Departments — AP50

Design: 100p, View of the University.

1956, Dec. 15 Unwmk. *Perf. 14½*

C190 AP50 20p green .35 .25
C191 AP50 100p dk vio bl 1.40 .80

25th anniversary of the Federico Santa Maria Technical University, Valparaiso.

A souvenir sheet contains one each of Nos. 299, C190-C191, imperf. It was not issued for postal use, though some served postally. Size: 127x160mm. Value, $125.

Mistral Type of Regular Issue, 1958

1958, Jan. 10 Engr. *Perf. 14*

C192 A144 100p green .25 .25

Ambrosio O'Higgins — AP51

1958, Mar. 23

C193 AP51 100p lt blue .40 .25

Founding of the city of Osorno, 500th anniv.

A souvenir sheet contains one each of Nos. 302 and C193, imperf. and printed in red brown. It was not issued for postal use, though some served postally. Size: 155x138mm. Value, $70.

Exhibition Type of Regular Issue

1958, Oct. 18 Unwmk.

C194 A146 50p dull green .45 .45

A souvenir sheet contains one each of Nos. 303 and C194, imperf. and printed in deep red. It was not issued for postal use, though some served postally. Size: 188x220mm. Value, $55.

Bank Type of Regular Issue, 1958

1958, Dec. 18 Engr. *Perf. 14*

C195 A147 50p redsh brown .25 .25

A souvenir sheet contains one each of Nos. 304 and C195, printed in dull violet, imperf. It was not issued for postal use, though some served postally. Value, $190.

Antarctic Types of Regular Issue

1958 Litho. *Perf. 14*

C199 A149 20p violet .50 .25

Engr.

C200 A150 500p dark blue 3.75 1.75

Symbols of Various Religions
AP52

Perf. 14½

1959, Jan. 23 Unwmk. Engr.
C206 AP52 50p dk car rose .30 .25

10th anniversary of the Universal Declaration of Human Rights.

Types of 1950-54

Designs: 50p, Plane silhouette over shore. 100p, Plane over map of Antarctica. 200p, Plane over natural arch rock.

Imprint: "Casa de Moneda de Chile"

1959 Litho. *Perf. 14*
C207 AP38 1p dk blue grn .85 .50
a. Wmk. 215 30.00
C208 AP38 10p emerald .55 .25
C209 AP38 20p red brown .35 .25
C210 AP38 50p yellow grn .35 .25
C211 AP38 100p car rose .35 .25
C212 AP38 200p brt blue .55 .25
Nos. C207-C212 (6) 3.00 1.75

Carlos Anwandter
AP53

1959, June 18 Engr. *Perf. 14*
C213 AP53 20p rose carmine .25 .25

Centenary of the German School in Valdivia, founded by Carlos Anwandter.

A souvenir sheet contains one each of Nos. 319 and C213, imperf. It was not issued for postal use, though some served postally. Value, $75.

IGY Type of Regular Issue, 1958

1959, Aug. 28 Unwmk. *Perf. 14*
C214 A148 50p green .70 .25

Ladrillero Type of Regular Issue

1959, Aug. 28 Litho.
C215 A154 50p green .50 .25

Barros Arana Type of Regular Issue

1959, Aug. 28
C216 A155 100p purple .50 .25

Red Cross Type of Regular Issue

1959, Oct. 6
C217 A156 50p red & blk .60 .25

WRY Type of Regular Issue, 1960

1960, Apr. 7 Unwmk. *Perf. 14½*
C218 A160 10c violet .35 .25

A souvenir sheet contains two stamps similar to Nos. 330 and C218, the 1c printed in blue, the 10c airmail in maroon. The sheet is imperf., printed on thin cardboard. Size: 160x204mm. Value, $125.

Type of Regular Issue, 1960-62, and

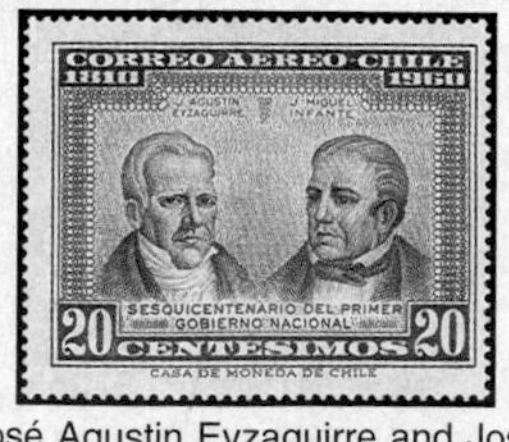

José Agustin Eyzaguirre and José Miguel Infante — AP54

Designs: 2c, Palace of Justice. 5c, National memorial. No. C220, Arms of Chile. No. C220A, José Gaspar Marín and J. Gregorio Argomedo. 50c, Archbishop J. I. Cienfuegos and Brother Camilo Henriquez. 1e, Bernardo O'Higgins.

1960-65 Unwmk. Engr. *Perf. 14½*
C218A AP54 2c mar & gray vio ('62) .25 .25
C219 A162 5c vio bl & dl pur ('61) .25 .25

Wmk. 215

C220 A161 10c dk brn & red brn .25 .25

Unwmk.

C220A AP54 10c vio brn & brn ('64) .40 .25
C220B AP54 20c dk bl & dl pur ('64) .25 .25
C220C AP54 50c bl grn & ind ('65) 1.00 .25
C220D A162 1e dk red & red brn ('63) 1.00 .40
Nos. C218A-C220D (7) 3.40 1.90

150th anniv. of the formation of the 1st Natl. Government.

A souvenir sheet contains two airmail stamps: a 5c brown similar to No. C219 (National Memorial) and a 10c green, type A161. The sheet is imperf., printed on heavy paper with papermaker's watermark. Size: 120x168mm. Value, $85.

Map and Rotary Emblem — AP55

Unwmk.

1960, Dec. 1 Litho. *Perf. 14*
C221 AP55 10c blue .50 .25

South American Rotary Regional Conference, Santiago, 1960.

A souvenir sheet contains one 10c maroon, type AP55, with brown marginal inscription. Size: 118x158mm. Value, $65.

The souvenir sheet was overprinted in green "El Mundo Unida Contra la Malaria" and the outline of a mosquito, and released in October, 1962. Value, $110.

Araucan Pine and Plane — AP56

Designs: 2m, Chilean flag and plane. 3m, Plane and dock crane. 4m, Plane above river (vignette like AP39). 5m, Blast furnace. 1c, Plane over mountain lake. 2c, Plane over cable cars. 5c, Plane silhouette over shore. 10c, Plane over map of Antarctica. 20c, Plane over natural arch rock.

Imprint: "Casa de Moneda de Chile"

1960-62 Litho. *Perf. 14*
C222 AP56 1m orange .25 .25
C223 AP56 2m yellow grn .25 .25
C224 AP56 3m violet .25 .25
C225 AP56 4m gray olive .25 .25
C226 AP56 5m brt bl grn .25 .25
C227 AP56 1c ultra .25 .25
C228 AP56 2c red brn ('61) .35 .25
C229 AP56 5c yel grn ('61) 1.75 .25
C230 AP56 10c car rose ('62) .45 .25
C231 AP56 20c brt bl ('62) .50 .25
Nos. C222-C231 (10) 4.55 2.50

Oil Derricks and Douglas DC-6 — AP57

Beechcraft Monoplane
AP58

5m, Train and plane. 2c, Jet plane & Easter Island statue. 5c, Control tower & plane. 10c, Comet airliner. 50c, Douglas DC-6.

Perf. 14x13½

1960-67 Unwmk. Litho.
C234 AP57 5m red brown .35 .35
C235 AP57 1c dull blue .35 .35
C236 AP57 2c ultra ('62) .35 .35
C237 AP57 5c rose red ('64) .35 .35
C238 AP58 10c ultra ('67) .35 .35
C239 AP58 20c car ('62) .35 .35
C240 AP58 50c green ('63) .35 .35
Nos. C234-C240 (7) 2.45 2.45

Stamps similar to type AP58, but inscribed in peso ($) currency, are listed as type AP49.

Congress Type of Regular Issue

1961, Oct. 5 *Perf. 14½*
C245 A164 10c gray green .95 .60

Soccer Type of Regular Issue, 1962

Designs: 5c, Goalkeeper and stadium, vert. 10c, Soccer players and globe.

1962, May 30 Unwmk. Engr.
C246 A165 5c rose lilac .25 .25
C247 A165 10c dk carmine .25 .25

A souvenir sheet of four contains one each of Nos. 340-341, C246-C247, imperf., with light brown marginal inscriptions. Size: 123x194mm. Sold for 7.50 escudos (face value, 22 centavos). Value $12.

Hunger Type of Regular Issue

20c, Mother with empty bowl, horiz.

1963, Mar. 21 Litho. *Perf. 14*
C248 A166 20c green .25 .25

Red Cross Type of Regular Issue

Design: 20c, Centenary emblem and plane silhouette, horiz.

1963, Sept. 6 Unwmk. *Perf. 14*
C249 A167 20c gray & red .25 .25

Fire Engine of 1860's
AP59

1963, Dec. 20 Litho. *Perf. 14½*
C250 AP59 30c red .50 .25

Centenary of the Santiago Fire Brigade.

Western Hemisphere
AP60

1964, Apr. 9 Unwmk. *Perf. 14½*
C254 AP60 4c ultra .40 .25

Issued in memory of President John F. Kennedy and to honor the Alliance for Progress.

Battle of Rancagua — AP61

1965, May 7 Engr. *Perf. 14½*
C255 AP61 5c dull grn & sepia .40 .25

Battle of Rancagua, 10/7/14, 150th anniv.

ITU Emblem, Old and New Communication Equipment
AP62

1965, May 7 Litho. *Perf. 14½x14*
C256 AP62 40c red & maroon .40 .25

ITU centenary.

Portrait Type of 1964

Portraits: No. C257, Enrique Molina. No. C258, Msgr. Carlos Casanueva.

1965, June Litho. *Perf. 14*
C257 A169 60c brt violet .30 .25
C258 A169 60c green .30 .25

See note after No. 346.

Skier Type of Regular Issue 1965

Design: 20c, Skier, horiz.

1965, Aug. 30 Unwmk. *Perf. 14*
C259 A172 20c ultra .30 .25

Fishing Boats, Angelmo Harbor
AP63

Aviators' Monument
AP64

1965
C260 AP63 40c brown .30 .25

Perf. 14x14½

C262 AP64 1e car rose .30 .25

Andrés Bello (1780?-1865), Venezuela-born Writer and Educator — AP65

1965, Nov. 29 Engr. Unwmk.
C263 AP65 10c dk car rose .35 .35

Skiers — AP66

1966, Apr. 6 Litho. *Perf. 14*
C264 AP66 4e dk bl & red brn 1.25 .25

World Skiing Championships, Partillo, Aug. 1966.

Basketball
AP67

1966, Apr. 28
C265 AP67 13c rose carmine .40 .25

International Basketball Championships.

Slalom
AP68

Perf. 14½x15

1966, July 20 Litho. Unwmk.
C266 AP68 75c rose car & lil .40 .25
C267 AP68 3e ultra & lt bl .40 .25

Intl. Skiing Championships, Partillo, August 1966. A souvenir sheet of 2 contains imperf. stamps similar to Nos. C266-C267. No gum. Size: 109x140mm. Value $36.

Ship Type of Regular Issue

1966 Litho. *Perf. 14½*
C268 A175 70c Prus grn & yel grn .35 .25

See note below No. 358.

ICY Type of Regular Issue

1966, Oct. 28 Unwmk. *Perf. 14½*
C269 A177 3e blue & carmine .50 .25

A souvenir sheet of 2 contains imperf. stamps similar to Nos. 360 and C269. No gum. Size: 111x140mm. Value $7.50.

Chilean Flag and Ships — AP69

1966, Nov. 21 Litho. *Perf. 14*
C270 AP69 13c dull red brn .40 .25

Centenary of the city of Antofagasta.

Pardo Type of Regular Issue

40c, Pardo & map of Chile's claim to Antarctica.

1967, Jan. 6 Unwmk. *Perf. 14½*
C271 A178 40c ultra .50 .25

See note below No. 361.

Family Type of Regular Issue

1967, Apr. 13 Litho. *Perf. 14*
C272 A179 80c brt bl & blk .35 .25

Ruben Dario and Title Page of "Azul" AP70

1967, May 15 Engr. *Perf. 14½*
C273 AP70 10c dark blue .30 .25

Ruben Dario (pen name of Felix Ruben Garcia Sarmiento, 1867-1916), Nicaraguan poet, newspaper correspondent and diplomat.

Tree Type of Regular Issue

1967, June 9 Litho.
C274 A180 75c grn & pale rose .35 .25

Lions Type of Regular Issue

1967 Litho. *Perf. 14*
C275 A181 1e purple & yel .40 .25
C276 A181 5e blue & yel 1.10 .30

A souvenir sheet without franking value contains 3 imperf. stamps, 20c, 1e and 5e, in violet blue and yellow. Size: 110x140mm. Value, $13.50.
Issue dates: 1e, July 12; 5e, Aug. 11.

Flag Type of Regular Issue

1967, Oct. 20 Unwmk. *Perf. 14½*
C277 A182 50c ultra & crimson .35 .25

ITY Emblem AP71

1967, Nov. 22 Litho. *Perf. 14½*
C278 AP71 30c lt vio bl & blk .35 .25

Issued for International Tourist Year, 1967.

Caro Type of Regular Issue, 1967

1967, Dec. 4 Engr. *Perf. 14½*
C279 A183 40c violet .70 .35

Type of Regular Issue, 1968

1968, Apr. 23 Litho. *Perf. 14½*
C280 A184 2e brt violet .60 .25

Sesquicentennial of the Battles of Chacabuco and Maipu. A souvenir sheet of 2 contains imperf. stamps similar to Nos. 367 and C280. Value, $12. A second sheet exists with the 2e in green and the 3e in brown. Size: 139½x100mm. Value, $12.

Farm Type of Regular Issue

1968, June 18 Unwmk.
C281 A185 50c blk, org & grn .35 .25

Juan I. Molina, Educator and Scientist AP72

1968, Aug. 27 Litho. *Perf. 14½*
C282 AP72 1e bright green .30 .25

Map of Chiloé Province — AP73

Perf. 14½

1968, Oct. 7 Unwmk. Litho.
C283 AP73 1e rose claret .35 .35

Anniversaries of the founding of five towns in Chiloé Province.

Auto Club Type of Regular Issue

1968, Nov. 10 Engr. *Perf. 14½x14*
C284 A189 5e ultra .35 .25

British Crown and Map of Chile — AP74

50c, Chilean coat of arms (horiz.; similar to type A161). 3e, British coat of arms, horiz.

1968, Nov. 12 Litho. *Perf. 14½*
C285 AP74 50c green & brn .25 .25
C286 AP74 3e bl & org brn .40 .25

Engr.

C287 AP74 5e purple & mag .60 .25
Nos. C285-C287 (3) 1.25 .75

Visit of Queen Elizabeth II of Great Britain, Nov. 11-18. A souvenir sheet of 3 contains imperf., lithographed stamps similar to Nos. C285-C287. Size: 124½x190mm. The souvenir sheet also publicizes the British-Chilean Philatelic Exhibition. Value, $20.

First Coin Minted in Chile and Coin Press AP75

Design: 1e, Chile No. 128.

1968, Dec. 31 Litho. *Perf. 14½*
C288 AP75 50c ocher & vio brn .30 .25
C289 AP75 1e lt bl & dp org .30 .25

225th anniversary of the founding of the State Mint (Casa de Moneda de Chile).
A souvenir sheet of 4 contains imperf. stamps similar to Nos. 373-374, C288-C289. Size: 150x119mm. Value, $10.

Satellite Type of Regular Issue

1969, May 20 Litho. *Perf. 14½*
C290 A191 2e rose lilac .30 .25

Red Cross Type of Regular Issue

1969, Sept. Litho. *Perf. 14½*
C291 A192 5e black & red .50 .25

A souvenir card contains 2 imperf. stamps similar to Nos. 376 and C291, with red marginal inscription. Size: 109x140mm. Value $5.

Dam Type of Regular Issue

1969, Nov. 18 Litho. *Perf. 14½*
C292 A193 3e blue .50 .25

Rodriguez Type of Regular Issue

1969, Nov. 24
C293 A194 30c brown .35 .25

EXPO '70 Type of Regular Issue

1969, Dec. 1 Litho. *Perf. 14*
C294 A195 5e red .35 .25

Bible Type of 1969

1969, Dec. 2 *Perf. 14½*
C295 A196 1e green .30 .25

ILO Type of Regular Issue

1969, Dec. 17 *Perf. 14½*
C296 A197 2e rose lil & blk .35 .25

Human Rights Year Type of 1969

1969, Dec. 18
C297 A198 4e brown & red .35 .35

A souvenir sheet of 2 contains imperf. stamps similar to Nos. 382 and C297. Size: 110x140mm. Value, $9.

Easter Island Type of 1970

1970, Jan. 26
C298 A199 50c dull grnsh bl .70 .25

Ship Type of Regular Issue

1970, Feb. 4 Litho. *Perf. 14½*
C299 A200 2e deep ultra .40 .25

Rotary Type of Regular Issue

1970, Mar. 18 Litho. *Perf. 14*
C300 A201 1e rose claret .35 .25

Gandhi Type of Regular Issue

1970, Apr. 1 Litho. *Perf. 14½*
C301 A202 1e red brown .40 .25

Education Year Type of 1970

1970, July 17 Litho. *Perf. 14½*
C302 A204 4e red brown .30 .25

National Shrine Type of 1970

1970, July 28 Litho. *Perf. 14½*
C303 A205 1e ultra .35 .25

Cancer Type of Regular Issue

1970, Aug. 11
C304 A206 2e brn & lt olive .40 .25

A few stampss are known inscribed "Correos de Chile" instead of "Correos Aereo Chile." Value $350.

Copper Type of Regular Issue

1970, Oct. 21 Litho. *Perf. 14½*
C305 A207 3e grn & lt red brn .50 .25

United Nations Type of 1970

1970, Oct. 22
C306 A208 5e dk car & grn .50 .25

Freighter Type of Regular Issue

1971, Jan. 18 Litho. *Perf. 14*
C307 A209 5e lt red brown .50 .25

No. C290 Surcharged in Red

1971, Jan. 21 Litho. *Perf. 14½*
C308 A191 52c on 2e rose lil .40 .25

Liberation Type of Regular Issue

1971, Feb. 3 *Perf. 14½*
C309 A210 1e gray bl & brn .40 .25

UNICEF Type of Regular Issue

1971, Feb. 11 Litho. *Perf. 14½*
C310 A211 2e blue & grn .30 .25

Boy Scout Type of Regular Issue

1971, Feb. 10 *Perf. 14*
C311 A212 5c dk car & ol .40 .25

Satellite Type of Regular Issue

1971, May 25 Litho. *Perf. 14½*
C312 A213 2e brown .40 .25

De Ercilla Type of Regular Issue

1972, Mar. 20 Engr. *Perf. 14*
C313 A221 2e Prussian blue .30 .25

A souvenir card contains impressions of Nos. 414 and C313 with black marginal inscription commemorating España 75 Philatelic Exhibition. Size: 165x220mm. Value $19.

AIR POST SEMI-POSTAL STAMPS

Catalogue values for unused stamps in this section are for Never Hinged items.

Type of Semi-Postal Stamps, 1961

Portraits: 10c+10c, Alonso de Ercilla. 20c+20c, Gabriela Mistral.

Perf. 13x12½

1961, Apr. 29 Photo. Unwmk.
CB1 SP3 10c + 10c salmon & choc 1.00 .30
CB2 SP3 20c + 20c gray & dp cl 1.00 .30

Printed without charge by the Spanish Mint as a gift to Chile. The surtax was to aid the 1960 earthquake victims and to increase teachers' salaries.

ACKNOWLEDGMENT OF RECEIPT STAMPS

AR1

1894 Unwmk. *Perf. 11½*
H1 AR1 5c brown .75 .50
a. Imperf., pair 3.00

The black stamp of design similar to AR1 inscribed "Avis de Paiement" was prepared for use on notices of payment of funds but was not regularly issued.

POSTAGE DUE STAMPS

D1

D2

Handstamped

1894 **Unwmk.** ***Perf. 13***

J1	D1	2c black, *straw*	15.00	8.00
J2	D1	4c black, *straw*	15.00	8.00
J3	D1	6c black, *straw*	15.00	8.00
J4	D1	8c black, *straw*	14.00	8.00
J5	D2	10c black, *straw*	15.00	8.00
J6	D1	16c black, *straw*	15.00	8.00
J7	D1	20c black, *straw*	15.00	8.00
J8	D1	30c black, *straw*	15.00	8.00
J9	D1	40c black, *straw*	15.00	8.00
		Nos. J1-J9 (9)	134.00	72.00
J1a	D1	2c black, *yellow*	85.00	80.00
J2a	D1	4c black, *yellow*	55.00	40.00
J3a	D1	6c black, *yellow*	80.00	35.00
J4a	D1	8c black, *yellow*	16.00	16.00
J5a	D2	10c black, *yellow*	16.00	16.00
J6a	D1	16c black, *yellow*	16.00	16.00
J7a	D1	20c black, *yellow*	16.00	16.00
J8a	D1	30c black, *yellow*	16.00	16.00
J9a	D1	40c black, *yellow*	16.00	16.00
		Nos. J1a-J9a (9)	316.00	251.00

Counterfeits exist.

D3

1895 **Litho.** ***Perf. 11***

J19	D3	1c red, *yellow*	7.50	3.00
J20	D3	2c red, *yellow*	7.50	3.00
J21	D3	4c red, *yellow*	6.00	3.00
J22	D3	6c red, *yellow*	7.50	3.00
J23	D3	8c red, *yellow*	4.50	3.00
J24	D3	10c red, *yellow*	4.50	4.50
J25	D3	20c red, *yellow*	4.50	2.25
J26	D3	40c red, *yellow*	4.50	3.00
J27	D3	50c red, *yellow*	4.50	3.00
J28	D3	60c red, *yellow*	9.00	4.50
J29	D3	80c red, *yellow*	9.00	6.00
J30	D3	1p red, *yellow*	9.50	6.50
		Nos. J19-J30 (12)	78.50	44.75

Nos. J19-J30 were printed in sheets of 100 (10x10) containing all 12 denominations.
Counterfeits of Nos. J19-J42 exist.

1896 ***Perf. 13½***

J31	D3	1c red, *straw*	.90	.50
J32	D3	2c red, *straw*	.90	.50
J33	D3	4c red, *straw*	1.10	.50
J34	D3	6c red, *straw*	2.50	1.00
J35	D3	8c red, *straw*	1.10	.60
J36	D3	10c red, *straw*	.90	.60
J37	D3	20c red, *straw*	.90	.60
J38	D3	40c red, *straw*	18.00	15.00
J39	D3	50c red, *straw*	18.00	15.00
J40	D3	60c red, *straw*	18.00	15.00
J41	D3	80c red, *straw*	25.00	17.50
J42	D3	100c red, *straw*	36.00	30.00
		Nos. J31-J42 (12)	123.30	96.80

D4

1898 ***Perf. 13***

J43	D4	1c scarlet	.50	.30
J44	D4	2c scarlet	1.25	.60
J45	D4	4c scarlet	.50	.30
J46	D4	10c scarlet	.50	.30
J47	D4	20c scarlet	.50	.30
		Nos. J43-J47 (5)	3.25	1.80

D5

1924 ***Perf. 11½, 12½***

J48	D5	2c blue & red	1.10	.90
J49	D5	4c blue & red	1.10	.90
J50	D5	8c blue & red	1.10	.90
J51	D5	10c blue & red	1.10	.90
J52	D5	20c blue & red	1.10	.60
J53	D5	40c blue & red	1.10	.90
J54	D5	60c blue & red	1.10	.90
J55	D5	80c blue & red	1.10	.90
J56	D5	1p blue & red	1.50	1.10
J57	D5	2p blue & red	2.60	1.90
J58	D5	5p blue & red	2.60	1.90
		Nos. J48-J58 (11)	15.50	11.80

Nos. J48-J58 were printed in sheets of 150 containing all 11 denominations, and a second printing was printed in sheets of 50 containing the five lower denominations, providing various se-tenants. Stamps from the second printing are of a slightly different shade of red.

All values of this issue exist imperforate, also with center inverted, but are not believed to have been regularly issued. Those with inverted centers sell for about 10 times normal stamps.

OFFICIAL STAMPS

For Domestic Postage

O1

Single-lined frame
Control number in violet

1907 **Unwmk.** ***Imperf.***

O1	O1	dl bl, "CARTA" org	22.50	17.50
O2	O1	red, "OFICIO" bl	22.50	17.50
O3	O1	vio, "PAQUETE" red	22.50	17.50
O4	O1	org, *bl*, "EP" vio	22.50	17.50
		Nos. O1-O4 (4)	90.00	70.00

The diagonal inscription in differing color indicates type of usage: CARTA for letters of ordinary weight; OFICIO, heavy letters to 100 grams; PAQUETE, parcels to 100 grams; E P (Encomienda Postal), heavier parcels; C (Certificado), as on No. O8, registration including postage.

Varieties include CARTA, PAQUETE and E P inverted, OFICIO omitted, etc.

Double-lined frame
Large control number in black
Perf. 11

O5	O1	bl, "CARTA" yel	8.00	7.00
O6	O1	red, "OFICIO" bl	8.00	5.25
O7	O1	brn, "PAQUETE" grn	8.00	5.25
O8	O1	grn, "C" red	110.00	82.50
		Nos. O5-O8 (4)	134.00	100.00

Nos. O5-O8 exist in tête bêche pairs; with CARTA, OFICIO or PAQUETE double or inverted, and other varieties.
Counterfeits of Nos. O1-O8 exist.

For Foreign Postage

Regular Issues of 1892-1909 Overprinted in Red — a

On Stamps of 1904-09

1907 ***Perf. 12***

O9	A14	1c green	7.50	7.50
a.		Inverted overprint	17.50	
O10	A12	3c on lp brn	14.00	13.00
a.		Inverted overprint	52.50	
O11	A14	5c ultra	10.00	9.50
a.		Inverted overprint	35.00	
O12	A15	10c gray & blk	10.50	10.50
O13	A15	15c vio & blk	14.00	13.00
O14	A15	20c org brn & blk	14.00	14.00
O15	A15	50c ultra & blk	45.00	45.00

On Stamp of 1892
Rouletted

O16	A6	1p dk brn & blk	110.00	87.50
		Nos. O9-O16 (8)	225.00	200.00

Counterfeits of Nos. O9-O16 exist.

Regular Issues of 1915-25 Overprinted in Red or Blue — b

1926 ***Perf. 13½x14, 14***

O17	A52	5c slate bl (R)	2.50	.50
O18	A50	10c bl & blk (R)	4.00	.75
O19	A39	20c org red & blk (Bl)	2.00	.40
O20	A42	50c dp grn & blk (Bl)	2.00	.40
O21	A43	1p grn & blk (R)	2.75	.70
O22	A43	2p ver & blk (Bl)	4.00	1.00
		Nos. O17-O22 (6)	17.25	3.75

Nos. O21 and O22 are overprinted vertically at each side.
Nos. O17 to O22 were for the use of the Biblioteca Nacional.

Regular Issue of 1915-25 Overprinted in Red — c

1928 ***Perf. 13½x14, 14***

O23	A50	10c bl & blk	6.50	2.00
O24	A39	20c brn org & blk	3.00	1.00
O25	A40	25c dl bl & blk	7.50	1.00
O26	A42	50c dp grn & blk	4.00	1.00
O27	A43	1p grn & blk	5.00	1.50
		Nos. O23-O27 (5)	26.00	6.50

The overprint on Nos. O23 to O26 is 16½mm high; on No. O27 it is 20mm.

Regular Issues of 1928-30 Overprinted in Red — d

On Stamp Inscribed: "Correos de Chile"

1930-31

O28	A50	10c bl & blk	3.00	1.50

Wmk. 215

On Stamps Inscribed: "Correos de Chile"

O29	A50	10c bl & blk	6.00	3.00
O30	A39	20c org red & blk	.75	.50
O31	A40	25c bl & blk	.75	.50
O32	A42	50c dp grn & blk	1.50	.75

On Stamps Inscribed: "Chile Correos"

O33	A42	50c dp grn & blk	1.50	.75
O34	A43	1p grn & blk	1.50	.75
		Nos. O28-O34 (7)	15.00	7.75

Same Overprint on No. 181

1933 ***Perf. 13½x14***

O35	A61	20c dk brn	.75	.25

Same Overprint in Red on No. 182

1935 **Wmk. 215**

O36	A62	10c deep blue	.75	.50

No. 163 Ovptd. Type "b" in Red Inscribed: "Correos de Chile"

1934

O37	A52	5c lt grn	.60	.50

Overprint "b" on No. 182

1935

O38	A62	10c dp bl	.50	.50

Same Overprint in Black on No. 181

1936 **Wmk. 215** ***Perf. 13½x14***

O39	A61	20c dk brn	10.00	.50

Overprint "b" in Red on No. 158

1938 ***Perf. 14***

O40	A43	1p grn & blk	2.50	1.00

Nos. 204 and 205 Overprinted Type "d" in Black

1939 ***Perf. 13½x14, 14***

O41	A78	50c violet	4.00	2.50
O42	A84	1p org brn	5.00	4.00

Stamps of 1938-40 Overprinted Type "b" in Black, Red or Blue

1940-46 ***Perf. 13½x14, 14***

O43	A78	10c sal pink ('45)	2.00	1.75
O44	A78	15c brn org	1.00	.40
O45	A78	20c lt bl (R) ('42)	1.50	.60
O46	A78	30c brn pink (Bl)	.75	.40
O47	A78	40c lt grn	.75	.40
O48	A78	50c vio ('45)	4.00	.75
O49	A84	1p org brn ('42)	2.50	.75
O50	A84	1.80p dp bl (R) ('45)	10.00	6.00
O51	A84	2p car lake ('42)	2.00	1.25
		Nos. O43-O51 (9)	24.50	12.30

Overprint "b" in Black on Nos. 223, 225

Unwmk.

O58	A84	1p brn org	2.50	1.50
O59	A84	2p car lake ('46)	5.00	2.00

Regular Issues of 1938-43 Overprinted Diagonally in Carmine, Black or Blue — e

Wmk. 215, Unwmkd.

1948-54 ***Perf. 13½x14, 14***

O60	A78	20c lt bl, #219 (C)	.75	.35
O61	A78	30c brt pink, #202 (Bl) ('54)	1.50	.50
O62	A78	40c brt grn, #203 ('54)	2.50	1.25
O63	A78	50c vio #222 ('49)	.75	.40
O64	A84	1p org brn, #205	2.50	1.00
O65	A84	2p car lake, #207 ('54)	1.00	.50
O66	A84	5p dk sl grn, #208 (C) ('51)	1.75	1.00
		Nos. O60-O66 (7)	10.75	5.00

Overprint "e" Diagonally on Nos. 265 and 275 in Red or Black

Wmk. 215, Unwmkd.

1953-55 ***Perf. 13½x14, 13x14***

O67	A126	1p dk bl grn, #265 (R)	1.00	.50
O68	A126	1p dk bl grn, #265 (Bk) ('55)	.75	.50
O69	A126	1p dk bl grn, #275 (R) ('55)	.75	.50
		Nos. O67-O69 (3)	2.50	1.50

Overprint "e" Horizontally on Nos. 207, 209 in Black or Blue

1955-56 **Wmk. 215** ***Perf. 14***

O70	A84	2p car lake ('56)	1.75	.75
O71	A84	10p rose vio (Bl)	2.75	1.75

Overprint "e" Horizontally on Nos. 293-295 and Types of 1956 Regular Issue in Black or Red

1956 **Unwmk.** ***Perf. 14x14½***

O72	A141	2p purple	1.00	.60
O73	A142	3p lt vio bl (R)	3.00	2.00
O74	A141	5p redsh brn	.75	.35
O75	A142	10p vio (19x22¼mm) (R)	3.00	1.75
a.		Perf. 13½x14 (19½x22½mm) ('58)	.50	.40
O76	A141	50p rose red	2.50	1.00

No. 310 Overprinted in Red Vertically, Reading Down, Similar to Type "e"

Size of Overprint: 21x2½mm

1958 **Litho.** ***Perf. 14***

O77	A149	10p vio blue	*200.00*	*30.00*

Overprint "e" Horizontally on No. 327 in Red

1960 **Unwmk.** ***Perf. 13x14***

O79	A157	5c blue	1.75	.70

POSTAL TAX STAMPS

Talca Issue.

A 10c blue postal tax stamp, inscribed "Bicentenario de Talca" and picturing a coat of arms, was issued in 1942. It was sold only in Talca and was required for a time on all domestic letters sent from that city. The tax helped pay for Talca's bicentenary celebration. Value 20 cents.

Nos. 326 and 347 Surcharged

1970 Unwmk. Litho. *Perf. 14x13*

RA1	A159 10c on 2c ultra	.25	.25
	Perf. 14x14½		
RA2	A170 10c on 6c rose lil	.25	.25

Chilean Arms — PT1

Perf. 14½x14

1970, Apr. 23 Litho. Unwmk.

RA3	PT1 10c blue	.30	.25

See No. RA6.

No. RA3 Surcharged in Red

a

b

1971-72

RA4	PT1 (a) 15c on 10c bl	.30	.25
RA5	PT1 (b) 15c on 10c bl ('72)	.30	.25

Type of 1970

1972, July Litho. *Perf. 14½x14*

RA6	PT1 15c rose red	.30	.25

No. RA6 Surcharged In Ultramarine

1972-73

RA7	PT1 20c on 15c rose red	.30	.25
RA8	PT1 50c on 15c rose red ('73)	.30	.25

No. RA8 has 9 bars instead of 8.

The surtax on Nos. RA1-RA8 was for modernization of postal system. Compulsory on all inland mail.

PARCEL POST POSTAL TAX STAMP

Pres. J. J. Prieto V. — PPT1

Unwmk.

1957, Apr. 8 Litho. *Perf. 14*

QRA1	PPT1 15p green	.35	.30

The surtax aided the Prieto Foundation. No. QRA1 was required on parcel post entering or leaving Chile.

CHINA

'chī-nə

LOCATION — Eastern Asia
GOVT. — Republic
AREA — 2,903,475 sq. mi.
POP. — 462,798,093 (1948)

10 Candareen = 1 Mace
10 Mace = 1 Tael
100 Cents = 1 Dollar (Yuan) (1897)

Watermarks

Wmk. 103 — Yin-Yang Symbol

Wmk. 261 — Character Yu (Post) Multiple

Issues of the Imperial Maritime Customs Post

Imperial Dragon — A1

1878 Unwmk. Typo. *Perf. 12½*
Thin Paper
Stamps printed 2½-3¼mm apart

1	A1	1c green	600.00	500.00
a.		1c dark green	700.00	550.00
2	A1	3c brown red	700.00	400.00
a.		3c vermilion	850.00	450.00
3	A1	5c orange	800.00	375.00
a.		5c bister orange	1,100.	500.00

Imperforate essays of Nos. 1-3 have an extra circle near the dragon's lower left foot. Examples with the circle completely or mostly removed are proofs or unfinished stamps.

1882
Thin or Pelure Paper
Stamps printed 4½mm apart

4	A1	1c green	650.00	375.00
a.		1c dark green	750.00	400.00
5	A1	3c brown red	1,200.	350.00
6	A1	5c orange yellow	25,000.	1,400.

1883 *Rough to smooth Perf. 12½*
Medium to Thick Opaque Paper
Stamps printed 2½ to 3¼mm apart

7	A1	1c green	700.00	450.00
a.		1c dark green	800.00	500.00
b.		1c light green	850.00	525.00
c.		Vert. pair, imperf. between	*160,000.*	
8	A1	3c brown red	1,200.	475.00
a.		3c vermilion	1,500.	375.00
b.		Vert. pair, imperf. between		*230,000.*
9	A1	5c yellow	2,200.	600.00
a.		5c chrome yellow	2,500.	850.00
b.		Horiz. pair, imperf. btwn.		*60,000.*

Nos. 1-9 were printed from plates of 25, 20 or 15 individual copper dies, but only No. 5 exists in the 15-die setting. Many different printings and plate settings exist. All values occur in a wide variety of shades and papers. The effect of climate on certain papers has produced the varieties on so-called toned papers in Nos. 1-15.

Value for No. 8b is for a damaged example.

Counterfeits, frequently with forged cancellations, occur in all early Chinese issues.

Imperial Dragon — A2

1885 Wmk. 103 *Perf. 12½*

10	A2	1c green	175.00	90.00
a.		Vert. pair, imperf. btwn.	*20,000.*	*17,500.*
b.		Horiz. pair, imperf. btwn.		—
11	A2	3c lilac	400.00	120.00
a.		Horiz. pair, imperf. btwn.	*22,000.*	*17,500.*
b.		Vert. pair, imperf. btwn.		*24,000.*
12	A2	5c grnsh yellow	375.00	120.00
a.		5c bister brown	675.00	150.00
b.		Vert. pair, imperf. btwn.	*24,000.*	*24,000.*
c.		Horiz. pair, imperf. btwn.		*52,500.*
		Nos. 10-12 (3)	950.00	330.00

1888 *Perf. 11½-12*

13	A2	1c green	90.00	50.00
14	A2	3c lilac	250.00	90.00
b.		Double impression		*1,100.*
15	A2	5c grnsh yellow	450.00	140.00
b.		Horiz. pair, imperf. vert.		*50,000.*
c.		Double impression	1,100.	1,100.
		Nos. 13-15 (3)	790.00	280.00

Nos. 10-15 were printed from plates made of 40 individual copper dies, arranged in two panes of 20 each. Several different settings exist of all values.

Imperforates of Nos. 13-15 are considered proofs by most authorities.

Stamps overprinted "Formosa" in English or Chinese are proofs.

For surcharges see Nos. 25-27, 75-77.

"Shou" and "Wu Fu" — A3

Dragon and Hydrangea Leaves — A4

"Pa Kua" Signs in Corners — A5

Dragon and Peony — A6

Carp, the Messenger Fish — A7

Dragon, "Pa Kua" and Immortelle A8

Dragons and "Shou" A9

Dragons and Giant Peony — A10

Junk on the Yangtse A11

1894 Lithographed in Shanghai

16	A3	1c orange red	60.00	*47.50*
a.		Vert. pair, imperf. btwn.	*2,250.*	*2,100.*
b.		Horiz. pair, imperf. btwn.	*17,500.*	*12,000.*
c.		Vert. pair, imperf. horiz.	*3,250.*	*3,250.*
17	A4	2c green	65.00	45.00
a.		Horiz. pair, imperf. btwn.	*3,750.*	*3,500.*
18	A5	3c orange	57.50	37.50
a.		Vert. pair, imperf. btwn.	*3,350.*	*3,500.*
b.		Horiz. pair, imperf. btwn.	*5,000.*	*3,800.*
19	A6	4c rose pink	200.00	*250.00*
a.		Horiz. pair, imperf. btwn.	*14,000.*	
20	A7	5c dull orange	350.00	*400.00*
a.		Horiz. pair, imperf. btwn.	*18,000.*	*18,000.*
21	A8	6c dark brown	190.00	60.00
a.		Vert. pair, imperf. btwn.	*24,000.*	
b.		Horiz. pair, imperf. btwn.	*12,500.*	
22	A9	9c dark green	250.00	120.00
a.		Imperf., pair	*2,250.*	
b.		Horiz. pair, imperf. vert.	*4,250.*	*3,750.*
c.		Vert. pair, imperf. horiz.	*4,250.*	
d.		Vert. pair, imperf. btwn.	*4,750.*	*4,250.*
e.		Tete beche pair, vert.	*1,650.*	*1,400.*
f.		Tete beche pair, imperf. horiz.	*5,500.*	
g.		Tete beche pair, imperf. vert.	*5,500.*	*4,750.*
h.		Vert. strip of 3, imperf. btwn.	*5,500.*	
i.		Tete beche pair, horiz.	*1,500.*	*1,300.*
23	A10	12c orange	600.00	250.00
24	A11	24c carmine	775.00	200.00
a.		Vert. pair, imperf. btwn.	*30,000.*	
		Nos. 16-24 (9)	2,547.	1,410.

60th birthday of Tsz'e Hsi, the Empress Dowager. All values exist in several distinct shades.

On Mar. 20, 1896, the Customs Post was changed, by Imperial Edict, effective Jan. 1, 1897, to a National Post and the dollar was adopted as the unit of currency.

Time was required to work out details of the Imperial Post and design new stamps. As a provisional measure, stocks of Nos. 16-24 were ordered surcharged with new values in dollars and cents. It is believed that only the Shanghai office stock of Nos. 16-24 (plus any reserve stock at the printers) was surcharged with small figures of value. Other post offices throughout China were instructed to return all unoverprinted stocks on receipt of the new surcharges.

Early in the year it was apparent that all stamps would be exhausted before the new issues were ready (Nos. 86-97), and since the stones from which Nos. 16-24 had been printed no longer existed, new stones were made from the original transfers. A printing from the new stones was made early in 1897 and surcharged with large figures of value spaced 2½mm below the Chinese characters. During the surcharging, sheets from the 1894 (original) printing were received from outlying post offices and surcharged as they arrived. A small quantity of the 1897 printing reached the public without surcharge (Nos. 16n-24n).

Additional stamps were still required and another printing was made from the new stones and surcharged with large figures, but in a new setting with 1½mm between the Chinese characters and the value. Additional sheets of the 1894 printing were received from the most distant post offices and were also surcharged with the 1½mm setting. Thus there are four different sets of the large-figure surcharges. All these stamps were regularly issued but no attempt was made by the post office to separate printings. Some values are difficult to distinguish as to printing, particularly in used condition.

See No. 73. For surcharges see Nos. 28-72, 74.

1897 Lithographed in Shanghai

16n	A3	1c pink	*1,200.*
17n	A4	2c olive green	*1,200.*
18n	A5	3c chrome yellow	*825.00*
p.		3c yellow buff	*1,000.*
19n	A6	4c pale rose	*875.00*
20n	A7	5c yellow	*975.00*
21n	A8	6c red brown	*1,000.*
22n	A9	9c yellowish green	*3,750.*
p.		9c emerald green	—
23n	A10	12c yellowish orange	*5,750.*
24n	A11	24c purplish red	*3,750.*

The colors of the 1897 printings are pale or dull; the gum is thin and white. The 1894 printing has a thicker, yellowish gum.

The set of 9 values on thick unwatermarked paper is a special printing of 5,000 sets ordered by P. G. von Mollendorf, a Customs official, for presentation purposes. Value, set $2,400.

For surcharges see Nos. 47-55, 65-72.

Issues of the Chinese Government Post

Preceding Issues Surcharged in Black

Small Numerals 2½mm Below Chinese Characters
Surcharged on Nos. 13-15

1897, Jan. 2 *Perf. 11½-12*

25	A2	1c on 1c	72.50	*85.00*
26	A2	2c on 3c	300.00	120.00
a.		Double surcharge	—	
27	A2	5c on 5c	100.00	57.50
		Nos. 25-27 (3)	472.50	262.50

Surcharged on Nos. 16-24

28	A5	½c on 3c	45.00	32.50
a.		"1" instead of "½"	350.00	350.00
b.		Horiz. pair, imperf. btwn.	*5,000.*	
c.		Vert. pair, imperf. horiz.	*5,000.*	*3,000.*
d.		Double surcharge	*12,000.*	*11,000.*
e.		Vert. pair, imperf. btwn.	*5,000.*	
29	A3	1c on 1c	27.50	25.00
a.		Inverted surcharge	*25,000.*	*5,250.*
30	A4	2c on 2c	32.50	22.50
a.		Horiz. pair, imperf. vert.	*4,000.*	
b.		Vert. pair, imperf. btwn.	*4,000.*	
c.		Double surcharge	*14,000.*	
d.		Inverted surcharge	—	*15,000.*
e.		Horiz. pair, imperf. btwn.	*2,000.*	
31	A6	4c on 4c	35.00	27.50
a.		Double surcharge	*30,000.*	*20,000.*
b.		Vert. pair, imperf. btwn.	*5,000.*	*5,000.*
c.		Horiz. pair, imperf. btwn.	*5,000.*	*5,000.*
32	A7	5c on 5c	42.50	19.00
a.		Vert. pair, imperf. btwn.	*15,000.*	*10,000.*
33	A8	8c on 6c	52.50	35.00
a.		Vert. pair, imperf. btwn.	*2,750.*	*2,250.*
b.		Vert. strip of 3, imperf. btwn.	*4,200.*	*2,100.*
c.		Horiz. pair, imperf. btwn.	*2,500.*	*2,500.*
34	A8	10c on 6c	87.50	70.00
b.		Vert. pair, imperf. btwn.	*7,500.*	*2,500.*
c.		Horiz. pair, imperf. vert.	*2,400.*	*2,400.*
35	A9	10c on 9c	450.00	175.00
a.		Double surcharge	*40,000.*	*40,000.*
b.		Inverted surcharge	*450,000.*	—
36	A10	10c on 12c	425.00	175.00
a.		Vert. pair, imperf. horiz.	*2,000.*	
b.		Vert. pair, imperf. btwn.	*2,200.*	*2,200.*
37	A11	30c on 24c	575.00	225.00
a.		Vert. pair, imperf. btwn.	*7,500.*	
		Nos. 28-37 (10)	1,772.	806.50

Small Numerals 4mm Below Chinese Characters

25a	A2	1c on 1c green	75.00	*85.00*
28f	A4	½c on 3c orange	60.00	60.00
29b	A3	1c on 1c vermilion	75.00	75.00
30f	A4	2c on 2c dark green	55.00	55.00
31d	A6	4c on 4c dark pink	55.00	55.00
32b	A7	5c on 5c dull orange	55.00	55.00
33d	A8	8c on 6c brown	55.00	37.50
35c	A9	10c on 9c dark green	425.00	350.00
37b	A11	30c on 24c dark red	500.00	500.00

Preceding Issues Surcharged in Black

Large Numerals
Numerals 2½mm below Chinese characters
Surcharged on Nos. 16-24

1897, Mar.

38	A5	½c on 3c	2,500.	850.00
b.		Inverted surcharge		*10,000.*
39	A3	1c on 1c	700.00	200.00
40	A4	2c on 2c	375.00	350.00
41	A6	4c on 4c	475.00	375.00
b.		Horiz. pair, imperf. btwn.	*11,000.*	
42	A7	5c on 5c	225.00	200.00
43	A8	8c on 6c	2,250.	1,750.
44	A9	10c on 9c	800.00	375.00
45	A10	10c on 12c	*35,000.*	2,750.
46	A11	30c on 24c	1,200.	*1,300.*
b.		2mm spacing between "30" and "cents."	*15,000.*	

Same Surcharge on Nos. 16n-24n

47	A5	½c on 3c	32.50	*40.00*
a.		"cen" for "cent"	850.00	850.00
b.		Vert. pair, imperf. btwn.	*2,100.*	*2,100.*
c.		Vert. pair, imperf. horiz.	1,750.	1,250.
d.		As "a" and "c"	*9,500.*	*9,500.*
e.		As "a" and "b"	*7,500.*	*7,500.*
f.		Horiz. pair, imperf. btwn.	*1,900.*	*1,900.*
48	A3	1c on 1c	27.50	22.50
a.		Horiz. pair, imperf. btwn.		*2,500.*
49	A4	2c on 2c	25.00	17.50
50	A6	4c on 4c	35.00	25.00
a.		Horiz. pair, imperf. btwn.	*3,250.*	*3,250.*
b.		Vert. pair, imperf. btwn.		*4,000.*
51	A7	5c on 5c	47.50	27.50
52	A8	8c on 6c	525.00	300.00
53	A9	10c on 9c	200.00	85.00
a.		10c on 9c emerald	210.00	87.50
b.		Pair, one without surcharge	1,100.	

54 A10 10c on 12c 375.00 90.00
55 A11 30c on 24c 750.00 325.00
a. 2mm spacing btwn "30" and "cents" *1,250.* 750.00
b. Vert. pair, imperf. btwn. *6,250.*

All recorded unused examples of No. 45 are flawed.

Numerals 1½mm below Chinese characters

1897, May

Surcharged on Nos. 16-24

56 A5 ½c on 3c org yel 500.00 425.00
57 A3 1c on 1c 350.00 275.00
58 A4 2c on 2c — *3,500.*
59 A6 4c on 4c 300.00 225.00
60 A7 5c on 5c 175.00 160.00
61 A8 8c on 6c 1,600. 1,350.
62 A9 10c on 9c 350.00 250.00
63 A10 10c on 12c 1,500. 1,100.
64 A11 30c on 24c *65,000.* —

Same Surcharge on Nos. 16n-24n

65 A5 ½c on 3c 25.00 *27.50*
a. Inverted surcharge *3,000.* 3,000.
b. ½mm spacing *1,500.* *1,200.*
66 A3 1c on 1c 27.50 22.50
67 A4 2c on 2c 30.00 25.00
a. Inverted surcharge *25,500.* *8,750.*
b. Vert. pair, imperf. btwn. *8,500.*
68 A6 4c on 4c 300.00 160.00
a. Inverted surcharge 2,500. 1,500.
69 A7 5c on 5c 300.00 140.00
70 A9 10c on 9c 210.00 95.00
a. Inverted surcharge 1,350. 1,100.
71 A10 10c on 12c 375.00 110.00
72 A11 30c on 24c *13,000.* 2,600.

Same Surcharge (1½mm Spacing) on Type A12, and

A12

A12a

Redrawn Designs Printed from New Stones

1897

73 A12 ½c on 3c yel 250.00 200.00
a. ½mm spacing *7,000.* *5,000.*
74 A12a 2c on 2c yel grn 60.00 45.00
a. Horiz. pair, imperf. btwn. *6,000.*

Nos. 73 and 74 were surcharged on stamps printed from new stones, which differ slightly from the originals. On No. 73 the numeral "3" and symbols in the four corner panels have been enlarged and strengthened. On No. 74, the numeral "2" has a thick, flat base.

Surcharged on Nos. 13-15

75 A2 1c on 1c green 500.00 *625.00*
76 A2 2c on 3c lilac 1,000. *1,000.*
77 A2 5c on 5c grnsh yel 350.00 *500.00*

Revenue Stamps Surcharged in Black

A13

a

b

c

d

e

f

g

1897 Unwmk. *Perf. 12 to 15*

78 A13 (a) 1c on 3c red 450.00 275.00
a. No period after "cent" 500.00 350.00
b. Central character with large "box" 525.00 525.00
79 A13 (b) 2c on 3c red 750.00 400.00
a. Inverted surcharge *25,000.* *12,000.*
b. Inverted "S" in "CENTS" 900.00 575.00
c. No period after "CENTS" 900.00 575.00
d. Comma after "CENTS" 850.00 500.00
e. Double surcharge *25,000.* *25,000.*
f. Dbl. surch., both inverted *50,000*
g. Double surch. (blk & grn) *220,000.*
80 A13 (c) 2c on 3c red 525.00 350.00
81 A13 (d) 4c on 3c red *100,000.* *75,000.*
a. Double surcharge (blk & vio) *250,000.* *250,000.*
82 A13 (e) 4c on 3c red 1,650. 600.00
83 A13 (f) $1 on 3c red *900,000.* —
a. No period after "r" —
84 A13 (g) $1 on 3c red 9,000. 3,500.
85 A13 (g) $5 on 3c red 90,000. 40,000.
a. Inverted surcharge *110,000.* *45,000.*

A few examples of the 3c red exist without surcharge; one canceled. Value, unused $60,000. No. 79 with green surcharge is a trial printing. Value for faulty upper left corner block, $190,000.

No. 79g is unique. The only canceled example of No. 83 is in a museum.

Dragon — A14

Carp — A15

Wild Goose — A16

"Imperial Chinese Post" Lithographed in Japan

Perf. 11, 11½, 12

1897, Aug. 16 Wmk. 103

86 A14 ½c purple brn 5.50 4.50
a. Horiz. pair, imperf. btwn. 650.00
87 A14 1c yellow 6.50 4.00
88 A14 2c orange 5.75 3.75
a. Vert. pair, imperf. horiz. 900.00
89 A14 4c brown 10.50 3.75
a. Horiz. pair, imperf. btwn. 1,000.
90 A14 5c rose red 12.00 3.75
91 A14 10c dk green 40.00 3.75
92 A15 20c maroon 85.00 17.50
93 A15 30c red 140.00 32.50
94 A15 50c yellow grn 100.00 45.00
a. 50c black green 1,150.
b. 50c blue green 1,300.
95 A16 $1 car & rose 275.00 200.00
a. Horiz. pair, imperf. vert. —
96 A16 $2 orange & yel 2,000. 1,200.
a. Horiz. pair, imperf. vert. —
97 A16 $5 yel grn & pink 1,500. 900.00

The inner circular frames and outer frames of Nos. 86-91 differ for each denomination.

No. 97 imperforate was not regularly issued. **Examples have been privately perforated and offered as No. 97.** Shades occur in most values of this issue.

A17

A18

A19

"Chinese Imperial Post" Engraved in London

1898 Wmk. 103 *Perf. 12 to 16*

98 A17 ½c chocolate 6.00 2.75
a. Vert. pair, imperf. btwn. 850.00 475.00
b. Vert. pair, imperf. horiz. 850.00 475.00
99 A17 1c ocher 6.50 2.75
a. Vert. pair, imperf. btwn. 300.00 250.00
b. Horiz. pair, imperf. btwn. 400.00 350.00
100 A17 2c scarlet 7.25 2.75
a. Vert. pair, imperf. btwn. 400.00 200.00
b. Horiz. pair, imperf. vert. 400.00 200.00
101 A17 4c orange brn 7.50 2.75
a. Vert. pair, imperf. btwn. 575.00
b. Horiz. pair, imperf. vert. 400.00 300.00
c. Horiz. pair, imperf. btwn. 700.00 600.00
d. Horiz. strip of 3, imperf. btwn. 2,250. 1,500.
102 A17 5c salmon 11.00 4.75
a. Vert. pair, imperf. btwn. 400.00 300.00
b. Horiz. pair, imperf. btwn. 775.00 500.00
c. Vert. pair, imperf. horiz. 600.00 500.00
d. 5c pale reddish orange 16.00 5.50
e. As "d," vert pair, imperf. btwn. 600.00 500.00
103 A17 10c dk blue grn 17.50 3.00
a. Vert. or horiz, pair, imperf. btwn — —
104 A18 20c claret 70.00 9.00
a. Horiz. pair, imperf. btwn. 850.00 750.00
b. Vert. pair, imperf. horiz. 850.00 750.00
c. Vert. pair, imperf. btwn. 900.00 800.00
105 A18 30c dull rose 60.00 14.00
a. Horiz. pair, imperf. btwn. *2,000.*
b. Vert. pair, imperf. horiz. *1,750.*
c. Vert. pair, imperf. btwn. *1,750.*
106 A18 50c lt green 85.00 19.00
a. Vert. pair, imperf. btwn. *2,250.*
107 A19 $1 red & pale rose 325.00 45.00
108 A19 $2 brn, red & yel 550.00 85.00
109 A19 $5 dp grn & sal 900.00 275.00
a. Horiz. pair, imperf. btwn. *77,500.*
b. Vert. pair, imperf. btwn. *8,500.*
Nos. 98-109 (12) 2,045. 465.75

No. 98 surcharged "B. R. A.-5-Five Cents" in three lines in black or green, was surcharged by British military authorities shortly after the Boxer riots for use from military posts in an occupied area along the Peking-Mukden railway. Usually canceled in violet.

See note following No. 122.

1900(?)-06 Unwmk. *Perf. 12 to 16*

110 A17 ½c brown 4.00 2.75
a. Horiz. pair, imperf. btwn. 400.00 400.00
b. Vert. pair, imperf. btwn. 400.00 400.00
111 A17 1c ocher 4.00 2.75
a. Horiz. pair, imperf. btwn. 350.00 350.00
b. Vert. pair, imperf. btwn. 350.00 350.00
c. Vert. pair, imperf. horiz. 350.00 350.00
112 A17 2c scarlet 5.25 2.75
a. Horiz. pair, imperf. btwn. 300.00 325.00
b. Vert. pair, imperf. btwn. 300.00 300.00
c. Vert. pair, imperf. horiz. 300.00 300.00
d. Horiz. pair, imperf. vert. 300.00 300.00
e. Vert. strip of 3, imperf. btwn. 1,250. 750.00
113 A17 4c orange brn 5.75 2.75
a. Horiz. pair, imperf. btwn. 300.00 300.00
b. Vert. pair, imperf. btwn. 300.00 300.00
114 A17 5c rose red 30.00 4.25
a. Vert. pair, imperf. btwn. 300.00 300.00
b. Vert. pair, imperf. horiz. 275.00 275.00
115 A17 5c orange 27.50 4.75
a. 5c yellow 200.00 27.50
b. Vert. pair, imperf. btwn. 475.00 475.00
c. Horiz. pair, imperf. btwn. 475.00 475.00
116 A17 10c green 20.00 2.75
a. Vert. pair, imperf. btwn. 425.00
b. Horiz. pair, imperf. btwn. 725.00
c. Vert. pair, imperf. horiz. 425.00
d. Vert. strip of 3, imperf. btwn. 700.00
117 A18 20c red brown 30.00 2.75
a. Horiz. pair, imperf. btwn. 600.00
b. Vert. pair, imperf. btwn. 500.00
c. Vert. pair, imperf. horiz. 500.00
118 A18 30c dull red 30.00 2.75
a. Vert. pair, imperf. btwn. 850.00
119 A18 50c yellow grn 55.00 2.75
a. Horiz. pair, imperf. btwn. 1,000.
120 A19 $1 red & pale rose ('06) 175.00 27.50
121 A19 $2 brn red & yel ('06) 375.00 60.00
122 A19 $5 dp grn & sal 600.00 240.00
Nos. 110-122 (13) 1,361. 358.50

See No. 124-130. For surcharges and overprints see Nos. 123, 134-177, J1-J6, Offices in Tibet 1-11.

Diagonal Half of No. 112 Surcharged on Stamp and Envelope

1903

123 A17 1c on half of 2c scarlet, on cover *1,600.*

Used Oct. 22 to Oct. 24. Value is for cover mailed to post office other than sending office (Foochow) and bearing backstamp showing arrival date. Locally addressed or unaddressed covers without backstamps properly used are worth approximately $1,000. Others are worth less.

Forgeries are plentiful, particularly on pieces of cover. Certificates of authenticity are mandatory.

1905-10

124 A17 2c green ('08) 3.00 2.50
a. Horiz. pair, imperf. btwn. 325.00 325.00
b. Vert. pair, imperf. btwn. 325.00 325.00
c. Horiz. pair, imperf. vert. 325.00 325.00
d. Horiz. strip of 4, imperf. btwn. 725.00 725.00
125 A17 3c slate grn ('10) 5.00 2.50
a. Horiz. pair, imperf. btwn. 250.00
b. Vert. pair, imperf. btwn. 250.00
126 A17 4c vermilion ('09) 6.00 2.25
127 A17 5c violet 7.50 2.50
a. 5c lilac 8.50 2.50
b. Horiz. pair, imperf. btwn. 450.00
c. Vert. pair, imperf. btwn. 1,000.
d. Vert. pair, imperf. horiz. 500.00
128 A17 7c maroon ('10) 16.00 8.75
129 A17 10c ultra ('08) 21.00 2.75
a. Horiz. pair, imperf. btwn. 400.00
b. Vert. pair, imperf. btwn. 400.00
c. Vert. pair, imperf. horiz. 400.00 400.00
130 A18 16c olive grn ('07) 60.00 17.50
Nos. 124-130 (7) 118.50 38.75

Temple of Heaven, Peking — A20

1909 *Perf. 14*

131 A20 2c orange & green 9.00 *8.00*
132 A20 3c orange & blue 12.00 *21.00*
133 A20 7c orange & brn vio 17.50 12.00
Nos. 131-133 (3) 38.50 *41.00*

1st year of the reign of Hsuan T'ung, who later became Henry Pu-yi and then Emperor Kang Teh of Manchukuo.

Stamps of 1902-10 Overprinted with Chinese Characters

Foochow Issue

Overprinted in Red or Black

1912 *Perf. 12 to 16*

134 A17 3c slate grn (R) 300. 160.
135 A19 $1 red & pale rose 2,900. 2,500.
136 A19 $2 brn red & yel 4,400. 3,500.
137 A19 $5 dp grn & sal 5,750. 4,000.

The overprint "Ling Shih Chung Li" or "Provisional Neutrality," signified that the P.O. was conducted neutrally by agreement between the Manchu and opposing forces.

Nanking Issue

Overprinted in Red or Black

138 A17 1c ocher (R) 275. 175.
139 A17 3c slate grn (R) 275. 175.
140 A17 7c maroon 500. 375.
141 A18 16c olive grn (R) 2,750. 2,500.
142 A18 50c yellow grn (R) 3,500. 2,250.
143 A19 $1 red & pale rose 3,750. 1,800.
144 A19 $2 brn red & yel 5,500. 4,400.
145 A19 $5 dp green & sal 12,750. 10,000.

Vertical overprint reads: "Chung Hwa Min Kuo" (Republic of China).

Stamps of this issue were also used in Shanghai and Hankow.

Additional values were overprinted but not issued. Excellent forgeries of the overprints of Nos. 134-145 exist.

Issues of the Republic

Overprinted in Black or Red

Overprinted by the Maritime Customs Statistical Department, Shanghai

146 A17 ½c brown 1.50 1.25
a. Inverted overprint 50.00 50.00
b. Double overprint 100.00
147 A17 1c ocher (R) 2.25 1.25
a. Vert. pair, imperf. horiz. 200.00 200.00
b. Inverted overprint 175.00 125.00
c. Double overprint 200.00 175.00
d. Horiz. pair, imperf. btwn. 300.00 250.00
e. Horiz. pair, imperf. vert. 175.00
f. Pair, one without overprint 175.00
148 A17 2c green (R) 2.50 1.75
a. Vert. pair, imperf. btwn. 350.00 300.00
149 A17 3c slate grn (R) 3.00 1.50
a. Inverted overprint 125.00 75.00
b. Horiz.. pair, imperf. btwn. 300.00 300.00
c. Vert. pair, imperf btwn. 300.00 300.00
d. Horiz. pair, imperf. vert. 125.00
e. Horiz. strip of 3, imperf btwn. 450.00
f. Horiz. strip of 5, imperf btwn. 975.00
150 A17 4c vermilion 4.75 1.75
a. Vert. pair, imperf. btwn. 800.00
151 A17 5c violet (R) 6.25 1.75
a. Horiz. pair, imperf. btwn.
152 A17 7c maroon 8.25 3.50
153 A17 10c ultra (R) 8.50 1.75
a. Double overprint 250.00
b. Pair, one without overprint 900.00
c. Brownish red overprint 22.50 9.00
d. Inverted overprint 275.00 275.00
154 A18 16c olive grn (R) 22.50 8.50
155 A18 20c red brown 19.00 5.00
156 A18 30c rose red 24.00 6.00
157 A18 50c yel grn (R) 40.00 6.00
158 A19 $1 red & pale rose 400.00 35.00
a. Inverted overprint *27,500.*
159 A19 $2 brn red & yel 275.00 70.00
a. Inverted overprint 600.00 600.00
160 A19 $5 dp grn & sal 650.00 500.00
Nos. 146-160 (15) 1,467. 645.00

Stamps with blue overprint similar to the preceding were not an official issue but were privately made by a printer in Tientsin.

Overprinted in Red

Overprinted by the Commercial Press, Shanghai

This type differs in that the top character is shifted slightly to right and the bottom character is larger and has small "legs".

161 A17 1c ocher 6.00 1.25
a. Inverted overprint 375.00 375.00
b. Vert. pair, imperf. btwn. 450.00
c. Double overprint 450.00
162 A17 2c green 34.00 2.25
a. Inverted overprint 1,100. 900.00
b. Vert. pair, imperf. btwn. 260.00
c. Horiz. pair, imperf. btwn. 300.00
d. Horiz. strip of 3, imperf. btwn. 475.00

Overprinted in Blue, Carmine or Black

Overprinted by Waterlow & Sons, London

163 A17 ½c brown (Bl) 1.75 1.25
a. Vert. pair, imperf. btwn. 1,400. 1,275.
164 A17 1c ocher (C) 1.75 1.25
a. Horiz. pair, imperf. btwn. 825.00
165 A17 2c green (C) 3.25 1.40
166 A17 3c slate grn (C) 3.75 1.50
a. Inverted overprint 1,750.
167 A17 4c vermilion (Bk) 5.00 1.75
168 A17 5c violet (C) 11.00 1.60
169 A17 7c maroon (Bk) 35.00 *37.50*
170 A17 10c ultra (C) 17.50 2.75
a. Vert. pair, imperf. btwn. 1,500. *2,600.*
171 A18 16c olive grn (R) 50.00 19.00
172 A18 20c red brn (Bk) 32.50 3.50
173 A18 30c dull red (Bk) 100.00 6.75
174 A18 50c yellow grn (R) 150.00 17.50
175 A19 $1 red & pale rose (Bk) 225.00 20.00
176 A19 $2 brn red & yel (Bk) 475.00 225.00
177 A19 $5 dp grn & sal (C) 750.00 525.00
Nos. 163-177 (15) 1,861. 865.75

Due to instructions issued to postmasters throughout China at the time of the Revolution, a number of them prepared unauthorized overprints using the same characters as the overprints prepared by the government. While many were made in good faith, some, like the blue overprints from Tientsin, were bogus, and the status of certain others is extremely dubious.

Dr. Sun Yat-sen — A21

1912, Dec. 14 *Perf. 14½*

178 A21 1c orange 4.75 *3.25*
179 A21 2c yellow grn 4.75 *3.25*
180 A21 3c slate grn 4.75 *3.25*
181 A21 5c rose lilac 9.50 3.25
182 A21 8c dp brown 9.50 5.00
183 A21 10c dull blue 9.50 5.00
184 A21 16c olive grn 27.50 17.50
185 A21 20c maroon 37.50 10.00
186 A21 50c dk green 100.00 40.00
187 A21 $1 brown red 260.00 60.00
188 A21 $2 yellow brn 750.00 300.00
189 A21 $5 gray 275.00 *225.00*
Nos. 178-189 (12) 1,492. 675.50

Honoring the leader of the Revolution.

President Yuan Shih-kai — A22

1912, Dec. 14

190 A22 1c orange 2.75 1.75
191 A22 2c yellow green 2.75 1.75
192 A22 3c slate green 2.75 1.75
193 A22 5c rose lilac 3.75 2.00
194 A22 8c deep brown 11.50 4.00
195 A22 10c dull blue 9.50 2.50
196 A22 16c olive green 10.00 *12.00*
197 A22 20c maroon 9.00 *10.00*
198 A22 50c dark green 55.00 *35.00*
199 A22 $1 brown red 160.00 55.00
200 A22 $2 yellow brown 200.00 65.00
201 A22 $5 gray 600.00 290.00
Nos. 190-201 (12) 1,067. 480.75

Honoring the 1st pres. of the Republic.

Junk — A24

Reaping Rice — A25

Gateway, Hall of Classics, Peking — A26

DESIGN A24

London Printing: Vertical shading lines under top panel fine, junk with clear diagonal shading lines on sails, right pennant of junk usually long, lines in water weak except directly under junk.

Peking Printing: Vertical shading lines under top panel and inner vertical frame line much heavier, water and sails of junk more evenly and strongly colored, white wave over "H" of "CHINA" pointed upward, touching the junk.

DESIGN A25

London: Front hat brim thick and nearly straight, left foot touches shadow.

Peking: Front hat brim thin and strongly upturned, left foot and sickle clearly outlined in white, shadow of middle tree lighter than those of the right and left trees.

DESIGN A26

London: Light colored walk clearly defined almost to the doorway, figure in right doorway "T" shaped with strong horizontal cross-bar, white panel in base of central tower rectangular, vertical stroke in top left character uniformly thick at its base, tree to right of doorway ends in minute dots.

Peking: Walk more heavily shaded near doorway, especially at right; figure in right doorway more like a "Y", white panel at base of central tower is a long oval, right vertical stroke in top left character incurved near its base, tree at right has five prominent dots at top.

London Printing: By Waterlow & Sons, London, perf. 14 to 15.

Peking Printing: By the Chinese Bureau of Engraving and Printing, Peking, perf. 14.

London Printing

1913, May 5 *Perf. 14-15*

202 A24 ½c black brn .75 .40
a. Horiz. or vert. pair, imperf. btwn. 200.00
203 A24 1c orange .75 .40
a. Horiz. pair, imperf. btwn. 250.00
b. Vert. pair, imperf. btwn. 175.00
c. Horiz. strip of 5, imperf. btwn 650.00
204 A24 2c yellow grn 2.75 .40
a. Horiz. pair, imperf. btwn. 400.00
205 A24 3c blue grn 6.75 .45
a. Horiz. pair, imperf. btwn. 200.00
b. Vert. pair, imperf. btwn. 400.00
206 A24 4c scarlet 9.50 .70
207 A24 5c rose lilac 30.00 .60
208 A24 6c gray 5.00 .90
209 A24 7c violet 22.50 8.75
210 A24 8c brown org 42.50 2.50
211 A24 10c dk blue 37.50 1.10
a. Horiz. pair, imperf. btwn. 375.00 375.00
b. Vert. pair, imperf. btwn. 400.00 300.00
212 A25 15c brown 32.50 5.75
213 A25 16c olive grn 17.50 2.25
214 A25 20c brown red 30.00 2.75
215 A25 30c brown vio 32.50 2.00
a. Horiz. pair, imperf. btwn. 400.00 400.00
216 A25 50c green 60.00 3.50
217 A26 $1 ocher & blk 150.00 5.00
218 A26 $2 blue & blk 275.00 17.50
219 A26 $5 scarlet & blk 425.00 125.00
220 A26 $10 yel grn & blk 1,375. 925.00
Nos. 202-220 (19) 2,555. 1,104.

First Peking Printing

1915 *Perf. 14*

221 A24 ½c black brn .80 .35
222 A24 1c orange .80 .35
223 A24 2c yellow grn 1.60 .35
224 A24 3c blue grn 1.75 .35
225 A24 4c scarlet 20.00 .35
226 A24 5c rose lilac 8.50 .35
a. Booklet pane of 4 140.00
227 A24 6c gray 16.00 .35
228 A24 7c violet 25.00 4.50
229 A24 8c brown org 14.00 .40
230 A24 10c dk blue 15.00 .70
a. Booklet pane of 4 140.00
231 A25 15c brown 42.50 4.50
232 A25 16c olive grn 17.50 .70
233 A25 20c brown red 18.50 .70
234 A25 30c brown vio 17.50 .70
235 A25 50c green 42.50 .80
236 A26 $1 ocher & blk 140.00 .85
237 A26 $2 blue & blk 350.00 5.00
a. Center inverted *200,000.* —
238 A26 $5 scarlet & blk 800.00 30.00
239 A26 $10 yel grn & blk 1,300. 250.00
Nos. 221-239 (19) 2,831. 301.30

1919

240	A24	1½c violet	3.75	.60
241	A25	13c brown	9.50	.70
242	A26	$20 yellow & blk	4,900.	3,250.

Nos. 226 and 230 overprinted in red with five characters in vertical column were for postal savings use.

The higher values of the 1913-19 issues are often overprinted with Chinese characters, which are the names of various postal districts. Stamps were frequently stolen while in transit to post offices. The overprints served to protect them, since the stamps could only be used in the districts for which they were overprinted.

Compare designs A24-A26 with designs A29-A31. For surcharges and overprints see Nos. 247, 288, B1-B3, Sinkiang 1-38.

Yeh Kung-cho, Hsu Shi-chang and Chin Yun-peng A27

1921, Oct. 10

243	A27	1c orange	6.00	1.75
244	A27	3c blue green	6.50	1.50
245	A27	6c gray	7.50	5.00
246	A27	10c blue	8.50	4.00
		Nos. 243-246 (4)	28.50	12.25

National Post Office, 25th anniversary.
For overprints see Sinkiang Nos. 39-42.

No. 224 Surcharged in Red

1922

247	A24	2c on 3c blue green	3.50	.70
a.		Inverted surcharge	*175,000.*	—

Second Peking Printing

A29

A30

A31

Types of 1913-19 Issues Re-engraved

Type A29: Most of the whitecaps in front of the junk have been removed and the water made darker. The shading lines have been removed from the arabesques and pearls above the top inscription. The inner shadings at the top and sides of the picture have been cut away.

Type A30: The heads of rice in the side panels have a background of crossed lines instead of horizontal lines. The Temple of Heaven is strongly shaded and has a door. There are rows of pearls below the Chinese characters in the upper corners. The arabesques above the top inscription have been altered and are without shading lines.

Type A31: The curved line under the inscription at top is single instead of double. There are four vertical lines, instead of eight, at each side of the picture. The trees at the sides of the temple had foliage in the 1913-19 issues, but now the branches are bare. There are numerous other alterations in the design.

1923 ***Perf. 14***

248	A29	½c black brown	1.75	.30
a.		Horiz. pair, imperf. btwn.	175.00	175.00
b.		Horiz. pair, imperf. vert.	150.00	150.00
249	A29	1c orange	1.00	.30
a.		Imperf., pair	125.00	
b.		Horiz. pair, imperf. vert.	125.00	
c.		Booklet pane of 6	90.00	
d.		Booklet pane of 4	45.00	
250	A29	1½c violet	3.50	.90
251	A29	2c yellow grn	2.00	.30
252	A29	3c blue green	6.00	.30
a.		Booklet pane of 6	80.00	
253	A29	4c gray	27.50	.80
254	A29	5c claret	4.00	.50
a.		Booklet pane of 4	100.00	
255	A29	6c scarlet	8.50	.50
256	A29	7c violet	8.50	.50
257	A29	8c orange	17.50	.50
258	A29	10c blue	14.50	.30
a.		Booklet pane of 6	120.00	
b.		Booklet pane of 2	150.00	
259	A30	13c brown	32.50	.60
260	A30	15c dp blue	10.00	.60
261	A30	16c olive grn	11.00	.60
262	A30	20c brown red	8.50	.40
263	A30	30c purple	32.50	.40
264	A30	50c dp green	60.00	.55
265	A31	$1 org brn & sep	65.00	.65
266	A31	$2 blue & red brn	85.00	1.00
267	A31	$5 red & slate	140.00	4.25
268	A31	$10 green & claret	675.00	65.00
269	A31	$20 plum & blue	1,300.	175.00
		Nos. 248-269 (22)	2,514.	254.25

Nos. 249 and 275 exist with webbing watermark from experimental printing.

To prevent speculation and theft, the dollar denominations were overprinted with single characters in red for use in Kwangsi ($1-$20) and Kweichow ($1-$5).

See Nos. 275, 324. For surcharges and overprints see Nos. 274, 289, 311, 325, 330, 339-340, Szechwan 1-3, Yunnan 1-20, Manchuria 1-20, Sinkiang 47-69, 114, C1-C4.

Temple of Heaven, Peking — A32

1923, Oct. 17 ***Perf. 14***

270	A32	1c orange	5.00	1.00
271	A32	3c blue green	5.50	2.25
272	A32	4c red	10.50	2.50
273	A32	10c blue	16.50	3.50
		Nos. 270-273 (4)	37.50	9.25

Adoption of Constitution, October, 1923.
For overprints see Sinkiang Nos. 43-46.

No. 253 Surcharged in Red

1925

274	A29	3c on 4c gray	3.50	.35
a.		Inverted surcharge	*300,000.*	*275,000.*
b.		Vert. pair, imperf. btwn.		

Junk Type of 1923

1926

275	A29	4c olive green	1.60	.25
a.		Horiz. pair, imperf. vert.	200.00	
b.		Horiz. pair, imperf. btwn.	200.00	
c.		Horiz. strip of 3, imperf. btwn.	250.00	

Marshal Chang Tso-lin — A34

1928, Mar. 1 ***Perf. 14***

276	A34	1c brown orange	1.50	1.50
277	A34	4c olive green	3.00	3.00
278	A34	10c dull blue	7.50	5.50
279	A34	$1 red	60.00	*65.00*
		Nos. 276-279 (4)	72.00	75.00

Assumption of office by Marshal Chang Tso-lin. The stamps of this issue were only available for postage in the Provinces of Chihli and Shantung and at the Offices in Manchuria and Sinkiang.

For overprints see Manchuria Nos. 21-24, Sinkiang 70-73.

President Chiang Kai-shek — A35

1929, May

280	A35	1c brown orange	1.00	.40
281	A35	4c olive green	1.50	.75
282	A35	10c dark blue	12.50	1.50
283	A35	$1 dark red	75.00	55.00
		Nos. 280-283 (4)	90.00	57.65

Unification of China.
For overprints see Yunnan Nos. 21-24, Manchuria 25-28, Sinkiang 74-77.

Sun Yat-sen Mausoleum, Nanking — A36

1929, May 30 ***Perf. 14***

284	A36	1c brown orange	1.25	.75
285	A36	4c olive green	1.00	1.25
286	A36	10c dark blue	7.00	2.50
287	A36	$1 dark red	70.00	35.00
		Nos. 284-287 (4)	79.25	39.50

The transfer of Dr. Sun Yat-sen's remains from Peiping to the mausoleum at Nanking.
For overprints see Yunnan Nos. 25-28, Manchuria 29-32, Sinkiang 78-81.

Nos. 224 and 252 Surcharged in Red

1930

288	A24	1c on 3c blue green	1.25	*2.25*
289	A29	1c on 3c blue green	1.00	.40
a.		No period after "Ct"	18.00	18.00

See Nos. 311, 325, 330.

Dr. Sun Yat-sen — A37

Type I

Type II

Type I — Double-lined circle in the sun.
Type II — Heavy, single-lined circle in the sun.

Printed by De la Rue & Co., Ltd., London

Perf. 11½x12½, 12½x13, 12½, 13½

1931, Nov. 12 **Type I** **Engr.**

290	A37	1c orange	.55	.30
291	A37	2c olive green	.65	.40
292	A37	4c green	1.10	.30
293	A37	20c ultra	1.40	.30
294	A37	$1 org brn & dk brn	12.00	.50
295	A37	$2 blue & org brn	35.00	3.00
296	A37	$5 dull red & blk	50.00	5.00
		Nos. 290-296 (7)	100.70	9.80

1931-37 **Type II**

297	A37	2c olive grn	.45	.25
298	A37	4c green	.65	.25
299	A37	5c green ('33)	.40	.25
300	A37	15c dk green	4.25	1.25
301	A37	15c scarlet ('34)	.45	.25
302	A37	20c ultra ('37)	.85	.25
303	A37	25c ultra	.45	.65
304	A37	$1 org brn & dk brn	14.00	.50
305	A37	$2 blue & org brn	25.00	1.25
306	A37	$5 dull red & blk	47.50	5.00
		Nos. 297-306 (10)	94.00	9.90

Stamps issued prior to 1933 were printed by a wet-paper process, and owing to shrinkage such stamps are 1-1½mm narrower than the later dry-printed stamps.

Early printings are perf. 12½x13. Nos. 304, 305 and 306 were later perf. 11½x12½.

See Nos. 631-635. For surcharges and overprints see Nos. 341, 343, 678, 682, 684-685, 689-691, 768, 843, 1N1, 2N1-2N5, 2N57-2N59, 2N83-2N84, 2N101-2N103, 2N116, 2N124-2N126, 3N1-3N5, 4N1-4N5, 5N1-5N4, 6N1-6N5, 7N1-7N4, 7N54, 8N2-8N3, 8N43-8N44, 8N54, 8N57, 8N69-8N71, 8N85, 9N1-9N5, Taiwan 19, 21-22, Northeastern Provinces 44, Szechwan 4-11, Yunnan 29-44, Sinkiang 82-97.

"Nomads in the Desert" — A38

1932 **Unwmk.** ***Perf. 14***

307	A38	1c deep orange	29.00	29.00
308	A38	4c olive green	29.00	29.00
309	A38	5c claret	29.00	29.00
310	A38	10c deep blue	29.00	29.00
		Nos. 307-310 (4)	116.00	116.00

Northwest Scientific Expedition of Sven Hedin. A small quantity of this issue was sold at face at Peking and several other cities. The bulk of the issue was furnished to Hedin and sold at $5 (Chinese) a set for funds to finance the expedition.

No. 252 Surcharged in Black Like 288

1932

311	A29	1c on 3c blue green	2.50	1.10

Martyrs Issue

Teng Keng A39

Ch'en Ying-shih A40

Chu Chih-hsin A45

Sung Chiao-jen A46

Huang Hsing A47

Liao Chung-kai A48

1932-34 ***Perf. 14***

312	A39	½c black brown	.25	.25
313	A40	1c orange ('34)	.25	.25
314	A39	2½c rose lilac ('33)	.25	.25
315	A48	3c dp brown ('33)	.25	.25
316	A45	8c brown orange	.50	.30
317	A46	10c dull violet	.60	.30
318	A45	13c blue green	.65	.30
319	A46	17c brown olive	.55	.30
320	A47	20c brown red	1.10	.30
321	A48	30c brown violet	1.50	.30
322	A47	40c orange	1.40	.35
323	A40	50c green ('34)	5.00	.50
		Nos. 312-323 (12)	12.30	3.65

Perfs. 12 to 13 and compound and with secret marks are listed as Nos. 402-439. No. 316 re-drawn is No. 485.

For overprints and surcharge see Nos. 342, 472, 474, 478-479, 486-487, 490, 531-536, 539-541, 544-549, 616, 619, 622-624, 647-659, 662-663, 665, 669, 672, 698, 704, 711, 713-715, 720-721, 831, 846-847, 867, 870, 872, 881-882, J120-J121, 1N14-1N15, 1N59, 2N6-2N9, 2N32-2N56, 2N60, 2N76-2N82, 2N85, 2N87-2N90, 2N107-2N115, 2N118, 2N121-2N123, 3N6-3N10, 3N34-3N55, 3N59, 4N6-4N9, 4N39-4N64, 4N69, 5N5-5N8, 5N34-5N60, 5N65, 6N6-6N8, 6N35-6N61, 6N66, 7N5-7N7, 7N30-7N53, 7N55, 7N59, 8N1, 8N4, 8N28-8N42, 8N45, 8N47-8N50, 8N60-8N61, 8N68, 8N73, 8N76-8N79, 8N89, 8N97, 8N99-8N100, 8N103-8N104, 9N72-9N77, Taiwan 14-17, 20, 28A, 74, Northeastern Provinces 6-8, 11, Szechwan 12-23, Yunnan 49-60, Sinkiang 102-113, 140-161, 197.

Junk Type of 1923

1933 *Perf. 14*

324	A29	6c brown	20.00	1.25

No. 275 Surcharged in Red Like 288

1933

325	A29	1c on 4c olive green	1.75	.35
a.		No period after "Ct"	21.00	21.00

Tan Yuan-chang — A49

1933, Jan. 9

326	A49	2c olive green	2.50	1.25
327	A49	5c green	4.00	.40
328	A49	25c ultra	10.00	1.75
329	A49	$1 red	72.50	35.00
		Nos. 326-329 (4)	89.00	38.40

Tan Yuan-chang, more commonly known as Tan Yen-kai, a prominent statesman in China since the revolution of 1912 and Pres. of the Executive Dept. of the Natl. Government. Placed on sale Jan. 9, 1933, the date of the ceremony in celebration of the completion of the Tan Yuan-chang Memorial Hall and Tomb at Mukden.

For overprints see Yunnan Nos. 45-48, Sinkiang 98-101.

No. 251 Surcharged in Red Like 288

1935 *Perf. 14*

330	A29	1c on 2c yellow grn	2.50	.25

Emblem of New Life Movement A50

Four Virtues of New Life A51

Lighthouse — A52

1936, Jan. 1

331	A50	2c olive green	1.75	.75
332	A50	5c green	2.00	.25
333	A51	20c dark blue	6.00	.70
334	A52	$1 rose red	40.00	11.00
		Nos. 331-334 (4)	49.75	12.70

"New Life" movement.

Methods of Mail Transportation A53

Maritime Scene — A54

Shanghai General Post Office — A55

Ministry of Communications, Nanking — A56

1936, Oct. 10

335	A53	2c orange	3.00	.70
336	A54	5c green	1.50	.25
337	A55	25c blue	4.75	.45
338	A56	$1 dk carmine	27.50	8.50
		Nos. 335-338 (4)	36.75	9.90

Founding of the Chinese PO, 40th anniv.

Nos. 260 and 261 Surcharged in Red

1936, Oct. 11

339	A30	5c on 15c dp blue	1.75	.50
340	A30	5c on 16c olive grn	3.00	1.00

No. 298 Surcharged in Red

1937

341	A37	1c on 4c green, type II	1.25	.50
a.		Upper left character missing		

Nos. 322 and 303 Surcharged in Black or Red

1938 *Perf. 12½, 14*

342	A47	8c on 40c orange (Bk)	2.00	.75
343	A37	10c on 25c ultra (R)	1.75	.30

Dr. Sun Yat-sen — A57

Type I

Type II

Type III

Type I — Coat button half circle. Six lines of shading above head. Top frame partially shaded with vertical lines.

Type II — Coat button complete circle. Nine lines of shading above head. Top frame partially shaded with vertical lines.

Type III — Coat button complete circle. Nine lines of shading above head. Top frame line fully shaded with vertical lines.

Printed by the Chung Hwa Book Co.

Type I

1938 **Unwmk.** **Engr.** *Perf. 12½*

344	A57	$1 henna & dk brn	85.00	12.00
345	A57	$2 dp blue & org brn	17.50	4.25
346	A57	$5 red & grnsh blk	150.00	19.00
		Nos. 344-346 (3)	252.50	35.25

1939 **Type II**

347	A57	$1 henna & dk brn	16.00	1.00
348	A57	$2 dp blue & org brn	18.00	4.00

1939-43 **Type III**

349	A57	2c olive green	.25	.25
350	A57	3c dull claret	.25	.25
351	A57	5c green	.25	.25
352	A57	5c olive green	.25	.25
353	A57	8c olive green	.25	.25
354	A57	10c green	.25	.25
355	A57	15c scarlet	1.25	*2.25*
356	A57	15c dk vio brn ('43)	17.50	*32.50*
357	A57	16c olive gray	1.75	.45
358	A57	25c dk blue	.35	*.75*
359	A57	$1 henna & dk brn	2.00	.75
360	A57	$2 dp blue & org brn	4.50	.55
a.		Imperf., pair	275.00	
361	A57	$5 red & grnsh blk	2.75	.50
362	A57	$10 dk green & dull pur	17.50	2.25
363	A57	$20 rose lake & dk blue	60.00	50.00
		Nos. 349-363 (15)	109.10	*91.50*

Several values exist imperforate, but these were not regularly issued. No. 361 imperforate is printer's waste.

See Nos. 368-401, 506-524. For surcharges and overprints see Nos. 440-448, 473, 475-477, 480-481, 482-484, 489, 537-538, 615, 618, 620, 660-661, 664, 666-668, 673-676, 680-681, 686, 688, 699-703, 707-709, 717, 719, 830, J67-J68, M2, M11-M12, 1N2-1N13, 1N23-1N42, 1N57-1N58, 2N10-2N31, 2N61-2N75, 2N86, 2N91-2N93, 2N117, 2N119-2N120, 3N11-3N33, 3N56-3N58, 3N60-3N61, 4N10-4N38, 4N65-4N68, 4N70-4N71, 5N9-5N33, 5N61-5N64, 5N66-5N68, 6N9-6N34, 6N62-6N65, 6N67-6N69, 7N8-7N29, 7N56-7N58, 7N60-7N61, 8N5-8N27, 8N46, 8N51-8N53, 8N55-8N56, 8N58-8N59, 8N62-8N67, 8N72, 8N74-8N75, 8N80-8N84, 8N86-8N88, 8N90, 8N95-8N96, 8N98, 8N101-8N102, 8N105-8N106, 9N6-9N71, 9N97, 9N99, Taiwan 78, 84, Northeastern Provinces 9-10, Sinkiang 115-139, 174-188, 196, 198.

Chinese and American Flags and Map of China — A58

Printed by American Bank Note Co.

Frame Engr., Center Litho.

1939, July 4 **Unwmk.** *Perf. 12*

Flag in Deep Rose and Ultramarine

364	A58	5c dark green	1.75	.50
365	A58	25c deep blue	1.75	.90
366	A58	50c brown	4.00	1.10
367	A58	$1 rose carmine	6.50	2.25
		Nos. 364-367 (4)	14.00	4.75

150th anniv. of the US Constitution.

Type of 1939-41 Re-engraved

2c, 1939-41

Re-engraved

8c, 1939-41

Re-engraved

1940 *Perf. 12½*

368	A57	2c olive green	.25	.25
369	A57	8c olive green	.25	.25

Type of 1938-41

Type III

1940 **Unwmk.** *Perf. 14*

370	A57	2c olive green	2.50	1.00
371	A57	5c green	5.00	2.10
372	A57	$1 henna & dk brn	110.00	19.00
373	A57	$2 dp blue & org brn	21.00	5.00
374	A57	$5 red & grnsh blk	26.00	16.50
375	A57	$10 dk grn & dull pur	72.50	12.50
		Nos. 370-375 (6)	237.00	56.10

See surcharge note following No. 363.

Type of 1939-41

1940 **Wmk. 261** *Perf. 12½*

Type III

376	A57	$1 henna & dk brn	7.00	*9.00*
377	A57	$2 dp blue & org brn	9.00	*9.00*
378	A57	$5 red & grnsh blk	10.00	*18.00*
379	A57	$10 dk green & dull pur	15.00	*30.00*
380	A57	$20 rose lake & dp blue	19.00	*30.00*
		Nos. 376-380 (5)	60.00	*96.00*

See surcharge note following No. 363.

Printed by the Dah Tung Book Co.

Five Cent

Type III - Characters joined

Secret Mark - Characters not joined

Eight Cent

Type III - Characters not joined

Secret Mark - Characters joined

Ten Cent

Type III - Characters sharp and well shaped

Secret Mark - Characters coarse and varying in thickness

Dollar Values

Type III

Secret Mark

1940 Unwmk. *Perf. 14*

Type III with Secret Marks

381	A57	5c green	.25	.25
382	A57	5c olive green	.25	.25
383	A57	8c olive green	.40	.25
a.		Without "star" in uniform button	1.50	*2.50*
384	A57	10c green	.25	.25
385	A57	30c scarlet	.35	.25
386	A57	50c dk blue	.45	.25
387	A57	$1 org brn & sepia	2.50	.25
388	A57	$2 dp blue & yel brn	1.00	.35
389	A57	$5 red & slate grn	1.00	.45
390	A57	$10 dk grn & dull pur	4.00	2.25
391	A57	$20 rose lake & dk blue	12.00	3.50
		Nos. 381-391 (11)	22.45	8.30

Type III with Secret Marks

1940 Wmk. 261 *Perf. 14*

392	A57	5c green	.25	.25
393	A57	5c olive green	.25	.25
394	A57	10c green	.35	.25
395	A57	30c scarlet	.25	.25
396	A57	50c dk blue	.55	.25
397	A57	$1 org brn & sepia	4.50	2.75
398	A57	$2 dp blue & yel brn	12.50	13.00
399	A57	$5 red & slate grn	11.50	*12.00*
400	A57	$10 dk grn & dull pur	16.00	*17.00*
401	A57	$20 rose lake & dk blue	25.00	20.00
		Nos. 392-401 (10)	71.15	66.00

Nos. 383, 384, 385, 397, 400 and 401 exist perf. 12½, but were not issued with this perforation.

See surcharge note following No. 363.

Types of 1932-34 Martyrs Issue with Secret Mark

1932-34 Issue. In the left Chinese character in bottom row, the two parts are not joined.

Secret Mark, 1940-41 Issue. The two parts are joined

Perf. 12½, 13 and Compound

1940-41 Wmk. 261

402	A39	½c olive blk	.25	.25
403	A40	1c orange	.25	.25
404	A46	2c dp blue ('41)	.25	.25
405	A39	2½c rose lilac	.25	.25
406	A48	3c dp yellow brn	.30	.25
407	A39	4c pale vio ('41)	.30	.25
408	A48	5c dull red org ('41)	.30	.25
409	A45	8c dp orange	.25	.25
410	A46	10c dull violet	.25	.25
411	A45	13c dp yellow grn	.35	.25
412	A48	15c brown car	.25	.25
413	A46	17c brown olive	.25	.25
414	A47	20c lt blue	.25	.25
415	A45	21c olive brn ('41)	1.10	*1.25*
416	A40	25c red vio ('41)	.25	.25
417	A46	28c olive ('41)	.30	.25
418	A48	30c brown car	.45	.25
a.		Vert. pair, imperf. btwn.	125.00	
419	A47	40c orange	.30	.25
420	A40	50c green	.30	.25

Unwmk.

421	A39	½c olive black	.25	.25
422	A40	1c orange	.25	.25
a.		Without secret mark	2.75	2.75
b.		Horiz. pair, imperf. vert.	110.00	
423	A46	2c dp blue	.25	.25
a.		Vert. pair, imperf. horiz.	100.00	
b.		Horiz. pair, imperf. between	160.00	
424	A39	2½c rose lilac	.25	.25
425	A48	3c dp yellow brn	.25	.25
426	A39	4c pale violet	.25	.25
427	A48	5c dull red org	.25	.25
428	A45	8c dp orange	.25	.25
429	A46	10c dull violet	3.25	.40
430	A45	13c dp yel grn	.25	.65
431	A48	15c brown car	.35	.60
432	A46	17c brn olive	.40	.25
433	A47	20c lt blue	.30	.25
a.		Vert. pair, imperf. horiz.	125.00	
b.		Horiz. pair, imperf. vert.	125.00	
434	A45	21c olive brn	.50	.35
435	A40	25c rose vio	.35	*.50*
436	A46	28c olive	.70	.50
437	A48	30c brown car	2.50	2.50
438	A47	40c orange	.35	.35
439	A40	50c green	3.50	.40
		Nos. 402-439 (38)	20.65	14.50

Several values exist imperforate, but they were not regularly issued.

Used values are for favor cancels. Postally used examples sell for more.

See surcharge note following No. 323.

Regional Surcharges.

The regional surcharges, Nos. 440-448, 482-484, 486-491, 525-549, have been listed according to the basic stamps, with black or red surcharges. The surcharges of the individual provinces, plus Hong Kong and Shanghai, are noted in small type. The numeral following each letter is the surcharge denomination. These surcharges are identified by the following letters:

a — Hong Kong	i — Kwangsi
b — Shanghai	j — Kwangtung
bx — Anhwei	k — Western Szechwan
c — Hunan	l — Yunnan
d — Kansu	m — Honan
e — Kiangsi	n — Shensi
f — Eastern Szechwan	o — Kweichow
g — Chekiang	p — Hupeh
h — Fukien	

Regional Surcharges on Stamps of 1939-40

Hong Kong — a4

Shanghai — b3

Hunan — c3

Kansu — d3

Kiangsi — e3

Eastern Szechwan — f3

Chekiang — g3

1940-41 Unwmk. *Perf. 12½, 14*

Carmine Surcharge

440	A57	4c on 5c ol grn (#382)	.60	.60
r.		Lower right character duplicated at left	30.00	32.50

Black Surcharge

441	A57	3c on 5c grn (#351) (b3)	1.25	*1.40*
442	A57	3c on 5c ol grn (#352) (c3, d3)	.65	*2.00*
443	A57	3c on 5c grn (#381) (b3)	.60	*1.25*
444	A57	3c on 5c ol grn (#382) (e3)	.70	*1.00*
r.		Lower left character duplicated at right (Kiangsi)	42.50	42.50
		(b3) Shanghai	.65	*1.40*
		(f3) Eastern Szechwan	.65	*1.60*

The Kansu surcharges of No. 442 are of 6 types. Differences include formation of top part of fen character (at left of "3"), fen with low right hook, height of "3" (5-4mm), space between upper and lower characters (6-9mm), etc.

1940-41 Wmk. 261 *Perf. 14*

445	A57	3c on 5c grn (#392) (e3)	.60	*1.40*
r.		Lower left character duplicated at right (Kiangsi)	35.00	35.00
		(b3, c3) Shanghai, Hunan	.60	*1.60*
446	A57	3c on 5c ol grn (#393) (f3)	.70	*1.75*
		(b3) Shanghai	.95	*1.75*
r.		Lower left character duplicated at right (f3)	60.00	65.00

Red Surcharge

447	A57	3c on 5c grn (#392) (g3)	1.25	3.25
448	A57	3c on 5c ol grn (#393) (g3)	6.00	6.00

Dr. Sun Yat-sen — A59

Printed by American Bank Note Co.

1941 Unwmk. Engr. *Perf. 12*

449	A59	½c sepia	.25	.30
450	A59	1c orange	.25	.25
451	A59	2c brt ultra	.25	.25
452	A59	5c green	.25	.25
453	A59	8c red orange	.60	.70
454	A59	8c turq green	.30	.25
455	A59	10c brt green	.25	.25
456	A59	17c olive	4.50	*12.00*
457	A59	25c rose violet	.30	1.00
458	A59	30c scarlet	.35	.25
459	A59	50c dk blue	.50	.25
460	A59	$1 brown & blk	.60	.25
461	A59	$2 blue & blk	.75	.25
a.		Center inverted	*180,000.*	
462	A59	$5 scarlet & blk	1.75	.65
463	A59	$10 green & blk	5.00	2.75
464	A59	$20 rose vio & blk	4.00	*6.00*
		Nos. 449-464 (16)	19.90	25.65

For surcharges see Nos. 488, 491, 542-543, 617, 621, 670, 677, 687, 705-706, 712, 716, 718, M1, M3-M4, 1N16-1N22, 1N43-1N56, 9N78-9N96, 9N98, 9N100.

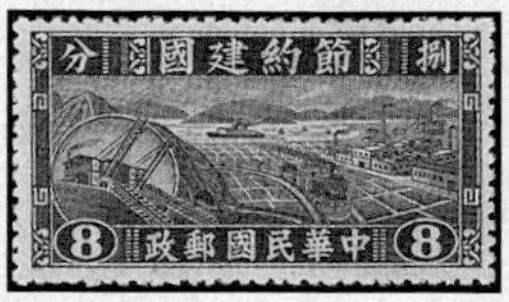

Industry and Agriculture — A60

1941, June 21 *Perf. 12½*

465	A60	8c green	.50	.50
466	A60	21c red brown	.65	.65
467	A60	28c dk olive grn	.85	.85
468	A60	33c vermilion	1.10	*1.50*
469	A60	50c dp ultra	1.25	1.25
470	A60	$1 dk violet	1.75	1.75
		Nos. 465-470 (6)	6.10	6.50

Souvenir Sheet

Imperf

Typo.

471	Sheet of 6	70.00	70.00
a.	A60 8c dull green	6.50	6.50
b.	A60 21c dark orange brown	6.50	6.50
c.	A60 28c dull yellow green	6.50	6.50
d.	A60 33c red	6.50	6.50
e.	A60 50c dull blue	6.50	6.50
f.	A60 $1 dark violet	6.50	6.50

The Thrift Movement and its aim to "Save for Reconstruction."

Issued in sheets measuring 155x171mm, without gum.

This sheet exists with additional blue marginal overprints in Russian, French and Chinese reading "Souvenir of the Exhibition of the Russian Philatelic Society in China, Shanghai, China, Feb. 28, 1943." Value, $800.

The overprinting was applied by the society, and when so overprinted this sheet had no franking power.

Stamps of 1939-41 Overprinted in Carmine or Blue

1941, Oct. 10 *Perf. 12½, 14, 13*

472	A40	1c dull orange	.25	*.60*
473	A57	2c olive grn (C)	.25	*.60*
474	A39	4c pale violet (C)	.25	*.60*
475	A57	8c ol grn (#369) (C)	.25	*.60*
476	A57	10c green (#354) (C)	.25	*.60*
477	A57	16c ol gray (#357) (C)	.25	*.60*
478	A45	21c olive brn (C)	.25	*.60*
479	A46	28c olive (C)	.60	*1.65*
480	A57	30c scarlet	1.00	*3.25*
481	A57	$1 hn & dk brn (#359)	4.00	*4.00*
		Nos. 472-481 (10)	7.35	*13.10*

Chinese Republic, 30th anniversary.

Kiangsi — e7

Eastern Szechwan — f7

Chekiang — g7

Fukien — h7

1941 Unwmk. *Perf. 12½, 14*

482	A57	7c on 8c (#353) (g7, h7)	1.00	1.10
483	A57	7c on 8c (#369) (f7)	1.00	.55

484 A57 7c on 8c (#383) (h7) 1.00 .90
(e7) Kiangsi 1.00 .90
(g7) Chekiang 1.00 1.10
r. Without "star" in uniform button 70.00

Type of 1932-34 Re-engraved

1941 Unwmk. ***Perf. 14***
485 A45 8c deep orange 13.00 *57.50*

The original stamps are 19½mm wide, the re-engraved 21mm.

Eleven other values of the Martyrs Issue and types A37 and A57 exist re-engraved, but were not issued.

Hunan — c1

Kiangsi — e1

Fukien — h1

Kwangsi — i1

Kwangtung — j1

1942 Red Surcharge
486 A39 1c on ½c blk brn (#312) (i1) 1.00 *1.75*
(c1) Hunan 2.00 *2.75*
487 A39 1c on ½c ol blk (#421) (e1) .75 1.60
(c1) Hunan .85 *2.00*
(i1) Kwangsi 1.65 *2.50*
(h1) Fukien 6.00 *9.50*
488 A59 1c on ½c sepia (#449) (j1) 1.00 *1.60*
(c1) Hunan 1.25 *2.50*

Hunan — c40

Eastern Szechwan — f40

Western Szechwan — k40

Yunnan — l40

Red Surcharge
489 A57 40c on 50c dk bl (#386) (f40) .75 1.25
(k40) Western Szechwan 4.25 *6.00*
(l40) Yunnan 3.75 *5.50*
r. Inverted surcharge (Yunnan) 110.00

Wmk. 261
490 A40 40c on 50c grn (#420) (c40) 1.75 *6.50*

Unwmk.
491 A59 40c on 50c dk bl (#459) (c40) 3.25 *8.25*

Dr. Sun Yat-sen — A62

Central Trust Printing

Perf. 10½-11, 11½-12½, 13 and Compounds

1942-43 Without Gum Typo.
492 A62 10c dp green ('43) .25 *1.50*
493 A62 16c dull ol brn 13.50 *47.50*
a. Perf 10½ 550.00 *550.00*
494 A62 20c dk ol grn ('43) .25 *1.50*
a. Perf. 11 13.50 11.00
495 A62 25c brown vio .25 *1.00*
496 A62 30c dull ver .25 *1.00*
a. Perf. 11 3.00 5.00
497 A62 40c dk red brn ('43) .25 *1.00*
a. Perf. 11x13 85.00
b. Perf. 11 14.00 14.00
498 A62 50c sage green .25 .25
a. Perf. 11 7.00 *13.50*
499 A62 $1 rose lake .35 .25
a. Perf. 11 40.00 40.00
500 A62 $1 dull grn ('43) .35 .35
501 A62 $1.50 dp blue ('43) .35 *.45*
a. Perf. 11 290.00 290.00
502 A62 $2 dk blue grn .35 .35
503 A62 $3 dk yel ('43) .35 .35
504 A62 $4 red brown .40 .45
505 A62 $5 cerise ('43) .35 .35
Nos. 492-505 (14) 17.50 56.30

Many shades and part-perforate varieties exist.

See Nos. 550 to 563 for other stamps of type A62 with secret mark and new values and colors. For surcharges and overprints see Nos. 525-530, 671, 683, 692-694, 696, 771, 773, 807-809, 811-820, 824-827, 832, 834-834A, 836, 848-850, 852-854, 857, 860-863, 876, 879, M5-M10, Taiwan 55, 86, 99, Kwangsi 6-7, Sinkiang 162-173, 194-195.

Type of 1938
Thin Paper Without Gum

1942-44 Unwmk. Engr. ***Imperf.***
506 A57 $10 red brown 1.75 1.25
507 A57 $20 blue grn 1.75 1.00
508 A57 $20 rose red ('44) 17.00 11.00
509 A57 $30 dull vio ('43) 1.25 1.00
510 A57 $40 rose red ('43) 1.40 1.00
511 A57 $50 blue 2.00 1.25
512 A57 $100 org brn ('43) 8.00 5.00

Rouletted
513 A57 $5 lilac gray ('44) 14.00 *14.00*
a. Rouletted x perf. 12½ 25.00 30.00
514 A57 $10 red brown 6.75 5.00
515 A57 $50 blue 7.25 6.00
a. Rouletted x imperf. 6.50 —
Nos. 506-515 (10) 61.15 46.50

1942-45 ***Perf. 12½ to 15***
516 A57 $4 dp blue ('43) .80 1.25
517 A57 $5 lil gray ('43) 1.75 1.25
518 A57 $10 red brown 1.75 1.25
519 A57 $20 blue grn ('43) 1.75 1.00
520 A57 $20 rose red ('45) 100.00 *125.00*
521 A57 $30 dull vio ('43) 1.25 1.00
522 A57 $40 rose ('43) 1.25 1.00
523 A57 $50 blue 5.50 2.50
524 A57 $100 org brn ('45) 110.00 *125.00*
Nos. 516-524 (9) 224.05 259.25

Beware of Nos. 508 and 512 with faked perforations that are offered as Nos. 520 and 524.

See surcharge note following No. 363.

No. 493 Overprinted in Black or Red

1942
525 A62 (i) 16c (Bk) 85.00 100.00
(c) Hunan 500.00
(k) Western Szechwan 190.00 190.00
(m) Honan 850.00 850.00
(n) Shensi 250.00 260.00
r. Perf. 10½ (Kwangsi) 550.00
s. Inverted ovpt. (Shensi) 300.00
526 A62 (d) 16c (R) 60.00 50.00
(bx) Anhwei 550.00 550.00
(e) Kiangsi 77.50 60.00
(f) Eastern Szechwan 120.00 75.00
(h) Fukien 300.00 225.00
(j) Kwangtung 675.00 675.00
(l) Yunnan 60.00 50.00
(o) Kweichow 275.00 200.00
(p) Hupeh, perf. 10½ 925.00 850.00
r. Perf. 10½ (E. Szechwan) 500.00
s. Horiz. pair, imperf. btwn (Yunnan) 650.00
t. Perf. 13 (Hupeh) — —

This overprint means "Domestic Ordinary Letter Surcharge Paid." It was applied in various sizes and types by 14 districts, 9 using red ink, 5 using black. (The Anhwei overprint comes in two types.) These overprinted stamps were briefly sold for $1.16 before the government ordered their sale suspended. The vertical bars and 50c surcharge of Nos. 527-528 were then applied.

Nos. 525-526 Surcharged "50 cents" and 2 Vertical Bars in Black or Red

Anhwei — bx

Hunan — c

Kansu — d

Kiangsi — e

Eastern Szechwan — f

Fukien — h

Kwangsi — i

Kwangtung — j

Western Szechwan — k

Yunnan — l

Honan — m

Shensi — n

Kweichow — o

Hupeh — p

1942 Unwmk.
527 A62 50c on 16c (Bk) (c,f) 3.25 3.00
(i) Kwangsi 6.00 6.00
(k) Western Szechwan 11.00 8.50
(m) Honan 11.50 10.00
(n) Shensi 4.25 *5.00*
r. Inverted surch. (W. Szech.) 250.00
s. "k" surcharge on #493 350.00
528 A62 50c on 16c (R) (p) 5.00 5.00
(bx) Anhwei 95.00 *300.00*
(d) Kansu 3.25 *5.00*
(e) Kiangsi 5.50 *10.00*
(h) Fukien 6.50 *8.50*
(j) Kwangtung 6.50 6.00
(l) Yunnan 6.50 8.00
(o) Kweichow 4.00 7.00
r. "o" surcharge inverted 300.00
s. "p" surch. on #526(f) 100.00 *47.50*

Many varieties of Nos. 527-528 exist, including narrow or wide spacing between the two top characters, or between the vertical bars, or both.

Surcharges on stamps perf. 10½ (basic No. 493a) usually sell at much higher prices.

No. 493 Surcharged in Black, Red or Carmine

General Issue

Hunan — c50

Eastern Szechwan — f50

Chekiang — g50

Kwangsi — i50

Kwangtung — j50

Western Szechwan — k50

Honan — m50

Shensi — n50

Kweichow — o50

1943 Unwmk.
529 A62 50c on 16c (Bk) (m50) 11.00 11.00
(n50) Shensi 11.00 11.00
r. Perf. 11x13 (Shensi) 95.00
530 A62 50c on 16c (C) 1.00 *2.00*
(c50) Hunan 3.00 6.00
(f50) Eastern Szechwan 3.75 2.75
(g50) Chekiang 42.50 *50.00*
(i50) Kwangsi 6.50 *7.50*
(j50) Kwangtung 5.00 *7.00*
(k50) Western Szechwan 5.00 *6.50*
(m50) Honan 8.50 *9.50*
(o50) Kweichow 11.00 13.00
r. Inverted surch. (Hunan) 65.00
s. "05" instead of "50" (Kweichow) 450.00

Many varieties of Nos. 529-530 exist, such as narrow or wide spacing horizontally or vertically between the overprinted Chinese characters.

Surcharges on No. 493a (perf. 10½) usually sell at much higher pricess.

The General Issue type, No. 530, was distributed to all head offices, which in turn supplied the post offices under their direction. It is surcharged in carmine; the other stamps listed under No. 530 are surcharged in red or carmine.

Hunan — c20

Kansu — d20

Kiangsi — e20

Eastern Szechwan — f20

Fukien — h20

Kwangsi — i20

Kwangtung — j20

Western Szechwan — k20

Yunnan — l20

Honan — m20

Shensi — n20

Kweichow — o20

Hupeh — p20

On No. 318

1943 Wmk. 261, Unwmkd.

531 A45 20c on 13c (k20) 2.25 *5.00*
(d20) Kansu 2.25 *6.00*
(n20) Shensi 3.50 *5.50*
532 A45 20c on 13c (i20;R) 1.00 *2.75*
(c20) Hunan 1,100.
(e20) Kiangsi 275.00
(j20) Kwangtung 85.00 95.00
(p20) Hupeh 2.00 *4.00*

On No. 411

533 A45 20c on 13c (n20) 2.25 *4.25*
(d20) Kansu 2.75 *7.50*
(k20) Western Szechwan 2.00 *7.50*
(l20) Yunnan 21.00 *35.00*
(m20) Honan 350.00
534 A45 20c on 13c (p20;R) 1.75 *5.25*
(c20) Hunan 2.50 1.75
(e20) Kiangsi 9.00 2.10
(f20) Eastern Szechwan 2.50 *2.75*
(h20) Fukien 9.50 *11.00*
(i20) Kwangsi 2.00 *2.75*
(j20) Kwangtung 22.00 22.00
(o20) Kweichow 3.75 *3.25*

On No. 430

535 A45 20c on 13c (l20) 2.25 *4.75*
(d20) Kansu 2.25 *2.75*
(k20) Western Szechwan 35.00 *42.50*
(m20) Honan 9.50 *9.25*
(n20) Shensi 3.50 *5.50*
536 A45 20c on 13c (f20;i20;R) 2.25 *3.50*
(c20) Hunan 11.00 *9.75*
(e20) Kiangsi 4.50 *4.00*
(j20) Kwangtung 2.25 *2.75*
(o20) Kweichow 2.25 *10.00*
(p20) Hupeh 2.25 *4.00*

On No. 357

537 A57 20c on 16c (k20) 2.25 *2.75*
(c20) Hunan 3.50 *13.50*
(d20) Kansu 3.50 *13.50*
(m20) Honan 11.00 *17.50*
(n20) Shensi 3.50 *13.50*
538 A57 20c on 16c (e20, o20; R) 2.25 *13.50*
(c20) Hunan 11.00 *17.50*
(i20) Kwangsi 11.00 *13.50*
(j20) Kwangtung 52.50 *55.00*

On No. 413

539 A46 20c on 17c (c20;R) 2.75 *4.25*
(i20) Kwangsi 2.25 *2.75*
(j20) Kwangtung 30.00 *42.50*

On No. 432

540 A46 20c on 17c (k20) 3.50 *5.50*
(d20) Kansu 3.50 *6.50*
(m20) Honan 40.00 *47.50*
541 A46 20c on 17c (e20;R) 2.25 *5.50*
(j20) Kwangtung 3.75 *15.00*
(o20) Kweichow 2.50 *6.75*

On No. 456

542 A59 20c on 17c (m20) 210.00 *275.00*
543 A59 20c on 17c (c20;R) 18.00 30.00

On No. 415

544 A45 20c on 21c (e20;R) 11.00 *12.00*

On No. 434

545 A45 20c on 21c (c20, k20) 2.25 *4.00*
(d20) Kansu 2.50 *6.75*
(l20) Yunnan 2.50 *4.00*
(m20) Honan 2.50 *9.25*
546 A45 20c on 21c (f20;R) 1.75 *4.25*
(e20) Kiangsi 1.75 *5.50*
(h20) Fukien 2.50 *4.75*
(i20) Kwangsi 2.75 *4.00*
(j20) Kwangtung 3.75 *5.00*
(o20) Kweichow 2.50 *2.75*
(p20) Hupeh 2.50 *5.50*

On No. 417

547 A46 20c on 28c (e20;R) 775.00 *725.00*

On No. 436

548 A46 20c on 28c (l20) 3.50 *6.25*
(d20) Kansu 17.50 *24.00*
(k20) Western Szechwan 25.00 *65.00*
(m20) Honan 40.00 *47.50*
549 A46 20c on 28c (e20;R) 1.75 *3.25*
(c20) Hunan 1.90 *4.75*
(h20) Fukien 3.50 *4.75*
(i20) Kwangsi 4.75 *4.75*
(j20) Kwangtung 4.25 *6.25*
(o20) Kweichow 4.75 *4.75*

Many varieties of Nos. 531-549 exist, such as narrow or wide spacing between the overprinted Chinese characters, and "20" higher or lower than illustrated.

Type of 1942-43
Pacheng Printing

1944-46 Unwmk. *Perf. 12*
Without Gum

550 A62 30c chocolate .40 *13.00*
551 A62 $1 green 4.00 *5.00*
552 A62 $2 dk vio brn .25 .25
a. Imperf., pair 30.00 25.00
553 A62 $2 dk bl grn .25 .25
a. Perf. 10½ 47.50 35.00
554 A62 $2 deep blue 1.75 *6.00*
555 A62 $3 lt yellow 1.60 .80
556 A62 $4 violet brn .25 .25
a. Imperf., pair 60.00
557 A62 $5 car ('46) .25 .25
a. Perf. 10½ 75.00 75.00
558 A62 $6 gray vio ('45) .25 *.40*
559 A62 $10 red brn ('45) .25 .25
a. Imperf., pair 60.00
560 A62 $20 dp ultra ('46) .25 .25
561 A62 $50 dk green ('46) 4.00 .25
562 A62 $70 lilac ('46) 5.00 .25
563 A62 $100 lt brown ('46) .30 .25
Nos. 550-563 (14) 18.80 *27.45*

In the Pacheng printing of the Central Trust type stamps, the secret mark "C" has been added below the lower left foliate ornament beneath the sun emblem. On the $3, it is below the right ornament. New values also include a "P" at right of sun emblem on the $6 and $10, and at right of necktie on the $20.

Seven different varieties of paper were used in the printing of Nos. 550-563. Some values exist on laid paper with elephant watermark in sheet.

See surcharge note following No. 505.

Dr. Sun Yat-sen — A63

1944-46 Unwmk. Typo. *Perf. 12½*
Without Gum

565 A63 40c brown red .35 .35
566 A63 $2 gray brown .35 .35
567 A63 $3 red .35 .35
a. $3 orange red 4.00 4.00
568 A63 $3 lt red brown ('45) .95 .75
569 A63 $6 pale lilac gray ('45) .35 .45
570 A63 $10 dull lake ('45) .35 .35
571 A63 $20 rose ('45) .35 .35
a. Perf. 16 400.00 400.00
572 A63 $50 lt brown ('46) .45 .55
573 A63 $70 rose violet ('46) .55 .55
Nos. 565-573 (9) 4.05 4.05

For surcharges see Nos. 772, 774, 828, 833, 835, 836A, 839, 842, 851, 864, 868, 873-875, 877, 880. Taiwan 81, 98, Sinkiang 200-201.

Allegory of Savings — A64

1944-45 Engr. *Perf. 13*
Without Gum

574 A64 $40 indigo ('45) .35 *.90*
575 A64 $50 yellow grn ('45) .35 .35
576 A64 $100 yellow brn .35 .35
577 A64 $200 dk green ('45) .35 .35
Nos. 574-577 (4) 1.40 1.95

All four values were printed on thick paper; the first three were also printed on thin paper.

For surcharges see Szechwan Nos. F1, F3.

A65

1944, Dec. 25 Litho.
Without Gum

578 A65 $2 deep green .70 *2.00*
579 A65 $5 fawn .70 *2.00*
580 A65 $6 dull rose vio 1.40 *3.50*
581 A65 $10 violet blue 2.75 *7.00*
582 A65 $20 carmine 5.25 *9.00*
Nos. 578-582 (5) 10.80 23.50

50th anniversary of the Kuomintang.

Dr. Sun Yat-sen — A66

1945, Mar. 12 Without Gum

583 A66 $2 gray green .45 *1.75*
584 A66 $5 red brown .55 *1.75*
585 A66 $6 dk vio blue .65 *2.25*
586 A66 $10 lt blue 1.00 *1.75*
587 A66 $20 rose 1.25 *4.00*
588 A66 $30 buff 2.00 *6.00*
Nos. 583-588 (6) 5.90 17.50

Death of Dr. Sun Yat-sen, 20th anniv.

Dr. Sun Yat-sen — A67

1945-46 Without Gum *Perf. 12½*

589 A67 $2 green .25 .35
590 A67 $5 dull green .25 .35
591 A67 $10 dk blue .25 .35
a. Imperf., pair 110.00
592 A67 $20 carmine ('46) .25 .35
a. Imperf., pair 110.00
Nos. 589-592 (4) 1.00 1.40

For surcharges see Nos. 695, 697, 837, 855, Taiwan 58, 82, 87-88.

Statue of Liberty, Map of China, Flags of Great Britain, China and United States, and Chiang Kai-shek
A68

Unwmk.
1945, July 7 Engr. *Perf. 12*
Flags in Dark Blue and Red

593 A68 $1 deep blue .50 .50
594 A68 $2 dull green .50 *1.00*
595 A68 $5 olive gray .50 *1.00*
596 A68 $6 brown 1.00 *1.25*
597 A68 $10 rose lilac 5.00 *7.00*
598 A68 $20 carmine rose 5.00 *9.50*
Nos. 593-598 (6) 12.50 *20.25*

Signing of a Treaty in 1943 between Great Britain, the US and China.

Pres. Lin Sen (1864-1943) — A69

1945, Aug. Unwmk. *Perf. 12*

599 A69 $1 dp ultra & blk .65 *2.00*
600 A69 $2 myrtle grn & blk .65 *2.00*
601 A69 $5 red & blk .65 *2.00*
602 A69 $6 purple & blk .90 *2.00*
603 A69 $10 choc & blk 4.00 *4.00*
604 A69 $20 olive grn & blk 4.25 *6.00*
Nos. 599-604 (6) 11.10 *18.00*

Pres. Chiang Kai-shek — A70

1945, Oct. 10
Flag in Rose Red and Violet Blue

605 A70 $2 green .45 *1.00*
606 A70 $4 dark blue .50 *1.00*
607 A70 $5 olive gray .50 *1.50*
608 A70 $6 bister brown 1.50 *2.25*
609 A70 $10 gray 4.00 *7.00*
610 A70 $20 red violet 5.00 *7.00*
Nos. 605-610 (6) 11.95 19.75

Inauguration of Chiang Kai-shek as president, Oct. 10, 1943.

President Chiang Kai-shek — A71

1945, Oct. 10 Typo. *Perf. 13*
Without Gum
Flag in Carmine and Blue

611 A71 $20 green & blue .25 .25
612 A71 $50 bister brn & bl .50 .50
613 A71 $100 blue .50 .40
614 A71 $300 rose red & blue .50 .40
Nos. 611-614 (4) 1.75 1.55

Victory of the Allied Nations over Japan.

C. N. C. Surcharges

The green surcharges on Nos. 615 to 621, and the surcharges on Nos. 647 to 721, and 768 to 774 represent Chinese National Currency and were applied at Shanghai.

Stamps of 1938-41 Srchd. in Black with Chinese Characters and New Value in Checkered Rectangle at Bottom, Resrchd. in Green

1945 *Perf. 12, 12½*

615	A57	10c on $20 on 3c (#350)	.25	*1.00*
616	A46	15c on $30 on 2c (#423)	.25	*1.00*
a.		Horiz. pair, imperf. between	90.00	
b.		Vert. pair, imperf. between	85.00	
617	A59	25c on $50 on 1c (#450)	.25	.90
618	A57	50c on $100 on 3c (#350)	.25	.50
619	A40	$1 on $200 on 1c (#422)	.25	.25
a.		Horiz. pair, imperf. between	90.00	
620	A57	$2 on $400 on 3c (#350)	.25	.30
621	A59	$5 on $1000 on 1c (#450)	.25	.25
		Nos. 615-621 (7)	1.75	4.20

The black (first) surcharges on Nos. 615 to 621 represent Nanking puppet government currency.

In the green surcharge, the characters at the left express the new value and are either two or four in number.

Types of 1932-34, Re-engraved, and Srchd. in Green with Horiz. Bar and Four or Five Chinese Characters and Ovptd. in Black

Perf. 14

622	A47	$10 on 20c brown red	8.00	*12.00*
623	A47	$20 on 40c orange	25.00	*29.00*
a.		Green surcharge inverted	60.00	
624	A48	$50 on 30c violet brn	18.50	*22.00*
		Nos. 622-624 (3)	51.50	*63.00*

These provisional surcharges were applied in Honan in National currency to stamps of the Hwa Pei (North China) government. The black overprint reads: "Hwa Pei."

The two-character "Hwa Pei" overprint was applied to various stamps in 1941-43 by the North China puppet government. See Nos. 8N1-8N53, 8N60-8N84.

Dr. Sun Yat-sen — A72

1945, Dec. **Typo.** *Perf. 12*
Without Gum

625	A72	$20 dp carmine	.25	.25
626	A72	$30 dp blue	.25	.25
627	A72	$40 orange	.60	1.25
628	A72	$50 green	1.00	.35
629	A72	$100 dk brown	.25	.25
630	A72	$200 brown violet	.25	.25
		Nos. 625-630 (6)	2.60	2.60

For surcharges see Nos. 810, 829, 838, 865, J110-J119, Taiwan 75, Kwangsi F2, Szechwan F2, F4, Yunnan 66-67, 71.

Type of 1931-37
Perf. 12½, 13x12½, 13½

1946 **Unwmk.**

631	A37	$1 dk violet	.30	*1.50*
632	A37	$2 olive green	.30	*3.00*
633	A37	$20 brt yellow grn	.30	*.55*
634	A37	$30 chocolate	.30	*.50*
635	A37	$50 red orange	.30	*.50*
		Nos. 631-635 (5)	1.50	6.05

$4 blue and $5 red values were prepared but not issued. Value $400.

For surcharges see Nos. 678, 684, 689-690, 768, 843.

Dr. Sun Yat-sen — A73

1946-47 **Engr.** *Perf. 14*
Without Gum

636	A73	$20 carmine	6.25	.25
637	A73	$30 dk blue ('47)	.35	.25
638	A73	$50 purple	.25	.25
639	A73	$70 red org ('47)	17.50	2.50
640	A73	$100 dk carmine	.25	.25
641	A73	$200 olive grn ('47)	.25	.25
642	A73	$500 brt bl grn ('47)	.35	.25
643	A73	$700 red brown ('47)	.25	.25
644	A73	$1000 rose lake	.35	.35
645	A73	$3000 blue	1.00	.40
646	A73	$5000 dp green & ver	1.00	.40
		Nos. 636-646 (11)	27.80	5.40

For surcharges see Nos. 679, 769, 775, 823, 837A, 844-845, 856, 866, 875A, 878, Taiwan 18, 23-28, 54, 76-77, 100, Northeastern Provinces 41-43, Fukien 5-6, Hunan 1, E1, Kwangsi 11, F2, Szechwan F5-F8, Sinkiang 202-204, People's Republic of China 3L53, 3L67-3L68, 6L28.

Stamps of 1932-41 Surcharged in Black

Perf. 12½, 13, 13x12, 14
Wmk. 261

647	A45	$20 on 8c (#409)	.25	*.65*
648	A39	$30 on ½c (#402)	2,000.	
649	A45	$50 on 21c (#415)	.25	*.25*
650	A45	$70 on 13c (#411)	.25	.25
651	A46	$100 on 28c (#417)	.25	*.65*

Unwmk.

652	A39	$3 on 2½c (#424)	7.50	6.25
653	A48	$10 on 15c (#431)	.25	.25
654	A45	$20 on 8c (#428)	.25	.25
655	A47	$20 on 20c (#433)	.35	.35
656	A39	$30 on ½c (#421)	.25	.25
657	A45	$50 on 21c (#434)	.40	*.55*
657A	A45	$70 on 13c (#318)	210.00	210.00
658	A45	$70 on 13c (#430)	.40	*.55*
659	A46	$100 on 28c (#436)	.40	.40

Forgeries of No. 648 exist.

Stamps and Types of 1931-1946 Surcharged in Black or Carmine

Perf. 12½, 13, 14

1946-47 **Wmk. 261**

660	A57	$50 on 5c green (#392)	.35	.85
661	A57	$50 on 5c ol grn (#393)	21.00	20.00
662	A48	$50 on 5c dl red org (#408)	.25	*1.25*
663	A40	$100 on 1c org (#403)	.25	*1.10*

Perf. 12, 12½, 12½x13, 13, 14

1946-47 **Unwmk.**

664	A57	$20 on 3c (#350)	.25	*.35*
665	A45	$20 on 8c (#428)	.25	.25
666	A57	$50 on 3c (#350)	.25	.25
667	A57	$50 on 5c (#352)	.25	.25
668	A57	$50 on 5c (#382)	.95	*1.75*
669	A48	$50 on 5c (#427)	.25	.25
670	A59	$50 on 5c (#452)	.25	.25
671	A62	$50 on $1 (#500)	.25	.25
672	A40	$100 on 1c (#422)	.25	.25
a.		Without secret mark (#422a)	67.50	67.50
673	A57	$100 on 3c (#350)	.25	.25
674	A57	$100 on 8c (#353)	14.00	14.00
675	A57	$100 on 8c (#369)	2.00	.35
676	A57	$100 on 8c (#383)	.35	.35
a.		Without "star" in uniform button (No. 383a)	25.00	16.00
677	A59	$100 on 8c (#454)	.25	.25
678	A37	$100 on $1 (#631)	.25	.25
679	A73	$100 on $20 (#636)	.35	.35
680	A57	$200 on 10c (#354)	.75	.25
681	A57	$200 on 10c (#384)	.40	1.10
682	A37	$200 on $4 dl bl	.50	.25
a.		Double surcharge	16.00	
683	A62	$250 on $1.50 (#501)	.30	*2.50*
a.		Perf. 11	250.00	250.00
684	A37	$250 on $2 (#632)	.50	.25
685	A37	$250 on $5 car	.50	.25
686	A57	$300 on 10c (#354)	.25	.25
687	A59	$300 on 10c (#455)	.25	.25
688	A57	$500 on 3c (#350)	.50	.25
689	A37	$500 on $20 (#633)	.25	.25
690	A37	$800 on $30 (#634)	.30	.25
691	A37	$1000 on 2c (#297)	.65	.35
692	A62	$1000 on $2 (#552)	.30	.25
a.		Imperf., pair	30.00	20.00
693	A62	$1000 on $2 (#553)	.25	.25
694	A62	$1000 on $2 (#554)	.25	*.55*
695	A67	$1000 on $2 (#589)	.25	.25
696	A62	$2000 on $5 (#557)	.30	.25
697	A67	$2000 on $5 dl grn (C) (#590)	.25	.25
		Nos. 664-697 (34)	27.15	27.66

Nos. 660-697 have a double row of dots in the surcharge box frame.

Nos. 682 and 685 were not issued without surcharge. No. 682 is perf. 13x13½; No. 685, perf. 12x12½.

The characters at the left express the new value and vary in number.

Stamps of 1938-41 Surcharged in Black

Perf. 12, 12½, 13, 14

1946 **Wmk. 261**

698	A45	$20 on 8c (#409)	200.00	175.00
699	A57	$50 on 5c (#392)	.25	*.65*
700	A57	$50 on 5c (#393)	.50	*1.25*

1946-48 **Unwmk.**

700A	A57	$20 on 5c (#381)	1,050.	
701	A57	$20 on 8c (#353)	.25	.35
702	A57	$20 on 8c (#369)	.35	.35
703	A57	$20 on 8c (#383)	.25	.50
a.		Without "star" in uniform button (No. 383a)	4.50	4.50
b.		Inverted surcharge	20.00	
c.		Dbl. surch., one on back	32.50	32.50
d.		Double surcharge	32.50	
704	A45	$20 on 8c (#428)	.25	.25
a.		Double surcharge	22.50	
705	A59	$20 on 8c (#453)	.25	.25
706	A59	$20 on 8c (#454)	.25	.25
a.		Inverted surcharge	13.00	
b.		Double surcharge	13.00	
707	A57	$50 on 5c (#351)	7.25	6.75
708	A57	$50 on 5c (#352)	.25	.25
a.		Inverted surcharge	27.50	
709	A57	$50 on 5c (#381)	.70	.70
710	A57	$50 on 5c (#382)	.50	.35
711	A48	$50 on 5c (#427)	.25	.25
a.		Inverted surcharge	27.50	
712	A59	$50 on 5c (#452)	.50	.25
a.		Double surcharge	16.00	

Stamps of 1939-41 Surcharged in Blue or Red

1946 **Wmk. 261** *Perf. 12½*

713	A40	$10 on 1c org (#403)	.25	.25
a.		Inverted surcharge	40.00	
714	A48	$20 on 3c dp yel brn (#406)	800.00	800.00

Forgeries of No. 714 exist.

1946 **Unwmk.** *Perf. 12, 12½, 13*

715	A40	$10 on 1c org (#422)	.25	.25
a.		Without secret mark (#422a)	10.00	12.00
b.		Inverted surcharge	8.00	10.00
716	A59	$10 on 1c org (#450)	.25	.25
a.		Double surcharge	27.50	
717	A57	$20 on 2c ol grn (R) (#368)	.25	.25
718	A59	$20 on 2c brt ultra (R) (#451)	.25	.25
a.		Inverted surcharge	20.00	
b.		Double surcharge	16.00	
719	A57	$20 on 3c dl cl (#350)	.25	.25
a.		Double surcharge	22.50	
720	A48	$20 on 3c dp yel brn (#425)	.25	.35
721	A39	$30 on 4c pale vio (R) (#426)	.25	.25
a.		Inverted surcharge	9.00	
		Nos. 715-721 (7)	1.75	1.85

President Chiang Kai-shek — A74

Perf. 10½-11½

1946, Oct. 31 **Engr.** **Unwmk.**

722	A74	$20 carmine	.50	.55
723	A74	$30 green	.50	.75
724	A74	$50 vermilion	.50	.65
725	A74	$100 yellow grn	.60	1.10
726	A74	$200 yellow org	.95	1.00
727	A74	$300 magenta	.95	.65
		Nos. 722-727 (6)	4.00	4.70

60th birthday of Chiang Kai-shek.

Printed by Dah Yeh Printing Co.; the earlier ones are gumless, the later ones gummed.

For stamps of Type A74 with additional characters on either side of the portrait see Taiwan Nos. 29-34, Northeastern Provinces 30-35.

Printed by Dah Tung Book Co.
Without Gum
Perf. 14

722a	A74	$20 carmine	1.10	1.60
723a	A74	$30 green	1.10	1.50
724a	A74	$50 vermilion	1.10	1.50
725a	A74	$100 yellow green	3.00	3.00
726a	A74	$200 yellow orange	2.00	2.00
727a	A74	$300 magenta	2.50	2.50
		Nos. 722a-727a (6)	10.80	12.00

Assembly House, Nanking A75

1946, Nov. 15 **Litho.** *Perf. 14*
Without Gum

728	A75	$20 green	.75	.40
729	A75	$30 blue	.75	.40
730	A75	$50 dk brown	.75	.40
a.		Horiz. pair, imperf. between	95.00	95.00
731	A75	$100 carmine	.75	.40
		Nos. 728-731 (4)	3.00	1.60

Convening of National Assembly.

For surcharges see Taiwan Nos. 10-13, Northeastern Provinces 26-29.

Entrance to Dr. Sun Yat-sen Mausoleum A76

1947, May 5 **Engr.**

732	A76	$100 dp green	.35	.35
733	A76	$200 deep blue	.35	.35
734	A76	$250 carmine	.35	.35
735	A76	$350 lt brown	.35	.35
736	A76	$400 dp claret	.35	.35
		Nos. 732-736 (5)	1.75	1.75

First anniversary of return of Chinese National Government to Nanking.

See Taiwan Nos. 35-39, Northeastern Provinces 36-40.

Dr. Sun Yat-sen — A77

1947 *Perf. 12½, 11½x12½*

737	A77	$500 olive green	.25	.25
738	A77	$1000 green & car	.25	.25
739	A77	$2000 dp blue & red brn	.30	.25
740	A77	$5000 org red & blk	.30	.25
		Nos. 737-740 (4)	1.10	1.00

For surcharge see Szechwan No. 50.

Confucius A78

Confucius' Lecturing School A79

Tomb of Confucius A80

Temple of Confucius A81

1947, Aug. 27 **Litho.** *Perf. 14*

Without Gum

741	A78	$500 carmine rose	.60	*.65*

Engr.

742	A79	$800 yellow brown	.50	*.80*
743	A80	$1250 blue green	.50	*1.25*
744	A81	$1800 blue	.50	*1.90*
		Nos. 741-744 (4)	2.10	4.60

Sun Yat-sen and Plum Blossoms — A82

1947-48 **Engr.** *Perf. 14*

Without Gum

745	A82	$150 dk blue	.25	*.25*
746	A82	$250 dp lilac	.35	.25
747	A82	$500 blue grn	.25	.25
748	A82	$1000 red	.25	.25
749	A82	$2000 vermilion	.25	.25
750	A82	$3000 blue	.25	.25
751	A82	$4000 gray ('48)	.25	.25
752	A82	$5000 dk brown	.25	.25
753	A82	$6000 rose lilac ('48)	.25	.25
754	A82	$7000 lt red brn ('48)	.25	.25
755	A82	$10,000 dp blue & car	1.10	.25
756	A82	$20,000 car & yel grn	.35	.25
757	A82	$50,000 grn & dk bl	1.25	.25
758	A82	$100,000 dl yel & ol grn ('48)	1.80	.25
759	A82	$200,000 vio brn & dp bl ('48)	2.25	.45
760	A82	$300,000 sep & org brn ('48)	2.25	.55
761	A82	$500,000 dk Prus grn & sep ('48)	3.00	.55
		Nos. 745-761 (17)	14.60	5.05

See Nos. 788-799. For similar type see Formosa A1. For surcharges see Nos. 770, 804-806, 821-822, 840-841, 858-859, 869, 871, 880A-880B, 885A-885E, 1025-1036, Taiwan 56-57, 59, 89, Fukien 1-4, 7-12, 19-23, Hunan 2-5, C1, F1, Kiangsi 1-3, C1, E1, F1-F2, Kwangsi 8-10, 12-17, Shensi 1-2, C1, E1, Szechwan 24-49, Yunnan 61-62, 69, 205-207, People's Republic of China 3L69-3L70, 3L76, 4L63-4L64, 6L22, 6L27, 6L29, 6L32.

Chinese Flag and Map of Taiwan — A83

1947, Oct. 25 **With Gum**

762	A83	$500 carmine	.35	*1.00*
763	A83	$1250 deep green	.35	*1.00*

Restoration of Taiwan to China, 2nd anniv.

Mobile Post Office — A84

Street-Corner Branch Post Office — A85

1947, Nov. 5

764	A84	$500 carmine	.25	*.50*
765	A85	$1000 lilac	.25	*.50*
766	A85	$1250 green	.25	*.85*
767	A84	$1800 deep blue	.25	*1.10*
		Nos. 764-767 (4)	1.00	2.95

Stamps and Type of 1943-47 Surcharged in Black or Green

1947-48 **Unwmk.** *Perf. 12½, 13, 14*

768	A37	$500 on $20 brt yel grn (#633)	.25	.25
769	A73	$1250 on $70 red org (#639)	.25	.25
770	A82	$1800 on $350 yel org	.25	.25
771	A62	$2000 on $3 dk yel ('48) (#503)	.50	.25
772	A63	$2000 on $3 red (#567)	.25	.25
a.		On #567a	6.50	2.25
773	A62	$3000 on $3 lt yel ('48) (#555)	.25	.25
774	A63	$3000 on $3 lt red brn (G) ('48) (#568)	.25	.25
		Nos. 768-774 (7)	2.00	1.75

Nos. 768-774 have a single row of dots in the surcharge box frame.

The characters at the left express the new value and vary in number.

No. 640 Surcharged

1948, Aug. *Perf. 14*

775	A73	$5000 on $100 dk car	7.00	*70.00*

No. 775 received its surcharge in Kwangsi for use in that province.

Map of China and Mail-carrying Vehicles A86

Rural Mail Delivery — A87

Early and Modern Mail Transportation A88

1947, Dec. 16 **Engr.** *Perf. 12*

776	A86	$100 violet	.25	*1.00*
777	A87	$200 brt green	.25	*1.00*
778	A87	$300 red brown	.25	*1.00*
779	A88	$400 scarlet	.25	*1.00*
780	A88	$500 brt vio blue	.25	*1.00*
		Nos. 776-780 (5)	1.25	5.00

Chinese Postal Administration, 50th anniv.

National Assembly Building and New Constitution A89

1947, Dec. 25 *Perf. 14*

Without Gum

781	A89	$2000 brt red	.50	.60
782	A89	$3000 blue	.50	.60
783	A89	$5000 deep green	.50	.60
		Nos. 781-783 (3)	1.50	1.80

1st anniv. of the adoption of China's new constitution, Dec. 25, 1946.

Chinese Stamps of 1947 and 1912 — A90

Perf. 14, Imperf.

1948, Mar. 20 **Litho.**

Without Gum

784	A90	$5000 dk car rose	1.00	*4.00*
a.		Vert. pair, imperf. btwn	40.00	
785	A90	$5000 dk green	1.00	*4.00*
a.		Vert. pair, imperf. btwn	40.00	

Stamp exhibitions at Nanking, Mar. 20 (No. 784), and at Shanghai, May 19 (No. 785).

Sun Yat-sen Memorial Hall, Taipei — A91

1948, Apr. 28 **Engr.** *Perf. 14*

786	A91	$5000 violet	.30	*1.25*
787	A91	$10000 red	.30	*1.25*

Restoration of Formosa to China, 3rd anniv.

Sun Yat-sen Type of 1947-48

1948 **Without Gum**

788	A82	$20000 rose pink	.50	.35
789	A82	$30000 chocolate	.25	.25
790	A82	$40000 green	.25	.25
791	A82	$50000 dp blue	.25	.25
792	A82	$100000 dull grn	.25	.25
793	A82	$200000 brn vio	.75	.25
794	A82	$300000 yel grn	2.75	1.00
795	A82	$500000 lil rose	1.25	.25
796	A82	$1000000 claret	.75	.25
797	A82	$2000000 vermilion	1.50	.25
798	A82	$3000000 ol bis	3.00	.55
799	A82	$5000000 ultra	6.00	.90
		Nos. 788-799 (12)	17.50	4.80

Zeros for "cents" omitted.

For surcharges see Nos. 841, 871, 880A-880B, 885A-885E, 1025-1028, 1031-1036.

Early Ship and Modern Hai Tien — A92

Passenger Ship Kiang Ya — A93

1948, Aug. 16 **Without Gum**

800	A92	$20000 blue	.60	*1.75*
801	A92	$30000 rose lilac	.60	*1.75*
802	A93	$40000 yel brown	.60	*2.75*
803	A93	$60000 vermilion	.60	*2.75*
		Nos. 800-803 (4)	2.40	9.00

75th anniversary of the China Merchants' Steam Navigation Company.

Type of 1947-48 Surcharged in Black

1948 **Unwmk.** *Perf. 14*

804	A82	$4000 on $100 car	.25	*25.00*
805	A82	$5000 on $100 car	.25	.25
806	A82	$8000 on $700 red brn	.35	*.90*
		Nos. 804-806 (3)	.85	26.15

Stamps of 1942-46 Surcharged in Black or Red

1948 *Perf. 12½, 13*

807	A62	$5000 on $1 (#500)	.25	.25
808	A62	$5000 on $1 (#551)	20.00	*20.00*
809	A62	$5000 on $2 (#502)	.25	.25
810	A72	$10000 on $20 (#625)	.25	.25
811	A62	$20000 on 10c (#492)	.25	.25
812	A62	$20000 on 50c (#498;R)	.25	*.50*
813	A62	$30000 on 30c (#496)	.25	*.50*
a.		Perf. 10½	22.00	22.00
		Nos. 807-813 (7)	21.50	22.00

Nos. 492, 556 and 558 Surcharged in Black or Carmine

1948

814	A62	$15,000 on 10c dp grn	.25	.25
815	A62	$15,000 on $4 vio brn	.25	.25
816	A62	$15,000 on $6 gray vio (C)	.25	.25
		Nos. 814-816 (3)	.75	.75

No. 498, 494 and 504 Surcharged in Black

1948 **Unwmk.** *Perf. 11½, 13*

817	A62	$15,000 on 50c, perf. 13	.25	*.50*
a.		Perf. 11½	10.00	10.00
818	A62	$40,000 on 20c dk ol grn	.25	*.90*
a.		Perf. 11	10.00	7.50
819	A62	$60,000 on $4 red brn	.45	*.50*
		Nos. 817-819 (3)	.95	1.90

Gold Yuan Surcharges

(Nos. 820-885E)

Stamps of 1942-47 Surcharged in Black, Carmine or Red

1948 *Perf. 14, 13, 11*

820	A62	½c on 30c (#496)	.25	*5.00*
821	A82	½c on $500 (Bk) (#747)	.25	.25
822	A82	½c on $500 (C) (#747)	.25	*.90*
823	A73	1c on $20 (#636)	.25	*2.25*
824	A62	2c on $1.50 (R) (#501)	.25	*3.25*
825	A62	3c on $5 (#505)	.25	*3.25*
826	A62	4c on $1 (#499)	.25	*3.25*

827	A62	5c on 50c (#498)	.25	.45
a.		Perf. 11	6.50	6.50
		Nos. 820-827 (8)	2.00	18.60

On No. 820-827, the position of the surcharged denomination and "Gold Yuan" characters varies, the aim being to obliterate the original denomination.

Stamps of 1940-48 Surcharged in Black, Violet, Carmine, Blue or Green

Perf. 12, 12½, 13, 14, 12½x13

1948-49

828	A63	5c on $20 (#571)	.25	*1.10*
829	A72	5c on $30 (C) (#626)	.25	*1.40*
a.		Double surcharge	17.50	
830	A57	10c on 2c (#368)	.25	*1.75*
831	A39	10c on 2½c (#424)	.25	*1.10*
832	A62	10c on 25c (V) (#495)	.25	*1.25*
833	A63	10c on 40c (#565)	.25	*1.40*
834	A62	10c on $1 (#500)	.25	*.35*
834A	A62	10c on $1 (#551)	275.00	*225.00*
835	A63	10c on $2 (#566)	.25	.25
836	A62	10c on $20 (C) (#560)	.25	.25
836A	A63	10c on $20 (#571)	300.00	*300.00*
837	A67	10c on $20 (#592)	.25	.25
837A	A73	10c on $20 (#636)	1.00	*3.50*
838	A72	10c on $30 (C) (#626)	.25	*1.50*
839	A63	10c on $70 (#573)	.25	.50
a.		Double surcharge	15.00	
840	A82	10c on $7000 (#754)	1.00	1.00
841	A82	10c on $20,000 (#788)	.25	*4.75*
842	A63	20c on $6 (#569)	.25	*.35*
843	A37	20c on $30 (#634)	.45	*4.75*
844	A73	20c on $30 (C) (#637)	.65	*3.75*
845	A73	20c on $100 (#640)	.25	*3.00*
a.		Inverted surcharge	22.00	
b.		Double surcharge	16.00	
846	A39	50c on ½c (#312)	75.00	75.00
847	A39	50c on ½c (#421)	.25	*.65*
a.		Inverted surcharge	30.00	
848	A62	50c on 20c (#494)	.25	*.50*
849	A62	50c on 30c (Bl) (#496)	.25	*1.40*
850	A62	50c on 40c (V) (#497)	.25	*.90*
a.		Perf. 11	9.00	*10.00*
851	A63	50c on 40c (V) (#565)	.25	*1.00*
852	A62	50c on $4 (#556)	1.00	*3.50*
853	A62	50c on $4 (Bl) (#556)	.25	*2.00*
854	A62	50c on $20 (C) (#560)	.25	.25
855	A67	50c on $20 (V) (#592)	.50	*1.50*
856	A73	50c on $20 (#636)	.25	*1.25*
857	A62	50c on $70 (C) (#562)	.30	.30
858	A82	50c on $6000 (#753)	2.00	*3.50*
859	A82	50c on $6000 (Bl) (#753)	.25	*1.50*
860	A62	$1 on 30c (#550)	.25	.25
a.		Perf. 11	22.00	22.00
861	A62	$1 on 40c (#497)	.25	.25
a.		Perf. 11	4.00	4.00
862	A62	$1 on $1 (#499)	.55	*2.00*
863	A62	$1 on $5 (#557)	.70	.40
864	A63	$2 on $2 (R) (#566)	.25	.25
865	A72	$2 on $20 (#625)	.25	.25
866	A73	$2 on $100 (#640)	.25	.25
867	A46	$5 on 17c (#432)	.90	.90
868	A63	$5 on $2 (#566)	.25	.25
869	A82	$5 on $3000 (C) (#750)	.25	*1.50*
870	A47	$8 on 20c (#433)	.50	.50
871	A82	$8 on $30,000 (C) (#789)	.25	*2.50*
872	A47	$10 on 40c (#438)	1.25	1.00
873	A63	$10 on $2 (G) (#566)	.25	.35
874	A63	$10 on $2 (C) (#566)	.25	.25
875	A63	$20 on $2 (C) (#566)	.25	.25
875A	A73	$20 on $20 (#636)	4.75	3.00
876	A62	$50 on 30c (#496)	.25	*.30*
877	A63	$50 on $2 (Bl) (#566)	.30	.25
878	A73	$80 on $20 (#636)	.25	*1.00*
879	A62	$100 on $1 (#551)	.25	*1.00*
a.		Perf. 11	*60.00*	*60.00*
880	A63	$100 on $2 (C) (#566)	.35	.35
880A	A82	$50,000 on $20,000 (#788)	1.40	.40
880B	A82	$100,000 on $30,000 (V) (#789)	2.75	.90

Wmk. 261

881	A39	10c on 2½c (#405)	.40	*4.00*
882	A39	50c on ½c (#402)	.25	*.85*
		Nos. 828-882 (61)	680.50	673.65

Characters at left express the new value. Style of characters and numerals varies.

Nos. Q7 to Q9 Surcharged in Black or Carmine

1948 Unwmk. *Perf. 12½*

883	PP2	$200 on $3000 red org	.70	.50
884	PP2	$500 on $5000 dk bl (C)	.70	.45
885	PP2	$1000 on $10,000 vio	.70	.50
		Nos. 883-885 (3)	2.10	1.45

Nos. 788-791 Surcharged in Gold Yuan in Red (Nos. 885A, 885D-885E) or Black (Nos. 885B-885C) at Foochow

1949, Apr. 30 Unwmk. *Perf. 14*

885A	$20,000 on $40,000	15.00	*21.00*
885B	$50,000 on $30,000	15.00	*21.00*
885C	$100,000 on $20,000	15.00	*21.00*
885D	$200,000 on $40,000	15.00	*21.00*
885E	$200,000 on $50,000	15.00	*21.00*
	Nos. 885A-885E (5)	75.00	*105.00*

Issued in Fukien Postal District.

Dr. Sun Yat-sen — A94

1949 Unwmk. Engr. *Perf. 14*

Without Gum

886	A94	$1 orange	.45	.65
887	A94	$10 green	.50	.65
888	A94	$20 vio brown	.45	.65
889	A94	$50 dk Prus grn	.45	.65
890	A94	$100 org brn	.45	.65
891	A94	$200 red org	.45	.65
892	A94	$500 rose lilac	.45	.65
893	A94	$800 car rose	.45	*2.50*
894	A94	$1000 blue	.45	.65

Redrawn

Engr.

Perf. 12½

895	A94	$10 green	.45	*5.00*
a.		Perf. 14	4.00	*8.00*
b.		Perf. 13	.45	*5.50*
896	A94	$20 violet brn	.45	*.55*
a.		Perf. 14	1.10	*4.50*
b.		Perf. 13	.45	*.90*
		Nos. 886-896 (11)	5.00	*13.25*

Small "T" at left of necktie on Nos. 895-896a.

Redrawn

1949 Litho. *Perf. 12½*

Without Gum

897	A94	$50 grnsh gray	.30	*2.75*
898	A94	$100 dk org brn	.30	*.50*
899	A94	$200 orange red	.60	*3.00*
900	A94	$500 rose lilac	.30	*.50*
901	A94	$1000 deep blue	.30	*.50*
902	A94	$2000 violet	.30	*1.50*
903	A94	$5000 light blue	.30	*.45*
904	A94	$10,000 sepia	.30	*.45*
905	A94	$20,000 apple grn	.30	*1.50*
906	A94	$50,000 rose pink	.30	*.45*
907	A94	$80,000 brn red	.70	*4.50*
908	A94	$100,000 bl grn	.45	.45
		Nos. 897-908 (12)	4.45	*16.55*

Diagonal lines have been added to the background of the redrawn design.

Zeros for "cents" omitted on No. 908.

See Nos. 973-981. For surcharges see Nos. 991-1006, 1057-1060, Fukien 13-17, Szechwan 51, Tsingtau 1-4, Yunnan 63-65, 68, 70, People's Republic of China 4L34-4L44, 4L48-4L60, 5L43-5L50, 5L54-5L59, 5L91-5L95, 6L1-6L16, 6L23-6L26, 6L30-6L31, 7L6-7L8, 7L13-7L16, 8L12-8L13, 8L48-8L51.

Plane, Train and Ship — A95

Gold Yuan Surcharge in Black or Other Colors on Revenue Stamps

Two types, 50c on $20:
I — Thick numerals in "20." Vertical stroke in lower right corner of vignette. (Dah Tung Book Co.)
II — Thin "20." No vertical stroke in corner. (Central Trust.)

Two types, $2 on $50, $10 on $30, $100 on $50 and $300 on $50:
III — "Y" in lower right corner of vignette. (Dah Yeh Printing Co.)
IV — No "Y" in corner. (Dah Tung, Central Trust or Chung Ming.)

Two types, $50 on $300 and $1000 on $100:
V — Projection on left frame column below foliate ornament. (Dah Yeh Printing Co.)
VI — No projection. (Dah Tung Book Co.)

Litho.; Nos. 923, 933, 935-936 Engr.

1949 *Perf. 12½, 13, 14*

Without Gum

913	A95	50c on $20 red brn, I	.25	*.50*
a.		50c on $20 brown, II	.25	*.50*
914	A95	$1 on $15 red org	.25	*9.00*
915	A95	$2 on $50 dk bl, IV (C)	.25	*1.00*
a.		Type III	.40	*1.25*
916	A95	$3 on $50 dk bl (Bl)	.25	*1.00*
917	A95	$3 on $50 dk bl	.25	*1.00*
918	A95	$5 on $600 brn	.25	*.90*
919	A95	$10 on $30 dk vio, III (Bl)	.25	*.45*
a.		Type IV	.70	*1.75*
b.		Double surcharge, IV		
920	A95	$15 on $20 org brn (Bl)	.25	*.45*
921	A95	$25 on $20 org brn (G)	.25	*.45*
922	A95	$50 on $50 dk bl (R O)	.25	*.45*
923	A95	$50 on $300 grn, VI (C)	.25	*.60*
a.		$50 on $300 yel grn, V (C)	.25	*.50*
924	A95	$80 on $50 dk bl (Dk Br)	.25	*1.25*
925	A95	$100 on $50 dk bl, IV	1.00	.60
a.		Type III	5.00	*17.50*
926	A95	$200 on $50 dk bl	.90	.90
927	A95	$200 on $500 brn (Bl)	.60	*.70*
928	A95	$300 on $50 dk bl, III (C)	1.25	1.25
a.		Type IV	1.75	*2.00*
929	A95	$300 on $50 dk bl (Br)	2.00	2.00
930	A95	$500 on $15 red org (Bl)	1.50	*4.25*
931	A95	$500 on $30 dk vio	.75	*3.00*
932	A95	$1000 on $50 dk bl (C)	9.00	9.00
933	A95	$1000 on $100 ol grn, V	3.00	*4.50*
a.		Type VI	14.00	*15.00*
934	A95	$1500 on $50 dk bl (Bl)	2.50	*3.00*
935	A95	$2000 on $300 grn (Bl)	.45	.65
a.		Horiz. pair, imperf. between		
936	A95	$5000 on $100 ol grn (C)	350.00	
		Nos. 913-936 (24)	375.95	
		Nos. 913-935 (23)	25.95	46.90

No. 936 was officially authorized, but never issued.

Key pattern of overprinted border inverted and in 2 or 3 detached sections at top and bottom in Blue, Black or Green

Without Gum

Type A95

1949 Hankow Prints Litho.

937	A95	$50 on $10 (Bk)	9.50	*11.00*
938	A95	$100 on $10	11.00	*14.00*
939	A95	$500 on $10 (Bk)	9.00	*6.50*
940	A95	$1000 on $10	7.00	7.00
941	A95	$5000 on $20	29.00	25.00
942	A95	$10,000 on $20 (Bk)	17.50	14.00
943	A95	$50,000 on $20	20.00	*25.00*
944	A95	$100,000 on $20 (Bk)	25.00	25.00
945	A95	$500,000 on $20	350.00	250.00
946	A95	$2,000,000 on $20 (G)	900.00	375.00
947	A95	$5,000,000 on $20	1,600.	750.00
		Nos. 937-944 (8)	128.00	127.50

The $10 stamp is slate green, the $20 red brown.

The basic revenue stamps of Nos. 915-947 were the work of several printers. There are three main types, differing in the bottom label. Nos. 922 and 925 are in a second type: Nos. 923 and 930 in a third. Varieties of paper, color and overprint exist.

Counterfeits exist of Nos. 945-947.

For surcharges and overprints see Nos. 960-970, C63, E13, F3, J122-J126, Hupeh 1-2, People's Republic of China 5L51-5L53, 6L17-6L21.

Redrawn Coarse Impression

1949 Litho. Without Gum

Size: 18¼x20¾mm

951	A94	$50 green	.40	*40.00*
952	A94	$1000 dp blue	.50	*2.00*
953	A94	$5000 carmine	.65	*2.00*
954	A94	$10,000 brown	4.00	*7.50*
955	A94	$20,000 orange	1.25	*2.00*
956	A94	$50,000 blue	3.00	3.50
957	A94	$200,000 violet	5.00	3.75
958	A94	$500,000 vio brn	6.00	3.00
		Nos. 951-958 (8)	20.80	*63.75*

Zeros for "cents" omitted on Nos. 957-958.

See surcharge note following No. 900.

Locomotive and Ship — A96

1949, May 1 Litho. *Perf. 12½*

Without Gum

959	A96	orange	5.00	2.50
a.		Rouletted	13.50	10.00

Nos. 959, C62, E12 and F2 were printed without denomination and sold at the daily rate of the yuan. This was necessitated by the gold yuan inflation.

For surcharges and overprints see Nos. 1130, 1213, Taiwan 97, Fukien 18, Kansu 1, People's Republic of China 24-29, 101-104, 4L31-4L33, 4L45-4L47, 4L61-4L62, 7L9-7L12, 8L52-8L54.

Revenue Stamps Overprinted in Black

1949, May *Perf. 12½, 13, 14*

Without Gum

960	A95	$30 dark violet	125.00	120.00

Engr.

961	A95	$200 violet brown	15.00	12.00
962	A95	$500 dark green	20.00	20.00
		Nos. 960-962 (3)	160.00	152.00

A similar overprint appears on Nos. C63, E13, F3, differing in 2nd and 3rd characters of bottom row.

Silver Yuan Surcharge in Black or Other Colors

1949 **Litho.**

963	A95	1c on $5000 brn (G)	8.50	5.50
964	A95	4c on $100 ol grn (Bl)	6.00	3.75
965	A95	4c on $3000 org)	6.00	2.00
966	A95	10c on $50 dk bl (RV)	8.50	2.75
967	A95	10c on $1000 car	8.50	3.25
a.		Inverted surcharge	60.00	
968	A95	20c on $1000 red (V)	8.50	5.00
b.		Inverted surcharge		
968A	A95	50c on $30 dk vio (C)	47.50	6.00
969	A95	50c on $50 dk bl (C)	21.00	2.75
970	A95	$1 on $50 dk bl	25.00	*35.00*
		Nos. 963-970 (9)	139.50	66.00

Nos. 963-965 and 967 are engraved.

Sun Type of 1949 Redrawn

Coarse Impression

1949 *Perf. 12½, 13 or Compound*

973	A94	1c apple green	29.00	*11.00*
974	A94	2c orange	9.00	*17.50*
975	A94	4c blue green	.35	*2.00*
976	A94	10c deep lilac	.35	*2.00*
977	A94	16c orange red	.75	*17.50*
978	A94	20c blue	.45	*5.50*
979	A94	50c dk brown	2.40	*48.00*
980	A94	100c deep blue	475.00	475.00
981	A94	500c scarlet	500.00	525.00
		Nos. 973-981 (9)	1,017.	1,103.

For surcharges see Nos. 1057-1060.

Flying Geese Over Globe — A97

1949, May **Litho.** *Perf. 12½*

Without Gum

984	A97	$1 brown org	15.00	*17.50*
985	A97	$2 blue	75.00	30.00
986	A97	$5 car rose	75.00	32.50
987	A97	$10 blue grn	75.00	65.00
		Nos. 984-987 (4)	240.00	145.00

Five other denominations — 10c, 16c, 50c, $20 and $50 — were also printed at Shanghai, but were not issued.

For surcharges see Nos. 1007-1011, 1042-1045, 1061-1063, People's Republic of China 49-56, 5LQ17-5LQ26, 7L17-7L18, 8L14-8L16.

Pigeons, Globe and Wreath A98

Engraved and Typographed

1949, Aug. 1 **Without Gum** *Imperf.*

988	A98	$1 org red & blk	12.00	*17.50*

75th anniv. of the UPU.

Exists with black denomination omitted.

Summer Palace, Peiping — A99

Bronze Bull and Kunming Lake — A100

Engraved and Typographed

1949, Aug. *Rouletted*

Without Gum

989	A99	15c org brn & grn	8.00	*9.50*
990	A100	40c dl grn & car	9.25	*9.50*
a.		2nd and 3rd characters at top transposed	160.00	200.00

Silver Yuan Surcharge in Black on 1949 Sun Yat-sen Issues

1949 *Perf. 12½, 14*

991	A94	1c on $100 org brn (890)	15.00	10.00
992	A94	1c on $100 dk org brn (898)	15.00	10.00
993	A94	2½c on $500 rose lil (892)	19.00	11.00
a.		Inverted surcharge	60.00	
994	A94	2½c on $500 rose lil (900)	21.00	12.00
995	A94	15c on $10 grn (887)	30.00	40.00
a.		Inverted surcharge	67.50	
996	A94	15c on $20 vio brn (896)	42.50	*65.00*
		Nos. 991-996 (6)	142.50	148.00

Silver Yuan Surcharge in Black or Carmine

997	A94	2½c on $50 grn (951)	2.75	3.75
998	A94	2½c on $50,000 bl (956)	7.50	3.75
999	A94	5c on $1000 dp bl (952) (C)	6.00	3.75
1000	A94	5c on $20,000 org (955)	4.00	3.25
1001	A94	5c on $200,000 vio (957) (C)	5.50	3.25
1002	A94	5c on $500,000 vio brn (958)	5.50	3.25
1003	A94	10c on $5000 car (953)	11.00	8.00
1004	A94	10c on $10,000 brn (954)	11.00	8.00
1005	A94	15c on $200 red org (891)	13.50	16.00
1006	A94	25c on $100 dk org brn (896)	27.50	30.00
		Nos. 997-1006 (10)	94.25	83.00

REPUBLIC OF CHINA

ri-ˈpə-blik of ˈchī-nə

(Taiwan)

LOCATION — Taiwan (since 1949) (Formosa)
GOVT. — Republic
AREA — 13,970 sq. mi.
POP. — 22,113,250 (1999 est.)
CAPITAL — Taipei

Stamps issued and used in Taiwan after Communist forces occupied the Chinese mainland include Taiwan Nos. 91-96, 101-103, J10-J17.

Catalogue values for unused stamps in this country are for Never Hinged items, beginning with Scott 1124 in the regular postage section, Scott B17 in the semi-postal section, Scott C69 in the airpost section, and Scott J142 in the postage due section.

Watermarks

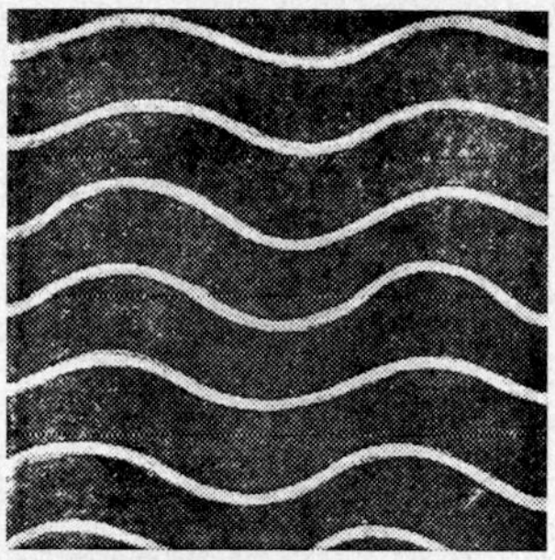

Wmk. 281 — Wavy Lines

Wmk. 323 — Seal Character (found with "Yu" in various arrangements)

Wmk. 368 — JEZ Multiple

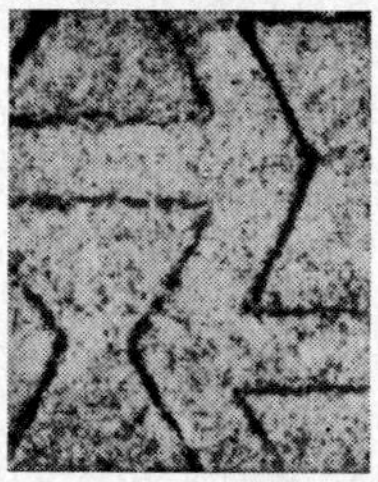

Wmk. 370 — Geometrical Design

Type of 1949 with Value Omitted Surcharged in Various Colors

1950, Jan. 1 **Unwmk.** *Perf. 12½*

1007	A97	$1 green (Bk)	225.00	14.00
1008	A97	$2 green (C)	260.00	25.00
1009	A97	$5 green (V)	2,750.	140.00
1010	A97	$10 green (Br)	3,750.	325.00
1011	A97	$20 green (Dk Bl)	6,500.	1,100.
		Nos. 1007-1011 (5)	13,485.	1,604.

Two printings of the $1 and $2 show minor differences.

Cheng Ch'eng-kung (Koxinga) — A101

1950, June 26 **Typo.** *Rouletted*

Without Gum

1012	A101	3c dk gray grn	4.00	1.10
1013	A101	10c orange brn	3.00	.30
1014	A101	15c orange yel	14.25	3.25
1015	A101	20c emerald	4.00	.25
1016	A101	30c claret	60.00	17.50
1017	A101	40c red orange	4.50	.30
1018	A101	50c chocolate	7.50	1.10
1019	A101	80c carmine	22.00	3.75
1020	A101	$1 ultra	18.50	1.10
1021	A101	$1.50 green	70.00	14.00
1022	A101	$1.60 blue	60.00	1.75
1023	A101	$2 red violet	25.00	1.40
1024	A101	$5 aqua	175.00	27.50
		Nos. 1012-1024 (13)	467.75	73.30

Part perf pairs exist of the 10c, 20c, 80c.

The 10c and 20c were reprinted from new plates. There are slight differences.

For surcharges see Nos. 1070-1072, 1105-1108, 1118-1119.

Nos. 751, 753, 788-791, 793, 795-799 Surcharged in Carmine or Black

1950 **Engr.** *Perf. 14*

1025	A82	3c on $30,000	3.75	2.25
1026	A82	3c on $40,000 (C)	3.25	2.25
1027	A82	3c on $50,000 (C)	3.25	3.00
1028	A82	5c on $200,000	3.75	2.50
1029	A82	10c on $4000	32.50	4.00
1030	A82	10c on $6000	24.00	4.00
1031	A82	10c on $20,000	24.00	4.00
1032	A82	10c on $2,000,000	24.00	4.00
1033	A82	20c on $500,000	35.00	4.00
1034	A82	20c on $1,000,000	60.00	8.00
1035	A82	30c on $3,000,000	90.00	10.00
1036	A82	50c on $5,000,000 (C)	150.00	10.00
		Nos. 1025-1036 (12)	453.50	58.00

Issued: Nos. 1025-1027, 3/6; No. 1028, 3/25; No. 1031, 6/10: Nos. 1029-1030, 1032, 1035-1036, 8/1; No. 1033-1034, 8/25.

Forgeries exist.

Inverted Surcharge

1029a	A82	10c on $4000	160.00
1030a	A82	10c on $6000	350.00
1031a	A82	10c on $20,000	200.00
1032a	A82	10c on $2,000,000	210.00
1033a	A82	20c on $500,000	275.00
1034a	A82	20c on $1,000,000	275.00

Allegory of Election A102

Perf. 12x12½, Imperf.

1951, Mar. 20 **Engr.** **Unwmk.**

Without Gum

1037	A102	40c carmine	15.00	2.00
a.		Horiz. pair, imperf. btwn.	85.00	
1038	A102	$1 dp blue	35.00	4.00
1039	A102	$1.60 purple	60.00	5.00
1040	A102	$2 brown	85.00	5.00
		Nos. 1037-1040 (4)	195.00	16.00

Souvenir Sheet

Imperf

1041	A102	$2 dp blue grn	*550.00*	*375.00*

Adoption of local self-government in Taiwan.

Design A97 Surcharged — A103

Surcharge in Various Colors

1951, July 19 *Perf. 12½*

Without Gum

1042	A103	$5 green (R Br)	110.00	12.50
1043	A103	$10 green (Bk)	225.00	14.00
1044	A103	$20 green (R)	950.00	35.00
1045	A103	$50 green (P)	1,600.	100.00
		Nos. 1042-1045 (4)	2,885.	161.50

Farmer and Scroll Announcing Tax Reduction — A104

1952, Jan. 1 Without Gum *Perf. 14*

1046	A104	20c red orange	11.00	1.50
1047	A104	40c dk green	15.00	2.75
1048	A104	$1 brown	25.00	6.50
1049	A104	$1.40 dp blue	40.00	4.50
1050	A104	$2 dk gray	110.00	40.00
1051	A104	$5 brown car	150.00	16.00
		Nos. 1046-1051 (6)	351.00	71.25

Land tax reduction of 37.5% in Taiwan.
Value, imperf. set, $1,100.

Pres. Chiang Kai-shek, Flag and Followers A105

Flag in Violet Blue and Carmine

1952, Mar. 1 Unwmk. *Perf. 14*

Without Gum

1052	A105	40c rose car	16.00	.50
a.		Vert. pair, imperf. btwn.	150.00	
1053	A105	$1 dp green	30.00	2.25
1054	A105	$1.60 brown org	60.00	1.10
a.		Horiz. pair, imperf. btwn.	320.00	
1055	A105	$2 brt blue	120.00	19.00
1056	A105	$5 violet brn	135.00	5.00
		Nos. 1052-1056 (5)	361.00	27.85

2nd anniv. of Chiang Kai-shek's return to the presidency.
Value, imperf. set, $495.
See Nos. 1064-1069.

Nos. 975-976, 978-979 Surcharged in Black

1952, Aug. 1 *Perf. 12½*

1057	A94	3c on 4c bl grn	6.25	5.25
1058	A94	3c on 10c dp lil	6.25	5.25
a.		Inverted surcharge		
1059	A94	3c on 20c blue	8.75	7.50
1060	A94	3c on 50c dk brn	10.00	8.75
		Nos. 1057-1060 (4)	31.25	26.75

Forgeries exist.

Geese Type of 1949 with Value Omitted Surcharged

1952, Dec. 8

1061	A97	$10 green (P)	100.00	16.00
1062	A97	$20 green (R)	300.00	27.50
1063	A97	$50 green (Bk)	2,750.	750.00
		Nos. 1061-1063 (3)	3,150.	793.50

Chiang Type of 1952 Redrawn

Perf. 12½

1953, Mar. 1 Engr. Unwmk.

Without Gum

Flag in Dark Blue & Carmine

1064	A105	10c red orange	5.00	1.50
1065	A105	20c green	1.05	1.50
1066	A105	40c rose pink	15.00	2.00
1067	A105	$1.40 blue	45.00	3.25
1068	A105	$2 brown	120.00	6.50
1069	A105	$5 rose violet	180.00	17.50
		Nos. 1064-1069 (6)	366.05	32.25

Chiang Kai-shek's return to presidency, 3rd anniv.

Many differences in redrawn design. Value, imperf. set, $495.

Nos. 1020, 1014, 1016 and 1022 Surcharged in Various Colors

1953 *Rouletted*

1070	A101	3c on $1 ultra (C)	2.00	.50
1070A	A101	10c on 15c org yel (G) ('54)	7.50	1.05
1071	A101	10c on 30c cl (Bl)	4.00	1.40
1072	A101	20c on $1.60 bl (Bk)	4.50	1.50
		Nos. 1070-1072 (4)	18.00	4.45

Chinese characters and ornamental device at bottom differ on each value.

Issued: No. 1071, 2/1; No. 1070, 5/25; No. 1072, 6/13; No. 1070A, 7/16.

Nurse & Patients — A106

Cross in Red, Burelage Color in Italics

1953, July 1 Litho. *Perf. 12½*

Without Gum

1073	A106	40c brown, *buff*	14.50	1.50
1074	A106	$1.60 blue, *bl*	35.00	1.40
1075	A106	$2 green, *yel*	55.00	2.25
1076	A106	$5 red org, *org*	95.00	10.00
		Nos. 1073-1076 (4)	199.50	15.15

Chinese Anti-Tuberculosis Association.

Chiang Kai-shek — A107

1953, Oct. 31 Engr. Without Gum

1077	A107	10c dk brown	5.75	.25
1078	A107	20c lilac	5.75	.25
1079	A107	40c dp green	5.75	.25
1080	A107	50c dp pink	8.00	.45
1081	A107	80c brown bis	22.00	2.00
1082	A107	$1 dp olive grn	10.00	.25
1083	A107	$1.40 dp blue	10.00	.25
1084	A107	$1.60 dp carmine	10.00	.25
1085	A107	$1.70 apple grn	10.00	1.10
1086	A107	$2 brown	12.00	.25
1087	A107	$3 dark blue	190.00	7.00
1088	A107	$4 aqua	12.00	.70
1089	A107	$5 red orange	18.00	.70
1090	A107	$10 dk green	80.00	3.25
1091	A107	$20 dk brn lake	100.00	10.00
a.		Souvenir folder	600.00	
		Nos. 1077-1091 (15)	499.25	26.95

67th birthday of Pres. Chiang Kai-shek.

No. 1091a contains Nos. 1077-1091 imperf, arranged in 3 sheets of 5 stamps each.

Silo Highway Bridge — A108

$1.60 and $5, Silo bridge, side view.

Without Gum

Various Frames

1954, Jan. 28 Unwmk. *Perf. 12½*

1092	A108	40c vermilion	20.00	2.50
1093	A108	$1.60 blue violet	100.00	3.00
1094	A108	$3.60 sepia	75.00	8.50
1095	A108	$5 magenta	175.00	22.50
a.		Souvenir folder	2,100.	
		Nos. 1092-1095 (4)	370.00	36.50

Opening of Silo bridge, 1st anniversary.

No. 1095a contains one sheet of 4 containing Nos. 1092-1095 imperforate. Beware of stapled folders.

Forest of Evergreens — A109

1954, Mar. 12 *Perf. 12x12½*

Without Gum

1096	A109	40c shown	17.00	1.50
1097	A109	$10 Nursery	126.50	10.00

Issued to publicize forest conservation.

Runner — A110

1954, Mar. 29 Without Gum

1098	A110	40c dp ultra	14.00	2.00
1099	A110	$5 carmine	100.00	10.00

11th Youth Day, Mar. 29, 1954.

Globe, Bridge and Ship — A111

1954, Oct. 21 *Perf. 12*

Without Gum

1100	A111	40c red orange	15.00	1.00
1101	A111	$5 deep blue	17.50	4.50

2nd Overseas Chinese Day, Oct. 21, 1954.

Ex-Prisoner with Broken Chains — A112

Designs: $1, Ex-prisoner with torch and flag, UN emblem. $1.60, Torch and date.

1955, Jan. 23

1102	A112	40c blue green	2.50	.65
a.		Vert. pair, imperf. btwn.	150.00	
1103	A112	$1 sepia	18.50	5.00
1104	A112	$1.60 lake	18.50	4.25
		Nos. 1102-1104 (3)	39.50	9.90

Honoring Chinese who fought on the side of the North Korean army, who, when released January 23, 1954, chose to return to the Republic of China.

Nos. 1019-1021, 1017 Surcharged in Brown, Blue or Green

a

b

c

1955 *Rouletted*

1105	A101(a)	3c on $1 (Br)	2.75	.50
1106	A101(b)	10c on 80c (Bl)	3.75	.50
1107	A101(b)	10c on $1.50 (Bl)	3.75	.50
1108	A101(c)	20c on 40c (G)	4.50	.85
		Nos. 1105-1108 (4)	14.75	2.35

Issued: No. 1105, 1108, 2/18; Nos. 1106-1107, 8/1.

Hand Planting Evergreen Tree — A113

Design: $50, Seedling and map of Taiwan.

1955, Apr. 1 *Perf. 12*

Without Gum

1109 A113 $20 dp carmine 32.50 1.25
1110 A113 $50 blue 80.00 5.75

Issued to publicize forest conservation.

Chiang Kai-shek, Flags, Building A114

1955, May 20 Engr. *Perf. 12*

Without Gum

1111 A114 20c olive 4.50 .40
1112 A114 40c blue green 4.00 .40
1113 A114 $2 car rose 10.75 1.25
1114 A114 $7 dp ultra 17.00 2.00
a. Souv. sheet of 4, #1111-1114, imperf. *325.00 200.00*
Nos. 1111-1114 (4) 36.25 4.05

First anniversary of Pres. Chiang Kai-shek's re-election.
No. 1114a is perf. 12 at right edge of sheet. Value is for sheet with right selvage.

Armed Forces Emblem — A115

1955, Sept. 3 Without Gum

1115 A115 40c dk blue 4.75 .50
1116 A115 $2 org ver 17.00 1.50
1117 A115 $7 bl grn 27.50 1.75
a. Sheet of 3, #1115-1117, imperf. *700.00 500.00*
Nos. 1115-1117 (3) 49.25 3.75

Armed Forces Day, Sept. 3.
No. 1117a is perf. 12 at right edge of sheet. Value is for sheet with right selvage.

Nos. 1017, 1018 and C64 Surcharged in Magenta

1955, Sept. 16 Typo. *Rouletted*

1118 A101 20c on 40c red org 5.00 .40
1119 A101 20c on 50c choc 5.00 .40
1120 AP6 20c on 60c dp blue 7.00 .50
Nos. 1118-1120 (3) 17.00 1.30

Flags of UN and China A116

1955, Oct. 24 Engr. *Perf. 11½*

Without Gum

1121 A116 40c dk blue 3.50 .55
1122 A116 $2 dk car rose 6.75 1.10
1123 A116 $7 slate green 11.50 1.90
Nos. 1121-1123 (3) 21.75 3.55

10th anniv. of the UN, Oct. 24, 1955.

Catalogue values for unused stamps in this section, from this point to the end of the section, are for Never Hinged items.

Pres. Chiang Kai-shek — A117

1955, Oct. 31 Photo. *Perf. 13½*

1124 A117 40c dk bl, red & brn 6.00 .60
1125 A117 $2 grn, red & dk bl 12.75 2.00
1126 A117 $7 brn, red & grn 19.00 3.00
a. Souv. sheet of 3, #1124-1126, imperf. *180.00 180.00*
Nos. 1124-1126 (3) 37.75 5.60

69th birthday of Pres. Chiang Kai-shek.
No. 1126a is perf. 12 at right edge of sheet. Value is for sheet with right selvage.

Birthplace of Sun Yat-sen — A118

1955, Nov. 12 Engr. *Perf. 12*

Without Gum

1127 A118 40c blue 3.25 .45
1128 A118 $2 red brown 8.00 1.00
1129 A118 $7 rose lake 10.00 2.00
Nos. 1127-1129 (3) 21.25 3.45

90th anniversary, birth of Sun Yat-sen.

No. 959a Surcharged in Bright Green

1956, Feb. 10 Litho. *Rouletted*

1130 A96 20c on orange .60 .25

See No. 1213.

China Map and Transportation Methods — A119

Wmk. 281

1956, Mar. 20 Engr. *Perf. 12*

Without Gum

1131 A119 40c dk carmine 2.00 .25
1132 A119 $1 intense blk 4.00 .65
1133 A119 $1.60 chocolate 5.50 .45
1134 A119 $2 dk green 8.75 1.00
Nos. 1131-1134 (4) 20.25 2.35

60th anniv. of the founding of the modern Chinese postal system.

Souvenir Sheets

Imperf

1135 A119 $2 magenta *60.00 30.00*
1136 A119 $2 red *60.00 30.00*

Exhib. for the 60th anniv. of the modern Chinese postal system, Mar. 20, 1956.

Children at Play — A120

1956, Apr. 4 Unwmk. *Perf. 12*

Without Gum

1137 A120 40c emerald 1.75 .25
1138 A120 $1.60 dk blue 3.50 .50
1139 A120 $2 dk carmine 5.75 1.00
Nos. 1137-1139 (3) 11.00 1.75

Children's Day, Apr. 4, 1956.

Early and Modern Locomotives A121

1956, June 9 Wmk. 281 Vert.

Without Gum

1140 A121 40c rose car 4.25 .40
1141 A121 $2 blue 6.00 .65
1142 A121 $8 green 10.00 1.75
Nos. 1140-1142 (3) 20.25 2.80

75th anniversary of Chinese Railroads.

Pres. Chiang Kai-shek
A122 A123

A124

Various Portraits of Chiang

Perf. 14½x13½, 14½ (A123), 13½x14½

1956, Oct. 31 Photo. Unwmk.

1143 A122 20c red orange 4.50 .25
1144 A122 40c carmine rose 6.75 .25
1145 A123 $1 brt ultra 9.00 .30
1146 A123 $1.60 red lilac 11.50 .25
1147 A124 $2 red brown 16.00 .50
1148 A124 $8 brt grnsh blue 35.00 .85
Nos. 1143-1148 (6) 82.75 2.40

70th birthday of Pres. Chiang Kai-shek.

Types of Special Delivery, Air Post and Registration Stamps of 1949 Surcharged in Black or Maroon

a

b

c

1956 Unwmk. Litho. *Rouletted*

Without Gum

1150 SD2(a) 3c red violet 1.25 .25
a. Perf. 12½ 3.50 .30
1151 AP5(b) 3c blue green (M) 1.25 .25
1152 R2(c) 10c bright red 1.25 .25
Nos. 1150-1152 (3) 3.75 .75

Issued: No. 1150, 4/25; No. 1151, 11/11; No. 1152, 12/25.

Telecommunications Emblem and Radio Tower — A125

Wmk. 281

1956, Dec. 28 Engr. *Perf. 12*

Without Gum

1153 A125 40c deep ultra 1.60 .25
1154 A125 $1.40 carmine 2.25 .25
1155 A125 $1.60 dark green 3.25 .25
1156 A125 $2 chocolate 4.25 .40
Nos. 1153-1156 (4) 11.35 1.15

Chinese telegraph service, 75th anniv.

Map of China — A126

Pin Perf., Perf. 12x12½

1957 Litho. Wmk. 281

Without Gum

1157 A126 3c brt blue .90 .25
1158 A126 10c violet 1.40 .25
1159 A126 20c red orange .90 .25
1160 A126 40c rose red 1.75 .25

Unwmk.

1161 A126 $1 orange brown 2.50 .25
1162 A126 $1.60 green 3.75 .25
Nos. 1157-1162 (6) 11.20 1.50

Map inscription reads: "Recovery of Mainland."
See Nos. 1177-1182.

Mother Instructing Mencius — A127

Design: $3, Mother tattooing Yueh Fei.

Without Gum

Unwmk.

1957, May 12 Engr. *Perf. 12*

1163 A127 40c green 1.50 .25
1164 A127 $3 redsh brown 2.75 .40

Issued to honor Mother's Day, 1957.

Badge of Chinese Boy Scouts — A128

1957, Aug. 11 Without Gum

1165 A128 40c lilac .80 .25
1166 A128 $1 green 1.75 .50
1167 A128 $1.60 dk blue 2.50 .25
Nos. 1165-1167 (3) 5.05 1.00

Cent. of the birth of Lord Baden-Powell and to publicize the World Scout Jubilee Jamboree, England, Aug. 1-12.

Globe, Radio Tower and Microphone A129

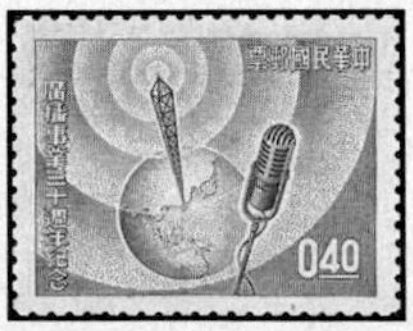

1957, Sept. 16 Without Gum

1168 A129 40c vermilion .60 .25
1169 A129 50c brt rose lilac 1.00 .25
1170 A129 $3.50 dark blue 1.75 .55
Nos. 1168-1170 (3) 3.35 1.05

30th anniv. of Chinese broadcasting.

Map of Taiwan — A130

1957, Oct. 26 **Without Gum**

1171 A130 40c blue green 3.25 .40
1172 A130 $1.40 lt ultra 6.25 1.75
1173 A130 $2 gray 8.50 1.90
Nos. 1171-1173 (3) 18.00 4.05

Start of construction on the Cross Island Highway, Taiwan.

Freighter "Hai Min" and River Boat "Kiang Foo" — A131

1957, Dec. 16 **Engr.** ***Perf. 12***
Without Gum

1174 A131 40c deep ultra .75 .25
1175 A131 80c rose lake 1.50 .95
1176 A131 $2.80 vermilion 2.25 1.40
Nos. 1174-1176 (3) 4.50 2.60

85th anniv. of the establishment of the China Merchants Steam Navigation Co.

Type of 1957
Pin Perf., Perf. 12x12½
1957, Dec. 25 **Typo.** **Unwmk.**
Without Gum
Dark Blue Frames

1177 A126 3c brt blue .30 .25
1178 A126 10c violet .55 .25
1179 A126 20c brick red .85 .25
1180 A126 40c rose red 1.00 .25
1181 A126 $1 dp org brn 3.25 .25
1182 A126 $1.60 dp green 4.00 .30
Nos. 1177-1182 (6) 9.95 1.55

Stamps with bars obliterating the face value are specimens.

Butterfly — A132

Various Insects in Natural Colors
Perf. 13½
1958, Mar. 20 **Unwmk.** **Photo.**

1183 A132 10c pale grn, grn & blk 1.25 .50
1184 A132 40c lem, pink, grn & blk 1.25 .50
1185 A132 $1 yel grn & mar 2.25 .60
1186 A132 $1.40 yel, org & blk 3.25 .75
1187 A132 $1.60 pale brn & dk pur 4.75 .90
1188 A132 $2 brt yel, org & blk 5.75 1.25
Nos. 1183-1188 (6) 18.50 4.50

Mme. Chiang Kai-shek Orchid — A133

Orchids: 20c, Formosan Wilson, horiz. $1.40, Klotzsch. $3, Fitzgerald, horiz.

Orchids in Natural Colors
1958, Mar. 20

1189 A133 20c chocolate 2.25 .40
1190 A133 40c purple 2.50 .40
1191 A133 $1.40 dk vio brn 4.50 .60
1192 A133 $3 dark blue 6.25 1.10
Nos. 1189-1192 (4) 15.50 2.50

World Health Organization Emblem — A134

1958, May 28 **Engr.** ***Perf. 12***
Without Gum

1193 A134 40c dark blue .50 .25
1194 A134 $1.60 brick red .65 .25
1195 A134 $2 deep red lilac .85 .40
Nos. 1193-1195 (3) 2.00 .90

10th anniv. of the WHO.

President's Mansion, Taipei — A135

Wmk. 323
1958, Sept. 20 **Engr.** ***Perf. 12***
Without Gum

1196 A135 $10 blue green 16.00 .30
a. Granite paper 12.00 .30
1197 A135 $20 car rose 24.00 .50
a. Granite paper 20.00 .50
1198 A135 $50 red brown 60.00 2.00
1199 A135 $100 dk blue 90.00 5.00
Nos. 1196-1199 (4) 190.00 7.80

Issued: Nos. 1196a, 1197a, 5/24/63.
See Nos. 1349-1351. For surcharge see No. J131.

Taiwan Farm Scene A136

1958, Oct. 1 **Unwmk.**
Without Gum

1200 A136 20c emerald 1.25 .25
1201 A136 40c black 1.50 .25
1202 A136 $1.40 brt magenta 2.75 .25
1203 A136 $3 ultra 4.50 .75
Nos. 1200-1203 (4) 10.00 1.50

10th anniversary of the Joint Commission on Rural Reconstruction.

Pres. Chiang Kai-shek A137

1958, Oct. 31 **Photo.** ***Perf. 13½***
1204 A137 40c multicolored 1.25 .45

Pres. Chiang Kai-shek on his 72nd birthday.

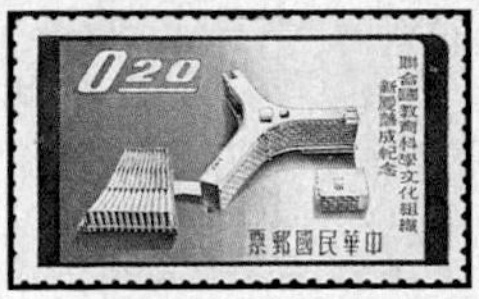

UNESCO Building, Paris A138

1958, Nov. 3 **Engr.** ***Perf. 12***
Without Gum

1205 A138 20c dark blue .35 .25
1206 A138 40c green .50 .25
1207 A138 $1.40 orange ver .70 .40
1208 A138 $3 red lilac 1.25 .55
Nos. 1205-1208 (4) 2.80 1.45

UNESCO Headquarters in Paris opening, Nov. 3.

Flame from Liberty Torch Encircling Globe — A139

1958, Dec. 10 **Unwmk.**
Without Gum

1209 A139 40c green .25 .25
1210 A139 60c gray brown .30 .25
1211 A139 $1 carmine .50 .25
1212 A139 $3 ultra .75 .40
Nos. 1209-1212 (4) 1.80 1.15

10th anniversary of the signing of the Universal Declaration of Human Rights.

No. 959a Surcharged in Bright Green

Rouletted
1958, Dec. 11 **Litho.** **Unwmk.**
Without Gum

1213 A96 20c on orange .55 .25

Ballot Box, Scales and Constitution — A140

1958, Dec. 25 **Engr.** ***Perf. 12***
Without Gum

1214 A140 40c green 1.25 .25
1215 A140 50c dull purple 1.75 .25
1216 A140 $1.40 car rose 2.00 .25
1217 A140 $3.50 dk blue 3.50 .75
Nos. 1214-1217 (4) 8.50 1.50

Adoption of the constitution, 10th anniv.

Chu Kwang Tower, Quemoy — A141

1959-60 **Wmk. 323** **Litho.** ***Perf. 12***
Without Gum

1218 A141 3c orange .50 .25
1218A A141 5c lt yel grn ('60) .60 .25
1219 A141 10c lilac .70 .25
1220 A141 20c ultra .90 .25
1221 A141 40c brown 1.10 .25
1222 A141 50c bluish grn 1.40 .25
1223 A141 $1 rose red 1.50 .25
1224 A141 $1.40 yel grn 2.10 .25
1225 A141 $2 gray grn 2.75 .25
1226 A141 $2.80 rose pink 4.00 .25
1227 A141 $3 slate blue 4.25 .25
Nos. 1218-1227 (11) 19.80 2.75

See Nos. 1270-1283.

ILO Emblem and Headquarters, Geneva — A142

1959, June 15 **Engr.** ***Perf. 12***
Without Gum

1228 A142 40c blue .40 .25
1229 A142 $1.60 dk brown .50 .25
1230 A142 $3 brt blue grn .75 .25
1231 A142 $5 orange ver 1.25 .50
Nos. 1228-1231 (4) 2.90 1.25

40th anniversary of the ILO.

Bugler and Tents A143

1959, July 8 **Unwmk.**
Without Gum

1232 A143 40c carmine .95 .25
1233 A143 50c dark blue 1.10 .25
1234 A143 $5 green 1.90 .55
Nos. 1232-1234 (3) 3.95 1.05

10th World Boy Scout Jamboree, Makiling National Park, Philippines, July 17-26.

Inscribed Stone, Mt. Tai-wu, Quemoy — A144

Map of Taiwan Straits A145

1959, Sept. 3 **Engr.** ***Perf. 12***
Without Gum

1235 A144 40c brown .90 .25
1236 A145 $1.40 ultra 1.00 .25
1237 A145 $2 green 1.75 .25
1238 A144 $3 dark blue 2.10 .30
Nos. 1235-1238 (4) 5.75 1.05

Defense of Quemoy and Matsu islands. For overprints see Nos. 1258-1259.

Pigeons Circling Globe A146

1959, Oct. 4 **Without Gum**

1239 A146 40c blue .45 .25
1240 A146 $1 rose carmine .80 .25
1241 A146 $2 gray brown 1.10 .25
1242 A146 $3.50 red orange 1.40 .50
Nos. 1239-1242 (4) 3.75 1.25

Intl. Letter Writing Week, Oct. 4-10.

National Taiwan Science Hall, Taipei — A147

1959, Nov. 12 Photo. *Perf. 13x13½*

1243 A147 40c shown 1.40 .25
1244 A147 $3 Front view 2.75 .70

Emblem A148

1959, Dec. 7 Engr. *Perf. 12*
Without Gum

1245 A148 40c blue green .40 .25
1246 A148 $1.60 red lilac .70 .25
1247 A148 $3 orange 1.10 .60
Nos. 1245-1247 (3) 2.20 1.10

Intl. Confederation of Free Trade Unions, 10th anniv.

Sun Yat-sen, Lincoln and Flags A149

Perf. 13½, 12
1959, Dec. 25 Photo. Unwmk.

1248 A149 40c multicolored .50 .25
1249 A149 $3 multicolored 1.25 .60

Issued to honor Sun Yat-sen and Abraham Lincoln as "Leaders of Democracy."

Mailman on Motorcycle Delivering Night Mail — A150

Postal Launch A151

1960, Mar. 20 Engr. *Perf. 11½*
Without Gum

1250 A150 $1.40 dk violet brn 1.50 .25
1251 A151 $1.60 ultra 1.50 .25

Issued to publicize the Prompt Delivery Service.

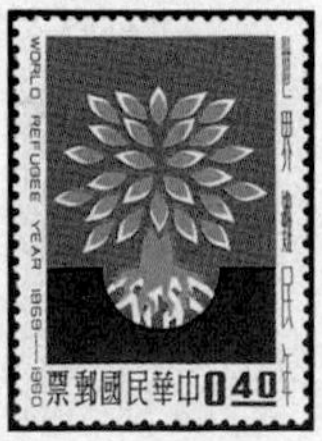

WRY Uprooted Oak Emblem — A152

1960, Apr. 7 Photo. *Perf. 13*

1252 A152 40c blk, red brn & emer .75 .25
1253 A152 $3 blk, red org & grn 1.40 .35

World Refugee Year, 7/1/59-6/30/60.

Cross Island Highway, Taiwan — A153

Design: $1, $2, Road through tunnel, vert.

Perf. 11½
1960, May 9 Engr. Unwmk.
Without Gum

1254 A153 40c green 1.25 .25
1255 A153 $1 dk blue 2.50 .30
1256 A153 $2 brown vio 2.50 .30
1257 A153 $3 brown 3.75 .40
a. Souv. sheet of 2, #1255, 1257, wmk. 323, imperf. *250.00 125.00*
Nos. 1254-1257 (4) 10.00 1.25

Opening of the Cross Island Highway, Taiwan.

Red Overprint on Nos. 1237-1238 Chinese and English: "Welcome U.S. President Dwight D. Eisenhower 1960"

1960, June 18 Unwmk. *Perf. 12*

1258 A145 $2 green 1.40 .30
a. Inverted overprint 2,250. 2,250.
1259 A144 $3 dk blue 1.75 .45

Eisenhower's visit to China, June 18, 1960.

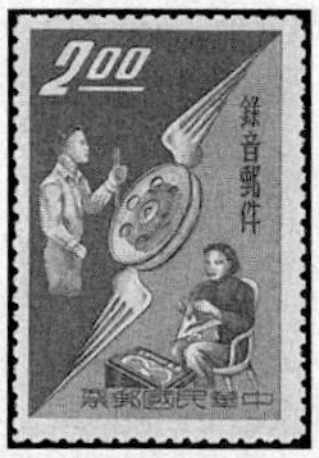

Phonopost — A154

1960, June 27 Without Gum

1260 A154 $2 red orange 1.75 .40

Phonopost Service of the Chinese armed forces.

Two Horses and Groom, by Han Kan — A155

Paintings from Palace Museum, Taichung: $1, Two Riders, by Wei Yen. $1.60, Flowers and Birds by Hsiao Yung, vert. $2, Pair of Mandarin Ducks by Monk Hui Ch'ung.

1960, Aug. 4 Photo. *Perf. 13*

1261 A155 $1 ol gray, blk & brn 4.00 .55
1262 A155 $1.40 bis brn, blk & fawn 8.00 1.00
1263 A155 $1.60 multicolored 9.00 1.75
1264 A155 $2 beige, blk & gray grn 14.00 3.25
Nos. 1261-1264 (4) 35.00 6.55

Chinese paintings, 7th-11th centuries.
For other painting types with large straight numerals in the upper corners and large Chinese characters on the side see A186, A241 and A285.

Youth Corps Flag and Summer Activities — A156

Design: $3, similar to 50c, horiz.

1960, Aug. 20 Engr. *Perf. 12*
Without Gum

1265 A156 50c slate green .50 .25
1266 A156 $3 copper brown 1.10 .45

Summer activities of China Youth Corps.

Reforestation A157

$2, Protection of forest. $3, Timber industry.

1960, Aug. 29 Photo. *Perf. 13½x13*

1267 A157 $1 multicolored 1.60 .25
1268 A157 $2 multicolored 2.25 .80
1269 A157 $3 multicolored 3.25 .60
a. Souvenir sheet of 3 27.50 20.00
Nos. 1267-1269 (3) 7.10 1.65

Fifth World Forestry Congress, Seattle, Washington, Aug. 29-Sept. 10.
No. 1269a contains Nos. 1267-1269 assembled as a triptych, 65½x40mm and imperf., but with simulated black perforations.

Chu Kwang Tower, Quemoy — A158

1960-61 Wmk. 323 Litho. *Perf. 12*
Without Gum

1270 A158 3c lt red brown .50 .25
1271 A158 40c pale violet .50 .25
1272 A158 50c orange ('61) .80 .25
1273 A158 60c rose lilac 1.00 .25
1274 A158 80c pale green 1.10 .25
1275 A158 $1 gray grn ('61) 1.25 .25
1276 A158 $1.20 gray olive 1.25 .25
1277 A158 $1.50 ultra 1.50 .25
1278 A158 $2 car rose ('61) 1.75 .25
1279 A158 $2.50 pale blue 1.90 .25
1280 A158 $3 bluish green 2.00 .25
1281 A158 $3.20 lt red brown 1.75 .25
1282 A158 $3.60 vio blue ('61) 3.75 .30
1283 A158 $4.50 vermilion 7.00 .35
Nos. 1270-1283 (14) 26.05 3.65

For surcharges see Nos. J132-J134.

Without Gum

1962-64 Granite Paper

1270a A158 3c light red brown .75 .25
1270B A158 10c emerald ('63) 2.25 .25
1271a A158 40c pale violet .75 .25
1274a A158 80c pale green .75 .25
1275a A158 $1 gray grn ('63) 12.00 .25
1278a A158 $2 carmine rose 6.00 .25
1281a A158 $3.20 red brn ('64) 15.00 .25
1282A A158 $4 brt blue grn 15.00 .25
1283a A158 $4.50 vermilion 21.00 .50
Nos. 1270a-1283a (9) 73.50 2.50

Two types of No. 1271a: I. Seven lines in "0" of "40." II. Eight lines in "0."

Sports — A159

Perf. 12½
1960, Oct. 25 Photo. Unwmk.

1284 A159 50c Diving 1.25 .25
1285 A159 80c Discus thrower 1.00 .25
1286 A159 $2 Basketball 2.50 .30
1287 A159 $2.50 Soccer 2.75 .55
1288 A159 $3 Hurdling 4.00 .75
1289 A159 $3.20 Runner 5.25 .80
Nos. 1284-1289 (6) 16.75 2.90

Bronze Wine Container, 1751-1111 B.C. — A160

Ancient Chinese Art Treasures: $1, Cauldron, 1111-771 B.C. $1.20, Porcelain vase, 960-1126 A.D. $1.50, Perforated tube, 1111-771 B.C. $2, Jug in shape of monk's cap, 1368-1661 A.D. $2.50, Jade flower vase, 1368-1661, A.D.

1961 Photo. *Perf. 13*

1290 A160 80c lt ol, blk & dk vio 3.00 .25
1291 A160 $1 sal, bl & blk 5.75 .35
1292 A160 $1.20 yel, brn & ultra 9.00 .50
1293 A160 $1.50 lil, bl & sep 7.00 1.10
1294 A160 $2 pale grn, dk grn & red brn 10.00 .70
1295 A160 $2.50 grnsh bl & dk vio 15.00 1.25
Nos. 1290-1295 (6) 49.75 4.15

Issue dates: Nos. 1290, 1292, 1295, Feb. 1. Nos. 1291, 1293-1294, May 1.

Flat Bowl, 1111-771 B.C. — A161

80c, Palace perfumer, 1662-1911. $1, Corn vase, 770-221 B.C. $2, Jade tankard, 960-1126 A.D. $4, Glazed washer, 1127-1279 A.D. $4.50, Jade chimera, 8 B.C.-206 A.D.

1961

1296 A160 80c pink, brn, bl & yel 2.25 .30
1297 A160 $1 cit, blk & brn 6.00 .60
1298 A161 $1.50 sal & ind 7.00 1.25
1299 A160 $2 bl, blk & rose 14.50 .75
1300 A161 $4 red, blk & bluish gray 17.00 1.25
1301 A161 $4.50 grnsh bl, blk & brn 35.00 3.00
Nos. 1296-1301 (6) 81.75 7.15

Issued: Nos. 1296-1298, 8/15; Nos. 1299-1301, 9/15.

1962

Designs: 80c, Topaz twin wine vessels, 1662-1911 A.D. $1, Squat pouring vase, 1751-1111 B.C. $2.40, Vase, 1368-1661 A.D. $3, Wine vase, 1751-1111 B.C. $3.20, Covered porcelain jar, 1662-1911 A.D. $3.60, Perforated disc, 206 B.C.-8 A.D.

1302 A160 80c crim, blk & ocher 2.00 .25
1303 A160 $1 blue & vio blk 2.50 .25
1304 A160 $2.40 hn brn, blk & bl 20.00 1.00
1305 A160 $3 blue, blk & pink 22.50 .90
1306 A160 $3.20 ultra, lt grn & red 20.00 .90
1307 A160 $3.60 yel, blk & brn 35.00 1.25
Nos. 1302-1307 (6) 102.00 4.55

Issue dates: Nos. 1303-1304, 1307, Jan. 15. Nos. 1302, 1305-1306, Feb. 15.

Farmer with Mechanized Plow — A162

1961, Feb. 4 Engr. *Perf. 12*
Without Gum
1308 A162 80c rose violet 1.40 .25
1309 A162 $2 green 3.25 .50
1310 A162 $3.20 vermilion 5.00 .35
Nos. 1308-1310 (3) 9.65 1.10

1961 agricultural census.

Madame Chiang Kai-shek and League Emblem — A163

Unwmk.
1961, Mar. 8 Photo. *Perf. 13*
Portrait in Black
1311 A163 80c lt grn & car rose 2.10 .30
1312 A163 $1 yel grn & car rose 4.00 .60
1313 A163 $2 org brn & car rose 4.00 .70
1314 A163 $3.20 lil & car rose 6.50 1.40
Nos. 1311-1314 (4) 16.60 3.00

10th anniversary of the Chinese Women's Anti-Aggression League.

Spiny Lobster and Mail Order Service Emblem — A164

1961, Mar. 20 Engr. *Perf. 11½*
Without Gum
1315 A164 $3 slate green 5.50 .40

Issued to publicize the mail order service for consumer goods.

Jeme Tien-yow and Pataling Tunnel — A165

$2, Jeme Tien-yow & 1909 locomotive.

1961, Apr. 26 *Perf. 11½*
Without Gum
1316 A165 80c lilac 1.50 .25
1317 A165 $2 black, horiz. 3.50 .60

Centenary of the birth of Jeme Tien-yow, builder of the Peking-Kalgan railroad.

Map of China inscribed: "Recovery of the Mainland" — A166

Pres. Chiang Kai-shek — A167

1961, May 20 Photo. *Perf. 13½*
1318 A166 80c multicolored 2.50 .25
1319 A167 $2 multicolored 5.00 1.25
a. Souvenir sheet of 2 20.00 20.00

1st anniversary of Pres. Chiang Kai-shek's 3rd term inauguration.

No. 1319a contains one each of Nos. 1318-1319, imperf. with simulated perforations. Without gum.

Convair 880-M, Biplane of 1921 and Flag — A168

1961, July 1 *Perf. 13x12½*
1320 A168 $10 multicolored 4.50 1.40

40th anniversary of civil air service.

Sun Yat-sen and Chiang Kai-shek — A169

Flag and Map of China — A170

Perf. 13½
1961, Oct. 10 Unwmk. Photo.
1321 A169 80c gray, lt brn & sl 1.60 .25
1322 A170 $5 gray, ultra, red & beige 4.25 1.60
a. Souvenir sheet of 2 16.00 16.00

50th anniv. of the Republic of China. No. 1322a contains one each of Nos. 1321-1322, imperf. with simulated perforations. No gum.

Green Lake — A171

Lotus Pond A172

Taiwan Scenery: $2, Sun-Moon Lake. $3.20, Wulai waterfalls.

Perf. 13½x14, 14x13½
1961, Oct. 31 Unwmk.
1323 A171 80c multicolored 4.00 .25
1324 A172 $1 multicolored 9.00 .90
1325 A172 $2 multicolored 12.00 .70
1326 A171 $3.20 multicolored 16.00 1.25
Nos. 1323-1326 (4) 41.00 3.10

Oil Refinery — A173

Designs: $1.50, Steel works. $2.50, Aluminum plant. $3.20, Fertilizer plant, horiz.

1961, Nov. 14 *Perf. 11½*
1327 A173 80c multicolored 2.00 .25
1328 A173 $1.50 multicolored 3.50 .80
1329 A173 $2.50 multicolored 5.00 .70
1330 A173 $3.20 multicolored 7.25 .65
Nos. 1327-1330 (4) 17.75 2.40

Chinese industrial development and the Golden Jubilee Convention of the Chinese Institute of Engineers, Nov. 13-16.

Atomic Reactor, Tsing-Hwa University A174

Atomic Reactor in Operation A175

Design: $3.20, Atomic symbol and laboratory, Tsing-Hwa, horiz.

1961-62 Photo. *Perf. 12½*
1331 A174 80c multicolored 2.25 .25
1332 A175 $2 multicolored 5.00 1.40
1333 A175 $3.20 multicolored 5.50 1.25
Nos. 1331-1333 (3) 12.75 2.90

Inauguration on Apr. 13, 1961, of the 1st Chinese atomic reactor at the National Tsing-Hwa University Institute of Nuclear Science.
Issued: 80c, 12/2; $2, $3.20, 3/20/62.

Microwave Reflector and Telegraph Wires — A176

Design: $3.20, Microwave parabolic antenna and mountains, horiz.

1961, Dec. 28 *Perf. 12½*
1334 A176 80c multicolored 1.50 .25
1335 A176 $3.20 multicolored 3.00 .80

80th anniv. of Chinese telecommunications.

Mechanical Postal Equipment and Twine Tying Machine — A176a

Wmk. 323
1962, Mar. 20 Engr. *Perf. 11½*
Without Gum
1336 A176a 80c chocolate 1.50 .45

Yu Shan Observatory A177

Observation Balloon, Earth and Cumulus Clouds A178

Design: $1, Map showing route of typhoon Pamela, Sept. 1961, horiz.

1962 Without Gum
1337 A177 80c brown .95 .25
1338 A178 $1 bluish black 1.90 .30
1339 A178 $2 green 2.50 .65
Nos. 1337-1339 (3) 5.35 1.20

Issue dates: 80c, $2, Mar. 23; $1, May 7.
World Meteorological Day, Mar. 23.

Child Receiving Milk, UN Emblem A179

1962, Apr. 4 Without Gum
1340 A179 80c rose red .85 .25
1341 A179 $3.20 green 2.50 .50
a. Souvenir sheet of 2 16.00 4.50

15th anniv. of UNICEF. No. 1341a contains one each of Nos. 1340-1341 imperf. with simulated perforations.

Malaria Eradication Emblem — A180

Unwmk.
1962, Apr. 7 Photo. *Perf. 13*
1342 A180 80c dk bl, red & lt grn .60 .25
1343 A180 $3.60 brn, pink & grn 1.60 1.00

WHO drive to eradicate malaria.

Yu Yu-jen — A181

1962, Apr. 24 *Perf. 13*
1344 A181 80c gray, blk & pink 2.00 .25

Issued to honor Yu Yu-jen, newspaper reporter, revolutionary leader and co-worker of Sun Yat-sen, on his 84th birthday.

Cheng Ch'eng-kung (Koxinga) — A182

1962, Apr. 29
1345 A182 80c deep claret 2.00 .25
1346 A182 $2 dark green 3.50 .55

300th anniversary (in 1961) of the recovery of Taiwan from the Dutch by Koxinga.

Emblem of Intl. Cooperative Alliance — A183

Clasped Hands Across Globe — A184

Wmk. 323

1962, July 7 Engr. *Perf. 12*

Without Gum

1347	A183	80c brown	.90	.25
1348	A184	$2 violet	2.00	.45

Intl. Cooperative Movement and 40th Intl. Cooperative Day, July 7, 1962.

Mansion Type of 1958

1962, July 20 Without Gum

1349	A135	$5 gray green	2.75	.25
1350	A135	$5.60 violet	3.75	.25
1351	A135	$6 orange	3.50	.25
		Nos. 1349-1351 (3)	10.00	.75

1963 Granite Paper

1349a	A135	$5 gray green	3.50	.25
1350a	A135	$5.60 violet	4.00	.25
1351a	A135	$6 orange	5.50	.25
		Nos. 1349a-1351a (3)	13.00	.75

"Art and Science" — A185

$2, "Education," book and UNESCO emblem, horiz. $3.20, "Communications," globes, horiz.

1962, Aug. 28 Wmk. 323 *Perf. 12*

Without Gum

1352	A185	80c lilac rose	.60	.25
1353	A185	$2 rose claret	1.50	.40
1354	A185	$3.20 yellow green	1.75	.30
		Nos. 1352-1354 (3)	3.85	.95

UNESCO activities in China.

Emperor T'ai Tsung, T'ang Dynasty, 627-649 A186

Emperors: $2, T'ai Tsu, Sung dynasty, 960-975. $3.20, T'ai Tsu, Yuan dynasty (Genghis Khan), 1206-27. $4, T'ai Tsu, Ming dynasty, 1368-98.

1962, Sept. 20 Photo. Unwmk.

1355	A186	80c multicolored	25.00	2.25
1356	A186	$2 multicolored	90.00	7.00
1357	A186	$3.20 multicolored	150.00	7.50
1358	A186	$4 multicolored	250.00	19.50
		Nos. 1355-1358 (4)	515.00	36.25

Lions International Emblem A187

1962, Oct. 8 *Perf. 13½*

1359	A187	80c multicolored	1.25	.25
1360	A187	$3.60 multicolored	2.50	.80
a.		Souvenir sheet of 2	18.00	9.00

45th anniv. of Lions Intl. No. 1360a contains one each of Nos. 1359-1360, imperf. with simulated perforations.

Pole Vaulting — A188

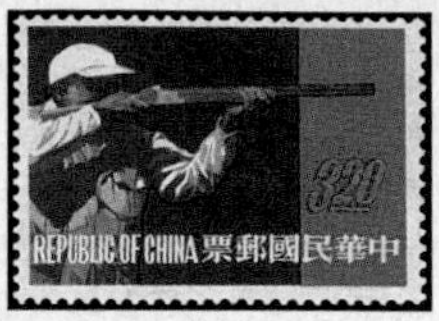

Shooting A189

1962, Oct. 25 Unwmk. *Perf. 13*

1361	A188	80c multicolored	1.00	.25
1362	A189	$3.20 multicolored	2.25	.40

Sports meet.

Young Farmers and 4-H Emblem — A190

Design: $3.20, 4-H emblem and rice.

Wmk. 323

1962, Dec. 7 Engr. *Perf. 12*

Without Gum

1363	A190	80c carmine	.75	.25
1364	A190	$3.20 green	2.25	.65
a.		Souvenir sheet of 2	18.00	11.00

10th anniv. of the 4-H Club in China. No. 1364a contains one each of Nos. 1363-1364, imperf. with simulated perforations.

Flag, Liner of China Merchants' Steam Navigation Co. — A191

Design: $3.60, Company's Pacific navigation chart and freighter, horiz.

Perf. 13½

1962, Dec. 16 Unwmk. Photo.

1365	A191	80c multicolored	1.60	.25
1366	A191	$3.60 multicolored	4.25	1.00

90th anniversary of the China Merchants' Steam Navigation Co., Ltd.

Farm Woman, Tractor and Plane Dropping Food over Mainland — A192

Perf. 12½

1963, Mar. 21 Unwmk. Photo.

1367	A192	$10 multicolored	4.00	1.00

FAO "Freedom from Hunger" campaign.

Torch, Young Couple and Martyrs' Monument, Canton A193

Wmk. 323

1963, Mar. 29 Engr. *Perf. 11½*

Without Gum

1368	A193	80c purple	1.00	.25
1369	A193	$3.20 green	2.00	.40

Issued for the 20th Youth Day.

Swallows, Pagoda and AOPU Emblem — A194

Designs: $2, Northern gannet, horiz. $6, Japanese crane and pine.

Unwmk.

1963, Apr. 1 Photo. *Perf. 13*

1370	A194	80c multicolored	5.00	.75
1371	A194	$2 multicolored	7.00	.65
1372	A194	$6 multicolored	10.50	2.10
		Nos. 1370-1372 (3)	22.50	3.50

1st anniversary of the formation of the Asian-Oceanic Postal Union, AOPU.

Refugee Girl (Li Ying) and Map of China — A195

Refugees Fleeing Mainland A196

Wmk. 323

1963, June 27 Engr. *Perf. 11½*

Without Gum

1373	A195	80c bluish black	1.40	.25
1374	A196	$3.20 dp claret	3.00	.30

1st anniv. of the evacuation of Chinese mainland refugees from Hong Kong to Taiwan. Designs from photographs of refugees.

Nurse and Red Cross A197

Design: $10, Globe and Red Cross.

Perf. 12½

1963, Sept. 1 Unwmk. Photo.

1375	A197	80c black & carmine	6.50	.30
1376	A197	$10 slate, gray & car	7.75	2.75

Centenary of International Red Cross.

Basketball Player, Stadium and Asian Cup — A198

$2, Hands reaching for ball and Asian cup.

Wmk. 323

1963, Nov. 20 Engr. *Perf. 12*

Without Gum

1377	A198	80c lilac rose	1.25	.25
1378	A198	$2 violet	2.40	.80

The 2nd Asian Basketball Championship, Taipei, Nov. 20.

UN Emblem, Torch and Men — A199

Scales and Men of Various Races A200

1963, Dec. 10 Wmk. 323 *Perf. 11½*

Without Gum

1379	A199	80c brt green	.80	.30
1380	A200	$3.20 maroon	1.50	.65

Universal Declaration of Human Rights, 15th anniversary.

Village and Orchids A201

"Kindle the Fire of Conscience" A202

Perf. 13½x13

1963, Dec. 17 Photo. Unwmk.

1381	A201	40c multicolored	3.50	.50
1382	A202	$4.50 multicolored	5.50	2.25

Contribution of the Good-People-Good-Deeds campaign to improve ethical standards.

Sun Yat-sen and Book, "Three Principles of the People" A203

1963, Dec. 25 *Perf. 13*

1383	A203	$5 blue & multi	10.00	1.50

"Land-to-the-Tillers" program, 10th anniv. An 80c was prepared but not issued.

Torch — A204

Hands Unchained — A205

Wmk. 323

1964, Jan. 23 Engr. *Perf. 11½*

Without Gum

1384	A204	80c red orange	.60	.25
1385	A205	$3.20 indigo	2.75	.35

Liberty Day, 10th anniversary.

Broadleaf Cactus — A206

Designs: $1, Crab cactus. $3.20, Nopalxochia. $5, Grizzly bear cactus.

Perf. 12½

1964, Feb. 27 Unwmk. Photo.

Plants in Original Colors

1386	A206	80c	dp plum & fawn	4.50	.25
1387	A206	$1	dk blue & car	7.75	.90
1388	A206	$3.20	green	11.50	.25
1389	A206	$5	lilac & yellow	12.50	1.10
	Nos. 1386-1389 (4)			36.25	2.50

Wu Chih-hwei — A207

Wmk. 323

1964, Mar. 25 Engr. *Perf. 11½*

Without Gum

1390	A207	80c	black brown	1.75	.25

Centenary of the birth of Wu Chih-hwei (1865-1953), politician and leader of the Kuomintang.

Chu Kwang Tower, Quemoy — A208

Perf. 13x12½

1964-66 Wmk. 323 Litho.

Granite Paper; Without Gum

1391	A208	3c	sepia	.25	.25
1392	A208	5c	brt yel grn ('65)	.25	.25
1393	A208	10c	yellow grn	.25	.25
1394	A208	20c	slate grn ('65)	.25	.25
1395	A208	40c	rose red	.25	.25
1396	A208	50c	brown	.25	.25
1397	A208	80c	orange ('65)	.25	.25
1398	A208	$1	violet ('65)	.25	.25
1399	A208	$1.50	brt lilac ('66)	2.50	.25
1400	A208	$2	lilac rose	.25	.25
1401	A208	$2.50	ultra ('65)	2.50	.25
1402	A208	$3	slate	2.50	.30
1403	A208	$3.20	brt blue	5.00	.25
1404	A208	$4	brt green	5.75	.25
	Nos. 1391-1404 (14)			20.50	3.55

Nurses Holding Candles A209

Florence Nightingale and Student Nurse — A210

1964, May 12 Engr. *Perf. 11½*

Without Gum

1406	A209	80c	violet blue	1.40	.25
1407	A210	$4	red	3.50	.50

Issued for Nurses Day.

Shihmen Reservoir A211

Designs: $1, Irrigation system. $3.20, Main dam and power plant. $5, Spillway.

Perf. 12½

1964, June 14 Unwmk. Photo.

1408	A211	80c	multicolored	2.25	.25
1409	A211	$1	multicolored	3.75	.45
1410	A211	$3.20	multicolored	7.00	.55
1411	A211	$5	multicolored	10.00	1.40
	Nos. 1408-1411 (4)			23.00	2.65

Completion of Shihmen Reservoir.

15th Century Ship, Modern Liner — A212

Wmk. 323

1964, July 11 Engr. *Perf. 11½*

Without Gum

1412	A212	$2	orange	1.25	.25
1413	A212	$3.60	brt green	1.90	.35

China's 10th Navigation Day.

Bananas A213

Unwmk.

1964, July 25 Photo. *Perf. 14*

1414	A213	80c	shown	*10.00*	1.00
1415	A213	$1	Oranges	*20.00*	2.00
1416	A213	$3.20	Pineapple	*23.50*	2.00
1417	A213	$4	Watermelon	*37.50*	5.00
	Nos. 1414-1417 (4)			*91.00*	10.00

Artillery, Warships, Jet Fighters A214

Wmk. 323

1964, Sept. 3 Engr. *Perf. 11½*

Without Gum

1418	A214	80c	dk blue	1.60	.25
1419	A214	$6	violet brown	4.25	.60

Issued for the 10th Armed Forces Day.

Unisphere, Flags of China and U.S. — A215

Chinese Pavilion, NY World's Fair — A216

1964, Sept. 10 Photo. Unwmk.

1420	A215	80c	violet & multi	2.75	.25
1421	A216	$5	blue & multi	6.25	.90

NY World's Fair, 1964-65. See Nos. 1450-1451.

Cowboy Carrying Calf, and Ranch — A217

Wmk. 323

1964, Sept. 24 Engr. *Perf. 11½*

Without Gum

1422	A217	$2	brown lake	1.60	.25
1423	A217	$4	dark violet blue	3.25	.80

Animal Protection Week, Sept. 24-30.

Bicycling — A218

Sports: $1, Runner. $3.20, Gymnast on rings. $10, High jump.

1964, Oct. 10 Without Gum

1424	A218	80c	violet blue	1.05	.25
1425	A218	$1	rose red	1.75	.25
1426	A218	$3.20	dull blue grn	2.25	.40
1427	A218	$10	lilac	4.00	2.00
	Nos. 1424-1427 (4)			9.05	2.90

18th Olympic Games, Tokyo, Oct. 10-25.

Xu Guangqi — A219

1964, Nov. 8 Engr. *Perf. 11½*

Without Gum

1428	A219	80c	indigo	2.75	.25

Issued to honor Xu Guangqi (1562-1633), scholar and statesman.

Pharmaceutical Industry — A220

Textile Industry A221

$2, Chemical industry. $3.60, Cement industry.

1964, Nov. 11 Photo. Unwmk.

1429	A220	40c	multi	2.75	.25
1430	A221	$1.50	multi	3.50	.70
1431	A220	$2	multi	5.50	.50
1432	A221	$3.60	multi	6.25	1.10
	Nos. 1429-1432 (4)			18.00	2.55

Dr. Sun Yat-sen — A222

1964, Nov. 24 Engr. Wmk. 323

Without Gum

1433	A222	80c	green	2.00	.30
1434	A222	$3.60	purple	5.25	1.00

Founding of the Kuomintang by Sun Yat-sen, 70th anniversary.

Eleanor Roosevelt and Scales of Justice — A223

Unwmk.

1964, Dec. 10 Photo. *Perf. 13*

1435	A223	$10	violet & brown	2.10	.40

Issued to honor Eleanor Roosevelt (1884-1962) on the 16th anniversary of the Universal Declaration of Human Rights.

Scales, Code Book and Plum Blossom — A224

Wmk. 323

1965, Jan. 11 Engr. *Perf. 11½*

Without Gum

1436	A224	80c	carmine rose	.55	.25
1437	A224	$3.20	dull slate grn	1.10	.65

The 20th Judicial Day.

Rotary Emblem and Mainspring — A225

1965, Feb. 23 Wmk. 323 *Perf. 11½*

Without Gum

1438	A225	$1.50	vermilion	.75	.25
1439	A225	$2	emerald	.90	.25
1440	A225	$2.50	blue	1.25	.40
	Nos. 1438-1440 (3)			2.90	.90

Rotary International, 60th anniversary.

Double Carp Design — A226

Wmk. 323

1965, Mar. 29 Engr. *Perf. 11½*

Granite Paper; Without Gum

1441	A226	$5	purple	12.50	1.25
1442	A226	$5.60	dp blue	21.00	2.00
1443	A226	$6	brown	19.00	1.25
1444	A226	$10	lilac rose	32.00	1.25
1445	A226	$20	rose car	35.00	2.00

1446 A226 $50 green 42.50 4.50
1447 A226 $100 crim rose 52.50 7.50
Nos. 1441-1447 (7) 214.50 19.75

New dies used to reprint Nos. 1444-1447, 8/20/67. Remainders of Nos. 1441-1447 issued with gum, 11/1/71.

Madame Chiang Kai-shek — A227

1965, Apr. 17 Photo. Unwmk.
1448 A227 $2 multicolored 18.00 1.00
1449 A227 $6 salmon & multi 32.50 4.00

Chinese Women's Anti-Aggression League, 15th anniversary.

Unisphere and Chinese Pavilion — A228

"100 Birds Paying Homage to Queen Phoenix" and Unisphere — A229

1965, May 8
1450 A228 $2 blue & multi 30.00 1.50
1451 A229 $10 red, ocher & bis 35.00 3.00

New York World's Fair, 1964-65.

ITU Emblem, Old and New Communication Equipment A230

Design: $5, similar to 80c, vert.

Perf. 13½x13, 13x13½
1965, May 17 Photo. Unwmk.
1452 A230 80c multicolored .80 .25
1453 A230 $5 multicolored 2.40 .75

Centenary of the ITU.

Red Sea Bream A231

Fish: 80c, White pomfret. $2, Skipjack, vert. $4, Moonfish.

1965, July 1 ***Perf. 13***
1454 A231 40c multicolored 2.25 .25
1455 A231 80c multicolored 3.50 .40
1456 A231 $2 multicolored 7.75 1.40
1457 A231 $4 multicolored 13.50 2.00
Nos. 1454-1457 (4) 27.00 4.05

Issued for Fishermen's Day.

Confucius — A232

Portraits: $2.50, Yueh Fei. $3.50, Wen Tien-hsiang. $3.60, Mencius.

Wmk. 323
1965-66 Engr. ***Perf. 11½***
Without Gum
1458 A232 $1 deep carmine 4.50 .35
1459 A232 $2.50 black brown 3.00 .35
1460 A232 $3.50 dark red 6.50 .75
1461 A232 $3.60 dark blue 7.75 .90
Nos. 1458-1461 (4) 21.75 2.35

The $2.50 and $3.50 have colored background.
Forgeries of No. 1461 exist.
Issued: Nos. 1458, 1461, 9/28/65; Nos. 1459-1460, 9/3/66.
See Nos. 1507-1508, design A251.

ICY Emblem — A233

Design: $6, ICY emblem, horiz.

Unwmk.
1965, Oct. 24 Photo. ***Perf. 13***
1462 A233 $2 brn, blk & gold 1.60 .25
1463 A233 $6 brt grn, red & gold 3.75 1.40

International Cooperation Year, 1965.

Street Crossing, Traffic Light — A234

Wmk. 323
1965, Nov. 1 Engr. ***Perf. 11½***
Without Gum
1464 A234 $1 brown violet 1.50 .55
1465 A234 $4 crimson rose 3.00 1.10

Issued to publicize traffic safety.

Sun Yat-sen — A235

Designs: $4, Dr. Sun Yat-sen, portrait at right. $5, Sun Yat-sen and flags, horiz.

Perf. 13½
1965, Nov. 12 Unwmk. Photo.
1466 A235 $1 multicolored 3.50 .25
1467 A235 $4 multicolored 1.10 1.00
1468 A235 $5 multicolored 13.00 2.50
Nos. 1466-1468 (3) 17.60 3.75

Children with New Year's Firecrackers A236

Dragon Dance, "Dragon Playing Ball" A237

1965, Dec. 1 Photo. ***Perf. 13***
1469 A236 $1 multi 5.50 .30
1470 A237 $4.50 multi 12.50 1.10

Lien Po from "Marshal and Prime Minister Reconciled" — A238

Facial Paintings for Chinese Operas: $3, Kuan Yü from "Reunion at Ku City." $4, Gen. Chang Fei from "The Battle of Chang Pan Hill." $6, Buddha from "The Flower-Scattering Angel."

1966, Feb. 15 Unwmk. ***Perf. 11½***
1471 A238 $1 olive & multi 10.75 1.00
1472 A238 $3 multicolored 20.00 2.00
1473 A238 $4 multicolored 38.00 4.00
1474 A238 $6 ver & multi 40.00 6.00
Nos. 1471-1474 (4) 108.75 13.00

Labels with a similar appearance to these stamps exist. These labels have the numbers 1 to 20 in the upper right corner, but lack the "00."

Postal Service Emblem Held by Carrier Pigeon — A239

Stone, Mt. Tai-wu, Quemoy, and Mailman A240

postal service emblem and: $3, Postal Museum. $4, Mailman climbing symbolic slope.

1966, Mar. 20 Photo. ***Perf. 12½***
1475 A239 $1 green & multi 1.75 .25
1476 A240 $2 multicolored 3.50 .30
1477 A240 $3 multicolored 4.25 .40
1478 A239 $4 multicolored 8.75 2.25
Nos. 1475-1478 (4) 18.25 3.20

China postal service, 70th anniversary.

Fishing on a Snowy Day, "Five Dynasties" (907-960) A241

Paintings from Palace Museum: $3.50, Calves on the Plain, Sung artist (960-1126). $4.50, Winter landscape, Sung artist (960-1126). $5, Magpies, by Lin Ch'un, Southern Sung dynasty (1127-1279).

1966, May 20 Photo. ***Perf. 13***
1479 A241 $2.50 blk, brn & red 11.50 .50
1480 A241 $3.50 bis brn, blk & gray 30.00 .75
1481 A241 $4.50 blk, buff & sl 42.50 1.90
1482 A241 $5 multicolored 55.00 2.75
Nos. 1479-1482 (4) 139.00 5.90

Inauguration of Pres. Chiang Kai-shek for a 4th term.

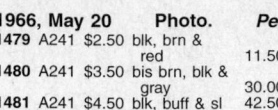

Dragon Boat Race A242

Lion Dance — A243

$4, Lady Chang O flying to the Moon.

1966 Unwmk.
1483 A242 $2.50 multi 5.50 .40
1484 A242 $4 multi 10.00 .50
1485 A243 $6 multi 20.00 1.00
Nos. 1483-1485 (3) 35.50 1.90

Dragon Boat, Mid-Autumn and Lunar New Year Festivals. Issued: $2.50, 6/23; $4, 9/29; $6, 11/26.

Flags of China and Argentina A244

1966, July 9 Photo. ***Perf. 13***
1486 A244 $10 multicolored 4.25 .60

Argentina's Independence. 150th anniv.

Lin Sen — A245

Wmk. 323
1966, Aug. 1 Engr. ***Perf. 11½***
Without Gum
1487 A245 $1 dk brown 2.00 .25

Centenary of the birth of Lin Sen (1867-1943), Chairman of the Nationalist Government of China (1931-43).

Flying Geese — A246

1966-67 ***Perf. 11½ Rough***
Granite Paper; Without Gum
1496 A246 $3.50 brown 1.10 .40
1497 A246 $4 vermilion 1.05 .40
1498 A246 $4.50 brt green 1.90 .45
1499 A246 $5 rose lilac 1.10 .40
1500 A246 $5.50 yel grn ('67) 2.25 .40
1501 A246 $6 brt blue 2.50 .50
1502 A246 $6.50 violet 2.25 .45
1503 A246 $7 black 1.25 .40
1504 A246 $8 car rose ('67) 1.90 .40
Nos. 1496-1504 (9) 15.30 3.80

The $4.50, $5, $6, $7 and $8 were reissued with gum in 1970-71.

Pres. Chiang Kai-shek in Chung San Robe — A247

$5, Chiang Kai-shek in marshal's uniform.

Unwmk.

1966, Oct. 31 Photo. *Perf. 13*

1505 A247 $1 multicolored 1.90 .30
1506 A247 $5 multicolored 6.25 1.60

Chiang Kai-shek's inauguration for a fourth term as president, May 20, 1966.

Famous Men Type of 1965-66 with Frame Line

Portraits: No. 1507, Tsai Yuan-pei (1868-1940), educator. No. 1508, Chiu Ching (1875-1907), woman educator and revolutionist.

1967 Wmk. 323 Engr. *Perf. 11½*
Without Gum

1507 A232 $1 violet blue 2.25 .25
1508 A232 $1 black 2.25 .25

Issue dates: No. 1507, Jan. 11. No. 1508, July 15.
No. 1507 is on granite paper.

Motorized Mailman and Microwave Station — A248

"Transportation" and Radar Weather Station — A249

Unwmk.

1967, Mar. 15 Photo. *Perf. 13*

1511 A248 $1 multicolored 1.40 .25
1512 A249 $5 multicolored 2.50 .90

Issued to publicize the progress in communication and transportation services.

Pres. Chiang Kai-shek and Chinese Flag — A250

Design: $4, Different frame.

1967, May 20 Litho. *Perf. 13*

1513 A250 $1 multicolored 1.90 .25
1514 A250 $4 multicolored 3.00 .90

First anniversary of President Chiang Kai-shek's 4th-term inauguration.

Chu Yuan, 332-295 B.C. — A251

Portraits: $2, Li Po (705-760). $2.50, Tu Fu (712-770). $3, Po Chu-i (772-846).

Granite Paper; Without Gum
Wmk. 323

1967, June 12 Engr. *Perf. 11½*

1515 A251 $1 black 1.10 .25
1516 A251 $2 brown 3.50 .25
1517 A251 $2.50 brown blk 4.75 .45
1518 A251 $3 grnsh black 7.00 .45
Nos. 1515-1518 (4) 16.35 1.40

Issued for Poets' Day.
See design A232.

Hotei, Wood Carving — A252

Handicrafts: $2.50, Vase and plate. $3, Dolls. $5, Palace lanterns.

Perf. 11½

1967, Aug. 12 Unwmk. Photo.

1519 A252 $1 gray & multi 3.00 .65
1520 A252 $2.50 multi 4.00 1.00
1521 A252 $3 multi 5.00 1.65
1522 A252 $5 multi 6.75 3.50
Nos. 1519-1522 (4) 18.75 6.80

Taiwan handicraft industry.

World Map — A253

Granite Paper; Without Gum
Wmk. 323

1967, Sept. 25 Engr. *Perf. 11½*

1523 A253 $1 vermilion .45 .25
1524 A253 $5 blue 1.10 .50

1st Conference of the World Anti-Communist League, WACL, Taipei, Sept. 25-29.

Players on Stilts: "The Fisherman and the Woodcutter" A254

Unwmk.

1967, Oct. 10 Photo. *Perf. 13*

1525 A254 $4.50 multi 1.90 .45

Issued for the 56th National Day.

Maroon Oriole — A255

Formosan Birds: $1, Formosan barbet, vert. $2.50, Formosan green pigeon. $3, Formosan blue magpie. $5, Crested serpent eagle, vert. $8, Mikado pheasants.

1967, Nov. 25 Photo. *Perf. 11*
Granite Paper

1526 A255 $1 multi 4.00 .25
1527 A255 $2 multi 5.50 .40
1528 A255 $2.50 multi 6.75 .50
1529 A255 $3 multi 8.00 .60
1530 A255 $5 multi 9.50 .70
1531 A255 $8 multi 11.50 1.25
Nos. 1526-1531 (6) 45.25 3.70

Chung Hsing Pagoda — A256

Buddha, Changhua A257

Designs: $2.50, Seashore, Yeh Liu Park. $5, National Palace Museum, Taipei.

Unwmk.

1967, Dec. 10 Photo. *Perf. 13*

1532 A256 $1 multi 1.50 .25
1533 A257 $2.50 multi 4.00 .50
1534 A257 $4 multi 5.00 .60
1535 A257 $5 multi 5.75 .90
Nos. 1532-1535 (4) 16.25 2.25

Issued for International Tourist Year 1967.

China Park, Manila, and Flags — A258

1967, Dec. 30 *Perf. 13½*

1536 A258 $1 multicolored .65 .25
1537 A258 $5 multicolored 2.25 .65

Sino-Philippine Friendship Year 1966-67.

Sun Yat-sen Building, Yangmingshan
A259 A259a

Perf. 13x12½

1968-75 Litho. Wmk. 323
Granite Paper

1538 A259 5c lt brown .60 .25
1539 A259 10c grnsh black .60 .25
1540 A259 50c brt rose lilac .60 .25
1541 A259 $1 vermilion .60 .25
1542 A259 $1.50 emerald 1.10 .70
1543 A259 $2 plum 1.05 .25
1544 A259 $2.50 blue 1.25 .25
1545 A259 $3 grnsh blue 1.40 .25
Nos. 1538-1545 (8) 7.20 2.45

See Nos. 1702-1709. For overprints see Nos. 1723-1725.

Coil Stamps

Perf. 13 Horiz.

Photo. Unwmk.

1546 A259a $1 carmine rose .55 .25
1547 A259a $1 vermilion .55 .25

Issued: 50c, $1, $2.50, 1/23/68; No. 1546, 3/20/70; No. 1547, 1/28/75; others 7/11/68.
Inscription on No. 1546 is in color with white background. On No. 1547 it is white with colored background.

Harvesting Sugar Cane — A260

Unwmk.

1968, Mar. 1 Photo. *Perf. 13*

1548 A260 $1 olive & multi 1.75 .25
1549 A260 $4 multicolored 3.00 .45

Jade Cabbage, 1662-1911 — A261

Ancient Art Treasures: $1.50, Jade battle axe. $2, Porcelain flower bowl, 960-1126 A.D., horiz. $2.50, Cloisonné enamel vase, 1723-1736 A.D. $4, Agate flower holder in shape of finger citrus, 1662-1911 A.D., horiz. $5, Sacrificial kettle, 1111-771 B.C.

1968, Mar. 29 Unwmk. *Perf. 13*

1550 A261 $1 rose & multi 2.25 .25
1551 A261 $1.50 blue & multi 3.25 .50
1552 A261 $2 blue & multi 3.50 .25
1553 A261 $2.50 dull rose & multi 4.25 .50
1554 A261 $4 pink & multi 5.50 .60
1555 A261 $5 blue & multi 6.50 .70
Nos. 1550-1555 (6) 25.25 2.80

For similar artifact designs inscribed "Republic of China," with single-color denominations in slanted numerals and the cents underlined, see types A276, A291, A323, A336, A384, A395, A411.
Artifact designs with denominations in outlined numerals begin with type A439.

View of City in Cathay (1) — A262

Views: No. 1557, City and wall of Forbidden City (2). No. 1558, Wall at right, bridge at left (3). No. 1559, Queen's ship landing at left (4). No. 1560, Palace (5). $5, City wall and gate. $8, Suburb around Great Bridge. Design from scroll "A City in Cathay," painted 1736.

1968, June 18 Photo. *Perf. 13½*
Size: 50x29mm

1556 A262 $1 multicolored 2.25 .40
1557 A262 $1 multicolored 2.25 .40
1558 A262 $1 multicolored 2.25 .40
1559 A262 $1 multicolored 2.25 .40
1560 A262 $1 multicolored 2.25 .40
a. Strip of 5, #1556-1560 10.00 10.00

Size: 60x31mm
Perf. 13x13½

1561 A262 $5 multicolored 12.00 2.10
1562 A262 $8 multicolored 21.00 2.75
Nos. 1556-1562 (7) 44.25 6.85

See Nos. 1610-1614. For similar designs see types A281, A299, A326, A343.

Entrance Gate, Taroko Gorge A263

$8, Sun Yat-sen Building, Yangmingshan.

1968, Feb. 12 Photo. *Perf. 13*

1563 A263 $5 multicolored 1.75 .35
1564 A263 $8 multicolored 3.00 .40

The 17th Annual Conference of the Pacific Area Travel Association.

Vice President Chen Cheng — A264

1968, Mar. 5

1565 A264 $1 brown & multi 1.60 .25

Vice President Chen Cheng (1898-1965).

Flying Geese — A265

Wmk. 323

1968, Mar. 20 Litho. *Perf. 12*

Granite Paper

1566 A265 $1 vermilion 9.00 .25

Souvenir Sheet

Imperf

1567 A265 $3 green 11.00 3.50

90th anniv. of Chinese postage stamps. No. 1567 contains one stamp with simulated perforations.

WHO Emblem and "20" — A266

1968, Apr. 7 Engr. *Perf. 12*

Granite Paper

1568 A266 $1 green .45 .25
1569 A266 $5 scarlet 1.25 .65

20th anniv. of WHO.

Symbolic Water Cycle — A267

Wmk. 323

1968, June 6 Litho. *Perf. 11½*

Granite Paper

1570 A267 $1 green & org .45 .25
1571 A267 $4 brt blue & org 1.40 .25

Hydrological Decade (UNESCO) 1965-74.

Broadcasting to Mainland China — A268

Dual Carriers for FM Broadcasting A269

Wmk. 323

1968, Aug. 1 Litho. *Perf. 12*

Granite Paper

1572 A268 $1 bl, vio bl & gray .55 .25
1573 A269 $4 lt ultra & ver 1.25 .25

40th anniv. of the Broadcasting Corp. of China, and the inauguration of frequency modulation broadcasting.

Human Rights Flame — A270

1968, Sept. 3 Granite Paper

1574 A270 $1 multicolored .60 .25
1575 A270 $5 multicolored 1.50 .25

International Human Rights Year 1968.

Crop Improvement and Extension Work — A271

Wmk. 323

1968, Sept. 30 Litho. *Perf. 12*

Granite Paper

1576 A271 $1 yel, bister & dk brn .45 .25
1577 A271 $5 yel, emer & dk grn 1.75 .50

Joint Commission on Rural Reconstruction, 20th anniversary.

Javelin — A272

Designs: $2.50, Weight lifting. $5, Pole vault, horiz. $8, Woman hurdling, horiz.

Unwmk.

1968, Oct. 12 Photo. *Perf. 13*

1578 A272 $1 multi .55 .25
1579 A272 $2.50 multi .80 .25
1580 A272 $5 multi 1.25 .25
1581 A272 $8 pink & multi 1.90 .35
Nos. 1578-1581 (4) 4.50 1.10

19th Olympic Games, Mexico City, 10/12-27.

Pres. Chiang Kai-shek and Whampoa Military Academy — A273

Designs: $2, Pres. Chiang Kai-shek reviewing forces of the Northern Expedition. $2.50, Suppression of bandits, reconstruction work and New Life Movement emblem. $3.50, Marco Polo Bridge near Peking and victory parade, Nanking. $4, Original copy of Constitution of Republic of China. $5, Nationalist Chinese flag flying over mainland China.

1968, Oct. 31 *Perf. 11½x12*

1582 A273 $1 multi .75 .30
1583 A273 $2 multi 1.00 .30
1584 A273 $2.50 multi 1.40 .45
1585 A273 $3.50 multi 1.75 .60
1586 A273 $4 multi 2.25 1.00
1587 A273 $5 multi 3.75 1.25
Nos. 1582-1587 (6) 10.90 3.90

Chiang Kai-shek's achievements for China.

Cock — A274

1968, Nov. 12 Litho. *Perf. 12*

Granite Paper

1588 A274 $1 pink & multi 17.00 1.00
1589 A274 $4.50 lilac & multi 40.00 6.00

Issued for use on New Year's greetings.

Flag — A275

1968, Dec. 25 Wmk. 323 *Perf. 12½*

Granite Paper

1590 A275 $1 multicolored .70 .25
1591 A275 $5 lt blue & multi 1.00 .75

Constitution of the Republic of China, 20th anniversary.

Jade Belt Buckle, 1662-1911 A276

Ancient Art Treasures: $1.50, Yellow jade vase, 960-1126 A.D., vert. $2, Cloisonne enamel square teapot, 1662-1911 A.D. $2.50, Kuei, sacrificial bronze vessel, 722-481 B.C. $4, Heavenly ball vase, 1368-1661 A.D., vert. $5, Gourd-shaped vase, 1662-1911 A.D., vert.

Unwmk.

1969, Jan. 15 Photo. *Perf. 13*

1592 A276 $1 dl rose & multi 1.10 .25
1593 A276 $1.50 rose & multi 2.00 .25
1594 A276 $2 brt rose & multi 2.50 .25
1595 A276 $2.50 lt blue & multi 2.75 .60
1596 A276 $4 tan & multi 3.00 .80
1597 A276 $5 pale blue & multi 3.00 1.00
Nos. 1592-1597 (6) 14.35 3.15

Servicemen and Savings Emblem A277

Wmk. 323

1969, Feb. 1 Engr. *Perf. 12*

Granite Paper

1598 A277 $1 dull red brown .35 .25
1599 A277 $4 deep blue 1.00 .55

Military Savings Program, 10th anniv.

Ti (Flute) A278

Musical Instruments: $2.50, Sheng (13 bamboo pipes connected at the base). $4, P'i p'a (lute). $5, Cheng (zither).

Unwmk.

1969, Mar. 16 Photo. *Perf. 13*

1600 A278 $1 buff & multi .55 .30
1601 A278 $2.50 lt ap grn & multi 1.25 .40
1602 A278 $4 pink & multi 1.60 .45
1603 A278 $5 lt grnsh bl & multi 2.25 .60
Nos. 1600-1603 (4) 5.65 1.75

Sun Yat-sen Building and Kuomintang Emblem A279

1969, Mar. 29 Litho. *Perf. 13½*

1604 A279 $1 multicolored .70 .25

10th Natl. Cong. of the Chinese Nationalist Party (Kuomintang), Mar. 29. A $2.50 stamp portraying Sun Yat-sen and Chiang Kai-shek was prepared but not issued.

Double Carp Design — A280

Perf. 13½x12½

1974 Engr. Wmk. 323

Granite Paper

1606 A280 $10 dark blue 2.50 .40
1607 A280 $20 dark brown 5.25 .40
1608 A280 $50 green 8.50 .75
1609 A280 $100 bright red 10.75 1.40
Nos. 1606-1609 (4) 27.00 2.95

1969 *Perf. 11½*

1606a A280 $10 3.25 .35
1607a A280 $20 4.25 .35
1608a A280 $50 11.00 .45
1609a A280 $100 17.00 .90
Nos. 1606a-1609a (4) 35.50 2.05

The 1969 issue is 27mm high; 1974, 28mm. See No. 1980.

Bridal Procession — A281

Designs: No. 1610, Musicians and standard bearer from bridal procession. $2.50, Emigrant farm family in oxcart. $5, Art gallery. $8, Roadside food stands. Designs from scroll "A City in Cathay," painted in 1736.

Perf. 13½

1969, May 20 Unwmk. Photo.

1610 A281 $1 multi 1.25 .35
1611 A281 $1 multi 1.25 .35
a. Pair, #1610-1611 2.75 2.75
1612 A281 $2.50 multi 4.00 1.00
1613 A281 $5 multi 4.25 .75
1614 A281 $8 multi 7.25 1.25
Nos. 1610-1614 (5) 18.00 3.70

ILO Emblem A282

Wmk. 323

1969, June 15 Engr. *Perf. 11½*

Granite Paper

1615 A282 $1 dark blue .70 .25
1616 A282 $8 dark carmine 1.50 .55

ILO, 50th anniversary.

Family at Dinner Table and Dressing A283

Designs: $2.50, Housecleaning and obeying traffic rules. $4, Recreation (music, fishing, basketball) and education.

Wmk. 323

1969, July 15 Engr. *Perf. 11½*

1617	A283	$1	brick red	.25	.25
1618	A283	$2.50	blue	.70	.35
1619	A283	$4	green	.80	.45
			Nos. 1617-1619 (3)	1.75	1.05

Model Citizen's Life Movement.

Pupils in Laboratory and Playing — A284

Design: $1, $5, Pupils with book and various school activities, horiz.

Granite Paper

1969, Sept. 1 Wmk. 323 *Perf. 11½*

1620	A284	$1	brt red	.25	.25
1621	A284	$2.50	brt green	.75	.30
1622	A284	$4	dk blue	1.00	.30
1623	A284	$5	brown	1.40	.55
			Nos. 1620-1623 (4)	3.40	1.40

Free 9-year education system, 1st anniv.

Wild Flowers and Pheasants, by Lu Chih (Ming) A285

Paintings: $2.50, Bamboo and birds, Sung dynasty. $5, Flowers and Birds, Sung dynasty. $8, Cranes and Flowers, by G. Castiglione, S.J. (1688-1766).

1969, Oct. 9 Photo. *Perf. 13½*

1624	A285	$1	multi	1.40	.35
1625	A285	$2.50	multi	3.50	.45
1626	A285	$5	multi	8.50	.75
1627	A285	$8	multi	11.50	1.10
			Nos. 1624-1627 (4)	24.90	2.65

Golden Scepter Rose — A286

Roses: $1, "Charles Mollerin," called black rose. $5, Peace. $8, Josephine Bruce.

1969, Oct. 31 Litho. *Perf. 14*

1628	A286	$1	lt vio & multi	1.25	.25
1629	A286	$2.50	lt bl & multi	3.75	.25
1630	A286	$5	dl org & multi	4.75	.35
1631	A286	$8	ap grn & multi	4.50	.70
			Nos. 1628-1631 (4)	14.25	1.55

Rocket and Radar Station — A287

Wmk. 323

1969, Nov. 21 Engr. *Perf. 11½*

1632	A287	$1	rose claret	1.50	.25

The 30th Air Defense Day.

Symbol of International Cooperation A288

1969, Nov. 25

1633	A288	$1	rose claret	.35	.25
1634	A288	$5	green	1.10	.35

5th General Assembly of the Asian Parliamentary Union, Taipei, Nov. 24-28.

Pekingese — A289

1969, Dec. 1 Litho. *Perf. 12*

Granite Paper

1635	A289	50c	red & multi	2.00	.50
1636	A289	$4.50	green & multi	10.00	2.00

Issued for use on New Year's greetings.

Satellite, Earth Station and Map of Taiwan A290

Unwmk.

1969, Dec. 28 Photo. *Perf. 13*

1637	A290	$1	brown & multi	.45	.25
1638	A290	$5	vio blue & multi	1.60	.35
1639	A290	$8	purple & multi	2.25	.65
			Nos. 1637-1639 (3)	4.30	1.25

Inauguration of the Communication Satellite Earth Station at Chin-Shan-Li, Dec. 28.

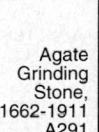

Agate Grinding Stone, 1662-1911 A291

Ancient Art Treasures: $1, Carved lacquer ware vase, 1662-1911, vert. $2, White jade Chin-li-chih melons, 1662-1911. $2.50, Black jade shepherd and ram, 206 B.C.-220 A.D. $4, Chien-lung twin porcelain vase, 1736-1796, vert. $5, Ju porcelain vase with 3 bulls, 960-1126, vert.

1970, Jan. 23

1640	A291	$1	lt grnsh bl & multi	.75	.25
1641	A291	$1.50	pale bl & multi	1.40	.25
1642	A291	$2	green & multi	1.60	.25
1643	A291	$2.50	pink & multi	2.75	.35
1644	A291	$4	ol bis & multi	3.00	.45
1645	A291	$5	ultra & multi	4.00	.80
			Nos. 1640-1645 (6)	13.50	2.35

Hsuan Chuang — A292

Chu Hsi — A293

Design: $2.50, Hua To.

1970 Wmk. 323 Engr. *Perf. 11½*

Granite Paper

1646	A292	$1	car rose	.70	.25
1647	A293	$2.50	blue grn	1.10	.25
1648	A293	$4	blue	1.75	.45
			Nos. 1646-1648 (3)	3.55	.95

Issued in memory of Hsuan Chuang (602-664), who propagated Buddhism in China; Chu Hsi (1130-1200), who developed Neo-Confucianism, and Hua To (3rd century A.D.) physician and surgeon.

Issued: $2.50, 3/17; others, 2/20.

EXPO '70 Pavilion, Emblem and Flags of Participants A294

Design: $5, Chinese pavilion, EXPO '70 emblem, exhibition and Chinese flags.

Unwmk.

1970, Mar. 13 Photo. *Perf. 13*

1649	A294	$5	org red & multi	.70	.25
1650	A294	$8	lt blue & multi	1.75	.70

EXPO '70 International Exhibition, Osaka, Japan, Mar. 15-Sept. 13.

Nimbus III and WMO Emblem A295

Design: $1, Agricultural meteorological station and tropical landscape, vert.

Perf. 14x13½, 13½x14

1970, Mar. 23 Litho. Wmk. 323

Granite Paper

1651	A295	$1	green & multi	.55	.25
1652	A295	$8	blue & multi	1.00	.65

10th Annual World Meteorological Day.

Martyrs' Shrine, Taipei A296

Shrine's Gate A297

Unwmk.

1970, Mar. 29 Photo. *Perf. 13*

1653	A296	$1	multicolored	.70	.25
1654	A297	$8	multicolored	1.75	.65

Completion of the Martyrs' Shrine in Northern Taipei, dedicated to the memory of 72 young revolutionaries who died Mar. 29, 1911.

Yueh Fei Fighting for Lost Territories A298

Characters from Chinese Operas: $2.50, Emperor Shun and stepmother. $5, The Lady Warrior Chin Liang-yu. $8, Kuan Yu and groom.

1970, May 4 Unwmk. *Perf. 13½*

1655	A298	$1	multi	1.10	.25
1656	A298	$2.50	multi	2.75	.55
1657	A298	$5	multi	3.75	.65
1658	A298	$8	multi	5.75	.80
			Nos. 1655-1658 (4)	13.35	2.25

A299

Three Horses Playing — A300

Horses: No. 1659, Barren tree at right. No. 1660, Horse standing in river. No. 1661, Tree trunk in lower left corner. No. 1662, Trees in left background. No. 1663, shown. $8, Groom roping horses. Designs from scroll "One Hundred Horses" by Lang Shih-ning (Giuseppe Castiglione, 1688-1766).

Perf. 13½

1970, June 18 Unwmk. Photo.

1659	A299	$1	multi	1.00	.25
1660	A299	$1	multi	1.00	.25
1661	A299	$1	multi	1.00	.25
1662	A299	$1	multi	1.00	.25
1663	A299	$1	multi	1.00	.25
a.			Strip of 5, #1659-1663	8.00	8.00
1664	A300	$5	bister & multi	9.75	2.00
1665	A300	$8	dl yel & multi	11.50	3.00
			Nos. 1659-1665 (7)	26.25	6.25

Lai-tsu Amusing his Old Parents — A301

Chinese Fairy Tales: No. 1667, Man disguised as deer, and hunters. No. 1668, Boy cooling his father's bed. No. 1669, Boy fishing through ice. No. 1670, Son reunited with old mother. No. 1671, Emperor tasting mother's medicine. No. 1672, Boy saving oranges for mother. No. 1673, Boy saving father from tiger.

Wmk. 323

1970, July 10 Litho. *Perf. 13½*

Granite Paper

1666	A301	10c	red & multi	.25	.25
1667	A301	10c	car rose & multi	.25	.25
1668	A301	10c	lt vio & multi	.25	.25
1669	A301	10c	gray & multi	.25	.25
1670	A301	10c	emerald & multi	.25	.25
1671	A301	50c	bister & multi	.45	.25
1672	A301	$1	sky blue & multi	.65	.35
1673	A301	$1	dp blue & multi	.55	.45
			Nos. 1666-1673 (8)	2.90	2.30

See Nos. 1726-1733.

Man's First Step onto Moon — A302

$1, Pres. Chiang Kai-shek's message brought to the moon. $5, Neil A. Armstrong, Michael Collins, Edwin E. Aldrin, Jr., and moon, horiz.

Perf. 13½x13, 13x13½

1970, July 21 Photo. Unwmk.

1674 A302 $1 yellow & multi 1.00 .25
1675 A302 $5 lt yel grn & multi 1.60 .45
1676 A302 $8 blue & multi 2.75 .70
Nos. 1674-1676 (3) 5.35 1.40

1st anniv. of man's 1st landing on the moon.

Asian Productivity Year Symbol A303

Wmk. 323

1970, Aug. 18 Litho. *Perf. 13½*

Granite Paper

1677 A303 $1 emerald & multi .65 .25
1678 A303 $5 blue & multi 1.25 .40

Issued to publicize Asian Productivity Year.

Flags of China and UN — A304

1970, Sept. 19 Wmk. 323 *Perf. 12*

Granite Paper

1679 A304 $5 blue, car & blk 1.75 .65

25th anniversary of the United Nations.

Postal Zone Map — A305

Postal Code Emblem A306

1970, Oct. 8 Litho.

1680 A305 $1 lt blue & multi .90 .25
1681 A306 $2.50 green & multi 1.10 .40

Issued to publicize the postal code system.

Eleventh Month Scroll — A307

Designs: A scroll series, "Activities of the 12 Months," painted on silk by a group of painters of the Ch'ien Lung court (1736-1796). Chinese number in parenthesis at right of denomination tells month.

Jan., Feb., Mar.
(一) (二) (三)

Perf. 13½x13

1970-71 Photo. Unwmk.

1682 A307 $1 multi 2.25 .40
1683 A307 $2.50 multi 5.00 1.00
1684 A307 $5 multi 8.50 1.40

Apr., May, June
(四) (五) (六)

1685 A307 $1 multi 2.25 .40
1686 A307 $2.50 multi 5.00 1.00
1687 A307 $5 multi 8.50 1.40

July, Aug., Sept.
(七) (八) (九)

1688 A307 $1 multi 2.25 .40
1689 A307 $2.50 multi 5.00 1.00
1690 A307 $5 multi 8.50 1.40

Oct., Nov., Dec.
(十) (一十) (二十)

1691 A307 $1 multi 2.25 .40
1692 A307 $2.50 multi 5.00 1.00
1693 A307 $5 multi 8.50 1.40
Nos. 1682-1693 (12) 63.00 11.20

Issued: Nos. 1691-1693, 10/21/70; Nos. 1682-1684, 1/14/71; Nos. 1685-1687, 4/26/71; Nos. 1688-1690, 8/27/71.

Family at Home A308

$4, Family of 5 going on an excursion, vert.

Perf. 13½x14, 14x13½

1970, Nov. 11 Litho. Wmk. 323

Granite Paper

1694 A308 $1 multicolored .70 .25
1695 A308 $4 yel grn & multi 1.50 .35

Issued to publicize family planning.

Piggy Bank — A309

1970, Dec. 1 *Perf. 12½x12*

Granite Paper

1696 A309 50c multi 3.25 .25
1697 A309 $4.50 blue & multi 5.00 .90

Issued for use on New Year's greetings.

Tibia Fusus Shells A310

Rare Taiwan Shells: $2.50, Harpeola kurodai. $5, Conus stupa kuroda. $8, Entemnotrochus rumphii.

1971, Feb. 25 *Perf. 13x13½*

1698 A310 $1 vio & multi .50 .25
1699 A310 $2.50 multi 1.90 .25
1700 A310 $5 org & multi 2.40 .45
1701 A310 $8 grn & multi 3.25 .65
Nos. 1698-1701 (4) 8.05 1.60

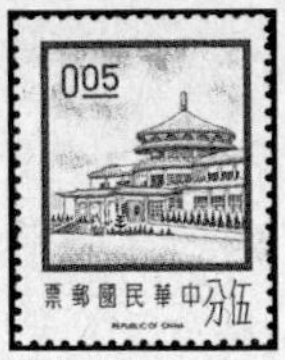

Sun Yat-sen Building, Yangmingshan A311

Perf. 13½x12½

1971 Litho. Wmk. 323

Granite Paper

1702 A311 5c brown .25 .25
1703 A311 10c dk gray .25 .25
1704 A311 50c brt rose lilac .95 .25
1705 A311 $1 vermilion 1.00 .25
1706 A311 $1.50 ultra 1.10 .25
1707 A311 $2 plum 1.25 .25
1708 A311 $2.50 emerald 1.40 .25
1709 A311 $3 aqua 1.90 .30
Nos. 1702-1709 (8) 8.10 2.05

Passbook and Postal Savings Certificate A312

$4, People and hand dropping coin into bank.

Perf. 13½x14

1971, Mar. 20 Litho. Wmk. 323

1712 A312 $1 yel grn & multi .65 .25
1713 A312 $4 ver & multi 1.50 .30

Publicizing Chinese Postal Savings Service.

Cooperation Emblem, Farmers — A313

Design: $8, Chinese teaching rice farming to Africans, horiz.

Unwmk.

1971, May 20 Photo. *Perf. 13*

1714 A313 $1 multicolored .65 .25
1715 A313 $8 multicolored 1.40 .70

Sino-African Technical Cooperation Committee, 10th anniversary.

Rock Monkey — A314

Taiwan Animals: $2, White-face flying squirrel. $3, Chinese pangolin. $5, Formosan sika deer. $2, $3, $5 are horiz.

1971, June 25 *Perf. 11½*

1716 A314 $1 gold & multi .40 .25
1717 A314 $2 gold & multi 1.25 .25
1718 A314 $3 gold & multi 1.75 .30
1719 A314 $5 gold & multi 2.50 .50
Nos. 1716-1719 (4) 5.90 1.30

Pitcher — A315

Designs: $2.50, Players at base, horiz. $4, Batter and catcher.

1971, July 29 Photo. *Perf. 13*

1720 A315 $1 multi .30 .25
1721 A315 $2.50 multi .50 .25
1722 A315 $4 multi .90 .25
Nos. 1720-1722 (3) 1.70 .75

Pacific Regional competition for the 1971 Little League World Series.

Nos. 1541, 1544-1545 Overprinted in Magenta or Red

Perf. 13x12½

1971, Sept. 9 Litho. Wmk. 323

Granite Paper

1723 A259 $1 vermilion (M) .30 .25
1724 A259 $2.50 blue (R) .60 .25
1725 A259 $3 grnsh blue (R) .60 .25
Nos. 1723-1725 (3) 1.50 .75

Chinese victory in 1971 Little League World Series, Williamsport, Pa., Aug. 24.

Fairy Tale Type of 1970

Chinese Fairy Tales (Filial Piety): No. 1726, Birds and elephant helping in rice field. No. 1727, Son gathering mulberries for mother. No. 1728, Son gathering firewood. No. 1729, Son, mother and bandits. No. 1730, Son carrying heavy burden. 50c, Son digging for bamboo shoots in winter. No. 1732, Man and wife working as slaves. No. 1733, Father, son and carriage.

1971, Sept. 22 *Perf. 13½*

Granite Paper

1726 A301 10c dp org & multi .25 .25
1727 A301 10c lilac & multi .25 .25
1728 A301 10c ocher & multi .25 .25
1729 A301 10c dp car & multi .25 .25
1730 A301 10c lt ultra & multi .25 .25
1731 A301 50c multicolored .30 .25
1732 A301 $1 emerald & multi .80 .25
1733 A301 $1 lt red brn & multi .80 .25
Nos. 1726-1733 (8) 3.15 2.00

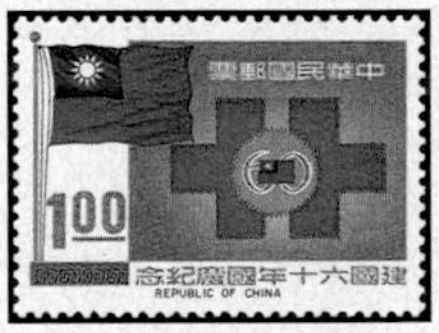

Flag of China, "Double Ten" and Anniversary Emblems A316

Designs (Flag of China and): $2.50, National anthem. $5, Gen. Chiang Kai-shek. $8, Sun Yat-sen.

1971, Oct. 10 Photo. *Perf. 13*

1734 A316 $1 orange & multi .40 .25
1735 A316 $2.50 multi 1.05 .25
1736 A316 $5 green & multi 1.25 .30
1737 A316 $8 olive & multi 1.25 .35
Nos. 1734-1737 (4) 3.95 1.15

60th National Day.

Bird in Flight (AOPU Emblem) A317

Perf. 13½x14

1971, Nov. 8 Litho. Wmk. 323

1738 A317 $2.50 yellow & multi .70 .25
1739 A317 $5 orange & multi .90 .25

Asian-Oceanic Postal Union Executive Committee Session, Taipei, Nov. 8-15.

"White Frost Hawk," by Lang Shih-ning A318

Dog Series I

Designs: $2, "Star-Glancing Wolf." $2.50, "Golden-Winged Face." $5, "Young Black Dragon." $8, "Young Gray Dragon."

Designs from painting series "Ten Prized Dogs," by Lang Shih-ning (Giuseppe Castiglione, 1688-1766).

Perf. 13½x13

1971, Nov. 16 Litho. Unwmk.

1740	A318	$1	Facing left	.70	.25
1741	A318	$2	Lying down	1.00	.25
1742	A318	$2.50	Scratching	1.25	.30
1743	A318	$5	Facing right	3.00	.50
1744	A318	$8	Looking back	5.00	1.00
			Nos. 1740-1744 (5)	10.95	2.30

Dog Series II

Designs: $1, "Black with Snow-white Paws." $2, "Yellow Leopard." $2.50, "Flying Magpie." $5, "Heavenly Lion." $8, "Mottled Tiger."

1972, Jan. 12

1745	A318	$1	Facing right	2.00	.25
1746	A318	$2	Walking	3.50	.25
1747	A318	$2.50	Sleeping	5.00	.30
1748	A318	$5	Facing left	10.00	.50
1749	A318	$8	Sitting	22.50	1.00
			Nos. 1745-1749 (5)	43.00	2.30

Squirrels — A319

Perf. 13½x12½

1971, Dec. 1 Wmk. 323

1750	A319		Block of 4	5.00	3.50
a.			50c in UL corner	.90	.25
b.			50c in UR corner	.90	.25
c.			50c in LL corner	.90	.25
d.			50c in LR corner	.90	.25
1751	A319		Block of 4	20.00	5.00
a.			$4.50 in UL corner	4.50	.60
b.			$4.50 in UR corner	4.50	.60
c.			$4.50 in LL corner	4.50	.60
d.			$4.50 in LR corner	4.50	.60

New Year 1972.

Flags of China and Jordan A320

1971, Dec. 16 *Perf. 13½*

Granite Paper

1752	A320	$5	multicolored	1.60	.25

50th anniversary of the founding of the Hashemite Kingdom of Jordan.

Cargo Ship "Hai King" — A321

$7, Ocean liner & map of Pacific Ocean, vert.

1971, Dec. 16 *Perf. 12½*

1753	A321	$4	grn, dk bl & red	.70	.45
1754	A321	$7	ocher & multi	1.10	.55

China Merchants Steam Navigation Co., cent.

Downhill Skiing, Olympic Rings A322

$5, Cross-country skiing. $8, Giant slalom.

1972, Feb. 3 *Perf. 13½*

1755	A322	$1	org, blk & bl	.30	.25
1756	A322	$5	yel grn, dp org & blk	.70	.25
1757	A322	$8	red, gray & blk	.80	.25
			Nos. 1755-1757 (3)	1.80	.75

11th Winter Olympic Games, Sapporo, Japan, Feb. 3-13.

Vase, 18th Century — A323

Porcelain Series I

Porcelain Masterworks of Ching Dynasty: $2, Covered jar. $2.50, Pitcher. $5, Vase with 5 openings and dragon design. $8, Covered jar with children design.

Perf. 11½

1972, Mar. 20 Photo. Unwmk.

1758	A323	$1	violet & multi	.70	.25
1759	A323	$2	plum & blue	1.50	.25
1760	A323	$2.50	org ver & bl	2.25	.25
1761	A323	$5	bis brn & bl	2.50	.46
1762	A323	$8	sl grn & multi	3.75	.45
			Nos. 1758-1762 (5)	10.70	1.65

See Nos. 1812-1821, 1864-1868.

Nine Flying Doves A324

Perf. 13½x14

1972, Apr. 1 Litho. Wmk. 323

1763	A324	$1	lt blue & blk	.55	.25
1764	A324	$5	lt violet & blk	1.60	.30

Asian-Oceanic Postal Union, 10th anniv.

"Dignity with Self-reliance" — A325

Perf. 13½x12½

1972-75 Litho. Wmk. 323

1765	A325	5c	brown & yel	.25	.25
1766	A325	10c	blue & org	.25	.25
1767	A325	20c	cl & yel grn ('75)	.25	.25
1768	A325	50c	lil & lil rose	.25	.25
1769	A325	$1	red & brt bl	.30	.25
1770	A325	$1.50	yel & dk bl	.40	.25
1771	A325	$2	maroon & org	.60	.25
1772	A325	$2.50	emer & ver	1.50	.25
1773	A325	$3	red & lt grn	1.10	.25
			Nos. 1765-1773 (9)	4.90	2.25

Souvenir Sheet

Imperf

1775	A325		Sheet of 2	5.00	2.25

No. 1775 commemorates ROCPEX '72 Philatelic Exhibition, Taipei, Oct. 24-Nov. 2. It contains 2 stamps similar to Nos. 1771 and 1773 with simulated perforations.

Issued: $1, $1.50, $2, $3, 5/20/72; 5c, 10c, 50c, $2.50, No. 1775, 10/24/72; 20c, 1975.

For overprints see Nos. 1787-1790.

Emperor Shih-tsung's Procession — A326

Messengers on Horseback — A327

Designs from scrolls depicting Emperor Shih-tsung's (reigned 1522-1566) journey to and from tombs at Cheng-tien. No. 1776 shows land journey departure and is designed from right to left. No. 1779 shows return trip by boat and is designed from left to right. The 5 stamps of Nos. 1776 and 1780 are numbered 1 to 5 in Chinese (see illustrations with Nos. 1682-1686 for numerals).

1972 Photo. Unwmk. *Perf. 13½*

1776			Strip of 5	3.50	3.00
a.	A326	$1	shown (1)	.55	.35
b.	A326	$1	Seven carriages (2)	.55	.35
c.	A326	$1	Carriage drawn by 23 horses (3)	.55	.35
d.	A326	$1	Procession (4)	.55	.35
e.	A326	$1	Emperor under 2 canopies (5)	.55	.35
1777	A327	$2.50	shown	2.25	.50
1778	A327	$5	Guards with flags, fans & spears	3.00	.50
1779	A327	$8	Sedan chair carried by 28 men	6.00	.60
1780			Strip of 5	3.50	3.00
a.	A326	$1	Three barges (1)	.55	.35
b.	A326	$1	Procession, sedan chairs (2)	.55	.35
c.	A326	$1	Two barges with trunks (3)	.55	.35
d.	A326	$1	Procession on land (4)	.55	.35
e.	A326	$1	Procession, 2 sedan chairs (5)	.55	.35
1781	A326	$2.50	Courtiers at city welcoming Emperor	2.25	.40
1782	A327	$5	Orchestra on horseback	3.00	.40
1783	A326	$8	Barges	3.75	.50
			Nos. 1776-1783 (8)	27.25	8.90

Issue dates: No. 1776-1779, June 14; Nos. 1780-1783, July 12.

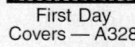

First Day Covers — A328

Magnifying Glass, Tongs, Gauge — A329

Design: $2.50, Sun Yat-sen stamp of 1971 (type A311) under magnifying glass.

Wmk. 323

1972, Aug. 9 Engr. *Perf. 12*

1784	A328	$1	dk vio blue	.25	.25
1785	A328	$2.50	brt green	.25	.25
1786	A329	$8	scarlet	.55	.25
			Nos. 1784-1786 (3)	1.05	.75

Promotion of philately. Printed in sheets of 40. Each sheet contains 4 blocks of 10 stamps surrounded by margins with inscriptions.

Nos. 1768-1770, 1772 Overprinted in Dark Blue or Red

Perf. 13½x12½

1972, Sept. 9 Litho. Wmk. 323

1787	A325	$1	red & brt bl (DB)	.25	.25
1788	A325	$1.50	yel & dk bl (R)	.40	.25
1789	A325	$2	mar & org (R)	.55	.25
1790	A325	$3	red & lt grn (DB)	.60	.25
			Nos. 1787-1790 (4)	1.80	1.00

China's championship victories in the Little League World Series, Gary, Ind., and in the Senior League World Series, Williamsport, Pa., Aug. 1972.

Emperor Yao (2357-2258 B.C.) — A330

Rulers: $4, Emperor Shun (ruled 2255-2208 B.C.). $4.50, Yu, the Great (ruled 2205-2198 B.C.). $5, King T'ang (ruled 1783-1754 B.C.). $5.50, King Wen (ruled 1171-1122 B.C.). $6, King Wu (ruled 1121-1114 B.C.). $7, Chou Kung (died 1105 B.C.). $8, Confucius (551-479 B.C.).

1972-73 Engr. *Perf. 12*

Granite Paper

1791	A330	$3.50	dk blue	.40	.25
1792	A330	$4	rose red	.60	.25
1793	A330	$4.50	bluish lil	.80	.25
1794	A330	$5	brt green	.40	.25
1795	A330	$5.50	dp claret ('73)	1.25	.25
1796	A330	$6	dp org ('73)	1.10	.25
a.			Perf. 13½x12½ ('76)	1.10	.30
1797	A330	$7	sepia ('73)	1.10	.25
a.			Perf. 13½x12½ ('76)	1.10	.30
1798	A330	$8	indigo ('73)	1.25	.25
a.			gray, perf. 13½x12½ ('76)	1.75	.35
			Nos. 1791-1798 (8)	6.90	2.00

In the first printing, Nos. 1791-1794, 1796-1798 measure 32mm high. In a 1974 reissue they are 33mm.

Mountain Climbing — A331

Designs (China Youth Corps emblem and): $2.50, Skiing (skiers forming circle). $4, Diving. $8, Parachute jumping.

Unwmk.

1972, Oct. 31 Photo. *Perf. 12*

1800	A331	$1	green & multi	.25	.25
1801	A331	$2.50	blue & multi	.50	.25
1802	A331	$4	orange & multi	.75	.25
1803	A331	$8	multicolored	1.25	.25
			Nos. 1800-1803 (4)	2.75	1.00

China Youth Corps, 20th anniversary.

JCI Emblem A332

1972, Nov. 12 Litho. Wmk. 323

1804	A332	$1	multicolored	.25	.25
1805	A332	$5	orange & multi	.40	.25
1806	A332	$8	multicolored	.70	.40
			Nos. 1804-1806 (3)	1.35	.90

27th Junior Chamber International (JCI) World Congress, Taipei, Nov. 12-19.

Electronic Mail Sorter — A333

Plane, Ship and Pier — A334

Progress of Communications System on Taiwan: $5, Highway overpass over railroad.

Wmk. 323

1972, Nov. 12 Engr. *Perf. 11½*

1807 A333 $1 red .25 .25
1808 A334 $2.50 blue .50 .25
1809 A334 $5 dk violet brn 1.10 .35
Nos. 1807-1809 (3) 1.85 .85

Cow and Calf (Parental Love) — A335

1972, Dec. 1 Litho. *Perf. 12*

1810 A335 50c red & blk 2.75 .30
1811 A335 $4.50 yel, red & brn 4.25 .90

New Year 1973. Printed in sheets of 80, divided into 4 panes of 20, separated by vertical and horizontal gutters 2 rows wide. 20 red chops meaning "Happy New Year" are printed in the gutters.

Porcelain Type of 1972 and

Stem Bowl with Dragons A336

Porcelain Series II

Porcelain Masterworks of Ming Dynasty: $1, Covered vase with fruits and flowers. $2, Vase with ornamental and floral design. $2.50, Vase imitating ancient bronze. $5, Flask with flowers of 4 seasons. $8, Garlic head vase.

1973 Photo. *Perf. 11½*

1812 A323 $1 gray & multi 1.10 .25
1813 A323 $2 lt brn & multi 1.60 .25
1814 A323 $2.50 brt grn & multi 2.25 .25
1815 A323 $5 ultra & multi 2.40 .35
1816 A323 $8 olive & multi 3.50 .60
Nos. 1812-1816 (5) 10.85 1.70

Porcelain Series III

Ming Porcelain: $2, Refuse container with dragons. $2.50, Covered jar with lotus. $5, Covered jar with horses. $8, Bowl with figures of immortals.

1817 A336 $1 gray & multi 1.10 .25
1818 A336 $2 lt vio & multi 1.60 .25
1819 A336 $2.50 dk red & multi 2.25 .25
1820 A336 $5 blue & multi 2.40 .35
1821 A336 $8 dp org & multi 3.50 .60
Nos. 1817-1821 (5) 10.85 1.70

Issued: Nos. 1812-1816, 1/10; Nos. 1817-1821, 3/24.

See Nos. 1864-1868.

Oyster Fairy and Fisherman's Dance — A337

$1, Kicking shuttlecock, vert. $5, Rowing boat over land. $8, Old man carrying young lady, vert.

1973, Feb. 7 Photo. *Perf. 11½*
Granite Paper

1822 A337 $1 multicolored .70 .25
1823 A337 $4 Shown 1.10 .25
1824 A337 $5 multicolored 1.25 .25
1825 A337 $8 multicolored 1.40 .40
Nos. 1822-1825 (4) 4.45 1.15

Chinese folklore popular entertainment.

Bamboo Boat A338

Taiwanese Handicrafts: $2.50, Painted marble vase, vert. $5, Painted glass plate. $8, Doll, bridegroom carrying bride on back, vert.

Perf. 13½x14½, 14½x13½

1973, Mar. 9 Photo.

1826 A338 $1 multi .25 .25
1827 A338 $2.50 multi .85 .25
1828 A338 $5 multi 1.25 .25
1829 A338 $8 multi 1.75 .40
Nos. 1826-1829 (4) 4.10 1.15

Federation Emblem, Cargo Hook, Crane — A339

Emblem, Tractor, New Buildings A340

Wmk. 323

1973, Apr. 2 Litho. *Perf. 12½*

1830 A339 $1 salmon & multi .40 .25
1831 A340 $5 blue & blk .75 .25

12th convention of International Federation of Asian and Western Pacific Contractors Association, Taipei, Apr. 2-10.

Pres. Chiang Kai-shek, Flag of China — A341

Design: $4, like $1 with different border.

Unwmk.

1973, May 20 Photo. *Perf. 12*

1832 A341 $1 yellow & multi .75 .25
1833 A341 $4 dk grn & multi 1.10 .50

First anniversary of Pres. Chiang Kai-shek's inauguration for a fifth term.

Lin Tse-hsü — A342

Wmk. 323

1973, June 3 Engr. *Perf. 12*

1834 A342 $1 sepia .75 .25

Lin Tse-hsü (1785-1850), Governor of Hunan and Kwantung, who destroyed large quantity of opium at Humen, Kwantung, June 3, 1839.

Willows and Palace Gate in the Morning — A343

Lady Watering Peonies, Stone Ornament A344

Design from scroll "Spring Morning in the Han Palace," by Chiu Ying. The five stamps of No. 1835 are numbered 1 to 5 and the five stamps of No. 1838 are numbered 6-10 in Chinese (see illustrations with Nos. 1682-1691 for numerals). The stamps are numbered and listed from right to left.

1973 Photo. Unwmk. *Perf. 11½*
Granite Paper

1835 Strip of 5 3.00 3.00
a. A343 $1 shown (1) .40 .25
b. A343 $1 Ladies feeding peacocks (2) .40 .25
c. A343 $1 Lady watering peonies (3) .40 .25
d. A343 $1 Pear tree in bloom (4) .40 .25
e. A343 $1 Lady musicians (5) .40 .25
1836 A344 $5 shown 2.25 .60
1837 A344 $8 Lady musicians 3.50 1.00
1838 Strip of 5 3.00 3.00
a. A343 $1 Ladies playing go (6) .40 .25
b. A343 $1 Various games (7) .40 .25
c. A343 $1 Talking and playing music (8) .40 .25
d. A343 $1 Artist painting portrait (9) .40 .25
e. A343 $1 Sentries guarding wall (10) .40 .25
1839 A344 $5 Ladies playing go 2.25 .60
1840 A344 $8 Girl chasing butterfly 3.50 1.00
Nos. 1835-1840 (6) 17.50 9.20

Issued: Nos. 1835-1837, 6/20; Nos. 1838-1840, 7/18.

Fan, Bamboo Design, by Hsiang Te-hsin — A345

Designs: Painted fans, Ming dynasty.

Perf. 12½x13

1973, Aug. 15 Photo. Wmk. 368

1841 A345 $1 bister & multi .50 .25
1842 A345 $2.50 bister & multi .95 .25
1843 A345 $5 bister & multi 1.75 .35
1844 A345 $8 bister & multi 2.75 .50
Nos. 1841-1844 (4) 5.95 1.35

See Nos. 1934-1937.

Little League Emblem — A346

Wmk. 370

1973, Sept. 9 Litho. *Perf. 13½*

1845 A346 $1 yel, car & dk bl .90 .25
1846 A346 $4 yel, grn & dk bl 1.60 .35

Chinese victory in Little League Twin Championships, Gary, Ind., and Williamsport, Pa.

INTERPOL Emblem — A347

Wmk. 370

1973, Sept. 11 Litho. *Perf. 12*

1847 A347 $1 blue & org .25 .25
1848 A347 $5 green & org .70 .25
1849 A347 $8 magenta & org 1.00 .40
Nos. 1847-1849 (3) 1.95 .90

Intl. Criminal Police Organization, 50th anniv.

Ch'iu Feng-chia — A348

Wmk. 323

1973, Oct. 5 Engr. *Perf. 11½*

1850 A348 $1 violet black .70 .25

2nd meeting of overseas Hakkas, Taipei, Oct. 5-7, and to honor Ch'iu Feng-chia (1864-1912), Hakka scholar, poet and revolutionist.

Tsengwen Reservoir A349

Tsengwen Dam — A350

Perf. 13½

1973, Oct. 31 Photo. Unwmk.

1851 Strip of 3 .90 .70
a. A349 $1 Upper shore .25 .25
b. A349 $1 shown .25 .25
c. A349 $1 Lower shore .25 .25

Perf. 12x11½

1852 A350 $5 shown .65 .30
1853 A350 $8 Spillway 1.00 .60
Nos. 1851-1853 (3) 2.55 1.60

Inauguration of Tsengwen Reservoir. No. 1851 printed in sheets of 15.

Tiger — A351

Wmk. 370

1973, Dec. 1 Litho. *Perf. 12½*

1854 A351 50c multi 1.10 .25
1855 A351 $4.50 multi 2.00 .50

New Year 1974.

"Snow-dotted Eagle," by Lang Shih-ning — A352

No. 1857, "Comfortable Ride." No. 1858, "Red Flower Eagle." No. 1859, "Cloud-running Steed." No. 1860, "Sky-running steed." $2.50, "Red Jade Seat." $5, "Thunderclap Steed." $8, "Arabian Champion." Designs from painting series "Ten Prized Horses," by Lang Shih-ning (Giuseppe Castiglione, 1688-1766).

1973 Litho. Unwmk. *Perf. 13*

1856	A352	50c shown	.75	.25
1857	A352	$1 Pinto, blk tail	1.00	.35
1858	A352	$1 Facing left	1.00	.35
1859	A352	$1 Facing right	1.00	.35
1860	A352	$1 Pinto, white tail	1.00	.35
a.		Horiz. or vert. strip of 4, #1857-1860	5.00	4.00
1861	A352	$2.50 Palomino	2.25	.60
1862	A352	$5 Grazing	3.75	1.00
a.		Souvenir sheet of 4	40.00	17.00
1863	A352	$8 Brown stallion	6.00	1.25
		Nos. 1856-1863 (8)	16.75	4.50

No. 1862a contains 4 stamps with simulated perforations similar to Nos. 1856-1857, 1861-1862.

Issued: 50c, $2.50, $5, 11/21; others 12/21.

Porcelain Types of 1972-73
Porcelain Series IV

Porcelain Masterworks of Sung Dynasty: $1, Vase. $2, Three-tiered vase. $2.50, Lotus-shaped bowl. $5, Incense burner. $8, Incense burner on stand.

1974, Jan. 16 Photo. *Perf. 11½*

1864	A323	$1 ultra & multi	.60	.25
1865	A336	$2 multicolored	1.10	.25
1866	A336	$2.50 red & multi	1.40	.25
1867	A336	$5 lilac & multi	1.60	.25
1868	A336	$8 green & multi	1.60	.50
		Nos. 1864-1868 (5)	6.30	1.50

Juggler — A353

Design: $8, Magician producing dishes from his robe, horiz.

1974, Feb. 6 Photo. *Perf. 11½*

1869	A353	$1 yellow & multi	.70	.25
1870	A353	$8 yellow & multi	1.60	.25

Taroko Gorge, Hualien — A354

Designs: $2.50, Luce Chapel, Tunghai University. $5, Tzu En Pagoda, Sun Moon Lake. $8, Goddess of Mercy, Keelung.

1974, Mar. 22 Photo. *Perf. 12*

1871	A354	$1 multi	.50	.25
1872	A354	$2.50 multi	1.10	.25
1873	A354	$5 multi	1.40	.25
1874	A354	$8 multi	2.00	.25
		Nos. 1871-1874 (4)	5.00	1.00

Taiwan landmarks.

Fighting Cocks (Brass) A355

Designs: $2.50, Grapes and bowl with fruit (imitation jade). $5, Fisherman (wood carving), vert. $8, Basket with plastic roses, vert.

Perf. 13½x14½, 14½x13½

1974, Apr. 10

1875	A355	$1 bl grn & multi	.30	.25
1876	A355	$2.50 brown & multi	.70	.25
1877	A355	$5 crimson & multi	1.00	.25
1878	A355	$8 multicolored	2.10	.40
		Nos. 1875-1878 (4)	4.10	1.15

Taiwanese handicraft products.

Sun Yat-sen Memorial Hall — A356

Taiwan landmarks: $2.50, Reaching-moon Tower, Cheng Ching Lake. $5, Orchid Island (boats). $8, Penghu Interisland Bridge.

1974, May 15 Photo. *Perf. 11½*
Granite Paper

1879	A356	$1 blue & multi	.30	.25
1880	A356	$2.50 blue & multi	.70	.25
1881	A356	$5 blue & multi	.90	.25
1882	A356	$8 blue & multi	1.25	.25
		Nos. 1879-1882 (4)	3.15	1.00

Pres. Chiang and Gate of Whampoa Military Academy A357

Marching Cadets and Entrance Gate — A358

Wmk. 323

1974, June 16 Engr. *Perf. 11½*

1883	A357	$1 carmine rose	.45	.25
1884	A358	$14 violet blue	.90	.40

50th anniversary of the founding of the Whampoa Military Academy.

Long-distance Runner and Olympic Rings — A359

$8, Women's relay race, Olympic rings.

1974, June 23 Litho. *Perf. 12½*

1885	A359	$1 blue, blk & red	.30	.25
1886	A359	$8 pink, blk & red	1.00	.40

80th anniv. of Intl. Olympic Committee.

The Boy Wang Ch'i Fighting Invaders — A360

Folk Tales: No. 1888, T'i Ying pleading for her father before the Emperor. No. 1889, Wen Yen-po flushing out ball caught in tree. No. 1890, Boy Wang Hua returning gold piece he found. No. 1891, Pu Shih, a rich sheep raiser and benefactor. No. 1892, K'ung Yung as a child choosing smallest pear. No. 1893, Tung Yu studying. No. 1894, Szu Ma-kuang saving playmate from drowning in water jar.

1974, July 15 Wmk. 370 *Perf. 13½*

1887	A360	50c olive & multi	.35	.25
1888	A360	50c ultra & multi	.35	.25
1889	A360	50c ocher & multi	.35	.25
1890	A360	50c red brn & multi	.35	.25
a.		Block of 4, #1887-1890	1.40	1.40
1891	A360	$1 green & multi	.75	.40
1892	A360	$1 lilac & multi	.75	.40
1893	A360	$1 blue & multi	.75	.40
1894	A360	$1 car & multi	.75	.40
a.		Block of 4, #1891-1894	3.00	3.00
		Nos. 1887-1894 (8)	4.40	2.60

For similar designs see A380, A427, A456, A495.

Myrtle, by Wei Sheng — A361

Silk Fan Paintings, Sung Dynasty (960-1279 A.D.): $2.50, Cabbage and Insects, by Hsu Ti. $5, Hibiscus, Cat and Dog, by Li Ti. $8, Pomegranate and Birds, by Wu Ping. Fans from National Palace Museum.

Perf. 13x12½

1974, Aug. 14 Photo. Wmk. 368

1895	A361	$1 multi	.25	.25
1896	A361	$2.50 multi	.85	.25
1897	A361	$5 multi	1.40	.25
1898	A361	$8 multi	2.00	.50
		Nos. 1895-1898 (4)	4.50	1.25

See Nos. 1950-1953.

Battle at Marco Polo Bridge, July 7, 1937 A362

Wmk. 370

1974, Sept. 3 Litho. *Perf. 13½*

1899	A362	$1 multicolored	.45	.25

Souvenir Sheet
Wmk. 323
Without Gum; Granite Paper

1900	Sheet of 8	9.00	9.00
a.	A362 $1, single stamp	.80	.80

20th Armed Forces Day. No. 1900 commemorates Armed Forces Stamp Exhibition, Sun Yat-sen Memorial Hall, Sept. 3-9.

Chrysanthemum A363

Designs: Various chrysanthemums.

Unwmk.

1974, Sept. 30 Photo. *Perf. 12*
Granite Paper

1901	A363	$1 lilac & multi	.25	.25
1902	A363	$2.50 multi	.70	.25
1903	A363	$5 orange & multi	.95	.25
1904	A363	$8 multi	1.60	.35
		Nos. 1901-1904 (4)	3.50	1.10

Rep. of China Pavilion, EXPO Emblem A364

Map of Fair Grounds, Chinese Flag A364a

Wmk. 370

1974, Oct. 10 Litho. *Perf. 13*

1905	A364	$1 multi	.25	.25
1906	A364a	$8 multi	.70	.40

EXPO '74, Spokane, Wash., May 4-Nov. 4. Theme, "Preserve the Environment."

Steel Mill, Kaohsiung A365

Taichung Harbor A366

Designs: $1, Taiwan North Link Railroad and map. $2, Oil refinery. $2.50, Electric train. $3.50, Taoyuan International Airport. $4, Taiwan North-South Highway and map. $4.50, Kaohsiung shipyard. $5, Su-ao Port.

Perf. 13x12½, 12½x13

1974, Oct. 31 Wmk. 323

1907	A365	50c lilac, yel & brn	.25	.25
1908	A365	$1 green & org	.25	.25
1909	A365	$2 blue & yel	.25	.25
1910	A365	$2.50 emer & org	.25	.25
1911	A366	$3 ocher & ultra	.25	.25
1912	A366	$3.50 sl grn & yel	.25	.25
1913	A366	$4 brown & yel	.25	.25
1914	A366	$4.50 ver & bl	.35	.25
1915	A366	$5 sepia & dk bl	.35	.25
		Nos. 1907-1915 (9)	2.45	2.25

Major construction projects.

See Nos. 2009-2017, 2068-2076. For overprints see Nos. 2064-2065, 2112-2113.

Agaricus Bisporus A367

Edible Mushrooms: $2.50, Pleurotus ostreatus. $5, Dictyophora indusiata. $8, Flammulina velutipes.

Perf. 11½

1974, Nov. 15 Unwmk. Photo.

1916	A367	$1 multi	.55	.25
1917	A367	$2.50 multi	.55	.25
1918	A367	$5 multi	1.00	.25
1919	A367	$8 multi	1.25	.30
		Nos. 1916-1919 (4)	3.35	1.05

9th Intl. Scientific Congress on the Cultivation of Edible Fungi, Taipei, Nov. 1974.

Batters and World Map — A368

Pitcher and Championship Banners — A369

Wmk. 323

1974, Nov. 24 Litho. *Perf. 13½*

1920	A368	$1	multicolored	.90	.25
1921	A369	$8	multicolored	.80	.35

China's victory in 1974 Little League Baseball World Series Triple Championships.

Rabbit — A370

Wmk. 323

1974, Dec. 10 Photo. *Perf. 12½*

1922	A370	50c	orange & multi	.60	.25
1923	A370	$4.50	brown & multi	2.10	.30

New Year 1975.

Acrobat with Iron Rod — A371

$5, Two acrobats spinning tops, horiz.

Granite Paper

1975, Jan. 15 Unwmk. *Perf. 11½*

1924	A371	$4	yellow & multi	.90	.40
1925	A371	$5	yellow & multi	1.40	.45

Children Watching Puppet Show — A372

Ceremonial New Year Greetings — A373

Designs from scroll "Festivals for the New Year," by Ting Kuan-p'eng. Nos. 1926a-1926e are numbered 1-5 in Chinese.

$5, Children buying firecrackers. $8, Children and man with trained monkey.

1975, Feb. 25 Photo. *Perf. 11½*

Granite Paper

1926	Strip of 5	3.75	2.50
a.	A372 $1 Ceremonial New Year Greetings (1)	.55	.25
b.	A372 $1 Man with trained monkey (2)	.55	.25
c.	A372 $1 Crowd and musicians (3)	.55	.25
d.	A372 $1 Picnic under a tree (4)	.55	.25
e.	A372 $1 shown (5)	.55	.25

1927	A373	$2.50	shown	2.50	.30
1928	A373	$5	multi	3.00	.55
1929	A373	$8	multi	5.25	.90
	Nos. 1926-1929 (4)			14.50	4.25

Sun Yat-sen Memorial Hall, Taipei A374

Sun Yat-sen's Handwriting — A375

Sun Yat-sen, Bronze Statue in Memorial Hall — A376

Sun Yat-sen Memorial Hall, St. John's University, NY A377

Perf. 13½x14, 14x13½

1975, Mar. 12 Litho.

1930	A374	$1	green & multi	.25	.25
1931	A375	$4	yel grn & multi	.55	.25
1932	A376	$5	yellow & multi	.80	.25
1933	A377	$8	gray & multi	1.10	.30
	Nos. 1930-1933 (4)			2.70	1.05

Dr. Sun Yat-sen (1866-1925), statesman and revolutionary leader.

Fan Type of 1973 Inscribed "Landscape" (1st Character, 2nd Row)

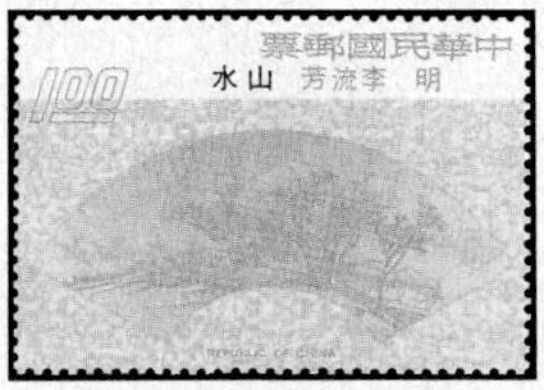

Painted fans, Ming Dynasty. Second row of inscription gives design description.

Perf. 12½x13

1975, Apr. 16 Photo. Wmk. 368

1934	A345	$1	bister & multi	.30	.25
1935	A345	$2.50	bister & multi	.95	.25
1936	A345	$5	bister & multi	2.00	.35
1937	A345	$8	bister & multi	2.25	.55
	Nos. 1934-1937 (4)			5.50	1.40

Yuan-chin coin, 1122-221 B.C. — A378

Ancient Chinese Coins: $4, Pan-liang, 221-207 B.C. $5, Five chu, 206 B.C.-220 A.D. $8, Five chu, 502-557 A.D.

Wmk. 323

1975, May 20 Litho. *Perf. 13*

1938	A378	$1	salmon & multi	.25	.25
1939	A378	$4	yellow & multi	.95	.25
1940	A378	$5	dl yel & multi	1.10	.25
1941	A378	$8	lt vio & multi	1.75	.25
	Nos. 1938-1941 (4)			4.05	1.00

The Cloth-bag Monk, by Chang Hung (1577-1668) A379

Chinese Paintings: $4, Lao-tzu Riding Buffalo, by Chao Pu-chih (1053-1110). $5, Portrait of Shih-te, by Wang Wen (1497-1576). $8, Splashed-ink Immortal, by Liang K'ai (early 13th century).

Perf. 11½

1975, June 18 Photo. Unwmk.

Granite Paper

1942	A379	$2	blk, buff & ver	.75	.25
1943	A379	$4	blk, gray & red	1.75	.25
1944	A379	$5	blk, yel & ver	2.75	.40
1945	A379	$8	tan, red & blk	3.75	.60
	Nos. 1942-1945 (4)			9.00	1.50

Chu Yin Reading by the Light of Fireflies — A380

Folk Tales: No. 1947, Hua Mu-lan going to war for her father. No. 1948, King Kou Chien tasting gall. $5, Chou Ch'u killing tiger.

Perf. 14x13½

1975, July 16 Litho. Wmk. 368

1946	A380	$1	olive & multi	.25	.25
1947	A380	$2	bis brn & multi	.40	.25
1948	A380	$2	lt grn & multi	.60	.25
1949	A380	$5	blue & multi	1.40	.30
	Nos. 1946-1949 (4)			2.65	1.05

See Nos. 2108-2111.

Cherry-Apple Blossoms, by Lin Ch'un — A381

Silk Fan Paintings, Sung Dynasty: $2, Spring Blossoms and Butterfly, by Ma K'uei. $5, Monkeys and Deer, by I Yüan-chih. $8, Tame Sparrow among Bamboo.

Perf. 13x12½

1975, Aug. 15 Litho. Wmk. 323

1950	A381	$1	multicolored	.30	.25
1951	A381	$2	multicolored	1.10	.25
1952	A381	$5	multicolored	1.50	.40
1953	A381	$8	multicolored	3.00	.80
	Nos. 1950-1953 (4)			5.90	1.70

See Nos. 2001-2004.

Gen. Chang Tzu-chung (1891-1940) A382

No. 1955, Maj. Gen. Kao Chih-hong (1908-37). No. 1956, Capt. Sha Shih-chiun (1896-1938). No. 1957, Maj. Gen. Hsieh Chin-yuan (1905-41). No. 1958, Lt. Yen Hai-wen (1916-37). No. 1959, Lt. Gen. Tai An-lan (1905-42).

Wmk. 323

1975, Sept. 3 Engr. *Perf. 12*

1954	A382	$2	carmine	.25	.25
1955	A382	$2	sepia	.25	.25
1956	A382	$2	dull green	.25	.25
1957	A382	$5	violet black	.30	.25
1958	A382	$5	violet blue	.30	.25
1959	A382	$5	dark blue	.30	.25
	Nos. 1954-1959 (6)			1.65	1.50

Martyrs of the resistance fight against Japan.

Lotus Pond with Willows, by Madame Chiang — A383

Paintings by Madame Chiang Kai-shek: $5, Sun Breaks through Mountain Clouds. $8, A Pair of Pine Trees. $10, Fishing and Farming.

Perf. 13½

1975, Oct. 31 Litho. Unwmk.

1960	A383	$2	multicolored	1.00	.25
1961	A383	$5	multicolored	2.25	.30
1962	A383	$8	multicolored	3.25	.40
1963	A383	$10	multicolored	4.50	.75
	Nos. 1960-1963 (4)			11.00	1.70

For similar design see type A404.

Cauldron with Phoenix Handles, 481-221 B.C. A384

Ancient Bronzes: $2, Rectangular cauldron, 1122-722 B.C., vert. $8, Flat jar, 481-221 B.C. $10, 3-legged wine vessel, 1766-1122 B.C., vert.

1975, Nov. 12 Photo. *Perf. 12*

1964	A384	$2	pink & multi	.25	.25
1965	A384	$5	lt blue & multi	.85	.25
1966	A384	$8	yellow & multi	1.10	.25
1967	A384	$10	lilac & multi	1.25	.30
	Nos. 1964-1967 (4)			3.45	1.05

For similar design see type A395. No. 1964 has 7 Chinese characters at left, No. 2005 has 4. No. 1967 has 4 characters at left, No. 2008 has 5.

Dragon, Nine-Dragon Wall, Peihai — A385

Wmk. 323

1975, Dec. 1 Litho. *Perf. 12½*

1968	A385	$1	orange & multi	.75	.30
1969	A385	$5	green & multi	1.50	.90

New Year 1976.

Techi Dam — A386

Design: $10, Panoramic view of Techi Dam.

1975, Dec. 17 Unwmk. *Perf. 13½*

1970	A386	$2	green & multi	.25	.25
1971	A386	$10	blue & multi	.55	.45

Completion of Techi Dam, Tachia River.

Biathlon and Olympic Rings — A387

Olympic Rings and: $5, Luge. $8, Skiing.

1976, Jan. 15 Litho. *Perf. 13½*

1972	A387	$2	blue & multi	.35	.25
1973	A387	$5	blue & multi	.65	.25
1974	A387	$8	blue & multi	1.00	.25
			Nos. 1972-1974 (3)	2.00	.75

12th Winter Olympic Games, Innsbruck, Austria, Feb. 4-15.

Chin, Oldest Chinese Instrument A388

Musical Instruments: $5, Se, c. 2900 B.C. $8, Standing kong-ho (harp). $10, Sleeping kong-ho.

1976, Feb. 11 Unwmk. *Perf. 14*

1975	A388	$2	yellow & multi	.35	.25
1976	A388	$5	orange & multi	.55	.25
1977	A388	$8	grnsh bl & multi	.80	.25
1978	A388	$10	multicolored	1.25	.30
			Nos. 1975-1978 (4)	2.95	1.05

For similar design see Type A407.

Double Carp Type of 1969

Perf. 13½x12½

1976, Dec. 15 Engr. Unwmk.

1980	A280	$14	carmine rose	2.25	.30

Mail Collecting A389

Mail Sorting — A390

Postal Service, 80th Anniv.: $8, Mail transport. $10, Mail delivery.

Wmk. 323

1976, Mar. 20 Litho. *Perf. 13½*

1984	A389	$2	yellow & multi	.30	.25
1985	A390	$5	green & multi	.55	.30
1986	A390	$8	blue & multi	.80	.30
1987	A389	$10	orange & multi	1.00	.40
a.			Souv. sheet of 4, #1984-1987	12.50	9.00
			Nos. 1984-1987 (4)	2.65	1.25

Pres. Chiang Kai-shek A391

People Paying Homage — A392

No. 1990, Pres. Chiang lying in state. No. 1991, Hearse leaving funeral chapel. $5, People along funeral route. $8, Spirit tablet in Tzuhu Guest House. $10, Tzuhu Guest House, Pres. Chiang's burial place.

1976, Apr. 4

1988	A391	$2	gray & multi	.25	.25
1989	A392	$2	gray & multi	.25	.25
1990	A392	$2	gray & multi	.25	.25
1991	A392	$2	gray & multi	.25	.25
1992	A392	$5	gray & multi	.40	.25
1993	A392	$8	gray & multi	.40	.25
1994	A392	$10	gray & multi	.50	.35
			Nos. 1988-1994 (7)	2.30	1.85

Pres. Chiang Kai-shek (1887-1975), first death anniversary.

Flags of China and US — A393

Wmk. 323

1976, May 29 Litho. *Perf. 13½*

1995	A393	$2	multicolored	.25	.25
1996	A393	$10	yellow & multi	.80	.40

American Bicentennial.

Coin, 12th Century B.C. — A394

Bronze Shovel Coins (pu): $5, Pointed-feet coin, 481-221 B.C. $8, Round-feet coin, 722-481 B.C. $10, Square-feet coin, 3rd-2nd centuries B.C.

1976, June 16

1997	A394	$2	salmon & multi	.25	.25
1998	A394	$5	lt blue & multi	.65	.25
1999	A394	$8	gray & multi	1.05	.30
2000	A394	$10	multicolored	1.60	.40
			Nos. 1997-2000 (4)	3.55	1.20

Fan Painting Type of 1975

Silk Fan Paintings, Sung Dynasty: $2, Hibiscus, by Li Tung. $5, Lilies, by Lin Ch'un. $8, Deer and Pine, by Mou Chung-fu. $10, Quail and Wild Flowers, by Li An-chung.

Perf. 13x12½

1976, July 14 Litho. Wmk. 323

2001	A381	$2	multicolored	.75	.25
2002	A381	$5	multicolored	1.75	.25
2003	A381	$8	multicolored	2.25	.30
2004	A381	$10	multicolored	3.50	.40
			Nos. 2001-2004 (4)	8.25	1.20

Cauldron, Shang Dynasty — A395

Ancient Bronzes: $5, 3-legged cauldron, Chou Dynasty (1122-722 B.C.). $8, Wine container, Chou Dynasty. $10, Wine vessel with spout, Shang Dynasty (1766-1122 B.C.).

1976, Aug. 25 Photo. *Perf. 11½*

Granite Paper

2005	A395	$2	rose & multi	.25	.25
2006	A395	$5	lt blue & multi	.95	.25
2007	A395	$8	yellow & multi	1.40	.25
2008	A395	$10	lilac & multi	1.50	.30
			Nos. 2005-2008 (4)	4.10	1.05

Construction Types of 1974

Designs: $1, Taiwan North Link railroad and map. $2, Railroad electrification. $3, Taichung Harbor. $4, Taiwan North-South Highway and map. $5, Steel Mill, Kaohsiung. $6, Taoyuan International Airport. $7, Kao-hsiung shipyard. $8, Oil refinery. $9, Su-ao Port.

Perf. 13½x12½, 12½x13½

1976 Litho. Wmk. 323

2009	A365	$1	carmine & grn	.25	.25
2010	A365	$2	orange & multi	.25	.25
2011	A366	$3	violet & multi	.25	.25
2012	A366	$4	carmine & multi	.25	.25
2013	A365	$5	green & brn	.25	.25
2014	A366	$6	brown & multi	.40	.25
2015	A366	$7	brown & multi	.50	.25
2016	A365	$8	carmine & grn	.60	.25
2017	A366	$9	olive & blue	.70	.25
			Nos. 2009-2017 (9)	3.45	2.25

Chiang Kai-shek and Mother A396

Sun Yat-sen and Chiang Kai-shek at Canton Station — A397

Design: $5, Chiang Kai-shek, portrait.

1976, Oct. 31 Litho. *Perf. 13½*

2023	A396	$2	multicolored	.35	.25
2024	A396	$5	multicolored	.80	.25
2025	A397	$10	multicolored	1.10	.40
			Nos. 2023-2025 (3)	2.25	.90

Pres. Chiang Kai-shek, 90th anniv. of birth.

Flags of Kuomintang and China A398

Sun Yat-sen and Chiang Kai-shek A399

1976, Nov. 12 *Perf. 13½x14*

2026	A398	$2	multicolored	.25	.25
2027	A399	$10	multicolored	.65	.45
a.			Souv. sheet of 2, #2026-2027	4.50	4.50

11th National Kuomintang Cong., Taipei.

Brazen Serpent — A400

1976, Dec. 15 Wmk. 323 *Perf. 12½*

2028	A400	$1	red, lilac & gold	.75	.25
2029	A400	$5	plum, yel & gold	1.75	.25

New Year 1977.

Bird and Plum Blossoms, by Ch'en Hung-shou A401

Chinese Paintings: $8, "Wintry Days" (pine), by Yang Wei-chen. $10, Rock and Bamboo, by Hsia Ch'ang.

Perf. 11½

1977, Jan. 12 Photo. Unwmk.

Granite Paper

2030	A401	$2	multicolored	1.00	.25
2031	A401	$8	multicolored	3.00	.25
2032	A401	$10	multicolored	3.75	.40
			Nos. 2030-2032 (3)	7.75	.90

Black-naped Orioles — A402

Birds of Taiwan: $8, Common Kingfisher. $10, Chinese pheasant-tailed jacana.

1977, Feb. 16 Litho.

2033	A402	$2	multicolored	.55	.25
2034	A402	$8	multicolored	1.10	.25
2035	A402	$10	multicolored	2.00	.35
			Nos. 2033-2035 (3)	3.65	.85

See Nos. 2163-2165.

Census Emblem, Industry and Commerce A403

Perf. 13½

1977, Mar. 16 Litho. Unwmk.

2036	A403	$2	red & multi	.25	.25
2037	A403	$10	purple & multi	.80	.40

Industry and Commerce Census.

Green Mountains Rising into Clouds, by Madame Chiang — A404

Landscapes, by Madame Chiang Kai-shek: $5, Boat in the Beauty of Spring. $8, Scholar beside Waterfall. $10, Water Rises to Meet the Bridge.

Perf. 11½

1977, Mar. 31 Unwmk. Photo.

Granite Paper

2038	A404	$2	multi	.55	.25
2039	A404	$5	multi	2.25	.25
2040	A404	$8	multi	2.75	.50
2041	A404	$10	multi	3.00	.60
	Nos. 2038-2041 (4)			8.55	1.60

League Emblem — A405

1977, Apr. 18 Litho. *Perf. 12½*

2042	A405	$2	carmine & multi	.25	.25
2043	A405	$10	green & multi	.80	.65

10th World Anti-Communist League Conference.

Blood Donation — A406

Design: $2, Donating blood, horiz.

1977, May 5 Wmk. 323 *Perf. 13½*

2044	A406	$2	red & black	.25	.25
2045	A406	$10	red & black	.80	.65

Blood donation movement.

San-hsien A407

Musical Instruments: $5, Tung-hsiao (bamboo flute). $8, Yang-chin (butterfly harpsichord). $10, Pai-hsiao (pipes). Background shows musician playing instrument.

Unwmk.

1977, June 21 Photo. *Perf. 14*

2046	A407	$2	multicolored	.35	.25
2047	A407	$5	multicolored	.60	.25
2048	A407	$8	multicolored	.80	.25
2049	A407	$10	multicolored	1.00	.30
	Nos. 2046-2049 (4)			2.75	1.05

Idea Leuconoe — A408

Protected Butterflies: $4, Hebomoia glaucippe formosana. $6, Stichophthalma howqua formosana. $10, Atrophaneura horishana.

1977, July 20 Litho. *Perf. 13½*

2050	A408	$2	ver & multi	.40	.25
2051	A408	$4	lt grn & multi	.90	.25
2052	A408	$6	lt bl & multi	1.40	.40
2053	A408	$10	yellow & multi	1.75	.50
	Nos. 2050-2053 (4)			4.45	1.40

National Palace Museum A409

Temple — A410

Children's Drawings: $2, Sea Goddess Festival. $4, Boats on Shore of Lan-yu.

Wmk. 323

1977, Aug. 27 Litho. *Perf. 13½*

2054	A409	$1	multicolored	.25	.25
2055	A409	$2	multicolored	.25	.25
2056	A409	$4	multicolored	.40	.25
2057	A410	$5	multicolored	.50	.25
	Nos. 2054-2057 (4)			1.40	1.00

8th Exhib. of World School Children's Art.

Carved Lacquer Plate, Wan-li Ware A411

Ancient Carved Lacquer Ware: $5, Bowl, Ching dynasty. $8, Round box, Ming dynasty. $10, Four-tiered box, Ching dynasty.

Perf. 13x14

1977, Sept. 28 Photo. Wmk. 368

2058	A411	$2	multicolored	.40	.25
2059	A411	$5	multicolored	.85	.25
2060	A411	$8	multicolored	1.75	.25
2061	A411	$10	multicolored	1.50	.30
	Nos. 2058-2061 (4)			4.50	1.05

Lions International, Emblem and Activities — A412

Unwmk.

1977, Oct. 8 Litho. *Perf. 13*

2062	A412	$2	multicolored	.25	.25
2063	A412	$10	multicolored	.55	.35

Intl. Association of Lions Clubs, 60th anniv.

Nos. 2069 and 2075 Overprinted in Claret

Perf. 13½x12½

1977, Sept. 9 Litho. Unwmk.

2064	A365	$2	orange & multi	.25	.25
2065	A365	$8	carmine & grn	.60	.30

Little League baseball championship.

Chinese Quality Mark — A413

Perf. 13x12½

1977, Oct. 14 Litho. Unwmk.

2066	A413	$2	red & multi	.50	.25
2067	A413	$10	blue & multi	2.00	.30

International Standardization Day.

Construction Types of 1974 Redrawn: Numerals Outlined

Designs as 1976 Issue.

Perf. 13½x12½, 12½x13½

1977 Litho. Unwmk.

Granite Paper

2068	A365	$1	car & dp grn	.25	.25
2069	A365	$2	ver & multi	.25	.25
2070	A366	$3	violet & multi	.25	.25
2071	A366	$4	carmine & multi	.25	.25
2072	A365	$5	green & multi	.30	.25
2073	A366	$6	sepia & multi	.30	.25
2074	A366	$7	sepia & multi	.35	.25
2075	A365	$8	red lil & multi	.40	.25
2076	A366	$9	olive & multi	.40	.25
	Nos. 2068-2076 (9)			2.75	2.25

Numerals are in solid color on Nos. 1907-1915, 2009-2017; in outline on Nos. 2068-2076.

For overprints see Nos. 2064-2065, 2112-2113.

Man and Heart — A414

Perf. 13½x12½

1977, Nov. 12 Litho. Wmk. 323

2077	A414	$2	multicolored	.25	.25
2078	A414	$10	multicolored	.80	.40

Physical health, cardiac care.

White Stallion — A415

New Year 1978: $5, Two horses, horiz. Designs from painting "100 Horses," by Lang Shih-ning.

Perf. 12½

1977, Dec. 1 Unwmk. Litho.

2079	A415	$1	red & multi	.50	.25
2080	A415	$5	emerald & multi	1.50	.55

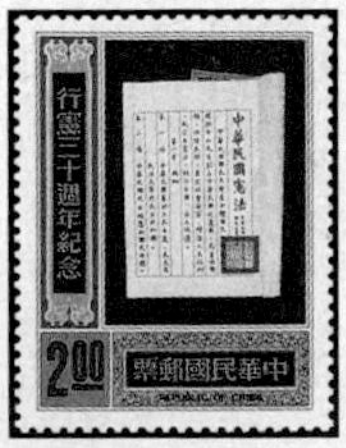

First Page of Constitution A416

Pres. Chiang Accepting Constitution, 1946 — A417

1977, Dec. 25 Litho. *Perf. 13½*

2081	A416	$2	multicolored	.25	.25
2082	A417	$10	multicolored	.80	.30

30th anniversary of the Constitution.

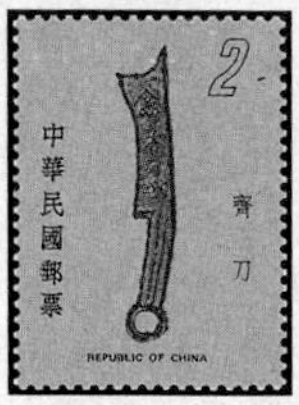

Knife Coin with 3 Characters, 403-221 B.C. — A418

Designs: Ancient knife coins.

1978, Jan. 18 Wmk. 323 *Perf. 13½*

2083	A418	$2	salmon & multi	.40	.25
2084	A418	$5	lt blue & blk	.90	.25
2085	A418	$8	lt gray & multi	1.00	.25
2086	A418	$10	tan & multi	1.25	.30
	Nos. 2083-2086 (4)			3.55	1.05

China No. 1 and Flag of China — A419

Designs: $5, No. 464 (Sun Yat-sen). $10, No. 1204 (Chiang Kai-shek).

1978, Feb. 21 Litho. *Perf. 13½*

2087	A419	$2	brown & multi	.55	.25
2088	A419	$5	blue & multi	.70	.25
2089	A419	$10	orange & multi	1.00	.40
a.		Souv. sheet of 3, #2087-2089		11.00	5.00
	Nos. 2087-2089 (3)			2.25	.90

Centenary of Chinese postage stamps.

Sun Yat-Sen Memorial Hall A420

China Nos. 2079 and 2 — A421

Perf. 14x12½, 12½x14

1978, Mar. 20 Wmk. 323

2090	A420	$2	multicolored	.25	.25
2091	A421	$10	multicolored	.50	.35

ROCPEX '78 Phil. Exhib., Taipei, Mar. 20-29.

Chiang Kai-shek with Revolutionary Army — A422

Pres. Chiang Kai-shek (1887-1975); $2, as young man, 1912, vert. $8, Making speech at Mt. Lu, July 17, 1937. $10, Reviewing Armed Forces on National Day, 1956, and Chinese flags, vert.

1978, Apr. 5 Wmk. 323 *Perf. 13½*

2092	A422	$2 violet & multi	.30	.25
2093	A422	$5 green & multi	.50	.25
2094	A422	$8 blue & multi	.75	.40
2095	A422	$10 vio blue & multi	1.00	.50
		Nos. 2092-2095 (4)	2.55	1.40

Nuclear Reactor and Plant — A423

Perf. 13½x12½

1978, Apr. 26 Unwmk.

2096 A423 $10 multicolored .70 .25

First nuclear power plant on Taiwan.

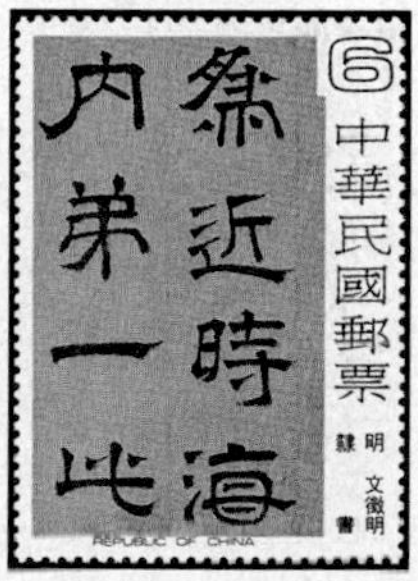

Poem by Wen Cheng-ming (1470-1559) A424

Chinese Calligraphy: $2, Letter by Wang Hsi-chih (307-365). $4, Eulogy by Chu Sui-liang (596-658). $8, From Autobiography of Huai-su, Tang Dynasty. $10, Poem by Ch'ang Piao, Sung Dynasty.

1978, May 20 Wmk. 323 *Perf. 13½*

2097	A424	$2 multicolored	*.85*	.25
2098	A424	$4 multicolored	*3.50*	.25
2099	A424	$6 multicolored	*3.50*	.50
2100	A424	$8 multicolored	*3.75*	.30
2101	A424	$10 multicolored	*5.00*	.55
		Nos. 2097-2101 (5)	*16.60*	1.85

Head and Dao Cancer Fund Emblem — A425

1978, June 15 Litho. *Perf. 13½*

2102	A425	$2 red, org & ol	.25	.25
2103	A425	$10 dk & lt bl & grn	.70	.35

Cancer prevention.

Carved Lacquer Vase, Ming Dynasty — A426

Ancient Carved Lacquer Ware: $2, Box with dragon and cloud design, Ch'ing dynasty, horiz. $5, Double box on legs, Ch'ing dynasty, horiz. $8, Round box with peonies, Ming dynasty, horiz.

1978, July 12

2104	A426	$2 gray olive & multi	.40	.25
2105	A426	$5 gray olive & multi	.50	.25
2106	A426	$8 gray olive & multi	.75	.25
2107	A426	$10 gray olive & multi	1.05	.30
		Nos. 2104-2107 (4)	2.70	1.05

Tsu Ti Practicing with his Sword — A427

Folk Tales: No. 2109, Pan Ch'ao, diplomat and governor. No. 2110, Tien Tan's "Fire Bull Battle." $5, Liang Hung-yu, a general's wife, who served as drummer in battle.

Wmk. 323

1978, Aug. 16 Litho. *Perf. 13½*

2108	A427	$1 multicolored	.25	.25
2109	A427	$2 bister & multi	.55	.25
2110	A427	$2 gray & multi	.90	.25
2111	A427	$5 multicolored	1.25	.25
		Nos. 2108-2111 (4)	2.95	1.00

For similar designs see types A456, A495.

Nos. 2071 & 2073 Overprinted in Red

1978, Sept. 9 *Perf. 12½x13*

2112	A366	$4 multicolored	.30	.25
2113	A366	$6 multicolored	.75	.30

Triple championships won by Chinese teams in Little League World Series. "1978" overprint on $4 at left, on $6 at right.

Ixias Pyrene A428

Protected Butterflies: $4, Euploea sylvestor swinhoei. $6, Cyrestis thyodamas formosana. $10, Byasa polyeuctes termessus.

1978, Sept. 20

2114	A428	$2 multicolored	.55	.25
2115	A428	$4 multicolored	.70	.25
2116	A428	$6 multicolored	1.05	.30
2117	A428	$10 multicolored	2.75	.45
		Nos. 2114-2117 (4)	5.05	1.25

Scout Symbols — A429

1978, Oct. 5 Litho. *Perf. 13½*

2118	A429	$2 multicolored	.40	.25
2119	A429	$10 multicolored	.65	.30

5th Chinese Boy Scout Jamboree, Cheng Ching Lake, Oct. 5-12.

Tropical Tomatoes — A430

Design: $10, Tropical tomatoes, horiz.

1978, Oct. 23 Wmk. 323

2120	A430	$2 multicolored	.30	.25
2121	A430	$10 multicolored	1.25	.40

International Symposium on Tropical Tomatoes, Taiwan, Oct. 23-28.

Sino-Saudi Bridge A431

Design: $6, Buttresses of bridge, flags of Taiwan and Saudi Arabia, horiz.

1978, Oct. 31

2122	A431	$2 multicolored	.35	.25
2123	A431	$6 multicolored	1.40	.30

Completion of Sino-Saudi Bridge over Cho-Shui River.

National Flag — A432

1978-80 *Perf. 13½*

2124	A432	$1 red & dk bl, I	.25	.25
a.		Bklt. pane of 16 ($5, $6, $8, $10, 3 $1, 9 $2)	7.75	
b.		Type II	.25	.25
2125	A432	$2 red & dk bl, I	.25	.25
a.		Bklt. pane of 15 + label	11.50	
b.		Type II	.25	.25
2126	A432	$3 yel grn & multi ('80)	.30	.25
2127	A432	$4 bis & multi ('80)	.35	.25
2128	A432	$5 dk grn & multi, I	.25	.25
a.		Type II	.25	.25
2129	A432	$6 brn org & multi	.30	.25
2130	A432	$7 dk brn & multi ('80)	.35	.25
2131	A432	$8 dk grn & multi, I	.45	.25
a.		Type II	.45	.25
2132	A432	$10 brt bl & multi ('79)	.60	.25
2133	A432	$12 brt rose lil & multi ('80)	.60	.25
		Nos. 2124-2133 (10)	3.70	2.50

Two types exist: I. Second line (red) below flag is same width as blue line. II. Second line is a hairline, notably thinner. The $3, $4, $7 and $12 were issued only in type II; $6, $10, Nos. 2134, 2124a, only in type I.

Nos. 2129-2133 have colorless inscriptions and denomination in a panel of solid color.

Nos. 2124a, 2125a have selvage inscribed in blue. 1980 printings are in green or red.

Coil Stamp

1980, Jan. 15 *Perf. 12 Horiz.*

2134 A432 $2 multicolored .25 .25

See Nos. 2288-2300. For overprints see Nos. 2540-2541.

Three Rams, by Emperor Hsuan-tsung A433

Wmk. 323

1978, Dec. 1 Litho. *Perf. 12½*

2135	A433	$1 multicolored	.30	.25
2136	A433	$5 multicolored	1.75	.40

New Year 1979.

Taoyuan International Airport — A434

$10, Passenger terminal, control tower.

1978, Dec. 31 *Perf. 13½*

2137	A434	$2 multi	.40	.25
2138	A434	$10 multi, horiz.	.70	.40

Completion of Taoyuan Intl. Airport.

Oracle Bones and Inscription, 1766-1123 B.C. — A435

Antiquities and Inscriptions: $5, Lehchi cauldron, 722-481 B.C. $8, Small seal (turtle), 206 B.C.-8 A.D. $10, Inscribed stone tablet, 175-183 A.D.

1979, Jan. 17

2139	A435	$2 multicolored	.60	.25
2140	A435	$5 multicolored	1.25	.30
2141	A435	$8 multicolored	2.25	.50
2142	A435	$10 multicolored	2.25	.65
		Nos. 2139-2142 (4)	6.35	1.70

Origin and development of Chinese characters.

Chihkan Tower, 1653 A436

Taiwan Scenery: $5, Shrine of Confucius, 1665. $8, Shrine of Koxinga, 1661. $10, Eternal Castle and moat.

1979, Feb. 11 Litho. *Perf. 13½*

2143	A436	$2 multicolored	.40	.25
2144	A436	$5 multicolored	.85	.25
2145	A436	$8 multicolored	1.10	.25
2146	A436	$10 multicolored	2.10	.25
		Nos. 2143-2146 (4)	4.45	1.00

Children Playing on Winter Day, Sung Dynasty — A437

1979, Mar. 8

2147	A437	Block of 4	14.00	9.25
a.		$5 in UL corner	3.50	.55
b.		$5 in UR corner	3.50	.55
c.		$5 in LL corner	3.50	.55
d.		$5 in LR corner	3.50	.55
e.		Souvenir sheet of 4, #2147, imperf.	*27.50*	16.00

No. 2147e has simulated perforations.

Lu Hao-tung — A438

Perf. 13x12½

1979, Mar. 29 Engr. Wmk. 323

2148 A438 $2 blue .50 .25

Lu Hao-tung (1868-1895), revolutionist.

Yellow Jade Brush Holder — A439

Ancient Brush Washers: $5, White jade, Ming Dynasty. $8, Dark green jade, Ch'ing Dynasty. $10, Bluish jade, Ch'ing Dynasty. All horiz.

Granite Paper

Unwmk.

1979, Apr. 12 Photo. *Perf. 12*

2149	A439	$2 multicolored	.25	.25
2150	A439	$5 multicolored	1.10	.25
2151	A439	$8 multicolored	1.50	.35
2152	A439	$10 multicolored	2.10	.50
		Nos. 2149-2152 (4)	4.95	1.35

For similar artifacts designs with single-color background and denominations in outlined numerals with the cents, see types A453, A469, A489, A523, A547, A582.

A440

A440a

Plum Blossoms, Natl. Flower

Perf. 13½x12½

1979-92 Engr. Wmk. 323

Granite Paper

2153	A440	$10 dk blue	1.60	.25
a.		Plain paper ('88)	2.50	.30
2154	A440	$20 brown	2.00	.25
b.		Plain paper ('87)	3.50	.60
2154A	A440	$40 brt car, plain paper ('85)	2.00	.25
2155	A440	$50 dull green	4.25	.25
a.		Plain paper ('87)	5.00	.55
2156	A440	$100 vermilion	6.00	.90
e.		Plain paper ('92)	6.00	3.25

Perf. 14x13½

2156A	A440a	$300 pur & red org ('83)	16.00	3.25
c.		Plain paper ('91)	18.00	3.25
2156B	A440a	$500 ver & brn ('82)	24.00	5.50
d.		Plain paper ('91)	26.00	5.50
		Nos. 2153-2156B (7)	55.85	10.65

Issued: Nos. 2156Ac, 2156Bd, May 1; No. 2156e, Jan. 7

City Houses and Garden — A441

Design: $10, Rural landscape, horiz.

Perf. 13x12½, 12½x13

1979, June 5 Litho.

2157	A441	$2 multicolored	.25	.25
2158	A441	$10 multicolored	.75	.35

Protection of the Environment.

Bankbook and Computer Department A442

Designs: $2, Children at counter, vert. $5, People standing in line, vert. $10, Hand putting coin in savings bank, symbolic tree.

1979, July 1 Wmk. 323 *Perf. 13½*

2159	A442	$2 multicolored	.30	.25
2160	A442	$5 multicolored	.45	.25
2161	A442	$8 multicolored	.65	.25
2162	A442	$10 multicolored	.80	.25
		Nos. 2159-2162 (4)	2.20	1.00

Postal savings, 60th anniversary.

Bird Type of 1977

Birds of Taiwan: $2, Swinoe's pheasant. $8, Steere's babbler. $10, Formosan yuhina.

1979, Aug. 8 *Perf. 11½*

2163	A402	$2 multicolored	.50	.25
2164	A402	$8 multicolored	1.25	.25
2165	A402	$10 multicolored	1.40	.35
		Nos. 2163-2165 (3)	3.15	.85

Rowland Hill, Penny Black A443

Perf. 13½x13

1979, Aug. 27 Litho. Wmk. 323

2166	A443	$10 multicolored	1.25	.35

Sir Rowland Hill (1795-1879), originator of penny postage.

Jar with Rope Design, Shang Dynasty — A444

Ancient Chinese Pottery: $5, Two-handled jar, Shang dynasty. $8, Red jar with "ears," Han dynasty. $10, Green glazed jar, Han dynasty.

1979, Sept. 12 *Perf. 13½*

2167	A444	$2 multicolored	.45	.25
2168	A444	$5 multicolored	1.40	.25
2169	A444	$8 multicolored	2.50	.25
2170	A444	$10 multicolored	2.75	.30
		Nos. 2167-2170 (4)	7.10	1.05

Children and IYC Emblem — A445

1979, Sept. 28 Litho. *Perf. 13½*

2171	A445	$2 multicolored	.35	.25
2172	A445	$10 multicolored	.70	.35

International Year of the Child.

Trade Symbols, Competition Emblem A446

1979, Dec. 9 Litho. *Perf. 13½*

2173	A446	$2 blue & multi	.25	.25
2174	A446	$10 green & multi	.80	.35

10th National Vocational Training Competition, Taichung, Dec. 9.

Trees on a Winter Plain, by Li Ch'eng A447

Paintings: $5, Bamboo, Wen T'ung. $8, Old tree, bamboo and rock, by Chao Meng-fu. $10, Twin Pines, by Li K'an.

1979, Nov. 21

2175	A447	$2 multicolored	.60	.25
2176	A447	$5 multicolored	1.25	.25
2177	A447	$8 multicolored	3.00	.40
2178	A447	$10 multicolored	4.25	.50
		Nos. 2175-2178 (4)	9.10	1.40

Monkey — A448

1979, Dec. 1 *Perf. 12½*

2179	A448	$1 yellow & multi	1.40	.25
2180	A448	$6 tan & multi	3.00	.50

New Year 1980.

Rotary Emblem and "75" — A449

Rotary Intl., 75th Anniv.: $12, Anniv. emblem.

1980, Feb. 23 Litho. *Perf. 13½*

2181	A449	$2 multicolored	.35	.25
2182	A449	$12 multi, vert.	.80	.35

Mt. Hohuan A450

Taiwan Landscapes (East-West Cross-Island Highway): $2, Tunnel of Nine Turns, vert. $12, Bridge, Tien Hsiang, vert.

1980, Mar. 1 Wmk. 323

2183	A450	$2 multicolored	.30	.25
2184	A450	$8 multicolored	1.00	.25
2185	A450	$12 multicolored	1.60	.35
		Nos. 2183-2185 (3)	2.90	.85

A451

1980, Mar. 29 Engr. *Perf. 13½x12½*

Granite Paper

2186	A451	$2 red brown	.55	.25

Shih Chien-Ju (1879-1900), revolutionist.

A452

$2, Chung-cheng Memorial Hall. $8, Quotation. $12, Bronze statue.

1980, Apr. 4 Litho. *Perf. 13½*

2187	A452	$2 multicolored	.25	.25
2188	A452	$8 multicolored	.50	.25
2189	A452	$12 multicolored	.60	.50
		Nos. 2187-2189 (3)	1.35	1.00

Chiang Kai-shek (1887-1975).

Melon-shaped Jade Brush Washer, Ming Dynasty — A453

Jade Pottery: $2, Jar with dragons, Sung dynasty, vert. $8, Monk's alms bowl, Ch'ing dynasty. $10, Yellow jade brush washer, Ch'ing dynasty.

1980, May 20 Photo. *Perf. 12*

Granite Paper

2190	A453	$2 multicolored	.45	.25
2191	A453	$5 multicolored	.90	.25
2192	A453	$8 multicolored	1.60	.25
2193	A453	$10 multicolored	2.00	.30
		Nos. 2190-2193 (4)	4.95	1.05

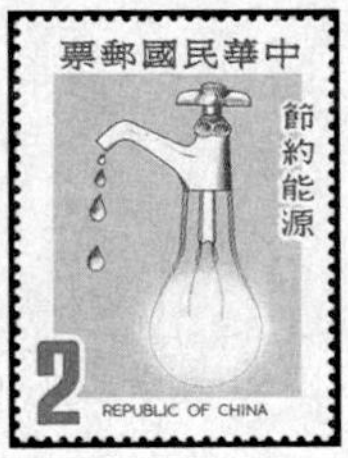
Energy Conservation A454

1980, July 15 Litho. *Perf. 13½*

2194	A454	$2 multicolored	.25	.25
2195	A454	$12 multicolored	.80	.40

A455

T'ang Dynasty pottery.

1980, Aug. 18 Litho. *Perf. 13½*

2196	A455	$2 Soldier	.45	.25
2197	A455	$5 Roosters	1.40	.25
2198	A455	$8 Horse	1.90	.25
2199	A455	$10 Camel	2.25	.30
		Nos. 2196-2199 (4)	6.00	1.05

A456

Folk Tales: $1, Grinding mortar into a needle. No. 2201, Confucius Returning Lost Article (shown). No. 2202, Wen Tien-hsiang in jail. $5, Sending coal in snow.

Perf. 14x13½

1980, Sept. 23 Litho. Wmk. 323

2200	A456	$1 multicolored	.25	.25
2201	A456	$2 multicolored	.30	.25
2202	A456	$2 multicolored	.80	.25
2203	A456	$5 multicolored	1.10	.30
		Nos. 2200-2203 (4)	2.45	1.05

Railroad Electrification A457

No. 2205, Taichung Harbor. No. 2206, Chiang Kai-shek Airport. No. 2207, Steel Mill. No. 2208, Sun Yat-sen Freeway. No. 2209, Nuclear power plant. No. 2210, Petrochemical plants. No. 2211, Su-ao Harbor. No. 2212, Kaohsiung shipyard. No. 2213, North link railroad.

1980, Oct. 10 ***Perf. 13½x14***

2204	A457	$2 shown	.50	.25
2205	A457	$2 multicolored	.50	.25
2206	A457	$2 multicolored	.50	.25
2207	A457	$2 multicolored	.50	.25
2208	A457	$2 multicolored	.50	.25
2209	A457	$2 multicolored	.50	.25
2210	A457	$2 multicolored	.50	.25
2211	A457	$2 multicolored	.50	.25
2212	A457	$2 multicolored	.50	.25
2213	A457	$2 multicolored	.50	.25
a.		Souv. sheet of 10, #2204-2213	9.50	9.50
b.		Block of 10, #2204-2213	4.50	4.50
		Nos. 2204-2213 (10)	5.00	2.50

Completion of major construction projects.

10th National Savings Day — A458

$2, Ancient coin and coin banks.

Wmk. 323

1980, Oct. 25 Litho. ***Perf. 13½***

2214	A458	$2 multicolored	.55	.25
2215	A458	$12 shown	1.10	.40

Landscape, by Ch'iu Ying, Ming Dynasty — A459

1980, Nov. 12 Litho. ***Perf. 13½***

2216	A459	Block of 4	10.75	5.25
a.		$5 in UL corner	2.50	.40
b.		$5 in UR corner	2.50	.40
c.		$5 in LL corner	2.50	.40
d.		$5 in LR corner	2.50	.40
e.		Souvenir sheet, imperf.	16.00	14.50

No. 2216e has simulated perforations.

Cock — A460

1980, Dec. 1 ***Perf. 12½***

2217	A460	$1 multicolored	.90	.25
2218	A460	$6 multicolored	2.75	.35
a.		Souv. sheet, 2 each #2217-2218	11.50	11.50

New Year 1981.

Faces, Flag, Census Form — A461

1980, Dec. 13 ***Perf. 13½***

2219	A461	$2 shown	.25	.25
2220	A461	$12 Buildings, horiz.	1.00	.40

1980 population and housing census.

TIROS-N Satellite — A462

Design: $10, Central weather bureau, horiz.

1981, Jan. 28 Litho. ***Perf. 13½***

2221	A462	$2 multicolored	.35	.25
2222	A462	$10 multicolored	1.00	.40

Completion of meteorological satellite ground station, Taipei.

"Happiness" A463

New Year 1981 (Calligraphy): No. 2224, Wealth. No. 2225, Longevity. No. 2226, Joy.

1981, Feb. 3 ***Perf. 13½x12½***

2223	A463	$5 multi, 5 at B	1.00	.25
2224	A463	$5 multi, 5 at R	1.00	.25
2225	A463	$5 multi, 5 at L	1.00	.25
2226	A463	$5 multi, 5 at T	1.00	.25
a.		Block of 4, #2223-2226	4.50	1.75

International Year of the Disabled — A464

1981, Feb. 19 Litho. ***Perf. 13½***

2227	A464	$2 multicolored	.25	.25
2228	A464	$12 multicolored	.70	.25

Mt. Ali — A465

1981, Mar. 1

2229	A465	$2 shown	.30	.25
2230	A465	$7 Oluanpi Beach	1.00	.25
2231	A465	$12 Sun Moon Lake	1.60	.30
		Nos. 2229-2231 (3)	2.90	.80

A $2 multicolored stamp for the 12th National Kuomintang Congress at Taipei was prepared for release Mar. 29, 1981, but not issued. It showed Sun Yat-sen, Chiang Kai-shek, flags of China and the Kuomintang and a map of China.

Children in Forest A467

Children's Day: Drawings.

1981, Apr. 4

2233	A467	$1 multicolored	.25	.25
2234	A467	$2 multicolored	.25	.25
2235	A467	$5 multicolored	.25	.25
2236	A467	$7 multicolored	.30	.25
		Nos. 2233-2236 (4)	1.05	1.00

Chiang Kai-shek Memorial Hall — A468

1981, Apr. 5 ***Perf. 12½x13½***

2237	A468	20c bluish lilac	.25	.25
a.		Photo. ('87)	.25	.25
2238	A468	40c crim rose	.25	.25
a.		Photo. ('87)	.25	.25
2239	A468	50c dull red brn	.25	.25
a.		Photo. ('88)	.25	.25
		Nos. 2237-2239 (3)	.75	.75

Chiang Kai-shek (1887-1975).
See Nos. 2601-2603.

Cloisonne Enamel Brush Washer, 15th Cent. A469

Cloisonne Enamel: $5, Ritual vessel, 15th cent., vert. $8, Plate, 17th cent. $10, Vase, Ming Dynasty, vert.

1981, May 20 Photo. ***Perf. 12***

Granite Paper

2240	A469	$2 multicolored	.50	.25
2241	A469	$5 multicolored	1.10	.25
2242	A469	$8 multicolored	1.25	.25
2243	A469	$10 multicolored	1.60	.30
		Nos. 2240-2243 (4)	4.45	1.05

For similar enamelware stamps see Nos. 2318-2321, 2348-2351, 2410-2413.

Early & Modern Locomotives A470

Wmk. 323

1981, June 9 Litho. ***Perf. 12½***

2244	A470	$2 shown	.45	.25
2245	A470	$14 Trains, horiz.	1.60	.40

Railroad service centenary.

Linnaeus Crab — A471

1981, June 14 ***Perf. 13½***

2246	A471	$2 De Haan crab, horiz.	.30	.25
2247	A471	$5 shown	.60	.25
2248	A471	$8 Miers crab, horiz.	.95	.25
2249	A471	$14 Rathbun crab	1.75	.30
		Nos. 2246-2249 (4)	3.60	1.05

Central Weather Bureau, 40th Anniv. — A472

1981, July 1 Litho. ***Perf. 13½***

2250	A472	$2 multicolored	.30	.25
2251	A472	$14 multicolored	1.25	.40

Scene from The Cowherd and the Weaving Maid — A473

Designs: Scenes from the Cowherd and the Weaving Maid.

1981, Aug. 6 Litho. ***Perf. 13½x14***

2252	A473	$2 multicolored	.50	.25
2253	A473	$4 multicolored	.80	.25
2254	A473	$8 multicolored	1.50	.25
2255	A473	$14 multicolored	2.25	.50
		Nos. 2252-2255 (4)	5.05	1.25

First Lasography Exhibition — A474

Lasography Designs.

1981, Aug. 15 ***Perf. 13½***

2256	A474	$2 multicolored	.25	.25
2257	A474	$5 multicolored	.30	.25
2258	A474	$8 multicolored	.65	.25
2259	A474	$14 multicolored	1.10	.50
		Nos. 2256-2259 (4)	2.30	1.25

Soccer Players — A475

1981, Sept. 9 Litho. ***Perf. 13½***

2260		$5 multicolored	.50	.25
2261		$5 multicolored	.50	.25
a.		A475 Pair, #2260-2261	1.10	.65

Sports Day.

A477

70th Anniv. of Republic: No. 2263, Eastward Expedition (soldiers on Hill). No. 2264, Northward Expedition (Chiang on horse). No. 2265, Resistance War with Japan (Chiang, fist raised). No. 2266, Suppression of Communist Rebels (Battle scene). No. 2267, Counter-offensive and unification. $8, Chiang Kai-shek. $14, Sun Yat-sen.

1981, Oct. 10 *Perf. 13½*

2262	A477	$2	multicolored	.25	.25
2263	A477	$2	multicolored	.25	.25
2264	A477	$2	multicolored	.25	.25
2265	A477	$2	multicolored	.25	.25
2266	A477	$3	multicolored	.25	.25
2267	A477	$3	multicolored	.25	.25
2268	A477	$8	multicolored	.45	.25
2269	A477	$14	multicolored	1.00	.45
a.			Souv. sheet of 8, #2262-2269	9.00	3.50
			Nos. 2262-2269 (8)	2.95	2.20

No. 2269a issued Oct. 25.

ROCPEX TAIPEI '81 Intl. Philatelic Exhibition, Taipei, Oct. 25-Nov. 2 A478

1981, Oct. 25

2270	A478	$2	multicolored	.25	.25
2271	A478	$14	multicolored	.50	.25

Nos. 2269a, 2270-2271 overprinted with four characters meaning "Best of Show" were not valid for postage. They were inserted in a special "ROCPEX" book, edition of 10,000. Value $25.

Boys Playing Games (#2272a) — A479

Designs: a.-j. "One Hundred Boys," Sung Dynasty scroll (each stamp is numbered from 1 to 10 in Chinese. See illustrations with Nos. 1682-1691 for numerals.) Two strips of 5 each in continuous design.

1981, Nov. 12

2272		Block of 10	16.50	16.50
a.-e.	A479	$2 single (top row)	1.50	.25
f.-j.	A479	$2 single (bottom row)	1.50	.25

New Year 1982 (Year of the Dog) — A480

Wmk. 323

1981, Dec. 1 **Litho.** *Perf. 12½*

2273	A480	$1	multicolored	1.25	.25
2274	A480	$10	multicolored	2.00	.40
a.			Souv. sheet, 2 ea #2273-2274	13.50	5.00

Information Week, Dec. 6-12 — A481

1981, Dec. 7 *Perf. 14x13½*

2275	A481	$2	multicolored	.55	.25

Telecommunications Centenary — A482

1981, Dec. 28 *Perf. 14x13½, 13½x14*

2276	A482	$2	Telephone, vert.	.25	.25
2277	A482	$3	Old, new phones	.25	.25
2278	A482	$8	Submarine cable	.40	.25
2279	A482	$18	Computers, vert.	.55	.30
			Nos. 2276-2279 (4)	1.45	1.05

Floral Arrangement A483

Various floral arrangements in Ming vases.

Wmk. 323

1982, Jan. 23 **Litho.** *Perf. 13½*

2280	A483	$2	multicolored	.25	.25
2281	A483	$3	multicolored	.35	.25
2282	A483	$8	multicolored	.75	.25
2283	A483	$18	multicolored	1.75	.50
			Nos. 2280-2283 (4)	3.10	1.25

Compare with designs A559, A584.

The Ku Cheng Reunion — A484

Designs: Opera scenes.

Wmk. 323

1982, Feb. 15 **Litho.** *Perf. 13½*

2284	A484	$2	multicolored	.55	.25
2285	A484	$3	multicolored	1.75	.25
2286	A484	$4	multicolored	1.90	.25
2287	A484	$18	multicolored	3.50	.60
			Nos. 2284-2287 (4)	7.70	1.35

Flag Type of 1978
Value Colorless in Colored Panel

1981 **Litho.** *Perf. 13½*

Panel Color

2288	A432	$1	dk blue	.30	.25
2289	A432	$1.50	lt olive	.30	.25
2290	A432	$2	dk olive bis	.30	.25
2291	A432	$3	red	.30	.25
2292	A432	$4	blue	.30	.25
2293	A432	$5	sepia	.30	.25
2294	A432	$6	orange	.40	.25
2295	A432	$7	green	.60	.25
2296	A432	$8	magenta	.75	.25
2297	A432	$9	olive grn	.95	.25
2298	A432	$10	dk purple	1.10	.25
2299	A432	$12	lilac	1.25	.25
2300	A432	$14	dk green	1.25	.30
			Nos. 2288-2300 (13)	8.10	3.30

Second line (red) below flag is a hairline, notably thinner.

For overprints see Nos. 2540-2541.

Robert Koch — A485

Wmk. 323

1982, Mar. 24 **Litho.** *Perf. 13½*

2309	A485	$2	multicolored	.25	.25

Tubercle Bacillus centenary.

Cheng Shih-liang, Revolutionary A486

1982, Mar. 29 **Engr.** *Perf. 13½x12½*

Granite Paper

2310	A486	$2	carmine rose	.25	.25

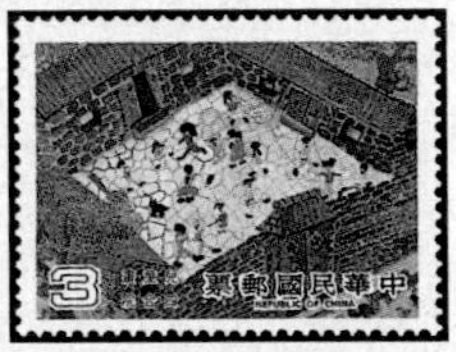

Children's Day A487

Designs: Various children's drawings.

1982, Apr. 4 **Litho.**

2311	A487	$2	multi, vert.	.40	.25
2312	A487	$3	multicolored	.60	.25
2313	A487	$5	multicolored	.80	.25
2314	A487	$8	multicolored	.80	.25
			Nos. 2311-2314 (4)	2.60	1.00

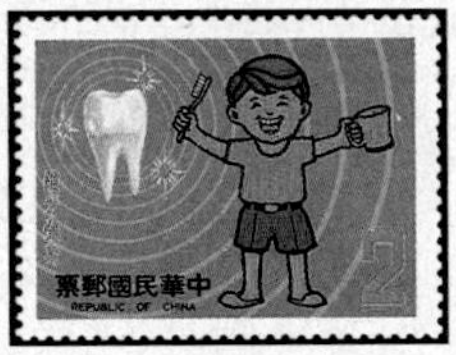

Dentists' Day A488

1982, May 4 **Litho.** *Perf. 13½*

2315	A488	$2	Tooth, boy	.30	.25
2316	A488	$3	Flossing, brushing	.60	.25
2317	A488	$10	Examination	1.10	.30
			Nos. 2315-2317 (3)	2.00	.80

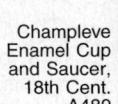

Champleve Enamel Cup and Saucer, 18th Cent. A489

Painted Enamelware: $5, Cloisonne gold-plated duck Ch'ien-lung period (1736-1795), vert. $8, Incense burner, K'ang-hsi period (1662-1722). $12, Cloisonne pitcher, Ch'ien-lung period, vert.

1982, May 20 **Photo.** *Perf. 12*

Granite Paper

2318	A489	$2	multicolored	.40	.25
2319	A489	$5	multicolored	.80	.25
2320	A489	$8	multicolored	2.00	.25
2321	A489	$12	multicolored	2.75	.25
			Nos. 2318-2321 (4)	5.95	1.00

See Nos. 2348-2351.

Poets' Day — A490

Tang Dynasty Poetry Illustrations (618-906): $2, Spring Dawn, by Meng Hao-Jan. $3, On Looking for a Hermit and Not Finding Him, by Chia Tao. $5, Summer Dying, by Liu Yu-Hsi. $18, Looking at the Snow Drifts on South Mountain, by Tsu Yung. Chinese characters are to the left of the denominations on Nos. 2322-2325, Nos. 2396-2399 have no characters to the left of the denominations.

Wmk. 323

1982, June 25 **Litho.** *Perf. 13½*

2322	A490	$2	multicolored	*2.25*	.25
2323	A490	$3	multicolored	*4.00*	.35
2324	A490	$5	multicolored	*6.25*	.75
2325	A490	$18	multicolored	*14.50*	1.50
			Nos. 2322-2325 (4)	*27.00*	2.85

See Nos. 2352-2355.

5th World Women's Softball Championship, Taipei, July 1-12 — A491

1982, July 2

2326	A491	$2	lt grn & multi	.65	.25
2327	A491	$18	tan & multi	1.25	.40

Scouting Year A492

$2, Crossing bridge, Baden-Powell. $18, Emblem, camp.

1982, July 18

2328	A492	$2	multicolored	.25	.25
2329	A492	$18	multicolored	.70	.40

Stamp in Tongs A493

$18, Album stamps magnified.

1982, Aug. 9

2330	A493	$2	shown	.65	.25
2331	A493	$18	multicolored	1.40	.40

Carved Lion, Tsu Shih Temple — A494

Tsu Shih Temple of Sanhsia Architecture: $3, Lion brackets, horiz. $5, Sub-lintels. $18, Tiled roof, horiz.

1982, Sept. 1 Litho. *Perf. 13½*

2332 A494 $2 multicolored .40 .25
2333 A494 $3 multicolored .55 .25
2334 A494 $5 multicolored 1.25 .25
2335 A494 $18 multicolored 1.75 .40
Nos. 2332-2335 (4) 3.95 1.15

Hsun Kuan Saving Hsiang-cheng City — A495

Designs: Scenes from The Thirty-Six Examples of Filial Piety, Folk Tale collection by Wu Yen-huan.

1982, Oct. 15 *Perf. 14x13½*

2336 A495 $1 multicolored .25 .25
2337 A495 $2 multicolored .50 .25
2338 A495 $3 multicolored .70 .25
2339 A495 $5 multicolored .80 .25
Nos. 2336-2339 (4) 2.25 1.00

30th Anniv. of China Youth Corps A496

1982, Oct. 31

2340 A496 $2 Riding .25 .25
2341 A496 $3 Raising flag, vert. .25 .25
2342 A496 $18 Mountain climbing .60 .40
Nos. 2340-2342 (3) 1.10 .90

Seated Lohan (Buddhist Saint) — A497

Paintings of Lohan, Hanging Scrolls by Liu Sung-nien, 13th cent.

Perf. 13x12½

1982, Nov. 12 Litho. Wmk. 323

2343 A497 $2 multicolored 1.25 .25
2344 A497 $3 multicolored 3.00 .25
2345 A497 $18 multicolored 7.75 .85
a. Souv. sheet, #2343-2345 *27.50* 13.00
Nos. 2343-2345 (3) 12.00 1.35

No. 2345a comes overprinted in red in the sheet margins. Value, unused $18, Used $12.

New Year 1983 (Year of the Boar) — A498

1982, Dec. 1 *Perf. 12½*

2346 A498 $1 multicolored 1.60 .25
2347 A498 $10 multicolored 2.75 .45
a. Souv. sheet, 2 ea #2346-2347 *14.50* 6.50

Enamelware Type of 1982

Designs: $2, Square basin, Ch'ing Dynasty (1644-1911). $3, Vase, Ch'ien-lung period (1736-1795). $4, Tea pot, Ch'ien-lung period. $18, Elephant vase, Ch'ing Dynasty.

1983, Jan. 5 Photo. *Perf. 12*
Granite Paper

2348 A489 $2 multi .50 .25
2349 A489 $3 multi, vert. .70 .25
2350 A489 $4 multi 1.25 .25
2351 A489 $18 multi, vert. 2.00 .50
Nos. 2348-2351 (4) 4.45 1.25

Poetry Illustration Type of 1982

Sung Dynasty Poetry: $2, Seeing the Flowers Fade Away. $3, River. $5, Freckled with Clouds is the Azure Sky. $11, Yielding Fine Fragrance in the Snow. Nos. 2352-2355 vert.

Wmk. 323

1983, Feb. 10 Litho. *Perf. 13½*

2352 A490 $2 multicolored *1.40* .25
2353 A490 $3 multicolored *5.25* .35
2354 A490 $5 multicolored *7.50* .50
2355 A490 $11 multicolored *11.00* .60
Nos. 2352-2355 (4) *25.15* 1.70

Mt. Jade, Taiwan — A499

$2, Wawa Valley, vert. $3, University Pond, vert.

1983, Mar. 1

2356 A499 $2 multicolored .70 .25
2357 A499 $3 multicolored 1.10 .25
2358 A499 $18 shown 1.75 .50
Nos. 2356-2358 (3) 3.55 1.00

400th Anniv. of Arrival of Matteo Ricci (1552-1610), Italian Missionary A500

Perf. 14x13½

1983, Apr. 3 Litho. Wmk. 323

2359 A500 $2 Globe .45 .25
2360 A500 $18 Great Wall 1.40 .35

Mandarin Phonetic Symbols, 70th Anniv. — A501

$2, Wu Ching-heng, inventor. $18, Children writing.

Wmk. 323

1983, May 22 Litho. *Perf. 13½*

2361 A501 $2 multicolored .45 .25
2362 A501 $18 multicolored 1.40 .30

Scenes from Lady White Snake Fairytale — A502

1983, June 15 *Perf. 14x13½*

2363 A502 $2 multicolored .60 .25
2364 A502 $3 lt blue & multi 1.10 .25
2365 A502 $3 orange & multi 1.10 .25
2366 A502 $18 multicolored 1.25 .50
Nos. 2363-2366 (4) 4.05 1.25

A503

Various bamboo carved objects: $2, Bamboo jug. $3, Tao-t'ieh motif vase. $4, Landscape sculpture. $18, Brush holder, Ming dynasty.

Nos. 2367-2369 Ch'ing dynasty.

Wmk. 323

1983, July 14 Litho. *Perf. 13½*

2367 A503 $2 multicolored .75 .25
2368 A503 $3 multicolored .90 .25
2369 A503 $4 multicolored 1.05 .25
2370 A503 $18 multicolored 2.25 .40
Nos. 2367-2370 (4) 4.95 1.15

A504

Wmk. 323

1983, Aug. 5 Litho. *Perf. 13½*

2371 A504 $2 Globe .55 .25
2372 A504 $18 Emblem .80 .35

World Communications Year.

Fishing Industry (Local Fish) A505

$2, Epinephelus tauvina. $18, Saurida undosquamis.

1983, Aug. 20

2373 A505 $2 multicolored .60 .25
2374 A505 $18 multicolored 2.25 .35

40th Journalists' Day — A506

1983, Sept. 1

2375 A506 $2 multicolored .55 .25

Views of Mongolia and Tibet — A507

1983, Sept. 15

2376 A507 $2 Village .55 .25
2377 A507 $3 Potala Palace 1.00 .25
2378 A507 $5 Sheep grazing 1.10 .25
2379 A507 $11 Camel caravan 1.75 .40
Nos. 2376-2379 (4) 4.40 1.15

2nd East Asian Bird Protection Conference, Oct. — A508

1983, Oct. 8 Litho. *Perf. 13½*

2380 A508 $2 Lanius cristatus, vert. .65 .25
2381 A508 $18 Butastur indicus 2.50 .40

A509

Plum Blossoms, photography by Hu Ch'ung-hsien.

1983, Oct. 31 Litho. *Perf. 14x13½*

2382 A509 $2 multicolored .35 .25
2383 A509 $3 multi, diff. .65 .25
2384 A509 $5 multi, diff. .70 .25
2385 A509 $11 multi, diff. 1.00 .30
Nos. 2382-2385 (4) 2.70 1.05

A510

$2, JCI and Congress emblems. $18, Globe and emblems, horiz.

1983, Nov. 6 *Perf. 13x13½, 13½x13*

2386 A510 $2 multicolored .25 .25
2387 A510 $18 multicolored .90 .40

Jaycees Intl., 38th World Congress, Taipei.

8th Asian-Pacific Cardiology Congress — A511

$18, Electrocardiogram.

1983, Nov. 27 Litho. *Perf. 13½*

2388 A511 $2 shown .30 .25
2389 A511 $18 multicolored 1.10 .65

New Year 1984 (Year of the Rat) — A512

1983, Dec. 1 Litho. *Perf. 12½*

2390 A512 $1 multicolored 1.75 .70
2391 A512 $10 multicolored 4.00 .45
a. Souv. sheet, 2 each #2390-2391 *30.00* 9.00

Literacy Week A513

1983, Dec. 17 Litho. *Perf. 13½*

2392 A513 $2 shown .35 .25
2393 A513 $18 Modern family, vert. 1.10 .55

World Freedom Day A514

1984, Jan. 23 Litho. *Perf. 13½*

2394 A514 $2 Korean War Patriots .35 .25
2395 A514 $18 Intl. support 1.40 .35

Drama Day — A515

Yuan Dynasty Poetry Illustrations by Tien-shih Lin (Poems by): $2, Kuan Yun-shih. $3, Po Pu. $5, Chang Ko-chiu. $18, Shang Cheng-shu. (See note with Nos. 2322-2325.)

1984, Feb. 15 Litho. *Perf. 13½*

2396 A515 $2 multicolored *1.90* .35
2397 A515 $3 multicolored *3.75* .45
2398 A515 $5 multicolored *6.50* .55
2399 A515 $18 multicolored *10.00* 1.40
Nos. 2396-2399 (4) *22.15* 2.75

A516

A517

A518

Arbor Day — A519

1984, Mar. 12 Litho. *Perf. 13½x14*

2400 A516 $2 multicolored .90 .25
2401 A517 $2 multicolored .90 .25
2402 A518 $2 multicolored .90 .25
2403 A519 $2 multicolored .90 .25
a. Block of 4, #2400-2403 5.00 3.25

Lin Chueh-min — A520

1984, Mar. 29 Engr. *Perf. 13x12½*
Granite Paper

2404 A520 $2 dark green .25 .25

Central News Agency, 60th Anniv. — A521

Perf. 14x13½
1984, Apr. 1 Litho. Wmk.

2405 A521 $2 Emblem .25 .25
2406 A521 $10 Emblem, satellite, dish antenna .70 .45

God of Longevity — A522

Paintings by Chang Ta-chien (1899-1983): $2, Five Auspicious Tokens. $18, Lotus Blossoms in Ink Splash.

Wmk. 323
1984, Apr. 20 Litho. *Perf. 11½*

2407 A522 $2 multicolored 1.50 .25
2408 A522 $5 multicolored 4.00 .25
2409 A522 $18 multicolored 6.00 .50
Nos. 2407-2409 (3) 11.50 1.00

Ch'ing Dynasty Enamelware A523

1984, May 20 Photo. *Perf. 12*
Granite Paper

2410 A523 $2 Cup, pot, plate, horiz. .40 .25
2411 A523 $3 Wine jug .80 .25
2412 A523 $4 Teapot 1.25 .25
2413 A523 $18 Candle holder 1.60 .45
Nos. 2410-2413 (4) 4.05 1.20

China Airlines World-wide Service Inauguration A524

1984, May 31 Litho. *Perf. 13½x14*

2414 A524 $2 Jet circling globe .25 .25
2415 A524 $7 Globe, jet .50 .25
2416 A524 $11 New York City .65 .30
2417 A524 $18 Amsterdam .85 .45
Nos. 2414-2417 (4) 2.25 1.25

30th Navigation Day A525

Perf. 13½x13
1984, July 11 Litho. Wmk. 323

2418 A525 $2 Container ship 1.10 .25
2419 A525 $18 Oil tanker 2.10 .35

1984 Summer Olympics — A526

Perf. 13½x14, 14x13½
1984, June 23

2420 A526 $2 Judo, horiz. .30 .25
2421 A526 $5 Archery .50 .65
2422 A526 $18 Swimming, horiz. 1.00 .80
Nos. 2420-2422 (3) 1.80 1.70

Alpine Plants — A527

$2, Gentiana arisanensis. $3, Epilobium nankotaizanense. $5, Adenophora uehatae. $18, Aconitum fukutomei.

1984, Aug. 8 *Perf. 13*

2423 A527 $2 multi .50 .25
2424 A527 $3 multi 1.00 .25
2425 A527 $5 multi 1.40 .25
2426 A527 $18 multi 2.00 .50
Nos. 2423-2426 (4) 4.90 1.25

The Eighteen Scholars, Sung Dynasty Hanging Scroll — A528

$2, Playing instruments. $3, Playing chess. $5, Practicing calligraphy. $18, Painting.

Wmk. 323
1984, Aug. 20 Litho. *Perf. 13*

2427 A528 $2 multicolored *2.40* .25
2428 A528 $3 multicolored *4.75* .35
2429 A528 $5 multicolored *7.00* .50
2430 A528 $18 multicolored *16.00* 1.00
Nos. 2427-2430 (4) *30.15* 2.10

Athletics Day — A529

1984, Sept. 9

2431 $5 Two players .90 .25
2432 $5 One player .90 .25
a. A529 Pair, #2431-2432 2.00 .90

A531

1984, Sept. 9

2433 A531 $10 "20," map of Asia .70 .25

Asian-Pacific Parliamentarians' Union, 20th anniv.

A532

1984, Oct. 10 Litho. *Perf. 12½*

2434 A532 $2 No. 1458 .25 .25
2435 A532 $5 No. 296 .60 .25
2436 A532 $18 Museum .90 .50
a. Souv. sheet of 3, #2434-2436 9.00 2.25
Nos. 2434-2436 (3) 1.75 1.00

Postal Museum opening.

Flag, Alliance Emblem — A533

1984, Oct. 16 *Perf. 13½*

2437 A533 $2 multicolored .45 .25

Grand Alliance for China's Reunification Under the Three Principles of the People Convention, Taipei, Oct. 16-17.

Veteran's Assistance A534

1984, Nov. 1 Litho. *Perf. 13½*

2438 A534 $2 Vignettes .45 .25

Pine Tree A535

Bamboo A535a

Plum Tree — A535b

1984-88

2439 A535 $2 multicolored .25 .25
2440 A535a $8 multicolored .75 .25
2441 A535b $10 pale yellow bister background .80 .25
a. Grayish tan background .40 .25
Nos. 2439-2441 (3) 1.80 .75

Issued: Nos. 2439-2440, 2441a, 11/12; No. 2441, 1/12/88.

See Nos. 2495-2503, 3303.

A536

1984, Dec. 1 *Perf. 12x12½*

2442 A536 $1 multicolored 1.10 .25
2443 A536 $10 multicolored 3.00 .30
a. Min. sheet, 2 ea #2442-2443 7.75 3.50

New Year 1985 (Year of the Ox).

Scales, Legal Codes — A537

1985, Jan. 11 Litho. *Perf. 13½*

2444 A537 $5 multicolored .65 .25

Judicial Day 1985.

Quemoy and Matsu Scenes A538

$2, Ku-kang Lake, Quemoy. $5, Kuang-hai Stone, Quemoy. $8, Sheng-li Reservoir, Matsu. $10, Tung-chu Lighthouse, Matsu.

1985, Jan. 23 Litho. *Perf. 13½x14*

2445 A538 $2 multicolored .30 .25
2446 A538 $5 multicolored .80 .25
2447 A538 $8 multicolored 1.05 .25
2448 A538 $10 multicolored 1.40 .25
Nos. 2445-2448 (4) 3.55 1.00

Sir Robert Hart (1835-1911) A539

1985, Feb. 15 Litho. *Perf. 14x13½*

2449 A539 $2 No. 1 .45 .25

Inspector General of Chinese Customs, 1863-1908, and founder of the Chinese Postal Service.

Lo Fu-hsing (1886-1914) A540

1985, Feb. 24 *Perf. 13x13½*

2450 A540 $2 multicolored .45 .25

Tsou Jung (1882-1905) A541

1985, Mar. 29 Engr. *Perf. 13½x12½*
Granite Paper

2451 A541 $3 green .45 .25

Chung-cheng Memorial Hall Main Gate — A542

1985, Apr. 5 Litho. *Perf. 13*

2452 A542 $2 shown .30 .25
2453 A542 $8 Tzuhu Memorial 1.10 .25
2454 A542 $10 Chiang Kai-shek, vert. 1.25 .30
Nos. 2452-2454 (3) 2.65 .80

Tenth death anniv. of Chiang Kai-shek.

A543

1985, May 8 Litho. *Perf. 13½*

2455 A543 $2 Carnation 1.00 .25
2456 A543 $2 Day lily 1.00 .25
a. Pair, #2455-2456 2.50 .80

Mother's Day.

Tunnel to Chi-chin Island — A544

1985, May 18

2457 A544 $5 multicolored .70 .25

Kaohsiung Cross-Harbor Tunnel, 1st anniv.

Girl Scouts, 75th Anniv. — A545

Wmk. 323

1985, June 1 Litho. *Perf. 13½*

2458 A545 $2 multicolored .25 .25
2459 A545 $18 multicolored 2.00 .30

The Book of Odes, Confucius A545a

1985, June 22 Litho. Wmk. 323

2460 A545a $2 Spring 1.25 .25
2461 A545a $5 Summer 2.40 .25
2462 A545a $8 Fall 4.75 .30
2463 A545a $10 Winter 6.00 .50
Nos. 2460-2463 (4) 14.40 1.30

Fruit — A546

Perf. 13½x14

1985, July 5 Litho. Wmk. 323

2464 A546 $2 Wax Jambo .70 .25
2465 A546 $3 Guava 1.25 .25
2466 A546 $5 Carambola 1.40 .25
2467 A546 $8 Litchi nut 1.50 .30
Nos. 2464-2467 (4) 4.85 1.05

Ch'ing Dynasty (1644-1911) Ivory Carvings — A547

$2, Dragon Boat. $3, Landscape. $5, Melon, water container. $18, Brush holder, vert.

1985, July 18 Wmk. 323 *Perf. 13½*

2468 A547 $2 multicolored .25 .25
2469 A547 $3 multicolored .60 .25
2470 A547 $5 multicolored .90 .25
2471 A547 $18 multicolored 1.10 .35
Nos. 2468-2471 (4) 2.85 1.10

T'ang Dynasty (618-907) Aristocrat — A548

Designs: $5, Sung Dynasty (960-1280) palace woman. $8, Yuan Dynasty (1280-1368) aristocrat. $11, Ming Dynasty (1368-1644) aristocrat.

1985, Aug. 1 Wmk. 323 *Perf. 13½*

2472 A548 $2 multicolored .55 .25
2473 A548 $5 multicolored 1.75 .25
2474 A548 $8 multicolored 2.50 .25
2475 A548 $11 multicolored 3.00 .30
Nos. 2472-2475 (4) 7.80 1.05

4th Asian Conf. on Costume, Aug. 3.
In the 2 rows of Chinese characters above the denomination, the right row has 3 characters and a dot on Nos. 2472-2475, 4 characters and a dot on Nos. 2549-2552. Nos. 2605-2608, 2660-2663 have solid black numerals.
See Nos. 2549-2552, 2605-2608, 2660-2663, 2721-2724, 2794-2797.

Social Welfare Program A549

Perf. 13½x14

1985, Aug. 15 Wmk. 323

2476 A549 $2 Heart, bird feeding young .45 .25

Historic Sites A550

$2, Taipei North Gate. $5, San Domingo Fort, Tamsui. $8, Lung Shun Temple, Lukang. $10, Confucius Temple, Changhua.

Wmk. 323

1985, Sept. 3 Litho. *Perf. 13½*

2477 A550 $2 multicolored .25 .25
2478 A550 $5 multicolored .65 .25
2479 A550 $8 multicolored .85 .25
2480 A550 $10 multicolored 1.10 .25
Nos. 2477-2480 (4) 2.85 1.00

Bonsai — A551

Perf. 13½x14

1985, Sept. 22 Wmk. 323

2481 A551 $2 Oak .35 .25
2482 A551 $5 Five-leaf pine .75 .25
2483 A551 $8 Lohan pine 1.00 .25
2484 A551 $18 Banyan 1.50 .50
Nos. 2481-2484 (4) 3.60 1.25

Trade Shows — A552

Taipei World Trade Center and show emblems: a, Sporting goods. b, Toys and gifts. c, Electronics. d, Machinery. Se-tenant in continuous design.

1985, Oct. 5 *Perf. 13½*

2485 A552 Strip of 4 3.50 1.25
a.-d. $2 any single .75 .25

Scenes of Modern Taiwan, Map, Flag A553

$18, Chiang Kai-shek, Triumphal Arch.

1985, Oct. 25

2486 A553 $2 shown 1.00 .25
2487 A553 $18 multicolored 2.00 .70

Defeat of Japanese army, end of World War II, and return of Taiwan to control of the Republic, 40th anniv.

7th Asian Conference on Mental Retardation A554

1985, Nov. 8 *Perf. 14x13½*

2488 A554 $2 multicolored .40 .25
2489 A554 $11 multicolored 1.50 .30

Sun Yat-sen and Birthplace
A555

1985, Nov. 12 *Perf. 13½*

2490 A555 $2 multicolored .40 .25
2491 A555 $18 multicolored 1.75 .40

Postal Life Insurance, 50th Anniv. — A556

1985, Dec. 1

2492 A556 $2 multicolored .45 .25

New Year 1986 (Year of the Tiger) — A557

1985, Dec. 1 *Perf. 12½*

2493 A557 $1 multicolored .60 .25
2494 A557 $10 multicolored 2.00 .35
a. Min. sheet, 2 ea #2493-2494 *11.00* 3.25

Flora Types of 1984

1986, Jan. 10 Litho. *Perf. 13½*

2495 A535 $1 multicolored .25 .25
2496 A535a $11 multicolored .65 .25
2497 A535b $18 multicolored .90 .25

1988, Feb. 12

2498 A535 $1.50 multicolored .25 .25
2499 A535a $7.50 multicolored .65 .25
2500 A535b $16 multicolored 1.25 .30

No. 2500 has value expressed in dollars and cents. For surcharge, see No. 3303.

1989, Feb. 24

2501 A535 $3 multicolored .25 .25
2502 A535a $16.50 multicolored 1.25 .30
2503 A535b $21 multicolored 1.60 .35
Nos. 2495-2503 (9) 7.05 2.45

Cultural Renaissance Movement — A558

Painting: Hermit Anglers on a Mountain Stream, Ming Dynasty, 1386-1644. Continuous design. (Each stamp is numbered from 1 to 5 in Chinese. See illustrations with Nos. 1682-1691 for numerals.)

1986, Jan. 28 Litho. *Perf. 13½*

2507 Strip of 5 9.00 7.00
a.-e. A558 $2 any single *1.50* .25

See No. 2604.

Floral Arrangements
A559

Wmk. 323

1986, Feb. 20 Litho. *Perf. 13½*

2517 A559 $2 denom. UL .35 .25
2518 A559 $5 denom. UR .75 .25
2519 A559 $8 shown .85 .25
2520 A559 $10 denom. UL 1.25 .25
Nos. 2517-2520 (4) 3.20 1.00

Compare with designs A483, A584.

Natl. Postal Service, 90th Anniv.
A560

$2, Unloading express mail at airport. $5, Motorcycle delivery. $8, Technological innovations. $10, Electronic sorting machine.

1986, Mar. 20

2521 A560 $2 multi .25 .25
2522 A560 $5 multi, vert. .35 .25
2523 A560 $8 multi, vert. .55 .25
2524 A560 $10 multi .65 .25
a. Souv. sheet of 4, #2521-2524 5.75 2.55
Nos. 2521-2524 (4) 1.80 1.00

Chen Tien-hua (1875-1905), Revolutionary
A561

1986, Mar. 29 Engr. *Perf. 13½x12½*
Granite Paper

2525 A561 $2 violet .55 .25

Yushan Natl. Park
A562

1986, Apr. 10 Litho. *Perf. 13½*

2526 A562 $2 multicolored .50 .25
2527 A562 $5 multi, diff. 1.25 .25
2528 A562 $8 multi, diff. 1.60 .25
2529 A562 $10 multi, diff. 2.00 .30
Nos. 2526-2529 (4) 5.35 1.05

Power Plants
A563

1986, Apr. 29

2530 A563 $2 Hydro-electric .30 .25
2531 A563 $8 Thermo-electric .80 .25
2532 A563 $10 Nuclear 1.10 .25
Nos. 2530-2532 (3) 2.20 .75

Economic prosperity through energy development.

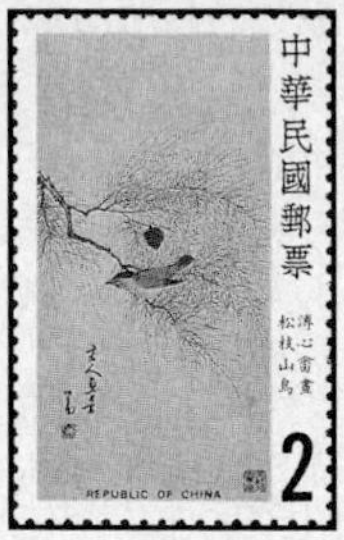

Paintings by P'u Hsin-yu (1896-1963)
A564

1986, May 22 *Perf. 11½*

2533 A564 $2 Bird 1.75 .25
2534 A564 $8 Landscape 3.50 .30
2535 A564 $10 Woman in forest 5.50 .35
Nos. 2533-2535 (3) 10.75 .90

Asian Productivity Org., 25th Anniv. — A565

1986, June 3 *Perf. 13x13½*

2536 A565 $2 multicolored .25 .25
2537 A565 $11 multicolored 1.00 .30

Natl. Productivity Center, 30th anniv.

Coral-reef Fish
A566

Designs: a, Chrysiptera starcki. b, Chelmon rostratus. c, Chaetodon xanthurus. d, Chaetodon quadrimaculatus. e, Chaetodon meyeri. f, Genicanthus semifasciatus. g, Genicanthus semifasciatus. h, Pomacanthus annularis. i, Lienardella fasciata. j, Balistapus undulatus.

1986, June 27 *Perf. 13½*

2538 Block of 10 6.50 4.00
a.-j. A566 $2 any single .60 .25

Protection of Intellectual Property Rights — A567

1986, June 12

2539 A567 $2 Macaw 1.40 .25

Nos. 2294, 2297 Surcharged

1986, July 9 Litho. *Perf. 13½*

2540 A432 $2 on $6 multi .25 .25
2541 A432 $8 on $9 multi .55 .25

60th Anniv. of northward expedition by the national revolutionary army.

Bridges
A568

$2, Tzu Mu, 1965. $5, Chang Hung, 1968. $8, Kuan Fu, 1977. $10, Kuan Tu, 1983.

1986, July 30

2542 A568 $2 multicolored .45 .25
2543 A568 $5 multicolored 1.10 .25
2544 A568 $8 multicolored 1.40 .25
2545 A568 $10 multicolored 2.00 .25
Nos. 2542-2545 (4) 4.95 1.00

Love between Liang Shanpo and Chu Yingtai, Folk Tale — A569

Cartoons by Huang Mu-ts'un: a, Yingtai disguised to go to school. b, Yingtai and Shanpo meet in class. c, The friends at pond. d, Yingtai summoned home for arranged marriage. e, Yingtai and Shanpo ascend to heaven as butterflies (each stamp is numbered from 1 to 5 in Chinese. See illustrations with Nos. 1682-1691 for numerals.)

1986, Aug. 12 *Perf. 12½*

2546 Strip of 5 4.00 2.00
a.-e. A569 $5 any single .60 .25

Social Awareness Campaign
A570

1986, Sept. 12 Litho. *Perf. 13½*

2547 A570 $2 Rainbow, children .30 .25
2548 A570 $8 Children, adults .70 .25

Folk Costumes — A571

Designs: $2, Shang Dynasty (1766-1122 B.C.) aristocrat. $5, Warring States (403-221 B.C.) aristocrat. $8, Later Han Dynasty (A.D. 25-221) empress. $10, Flying ribbons gown, Wei and Tsin Dynasties (A.D. 221-420) aristocrat.

1986, Sept. 23 Litho. *Perf. 13½*

2549 A571 $2 multicolored .85 .25
2550 A571 $5 multicolored 1.40 .25
2551 A571 $8 multicolored 1.75 .25
2552 A571 $10 multicolored 2.75 .25
Nos. 2549-2552 (4) 6.75 1.00

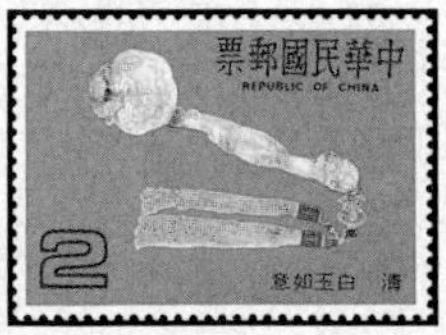

Ch'ing Dynasty Ju-i Scepters
A572

1986, Oct. 10 Photo. *Perf. 14x14½*

2553 A572 $2 White jade .25 .25
2554 A572 $3 Red coral .45 .25
2555 A572 $4 Redwood and gems .60 .25
2556 A572 $18 Gilded wood 1.60 .40
Nos. 2553-2556 (4) 2.90 1.15

See Nos. 2582-2585.

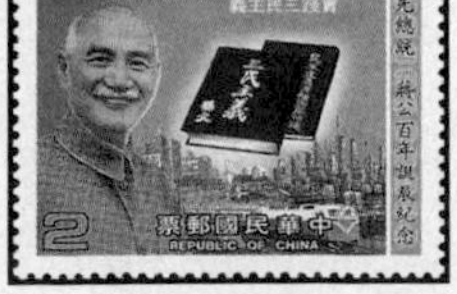

Chiang Kai-shek
A573

Portrait and: $5, Map and flag. $8, Emblem. $10, Flags on globe.

1986, Oct. 31 Litho. *Perf. 13½*

2557 A573 $2 multicolored .25 .25
2558 A573 $5 multicolored .85 .25
2559 A573 $8 multicolored 1.10 .25
2560 A573 $10 multicolored 1.40 .25
a. Souv. sheet of 4, #2557-2560 9.00 2.50
Nos. 2557-2560 (4) 3.60 1.00

Cultural Heritage A574

Architecture: $2, Chin-Kuang Fu land development and defense fund building, 1826. $5, Erh-sha-wan Gun Emplacement, Keelung, 1841, restored 1979. $8, Fort Hsi T'ai, 1886. $10, Matsu Temple, Peng-hu, renovated 1563-1624.

1986, Nov. 14 Litho. *Perf. 13½*

2561 A574 $2 multicolored .40 .25
2562 A574 $5 multicolored .95 .25
2563 A574 $8 multicolored 1.10 .25
2564 A574 $10 multicolored 1.40 .30
Nos. 2561-2564 (4) 3.85 1.05

New Year 1987 (Year of the Hare) — A575

1986, Dec. 1 *Perf. 12½*

2565 A575 $1 dl pink & multi .50 .25
2566 A575 $10 pale grn & multi 2.25 .30
a. Souv. sheet, 2 each #2565-2566 *14.50* 3.50

Kenting, 1st Natl. Park A576

1987, Jan. 8 Litho. *Perf. 13½*

2567 A576 $2 Garden .45 .25
2568 A576 $5 Shore rocks 1.10 .25
2569 A576 $8 Shore and hill 1.40 .25
2570 A576 $10 Shore and rocks, diff. 2.00 .30
Nos. 2567-2570 (4) 4.95 1.05

Folk Art — A577

Puppets: $2, Hand puppet. $5, Marionette. $18, Shadow puppet.

1987, Feb. 12 Litho. *Perf. 14x13½*

2571 A577 $2 multicolored .35 .25
2572 A577 $5 multicolored 1.00 .25
2573 A577 $18 multicolored 1.75 .40
Nos. 2571-2573 (3) 3.10 .90

Speedpost A578

1987, Mar. 20 Litho. *Perf. 14x13½*

2574 A578 $2 multicolored .35 .25
2575 A578 $18 multicolored 1.25 .40

Stamp Day.

Wu Yueh (1878-1905), Revolutionary A579

1987, Mar. 29 Engr. *Perf. 13½x12½*

2576 A579 $2 orange 1.10 .25

Landscapes Painted by Madame Chiang Kai-shek — A580

$2, Singing Creek with Bamboo Orchestra. $5, Mountains Draped in Clouds. $8, Vista of Tranquility. $10, Mountains after a Snowfall.

1987, Apr. 10 Litho. *Perf. 13½*

2577 A580 $2 blk, buff & ver .45 .25
2578 A580 $5 blk, buff & ver 1.25 .25
2579 A580 $8 blk, buff & ver 2.75 .30
2580 A580 $10 blk, buff & ver 3.75 .45
Nos. 2577-2580 (4) 8.20 1.25

Stone Sculptures — A581

Designs: a, Head of a Bodhisattva, sandstone, Northern Wei Dynasty (386-534). b, Standing Buddha, limestone, Northern Ch'i Dynasty (550-577). c, Head of a Bodhisattva, sandstone, T'ang Dynasty (618-907). d, Seated Buddha, alabaster, T'ang Dynasty.

1987, Apr. 23

2581 Strip of 4 3.50 2.25
a.-d. A581 $5 any single .70 .30

No. 2581a shows seven Chinese characters at left; No. 2581c shows five.

Ju-i Scepters, Ch'ing Dynasty A582

1987, May 7 Photo. *Perf. 14x14½*

2582 A582 $2 Silver and gems .55 .25
2583 A582 $3 Gold and gems 1.40 .25
2584 A582 $4 Gilded, jade and inlaid gems 2.10 .25
2585 A582 $18 Gilded, inlaid malachite 3.00 .45
Nos. 2582-2585 (4) 7.05 1.20

Feitsui Reservoir Inauguration A583

1987, June 6 Litho. *Perf. 13½x14*

2586 A583 $2 Reservoir .45 .25
2587 A583 $18 Hsintien Stream, reservoir 1.75 .45

Flower Arrangements by Huang Yung-ch'uan A584

1987, June 19 *Perf. 13½*

2588 A584 $2 denom. LL .25 .25
2589 A584 $5 denom. LL .70 .25
2590 A584 $8 Flowers in brown vase .90 .25
2591 A584 $10 denom. UR 1.00 .25
Nos. 2588-2591 (4) 2.85 1.00

Compare with designs A483, A559.

Lions Club Intl. 70th Annual Convention, Taipei — A585

1987, July 1

2592 A585 $2 multicolored .30 .25
2593 A585 $18 multicolored 1.40 .50

Sino-Japanese War, 50th Anniv. — A586

$1, Battle front. $2, Chiang Kai-shek giving speech. $5, Public donating funds. $6, Troops marching. $8, Signing of peace treaty. $18, Parade.

1987, July 7 *Perf. 14x13½*

2594 A586 $1 multicolored .25 .25
2595 A586 $2 multicolored .40 .25
2596 A586 $5 multicolored .45 .25
2597 A586 $6 multicolored .60 .25
2598 A586 $8 multicolored .85 .25
2599 A586 $18 multicolored 1.00 .40
Nos. 2594-2599 (6) 3.55 1.65

Wang Yun-wu (1888-1979), Lexicographer A587

1987, Aug. 14 *Perf. 13½*

2600 A587 $2 gray black .55 .25

Memorial Hall Type of 1981

Perf. 12½x13½

1987, Sept. 24 Photo.

2601 A468 10c lake .25 .25
2602 A468 30c brt green .25 .25
2603 A468 60c brt blue .25 .25
Nos. 2601-2603 (3) .75 .75

A588

Cultural Renaissance Movement — A589

Scroll, 1543, by Weng Chen-ming (1470-1559), a copy of Chao Po-su's *Red Cliff.* Nos. 2604a-2604e and 2604f-2604j are printed in continuous designs. (Each stamp is numbered from 1 to 10 in Chinese. See illustrations with Nos. 1682-1691 for numerals.)

1987, Sept. 22 Engr. *Perf. 13½*

2604 Block of 10 13.50 13.50
a.-e. A588 $3 any single 1.00 .25
f.-j. A589 $3 any single 1.00 .25

Folk Costumes — A590

$1.50, Han woman, early Ch'ing Dynasty (1644-1911). $3, Wife of a Ch'ing Dynasty Manchu Bannerman. $7.50, Urban woman wearing Manchu ch'i-p'ao dress, c. 1912. $18, Short jacket over long skirt, c. 1920.

1987, Oct. 2 Litho.

2605 A590 $1.50 multicolored *1.25* .25
2606 A590 $3 multicolored *1.50* .25
2607 A590 $7.50 multicolored *1.75* .25
2608 A590 $18 multicolored *2.10* .50
Nos. 2605-2608 (4) *6.60* 1.25

Nos. 2605-2608 have 3 groups of 2 smaller Chinese characters above denomination. Nos. 2660-2663 have 2 groups of 2 and 4 characters.

A591

$3, Ta Chen Tian temple, Taichung. $18, Confucius.

1987, Nov. 12 *Perf. 13½x14*

2609 A591 $3 multicolored .45 .25
2610 A591 $18 multicolored 1.75 1.10

Intl. Symposium on Confucianism, Taipei, Nov. 12-17.

A592

1987, Dec. 1 *Perf. 12½*

2611 A592 $1.50 multicolored .60 .25
2612 A592 $12 multicolored 2.50 .45
a. Souv. sheet, 2 ea #2611-2612 11.00 2.50

New Year 1988 (Year of the Dragon).

Constitution, 40th Anniv. — A593

1987, Dec. 25 Litho. *Perf. 13½*

2613 A593 $3 multicolored .25 .25
2614 A593 $16 multi, diff. 1.10 .55

Prevent Hypertension Campaign A594

1988, Jan. 8 *Perf. 12½x13½*

2615 A594 $3 multicolored .45 .25

Fruit Tree Blossoms — A595

No. 2616, Prunus mume. No. 2617, Prunus armeniaca. No. 2618, Prunus persica.
No. 2619, Paeonia suffruticosa. No. 2620, Punica granatum. No. 2621, Nelumbo nucifera.
No. 2622, Impatiens balsamina. No. 2623, Osmanthus fragrans. No. 2624, Chrysanthemum morifolium.
No. 2625, Hibiscus mutabilis. No. 2626, Camellia japonica. No. 2627, Narcissus tazetta.

Wmk. 323

1988, Feb. 4 Litho. *Perf. 13½*

2616 A595 $3 multi 1.50 .25
2617 A595 $7.50 multi 1.75 .30
2618 A595 $12 multi 2.25 .50
a. Min. sheet of 3, #2616-2618 *22.50 22.50*

Wmk. 323

1988, May 5 Litho. *Perf. 13½*

2619 A595 $3 multi .45 .25
2620 A595 $7.50 multi 1.40 .30
2621 A595 $12 multi 1.60 .50
a. Min. sheet of 3, #2619-2621 *13.50 13.50*

Wmk. 323

1988, Aug. 9 Litho. *Perf. 13½*

2622 A595 $3 multi .40 .25
2623 A595 $7.50 multi 1.25 .30
2624 A595 $12 multi 1.50 .50
a. Min. sheet of 3, #2622-2624 *12.00 12.00*

Wmk. 323

1988, Nov. 7 Litho. *Perf. 13½*

2625 A595 $3 multi .40 .25
2626 A595 $7.50 multi 1.75 .30
2627 A595 $12 multi 2.10 .50
a. Min. sheet of 3, #2625-2627 *12.50 12.50*
Nos. 2616-2627 (12) 16.35 4.20

Tourism Day — A596

Folk art: $3, Modeled dough figurines. $7.50, Blown sweet-malt sugar candy. $16, Sugar paintings.

Perf. 13½x14

1988, Mar. 2 Litho. Wmk. 323

2628 A596 $3 multicolored .75 .30
2629 A596 $7.50 multicolored 1.50 .45
2630 A596 $16 multicolored 2.75 1.05
Nos. 2628-2630 (3) 5.00 1.80

A597

Perf. 13½x12½

1988, Mar. 29 Engr. Wmk. 323

2631 A597 $3 brown .40 .25

Hsu Hsi-lin (1873-1907), hero of the revolution.

A598

$1.50, Biotechnology. $3, Energy resources. $7, Immunization. $7.50, Automation. $10, Telecommunications. $12, Laser technology. $16, Micro-optics. $16.50, Agricultural research.

1988 Litho. *Perf. 13½*

2632 A598 $1.50 multicolored .25 .25
2633 A598 $3 multicolored .30 .25
2634 A598 $7 multicolored .45 .25
2635 A598 $7.50 multicolored .45 .25
2636 A598 $10 multicolored .60 .40
2637 A598 $12 multicolored .65 .40
2638 A598 $16 multicolored .95 .65
2639 A598 $16.50 multicolored 1.25 .65
Nos. 2632-2639 (8) 4.90 3.10

Industrialization by technological development. Issued: $3, $7.50, $10, $16, Apr. 22; others, May 9.

Police Day A599

Wmk. 323

1988, June 15 Litho. *Perf. 13½*

2640 A599 $3 Traffic control .25 .25
2641 A599 $12 Rescue operations .80 .40

Amphibians A600

$1.50, Microhyla butleri. $3, Rana taipehensis. $7.50, Microhyla inornata. $16, Rhacophorus smaragdinus.

1988, July 8 *Perf. 13½x14*

2642 A600 $1.50 multicolored *1.10* .25
2643 A600 $3 multicolored *1.75* .25
2644 A600 $7.50 multicolored *2.25* .35
2645 A600 $16 multicolored *3.00* .75
Nos. 2642-2645 (4) *8.10* 1.60

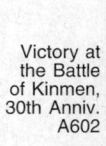

China Broadcasting Corp. (BBC), 60th Anniv. — A601

Wmk. 323

1988, Aug. 1 Litho. *Perf. 13½*

2646 A601 $3 multicolored .45 .25

Victory at the Battle of Kinmen, 30th Anniv. A602

Designs: $1.50, Chiang Kai-shek and artillery commander. $3, With troops. $7.50, Cannon. $12, Tanks.

1988, Aug. 23

2647 A602 $1.50 multicolored .40 .25
2648 A602 $3 multicolored .50 .25
2649 A602 $7.50 multicolored .55 .25
2650 A602 $12 multicolored .80 .40
Nos. 2647-2650 (4) 2.25 1.15

Sports Promotion — A603

Nos. 2651-2652, Basketball. Nos. 2653-2654, Baseball.

1988, Sept. 9

2651 $5 Players .90 .25
2652 $5 Players .90 .25
a. A603 Pair, #2651-2652 1.90 1.10
2653 $5 Batter .90 .25
2654 $5 Catcher .90 .25
a. A603 Pair, #2653-2654 1.90 1.10
Nos. 2651-2654 (4) 3.60 1.00

Nos. 2652a, 2654a have continuous designs.

Yangmingshan Natl. Park — A604

$1.50, Volcanic crater. $3, Lake. $7.50, Tatun Volcanic Range. $16, Dormant volcano.

1988, Sept. 16

2655 A604 $1.50 multicolored *.25* .25
2656 A604 $3 multicolored *.45* .25
2657 A604 $7.50 multicolored *.85* .25
2658 A604 $16 multicolored *1.60* .55
Nos. 2655-2658 (4) *3.15* 1.30

Lofty Mount Lu, a Hanging Scroll, 1467, By Shen Chou (1427-1509) — A605

Painting details: a, UL. b, UR. c, LL. d, LR.

Wmk. 323

1988, Oct. 19 Litho. *Perf. 11½*

2659 A605 Block of 4 *7.00* 5.00
a.-d. $5 any single *1.50* .35

Folk Costumes — A606

Designs: $2, Shang Dynasty (1766-1122 B.C.) nobleman. $3, Warring States (403-221) B.C.) ruler. $7.50, Wei-Chin Period (221-420) official. $12, Northern Dynasties (502-581) official.

Perf. 13½x14

1988, Nov. 23 Litho. Wmk. 323

2660 A606 $2 multicolored *.50* .25
2661 A606 $3 multicolored *.85* .25
2662 A606 $7.50 multicolored *1.75* .35
2663 A606 $12 multicolored *2.40* .55
Nos. 2660-2663 (4) *5.50* 1.40

Nos. 2721-2724 have groups of 2 and 6 Chinese characters above denomination; Nos. 2660-2663 groups of 2 and 4; Nos. 2794-2797 groups of 1 and 5.

A607

1988, Dec. 1 *Perf. 12½*

2664 A607 $2 multicolored *.55* .25
2665 A607 $13 multicolored *4.25* .60
a. Souv. sheet, 2 each #2664-2665 *14.50* 14.50

New Year 1989 (Year of the Snake).

A608

Wmk. 323

1989, Jan. 4 Litho. *Perf. 13½*

2666 A608 $3 black .55 .25

Tai Ch'uan-hsien (1890-1949), party leader.

Pres. Chiang Ching-kuo (1910-88) A609

1989, Jan. 13

2667 A609 $3 shown .25 .25
2668 A609 $6 Suffrage .40 .25
2669 A609 $7.50 Industry .60 .30
2670 A609 $16 Children .95 .65
Nos. 2667-2670 (4) 2.20 1.45

Ni Ying-tien (1884-1910), Revolution Leader — A610

Perf. 13½x12½

1989, Mar. 28 Engr. Wmk. 323

2671	A610	$3 black	.45	.25

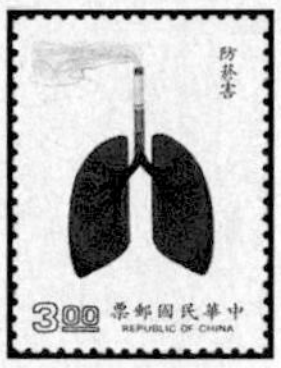

Stop Smoking — A611

Perf. 13½x12½

1989, Apr. 7 Litho. Wmk. 323

2672	A611	$3 multicolored	.45	.25

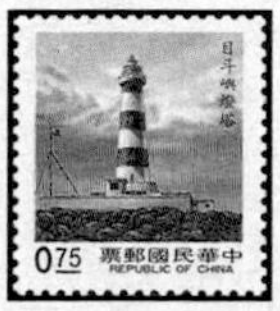

Lighthouses — A612

75c, Mu Tou Yu. $2, Lu Tao. $2.25, Pen Chia Yu.$3, Pitou Chiao. $4.50, Tungyin Tao. $6, Chilai Pi. $7, Fukwei Chiao. $7.50, Hua Yu. $9, Oluan Pi. $10, Kaohsiung. $10.50, Yuweng Tao. $12, Tungchu Tao. $13, Yeh Liu. $15, Tungchi Yu. $16.50, Chimei Yu.

1989-91 *Perf. 13½*

2673	A612	75c multi	.40	.25
2674	A612	$2 multi	.40	.25
2675	A612	$2.25 multi	.40	.25
2676	A612	$3 multi	.60	.25
2677	A612	$4.50 multi	.75	.25
2678	A612	$6 multi	.80	.25
2679	A612	$7 multi	.90	.35
2680	A612	$7.50 multi	.95	.35
2681	A612	$9 multi	1.00	.25
2682	A612	$10 multi	1.05	.45
2683	A612	$10.50 multi	1.10	.35
2683A	A612	$12 multi	1.60	.55
2683B	A612	$13 multi	2.00	.45
2683C	A612	$15 multi	2.10	.80
2684	A612	$16.50 multi	2.40	.75
		Nos. 2673-2684 (15)	16.45	5.80

Issued: $7, $15, 5/19/90; $6, $12, 1/9/91; $2, $3, $7.50, $10, $16.50, 5/20/91; others, 1989.

See Nos. 2811-2823.

1st Natl. Wealth Survey A613

1989, May 18 Litho. *Perf. 13½*

2685	A613	$3 multicolored	.30	.25

Ch'u Ts'u Collection of Poems, 722-481 B.C. — A614

Designs: $3, Man overlooking fields. $7.50, Man, woman on path. $12, Man holding staff. $16, Man, stallion, stone gate. Excerpts: $3, "I once tended nine fields of orchids; Also I had planted a hundred rods of melilotus" (Li Sao). $7.50, "No grief is greater than parting of the living; No joy is more than making new friends" (Chiu Ko, shao ssu ming). $12, "Since my heart is straight and good, Why should I be chagrined at living remote and neglected?" (Chiu Chang, she chiang). $16, "The steed will not gallop itself into servitude; The phoenix has no appetite for slave food." (Chiu Pien).

1989, June 7 Photo. *Perf. 11½x12*

Granite Paper

2686	A614	$3 multicolored	.45	.25
2687	A614	$7.50 multicolored	1.10	.45
2688	A614	$12 multicolored	2.10	.70
2689	A614	$16 multicolored	2.50	1.00
		Nos. 2686-2689 (4)	6.15	2.40

Compare with types A629, A663. Nos. 2686-2689 have two Chinese characters near denomination. Nos. 2725-2728 have groups of 3 and 4 characters.

Taipei Subway Inauguration — A615

1989, June 27 Litho. *Perf. 13½*

2690	A615	$3 Subway tunnel	.40	.25
2691	A615	$16 Entering underground	1.75	.90

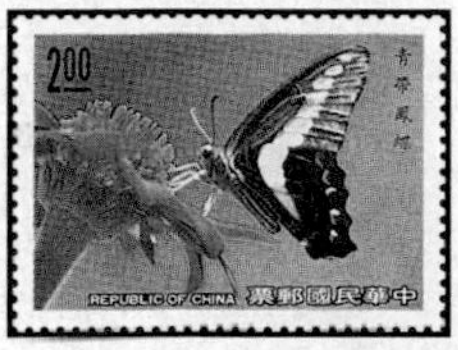

A616

A616a

A616b

Butterflies A616c

$2, Graphium sarpedon connectens. $3, Papilo memnon heronus. $7.50, Princeps demoleus libanius. $9, Pachliopa aristolochiae interpositas.

Wmk. 323

1989, July 14 Litho. *Perf. 13½*

2692	A616	$2 multicolored	.45	.25
2693	A616a	$3 multicolored	.85	.30
2694	A616b	$7.50 multicolored	2.00	.40
2695	A616c	$9 multicolored	2.50	.50
		Nos. 2692-2695 (4)	5.80	1.45

Compare with design A627.

Ch'ing Dynasty Teapots from I-Hsing of Kiangsu, 1644-1911 A617

1989, July 28 *Perf. 13½x14*

2696	A617	$2 multicolored	.30	.25
2697	A617	$3 multi, diff.	.90	.25
2698	A617	$12 multi, diff.	2.25	.50
2699	A617	$16 multi, diff.	2.25	.70
		Nos. 2696-2699 (4)	5.70	1.70

For stamps with teapot designs and solid black denominations see Nos. 2760-2764.

Intl. Seminar on Fan Chung-yen (989-1052), Military Leader and Civil Service Reformer — A618

Perf. 14x13½

1989, Sept. 1 Litho. Wmk. 323

2700	A618	$12 multicolored	1.25	.55

Autumn Colors on the Ch'iao and Hua Mountains, 14th Cent., by Ch'iao Meng-fu A619

a, Right side of mountain, trees. b, Trees, left side of mountain. c, House, trees. d, shown.

Wmk. 323

1989, Oct. 5 Litho. *Perf. 13½*

2701	Strip of 4	10.00	4.75
a.-d.	A619 $7.50 any single	2.25	.55

Social Welfare A619a

1989, Nov. 3 Litho. *Perf. 13½*

2701E	A619a	$3 multicolored	.45	.25

Taroko Natl. Park — A620

Designs: $2, Marble gorge, Liwu River. $3, Hohuan Mountain. $12, Waterfall, Cirque of Nanhu. $16, Chingshui Cliff.

Wmk. 323

1989, Nov. 28 Litho. *Perf. 13½*

2702	A620	$2 multicolored	.25	.25
2703	A620	$3 multicolored	.45	.35
2704	A620	$12 multicolored	1.00	.55
2705	A620	$16 multicolored	1.25	.70
		Nos. 2702-2705 (4)	2.95	1.85

New Year 1990 (Year of the Horse) — A621

1989, Dec. 1 *Perf. 12½*

2706	A621	$2 multicolored	.45	.25
2707	A621	$13 multicolored	1.75	.80
a.		Souv. sheet, 2 ea #2706-2707	8.00	3.00

Yu Lu — A622

Men Shen, "guardian spirits" (likenesses of legendary beings placed on residence doors at the new year): No. 2708, Yu Lu. No. 2709, Shen Shu. No. 2710, Wei-ch'ih Ching-te. No. 2711, Ch'in Shu-pao.

Wmk. 323

1990, Jan. 19 Litho. *Perf. 13½*

2708	A622	$3 shown	1.25	.25
2709	A622	$3 "$3" at LR	1.25	.25
a.		Pair, #2708-2709	2.50	2.00
2710	A622	$7.50 "$7.50" at LL	3.00	.50
2711	A622	$7.50 "$7.50" at LR	3.00	.50
a.		Pair, #2710-2711	6.00	5.00
		Nos. 2708-2711 (4)	8.50	1.50

Nos. 2709a, 2711a have continuous designs.

A623

Scenery — A624

Designs: $2, Lishan House, Pear Mountain. $18, Tayu Pass, Tayuling, vert.

Wmk. 323

1990, Feb. 10 Litho. *Perf. 13½*

2712	A623	$2 multicolored	.50	.25
2713	A624	$18 multicolored	2.00	1.00

Labor Insurance System, 40th Anniv. — A625

1990, Mar. 1

2714	A625	$3 multicolored	.60	.25

Liquefied Natural Gas A626

$3, Terminal, Yung-an Hsiang of Kaohsiung. $16, Container ship, map, refinery.

1990, Mar. 31 Litho. *Perf. 13½*

2715	A626	$3 multi	.50	.25
2716	A626	$16 multi, vert.	1.50	.65

A627

A627a

A627b

Butterflies
A627c

$2, Salatura genutia. $3, Hypolimnas misippus. $7.50, Pieris canidia. $9, Precis almana.

1990, Apr. 20

2717	A627	$2	multicolored	.45	.25
2718	A627a	$3	multicolored	.45	.25
2719	A627b	$7.50	multicolored	1.25	.35
2720	A627c	$9	multicolored	1.75	.45
	Nos. 2717-2720 (4)			3.90	1.30

Compare with design A616.

Folk Costumes — A628

$2, Official, Sui & T'ang Dynasties (589-907). $3, Official, T'ang & Sung Dynasties (618-1280). $7.50, Royal guardsman, Chin & Yuan Dynasties (1115-1368). $12, Highest ranking civil official, Ming Dynasty (1368-1644).

1990, May 10 Litho. *Perf. 13½*

2721	A628	$2	multicolored	.35	.25
2722	A628	$3	multicolored	.75	.25
2723	A628	$7.50	multicolored	1.50	.30
2724	A628	$12	multicolored	1.60	.55
	Nos. 2721-2724 (4)			4.20	1.35

See note after No. 2663.

Yueh Fu Classical Poetry
A629

Lyrics from Tzu-yeh folk songs, Six Dynasties (222-589): $3, Spring Song at Midnight. $7.50, Summer Song at Midnight. $12, Autumn Song at Midnight. $16, Winter Song at Midnight.

Wmk. 323

1990, June 27 Litho. *Perf. 11½*

Granite Paper

2725	A629	$3	shown	.50	.25
2726	A629	$7.50	Couple, river	1.25	.35
2727	A629	$12	Washing clothes, river	3.00	.55
2728	A629	$16	River in winter	4.25	.80
	Nos. 2725-2728 (4)			9.00	1.95

Compare with designs A614 and A663.

Bonsai
A630

Designs: $3, Pinus thunbergii parl. $6.50, Ehretia microphylla lamk. $12, Buxus harlandii hance. $16, Celtis sinensis pers.

1990, July 20 Litho. *Perf. 13½*

2729	A630	$3	multicolored	.30	.25
2730	A630	$6.50	multicolored	.70	.30
2731	A630	$12	multicolored	1.00	.70
2732	A630	$16	multicolored	1.50	.80
	Nos. 2729-2732 (4)			3.50	2.05

Snuff Bottles — A631

1990, Aug. 9

2733	A631	$3	Bamboo stem shaped	.40	.25
2734	A631	$6	Peony motif	.75	.30
2735	A631	$9	Amber	1.05	.45
2736	A631	$16	White jade	2.10	.80
	Nos. 2733-2736 (4)			4.30	1.80

Formosan Firecrest
A632

$3, Laughing thrush. $7.50, White-eared sibia. $16, Yellow tit.

1990, Aug. 20 Litho. *Perf. 13½*

2737	A632	$2	shown	.40	.25
2738	A632	$3	multicolored	.40	.25
2739	A632	$7.50	multicolored	1.00	.25
2740	A632	$16	multicolored	2.25	.60
	Nos. 2737-2740 (4)			4.05	1.35

Sports — A633

1990, Sept. 8 Litho. *Perf. 13½*

2741	A633	$2	Sprint	.30	.25
2742	A633	$3	Long jump	.30	.25
2743	A633	$7	Pole vault	1.10	.30
2744	A633	$16	High hurdle	1.50	.60
	Nos. 2741-2744 (4)			3.20	1.40

Flying Tigers, 50th Anniv.
A634

1990, Sept. 26 Litho. *Perf. 13½*

2745	A634	$3	multicolored	1.25	.25

Children's Drawings
A635

1990, Oct. 9

2746	A635	$2	Cat	.30	.25
2747	A635	$3	Peacocks	.30	.25
2748	A635	$7.50	Chickens	.90	.30
2749	A635	$12	Cattle	1.40	.50
	Nos. 2746-2749 (4)			2.90	1.30

National Theater
A636

Photo. & Engr.

1990, Oct. 30 *Perf. 13½*

2750	A636	$3	shown	.40	.25
2751	A636	$12	Natl. concert hall	1.60	.80

A637

Ancient money.

1990, Nov. 5 Litho. *Perf. 13x13½*

2752	A637	$2	Shell	.40	.25
2753	A637	$3	Oyster	.40	.25
2754	A637	$6.50	Bone	.60	.35
2755	A637	$7.50	Jade	.80	.40
2756	A637	$9	Bronze	.90	.50
	Nos. 2752-2756 (5)			3.10	1.75

A638

1990, Dec. 1 *Perf. 12½*

2757	A638	$2	multicolored	.70	.25
2758	A638	$13	multicolored	2.75	.80
a.	Souv. sheet, 2 ea #2757-2758			9.50	2.50

New Year 1991 (Year of the Sheep).

Hu Shih (1891-1962), Educator — A639

Wmk. 323

1990, Dec. 17 Engr. *Perf. 13½*

2759	A639	$3	purple	.50	.25

Teapots, Natl. Palace Museum
A640

Teapots: $2, Blue phoenix, Ming Dynasty. $3, Dragon handle and spout, Ming Dynasty. $9, Blue landscape, flowered top, Ch'ing Dynasty. $12, Rectangular, passion flower motif, Ch'ing Dynasty. $16, Rectangular, flower motif, Ch'ing Dynasty.

1991, Jan. 18 Photo. *Perf. 12*

Granite Paper

2760	A640	$2	yel, blk & blue	.40	.25
2761	A640	$3	brt yel grn & blk	.60	.40
2762	A640	$9	pink & multi	1.00	.60
2763	A640	$12	violet & multi	1.40	.80
2764	A640	$16	lt blue & multi	1.60	1.20
	Nos. 2760-2764 (5)			5.00	3.25

God of Happiness
A641

God of Joy — A642

1991, Feb. 7 Litho. *Perf. 13½*

2765	A641	$3	shown	.60	.25
2766	A641	$3	God of Wealth	.60	.25
2767	A642	$7.50	shown	1.40	.30
2768	A642	$7.50	God of Longevity	1.40	.30
	Nos. 2765-2768 (4)			4.00	1.10

Perf. 13½ Vert.

2765a	A641	$3	*1.50*	.25
2766a	A641	$3	*1.50*	.25
2767a	A642	$7.50	*1.50*	.25
2768a	A642	$7.50	*1.50*	.25
b.	Bklt. pane of 8, 2 each #2765a-2768a + label		*14.00*	

Native Plants
A643

Designs: $2, Petasites formosanus. $3, Heloniopsis acutifolia. $7.50, Disporum shimadai. $9, Viola nagasawai.

1991, Mar. 12 Litho. *Perf. 13½*

2769	A643	$2	multicolored	.40	.25
2770	A643	$3	multicolored	.50	.25
2771	A643	$7.50	multicolored	.80	.30
2772	A643	$9	multicolored	.90	.35

1991, June 12

Designs: $2, Gaultheria itoana. $3, Lysionotus montanus. $7.50, Leontopodium microphyllum. $9, Gentiana flavo-maculata.

2773	A643	$2	multicolored	.30	.25
2774	A643	$3	multicolored	.50	.25
2775	A643	$7.50	multicolored	1.25	.30
2776	A643	$9	multicolored	1.50	.35

1991, Sept. 12

Designs: $3.50, Rosa transmorrisonensis. $5, Impatiens devolii. $9, Impatiens uniflora. $12, Impatiens tayemonii.

2777	A643	$3.50	multicolored	.50	.25
2778	A643	$5	multicolored	.70	.25
2779	A643	$9	multicolored	1.25	.35
2780	A643	$12	multicolored	1.50	.45

1991, Dec. 12

Designs: $3.50, Kalanchoe garambiensis. $5, Pieris taiwanensis. $9, Pleione formosana. $12, Elaeagnus oldhamii.

2781	A643	$3.50	multicolored	.50	.25
2782	A643	$5	multicolored	.70	.25
2783	A643	$9	multicolored	.90	.60
2784	A643	$12	multicolored	1.25	.70
	Nos. 2769-2784 (16)			13.45	5.40

Hsiung Cheng-Chi (1887-1910), Revolutionary
A644

1991, Mar. 28 Engr. *Perf. 13½x12½*

2785	A644	$3	blue	.50	.25

Republic of China, 80th Anniv.
A645

$3, Agriculture. $7.50, Science & technology. $12, Cultural activities. $16, Transportation.

1991, Mar. 28 Litho. *Perf. 13½*

2786 A645 $3 multicolored .40 .25
2787 A645 $7.50 multicolored .80 .40
2788 A645 $12 multicolored 1.40 .70
2789 A645 $16 multicolored 1.60 .90
Nos. 2786-2789 (4) 4.20 2.25

Children's Toys — A646

1991, Apr. 20 Litho. *Perf. 13½*

2790 A646 $3 Bamboo pony .50 .30
2791 A646 $3 Woven-grass grasshopper .50 .30
2792 A646 $3 Top .50 .30
2793 A646 $3 Pinwheels .50 .30
a. Souv. sheet of 4, #2790-2793 *8.00* 5.00
Nos. 2790-2793 (4) 2.00 1.20

See Nos. 2840-2843. Compare with designs A676, A696.

Perf. 13½ Vert.

2790a A646 $3 *1.25* .30
2791a A646 $3 *1.25* .30
2792a A646 $3 *1.25* .30
2793b A646 $3 *1.25* .30
c. Bklt. pane, 2 each #2790a-2793b + label *10.00*
Nos. 2790a-2793b (4) *5.00* 1.20

Folk Costumes — A647

Ch'ing Dynasty (1644-1911): $2, Winter court hat, Mang robe. $3, Summer court hat, surcoat. $7.50, Winter overcoat. $12, Common hat, traveling robe.

1991, June 29 Litho. *Perf. 13½*

2794 A647 $2 multicolored .50 .25
2795 A647 $3 multicolored .65 .25
2796 A647 $7.50 multicolored 1.60 .30
2797 A647 $12 multicolored 2.25 .45
Nos. 2794-2797 (4) 5.00 1.25

See note after No. 2663.
Nos. 2794-2797 have groups of one and five Chinese characters.

Traffic Safety Year
A648

1991, July 17 Litho. *Perf. 13½*

2798 A648 $3 shown .30 .25
2799 A648 $7.50 Don't drink & drive .90 .35

Cloisonne Enamel Lions, Ch'ing Dynasty (1644-1911)
A649 A649a

1991, July 20 Litho. *Perf. 12½*

2800 A649 yel grn & multi .70 .25
2801 A649a violet & multi 2.75 .75
Nos. 2800-2801 (2) 3.45 1.00

No. 2800 paid basic domestic rate, No. 2801 paid basic express mail rate on date of issue.

Fruits — A650

1991, Aug. 10 Litho. *Perf. 14x13½*

2802 A650 $3 Strawberry .40 .25
2803 A650 $7.50 Grapes .70 .50
2804 A650 $9 Mango .90 .60
2805 A650 $16 Sugar apple 1.50 .90
Nos. 2802-2805 (4) 3.50 2.25

Birds — A651

Designs: a, Myiophoneus insularis. b, Cinclus pallasii. c, Aix galericulata. d, Nycticorax nycticorax. e, Egretta garzetta. f, Rhyacornis fuliginosus. g, Enicurus scouleri. h, Motacilla cinerea. i, Alcedo atthis. j, Motacilla alba.

1991, Aug. 24 *Perf. 13½*

2806 Block of 10 7.00 4.00
a.-j. A651 $5 any single .50 .30

Outdoor Activities
A652

Wmk. 323

1991, Sept. 27 Litho. *Perf. 13½*

2807 A652 $2 Rock climbing .30 .25
2808 A652 $3 Fishing .40 .25
2809 A652 $7.50 Bird watching .85 .35
2810 A652 $10 Playing in water 1.25 .50
Nos. 2807-2810 (4) 2.80 1.35

Intl. Federation of Camping and Caravaning, 1991 Rally.

Lighthouse Type of 1989
Inscription Panel in Blue

1991-92 *Perf. 13½*

2811 A612 50c like #2683C .30 .25
2812 A612 $1 like #2674 .40 .25
2813 A612 $3.50 like #2678 .50 .25
2814 A612 $5 like #2679 .60 .25
a. Booklet pane of 10 7.00
2815 A612 $7 like #2676 .60 .25
2816 A612 $9 like #2681 .90 .35
2817 A612 $10 like #2682 1.10 .40
2818 A612 $12 like #2683A 1.25 .50
a. $12 Bklt. pane of 5 + label 7.00
2819 A612 $13 like #2675 1.25 .50
2820 A612 $19 like #2680 1.90 .80
2821 A612 $20 like #2683B 2.00 .80
2822 A612 $26 like #2683 2.10 1.10
2823 A612 $28 like #2684 2.10 1.10
Nos. 2811-2823 (13) 15.00 6.80

Issued: 50c, $3.50, $5, $12, 10/2; No. 2818a, 9/26/92; $1, $19, $20, 3/2/92; $26, $28, 5/20/92; $7, $9, $10, $13, 8/21/92.

Peacocks by Lan Shih-ning (Giuseppe Castiglione, 1688-1768)
A653

$20, Peacock spreading tail feathers.

Perf. 12x11½

1991, Oct. 30 Photo. Unwmk.

Granite Paper

2826 A653 $5 multicolored .80 .50
2827 A653 $20 multicolored 3.00 1.00
a. Souvenir sheet of 1 6.00 5.00

New Year 1992 (Year of the Monkey) — A654

Wmk. 323

1991, Nov. 30 Litho. *Perf. 12½*

2828 A654 $3.50 orange & multi .40 .25
2829 A654 $13 tan & multi 1.50 .60
a. Souv. sheet, 2 ea #2828-2829 6.00 2.00

Chinese Books
A655

Wmk. 323

1992, Jan. 17 Litho. *Perf. 13½*

2830 A655 $3.50 Scroll .30 .25
2831 A655 $5 Fold bindings .50 .25
2832 A655 $9 Butterfly bindings .90 .35
2833 A655 $15 String bindings 1.50 .65
Nos. 2830-2833 (4) 3.20 1.50

Good Fortune and Satisfaction
A656

Five Blessings Upon the House — A657

Nienhwa paintings: No. 2835, Peace in the Wake of Firecrackers. No. 2837, An Abundance for Every Year.

1992, Jan. 27 Litho. *Perf. 13½*

2834 A656 $5 multicolored .40 .25
2835 A656 $5 multicolored .40 .25
2836 A657 $12 multicolored 1.10 .60
2837 A657 $12 multicolored 1.10 .60
a. Bklt. pane, 2 each #2834-2837 + label *10.00*
Nos. 2834-2837 (4) 3.00 1.70

Lunar New Year.

A658

Lunar New Year: a, like #2664. b, like #2611. c, like #2565. d, like #2493. e, like #2442. f, like #2390. g, like #2346. h, like #2273. i, like #2217. j, like #2828. k, like #2757. l, like #2706.

Wmk. 323

1992, Feb. 18 Litho. *Perf. 12½*

2838 A658 $5 Block of 12, #a.-l., ver & multi 6.50 3.00
m. Sheet of 12, #2838a-2838 l 6.75 3.25

A659

Trees: a, Chamaecyparis formosensis. b, Chamaecyparis taiwanensis. c, Calocedrus formosana. d, Cunninghamia konishii. e. Taiwania crypto- merioides.

1992, Mar. 12 *Perf. 13½*

2839 A659 $5 Strip of 5, #a.-e. 3.50 1.50

Children's Toys Type of 1991

1992, Apr. 29 Litho. *Perf. 13½*

2840 A646 $5 Walking on iron pots .70 .25
a. Perf. 13½ vert. .70 .25
2841 A646 $5 Chopstick gun .70 .25
a. Perf. 13½ vert. .70 .25
2842 A646 $5 Hoop rolling .70 .25
a. Perf. 13½ vert. .70 .25
2843 A646 $5 Grass fighting .70 .25
a. Sheet of 4, #2840-2843 *5.75* *5.75*
b. As "a," imperf. (simulated perfs), red inscription in sheet margin *11.50* *11.50*
c. Perf. 13½ vert. .70 .25
d. Bklt. pane, 2 each #2840a-2842a, 2843c + label 5.75
Nos. 2840-2843 (4) 2.80 1.00

Issue date: No. 2843b, May 15.

A660

Mother and son in: $3.50, Spring. $5, Summer. $9, Autumn. $10, Winter.

Wmk. 323

1992, May 9 Litho. *Perf. 13½*

2844 A660 $3.50 multicolored .35 .25
2845 A660 $5 multicolored .70 .25
2846 A660 $9 multicolored 1.25 .40
2847 A660 $10 multicolored 1.40 .45
Nos. 2844-2847 (4) 3.70 1.35

Parent-child relationships.

A661

Glassware Decorated with Enamel — Vases: $3.50, Faceted, decorated with bats and longevity characters. $5, Double-lobed, with children at play. $7, Flowered. $17, Tutoring scene.

Wmk. 323

1992, June 25 Litho. *Perf. 13½*

Background colors

2848 A661 $3.50 pink .30 .25
2849 A661 $5 green .45 .25
2850 A661 $7 bister .70 .30
2851 A661 $17 blue 2.00 .70
Nos. 2848-2851 (4) 3.45 1.50

Stone Lion of Lugouqiao A662

Various stone lions.

Wmk. 323

1992, July 7 Engr. *Perf. 13½*

2852 A662 $5 olive grn & pur .60 .25
2853 A662 $5 blue & brown .60 .25
2854 A662 $12 org & olive grn 1.40 .50
2855 A662 $12 purple & black 1.40 .50
Nos. 2852-2855 (4) 4.00 1.50

Compare with designs A614, A629, A663.

Ku Shih Classical Poetry — A663

Excerpts: $3.50, "Flesh and body are as closely linked as leaves to a tree." $5, "Once a man and woman get married, conjugal love will last forever without doubt." $9, "Man takes pains to uphold virtue." $15, "Tartar horses lean toward the northern wind."

1992, Aug. 8 Litho.

2856 A663 $3.50 Children playing near tree .30 .25
2857 A663 $5 Man & woman .70 .25
2858 A663 $9 Couple near stream 1.25 .35
2859 A663 $15 Horse, tree 1.75 .60
Nos. 2856-2859 (4) 4.00 1.45

Life in the Countryside A664

Scenes of temple fair: a, Two women, man beating drum, crowd. b, Vendor with basket. c, People playing musical instruments. d, Man with food cart. e, Women with umbrella, basket.

Wmk. 323

1992, Sept. 22 Litho. *Perf. 11½*

2860 A664 $5 Strip of 5, #a.-e. 5.00 3.50

Silk Tapestries A665

Ming Dynasty Silk Tapestry Drawing on Life: $5, Two Birds Perched on a Red Camellia Branch. $12, Two Birds Playing on a Peach Branch.

1992, Oct. 9 Litho. *Perf. 11½*

Granite Paper

2861 A665 $5 multicolored .70 .25
2862 A665 $12 multicolored 1.90 .60
a. Sheet of 2, #2861-2862 3.00 1.00

Chinese Opera A666

Actors, props: $3.50, Nin Hsiang-ju's carting to a party from "The General and Premier." $5, Hsao En rowing a boat from "The Lucky Pearl." $9, Wang Chao-chun making peace with the frontier from "Chao-chun Serves as an Envoy." $12, Scene with red sedan chair from "Escort to the Wedding."

Wmk. 323

1992, Oct. 21 Litho. *Perf. 13½*

2863 A666 $3.50 multicolored .30 .25
2864 A666 $5 multicolored .65 .25
2865 A666 $9 multicolored 1.05 .40
2866 A666 $12 multicolored 1.00 .55
Nos. 2863-2866 (4) 3.00 1.45

Alishan Forest Railway — A667

1992, Nov. 5 *Perf. 11½*

2867 A667 $5 Steam engine .70 .25
2868 A667 $15 Diesel engine 1.50 .65

Endangered Mammals of Taiwan A668

Designs: a, Lutra lutra chinensis. b, Pteropus dasymallus formosus. c, Neofelis nebulosa brachyurus. d, Selenarctos thibetanus formosanus.

Perf. 11½x12

1992, Nov. 25 Photo. Unwmk.

Granite Paper

2869 A668 $5 Block of 4, #a.-d. 3.50 1.50

New Year 1993 (Year of the Rooster) — A669

Design: $13, Rooster facing left.

Wmk. 323

1992, Dec. 1 Litho. *Perf. 12½*

2870 A669 $3.50 red & multi .50 .25
a. Perf. 13½ vert. .50 .25
2871 A669 $13 pur & multi 1.25 .45
a. Souv. sheet, 2 ea #2870-2871 4.00 4.00
b. As "a" with added inscription in border 4.00 4.00
c. Bklt. pane, 5 ea #2870-2871 9.25
d. Perf. 13½ vert. 1.25 .50
e. Booklet pane, 6 each #2870a, 2871d + label 10.75

Inscription on No. 2871b reads "Philippine Stamp Exhibition 1992-Taipei" in English and Chinese.

Johann Adam Schall von Bell (1592-1666), Astronomer and Missionary — A670

1992 Dec. 10 *Perf. 11½*

2872 A670 $5 multicolored 1.00 .25

Traditional Nienhwas of Window Frames — A671

Wmk. 323

1993, Jan. 7 Litho. *Perf. 11½*

Background Color

2873 A671 $5 brt green .25 .25
2874 A671 $5 red lilac .25 .25
2875 A671 $12 yellow .65 .40
2876 A671 $12 red .65 .40
Nos. 2873-2876 (4) 1.80 1.30

Lunar New Year.

Perf. 13½ Vert.

2873a A671 $5 *1.00* .45
2874a A671 $5 *1.00* .45
2875a A671 $12 *1.00* .45
2876a A671 $12 *1.00* .45
b. Booklet pane, 2 each #2873a-2876a + label *9.00*

Nos. 2873a-2876a are 29x43mm.

Traditional Crafts A672

1993, Jan. 16

2877 A672 $3.50 Clip & paste moldings .30 .25
2878 A672 $5 Lanterns .40 .25
2879 A672 $9 Pottery jars .80 .40
2880 A672 $15 Oil paper umbrella 1.25 .65
Nos. 2877-2880 (4) 2.75 1.55

Chinese Creation Story — A673

Designs: $3.50, Pan Gu's creation of the universe, vert. $5, Pan Gu transmitted himself into all creatures. $9, Nu Wa created human beings with pestled earth. $19, Nu Wa mended sky with smelted stone, vert.

1993, Feb. 6 *Perf. 12x11½, 11½x12*

2881 A673 $3.50 multicolored .30 .25
2882 A673 $5 multicolored .50 .25
2883 A673 $9 multicolored .90 .65
2884 A673 $19 multicolored 1.75 1.40
Nos. 2881-2884 (4) 3.45 2.55

Lucky Animals — A674

Wmk. 323

1993, Mar. 2 Litho. *Perf. 13½*

2885 A674 $3.50 Mandarin duck .30 .25
2886 A674 $5 Chinese unicorn .45 .25
2887 A674 $10 Deer .90 .50
2888 A674 $15 Crane 1.40 1.25
Nos. 2885-2888 (4) 3.05 2.25

See Nos. 2920-2923.

Water Plants — A675

$5, Nymphaea x hybrida. $9, Nuphar shimadai. $12, Eichhornia crassipes.

1993, Mar. 12 *Perf. 11½*

2889 A675 $5 multicolored .60 .25
2890 A675 $9 multicolored 1.00 .40
2891 A675 $12 multicolored 1.25 .50
Nos. 2889-2891 (3) 2.85 1.15

A676

No. 2892, Sandbag tossing. No. 2893, Bamboo dragonfly twisting. No. 2894, Rubber band skipping. No. 2895, Waist-strength dueling.

1993 Litho. Wmk. 323 *Perf. 11½*

2892 A676 $5 multicolored .50 .30
2893 A676 $5 multicolored .50 .30
2894 A676 $5 multicolored .50 .30
2895 A676 $5 multicolored .50 .30
a. Souv. sheet, #2892-2895 3.25 3.25
b. As "a," with green & black inscriptions in border 3.25 3.25
c. As "a," with red inscription in border 3.25 3.25
Nos. 2892-2895 (4) 2.00 1.20

Inscriptions on No. 2895b read "AUSTRALIAN STAMP EXHIBITION 1993-TAIPEI" in Chinese and English.

Inscription on No. 2895c reads "Chinese Stamp Exhibition-Thailand" in Chinese.

Nos. 2895b-2895c each have perforations extending into the margin at top (No. 2895c) or bottom (No. 2895b).

Issue dates: Nos. 2892-2895, 2895a, Apr. 20; No. 2895b, Apr. 23; No. 2895c, Apr. 30.

Perf. 13½ Vert.

2892a	A676	$5	*1.00*	.30
2893a	A676	$5	*1.00*	.30
2894a	A676	$5	*1.00*	.30
2895d	A676	$5	*1.00*	.30
e.	Bklt. pane, 2 each #2892a-2894a, 2895d + label		*8.50*	

A677

Yangtze River A678

Designs: No. 2896, Source on Ching-Kang-Chang Plateau. No. 2897, Abrupt bend, Chinsha River. No. 2898, Narrow waterway, Roaring Tiger Gorge, Chinsha River. No. 2899, Sheer cliffs, Chuntang Gorge. $9, Three Small Gorges (Dragon Gate, Pawu, and Titsui).

Perf. 13x13½

1993, May 15 Litho. Wmk. 323

2896	A677	$3.50	shown	.30	.25
2897	A677	$3.50	multicolored	.30	.25
2898	A678	$5	shown	.55	.25
2899	A677	$5	multicolored	.55	.25
2900	A677	$9	multicolored	1.05	.40
	Nos. 2896-2900 (5)			2.75	1.40

Environmental Protection
A679 A680

Children's paintings: $5, No More Noise Pollution, by Yen Chao-min. $17, Clothing My Hometown with Green, by Hu Hui-chun.

Perf. 12½x13½, 13½x12½

1993, June 5

2901	A679	$5	multicolored	.50	.30
2902	A680	$17	multicolored	1.50	1.25

Ch'eng-hua Porcelain, Natl. Palace Museum A681

Cups decorated in tou-ts'ai: $3.50, Human figures. $5, Chickens. $7, Flowers and fruits. $9, Dragon.

1993, June 30 *Perf. 12*

2903	A681	$3.50	multicolored	.30	.25
2904	A681	$5	multicolored	.55	.30
2905	A681	$7	multicolored	.75	.50
2906	A681	$9	multicolored	.90	.80
	Nos. 2903-2906 (4)			2.50	1.85

Vocational Training A682

$3.50, Graphic artist. $5, Computer operator. $9, Carpenter. $12, Welder.

Wmk. 323

1993, July 24 Litho. *Perf. 12½*

2907	A682	$3.50	multicolored	.30	.25
2908	A682	$5	multicolored	.40	.30
2909	A682	$9	multicolored	.75	.60
2910	A682	$12	multicolored	1.05	.90
	Nos. 2907-2910 (4)			2.50	2.05

Parent-Child Relationship A683

Silhouettes: $3.50, Adult carrying child on shoulders. $5, Father playing flute for daughter. $9, Father teaching daughter. $10, Father, adult son enjoying wildlife.

Wmk. 323

1993, Aug. 4 Litho. *Perf. 11½*

Background Color

2911	A683	$3.50	tan	.30	.25
2912	A683	$5	green	.45	.30
2913	A683	$9	lilac	.95	.70
2914	A683	$10	red brown	1.10	.80
	Nos. 2911-2914 (4)			2.80	2.05

Souvenir Sheet

Taipei '93, Asian Intl. Philatelic Exhibition — A684

Enjoying Antiques, by Tu Chin, 15th cent: a, Man carrying stick. b, Man selecting antiques from table. c, Man seated in chair. d, Two people at table.

Perf. 12x11½

1993, Aug. 14 Photo. Unwmk.

Granite Paper

2915	A684	$5	Sheet of 4, #a.-d.	3.75	3.00

Persimmon A685 Loquat A686

1993, Sept. 10 Litho. *Perf. 12½*

2916	A685	$5	shown	.50	.30
2917	A685	$5	Peach	.50	.30
2918	A686	$12	shown	1.25	.90
2919	A686	$12	Papaya	1.25	.90
	Nos. 2916-2919 (4)			3.50	2.40

Lucky Animals Type of 1993

Wmk. 323

1993, Sept. 29 Litho. *Perf. 13½*

2920	A674	$1	Blue dragon	.30	.30
2921	A674	$2.50	White tiger	.30	.30
2922	A674	$9	Linnet	.85	.50
2923	A674	$19	Black tortoise	1.75	1.10
	Nos. 2920-2923 (4)			3.20	2.20

Taiwan Area Games, Taoyuan — A687

Designs: a, Taekwondo. b, Pommel horse.

Wmk. 323

1993, Oct. 20 Litho. *Perf. 12½*

2924	A687	$5	Pair, #a.-b.	1.25	.80

Stone Lions — A688

Stone lions from: $3.50, Taipei New Park. $5, Hsinchu City Council. $9, Hsinchu City God Temple. $12, Fort Providentia, Tainan.

1993, Oct. 30

2925	A688	$3.50	multicolored	.30	.30
2926	A688	$5	multicolored	.45	.30
2927	A688	$9	multicolored	.90	.55
2928	A688	$12	multicolored	1.25	.75
	Nos. 2925-2928 (4)			2.90	1.90

Syrmaticus Mikado A689

Designs: a, Hatchling. b, Mother with chicks. c, Immature female, male. d, Adult female, male (profile, showing plumage).

Perf. 11½

1993, Nov. 17 Photo. Unwmk.

Granite Paper

2929	A689	$5	Strip of 4, #a.-d.	2.75	2.00

New Year 1994 (Year of the Dog) — A690

Design: $13, Dog facing left.

Wmk. 323

1993, Dec. 1 Litho. *Perf. 12½*

2930	A690	$3.50	red & multi	.30	.30
a.	Perf. 13½ vert.			.30	.30
b.	As "a," bklt. pane of 12 + label			3.75	
2931	A690	$13	green & multi	1.40	.70
a.	Souv. sheet, 2 ea #2930-2931			3.75	2.00
b.	As "a," overprinted in red			3.75	2.00

No. 2931b is inscribed in Chinese for Kaohsiung Kuo-kuang Stamp Exhibition-1993, and has additional perforations extending into top and bottom margins.

Asian Vegetable Research and Development Center, 20th Anniv. — A691

1993, Dec. 7

2932	A691	$5	shown	.40	.30
2933	A691	$13	Researchers in field	1.40	.90

Formation of Constitutional Court — A692

Wmk. 323

1994, Jan. 11 Litho. *Perf. 12½*

2934	A692	$5	multicolored	.50	.30

Paper Making — A693

Designs: No. 2935, Cutting bamboo. No. 2936, Cooking bamboo. No. 2937, Pouring syrup into wooden panel. No. 2938, Stacking panel. No. 2939, Drying paper.

1994, Jan. 24 *Perf. 12x12½*

2935	A693	$3.50	multicolored	.30	.25
2936	A693	$3.50	multicolored	.30	.25
2937	A693	$5	multicolored	.60	.25
2938	A693	$5	multicolored	.60	.25
2939	A693	$12	multicolored	1.25	.80
	Nos. 2935-2939 (5)			3.05	1.80

See Nos. 2993-2997, 3071-3075, 3098-3102, 3174-3177.

Flowers — A694

$5, Olivia miniata. $12, Cymbidium sinense. $19, Primula malacoides.

1994, Feb. 17 *Perf. 12½*

2940	A694	$5	multicolored	.40	.30
2941	A694	$12	multicolored	1.25	.80
2942	A694	$19	multicolored	1.90	1.40
	Nos. 2940-2942 (3)			3.55	2.50

Kinmen Wind Lion Lords — A695

Various Wind Lion Lords.

1994, Mar. 18 Litho. *Perf. 12½*

2943	A695	$5	green & multi	.50	.30
2944	A695	$9	yellow & multi	.80	.50
2945	A695	$12	org yel & multi	1.25	.70
2946	A695	$17	blue & multi	1.50	1.00
	Nos. 2943-2946 (4)			4.05	2.50

Children at Play — A696

No. 2947, Playing with paper boat. No. 2948, Fighting with water gun. No. 2949, Throwing paper airplane. No. 2950, Playing "train" with rope.

Wmk. 323

1994, Apr. 2 Litho. *Perf. 12½*

2947	A696	$5	multicolored	.50	.30
2948	A696	$5	multicolored	.50	.30
2949	A696	$5	multicolored	.50	.30
2950	A696	$5	multicolored	.50	.30
a.	Souv. sheet, #2947-2950			2.75	1.50
	Nos. 2947-2950 (4)			2.00	1.20

Perf. 13½ Vert.

2947a	A696	$5	.50	.30
2948a	A696	$5	.50	.30
2949a	A696	$5	.50	.30
2950b	A696	$5	.50	.30
c.	Bklt. pane, 2 ea #2947a-2949a, 2950b + label		4.50	1.50
	Nos. 2947a-2950b (4)		2.00	1.20

A697

Life in the countryside: $5, Playing chess. $10, Playing musical instruments. $12, Telling stories. $19, Drinking tea.

Wmk. 323

1994, Apr. 25 Litho. *Perf. 12½*

2951	A697	$5 multicolored		.40	.30
2952	A697	$10 multicolored		1.00	.60
2953	A697	$12 multicolored		1.25	.85
2954	A697	$19 multicolored		1.90	1.25
		Nos. 2951-2954 (4)		4.55	3.00

A698

Mother, baby birds: $5, Malay bittern. $7, Little tern, horiz. $10, Common noddy, horiz. $12, Muller's barbet.

1994, May 7

2955	A698	$5 multicolored	.40	.35
2956	A698	$7 multicolored	.70	.40
2957	A698	$10 multicolored	1.10	.70
2958	A698	$12 multicolored	1.25	.75
		Nos. 2955-2958 (4)	3.45	2.20

A699

Protection of Intellectual Property Rights: $5, Palm-shaped book. $15, Human head, computer disk.

Wmk. 323

1994, May 28 Litho. *Perf. 12½*

2959	A699	$5 multicolored	.60	.30
2960	A699	$15 multicolored	1.60	.90

A700

Designs: $5, Care for Lost Children. $17, Care for the aged.

1994, June 11

2961	A700	$5 multicolored	.30	.25
2962	A700	$17 multicolored	1.10	.75

Intl. Olympic Committee, Cent. — A701

1994, June 23

2963	A701	$5 shown	.50	.30
2964	A701	$15 Sporting events	1.50	.90

A702

Shei-pa Natl. Park: $5, Tapachienshan. $7, Shei-san Landslide Scar. $10, Holy Ridge. $17, Shiah-tsuei Lake.

Wmk. 323

1994, July 1 Litho. *Perf. 12½*

2965	A702	$5 multicolored	.55	.30
2966	A702	$7 multicolored	.70	.45
2967	A702	$10 multicolored	1.10	.60
2968	A702	$17 multicolored	1.75	1.10
		Nos. 2965-2968 (4)	4.10	2.45

A703

$5, Portrait of Chien Mu (b. 1895), educator.

1994, July 30 *Perf. 11½x12*

2969	A703	$5 multicolored	.50	.30

Intl. Year of the Family A704

$5, Rainbow, window. $15, Globe, house.

1994, Aug. 25 *Perf. 11½*

2970	A704	$5 multicolored	.50	.30
2971	A704	$15 yel & multi	1.50	.90

Invention Myths — A705

Designs: $5, Sueirenjy digging wood to obtain fire. $10, Fushijy drawing Pa-Kua. $12, Shennungjy making agricultural tools. $15, Tsang-jier creating written characters.

1994, Sept. 17 Photo. *Perf. 11½*

Granite Paper

2972	A705	$5 multicolored	.50	.30
2973	A705	$10 multicolored	1.05	.65
2974	A705	$12 multicolored	1.25	.90
2975	A705	$15 multicolored	1.60	1.05
		Nos. 2972-2975 (4)	4.40	2.90

A706

Design: $5, Dr. Lin Yutang, linguist, writer, 100th birthday.

Wmk. 323

1994, Oct. 8 Litho. *Perf. 12½*

2976	A706	$5 multicolored	.50	.30

A707

$5, Cheng Ho's ship. $17, Chart, ship, Cheng Ho.

1994, Oct. 17

2977	A707	$5 multicolored	.50	.30
2978	A707	$17 multicolored	1.50	.90

World Trade Week.

Sun Yat-sen, Founding of Kuomintang, Cent. — A708

Design: $19, Democratic elections, factories, economic development.

Wmk. 323

1994, Nov. 24 Litho. *Perf. 12½*

2979	A708	$5 multicolored	.50	.30
2980	A708	$19 multicolored	1.75	1.10

A709

1994, Nov. 29

2981	A709	$3.50 Facing right	.40	.30
a.		Perf. 13½ vert.	.40	.30
b.		As "a," booklet pane of 6	2.50	
		Complete booklet, 2 #2981b + label	5.00	
2982	A709	$13 Facing left	1.40	.90
a.		Souv. sheet, 2 ea #2981-2982	3.50	2.40

New Year 1995 (Year of the Boar).

A710

$5, Portrait. $15, Greeting farm family.

1994, Dec. 24 Litho. *Perf. 12½*

2983	A710	$5 multicolored	.50	.30
2984	A710	$15 multicolored	1.50	.90

Pres. Yen Chia-kan, 1st death anniv.

Horse's Back Roofline A711

Swallow's Tail Roofline — A711a

Talisman (Stove & Bowl) Roofline — A711b

Cylinder-Shaped Brick Roofline — A711c

Traditional Architecture: Roof lines.

Perf. 12½x12

1995, Jan. 10 Litho. Wmk. 323

2985	A711	$5 multicolored	.45	.30
2986	A711a	$5 multicolored	.45	.30
2987	A711b	$12 multicolored	1.25	.75
2988	A711c	$19 multicolored	1.90	1.25
		Nos. 2985-2988 (4)	4.05	2.60

See Nos. 3079-3082, 3113-3116, 3187-3190, 3235-3238.

Ancient Chinese Engravings — A712

Various floral designs.

1995, Jan. 24 *Perf. 13½*

Denomination in Black

2989	A712	$3.50 multicolored	.30	.25
2990	A712	$5 multicolored	.60	.30
2991	A712	$19 multicolored	1.75	1.25
2992	A712	$26 multicolored	2.75	1.75
		Nos. 2989-2992 (4)	5.40	3.55

See Nos. 3018-3021, 3044-3047, 3076-3078, 3178-3181, 3221-3226, 3254-3256, 3299-3300.

Ancient Skills Type of 1994

Methods of irrigation: No. 2993, Water wheel. No. 2994, Gear-driven bucket lift. $5, Pedal-powered hoist. $12, Hand-cranked hoist. $13, Using pole with counter-weight to raise bucket.

Perf. 12x11½

1994, Feb. 14 Litho. Wmk. 323

2993	A693	$3.50 multicolored	.30	.25
2994	A693	$3.50 multicolored	.30	.25
2995	A693	$5 multicolored	.50	.30
2996	A693	$12 multicolored	1.25	.85
2997	A693	$13 multicolored	1.40	.95
		Nos. 2993-2997 (5)	3.75	2.60

Beauties on an Outing, by Lee Gong-lin — A713

a, Two riders. b, Rider on black horse, woman with child on horse. c, Three riders. d, One rider.

Unwmk.

1995, Mar. 3 Photo. *Perf. 12*

Granite Paper

2998	A713	$9 Strip of 4, #a.-d.	4.00	2.50
e.		Souv. sheet, #2998b-2998c	2.00	1.25

No. 2998 is a continuous design.

Natl. Health Insurance Plan — A714

Perf. 11½x12½

1995, Mar. 1 Litho. Wmk. 323

2999	A714	$12 multicolored	1.25	.80

Flowers — A715

$5, Lilium speciosum. $12, Haemanthus multiflorus. $19, Hyacinthus orientalis.

1995, Mar. 20 Litho. *Perf. 12½*

3000	A715	$5 multicolored		.40	.30
3001	A715	$12 multicolored		.90	.75
3002	A715	$19 multicolored		1.90	1.25
		Nos. 3000-3002 (3)		3.20	2.30

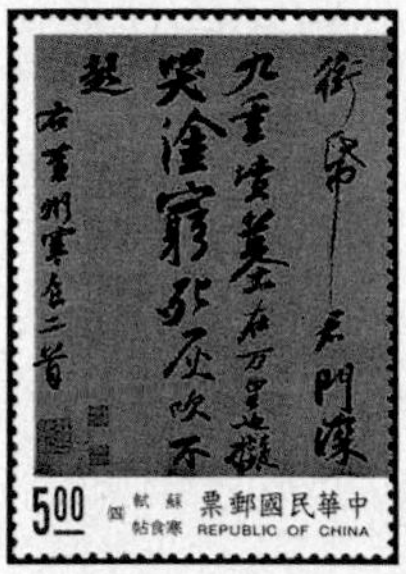

Chinese Calligraphy A716

Cold Food Observance, poem by Su Shih, red inscriptions at: a, Lower left. b, Middle. c, Upper right. d, Right half of design.

1995, Apr. 6 *Perf. 13½*

3003	Strip of 4	4.00	2.50
a.-d.	A716 $5 any single	.50	.30

Paintings by Tsou I Kuei's — A717

1995, May 5 Photo. *Die Cut*

Self-Adhesive

3004	A717	$5 Red peony	.60	.25
3005	A717	$5 Pink peony	.60	.25
a.		Bklt. pane, 9 ea #3004-3005	10.75	

By its nature, No. 3005a is a complete booklet. The peelable backing serves as a booklet cover.

Campaign Against Illegal Drugs — A718

Wmk. 323

1995, June 1 Litho. *Perf. 12½*

3006	A718	$5 shown	.50	.30
3007	A718	$15 Arm, hypodermic needle	1.25	.90

Natl. Taiwan University Hospital, Cent. — A719

Designs: $5, Medical treatment, old hospital. $19, Medical research, new hospital.

1995, June 20

3008	A719	$5 multicolored	.70	.30
3009	A719	$19 multicolored	1.75	1.25

East Coast Scenes A720

Designs: No. 3010, Green hills above Chichi Bay. No. 3011, Rocky promontory, Shihyuesan. $12, Hsiaoyehlieu. $15, Changhong Bridge.

Wmk. 323

1995, July 1 Litho. *Perf. 12½*

3010	A720	$5 multicolored	.50	.30
3011	A720	$5 multicolored	.50	.30
3012	A720	$12 multicolored	1.25	.80
3013	A720	$15 multicolored	1.75	1.10
		Nos. 3010-3013 (4)	4.00	2.50

Oncorhynchus Masou Formosanus A721

Designs: $5, Mating. $7, Female digging a spot to lay eggs. $10, Hatching of fry. $17, Fry swimming in river.

Perf. 14x14½

1995, July 27 Litho. Unwmk.

3014	A721	$5 multicolored	.50	.30
3015	A721	$7 multicolored	.75	.50
3016	A721	$10 multicolored	.95	.75
3017	A721	$17 multicolored	1.75	1.25
		Nos. 3014-3017 (4)	3.95	2.80

Ancient Chinese Engraving Type

Various pictures of birds on tree branches.

Wmk. 323

1995, Aug. 18 Litho. *Perf. 13½*

Denomination in Black

3018	A712	$2.50 multicolored	.35	.35
3019	A712	$7 multicolored	.80	.45
3020	A712	$13 multicolored	1.40	1.00
3021	A712	$28 multicolored	3.50	2.00
		Nos. 3018-3021 (4)	6.05	3.80

Marine Life — A722

No. 3022, Tubastraea aurea. No. 3023, Chromodoris elizabethina. $5, Spirobranchus gigateus. $17, Himerometra magnipinna.

Wmk. 323

1995, Sept. 7 Litho. *Perf. 12½*

3022	A722	$3.50 multicolored	.35	.30
3023	A722	$3.50 multicolored	.35	.30
3024	A722	$5 multicolored	.65	.40
3025	A722	$17 multicolored	1.90	1.00
		Nos. 3022-3025 (4)	3.25	2.00

Louis Pasteur (1822-95) — A723

1995, Sept. 20

3026	A723	$17 multicolored	2.00	1.00

Natl. Palace Museum, 70th Anniv. A724

Designs: No. 3027, Painting, "Strange Peaks and Myriad Trees." No. 3028, Greenish blue porcelain vase, vert. $5, Bronze X Fu-K'uei Ting vessel, vert. $26, Calligraphy of quatrain in seven-character verse, "The Fragrance of Flowers."

Perf. 12x11½, 11½x12

1995, Oct. 9 Photo. Unwmk.

3027	A724	$3.50 multicolored	.30	.25
3028	A724	$3.50 multicolored	.30	.25
3029	A724	$5 multicolored	.50	.25
3030	A724	$26 multicolored	2.40	1.50
		Nos. 3027-3030 (4)	3.50	2.25

A725

End of World War II, 50th Anniv.: $5, Chinese soldiers in battle. $19, Flag, outline map of Taiwan, presidential mansion.

Perf. 11½x12

1995, Oct. 24 Litho. Wmk. 323

3031	A725	$5 multicolored	.60	.25
3032	A725	$19 multicolored	1.90	.65
a.		Souvenir sheet, #3031-3032	2.50	.90

A726

Sea Turtles: No. 3033, Chelonia mydas. No. 3034, Caretta caretta. No. 3035, Lepidochelys olivacea. No. 3036, Eretmochelys imbricata.

Wmk. 323

1995, Nov. 10 Litho. *Perf. 12½*

3033	A726	$5 multicolored	.70	.25
3034	A726	$5 multicolored	.70	.25
3035	A726	$5 multicolored	.70	.25
3036	A726	$5 multicolored	.70	.25
		Nos. 3033-3036 (4)	2.80	1.00

Taiwan Agricultural Research Institute, Cent. — A727

Perf. 12x11½

1995, Nov. 22 Litho. Wmk. 323

3037	A727	$5 In rice field	.75	.25
3038	A727	$28 In anthurium field	2.50	.90

New Year 1996 (Year of the Rat) — A728

Designs: $3.50, $13, Different stylized rats.

Wmk. 323

1995, Dec. 1 Litho. *Perf. 12½*

3039	A728	$3.50 pink & multi	.30	.25
a.		Perf. 13½ vert.	.30	.25
b.		As "a," booklet pane of 6	1.60	
		Complete booklet, 2 #3039b + gutter	3.25	
3040	A728	$13 olive & multi	.90	.45
a.		Souv. sheet, 2 ea #3039-3040	3.75	1.10

Traditional Wedding Ceremony A729

Designs: $5, Escorting bride. $12, Kowtowing Heaven, Earth, and ancestors. $19, Seated in bridal chamber.

1996, Jan. 10

3041	A729	$5 multicolored	.40	.25
3042	A729	$12 multicolored	1.25	.50
3043	A729	$19 multicolored	2.25	.75
		Nos. 3041-3043 (3)	3.90	1.50

Ancient Chinese Engraving Type

Various pictures of fruit.

Wmk. 323

1996, Jan. 25 Litho. *Perf. 13½*

Denomination in Black

3044	A712	$9 multicolored	.90	.40
3045	A712	$12 multicolored	1.25	.65
3046	A712	$15 multicolored	1.50	.75
3047	A712	$17 multicolored	1.75	.85
		Nos. 3044-3047 (4)	5.40	2.65

Scenic Dwelling at Chü-Ch'ü, by Wang Meng, Yüan Dynasty — A730

Denominations: a, UL. b, UR. c, LL. d, LR.

Perf. 12½x12

1996, Feb. 15 Litho. Unwmk.

3048	A730	Block of 4, #a.-d.	4.00	3.00
a.-d.		$5 any single	.85	.75

A731

Flowers: $5, Bougainvillea spectabilis. $12, Wisteria sinensis. $19, Merremia tuberosa.

1996, Mar. 8 Unwmk. *Perf. 12½*

3049	A731	$5 multicolored	.50	.25
3050	A731	$12 multicolored	1.25	.60

Wmk. 323

3051	A731	$19 multicolored	1.75	.90
		Nos. 3049-3051 (3)	3.50	1.75

A732

Chinese Postal Service, Cent.: $5, Mailboxes. $9, Instruments of measurement. $12, Methods of mail transport. $13, Computers, plastic card.

Wmk. 323

1996, Mar. 20 Litho. *Perf. 13½*

3052	A732	$5 multicolored	.55	.25
3053	A732	$9 multicolored	.90	.50
3054	A732	$12 multicolored	1.05	.60
3055	A732	$13 multicolored	1.25	.70
a.		Souvenir sheet, #3052-3055	3.75	1.90
		Nos. 3052-3055 (4)	3.75	2.05

Natl. Chiao Tung University, Cent. — A733

Wmk. 323

1996, Apr. 8 Litho. *Perf. 12½*

3056	A733	$19 multicolored	1.75	.90

Penghu Natl. Scenic Areas — A734

No. 3057, Chimei Giant Lion. No. 3058, Chipei Beach. $12, Tungpan Yu. $17, Tingkou Yu.

1996, May 1

3057	A734	$5 multicolored	.40	.25
3058	A734	$5 multicolored	.40	.25
3059	A734	$12 multicolored	1.10	.45
3060	A734	$17 multicolored	1.60	.65
		Nos. 3057-3060 (4)	3.50	1.60

Tzu-Chi Buddhist Compassionate Relief Foundation — A735

$5, Hand holding people. $19, Lotus blossom, sick person.

Wmk. 323

1996, May 11 Litho. *Perf. 13*

3061	A735	$5 multicolored	.50	.30
3062	A735	$19 multicolored	2.75	1.00

First Democratic Presidential Election A736

New Pres., Vice Pres. and: $3.50, Natl. flag. $5, Presidential office building. $13, Development of Asia-Pacific Operations Hub project. $15, Greeting people at fair.

1996, May 20 Wmk. 323 *Perf. 12½*

3063	A736	$3.50 multicolored	.30	.25
3064	A736	$5 multicolored	.55	.25
3065	A736	$13 multicolored	1.25	.50
3066	A736	$15 multicolored	1.40	.55
a.		Souvenir sheet, #3063-3066	3.50	1.40
		Nos. 3063-3066 (4)	3.50	1.55

South China Sea Archipelago A737

Outline map of region, Interior Dept. monuments on: $5, Pratas Isl. $17, Itu Aba Isl.

1996, June 5 Wmk. 323 *Perf. 12½*

3067	A737	$5 multicolored	.50	.25
3068	A737	$17 multicolored	1.75	.65
a.		Souvenir sheet, #3067-3068	1.65	.85

Modern Olympic Games, Cent. — A738

Perf. 12½x12

1996, June 22 Litho. Wmk. 323

3069	A738	$5 Gymnast, cyclist	.60	.25
3070	A738	$15 Early Greek athletes	1.60	.55

Ancient Skills Type of 1994

Manufacturing silk: No. 3071, Feeding silkworms. No. 3072, Picking out cocoons. $7, Reeling raw silk. $10, Degumming raw silk. $13, Weaving silk.

1996, July 5 *Perf. 12*

3071	A693	$5 multicolored	.50	.25
3072	A693	$5 multicolored	.50	.25
3073	A693	$7 multicolored	.60	.30
3074	A693	$10 multicolored	1.00	.60
3075	A693	$13 multicolored	1.40	.70
		Nos. 3071-3075 (5)	4.00	2.10

Ancient Chinese Engraving Type

1996, Aug. 5 *Perf. 13½*

Denomination in Black

3076	A712	$1 Bamboo	.50	.25
3077	A712	$10 Orchid	.90	.60
3078	A712	$20 Plum tree branch	2.00	1.00
		Nos. 3076-3078 (3)	3.40	1.85

A738a

A738b

A738c

Column and Beam Construction — A738d

Perf. 12x11½

1996, Aug. 22 Litho. Wmk. 323

3079	A738a	$5 Tou-kung (lion)	.55	.30
3080	A738b	$5 Chiue-ti	.55	.30
3081	A738c	$10 Bu-tong	1.00	.50
3082	A738d	$19 Dye-tou	1.90	.90
		Nos. 3079-3082 (4)	4.00	2.00

Motion Pictures, Cent. — A739

Chinese movies: No. 3083, Princess Iron Fan, first full-length animated film, 1941. No. 3084, Chin Shan Bi Xie, 1957. $5, Oyster Girl, 1964. $19, City of Sadness, 1989.

1996, Sept. 17 Litho. *Perf. 12½x12*

3083	A739	$3.50 multicolored	.30	.25
3084	A739	$3.50 multicolored	.30	.25
3085	A739	$5 multicolored	.60	.25
3086	A739	$19 multicolored	1.75	.70
		Nos. 3083-3086 (4)	2.95	1.45

Winning Pictures from Children's Stamp Design Contest A740

Denomination triangle color, location: a, Red, LR. b, Red, LL. c, Green, LR. d, Green, LL. e, Pink, LL. f, Red, UR. g, Red, UL. h, Green, UR. i, Green, UL. j, Pink, UL. k, Purple, LR. l, Purple, LL. m, Tan, LR. n, Tan, LL. o, Pink, LR. p, Purple, UR. q, Purple, UL. r, Tan, UR. s, Tan, UL. t, Pink, UR.

Perf. 12½x12

1996, Oct. 9 Litho. Unwmk.

3087	A740	$5 Sheet of 20, #a.-t.	15.00	6.00

A741

Ancient Chinese paintings: $5, Autumn Scene with Wild Geese. $7, Reeds and Wild Geese. $13, Wild Geese Gathering on a Shore of Reeds. $15, Wild Geese on a Bank in Autumn.

1996, Oct. 21 Photo. *Perf. 12*

Granite Paper

3088	A741	$5 multicolored	.55	.25
3089	A741	$7 multicolored	.70	.25
3090	A741	$13 multicolored	1.25	.50
3091	A741	$15 multicolored	1.50	.55
a.		Souv. sheet, #3088-3091	4.50	2.00
		Nos. 3088-3091 (4)	4.00	1.55

10th Asian Intl. Philatelic Exhib., Taipei '96.

A742

Designs: $5, Computerized letters, numbers, bar coding. $26, Globe, graph line.

Perf. 12½x12

1996, Nov. 1 Litho. Wmk. 323

3092	A742	$5 multicolored	.60	.30
3093	A742	$26 multicolored	2.75	1.40

Merchant's Day, 50th Anniv.

A743

Caring for the Handicapped: $5, Woman in wheelchair working at computer. $19, Handicapped child painting picture.

Wmk. 323

1996, Nov. 15 Litho. *Perf. 12½*

3094	A743	$5 multicolored	.70	.30
3095	A743	$19 multicolored	1.75	.90

A744

1996, Dec. 2

3096	A744	$3.50 gray & multi	.40	.25
a.		Perf. 13½ vert.	.40	.25
b.		As "a," booklet pane of 6	2.40	
		Complete booklet, 2 #3096b + gutter	4.80	
3097	A744	$13 blue & multi	1.60	.55
a.		Souv. sheet, 2 ea #3096-3097	4.00	1.50
b.		As "a," overprinted	4.00	1.50

New Year 1997 (Year of the Ox).

No. 3097b overprinted in red lilac in sheet margin with Chinese inscription for Kaohsiung Intl. Stamp Exhibition for Chinese Postal Service cent.

Ancient Skills Type of 1994

Making porcelain: No. 3098, Pounding stone, looking at bottom of bowl. No. 3099, Painting, shaping. $7, Painting. $10, Glazing. $13, Firing.

Perf. 11½x12

1997, Jan. 15 Litho. Wmk. 323

3098	A693	$5 multicolored	.50	.25
3099	A693	$5 multicolored	.50	.25
3100	A693	$7 multicolored	.80	.25
3101	A693	$10 multicolored	1.00	.40
3102	A693	$13 multicolored	1.25	.50
		Nos. 3098-3102 (5)	4.05	1.65

Carp Encircled By Dragons — A745

Perf. 13x12½

1997, Feb. 14 Engr. Wmk. 323

3103	A745	$50 carmine	5.00	2.50
3104	A745	$60 dark blue	6.00	3.00
3105	A745	$70 red orange	7.00	3.50
3106	A745	$100 olive green	10.00	5.00
		Nos. 3103-3106 (4)	28.00	14.00

See Nos. 3131-3132, 3252-3253, 3369-3370, 3426, 3871.

Feb. 28, 1947 Rebellion, 50th Anniv. — A746

Perf. 12x11½

1997, Feb. 28 Litho. Wmk. 323

3107	A746	$19 Memorial	1.75	.90

Woody Plants — A747

$5, Rhododendron x mucronatum. $12, Hibiscus rosa-sinensis. $19, Hydrangea macrophylla.

Wmk. 323

1997, Mar. 12 Litho. *Perf. 12½*

3108	A747	$5 multicolored	.60	.30
3109	A747	$12 multicolored	1.40	.60
3110	A747	$19 multicolored	2.00	.90
		Nos. 3108-3110 (3)	4.00	1.80

Water Resource Protection
A748 A749

1997, Mar. 22 *Perf. 12½*

3111	A748	$5 multicolored	.60	.30
3112	A749	$19 multicolored	2.00	.90

A749a

A749b

A749c

Traditional Architecture — A749d

Perf. 12x12½

1997, Apr. 9 Litho. Wmk. 323

3113 A711 $5 Door .50 .30
3114 A711 $5 Gable wall .50 .30
3115 A711 $10 Carved brick 1.25 .60
3116 A711 $19 Column dragon 1.75 .80
Nos. 3113-3116 (4) 4.00 2.00

Insects — A750

Designs: $5, Dorcus formosanus. $7, Phyllophorina kotoshoensis. $10, Troides magellanus. $17, Megacrania tsudai.

1997, Apr. 25 Photo. *Perf. 11½*
Granite Paper

3117 A750 $5 multicolored .50 .30
3118 A750 $7 multicolored .80 .40
3119 A750 $10 multicolored 1.10 .60
3120 A750 $17 multicolored 1.75 .90
Nos. 3117-3120 (4) 4.15 2.20

Minerals A751

Wmk. 323

1997, May 8 Litho. *Perf. 13*

3121 A751 $5 Aragonite .50 .30
3122 A751 $5 Alunite .50 .30
3123 A751 $12 Enargite 1.25 .60
3124 A751 $19 Hokutolite 1.75 .80
Nos. 3121-3124 (4) 4.00 2.00

Nanyashan Outlook A752

1997, May 31 *Perf. 12½*

3125 A752 $5 shown .55 .25
3126 A752 $5 Pitou coastline .55 .25
3127 A752 $12 Stone pillars, Nanya 1.25 .60
3128 A752 $19 Tsaoling trail 1.25 .60
Nos. 3125-3128 (4) 3.60 1.70

A753

Around-The-Island Railway System: $5, Cliffs at Chingshuei, Northern Loop Line. $28, Southbound train passing through tunnel, Central Mountain area.

Wmk. 323

1997, June 12 Litho. *Perf. 13½*

3129 A753 $5 multicolored .70 .30
3130 A753 $28 multicolored 2.40 .90

Carp Type

1997, July 3 Engr. *Perf. 13*

3131 A745 $300 vio & dark blue 30.00 15.00
3132 A745 $500 dk red & mag 45.00 25.00

Electronic Industry's Use of Integrated Circuits A754

$5, Integrated circuit for computer & telecommunications industry. $26, Wafer linked to portable computer, cellular phone, electronic synthesizer.

1997, July 16 Litho. *Perf. 12½x12*

3133 A754 $5 multicolored .60 .30
3134 A754 $26 multicolored 2.75 1.25

Chinese Martial Arts — A755

Various stances in martial arts.

Wmk. 323

1997, Aug. 8 Litho. *Perf. 13*

3135 A755 $5 shown .50 .30
3136 A755 $5 multi, vert. .50 .30
3137 A755 $9 multicolored .80 .40
3138 A755 $19 multi, vert. 1.75 .80
Nos. 3135-3138 (4) 3.55 1.80

Chinese Classical (Yuan) Opera — A756

Designs: No. 3139, Chang Shen playing musical instrument, Tsuei Ying-ying listening outside, from "Hsi Hsiang Chi." No. 3140, Kuan Gung standing on ferry and holding large knife, enemies in distance, from "Dan Daw Huel." $12, Abduction of Wang Chao-juin on horseback, from "Han Guong Chiou." $15, Emperor Tang Ming Huang envisioning concubine, Makueibo, from "Wu Tong Yu."

1997, Aug. 22

3139 A756 $5 multicolored .50 .30
3140 A756 $5 multicolored .50 .30
3141 A756 $12 multicolored 1.00 .50
3142 A756 $15 multicolored 1.50 .70
Nos. 3139-3142 (4) 3.50 1.80

Sports — A757

1997, Sept. 9 *Perf. 12½*

3143 A757 $5 Badminton .50 .30
3144 A757 $12 Bowling 1.25 .60
3145 A757 $19 Tennis 1.60 .90
Nos. 3143-3145 (3) 3.35 1.80

Ming Dynasty Novel "Journey to the West" — A758

Episodes from novel: No. 3146, "Palm of Buddha," man making inscription while holding pole. No. 3147, "The pilgrimage of T'ang Monk," characters traveling west, one on horse. $5, "The Flaming Mountain," people fighting, fire in background. $20, "The Cobweb Cave," man using pole to fight, spider in cobweb.

1997, Sept. 24 Photo. *Perf. 11½x12*
Granite Paper

3146 A758 $3.50 multicolored .50 .30
3147 A758 $3.50 multicolored .50 .30
3148 A758 $5 multicolored .60 .40
3149 A758 $20 multicolored 1.60 .80
Nos. 3146-3149 (4) 3.20 1.80

Opening of Second Northern Freeway A759

Designs: $5, Bitan Bridge crossing, Shindian River. $19, Hsinchu interchange.

Wmk. 323

1997, Aug. 26 Litho. *Perf. 13*

3150 A759 $5 multicolored .60 .25
3151 A759 $19 multicolored 1.75 .80

Illustrations from Ching Dynasty Bird Manual A760

Various birds.

1997, Oct. 9 Photo. *Perf. 11½*
Granite Paper

3152 A760 $5 Sheet of 20, #a.-t. 12.00 9.50

Compare with Nos. 3268-3269.

New Year 1998 (Year of the Tiger) — A761

Wmk. 323

1997, Dec. 1 Litho. *Perf. 12½*

3153 A761 $3.50 pink & multi .30 .25
a. Perf. 14 vert. .30 .25
b. As "a," booklet pane of 6 1.90
Complete booklet, 2 #3153b + gutter 3.80
3154 A761 $13 yellow & multi 1.00 .45
a. Souv. sheet, 2 ea #3153-3154 2.60 1.10

Pres. Chiang Ching-kuo (1910-88) A762

1998, Jan. 13 Engr. *Perf. 13½*

3155 A762 $5 Portrait, vert. .50 .30

Perf. 11½

3156 A762 $19 shown 1.25 .90

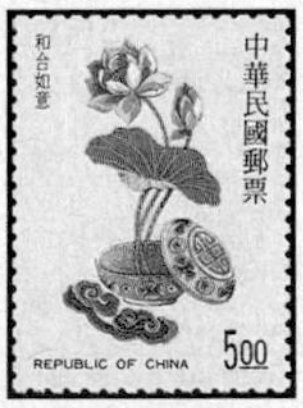

A763

Common Chinese Expressions of Good Fortune, designs: No. 3157, "Happy Occasion of Abundance," fish, vase with pictures of sun and sea. No. 3158, "Harmonious Union as One," flower with two blooms. No. 3159, "Honor and Wealth," flowers growing in pot, vase of flowers. No. 3160, "All is Lucky," bowl of fruit, vase with branch of fruit blossoms.

Perf. 11½x12

1998, Jan. 23 Litho. Wmk. 323
Background Color

3157 A763 $5 pink .50 .25
3158 A763 $5 beige .50 .25
a. Pair, 3157-3158 1.00 .30
3159 A763 $12 light yellow .90 .35
3160 A763 $12 tan .90 .35
a. Pair, #3159-3160 1.80 .70
Nos. 3157-3160 (4) 2.80 1.20

A764

Herbaceous Flowers: $5, Gaillardia pulchella. $12, Kalanchoe blossfeldiana. $19, Portulaca oleracea.

Wmk. 323

1998, Mar. 1 Litho. *Perf. 12½*

3161 A764 $5 multicolored .40 .25
3162 A764 $12 multicolored .80 .50
3163 A764 $19 multicolored 1.75 .80
Nos. 3161-3163 (3) 2.95 1.55

Emperor Shih-tzu, on Hunting Expedition, by Liu Kuan-tao A765

$5, Horseman drawing bow. $19, Emperor Shih-tzu leading hunting party on horseback.

1998, Mar. 20 Photo. *Perf. 12*
Granite Paper

3164 A765 $5 multicolored 1.00 .25

Size: 64x40mm

3165 A765 $19 multicolored 2.00 .60
a. Souvenir sheet, #3164-3165 3.00 1.25

No. 3165a is a continuous design.

Children's Folk Rhymes A766

No. 3166, "A Frog Has One Mouth." No. 3167, "A Little Mouse Climbs an Oil Lamp." $12, "Fireflies." $19, "Egrets."

Wmk. 323

1998, Apr. 4 Litho. *Perf. 11½*

3166 A766 $5 multicolored .50 .30
3167 A766 $5 multicolored .50 .30
3168 A766 $12 multicolored .75 .60
3169 A766 $19 multicolored 1.75 .80
Nos. 3166-3169 (4) 3.50 2.00

Copyright Law in Taiwan, 70th Anniv. A767

1998, Apr. 30

3170 A767 $19 multicolored 1.75 .80

A768

Portraits of Mythological Character, Chung K'uei: $5, Making ghosts work for him, from Kung Kai's "Chung K'uei Moving," Song Dynasty. $20, Dancing beside small ghost, from "An Auspicious Occasion," Ming Dynasty.

1998, May 15 Photo. *Perf. 11½*
Granite Paper

3171	A768	$5 multicolored		1.25	.25
3172	A768	$20 multicolored		2.25	.80

A769

Wmk. 323
1998, May 25 Litho. *Perf. 11½*

3173	A769	$15 multicolored	1.25	.60

Intl. Law Assoc., 125th anniv.

Ancient Skills Type of 1994

Ships and methods of transport, horiz.: $5, Grain barge. $7, Six-oared boat. $10, One-wheeled carriage. $13, Southern Chinese one-man push cart.

1998, June 10 *Perf. 12x11½*

3174	A693	$5 multicolored	.50	.25
3175	A693	$7 multicolored	.60	.25
3176	A693	$10 multicolored	.80	.30
3177	A693	$13 multicolored	1.00	.40
		Nos. 3174-3177 (4)	2.90	1.20

Ancient Chinese Engravings Type of 1995 Redrawn with Chinese Inscription Reading Left to Right

Various floral designs. Denominations do not include two zeros.

Wmk. 323
1998, July 8 Litho. *Perf. 13½*
Denomination in Red

3178	A712	$7 like #2989	.55	.30
3179	A712	$19 like #2990	1.60	.75
3180	A712	$20 like #2991	1.75	.85
3181	A712	$26 like #2992	2.10	1.05
		Nos. 3178-3181 (4)	6.00	2.95

Novel, "Red Chamber Dream," by Tsao Hsueh-chin
A770

Scenes from love story: No. 3182, Chia Pao-yu visits the garden (with group of women). No. 3183, Lin Tai-yu buries flowers (with hoe). $5, Hsueh Pao-chai plays with butterflies. $20, Shih Hsiang-yun in a drunken sleep (on bench).

1998, July 16 *Perf. 11x11½*

3182	A770	$3.50 multicolored	.25	.25
3183	A770	$3.50 multicolored	.25	.25
3184	A770	$5 multicolored	.40	.25
3185	A770	$20 multicolored	1.60	.75
		Nos. 3182-3185 (4)	2.50	1.50

20th Asia Pacific Jamboree, 8th Taiwan Jamboree — A771

1998, Aug. 5 Litho. *Perf. 11*

3186	A771	$5 Emblem	.30	.25
3186A	A771	$5 Tents	.30	.25
b.		Pair, #3186-3186A	1.00	.50

Traditional Architecture Type of 1995

Terraces set on raised platforms: No. 3187, Spirit way (carved stone ramp between two staircases). No. 3188, Octagonal base of a column. $10, Carved cornerstone. $19, Carved stone drainage spout.

Perf. 11½x12
1998, Aug. 26 Litho. Wmk. 323

3187	A711	$5 multi, vert.	.50	.25
3188	A711	$5 multi, vert.	.50	.25
3189	A711	$10 multi, vert.	.80	.30
3190	A711	$19 multi, vert.	1.25	.55
		Nos. 3187-3190 (4)	3.05	1.35

Sports Stamps — A772

Table tennis: No. 3191, Player awaiting serve. No. 3192, Player serving.
Rugby: No. 3193, Two players. No. 3194, Three players.

Wmk. 323
1998, Sept. 9 Litho. *Perf. 11½*
Denomination Color

3191		$5 green	.40	.25
3192		$5 red	.40	.25
a.	A772	Pair, #3191-3192	.80	.30
3193		$7 red	.50	.25
3194		$7 blue	.50	.25
a.	A772	Pair, #3193-3194	1.00	.40
		Nos. 3191-3194 (4)	1.80	1.00

Chinese Fables
A773

Designs: No. 3195, "A Frog in a Well." No. 3196, "The Fox Borrows the Tiger's Ferocity." $12, "Adding Legs to a Drawing of a Snake." $19, "The Snipe and the Clam are at a Deadlock."

Wmk. 323
1998, Sept. 25 Litho. *Perf. 11½*

3195	A773	$5 multicolored	.50	.30
3196	A773	$5 multicolored	.50	.30
3197	A773	$12 multicolored	1.00	.50
3198	A773	$19 multicolored	1.50	.70
		Nos. 3195-3198 (4)	3.50	1.80

Kinmen National Park
A774

No. 3199, Taiwushan mountain area. No. 3200, Kunningtou Cliff, beach. $12, Teyueh Tower, Huang Hui-huang's house, Shuitou village. $19, Putou Beach, Liehyu Coast.

1998, Oct. 16

3199	A774	$5 multicolored	.50	.30
3200	A774	$5 multicolored	.50	.30
3201	A774	$12 multicolored	1.10	.50
3202	A774	$19 multicolored	1.75	.70
		Nos. 3199-3202 (4)	3.85	1.80

Birds — A775

Spizaetus nipalensis: No. 3203, On tree branch. No. 3204, In flight.
Spilornis cheela: No. 3205, On tree branch. No. 3206, In flight.
Ictinaetus malayensis: No. 3207, On tree branch. No. 3208, In flight.
Milvus migrans: No. 3209, Perched on rock. No. 3210, In flight.

1998, Oct. 30 Litho. *Perf. 11½*

3203		$5 multicolored	.40	.25
3204		$5 multicolored	.40	.25
a.	A775	Pair, #3203-3204	.80	.30
3205		$5 multicolored	.40	.25
3206		$5 multicolored	.40	.25
a.	A775	Pair, #3205-3206	.80	.30
3207		$10 multicolored	.80	.30
3208		$10 multicolored	.80	.30
a.	A775	Pair, #3207-3208	1.60	.60
3209		$10 multicolored	.80	.30
3210		$10 multicolored	.80	.30
a.	A775	Pair, #3209-3210	1.60	.60
		Nos. 3203-3210 (8)	4.80	2.20

Ancient Jade Carvings
A776

No. 3211, 2 men mining jade on a mountain. No. 3212, Mountain with 2 pavilions, stream. $7, Figures washing an elephant. $26, Mountain, trees, men.

Perf. 11½x12, 12x11½
1998, Nov. 13 Photo.
Granite Paper

3211	A776	$5 multi	.40	.30
3212	A776	$5 multi, vert.	.40	.30
3213	A776	$7 multi	.60	.30
3214	A776	$26 multi, vert.	2.00	1.00
a.		Souvenir sheet, #3211-3214	4.50	2.00

New Year 1999 (Year of the Rabbit)
A777 A778

Wmk. 323
1998, Dec. 2 Litho. *Perf. 12½*

3215	A777	$3.50 multicolored	.40	.25
a.		Perf. 14 vert.	.40	.25
b.		As "a," booklet pane of 6	2.50	
		Complete bklt., 2 #3215b + gutter	5.00	
3216	A778	$13 multicolored	1.40	.40
a.		Souv. sheet, 2 ea #3215-3216	4.00	2.50
b.		As "a," ovptd. in margin, perf. 12½x11¾	4.00	2.50

No. 3216b was issued 1/30/99 and is inscribed in sheet margin, "ALLIANCE '99 INT'L. FAIR OF PRODUCTS & TRAVEL / Jan. 30-Feb. 1, 1999" and four lines of Chinese text.

Common Expressions of Good Fortune — A779

Expressions, designs: No. 3217, "To have prosperous descendants," gourd on a vine. No. 3218, "A good marriage that soon brings sons," pair of Mandarin ducks, lotus flowers, seeds. No. 3219, "Prosperity from start to finish," egret, flowers. No. 3220, "Reunion and abundance," fish surrounded by flowers.

Perf. 11½x12
1999, Jan. 6 Litho. Wmk. 323

3217	A779	$5 multicolored	.50	.25
3218	A779	$5 multicolored	.50	.25
3219	A779	$12 multicolored	1.00	.50
3220	A779	$12 multicolored	1.00	.50
		Nos. 3217-3220 (4)	3.00	1.50

Ancient Chinese Engravings Type of 1995 Redrawn with Chinese Inscription Reading Left to Right; No Zeros

Various pictures of birds on tree branches, bamboo and orchid.

1999, Jan. 20 *Perf. 13½*
Denomination in Red

3221	A712	$1 like #3018	.25	.25
3222	A712	$3.50 like #3019	.30	.25
3223	A712	$5 like #3020	.40	.25
3224	A712	$10 like #3021	.75	.35
3225	A712	$12 like #3076	1.00	.40
3226	A712	$28 like #3077	2.25	1.10
		Nos. 3221-3226 (6)	4.95	2.60

Indoor Potted Plants — A781

$5, Sinningia speciosa. $12, Saintpaulia x hybrida. $19, Anthurium scherzerianum.

Perf. 12½
1999, Feb. 10 Litho. Unwmk.

3228	A781	$5 multicolored	.40	.25
3229	A781	$12 multicolored	.90	.40
3230	A781	$19 multicolored	1.60	.80
		Nos. 3228-3230 (3)	2.90	1.45

Ancient Chinese Painting, "Joy in Peacetime"
A782

No. 3231, Woman holding child, boy with small elephant. No. 3232, Boy carrying lantern, crane on leash, people under tree. $7, Family, children playing with toy animals on wheels. $26, Women in front of steps, children playing with toys, boy on edge of balcony.

1999, Mar. 2 Photo. *Perf. 12*
Granite Paper

3231	A782	$5 multicolored	.40	.25
3232	A782	$5 multicolored	.40	.25
3233	A782	$7 multicolored	.55	.25
3234	A782	$26 multicolored	1.75	.80
a.		Souvenir sheet, 3231-3234	2.00	1.75
		Nos. 3231-3234 (4)	3.10	1.55

A782a

A782b

A782c

Traditional Architecture — A782d

Decorative features: No. 3235, Hanging cylinder with carving of woman and deer. No. 3236, Taishi screen. $10, Xuanyu (decorative element on gable). $19, Wood carving.

1999, Mar. 20 Litho. Wmk. 323
3235 A782a $5 multicolored .40 .25
3236 A782b $5 multicolored .40 .25
3237 A782c $10 multicolored .75 .30
3238 A782d $19 multicolored 1.50 .60
Nos. 3235-3238 (4) 3.05 1.40

Children's Folk Rhymes A783

Titles: No. 3239, "Baby Sleep." No. 3240, "Be Brave." $12, "Rock, Rock, Rock." $19, "Buggie Flies."

Perf. 11½x11
1999, Apr. 2 Litho. Unwmk.
3239 A783 $5 multicolored .50 .25
3240 A783 $5 multicolored .50 .25
3241 A783 $12 multicolored 1.00 .35
3242 A783 $19 multicolored 1.40 .55
Nos. 3239-3242 (4) 3.40 1.40

Taiwan's Aboriginal Culture A784

Celebrations wearing traditional costumes: a, Dancing in row, mountain in background, Atayal Ancestor Festival. b, People wearing hip bells, Saisiat Festival of the Dwarfs. c, Standing arm in arm in circle, Bunun eight-part contrapuntal vocals. d, Row of people standing inside building, Tsou Victory Festival. e, Group outside before large display board, Rukai Harvest Festival. f, Holding bamboo poles in air, Paiwan "Maleveq" Bamboo Festival. g, Men walking while holding millet leaves in air, Puyuma Harvest Ceremony. h, Women dancing in row, tree in background, Ami Harvest Ceremony. i, Holding boat in air, Yami Boat Ceremony.

Block of 9
1999, Apr. 22 ***Perf. 13***
3243 A784 $5 #a.-i. + label 6.00 5.50

No. 3243 was issued in sheets of 2 blocks + 2 labels. The labels contain the upper and lower halves of Taiwan. The lower block of 9 is in reverse order.

Intl. Council of Nurses, Cent. A785

1999, May 12 Litho. ***Perf. 11½***
3244 A785 $5 shown .50 .25
3245 A785 $17 Nurse, world map 1.40 .50

Chinese Classical Opera — A786

Legends of the Ming Dynasty: No. 3246, Fan Li watching Hsi-shih wash yarn, "Wuan Sha Chi.". No. 3247, Tsai Pochieh, Niu looking at moon, Chao Waniang with pipa (stringed instrument) on her back, "The Story of a Pipa." $12, Hung Funu surprising Li Ching, "The Story of Hung Fu." $15, Jueilan setting up incense table, "Paiyueh Pavilion."

1999, May 27 ***Perf. 13***
3246 A786 $5 multicolored .45 .25
3247 A786 $5 multicolored .50 .25
3248 A786 $12 multicolored 1.10 .35
3249 A786 $15 multicolored 1.40 .45
a. Souvenir sheet, #3246-3249 3.50 1.75
b. As "a," imperf., with added inscription 3.50 1.75
Nos. 3246-3249 (4) 3.45 1.30

No. 3249b was issued 7/23 and is inscribed in sheet margin with exhibition emblem, two lines of Chinese text and "TAIPEI INTERNATIONAL STAMP EXHIBITION 1999 (INVITATIONAL)."

New Taiwan Dollar, 50th Anniv. A787

1999, June 15 ***Perf. 11½***
3250 A787 $5 Coins .50 .25
3251 A787 $25 Currency 2.00 .75

Carp Type of 1997 Redrawn With Denominations at Right

1999, July 1 Engr. ***Perf. 13½x12½***
3252 A745 $50 green 4.00 3.00
3253 A745 $100 brown 9.00 4.00

Ancient Chinese Engravings Type of 1995 Redrawn with Chinese Inscription Reading Left to Right

Perf. 13½
1999, July 15 Litho. Unwmk.
Denomination in Red
3254 A712 50c like #3044 .25 .25
3255 A712 $6 like #3045 .50 .25
3256 A712 $25 like #3046 1.75 .75
Nos. 3254-3256 (3) 2.50 1.25

Father's Day A788

Designs: $5, Children with large present, silhouette of their father. $25, Father teaching son how to ride bicycle, girl.

1999, Aug. 8 ***Perf. 11½***
3257 A788 $5 multicolored .50 .30
3258 A788 $25 multicolored 2.00 1.25

Chinese Gourmet Food A789

Dish, region: a, Peony lobster, Taiwan. b, "Buddha Jumps the Wall" steamed seafood (with blue & white teapot, bowl), Fukien. c, Hors d'oeuvres shaped as star, Canton. d, "Dongpo Pork" (on yellow plate, bowl), Kiangsu and Chekiang. e, "Stewed Fish Jaws" (surrounded by strawberries, pineapple), Shanghai. f, "Beggar's Chicken" (with napkin), Hunan. g, "Carp Jumping over Dragon's Gate," Szechwan. h, "Peking Duck" (in footed dish), Beijing.

Perf. 11½x11¼
1999, Aug 20 Litho. Unwmk.
3259 A789 $5 Block of 8, #a.-h. 3.25 1.60

Outdoor Activities — A790

1999, Sept. 9 ***Perf. 11¼x11½***
3260 A790 $5 Diving .40 .30
3261 A790 $6 Rafting .50 .40
3262 A790 $10 Surfing .90 .50
3263 A790 $25 Windsurfing 2.25 .50
Nos. 3260-3263 (4) 4.05 1.70

Taiwanese Opera A791

1999, Oct. 15 Litho. ***Perf. 11½x11¼***
3264 A791 $5 Stage, audience .40 .30
3265 A791 $6 Dressing room .50 .40
3266 A791 $10 Actress, tents .90 .50
3267 A791 $25 Actress as clown 2.25 .80
Nos. 3264-3267 (4) 4.05 2.00

Illustrations from Ching Dynasty Bird Manual A792

No. 3268, Yellow-headed parrot. No. 3269, Blue-winged parrotlet (4 characters at LL). $12, African gray parrot (5 characters at UL). $25, King parrot (5 characters at UL).

1999, Nov. 11 Litho. ***Perf. 11½***
3268 A792 $5 multicolored .50 .30
3269 A792 $5 multicolored .50 .30
3270 A792 $12 multicolored 1.25 .50
3271 A792 $25 multicolored 2.40 1.10
Nos. 3268-3271 (4) 4.65 2.20

Compare with No. 3152.
See Nos. 3316-3319, 3379-3381, 3510-3512.

New Year 2000 (Year of the Dragon)
A793 A794

1999, Dec. 1 Litho. ***Perf. 12½***
3272 A793 $3.50 multicolored .30 .25
a. Perf. 13¼ vert. .30 .25
b. As "a," booklet pane of 6 1.60
Complete booklet, 2 #3272b + gutter 3.50
3273 A794 $13 multicolored 1.00 .40
a. Souv. sheet, 2 ea #3272-3273 2.50 1.50

Millennium A795

No. 3274, ROCSAT-1. No. 3275, Deer. $12, Train. $15, Dove, St. Peter's Basilica.

1999, Dec. 31 Litho. ***Perf. 11½***
3274 A795 $5 multicolored .50 .30
3275 A795 $5 multicolored .50 .30
3276 A795 $12 multicolored 1.10 .50
3277 A795 $15 multicolored 1.40 .70
a. Souvenir sheet of 4, #3274-3277, perf. 12 3.50 1.75
b. Souvenir sheet of 4, #3274-3277, imperf. 3.50 1.75
Nos. 3274-3277 (4) 3.50 1.80

Taipei 2000 Stamp Exhibition (No. 3277b). No. 3277b has simulated perforations.

Calligraphy Tools A796

Designs: No. 3278, "Colored Cloud Dragon" writing brushes of Ming Emperor Chia-Ching. No. 3279, "Imperial Dragon Fragrance" Ink stick of Ming Emperor Lung-Ching, vert. $7, "Clear Heart House" calligraphic work by Tsai Hsiang, Sung Dynasty, vert. $26, Celadon toad inkstone, Sung Dynasty.

2000, Jan. 12 Photo. ***Perf. 11¾***
Granite Paper
3278 A796 $5 multicolored .40 .30
3279 A796 $5 multicolored .50 .30
3280 A796 $7 multicolored .65 .40
3281 A796 $26 multicolored 2.40 1.00
Nos. 3278-3281 (4) 3.95 2.00

Opening of Second Southern Freeway A797

Designs: $5, $25, Kaoping River bridge. $12, Interchange.

2000, Feb. 2 Litho. ***Perf. 13x13¼***
3282 A797 $5 multi .60 .30
3283 A797 $12 multi 1.20 .50

Souvenir Sheet
Perf. 12
3284 A797 $25 multi 2.50 1.25

No. 3284 contains one 80x30mm stamp.

Seasons A798

Spring — No. 3285: a, Buds on tree. b, Farmer plowing. c, Cranes. d, Farmers planting. e, Basket of offerings to dead ancestors. f, Farmer's clothing.
Summer — No. 3286: a, Rice seedlings. b, Water wheel. c, Ripened rice. d, Cicada on tree. e, Palm leaf fan. f, Watermelons.
Autumn — No. 3287: a, Farmers in field. b, Granary. c, Dew on grass. d, Reddened maple leaves. e, Leafless tree. f, Hoarfrost on leaves.
Winter — No. 3288: a, Jar on table. b, Snow-covered pine trees. c, Snow-covered mountains. d, Bowl of rice balls. e, Snow-covered plum blossoms. f, House and village.

2000, Feb. 3 ***Perf. 11¾***
3285 A798 $5 Strip of 6, #a-f 3.00 1.75
3286 A798 $5 Strip of 6, #a-f 3.00 1.75
3287 A798 $5 Strip of 6, #a-f 3.00 1.75
3288 A798 $5 Strip of 6, #a-f 3.00 1.75
Nos. 3285-3288 (4) 12.00 7.00

Issued: No. 3285, 2/3; No. 3286, 5/5; No. 3287, 8/4; No. 3288, 11/3.

Soochow University, Cent. A799

Designs: $5 School gate. $25, Justice statue at Law School.

2000, Mar. 16 *Perf. 13x13¼*
3289 A799 $5 multi .50 .30
3290 A799 $25 multi 2.40 1.25

Novel "The Romance of the Three Kingdoms" A800

No. 3291, Gathering of Liu Bei, Guan Yu and Chang Fei. No. 3292, Guan Yu reading. $5, Three visits to the thatched cottage. $20, Filling boats with straw for making arrows.

2000, Apr. 12 Litho. *Perf. 11½*
3291 A800 $3.50 multi .60 .30
3292 A800 $3.50 multi .60 .30
3293 A800 $5 multi .80 .40
3294 A800 $20 multi 1.75 .70
a. Souv. sheet, #3291-3294, perf. 12 3.75 3.25
Nos. 3291-3294 (4) 3.75 1.70

Inauguration of New President and Vice-president — A801

a, Pres. Chen Shui-bian, Vice-pres. Lu Hsiu-lien. b, Presidential Office Building.

2000, May 20 Litho. *Perf. 11¾*
3295 A801 $5 Pair, #a-b .75 .30
c. Souvenir sheet, 2 #3295 2.50 1.00

Tropic of Cancer Monuments A802

2000, June 21 *Perf. 13*
3296 A802 $5 Hsialiao .40 .30
3297 A802 $12 Wuho 1.25 .60
3298 A802 $25 Chingpu 2.25 1.10
Nos. 3296-3298 (3) 3.90 2.00

Ancient Chinese Engravings Type of 1995 Redrawn with Chinese Inscription Reading Left to Right

2000, July 5 Litho. *Perf. 13½*

Denomination in Red

3299 A712 $32 like #3046 2.75 1.75
3300 A712 $34 like #3078 3.25 1.75

Sacred Trees — A803

Designs: $5, Taiwan Giant, Miaoli County. $39, Sleeping Moon, Chiayi County.

2000, July 20 Litho. *Perf. 11¼x11½*
3301 A803 $5 multi .40 .30
3302 A803 $39 multi 3.25 1.50

No. 2499 Surcharged in Red

2000, Aug. 24 Litho. *Perf. 13½*
3303 A535a $3.50 on $7.50 multi .75 .30

Poisonous Plants — A804

Designs: No. 3304, $5, Lycoris radiata. No. 3305, $5, Cerbera manghas. $12, Abrus precatorius. $20, Nerium indicum.

2000, Sept. 8 Litho. *Perf. 13*
3304-3307 A804 Set of 4 4.25 2.00

Sept. 21, 1999 Earthquake, 1st Anniv. — A805

Designs: $5, Map, seismograph reading. $12, Rescue workers. $25, Earthquake preparedness.

2000, Sept. 21 *Perf. 11¼x11½*
3308-3310 A805 Set of 3 4.25 2.00

Dragonflies A806

Designs: Nos. 3311, 3315a, $5, Lamelligomphus formosanus. Nos. 3312, 3315b, $5, Anotogaster sieboldii, vert. Nos. 3313, 3315c, $12, Trithemis festiva, vert. Nos. 3314, 3315d, $12, Neurothemis ramburii.

2000, Oct. 11 *Perf. 13*
3311-3314 A806 Set of 4 3.50 1.50

Souvenir Sheet

Stamps Without White Margins

Perf. 11¾

3315 A806 Sheet of 4, #a-d 3.50 1.50

Bird Manual Type of 1999

No. 3316, $5, Corn bunting (2 characters at UR). No. 3317, $5, Brambling (3 characters at UL). $12, Bali mynah (3 characters at LR). $25, Indian grackle (2 characters at LR).

2000, Oct. 26 *Perf. 11½*
3316-3319 A792 Set of 4 4.50 2.00

Compare No. 3317 with No. 3378.

Tamkang University, 50th Anniv. A807

$5, Palace Lamp Boulevard, classroom buildings. $25, Maritime Museum, Scroll Plaza.

2000, Nov. 8 *Perf. 13*
3320-3321 A807 Set of 2 3.00 1.50

A808

New Year 2001 (Year of the Snake) — A809

2000, Dec. 1 *Perf. 12½*
3322 A808 $3.50 multi .50 .25
a. Perf. 13¼ vert. .50 .25
b. As "a," booklet pane of 6 3.00
Booklet, 2 #3322b + gutter 6.00
3323 A809 $13 multi 1.25 .40
a. Souv. sheet, 2 ea #3322-3323 3.50 1.50
b. As "a," with added marginal inscription in red 3.50 1.50

Added marginal inscription of No. 3323b reads in Chinese "Turn-of-the-Century Intl. Stamp Exhibition, Kaohsiung / Dec. 25, 2000-Jan. 3, 2001" in red

Issued: No. 3323b, 12/25/00.

Establishment of Trade Links with People's Republic of China — A810

Ships in Taiwan Strait and: $9, Building. $25, Obelisk.

2001, Jan. 1 Litho. *Perf. 11½*
3324-3325 A810 Set of 2 3.00 2.50

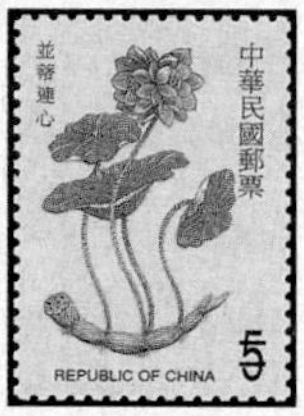

A811

Common Chinese expressions of good fortune: No. 3326, $5, "Marital bliss," twin lotus blossoms on one stalk (pink background). No. 3327, $5, "Success in one's career," longan, lichee and walnuts (light green background). No. 3328, $12, "Producing many offspring," split pomegranates (buff background). No. 3329, $12, "Growing old together with wealth and high position," bulbuls flying around peonies (light orange background).

2001, Jan. 2 *Perf. 11¾x12¼*
3326-3329 A811 Set of 4 3.00 2.50

See Nos. 3404-3407.

Zodiac Signs A812

Designs: No. 3330, $5, Aquarius. No. 3331, $12, Gemini. No. 3332, $25, Libra. No. 3333, $5, Capricorn. No. 3334, $12, Taurus. No. 3335, $25, Virgo. No. 3336, $5, Aries. No. 3337, $12, Leo. No. 3338, $25, Sagittarius. No. 3339, $5, Pisces. No. 3340, $12, Cancer. No. 3341, $25, Scorpio.

2001 *Perf. 12*
3330-3341 A812 Set of 12 18.00 12.00

Values are for stamps with surrounding selvage.

Issued: Nos. 3330-3332, 2/14. Nos. 3333-3335, 4/20. Nos. 3336-3338, 7/25. Nos. 3339-3341, 11/8.

Fruit — A813

2001-05 Litho. *Perf. 12½x13¼*
3342 A813 $1 Plums .25 .25
3343 A813 $3.50 Tangerines .35 .25
a. "Republic of China" 12½mm long ('05) .35 .25
3344 A813 $5 Apples .45 .25
3345 A813 $7 Pears .65 .25
3346 A813 $12 Guavas 1.05 .65
3347 A813 $20 Longans 1.60 1.00
a. "Republic of China" 12½mm long ('05) 1.60 .85
3348 A813 $25 Cantaloupes 2.00 1.05
3349 A813 $40 Grapefruit 3.75 3.25
Nos. 3342-3349 (8) 10.10 6.95

Issued: $5, $7, $12, $25, 2/23. $1, $3.50, $20, $40, 8/23. Nos. 3343a, 3347a, 5/16/05.

"Republic of China" on Nos. 3343 and 3347 is 12mm long and is in taller letters.

See Nos. 3408-3411, 3472-3475.

Mount Jade A814

Designs: No. 3350, $5, Main peak (shown). No. 3351, $5, Western peak, flowers in foreground. $12, Northern peak. $25, Eastern peak.

2001, Mar. 8 Litho. *Perf. 11½x11¼*
3350-3353 A814 Set of 4 4.50 3.75

Compare Type A814 with Types A834-A837, A855-A858.

Children's Rhymes A815

Designs: No. 3354, $5, Little Ball (blue background). No. 3355, $5, Point to the Water Vat (pink background). $12, Pangolin. $25, Shake and Stamp.

2001, Apr. 4
3354-3357 A815 Set of 4 4.50 3.75

Buddhist Statues — A816

Designs: $5, Sakyamuni Buddha, Northern Wei Dynasty. $9, Seated Buddha, Tang Dynasty. $12, Mahavairocana Buddha, Sung Dynasty.

2001, May 11 *Perf. 11¼x11½*
3358-3360 A816 Set of 3 2.50 2.00
3360a Souvenir sheet, #3358-3360, perf. 12 2.50 2.50

Agricultural Implements — A817

Designs: $5, Rice wind drum. $7, Plow. $10, Bamboo rice baskets. $25, Coir rainwear.

2001, May 25 *Perf. 11½x11¼*
3361-3364 A817 Set of 4 4.50 3.75

Dr. George Leslie Mackay (1844-1901) A818

2001, June 1 *Perf. 11¼x11½*
3365 A818 $25 multi 2.25 2.00

2001 Kiwanis International Convention A819

Designs: $5, Girl, Earth. $25, Mother and child, map.

2001, June 22 *Perf. 13*
3366-3367 A819 Set of 2 2.50 2.00

Kites — A820

No. 3368: a, Dragon. b, Phoenix. c, Tiger. d, Fish.

2001, July 13 *Perf. 11¼x11½*
3368 Horiz. strip of 4 2.00 1.60
a.-d. A820 $5 Any single .45 .80

Carp Encircled by Dragons Type of 1997 With Denominations at Right

2001, Aug. 3 **Engr.** *Perf. 13*
Size: 25x33mm
3369 A745 $300 red vio & dk bl 20.00 10.00
3370 A745 $500 red & brown 45.00 20.00

Rapid Transit A821

Designs: $5, Train, transit system emblem. $12, Passengers in station, fare card. $25, Chientan Station.

2001, Aug. 14 **Litho.** *Perf. 13*
3371-3372 A821 Set of 2 1.75 1.00

Souvenir Sheet

Perf. 13¾
3373 A821 $25 multi 2.75 1.50

No. 3373 contains one 85x42mm stamp.

Fables — A822

Designs: No. 3374, $5, Now Three, Now Four (man and monkeys). No. 3375, $5, Selling the All-Penetrating Sword and Unyielding Shield (men watching man with sword and shield). $12, Waiting by the Tree for the Rabbit. $25, An Old Fool Moves Mountains.

2001, Sept. 6 **Litho.** *Perf. 11½*
3374-3377 A822 Set of 4 3.75 3.00

Bird Manual Type of 1999 and

Siberian Rubythroat A823

Designs: No. 3379, Waxwing (3 characters at UR). $12, White-rumped munia (2 characters at R). $25, Great barbet (3 characters at LL).

2001, Sept. 28 **Litho.** *Perf. 11½*
3378 A823 $5 shown .60 .40
3379 A792 $5 multi .60 .40
3380 A792 $12 multi 1.10 .60
3381 A792 $25 multi 2.00 1.60
Nos. 3378-3381 (4) 4.30 3.00

Republic of China, 90th Anniv. A824

Designs: No. 3382, $5, Terminal, Chiang Kai-shek Intl. Airport. No. 3383, $5, Electronic products made in Republic of China. $12, Dancers at National Theater. $15, Dolphins.

2001, Oct. 9 **Litho.** *Perf. 11½*
3382-3385 A824 Set of 4 3.25 2.50

2001 National Games — A825

Athletes and: $5, Torch. $25, Map.

2001, Oct. 18 **Litho.** *Perf. 12½*
3386-3387 A825 Set of 2 2.50 2.00

34th Baseball World Cup A826

Emblem, map and: No. 3388, $5, Pitcher. No. 3389, $5, Batter. $12, Catcher. $20, Runner sliding.

2001, Oct. 30 *Perf. 11½*
3388-3391 A826 Set of 4 3.75 3.00
3391a Souvenir sheet, #3388-3391, perf. 12 3.75 3.00

Puppet Theater A827

Designs: $5, Mozhaonu, from "Thunder Storm." $6, Taiyangnu, from "Rising Winds, Surging Clouds." $10, Kuangdao, from "Thunder Crazy Sword." $25, Chin Chia-chien, from "Thunder Golden Light."

2001, Nov. 16 **Litho.** *Perf. 11½*
3392-3395 A827 Set of 4 4.50 3.00

National Defense Medical Center, Cent. A828

Designs: $5, Medical students, old medical school building. $25, Doctors, new medical school building.

2001, Nov. 23 *Perf. 13*
3396-3397 A828 Set of 2 2.50 2.00

New Year 2002 (Year of the Horse) — A829

Horse and: $3.50, Clouds. $13, Flowers.

2001, Dec. 3 **Litho.** *Perf. 12½*
3398 A829 $3.50 multi .50 .30
a. Perf. 13¾ vert. .50 .30
b. Booklet pane, 12 #3398a 4.50 —
Booklet, #3398b 5.00
3399 A829 $13 multi 1.50 1.00
a. Souvenir sheet, 2 each #3398-3399 4.00 2.50

Paul Cardinal Yu Pin (1901-78) — A830

2001, Dec. 7 *Perf. 11½*
3400 A830 $25 multi 2.25 .90
a. Souvenir sheet of 1, perf. 12 2.25 1.60

Greetings A831

No. 3401: a, Pink chrysanthemums, red background. b, White lilies, red background. c, Pink flowers, yellow background. d, Red orange flowers, yellow background. e, Pink flowers, green background. f, Coral roses, blue green background. g, Star and wreath, blue background. h, Poinsettias, blue background. i, Red violet flowers, purple background. j, Yellow flowers, purple background.

2001, Dec. 12 *Perf. 12½*
3401 Sheet of 10 + 10 labels 4.50 3.00
a.-j. A831 $5 Any single .45 .30

Labels could be personalized for an additional fee.

Sheets with blank (unprinted) labels were not released.

Fu Hsing Kang College, 50th Anniv. A832

Designs: $5, Students with flags. $25, Tower, administration building, statue of students.

2002, Jan. 4 *Perf. 11½*
3402-3403 A832 Set of 2 2.50 2.00

Expressions of Good Fortune Type of 2001

Designs: No. 3404, $5, "Continuously produce good offspring," lotus and sweet osmanthus flowers in a vase (gradiated pink background). No. 3405, $5, "A high, moral gentleman," orchid and sweet osmanthus in containers (gradiated green background). No. 3406, $12, "A hall full of the rich and famous," flowering crabapple in a vase (gradiated orange background). No. 3407, $12, "Safe and peaceful in all seasons," roses in vase (gradiated purple background).

2002, Jan. 16 *Perf. 11¾x12¼*
3404-3407 A811 Set of 4 3.50 2.00

Fruit Type of 2001

2002-05 **Litho.** *Perf. 12½x13¼*
3408 A813 $6 Avocados .45 .25
3409 A813 $10 Lichees .90 .35
a. "Republic of China" 12½mm long ('05) .75 .35
3410 A813 $17 Dates 1.50 .60
a. "Republic of China" 12½mm long ('05) 1.25 .65
3411 A813 $32 Passion fruit 2.75 1.05
a. "Republic of China" 12½mm long ('05) 2.50 1.25
Nos. 3408-3411 (4) 5.60 2.25

Issued: Nos. 3408-3411, 2/8/02; 3409a, 3410a, 3411a, 5/16/05.

"Republic of China" on Nos. 3409-3411 is 12mm long and is in taller letters.

Folk Traditions A833

Designs: No. 3412, $5, Release of sky lanterns (orange background). No. 3413, $5, Fireworks display (blue background). $10, Matsu procession (lilac background). $20, Dragon boat race (pink background).

2002, Feb. 26 **Litho.** *Perf. 12½*
3412-3415 A833 Set of 4 4.00 3.00

See Nos. 3440-3443.

Winter, Mount Hsueh A834

North Ridge, Mount Hsueh A835

Autumn, Mount Hsueh A836

Glacial Cirques, Mount Hsueh A837

2002, Mar. 20 *Perf. 11½*
3416 A834 $5 multi .40 .40
3417 A835 $5 multi .40 .40
3418 A836 $12 multi 1.00 .90
3419 A837 $25 multi 2.00 1.75
Nos. 3416-3419 (4) 3.80 3.45

Compare with Types A814, A855-A858.

Novel "The Romance of the Three Kingdoms" A838

Designs: No. 3420, $3.50, Three heroes battling Lu Bu (warriors on horseback). No. 3421, $3.50, To the rescue of his master's family (one warrior on horseback). $5, Scraping away the poison from the bone (medicinal bleeding). $20, Playing a lute to make the enemy retreat (horseman and gate).

2002, Apr. 4

3420-3423 A838 Set of 4 5.00 2.10
a. Souvenir sheet, #3420-3423, perf. 12 5.00 5.00

Endangered Bird Thalasseus Bernsteini — A839

No. 3424: a, Two birds in flight. b, Bird in flight heading left. c, Bird landing on rock carrying fish. d, Bird on rock with beak open. e, Adult feeding chick. f, Bird diving. g, Bird landing with bill open. h, Bird standing on rock, looking left. i, Adult with chick. j, Adult on nest. $25, Bird in flight.

2002, May 15 Litho. ***Perf. 11½***

3424 A839 $5 Sheet of 10, #a-j 5.00 4.00

Souvenir Sheet

Perf. 12

3425 A839 $25 multi 3.00 2.00

No. 3424 contains ten 40x30mm stamps.

Dragon & Carp Type of 1997 Redrawn With Denomination at Right

2002, June 5 Engr. ***Perf. 13¼x12½***

3426 A745 $80 brown 6.00 3.50

Porcelain Bowls A840

Ching Dynasty bowls depicting: No. 3427, $5, Peacock (salmon background). No. 3428, $5, Lotus flowers (blue green background). $7, Peonies. $32, Sparrows and bamboo.

2002, June 21 Litho. ***Perf. 11½***

3427-3430 A840 Set of 4 4.25 3.75

Flowers — A841

Designs: $5, Matthiola incana. $12, Gardenia jasminoides. $25, Michelia figo.

2002, July 5 ***Perf. 13***

3431-3433 A841 Set of 3 3.25 1.50

Cetaceans A842

Designs: No. 3434, $5, Megaptera novaeangliae, whaling ship. No. 3435, $5, Tursiops truncatus, people on shore attracting cetacean. $10, Orcinus orca, boat following cetaceans. $25, Grampus griseus, people rescuing beached dolphin.

2002, July 25 Litho. ***Perf. 11½x11¼***

3434-3437 A842 Set of 4 4.50 1.75
a. Souvenir sheet, #3434-3437, perf. 12 4.50 3.25

Intl. Paralympic Committee World Table Tennis Championships — A843

Player: No. 3438, $5, On crutches. No. 3439, $5, In wheelchair.

2002, Aug. 13 ***Perf. 11½x11¼***

3438-3439 A843 Set of 2 1.25 .80

Folk Traditions Type of 2002

Designs: No. 3440, $5, Launching of water lanterns (green background). No. 3441, $5, Snatching flags for good luck (yellow background). $10, Worship of the just (blue background). $20, Burning the Prince's boat (red orange background).

2002, Aug. 22 ***Perf. 12½***

3440-3443 A833 Set of 4 3.25 2.75

Republic of China — Vatican City Diplomatic Relations, 60th Anniv. A844

Designs: $5, Chinese and Vatican flags, Chinese Presidential building, St. Peter's Basilica. $17, Flags, doves, Celso Cardinal Costantini.

2002, Sept. 20 ***Perf. 11½x11¼***

3444-3445 A844 Set of 2 2.00 1.25

Bird Manual Type of 1999 and

White-rumped Munia — A845

Designs: No. 3446, $5, Vernal hanging parrot (3 characters at LL). $12, White-headed greenfinch (4 characters at LL). $25, Yunnan greenfinch (2 characters at UL).

2002, Oct. 9

3446 A792 $5 multi .50 .40
3447 A845 $5 multi .50 .40
3448 A792 $12 multi .90 .80
3449 A792 $25 multi 1.90 1.75
Nos. 3446-3449 (4) 3.80 3.35

Taiwanese Opera A846

Designs: $5, Liang Shan-po and Chu Yingtai. $6, Hsueh Ting-shan and Fan Li-hua. $10, Hsueh Ping-kuei and Wang Pao-chuan. $25, The Living Buddha Chikung.

2002, Oct. 25

3450-3453 A846 Set of 4 3.50 1.50

Koalas — A847

Designs: No. 3454, $5, Adult with cub. No. 3455, $5, Adult on branch. $9, Adult with head on branch. $21, Adult with cub, diff.

2002, Nov. 15 ***Perf. 11¼x11½***

3454-3457 A847 Set of 4 3.50 1.60
a. Souvenir sheet, #3454-3457, perf. 12 3.50 2.75

Knots A848

Nos. 3458-3459 — Various knots (Denomination location, denomination color and background color): a, UL, orange, light orange. b, UL, purple, yellow. c, UL, green, light green. d, UL, yellow, light blue. e, UL, blue, pink. f, UR, orange, light orange. g, UR, red violet, yellow. h, UR, blue, light green. i, UR, yellow, light blue. j, UR, red violet, pink.

No. 3460 (yellow denominations, olive green background): a, Like #3458a. b, Like #3458b. c, Like #3458c, d, Like #3458d, e, Like #3458e. f, Like #3458f. g, Like #3458g. h, Like #3458h. i, Like #3458i. j, Like #3458j.

2002, Nov. 22 Litho. ***Perf. 12½***

3458 Block of 10 2.25 1.20
a.-j. A848 $3.50 Any single .25 .25
k. Sheet of 10 #3458f + 10 attached labels 12.00 12.00
l. Sheet of 10 #3458g + 10 attached labels 12.00 12.00
m. Sheet of 10 #3458h + 10 attached labels 12.00 12.00
n. Sheet of 10 #3458i + 10 attached labels 12.00 12.00
o. Sheet of 10 #3458j + 10 attached labels 12.00 12.00
p. Sheet , #3458a-3458j + 10 attached labels 12.00 12.00
q. Sheet, #3458a, 3458b, 3458d, 3458f, 3458g, 3458i + 6 attached labels ('04) 8.50 8.50
3459 Block of 10 3.50 1.75
a.-j. A848 $5 Any single .35 .25
k. Sheet of 10 #3459a + 10 attached labels 12.50 12.50
l. Sheet of 10 #3459b + 10 attached labels 12.50 12.50
m. Sheet of 10 #3459c + 10 attached labels 12.50 12.50
n. Sheet of 10 #3459d + 10 attached labels 12.50 12.50
o. Sheet of 10 #3459e + 10 attached labels 12.50 12.50
p. Sheet of 10 #3459f + 10 attached labels 12.50 12.50
q. Sheet of 10 #3459g + 10 attached labels 12.50 12.50
r. Sheet of 10 #3459h + 10 attached labels 12.50 12.50
s. Sheet of 10 #3459i + 10 attached labels 12.50 12.50
t. Sheet of 10 #3459j + 10 attached labels 12.50 12.50
3460 Block of 10 17.50 8.50
a.-j. A848 $25 Any single 1.75 .80
k. Sheet of 10 #3460a + 10 attached labels 24.00 24.00
l. Sheet of 10 #3460b + 10 attached labels 24.00 24.00
m. Sheet of 10 #3460c + 10 attached labels 24.00 24.00
n. Sheet of 10 #3460d + 10 attached labels 24.00 24.00
o. Sheet of 10 #3460e + 10 attached labels 24.00 24.00
p. Sheet, #3460a-3460j + 10 attached labels 24.00 24.00
Nos. 3458-3460 (3) 23.25 11.45

Nos. 3458k-3458p sold for $185 each; Nos. 3459k-3459u for $200 each; Nos. 3460k-3460p for $400 each. Labels, which were personalized, were separated from stamps on Nos. 3458k-3458p, 3459k-3459u, 3460k-3460p by vertical rows of simulated perforations.

No. 3458q sold for $141 and has labels, which could be personalized, that are separated from the stamps by simulated perforations. Issued 9/30/04.

New Year 2003 (Year of the Ram) — A849

Designs: $3.50, Yellow ram. $13, Red ram.

2002, Dec. 2 Litho. ***Perf. 12¼***

3461 A849 $3.50 multi .40 .25
a. Perf. 12¼ Vert. .40 .25
b. As "a," booklet pane of 6 2.25 —
Booklet, 2 #3461b 5.25
3462 A849 $13 multi 1.10 .40
a. Souvenir sheet, 2 each #3461-3462 3.00 1.50
b. As "a," with Chinese text in red in L & R sheet margins 3.00 1.50

Issued: No. 3462b, 1/1/03. Chinese text in left and right sheet margins on No. 3462b commemorates the establishment of Chunghwa Post Co., Ltd.

Street Scene on a Summer Day, by Chen Cheng-po A850

Girl in the White Dress, by Li Mei-shu — A851

Courtyard with Banana Trees, by Liao Chi-chun — A852

Sunrise, by Kuo Po-chuan A853

Perf. 11½x11¼, 11¼x11½

2002, Dec. 6

3463 A850 $5 multi .40 .25
3464 A851 $5 multi .40 .25
3465 A852 $10 multi .75 .30
3466 A853 $20 multi 1.60 .55
Nos. 3463-3466 (4) 3.15 1.35

Admission to World Trade Organization, 1st Anniv. — A854

2003, Jan. 1 Litho. ***Perf. 11½x11¼***

3467 A854 $17 multi 2.75 1.10

Spring on Wuyen Peak A855

Glacial Cirques, Mt. Nanhu
A856

Mt. Nanhu
A857

Snow on Mt. Chungyang Chien
A858

2003, Jan. 23

3468	A855	$5 multi	.40	.25
3469	A856	$5 multi	.40	.25
3470	A857	$12 multi	.90	.35
3471	A858	$25 multi	1.60	.70
		Nos. 3468-3471 (4)	3.30	1.55

Compare with Types A814, A834-A837.

Fruit Type of 2001

2003-05 Litho. *Perf. 12½x13¼*

3472	A813	$9 Rose apples	.60	.25
a.		"Republic of China" 12½mm long ('05)	.60	.30
3473	A813	$13 Kumquats	.90	.40
3474	A813	$15 Lemons	1.10	.45
a.		"Republic of China" 12½mm long ('05)	.95	.50
3475	A813	$34 Coconuts	2.00	1.00

Issued: Nos. 3472-3475, 2/14/03; 3472a, 3474a, 5/16/05.

"Republic of China" on Nos. 3472 and 3474 is 12mm long and is in taller letters.

Love — A859

Hearts and: No. 3476, $5, Woman tending to man in wheelchair. No. 3477, $5, Family. $10, Landscape. $25, Girl and dogs.

2003, Mar. 20 *Perf. 11¼x11½*

3476-3479 A859 Set of 4 3.50 2.50

Puppet Theater
A860

Designs: No. 3480, $5, *Journey to the West* performed on outdoor stage. No. 3481, $5, Puppets on television. $10, *Mysteries of the Wolf Castle* performed at the National Opera House. $25, Screening of movie, *Legend of the Sacred Stone.*

2003, Apr. 3 *Perf. 11½x11¼*

3480-3483 A860 Set of 4 3.50 2.50

Merops Philippinus
A861

Designs: Nos. 3484, 3488a, $5, Foraging. Nos. 3485, 3488b, $5, Roosting. Nos. 3486, 3488c, $10, Bathing. Nos. 3487, 3488d, $20, Feeding chick.

2003, May 8 *Perf. 12½*

With White Frame

3484-3487 A861 Set of 4 3.00 2.25

Souvenir Sheet

Without White Frame

3488 A861 Sheet of 4, #a-d 3.00 2.25

No. 3488 contains four 33x25mm stamps.

Furniture — A862

Designs: No. 3489, $5, Wash basin stand. No. 3490, $5, Canopy bed. $12, Taishi chair. $20, Pahsien table.

2003, May 22 *Perf. 11¼x11½*

3489-3492 A862 Set of 4 3.25 1.50

Folktale "Eight Immortals Cross the Sea" — A863

Immortal: No. 3493, $5, Riding catfish. No. 3494, $5, On donkey. $10, Holding fan. $25, In brown robe.

2003, June 12

3493-3496 A863 Set of 4 3.50 1.50

See Nos. 3535-3538.

Moths
A864

Designs: No. 3497, $5, Antitrygodes divisaria perturbata. No. 3498, $5, Vamuna virilis. $12, Sinna extrema. $20, Thyas juno.

2003, June 26 *Perf. 11½x11¼*

3497-3500 A864 Set of 4 3.25 1.50

Dragonflies
A865

Designs: Nos. 3501, 3505a, $5, Acisoma panorpoides panorpoides. Nos. 3502, 3505b, $5, Sympetrum eroticu ardens, vert. Nos. 3503, 3505c, $10, Anax parthenope julius. Nos. 3504, 3505d, $17, Rhyothemis variegata arria, vert.

2003, July 25 *Perf. 12½*

With White Frames

3501-3504 A865 Set of 4 3.25 1.50

Souvenir Sheet

Without White Frames

Perf. 11¾

3505 A865 Sheet of 4, #a-d 3.25 1.50

Stamp size: Nos. 3505a, 3505c, 33x25mm; Nos. 3505b, 3505d, 25x33mm.

Greetings
A866

No. 3506: a, Cranes. b, Wood carving and red plate. c, Fish and coin. d, Bamboo. e, Wood carving of bird.

No. 3507: a, Vase with tasseled rope. b, Like #3506a. c, Like #3506b. d, Three brown containers. e, Like #3508. f, Dragon. g, Like #3506c. h, Like #3506d. i, Horse and rider. j, Like #3506e.

No. 3508, Vase with flowers.

2003, Aug. 9 *Perf. 12½*

3506	Horiz. strip of 5	1.25	.65
a.-e.	A866 $3.50 Any single	.25	.25
f.	Sheet of 10 #3506a+ 10 attached labels	12.00	12.00
g.	Sheet of 10 #3506b+ 10 attached labels	12.00	12.00
h.	Sheet of 10 #3506c + 10 attached labels	12.00	12.00
i.	Sheet of 10 #3506d + 10 attached labels	12.00	12.00
j.	Sheet of 10 #3506e + 10 attached labels	12.00	12.00
k.	Sheet , 2 each #3506a-3506e + 10 attached labels	12.00	12.00
3507	Block of 10	3.50	1.75
a.-j.	A866 $5 Any single	.35	.25
k.	Sheet of 10 #3507a + 10 attached labels	12.50	12.50
l.	Sheet of 10 #3507b + 10 attached labels	12.50	12.50
m.	Sheet of 10 #3507c + 10 attached labels	12.50	12.50
n.	Sheet of 10 #3507d + 10 attached labels	12.50	12.50
o	Sheet of 10 #3507e + 10 attached labels	12.50	12.50
p.	Sheet of 10 #3507f + 10 attached labels	12.50	12.50
q.	Sheet of 10 #3507g + 10 attached labels	12.50	12.50
r.	Sheet of 10 #3507h + 10 attached labels	12.50	12.50
s.	Sheet of 10 #3507i + 10 attached labels	12.50	12.50
t.	Sheet of 10 #3507j + 10 attached labels	12.50	12.50
u.	Sheet, #3507a-3507j + 10 attached labels	12.50	12.50
v.	Sheet, #3507d, 3507e, 3507f, 3507g, 3507h, 3507j + 6 attached labels ('04)	9.00	9.00
3508	A866 $12 multi	.85	.45
a.	Sheet of 10 #3508 + 10 attached labels	17.00	17.00
	Nos. 3506-3508 (3)	5.60	2.85

Nos. 3506f-3506k sold for $185 each; Nos. 3507k-3507u for $200 each; No. 3508a for $270 each. Labels, which were personalized, were separated from stamps on Nos. 3506f-3506k, 3507k-3507u, 3508a by vertical rows of simulated perforations.

No. 3507v sold for $150 and has labels, which could be personalized, that are separated from the stamps by simulated perforations. Issued 5/30/04.

Bird Manual Type of 1999 and

White-throated Laughing Thrush — A867

Designs: No. 3510, Great mynah (2 characters at LR). $12, Yellow-legged buttonquail (3 characters at UL). $25, Crested lark (4 characters at L).

Perf. 11½x11¼

2003, Sept. 10 Litho.

3509	A867	$5 multi	.40	.25
3510	A792	$5 multi	.40	.25
3511	A792	$12 multi	.90	.35
3512	A792	$25 multi	1.75	.75
		Nos. 3509-3512 (4)	3.45	1.60

Chungshan Park, Taichung
A868

Tourist attractions: No. 3514, $5, Dongshan River Bridge, Ilan. $11, Badlands, Tianliao. $20, Sansiantai, Chenggong.

2003, Oct. 28 Litho. *Perf. 11½*

3513-3516 A868 Set of 4 3.00 1.25

Chungshan Park, cent. (No. 3513).

Veterans Day, 25th Anniv.
A869

Veterans Affairs Commission insignia and: $5, Veterans building Central Cross-Island Highway. $25, Veterans, homes and hospital for veterans.

2003, Oct. 31

3517-3518 A869 Set of 2 2.00 .90

The Back Yard, by Lu Tie-jhou — A870

A Gold Mine Tower: Jioufen, by Lin Ke-gong — A871

Leisurely, by Chen Jin — A872

East Gate, by Li Ze-fan
A873

2003, Nov. 20

3519	A870	$5 multi	.40	.25
3520	A871	$5 multi	.40	.25
3521	A872	$10 multi	.75	.30
3522	A873	$20 multi	1.50	.60
		Nos. 3519-3522 (4)	3.05	1.40

New Year 2004 (Year of the Monkey) — A874

Monkey holding fruit: $3.50, With tail. $13, In hand.

2003, Dec. 1 *Perf. 12¼*

3523-3524	A874	Set of 2	1.40	.70
3523a		Perf. 12¼ vert.	.35	.25
3524a		Sheet, 2 each #3523-3524	2.50	1.60
3523b		Booklet pane, 12 #3523a	6.50	—
		Complete booklet, #3523b	7.25	

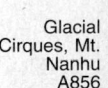

Springs
A875

Designs: No. 3525, $5, Yangmingshan Hot Springs, fumaroles (light orange background). No. 3526, $5, Suao Cold Springs, Nanfangao Bridge (light blue background). $10, Guanziling Murky Hot Spring, Shuei Huo Tong Yuan. $25, Green Island Seabed Hot Springs, Green Island Lighthouse.

2003, Dec. 14 *Perf. 13*

3525-3528 A875 Set of 4 3.50 1.50
3528a Souvenir sheet, #3525-3528 3.50 2.00

Completion of Highway 3 — A876

Designs: $5, Jhonggang Interchange. $25, Cingshuei Service Area.
$20, Cingshuei Service Area, diff.

2004, Jan. 8 **Litho.** *Perf. 12½*

3529-3530 A876 Set of 2 2.25 .90

Souvenir Sheet

Perf. 11½x11¼

3531 A876 $20 multi 1.50 1.25

No. 3531 contains one 80x30mm stamp.

Flowers — A877

Designs: No. 3532, $5, Lilium formosanum. No. 3533, $5, Hippeastrum x hybridum. $12, Fressia x hybrida.

2004, Jan. 17 *Perf. 12¼*

3532-3534 A877 Set of 3 1.75 .70
3534a Souvenir sheet, #3532-3534, perf. 13 1.75 1.25
3534b As "a," with Taiwan Flower Expo emblem and text added in margin 1.75 1.25

Eight Immortals Cross the Sea Type of 2003

Immortal: No. 3535, $5, With crane and flute. No. 3536, $5, With lotus flower. $10, Holding stick, wearing red robe. $25, Carrying flower basket.

2004, Feb. 25 *Perf. 11¼x11½*

3535-3538 A863 Set of 4 3.50 1.50

Red Cross Society, Cent. — A878

No. 3539: a, Heart, stylized people with arms raised. b, Heart, stylized people doing Red Cross activities.

2004, Mar. 9 *Perf. 11¼x11½*

3539 A878 $5 Horiz. pair, #a-b 1.00 .50

A Young Girl From Lu Kai, by Yan Shui-long
A879

Old Street in Taipei, by Yang San-lang
A880

Happy Farmers, by Lee Shih-chiao
A881

Fish Shop, by Liu Chi-hsiang
A882

Perf. 11¼x11½, 11½x11¼

2004, Mar. 25

3540 A879 $5 multi .40 .25
3541 A880 $5 multi .40 .25
3542 A881 $10 multi .80 .30
3543 A882 $20 multi 1.40 .60
Nos. 3540-3543 (4) 3.00 1.40

Butterflies
A883

Designs: No. 3544, $5, Parantica sita niphonica. No. 3545, $5, Choaspes benjaminii formosanus. $17, Junonia almana. $20, Artipe eryx horiella.

2004, Apr. 21 *Perf. 11½x11¼*

3544-3547 A883 Set of 4 3.50 1.50

Yijhen Folk Art Performers
A884

Designs: No. 3548, $5, Eight Generals (buff background). No. 3549, $5, Song Jiang Battle Array (grayish blue background). $11, Drum Dance. $25, Stilt walkers.

2004, May 11

3548-3551 A884 Set of 4 3.50 1.50

Inauguration of Pres. Chen Shiu-bian and Vice-President Hsiu-lien Annette Lu — A885

No. 3552 — President, Vice-President and: a, Map of Taiwan, flag, crowd. b, Map of People's Republic of China and Taiwan, handshake, flowers. c, Buildings, crowd. d, Train, highway, buildings.
$12, President, Vice-President, buildings, train, highway.

2004, May 20 *Perf. 12½*

3552 Horiz. strip of 4 1.75 .70
a.-d. A885 $5 Any single .40 .25

Souvenir Sheet

Perf. 12

3553 A885 $12 multi 1.50 1.25

No. 3553 contains one 80x30mm stamp.

Opening of Movie, *Harry Potter and the Prisoner of Azkaban* — A886

No. 3554: a, $5, Harry, messenger owl, Hedwig, with letter. b, $5, Hedwig, rose background. c, $5, Harry riding Hippogriff. d, $5, Hippogriff, green background. e, $5, Harry, Monster Book of Monsters. f, $25, Crookshanks the Cat.

No. 3555: a, $5, Harry playing quidditch. b, $5, Harry playing quidditch, Dementors. c, $5, Harry and Hermoine riding Hippogriff. d, $5, Harry holding wand, Hogwarts. e, $5, Harry practicing Patronus Charm to repel Dementors. f, $25, Harry thrusting wand.

2004, June 4 *Perf. 12*

Sheets of 6, #a-f

3554-3555 A886 Set of 2 10.00 6.00

Postal administrators said that Nos. 3554-3555 would not be not sold directly to customers at foreign addresses. The sheets were made available abroad through Canada Post's philatelic agency, and also were sent to foreign standing order customers.

Old Train Stations
A887

Designs: No. 3556, $5, Keelung Station, rickshaws. No. 3557, $5, Taipei Station, automobile. $15, Hsinchu Station, ox and cart. $25, Taichung Station, wagons.

2004, June 9 *Perf. 13½x13¾*

3556-3559 A887 Set of 4 3.50 1.50

Compare Type A887 with Types A926-A929.

Iron Fort, Nangan Island
A888

Cinbi, Beigan Island
A889

Fujheng, Tungchu Island
A890

Lienyuyikeng, Tungyin Island — A891

2004, July 1 **Litho.** *Perf. 11½x11¼*

3560 A888 $5 multi .40 .25
3561 A889 $5 multi .40 .25
3562 A890 $9 multi .70 .25
3563 A891 $25 multi 1.90 .75
Nos. 3560-3563 (4) 3.40 1.50

Matsu National Scenic Area.

Crabs
A892

Designs: No. 3564, $3.50, Uca formosensis. No. 3565, $3.50, Uca borealis. $5, Uca arcuata. $25, Uca lactea.

2004, July 21

3564-3567 A892 Set of 4 2.50 1.10

Souvenir Sheet

Listening to the Lute, Attributed to Li Sung — A893

No. 3568: a, $5, Lute player. b, $25, Scholar and woman.

2004, Aug. 6 *Perf. 12*

3568 A893 Sheet of 2, #a-b 2.50 2.50

Souvenir Sheet

Taipei 2005 Intl. Stamp Exhibition — A894

No. 3569: a, $5, Sun Moon Lake. b, $25, Mt. Ali.

2004, Aug. 27 ***Perf. 11½x11¼***

3569	A894	Sheet of 2, #a-b	3.00	3.00

Intl. Day of Peace A895

2004, Sept. 21 ***Perf. 12¼x11¾***

3570	A895	$15 multi	1.25	.55

Souvenir Sheets

Hello Kitty — A896

No. 3571, oval stamps: a, $5, Dear Daniel, donuts. b, $15, Hello Kitty, Taipei 101 Building.
No. 3572, rectangular stamps: a, $5, Hello Kitty, bird, horiz. b, $15, Dear Daniel, Fisherman's Wharf, Danshuei.

2004, Sept. 24 ***Perf.***

3571	A896	Sheet of 2, #a-b	1.75	1.25

Perf. 12

3572	A896	Sheet of 2, #a-b	1.75	1.25

Sayings With Numbers Greeting Stamps

One Sea of Smooth Sailing A897

Two Lions Bring Good Fortune A898

Three Goats of Auspiciousness — A899

Safety in All Four Seasons A900

Five Blessings at the Door A901

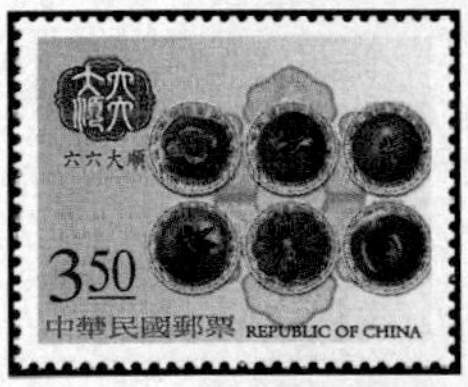

Six is Silky Smooth A902

Married for Seven Lives A903

Eight Immortals Wish for Your Perfection A904

Nine Means Success A905

Ten is All Around Perfection A906

2004, Oct. 10 ***Perf. 12½***

3573	Block of 10	3.25	1.10
a.	A897 $3.50 multi	.30	.25
b.	A898 $3.50 multi	.30	.25
c.	A899 $3.50 multi	.30	.25
d.	A900 $3.50 multi	.30	.25
e.	A901 $3.50 multi	.30	.25
f.	A902 $3.50 multi	.30	.25
g.	A903 $3.50 multi	.30	.25
h.	A904 $3.50 multi	.30	.25
i.	A905 $3.50 multi	.30	.25
j.	A906 $3.50 multi	.30	.25

Changed Colors

3574	Block of 10	4.25	1.50
a.	A897 $5 multi	.40	.25
b.	A898 $5 multi	.40	.25
c.	A899 $5 multi	.40	.25
d.	A900 $5 multi	.40	.25
e.	A901 $5 multi	.40	.25
f.	A902 $5 multi	.40	.25
g.	A903 $5 multi	.40	.25
h.	A904 $5 multi	.40	.25
i.	A905 $5 multi	.40	.25
j.	A906 $5 multi	.40	.25
k.	Sheet, #3574a-3574j + 10 attached labels ('04)	11.00	11.00

No. 3574k sold for $170 and has labels, which could be personalized, that are separated from the stamps by simulated perforations. Issued 10/10/04.

Kaohsiung Medical University, 50th Anniv. A907

Designs: No. 3575, $5, University gate and buildings. No. 3576, $5, Building, researcher, beaker, mosquito and snake.

2004, Oct. 16 ***Perf. 12½***

3575-3576	A907	Set of 2	1.00	.50

Main Peak, Mt. Cilai A908

North Peak, Mt. Cilai A909

South Peak, Mt. Cilai A910

Grasslands, Mt. Cilai — A911

2004, Oct. 16 ***Perf. 11½x11¼***

3577	A908	$5 multi	.35	.25
3578	A909	$5 multi	.35	.25
3579	A910	$12 multi	.95	.35
3580	A911	$25 multi	1.90	.75
		Nos. 3577-3580 (4)	3.55	1.60

Sports In Which Taiwanese Athletes Won Medals At 2004 Summer Olympics A912

Designs: No. 3581, $5, Women's Taekwondo. No. 3582, $5, Men's Taekwondo, vert. $9, Archery. $12, Athletes on winner's platform, vert.

Perf. 11¼x11½, 11½x11¼

2004, Oct. 22

3581-3584	A912	Set of 4	2.50	1.25

Platalea Minor A913

Designs: No. 3585, $2.50, Pair in flight. No. 3586, $2.50, Pair standing on one leg. $15, With wings spread. $25, Foraging for food.
$20, Birds in water.

2004, Oct. 30 ***Perf. 13½x13¼***

3585-3588	A913	Set of 4	3.50	1.65

Souvenir Sheet

3589	A913	$20 multi	2.25	1.00

No. 3589 contains one 80x30mm stamp.

Pres. Yen Chia-kan (1905-93) A914

2004, Nov. 5 ***Perf. 13¼x13½***

3590	A914	$12 multi	1.10	.45

New Year 2005 (Year of the Cock) — A915

Designs: $3.50, Cock on lantern. $13, Lanterns, cock
$5, Cock, hen and chick, horiz.

2004, Nov. 10 ***Perf. 12¼x11¾***

3591-3592	A915	Set of 2	1.25	.90

Souvenir Sheet

Perf. 11¾x11¼

3593	A915	$5 multi	.60	.45

No. 3593 contains one 46x26mm stamp.

Prefectural Hall, Chiayi A916

East Gate, Chiayi A917

2004, Nov. 20 ***Perf. 13½x13¼***

3594	A916	$5 multi	.50	.30
3595	A917	$5 multi	.50	.30

Chiayi, 300th anniv.

Embroidered Squares for Ching Dynasty Civil Official Court Dresses — A918

Designs: No. 3596, $3.50, Manchurian crane (orange background). No. 3597, $3.50, Golden pheasant (green background). $5, Peacock. $25, Goose.

2005, Jan. 20 Litho. ***Perf. 11½x11¼***

3596-3599 A918 Set of 4 2.40 1.25

See Nos. 3727-3730.

Greetings A919

No. 3600 — Cartoon balloon with various keyboard characters creating faces and backgrounds with: a, Hands. b, Envelopes. c, Hearts. d, Flowers.

2005, Jan. 31 ***Perf. 12½***

3600	Horiz. strip of 4	1.60	.85
a.-d.	A919 $5 Any single	.40	.25
e.	Sheet, #3600a-3600d + 4 attached labels	11.50	11.50

No. 3600e sold for $140 and has labels, which could be personalized, that are separated from the stamps by simulated perforations. Sheets exist with various arrangements of stamps and positions of labels respective to the stamps (at left, above or below).

Rotary International, Cent. — A920

Rotary emblem and: $5, Map of Taiwan. $12, Dove.

2005, Feb. 23 ***Perf. 13½x13¼***

3601-3602 A920 Set of 2 1.25 1.00

Mangroves A921

Designs: No. 3603, $3.50, Kandelia obovata. No. 3604, $3.50, Rhizophora stylosa. No. 3605, $5, Avicennia marina. No. 3606, $5, Lumnitzera racemosa.

2005, Mar. 10 ***Perf. 11½x11¼***

3603-3606 A921 Set of 4 1.25 1.00

Longshan Temple, Mengjia A922

Lin Ben Yuan Garden, Banciao A923

Designs: $13, Chaotain Temple, Beigang. $15, Fort Anping, Tainan.

2005, Mar. 18

3607	A922	$5 multi		.35	.25
3608	A923	$5 multi		.35	.25
3609	A923	$13 multi		.85	.40
3610	A923	$15 multi		.95	.45
		Nos. 3607-3610 (4)		2.50	1.35

Souvenir Sheet

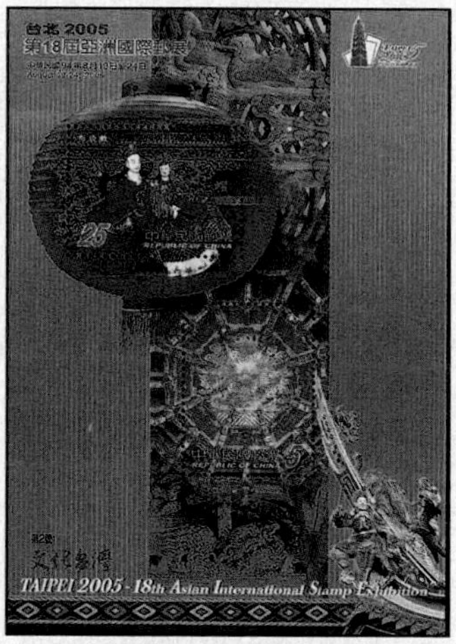

Taipei 2005 Intl. Stamp Exhibition — A924

No. 3611: a, $5, Wood carving, Mandarin Ducks Playing in a Lotus Pond. b, $25, Hand puppets, horiz.

2005, Apr. 19 ***Perf. 12***

3611 A924 Sheet of 2, #a-b 3.00 3.00

Coral Reef Fish A925

Designs: No. 3612, $5, Rhinomuraena quaesita. No. 3613, $5, Pomacanthus semicirculatus. $12, Forcipiger flavissimus. $25, Pterois volitans.

2005, May 16 ***Perf. 11½x12***

3612-3615 A925	Set of 4	3.50	1.75
a.	Sheet, 2 each #3612-3615	7.00	7.00

Changhua Train Station, 1918 A926

Chiayi Train Station, 1933 A927

Tainan Train Station, 1936 A928

Kaohsiung Train Station, 1941 A929

2005, June 9 ***Perf. 13½x13¾***

3616	A926	$5 multi	.40	.25
3617	A927	$5 multi	.40	.25
3618	A928	$15 multi	1.10	.50
3619	A929	$25 multi	1.75	.80
		Nos. 3616-3619 (4)	3.65	1.80

Compare with type A887.

Novel "The Romance of the Three Kingdoms" A930

Designs: No. 3620, $3.50, Mayhem in the Fengyi Pavilion (man and woman near pavilion railing). No. 3621, $3.50, Deterring the Enemy in Changban (horse and rider on bridge). $5, Releasing Tsao Tsao (rider on horse near flag). $20, A Trick in the Bag (man in bed holding bag).

Perf. 11½x11¼

2005, June 23 **Litho.**

3620-3623 A930	Set of 4	2.50	2.00
3623a	Souvenir sheet, #3620-3623	2.50	2.00

Lifeline Suicide Prevention Hotline — A931

2005, July 1 ***Perf. 12x11½***

3624 A931 $12 multi 1.25 .90

Albert Einstein's Theory of Relativity, Cent. — A932

2005, July 1

3625 A932 $15 multi 1.25 .60

Souvenir Sheets

Mickey Mouse — A933

No. 3626: a, $5, At ship's wheel, in *Steamboat Willie*. b, $25. As wizard, in *Fantasia*.

No. 3627: a, $5, Holding sword, in *The Prince and the Pauper*. b, $25. With Pluto, in *Mickey's Twice Upon a Christmas*.

2005, Aug. 3 ***Perf. 12***

Sheets of 2, #a-b

3626-3627 A933 Set of 2 4.00 2.00

Rooster-shaped Wine Vessel — A934

2005, Aug. 19 ***Perf. 11¼x11½***

3628	A934 $15 multi	.95	.45
a.	Sheet of 6, perf. 12	5.75	3.00

Taipei 2005 Intl. Stamp Exhibition.

Souvenir Sheets

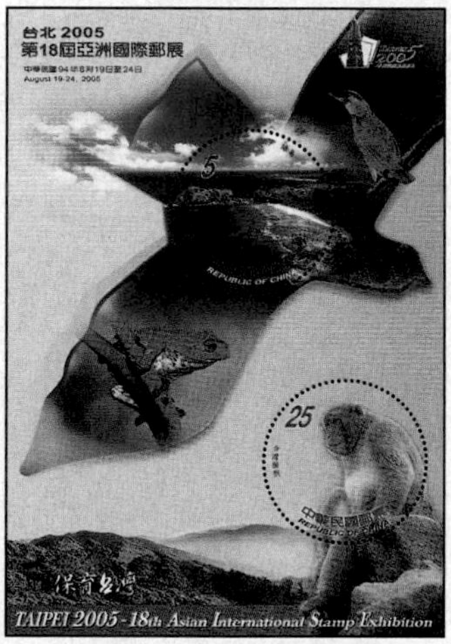

A935

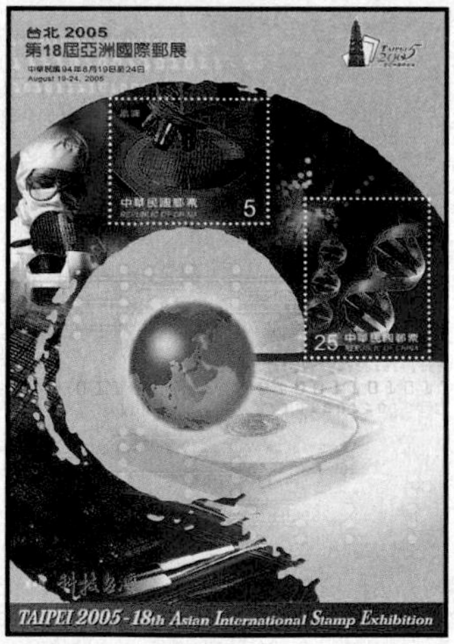

A936

A937

A938

A939

Taipei 2005 Intl. Stamp Exhibition — A940

No. 3629: a, $5, Green Island and shoreline. b, $25, Formosan rock monkey.
No. 3630: a, $5, Microscope. b, $25, DNA double helices, vert.
No. 3631: a, $5, Flowers. $25, Fruit.
No. 3632: a, $5, Ear Shooting Ceremony, vert. b, $25, Dragon boat in race.
No. 3633: a, $5, Bowl of food and ladle. b, $25, Rice cakes.
No. 3634: a, $5, Royal empress angelfish. b, $25, Red horny coral.

2005 *Perf.*
3629 A935 Sheet of 2, #a-b 2.50 .95

Perf. 13½x13, 13x13½
3630 A936 Sheet of 2, #a-b 2.50 .95

Perf. 13½
3631 A937 Sheet of 2, #a-b 2.50 .95

Perf. 13¼x13½, 13½x13¼
3632 A938 Sheet of 2, #a-b 2.50 .95

Perf. 12
3633 A939 Sheet of 2, #a-b 2.50 .95

Perf.
3634 A940 Sheet of 2, #a-b 2.50 .95
Nos. 3629-3634 (6) 15.00 5.70

Issued: No. 3629, 8/19; No. 3630, 8/20; No. 3631, 8/21; No. 3632, 8/22; No. 3633, 8/23; No. 3634, 8/24. No. 3629 contains two 38mm diameter stamps. No. 3634 contains two 43x33mm oval stamps.

Novel, "Journey to the West" — A941

Designs: No. 3635, $3.50, Stone Monkey (monkeys at waterfall). No. 3636, $3.50, Buddhist Baby in the River. $5, Making a Pass at Chang E. $20, Taming the Monster of the River of Flowing Sands.

2005, Sept. 15 *Perf. 11¼x11½*
3635-3638 A941 Set of 4 2.40 1.90

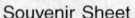

Souvenir Sheet

Kaohsiung 2005 Intl. Stamp Exhibition — A942

No. 3639: a, $5, Loyalty and Filial Piety, by Cian Syuan, vert. b, Gilt scepter.

Perf. 13¼x13½, 13½x13¼
2005, Oct. 7
3639 A942 Sheet of 2, #a-b 2.00 2.00

Souvenir Sheets

A943

Opening of Movie, *Harry Potter and the Goblet of Fire* — A944

No. 3640: a, $5, Triwizard Cup. b, $5, Harry and Hungarian Horntail. c, $5, Golden Egg. d, $5, Harry swimming. e, $5, Harry summoning Firebolt with wand. f, $25, Harry and Triwizard Cup.
No. 3641: a, $5, Hungarian Horntail. b, $5, Harry on Firebolt. c, $5, Voldemort's snake, Nagini. d, $5, Grindylows. e, $5, Dumbledore's phoenix, Fawkes. f, $25, Merchieftainess.

2005, Nov. 18 *Perf. 12*
3640 A943 Sheet of 6, #a-f 5.00 2.50
3641 A944 Sheet of 6, #a-f 5.00 2.50

New Year 2006 (Year of the Dog) — A945

Designs: $3.50, Dog at left. $13, Dog at lower right.
$12, Three dogs, horiz.

2005, Dec. 1 *Perf. 12¼x11¾*
3642-3643 A945 Set of 2 1.25 1.00

Souvenir Sheet

Perf. 11¾x11¼
3644 A945 $12 multi 1.25 .70

No. 3644 contains one 46x26mm stamp.

Pets — A946

Designs: $3.50, Siberian husky. $5, Golden retriever. $12, Himalayan cat. $25, Scottish fold cat.

Perf. 13½x12½
2005, Dec. 22 **Litho.**
Country Name in Green
3645 A946 $3.50 multi .30 .25
3646 A946 $5 multi .40 .25
3647 A946 $12 multi .80 .35
3648 A946 $25 multi 1.50 .75
Nos. 3645-3648 (4) 3.00 1.60

See Nos. 3652-3655, 3685-3688 3712-3715.

Tea Ceremony — A947

No. 3649: a, Preparation of tea set (dull orange panel). b, Placing of tea leaves in pot (lemon panel). c, Pouring hot water over pots and cups (light green panel). d, Drying of pot and pouring of tea (blue geen panel). e, Smelling and drinking of tea (gray blue panel).

2006, Jan. 26 *Perf. 13½*
3649 A947 Horiz. strip of 5 2.00 1.00
a.-e. $5 Any single .40 .25

Taipei 101 Building — A948

Designs: $5, In day. $12, At night.

2006, Feb. 23 *Perf. 12*
3650-3651 A948 Set of 2 1.25 .70

Pets Type of 2005

Designs: $2.50, Labrador retriever. $7, St. Bernard. $10, Siamese cat. $32, Persian cat.

2006, Mar. 8 *Perf. 13½x12½*
Country Name in Blue
3652 A946 $2.50 multi .25 .25
3653 A946 $7 multi .45 .25
3654 A946 $10 multi .60 .30
3655 A946 $32 multi 2.00 1.00
Nos. 3652-3655 (4) 3.30 1.80

See Nos. 3712-3715.

King Penguins A949

Aptenodytes patagonicus: No. 3656, $5, Adult and juvenile. No. 3657, $5, Courtship. $9, Swimming and diving, horiz. $12, Gliding and preening, horiz.
$15, Colony, horiz.

Perf. 11¼x11½, 11½x11¼
2006, Mar. 26
3656-3659 A949 Set of 4 2.40 2.00

Souvenir Sheet

Perf. 12
3660 A949 $15 multi 1.60 1.00

No. 3660 contains one 80x30mm stamp.

Miniature Sheet

Children's Art — A950

No. 3661 — Winning drawings in children's stamp design competition: a, Birds with black bills. b, People with red faces. c, Pheasants. d, Chinese celebration. e, Fishing boats and catch. f, People with large flowers and fruit. g, Man painting Chinese lantern. h, Bridge and ducks. i, Train. j, Bees and flowers. k, People with black faces. l, Boy on ladder. m, People and chickens. n, Ring of people around dancers and musicians. o, People and large lions. p, Two cats. q, People and cow. r, Whale and fish. s, People with white faces bending backwards. t, Bus.

2006, Apr. 4 ***Perf. 11½***

3661 A950 $5 Sheet of 20, #a-t 6.50 3.50

Fireflies A951

Designs: No. 3662, $5, Pyrocoelia analis. No. 3663, $5, Diaphanes citrinus. No. 3664, $5, Diaphanes niveus. No. 3665, $5, Diaphanes formosus.

2006, May 25 ***Perf. 13½x13¼***

3662-3665 A951 Set of 4 1.60 .75

Souvenir Sheet

Completion of Nangang to Suao Section of National Expressway 5 — A952

2006, June 16 Litho. ***Perf. 11½***

3666 A952 $12 multi 1.50 .80

Souvenir Sheets

Winnie the Pooh — A953

No. 3667: a, $5, Winnie the Pooh pushing Piglet in wheelbarrow. b, $25, Winnie the Pooh, Piglet and Tigger floating in inner tube.

No. 3668: a, $5, Winnie the Pooh and Piglet running in autumn. b, $25, Winnie the Pooh and Tigger ice fishing.

2006, June 21 ***Perf. 12***

Sheets of 2, #a-b

3667-3668 A953 Set of 2 4.00 2.00

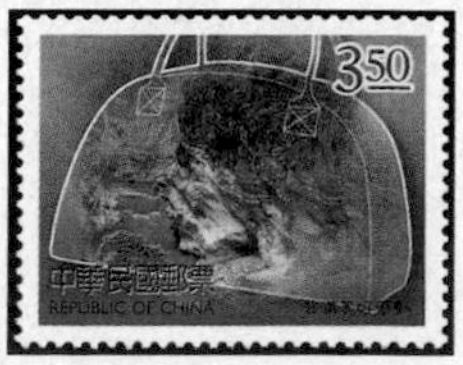

Tourism Greeting Stamps A954

Designs: Nos. 3669a, 3670a, Satchel and cliff. Nos. 3669b, 3670b, Camera and boat. Nos. 3669c, 3670c, Notebook, pen and bridge. No. 3669d, 3670d, Sailboat and rock. No. 3669e, 3670e, Heart and train.

2006, June 30 ***Perf. 12½***

3669 Horiz. strip of 5 1.50 .55
a.-e. A954 $3.50 Any single .30 .25
f. Sheet, 2 each #3669a-3669e, + 5 labels 7.00 —
3670 Horiz. strip of 5 2.00 .80
a.-e. A954 $5 Any single .40 .25
f. Sheet, 2 each #3670a-3670e, + 5 labels 7.00 —

Nos. 3669f and 3670f each sold for $100. Labels could be personalized.

Fish A955

Designs: No. 3671, $5, Amphiprion ocellaris. No. 3672, $5, Zanclus cornutus. No. 3673, $12, Coris gaimard. No. 3674, $12, Oxycirrhites typus.

2006, July 14 ***Perf. 11½***

3671-3674 A955 Set of 4 2.40 2.00
3674a Miniature sheet, 2 each #3671-3674, perf. 11½x12 4.75 4.75

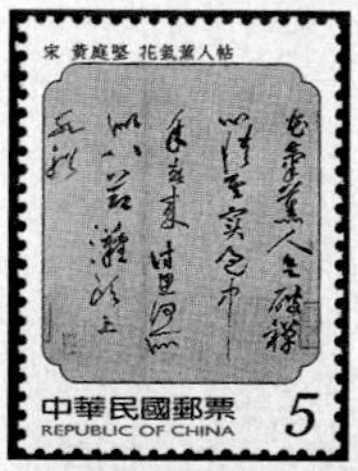

A956

Sung Dynasty Calligraphy and Painting — A957

Designs: $5, Poem by Huang T'ing-chien. $9, Calligraphy on silk, by Mi Fu. Nos. 3677, 3679a, $12, Detail of magpie in flight, from Magpies and Hare, by Ts'ui Po. Nos. 3678, 3679b, $15, Detail of magpie on branch, from Magpies and Hare.

2006, Aug. 4 ***Perf. 11½***

Denominations in Black

3675-3678 A956 Set of 4 2.75 1.40

Souvenir Sheet

Denominations in Black and Orange

Perf. 12½

3679 A957 Sheet of 2, #a-b 2.25 1.10

Dragonflies A958

Designs: Nos. 3680, 3684a, $5, Crocothemis servilia servilia. Nos. 3681, 3684b, $5, Orthetrum, pruinosum neglectum, vert. Nos. 3682, 3684c, $12, Diplacodes trivialis, vert. No. 3683, 3684d, $12, Orthetrum sabina sabina.

Perf. 13x13¼, 13¼x13

2006, Aug. 16 With White Frames

3680-3683 A958 Set of 4 2.40 2.00

Souvenir Sheet

Without White Frames

Perf. 11¾

3684 A958 Sheet of 4, #a-d 2.40 2.00

Pets Type of 2005

Designs: $1, Yorkshire terrier. $9, Pomeranian. $15, Abyssinian cat. $20, Norwegian Forest cat.

2006, Aug. 30 ***Perf. 13½x12½***

Country Name in Blue

3685 A946 $1 multi .25 .25
3686 A946 $9 multi .55 .25
3687 A946 $15 multi .90 .45
3688 A946 $20 multi 1.25 .60
Nos. 3685-3688 (4) 2.95 1.55

Aerial Activities — A959

Designs: No. 3689, $3.50, Paragliding. No. 3690, $3.50, Hang gliding, horiz. $12, Ultralight aircraft, horiz. $15, Parasailing.

2006, Sept. 15 ***Perf. 13½***

3689-3692 A959 Set of 4 2.75 1.50

Pitta Nympha — A960

Designs: Nos. 3693, 3697a, $5, On branch. Nos. 3694, 3697b, $5, In flight, horiz. Nos. 3695, 3697c, $10, With young at nest, horiz. Nos. 3696, 3697d, $10, With insect in beak.

Perf. 13¼x13, 13x13¼

2006, Sept. 30 With White Frames

3693-3696 A960 Set of 4 2.25 1.10

Souvenir Sheet

Without White Frames

Perf. 11¾

3697 A960 Sheet of 4, #a-d 2.25 1.10

Cetaceans A961

Designs: No. 3698, $5, Stenella attenuata. No. 3699, $5, Stenella longirostris. $10, Feresa attenuata. $15, Physeter macrocephalus.

Perf. 13x12 Syncopated

2006, Oct. 18 Litho.

3698-3701 A961 Set of 4 2.50 1.50
3701a Souvenir sheet, #3698-3701 2.50 1.50

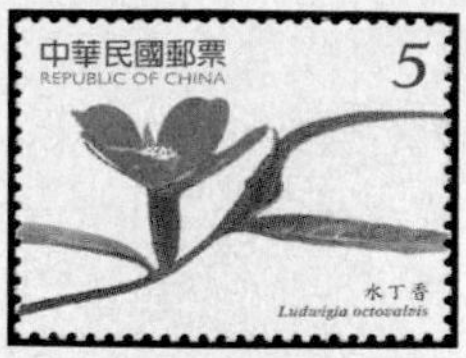

Flowers A962

Designs: No. 3702, $5, Ludwigia octovalvis. No. 3703, $5, Hygrophila pogonocalyx, vert. $12, Titanotrichum oldhamii, vert.

2006, Nov. 8 ***Perf. 11½***

3702-3704 A962 Set of 3 1.60 .80

Scenic Areas — A963

Designs: No. 3705, $5, Jhongshan Building, Yangmingshan National Park. No. 3706, $5, Taroko Gorge, vert. $9, Queen's Head Rock, vert. $12, Sun Moon Lake.

2006, Nov. 11 ***Perf. 12½***

3705-3708 A963 Set of 4 2.25 1.10

A964

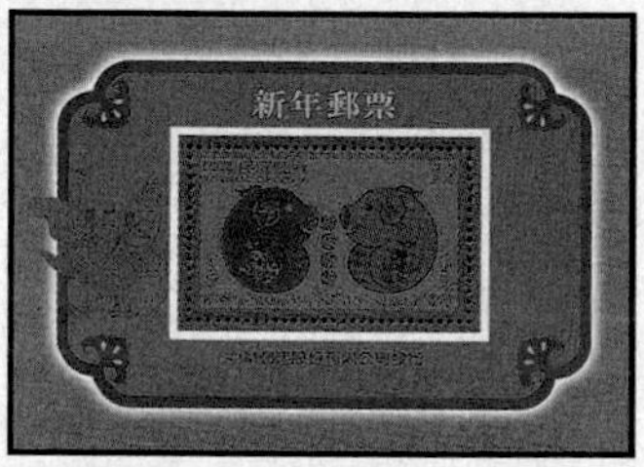

New Year 2007 (Year of the Pig) — A965

Designs: $3.50, Pig on drum. $13, Pig and drums.

2006, Dec. 1 ***Perf. 12¼x11¾***

3709-3710 A964 Set of 2 1.25 .60

Souvenir Sheet

Perf. 11½x11¼

3711 A965 $12 multi 1.25 .60

Pets Type of 2005

Designs: 50c, Border collie. $13, Beagle. $17, American Shorthair cat. $34, Maine Coon cat.

2006, Dec. 18 ***Perf. 13½x12½***

Country Name in Green

3712 A946 50c multi .25 .25
3713 A946 $13 multi .80 .40
3714 A946 $17 multi 1.10 .55
3715 A946 $34 multi 2.10 1.10
Nos. 3712-3715 (4) 4.25 2.30

Inauguration of High Speed Rail Line — A966

No. 3716: a, 700T Series train. b, Hsinchu Station.

2006, Dec. 25 ***Perf. 11½***

3716 A966 $12 Horiz. pair, #a-b 1.50 .75

Orchids — A967

Designs: $3.50, Phaius tankervilleae. $5, Spiranthes sinensis. $12, Vanda x hybrida. $25, Cattleya sp.

2007, Jan. 10 Litho. ***Perf. 13½x12½***

3717	A967	$3.50 multi	.25	.25
3718	A967	$5 multi	.30	.25
3719	A967	$12 multi	.75	.35
3720	A967	$25 multi	1.50	.75
	Nos. 3717-3720 (4)		2.80	1.60

See Nos. 3751-3754, 3768-3771.

Ching Dynasty Jewelry A968

Designs: No. 3721, $5, Earrings. No. 3722, $5, Hairpin. $12, Fingernail guard. $25, Ring.

2007, Jan. 17 ***Perf. 11½***

3721-3724 A968 Set of 4 3.00 1.50

Valentine's Day — A969

Heart and faces in: $5, White. $20, Red.

2007, Feb. 6

3725-3726 A969 Set of 2 1.50 .75

Embroidered Squares Type of 2005

Embroidered squares for Ching Dynasty military officials: No. 3727, $3.50, Cilin (light green background). No. 3728, $3.50, Lion (light orange background). $5, Leopard (bright orange background). $25, Tiger (light blue background).

2007, Feb. 16 ***Perf. 11½x11¼***

3727-3730 A918 Set of 4 2.25 1.10

Feb. 28, 1947 Massacre Memorial Museum A970

2007, Feb. 28

3731 A970 $5 multi 4.00 .25

Bridges A971

Designs: No. 3732, $5, Kanjin Bridge, Taoyuan (green panel). No. 3733, $5, Fusing Bridge, Luofu (purple panel). $12, MacArthur Second Bridge, Taipei. $15, Dajhih Bridge, Taipei.

2007, Apr. 12 Litho. ***Perf. 11½x12***

3732-3735 A971 Set of 4 2.25 1.10

See Nos. 3808-3811.

Lesser Panda A972

Panda: No. 3736, $5, Eating bamboo. No. 3737, $5, Resting on rock. No. 3738, $10, Walking near tree, vert. No. 3739, $10, Scratching on rock, vert.
$12, Two pandas, vert.

Perf. 11½x11¼, 11¼x11½

2007, Apr. 25

3736-3739 A972 Set of 4 1.90 .95

Souvenir Sheet

Perf. 12

3740 A972 $12 multi .75 .35

No. 3740 contains one 40x50mm stamp.

Dharma Drum Mountain Intl. Buddhist Educational Complex — A973

Chung Tai Chan Monastery A974

Fo Guang Shan Monastery A975

Tzu Chi Foundation Building — A976

2007, May 24 ***Perf. 13¼x13***

3741	A973	$5 multi	.30	.25
3742	A974	$5 multi	.30	.25
3743	A975	$5 multi	.30	.25
3744	A976	$5 multi	.30	.25
	Nos. 3741-3744 (4)		1.20	1.00

Dahlia and Butterflies A977

Iris and Butterfly A978

Clematis and Ladybugs A979

Tung Blossom and Butterflies A980

Rose and Butterfly A981

Sunflower and Insects — A982

Bird-of-Paradise Flower and Butterfly A983

Lotus and Butterflies A984

English Daisies and Dragonfly A985

Balloon Flower and Dragonfly A986

2007, May 28 ***Perf. 12½***

3745		Block of 10	2.10	1.10
a.	A977	$3.50 multi	.25	.25
b.	A978	$3.50 multi	.25	.25
c.	A979	$3.50 multi	.25	.25
d.	A980	$3.50 multi	.25	.25
e.	A981	$3.50 multi	.25	.25
f.	A982	$3.50 multi	.25	.25
g.	A983	$3.50 multi	.25	.25
h.	A984	$3.50 multi	.25	.25
i.	A985	$3.50 multi	.25	.25
j.	A986	$3.50 multi	.25	.25

Changed Colors

3746		Block of 10	3.00	1.50
a.	A977	$5 multi	.30	.25
b.	A978	$5 multi	.30	.25
c.	A979	$5 multi	.30	.25
d.	A980	$5 multi	.30	.25
e.	A981	$5 multi	.30	.25
f.	A982	$5 multi	.30	.25
g.	A983	$5 multi	.30	.25
h.	A984	$5 multi	.30	.25
i.	A985	$5 multi	.30	.25
j.	A986	$5 multi	.30	.25

Food Preparation Implements — A987

Designs: No. 3747, $5, Rice bucket and shelf (light blue background). No. 3748, $5, Steamer (green background). No. 3749, $12, Rice baskets (tan background). No. 3750, $12, Dinnerware (lilac background).

2007, June 28 ***Perf. 11½x11¼***

3747-3750 A987 Set of 4 2.10 1.10

Orchids Type of 2007 Inscribed "Taiwan" Instead of "Republic of China"

Designs: $1, Paphiopedilum sp. $2.50, Phalaenopsis aphrodite. $10, Dendrobium sp. $32, Oncidium x hybridum.

2007, July 12 ***Perf. 13½x12½***

3751	A967	$1 multi	.25	.25
3752	A967	$2.50 multi	.25	.25
3753	A967	$10 multi	.60	.30
3754	A967	$32 multi	2.00	1.00
	Nos. 3751-3754 (4)		3.10	1.80

End of Martial Law, 20th Anniv. — A988

2007, July 15 ***Perf. 11¼x11½***

3755 A988 $12 multi .75 .35

Fish A989

Designs: No. 3756, $5, Nemateleotris magnifica. No. 3757, $5, Balistoides conspicillum. $12, Paracanthurus hepatus. $25, Cetoscarus bicolor.

2007, July 27 ***Perf. 11½x11¼***

3756-3759 A989 Set of 4 5.50 1.60

Chiang Wei-shui (1890-1931), Political and Social Leader — A990

2007, Aug. 6 Engr. ***Perf. 11¼x11½***

3760 A990 $25 brown 1.50 .75

Taiwan - African Heads of State Summit, Taipei A991

2007, Sept. 9 Litho. ***Perf. 11½x11¼***

3761 A991 $12 multi .90 .55

Miniature Sheet

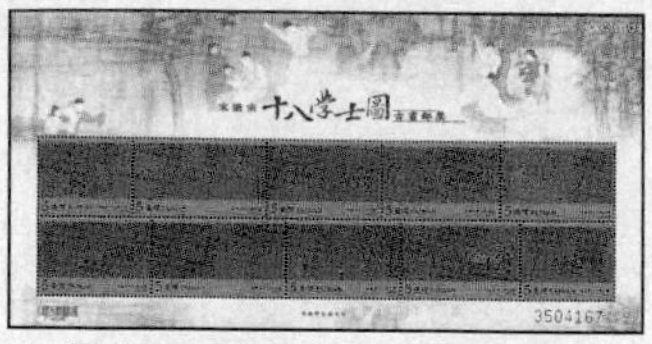

Eighteen Scholars of T'ang, by Emperor Hui-tsung. — A992

No. 3762 — Various portions of painting numbered: a, (10-5), 36x30mm. b, (10-4), 51x30mm. c, (10-3), 43x30mm. d, (10-2), 45x30mm. e, (10-1), 43x30mm. f, (10-10), 43x30mm. g, (10-9), 51x30mm. h, (10-8), 43x30mm. i, (10-7), 45x30mm. j, (10-6), 36x30mm.

2007, Sept. 21 ***Perf. 13¼***

3762 A992 Sheet of 10 3.00 1.50
a.-j. $5 Any single .30 .25

Doves — A993

2007, Sept. 28 ***Perf. 11¼x11½***

3763 A993 $5 multi .60 .30

Portions of the design were applied by a thermographic process producing a shiny, raised effect.

Shells A994

Designs: No. 3764, $5, Marchia loebbeckei. No. 3765, $5, Harpa major. No. 3766, $12, Epitonium scalare. No. 3767, $12, Cypraea aurantium.

2007, Oct. 11 Litho. ***Perf. 11½x11¼***

3764-3767 A994 Set of 4 2.10 1.10

Orchids Type of 2007 Inscribed "Taiwan" Instead of "Republic of China"

Designs: $7, Ascocentrum sp. $9, Arundina graminifolia. $15, Vanda teres. $20, Epidendrum sp.

2007, Oct. 24 ***Perf. 13½x12½***

3768 A967 $7 multi .45 .25
3769 A967 $9 multi .55 .30
3770 A967 $15 multi .95 .45
3771 A967 $20 multi 1.25 .60
Nos. 3768-3771 (4) 3.20 1.60

Birds — A995

Designs: $3.50, Pericrocotus solaris. $5, Parus varius. $12, Luscinia calliope. $25, Phoenicurus auroreus.

2007, Nov. 3

3772 A995 $3.50 multi .25 .25
3773 A995 $5 multi .30 .25
3774 A995 $12 multi .75 .35
3775 A995 $25 multi 1.60 .80
Nos. 3772-3775 (4) 2.90 1.65

See Nos. 3792-3795, 3819-3822, 3845-3848.

Outdoor Activities — A996

Designs: No. 3776, $5, Speed walking. No. 3777, $5, Cycling. $12, Skateboarding. $25, Rollerblading.

2007, Nov. 9 ***Perf. 11½***

3776-3779 A996 Set of 4 3.00 1.50

Scouting, Cent. — A997

2007, Nov. 28 ***Perf. 12½***

3780 A997 $12 multi .75 .35

A998

New Year 2008 (Year of the Rat) — A999

2007, Dec. 3 ***Perf. 12½x11¾***

3781 A998 $3.50 Rat at left .30 .25
3782 A998 $13 Rat at right .90 .40

Souvenir Sheet

Perf. 12½

3783 A999 $12 multi 1.25 .60

Democracy Movement Leaders A1000

Designs: No. 3784, Lei Chen (1897-1979), publisher. No. 3785, Fu Jheng (1927-91), editor. No. 3786, Kuo Yu Shing (1908-85), politician. No. 3787, Huang Hsin Chieh (1928-99), politician.

2007, Dec. 10 Engr. ***Perf. 11½***

3784 A1000 $5 brown .30 .25
3785 A1000 $5 green .30 .25
3786 A1000 $5 claret .30 .25
3787 A1000 $5 brown black .30 .25
Nos. 3784-3787 (4) 1.20 1.00

Liou Family Compound, Shangfangliao — A1001

Lin Family Mansion, Banciao — A1002

Li Teng-fang Compound, Dasi — A1003

Siao Family Compound, Jiadong — A1004

2008, Jan. 23 Litho. ***Perf. 12***

3788 A1001 $5 multi .30 .25
3789 A1002 $5 multi .30 .25
3790 A1003 $5 multi .30 .25
3791 A1004 $12 multi .75 .40
Nos. 3788-3791 (4) 1.65 1.15

Birds Type of 2007

Designs: $1, Dicrurus aeneus. $2.50, Lanius schach. $10, Dendrocitta formosae. $32, Pycnonotus sinensis.

2008, Jan. 30 ***Perf. 13½x12½***

3792 A995 $1 multi .25 .25
3793 A995 $2.50 multi .25 .25
3794 A995 $10 multi .65 .30
3795 A995 $32 multi 2.00 1.00
Nos. 3792-3795 (4) 3.15 1.80

A1005

Puppet Theater — A1006

No. 3796: a, Mirror Man, denomination at UL. b, Old Oddball, denomination at UR.

No. 3797: a, Shih Yan-wun, denomination at UL. b, Dragon Lady of the Bitter Sea, denomination at UR.

2007, Feb. 4 ***Perf. 11½***

3796 A1005 $5 Horiz. pair, #a-b .65 .30
3797 A1006 $5 Horiz. pair, #a-b .65 .30
c. Souvenir sheet, #3796-3797, perf. 11½x11 1.30 .60

Syrmaticus Mikado — A1007

Litho. & Engr.

2008, Mar. 7 ***Perf. 12***

3798 A1007 $25 multi 1.75 .85

Taipei 2008 Intl. Stamp Exhibition A1008

Paintings: $5, Plum Blossoms and Solitary Bird, by Pien Wen-chin. $9, Apricot Blossoms and Peacocks, by Lu Chi. $13, Wild Duck by a Brook, by Ch'en Lin. $15, Bamboo and Shrike, by Li An-chung.

2008, Mar. 7 Litho. ***Perf. 12½***

3799-3802 A1008 Set of 4 2.75 1.40
3802a Souvenir sheet, #3799-3802, perf. 12½ syncopated 2.75 1.40

Miniature Sheets

A1009

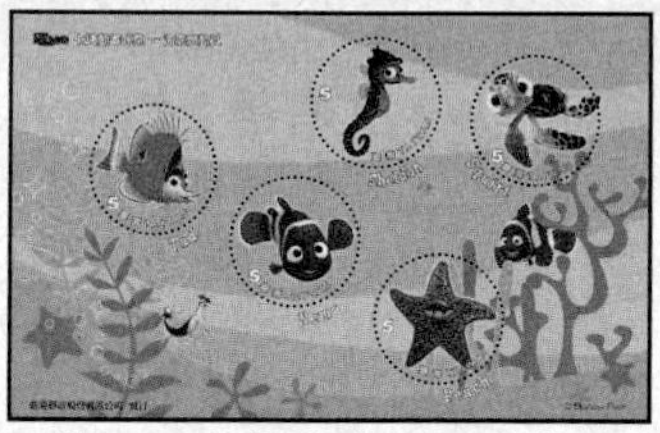

Characters From Animated Film, "Finding Nemo" — A1010

No. 3803: a, Turtles (32mm diameter). b, Dory (26x34mm). c, Bubbles (32mm diameter). d, Nemo (34x26mm). e, Pearl (32mm diameter).

No. 3804 (all stamps 32mm diameter): a, Sheldon. b, Squirt. c, Tad. d, Nemo. e, Peach.

Perf. 13x13½ (#3803b), 13½x13 (#3803d)

2008, Apr. 3

3803 A1009 $5 Sheet of 5, #a-e 1.75 .85
3804 A1010 $5 Sheet of 5, #a-e 1.75 .85

Cactus Flowers — A1011

Designs: No. 3805, $5, Hylocerus undatus. No. 3806, $5, Thelocactus bicolor. $12, Rhipsalidopsis gaertneri.

2008, Apr. 30 Litho. *Perf. 11¼x11½*
3805-3807 A1011 Set of 3 1.50 .75

Bridges Type of 2007 Inscribed "Taiwan"

Designs: No. 3808, $5, Wurih Bridge, Taichung. No. 3809, $5, Jilu Bridge, Nantou, at night. $12, Shueiyun Bridge, Shueili. $15, Sindong Bridge, Miaoli.

2008, May 12 *Perf. 11½x11¼*
3808-3811 A971 Set of 4 2.50 1.25

A1012

A1013

A1014

Inauguration of President Ma Ying-jeou and Vice-president Vincent C. Siew — A1015

2008, May 20 *Perf. 13½x13¼*
3812 A1012 $5 multi .35 .25
3813 A1013 $5 multi .35 .25
3814 A1014 $13 multi .85 .45
3815 A1015 $15 multi 1.00 .50
a. Miniature sheet, #3812-3815, perf. 12 2.60 1.40
Nos. 3812-3815 (4) 2.55 1.45

Yellow Tiger Flag A1016

Portrait of Jheng Cheng-gong A1017

2008, May 29 *Perf. 12½*
Stamps With White Frames
3816 A1016 $5 multi .35 .25
3817 A1017 $25 multi 1.75 .85

Souvenir Sheet
Perf. 13½
Stamps Without White Frames
3818 Sheet of 2 2.10 1.10
a. A1016 $5 multi .35 .25
b. A1017 $25 multi 1.75 .85

National Taiwan Museum, cent.

Birds Type of 2007

Designs: $7, Streptopelia orientalis. $15, Passer montanus. $20, Pica pica. $34, Zosterops japonicus.

2008, June 5 *Perf. 13½x12½*
3819 A995 $7 multi .50 .25
3820 A995 $15 multi 1.00 .50
3821 A995 $20 multi 1.40 .70
3822 A995 $34 multi 2.25 1.10
Nos. 3819-3822 (4) 5.15 2.55

Stag Beetles — A1018

Designs: No. 3823, $5, Neolucanus swinhoei. No. 3824, $5, Dorcus schenklingi. $10, Lucanus datunensis. $12, Cyclommatus asahinai.

2008, June 5 *Perf. 12¼*
3823-3826 A1018 Set of 4 2.10 1.10

Shells A1019

Designs: No. 3827, $5, Murex troscheli. No. 3828, $5, Lambis chiragra. No. 3829, $12, Spondylus regius. No. 3830, $12, Cymatium pyrum.

2008, July 9 Litho. *Perf. 13½*
3827-3830 A1019 Set of 4 2.25 1.10

Urocissa Caerulea A1020

Designs: Nos. 3831, 3835a, $5, Adults feeding hatchlings in nest. Nos. 3832, 3835b, $5, Bird holding snake in beak. Nos. 3833, 3835c, $12, Bird in flight. Nos. 3834, 3835d, $12, Bird on branch with spread wings.

2008, July 9 *Perf. 13x13¼*
Stamps With White Frames
3831-3834 A1020 Set of 4 2.25 1.10

Souvenir Sheet
Stamps Without White Frames
Perf. 11¾
3835 A1020 Sheet of 4, #a-d 2.25 1.10

No. 3835 contains four 34x25mm stamps.

Miniature Sheet

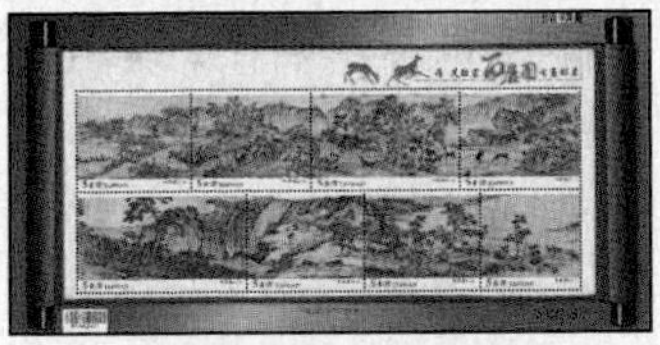

A Hundred Deers, by Ignace Sichelbart — A1021

No. 3836 — Parts of painting numbered: a, 8-1 (45x38mm). b, 8-2 (55x38mm). c, 8-3 (45x38mm). d, 8-4 (43x38mm). e, 8-5 (37x38mm). f, 8-6 (43x38mm). g, 8-7 (43x38mm). h, 8-8 (65x38mm).

2008, July 16 *Perf. 13¼*
3836 A1021 Sheet of 8, #a-h 2.60 1.40
a.-h. $5 Any single .30 .25

Items From Aboriginal Culture — A1022

Designs: $5, Paiwan earthenware pot. No. 3838, $12, Ami lover's bag (orange background). No. 3839, $12, Rukai men's head-dress (green background). $25, Bunun men's neck ornament.

2008, Aug. 1 *Perf. 11¼x11½*
3837-3840 A1022 Set of 4 3.50 1.75

Miniature Sheet

Yimin Festival — A1023

No. 3841: a, Erection of lantern poles. b, Bowl of congee, spoon, flowers. c, Sinpu Yimin Temple, horiz. d, Pig competition, horiz.

2008, Aug. 20 Litho. *Perf. 12½*
3841 A1023 $5 Sheet of 4, #a-d 1.25 .65

New Year 2009 (Year of the Ox) — A1024

Designs: $3.50, Head of ox. $13, Ox. $12, Ox in water, horiz.

2008, Dec. 1 *Perf. 12¼x11¾*
3842-3843 A1024 Set of 2 1.00 .50

Souvenir Sheet
Perf. 11¾x11¼
3844 A1024 $12 multi .75 .35

No. 3844 contains one 50x30mm stamp.

Birds Type of 2007 Inscribed "Republic of China (Taiwan)"

Designs: 50c, Rostratula benghalensis. $9, Turdus poliocephalus. $13, Amaurornis phoenicurus. $17, Cettia acanthizoides.

2009, Jan. 15 *Perf. 13½x12½*
3845 A995 50c multi .25 .25
3846 A995 $9 multi .55 .25
3847 A995 $13 multi .80 .40
3848 A995 $17 multi 1.00 .50
Nos. 3845-3848 (4) 2.60 1.40

Giant Pandas in Taipei Zoo A1025

Designs: $5, Tuan Tuan on log bridge. $9, Yuan Yuan eating.
$25, Tuan Tuan and Yuan Yuan.

2009, Jan. 20 *Perf. 11½x11¼*
3849-3850 A1025 Set of 2 .85 .40

Souvenir Sheet
Perf. 12
3851 A1025 $25 multi 1.50 1.00

No. 3851 contains one 50x40mm stamp.

Ceremonial Objects A1026

Designs: No. 3852, $5, Gift basket with handle, two women in background. No. 3853, $5, Wooden box, men carrying box in background. No. 3854, $12, Bridal sedan chair, wedding procession in background. No. 3855, $12, Candlesticks, bride and groom holding incense sticks in background.

2009, Feb. 10 *Perf. 11½x11¼*
3852-3855 A1026 Set of 4 2.25 1.10

Shells A1027

Designs: No. 3856, $5, Strombus sinuatus. No. 3857, $5, Hydatina amplustre. No. 3858, $12, Cymatium hepaticum. No. 3859, $12, Mitra mitra.

2009, Feb. 26 *Perf. 13½*
3856-3859 A1027 Set of 4 2.25 1.10

Flowers — A1028

Designs: $3.50, Lantana camara. $5, Murraya paniculata. $12, Tabebuia chrysantha. $25, Hibiscus sabdariffa.

2009, Mar. 12 *Perf. 13½x12½*
3860 A1028 $3.50 multi .25 .25
3861 A1028 $5 multi .30 .25
3862 A1028 $12 multi .75 .35
3863 A1028 $25 multi 1.50 .75
Nos. 3860-3863 (4) 2.80 1.60

See Nos. 3890-3893, 3905-3908, 3934-3937.

Opening of Red and Orange Lines of Kaohsiung Mass Rapid Transit System A1029

Train and: $5, Central Park Station. $25, World Games Station.

2009, Apr. 7 *Perf. 11½x11¼*
3864-3865 A1029 Set of 2 2.00 1.00

A1030

Pres. Chiang Ching-kuo (1910-88) — A1031

Pres. Chiang: No. 3866, $5, Wearing hat (gray panel). No. 3877, $5, Wearing suit and tie (dull purple panel). $10, Holding cane (blue panel), horiz. $12, Holding baby (brown panel), horiz.

Perf. 11¼x11½, 11½x11¼

2009, Apr. 13

3866-3869 A1030 Set of 4 1.90 .95

Souvenir Sheet

3870 A1031 $25 shown 1.60 .75

Carp Encircled By Dragons Type of 1997 With Denominations at Lower Right and Inscribed "Republic of China (Taiwan)"

2009, May 20 Engr. *Perf. 13¼x12½*

3871 A745 $50 blue 3.25 1.60

Miniature Sheet

Butterflies — A1032

No. 3872: a, $5, Papilio xuthus (butterfly cutout at LL). b, $5, Troides aeacus formosanus (butterfly cutout at LR). c, $12, Graphium agamemnon (butterfly cutout at UL). d, Papilio paris nakaharai (butterfly cutout at UR).

2009, June 25 Litho. *Perf. 11½x12*

3872 A1032 Sheet of 4, #a-d 2.10 1.10

2009 World Games, Kaohsiung — A1033

Designs: $5, Kaohsiung Arena and World Games mascots Kao Mei and Syong Ge. $12, Main Stadium and World Games emblem.

2009, July 16 *Perf. 12*

3873-3874 A1033 Set of 2 1.10 .55

3874a Souvenir sheet, #3873-3874 1.10 .55

Ancient Art Treasures — A1034

Designs: No. 3875, $5, Two Qing Dynasty gold gourds. No. 3876, $5, Gold bowl used by Emperor Qianlong. No. 3877, $12, Mughal Empire inlaid round urn. No. 3878, $12, Qing Dynasty gilt ewer.

2009, July 20 *Perf. 12¼*

3875-3878 A1034 Set of 4 2.10 1.10

3878a Souvenir sheet, #3875-3878, perf. 12¼x11¾ 2.10 1.10

Sites in Kinmen — A1035

Designs: $5, Guningtou. $9, Zhaishan Tunnel. No. 3881, $10, Interior of Qingtian Hall. No. 3882, $10, Lake Taihu.

2009, July 29 *Perf. 12½*

3879-3882 A1035 Set of 4 2.10 1.10

Paintings by Lin Yu-shan (1907-2004) — A1036

No. 3883: a, $5, On the Way Home. b, $25, Two Heads of Cattle.

2009, Aug. 7 Litho. *Perf. 12½x12*

3883 A1036 Horiz. pair, #a-b, + central label 1.90 .95

Nursery Rhymes — A1037

Designs: No. 3884, $5, Little Girl and Her Doll (blue denomination). No. 3885, $5, Kingdom of Dolls (king and soldier on horses, yellow denomination). No. 3886, $5, Train, horiz. (red denomination). No. 3887, $5, Thunder Shower, horiz. (fish, fireflies, lotus flower, denomination in orange).

2009, Aug. 26 *Perf. 12¼*

3884-3887 A1037 Set of 4 1.25 .60

21st Summer Deaflympics, Taipei — A1038

Designs: $5, Badminton, running. $25, Taekwondo, tennis.

2009, Sept. 5 *Perf. 11½*

3888-3889 A1038 Set of 2 1.90 .95

Flowers Type of 2009

Designs: $1, Calliandra emarginata. $2.50, Bombax ceiba. $10, Delonix regia. $32, Spathodea campanulata.

2009, Oct. 14 Litho. *Perf. 13½x12½*

3890 A1028 $1 multi .25 .25
3891 A1028 $2.50 multi .25 .25
3892 A1028 $10 multi .65 .30
3893 A1028 $32 multi 2.00 1.00
Nos. 3890-3893 (4) 3.15 1.80

Greetings A1039

No. 3894: a, Necklace (orange background). b, Gift boxes (pink background). c, Bouquet of roses (yellow background). d, Lollipop and candy (light blue background). e, Balloons (orange red background). f, Champagne flutes (blue violet background). g, Hearts (yellow green background). h, Cake and strawberry (red background). i, Sparklers (red violet background). j, Four-leaf clover (green background).

No. 3895: a, Necklace (orange red background). b, Gift boxes (yellow green background). c, Bouquet of roses (pink background). d, Lollipop and candy (yellow background). e, Balloons (red background). f, Champagne flutes (red violet background). g, Hearts (orange background). h, Cake and strawberry (green background). i, Sparklers (blue background). j, Four-leaf clover (yellow background).

2009, Nov. 12 *Perf. 12½*

3894 Block of 10 2.50 1.25
a.-j. A1039 $3.50 Any single .25 .25
3895 Block of 10 3.00 1.50
a.-j. A1039 $5 Any single .30 .25

Nos. 3894 and 3895 were each printed in sheets containing two blocks + 5 labels.

Ferns — A1040

Designs: $5, Asplenium nidus. $9, Cyathea spinulosa. $12, Cyathea lepifera. $25, Cibotium taiwanense.

2009, Nov. 26 *Perf. 11¼x11½*

3896-3899 A1040 Set of 4 3.25 1.60

3899a Souvenir sheet, #3896-3899 3.25 1.60

See Nos. 4060-4063.

A1041

New Year 2010 (Year of the Tiger) — A1042

Tiger at: $3.50, Left. $13, Right.

2009, Dec. 1 *Perf. 12¼x12½*

3900-3901 A1041 Set of 2 1.10 .55

Souvenir Sheet

Perf. 12½

3902 A1042 $12 multi .75 .35

Anti-Corruption Day — A1043

Background color: $5, Light blue. $25, Lilac.

2009, Dec. 9 Litho. *Perf. 11½*

3903-3904 A1043 Set of 2 1.90 .95

Flowers Type of 2009

Designs: $7, Michelia champaca. $15, Duranta repens. $20, Ixora chinensis. $34, Lagerstroemia speciosa.

2010, Jan. 20 *Perf. 13½x12½*

3905 A1028 $7 multi .45 .25
3906 A1028 $15 multi .95 .45
3907 A1028 $20 multi 1.25 .65
3908 A1028 $34 multi 2.25 1.10
Nos. 3905-3908 (4) 4.90 2.45

Lin An-tai Historical Home, Taipei — A1044

Li Family Compound, Luzhou — A1045

Lin Family Compound, Wufeng — A1046

Xiaoyun Villa, Shengang — A1047

2010, Feb. 9 *Perf. 13½x13¼*

3909 A1044 $5 multi .35 .25
3910 A1045 $5 multi .35 .25
3911 A1046 $5 multi .35 .25
3912 A1047 $12 multi .75 .35
Nos. 3909-3912 (4) 1.80 1.10

Little Taiwan, Qimei Islet A1048

Whale Arch, Xiaomen Islet A1049

Scenery of Penghu Islands: No. 3914, Basalt rocks, Xiaomen Islet. No. 3916, Heart-shaped stone weir, Qimei Islet.

2010, Feb. 24 *Perf. 13½*

3913 A1048 $5 shown .35 .25
3914 A1048 $5 multi .35 .25
3915 A1049 $10 shown .65 .30
3916 A1049 $10 multi .65 .30
Nos. 3913-3916 (4) 2.00 1.10

Bridges A1050

Designs: No. 3917, $5, Jinde Bridge, Donggang (shown). No. 3918, $5, Qigu River Bridge, Tainan. No. 3919, $12, Anyi Bridge,

Tainan. No. 3920, $12, Wangyue Bridge, Tainan (blue bridge at night).

2010, Mar. 10 ***Perf. 11½***
3917-3920 A1050 Set of 4 2.25 1.10

Mushrooms
A1051

Designs: Nos. 3921, 3925a, $5, Dictyphora multicolor. Nos. 3922, 3925b, $5, Pleurotus salmoneostramineus. Nos. 3923, 3925c, $12, Pseudocolus fusiformis. Nos. 3924, 3925d, $12, Coprinus disseminatus.

2010, Mar. 25 ***Perf. 13***
Stamps With White Frames
3921-3924 A1051 Set of 4 2.25 1.10
Miniature Sheet
Stamps Without White Frames
Perf. 11¾
3925 A1051 Sheet of 4, #a-d 2.25 1.10

Crabs
A1052

Designs: No. 3926, $5, Cardisoma carnifex. No. 3927, $5, Scandarma lintou. $10, Sesarmops intermedius. $25, Gecarcoidea lalandii.

2010, Apr. 15 ***Perf. 11½***
3926-3929 A1052 Set of 4 3.00 1.50

Scenes From *The Romance of the Three Kingdoms*
A1053

Designs: No. 3930, $3.50, Shooting an Arrow at the Halberd Beside the Gate of the Camp (shown). No. 3931, $3.50, Commenting on Heroes Over Wine. $5, Zhou Yu's Anger at Being Tricked by Zhuge Liang Three Times. $20, Holding Meng Huo Captive Seven Times.

2010, Apr. 29 ***Perf. 11½***
3930-3933 A1053 Set of 4 2.10 1.10
3933a Sheet of 4, #3930-3933, perf. 12 2.10 1.10

Flowers Type of 2009

Designs: 50c, Bauhinia variegata. $9, Euphorbia milii. $13, Brunfelsia hopeana. $17, Plumeria rubra.

2010, May 12 Litho. ***Perf. 13½x12½***
3934 A1028 50c multi .25 .25
3935 A1028 $9 multi .55 .30
3936 A1028 $13 multi .80 .40
3937 A1028 $17 multi 1.10 .55
Nos. 3934-3937 (4) 2.70 1.50

Long-horned Beetles
A1054

Designs: 75c, Erythrus formosanus. $2.50, Rosalia formosa conviva. $5, Aphrodisium faldermannii yuagii. $25, Anoplophora horsfieldi tonkinensis.

2010, May 21 ***Perf. 12½x13½***
3938 A1054 75c multi .25 .25
3939 A1054 $2.50 multi .25 .25
3940 A1054 $5 multi .30 .25
3941 A1054 $25 multi 1.60 .80
Nos. 3938-3941 (4) 2.40 1.55

See Nos. 3976-3979, 4027-4030, 4134-4137.

Girl Scouts, Cent. — A1055

Emblems and: $5, Two doves, stylized globe. $25, Dove, ribbon hearts.

2010, June 1 ***Perf. 12½***
3942-3943 A1055 Set of 2 1.90 .95

Souvenir Sheet

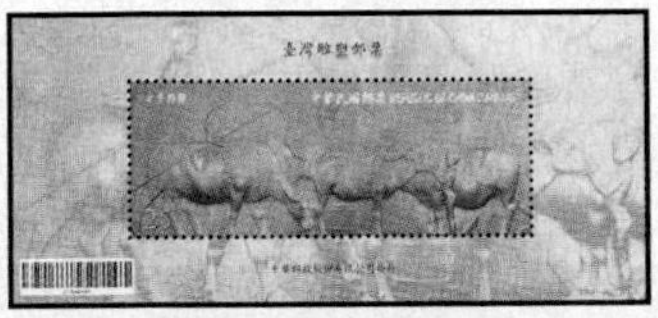
Water Buffaloes, Sculpture by Huang Tu-shui (1895-1930) — A1056

Litho. & Embossed
2010, June 22 ***Perf. 11½x11¼***
3944 A1056 $25 multi 1.60 .80

A1057

Scenes From Novel "Journey to the West" — A1058

Designs: No. 3945, Complete Enlightenment. No. 3946, Sun Wukong Wreaks Havoc in Heaven. $12, Dreaming of Beheading the Jing River Dragon King. $25, Stealing the Ginseng Fruits.

2010, July 7 Litho. ***Perf. 11¼x11½***
3945 A1057 $5 multi .35 .25
3946 A1058 $5 multi .35 .25
3947 A1058 $12 multi .75 .35
3948 A1058 $25 multi 1.60 .80
Nos. 3945-3948 (4) 3.05 1.65

Compare with Nos. 4003-4006.

Lighthouses
A1059

Designs: No. 3949, $5, Chilung Tao Lighthouse (denomination in yellow). No. 3950, $5, Wenkan Tui Lighthouse (denomination in blue). $10, Paisha Chia Lighthouse (denomination in lilac), horiz. $25, Liuchiu Yu Lighthouse (denomination in light green), horiz.

Perf. 11¼x11½, 11½x11¼
2010, July 28
3949-3952 A1059 Set of 4 3.00 1.50

See Nos. 4160-4163.

Modern Taiwanese Paintings — A1060

No. 3953: a, $5, Bamboo Grove in Early Summer, by Tsai Yun-yan. b, $25, Pear Espalier, by Lu Yun-sheng.

2010, Aug. 9 ***Perf. 12x12½***
3953 A1060 Horiz. pair, #a-b, + central label 1.90 .95

Souvenir Sheet

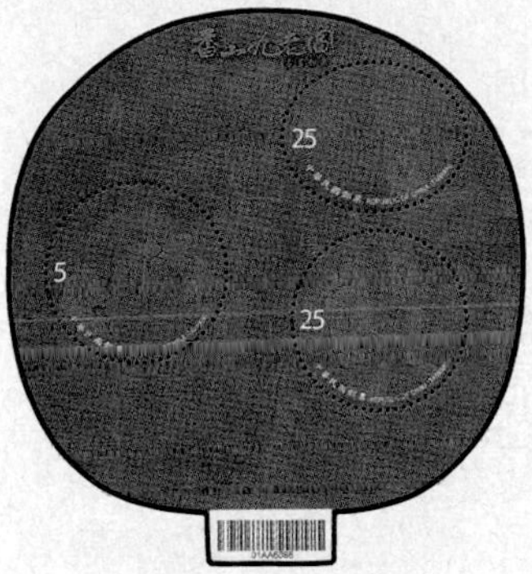
Nine Elders of Mt. Hsiang, by Unknown Painter — A1061

No. 3954: a, $5, Servant and elders playing game (35mm diameter). b, $25, Three elders and dancer (35mm diameter). c, $25, Elders in bamboo grove (37x29mm oval stamp).

2010, Sept. 9 ***Perf.***
3954 A1061 Sheet of 3, #a-c 3.50 1.75

Stamps Depicting Educators
A1062

Designs: $5, Republic of China No. 1648 (Chu Hsi). $25, Republic of China No. 1798 (Confucius).

Perf. 11¼x11½
2010, Sept. 28 **Litho.**
3955-3956 A1062 Set of 2 1.90 .95

Shells
A1063

Designs: No. 3957, $5, Thatcheria mirabilis. No. 3958, $5, Tibia martinii. No. 3959, $12, Stellaria solaris. No. 3960, $12, Rapa rapa.

2010, Oct. 4 ***Perf. 11½x11¼***
3957-3960 A1063 Set of 4 2.25 1.10

Bridges
A1064

Designs: No. 3961, $5, Lizejian Bridge, Yilan (shown). No. 3962, $5, Taroko Bridge, Hualien. $12, Hongye Bridge, Taitung. $15, Pudu Bridge, Hualien.

2010, Oct. 20
3961-3964 A1064 Set of 4 2.50 1.25

National Taipei University of Technology, Cent. — A1065

No. 3965: a, $5, Building, old gate. b, $25, Sixth Instructional Building, Technology Building, new gate.

2010, Nov. 1 ***Perf. 12½***
3965 A1065 Horiz. pair, #a-b 2.00 1.00

A1066

A1067

A1068

A1069

A1070

A1071

A1072

A1073

A1074

A1075

A1076

A1077

A1078

A1079

A1080

A1081

A1082

A1083

A1084

2010, Nov. 6 Litho. ***Perf. 13½x13¼***

3966	Sheet of 9	3.25	1.60
a.	A1066 $5 multi	.35	.25
b.	A1067 $5 multi	.35	.25
c.	A1068 $5 multi	.35	.25
d.	A1069 $5 multi	.35	.25
e.	A1070 $5 multi	.35	.25
f.	A1071 $5 multi	.35	.25
g.	A1072 $5 multi	.35	.25
h.	A1073 $5 multi	.35	.25
i.	A1074 $5 multi	.35	.25

Perf. 13¼x13½

3967	Sheet of 10	3.50	1.75
a.	A1075 $5 multi	.35	.25
b.	A1076 $5 multi	.35	.25
c.	A1077 $5 multi	.35	.25
d.	A1078 $5 multi	.35	.25
e.	A1079 $5 multi	.35	.25
f.	A1080 $5 multi	.35	.25
g.	A1081 $5 multi	.35	.25
h.	A1082 $5 multi	.35	.25
i.	A1083 $5 multi	.35	.25
j.	A1084 $5 multi	.35	.25

Taipei International Flora Expo.

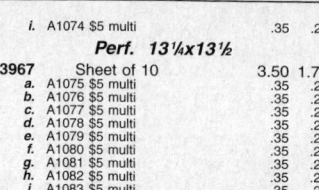

Qing Dynasty Gilt Copper Censers A1085

Censer with: No. 3968, $5, Turquoise inlays (shown). No. 3969, $5, Lotus flower designs. $10, Glass and enamel inlays. $25, White jade, turquoise and glass inlays.

2010, Nov. 18 ***Perf. 11½***

3968-3971	A1085	Set of 4	3.00	1.50
3971a		Souvenir sheet of 4, #3968-3971, perf. 12	3.00	1.50

New Year 2011 (Year of the Rabbit) A1086

Designs: $3.50, Two rabbits. $13, One rabbit.
$12, One rabbit, diff.

2010, Dec. 1 ***Perf. 12¼***

3972-3973	A1086	Set of 2	1.10	.55

Souvenir Sheet

Perf. 12½

3974	A1086 $12 multi	.80	.40

No. 3974 contains one 61x37mm stamp.

Miniature Sheet

Fireworks Displays — A1087

No. 3975: a, $5, Double Tenth Day display, Taipei (30x30mm). b, $5, New Year's display at Taipei 101 Building (24x48mm). c, $25, Lantern Festival display, Kaohsiung (30x30mm). d, $25, Dragon Boat Festival display, Longtan (24x48mm).

Litho. With Hologram

2011, Jan. 1 ***Perf. 13¼***

3975	A1087	Sheet of 4, #a-d	4.25	2.10

Long-horned Beetles Type of 2010

Designs: $1, Aeolesthes oenochrous. $3.50, Doliops similis. $10, Thermistis taiwanensis. $32, Dorysthenes pici.

2011, Jan. 26 Litho. ***Perf. 12½x13½***

3976	A1054 $1 multi	.25	.25
3977	A1054 $3.50 multi	.25	.25
3978	A1054 $10 multi	.70	.35
3979	A1054 $32 multi	2.25	1.10
	Nos. 3976-3979 (4)	3.45	1.95

Valentine's Day — A1088

Quick response code and: $5, Outline of heart. $25, Heart.

2011, Feb. 14 ***Perf. 12½***

3980-3981	A1088	Set of 2	2.10	1.10

Values are for stamps with surrounding selvage.

Fish A1089

Designs: No. 3982, $5, Candidia barbatus. No. 3983, $5, Opsariichthys pachycephalus. $12, Spinibarbus hollandi. $25, Squalidus banarescui.

2011, Mar. 18 ***Perf. 13½x13¼***

3982-3985	A1089	Set of 4	3.25	1.60

Miniature Sheet

Butterflies — A1090

No. 3986: a, $5, Euploea eunice hobsoni (butterfly cutout at LL). b, $5, Euploea sylvester swinhoei (butterfly cutout at LR). c, $12, Euploea tulliolus koxinga (denomination at LL). d, $12, Euploea mulciber barsine (denomination at LR).

2011, Apr. 8 ***Perf. 12½x12***

3986	A1090	Sheet of 4, #a-d	2.40	1.25

National Tsing Hua University, Cent. A1091

Designs: $5, Second campus gate, old library building. $25, Current campus gate, Humanities and Social Sciences Building.

2011, Apr. 20 ***Perf. 12½***

3987-3988	A1091	Set of 2	2.10	1.10

Alpine Flowers — A1092

Designs: No. 3989, $5, Gentiana scabrida var. punctulata. No. 3990, $5, Euphrasia transmorrisonensis. No. 3991, $10, Clematis montana, horiz. No. 3992, $10, Cypripedium formosanum, horiz.

2011, May 16 ***Perf. 12***

3989-3992	A1092	Set of 4	2.10	1.10

A Singularly Harmonious Vibration — A1093

Double Happiness A1094

Blessings From the Three Stars A1095

Four is for Everything Goes as One Wishes A1096

Bumper Crops of All Five Grains A1097

Spring in All Six Directions A1098

Seven is for a Match Made in Heaven A1099

The Eight Immortals Wish for Your Longevity A1100

Nine Similes and Three Abundances — A1101

Ten Complete A1102

No. 3993 — Color of denomination: a, Blue green. b, Pink. c, Gray. d, Orange red. e, Red violet. f, Red. g, Blue gray. h, Purple. i, Green. j, Olive green.

No. 3994 — Color of denomination: a, Olive green. b, Gray. c, Pink. d, Purple. e, Red. f, Blue gray. g, Orange red. h, Green. i, Red violet. j, Blue green.

2011, May 27 ***Perf. 12½***

3993		Block of 10	2.50	1.25
	a.	A1093 $3.50 multi	.25	.25
	b.	A1094 $3.50 multi	.25	.25
	c.	A1095 $3.50 multi	.25	.25
	d.	A1096 $3.50 multi	.25	.25
	e.	A1097 $3.50 multi	.25	.25
	f.	A1098 $3.50 multi	.25	.25
	g.	A1099 $3.50 multi	.25	.25
	h.	A1100 $3.50 multi	.25	.25
	i.	A1101 $3.50 multi	.25	.25
	j.	A1102 $3.50 multi	.25	.25
3994		Block of 10	3.50	1.75
	a.	A1093 $5 multi	.35	.25
	b.	A1094 $5 multi	.35	.25
	c.	A1095 $5 multi	.35	.25
	d.	A1096 $5 multi	.35	.25
	e.	A1097 $5 multi	.35	.25
	f.	A1098 $5 multi	.35	.25
	g.	A1099 $5 multi	.35	.25
	h.	A1100 $5 multi	.35	.25
	i.	A1101 $5 multi	.35	.25
	j.	A1102 $5 multi	.35	.25

Sea Slugs A1103

Designs: No. 3995, $5, Mexichromis multituberculata. No. 3996, $5, Chromodoris willani. $12, Gymnodoris ceylonica. $25, Glossodoris averni.

2011, June 8 ***Perf. 12½***

3995-3998	A1103	Set of 4	3.25	1.60

Owls — A1104

Designs: No. 3999, $5, Asio otus. No. 4000, $5, Otus sunia. $10, Strix aluco. $25, Glaucidium brodiei.

2011, July 7 Engr. ***Perf. 12¾x12½***

3999-4002	A1104	Set of 4	3.25	1.60

See Nos. 4051-4054, 4122-4125.

Swindling Treasures A1105

Red Boy — A1106

Crossing the River on a Turtle's Back — A1107

Achieving Nirvana — A1108

2011, July 21 **Litho.**

4003	A1105	$5 multi	.35	.25
4004	A1106	$5 multi	.35	.25
4005	A1107	$12 multi	.85	.40
4006	A1108	$25 multi	1.75	.85
		Nos. 4003-4006 (4)	3.30	1.75

Scenes from Novel "Journey to the West." Compare with Nos. 3945-3948.

Atayal Facial Tattoos A1109

2011, Aug. 1 ***Perf. 12½***

4007	A1109	$25 multi	1.75	.85

Souvenir Sheet

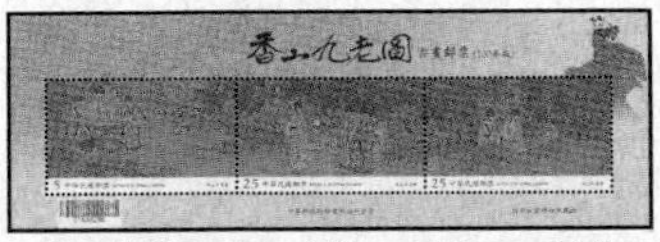
Scroll Painting, "Nine Elders of Mt. Hsiang" — A1110

No. 4008: a, $5, Three elders and attendant at game table. b, $25, Three elders and three attendants dancing. c, $25, Two elders reading, attendant, tree in foreground.

2011, Sept. 9 ***Perf. 13½x13¼***

4008	A1110	Sheet of 3, #a-c	3.75	1.90

National Palace Museum A1111

Taipei 101 Building A1112

Sun Moon Lake A1113

Yushan (Jade Mountain) A1114

Alishan A1115

Love River, Kaohsiung A1116

Beach, Kenting A1117

Day Lilies in Liushidan Mountains A1118

Taroko National Park A1119

Jiufen A1120

2011, Sept. 27 ***Perf. 12½***

4009		Block of 10	2.50	1.25
	a.	A1111 $3.50 multi	.25	.25
	b.	A1112 $3.50 multi	.25	.25
	c.	A1113 $3.50 multi	.25	.25
	d.	A1114 $3.50 multi	.25	.25
	e.	A1115 $3.50 multi	.25	.25
	f.	A1116 $3.50 multi	.25	.25
	g.	A1117 $3.50 multi	.25	.25
	h.	A1118 $3.50 multi	.25	.25
	i.	A1119 $3.50 multi	.25	.25
	j.	A1120 $3.50 multi	.25	.25
4010		Block of 10	3.50	1.75
	a.	A1111 $5 multi	.35	.25
	b.	A1112 $5 multi	.35	.25
	c.	A1113 $5 multi	.35	.25
	d.	A1114 $5 multi	.35	.25
	e.	A1115 $5 multi	.35	.25
	f.	A1116 $5 multi	.35	.25
	g.	A1117 $5 multi	.35	.25
	h.	A1118 $5 multi	.35	.25
	i.	A1119 $5 multi	.35	.25
	j.	A1120 $5 multi	.35	.25

Travel destinations. Nos. 4009 and 4010 were each printed in sheets containing two blocks + 5 labels.

A1121

Republic of China, Cent. — A1122

No. 4011: a, Flag of Republic of China, Sun Yat-sen, doves over buildings. b, Presidential Office Building, bananas, pineapple, sugar cane. c, Building, highway bridge, airplane, ship. d, Train, silicon wafers, satellite dish. No. 4012, Flag of Republic of China, Presidential Office Building, Sun Yat-sen.

Perf. 12½x13¼ Syncopated

2011, Oct. 10 **Litho.**

4011		Horiz. strip of 4	3.25	1.60
	a.-b.	A1121 $5 Either single	.35	.25
	c.	A1121 $10 multi	.65	.35
	d.	A1121 $25 multi	1.75	.85

Souvenir Sheet

Litho. With Foil Application

Perf. 13¼

4012	A1122	$25 multi	1.75	.85

The syncopation between Nos. 4011a and 4011b is a rectangle, and oval between Nos. 4011b and 4011c and 4011c and 4011d.

Plum Blossoms A1123

Perf. 13¼x13½

2011, Oct. 10 **Litho. & Engr.**

4013	A1123	$100 multi	6.75	3.25

No. 4013 was printed in sheets of 10 + 8 labels.

Scouting in China, Cent. — A1124

Scout and: $5, City. $12, Mountain, horiz.

Perf. 12¾x12½, 12½x12¾

2011, Nov. 1 **Litho.**

4014-4015	A1124	Set of 2	1.25	.60

Railway Branch Lines — A1125

No. 4016: a, $5, Shalun Branch Line (denomination in pink). b, $5, Jiji Branch Line (denomination in orange). c, $12, Neiwan Branch Line (denomination in blue). d, $12, Liujia Branch Line (denomination in pink). e, $15, Pingxi Branch Line.

2011, Nov. 12 ***Perf. 12½***

4016 Vert. strip of 5 3.50 1.75
a.-b. A1125 $5 Either single .35 .25
c.-d. A1125 $12 Either single .80 .40
e. A1125 $15 multi 1.00 .50

New Year 2012 (Year of the Dragon) A1126

Designs: $3.50, Two dragons. $13, Dragon facing left.
$12, Dragon facing right.

2011, Dec. 1 ***Perf. 13***

4017-4018 A1126 Set of 2 1.10 .55

Souvenir Sheet

Perf. 12½

4019 A1126 $12 multi .80 .40

No. 4019 contains one 64x40mm stamp.

Souvenir Sheet

Alishan Forest Railway, Cent. — A1127

No. 4020: a, $5, Diesel engine, tunnel. b, $25, Steam engine.

2011, Dec. 25 ***Perf. 12½x12¾***

4020 A1127 Sheet of 2, #a-b 2.00 1.00

Berries — A1128

Designs: $3.50, Actinidia callosa. $5, Synsepalum dulcificum. $12, Solanum americanum. $25, Solanum verbascifolium.

2012, Jan. 12 ***Perf. 13¼x12½***

4021 A1128 $3.50 multi .25 .25
4022 A1128 $5 multi .35 .25
4023 A1128 $12 multi .85 .40
4024 A1128 $25 multi 1.75 .85
Nos. 4021-4024 (4) 3.20 1.75

See Nos. 4084-4087, 4106-4109, 4164-4167..

A1129

Roses — A1130

No. 4025: a, Rose. b, Rose, stem and leaves.
$32, Two roses.

Litho. & Embossed

2012, Feb. 10 ***Perf. 14½***

4025 A1129 Horiz. pair + central label 2.60 1.25
a. $12 multi .85 .40
b. $25 multi 1.75 .85

Souvenir Sheet

Litho.

Perf.

4026 A1130 $32 multi 2.25 1.10

No. 4026 is impregnated with a rose scent.

Long-horned Beetles Type of 2010

Designs: $7, Leptura formosomontana formosomontana. $12, Pyrestes curticornis. $15, Anaglyptus meridionalis. $20, Anoplophora albopicta.

2012, Mar. 9 Litho. ***Perf. 12½x13½***

4027 A1054 $7 multi .50 .25
4028 A1054 $12 multi .85 .40
4029 A1054 $15 multi 1.00 .50
4030 A1054 $20 multi 1.40 .70
Nos. 4027-4030 (4) 3.75 1.85

Mushrooms A1131

Designs: Nos. 4031, 4035a, $5, Amanita rubrovolvata. Nos. 4032, 4035b, $5, Entoloma murraii. Nos. 4033, 4035c, $12, Geastrum sessile. Nos. 4034, 4035d, $12, Clavulinopsis miyabeana.

2012, Mar. 23 ***Perf. 13¼x13***

Stamps With White Frames

4031-4034 A1131 Set of 4 2.40 1.25

Souvenir Sheet

Stamps Without White Frames

Perf. 12¾x13

4035 A1131 Sheet of 4, #a-d 2.40 1.25

No. 4035 contains four 26x34mm stamps.

Fish A1132

Designs: No. 4036, $5, Formosania lacustre. No. 4037, $5, Tanakia himantegus. $12, Channa asiatica. $25, Sinogastromyzon puliensis.

2012, Apr. 11 ***Perf. 12½x13¼***

4036-4039 A1132 Set of 4 3.25 1.60

Scenes From Novel "Outlaws of the Marsh" A1133

Designs: No. 4040, $5, Demons Released (denomination at LL). No. 4041, $5, Slaying the Tiger on Jingyang Ridge (denomination at LR). $10, Mountain God Temple on a Stormy Night. $25, Knocking the Lord of the West Dead.

2012, Apr. 25 ***Perf. 12½x12¾***

4040-4043 A1133 Set of 4 3.25 1.60

See Nos. 4110-4113.

"A Match Made in Heaven" A1134

"One Child After Another" A1135

Congratulatory greetings: $5, "The Hall is Packed with Wealth and Riches." $12, "A Family Experinces Two Joys."

2012, May 4 ***Perf. 13***

4044 A1134 $3.50 multi .25 .25
4045 A1135 $3.50 multi .25 .25
4046 A1135 $5 multi .35 .25
4047 A1135 $12 multi .80 .40
Nos. 4044-4047 (4) 1.65 1.15

Booklet Stamp

Perf. 13½ Vert.

4048 A1135 $5 multi .35 .25
a. Booklet pane of 12 4.25 —
Complete booklet, #4048a 4.25

Inauguration of President Ma Ying-jeou and Vice President Wu Den-yih — A1136

No. 4049 — President, Vice president and: a, Flag and Presidental Palace. b, Taipei 101 building, train, ship and airplane. c, Children, dancers, National Theater. d, Map of Taiwan, stylized globe. $32, President, Vice President, flag, Presidential Palace, plum blossoms, horiz.

2012, May 20 ***Perf. 13¼x13½***

4049 Horiz. strip of 4 2.40 1.25
a.-b. A1136 $5 Either single .35 .25
c.-d. A1136 $12 Either single .80 .40

Souvenir Sheet

Perf. 13½x13¼

4050 A1136 $32 multi 2.25 1.10

No. 4050 contains one 80x30mm stamp.

Owls Type of 2011

Designs: No. 4051, $5, Asio flammeus. No. 4052, $5, Otus spilocephalus. $10, Strix leptogrammica. $25, Ninox scutulata.

2012, June 6 Engr. ***Perf. 12¾x12½***

4051-4054 A1104 Set of 4 3.00 1.50

Festivals A1137

Designs: No. 4055, $5, Chinese New Year (fireworks and calligraphic couplets). No. 4056, $5, Lantern Festival (lanterns and sandals). $10, Dragon Boat Festival (herb sachets and covered wine containers). $25, Mid-autumn Festival (Jade Hare, Lady Chang'e, moon cakes).

2012, June 20 Litho. ***Perf. 12½***

4055-4058 A1137 Set of 4 3.00 1.50

Miniature Sheet

Bees and Wasps — A1138

No. 4059: a, $5, Phimenes flavopictus. b, $5, Xanthopimpla pedator. c, $5, Vespa ducalis. d, $10, Apis mellifera. e, $10, Xylocopa tranquebarorum. f, $10, Apis cerana.

2012, July 12 ***Perf. 13***

4059 A1138 Sheet of 6, #a-f 3.00 1.50

Ferns Type of 2009

Designs: No. 4060, $5, Polystichum lepidocaulon. No. 4061, $5, Bolbitis heteroclita. $10, Adiantum malesianum, horiz. $25, Asplenium prolongatum, horiz.

Perf. 12¾x12½, 12½x12¾

2012, July 25

4060-4063 A1040 Set of 4 3.00 1.50
4063a Sheet of 4, #4060-4063, perf. 12, + label 3.00 1.50

Familial Bonds A1139

Silhouettes of: $5, Father and daughter. $7, Mother and son. $10, Mother, father and child. $12, Grandparents and child.

2012, Aug. 24 ***Perf. 12½x13¼***

4064-4067 A1139 Set of 4 2.40 1.25

Miniature Sheet

Teas and Tourist Attractions — A1140

No. 4068: a, Baozhong tea, Pinglin Tea Museum (bright yellow frame). b, Tieguanyin tea, Maokong Funicular (yellow orange frame). c, Black tea, Sun Moon Lake Wharf (orange frame). d, Oolong tea, Alishan Forest train (bister frame). e, Oriental Beauty tea, Emei Lake Suspension Bridge (red brown frame).

2012, Sept. 12 ***Perf. 12½***

4068 A1140 $10 Sheet of 5, #a-e 3.50 1.75

Nos. 4068a-4068e each have a cut-out of a teapot under the denomination.

Cotton Rose — A1141

Bird-of-Paradise Flower — A1142

Clary Sage — A1143

Dancing Lady Orchid — A1144

Zinnia — A1145

Marigold A1146

Chinese Hibiscus — A1147

Fragrant Olive — A1148

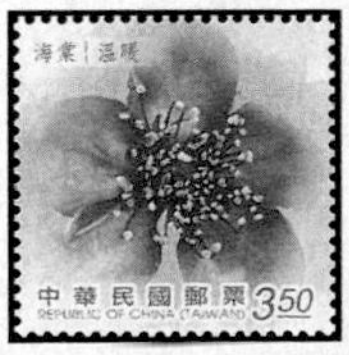
Flowering Crab Apple — A1149

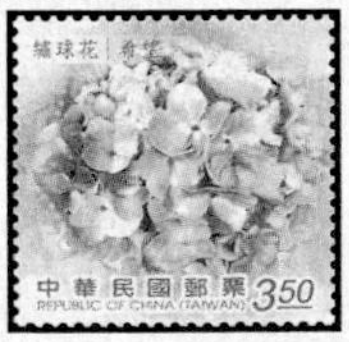
Hydrangea A1150

2012, Sept. 28 ***Perf. 13¼***

4069	Block of 10	2.50	1.25
a.	A1141 $3.50 multi	.25	.25
b.	A1142 $3.50 multi	.25	.25
c.	A1143 $3.50 multi	.25	.25
d.	A1144 $3.50 multi	.25	.25
e.	A1145 $3.50 multi	.25	.25
f.	A1146 $3.50 multi	.25	.25
g.	A1147 $3.50 multi	.25	.25
h.	A1148 $3.50 multi	.25	.25
i.	A1149 $3.50 multi	.25	.25
j.	A1150 $3.50 multi	.25	.25
4070	Block of 10	3.50	1.75
a.	A1141 $5 multi	.35	.25
b.	A1142 $5 multi	.35	.25
c.	A1143 $5 multi	.35	.25
d.	A1144 $5 multi	.35	.25
e.	A1145 $5 multi	.35	.25
f.	A1146 $5 multi	.35	.25
g.	A1147 $5 multi	.35	.25
h.	A1148 $5 multi	.35	.25
i.	A1149 $5 multi	.35	.25
j.	A1150 $5 multi	.35	.25

Miniature Sheets

A1151

Characters From *Toy Story* — A1152

No. 4071: a, $5, Mr. Pricklepants, Peas-in-a-Pod (40x30mm). b, $5, Aliens (35mm diameter). c, $5, Trixie, Buttercup (40x30mm). d, $12, Lotso-Huggin Bear (30x40mm). e, $12, Woody (35mm diameter).

No. 4072: a, $5, Woody on Bullseye (35mm diameter). b, $5, Rex (35mm diameter). c, $5, Hamm (35mm diameter). d, $12, Buzz Lightyear (35mm diameter). e, $12, Jessie (30x40mm).

Serpentine Die Cut (round stamps), Serpentine Die Cut 14x13½ (horiz. stamps), Serpentine Die Cut 13½x14 (vert. stamps)

2012, Oct. 23 **Self-Adhesive**

4071	A1151	Sheet of 5, #a-e	2.75	1.40
4072	A1152	Sheet of 5, #a-e	2.75	1.40

Protected Mammals A1153

Designs: No. 4073, $5, Paguma larvata taivana. No. 4074, $5, Mustela nivalis formosana. $10, Martes flavigula chrysopila. $25, Viverricula indica pallida.

2012, Nov. 7 **Litho.** ***Perf. 12½x13¼***

4073-4076	A1153	Set of 4	3.25	1.60

A1154

Three Friends and a Hundred Birds, by Pien Wen-chin (c. 1356-c. 1428) — A1155

No. 4077 — Details from painting of various birds in tree: a, $5. b, $10. c, $12.
$70, Entire painting.

2012, Nov. 22 ***Perf. 13¼x13***

4077	A1154	Sheet of 3, #a-c	1.90	.95

Souvenir Sheet
Silk-Faced Paper
Perf. 14x14¼

4078	A1155	$70 multi	5.00	2.50

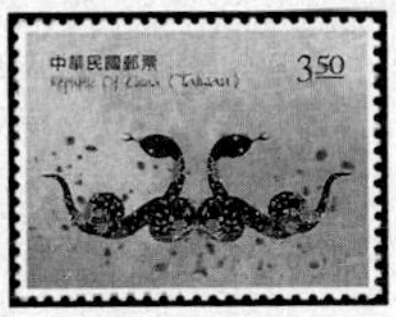
New Year 2013 (Year of the Snake) A1156

Designs: $3.50, Two snakes. $13, Snake, head at left.
$12, Snake, head at right.

2012, Dec. 3 ***Perf. 13***

4079-4080	A1156	Set of 2	1.25	.60

Souvenir Sheet
Perf. 12½

4081	A1156	$12 multi	.85	.45

No. 4081 contains one 64x40mm stamp.

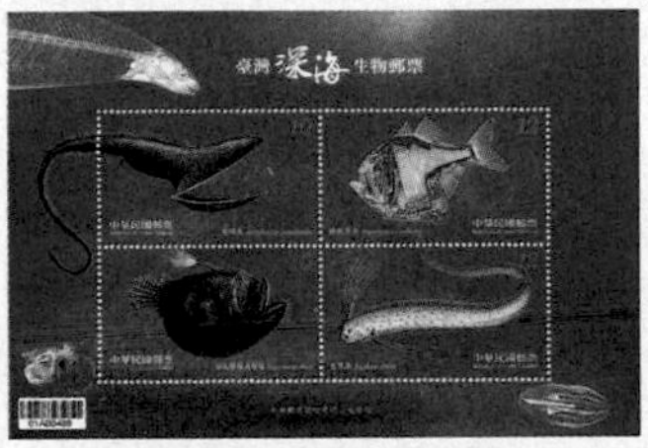
Marine Life — A1157

No. 4082: a, $10, Eurypharynx pelecanoides. b, $10, Bufoceratias shaoi. c, $12, Argyropelecus aculeatus. d, $12, Regalecus glesne.
$25, Histioteuthis celetaria pacifica, vert.

Litho., Litho. With Foil Application (#4082c)

2012, Dec. 12 ***Perf. 14x13¼***

4082	A1157	Sheet of 4, #a-d	3.00	1.50

Souvenir Sheet
Perf. 13¼x14

4083	A1157	$25 multi	1.75	.85

Berries Type of 2012

Designs: $2.50, Rhodomyrtus tomentosa. $7, Ardisia squamulosa. $10, Hylocereus undatus. $32, Mahonia japonica.

2013, Jan. 17 **Litho.** ***Perf. 13¼x12½***

4084	A1128	$2.50 multi	.25	.25
4085	A1128	$7 multi	.50	.25
4086	A1128	$10 multi	.70	.35
4087	A1128	$32 multi	2.25	1.10
	Nos. 4084-4087 (4)		3.70	1.95

Chinese Dishes — A1158

No. 4088 — Chopsticks and: a, Kung Pao Chicken, bowl of rice, spoon. b, Mud Crab with Glutinous Rice Cake, cup of green tea, salt shaker. c, Three-cup Chicken, bowl of sauce, salt shaker. d, Hakka Stir-fry, bowl of rice, salt shaker.

2013, Jan. 31 ***Perf. 13¼x13***

4088	A1158	$5 Horiz. strip of 4, #a-d	1.40	.70

Compare with Type A1176.

St. Valentine's Day — A1159

Designs: $12, Colored roses. $25, White roses.

Litho. & Embossed

2013, Feb. 4 ***Perf. 13¼x13½***

4089-4090	A1159	Set of 2	2.50	1.25
4090a		Souvenir sheet of 2, #4089-4090	2.50	1.25

Grain Farming — A1160

Designs: $5, Oryza sativa. $7, Setaria italica. $10, Zea mays. $25, Triticum aestivum.

2013, Mar. 5 **Litho.** ***Perf. 12½***

4091-4094	A1160	Set of 4	3.25	1.60

A1161

A1162

A1163

A1164

A1165

Qing Dynasty Embroidery — A1166

2013, Mar. 20 Litho. *Perf. 14*

4095 A1161 $10 multi .70 .35
4096 A1162 $10 multi .70 .35
4097 A1163 $10 multi .70 .35
4098 A1164 $10 multi .70 .35
4099 A1165 $10 multi .70 .35
Nos. 4095-4099 (5) 3.50 1.75

Litho. & Embossed With Foil Application

Souvenir Sheet
Silk-Faced Paper

Perf. 13x13¼

4100 A1166 $100 multi 6.75 3.50

Children at Play — A1167

Children: No. 4101, $5, Carrying lantern. No. 4102, $5, Flying paper airplanes. No. 4103, $5, With pinwheels. No. 4104, $5, With spinning top. No. 4105, $5, With hand puppets.

2013, Apr. 2 Litho. *Perf. 12½*

4101-4105 A1167 Set of 5 1.75 .85
4105a Booklet pane of 10, 2 each #4101-4105, perf. 12½ on 3 sides 3.50 —
Complete booklet, #4105a 3.50

See Nos. 4168-4172.

Berries Type of 2012

Designs: $1, Ribes formosanum. $15, Garcinia subelliptica. $17, Coffea arabica. $20, Smilax ocreata.

2013, Apr. 17 *Perf. 13¼x12½*

4106 A1128 $1 multi .25 .25
4107 A1128 $15 multi 1.00 .50
4108 A1128 $17 multi 1.25 .60
4109 A1128 $20 multi 1.40 .70
Nos. 4106-4109 (4) 3.90 2.05

Capturing Daming Prefecture by Ruse A1168

Heavenly Inscriptions on Stele A1169

Lianshan Outlaws Granted Imperial Amnesty A1170

Successful Expedition Against Liao Empire A1171

2013, May 10 *Perf. 12½x12¾*

4110 A1168 $5 multi .35 .25
4111 A1169 $5 multi .35 .25
4112 A1170 $10 multi .70 .35
4113 A1171 $25 multi 1.75 .85
Nos. 4110-4113 (4) 3.15 1.70

Scenes from novel "Outlaws of the Marsh." Compare with Nos. 4040-4043.

Congratulations — A1172

Designs: No. 4114, $3.50, Tropical fish. No. 4115, $3.50, Swans. No. 4116, $5, Penguins. No. 4117, $5, Mandarin ducks.

2013, May 22 *Perf. 12½*

4114-4117 A1172 Set of 4 1.25 .60

Values are for stamps with surrounding selvage.

Herbs — A1173

Designs: No. 4118, $5, Mentha x piperita. No. 4119, $5, Rosmarinus officinalis. $12, Salvia elegans. $15, Artemisia indica.

2013, June 11

4118-4121 A1173 Set of 4 2.50 1.25

See Nos. 4179-4182, 4244-4247.

Owls Type of 2011

Designs: No. 4122, $5, Otus lettia. No. 4123, $5, Tyto longimembris. $10, Ketupa flavipes. $25, Otus elegans botelensis.

Perf. 12¾x12½

2013, June 26 Engr.

4122-4125 A1104 Set of 4 3.00 1.50

Vases — A1174

Designs: $12, Ming Dynasty vase with "One Hundred Deer" design. $25, Qing Dynasty vase with "One Hundred Boys" design.

2013, July 10 Litho.

4126-4127 A1174 Set of 2 2.50 1.25
4127a Souvenir sheet of 2, #4126-4127 2.50 1.25

Mushrooms A1175

Designs: Nos. 4128, 4132a, $5, Ramaria botrytis. Nos. 4129, 4132b, $5, Morchella elata. Nos. 4130, 4132c, $12, Gomphus floccosus. Nos. 4131, 4132d, $12, Aleuria aurantia.

2013, July 24 *Perf. 12½*

Stamps With White Frames

4128-4131 A1175 Set of 4 2.25 1.10

Souvenir Sheet
Stamps Without White Frames

Perf. 12½x13

4132 A1175 Sheet of 4, #a-d 2.25 1.10

No. 4132 contains four 26x34mm stamps.

Chinese Dishes — A1176

No. 4133 — Chopsticks and: a, Stinky tofu, condiment bowl at UL. b, Taiwanese meatball, two sauce bottles at UL. c, Oyster omelet, teapot and condiment bowl at UL. d, Braised pork rice, salt and pepper shakers at UL.

2013, Aug. 16 *Perf. 13¼x13*

4133 A1176 $5 Horiz. strip of 4, #a-d 1.40 .70

Compare with Type A1158.

Long-horned Beetles Type of 2010

Designs: No. 4134, Parandra lanyuana. No. 4135, Bunothorax takasagoensis. $10, Oplatocera mandibulata. $25, Cyrtoclytus kusumai.

2013, Aug. 28 *Perf. 12½x13½*

4134 A1054 $5 multi .35 .25
4135 A1054 $5 multi .35 .25
4136 A1054 $10 multi .70 .35
4137 A1054 $25 multi 1.75 .85
Nos. 4134-4137 (4) 3.15 1.70

Soong May-ling (Madame Chiang) (1898-2003), First Lady — A1177

2013, Sept. 12 *Perf. 12¾x12½*

4138 A1177 $12 multi .80 .40

A1178

Emperor Gaozong Era Artifacts — A1179

No. 4139: a, Qing Dynasty gourd-shaped vase. b, Qing Dynasty carved red lacquer bowl, horiz. c, Northern Song Dyanasty plate with celadon glaze, horiz. d, Qing Dynasty jade bear-shaped vessel.

$25, Qing Dynasty New Year's silk tapestry scroll.

2013, Oct. 8 Litho. *Perf. 12*

4139 A1178 Sheet of 4 + label 2.50 1.25
a. $5 multi .35 .25
b.-c. $10 Either single .65 .30
d. $12 multi .85 .40

Souvenir Sheet

Perf. 12¾x12½

4140 A1179 $25 multi 1.75 .85

Presidential Office Building, Taipei — A1180

Sun Yat-sen Memorial Hall, Taipei — A1181

National Palace Museum, Taipei — A1182

Taipei 101 Building — A1183

Chiang Kai-shek Memorial Hall, Taipei — A1184

Jiufen — A1185

Alishan — A1186

Qingshui Cliff — A1187

Queen's Head Rock Formation A1188

Sun Moon Lake — A1189

2013, Oct. 22 Litho. *Perf. 13¼*

4141 Block of 6 2.10 1.10
a. A1180 $5 multi .35 .25
b. A1181 $5 multi .35 .25
c. A1182 $5 multi .35 .25
d. A1183 $5 multi .35 .25
e. A1184 $5 multi .35 .25
f. A1185 $5 multi .35 .25
4142 Block of 4 3.50 1.60
a. A1186 $12 multi .85 .40
b. A1187 $12 multi .85 .40
c. A1188 $12 multi .85 .40
d. A1189 $12 multi .85 .40

Bicycle Paths — A1190

Bicyclist on: No. 4143, $5, Yangguang Bridge on Xindian River Bicycle Path, New Taipei City (pale orange panel). No. 4144, $5, Bali Zuoan Bicycle Path, New Taipei City (pink panel). No. 4145, $10, Sankeng Bicycle Path, Taoyuan (green panel). No. 4146, $10, Hsinchu Coast Bicycle Path (yellow panel).

2013, Nov. 8 Litho. *Perf. 13¼x13*

Stamp + Label

4143-4146 A1190 Set of 4 2.10 1.10

Dragon and Phoenix — A1191

2013, Nov. 15 Engr. *Perf. 13¼x12½*

4147 A1191 $50 car & rose 3.50 1.75

Qing Dynasty Bowl, 1723-35 A1192

Wash Bowl, Southern Song to Yuan Dynasties, 13th-14th Cent. A1193

Ming Dynasty Jar With Lid, 1465-87 A1194

12th Cent. Ding Ware Pillow A1195

Ming Dynasty Flower Holder A1196

Qing Dynasty Covered Box, 1874-1908 A1197

Qing Dynasty Jadeite Cabbage and Insects Figurine A1198

Ru Ware Warming Bowl, 11th-12th Cent. A1199

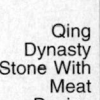

Qing Dynasty Stone With Meat Design A1200

Western Zhoud Dynasty Mao-gong Ding (Ritual Vessel) A1201

2013, Nov. 22 Litho. *Perf. 12½*

4148 Block of 6 2.10 1.10
a. A1192 $5 multi .35 .25
b. A1193 $5 multi .35 .25
c. A1194 $5 multi .35 .25
d. A1195 $5 multi .35 .25
e. A1196 $5 multi .35 .25
f. A1197 $5 multi .35 .25
4149 Block of 4 3.50 1.60
a. A1198 $12 multi .85 .40
b. A1199 $12 multi .85 .40
c. A1200 $12 multi .85 .40
d. A1201 $12 multi .85 .40

Items in National Palace Museum.

New Year 2014 (Year of the Horse) A1202

Designs: $3.50, Horse with leg lifted. $13, Horse leaping.
$12, Two leaping horses.

2013, Dec. 2 Litho. *Perf. 13*

4150-4151 A1202 Set of 2 1.10 .55

Souvenir Sheet

Perf. 12½

4152 A1202 $12 multi .85 .40

No. 4152 contains one 64x40mm stamp.

Corals A1203

Designs: $3.50, Dendronephthya gigantea. $5, Pavona cactus. $10, Acropora granulosa. $15, Melithaea ochracea.

2014, Jan. 8 Litho. *Perf. 12½x13¼*

4153-4156 A1203 Set of 4 2.25 1.10

See Nos. 4257-4260.

Chinese Desserts A1204

No. 4157: a, Pineapple-filled shortcrust pastries, orange shopping bag and box. b, Mochi, green shopping bag and box. c, Sun cakes, red shopping bag and box. d, Egg yolk pastries, rose lilac shopping bag and box.

2014, Jan. 22 Litho. *Perf. 13¼x13*

4157 A1204 $5 Horiz. strip of 4, #a-d 1.40 .70

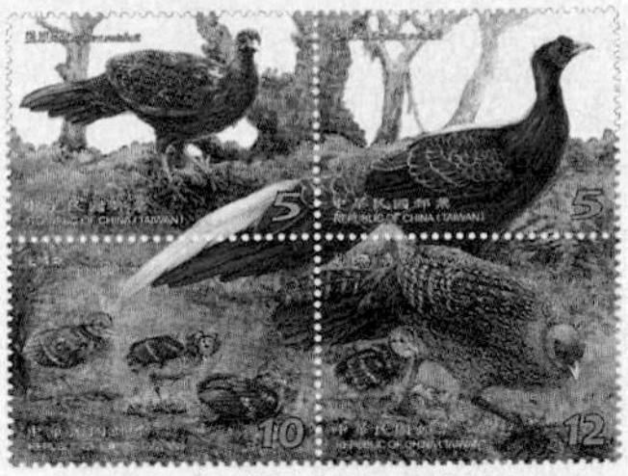

Lophura Swinhoii — A1205

No. 4158: a, Immature male. b, Head of mature male. c, Chicks. d, Hen and chick. $25, Male and female.

Perf. 12½x13¼

2014, Feb. 20 Litho.

4158 A1205 Block of 4 2.25 1.25
a.-b. $5 Either single .35 .25
c. $10 multi .65 .35
d. $12 multi .80 .40

Souvenir Sheet

Perf. 13½

4159 A1205 $25 multi 1.75 .85

No. 4159 contains one 80x50mm stamp.

Lighthouses Type of 2010

Designs: No. 4160, $5, Fangyuan Lighthouse (denomination in rose), horiz. No. 4161, $5, Chamu Yu Lighthouse (denomination in blue), horiz. $10, Lanyu Lighthouse (denomination in purple), horiz. $25, Sandiaojiao Lighthouse (denomination in yellow), horiz.

2014, Mar. 6 Litho. *Perf. 12½x12¾*

4160-4163 A1059 Set of 4 3.00 1.50

Berries Type of 2012

Designs: No. 4164, Lycium chinense. No. 4165, Dianella ensifolia. $15, Ampelopsis brevipedunculata var. hancei. $34, Diplocylos palmatus.

Perf. 13¼x12½

2014, Mar. 27 Litho.

4164 A1128 $5 multi .35 .25
4165 A1128 $5 multi .35 .25
4166 A1128 $15 multi 1.00 .50
4167 A1128 $34 multi 2.25 1.10
Nos. 4164-4167 (4) 3.95 2.10

Children at Play Type of 2013

Designs: No. 4168, $5, Boy on hobby horse. No. 4169, $5, Children playing with bamboo helicopters. No. 4170, $5, Child flying kite. No. 4171, $5, Children playing marbles. No. 4172, $5, Children with Lion Dance costumes.

2014, Apr. 2 Litho. *Perf. 12½*

4168-4172 A1167 Set of 5 1.75 .85
4172a Booklet pane of 10, 2 each #4168-4172, perf. 12½ on 3 sides 3.50 —
Complete booklet, #4172a 3.50

Children at Play Bathing a Buddha, Scroll Painting by Su Hanchen A1206

Children Playing in an Autumn Garden, Scroll Painting by Su Hanchen A1207

Children Playing in Summer, Scroll Painting by Unknown Artist — A1208

Children Playing in Autumn, Scroll Painting by Unknown Artist — A1209

Children Painting in Winter, Scroll Painting by Unknown Artist — A1210

2014, Apr. 30 Litho. *Perf. 13¼x12½*

4173	A1206	$5 multi		.35	.25
4174	A1207	$5 multi		.35	.25
4175	A1208	$10 multi		.70	.35
4176	A1209	$10 multi		.70	.35
4177	A1210	$12 multi		.80	.40
	Nos. 4173-4177 (5)			2.90	1.60

"The Swan Goose Carries a Message" — A1211

Perf. 13½x13¼

2014, May 9 Litho. & Engr.

4178 A1211 $9 multi .60 .30

See People's Republic of China No.

Herbs Type of 2013

Designs: $3.50, Foeniculum vulgare. $5, Perilla frutescens. $12, Lavandula angustifolia. $25, Ocimum basilicum.

2014, June 11 Litho. *Perf. 12½*

4179-4182 A1173 Set of 4 3.00 1.50

Souvenir Sheet

Electrification of the Hua-tung Railway — A1212

No. 4183: a, $5, Trains in Hualien Station. b, $12, Train and Kecheng bridge. c, $25, Train exiting Shanli Tunnel.

Perf. 12½x12¾

2014, June 28 Litho.

4183 A1212 Sheet of 3, #a-c 3.00 1.50

Cuichi Pond A1213

Tunlu Pond A1214

Designs: $10, Qicai Lake. $12, Jiaming Lake.

2014, July 17 Litho. *Perf. 13¼*

4184	A1213	$5 multi		.35	.25
4185	A1214	$5 multi		.35	.25
4186	A1214	$10 multi		.70	.35
4187	A1214	$12 multi		.80	.40
	Nos. 4184-4187 (4)			2.20	1.25

National Taiwan Library, Cent. — A1215

2014, Aug. 9 Litho. *Perf. 12½*

4188 A1215 $12 multi .80 .40

Jugang Tower and Residential Buildings, Kinmen — A1216

Wentai Pagoda and Buildings, Kinmen — A1217

2014, Aug. 28 Litho. *Perf. 12½*

4189	Horiz. pair	1.10	.65
a.	A1216 $5 multi	.35	.25
b.	A1217 $12 multi	.80	.40

Kinmen County, cent.

Miniature Sheet

Museums — A1218

No. 4190: a, $5, National Taiwan Museum of Fine Arts (modern building with lawn), Taichung. b, $5, National Taiwan Museum, Taipei (building with 6 pillars). c, $5, National Museum of Taiwan Literature (building with domes at sides). d, $5, National Museum of Taiwan History (building with solar panels). e, $12, National Palace Museum, vert.

2014, Sept. 10 Litho. *Perf. 12½*

4190 A1218 Sheet of 5, #a-e, + 4 labels 2.10 1.10

Blue and White Porcelain A1219

Designs: $5, Qing Dynasty dish with floral design. $10, Ming Dynasty jar with peony design. $12, Ming Dynasty jar with dragon design. $20, Qing Dynasty vase depicting women.

$25, Qing Dynasty plate with bird and flowers design, horiz.

Litho. & Embossed

2014, Sept. 19 *Perf. 13¾x13½*

4191-4194 A1219 Set of 4 3.25 1.60

Souvenir Sheet

Perf. 13½x13¾

4195 A1219 $25 multi 1.75 .85

Miniature Sheet

Taipei 2015 Asian International Stamp Exhibition — A1220

No. 4196: a, $5, Pink azalea blossoms in spring, Mt. Hehuan. b, $5, Tung trees in summer, Pingxi Railway. c, $10, Maple trees in autumn, Wuling Farm. d, $25, Cherry blossoms in winter, Mt. Xue.

2014, Oct. 3 Litho. *Perf. 12½*

4196 A1220 Sheet of 4, #a-d, + 4 labels 3.00 1.50

Miniature Sheet

Taipei Zoo, Cent. — A1221

No. 4197: a, $5, Formosan serow (30x40mm). b, $5, Formosan pangolin (40x30mm). c, $10, Asian elephant (55x38mm). d, $10, Formosan black bear (30x40mm). e, $12, Bengal tiger (55x38mm). f, $12, Giant pandas (38x55mm).

Perf. 13¼x12½, 12½x13¼

2014, Oct. 16 Litho.

4197 A1221 Sheet of 6, #a-f 3.50 1.75

Scenes From Novel "The Dream of Red Mansions," by Cao Xueqin A1222

Designs: No. 4198, $5, Women standing around seated man. No. 4199, $5, Woman and five men looking at garden. $10, Visit of Yuanchun at Lantern Festival. $25, Baochai chasing butterflies.

2014, Oct. 27 Litho. *Perf. 13x13½*

4198-4201 A1222 Set of 4 3.00 1.50

See Nos. 4228-4231.

Flowers in Koji Pottery Vases — A1223

Large vases with: No. 4202, $5, Peonies (yellow green panel). No. 4203, $5, Lotuses (blue panel). $10, Chrysanthemums (orange panel). $25, Camellias (pink lilac panel).

2014, Nov. 14 Litho. *Perf. 13½*

4202-4205 A1223 Set of 4 3.00 1.50

Bride and Groom In Chinese Attire A1224

Bride and Groom in Western Attire A1225

Bride and groom with: No. 4206, Red ribbon. No. 4207, Angels and flowers. No. 4208, Red streamer and bow. No. 4209, Hearts and horses.

2014, Nov. 21 Litho. *Perf. 12½*

4206	A1224	$3.50	multi	.25	.25
4207	A1225	$3.50	multi	.25	.25
4208	A1224	$5	multi	.35	.25
4209	A1225	$5	multi	.35	.25
	Nos. 4206-4209 (4)			1.20	1.00

New Year 2015 (Year of the Ram) — A1226

Designs: $3.50, Bright pink ram. $13, Purple ram.
$12, Two rams.

2014, Dec. 1 Litho. *Perf. 13*

4210-4211 A1226 Set of 2 1.10 .55

Souvenir Sheet

Perf. 12½

4212 A1226 $12 multi .80 .40

No. 4212 contains one 64x40mm stamp.

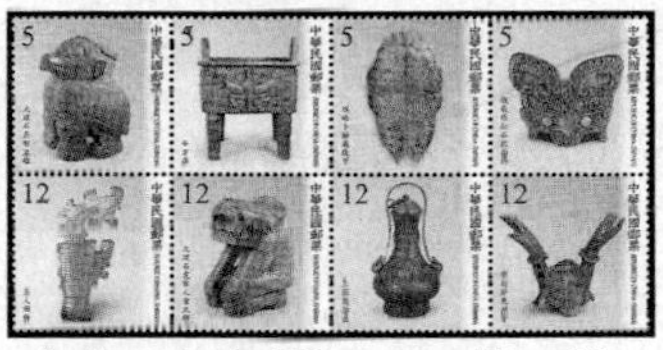
Archaeological Treasures From Yin Ruins — A1227

No. 4213: a, Marble figurine depicting owl, rose brown background. b, Cauldron with handles, light blue background. c, Oracle bone, rose brown background. d, Mask for horse with turquoise inlays, gray blue background. e, Figurine of human head with crest, light blue background. f, Anthropomorphic figurine with tiger's head, rose brown background. g, Wine container with detachable cap, gray blue background. h, Deer skull with inscriptions, rose brown background.

2014, Dec. 10 Litho. *Perf. 12½*

4213	A1227 Block of 8		4.25	2.10
a.-d.	$5 Any single		.25	.25
e.-h.	$12 Any single		.80	.40
i.	Souvenir sheet of 8, #4213a-4213h + 4 labels		4.25	2.10

Jellyfish — A1228

Designs: $5, Pelagia noctiluca. $7, Physophora hydrostatica. $10, Mastigias papua. $12, Cyanea capillata.

2015, Jan. 8 Litho. *Perf. 13¼x13*

4214-4217 A1228 Set of 4 2.25 1.10

Legumes A1229

Designs: $5, Arachis hypogaea. $7, Vigna angularis. $10, Glycine max. $25, Vigna radiata.

2015, Jan. 28 Litho. *Perf. 13¼x12½*

4218-4221 A1229 Set of 4 3.00 1.50

Animals — A1230

Nos. 4222 and 4223: a, Rabbits. b, Squirrels. c, Dogs. d, Bears. e, Elephants. f, Cats. g, Deer. h, Sheep. i, Zebras. j, Giraffes.

2015, Feb. 12 Litho. *Perf. 13¼*

4222	Block of 10	2.50	1.25
a.-j.	A1230 $3.50 Any single	.25	.25
4223	Block of 10	3.50	1.75
a.-j.	A1230 $5 Any single	.35	.25

Bo Le Appraises the Horse A1231

The Ambition of a Swan A1232

Adept With Both the Pen and the Sword A1233

Tiny Blade of Grass and Spring Sun A1234

Perf. 12½x12¾

2015, Mar. 20 Litho.

4224	A1231	$5	multi	.35	.25
4225	A1232	$5	multi	.35	.25
4226	A1233	$5	multi	.35	.25
4227	A1234	$5	multi	.35	.25
	Nos. 4224-4227 (4)			1.40	1.00

Chinese idioms.

Daiyu Burying the Flowers A1235

Tanchun Starting a Poetry Club A1236

Grandmother Liu Touring Daguanyuan — A1237

Miaoyu Tasting Tea A1238

2015, Mar. 30 Litho. *Perf. 13x13¼*

4228	A1235	$5	multi	.35	.25
4229	A1236	$5	multi	.35	.25
4230	A1237	$10	multi	.65	.30
4231	A1238	$25	multi	1.60	.80
	Nos. 4228-4231 (4)			2.95	1.60

Scenes from "The Dream of Red Mansions," by Cao Xueqin. Compare with Nos. 4198-4201.

Teresa Teng (1953-95), Singer — A1239

Various photographs of Teng with panel color of: $5, Pink. $9, Orange. $13, Dull rose. $15, Lilac.

2015, Apr. 15 Litho. *Perf. 12½*

4232-4235 A1239 Set of 4 2.75 1.40

Control Yuan Building, Cent. — A1240

2015, Apr. 24 Litho. *Perf. 13¼*

4236 A1240 $25 multi 1.75 .85

Taipei 2015 Intl. Stamp Exhibition — A1241

No. 4237: a, Dragon. b, Geese.

2015, Apr. 24 Litho. *Perf. 14*

4237	A1241 Horiz. pair + central label	2.10	1.10
a.	$5 multi	.35	.25
b.	$25 multi	1.75	.85
c.	Souvenir sheet of 4, 2 each #4237a-4237b, perf. 13¼x13½ syncopated	4.25	2.25

Black-faced Spoonbills on Zengwen River — A1242

Black-winged Stilt, Sicao Wetlands A1243

2015, Apr. 25 Litho. *Perf. 14*

4238	A1242 $10 multi	.65	.30
4239	A1243 $25 multi	1.75	.85
a.	Horiz. pair, #4238-4239, + central label	2.40	1.25
b.	Vert. pair, #4238-4239, no label	2.40	1.25

Taipei 2015 Intl. Stamp Exhibition. Nos 4238-4239 were printed in sheets of 16 (8 of each stamp) + 9 labels.

A1244

Taipei 2015 Intl. Stamp Exhibition — A1245

No. 4240: a, Family, child playing with blocks. b, Family on bicycle.

No. 4241: a, Family, child playing with blocks at left, on bicycle at right. b, Family, child playing with blocks at right, on bicycle at left.

2015, Apr. 26 Litho. *Perf. 12¾x12½*

4240	A1244 Horiz. pair + central label	2.10	1.10
a.	$5 multi	.35	.25
b.	$25 multi	1.75	.85

Souvenir Sheet

4241	A1245 Sheet of 2	3.50	1.75
a.-b.	$25 Either single	1.75	.85

Taipei 2015 Intl. Stamp Exhibition — A1246

No. 4242: a, Sky Lantern Festival, Pingxi. b, Xiao Liuqiu coral island.

2015, Apr. 27 Litho. *Perf. 14*

4242	A1246 Horiz. pair + central label	2.60	1.25
a.	$12 multi	.80	.40
b.	$25 multi	1.75	.85

Taipei 2015 Intl. Stamp Exhibition — A1247

No. 4243 — Scroll paintings: a, Literary Gathering, by Emperor Huizong. b, Elegant Gathering in the Western Garden, by Zhao Mengfu.

2015, Apr. 28 Litho. ***Perf. 13¼x12½***

4243	A1247	Horiz. pair + central label	2.40	1.25
a.		$9 multi	.60	.30
b.		$25 multi	1.75	.85
c.		Souvenir sheet of 2, #4243a-4243b, + label	2.40	1.25

Herbs Type of 2013

Designs: $3.50, Allium schoenoprasum. $5, Borago officinalis. $12, Tropaeolum majus. $25, Chamaemelum nobile.

2015, June 11 Litho. ***Perf. 12½***

4244-4247 A1173 Set of 4 3.00 1.50

Liberation of Taiwan in World War II, 70th Anniv. — A1248

Designs: No. 4248, $3.50, Soldiers carrying flags. No. 4249, $3.50, Farm woman holding sheaf of rice, Shimen Reservoir. No. 4250, $5, People cheering Chiang Kai-shek, horiz. No. 4251, $5, Crowd in plaza celebrating Taiwan Retrocession Day, 1963, horiz.

2015, July 7 Litho. ***Perf. 12½***

4248-4251 A1248 Set of 4 1.10 .55

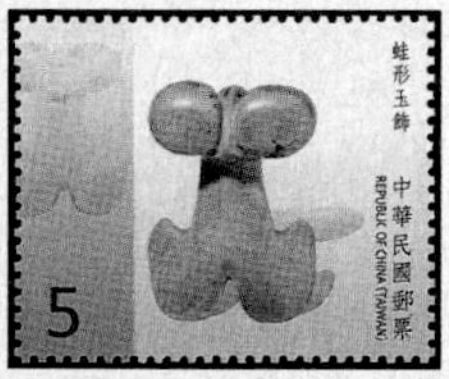

A1249

Prehistoric Artifacts — A1250

Designs: $5, Frog-shaped jade ornament. $7, Jade tubes. $9, Circular jade bangle. $12, String of jade beads.
$20, Jade earring.

2015, Aug. 21 Litho. ***Perf. 12½***

4252-4255 A1249 Set of 4 2.10 1.10

Souvenir Sheet

4256 A1250 $20 multi 1.25 .60

Corals Type of 2014

Designs: $3.50, Montipora foliosa. $5, Sarcophyton ehrenbergi. $10, Ellisella robusta. $15, Stylaster gracilis.

2015, Sept. 10 Litho. ***Perf. 12½***

4257-4260 A1203 Set of 4 2.10 1.10

A1251

Paintings by Giuseppe Castiglione (Lang Shining) — A1252

Designs: No. 4261, $5, Gathering of Auspicious Signs (flowers in vase). No. 4262, $5, Long-haired Dog Beneath Blossoms. No. 4263, $9, Ayusi Sweeping Bandits with a Lance, horiz. No. 4264, $9, Cochin Lemur, horiz.
No. 4265 — Golden Pheasant in Spring: a, $12. b, $70.

2015, Oct. 8 Litho. ***Perf. 13¼***

4261-4264 A1251 Set of 4 1.75 .85

Souvenir Sheet
Silk-Faced Paper

4265 A1252 Sheet of 2, #a-b 5.00 2.50

Sun Yat-sen (1866-1925), First President of Republic of China — A1253

Various depictions of Sun Yat-sen: $5, $12, horiz.

2015, Nov. 12 Litho. ***Perf. 12½***

4266-4267 A1253 Set of 2 1.10 .55

Rail Tourism — A1254

Designs: $5, Yuli-Taitung Summer Formosa train, railroad bridge. $10, South Link Line train, bridge near coast. $15, Jiji Line Evolution No. 1001 train, bicyclists.

2015, Nov. 25 Litho. ***Perf. 13x13¼***

4268-4270 A1254 Set of 3 1.90 .95

New Year 2016 (Year of the Monkey) A1255

Designs: $3.50, Monkey facing right. $13, Monkey facing left.
$12, Two monkeys.

2015, Dec. 1 Litho. ***Perf. 13***

4271-4272 A1255 Set of 2 1.00 .50

Souvenir Sheet
Perf. 12½

4273 A1255 $12 multi .75 .35

No. 4273 contains one 64x40mm stamp.

A1256

Opening of National Palace Museum Southern Branch — A1257

Designs: $5, Right-spiraling conch, Qing dynasty. $10, Jade bowl with handles and lid. $12, Hanging scroll with deities Good Fortune, Wealth and Long Life.
No. 4277: a, Board from Tibetan Kangyar with text and two deities. b, Board from Tibetan Kangyar with five deities.

Perf. 14¼x14½

2015, Dec. 10 Litho.

4274-4276 A1256 Set of 3 1.75 .85

Souvenir Sheet
Perf. 14¾

4277 A1257 $25 Sheet of 2, #a-b 3.00 1.50

SEMI-POSTAL STAMPS

SP1

Red or Blue Surcharge

1920, Dec. 1 Unwmk. ***Perf. 14, 15***

B1	SP1	1c on 2c green	5.00	2.00
B2	SP1	3c on 4c scar (B)	8.00	3.00
B3	SP1	5c on 6c gray	12.00	5.00
		Nos. B1-B3 (3)	25.00	10.00

The surcharge represents the actual franking value. The extra cent helped victims of the 1919 Yellow River flood.

War Refugees SP2

Black Surcharge

1944, Oct. 10 Engr. ***Perf. 12***

B4	$2 +$2 on 50c + 50c	2.00	2.00
B5	$4 +$4 on 8c + 8c	2.00	2.00
B6	$5 +$5 on 21c + 21c	2.00	2.00
B7	$6 +$6 on 28c + 28c	4.00	4.00
B8	$10 +$10 on 33c + 33c	5.00	5.00
B9	$20 +$20 on $1 + $1	6.00	6.00
a.	Sheet of 6, #B4-B9	85.00	60.00
	Nos. B4-B9 (6)	21.00	21.00

The borders of each stamp differ slightly in design. The surtax was for war refugees.
Nos. B4-B8 exist without surcharge, but were not regularly issued.

Great Wall of China — SP4

1948, July 5 Litho. ***Perf. 14, Imperf.***

Without Gum

Cross in Carmine

B11	SP4	$5000 + $2000 vio	.50	*2.50*
B12	SP4	$10,000 + $2000 brn	.50	*2.50*
B13	SP4	$15,000 + $2000 gray	.50	*2.50*
a.		Cross omitted		
		Nos. B11-B13 (3)	1.50	*7.50*

The surtax was for anti-tuberculosis work.
Fakes of B13a exist with cross chemically removed. No genuine used copies are known.

Republic of China (Taiwan)

Chinese Refugee Family — SP5

1954, Oct. 1 Engr. ***Perf. 12***

Without Gum

B14	SP5	40c + 10c dp bl	25.00	5.00
B15	SP5	$1.60 + 40c lil rose	67.50	26.00
B16	SP5	$5 + $1 red	125.00	110.00
		Nos. B14-B16 (3)	217.50	141.00

The surtax was used to aid in the evacuation of Chinese from North Viet Nam.

Catalogue values for unused stamps in this section, from this point to the end of the section, are for Never Hinged items.

Sept. 21, 1999 Earthquake Relief — SP6

a, Damaged buildings, map, rescue workers. b, Hands, heart, earthquake fault.

1999, Nov. 1 Litho. ***Imperf.***

Sheet of 2

B17 SP6 $25 +$25, #a.-b. 9.00 9.00

No. B17 has simulated perforations.

Souvenir Sheet

Typhoon Morakot Relief — SP7

No. B18: a, Map of Taiwan surrounded by clouds, rescuers and rafts. b, House, construction equipment and workers.

2009, Oct. 9 Litho. ***Imperf.***

B18 SP7 $25 +$25 Sheet of 2, #a-b 7.00 7.00

No. B18 has simulated perforations.

AIR POST STAMPS

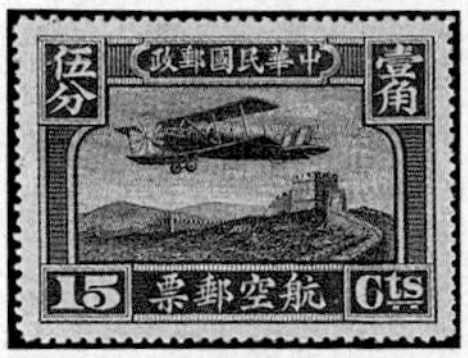

Curtiss "Jenny" over Great Wall (Bars of Republic flag on tail) — AP1

Unwmk.

1921, July 1 Engr. *Perf. 14*

C1 AP1 15c bl grn & blk 50.00 50.00
C2 AP1 30c scar & blk 50.00 50.00
C3 AP1 45c dull vio & blk 50.00 50.00
C4 AP1 60c dk blue & blk 65.00 65.00
C5 AP1 90c ol grn & blk 72.50 72.50
Nos. C1-C5 (5) 287.50 287.50

(Nationalist sun emblem on tail) — AP2

1929, July 5

C6 AP2 15c blue grn & blk 10.00 3.00
C7 AP2 30c dk red & blk 15.00 5.00
C8 AP2 45c dk vio & blk 24.00 10.00
C9 AP2 60c dk blue & blk 27.50 12.00
C10 AP2 90c ol grn & blk 27.50 18.00
Nos. C6-C10 (5) 104.00 48.00

Junkers F-13 over Great Wall AP3

1932-37

C11 AP3 15c gray grn .70 .45
C12 AP3 25c orange ('33) 5.00 3.00
C13 AP3 30c red 10.00 2.50
C14 AP3 45c brown vio 1.00 .45
C15 AP3 50c dk brown ('33) 1.00 .45
C16 AP3 60c dk blue 1.00 .45
C17 AP3 90c olive grn 1.00 .60
C18 AP3 $1 yellow grn ('33) 1.50 .45
C19 AP3 $2 brown ('37) 1.50 .80
C20 AP3 $5 brown car ('37) 4.00 3.00
Nos. C11-C20 (10) 26.70 12.15

See #C21-C40. For surcharges and overprints see #C41-C52, C54-C60, 9N111-9N114, 9NC1-9NC7, Szechwan C1, C3-C6, Sinkiang C5-C19.

Type of 1932-37, with secret mark

1932-37 Issue. Lower part of left character joined

Secret Mark, 1940-41 Issue. Separated.

Perf. 12, 12½, 12½x13, 13

1940-41 Wmk. 261

C21 AP3 15c gray green 1.00 .60
C22 AP3 25c yellow org 1.25 .80
C23 AP3 30c red 1.00 .60
a. Vert. pair, imperf. between 500.00
C24 AP3 45c dull rose vio ('41) 1.00 .60
C25 AP3 50c brown 1.00 .60
C26 AP3 60c dp blue ('41) 1.00 .60
C27 AP3 90c olive ('41) 1.00 .70
C28 AP3 $1 apple grn ('41) 1.00 .70
C29 AP3 $2 lt brown ('41) 1.00 .70
C30 AP3 $5 lake 2.50 1.20
Nos. C21-C30 (10) 11.75 7.10

Unwmk.

Perf. 12½, 13, 13½

C31 AP3 15c gray green ('41) .70 .30
C32 AP3 25c lt orange ('41) .70 .30
C33 AP3 30c lt red ('41) .70 .30
C34 AP3 45c dl rose vio ('41) .70 .45
C35 AP3 50c brown .70 .60
C36 AP3 60c blue ('41) .70 .60
C37 AP3 90c lt olive ('41) .70 .60
C38 AP3 $1 apple grn ('41) .70 .70
C39 AP3 $2 lt brown ('41) 3.00 1.50
C40 AP3 $5 lake ('41) 2.00 1.25
Nos. C31-C40 (10) 10.60 6.60

For surcharges see note following No. C20.

Nos. C11 and C12 Surcharged

1946, May 2 Unwmk. *Perf. 14*

C41 AP3 $53 on 15c 1.50 *1.25*
C42 AP3 $73 on 25c 2,000. —

Forgeries of No. C42 exist.

On Nos. C23, C21, C22, C29 and C30

Perf. 13, 13x12, 12½

Wmk. 261

C43 AP3 $23 on 30c red .70 *.70*
C44 AP3 $53 on 15c gray grn 20.00 *25.00*
C45 AP3 $73 on 25c yel org .70 *.70*
C46 AP3 $100 on $2 lt brown 1.25 *.50*
C47 AP3 $200 on $5 lake .70 *.70*
Nos. C43-C47 (5) 23.35 27.60

On Nos. C33, C31, C32, C39 and C40

Perf. 13, 13x12, 13x12½, 12½

Unwmk.

C48 AP3 $23 on 30c lt red .60 *1.00*
a. Inverted surcharge 450.00
b. "2300" omitted 50.00
c. Last character (kuo) of surch. omitted 120.00
C49 AP3 $53 on 15c gray grn .60 *1.00*
a. Horiz. pair, imperf. btwn. 1,500. 675.00
C50 AP3 $73 on 25c lt org .60 *1.50*
a. Inverted surcharge 1,200.
C51 AP3 $100 on $2 lt brn .60 *.60*
C52 AP3 $200 on $5 lake .60 .40
a. Inverted surcharge 500.00
Nos. C48-C52 (5) 3.00 4.50

The surcharges on Nos. C41-C52 represent Chinese natl. currency and were applied at Shanghai.

Douglas DC-4 over Sun Yat-sen Mausoleum, Nanking — AP4

1946, Sept. 10 Litho. *Perf. 14*

Without Gum

C53 AP4 $27 blue .65 *1.00*

For surcharges see Nos. C61, Szechwan C2.

No. C23 Surcharged in Black

Perf. 13x12

1948, May 18 Wmk. 261

C54 AP3 $10,000 on 30c red .60 *1.00*

Same, in Black or Carmine, on Nos. C33, C32, C37, C36, C18 and C38

Unwmk.

Perf. 12½, 13x12½, 14

C55 AP3 $10,000 on 30c lt red .60 *.75*
C56 AP3 $20,000 on 25c lt org .60 *.75*
C57 AP3 $30,000 on 90c lt ol (C) .60 *1.00*
C58 AP3 $50,000 on 60c blue (C) .60 *1.00*
C59 AP3 $50,000 on $1 yel grn (C) (#C18) 175.00 150.00
C60 AP3 $50,000 on $1 ap grn (C) (#C38) .60 *.90*

No. C53 Surcharged in Black

Perf. 14

C61 AP4 $10,000 on $27 bl .75 *3.00*
Nos. C54-C61 (8) 179.35 158.40

Douglas DC-4 and Arrow — AP5

Perf. 12½

1949, May 2 Unwmk. Litho.

Without Gum

C62 AP5 blue green 7.00 *7.00*
a. Rouletted 12.00 *17.50*

See note after No. 959.

For overprints see Taiwan No. C1, Fukien No. C1, Kansu No. C1, PRC Nos. 26, 102.

Revenue Stamp Overprinted in Blue

1949, May Engr. *Perf. 14*

C63 A95 $100 olive green 125.00 110.00

See note after No. 962.

Republic of China (Taiwan)

Cheng Ch'eng-kung (Koxinga) — AP6

Rouletted

1950, Sept. 26 Unwmk. Typo.

Without Gum

C64 AP6 60c deep blue 14.00 7.00

For surcharge see No. 1120.

Plane over City Gate, Taipei — AP7

Jet Planes above Chung Shan Bridge — AP8

Two Doves Near Koxinga Shrine — AP9

1954 Engr. *Perf. 11½*

Without Gum

C65 AP7 $1 dk brown 11.00 1.00
a. Vert. pair, imperf. btwn. 200.00
C66 AP8 $1.60 olive blk 14.00 .80
a. Vert. pair, imperf. btwn. 140.00
b. Horiz. pair, imperf. btwn. 100.00 110.00
C67 AP9 $5 grnsh blue 20.00 1.75
Nos. C65-C67 (3) 45.00 3.55

Issued: No. C66, 8/14; Nos. C65, C67, 9/1.

No. C67 Surcharged in Red

1958, Dec. 11 Without Gum

C68 AP9 $3.50 on $5 grnsh bl 4.00 1.50

Catalogue values for unused stamps in this section, from this point to the end of the section, are for Never Hinged items.

Sea Gull — AP10

1959, Mar. 20 Photo. *Perf. 13*

C69 AP10 $8 blue, gray & blk 5.50 .40

Sabre Jets in Bomb Burst Formation — AP11

Plane Formations: $2, Loop, horiz. $5, Diamond formation passing over grounded plane, horiz.

1960, Feb. 29 Unwmk. *Perf. 13*

C70 AP11 $1 multicolored 6.50 .50
C71 AP11 $2 multicolored 6.00 .50
C72 AP11 $5 multicolored 10.00 .60
Nos. C70-C72 (3) 22.50 1.60

Issued to honor the Chinese Air Force and the "Thunder Tiger" aerobatic team.

Jet Airliner over Pitan Bridge AP12

Designs: $6, Jet over Tropic of Cancer monument, Kiai, vert. $10, Jet over Lion Head mountain, Sinchu, vert.

1963, Aug. 14 Photo. *Perf. 13*

C73 AP12 $2.50 multi 7.25 .25
C74 AP12 $6 multi 12.50 .40
C75 AP12 $10 multi 16.00 .65
Nos. C73-C75 (3) 35.75 1.30

Boeing 727 over Chilin Pavilion, Grand Hotel — AP13

Design: $8, Boeing 727 over National Palace Museum, Taipei.

1967, Apr. 1 Unwmk. *Perf. 13*

C76 AP13 $5 multicolored 3.75 .25
C77 AP13 $8 multicolored 5.50 .50

Wild Geese Flying over Mountains — AP14

Wild Geese flying over: $5, The sea. $8, The land, horiz.

1969, Aug. 14 Photo. *Perf. 13*

C78	AP14	$2.50 multicolored	3.00	.25
C79	AP14	$5 multicolored	4.75	.45
C80	AP14	$8 multicolored	5.75	.60
	Nos. C78-C80 (3)		13.50	1.30

Presidential Palace and Tzu-Ch'iang Squadron AP15

1980, June 18 Litho. *Perf. 13½*

C81	AP15	$5 shown	.25	.25
C82	AP15	$7 China Airlines jet	.70	.30
C83	AP15	$12 China flag, jet	1.00	.50
	Nos. C81-C83 (3)		1.95	1.05

Civil Aeronautics Administration, 37th Anniv. — AP16

Jet Airliners over: $7, Chiang Kai-shek Intl. Airport, vert. $11, Chung Cheng Memorial Hall. $18, Sun Yat-sen Memorial Hall.

Perf. 14x13½, 13½x14

1984, Jan. 20 Litho.

C84	AP16	$7 multicolored	.50	.25
C85	AP16	$11 multicolored	.80	.40
C86	AP16	$18 multicolored	1.00	.60
	Nos. C84-C86 (3)		2.30	1.25

Airplane AP17

1987, Aug. 4 Litho. *Perf. 13½*

C87	AP17	$9 multicolored	.60	.40
C88	AP17	$14 multicolored	.95	.55
C89	AP17	$18 multicolored	1.25	.65
	Nos. C87-C89 (3)		2.80	1.60

SPECIAL DELIVERY STAMPS

Used values of Nos. E1-E8 are for mailer's receipts. Complete unused strips of four are exceptionally scarce because the first section (#1) was to remain in the P.O. booklet.

The mailer received the righthand section (#4), usually canceled, as a receipt. The middle two sections were canceled and attached to the letter. Upon arrival at the destination P.O. they were canceled again, usually on the back, with the righthand copy (#3) retained by that P.O. The lefthand copy (#2) was signed by the recipient and returned to the original P.O. as evidence of delivery. Sections 2 and 3 usually are thin or badly damaged.

Unused strips of three (#2-4) can be found of Nos. E3-E8.

Design: Dragon in irregular oval. Stamp 8x2½ inches, divided into four parts by perforation or serrate rouletting.

"Chinese Imperial Post Office" in lines, repeated to form the background which is usually lighter in color than the rest of the design.

Dragon's head facing downward

Background with period after "POSTOFFICE."

No Date

1905 Unwmk. *Perf. 11*

E1	10c grass green	*12,000.*	500.00

Serrate Roulette in Black

E2	10c deep green	*15,000.*	500.00

Type, E3-E8

Dragon's head facing forward

Background with no period after "POSTOFFICE"

No Date

1907-10

E3	10c light bluish green	*2,000.*	250.00

Background with date at bottom

1909-11

E4	10c green (Feby 1909)	*1,750.*	200.00
E5	10c bl grn (Jan. 1911)	1,600.	150.00

"IMPERIAL POST OFFICE" in serifed letters repeated to form the background.

No Date, No Border

Background of 30 or 28 lines

1912

E6	10c green (30 lines)	1,400.	130.00
a.	28 lines	1,600.	800.00

Background of 35 lines of sans-serif letters

Colored Border

E8	10c green	1,600.	190.00

On No. E8 the medallion in the third section has Chinese characters in the background instead of the usual English inscriptions. E6 and E8 occur with many types of four-character overprints reading "Republic of China," applied locally but unofficially at various post offices.

Type, E9, E10

Design: Wild Goose. Stamp 7½x2¾ inches, divided into five parts.

"CHINESE POST OFFICE" in sans-serif letters, repeated to form the background of 28 lines. With border.

Serrate Roulette in Black

1913

E9	10c green	900.00	110.00

Unused values for Nos. E9-E10 are for complete strips of five parts. Used values are for single parts.

"CHINESE POST OFFICE" in antique letters, forming a background of 29 or 30 lines. No border.

1914 Serrate Roulette in Green

E10	10c green	325.00	50.00

On No. E9 the background is in sans-serif capitals, the Chinese and English inscriptions are on white tablets and the serial numbers are in black.

On No. E10 the background is in antique capitals and extends under the inscriptions. The serial numbers are in green.

NOTE:

In February, 1916, the Special Delivery Stamps were demonetized and became merely receipts without franking value. To mark this, four of the five sections of the stamp had the letters A, B, C, D either handstamped or printed on them.

SD1

1941 Unwmk. Typo. *Rouletted*

Without Gum

E11	SD1 ($2) car & yel	35.00	32.50

Motorcycle Messenger — SD2

1949, July Litho. *Perf. 12½*

Without Gum

E12	SD2 red violet	9.00	*20.00*
a.	Rouletted	12.00	*21.00*

See note after No. 959.

For surcharge and overprints see Nos. 1150, Taiwan E1, Fukien E1.

Revenue Stamp Overprinted in Purple Brown

1949 Without Gum

E13	A95 $10 grnsh gray	55.00	55.00

See note after No. 962.

REGISTRATION STAMPS

R1

1941 Unwmk. Typo. *Rouletted*

Without Gum

F1	R1 ($1.50) green & buff	21.00	21.00

Mountain Scene — R2

1949, July Litho. *Perf. 12½*

Without Gum

F2	R2 carmine	10.00	*15.00*
a.	Rouletted	12.00	*18.00*

See note after No. 959.

For surcharge and overprints see Nos. 1152, Taiwan F1, Fukien F1, PRC 103.

Revenue Stamp Overprinted in Carmine

1949

F3	A95 $50 dark blue	35.00	24.00

See note after No. 962.

POSTAGE DUE STAMPS

Regular Issue of 1902-03 Overprinted in Black

1904 Unwmk. *Perf. 14 to 15*

J1 A17 ½c chocolate 14.00 6.00
J2 A17 1c ocher 14.00 5.00
J3 A17 2c scarlet 17.00 6.00
J4 A17 4c red brn 18.00 7.00
J5 A17 5c salmon 20.00 12.00
J6 A17 10c dk blue grn 33.00 20.00
a. Vert. pair, imperf. btwn. *2,000. 2,000.*
Nos. J1-J6 (6) 116.00 56.00

D1

1904 Engr.

J7 D1 ½c blue 7.00 4.00
a. Horiz. pair, imperf. btwn. 3,000. 2,000.
J8 D1 1c blue 12.00 4.00
J9 D1 2c blue 12.00 4.00
a. Horiz. pair, imperf. btwn. 2,000. 1,800.
J10 D1 4c blue 15.00 6.00
J11 D1 5c blue 18.00 7.00
J12 D1 10c blue 20.00 9.00
J13 D1 20c blue 50.00 12.00
J14 D1 30c blue 70.00 40.00
Nos. J7-J14 (8) 204.00 86.00

Arabic numeral of value at left on Nos. J12-J14.

1911

J15 D1 1c brown 25.00 *18.00*
J16 D1 2c brown 40.00 32.50

The ½c, 4c, 5c and 20c in brown exist but were not issued as they arrived in China after the downfall of the Ching dynasty.

Issues of 1904 Overprinted in Red

1912

J19 D1 ½c blue 700. *1,000.*
J20 D1 4c blue 900. *1,100.*
J21 D1 5c blue 1,000. *1,100.*
J22 D1 10c blue 1,500. 1,100.
J23 D1 20c blue 3,000. *3,200.*
J24 D1 30c blue 3,000. *3,200.*

Nos. J15-J16 exist with this overprint, but were not regularly issued.

Nos. J1-J14 Overprinted in Red

1912

J25 D1 ½c blue 5.00 3.00
J26 D1 1c brown 6.00 3.00
a. Horiz. pair, imperf. btwn. 3,000. 3,000.
b. Inverted overprint 550.00 550.00
J27 D1 2c brown 8.00 4.00
J28 D1 4c blue 15.00 6.00
J29 D1 5c blue 275.00 *300.00*
J30 D1 5c brown 20.00 *10.00*
a. Inverted overprint 320.00 *340.00*
J31 D1 10c blue 25.00 *13.00*
J32 D1 20c blue 27.00 17.00
J33 D1 30c blue 35.00 30.00
Nos. J25-J33 (9) 416.00 386.00

Issues of 1904 Overprinted in Black

1912

J34 D1 ½c blue 15.00 10.00
J35 D1 ½c brown 8.00 3.00
J36 D1 1c brown 8.00 3.00
a. Inverted overprint 350.00 350.00
J37 D1 2c brown 10.00 *5.00*
J38 D1 4c blue 20.00 *9.50*
J39 D1 5c brown 27.50 *14.00*
a. Horiz. pair, imperf. btwn. *3,800. 3,800.*
J40 D1 10c blue 45.00 *27.50*
J41 D1 20c brown 65.00 *100.00*
J42 D1 30c blue 75.00 65.00
Nos. J34-J42 (9) 273.50 237.00

D4

Printed by Waterlow & Sons

1913, May *Perf. 14, 15*

J43 D4 ½c blue 3.00 1.50
a. Horiz. pair, imperf. btwn. *4,000. 3,000.*
J44 D4 1c blue 3.50 1.50
J45 D4 2c blue 5.00 3.00
J46 D4 4c blue 8.00 3.00
J47 D4 5c blue 12.00 6.00
J48 D4 10c blue 17.50 8.00
J49 D4 20c blue 27.50 13.00
J50 D4 30c blue 35.00 15.00
Nos. J43-J50 (8) 111.50 51.00

Printed by the Chinese Bureau of Engraving & Printing

1915 Re-engraved *Perf. 14*

J51 D4 ½c blue 3.00 *1.00*
J52 D4 1c blue 3.75 .65
J53 D4 2c blue 4.00 .65
J54 D4 4c blue 5.00 .75
J55 D4 5c blue 7.00 1.50
J56 D4 10c blue 11.00 2.50
J57 D4 20c blue 17.50 8.00
J58 D4 30c blue 50.00 20.00
Nos. J51-J58 (8) 101.25 35.05

In the upper part of the stamps of type D4 there is an ornament of five marks like the letter "V". Below this is a curved label with an inscription in Chinese characters. On the 1913 stamps there are two complete background lines between the ornament and the label. The 1915 stamps show only one unbroken line at this place. There are other minute differences in the engraving of the stamps of the two issues.

D5

1932 *Perf. 14*

J59 D5 ½c orange .60 *.30*
J60 D5 1c orange .60 *.30*
J61 D5 2c orange .60 *.30*
J62 D5 4c orange .60 *.30*
J63 D5 5c orange 1.50 *1.50*
J64 D5 10c orange 2.00 2.00
J65 D5 20c orange 2.75 3.00
J66 D5 30c orange 4.00 *4.00*
Nos. J59-J66 (8) 12.65 11.70

See Nos. J69-J79. For surcharges see Nos. 1NJ1, 9NJ1-9NJ4.

Regular Stamps of 1939 Overprinted in Black or Red

1940

J67 A57 $1 henna & dk brn (Bk) 8.00 *25.00*
J68 A57 $2 dl bl & org brn (R) 12.00 *25.00*

Type of 1932
Printed by The Commercial Press, Ltd.
Perf. 12½, 12½x13, 13

1940-41 Engr.

J69 D5 ½c yellow orange .80 *1.00*
J70 D5 1c yellow orange .80 *1.00*
J71 D5 2c yellow orange ('41) .80 *1.00*
J72 D5 4c yellow orange .80 *1.00*
J73 D5 5c yellow orange ('41) 1.20 *1.00*
J74 D5 10c yellow orange ('41) .80 *1.00*
J75 D5 20c yellow orange ('41) .80 *1.00*
J76 D5 30c yellow orange .80 *1.00*
J77 D5 50c yellow orange 1.00 *1.00*
J78 D5 $1 yellow orange 1.20 *1.00*
J79 D5 $2 yellow orange 1.50 *2.00*
Nos. J69-J79 (11) 10.50 *12.00*

For surcharge see No. 1NJ1.

D6

Thin Paper Without Gum

1944 Typo. *Perf. 13*

J80 D6 10c bluish green .80 *3.00*
J81 D6 20c light chalky blue .80 *3.00*
J82 D6 40c dull rose .80 *3.00*
J83 D6 50c bluish green .80 *3.00*
J84 D6 60c dull blue .80 *3.00*
J85 D6 $1 dull rose .80 *2.00*
J86 D6 $2 lilac brown .80 *2.00*
Nos. J80-J86 (7) 5.60 *19.00*

D7

1945 Without Gum Unwmk.

J87 D7 $2 rose carmine .80 *2.00*
J88 D7 $6 rose carmine .80 *2.00*
J89 D7 $8 rose carmine .80 *2.00*
J90 D7 $10 rose carmine .80 *2.00*
J91 D7 $20 rose carmine .80 *2.00*
J92 D7 $30 rose carmine 1.00 *2.00*
Nos. J87-J92 (6) 5.00 *12.00*

For surcharges see Nos. J102-J109.

D8

Thin Paper Without Gum

1947 Litho. *Perf. 14*

J93 D8 $50 plum .80 *2.00*
J94 D8 $80 plum .80 *2.00*
J95 D8 $100 plum .80 *2.00*
J96 D8 $160 plum .80 *2.00*
J97 D8 $200 plum .80 *2.00*
J98 D8 $400 violet brown .80 *2.00*
J99 D8 $500 violet brown .80 *2.00*
a. Vert. pair, imperf. between 80.00
J100 D8 $800 violet brown .80 *2.00*
J101 D8 $2000 violet brown .80 *2.00*
Nos. J93-J101 (9) 7.20 *18.00*

Type of 1945, Redrawn Surcharged in Black

Without Gum
Deep claret

1948 Engr. *Perf. 13½x14*

J102 D7 $1000 on $20 .70 *2.50*
J103 D7 $2000 on $30 .70 *2.50*
J104 D7 $3000 on $50 .70 *2.50*
J105 D7 $4000 on $100 .70 *2.00*
J106 D7 $5000 on $200 .70 *2.00*
J107 D7 $10,000 on $300 .70 *1.00*
J108 D7 $20,000 on $500 .70 *1.00*
J109 D7 $30,000 on $1000 .70 *1.00*
Nos. J102-J109 (8) 5.60 *14.50*

There are many differences in the redrawn design.

No. 627 Surcharged in Black

1949 *Perf. 12*

J110 A72 1 (c) on $40 org .70 *10.00*
J111 A72 2 (c) on $40 org .70 *10.00*
J112 A72 5 (c) on $40 org .70 *10.00*
J113 A72 10 (c) on $40 org .70 *10.00*
J114 A72 20 (c) on $40 org .70 *10.00*
J115 A72 50 (c) on $40 org .70 *10.00*
J116 A72 $1 on $40 org .70 *10.00*
J117 A72 $2 on $40 org .70 *10.00*
J118 A72 $5 on $40 org 1.00 *10.00*
J119 A72 $10 on $40 org 1.00 *5.00*
Nos. J110-J119 (10) 7.60 *95.00*

Republic of China (Taiwan)

No. 438 Surcharged in Green or Black

1951 Unwmk. *Perf. 12½*

J120 A47 40c on 40c org (G) 18.00 *24.00*
J121 A47 80c on 40c org (Bk) 18.00 *24.00*

Revenue Stamps Surcharged in Various Colors

1953 Unwmk. *Perf. 12½, 14*
Without Gum

J122 A95 10c on $50 dk bl (O) 18.00 4.50
J123 A95 20c on $100 ol grn (Dk Br) 18.00 4.50
J124 A95 40c on $20 org brn 20.00 1.50
J125 A95 80c on $500 sl grn (Dk Bl) 30.00 2.50
J126 A95 $1 on $30 dk vio (G) 30.00 8.25
Nos. J122-J126 (5) 116.00 21.25

D9

1956 Unwmk. Litho. *Perf. 12½*
Without Gum

J127 D9 20c rose car, & lt bl 1.25 .25
J128 D9 40c green & buff 1.75 .25
J129 D9 80c brown & gray 3.50 .40
J130 D9 $1 ultra & pink 4.00 .40
Nos. J127-J130 (4) 10.50 1.30

No. 1197 Surcharged in Dark Violet

Wmk. 323

1961, Dec. 28 Engr. *Perf. 12*
Without Gum

J131 A135 $5 on $20 car rose 1.75 .50

Nos. 1274, 1282-1283 Surcharged in Black, Carmine Rose or Blue

1964-65 Litho.

J132 A158 10c on 80c pale grn .25 .25
J133 A158 20c on $3.60 vio bl (CR) ('65) .30 .25
J134 A158 40c on $4.50 ver (B) ('65) .65 .25
Nos. J132-J134 (3) 1.20 .75

D10

1966-76 Wmk. 323 ***Perf. 12½***

Granite Paper; Without Gum

J135	D10	10c dk brn & lil	.25	.25
J136	D10	20c blue & yel	.40	.25
J137	D10	50c vio bl & lt bl ('70)	.65	.25
J138	D10	$1 purple & sal	.50	.25
J139	D10	$2 grn & lt bl	.65	.25
J140	D10	$5 red & sal	1.25	.30
a.		$5 org red & pale yel	1.25	.30
J141	D10	$10 lil rose & pink ('76)	*22.50*	1.00
		Nos. J135-J141 (7)	*26.20*	2.55

The 50c, $10 and No. J140a are gummed. The $1 and $2 were reissued with gum in 1968 and 1973 respectively. No. J140a and the $10 are on ordinary paper.

Catalogue values for unused stamps in this section, from this point to the end of the section, are for Never Hinged items.

D11

1984-88 Litho. ***Perf. 12½***

J142	D11	$1 rose & violet	.25	.25
J143	D11	$2 yellow & blue	.25	.25
J144	D11	$3 pale grn & brt rose lil	.25	.25
J145	D11	$5 blue & yellow	.25	.25
J146	D11	$5.50 rose lil & brt blue	.40	.35
J147	D11	$7.50 bister yel & dp violet	.60	.45
J148	D11	$10 yel & lil rose	.50	.30
J149	D11	$20 sky blue & citron	1.60	1.25
		Nos. J142-J149 (8)	4.10	3.35

Issued: $3, $5.50, $7.50, $20, Apr. 1, 1988; others, Mar. 15, 1984.

D12

1998, Sept. 30 Litho. ***Perf. 12½***

Background Color

J150	D12	50c orange yellow	.25	.25
J151	D12	$1 pink	.25	.25
J152	D12	$2 deep pink	.25	.25
J153	D12	$5 yellow green	.40	.25
J154	D12	$10 blue	.75	.30
J155	D12	$20 green	1.60	.60
		Nos. J150-J155 (6)	3.50	1.90

Lotus Flower, Peach, Bats, Coins and Chinese Characters — D13

Perf. 12½x12¼

2008, Nov. 12 Litho.

Denomination Color

J156	D13	$1 dark red	.25	.25
J157	D13	$3 green	.25	.25
J158	D13	$5 olive green	.30	.25
J159	D13	$10 purple	.60	.30
J160	D13	$20 bister	1.25	.60
		Nos. J156-J160 (5)	2.65	1.65

Type of 2008

Die Cut Perf. 22

2015, Oct. 28 Litho.

Self-Adhesive

Denomination Color

J161	D13	50c red brown	.25	.25
J162	D13	$2 dark blue	.25	.25

PARCEL POST STAMPS

PP1

PP2

PP3

1945-48 Unwmk. Engr. ***Perf. 13***

Without Gum

Q1	PP1	$500 green	12.00	1.00
Q2	PP1	$1000 blue	12.00	1.00
Q3	PP1	$3000 rose red	22.50	1.60
Q4	PP1	$5000 brown	150.00	30.00
Q5	PP1	$10,000 lil gray	270.00	50.00
Q6	PP1	$20,000 red org	*5,000.*	
		Nos. Q1-Q5 (5)	466.50	83.60

No. Q6 was prepared but not issued.

For surcharges see People's Republic of China Nos. 5LQ1-5LQ2, 5LQ27-5LQ28.

Perf. 12½

Q7	PP2	$3000 red org	30.00	2.00
Q8	PP2	$5000 dk blue	40.00	2.00
Q9	PP2	$10,000 violet	45.00	5.00
Q10	PP2	$20,000 dk red	50.00	5.00

Perf. 13½

Q11	PP3	$1000 org yel	9.00	1.50
Q12	PP3	$3000 bl grn	9.00	1.50
Q13	PP3	$5000 org red	9.00	1.50
Q14	PP3	$7000 dl blue	9.00	1.50
Q15	PP3	$10,000 car rose	10.00	2.00
Q16	PP3	$30,000 olive	10.00	2.00
Q17	PP3	$50,000 indigo	10.00	2.00
Q18	PP3	$70,000 org brn	14.00	4.00
Q19	PP3	$100,000 dp plum	14.00	4.00

Denomination Tablet Without Inner Frame

Q20	PP3	$200,000 dk grn	18.50	4.00
Q21	PP3	$300,000 pink	18.50	4.00
Q22	PP3	$500,000 vio brn	18.50	4.00
Q23	PP3	$3,000,000 sl bl	20.00	7.00
Q24	PP3	$5,000,000 lilac	20.00	7.00
Q25	PP3	$6,000,000 ol gray	22.00	10.00
Q26	PP3	$8,000,000 scar	22.00	11.00
Q27	PP3	$10,000,000 sage grn	25.00	14.00
		Nos. Q11-Q27 (17)	258.50	81.00

Zeros for "cents" omitted on Nos. Q23-Q27.

See Taiwan Nos. Q1-Q5. For surcharges see Nos. 883-885, Northeastern Provinces Q1, Szechwan Q1, People's Republic of China 3LQ1-3LQ9, 5LQ3-5LQ16, 5LQ29-5LQ30.

#Q11-Q15, Q23-Q24 Surcharged in Black or Carmine (#Q35)

1949 Unwmk. ***Perf. 13½***

Q32	PP3	$10 on $3000	5.00	1.00
Q33	PP3	$20 on $5000	5.00	1.00
Q34	PP3	$50 on $10,000	5.00	1.00
Q35	PP3	$100 on $3,000,000	8.00	2.00
Q36	PP3	$200 on $5,000,000	12.00	2.00
Q37	PP3	$500 on $1000	22.50	.25
Q38	PP3	$1000 on $7000	22.50	.30
		Nos. Q32-Q38 (7)	80.00	7.55

5 characters in each line on Nos. Q33-Q38.

MILITARY STAMPS

No. 454 Overprinted in Dull Red

1943-44 Unwmk. ***Perf. 12***

M1	A59	8c turquoise green	6.00	*9.00*

Nos. 383, 453-454 Overprinted in Red or Black

6mm between characters

Perf. 14, 12½

M2	A57	8c olive green	6.00	*9.00*
a.		8mm between characters	6.00	*9.00*
M3	A59	8c red orange (B)	550.00	
M4	A59	8c turquoise green	12.00	10.00

Forgeries of No. M3 abound.

No. 493 Overprinted in Red

Perf. 13

M5	A62	16c dull olive brn	11.00	9.00
a.		Perf. 10½-11	300.00	

No. M5 overprinted in black is a proof.

Stamps of 1942-44 Overprinted in Carmine or Black

M6	A62	50c sage green (C)	6.00	*7.00*
M7	A62	$1 rose lake	8.00	*9.00*
M8	A62	$1 dull green	8.00	*9.00*
M9	A62	$2 dk blue grn (C)	10.00	*14.00*
M10	A62	$2 dk vio brn ('44)	200.00	150.00
		Nos. M6-M10 (5)	232.00	189.00

Nos. 383 and 357 Overprinted in Red

1944 ***Perf. 12, 14***

M11	A57	8c olive green	6.00	*10.00*
a.		Right character inverted	1,000.	
M12	A57	16c olive gray	90.00	90.00

Anti-Aircraft Guns — M1

1945, Jan. 1 Typo. ***Perf. 12½***

Thin Paper Without Gum

M13	M1	rose	3.00	*10.00*

For overprints see Northeastern Provinces Nos. M2-M3.

TAIWAN

(Formosa)

100 Sen = 1 Yen

100 Cents = 1 Dollar

Stamps and Types of Japan (Taiwan) Overprinted in Black

Stamps Divided by Lines of Colored Dashes

Values in Sen and Yen

1945 Unwmk. Litho. ***Imperf.***

Without Gum

1	A1	3s carmine	2.50	10.00
2	A1	5s blue grn	2.50	2.00
3	A1	10s pale blue	2.50	.55
a.		Inverted overprint	375.00	
b.		Double overprint	375.00	
4	A1	30s dk blue	14.00	10.00
5	A1	40s violet	14.00	7.00
6	A1	50s gray brn	10.00	5.00
7	A1	1y olive grn	12.00	5.00

Same Overprint on Types of Japan

8	A99	5y gray grn	24.00	18.00
9	A100	10y brown vio	45.00	45.00
a.		Inverted overprint	375.00	
		Nos. 1-9 (9)	126.50	102.55

The basic stamps of this issue were prepared by Japanese authorities for Taiwan use before the end of World War II when the island reverted to Chinese control. They are printed on crude buff or white wove paper. The overprint translates: "For Use in Taiwan, Chinese Republic."

A second overprinting of Nos. 2-3 was made with a different font.

China, Nos. 728-731, Srchd. in Black

1946 Without Gum ***Perf. 14***

10	A75	70s on $20 green	3.50	*5.50*
a.		Inverted surcharge	*1,200.*	
11	A75	1y on $30 blue	3.50	*5.50*
12	A75	2y on $50 dk brn	3.50	*5.75*
13	A75	3y on $100 car	3.75	*5.75*
		Nos. 10-13 (4)	14.25	*22.50*

Convening of the Chinese Natl. Assembly.

China Issues and Types of 1940-1946 Srchd. in Black — a

Perf. 12½, 12½x13, 13, 13x12½, 14

1946-47

Nos. 18, 23-28 Without Gum

14	A46	2s on 2c dp bl	.80	*1.50*
15	A48	5s on 5c dl red org	.80	*1.00*
16	A39	10s on 4c pale vio	.80	*1.50*
17	A48	30s on 15c brn car	.80	*1.00*
18	A73	50s on $20 car	.80	*1.00*
19	A37	65s on $20 brt yel grn	1.00	*2.00*
20	A47	1y on 20c lt bl	.80	*2.00*
a.		Inverted surcharge	*950.00*	
21	A37	1y on $30 choc	1.00	*1.75*
22	A37	2y on $50 red org	1.50	2.00
23	A73	3y on $100 dk car	.80	*2.00*
24	A73	5y on $200 ol grn	.80	*2.00*
25	A73	10y on $500 brt bl grn	.80	*1.50*
26	A73	20y on $700 red brn	1.00	1.00
27	A73	50y on $1000 rose lake	2.00	1.50
28	A73	100y on $3000 blue	2.75	1.60
		Nos. 14-28 (15)	16.45	*23.35*

The bottom line of the surcharge expresses the new value and consists of 2, 3 or 4 characters.

Nos. 14, 18-19, 21-28 issued in 1947.

Same Surcharge on China No. 412

1947 Wmk. 261 *Perf. 13*

28A	A48	30s on 15c brn car	135.00	150.00

Type of China, 1946, with additional inscription on both sides of head

1947 Unwmk. Engr. *Perf. 11, 11½*

29	A74	70c carmine	3.50	*4.75*
30	A74	$1 green	3.50	*4.75*
31	A74	$2 vermilion	3.50	*4.75*
32	A74	$3 yel grn	3.50	*4.75*
33	A74	$7 yel org	3.50	*4.75*
34	A74	$10 magenta	3.50	*4.75*
		Nos. 29-34 (6)	21.00	*28.50*

60th birthday of Chiang Kai-shek.

Type of China, 1947, with additional inscription above value

1947 *Perf. 14*

35	A76	50c deep green	3.50	*5.50*
36	A76	$3 deep blue	3.50	*5.50*
37	A76	$7.50 carmine	3.50	*5.50*
38	A76	$10 light brown	3.50	*5.50*
39	A76	$20 deep claret	3.50	*5.50*
		Nos. 35-39 (5)	17.50	*27.50*

First anniversary of return of Chinese National Government to Nanking.

Dr. Sun Yat-sen — A3

1947, July 10 Without Gum

40	A3	$1 dk brown	1.00	2.50
41	A3	$2 org brn	1.20	2.00
42	A3	$3 blue grn	1.20	2.00
43	A3	$5 vermilion	2.50	*2.75*
44	A3	$9 deep blue	1.00	1.20
45	A3	$10 brt rose car	1.00	.80
46	A3	$20 deep green	.85	.70
47	A3	$50 rose lilac	.85	.60
48	A3	$100 blue	.85	.60
49	A3	$200 dark red	.85	.60
		Nos. 40-49 (10)	11.30	13.75

The 30c gray and $7.50 orange were not regularly issued without surcharge. Value for the two stamps, $450.

See Nos. 63-68. For overprint and surcharges see Nos. 51-53, 69-73, 102, J10-J17.

Type of 1947 Surcharged in Black — b

1948 Unwmk. *Perf. 14*

51	A3	$25 on $100 blue	2.50	*3.00*
52	A3	$500 on $7.50 org	6.75	3.50
53	A3	$1000 on 30c gray	14.00	9.00
		Nos. 51-53 (3)	23.25	15.50

Stamps of China, 1943-48, Surcharged Type "a" in Black or Carmine

1948-49 *Perf. 12½, 14*

Without Gum

54	A73	$5 on $70 red org (#639)	1.00	*2.50*
55	A62	$10 on $3 dk yel (#555)	4.50	*3.50*
56	A82	$10 on $150 dk bl (C) (#745)	1.20	*1.75*
57	A82	$20 on $250 dp lil (C) (#746)	1.10	*1.20*
58	A67	$100 on $20 car (#592)	1,600.	—
59	A82	$1000 on $20,000 rose pink ('49) (#788)	6.50	3.50
		Nos. 54-59 (6)	1,614.	12.45

The bottom line of the surcharge expresses the new value and consists of 2 or 3 characters.

Forgeries of No. 58 abound.

Type of 1947

1949 Engr. *Perf. 14*

63	A3	$25 olive grn	1.20	1.00
64	A3	$5000 ocher	10.00	2.00
65	A3	$10,000 apple grn	10.00	5.00
66	A3	$20,000 ol bister	10.00	5.00
67	A3	$30,000 indigo	10.00	2.00
68	A3	$40,000 violet brn	9.00	2.00
		Nos. 63-68 (6)	50.20	17.00

For overprint and surcharges see Nos. 101, 103, J12.

No. 42 and type of 1947 Surcharged Type "b" in Black, Carmine Violet or Red Violet

1949

69	A3	$300 on $3 bl grn	1.75	1.00
70	A3	$1000 on $3 bl grn (C)	3.00	1.00
71	A3	$2000 on $3 bl grn (V)	2.50	1.00
72	A3	$3000 on $3 bl grn (RV)	12.00	4.25
73	A3	$3000 on $7.50 org	120.00	5.50
		Nos. 69-73 (5)	139.25	12.75

For overprints see Nos. J10-J11.

Stamps of China, 1940-47, Surcharged Type "a" in Black or Carmine

Perf. 12½, 13x13½, 14

74	A39	$2 on 2½c rose lil (#424)	.80	.80
75	A72	$5 on $40 org (#627)	1.00	*2.00*
76	A73	$5 on $50 pur (C) (#638)	1.00	1.50
77	A73	$5 on $100 dk car (#640)	1.25	.80
78	A57	$20 on 2c ol grn (#368)	1.00	1.75
81	A63	$100 on $20 rose (#571)	1.10	.50
82	A67	$200 on $10 dk bl (C) (#591)	8.00	1.75
84	A57	$500 on $30 dl vio (#521)	18.00	5.00
86	A62	$800 on $4 red brn (#504)	15.00	6.00
87	A67	$5000 on $10 dk bl (#591)	18.00	5.00
88	A67	$10,000 on $20 car (#592)	18.00	4.00
89	A82	$200,000 on $3000 bl (C) (#750)	900.00	50.00
		Nos. 74-89 (12)	983.15	79.10

Northeastern Provinces No. 47, Surcharged in Green, Red Violet, Black or Blue

1949-50

91	A2	2c on $44 (G)	62.50	6.00
92	A2	5c on $44 (RV) ('50)	57.50	7.00
a.		Violet surcharge	85.00	11.50
93	A2	10c on $44 (RV) ('50)	75.00	6.00
94	A2	20c on $44 (Bk) ('50)	100.00	7.00
a.		Double surcharge	200.00	
95	A2	30c on $44 (Bl) ('50)	110.00	14.00
96	A2	50c on $44 (Bl) ('50)	130.00	17.00
		Nos. 91-96 (6)	535.00	57.00

There were two printings of Nos. 91-93, with minor differences.

China 959a, Overprinted in Black

Overprint 15mm Wide

1949 Unwmk. *Rouletted 9½*

97	A96	orange	5.50	1.75

China Nos. 567, 498 and 640 Surcharged Type "a" in Black

1948-49 Unwmk. *Perf. 12½, 13, 14*

98	A63	$20 on $3 red	3.50	2.50
99	A62	$50 on 50c sage grn	3.75	5.00
a.		Perf. 11	50.00	75.00
100	A73	$600 on $100 dk car	6.50	3.50
		Nos. 98-100 (3)	13.75	11.00

Botton line of surcharge consists of 3 characters.

No. 99 has two settings of surcharge: I. Spacing 10mm between rows of characters. II. Spacing 12mm.

#67, 47 and 68 Surcharged in Violet (#101) or Black

1949 *Perf. 14*

101	A3	2c on $30,000 ind	52.50	30.00
102	A3	10c on $50 rose lil	52.50	6.75
103	A3	10c on $40,000 vio brn	125.00	30.00
		Nos. 101-103 (3)	230.00	66.75

Numerals slightly larger on Nos. 101-103.

For similar surcharges on China type A82 see China Nos. 1025-1036.

AIR POST STAMP

China No. C62a, Overprinted in Black

Overprint 15mm Wide

1949 Unwmk. *Rouletted 9½*

C1	AP5	blue green	2.50	2.50

SPECIAL DELIVERY STAMP

China No. E12a, Overprinted in Black

Overprint 12½mm Wide

1950 Unwmk. *Rouletted 9½*

E1	SD2	red violet	10.00	4.50

REGISTRATION STAMP

China No. F2a Overprinted in Black

Overprint 12mm Wide

1950 Unwmk. *Rouletted 9½*

F1	R2	carmine	10.00	4.50

POSTAGE DUE STAMPS

D1

Unwmk.

1948, Feb. 10 Litho. *Perf. 14*

Without Gum

J1	D1	$1 blue	2.50	*5.00*
J2	D1	$3 blue	2.50	*5.75*
J3	D1	$5 blue	2.50	*5.75*
J4	D1	$10 blue	2.50	*7.75*
J5	D1	$20 blue	2.50	*4.75*
		Nos. J1-J5 (5)	12.50	*29.00*

Nos. J1-J4 Surcharged in Carmine

1948, Dec. 4

J6	D1	$50 on $1 blue	24.00	*13.00*
J7	D1	$100 on $3 blue	24.00	*13.00*
J8	D1	$300 on $5 blue	24.00	*13.00*
J9	D1	$500 on $10 blue	24.00	*13.00*
		Nos. J6-J9 (4)	96.00	*52.00*

Nos. 70, 72 and 64 Handstamped in Violet

1949, Aug. 5

J10	A3	$1000 on $3 bl grn	35.00	22.00
J11	A3	$3000 on $3 bl grn	54.00	29.00
J12	A3	$5000 ocher	120.00	70.00
		Nos. J10-J12 (3)	209.00	121.00

No. 48 Surcharged in Various Colors

1950

J13	A3	4c on $100 bl (Br)	12.00	10.00
J14	A3	10c on $100 bl (RV)	22.50	*26.00*
J15	A3	20c on $100 bl (Bk)	10.00	*22.50*
J16	A3	40c on $100 bl (C)	47.50	*90.00*
J17	A3	$1 on $100 bl (Bl)	35.00	*47.50*
		Nos. J13-J17 (5)	127.00	*196.00*

PARCEL POST STAMPS

Type of China, Parcel Post Stamps of 1945-48 With Added Inscription

1949 Unwmk. Engr. *Perf. 14*

Q1	PP3	$100 bluish grn	*265.00*	1.00
Q2	PP3	$300 rose car	*265.00*	1.00
Q3	PP3	$500 olive green	*265.00*	1.00
Q4	PP3	$1000 slate	*265.00*	1.00
Q5	PP3	$3000 deep plum	*265.00*	1.00
		Nos. Q1-Q5 (5)	*1,325.*	5.00

Chinese characters in lower corners have colorless background; denomination tablet in color.

OCCUPATION STAMPS

Issued Under Japanese Occupation

Unused values for Japanese occupation issues are for never hinged examples.

Canceled Stamps

Postally used stamps of the Japanese occupation generally have heavy, smudgy cancels.

Kwangtung

China No. 297 Overprinted in Black

1942 Unwmk. *Perf. 12½*

1N1	A37	2c olive green	8.00	8.00
a.		Inverted overprint	120.00	165.00

Same Overprint in Red or Black on Stamps of China, 1939-41

Perf. 12½, 14

1N2 A57 3c dl cl (#350) 2.75 2.75
1N3 A57 8c ol grn (#383) 2.75 2.75
1N4 A57 10c grn (#354) (R) 2.50 2.75
1N5 A57 10c grn (#384) (R) 3.50 3.50
1N6 A57 16c ol gray (#357) 4.75 7.25
1N7 A57 30c scar (#385) 4.00 2.75
1N8 A57 50c dk bl (#386) (R) 5.00 8.00
1N9 A57 $1 org brn & sep (#387) 10.00 10.00
1N10 A57 $2 dp bl & yel brn (#388) 10.00 9.50
1N11 A57 $5 red & sl grn (#389) 11.00 10.00
1N12 A57 $10 dk grn & dl pur (#390) 20.00 20.00
1N13 A57 $20 rose lake & dk bl (#391) 13.00 13.00

Same Overprint on China Nos. 422 and 433

Perf. 12½

1N14 A40 1c orange 2.00 2.40
a. Inverted overprint 87.50 80.00
1N15 A47 20c lt blue 4.00 5.00

Same Overprint on Stamps of China, 1941

Perf. 12

1N16 A59 1c orange 2.50 3.75
1N17 A59 5c green 2.50 3.75
1N18 A59 8c turq green 2.75 3.75
1N19 A59 10c brt green 3.25 3.75
1N20 A59 17c olive 4.00 6.00
1N21 A59 30c scarlet 6.00 7.00
1N22 A59 50c dark blue 4.00 4.00
Nos. 1N1-1N22 (22) 128.25 139.65

Stamps of China, 1939-41 Overprinted in Black

1942 *Perf. 12½, 14*

1N23 A57 2c olive grn (#368) 1.00 2.00
1N24 A57 3c dl claret (#350) 1.00 2.00
1N25 A57 5c olive grn (#352) 1.00 1.25
1N26 A57 8c olive grn (#353) 300.00 —
1N27 A57 8c olive grn (#369) 1.00 1.00
1N28 A57 10c green (#354) 1.50 2.00
1N29 A57 16c ol gray (#357) 1.50 3.00
1N30 A57 25c dk bl (#358) 2.00 4.00
1N31 A57 30c scarlet (#385) 2.00 3.00
1N32 A57 50c dk blue (#386) 2.25 2.75
1N33 A57 $1 org brn & sep (#387) 13.00 17.00
1N34 A57 $2 dp bl & yel brn (#388) 13.00 14.00
1N35 A57 $5 red & sl grn (#389) 14.00 17.00
1N36 A57 $10 dk grn & dl pur (#390) 20.00 20.00
1N37 A57 $20 rose lake & dk bl (#391) 14.00 27.50
Nos. 1N23-1N25,1N27-1N37 (14) 87.25 116.50

No. 1N26 is valued in fine condition.

Same Overprint on China Nos. 397-401

1942 **Wmk. 261** *Perf. 14*

1N38 A57 $1 org brn & sep 9.00 9.00
1N39 A57 $2 dp bl & yel brn 9.00 13.00
1N40 A57 $5 red & sl grn 11.00 14.00
1N41 A57 $10 dk grn & dl pur 22.50 22.50
1N42 A57 $20 rose lake & dk bl 22.50 24.00
Nos. 1N38-1N42 (5) 74.00 82.50

Same Overprint on Stamps of China, 1941

1942 **Unwmk.** *Perf. 12*

1N43 A59 2c brt ultra 1.00 2.00
1N44 A59 5c green 1.00 2.00
1N45 A59 8c red org 2.00 3.00
1N46 A59 8c turq grn 2.00 3.00
1N47 A59 10c brt green 2.00 5.00
1N48 A59 17c olive 2.00 5.00
1N49 A59 25c rose vio 2.00 4.00
1N50 A59 30c scarlet 2.00 3.00
1N51 A59 50c dk blue 3.00 3.00
1N52 A59 $1 brn & blk 7.00 8.00
1N53 A59 $2 bl & blk 7.00 8.75
1N54 A59 $5 scar & blk 13.00 13.00
1N55 A59 $10 grn & blk 17.00 17.00
1N56 A59 $20 rose vio & blk 11.00 20.00
Nos. 1N43-1N56 (14) 72.00 96.75

China Nos. 354 and 369 Surcharged in Black

1945 **Unwmk.** *Perf. 12½*

1N57 A57 $200 on 10c grn 165.00 110.00
1N58 A57 $400 on 8c ol grn 165.00 110.00

China No. 422 Surcharged in Black

1945

1N59 A40 $400 on 1c org 750.00 600.00

Forgeries exist.

OCCUPATION POSTAGE DUE STAMPS

China, No. J79 Surcharged Diagonally with New Value Between Parallel Lines in Black

1945 **Unwmk.** *Perf. 12½*

1NJ1 D5 $100 on $2 yel org 825.00 900.00
a. Inverted surcharge 1,100. 1,100.

MENG CHIANG (Inner Mongolia)

Nos. 297-298, 301-303 Overprinted

Characters 4mm High — I

Characters 5mm High — II

1941 **Engr.** **Unwmk.**

2N1 A37 2c #297, I 3.00 2.00
a. Type II 2.00 2.00
2N2 A37 4c #298, II 45.00 —
a. Type I 60.00 55.00
2N3 A37 15c #301, I 6.00 5.50
a. Type II 40.00 6.00
2N4 A37 20c #302, II 8.75 8.75
a. Type I 12.00 16.00
2N5 A37 25c #303, II 12.00 14.00
a. Type I 92.50 92.50
Nos. 2N1-2N5 (5) 74.75 30.25

For surcharge see No. 2N116.

On Nos. 312, 314, 318, 321

1941 *Perf. 14*

2N6 A39 ½c #312, I 14.00 17.50
a. Type II 32.50 —
2N7 A39 2½c #314, II 4.00 3.75
a. Type I 7.25 8.75
2N8 A45 13c #318, II 4.00 6.00
a. Type I 120.00 110.00
2N9 A48 30c #321, II 87.50 92.50
Nos. 2N6-2N9 (4) 109.50 119.75

On Stamps of 1939-41

1941 *Perf. 12½*

2N10 A57 2c #368, II 2.40 3.00
2N11 A57 3c #350, II 1.00 1.00
a. Type I 2.00 2.00
2N12 A57 5c #352, II 2.10 2.50
a. Type I 2.75 6.00
2N13 A57 8c #353, I 2.00 2.00
a. Type II 2.00 2.00
2N14 A57 8c #369, II 17.50 11.00
2N15 A57 10c #354, II 3.00 2.25
2N16 A57 16c #357, II 6.00 6.00
2N17 A57 $1 #359, II 25.00 25.00
a. Type I 440.00 440.00
b. #347, I 87.50 80.00
2N18 A57 $5 #361, II 100.00 92.50
Nos. 2N10-2N18 (9) 159.00 145.25

For surcharges see Nos. 2N117, 2N119.

On Stamps of 1940 with Secret Marks

1941 **Unwmk.** *Perf. 14*

2N19 A57 5c #382, II 2.00 2.00
2N20 A57 8c #383, I 3.25 3.25
a. Type II 55.00 —
2N21 A57 10c #384, II 2.25 2.00
a. Type I 4.00 4.00
2N22 A57 30c #385, II 3.00 4.00
a. Type I 5.00 5.00
2N23 A57 50c #386, I 7.25 7.25
a. Type II 7.25 7.25
2N24 A57 $1 #387, I 22.50 17.50
a. Type II 25.00 29.00
2N25 A57 $2 #388, I 25.00 22.50
a. Type II 35.00 32.50
2N26 A57 $5 #389, I 42.50 45.00
a. Type II 87.50 —
2N27 A57 $10 #390, II 87.50 87.50
a. Type I 87.50 87.50
2N28 A57 $20 #391, II 120.00 120.00
a. Type I 120.00 110.00
Nos. 2N19-2N28 (10) 315.25 311.00

For surcharge see No. 2N120.

On Stamps of 1940 with Secret Marks

1941 **Wmk. 261** *Perf. 14*

2N29 A57 10c #394, II 4.50 4.50
2N30 A57 30c #395, II 5.00 6.00
a. Type I 120.00 110.00
2N31 A57 50c #396, II 8.00 9.00
Nos. 2N29-2N31 (3) 17.50 19.50

On Stamps of 1940-41 (Martyrs) with Secret Marks

Perf. 12½, 13 & Compound

1941 **Wmk. 261**

2N32 A39 ½c #402, II 12.00 14.00
2N33 A40 1c #403, II 3.00 2.00
a. Type I 4.00 3.50
2N34 A39 2½c #405, I 80.00 72.50
a. Type II 80.00 80.00
2N35 A48 3c #406, II 5.00 4.00
2N36 A46 10c #410, I 12.50 12.50
a. Type II 17.50 —
2N37 A46 17c #413, II 62.50 —
a. Type I 80.00 80.00
2N38 A40 25c #416, II 8.00 10.00
2N39 A48 30c #418, II 72.50 77.50
a. Type I 77.50 87.50
2N40 A47 40c #419, II 7.00 7.00
a. Type I 12.00 13.00
2N41 A40 50c #420, I 13.00 14.00
a. Type II 60.00 —

Unwmk.

2N42 A39 ½c #421, II 2.00 3.00
a. Type I 5.00 5.00
2N43 A40 1c #422, I 2.00 2.00
a. Type II 4.25 3.50
2N44 A46 2c #423, I 6.00 6.00
2N45 A48 3c #425, II 4.00 3.50
a. Type I 4.00 4.00
2N46 A39 4c #426, II 2.00 2.00
2N47 A45 8c #428, II 16.00 —
a. Type I 100.00
2N48 A46 10c #429, I 24.00 24.00
a. Type II 72.50 —
2N49 A45 13c #430, I 6.50 7.25
a. Type II 24.00 —
2N50 A48 15c #431, II 5.00 5.00
2N51 A46 17c #432, II 5.00 5.00
a. Type I 6.00 6.00
2N52 A47 20c #433, II 5.00 5.00
a. Type I 6.00 7.00
2N53 A45 21c #434, II 5.00 5.00
2N54 A40 25c #435, I 5.00 8.00
2N55 A46 28c #436, II 5.00 7.00
2N56 A40 50c #439, I 18.00 18.00
a. Type II 8.00 9.00
Nos. 2N42-2N56 (15) 110.50 100.75

For surcharges see Nos. 2N114-2N115, 2N118, 2N121-2N122.

China Nos. 297-298, 302 Surcharged in Black

1942 **Unwmk.** *Perf. 12½, 13*

2N57 A37 1c on 2c ol grn 55.00 55.00
2N58 A37 2c on 4c grn 14.00 14.00
2N59 A37 10c on 20c ultra 85.00 42.50
Nos. 2N57-2N59 (3) 154.00 111.50

Same, on China No. 313

Perf. 14

2N60 A40 ½c on 1c org 62.50 35.00

Same, on Stamps of China, 1938-41

Perf. 12½

2N61 A57 1c on 2c (#368) 2.00 1.25
2N62 A57 4c on 8c (#353) 14.00 13.00
a. Inverted surcharge 47.50 —
2N63 A57 4c on 8c (#369) 8.00 7.00
2N64 A57 5c on 10c (#354) 3.00 3.00
2N65 A57 8c on 16c (#357) 9.00 7.00
2N66 A57 50c on $1 (#359) 13.00 17.50
a. On No. 347 220.00 220.00
b. On No. 344 660.00 —
2N67 A57 $1 on $2 (#360) 87.50 72.50
Nos. 2N61-2N67 (7) 136.50 121.25

No. 2N66b was issued without gum.

Same, on Stamps of China, 1940

Perf. 14

2N68 A57 4c on 8c (#383) 3.00 1.50
2N69 A57 15c on 30c (#385) 7.25 10.00
a. Inverted surcharge 55.00 55.00
2N70 A57 25c on 50c (#386) 9.00 10.00
2N71 A57 50c on $1 (#387) 25.00 18.00
2N72 A57 $1 on $2 (#388) 25.00 18.00
2N73 A57 $5 on $10 (#390) 70.00 62.50
2N74 A57 $10 on $20 (#391) 130.00 110.00
Nos. 2N68-2N74 (7) 269.25 230.00

Same, on China No. 395

1942 **Wmk. 261** *Perf. 14*

2N75 A57 15c on 30c scar 140.00 100.00

Same, on China Nos. 418 and 419

Perf. 12½, 13

2N76 A48 15c on 30c brn car 47.50 47.50
2N77 A47 20c on 40c org 17.00 13.50
Nos. 2N75-2N77 (3) 204.50 161.00

Same, on Stamps of China, 1940-41

1942 **Unwmk.**

2N78 A40 ½c on 1c org 3.00 3.00
2N79 A39 2c on 4c pale vio 6.00 6.00
2N80 A47 10c on 20c lt bl 6.00 6.00
2N81 A47 20c on 40c org 17.50 14.50
2N82 A40 25c on 50c grn 24.00 24.00
Nos. 2N78-2N82 (5) 56.50 53.50

Same Surcharge on "New Peking" Prints

Perf. 14

2N83 A37 1c on 2c ol grn 14.50 25.00
2N84 A37 2c on 4c dl grn 1.00 1.00
2N85 A46 5c on 10c dl vio 5.00 9.00
2N86 A57 8c on 16c ol gray 2.00 2.75
2N87 A47 10c on 20c red brn 5.00 7.25
2N88 A48 15c on 30c brn car 4.00 4.00
2N89 A47 20c on 40c org 9.00 10.00
2N90 A40 25c on 50c grn 6.00 6.00
2N91 A57 50c on $1 org brn & sep 14.50 14.50
2N92 A57 $1 on $2 dp bl & org brn 40.00 45.00
2N93 A57 $5 on $10 dk grn & dl pur 80.00 80.00
Nos. 2N83-2N93 (11) 181.00 204.50

The "New Peking" printings were made by the Chinese Bureau of Engraving and Printing for use in Japanese controlled areas of North China. They are on thin, poor quality paper, with dull gum or without gum and there are slight alterations in the designs.

Dragon-Carved Pillar and Doves — A1

Wmk. Characters in Circle in Sheet

1943 **Engr.** *Perf. 12xPin-perf. 12*

2N94 A1 4f deep orange 4.00 4.00
2N95 A1 8f dark blue 4.00 4.00

5th anniv. of the Inner Mongolia post and telegraph service.

The watermark, which is 40mm in diameter and covers four stamps, occurs three times in the sheet.

Mining Coal — A2

1943 Unwmk. Photo. *Perf. 12*

2N96	A2	4f Prus green	4.00	*5.00*
2N97	A2	8f brown red	4.00	*5.00*

2nd anniv. of the "Greater East Asia War."

Flying Horse — A3

Yun Wang — A4

1944 *Perf. 12½x12, 12x12½*

2N98	A3	4f rose	3.00	*5.00*
2N99	A4	8f dull blue	3.00	*5.00*

5th anniv. of the founding of the Federal Autonomous Government of Mongolia, Sept. 1, 1939.

Industrial Plant — A5

1944, Dec. 8 Photo. *Perf. 12x12½*

2N100	A5	8f red brown	4.00	*6.00*

3rd anniv. of the "Greater East Asia War" and to encourage production increase.

New Peking Printings of 1942 Overprinted in Black

1945 Unwmk. Engr. *Perf. 14*

Without Gum

2N101	A37	2c olive grn	12.00	—
2N102	A37	4c dull grn	20.00	—
2N103	A37	5c green	21.00	*27.50*
2N104	A57	$1 org brn & sep	8.00	8.00
2N105	A57	$2 dp bl & org brn	19.00	19.00
2N106	A57	$5 red & grnsh blk	50.00	50.00

Same Overprint on New Peking Printings of Martyrs Issue

2N107	A40	1c orange	2.00	*2.00*
2N108	A45	8c dp orange	3.00	*3.00*
2N109	A46	10c dl violet	3.00	*3.00*
2N110	A47	20c red brown	3.00	*3.00*
2N111	A48	30c brown car	3.00	*3.00*
2N112	A47	40c orange	2.00	*2.00*
2N113	A40	50c green	8.00	*8.00*

For surcharges see Nos. 2N123-2N127.

Stamps of Meng Chiang, 1941, Surcharged in Red or Black

50c

10c

$1

1945

2N114	A39	10c on ½c ol blk (#2N42, II, R)	4.00	*4.00*
a.		On #2N42a, I	7.25	*8.00*
2N115	A40	10c on 1c org (#2N43a, II, R)	2.00	*2.00*
a.		Without secret mark (China #422a)	40.00	*40.00*
b.		On #2N43, I	3.00	*3.50*
2N116	A37	50c on 2c ol grn (#2N1a, II, B)	29.00	*35.00*
b.		On #2N1, I	29.00	*35.00*
2N117	A57	50c on 2c ol grn (#2N10, II, B))	1.40	*2.00*
2N118	A39	50c on 4c pale vio (#2N46, II, R)	2.00	*2.00*
2N119	A57	50c on 5c ol grn (#2N12, II, R)	1.00	*1.10*
a.		On #2N12a, I	12.50	*12.50*
2N120	A57	50c on 5c ol grn (#2N19, II, R)	1.50	*2.10*
		Nos. 2N114-2N120 (7)	40.90	*48.20*

Same Surcharge on #2N32, 2N33

1945 Wmk. 261

2N121	A39	10c on ½c ol blk, II (R)	29.00	*35.00*
2N122	A40	10c on 1c orange, II (R)	6.00	*6.00*
a.		On #2N33a, I	35.00	—

Same Surcharge on Nos. 2N107, 2N101-2N103 and 2N108

1945 Unwmk.

2N123	A40	10c on 1c org (R)	2.00	*2.00*
2N124	A37	50c on 2c ol grn (Bk)	5.00	*5.00*
2N125	A37	50c on 4c dl grn (R)	10.00	*10.00*
2N126	A37	50c on 5c green	1.00	*2.00*
2N127	A45	$1 on 8c dp org (R)	4.00	*6.00*
		Nos. 2N123-2N127 (5)	22.00	*25.00*

NORTH CHINA

Honan

Nos. 297-298, 301-303 Overprinted

I

II

1941 Engr. Unwmk.

3N1	A37	2c #297, II	18.00	18.00
a.		Type I	30.00	30.00
3N2	A37	4c #298, I	9.00	7.25
a.		Type II	32.50	32.50
3N3	A37	15c #301, I	2.50	*3.00*
a.		Type II	40.00	3.00
3N4	A37	20c #302, I	11.00	8.00
3N5	A37	25c #303, II	24.00	24.00
		Nos. 3N1-3N5 (5)	64.50	60.25

1941 *Perf. 14*

3N6	A39	½c #312, I	3.00	*3.50*
a.		Type II	40.00	—
3N7	A39	2½c #314, I	3.00	*3.00*
a.		Type II	3.00	3.00
3N8	A45	13c #318, II	3.00	3.00
a.		Type I	100.00	100.00
3N9	A48	30c #321, II	18.00	*18.00*
3N10	A47	40c #322, II	100.00	100.00
		Nos. 3N6-3N10 (5)	127.00	127.50

On Stamps of 1939-41

1941 *Perf. 12½*

3N11	A57	2c #368, II	2.00	2.00
3N12	A57	3c #350, I	2.00	2.00
a.		Type II	3.00	2.00
3N13	A57	5c #352, II	4.00	2.00
a.		Type I	2.40	2.40
3N14	A57	8c #353, II	4.00	2.00
a.		Type I	2.00	1.50
3N15	A57	10c #354, II	6.00	*4.25*
3N16	A57	16c #357, II	2.00	*3.00*
3N17	A57	$1 #359, II	20.00	20.00
a.		Type I	325.00	325.00
b.		On #347, I	80.00	75.00
3N18	A57	$5 #361, II	80.00	80.00
		Nos. 3N11-3N18 (8)	120.00	115.25

For overprints see Nos. 3N56, 3N58, 3N61.

On Stamps of 1940 with Secret Marks

1941 Unwmk. *Perf. 14*

3N20	A57	5c #382, II	4.00	3.00
3N21	A57	8c #383, II	4.00	*1.00*
3N22	A57	10c #384, II	4.00	2.00
3N23	A57	30c #385, I	8.00	9.00
a.		Type II	11.00	11.00
3N24	A57	50c #386, I	6.00	*6.00*
a.		Type II	18.00	*17.00*
3N25	A57	$1 #387, I	15.00	*15.00*
a.		Type II	80.00	80.00
3N26	A57	$2 #388, I	18.00	*18.00*
a.		Type II	24.00	*24.00*
3N27	A57	$5 #389, I	40.00	29.00
a.		Type II	62.50	57.50
3N28	A57	$10 #390, II	65.00	62.50
a.		Type I	195.00	195.00
3N29	A57	$20 #391, II	125.00	*140.00*
a.		Type I	125.00	*140.00*
		Nos. 3N20-3N29 (10)	289.00	*285.50*

On Stamps of 1940 with Secret Marks

1941 Wmk. 261 *Perf. 14*

3N30	A57	5c #392, II	24.00	14.50
3N31	A57	5c #393, II	15.00	10.00
3N32	A57	30c #395, I	32.50	29.00
a.		Type II	40.00	40.00
3N33	A57	50c #396, II	75.00	*67.50*
		Nos. 3N30-3N33 (4)	146.50	121.00

On Stamps of 1940-41 (Martyrs) with Secret Marks

Perf. 12½, 13 & Compound

1941 Wmk. 261

3N34	A39	½c #402, II	3.00	*3.50*
3N35	A40	1c #403, II	3.00	2.00
a.		Type I	3.00	3.00
3N36	A39	2½c #405, II	13.50	*17.00*
3N37	A46	10c #410, II	15.00	*18.50*
a.		Type I	35.00	35.00
3N38	A45	13c #411, II	5.00	5.00
3N39	A46	17c #413, II	5.00	5.00
a.		Type I	13.00	9.00
3N40	A40	25c #416, II	5.00	5.00
3N41	A47	40c #419, II	6.00	6.00
a.		Type I	20.00	20.00
		Nos. 3N34-3N41 (8)	55.50	*62.00*

Unwmk.

3N42	A39	½c #421, II	3.00	2.00
a.		Type I	4.50	4.50
3N43	A40	1c #422, I	3.00	2.50
a.		Type II	4.50	4.50
3N44	A46	2c #423, I	15.00	15.00
3N45	A48	3c #425, I	1.50	*2.50*
3N46	A39	4c #426, II	4.00	4.00
3N47	A46	10c #429, I	50.00	50.00
3N48	A45	13c #430, II	4.00	3.50
a.		Type I	25.00	25.00
3N49	A48	15c #431, II	4.50	4.50
3N50	A46	17c #432, II	4.50	4.50
a.		Type I	20.00	20.00
3N51	A47	20c #433, II	5.00	4.00
a.		Type I	62.50	50.00
3N52	A45	21c #434, II	5.00	5.00
3N53	A40	25c #435, I	8.00	7.00
3N54	A46	28c #436, II	5.00	5.00
		Nos. 3N42-3N54 (13)	112.50	109.50

For overprints see Nos. 3N55, 3N59.

Overprinted in Red

1942

3N55	A39	4c #3N46	6.00	*6.00*
3N56	A57	8c #3N14	40.00	*40.00*
3N57	A57	8c #369, II	21.00	*21.00*
		Nos. 3N55-3N57 (3)	67.00	*67.00*

The fall of Singapore.

Overprinted in Red

1942

3N58	A57	2c #3N11	15.00	*15.00*
3N59	A39	4c #3N46	20.00	*25.00*
3N60	A57	8c #369, II	72.50	*72.50*
3N61	A57	8c #3N14	65.00	*72.50*
		Nos. 3N58-3N61 (4)	172.50	185.00

Formation of Manchukuo, 10th anniv.

Hopei

On Stamps of 1940-41 (Martyrs) with Secret Marks

I

II

1941 Engr. Unwmk.

4N1	A37	2c #297, II	3.00	3.00
a.		Type I	11.00	11.00
4N2	A37	4c #298, I	4.50	4.50
a.		Type II	85.00	—
4N3	A37	15c #301, II	5.00	3.00
a.		Type I	4.25	4.00
4N4	A37	20c #302, II	87.50	62.50
4N5	A37	25c #303, II	85.00	8.75
a.		Type I	95.00	90.00
		Nos. 4N1-4N5 (5)	185.00	*81.75*

On Nos. 312, 314, 318, 321

1941 *Perf. 14*

4N6	A39	½c #312, II	3.00	*2.00*
a.		Type I	100.00	100.00
4N7	A39	2½c #314, II	3.00	2.00
a.		Type I	3.00	*2.00*
4N8	A45	13c #318, II	5.00	4.00
a.		Type I	5.00	4.00
4N9	A48	30c #321, II	7.00	*7.00*
		Nos. 4N6-4N9 (4)	18.00	*15.00*

On Stamps of 1939-41

1941 *Perf. 12½*

4N10	A57	2c #368, II	4.00	3.00
4N11	A57	2c #349, II	2.00	*2.00*
4N12	A57	3c #350, II	3.00	2.00
a.		Type I	3.00	2.00
4N13	A57	5c #352, II	2.00	2.00
a.		Type I	2.25	2.00
4N14	A57	8c #353, II	2.00	1.00
a.		Type I	2.00	1.60
4N15	A57	8c #369, II	4.00	3.75
4N16	A57	10c #354, II	2.00	1.00
4N17	A57	16c #357, II	4.00	2.00
4N18	A57	$1 #359, II	175.00	165.00
a.		On #347, I	250.00	—
4N19	A57	$2 #360, II	62.50	55.00
a.		Type I	65.00	65.00
4N20	A57	$5 #361, I	65.00	65.00
a.		Type II	75.00	75.00
4N21	A57	$10 #362, II	200.00	200.00
4N22	A57	$20 #363, II	450.00	450.00
		Nos. 4N10-4N22 (13)	975.50	951.75

For overprints see Nos. 4N66-4N68, 4N70.

On Stamps of 1940 with Secret Marks

1941 Unwmk. *Perf. 14*

Type II

4N24	A57	5c #382	2.00	1.00
4N25	A57	8c #383	65.00	45.00
4N26	A57	10c #384	4.00	3.00
4N27	A57	30c #385	4.00	3.00
4N28	A57	50c #386	4.00	3.00
4N29	A57	$1 #387	11.00	6.00
4N30	A57	$2 #388	45.00	20.00
4N31	A57	$5 #389	55.00	50.00
4N32	A57	$10 #390	65.00	55.00
4N33	A57	$20 #391	75.00	*72.50*
		Nos. 4N24-4N33 (10)	330.00	258.50

For overprints see Nos. 4N65, 4N71.

Type I

4N24a	A57	5c	2.00	1.50
4N25a	A57	8c	70.00	70.00
4N26a	A57	10c	3.00	2.40
4N28a	A57	50c	4.00	3.00
4N29a	A57	$1	11.00	6.00
4N30a	A57	$2	45.00	32.50
4N31a	A57	$5	55.00	55.00
4N32a	A57	$10	75.00	65.00
4N33a	A57	$20	110.00	110.00
		Nos. 4N24a-4N33a (9)	375.00	345.40

On Stamps of 1940 with Secret Marks

1941 Wmk. 261 *Perf. 14*

4N34	A57	5c #392, II	2.00	2.00
4N35	A57	5c #393, II	2.00	2.00
4N36	A57	10c #394, II	4.00	2.00
4N37	A57	30c #395, II	10.00	5.00
a.		Type I	15.00	14.00
4N38	A57	50c #396, II	5.00	5.00
		Nos. 4N34-4N38 (5)	23.00	16.00

On Stamps of 1940-41 (Martyrs) with Secret Marks

Perf. 12½, 13 & Compound

1941 Wmk. 261

4N39	A39	½c #402, II	3.00	3.00
4N40	A40	1c #403, I	2.00	2.00
a.		Type II	3.00	3.00
4N41	A46	2c #404, II	4.00	*2.00*
4N42	A39	2½c #405, II	4.00	*4.00*
4N43	A48	3c #406, II	4.00	*3.00*

4N44 A46 10c #410, II 5.00 4.00
a. Type I 4.00 5.00
4N45 A45 13c #411, II 4.00 4.00
4N46 A46 17c #413, II 5.00 3.50
a. Type I 4.25 4.25
4N47 A40 25c #416, II 5.00 5.00
4N48 A48 30c #418, II 25.00 22.50
a. Type I 50.00 50.00
4N49 A47 40c #419, II 6.00 4.00
a. Type I 6.00 5.75
Nos. 4N39-4N49 (11) 67.00 57.00

Unwmk.

4N50 A39 ½c #421, II 3.00 2.00
a. Type I 3.00 2.25
4N51 A40 1c #422, II 3.00 2.00
a. Type I 3.00 2.00
4N52 A46 2c #423 3.00 2.00
4N53 A48 3c #425, I 3.00 2.00
a. Type II 3.50 4.25
4N54 A39 4c #426, II 3.00 2.50
4N55 A45 8c #428, II 4.00 2.50
a. Type I 5.00 3.50
4N56 A46 10c #429, II 5.00 3.00
4N57 A45 13c #430, I 5.00 4.00
a. Type II 4.50 4.50
4N58 A48 15c #431, II 5.75 5.75
4N59 A46 17c #432, II 8.00 5.00
a. Type I 8.00 6.00
4N60 A47 20c #433, II 6.00 4.00
a. Type I 6.00 5.00
4N61 A45 21c #434, II 6.00 5.00
4N62 A40 25c #435, I 6.00 5.00
a. Type II 5.00 5.00
4N63 A46 28c #436, II 5.00 4.00
Nos. 4N50-4N63 (14) 65.75 48.75

For overprints see Nos. 4N64, 4N69.

Honan Singapore Overprint in Red

1942

4N64 A39 4c #4N54 5.00 6.00
4N65 A57 8c #4N25 8.00 10.00
4N66 A57 8c #4N14 10.00 14.00
4N67 A57 8c #4N15 11.00 15.00
Nos. 4N64-4N67 (4) 34.00 45.00

Honan Anniv. of Manchukuo Overprint in Red

1942

4N68 A57 2c #4N10 16.00 17.00
4N69 A39 4c #4N54 7.00 8.25
4N70 A57 8c #4N14 90.00 90.00
4N71 A57 8c #4N25 15.00 17.00
Nos. 4N68-4N71 (4) 128.00 132.25

Shansi

Nos. 297-298, 301, 303 Overprinted

I

II

1941 Engr. Unwmk.

5N1 A37 2c #297, II 65.00 65.00
a. Type I 87.50 55.00
5N2 A37 4c #298, I 62.50 62.50
a. Type II 125.00 —
5N3 A37 15c #301, II 5.25 6.75
a. Type I 9.00 11.00
5N4 A37 25c #303, II 9.00 13.50
a. Type I 62.50 67.50
Nos. 5N1-5N4 (4) 141.75 147.75

On Nos. 312, 314, 318, 321

1941 Perf. 14

5N5 A39 ½c #312, II 55.00 55.00
a. Type I 4.00 4.00
5N6 A39 2½c #314, II 3.00 3.00
a. Type I 4.00 4.00
5N7 A45 13c #318, II 4.00 4.00
a. Type I 240.00 240.00
5N8 A48 30c #321, II 10.00 12.00
Nos. 5N5-5N8 (4) 72.00 74.00

On Stamps of 1939-41

1941 Perf. 12½

5N9 A57 2c #368, II 2.00 2.00
5N10 A57 3c #350, II 2.00 2.00
a. Type I 15.00 15.00
5N11 A57 5c #352, II 4.00 3.50
a. Type I 5.00 5.00
5N12 A57 8c #353, II 1.50 1.50
a. Type I 4.00 3.50
5N13 A57 8c #369, II 42.50 25.00
5N14 A57 10c #354, II 17.00 8.00
5N15 A57 16c #357, II 5.00 5.00
5N16 A57 $1 #359, II 20.00 17.00
5N17 A57 $2 #360, II 50.00 50.00
5N18 A57 $5 #361, II 72.50 57.50
Nos. 5N9-5N18 (10) 216.50 171.50

For overprints see Nos. 5N62-5N64, 5N66-5N67.

On Stamps of 1940 with Secret Marks

1941 Unwmk. Perf. 14

5N19 A57 5c #382, II 3.00 2.00
5N20 A57 8c #383, II 3.00 2.00
5N21 A57 10c #384, I 4.00 2.00
a. Type II 32.50 5.00
5N22 A57 30c #385, II 5.00 4.00
a. Type I 5.00 3.00
5N23 A57 50c #386, I 6.00 5.00
a. Type II 5.75 5.75
5N24 A57 $1 #387, I 18.00 14.00
a. Type II 45.00 37.50
5N25 A57 $2 #388, II 27.50 25.00
a. Type I 25.00 25.00
5N26 A57 $5 #389, II 32.50 32.50
a. Type I 97.50 97.50
5N27 A57 $10 #390, II 70.00 70.00
a. Type I 75.00 75.00
5N28 A57 $20 #391, II 70.00 70.00
a. Type I 125.00 135.00
Nos. 5N19-5N28 (10) 239.00 226.50

For overprints see Nos. 5N61, 5N68.

On Stamps of 1940 with Secret Marks

1941 Wmk. 261 Perf. 14

5N29 A57 5c #392, II 4.00 3.00
5N30 A57 5c #393, II 3.00 2.00
5N31 A57 10c #394, II 4.00 3.00
5N32 A57 30c #395, I 80.00 80.00
5N33 A57 50c #396, I 15.00 11.00
Nos. 5N29-5N33 (5) 106.00 99.00

On Stamps of 1940-41 (Martyrs) with Secret Marks

Perf. 12½, 13 & Compound

1941 Wmk. 261

5N34 A39 ½c #402, II 3.00 3.00
5N35 A40 1c #403, II 3.00 2.00
a. Type I 3.00 2.00
5N36 A46 2c #404, II 5.00 5.00
5N37 A39 2½c #405, I 9.00 10.50
5N38 A46 10c #410, I 9.75 9.75
5N39 A45 13c #411, II 5.00 5.00
5N40 A46 17c #413, I 32.50 32.50
5N41 A40 25c #416, II 5.00 5.00
5N42 A48 30c #418, I 150.00 150.00
a. Type II 150.00 150.00
5N43 A47 40c #419, II 6.00 6.00
a. Type I 37.50 37.50
5N44 A40 50c #420, II 7.50 7.50
a. Type I 42.50 42.50
Nos. 5N34-5N44 (11) 235.75 236.25

Unwmk.

5N45 A39 ½c #421, II 3.00 3.75
a. Type I 5.25 5.75
5N46 A40 1c #422, I 3.00 3.00
a. Type II 3.00 3.00
5N47 A46 2c #423, II 4.00 4.00
5N48 A48 3c #425, I 11.00 9.00
5N49 A39 4c #426, II 5.00 5.00
5N50 A45 8c #428, I 17.00 15.00
a. Type II 21.00 21.00
5N51 A46 10c #429, I 50.00 50.00
a. Type II 57.50 57.50
5N52 A45 13c #430, I 22.50 20.00
a. Type II 22.50 22.50
5N53 A48 15c #431, II 6.75 6.75
5N54 A46 17c #432, II 6.00 6.00
a. Type I 6.00 5.50
5N55 A47 20c #433, II 6.00 6.00
a. Type I 6.00 4.00
5N56 A45 21c #434, II 6.00 6.00
5N57 A40 25c #435, I 6.00 5.00
5N58 A46 28c #436, II 6.00 6.00
5N59 A40 50c #439, II 17.00 15.00
Nos. 5N45-5N59 (15) 169.25 160.50

For overprints see Nos. 5N60, 5N65.

Honan Singapore Overprint in Red

1942

5N60 A39 4c #5N49 6.00 7.00
5N61 A57 8c #5N20 18.00 22.50
5N62 A57 8c #5N12 18.00 18.00
5N63 A57 8c #5N13 50.00 55.00
Nos. 5N60-5N63 (4) 92.00 102.50

Honan Anniv. of Manchukuo Overprint in Red

1942

5N64 A57 2c #5N9 11.50 17.00
5N65 A39 4c #5N49 13.50 17.00
5N66 A57 8c #5N12 62.50 62.50
5N67 A57 8c #5N13 72.50 85.00
5N68 A57 8c #5N20 55.00 55.00
Nos. 5N64-5N68 (5) 215.00 236.50

Shantung

Nos. 297-298, 301-303 Overprinted

I

II

1941 Engr. Unwmk.

6N1 A37 2c #297, II 2.00 2.00
a. Type I 5.00 5.00
6N2 A37 4c #298, II 8.00 7.25
a. Type I 9.25 8.00
6N3 A37 15c #301, II 2.50 2.50
a. Type I 4.00 3.50
6N4 A37 20c #302, II 5.00 5.00
6N5 A37 25c #303, II 7.25 7.25
a. Type I 265.00 225.00
Nos. 6N1-6N5 (5) 24.75 24.00

On Nos. 312, 314, 318

1941 Perf. 14

6N6 A39 ½c #312, II 3.00 2.00
a. Type I 3.00 2.00
6N7 A39 2½c #314, II 3.00 2.10
a. Type I 3.00 2.00
6N8 A45 13c #318, II 6.00 3.00
a. Type I 25.00 25.00
Nos. 6N6-6N8 (3) 12.00 7.10

On Stamps of 1939-41

1941 Perf. 12½

6N9 A57 2c #349, II 2.00 2.00
6N10 A57 2c #368, II 2.00 2.00
6N11 A57 3c #350, II 2.00 2.00
a. Type I 2.00 1.50
6N12 A57 5c #352, II 2.00 2.00
a. Type I 2.00 1.50
6N13 A57 8c #353, II 2.00 2.00
a. Type I 2.00 1.00
6N14 A57 8c #369, II 2.00 2.00
6N15 A57 10c #354, II 2.00 2.00
6N16 A57 16c #357, II 5.50 7.50
6N17 A57 $1 #359, II 18.00 13.00
a. Type I 425.00 425.00
b. On No. 347, I 62.50 57.50
6N18 A57 $5 #361, II 60.00 55.00
Nos. 6N9-6N18 (10) 97.50 89.50

For overprints see Nos. 6N62, 6N64-6N65, 6N67-6N68.

On Stamps of 1940 with Secret Marks

1941 Unwmk. Perf. 14

6N20 A57 5c #382, II 2.00 1.25
6N21 A57 8c #383, II 2.00 1.00
a. Type I 3.00 1.50
6N22 A57 10c #384, II 3.00 2.00
6N23 A57 30c #385, II 3.00 2.00
a. Type I 7.00 7.50
6N24 A57 50c #386, I 6.75 6.75
a. Type II 9.00 8.00
6N25 A57 $1 #387, II 6.75 5.00
a. Type I 20.00 22.50
6N26 A57 $2 #388, II 15.00 15.00
a. Type I 24.50 27.50
6N27 A57 $5 #389, II 30.00 30.00
a. Type I 42.50 40.00
6N28 A57 $10 #390, II 67.50 67.50
a. Type I 72.50 72.50
6N29 A57 $20 #391, II 97.50 97.50
a. Type I 100.00 125.00
Nos. 6N20-6N29 (10) 233.50 228.00

For overprints see Nos. 6N63, 6N69.

On Stamps of 1940 with Secret Marks

1941 Wmk. 261 Perf. 14

6N30 A57 5c #392, II 3.00 2.00
6N31 A57 5c #393, II 3.00 2.00
6N32 A57 10c #394, II 10.00 8.00
6N33 A57 30c #395, II 11.00 7.00
a. Type I 25.00 25.00
6N34 A57 50c #396, II 10.00 4.25
a. Type I 12.00 11.50
Nos. 6N30-6N34 (5) 37.00 23.25

On Stamps of 1940-41 (Martyrs) with Secret Marks

Perf. 12½, 13 & Compound

1941 Wmk. 261

6N35 A39 ½c #402, II 3.00 3.00
6N36 A40 1c #403, II 3.00 2.00
a. Type I 3.00 2.00
6N37 A39 2½c #405, II 17.00 17.00
6N38 A46 10c #410, I 7.00 4.00
6N39 A45 13c #411, II 6.00 5.00
6N40 A46 17c #413, II 5.00 5.00
a. Type I 11.00 11.00
6N41 A40 25c #416, II 5.00 5.00
6N42 A48 30c #418, I 37.50 37.50
6N43 A47 40c #419, II 6.00 6.00
a. Type I 37.50 37.50
6N44 A40 50c #420, II 9.00 9.00
Nos. 6N35-6N44 (10) 98.50 93.50

Unwmk.

6N45 A39 ½c #421, II 3.00 2.00
a. Type I 4.25 4.25
6N46 A40 1c #422, II 3.00 2.00
a. Type I 3.25 3.25
b. On No. 422a, II 97.50 97.50
6N48 A46 2c #423, II 5.00 2.50
6N49 A48 3c #425, I 4.25 5.00
a. Type II 5.00 6.75
6N50 A39 4c #426, II 5.00 3.00
6N51 A45 8c #428, II 4.00 3.50
a. Type I 40.00 40.00
6N52 A46 10c #429, I 15.00 15.00
6N53 A45 13c #430, I 4.50 4.50
a. Type II 4.50 4.50
6N54 A48 15c #431, II 5.00 5.00
6N55 A46 17c #432, II 5.00 4.00
a. Type I 5.00 5.00
6N56 A47 20c #433, II 5.00 4.50
a. Type I 6.75 6.75
6N57 A45 21c #434, II 5.00 5.00
6N58 A40 25c #435, I 7.00 5.75
6N59 A46 28c #436, II 5.00 4.00
6N60 A40 50c #439, II 55.00 55.00
Nos. 6N45-6N60 (15) 130.75 120.75

For overprints see Nos. 6N61, 6N66.

Honan Singapore Overprint in Red

1942

6N61 A39 4c #6N50 5.00 5.00
6N62 A57 8c #6N13 24.50 30.00
6N63 A57 8c #6N21 24.50 24.50
6N64 A57 8c #6N14 40.00 40.00
Nos. 6N61-6N64 (4) 94.00 99.50

Honan Anniv. of Manchukuo Overprint in Red

1942

6N65 A57 2c #6N10 9.00 9.00
6N66 A39 4c #6N50 11.00 11.00
6N67 A57 8c #6N13 30.00 30.00
6N68 A57 8c #6N14 65.00 72.50
6N69 A57 8c #6N21 32.50 37.50
Nos. 6N65-6N69 (5) 147.50 160.00

Supeh

Nos. 297-298, 301-302 Overprinted

I

II

1941 Engr. Unwmk.

7N1 A37 2c #297, I 13.00 13.00
a. Type II 15.00 15.00
7N2 A37 4c #298, I 57.50 57.50
a. Type II 110.00
7N3 A37 15c #301, II 6.00 6.00
a. Type I 6.00 6.00
7N4 A37 20c #302, II 8.00 6.00
Nos. 7N1-7N4 (4) 84.50 82.50

On Nos. 312, 314, 318

1941 Perf. 14

7N5 A39 ½c #312, I 4.25 4.25
7N6 A39 2½c #314, II 4.00 4.00
a. Type I 4.00 4.00
7N7 A45 13c #318, II 5.00 5.00
a. Type I 160.00 160.00
Nos. 7N5-7N7 (3) 13.25 13.25

On Stamps of 1939-41

1941 Perf. 12½

7N8 A57 2c #368, II 3.00 3.00
7N9 A57 3c #350, II 3.00 3.00
a. Type I 24.50 24.50
7N10 A57 5c #352, II 4.00 4.00
a. Type I 6.00 4.00
7N11 A57 8c #353, I 6.00 4.00
a. Type II 6.00 4.00
7N12 A57 8c #369, II 50.00 42.50
7N13 A57 10c #354, II 5.00 5.00
7N14 A57 16c #357, II 5.00 5.00
7N15 A57 $1 #359, II 18.00 18.00
a. On No. 347, I 210.00 210.00
Nos. 7N8-7N15 (8) 94.00 84.50

For overprints see Nos. 7N56-7N58, 7N60-7N61.

On Stamps of 1940 with Secret Marks

1941 Unwmk. Perf. 14

7N17 A57 5c #382, II 4.00 4.00
7N18 A57 8c #383, II 4.00 2.00
7N19 A57 10c #384, I 4.25 4.25
a. Type II 4.25 4.25
7N20 A57 30c #385, I 5.00 5.00
a. Type II 8.00 9.00
7N21 A57 50c #386, II 5.00 5.50
a. Type I 7.00 7.00

7N22 A57 $1 #387, I 24.50 *30.00*
a. Type II 50.00 *50.00*
7N23 A57 $2 #388, II 29.00 29.00
a. Type I 32.50 *40.00*
7N24 A57 $5 #389, I 50.00 50.00
a. Type II 100.00 100.00
7N25 A57 $10 #390, I 80.00 80.00
a. Type II 90.00 90.00
7N26 A57 $20 #391, II 100.00 *100.00*
a. Type I 100.00 *110.00*
Nos. 7N17-7N26 (10) 305.75 *309.75*

On Stamps of 1940 with Secret Marks

1941 **Wmk. 261** ***Perf. 14***

7N27 A57 10c #395, II 6.00 6.00
7N28 A57 30c #395, I 17.00 *17.00*
7N29 A57 50c #396, I 18.00 *18.50*
Nos. 7N27-7N29 (3) 41.00 *41.50*

On Stamps of 1940-41 (Martyrs) with Secret Marks

Perf. 12½, 13 & Compound

1941 **Wmk. 261**

7N30 A39 ½c #402, II 5.75 5.75
7N31 A40 1c #403, I 4.00 4.00
a. Type II 3.50 3.50
7N32 A46 2c #404, II 3.00 3.00
7N33 A39 2½c #405, I 32.50 32.50
7N34 A46 10c #410, I 19.50 19.50
7N35 A45 13c #411, II 6.75 6.75
7N36 A46 17c #413, II 5.75 5.75
a. Type I 100.00 100.00
7N37 A40 25c #416, II 6.00 6.00
7N38 A48 30c #418, I 14.50 14.50
7N39 A47 40c #419, II 6.00 6.00
a. Type I 9.00 9.00
7N40 A40 50c #420, I 100.00 100.00
Nos. 7N30-7N40 (11) 203.75 203.75

Unwmk.

7N41 A39 ½c #421, II 4.25 4.25
a. Type I 5.75 5.75
7N42 A40 1c #422, II 3.00 2.00
7N43 A46 2c #423, I 14.50 14.50
7N44 A48 3c #425, I 5.00 5.00
7N45 A39 4c #426, II 11.00 11.00
7N46 A46 10c #429, I 50.00 50.00
7N47 A45 13c #430, I 6.75 *7.50*
7N48 A48 15c #431, II 7.50 7.00
7N49 A46 17c #432, II 8.00 8.00
a. Type I 6.75 6.75
7N50 A47 20c #433, II 7.00 7.00
a. Type I 6.75 6.75
7N51 A45 21c #434, II 7.00 7.00
7N52 A40 25c #435, I 7.00 7.00
a. Type II 18.00 18.00
7N53 A46 28c #436, II 6.75 6.75
Nos. 7N41-7N53 (13) 137.75 137.00

For overprints see Nos. 7N55, 7N59.

Honan Singapore Overprint in Red

1942

7N54 A37 4c #298, II 95.00 *110.00*
7N55 A39 4c #7N45 11.00 *13.00*
7N56 A57 8c #7N11a 40.00 *40.00*
7N57 A57 8c #7N12 20.00 *20.00*
Nos. 7N54-7N57 (4) 166.00 *183.00*

Honan Anniv. of Manchukuo Overprint in Red

1942

7N58 A57 2c #7N8 17.00 *24.50*
7N59 A39 4c #7N45 16.00 *17.00*
7N60 A57 8c #7N11a 130.00 *130.00*
7N61 A57 8c #7N12 90.00 *97.50*
Nos. 7N58-7N61 (4) 253.00 *269.00*

North China

For use in Honan, Hopei, Shansi, Shantung and Supeh (Northern Kiangsu)

Stamps of China, 1931-37 Surcharged North China (Hwa Pei) and Half of Original Value

1942 **Unwmk.** ***Perf. 14, 12½***

8N1 A40 ½c on 1c (#313) 2.00 *2.50*
8N2 A37 1c on 2c (#297) .75 .45
8N3 A37 2c on 4c (#298) 1.50 1.25
8N4 A45 4c on 8c (#316) 150.00

Same Surcharge on Stamps of 1938-41

Perf. 12½

8N5 A57 1c on 2c (#349) 5.00 *7.50*
8N6 A57 1c on 2c (#368) .50 .30
8N7 A57 4c on 8c (#353) 2.10 1.25
8N8 A57 4c on 8c (#369) .60 .35
8N9 A57 5c on 10c grn .65 .50
8N10 A57 8c on 16c ol gray 2.00 .80
8N11 A57 50c on $1 (#359) 8.00 8.00
8N12 A57 50c on $1 (#344) 575.00 575.00
8N13 A57 50c on $1 (#347) 110.00 110.00
8N14 A57 $1 on $2 (#360) 12.50 12.50
8N15 A57 $1 on $2 (#345) 32.50 32.50
8N16 A57 $1 on $2 (#348) 155.00 155.00

No. 8N12 was issued without gum.
For overprint see No. 8N58.

Same Surcharge on China Nos. 383-388, 390-391

Perf. 14

8N17 A57 4c on 8c ol grn .65 .65
8N18 A57 5c on 10c grn 1.25 2.00
8N19 A57 15c on 30c scar 1.50 1.25
a. Inverted surcharge 80.00 80.00
8N20 A57 25c on 50c dk bl 2.00 1.75
8N21 A57 50c on $1 org brn & sep 4.50 4.50
8N22 A57 $1 on $2 dp bl & yel brn 5.75 5.75
8N23 A57 $5 on $10 dk grn & dl pur 50.00 50.00
8N24 A57 $10 on $20 rose lake & dk bl 50.00 60.00
Nos. 8N17-8N24 (8) 115.65 125.90

For overprint see No. 8N55.

Same Surcharge on China Nos. 394-396

Wmk. 261

8N25 A57 5c on 10c grn .85 *1.50*
8N26 A57 15c on 30c scar 3.50 *5.00*
8N27 A57 25c on 50c dk bl 1.50 1.50
Nos. 8N25-8N27 (3) 5.85 *8.00*

Same Surcharge on Stamps of 1940-41

1942 **Wmk. 261** ***Perf. 12½, 13***

8N28 A40 ½c on 1c org .30 .25
8N29 A46 1c on 2c dp bl 2.50 2.50
8N30 A45 4c on 8c dp org 20.00 *24.50*
8N31 A46 5c on 10c dl vio 2.50 *3.00*
8N32 A48 15c on 30c brn car 9.75 9.75
8N33 A47 20c on 40c org 5.75 2.10
8N34 A40 25c on 50c grn 5.00 5.00
Nos. 8N28-8N34 (7) 45.80 47.10

Unwmk.

8N35 A40 ½c on 1c org (#422) .30 .25
a. ½c on 1c org (#422a) 37.00 37.00
8N36 A46 1c on 2c dp bl 1.40 1.40
8N37 A39 2c on 4c pale vio 1.00 .85
8N38 A45 4c on 8c dp org 1.25 2.00
8N39 A46 5c on 10c dl vio 3.00 3.00
8N40 A47 10c on 20c lt bl 3.75 .75
8N41 A47 20c on 40c org 4.00 1.00
8N42 A40 25c on 50c grn 32.50 32.50
Nos. 8N35-8N42 (8) 47.20 41.75

Same Surcharge on "New Peking" Prints

Perf. 14

8N43 A37 1c on 2c ol grn .35 .25
8N44 A37 2c on 4c dl grn .90 .25
a. Inverted surcharge 42.50
8N45 A45 4c on 8c dp org .65 .25
8N46 A57 8c on 16c ol gray .35 .25
8N47 A47 10c on 20c red brn 1.75 1.50
8N48 A48 15c on 30c brn car .85 .85
8N49 A47 20c on 40c org 2.10 .30
a. Inverted surcharge 55.00
8N50 A40 25c on 50c grn 1.75 1.50
8N51 A57 50c on $1 org brn & sep 3.50 3.50
8N52 A57 $1 on $2 dp bl & org brn 5.75 3.50
8N53 A57 $5 on $10 dk grn & dl pur 24.50 24.50
Nos. 8N43-8N53 (11) 42.45 *36.65*

See note after No. 2N93. For overprints see #8N54, 8N56-8N57, 8N59.

Nos. 8N44, 8N17 and 8N46 with Additional Overprint in Red

1943 **Unwmk.** ***Perf. 14***

8N54 A37 2c on 4c dl grn .30 *1.00*
8N55 A57 4c on 8c ol grn 1.50 *1.75*
8N56 A57 8c on 16c ol gray 1.50 *2.00*
Nos. 8N54-8N56 (3) 3.30 *4.75*

Return of the Foreign Concessions to China.

Nos. 8N44, 8N8 and 8N46 with Additional Overprint in Red

1943, Aug. 15 ***Perf. 14, 12½***

8N57 A37 2c on 4c dl grn .45 *.85*
8N58 A57 4c on 8c ol grn .45 *1.00*
8N59 A57 8c on 16c ol gray .50 *.85*
Nos. 8N57-8N59 (3) 1.40 *2.70*

North China Postal Service, 5th anniv.

Stamps of China, 1934-41, Overprinted in Black

1943, Nov. 1

8N60 A40 1c org (#313) .85 .85
8N61 A40 1c org (#422) .85 .75
8N62 A57 10c grn (#354) .50 .45
8N63 A57 $2 dp bl & yel brn (#388) 30.00 30.00
8N64 A57 $5 red & grnsh blk (#361) 20.00 20.00
8N65 A57 $5 red & sl grn (#389) 9.75 9.75
8N66 A57 $10 dk grn & dl pur (#390) 14.50 14.50
8N67 A57 $20 rose lake & dk bl (#391) 90.00 *110.00*
Nos. 8N60-8N67 (8) 166.45 *186.30*

Same Overprint on "New Peking" Prints

8N68 A40 1c orange .30 .25
8N69 A37 2c olive grn .30 *.75*
8N70 A37 4c dull green .30 *1.50*
8N71 A37 5c green .60 *.75*
8N72 A57 9c olive grn .35 *.60*
8N73 A46 10c dl violet .35 *.75*
8N74 A57 16c olive gray .30 *.45*
8N75 A57 18c olive gray .30 *.45*
8N76 A47 20c henna .50 *.60*
8N77 A48 30c brown car .45 .45
8N78 A47 40c brt orange .45 *.75*
a. Inverted overprint 42.50 42.50
8N79 A40 50c green 2.50 2.50
8N80 A57 $1 org brn & sep 4.25 1.25
8N81 A57 $2 bl & org brn 2.50 1.05
8N82 A57 $5 red & sl grn 5.00 *7.50*
8N83 A57 $10 dk grn & dl pur 9.00 9.00
8N84 A57 $20 rose lake & dk bl 10.00 *12.50*
Nos. 8N68-8N84 (17) 37.45 *41.10*

See note after No. 2N93. For overprints see Nos. 8N85-8N90, 8N95-8N106.

Nos. 8N70 and 8N62 with Additional Overprint in Red

1944, Jan. 9

8N85 A37 4c dull green .35 *1.05*
8N86 A57 10c green .35 *.75*

1st anniv. of the declaration of war against the Allies by North China.

Nos. 8N72, 8N75, 8N79 and 8N80 with Additional Overprint in Red

1944, Mar. 30

8N87 A57 9c olive green .55 *1.50*
8N88 A57 18c olive gray 1.00 *3.00*
8N89 A40 50c green 5.75 *7.50*
8N90 A57 $1 org brn & sepia 2.10 *3.00*
a. Red overprint inverted 37.00 37.00
Nos. 8N87-8N90 (4) 9.40 *15.00*

North China Political Council, 4th anniv.

Shanghai-Nanking Nos. 9N101-9N104 Surcharged North China (Hwa Pei) and New Value in Red or Black

a

b

c

d

1944 ***Perf. 12½x12, 12x12½***

8N91 OS1 (a) 9c on 50c org 1.40 1.75
8N92 OS1 (b) 18c on $1 grn (R) 1.50 2.10
a. Double surcharge 37.00 37.00
8N93 OS2 (c) 36c on $2 dp bl (R) 1.75 2.10
8N94 OS2 (d) 90c on $5 car rose 2.10 2.50
Nos. 8N91-8N94 (4) 6.75 8.45

Nos. 8N72, 8N75, 8N79 and 8N80 Overprinted in Red or Blue

1944, Aug. 15

8N95 A57 9c olive grn .90 *1.50*
8N96 A57 18c olive gray .90 *3.00*
8N97 A40 50c green 1.50 *2.10*
8N98 A57 $1 org brn & sep (Bl) 3.50 *4.00*
Nos. 8N95-8N98 (4) 6.80 *10.60*

6th anniv. of the General P.O. Dept. of North China.

North China Nos. 8N76, 8N79-8N81 Overprinted in Blue or Black

1944, Dec. 5

8N99 A47 20c henna (Bl) 3.00 *3.50*
8N100 A40 50c green (Bl) 3.00 *3.50*
8N101 A57 $1 org brn & sep (Bl) 5.75 *6.75*
8N102 A57 $2 bl & org brn 1.75 *1.75*
Nos. 8N99-8N102 (4) 13.50 *15.50*

Death of Wang Ching-wei, puppet ruler of China.

North China Nos. 8N76, 8N79-8N81 Overprinted in Red or Black

1945

8N103 A47 20c henna 3.00 *4.00*
8N104 A40 50c green (R) 9.00 9.00
8N105 A57 $1 org brn & sep 3.25 *3.50*
8N106 A57 $2 bl & org brn 5.75 2.00
Nos. 8N103-8N106 (4) 21.00 *18.50*

2nd anniv. of the declaration of war.

Shanghai-Nanking Nos. 9N105-9N106 Surcharged in Red

1945 *Perf. 12x12½*

8N107	OS3 50c on $3 lt org	.65	.85
8N108	OS3 $1 on $6 blue	.65	.85

Return of the foreign concessions in Shanghai.

Dragon Pillar — OS1

Designs: $2, Long Bridge and White Pagoda. $5, Tower in Imperial City. $10, Marble Boat, Summer Palace.

1945 Unwmk. Litho. *Perf. 14*

Various Papers

8N109	OS1 $1 dull yellow	1.50	1.50
8N110	OS1 $2 deep blue	.30	*1.50*
8N111	OS1 $5 carmine	1.05	.75
8N112	OS1 $10 dull green	.50	*1.10*
	Nos. 8N109-8N112 (4)	3.35	*4.85*

North China Political Council, 5th anniv.

Dr. Sun Yat-sen — OS2

Various Papers

1945 **Without Gum**

8N113	OS2 $1 bister	.30	.25
8N114	OS2 $2 dark blue	1.10	.25
8N115	OS2 $5 fawn	2.50	2.50
8N116	OS2 $10 sage green	2.50	.75
8N117	OS2 $20 dull violet	2.50	1.75
8N118	OS2 $50 brown	50.00	*57.50*
	Nos. 8N113-8N118 (6)	58.90	*63.00*

Nos. 8N113-8N118 without "Hwa Pei" overprint are proofs.

Wutai Mountain, Shansi — OS3

Designs: $10, Kaifeng Iron Pagoda. $20, International Bridge, Tientsin. $30, Taishan Mountain, Shantung. $50, General Post Office, Peking.

Various Papers

1945, Aug. 15 **Without Gum**

8N119	OS3 $5 gray green	.30	*1.05*
8N120	OS3 $10 dull brown	.75	*1.05*
8N121	OS3 $20 dull purple	.55	*1.50*
8N122	OS3 $30 slate blue	1.10	*1.50*
8N123	OS3 $50 carmine	2.50	3.00
	Nos. 8N119-8N123 (5)	5.20	*8.10*

North China Postal Directorate, 7th anniv.

SHANGHAI AND NANKING

China Nos. 299-303 Surcharged

a

b

Surcharged Type "b"

1942-45 Unwmk. *Perf. 12½, 13½*

9N1	A37 $6 on 5c green	.90	*1.25*
9N2	A37 $20 on 15c scar	.45	*.90*
9N3	A37 $500 on 15c dk grn	.30	*1.25*
9N4	A37 $1000 on 20c ultra	3.50	3.50
9N5	A37 $1000 on 25c ultra	3.50	3.50
	Nos. 9N1-9N5 (5)	8.65	*10.40*

A $1000 on 20c ultramarine, No. 293, exists.

Surcharged Type "a" (Nos. 9N6-9N10) or Type "b" (Nos. 9N11-9N40) on Type A57 Stamps of 1939-41

Perf. 12½

9N6	25c on 5c (#352)	2.50	*4.00*
9N7	30c on 2c (#368)	.25	*.30*
9N8	50c on 3c (#350)	.30	*.35*
9N9	50c on 5c (#352)	.30	.30
9N10	50c on 8c (#353)	.30	*.45*
9N11	$1 on 8c (#353)	.30	.25
9N12	$1 on 8c (#369)	14.50	14.50
9N13	$1 on 15c (#356)	.30	.25
9N14	$1.30 on 16c (#357)	.30	*.50*
9N15	$1.50 on 3c (#350)	.30	*.50*
9N16	$2 on 5c (#352)	1.40	1.40
9N17	$2 on 10c (#354)	.30	*.35*
9N18	$3 on 15c (#356)	.30	*.35*
9N19	$4 on 16c (#357)	.50	.30
9N20	$5 on 15c (#356)	.30	.30
9N21	$6 on 5c (#351)	.75	*1.75*
a.	Perf. 14 (#371)	62.50	62.50
9N22	$6 on 5c (#352)	.30	*.45*
9N23	$6 on 8c (#353)	.50	*1.25*
9N24	$6 on 8c (#369)	*990.00*	*990.00*
9N25	$6 on 10c (#354)	.30	.30
9N26	$10 on 10c (#354)	.30	.35
9N27	$10 on 16c (#357)	.60	.30
9N28	$20 on 3c (#350)	.30	*.50*
9N29	$20 on 15c (#355)	1.40	*3.00*
9N30	$20 on 15c (#356)	.50	.50
9N31	$20 on $2 (#360)	1.75	*3.50*
9N32	$100 on 3c (#350)	.60	.50
9N33	$500 on 8c (#353)	3.00	*5.50*
9N34	$500 on 8c (#369)	42.50	*57.50*
9N35	$500 on 10c (#354)	3.00	*4.25*
9N36	$500 on 15c (#355)	1.50	*3.00*
9N37	$500 on 15c (#356)	1.25	*2.50*
9N38	$500 on 16c (#357)	1.50	*5.00*
9N39	$1000 on 25c (#358)	1.50	*3.00*
9N40	$2000 on $5 (#361)	1.75	*3.00*
	Nos. 9N1-9N23,9N25-9N40 (39)	94.10	*130.65*

Nos. 381-391 (Type A57) Surcharged with Type "b"

Perf. 14

9N41	$1 on 8c ol grn	.30	*.35*
9N42	$1.70 on 30c scar	.35	*.75*
a.	Perf. 12½	4.00	4.00
9N43	$2 on 5c ol grn	.50	*1.50*
9N44	$2 on $1 org brn & sep	1.25	*3.00*
9N45	$3 on 8c ol grn	.75	*.75*
a.	$3 on 8c olive green (#383a)	42.50	42.50
b.	"3" with flat top	.50	.50
9N46	$6 on 5c grn	.50	*.60*
9N47	$6 on 5c ol grn	.50	*1.00*
9N48	$6 on 8c ol grn	.45	*.85*
9N49	$10 on 10c grn	.50	*2.50*
a.	Perf. 12½	2.50	*7.50*
9N50	$20 on $2 dp bl & yel brn	1.50	*1.50*
9N51	$50 on 30c scar	.90	*1.00*
9N52	$50 on 50c dk bl	.80	*.80*
9N53	$50 on $5 red & sl grn	1.10	1.10
9N54	$50 on $20 rose lake & dk bl	2.50	*3.00*
9N55	$100 on $10 dk grn & dl pur	2.00	*2.00*
9N56	$200 on $20 rose lake & dk bl	.75	*1.25*
9N57	$500 on 8c ol grn	13.50	*16.00*
a.	$500 on 8c ol grn (#383a)	30.50	30.00
9N58	$500 on 10c grn	3.00	*4.25*
9N59	$1000 on 30c scar	2.50	*3.50*
9N60	$1000 on 50c dk bl	1.25	*1.75*
9N61	$1000 on $2 dp bl & yel brn	3.00	*9.75*
9N62	$2000 on $5 red & sl grn	1.50	*2.00*

China Nos. 392-395 and 399-401 (Type A57) Surcharged with Type "b"

1942-45 Wmk. 261 *Perf. 14*

9N63	$2 on $1 org brn & sep, perf. 12½	1.00	*1.75*
9N64	$6 on 5c grn	.50	*1.05*
9N65	$6 on 5c ol grn	1.40	*2.00*
9N66	$50 on $5 red & sl grn	.85	*1.25*
a.	Numeral tablet violet	1.00	*1.25*
9N67	$100 on $10 dk grn & dl pur	.50	*.75*
9N68	$200 on $20 rose lake & dk bl	.60	*.75*
9N69	$500 on 10c grn	2.50	*3.00*
9N70	$1000 on 30c scar	3.50	*4.00*
9N71	$5000 on $10 dk grn & dl pur, perf. 12½	8.00	*9.75*
a.	Perf. 14	125.00	125.00
	Nos. 9N41-9N71 (31)	58.25	*83.50*

Nos. 9N63 and 9N71 were not issued without surcharge. A $50 on 30c scarlet exists.

Same Surch. on Stamps of 1940-41

Perf. 12½, 13

Wmk. 261

9N72	A46 $30 on 2c dp bl	150.00	150.00

A $7.50 on ½c and a $15 on 1c are known.

Unwmk.

9N73	A39 $7.50 on ½c ol blk	2.50	*3.00*
9N74	A40 $15 on 1c org	.35	*1.50*
a.	Without secret mark	62.50	62.50
9N75	A46 $30 on 2c dp bl	1.40	*2.00*
9N76	A40 $200 on 1c org	.30	*.35*
9N77	A45 $200 on 8c dp org	.85	*1.25*
	Nos. 9N73-9N77 (5)	5.40	*8.10*

Surcharged Type "a" (Nos. 9N78-9N81) or Type "b" (Nos. 9N82-9N96) on Type A59 Stamps of 1941

Perf. 12

9N78	5c on ½c sepia	.25	*.35*
9N79	10c on 1c orange	.25	*.35*
9N80	20c on 1c orange	.25	*.50*
9N81	40c on 5c green	.25	*.50*
9N82	$5 on 5c green	.25	*.35*
9N83	$10 on 10c brt grn	.25	*.35*
9N84	$50 on ½c sepia	.25	*.35*
9N85	$50 on 1c orange	.45	*.50*
9N86	$50 on 17c olive	.45	*.60*
9N87	$200 on 5c green	.45	*.50*
9N88	$200 on 8c turq grn	.25	*.30*
9N89	$200 on 8c red org	.45	*.75*
9N90	$500 on $5 scar & blk	.50	*.50*
9N91	$1000 on 1c orange	.45	*.65*
9N92	$1000 on 25c rose vio	.50	*.65*
9N93	$1000 on 30c scarlet	1.25	.65
9N94	$1000 on $2 bl & blk	1.25	*1.25*
9N95	$1000 on $10 grn & blk	.50	*.65*
9N96	$2000 on $5 scar & blk	1.25	*1.25*
	Nos. 9N78-9N96 (19)	9.50	*11.00*

Stamps of China 1939-41 Surcharged in Red or Blue

1943 Unwmk. *Perf. 12, 12½*

9N97	A57 25c on 5c grn	.25	*1.50*
9N98	A59 50c on 8c red org (Bl)	.25	*.60*
9N99	A57 $1 on 16c ol gray	.25	*1.75*
9N100	A59 $2 on 50c dk bl	.25	*.60*
	Nos. 9N97-9N100 (4)	1.00	*4.45*

Return of the foreign concessions in Shanghai.

Wheat and Cotton — OS1

Purple Mountain, Nanking OS2

Perf. 12½x12, 12x12½

1944 Engr. Unwmk.

9N101	OS1 50c orange	.90	*1.10*
9N102	OS1 $1 green	.90	*1.10*
9N103	OS2 $2 deep blue	.90	*1.10*
9N104	OS2 $5 carmine rose	.90	*1.10*
	Nos. 9N101-9N104 (4)	3.60	*4.40*

Puppet government at Nanking, 4th anniv.

For surcharges see Nos. 8N91-8N94, 9N107-9N110.

Map of Foreign Concessions in Shanghai — OS3

1944 *Perf. 12x12½*

9N105	OS3 $3 lt orange	.90	*1.10*
9N106	OS3 $6 blue	.90	*1.10*

1st anniversary of the return of the foreign concessions in Shanghai.

For surcharges see Nos. 8N107-8N108.

Nos. 9N101-9N104 Surcharged in Black with Type "b"

1945, Mar. 30

9N107	OS1 $15 on 50c orange	.90	*1.10*
9N108	OS1 $30 on $1 green	.90	*1.10*
9N109	OS2 $60 on $2 dp blue	.90	*1.10*
9N110	OS2 $200 on $5 car rose	.90	*1.10*
	Nos. 9N107-9N110 (4)	3.60	*4.40*

China Nos. C31, C32, C36 and C38 Srchd. in Red, Green, Orange or Carmine

1945 *Perf. 12½, 13*

9N111	AP3 $150 on 15c (R)	.45	*.90*
9N112	AP3 $250 on 25c (G)	.45	*.90*
9N113	AP3 $600 on 60c (O)	.45	*.90*
9N114	AP3 $1,000 on $1 (C)	.45	*.90*
	Nos. 9N111-9N114 (4)	1.80	*3.60*

Issue as air raid precaution propaganda.

AIR POST STAMPS

China Nos. C35 and C38 Surcharged in Black

The surcharges on Nos. 9NC1-9NC7 were in Japanese currency because all air mail then was carried by Japanese planes.

The surcharges translate: (10c) "Airmail fee for postcard within the nation has been paid." (20c) "Airmail fee for letter within the nation has been paid."

1941 Unwmk. *Perf. 12½*

9NC1	AP3 10(s) on 50c brown	.55	*.40*
9NC2	AP3 20(s) on $1 apple grn	.90	*.90*

Two types of surcharge exist on No. 9NC1.

Similar Surcharge on No. C28

1941 Wmk. 261 *Perf. 13*

9NC3	AP3 20(s) on $1 ap grn	18.00	18.00

Nos. C37 and C39 Surcharged

The surcharges translate: (18c and 25c) "Airmail fee for postcard to Japan has been paid." (35c) "Airmail fee for letter to Japan has been paid."

1941 Unwmk. *Perf. 12½, 13*

9NC4	AP3 18(s) on 90c lt olive	.55	*.60*
9NC5	AP3 25(s) on 90c lt olive	.45	*.60*
9NC6	AP3 35(s) on $2 lt brown	.45	*.60*
	Nos. 9NC4-9NC6 (3)	1.45	*1.80*

No. 9NC6 with Additional Surcharge in Red

Perf. 12½

9NC7	AP3 60(s) on 35(s) on $2	.45	*.55*

POSTAGE DUE STAMPS

Postage Due Stamps of China 1932 Surcharged in Black

1945 Unwmk. *Perf. 14*

9NJ1 D5 $1 on 2c org .90 *1.75*
9NJ2 D5 $2 on 5c org .90 *1.75*
9NJ3 D5 $5 on 10c org .90 *1.75*
9NJ4 D5 $10 on 20c org .90 *3.00*
Nos. 9NJ1-9NJ4 (4) 3.60 *8.25*

Northeastern Provinces

With the end of World War II and the collapse of Manchukuo, the Northeastern Provinces reverted to China. In many Manchurian towns and cities, the Manchukuo stamps were locally handstamped in ideograms: "Republic of China," "China Postal Service" or "Temporary Use for China." A typical example is shown above.

Dr. Sun Yat-sen — A1

Black Surcharge

1946, Feb. Unwmk. Typo. *Perf. 14*

1 A1 50c on $5 red .35 *1.40*
2 A1 50c on $10 green .90 *2.10*
3 A1 $1 on $10 green .35 *1.75*
4 A1 $2 on $20 brown vio .35 *1.40*
5 A1 $4 on $50 brown .35 *1.10*
Nos. 1-5 (5) 2.30 *7.75*

The two characters at left express the new value.

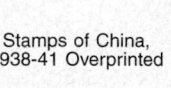

Stamps of China, 1938-41 Overprinted

1946, Apr. *Perf. 12½, 13, 13½, 14*

6 A40 1c org (#422) .35 *3.75*
7 A48 3c dp yel brn (#425) .35 *3.75*
8 A48 5c dl red org (#427) .35 *4.75*
9 A57 10c grn (#354) .35 *3.75*
10 A57 10c grn (#384) .35 *3.75*
11 A47 20c lt bl (#433) .35 *3.75*
a. Horiz. pair, imperf. btwn 100.00
Nos. 6-11 (6) 2.10 *23.50*

Dr. Sun Yat-sen — A2

1946, July Engr. *Perf. 14*
Without Gum

12 A2 5c lake .35 *3.50*
13 A2 10c orange .35 *3.50*
14 A2 20c yel grn .35 *4.00*
15 A2 25c blk brn .35 *3.50*
16 A2 50c red org .35 *2.75*
17 A2 $1 blue .35 *2.25*
18 A2 $2 dk vio .35 *2.75*
19 A2 $2.50 indigo .35 *3.50*
20 A2 $3 brown .35 *2.75*
21 A2 $4 org brn .35 *3.50*
22 A2 $5 dk grn .35 *2.75*
23 A2 $10 crimson .35 *1.75*
24 A2 $20 olive .35 *1.40*
25 A2 $50 blue vio .40 *1.00*
Nos. 12-25 (14) 4.95 *38.90*

Two types of $4, $10, $20 and $50: I- Character *kuo* directly left of sun emblem is open at upper and lower left corners of "box." Diagonal stroke from top center to lower right has no hook at bottom. II- Character is closed at left corners. Diagonal stroke has hook at bottom.

See Nos. 47-52, 61-63. For surcharges see Nos. M1, Taiwan 91-96, People's Republic of China 35-48, 3L37-3L52, 3L55-3L66, 3L71-3L75.

China Nos. 728-731 Surcharged in Black

1946

26 A75 $2 on $20 green .35 *3.25*
27 A75 $3 on $30 blue .35 *3.25*
28 A75 $5 on $50 dark brown .35 *3.25*
29 A75 $10 on $100 carmine .35 *3.25*
Nos. 26-29 (4) 1.40 *13.00*

Convening of Chinese National Assembly.

Type of China, 1946, with added inscriptions on both sides of head

1947 Engr. *Perf. 11, 11½*

30 A74 $2 carmine .65 *4.00*
31 A74 $3 green 1.10 *4.00*
32 A74 $5 vermilion 1.10 *4.00*
33 A74 $10 yel grn 1.10 *4.00*
34 A74 $20 yel org 1.40 *4.00*
35 A74 $30 magenta 1.40 *4.00*
Nos. 30-35 (6) 6.75 *24.00*

60th birthday of Chiang Kai-shek.

Type of China, 1947, with additional inscription above value

1947 Unwmk. Engr. *Perf. 14*

36 A76 $2 deep green .65 *2.00*
37 A76 $4 deep blue .65 *2.00*
38 A76 $6 carmine .65 *2.00*
39 A76 $10 lt brown .65 *2.00*
40 A76 $20 deep claret .65 *2.00*
Nos. 36-40 (5) 3.25 *10.00*

First anniversary of return of Chinese National Government to Nanking.

China Nos. 644 to 646 and 634 Surcharged in Black

1947 *Perf. 12½, 14*

41 A73 $100 on $1000 rose lake 1.10 *4.25*
42 A73 $300 on $3000 bl 1.10 *4.25*
43 A73 $500 on $5000 dp grn & ver .55 *5.00*
44 A37 $500 on $30 choc 1.00 *4.25*
Nos. 41-44 (4) 3.75 *17.75*

Type of 1946

1947 Engr. *Perf. 14*
Without Gum

47 A2 $44 dk car rose *40.00 57.50*
48 A2 $100 dp grn .35 *.70*
49 A2 $200 rose brn .35 *1.40*
50 A2 $300 bluish grn .35 *2.75*
51 A2 $500 rose car .35 *.70*
52 A2 $1000 dp orange .35 *.60*
Nos. 47-52 (6) *41.75 63.65*

For surcharges see note following No. 25.

Stamps and Types of 1946-47 Surcharged in Black or Red

1948 Unwmk. *Perf. 14*

53 A2 $1500 on 20c yel grn .90 *4.50*
54 A2 $3000 on $1 blue .45 *5.00*
55 A2 $4000 on 25c blk brn (R) .45 *4.00*
56 A2 $8000 on 50c red org .45 *3.25*
57 A2 $10,000 on 10c org .55 *3.25*
58 A2 $50,000 on $109 dk grn (R) 1.00 *6.25*
59 A2 $100,000 on $65 dl grn .90 *6.25*
60 A2 $500,000 on $22 gray (R) 1.50 *6.25*
Nos. 53-60 (8) 6.20 *38.75*

Type of 1946

1947, Nov. 5 Without Gum

61 A2 $22 gray 80.00 85.00
62 A2 $65 dull green 80.00 100.00
63 A2 $109 dark green 85.00 100.00
Nos. 61-63 (3) 245.00 285.00

For surcharges see note following No. 25.

POSTAGE DUE STAMPS

D1

1947 Unwmk. Engr. *Perf. 14*
Without Gum

J1 D1 10c dark blue .55 *7.75*
J2 D1 20c dark blue .55 *7.75*
J3 D1 50c dark blue .55 *5.75*
J4 D1 $1 dark blue .25 *4.25*
J5 D1 $2 dark blue .25 *5.50*
J6 D1 $5 dark blue .25 *5.50*
Nos. J1-J6 (6) 2.40 *36.50*

Nos. J4-J6 are known on paper with the papermaker's watermark, "COSMOS BOND."

Nos. J1 to J3 Surcharged in Red

1948

J7 D1 $10 on 10c dark blue .35 *9.00*
J8 D1 $20 on 20c dark blue .35 *9.00*
J9 D1 $50 on 50c dark blue .35 *9.00*
Nos. J7-J9 (3) 1.05 *27.00*

The surcharge reads "Changed to . . . dollars." Characters at the left express the new value and vary on each denomination.

MILITARY STAMPS

No. 16 Surcharged in Black

1947 Unwmk. *Perf. 14*

M1 A2 $44 on 50c red org 11.00 *40.00*

The surcharge reads: "Army Post. Temporarily for 44 dollars."

China No. M13 Overprinted in Black

Thin Paper Without Gum
Perf. 12½

M2 M1 rose 2.75 *18.00*

China No. M13 Overprinted in Black

M3 M1 rose 62.50 62.50

PARCEL POST STAMP

China No. Q25 Surcharged in Black

1948 Unwmk. Engr. *Perf. 13½*
Without Gum

Q1 PP3 $500,000 on $5,000,000 lil 180.00

Used value is for CTO.

The use of this handstamp from Anhwei has not been verified.

FUKIEN PROVINCE

Stamps of China, 1945-49, Surcharged

1949 Engr. *Perf. 14*
Without Gum

1 A82 1c on $500 bl grn 10.00 *6.25*
2 A82 1c on $7000 lt red brn 15.00 *22.50*
3 A82 2c on $2,000,000 ver 5.00 *6.75*
4 A82 2½c on $50,000 dp bl 35.00 35.00
5 A73 4c on $100 dk car 4.50 4.50
6 A73 10c on $200 ol grn 7.25 9.00
7 A82 10c on $3000 bl 5.50 *4.50*
8 A82 10c on $4000 gray 7.25 *10.75*
9 A82 10c on $6000 rose lil 4.50 *6.25*
10 A82 10c on $100,000 dl grn 5.75 *6.75*
11 A82 10c on $1,000,000 cl 5.75 *6.25*
12 A82 40c on $200,000 brn vio 9.00 *10.00*
Nos. 1-12 (12) 114.50 128.50

The surcharge on No. 2 is handstamped and in slightly larger characters.

Issue dates: No. 2, May 10; others, June.

China Nos. 973, 975-978 Overprinted

1949, June Litho. *Perf. 12½, 13*

13 A94 1c apple grn 18.00 5.50
14 A94 4c blue green 5.50 2.00
15 A94 10c deep lilac 55.00 27.50
16 A94 16c orange red 11.00 *27.50*
17 A94 20c blue 55.00 27.50
Nos. 13-17 (5) 144.50 90.00

Same Overprint on China No. 959

1949, July Litho. *Perf. 12½*

18 A96 orange 72.50 72.50

Same Overprint on Fukien Nos. 1, 3-4, 8, 11 in Black or Red

1949, June Engr. *Perf. 14*

19 A82 1c on $500 bl grn 150.00 150.00
20 A82 2c on $2,000,000 ver 55.00 55.00
21 A82 2½c on $50,000 dp bl 90.00 90.00
22 A82 10c on $4000 gray 37.50 37.50
23 A82 10c on $1,000,000 cl 145.00 145.00
Nos. 19-23 (5) 477.50 477.50

AIR POST STAMP

China #C62 Overprinted as #13-17

1949, July Litho. *Perf. 12½*

C1 AP5 blue green 72.50 37.50

SPECIAL DELIVERY STAMP

China #E12 Overprinted as #13-17

1949, July Litho. *Perf. 12½*

E1 SD2 red violet 50.00 35.00

REGISTRATION STAMP

China #F2 Overprinted as #13-17

1949, July Litho. *Perf. 12½*

F1 R2 carmine 50.00 35.00

HUNAN PROVINCE

China No. 640 Surcharged

1949, May Engr. *Perf. 14*

1 A73 on $100 dk car 14.50 8.50

The first printing of surcharge on No. 1 is in smaller characters.

China Nos. 797, 788, 750, 747 Surcharged

1949, May Engr. *Perf. 14*

2 A82 1c on $2,000,000 ver 27.50 27.50
3 A82 2c on $20,000 rose pink 27.50 27.50
4 A82 5c on $3000 blue 35.00 *40.00*
5 A82 10c on $500 blue grn 30.00 27.50
Nos. 2-5 (4) 120.00 122.50

AIR POST STAMP

China No. 790 Surcharged

1949, May Engr. *Perf. 14*

C1 A82 On $40,000 green 22.50 *24.00*

SPECIAL DELIVERY STAMP

China No. 637 Surcharged as No. F1 in Red

1949, May Engr. *Perf. 14*

E1 A73 On $30 dark blue 27.50 27.50

REGISTRATION STAMP

China No. 754 Surcharged

1949, May Engr. *Perf. 14*

F1 A82 On $7000 lt red brn 27.50 27.50

HUPEH PROVINCE

China Type A95 Surcharged

1949, May Litho.

1 A95 1c on $20 red brn 67.50 67.50
2 A95 10c on $20 red brn 67.50 67.50

KANSU PROVINCE

China No. 959 Handstamped in Purple

1949, Aug. Litho. *Perf. 12½*

1 A96 orange *1,100.*

AIR POST STAMP

Same Handstamp Overprinted on China No. C62 in Red

1949, Aug. Litho. *Perf. 12½*

C1 AP5 blue green *1,100.*

Counterfeits exist.

KIANGSI PROVINCE

China Nos. 789-791 Surcharged

1949 Engr. *Perf. 14*

1 A82 On $30,000 choc 57.50 55.00
2 A82 On $40,000 green 57.50 55.00
3 A82 On $50,000 dp bl 57.50 55.00
Nos. 1-3 (3) 172.50 165.00

AIR POST STAMP

Similar Surcharge on China No. 754

1949 Engr. *Perf. 14*

C1 A82 On $7000 lt red brn 62.50 62.50

Third and fourth characters in right column of surcharge read "Air Mail" in Chinese on No. C1, "Registered" on Nos. F1-F2.

SPECIAL DELIVERY STAMP

Similar Surcharge on China No. 750

1949 Engr. *Perf. 14*

E1 A82 On $3000 blue 67.50 45.00

See note below No. C1.

REGISTRATION STAMPS

Similar Surcharge on China Nos. 747 and 754

1949 Engr. *Perf. 14*

F1 A82 On $500 bl grn 67.50 45.00
F2 A82 On $7000 lt red brn 67.50 55.00

KWANGSI PROVINCE

China Nos. 811 and 818 Also Surcharged in Red

1949, May 21 Typo.

6 A62 5c on $20,000 on 10c dp grn 30.00 30.00
7 A62 5c on $40,000 on 20c dk ol grn 67.50 67.50

China Stamps of 1946-48 Surcharged in Black or Red

a

b

1949 Engr. *Perf. 14*

Type "a" Surcharge

8 A82 ½c on $500,000 lil rose 40.00 27.50
9 A82 1c on $200,000 brn vio 35.00 12.00
10 A82 2c on $300,000 yel grn 120.00 72.50
11 A73 5c on $3000 blue 35.00 20.00
12 A82 5c on $3000 blue 18.00 11.00
13 A82 5c on $40,000 grn 35.00 20.00

Type "b" Surcharge

14 A82 13c on $50,000 dp bl (R) 25.00 16.00
15 A82 13c on $50,000 dp bl 100.00 25.00
16 A82 17c on $7000 lt red brn 27.50 27.50
17 A82 21c on $100,000 dl grn 32.50 29.00
Nos. 8-17 (10) 468.00 260.50

SHENSI PROVINCE

China Nos. 747, 750 Surcharged

1949, May Engr. *Perf. 14*

1 A82 On $500 bl grn 45.00 45.00
2 A82 On $3000 blue 45.00 45.00

AIR POST STAMP

Similar Surcharge on China No. 754

1949, May Engr. *Perf. 14*

C1 A82 On $7000 lt red brn 55.00 55.00

SPECIAL DELIVERY STAMP

Similar Surcharge on China No. 746 in Red

1949, May Engr. *Perf. 14*

E1 A82 On $250 dp lil 62.50 62.50

REGISTRATION STAMPS

Similar Surcharge on China Nos. 626, 637 in Red

1949, May Typo. *Perf. 12*

F1 A72 on $30 dp bl 62.50 62.50
F2 A73 on $30 dk bl 55.00 55.00

SZECHWAN PROVINCE

Re-engraved Issue of China, 1923, Overprinted

1933 Unwmk. *Perf. 14*

1 A29 1c orange 11.00 1.00
2 A29 5c claret 11.00 1.40
3 A30 50c deep green 32.50 6.75
Nos. 1-3 (3) 54.50 9.15

The overprint reads "For use in Szechwan Province exclusively."

Same on Sun Yat-sen Issue of 1931-37 Type II

1933-34 *Perf. 12½*

4 A37 2c olive grn 2.00 1.00
5 A37 5c green 22.50 2.40
6 A37 15c dk green 7.75 3.50
7 A37 15c scar ('34) 9.00 12.00
8 A37 25c ultra 7.50 1.75
9 A37 $1 org brn & dk brn 22.50 4.00
10 A37 $2 bl & org brn 55.00 6.75
11 A37 $5 dl red & blk 125.00 37.50
Nos. 4-11 (8) 251.25 68.90

Same on Martyrs Issue of 1932-34

1933 *Perf. 14*

12 A39 ½c black brn .80 .80
13 A40 1c orange 1.25 .55
14 A39 2½c rose lilac 3.50 3.75
15 A48 3c deep brown 3.00 3.00
16 A45 8c brown org 1.75 1.50

17	A46	10c dull violet	4.50	.65
18	A45	13c blue green	5.00	1.00
19	A46	17c brown olive	5.50	1.40
20	A47	20c brown red	8.50	1.00
21	A48	30c brown violet	6.75	1.00
22	A47	40c orange	18.00	1.40
23	A40	50c green	37.50	2.10
		Nos. 12-23 (12)	96.05	18.05

Stamps of China, 1947-48, Surcharged

1949 Engr. *Perf. 14*

24	A82	on $150 dk bl	72.50	55.00
25	A82	on $250 dp lil	72.50	55.00
26	A82	on $500 bl grn	21.00	12.50
27	A82	on $1000 red	55.00	42.50
28	A82	on $2000 ver	21.00	9.50
29	A82	on $3000 blue	21.00	9.50
30	A82	on $4000 gray	21.00	9.50
31	A82	on $5000 dk brn	62.50	*62.50*
32	A82	on $6000 rose lil	21.00	21.00
33	A82	on $7000 lt red brn	55.00	45.00
34	A82	on $10,000 dk bl & car	30.50	16.00
35	A82	on $20,000 rose pink	22.50	16.00
36	A82	on $30,000 choc	29.00	22.50
37	A82	on $50,000 grn & dk bl	29.00	25.00
38	A82	on $50,000 dp bl	29.00	22.50
39	A82	on $100,000 dl yel & ol	29.00	22.50
40	A82	on $100,000 dl grn	29.00	25.00
41	A82	on $200,000 vio brn & dp bl	29.00	22.50
42	A82	on $200,000 brn vio	29.00	22.50
43	A82	on $300,000 sep & org brn	40.00	27.50
44	A82	on $300,000 yel grn	55.00	40.00
45	A82	on $500,000 dk Prus grn & sep	29.00	22.50
46	A82	on $1,000,000 claret	55.00	40.00
47	A82	on $2,000,000 ver	29.00	27.50
48	A82	on $3,000,000 ol bis	29.00	27.50
49	A82	on $5,000,000 ultra	110.00	67.50
		Nos. 24-49 (26)	1,025.	769.00

Several of Nos. 24-49 exist with inverted surcharge and a few with bottom character of left row repeated in right row, same position.

Counterfeits exist.

China No. 737 Surcharged in Black

1949 *Perf. 12½*

50	A77	2c on $500 ol grn	40.00	*55.00*

China No. 975 Handstamp Surcharged in Purple

1949 Litho.

51	A94	2½c on 4c bl grn	55.00	*40.00*

AIR POST STAMPS

China Nos. C55-C58, C60-C61 Surcharged

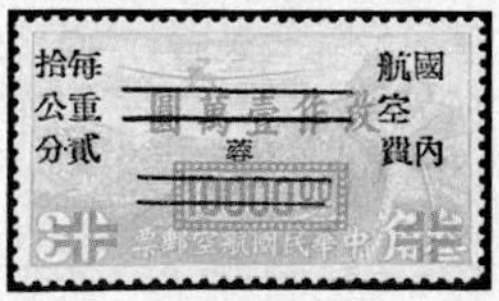

Perf. 12½, 13x12½, 14

1949, July Unwmk.

C1	AP3	On $10,000 on 30c	9.00	9.00
a.		On #C54		500.00
C2	AP4	On $10,000 on $27	14.50	*20.00*
a.		Second surcharge inverted	250.00	
b.		On #C53	125.00	
C3	AP3	On $20,000 on 25c	14.50	*16.00*
C4	AP3	On $30,000 on 90c	16.00	*27.50*
C5	AP3	On $50,000 on 60c	125.00	*155.00*
C6	AP3	On $50,000 on $1	17.00	*24.00*
		Nos. C1-C6 (6)	196.00	*251.50*

REGISTRATION STAMPS

Stamps of China, 1944-47, Surcharged

Engraved; Typographed (A72)

1949 *Perf. 12, 13, 14*

F1	A64	On $100 yel brn	77.50
F2	A72	On $100 dk brn	77.50
F3	A64	On $200 dk grn	155.00
F4	A72	On $200 brn vio	72.50
F5	A73	On $200 ol grn	77.50
F6	A73	On $500 brt bl grn	155.00
F7	A73	On $700 red brn	275.00
F8	A73	On $5000 dp grn & ver	120.00
		Nos. F1-F8 (8)	1,010.

PARCEL POST STAMP

China No. Q10 Surcharged

1949 Engr. *Perf. 12½*

Q1	PP2	1c on $20,000 dk red	—	—

TSINGTAU PROVINCE

China Nos. 890, 903, 900, 894 Handstamp Surcharged in Purple (#1-2), Blue (#3) or Red (#4)

Engraved; Lithographed

1949, May *Perf. 14, 12½*

1	A94	1c on $100 org brn	100.00	90.00
2	A94	4c on $5000 lt bl	100.00	90.00
3	A94	6c on $500 rose lil	100.00	90.00
4	A94	10c on $1000 bl	100.00	90.00
		Nos. 1-4 (4)	400.00	360.00

YUNNAN PROVINCE

Stamps of China, 1923-26, Overprinted

The overprint reads "For exclusive use in the Province of Yunnan." It was applied to prevent stamps being purchased in the depreciated currency of Yunnan and used elsewhere.

1926 Unwmk. *Perf. 14*

1	A29	½c blk brn	1.10	.35
2	A29	1c orange	1.75	.35
3	A29	1½c violet	3.75	4.25
4	A29	2c yellow grn	2.75	.50
5	A29	3c blue green	2.75	.35
6	A29	4c olive grn	3.50	.50
7	A29	5c claret	3.50	.50
8	A29	6c red	5.25	1.25
9	A29	7c violet	5.50	1.90
10	A29	8c brown org	4.75	1.40
11	A29	10c dark blue	3.00	.30
12	A30	13c brown	1.75	1.90
13	A30	15c dark blue	1.75	1.90
14	A30	16c olive grn	3.50	1.90
15	A30	20c brown red	8.50	3.25
16	A30	30c brown vio	5.25	5.75
17	A30	50c deep green	5.50	5.75
18	A31	$1 org brn & sep	20.50	14.00
19	A31	$2 blue & red brn	35.00	14.00
20	A31	$5 red & slate	240.00	260.00
		Nos. 1-20 (20)	359.35	320.10

Unification Issue of China, 1929, Overprinted in Red

1929 *Perf. 14*

21	A35	1c brown org	2.25	2.25
22	A35	4c olive grn	3.75	*5.75*
23	A35	10c dark blue	12.00	9.00
24	A35	$1 dark red	120.00	90.00
		Nos. 21-24 (4)	138.00	107.00

Similar Overprint in Black on Sun Yat-sen Mausoleum Issue

Characters 15½-16mm apart

25	A36	1c brown orange	2.25	2.00
26	A36	4c olive green	2.25	*3.75*
27	A36	10c dark blue	9.00	8.50
28	A36	$1 dark red	77.50	*67.50*
		Nos. 25-28 (4)	91.00	*81.75*

London Print Issue of China, 1931-37, Overprinted

1932-34 Unwmk. *Perf. 12½*

Type I (double circle)

29	A37	1c orange	4.00	2.75
30	A37	2c olive grn	5.00	*5.50*
31	A37	4c green	3.25	*5.50*
32	A37	20c ultra	3.25	*3.00*
33	A37	$1 org brn & dk brn	50.00	*55.00*
34	A37	$2 bl & org brn	82.50	*85.00*
35	A37	$5 dl red & blk	250.00	*295.00*
		Nos. 29-35 (7)	398.00	*451.75*

Type II (single circle)

36	A37	2c olive grn	26.00	26.00
37	A37	4c green	17.00	10.75
38	A37	5c green	15.00	10.00
39	A37	15c dk green	8.00	*8.75*
40	A37	15c scar ('34)	8.00	*10.00*
41	A37	25c ultra	11.00	*11.50*
42	A37	$1 org brn & dk brn	67.50	67.50
43	A37	$2 bl & org brn	125.00	125.00
44	A37	$5 dl red & blk	260.00	260.00
		Nos. 36-44 (9)	537.50	529.50

Nos. 36-39, 41-44 were overprinted in London as well as in Peking. The London overprints are 11mm in length; the Peking overprints are 12mm in length. There are other minor differences. Value of London overprints is significantly more than the Peking overprints, which are valued above.

Tan Yuan-chang Issue of China, 1933, Overprinted

1933 *Perf. 14*

45	A49	2c olive green	1.75	1.75
46	A49	5c green	3.00	2.40
47	A49	25c ultra	5.25	*5.50*
48	A49	$1 red	80.00	65.00
		Nos. 45-48 (4)	90.00	74.65

Martyrs Issue of China, 1932-34, Overprinted

1933

49	A39	½c blk brown	1.75	1.60
50	A40	1c orange	3.50	2.75
51	A39	2½c rose lilac	4.00	4.50
52	A48	3c deep brown	6.25	2.25
53	A45	8c brown org	2.75	2.75
54	A46	10c dull vio	4.00	4.50
55	A45	13c blue grn	2.50	1.10
56	A46	17c brn olive	12.50	12.50
57	A47	20c brown red	3.25	3.25
58	A48	30c brown vio	10.00	10.00
59	A47	40c orange	47.50	47.50
60	A40	50c green	47.50	47.50
		Nos. 49-60 (12)	145.50	140.20

China No. 324 was overprinted with characters arranged vertically, like Sinkiang No. 114, but was not issued.

China Stamps of 1945-49 Surcharged in Black or Blue

Engraved; Lithographed; Typographed

1949 *Perf. 12, 12½, 14*

61	A82	1c on $200,000 brn vio	19.00	19.00
62	A82	1.2c on $40,000 grn	19.00	*21.00*
63	A94	6c on $200 red org	19.00	19.00
64	A94	10c on $20,000 org	19.00	*21.00*
65	A94	12c on $50 dk Prus grn (Bl)	19.00	19.00
66	A72	12c on $50 grnsh gray (Bl)	19.00	19.00
67	A72	12c on $200 brn vio (Bl)	19.00	*21.00*
68	A94	30c on $20 vio brn	19.00	19.00
69	A82	$1.20 on $100,000 dl grn	30.00	*35.00*
		Nos. 61-69 (9)	182.00	193.00

China No. 888 and 630 Surcharged

1949 Engr. *Perf. 14*

70	A94	4c on $20 vio brn	360.00	225.00

Typo. *Perf. 12*

71	A72	12c on $200 brn vio	310.00	200.00

MANCHURIA

Kirin and Heilungkiang Issue

Stamps of China, 1923-26, Overprinted

The overprint reads: "For use in Ki-Hei District" the two names being abbreviated.

The intention of the overprint was to prevent the purchase of stamps in Manchuria, where the currency was depreciated, and their resale elsewhere.

1927 Unwmk. *Perf. 14*

1	A29	½c black brn	1.90	.35
2	A29	1c orange	1.90	.35
3	A29	1½c violet	2.50	1.90
4	A29	2c yellow grn	2.50	1.90
5	A29	3c blue grn	1.75	.75
6	A29	4c olive grn	.85	.35
7	A29	5c claret	1.75	.35
8	A29	6c red	2.50	1.90
9	A29	7c violet	5.25	1.90
10	A29	8c brown org	3.50	1.90
11	A29	10c dk blue	1.90	.50
12	A30	13c brown	4.00	3.00
13	A30	15c dk blue	4.00	3.00
14	A30	16c olive grn	4.00	2.75
15	A30	20c brown red	6.00	3.50
16	A30	30c brown vio	8.75	3.50
17	A30	50c dp green	12.00	4.25
18	A31	$1 org brn & sep	26.00	8.75
19	A31	$2 bl & red brn	70.00	19.00
20	A31	$5 red & slate	325.00	325.00
		Nos. 1-20 (20)	486.05	384.90

Several values of this issue exist with inverted overprint, double overprint and in pairs with one overprint omitted. These "errors" were not regularly issued. Forgeries also exist.

Chang Tso-lin Stamps of 1928 Overprinted in Red or Blue

1928 *Perf. 14*

21	A34	1c brown org (R)	2.75	1.75
22	A34	4c olive grn (R)	1.75	1.75
23	A34	10c dull blue (R)	5.00	3.75
24	A34	$1 red (Bl)	50.00	45.00
		Nos. 21-24 (4)	59.50	52.25

Unification Issue of China, 1929, Overprinted in Red as in 1928

1929

25	A35	1c brown orange	2.00	2.00
26	A35	4c olive green	3.75	3.25
27	A35	10c dark blue	13.00	12.50
28	A35	$1 dark red	110.00	*100.00*
		Nos. 25-28 (4)	128.75	*117.75*

Similar Overprint in Black on Sun Yat-sen Mausoleum Issue of China Characters 15-16mm apart

1929 *Perf. 14*

29	A36	1c brown orange	2.25	*2.50*
30	A36	4c olive green	2.75	*3.00*
31	A36	10c dark blue	8.50	5.25
32	A36	$1 dark red	85.00	65.00
		Nos. 29-32 (4)	98.50	75.75

SINKIANG

Stamps of China, 1913-19, Overprinted in Black or Red

The first character of overprint is ½mm out of alignment, to the left, and the overprint measures 16mm.

1915 Unwmk. *Perf. 14*

1	A24	½c black brn	1.75	.95
2	A24	1c orange	1.75	.70
3	A24	2c yellow grn	2.40	1.25
4	A24	3c slate grn	2.40	.65
5	A24	4c scarlet	4.75	1.10
6	A24	5c rose lilac	3.50	.95
7	A24	6c gray	6.50	2.75
8	A24	7c violet	6.50	*8.50*
9	A24	8c brown orange	5.50	5.50
10	A24	10c dark blue	5.50	2.75
11	A25	15c brown	6.50	3.50
12	A25	16c olive grn	13.00	9.25
13	A25	20c brown red	13.00	7.25
14	A25	30c brown violet	14.50	11.00
15	A25	50c deep green	40.00	18.50
16	A26	$1 ocher & blk (R)	145.00	62.50
a.		Second & third characters of overprint transposed	*70,000.*	
		Nos. 1-16 (16)	272.55	137.10

Stamps of China, 1913-19, Overprinted in Black or Red

The five characters of overprint are correctly aligned and measure 15½mm.

1916-19

17	A24	½c black brn	2.00	2.40
18	A24	1c orange	3.25	1.75
19	A24	1½c violet	4.50	4.00
20	A24	2c yellow grn	3.25	1.75
21	A24	3c slate grn	5.50	.70
22	A24	4c scarlet	5.50	1.25
23	A24	5c rose lilac	5.50	.90
24	A24	6c gray	8.00	1.25
25	A24	7c violet	8.00	*11.00*
26	A24	8c brown org	8.75	8.50
27	A24	10c dark blue	8.75	1.25
28	A25	13c brown	4.75	*8.00*
29	A25	15c brown	6.00	*8.50*
30	A25	16c olive grn	5.50	4.00
31	A25	20c brown red	4.50	3.00
32	A25	30c brown vio	6.75	6.00
33	A25	50c deep green	9.25	5.50
34	A26	$1 ocher & blk (R)	29.00	11.00
35	A26	$2 dk bl & blk (R)	27.50	12.00
36	A26	$5 scar & blk (R)	110.00	37.50
37	A26	$10 yel grn & blk (R)	275.00	175.00
38	A26	$20 yel & blk (R)	1,435.	875.00
		Nos. 17-38 (22)	1,976.	1,180.

For overprint see No. C4.

China Nos. 243-246 Overprinted

1921 *Perf. 14*

39	A27	1c orange	1.75	1.75
40	A27	3c blue green	3.50	3.50
41	A27	6c gray	13.50	13.50
42	A27	10c blue	80.00	80.00
		Nos. 39-42 (4)	98.75	98.75

Constitution Issue of China, 1923, Overprinted

1923

43	A32	1c orange	1.55	1.55
44	A32	3c blue green	6.50	6.50
45	A32	4c red	9.75	9.75
46	A32	10c blue	27.50	27.50
		Nos. 43-46 (4)	45.30	45.30

Stamps of China, 1923-26, Overprinted as in 1916-19, in Black or Red

1924

Re-engraved

47	A29	½c black brn	1.50	*3.00*
48	A29	1c orange	1.50	1.25
49	A29	1½c violet	2.75	*5.00*
50	A29	2c yellow grn	4.25	1.40
51	A29	3c blue grn	4.25	1.25
52	A29	4c gray	4.25	*6.75*
53	A29	5c claret	1.40	1.00
54	A29	6c red	7.50	2.75
55	A29	7c violet	8.50	7.50
56	A29	8c org brn	17.00	*15.00*
57	A29	10c dark blue	6.75	1.90
58	A30	13c red brown	6.00	*8.50*
59	A30	15c deep blue	8.75	6.75
60	A30	16c olive grn	10.00	9.75
61	A30	20c brown red	8.50	6.25
62	A30	30c brown vio	9.75	6.75
63	A30	50c deep green	10.00	6.75
64	A31	$1 org brn & sep (R)	18.00	8.50
65	A31	$2 bl & red brn (R)	40.00	12.00
66	A31	$5 red & slate (R)	95.00	19.00
67	A31	$10 grn & claret (R)	300.00	170.00
68	A31	$20 plum & bl (R)	425.00	325.00
		Nos. 47-68 (22)	990.65	626.05

See #69, 114. For overprints see #C1-C3.

Same Overprint on China No. 275

1926

69	A29	4c olive green	5.50	5.50

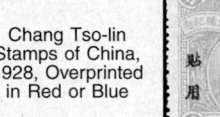

Chang Tso-lin Stamps of China, 1928, Overprinted in Red or Blue

1928 *Perf. 14*

70	A34	1c brn org (R)	1.75	1.75
71	A34	4c ol grn (R)	2.75	2.75
72	A34	10c dull bl (R)	6.50	6.50
73	A34	$1 red (Bl)	55.00	55.00
		Nos. 70-73 (4)	66.00	66.00

Unification Issue of China, 1929, Overprinted in Red as in 1928

1929

74	A35	1c brown org	2.75	2.75
75	A35	4c olive grn	4.75	4.75
76	A35	10c dk blue	11.50	11.50
77	A35	$1 dk red	90.00	90.00
		Nos. 74-77 (4)	109.00	109.00

Similar Overprint in Black on Sun Yat-sen Mausoleum Issue of China Characters 15mm apart

1929 *Perf. 14*

78	A36	1c brown org	2.25	2.25
79	A36	4c olive grn	3.50	*3.50*
80	A36	10c dark blue	8.00	*8.00*
81	A36	$1 dark red	95.00	95.00
		Nos. 78-81 (4)	108.75	108.75

Stamps of Sun Yat-sen Issue of 1931-37 Overprinted

1932 Type I *Perf. 12½*

82	A37	1c orange	1.75	*4.00*
83	A37	2c olive grn	4.25	*5.75*
84	A37	4c green	2.50	*6.50*
85	A37	20c ultra	4.00	*8.25*
86	A37	$1 org brn & dk brn	12.00	*20.00*
87	A37	$2 bl & org brn	35.00	*42.50*
88	A37	$5 dl red & blk	40.00	*60.00*
		Nos. 82-88 (7)	99.50	*147.00*

No. 83 was overprinted in Shanghai in 1938. The overprint differs in minor details.

1932-38 Type II

89	A37	2c olive grn	.45	*2.00*
90	A37	4c green	1.25	*4.00*
91	A37	5c green	.80	*4.00*
92	A37	15c dk green	1.10	*4.00*
93	A37	15c scar ('34)	1.10	*4.00*
93A	A37	20c ultra ('38)	.80	*2.75*
94	A37	25c ultra	1.25	*4.00*
95	A37	$1 org brn & dk brn	9.50	*11.00*
96	A37	$2 bl & org brn	20.00	*32.50*
97	A37	$5 dl red & blk	40.00	*65.00*
		Nos. 89-97 (10)	76.25	*133.25*

Nos. 89, 90 and 94 were overprinted in London, Peking and Shanghai. Nos. 92, 95-97 exist with London and Peking overprints. Nos. 91 and 93 exist with Peking and Shanghai overprints. No. 93A is a Shanghai overprint. The overprints differ in minor details.

Tan Yuan-chang Issue of China, 1933, Overprinted as in 1928

1933 *Perf. 14*

98	A49	2c olive grn	3.75	3.75
99	A49	5c green	4.75	4.75
100	A49	25c ultra	15.00	15.00
101	A49	$1 red	75.00	65.00
		Nos. 98-101 (4)	98.50	88.50

Stamps of China Martyrs Issue of 1932-34 Overprinted

1933-34

102	A39	½c black brown	.25	*3.50*
103	A40	1c orange	1.10	*4.25*
104	A39	2½c rose lilac	.25	*3.25*
105	A48	3c deep brown	.25	*3.25*
106	A45	8c brown orange	.75	*3.50*
107	A46	10c dull violet	.25	*3.25*
108	A45	13c blue green	.25	*4.50*
109	A46	17c brown olive	.25	*2.50*
110	A47	20c brown red	1.10	*6.50*
111	A48	30c brown violet	.40	*4.50*
112	A47	40c orange	.60	*3.25*
113	A40	50c green	.70	*2.50*
		Nos. 102-113 (12)	6.15	*44.75*

Nos. 102-113 were originally overprinted in Peking. In 1938, Nos. 103-105, 108-112 were overprinted in Shanghai. The two overprints differ in minor details. No. 105, Shanghai overprint, is scarce. Value $35.

China No. 324 Overprinted as in 1916-19

1936 *Perf. 14*

114	A29	6c brown	20.00	*20.00*

Stamps of China, 1939-40 Overprinted in Black Type III

1940-45 Unwmk. *Perf. 12½*

115	A57	2c olive green	.85	*1.00*
116	A57	3c dull claret ('41)	.25	*1.50*
117	A57	5c green	.25	*1.50*
118	A57	5c olive green	.25	*1.50*
119	A57	8c olive green ('41)	.25	*.75*
120	A57	10c green ('41)	.25	*1.10*
121	A57	15c scarlet	.55	*2.50*
122	A57	16c olive gray ('41)	.40	*1.00*
123	A57	25c dark blue	.55	*2.75*
124	A57	$1 hn & dk brn (type II)	6.25	*11.00*
125	A57	$2 dp bl & org brn (type I)	4.50	*11.00*
126	A57	$5 red & grnsh blk	26.00	*32.50*
		Nos. 115-126 (12)	40.35	*68.10*

Perf. 14

With Secret Marks

127	A57	8c ol grn (#383a)	1.10	*1.65*
a.		On #383	19.00	*22.50*
128	A57	10c green ('41)	10.00	*13.00*
129	A57	30c scarlet ('45)	.30	*1.10*
130	A57	50c dk blue ('45)	.55	*1.75*
131	A57	$1 org brn & sep	.55	*2.25*
132	A57	$2 dp bl & org brn	.55	*2.25*
133	A57	$5 red & sl grn	.65	*3.75*
134	A57	$10 dk grn & dl pur	1.90	*2.75*
135	A57	$20 rose lake & dk bl	3.50	*5.50*
		Nos. 127-135 (9)	19.10	*34.00*

Wmk. Character Yu (Post) (261)

Perf. 14

136	A57	5c olive green	.30	*2.50*
137	A57	10c green	.35	*3.75*
138	A57	30c scarlet	.35	*5.00*
139	A57	50c dark blue	.45	*2.50*
		Nos. 136-139 (4)	1.45	*13.75*

Martyrs Issue, 1940-41, Overprinted in Black

Perf. 12, 12½, 13, 13x12, 13½x13

1941-45 Wmk. 261

140	A40	1c orange	.35	*2.40*
141	A39	2½c rose lilac	.35	*4.50*
142	A45	8c dp org ('45)	5.75	12.00
143	A46	10c dull vio	.45	*3.00*
144	A45	13c dp yel grn	1.00	*5.50*
145	A46	17c brown olive	1.00	*5.25*
146	A40	25c red vio ('45)	2.00	*7.25*
147	A47	40c orange ('45)	3.50	*9.25*
		Nos. 140-147 (8)	14.40	*49.15*

Unwmk.

148	A39	½c olive blk	.35	*3.25*
149	A40	1c orange ('45)	.35	*2.40*
150	A46	2c dp blue ('45)	3.25	*3.75*
151	A48	3c dp yel brn	.35	*4.50*
152	A39	4c pale vio ('45)	.35	*4.50*
153	A45	8c dp orange	.35	*5.50*
154	A45	13c dp yel grn ('45)	.65	*4.00*
155	A48	15c brn car ('45)	.35	*4.00*
156	A46	17c brn ol ('45)	1.00	*4.50*
157	A47	20c lt blue ('45)	.35	*3.25*
158	A45	21c ol brn ('45)	1.25	*4.50*
159	A46	28c olive ('45)	1.45	*5.50*
160	A47	40c orange ('45)	3.00	*14.00*
161	A40	50c green ('45)	2.00	*7.00*
		Nos. 148-161 (14)	15.05	*70.65*

Stamps of China, 1942-43 Overprinted in Carmine, Black or Red

1944 Without Gum *Perf. 12½, 13*

162	A62	10c dp grn (C)	1.75	*7.75*
163	A62	20c dk ol grn (C)	2.00	*7.75*
164	A62	25c violet brn	.30	*8.50*
165	A62	30c dk orange	.95	*9.00*
166	A62	40c red brown	.30	*8.50*
167	A62	50c sage green	.30	*5.00*
a.		Perf. 11	16.00	24.00
168	A62	$1 rose lake	3.75	5.00
169	A62	$1 dull green	.30	*8.50*
170	A62	$1.50 dp bl (C)	.30	*9.50*
171	A62	$2 dk bl grn (R)	2.40	*7.00*
172	A62	$3 yellow	.30	*12.00*
173	A62	$5 cerise	2.40	*11.00*
		Nos. 162-173 (12)	15.05	*99.50*

For surcharges see Nos. 194-195.

Same Overprint on Stamps of China, 1942-43, in Black

1944-46 *Imperf.*

174	A57	$10 red brown	140.00	125.00
175	A57	$20 rose red	6.75	*17.00*
176	A57	$30 dull vio	5.00	*17.00*
177	A57	$40 rose red	5.00	*17.00*
178	A57	$50 blue ('46)	1,080.	*1,170.*
179	A57	$100 orange brn	14.50	*22.50*

Perf. 13½

180	A57	$4 dp blue	2.00	*13.50*
181	A57	$5 lilac gray	3.50	*13.50*
182	A57	$10 red brn	3.50	*13.50*
183	A57	$20 blue grn	2.00	*15.00*
184	A57	$20 rose red	140.00	140.00
185	A57	$30 dull vio	4.00	*17.00*
186	A57	$40 rose	4.00	*16.00*
187	A57	$50 blue	4.50	*17.00*
188	A57	$100 orange brn	160.00	140.00
		Nos. 174-177,179-188 (14)	494.75	*584.00*

Beware of trimmed examples of Nos. 182 and 187 offered as Nos. 174 and 178.

Nos. 162 and 164 Surcharged in Black

1944, Aug. 1

194	A62	12c on 10c dp grn	9.00	*27.50*
195	A62	24c on 25c brn vio	9.00	*27.50*

Stamps of China, 1940-41, Overprinted in Black at Chengtu, Szechwan

1943

196	A57	10c green (#354)	25.00	*30.00*
197	A47	20c lt blue (#433)	25.00	*30.00*

Wmk. 261 *Perf. 14*

198	A57	50c dk blue (#396)	25.00	*30.00*

China Nos. 565 and 567 Overprinted in Black

1945 Unwmk. *Perf. 12½*

200	A63	40c brown red	.45	20.00
201	A63	$3 red	.45	18.00

China Nos. 640-642, 788, 751, 753 Surcharged in Black or Red

1949 Engr. *Perf. 14*

202	A73	1c on $100 dk car	29.00	*35.00*
203	A73	3c on $200 ol grn (R)	29.00	*35.00*
204	A73	5c on $500 brt bl grn (R)	29.00	*35.00*
205	A82	10c on $20,000 rose pink	25.00	*30.00*
206	A82	50c on $4000 gray (R)	100.00	100.00
207	A82	$1 on $6000 rose lil	110.00	110.00
		Nos. 202-207 (6)	322.00	*345.00*

AIR POST STAMPS

Sinkiang Nos. 53, 57, 59, 32 Overprinted in Red

1932-33 Unwmk. *Perf. 14*

C1	A29	5c claret ('33)	400.00	290.00
C2	A29	10c dark blue ('33)	400.00	225.00
C3	A30	15c deep blue	2,700.	775.00
C4	A25	30c brown violet	1,170.	990.00

Counterfeits exist of Nos. C1-C4.

Air Post Stamps of China, 1932-37 Handstamped in Dull Red

1942

C5	AP3	15c gray green	7.25	*9.00*
C6	AP3	25c orange	425.00	375.00
C7	AP3	30c red	15.50	*27.50*
C8	AP3	45c brown vio	11.00	*18.00*
C9	AP3	50c dk brown	45.00	*50.00*
C10	AP3	60c dk blue	11.00	*21.00*
C11	AP3	90c olive grn	57.50	*80.00*
C12	AP3	$1 yellow grn	12.00	*20.00*
		Nos. C5-C12 (8)	584.25	*600.50*

Same Handstamped Overprint on Air Post Stamps of China, 1940-41 in Dull Red

1942 Wmk. 261 *Perf. 12½, 13, 13½*

C13	AP3	15c gray green	6.75	*15.00*
C14	AP3	25c yellow orange	6.75	*17.00*

1942 Unwmk.

C15	AP3	25c light orange	6.75	13.50
C16	AP3	30c light red	6.75	13.50
C17	AP3	50c brown	9.00	15.00
C18	AP3	$2 light brown	42.50	42.50
C19	AP3	$5 lake	42.50	42.50
		Nos. C15-C19 (5)	107.50	127.00

Twelve values exist with this overprint in black. Their status has not been determined. Inverted overprints exist in both red and black.

Official Perforated Characters

For use on official mail, various Sinkiang stamps were perforated with an arrangement of four Chinese characters ("For Official Business Only"). These include Nos. 1-38, 47-69, 114.

OFFICES IN TIBET

12 Pies = 1 Anna
16 Annas = 1 Rupee

Stamps of China, Issues of 1902-10, Surcharged

1911 Unwmk. *Perf. 12 to 16*

1	A17	3p on 1c ocher	27.50	*45.00*
a.		Inverted surcharge	*3,500.*	
2	A17	½a on 2c grn	27.50	*45.00*
3	A17	1a on 4c ver	27.50	*45.00*
4	A17	2a on 7c mar	27.50	*45.00*
5	A17	2½a on 10c ultra	35.00	*55.00*
6	A18	3a on 16c ol grn	70.00	*80.00*
a.		Large "S" in "Annas"	*1,250.*	
7	A18	4a on 20c red brn	70.00	*80.00*
8	A18	6a on 30c rose red	125.00	*140.00*
9	A18	12a on 50c yel grn	325.00	*400.00*
10	A19	1r on $1 red & pale rose	900.00	*900.00*
11	A19	2r on $2 red & yel	1,620.	*1,800.*
		Nos. 1-11 (11)	3,255.	3,635.

Beware of fake overprints.

PEOPLE'S REPUBLIC OF CHINA

'pē-pəls ri-'pə-blik of 'chī-nə

LOCATION — Eastern Asia
GOVT. — Communist Republic
POP. — 1,339,724,852 (2010 est.)
CAPITAL — Beijing (Peking)

The communists completed their conquest of all mainland China in 1949. They established the Central Government and General Postal Administration in Peking. They ordered all but two regions to stop selling regional issues by June 30, 1950, extending validity one year from that date. The Northeast and Port Arthur-Dairen regions were exempted because their currency had a different value. These two regions stopped using separate issues at the end of 1950. Thereafter unified issues were used throughout mainland China.

On July 1, 1997 Hong Kong returned to Chinese control as an administrative district. Hong Kong stamps issued under Chinese rule will continue to be listed under "Hong Kong."

Reprints

After currency revaluation Mar. 1, 1955, reprints were prepared and put on sale by the Philatelic Agency in order to supply stocks of exhausted issues for collectors. Minor differences in design or paper distinguish the reprints. They are of commemorative and special issues up to the gymnastics set of 1952. Reprints are less expensive. Values are for original issues. Reprint distinctions are footnoted.

Used Stamps

Most used stamps before 1970 exist primarily canceled to order. Postally used stamps generally sell for ½ the unused value.

Beginning in 1987 the PRC stopped furnishing quantities of used stamps to the philatelic market. When available, used stamps of these issues sell for the same or more than unused stamps.

PRC Issue Numbers

Commemorative issues, beginning in 1949, and special issues, beginning in 1951, bear 4 numbers in lower margin: 1. Issue number. 2. Total of stamps in set. 3. Position of stamp in set. 4. Cumulative number of stamp (usually in parenthesis). A fifth number, the year of issue, was added in 1952.

The numbering system varies at times, with all numbers omitted on Scott 938-1046.

In certain sets listings include parenthetically the position-in-set number. During some periods these parentheses in listings hold the stamp's cumulative number. Issue numbers are noted when one or more designs are not illustrated.

Gum

All stamps to the beginning of 1960 were issued without gum, except as noted. After that date, most stamps have gum, which is translucent and almost invisible. Catalogue values are for stamps with fresh, untoned paper and gum. Stamps with toned paper or gum sell for approximately 20% to 50% less. All issues are unwatermarked, unless otherwise noted.

100 fen = 1 yuan ($)

Catalogue values for unused stamps in this country are for Never Hinged items, beginning with Scott 487 in the regular postage section, Scott B1 in the semi-postal section.

Syncopated Perforations

Type A (1st stamp No. 2880): On the two shorter sides, an oval hole equal in width to three holes is centered.

Lantern and Gate of Heavenly Peace — A1

Original

Reprint

Reprints have altered ornament on lantern base. On originals, it is a full oval; on reprints, only a partial circle. Value, set: unused $12; used $3.

1949, Oct. 8 Litho. *Perf. 12½*

1	A1	$30 blue	9.00	7.00
2	A1	$50 rose red	10.00	7.00
3	A1	$100 green	13.00	7.00
4	A1	$200 maroon	13.00	7.00
		Nos. 1-4 (4)	45.00	28.00

1st session of Chinese People's Consultative Political Conference. See Nos. 1L121-1L124.

Globe and Hand Holding Hammer — A2

Original

Reprint

Reprints show heavier shading on index finger and thumb. Value, set $8 unused or $3 used.

1949, Nov. 16

5	A2	$100 carmine	28.50	9.50
6	A2	$300 slate green	28.50	9.50
7	A2	$500 dark blue	28.50	9.50
		Nos. 5-7 (3)	85.50	28.50

Asiatic and Australasian Congress of the World Federation of Trade Unions, Peking.

The $100, imperf., is of dubious status.

See Nos. 1L133-1L135.

Conference Hall, Peking — A3

Mao Tse-tung on Rostrum A4

Original

Reprint

Nos. 8-9: First character in top inscription shows a square, reprints an oblong.

Nos. 10-11: Originals have heavy cross-hatching and lines which touch back of head and top of rostrum. Reprints have lighter lines which do not touch head or top of rostrum. Reprints, value set $25 unused, $9 used.

1950, Feb. 1 Engr. *Perf. 14*

8	A3	$50 red	12.50	8.00
9	A3	$100 blue	12.50	8.00
10	A4	$300 red brown	14.00	11.00
11	A4	$500 green	20.00	17.50
		Nos. 8-11 (4)	59.00	44.50

Chinese People's Consultative Political Conference. See Nos. 1L136-1L139.

Gate of Heavenly Peace (actual size) — A5

First Issue: Top line of shading broken at right.

1950, Feb. 10 Litho. *Perf. 12½*

12	A5	$200 green	15.00	2.25
13	A5	$300 brown red	1.00	*1.25*
14	A5	$500 red	1.00	.60
15	A5	$800 orange	100.00	1.75
16	A5	$1000 dull violet	4.00	.75
17	A5	$2000 olive	19.00	2.75
18	A5	$5000 brt pink	1.00	*2.25*
19	A5	$8000 blue	.75	*20.00*
20	A5	$10,000 brown	1.00	*2.75*
		Nos. 12-20 (9)	142.75	*34.35*

1950, June 9 Typo.

Second Issue: Top line of shading extends to frame line at right.

21	A5	$1000 dull violet	1.75	1.25
22	A5	$3000 red brown	1.50	1.00
23	A5	$10,000 brown	1.00	*1.25*
		Nos. 21-23 (3)	4.25	*3.50*

Other Gate of Heavenly Peace issues are illustrated where they are listed. See A10, A13, A14 and A42 for similar designs.

For similar types with Chinese characters in upper right corner see Northeast China A28, A29, Port Arthur & Darien A11, North China A8.

China Nos. 959, C62, E12, F2 Surcharged in Blue, Black, Green or Red

Rouletted, Perf. 12½ (#27, 29)

1950, Mar. Litho.

24	SD2	$100 on red vio (Bl)	.70	*2.25*
a.		Perf. 12½	7.50	3.25
25	R2	$200 on red (Bk)	3.00	1.75
a.		Perf. 12½	52.50	3.25
26	AP5	$300 on bl grn (Bk)	.50	*1.25*
a.		Perf. 12½	1.10	1.25
27	A96	$500 on org (Gr)	.75	.50
a.		Perf. 14	60.00	50.00
28	A96	$800 on org (R)	4.00	1.00
a.		Perf. 12½	30.00	4.00
b.		Perf. 14	*850.00*	75.00
29	A96	$1000 on org (Bk)	.50	.50
a.		Perf. 14	.50	.50
		Nos. 24-29 (6)	9.45	7.25

Harvesters with Ox — A6

1950, May

30	A6	$20,000 on $10,000 red	*675.00*	120.00

No. 30 is surcharged on an unissued stamp of East China. Value, without surcharge (unissued) *$1,500.*

Flag, Mao Tse-tung, Gate of Heavenly Peace — A7

Original

Reprint

Originals have a single curved line in jacket button, reprints have an extra dot in button. Value, set unused $42.50 used $16.

1950, July 1 *Perf. 14*

Yellow Stars

31	A7	$800 green & red	60.00	17.50
32	A7	$1000 brn & red	90.00	22.50
33	A7	$2000 dk brn & red	110.00	22.50
34	A7	$3000 dk blue & red	160.00	32.50
		Nos. 31-34 (4)	420.00	95.00

Inauguration of the People's Republic, Oct. 1, 1949. See Nos. 1L150-1L153.

Sun Yat-sen Stamps of Northeastern Provinces Surcharged in Red, Black or Blue

1950, July 1 Engr.

35	A2	$50 on 20c yel grn	10.00	*7.00*
36	A2	$50 on 25c blk brn	5.00	5.00
37	A2	$50 on 50c red org (Bk)	2.25	3.00
38	A2	$100 on $2.50 ind	1.50	*2.50*
39	A2	$100 on $3 brn (Bk)	2.50	*5.00*
40	A2	$100 on $4 org brn, Type II (Bl)	4.00	*10.00*
a.		Type I	*800.00*	*275.00*
41	A2	$100 on $5 dk grn (Bk)	7.00	3.75
42	A2	$100 on $10 crim, Type II (Bl)	37.50	13.00
a.		Type I	*7,500.*	—
43	A2	$400 on $20 ol, Type II (Bl)	75.00	50.00
a.		Type I	*1,000.*	*300.00*
44	A2	$400 on $44 dk car rose (Bl)	3.50	*8.50*
45	A2	$400 on $65 dl grn	150.00	80.00
46	A2	$400 on $100 dp grn	30.00	11.50
47	A2	$400 on $200 rose brn (Bk)	80.00	22.50
48	A2	$400 on $300 bluish grn	100.00	30.00
		Nos. 35-48 (14)	508.25	251.75

Flying Geese Type of China Surcharged in Red, Blue, Green, Brown or Black

1950, Aug. 1 *Perf. 12½, Imperf.*

49	A97	$50 on 10c dk bl (R)	.25	.40
50	A97	$100 on 16c ol, imperf. (Bl)	.35	.45
51	A97	$100 on 50c dl grn, imperf. (Bl)	.35	.35
52	A97	$200 on $1 org (G)	.45	.30
53	A97	$200 on $2 bl (Br)	6.25	.90
54	A97	$400 on $5 car rose (Bk)	.50	.50
55	A97	$400 on $10 bl grn (Bk)	.45	*1.50*
56	A97	$400 on $20 pur (Bk)	1.10	*2.75*
		Nos. 49-56 (8)	9.70	7.15

Dove of Peace, by Picasso — A8

1950, Aug. 1 Engr. *Perf. 14*

57	A8	$400 brown	27.50	7.00
58	A8	$800 green	27.50	7.00
59	A8	$2000 blue	47.50	12.00
		Nos. 57-59 (3)	102.50	26.00

World Peace Campaign. See Nos. 1L154-1L156.

Paper of originals appears bright under ultraviolet lamp. That of reprints looks dull. Value, set unused $8.50 used $4.

Chinese Flag and "1" — A9

$800

Original

Reprint

Reprints are a brighter red, leaves beside "1" are gray brown instead of reddish brown. On the $800 the arrangement of dots in background differs in relationship to large star. Value, set unused $25 used $10.

1950 Engr. & Litho.

Flag in Red & Yellow

60	A9	$100 purple	40.00	13.00
61	A9	$400 red brown	42.50	15.00
62	A9	$800 green	55.00	11.00
63	A9	$1000 lt olive	92.50	22.00
64	A9	$2000 blue	100.00	45.00
		Nos. 60-64 (5)	330.00	106.00

1st anniv. of the Chinese People's Republic. Size of $800: 38x46mm; others 26x32mm.

Issue dates: No. 62, Oct. 1; others Oct. 31. See Nos. 1L157-1L161.

Gate of Heavenly Peace (actual size) — A10

Third Issue: Cloud almost touches character at upper left. Cloud breaks inner frame line at top.

1950 Litho.

65	A10	$100 lt grnsh bl	37.50	12.50
66	A10	$200 green	275.00	21.00
67	A10	$300 dk carmine	2.50	*5.00*
68	A10	$400 grnsh gray	8.00	*4.00*
69	A10	$500 carmine	1.25	*3.50*
70	A10	$800 orange	8.00	1.00
71	A10	$2000 gray olive	3.00	2.25
		Nos. 65-71 (7)	335.25	*49.25*

Issued: $800, 10/8; $500, $2000, 12/1; others, 10/6.

"Communication" and Map of China — A11

Original

Reprint

Originals have 3 lines below horizontal bar (2nd character); reprints have four. Value, set unused $3.25, used $1.50.

1950, Nov. 1 Litho.

72	A11	$400 green & brn	35.00	11.00
73	A11	$800 carmine & grn	40.00	9.00

First All-China Postal Conference, Peking. See Nos. 1L162-1L163.

Stalin and Mao Tse-tung — A12

1950, Dec. 1 Engr. *Perf. 14*

74	A12	$400 red	21.00	12.00
75	A12	$800 dp green	21.00	10.00
76	A12	$2000 dk blue	32.50	12.00
		Nos. 74-76 (3)	74.50	34.00

Signing of Sino-Soviet Treaty of Friendship, Alliance and Mutual Assistance. See Nos. 1L176-1L178.

Paper of originals appears bright under ultraviolet lamp. That of reprints looks dull. Value, set unused $18.50, used $7.

East China Issue of 1949 Surcharged in Red, Black, Brown or Blue

Train and Postal Runner — A12a

1950, Dec. Litho. *Perf. 12½*

77	A12a	$50 on $10 dp ultra (R)	.30	.30
78	A12a	$100 on $15 org ver (Bk)	.30	.30
a.		$100 on $15 red (Bk), perf. 14	1.00	.85
79	A12a	$300 on $50 car (Bk)	.40	.30
80	A12a	$400 on $1600 vio bl (Br)	2.50	1.00

81	A12a	$400 on $2000 brn vio (Bl)	1.00	.70
		Nos. 77-81 (5)	4.50	2.60

East China Issue of 1949 Surcharged in Red or Black

Chairman Mao — A12b

1950, Dec.

82	A12b	$50 on $10 ultra (R)	.45	.25
83	A12b	$400 on $15 ver (Bk)	.60	.30
84	A12b	$400 on $2000 grn (Bk)	2.25	.90
		Nos. 82-84 (3)	3.30	1.45

(actual size) — A13

Fourth Issue: Similar to 3rd issue, but large cloud does not break inner frame line at top.

1950-51 **Litho.**

85	A13	$100 lt blue	.80	1.75
86	A13	$200 dull green	11.00	4.25
87	A13	$300 dull lilac	.65	*5.25*
88	A13	$400 gray grn	9.00	1.50
89	A13	$500 carmine	.75	1.50
90	A13	$800 orange	77.50	6.75
a.		Imperf., pair	—	
91	A13	$1000 violet	1.00	*2.75*
92	A13	$2000 olive	290.00	8.00
93	A13	$3000 brown	.90	*6.00*
94	A13	$5000 pink	.90	*4.50*
		Nos. 85-94 (10)	392.50	*42.25*

Issued: $200, $300, $500, $800, $2000, $5000, 12/22/50; others 6/8/51.

(actual size) — A14

Fifth Issue: Colored network on surface in salmon.

1951, Jan. 18 **Engr.** ***Perf. 14***

95	A14	$10,000 brown	2.50	*35.00*
96	A14	$20,000 olive	3.50	*15.00*
97	A14	$30,000 green	82.50	*110.00*
98	A14	$50,000 violet	110.00	55.00
99	A14	$100,000 scarlet	2,750.	350.00
100	A14	$200,000 blue	3,800.	675.00
		Nos. 95-100 (6)	6,748.	1,240.

Unit Issue of China Surcharged

1951, May 2 **Litho.** ***Perf. 12½***

101	SD2	$5 on rose lilac	3.75	*3.25*
102	AP5	$10 on brt grn	2.25	*3.25*
103	R2	$15 on red	1.50	*1.75*
104	A96	$25 on orange	1.50	*1.75*
		Nos. 101-104 (4)	9.00	10.00

Issued for use in Northeast China, but available for use throughout China. Nos. 101-104 rouletted were sold for philatelic purposes only. Value, set unused $10, used $8.

Chairman Mao Tse-tung — A15

1951, July 1 **Engr.** ***Perf. 14***

105	A15	$400 chestnut	10.00	6.50
106	A15	$500 deep green	12.00	6.50
107	A15	$800 crimson	14.50	6.50
		Nos. 105-107 (3)	36.50	19.50

Chinese Communist Party, 30th anniv.

Reprints are on whiter, thinner and harder paper. Value, set unused $21.50, used $12.

Picasso Dove — A16

1951, Aug. 15 ***Perf. 12½***

108	A16	$400 orange brn	25.00	13.00
109	A16	$800 blue grn	25.00	13.00
110	A16	$1000 dull vio	25.00	13.00
		Nos. 108-110 (3)	75.00	39.00

Reprints are perf 14. Value, set unused $30, used $9.50.

Remittance Stamp of China Surcharged in Carmine or Black

(same size) — A17

Engraved, Commercial Press

1951, Sept. ***Perf. 12½***

111	A17	$50 on $2 bl grn (C)	1.50	*1.00*

Rouletted 9½

Typo., Kang Hwa Printing Co.

112	A17	$50 on $2 gray bl (C)	4.25	*5.25*
113	A17	$50 on $5 red org (Bk)	1.50	*1.50*
114	A17	$50 on $50 gray (C)	5.00	*5.25*

Perf. 13

Lithographed, Central Trust Co.

115	A17	$50 on $50 gray blk (C)	1.00	*1.00*

Perf. 11½x10

Lithographed, Chung Hwa Book Co.

116	A17	$50 on $50 gray (C)	3.00	1.25
a.		Perf. 11½	2.00	1.25
		Nos. 111-116 (6)	16.25	*15.25*

National Emblem — A18

Engraved; Background Network Lithographed in Yellow

1951, Oct. 1 ***Perf. 14***

117	A18	$100 Prus blue	12.50	7.00
118	A18	$200 brown	12.50	7.00
119	A18	$400 orange	12.50	7.00
120	A18	$500 green	17.50	7.00
121	A18	$800 carmine	18.50	7.00
		Nos. 117-121 (5)	73.50	35.00

Reprints exist but are difficult to distinguish; paper whiter, and colors slightly brighter. Value, set unused or used $20.

Rough Perfs

Rough perforations are normal on many early issues. These include Nos. 122-123, 136-140, 155-176, 239-240, 299-300, 453-456, 467-482, 629-634, 684-707, 737-745 and probably others.

Lu Hsun and Quotation A19

Original

Reprint

Reprints have dot in triangle at lower right; no dot in original. Value, set unused $6.50, used $2.25.

1951, Oct. 19 **Litho.** ***Perf. 12½***

122	A19	$400 lilac	11.00	6.00
123	A19	$800 green	15.00	6.00

15th anniversary of the death of Lu Hsun (1881-1936), writer.

Peasant Uprising, Chintien — A20

Design: Nos. 126-127, Coin of Taiping Regime and decrees of peasant government.

Original

Reprint

Reprints of Nos. 124-125 have additional short stroke at upper left.

Original

Reprint

Reprints of Nos. 126-127 have two short strokes on scale near tail of right dragon on coin. Value, Nos. 124-127 unused $10, used $4.25.

1951, Dec. 15 **Engr.** ***Perf. 14***

124	A20	$400 green	15.00	7.00
125	A20	$800 scarlet	12.00	7.00
126	A20	$800 orange	12.00	7.00
127	A20	$1000 deep blue	20.00	7.00
		Nos. 124-127 (4)	59.00	28.00

Centenary of Taiping Peasant Rebellion.

Old and New Methods of Agriculture — A21

Original

Reprint

One short horizontal line between legs of plower; 2 lines in reprints. Value, set unused $9.50, used $4.

1952, Jan. 1

128	A21	$100 scarlet	11.00	6.75
129	A21	$200 bright blue	11.00	6.75
130	A21	$400 deep brown	11.00	6.75
131	A21	$800 green	11.00	6.75
		Nos. 128-131 (4)	44.00	27.00

Agrarian reform.

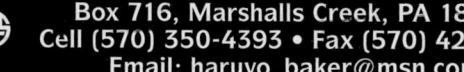

Potala Monastery, Lhasa — A22

Nos. 134-135, Farmer plowing with yaks.

1952, Mar. 15 ***Perf. 12½***

132	A22	$400 vermilion		16.00	7.50
133	A22	$800 claret		16.00	7.50
134	A22	$800 blue grn		16.00	7.50
135	A22	$1000 dull vio		16.00	7.50
		Nos. 132-135 (4)		64.00	30.00

Liberation of Tibet.

Reprints, perf 14, have a small Chinese character at lower left of the vignette which is missing in the original. Value, set unused $22, used $7.

Children of Four Races — A23

1952, Apr. 12 **Litho.**

136	A23	$400 dull grn	1.50	.35
137	A23	$800 vio blue	1.75	.45

Intl. Child Protection Conf., Vienna.

Hammer and Sickle on Numeral 1 — A24

Labor Day: No. 139, Dove rising from worker's hand. No. 140, Dove, hammer, wheat & chimneys.

1952, May 1

138	A24	$800 scarlet	2.50	.40
139	A24	$800 blue grn	2.50	.40
140	A24	$800 orange brn	2.50	.40
		Nos. 138-140 (3)	7.50	1.20

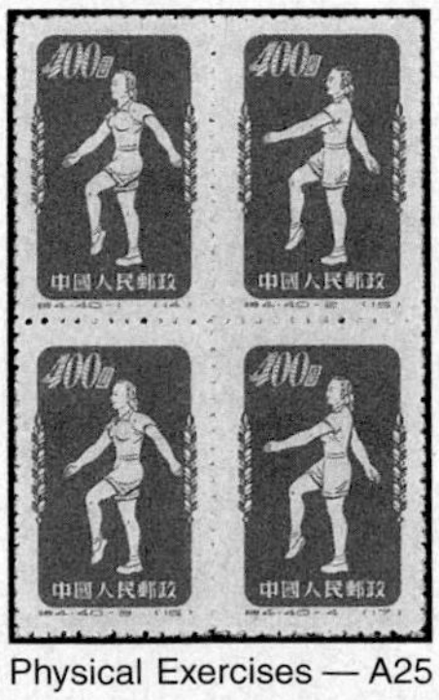

Physical Exercises — A25

Stamps printed in blocks of four for each color, each block representing a specific setting-up exercise; exercises coincided with a national radio program. Where exercise positions are identical within the block, the serial number in the LL margin of each stamp (and in parenthesis in the listings below) is the only means of differentiation.

1952, June 20

141	A25	Block of 4	160.00	60.00
a.		$400 vermilion (1)	9.00	4.75
b.		$400 vermilion (2)	9.00	4.75
c.		$400 vermilion (3)	9.00	4.75
d.		$400 vermilion (4)	9.00	4.75
142	A25	Block of 4	160.00	60.00
a.		$400 blue (5)	9.00	4.75
b.		$400 blue (6)	9.00	4.75
c.		$400 blue (7)	9.00	4.75
d.		$400 blue (8)	9.00	4.75
143	A25	Block of 4	160.00	60.00
a.		$400 brown red (9)	9.00	4.75
b.		$400 brown red (10)	9.00	4.75
c.		$400 brown red (11)	9.00	4.75
d.		$400 brown red (12)	9.00	4.75
144	A25	Block of 4	160.00	60.00
a.		$400 yellow green (13)	9.00	4.75
b.		$400 yellow green (14)	9.00	4.75
c.		$400 yellow green (15)	9.00	4.75
d.		$400 yellow green (16)	9.00	4.75
145	A25	Block of 4	160.00	60.00
a.		$400 red orange (17)	9.00	4.75
b.		$400 red orange (18)	9.00	4.75
c.		$400 red orange (19)	9.00	4.75
d.		$400 red orange (20)	9.00	4.75
146	A25	Block of 4	160.00	60.00
a.		$400 dull blue (21)	9.00	4.75
b.		$400 dull blue (22)	9.00	4.75
c.		$400 dull blue (23)	9.00	4.75
d.		$400 dull blue (24)	9.00	4.75
147	A25	Block of 4	160.00	60.00
a.		$400 orange (25)	9.00	4.75
b.		$400 orange (26)	9.00	4.75
c.		$400 orange (27)	9.00	4.75
d.		$400 orange (28)	9.00	4.75
148	A25	Block of 4	160.00	60.00
a.		$400 dull purple (29)	9.00	4.75
b.		$400 dull purple (30)	9.00	4.75
c.		$400 dull purple (31)	9.00	4.75
d.		$400 dull purple (32)	9.00	4.75
149	A25	Block of 4	160.00	60.00
a.		$400 yellow bister (33)	9.00	4.75
b.		$400 yellow bister (34)	9.00	4.75
c.		$400 yellow bister (35)	9.00	4.75
d.		$400 yellow bister (36)	9.00	4.75
150	A25	Block of 4	160.00	60.00
a.		$400 sky blue (37)	9.00	4.75
b.		$400 sky blue (38)	9.00	4.75
c.		$400 sky blue (39)	9.00	4.75
d.		$400 sky blue (40)	9.00	4.75
		Nos. 141-150 (10)	1,600.	600.00

Originals are on thin gray paper, colors darker. Reprints on thicker white paper, colors brighter. Value, set of blocks unused $52.50, used $47.50.

Hunting, Wei Dynasty, A.D. 386-580 A26

Designs from Murals in Cave Temples at Tunhuang, Kansu Province: No. 152, Lady attendants, Sui Dynasty, 581-617 A.D. No. 153, Gandharvas (mythology), Tang Dynasty, 618-906. No. 154, Dragon, Tang Dynasty.

1952, July 1 **Engr.**

151	A26	$800 slate green (1)	2.40	.55
152	A26	$800 chocolate (2)	2.40	.55
a.		Vert. pair, imperf. between	360.00	
153	A26	$800 indigo (3)	2.40	.55
154	A26	$800 dk vio (4)	2.40	.55
		Nos. 151-154 (4)	9.60	2.20

"Glorious Mother Country," 1st series.

Marco Polo Bridge, near Peking A27

Designs: No. 156, Cavalry passing through Great Wall. No. 157, Departure of New Fourth Army. No. 158, Mao Tse-tung and Gen. Chu Teh planning counter-attack.

1952, July 7 **Litho.** ***Perf. 14***

155	A27	$800 brt blue	4.00	.50
156	A27	$800 blue grn	4.00	.50
157	A27	$800 plum	4.00	.50
158	A27	$800 scarlet	4.00	.50
		Nos. 155-158 (4)	16.00	2.00

15th anniversary of war against Japan.

Soldier and Tanks — A28

No. 159, Soldier, sailor & airman, vert. No. 161, Sailor & warships. No. 162, Airman & planes.

1952, Aug. 1 **Engr.** ***Perf. 12½***

159	A28	$800 carmine	2.50	.50
160	A28	$800 deep green	2.50	.50
161	A28	$800 purple	2.50	.50
162	A28	$800 orange brown	2.50	.50
		Nos. 159-162 (4)	10.00	2.00

25th anniv. of People's Liberation Army.

Huai River Sluice Dam — A29

No. 164, Train on the Chengtu-Chungking Railway. No. 165, Oil refinery and derricks in the Northwest. No. 166, Mechanized state farm.

1952, Oct. 1 ***Perf. 14***

163	A29	$800 dk violet	3.00	.60
164	A29	$800 red	3.00	.60
165	A29	$800 dk vio brn	3.00	.60
166	A29	$800 dp green	3.00	.60
		Nos. 163-166 (4)	12.00	2.40

"Glorious Mother Country," 2nd series.

Doves and Globe A30

Designs: Nos. 167-168, Picasso dove over Pacific, vert. $2500, as No. 169.

1952, Oct. 2 ***Perf. 14***

167	A30	$400 maroon	2.00	.35
168	A30	$800 red	2.00	.35
169	A30	$800 brown orange	2.00	.35
170	A30	$2500 deep green	2.00	.55
		Nos. 167-170 (4)	8.00	1.60

Peace Conf. of the Asian and Pacific Regions.

Volunteers on the March — A31

No. 172, Chinese peasants loading supplies. No. 173, Volunteers attacking across river. No. 174, Meeting of Chinese & Korean troops.

1952, Oct. 25

171	A31	$800 blue green (1)	3.75	.40
172	A31	$800 vermilion (2)	3.75	.40
173	A31	$800 violet (3)	3.75	.40
174	A31	$800 lake brown (4)	3.75	.40
		Nos. 171-174 (4)	15.00	1.60

2nd anniv. of Chinese Volunteers in Korea.

Woman Textile Worker A32

Design: No. 176, Farm woman with sickle.

1953, Mar. 10

175	A32	$800 carmine	1.75	.40
176	A32	$800 emerald	1.75	.40

International Women's Day.

Textile Worker — A33

$200, Shepherdess. $250, Stone lion. $800, Lathe operator. $1600, Coal miners. $2000, Corner tower of Forbidden City, Peking.

1953 **Litho.** ***Perf. 14, 12½ ($250)***

177	A33	$50 magenta	1.00	.25
178	A33	$200 emerald	1.50	.45
179	A33	$250 ultra	5.00	2.75
180	A33	$800 blue grn	1.00	.25
181	A33	$1600 gray	1.00	.50
182	A33	$2000 red org	2.00	.35
		Nos. 177-182 (6)	11.50	4.55

Issued: Nos. 177-181, Mar. 25; No. 182, May 23.

Karl Marx — A34

1953, May 20 **Engr.** ***Perf. 14***

183	A34	$400 dk brown	2.75	.50
184	A34	$800 slate grn	2.75	.50

135th anniv. of the birth of Karl Marx.

Workers and Banners — A35

1953, June 25

185	A35	$400 Prus blue	2.25	.40
186	A35	$800 carmine	2.25	.40

7th All-China Trade Union Congress.

Picasso Dove — A36

1953, July 25

187	A36	$250 blue grn	1.75	.40
188	A36	$400 orange brn	2.25	.45
189	A36	$800 purple	3.00	.65
		Nos. 187-189 (3)	7.00	1.50

World Peace.

Groom, Wei Dynasty, 386-580 A37

Scenes from Tunhuang Murals: No. 191, Court Players, Wei Dynasty. No. 192, Battle Scene, Sui Dynasty, 581-617. No. 193, Ox-drawn palanquin, Tang Dynasty, 618-906.

1953, Sept. 1

190	A37	$800 dp green (1)	2.00	.50
191	A37	$800 red org (2)	2.00	.50
192	A37	$800 Prus blue (3)	2.00	.50
193	A37	$800 carmine (4)	2.00	.50
		Nos. 190-193 (4)	8.00	2.00

"Glorious Mother Country," 3rd series.

Stalin and Mao on Kremlin Terrace A38

Statue of Stalin at Volga-Don Canal — A39

Designs: No. 195, Lenin proclaiming Soviet power. No. 197, Stalin as orator.

1953, Oct. 5

194	A38	$800 green (1)	2.50	1.25
195	A38	$800 carmine (2)	2.50	1.25
196	A39	$800 brt blue (3)	3.50	1.25
197	A39	$800 org brn (4)	4.50	2.00
		Nos. 194-197 (4)	13.00	5.75

Russian October Revolution, 35th anniv.

Stamps in same designs with two additional characters meaning "Soviet" in the single-line Chinese inscription, and in different colors, were unofficially released at several small post offices in Hunan, Fukien and Canton areas in February, 1953, but were withdrawn after only a small number had been sold. Value, set $47,500. unused, $20,000 canceled.

Compass, 3rd Century B.C. A40

No. 199, Seismoscope, later Han Dynasty. No. 200, Drum cart to measure distance, Chin Dynasty. No. 201, Armillary sphere, Ming Dynasty.

1953, Dec. 1

198	A40	$800 indigo (1)	2.50	.90
199	A40	$800 dk green (2)	2.50	.90
200	A40	$800 dk blue (3)	2.50	.90
201	A40	$800 choc (4)	2.50	.90
		Nos. 198-201 (4)	10.00	3.60

Major inventions by ancient and medieval Chinese scientists.

"Glorious Mother Country," 4th series.

Francois Rabelais — A41

Designs: $400, Jose Marti, Cuban revolutionary. $800, Chu Yuan (350-275 B.C.), philosopher. $2200, Nicolaus Copernicus, astronomer.

1953, Dec. 30

202	A41	$250 slate grn (3)	1.80	.40
203	A41	$400 brown blk (4)	1.80	.40
204	A41	$800 indigo (1)	1.80	.40
205	A41	$2200 choc (2)	1.80	.40
		Nos. 202-205 (4)	7.20	1.60

(same size) Gate of Heavenly Peace — A42

Sixth Issue: Inscription at upper right.

1954, Apr. 16 **Litho.**

206	A42	$50 carmine	.50	.30
207	A42	$100 lt blue	.50	.30
208	A42	$200 green	.50	.25
209	A42	$250 ultra	3.75	.80
210	A42	$400 gray grn	1.00	.25
211	A42	$800 orange	.50	.25
212	A42	$1600 gray	.50	*.65*
213	A42	$2000 olive	1.25	.50
		Nos. 206-213 (8)	8.50	3.30

Textile Plant, Harbin — A43

Designs: $200, Tangku Harbor. $250, Tienshui-Lanchow railroad bridge, Kansu Province. $400, Heavy machine-building plant, Taiyuan, Shansi. No. 218, Automatic blast, furnace, Anshan, Manchuria. No. 219, Fushun open-cut coal mine. $2000, Automatic power plant, Northeast. $3200, Prospecting in Tayeh district, Hupeh.

1954, May 1 **Engr.**

214	A43	$100 brown olive	1.50	1.00
215	A43	$200 blue green	3.00	1.00
216	A43	$250 violet	1.50	.50
217	A43	$400 black	1.50	1.00
218	A43	$800 claret	1.50	.50
219	A43	$800 indigo	1.50	.50
220	A43	$2000 red	2.00	.50
221	A43	$3200 dark brown	2.00	1.00
		Nos. 214-221 (8)	14.50	6.00

Economic progress.

Lenin — A44

$400, Lenin and Stalin Monument, Gorki, horiz. $2000, Lenin proclaiming Soviet power.

1954, June 30 **Engr.**

222	A44	$400 deep green	2.00	1.50
223	A44	$800 dark brown	3.00	1.25
224	A44	$2000 deep carmine	3.50	1.00
		Nos. 222-224 (3)	8.50	3.75

30th anniversary of the death of Lenin.

Pottery Vessels, Neolithic Period, 2000 B. C. — A45

Archeological Treasures: No. 226, Stone clime, Shang Dynasty, c. 1200 B.C. No. 227, Kuo Chi Tsu-pai bronze basin, Middle Chou Dynasty, 816 B.C. No. 228, Lacquered box and wine cup, Warring States Period, 403-221 B.C.

1954, Aug. 25

225	A45	$800 brown	1.90	.40
226	A45	$800 indigo	1.90	.40
227	A45	$800 Prus bl	1.90	.40
228	A45	$800 car	1.90	.40
		Nos. 225-228 (4)	7.60	1.60

"Glorious Mother Country," 5th series.

Pipe Production, Anshan Steel Mill — A46

Design: $800, Rolling mill, Anshan.

1954, Oct. 1

229	A46	$400 Prus green	3.25	.60
230	A46	$800 vio brown	3.25	.60

Stalin Statue, by Tomsky — A47

Designs: $800, Stalin portrait. $2000, Stalin viewing hydroelectric plant.

1954, Oct. 15 **Size: 21x45mm**

231	A47	$400 black	1.50	.70

Size: 26x37mm

232	A47	$800 black brown	2.50	.70

Size: 42x26mm

233	A47	$2000 deep red	4.00	.95
		Nos. 231-233 (3)	8.00	2.35

First anniversary of the death of Stalin.

Exhibition Building, Peking — A48

1954, Nov. 7

234	A48	$800 brown, *cream*	37.50	7.50
a.		Size: 53½x24mm	50.00	12.00

Russian Economic and Cultural Exhibition, Peking. No. 234 measures 52½x24½mm.

Apprentices and Lathe — A49

Progress in Technology: $800, Heavy machinery and workers.

1954, Dec. 15

235	A49	$400 dk olive grn	3.25	.50
236	A49	$800 bright red	3.25	.60

Woman Worker Voting — A50

People Celebrating Opening of Congress — A51

1954, Dec. 30

237	A50	$400 deep claret	2.75	.75
238	A51	$800 bright red	4.25	1.00

First National Congress.

Flags, Worker and Woman Holding Constitution — A52

1954, Dec. 30

239	A52	$400 brown, *buff*	2.50	.40
240	A52	$800 brt red, *yel*	4.00	.60

Adoption of Constitution.

High-tension Pylon — A53

1955, Feb. 25

241	A53	$800 dk Prus bl	6.50	1.10

Development of electric power.

Factory Health Workers and Red Cross A54

1955, June 25 **Engr.; Cross Typo.**

242	A54	8f dp grn & red	18.00	2.50

50th anniversary of Chinese Red Cross.

Stalin and Mao in Kremlin A55

Soviet Specialist and Chinese Worker — A56

1955, July 25 **Engr.**

243	A55	8f brown red	20.00	1.00
244	A56	20f olive blk	27.50	2.75

5th anniv. of Sino-Soviet Friendship Treaty.

Chang Heng (78-139), Astronomer — A57

Portraits of Scientists: No. 246, Tsu Chung-chih (429-500), mathematician. No. 247, Chang Sui (683-727), astronomer. No. 248, Li Shih-chen (1518-1593), physician and pharmacologist.

1955, Aug. 25 ***Perf. 14***

245	A57	8f sepia, *buff*	6.00	1.00
a.		Min. sheet, sepia, *white*	65.00	20.00
246	A57	8f dp grn, *buff*	6.00	1.00
a.		Min. sheet, deep green, *white*	65.00	20.00
247	A57	8f black, *buff*	6.00	1.00
a.		Min. sheet, blk, *white*	65.00	20.00
248	A57	8f claret, *buff*	6.00	1.00
a.		Min. sheet, claret, *white*	65.00	20.00
		Nos. 245-248 (4)	24.00	4.00

Miniature sheets contain one imperf. stamp.

Steel Pouring Ladle A58

No. 250, High tension line (2). No. 251, Mechanized coal mining (3). No. 252, Tank cars and derricks (4). No. 253, Heavy machine shop (5). No. 254, Soldier on guard (6). No. 255, Spinning machine (7). No. 256, Workers discussing 5-year plan (8). No. 257, Combine harvester (9). No. 258, Milk production (10). No. 259, Dam (11). No. 260, Pottery industry (12). No. 261, Truck (13). No. 262, Ship at dock (14). No. 263, Geological survey (15). No. 264, Higher education (16). No. 265, Family (17). No. 266, Workers' rest home (18).

1955-56 **Litho.**

Position-in-set number in ( )

249	A58	8f shown (1)	4.00	.85
250	A58	8f multicolored	4.00	.85
251	A58	8f multicolored	4.00	.85
252	A58	8f multicolored	4.00	.85
253	A58	8f multicolored	4.00	.85
254	A58	8f multicolored	4.00	.85
255	A58	8f multicolored	4.00	.85
256	A58	8f multicolored	4.00	.85
257	A58	8f multicolored	4.00	.85
258	A58	8f multicolored	4.00	.85
259	A58	8f multicolored	4.00	.85
260	A58	8f multi ('56)	4.00	.85
261	A58	8f multicolored	4.00	.85
262	A58	8f multicolored	4.00	.85
263	A58	8f multicolored	4.00	.85
264	A58	8f multicolored	4.00	.85
265	A58	8f multicolored	4.00	.85
266	A58	8f multi ('56)	4.00	.85
		Nos. 249-266 (18)	72.00	15.30

1st 5 Year Plan. Issued: Nos. 249-257, 10/1; Nos. 258-259, 261-265, 12/15; Nos. 260, 266, 2/24/56.

Lenin — A59

1955, Dec. 15 **Engr.** ***Perf. 14***

267	A59	8f dk blue grn	22.50	1.50
268	A59	20f dk rose car	27.50	2.50

85th anniversary of the birth of Lenin.

Engels — A60

1955, Dec. 15

269	A60	8f deep orange	20.00	1.50
270	A60	20f brown	32.50	2.50

135th anniversary of the birth of Friedrich Engels (1820-1895), German socialist.

Storming Lu Ting Bridge — A61

Crossing Great Snow Mountains A62

1955, Dec. 30

271	A61	8f dark red	20.00	1.00
272	A62	8f dark blue	30.00	3.50

Long March of Chinese Communist army, 20th anniversary.

Miner — A63

Gate of Heavenly Peace — A64

Designs: 1f, Machinist. 2f, Airman. 2½f, Nurse. 4f, Soldier. 8f, Steel worker. 10f, Scientist. 20f, Farm woman. 50f, Sailor.

1955-56 **Litho.** ***Perf. 14***

273	A63	½f orange brn	1.75	.35
274	A63	1f purple	1.75	.35
275	A63	2f green	2.50	.35
276	A63	2½f blue ('56)	4.00	.35
277	A63	4f gray olive	2.50	.35
278	A63	8f red org (Peking printing)	4.00	.75
a.		Perf. 12½ (Shanghai printing)	475.00	55.00
279	A63	10f claret ('56)	21.00	.40
280	A63	20f dp blue	8.00	.50
281	A63	50f gray	7.00	.60
		Nos. 273-281 (9)	52.50	4.00

Engr.

282	A64	$1 claret ('56)	2.50	.40
283	A64	$2 sepia ('55)	4.25	.40
284	A64	$5 indigo ('56)	9.00	.70
285	A64	$10 dp org ('56)	14.00	7.50
286	A64	$20 gray vio ('56)	17.50	*22.50*
		Nos. 282-286 (5)	47.25	31.50

Nos. 282-286 are the 7th Gate Issue. Used values for Nos. 282-286 are for postally used examples.

Trucks, Mountains, Highway Map — A65

Suspension Bridge over Tatu River — A66

No. 289, 1st truck arriving in Lhasa, & the Potala.

1956, Mar. 10 **Engr.**

287	A65	4f dp blue	2.40	.50
288	A66	8f dk brown	2.40	.50
289	A65	8f carmine	2.40	.75
		Nos. 287-289 (3)	7.20	1.75

Completion of Sikang-Tibet and Chinghai-Tibet Highways.

Summer Palace and Marble Boat A67

Famous Views of Imperial Peking: No. 291, Peihai Park with Jade Belt Marble Bridge. No. 292, Gate of Heavenly Peace. No. 293, Temple of Heaven. No. 294, Great Throne Hall, Forbidden City.

1956-57

290	A67	4f car rose (1)	8.00	.90
291	A67	4f blue grn (2)	8.00	.90
292	A67	8f red org (3) ('57)	24.00	.90
293	A67	8f Prus blue (4)	8.00	.90
294	A67	8f yellow brn (5)	8.00	2.40
		Nos. 290-294 (5)	56.00	6.00

Issued: No. 292, 2/20/57; others, 6/15/56.

No. 292 exists with sun rays in background. Values: unused, $250,000; used, $80,000.

Salt Making A68

Designs: No. 296, Dwelling of the Eastern Han period. No. 297, Duck hunting and harvesting. No. 298, Carriage crossing bridge.

1956, Oct. 1

295	A68	4f gray olive	2.00	.35
296	A68	4f slate blue	2.00	.35
297	A68	8f gray brown	2.00	.35
298	A68	8f sepia	2.00	.35
		Nos. 295-298 (4)	8.00	1.40

Murals, Tung Han Dynasty, 250 B.C.-220 A.D., found near Chengtu.

Ancient Coins and "Save" A69

1956, Oct. 1

299	A69	4f yellow brown	9.50	1.50
300	A69	8f rose red	14.00	1.50

Promotion of saving.

Gate of Heavenly Peace — A70

1956, Nov. 10

301	A70	4f dk green	12.00	.55
302	A70	8f brt red	16.00	.80
303	A70	16f dk carmine	27.50	.90
		Nos. 301-303 (3)	55.50	2.25

8th National Congress of the Communist Party of China.

Sun Yat-sen — A71

1956, Nov. 12

304	A71	4f brown, *cream*	22.50	2.00
305	A71	8f dp blue, *cream*	32.50	3.50

90th anniversary of birth of Sun Yat-sen.

Weight Lifting — A72

1957, Mar. 20 **Litho.** ***Perf. 12½***

Hibiscus red and green; inscription brown

306	A72	4f Shot put (2)	3.25	.25
307	A72	4f shown (5)	3.25	.25
308	A72	8f Track (1)	3.25	.75
309	A72	8f Soccer (3)	3.25	.50
310	A72	8f Bicycling (4)	3.25	.75
		Nos. 306-310 (5)	16.25	2.50

First National Workers' Sports Meeting.

Truck Factory No. 1, Changchun — A73

China's truck industry: 8f, Trucks rolling off assembly line.

1957, May 1 **Engr.** ***Perf. 14***

311	A73	4f light brown	2.75	.55
312	A73	8f slate green	3.75	.60

Nanchang Uprising — A74

No. 314, Mao and Chu Teh at Chingkanshan. No. 315, Crossing Yellow River. No. 316, Liberation of Nanking, 4/23/49.

1957

313	A74	4f blk vio (1)	32.50	3.00
314	A74	4f slate grn (2)	32.50	2.50
315	A74	8f red brn (3)	32.50	2.50
316	A74	8f dp blue (4)	32.50	2.00
		Nos. 313-316 (4)	130.00	10.00

People's Liberation Army, 30th anniv. Issued: Nos. 313, 315, 8/10; No. 314, 8/30; No. 316, 12/30.

Congress Emblem — A75

1957, Sept. 30

317	A75	8f chocolate	9.00	1.00
318	A75	22f indigo	12.00	1.00

4th Intl. Trade Union Cong., Leipzig, 10/4-15.

Yangtze River Bridge A76

20f, Road leading to and over bridge.

1957, Oct. 1

319	A76	8f	scarlet	2.25	.60
320	A76	20f	slate blue	5.50	.60

Completion of Yangtze River Bridge at Wuhan.

Fireworks over Kremlin — A77

Designs: 8f, Hammer and sickle over globe and broken chain. 20f, Stylized dove and olive branch. 22f, Hands of three races holding book with Marx and Lenin. 32f, Star and pylon.

1957, Nov. 7

321	A77	4f	brt red	4.50	.75
322	A77	8f	chocolate	6.00	.75
323	A77	20f	dp green	10.00	.75
324	A77	22f	red brown	12.00	1.25
325	A77	32f	dp blue	25.00	2.00
			Nos. 321-325 (5)	57.50	5.50

40th anniv. of Russian October Revolution.

Map of Yellow River Basin A78

No. 327, Sanmen Gorge dam & powerhouse. No. 328, Ocean liner on Yellow River. No. 329, Dam, irrigation canals & tree-bordered fields.

1957, Dec. 30

326	A78	4f	deep orange (1)	18.00	2.00
327	A78	4f	deep blue (2)	18.00	2.25
328	A78	8f	deep lake (3)	30.00	2.75
329	A78	8f	blue green (4)	30.00	2.75
			Nos. 326-329 (4)	96.00	9.75

Yellow River control plan.

Old Man and Young Drummer — A79

1957, Dec. 30 **Litho.**

330	A79	8f	shown (1)	2.25	.30
331	A79	8f	Plowman (2)	2.25	.30
332	A79	8f	Woman planting tree (3)	2.25	.30
333	A79	8f	Harvest (4)	2.25	.30
			Nos. 330-333 (4)	9.00	1.20

Agricultural cooperation.

Train on Bridge, Ship and Train — A80

Designs (Congratulatory Banner and): 4f, Crane, dove and flowers. 8f, Crane with hot ingots, cotton bolls and wheat.

1958, Jan. 30 **Engr.**

334	A80	4f	emer, *cream*	2.25	1.50
335	A80	8f	red, *cream*	2.25	1.50
336	A80	16f	ultra, *cream*	2.25	1.50
			Nos. 334-336 (3)	6.75	4.50

Fulfillment of First Five-Year Plan.

Sungyu Pagoda, Honan — A81

Ancient Pagodas: No. 338, Chienhsun Pagoda, Yunnan. No. 339, Sakyamuni Pagoda, Shansi. No. 340, Flying Rainbow Pagoda, Shansi.

1958, Mar. 15 **Engr.**

337	A81	8f	sepia (1)	5.00	.60
338	A81	8f	Prus blue (2)	5.00	.40
339	A81	8f	maroon (3)	5.00	.60
340	A81	8f	dp green (4)	5.00	.80
			Nos. 337-340 (4)	20.00	2.40

Trilobite, Kaoli — A82

Designs: 8f, Lufeng dinosaur. 16f, Choukoutien sino-megaceros.

1958, Apr. 15

341	A82	4f	blue	2.75	.40
342	A82	8f	sepia	4.00	.40
343	A82	16f	slate green	3.25	.40
			Nos. 341-343 (3)	10.00	1.20

Prehistoric animals of China.

Heroes Monument A83

1958, May 1

344	A83	8f	scarlet	40.00	4.50
a.			Souvenir sheet, imperf.	*275.00*	100.00

Unveiling of People's Heroes Monument, Peking. No. 344a issued May 30.

Karl Marx — A84

Design: 22f, Marx Speaking to German Workers' Educational Association, London, painting by Zhukow.

1958, May 5

345	A84	8f	chocolate	20.00	1.50
346	A84	22f	dk green	25.00	3.00

Karl Marx (1818-83), 140th birth anniv.

Cogwheels and Factories — A85

1958, May 25

347	A85	4f	brt grnsh bl	30.00	2.50
348	A85	8f	red lilac	30.00	3.25

8th All-China Trade Union Cong., Peking.

Dove over Globe — A86

1958, June 1

349	A86	8f	violet blue	8.00	1.50
350	A86	20f	blue green	17.50	3.00

4th Congress of the Intl. Democratic Women's Federation, Vienna, June 1958.

Mother and Child — A87

Children's Day: No. 352, Watering sunflowers. No. 353, Playing hide-and-seek. No. 354, Sailing toy boat.

1958, June 1 **Litho.**

351	A87	8f	green & multi (1)	25.00	2.25
352	A87	8f	green & multi (2)	25.00	2.25
353	A87	8f	green & multi (3)	25.00	2.25
a.			Red omitted	—	—
354	A87	8f	green & multi (4)	25.00	2.25
			Nos. 351-354 (4)	100.00	9.00

Kuan Han-ching A88

Designs (Operas): 4f, "Dream of Butterflies." 20f, "The Riverside Pavilion."

1958, June 20 **Engr.**

355	A88	4f	indigo, *cr*	30.00	2.25
356	A88	8f	brown, *cr*	35.00	4.50
357	A88	20f	black, *cr*	50.00	2.25
a.			Souvenir sheet of 3, *ivory*	550.00	140.00
			Nos. 355-357 (3)	115.00	9.00

700th anniversary of publication of works of Kuan Han-ching (1210-1280), dramatist. No. 357a contains 3 imperf. stamps similar to Nos. 355-357. Size: 130x100mm. Issued June 28.

Planetarium A89

20f, Telescope and stars over Peking.

1958, June 25

358	A89	8f	dk green	10.00	2.00
359	A89	20fr	indigo	12.00	3.00

First Chinese planetarium, Peking.

Marx and Engels — A90

8f, Cover of 1st edition of the Communist Manifesto.

1958, July 1

360	A90	4f	dk red vio	30.00	3.25
361	A90	8f	Prus blue	35.00	2.00

110th anniversary of publication of the Communist Manifesto.

Wild Goose and Broadcasting Tower — A91

1958, July 10

362	A91	4f	ultra	17.50	3.50
363	A91	8f	deep green	20.00	1.75

1st Conference of the Ministers of Posts and Telecommunications of Socialist Countries, Moscow, Dec. 3-17, 1957.

Peony and Doves — A92

8f, Olive branch with ribbon & clouds. 22f, Atomic energy symbol over factories.

1958, July 20

364	A92	4f	red	20.00	3.00
365	A92	8f	green	15.00	2.50
366	A92	22f	red brown	27.50	4.75
			Nos. 364-366 (3)	62.50	10.25

Congress for Disarmament and International Cooperation, Stockholm, July 17-22.

Bronze Weather Vane — A93

Designs: No. 368, Weather balloon. No. 369, Typhoon tower and weather map of Asia.

1958, Aug. 25

367	A93	8f	yel bis & blk (1)	2.25	.40
368	A93	8f	blue & blk (2)	2.25	.40
369	A93	8f	brt grn & blk (3)	2.25	.40
			Nos. 367-369 (3)	6.75	1.20

Meteorological services in ancient and modern China.

"5" Encircling IUS Emblem — A94

1958, Sept. 4

370 A94 8f rose lilac 25.00 2.00
371 A94 22f dp blue grn 37.50 4.50

Intl. Union of Students, 5th Cong., Peking, 9/4-13.

Nos. 370-371 exist with incorrect inscription. Values; unused set, $175,000, used set, $125,000.

Telegraph Building, Peking A95

1958, Sept. 29

372 A95 4f greenish black 5.25 .75
373 A95 8f rose red 5.25 .75

Opening of Telegraph Building, Peking.

Exhibition Emblem and Exhortation A96

Designs: No. 375, Dragon over clouds signifying "aiming high." No. 376, Flying horses, signifying "great leap forward" in production.

1958, Oct. 1

374 A96 8f slate grn (1) 20.00 1.25
375 A96 8f rose car (2) 20.00 1.25
376 A96 8f red brown (3) 20.00 2.25
Nos. 374-376 (3) 60.00 4.75

National Exhibition of Industry and Communications, Peking.

Worker and Excavator A97

Design: 8f, Completed dam and pylon.

1958, Oct. 25

377 A97 4f dark brown 3.25 .50
378 A97 8f deep Prussian blue 5.25 .50

13 Ming Tombs Reservoir completion.

Sputnik 3 in Orbit — A98

Designs: 4f, Sputnik over armillary sphere. 10f, Trajectories of 3 Sputniks over earth.

1958, Oct. 30

379 A98 4f scarlet 6.00 .75
380 A98 8f dp violet bl 6.00 1.00
381 A98 10f dp green 8.00 2.50
Nos. 379-381 (3) 20.00 4.25

Anniversary of first earth satellite launched by the USSR.

Chinese and North Korean Soldiers A99

Designs: No. 383, Chinese soldier embracing Korean woman. No. 384, Chinese girl presenting flowers to returning soldier.

1958, Nov. 20

382 A99 8f brt purple (1) 7.00 1.00
383 A99 8f chestnut (2) 6.25 .60
384 A99 8f rose car (3) 6.25 .60
Nos. 382-384 (3) 19.50 2.20

Return of the Chinese Volunteers from Korea.

Forest and Mountains A100

Afforestation: No. 386, Mounted forest patrol. No. 387, Mechanized lumbering, horiz. No. 388, Tree-planting: "Turning the Country Green," horiz.

1958, Dec. 15

385 A100 8f dp blue grn (1) 4.00 .85
386 A100 8f slate grn (2) 4.00 .85
387 A100 8f dk purple (3) 4.00 .85
388 A100 8f indigo (4) 4.00 .85
Nos. 385-388 (4) 16.00 3.40

Peony — A101

Designs: 3f, Lotus. 5f, Chrysanthemums.

1958, Sept. 25 **Litho.**

389 A101 1½f lilac rose 4.25 .75
390 A101 3f blue grn 9.00 2.25
391 A101 5f dp orange 5.00 .45
Nos. 389-391 (3) 18.25 3.45

Atomic Reactor A102

1958, Dec. 30 **Engr.**

392 A102 8f shown 16.00 1.75
393 A102 20f Cyclotron 25.00 2.50

Inauguration of China's first atomic reactor and cyclotron, Peking.

Children Launching Model Planes — A103

8f, Gliders over trees. 10f, Parachutists descending. 20f, Small monoplanes in mid-air.

1958, Dec. 30

394 A103 4f carmine 2.00 .50
395 A103 8f dp slate grn 2.00 .50
396 A103 10f dk brown 3.00 .50
397 A103 20f Prus blue 4.00 .50
Nos. 394-397 (4) 11.00 2.00

Sports-aviation publicity.

Camel Carrying Load — A104

Designs: No. 399, Pomegranates. No. 400, Rooster. No. 401, Theatrical figure.

1959, Jan. 1

398 A104 8f vio & blk (1) 18.00 .90
399 A104 8f dp bl grn & blk (2) 18.00 .90
400 A104 8f red & blk (3) 18.00 .90
401 A104 8f dp bl & blk (4) 18.00 .90
Nos. 398-401 (4) 72.00 3.60

Paper cut-outs (folk art).

Red Flag, Mao and Workers — A105

Designs: 8f, Traditional and modern blast furnaces. 10f, Steel works and workers.

1959

402 A105 4f brt red 30.00 1.50
403 A105 8f lake 30.00 2.00
404 A105 10f deep red 35.00 2.25
Nos. 402-404 (3) 95.00 5.75

"Great Leap Forward" in steel production. Issue dates: 4f, 8f, Feb. 19; 10f, May 25.

Women Workers and Atomic Model — A106

Design: 22f, Chinese and Soviet women holding banners dated "3.8."

1959, Mar. 8

405 A106 8f emerald, *cr* 3.00 .50
406 A106 22f magenta, *cr* 4.00 .50

International Women's Day.

Natural History Museum A107

1959, Apr. 1

407 A107 4f greenish blue 3.00 .50
408 A107 8f olive brown 3.00 .50

Opening of Museum of Natural History, Peking.

Wheat — A108

Designs on Chinese Flag: No. 410, Rice. No. 411, Cotton bolls. No. 412, Soybeans, rapeseed and peanuts.

1959, Apr. 25

409 A108 8f red (1) 2.50 .50
410 A108 8f red (2) 2.50 .50
411 A108 8f red (3) 2.50 .50
412 A108 8f red (4) 2.50 .50
a. Block of 4, #409-412 50.00 6.00

Successful harvest, 1958.

A109

Designs: 4f, Marx, Lenin and workers. 8f, Black, yellow and white fists holding banner. 22f, Steel workers parading with banners dated "5.1."

1959, May 1

413 A109 4f ultra 6.00 1.50
414 A109 8f red 10.00 1.50
415 A109 22f emerald 20.00 2.25
Nos. 413-415 (3) 36.00 5.25

International Labor Day.

A110

8f, Peking airport. 10f, Plane loading on runway.

1959, June 20

416 A110 8f lilac & blk 25.00 2.75
417 A110 10f ol gray & blk 32.50 2.25

Opening of new Peking Airport.

Students with Marx-Lenin Banners A111

Design: 8f, Workers with banners of Mao.

1959, July 1 **Photo.** ***Perf. 11x11½***

418 A111 4f gray, red & dk brn 30.00 11.00
419 A111 8f bis, red & dk brn 55.00 7.50

40th anniv. of the May 4th students' uprising.

Frederick Joliot-Curie — A112

22f, Three races, dove and olive branch.

1959, July 25 **Engr.** ***Perf. 11½***

420 A112 8f violet brn 10.00 2.00
421 A112 22f dk violet 20.00 3.50

10th anniv. of the World Peace Movement.

Stamp Printing Plant, Peking A113

1959, Aug. 15 ***Perf. 11x11½***

422 A113 8f dp blue grn 15.00 2.00

Sino-Czechoslovak cooperation in stamp production.

Table Tennis — A114

1959, Aug. 30 **Litho.** ***Perf. 14***

423 A114 4f black & blue 8.50 .75
424 A114 8f black & red 6.50 .75

25th World Table Tennis Championships, Dortmund, German Democratic Republic.

Soviet Space Rocket — A115

1959, Sept. 10 Photo. *Perf. 11½*

425 A115 8f Prus bl, red & blk 22.00 3.00

Launching of first Russian space rocket, Jan. 2, 1959.

Backyard Steel Production — A116

Designs: No. 426, Sun rising over "industry and agriculture." No. 428, Farming. No. 429, Trade. No. 430, Education. No. 431, Militia. No. 432, Communal dining. No. 433, Nursery. No. 434, Care for the aged. No. 435, Health services. No. 436, Flutist; culture and sports. No. 437, Flower symbolizing unity of industry, agriculture, trade, education and armed forces.

Position-in-set number in ( ).

1959, Sept. 25 Engr.

426 A116 8f rose (1) 5.00 .75
427 A116 8f violet brn (2) 5.00 .75
428 A116 8f dp orange (3) 5.00 .75
429 A116 8f slate grn (4) 5.00 .75
430 A116 8f dp blue (5) 5.00 .75
431 A116 8f olive (6) 5.00 .75
432 A116 8f indigo (7) 5.00 .75
433 A116 8f lilac rose (8) 5.00 .75
434 A116 8f gray blk (9) 5.00 .75
435 A116 8f emerald (10) 5.00 .75
436 A116 8f dk violet (11) 5.00 .75
437 A116 8f red (12) 5.00 .75
Nos. 426-437 (12) 60.00 9.00

First anniversary of Peoples' Communes.

Mao and Gate of Heavenly Peace — A117

Designs: No. 439, Marx, Lenin and Kremlin. 22f, Dove over globe.

Perf. 11½ x 11

1959, Sept. 28 Photo.

With Gum

438 A117 8f lt brown & red 60.00 3.75
439 A117 8f dull blue & red 28.00 2.25
440 A117 22f blue grn & red 28.00 6.00
Nos. 438-440 (3) 116.00 12.00
Set, never hinged 170.00

National Emblem A118

1959, Oct. 1 Litho. *Perf. 14*

441 A118 4f pale grn, red & gold 10.00 2.00
442 A118 8f gray, red & gold 12.00 2.50
443 A118 10f lt blue, red & gold 20.00 4.00
444 A118 20f pale brn, red & gold 35.00 5.00
Nos. 441-444 (4) 77.00 13.50

Blast Furnaces — A119

No. 446, Large coal mine. No. 447, Planer, Wuhan heavy machinery plant. No. 448, Wuhan Yangtze River Bridge. No. 449, Combine harvester. No. 450, Hsinankiang hydroelectric station. No. 451, Spinning machine. No. 452, Kirin chemical fertilizer plant.

Engraved and Photogravure

1959, Oct. 1 *Perf. 11½ x 11*

With Gum

445 A119 8f brown & rose red (1) 4.50 1.40
446 A119 8f brown & gray (2) 4.50 1.40
447 A119 8f brown & yel brn (3) 4.50 1.40
448 A119 8f brown & stl bl (4) 4.50 1.40
449 A119 8f brown & org (5) 4.50 1.40
450 A119 8f brown & ol (6) 4.50 1.40
451 A119 8f brown & bl grn (7) 4.50 1.40
452 A119 8f brown & vio (8) 4.50 1.40
Nos. 445-452 (8) 36.00 11.20
Set, never hinged 62.50

Celebration at Gate of Heavenly Peace — A120

Designs: 10f, Workers and factory, vert. 20f, People rejoicing, vert.

1959, Oct. 1 Litho. *Perf. 14*

453 A120 8f cream & multi 10.00 3.00
454 A120 10f cream & multi 18.00 3.50
455 A120 20f cream & multi 22.50 5.50
Nos. 453-455 (3) 50.50 12.00

Mao Proclaiming Republic — A121

1959, Oct. 1 Engr.

456 A121 20f deep carmine 275.00 90.00

Nos. 438-456 commemorate 10th anniversary of the Proclamation of the People's Republic of China.

A122

Designs: No. 457, Pioneers' emblem. No. 458, Pioneer Bugler. No. 459, Schoolgirl. No. 460, Girl using rain gauge. No. 461, Boy planting tree. No. 462, Girl figure skater.

1959, Nov. 10 Photo. *Perf. 11½*

457 A122 4f red yel & blk (1) 12.00 .95
458 A122 4f Prus bl & red (2) 12.00 .95
459 A122 8f brn & red (3) 12.00 .95
460 A122 8f dk bl & red (4) 12.00 .95
461 A122 8f red & grn (5) 12.00 .95
462 A122 8f mag & red (6) 12.00 .95
Nos. 457-462 (6) 72.00 5.70

10th anniversary of the Young Pioneers. Black inscription on No. 457 engraved.

A123

4f, Exhibition emblem, communications symbols. 8f, Exhibition emblem & chimneys.

1959, Dec. 1 Engr.

463 A123 4f dark blue 3.75 .50
464 A123 8f red 3.75 .50

Exhibition of Industry and Communications, Peking.

Palace of Nationalities A124

Engraved, Frame Lithographed

1959, Dec. 10 *Perf. 14*

465 A124 4f red & blk 13.00 1.00
466 A124 8f brt grn & blk 17.50 1.50

Inauguration of the Cultural Palace of Nationalities, Peking.

Athletes' Monument and Track — A125

Sports: No. 468, Parachuting. No. 469, Marksmanship. No. 470, Diving. No. 471, Table tennis. No. 472, Weight lifting. No. 473, High jump. No. 474, Rowing. No. 475, Track. No. 476, Basketball. No. 477, Traditional Chinese fencing. No. 478, Motorcycling. No. 479, Gymnastics. No. 480, Bicycling. No. 481, Horsemanship. No. 482, Soccer.

1959, Dec. 28 Litho.

467 A125 8f bis, blk & gray (1) 7.25 1.00
468 A125 8f dl bl, blk & gray (2) 7.25 1.00
469 A125 8f red brn & blk (3) 7.25 1.00
470 A125 8f grn, blk & brn (4) 7.25 1.00
471 A125 8f brt grn, blk, brn & gray (5) 7.25 1.00
472 A125 8f gray, blk & brn (6) 7.25 1.00
473 A125 8f dl bl, blk & brn (7) 7.25 1.00
474 A125 8f Prus grn, blk & brn (8) 7.25 1.00
475 A125 8f org, blk & brn (9) 7.25 1.00
476 A125 8f dl vio, blk & brn (10) 7.25 1.00
477 A125 8f lt ol, blk & brn (11) 7.25 1.00
478 A125 8f bl, blk & gray (12) 7.25 1.00
479 A125 8f gray bl, blk, grn, & bl (13) 7.25 1.00
480 A125 8f gray, blk, brn, & vio (14) 7.25 1.00
481 A125 8f red org, blk, brn, & gray (15) 7.25 1.00
482 A125 8f lt gray, blk, brn, & red (16) 7.25 1.00
Nos. 467-482 (16) 116.00 16.00

First National Sports Meeting, Peking.

Wheat and Main Pavilion A126

Designs (Pavilion and): 8f, Meteorological symbols. 10f, Domestic animals. 20f, Fish.

1960, Jan. 20 Engr. & Litho.

Cream Background

483 A126 4f black & org 2.50 .50
484 A126 8f black & dull bl 2.50 .50
485 A126 10f black & org brn 2.50 .50
486 A126 20f black & grnsh bl 2.50 .50
Nos. 483-486 (4) 10.00 2.00

Opening of the National Agricultural Exhibition Halls, Peking.

With Gum

From No. 487 onward all stamps were issued with gum except as noted.

Catalogue values for unused stamps in this section, from this point to the end of the section, are for Never Hinged items.

Conference Hall, Tsunyi A127

Designs: 8f, Mao addressing conference. 10f, Crossing Chinsha River.

Engraved (4f, 10f); Photogravure (8f)

1960, Jan. 25 *Perf. 11x11½*

487 A127 4f violet & blue 60.00 10.00
488 A127 8f red & multi 80.00 6.00
489 A127 10f slate green 130.00 12.00
Nos. 487-489 (3) 270.00 28.00

25th anniversary of the Communist Party Conference at Tsunyi.

Clara Zetkin (1857-1933) A128

8f, Mother, child and dove. 10f, Woman tractor driver. 22f, Women of three races.

1960, Mar. 8 Photo. *Perf. 11½x11*

490 A128 4f black & multi 7.00 .50
491 A128 8f black & multi 11.00 .75
492 A128 10f black & multi 12.00 1.00
493 A128 22f black & multi 15.00 2.00
Nos. 490-493 (4) 45.00 4.25

50th anniv. of International Women's Day.

Chinese and Russian Workers — A129

Designs: 8f, Chinese and Russian flags. 10f, Chinese and Russian soldiers.

1960, Mar. 10

494 A129 4f dk brown 30.00 5.00
495 A129 8f red, yel & blk 40.00 2.00
496 A129 10f dp blue 50.00 8.00
Nos. 494-496 (3) 120.00 15.00

10th anniv. of Sino-Soviet Treaty of Friendship. Black inscription engraved on No. 495.

Flags of Hungary and China A130

Design: 8f, Parliament Building, Budapest.

1960, Apr. 4 ***Perf. 11 x 11½***

497 A130 8f yel, blk, red & grn 55.00 7.25
498 A130 8f blue, red & blk 60.00 7.25

15th anniv. of the liberation of Hungary.

Lenin Speaking — A131

Designs: 8f, Portrait of Lenin. 20f, Lenin talking with Smolny Palace guard.

Engraved (4f, 20f); Engraved and Photogravure (8f)

1960, Apr. 22 ***Perf. 11½ x 11***

499 A131 4f violet brn 28.00 1.75
500 A131 8f org red & blk 35.00 3.00
501 A131 20f dk brown 45.00 4.00
Nos. 499-501 (3) 108.00 8.75

90th anniversary of the birth of Lenin.

Lunik 2, Moon and Russian Arms — A132

Design: 10f, Lunik 3 over moon.

1960, Apr. 30 **Engr.** ***Perf. 11½***

502 A132 8f red 11.00 1.75
503 A132 10f green 15.00 1.75

Russian space flights.

Pioneers and Flags of Czechoslovakia and China — A133

View of Prague with Charles Bridge A134

Perf. 11½x11; 11x11½

1960, May 9 **Photo.**

504 A133 8f yellow & multi 40.00 6.00
505 A134 8f deep green 40.00 6.00

Liberation of Czechoslovakia, 15th anniv.

Nostril Bouquet A135

Various goldfish: No. 507, Black-back dragon eye (2). No. 508, Bubble eye (3). No. 509, Red tiger head (4). No. 510, Pearl scale (5). No. 511, Blue dragon eye (6). No. 512, Skyward eye (7). No. 513, Red cap (8). No. 514, Purple cap (9). No. 515, Red head (10). No. 516, Red and white dragon eye (11). No. 517, Red dragon eye (12).

1960, June 1 ***Perf. 11x11½***

506 A135 4f shown (1) 47.50 5.50
507 A135 4f multi 47.50 5.50
508 A135 4f multi 47.50 5.50
509 A135 4f multi 47.50 5.50
510 A135 8f multi 125.00 5.50
511 A135 8f multi 80.00 5.50
512 A135 8f multi 80.00 5.50
513 A135 8f multi 30.00 8.00
514 A135 8f multi 30.00 8.00
515 A135 8f multi 30.00 8.00
516 A135 8f multi 90.00 8.00
517 A135 8f multi 50.00 15.00
Nos. 506-517 (12) 705.00 85.50

Unused values for Nos. 506-517 are for examples with untoned gum.

Sow with Litter A136

No. 519, Pig being inoculated. No. 520, Pigs. No. 521, Pig and mechanized feeding. No. 522, Pig and bales.

1960, June 15

518 A136 8f red & blk (1) 57.50 9.00
519 A136 8f dp grn & blk (2) 57.50 9.00
520 A136 8f lil rose & blk (3) 57.50 9.00
521 A136 8f lt yel grn & blk (4) 57.50 9.00
522 A136 8f org & blk (5) 57.50 11.00
Nos. 518-522 (5) 287.50 47.00

Flag Inscribed "Serving the Workers" — A137

Design: 8f, Inscribed stone seal.

1960, July 30 **Photo.** ***Perf. 11½x11***

523 A137 4f lt grn, red, pink & brn 47.50 5.00

Photogravure & Engraved

524 A137 8f pale bl, red & bis 60.00 7.00

3rd Natl. Cong. for Literature and Arts, Peking.

Flowers, Flags of North Korea and China — A138

Design: 8f, Flying horse of Korea.

1960, Aug. 15 **Photo.**

525 A138 8f red & multi 50.00 9.00
526 A138 8f ultra, red & indigo 65.00 14.00

15th anniversary of the liberation of Korea.

Railroad Station, Peking — A139

Design: 10f, Train arriving at station.

1960, Aug. 30 ***Perf. 11½***

527 A139 8f blue, cream & brn 47.50 15.00
528 A139 10f bluish grn, cr & ind 67.50 17.00

Opening of new Peking Railroad Station.

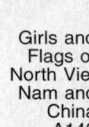

Girls and Flags of North Viet Nam and China A140

Lake of the Returning Sword, Hanoi — A141

1960, Sept. 2 ***Perf. 11x11½, 11½x11***

529 A140 8f red & multi 18.00 3.00
530 A141 8f red, gray grn & gray 18.00 3.00

15th anniversary of the Democratic Republic of North Viet Nam.

Worker and Fresh-air Installation — A142

Designs: No. 532, Exterminator. No. 533, Window cleaning. No. 534, Medical examination of child. No. 535, Physical exercise.

1960, Sept. 10 ***Perf. 11½***

531 A142 8f black & orange (1) 11.50 1.00
532 A142 8f indigo & slate (2) 11.50 1.00
533 A142 8f brown & blue (3) 11.50 1.00
534 A142 8f maroon & ocher (4) 11.50 1.00
535 A142 8f indigo & brt grn (5) 11.50 1.00
Nos. 531-535 (5) 57.50 5.00

National health campaign.

Great Hall of the People — A143

Design: 10f, Inside view.

1960, Oct. 1

536 A143 8f yellow & multi 47.50 15.00
537 A143 10f brown & multi 67.50 17.00

Completion of the Great Hall of the People, Peking.

Dr. Norman Bethune — A144

No. 539, Dr. Bethune operating on a soldier.

Photo. (No. 538); Engr. (No. 539)

1960, Nov. 20 ***Perf. 11½x11***

538 A144 8f red & multi 24.00 3.00
539 A144 8f sepia 24.00 2.00

Dr. Norman Bethune (1890-1939), Canadian surgeon with 8th Route Army.

Engels Addressing Congress at The Hague — A145

1960, Nov. 28 **Engr.**

540 A145 8f shown 47.50 2.75

Photo.

541 A145 10f Portrait of Engels 52.50 8.00

140th anniversary of the birth of Friedrich Engels (1820-1895), German Socialist.

"Hwang Shi Ba" — A146

1960-61 **Photo.**

Various Chrysanthemums in Natural Colors

542 A146 4f bl gray (1) 20.00 3.50
543 A146 4f pink (2) 20.00 3.50
544 A146 8f dk gray (3) 22.50 3.50
545 A146 8f dp blue (4) 22.50 3.50
546 A146 8f green (5) 22.50 3.50
547 A146 8f magenta (6) 22.50 3.50
548 A146 8f olive (7) 22.50 3.50
549 A146 8f grnsh bl (8) 22.50 3.50
550 A146 10f gray (9) 27.50 5.00
551 A146 10f choc (10) 27.50 5.00
552 A146 20f dp blue (11) 45.00 6.00
553 A146 20f brt red (12) 45.00 6.00
554 A146 22f olive bis (13) 100.00 12.00
555 A146 22f carmine (14) 100.00 12.00
556 A146 30f grnsh gray (15) 100.00 14.00
557 A146 30f brt pink (16) 67.50 9.00
558 A146 35f dp green (17) 67.50 9.00
559 A146 52f brt lilac rose (18) 67.50 17.50
Nos. 542-559 (18) 822.50 123.50

Issued: Nos. 548-550, 557-559, 12/10/60; Nos. 545-547, 554-556, 1/18/61; Nos. 542-544, 2/24/61.

Freighter — A147

1960, Dec. 15 ***Perf. 11½***

Without Gum

560 A147 8f deep blue 12.50 2.00

1st 10,000-ton Chinese-built freighter, launching.

Pantheon, Paris — A148

Design: 8f, Proclamation of the Commune.

Engraved and Photogravure

1961, Mar. 18 ***Perf. 11½x11***

561 A148 8f gray blk & red 40.00 6.00
562 A148 8f brown & red 40.00 7.00

90th anniversary of the Paris Commune.

Championship Symbol and Jasmine — A149

Designs: 10f, Table tennis racket and ball; Temple of Heaven. 20f, Table tennis match. 22f, Peking workers' gymnasium.

1961, Apr. 5 Photo. *Perf. 11*

563	A149 8f multicolored	7.50	.75
564	A149 10f multicolored	8.50	1.00
565	A149 20f multicolored	9.50	1.50
566	A149 22f multicolored	11.00	2.00
a.	Souv. sheet, #563-566	*1,000.*	*800.00*
	Nos. 563-566 (4)	36.50	5.25

26th World Table Tennis Championships, Peking.

Jeme Tien-yow — A150

Design: 10f, Train and tunnel, Peking-Changchow Railroad.

1961, June 20 *Perf. 11½x11*

567	A150 8f ol grn & blk	7.50	1.00
568	A150 10f org brn & brn	24.00	4.00

Centenary of the birth of Jeme Tien-yow, railroad construction engineer.

Congress Building, Shanghai — A151

Designs: 8f, August 1st Building, Nanchang. 10f, Provisional Central Government Office, Juikin. 20f, Pagoda Hill, Yenan. 30f, Gate of Heavenly Peace, Peking.

1961, July 1 *Perf. 11½*

569	A151 4f gold, red & cl	50.00	5.00
570	A151 8f gold, red & bl grn	50.00	3.00
571	A151 10f gold, red & yel brn	60.00	5.00
572	A151 20f gold, red & ultra	90.00	7.00
573	A151 30f gold, red & org red	100.00	17.50
	Nos. 569-573 (5)	350.00	37.50

40th anniv. of the Chinese Communist Party.

August 1 Building, Nanchang — A152

3f, 4f, 5f, Trees & Sha Cho Pa Building, Juikin. 8f, 10f, 20f, Pagoda Hill, Yenan. 22f, 30f, 50f, Gate of Heavenly Peace, Peking.

1961-62 Engr. *Perf. 11*

Without Gum

Size: 24x16mm

574	A152 1f vio blue	15.00	.50
575	A152 1½f maroon	35.00	2.50
576	A152 2f indigo	17.50	1.00
577	A152 3f dull vio	52.50	3.00
578	A152 4f green	4.00	.65
579	A152 5f gray	4.00	.40
580	A152 8f sepia	4.00	.35
581	A152 10f brt lil rose	10.00	.35
582	A152 20f grnsh bl	3.00	.35
583	A152 22f brown	2.00	.35
584	A152 30f blue	3.00	.35
585	A152 50f vermilion	3.00	.35
	Nos. 574-585 (12)	153.00	10.15

Issued: 1f, 1½f, 5f, 7/20/62; others 7/20/61.
See Nos. 647-654, 1059-1064.

Flowers, Flags of Mongolia and China A153

Design: 10f, Parliament, Ulan Bator, and statue of Sukhe Bator.

1961, July 11 Photo. *Perf. 11x11½*

586	A153 8f crim, ultra & yel	120.00	15.00
587	A153 10f orange, blk & yel	160.00	30.00

40th anniv. of the Mongolian People's Republic.

Military Museum — A154

Photo. & Engr.

1961, Aug. 1 *Perf. 11½*

588	A154 8f gray bl, brn & grn	85.00	3.00
a.	Inscribed series "(229)" (error)	150.00	11.00
589	A154 10f gray, blk & grn	90.00	5.00

Opening of the People's Revolutionary Military Museum.

Uprising at Wuchang A155

Sun Yat-sen — A156

Perf. 11x11½, 11½x11

1961, Oct. 10 Photo.

590	A155 8f gray & blk	55.00	4.50
591	A156 10f tan & black	75.00	5.00

50th anniversary of the 1911 Revolution.

Donkey — A157

Designs: 8f, 10f, 20f, 22f, Horses; 30f, 50f, Camels. Ceramic statuettes from Tang Dynasty (618-906) graves.

1961, Nov. 10 *Perf. 11½x11*

Statuettes in Original Colors

592	A157 4f dull blue	20.00	2.75
593	A157 8f gray green	20.00	2.75
594	A157 8f dp purple	20.00	2.75
595	A157 10f dp blue	20.00	2.75
596	A157 20f olive	20.00	2.75
597	A157 22f blue grn	30.00	4.00
598	A157 30f red brown	50.00	6.00
599	A157 50f slate	50.00	6.00
	Nos. 592-599 (8)	230.00	29.75

Rejoicing Tibetans — A158

Designs: 8f, Woman sower. 10f, Celebration of bumper crop. 20f, People's representatives. 30f, Tibetan children.

1961, Nov. 25

600	A158 4f brn & ocher	40.00	3.25
601	A158 8f brn & lt bl grn	32.50	3.25
602	A158 10f brn & yel	50.00	3.25
603	A158 20f brn & rose	100.00	6.50
604	A158 30f brn & bluish gray	160.00	10.00
	Nos. 600-604 (5)	382.50	26.25

Rebirth of the Tibetan people.

Lu Hsun — A159

1962, Feb. 26

605	A159 8f red brown & blk	5.75	1.50

80th anniv. of the birth of Lu Hsun, writer.

An Chi Bridge, Chao Hsien — A160

Bridges of Ancient China: 8f, Pao Tai, Soochow. 10f, Chu Pu, Kwan Hsien. 20f, Chen Yang, San Kiang.

1962, May 15 *Perf. 11*

606	A160 4f dk gray blue	5.00	.80
607	A160 8f dp green	5.00	.80
608	A160 10f brown	20.00	2.50
609	A160 20f grnsh blue	20.00	2.50
	Nos. 606-609 (4)	50.00	6.60

Tu Fu — A161

4f, Tu Fu memorial pavilion, Chengtu.

1962, May 25 *Perf. 11½x11*

610	A161 4f ol bis & blk	65.00	2.25
611	A161 8f grnsh bl & blk	75.00	4.50

Poet Tu Fu, 1,250th anniversary of birth.

Cranes and Bamboo — A162

10f, Two cranes in flight. 20f, Crane on rock.

1962, June 10

612	A162 8f tan & multi	22.00	3.00
613	A162 10f blue & multi	40.00	4.00
614	A162 20f bister & multi	55.00	6.00
	Nos. 612-614 (3)	117.00	13.00

"The Sacred Crane," from paintings by Chen Chi-fo.

Cuban Soldier and Flag A163

Designs: 10f, Sugar cane worker. 22f, Militiaman and woman.

1962, July 10 *Perf. 11x11½*

615	A163 8f car, rose & blk	40.00	6.00
616	A163 10f green & blk	70.00	10.00
617	A163 22f ultra & blk	160.00	40.00
	Nos. 615-617 (3)	270.00	56.00

Support of Cuba.

Torch and Map of Algeria — A164

Design: 22f, Algerian soldiers and flag.

1962, July 10 *Perf. 11½x11*

618	A164 8f dp brown & red org	3.00	1.25
619	A164 22f ocher & dp brn	8.75	1.75

Support of Algeria.

Mei Lan-fang — A165

Designs (Mei Lan-fang in Women's Roles): No. 621, Beating drum. No. 622, With fan. 10f, Lady Yu with swords. 20f, With bag. 22f, Heavenly Maiden, horiz. 30f, With spinning wheel, horiz. 50f, Kneeling, horiz. $3, Scene from opera "Drunken Beauty."

1962 *Perf. 11½x11, 11x11½*

620	A165 4f tan & multi	225.00	45.00
621	A165 8f tan & multi	150.00	15.00
622	A165 8f gray & multi	150.00	15.00
623	A165 10f gray & multi	225.00	15.00
624	A165 20f lt grn & multi	225.00	30.00
625	A165 22f cream & multi	325.00	50.00
626	A165 30f lt blue & multi	325.00	60.00
627	A165 50f buff & multi	325.00	60.00
	Nos. 620-627 (8)	1,950.	290.00

Souvenir Sheet

Perf. 11

628	A165 $3 brown & multi	*18,000.*	*6,500.*

Stage art of Mei Lan-fang, actor.
Issued: 4f, 8f, 10f, 8/8; $3, 9/15; others 9/1.
Nos. 620-627 exist imperf. Value, set unused $7,000, used $2,000.
No. 628 contains one 48x58mm stamp and almost always has some faults. Values above are for fault-free examples. Value for No. 628 with small faults, unused $9,000. Excellent forgeries exist.

Flower Drum Dance, Han — A166

Folk Dances: 8f, Ordos, Mongolia. 10f, Catching shrimp, Chuang. 20f, Friend, Yi. 30f, Fiddle dance, Tibet. 50f, Tambourine dance, Uighur.
Cumulative numbers 246-251 at lower right.

1962, Oct. 15 Litho. *Perf. 12½*
Without Gum

629	A166	4f cream & multi	3.00	.60
630	A166	8f cream & multi	3.00	.60
631	A166	10f cream & multi	3.00	.60
632	A166	20f cream & multi	4.00	1.00
633	A166	30f cream & multi	6.00	1.50
634	A166	50f cream & multi	8.00	2.00
		Nos. 629-634 (6)	27.00	6.30

See Nos. 696-707.

Soldiers Storming Winter Palace — A167

Design: 8f, Lenin leading soldiers, vert.

1962, Nov. 7 Photo. *Perf. 11½*

635	A167	8f black & red	80.00	6.00
636	A167	20f slate grn & red	165.00	13.00

45th anniversary of the Russian Revolution.

Monument and Map of Albania — A168

Design: 10f, Albanian flag and Girl Pioneer.

1962, Nov. 28 *Perf. 11½x11*

637	A168	8f Prus blue & sepia	4.00	1.25
638	A168	10f red, yel, & blk	5.50	1.25

50th anniversary of Albanian independence.

Tsai Lun, Inventor of Papermaking A169

Designs: No. 640, Paper making. No. 641, Sun Szu-miao, physician. No. 642, Writing medical treatise. No. 643, Shen Ko, geologist. No. 644, Making field notes. No. 645, Kuo Shou-chin, astronomer. No. 646, Astronomical instrument.
Cumulative numbers 297-304 at lower right.

1962, Dec. 1 *Perf. 11½x11*

639	A169	4f multicolored	10.00	1.00
640	A169	4f multicolored	10.00	1.00
641	A169	8f multicolored	12.00	1.25
642	A169	8f multicolored	12.00	1.25
643	A169	10f multicolored	12.00	4.00
644	A169	10f multicolored	12.00	4.00
645	A169	20f multicolored	22.50	7.50
646	A169	20f multicolored	22.50	7.50
		Nos. 639-646 (8)	113.00	27.50

Scientists of ancient China.

No. 639 exists with an extra character in the inscription. Value, unused *$15,000*, used *$5,000*.

Building Type of 1961

Designs: 1f, 2f, Building, Nanchang. 3f, 4f, Trees and Sha Cho Pa Building. 8f, 10f, 20f, Pagoda Hill, Yenan. 30f, Gate of Heavenly Peace, Peking.

1962, Jan. Litho. *Rough Perf. 12½*
Size: 21x16mm
Without Gum

647	A152	1f ultra	.80	.25
648	A152	2f greenish gray	.80	.25
649	A152	3f violet gray	.80	.25
650	A152	4f green	.80	.25
651	A152	8f dk olive, perf. 14	1.75	.25
b.		Perf. 11x11½	9.00	
652	A152	10f brt rose lilac	3.75	.30
653	A152	20f slate blue	3.75	.55
654	A152	30f dull blue	4.25	.65
		Nos. 647-654 (8)	16.70	2.75

Tank Monument, Havana A170

Crowd in Peking — A171

Designs: No. 656, Cuban revolutionaries. No. 658, Crowd in Havana. No. 659, Cuban soldier. No. 660, Castro and Cuban flag.

Perf. 11½, 11x11½
1963, Jan. 1 Photo.

655	A170	4f red & blk brn	60.00	2.50
656	A170	4f green & blk	60.00	2.50
657	A171	8f dull red & brn	100.00	6.00
658	A171	8f dull red & brn	120.00	14.00
659	A170	10f ocher & blk	110.00	16.00
660	A170	10f red, blue & blk	130.00	*60.00*
		Nos. 655-660 (6)	580.00	*101.00*

4th anniversary of the Cuban revolution.

Green Dragontail — A172

No. 661, Tibetan clouded yellow (1). No. 662, Tritailed glory (2). No. 663, Neumogeni jungle queen (3). No. 664, Washan swordtail (4). No. 665, Striped ringlet (5). No. 667, Dilunulated peacock (7). No. 668, Yamfly (8). No. 669, Golden kaiser-i-hind (9). No. 670, Mushaell hairstreak (10). No. 671, Yellow orange-tip (11). No. 672, Great jay (12). No. 673, Striped punch (13). No. 674, Hainan violet-beak (14). No. 675, Omeiskipper (15). No. 676, Philippines birdwing (16). No. 677, Richtofenis red apollo (17). No. 678, Blue-banded king crow (18). No. 679, Solskyi copper (19). No. 680, Yunnan clipper (20).

1963 Without Gum *Perf. 11*

661	A172	4f multi	13.00	2.00
662	A172	4f multi	13.00	2.00
663	A172	4f multi	13.00	2.00
664	A172	4f multi	13.00	2.00
665	A172	4f multi	13.00	2.00
666	A172	8f shown (6)	15.00	2.00
667	A172	8f multi	15.00	2.00
668	A172	8f multi	15.00	2.00
669	A172	8f multi	15.00	2.00
670	A172	8f multi	15.00	2.00
671	A172	10f multi	22.50	3.25
672	A172	10f multi	22.50	3.25
673	A172	10f multi	22.50	3.25
674	A172	10f multi	22.50	*3.25*
675	A172	10f multi	22.50	3.25
676	A172	20f multi	27.50	6.00
677	A172	20f multi	27.50	6.00
678	A172	22f multi	27.50	6.00
679	A172	30f multi	35.00	12.00
680	A172	50f multi	35.00	12.00
		Nos. 661-680 (20)	405.00	78.25

Issued: Nos. 666-675, July 15; others Apr. 5.

Karl Marx — A173

Designs: No. 682, "Workers of the World, Unite" on cover of first edition of Communist Manifesto. No. 683, Marx and Engels.

1963, May 5 *Perf. 11½*
Without Gum

681	A173	8f black, gold & sal (1)	27.50	4.00
682	A173	8f gold & red (2)	27.50	4.00
683	A173	8f gold & choc (3)	27.50	4.00
		Nos. 681-683 (3)	82.50	12.00

145th anniversary of birth of Karl Marx (1818-1883), German political philosopher.

Child with Top — A174

Child: No. 685, eating berries. No. 686, as traffic policeman. No. 687, with windmill. No. 688, listening to caged cricket. No. 689, with sword. No. 690, embroidering. No. 691, with umbrella. No. 692, playing with sand. No. 693, playing table tennis. No. 694, learning to add. No. 695, with kite.

1963, June 1 Litho. *Perf. 12½*
Without Gum
Multicolored Designs

684	A174	4f grnsh gray (1)	5.50	.65
685	A174	4f tan (2)	5.50	.65
686	A174	8f gray (3)	5.50	.65
687	A174	8f blue (4)	5.50	.65
688	A174	8f tan (5)	5.50	.65
689	A174	8f dp gray (6)	5.50	.65
690	A174	8f citron (7)	5.50	1.00
691	A174	8f gray (8)	5.50	1.00
692	A174	10f green (9)	8.00	2.00
693	A174	10f violet (10)	8.00	2.00
694	A174	20f bister (11)	15.00	3.50
695	A174	20f green (12)	15.00	3.50
		Nos. 684-695 (12)	90.00	16.90

Children's Day. Value, imperf set unused $300, used $150.

Dance Type of 1962

Folk Dances: 4f, Weavers' dance, Puyi. 8f, Kazakh. 10f, Olunchun. 20f, Labor dance, Kaochan. 30f, Reed pipe dance, Miao. 50f, Fan dance, Korea.
Cumulative numbers 261-266 at lower right.

1963, June 15 *Perf. 12½*
Without Gum

696	A166	4f cream & multi	3.00	.40
697	A166	8f cream & multi	3.00	.50
698	A166	10f cream & multi	4.00	.60
699	A166	20f cream & multi	5.00	1.75
700	A166	30f cream & multi	5.00	1.75
701	A166	50f cream & multi	8.00	3.25
		Nos. 696-701 (6)	28.00	8.25

1963, June 30 Without Gum

Folk Dances: 4f, "Wedding Ceremony," Yu. 8f, "Encircling Mountain Forest," Pai. 10f, Long drum dance, Yao. 20f, Third day of the third month dance, Li. 30f, Knife dance, Kawa. 50f, Peacock dance, Thai.

Cumulative numbers 279-284 at lower right.

702	A166	4f cream & multi	3.00	.40
703	A166	8f cream & multi	3.00	.50
704	A166	10f cream & multi	3.00	.60
705	A166	20f cream & multi	6.00	1.25
706	A166	30f cream & multi	6.00	1.25
707	A166	50f cream & multi	6.00	1.25
		Nos. 702-707 (6)	27.00	5.25

Giant Panda Eating Apples — A175

Designs: No. 709, Giant panda eating bamboo shoots. 10f, Two pandas, horiz.

1963, Aug. 5 Photo. *Perf. 11½x11*
Size: 28x38mm

708	A175	8f pale blue & blk	35.00	2.50
709	A175	8f pale blue & blk	55.00	7.50

Size: 50x29mm
Perf. 11½

710	A175	10f olive & blk	37.50	2.50
		Nos. 708-710 (3)	127.50	12.50

Value, imperf set unused $300, used $130.

Table Tennis Player — A176

No. 712, Trophies won by Chinese team.

1963, Sept. 10 Engr. *Perf. 11½*

711	A176	8f dk olive grn	30.00	2.50
712	A176	8f brown	30.00	2.50

27th World Table Tennis Championships.

Snub-nosed Langur — A177

Designs: 10f, Two monkeys playing. 22f, Two monkeys grooming.

1963, Sept. 23 Photo. *Perf. 11½x11*

713	A177	8f gray & multi	18.00	1.75
714	A177	10f gray & multi	18.00	1.75
715	A177	22f gray & multi	32.50	7.25
		Nos. 713-715 (3)	68.50	10.75

Value, imperf set unused $300, used $100.

Jade-green Screen Mountain — A178

Hwang Shan Landscapes (Yellow Mountains), Anhwei Province: No. 717, "Guests Welcoming Pines" (2). No. 718, Pines and

Rock Behind the Sea (3). No. 719, Terrace of Keeping Cool (4). No. 720, Mount of Heavenly Capital (5). No. 721, Mount of Scissors (6). No. 722, Forest of Ten Thousand Pines (7). No. 723, "Brush Blooming in Dream" (8). No. 724, Mount of Lotus Flower (9). No. 725, Cumulus Cloud over West Sea (10). No. 726, Old Pines of Hwang Shan (11). No. 727, "Watching the Clouds over West Sea" (12). No. 728, Mount of Stalagmites (13). No. 729, "Stone Monkey Watching the Sea" (14). No. 730, Forest of Lions (15). No. 731, Three Fairy Tales of Pen Lai (16).

Nos. 724-731 horiz.

Engraved and Photogravure

1963, Oct. 15 *Perf. 11½*

716	A178	4f shown (1)	37.50	5.50
717	A178	4f multi	37.50	5.50
718	A178	4f multi	37.50	5.50
719	A178	4f multi	37.50	5.50
720	A178	8f multi	30.00	5.00
721	A178	8f multi	30.00	5.00
722	A178	8f multi	30.00	5.00
723	A178	8f multi	30.00	5.00
724	A178	10f multi	60.00	9.00
725	A178	10f multi	60.00	9.00
726	A178	10f multi	60.00	9.00
727	A178	10f multi	60.00	9.00
728	A178	20f multi	80.00	12.00
729	A178	22f multi	80.00	12.00
730	A178	30f multi	150.00	37.50
731	A178	50f multi	150.00	50.00
		Nos. 716-731 (16)	970.00	189.50

Soccer Player — A179

Athletes and Banners — A180

No. 733, Discus, women's. No. 734, Diving, men's. No. 735, Gymnastics, women's.

Engraved and Photogravure

1963, Nov. 17 *Perf. 11*

732	A179	8f gray, red & blk (1)	20.00	1.75
733	A179	8f gray, ultra & blk (2)	20.00	1.75
734	A179	8f lt grn, brn & blk (4)	20.00	1.75
735	A179	8f gray, lil rose & blk (5)	20.00	1.75

Photo.

Perf. 11½

736	A180	10f red & multi (3)	65.00	5.50
		Nos. 732-736 (5)	145.00	12.50

Games of the Newly Emerging Forces, Djakarta.

Clay Rooster and Goat — A181

Chinese Folk Toys: No. 738, Cloth camel. No. 739, Cloth tigers. No. 740, Clay ox and rider. No. 741, Cloth rabbit, wooden doll, clay roosters. No. 742, Straw rooster. No. 743, Cloth donkey and bird. No. 744, Clay lion. No. 745, Cloth tiger and tumbler doll.

1963, Dec. 10 Litho. *Perf. 11½*

Toys Multicolored; Without Gum

737	A181	4f bister (1)	2.00	.80
738	A181	4f gray (4)	2.00	.80
739	A181	4f lt blue (7)	2.00	.80
740	A181	8f bister (2)	2.00	.80
741	A181	8f gray (5)	2.00	.80
742	A181	8f lt blue (8)	2.00	.80
743	A181	10f bister (3)	4.00	.80
744	A181	10f gray (6)	4.00	.80
745	A181	10f lt blue (9)	4.00	.80
		Nos. 737-745 (9)	24.00	7.20

Armed Vietnamese Family — A182

Liberation of South Viet Nam: No. 747, Militia with Vietnamese flag.

1963, Dec. 20 Photo. *Perf. 11½x11*

746	A182	8f tan, blk & red	9.00	1.50
747	A182	8f red & multi	9.00	1.50

Flags of Cuba and China — A183

Design: No. 749, Boy waving Cuban flag.

1964, Jan. 1

748	A183	8f red, yel, bl & ind	70.00	7.00
749	A183	8f multicolored	70.00	7.00

5th anniversary of the liberation of Cuba.

Woman Driving Tractor — A184

Woman of the People's Commune: No. 751, harvesting. No. 752, pickling cotton. No. 753, picking fruit. No. 754, reading book. No. 755, on guard duty.

1964, Mar. 8

750	A184	8f ol, pink & brn (1)	5.00	1.00
751	A184	8f brn yel & org (2)	5.00	1.00
752	A184	8f gray & multi (3)	5.00	1.00
753	A184	8f black, org & bl (4)	5.00	1.00
754	A184	8f green & multi (5)	5.00	2.00
755	A184	8f lilac & multi (6)	5.00	2.00
		Nos. 750-755 (6)	30.00	8.00

Chinese and African Men A185

Design: No. 757, African drummer.

1964, Apr. 12 Photo. *Perf. 11*

756	A185	8f red & multi	4.75	.90
757	A185	8f black & dk brn	4.75	.90

African Freedom Day.

Marx, Engels, Lenin and Stalin — A186

Design: No. 759, Banners and workers.

1964, May 1 *Perf. 11½*

758	A186	8f gold, red & blk	*55.00*	*7.50*
759	A186	8f gold, red & blk	*55.00*	*7.50*

Labor Day.

Orchard, Yenan A187

Yenan, Shrine of the Chinese Revolution: No. 761, Central Auditorium, Yang Chia Ling. No. 762, Mao's office and residence. No. 763, Auditorium, Wang Chia Ping. No. 764, Border Region Assembly Hall. No. 765, Pagoda Hill and Bridge.

1964, July 1 Photo. *Perf. 11x11½*

760	A187	8f multicolored (1)	12.00	2.00
761	A187	8f multicolored (2)	12.00	2.00
762	A187	8f multicolored (3)	12.00	2.00
763	A187	8f multicolored (4)	12.00	2.00
764	A187	8f multicolored (5)	12.00	2.00
765	A187	52f multicolored (6)	90.00	20.00
		Nos. 760-765 (6)	150.00	30.00

Map and Flag of Viet Nam — A188

1964, July 20 *Perf. 11½*

766	A188	8f multicolored	55.00	6.00

Victory in South Viet Nam.

Alchemist's Glowing Crucible — A189

No. 768, Night-shining jade (2). No. 769, Purple Kuo's cap (3). No. 770, Chao pink (4). No. 771, Yao yellow (5). No. 772, Twin beauty (6). No. 773, Ice-veiled ruby (7). No. 774, Gold-sprinkled Chinese ink (8). No. 775, Cinnabar jar (9). No. 776, Lan Tien jade (10). No. 777, Imperial robe yellow (11). No. 778, Hu red (12). No. 779, Pea green (13). No. 780, Wei purple (14). No. 781, Intoxicated celestial peach (15).

No. 782, Glorious crimson & great gold pink.

1964, Aug. 5 *Perf. 11½x11*

767	A189	4f shown (1)	17.50	2.00
768	A189	4f multi	17.50	2.00
769	A189	8f multi	10.00	2.00
770	A189	8f multi	10.00	2.00
771	A189	8f multi	10.00	2.00
772	A189	8f multi	10.00	2.00
773	A189	8f multi	10.00	2.00
774	A189	10f multi	17.50	2.00
775	A189	10f multi	17.50	2.00
776	A189	10f multi	17.50	2.00
777	A189	10f multi	17.50	2.00
778	A189	10f multi	17.50	2.00
779	A189	20f multi	65.00	*15.00*
780	A189	43f multi	100.00	*20.00*
781	A189	52f multi	175.00	*30.00*
		Nos. 767-781 (15)	512.50	*89.00*

Souvenir Sheet

Perf. 11½

Without Gum

782	A189	$2 multi	*2,500.*	*800.00*

No. 782 contains one 48x59mm stamp.

Wine Cup — A190

Sacrificial bronze vessels of Yin dynasty, prior to 1050 B.C.: No. 784, Ku beaker (2). No. 785, Kuang wine urn (3). No. 786, Chia wine cup (4). No. 787, Tsun wine vessel (5). No. 788, Yu wine urn (6). No. 789, Tsun wine vessel (7). No. 790, Ceremonial cauldron (8).

Engraved and Photogravure

1964, Aug. 25 *Perf. 11½x11*

783	A190	4f shown (1)	12.50	1.75
784	A190	4f multi	12.50	1.75
785	A190	8f multi	10.00	1.75
786	A190	8f multi	10.00	1.75
787	A190	10f multi	25.00	2.00
788	A190	10f multi	25.00	2.00
789	A190	20f multi	45.00	4.50
790	A190	20f multi	45.00	4.50
		Nos. 783-790 (8)	185.00	20.00

Grain Harvest — A191

Designs: No. 792, Students planting trees. No. 793, Study period. No. 794, Scientific experimentation.

1964, Sept. 26 **Photo.**

791	A191	8f multicolored (1)	7.00	1.00
792	A191	8f multicolored (2)	7.00	1.00
793	A191	8f multicolored (3)	7.00	1.00
794	A191	8f multicolored (4)	7.00	1.00
		Nos. 791-794 (4)	28.00	4.00

Youth helping in agriculture.

Marx, Engels, Trafalgar Square, London — A192

1964, Sept. 28 *Perf. 11½*

795	A192	8f red, gold & red brn	130.00	30.00

Centenary of the First International.

Gold Ink

Stamps with gold ink often show some tarnishing. Values are for untarnished gold color. Tarnished stamps will sell for less.

People with Banners — A193

No. 797, Gate of Heavenly Peace and Chinese flag. No. 798, People with banners, facing left.

1964, Oct. 1

796 A193 8f cream & multi (1) 40.00 5.50
797 A193 8f cream & multi (2) 40.00 5.50
798 A193 8f cream & multi (3) 40.00 5.50
a. Souvenir sheet of 3 *3,700.* *1,400.*
b. Strip of 3, #796-798 300.00 80.00
Nos. 796-798 (3) 120.00 16.50

15th anniv. of the People's Republic.

No. 798a contains No. 798b in continuous design without separating perfs. No. 798a almost always has disturbed gum, with interleaving paper sticking to it, or tarnished gilt. Such examples sell for considerably less than the very fine example valued above.

Values for No. 798b are for an unfolded strip.

Oil Derricks — A194

Oil industry: 4f, Geological surveyors and truck, horiz. 8f, "Christmas tree" and extraction accessories. 10f, Oil refinery. 20f, Tank cars, horiz.

1964, Oct. 1

799 A194 4f lt blue & multi 100.00 10.00
800 A194 8f shown 120.00 15.00
801 A194 8f lilac & multi 80.00 6.50
802 A194 10f slate & multi 80.00 6.50
803 A194 20f brown & multi 150.00 25.00
Nos. 799-803 (5) 530.00 63.00

Albanian and Chinese Flags A195

10f, Enver Hoxha and Albanian coat of arms.

1964, Nov. 29 ***Perf. 11x11½***

804 A195 8f red & multi 32.50 10.00
805 A195 10f red, yel & blk 50.00 20.00

20th anniv. of the liberation of Albania.

Power Dam Construction A196

No. 807, Installation of turbogenerator rotor. No. 808, Main dam. 20f, Pylon.

1964, Dec. 15 ***Perf. 11½***

806 A196 4f multicolored 110.00 12.00
807 A196 8f multicolored 75.00 5.00
808 A196 8f multicolored 110.00 5.00
809 A196 20f multicolored 190.00 27.50
Nos. 806-809 (4) 485.00 49.50

Hsin An Kiang Dam and hydroelectric power station.

Fertilizer Industry — A197

Chemical Industry: No. 811, Plastics. No. 812, Medicines. No. 813, Rubber. No. 814, Insecticides. No. 815, Industrial acids. No. 816, Industrial alkaloids. No. 817, Synthetic fibers.

1964, Dec. 30 **Photo. & Engr.**

810 A197 8f red & blk (1) 10.00 1.50
811 A197 8f yel grn & blk (2) 10.00 1.50
812 A197 8f brown & blk (3) 10.00 1.50
813 A197 8f lilac rose & blk (4) 10.00 1.50
814 A197 8f blue & blk (5) 10.00 1.50
815 A197 8f orange & blk (6) 10.00 1.50
816 A197 8f violet & blk (7) 10.00 1.50
817 A197 8f brt green & blk (8) 10.00 1.50
Nos. 810-817 (8) 80.00 12.00

Mao Studying Map — A198

Mao Tse-tung — A199

Design: No. 819, Victory at Lushan Pass.

1965, Jan. 31 **Photo.** ***Perf. 11***

818 A198 8f red & multi 90.00 20.00
819 A198 8f red & multi 90.00 20.00

Perf. 11½x11

820 A199 8f gold & multi 130.00 35.00
Nos. 818-820 (3) 310.00 75.00

Tsunyi Conference, 30th anniversary.

Conference Hall, Bandung — A200

No. 822, Asians and Africans applauding.

1965, Apr. 18 ***Perf. 11½x11***

821 A200 8f cream & multi 4.00 .75
822 A200 8f cream & multi 4.00 1.00

10th anniversary of the Bandung, Indonesia, Conference, Apr. 1955.

Lenin — A201

1965, Apr. 25 ***Perf. 11½***

823 A201 8f red, choc & salmon 27.50 5.00

95th anniversary of the birth of Lenin.

Chinese Player — A202

No. 825, European woman (2). No. 826, Chinese woman (3). No. 827, European man (4).

1965, Apr. 25 ***Perf. 11½***

824 A202 8f shown (1) .85 .35
825 A202 8f multi .85 .35
826 A202 8f multi .85 .35
827 A202 8f multi .85 .35
a. Block of 4, #824-827 10.00 4.50

28th World Table Tennis Championships, Ljubljana, Yugoslavia, Apr. 15-25.

Climbers on Mt. Minya Konka — A203

Mountain Climbers: No. 829, on Muztagh Ata. No. 830, on Mt. Jolmo Lungma (Mt. Everest). No. 831, Women camping on Kongur Tiubie Tagh. No. 832, on Shisha Pangma.

1965, May 25 **Photo. & Engr.**

828 A203 8f blue, blk & ol (1) 16.00 2.00
829 A203 8f blue, blk & ol (2) 16.00 2.00
830 A203 8f ultra, blk & gray (3) 16.00 2.00
831 A203 8f lt bl, blk & yel gray (4) 16.00 2.00
832 A203 8f ultra, blk & gray (5) 16.00 2.00
Nos. 828-832 (5) 80.00 10.00

Chinese mountaineering achievements, 1957-64.

Marx and Lenin — A204

1965, June 21 **Photo.** ***Perf. 11½x11***

833 A204 8f red, yel & blk 24.00 4.00

Postal Ministers' Congress, Peking.

Tseping Valley A205

Chingkang Mountains, Cradle of the Chinese Revolution: No. 835, San Wan Tsun (2). No. 836, Octagon Bldg., Mao Ping (3). No. 837, River and Bridge at Lung Shih (4). No. 838, Ta Ching Tsun (5). No. 839, Bridge across the Lung Yuan (6). No. 840, Hwang Yang Mountain (7). No. 841, Chingkang peaks (8).

1965, July 1 ***Perf. 11x11½***

834 A205 4f shown (1) 35.00 9.00
835 A205 8f multi 20.00 3.00
836 A205 8f multi 20.00 3.00
837 A205 8f multi 40.00 3.00
838 A205 8f multi 40.00 3.00
839 A205 10f multi 55.00 3.00
840 A205 10f multi 55.00 10.00
841 A205 52f multi 45.00 17.50
Nos. 834-841 (8) 310.00 51.50

Soldiers with Books — A206

No. 843, Soldiers reading Little Red Books (2). No. 844, With shell and artillery (3). No. 845, Rifle instruction (4). No. 846, Sewing jacket (5). No. 847, Bayonet charge (6). No. 848, With Banner (7). No. 849, Military band (8).

1965, Aug. 1 ***Perf. 11½***

Without Gum

842 A206 8f shown (1) 42.50 7.00
843 A206 8f multi 42.50 7.00
844 A206 8f multi 42.50 7.00
845 A206 8f multi 42.50 7.00
846 A206 8f multi 42.50 7.00
847 A206 8f multi 42.50 10.00
848 A206 8f multi 42.50 10.00
849 A206 8f multi 42.50 10.00
Nos. 842-849 (8) 340.00 65.00

People's Liberation Army. Nos. 846-849 vertical.

"Welcome to Peking" — A207

No. 851, Chinese and Japanese young men. No. 852, Chinese and Japanese girls. No. 853, Musical entertainment. No. 854, Emblem of meeting.

1965, Aug. 25 ***Perf. 11½x11***

850 A207 4f yellow & multi 2.00 1.00
851 A207 8f pink & multi 2.00 1.00
852 A207 8f multicolored 2.50 1.00
853 A207 10f multicolored 4.50 2.00
854 A207 22f lt blue & multi 9.50 3.50
Nos. 850-854 (5) 20.50 8.50

Chinese-Japanese Youth Meeting, Peking.

North Vietnamese Soldier — A208

Peoples of the World — A209

Designs: No. 856, Soldier with guns. No. 857, Soldier giving victory salute.

1965, Sept. 2 ***Perf. 11½x11***

855 A208 8f red & red brn (1) 5.00 1.25
856 A208 8f red & blk (2) 5.00 1.25
857 A208 8f red & vio brn (3) 5.00 1.25

Perf. 11½

858 A209 8f black & red (4) 6.00 1.75
Nos. 855-858 (4) 21.00 5.50

Struggle of the people of Viet Nam.

Mao Tse-tung at His Desk — A210

Crossing Yellow River A211

Victory Monument A212

Design: No. 862, Recruits in cart.

1965, Sept. 3 *Perf. 11*

859 A210 8f red & multi (1) 60.00 17.50

Perf. 11x11½, 11½x11

860 A211 8f red & dk grn (2) 40.00 4.00
861 A212 8f red & dk brn (3) 40.00 4.00
862 A211 8f red & dk grn (4) 40.00 4.00
Nos. 859-862 (4) 180.00 29.50

20th anniversary of victory over Japan.

2nd National Games — A213

National Games Opening Ceremonies — A214

Perf. 11½x11, 11 (A214)

1965, Sept. 28

863 A213 4f Soccer (1) 20.00 2.00
864 A213 4f Archery (2) 20.00 2.00
865 A213 8f Javelin (3) 20.00 2.00
866 A213 8f Gymnastics (4) 20.00 2.00
867 A213 8f Volleyball (5) 20.00 2.00
868 A214 10f shown (6) 50.00 4.00
869 A213 10f Bicycling (7) 55.00 4.50
870 A213 20f Diving (8) 60.00 7.50
871 A213 22f Hurdles (9) 60.00 7.50
872 A213 30f Weight lifting (10) 70.00 18.00
873 A213 43f Basketball (11) 70.00 18.00
Nos. 863-873 (11) 465.00 69.50

Government Building — A215

1½f, 5f, 22f, Gate of Heavenly Peace. 2f, 8f, 30f, People's Hall. 3f, 10f, 50f, Military Museum.

1965-66 *Perf. 11½x11*

Without Gum

874 A215 1f brown .35 .30
875 A215 1½f red lilac .45 *.30*
876 A215 2f green .45 .30
877 A215 3f blue grn .50 .30
878 A215 4f brt blue .60 .30
879 A215 5f vio brn ('66) 2.00 .30
880 A215 8f rose red .75 .30
881 A215 10f gray olive 1.75 .30
882 A215 20f violet 2.00 .30
883 A215 22f orange 2.00 .30
884 A215 30f yellow grn 4.00 .40
885 A215 50f dp blue ('66) 11.00 2.75
Nos. 874-885 (12) 25.85 *6.15*

Textile Workers — A216

1965, Nov. 30

886 A216 8f shown (1) 30.00 3.50
887 A216 8f Machine shop (2) 30.00 3.50
888 A216 8f Welder (3) 30.00 3.50
889 A216 8f Students (4) 30.00 3.50
890 A216 8f Militia (5) 30.00 3.50
Nos. 886-890 (5) 150.00 17.50

Women workers.

Soccer — A217

Children's Sports: No. 892, Racing. No. 893, Tobogganing and skating. No. 894, Gymnastics. No. 895, Swimming. No. 896, Rifle practice. No. 897, Jumping rope. No. 898, Table tennis.

1966, Feb. 25 *Perf. 11*

891 A217 4f emerald & multi (1) 1.50 .45
892 A217 4f yel brown & multi (2) 1.50 .45
893 A217 8f blue & multi (3) 1.50 .45
894 A217 8f yellow & multi (4) 1.50 .55
895 A217 8f grnsh bl & multi (5) 1.50 .55
896 A217 8f green & multi (6) 1.50 .55
897 A217 10f orange & multi (7) 4.50 1.25
898 A217 52f grnsh gray & multi (8) 14.00 5.75
Nos. 891-898 (8) 27.50 10.00

Mobile Transformer A218

New Industrial Machinery: No. 900, Electron microscope, vert. No. 901, Lathe. No. 902, Vertical boring and turning machine, vert. No. 903, Gear-grinding machine. No. 904, Hydraulic press. No. 905, Milling machine. No. 906, Electron accelerator, vert.

Perf. 11x11½, 11½x11

1966, Mar. 30 **Photo. & Engr.**

899 A218 4f yellow & blk (1) 32.50 3.00
900 A218 8f blk & lt ultra (2) 32.50 2.00
901 A218 8f sal pink & blk (3) 32.50 2.00
902 A218 8f olive & blk (4) 32.50 2.00
903 A218 8f rose lil & blk (5) 32.50 2.00
904 A218 10f gray & blk (6) 42.50 8.00
905 A218 10f bl grn & blk (7) 42.50 10.00
906 A218 22f lilac & blk (8) 50.00 7.50
Nos. 899-906 (8) 297.50 36.50

Military and Civilian Workers A219

Women in Various Occupations: No. 908, Train conductor. No. 909, Red Cross worker. No. 910, Kindergarten teacher. No. 911, Road sweeper. No. 912, Hairdresser. No. 913, Bus conductor. No. 914, Traveling saleswoman. No. 915, Canteen worker. No. 916, Rural mail carrier.

1966, May 10 *Perf. 11x11½*

907 A219 8f red & multi (1) 2.50 1.00
908 A219 8f pale grn & multi (2) 2.50 1.00
909 A219 8f yellow & multi (3) 2.50 1.00
910 A219 8f green & multi (4) 2.50 1.00
911 A219 8f salmon & multi (5) 2.50 1.00
912 A219 8f pale bl & bl (6) 2.50 1.00
913 A219 8f yellow & multi (7) 2.50 1.00
914 A219 8f tan & multi (8) 2.50 1.00
915 A219 8f yel grn & multi (9) 2.50 1.00
916 A219 8f green & multi (10) 2.50 1.00
Nos. 907-916 (10) 25.00 10.00

Statue "Thunderstorm" — A220

22f, Open book and association emblem.

1966, June 27 *Perf. 11*

917 A220 8f red & black 10.00 3.00
918 A220 22f red, gold & yel 25.00 4.50

Afro-Asian Writers' Assoc. Conf., Peking.

Sun Yat-sen — A221

1966, Nov. 12 *Perf. 11½x11*

919 A221 8f sepia & lt buff 90.00 27.50

Birth centenary of Sun Yat-sen.

Athletes Holding Portrait of Mao — A222

Two Women Athletes with Little Red Book A223

No. 921, Athletes holding Little Red Books. No. 923, Athletes reading Mao texts.

1966, Dec. 31 *Perf. 11*

920 A222 8f red & multi (1) 80.00 15.00
921 A222 8f red & multi (2) 60.00 15.00

Perf. 11x11½

922 A223 8f blue & multi (3) 75.00 17.00
923 A223 8f blue & multi (4) 75.00 17.00
Nos. 920-923 (4) 290.00 64.00

1st Athletic Games of the New Emerging Nations.

Appreciation of Lu Hsun by Mao — A224

Designs: No. 925, Portrait of Lu Hsun. No. 926, Lu Hsun's handwriting (3 vert. rows).

Engr. & Photo.; Photo. (#925)

1966, Dec. 31 *Perf. 11½*

924 A224 8f red & black (1) 85.00 22.50
925 A224 8f red & multi (2) 110.00 22.50
926 A224 8f red & black (3) 85.00 22.50
Nos. 924-926 (3) 280.00 67.50

Lu Hsun, Revolutionary writer (1881-1936).

"Be Resolute ...," by Mao Tse-tung — A225

Designs: No. 928, Drilling crew fighting natural gas fire, horiz. No. 929, Attempt to close fire-engulfed valve.

Sizes: Nos. 927, 929, 26x38mm; No. 928, 49x29mm

Perf. 11½x11, 11½ (No. 928)

1967, Mar. 10 **Photo.**

927 A225 8f red, gold & blk 60.00 17.50
928 A225 8f brick red & blk 60.00 17.50
929 A225 8f brick red & blk 60.00 17.50
Nos. 927-929 (3) 180.00 52.50

Heroic oil well firefighters.

Liu Ying-chun A226

No. 931, With book by Mao (2). No. 932, Holding bridle of horse (3). No. 933, With film slide (4). No. 934, Lecturing (5). No. 935, Fatal attempt to stop runaway horse (6).

1967, Mar. 25 *Perf. 11½x11*

930 A226 8f shown (1) 60.00 17.50
931 A226 8f multi 60.00 17.50
932 A226 8f multi 60.00 17.50
933 A226 8f multi 60.00 17.50
934 A226 8f multi 60.00 17.50
935 A226 8f multi 60.00 17.50
Nos. 930-935 (6) 360.00 105.00

In memory of soldier Liu Ying-chun, hero.

Third 5-Year Plan — A227

Design: No. 936, Banners, 3 workers and male soldier facing right (industrial growth). No. 937, Banners, 3 workers and female militia member facing left (agricultural growth).

1967, Apr. 15 ***Perf. 11***

936	A227	8f	red & multi	105.00	20.00
937	A227	8f	red & multi	105.00	20.00

Third Five-Year Plan.

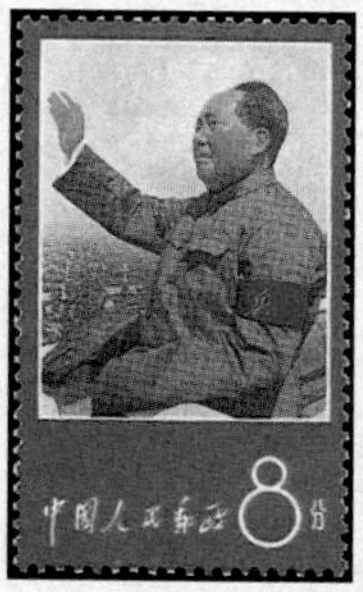

Mao Tse-tung — A228

Thoughts of Mao — A229

1967, Apr. 20 ***Perf. 11½***

938	A228	8f	red & multi	90.00	60.00

Red & Gold

939	A229	8f	39 characters	95.00	60.00
940	A229	8f	50 characters	95.00	60.00
941	A229	8f	39 characters in 6 lines	95.00	60.00
942	A229	8f	53 characters	95.00	60.00
943	A229	8f	46 characters	95.00	60.00
a.			Strip of 5, #939-943	1,600.	675.00

Gold & Red

944	A229	8f	41 characters	140.00	100.00
945	A229	8f	49 characters	140.00	100.00
946	A229	8f	35 characters	140.00	140.00
947	A229	8f	22 characters	140.00	100.00
948	A229	8f	29 characters	140.00	100.00
a.			Strip of 5, #944-948	2,500.	800.00
			Nos. 938-948 (11)	1,265.	900.00

Thoughts of Mao Tse-tung.

Values for Nos. 943a and 948a are for unfolded strips without tarnishing. Strips with folds and/or tarnishing sell for much less.

For Nos. 938-1046, beware of forgeries, removed cancels and repairs. No numbers appear below design on Nos. 938-1046.

Gate of Heavenly Peace and Text from C. C. P. Communique Praising Mao — A230

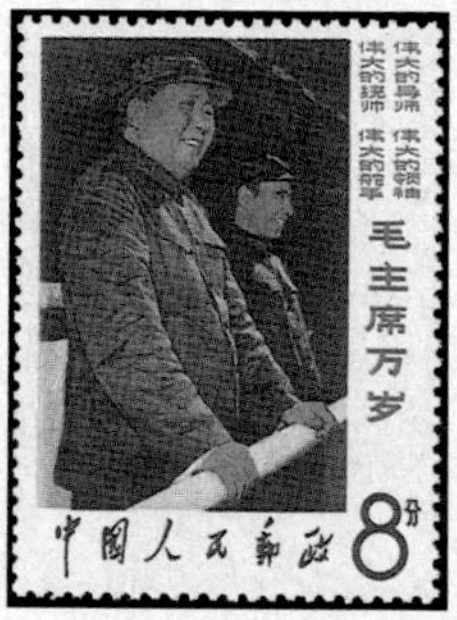

Mao and Lin Piao A231

No. 950, Mao and poem. No. 951, Mao among people of various races. No. 952, Mao facing left and Red Guards with books. No. 953, Mao with upraised right hand. No. 955, Mao leaning on rail, horiz. 10f, Mao and Lin Piao in discussion, horiz.

Engraved and Photogravure

1967 ***Perf. 11x11½***

Size: 36x56mm

949	A230	4f	yel, red & mar	100.00	45.00

Photo.

950	A230	8f	yel, brn, & red	110.00	45.00
951	A230	8f	yel, red & multi	110.00	45.00
952	A230	8f	yel, red & multi	110.00	45.00

Size: 36x50mm, 50x36mm

Perf. 11

953	A231	8f	black & multi	160.00	45.00
954	A231	8f	black & multi	400.00	175.00
955	A231	8f	lt blue & multi	90.00	45.00
956	A231	10f	black & multi	400.00	175.00
			Nos. 949-956 (8)	1,480.	620.00

"Mao Tse-tung Our Great Teacher."

Issued: Nos. 949-953, 5/1; Nos. 954-956, 9/20.

Mao Text (4 lines) — A232

Parade of Supporters — A233

Design: No. 958, Mao text (5 lines).

Engraved and Photogravure

1967, May 23 ***Perf. 11½***

957	A232	8f	black, red & yel	300.00	125.00
958	A232	8f	black, red & yel	375.00	150.00

Photo.

Perf. 11

959	A233	8f	multicolored	375.00	150.00
			Nos. 957-959 (3)	1,050.	425.00

25th anniversary of Mao Tse-tung's "Talks on Literature and Art" in Yenan.

A stamp was prepared in August 1967 for the 50th anniversary of the Autumn Harvest March. It was not issued, but a few examples have entered the marketplace. It depicts Mao Tse-tung on the left and Lin Piao on the right, against a blue sky. A cut example comprising the right half of the stamp was sold in a Jan. 2010 Hong Kong auction for the equivalent of U.S. $285,000. Presumably, an intact example would sell for far more.

Mao Tse-tung — A234

1967 **Engr.** ***Perf. 11***

960	A234	4f	brown	60.00	*27.50*
961	A234	8f	carmine	240.00	*50.00*
962	A234	35f	dk brown	30.00	*11.50*
963	A234	43f	vermilion	30.00	*11.50*
964	A234	52f	carmine	35.00	*15.00*
			Nos. 960-964 (5)	395.00	*115.50*

46th anniv. of Chinese Communist Party. Issue dates: 8f, July 1; others Sept.

Mao, "Sun of the Revolution" — A235

No. 966, Mao and people of various races.

1967, Oct. 1 ***Perf. 11½x11***

965	A235	8f	multicolored	*75.00*	*35.00*
966	A235	8f	multicolored	*200.00*	*75.00*

People's Republic of China, 18th anniv.

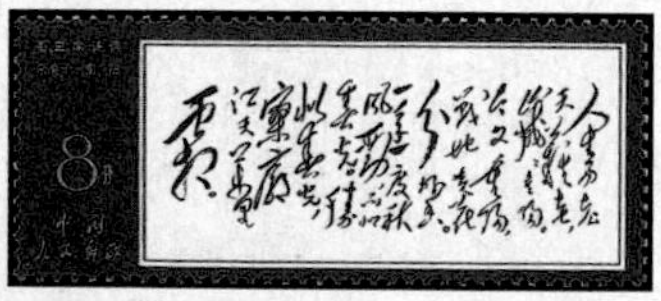

"September 9" — A236

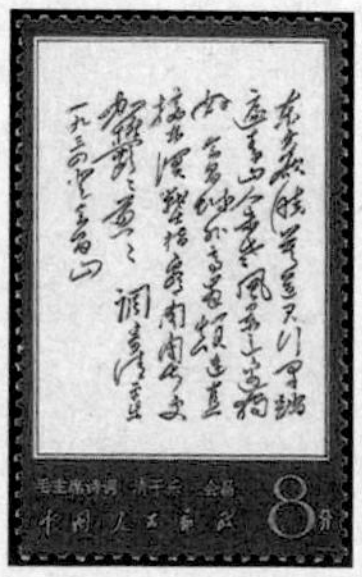

"Huichang" A237

"Peitaiho" A238

Reply to Comrade Kuo Mo-jo — A239

Mao Tse-tung Writing Poems — A240

Poems by Mao: No. 967, "The Long March." No. 968, "Liupanshan." No. 969, shown. No. 970, "The Cave of the Fairies." No. 971, "Snow." No. 972, "Lushan Pass." No. 975, "Conquest of Nanking." No. 976, "The Yellow Crane Pavilion." No. 977, "Swimming." No. 979, "Changsha."

1967-68 **Photo.** ***Perf. 11***

Size: 79x18½mm

967	A236	4f	9 characters, UL panel	135.00	100.00
968	A236	4f	11 characters, UL panel	135.00	30.00

Size: 60x24mm

Perf. 11½

969	A236	8f	shown, 10 characters in UL panel	100.00	50.00
970	A236	8f	21 characters in UL panel	125.00	50.00
971	A236	8f	11 characters in UL panel	110.00	65.00
972	A236	8f	9 characters in UL panel	110.00	65.00

Size: 29x50mm

973	A237	8f	shown	650.00	175.00
974	A238	8f	shown	850.00	275.00
975	A238	8f	3 rows in bottom panel	600.00	190.00
976	A238	8f	2 rows in bottom panel	300.00	160.00

Size: 52x38mm

Perf. 11

977	A239	8f	3 short vert. rows, at left of poem	450.00	175.00
978	A239	10f	shown	60.00	30.00
979	A239	10f	undivided text	150.00	30.00
980	A240	10f	red, yel & multi	150.00	50.00
			Nos. 967-980 (14)	3,925.	1,445.

Issued: Nos. 969-970, 980, 10/1; Nos. 973-974, 977, 5/20/68; others 7/20/68.

Lin Piao's Epigram on Mao Tse-tung
A241

1967, Dec. 26 Photo. *Perf. 11x11½*

981	A241	8f red & gold	45.00	15.00

Mao and Parade of Artists — A242

"Raid on White Tiger Regiment" — A243

"Red Detachment of Women" — A244

No. 983, "The Red Lantern," vert. No. 985, "Shachiapang" (women & soldier). No. 986, "On the Dock". No. 987, "Taking Bandits' Fort". No. 989, "The White-haired Girl". No. 990, Mao with Orchestra & Chorus (50x36mm).

1968 *Perf. 11½x11; 11 (983, 990)*

982	A242	8f shown (56x36mm)	140.00	30.00
983	A242	8f multi	140.00	35.00
984	A243	8f shown	140.00	40.00
985	A243	8f multi	140.00	40.00
986	A243	8f multi	140.00	40.00
987	A243	8f multi	140.00	40.00
988	A244	8f shown	190.00	70.00
989	A244	8f multi	140.00	55.00
990	A242	8f multi	140.00	45.00
		Nos. 982-990 (9)	1,310.	395.00

Mao's direction for revolutionary literature and art. Issued: Nos. 982-987, Jan. 30; Nos. 988-990, May 1.

"Unite still more closely . . ." — A245

1968, May 31 Photo. *Perf. 11*

991	A245	8f red, gold & red brn	300.00	100.00

Mao Tse-tung's statement of support of Afro-Americans.

Statement about Cultural Revolution
A246

Directives of Chairman Mao: No. 993, Experiences of Revolutionary Committee. No. 994, Leadership role of Revolutionary Committee. No. 995, Basic principle of reform. No. 996, Purpose of Cultural Revolution.

1968, July 20 Photo. *Perf. 11½*
No. of Lines Over Signature

992	A246	8f shown	500.00	275.00
993	A246	8f 5	500.00	275.00
994	A246	8f 4½	500.00	275.00
995	A246	8f 4	500.00	275.00
996	A246	8f 8	500.00	275.00
a.		Strip of 5, #992-996	*5,750.*	2,250.
		Nos. 992-996 (5)	2,500.	1,375.

Value for No. 996a is for an unfolded strip.

Lin Piao's Statement, July 26, 1965 — A247

1968, Aug. 1 Engr. & Photo.

997	A247	8f red, gold & blk	40.00	12.50

Chinese People's Liberation Army, 41st anniv.

Mao Tse-tung Going to An Yuan, 1921
A248

1968, Aug. 1 *Perf. 11x11½*

998	A248	8f multicolored	250.00	55.00

Shade varieties include varying amount of red in clouds.

An 8f stamp was prepared in Sept. 1968, showing black writing on a red background, regarding Chairman Mao's inscriptions to Japanese Labor Friends. It was not issued, but a few examples have reached the marketplace. Value, *$175,000.*

Directive of Chairman Mao — A249

1968, Nov. 30 *Perf. 11½*

999	A249	8f red & blk brn	*260.00*	55.00

China Map, Worker, Farmer and Soldier
999A

1968, Nov. Photo. *Perf. 11½x11*

999A	A249a	8f red, bl & bis	*125,000.*	*90,000.*

Map inscribed: "The entire nation is red." Issued in Canton and quickly withdrawn because Taiwan appears white instead of red.

No. 999A most often is found repaired. Values are for sound, unrepaired examples.

Counterfeits exist.

Two values were prepared to celebrate the Great Victory of the Cultural Revolution but were not issued, although a few examples have entered the marketplace. Values for sound stamps: 8f, Mao Tse-tung and Lin Piao, $300,000; 8f, map and workers, $1,150,000.

Woman, Miner and Soldier Holding Little Red Book
A250

1968, Dec. 26 *Perf. 11x11½*

1000	A250	8f multicolored	65.00	18.00

Canceled-to-order
From about this point on stamps are valued postally used.

Yangtze Bridge, Nanking
A251

Road across Bridge — A252

No. 1003, Side view. 10f, Aerial view.

Lithographed, *Perf. 11½x11 (A251);*
Photogravure, *Perf. 11½ (A252)*

1969 Without Gum

1001	A251	4f multicolored	8.00	3.00
1002	A252	8f multicolored	68.00	10.00
1003	A252	8f multicolored	20.00	6.00
1004	A251	10f multicolored	6.00	3.00
		Nos. 1001-1004 (4)	102.00	22.00

Inauguration of Yangtze Bridge at Nanking on Dec. 29, 1968.

Singer and Pianist
A253

(Piano Music from the Opera, "The Red Lantern"): No. 1006, Woman singer and pianist.

1969, Aug. Photo. *Perf. 11x11½*
Without Gum

1005	A253	8f multicolored	20.00	13.00
1006	A253	8f multicolored	115.00	21.00

Harvest
A254

No. 1008, Two harvesters. No. 1009, Harvesters with Little Red Books. No. 1010, Red Cross Worker examining baby.

1969, Oct. Without Gum

1007	A254	4f shown	15.00	3.50
a.		Brown omitted	50.00	50.00
1008	A254	8f multi	70.00	9.00
1009	A254	8f multi	90.00	20.00
1010	A254	10f multi	10.00	4.00
		Nos. 1007-1010 (4)	185.00	36.50

Agriculture students.

Armed Forces and Slogan — A255

Guarding the Coast — A256

Designs: No. 1013, 43f, Snow patrol, vert.

1969, Oct. Without Gum *Perf. 11½*

1011	A255	8f red & multi	60.00	*16.00*
a.		Bayonets omitted	300.00	85.00
1012	A256	8f blue & multi	15.00	*5.00*
1013	A256	8f blue & multi	15.00	*5.00*
1014	A256	35f black & multi	12.00	*5.00*
1015	A256	43f black & multi	15.00	*7.50*
		Nos. 1011-1015 (5)	117.00	*38.50*

Defense of Chen Pao-tao (Damansky Islands) in Ussuri River.

Farm Woman
A257

Designs: 8f, Foundry worker. 10f, Soldier.

1969, Dec. *Perf. 10; 11½*
Without Gum

1016	A257	4f ver & dk pur	2.50	*.75*
a.		Perf 11½	7.50	1.50

1017	A257	8f ver & dk brn	3.00	.75
a.		Perf 11½	4.50	1.50
1018	A257	10f ver & blk	5.00	*1.50*
a.		Perf 11½	—	*900.00*
		Nos. 1016-1018 (3)	10.50	*3.00*

Perforation

Nos. 1016-1018 and some succeeding issues bear two kinds of perforation: clean (Peking) and rough (Shanghai).

Building — A258

Communist Party Building, Shanghai A259

Agriculture Building, Canton — A260

Foundry Worker — A261

Type I

Two types of 8f Gate of Heavenly Peace:
I — Strong, definite halo around sun.
II — Halo missing, white shades gradually into red.

No. 1022, 1929 Party Day House, Pu Tien. No. 1023, Mao's Home and Office, Yunnan. No. 1024, Woman Tractor Driver. No. 1025, Gate of Heavenly Peace. No. 1026, Heroes Monument. No. 1027, Pagoda Hill, Yenan. No. 1028, Gate of Heavenly Peace (no sun). No. 1029, Monument, Tsu Ping. No. 1030, Conference Hall, Tsunyi. No. 1031, Highway ('72). No. 1032, Shao Shan Village, Birthplace of Mao. No. 1033, Conference Hall. No. 1034, Chingkang Peaks. No. 1035, as 4f, different view. No. 1036, People's Hall, Peking.

1969-72 Photo. *Perf. 10, 11½*
Without Gum

1019	A258	1f shown	.40	.30
1020	A259	1½f shown	1.50	1.00
a.		Perf. 11½	8.00	4.00
1021	A260	2f shown	.40	.30
1022	A260	3f multi	1.00	.30
1023	A260	4f multi	.55	.30
1024	A261	5f multi	2.50	.75
1025	A260	8f multi, type II	.90	.40
a.		Type I	2.50	1.25
1026	A259	8f multi	3.50	1.50
a.		Perf. 11½	7.50	3.50
1027	A260	8f multi	7.50	*3.25*
1028	A260	8f multi	1.00	.40
1029	A260	10f multi	1.00	.40
1030	A259	20f multi	5.50	1.75
a.		Perf. 11½	22.50	5.50
1031	A260	20f multi	2.00	.55
1032	A260	22f multi	2.00	.60
1033	A260	35f multi	2.50	.60
1034	A260	43f multi	3.50	.70
1035	A259	50f multi	2.00	.50
1036	A260	52f multi	6.00	.85
1037	A261	$1 shown ('70)	12.00	1.75
		Nos. 1019-1037 (19)	55.75	16.20

Kin Hsün-hua A262

1970, Jan. Without Gum *Perf. 11½*

1045	A262	8f red & black	32.50	*17.50*
a.		8f red & gray brown	40.00	15.00

Death of Kin Hsün-hua in Kirin border flood.

Mounted Patrol — A263

1970, Aug. 1 Without Gum

1046	A263	8f yel grn & multi	22.50	9.00

People's Liberation Army, 43rd anniv.

Commemorative stamps from Nos. 1047 to 1142 and 1211-1214, carry a cumulative number in parentheses at lower left and the year at lower right. Where such numbers help to identify, they are quoted in parentheses.

Cpl. Yang Tse-jung — A264

Ensemble A265

No. 1048, Armed guards (2). No. 1049, Yang leaping through forest (3). No. 1051, Yang in folk costume (5). No. 1052, Four actors (6).

1970, Aug. 1 *Perf. 11½x11, 11x11½*
Without Gum

1047	A264	8f shown (1)	45.00	11.00
1048	A264	8f multi	12.50	3.50
1049	A264	8f multi	20.00	6.00
1050	A265	8f shown (4)	85.00	15.00
1051	A265	8f multi	15.00	3.75
1052	A265	8f multi	22.50	8.50
		Nos. 1047-1052 (6)	200.00	47.75

Scenes from opera "Taking Tiger Mountain by Strategy." Nos. 1048, 1052, horizontal.

Frontier Guard A266

1971, Jan. Litho. *Perf. 10*
Without Gum

1053	A266	4f multicolored	6.00	1.75
a.		Perf. 11½	5.50	1.75
b.		Perf. 11½x10	5.00	2.75
c.		Perf. 10x11½	5.75	3.25

Banner of the Commune A267

Street Battle, Paris, 1871 A268

10f, Proclamation of the Commune. 22f, Rally.

Perf. 11½x11, 11x11½
1971, Mar. 18 Litho. & Engr.
Without Gum

1054	A267	4f sal & multi	42.50	18.00
1055	A268	8f ver, pink & brn	265.00	55.00
1056	A267	10f ver, pink & dk brn	17.50	11.00
1057	A268	22f ver, pink & dk brn	11.50	10.00
		Nos. 1054-1057 (4)	336.50	94.00

Centenary of the Paris Commune.

Redrawn Building Type of 1961

Designs: 2f, 3f, August 1 building, Nanchang. 4f, 52f, Gate of Heavenly Peace, Peking. 10f, 20f, Pagoda Hill, Yenan.

1971, July 1 Litho. *Perf. 11x11½*
Size: 21x16mm
Without Gum

1059	A152	2f slate green	2.00	.75
1060	A152	3f sepia	3.00	1.25
1061	A152	4f brt pink	5.00	2.00
1062	A152	10f brt rose lil	1.50	1.25
1063	A152	20f dk blue grn	3.75	1.25
1064	A152	52f orange	2.50	3.00
		Nos. 1059-1064 (6)	17.75	9.50

Paper of Nos. 1059-1064 is white. That of Nos. 647-654 is toned.

Communist Party Building, Shanghai — A269

People and Factories — A270

Designs: No. 1068, Peasant Movement Training Institute. No. 1069, Ching Kang Peaks. No. 1070, Conference Building, Tsunyi. No. 1071, Pagoda Hill, Yenan. No. 1073, People and People's Hall, Peking. No. 1074, People and Pagoda Hill, Yenan. 22f, Gate of Heavenly Peace, Peking.

1971, July 1 Photo. *Perf. 11½*
Red and Gold Frame
Without Gum

1067	A269	4f vermilion (12)	27.50	5.00
1068	A269	4f brt grn (13)	27.50	5.00
1069	A269	8f grnsh bl & red (14)	35.00	5.00
1070	A269	8f ol blk (15)	45.00	5.00
1071	A269	8f bis, grn & red (16)	45.00	5.00
1072	A270	8f yel, red & multi (18)	45.00	8.00
1073	A270	8f yel, red & multi (19)	45.00	8.00
1074	A270	8f yel, red & multi (20)	45.00	8.00
a.		Strip of 3, #1072-1074	250.00	75.00
1075	A269	22f red, gold & brn (17)	22.50	9.00
		Nos. 1067-1075 (9)	337.50	58.00

50th anniv. of the Chinese Communist Party. No. 1074a has a continuous design and is valued as an unfolded strip.

Chinese Welcome A271

No. 1077, Chinese & African players. No. 1078, Chinese & African girl players. 43f, Games' emblem.

1971, Nov. 3 Litho. *Perf. 11½*
Without Gum

1076	A271	8f lil rose & multi	22.50	5.75
1077	A271	8f lt yellow & multi	22.50	5.75
1078	A271	8f dk grn & multi	22.50	5.75
1079	A271	43f grn, gold & org	85.00	16.00
		Nos. 1076-1079 (4)	152.50	33.25

Afro-Asian Table Tennis Games, Peking.

Enver Hoxha — A272

No. 1081, Party's birthplace. No. 1082, Albanian flag. 52f, Albanian partisans, horiz.

1971, Nov. 3 Photo. *Perf. 11*
Without Gum

1080	A272	8f Prus blue & multi	32.50	7.00
1081	A272	8f buff & multi	20.00	6.00
1082	A272	8f red, yel & multi	20.00	6.00
1083	A272	52f lt blue & multi	35.00	9.00
		Nos. 1080-1083 (4)	107.50	28.00

30th anniversary of the founding of Albanian Communist Party.

Yenan Pagoda and 1942 Meeting House A273

No. 1085, Uniformed choir (34). No. 1086, "Brother & Sister" (35). No. 1087, Outdoor performance (36). No. 1088, "The Red Signal Lantern" (37). No. 1089, Dancer from "The Red Company of Women" (38).

1972, May 23 Photo. *Perf. 11*
Without Gum

1084 A273 8f shown (33) 25.00 7.50
1085 A273 8f multi 25.00 7.50
1086 A273 8f multi 25.00 7.50
1087 A273 8f multi 25.00 7.50
1088 A273 8f multi 25.00 7.50
1089 A273 8f multi 25.00 7.50
Nos. 1084-1089 (6) 150.00 45.00

30th anniversary of the publication of the Discussions on Literature and Art at the Yenan Forum.

Various Ball Games — A274

Workers' Gymnastics A275

No. 1092, Tug of war (41). No. 1093, Mountain climbers and tents (42). No. 1094, Children diving & swimming (43).

1972, June 10

1090 A274 8f shown (39) *45.00* 4.00
1091 A275 8f shown (40) *22.50* 4.00
1092 A275 8f multi *22.50* 4.00
1093 A275 8f multi *20.00* 4.00
1094 A275 8f multi *22.50* 4.00
Nos. 1090-1094 (5) 132.50 20.00

10th anniversary of Mao Tse-tung's edict on physical culture.

Ocean Freighter Fenglei — A276

No. 1096, Tanker Taching No. 30 (30). No. 1097, Cargo-passenger ship Changzeng (31). No. 1098, Dredger Xienfeng (32).

1972, July 10 Photo. *Perf. 11½*
Without Gum

1095 A276 8f shown (29) 70.00 11.00
1096 A276 8f multi 20.00 9.00
1097 A276 8f multi 20.00 9.00
1098 A276 8f multi 47.50 11.00
Nos. 1095-1098 (4) 157.50 40.00

Table Tennis Players' Welcome A277

No. 1099, Championship emblem, vert. (45). No. 1101, Table tennis (47). No. 1102, Women from different countries, vert. (48).

1972, Sept. 2 *Perf. 11½x11, 11x11½*
Without Gum

1099 A277 8f multi 12.50 5.00
1100 A277 8f shown (46) 35.00 5.00
1101 A277 8f multi 22.50 5.00
1102 A277 22f multi 20.00 6.00
Nos. 1099-1102 (4) 90.00 21.00

First Asian table tennis championships.

Wang Chin-hsi — A278

Engraved and Photogravure

1972, Dec. 25 *Perf. 11½x11*
1103 A278 8f multicolored (44) 65.00 25.00

Wang Chin-hsi, the Iron Man, fighter for the working class.

Workers on Cliffs along Canal — A279

No. 1105, Canal flowing through tunnel (50). No. 1106, Bridge (51). No. 1107, Canal along cliffs (52).

1972, Dec. 30

1104 A279 8f multi (49) 30.00 7.00
1105 A279 8f multicolored 30.00 7.00
1106 A279 8f multicolored 40.00 10.00
1107 A279 8f multicolored 40.00 10.00
Nos. 1104-1107 (4) 140.00 34.00

Construction of Red Flag Canal, Linhsien county, Honan.

Giant Panda — A280

Designs: Pandas in various positions. The 8f stamps are horizontal.

Perf. 11½x11, 11x11½
1973, Jan. 15 Photo.
Designs in Black and Red

1108 A280 4f lt yel grn (61) 9.00 8.00
1109 A280 8f buff (59) 9.00 6.00
1110 A280 8f lt tan (60) 9.00 6.00
1111 A280 10f pale grn (58) 100.00 18.00
1112 A280 20f pale bl gray (57) 50.00 10.00
1113 A280 43f pale lil (62) 15.00 14.00
Nos. 1108-1113 (6) 192.00 62.00

Woman Coal Miner — A281

No. 1115, Committee member (64). No. 1116, Telephone line worker (65).

1973, Mar. 8 Photo. *Perf. 11½x11*

1114 A281 8f shown (63) 28.00 6.00
1115 A281 8f multi 20.00 7.00
1116 A281 8f multi 20.00 6.00
Nos. 1114-1116 (3) 68.00 19.00

Intl. Working Women's Day. Designs are after paintings from an exhib. for 30th anniv. of the Yenan Forum on Literature and Art.

Dancing Girl — A282

No. 1118, Musician, boy (87). No. 1119, Girl with scarf (88). No. 1120, Boy with tambourine (89). No. 1121, Girl with drum (90).

1973, June 1 Photo. *Perf. 11*

1117 A282 8f shown (86) 3.25 1.75
1118 A282 8f multi 3.25 1.75
1119 A282 8f multi 3.25 1.75
1120 A282 8f multi 3.25 1.75
1121 A282 8f multi 3.25 1.75
a. Strip of 5, #1117-1121 60.00 22.50
Nos. 1117-1121 (5) 16.25 8.75

Values for No. 1121a are for an unfolded strip.

Tournament Emblem — A283

No. 1123, Visitors from Asia, Africa and Latin America arriving by plane (92). No. 1124, Woman player (93). No. 1125, African, Asian & Latin American women (94).

1973, Aug. 25 Photo. *Perf. 11½*

1122 A283 8f multi (91) 18.00 3.00
1123 A283 8f multicolored 14.00 3.00
1124 A283 8f multicolored 14.00 3.00
1125 A283 22f multicolored 14.00 3.00
Nos. 1122-1125 (4) 60.00 12.00

Asian, African and Latin American Table Tennis Friendship Invitational Tournament.

The White-haired Girl — A284

Designs: Scenes from the ballet "The White-haired Girl." Nos. 1126, 1129 vert.

1973, Sept. 25 Photo. *Perf. 11½*

1126 A284 8f multi (53) 40.00 12.00
1127 A284 8f multi (54) 50.00 12.00
1128 A284 8f multi (55) 40.00 12.00
1129 A284 8f multi (56) 45.00 12.00
Nos. 1126-1129 (4) 175.00 48.00

Fair Building, Canton — A285

1973, Oct. 15 Photo. *Perf. 11*
1130 A285 8f multicolored (95) 27.50 3.00

Export Commodities Fall Fair, Canton.

Teapot with Blue Phoenix Design — A286

Excavated Works of Art: No. 1132, Silver pot with horse design. No. 1133, Black pottery horse. No. 1134, Woman, clay figurine. No. 1135, Carved stone pillar base. No. 1136, Galloping bronze horse. No. 1137, Bronze inkwell (toad). No. 1138, Bronze lamp, Chang Hsin Palace. No. 1139, Bronze tripod. No. 1140, Square bronze pot. 20f, Bronze wine vessel. 52f, Painted red clay tripod.

1973, Nov. 20 *Perf. 11½*

1131 A286 4f ol bis & multi (66) 5.50 .75
1132 A286 4f ver & multi (67) 5.50 .75
1133 A286 8f yel grn & multi (68) 4.50 .75
1134 A286 8f brt rose & multi (69) 4.50 .75
1135 A286 8f lt vio & multi (70) 4.50 .75
1136 A286 8f yel bis & multi (71) 4.50 .75
1137 A286 8f lt bl & multi (72) 4.50 .75
1138 A286 8f gray & multi (73) 4.50 .75
1139 A286 10f yel bis & multi (74) 4.50 .75
1140 A286 10f dp org & multi (75) 4.50 .75
1141 A286 20f lil & multi (76) 9.00 2.00
1142 A286 52f grn & multi (77) 14.50 4.00
Nos. 1131-1142 (12) 70.50 13.50

Marginal Markings

Marginal inscriptions on stamps of 1974-91 start at lower left with "J" for commemoratives and "T" for "special issues," followed by three numbers indicating (a) set sequence for the year, (b) total of stamps in set, and (c) number of stamp within set. At right appears the year date. Listings include the "c" number parenthetically. The "a" number is included only when it will help identify stamps not illustrated.

Example: T26 (6-3), the 3rd stamp of 6 from the 26th special set. Set numbers and or positions will be shown only when they help identify a stamp. An illustrated single stamp set will not have these numbers in the listings.

Woman Gymnast — A287

Designs: No. 1144, Gymnast on rings. No. 1145, Aerial split over balance beam, woman. No. 1146, Gymnast on parallel bars. No. 1147, Uneven bars, woman. No. 1148, Gymnast on horse. T.1.

1974, Jan. 1 Photo. *Perf. 11½x11*

1143 A287 8f lt grn & multi (1) 10.00 3.50
1144 A287 8f lt vio & multi (2) 10.00 3.50
1145 A287 8f lt blue & multi (3) 10.00 3.50
1146 A287 8f sal & multi (4) 12.50 4.50
1147 A287 8f yel & multi (5) 10.00 4.50
1148 A287 8f lil rose & multi (6) 12.50 4.50
Nos. 1143-1148 (6) 65.00 24.00

Girls Twirling Bamboo Diabolos — A288

Designs: No. 1149, Lion Dance, vert. No. 1150, Handstand on chairs, vert. No. 1152, Men balancing jar. No. 1153, Plate spinning, vert. No. 1154, Twirling umbrella, vert. T.2.

1974, Jan. 21 *Perf. 11*

1149 A288 8f brn & multi (1) 7.00 2.75
1150 A288 8f Prus bl & multi (2) 7.00 2.75
1151 A288 8f lilac & multi (3) 10.00 2.75
1152 A288 8f dull bl & multi (4) 7.00 2.75
1153 A288 8f ol grn & multi (5) 7.00 2.75
1154 A288 8f gray & multi (6) 10.00 2.75
Nos. 1149-1154 (6) 48.00 16.50

Traditional acrobatics.

Shao Shan — A289

Site of 1st National Communist Party Congress — A289a

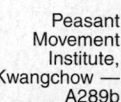

Peasant Movement Institute, Kwangchow — A289b

Headquarters of Nanchang Uprising — A289c

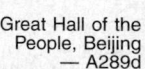

Great Hall of the People, Beijing — A289d

View of Wen Chia Shih — A289e

Tien An Men, Beijing — A289f

Tzeping in Chingkang Mountains — A289g

Site of Kutien Meeting — A289h

Tsunyi Conference Site — A289i

Yenan (bridge) — A289j

Hsi Pai Ho, Communist Party Meeting Site — A289k

Fairy Cave, Lushan — A289l

Monument to People's Heroes — A289m

Transportation by Railroad — A289n

Trucks on Mountain Road — A289o

1973-74 Litho. *Perf. 11*
Without Gum

1163	A289	1f sl grn & pale grn	.65	.35
1164	A289a	1½f car & buff	.65	.35
1165	A289b	2f dk blue & pale grn	.70	.35
1166	A289c	3f dk ol & yel	.70	.35
1167	A289d	4f red & yel	1.00	.35
1168	A289e	5f brn & lt yel	.80	.35
1169	A289f	8f dull mag & buff	.80	.35
a.		Perf. 11½x12	15.00	
1170	A289g	10f blue & buff	.80	.40
1171	A289h	20f dk red & buff	1.50	.40
1172	A289i	22f vio & lt yel	5.00	1.90
1173	A289j	35f mar & lt yel	3.50	1.75
1174	A289k	43f red brn & buff	4.50	2.00
1175	A289l	50f dk blue & pink	3.00	.50
1176	A289m	52f sepia & buff	3.00	.50

Photogravure & Engraved

1177	A289n	$1 multicolored ('73)	5.00	1.25
1178	A289o	$2 multicolored	6.00	1.25
		Nos. 1163-1178 (16)	37.60	12.40

Capital Stadium — A290

Design: 8f, Hotel Peking.

1974, Dec. 1 Photo. *Perf. 11*
Without Gum

1179	A290	4f black & yel grn	.75	.25
1180	A290	8f black & ultra	.60	.25

"Veteran Secretary" — A291

Well Diggers — A292

Designs: Nos. 1183-1186 horizontal. T.3.

1974, Apr. 20 Photo. *Perf. 11*

1181	A291	8f shown (1)	4.00	2.25
1182	A292	8f shown (2)	4.00	2.25
1183	A291	8f Spring hoeing (3)	5.00	2.25
1184	A291	8f Farmers (4)	5.00	2.25
1185	A292	8f Farm (5)	5.00	2.25
1186	A291	8f Bumper crops (6)	5.00	2.50
		Nos. 1181-1186 (6)	28.00	13.75

Paintings by farmers of Huhsien County, shown at exhibition in Peking.

Mailman on Motorcycle — A293

1974, May 15 Photo. *Perf. 11*

1187	A293	8f shown (1)	10.00	4.50
1188	A293	8f People of the world (2)	10.00	3.50
1189	A293	8f Great Wall (3)	15.00	3.50
		Nos. 1187-1189 (3)	35.00	11.50

Centenary of the UPU. J.1.

Barefoot Doctor Inoculating Children A294

Designs (Barefoot Doctors): No. 1191, Crossing stream at night to reach patient, vert. No. 1192, Gathering herbs, vert. No. 1193, Acupuncture treatment for farmer in the field.

Perf. 11x11½, 11½x11
1974, June 26 Photo.

1190	A294	8f multicolored (82)	15.00	2.00
1191	A294	8f multicolored (83)	20.00	3.00
1192	A294	8f multicolored (84)	17.50	2.00
1193	A294	8f multicolored (85)	15.00	2.00
		Nos. 1190-1193 (4)	67.50	9.00

Steel Worker Wang Chin-hsi — A295

No. 1195, Workers studying Mao's writings around campfire. No. 1196, Drilling for oil in winter. No. 1197, Scientific industrial management. No. 1198, Oil derricks and farms. T.4.

1974, Sept. 30 Photo. *Perf. 11*

1194	A295	8f multi (5-1)	6.00	1.50
1195	A295	8f multi (5-2)	5.50	1.50
1196	A295	8f multi (5-3)	5.50	1.50
1197	A295	8f multi (5-4)	5.50	1.50
1198	A295	8f multi (5-5)	6.00	1.50
		Nos. 1194-1198 (5)	28.50	7.50

Workers of Taching as examples of achievement.

Members of Tachai Commune — A296

No. 1200, Farmers leveling mountains and fields in winter. No. 1201, Scientific farming. No. 1202, Trucks carrying surplus harvest. No. 1203, Young workers with banner. T.5.

1974, Sept. 30

1199	A296	8f multi (5-1)	5.00	1.50
1200	A296	8f multi (5-2)	5.00	1.50
1201	A296	8f multi (5-3)	5.00	1.50
1202	A296	8f multi (5-4)	6.00	1.50
1203	A296	8f multi (5-5)	6.00	1.50
		Nos. 1199-1203 (5)	27.00	7.50

Farmers of Tachai as examples of achievement.

Arms of Republic and Members of Ethnic Groups — A297

1974, Oct. 1

1204	A297	8f multi (1-1)	37.50	8.50

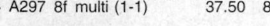

Taching Steel Worker — A298

Designs: No. 1206, Tachai farm woman. No. 1207, Soldier, planes and ships. J.3.

1974, Oct. 1

1205	A298	8f multi (3-1)	4.50	2.00
1206	A298	8f multi (3-2)	4.50	2.00
1207	A298	8f multi (3-3)	4.50	2.00
a.		Strip of 3, #1205-1207	25.00	12.00

People's Republic of China, 25th anniv.

Values for No. 1207a are for an unfolded strip.

Export Commodities Fair Building, Canton — A299

1974, Oct. 15

1208	A299	8f multicolored	12.00	2.00

Chinese Export Commodities Fair, Canton.

Guerrillas' Monument, Permet, Albania — A300

Albanian Patriots and Coat of Arms — A301

1974, Nov. 29 Photo. *Perf. 11½x11*

1209	A300	8f multicolored	8.50	2.00
1210	A301	8f multicolored	8.50	2.00

Albania's liberation, 30th anniversary.

Water-cooled Generator — A302

Industrial Products: No. 1212, Motorized rice sprouts transplanter. No. 1213, Universal cylindrical grinding machine. No. 1214, Open-air rock drill, vert. All dated 1973.

Photogravure and Engraved

1974, Dec. 23 ***Perf. 11***

1211 A302 8f vio & multi (78) 75.00 11.00
1212 A302 8f yel grn & multi (79) 100.00 25.00
1213 A302 8f ver & multi (80) 75.00 11.00
1214 A302 8f blue & multi (81) 150.00 25.00
Nos. 1211-1214 (4) 400.00 72.00

Congress Delegates — A303

Designs: No. 1216, Red flags, constitution and flowers. No. 1217, Worker, farmer and soldier, agriculture and industry.

1975, Jan. 25 **Photo.** ***Perf. 11½***

1215 A303 8f gold & multi (3-1) 16.00 4.00
1216 A303 8f gold & multi (3-2) 20.00 4.00
1217 A303 8f gold & multi (3-3) 25.00 10.00
Nos. 1215-1217 (3) 61.00 18.00

Fourth National People's Congress, Peking.

Teacher Studying Revolutionary Works — A304

No. 1219, Teacher, children and horse. No. 1220, Outdoors class. No. 1221, Class held in boat. T.9.

1975, Mar. 8 **Photo.** ***Perf. 11***

1218 A304 8f multi (4-1) 17.50 5.00
1219 A304 8f multi (4-2) 27.50 6.00
1220 A304 8f multi (4-3) 20.00 5.00
1221 A304 8f multi (4-4) 17.50 4.00
Nos. 1218-1221 (4) 82.50 20.00

Rural women teachers and for International Working Women's Day.

"Broadsword," Encounter Position — A305

No. 1223, Exercise with 2 swords (woman). No. 1224, Graceful boxing (woman). No. 1225, Man leaping with spear. No. 1226, Woman holding fighting staff. 43f, 2 women with spears against man with 3-section staff.

1975, June 10 **Photo.** ***Perf. 11x11½***

Size: 39x29mm

1222 A305 8f (6-1) 6.00 2.25
1223 A305 8f (6-2) 7.00 2.25
1224 A305 8f (6-3) 5.00 2.25
1225 A305 8f (6-4) 5.00 2.25
1226 A305 8f (6-5) 6.00 2.25

Size: 59x29mm

1227 A305 43f red & multi (6-6) 12.00 8.00
Nos. 1222-1227 (6) 41.00 19.25

Wushu ("Kung Fu"), self-defense exercises. Tête bêche in sheets of 50 (5x10). Value, set of pairs $120.

Mass Judgment and Criticisms — A306

No. 1229, Brigade leader writing wall newspaper. No. 1230, Study and criticism on battlefield, horiz. No. 1231, Former "slave" led into battle by criticism of Lin Piao and Confucius, horiz. T.8.

Perf. 11½x11, 11x11½

1975, Aug. 20 **Photo.**

1228 A306 8f red & multi (4-1) 20.00 4.00
1229 A306 8f red & multi (4-2) 20.00 4.00
1230 A306 8f red & multi (4-3) 18.50 4.00
1231 A306 8f red & multi (4-4) 20.00 4.00
Nos. 1228-1231 (4) 78.50 16.00

Campaign to encourage criticism of Lin Piao and Confucius.

Athletes Studying Theory of Dictatorship of Proletariat — A307

3rd National Sports Meet: No. 1232, Women athletes leading parade, vert. No. 1234, Women volleyball players. No. 1235, Runner, soldier, farmer and worker, vert. No. 1236, Young athlete and various sports. No. 1237, Athletes of various races and horse race. 35f, Children and diving tower, vert. J.6.

1975, Sept. 12 **Photo.** ***Perf. 11½***

1232 A307 8f multi (7-1) 4.50 1.00
1233 A307 8f multi (7-2) 8.50 1.00
1234 A307 8f multi (7-3) 18.50 2.00
1235 A307 8f multi (7-4) 4.50 1.00
1236 A307 8f multi (7-5) 4.50 1.00
1237 A307 8f multi (7-6) 4.50 1.00
1238 A307 35f multi (7-7) 4.50 3.00
Nos. 1232-1238 (7) 49.50 10.00

Mountaineers A308

Mt. Everest A309

Design: No. 1240, Mountaineers raising Chinese flag on summit, horiz. T.15.

1975 **Photo.** ***Perf. 11½x11, 11x11½***

1239 A308 8f multi (3-2) 2.50 1.00
1240 A308 8f multi (3-3) 2.50 1.00
1241 A309 43f multi (3-1) 4.00 1.25
Nos. 1239-1241 (3) 9.00 3.25

Chinese Mt. Everest expedition.

Agricultural Workers with Book — A310

No. 1243, Workers carrying load. No. 1244, Woman driving harvester combine. J.7.

1975, Oct. 1 ***Perf. 11½***

1242 A310 8f multi (3-1) 9.00 1.75
1243 A310 8f multi (3-2) 9.00 1.75
1244 A310 8f multi (3-3) 13.00 1.75
Nos. 1242-1244 (3) 31.00 5.25

National Conference to promote learning from Tachai's achievements in agriculture.

Girl Giving Boy Red Scarf — A311

Designs (Children): No. 1246, Putting up wall posters criticizing Lin Piao and Confucius. No. 1247, Studying. No. 1248, Harvesting. 52f, Physical training. T.14.

1975, Dec. 1 **Photo.** ***Perf. 11½***

1245 A311 8f multi (5-1) 4.00 1.25
1246 A311 8f multi (5-2) 4.00 1.25
1247 A311 8f multi (5-3) 4.00 1.25
1248 A311 8f multi (5-4) 4.00 1.25
1249 A311 52f multi (5-5) 8.00 2.50
Nos. 1245-1249 (5) 24.00 7.50

Moral, intellectual and physical progress of Chinese children.

Woman Plowing Rice Field A312

No. 1251, Mechanized rice planting. No. 1252, Drainage and irrigation. No. 1253, Woman spraying insecticide over cotton field. No. 1254, Combine. T.13.

1975, Dec. 15 ***Perf. 11***

1250 A312 8f multi (5-1) 7.00 1.75
1251 A312 8f multi (5-2) 7.00 1.75
1252 A312 8f multi (5-3) 5.00 1.75
1253 A312 8f multi (5-4) 5.00 1.75
1254 A312 8f multi (5-5) 5.00 1.75
Nos. 1250-1254 (5) 29.00 8.75

Priority program of farm mechanization.

Farmland and Irrigation Canal — A313

Designs of Nos. 1255-1270 numbered J.8.: No. 1256, Irrigation canal (16-2). No. 1257, Fertilizer plant (16-3). No. 1258, Textile plant (16-4). No. 1259, Anshan Iron and Steel Co. (16-5). No. 1260, Coal freight trains (16-6). No. 1261, Hydroelectric station (16-7). No. 1262, Ship building (16-8). No. 1263, Oil industry (16-9). No. 1264, Pipe line and port (16-10). No. 1265, Train on viaduct (16-11). No. 1266, Scientific research (16-12). No. 1267, Classroom (16-13). No. 1268, Health Center (16-14). No. 1269, Apartment houses (16-15). No. 1270, Department store (16-16).

1976 **Photo.** ***Perf. 11½***

1255 A313 8f shown (16-1) 8.00 2.25
1256 A313 8f multi 8.00 2.25
1257 A313 8f multi 15.00 2.25
1258 A313 8f multi 8.00 2.25
1259 A313 8f multi 8.00 2.25
1260 A313 8f multi 10.00 2.25
1261 A313 8f multi 10.00 2.25
1262 A313 8f multi 10.00 2.25
1263 A313 8f multi 10.00 2.25
1264 A313 8f multi 10.00 2.25
1265 A313 8f multi 10.00 2.25
1266 A313 8f multi 8.00 2.25
1267 A313 8f multi 24.00 5.50
1268 A313 8f multi 8.00 2.25
1269 A313 8f multi 8.00 2.25
1270 A313 8f multi 24.00 5.50
Nos. 1255-1270 (16) 179.00 42.50

Nos. 1255-1270 commemorate fulfillment of 4th Five-year Plan.

Issued: Nos. 1255-1259, 2/20; Nos. 1260-1264, 4/9; Nos. 1265-1270, 6/12.

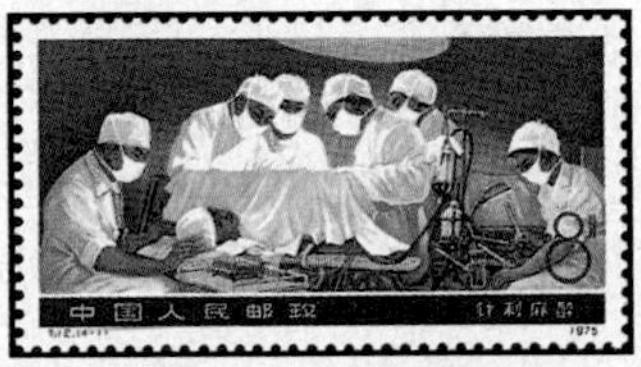

Heart Surgery with Acupuncture Anesthesia — A314

Operating Room and: No. 1272, Man driving tractor with severed arm restored. No. 1273, Man exercising broken arm in cast. No. 1274, Patient threading needle after cataract operation. T.12.

1976, Apr. 9 **Photo.** ***Perf. 11½***

1271 A314 8f brn & multi (4-1) 8.00 2.00
1272 A314 8f yel grn & multi (4-2) 15.00 3.00
1273 A314 8f bl grn & multi (4-3) 8.00 1.75
1274 A314 8f vio bl & multi (4-4) 8.00 1.75
Nos. 1271-1274 (4) 39.00 8.50

Achievements in medical and health services.

Students in May 7 School — A315

Designs: No. 1276, Students as farm workers. No. 1277, Production brigade. J.9.

1976, May 7 **Photo.** ***Perf. 11½***

1275 A315 8f multi (3-1) 12.00 2.00
1276 A315 8f multi (3-2) 5.00 2.00
1277 A315 8f multi (3-3) 11.00 2.00
Nos. 1275-1277 (3) 28.00 6.00

Chairman Mao's May 7 Directive, 10th anniv.

Mass Training in Swimming — A316

No. 1279, Swimmers crossing Yangtze River. No. 1280, Swimmers walking into the surf. J.10.

1976, July 16 **Photo.** ***Perf. 11½***

Size: 47x27mm

1278 A316 8f multi (3-1) 8.00 2.00

Size: 35x27mm

1279 A316 8f multi (3-2) 8.00 2.00
1280 A316 8f multi (3-3) 8.00 2.00
Nos. 1278-1280 (3) 24.00 6.00

Chairman Mao's swim in Yangtze River, 10th anniversary.

Workers, Peasants and Soldiers Going to College — A317

No. 1282, Classroom. No. 1283, Instruction on construction site. No. 1284, Computer room. No. 1285, Graduates returning home. T.18.

1976, Sept. 6 **Photo.** ***Perf. 11½***

1281	A317	8f multi (5-1)		10.00	2.50
1282	A317	8f multi (5-2)		11.00	2.50
1283	A317	8f multi (5-3)		13.00	3.50
1284	A317	8f multi (5-4)		13.00	3.50
1285	A317	8f multi (5-5)		11.00	2.50
		Nos. 1281-1285 (5)		58.00	14.50

Success of proletarian education system.

Power Line Repair by Woman — A318

No. 1287, Insulator repair. No. 1288, Cherry picker. No. 1289, Transformer repair. T.16.

1976, Sept. 15

1286	A318	8f multi (4-1)	9.00	1.75
1287	A318	8f multi (4-2)	9.00	1.75
1288	A318	8f multi (4-3)	6.00	1.75
1289	A318	8f multi (4-4)	6.00	1.75
		Nos. 1286-1289 (4)	30.00	7.00

Maintenance of high power lines.

Lu Hsun A319

No. 1291, Lu Hsun sick, writing in bed. No. 1292, Lu Hsun with worker, soldier and peasant. J.11.

Photo. & Engr.

1976, Oct. 19 ***Perf. 11x11½***

1290	A319	8f multi (3-1)	5.00	2.00

Photo.

1291	A319	8f multi (3-2)	14.00	3.50
1292	A319	8f multi (3-3)	7.50	2.00
		Nos. 1290-1292 (3)	26.50	7.50

Lu Hsun (1881-1936), writer and revolutionary leader.

Old Farmer Tying Towel on Student's Head — A320

Designs: No. 1294, Student teaching farm woman, horiz. No. 1295, Students climbing mountain for new water resources. No. 1296, Student testing wheat, horiz. 10f, Student feeding lamb. 20f, Frontier guards, horiz. T.17.

1976, Dec. 22 **Photo.** ***Perf. 11½***

1293	A320	4f multi (6-1)	4.50	.75
1294	A320	8f multi (6-2)	4.50	.85
1295	A320	8f multi (6-3)	4.50	.85
1296	A320	8f multi (6-4)	10.00	3.00
1297	A320	10f multi (6-5)	7.00	.85
1298	A320	20f multi (6-6)	8.00	2.50
		Nos. 1293-1298 (6)	38.50	8.80

Students' efforts to help poor country people.

Mao's Home, Shaoshan — A321

Shaoshan, Mao's birthplace: No. 1300, School building. No. 1301, Farmers' Association building. 10f, Railroad station. T.11.

1976, Dec. 26 ***Perf. 11***

1299	A321	4f multi (4-1)	3.50	1.50
1300	A321	8f multi (4-2)	3.50	1.50
1301	A321	8f multi (4-3)	6.25	1.50
1302	A321	10f multi (4-4)	3.50	1.50
		Nos. 1299-1302 (4)	16.75	6.00

Chou En-lai — A322

No. 1304, Chou giving report at 10th Party Congress. No. 1305, Chou with Wang Chin-hsi, famous oil worker, horiz. No. 1306, Chou with people of Tachai, 1973, horiz. J.13.

1977, Jan. 8 **Photo.** ***Perf. 11½***

1303	A322	8f multi (4-1)	3.75	1.25
1304	A322	8f multi (4-2)	5.00	1.25
1305	A322	8f multi (4-3)	3.75	1.25
1306	A322	8f multi (4-4)	10.00	1.25
		Nos. 1303-1306 (4)	22.50	5.00

Premier Chou En-lai (1898-1976), a founder of Chinese Communist Party, 1st death anniversary.

Liu Hu-lan, an Inspiration A323

Liu Hu-lan, Chinese heroine: No. 1307, Liu Hu-lan monument. No. 1308, Mao Tse-tung quotation: "A great life-a glorious death." J.12.

1977, Jan. 31

1307	A323	8f multi (3-1)	16.00	4.00
1308	A323	8f multi (3-2)	5.00	2.00
1309	A323	8f multi (3-3)	5.00	2.00
		Nos. 1307-1309 (3)	26.00	8.00

Uprising in Taiwan A324

Design: 10f, Gate of Heavenly Peace, Peking; Sun Moon Lake, Taiwan, Taiwanese people holding PRC flag. J.14.

1977, Feb. 28 **Photo.** ***Perf. 11***

1310	A324	8f multi (2-1)	9.00	1.25
1311	A324	10f multi (2-2)	11.00	1.75

Uprising of the people of Taiwan, 2/28/47.

Sharpshooters — A325

Militia Women: No. 1313, Women horseback riders. No. 1314, Underground defense tunnel. T.10.

1977, Mar. 8 ***Perf. 11½***

1312	A325	8f multi (3-1)	7.00	3.00
1313	A325	8f multi (3-2)	7.00	3.00
1314	A325	8f multi (3-3)	10.00	3.00
		Nos. 1312-1314 (3)	24.00	9.00

Coal Mining — A326

Sheepherding — A326a

Export (Loading Railroad Car onto Ship) — A326b

Forestry — A326c

Hydroelectric Station — A326d

Fishery — A326e

Combine in Field — A326f

Radio Tower, Mail Truck — A326g

Steel Production — A326h

Trucks on Mountain Road — A326i

Textiles — A326j

Tractor Assembly Line — A326k

Offshore Oil Rigs, Birds, Setting Sun — A326l

Railroad Bridge, Yangtze Gorge — A326m

No numbers.

1977 **Photo.** ***Perf. 11½***

1315	A326	1f yel grn, red & blk	.45	.30
1316	A326a	1½f bl grn, yel grn & brn	.50	.30
1317	A326b	2f org, bl & blk	.50	.30
1318	A326c	3f ol & dk grn	.60	.30
1319	A326d	4f lil, org & blk	.85	.30
1320	A326e	5f lt ol & ultra	.85	.30
1321	A326f	8f red & yel	.85	.30
1322	A326g	10f lt grn, org & bl	.85	.30
1323	A326h	20f org, yel & brn	.95	.30
1324	A326i	30f bl, gray grn & blk	1.25	.30
1325	A326j	40f multicolored	1.40	.35
1326	A326k	50f cit, red & blk	1.25	.35
1327	A326l	60f pur, lt & dk org	1.25	.45
1328	A326m	70f blue & multi	2.00	.75
		Nos. 1315-1328 (14)	13.55	4.90

Nos. 1316, 1317 and 1325 exist imperf. Value, pair each $1,000.

Address by Party Committee A327

Designs: No. 1330, Planting new rice fields. No. 1331, Farmers reading wall newspaper. No. 1332, Land reclamation. T.22.

1977, Apr. 9 ***Perf. 11x11½***

1329	A327	8f multi (4-1)	4.50	1.00
1330	A327	8f multi (4-2)	4.50	1.00
1331	A327	8f multi (4-3)	4.50	1.00
1332	A327	8f multi (4-4)	4.50	1.00
		Nos. 1329-1332 (4)	18.00	4.00

Building Tachai-type communities throughout China.

Worker at Microphone — A328

Designs: No. 1334, Drilling for oil during snowstorm. No. 1335, Crowd advancing under Red banner. No. 1336, Workers, industrial complex, rocket blast-off. J.15.

1977, Apr. 25 ***Perf. 11***

1333	A328	8f multi (4-1)	7.00	1.25
1334	A328	8f multi (4-2)	7.00	1.25
1335	A328	8f multi (4-3)	7.00	1.25
1336	A328	8f multi (4-4)	7.00	1.25
		Nos. 1333-1336 (4)	28.00	5.00

Conference on learning from Taching workers in industry.

Mongolians Hailing Anniversary A329

10f, Iron and steel complex, iron ore train. 20f, Cattle grazing in improved pasture. J.16.

1977, May 1 ***Perf. 11x11½***

1337	A329 8f multi (3-1)	5.00	.75
1338	A329 10f multi (3-2)	1.50	.55
1339	A329 20f multi (3-3)	3.00	1.00
	Nos. 1337-1339 (3)	9.50	2.30

30th anniversary of Inner Mongolian Autonomous Region.

1877 Flag of Romania and Oak Leaves — A330

Mihai Viteazu Memorial (16th Century Hero) — A331

10f, Battle of Smirdan, by N. Grigorescu. J.17.

1977, May 9 **Photo.** ***Perf. 11***

1340	A330 8f multi (3-1)	5.00	1.25
1341	A331 10f multi (3-2)	1.00	1.00
1342	A331 20f multi (3-3)	1.00	1.00
	Nos. 1340-1342 (3)	7.00	3.25

Centenary of Romanian independence.

Yenan "Let 100 Flowers Bloom" A332

No. 1344, Hammer, sickle, gun & flowers; "Proletarian revolutionary literature will prosper." J.18.

1977, May, 23

1343	A332 8f grn, red & gold	1.75	.65
1344	A332 8f lt brn, red & gold	1.75	.65

Yenan Forum on Literature & Art, 35th anniv.

Zhu De — A333

Designs: No. 1346, Zhu De, last address to Congress. No. 1347, Zhu De at his desk, horiz. No. 1348, Zhu De on horseback as commander of Red Army. J.19.

1977, July 6 **Photo.** ***Perf. 11½***

1345	A333 8f multi (4-1)	1.50	.45
1346	A333 8f multi (4-2)	1.50	.45
1347	A333 8f multi (4-3)	2.00	.55
1348	A333 8f multi (4-4)	2.00	.55
	Nos. 1345-1348 (4)	7.00	2.00

Zhu De (1886-1976), Commander of Red Army, Chairman of National People's Congress.

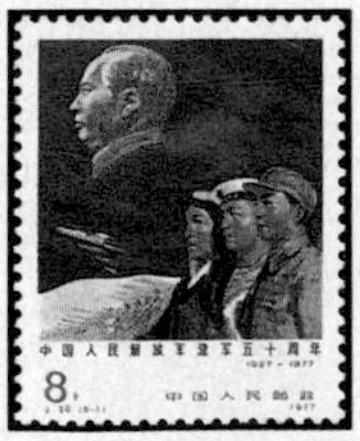
Military under Mao's Banner — A334

No. 1350, Red Flag, Soldiers, Chingkang Mountains. No. 1351, Guerrilla fighters returning to base. No. 1352, Guerrillas crossing Yangtze. No. 1353, National defense. J.20.

1977, Aug. 1

1349	A334 8f multi (5-1)	7.00	1.50
1350	A334 8f multi (5-2)	3.50	1.50
1351	A334 8f multi (5-3)	5.50	1.50
1352	A334 8f multi (5-4)	5.50	1.50
1353	A334 8f multi (5-5)	4.00	1.50
	Nos. 1349-1353 (5)	25.50	7.50

Liberation Army Day, 50th anniversary of People's Army.

Gate of Heavenly Peace, People and Red Flags — A335

Designs: No. 1355, People marching under Red Flag with Mao's portrait. No. 1356, People marching under Red Flag with hammer and sickle. J.23.

1977, Aug. 22 **Photo.** ***Perf. 11½x11***

1354	A335 8f multi (3-1)	15.00	4.00
1355	A335 8f multi (3-2)	15.00	4.00
1356	A335 8f multi (3-3)	15.00	4.00
	Nos. 1354-1356 (3)	45.00	12.00

11th National Congress of the Communist Party of China.

Chairman Mao — A336

Designs (Mao Portraits): No. 1358, as young man in Shansi. No. 1359, addressing Communist Party in Plenary Session. No. 1360, Proclaiming People's Republic at Gate of Heavenly Peace. No. 1361, at airport with Chou En-lai and Zhu De, horiz. No. 1362, Reviewing Army as old man. J.21.

1977, Sept. 9 **Photo.** ***Perf. 11½***

1357	A336 8f multi (6-1)	4.00	1.25
1358	A336 8f multi (6-2)	4.00	1.25
1359	A336 8f multi (6-3)	4.00	1.25
1360	A336 8f multi (6-4)	4.00	1.25
1361	A336 8f multi (6-5)	6.00	1.25
1362	A336 8f multi (6-6)	4.00	1.25
	Nos. 1357-1362 (6)	26.00	7.50

Mao-Tse-tung (1893-1976), first death anniversary.

Mao Memorial Hall — A337

Completion of Mao Memorial Hall: No. 1364, Chairman Hua's inscription. J.22.

1977, Sept. 9

1363	A337 8f lt ultra & multi	5.00	1.50
1364	A337 8f lt grn, tan & gold	7.50	2.25

Tractors Moving Drilling Tower — A338

No. 1366, Shui Pow Tsi oil well and women workers. No. 1367, Construction of oil pipe line, Taching, and silos. No. 1368, Tung Fang Hung oil refinery, Peking. No. 1369, Taching oil loaded into tanker in harbor. 20f, Off-shore drilling platform "Pohai No. 1." T.19.

1978, Jan. 31 **Photo.** ***Perf. 11***

1365	A338 8f multi (6-1)	2.00	.75
1366	A338 8f multi (6-2)	2.00	.75
1367	A338 8f multi (6-3)	2.00	.75
1368	A338 8f multi (6-4)	4.00	.75
1369	A338 8f multi (6-5)	4.00	.75
1370	A338 20f multi (6-6)	4.00	2.00
	Nos. 1365-1370 (6)	18.00	5.75

Development of Chinese oil industry.

"Army Teaching Militia" — A339

No. 1372, "Army helping with rice planting." T.23.

1978, Feb. 5 **Photo.** ***Perf. 11***

1371	A339 8f multi (2-1)	4.50	1.25
1372	A339 8f multi (2-2)	4.50	1.25

Army and people working as a family.

Red Flags, Mao Tse-tung — A340

Constitution and Red Flags — A341

No. 1375, Atom symbol over symbols of agriculture & industry. All designs include Great Hall of the People, Peking, & flowers. J.24.

1978, Feb. 26

1373	A340 8f multi (3-1)	4.00	.85
1374	A341 8f multi (3-2)	4.00	.85
1375	A340 8f multi (3-3)	4.00	.85
	Nos. 1373-1375 (3)	12.00	2.55

5th National People's Congress.

Mao's Eulogy for Lei Feng — A342

Lei Feng, Studying Mao's Works — A343

No. 1377, Chairman Hua's thoughts (5 lines). J.26.

1978, Mar. 5

1376	A342 8f gold & red (3-1)	8.00	2.00
1377	A342 8f gold & red (3-2)	8.00	2.00
1378	A343 8f multicolored (3-3)	8.00	2.00
	Nos. 1376-1378 (3)	24.00	6.00

Lei Feng (1940-1962), communist fighter; 15th anniversary of Chairman Mao's eulogy "Learn from Comrade Lei Feng."

Hsiang Ching-yu — A344

Yang Kai-hui — A345

1978, Mar. 8

1379	A344 8f multi (2-1)	4.00	1.00
1380	A345 8f multi (2-2)	4.00	1.00

Hsiang Ching-yu, pioneer of Women's Movement, executed 1928; Yang Kai-hui, communist fighter, executed 1930. J.27.

A346

A346a

A346b

No. 1381, Conference emblem. No. 1382, Banners symbolizing industry, agriculture, defense & science. No. 1383, Red flag, atom symbol & globe. J.25.

1978, Mar. 18 **Litho.** ***Perf. 11½x11***

1381	A346 8f gold & red (3-1)	3.00	.90
1382	A346a 8f multi (3-2)	3.00	.90
1383	A346b 8f multi (3-3)	3.00	.90
a.	Souvenir sheet of 3	*475.00*	*200.00*
	Nos. 1381-1383 (3)	9.00	2.70

Natl. Science Conf. No. 1383a contains Nos. 1381-1383 with simulated perforations. Sold for 50f.

Release of Weather Balloon A347

Weather Observations: No. 1385, Radar station, typhoon watch. No. 1386, Computer, weather maps. No. 1387, Local weather observers. No. 1388, Rockets intercepting hail clouds. T.24.

1978, Apr. 25 Photo. *Perf. 11x11½*

1384	A347 8f multi (5-1)	1.50	.70
1385	A347 8f multi (5-2)	1.50	.70
1386	A347 8f multi (5-3)	1.50	.70
1387	A347 8f multi (5-4)	1.50	.70
1388	A347 8f multi (5-5)	1.50	.70
	Nos. 1384-1388 (5)	7.50	3.50

Galloping Horse — A348

Designs: Galloping Horses, by Hsu Peihung (1895-1953). 40f, 50f, 60f, 70f, $5, horiz. T.28.

1978, May 5 *Perf. 11½x11, 11x11½*

1389	A348 4f multi (10-1)	3.00	1.00
1390	A348 8f multi (10-2)	3.00	1.00
1391	A348 8f multi (10-3)	3.00	1.00
1392	A348 10f multi (10-4)	4.00	1.00
1393	A348 20f multi (10-5)	4.00	1.00
1394	A348 30f multi (10-6)	8.50	2.00
1395	A348 40f multi (10-7)	6.50	1.75
1396	A348 50f multi (10-8)	25.00	3.00
1397	A348 60f multi (10-9)	8.00	2.00
1398	A348 70f multi (10-10)	7.00	2.00
	Nos. 1389-1398 (10)	72.00	15.75

Souvenir Sheet

1399	A348 $5 multicolored	*575.00*	200.00

No. 1399 contains one stamp showing 4 horses, size: 89x39mm.

Children Playing Soccer — A349

Designs: No. 1401, Children on the beach. No. 1402, Little girls dancing. No. 1403, Children taking long walks. 20f, Children exercising for good health. T.21.

Size: 22x27mm

1978, June 1 *Perf. 11½*

1400	A349 8f multi (5-2)	1.00	.50
1401	A349 8f multi (5-3)	1.00	.50
1402	A349 8f multi (5-4)	1.00	.50
1403	A349 8f multi (5-5)	1.00	.50

Size: 48x28mm

1404	A349 20f multi (5-1)	1.25	.80
	Nos. 1400-1404 (5)	5.25	2.80

Build up your health while young.

Synthetic Fiber Feeder A350

Designs: No. 1406, Drawing out threads. No. 1407, Weaving. No. 1408, Dyeing and printing. No. 1409, Finished products. T.25.

1978, June 15 Photo. *Perf. 11½*

1405	A350 8f multi (5-1)	1.00	.60
1406	A350 8f multi (5-2)	1.00	.60
1407	A350 8f multi (5-3)	1.00	.60
1408	A350 8f multi (5-4)	1.00	.60
1409	A350 8f multi (5-5)	1.00	.60
a.	Strip of 5, #1405-1409	11.00	11.00
	Nos. 1405-1409 (5)	5.00	3.00

Chemical fiber industry. No. 1409a has continuous design. No. 1409a is valued as an unfolded strip. Folded strips sell for less.

Conference Emblem A351

"Develop Economy and Ensure Supplies" A352

1978, June 20 *Perf. 13*

1410	A351 8f multi (2-1)	1.75	.55
1411	A352 8f multi (2-2)	1.75	.55

Natl. Conf. on Learning from Taching and Tachai in Finance and Trade. J.28.

New Pastures, Mongolia — A353

Designs: No. 1413, Kazakh shepherds selecting sheep for breeding. No. 1414, Mechanized shearing of sheep, Tibet, T.27.

1978, June 30 Photo. *Perf. 11½*

1412	A353 8f multi (3-1)	3.00	.80
1413	A353 8f multi (3-2)	3.00	.80
1414	A353 8f multi (3-3)	3.00	.80
	Nos. 1412-1414 (3)	9.00	2.40

Learning from Tachai in developing animal husbandry and new pastoral areas.

Coke Oven — A354

Iron and Steel Industry: No. 1416, Iron furnace. No. 1417, Pouring steel. No. 1418, Steel rolling. No. 1419, Finished iron and steel products. T.26.

1978, July 22

1415	A354 8f multi (5-1)	2.25	.50
1416	A354 8f multi (5-2)	2.25	.50
1417	A354 8f multi (5-3)	2.25	.50
1418	A354 8f multi (5-4)	2.25	.50
1419	A354 8f multi (5-5)	2.25	.50
	Nos. 1415-1419 (5)	11.25	2.50

Iron Fist to Prevent Revisionism A355

No. 1421, "Carrying forward revolutionary tradition." No. 1422, "Strenuous training in military skills to wipe out enemy." T.32.

1978, Aug. 1 Photo. *Perf. 11½*

1420	A355 8f multi (3-1)	3.50	.70
1421	A355 8f multi (3-2)	3.50	.70
1422	A355 8f multi (3-3)	3.50	.70
	Nos. 1420-1422 (3)	10.50	2.10

"Learn from Hard-boned 6th Company." (A military unit since 1939).

Jug in Shape of Sheep — A356

Arts and Crafts: 4f, Giant lion (toy; horiz.). No. 1425, Rhinoceros (lacquer ware; horiz). 10f, Cat (embroidery). 20f, Bag (weaving; horiz.). 30f, Teapot in shape of peacock (cloisonné). 40f, Plate with lotus, and swan-shaped box (lacquer ware; horiz.). 50f, Dragon flying in sky (ivory). 60f, Sun rising (jade; horiz.). 70f, Flight to human world (ivory). $3, Flying fairies (arts and crafts; horiz.). T.29.

1978, Aug. 26

1423	A356 4f multi (10-1)	.95	.45
1424	A356 8f multi (10-2)	.95	.45
1425	A356 8f multi (10-3)	.95	.45
1426	A356 10f multi (10-4)	.95	.55
1427	A356 20f multi (10-5)	.95	.55
1428	A356 30f multi (10-6)	2.00	.80
1429	A356 40f multi (10-7)	2.50	1.10
1430	A356 50f multi (10-8)	6.00	2.75
1431	A356 60f multi (10-9)	3.50	2.75
1432	A356 70f multi (10-10)	3.50	1.60
	Nos. 1423-1432 (10)	22.25	11.45

Souvenir Sheet

1433	A356 $3 multi	*300.00*	175.00

No. 1433 contains one 85x36mm stamp.

Women, Atom Symbol, Rocket and Wheat A357

1978, Sept. 8 Photo. *Perf. 11*

1434	A357 8f multicolored	2.00	1.00

4th National Women's Congress.

Ginseng — A358

Medicinal Plants: No. 1436, Horn of plenty. No. 1437, Blackberry lily. No. 1438, Balloon-flower. 55f, Rhododendron dauricum. T.30.

1978, Sept. 15

1435	A358 8f multi (5-1)	1.00	.35
1436	A358 8f multi (5-2)	1.00	.35
1437	A358 8f multi (5-3)	1.00	.35
1438	A358 8f multi (5-4)	1.00	.35
1439	A358 55f multi (5-5)	4.00	1.25
	Nos. 1435-1439 (5)	8.00	2.65

Flag, Wheat, Cogwheel, Plane, Atom Symbols — A359

1978, Oct. 11 Photo. *Perf. 11*

1440	A359 8f multicolored	3.50	1.00

9th National Trade Union Congress.

Youth League Emblem A360

1978, Oct. 16

1441	A360 8f multicolored	3.50	1.00

10th Natl. Communist Youth League Cong.

Chinese and Japanese Girls Exchanging Gifts A361

Great Wall and Mt. Fuji A362

1978, Oct. 22

1442	A361 8f multicolored	1.50	.75
1443	A362 55f multicolored	2.50	1.50

Signing of Sino-Japanese Peace and Friendship Treaty.

Moslem, Chinese and Mongolian People — A363

No. 1445, Loading coal at Holan Mountain. 10f, Irrigated rice fields & boxthorn. J.29.

1978, Oct. 25

1444	A363 8f multi (3-1)	2.50	1.00
1445	A363 8f multi (3-2)	2.50	1.00
1446	A363 10f multi (3-3)	3.00	1.00
	Nos. 1444-1446 (3)	8.00	3.00

20th anniversary of founding of Ningsia Moslem Autonomous Region.

Chinsha River Bridge, West Szechuan A364

Highway Bridges: No. 1448, Hsinhong bridge, Wuhsi. No. 1449, Chiuhsikou bridge, Fengdu. No. 1450, Chinsha River bridge, West Szechuan. 60f, Shangyeh bridge, Sanmen. $2, Hsiang-kiang River bridge. T.31.

1978, Nov. 1 Photo. *Perf. 11½x11*

1447	A364 8f multi (5-1)	1.50	.40
1448	A364 8f multi (5-2)	1.50	.40
1449	A364 8f multi (5-3)	1.50	.40
1450	A364 8f multi (5-4)	1.50	.40
1451	A364 60f multi (5-5)	3.00	1.25
	Nos. 1447-1451 (5)	9.00	2.85

Souvenir Sheet

1452	A364 $2 multi	*325.00*	175.00

No. 1452 contains one 86x37mm stamp.

Mechanical Transplanting of Rice Seedlings A365

Paintings: No. 1454, Spraying fields. No. 1455, Seed selection. No. 1456, Trade. No. 1457, Delivery of public grain in city. T.34.

1978, Nov. 30 *Perf. 11½*

1453 A365 8f multi (5-1) 3.00 1.50
1454 A365 8f multi (5-2) 3.00 1.50
1455 A365 8f multi (5-3) 3.00 1.50
1456 A365 8f multi (5-4) 3.00 1.50
1457 A365 8f multi (5-5) 3.00 1.50
a. Strip of 5, #1453-1457 22.50 16.50

Agricultural progress. No. 1457a has a continuous design. Value is for unfolded strip. Folded strips are worth less.

Dancers and Fireworks — A366

Designs: No. 1459, Industry, vert. 10f, Agriculture, vert. J.33.

1978, Dec. 11 **Photo.** *Perf. 11*

1458 A366 8f multi (3-1) 4.00 1.00
1459 A366 8f multi (3-2) 3.00 1.00
1460 A366 10f multi (3-3) 1.50 1.00
Nos. 1458-1460 (3) 8.50 3.00

20th anniversary of Kwangsi Chuang Autonomous Region.

Miners with Pneumatic Drill A367

Mine Development: 4f, Old Tibetan peasant reporting to surveyor. 10f, Open-cut mining with power shovel. 20f, Loaded electric train in pit. T.20.

1978, Dec. 29 **Photo. & Engr.**

1461 A367 4f multi (4-1) 2.50 1.00
1462 A367 8f multi (4-2) 3.50 1.75
1463 A367 10f multi (4-3) 2.50 1.00
1464 A367 20f multi (4-4) 2.50 1.00
Nos. 1461-1464 (4) 11.00 4.75

A368

Golden Pheasants: 4f, Roosting on rock. 8f, In flight. 45f, Seeking food. T.35.

1979, Jan. 25 **Photo.** *Perf. 11½*

1465 A368 4f multi (3-1) 2.00 1.00
1466 A368 8f multi (3-2) 2.50 2.00
1467 A368 45f multi (3-3) 4.00 3.00
Nos. 1465-1467 (3) 8.50 6.00

A369

1979, Mar. 14 **Photo.** *Perf. 11½x11*

1468 A369 8f Albert Einstein, equation 2.50 1.25

Phoenix Battling Monster, Praying Woman A370

60f, Man riding dragon to heaven. Designs from silk paintings found in Changsha tomb, Warring States Period (475-221 B.C.). T.33.

1979, Mar. 29 *Perf. 11*

1469 A370 8f multi (2-1) 2.50 1.50
1470 A370 60f multi (2-2) 3.50 1.50

Summer Palace — A371

Photo., Photo. & Engr. ($5)

1979-80 *Perf. 13*

1471 A371 $1 Pagoda ('80) .80 .35
1472 A371 $2 Shown 1.50 .70
1473 A371 $5 Temple, Beihai Park 4.50 1.50
Nos. 1471-1473 (3) 6.80 2.55

Issued: $2, June 16, 1979.

Hammer and Sickle "51" and Bars from "International" — A372

1979, May 1 **Photo.** *Perf. 11*

1474 A372 8f multicolored 2.00 1.00

International Labor Day, 90th anniv.

"Tradition of May 4th Movement" A373

Young Woman, Rocket, Antenna, Nuclear Reactor A374

1979, May 4

1475 A373 8f multicolored 1.25 .65
1476 A374 8f multicolored 1.25 .65

60th anniversary of May 4th Movement.

IYC Emblem, Children Holding Balloons — A375

Children of Three Races, IYC Emblem — A376

1979, May 25 *Perf. 11½*

1477 A375 8f multicolored 1.75 1.00
1478 A376 60f multicolored 11.00 4.50

International Year of the Child.

Great Wall in Spring A377

Designs (The Great Wall): No. 1480, in summer. No. 1481, in autumn. 60f, in winter. $2, Guard tower. T.38.

1979, June 25 **Photo.** *Perf. 11*

1479 A377 8f multi (4-1) 2.00 .95
1480 A377 8f multi (4-2) 2.00 .95
1481 A377 8f multi (4-3) 2.00 1.00
1482 A377 60f multi (4-4) 10.00 4.50
Nos. 1479-1482 (4) 16.00 7.40

Souvenir Sheet

1483 A377 $2 multi *145.00* 80.00

For overprint see No. 1492.

Roaring Tiger — A379

Manchurian Tiger: 8f, Two young tigers. 60f, Tiger at rest. T.40.

1979, July 20 *Perf. 11½x11*

1484 A379 4f multi (3-1) 3.50 1.00
1485 A379 8f multi (3-2) 2.00 1.00
1486 A379 60f multi (3-3) 3.00 1.75
Nos. 1484-1486 (3) 8.50 3.75

Mechanical Harvesting — A380

Work of the Communes: No. 1488, Forestry. No. 1489, Raising ducks. No. 1490, Women weaving baskets. 10f, Fishing. T.39.

1979, Aug. 10 *Perf. 11½*

1487 A380 4f multi (5-1) 6.00 2.00
1488 A380 8f multi (5-2) 3.25 1.00
1489 A380 8f multi (5-3) 3.25 1.00
1490 A380 8f multi (5-4) 3.25 1.00
1491 A380 10f multi (5-5) 4.00 1.75
Nos. 1487-1491 (5) 19.75 6.75

No. 1483 Overprinted with Gold Inscription and "1979"

Souvenir Sheet

1979, Aug. 25 **Photo.** *Perf. 11*

1492 A377 $2 multicolored *650.00 225.00*

31st International Stamp Exhibition, Riccione, Italy. J41 (1-1).
Forged overprints exist.

Games Emblem, Sports — A381

No. 1494, Soccer, badminton, high jump, speed skating. No. 1495, Fencing, skiing, gymnastics, diving. No. 1496, Motorcycling, table tennis, basketball, archery. No. 1497, Emblem only. J.43.

1979, Sept. 15 *Perf. 11½x11*

1493 A381 8f multi (4-1) 1.00 .80
1494 A381 8f multi (4-2) 1.00 .80
1495 A381 8f multi (4-3) 1.00 .80
1496 A381 8f multi (4-4) 1.00 .80
a. Block of 4, #1493-1496 6.00 4.00

Souvenir Sheet

Perf. 11½

1497 A381 $2 multi, vert. *85.00 45.00*

4th National Games. Size of stamp in No. 1497: 22x26mm.

Flag and Rainbow — A382

Design: No. 1499, Flag and mountains.

1979, Oct. 1 **Photo.** *Perf. 11½*

1498 A382 8f multicolored 2.25 1.00
1499 A382 8f multicolored 5.00 1.50

National Emblem — A383

1979, Oct. 1 **Photo.** *Perf. 11½*

1500 A383 8f multicolored 4.00 1.50

Souvenir Sheet

1501 A383 $1 multicolored *80.00* 32.50

Dancers — A384

Designs: Nos. 1503-1505, various dances. J.47.

1979, Oct. 1 **Photo.** *Perf. 11½*

1502 A384 8f multi (4-1) .85 .40
1503 A384 8f multi (4-2) .85 .40
1504 A384 8f multi (4-3) .85 .40
1505 A384 8f multi (4-4) .85 .40
a. Block of 4, #1502-1505 7.00 5.00

Tractor, Aerial Crop Spraying, Irrigation — A385

No. 1507, Gear, computers. No. 1508, Rocket, submarine, jets. No. 1509, Atom symbol. J.48.

1979, Oct. 1 Photo. *Perf. 11½*

1506	A385 8f multi (4-1)		2.50	.90
1507	A385 8f multi (4-2)		2.50	.90
1508	A385 8f multi (4-3)		1.50	.80
1509	A385 8f multi (4-4)		2.00	.80
	Nos. 1506-1509 (4)		8.50	3.40

National Anthem A386

1979, Oct. 1 Engr. *Perf. 11*

1510	A386 8f multicolored	11.00	2.00

Exhibition Emblem — A387

1979, Oct. 3

1511	A387 8f multicolored	1.25	.90

Junior National Scientific and Technological Exhibition.

Children Flying Model Planes — A388

No. 1513, Girls and microscope. No. 1514, Children and telescope. No. 1515, Boy catching butterflies. No. 1516, Girl taking meteorological readings. No. 1517, Boys sailing model boat. No. 1518, Girl with book. T.41.

1979, Oct. 3

1512	A388 8f multi (6-1)	1.50	.70
1513	A388 8f multi (6-2)	1.50	.70
1514	A388 8f multi (6-3)	1.50	.70
1515	A388 8f multi (6-4)	1.50	.70
1516	A388 8f multi (6-5)	1.50	.70
1517	A388 60f multi (6-6)	7.00	3.00
	Nos. 1512-1517 (6)	14.50	6.50

Souvenir Sheet

Perf. 11

1518	A388 $2 multi	*1,600.*	900.00

Study Science from Childhood. No. 1518 contains one stamp, size: 90x40mm.

Yu Shan Mountain A389

Taiwan Landscapes: No. 1520, Sun and Moon Lake. No. 1521, Chihkan Tower. No. 1522, Suao-Hualien Highway. 55f, Tian Xiang Falls. 60f, Banping Mountain. T.42.

1979, Oct. 20 Photo. *Perf. 11x11½*

1519	A389 8f multi (6-1)	1.50	.85
1520	A389 8f multi (6-2)	1.50	.85
1521	A389 8f multi (6-3)	1.50	.85
1522	A389 8f multi (6-4)	1.50	.85
1523	A389 55f multi (6-5)	4.00	1.50
1524	A389 60f multi (6-6)	11.00	3.00
	Nos. 1519-1524 (6)	21.00	7.90

Arts Symbols A390

8f, Seals and modernization symbols. J.39.

1979, Oct. 30

1525	A390 4f multicolored	1.25	.65
1526	A390 8f multicolored	2.00	.85

4th Natl. Cong. of Literary and Art Workers.

Train in Tunnel A391

Railroads: No. 1528, Mountain bridge. No. 1529, Freight train. T.36.

1979, Oct. 30 Photo. & Engr.

1527	A391 8f multi (3-1)	3.00	1.00
1528	A391 8f multi (3-2)	3.00	1.25
1529	A391 8f multi (3-3)	3.00	1.50
	Nos. 1527-1529 (3)	9.00	3.75

Chrysanthemum Petal — A392

Camellias: No. 1531, Lion head. No. 1532, Camellia chryantha. 10f, Small osmanthus leaf. 20f, Baby face. 30f, Cornelian. 40f, Peony camellia. 50f, Purple gown. 60f, Dwarf rose. 70f, Willow leaf spinel pink. $2, Red jewelry. T.37.

1979, Nov. 10 Photo. *Perf. 11x11½*

1530	A392 4f multi (10-1)	5.25	1.00
1531	A392 8f multi (10-2)	1.75	.65
1532	A392 8f multi (10-3)	1.75	.65
1533	A392 10f multi (10-4)	1.75	.65
1534	A392 20f multi (10-5)	1.75	1.00
1535	A392 30f multi (10-6)	14.00	3.00
1536	A392 40f multi (10-7)	2.75	1.25
1537	A392 50f multi (10-8)	1.50	1.00
1538	A392 60f multi (10-9)	3.25	1.00
1539	A392 70f multi (10-10)	3.50	1.00
	Nos. 1530-1539 (10)	37.25	11.20

Souvenir Sheet

Perf. 11½x11

1540	A392 $2 multi	*240.00*	*140.00*

No. 1540 contains one 86x36mm stamp.

No. 1540 Overprinted and Numbered in Gold in Margin

Souvenir Sheet

1979, Nov. 10

1541	A392 $2 multicolored	*450.00*	*160.00*

People's Republic of China Phil. Exhib., Hong Kong, 1979. J.42 (1-1).

Forged overprints exist.

Norman Bethune Treating Soldier — A393

Design: 70f, Bethune statue.

1979, Nov. 12

1542	A393 8f multi (2-2)	1.50	.45
1543	A393 70f multi (2-1)	4.50	2.00

Dr. Norman Bethune, 40th death anniv. J.50.

Central Archives Hall A394

Intl. Archives Weeks: No. 1545, Gold archive cabinet, vert. 60f, Pavilion. J.51.

Perf. 11x11½, 11½x11

1979, Nov. 26 Photo.

1544	A394 8f multi (3-1)	2.00	1.00
1545	A394 8f multi (3-2)	2.00	1.00
1546	A394 60f multi (3-3)	11.00	2.25
	Nos. 1544-1546 (3)	15.00	4.25

Monkey King in Waterfall Cave — A395

Monkey King, Scenes from Pilgrimage to the West (Novel): No. 1548, Fighting Necha, son of Prince Li. No. 1549, In Mother Queen's peach orchard. No. 1550, In the alchemy furnace. 10f, Subduing the white bone demon. 20f, With palm leaf fan. 60f, In cobweb cave. 70f, Walking on scripture-seeking route. T.43.

1979, Dec. 1 *Perf. 11½x11*

1547	A395 8f multi (8-1)	5.00	1.75
1548	A395 8f multi (8-2)	5.00	1.75
1549	A395 8f multi (8-3)	5.00	1.75
1550	A395 8f multi (8-4)	5.00	1.75
1551	A395 10f multi (8-5)	7.00	1.75
1552	A395 20f multi (8-6)	7.00	1.75
1553	A395 60f multi (8-7)	30.00	10.00
1554	A395 70f multi (8-8)	18.00	6.00
	Nos. 1547-1554 (8)	82.00	26.50

Stalin Delivering Speech A396

Joseph Stalin (1879-1953): No. 1555, Portrait of Stalin, vert. J.49.

Perf. 11x11½, 11½x11

1979, Dec. 21 Engr.

1555	A396 8f brown (2-1)	1.25	1.00
1556	A396 8f black (2-2)	1.75	1.00

A397

No. 1557, Peony (16-1). No. 1558, Squirrels and grapes (16-2). No. 1559, Crabs candle and wine (16-3). No. 1560, Tadpoles in mountain spring (16-4). No. 1561, Chicks (16-5). No. 1562, Lotus (16-6). No. 1563, Red plum (16-7). No. 1564, Kingfisher (16-8). No. 1565, Bottle gourd (16-9). No. 1566, Voice of autumn (16-10). No. 1567, Wisteria (16-11). No. 1568, Chrysanthemums (16-12). No. 1569, Shrimp (16-13). No. 1570, Litchi (16-14). No. 1571, Cabbages, mushrooms (16-15). No. 1572, Peaches (16-16).

No. 1573, Hyacynth.

1980 Photo. *Perf. 11½*

1557	A397 4f multi	2.50	1.00
1558	A397 4f multi	2.50	1.00
1559	A397 8f multi	2.00	.75
1560	A397 8f multi	2.00	.75
1561	A397 8f multi	2.00	.75
1562	A397 8f multi	2.00	.75
1563	A397 8f multi	2.00	.75
1564	A397 8f multi	2.00	.75
1565	A397 10f multi	5.00	1.75
1566	A397 20f multi	5.00	1.75
1567	A397 30f multi	6.00	2.00
1568	A397 40f multi	30.00	8.00
1569	A397 50f multi	7.50	2.00
1570	A397 55f multi	7.50	3.00
1571	A397 60f multi	37.50	8.00
1572	A397 70f multi	15.00	5.00
	Nos. 1557-1572 (16)	130.50	38.00

Souvenir Sheet

1573	A397 $2 multi	*290.00*	*140.00*

Qi Baishi paintings. Issued: Nos. 1557-1560, 1569-1572, 1/15; others, 5/20. No. 1573 contains one 37½x61mm stamp. T. 44.

A398

Opera Masks: No. 1574, Meng Liang Mask from Hongyang Cave Opera. No. 1575, Li Kui, from Black Whirlwind. No. 1576, Huang Gai, from Meeting of Heroes. No. 1577, 10f, Lu Zhishen, from Wild Boar Forest. 20f, Lian Po, from Reconciliation between the General and Minister. 60f, Zhang Fei, from Reed Marsh. 70f, Dou Erdun, from Stealing the Emperor's Horse, T. 45.

1980, Jan. 25 *Perf. 11½x11*

1574	A398 4f multi (8-1)	4.25	1.25
1575	A398 4f multi (8-2)	25.00	5.50
1576	A398 8f multi (8-3)	3.00	1.25
1577	A398 8f multi (8-4)	3.00	1.75
1578	A398 10f multi (8-5)	4.00	1.75
1579	A398 20f multi (8-6)	4.00	1.75
1580	A398 60f multi (8-7)	7.00	3.00
1581	A398 70f multi (8-8)	8.00	4.00
	Nos. 1574-1581 (8)	58.25	20.25

A set of eight similar to Nos. 1574-1581 was prepared but not issued in 1964. The unissued stamps are dated "1964" in the bottom margin. Sound examples appear rarely in the marketplace and sell for $125,000 or more.

Speed Skating, Olympic Rings — A399

Olympic Rings and: No. 1582, Chinese flag. No. 1584, Figure skating. 60f, Downhill skiing. J.54.

1980, Feb. 13

1582	A399	8f multi (4-1)		2.25	.70
1583	A399	8f multi (4-2)		2.25	.70
1584	A399	8f multi (4-3)		2.25	.70
1585	A399	60f multi (4-4)		8.00	3.00
		Nos. 1582-1585 (4)		14.75	5.10

13th Winter Olympic Games, Lake Placid, NY, Feb. 12-24.

Monkey, New Year — A400

Engraved and Photogravure

1980, Feb. 15 ***Perf. 11½***

1586	A400	8f multicolored	*1,800.*	*550.00*

Excellent forgeries of No. 1586 exist.

Clara Zetkin — A401

Photogravure & Engraved

1980, Mar. 8 ***Perf. 11½x11***

1587	A401	8f black & yellow	2.50	1.10

International Working Women's Day, 70th anniv., founded by Clara Zetkin (1857-1933).

Orchard A402

Afforestation: 8f, Trees lining highway. 10f, Aerial seeding. 20f, Trees surrounding factory. T.48.

1980, Mar. 12 ***Perf. 11x11½***

1588	A402	4f multi (4-1)	3.25	.75
1589	A402	8f multi (4-2)	3.25	.75
1590	A402	10f multi (4-3)	1.50	.55
1591	A402	20f multi (4-4)	1.50	.55
		Nos. 1588-1591 (4)	9.50	2.60

Apsaras, Symbols of Modernization — A403

1980, Mar. 15 Photo. ***Perf. 11½***

1592	A403	8f multicolored	2.75	1.40

2nd National Conference of the Scientific and Technical Association of China.

Mail Transport (T.49) — A404

1980, Mar. 20 ***Perf. 11x11½***

1593	A404	2f Ship (4-1)	1.75	1.50
1594	A404	4f Bus (4-2)	5.50	2.00
1595	A404	8f Train (4-3)	4.75	2.00
1596	A404	10f Jet (4-4)	3.75	2.25
		Nos. 1593-1596 (4)	15.75	7.75

Forgeries exist.

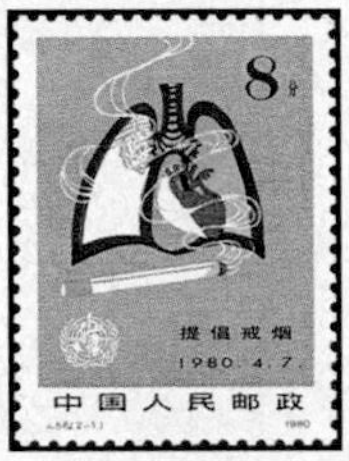

Lungs, Heart, Cigarette, WHO Emblem — A405

1980, Apr. 7 ***Perf. 11½x11***

1597	A405	8f shown (2-1)	2.00	.60
1598	A405	60f Faces (2-2)	14.00	3.50

Fight against cigarette smoking. J.56.

Statue of Chien Chen (688-763) — A406

Loan to China by Japan of statue of Chien Chen (Jian Zhen), Buddhist missionary to Japan (754-763): No. 1600, Chien Chen Memorial Hall, Yangchou, horiz. 60f, Chien Chen's ship, horiz. His name in Japan is Ganjin. J.55.

1980, Apr. 13 ***Perf. 11x11½, 11½x11***

1599	A406	8f multi (3-1)	4.00	1.10
1600	A406	8f multi (3-2)	4.00	1.10
1601	A406	60f multi (3-3)	35.00	7.75
		Nos. 1599-1601 (3)	43.00	9.95

Lenin's 110th Birthday — A407

Photogravure and Engraved

1980, Apr. 22 ***Perf. 11½x11***

1602	A407	8f multicolored	3.00	1.10

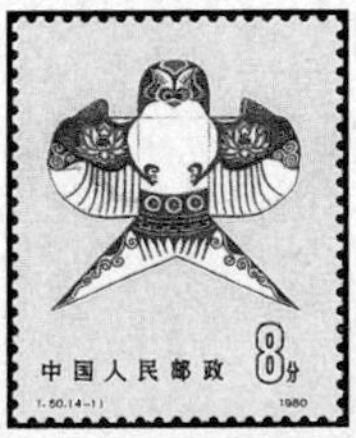

Swallow Chick Kite — A408

Kites. T.50: No. 1604, Slender-swallow (4-2). No. 1605, Semi-slender swallow (4-3). No. 1606, Dual swallows (4-4).

1980, May 10 Photo. ***Perf. 11½***

1603	A408	8f shown (4-1)	5.50	1.75
1604	A408	8f multi	5.50	1.75
1605	A408	8f multi	5.50	1.75
1606	A408	70f multi	30.00	6.25
		Nos. 1603-1606 (4)	46.50	11.50

Hare Running from Fallen Papaya A409

1980, June 1 Photo. ***Perf. 11x11½***

1607	Strip of 4 + label	17.50	17.50
a.	A409 8f shown (4-1)	2.00	1.60
b.	A409 8f Hare fox, monkey running away (4-2)	2.00	1.60
c.	A409 8f Lion instructing animals (4-3)	2.00	1.60
d.	A409 8f Discovery of fallen papaya (4-4)	2.00	1.60
e.	Bklt. pane, 2 #1607	*500.00*	
	Complete booklet	*900.00*	

Gu Dong fairy tale. T.51.

Beware of complete booklets of No. 1607e with forged booklet covers.

Terminal Building, Jets — A410

1980, June 20 ***Perf. 11½***

1608	A410	8f Shown (2-1)	4.00	1.25
1609	A410	10f Runways, jets (2-2)	4.00	1.25

Peking Intl. Airport opening. T.47.

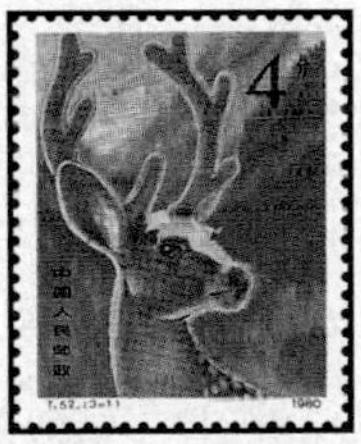

Sika Stag — A411

1980, July 18 Photo. ***Perf. 11½***

1610	A411	4f Shown (3-1)	2.25	1.40
1611	A411	8f Doe and fawn (3-2)	2.25	1.40
1612	A411	60f Herd (3-3)	11.00	5.25
		Nos. 1610-1612 (3)	15.50	8.05

T.52.

White Lotus — A412

No. 1614, Rose-tipped snow (4-2). No. 1615, Buddha's seat (4-3). No. 1616, Variable charming face (4-4).

No. 1617, Fresh lotus on rippling water.

1980, Aug. 4

1613	A412	8f Shown (4-1)	5.00	2.00
1614	A412	8f multi	5.00	2.00
1615	A412	8f multi	5.00	2.00
1616	A412	70f multi	55.00	8.00
		Nos. 1613-1616 (4)	70.00	14.00

Souvenir Sheet

1617	A412	$1 multi	*300.00*	*140.00*

No. 1617 contains one 48x88mm stamp. T.54.

Pearl Cave, Sword-cut Stone Sculptures — A413

Guilin Landscapes: No. 1619, Three mountains, distant views. No. 1620, Nine-horse fresco hill. No. 1621, Egrets around aged banyan. No. 1622, Western hills at sunset, vert. No. 1623, Moonlight on Lijiang River, vert. 60f, Springhead, ancient ferry, vert. 70f, Scenic path, Yangshue, vert. T.53.

1980, Aug. 30 Photo. ***Perf. 11½***

1618	A413	8f multi (8-1)	2.00	1.00
1619	A413	8f multi (8-2)	2.00	1.00
1620	A413	8f multi (8-3)	2.00	1.00
1621	A413	8f multi (8-4)	2.00	1.00
1622	A413	8f multi (8-5)	2.00	1.00
1623	A413	8f multi (8-6)	2.00	1.00
1624	A413	60f multi (8-7)	20.00	4.00
1625	A413	70f multi (8-8)	25.00	5.00
		Nos. 1618-1625 (8)	57.00	15.00

Entrance Gate and Good Fairies A414

Great Wall, Symbols of Chicago, San Francisco and New York A415

1980, Sept. 13 Photo. ***Perf. 11x11½***

1626	A414	8f multicolored	2.00	.90
1627	A415	70f multicolored	14.00	3.75

Exhibitions of the People's Republic of China in San Francisco, Chicago and New York, Sept.-Dec. Sheets of 12 were sold only at the US exhibitions at increasing prices. Value, set of two sheets of 12, $1,500.

Romanian Flag, Warrior and Scroll — A416

1980, Sept. 20 Photo. ***Perf. 11½x11***

1628	A416	8f multicolored	2.75	1.50

2050th anniv. of Dacia, 1st independent Romanian state.

UNESCO Exhibition of Drawings and Paintings (J.60) — A417

No. 1629, Sea of Clouds, by Liu Haisu (3-1). No. 1630, Oriole and Magnolia, by Yu Feian, vert., (3-2). No. 1631, Camels, by Wu Zuoren (3-3).

1980, Oct. 8 ***Perf. 11½***

1629	A417	8f multi	2.00	.80
1630	A417	8f multi	2.00	.80
1631	A417	8f multi	2.00	.80
		Nos. 1629-1631 (3)	6.00	2.40

Scenes from Tarrying Garden (T.56) — A418

No. 1632, Quxi Tower (4-1). No. 1633, Yuancui Pavilion (4-2). No. 1634, Hanbi Shanfang (4-3). No. 1635, Guanyun Peak (4-4).

1980, Oct. 25 Photo. *Perf. 11½*

1632	A418	8f multi	*7.00*	4.00
1633	A418	8f multi	*7.00*	4.00
1634	A418	10f multi	*11.00*	4.00
1635	A418	60f multi	*60.00*	17.50
		Nos. 1632-1635 (4)	*85.00*	29.50

Xu Guangqi (1562-1633), Agronomist A419

Scientists of Ancient China: No. 1637, Li Bing, hydraulic engineer, 3rd century B.C. No. 1638, Jia Sixie, agronomist, 5th century. 60f, Huang Daopo, textile expert, 13th century. J.58.

Photogravure and Engraved

1980, Nov. 20 *Perf. 11½x11*

1636	A419	8f multi (4-1)	6.50	2.00
1637	A419	8f multi (4-2)	6.50	2.00
1638	A419	8f multi (4-3)	6.50	2.00
1639	A419	60f multi (4-4)	40.00	11.00
		Nos. 1636-1639 (4)	59.50	17.00

Shooting, Olympic Rings — A420

1980, Nov. 26 Photo.

1640	A420	4f shown (5-1)	2.25	.45
1641	A420	8f Gymnastics (5-2)	2.25	.45
1642	A420	8f Diving (5-3)	2.25	.45
1643	A420	10f Volleyball (5-4)	2.25	.75
1644	A420	60f Archery (5-5)	14.00	2.75
		Nos. 1640-1644 (5)	23.00	4.85

Return to International Olympic Committee, 1st anniversary. J.62.

Chinese River Dolphin A421

Photogravure & Engraved

1980, Dec. 25 *Perf. 11x11½*

1645	A421	8f shown (2-1)	2.00	.50
a.		Booklet pane of 6	50.00	
1646	A421	60f Dolphins (2-2)	8.00	1.75
a.		Booklet pane of 1	50.00	

Stamps from No. 1645a have straight edges on top or bottom.

Cock — A422

Photogravure & Engraved

1981, Jan. 5 *Perf. 11½*

1647	A422	8f multicolored	32.50	6.00
a.		Booklet pane of 12	275.00	
		Complete booklet	300.00	

New Year 1981.

Stamps from booklet pane have straight edges on top or bottom.

Early Morning in Xishuang Bana (T.55) A423

No. 1649, Dai mountain village (6-2). No. 1650, Rainbow over Lanchang River (6-3). No. 1651, Ancient temple vert. (6-4). No. 1652, Moonlit night, vert. (6-5). No. 1653, Phoenix tree, vert. (6-6).

Perf. 11x11½, 11½x11

1981, Jan. 20 Photo.

1648	A423	4f shown (6-1)	8.00	1.50
1649	A423	4f multi	3.00	.75
1650	A423	8f multi	3.00	.75
1651	A423	8f multi	3.00	.75
1652	A423	8f multi	3.00	.75
1653	A423	60f multi	15.00	3.50
		Nos. 1648-1653 (6)	35.00	8.00

Flower Basket Palace Lantern — A424

Designs: Palace lanterns. T.60.

1981, Feb. 19 Photo. *Perf. 11½*

1654	A424	4f multi (6-1)	2.00	1.00
1655	A424	8f multi (6-2)	2.00	1.00
1656	A424	8f multi (6-3)	2.00	1.00
1657	A424	8f multi (6-4)	2.00	1.00
1658	A424	20f multi (6-5)	4.50	3.50
1659	A424	60f multi (6-6)	25.00	7.50
		Nos. 1654-1659 (6)	37.50	15.00

Crossing River, Scene from Marking the Gunwale A425

Scenes from Marking the Gunwale fable. T.59: No. 1660, Text (5-1). No. 1662, Dropping sword in water (5-3). No. 1663, Marking gunwale (5-4). No. 1664, Searching for sword (5-5).

1981, Mar. 10 Photo. *Perf. 11x11½*

1660	A425	8f multi	2.00	1.25
1661	A425	8f shown (5-2)	2.00	1.25
1662	A425	8f multi	2.00	1.25
1663	A425	8f multi	2.00	1.25
1664	A425	8f multi	2.00	1.25
a.		Bklt. pane, 2 each #1660-1664	50.00	
		Complete booklet, #1664a	55.00	
b.		Strip of 5, #1660-1664	16.00	10.00

Chinese Juniper A426

Designs: Miniature landscapes. T.61: No. 1665, Chinese elm, vert. (6-1). No. 1666, Juniper, vert. (6-2). No. 1667, Maidenhair tree, vert. (6-3). No. 1669, Persimmon (6-5). No. 1670, Juniper (6-6).

1981, Mar. 31 *Perf. 11½*

1665	A426	4f multi	3.25	1.40
1666	A426	8f multi	2.25	1.10
1667	A426	8f multi	2.25	1.10
1668	A426	10f shown (6-4)	2.25	1.10
1669	A426	20f multi	2.25	1.25
1670	A426	60f multi	14.00	4.25
		Nos. 1665-1670 (6)	26.25	10.20

Vase with Tiger-shaped Handles — A427

Cizhou Kiln Ceramic Pottery: 4f, Vase with 2 tigers, Song Dynasty. No. 1672, Black glazed jar, Jin Dynasty. No. 1673, Amphora. No. 1674, Jar with 2 phoenixes (Yuan Dynasty). 10f, Flat flask, Yuan Dynasty. T.62.

1981, Apr. 15 Photo. *Perf. 11½x11*

1671	A427	4f multi, vert. (6-1)	1.50	.80
1672	A427	8f multi (6-2)	1.50	.80
1673	A427	8f multi, vert. (6-3)	1.50	.80
1674	A427	8f multi (6-4)	1.50	.80
1675	A427	10f multi (6-5)	1.50	.80
1676	A427	60f multi (6-6)	7.50	3.50
		Nos. 1671-1676 (6)	15.00	7.50

Panda and Colored Stamps — A428

1981, Apr. 29 Photo. *Perf. 11½x11*

1677	A428	8f shown (2-1)	.45	.30
1678	A428	60f Boat, bird (2-2)	3.00	1.60
a.		Booklet pane (8 #1677, souv. sheet with 1677-1678)	20.00	
		Complete booklet, #1678a	22.50	

Qinchuan Steer A429

Cattle Breeds: No. 1680, Binhu buffalo. No. 1681, Yak. No. 1682, Black and white dairy cows. 10f, Pasture red cow. 55f, Simmental cross-breed. T.63.

1981, May 5 *Perf. 11x11½*

1679	A429	4f multi (6-1)	1.75	1.00
1680	A429	8f multi (6-2)	2.75	1.25
1681	A429	8f multi (6-3)	2.50	1.25
1682	A429	8f multi (6-4)	2.00	1.00
1683	A429	10f multi (6-5)	2.00	1.00
1684	A429	55f multi (6-6)	3.00	1.00
		Nos. 1679-1684 (6)	14.00	6.50

Mail Delivery Slogan — A430

1981, May 9 *Perf. 11*

1685	A430	8f multicolored	1.25	.30

13th World Telecommunications Day — A431

1981, May 17 *Perf. 11½x11*

1686	A431	8f multicolored	1.50	.35

Construction Worker — A432

1981, May 20 *Perf. 11½*

1687	A432	8f shown (4-1)	1.40	.55
1688	A432	8f Miner (4-2)	1.40	.55
1689	A432	8f Children crossing street (4-3)	1.40	.55
1690	A432	8f Farm worker (4-4)	1.40	.55
		Nos. 1687-1690 (4)	5.60	2.20

National Safety Month. J.65.

Telephone Building, Peking — A433

1981, June 5 Engr. *Perf. 11½x11*

1691	A433	8f violet brown	1.25	.65

Swaythling Cup, Men's Team Table Tennis — A434

36th World Table Tennis Championships Victory — No. 1692: a, St. Bride Vase, men's singles (7-3). b, Iran Cup, men's doubles (7-4). c, G. Geist Prize, women's singles (7-5). d, W.J. Pope Trophy, women's doubles (7-6). e, Heydusek Prize, mixed doubles (7-7). No. 1694, Marcel Corbillon Cup, women's team. Nos. 1693-1694 printed in sheets of 16 (8 each) + 2 labels. J.71.

1981, June 30 Photo. *Perf. 11½x11*

1692		Strip of 5	6.50	3.75
a.-e.		A434 8f multi	.45	.25
1693	A434	20f multi (7-1)	1.75	.85
1694	A434	20f multi (7-2)	1.75	.85

Chinese Communist Party, 60th Anniv. A435

1981, July 1 Photo. *Perf. 11x11½*

1695	A435	8f multicolored	1.50	.60

Hanpo Pass, Lushan Mountains (T.67) A436

No. 1696, Five-veteran Peak, vert. (7-1). No. 1698, Yellow Dragon Pool, vert. (7-3). No. 1699, Sunlit Peak (7-4). No. 1700, Three-layer Spring, vert. (7-5). No. 1701, Stone and pines (7-6). No. 1702, Dragon-head Cliff, vert. (7-7).

Photogravure & Engraved

1981, July 20 *Perf. 12½x12*

1696	8f multi	3.00	.70
1697	8f shown (7-2)	3.00	.70
1698	8f multi	3.00	.70
1699	8f multi	3.00	.70
1700	8f multi	3.00	.70
1701	8f multi	3.00	.70
1702	60f multi	30.00	5.00
	Nos. 1696-1702 (7)	48.00	9.20

Tremella Fuciformis A437

Edible mushrooms. T.66: No. 1704, Dictyophora indusiata (6-2). No. 1705, Hericium erinaceus (6-3). No. 1706, Russula rubra (6-4). No. 1707, Lentinus edodes (6-5). No. 1708, Agaricus bisporus (6-6).

1981, Aug. 6 Photo. *Perf. 11½*

1703	A437	4f shown (6-1)	1.00	.50
1704	A437	8f multi	1.00	.50
1705	A437	8f multi	1.00	.50
1706	A437	8f multi	1.00	.50
1707	A437	10f multi	1.00	.50
1708	A437	70f multi	8.00	2.25
		Nos. 1703-1708 (6)	13.00	4.75

Quality Month (J.66) — A438

1981, Sept. 1 Photo. *Perf. 11½x11*

1709	A438	8f Silver medal (2-1)	2.50	.55
1710	A438	8f Gold medal (2-2)	2.50	.55

Lunan Stone Forest, Yunn — A439

Designs: Views of limestone formations, Lunan Stone Forest. Nos. 1711-1713 horiz. T.64.

1981, Sept. 18 *Perf. 11½*

1711	A439	8f multi (5-1)	1.50	.60
1712	A439	8f multi (5-2)	1.50	.60
1713	A439	8f multi (5-3)	1.50	.60
1714	A439	10f multi (5-4)	1.50	.60
1715	A439	70f multi (5-5)	14.00	4.75
		Nos. 1711-1715 (5)	20.00	7.15

Lu Xun, Writer, Birth Centenary (J.67) A440

1981, Sept. 25

1716	A440	8f shown (2-1)	2.25	.40
1717	A440	20f Portrait (diff.) (2-2)	3.50	1.50

Sun Yat-sen and Text A441

70th Anniv. of 1911 Revolution: No. 1719, 72 Martyrs Grave, Huang Hua Gang. No. 1720, Hubei Provincial Government Headquarters, 1911. J.68.

1981, Oct. 10 Photo. *Perf. 11x11½*

1718	A441	8f multi (3-1)	2.00	.45
1719	A441	8f multi (3-2)	2.00	.45
1720	A441	8f multi (3-3)	2.00	.45
		Nos. 1718-1720 (3)	6.00	1.35

Asian Conference of Parliamentarians on Population and Development, Peking, Oct. 27 (J.73) — A442

1981, Oct. 27 *Perf. 11½x11, 11x11½*

1721	A442	8f Tree, vert. (2-1)	.75	.30
1722	A442	70f shown (2-2)	1.40	.75

Xishuang Banna — A443

Mt. Hua — A443a

Mt. Tai — A443b

Huang Guo Shu Falls — A443c

Hainan Island — A443d

Tiger Hill, Suzhou — A443e

Great Wall — A443f

Immense Forest — A443g

Mt. Tian — A443h

Grassland, Inner Mongolia — A443i

Stone Forest — A443j

Banping Mountain — A443k

Mt. Qomolangma — A443l

Seven-Star Crag — A443m

Three Gorges, Changjiang River — A443n

Guilin landscape — A443o

Mt. Huangshan — A443p

Nos. 1731-1739 are horizontal.

Perf. 11¼, 13x13¼ (#1726, 1729), 13¼x13 (#1731)

1981-83 Engr.

1723	A443	1f blue green	.25	.25
1724	A443a	1½f red orange	.25	.25
1725	A443b	2f gray green	.25	.25
1726	A443c	3f red brown	.30	.25
1727	A443d	4f purple	.30	.25
1728	A443e	5f brown	.35	.25
1729	A443f	8f blue	.35	.25
1730	A443g	10f purplish brn	.35	.25
1731	A443h	20f blue green	.35	.25
1732	A443i	30f light brown	.35	.25
1733	A443j	40f blue black	.45	.25
1734	A443k	50f violet	.60	.25
1735	A443l	70f greenish blk	.75	.40
1736	A443m	80f rose lake	.85	.55
1737	A443n	$1 violet black	1.00	.60
1738	A443o	$2 green	1.75	1.25
1739	A443p	$5 Prussian blue	4.00	2.25
		Nos. 1723-1739 (17)	12.50	8.05

Issued: Nos. 1737-1739, 10/9/82; Nos. 1732, 1734-1736 4/1/83.

Photo.

Perf. 11½

1726a	A443	3f tan & brown	.25	.25
1727a	A443	4f pink & purple	.25	.25
1727b		Perf. 11½x11	10.00	10.00
1729a	A443	8f blue	.35	.25
1730a	A443	10f dark brown	.55	.40
1731a	A443	20f blue green	1.25	.75
		Nos. 1726a-1731a (5)	2.65	1.90

Nos. 1727a, 1729a, 1730a exist tagged. Values 10-15% higher.

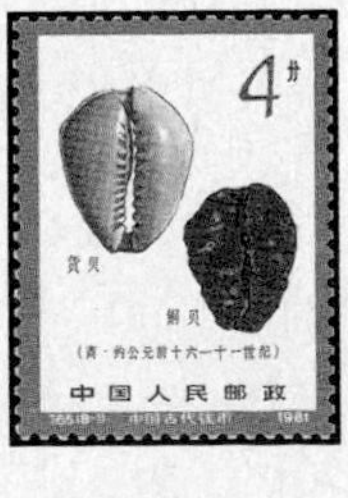
Cowrie Shell and Shell-shaped Coin — A444

Ancient Coins. T.65.

Photogravure and Engraved

1981, Oct. 29 *Perf. 11½x11*

1740	A444	4f shown (8-1)	1.50	.50
1741	A444	4f Shovel (8-2)	1.50	.50
1742	A444	8f Shovel, diff. (8-3)	1.50	.50
1743	A444	8f Shovel, diff. (8-4)	2.00	.50
1744	A444	8f Knife (8-5)	2.00	.50
1745	A444	8f Knife (8-6)	2.00	.50
1746	A444	60f Knife, diff. (8-7)	9.00	2.50
1747	A444	70f Gong (8-8)	12.00	3.00
		Nos. 1740-1747 (8)	31.50	8.50

See Nos. 1765-1772.

A445

1981, Nov. 10 Photo. *Perf. 11½x11*

1748	A445	8f multicolored	1.00	.40

Intl. Year of the Disabled.

A446

Twelve Beauties, from The Dream of Red Mansions, by Cao Xueqin: No. 1749, Daiyu (12-1). No. 1750, Baochai (12-2). No. 1751, Yuanchun (12-3). No. 1752, Yingchun (12-4). No. 1753, Tanchun (12-5). No. 1754, Xichun (12-6). No. 1755, Xiangyuh (12-7). No. 1756, Liwan (12-8). No. 1757, Xifeng (12-9). No. 1758, Sister Qiao (12-10). No. 1759, Keqing (12-11). No. 1760, Miaoyu (12-12).

No. 1761, Baoyu, Daiyu.

1981-82 Photo. *Perf. 11*

1749	A446	4f multi	5.00	.95
1750	A446	4f multi	3.00	.95
1751	A446	8f multi	4.00	1.50
1752	A446	8f multi	3.00	1.00
1753	A446	8f multi	3.00	1.00
1754	A446	8f multi	3.00	1.00
1755	A446	8f multi	3.00	1.25
1756	A446	10f multi	3.00	1.25
1757	A446	20f multi	3.00	1.25
1758	A446	30f multi	5.00	1.75
1759	A446	40f multi	22.50	6.00
1760	A446	80f multi	8.00	2.75
		Nos. 1749-1760 (12)	65.50	20.65

Souvenir Sheet

1761	A446	$2 multi	*260.00*	*120.00*

No. 1761 contains one 59x39mm stamp. Issued: Nos. 1749, 1751, 1753, 1755, 1757, 1759, 1761, 11/20/81; others, 4/24/82. T.69.

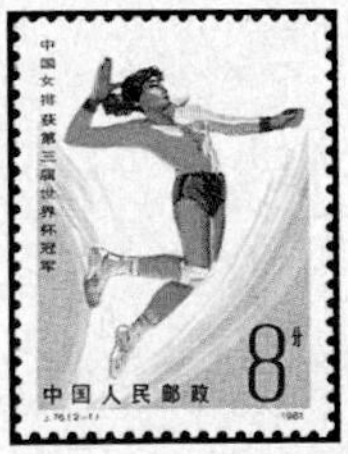
A447

8f, Girl playing (2-1). 20f, Girl holding trophy (2-2).

1981, Dec. 21 Photo.

1762	A447	8f multi	.60	.30
1763	A447	20f multi	1.10	.55

Women's team victory in 3rd World Cup Volleyball Championship (J.76).

A448

Photogravure & Engraved

1982, Jan. 5 ***Perf. 11½***

1764 A448 8f multicolored	6.00	2.00
a. Booklet pane of 10 + label	30.00	
Complete booklet, #1764a	32.50	*32.50*

New Year 1982 (Year of the Dog).
Stamps from No. 1764a have straight edges at top or bottom.

Coin Type of 1981

No. 1765, Guilian mask (8-1). No. 1766, Shu shovel (8-2). No. 1767, Xia zhuan shovel (8-3). No. 1768, Han Dan shovel (8-4). No. 1769, Knife (8-5). No. 1770, Ming knife (8-6). No. 1771, Jin hua knife (8-7). No. 1772, Yi Liu Hua coin (8-8).

1982, Feb. 12

1765 A444 4f multi	1.10	.55
1766 A444 4f multi	1.10	.55
1767 A444 8f multi	1.10	.55
1768 A444 8f multi	1.10	.55
1769 A444 8f multi	1.10	.55
1770 A444 8f multi	1.10	.70
1771 A444 70f multi	4.00	2.00
1772 A444 80f multi	5.00	2.50
Nos. 1765-1772 (8)	15.60	7.95

T.71.

Nie Er (1912-1935), Natl. Anthem Composer — A449

1982, Feb. 15 ***Perf. 11x11½***

1773 A449 8f multicolored	2.00	.50

Intl. Drinking Water and Sanitation Decade, 1981-1990 A450

1982, Mar. 1 ***Perf. 11½x11***

1774 A450 8f multicolored	1.00	.50

TB Bacillus Centenary A451

1982, Mar. 24 ***Perf. 11x11½***

1775 A451 8f multicolored	1.50	.50

Fire Control (T.76) — A452

1982, May 8 Photo. ***Perf. 11½x11***

1776 A452 8f Water hoses (2-1)	1.50	.50
1777 A452 8f Chemical extinguisher (2-2)	1.50	.50

Syzygy of the Nine Planets, Mar. 10 and May 16 — A453

1982, May 16 ***Perf. 11½***

1778 A453 8f multicolored	2.00	.60

Medicinal Herbs — A454

No. 1779, Hemerocallis flava (6-1). No. 1780, Fritillaria unibracteata (6-2). No. 1781, Aconitum carmichaeli (6-3). No. 1782, Lilium brownii (6-4). No. 1783, Arisaema (6-5). No. 1784, Paeonia lactiflora (6-6).
No. 1785, Iris tectorum maxim.

1982, May 20 ***Perf. 11½x11***

1779 A454 4f multi	.65	.45
1780 A454 8f multi	.65	.45
1781 A454 8f multi	.65	.45
1782 A454 10f multi	1.40	.65
1783 A454 20f multi	1.75	.75
1784 A454 70f multi	5.25	1.50
Nos. 1779-1784 (6)	10.35	4.25

Souvenir Sheet

1785 A454 $2 multi	27.50	17.50

No. 1785 contains one 89x39mm stamp. Nos. 1779-1784 numbered T.72.

Soong Ching Ling (1893-1981), Sun Yat-sen's Widow — A455

8f, Addressing Consultative Conf. (2-1). 20f, Portrait (2-2).

1982, May 29 ***Perf. 11½***

1786 A455 8f multi	1.00	.45
1787 A455 20f multi	4.00	1.40

J.82.

Sable (T.68) A456

1982, June 20 Photo. ***Perf. 11½***

1788 A456 8f shown (2-1)	1.25	.55
1789 A456 80f Sable, diff. (2-2)	5.00	3.50
a. Bklt. pane of 8, 6 8f plus sheetlet of 2 (8f, 80f)	37.50	
Complete booklet, #1789a	44.00	

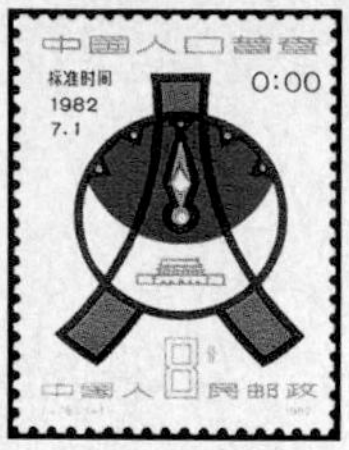
A457

1982, June 30 ***Perf. 11½x11***

1790 A457 8f multicolored	1.75	.40

Natl. census, July 1.

A458

1982, July 25 Photo. ***Perf. 11½x11***

1791 A458 8f multicolored	1.40	.40

2nd UN Conference on Peaceful Uses of Outer Space, Vienna, Aug. 9-21.

Strolling in Autumn Woods, by Shen Zhou, Ming Dynasty — A459

Fan Paintings (Ming or Qing Dynasty): No. 1793, Jackdaw on Withered Tree, by Tang Yin. No. 1794 Bamboo and Sparrows, by Zhou Zhimian. 10f, Writing Poem under Pine, by Chen Hongshou and Bai Han. 20f, Chrysanthemums, by Yun Shouping, Qing. 70f, Birds, Crape Myrtle and Chinese Parasol, by Wang Wu, Qing. T.77.

1982, July 31 ***Perf. 11½***

1792 A459 4f multi (6-1)	3.00	.80
1793 A459 8f multi (6-2)	1.25	.70
1794 A459 8f multi (6-3)	1.25	.70
1795 A459 10f multi (6-4)	2.00	.70
1796 A459 20f multi (6-5)	2.00	.80
1797 A459 70f multi (6-6)	6.00	2.25
Nos. 1792-1797 (6)	15.50	5.95

A460

1982, Aug. 25 ***Perf. 11½x11***

1798 A460 8f multicolored	.80	.35

60th anniv. of Chinese Geological Society.

A461

1982, Aug. 25 Photo. ***Perf. 11½x11***

1799 A461 4f Orpiment (4-1)	.75	.30
1800 A461 8f Stibnite (4-2)	.75	.30
1801 A461 10f Cinnabar (4-3)	1.50	.30
1802 A461 20f Wolframite (4-4)	1.50	.55
Nos. 1799-1802 (4)	4.50	1.45

T.73.

Souvenir Sheet

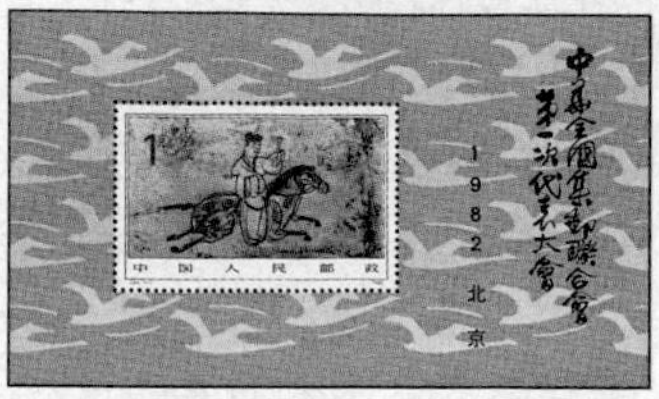
Messenger, Tomb Mural, Jiayu Pass, Wei-Jin Period — A462

1982, Aug. 25

1803 A462 $1 multicolored	27.50	12.00

All-China Philatelic Federation, 1st Cong.

12th Natl. Communist Party Congress A463

1982, Sept. 1 ***Perf. 11½***

1804 A463 8f multicolored	1.75	.45

Hoopoe — A464

No. 1806, Swallows (5-2). No. 1807, Oriole (5-3). No. 1808, Chickadees (5-4). No. 1809, Woodpecker (5-5).
No. 1810, Cuckoos.

1982, Sept. 10 ***Perf. 11½x11***

1805 A464 8f shown (5-1)	1.25	.40
1806 A464 8f multi	1.25	.40
1807 A464 8f multi	1.25	.40
1808 A464 20f multi	3.25	.80
1809 A464 70f multi	9.00	3.25
Nos. 1805-1809 (5)	16.00	5.25

Souvenir Sheet

1810 A464 $2 multi	52.50	18.50

No. 1810 contains one 56x36mm stamp. T.79.

Japan-China Relations Normalization, 10th Anniv. — A465

Flower Paintings: 8f, Plum blossoms, by Guan Shanyue. 70f, Hibiscus, by Xiao Shufang. J.84.

1982, Sept. 29 *Perf. 11*
1811 A465 8f multi (2-1) 1.25 .30
1812 A465 70f multi (2-2) 2.50 .95

World Food Day — A466

1982, Oct. 16 *Perf. 11½*
1813 A466 8f multicolored 1.25 .40

Guo Morou (1892-1978), Acad. of Sciences Pres. — A467

Designs: Portraits. J.87.

1982, Nov. 16 Photo. *Perf. 11½x11*
1814 A467 8f multi (2-1) .60 .30
1815 A467 20f multi (2-2) 1.50 .50

Bodhisattva, 11th Cent. Sculpture — A468

Liao Dynasty Buddha Sculptures, Lower Huayan Monastery. T.74.

1982, Nov. 19 *Perf. 11*
1816 A468 8f multi (4-1) 1.25 .40
1817 A468 8f multi (4-2) 1.25 .40
1818 A468 8f multi (4-3) 1.75 .40
1819 A468 70f multi (4-4) 4.50 2.75
Nos. 1816-1819 (4) 8.75 3.95

Souvenir Sheet

Perf. 11x11½

1820 A468 $2 multicolored 55.00 20.00

No. 1820 contains one 36x55mm stamp.

Dr. D.S. Kotnis, Indian Physician in 8th Army (J.83) A469

Perf. 11½x11, 11x11½

1982, Dec. 9 **Photo.**
1821 A469 8f Portrait, vert. (2-1) .55 .25
1822 A469 70f Riding horse (2-2) 2.25 1.50

11th Communist Youth League Natl. Congress A470

1982, Dec. 20 *Perf. 11x11½*
1823 A470 8f multicolored 1.50 .50

Bronze Wine Container — A471

Western Zhou Dynasty Bronze (1200-771 B.C.): No. 1825, Three-legged cooking pot. No. 1826, Food bowl. No. 1827, Three-legged cooking pot (diff.). No. 1828, Animal-shaped wine container. 10f, Wine container with lid. 20f, Round food bowl. 70f, Square wine container. T.75.

Photogravure & Engraved

1982, Dec. 25 *Perf. 11*
1824 A471 4f multi (8-1) 1.75 .80
1825 A471 4f multi (8-2) 1.75 .80
1826 A471 8f multi (8-3) 1.75 .80
1827 A471 8f multi (8-4) 3.00 1.25
1828 A471 8f multi (8-5) 1.75 .80
1829 A471 10f multi (8-6) 2.75 .80
1830 A471 20f multi (8-7) 3.50 1.50
1831 A471 70f multi (8-8) 17.50 4.50
Nos. 1824-1831 (8) 33.75 11.25

A472

1983, Jan. 5 *Perf. 11½*
1832 A472 8f multicolored 20.00 4.50
a. Booklet pane of 12 50.00 *70.00*
Complete booklet, #1832a 70.00

New Year 1983 (Year of the Pig).
Stamps from No. 1832a have straight edges at top or bottom and sell for less as singles than No. 1832.

A473

Stringed Instruments (T.81).

1983, Jan. 20 *Perf. 11½x11, 11x11½*
1833 A473 4f Konghou (5-1) 3.75 1.25
1834 A473 8f Ruan (5-2) 3.75 1.25
1835 A473 8f Qin, horiz. (5-3) 3.75 1.25
1836 A473 10f Piba (5-4) 3.75 1.25
1837 A473 70f Sanxian (5-5) 29.00 8.00
Nos. 1833-1837 (5) 44.00 13.00

A474

No. 1838, Memorial Tower, Zhengzhou (2-1). No. 1839, Monument, Jiangan (2-2).

1983, Feb. 7 Photo. *Perf. 11½x11*
1838 A474 8f multi .80 .40
1839 A474 8f multi 1.00 .40

60th Anniv. of Peking-Hankow Railroad Workers' Strike (J.89).

The Western Chamber, Traditional Opera, by Wang Shifu (1271-1368) A475

Scenes from the opera.

1983, Feb. 21 Photo. *Perf. 11x11½*
1840 A475 8f multi (4-1) 3.50 2.00
1841 A475 8f multi (4-2) 3.50 2.00
1842 A475 10f multi (4-3) 6.00 2.50
1843 A475 80f multi (4-4) 27.50 7.50
Nos. 1840-1843 (4) 40.50 14.00

Souvenir Sheet

Photogravure and Engraved

Perf. 12

1844 A475 $2 multicolored 120.00 60.00

No. 1844 contains one 27x48mm stamp. T.82.

Karl Marx (1818-1883) (J.90) — A476

Photogravure & Engraved

1983, Mar. 14 *Perf. 11½x11*
1845 A476 8f Portrait (2-1) .60 .35
1846 A476 20f Making speech (2-2) 1.25 .55

Tomb of the Yellow Emperor (T.84) A477

8f, Tomb, vert. (3-1). 10f, Hall of Founder of Chinese Culture (3-2). 20f, Cypress tree, vert. (3-3).

Photogravure & Engraved

1983, Apr. 5 *Perf. 11½*
1847 A477 8f multi 1.50 .75
1848 A477 10f multi 2.00 .75
1849 A477 20f multi 3.25 1.10
Nos. 1847-1849 (3) 6.75 2.60

World Communications Year — A478

1983, Apr. 28 Photo. *Perf. 11½*
1850 A478 8f multicolored 1.50 .60

Male Chinese Alligator (T.85) — A479

Photogravure & Engraved

1983, May 24 *Perf. 11*
1851 A479 8f shown (2-1) 1.10 .55
1852 A479 20f Female, hatching eggs (2-2) 1.90 .90

Kitten, by Tan Arxi — A480

Various children's drawings. T.86.

1983, June 1 *Perf. 11½x11*
1853 A480 8f multi (4-1) .50 .30
1854 A480 8f multi (4-2) .50 .30
1855 A480 8f multi (4-3) .50 .30
1856 A480 8f multi (4-4) .50 .30
Nos. 1853-1856 (4) 2.00 1.20

6th Natl. People's Congress (J.94) A481

1983, June 6 *Perf. 11x11½*
1857 A481 8f Hall (2-1) 1.25 .50
1858 A481 20f Natl. anthem score (2-2) 3.25 .90

Terra Cotta Figures, Qin Dynasty (221-207 BC) A482

No. 1859, Soldiers (4-1). No. 1860, Heads (4-2). No. 1861, Soldiers, horses (4-3). No. 1862, Excavation site (4-4).
No. 1863, Soldier leading horse.

1983, June 30
1859 A482 8f multi 1.10 .70
1860 A482 8f multi 1.10 .70
1861 A482 10f multi 1.75 .85
1862 A482 70f multi 5.00 3.25
a. Bklt. pane of 8 (#1859, 3 #1860, 3 #1861, #1862) *35.00 25.00*
Nos. 1859-1862 (4) 8.95 5.50

Souvenir Sheet

1863 A482 $2 multi *55.00 32.50*
a. Booklet pane of 1 *55.00*
Complete booklet, #1862a, #1863a 95.00 *65.00*

No. 1863 contains one 59x39mm stamp. T.88.

A483

Female roles in Peking opera (T.87) — 4f, Sun Yujiao (8-1). No. 1865, 8f, Chen Miaochang (8-2). No. 1866, 8f, Bai Suzhen (8-3). No. 1867, 8f, Sister Thirteen (8-4). 10f, Qin Xianglian (8-5). 20f, Yang Yuhuan (8-6). 50f, Cui Yingying (8-7). 80f, Mu Guiying (8-8).

1983, July 20 Photo. *Perf. 11*
1864 A483 4f multi 2.75 .95
1865 A483 8f multi 2.75 .95
1866 A483 8f multi 2.75 .95

1867	A483	8f multi	2.75	.95
1868	A483	10f multi	2.75	.95
1869	A483	20f multi	2.75	.95
1870	A483	50f multi	15.00	4.00
1871	A483	80f multi	20.00	6.50
		Nos. 1864-1871 (8)	51.50	16.20

A484

Paintings by Liu Lingcang.

1983, Aug. 10 Photo. *Perf. 11½*

1872	A484	8f Li Bai (4-1)	2.25	.45
1873	A484	8f Du Fu (4-2)	2.25	.45
1874	A484	8f Han Yu (4-3)	2.25	.45
1875	A484	70f Liu Zongyuan (4-4)	13.00	3.50
		Nos. 1872-1875 (4)	19.75	4.85

Poets and philosophers of ancient China (J.92).

5th Natl. Women's Congress — A485

1983, Sept. 1 Photo. *Perf. 11½*

1876	A485	8f multicolored	1.25	.40

5th National Games (J.93) — A486

1983, Sept. 16 Photo. *Perf. 11½*

1877	A486	4f Emblem (6-1)	.85	.35
1878	A486	8f Gymnast (6-2)	.85	.35
1879	A486	8f Badminton (6-3)	.85	.35
1880	A486	8f Diving (6-4)	.85	.35
1881	A486	20f High jump (6-5)	1.50	.40
1882	A486	70f Wind surfing (6-6)	5.50	2.25
		Nos. 1877-1882 (6)	10.40	4.05

Family Planning (T.91) A487

1983, Sept. 19 *Perf. 11x11½*

1883	A487	8f One child (2-1)	.60	.30
1884	A487	8f Cultivated land (2-2)	.60	.30

10th Intl. Trade Union Congress — A488

1983, Oct. 18 Litho. *Perf. 11½*

1885	A488	8f multicolored	.90	.40

Swans (T.83) A489

Perf. 11x11½ on 3 sides

1983, Nov. 18 Photo.

1886	A489	8f (4-1)	.35	.30
1887	A489	8f (4-2)	1.40	.55
1888	A489	10f (4-3)	1.40	.55
1889	A489	80f (4-4)	3.00	1.90
a.		Booklet pane, 7 #1886, 1 each #1887-1889	30.00	*20.00*
		Complete booklet, #1889a	55.00	*27.50*
		Nos. 1886-1889 (4)	6.15	3.30

A490

Various photos. J.96.

1983, Nov. 24 Photo. *Perf. 11½*

1890	A490	8f multi (4-1)	1.40	.50
1891	A490	8f multi (4-2)	1.40	.50
1892	A490	8f multi (4-3)	1.40	.50
1893	A490	8f multi (4-4)	1.40	.50
		Nos. 1890-1893 (4)	5.60	2.00

85th birth anniv. of Liu Shaoqi, political leader.

A491

1983, Nov. 29 Photo. *Perf. 11½*

1894	A491	8f No. 117 (2-1)	.55	.30
1895	A491	20f No. 4L1 (2-2)	.75	.40

CHINAPEX '83 Natl. Philatelic Exhibition (J.99).

A492

Various portraits. J.97.

1983, Dec. 26 Photo. *Perf. 11½*

1896	A492	8f 1925 (4-1)	1.25	.35
1897	A492	8f 1945 (4-2)	1.25	.35
1898	A492	10f 1952 (4-3)	5.75	1.00
1899	A492	20f 1961 (4-4)	3.50	.60
		Nos. 1896-1899 (4)	11.75	2.30

90th birth anniv. of Mao Tse-tung.

A493

Photogravure and Engraved

1984, Jan. 5 *Perf. 11½*

1900	A493	8f multicolored	7.00	2.50
a.		Booklet pane of 12	*80.00*	*30.00*
		Complete booklet, #1900a	110.00	*92.50*

New Year 1984 (Year of the Rat).

Stamps from No. 1900a have straight edge at top or bottom.

Beauties Wearing Flowers — A494

Portions of painting by Zhou Fang (Tang Dynasty). T.89.

1984, Mar. 24 Photo. *Perf. 11*

1901	A494	8f multi (3-1)	1.75	.40
1902	A494	10f multi (3-2)	2.75	.60
1903	A494	70f multi (3-3)	8.50	3.00
		Nos. 1901-1903 (3)	13.00	4.00

Souvenir Sheet

1904	A494	$2 Entire painting	*180.00*	55.00

No. 1904 contains one 162x40mm stamp.

Chinese Roses (T.93) — A495

No. 1905, Spring of Shanghai (6-1). No. 1906, Rosy Dawn of Pujiang River (6-2). No. 1907, Pearl (6-3). No. 1908, Black whirlwind (6-4). No. 1909, Yellow flower in battlefield (6-5). No. 1910, Blue Phoenix (6-6).

1984, Apr. 20 Photo. *Perf. 11½*

1905	A495	4f multi	.90	.30
1906	A495	8f multi	.90	.30
1907	A495	8f multi	.90	.30
1908	A495	10f multi	.90	.35
1909	A495	20f multi	2.00	.45
1910	A495	70f multi	4.50	1.40
		Nos. 1905-1910 (6)	10.10	3.10

Ren Bishi (1904-50), Statesman A496

1984, Apr. 30 *Perf. 11½x11*

1911	A496	8f multicolored	.75	.30

Crested Ibis (T.94) A497

1984, May 15 Photo. *Perf. 11x11½*

1912	A497	8f Flying (3-1)	.80	.25
1913	A497	8f Wading (3-2)	.80	.25
1914	A497	80f Perching (3-3)	2.50	1.50
		Nos. 1912-1914 (3)	4.10	2.00

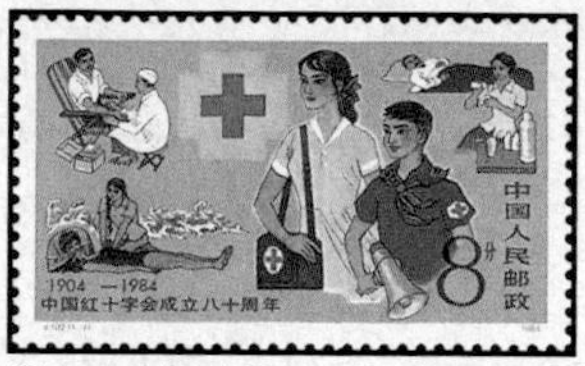

Chinese Red Cross Society, 80th Anniv. — A498

1984, May 29 *Perf. 11½*

1915	A498	8f multicolored	.85	.30

Gezhou Dam, Yangtze River (T.95) — A499

1984, June 15 Photo.

1916	A499	8f Dam (3-1)	.50	.35
1917	A499	10f Bridge, vert. (3-2)	.75	.40
1918	A499	20f Lock Gate #2 (3-3)	1.60	.75
		Nos. 1916-1918 (3)	2.85	1.50

Zhuo Zheng Garden, Suzhou (T.96) — A500

No. 1919, Inverted Image Tower (4-1). No. 1920, Loquat Garden (4-2). No. 1921, Water Court, Xiao Cang Lang (4-3). No. 1922, Yuan-xiang Hall, Yiyu Study (4-4).

Photogravure & Engraved

1984, June 30 *Perf. 11½x11*

1919	A500	8f multi	.75	.45
1920	A500	8f multi	.75	.45
1921	A500	10f multi	.85	.45
1922	A500	70f multi	2.25	1.50
		Nos. 1919-1922 (4)	4.60	2.85

1984 Summer Olympics A501

1984, July 28 Photo. *Perf. 11½*

1923	A501	4f Shooting (6-1)	.35	.25
1924	A501	8f High jump (6-2)	.40	.25
1925	A501	8f Weight lifting (6-3)	.40	.25
1926	A501	10f Gymnastics (6-4)	.45	.25
1927	A501	20f Volleyball (6-5)	.50	.30
1928	A501	80f Diving (6-6)	1.25	.40
		Nos. 1923-1928 (6)	3.35	1.70

Souvenir Sheet

1929	A501	$2 Athletes, rings	14.00	7.00

No. 1929 contains one 61x38mm stamp. J.103.

Calligraphy — A502

Artworks by Wu Changshuo. T.98: No. 1931, A Pair of Peaches (8-2). No. 1932, Lotus (8-3). No. 1933, Wisteria (8-4). No. 1934, Peony (8-5). No. 1935, Chrysanthemum (8-6). No. 1936, Plum Blossom (8-7). No. 1937, Seal Cutting (8-8).

1984, Aug. 27 Photo. *Perf. 11½*

1930 A502 4f shown (8-1) .90 .35
1931 A502 4f multi .90 .35
1932 A502 8f multi 2.00 .35
1933 A502 8f multi .80 .35
1934 A502 8f multi 8.00 2.00
1935 A502 10f multi 1.75 .60
1936 A502 20f multi 2.00 .60
1937 A502 70f multi 4.75 2.00
Nos. 1930-1937 (8) 21.10 6.60

Luanhe River Water Diversion Project (T.97) — A503

Perf. 11½x11, 11 (#1939)

1984, Sept. 11 Photo.

1938 A503 8f multi (3-1) .40 .30
1939 A503 10f multi, horiz. (3-2) .40 .30
1940 A503 20f multi (3-3) .60 .40
Nos. 1938-1940 (3) 1.40 1.00

Chinese-Japanese Youth (J.104) — A504

1984, Sept. 24 Photo. *Perf. 11½*

1941 A504 8f Neighbors (3-1) .35 .30
1942 A504 20f Planting tree (3-2) .55 .30
1943 A504 80f Dancing (3-3) 1.10 .70
Nos. 1941-1943 (3) 2.00 1.30

People's Republic, 35th Anniv. (J.105) — A505

No. 1944, Engineer (5-1). No. 1945, Farm woman (5-2). No. 1946, Scientist (5-4). No. 1947, Soldier (5-5). No. 1948, Cranes (5-3).

1984, Oct. 1 Photo. *Perf. 11½x11*

Size: 26x35mm

1944 A505 8f multi .45 .30
1945 A505 8f multi .45 .30
1946 A505 8f multi .45 .30
1947 A505 8f multi .45 .30

Size: 36x48mm

Perf. 11

1948 A505 20f multi 2.25 1.00
Nos. 1944-1948 (5) 4.05 2.20

110th Birth Anniv. of Chen Jiageng (J.106) A506

8f, Chen Jiageng (2-1). 80f, Jimei School (2-2).

1984, Oct. 21 Photo. *Perf. 12½x12*

1949 A506 8f multi .65 .25
1950 A506 80f multi 2.10 .40

The Maiden's Study A507

Scenes from The Peony Pavilion, by Tang Xianzu. T.99: No. 1952, In the dreamland (4-2). No. 1953, Du Liniang drawing self-portrait (4-3). No. 1954, Married to Liu Mengmai (4-4).
No. 1955, Playing in the garden.

Photogravure & Engraved

1984, Oct. 30 *Perf. 11*

1951 A507 8f shown (4-1) .75 .50
1952 A507 8f multi .75 .50
1953 A507 20f multi 1.60 .90
1954 A507 70f multi 3.25 2.60
Nos. 1951-1954 (4) 6.35 4.50

Souvenir Sheet

Perf. 11½

1955 A507 $2 multi *45.00 25.00*

No. 1955 contains one 90x60mm stamp.

Emei Shan Mountain Scenery (T.100) — A508

No. 1956, Baoguo Temple (6-1). No. 1957, Leiyin Temple (6-2). No. 1958, Hongchun Lawn (6-3). No. 1959, Elephant bath (6-4). No. 1960, Woyun Temple (6-5). No. 1961, Shining Cloud Sea at Jinding (6-6).

1984, Nov. 16 *Perf. 11*

1956 A508 4f multi 1.10 .55
1957 A508 8f multi .75 .40
1958 A508 8f multi .45 .45
1959 A508 10f multi 1.00 .55
1960 A508 20f multi 2.00 1.25
1961 A508 80f multi 6.00 2.75
Nos. 1956-1961 (6) 11.30 5.95

A509

Portraits: 8f, During the Long March (3-1). 10f, At 7th Natl. Party Congress (3-2). 20f, In motorcade (3-3).

1984, Dec. 15 Photo. *Perf. 11½x11*

1962 A509 8f multi .35 .35
1963 A509 10f multi .45 .40
1964 A509 20f multi .65 .40
Nos. 1962-1964 (3) 1.45 1.15

Former party secretary Ren Bishi (1904-50).

Flower Arrangement A510

1984, Dec. 25 *Perf. 11*

1965 A510 8f multi .75 .40

Chinese insurance industry.

New Year 1985 (Year of the Ox) — A511

Photogravure & Engraved

1985, Jan. 5 *Perf. 11½*

1966 A511 8f T.102 2.25 .55
a. Bklt. pane of 4 + 8 plus label 24.00 12.00
Complete booklet, #1966a 35.00

Stamps from No. 1966a have straight edge at top or bottom.

Zunyi Meeting, 50th Anniv. — A512

Paintings: 8f, The Zunyi Meeting, by Liu Xiangping. 20f, The Red Army Successfully Arrived in Northern Shaanxi, by Zhao Yu. J.107.

1985, Jan. 15 Photo. *Perf. 11x11½*

1967 A512 8f multi (2-1) 1.10 .40
1968 A512 20f multi (2-2) 1.90 .80

A513

Lantern Folk Festival: No. 1969, Lotus of Good Luck. No. 1970, Auspicious dragon and phoenix. No. 1971, A hundred flowers blossoming. 70f, Prosperity and affluence. T.104.

1985, Feb. 28 *Perf. 11½*

1969 A513 8f multi (4-1) 1.60 .55
1970 A513 8f multi (4-2) 1.60 .55
1971 A513 8f multi (4-3) 1.60 .55
1972 A513 70f multi (4-4) 5.00 1.60
Nos. 1969-1972 (4) 9.80 3.25

A514

1985, Mar. 8

1973 A514 20f multicolored .80 .45

UN Decade for Women (1976-85).

Mei (Prunus mume) (T.103) — A515

No. 1974, Green calyx (6-1). No. 1975, Pendant mei (6-2). No. 1976, Contorted dragon (6-3). No. 1977, Cinnabar (6-4). No. 1978, Versicolor mei (6-5). No. 1979, Apricot mei (6-6).

No. 1980, Duplicate and condensed fragrance mei.

1985, Apr. 5 *Perf. 11*

1974 A515 8f multi 1.10 .35
1975 A515 8f multi 1.10 .35
1976 A515 8f multi 1.10 .35
1977 A515 10f multi 2.10 .35
1978 A515 20f multi 3.25 .75
1979 A515 80f multi 8.25 2.25
Nos. 1974-1979 (6) 16.90 4.40

Souvenir Sheet

Perf. 11½

1980 A515 $2 multi *45.00 25.00*

No. 1980 contains one 93x52mm stamp.

Huizo Guild Hall, Guangzhou — A516

1985, May 1 Photo. *Perf. 11*

1981 A516 8f multi .80 .40

All-China Fed. of Trade Unions.

A517

1985, May 4 Photo.

1982 A517 20f multicolored 1.00 .35

Intl. Youth Year.

A518

Paintings of giant pandas: 8f, 20f, 50f, 80f, by Han Meilin; $3, by Wu Zuoren. T.106.

1985, May 24 *Perf. 11½*

1983 A518 8f multi (4-1), vert. 1.25 .35
1984 A518 20f multi (4-2) 1.50 .40
1985 A518 50f multi (4-3), vert. 1.50 .50
1986 A518 80f multi (4-4) 4.00 .70
Nos. 1983-1986 (4) 8.25 1.95

Souvenir Sheet

Perf. 11x11½

1987 A518 $3 multi, vert. 5.25 3.00
a. Ovptd. in sheet margin 8.00

No. 1987 contains one 39x59mm stamp.
No. 1987a ovptd. in sheet margin with panda hologram, PJZ-4 and horizontal Chinese inscription in gold. Issued 10/9/96.
No. 1987a was sold in a mount affixed to a small card.

Xian Xinghai (1905-1945), Composer A519

Design: Bust, by Cao Chongen and music from The Yellow River Cantata.

1985, June 13 Photo. *Perf. 11½x11*
1988 A519 8f multicolored 1.10 .45

Agnes Smedley, 1892-1950 (3-1) — A520

American journalists: 20f, Anna Louise Strong, 1885-1970 (3-2). 80f, Edgar Snow, 1905-1972 (3-3). J.112.

1985, June 25
1989 A520 8f multicolored .35 .30
1990 A520 20f multicolored .45 .30
1991 A520 80f multicolored .90 .60
Nos. 1989-1991 (3) 1.70 1.20

Zheng He's West Seas Expedition, 580th Anniv. — A521

No. 1992, Portrait of the navigator. No. 1993, Peace envoy. 20f, Trade, cultural exchange. 80f, Honored for navigational feats. J.113.

1985, July 11 *Perf. 11½*
1992 A521 8f multi (4-1) .55 .30
1993 A521 8f multi (4-2) .55 .30
1994 A521 20f multi (4-3) 1.10 .45
1995 A521 80f multi (4-4) 2.60 .90
Nos. 1992-1995 (4) 4.80 1.95

Xu Beihong, 1895-1953, Painter (J.114) A522

1985, July 19 *Perf. 11½x11, 11x11½*
1996 A522 8f Self-portrait (2-1), vert. .50 .30
1997 A522 20f shown (2-2) 1.10 .40

A523

Designs: 8f, Lin Zexu, 1785-1850, statesman, patriot. 80f, Burning opium at Humen, bas-relief.

1985, Aug. 30 *Perf. 11*
1998 A523 8f multi (2-1) .45 .35

Size: 51x22mm

1999 A523 80f multi (2-2) 1.25 .45

Lin Zexu's ban of the opium trade catalyzed the Anglo-Chinese Opium Wars. J.115.

A524

8f, Prosperity (3-1). 10f, Celebration (3-2). 20f, Abundant Harvest (3-3).

1985, Sept. 1 *Perf. 11½x11*
2000 A524 8f multi .65 .30
2001 A524 10f multi .85 .35
2002 A524 20f multi 1.75 .55
Nos. 2000-2002 (3) 3.25 1.20

Tibet Autonomous Region, 20th anniv. (J.116).

End of World War II, 40th Anniv. A525

Woodcuts by Wu Biduan: 8f, The Chinese Army Rose Against the Japanese Agressors at Logouqiao (2-1). 80f, The Eighth Route Army and Militia Fought Around the Great Wall (2-2). J.117.

1985, Sept. 3 *Perf. 11*
2003 A525 8f multi .50 .30
2004 A525 80f multi .95 .55

2nd Natl. Worker's Games, Sept. 8-15, Beijing A526

Competitors from various events and: 8f, Men's bicycling (2-1). 20f, Women hurdlers (2-2). J.118.

1985, Sept. 8 *Perf. 11x11½*
2005 A526 8f multi .75 .65
2006 A526 20f multi 1.10 .90

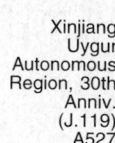

Xinjiang Uygur Autonomous Region, 30th Anniv. (J.119) A527

8f, Oasis in the Gobi, woman (3-1). 10f, Oil field, Lake Tianchi (3-2). 20f, Tianshan pasture, woman (3-3).

1985, Oct. 1 Photo. *Perf. 11½*
2007 A527 8f multi .35 .35
2008 A527 10f multi .40 .35
2009 A527 20f multi .70 .40
Nos. 2007-2009 (3) 1.45 1.10

Size of No. 2008, 60x30mm.

1st Natl. Youth Games, Oct. 6-15, Zhengzhou (J.121) — A528

8f, Girls' track & field (2-1). 20f, Boys' basketball (2-2).

1985, Oct. 6 *Perf. 11½x11*
2010 A528 8f multi .40 .30
2011 A528 20f multi .65 .55

Forbidden City Main Buildings — A529

1985, Oct. 10 *Perf. 11½*
2012 A529 8f multi (4-1) .35 .30
2013 A529 8f multi (4-2) .35 .30
2014 A529 20f multi (4-3) .35 .30
2015 A529 80f multi (4-4) .70 .70
a. Vert. strip of 4, #2012-2015 2.75 2.75

Palace Museum, 60th anniv. J.120.

Zou Taofen (1895-1935), Journalist (J.122) — A530

1985, Nov. 5 *Perf. 11½x11*
2016 A530 8f Portrait (2-1) .35 .35
2017 A530 20f Epitaph by Zhou Enlai (2-2) .35 .35
a. Pair, #2016-2017 1.00 .90

December 9th Revolution, 50th Anniv. — A531

1985, Dec. 9 *Perf. 11½*
2018 A531 8f Memorial Pavilion .90 .30

New Year 1986 — A532

Photogravure & Engraved

1986, Jan. 5 *Perf. 11½*
2019 A532 8f multicolored 1.10 .50
a. Bklt. pane of 4 + 8 with label btwn *5.50*
Complete booklet, #2019a 20.00

Natl. Space Industry — A533

4f, 1st experimental satellite. No. 2021, Recoverable satellite. No. 2022, Underwater rocket launch. 10f, Rocket launch. 20f, Earth satellite receiver. 70f, Satellite trajectory diagram. T.108.

1986, Feb. 1 Photo.
2020 A533 4f multi (6-1) .65 .35
2021 A533 8f multi (6-2) .65 .35
2022 A533 8f multi (6-3) .65 .35
2023 A533 10f multi (6-4) .65 .40
2024 A533 20f multi (6-5) 1.50 .40
2025 A533 70f multi (6-6) 3.25 .80
Nos. 2020-2025 (6) 7.35 2.65

Dong Biwu (1886-1975), Party Founder (J.123) — A534

Photogravure and Engraved

1986, Mar. 5 *Perf. 11½x11*
2026 A534 8f 1975 (2-1) .90 .30
2027 A534 20f 1945 (2-2) 1.10 .65

Lin Boqu (1886-1960), Party Leader (J.124) — A535

1986, Mar. 20
2028 A535 8f shown (2-1) .65 .30
2029 A535 20f Lin standing (2-2) .85 .50

Marshal He Long (1896-1969), Revolution Leader (J.126) — A536

1986, Mar. 22 *Perf. 11x11½*
2030 A536 8f shown (2-1) 1.00 .30
2031 A536 20f On horseback (2-2) 1.25 .45

Halley's Comet — A537

1986, Apr. 11 Photo. *Perf. 11½*
2032 A537 20f dk bl & gray 1.00 .30

White Crane (T.110) A538

8f, Two cranes (3-1). 10f, One flying (3-2), vert. 70f, Four cranes (3-3), vert. $2, Flock.

1986, May 22 *Perf. 11x11½, 11½x11*
2033 A538 8f multi .90 .30
2034 A538 10f multi .90 .30
2035 A538 70f multi 2.40 .75
Nos. 2033-2035 (3) 4.20 1.35

Souvenir Sheet

2036 A538 $2 multi *9.00 4.50*

No. 2036 contains one 116x25mm stamp.

Li Weihan (1896-1984), Party Leader (J.127) — A539

1986, June 2 *Perf. 11x11½*
2037 A539 8f Portrait (2-1) .50 .30
2038 A539 20f Writing (2-2) .65 .50

Intl. Peace Year A540

1986, June 16 *Perf. 11*
2039 A540 8f multi 1.00 .30

Mao Dun (1896-1981), Writer (J.129) — A541

1986, July 4 *Perf. 11x11½*
2040 A541 8f Portrait (2-1) .50 .30
2041 A541 20f Portrait, diff. (2-2) .65 .50

Wang Jiaxiang (1906-1974), Party Leader (J.130) — A542

1986, Aug. 15
2042 A542 8f Portrait (2-1) .50 .30
2043 A542 20f Portrait, diff. (2-2) .65 .50

Teacher's Day A543

1986, Sept. 10 *Perf. 11*
2044 A543 8f multi 1.00 .30

Magnolia Liliflora (T.111) A544

No. 2045, Blossom (3-1). No. 2046, Two blossoms (3-2). No. 2047, Blossom, diff. (3-3). No. 2048, Three blossoms.

1986, Sept. 23 *Perf. 11x11½*
2045 A544 8f multi .45 .40
2046 A544 8f multi .45 .40
2047 A544 70f multi 2.60 2.40
Nos. 2045-2047 (3) 3.50 3.20

Souvenir Sheet

2048 A544 $2 multi *13.50 8.00*

No. 2048 contains one 132x70mm stamp.

Inner Mongolia — A545

Tibet — A545a

Northeastern China — A545b

Hunan — A545c

So. Yangtze River — A545d

Beijing — A545e

Yunnan — A545f

Shanghai — A545g

Anhui — A545h

No. Shaanxi — A545i

Sichuan — A545j

Taiwan — A545k

Fujian — A545l

Zhejiang — A545m

Folk Houses.

Perf. 13x13½, 11x11½, (1½f, 3f, #2057-2062)

1986, Apr. 1 **Photo.**
2049 A545 1f multi .25 .25
2050 A545a 1½f multi .25 .25
2051 A545b 2f multi .25 .25
2052 A545c 3f multi .25 .25
2053 A545d 4f multi .25 .25
2054 A545e 8f multi .25 .25
2055 A545f 10f multi .25 .25
2056 A545g 20f multi .25 .25
2057 A545h 30f multi .30 .25
2058 A545i 40f multi .40 .30
2059 A545j 50f multi .60 .40
2060 A545k 90f multi .80 .55
2061 A545l $1 multi .85 .65
2062 A545m $1.10 multi .90 .75
Nos. 2049-2062 (14) 5.85 4.90

Issue dates: 3f, Dec. 25; 4f, $1, Oct. 15; 20f, 50f, Sept. 10; 40f, Nov. 15; others, Apr. 1.
Postal forgeries of No. 2056 exist.
See Nos. 2198-2204.

1989-90 **Photo.**
2055a Perf. 11x11½ ('89) 1.00 1.00
2056a Perf. 11x11½ ('89) 1.50 1.00
2057a Perf. 13x13½ ('90) .65 .35
2058a Perf. 13x13½ 9.00 *4.50*
2059a Perf. 13x13½ ('89) 1.10 .60
2061a Perf. 13x13½ ('90) 2.25 1.25
Nos. 2055a-2061a (6) 15.50 8.70

Souvenir Sheet

All-China Philatelic Federation, 2nd Congress — A546

1986, Oct. 17 **Litho.** *Perf. 11½*
2063 A546 $2 Jade lion *8.50 3.50*

Leaders of the 1911 Revolution (J.132) A547

1986, Oct. 10 **Photo.** *Perf. 11x11½*
2064 A547 8f Sun Yat-sen (3-1) 1.00 .40
2065 A547 10f Huang Xing (3-2) 1.40 .80
2066 A547 40f Zhang Taiyan (3-3) 3.00 1.60
Nos. 2064-2066 (3) 5.40 2.80

Souvenir Sheet

Sun Yat-sen (1866-1925) — A548

1986, Nov. 12 *Perf. 11½*
2067 A548 $2 multicolored *16.00 6.50*

Marshal Zhu De (1886-1976) (J.134) — A549

Designs: 20f, Orating.

1986, Dec. 1 **Engr.** *Perf. 11½x11*
2068 A549 8f sepia (2-1) 2.75 .35
2069 A549 20f myrtle grn (2-2) 5.00 .55

Sports of Ancient China A550

Stone carvings. T.113.

Perf. 11½x11, 11x11½

1986, Dec. 20 **Photo.**
2070 A550 8f Archery (4-1), vert. .65 .35
2071 A550 8f Weiqi (4-2) .65 .35
2072 A550 10f Golf (4-3) .95 .45
2073 A550 50f Soccer (4-4), vert. 4.00 2.00
Nos. 2070-2073 (4) 6.25 3.15

A551

Photogravure & Engraved

1987, Jan. 5 *Perf. 11½*
2074 A551 8f blk, dk pink & yel grn 1.40 .45
a. Bklt. pane of 4 + 8 + label *16.00* —
Complete booklet, #2074a 30.00

New Year 1987 (Year of the Hare).

A552

8f, Traveling (3-1). 20f, Cave writing (3-2). 40f, Mountain climbing (3-3).

1987, Feb. 20 **Photo.** *Perf. 11½*
2075 A552 8f multi .75 .35
2076 A552 20f multi 2.50 1.40
2077 A552 40f multi 4.50 2.25
Nos. 2075-2077 (3) 7.75 4.00

Xu Xiake (1587-1621), Ming Dynasty geographer (J.136).

Birds of Prey (T.114) — A553

No. 2078, Kite (4-1). No. 2079, Sea eagle (4-2), vert. No. 2080, Vulture (4-3), vert. No. 2081, Buzzard (4-4).

1987, Mar. 20
2078 A553 8f multi .60 .40
2079 A553 8f multi .60 .40
2080 A553 10f multi .95 .40
2081 A553 90f multi 6.00 1.40
Nos. 2078-2081 (4) 8.15 2.60

Liao Zhongkai (1877-1925), National Party Leader (J.137) — A554

20f, Liao, He Xiangning (2-2).

1987, Apr. 23 *Perf. 11½x11*
2082 A554 8f shown (2-1) 1.00 .30
2083 A554 20f multi 2.00 .35

Kites (T.115) — A555

1987, Apr. 1
2084 A555 8f Hawk (4-1) .75 .35
2085 A555 8f Dragon (4-2) .75 .35
a. Pair, #2084-2085 2.75 2.25
2086 A555 30f Symbolic octagon (4-3) 2.00 .95
2087 A555 30f Phoenix (4-4) 2.00 .95
a. Pair, #2086-2087 5.25 4.00
Nos. 2084-2087 (4) 5.50 2.60

Nos. 2085a, 2087a have continuous designs.

A556

Portraits of Ye Jianying (1897-1986), central committee vice chairman (J.138).

1987, Apr. 28
2088 A556 8f multi (3-3) 1.00 .40
2089 A556 10f multi (3-2) 1.50 .50
2090 A556 30f multi (3-1) 5.50 1.90
Nos. 2088-2090 (3) 8.00 2.80

Caves of the Thousand Buddhas, Dunhuang, Gansu Province — A557

Wall Paintings: 8f, Worshipping Bodhisattvas, Northern Liang Dynasty. 10f, Deer King Jatka, Northern Wei Dynasty. 20f, Heavenly Musicians, Northern Wei Dynasty. 40f, Flying Devata, Northern Wei Dynasty. $2, Mahasattva Jataka. T.116.

1987, May 20 *Perf. 11½*
2091 A557 8f multi (4-1) .55 .30
2092 A557 10f multi (4-2) .65 .35
2093 A557 20f multi (4-3) 1.75 .85
2094 A557 40f multi (4-4) 3.00 1.40
Nos. 2091-2094 (4) 5.95 2.90

Souvenir Sheet

2095 A557 $2 multi *27.50 15.00*

No. 2095 contains one 92x73mm stamp.
See Nos. 2149-2152, 2283-2286, 2407-2411, 2505-2508, 2704-2707.

Children's Day Festival A558

Children's drawings: No. 2096, Happy Holiday, by Yan Qinghui, age 7. No. 2097, Peace and Happiness, by Liu Yuan, age 7. T.117.

1987, June 1 *Perf. 12½x12*
2096 A558 8f shown (2-1) 1.25 .25
2097 A558 8f multi, vert. (2-2) 1.60 .45

Rural Development A559

No. 2098, Village, southeast China (4-1). No. 2099, Market (4-2). No. 2100, Dairy industry (4-3). No. 2101, Theater (4-4).

1987, June 25 *Perf. 11½*
2098 A559 8f multi .60 .45
2099 A559 8f multi .60 .45
2100 A559 10f multi .85 .60
2101 A559 20f multi 1.75 1.25
Nos. 2098-2101 (4) 3.80 2.75

Nos. 2099-2100 horiz. T.118.

Postal Savings Bank Inauguration A560

1987, July 1
2102 A560 8f multicolored 2.00 .35

Esperanto Language Movement, Cent. — A561

1987, July 26
2103 A561 8f lt olive grn, blk & brt blue 1.75 .40

People's Liberation Army, 60th Anniv. (J.140) A562

No. 2104, Flag, Great Wall (4-1). No. 2105, Rocket launch, soldier, village (4-2). No. 2106, Submarine, sailor (4-3). No. 2107, Aircraft, pilot (4-4).

1987, Aug. 1 *Perf. 11*
2104 A562 8f multi .75 .35
2105 A562 8f multi .75 .35
2106 A562 10f multi 1.75 .40
2107 A562 30f multi 2.50 .65
Nos. 2104-2107 (4) 5.75 1.75

Intl. Year of Shelter for the Homeless A563

1987, Aug. 20 *Perf. 11*
2108 A563 8f gray, dk car rose & blk 1.00 .30

Chinese Art Festival, Sept. 5-25, Beijing — A564

1987, Sept. 5 *Perf. 11*
2109 A564 8f brt red, gold & blk 3.00 .40

Fairy Tales — A565

4f, Pan Gu inventing the universe. No. 2111, Nu Wa creating man. No. 2112, Yi shooting nine suns. 10f, Chang'e flying to the moon. 20f, Kua Fu pursuing the sun. 90f, Jing Wei filling the sea. T.120.

1987, Sept. 25 *Perf. 11½*
2110 A565 4f multi (6-1) .55 .30
2111 A565 8f multi (6-2) .65 .30
2112 A565 8f multi (6-3) .65 .30
2113 A565 10f multi (6-4) .80 .30
2114 A565 20f multi (6-5) 1.10 .50
2115 A565 90f multi (6-6) 2.50 1.50
Nos. 2110-2115 (6) 6.25 3.20

Communist Party of China, 13th Natl. Congress A566

1987, Oct. 25 *Perf. 11*
2116 A566 8f multicolored 1.25 .50

Yellow Crane Tower (T.121) A567

No. 2118, Yue Yang Tower (4-2). No. 2119, Teng Wang Pavilion (4-3). No. 2120, Peng Lai Pavilion (4-4).

1987, Oct. 30
2117 A567 8f shown (4-1) .50 .25
2118 A567 8f multi .50 .30
2119 A567 10f multi .65 .45
2120 A567 90f multi 3.75 3.50
a. Min. sheet of 4, #2117-2120 *17.00 10.00*
Nos. 2117-2120 (4) 5.40 4.50

No. 2120a sold for $1.50.

6th Natl. Games (J.144) — A568

1987, Nov. 20 *Perf. 11½x11*
2121 A568 8f Pole vault (4-1) .35 .25
2122 A568 8f Softball (4-2) .35 .25
2123 A568 30f Weight lifting (4-3) .60 .35
2124 A568 50f Diving (4-4) 1.00 .55
Nos. 2121-2124 (4) 2.30 1.40

Souvenir Sheet

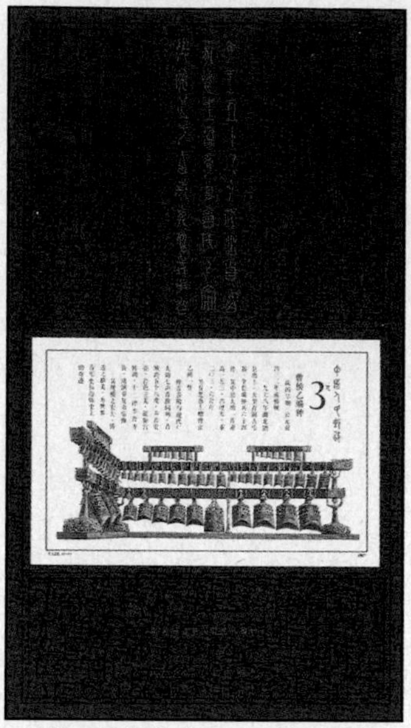

Bronze Bells from the Tomb of Marquis Yi of the Zeng State (c. 433 B.C.), Hubei Province — A569

1987, Dec. 10 **Litho.** *Imperf.*
2125 A569 $3 multicolored *9.50 4.50*

Classic Literature — A570

Outlaws of the Marsh: 8f, Shi Jin practicing martial arts. 10f, Sagacious Lu, the "Tattooed Monk," uprooting a willow tree. 30f, Lin Chong seeking shelter from snow storm at the Mountain Spirit Temple. 50f, Song Jiang helps Ward Chief Chao Gai flee. $2, Outlaws of the Marsh capture treasures. T.123.

1987, Dec. 20 **Photo.** *Perf. 11*
2126 A570 8f multi (4-1) .60 .25
2127 A570 10f multi (4-2) .80 .25
2128 A570 30f multi (4-3) 2.50 .70
2129 A570 50f multi (4-4) 3.50 1.50
Nos. 2126-2129 (4) 7.40 2.70

Souvenir Sheet

Perf. 11½x11

2130 A570 $2 multi *30.00 16.00*

No. 2130 contains one 90x60mm stamp.
See Nos. 2216-2219, 2373-2377, 2449-2452, 2822-2826, 2889-2893.

New Year 1988 (Year of the Dragon) — A571

Photo. & Engr.

1988, Jan. 5 *Perf. 11½*
2131 A571 8f multicolored *3.25* .55
a. Bklt. pane of 4 + 8 with label between *38.00* —
Complete booklet, #2131a *55.00*

Cai Yuanpei (1868-1940), Education Reformer ((J.145) — A572

1988, Jan. 11 Photo. *Perf. 11½x11*

2132	A572 8f shown (2-1)	.70	.25
2133	A572 20f Seated (2-2)	1.10	.50

Tao Zhu (1908-1969), Party Leader (J.146) — A573

1988, Jan. 16 *Perf. 11x11½*

2134	A573 8f shown (2-1)	1.25	.30
2135	A573 20f Tao, diff. (2-2)	1.60	.55

Folklore (T.125) A574

1988, Feb. 10

2136	A574 8f shown (4-1)	.45	.25
2137	A574 10f multi, diff. (4-2)	.60	.25
2138	A574 20f multi, diff. (4-3)	.75	.40
2139	A574 30f multi, diff. (4-4)	1.50	.70
	Nos. 2136-2139 (4)	3.30	1.60

A575

1988, Mar. 25 Photo. *Perf. 11½*

2140	A575 8f multicolored	1.00	.30

7th Natl. People's Congress.

A576

8f, Wuzhi Mountain (4-1). 10f, Wanquan River (4-2). 30f, "End of the Earth" (4-3). $1.10, "Deer Turning Its Head" (4-4).

1988, Apr. 20 Photo. *Perf. 11½*

2141	A576 8f multi	.50	.25
2142	A576 10f multi	.65	.25
2143	A576 30f multi	.90	.30
2144	A576 $1.10 multi	1.20	.50
	Nos. 2141-2144 (4)	3.25	1.30

Establishment of Hainan Province (J.148).

Modern Scientists A577

Designs: 8f, Li Siguang, geologist. 10f, Zhu Kezhen, meteorologist and geographer. 20f, Wu Youxun, physicist. 30f, Hua Luogeng, mathematician. J.149.

1988, Apr. 28 *Perf. 11x11½*

2145	A577 8f multi (4-1)	.55	.25
2146	A577 10f multi (4-2)	.65	.25
2147	A577 20f multi (4-3)	.85	.30
2148	A577 30f multi (4-4)	1.50	.60
	Nos. 2145-2148 (4)	3.55	1.40

Wall Paintings Type of 1987

Caves of the Thousand Buddhas, Dunhuang, Gansu Province: No. 2149, Hunting, Western Wei Dynasty. No. 2150, Fishing, Western Wei Dynasty. 10f, Farming, Northern Zhou Dynasty. 90f, Building a Pagoda, Northern Zhou Dynasty. T.126.

1988, May 25 *Perf. 11½x11*

2149	A557 8f multi (4-1)	.55	.25
2150	A557 8f multi (4-2)	.55	.25
2151	A557 10f multi (4-3)	.75	.30
2152	A557 90f multl (4-4)	2.60	.75
	Nos. 2149-2152 (4)	4.45	1.55

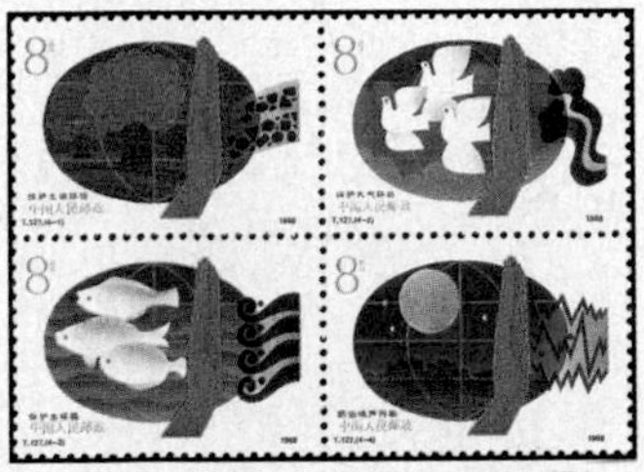

Environmental Protection — A578

1988, June 5 Photo. *Perf. 11*

2153	8f Soil (4-1)	.55	.30
2154	8f Air (4-2)	.55	.30
2155	8f Water (4-3)	.55	.30
2156	8f Prevent noise pollution (4-4)	.55	.30
a.	A578 Block of 4, #2153-2156	4.25	1.75

Souvenir Sheet

China Nos. 1-3 — A579

Photo. & Engr.

1988, July 2 *Perf. 13*

2157	A579 $3 multicolored	*11.00*	*7.00*

Postage stamps of China, 110th anniv.

11th Asian Games (in 1990), Beijing (J.151) A580

1988, July 20 Photo. *Perf. 11x11½*

2158	A580 8f Emblem (2-1)	.35	.25
2159	A580 30f Character trade-mark (2-2)	.75	.45

See No. 2300a.

Signing of the Sino-Japanese Peace Treaty, 10th Anniv. (J.152) — A581

1988, Aug. 12 Photo. *Perf. 11*

2160	A581 8f Peony (2-1)	.30	.25
2161	A581 $1.60 Sakura (2-2)	.90	.50
a.	Pair, #2160-2161	3.25	1.50

Achievements in Construction — A582

Designs: 8f, Coal-loading wharf, Ch'in-huang-tao Port. 10f, Ethylene refinery, Qilu. 20f, Pao-shan steel plant, Shanghai. 30f, Central Television Broadcasting Station. T.128.

1988, Sept. 2 Photo. *Perf. 11*

2162	A582 8f multi (4-1)	.50	.25
2163	A582 10f multi (4-2)	.75	.30
2164	A582 20f multi (4-3)	.90	.35
2165	A582 30f multi (4-4)	1.00	.45
	Nos. 2162-2165 (4)	3.15	1.35

See Nos. 2221-2224, 2279-2282, 2354-2357.

Mt. T'ai Shan, Shantung Province (T.130) — A583

8f, T'ai Shan Temple (4-1). 10f, Ladder to Heaven (4-2). 20f, Daguang peak (4-3). 90f, Sun-watching peak (4-4).

1988, Sept. 14 Photo. & Engr.

2166	A583 8f multi	.40	.25
2167	A583 10f multi	.50	.40
2168	A583 20f multi	.90	.50
2169	A583 90f multi	3.75	1.40
	Nos. 2166-2169 (4)	5.55	2.55

Liao Chengzhi (1908-1983), Party Leader (J.153) — A584

1988, Sept. 25 Photo. *Perf. 11½x11*

2170	A584 8f shown (2-1)	.40	.25
2171	A584 20f Writing (2-2)	.75	.45

Marshal Peng Dehuai (1898-1974), Party Leader (J.155) — A585

1988, Oct. 24 Photo. *Perf. 11x11½*

2172	A585 8f shown (2-1)	.45	.25
2173	A585 20f Peng in uniform (2-2)	1.25	.60

1st Natl. Farmers' Games (J.154) A586

1988, Oct. 9 Photo. *Perf. 11½*

2174	A586 8f Cycling (2-1)	.35	.25
2175	A586 20f Javelin (2-2)	.65	.40

Literary Masterpieces — A587

The Romance of the Three Kingdoms, by Luo Guanzhong, 14th cent.: No. 2176, Three heroes' sworn brotherhood (4-1). No. 2177, Battle between Lu Bu and the heroes, vert. (4-2). No. 2178, Struggle between man and woman at Fengyi Pavilion (4-3). No. 2179, Two noblemen, vert. (4-4). No. 2180, Guan Yu's battle through five passes. T.131.

Perf. 11½x11, 11x11½

1988, Nov. 25 Photo.

2176	A587 8f multicolored	.40	.25
2177	A587 8f multicolored	.40	.30
2178	A587 30f multicolored	1.10	.60
2179	A587 50f multicolored	1.40	1.00
	Nos. 2176-2179 (4)	3.30	2.15

Souvenir Sheet

Perf. 11

2180	A587 $3 multicolored	*27.50*	*14.50*

See Nos. 2310-2313, 2403-2406, 2539-2543.

A588

1988, Dec. 5 Photo. *Perf. 11*

2181	A588 20f multicolored	1.00	.30

Intl Volunteers' Day.

A589

Milu, *Elaphurus davidianus* (T.132).

1988, Dec. 20 Photo. *Perf. 11½x11*

2182	A589 8f Buck (2-1)	1.10	.25
2183	A589 40f Herd (2-2)	3.00	2.00

Exist imperf. Value, pairs each $6.50.

Orchids (T.129) — A590

8f, Da yi pin (4-1). 10f, Dragon (4-2). 20f, Large phoenix tail (4-3). 50f, Silver-edged black (4-4).

Red lotus petal.

1988, Dec. 25 ***Perf. 12***

2184	A590	8f multi	.70	.30
2185	A590	10f multi	.85	.35
2186	A590	20f multi	1.10	.45
2187	A590	50f multi	1.40	.95
a.		Strip of 4, #2184-2187	6.50	3.75
		Nos. 2184-2187 (4)	4.05	2.05

Souvenir Sheet

Perf. 11½x11

2188	A590	$2 multi	*15.00*	*8.00*

No. 2188 contains one 55x37mm stamp.

A591

Grotto Statuary: $2, Buddha. $5, Warrior, Longmen Grotto, Henan. $10, Goddess. $20, Woman and birds.

Photo & Engr.

1988-89 ***Perf. 11½x11***

2189	A591	$2 buff & reddish blk	1.40	.30
2190	A591	$5 buff & grnh blk	1.75	.65
2191	A591	$10 buff & brn blk	2.75	1.25
a.		Souv. sheet of 1, buff & sep	*20.00*	—
2192	A591	$20 buff & indigo	6.75	2.50
		Nos. 2189-2192 (4)	12.65	4.70

Issued: $2, 11/30; $5, 8/10; $10, 10/15; $20, 10/20.

No. 2191a released on Oct. 12, 1989, for the China Natl. Philatelic Exhibition and the 40th anniv. of the People's Republic.

Nos. 2189-2192, 2191a are almost always found with small ink spots on the stamps. Values are for stamps in this condition.

A592

Photo. & Engr.

1989, Jan. 5 ***Perf. 11½***

2193	A592	8f multicolored	3.25	.30
a.		Bklt. pane of 4+8 with label between	*17.50*	—
		Complete booklet, #2193a	*26.00*	

New Year 1989 (Year of the Snake).

Stamps from No. 2193a have one or two straight edges and sell for less as singles than No. 2193.

Qu Qiubai (1899-1935), Party Leader (J.157) — A593

1989, Jan. 29 Photo. ***Perf. 11x11½***

2194	A593	8f multi (2-1)	.45	.35
2195	A593	20f multi, diff. (2-2)	.75	.55

Brown-eared Pheasant, *Crossoptilon mantchuricum* (T.134) — A594

1989, Feb. 21 ***Perf. 11½***

2196	A594	8f multi (2-1)	.45	.25
2197	A594	50f multi, diff. (2-2)	.80	.40

Folk Houses Type of 1986

1989-91 Photo. ***Perf. 13x13½***

2198	A545	5f Shandong	.25	.25
2199	A545	15f Guangxi	.25	.25
2200	A545	25f Ningxia	.30	.25
2201	A545	80f Shanxi	.60	.25
2202	A545	$1.30 Qinghai	.60	.40
2203	A545	$1.60 Guizhou	.75	.40
2204	A545	$2 Jiangxi	1.00	.40
		Nos. 2198-2204 (7)	3.75	2.20

Issued: 5f, 6/10/91; 15f, 11/25/90; 25f, 11/10/90; 80f, 9/20/90; $1.30, $1.60, 3/10/89; $2, 4/25/91.

Silk Painting Excavated from Han Tomb No. 1 at Mawangdui, Changsha (T.135) A595

8f, In the Heavens (3-1). 20f, On the Earth, vert. (3-2). 30f, In the Netherworld, vert. (3-3). $5, Entire painting.

1989, Mar. 25 Photo. ***Perf. 11x11½***

2208	A595	8f multi	.55	.25
a.		Perf. 11½	5.50	5.50
2209	A595	20f multi	.55	.25
a.		Perf. 11½	5.50	5.50
2210	A595	30f multi	.55	.25
a.		Perf. 11½	5.50	5.50
		Nos. 2208-2210 (3)	1.65	.75

Textured Paper, Without Gum

Size: 90x165mm

Imperf

2211	A595	$5 multi	*4.50*	*3.25*

Prevention and Resistance of Cancer (T.136) — A596

1989, Apr. 7 Litho. ***Perf. 12***

2212	A596	8f shown (2-1)	.35	.25
2213	A596	20f Woman's thermogram (2-2)	.65	.30

May Fourth Movement, 70th Anniv. (J.158) A597

1989, May 4 Photo. ***Perf. 11***

2214	A597	8f Bas-relief	.60	.30

Interparliamentary Union, Cent. — A598

1989, June 29 Photo. ***Perf. 11x11½***

2215	A598	20f multi	.80	.30

Literature Type of 1987

Outlaws of the Marsh: 8f, Wu Song slaying a tiger on Jingyang Ridge. 10f, Qin Ming dodging arrows. 20f, Hua Rong shooting a wild goose on Mt. Liangshan. $1.30, Li Kui fighting Zhang Shun from a junk. T.138.

1989, July 25 Photo. ***Perf. 11***

2216	A570	8f multi (4-1)	.30	.25
2217	A570	10f multi (4-2)	.30	.25
2218	A570	20f multi (4-3)	.40	.35
2219	A570	$1.30 multi (4-4)	.75	.50
		Nos. 2216-2219 (4)	1.75	1.35

Asia-Pacific Telecommunity, 10th Anniv. — A599

1989, Aug. 4 Litho. ***Perf. 12***

2220	A599	8f multi	.55	.25

Type of 1988

Achievements in Engineering and Construction: 8f, Beijing Intl. Telecommunications Building, vert. 10f, Xi Qu Coal Mine, Gu Jiao, Shanxi Province. 20f, Long Yang Gorge Hydroelectric Power Station, Qinghai Province. 30f, Da Yao Shan Tunnel of the Guangzhou-Heng Yang Railway. T.139.

1989, Aug. 10 Photo. ***Perf. 11***

2221	A582	8f multi (4-1)	.30	.25
2222	A582	10f multi (4-2)	.30	.25
2223	A582	20f multi (4-3)	.30	.30
2224	A582	30f multi (4-4)	.35	.30
		Nos. 2221-2224 (4)	1.25	1.10

Mt. Huashan — A601

Designs: 8f, Five prominent peaks. 10f, View from atop Huashan. 20f, 1000-foot precipice. 90f, Blue Dragon Ridge. T.140.

1989, Aug. 25 Photo. & Engr.

2225	A601	8f multi (4-1)	.40	.25
2226	A601	10f multi (4-2)	.50	.25
2227	A601	20f multi (4-3)	.60	.35
2228	A601	90f multi (4-4)	1.35	.55
		Nos. 2225-2228 (4)	2.85	1.40

Modern Art — A602

Paintings: 8f, *The Fable of the White Snake,* by Ye Qianyu. 20f, *Li River in Fine Rain,* by Li Keran. 50f, *Marching Together,* by Wu Zuoren. T.141

1989, Sept. 1 Photo.

2229	A602	8f multi (3-1)	.50	.25
2230	A602	20f multi (3-2)	.60	.25
2231	A602	50f multi (3-3)	1.25	.40
		Nos. 2229-2231 (3)	2.35	.90

People's Political Conference A603

1989, Sept. 21 ***Perf. 12***

2232	A603	8f No. 2	.80	.30

A604

Confucius (551-479 B.C.) — A605

Designs: 8f, The lecture in the Apricot Temple, Qufu. $1.60, Confucius riding in an ox cart. J.162.

1989, Sept. 28 Photo. ***Perf. 11***

2233	A604	8f shown (2-1)	1.00	.40
2234	A604	$1.60 multi (2-2)	3.00	1.00

Souvenir Sheet
Without Gum

Litho. ***Imperf.***

2235	A605	$3 multicolored	*6.00*	*4.25*

A606

Gate of Heavenly Peace — A607

1989, Oct. 1 Photo. ***Perf. 11x11½***

2236	A606	8f shown (4-1)	.30	.25
2237	A606	10f Flowers (4-2)	.35	.25
2238	A606	20f Five stars (4-3)	.45	.25
2239	A606	40f Construction (4-4)	.75	.25
		Nos. 2236-2239 (4)	1.85	1.00

Souvenir Sheet
Without Gum

Litho. ***Imperf.***

2240	A607	$3 shown	4.00	2.25

PRC, 40th anniv. J.163.

Photography, Sesquicentennial — A608

1989, Oct. 15 Photo. ***Perf. 11***

2241	A608	8f multicolored	.75	.30

Li Dazhao (1889-1927), Party Leader (J.164) — A609

1989, Oct. 29 Photo. *Perf. 11*

2242	A609 8f Li, soldiers (2-1)	.75	.30
a.	Perf. 11½	6.00	6.00
2243	A609 20f Li, text (2-2)	1.25	.30
a.	Perf. 11½	6.00	6.00

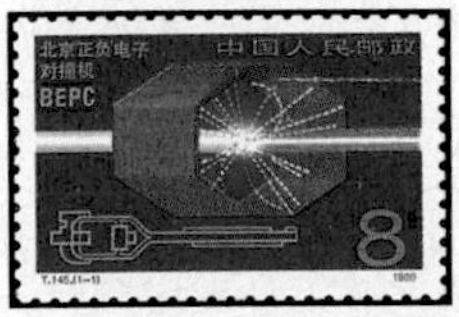

Positron Collider Produced in Beijing A610

1989, Nov. 1 *Perf. 11*

2244	A610 8f multicolored	.90	.60

Rocket Defense A611

Designs: 4f, Transporting 3 rockets. 8f, Disassembled rocket on transport. 10f, Launch, vert. 20f, Stage separation in space. T.143.

1989, Nov. 15 Litho. *Perf. 12*

2245	A611 4f multicolored (4-1)	.35	.30
2246	A611 8f multicolored (4-2)	.50	.35
2247	A611 10f multicolored (4-3)	.65	.40
2248	A611 20f multicolored (4-4)	.85	.55
	Nos. 2245-2248 (4)	2.35	1.60

A612

Views of West Lake (T.144) — A613

1989, Nov. 25 Photo. *Perf. 11x11½*

2249	A612 8f multi (4-1)	.50	.30
2250	A612 10f multi, diff. (4-2)	.65	.30
2251	A612 30f multi, diff. (4-3)	.85	.35
2252	A612 40f multi, diff. (4-4)	1.10	.40
	Nos. 2249-2252 (4)	3.10	1.35

Souvenir Sheet

Perf. 11½x11

2253	A613 $5 multicolored	8.00	2.50

11th Asian Games A614

Various stadiums. J.165.

1989, Dec. 15 *Perf. 11x11½*

2254	A614 8f multi (4-1)	.30	.25
2255	A614 10f multi (4-2)	.30	.25
2256	A614 30f multi (4-3)	.30	.25
2257	A614 $1.60 multi (4-4)	.55	.40
	Nos. 2254-2257 (4)	1.45	1.15

See Nos. 2295-2300.

A615

Photo & Engr.

1990, Jan. 5 *Perf. 11½*

2258	A615 8f multicolored	1.60	.35
a.	Bklt. pane of 12 + 4 labels	*20.00*	—
	Complete booklet, #2258a	22.00	
b.	As. No. 2258, perf. 11½x11	16.00	16.00

New Year 1990 (Year of the Horse).

Stamps from No. 2258a have straight edges at top or bottom and sell for less as singles than No. 2258.

Narcissus (T.147) — A616

1990, Feb. 10 Photo. *Perf. 11x11½*

2259	A616 8f multi (4-1)	.25	.25
2260	A616 20f multi, diff. (4-2)	.30	.30
2261	A616 30f multi, diff. (4-3)	.45	.30
2262	A616 $1.60 multi, diff. (4-4)	.55	.40
	Nos. 2259-2262 (4)	1.55	1.25

Norman Bethune (1890-1939), Surgeon (J.166) — A617

Litho. & Engr.

1990, Mar. 3 *Perf. 11x11½*

2263	A617 8f In Canada (2-2)	.30	.25
2264	A617 $1.60 In China (2-1)	.60	.50
a.	Pair, #2263-2264	1.60	1.25

See Canada Nos. 1264-1265.

Intl. Women's Day — A618

1990, Mar. 8 Photo. *Perf. 11½x11*

2265	A618 20f multicolored	.60	.30

Afforestation (T.148) — A619

8f, Bird, flora (4-1). 10f, Buildings (4-2). 20f, Great Wall, forest, (4-3). 30f, Bushes, evergreens (4-4).

1990, Mar. 12 *Perf. 11*

2266	A619 8f multi	.30	.25
2267	A619 10f multi	.30	.25
2268	A619 20f multi	.45	.25
2269	A619 30f multi	.55	.25
	Nos. 2266-2269 (4)	1.60	1.00

Pottery (T.149) — A620

1990, Apr. 10 Litho. *Perf. 12*

2270	A620 8f multi (4-1)	.25	.25
2271	A620 20f multi (4-2)	.30	.25
2272	A620 30f multi (4-3)	.50	.30
2273	A620 50f multi (4-4)	.65	.30
	Nos. 2270-2273 (4)	1.70	1.10

Li Fuchun (1900-1975), Party Leader (J.168) — A621

1990, May 22 Photo. *Perf. 11x11½*

2274	A621 8f shown	.40	.30
2275	A621 20f In uniform (2-2)	.60	.35

Bronze Head — A622

Bronze treasures from Emperor Qin Shi Huang Mausoleum: 50f, Horse head. $5, Chariots. T.151.

1990, June 20 Photo. *Perf. 11½x11*

2276	A622 8f shown (2-1)	.45	.25
2277	A622 50f multicolored (2-2)	.75	.35

Miniature Sheet

Size: 141x79mm

2278	A622 $5 multicolored	*9.50*	*4.50*

Achievements Type of 1988

Designs: 8f, 2nd automobile factory. 10f, Yizheng Joint Corporation of Chemical Fiber Industry. 20f, Shengli Oil Field. 30f, Qinshan Nuclear Power Station. T.152.

1990, June 30 Litho. *Perf. 12*

2279	A582 8f shown (4-1)	.30	.25
2280	A582 10f multicolored (4-2)	.30	.25
2281	A582 20f multicolored (4-3)	.45	.25
2282	A582 30f multicolored (4-4)	.60	.30
	Nos. 2279-2282 (4)	1.65	1.05

Wall Paintings Type of 1987

8f, Flying Devatas. 10f, Worshipping Bodhisatva. 30f, Savior Avolokitesvara. 50f, Indra. T.150.

1990, July 10 *Perf. 11½x11*

2283	A557 8f multi (4-1)	.30	.25
2284	A557 10f multi, vert. (4-2)	.30	.25
2285	A557 30f multi, vert. (4-3)	.40	.30
2286	A557 50f multi (4-4)	.80	.40
	Nos. 2283-2286 (4)	1.80	1.20

Snow Leopard (Uncia Uncia) (T.153) A624

1990, July 20 Photo. *Perf. 11½*

2287	A624 8f multicolored (2-1)	.45	.25
2288	A624 50f multicolored (2-2)	.80	.30

Chinese Soviet Post Stamp of 1931 A625

Design: 20f, Chinese Red Post issue of West Fukien, 1929. J.169.

1990, Aug. 1 Litho. *Perf. 12*

2289	A625 8f multi (2-1)	.40	.25
2290	A625 20f multi, diff. (2-2)	.80	.25

Zhang Wentian (1900-1990) (J.170) — A626

1990, Aug. 30 *Perf. 11x11½*

2291	A626 8f shown (2-1)	.35	.25
2292	A626 20f multi, diff. (2-2)	.75	.25

Intl. Literacy Year — A627

1990, Sept. 8 *Perf. 11½x11*

2293	A627 20f multicolored	.75	.30

Chinese Films — A628

1990, Sept. 21 Litho. *Perf. 11*

2294	A628 20f multicolored	.90	.25

11th Asian Games, Beijing (J.172) A629

4f, Running (6-1). 8f, Gymnastics (6-2). 10f, Karate (6-3). 20f, Volleyball (6-4). 30f, Swimming (6-5). $1.60, Shooting (6-6).

1990, Sept. 22 *Perf. 11x11½*

2295	A629 4f multi	.25	.25
2296	A629 8f multi	.25	.25
2297	A629 10f multi	.30	.25
2298	A629 20f multi	.30	.25
2299	A629 30f multi	.40	.30
2300	A629 $1.60 multi	.90	.65
a.	Souv. sheet of 12, #2158-2159, 2254-2257, 2295-2300	*9.00*	*6.00*
	Nos. 2295-2300 (6)	2.40	1.95

Souvenir Sheet

Sportphilex '90, Beijing — A629a

1990, Sept. 21 Litho. *Perf. 11½*
2300B A629a $10 multi *22.50 11.00*

No. 2300B exists imperf. Value, *$700.*

Modern Scientists A630

Designs: 8f, Lin Qiaozhi, obstetrician. 10f, Zhang Yuzhe, astronomer. 20f, Hou Debang, chemist. 30f, Ding Ying, agronomist. J.173.

1990, Oct. 10 Litho. *Perf. 12*
2301 A630 8f multicolored (4-1) .45 .25
2302 A630 10f multicolored (4-2) .45 .25
2303 A630 20f multicolored (4-3) .80 .25
2304 A630 30f multicolored (4-4) .85 .25
Nos. 2301-2304 (4) 2.55 1.00

Mt. Hengshan — A631

Designs: 8f, Towering Temple. 10f, South Sacred Mountain. 20f, Forested mountainside. 50f, Imposing Zhurong Peak. T.155.

Photo. & Engr.

1990, Nov. 5 *Perf. 11*
2305 A631 8f multicolored (4-1) .50 .30
2306 A631 10f multicolored (4-2) .70 .30
2307 A631 20f multicolored (4-3) 1.00 .35
2308 A631 50f multicolored (4-4) 1.60 .45
Nos. 2305-2308 (4) 3.80 1.40

See Nos. 2342-2345, 2628-2631.

Souvenir Sheet

China Philatelic Federation, 3rd Congress — A632

1990, Nov. 28 *Perf. 11½x11*
2309 A632 $2 multicolored 5.50 4.00

Two types of No. 2309 exist. Either two or three of the horizontal bars in seventh character from top right are connected at left side. Value for No. 2309 is for the first type. Examples with three bars connected, value $7.

Literature Type of 1988

Romance of the Three Kingdoms by Luo Guanzhong: No. 2310, Night Attack on Wuchao. No. 2311, Making Three Calls at the Thatched Cottage. 30f, Rescuing the Master Single-handedly. 50f, Turning the Changban Bridge Upside Down. T.157.

1990, Dec. 10 Photo. *Perf. 11½x11*
2310 A587 20f multicolored (4-1) .30 .25
2311 A587 20f multi, vert. (4-2) .30 .25
2312 A587 30f multicolored (4-3) .35 .30
2313 A587 50f multi, vert. (4-4) .55 .35
Nos. 2310-2313 (4) 1.50 1.15

Han Xizai's Night Revels by Gu Hongzhong — A633

Designs: a, Guests enjoying food, music (5-1). b, Music and dance (5-2). c, Hand washing (5-3). d, Musicians (5-4). e, Guests departing (5-5). T.158.

1990, Dec. 20 Litho. *Perf. 12*
2314 Strip of 5 5.00 3.25
a.-e. A633 50f any single .70 .40

New Year 1991 (Year of the Sheep) — A634

Photo. & Engr.

1991, Jan. 5 *Perf. 11½*
2315 A634 20f multicolored 2.50 .50
a. Bklt. pane of 12 + label 17.50 —
Complete booklet, #2315a 19.00

Stamps from No. 2315a have straight edges at top or bottom and sell for less as singles than No. 2315.

Dujiangyan Irrigation Project — A635

Designs: 20f, Yuzui, flood control. 50f, Feishayan, drainage. 80f, Baopingkou, water volume control. T.156.

1991, Feb. 20 Photo. *Perf. 11½x11*
2316 A635 20f multicolored .55 .25
2317 A635 50f multicolored 1.25 .50
2318 A635 80f multicolored 2.25 .90
Nos. 2316-2318 (3) 4.05 1.65

A636

1991, Mar. 18
2319 A636 20f multicolored .75 .30

Paris Commune, 120th anniv.

A637

1991, Apr. 20 Photo. *Perf. 10*
2320 A637 20f multi (2-1) .45 .30
a. Perf. 11½x11 1.50 .90

Perf. 11½x11
2321 A637 50f Child & adult hands (2-2) .55 .30

Family planning (T.160).

Horned Animals (T.161) A638

No. 2322, Saiga tatarica (4-1). No. 2323, Budorcas taxicolor (4-2). No. 2324, Ovis ammon (4-3). No. 2325, Capra ibex (4-4).

1991, May 10 *Perf. 11x11½*
2322 A638 20f multi .30 .25
2323 A638 20f multi .30 .25
a. Perf. 11 7.00 7.00
2324 A638 50f multi .50 .30
a. Perf. 11 17.50 17.50
2325 A638 $2 multi .75 .35
Nos. 2322-2325 (4) 1.85 1.15

No. 2322 exists imperf. Value, pair *$140.*

A639

25f, Song and dance (2-1). 50f, Golden bridge (2-2).
$2, PRC No. 132, cranes.

1991, May 23 Photo. *Perf. 11*
2326 A639 25f multi .45 .30
2327 A639 50f multi .70 .35

Souvenir Sheet

2328 A639 $2 multi *15.00 5.00*

Occupation of Tibet, 40th anniv. (J.176).

A640

1991, June 22 *Perf. 11½x11*
2329 A640 20f multicolored .60 .30

Antarctic Treaty, 30th anniv.

Rhododendrons — A641

Varieties of rhododendrons. T.162: No. 2330, Delavayi (8-1). No. 2331, Molle (8-2). No. 2332, Simsii (8-3). No. 2333, Fictolacteum (8-4). No. 2334, Agglutinatum, vert. (8-5). No. 2335, Fortunei, vert. (8-6). No. 2336, Giganteum, vert. (8-7). No. 2337, Rex, vert. (8-8).
$5, Wardii.

1991, June 25 Litho. *Perf. 12*
2330 A641 10f multi .40 .25
2331 A641 15f multi .40 .25
2332 A641 20f multi .40 .25
2333 A641 20f multi .40 .30
2334 A641 50f multi .80 .30
2335 A641 80f multi 1.25 .40
2336 A641 90f multi 1.40 .60
2337 A641 $1.60 multi 2.50 .75
Nos. 2330-2337 (8) 7.55 3.10

Souvenir Sheet

Perf. 11½
2338 A641 $5 multi *11.50 8.50*

No. 2338 contains one 80x40mm stamp.

Chinese Communist Party, 70th Anniv. (J.178) A642

1991, July 1 Photo. *Perf. 11x11½*
2339 A642 20f shown (2-1) 1.00 .30
2340 A642 50f Hammer and sickle (2-2) 1.50 .50

Peasant Uprising, 209B.C. A643

1991, July 7
2341 A643 20f brown .60 .25

Mt. Hengshan Type of 1990

Designs: No. 2342, Monastery on mountainside. No. 2343, Snow-covered mountain top. 55f, Inscription carved into mountainside. 80f, Hidden monastery. T.163.

Photo. & Engr.

1991, July 20 *Perf. 11*
2342 A631 20f multi (4-1) .30 .25
2343 A631 20f multi (4-2) .30 .25
2344 A631 55f multi (4-3) .70 .30
2345 A631 80f multi (4-4) .95 .45
Nos. 2342-2345 (4) 2.25 1.25

Intl. Union for Quaternary Research, 13th Conf. A644

1991, Aug. 2 Photo. *Perf. 11x11½*
2346 A644 20f multicolored .70 .30
a. Perf. 11½ *13.00 13.00*

Chengde Mountain Resort — A645

Ch'ing Dynasty Royal Gardens: 15f, Pine valleys. 20f, Mid-lake pavilion. 90f, Islet, maple trees. $2, Chengde Royal Summer Resort. T.164.

1991 *Perf. 11½x11*
2347 A645 15f multi (3-1) .30 .25
2348 A645 20f multi (3-2) .40 .30
2349 A645 90f multi (3-3) .90 .60
Nos. 2347-2349 (3) 1.60 1.15

Souvenir Sheet

2350 A645 $2 multicolored *6.50 3.75*

No. 2350 contains one 90x40mm stamp. Issue dates: $2, Aug. 19; others, Aug. 10.

A646

Chen Yi, (b. 1901), party leader (J.181).

1991, Aug. 26 Photo. Perf. 11½x11

2351 A646 20f shown (2-1) .50 .25
2352 A646 50f Verse (2-2) .90 .40

A647

1991, Sept. 14

2353 A647 80f Disaster relief .55 .30

Achievements Type of 1988

20f, Luoyang glassworks. 25f, Urumchi chemical fertilizer project. 55f, Dalian expressway, Shenyang. 80f, Xichang satellite launching center. T.165.

1991, Sept. 20 Litho. Perf. 12

2354 A582 20f multi (4-1) .30 .25
2355 A582 25f multi (4-2) .30 .30
2356 A582 55f multi (4-3) .65 .35
2357 A582 80f multi (4-4) .75 .45
Nos. 2354-2357 (4) 2.00 1.35

Revolutionary Heroes — A648

Designs: No. 2358, Xu Xilin (1873-1907). No. 2359, Qiu Jin (1879-1907). No. 2360, Song Jiaoren (1882-1913). J.182.

Perf. 10 (#2358), 11x11½

1991, Oct. 10 Photo.

2358 A648 20f multi (3-1) .85 .40
a. Perf. 11x11½ 5.00 1.50
2359 A648 20f multi (3-2) .60 .30
2360 A648 20f multi (3-3) .60 .30
Nos. 2358-2360 (3) 2.05 1.00

Jingdezhen Chinaware A649

Designs: 15f, Glazed wine pot and warming bowl, Song Dynasty, vert. No. 2362, Porcelain vase, Yuan Dynasty, vert. No. 2363, Jar, Ming Dynasty. 25f, Porcelain vase, Ch'ing Dynasty, vert. 50f, Modern underglazed plate, vert. $2, Modern octagonal eggshell bowl, T.166.

Perf. 11¼x11½, 11½x11¼ (#2363, 2366)

1991, Oct. 11 Photo.

2361 A649 15f multi (6-1) .40 .25
2362 A649 20f multi (6-2) .40 .25
2363 A649 20f multi (6-3) .40 .25
2364 A649 25f multi (6-4) .40 .25
2365 A649 50f multi (6-5) .40 .30
2366 A649 $2 multi (6-6) 1.00 .50
Nos. 2361-2366 (6) 3.00 1.80

Perf. 11¼x11, 11x11¼ (#2363a, 2366a)

1991

2361a A649 15f multi .55 .25
2362a A649 20f multi .55 .25
2363a A649 20f multi .55 .25
2364a A649 25f multi .55 .30
2365a A649 50f multi .55 .30
2366a A649 $2 multi 1.00 .55
Nos. 2361a-2366a (6) 3.75 1.90

Tao Xingzhi, Educator, Birth Cent. (J.183) — A650

1991, Oct. 18 Litho. Perf. 12

2367 A650 20f shown (2-1) .40 .25
2368 A650 50f Wearing robe (2-2) .60 .35

Xu Xiangqian, Revolutionary Leader, 90th Birth Anniv. (J.184) — A651

1991, Nov. 8 Perf. 11x11½

2369 A651 20f shown (2-1) .45 .30
2370 A651 50f In uniform (2-2) .65 .40

1st Women's Soccer World Championships, Guangdong Province (J.185) — A652

Designs: 50f, Woman kicking soccer ball.

1991, Nov. 16 Perf. 11½x11

2371 A652 20f red & multi (2-1) .40 .30
2372 A652 50f grn & multi (2-2) .50 .35

Literature Type of 1987

Outlaws of the Marsh: 20f, Dai Zong sends a false letter from Liangshan Marsh. No. 2374, Ten feet of steel alone captures Stumpy Tiger Wang. No. 2375, Mistress Gu breaks open the jail in Dengzhou to rescue the Xie Brothers. 90f, Sun Li offers a plan to attack Zhu Family manor. $3, Mount Liangshan gallants raid the execution grounds. T.167.

1991, Nov. 19 Perf. 11

2373 A570 20f multi (4-1) .30 .25
2374 A570 25f multi (4-2) .40 .30
2375 A570 25f multi (4-3) .45 .35
2376 A570 90f multi (4-4) 1.60 .55
Nos. 2373-2376 (4) 2.75 1.45

Souvenir Sheet

Perf. 11x11½

2377 A570 $3 multicolored *10.00 5.50*

No. 2377 contains one 60x90mm stamp.

Beginning with No. 2378 stamps are inscribed "CHINA" and are numbered chronologically with the year followed by the number of the set. Additional numbers in parentheses indicate the number and position of each stamp in a set. We will note these only when helpful in identifying stamps.

New Year 1992, Year of the Monkey

A653 A654

Photo. & Engr.

1992, Jan. 25 Perf. 11½

2378 A653 20f Monkey, peach .40 .30
2379 A654 50f Magpies, plum branches .70 .35

Storks — A655

1992, Feb. 20 Photo. Perf. 11x11½

2380 A655 20f Ciconia nigra .30 .25
2381 A655 $1.60 Ciconia ciconia .80 .45

Conifers — A656

Designs: 20f, Metasequoia glyptostroboides. 30f, Cathaya argyrophylla. 50f, Taiwania flousiana. 80f, Abies beshanzuensis.

1992, Mar. 10 Litho. Perf. 12½

2382 A656 20f multicolored .30 .25
2383 A656 30f multicolored .30 .25
2384 A656 50f multicolored .35 .30
2385 A656 80f multicolored .55 .35
Nos. 2382-2385 (4) 1.50 1.15

Marine Life A660

20f, Pagrosomus major. 25f, Penaeus chinesis. 50f, Chlamys farreri. 80f, Laminaria japonica.

1992, Apr. 15 Photo. Perf. 11

2386 A660 20f multi .25 .25
2387 A660 25f multi .25 .25
2388 A660 50f multi .35 .25
2389 A660 80f multi .40 .30
Nos. 2386-2389 (4) 1.25 1.05

Publication of "Discussions on Literature and Art at the Yenan Forum," 50th Anniv. — A661

1992, May 23 Photo. Perf. 11½x11

2390 A661 20f org, blk & red .90 .30

A662

1992, June 5 Litho. Perf. 12

2392 A662 20f multicolored .95 .30

UN Conf. on Human Development, 20th anniv.

A663

Insects: 20f, Coccinella septempunctata. 30f, Sympetrum croceolum. 50f, Chrysopa septempunctata. $2, Tenodera aridifolia sinensis.

1992, June 28

2393 A663 20f multicolored .90 .25
2394 A663 30f multicolored .35 .30
2395 A663 50f multicolored .40 .35
2396 A663 $2 multicolored 1.10 .55
Nos. 2393-2396 (4) 2.15 1.45

1992 Summer Olympics, Barcelona A664

20f, Basketball, vert. 25f, Women's gymnastics. 50f, Women's diving. 80f, Weight lifting, vert.
$5, Runners.

1992, July 25 Photo. Perf. 11

2397 A664 20f multi .30 .25
2398 A664 25f multi .35 .25
2399 A664 50f multi .40 .30
2400 A664 80f multi .50 .35
Nos. 2397-2400 (4) 1.55 1.15

Souvenir Sheet

2401 A664 $5 multi 2.75 2.25

No. 2401 contains one 54x40mm stamp.

Intl. Space Year — A665

1992, Aug. 18 Litho. Perf. 12

2402 A665 20f multicolored .80 .30

Literature Type of 1988

Romance of the Three Kingdoms by Luo Guanzhong: 20f, Verbal battle with scholars. 30f, Goading Sun Quan with sarcasm, vert. 50f, Jiang Gan stealing the letter. $1.60, Gathering arrows with straw-covered boats, vert.

Perf. 11½x11, 11x11½

1992, Aug. 25 Photo.

2403 A587 20f multi .30 .25
2404 A587 30f multi .35 .30
2405 A587 50f multi .40 .35
2406 A587 $1.60 multi .85 .45
Nos. 2403-2406 (4) 1.90 1.35

Wall Paintings Type of 1987

20f, Bodhisattva, vert. 25f, Musical performance, vert. 55f, Flight of a dragon. 80f, Envoy to the western regions. $5, Avalokitesvara-Bodhisattva, vert.

1992, Sept. 15 *Perf. 11*
2407 A557 20f multicolored .30 .25
2408 A557 25f multicolored .35 .30
2409 A557 55f multicolored .40 .35
2410 A557 80f multicolored .65 .40
Nos. 2407-2410 (4) 1.70 1.30

Souvenir Sheet
Perf. 11½

2411 A557 $5 multicolored *3.00 2.25*

No. 2411 contains one 52x70mm stamp.

Normalization of Diplomatic Relations Between China and Japan, 20th Anniv. — A666

20f, Cranes, Great Wall of China, Mt. Fuji. $2, Japanese, Chinese children, dove.

1992, Sept. 29 Photo. *Perf. 11x11½*
2412 A666 20f multicolored .25 .25
2413 A666 $2 multicolored .95 .55

A667

Statue of Mazu, Chinese Goddess of the Sea.

1992, Oct. 4 Litho. *Perf. 12*
2414 A667 20f multicolored .60 .30

A667a

1992, Oct. 12 Photo. *Perf. 11½x11*
2414A A667a 20f multicolored 1.50 .30

14th Chinese Communist Party Congress.

Jiao Yulu (1922-1964), Communist Party Leader — A668

1992, Oct. 28 Litho. *Perf. 12*
2415 A668 20f multicolored .60 .30

Famous Men A669

Designs: 20f, Xiong Qinglai, mathematician. 30f, Tang Feifan, microbiologist. 50f, Zhang Xiaoqian, physician. $1, Liang Sicheng, architect.

1992, Nov. 20
2416 A669 20f multicolored .30 .25
2417 A669 30f multicolored .35 .25
2418 A669 50f multicolored .45 .30
2419 A669 $1 multicolored .80 .35
Nos. 2416-2419 (4) 1.90 1.15

Luo Ronghuan, Leader of People's Army, 90th Anniv. of Birth A670

1992, Nov. 26 Photo. *Perf. 11x11½*
2420 A670 20f In dress uniform .45 .30
2421 A670 50f In field uniform .75 .40

Constitution of the People's Republic of China, 10th Anniv. — A671

1992, Dec. 4 *Perf. 11½x11*
2422 A671 20f multicolored .80 .30

Liu Bocheng, Leader of People's Army, Birth Cent. A672

Designs: 20f, In dress uniform. 50f, During period of Long March, vert.

1992, Dec. 4 *Perf. 11x11½, 11½x11*
2423 A672 20f multicolored .45 .30
2424 A672 50f multicolored .75 .40

Quingtian Stone Carvings — A673

1992, Dec. 15 Litho. *Perf. 12*
2425 A673 10f Spring .25 .25
2426 A673 20f Chinese sorghum .25 .25
2427 A673 40f Harvest .30 .25
2428 A673 $2 Blooming flowers, full moon .50 .30
Nos. 2425-2428 (4) 1.30 1.05

New Year 1993 (Year of the Rooster)
A674 A675

Photo. & Engr.

1993, Jan. 5 *Perf. 11½*
2429 A674 20f red & black .50 .25
2430 A675 50f red, white & blk .70 .30

Madam Song Qingling, Chinese Communist Leader, Birth Cent. A676

1993, Jan. 20 Photo. *Perf. 11x11½*
2431 A676 20f Portrait .35 .30
a. Perf. 11 5.00 5.00
2432 A676 $1 With children .65 .45
a. Perf. 11 5.00 5.00

No. 2431 exists imperf. Value, pair $140.

Camelus Bactrianus Ferus A677

1993, Feb. 20 Litho. *Perf. 12*
2433 A677 20f shown .30 .25
2434 A677 $1.60 Adult, young .70 .35

8th Natl. People's Congress A678

1993, Mar. 15 Litho. *Perf. 12*
2435 A678 20f multicolored .80 .30

A679

Game of Weiqi (Go): 20f, Painting of players of ancient times. $1.60, Game board showing Chinese-style position.

1993, Apr. 30 Litho. *Perf. 12*
2436 A679 20f multi .30 .25
2437 A679 $1.60 multi .60 .40

A680

20th Cent. Revolutionaries: 20f, Li Jishen (1885-1959), horiz. 30f, Zhang Lan (1872-1955). 50f, Shen Junru (1875-1963). $1, Huang Yanpei (1878-1965), horiz.

1993, May 15 Litho. *Perf. 12*
2438 A680 20f multi .30 .25
2439 A680 30f multi .30 .25
2440 A680 50f multi .35 .30
2441 A680 $1 multi .50 .35
Nos. 2438-2441 (4) 1.45 1.15

See Nos. 2483-2486.

A681

1993, May 9 Photo. *Perf. 12*
2442 A681 50f Runner (2-1) .35 .25
2443 A681 50f Mascot (2-2) .35 .25
a. Pair, #2442-2443 .85 .75

First East Asian Games. No. 2443a printed in continuous design.

A682

Bamboo: 20f, Phyllostachys nigra. 30f, Phyllostachys aureosulcata spectabilis. 40f, Bambusa ventricosa. $1, Pseudosasa amabilis. $5, Phyllostachys heterocycla pubescens, horiz.

1993, June 15 Litho. *Perf. 12½*
2444 A682 20f multi .35 .25
2445 A682 30f multi .45 .25
2446 A682 40f multi .55 .30
2447 A682 $1 multi .75 .35
Nos. 2444-2447 (4) 2.10 1.15

Souvenir Sheet
Photo.
Perf. 11

2448 A682 $5 multicolored 3.00 2.25
a. As #2448, added inscription 7.50 7.50

No. 2448 contains one 54x40mm stamp.

No. 2448a is inscribed in sheet margin with hologram of panda at left, Chinese inscription for CHINA '96 and PJZ-3 at bottom, and flag and tagged security emblem at right. Soaking in water may affect the hologram. Issued: May 10, 1996.

Literature Type of 1987

Outlaws of the Marsh: 20f, Chai Jin is trapped in Gaotang. 30f, Shi Qian steals armor. 50f, Xu Ning teaches how to use barbed lance. $2, Shi Xiu leaps from building to rescue condemned man from execution.

1993, Aug. 20 Photo. *Perf. 11*
2449 A570 20f multi .35 .25
2450 A570 30f multi .40 .25
2451 A570 50f multi .55 .30
2452 A570 $2 multi 1.00 .45
Nos. 2449-2452 (4) 2.30 1.25

Changbai Mountains — A683

1993, Sept. 3 *Perf. 11½x11*
2453 A683 20f Tianchi .25 .25
2454 A683 30f Alpine tundra .30 .25
2455 A683 50f Waterfall .35 .30
2456 A683 $1 Mixed forest .45 .35
Nos. 2453-2456 (4) 1.35 1.15

Seventh Natl. Games — A684

1993, Sept. 4
2457 A684 20f multicolored .75 .30

Longmen Grottoes — A685

Designs: 20f, Rocana, Ancestor Worshipping Temple. 30f, Sakyamuni, Middle Binyang Cave, Northern Wei. 50f, Maharaja, devas treading on Yaksha. $1, Bodhisattva at the left side of Rocana, Guyang Cave, Northern Wei. $5, Ancestor Worshipping Temple.

1993, Sept. 5 Litho. *Perf. 12*

2458 A685 20f multi .30 .25
2459 A685 30f multi .35 .25
2460 A685 50f multi .50 .30
2461 A685 $1 multi .95 .45
Nos. 2458-2461 (4) 2.10 1.25

Souvenir Sheets

2462 A685 $5 multicolored *3.00 3.00*
a. Overprinted in gold *10.00 6.50*
b. Overprinted in silver *6.00 4.00*

No. 2462 contains one 120x40mm stamp.

Overprint in margin of No. 2462a includes Chinese characters and "PJZ-1." Bangkok '95 (No. 2462a). No. 2462a sold for $6.

No. 2462a exists with serial number inscribed in sheet margin. The same number is inscribed on Thailand No. 1615b. These were sold as a set. Value for the two sheets with matching numbers, $26.50.

Sheet margin of No. 2462b contains silver lettering in Chinese for Thailand stamp exhibition and "PJZ-7." No. 2462b exists with serial number inscribed in sheet margin. Value: *$11.50.*

Issued: No. 2462a, 8/95; No. 2462b, 12/5/97.

Honey Bees A686

10f, Queen and two bees. 15f, Extracting nectar. 20f, Two Zhonghua bees. $2, Two bees in flight.

1993, Sept. 21 Photo. *Perf. 11½*

2463 A686 10f multi .30 .25
a. Perf. 11x11½ 5.00 5.00
2464 A686 15f multi .30 .25
a. Perf. 11x11½ 5.00 5.00
2465 A686 20f multi .30 .30
2466 A686 $2 multi .75 .50
Nos. 2463-2466 (4) 1.65 1.30

Lacquerware — A687

1993, Oct. 20 Photo. *Perf. 12*

2467 A687 20f Bowl .25 .25
2468 A687 30f Duck .30 .25
2469 A687 50f Round tray .35 .25
2470 A687 $1 Lidded box .40 .30
Nos. 2467-2470 (4) 1.30 1.05

Paintings, by Zheng Banqiao — A688

Designs: 10f, Bamboo, rock on fan. No. 2472, Orchard. No. 2473, Orchard, bamboo, rock on scroll, vert. 30f, Bamboo, rock on scroll, vert. 50f, Vase and chrysanthemums. $1.60, Chinese calligraphy on fan.

1993, Nov. 22 Litho. *Perf. 12½*

2471 A688 10f multi (6-1) .30 .25
2472 A688 20f multi (6-2) .30 .25
2473 A688 20f multi (6-3) .30 .25
2474 A688 30f multi (6-4) .40 .30
2475 A688 50f multi (6-5) .40 .30
2476 A688 $1.60 multi (6-6) .60 .35
Nos. 2471-2476 (6) 2.30 1.70

No. 2476 exists imperf. Value, pair *$240.*

A689

1993, Nov. 26 *Perf. 12*

2477 A689 20f multicolored .60 .30

Yang Hucheng, birth cent.

A690

Mao Tse-tung (1893-1976).

1993 Photo. *Perf. 11½*

2478 A690 20f shown *1.75* .35
2479 A690 $1 Portrait, seated *4.75* .55

Souvenir Sheet

2480 A690 $5 Standing by Great Wall *4.00 3.00*
a. Overprinted in gold in margin *7.50 6.00*

No. 2480 contains one 48x58mm stamp. No. 2480a sold for $8.

No. 2478 exists imperf. Value, pair *$350.*

Issued: $5, 11/16; 20f, $1, 12/26; No. 2480a, 4/9/99.

New Year 1994 (Year of the Dog)
A691 A692

1994, Jan. 5 Photo. *Perf. 11½*

2481 A691 20f multi .45 .25
2482 A692 50f yel, red & blk .65 .35

20th Cent. Revolutionaries Type

Designs: No. 2483, Chen Qiyou, horiz. No. 2484, Chen Shutong. No. 2485, Ma Xulun. No. 2486, Xu Deheng, horiz.

1994, Feb. 25 Litho. *Perf. 12*

2483 A680 20f blk & brn (4-1) .35 .30
2484 A680 20f blk & brn (4-2) .35 .30
2485 A680 50f blk & brn (4-3) .40 .30
2486 A680 50f blk & brn (4-4) .40 .30
Nos. 2483-2486 (4) 1.50 1.20

Sturgeon — A693

20f, Huso dauricus. 40f, Acipenser sinensis. 50f, Psephurus gladius. $1, Acipenser dabryanus.

1994, Mar. 18 Litho. *Perf. 12½*

2487 A693 20f multi .40 .25
2488 A693 40f multi .45 .25
2489 A693 50f multi .55 .30
2490 A693 $1 multi .75 .40
Nos. 2487-2490 (4) 2.15 1.20

Afforestation Campaign — A694

Designs: 15f, Sand dunes. 20f, Flowers on sand dune. 40f, Forest of poplars. 50f, Oasis.

1994, Apr. 21 Litho. *Perf. 12*

2491 A694 15f multi .25 .25
2492 A694 20f multi .30 .25
2493 A694 40f multi .35 .25
2494 A694 50f multi .40 .30
Nos. 2491-2494 (4) 1.30 1.05

Teapots — A695

Style of teapot: 20f, Round, three-legged. 30f, Square, four-legged. 50f, Eight diagrams. $1, Round-eared.

1994, May 5 Litho. *Perf. 12*

2495 A695 20f multi .30 .25
2496 A695 30f multi .35 .25
2497 A695 50f multi .40 .30
2498 A695 $1 multi .85 .35
Nos. 2495-2498 (4) 1.90 1.15

Huangpu Military School, 70th Anniv. A696

1994, June 16 Litho. *Perf. 12*

2499 A696 20f multicolored .65 .30

Intl. Olympic Committee, Cent. A697

1994, June 23

2500 A697 20f multicolored .60 .25

Ancient Chinese Writers — A698

Designs: 20f, Tao Yuanming holding basket of flowers. 30f, Cao Zhi holding sword at side. 50f, Si Maqian writing on scroll. $1, Qu Yuan walking away with sword under arm.

1994, June 25

2501 A698 20f multi .25 .25
2502 A698 30f multi .30 .25
2503 A698 50f multi .35 .30
2504 A698 $1 multi .55 .35
Nos. 2501-2504 (4) 1.45 1.15

Wall paintings Type of 1987

10f, Flying Devata. 20f, Vimalakirti. 50f, Z. Yichao on the march. $1.60, Sorceresses.

1994, July 16 Photo. *Perf. 11*

2505 A557 10f multi .25 .25
2506 A557 20f multi .30 .25
2507 A557 50f multi .35 .30
2508 A557 $1.60 multi .55 .35
Nos. 2505-2508 (4) 1.45 1.15

Zhaojun's Marriage to Xiongnu — A699

1994, Aug. 25 Photo. *Perf. 11½x11*

2509 A699 20f Zhaojun .35 .30
2510 A699 50f Leaving home .65 .35

Souvenir Sheet

Perf. 11½

2511 A699 $3 Wedding 3.25 3.25

No. 2511 contains one 85x46mm stamp.

Sixth Far East and South Pacific Games for the Disabled, Beijing — A700

1994, Sept. 4 Litho. *Perf. 12*

2512 A700 20f multicolored 1.00 .25

Wulingyuan State Forest Park — A701

20f, South Gate to Heaven. 30f, Shentangwan. 50f, No. One Bridge. $1, Writing-brush Peak. $3, Picturesque corridor.

1994, Sept. 25 Litho. *Perf. 12*

2513 A701 20f multi, vert. .35 .25
2514 A701 30f multi, vert. .45 .30
2515 A701 50f multi .55 .40
2516 A701 $1 multi .90 .50
Nos. 2513-2516 (4) 2.25 1.45

Souvenir Sheet

Perf. 11½x12

2517 A701 $3 multicolored *3.25 2.75*

No. 2517 contains one 50x36mm stamp.

Wuyi Mountains — A702

Designs: a, Jade-girl Peak (4-1). b, Ninebend Brook (4-2). c, Guadun Village (4-3). d, Alpine Grassland (4-4).

1994, Sept. 30 *Perf. 12*

2518 Strip of 4 2.00 1.50
a.-d. A702 50f any single .40 .25

No. 2518 exists imperf. Value, $225.

Listening to the Rapids, by Fu Baoshi (1904-65) A703

Paintings: No. 2520, Appreciating a Painting. No. 2521, Dadi's Thatched Hut. 40f, Playing the Ruan. 50f, At Hupao. $1, The Road to Shanyin.

1994, Oct. 5

2519	A703 10f multi (6-1)		.30	.25
2520	A703 20f multi (6-2)		.30	.25
2521	A703 20f multi (6-3)		.30	.25
2522	A703 40f multi (6-4)		.35	.30
2523	A703 50f multi (6-5)		.50	.35
2524	A703 $1 multi (6-6)		.90	.40
	Nos. 2519-2524 (6)		2.65	1.80

Cranes — A704

20f, Whooping crane. $2, Black-necked crane.

Photo. & Engr.

1994, Oct. 9 ***Perf. 11x11½***

2528	A704 20f multi	.35	.25
2529	A704 $2 multi	.65	.50

See US Nos. 2867-2868.

Souvenir Sheet

UPU, 120th Anniv. — A705

1994, Oct. 9 **Litho.** ***Perf. 12***

2530	A705 $3 multicolored	3.00	2.00
a.	Ovptd. in sheet margin	4.00	3.00

No. 2530a ovptd. in sheet margin with UPU hologram, vertical Chinese inscription in gold. Issued: July 18, 1996.

Gorges of Yangtze River — A706

Designs: 10f, Baidicheng. No. 2532, Qutang Gorge. No. 2533, Wuxia Gorge. 30f, Goddess Peak. 50f, Xiling Gorge. $1, Qu Yuan Memorial Temple.
$5, The Three Gorges.

1994, Nov. 4 **Photo.** ***Perf. 12***

2531	A706 10f multi (6-1)	.30	.25
2532	A706 20f multi (6-2)	.30	.25
2533	A706 20f multi (6-3)	.30	.25
2534	A706 30f multi (6-4)	.30	.25
2535	A706 50f multi (6-5)	.35	.30
2536	A706 $1 multi (6-6)	.40	.35
	Nos. 2531-2536 (6)	1.95	1.65

Souvenir Sheet

Perf. 11½x11

2537	A706 $5 multicolored	3.50	2.75

No. 2537 contains one 116x35mm stamp.

Souvenir Sheet

All-China Philatelic Federation, 4th Congress — A707

1994, Nov. 17 **Litho.** ***Perf. 11***

2538	A707 $3 multicolored	2.25	1.50

Literature Type of 1988

Romance of the Three Kingdoms by Luo Guanzhong: 20f, Composing a poem with a lance in hands. 30f, Liu Bei's marriage, vert. 50f, Overwhelming Xiaoyaojin with prowess. $1, Campsites burned, vert.
$5, Fierce battle at Chibi.

Perf. 11½x11, 11x11½

1994, Nov. 24 **Photo.**

2539	A587 20f multicolored	.25	.25
2540	A587 30f multicolored	.30	.25
2541	A587 50f multicolored	.35	.30
2542	A587 $1 multicolored	.40	.35
	Nos. 2539-2542 (4)	1.30	1.15

Souvenir Sheet

Perf. 11

2543	A587 $5 multicolored	5.25	4.00

No. 2543 contains one 158x36mm stamp.

Special Economic Zones A708

Designs: a, Shenzhen (5-1). b, Zhuhai (5-2). c, Shantou (5-3). d, Xiamen (5-4). e, Hainan (5-4).

1994, Dec. 10 **Litho.** ***Perf. 12***

2544	A708 50f Strip of 5, #a.-e.	3.50	*2.00*

Pagodas of Ancient China — A709

Designs: No. 2545, Dayan Pagoda, Cien Temple. No. 2546, Zhenguo Pagoda, Kaiyuan Temple. 50f, Liuhe Pagoda, Kaihua Temple. $2, Youguo Temple.

Photo. & Engr.

1994, Dec. 15 ***Perf. 11½x11***

2545	20f tan, brn & blk (4-1)	.30	.25
2546	20f tan, brn & blk (4-2)	.35	.25
2547	50f tan, brn & blk (4-3)	.40	.25
2548	$2 tan, brn & blk (4-4)	.75	.30
a.	Souvenir sheet of 4, #2545-2548	*5.00*	*4.50*
	Nos. 2545-2548 (4)	1.80	1.05

No. 2548a sold for $5.

New Year 1995 (Year of the Boar)
A711 A712

Photo. & Engr.

1995, Jan. 5 ***Perf. 11½***

2550	A711 20f multicolored	.75	.25
2551	A712 50f multicolored	.85	.30

Winter Scenes A713

Designs: 20f, Snow willows, Cold River. 50f, Ice & snow on jade trees, vert.

1995, Jan. 12 **Litho.** ***Perf. 12***

2552	A713 20f multicolored	.35	.25
2553	A713 50f multicolored	.65	.30

Mt. Dinghushan — A714

Designs: 15f, Topographical map. No. 2555, Stream flowing down from mountain. No. 2556, Buildings on mountain side. $2.30, Silver pheasants.

1995, Feb. 15 **Litho.** ***Perf. 12½***

2554	A714 15f multi (4-1)	.30	.25
2555	A714 20f multi (4-2)	.45	.30
2556	A714 20f multi (4-3)	.45	.30
2557	A714 $2.30 multi (4-4)	1.25	.35
	Nos. 2554-2557 (4)	2.45	1.20

World Summit for Social Development, Copenhagen — A715

1995, Mar. 6 **Photo.** ***Perf. 11x11½***

2558	A715 20f multicolored	3.00	.40

Owls — A716

1995, Mar. 22 **Photo.** ***Perf. 11½***

2559	A716 10f Eagle owl	.40	.30
2560	A716 20f Long-eared owl	.50	.30
2561	A716 50f Snowy owl	.65	.40
2562	A716 $1 Grass owl	1.25	.50
	Nos. 2559-2562 (4)	2.80	1.50

Sweet Osmanthus A717

No. 2563, Thunbergii (4-1). No. 2564, Latifolius (4-2). No. 2565, Aurantiacus (4-3). No. 2566, Semperflorens (4-4).

1995, Apr. 14 **Litho.** ***Perf. 12***

2563	A717 20f multicolored	.35	.25
2564	A717 20f multicolored	.35	.25
2565	A717 50f multicolored	.45	.30
2566	A717 $1 multicolored	.90	.45
	Nos. 2563-2566 (4)	2.05	1.25

A souvenir sheet of 4, Nos. 2563-2566, exists, both perf and imperf. Value, perf $5., imperf. $75.

43rd World Table Tennis Championships, Tianjin — A718

1995, May 1 **Litho.** ***Perf. 12***

2567	A718 20f Athlete	.35	.25
2568	A718 50f Arena	.55	.30
a.	Souv. sheet of 2, #2567-2568	*20.00*	*14.00*

No. 2568a sold for $7. Issued 8/14/95.

Spring Outing — A719

Designs: No. 2569, Group riding horses. No. 2570, Three riding horses.

1995, May 23 **Litho.** ***Perf. 12***

2569	A719 50f multi (2-1)	.75	.35
2570	A719 50f multi (2-2)	.75	.35
a.	Pair, #2569-2570	2.75	1.25

No. 2570a is a continuous design.

Shadow Play — A720

Various costumed characters.

1995, June 8 **Photo.** ***Perf. 12x12½***

2571	A720 20f multi (4-1)	.30	.25
2572	A720 40f multi (4-2)	.30	.25
2573	A720 50f multi (4-3)	.40	.30
2574	A720 50f multi (4-4)	.40	.30
	Nos. 2571-2574 (4)	1.40	1.10

Highway Interchanges, Beijing — A721

1995, June 20 **Photo.** ***Perf. 11½x11***

2575	A721 20f Siyuan	.30	.25
2576	A721 30f Tianningsi	.35	.25
2577	A721 50f Yuting	.40	.25
2578	A721 $1 Anhui	.55	.30
	Nos. 2575-2578 (4)	1.60	1.05

Diplomatic Relations Between China & Thailand, 20th Anniv. — A722

No. 2579, Elephants walking right into water. No. 2580, Elephants walking left into water.

1995, July 1

2579 A722 $1 multi (2-1) .35 .30
2580 A722 $1 multi (2-2) .35 .30
a. Pair, #2579-2580 1.00 .85

No. 2580a is a continuous design.

Taihu Lake A723

Lake scenes: No. 2581, Yellow trees. No. 2582, Structures on bank, boats, hills. No. 2583, Structures across inlet. No. 2584, Red trees, home. 230f, Winter scene. 500f, Houses on cliff, lighthouse.

1995, July 20 Photo. *Perf. 11½*

2581 A723 20f multi (5-1) .25 .25
2582 A723 20f multi (5-2) .30 .25
2583 A723 50f multi (5-3) .45 .30
2584 A723 50f multi (5-4) .45 .30
2585 A723 230f multi (5-5) 1.10 .70
Nos. 2581-2585 (5) 2.55 1.80

Souvenir Sheet

Perf. 11

2586 A723 500f multicolored 3.50 2.75
a. Ovptd. in sheet margin 8.50 7.00

No. 2586 contains one 90x60mm stamp with continuing design.

No. 2586a issued 3/24/97. Gold overprint in sheet margin contains an emblem, Chinese inscription saying "Hong Kong Returns to China" and "PJZ-5."

Posts of Ancient China A724

1995, Aug. 17 Photo. *Perf. 12*

2587 A724 20f Yucheng .35 .25
2588 A724 50f Jimingshan .55 .30

Shaolin Temple, 1500th Anniv. A725

No. 2589, Entrance (4-1). No. 2590, Pagoda Forest (4-2). No. 2591, Martial arts (4-3). No. 2592, Historical rescue (4-4).

1995, Aug. 30

2589 A725 20f multicolored .60 .25
2590 A725 20f multicolored .60 .25
2591 A725 50f multicolored .70 .30
2592 A725 100f multicolored 1.50 .50
Nos. 2589-2592 (4) 3.40 1.30

Cultural Relics of Tibet — A726

1995, Sept. 1

2593 A726 20f Jar .25 .25
2594 A726 30f Casque .30 .25
2595 A726 50f Celestial motion chart .35 .25
2596 A726 100f Pearl mandala .40 .30
Nos. 2593-2596 (4) 1.30 1.05

Wildlife A727

1995, Sept. 1 *Perf. 11x11½*

2597 A727 20f Koalas .30 .25
2598 A727 $2.90 Pandas 1.10 .85

See Australia No. 1459.

End of World War II, 50th Anniv. A728

10f, July 7th event. No. 2600, Victory at Taier village. No. 2601, Soldier, hundred-regiment battle. No. 2602, Guerrilla war. No. 2603, Troops on parade, joining forces at Mangyo. 60f, Aircraft donated by Chinese living abroad. No. 2605, Taiwan recovered. No. 2606, Japanese surrender aboard USS Missouri.

1995, Sept. 3

2599 A728 10f multi (8-1) .25 .25
2600 A728 20f multi (8-2) .30 .25
2601 A728 20f multi (8-3) .30 .25
2602 A728 50f multi (8-4) .35 .30
2603 A728 50f multi (8-5) .35 .30
2604 A728 60f multi (8-6) .40 .35
2605 A728 100f multi (8-7) .55 .40
2606 A728 100f multi (8-8) .55 .40
Nos. 2599-2606 (8) 3.05 2.50

4th World Conference on Women, Beijing A729

Symbols of: 15f, Equality. 20f, Development. 50f, Peace. 60f, Friendship.

1995, Sept. 4 *Perf. 12*

2607 A729 15f multi .25 .25
2608 A729 20f multi .30 .25
2609 A729 50f multi .35 .25
2610 A729 60f multi .40 .30
Nos. 2607-2610 (4) 1.30 1.05

The Great Wall — A730

230f, Shanhaiguan Pass. 290f, Jinshanling.

1995, Oct. 5 Photo. *Perf. 12½*

2611 A730 60f shown .25 .25
2612 A730 230f multicolored .75 .30
2613 A730 290f multicolored .95 .35
Nos. 2611-2613 (3) 1.95 .90

See Nos. 2755, 2792-2795, 2907-2910, 2934-2941, 2952-2955.

Jiuhua Mountains A731

10f, Sunrise at Peak Terrace, horiz. No. 2615, Hall of Meditation. No. 2616, Temple of Bodhisattva, horiz. No. 2617, Sunset at Zhiyuan, horiz. No. 2618, Great Rock. No. 2619, Phoenix Pine, horiz.

1995, Oct. 9 *Perf. 12*

2614 A731 10f multi (6-1) .30 .25
2615 A731 20f multi (6-2) .30 .25
2616 A731 20f multi (6-3) .30 .25
2617 A731 50f multi (6-4) .40 .30
2618 A731 50f multi (6-5) .40 .30
2619 A731 290f multi (6-6) 1.25 .45
Nos. 2614-2619 (6) 2.95 1.80

Motion Pictures, Cent. A732

Projector and: 20f, Black and white film. 50f, Color film.

1995, Oct. 13

2620 A732 20f blue & black .35 .25
2621 A732 50f multicolored .65 .30

UN, 50th Anniv. A733

Designs: 20f, UN flag, Headquarters. 50f, Stylized flags, UN emblem, "50."

1995, Oct. 24 Litho.

2622 A733 20f multi .50 .25
2623 A733 50f multi 1.25 .30

Sanqing Mountains — A734

No. 2624, Good Fortune Land. No. 2625, Sichun Goddess. 50f, Bodhisattva Enjoys Music. 100f, Huge Boa out of Mountain.

1995, Nov. 1 Photo. *Perf. 12*

2624 A734 20f multi (4-1) .30 .25
2625 A734 20f multi (4-2) .30 .25
2626 A734 50f multi, vert. (4-3) .35 .25
2627 A734 100f multi, vert. (4-4) .45 .40
Nos. 2624-2627 (4) 1.40 1.15

Mt. Hengshan Type of 1990

Songshan Mountains: 20f, Ancient Temple of Mount Song. 50f, Moon waiting at Songmen Gate. 60f, Shaolin Temple. $1, Panorama view of Mt. Song.

Photo. & Engr.

1995, Nov. 10 *Perf. 11*

2628 A631 20f multi .30 .25
2629 A631 50f multi .40 .25
2630 A631 60f multi .50 .30
2631 A631 $1 multi 1.10 .40
Nos. 2628-2631 (4) 2.30 1.20

Scenic Views of Hong Kong — A735

Designs: 20f, Victoria Harbor. 50f, Central Plaza at night. 60f, Hong Kong Cultural Center. 290f, Repulse Bay.

1995, Nov. 28 Photo. *Perf. 12*

2632 A735 20f multi .25 .25
2633 A735 50f multi .30 .25
2634 A735 60f multi .35 .30
2635 A735 290f multi 1.10 .40
Nos. 2632-2635 (4) 2.00 1.20

No. 2635 exists imperf. Value, pair *$140.*

Sun Zi's Art of War — A736

Drawings depicting: No. 2637, Discussing strategy. 30f, Capturing Ying. 50f, Battle at Ailing. 100f, Meeting of sovereigns, Huangchi.

1995, Dec. 4 *Perf. 11x11½*

2636 A736 20f multi (5-1) .30 .25
2637 A736 20f multi (5-2) .30 .25
2638 A736 30f multi (5-3) .40 .30
2639 A736 50f multi (5-4) .50 .35
2640 A736 100f multi (5-5) 1.00 .45
Nos. 2636-2640 (5) 2.50 1.60

New Year 1996 (Year of the Rat)
A737 A738

Photo. & Engr.

1996, Jan. 5 *Perf. 11½*

2641 A737 20f multi .80 .25
2642 A738 50f multi 1.75 .40

3rd Asian Winter Games A739

No. 2643, Speed skating. No. 2644, Ice hockey. No. 2645, Figure skating. No. 2646, Skiing.

1996, Feb. 4 Litho. *Perf. 12*

2643 A739 50f multi (4-1) .30 .25
2644 A739 50f multi (4-2) .30 .25
2645 A739 50f multi (4-3) .30 .25
2646 A739 50f multi (4-4) .30 .25
a. Block of 4, #2643-2646 1.50 1.00

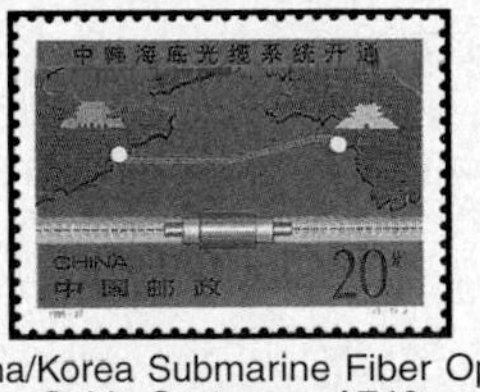

China/Korea Submarine Fiber Optic Cable System — A740

1996, Feb. 8 Litho. *Perf. 12*

2647 A740 20f multicolored .60 .25

First day covers are dated 12/15/95.
See Korea No. 1863.

Shenyang Imperial Palace — A741

Designs: No. 2648, Buildings, denomination UL. No. 2649, Buildings, denomination LR.

1996, Mar. 18 Photo. *Perf. 12*

2648 A741 50f multi (2-1) .35 .25
2649 A741 50f multi (2-2) .35 .25
a. Pair, Nos. 2648-2649 1.00 .75

China Post, Cent. A742

Post Office buildings: 10f, Tianjin Posts Bureau. 20f, Beijing Postal Administration. 50f, Directorate of Posts of China. 100f, Beijing postal hub.
500f, China #78-85.

1996, Mar. 20 *Perf. 11½*

2650 A742 10f multi .30 .25
2651 A742 20f multi .45 .25
2652 A742 50f multi .50 .30
2653 A742 100f multi .65 .40
Nos. 2650-2653 (4) 1.90 1.20

Souvenir Sheet

Perf. 11

2654 A742 500f multicolored *5.50* 4.75

No. 2654 contains one 89x59mm stamp.

Huang Binhong, Artist — A743

No. 2655, Calligraphy. No. 2656, Landscape. 40f, Qingcheng Mts. No. 2658, View from Xiing. No. 2659, Colored landscape. 230f, Flowers.

1996, Apr. 5 *Perf. 11½*

2655 A743 20f multi (6-1) .30 .25
2656 A743 20f multi (6-2) .30 .25
2657 A743 40f multi (6-3) .50 .30
2658 A743 50f multi (6-4) .60 .30
2659 A743 50f multi (6-5) .60 .35
2660 A743 230f multi (6-6) 2.40 .55
Nos. 2655-2660 (6) 4.70 2.00

Aircraft — A744

1996, Apr. 17 *Perf. 12*

2661 A744 20f F-8 (4-1) .30 .25
2662 A744 50f A-5 (4-2) .55 .30
2663 A744 50f Yun-7 (4-3) .55 .30
2664 A744 100f Yun-12 (4-4) .90 .45
Nos. 2661-2664 (4) 2.30 1.30

Potted Landscapes — A745

Nos. 2665-2666, Lijing & Divine Peak. Nos. 2667-2668, Melting Snow & Eagle Rock. Nos. 2668-2669, Manch & Rosy Clouds.

1996, Apr. 18

2665 A745 20f multi (6-1) .25 .25
2666 A745 20f multi (6-2) .25 .25
a. Pair, #2665-2666 .75 .60
2667 A745 50f multi (6-3) .35 .25
2668 A745 50f multi (6-4) .35 .25
a. Pair, #2667-2668 1.00 .80
2669 A745 100f multi (6-5) .50 .40
2670 A745 100f multi (6-6) .50 .40
a. Pair, #2669-2670 1.60 1.40
Nos. 2665-2670 (6) 2.20 1.80

Iron Trees — A746

No. 2671, Cycas revoluta. No. 2672, Cycas panzhihuaensis. 50f, Cycas pectinata. 230f, Cycas multipinnata.

1996, May 2 Litho. *Perf. 12*

2671 A746 20f multi (4-1) .30 .25
2672 A746 20f multi (4-2) .30 .25
2673 A746 50f multi (4-3) .35 .25
2674 A746 230f multi (4-4) .80 .40
Nos. 2671-2674 (4) 1.75 1.15

Nos. 2671-2674 exist imperf. Value, set of pairs *$325.*

China-San Marino Relations, 25th Anniv. A747

1996, May 6 Photo. *Perf. 12*

2675 A747 100f Great Wall of China (2-1) .40 .30
2676 A747 100f Mt. Titano (2-2) .40 .30
a. Pair, #2675-2676 1.00 .80

See San Marino Nos. 1356-1357.

Artifacts from Hemudu Ruins — A748

Designs: 20f, Agricultural tool. 50f, Pile to support building. 100f, Paddles for boats. 230f, Bird and sun carved in wood.

1996, May 12 Litho. *Perf. 12*

2677 A748 20f multi .30 .25
2678 A748 50f multi .35 .25
2679 A748 100f multi .40 .30
2680 A748 230f multi .85 .40
Nos. 2677-2680 (4) 1.90 1.20

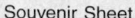

Souvenir Sheet

CHINA '96, 9th Asian Intl. Philatelic Exhibition — A749

1996, May 18 *Perf. 11½x12*

2681 A749 500f multicolored *6.25* 4.25
a. Overprinted in gold *8.50* 7.50

No. 2681 exists imperf. Value, $18.
Overprint in margin of No. 2681a includes Chinese characters, Shanghai '97 exhibition emblem, and "PJZ-6." Issued in 1998.

Children's Activities A750

Designs: 20f, Singing, playing musical instruments. 30f, Pushing child in wheelchair, holding umbrella. 50f, Placing flag on South Pole, penguins. 100f, Planting tree.

1996, June 1 *Perf. 12*

2682 A750 20f multi .25 .25
2683 A750 30f multi .30 .25
2684 A750 50f multi .35 .25
2685 A750 100f multi .45 .30
Nos. 2682-2685 (4) 1.35 1.05

Modern Olympic Games, Cent. — A751

1996, June 23 Photo. *Perf. 12*

2686 A751 20f multicolored .85 .30

Protection of Land A752

Stylized designs representing: 20f, Making use of land. 50f, Protection of farmland.

1996, June 25 *Perf. 11x11½*

2687 A752 20f multi .40 .25
2688 A752 50f multi .60 .30

A753

Military Terraces — A754

1996, July 9 Litho. *Perf. 12*

2689 A753 20f multi .40 .25
2690 A754 50f multi .60 .30

Vehicles — A755

No. 2691, Red Flag, 4-door limousine. No. 2692, Dongfeng, stake truck. 50f, Jiefang, 4-door truck. 100f, Beijing, canvas-topped jeep.

1996, July 15 Photo. *Perf. 12*

2691 A755 20f multi (4-1) .30 .25
2692 A755 20f multi (4-2) .30 .25
2693 A755 50f multi (4-3) .40 .25
2694 A755 100f multi (4-4) .60 .35
Nos. 2691-2694 (4) 1.60 1.10

New Tangshan Built Following 1976 Earthquake — A756

1996, July 28 *Perf. 11½*

2695 A756 20f Farm cottages (4-1) .25 .25
2696 A756 50f Factory (4-2) .35 .25
2697 A756 50f Street (4-3) .35 .25
2698 A756 100f Port (4-4) .45 .30
Nos. 2695-2698 (4) 1.40 1.05

30th Intl. Geological Conference — A757

1996, Aug. 4 Litho. *Perf. 12*

2699 A757 20f multicolored .70 .30

Tianchi Lake, Tianshan Mountains — A758

20f, High mountain lake. No. 2701, Splendid Waterfalls. No. 2702, Snow-capped peaks. 100f, Lakeside scenery.

1996, Aug. 8

2700 A758 20f multi (4-1) .25 .25
2701 A758 50f multi, vert. (4-2) .35 .25
2702 A758 50f multi, vert. (4-3) .35 .25
2703 A758 100f multi (4-4) .50 .30
Nos. 2700-2703 (4) 1.45 1.05

Wall Paintings Type of 1987

10f, Illustration of Mount Wutai. 20f, King of Khotan, vert. 50f, Savior Avalokitesvara. 100f, Worshipping Bodhisattvas.
$5, Thousand Arm Avalokitesvara.

1996, Aug. 15 Photo. *Perf. 11*

2704 A557 10f multi, vert. .30 .25
2705 A557 20f multi .35 .25
2706 A557 50f multi .40 .30
2707 A557 100f multi .60 .40
Nos. 2704-2707 (4) 1.65 1.20

Souvenir Sheet

2708 A557 500f multicolored 6.25 4.00

No. 2708 contains one 46x102mm stamp.

Mausoleums of Western Xia — A759

Designs: No. 2709: Mausoleum terrace. No. 2710, Ornament on Divine Gate. 50f, Stele. 100f, Stele remnant, Shouling.

1996, Aug. 22 Photo. *Perf. 11½*

2709 A759 20f multi (4-1) .25 .25
2710 A759 20f multi (4-2) .25 .25
2711 A759 50f multi (4-3) .35 .25
2712 A759 100f multi (4-4) .50 .30
Nos. 2709-2712 (4) 1.35 1.05

Railways in China — A760

Designs: 15f, Datong-Quinhuangdao Railway. 20f, Lanzhou-Xinjiang Two-Track Railway. 50f, Beijing-Kowloon Railway. 100f, Beijing Western Railway Station

1996, Sept. 1

2713 A760 15f multi .40 .25
2714 A760 20f multi .60 .25
2715 A760 50f multi .60 .30
2716 A760 100f multi 1.25 .55
Nos. 2713-2716 (4) 2.85 1.35

A761

Chinese Archives: No. 2717, Archives on tortoise shells, Shang Dynasty. No. 2718, Archives on wood slips, Han Dynasty. 50f, Iron scrolls, Ming Dynasty. 100f, Books of Ch'ing Dynasty.

1996, Sept. 2 Litho. *Perf. 12*

2717 A761 20f multi (4-1) .60 .25
2718 A761 20f multi (4-2) .60 .25
2719 A761 50f multi (4-3) .80 .30
2720 A761 100f multi (4-4) 1.75 .45
Nos. 2717-2720 (4) 3.75 1.25

A762

1996, Sept. 10 *Perf. 12*

2721 A762 20f Portrait .45 .25
2722 A762 50f In uniform .75 .35

Ye Ting (1896-1946), co-founder of Chinese People's Liberation Army.

96th Conference of Inter-Parliamentary Union — A763

1996, Sept. 16 *Perf. 11½*

2723 A763 20f multi .80 .25

Shanghai — A764

No. 2724, Communication (6-1). No. 2725, Lujiazui (6-2). No. 2726, Jinqiao (6-3). No. 2727, Zhanghiang (6-4). No. 2728, Waigaoqiao (6-5). No. 2729, Residential (6-6).
No. 2730, Panoramic view.

Photo. & Engr.

1996, Sept. 21 *Perf. 11½*

2724 A764 10f multicolored .25 .25
2725 A764 20f multicolored .35 .25
2726 A764 20f multicolored .40 .25
2727 A764 50f multicolored .45 .30
2728 A764 60f multicolored .50 .30
2729 A764 100f multicolored .90 .35
Nos. 2724-2729 (6) 2.85 1.70

Souvenir Sheet
Perf. 11

2730 A764 500f multicolored 7.50 6.50
a. Margin ovptd. 18.00 10.00

No. 2730 contains one 90x45mm stamp.
No. 2730a issued 10/20/01. It is inscribed in margin with multicolored emblems and gold "PJZ-14," "APEC CHINA 2001," and Chinese characters.

Space Navigation — A765

1996, Oct. 7 Litho. *Perf. 12*

2731 A765 20f Rocket lift-off .45 .25
2732 A765 100f Satellite in orbit .65 .35

Singapore Waterfront — A766

Design: 290f, Panmen, Suzhou, China.

1996, Oct. 9 Photo. *Perf. 11½*

2733 A766 20f multi .30 .25
2734 A766 290f multi 1.00 .40

See Singapore Nos. 768-769.

Victory of Long March, 60th Anniv. — A767

Designs: 20f, Red Army through Marshland. 50f, Reunion of Three Armies.

1996, Oct. 22 Litho. *Perf. 12*

2735 A767 20f multi .60 .35
2736 A767 50f multi 1.20 .60

Colored Sculpture of Tianjin A768

Designs: 20f, The Two Immortals. No. 2738, Making Candy. No. 2739, Returning from Fishing. 100f, Xi Ohun In Painting.

1996, Nov. 5 Photo. *Perf. 11½*

2737 A768 20f multi (4-1) .25 .25
2738 A768 50f multi (4-2) .30 .25
2739 A768 50f multi (4-3) .30 .25
2740 A768 100f multi (4-4) .35 .30
Nos. 2737-2740 (4) 1.20 1.05

Hong Kong A769

20f, Bank of China. 40f, Container Terminal. 60f, Kai Tak Airport. 290f, Stock Exchange.

1996, Dec. 19 Litho. *Perf. 12*

2741 A769 20f multi (4-1) .25 .25
2742 A769 40f multi (4-2) .30 .25
2743 A769 60f multi (4-3) .40 .25
2744 A769 290f multi (4-4) 1.25 .35
Nos. 2741-2744 (4) 2.20 1.10

Nos. 2741-2744 exist imperf. Value, set of pairs *$700.*

A770

1997, Jan. 1

2745 A770 50f Visit China 1.00 .25

A771

1997, Jan. 1

2746 A771 50f multicolored 1.00 .25

First natl. agricultural census.

New Year 1997 (Year of the Ox)
A772 A773

Photo. & Engr.

1997, Jan. 5 *Perf. 11½*

2747 A772 50f multi (2-2) .75 .30
2748 A773 150f multi (2-1) 1.75 .60

Paintings by Pan Tianshou (1897-1971) A774

No. 2749, Pines on the Yellow Mountain. No. 2750, Rosy Clouds of Dawn. No. 2751, Clearing Up after Mould Rains. No. 2752, Chrysanthemum and Bamboo. No. 2753, Sleeping Cat. No. 2754, A Corner of Lingyan Brook.

1997, Mar. 14 Photo. *Perf. 11½*

2749 A774 50f multi (6-1) .30 .25
2750 A774 50f multi (6-2) .30 .25
2751 A774 100f multi (6-3) .75 .35
2752 A774 100f multi (6-4) .75 .35
2753 A774 150f multi (6-5) 1.40 .40
2754 A774 150f multi (6-6) 1.40 .40
Nos. 2749-2754 (6) 4.90 2.00

Great Wall Type of 1995

1997, Apr. 1 Photo. *Perf. 13x12*

2755 A730 50f multicolored .25 .25

A776

Tea: No. 2756, People forming circle beside tea tree. No. 2757, Statue of tea sage. No. 2758, Tea utensils, horiz. No. 2759, Painting of tea party, horiz.

1997, Apr. 8 Litho. *Perf. 12*

2756 A776 50f multi (4-1) .50 .25
2757 A776 50f multi (4-2) .50 .25
2758 A776 150f multi (4-3) .90 .40
2759 A776 150f multi (4-4) .90 .40
Nos. 2756-2759 (4) 2.80 1.30

A777

Stylized designs depicting: No. 2760, Celebration. No. 2761, Unity (group of people), horiz. 200f, Advance (horses running), horiz.

1997, May 1 Photo. *Perf. 11½*

2760 A777 50f multi (3-1) .35 .25
2761 A777 50f multi (3-2) .35 .25
2762 A777 200f multi (3-3) .95 .35
Nos. 2760-2762 (3) 1.65 .85

Inner Mongolia Autonomous Region, 50th anniv.

Pheasants
A778

Designs: 50f, Chinese copper pheasant. 540f, Common pheasant.

Litho. & Engr.

1997, May 9 *Perf. 11½x11*

2763 A778 50f multi (2-1) .35 .25
2764 A778 540f multi (2-2) 2.25 .90

See Sweden Nos. 2225-2226.

Dong Architecture
A779

No. 2765, Zengchong Drum Tower. No. 2766, Bai'er Drum Tower. No. 2767, Wind and Rain Bridge over the River, horiz. No. 2768, Wind and Rain Bridge in the Field, horiz.

1997, June 2 Litho. *Perf. 12*

2765 A779 50f multi (4-1) .25 .25
2766 A779 50f multi (4-2) .25 .25
a. Pair, #2765-2766 .75 .60
2767 A779 150f multi (4-3) .50 .30
2768 A779 150f multi (4-4) .50 .30
a. Pair, #2767-2768 1.25 1.10
Nos. 2765-2768 (4) 1.50 1.10

Maiji
Grottoes — A780

Statues: No. 2769, Buddha and Xieshi Bodhisattva. No. 2770, Xieshi Bodhisattva and his disciple. 100f, Maid. No. 2772, Buddha. No. 2773, Xieshi Bodhisattva. 200f, Provider.

1997, June 13

2769 A780 50f multi (6-1) .30 .25
2770 A780 50f multi (6-2) .30 .25
2771 A780 100f multi (6-3) .40 .25
2772 A780 150f multi (6-4) .55 .30
2773 A780 150f multi (6-5) .55 .30
2774 A780 200f multi (6-6) .70 .35
Nos. 2769-2774 (6) 2.80 1.70

A780a

A781

Texts surrounded by flowers: 50f, Sino-British Joint Declaration. 150f, Basic Law of the Hong Kong Special Adminstrative Region. 800f, Deng Xiaoping.

1997, July 1 Litho. *Perf. 12*

2774A A780a 50f multi (2-1) .35 .25
2774B A780a 150f multi (2-2) .95 .65

Souvenir Sheets

2774C A781 800f multi 4.25 3.50
d. Overprinted in sheet margin 7.00 5.00

Litho. (stamp) & Embossed (margin)

Perf. 13½

2775 A781 $50 gold & multi *45.00 45.00*
a. Overprinted in margin *47.50 47.50*

Deng Xiaoping (1904-97), return of Hong Kong to China.

No. 2775 was released in special souvenir folder.

No. 2744C exists imperf. Value, *$500.*

No. 2774Cd contains gold Chinese inscription for Hong Kong's Return Exhibition Tour, emblem, and "PJZ-8" in sheet margin. Issued: 6/19/98.

Overprint in margin on No. 2775a is Chinese inscription, "2000-1" and "(2-1)J." Issued: 1/1/00.

Ancient Temples of Wutai Mountain — A782

Designs: 40f, Taihuai Township. No. 2777, Nanchan Temple. No. 2778, Foguang Temple. No. 2779, Xiantong Temple. No. 2780, Bodhisattva Summit. 200f, Zhenhai Temple.

1997, July 26 Litho. *Perf. 12*

2776 A782 40f multi (6-1) .25 .25
2777 A782 50f multi (6-2) .30 .25
2778 A782 50f multi (6-3) .30 .25
2779 A782 150f multi (6-4) .55 .30
2780 A782 150f multi (6-5) .55 .30
2781 A782 200f multi (6-6) .70 .35
Nos. 2776-2781 (6) 2.65 1.70

Chinese People's Liberation Army, 70th Anniv. — A783

No. 2782, Land Force. No. 2783, Naval Force. No. 2784, Air Force. No. 2785, Strategic Missile Troops. 200f, Joint military maneuvers.

1997, Aug. 1

2782 A783 50f multi (5-1) .45 .30
2783 A783 50f multi (5-2) .45 .30
2784 A783 50f multi (5-3) .45 .30
2785 A783 50f multi (5-4) .45 .30
2786 A783 200f multi (5-5) 2.00 .90
Nos. 2782-2786 (5) 3.80 2.10

Shoushan Stone Carvings A784

Designs: No. 2787, "Rhythm of Autumn," vert. No. 2788, "Rhinoceros under Sunshine,", vert. No. 2789, "Jade's Fragrance," (basket of fruit). No. 2790, "Drunken Joy."
800f, Qianlong's Chain Seals.

1997, Aug. 17 Litho. *Perf. 12*

2787 A784 50f multi (4-1) .30 .25
2788 A784 50f multi (4-2) .30 .25
2789 A784 150f multi (4-3) .55 .30
2790 A784 150f multi (4-4) .55 .30
Nos. 2787-2790 (4) 1.70 1.10

Souvenir Sheet

2791 A784 800f multi 5.00 4.50

No. 2791 contains one 60x60mm stamp.

Great Wall Type of 1995

Gates: 30f, Huangyaguan. 100f, Badaling. 150f, Joyongguan. 200f, Zijingguan.

1997, Sept. 1 Photo. *Perf. 13x12*

2792 A730 30f yellow & black .25 .25
2793 A730 100f vermilion & black .40 .25
2794 A730 150f green & black .55 .25
2795 A730 200f red & black .70 .30
Nos. 2792-2795 (4) 1.90 1.05

Communist Party of China, 15th Natl. Congress A785

1997, Sept. 12 Litho. *Perf. 12*

2796 A785 50f multicolored 1.00 .40

A786

No. 2797, China Rose. No. 2798, New Zealand Monthly Rose.

1997, Oct. 9 Photo. *Perf. 11½*

2797 150f multi (2-1) .65 .30
2798 150f multi (2-2) .65 .30
a. A786 Pair, #2797-2798 1.90 1.50

See New Zealand Nos. 1469-1470.

Eighth Natl. Games A788

1997, Oct. 12 Litho. *Perf. 12*

2799 A788 50f Athletes (2-1) .35 .25
2800 A788 150f Stadium)2-2) .65 .40
a. Souv. sheet, #2799-2800 5.25 4.00

No. 2800a sold for 300f.

Temple of Heaven, Beijing — A789

No. 2801, Hall of Prayers for Bumper Harvests. No. 2802, Imperial Vault of Heaven. No. 2803, Circular Mound Altar. No. 2804, Fasting Palace.

1997, Oct. 16 Litho. *Perf. 12*

2801 A789 50f multi (4-1) .35 .25
2802 A789 50f multi (4-2) .35 .25
a. Pair, #2801-2802 .85 .75
2803 A789 150f multi (4-3) .55 .30
2804 A789 150f multi (4-4) .55 .30
a. Pair, #2803-2804 1.40 1.10
Nos. 2801-2804 (4) 1.80 1.10

Mt. Huangshan — A790

a, Mt. Huangshan at sunrise (8-1). b, Xihai Peaks (8-2). c, Flying Rock in surging clouds (8-3). d, Beihai in drifting clouds (8-4). e, Yuping Peak (8-5). f, Mystical stone (8-6). g, Tiandu Peak over clouds (8-7). h, Fabled Abode of Immortals (8-8).

1997, Oct. 20 Photo. *Perf. 11½*

Sheet of 8 + Label

2805 A790 200f #a.-h. 12.00 9.00

Nos. 2805d, 2805e are each 36x46mm.
22nd UPU Congress, Beijing, 1999.

City Wall of Xi'an A791

Designs: No. 2806, Surrounding tower. No. 2807, Arrow Tower. No. 2808, Watch Tower. No. 2809, Corner Tower.

1997, Oct. 24 Litho. *Perf. 12*

2806 A791 50f multi (4-1) .30 .25
2807 A791 50f multi (4-2) .30 .25
2808 A791 150f multi (4-3) .55 .35
2809 A791 150f multi (4-4) .55 .35
Nos. 2806-2809 (4) 1.70 1.20

Three Gorges Dam Project on Yangtze River — A792

No. 2810, New channel being opened to navigation. No. 2811, Damming Yangtze River.

1997, Nov. 8 Photo. *Perf. 11½*

2810 A792 50f multi (2-1) .35 .25
2811 A792 50f multi (2-2) .35 .25
a. Pair, #2810-2811 1.00 .75

Macao Landmarks — A793

50f, Ma Kok Temple. 100f, Lin Fong Temple. 150f, St. Paul's Ruins. 200f, Guia Lighthouse.

1997, Nov. 11 Litho. *Perf. 12*

2812 A793 50f multi (4-1) .25 .25
2813 A793 100f multi (4-2) .40 .25
2814 A793 150f multi (4-3) .50 .35
2815 A793 200f multi (4-4) .65 .40
Nos. 2812-2815 (4) 1.80 1.25

Steel Production Exceeds 100 Million Tons in 1996 A794

50f, Ancient method of producing steel. 150f, Modern mill, pouring steel from smelter.

1997, Nov. 25

2816 A794 50f multi (2-1) .40 .25
2817 A794 150f multi (2-2) .90 .40

Telecommunications — A795

Stylized designs: No. 2818, Digital transmissions. No. 2819, Computer, "X-changing" data. No. 2820, Computer receiving signals, Chinese landmarks. No. 2821, Cellular phone transmission, man's head.

1997, Dec. 10

2818 A795 50f multi (4-1) .30 .25
2819 A795 50f multi (4-2) .30 .25
2820 A795 150f multi (4-3) .55 .35
2821 A795 150f multi (4-4) .55 .35
Nos. 2818-2821 (4) 1.70 1.20

Literature Type of 1987

Outlaws of the Marsh: 40f, Huyan Zhuo coaxes Guan Sheng in a moonlit night. No. 2823, Lu Junyi captures Shi Wengong. No. 2824, Yan Qing defeats sky supporting pillar. 150f, Thunderbolt defeats Imperial Army.
800f, Heroes of Mount Liangshan take seats in order of rank.

1997, Dec. 22 Photo. *Perf. 11*

2822 A570 40f multi (4-1) .30 .25
2823 A570 50f multi (4-2) .35 .30
2824 A570 50f multi (4-3) .35 .30
2825 A570 150f multi (4-4) .80 .40
Nos. 2822-2825 (4) 1.80 1.25

Souvenir Sheet

2826 A570 800f multicolored 3.50 3.25

No. 2826 contains one 60x90mm stamp.

New Year 1998 (Year of the Tiger)
A796 A797

Photo. & Engr.

1998, Jan. 5 *Perf. 11½*

2827 A796 50f multi (2-1) .60 .25
2828 A797 150f multi (2-2) 1.40 .40

Gardens of Lingnan — A798

1998, Jan. 18 Litho. *Perf. 12*

2829 A798 50f Keyaun (4-1) .30 .25
2830 A798 50f Liangyuan (4-2) .30 .25
2831 A798 100f Qinghui (4-3) .40 .30
2832 A798 200f Yuyin Villa (4-4) .70 .35
Nos. 2829-2832 (4) 1.70 1.15

Deng Xiaoping (1904-97) — A799

No. 2833, At middle age. No. 2834, During Liberation War. No. 2835, With Mao Tse-tung. 100f, As Chairman of Central Military Commission. 150f, Making speech on 35th anniversary of People's Republic. 200f, Making speech, hand raised, 1992.

1998, Feb. 19 Photo. *Perf. 11½*

2833 A799 50f multi (6-1) .50 .25
2834 A799 50f multi (6-2) .50 .25
2835 A799 50f multi (6-3) .50 .25
2836 A799 100f multi (6-4) .75 .30
2837 A799 150f multi (6-5) 1.00 .40
2838 A799 200f multi (6-6) 1.25 .55
Nos. 2833-2838 (6) 4.50 2.00

Chinese People's Police — A800

Designs: 40f, Golden shield. No. 2840, Blitz operation. No. 2841, Cooperation between police and people. 100f, Traffic control. 150f, Fire police. 200f, Border guards.

1998, Feb. 28 Litho. *Perf. 12*

2839 A800 40f multi (6-1) .25 .25
2840 A800 50f multi (6-2) .30 .25
2841 A800 50f multi (6-3) .30 .25
2842 A800 100f multi (6-4) .40 .30
2843 A800 150f multi (6-5) .55 .30
2844 A800 200f multi (6-6) .70 .35
Nos. 2839-2844 (6) 2.50 1.70

A801

1998, Mar. 5

2845 A801 50f multi (1-1) 1.00 .25

Ninth Natl. People's Congress, Beijing.

A802

Chou En-lai (1898-1976), Communist Party leader: No. 2846, In military uniform on horse. No. 2847, As First Premier, walking. No. 2848, As diplomat wearing lei. No. 2849, Standing and applauding.

1998, Mar. 5 Photo. *Perf. 11½*

2846 A802 50f multi (4-1) 1.00 .25
2847 A802 50f multi (4-2) 1.00 .25
2848 A802 150f multi (4-3) 1.40 .50
2849 A802 150f multi (4-4) 1.40 .50
Nos. 2846-2849 (4) 4.80 1.50

Nine-Village Valley — A803

Designs: No. 2850, Fangcao Lake. No. 2851, Wuhua Lake. No. 2852, Shuzheng Waterfalls. No. 2853, Nuorilang Waterfalls.
No. 2854, Long Lake.

1998, Mar. 26 Litho. *Perf. 12*

2850 A803 50f multi (4-1) .30 .25
2851 A803 50f multi (4-2) .30 .25
2852 A803 150f multi (4-3) .50 .35
2853 A803 150f multi (4-4) .50 .35
Nos. 2850-2853 (4) 1.60 1.20

Souvenir Sheet

2854 A803 800f multicolored 3.25 3.00

No. 2854 contains one 93x52mm stamp.

Dai Architecture — A804

No. 2855, Building on stilts. No. 2856, Well. No. 2857, Pavilion. No. 2858, Pagoda.

1998, Apr. 12 Photo. *Perf. 11½*

2855 A804 50f multi (4-1) .30 .25
2856 A804 50f multi (4-2) .30 .25
2857 A804 150f multi (4-3) .55 .35
2858 A804 150f multi (4-4) .55 .35
Nos. 2855-2858 (4) 1.70 1.20

Construction, Hainan Special Economic Zone — A805

No. 2859, Urban construction, Haikou. No. 2860, Economic development zone, Yangpu. No. 2861, Phoenix Intl. Airport, Sanya. No. 2862, Natl. tourism and resort zone, Yalongwan.

1998, Apr. 13 Litho. *Perf. 12*

2859 A805 50f multi (4-1) .25 .25
2860 A805 50f multi (4-2) .25 .25
a. Pair, #2859-2860 .75 .65
2861 A805 150f multi (4-3) .55 .30
2862 A805 150f multi (4-4) .55 .30
a. Pair, #2861-2862 1.25 1.00
Nos. 2859-2862 (4) 1.60 1.10

Ancient Academies — A806

Designs: No. 2863, Yingtian. No. 2864, Songyang. No. 2865, Yuelu. No. 2866, Bailu.

1998, Apr. 29

2863 A806 50f multi (4-1) .30 .25
2864 A806 50f multi (4-2) .30 .25
2865 A806 150f multi (4-3) .55 .35
2866 A806 150f multi (4-4) .55 .35
Nos. 2863-2866 (4) 1.70 1.20

Beijing University, Cent. A807

1998, May 4 Litho. *Perf. 12*

2867 A807 50f multicolored 1.00 .25

22nd UPU Congress, Beijing A808

1998, May 15 Litho. *Perf. 12*

2868 A808 50f Emblem (2-1) .25 .25
2869 A808 540f Emblem, vert. (2-2) 1.75 .85

Shennongjia Nature Reserve — A809

No. 2870, Mountain peaks. No. 2871, River, gorge. No. 2872, Primitive forest. No. 2873, Grasslands.

1998, June 6

2870 A809 50f multi (4-1) .30 .25
2871 A809 50f multi (4-2) .30 .25
2872 A809 150f multi (4-3) .55 .35
2873 A809 150f multi (4-4) .55 .35
Nos. 2870-2873 (4) 1.70 1.20

Chongqing — A810

1998, June 18 Litho. *Perf. 12*

2874 A810 50f Great Hall (2-1) .40 .25
2875 A810 150f Port (2-2) .70 .45

Xilinguole Grassland — A811

Designs: No. 2876, Sheep grazing, sheep herders. No. 2877, Cattle grazing, flowers. 150f, Poplar and birch forest, deer.
800f, Xilinguole River Bend.

1998, June 24

2876 A811 50f multi (3-1) .30 .25
2877 A811 50f multi (3-2) .30 .25
2878 A811 150f multi (3-3) .55 .35
Nos. 2876-2878 (3) 1.15 .85

Souvenir Sheet

2879 A811 800f multicolored 3.25 3.00

No. 2879 contains one 56x36mm stamp.

Paintings, by He Xiangning (1878-1972) — A812

Perf. 12½ Syncopated Type A (2 Sides)

1998, June 27 Photo.

2880 A812 50f Tiger (3-1) .50 .25
2881 A812 100f Lion, vert. (3-2) .80 .35
2882 A812 150f Plum blossom, vert. (3-3) 1.00 .50
Nos. 2880-2882 (3) 2.30 1.10

Jingpo Lake — A813

Views of lake: No. 2883, Bridge, houses on cliff, boat. No. 2884, Islands, boats at shore. No. 2885, Boat, island. No. 2886, Waterfalls.

1998, Aug. 15 Litho. *Perf. 12*

2883 A813 50f multi (4-1) .30 .25
2884 A813 50f multi (4-2) .30 .25
2885 A813 50f multi (4-3) .30 .25
2886 A813 50f multi (4-4) .30 .25
a. Strip of 4, #2883-2886 1.50 1.25

Würzburg Palace — A814

Puning Temple, Chengde — A815

1998, Aug. 20 Litho. *Perf. 12*

2887 A814 50f multi (2-1) .35 .25
2888 A815 540f multi (2-2) 1.90 1.40

See Germany Nos. 2012-2013.

Literature Type of 1987

Romance of the Three Kingdoms: No. 2889, Liu Bei finds a guardian for his heir at Baidi City. No. 2890, Zhuge Liang leads his army home, vert. 100f, Death of Zhuge Liang. 150f, Three Kingdoms united under the reign of Jin, vert.

800f, The Stratagem of Empty City.

1998, Aug. 26 Photo. *Perf. 11½*

2889 A570 50f multi (4-1) .25 .25
2890 A570 50f multi (4-2) .25 .25
2891 A570 100f multi (4-3) .40 .35
2892 A570 150f multi (4-4) .60 .55
Nos. 2889-2892 (4) 1.50 1.40

Souvenir Sheet

2893 A570 800f multicolored 7.25 4.25

No. 2893 contains one 158x37mm stamp.

Flood Victims Relief — A816

1998, Sept. 10 Photo. *Perf. 13x13½*

2894 A816 50f + 50f label .60 .40

The Louvre, France A817

Design: 200f, Hall of Heavenly Peace, Imperial Palace, China.

1998, Sept. 12 Photo. *Perf. 13x13½*

2895 A817 50f multi (2-1) .35 .25
2896 A817 200f multi (2-2) .85 .55

See France Nos. 2669-2670.

Cliff Paintings of Helan Mountains — A818

1998, Sept. 23 Litho. *Perf. 12*

2897 A818 50f Human face (3-1) .30 .25
2898 A818 100f Hunting (3-2) .40 .35
2899 A818 150f Ox (3-3) .55 .45
Nos. 2897-2899 (3) 1.25 1.05

Longquan Pottery and Porcelain — A819

Designs: No. 2900, Vase with five spouts. No. 2901, Vase with phoenix ears. No. 2902, Double gourd vase. 150f, Ewer.

1998, Oct. 13

2900 A819 50f multi (4-1) .30 .25
2901 A819 50f multi (4-2) .30 .25
2902 A819 50f multi (4-3) .30 .25
2903 A819 150f multi (4-4) .65 .50
Nos. 2900-2903 (4) 1.55 1.25

Mausoleum of Yandi A820

Designs: 50f, Meridian Gate. 100f, Saluting Pavilion. 150f, Tomb.

1998, Oct. 28 Litho. *Perf. 12*

2904 A820 50f multi (3-1) .25 .25
2905 A820 100f multi (3-2) .35 .30
2906 A820 150f multi (3-3) .50 .40
a. Souvenir sheet, #2904-2906 2.40 2.00
Nos. 2904-2906 (3) 1.10 .95

Great Wall Type of 1995

10f, Jiumenko Pass. 300f, Niagziguan Pass. 420f, Pianguan Pass. 500f, Bianjing Tower.

1998, Nov. 1 Photo. *Perf. 13x12*

2907 A730 10f apple green & black .25 .25
2908 A730 300f olive & black 1.00 .75
2909 A730 420f brn org & blk 1.50 1.00
2910 A730 500f blue, black & brown 1.75 1.25
Nos. 2907-2910 (4) 4.50 3.25

Major Campaigns in Liberation War — A821

No. 2911, Making plans. No. 2912, Conquering Jinzhou. No. 2913, Battle in Huaihai. No. 2914, Liberating Beijing. 150f, People moving supplies.

1998, Nov. 14 Litho. *Perf. 12*

2911 A821 50f red & multi (5-1) .55 .25
2912 A821 50f gray & multi (5-2) .55 .25
2913 A821 50f org yel & multi (5-3) .55 .25
2914 A821 50f org & multi (5-4) .55 .25
2915 A821 150f brn org & multi (5-5) 1.25 .75
Nos. 2911-2915 (5) 3.45 1.75

Liu Shaoqi (1898-1969), Communist Party Leader — A822

Various portraits.

1998, Nov. 24 Photo. *Perf. 11½*

2916 A822 50f multi (4-1), vert. .35 .25
2917 A822 50f multi (4-2), vert. .35 .25
2918 A822 50f shown (4-3) .35 .25
2919 A822 150f multi (4-4) 1.10 .50
Nos. 2916-2919 (4) 2.15 1.25

Chillon Castle, Lake Geneva A823

Bridge 24, Slender West Lake, Yangzhou A824

1998, Nov. 25 *Perf. 11x11½*

2920 A823 50f multi (2-1) .35 .25
2921 A824 540f multi (2-2) 1.90 1.40

See Switzerland Nos. 1037-1039.

Lingqu Canal — A825

No. 2922, Dam. No. 2923, Bridge over canal, vert. 150f, Boat approaching lock, vert.

1998, Dec. 1 Litho. *Perf. 12*

2922 A825 50f multi (3-1) .30 .25
2923 A825 50f multi (3-2) .30 .25
2924 A825 150f multi (3-3) .60 .45
Nos. 2922-2924 (3) 1.20 .95

Buildings in Macao — A826

Designs: 50f, Building complex, Nanwan. 100f, Friendship Bridge. 150f, Macao Stadium. 200f, Macao Intl. Airport.

1998, Dec. 12 Litho. *Perf. 12*

2925 A826 50f multi (4-1) .25 .25
2926 A826 100f multi (4-2) .40 .30
2927 A826 150f multi (4-3) .55 .40
2928 A826 200f multi (4-4) .70 .60
Nos. 2925-2928 (4) 1.90 1.55

11th Communist Party Congress, 20th Anniv. — A827

50f, Deng Xiaoping (2-1). 150f, Handbill, buildings (2-2).

1998, Dec. 18

2929 A827 50f multicolored .65 .25
2930 A827 150f multicolored 1.25 .45

Fish of the Coral Reef A828

a, Pomacanthus imperator (8-1). b, Plectropomus maculatus (8-2). c, Chaetodon plebeius (8-3). d, Chaetodon chrysurus (8-4), vert. e, Heniochus acuminatus (8-5), vert. f, Lutjanus sebae (8-6). g, Balistoides conspicillum (8-7). h, Pygoplites diancanthus (8-8).

1998, Dec. 22 Photo. *Perf. 11½*

Sheet of 8

2931 A828 200f #a.-h. + label 6.00 6.00
i. As No. 2931, with margin ovptd. in gold *10.00 10.00*

UPU, 22nd Congress, Beijing '99 World Philatelic Exhibition.

Nos. 2931d-2931e are each 40x49mm.

No.2931i issued 7/15/00. No. 2931i inscribed in margin in gold "PJZ-12" , "1997-1999" and Chinese characters. Inscription for best philatelic item from 1997-99.

New Year 1999 (Year of the Rabbit)

A829 A830

Photo. & Engr.

1999, Jan. 5 *Perf. 11½*

2932 A829 50f Stylized rabbit (2-1) 1.00 .25
2933 A830 150f Symbol for rabbit (2-2) 1.50 .50

Great Wall Type of 1995

5f, Hushan Section. 20f, Shanhaiguan Pass. 40f, Jinshanling Section. 80f, Mutianyu Section. 270f, Pingxingguan Pass. 320f, Desheng Pass. 440f, Yanmen Pass. 540f, Zhenbei Tower.

1999, Mar. 1 Photo. *Perf. 13x12*

2934 A730 5f bl, blk & bl grn .25 .25
2935 A730 20f vio & blk .40 .25
2936 A730 40f pink & blk .45 .30
2937 A730 80f grn, blk & ol .60 .40
2938 A730 270f grn, blk & brn 1.50 .65
2939 A730 320f vio, blk & bwn 2.00 1.10
2940 A730 440f red brn, blk & bwn 3.75 2.00
2941 A730 540f blue & black 3.50 1.50
Nos. 2934-2941 (8) 12.45 6.45

Stone Carvings of the Han Dynasty A831

No. 2942, Plowing fields with oxen. No. 2943, Group weaving. No. 2944, Three figures dancing in front of fire. No. 2945, Horses, carriage. No. 2946, Group in assassination attempt. No. 2947, Goddess Chang'e.

1999, Mar. 16 *Perf. 12*

2942 A831 50f dark green & blk .25 .25
2943 A831 50f brown & blk .25 .25
2944 A831 50f dark blue & blk .25 .25
2945 A831 150f dark brown & blk .55 .45
2946 A831 150f brown olive & blk .55 .45
2947 A831 150f dark purple & blk .55 .45
Nos. 2942-2947 (6) 2.40 2.10

A832

Chinese Ceramics (Porcelain from the Jun Kiln): 80f, Halberd-shaped cup. 100f, Cup. 150f, Dual-handled stove. 200f, Dual-handled vase with base.

1999, Apr. 8 Photo. *Perf. 11½*

2948 A832 80f multi (4-1) .30 .25
2949 A832 100f multi (4-2) .40 .30
2950 A832 150f multi (4-3) .60 .45
2951 A832 200f multi (4-4) .85 .60
Nos. 2948-2951 (4) 2.15 1.60

Great Wall Type of 1995

Designs: 60f, Huanghua Tower. $10, Huama section. $20, Sanguankou Pass. $50 Jiayuguan Pass.

1999, May 1 Photo. *Perf. 13x12*

2952 A730 60f multicolored .30 .30

Size: 28x22mm

Perf. 11½

Photo. & Engr.

2953 A730 $10 multicolored 4.00 3.00
2954 A730 $20 multicolored 8.00 5.75
2955 A730 $50 multicolored 17.50 14.50
Nos. 2952-2955 (4) 29.80 23.55

A833

1999, May 1 Litho. *Perf. 12*

2956 A833 80f shown (2-1) .40 .25
2957 A833 200f Tree (2-2) .80 .55

Kunming World Horticultural Fair.

Red Deer A834

1999, May 18 Litho. *Perf. 11x11½*

2958 A834 80f Bucks .35 .25
2959 A834 80f Does .35 .25
a. Pair, #2958-2959 .80 .70

See Russia No. 6514.

Beauty of Putuo Mountain — A835

No. 2960, Puji Temple (6-1). No. 2961, Nantian Gate, vert. (6-2). No. 2962, 100-step Sand (6-3). No. 2963, Pantuo Rock (6-4). No. 2964, Fanyin Cave, vert. (6-5). No. 2965, Fayu Temple (6-6).

1999, June 3 Litho. *Perf. 12*

2960 A835 30f multicolored .25 .25
2961 A835 60f multicolored .30 .25
2962 A835 60f multicolored .30 .25
2963 A835 80f multicolored .35 .30
2964 A835 80f multicolored .35 .30
2965 A835 280f multicolored .95 .75
Nos. 2960-2965 (6) 2.50 2.10

Fang Zhimin (1899-1935), Revolutionary A836

1999, Aug. 21 Photo. *Perf. 11¼*

2966 A836 80f Close-up (2-1) .50 .35
2967 A836 80f Standing (2-2) .50 .35

Souvenir Sheet

China 1999 World Philatelic Exhibition — A837

1999, Aug. 21 *Perf. 11½x11¼*

2968 A837 800f multicolored 4.50 4.00

Exists overprinted in upper corners in gold. Value, $10.

A838

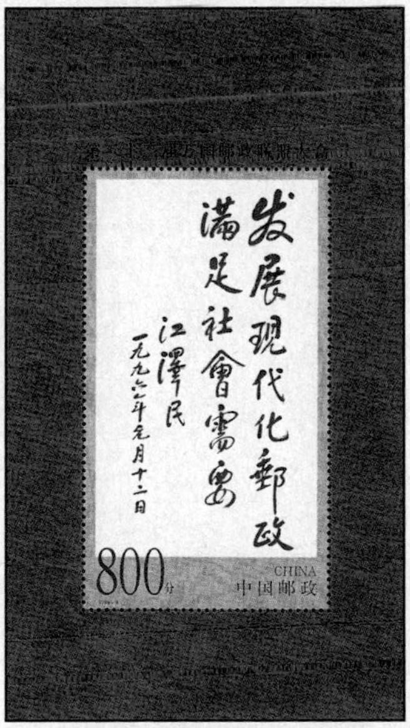

22nd UPU Congress — A839

Congress sites: 80f, 1st, Bern. 540f, 22nd, Beijing.
800f, Inscription by Pres. Jiang Zemin.

1999, Aug. 23 Litho. *Perf. 12*

2969 A838 80f multi (2-1) .35 .25
2970 A838 540f multi (2-2) 2.00 1.40

Souvenir Sheet

Perf. 12¼

2971 A839 800f multicolored 5.50 5.00

UPU, 125th Anniv. — A840

1999, Sept. 7 Litho. *Perf. 12*

2972 A840 80f multicolored .65 .35

Intl. Year of the Elderly — A841

1999, Sept. 9

2973 A841 80f multicolored .80 .25

Chinese People's Political Consultative Conference, 50th Anniv. — A842

1999, Sept. 21

2974 A842 60f Building (2-1) .75 .25
2975 A842 80f Mao Zedong, vert. (2-2) 2.00 .35

Ethnic Groups in China — A843

Designs (stamp number following "56-" at LR): a, Han (1). b, Mongols (2). c, Hui (3). d, Tibetans (4). e, Uygurs (5) f, Miao (6). g, Yi (7). h, Zhuang (8). i, Bouyei (9). j, Koreans (10). k, Manchu (11). l, Dongs (12). m, Yao (13). n, Bai (14). o, Tujia (15). p, Hani (16). q, Kazak (17). r, Dai (18). s, Li (19). t, Lisu (20). u, Va (21). v, She (22). w, Gaoshan (23). x, Lahu (24). y, Shui (25). z, Dongxiang (26). aa, Naxi (27). ab, Jingpo (28). ac, Kirgiz (29). ad, Tu (30). ae, Daur (31). af, Mulam (32). ag, Qiang (33). ah, Blang (34). ai, Salas (35). aj, Maonan (36). ak, Gelao (37). al, Xibe (38). am, Achang (39). an, Pumi (40). ao, Tajiks (41). ap, Nu (42). aq, Uzbeks (43). ar, Russians (44). as, Ewenki (45). at, De'ang (46). au, Bonan (47). av, Yugur (48). aw, Jing (49). ax, Tartars (50). ay, Drung (51). az, Oroqen (52). ba, Hezhe (53). bb, Moiba (54). bc, Lhoba (55). bd, Jino (56).

1999, Oct. 7 Photo. *Perf. 13¼*

2976 A843 80f Sheet of 56, #a.-bd. 22.50 18.00

Mountains — A844

1999, Oct. 5 *Perf. 11½x11¼*

2977 A844 80f Lushan (2-1) .55 .30
2978 A844 80f Kuryongyon (2-2) .55 .30

Project Hope, 10th Anniv. — A845

1999, Oct. 30 Photo. *Perf. 11½*

2979 A845 80f multi .75 .30

Scientific and Technological Achievements — A846

Designs: No. 2980, Cambrian era fossil. No. 2981, Underwater robot. No. 2982, Best result of Goldbach conjecture, vert. No. 2983, 2.16m telescope, vert.

1999, Nov. 1 Litho. *Perf. 12*

2980 A846 80f multi (4-1) .60 .30
2981 A846 80f multi (4-2) .60 .30
a. Pair, #2980-2981 4.25 2.00
2982 A846 80f multi (4-3) .60 .30
2983 A846 80f multi (4-4) .60 .30
a. Pair, #2982-2983 4.25 2.00
Nos. 2980-2983 (4) 2.40 1.20

Li Lisan (1899-1967), Minister of Labor — A847

1999, Nov. 19 Photo. *Perf. 11½*

2984 A847 80f As young man (2-1) .50 .30
2985 A847 80f Wearing glasses (2-2) .50 .30

Return of Macao to China — A848

Designs: 80f, Sino-Portuguese declaration, flower. 150f, Basic Law of Macao Special Administrative Region, Great Wall.
800f, $50, Deng Xiaoping.

1999-2000 Photo. *Perf. 11¾x11½*

2986 A848 80f multi (2-1) .55 .25
2987 A848 150f multi (2-2) .75 .50

Souvenir Sheets

Perf. 13

2988 A848 800f multi 4.25 3.75

Litho. (stamp) & Embossed (margin)
Perf. 12

2989 A848 $50 multi *15.00 15.00*
a. Overprinted in margin *37.50 37.50*

No. 2988 contains one 60x50mm stamp with star-shaped perforations in the corners.
Overprint in margin on No. 2989a is Chinese inscription, "2000-1" and "(2-2)J."
Issued: No. 2989a, 1/1/00; others, 12/20/99.

Nie Rongzhen (1899-1992), Military Leader — A849

1999, Dec. 29 Litho. *Perf. 12*

2990 A849 80f In uniform (2-1) .75 .30
2991 A849 80f Seated (2-2) .75 .30

Millennium — A850

No. 2992, Sun Yat-sen, #590. No. 2993, #2214. No. 2994, #2339. No. 2995, #2601. No. 2996, Mao Zedong, #456. 200f, #2248. 260f, #2730. 280f, Deng Xiaoping, #2774C.

1999, Dec. 31 Litho. *Perf. 12*

2992 A850 60f multi (8-1) .30 .25
2993 A850 60f multi (8-2) .30 .25
2994 A850 80f multi (8-3) .40 .25
2995 A850 80f multi (8-4) .40 .25
2996 A850 80f multi (8-5) .40 .25
2997 A850 200f multi (8-6) .85 .40
2998 A850 260f multi (8-7) .95 .50
2999 A850 280f multi (8-8) 1.10 .60
Nos. 2992-2999 (8) 4.70 2.75

New Year 2000 (Year of the Dragon) — A851

Photo. & Engr.

2000, Jan. 5 *Perf. 11½x11¾*

3000 A851 80f Dragon (2-1) *10.00* .90
3001 A851 $2.80 Rising sun (2-2) *15.00* 1.40

A852

Spring Festival: No. 3002, Welcoming the Spring Festival. No. 3003, Bidding farewell to outgoing year. $2.80, Offering sacrifices to god of land.
$8, Family reunion, horiz.

2000, Jan. 29 Photo. *Perf. 11¼*

3002 A852 80f multi (3-1) .75 .25
3003 A852 80f multi (3-2) .75 .25
3004 A852 $2.80 multi (3-3) 2.50 .80
Nos. 3002-3004 (3) 4.00 1.30

Souvenir Sheet
Perf. 11¼x11

3005 A852 $8 multi *6.00 6.00*
a. Ovptd. in sheet margin *8.50 8.50*

No. 3005 contains one 90x60mm stamp.
No. 3005a contains gold Chinese inscription for New Century Philatelic Exhibition, "2000," and "PJZ-11" in sheet margin. Issued: 4/28.

A853

Wildlife.

2000, Feb. 25 Photo. *Perf. 13¼x13*

3006 A853 Sheet of 10 + 2 labels 8.00 8.00
a. 30f Nipponia nippon .25 .25
b. 60f Teinopalpus aureus .25 .25
c. 80f Ailuropoda melanoleuca .30 .25
d. $1 Crossoptilon manichuricum .35 .25
e. $1.50 Acipenser sinensis .50 .35
f. $2 Rhinopithecus roxellanae .65 .45
g. $2.60 Lipotes vexillifer .85 .60
h. $2.80 Grus japonensis .90 .65
i. $3.70 Panthera tigris 1.25 .85
j. $5.40 Alligator sinensis 1.90 1.40

Cultural Relics — A854

Designs; 60f, Neolithic Age jade dragon. No. 3008, Dragon-shaped ornament. No. 3009, Carved tile with dragon. No. 3010, Copper mirror with dragon. No. 3011, Bronze dragon. $2.80, Dragon on sandalwood throne.

2000, Mar. 7 Litho. *Perf. 12*

3007 A854 60f multi (6-1) 1.00 .25
3008 A854 80f multi (6-2) 1.50 .40
3009 A854 80f multi (6-3) 1.50 .40
3010 A854 80f multi (6-4) 1.50 .40
3011 A854 80f multi (6-5) 1.50 .40
3012 A854 $2.80 multi (6-6) 5.00 2.50
Nos. 3007-3012 (6) 12.00 4.35

Yangtze River Highway Bridges — A855

2000, Mar. 26 Litho. *Perf. 12*

3013 A855 80f Wanxian (4-1) .45 .30
3014 A855 80f Huangshi (4-2) .45 .30
3015 A855 80f Tongling (4-3) .45 .30
3016 A855 $2.80 Jiangyin (4-4) 1.75 .75
Nos. 3013-3016 (4) 3.10 1.65

Landscapes in Dali — A856

Designs: No. 3017, Cangshan Mountain and Erhai Lake. No. 3018, Pagodas at Chongsheng Temple. No. 3019, Jizu Mountain. $2.80, Shibao Mountain.

Perf. 11¾x11½

2000, Apr. 19 Photo.

3017 A856 80f multi (4-1) .30 .25
3018 A856 80f multi (4-2) .30 .25
3019 A856 80f multi (4-3) .30 .25
3020 A856 $2.80 multi (4-4) 1.00 .70
Nos. 3017-3020 (4) 1.90 1.45

Legend of Mulan — A857

Mulan: No. 3021, Weaving cloth. No. 3022, Joining army. No. 3023, On expedition. No. 3024, Returning home.

2000, Apr. 30 Litho. *Perf. 12*

3021 A857 80f multi (4-1) .35 .30
3022 A857 80f multi (4-2) .35 .30
3023 A857 80f multi (4-3) .35 .30
3024 A857 80f multi (4-4) .35 .30
a. Strip, #3021-3024 *2.50 2.50*

Taer Lamasery A858

No. 3025, Good Luck Treasure Pagoda. No. 3026, Big Golden Tile Palace. No. 3027, Big Scripture Hall. $2.80, Banqen residence.

2000, May 5

3025 A858 80f multi (4-1) .35 .30
3026 A858 80f multi (4-2) .35 .30
3027 A858 80f multi (4-3) .35 .30
3028 A858 $2.80 multi (4-4) 1.00 .75
Nos. 3025-3028 (4) 2.05 1.65

Cai Chang and Li Fuchun A859

2000, May 22

3029 A859 80f multi .90 .30

Stampin' the Future Children's Stamp Design Contest Winners — A860

Various children's drawings: No. 3030, 30f, (8-1). No. 3031, 60f, (8-2). No. 3032, 60f, (8-3). No. 3033, 80f, (8-4). No. 3034, 80f, (8-5). No. 3035, 80f, (8-6). $2.60, (8-7). $2.80, (8-8).

Perf. 11½x11¼

2000, June 1 Photo.

3030-3037 A860 Set of 8 3.75 2.50

Chen Yun (1905-95), Statesman A861

No. 3038, 80f, As a young man (4-1). No. 3039, 80f, In uniform, vert. (4-2). No. 3040, 80f, In black jacket, vert. (4-3). $2.80, As old man (4-4).

Perf. 13x13¼, 13¼x13

2000, June 13

3038-3041 A861 Set of 4 2.75 1.50

Pots A862

Designs: No. 3042, 80f, Wine vessel (2-1). No. 3043, 80f, Horse milk pot (2-2).

2000, June 28 Litho. *Perf. 12*

3042-3043 A862 Set of 2 1.00 .50

See Kazakhstan No. 305.

Laoshan Mountain — A863

No. 3044, 80f, Huge Peak (4-1). No. 3045, 80f, Yangkou Bay (4-2). No. 3046, 80f, Beijiu Lake (4-3). $2.80, Taiqing Palace (4-4).

Perf. 11½x11¼

2000, July 15 Photo.

3044-3047 A863 Set of 4 2.00 1.75
3047a Souvenir sheet, #3044-3047 *6.00 6.00*

Souvenir Sheet

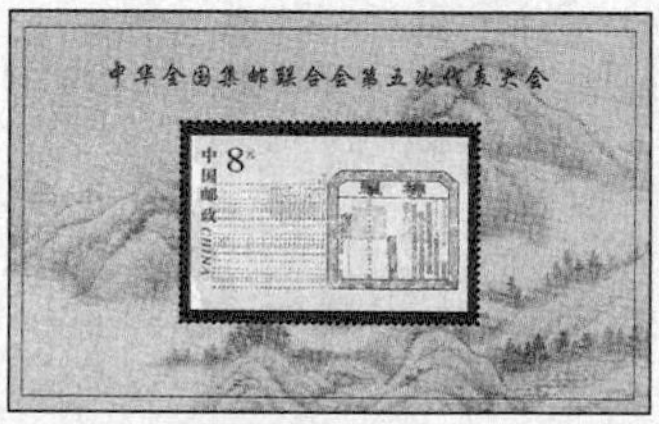

All-China Philatelic Federation, Fifth Congress — A864

2000, July 18 Litho. *Perf. 12*

3048 A864 $8 multi 6.00 5.50
a. Margin ovptd. in gold 8.50 7.50

No. 3048a issued 9/21/01. It is inscribed in margin in gold "PJZ-13," "2001," with Chinese characters and Nanjing 2001 Philatelic Exhibition mascot.

Small Carp Leap Through Dragon Gate Legend — A865

No. 3049: a, Grandma Carp tells a story (5-1). b, Small Carp look for Dragon Gate (5-2). c, Help from Uncle Crab (5-3). d, Small Carp leap through Dragon Gate (5-4). e, Aunt Swallow passes on a letter (5-5).

2000, Aug. 8 Photo. *Perf. 11½*

3049 A865 80f Horiz. strip of 5, #a-e 2.75 2.40
f. Booklet pane, #3049 + 2 labels, perf. 12 11.00
Booklet, #3049f 12.50

Shenzhen Special Economic Zone — A866

No. 3050: a, 80f, Financial Center district (5-1). b, 80f, China Intl. Exhibition Center (5-2). c, 80f, Yantian Harbor area (5-3). d, 80f, Shenzhen Bay tourist area (5-4). e, $2.80, Shekou industrial district (5-5).

2000, Aug. 26 Litho. *Perf. 12*

3050 A866 Horiz. strip of 5, #a-e 2.75 2.50

2000 Summer Olympics, Sydney — A867

2000, Sept. 15 Photo. ***Perf. 13¼x13***

3051 A867 $8 multi		*4.25*	*4.25*
a.	Sheet of 2	*50.00*	*50.00*

No. 3051a issued 10/31/00.

Beaches — A868

a, Coconuts Bay, PRC (2-1). b, Varadero Beach, Cuba (2-2).

2000, Sept. 26 Litho. ***Perf. 12***

3052 A868 Pair		.90	.75
a.-b.	80f Any single	.85	.25

See Cuba Nos. 4108-4109.

Masks and Puppets A869

No. 3053, Tan background (2-1). No. 3054, Violet blue background (2-2).

2000, Oct. 9 Photo. ***Perf. 13x13½***

3053-3054 A869 80f Set of 2 1.00 .60

See Brazil Nos. 2767-2768.

Relics from the Tomb of Prince Jing of Zhongshan — A870

No. 3055, 80f, Eternal Fidelity palace lamp (4-1). No. 3056, 80f, Bronze pot (4-2). No. 3057, 80f, Boshan incense burner (4-3). $2.80, Cup (4-4).

2000, Oct. 20 ***Perf. 13½x13¼***

3055-3058 A870 Set of 4 2.25 1.75

Ancient Thinkers — A871

No. 3059, 60f, Confucius (6-1). No. 3060, 80f, Mencius (6-2). No. 3061, 80f, Lao Zi (6-3). No. 3062, 80f, Zhuang Zi (6-4). No. 3063, 80f, Mo Zi (6-5). $2.80, Xun Zi (6-6).

Photo. & Engr.

2000, Nov. 11 ***Perf. 11¼x11***

3059-3064 A871 Set of 6 9.50 3.00

Test of Shenzhou Spacecraft, 1st Anniv. — A872

No. 3065: a, Launch (2-1). b, In orbit (2-2).

2000, Nov. 20 Photo. ***Perf. 11½***

3065 A872 Pair		*5.00*	*4.00*
a.-b.	80f Any single	1.00	.35
c.	Sheet, 6 #3065	*45.00*	*45.00*

World Meteorological Organization, 50th Anniv. — A873

Designs: No. 3066, 80f, Weather satellite (4-1). No. 3067, 80f, Weather measuring equipment on Qinghai-Tibetan Plateau (4-2). No. 3068, 80f, Weather-predicting computer (4-3). $2.80, Airplane for cloud seeding (4-4).

2000, Nov. 22 Litho. ***Perf. 12***

3066-3069 A873 Set of 4 2.00 1.50

Flowers — A874

No. 3070, 80f, Scarlet kaffir lily (4-1). No. 3071, 80f, Noble clivia (4-2). No. 3072, 80f, Golden striated lily (4-3). $2.80, White kaffir lily (4-4).

Perf. 11¼x11½

2000, Dec. 12 Photo.

3070-3073 A874	Set of 4	3.25	1.75
3073a	Souv. sheet, #3070-3073	6.00	6.00

Ancient Bells — A875

No. 3074, 80f, Jingshu bell (4-1). No. 3075, 80f, Su chime bell (4-2). No. 3076, 80f, Jingyun bell (4-3). $2.80, Qianlong bell (4-4).

2000, Dec. 31 ***Perf. 11¼x11½***

3074-3077 A875 Set of 4 2.25 1.60

Advent of New Millennium A876

Designs: 60f, Sun, moon, date, time, building (5-1). No. 3079, 80f, Dove, Earth (5-2). No. 3080, 80f, Map, leaf, infant's hands (5-3). No. 3081, 80f, Circuitboard, head, Earth, horiz. (5-4). $2.80, Moon, stars, sundial (5-5).

2001, Jan. 1 Litho. ***Perf. 12***

3078-3082 A876 Set of 5 5.00 2.00

New Year 2001 (Year of the Snake) — A877

Snake and: 80f, Flower (2-1). $2.80, Chinese character for snake (2-2).

Photo. & Engr.

2001, Jan. 5 ***Perf. 11½x11¾***

3083 A877 80f multi		2.75	.75
a.	Sheet of 6	*17.50*	*17.50*
3084 A877 $2.80 multi		3.25	1.25
a.	Sheet of 6	*24.00*	*24.00*

Clown Roles in Peking Opera — A878

Designs: No. 3085, 80f, Tang Qin (6-1). No. 3086, 80f, Lin Lihua (6-2). No. 3087, 80f, Gao Llshi (6-3). No. 3088, 80f, Jiang Gan (6-4). No. 3089, 80f, Yang Xiangwu (6-5). $2.80, Shi Qian (6-6).

2001, Feb. 15 Photo. ***Perf. 11½x11***

3085-3090 A878 Set of 6 2.75 2.00

Wildlife — A879

2001, Mar. 16 ***Perf. 13¼x13***

3091	Sheet of 10 + 2 labels	*10.00*	*9.00*
a.	A879 30f Budorcas taxicolor	.25	.25
b.	A879 60f Psephurus gladius	.40	.40
c.	A879 60f Elaphurus davidianus	.40	.40
d.	A879 80f Acipenser dabryanus	.50	.50
e.	A879 80f Capra ibex	.50	.50
f.	A879 80f Haliaeetus pelagicus	.50	.50
g.	A879 80f Camelus bactrianus	.50	.50
h.	A879 $1 Uncia uncia	.65	.65
i.	A879 $2.60 Martes zibellina	1.75	1.75
j.	A879 $5.40 Saiga tatarica	3.50	3.50

Ancient Towns — A880

Designs: No. 3092, 80f, Zhouzhuang, Kunshan (6-1). No. 3093, 80f, Tongli, Wujiang (6-2). No. 3094, 80f, Wuzhen, Tongxiang (6-3). No. 3095, 80f, Nanxun, Huzhou (6-4). No. 3096, 80f, Luzhi, Wuxian (6-5). $2.80, Xitang, Jiashan (6-6).

2001, Apr. 7 Photo. ***Perf. 11½x11¼***

3092-3097 A880	Set of 6	2.75	2.50
3097a	Booklet pane, #3092-3097 + 6 labels	*9.00*	
	Booklet, #3097a	*11.50*	

Strange Stories From a Chinese Studio, by Pu Songling A881

Designs: 60f, Ying Ning (4-1). No. 3099, 80f, A Bao (4-2). No. 3100, 80f, Mask of Evildoer (4-3). $2.80, Stealing Peach (4-4).
$8, Taoist Priest from Laoshan.

2001, Apr. 21 ***Perf. 11½***

3098-3101 A881 Set of 4 2.25 2.00

Souvenir Sheet

Perf. 13½x13

3102 A881 $8 multi *10.00* *10.00*

No. 3102 contains one 90x60mm stamp.

Yongle Temple Murals A882

No. 3103: a, Lady Queen Mother (4-1). b, Jade Lady Presenting Treasure (4-2). c, Celestial Worthy of the East (4-3). d, Venus and Mercury (4-4).

2001, May 5 Litho. ***Perf. 12***

3103	Horiz. strip of 4	2.50	2.50
a.	A882 60f multi	.30	.25
b.-c.	A882 80f Any single	.40	.35
d.	A882 $2.80 multi	1.10	.95

Mount Wudang — A883

Designs: 60f, Nanyan Hall (3-1). No. 3105, 80f, Zixiao Temple (3-2). No. 3106, 80f, Taizi Slope (3-3).
$8, Golden Crown in spring.

Perf. 11¼x11½

2001, May 26 Photo.

3104-3106 A883 Set of 3 2.50 1.10

Souvenir Sheet

Perf. 12¼x12½

3107 A883 $8 multi + label *7.00* *7.00*

No. 3107 contains one 47x71mm stamp.

Ancient Chinese Receptacles A884

Designs: No. 3108, 80f, Earthenware vase. No. 3109, 80f, Porcelain coffee pot.

2001, June 12 ***Perf. 11¼x11½***

3108-3109 A884 Set of 2 1.00 .60

See Belgium Nos. 1858-1859.

Dragon Boat Festival A885

Designs: No. 3110, Dragon boat race (3-1). No. 3111, Making Zongzi (3-2). $2.80, Expelling five poisons (3-3).

2001, June 25 Photo. *Perf. 13x13½*

3110 A885 80f multi .50 .30
a. Sheet of 9 *9.50* —
3111 A885 80f multi .50 .30
a. Sheet of 9 *9.50* —
3112 A885 $2.80 multi 1.25 1.00
a. Sheet of 9 *32.50* —
Nos. 3110-3112 (3) 2.25 1.60

Nos. 3110-3112 each issued in sheets of 40.

Early Leaders of the Communist Party — A886

Designs: No. 3113, 80f, Wang Jinmei (5-1). No. 3114, 80f, Zhao Shiyan (5-2). No. 3115, 80f, Deng Enming (5-3). No. 3116, 80f, Cai Hesen (5-4). No. 3117, 80f, He Shuheng (5-5).

2001, June 28 *Perf. 11¼x11*

3113-3117 A886 Set of 5 3.50 2.00

Communist Party, 80th Anniv. A887

2001, July 1 Photo. *Perf. 13x13¼*

3118 A887 80f multi 2.00 .40
a. Sheet of 8 *40.00* —

No. 3118 issued in sheets of 40.

Emblem of 2008 Summer Olympics, Beijing — A888

2001, July 14 *Perf. 13x13¼*

3119 A888 80f multi + label .90 .60
a. Sheet of 36 + 39 labels *40.00* —

No. 3119 printed in sheets of 12 stamp + label pairs with one large central label. See Hong Kong No. 940, Macao No. 1067.

No. 3119a contains 12 each of No. 3119, Hong Kong No. 940 (with different adjacent label), and Macao No. 1067 (with different adjacent label).

Waterfalls A889

Designs: No. 3120, 80f, Yinlianzhuitan (3-1). No. 3121, 80f, Doupotang, horiz. (3-2). No. 3122, 80f, Dishuitan (3-3).
$8, Huangguoshu.

Perf. 12¼x12, 12x12¼

2001, July 22 Litho.

3120-3122 A889 Set of 3 1.50 1.00

Souvenir Sheet

Perf. 12

3123 A889 $8 multi *7.00 7.00*

No. 3123 contains one 40x60mm stamp.

Beidaihe Beach — A890

Designs: 60f, Pigeon Nest (4-1). No. 3125, 80f, Zhonghai Beach (4-2). No. 3126, 80f, Lianfeng Hill (4-3). $2.80, Tiger Stone (4-4).

2001, Aug. 5 Litho. *Perf. 12*

3124-3127 A890 Set of 4 2.00 1.75

21st Universiade A891

Emblem, "2001" and: 60f, Concentric circles (3-1). 80f, Runners (3-2). $2.80, Hemispheres of globe (3-3).

2001, Aug. 22 Litho.

3128-3130 A891 Set of 3 1.75 1.40
3129a Sheet of 20 +20 labels *22.50*

No. 3129a exists with different margin designs.

Sheets of four No. 3129 plus four labels were not placed on sale but were included with 2001 year sets. Uncut sheets containing two of these sheets also exist.

Datong River Diversion Project — A892

Designs: No. 3131, 80f, Sluice gates (4-1). No. 3132, 80f, Xianming Gorge water pipeline (4-2). No. 3133, 80f, Tunnel (4-3). $2.80, Zhuanglang River Aqueduct (4-4).

2001, Aug. 26

3131-3134 A892 Set of 4 2.25 1.75

Wuhu Bridge — A893

View from: 80f, Shore (2-1). $2.80, Roadway (2-2).

Photo. & Engr.

2001, Sept. 20 *Perf. 11½x11¼*

3135-3136 A893 Set of 2 1.60 1.25

Orchids A894

Designs: No. 3137, 80f, Paphiopedilum malipoense (4-1). No. 3138, 80f, Paphiopedilum dianthum (4-2). No. 3139, 80f, Paphiopedilum markianum (4-3). $2.80, Paphiopedilum appletonianum (4-4).

2001, Sept. 28 Photo. *Perf. 12½*

3137-3140 A894 Set of 4 2.25 2.00
3140a Souvenir sheet, #3137-3140 *6.00*

Ancient Gold Masks — A895

Designs: No. 3141, 80f, Mask of San Xing Dui (2-1). No. 3142, 80f, Funerary mask of King Tutankhamun, Egypt (2-2).

2001, Oct. 12 *Perf. 11¾x11½*

3141-3142 A895 Set of 2 2.25 1.25

See Egypt Nos. 1807-1808.

People's Republic of China as 2001 Asia-Pacific Economic Cooperation Head — A896

2001, Oct. 20 Litho. *Perf. 12*

3143 A896 80f multi .90 .35

Souvenir Sheet

Ertan Hydroelectric Plant — A897

2001, Oct. 20 Litho. *Perf. 12¼*

3144 A897 $8 multi *3.75 3.75*

Horses, Zhaoling Mausoleum A898

Horse: a, Facing right, galloping (6-1). b, Facing right, galloping, diff. (6-2). c, Facing right, walking (6-3). d, With attendant (6-4). e, Facing left, walking (6-5). f, Facing left, galloping (6-6).

2001, Oct. 28 Photo. *Perf. 12*

Fawn Background

3145 Horiz. strip of 6 3.50 3.00
a. A898 60f multi .30 .25
b.-e. A898 80f multi .40 .30
f. A898 $2.80 multi 1.00 .90
g. Sheet, 2 each #3145a-3145c, white background, photo. & embossed *16.00* —
h. Sheet, 2 each #3145d-3145f, white background, photo. & embossed *16.00* —

Sailing Ships — A899

No. 3146: a, Chinese junk, 13th cent. (2-1). b, Portuguese caravel, 15th cent. (2-2).

2001, Nov. 8 *Perf. 13x13¼*

3146 A899 80f Horiz. pair, #a-b 1.40 1.00

See Portugal No. 2454.

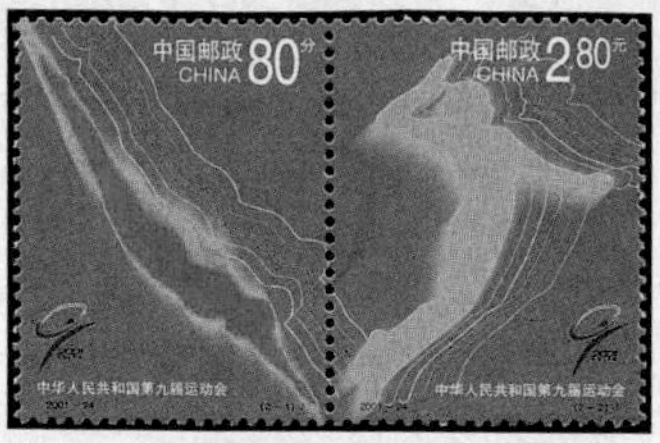

9th Natl. Games — A900

No. 3147: a, 80f, Diving (2-1). b, $2.80, Volleyball (2-2).

2001, Nov. 11 Litho. *Perf. 12*

3147 A900 Horiz. pair, #a-b 1.50 1.50
c. Souvenir sheet, #3147 *3.75 3.75*

Liupan Shan Mountains — A901

Various landscapes: No. 3148, 80f (4-1). No. 3149, 80f (4-2). No. 3150, 80f (4-3). $2.80, (4-4).

Photo. & Engr.

2001, Nov. 24 *Perf. 11¼x11½*

3148-3151 A901 Set of 4 2.25 2.00

Xiu Xian and the White Snake — A902

Designs: No. 3152, Women, umbrella (4-1). No. 3153, Three men (4-2). No. 3154, Man with sword, man with bowl (4-3). $2.80, Women on bridge (4-4).

Perf. 11½, 11½x11 (#3153-3154)

2001, Dec. 5 Photo.

3152 A902 80f multi .40 .30
a. Booklet pane of 1 *1.10* —
3153 A902 80f multi .40 .30
a. Booklet pane of 1 *1.10* —
3154 A902 80f multi .40 .30
a. Booklet pane of 1 *1.10* —
3155 A902 $2.80 multi 1.25 .90
a. Booklet pane of 1 *4.00* —
Booklet, #3152a-3155a *7.50*
Nos. 3152-3155 (4) 2.45 1.80

Admission to World Trade Organization A903

2001, Dec. 11 Photo. *Perf. 13¼x13*

3156 A903 80f multi 1.40 1.25

Koxinga's Recovery of Taiwan from the Dutch, 340th Anniv. — A904

Koxinga and: No. 3157, 80f, Warriors, ships (3-1). No. 3158, 80f, Warriors, horse (3-2). $2.80, People, trees (3-3).

Perf. 11½x11¼

2001, Dec. 13 **Photo.**
3157-3159 A904 Set of 3 2.00 1.75

Souvenir Sheet

Qinhai - Tibet Railway — A905

2001, Dec. 29 ***Perf. 13¼***
3160 A905 $8 multi 5.00 5.00

New Year 2002 (Year of the Horse) — A906

Designs: 80f, Ceramic horse (2-1). $2.80, Flowers, Chinese symbol for horse (2-2).

Photo. & Engr.

2002, Jan. 5 ***Perf. 11½***
3161-3162 A906 Set of 2 5.50 2.75

Nos. 3161-3162 each exist in a miniature sheet of six. Value, each $20.

Art of Badashanren (1626-1705) A907

Designs: 60f, Two Eagles (6-1). No. 3164, 80f, Pine Tree (6-2). No. 3165, 80f, Lotus Flowers (6-3). No. 3166, 80f, Chysanthemum in Vase (6-4). $2.60, Two Magpies on a Rock (6-5). $2.80, Landscape After Dong Yuan (6-6).

Perf. 11¼x11½

2002, Jan. 20 **Photo.**
3163-3168 A907 Set of 6 4.25 4.00

Environmental Protection — A908

Designs: 5f, Keeping birth rate low. 10f, Forest conservation. 30f, Conservation of mineral resources. 60f, Preventing air pollution. 80f, Conservation of water. $1.50, Conservation of ocean resources.

Perf. 12¾x13¼ Syncopated

2002			**Photo.**	
3169 A908	5f multi		.25	.25
3170 A908	10f multi		.30	.25
3171 A908	30f multi		.30	.25
3172 A908	60f multi		.35	.25
3173 A908	80f multi		.40	.25
3174 A908	$1.50 multi		.75	.40
	Nos. 3169-3174 (6)		2.35	1.65

Issued: 10f, 60f, 2/1; others, 4/1. See Nos. 3334-3335.

Birds — A909

Designs: 80f, Yellow-bellied tragopan. $1, Biddulph's ground jay. $2, Taiwan blue magpies. $4.20, Alashan redstart. $5.40, Kozlov's bunting.

2002		***Perf. 13¼***	
3175 A909	80f multi	.40	.30
a.	Booklet pane of 10 +2 labels	4.00	
	Booklet, #3175a	4.00	
3176 A909	$1 multi	.50	.35
3177 A909	$2 multi	.90	.65
3178 A909	$4.20 multi	1.60	1.25
3179 A909	$5.40 multi	2.00	1.50
	Nos. 3175-3179 (5)	5.40	4.05

Issued: 80f, $1, $2, 2/1; Nos. 3178, 3179, 4/1. No. 3175a, 12/7.
See Nos. 3336-3337, 3547-3548.

Flowers — A910

No. 3180: a, Camellia nitidissima (2-1). b, Couroupita guianensis (2-2).

2002, Feb. 5 ***Perf. 13¼x13***
3180 A910 80f Horiz. pair, #a-b 1.10 .85

See Malaysia Nos. 861-864.

Musical Instruments A911

Designs: 60f, Yaqin (5-1). No. 3182, 80f, Erhu (5-2). No. 3183, 80f, Banhu (5-3). No. 3184, 80f, Satar (5-4). $2.80, Matouqin (5-5).

2002, Feb. 23 **Litho.** ***Perf. 12***
3181-3185 A911 Set of 5 2.75 2.00

Souvenir Sheet

The Royal Carriage, by Yan Liben — A912

2002, Mar. 16 **Photo.**
3186 A912 $8 multi 12.00 9.00

Song Dynasty Pottery and Porcelain from Ruyao Kilns A913

Designs: 60f, Wine vessel (4-1). No. 3188, 80f, Three-legged basin (4-2). No. 3189, 80f, Bowl (4-3). $2.80, Dish (4-4).

2002, Mar. 30 **Litho.**
3187-3190 A913 Set of 4 2.50 2.00

Strange Stories from a Chinese Studio, by Pu Songling A914

No. 3191: a, 60f, Xi Fangping (4-1). b, 80f, Pianpian (4-2).
No. 3192: a, 80f, Tian Qilang (4-3). b, $2.80, Bai Qiulian (4-4).

2002, Apr. 21 **Photo.** ***Perf. 11½***
3191 A914 Vert. pair, #a-b 1.00 .90
3192 A914 Horiz. pair, #a-b 1.60 1.25

Qianshan Mountain — A915

No. 3193: a, Wuliang Taoist Temple (4-1). b, Maitreya Peak (4-2). c, Longquan Temple (4-3). d, Terrace of Immortals (4-4).

2002, Apr. 26		***Perf. 12***	
3193 A915	Horiz. strip of 4	2.25	2.00
a.-c.	80f Any single	.30	.25
d.	$2.80 multi	.90	.70

Ancient City of Lijiang — A916

Designs: No. 3194, 80f, Sifang Street (3-1). No. 3195, 80f, Stream, vert. (3-2). $2.80, House of Naxi people (3-3).

2002, May 1 ***Perf. 11½***
3194-3196 A916 Set of 3 4.25 2.00
a. Souvenir sheet, #3194-3196 5.50 5.00

No. 3196a sold for $6.60.

Ruyi (Good Luck Symbol) — A917

2002, May 10 **Litho.** ***Perf. 12***
3197 A917 80f multi + label .60 .30

Exists in miniature sheet of 4 + 4 vert. labels (value $6) and in sheet of 16 + 16 horiz. labels (value $20).

Stamps with Attached Labels

Starting with No. 3197, stamps listed as having attached labels are known to have been issued in dozens of different sheets having various margin and label designs, various numbers of stamps and labels in the sheets, and different stamp and label combinations. Little information has been made available about these sheets, and all seem to have been sold for prices significantly above face value. Labels on these sheets do not seem to have been personalizable with personal photos but have illustrations with approved designs.

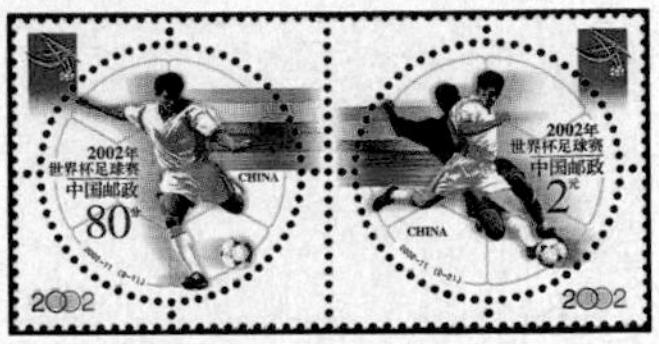

2002 World Cup Soccer Championships, Japan and Korea — A918

No. 3198: a, 80f, Player (2-1). b, $2.80, Players (2-2).

2002, May 16 **Photo.** ***Perf. 12¼***
3198 A918 Horiz. pair, #a-b 1.50 1.25

A souvenir sheet containing People's Republic of China No. 3198, Hong Kong Nos. 978a-978b and Macao 1091a-1091b exists, and sold for premium over face value. Value $17.50.

Lighthouses A919

Nautical charts and: No. 3199, 80f, Maota Pagoda Lighthouse (5-1). No. 3200, 80f, Jiangxin Pagoda Lighthouses (5-2). No. 3201, 80f, Huaniaoshan Lighthouse (5-3). No. 3202, 80f, Laotieshan Lighthouse (5-4). No. 3203, 80f, Lin'gao Lighthouse (5-5).

Photo. & Engr.

2002, May 18 ***Perf. 11½x11***
3199-3203 A919 Set of 5 2.25 1.50

Yellow River Dams A920

Designs: No. 3204, 80f, Lijia Gorge (4-1). No. 3205, 80f, Liujia Gorge (4-2). No. 3206, 80f, Qingtong Gorge (4-3). No. 3207, 80f, Sanmen Gorge (4-4).
$8, Xiaolangdi, vert.

2002, June 8 **Photo.** ***Perf. 12***
3204-3207 A920 Set of 4 1.60 1.25

Souvenir Sheet

Perf. 13x13¼

3208 A920 $8 multi 3.50 3.00

No. 3208 contains one 40x60mm stamp.

Dazu Stone Carvings — A921

Designs: No. 3209, 80f, Avalokitesvara of the Sun and Moon, North Mountain (4-1). No. 3210, 80f, Samantabhadra, North Mountain (4-2). No. 3211, 80f, Three Avatamasaka Sages, Holy Summit Mountain (4-3). No. 3212, 80f, Statue in Cave of the Three Emperors, Stone Gate Mountain (4-4).

$8, Avalokitesvara of a Thousand Hands, Holy Summit Mountain.

2002, June 18 Litho. *Perf. 12*
3209-3212 A921 Set of 4 1.40 1.00

Souvenir Sheet

Photo.

Perf. 13x13¼

3213 A921 $8 multi 3.25 2.75

No. 3213 contains one 40x60mm stamp.

Desert Flowers A922

No. 3214: a, Ammopiptanthus mongolicus (4-1). b, Calligonum rubicandum (4-2). c, Hedysarum scoparium (4-3). d, Tamarix leptostachys (4-4).

2002, June 29 Photo. *Perf. 13x13¼*
3214 Vert. strip of 4 1.75 1.50
a.-c. A922 80f Any single .35 .25
d. A922 $2 multi .70 .60

Antarctic Scenes A923

Designs: No. 3215, 80f, Penguins (3-1). No. 3216, 80f, Aurora Australis (3-2). $2, Bird, Grove Mountains (3-3).

2002, July 15 Litho. *Perf. 12*
3215-3217 A923 Set of 3 1.75 1.25

Qinghai Lake — A924

Designs: No. 3218, 80f, Lake shore (3-1). No. 3219, 80f, Birds on rock (3-2). $2.80, View of lake and birds (3-3).

2002, July 20
3218-3220 A924 Set of 3 1.75 1.40

Early Communist Party Leaders — A925

Designs: No. 3221, 80f, Huang Gonglue (1898-1931) (5-1). No. 3222, 80f, Xu Jishen (1901-31) (5-2). No. 3223, 80f, Cai Shengxi (1906-32) (5-3). No. 3224, 80f, Wei Baqun (1894-1932) (5-4). No. 3225, 80f, Liu Zhidan (1903-36) (5-5).

2002, Aug. 1 Photo.
3221-3225 A925 Set of 5 3.25 2.00

Scientists of Ancient China — A926

Designs: No. 3226, 80f, Bian Que (4-1). No. 3227, 80f, Liu Hui (4-2). No. 3228, 80f, Su Song (4-3). No. 3229, 80f, Song Yingxing (4-4).

Photo. & Engr.

2002, Aug. 20 *Perf. 11¼x11*
3226-3229 A926 Set of 4 1.75 1.25

Yandangshan Mountain — A927

Designs: No. 3230, 80f, Xianshengmen Gate (4-1). No. 3231, 80f, Dalongqui Pond (4-2). No. 3232, 80f, Beidou Cave, horiz. (4-3). No. 3233, 80f, Guanyin Peak, horiz. (4-4).

2002, Sept. 7 Litho. *Perf. 12¾*
3230-3233 A927 Set of 4 1.50 1.25

Mid-Autumn Festival — A928

Designs: No. 3234, 80f, Family reunion (3-1). No. 3235, 80f, People looking at Moon (3-2). $2, The Moon as a matchmaker (3-3).

2002, Sept. 21 *Perf. 12*
3234-3236 A928 Set of 3 1.75 1.40

Each printed in sheets of 20. Sheets of nine containing three of each stamp exist with a decorative border (value $25) and a border with Chinese text for the Beijing 2002 Stamp Exhibition (value $55).

Peng Zhen (1902-97) — A929

Designs: No. 3237, 80f, Head of Peng Zhen (2-1). No. 3238, 80f, Peng Zhen standing (2-2).

2002, Oct. 12 *Perf. 11¾x12*
3237-3238 A929 Set of 2 1.10 .60

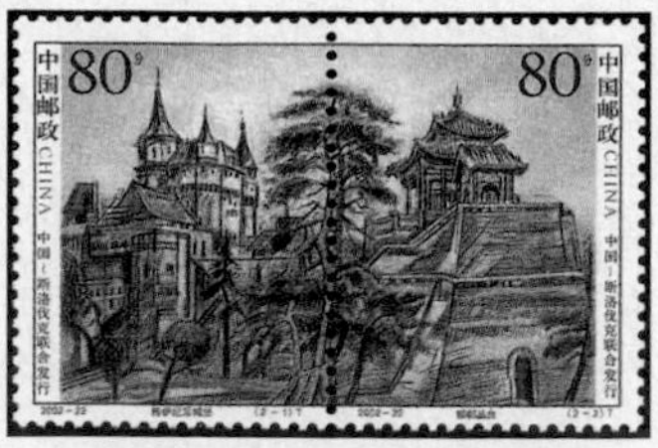

Architecture in Slovakia and China — A930

No. 3239: a, Bojnice Castle, Slovakia (2-1). b, Handan Congtai Pavilion, China (2-2).

Photo. & Engr.

2002, Oct. 12 *Perf. 11¼x11*
3239 A930 80f Horiz. pair, #a-b .80 .60

See Slovakia No. 410.

Dong Yong and Lady — A931

No. 3240: a, Dong Yong's filial love moves immortals (5-1). b, Dong Yong marries seventh immortal maiden (5-2). c, Immortal maiden weaving brocade (5-3). d, Dong Yong returns home (5-4). e, Everlasting love (5-5).

2002, Oct. 26 Litho. *Perf. 13¼x13*
3240 Horiz. strip of 5 2.25 2.00
a.-d. A931 80f Any single .35 .25
e. A931 $2 multi .70 .50

Nos. 3240a-3240e exist in booklet panes of one that made up a booklet that had limited distribution to people with standing order accounts.

Flower — A932

2002, Nov. 8 Litho. *Perf. 12*
3241 A932 80f multi + label .60 .50

Exists in a miniature sheet of 4 + 4 labels.

Souvenir Sheet

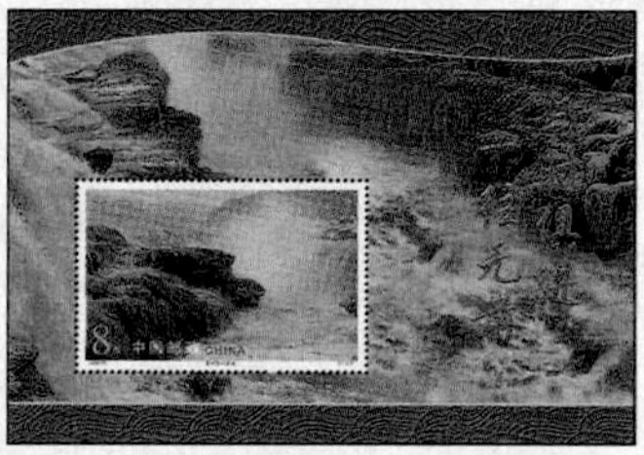

Hukou Waterfall — A933

Photo. (Margin Photo. & Embossed)

2002, Nov. 8 *Perf. 13¼x13*
3242 A933 $8 multi *19.50 10.00*

Museums — A934

Designs: No. 3243, 80f, Shanxi History Museum (5-1). No. 3244, 80f, Shanghai Museum (5-2). No. 3245, 80f, Henan Museum (5-3). No. 3246, 80f, Tibet Museum (5-4). No. 3247, 80f, Tianjin Natural Museum.

2002, Nov. 9 Photo. *Perf. 12¾*
3243-3247 A934 Set of 5 2.00 1.50

Martial Arts A935

No. 3248: a, Kung Fu (2-1). b, Taekwondo (2-2)

2002, Nov. 20 Photo. *Perf. 12*
3248 A935 80f Vert. pair, #a-b 1.10 .80

No. 3248 is a joint issue with South Korea No. 2109.

Gibbons — A936

Designs: No. 3249, 80f, Hylobates lar (4-1). No. 3250, 80f, Hylobates leucogenys (4-2). No. 3251, 80f, Hylobates concolor (4-3). $2, Hylobates hoolock (4-4).

Photo. & Engr.

2002, Dec. 7 *Perf. 11¼x11*
3249-3252 A936 Set of 4 1.75 1.40

New Year 2003 (Year of the Ram) — A937

Designs: 80f, Ram (2-1). $2, Chinese symbol (2-2).

Photo. & Engr.

2003, Jan. 5 *Perf. 11½*
3253-3254 A937 Set of 2 7.50 3.75

Sheets of 8 + central label of Nos. 3253-3254 exist. Value, each $65. Sheets of 6 of Nos. 3253-3254 also exist. Value, each $45.

Yangliuqing New Year Woodprints A938

Designs: No. 3255, 80f, Five boys wrestling for a lotus (4-1). No. 3256, 80f, Zhong Kui, vert. (4-2). No. 3257, 80f, Steaing the herb of immortality (4-3). $2, Wealth in a jade hall (4-4).

2003, Jan. 25 Photo. *Perf. 12*
3255-3258 A938 Set of 4 4.25 3.00

A sheet containing two each Nos. 3255-3258 exists. Value $22.50.

Seal Characters A939

Designs: No. 3259, 80f, 24 characters (2-1). No. 3260, 80f, 12 characters (2-2).

2003, Feb. 22 **Litho.**
3259-3260 A939 Set of 2 4.50 1.25

A sheet exists containg four each Nos. 3259-3260. Value $50.

Knot A940

2003, Feb. 3
3261 A940 80f multi + label 1.00 .60

Exists in sheets of 4 stamps + 4 labels. Value $20.
Perf 12¾ examples come from a sheetlet containing four examples with labels below the stamps that also contain four No. 3375. The sheetlet sold for $15.

Lilies A941

Designs: 60f, Lilium taliense (4-1). No. 3263, 80f, Lilium lankongense (4-2). No. 3264, 80f, Lilium distichum (4-3). $2, Lilium lophophorum (4-4).
$8, Lilium leucanthum.

2003, Mar. 5 **Photo.** ***Perf. 13x13¼***
3262-3265 A941 Set of 4 4.25 2.50

Souvenir Sheet

Perf. 13¼

3266 A941 $8 multi 2.00 1.25

Nos. 3262-3265 each exist in sheets of 10. Value, set of 4, $25.
No. 3266 contains one 75x53mm stamp.

Arch Bridges — A942

Designs: No. 3267, 80f, Maple Bridge (4-1). No. 3268, 80f, Xiaoshang Bridge (4-2). No. 3269, 80f, Lugouqiao Bridge (4-3). No. 3270, 80f, Double Dragon Bridge (4-4).

Photo. & Engr.

2003, Mar. 29 ***Perf. 11½***
3267-3270 A942 Set of 4 2.00 1.25

A sheet of 8 exists for each of Nos. 3267-3270. Value, set of 2, $70.

Chinese and Iranian Buildings A943

Designs: No. 3271, 80f, Bell Tower, Xian, China (2-1). No. 3272, 80f, Mosque, Isfahan, Iran (2-2).

2003, Apr. 15 **Photo.** ***Perf. 13x13¼***
3271-3272 A943 Set of 2 2.75 1.50

See Iran No. 2856.
A sheet exists containing 4 each Nos. 3271-3272. Value $15.

Souvenir Sheet

Leshan Giant Buddha — A944

Photo. & Engr.

2003, Apr. 28 ***Perf. 12***
3273 A944 $8 multi 3.75 3.25

Gulangyu Island — A945

No. 3274: a, Eight Diagram Building (3-1). b, Sunlight Rock (3-2). c, Shuzhuang Park (3-3)

2003, May 2 **Photo.** ***Perf. 12***

3274	Horiz. strip of 3	1.80	1.50
a.-b.	A945 80f Either single	.35	.25
c.	A945 $2 multi	.75	.60
d.	Souvenir sheet, #3274	3.50	3.00

A souvenir sheet exists containing 3 No. 3274. Value $45.

Campaign to Combat Epidemic of Severe Acute Respiratory Syndrome — A946

2003, May 19 ***Perf. 13¼x13***
3275 A946 80f multi *37.50 15.00*

Beware of counterfeits of No. 3275.

Strange Stories from a Chinese Studio, by Pu Songling A947

Designs: 10f, Xiang Yu (6-1). 30f, Tiger of Zhaocheng (6-2). 60f, Huanniang (6-3). 80f, Ah Xiu (6-4). $1.50, Wang Gui'an (6-5). $2, Goddess (6-6).
$8, Princess of Dongting Lake, horiz.

2003, May 16 ***Perf. 12***
3276-3281 A947 Set of 6 2.75 2.25

Souvenir Sheet

Perf. 13¼x13

3282 A947 $8 multi 5.50 5.50

No. 3282 contains one 90x60mm stamp.
Sheets exist containing 4 each of Nos. 3276-3277, 3278-3279 and 3280-3281. Value, set $42.50

1976 Meteorite Shower Over Jilin — A948

Designs: No. 3283, 80f, Meteorites falling (3-1). No. 3284, 80f, Dispersal of meteorites (3-2). $2, Meteorite (3-3).

2003, June 21 **Litho.**
3283-3285 A948 Set of 3 2.00 1.25

A sheet exists containing 3 each of Nos. 3283-3285. Value $45.

Master-of-Nets Garden, Suzhou — A949

No. 3286: a, 80f, Late Spring Cottage (4-1). b, 80f, Pavilion Greeting the Moon and Breeze (4-2). c, 80f, Veranda of Bamboo (4-3). d, $2, Hall of Ten Thousand Volumes (4-4).

2003, June 29 **Photo.** ***Perf. 12¾***
3286 A949 Horiz. strip of 4, #a-d 3.25 2.50

A sheet exists containing 2 No. 3286. Value $42.

Tibetan Antelopes A950

Designs: 80f, Antelopes and mountain (2-1). $2, Antelope's head, adult with young (2-2).

Photo. & Engr.

2003, July 20 ***Perf. 11x11¼***
3287-3288 A950 Set of 2 1.50 1.50

Sheets exist containing 3 each of Nos. 3287-3288. Value, set $34.

Kongtong Mountain — A951

No. 3289: a, 80f, Town of Huangcheng (4-1). b, 80f, Gorge of Playing the Zither (4-2). c, 80f, Pagoda Courtyard (4-3). d, $2, Peak of Thunder (4-4).

2003, July 26 **Litho.** ***Perf. 12***
3289 A951 Block of 4, #a-d 2.25 2.00

A sheet exists containing 2 No. 3289. Value, $50.

Sailing Ship — A952

2003, Aug. 5
3290 A952 80f multi + label 1.00 1.00

No. 3290 exists in sheets of 4 stamps + 4 labels. Value $7.

Powered Flight, Cent. — A953

Designs: 80f, Foreign airplanes (2-1). $2, Chinese airplanes (2-2).

2003, Aug. 9 **Photo.** ***Perf. 12¾***
3291-3292 A953 Set of 2 1.75 1.25

A sheet exists containing 6 each of Nos. 3291-3292. Value, $38.

Jinci Temple Painted Statues — A954

Designs: No. 3293, 80f, Ruyi maid (4-1). No. 3294, 80f, Maid holding a towel (4-2). No. 3295, 80f, Maid carrying a royal seal (4-3). $2, Maid singing and dancing (4-4).

2003, Aug. 16 ***Perf. 11¾x12***
3293-3296 A954 Set of 4 4.00 1.50

Sheets exist containing four each of Nos. 3293-3294 and 3295-3296. Value, set of 2 sheets $45.

Three Gorges Project — A955

Designs: No. 3297, 80f, Dam and reservoir (3-1). No. 3298, 80f, Ship locks (3-2). $2, Power plant and high tension wire towers (3-3).

2003, Aug. 20 **Litho.** ***Perf. 12***
3297-3299 A955 Set of 3 1.90 1.40

A sheet exists containing 3 each of Nos. 3297-3299. Value, $22.

Traditional Sports of Ethnic Minorities A956

Designs: No. 3300, 80f, Wrestling (4-1). b, No. 3301, 80f, Archery (4-2). No. 3302, 80f, Horse racing (4-3). No. 3303, 80f, Swinging (4-4).

2003, Sept. 5 **Photo.** ***Perf. 13x13½***

3300-3303	A956 Set of 4	1.50	1.10
3303a	Souvenir sheet, #3300-3303	2.50	2.00

No. 3303a sold for $5. Sheets exist containing four each of No. 3300-3301 and 3302-3303. Value, set $30.

Tiananmen Gate, Beijing — A957

2003, Sept. 10 **Litho.** ***Perf. 12***
3304 A957 80f multi + label .90 .45

Two different sheets each containing four examples of No. 3304 were included in a souvenir folder sold only at the International Stamp and Coin Expo in Beijing in 2004. Value, set of 2 $8. Two additional sheets of four stamps + four labels, perf. 12½, exist. Value, set of 2 $30.

General Yue Fei (1103-42) — A958

Designs: No. 3305, 80f, Mother tattooing "Loyalty to the Country" on Yue Fei's back (3-1). No. 3306, 80f, Yue Fei standing with sword (3-2). $2, Yue Fei seated (3-3).

2003, Sept. 25
3305-3307 A958 Set of 3 1.75 1.25

A sheet exists containing 3 each of Nos. 3305-3307. Value, $39.

Souvenir Sheet

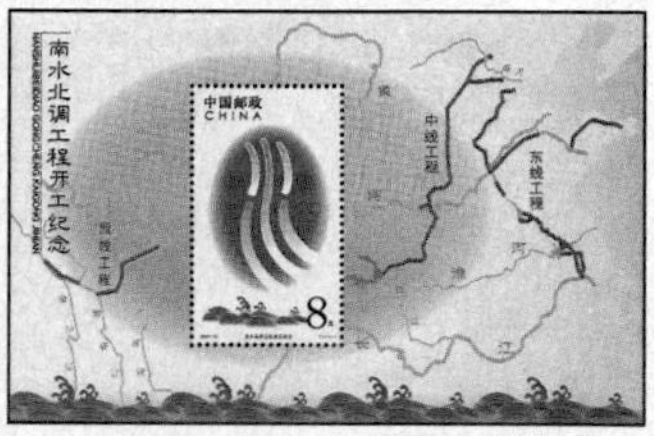

Water Diversion Projects — A959

2003, Sept. 26 Photo. *Perf. 12¾*
3308 A959 $8 multi 3.00 2.50

Book Printing — A960

Designs: No. 3309, 80f, Ritual of Zhou, China (2-1). No. 3310, 80f, Hungarian Illuminated Chronicle, 1473 (2-2).

2003, Sept. 30 Litho. *Perf. 12*
3309-3310 A960 Set of 2 1.50 1.00

Nos. 3309-3310 have large perforation holes at the stamp corners. A sheet exists containing 4 each of Nos. 3309-3310 in se-tenant pairs. Value, $40.

See Hungary Nos. 3863-3864.

Double Ninth Festival — A961

Designs: No. 3311, 80f, Climbing mountain (3-1). No. 3312, 80f, Enjoying the beauty of chrysanthemums (3-2). $2, Playing chess and drinking wine (3-3).

2003, Oct. 4 Photo. *Perf. 11½*
3311-3313 A961 Set of 3 1.75 1.25

A sheet exists containing 3 each of Nos. 3311-3313 in strips of 3. Value, $16.

Launch of First Manned Chinese Spacecraft A962

No. 3314: a, 80f, Astronaut, Shenzhou spacecraft (2-1). b, $2, Yang Liwei, flag (2-2).

2003, Oct. 16 *Perf. 13x13¼*
3314 A962 Pair, #a-b 11.50 7.50

A booklet containing No. 3314, Hong Kong No. 1062 and Macao No. 1128 exists. The booklet sold for a premium over face value. Value, $20.

Folktale of Liang Shanbo and Zhu Yingtai — A963

Designs: No. 3315, 80f, Zhu Yingtai, disguised as a man, and Liang Shanbo become sworn brothers at Caoqiao (5-1). No. 3316, 80f, Classmates for three years (5-2). No. 3317, 80f, Bidding farewell (5-3). No. 3318, 80f, Sad parting on the terrace (5-4). $2, Turning into butterflies (5-5).

2003, Oct. 18 *Perf. 12*
3315-3319 A963 Set of 5 3.00 1.75

A booklet containing booklet panes of 1 of each of Nos. 3315-3319 exists. Value, $7.50. A sheet exists containing 2 each of Nos. 3315-3319. Value, $25.

China 2003 Intl. Stamp Exhibition, Mianyang A964

2003, Nov. 20 Photo. *Perf. 13¼*
3320 A964 80f multi 1.00 .60

World AIDS Day — A965

2003, Dec. 1 *Perf. 11¼x11*
3321 A965 80f multi 2.00 1.00

Mao Zedong (1893-1976) — A966

Mao: No. 3322, 80f, Seated in folding chair (4-1). No. 3323, 80f, Standing (4-2). No. 3324, 80f, Seated on bench (4-3). No. 3325, 80f, Seated at desk (4-4).

Litho. & Engr.

2003, Dec. 6 *Perf. 12*
3322-3325 A966 Set of 4 16.00 9.00

A sheet exists containing 2 each of Nos. 3322-3325 in se-tenant strips of 4. Value, $100.

Bronze Objects of Eastern Zhou Dyansty — A967

Designs: No. 3326, 60f, Square plate with turtle and fish patterns (8-1). No. 3327, 60f, Gui of the Duke of Qin (handled bowl with lid) (8-2). No. 3328, 80f, Iron-footed tripod of the King of Zhongshan (8-3). No. 3329, 80f, Gourd-shaped ladle of Yi, the Marquis of Zeng (8-4). No. 3330, 80f, Divine animal wine vessel, vert. (8-5). No. 3331, 80f, Wine vessel with phoenix pattern, vert. (8-6). $1, Square pot with lotus and cranes design, vert. (8-7). $2, Tripod with a dragon-shaped handle, vert. (8-8).

Perf. 11½x11¼, 11¼x11½

2003, Dec. 13 Photo. & Engr.
3326-3333 A967 Set of 8 6.25 3.00

A sheet of 8 No. 3328 exists. Value, $45.

Environmental Protection Type of 2002

Designs: 50f, Prevention and control of desertification. $4.50, Protection of biodiversity.

Perf. 12¾x13¼ Syncopated

2004, Jan. 1 Photo.
3334 A908 50f multi .35 .35
3335 A908 $4.50 multi 1.50 .90

Bird Type of 2002

Designs: $5, Yellow-bellied tit. $6, Yunnan nuthatch.

2004, Jan. 1 *Perf. 13¼*
3336 A909 $5 multi 1.75 1.60
3337 A909 $6 multi 2.00 1.90

New Year 2004 (Year of the Monkey) A968

2004, Jan. 5 *Perf. 13 Syncopated*
3338 A968 80f multi 2.50 1.25
a. Booklet pane of 10 25.00 —
Complete booklet, #3338a 27.00

Sheets of 4 and sheets of 6 exist. Value, set $70.

Taohuawu New Year Pictures — A969

Designs: No. 3339, 80f, Feelings of Pipa (4-1). No. 3340, 80f, Kylin Bringing a Son (4-2). No. 3341, 80f, Liu Hai Playing with the Golden Toad (4-3). $2, Ten Beauties Playing Football (4-4).

2004, Jan. 14 Litho. *Perf. 12*
3339-3342 A969 Set of 4 1.50 1.25
3342a Souvenir sheet, #3339-3342 7.00 5.50

A sheet of 2 each of Nos. 3339-3342 in se-tenant blocks of 4 exists. Value, $12.

Deng Yingchao (1904-92), Communist Party Leader — A970

No. 3343: a, Holding book. b, Portrait.

2004, Feb. 4 Litho. & Engr.
3343 A970 80f Vert. pair, #a-b 1.25 1.25

Suzhou Industrial Park, 10th Anniv. A971

2004, Mar. 1 Photo. *Perf. 13x13¼*
3344 A971 80f multi 1.00 .50

See Singapore No. 1084.

Red Cross Society, Cent. — A972

2004, Mar. 10 *Perf. 11¼x11*
3345 A972 80f multi .70 .35

Stories Explaining Chinese Idioms A973

Idioms: No. 3346, 80f, Trying to learn the Handan walk (4-1). No. 3347, 80f, Lord Ye's love for dragon (4-2). No. 3348, 80f, Filling a position in a Yu band (4-3). No. 3349, 80f, When the snipe and the clam grapple (4-4).

Perf. 12½x13¼ Syncopated

2004, Apr. 2
3346-3349 A973 Set of 4 1.75 1.25

A sheet of 2 each of Nos. 3346-3349 in se-tenant strips of 4 exists. Value, $15.

Peacocks — A974

Designs: No. 3350, 80f, Blue peacock (2-1). No. 3351, 80f, Albino peacock, vert. (2-2). $6, Green peacocks.

2004, Apr. 13 *Perf. 12¾*
3350-3351 A974 Set of 2 .80 .60

Souvenir Sheet
Perf. 13¼x13

3352 A974 $6 multi 4.00 3.25

No. 3352 contains one 60x40mm stamp

Nanxi River — A975

No. 3353: a, River and mountain (4-1). b, Tree and boat in foreground, mountains in background (4-2). c, Rocks, boat in river (4-3). d, Boat, spit of land with trees (4-4).

2004, Apr. 24 Photo. *Perf. 12¾*

3353	Horiz. strip of 4	2.00	1.60
a.	A975 60f multi	.30	.25
b.-c.	A975 80f Either single	.40	.30
d.	A975 $2 multi	.75	.55

Danxia Mountain — A976

Designs: 60f, Sengmao Peak (4-1). No. 3355, 80f, Xianlong Lake (4-2). No. 3356, 80f, Chahu Peak (4-3). $2, Jinjiang River (4-4).

2004, May 1 Litho. & Engr. *Perf. 12*

3354-3357 A976 Set of 4 1.75 1.40

Economic and Technological Development Zones, 20th Anniv. — A977

2004, May 4 Litho.

3358 A977 80f multi .80 .50

Exists in a sheet of 8 stamps + 8 labels. Value, $6.

Hometowns of Returned Chinese — A978

Designs: No. 3359, 80f, Xinglong Overseas Chinese Farm (4-1). No. 3360, 80f, Jinan University (4-2). No. 3361, 80f, Fuqing Rongqiao Development Zone (4-3). No. 3362, 80f, Kaiping (4-4).

2004, May 15 Photo. *Perf. 11x11¼*

3359-3362 A978 Set of 4 1.40 1.10

Sima Guang Breaking the Vat — A979

Designs: No. 3363, 80f, Sima Guang falling into water (3-1). No. 3362, 80f, Breaking vat (3-2). No. 3363, $2, Rescued (3-3).

2004, June 1 *Perf. 12*

3363-3365 A979 Set of 3 1.40 1.25

A sheet of 2 each of Nos. 3363-3365 exists. Value, $18.

Scenes of Villages of Southern Anhui Province A980

Designs: No. 3366, 80f, Archway (4-1). No. 3367, 80f, Old buildings (4-2). No. 3368, 80f, Buildings on South Lake (4-3). No. 3369, 80f, Moon Pond (4-4).

Photo. & Engr.

2004, June 25 *Perf. 11x11¼*

3366-3369 A980 Set of 4 1.40 1.25

Liu Yi Delivering a Letter — A981

Designs: No. 3370, 80f, Dragon Princess asking Liu Yi to deliver a letter (4-1). No. 3371, 80f, Delivering letter to Dongting Lake (4-2). No. 3372, 80f, Family reunion (4-3). $2, Couple embracing (4-4).

2004, July 17 Photo. *Perf. 13¼x13*

3370	A981 80f multi	.35	.30
a.	Booklet pane of 1	.75	—
3371	A981 80f multi	.35	.30
a.	Booklet pane of 1	.75	—
3372	A981 80f multi	.35	.30
a.	Booklet pane of 1	.75	—
3373	A981 $2 multi	.75	.30
a.	Booklet pane of 1	2.00	—
	Complete booklet, #3370a-3373a	4.50	
	Nos. 3370-3373 (4)	1.80	1.20

Complete booklet sold for $6.

Souvenir Sheet

Eight Immortals Crossing the Sea — A982

2004, July 30 *Perf. 12 Syncopated*

3374 A982 $6 multi 4.50 4.00

Peony — A983

2004, July 31 Litho. *Perf. 12¾*

3375 A983 80f multi + label .65 .45

Perf 12¾ examples come from a sheet containing four examples with labels below the stamps that also contain four No. 3261. The sheetlet sold for $15. Value, $17.50.

2004 Summer Olympics, Athens — A984

Olympic rings and: No. 3376, 80f, Parthenon, Athens (2-1). No. 3377, 80f, Hall of Good Harvest, Temple of Heaven, Beijing.

2004, Aug. 13 Photo. *Perf. 12¾*

3376-3377 A984 Set of 2 1.00 1.00

Perf. 12¾ examples come from a sheet containing four examples with labels below the stamps that also contain four No. 3261. The sheetlet sold for $15. Value, $17.50.

See Greece Nos. 2124-2125.

Deng Xiaoping (1904-97), Chinese Leader — A985

Designs: No. 3378, 80f, Walking (2-1). No. 3379, 80f, Saluting, horiz. (2-2), $6, Seated.

2004, Aug. 22 *Perf. 12 Syncopated*

3378-3379 A985 Set of 2 2.00 1.10

Souvenir Sheet
Perf. 13 Syncopated

3380 A985 $6 multi 3.50 3.25

No. 3380 contains one 47x57mm stamp.

South China Tiger A986

Designs: 80f, Head (2-1), $2, Adult and young (2-2).

2004, Aug. 23 Litho. *Perf. 12*

3381-3382 A986 Set of 2 1.40 1.10

A sheet of 4 each of Nos. 3381-3382 in se-tenant pairs exists. Value, $17.50.

People's Congress, 50th Anniv. — A987

Designs: No. 3383, 80f, Congress members arriving at Huairentang Hall of Zhongnanhai (2-1). No. 3384, 80f, Interior of Great Hall of the People (2-2).

2004, Sept. 15 *Perf. 13¼*

3383-3384 A987 Set of 2 1.25 1.00

A sheet containing 3 pairs of Nos. 3383-3384 exists. Value, $15.

Bloodstone Seals A988

No. 3385: a, 80f, Seal of Emperor Qianlong (2-1). b, $2, Seal of Emperor Jiaqing (2-2).

Litho. & Embossed

2004, Sept. 17 *Perf. 13x13¼*

3385 A988 Pair, #a-b 1.50 1.10

Celery Wormwood A989

Designs: No. 3386, 80f, Purple flowers (4-1). No. 3387, 80f, Blue flowers (4-2). No. 3388, 80f, Red flowers (4-3). $2, Yellow flowers (4-4).

2004, Sept. 19 Photo. *Perf. 13¼x13*

3386-3389 A989 Set of 4 1.75 1.50

A sheet containing 2 strips of 3386-3389 exists. Value, $15.

Chinese and Romanian Handicrafts A990

Designs: No. 3390, 80f, Drum with tigers and birds, China (2-1). No. 3391, 80f, Cucuteni pottery jar, Romania (2-2).

2004, Sept. 22 *Perf. 13 Syncopated*

3390-3391 A990 Set of 2 1.10 1.00

A sheet containing 4 pairs of Nos. 3390-3391 exists.

See Romania No. 4668.

National Symbols A991

Designs: No. 3392, 80f, Flag (2-1). No. 3393, 80f, Arms, vert. (2-2).

Perf. 13¼x13 Syncopated, 13x13¼ Syncopated

2004, Sept. 30

3392-3393 A991 Set of 2 3.00 2.50

A sheet of 4 self-adhesive examples of both Nos. 3392 and 3393 was included in a souvenir folder sold only at the International Stamp and Coin Expo in Beijing in 2004. Value, $35.

Landscapes of Chinese Borderlands — A992

Designs: No. 3394, 80f, Forest, Xing'an Mountains (12-1). No. 3395, 80f, Lake in Yalu River Basin (12-2). No. 3396, 80f, Reefs in Yellow Sea (12-3). No. 3397, 80f, Zhoushan Archipelago (12-4). No. 3398, 80f, Coast of Taiwan (12-5). No. 3399, 80f, Xisha Islands (12-6). No. 3400, 80f, Karst landscape, Southern Guangxi (12-7). No. 3401, 80f, Rain forest, Southern Yunnan (12-8). No. 3402, 80f, Mt. Qomolangma (12-9). No. 3403, 80f, Pamirs (12-10). No. 3404, 80f, Badain Jaran Desert (12-11). No. 3405, 80f, Hulun Buir Steppe (12-12).

2004, Oct. 1 ***Perf. 12¾***

3394-3405 A992 Set of 12 3.75 3.00
3405a Sheet of 12, #3394-3405 + central label 10.00 7.50

Buildings in China and Spain — A993

Designs: No. 3406, 80f, Jinmao Tower, China (2-1). No. 3407, 80f, Park Guell, Spain.

2004, Oct. 8 ***Perf. 13¼x13***

3406-3407 A993 Set of 2 1.25 .90

See Spain Nos. 3319-3320.

Miniature Sheet

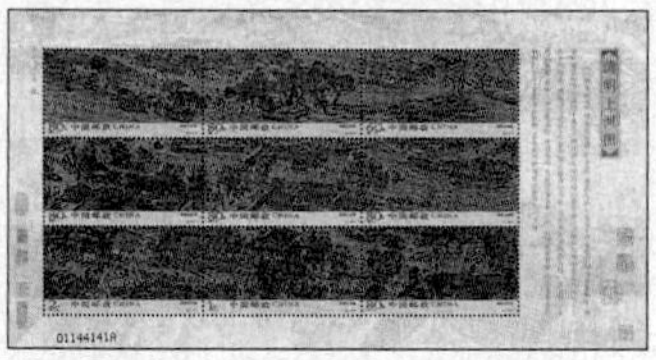

The Festival of Pure Brightness on the River, by Zhang Zeduan — A994

No. 3408 — Various details from painting: a, 60f, Trees (9-1). b, 80f, Trees, people on horseback (9-2). c, 80f, Buildings, boats on river (9-3). d, 80f, Buildings, boats on river, diff. (9-4). e, 80f, Bridge (9-5). f, 80f, Buildings, boats on river (9-6). g, 80f, Buildings (9-7). h, $1, Tower (9-8). i, $2, Intersection (9-9).

Litho. & Engr.

2004, Oct. 18 ***Perf. 12***

3408 A994 Sheet of 9, #a-i 18.00 15.00

Phoenix — A995

2004, Nov. 1 Litho. ***Perf. 12¾***

3409 A995 80f multi + label .80 .30

A sheet of 4 No. 3409 + label exists. Value, $6.

A sheet of 10 serpentine die cut 12¼ self-adhesive stamps like No. 3409 + 10 labels depicting Snoopy for 25 yuan. Value, $15.

Pavilions — A996

Designs: No. 3410, 80f, Aiwan (4-1). No. 3411, 80f, Pipa (4-2). No. 3412, 80f, Lan (4-3). No. 3413, 80f, Zuiweng (4-4).

2004, Nov. 6 Photo. ***Perf. 13¼x13***

3410-3413 A996 Set of 4 1.40 .90

A sheet of 2 each of Nos. 3410-3413 exists. Value, $13.

Ancient Calligraphy A997

Designs: No. 3414, 80f, Yiying stele (4-1). No. 3415, 80f, Zhangqian stele (4-2). No. 3416, 80f, Caoquan stele (4-3). No. 3417, 80f, Shimen song (4-4).

Photo. & Engr.

2004, Dec. 5 ***Perf. 11¼x11***

3414-3417 A997 Set of 4 2.50 .90

A sheet of 2 each of Nos. 3414-3417 exists. Value, $10.

New Year 2005 (Year of the Rooster) A998

Perf. 13 Syncopated

2005, Jan. 5 Photo.

3418 A998 80f multi 1.00 .35
a. Booklet pane of 10 10.00 —
Complete booklet, #3418a 10.00

No. 3418 exists in sheets of 4 and 6. Value, $17 each.

Tarim-Baihe Gas Pipeline — A999

No. 3419: a, 80f, Derrick (2-1). b, $3, Pipes (2-2).

2005, Jan. 8 Litho. ***Perf. 12***

3419 A999 Horiz. pair, #a-b 2.00 1.25

Historic Structures in Taiwan A1000

No. 3420: a, North Gate, Taipei City Wall (5-1). b, Confucian Temple (5-2). c, Longshan Temple, Lugang (5-3). d, Erkunshen Cannon Fort, Tainan (5-4). e, Matsu Temple, Penghu (5-5).

Perf. 13 Syncopated

2005, Jan. 30 Litho. & Engr.

3420 Vert. strip of 5 2.25 1.75
a.-d. A1000 80f Any single .30 .25
e. A1000 $1.50 multi .60 .45

Yangjiabu New Year Woodprints A1001

Designs: No. 3421, 80f, Door God (4-1). No. 3422, 80f, Abundance for year (4-2). No. 3423, 80f, Good news on New Year's Day (4-3). No. 3424, 80f, Goddess strewing flowers from heaven (4-4).

2005, Feb. 1 Litho. ***Perf. 13¼x13***

3421-3424 A1001 Set of 4 1.50 .95
3424a Souvenir sheet, #3421-3424 4.50 2.50

No. 3424a sold for $4.80. A miniature sheet containing 2 of each stamp exists. Value, $12.

Magnolias A1002

Designs: No. 3425, 80f, Magnolia denudata (4-1). No. 3426, 80f, Magnolia delavayi (4-2). No. 3427, 80f, Magnolia grandiflora (4-3). No. 3428, 80f, Magnolia liliflora (4-4).

2005, Mar. 5 Photo. ***Perf. 13x13¼***

3425-3428 A1002 Set of 4 2.50 1.10

Great Wall of China — A1003

2005, Apr. 1 Litho. ***Perf. 12¾***

3429 A1003 80f multi + label .60 .30

See note following No. 3462. See No. 3846A.

Earth Day — A1004

2005, Apr. 22 Photo. ***Perf. 13¼***

3430 A1004 80f multi .80 .30

A ring of syncopated perforations surrounds the vignette.

Jigong Mountains A1005

No. 3431: a, Mountain at daybreak (4-1). b, Garden in clouds (4-2). c, Moon Pond (4-3). d, Black Dragon Waterfall (4-4).

Perf. 12½ Syncopated

2005, Apr. 28 Litho.

3431 Horiz. strip of 4 1.50 1.25
a.-d. A1005 80f Any single .35 .25

All-China Federation of Trade Unions, 80th Anniv. — A1006

2005, May 1 ***Perf. 12***

3432 A1006 80f multi 3.50 .40

Paintings of Flower Arrangements A1007

Designs: No. 3433, 80f, Magnolia Flowers, by Chen Hongshou (2-1). No. 3434, 80f, Flower Vase in a Window Niche, by Ambrosius Bosschaert the Elder (2-2).

Perf. 12½ Syncopated

2005, May 18 Photo.

3433-3434 A1007 Set of 2 1.25 .50

See Liechtenstein Nos. 1315-1316.

Dalian Bay Area Views — A1008

No. 3435: a, Tiger Beach (4-1). b, Bangchui Island (4-2). c, Golden Pebble Beach (4-3). d, Lushunkou (4-4).

2005, May 21 ***Perf. 12¾ Syncopated***

3435 Horiz. strip of 4 1.50 1.25
a.-d. A1008 80f Any single .35 .25

Fudan University, Cent. A1009

Litho., Engr. & Embossed

2005, May 27 ***Perf. 12***

3436 A1009 80f multi .80 .25

Hans Christian Andersen (1805-75), Author A1010

No. 3437 — Fairy tales by Andersen: a, The Emperor's New Clothes (5-1). b, The Little Mermaid (5-2). c, Thumbelina (5-3). d, The Little Match Girl (5-4). e, The Ugly Duckling (5-5).

Perf. 13¼ Syncopated

2005, June 1 — Photo.

3437 Horiz. strip of 5 2.00 1.40
a.-e. A1010 60f Any single .30 .25
f. Booklet pane of 1, #3437a .50 —
g. Booklet pane of 1, #3437b .50 —
h. Booklet pane of 1, #3437c .50 —
i. Booklet pane of 1, #3437d .50 —
j. Booklet pane of 1, #3437e .50 —
Complete booklet, #3437f-3437j 5.00

The complete booklet sold for $6.

A sheet of ten serpentine die cut 10 self-adhesive stamps containing two of each of the designs of Nos. 3437a-3437e and ten labels exists. Value, $12.

Voyages of Admiral Zheng He, 600th Anniv. — A1011

No. 3438: a, Admiral Zheng He (3-1). b, Building, map of voyages (3-2). c, Compass, drawing of ship (3-3)
$6, Ship, horiz.

2005, June 28 — Litho.

3438 Horiz. strip of 3 1.50 1.00
a.-c. A1011 80f Any single .30 .25

Souvenir Sheet

3439 A1011 $6 multi 3.00 2.50

No. 3439 contains one 70x50mm stamp.

Nantong Museum — A1012

No. 3440: a, Southern Hall (2-1). b, Central Hall (2-2).

Photo. & Engr.

2005, July 16 ***Perf. 12½x12¾***

3440 A1012 80f Horiz. pair, #a-b 1.10 .75

Xianghai National Nature Reserve — A1013

Designs: No. 3441, 80f, Red-crowned cranes in nest (4-1). No. 3442, 80f, Three birds in flight, trees (4-2). No. 3443, 80f, Birds at lake (4-3). No. 3444, 80f, Eagles flying above steppe (4-4).

2005, July 30 — Photo. ***Perf. 12¾***

3441-3444 A1013 Set of 4 1.50 .90

Miniature Sheet

People's Army Generals — A1014

No. 3445: a, Yang Jingyu (5-1). b, Zuo Quan (5-2). c, Peng Xuefeng (5-3). d, Luo Binghui (5-4). e, Guan Xiangying (5-5).

2005, Aug. 1 ***Perf. 12***

3445 A1014 80f Sheet of 10, 2 each #a-e 7.00 4.75

End of World War II, 60th Anniv. — A1015

No. 3446: a, Soldiers with machine guns (4-1). b, Bugler (4-2). c, Soldier holding gun, troops landing in Normandy (4-3). d, Conquering Berlin (4-4).
$6, Dove, vert.

Perf. 12¾ Syncopated

2005, Aug. 15 — Litho.

3446 A1015 80f Block of 4, #a-d 1.50 .90

Souvenir Sheet

Photo.

Perf. 12¾

3447 A1015 $6 multi 3.00 2.00

Tibet Autonomous Region, 40th Anniv. — A1016

2005, Aug. 26 — Photo. ***Perf. 13¼***

3448 A1016 80f multi 1.00 .30

Chinese Motion Pictures, Cent. — A1017

2005, Aug. 28 — Litho. ***Perf. 12¾x13***

3449 A1017 80f multi .70 .25

Exists in a sheet of 8 stamps + 8 labels.

"Five Happinesses Arrive" — A1018

2005, Sept. 16 ***Perf. 12¾***

3450 A1018 80f multi + label 1.00 .35

See note following No. 3462.

Fanjing Mountain Nature Reserve A1019

No. 3451: a, Golden Summit (4-1). b, Mushroom Rock (4-2). c, Forest (4-3). d, Heiwan River (4-4).

2005, Sept. 18 — Photo. ***Perf. 13x13¼***

3451 Horiz. strip of 4 1.75 1.40
a.-d. A1019 80f Any single .35 .25

Farm Technology A1020

Sheep and: No. 3452, 80f, Chinese water wheel (2-1). No. 3453, 80f, Dutch windmill (2-2).

2005, Sept. 22 ***Perf. 12***

3452-3453 A1020 Set of 2 1.40 .50

See Netherlands Nos. 1203-1204.

Miniature Sheet

People's Liberation Army Generals — A1021

No. 1021: a, Su Yu (10-1). b, Xu Haidong (10-2). c, Huang Kecheng (10-3). d, Chen Geng (10-4). e, Tan Zheng (10-5). f, Xiao Jinguang (10-6). g, Zhang Yunyi (10-7). h, Luo Ruiqing (10-8). i, Wang Shusheng (10-9). j, Xu Guangda (10-10).

Litho. & Engr.

2005, Sept. 27 ***Perf. 13¼x13***

3454 A1021 80f Sheet of 10, #a-j 4.75 3.25

Miniature Sheet

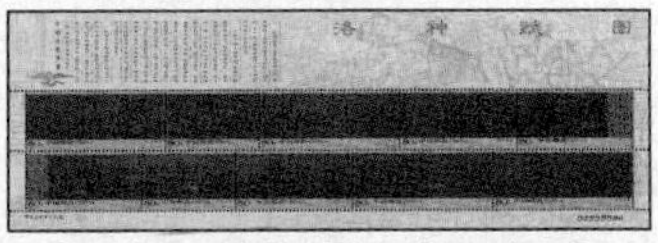

Goddess of the River Luo, by Gu Kaizhi — A1022

Various painting details with width of: a, 50mm (10-1). b, 50mm (10-2). c, 60mm (10-3). d, 40mm (10-4). e, 60mm (10-5). f, 60mm (10-6). g, 60mm (10-7). h, 50mm (10-8). i, 40mm (10-9). j, 50mm (10-10).

2005, Sept. 28 ***Perf. 12***

3455 A1022 80f Sheet of 10, #a-j 12.00 8.50

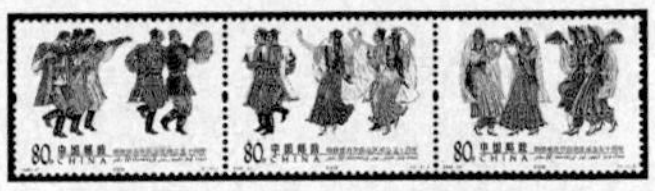

Xinjiang Uygur Autonomous Region, 50th Anniv. — A1023

No. 3456: a, Male dancers and musicians (3-1). b, Male and female dancers (3-2). c, Women carrying plates of food (3-3).

Perf. 12x12½ Syncopated

2005, Oct. 1 — Litho.

3456 A1023 Horiz. strip of 3 1.25 1.00
a.-c. 80f Any single .30 .25

Souvenir Sheet

10th National Games, Jiangsu Province — A1024

2005, Oct. 12 — Photo. ***Perf. 12¾***

3457 A1024 $6 multi 2.50 2.00

Wild Cats A1025

Designs: No. 3458, 80f, Panthera pardus orientalis (2-1). No. 3459, 80f, Puma concolor (2-2).

2005, Oct. 13 — Photo. ***Perf. 13x13¼***

3458-3459 A1025 Set of 2 1.20 .50

See Canada Nos. 2122-2123.

"Be Safe Every Year" — A1026

2005, Nov. 6 — Litho. ***Perf. 13¼***

3460 A1026 80f red & blk + label 3.50 1.00

A serpentine die cut 10 self-adhesive stamp of type A1026 exists. Value, $22.50.

Relics From Chengtoushan Archaeological Site — A1027

2005, Nov. 6 — Photo. ***Perf. 12½***

3461 A1027 80f multi .70 .25

"Beam With Delight" — A1028

2005, Nov. 11 Litho. *Perf. 12¾*
3462 A1028 80f multi + label 1.10 .25

A sheet of 2 each of Nos. 3429, 3450 and 3462 exists. Value, $6.

2008 Summer Olympics, Beijing — A1029

Designs: No. 3463, Beijing Olympics emblem, Olympic rings (6-1).
No. 3464 — Beijing Olympic mascots with emblem on chest: a, Beibei (6-2). b, Jingjing (6-3). c, Huanhuan (6-4). d, Yingying (6-5). e, Nini (6-6).
No. 3465: a, Like #3463. b, Like #3464a. c, Like #3464b. d, Like #3464c. e, Like #3464d. f, Like #3464e.

2005, Nov. 12 Photo. *Perf. 13¼x13*
3463 A1029 80f multi .50 .25
3464 A1029 80f Horiz. strip of 5, #a-e 11.00 8.50

Self-Adhesive
Serpentine Die Cut 11¾

3465 A1029 80f Sheet, 2 each #a-f *40.00 40.00*

A sheet of 5 30x30mm stamps with the Beijing Olympics emblem and Olympic rings was issued in 2008. Value, $15.

New Year 2006 (Year of the Dog) A1030

Perf. 13 Syncopated

2006, Jan. 5 Photo.
3466 A1030 80f multi 1.00 .25
a. Sheet of 6 *10.00 7.25*
b. Booklet pane of 10 5.00 —
Complete booklet, #3466b 6.00

A sheet of 4 exists that was a giveaway for standing-order customers. Value, $9.

Wuqiang New Year Woodprints A1031

Designs: No. 3467, 80f, Being Safe All Year Round (4-1). No. 3468, 80f, Five Blessings Approach Your Door (4-2). No. 3469, 80f, Flower of Prosperity Blossoms (4-3). No. 3470, 80f, Lion Rolling the Embroidered Ball (4-4).

Litho. & Engr.
2006, Jan. 22 *Perf. 12*
3467-3470 A1031 Set of 4 1.75 1.00
3470a Souvenir sheet, #3467-3470 4.50 2.50
3470b Souvenir sheet, 2 each #3467-3470 *9.00 6.00*

Lanterns A1032

Designs: No. 3471, 80f, Fish lantern (5-1). No. 3472, 80f, Chinese white cabbage lantern (5-2). No. 3473, 80f, Lotus lantern (5-3). No. 3474, 80f, Dragon and phoenix lantern (5-4). $1.50, Butterfly lantern (5-5).

2006, Feb. 12 Photo. *Perf. 13¼x13*
3471-3475 A1032 Set of 5 4.50 2.50
3475a Sheet, 2 each #3471-3475 *12.00 6.00*

Abolition of Agricultural Tax — A1033

Perf. 13½ Syncopated

2006, Feb. 22
3476 A1033 80f multi 7.00 1.25

Lijiang River — A1034

No. 3477: a, Yangdi (4-1). b, Langshi (4-2). c, Huangbu (4-3). d, Xingping (4-4).

2006, Feb. 25 *Perf. 12¾*
3477 A1034 Horiz. strip of 4 3.75 1.75
a.-d. 80f Any single .60 .25

Relic Plants — A1035

Designs: No. 3478, 80f, Ginkgo biloba (4-1). No. 3479, 80f, Glyptostrobus pensilis (4-2). No. 3480, 80f, Davidia involucrata (4-3). No. 3481, 80f, Liriodendron chinense (4-4).

Perf. 12x12¼ Syncopated

2006, Mar. 12 Litho.
3478-3481 A1035 Set of 4 5.00 1.50

Dogs A1036

Designs: Nos. 3482, 3486a, 80f, Pekingese (4-1). Nos. 3483, 3486b, 80f, Pug, vert. (4-2). Nos. 3484, 3486c, 80f, Chow chow (4-3). Nos. 3485, 3486d, 80f, Tibetan mastiff, vert. (4-4).

Perf. 13¼ Syncopated

2006, Mar. 19 Litho. & Engr.
3482-3485 A1036 Set of 4 2.00 1.40

Self-Adhesive
Serpentine Die Cut 11¾ on 2 Sides

3486 A1036 80f Sheet, 2 each #3486a-3486d 11.00 *7.00*

Qingcheng Mountain A1037

Designs: 60f, Remote mountain gate (4-1). No. 3488, 80f, Winding path (4-2). No. 3489, 80f, Ancient temple (4-3). No. 3490, 80f, Spring (4-4).

2006, Apr. 12 *Perf. 13¼ Syncopated*
3487-3490 A1037 Set of 4 3.50 1.50

Statues in Yungang Grottoes — A1038

Designs: No. 3491, 80f, Sakyamuni (4-1). No. 3492, 80f, Bodhisattva (4-2). No. 3493, 80f, Head of Bodhisattva (4-3). No. 3494, 80f, Xieshi Bodhisattva (4-4).
$6, Sakyamuni, diff.

Perf. 13¼x13½ Syncopated

2006, Apr. 13 Photo.
3491-3494 A1038 Set of 4 5.00 1.00

Souvenir Sheet
Perf. 13 Syncopated

3495 A1038 $6 multi 3.50 3.00

No. 3495 contains one 40x60mm stamp.

Tianzhu Mountain — A1039

Designs: 60f, Green Dragon Mountain Stream (4-1). No. 3497, 80f, Taoist Practice Terrace (4-2). No. 3498, 80f, Sanzu Temple (4-3). No. 3499, 80f, Qingtian Peak (4-4).

2006, Apr. 22 *Perf. 11½x11¼*
3496-3499 A1039 Set of 4 2.50 1.00

Scientists A1040

Designs: No. 3500, 80f, Liang Xi (1883-1958), forester (4-1). No. 3501, 80f, Mao Yisheng (1896-1989), civil engineer (4-2). No. 3502, 80f, Yan Jici (1900-96), physicist (4-3). No. 3503, 80f, Zhou Peiyuan (1902-93), physicist (4-4).

Litho. & Engr.
2006, May 13 *Perf. 12*
3500-3503 A1040 Set of 4 6.25 2.25

Lighthouses — A1041

No. 3504: a, Dagu Lighthouse (4-1). b, Guishan Island Lighthouse (4-2). c, Wusongkou Lighthouse (4-3). d, Mulantou Lighthouse (4-4).

2006, May 22 Photo. *Perf. 12¾*
3504 A1041 Horiz. strip of 4 3.25 2.25
a.-d. 80f Any single .50 .25

Chinese Space Program, 50th Anniv. — A1042

No. 3505: a, Geospace Double Star Exploration (2-1). b, Shenzhou 6 (2-2).

Perf. 12x11¼ Syncopated

2006, June 8 Litho.
3505 A1042 80f Horiz. pair, #a-b 2.25 1.25

Silver and Gold Objects — A1043

Designs: No. 3506, 80f, Jeeweled Qing Dynasty cup, China (2-1). No. 3507, 80f, Tankard with Biblical designs, by Peter Rohde, Poland.

2006, June 20 Photo. *Perf. 13¼x13*
3506-3507 A1043 Set of 2 2.00 .65

See Poland No. 3829.

Olympic Rings and Emblem of 2008 Summer Olympics, Beijing — A1043a

2006, June 23 Litho. *Perf. 12*
3507A A1043a 80f multi + label 1.25 .45

Printed in sheets of 15 stamps + 15 labels, sheets of 5 stamps + 5 labels, sheets of 4 stamps + 4 labels to right of stamps, sheets of 4 stamps + 4 labels below stamps, and sheets of 8 stamps + 8 labels. Value, set of 5 sheets $50.

Early Communist Leaders A1044

Designs: No. 3508, 80f, Gao Junyu (1896-1925) (5-1). No. 3509, 80f, Wang Hebo (1882-1927) (5-2). No. 3510, 80f, Su Zhaozheng (1885-1929) (5-3). No. 3511, 80f, Peng Pai (1896-1929) (5-4). No. 3512, 80f, Deng Xhongxia (1894-1933) (5-5).

2006, June 30 Litho. & Engr.
3508-3512 A1044 Set of 5 *30.00 17.50*

Opening of Qinghai-Tibet Railway — A1045

Designs: No. 3513, 80f, Bridge across Kekexili, antelopes (3-1). No. 3514, 80f, Train crossing Danggula Mountains, cattle (3-2). No. 3515, 80f, Lhasa Railway Station, birds (3-3).

Perf. 12½x12 Syncopated

2006, July 1 **Litho.**

3513-3515 A1045 Set of 3 7.25 2.50

Kanasi Nature Reserve — A1046

Designs: No. 3516, 80f, Kanasi Lake (4-1). No. 3517, 80f, Crouching Dragon Bend (4-2). No. 3518, 80f, Celestial Bend (4-3). No. 3519, 80f, Moon Bend (4-4).

2006, July 8 **Photo.** ***Perf. 12¾***

3516-3519 A1046 Set of 4 6.50 2.25

Earthquake Protection and Damage Mitigation A1047

2006, July 26 ***Perf. 13½x13***

3520 A1047 80f multi 4.25 .75

2008 Summer Olympics, Beijing — A1048

Designs: Nos. 3521, 3525a, 60f, Basketball (4-1). Nos. 3522, 3525b, 80f, Fencing (4-2). Nos. 3523, 3525c, Sailing (4-3). Nos. 3524, 3525d, $3, Gymnastics (4-4).

2006, Aug. 8 **Photo.** ***Perf. 13¼x13***

3521-3524 A1048 Set of 4 3.25 2.00

Self-Adhesive

Serpentine Die Cut 11¾

3525 A1048 Sheet of 8, 2 each #a-d 16.00 *11.00*

Portions of the designs of Nos. 3525a-3525d were applied by a thermographic process, producing a shiny, raised effect.

Treasures of the Study — A1049

Designs: No. 3526, 80f, Brushes (4-1). No. 3527, 80f, Ink (4-2). No. 3528, 80f, Paper (4-3). No. 3529, 80f, Ink stone (4-4).

Perf. 12x12½ Syncopated

2006, Sept. 10 **Litho.**

3526-3529 A1049 Set of 4 8.00 3.00

A sheet of 2 each of Nos. 3526-3529 exists. Value, $60.

All-China Federation of Returned Overseas Chinese, 50th Anniv. A1050

Perf. 12½x12 Syncopated

2006, Sept. 25

3530 A1050 80f multi 1.00 .30

Musical Instruments — A1051

Designs: No. 3531, 80f, Seven-stringed qin, China (2-1). No. 3532, 80f, Bösendorfer piano, Austria (2-2).

Perf. 13x12½ Syncopated

2006, Sept. 26 **Litho.**

3531-3532 A1051 Set of 2 2.50 .60

See Austria Nos. 2066-2067.

Chinese Export Commodities Fair — A1052

Perf. 13½x13¼ Syncopated

2006, Oct. 15 **Photo.**

3533 A1052 80f multi 1.00 .25

Long March, 70th Anniv. — A1053

Designs: No. 3534, 80f, Setting Out (4-1). No. 3535, 80f, Zunyi Conference (4-2). No. 3536, 80f, Speedily Occupy the Luding Bridge (4-3). No. 3537, 80f, The Red Army Through the Marshland (4-4).

$6, Reunion.

2006, Oct. 22 ***Perf. 13x13¼***

3534-3537 A1053 Set of 4 3.75 1.75

Souvenir Sheet

3538 A1053 $6 multi 4.50 3.75

No. 3538 contains one 80x50mm stamp. A souvenir sheet of one of No. 3535 exists.

No. 3538 exists imperf.

Dialogue With ASEAN, 15th Anniv. A1054

Perf. 12½x12 Syncopated

2006, Oct. 30 **Litho.**

3539 A1054 80f multi 1.50 .30

"Enjoying Prosperity Year After Year" A1055

"Happy New Year" — A1055a

Perf. 12¾ Syncopated

2006, Nov. 1 **Photo.**

3540 A1055 80f multi .30 .25

3541 A1055a $3 multi 1.10 .85

A souvenir sheet containing Nos. 3540-3541 exists. Value, $12.

See note following No. 3628. See Nos. 3708a, 3869b, 3978a, 4238a.

Beijing Summit of Forum on China-Africa Cooperation — A1056

2006, Nov. 3 **Litho.** ***Perf. 13¼***

3542 A1056 80f multi 1.25 .25

Buildings Associated With Dr. Sun Yat-sen (1826-1925) A1057

Designs: No. 3543, 80f, Sun Yat-sen Villa (4-1). No. 3544, 80f, Mausoleum (4-2). No. 3545, 80f, Sun Yat-sen Memorial Hall (4-3). No. 3546, 80f, Sun Yat-sen University (4-4).

Perf. 13¼ Syncopated

2006, Nov. 12 **Litho. & Engr.**

3543-3546 A1057 Set of 4 5.00 1.75

Birds Type of 2002

Designs: 40f, Chinese monal pheasant. $1.20, Taiwan yuhinas.

Perf. 13½ Syncopated

2006, Nov. 15 **Photo.**

3547 A909 40f multi .30 .25

3548 A909 $1.20 multi .45 .35

Heavenly Steed, Silk Roll Painting — A1058

No. 3549: a, Horse and rider. b, People looking at horse.

2006, Dec. 3 **Photo.** ***Perf. 12¾***

3549 A1058 $1.20 Horiz. pair, #a-b 2.00 1.25

Wu Lanfu (1906-88), Politician A1059

2006, Dec. 23 ***Perf. 13¼x13***

3550 A1059 $1.20 multi *11.50 4.00*

Trains — A1060

Designs: No. 3551, $1.20, Locomotive, blue background (4-1). No. 3552, $1.20, Locomotive, red brown background (4-2). No. 3553, $1.20, Box car (4-3). No. 3554, $1.20, Log cars and gateway (4-4).

$6, Locomotive and city skyline.

2006, Dec. 28 ***Perf. 13x13¼***

3551-3554 A1060 Set of 4 *27.50 12.00*

Souvenir Sheet

Perf. 13¼x13

3555 A1060 $6 multi *16.00 12.00*

No. 3555 contains one 90x40mm stamp.

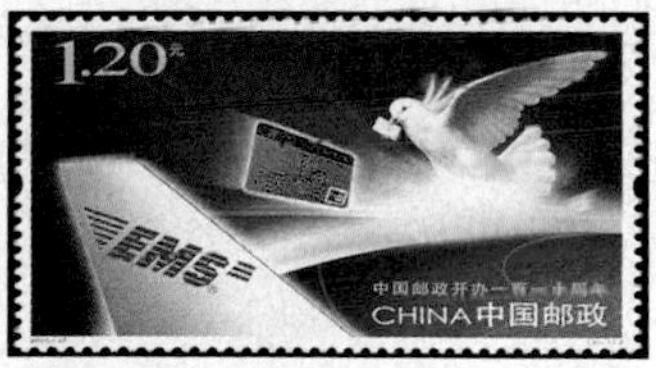

China Post, 110th Anniv. — A1061

Perf. 12x11½ Syncopated

2006, Dec. 30 **Litho.**

3556 A1061 $1.20 multi 1.50 .60

A sheet containing 6 No. 3556 exists. Value, $8.50.

New Year 2007 (Year of the Pig) — A1062

Perf. 13 Syncopated

2007, Jan. 5 **Photo.**

3557 A1062 $1.20 multi 1.00 .35

a. Souvenir sheet of 6 12.00 *6.00*

b. Booklet pane of 10 6.00 —

Complete booklet, #3557b 6.25

A sheet containing 4 No. 3557 exists. Value, $12.50.

6th Asian Winter Games — A1063

Perf. 12x12½ Syncopated

2007, Jan. 28 **Litho.**

3558 A1063 $1.20 multi 2.00 .35

Shiwan Pottery Figurines A1064

Designs: No. 3559, $1.20, Ta Xue Xun Mei (2-1). No. 3560, $1.20, Wang Zhaojun Chu Sai (2-2).

2007, Feb. 3 **Photo.** ***Perf. 13¼x13***

3559-3560 A1064 Set of 2 1.00 .65

3560a Miniature sheet, 4 each #3559-3560 8.00 3.50

"Divine Birds of the Sun" — A1065

2007, Feb. 9 **Litho.** ***Perf. 12***

3561 A1065 $1.20 multi + label .65 .35

Printed in sheets of 6 + 6 labels (value, $11), 8 + 8 labels and 15 + 15 labels (value, $20).

Mianzhu New Year Woodcuts A1066

Designs: No. 3562, $1.20, Zuo Zuo Ti Dao (4-1). No. 3563, $1.20, Mu Guiying (4-2). No. 3564, $1.20, Shuang Xi Tong Zi (4-3). No. 3565, $1.20, Zhang Xian She Gou (4-4).

Perf. 12x11½ Syncopated

2007, Feb. 10 **Litho. & Engr.**

3562-3565 A1066 Set of 4 2.25 1.50

3565a Souvenir sheet of 4, #3562-3565 3.00 2.50

3565b Miniature sheet of 8, 2 each #3562-3565 10.00 8.00

A lithographed sheet similar to No. 3565b on a textured silk-faced paper exists.

Beijing Opera — A1067

Designs: 80f, Lin Xiangru (6-1). No. 3567, $1.20, Song Shijie (6-2). No. 3568, $1.20, Zhou Yu (6-3). No. 3569, $1.20, Xu Xian (6-4). No. 3570, $1.20, Gao Chong (6-5). No. 3571, $1.20, Ren Tanghui (6-6).

2007, Mar. 10 **Photo.** ***Perf. 13¼x13***

3566-3571 A1067 Set of 6 2.75 2.00

Postal Savings Bank — A1068

2007, Mar. 20 ***Perf. 12¾***

3572 A1068 $1.20 multi .65 .35

a. Miniature sheet of 8 *9.00 4.50*

Writings of Li Keran A1069

Designs: No. 3573, $1.20, Man viewing waterfall (6-1). No. 3574, $1.20, Mountains with red-leaved trees (6-2). No. 3575, $1.20, People looking at scroll (6-3). No. 3576, $1.20, Crane flying above man under tent (6-4). No. 3577, $1.20, Cattle and driver in pond (6-5). No. 3578, $1.20, Raining in Jiangnan (6-6).

Perf. 13x13¼ Syncopated

2007, Mar. 26

3573-3578 A1069 Set of 6 4.50 2.25

Modern Chinese Drama, Cent. A1070

Perf. 13 Syncopated

2007, Apr. 6 **Litho.**

3579 A1070 $1.20 multi .60 .35

Yangzhou Garden — A1071

No. 3580: a, He Garden (3-1). b, Ge Garden (3-2). c, Xu Garden (3-3).

Perf. 12x11½ Syncopated

2007, Apr. 8

3580 A1071 Horiz. strip of 3 1.75 1.40

a.-c. $1.20 Any single .50 .35

Dances — A1072

Designs: No. 3581, $1.20, Dragon dance (2-1). No. 3582, $1.20, Lion dance (2-2).

2007, Apr. 13 **Litho.** ***Perf. 12¾x13***

3581-3582 A1072 Set of 2 1.40 .70

See Indonesia No. 2100.

Torch Relay for 2008 Summer Olympics, Beijing — A1073

2007, Apr. 27 ***Perf. 12***

3583 A1073 $1.20 multi + label 1.75 .60

a. Sheet of 4 + 4 labels 3.00 2.50

Inner Mongolia Autonomous Region, 60th Anniv. — A1074

Designs: No. 3584, $1.20, Horsemen, wrestlers, archer (2-1). No. 3585, $1.20, Seven women (2-2).

Perf. 12½x12 Syncopated

2007, May 1

3584-3585 A1074 Set of 2 1.00 .70

3585a Souvenir sheet, #3584-3585 2.75 2.25

Mausoleums of Qing Emperors A1075

Designs: No. 3586, $1.20, Zhaoling Mausoleum (3-1). No. 3587, $1.20, Xiaoling Mausoleum (3-2). No. 3588, Tailing Mausoleum (3-3).

2007, May 12 **Photo.** ***Perf. 12¾***

3586-3588 A1075 Set of 3 1.25 1.00

Tongji University, Cent. A1076

2007, May 20 ***Perf. 12½ Syncopated***

3589 A1076 $1.20 multi .60 .40

Kong Rong and Pears — A1077

Nos. 3590 and 3591: a, Denomination at LL (2-1). b, Denomination at LR (2-2).

2007, June 1 ***Perf. 13¼x13***

3590 A1077 $1.20 Horiz. pair, #a-b 1.00 .85

Self-Adhesive

Booklet Stamps

Serpentine Die Cut 11¾

3591 A1077 $1.20 Horiz. pair, #a-b .85 .85

c. Booklet pane, 4 #3591 5.00

Chongqing — A1078

No. 3592: a, City skyline (2-1). b, City and highway interchange (2-2).

Perf. 12x11½ Syncopated

2007, June 8 **Litho.**

3592 A1078 $1.20 Horiz. pair, #a-b 1.10 .90

Wudalianchi Natl. Park — A1079

No. 3593: a, Heilong Mountain (3-1). b, Sanchi Pool (3-2). c, Sea of Rock (3-3).

2007, June 19 **Photo.** ***Perf. 12¾***

3593 A1079 Horiz. strip of 3 1.75 1.25

a.-c. $1.20 Any single .45 .35

Return of Hong Kong, 10th Anniv. A1080

Designs: No. 3594, $1.20, Flags of People's Republic of China and Hong Kong, doves, monument (3-1). No. 3595, $1.20, "CEPA" and stylized buildings (3-2). No. 3596, $1.20, Hong Kong buildings, bridge (3-3).

Perf. 13¼x12¾ Syncopated

2007, July 1

3594-3596 A1080 Set of 3 1.40 1.00

A souvenir sheet containing Nos. 3594-3596 and Hong Kong No. 1275 sold for $12.95 in Hong Kong currency. Value, $27.50.

Pres. Yang Shangkun (1907-98) A1081

Designs: No. 3597, $1.20, Standing in uniform (2-1). No. 3598, $1.20, Seated at desk, horiz. (2-2).

Perf. 11½x11, 11x11½

2007, July 5 **Photo. & Engr.**

3597-3598 A1081 Set of 2 3.25 .85

Nanji Islands Marine Reserve — A1082

Shells and: No. 3599, $1.20, Sanpanwei (3-1). No. 3600, $1.20, Longchuanjiao (3-2). No. 3601, $1.20, Dashaao (3-3).

Perf. 12¾x12½ Syncopated

2007, July 10 **Photo.**

3599-3601 A1082 Set of 3 1.60 1.00

Emblem of People's Liberation Army — A1083

2007, July 15 **Litho.** ***Perf. 12***

3602 A1083 $1.20 multi + label 1.25 .45

Souvenir Sheet

All-China Philatelic Federation, 6th Congress — A1084

Perf. 12½ Syncopated

2007, July 28 **Litho. & Engr.**

3603 A1084 $6 multi 3.75 2.25

A sheet of 2 No. 3603 exists. Value, $9.

People's Liberation Army, 80th Anniv. — A1085

Designs: No. 3604, $1.20, Soldiers saluting (4-1). No. 3605, $1.20, Soldier carrying sack (4-2). No. 3606, $1.20, Soldier with rifle (4-3). No. 3607, $1.20, Soldiers wearing UN Peacekeeper berets (4-4).

Perf. 13¼x12½ Syncopated

2007, Aug. 1 **Photo.**

3604-3607 A1085 Set of 4 3.25 2.00

A sheet of eight (two each Nos. 3604-3607) exists. Value, $10.

Olympic Sports — A1086

Designs: Nos. 3608, 3614a, $1.20, Diving (6-1). Nos. 3609, 3614b, $1.20, Shooting (6-2). Nos. 3610, 3614c, $1.20, Athletics (6-3). Nos. 3611, 3614d, $1.20, Volleyball (6-4). Nos. 3612, 3614e, $1.20, BMX bicycling (6-5). Nos. 3613, 3614f, $1.20, Weight lifting (6-6).

2007, Aug. 8 **Photo.** ***Perf. 13¼x13***

3608-3613 A1086 Set of 6 3.50 2.25

3613a Sheet of 10, #3521-3524, 3608-3613, + label 12.00 12.00

Self-Adhesive

Serpentine Die Cut 11¾

3614 Miniature sheet of 12, 2 each #a-f *18.50*

a.-f. A1086 $1.20 Any single .40 .30

No. 3613a sold for $18.60.

Tengchong Volcano Area — A1087

Designs: No. 3615, $1.20, Rehai (3-1). No. 3616, $1.20, Volcanoes, vert. (3-2). No. 3617, $1.20, Shenzhu Valley, vert. (3-3).

Perf. 12x12½ Syncopated, 12½x12 Syncopated

2007, Aug. 18

3615-3617 A1087 Set of 3 1.50 1.00

Nos. 3615-3617 were printed together in a sheet of 15 stamps + a horizontal label. The first row consists of the label and 2 No. 3615; the second row, 3 No. 3615; the third row, 5 No. 3616; and the fourth row, 5 No. 3617.

Jin Hu — A1088

No. 3618: a, Da Chibi (2-1). b, Maoer Mountain (2-2).

Perf. 12¾ Syncopated

2007, Sept. 2 **Litho.**

3618 A1088 $1.20 Horiz. pair, #a-b 1.10 .95

2007 Women's Soccer World Cup, People's Republic of China A1089

2007, Sept. 10 **Photo.** ***Perf. 13¼***

3619 A1089 $1.20 multi 1.10 .75

Values are for stamps with surrounding selvage.

2007 World Summer Special Olympics, Shanghai — A1090

2007, Oct. 2 ***Perf. 13¼***

3620 A1090 $1.20 multi .70 .40

Historic Sites in Three Gorges Reservoir Area — A1091

Designs: No. 3621, $1.20, Zhang Fei Temple (4-1). No. 3622, $1.20, Shibaozhai Village, vert. (4-2). No. 3623, $1.20, Ancient Dachang, vert. (4-3). No. 3624, $1.20, Quyuan's Grave (4-4).

Perf. 13¼ Syncopated

2007, Oct. 13 **Litho. & Engr.**

3621-3624 A1091 Set of 4 2.00 1.50

17th Natl. Communist Party Congress — A1092

Designs: No. 3625, $1.20, Memorial for First Natl. Communist Party Congress (2-1). No. 3626, $1.20, Site of Second Plenary Session of the Seventh Central Committee.
$6, Dove and monument.

Perf. 13¼x13 Syncopated

2007, Oct. 15 **Photo.**

3625-3626 A1092 Set of 2 2.75 1.00

Souvenir Sheet

Perf. 13¼x13

3627 A1092 $6 multi 5.00 3.25

No. 3627 contains one 60x40mm stamp.
A souvenir sheet of 2 of Nos. 3625-3626 exists. Value, $50.

"Happiness" A1093

Perf. 12¾ Syncopated

2007, Nov. 1 **Photo.**

3628 A1093 $1.20 multi .45 .40

A sheet containing Nos. 3628, 3541 and four labels exists. Value, $14.

Ancient Calligraphy A1094

Designs: No. 3629, $1.20, Proclamation (6-1). No. 3630, $1.20, Zhang Menglong Stele (6-2). No. 3631, $1.20, Inscription for Sweet Spring at Jiucheng Palace (6-3). No. 3632, $1.20, Preface for Sacred Religion at Wild Goose Pagoda (6-4). No. 3633, $1.20, Yan Qinli Stele (6-5). No. 3634, $1.20, Mysterious Pagoda Stele (6-6).

Perf. 12x11½ Syncopated

2007, Nov. 5 **Litho.**

3629-3634 A1094 Set of 6 3.25 2.25

A sheet containing 2 each of lithographed and embossed examples of Nos. 3629-3634 exists. Value, $10.

Mountains — A1095

Designs: No. 3635, $1.20, Mount Gongga, People's Republic of China (2-1). No. 3636, $1.20, Popocatepetl, Mexico (2-2).

Perf. 12¾ Syncopated

2007, Nov. 22

3635-3636 A1095 Set of 2 2.25 .75

See Mexico Nos. 2561-2562.

Launch of China's First Lunar Probe A1096

2007, Nov. 26 **Litho. & Embossed**

3637 A1096 $1.20 multi 3.75 1.75

Emblem of Expo 2010, Shanghai A1097

Mascot of Expo 2010 — A1098

Perf. 11½ Syncopated

2007, Dec. 19 **Litho.**

3638 A1097 $1.20 multi .60 .45

a. Booklet pane of 1 .70 —

3639 A1098 $1.20 multi .60 .45

a. Booklet pane of 1 .70 —

b. Booklet pane of 10, 5 each #3638-3639 7.00 —

Complete booklet, #3638a, 3639a, 3639b 7.00

Venues at 2008 Summer Olympics, Beijing — A1099

Designs: 80f, China Agricultural University Gymnasium (6-1). No. 3641, $1.20, Laoshan Mountain Bike Course (6-2). No. 3642, $1.20, National Indoor Stadium (6-3). No. 3643, $1.20, Beijing University Gymnasium (6-4). No. 3644, $1.20, National Aquatics Center (6-5). No. 3645, $3, Qingdao Olympic Sailing Center (6-6).
$6, National Stadium.

2007, Dec. 20 **Photo.** ***Perf. 13x13¼***

3640-3645 A1099 Set of 6 3.50 2.75

Souvenir Sheet

Perf. 13

3646 A1099 $6 multi 5.75 4.00

No. 3646 contains one pentagonal 65x62mm stamp.
A self-adhesive sheet of 2 each of Nos. 3640-3645 exists. Value, $12.

New Year 2008 (Year of the Rat) A1100

Perf. 12¾ Syncopated

2008, Jan. 5 **Photo.**

3647 A1100 $1.20 multi .80 .40

a. Booklet pane of 10 8.00 —

Complete booklet, #3647a 8.00

Miniature sheets containing 4 and 6 stamps exist. Value, each $11.

Zhuxian New Year Woodprints A1101

Designs: No. 3648, $1.20, Gate guardian (4-1). No. 3649, $1.20, Woman lecturing son (4-2). No. 3650, $1.20, Come back with fruitful result (4-3). No. 3651, $1.20, Chivalrous women (4-4).

2008, Jan. 15 Photo. ***Perf. 13¼x13***
3648-3651 A1101 Set of 4 1.75 1.50
3651a Souvenir sheet of 4, #3648-3651 3.00 2.25

No. 3651a sold for $7.20. A miniature sheet containing two each of Nos. 3648-3651 exists. Value, $7.50.

Beijing Opera Characters A1102

Designs: 80f, Zhang Fei (6-1). No. 3653, $1.20, Cao Cao (6-2). No. 3654, $1.20, Bao Zheng (6-3). No. 3655, $1.20, Lian Po (6-4). No. 3656, $1.20, Xu Yanzhao (6-5). No. 3657, $1.20, Yang Yansi (6-6).

Perf. 12x11½ Syncopated
2008, Feb. 23 **Litho.**
3652-3657 A1102 Set of 6 3.00 2.25

Miniature Sheet

Birds — A1103

No. 3658: a, Urocissa caerulea (6-1). b, Emberiza koslowi (6-2). c, Tragopan caboti (6-3). d, Garrulax sukatschewi (6-4). e, Chrysolophus pictus (6-5). f, Podoces biddulphi (6-6).

2008, Feb. 28 Photo. ***Perf. 13¼x13***
3658 A1103 $1.20 Sheet of 6, #a-f 5.00 3.25

11th National People's Congress — A1104

2008, Mar. 5
3659 A1104 $1.20 multi .65 .40

Olympic Torch Relay — A1105

Designs: $1.20, Lighting of torch in Greece, mascot holding torch (2-1). $3, Torch, torch bearer, vert. (2-2).

2008, Mar. 5 Photo. ***Perf. 13¼***
3660-3661 A1105 Set of 2 2.00 1.25
3661a Souvenir sheet, #3660-3661 *9.00 4.50*

No. 3661a sold for $6.30. A sheet containing 4 self-adhesive examples each of Nos. 3660-3661 exists. Value, $15.

Suzhou-Nantong Yangtze River Bridge — A1106

No. 3662 — Denomination at: a, Left (2-1). b, Right (2-2).

2008, Apr. 12 ***Perf. 13¼***
3662 A1106 $1.20 Horiz. pair, #a-b 1.10 .90

Boao Forum For Asia — A1107

No. 3663: a, Dongyu Island (2-1). b, Forum venue (2-2).

Perf. 12x11½ Syncopated
2008, Apr. 13 **Litho.**
3663 A1107 $1.20 Horiz. pair, #a-b 1.10 .90

Qiandao Lake — A1108

No. 3664 — Islands with denomination at: a, Left (2-1). b, Right (2-2).

2008, Apr. 16 ***Perf. 12¾ Syncopated***
3664 A1108 $1.20 Horiz. pair, #a-b 1.10 .90
c. Souvenir sheet, #3664 3.25 2.75

No. 3664c sold for $3.60.

A1109

Olympic Expo, Beijing — A1110

2008, Apr. 30 Photo. ***Perf. 11¼x11***
3665 A1109 $1.20 multi .75 .40

Litho.
Perf. 12½
3666 A1110 $1.20 multi .75 .40

A circle of perforations surrounds the circular design on No. 3665.

Summer Palace — A1111

Designs: No. 3667, $1.20, Shiqikong Bridge (6-1). No. 3668, $1.20, Corridor (6-2). No. 3669, $1.20, Boat (6-3). No. 3670, $1.20, Garden of Harmonious Pleasures (6-4). No. 3671, $1.20, Yudai Bridge (6-5). No. 3672, $1.20, Houhu Lake (6-6).
$6, Tower of the Fragrance of Buddha, vert.

Litho. & Engr.
2008, May 10 ***Perf. 12***
3667-3672 A1111 Set of 6 3.25 2.10

Souvenir Sheet
Perf. 12x11¾
3673 A1111 $6 multi 3.00 2.00

No. 3673 contains one 50x62mm stamp.

Cao Chong Weighs the Elephant A1112

Cao Chong: Nos. 3674, 3676, $1.20, Marking water level on boat carrying elephant (2-1). Nos. 3675, 3677, $1.20, Replacing elephant with weighable objects (2-2).

2008, June 1 Photo. ***Perf. 13x13¼***
3674-3675 A1112 Set of 2 1.00 1.00

Booklet Stamps
Self-Adhesive
Serpentine Die Cut 11¾
3676-3677 A1112 Set of 2 .85 —
3677a Booklet pane of 8, 4 each #3676-3677 3.50 —
Complete booklet, #3677a 4.00

Temples A1113

Designs: No. 3678, $1.20, White Horse Temple, China (2-1). No. 3679, $1.20, Maha Bodhi Temple, India (2-2).

2008, June 6 ***Perf. 13¼x13***
3678-3679 A1113 Set of 2 1.25 .75

See India No. 2246.

Development on the Taiwan Strait — A1114

Designs: No. 3680, $1.20, Minjiang River development (4-1). No. 3681, $1.20, Port of Xiamen (4-2). No. 3682, $1.20, Exhibition Hall (4-3). No. 3683, $1.20, Fujian-Taiwan Kinship Museum (4-4).

2008, June 18 ***Perf. 12¾***
3680-3683 A1114 Set of 4 1.75 1.50

A sheet containing 2 each of Nos. 3680-3683 + 1 label exists. Value, $7.

Second Land Survey — A1115

Designs: No. 3684, $1.20, Satellite, rural land survey (2-1). No. 3685, $1.20, Theodolite, urban land survey (2-2).

Perf. 12¾x12½
2008, June 25 **Litho.**
3684-3685 A1115 Set of 2 .85 .75

Qiuci Grotto Murals A1116

Designs: No. 3686, $1.20 Heavenly Kings (4-1). No. 3687, $1.20, Bodhisattva (4-2). No. 3688, $1.20, Flying Apsaras, horiz. (4-3). No. 3689, $1.20, Maitreya Preaching, horiz. (4-4).

2008, July 6 Photo. ***Perf. 13¼***
3686-3689 A1116 Set of 4 2.00 1.50

General Qi Jiguang (1528-88) A1117

Qi Jiguang: No. 3690, $1.20, Standing (2-1). No. 3691, $1.20, On horse (2-2).

Perf. 12x12½ Syncopated
2008, July 19 **Litho.**
3690-3691 A1117 Set of 2 1.25 .90

Opening of 2008 Summer Olympics, Beijing — A1118

2008, Aug. 8 Photo. ***Perf. 13¼***
3692 A1118 $1.20 multi 2.25 .50

A sheet of 8 self-adhesive stamps similar to No. 3692 exists. Value, $11. A sheet of 8 stamps with a holographic background exists. Value, $35.

Olympex 2008 Philatelic Exhibition, Beijing — A1119

Designs: No. 3693, $1.20, Greece #127 (2-1). No. 3694, $1.20, Portugal #RA14 (2-2).
$6, Greece #127, gold medal and mascots of 2004 Summer Olympics.

2008, Aug. 8 Photo. *Perf. 13¼x13*
3693-3694 A1119 Set of 2 1.75 .85

Souvenir Sheet
Litho.
Perf.

3695 A1119 $6 multi 4.50 3.50

No. 3695 contains one 56mm diameter stamp. No. 3695 exists on silk paper. Value, $20.

2008 Summer Olympics Gold Medal A1119a

2008, Aug. 9 Litho. *Perf. 12*
3695A A1119a $1.20 multi + label *4.00 4.00*

Labels could be personalized. No. 3695A was printed in sheets of various sizes, with many sheets having pre-printed labels depicting Olympic athletes.

Closing of 2008 Summer Olympics A1120

Designs: No. 3696, $1.20, National Stadium, Beijing (4-1). No. 3697, $1.20, Tower, Forbidden City, Beijing (4-2). No. 3698, $1.20, Millennium Wheel, London (4-3). No. 3699, $1.20, Tower of London (4-4).

2008, Aug. 24 Photo. *Perf. 13¼*
3696-3699 A1120 Set of 4 4.00 2.25

A sheet containing 3 self-adhesive examples each of Nos. 3696-3699 exists. Value, $11.

China Central Television, 50th Anniv. A1121

Perf. 13½x13 Syncopated
2008, Sept. 2
3700 A1121 $1.20 multi .85 .40

Emblem of 2008 Paralympic Games, Beijing — A1122

Paralympic Games Mascot — A1123

2008, Sept. 6 *Perf. 13¼x13*
3701 A1122 $1.20 multi .75 .40
3702 A1123 $1.20 multi .75 .40

University of Science and Technology, 50th Anniv. — A1124

Perf. 12x11¼ Syncopated
2008, Sept. 20 Litho.
3703 A1124 $1.20 multi 1.50 .40

Ningxia Hui Autonomous Region, 50th Anniv. — A1125

No. 3704: a, Windmills (3-1). b, Trees and wildlife in desert (3-2). c, People holding flower bouquets (3-3).

Perf. 13¼x12¾ Syncopated
2008, Sept. 23 Photo.
3704 A1125 Horiz. strip of 3 1.40 1.25
a. 80f multi .25 .25
b.-c. $1.20 Either single .45 .35

Airports — A1126

No. 3705: a, Beijing Capital International Airport (3-1). b, Shanghai Pudong International Airport (3-2). c, Guangzhou Baiyun International Airport (3-3).

2008, Sept. 28 *Perf. 12¾*
3705 Vert. strip of 3 2.00 1.50
a.-c. A1126 $1.20 Any single .45 .35

Guangxi Zhuang Autonomous Region, 50th Anniv. — A1127

No. 3706: a, Dancers (3-1). b, Building (3-2). c, Port (3-3).

Perf. 12¾ Syncopated
2008, Oct. 18 Litho.
3706 A1127 Horiz. strip of 3 1.25 1.25
a. 80f multi .25 .25
b.-c. $1.20 Either single .45 .35

Happy New Year Type of 2006 and

"Blossom of Fortune" A1128

Perf. 11¾ Syncopated
2008, Oct. 9 Litho.
3707 A1128 $1.20 multi .50 .35

Souvenir Sheet

3708 Sheet of 2, #3707, 3708a *12.00 8.00*
a. A1055a $3 gold & multi *6.25 6.25*

Seventh Asia-Europe Meeting, Beijing — A1129

Perf. 12x11¼ Syncopated
2008, Oct. 24
3709 A1129 $1.20 multi .80 .40
a. Miniature sheet of 12 6.75 6.75

"Harmony" — A1130

2008, Dec. 3 *Perf. 12*
3710 A1130 $1.20 multi + label .50 .40

Expo 2010, Shanghai — A1131

2008, Dec. 13 *Perf. 12*
3711 A1131 $1.20 multi + label .60 .45

Compare with Type A1097.

A1132

Reform in China, 30th Anniv. — A1133

Perf. 12x11¼ Syncopated
2008, Dec. 18 Litho.
3712 A1132 $1.20 multi 1.00 .60
a. Miniature sheet of 8 5.00 5.00

Souvenir Sheet
Photo.
Perf.

3713 A1133 $6 multi + label 3.75 3.75

A sheet containing 2 examples of No. 3713 exists. Value, $35.

New Year 2009 (Year of the Ox) — A1134

Perf. 13 Syncopated
2009, Jan. 5 Photo.
3714 A1134 $1.20 multi 1.00 .45
a. Miniature sheet of 6 17.00 5.00
b. Booklet pane of 10 8.00 —
Complete booklet, #3714b 8.50

A sheet of 4 No. 3714 exists. Value, $7.

Bo Yibo (1908-2007), Politician A1135

Bo Yibo: No. 3715, $1.20, Standing (2-1). No. 3716, $1.20, Seated, horiz. (2-2).

2009, Jan. 15 *Perf. 13¼x13, 13x13¼*
3715-3716 A1135 Set of 2 1.25 .90

Zhangzhou New Year Woodprints A1136

Designs: No. 3717, $1.20, Lion holding a sword in mouth (4-1). No. 3718, $1.20, The coming flood of wealth, vert. (4-2). No. 3719, $1.20, Goddess sending children, vert. (4-3). No. 3720, $1.20, Rat marrying off its daughter (4-4).

2009, Jan. 18 *Perf. 12*
3717-3720 A1136 Set of 4 1.75 1.50
3720a Souvenir sheet, #3717-3720 + label 2.50 2.50
3720b Miniature sheet of 8, 2 each #3717-3720 4.50 4.50

A1137

24th Winter Universiade, Harbin — A1138

2009, Feb. 18 Litho. *Perf. 12¾*
3721 A1137 $1.20 multi .40 .40
3722 A1138 $1.20 multi .40 .40

Electric Power Grid Construction — A1139

No. 3723: a, Power station (3-1). b, Transmission towers and power lines (3-2). c, Light bulb, city skyline (3-3).

Perf. 12x12½ Syncopated

2009, Feb. 24

3723 A1139 $1.20 Horiz. strip of 3, #a-c 1.25 1.25

Paintings by Shi Tao (1642-1707) A1140

No. 3724: a, Chaohu Lake (30x55mm) (6-1). b, Enjoying Fountain Sound (25x55mm) (6-2). c, Double Chrysanthemums (30x55mm) (6-3). d, Plum Blossoms and Bamboo (25x55mm) (6-4). e, Horse and its Owner (30x55mm) (6-5). f, Lotus (25x55mm) (6-6).

2009, Mar. 22 Litho. *Perf. 12½x13*

3724 Horiz. strip of 6 5.50 2.75
a. A1140 80f multi .35 .25
b.-f. A1140 $1.20 Any single .65 .45

A1141

China 2009 World Stamp Exhibition, Luoyang — A1142

Designs: No. 3725, $1.20, Vase (2-1). No. 3726, $1.20, Jar with stopper (2-2).
$6, National Beauty and Heavenly Fragrance.

Perf. 12¾ Syncopated

2009, Apr. 10 Litho. & Embossed

3725-3726 A1141 Set of 2 1.10 .85

Souvenir Sheet

Litho.

Perf. 13 Syncopated

3727 A1142 $6 multi 4.50 3.50

Nos. 3725 and 3726 both exist in sheets of 4. Value, set $6.50.
No. 3727 exists in a sheet of 2. Value, $16.

China at World Expos A1143

Scenes from Expos from: No. 3728, $1.20, 1904, 1915, 1926, 1933 (red panel) (4-1). No. 3729, $1.20, 1982, 1982 (brown panel) (4-2). No. 3730, $1.20, 1999 (green panel) (4-3). No. 3731, $1.20, 2010 (blue panel) (4-4).

Perf. 13¼x12¾ Syncopated

2009, May 1 Photo.

3728-3731 A1143 Set of 4 2.00 2.00
3731a Miniature sheet of 8, 2 each #3728-3731 7.00 7.00

Fenghuang — A1144

No. 3732: a, North Gate (3-1). b, Rainbow Bridge (3-2). c, Street (3-3).

Perf. 12¾ Syncopated

2009, May 23 Litho.

3732 A1144 Horiz. strip of 3 1.25 1.25
a.-c. $1.20 Any single .40 .35

Children's Art — A1145

Designs: Nos. 3733, 3737, 80f, Love for the Motherland (yellow orange panel) (4-1). Nos. 3734, 3738, $1.20, Happy Life, horiz. (red panel) (4-2). Nos. 3735, 3739, $1.20, Peace Lovers (blue panel) (4-3). Nos. 3736, 3740, $1.20, Enthusiasm for Science, horiz. (green panel) (4-4).

Perf. 13¼x13, 13x13¼

2009, June 1 Photo.

3733-3736 A1145 Set of 4 1.60 1.40

Booklet Stamps

Self-Adhesive

Serpentine Die Cut 12

3737-3740 A1145 Set of 4 1.40 1.40
3740a Booklet pane of 8, 2 each #3737-3740 3.00

Hangzhou Bay Bridge — A1146

No. 3741: a, Bridge. b, Marine platform.

2009, June 18 Litho. *Perf. 12*

3741 A1146 $1.20 Horiz. pair, #a-b 1.00 .80

Li Xiannian (1909-92), People's Republic of China President A1147

Designs: No. 3742, $1.20, Wearing army uniform and cap (3-1). No. 3743, $1.20, Wearing gray suit with collar buttoned (3-2). No. 3744, $1.20, Wearing gray suit and eyeglasses (3-3).

2009, June 23 Photo. *Perf. 13¼x13*

3742-3744 A1147 Set of 3 1.50 1.25

A1148

16th Asian Games, Guangzhou — A1149

2009, June 30 Photo. *Perf. 13¼*

3745 A1148 $1.20 multi .60 .50
3746 A1149 $1.20 multi .60 .50

A sheet containing four each of Nos. 3745-3746 exists.

Great Hall of the People — A1150

Designs: No. 3747, East Gate (2-1). No. 3748, Great Auditorium (2-2).

2009, July 18 Litho. *Perf. 13¼x12½*

3747 A1150 $1.20 multi .55 .45
3748 A1150 $1.20 multi .55 .45
a. Booklet pane of 2, #3747-3748 1.10 —
b. Booklet pane of 8, 4 each #3747-3748 4.50 —
Complete booklet, #3748a, 3748b 4.50

Sanjiangyuan Nature Reserve — A1151

No. 3749: a, Geladandong (3-1). b, Eling Lake (3-2). c, Dza Chu (3-3).

Perf. 13¼x12½ Syncopated

2009, July 25 Photo.

3749 A1151 Horiz. strip of 3 1.40 1.25
a.-c. $1.20 Any single .40 .35

Flag, 60th Anniv. — A1152

2009, Aug. 2 Litho. *Perf. 13¼*

3750 A1152 $1.20 multi + label .80 .60

A souvenir sheet of 4 No. 3750 + one label exists.

Labrang Lamasery A1153

No. 3751: a, Grand Sutra Hall (2-1). b, Gongtang Pagoda (2-2).

Perf. 13x12¾ Syncopated

2009, Aug. 2

3751 A1153 $1.20 Vert. pair, #a-b .80 .80

Stork Tower A1154

Golden Gate A1155

2009, Aug. 14 Photo.

3752 A1154 $1.20 multi .55 .40
3753 A1155 $1.20 multi .55 .40

A1156

Huang Long Scenic Area — A1157

Designs: No. 3754, $1.20, Guest Welcome Ponds (3-1). No. 3755, $1.20, Waterfall (3-2). No. 3756, $1.20, Erdao Lake (3-3).
$6, Five-color Ponds.

2009, Aug. 27 *Perf. 12¾*

3754-3756 A1156 Set of 3 1.25 1.10

Souvenir Sheet

Perf. 13¼x12¾ Syncopated

3757 A1157 $6 multi 2.25 2.25

A miniature sheet containing 2 each of Nos. 3754-3756 exists. Value, $6.

National Library of China — A1158

Books and: No. 3758, $1.20, Old building (2-1). No. 3759, $1.20, Modern building (2-2).

2009, Sept. 9 ***Perf. 13¼ Syncopated***
3758-3759 A1158 Set of 2 1.10 1.10

Miniature Sheet

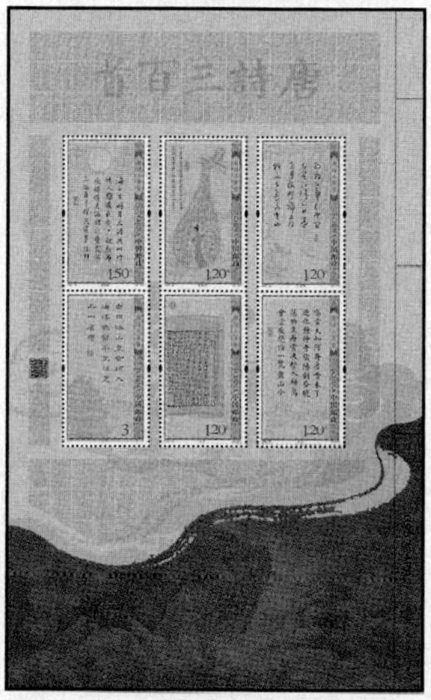

Tang Poems — A1159

No. 3760: a, $1.20, Downstream to Jiangling, by Il Bai (boat near rocks) (6-1). b, $1.20, A View of Taishan Mountain, by Du Fu (mountains) (6-2). c, $1.20, The Song of Pipa, by Bai Juyi (musician) (6-3). d, $1.20, To One Unnamed, by Li Shangyin (book) (6-4). e, $1.50, Looking at the Moon and Thinking of One Far Away, by Zhang Jiulin (Moon) (6-5). f, $3, On the Stork Tower, by Wang Zhihuan (Stork Tower) (6-6).

Litho., Engr. & Silk-screened
Perf. 12¾x13¼ Syncopated
2009, Sept. 13
3760 A1159 Sheet of 6, #a-f 6.50 6.50

Lanzhoui University, Cent. A1160

Perf. 13x12½ Syncopated
2009, Sept. 17 **Litho.**
3761 A1160 $1.20 multi .55 .50

Chinese People's Political Consultative Conference, 60th Anniv. — A1161

Flowers and: No. 3762, $1.20, Conference emblem (2-1). No. 3763, $1.20, Conference venue, horiz. (2-2).

Perf. 13¼ Syncopated
2009, Sept. 17
3762-3763 A1161 Set of 2 1.10 1.10

A1162

Beijing-Hangzhou Grand Canal — A1163

Designs: No. 3764, $1.20, Lantern Lighting Pagoda (6-1). No. 3765, $1.20, Boats and Tianhou Temple (6-2). No. 3766, $1.20, Shanshan Guild Hall (6-3). No. 3767, $1.20, Qingjiang Water Gate (6-4). No. 3768, $1.20, Boats and Wenfeng Pagoda (6-5). No. 3769, $1.20, Gongchen Bridge (6-6).
$6, Canal.

Perf. 13x13¼ Syncopated
2009, Sept. 26 **Photo.**
3764-3769 A1162 Set of 6 3.25 2.10

Souvenir Sheet
Perf. 13¼ Syncopated
3770 A1163 $6 multi 3.00 3.00

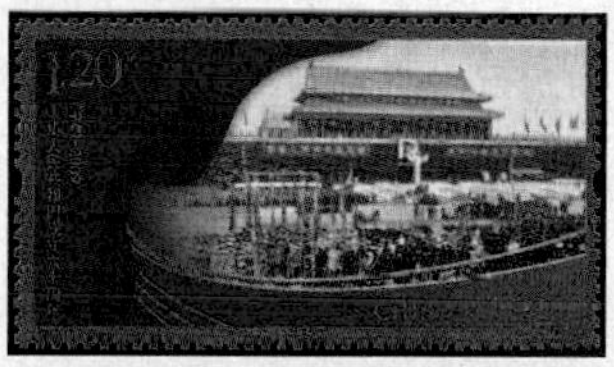

A1164

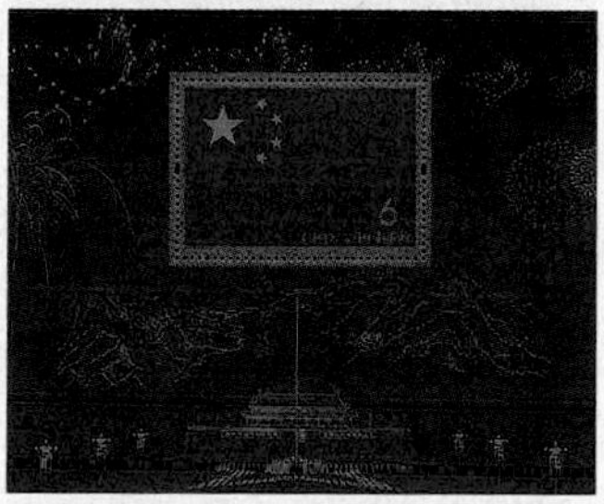

People's Republic of China, 60th Anniv. — A1165

Designs: No. 3771, $1.20, Marchers (4-1). No. 3772, $1.20, Tractors pulling floats bearing Chinese symbols (4-2). No. 3773, $1.20, Flag, emblems of Macao and Hong Kong (4-3). No. 3774, $1.20, Olympic rings and torch (4-4).
$6, Flag.

Perf. 13x12½ Syncopated
2009, Oct. 1
3771-3774 A1164 Set of 4 1.80 1.50

Souvenir Sheet
Perf. 13¼x13½ Syncopated
3775 A1165 $6 multi 4.25 3.50

A miniature sheet containing two each of Nos. 3771-3774 exists.

National Day Parade — A1166

Designs: No. 3776, $1.20, Infantry Group (red background) (4-1). No. 3777, $1.20, Army and 2nd Artillery Group (green background) (4-2). No. 3778, $1.20, Navy Equipment Group (blue background) (4-3). No. 3779, $1.20, Air Group (orange background) (4-4).

Perf. 13¼x12½ Syncopated
2009, Oct. 1
3776-3779 A1166 Set of 4 2.25 2.00

A miniature sheet containing two each of Nos. 3776-3779 exists. Value, $9.

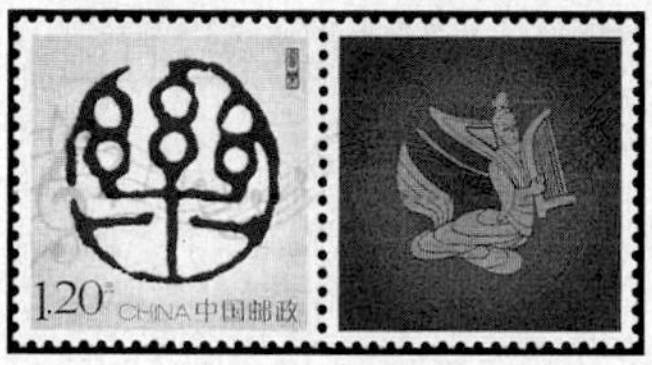

"Music" — A1167

2009, Sept. 29 **Litho.** ***Perf. 12***
3780 A1167 $1.20 multi + label .75 .35

See Stamps With Attached Labels note after No. 3197.

"Happiness With the Spring" — A1168

2009, Oct. 9 ***Perf. 13 Syncopated***
3781 A1168 $1.20 multi .75 .35

A souvenir sheet containing Nos. 3781 and 3708a exists.

A1169

11th National Games, Shandong A1170

Perf. 13¼x13 Syncopated
2009, Oct. 16
3782 A1169 $1.20 multi .35 .35
3783 A1170 $1.20 multi .35 .35
a. Souvenir sheet, #3782-3783 1.25 1.25

No. 3783a sold for $3.60.

Ancient Academies A1171

Designs: No. 3784, $1.20, Stone Drum Academy (4-1). No. 3785, $1.20, Anding Academy (4-2). No. 3786, $1.20, Ehu Academy (4-3). No. 3787, $1.20, Dongpo Academy (4-4).

Perf. 13¼ Syncopated
2009, Nov. 15 **Photo.**
3784-3787 A1171 Set of 4 1.40 1.40

A souvenir sheet containing two each of Nos. 3784-3787 exists.

Guangji Bridge — A1172

No. 3788: a, Building at left on shore, bridge, ships (3-1). b, Ships, central part of bridge (3-2). c, Bridge, building at right on shore (3-3).

Perf. 12¾ Syncopated
2009, Nov. 16 **Litho.**
3788 A1172 Horiz. strip of 3 1.10 1.10
a.-c. $1.20 Any single .35 .35

Ma Lianliang (1901-66), Opera Performer, in Kong Ming Borrows the East Wing — A1173

Ma Lianliang in Zhao the Orphan — A1174

Perf. 13¼x13½ Syncopated
2009, Nov. 28 **Photo.**
3789 A1173 $1.20 multi .50 .35
3790 A1174 $1.20 multi .50 .35

Return of Macao to China, 10th Anniv. A1175

Doves and: No. 3791, $1.20, Golden Lotus sculpture, flags of People's Republic of China and Macao (3-1). No. 3792, $1.20, "CEPA," buildings (3-2). $1.50, Bridge, buildings (3-3).

Perf. 13¼x13 Syncopated
2009, Dec. 20
3791-3793 A1175 Set of 3 1.25 1.25
3793a Souvenir sheet, #3791-3793, Macao #1302a-1302c 2.40 2.40

See Macao Nos. 1302-1303. No. 3793a was not offered for sale in Macao.

16th Asian Games, Guangzhou — A1176

2009, Dec. 25 **Litho.** ***Perf. 12***
3794 A1176 $1.20 multi + label 1.00 .40

Compare with Type A1148. See Stamps With Attached Labels note after No. 3197.

Gutian Conference, 80th Anniv. — A1177

Perf. 13¼x13 Syncopated

2009, Dec. 28

3795 A1177 $1.20 multi .80 .35

Ballet Dancers in Red Detachment of Women — A1178

Designs: No. 3796, $1.20, Dancer in red (2-1). No. 3797, $1.20, Dancers in blue (2-2).

2010, Jan. 1 Photo. *Perf. 13¼*

3796-3797 A1178 Set of 2 2.75 1.00

New Year 2010 (Year of the Tiger) A1179

2010, Jan. 5 *Perf. 12¾ Syncopated*

3798 A1179 $1.20 multi 1.00 .40
- *a.* Booklet pane of 10 4.00 —
- Complete booklet, #3798a 5.00

No. 3798 exists in sheets of 4 and 6.

Gen. Song Renqiong (1909-2005) — A1180

Designs: No. 3799, $1.20, Wearing cap (2-1). No. 3800, $1.20, Reading book (2-2).

Perf. 13 Syncopated

2010, Jan. 8 Litho.

3799-3800 A1180 Set of 2 1.00 .70

Expo 2010, Shanghai — A1181

Designs: 80f, Expo Center (4-1). No. 3802, $1.20, China Pavilion (4-2). No. 3803, $1.20, Expo Performance Center (4-3). $3, Theme Pavilion (4-4).

$6, Shanghai Expo Park, vert.

Perf. 13¼x13 Syncopated

2010, Jan. 21 Photo.

3801-3804 A1181 Set of 4 2.00 2.00

Souvenir Sheet

Perf. 13x12¾ Syncopated

3805 A1181 $6 multi 5.50 4.50

No. 3805 contains one 30x75mm stamp. A sheet containing two each of Nos. 3801-3804 exists. A sheet containing two examples of No. 3805 exists.

Liangping New Year Woodprints A1182

Designs: No. 3806, $1.20, Gate god (4-1). No. 3807, $1.20, Stealing the immortal grass (4-2). No. 3808, $1.20, Peace leads to happiness (4-3). No. 3809, $1.20, Exiting the pass with a stolen token (4-4).

2010, Feb. 6 *Perf. 13¼x13*

3806-3809 A1182 Set of 4 1.40 1.40
- *3809a* Souvenir sheet, #3806-3809 + label 2.50 2.50
- *3809b* Souvenir sheet of 8, 2 each #3806-3809 on fabric-faced paper *10.00 8.00*
- *3809c* As "b," plain paper *6.25 6.25*

No. 3809a sold for $7.20.

Intl. Women's Day, Cent. — A1183

Perf. 13¼x13 Syncopated

2010, Mar. 8

3810 A1183 $1.20 multi .50 .40

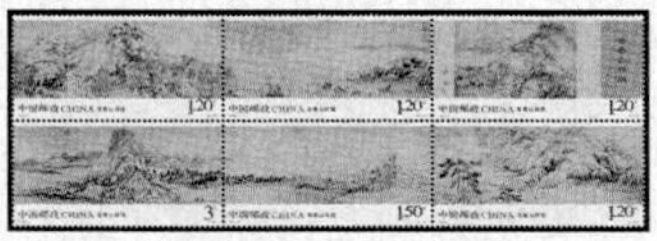

Dwelling in Fuchun Mountains, Painting by Huang Gongwang — A1184

No. 3811 — Various parts of painting with inscription: a, (6-1). b, (6-2). c, (6-3). d, (6-4). e, (6-5). f, (6-6).

2010, Mar. 20 *Perf. 13¼*

3811 A1184 Block of 6 17.50 15.00
- *a.-d.* $1.20 Any single .60 .35
- *e.* $1.50 multi .75 .50
- *f.* $3 multi 1.25 .95

Tomb Sweeping Festival — A1185

Designs: No. 3812, $1.20, Ancestor worship (3-1). No. 3813, $1.20, Spring outing (3-2). No. 3814, $1.20, Planting willows (3-3).

Perf. 13¼x13½ Syncopated

2010, Apr. 5 Litho.

3812-3814 A1185 Set of 3 1.10 1.10

A sheet containing three each of Nos. 3812-3814 exists.

Idioms — A1186

Designs: No. 3815, $1.20, The foolish old man removes the mountains (4-1). No. 3816, $1.20, Sleeping on brushwood and tasting gall (4-2). No. 3817, $1.20, Mao Sui recommending himself (4-3). No. 3818, $1.20, Rising to practice swordplay upon hearing the rooster crow (4-4).

Perf. 13¼x13½ Syncopated

2010, Apr. 18 Photo.

3815-3818 A1186 Set of 4 1.40 1.40

Opening of Expo 2010, Shanghai A1187

2010, May 1 *Perf. 13¼ Syncopated*

3819 A1187 $1.20 multi 1.00 .40

A sheet of six exists.

A1188

A1189

Ancient Calligraphy — A1190

No. 3820 — Preface to the Orchid Pavilion: a, Denomination at right (6-1). b, Denomination at left (6-2).

No. 3821 — Poems Composed During the Cold Food Festival in Huangzhou: a, Denomination at right (6-3). b, Denomination at left (6-4).

No. 3822 — Elegiac Lament for My Nephew: a, Denomination at right (6-5). b, Denomination at left (6-6).

2010, May 15 *Perf. 13x13¼*

3820 A1188 $1.20 Horiz. pair, #a-b .70 .70

3821 A1189 $1.20 Horiz. pair, #a-b .70 .70

3822 A1190 $1.20 Horiz. pair, #a-b .70 .70

Nos. 3820-3822 (3) 2.10 2.10

A sheet containing two each Nos. 3820-3822 exists.

Tenth Global Travel and Tourism Summit, Beijing — A1191

2010, May 25 *Perf. 13¼ Syncopated*

3823 A1191 $1.20 multi 3.50 .50

Wen Yanbo's Ball Goes Into Hole in Tree A1192

Wen Yanbo Retrieves Ball With Water A1193

2010, June 1 *Perf. 13 Syncopated*

3824 A1192 $1.20 multi .35 .35

3825 A1193 $1.20 multi .35 .35
- *a.* Booklet pane of 2, #3824-3825 .70 —
- *b.* Booklet pane of 8, 4 each #3824-3825 3.00 —
- Complete booklet, #3825a, 3825b 4.00

A1194

Environmental Protection A1195

Perf. 13¼x13½ Syncopated

2010, June 5

3826 A1194 $1.20 multi 1.25 .40

3827 A1195 $1.20 multi 1.25 .40

Kunqu Opera — A1196

Designs: No. 3828, $1.20, Washing the Silken Gauze (3-1). No. 3829, $1.20, The Peony Pavilion (3-2). No. 3830, $1.20, The Palace of Long Life (3-3).

Perf. 13¼ Syncopated

2010, June 12 **Photo.**
3828-3830 A1196 Set of 3 1.10 1.10

A miniature sheet containing 3 each of Nos. 3828-3830 exists.

Pearl River Scenes — A1197

Designs: No. 3831, $1.20, Five Goats Statue, Guangzhou (4-1). No. 3832, $1.20, Guangzhou Center for the Performing Arts (4-2). No. 3833, $1.20, Guangzhou skyline (4-3). No. 3834, $1.20, Guangzhou Intl. Convention and Exhibition Center (4-4).

Perf. 13¼x13 Syncopated

2010, June 28
3831-3834 A1197 Set of 4 1.40 1.40
3834a Souvenir sheet of 8, 2 each #3831-3834 *4.75 4.75*

Loulan — A1198

Designs: No. 3835, $1.20, Ruins of Buddhist stupa (2-1). No. 3836, $1.20, Ruins of building (2-2).

2010, July 3 **Litho.**
3835-3836 A1198 Set of 2 .70 .70

Maritime Day — A1199

Perf. 13½x13 Syncopated

2010, July 11 **Photo.**
3837 A1199 $1.20 multi .80 .35

Composers — A1200

Designs: No. 3838, $1.20, Johann Sebastian Bach (1685-1750) (4-1). No. 3839, $1.20, Joseph Haydn (1732-1809) (4-2). No. 3840, $1.20, Wolfgang Amadeus Mozart (1756-91) (4-3). $4.50, Ludwig van Beethoven (1770-1827) (4-4).

Perf. 13¼x12¾ Syncopated

2010, July 25 **Litho. & Engr.**
3838-3841 A1200 Set of 4 2.40 2.40

Legend of the Cowherd and the Weaving Maid — A1201

Designs: No. 3842, Dress-linked affection (4-1). No. 3843, Happy lovers (4-2). No. 3844, Carrying children to chase wife (4-3). No. 3845, Heavenly reunion (4-4).

Perf. 13¼x13¾ Syncopated

2010, Aug. 16 **Photo.**
3842 A1201 $1.20 multi .40 .35
a. Booklet pane of 1 + 5 labels .60 —
3843 A1201 $1.20 multi .40 .35
a. Booklet pane of 1 + 5 labels .60 —
3844 A1201 $1.20 multi .40 .35
a. Booklet pane of 1 + 5 labels .60 —
3845 A1201 $1.20 multi .40 .35
a. Booklet pane of 1 + 5 labels .60 —
Complete booklet, #3842a-3845a 3.00
Nos. 3842-3845 (4) 1.60 1.40

Complete booklet sold for $8.

2010 Asian Para Games, Guangzhou — A1202

2010, Sept. 3 ***Perf. 13***
3846 A1202 $1.20 multi .80 .35

Values are for stamp with adjacent selvage.

Great Wall Type of 2005

2010, Sept. 3 **Litho.** ***Perf. 12***
3846A A1003 $1.20 multi + label *5.00 5.00*

See note following No. 3462.

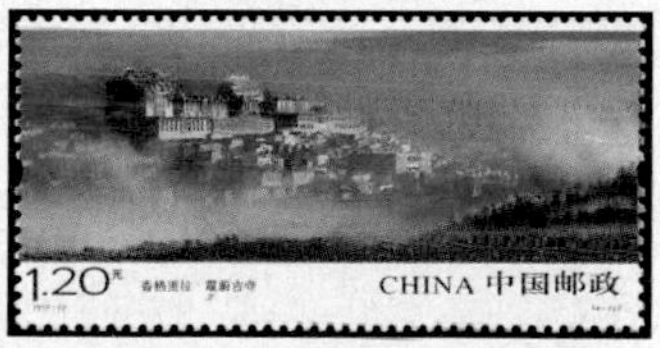

A1203

Shangri-La (Zhongdian) — A1204

Designs: No. 3847, $1.20, Songzanlin Lamasery (4-1). No. 3848, $1.20, Napa Lake and grassland (4-2). No. 3849, $1.20, Pudacuo National Park (4-3). No. 3850, $1.20, Dukezong (4-4).
$6, Meili Snow Mountain.

Perf. 13¼x13 Syncopated

2010, Sept. 13
3847-3850 A1203 Set of 4 1.50 1.50

Souvenir Sheet

Perf. 13¼x13¾ Syncopated

3851 A1204 $6 multi 2.50 1.90

Confucius and Buildings — A1205

No. 3852: a, $1.20, Confucius and temple (3-1). b, $1.20, Family home of Confucius (3-2). c, $3, Cemetery of Confucius (3-3).

Perf. 13¼ Syncopated

2010, Sept. 28 **Litho.**
3852 A1205 Horiz. strip of 3, #a-c 2.00 1.60
d. Souvenir sheet, #3852a-3852c 3.00 3.00

Huai River Water Control Project — A1206

Designs: No. 3853, $1.20, Nanwan Reservoir (4-1). No. 3854, $1.20, Linhuaigang Water Control Project (4-2). No. 3855, $1.20, Huai River Outflow Project (4-3). No. 3856, $1.20, Nansi Lake Water Control Project (4-4).

Perf. 12¾x13 Syncopated

2010, Oct. 14
3853-3856 A1206 Set of 4 1.50 1.50

Flora — A1207

Drawings of: No. 3857, $1.20, Plum blossom (4-1). No. 3858, $1.20, Orchid (4-2). No. 3859, $1.20, Bamboo (4-3). No. 3860, $1.20, Chrysanthemums (4-4).

2010, Oct. 18 ***Perf. 13¼ Syncopated***
3857-3860 A1207 Set of 4 2.50 1.50
3860a Souvenir sheet of 8, 2 each #3857-3860 *20.00 15.00*

Zhu Xi (Chu Hsi) (1130-1200), Philosopher A1208

Designs: No. 3861, $1.20, Portrait of Zhu Xi (2-1). No. 3862, $1.20, Zhu Xi, student and horse (2-2).

Perf. 13¼x13½ Syncopated

2010, Oct. 22 **Litho. & Engr.**
3861-3862 A1208 Set of 2 1.00 .75

2010 Asian Games, Guangzhou A1209

Designs: 80f, Badminton (6-1). No. 3864, $1.20, Wushu (6-2). No. 3865, $1.20, Hurdles (6-3). No. 3866, $1.20, Equestrian (6-4). No. 3867, $1.20, Dragon boat racing (6-5). $3, Weiqi (6-6).

Perf. 13¼ Syncopated

2010, Nov. 12 **Photo.**
3863-3868 A1209 Set of 6 2.60 2.60
3868a Sheet of 12, 2 each #3863-3868 *8.00 8.00*

Souvenir Sheet

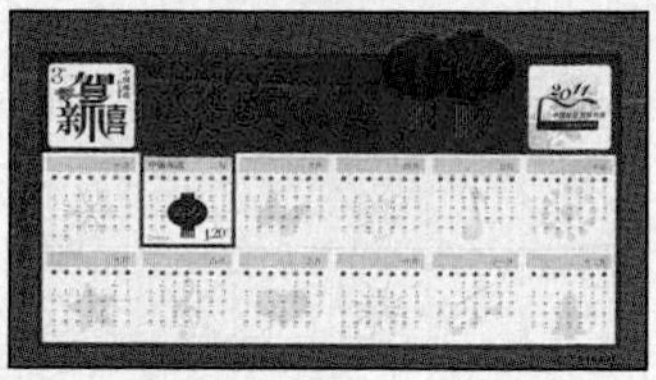

New Year 2011 — A1210

No. 3869: a, $1.20, Chinese lantern, calendar for February 2011. b, $3, Like #3541, with copper frame.

Serpentine Die Cut 12¼

2010, Oct. 9 **Self-Adhesive** **Litho.**
3869 A1210 Sheet of 2, #a-b, + 13 labels *4.75 4.75*

Traditional Chinese Medicine Stores — A1211

Designs: No. 3870, $1.20, Tongren Tang (4-1). No. 3871, $1.20, Huqing Yu Tang (4-2). No. 3872, $1.20, Lei Yongshang (4-3). No. 3873, $1.20, Chen Liji (4-4).

Perf. 13¼ Syncopated

2010, Nov. 20 **Photo.**
3870-3873 A1211 Set of 4 1.50 1.50

High-speed Train — A1212

Perf. 13¼x12¾ Syncopated

2010, Dec. 7 **Photo.**
3874 A1212 $1.20 multi 1.50 .80

Chinese Capital Markets A1213

Bar graph and: No. 3875, $1.20, Bull, computers at capital market (2-1). No. 3876, $1.20, City, satellite dish, train (2-2).

Perf. 13¼ Syncopated

2010, Dec. 12 **Litho.**
3875-3876 A1213 Set of 2 1.75 1.25
3876a Souvenir sheet of 8, 4 each #3875-3876 *30.00 20.00*

New Year 2011 (Year of the Rabbit) A1214

Perf. 13 Syncopated

2011, Jan. 5 **Photo.**

3877	A1214 $1.20 multi		.80	.60
a.	Booklet pane of 10		8.00	—
	Complete booklet, #3877a		8.00	
b.	Souvenir sheet of 6		*12.50*	*10.00*

A souvenir sheet containing 4 No. 3877 exists.

Fengxiang New Year Woodprints A1215

Designs: No. 3878, $1.20, General Yuchi Jingde (4-1). No. 3879, $1.20, Fortune boy (4-2). No. 3880, $1.20, Beauties (4-3). No. 3881, $1.20, Fortune flower vase (4-4).

Perf. 13¼x13¾ Syncopated

2011, Jan. 10 **Litho.**

3878-3881 A1215 Set of 4 1.50 1.50

Sheet of eight containing two each Nos. 3878-3881 on plain and fabric-faced paper exist.

Early Leaders of the Communist Party of China — A1216

Designs: No. 3882, $1.20, Chen Yannian (1898-1927) (5-1). No. 3883, $1.20, Zhang Tailei (1898-1927) (5-2). No. 3884, $1.20, Luo Yinong (1902-28) (5-3). No. 3885, $1.20, Yun Daiying (1895-1931) (5-4). No. 3886, $1.20, Xiang Ying (1898-1941) (5-5).

2011, Feb. 21

3882-3886 A1216 Set of 5 1.90 1.90

Liangzhu Jade — A1217

Designs: No. 3887, $1.20, Cong (carved block of jade) (2-1). No. 3888, $1.20, Bi (ring of jade) (2-2).

2011, Mar. 8 **Photo.**

3887-3888 A1217 Set of 2 .75 .75

Scenes From "The Scholars," Novel by Wu Jingzi — A1218

Designs: 80f, Lotus painter Wang Mian (6-1). No. 3890, $1.20, Fanjin passing the Imperial exam (6-2). No. 3891, $1.20, Two lamp wicks (6-3). No. 3892, $1.20, Ma Er tours West Lake (6-4). No. 3893, $1.20, Mr. and Mrs. Du Shaoqing (6-5). No. 3894, $1.20, Shen Qunzhi selling writings by Sheli Bridge (6-6).

2011, Mar. 21

3889-3894 A1218 Set of 6 2.10 2.10

A sheet of 12 containing two each of Nos. 3889-3894 exists.

Chinese Calligraphy A1219

Designs: No. 3895, $1.20, Pingfu Tie, by Lu Ji (4-1). No. 3896, $1.20, Chuyue Tie, by Wang Xizhi (4-2). No. 3897, $1.20, Gushi Si Tie, by Zhangxu (4-3). No. 3898, $1.20, Zixu Tie, by Huaisu (4-4).

2011, Apr. 15 ***Perf. 13¼ Syncopated***

3895-3898 A1219 Set of 4 1.50 1.50

A sheet of eight containing two each Nos. 3895-3896, printed on rice paper exists.

Military Aircraft — A1220

Designs: No. 3899, $1.20, J-10 fighter (3-1). No. 3900, $1.20, JH-7 fighter (3-2). No. 3901, $1.20, AC313 helicopter (3-3).

Perf. 13¼x12¾ Syncopated

2011, Apr. 17 **Litho.**

3899-3901 A1220 Set of 3 1.50 1.25

World Reading Day A1221

2011, Apr. 23 ***Perf. 13 Syncopated***

3902 A1221 $1.20 multi .60 .50

Tsinghua University, Cent. A1222

2011, Apr. 24 **Litho. & Embossed**

3903 A1222 $1.20 multi .80 .50

Expo 2011, Xi'an — A1223

Designs: $1.20, Emblem (2-1). $3, Mascot (2-2).

Perf. 13¼x13¾ Syncopated

2011, Apr. 28 **Photo.**

3904-3905 A1223 Set of 2 1.40 1.40

26th Summer Universiade, Shenzhen — A1224

No. 3906: a, $1.20, Emblem (50x30mm, 4-1). b, $1.20, Mascot (30x30mm, 4-2).
No. 3907: a, $1.20, Shenzhen Universiade Sports Center (50x30mm, 4-3). b, $3, Torch, Chinese and English text (30x30mm, 4-4).

2011, May 4 **Litho.** ***Perf. 13¼***
Horiz. Pairs, #a-b

3906-3907	A1224 Set of 2	2.10	2.10
3907a	Sheet of 8 2 each #3906a-3906b, 3907a-3907b	*6.50*	*5.50*

Cloud Brocade A1225

Designs: No. 3908, $1.20, Dragon (3-1). No. 3909, $1.20, Crane insignia of first-rank civil official (3-2). No. 3910, $1.20, Fish (Double happiness, 3-3).

Perf. 13¼x12¾

2011, May 10 **Photo.**

3908-3910	A1225 Set of 3	1.50	1.25
3910a	Souvenir sheet of 3, #3908-3910, + 3 labels	*5.50*	*3.50*

Emblem of Communist Party of China — A1226

2011, May 21 **Litho.** ***Perf. 13¼***

3911 A1226 $1.20 multi + label 1.00 .75

See Stamps With Attached Labels note after No. 3187.

Liberation of Tibet, 60th Anniv. — A1227

Designs: No. 3912, $1.20, Potala Palace, Chinese soldiers, Tibetans and livestock (3-1). No. 3913, $1.20, Airplane over building, dancers (3-2). No. 3914, $1.20, Building, dancers (3-3).

Perf. 13¼x13¾ Syncopated

2011, May 23 **Photo.**

3912-3914 A1227 Set of 3 1.50 1.25

Scientists A1228

Designs: No. 3915, $1.20, Bei Shizhang (1903-2009), biologist (4-1). No. 3916, $1.20, Qian Xuesen (1911-2009), rocket scientist (4-2). No. 3917, $1.20, Hou Xianglin (1912-2008), chemical engineer (4-3). No. 3918, $1.20, Qian Sanqiang (1913-92), nuclear physicist (4-4).

Perf. 13x12¾ Syncopated

2011, May 25

3915-3918 A1228 Set of 4 1.50 1.50

Ming and Qing Dynasty Furniture — A1230

No. 3919: a, 80f, Qing Dynasty rosewood-embedded copper dragon throne (6-1). b, $1.20, Ming Dynasy pearwood folding chair (6-2).
No. 3920: a, $1.20, Ming Dynasty pearwood official's armchair with carved Chinese characters (6-3). b, $1.20, Ming Dynasty pearwood armchair with carved dragons (6-4).
No. 3921: a, $1.20, Qing Dynasty rosewood-embedded marble armchair (6-5). b, $1.20, Ming Dynasty marble-embedded rosewood drum stool (6-6).

Perf. 13¼x13¾ Syncopated

2011, June 20 **Litho.**

3919	A1230 Horiz. pair, #a-b	.65	.65
c.	Booklet pane, #3919a-3919b + 2 labels	*.90*	—
3920	A1230 $1.20 Horiz. pair, #a-b	.75	.75
c.	Booklet pane, #3920a-3920b + 2 labels	*1.10*	—
3921	A1230 $1.20 Horiz. pair, #a-b	.75	.75
c.	Booklet pane, #3921a-3921b + 2 labels	*1.10*	—
d.	Booklet pane, #3919a-3919b, 3920a-3920b, 3921a-3921b	*3.25*	—
	Complete booklet, #3919c, 3920c, 3921c, 3921d	*6.50*	
	Nos. 3919-3921 (3)	2.15	2.15

A1231

Communist Party of China, 90th Anniv. — A1232

Flag of the Communist Party of China and: No. 3922, $1.20, People and building (6-1). No. 3923, $1.20, Soldiers and monument (6-2). No. 3924, $1.20, Sculpture and building (6-3). No. 3925, $1.20, City skyline, sculpture of bull (6-4). No. 3926, $1.20, City skyline and modern building (6-5). No. 3927, $1.20, Beijing National Stdium, Chinese Pavilion, Shanghai (6-6).
$6, Flag of the Communist Party of China.

2011, June 22 Photo. *Perf. 13¼*
3922-3927 A1231 Set of 6 2.50 2.50
3924a Sheet of 6, 2 each #3922-3924 *8.75 8.75*
3927a Sheet of 6, 2 each #3925-3927 *8.75 8.75*

Souvenir Sheet
Perf. 13¼x13
3928 A1232 $6 multi 3.50 2.75

Opening of Beijing-Shanghai High Speed Railway — A1233

Perf. 13¼x12¾ Syncopated
2011, June 30
3929 A1233 $1.20 multi 1.75 .90

Cycling — A1234

Designs: No. 3930, $1.20, Cyclists on bike path (2-1). No. 3931, $1.20, Cyclists racing (2-2).

2011, July 2 Litho.
3930-3931 A1234 Set of 2 1.00 .80

Folk Vocal Arts — A1235

Designs: No. 3932, $1.20, Xiangsheng (4-1). No. 3933, $1.20, Singer with drum (4-2). No. 3934, $1.20, Pingtan (4-3). No. 3935, $1.20, Performer in black robe (4-4).

2011, July 8 *Perf. 13¼ Syncopated*
3932-3935 A1235 Set of 4 1.50 1.50
3935a Sheet of 8, 4 each #3932-3935 *9.50 9.50*

Chinese Culture Abroad — A1236

No. 3936: a, Chinese Festival, London Eye (4-1). b, Chinese Benevolent Association sculpture and building, Buddhist temple, modern building (4-2). c, Chinatown, Transamerica Pyramid, San Francisco (4-3). d, Chinese school building, mountain (4-4).

Perf. 13¼x13¾ Syncopated
2011, July 10
3936 Horiz. strip of 4 2.60 2.60
a.-c. A1236 $1.20 Any single .40 .40
d. A1236 $4.50 multi 1.40 1.40

Cargo Ships — A1237

No. 3937: a, Cosco Asia container ship (4-1). b, Xinsheng Hai bulk transport ship (4-2).

Perf. 13¼x12¾ Syncopated
2011, Aug. 8 Photo.
3937 A1237 $1.20 Horiz. pair, #a-b 1.00 .85

Peonies — A1238

Lilies — A1239

Sunflowers — A1240

Chinese Rose — A1241

Carnations — A1242

Camellias — A1243

Azalea Flowers — A1244

Lotus Flowers — A1245

Plum Blossoms — A1246

Magnolia Blossoms — A1247

2011, Sept. 1 Litho. *Perf. 12*
3938 A1238 $1.20 multi + label .65 .50
3939 A1239 $1.20 multi + label .65 .50
3940 A1240 $1.20 multi + label .65 .50
3941 A1241 $1.20 multi + label .65 .50
3942 A1242 $1.20 multi + label .65 .50
3943 A1243 $1.20 multi + label .65 .50
3944 A1244 $1.20 multi + label .65 .50
3945 A1245 $1.20 multi + label .65 .50
3946 A1246 $1.20 multi + label .65 .50
3947 A1247 $1.20 multi + label .65 .50
Nos. 3938-3947 (10) 6.50 5.00

See Stamps With Attached Labels note after No. 3197.

Traditional Games of Ethnic Minorities A1248

No. 3948, $1.20: a, Men in board shoe race (4-1). b, Women with bamboo poles (4-2).
No. 3949, $1.20: a, Top spinning (4-3). b, Stilt racing (4-4).

Perf. 13x12¾ Syncopated
2011, Sept. 10 Photo.
Vert. Pairs, #a-b
3948-3949 A1248 Set of 2 1.50 1.50

A1249

Lord Guan Yu (?-219) — A1250

Lord Guan Yu: No. 3950, $1.20, On horse (2-1). No. 3951, $1.20, Seated, reading annals (2-2).

Perf. 13x13¼ Syncopated
2011, Sept. 12
3950-3951 A1249 Set of 2 2.75 1.00

Souvenir Sheet
Perf. 13¼x13 Syncopated
3952 A1250 $6 multi 6.50 6.00

A limited edition souvenir sheet of 6 containing three each Nos. 3950-3951 exists.

Details From the Scroll of the 87 Immortals A1251

Various details with stamps numbered: No. 3953, $1.20, (6-1). No. 3954, $1.20, (6-2). No. 3955, $1.20, (6-3). No. 3956, $1.20, (6-4). $1.50, (6-5). $3, (6-6).

Perf. 13¼ Syncopated
2011, Sept. 26 Litho.
3953-3958 A1251 Set of 6 3.00 3.00
3958a Booklet pane of 6, #3953-3958 *4.00* —
Complete booklet, #3958a *6.50*

A1252

Chinese Revolution, Cent. — A1253

Designs: No. 3959, $1.20, Wuchang Uprising (2-1). No. 3960, $1.20, Revolution leaders (2-2).
$6, Dr. Sun Yat-sen (1866-1925), leader of revolution.

Perf. 13¼x13 Syncopated

2011, Oct. 10 **Photo.**

3959-3960 A1252 Set of 2 1.00 .85
3960a Sheet of 8, 4 each #3959-3960 *8.00 7.00*

Souvenir Sheet

Perf. 13¼x12¾ Syncopated

3961 A1253 $6 multi 2.00 2.00

A1254

Rebuilding Efforts After May 12, 2008 Sichuan Earthquake — A1255

Designs: No. 3962, $1.20, Clock, rebuilt town (4-1). No. 3963, $1.20, Sculpture, rebuilt sections of ancient town (4-2). No. 3964, $1.20, Sculpture, buildings (4-3). No. 3965, $1.20, Flag, sculpture, rebuilt village (4-4).
$6, Rebuilt town, sculpture, wind generators.

Perf. 13¼ Syncopated

2011, Oct. 13 **Litho.**

3962-3965 A1254 Set of 4 1.50 1.50

Souvenir Sheet

Perf. 13 Syncopated

3966 A1255 $6 multi 2.00 2.00

A1256

Tianjin Binhai New Area — A1257

Building and: No. 3967, $1.20, New downtown (3-1). No. 3968, $1.20, Yujiabao Financial District (3-2). No. 3969, $1.20, Map of National Animation Industry Park (3-3).
$6, Port, crane, container ship.

Perf. 13¼x12¾ Syncopated

2011, Oct. 21 **Photo.**

3967-3969 A1256 Set of 3 1.25 1.25

Souvenir Sheet

Perf. 13x13¾ Syncopated

3970 A1257 $6 multi 1.90 1.90

A1258

China 2011 Intl. Philatelic Exhibition, Wuxi — A1259

Designs: No. 3971, $1.20, Flat-sided container with spout and handle (2-1). No. 3972, $1.20, A-fu (2-2).
$6, Yu Zhuang Qiu, by Ni Zan.

Perf. 13¼x13¾ Syncopated

2011, Oct. 10

3971-3972 A1258 Set of 2 .75 .75
3972a Sheet of 8, 4 each #3971-3972 + label *6.50 6.50*

Souvenir Sheet

Perf. 13¼x13 Syncopated

3973 A1259 $6 multi 1.90 1.90

Xinhua News Agency, 80th Anniv. A1260

Various buildings: No. 3974, $1.20, Red electric wave (4-1). No. 3975, $1.20, Anti-Japanese War (4-2). No. 3976, $1.20, War of Liberation (4-3). No. 3977, $1.20, Going global (4-4).

Perf. 13¼ Syncopated

2011, Nov. 7 **Litho.**

3974-3977 A1260 Set of 4 1.50 1.50

Bird on Branch A1261

2011, Oct. 9 ***Perf. 11¾ Syncopated***

3978 A1261 $1.20 multi .40 .40
a. Souvenir sheet of 2, #3708a, 3978 *3.75 3.75*

Armillary Spheres A1262

Designs: No. 3980, $1.20, Simplified armillary sphere built by Guo Shoujing, 1276 (2-1). No. 3981, $1.20, Equatorial armillary sphere built by Tycho Brahe, 1595 (2-2).

Perf. 13¼x12¾ Syncopated

2011, Dec. 10 **Litho. & Engr.**

3980-3981 A1262 Set of 2 1.00 .90

See Denmark Nos. 1576-1577.

New Year 2012 (Year of the Dragon) A1263

Perf. 12¾ Syncopated

2012, Jan. 5 **Photo.**

3982 A1263 $1.20 multi 1.50 1.00
a. Booklet pane of 10 15.00 —
Complete booklet, #3982a 16.00

Limited edition sheets of 4 and 6 stamps exist.

Bank of China, Cent. — A1264

Designs: $1.20, Old bank building (2-1). $1.50, Modern bank building (2-2).

2012, Feb. 5 ***Perf. 13 Syncopated***

3983-3984 A1264 Set of 2 3.50 2.00

Emblem and Building of Zhonghua Book Company A1265

Perf. 13¼x13¾ Syncopated

2012, Feb. 23 **Litho.**

3985 A1265 $1.20 multi .70 .50

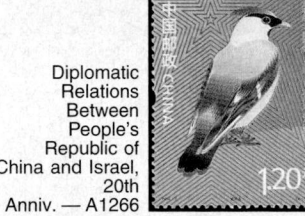

Diplomatic Relations Between People's Republic of China and Israel, 20th Anniv. — A1266

Designs: No. 3986, $1.20, Waxwing, five-pointed star (2-1). No. 3987, $1.20, White dove, Star of David (2-2).

2012, Mar. 20 **Litho. & Embossed**

3986-3987 A1266 Set of 2 2.50 1.50

See Israel Nos. 1923-1924.

Asian-Pacific Postal Union, 50th Anniv. — A1267

2012, Apr. 1 **Photo.** ***Perf. 13x13¼***

3988 A1267 $1.20 multi .80 .80

Musicians A1268

Designs: No. 3989, $1.20, Xiao Youmei (1884-1940) (4-1). No. 3990, $1.20, Liu Tianhua (1895-1932) (4-2). No. 3991, $1.20, He Lvting (1903-99) (4-3). No. 3992, $1.20, Ma Sicong (1912-87) (4-4).

2012, Apr. 15 ***Perf. 13 Syncopated***

3989-3992 A1268 Set of 4 1.60 1.60

Chinese Characters A1269

Embellished character for: No. 3993, $1.20, Good luck (fu) (4-1). No. 3994, $1.20, Richness (lu) (4-2). No. 3995, $1.20, Longevity (shou) (4-3). No. 3996, $1.20, Happiness (xi) (4-4).

Litho With Foil Application

2012, Apr. 27

3993-3996 A1269 Set of 4 4.50 2.50
3996a Souvenir sheet of 8, 2 each #3993-3996 *13.00 13.00*

Communist Youth League, 90th Anniv. A1270

Designs: 80f, Building, flag of Youth League (2-1). $1.20, Emblem, Great Wall of China, boy and girl (2-2).

Perf. 13x12¾ Syncopated

2012, May 4 **Photo.**

3997-3998 A1270 Set of 2 .65 .65
3998a Souvenir sheet of 8, 4 each #3997-3998 *4.50 4.50*

International Nurses Day — A1271

2012, May 12

3999 A1271 $1.20 multi .40 .40

Nanjing University, 110th Anniv. — A1272

Perf. 13¼x13¾ Syncopated

2012, May 20 **Litho.**

4000 A1272 $1.20 multi .40 .40

Publication of *Talks at Yan'an Forum on Literature and Art,* 70th Anniv. — A1273

Flowers and: No. 4001, $1.20, Former building of Chinese Communist Party Central Committee (2-1). No. 4002, $1.20, National Performing Arts Center, Beijing (2-2).

2012, May 23 **Photo.**
4001-4002 A1273 Set of 2 1.00 .80

Tables — A1274

No. 4003: a, Ming Dynasty pear wood drawing table (50x30mm) (4-1). b, Qing Dynasty square pear wood table (40x30mm) (4-2).
No. 4004: a, Ming Dynasty pear wood incense stand with base (40x30mm) (4-3). b, Ming Dynasty rock wood table (50x30mm) (4-4).

Perf. 13¼x13 Syncopated
2012, June 9 **Litho. & Embossed**

4003	A1274 $1.20 Horiz. pair, #a-b	.75	.75
c.	Booklet pane of 1 #4003a + 2 labels	.40	—
d.	Booklet pane of 1 #4003b + 2 labels	.40	—
4004	A1274 $1.20 Horiz. pair, #a-b	.75	.75
c.	Booklet pane of 1 #4004a + 2 labels	.40	—
d.	Booklet pane of 1 #4004b + 2 labels	.40	—
e.	Booklet pane of 4, #4003a-4003b, 4004a-4004b	1.50	—
	Complete booklet, #4003c, 4003d, 4004c, 4004d, 4004e	3.25	

Third Asian Beach Games, Haiyang A1275

Designs: No. 4005, $1.20, Beach volleyball (3-1). No. 4006, $1.20, Inline skating (3-2). No. 4007, $1.20, Waterskiing (3-3).

Perf. 13¼ Syncopated
2012, June 16 **Photo.**
4005-4007 A1275 Set of 3 1.25 1.25

Rocket Launch and Spacecraft — A1276

2012, June 25 **Litho.** ***Perf. 12***
4008 A1276 $1.20 multi + label .40 .40

See Stamps With Attached Labels note after No. 3197.

Places in People's Republic of China — A1277

Designs: No. 4009, $1.20, Jingangshan Mountain (6-1). No. 4010, $1.20, Ruijin (6-2). No. 4011, $1.20, Zunyi (6-3). No. 4012, $1.20, Huining (6-4). No. 4013, $1.20, Yan An (6-5). No. 4014, $1.20, Xibaipo (6-6).

Perf. 13¼x12¾ Syncopated
2012, June 30 **Litho. & Engr.**
4009-4014 A1277 Set of 6 2.25 2.25
4014a Sheet of 12, 2 each #4009-4014 5.75 5.75

Full Coverage in Insurance Systems A1278

Perf. 13¼x13¾ Syncopated
2012, July 1 **Photo.**
4015 A1278 $1.20 gold & red 1.50 .75

Emblem of Chinese Olympic Committee — A1279

2012, July 17 **Litho.** ***Perf. 12***
4016 A1279 $1.20 multi + label 1.00 .70

See Stamps With Attached Labels note after No. 3197.

National Museum and Stamps — A1280

No. 4017 — Museum and: a, $1.20, People's Republic of China #787. b, $3, People's Republic of China #790.

Perf. 13¼ Syncopated
2012, July 8 **Litho. & Engr.**
4017 A1280 Horiz. pair, #a-b 1.40 1.40

2012 Summer Olympics, London A1281

Designs: No. 4018, $1.20, Soccer (4-1). No. 4019, $1.20, Tennis (4-2). No. 4020, $1.20, Equestrian (4-3). No. 4021, $1.20, Hurdles (4-4).

Perf. 13¼x13 Syncopated
2012, July 27 **Photo.**
4018-4021 A1281 Set of 4 1.50 1.50
4021a Sheet of 8, 2 each #4018-4021 6.25 6.25

Generals A1282

Designs: No. 4022, $1.20, Zhao Bosheng (1897-1933) (5-1). No. 4023, $1.20, Duan Dechang (1904-33) (5-2). No. 4024, $1.20, Xie Zichang (1897-1935) (5-3). No. 4025, $1.20, Zeng Zhongsheng (1900-35) (5-4). No. 4026, $1.20, Dong Zhentang (1895-1937) (5-5).

Perf. 13¼x13¾ Syncopated
2012, Aug. 1
4022-4026 A1282 Set of 5 1.90 1.90

A1283

Silk Road — A1284

Designs: No. 4027, $1.20, Buildings, figurines of camel and man (4-1). No. 4028, $1.20, Building, horse figurine (4-2). No. 4029, $1.20, Mountains, pitcher (4-3). No. 4030, $1.20, Cliff buildings, horse and rider figurine (4-4).

Perf. 13¼x12¾ Syncopated
2012, Aug. 1
4027-4030 A1283 Set of 4 1.50 1.50
4030a Sheet of 8, 2 each #4027-4030 *7.25* *7.25*

Souvenir Sheet
Perf. 13¼ Syncopated
4031 A1284 $6 shown 1.90 1.90

Liu Sanjie — A1285

Designs: No. 4032, $1.20, Song fairy (4-1). No. 4033, $1.20, Singing, horiz. (4-2). No. 4034, $1.20, Couple with embroidered ball, horiz. (4-3). No. 4035, $1.20, Riding a carp to heaven (4-4).

Perf. 13¼x13½ Syncopated, 13 Syncopated
2012, Aug. 23

4032-4035	A1285 Set of 4	1.50	1.50
4032a	Booklet pane of 1	.65	—
4033a	Booklet pane of 1	.65	—
4034a	Booklet pane of 1	.65	—
4035a	Booklet pane of 1	.65	—
	Complete booklet, #4032-4035a	2.60	

Complete booklet sold for $8.

Hetian Jade A1286

Designs: No. 4036, $1.20, Figurine of dragon (4-1). No. 4037, $1.20, Bi with grain design, vert. (4-2). No. 4038, $1.20, Cup on plate (4-3). No. 4039, $1.20, Figurine of children washing elephant, vert. (4-4).

Litho. & Embossed
2012, Aug. 28 ***Perf. 12***
4036-4039 A1286 Set of 4 1.50 1.50
4039a Souvenir sheet of 4, #4036-4039 + label 2.40 2.40

A1287

Sanxingdui Bronze Relics — A1288

Designs: No. 4040, $1.20, Mask (2-1). No. 4041, $1.20, Statue of person kneeling (2-2). $6, Statue of person standing.

Perf. 13¼x13½ Syncopated
2012, Sept. 26 **Litho.**
4040-4041 A1287 Set of 2 .80 .80

Souvenir Sheet
Perf. 13x13¼
4042 A1288 $6 multi 1.90 1.90

Miniature Sheet

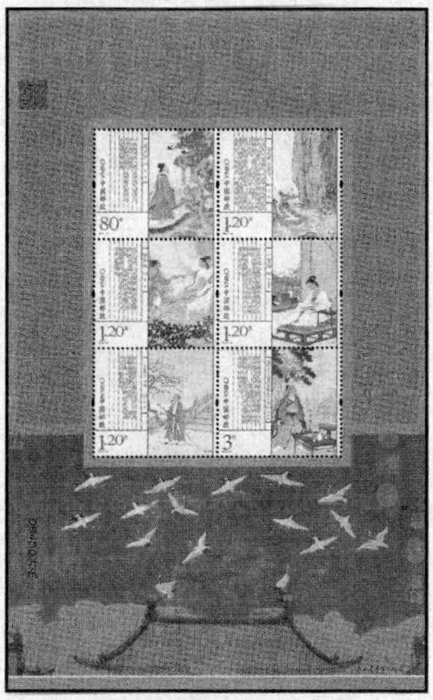
Song Poetry — A1289

No. 4043: a, 80f, Sand of Silk Washing, by Yan Shu (6-1). b, $1.20, Meditating on the Past at Chibi, by Su Shi (6-2). c, $1.20, Fairy of the Magpie Bridge, by Qin Guan (6-3). d, $1.20, A Twig of Plum Blossoms (6-4). e, $1.20, Ode to the Plum Blossom, by Lu You (6-5). f, $3, This Unconstrained Poem to Chen Tongfu, by Xin Qiji (6-6).

Perf. 13x13¼ Syncopated
2012, Aug. 31
4043 A1289 Sheet of 6, #a-f 3.75 3.75

Yanbian Culture — A1290

Designs: No. 4044, $1.20, Harvest Dance (3-1). No. 4045, $1.20, Dancers (3-2). No. 4046, $1.20, Hymn for harmony (3-3).

Perf. 13¼x13 Syncopated

2012, Sept. 3 **Photo.**

4044-4046	A1290	Set of 3	1.25	1.25
4046a		Sheet of 9, 3 each #4044-4046	*3.75*	*3.75*

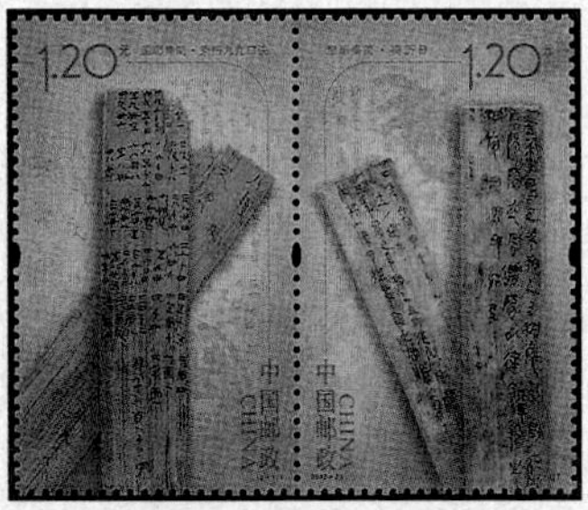

Qin Dynasty Liye Bamboo Slips — A1291

No. 4047: a, Multiplication table, denomination at UL (2-1). b, Calendar, denomination at UR (2-2).

Perf. 13¼ Syncopated

2012, Sept. 13

4047	A1291	$1.20 Horiz. pair, #a-b	.80	.80

"Good Fortune" A1292

Perf. 11¾ Syncopated

2012, Oct. 9 **Litho.**

4048	A1292	$1.20 multi	.40	.40
a.		Souvenir sheet of 2, #3708a, 4048	*1.90*	*1.90*

Porcelain Objects From Dehua Kiln — A1293

No. 4049, $1.20: a, Three-legged pot with dragon decoration (4-1). b, Vase with handles (4-2).

No. 4050, $1.20: a, Seated Guanyin figurine (4-3). b, Bodhidharma figurine (4-4).

Perf. 13¼ Syncopated

2012, Oct. 20 **Photo.**

Horiz. Pairs, #a-b

4049-4050	A1293	Set of 2	1.60	1.60

History of Merchants — A1294

Designs: No. 4051, $1.20, Steamship, 1872 (3-1). No. 4052, $1.20, Shekou skyline (3-2). $1.50, Hong Kong skyline (3-3)

Perf. 13¼x13 Syncopated

2012, Oct. 26 **Litho.**

4051-4053	A1294	Set of 3	1.25	1.25
4053a		Souvenir sheet of 6, 2 each #4051-4053	*4.75*	*4.75*

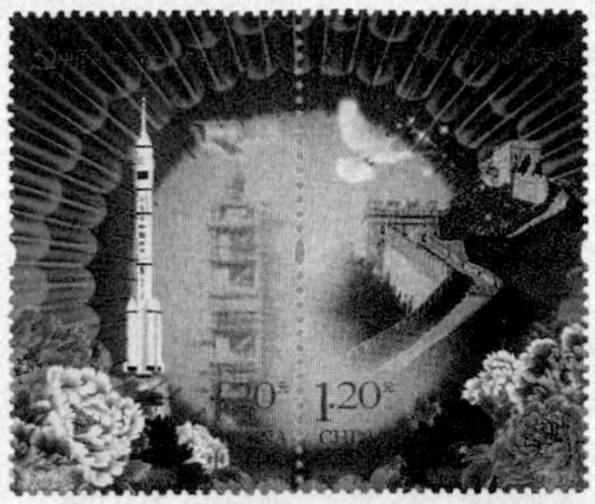

A1295

18th National Congress of Chinese Communist Party — A1296

No. 4054: a, Rocket launch (2-1). b, Great Wall of China (2-2).

Perf. 13¼ Syncopated

2012, Nov. 8 **Photo.**

4054	A1295	$1.20 Horiz. pair, #a-b	.80	.80

Souvenir Sheet

Perf. 13 Syncopated

4055	A1296	$6 multi	2.00	2.00

A sheet containing four No. 4054 exists.

Bridges — A1297

Designs: No. 4056, $1.20, Taizhou Yangtze River Bridge (2-1). No. 4057, $1.20, Bosporus Bridge, Istanbul, Turkey (2-2).

Perf. 13¼x13 Syncopated

2012, Nov. 26 **Litho.**

4056-4057	A1297	Set of 2	.80	.80

See Turkey No. 3319.

Auditing — A1298

No. 4058: a, Three-legged pot, bas-relief (4-1). b, Imperial Chinese chop (4-2). c, Auditing document of Communist era with red circular seal, building, star, hammer and sickle (4-3). d, Modern auditing documents, building (4-4).

Perf. 13 Syncopated

2012, Nov. 30 **Photo.**

4058	A1298	Horiz. strip of 4	1.60	1.60
a.-d.		$1.20 Any single	.40	.40

Confucius Institute — A1299

No. 4059: a, $1.20, Stylized dove and globe (2-1). b, $3, Panda (2-2).

2012, Dec. 1

4059	A1299	Horiz. pair, #a-b	1.40	1.40

Constitution of People's Republic of China, 30th Anniv. — A1300

Perf. 13½x13¼ Syncopated

2012, Dec. 4 **Litho.**

4060	A1300	$1.20 multi	.40	.40

New Year 2013 (Year of the Snake) A1301

Perf. 12¾ Syncopated

2013, Jan. 5 **Photo.**

4061	A1301	$1.20 multi	*.40*	*.40*
a.		Booklet pane of 10	*8.75*	—
		Complete booklet, #4061a	*8.75*	

A limited edition sheet of 6 stamps exists.

Offshore Oil Exploration — A1302

Designs: No. 4062, $1.20, Exploration ship (3-1). No. 4063, $1.20, Offshore drilling rig (3-2). $3, Production ship (3-3).

Perf. 13¼x13 Syncopated

2013, Jan. 18

4062-4064	A1302	Set of 3	1.75	1.75

Heart and Flowers — A1303

2013, Feb. 28 **Litho.** ***Perf. 12***

4065	A1303	$1.20 multi + label	.40	.40

See Stamps With Attached Labels note after No. 3197.

Lanterns — A1304

2013, Mar. 3

4066	A1304	$1.20 multi + label	.40	.40

See Stamps With Attached Labels note after No. 3197.

12th National People's Congress A1305

Perf. 13¼x13½ Syncopated

2013, Mar. 5 **Photo.**

4067	A1305	$1.20 multi	.40	.40
a.		Souvenir sheet of 6	4.50	4.50

Mao Zedong's Instruction to Follow Examples of Comrade Lei Feng, 50th Anniv. — A1306

Lei Feng (1940-62), model soldier: 80f, Holding gun (4-1). No. 4069, $1.20, Studying book (4-2). No. 4070, $1.20, Polishing object (4-3). No. 4071, $1.20, Holding baby (4-4).

Perf. 13¼ Syncopated

2013, Mar. 5 **Litho. & Engr.**

4068-4071	A1306	Set of 4	1.40	1.40
4071a		Sheet of 8, 2 each #4068-4071	*5.50*	*5.50*

Party School of the Central Committee, 80th Anniv. A1307

Perf. 13 Syncopated

2013, Mar. 13 **Litho.**

4072	A1307	$1.20 multi	.40	.40

Peach Blossoms A1308

Various peach blossoms in decorative frames: No. 4073, 80f, (12-1). No. 4074, 80f, (12-2). No. 4075, $1.20. (12-3). No. 4076, $1.20, (12-4). No. 4077, $1.20, (12-5). No. 4078, $1.20 (12-6). No. 4079, $1.20, (12-7). No. 4080, $1.20, (12-8). No. 4081, $1.20, (12-9). No. 4082, $1.20 (12-10). No. 4083, $1.20, (12-11). $1.50, (12-12).

Perf. 13¼x13 Syncopated

2013, Mar. 16 **Photo.**

4073-4084	A1308	Set of 12	4.50	4.50
4078a		Sheet of 12, 2 each #4073-4078	*5.50*	*5.50*
4084a		Sheet of 12, 2 each #4079-4084	*6.50*	*6.50*

World Water Day — A1309

2013, Mar. 22
4085 A1309 $1.20 multi .40 .40

Painting of Women Producing Silk — A1310

Details from painting: No. 4086, $1.20, Women beating silk in basin (3-1). No. 4087, $1.20, Women working silk thread (3-2). No. 4088, $1.20, Women pulling silk cloth (3-3).
$6, Entire painting.

Perf. 13 Syncopated
2013, Apr. 13 **Litho.**
4086-4088 A1310 Set of 3 1.25 1.25

Souvenir Sheet
Perf. 13½ Syncopated
4089 A1310 $6 multi 2.00 2.00

No. 4089 contains one 59x37mm stamp.

Cloisonné Ware — A1311

Designs: 80f, Yuan Dynasty three-legged pot (6-1). No. 4091, $1.20, Ming Dynasty container (6-2). No. 4092, $1.20, Qing Dynasty Zun vessel (6-3). No. 4093, $1.20, Qing Dynasty pot with spout and handle (6-4). No. 4094, $1.20, Hanging vase with handle (6-5). $3, Ming Dynasty bottle vase (6-6).

Perf. 13¼x13½ Syncopated
2013, Apr. 21
4090-4095 A1311 Set of 6 3.00 3.00
4095a Sheet of 12, 2 each #4090-4095 *7.75 7.75*

Souvenir Sheet

7th Congress of All-China Philatelic Federation — A1312

2013, Apr. 25 **LItho. & Embossed**
4096 A1312 $6 multi 2.00 2.00

Earthquake Relief A1313

Perf. 13x12½ Syncopated
2013, May 3 **Photo.**
4097 A1313 $1.20 multi *7.50 7.50*

Mother's Day — A1314

Litho. With Foil Application
Perf. 13x12¾ Syncopated
2013, May 11
4098 A1314 $1.20 multi .40 .40

Galloping Horse — A1315

2013, May 19 **Litho.** ***Perf. 12***
4099 A1315 $1.20 multi + label .40 .40

See Stamps With Attached Labels note after No. 3197.

Town Scenes A1316

Designs: No. 4100, $1.20, Qiantong (8-1). No. 4101, $1.20, Laitan (8-2). No. 4102, $1.20, Heping (8-3). No. 4103, $1.20, Jingziuan (8-4). No. 4104, $1.20, Heshun (8-5). No. 4105, $1.20, Tangjiawan (8-6). No. 4106, $1.20, Lizhuang (8-7). No. 4107, $1.20, Jingsheng (8-8).

Perf. 13¼x12¾ Syncopated
2013, May 19 **Litho. & Engr.**
4100-4107 A1316 Set of 8 3.25 3.25

Zhangjiajie Tianzi Mountain A1317

Xiapu Beaches A1318

Qilian Yu Island Group, Paracel Islands A1319

Panjin Red Beach A1320

Longsheng Terraced Fields A1321

Fields and Irrigation Canals, Xinghua A1322

Perf. 13x12¾ Syncopated
2013, May 19 **Photo.**

4108	A1317	80f	multi	.25	.25
4109	A1318	80f	multi	.25	.25
4110	A1319	$1.20	multi	.40	.40
4111	A1320	$1.20	multi	.40	.40
4112	A1321	$1.50	multi	.50	.50
4113	A1322	$3	multi	1.00	1.00
	Nos. 4108-4113 (6)			2.80	2.80

Tadpoles and Pond Life A1323

No. 4114 — Tadpoles and: a, Shrimp. b, Goldfish. c, Crab. d, Turtles. e, Frog.

Perf. 13x12½ Syncopated
2013, June 1 **Photo.**
4114 Horiz. strip of 5 1.90 1.90
a. A1323 80f multi .25 .25
b.-e. A1323 $1.20 Any single .40 .40
f. Booklet pane of 5, #4114a-4114e 1.90 —
Complete booklet, #4114f 1.90

Gold and Bronze Statues of Buddha — A1324

Buddha statue from: 80f, Five Dynasties period (6-1). No. 4116, $1.20, Song Dynasty (6-2). No. 4117, $1.20, Ming Dynasty (6-3). No. 4118, $1.20, Ming Dynasty, diff. (6-4). No. 4119, $1.20, Ming Dynasty, diff. (6-5). No. 4120, $1.20, Ming Dynasty, diff. (6-6).
$6, Five Buddha statues.

Perf. 13¼ Syncopated
2013, June 16 **Litho.**
4115-4120 A1324 Set of 6 2.25 2.25

Souvenir Sheet
Perf. 13 Syncopated
4121 A1324 $6 multi 2.00 2.00

No. 4121 contains one 74x83mm stamp.

Four Arts of Chinese Scholars A1325

Designs: No. 4122, $1.20, Scholar playing a qin (4-1). No. 4123, $1.20, Scholars playing game of Go (4-2). No. 4124, $1.20, Scholars learning calligraphy (4-3). No. 4125, $1.20, Scholar and wall painting (4-4).

Perf. 13¼ Syncopated
2013, July 13 **Litho.**
4122-4125 A1325 Set of 4 1.60 1.60

Longhu Mountain — A1326

No. 4126: a, Elephant Trunk Hill (3-1). b, Rocks of Immortals (3-2). c, Zhengyi Taoist Abbey (3-3).
$6, Longhu Mountain and lake, horiz.

Perf. 13¼ Syncopated
2013, July 27 **Photo.**
4126 A1326 $1.20 Horiz. strip of 3, #a-c 1.25 1.25

Souvenir Sheet
Perf. 13x13½ Syncopated
4127 A1326 $6 multi 2.00 2.00

Ship — A1327

Stars — A1328

Knot — A1329

Painting of Bamboo — A1330

Die Cut Perf. 12¾ Syncopated
2013, Aug. 8 **Photo.**
Self-Adhesive
4128 A1327 80f multi .25 .25

Die Cut Perf. 13¼x13 Syncopated

4129	A1328	$1.20	multi	.40	.40
4130	A1329	$2.40	multi	.80	.80
4131	A1330	$3	multi	1.00	1.00
	Nos. 4128-4131 (4)			2.45	2.45

Mascot of 2014 Youth Olympic Games, Nanjing — A1331

2013, Aug. 15 **Litho.** ***Perf. 12***
4132 A1331 $1.20 multi + label .40 .40

See Stamps With Attached Labels note after No. 3197.

China-ASEAN Expo, 10th Anniv. — A1332

Perf. 13¼x12¾ Syncopated

2013, Aug. 15 **Photo.**
4133 A1332 $1.20 multi .40 .40

Cats
A1333

Cat breed: No. 4134, $1.20, Chinese Li Hua (4-1). No. 4135, $1.20, Maine Coon (4-2). No. 4136, $1.20, Abyssinian, vert. (4-3). No. 4137, $1.20, Exotic shorthair, vert. (4-4).

Perf. 13 Syncopated, 13¼x13¾ Syncopated (#4136-4137)

2013, Aug. 18 **Litho. & Engr.**
4134-4137 A1333 Set of 4 1.60 1.60

Sun and Peonies — A1334

2013, Aug. 26 **Litho.** ***Perf. 12***
4138 A1334 $1.20 multi + label .40 .40

See Stamps with Attached Labels note after No. 3197.

12th National Games, Liaoning — A1335

Designs: No. 4139, $1.20, Rhythmic gymnastics (2-1). No. 4140, $1.20, Fencing (2-2).

Perf. 13¼x13 Syncopated

2013, Aug. 31 **Litho.**
4139-4140 A1335 Set of 2 .80 .80
4140a Souvenir sheet of 2, #4139-4140 *1.40 1.40*

Wei Guoqing (1913-89), Political and Military Leader — A1336

Wei Guoqing: No. 4141, $1.20, Wearing army cap (2-1). No. 4142, $1.20, Without cap (2-2).

Perf. 13¼x13¾ Syncopated

2013, Sept. 2 **Litho.**
4141-4142 A1336 Set of 2 .80 .80

Yu Yuan Garden, Shanghai — A1337

Designs: 80f, Zigzag Bridge and Mid-lake Pavilion (4-1). No. 4144, $1.20, Grand Rockery (4-2). No. 4145, $1.20, Yuan-yu Building (4-3). No. 4146, $1.20, Exquisite Jade Rock (4-4).

Perf. 13¼x12¾ Syncopated

2013, Sept. 7 **Litho. & Engr.**
4143-4146 A1337 Set of 4 1.50 1.50

Nanhua Temple — A1338

No. 4147: a, Cao Xi Gate (4-1). b, Mahavira Hall (4-2). c, Ling Zhao Pagoda (4-3). d, Liu Zu Hall (4-4).

Perf. 13¼x13 Syncopated

2013, Sept. 7 **Photo.**
4147 Horiz. strip of 4 1.60 1.60
a.-d. A1338 $1.20 Any single .40 .40

Poets — A1339

Designs: No. 4148, $1.20, Jia Yi (200 B.C.-168 B.C.) (4-1). No. 4149, $1.20, Sima Xiangru (179 B.C.-118 B.C.) (4-2). No. 4150, $1.20, Yang Xiong (53 B.C.-18 A.D.) (4-3). No. 4151, $1.20, Ban Gu (32-92) (4-4).

Perf. 13¼ Syncopated

2013, Sept. 15 **Photo.**
4148-4151 A1339 Set of 4 1.60 1.60

Table Tennis — A1340

Players: No. 4152, $1.20, Woman (2-1). No. 4153, $1.20, Man (2-2).

Perf. 13½x13 Syncopated

2013, Sept. 27 **Photo.**
4152-4153 A1340 Set of 2 .80 .80

See Sweden No. 2715.

Chinese Technical Achievements — A1341

Designs: 80f, Rendezvous of Shenzhou and Tiangong spacecraft (4-1). No. 4155, $1.20, Beidou Navigation Satellite System (4-2). No. 4156, $1.20, Liaoning Aircraft Carrier (4-3). No. 4157, $1.20, Jiaolong Manned Submersible (4-4).

Perf. 13x12¾ Syncopated

2013, Sept. 29 **Photo.**
4154-4157 A1341 Set of 4 1.50 1.50
4157a Souvenir sheet of 4, #4154-4157 1.50 1.50

Fish and Flowers
A1342

Perf. 12¾x12 Syncopated

2013, Oct. 9 **Litho.**
4158 A1342 $1.20 multi .40 .40
a. Souvenir sheet of 2, #3708a, 4158, perf. 11¾ syncopated 2.50 2.50

Tenth China Art Festival
A1343

Perf. 13¼x13 Syncopated

2013, Oct. 11 **Litho.**
4159 A1343 $1.20 multi .40 .40

Xi Zhongxun (1913-2002), Communist Party Official — A1344

Xi Zhnongxun: No. 4160, $1.20, As young man in military uniform (2-1). No. 4161, $1.20, As older man (2-2).

Perf. 13¼x13½ Syncopated

2013, Oct. 15 **Litho. & Engr.**
4160-4161 A1344 Set of 2 .80 .80

21st Intl. Congress of Supreme Audit Institutions, Beijing — A1345

No. 4162: a, Congress emblem, Gate of Heavenly Peace (2-1). b, Emblem of Intl. Organization of Supreme Audit Institutions, Great Wall of China (2-2)

Perf. 13¼ Syncopated

2013, Oct. 22 **Litho.**
4162 A1345 $1.20 Horiz. pair, #a-b .80 .80

Hybrid Rice — A1346

No. 4163: a, Seed production (2-1). b, Stalk of rice, rice bowl (2-2).

2013, Oct. 25 **Litho.** ***Perf. 13¼x13¾***
4163 A1346 $1.20 Horiz. pair, #a-b .80 .80

Mao Zedong (1893-1976), Chairman of People's Republic of China — A1347

Various paintings of Mao Zedong: No. 4164, $1.20, With boats in background (4-1). No. 4165, $1.20, With opened overcoat (4-2). No. 4166, $1.20, With arm extended, vert. (4-3). No. 4167, $1.20, Watching waves come ashore (4-4).

Perf. 13¼ Syncopated

2013, Nov. 16 **Litho.**
4164-4167 A1347 Set of 4 1.60 1.60

Wuhan University, 120th Anniv.
A1348

Perf. 13 Syncopated

2013, Nov. 29 **Litho.**
4168 A1348 $1.20 multi .40 .40

Chinese Junk — A1349

2013, Nov. 22 **Litho.** ***Perf. 12***
4169 A1349 $1.20 multi + label .40 .40

See Stamps With Attached Labels note under No. 3197.

First Moon Landing by Chinese Space Vehicles — A1350

No. 4170: a, $1.20, Chang'e 3 Lander (2-1). b, $1.50, Yutu Moon Rover (2-2).

Perf. 13¼x13 Syncopated

2014, Jan. 1 **Photo.**
4170 A1350 Horiz. pair, #a-b .90 .90

New Year 2014 (Year of the Horse)
A1351

Perf. 12¾ Syncopated

2014, Jan. 5 **Photo.**
4171 A1351 $1.20 multi .40 .40
a. Booklet pane of 10 4.00 —
Complete booklet, #4171a 4.00

Diplomatic Relations Between France and People's Republic of China, 50th Anniv. — A1352

Desings: No. 4172, $1.20, Qinhuai River, Nanjing (2-1). No. 4173, $1.20, Seine River, Paris (2-2).

Perf. 13x12½ Syncopated

2014, Jan. 27 — Litho. & Engr.

4172-4173 A1352 Set of 2 .80 .80

See France Nos. 4587-4588.

Birds of Prey — A1353

Designs: No. 4174, $1.20, Aquila heliaca (4-1). No. 4175, $1.20, Circus cyaneus, horiz. (4-2). No. 4176, $1.50, Accipiter gentilis, horiz. (4-3). No. 4177, $1.50, Falco tinnunculus (4-4).

Perf. 12¾ Syncopated (vert. stamps), 13x12½ Syncopated

2014, Feb. 23 — Litho. & Engr.

4174-4177 A1353 Set of 4 1.75 1.75

Bathing Horses, by Zhao Mengfu (1254-1322) — A1354

No. 4179: a, 7 horses and rider. (50x38mm) (3-1). b, 5 horses, 3 riders, 3 grooms, Chinese text (57x38mm) (3-2). c, 2 horses, 2 men (50x38mm) (3-3).
$6, Entire painting.

Perf. 13¼ Syncopated

2014, Mar. 1 — Litho.

4178 Horiz. strip of 3 1.40 1.40
a.-b. A1354 $1.20 Either single .40 .40
c. A1354 $1.50 multi .50 .50

Souvenir Sheet

Perf. 13½x14 Syncopated

4179 A1354 $6 multi 2.00 2.00

No. 4179 contains one 153x31mm stamp.

Strengthening of Consumer Rights in China — A1355

Designs: No. 4180, $1.20, Scales, book and Consumer Rights Day emblem (2-1). No. 4181, $1.20, Hands, bowl, shirt, house, steering wheel. (2-2).

Perf. 13¼x13¾ Syncopated

2014, Mar. 15 — Litho.

4180-4181 A1355 Set of 2 .80 .80

Internet Life — A1356

Designs: No. 4182, $1.20, Internet icons, man and woman touching hands (4-1). No. 4183, $1.20, Computer screen, mouse, man pushing shopping cart with Internet icons (4-2). No. 4184, $1.20, Hand holding smart phone showing picture of man on laptop computer (4-3). $1.50, Clouds with Internet icons, people on hills (4-4).

Perf. 13¼x13½ Syncopated

2014, Apr. 20 — Photo.

4182-4185 A1356 Set of 4 1.75 1.75

Theme Pavilion and Emblem A1357

Botanical Pavilion and Mascot A1358

Perf. 13 Syncopated

2014, Apr. 25 — Photo.

4186 A1357 $1.20 multi (2-1) .40 .40
4187 A1358 $1.20 multi (2-2) .40 .40

Intl. Horticultural Exposition, Qingdao.

Chinese People's Association for Friendship With Foreign Countries, 60th Anniv. — A1359

Perf. 13¼ Syncopated

2014, May 3 — Litho.

4188 A1359 $1.20 multi .40 .40

Wild Goose Delivering Letters — A1360

Perf. 13¼x13 Syncopated

2014, May 10 — Litho. & Engr.

4189 A1360 $1.20 multi .40 .40

Buddhist Art — A1361

Designs: No. 4190, $1.20, Sakyamuni Buddha (4-1). No. 4191, $1.20, Amitayus Buddha (4-2). No. 4192, $1.20, Green Tara (4-3). No. 4193, $1.20, White Tara (4-4).
$6, Sahasra-bhuja Sahasra-netra Avalokitesvara.

Perf. 13¼x13 Syncopated

2014, May 18 — Litho.

4190-4193 A1361 Set of 4 1.60 1.60

Souvenir Sheet

Perf. 13x13¼ Syncopated

4194 A1361 $6 multi 1.90 1.90

No. 4194 contains one 66x108mm stamp.

Birds In Bamboo Forest — A1362

2014, May 28 — Litho. — *Perf. 12*

4195 A1362 $1.20 multi + label .40 .40

See Stamps With Attached Labels note after No. 3197.

Premiere of Animated Movie *The Monkey King* — A1363

Designs: No. 4196, 80f, Monkey King seeking weapon in Dragon King's palace (6-1). No. 4197, 80f, Horses in water and in flight (6-2). No. 4198, $1.20, Monkey King, other monkeys, banner (6-3). No. 4199, $1.20, Monkey King in peach tree (6-4). No. 4200, $1.20, Monkey King in battle (6-5). No. 4201, $1.20, Monkey King breaking picture frame (6-6).

Perf. 13¼x12¾ Syncopated

2014, June 1 — Photo.

4196-4201 A1363 Set of 6 2.10 2.10
4201a Booklet pane of 6, #4196-4201 2.10 —
Complete booklet, #4201a 2.10

Huangpu Military Academy, 90th Anniv. — A1364

Perf. 13¼x12¾ Syncopated

2014, June 16 — Litho. & Engr.

4202 A1364 $1.20 multi .40 .40

The Dream of Red Mansions, Novel by Cao Xueqin A1365

Scenes from novel: No. 4203, $1.20, Lady Dowager sends for her motherless granddaughter (4-1). No. 4204 $1.20, Confounded monk ends a confounding case (4-2). No. 4205, $1.20, Grandmother Liu saw Madam Phoenix first (4-3). $1.50, Baoyu recognizes the gold locket (4-4).
$6, Spirit of Baoyu.

Perf. 13 Syncopated

2014, June 21 — Photo.

4203-4206 A1365 Set of 4 1.75 1.75

Souvenir Sheet

4207 A1365 $6 multi 2.00 2.00

No. 4207 contains one 45x70mm stamp.

Huangmei Opera — A1366

Designs: 80f, A Happy Marriage with a Fairy (3-1). No. 4209, $1.20, Royal Son-in-law (3-2). No. 4210, $1.20, Collecting Grass for Pig (3-3).

Perf. 13¼ Syncopated

2014, July 6 — Litho.

4208-4210 A1366 Set of 3 1.10 1.10

Fruit — A1367

Designs: No. 4211, $1.20, Apples (4-1). No. 4212, $1.20, Peaches (4-2). No. 4213, $1.50, Pomegranates (4-3). No. 4214, $1.50, Kumquats (4-4).

Perf. 13¼x13 Syncopated

2014, July 15 — Litho.

4211-4214 A1367 Set of 4 1.75 .75

2014 Youth Olympic Games, Nanjing — A1368

Perf. 13¼x13½ Syncopated

2014, Aug. 16 — Litho.

4215 A1368 $1.20 multi .40 .40

Basin — A1369

2014, Aug. 20 Litho. *Perf. 12*
4216 A1369 $1.20 multi + label .40 .40

See Stamps With Attached Labels note after No. 3197.

Deng Xiaoping (1904-97), Leader of People's Republic of China A1370

Deng Xiaoping: No. 4217, $1.20, In military uniform, Red Army flag (4-1). No. 4218, $1.20, At lectern, United Nations Building and flag (4-2). No. 4219, $1.50, Reading speech, microphones, teapot, flag of Chinese Communist Party (4-3). No. 4220, $1.50, With extended arm, flag of People's Republic of China (4-4)

Perf. 13 Syncopated

2014, Aug. 22 Litho.
4217-4220 A1370 Set of 4 1.75 1.75

Zhuge Liang (181-234), Chancellor of Shu Han — A1371

Designs: No. 4221, $1.20, Zhuge Liang standing (2-1). No. 4222, $1.20, Zhuge Liang writing (2-2).
$6, Zhuge Liang standing, diff.

Perf. 13¼ Syncopated

2014, Aug. 28 Litho.
4221-4222 A1371 Set of 2 .80 .80

Souvenir Sheet

4223 A1371 $6 multi 2.00 2.00

No. 4223 contains one 38x62mm stamp.

Teacher's Day — A1372

Designs: $1.20, Candles in hot-air balloon basket, eyeglasses and book on desk (2-1). $1.50, Tree with symbols of education, stylized faces (2-2).

Perf. 13¼x13¾ Syncopated

2014, Sept. 10 Photo.
4224-4225 A1372 Set of 2 .90 .90

Miniature Sheet

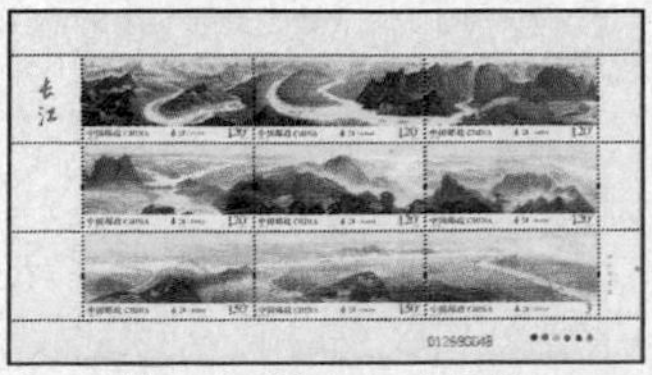

Yangtze River — A1373

No. 4226: a, $1.20, River running through mountains (9-1). b, $1.20, River passing Chongqing (9-2). c, $1.20, Three Gorges (9-3). d, $1.20, Hubei and Hunan (9-4). e, $1.20, Mount Lu and Jiujiang River (9-5). f, $1.20, Yellow Mountain (9-6). g, $1.50, Bridges over river (9-7). h, $1.50, River passing towns (9-8). i, $3, River running into sea (9-9).

Perf. 13¼x12¾ Syncopated

2014, Sept. 13 Photo.
4226 A1373 Sheet of 9, #a-i 4.50 4.50

People's Congress, 60th Anniv. — A1374

60th anniv. emblem and: No. 4227, $1.20, Building and people (2-1). No. 4228, $1.20, Great Hall of the People and flags (2-2).

Perf. 12¾x12½ Syncopated

2014, Sept. 15 Litho.
4227-4228 A1374 Set of 2 .80 .80

National Rejuvenation — A1375

Ribbons and: 80f, Buildings, flags and ship (4-1). No. 4230, $1.20, Buildings, construction cranes, harvesters (4-2). No. 4231, $1.20, China Central Television Building, Ferris wheel, buildings, dancers (4-3). No. 4232, $1.20, Ethnic dancers and musicians, buildings (4-4).

Perf. 13 Syncopated

2014, Sept. 20 Photo.
4229-4232 A1375 Set of 4 1.50 1.50
4232a Souvenir sheet of 4, #4229-4232 1.50 1.50

Filial Piety — A1376

Designs: No. 4233, $1.20, Yu Shun, elephants and birds (4-1). No. 4234, $1.20, Wife of Jiang Shi holding tray with bowl and plate, carp jumping from spring (4-2). No. 4235, $1.50, Hua Mulan with spear on horseback (4-3). No. 4236, $1.50, Sun Simao studying medicine (4-4).

Perf. 13¼ Syncopated

2014, Sept. 30 Litho. & Engr.
4233-4236 A1376 Set of 4 1.75 1.75

A1377

A1378

Xinjiang Production and Construction Corps, 60th Anniv. — A1379

Perf. 13 Syncopated

2014, Oct. 7 Litho.
4237 Horiz. strip of 3 1.25 1.25
a. A1377 $1.20 multi .40 .40
b. A1378 $1.20 multi .40 .40
c. A1379 $1.20 multi .40 .40

Calabash — A1380

Perf. 12¾ Syncopated

2014, Oct. 9 Litho.
4238 A1380 $1.20 multi .40 .40
a. Souvenr sheet of 2, #3869b (perf. 12 syncopated), #4238 1.40 1.40

Scientists A1381

Designs: No. 4239, $1.20, Wang Ganchang (1907-98), nuclear physicist (6-1). No. 4240, $1.20, Zhou Jiuzhang (1907-68), spacecraft engineer (6-2). No. 4241, $1.20, Guo Yonghuai (1909-68), physicist (6-3). No. 4242, $1.20, Deng Jiaxian (1924-86), nuclear physicist (6-4). No. 4243, $1.20, Zhu Guangya (1924-2011), nuclear physicist (6-5). No. 4244, $1.20, Wang Xuan (1937-2006), computer scientist (6-6).

Perf. 13¼ Syncopated

2014, Oct. 16 Photo.
4239-4244 A1381 Set of 6 2.40 2.40

Sail Your Dreams — A1382

2014, Oct. 31 Litho. *Perf. 13¼*
4245 A1382 $1.20 multi + label .40 .40

See Stamps With Attached Labels note after No. 3197.

Meeting of Leaders of Asia-Pacific Economic Cooperation, Beijing — A1383

2014, Nov. 10 Litho. *Perf. 13¼x13*
4246 A1383 $1.20 multi .40 .40

10th China Intl. Aviation and Aerospace Exhibition — A1384

No. 4247: a, Helicopter, airplanes, city skyline (2-1). b, Space Station, rockets, astronaut (2-2).

2014, Nov. 11 Litho. *Perf. 13¼x13*
4247 A1384 $1.20 Horiz. pair, #a-b .80 .80

Chinese Character for "Congratulations" — A1385

2014, Nov. 12 Litho. *Perf. 12*
4248 A1385 $1.20 multi + label .40 .40

See Stamps With Attached Labels note after No. 3197.

Chinese Arctic and Antarctic Research Expeditions, 30th Anniv. — A1386

No. 4249: a, $1.20, Map of Antarctica, research expedition station, buildings, penguins (2-1). b, $1.50, Map of Arctic region, ship, buildings and polar bears (2-2).

Perf. 13x12¾ Syncopated

2014, Nov. 20 Litho.
4249 A1386 Vert. pair, #a-b .90 .90

Double Happiness — A1387

2014, Dec. 1 Litho. *Perf. 13¼x13*
4250 A1387 $3 multi 1.00 1.00

Values are for stamp with surrounding selvage.

Miniature Sheet

Yuan Dramatic Works — A1388

No. 4251: a, 80f, Sand and Sky — Autumn Thoughts, by Ma Zhiyuan (6-1). b, $1.20, Sheep on the Slope — Meditation on the Past at Tong Pass, by Zhang Yanghao (6-2). c, $1.20, Dou E Yuan, by Guan Hanqing (6-3). d, $1.20, Over the Wall, by Bai Pu (6-4). e, $1.50, The Orphan of Zhao, by Ji Junxiang (6-5). f, $3, Premature Death of a Beautiful Young Girl, by Zheng Guangzu (6-6).

Litho. & Engr.

2014, Dec. 1 ***Perf. 13¼***

4251 A1388 Sheet of 6, #a-f 3.00 3.00

New Year 2015 (Year of the Ram) A1389

Perf. 13 Syncopated

2015, Jan. 5 **Photo.**

4252 A1389 $1.20 multi .40 .40
a. Booklet pane of 10 4.00 —
Complete booklet, #4252a 4.00

Greeting Chinese New Year A1390

Perf. 13 Syncopated

2015, Jan. 10 **Litho.**

4253 A1390 $1.20 multi .40 .40

Zunyi Conference, 80th Anniv. — A1391

Designs: No. 4254. $1.20, Conference site (2-1). No. 4255, $1.20, Conference participants (2-2).

Perf. 13¼x13 Syncopated

2015, Jan. 15 **Litho.**

4254-4255 A1391 Set of 2 .80 .80

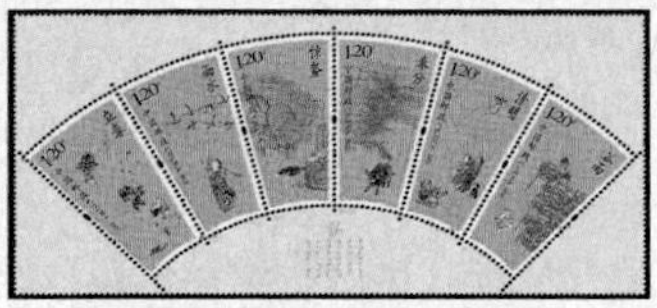

24 Solar Terms — A1392

No. 4256: a, Beginning of Spring (children and flowers) (6-1). b, Rain water (fisherman and birds). (6-2). c, Waking of insects (cowherd and bulls) (6-3). d, Spring equinox (boy on bull) (6-4). e, Pure brightness (kite flying) (6-5). f, Grain rain (women tending to vegetables on racks, rabbits) (6-6).

Perf. 13 Syncopated

2015, Feb. 4 **Photo.**

4256 A1392 $1.20 Block of 6, #a-f 2.40 2.40

Values are for stamps with surrounding selvage.

Court Ladies Swinging Fans, by Zhou Fang — A1393

No. 4257 — Painting details numbered: a, (3-1). b, (3-2). c, (3-3).
$6, Entire painting.

Perf. 13¼x13 Syncopated

2015, Mar. 22 **Litho.**

4257 Horiz. strip of 3 1.40 1.40
a.-b. A1393 $1.20 Either single .40 .40
c. A1393 $1.50 multi .50 .50

Souvenir Sheet

Perf. 12¾x12½ Syncopated

4258 A1393 $6 multi 2.00 2.00

No. 4258 contains one 157x28mm stamp.

Writers — A1394

Designs: No. 4259, $1.20, Tang Xianzu (1550-1616) (6-1). No. 4260, $1.20, Feng Menglong (1574-1645) (6-2). No. 4261, $1.20, Pu Songling (1640-1715) (6-3). No. 4262, $1.20, Hong Sheng (1645-1704) (6-4). No. 4263, $1.20, Kong Shangren (1648-1718) (6-5). No. 4264, $1.20, Cao Xueqin (c.1715-c.1763) (6-6).

Perf. 13 Syncopated

2015, Apr. 4 **Litho. & Engr.**

4259-4264 A1394 Set of 6 2.40 2.40

Slender West Lake — A1395

Designs: No. 4265, $1.20, Lotus Bridge (3-1). No. 4266, $1.20, Twenty-four Bridge (3-2). $1.50, White Pagoda (3-3).

Perf. 13¼x13 Syncopated

2015, Apr. 18 **Litho. & Engr.**

4265-4267 A1395 Set of 3 1.25 1.25

Scenes from *Journey to the West*, by Wu Cheng'en A1396

Designs: No. 4268, $1.20, Great sage equalling heaven (4-1). No. 4269, $1.20, Sun Wukong surrendered to Buddha (4-2). No. 4270, $1.50, Tang monk makes vows to go to the West (4-3). No. 4271, $1.50, Tang monk disciples Monkey King (4-4).
$6, Making havoc in heaven.

Perf. 13¼ Syncopated

2015, May 3 **Litho.**

4268-4271 A1396 Set of 4 1.75 1.75

Souvenir Sheet

Photo.

Perf. 13¼x13 Syncopated

4272 A1396 $6 multi 2.00 2.00

Vacation Activities A1397

Designs: 80f, Man taking photograph. $1.20, Family in automobile on bridge. $3, Backpacking.

Die Cut Perf. 12½ Syncopated

2015, May 19 **Photo.**

Self-Adhesive

4273 A1397 80f multi .25 .25
4274 A1397 $1.20 multi .40 .40
4275 A1397 $3 multi 1.00 1.00
Nos. 4273-4275 (3) 1.65 1.65

World Metrology Day — A1398

Perf. 13¼x12¾ Syncopated

2015, May 20 **Litho.**

4276 A1398 $1.20 multi .40 .40

Ships — A1399

Designs: No. 4277, $1.20, Space tracking ship (4-1). No. 4278, $1.20, Liquified natural gas tanker (4-2). No. 4279, $1.20, Floating Production Storage and Offloading ship (4-3). $1.50, Guided missile destroyer (4-4).

Perf. 13¼x12¾ Syncopated

2015, June 3 **Litho.**

4277-4280 A1399 Set of 4 1.75 1.75

World Environment Day — A1400

Perf. 13¼x12¾ Syncopated

2015, June 5 **Photo.**

4281 A1400 $1.20 multi .40 .40

Father's Day — A1401

Litho. With Foil Application

Perf. 13¼x13 Syncopated

2015, June 13

4282 A1401 $1.20 multi .40 .40

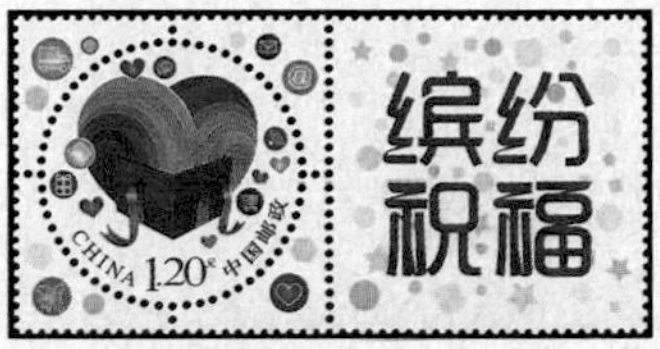

Rainbows, Hearts and Gift Box — A1402

2015, June 18 **Litho.** ***Perf. 13¼***

4283 A1402 $1.20 multi + label .40 .40

See Stamps With Attached Labels note after No. 3197.

Qiantang River Tidal Bores — A1404

No. 4285: a, Crossing bores (3-1). b, Spectators watching wave (3-2). c, Spectators watching reverse bore (3-3).

Perf. 13¼x12¾ Syncopated

2015, July 1 **Litho. & Engr.**

4285 Horiz. strip of 3 1.40 1.40
a.-b. A1404 $1.20 Either single .40 .40
c. A1404 $1.50 multi .50 .50

Peace Dove — A1405

2015, July 3 **Litho.** ***Perf. 13¼***

4286 A1405 $1.20 multi + label .40 .40

See Stamps With Attached Labels note after No. 3197.

Qingyuan Mountain — A1406

Designs: 80f, Sky Lake (3-1). No. 4288, $1.20, Rock carvings (3-2). No. 4289, $1.20, Statue of Lao Zi (3-3).

Perf. 13¼x12¾ Syncopated

2015, July 18 **Litho. & Engr.**

4287-4289 A1406 Set of 3 1.10 1.10

Stylized Athletes — A1407

2015, July 20 Litho. *Perf. 13¼*
4290 A1407 $1.20 multi + label .40 .40

See Stamps With Attached Labels note after No. 3197.

Happiness of the People A1408

Buildings and: 80f, Fruit sellers, machine (4-1). No. 4292, $1.20, Bus, medical care (4-2). No. 4293, $1.20, Automobile, person in wheelchair, voters (4-3). No. 4294, $1.20, Ferris wheel, tai chi, woman pushing baby carriage (4-4).

Perf. 13x12¾ Syncopated
2015, July 25 Photo.
4291-4294 A1408 Set of 4 1.40 1.40
4294a Souvenir sheet of 4, #4291-4294 1.40 1.40

Lord Bao (999-1062), Government Official A1410

Designs: No. 4296, $1.20, Lord Bao throwing inkstone into water (2-1). No. 4297, $1.20, Case of Chen Shimei (2-2).
$6, Lord Bao seated.

Perf. 13¼ Syncopated
2015, Aug. 8 Photo.
4296-4297 A1410 Set of 2 .75 .75

Souvenir Sheet
Perf. 13¼x13½ Syncopated
4298 A1410 $6 multi 1.90 1.90

No. 4298 contains one 60x67mm stamp.

Mandarin Ducks A1411

Perf. 13x12¾ Syncopated
2015, Aug. 20 Litho. & Engr.
4299 A1411 $1.20 multi .40 .40

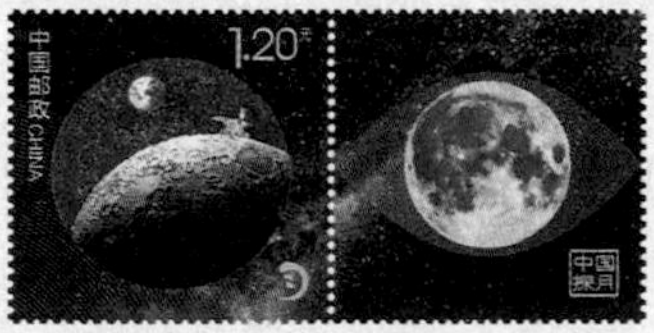

Lunar Exploration by China — A1412

2015, Aug. 20 Litho. *Perf. 13¼*
4300 A1412 $1.20 multi + label .40 .40

See Stamps With Attached Labels note after No. 3197.

Miniature Sheet

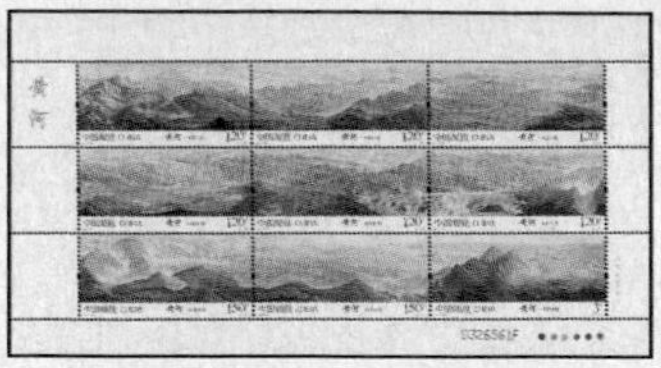

Yellow River — A1413

No. 4301: a, $1.20, Beginning of river (9-1). b, $1.20, Nine Bays (9-2). c, $1.20, River bend in Hinterland (9-3). d, $1.20, Great bend (9-4). e, $1.20, River approaching Hukou Waterfalls (9-5). f, $1.20, Hukou Waterfalls and Sanjing (9-6). g, $1.50, Helou area (9-7). h, $1.50, Zhongshou Plain (9-8). i, $3, Mountains and buildings in foreground (9-9).

Perf. 13¼x12¾ Syncopated
2015, Aug. 23 Photo.
4301 A1413 Sheet of 9, #a-i 4.25 4.25

Tibet Autonomous Region, 50th Anniv. — A1414

No. 4302: a, Tibetans, symbols of Tibet, cranes and mountains (3-1). b, Tibetans, doves, buildings (3-2). c, Tibetan family, house, symbols of Tibet (3-3).

Perf. 13¼x12¾ Syncopated
2015, Sept. 1 Photo.
4302 Horiz. strip of 3 1.25 1.25
a.-c. A1414 $1.20 Any single .40 .40

Victory in World War II, 70th Anniv. — A1415

Soldiers and: No. 4303, 80f, September 18 Memorial Museum (13-1). No. 4304, 80f, Northeast China Revolutionary Martyrs Memorial Hall (13-2). No. 4305, $1.20, Museum of the War of Chinese People's Resistance Against Japanese Aggression (13-3). No. 4306, $1.20, Shanghai Songhu Anti-Japanese War Memorial Hall (13-4). No. 4307, $1.20, Museum of Victims in the Nanjing Massacre by Japanese Invaders (13-5). No. 4308, $1.20, Taierzhuang Campaign Memorial Hall (13-6). No. 4309, $1.20, Yan'an Revolutionary Memorial Hall (13-7). No. 4310, $1.20, Memorial Hall of Former Site of the Eighth Route Army Headquarters (13-8). No. 4311, $1.20, Hundred Regiments Offensive Memorial Hall (13-9). No. 4312, $1.20, Pingxingguan Victory Memorial Hall (13-10). No. 4313, $1.20, Museum of Tunnel Warfare at Ranzhuang (13-11). No. 4314, $1.20, New Fourth Army Memorial Hall (13-12). No. 4315, $1.20, Memorial Hall of Anti-Japanese War in Western Yunnan (13-13).
$6, Statue of soldier with sword, vert.

Perf. 13¼x13 Syncopated
2015, Sept. 3 Photo.
4303-4315 A1415 Set of 13 4.75 4.75

Souvenir Sheet
4316 A1415 $6 multi 1.90 1.90

No. 4316 contains one 50x60mm stamp.

SEMI-POSTAL STAMPS

Catalogue values for unused stamps in this section are for Never Hinged items.

Girl Holding Ball — SP1

1984, Feb. 16 Photo. *Perf. 11½*
B1 SP1 8f + 2f shown (2-1) 1.25 .30
B2 SP1 8f + 2f Boy, panda (2-2) 1.25 .30

Surtax for China Children's Fund. T.92.

Hands Reading Braille — SP2

No. B4, Sign language, lip reading. No. B5, Artificial limb. No. B6, Handicapped person in wheelchair.

1985, Mar. 15 Photo. *Perf. 11½*
B3 SP2 8f + 2f shown (4-1) 1.00 .60
B4 SP2 8f + 2f multi (4-2) 1.00 .60
B5 SP2 8f + 2f multi (4-3) 1.00 .60
B6 SP2 8f + 2f multi (4-4) 1.00 .60
Nos. B3-B6 (4) 4.00 2.40

Surtax for China Welfare Fund. T.105.

Children (T.137) SP3

No. B7, Friends. No. B8, Penguins. No. B9, Bird, Moon, Sun. No. B10, Girl, boy playing ball.

1989, June 1 Litho. *Perf. 12*
B7 SP3 8f +4f multi (4-1) .25 .25
B8 SP3 8f +4f multi (4-2) .25 .25
B9 SP3 8f +4f multi (4-3) .25 .25
B10 SP3 8f +4f multi (4-4) .25 .25
a. Strip of 4, #B7-B10 1.50 1.50

Intl Children's Day, 40th anniv., and 10th Intl. Year of the Child. Surtax for China Children's Fund.

Sichuan Earthquake Relief — SP4

2008, May 20 Photo. *Perf. 13x13¼*
B11 SP4 $1.20 + $1 multi + label *18.00 4.00*

AIR POST STAMPS

Mail Plane and Temple of Heaven — AP1

1951, May 1 Engr. *Perf. 12½*
Without Gum
C1 AP1 $1000 carmine 1.00 .40
C2 AP1 $3000 green 1.00 .40
C3 AP1 $5000 orange 1.00 .40
a. Pair, imperf. between 600.00 —
C4 AP1 $10,000 vio brn & grn 3.00 1.00
C5 AP1 $30,000 dk bl & brn 24.00 4.25
Nos. C1-C5 (5) 30.00 6.45

Planes at Airport — AP2

Designs: 28f, Plane over winding mountain highway. 35f, Plane over railroad yard. 52f, Plane over ship.

1957-58 Without Gum *Perf. 14*
C6 AP2 16f indigo 16.00 1.00
C7 AP2 28f olive black 16.00 1.00
C8 AP2 35f slate 16.00 5.00
C9 AP2 52f Prus blue ('58) 16.00 2.00
Nos. C6-C9 (4) 64.00 9.00

POSTAGE DUE STAMPS

Grain and Cogwheel — D1

1950, Sept. 1 Typo. *Perf. 12½*
Without Gum
J1 D1 $100 steel blue .25 .25
J2 D1 $200 steel blue .25 .25
J3 D1 $500 steel blue .25 .25
J4 D1 $800 steel blue 25.00 1.00
J5 D1 $1000 steel blue .45 .40
J6 D1 $2000 steel blue .70 .40
J7 D1 $5000 steel blue .70 .60
J8 D1 $8000 steel blue .70 1.00
J9 D1 $10,000 steel blue 2.00 2.00
Nos. J1-J9 (9) 30.30 6.15

D2

1954, Aug. 18 Litho. *Perf. 14*
Without Gum
J10 D2 $100 red 1.50 .25
J11 D2 $200 red .75 .25
J12 D2 $500 red 1.50 .25
J13 D2 $800 red .60 .25
J14 D2 $1600 red .75 .25
Nos. J10-J14 (5) 5.10 1.25

MILITARY STAMP

Red Star, 8-1 in Center — M1

1953, Aug. Litho. *Perf. 14*
Without Gum
M1 M1 $800 yel, org & red *300.00 125.00*

This stamp also was printed in deep purple, orange & red (value, *$3,000.*), and blue, orange & red (value, *$240,000*). These were not issued.

While it has been assumed for many years that each color was for a separate branch of the armed forces (army, air force and navy), there is no documentation to support that theory. Quantities printed also do not correspond to the number of servicemen in each branch.

M2

1995 **Litho.** ***Perf. 12***

M4 M2 20f multicolored 6.50 *2.00*

NORTHEAST CHINA

The Northeast Liberation Area included the provinces of Liaoning, Kirin, Jehol and Heilungkiang, the area generally known as Manchuria under the Japanese. The first post war issues were local overprints on stamps of Manchukuo. In early 1946, a Ministry of Posts and Telegraphs served the areas already liberated, and in August, 1946, a Communications Committee of the Political Council was established. In June, 1947, these postal services were subordinated to the Harbin General Post Office, and this was extended to Changchun on Oct. 22, 1948, and to Mukden on Nov. 4, 1948. It was rapidly extended to cover all Manchuria.

Rough Perfs
Rough perforations are normal on most regional issues.

All Stamps Issued without Gum

Mao Tse-tung
A1 A2

1946, Feb. Unwmk. Litho. *Perf. 11*

1L1 A1 $1 violet 22.50 12.00
1L2 A2 $2 vermilion 2.50 1.00
1L3 A2 $5 orange 2.75 1.00
a. Booklet pane of 6 250.00
1L4 A2 $10 blue 3.00 1.25
a. Booklet pane of 6 250.00
Nos. 1L1-1L4 (4) 30.75 15.25

Value, imperf set $125.

For surcharges see Nos. 1L20-1L23, 1L49-1L50, 1L89, 1L91, 1L93.

Map of China, Lion, Hyena and Chiang Kai-shek — A3

1946, Dec. 12 ***Perf. 10½***

1L5 A3 $1 violet 2.25 1.50
1L6 A3 $2 orange 2.25 1.50
1L7 A3 $5 org brn 7.50 7.00
1L8 A3 $10 lt grn 12.00 10.00
a. Imperf., pair 60.00
Nos. 1L5-1L8 (4) 24.00 20.00

10th anniversary of the capture of Chiang Kai-shek at Sian.

Railroad Workers, Chengchow A4

1947, Feb. 7 ***Perf. 10½***

1L9 A4 $1 pink 2.00 *2.00*
1L10 A4 $2 dull grn 2.00 *2.00*
1L11 A4 $5 pink 3.50 2.25
1L12 A4 $10 dull grn 7.00 5.50
Nos. 1L9-1L12 (4) 14.50 11.75

24th anniversary of the Chengchow railroad workers' strike and massacre.

Women (Worker, Soldier and Farmer) — A5

Wmk. Chinese Characters in Sheet

1947, Mar. 8 ***Perf. 10½x11***

1L13 A5 $5 brick red 5.00 2.00
1L14 A5 $10 brown 5.00 2.00

International Women's Day, March 8. Exists imperf.

Same Overprinted in Green ("Northeast Postal Service")

1947, Mar. 18

1L15 A5 $5 brick red 9.50 6.00
1L16 A5 $10 brown 9.50 6.00

Exists imperf.

Children Carrying Banner — A6

1947, Apr. 4 ***Perf. 11x10½***

Granite Paper

1L17 A6 $5 rose red 7.00 5.00
1L18 A6 $10 lt green 12.00 9.50
1L19 A6 $30 orange 17.50 11.00
Nos. 1L17-1L19 (3) 36.50 25.50

Children's Day.

Nos. 1L1-1L2 Surcharged in Red, Brown, Black, Blue or Green

1947, Apr. Unwmk. *Perf. 11*

1L20 A1 $50 on $1 vio (R) 30.00 32.50
a. Brown surcharge 30.00 32.50
1L21 A2 $50 on $2 ver 30.00 32.50
a. Brown surcharge 30.00 32.50
1L22 A1 $100 on $1 vio 30.00 32.50
a. Green surcharge 30.00 32.50
1L23 A2 $100 on $2 ver (Bl) 30.00 32.50
a. Green surcharge 30.00 32.50
Nos. 1L20-1L23 (4) 120.00 130.00

Farmer and Worker — A7

Wmk. Chinese Characters in Sheet

1947, May 1 ***Perf. 10½x11***

Granite Paper

1L24 A7 $10 orange red 6.00 6.00
1L25 A7 $30 ultra 10.00 10.00
1L26 A7 $50 gray green 6.50 6.50
Nos. 1L24-1L26 (3) 22.50 22.50

Labor Day. Value, imperf. pairs, set $425.

Ax Severing Chain — A8

1947, May 4 ***Perf. 11***

1L27 A8 $10 brt green 8.00 8.00
1L28 A8 $30 brown 8.00 8.00
1L29 A8 $50 violet 10.00 10.00
Nos. 1L27-1L29 (3) 26.00 26.00

28th anniversary of the students' revolt at Peking University against the 1918 peace treaty. Value, imperf. pairs, set $525.

Workers with Banner: "Oppose Imperialist Aggression" — A9

1947, May 30 ***Perf. 10½x11***

Banner in Red

1L30 A9 $2 brt lilac 7.50 *8.00*
1L31 A9 $5 brt green 7.50 *8.00*
1L32 A9 $10 yellow 9.50 *9.00*
1L33 A9 $20 violet 9.00 *8.50*
1L34 A9 $30 red brown 9.00 *8.50*
1L35 A9 $50 dk blue 12.00 8.50
1L36 A9 $100 brown 15.00 8.50
a. Souvenir sheet of 7 375.00
Nos. 1L30-1L36 (7) 69.50 59.00

22nd anniversary of the Shanghai-Nanking Road incident. No. 1L36a is on granite paper and contains 7 imperf. stamps similar to Nos. 1L30-1L36. Size: 215x158mm. Value, imperf. pairs, ordinary paper, set $1,300.

Mao and Communist Flag — A10

1947, July 1 ***Perf. 10½x11***

1L37 A10 $10 red 20.00 *24.00*
1L38 A10 $30 brt lilac 20.00 *24.00*
1L39 A10 $50 rose brn 60.00 *65.00*
1L40 A10 $100 vermilion 70.00 *80.00*
Nos. 1L37-1L40 (4) 170.00 *193.00*

26th anniversary of the founding of the Chinese Communist Party.

Hand Holding Rifle — A11

1947, July 7 ***Perf. 10½***

1L41 A11 $10 orange 10.00 *12.00*
1L42 A11 $30 green 10.00 *12.00*
1L43 A11 $50 dull blue 15.00 14.00
1L44 A11 $100 brown 20.00 18.00
a. Souvenir sheet of 4 475.00 *400.00*
Nos. 1L41-1L44 (4) 55.00 56.00

10th anniversary of the start of Sino-Japanese War. No. 1L44a contains 4 imperf. stamps similar to Nos. 1L41-1L44. Size: 149x107mm.

Exist imperf. Value, set of pairs $1,100.

White Mountain and Black Water, Northeast China — A12

Wmk. Zigzag Lines (141)

1947, Aug. 15 ***Perf. 10½***

1L45 A12 $10 brown org 5.50 *8.50*
1L46 A12 $30 lt ol grn 5.50 *8.50*
1L47 A12 $50 blue grn 17.50 *16.00*
1L48 A12 $100 sepia 27.50 *22.50*
Nos. 1L45-1L48 (4) 56.00 *55.50*

2nd anniversary of the reoccupation of Northeast China and the surrender of Japan. Exist imperf. Value, set of pairs $700.

Nos. 1L1-1L2 Surcharged in Black, Red, Green or Blue

1947, Aug. 29 Unwmk. *Perf. 11*

1L49 A1 $5 on $1 vio 40.00 40.00
a. Red surcharge 40.00 40.00
b. Green surcharge 40.00 40.00
1L50 A2 $10 on $2 ver 40.00 40.00
a. Blue surcharge 40.00 40.00
b. Green surcharge 40.00 40.00

Map of Manchuria — A13

1947, Sept. 18 **Unwmk.**

White Paper

1L51 A13 $10 gray green 7.00 10.00
1L52 A13 $20 rose lilac 7.00 10.00
1L53 A13 $30 black brown 13.00 10.00
1L54 A13 $50 carmine 13.00 10.00
Nos. 1L51-1L54 (4) 40.00 40.00

16th anniversary of Japanese attack on Mukden, Sept. 18, 1931.

Northeast Political Council Offices — A14

1947, Oct. 10 ***Perf. 10½***

1L55 A14 $10 yel orange 50.00 50.00
1L56 A14 $20 rose red 50.00 50.00
1L57 A14 $100 brown 110.00 110.00
Nos. 1L55-1L57 (3) 210.00 210.00

35th anniversary of the founding of the Chinese Republic.

Mao Tse-tung (Value figures repeated) — A15

1947, Oct. 10 White Paper *Perf. 11*

1L58 A15 $1 brown 3.50 1.50
1L59 A15 $5 gray green 2.50 1.50
1L60 A15 $10 brt green 18.00 9.00
1L61 A15 $15 bluish lilac 18.00 9.00
1L62 A15 $20 brt rose 1.00 1.50
1L63 A15 $30 green 1.00 2.00
1L64 A15 $50 black brown 25.00 13.50
1L65 A15 $90 blue 6.50 4.00
Nos. 1L58-1L65 (8) 75.50 42.00

Newsprint

1L66 A15 $100 red .80
a. White paper 8.00 5.00
1L67 A15 $500 red orange 40.00 17.50
a. White paper 32.50 30.00

Type A22 resembles A15, but has "YUAN" at upper right.

The $1, $90 were also printed on newsprint.
See footnote following No. 1L72.
See Nos. 1L68-1L72. For surcharges see Nos. 1L84-1L88, 1L90, 1L92, 1L94.

White Paper

1947, Nov. **Redrawn**

1L68	A15	$50 lt grn	1.00	*1.50*
1L69	A15	$150 red org, wmkd. Chinese characters	2.25	1.50
a.		Unwatermarked	2.75	
1L70	A15	$250 bluish lil	.90	*1.50*
a.		Wmkd. Chinese characters	1.25	*1.50*

Nos. 1L69 and 1L69a exist in same sheet.

1947, Dec. **Unwmk.** **Newsprint**

1L71	A15	$300 green	55.00	30.00
1L72	A15	$1000 yellow	1.50	1.50
a.		White paper	1.50	1.50
		Nos. 1L68-1L72 (5)	60.65	36.00

Panel below portrait 8½x3mm on Nos. 1L68-1L70; 7x3mm on No. 1L58-1L67. Nos. 1L68-1L70 have different ornamental border. Nos. 1L71-1L72 without zeros for cents.
For surcharges see Nos. 1L90, 1L92, 1L94.

Hand Holding Torch — A16

1947, Dec. 12 **Unwmk.** ***Perf. 11***
White Paper

1L73	A16	$30 rose red	17.50	*17.50*
1L74	A16	$90 dk bl	19.00	*17.50*
1L75	A16	$150 green	21.00	17.50
		Nos. 1L73-1L75 (3)	57.50	52.50

11th anniversary of the capture of Chiang Kai-shek at Sian.

Tomb of Gen. Li Chao-lin — A17

1948, Mar. 9 **Unwmk.** ***Perf. 10½x11***

1L76	A17	$30 green	24.00	24.00
a.		Granite paper, wmkd.	24.00	24.00
1L77	A17	$150 vio gray	24.00	24.00
a.		Granite paper, wmkd.	24.00	24.00

2nd anniversary of the assassination of Gen. Li Chao-lin, Commander of 3rd Army.

Globe and Banner — A18

Wmk. Chinese Characters in Sheet

1948, May 1 ***Perf. 11x10½***

1L78	A18	$50 red	17.00	*13.00*
1L79	A18	$150 green	9.50	*20.00*
1L80	A18	$250 lilac	9.50	*40.00*
		Nos. 1L78-1L80 (3)	36.00	*73.00*

Labor Day.

Student, Torch and Banner — A19

1948, May 4 **Unwmk.** ***Perf. 10½x11***
Granite paper

1L81	A19	$50 green	21.00	20.00
1L82	A19	$150 brown	21.00	*25.00*
1L83	A19	$250 red	25.00	*30.00*
		Nos. 1L81-1L83 (3)	67.00	75.00

Youth Day, May 4.

Nos. 1L58, 1L61, 1L59, 1L63, 1L65, 1L2-1L4, 1L68-1L69, 1L71 Srchd. in Black, Blue, Red or Green

1948-49 ***Perf. 11***

1L84	A15	$100 on $1	75.00	90.00
a.		Blue surcharge	50.00	50.00
1L85	A15	$100 on $15	28.00	28.00
a.		Blue surcharge	50.00	50.00
1L86	A15	$300 on $5 (R)	55.00	42.50
1L87	A15	$300 on $30 (R)	20.00	20.00
1L88	A15	$300 on $90 (R)	15.00	15.00
1L89	A2	$500 on $2	12.00	12.00
1L90	A15	$500 on $50 (R, '49)	30.00	25.00
1L91	A2	$1500 on $5 (Bl)	12.00	10.00
1L92	A15	$1500 on $150 (G; '49)	25.00	25.00
a.		Blue surcharge	50.00	50.00
1L93	A2	$2500 on $10 (R)	15.00	15.00
1L94	A15	$2500 on $300 ('49)	20.00	20.00
		Nos. 1L84-1L94 (11)	307.00	302.50

Crane Operator — A20

Wmk. Chinese Characters in Sheet

1948, May ***Perf. 11***

1L95	A20	$100 red & pink	4.50	2.00
1L96	A20	$300 vio brn & yel	7.50	2.75
1L97	A20	$500 bl & grn	11.00	3.50
		Nos. 1L95-1L97 (3)	23.00	8.25

6th All-China Labor Conference, Harbin.

Farmer, Worker and Soldier Saluting — A21

1948, Dec. 3 **Unwmk.** ***Perf. 11x10½***
White paper

1L98	A21	$500 vermilion	17.50	16.00
1L99	A21	$1500 brt grn	20.00	18.00
1L100	A21	$2500 brown	32.50	30.00
		Nos. 1L98-1L100 (3)	70.00	64.00

Liberation of Northeast China.
Values for Nos. 1L98-1L100 are for fine stamps.

Mao Tse-tung ("YUAN" at upper right) — A22

1949, Feb. ***Perf. 11***

1L101	A22	$300 olive	.90	*1.25*
1L102	A22	$500 orange	8.50	*9.00*
1L103	A22	$1500 bl grn	.90	*1.25*
1L104	A22	$4500 brown	.90	*1.25*
1L105	A22	$6500 dk bl	.90	*1.25*
		Nos. 1L101-1L105 (5)	12.10	*14.00*

See type A15. For surcharges see Nos. 1L126-1L129, 1L131-1L132.

Workers, Globe and Flag — A23

1949, May 1 ***Perf. 11½***

1L106	A23	$1000 red & dl bl	.65	*1.10*
1L107	A23	$1500 red & pale bl	.65	*1.10*
1L108	A23	$4500 rose & ol brn	.85	*1.10*
1L109	A23	$6500 dl org & grn	.85	*1.10*
1L110	A23	$10,000 mar & ultra	4.00	*4.25*
		Nos. 1L106-1L110 (5)	7.00	*8.65*

Labor Day.

Fields and Factories — A24

1949 ***Perf. 10, 11***

1L111	A24	$5000 Prus bl	7.75	5.25
1L112	A24	$10,000 org brn	.60	*1.75*
1L113	A24	$50,000 green	.90	*2.50*
1L114	A24	$100,000 violet	1.25	*13.00*
		Nos. 1L111-1L114 (4)	10.50	*22.50*

Production in agriculture and industry.

Workers with Flags — A25

1949, July 1 ***Perf. 11***

1L115	A25	$1500 vio, lt bl & red	1.50	*2.25*
1L116	A25	$4500 dk brn, lt bl & ver	1.50	*2.25*
1L117	A25	$6500 gray, lt bl & rose red	3.25	*5.50*
		Nos. 1L115-1L117 (3)	6.25	*10.00*

28th anniversary of the founding of the Chinese Communist Party.

Heroes' Monument, Harbin — A26

1949, Aug. 15 ***Perf. 11½x11***

1L118	A26	$1500 brick red	1.50	*3.25*
1L119	A26	$4500 yel grn	2.00	*3.25*
1L120	A26	$6500 lt blue	4.00	*3.25*
		Nos. 1L118-1L120 (3)	7.50	*9.75*

4th anniversary of the Reoccupation, and the surrender of Japan.

"Northeast Postal Service"

The following commemorative issues are similar to those of the People's Republic of China, with the 4 characters shown added in different sizes and various arrangements.

Reprints were also issued similar to those of the PRC.

Chinese Lantern Type of PRC, 1949

1949, Sept. 12 **Litho.** ***Perf. 12½***

1L121	A1	$1000 dp blue	35.00	11.00
1L122	A1	$1500 scarlet	35.00	13.00
1L123	A1	$3000 green	65.00	*17.50*
1L124	A1	$4500 maroon	65.00	*17.50*
		Nos. 1L121-1L124 (4)	200.00	*59.00*

Reprints exist. Value, set $14.

Factory — A27

1949, Oct. ***Perf. 11x10½***

1L125	A27	$1500 orange	1.50	*1.75*

For surcharge see No. 1L130.

Nos. 1L101, 1L103-1L105, 1L125 Surcharged in Black or Green

1949, Nov. 20

1L126	A22	$2000 on $300	37.50	*17.00*
1L127	A22	$2000 on $4500 (G)	50.00	*40.00*
1L128	A22	$2500 on $1500	.70	*7.50*
1L129	A22	$2500 on $6500	37.50	*35.00*
1L130	A27	$5000 on $1500	.60	*2.00*
1L131	A22	$20,000 on $4500	.40	*7.00*
1L132	A22	$35,000 on $300	.50	*11.00*
		Nos. 1L126-1L132 (7)	127.20	*119.50*

Globe and Hammer Type of PRC

1949, Nov. 15 ***Perf. 12½***

1L133	A2	$5000 crimson	650.00	250.00
1L134	A2	$20,000 dp green	950.00	275.00
1L135	A2	$35,000 vio blue	1,250.	325.00
		Nos. 1L133-1L135 (3)	2,850.	850.00

Reprints, value; Nos. 1L133-1L134, each $2; No. 1L135, $575.

Mao and Conference Hall Types of PRC

1950, Feb. 1 ***Perf. 14***

1L136	A3	$1000 vermilion	35.00	29.00
1L137	A3	$1500 dp blue	35.00	29.00
1L138	A4	$5000 dk vio brn	60.00	45.00
1L139	A4	$20,000 green	60.00	*55.00*
		Nos. 1L136-1L139 (4)	190.00	158.00

Reprints exist. Value, set $13.

Gate of Heavenly Peace — A28

1950 ***Perf. 10½***
Narrow horizontal shading

1L140	A28	$500 olive	2.00	.60
1L141	A28	$1000 orange	2.25	.60
1L142	A28	$1000 lil rose	4.00	.60
1L143	A28	$2000 gray grn	1.75	.35
1L144	A28	$2500 yellow	4.50	.35
1L145	A28	$5000 dp org	35.00	.35
1L146	A28	$10,000 brn org	2.50	.65
1L147	A28	$20,000 vio brn	1.50	.35
1L148	A28	$35,000 dp blue	1.50	.45
1L149	A28	$50,000 brt grn	22.50	1.00
		Nos. 1L140-1L149 (10)	77.50	5.30

See A29.

Flag and Mao Type of PRC

1950, July 1 ***Perf. 14***
Yellow Stars

1L150	A7	$5000 grn & red	200.00	115.00
1L151	A7	$10,000 brn & red	225.00	115.00
1L152	A7	$20,000 dk brn & red	225.00	115.00
1L153	A7	$30,000 dk vio bl & red	375.00	150.00
		Nos. 1L150-1L153 (4)	1,025.	495.00

Reprints exist. Value, set $55.

Picasso Dove Type of PRC

1950, Aug. 1 **Engr.** ***Perf. 14***

1L154	A8	$2500 brown	16.00	*20.00*
1L155	A8	$5000 green	21.00	20.00
1L156	A8	$20,000 blue	28.00	20.00
		Nos. 1L154-1L156 (3)	65.00	60.00

Reprints exist. Value, set $6.

Flag Type of PRC

1950, Oct. 1 **Engr. & Litho.**

Flag in Red & Yellow

1L157 A9 $1000 purple 175.00 40.00
1L158 A9 $2500 org brn 190.00 42.50
1L159 A9 $5000 dp grn 200.00 55.00
1L160 A9 $10,000 olive 210.00 57.50
1L161 A9 $20,000 blue 250.00 95.00
Nos. 1L157-1L161 (5) 1,025. 290.00

Size of No. 1L159: 38x47mm, others 26x33mm.

Reprints exist. Value, set $40.

Postal Conference Type of PRC

1950, Nov. 1 **Litho.**

1L162 A11 $2500 grn & dp org 45.00 20.00
1L163 A11 $5000 car & grn 45.00 20.00

Reprints exist. Value, set, $5.

Gate of Heavenly Peace — A29

1950-51 ***Perf. 10½***

Wide horizontal shading

1L164 A29 $5000 orange 15.00 *11.00*
1L165 A29 $30,000 scarlet 9.00 *20.00*
1L166 A29 $100,000 violet 16.00 *24.00*

Wmk. Zigzag Lines (141)

1L167 A29 $250 brown 1.75 *2.50*
1L168 A29 $500 olive 1.75 *2.50*
1L169 A29 $1000 lil rose 2.00 *4.00*
1L170 A29 $2000 dl grn ('51) 3.00 *4.00*
1L171 A29 $2500 yellow 1.75 *4.00*
1L172 A29 $5000 orange 3.75 *4.00*
1L173 A29 $10,000 brn org ('51) 2.50 *4.00*
1L174 A29 $12,500 maroon 1.75 *4.00*
1L175 A29 $20,000 dp brn ('51) 2.75 *7.50*
Nos. 1L164-1L175 (12) 61.00 *91.50*

A $50,000 green was prepared, but not issued. Value $200.

Stalin and Mao Tse-tung Type of PRC

Unwmk.

1950, Dec. 1 **Engr.** ***Perf. 14***

1L176 A12 $2500 red 24.00 17.50
1L177 A12 $5000 dp green 29.00 17.50
1L178 A12 $20,000 dk blue 29.00 17.50
Nos. 1L176-1L178 (3) 82.00 52.50

Reprints exist. Value, set $16.

NORTHEAST CHINA PARCEL POST STAMPS

Locomotive — PP1

1951 **Litho.** ***Perf. 10½***

1LQ1 $100,000 purple *500.00*

Imperf

1LQ2 $300,000 brown *1,350.*
1LQ3 $500,000 grnsh bl *2,000.*
1LQ4 $1,000,000 ver *3,750.*

Value, Nos. 1LQ2-1LQ4 perf. 10½, $2,650.

For similar type see North China PP1.

PORT ARTHUR AND DAIREN

The Liaoning Postal Administration was established on April 1, 1946, in accordance with the Sino-Soviet Treaty, but was renamed one week later the Port Arthur and Dairen Postal Administration. On Apr. 3, 1947, it was combined with telecommunications and renamed the Kwantung Post and Telegraph General Administration.

On May 1, 1949, the name was again changed to Port Arthur and Dairen Post and Telegraph Administration. Postal tariffs were based on local currency and both Manchukuo and Japanese stamps were overprinted for use.

Gum

Nos. 2L1-2L35, 2L37-2L55 and 2L62-2L66 were issued with gum.

Manchukuo Nos. 162 and 94 Handstamp Surcharged in Violet ("Liaoning Post")

1946, Mar. 15

2L1 A19 20f on 30f buff 72.50 72.50
2L2 A18 1y on 12f org 37.50 37.50

Same Surcharge on Japan Nos. 260, 337, 195, 244, 263, 342 in Violet, Red or Black

1946, Apr. 1

2L3 A85 20f on 3s grn (V) 19.50 *21.00*
2L4 A151 1y on 17s gray vio (R) 16.00 *18.00*
2L5 A57 5y on 6s car 30.00 27.50
2L6 A57 5y on 6s crim 30.00 27.50
2L7 A88 5y on 6s org 22.00 20.00
2L8 A154 15y on 40s dk vio 110.00 *125.00*
Nos. 2L1-2L8 (8) 337.50 349.00

Surcharge sideways on Nos. 2L5-2L6.

Japan Nos. 260 and 263 Surcharged

1946, Apr.

2L9 A85 1y on 3s grn —
2L10 A88 5y on 6s org —

Sha Ho Kow (suburb of Dairen) issue. The status of this issue is in question.

Manchukuo Nos. 84, 88 and 98 Handstamp Surcharged in Green, Red or Black

1946, May 1

2L11 A16 1y on 1f red brn (G) 18.00 *24.00*
2L12 A18 5y on 4f lt ol grn (R) 24.00 *32.50*
2L13 A19 15y on 30f chnt brn 52.50 *62.50*
Nos. 2L11-2L13 (3) 94.50 *119.00*

Transfer of postal administration and Labor Day.

Manchukuo Nos. 159, 86 and 94 Surcharged in Green, Red or Black

1946, July 7

2L14 A17 1y on 6f crim rose (G) 11.50 *20.00*
2L15 A17 5y on 2f lt grn (R) 52.50 *85.00*
2L16 A18 15y on 12f dp org 110.00 110.00
Nos. 2L14-2L16 (3) 174.00 215.00

Outbreak of war with Japan, 9th anniv.

Manchukuo Nos. 94, 84 and 158 Surcharged in Black, Green or Red

1946, Aug. 15

2L17 A18 1y on 12f dp org 22.50 *27.50*
2L18 A16 5y on 1f red brn (G) 52.50 50.00
2L19 A10 15y on 5f gray blk (R) 110.00 100.00
Nos. 2L17-2L19 (3) 185.00 177.50

Surrender of Japan, first anniversary.

Manchukuo Nos. 159, 94 and 86 Surcharged in Green, Black or Red

1946, Oct. 10

2L20 A17 1y on 6f crim rose (G) 32.50 30.00
2L21 A18 5y on 12f dp org 57.50 55.00
2L22 A17 15y on 2f lt grn (R) 110.00 100.00
Nos. 2L20-2L22 (3) 200.00 185.00

35th anniversary of Chinese revolution.

Manchukuo Nos. 84, 159 and 94 Surcharged in Black, Green or Blue

1946, Oct. 19

2L23 A16 1y on 1f red brn 50.00 50.00
2L24 A17 5y on 6f crim rose (G) 100.00 100.00
2L25 A18 15y on 12f dp org (Bl) 135.00 135.00
Nos. 2L23-2L25 (3) 285.00 285.00

10th anniversary of the death of Lu Hsun (1881-1936), writer.

Manchukuo Nos. 86, 159 and 95 Surcharged in Red, Green or Black

1947, Feb. 20

2L26 A17 1y on 2f lt grn (R) 85.00 85.00
2L27 A17 5y on 6f crim rose (G) 175.00 175.00
2L28 A18 15y on 13f dk red brn 325.00 325.00
Nos. 2L26-2L28 (3) 585.00 585.00

29th anniversary of the Red (USSR) Army.

Manchukuo Nos. 86, 159 and 162 Surcharged in Red, Green or Black

1947, May 1

2L29 A17 1y on 2f lt grn (R) 24.00 24.00
2L30 A17 5y on 6f crim rose (G) 67.50 65.00
2L31 A19 15y on 30f buff 110.00 100.00
Nos. 2L29-2L31 (3) 201.50 189.00

Labor Day.

Manchukuo Nos. 86, 88, 98 and 162 Surcharged ("Kwantung Postal Service, China")

1947, Sept. 15

2L32 A17 5y on 2f lt grn 40.00 40.00
2L33 A18 15y on 4f lt ol grn 65.00 62.50
2L34 A19 20y on 30f red brn 100.00 95.00
2L35 A19 20y on 30f buff 110.00 100.00
Nos. 2L32-2L35 (4) 315.00 297.50

Manchukuo Nos. 86 and 159 Surcharged in Red and Green

Sacred Golden Kite (same size) — A1

1948, Feb. 20

2L36 A17 10y on 2f lt grn (R) 150.00 150.00
2L37 A17 20y on 6f crim rose (G) 190.00 190.00
2L38 A1 100y on bl & red brn 800.00 800.00

30th anniversary of the Red (USSR) Army. No. 2L38 is on an ungummed label for the 2600th anniv. of the Japanese Empire.

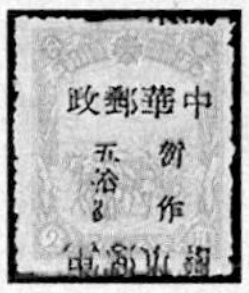

Japan No. 260 and Manchukuo Nos. 84, 86 and 88 Surcharged in Red, Blue or Black

1948, July

2L39 A85 5y on 3s grn (R) 125.00 125.00
2L40 A16 10y on 1f red brn (Bl) 250.00 250.00
2L41 A17 50y on 2f lt grn 500.00 500.00
2L42 A18 100y on 4f lt ol grn (R) 900.00 900.00

Smaller Characters on Bottom Line

2L43 A17 10y on 2f lt grn (R) 300.00 250.00
2L44 A16 50y on 1f red brn 350.00 300.00

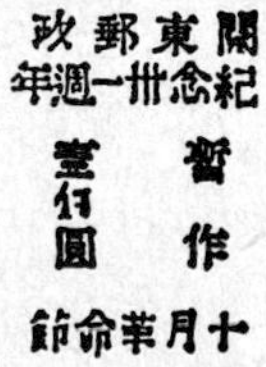

Stamps of Manchukuo Nos. 84, 86 and 88 Surcharged in Blue, Red or Black

1948, Nov. 1

2L45 A16 10y on 1f red brn (Bl) 275.00 600.00
2L46 A17 50y on 2f lt grn (R) 450.00 600.00
2L47 A18 100y on 4f lt ol grn 1,100. 600.00

31st anniversary of the Russian Revolution.

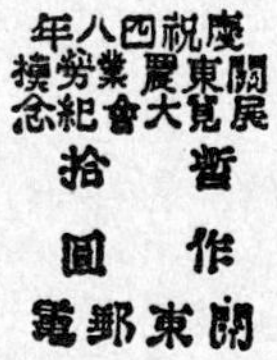

Manchukuo Nos. 86 and 161 Surcharged in Red or Green

1948, Nov. 15

2L48 A17 10y on 2f lt grn 1,050. 1,050.
2L49 A17 50y on 20f brn (G) 1,200. 1,200.

Kwantung Agricultural and Industrial Exhibition.

Manchukuo Nos. 86, 88 and 161 Surcharged in Red, Black or Green

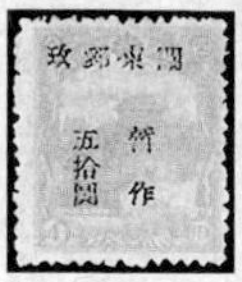

1949, Jan.

2L50 A17 20y on 2f lt grn (R) 500.00
2L51 A18 50y on 4f lt ol grn 700.00
2L52 A17 100y on 20f brn (G) 700.00

Without Gum

From No. 2L56 onward all stamps were issued without gum except as noted.

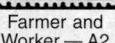

Farmer and Worker — A2

Train and Ship — A3

Ship at Dock (No. 2L55) — A4

(No. 2L56)

1949 **Litho.** ***Perf. 11, 11½***

2L53 A2 5y pale grn 3.00 *5.00*
2L54 A3 10y orange 20.00 20.00
2L55 A4 50y vermilion 22.50 22.50
2L56 A4 50y red (redrawn) 24.00 24.00
Nos. 2L53-2L56 (4) 69.50 71.50

Issue dates: No. 2L56, July 7; others Apr. 1.
For surcharges see Nos. 2L62-2L66.

Worker, Flag and Means of Transport A5

1949, May 1 ***Perf. 11***

2L57 A5 10y rose pink 55.00 *55.00*
a. 10y vermilion 75.00 75.00

Labor Day. No. 2L57a is from a worn plate.

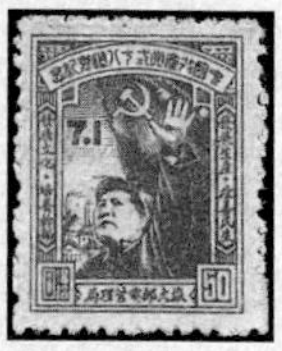

Mao Tse-tung and Red Flag — A6

1949, July 1

2L59 A6 50y red 45.00 45.00

28th anniversary of the founding of the Chinese Communist Party.

Heroes Monument, Dairen — A7

1949, Sept.

2L60 A7 10y red, bl & olive 45.00 45.00
a. 10y red, blue & pale blue 100.00 85.00

4th anniversary of victory over Japan and opening of the Dairen Industrial Fair.

Nos. 2L53-2L54 Surcharged in Red or Black

a

b

c

1949, Sept. **With Gum**

2L62 A2(a) 7y on 5y (R) 40.00 40.00
2L63 A2(a) 7y on 5y 40.00 40.00
2L64 A2(b) 50y on 5y (R) 95.00 95.00
2L65 A3(b) 100y on 10y 500.00 400.00
2L66 A3(c) 500y on 10y (R) 650.00 475.00
Nos. 2L62-2L66 (5) 1,325. 1,050.

Size of surcharge on No. 2L63: 16x19mm.
A 500y on 5y, red surcharge "c," and a 500y on 10y orange, surcharge "b" were prepared but not issued.

Stalin and Lenin — A8

1949, Nov. 7 ***Perf. 11x11½***

2L68 A8 10y dl bl grn (shades) 100.00 *65.00*

32nd anniversary of the Russian Revolution.

Workers Saluting Mao, Star and Flag — A9

1949, Nov. 16 ***Perf. 11***

2L69 A9 35y dk bl, red, & yel *120.00* 75.00

Founding of the People's Republic of China.

Stalin — A10

1949, Dec. 20 ***Perf. 11½***

2L70 A10 20y dull magenta *90.00 110.00*
2L71 A10 35y rose red *90.00 110.00*

70th birthday of Stalin.

Gate of Heavenly Peace — A11

1950, Mar. 10 **Typo.** ***Perf. 10½***

2L72 A11 10y Prus blue *425.00 400.00*
2L73 A11 20y dull grn *225.00 150.00*
2L74 A11 35y red *15.00 20.00*
2L75 A11 50y deep pur *15.00 25.00*
2L76 A11 100y lilac rose *55.00 55.00*
Nos. 2L72-2L76 (5) *735.00 650.00*

NORTH CHINA

The North China Liberation Area included the provinces of Hopeh, Chahar, Shansi and Suiyuan. The original postal service, begun in the Shansi-Hopeh-Chahar Border Area in December, 1937, became the North China Postal and Telegraph Administration in May, 1949.

All Stamps Issued without Gum Except as Noted

Large Victory Issue

Cavalry Man Holding Nationalist Flag — A1

Wmk. Wavy Lines

1946, Mar. ***Perf. 10½***

Granite Paper

Size: 34½x42mm

3L1 A1 $1 red brown 4.50 4.50
a. Newsprint 10.00 12.00
3L2 A1 $2 gray grn 4.50 4.50
3L3 A1 $4 vermilion 5.00 5.00
3L4 A1 $5 vio brn 16.00 6.00
3L5 A1 $8 vio bl 16.00 6.00
3L6 A1 $10 dp car 5.00 5.00
3L7 A1 $12 yellow 15.00 15.00
3L8 A1 $20 lt green 34.00 34.00
Nos. 3L1-3L8 (8) 100.00 80.00

Defeat of Japan.

Small Victory Issue

Perf. 10½x10, 9½ rough

1946, May **Unwmk.**

Granite paper

Size: 20x21mm

3L9 A1 $1 red org 1.60 *2.25*
3L10 A1 $2 green 2.50 2.25
3L11 A1 $3 lt lilac 4.75 *8.50*
3L12 A1 $5 dull pur 6.25 .40
3L13 A1 $8 dk blue 13.50 *17.50*
3L14 A1 $10 rose red 2.50 *4.50*
3L15 A1 $15 purple *77.50 67.50*
3L16 A1 $20 green 4.75 *6.25*
3L17 A1 $30 brt grnsh bl 4.00 *7.25*
3L18 A1 $40 brt rose lilac 4.75 3.25
3L19 A1 $50 brown *36.00* .75
3L20 A1 $60 myrtle green *67.50* 1.60

Wmk. Wavy Lines

3L21 A1 $100 orange 9.00 *4.50*
3L22 A1 $200 dull blue 12.00 *4.50*
3L23 A1 $500 rose 57.50 *70.00*
Nos. 3L9-3L23 (15) *304.10 201.00*

North China Postal and Telegraph Administration

Charging Infantrymen A2

Agriculture and Industry A3

1949, Jan. **Unwmk.** ***Imperf.***

White Paper

3L24 A2 50c brown lake 3.50 3.00
3L25 A2 $1 Prussian blue 3.50 3.50

Newsprint

3L26 A2 $2 apple green 3.50 3.50
3L27 A2 $3 dull violet 3.50 3.50
3L28 A2 $5 brown 3.50 3.50
3L29 A3 $6 deep rose 3.50 1.25
a. White paper 3.50 3.50
3L30 A2 $10 blue grn 1.25 *2.00*
3L31 A2 $12 dp car 3.75 3.50
Nos. 3L24-3L31 (8) 26.00 23.75

No. 3L29 issued in Peking, others in Tientsin.

Remittance Stamps of China Surcharged

A4

壹
$1

叁
$3

1949, Jan. **Engr.** ***Perf. 13***

Small Central Characters

3L32 A4 50c on $50 brn blk 3.25 *3.50*
3L33 A4 $1 on $50 gray blk 5.50 *2.75*
3L34 A4 $3 on $50 gray 5.50 2.50

Large Central Characters

3L35 A4 50c on $50 blk 2.50 1.60
3L36 A4 $6 on $20 dk vio brn 7.50 1.60
Nos. 3L32-3L36 (5) 24.25 11.95

Issued in Tientsin.
For surcharges see Nos. 3LQ10-3LQ21.

Sun Yat-sen Type A2 of Northeastern Provinces and China No. 640 Srchd. in Black, Red, Green or Blue

#3L37-3L45, 3L47-3L50, 3L52

#3L46, 3L51, 3L53

c

Type "b," bottom character of left vertical row (yuan) differs. Type "c," top character of right vertical row differs.

1949, Mar. 7 ***Perf. 14***

3L37 A2 50c on 5c lake .85 *2.75*
3L38 A2 $1 on 10c org .85 *2.25*
3L39 A2 $2 on 20c yel grn 80.00 25.00
3L40 A2 $3 on 50c red org .85 *1.75*
3L41 A2 $4 on $5 dk grn 9.50 2.25
3L42 A2 $6 on $10 crim 2.75 *2.25*
3L43 A2 $10 on $300 bluish grn 6.00 *3.25*
3L44 A2 $12 on $1 bl 4.00 *3.25*
3L45 A2 $18 on $3 brn 7.00 *1.75*
3L46 A2 $20 on 50c red org (Bl) 2.75 1.50
3L47 A2 $20 on $20 ol, II 5.50 *4.50*
a. Type I 20.00 *13.50*
3L48 A2 $30 on $2.50 ind (R) 7.00 *4.00*
3L49 A2 $40 on 25c blk brn (R) 9.00 *6.25*
3L50 A2 $50 on $109 dk grn (R) 17.50 9.00
3L51 A2 $80 on $1 bl (R) 22.50 4.50
3L52 A2 $100 on $65 dl grn (R) 30.00 9.00
3L53 A73 $100 on $100 dk car, surch. 16mm wide (Bl) 30.00 3.25
a. Surcharge 14mm wide 30.00 10.00

1949, Apr.

3L55 A2 (c) $2 on 20c yel grn 1.75 *3.25*
3L56 A2 (c) $3 on 50c red org .85 *2.25*
3L57 A2 (c) $4 on $5 dk grn 7.00 4.25
3L58 A2 (c) $6 on $10 crim, I 4.50 4.25
a. Type II 15.00 10.00
3L59 A2 (c) $12 on $1 blue 1.75 *1.75*

d

e

1949, Apr. **Type "d"**

3L60	A2	$1 on 25c blk grn (G)	.50	*1.25*
3L61	A2	$10 on $300 bluish grn (R)	13.00	5.75
3L62	A2	$20 on 50c red org (G)	26.00	*25.00*
3L63	A2	$20 on $20 ol (R)	11.00	4.25
3L64	A2	$40 on 25c blk brn (R)	11.00	5.00
3L65	A2	$50 on $109 dk grn, surch. 15mm wide (R)	13.00	*13.00*
a.		Surcharge 13mm wide	30.00	*30.00*
3L66	A2	$80 on $1 bl (R)	8.00	6.50

Type "d" On Stamps on China

3L67	A73	$100 on $100 dk car (G)	65.00	35.00
3L68	A73	$300 on $700 red brn (Bl)	20.00	12.50
3L69	A82	$500 on $500 bl grn (R)	20.00	4.50
3L70	A82	$3000 on $3000 bl (R)	20.00	8.25

Type "e" On Stamps of Northeastern Provinces

1949, Aug.

3L71	A2	$10 on $10 crim, II (Bl)	8.00	3.50
a.		Type I	12.50	12.00
3L72	A2	$30 on 20c yel grn (R)	8.00	2.25
3L73	A2	$50 on $44 dk car rose (Bl)	8.00	1.25
3L74	A2	$100 on $3 brn (Bl)	14.00	6.50
3L75	A2	$200 on $4 org brn, II (Bl)	40.00	24.00
a.		Type I	1,100.	450.00

On China No. 754 in Blue

3L76	A82	$10 on $7000 lt red brn	12.50	8.50
		Nos. 3L37-3L76 (39)	549.90	*269.25*

Overprints on Nos. 3L71 and 3L76 have 2 characters in center row.

Farmer and Worker on Globe — A5

1949, May 1 **Engr.** ***Perf. 14***

3L77	A5	$20 crimson	9.50	9.50
3L78	A5	$40 dark blue	9.50	9.50
3L79	A5	$60 brown org	9.50	9.50
3L80	A5	$80 dk green	9.50	9.50
3L81	A5	$100 purple	9.50	9.50
		Nos. 3L77-3L81 (5)	47.50	47.50

Labor day. Exists imperf. Value, set $50. Also issued in blocks of 4, imperf between. Value, unused or used, $17.50.

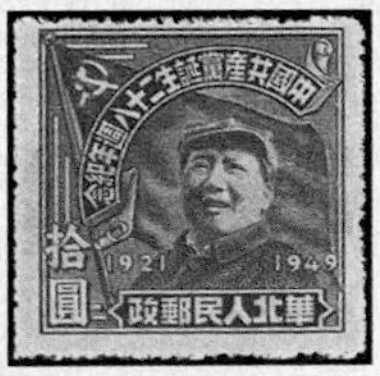
Mao Tse-tung (Chinese Numeral) — A6

Mao Tse-tung (Arabic Numeral) — A7

1949, July 1 ***Perf. 14***

3L82	A6	$10 red	8.00	*5.00*
3L83	A7	$20 dk blue	2.00	*3.50*
3L84	A6	$50 orange	13.00	5.50
3L85	A7	$80 dk green	5.50	*5.00*
3L86	A6	$100 purple	10.00	2.75
3L87	A7	$120 olive	2.00	*5.00*
3L88	A6	$140 vio brn	10.00	6.50
		Nos. 3L82-3L88 (7)	50.50	33.25

28th anniv. of the founding of the Chinese Communist Party. Value, imperf, set $150.

Gate of Heavenly Peace — A8

1949, Nov. 26 **Litho.** ***Perf. 12½***

3L89	A8	$50 orange	*1.00*	*7.00*
3L90	A8	$100 crimson	.50	*2.00*
3L91	A8	$200 green	2.00	*2.00*
3L92	A8	$300 rose brn	15.00	4.50
3L93	A8	$400 blue	15.00	4.50
3L94	A8	$500 brown	15.00	2.50
3L95	A8	$700 violet	8.00	7.00
		Nos. 3L89-3L95 (7)	56.50	29.50

Farmers and Factory — A9

1949, Dec. **Engr.** ***Perf. 14***

3L96	A9	$1000 orange	19.00	6.00
3L97	A9	$3000 dark blue	1.00	*1.50*
3L98	A9	$5000 crimson	1.00	*2.75*
3L99	A9	$10,000 red brown	1.00	*5.75*
		Nos. 3L96-3L99 (4)	22.00	*16.00*

NORTH CHINA PARCEL POST STAMPS

Parcel Post Stamps of China Nos. Q23-Q27 (Type PP3) Srchd. in Red, Black (#3LQ6-3LQ9) or Blue (#3LQ2)

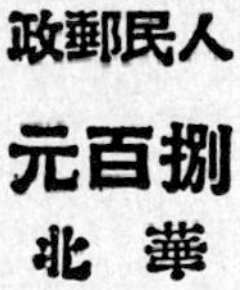
a

b

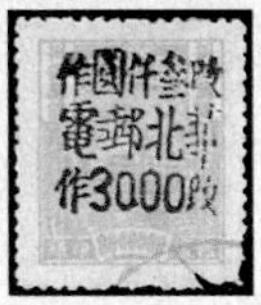
c

1949, June

Surcharged Type "a"

3LQ1	$300 on $6,000,000	55.00
3LQ2	$400 on $8,000,000	55.00
3LQ3	$500 on $10,000,000	55.00
3LQ4	$800 on $5,000,000	55.00
3LQ5	$1000 on $3,000,000	75.00

Surcharged Type "b"

3LQ6	$500 on $3,000,000	75.00
3LQ7	$1000 on $5,000,000	90.00

Surcharged Type "c"

3LQ8	$3000 on $8,000,000	225.00
3LQ9	$5000 on $10,000,000	300.00
	Nos. 3LQ1-3LQ9 (9)	985.00

Nos. 3LQ8-3LQ9 have large numerals unboxed.

Remittance Stamps of China (like North China Type A4) Surcharged in Black or Red

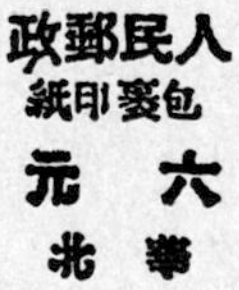
a

b

Peking Surcharge "a"

1949, June **Litho.** ***Perf. 13***

3LQ10	$6 on $5 ver	11.00	3.50
3LQ11	$20 on $50 gray	11.00	3.50
3LQ12	$50 on $20 dk vio brn	11.00	3.50
3LQ13	$100 on $10 ol grn	11.00	7.00

Tientsin Surcharge "b"

Engr. ***Perf. 14***

3LQ14	$20 on $1 brn org	14.00	6.00
a.	Perf. 12½	22.50	7.50
3LQ15	$30 on $2 dk grn	14.00	5.00
a.	Red surcharge	22.50	11.00
3LQ16	$30 on $10 ol grn	*125.00*	*42.50*
3LQ17	$100 on $10 gray grn (R)	14.50	6.00

Litho.

Perf. 13

3LQ18	$50 on $5 red	14.00	6.00

Engr.

Perf. 14

3LQ19	$20 on $1 org brn	40.00	17.00

Perf. 12½

3LQ20	$100 on $10 yel grn (R)	65.00	30.00

Typo.

Roulette 9½

3LQ21	$30 on $2 bl grn (R)	50.00	20.00

The surcharge on No. 3LQ19 is without first and last lines.

Nos. 3LQ14, 3LQ14a, 3LQ15, 3LQ15a, 3LQ16-3LQ17, 3LQ19-3LQ20 issued with gum.

Locomotive — PP1

1949, Nov. **Engr.** ***Perf. 14***

3LQ22	PP1	$500 crimn	17.50	*17.50*
3LQ23	PP1	$1000 dp bl	*175.00*	50.00
3LQ24	PP1	$2000 green	*250.00*	75.00
3LQ25	PP1	$5000 dp ol	*350.00*	125.00
3LQ26	PP1	$10,000 orange	*650.00*	250.00
3LQ27	PP1	$20,000 red brn	*1,400.*	750.00
3LQ28	PP1	$50,000 brn pur	*3,000.*	1,200.
		Nos. 3LQ22-3LQ28 (7)	5,842.	2,467.

NORTHWEST CHINA

The Northwest China Liberation Area consisted of the provinces of Sinkiang, Tsinghai, Ningsia and the western part of Shensi. The area was first established as the Shensi-Kansu-Ningsia Border Area in October, 1936, after the Long March to Yenan. Remote Sinkiang was not included until late 1949.

All Stamps Issued without Gum

Pagoda on Yenan Hill — A1

1945, Mar. **Litho.** ***Imperf.***

4L1	A1	$1 green	26.00
4L2	A1	$5 dk blue	150.00
4L3	A1	$10 rose red	25.00
4L4	A1	$50 dull pur	30.00
4L5	A1	$100 yel org	55.00
		Nos. 4L1-4L5 (5)	286.00

Rouletted 9

4L1a	A1	$1	95.00
4L2a	A1	$5	160.00
4L3a	A1	$10	100.00

First issue; denomination in Chinese and Arabic. Heavy shading at top of vignette. Columns at sides.

See types A2, A3 and A4. For surcharges see Nos. 4L6-4L10, 4L23.

Nos. 4L1-4L2 Surcharged in Red

a

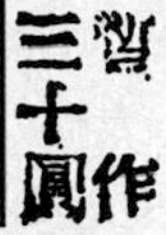
b

c

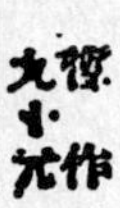
d

1946, Nov.

4L6	A1	(a) $30 on $1 grn	35.00	
4L7	A1	(b) $30 on $1 grn	*160.00*	
a.		Rectangular lower left character	*1,000.*	
4L8	A1	(c) $30 on $1 grn	20.00	
4L9	A1	(b) $60 on $1 grn	2,500.	
4L10	A1	(d) $90 on $5 dk bl	37.50	

Surcharge on Nos. 4L7a is type "b" as illustrated. Surcharge on No. 4L7 differs from "b," having lower left character as in type "a."

Surcharge on No. 4L9 the upper left surcharge character differs from that shown in "b."

Pagoda on Yenan Hill — A2

1948, June

4L11	A2	$100 buff	175.00
4L12	A2	$300 rose pink	8.00
4L13	A2	$500 red	8.50
4L14	A2	$1000 blue	8.00
4L15	A2	$2000 yel grn	24.00
4L16	A2	$5000 dull pur	22.50
		Nos. 4L11-4L16 (6)	246.00

Second issue; denominations in Chinese only. Many shades and proofs exist.

For surcharge see No. 4L24.

Pagoda on Yenan Hill (same size) — A3

1948, Dec.

4L17	A3	10c yel org	2.00
4L18	A3	20c lemon	2.00
4L19	A3	$1 dk blue	2.00
4L20	A3	$2 vermilion	2.00
4L21	A3	$5 pale bl grn	11.00
4L22	A3	$10 violet	18.00
		Nos. 4L17-4L22 (6)	37.00

Third issue; ornamental border at sides. Many shades exist.

Nos. 4L2 and 4L13 Surcharged in Red or Black

1949, Jan.

4L23	A1	$1 on $5 dk bl	80.00	80.00
4L24	A2	$2 on $500 red	40.00	40.00

Pagoda on Yenan Hill — A4

1949, May 1

4L25 A4 50c yel to olive .85 *2.00*
4L26 A4 $1 dl bl to indigo .85 *2.00*
4L27 A4 $3 ol yel to org yel .85 *2.00*
4L28 A4 $5 blue green 2.25 *3.00*
a. Upper left character as on #4L25
4L29 A4 $10 vio to dp vio 7.50 *9.00*
4L30 A4 $20 pink to rose red 13.50 *20.00*
Nos. 4L25-4L30 (6) 25.80 *38.00*

Fourth issue; light shading at top of vignette, columns without ornaments at sides. Many shades exist.

China Nos. 959, F2 and E12 Overprinted ("People's Post, Shensi")

1949, June 13 Engr. *Perf. 12½*

4L31 A96 orange 25.00 16.00
4L32 R2 carmine 35.00 35.00
4L33 SD2 red vio 35.00 35.00
Nos. 4L31-4L33 (3) 95.00 86.00

Stamps of China, Sun Yat-sen Type A94 of 1949, Overprinted in Black or Red ("People's Post, Shensi")

Lithographed; Engraved

1949, July 1 *Perf. 14, 12½*

4L34 $10 green (887) 1.25 1.25
4L35 $20 vio brn (888) 1.25 *2.25*
4L36 $20 vio brn (896) 1.25 1.25
4L37 $50 dk Prus grn (889; R) 6.00 5.25
4L38 $50 grn (951) 6.00 5.25
4L39 $100 org brn (890) 14.50 6.25
4L40 $500 ros lil (892) 20.00 6.25
4L41 $1000 dp bl (952; R) 27.50 15.00
4L42 $2000 vio (902;R) 30.00 18.00
4L43 $5000 car (953) 45.00 37.50
4L44 $10,000 brn (954) 80.00 75.00
Nos. 4L34-4L44 (11) 232.75 173.25

Kansu-Ningsia-Tsinghai Area, Lanchow Overprints

China Nos. 959a, F2 and E12 Overprinted ("People's Post, Kansu")

1949, Oct. Engr. *Rouletted*

4L45 A96 orange 22.50 22.50

Perf. 12½

4L46 R2 carmine 32.50 32.50
4L47 SD2 red vio 32.50 32.50
Nos. 4L45-4L47 (3) 87.50 87.50

Stamps of China, Sun Yat-sen Type A94 of 1949, Overprinted ("People's Post, Kansu")

Engraved; Lithographed

1949, Oct. *Perf. 14, 12½*

4L48 $10 grn (887) 2.25 2.25
4L49 $20 vio brn (888) 2.25 3.25
4L50 $50 dk Prus grn (889) 5.25 *8.25*
4L51 $100 org brn (890) 3.50 3.25
4L52 $100 dk org brn (898) 5.25 *6.00*
4L53 $200 red org (891) 6.50 5.25
4L54 $500 rose lil (892) 6.50 5.25
4L55 $1000 blue (894) 3.50 3.25
4L56 $1000 dp bl (901) 6.50 *7.50*
4L57 $2000 vio (902) 11.00 *15.00*
4L58 $5000 lt bl (903) 22.00 *27.50*
4L59 $10,000 sepia (904) 30.00 *37.50*
4L60 $20,000 ap grn (905) 60.00 *72.50*
Nos. 4L48-4L60 (13) 164.50 196.75

No. 4L54-4L60 exist with wider spaced overprints.

China Nos. 959, F2 and 791-792 Surcharged in Black or Red ("People's Post, Sinkiang")

1949, Oct.

4L61 A96 $1 on org 12.00 *13.50*
4L62 R2 $3 on car 18.00 *20.00*
4L63 A82 10c on $50,000 dp bl (R) 40.00 40.00
4L64 A82 $1.50 on $100,000 dl grn (R) 80.00 80.00
Nos. 4L61-4L64 (4) 150.00 153.50

Northwest People's Post

Mao Tse-tung — A5

Great Wall — A6

1949, Oct. 15 Litho. *Imperf.*

4L65 A5 $50 rose 7.00 *3.75*
a. $200 cliche in $50 plate *225.00*
4L66 A6 $100 dark blue 1.75 *2.00*
4L67 A5 $200 orange 6.50 *6.00*
4L68 A6 $400 sepia 12.00 *7.50*
Nos. 4L65-4L68 (4) 27.25 *19.25*

EAST CHINA

The East China Liberation Area included the provinces of Shantung, Kiangsu, Chekiang, Anhwei and Fukien. The original postal service established in Shantung in 1941, became the East China Posts and Telegraph General Office in July, 1948.

All Stamps Issued without Gum

Mao Tse-tung — A1

1948, Mar. Litho. *Perf. 10½*

5L1 A1 $50 yel org 2.00 1.75
5L2 A1 $100 dp rose 6.00 3.00
5L3 A1 $200 dk vio bl 6.00 3.00
5L4 A1 $300 brt grn 7.50 3.00
5L5 A1 $500 dp blue 2.50 3.00
5L6 A1 $800 vermilion 7.50 2.50
5L7 A1 $1000 dk blue 12.00 12.00
5L8 A1 $5000 rose 30.00 30.00
5L9 A1 $10,000 dp car 75.00 75.00
Nos. 5L1-5L9 (9) 148.50 133.25

Many varieties, including unissued imperforates exist.

Transportation and Tower — A2

Perf. 9 to 11 and compound

1949, Apr. Litho.

5L10 A2 $1 yel grn .95 .25
5L11 A2 $2 blue grn .60 .25
5L12 A2 $3 dull red .60 .25
5L13 A2 $5 pale brn (ovpt. 4x4mm) .60 .25
a. Without overprint 65.00 65.00
b. Overprint 3x3mm 1.25 1.00
c. As "b," purple overprint 65.00
5L14 A2 $10 ultra .90 .25
5L15 A2 $13 brt vio .60 .25
5L16 A2 $18 brt blue .60 .25
5L17 A2 $21 vermilion .90 .25
5L18 A2 $30 gray .60 .60
5L19 A2 $50 crimson 2.25 *1.50*
5L20 A2 $100 olive 27.50 22.00
Nos. 5L10-5L20 (11) 36.10 26.10

Seventh anniv. of Shantung Communist Postal Administration. The overprint on the $5, character "yu" meaning "Posts," obliterates Japanese flag on tower, erroneously included in design. Value, imperfs. of Nos. 5L10-5L12, 5L13c, 5L14-5L20 on different paper, set $150.

Train and Postal Runner (1949.2.7) — A3

1949, Apr. Litho. *Perf. 8 to 11*

5L21 A3 $1 brt emer .25 *1.50*
5L22 A3 $2 blue grn .25 *1.50*
5L23 A3 $3 dk red .25 *1.50*
5L24 A3 $5 brown .35 *2.00*
5L25 A3 $10 ultra .60 *2.25*
5L26 A3 $13 brt vio .35 *1.75*
5L27 A3 $18 brt blue .35 *1.75*
5L28 A3 $21 vermilion 3.50 *4.00*
5L29 A3 $30 slate .35 *2.25*
5L30 A3 $50 crimson .45 *2.25*
5L31 A3 $100 olive 2.00 *3.50*
Nos. 5L21-5L31 (11) 8.70 24.25

7th anniv. of Shantung P. O., Feb. 7. Imperf. sets were sold by the Philatelic Dept., Tientsin P.O. Value $40. See Nos. 5L69-5L76. For surcharges see People's Republic of China Nos. 77-81.

Mao, Soldiers, Map — A4

Perf. 9½ to 11 and comp.

1949, Apr.

5L32 A4 $1 brt emer .40 .25
5L33 A4 $2 blue grn .40 .25
5L34 A4 $3 dull red .40 .25
5L35 A4 $5 brown .40 .25
5L36 A4 $10 ultra .60 .25
5L37 A4 $13 brt vio .60 .40
5L38 A4 $18 brt blue .60 .40
5L39 A4 $21 vermilion .60 .40
5L40 A4 $30 gray .60 .50
5L41 A4 $50 crimson .60 .50
5L42 A4 $100 olive 6.75 5.00
Nos. 5L32-5L42 (11) 11.95 8.45

Victory of Hwai-Hai (Hwaiying and Haichow). Imperf. sets were sold by the Philatelic Dept., Tientsin P.O. Value, set $100.

Stamps of China, Sun Yat-sen Type of 1949, Surcharged in Red or Black

(Nanking) — a

(Wuhu) — b

1949, May 4 Engr. *Perf. 12½*

5L43 A94 (a) $1 on $10 grn (895, R) 1.00 .75
a. Perf. 13 3.25 3.00
5L44 A94 (a) $3 on $20 vio brn (896) 3.00 1.50
a. Perf. 13 3.00 4.50
b. Perf. 14 5.75 5.50
c. Surcharge inverted 200.00

Sun Yat-sen Type A94 Surcharged Type "b"

Lithographed, Engraved

1949, May *Perf. 12½, 14*

5L45 $30 on $1000 dp bl (901 10.00 7.50
5L46 $30 on $1000 bl (894) 10.00 7.50
5L47 $50 on $200 org red (899) 10.00 7.50
5L48 $100 on $5000 lt bl (903, R) 22.50 20.00
5L49 $300 on $10,000 sep (904, R) 67.50 60.00
5L50 $500 on $200 org red (899) 100.00 85.00
Nos. 5L45-5L50 (6) 220.00 187.50

Many varieties exist.

China Nos. 913a and 913 Srchd. in Blue, Green, Black or Red, (East China)

1949, May Litho. *Perf. 12½*

5L51 A95 $5 on 50c on $20 brn, II (B) 17.50 16.00
a. Green surcharge 100.00 *100.00*
5L52 A95 $10 on 50c on $20 brn, II 17.50 16.00
5L53 A95 $20 on 50c on $20 red brn, II (R) 17.50 16.00
a. Type I (R) 21.00 21.00
Nos. 5L51-5L53 (3) 52.50 48.00

Stamps of China, Sun Yat-sen Type of 1949, Srchd. in Black or Red, (Hangchow)

Engr., Litho. (No. 5L57)

1949, June 25 *Perf. 14, 12½*

5L54 A94 $1 on $1 org (886) 4.00 4.00
5L55 A94 $3 on $20 vio brn (896, R) 2.00 2.00
5L56 A94 $5 on $100 org brn (890) 7.50 7.50
5L57 A94 $5 on $100 dk org brn (898) 5.00 5.00
5L58 A94 $10 on $50 dk Prus grn (889, R) 24.00 24.00
5L59 A94 $13 on $10 grn (895) 2.75 *2.75*
Nos. 5L54-5L59 (6) 45.25 45.25

East China Liberation Area

Maps of Shanghai and Nanking — A5

1949, May 30 Litho. *Perf. 8½ to 11*

5L60 A5 $1 orange ver .30 *3.50*
5L61 A5 $2 blue green .30 *3.50*
5L62 A5 $3 brt violet .40 *3.50*
5L63 A5 $5 violet brn .40 *.50*
5L64 A5 $10 ultra .40 *1.00*
5L65 A5 $30 slate .40 *3.00*
5L66 A5 $50 carmine .40 *3.00*
5L67 A5 $100 olive .40 *1.00*
5L68 A5 $500 orange 15.00 8.00
Nos. 5L60-5L68 (9) 18.00 *27.00*

Liberation of Shanghai and Nanking. Many shades, paper and perforation varieties and imperfs. exist.

Train and Postal Runner Type Dated "1949"

1949, July-1950, Feb. *Perf. 12½, 14*

5L69 A3 $10 dp ultra .25 *.25*
5L70 A3 $15 orange ver .25 *.45*
a. $15 red, perf. 14 .50 .30
5L71 A3 $30 slate green .25 .25
a. Perf. 12½ .50 .30
5L72 A3 $50 carmine .25 *.50*
5L73 A3 $60 bl grn, perf. 14 .25 *1.50*
5L74 A3 $100 ol, perf. 14 8.00 2.00
5L75 A3 $1600 vio bl ('50) .90 *4.00*
5L76 A3 $2000 brn vio ('50) 1.00 *4.00*
Nos. 5L69-5L76 (8) 11.15 *12.95*

Chu Teh, Mao, Troops with Flags — A7

1949, Aug. 17 *Perf. 12½*

5L77	A7	$70 orange	.40	*.35*
5L78	A7	$270 crimson	.50	*.35*
5L79	A7	$370 emerald	.60	.50
5L80	A7	$470 vio brn	1.00	.60
5L81	A7	$570 blue	.50	*.50*
		Nos. 5L77-5L81 (5)	3.00	2.30

22nd anniv. of the People's Liberation Army.
For similar type see Southwest China A1.

Mao Tse-tung — A8

1949, Oct.

5L82	A8	$10 dk blue	8.00	*15.00*
5L83	A8	$15 vermilion	10.00	*15.00*
5L84	A8	$70 brown	.50	.50
5L85	A8	$100 vio brn	.50	.50
5L86	A8	$150 orange	.50	.50
5L87	A8	$200 grnsh gray	.50	.50
5L88	A8	$500 gray bl	.50	.50
5L89	A8	$1000 rose	.50	.50
5L90	A8	$2000 emerald	.50	.50
		Nos. 5L82-5L90 (9)	21.50	*33.50*

For surcharges see People's Republic of China Nos. 82-84.

Stamps of China, Sun Yat-sen Type of 1949 Surcharged in Black or Red

1949, Nov. **Litho.** *Perf. 12½*

5L91	A94	$400 on $200 org red (899)	22.50	1.50
5L92	A94	$1000 on $50 grnsh gray (897, R)	2.25	.70
5L93	A94	$1200 on $100 dk org brn (898)	.30	*1.50*
5L94	A94	$1600 on $20,000 ap grn (905)	.30	*3.00*
5L95	A94	$2000 on $1000 dp bl (952,R)	.30	*.75*
a.		Perf. 14	45.00	25.00
		Nos. 5L91-5L95 (5)	25.65	*7.45*

EAST CHINA PARCEL POST STAMPS

Parcel Post Stamps of China 1945-48 Surcharged, (Shantung)

1949, Aug. 1 **Engr.** *Perf. 13*

5LQ1	PP1	$200 on $500 grn	*10.00*	8.00
5LQ2	PP1	$500 on $1000 bl	30.00	18.00

Type PP3 *Perf. 13½*

5LQ3	$200 on $200,000 dk grn	32.50	16.00
5LQ4	$200 on $10,000,000 sage grn	32.50	14.00
5LQ5	$500 on $7000 dl bl	65.00	40.00
5LQ6	$500 on $50,000 indigo	12.00	10.00
5LQ7	$1000 on $10,000 car rose	12.00	10.00
5LQ8	$1000 on $100,000 dk rose brn	37.50	18.00
5LQ9	$1000 on $300,000 pink	12.00	10.00
5LQ10	$1000 on $500,000 vio brn	90.00	45.00
5LQ11	$1000 on $8,000,000 org ver	15.00	12.00
5LQ12	$2000 on $5,000,000 dl vio	30.00	30.00
5LQ13	$2000 on $6,000,000 brn blk	55.00	35.00
5LQ14	$3000 on $30,000 ol	60.00	35.00
5LQ15	$3000 on $70,000 org brn	30.00	24.00
5LQ16	$5000 on $3,000,000 dl bl	90.00	52.50
	Nos. 5LQ1-5LQ16 (16)	613.50	377.50

China Type A97, No. 987 Surcharged

1949, Sept. 7 **Litho.** *Perf. 12½*

5LQ17	$200 on $10	35.00	15.00
5LQ18	$500 on $10	35.00	15.00
5LQ19	$1000 on $10	35.00	15.00
5LQ20	$2000 on $10	50.00	32.50
5LQ21	$5000 on $10	75.00	50.00
5LQ22	$10,000 on $10	150.00	75.00
	Nos. 5LQ17-5LQ22 (6)	380.00	202.50

Flying Geese Type of China, 1949, and China Nos. 984-986 Surcharged in Red or Black

1950, Jan. 28

5LQ23	A97	$5000 on 10c bl vio (R)	30.00	25.00
5LQ24	A97	$10,000 on $1 brn org	45.00	40.00
5LQ25	A97	$20,000 on $2 bl	75.00	70.00
5LQ26	A97	$50,000 on $5 car rose	130.00	130.00
		Nos. 5LQ23-5LQ26 (4)	280.00	265.00

Parcel Post Stamps of China Type PP3, Nos. Q1-Q2, Q12-Q13 Surcharged in Red or Black

1950, Jan. 28 **Engr.** *Perf. 13, 13½*

5LQ27	$5000 on $500 grn (R)	.75	*15.00*
5LQ28	$10,000 on $1000 bl (R)	80.00	65.00
5LQ29	$20,000 on $3000 bl grn	140.00	110.00
5LQ30	$50,000 on $5000 org red	7.50	*75.00*
	Nos. 5LQ27-5LQ30 (4)	228.25	265.00

CENTRAL CHINA

The Central Chinese Liberation Area included the provinces of Honan, Hupeh, Hunan and Kiangsi. The area was established between August and September, 1949, following the occupation of Hankow by Red Army forces.

All Stamps Issued without Gum

Hupeh Postal and Telegraph Administration

Stamps of China, Sun Yat-sen Type A94 of 1949, Surcharged ("Chinese P.O., Temporary Use")

Engraved; Lithographed

1949, June 4 *Perf. 14, 12½*

Thin parallel lines

6L1	$1 on $200 red org (891)	4.00	*4.50*
6L2	$6 on $10,000 sep (904)	4.00	*4.50*
6L3	$15 on $1 org (886)	4.00	*4.50*
6L4	$30 on $100 org brn (890)	7.50	6.00
6L5	$30 on $100 dk org brn (898)	4.00	*4.50*
6L6	$50 on $20 vio brn (896)	25.00	14.00
6L7	$80 on $1000 dp bl (901)	5.50	5.00

Thick parallel lines

6L8	$1 on $200 red org (891)	7.00	7.00
6L9	$3 on $5000 lt bl (903)	3.50	*4.00*
6L10	$10 on $500 rose lil (892)	3.50	*4.00*
6L11	$10 on $500 rose lil (900)	5.25	*5.75*
6L12	$50 on $20 vio brn (888)	7.00	*7.50*
6L13	$50 on $20 vio brn (896)	4.00	*5.00*
6L14	$80 on $1000 bl (894)	6.50	5.00
6L15	$80 on $1000 dp bl (901)	27.00	16.00
6L16	$100 on $50 dk Prus grn (903)	5.00	*6.00*
	Nos. 6L1-6L16 (16)	122.75	103.25

Kiangsi Postal and Telegraph Administration.

Central Trust Revenue Stamps of China Surcharged ("People's Post, Kiangsi")

(same size) — A1

$30

$60

1949, June 20 **Engr.** *Perf. 12½*

6L17	A1	$3 on $30 pur	2.50	3.00
6L18	A1	$15 on $15 red org	7.00	3.00
6L19	A1	$30 on $50 dk bl	7.00	3.00
6L20	A1	$60 on $50 dk bl	7.00	3.00
6L21	A1	$130 on $15 red org	4.00	3.00

The $15 surcharge has 3 characters in left vertical row, the $130 surcharge has 5.

Same Surcharge on Sun Yat-sen Issues of China, 1945-49

Engraved, Lithographed *Perf. 14, 12½*

6L22	A82	$1 on $250 dp lil (746)	6.50	6.50
6L23	A94	$5 on $1000 dp bl (901)	6.50	6.50
6L24	A94	$5 on $2000 vio (902)	6.50	6.50
6L25	A94	$5 on $5000 lt bl (903)	3.50	4.00
6L26	A94	$10 on $1000 bl (894)	6.50	6.50
6L27	A82	$20 on $4000 gray	4.50	4.00
6L28	A73	$30 on $100 dk car	6.50	6.50
6L29	A82	$30 on $20,000 rose pink	4.50	4.00
6L30	A94	$80 on $500 rose lil (900)	4.00	4.00
6L31	A94	$100 on $1000 dp bl (901)	3.50	4.00
6L32	A82	$200 on $250 dp lil	4.50	4.50
		Nos. 6L17-6L32 (16)	84.50	72.00

Central China Posts and Telegraph Administration

Farmer, Soldier and Worker
A2 A3

I — Top white line of square character (yuan) at upper left does not touch left vertical stroke. No gap in shading between soldier's feet.

II — Top line connects with left vertical stroke. Gap in shading between feet.

Perf. 10 to 11½ & Comp.

1949 **Litho.**

6L33	A2	$1 orange	10.00	5.00
6L34	A2	$3 brn org	6.00	5.00
6L35	A2	$6 emerald	7.50	5.00
6L36	A3	$7 yel brn	1.00	*3.00*
6L37	A2	$10 bl grn	.25	*.35*
6L38	A3	$14 org brn	35.00	27.50
6L39	A2	$15 ultra	2.00	*2.50*
6L40	A2	$30 grn, type I	.25	*.40*
a.		Type II	.80	.70
6L41	A3	$35 gray bl	25.00	*25.00*
6L42	A2	$50 rose vio	12.00	12.00
6L43	A3	$70 dp grn	.70	.25
6L44	A2	$80 pink	.90	*3.00*
6L45	A3	$100 bl grn	.80	*2.00*
6L46	A3	$220 rose red	4.00	*2.00*
		Nos. 6L33-6L46 (14)	105.40	93.00

Nos. 6L33 and 6L34 exist imperf. Value, each $13.50.
For surcharges & overprints see Nos. 6L63-6L65, 6L66-6L73, 6L75, 6L90-6L98, 6L100-6L108.

Star Enclosing Map of Hankow Area — A4

Two types of $500:
I — Thick numerals of "500." No period after "500."
II — Thin numerals and period.

Two types of $1000:
I — No period after "1000."
II — Period after "1000."

1949, July

6L48	A4	$110 org brn	1.00	*1.25*
6L49	A4	$130 violet	5.00	3.00
6L50	A4	$200 dp org	.50	*.50*
6L51	A4	$290 brown	1.75	1.25
6L52	A4	$370 dk bl	1.75	1.25
6L53	A4	$500 lt bl, I	7.50	1.50
a.		$500 blue, II	20.00	7.00
6L54	A4	$1000 dull red, II	20.00	2.00
a.		$1000 dark red, I	27.50	8.00
6L55	A4	$5000 brown	5.00	5.00
6L56	A4	$10,000 brt pink	6.00	6.00
		Nos. 6L48-6L56 (9)	48.50	21.75

For surcharges and overprints see Nos. 6L74, 6L76-6L81, 6L99, 6L109.

Hankow River Customs Building A5

River Wall, Wuchang — A6

Design: $290, $370, River scene, Hanyang.

1949, Aug. 16 *Perf. 11*

6L57	A5	$70 green	3.00	2.00
6L58	A5	$220 crimson	3.00	2.00
6L59	A5	$290 brown	3.00	2.00
6L60	A5	$370 brt blue	3.00	2.00
6L61	A6	$500 purple	7.00	*3.00*
6L62	A6	$1000 vermilion	7.00	*2.00*
		Nos. 6L57-6L62 (6)	26.00	*13.00*

Liberation of Hankow, Wuchang and Hanyang.
Exist imperf. About the same value.
For overprints see Nos. 6L82-6L87.

Nos. 6L35, 6L39 and 6L40 Surcharged in Red ("Honan Renminbi Currency")

1949, July

6L63	A2	$7 on $6 emer	7.00	7.00
6L64	A2	$14 on $15 ultra	7.50	*7.50*
6L65	A2	$70 on $30 grn	9.00	*10.00*
		Nos. 6L63-6L65 (3)	23.50	24.50

Surcharge shown is for $70. The $7 has 5 characters in left column and no bottom line.

Issues of 1949 Overprinted ("Honan Renminbi Currency")

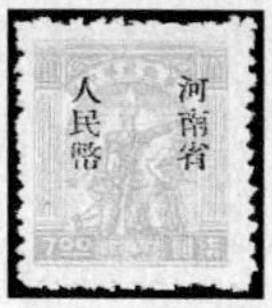

1949, Aug.

6L66	A2	$3	brn org	.95	.90
6L67	A3	$7	yel brn	.95	.90
6L68	A2	$10	bl grn	1.90	1.90
6L69	A3	$14	org brn	1.90	*3.00*
6L70	A2	$30	yel grn (6L40a)	2.00	*3.00*
6L71	A3	$35	gray bl	.95	*5.00*
6L72	A2	$50	rose vio	7.00	5.00
6L73	A3	$70	dp grn	2.00	*3.75*
6L74	A4	$110	org brn	7.00	7.00
6L75	A3	$220	rose red	6.00	6.00
6L76	A4	$290	brown	6.00	6.00
6L77	A4	$370	blue	10.00	10.00
6L78	A4	$500	bl, II	12.00	*14.00*
6L79	A4	$1000	dk red, I	25.00	*30.00*
6L80	A4	$5000	brown	100.00	*110.00*
6L81	A4	$10,000	brt pink	200.00	*225.00*
			Nos. 6L66-6L81 (16)	383.65	431.45

Width of the overprint varies slightly.

Nos. 6L57-6L62 Overprinted ("Honan Renminbi Currency")

1949, Aug. ***Perf. 11***

6L82	A5	$70	green	2.50	*3.00*
6L83	A5	$220	crimson	4.00	*4.25*
6L84	A5	$290	brown	4.00	*4.25*
6L85	A5	$370	brt bl	6.00	*6.50*
6L86	A6	$500	purple	6.00	*6.50*
6L87	A6	$1000	vermilion	8.00	*8.50*
			Nos. 6L82-6L87 (6)	30.50	33.00

Width of overprint on Nos. 6L82-6L85, 7mm; on Nos. 6L86-6L87, 12mm.

Exist imperf. About the same value.

Changchow Issue Surcharged in Red ("Honan Renminbi Currency")

(same size) Mao Tse-tung — A7

1949, Sept. ***Perf. 10***

6L88	A7	$290 on $30 yel grn	30.00	*32.50*
6L89	A7	$370 on $30 yel grn	37.50	*50.00*

Issues of 1949 Surcharged

1950, Jan.

6L90	A2	$200 on $1	.55	*1.75*
6L91	A2	$200 on $3	3.00	1.60
6L92	A2	$200 on $6	.55	*1.75*
6L93	A3	$200 on $7	3.00	1.60
6L94	A3	$200 on $14	3.00	1.60
6L95	A3	$200 on $35	3.25	2.40
6L96	A3	$200 on $70	3.00	1.60
6L97	A2	$200 on $80	3.00	1.60
6L98	A3	$200 on $220	3.00	1.60
6L99	A4	$200 on $370	.50	*1.75*
6L100	A3	$300 on $70	.50	*2.50*
6L101	A2	$300 on $80	.50	*1.75*
6L102	A3	$300 on $220	.25	*1.75*
6L103	A2	$1200 on $3	27.50	27.50
6L104	A3	$1200 on $7	5.25	5.00
6L105	A3	$1500 on $14	7.00	6.75
6L106	A2	$2100 on $1	35.00	35.00
6L107	A2	$2100 on $6	35.00	35.00
6L108	A3	$2100 on $35	10.00	9.00
6L109	A4	$5000 on $370	4.50	4.50
		Nos. 6L90-6L109 (20)	148.35	146.00

Two types of surcharge exist, differing in spacing of characters in top row.

CENTRAL CHINA PARCEL POST STAMPS

Star and Map of Hankow — PP1

1949, Nov. **Litho.** ***Perf. 11, 11½***

6LQ1	PP1	$5000	brown	4.50	*5.75*
6LQ2	PP1	$10,000	scarlet	19.00	17.00
6LQ3	PP1	$20,000	dk sl grn	9.50	*18.00*
6LQ4	PP1	$50,000	vermilion	5.00	*35.00*
			Nos. 6LQ1-6LQ4 (4)	38.00	*75.75*

SOUTH CHINA

The South China Liberation Area included the provinces of Kwangtung and Kwangsi and Hainan Island. The South China Postal and Telegraph Administration was organized on or about Nov. 4, 1949.

All Stamps Issued without Gum

Pearl River Bridge, Canton — A1

1949, Nov. 4 **Litho.** ***Imperf.***

7L1	A1	$10	green	.85	*.50*
7L2	A1	$20	sepia	.85	*.50*
7L3	A1	$30	violet	.85	*.50*
7L4	A1	$50	carmine	.85	*.50*
7L5	A1	$100	ultramarine	1.50	*.50*
			Nos. 7L1-7L5 (5)	4.90	2.50

For surcharges see Nos. 7L19-7L23.

China Nos. 993-995 With Additional Overprint in Red ("Liberation of Swatow")

1949, Nov. 9

7L6	A94	2½c on $500 rose lil (993)	35.00	35.00
a.		Handstamped	80.00	80.00
7L7	A94	2½c on $500 rose lil (994)	40.00	40.00
a.		Handstamped	95.00	95.00
7L8	A94	15c on $10 grn (995)	50.00	50.00
a.		Handstamped	175.00	175.00

On Unit Issues of China, 1949

7L9	A96	org (959)	19.00	12.50
7L10	AP5	bl grn (C62)	24.00	*27.50*
7L11	SD2	red vio (E12)	24.00	*27.50*
7L12	R2	car (F2)	20.00	*27.50*

On Sun Yat-sen and Flying Geese Issues of China

7L13	A94	2c org (974)	150.00	*200.00*
7L14	A94	4c bl grn (975)	300.00	*400.00*
7L15	A94	10c dp lil (976)	20.00	*20.00*
7L16	A94	20c bl (978)	40.00	*32.50*
7L17	A97	$1 brn org (984)	45.00	30.00
7L18	A97	$10 bl grn (987)	450.00	400.00
		Nos. 7L6-7L18 (13)	1,217.	1,302.

Forgeries exist of Nos. 7L13-7L14, 7L18.

Nos. 7L1-7L3 Surcharged in Red or Green

1950, Jan.

7L19	A1	$300 on $30 vio (R)	2.50	2.00
7L20	A1	$500 on $20 brn (R)	2.50	3.00
7L21	A1	$800 on $30 vio (G)	3.00	4.00
7L22	A1	$1000 on $10 gray grn (R)	3.50	3.00
7L23	A1	$1000 on $20 brn (R)	3.50	2.25
		Nos. 7L19-7L23 (5)	15.00	14.25

SOUTHWEST CHINA

The Southwest China Liberation Area included the provinces of Kweichow, Szechwan, Yunnan, Sikang and Tibet. The Southwest Postal and Telegraph Administration was organized on or about Nov. 15, 1949 after the liberation of Kweiyang, capital of Kweichow Province.

All Stamps Issued without Gum

Chu Teh, Mao and Troops — A1

1949, Dec. **Litho.** ***Perf. 12½***

8L1	A1	$10	deep blue	4.00	*4.25*
8L2	A1	$20	rose claret	.45	*2.00*
8L3	A1	$30	dp org	.60	*2.00*
8L4	A1	$50	gray grn	1.00	*2.00*
8L5	A1	$100	carmine	.90	*1.50*
8L6	A1	$200	blue	1.25	*1.50*
8L7	A1	$300	bl vio	1.50	*2.00*
8L8	A1	$500	dk gray	3.00	2.50
8L9	A1	$1000	pale pur	11.00	6.00
8L10	A1	$2000	green	20.00	*20.00*
8L11	A1	$5000	orange	57.50	*60.00*
			Nos. 8L1-8L11 (11)	101.20	*103.75*

For surcharges and overprints see Nos. 8L21-8L29, 8L40-8L47, 8L55.

China Nos. 974-975, 984, 986-987 Surcharged ("Kweichow People's Post")

1949, Dec. 1 ***Perf. 12½***

8L12	A94	$20 on 2c org	8.00	*10.00*
8L13	A94	$50 on 4c bl grn	12.00	12.00
8L14	A97	$100 on $1 brn org	20.00	15.00
8L15	A97	$400 on $5 car rose	40.00	*45.00*
8L16	A97	$2000 on $10 bl grn	140.00	95.00
		Nos. 8L12-8L16 (5)	220.00	177.00

Map of China, Flag Planted in Southwest — A2

1950, Jan. **Litho.** ***Perf. 9 to 11½***

8L17	A2	$20	dark blue	1.25	*2.50*
8L18	A2	$30	green	2.75	*2.50*
8L19	A2	$50	red	1.75	*3.50*
8L20	A2	$100	brown	2.75	*3.50*
			Nos. 8L17-8L20 (4)	8.50	*12.00*

Liberation of the Southwest.

For surcharges see Nos. 8L30-8L39, 8L56-8L59.

Nos. 8L5-8L6 Surcharged

No. 8L22

$300

$1200

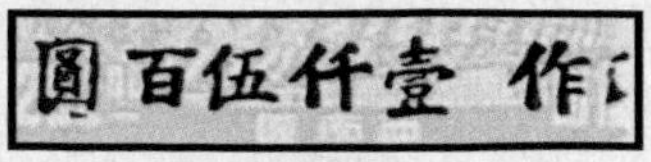

$1500

$2000

Perf. 12½

8L21	A1	$300 on $100 car	3.50	4.00
8L22	A1	$500 on $100 car	3.50	4.00
8L23	A1	$1200 on $100 car	7.00	7.00
8L24	A1	$1500 on $200 bl	7.00	7.00
8L25	A1	$2000 on $200 bl	11.00	10.00
		Nos. 8L21-8L25 (5)	32.00	32.00

Nos. 8L5-8L6 Overprinted ("East Szechwan")

1950, Jan.

8L26	A1	$100	carmine	9.00	9.00
8L27	A1	$200	blue	9.00	9.00

Nos. 8L5-8L6 Handstamp Surcharged

1950, Jan.

8L28	A1	$1200 on $100 car	15.00	*27.50*
8L29	A1	$1500 on $200 bl	40.00	*27.50*

Many varieties, including wide and narrow settings, exist.

Nos. 8L17-8L20 Surcharged in Black or Red

$60

$150

$300

$1500

$3000

$5000

$10,000

$20,000

$50,000

1950 *Perf. 9 to 11½*

8L30	A2	$60 on $30	12.00	9.00
8L31	A2	$150 on $30	12.00	9.00
8L32	A2	$300 on $20 (R)	2.00	*4.00*
8L33	A2	$300 on $100	12.00	9.00
8L34	A2	$1500 on $100	72.50	22.50
8L35	A2	$3000 on $50	7.75	*22.50*
8L36	A2	$5000 on $50	3.50	*22.50*
8L37	A2	$10,000 on $50	120.00	42.50
8L38	A2	$20,000 on $50	4.00	*42.50*
8L39	A2	$50,000 on $50	5.75	*60.00*
		Nos. 8L30-8L39 (10)	251.50	243.50

Nos. 8L5-8L7 Overprinted ("West Szechwan")

1950, Jan. *Perf. 12½*

8L40	A1	$100 carmine	22.50	*24.00*
8L41	A1	$200 pale blue	30.00	*32.50*
8L42	A1	$300 blue violet	40.00	*42.50*
		Nos. 8L40-8L42 (3)	92.50	99.00

Nos. 8L4-8L7 Surcharged

No. 8L43

No. 8L44

No. 8L45

No. 8L46

No. 8L47

1950, Jan.

8L43	A1	$500 on $100	8.75	8.75
a.		Narrow spacing	70.00	60.00
8L44	A1	$800 on $100	8.75	8.75
8L45	A1	$1000 on $50	11.00	11.00
8L46	A1	$2000 on $200	22.50	27.50
8L47	A1	$3000 on $300	35.00	45.00
		Nos. 8L43-8L47 (5)	86.00	101.00

Two lines of surcharge 7mm apart on No. 8L43, 4mm on No. 8L43a.

China Nos. 975 and 977 Surcharged

No. 8L48

No. 8L50

Perf. 12½, 13 or Compound

1950, Jan.

8L48	A94	$100 on 4c	7.50	*13.50*
8L49	A94	$200 on 4c	12.00	*22.50*
8L50	A94	$800 on 16c	67.50	67.50
8L51	A94	$1000 on 16c	300.00	*375.00*
		Nos. 8L48-8L51 (4)	387.00	478.50

Unit Issue of China Overprinted ("Southwest People's Post")

1950, Jan. **Engr.** ***Rouletted***

8L52	A96	orange	150.00	175.00
a.		Perf. 12½	225.00	250.00

Perf. 12½

8L53	SD2	red violet	225.00	250.00
8L54	R2	carmine	225.00	250.00
		Nos. 8L52-8L54 (3)	600.00	675.00

On No. 8L54, space between overprint columns is 3mm and right column is raised to height of left.

Nos. 8L3, 8L17-8L20 Surcharged in Black or Red

1950, Mar. *Perf. 12½, 9 to 11½*

8L55	A1	$800 on $30	45.00	45.00
8L56	A2	$1000 on $50	9.00	*12.00*
8L57	A2	$2000 on $100	13.50	*18.00*
8L58	A2	$4000 on $20 (R)	35.00	*40.00*
8L59	A2	$5000 on $30	55.00	55.00
		Nos. 8L55-8L59 (5)	157.50	*170.00*

CHRISTMAS ISLAND

ˈkris-məs ˈī-lənd

LOCATION — In the Indian Ocean, 230 miles south of Java
GOVT. — A territory of Australia
AREA — 52 sq. mi.
POP. — 2,373 (1999 est.)

Australia took over Christmas Island from Singapore in 1958.

Catalogue values for all unused stamps in this country are for Never Hinged items.

Queen Elizabeth II — A1

Engr.; Name and Value Typo. in Black

1958, Oct. 15 **Unwmk.** ***Perf. 14½***

1	A1	2c yellow orange	.45	.80
2	A1	4c brown	.55	.35
3	A1	5c lilac	.55	.50
4	A1	6c dull blue	1.75	.35
5	A1	8c gray brown	3.25	.50
6	A1	10c violet	2.50	.35
7	A1	12c carmine rose	3.50	2.00
8	A1	20c ultramarine	2.50	2.00
9	A1	50c yellow green	3.50	2.00
10	A1	$1 greenish blue	3.75	2.00
		Nos. 1-10 (10)	22.30	10.85
		Set, hinged	11.00	

Map of Island — A2

Island Scene — A3

4c, Moonflower. 5c, Robber crab. 8c, Phosphate train. 10c, Crane loading phosphate. 12c, Flying fish cove. 20c, Loading ship. 50c, Frigate bird. $1, Yellow-billed tropic bird.

Perf. 14x14½, 14½x14

1963, Aug. 28 **Engr.**

11	A2	2c orange	1.00	.55
12	A2	4c red brown	.40	.25
13	A2	5c rose lilac	.40	.35
14	A3	6c slate	.35	*.45*
15	A2	8c black	2.00	.45
16	A2	10c violet	.35	.25
17	A3	12c dull red	.30	.40
18	A3	20c dark blue	1.00	.35
19	A3	50c green	1.25	.35

Size: 35x21mm

20	A3	$1 orange yellow	1.75	.45
		Nos. 11-20 (10)	8.80	3.85
		Set, hinged	6.50	

"Simpson and His Donkey" by Wallace Anderson — A3a

1965, Apr. 14 **Photo.** ***Perf. 13½x13***

21	A3a	10c brt grn, sepia & blk	.55	*1.25*

ANZAC issue. See note after Australia No. 387.

Moorish Goddess A4

Fish: 1c, Golden striped grouper. 3c, Forceps fish. 4c, Queen triggerfish. 5c, Regal angelfish. 9c, Surgeonfish. 10c, Turkeyfish. 15c, Saddleback butterflyfish. 20c, Clown butterflyfish. 30c, Ghost pipefish. 50c, Lined surgeonfish. $1, Meyer's butterflyfish.

1968-70 **Photo.** ***Perf. 13½***

22	A4	1c multicolored	.55	.55
23	A4	2c multicolored	.75	.25
24	A4	3c multicolored	.75	.35
25	A4	4c multicolored	.75	.25
a.		Dark blue ("4c") omitted	3,000.	
26	A4	5c multicolored	.75	.30
27	A4	9c multicolored	.75	.60
28	A4	10c multicolored	.75	.30
29	A4	15c multicolored	8.75	3.50
30	A4	20c multicolored	1.75	.90
31	A4	30c multicolored	8.75	3.50
32	A4	50c multicolored	2.75	*2.75*
33	A4	$1 multicolored	2.75	*2.75*
		Nos. 22-33 (12)	29.80	16.00
		Set, hinged	20.00	

Issued: 15c, 30c, 12/14/70; others, 5/6/68.

Christmas Issues

"Hark the Herald Angels Sing" — A5

1969, Nov. 10 **Photo.** ***Perf. 13½***

34	A5	5c dk blue, gold, buff & red	.35	.35

A6

3c, The Ansidei Madonna, by Raphael. 5c, Virgin and Ohild, by Morando.

1970, Oct. 26 **Photo.** ***Perf. 14x14½***

35	A6	3c gold & multi	.25	.25
36	A6	5c silver & multi	.25	.25

A7

5c, Adoration of the Shepherds, Seville School. 20c, Adoration of the Shepherds, by Guido Reni.

1971, Oct. 4

37	A7	6c black & multi	.50	.50
38	A7	20c dark blue & multi	1.15	1.15

"Flying Fish," 1887 — A8

Ships and Map of Christmas Island: 1c, "Eagle," 1714. 2c, "Redpole," 1890. 3c, "Hoi Houw," 1959. 4c, "Pigot," 1771. 5c, "Valetta," 1968. 7c, "Asia," 1805. 8c, "Islander," 1929-60. 9c, "Imperieuse," 1888 (incorrectly inscribed "Imperious"). 10c, "Egeria," 1887. 20c, "Thomas," 1615. 25c, "Gordon," 1864. 30c, "Cygnet," 1688. 35c, "Triadic," 1958. 50c, "Amethyst," 1857. $1, "Royal Mary," 1643.

1972-73 **Photo.** ***Perf. 14½x13½***

39	A8	1c yel green & multi	.30	*.55*
40	A8	2c lt red brn & multi	.35	*.65*
41	A8	3c dp rose & multi	.35	*.70*
42	A8	4c multicolored	.45	*.70*
43	A8	5c multicolored	.45	*.70*
44	A8	6c lilac & multi	.45	*.70*
45	A8	7c lt green & multi	.45	*.70*
46	A8	8c blue & multi	.50	*.70*
47	A8	9c org & multi	.75	*.65*
48	A8	10c lem & multi	.45	*.50*
49	A8	20c tan & multi	.50	*.80*
50	A8	25c multicolored	.60	*1.60*
51	A8	30c multicolored	.75	*1.00*
52	A8	35c tan & multi	.80	*1.00*
53	A8	50c ultra & multi	.90	*1.60*
54	A8	$1 yellow & multi	1.25	*1.90*
		Nos. 39-54 (16)	9.30	*14.45*

Issued: 6c, 7c, 8c, 20c, 2/5/72; 1c, 2c, 3c, $1, 6/5/72; 4c, 5c, 9c, 50c, 2/6/73; 10c, 25c, 30c, 35c, 6/4/73.

A9 "Peace" A9a "Joy"

1972, Oct. 2 Litho. *Perf. 14½*

55	A9	3c black & multi	.50	.50
56	A9a	3c black & multi	.50	.50
a.		Pair, #55-56	1.25	1.25
57	A9	7c black & multi	.65	.65
58	A9a	7c black & multi	.65	.65
a.		Pair, #57-58	1.50	1.50
		Nos. 55-58 (4)	2.30	2.30

Mother and Child, Christmas Island Map — A10

1973, Oct. 2 Photo. *Perf. 14½x13½*

59	A10	7c blue & multi	.60	.60
60	A10	25c brt green & multi	1.75	1.75

Christmas.

Mother and Child with Star and Cross — A11

1974, Oct. 2 Photo. *Perf. 13½x14½*

61	A11	7c black & lilac rose	.55	.55
62	A11	30c black & yellow	1.60	*2.00*

Christmas.

Flight into Egypt — A12

1975, Oct. 2 Photo. *Perf. 14½x13½*

63	A12	10c gold, black & yel	.40	.40
64	A12	35c gold, vio blk & rose	.90	*1.25*

Christmas.

Star of Bethlehem and Dove
A13 A14

1976, Oct. 2 Photo. *Perf. 13½*

65	A13	10c red & multi	.25	.35
66	A14	10c red & multi	.25	.35
a.		Pair, #65-66	.90	*1.50*
67	A13	35c blue & multi	.40	.55
68	A14	35c blue & multi	.40	.55
a.		Pair, #67-68	1.10	*1.75*
		Nos. 65-68 (4)	1.30	1.80

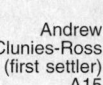

Christmas.

Andrew Clunies-Ross (first settler) A15

Famous Visitors: 1c, William Dampier, explorer, buccaneer. 2c, Capt. Willem de Vlamingh, Dutch explorer. 3c, Vice Adm. John F. L. P. Maclear, Royal Navy. 4c, John Murray, oceanographer, scientist. 5c, Adm. Pelham Aldrich and crew collecting specimen. 7c, Joseph Jackson Lister, naturalist, and arenga listeri plant. 8c, Adm. William Henry May. 9c, Henry Nicholas Ridley, botanist. 10c, George Clunies-Ross, pioneer phosphate miner. 20c, Capt. Joshua Slocum. 45c, Charles William Andrews, zoologist, and frigate birds. 50c, Karl Richard Hanitsch, zoologist, and fruit pigeon. 75c, Victor W. W. Saunders Purcell, Sinologist. $1, Fam Choo Beng, educator. $2, Harold Spencer-Jones, astronomer.

1977-78 Photo. *Perf. 14x13½*

69	A15	1c multicolored	.25	*.80*
70	A15	2c multicolored	.25	*.90*
71	A15	3c multicolored	.25	*.90*
72	A15	4c multicolored	.25	*.90*
73	A15	5c multicolored	.30	*.40*
74	A15	6c multicolored	.30	*.70*
75	A15	7c multicolored	.30	*.45*
76	A15	8c multicolored	.30	*.75*
77	A15	9c multicolored	.35	*1.75*
78	A15	10c multicolored	.30	*.55*
79	A15	20c multicolored	.35	*.70*
80	A15	45c multicolored	.65	.45
81	A15	50c multicolored	.90	*2.00*
82	A15	75c multicolored	.70	*1.25*
83	A15	$1 multicolored	.80	*1.25*
84	A15	$2 multicolored	1.30	*2.00*
		Nos. 69-84 (16)	7.55	*15.75*

Issued: 1c, 6c, 9c, $1, 4/30/77; 2c, 3c, 4c, $2, 2/22/78; 5c, 7c, 45c, 50c, 5/31/78; 8c, 10c, 20c, 75c, 9/1/78.

Australian Arms, Map of Christmas Island — A16

1977, June 2 Litho. *Perf. 14½x13½*

85	A16	45c multicolored	.50	.50

25th anniv. of reign of Elizabeth II.

Souvenir Sheet

The Twelve Days of Christmas — A17

Twelve Days of Christmas: a, Partridge in a pear tree. b, 2 turtle doves. c, 3 French hens. d, 4 calling birds. e, 5 gold rings. f, 6 geese. g, 7 swans. h, 8 maids a-milking. i, 9 ladies dancing. j, 10 lords a-leaping. k, 11 pipers piping. l, 12 drummers drumming.

Unwmk.

1977, Oct. 20 Litho. *Perf. 14*

86	A17	Sheet of 12	1.50	*2.00*
a.-l.		10c, any single	.25	.25
m.		Wmk. 373 ('78)	2.75	*3.75*

Christmas.

Common Design Types pictured following the introduction.

Elizabeth II Coronation Anniversary

Common Design Types

Souvenir Sheet

1978, Apr. 21 Litho. *Perf. 15*

87		Sheet of 6	3.50	*4.00*
a.		CD326 45c White swan of Bohun	.55	*.60*
b.		CD327 45c Elizabeth II	.55	*.60*
c.		CD328 45c Abbott's booby	.55	*.60*

No. 87 contains 2 se-tenant strips of Nos. 87a-87c, separated by horizontal gutter with commemorative and descriptive inscriptions.

Souvenir Sheet

The Song of Christmas — A18

Song of Christmas: a, Christ Child. b, Herald angels. c, Redeemer. d, Israel. e, Star. f, Three Wise Men. g, Manger. h. "All He stands for." i, "Shepherds came."

1978, Oct. 2 Litho. *Perf. 14*

88	A18	Sheet of 9	1.50	*1.75*
a.-i.		10c single stamp	.25	.25

Christmas. Each stamp design incorporates one letter of "Christmas."

IYC Emblem, Oriental Children — A19

Design: IYC emblem and children of different races holding hands, continuous design.

1979, Apr. 20 Litho. *Perf. 14*

89		Strip of 5	1.50	2.25
a.-e.		A19 20c single stamp	.25	.45

International Year of the Child.

Rowland Hill and No. 25 A20

Sir Rowland Hill (1795-1879), originator of penny postage, and Christmas Island stamps: a, #1. b, #11. c, #21. d, #25. e, #34.

1979, Aug. 27 Litho. *Perf. 13x13½*

90		Strip of 5	1.10	1.75
a.-e.		A20 20c any single	.25	.40

Three Kings Bearing Gifts — A21

Christmas: 55c, Virgin and Child, globe.

1979, Oct. 22 Litho. *Perf. 14x14½*

91	A21	20c multicolored	.25	*.30*
92	A21	55c multicolored	.45	*.70*

25 Years of Golf — A22

1980, Feb. 12 Litho. *Perf. 14½x14*

93	A22	20c shown	.35	.55
94	A22	55c Clubhouse	.95	1.40

Surveyor, Phosphate Industry A23

1980-81 Litho. *Perf. 14x14½*

95	A23	15c shown	.25	.25
96	A23	22c Drilling for samples	.25	.25
97	A23	40c Sample analysis	.30	.30
98	A23	55c Mine planning	.45	.45
99	A23	15c Jungle clearing	.25	.25
100	A23	22c Overburden removal	.25	.25
101	A23	40c Open cut mining	.30	.30
102	A23	55c Restoration	.45	.45
103	A23	22c Screening and stockpiling	.30	.30
104	A23	28c Loading train	.35	.35
105	A23	40c Rail transport	.45	.45
106	A23	60c Drying	.55	.55
107	A23	22c Crushing	.30	.30
108	A23	28c Pipeline	.35	.35
109	A23	40c Bulk storage	.45	.45
110	A23	60c Loading ship	.55	.55
		Nos. 95-110 (16)	5.80	5.80

Issued: Nos. 96-98, 5/5/80; Nos. 99-102, 7/14/80; Nos. 103-106, 2/9/81; NOs. 107-110, 5/4/81.

Souvenir Sheet

Christmas — A24

1980, Oct. 6 Litho. *Perf. 13½x13*

111	A24	Sheet of 6	1.60	*2.25*
a.		15c Angel	.25	.25
b.		22c Virgin and child	.25	.35
c.		60c Angel	.30	.35
d.		15c Angel holding soldier	.25	.35
e.		22c Kneeling woman and man	.25	.35
f.		60c Chinese, Indian, European children	.30	.35

Christmas. No. 111 contains 2 strips of 3 (Nos. 111a-111c and 111d-111f) with gutter between.

Cryptoblepharus Egeriae — A25

Designs: Reptiles.

1981, Aug. 10 Litho. *Perf. 13x13½*

112	A25	24c shown	.25	.25
113	A25	30c Emoia nativitata	.30	.30
114	A25	40c Lepidodactylus listeri	.45	.45
115	A25	60c Cyrtodactylus nov.	.55	.55
		Nos. 112-115 (4)	1.55	1.55

Souvenir Sheet

Christmas — A26

1981, Oct. 19 Litho. *Perf. 14½x14*

116	A26	Sheet of 4	1.60	*2.00*
a.		18c Angels, star	.25	*.30*
b.		24c Nativity	.25	*.35*
c.		40c Children praying to Jesus	.50	*.60*
d.		60c Children praying	.55	*.75*

Reef Heron A27

2c, Noddies. 3c, Glossy swiftlet. 4c, Imperial pigeon. 5c, Christmas Isld. silvereyes. 10c, Thrush. 25c, Silver bosunbird. 30c, Christmas Isld. emerald doves. 40c, Brown boobies. 50c, Red-footed boobies. 65c, Christmas Isld. frigatebird. 75c, Golden bosunbirds. 80c, Nankeen kestrel, vert. $1, Christmas Isld. hawk owl, vert. $2, Goshawk, vert. $4, Abbott's boobies, vert.

1982-83 Litho. *Perf. 14*

117	A27	1c	shown	.65	.25
118	A27	2c	multicolored	.65	.25
119	A27	3c	multicolored	.65	.75
120	A27	4c	multicolored	.65	.75
121	A27	5c	multicolored	.80	.95
122	A27	10c	multicolored	.65	.75
123	A27	25c	multicolored	1.00	.75
124	A27	30c	multicolored	.70	.75
125	A27	40c	multicolored	.70	.60
126	A27	50c	multicolored	.70	.60
127	A27	65c	multicolored	.70	.60
128	A27	75c	multicolored	.85	.75
129	A27	80c	multicolored	1.00	*2.00*
130	A27	$1	multicolored	2.00	2.25
131	A27	$2	multicolored	1.75	*4.00*
132	A27	$4	multicolored	2.75	3.00
			Nos. 117-132 (16)	16.20	19.00

Issued: 1c, 2c, 25c $4, 3/8; 3c, 4c, 10c, $2, 6/14; 40c, 50c, 65c, 75c, 8/23; 5c, 30c, 80c, $1, 2/21/83.

Christmas — A28

Paper sculptures.

1982, Oct. 18 Litho. & Embossed

135	A28	27c	Joseph	.30	.30
136	A28	50c	Angel	.40	.40
137	A28	75c	Mary, Baby Jesus	.50	.65
a.			Strip of 3, #135-137	1.30	1.60

25th Anniv. of Boat Club — A29

Designs: Various boating activities.

Perf. 14x14½, 14½x14

1983, May 2 Litho.

138	A29	27c	multicolored	.30	.30
139	A29	35c	multicolored	.30	.30
140	A29	50c	multi, horiz.	.45	.45
141	A29	75c	multi, horiz.	.45	.45
			Nos. 138-141 (4)	1.50	1.50

25th Anniv. of Australian Territory A30

24c, Maps. golden bosun bird, kangaroo. 30c, Map, flag. 85c, Boeing 727, maps.

1983, Oct. 1 Litho. *Perf. 14*

142	A30	24c	multicolored	.70	.45
143	A30	30c	multicolored	.80	.80
144	A30	85c	multicolored	1.60	2.00
			Nos. 142-144 (3)	3.10	3.25

Christmas — A31

Designs: Christmas candles.

1983, Oct. 31 Litho. *Perf. 13½x13*

145	A31	24c	multicolored	.25	.30
146	A31	30c	multicolored	.35	.50
147	A31	85c	multicolored	.75	1.50
			Nos. 145-147 (3)	1.35	2.30

Red Land Crab — A32

1984, Feb. 20 Litho. *Perf. 14x14½*

148	A32	30c	Feeding	.30	.30
149	A32	40c	Migration	.40	.40
150	A32	55c	Developmental stages	.40	.40
151	A32	85c	Adult female, young	.80	.80
			Nos. 148-151 (4)	1.90	1.90

Local Fungi — A33

30c, Leucocoprinus fragilissimus. 40c, Microporus xanthopus. 45c, Trogia anthidepas. 55c, Haddowia longipes. 85c, Phillipsia domingensis.

1984, Apr. 30 *Perf. 13½x14½*

152	A33	30c	multicolored	.45	.45
153	A33	40c	multicolored	.50	.50
154	A33	45c	multicolored	.65	.65
155	A33	55c	multicolored	.75	.75
156	A33	85c	multicolored	.95	.95
			Nos. 152-156 (5)	3.30	3.30

Cricket on Christmas Isld., 25th Anniv. A34

1984, July 23 Litho. *Perf. 14*

157	A34	30c	Runout	.50	*.75*
158	A34	40c	Catch at point	.55	*1.00*
159	A34	55c	Batsman	.65	*1.25*
160	A34	85c	Batsman hitting	.75	*1.50*
			Nos. 157-160 (4)	2.45	*4.50*

Souvenir Sheet

Christmas; Ausipex '84 A35

1984, Sept. 21 Litho. *Perf. 13½*

161		Sheet of 3 + 3 labels	2.60	2.60
a.		A35 30c Father Christmas arriving	.45	.45
b.		A35 55c Distributing gifts	.75	.75
c.		A35 85c Waving good-bye	1.25	1.25

Crabs A36

No. 162, Birgus latro. No. 163, Cardiosoma hirtipes. No. 164, Gecarcoidea natalis. No. 165, Ocypode ceratophthalma. No. 166, Ceonobita rugosa. No. 167, Metasesarma rousseauxi. No. 168, Coenobita brevimana. No. 169, Geograpsus stormi. No. 170, Grapsus tenuicrustatus. No. 171, Geograpsus grayi. No. 172, Ocypode cordimana. No. 173, Geograpsus crinipes.

1985 Litho. *Perf. 13x13½*

162	A36	30c	multicolored	1.00	.90
163	A36	33c	multicolored	1.00	.90
164	A36	33c	multicolored	1.10	1.00
165	A36	40c	multicolored	1.10	1.00
166	A36	45c	multicolored	1.10	1.25
167	A36	45c	multicolored	1.25	1.50
168	A36	55c	multicolored	1.25	1.50
169	A36	60c	multicolored	1.75	1.75
170	A36	60c	multicolored	2.25	2.50
171	A36	85c	multicolored	2.50	2.50
172	A36	90c	multicolored	2.50	*3.25*
173	A36	90c	multicolored	3.00	*4.00*
			Nos. 162-173 (12)	19.80	22.05

Issued: 30c, 40c, 55c, 85c, 1/30; Nos. 163, 166, 169, 172, 4/29; Nos. 164, 167, 170, 173, 7/22.

Once in Royal David's City — A37

Songs: 33c, While Shepherds Watched Their Flocks by Night. 45c, Away in a Manger. 60c, We Three Kings of Orient Are. 90c, Hark! The Herald Angels Sing.

1985, Oct. 28 Litho. *Perf. 14x14½*

174	A37	27c	multicolored	.80	*1.25*
175	A37	33c	multicolored	.90	*1.40*
176	A37	45c	multicolored	1.10	*1.50*
177	A37	60c	multicolored	1.20	*1.60*
178	A37	90c	multicolored	1.30	*1.75*
a.			Strip of 5, #174-178	6.75	*9.00*
			Nos. 174-178 (5)	5.30	*7.50*

Christmas.

Halley's Comet A38

33c, Over island. 45c, Edmond Halley. 60c, Over phosphate shipping. 90c, Over Flying Fish Cove.

1986, Apr. 30 Litho. *Perf. 14*

179	A38	33c	multicolored	.40	*.70*
180	A38	45c	multicolored	.50	*1.10*
181	A38	60c	multicolored	.75	*2.10*
182	A38	90c	multicolored	1.10	*2.50*
			Nos. 179-182 (4)	2.75	*6.40*

Indigenous Flowers — A39

1986, June 30 Litho. *Perf. 14*

183	A39	33c	Ridley's orchid	.85	.55
184	A39	45c	Hanging flower	.60	*.85*
185	A39	60c	Hoya	.60	*1.50*
186	A39	90c	Sea hibiscus	.70	*2.00*
			Nos. 183-186 (4)	2.75	*4.90*

Royal Wedding Issue, 1986

Common Design Type

Designs: 33c, Couple in Buckingham Palace garden. 90c, Andrew operating helicopter.

1986, July 23 Litho. *Perf. 14½x14*

187	CD338	33c	multicolored	.45	*.45*
188	CD338	90c	multicolored	1.00	*1.75*

Christmas A40

Santa Claus at Christmas Island.

1986, Sept. 30 Litho. *Perf. 13x13½*

189	A40	30c	Speedboating	.80	.60
190	A40	36c	At the beach	.95	.60
191	A40	55c	Fishing	1.40	1.50
192	A40	70c	Golfing	2.50	*3.50*
193	A40	$1	Sleeping in hammock	2.50	*4.00*
			Nos. 189-193 (5)	8.15	10.20

Visiting Ships, Cent. A41

1987, Jan. 21 *Perf. 14½*

194	A41	36c	Flying Fish	1.00	.80
195	A41	90c	Egeria	1.90	2.50

Wildlife A42

1c, Blind snake. 2c, Blue-tailed skink. 3c, Insectivorous bat. 5c, Green cricket. 10c, Christmas Is. fruit bat. 25c, Gecko. 30c, Praying mantis. 36c, Hawk owl. 40c, Bull-mouth helmet shell. 41c, Nudibranch. 50c, Textile cone shell. 65c, Brittle-stars. 75c, Royal angelfish. 90c, Christmas Is. white butterfly. $1, Mimic butterfly. $2, Shrew. $5, Green turtle.

1987-89 Litho. *Perf. 14*

196	A42	1c	multicolored	.40	.90
197	A42	2c	multicolored	.40	.90
198	A42	3c	multicolored	.75	.90
199	A42	5c	multicolored	1.10	.90
200	A42	10c	multicolored	.90	.90
201	A42	25c	multicolored	.90	1.00
202	A42	30c	multicolored	1.00	1.25
203	A42	36c	multicolored	2.25	1.75
204	A42	40c	multicolored	1.50	2.75
204A	A42	41c	multi ('89)	3.25	1.00
205	A42	50c	multicolored	1.60	2.75
206	A42	65c	multicolored	1.00	*1.25*
207	A42	75c	multicolored	1.00	*1.75*
208	A42	90c	multicolored	3.25	3.00
209	A42	$1	multicolored	3.25	3.00
210	A42	$2	multicolored	3.25	*6.50*

211 A42 $5 multicolored 4.00 *6.50*
a. Sheet of 16, #196-204, 205-211 *47.50 47.50*
Nos. 196-211 (17) 29.80 37.00

Issued: 1c, 2c, 25c, $5, 3/25; 3c, 10c, 36c, $2, 6/24; 40c, 50c, 65c, 75c, 8/26; 5c, 30c, 90c, $1, 3/1/88; 41c, 9/1/89.

Stamps contained in No. 211a inscribed "1988" at bottom.

For overprint see Nos. 246-247.

Souvenir Sheet

Santa Claus Delivering Presents — A43

1987, Oct. 7 Litho. *Perf. 13½*

212 A43 Sheet of 4 5.50 5.50
a. 30c multicolored .60 .60
b. 37c multicolored .65 .65
c. 90c multicolored 1.75 1.75
d. $1 multicolored 1.90 1.90

Christmas. Nos. 212a-212d printed in a continuous design.

Australia Bicentennial A44

Designs: a, First Fleet sighted by 5 Aborginals on land. b, Four Aboriginals on land, one in canoe. c, Ships entering bay, kangaroos. d, Europeans land. e, Flag raising.

1988, Jan. 26 Litho. *Perf. 13*

213 Strip of 5 10.00 10.00
a.-e. A44 37c any single 1.75 1.75

Nos. 213a-213e printed in a continuous design. See Cocos Islands No. 172.

Annexation of the Island, Cent. — A45

37c, Capt William Henry May. 53c, Annexation ceremony. 95c, HMS Imperieuse. $1.50, Building cairn of stones.

1988, June 8 Litho. *Perf. 14½*

214 A45 37c multicolored .65 .65
215 A45 53c multicolored .90 .90
216 A45 95c multicolored 1.50 1.50
217 A45 $1.50 multicolored 2.00 2.00
Nos. 214-217 (4) 5.05 5.05

Settlement of Christmas Is., Cent. — A46

Transportation: 37c, Horse and cart, 1910. 55c, Phosphate mining, 1910. 70c, Steam locomotive, 1914. $1, Arrival of first aircraft, 1957.

1988, Aug. 24 Litho. *Perf. 14½*

218 A46 37c multicolored .95 .55
219 A46 55c multicolored 1.40 .75
220 A46 70c multicolored 1.40 1.00
221 A46 $1 multicolored 2.25 1.60
Nos. 218-221 (4) 6.00 3.90

Christmas Presents — A47

32c, Bucket, shovel, boat. 39c, Snorkeling equipment. 90c, Toy soldier, doll, stuffed animals. $1, Race car, truck, plane.

1988, Nov. 15 *Perf. 14x14½*

222 A47 32c multicolored .50 .50
223 A47 39c multicolored .60 .60
224 A47 90c multicolored 1.25 1.25
225 A47 $1 multicolored 1.50 1.00
Nos. 222-225 (4) 3.85 3.35

Chinese New Year — A48

1989, Jan. 31 *Perf. 14½*

226 A48 39c Good harvest .70 .70
227 A48 70c Prosperity 1.00 1.00
228 A48 90c Good fortune 1.25 1.25
229 A48 $1 Progress 1.50 1.50
Nos. 226-229 (4) 4.45 4.45

Sir John Murray (1841-1914), Oceanographer — A49

39c, Portrait. 80c, Murray Hill (map). $1, Murray's equipment. $1.10, HMS Challenger.

1989, Mar. 16 *Perf. 14½x14*

230 A49 39c multicolored .70 .70
231 A49 80c multicolored 1.25 1.25
232 A49 $1 multicolored 1.60 1.60
233 A49 $1.10 multicolored 1.90 1.90
Nos. 230-233 (4) 5.45 5.45

Malay-Hari Raya Folk Celebration — A50

39c, Children. 55c, Tambourine player. 80c, Girl. $1.10, Minaret.

1989, May 31 *Perf. 14*

234 A50 39c multicolored .50 .50
235 A50 55c multicolored .85 .85
236 A50 80c multicolored 1.10 1.10
237 A50 $1.10 multicolored 1.75 1.75
Nos. 234-237 (4) 4.20 4.20

Ferns — A51

41c, Huperzia phlegmaria. 65c, Asplenium polydon. 80c, Davallia denticulata. $1.10, Asplenium nidus.

1989, Aug. 16

238 A51 41c multicolored .90 .90
239 A51 65c multicolored 1.25 1.25
240 A51 80c multicolored 1.40 1.25
241 A51 $1.10 multicolored 2.10 2.10
Nos. 238-241 (4) 5.65 5.50

Christmas — A52

Biblical scenes: 36c, Joseph. 41c, Manger. 80c, Shepherds see star. $1.10, Magi riding camels.

1989, Oct. 4 Litho. *Perf. 14½x15*

242 A52 36c multicolored .65 .55
243 A52 41c multicolored .70 .60
244 A52 80c multicolored 1.75 .90
245 A52 $1.10 multicolored 1.90 1.25
Nos. 242-245 (4) 5.00 3.30

Nos. 204A and 209 Overprinted

1989, Oct. 18 Litho. *Perf. 14*

246 A42 41c multicolored *1.40* .60
247 A42 $1 multicolored *4.75* 1.40

STAMPSHOW '89, Melbourne.
No. 247 is dated "1989."

1st Sighting of Christmas Is., 375th Anniv. — A53

Sightings of the island: 41c, John Milward, master of the British East India ship *Thomas,* 1615. $1.10, William Mynors, captain of *Royal Mary,* 1643.

1990, Jan. 31 Litho. *Perf. 14x15*

248 A53 41c multicolored 2.00 .50
249 A53 $1.10 multicolored 2.40 1.50

Transport Through the Ages — A55

1c, Phosphate transport. 2c, Phosphate train. 3c, Rail car, vert. 5c, Road train. 10c, Trishaw, vert. 15c, Terex. 25c, Long bus. 30c, Passenger rake, vert. 40c, Passenger barge, vert. 50c, Kolek canoe. 65c, Flying doctor, ambulance. 75c, Tradestore van. 90c, Vintage truck. $1, Water tanker. $2, Traction engine. $5, Steam locomotive, flat car.

Perf. 14x13½, 13½x14

1990 Litho. Unwmk.

254 A55 1c multicolored .25 .25
255 A55 2c multicolored .45 .45
256 A55 3c multicolored .30 .30
257 A55 5c multicolored .50 .50
258 A55 10c multicolored .45 .45
259 A55 15c multicolored .75 .75
260 A55 25c multicolored .40 .40
261 A55 30c multicolored .40 .40
262 A55 40c multicolored .45 .45
263 A55 50c multicolored .65 .65
264 A55 65c multicolored 3.75 1.75
265 A55 75c multicolored 1.75 1.75
266 A55 90c multicolored 1.75 1.75
267 A55 $1 multicolored 1.90 1.90
268 A55 $2 multicolored 2.50 2.50
269 A55 $5 multicolored 3.50 *3.75*
Nos. 254-269 (16) 19.75 18.00

Issued: 1c, 3c, 10c, 25c, 30c, 40c, 50c, $5, Apr. 18; others, Aug. 22.

World Wildlife Fund — A56

Abbott's boobies *(Sula abbotti):* 20c, Adult (facing left). 29c, Adult (facing right). No. 273, Adults, nest, hatchling. No. 274a, Adult landing on tree branch. No. 274b, Adult resting on branch. No. 274c, Adult, young in nest.

Perf. 14x14½

1990, June 6 Litho. Unwmk.

270 A56 10c shown 1.25 1.25
271 A56 20c multicolored 1.75 1.75
272 A56 29c multicolored 2.00 2.00
273 A56 41c multicolored 3.25 3.25
Nos. 270-273 (4) 8.25 8.25

Souvenir Sheet

Perf. 14½

274 Sheet of 3 8.25 8.25
a.-c. A56 41c any single 2.50 2.50
d. Overprinted in purple *13.50 13.50*
e. Overprinted in green *17.50 17.50*

No. 274d overprint reads "WORLD STAMP EXHIBITION / AUCKLAND, NEW ZEALAND, 24 AUGUST-2 SEPTEMBER 1990."

No. 274e overprint reads "BIRDPEX '90 National Philatelic Exhibition / University of Canterbury Christchurch NZ 6-9 Dec 1990 / In Conjunction / With The 20th International Ornithological Congress" and Bird's head.

Issued: No. 274d, Aug. 24; No. 274e, Dec. 6.

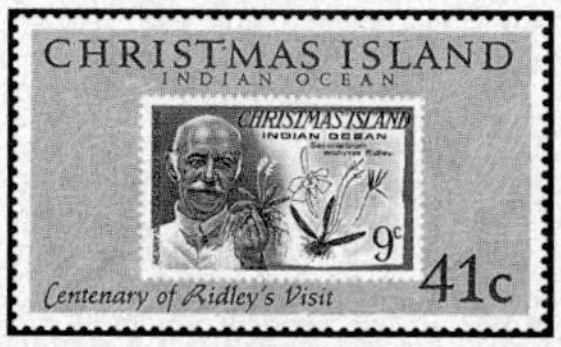

Centenary of Visit by Botanist Henry Ridley — A57

1990, July 11 Litho. *Perf. 14½*

275 A57 41c No. 77 .85 *.90*
276 A57 75c Ridley, vert. 1.30 *2.00*

Christmas A58

Flowers: 38c, Corymborkus veratrifolia. 43c, Hoya aldrichii. 80c, Quisqualis indica. $1.20, Barringtonia racemosa.

1990, Oct. 3 Litho. *Perf. 14½*

294 A58 38c multicolored 1.00 1.00
295 A58 43c multicolored 1.30 1.10
296 A58 80c multicolored 2.10 2.25
297 A58 $1.20 multicolored 3.00 *3.75*
Nos. 294-297 (4) 7.40 8.10

1st Phosphate Mining Lease, Cent. — A59

1991, Feb. 13 Litho. *Perf. 14½*

298 A59 43c Freighter 1.15 1.15
299 A59 43c Loading rail cars 1.15 1.15
300 A59 85c Shay locomotive 1.30 1.30
301 A59 $1.20 Bucket shovel 1.90 1.90
302 A59 $1.70 Reforestation 2.25 2.25
a. Strip of 5, #298-302 8.00 8.00
Nos. 298-302 (5) 7.75 7.75

Island Police Force — A60

No. 303, Community relations. No. 304, Traffic control. 90c, Customs and quarantine. $1.20, Search and rescue.

1991, Apr. 17 Litho. *Perf. 14½*

303 A60	43c multicolored	1.75	1.75
304 A60	43c multicolored	1.75	1.75
305 A60	90c multicolored	2.50	2.50
306 A60	$1.20 multicolored	3.25	3.25
a.	Souvenir sheet of 4, #303-306	9.25	9.25
	Nos. 303-306 (4)	9.25	9.25

Maps — A61

75c, Goos Atlas, 1666. $1.10, Apres De Manevillette, 1745. $1.20, Comberford, 1667.

1991, June 19 Litho. *Perf. 14*

307 A61	43c shown, 1991	1.10	1.10
308 A61	75c multicolored	2.10	2.10
309 A61	$1.10 multicolored	2.75	2.75
310 A61	$1.20 multicolored	3.00	3.00
	Nos. 307-310 (4)	8.95	8.95

Trees A62

43c, Bruguiera gymnorrhiza. 70c, Syzygium operculatum. 85c, Ficus microcarpa. $1.20, Arenga listeri.

1991, Aug. 21 Litho. *Perf. 14*

311 A62	43c multicolored	1.25	1.25
312 A62	70c multicolored	1.75	1.75
313 A62	85c multicolored	2.00	2.00
314 A62	$1.20 multicolored	2.25	2.25
	Nos. 311-314 (4)	7.25	7.25

Christmas A63

Drawings of "What Christmas Means to Me" by: No. 315a, S'ng Yen Luiw. b, Liew Ann Nee. c, Foo Pang Chuan. d, Too Lai Peng. e, Jesamine Wheeler. 43c, Ho Puay Ha. $1, Ng Hooi Hua. $1.20, Yani Kawi.

1991, Oct. 2 Litho. *Perf. 14½*

315	Strip of 5	4.25	4.25
a.-e.	A63 38c any single	.75	.75
316 A63	43c multicolored	.85	.70
317 A63	$1 multicolored	1.90	1.90
318 A63	$1.20 multicolored	2.10	2.10
	Nos. 315-318 (4)	9.10	8.95

A64

War Time Evacuation, 50th Anniv.: No. 319, Conference to decide upon evacuation. No. 320, Europeans awaiting barge. $1.05, Barge approaching waiting ship. $1.20, Remaining population waving to TSS Islander.

1992, Feb. 19 Litho. *Perf. 14½*

319 A64	45c multicolored	1.25	1.25
320 A64	45c multicolored	1.25	1.25
321 A64	$1.05 multicolored	2.60	2.60
322 A64	$1.20 multicolored	2.75	2.75
	Nos. 319-322 (4)	7.85	7.85

Shells — A65

5c, Cypraea tigris. 10c, Cypraea caputserpentis. 15c, Lambis scorpius. 20c, Chlamys pallium. 25c, Engina mendicaria. 30c, Drupa ricinus. 40c, Distorsio reticulata. 45c, Turbo petholatus. 50c, Cantharus pulcher. 60c, Conus capitaneus. 70c, Turbo lajonkairii. 80c, Lambis chiragra. 90c, Angaria delphinus. $1, Vasum ceramicum. $2, Tonna perdix. $5, Drupa rubusidaea.

1992 Litho. *Perf. 15x14½*

326	A65	5c multicolored	.60	.90
327	A65	10c multicolored	.90	.80
328	A65	15c multicolored	1.40	.80
329	A65	20c multicolored	1.40	.80
330	A65	25c multicolored	1.40	.80
331	A65	30c multicolored	1.40	.80
332	A65	40c multicolored	1.40	.80
333	A65	45c multicolored	1.75	.90
334	A65	50c multicolored	1.75	.90
335	A65	60c multicolored	2.25	1.00
336	A65	70c multicolored	2.75	1.25
337	A65	80c multicolored	2.75	1.75
338	A65	90c multicolored	2.75	2.00
339	A65	$1 multicolored	2.75	2.10
340	A65	$2 multicolored	2.00	3.50
341	A65	$5 multicolored	5.00	5.50
		Nos. 326-341 (16)	32.25	24.60

Issued: 10c, 20c, 30c, 45c, 60c, 80c, $1, $2, 4/15; 5c, 15c, 25c, 40c, 50c, 70c, 90c, $5, 8/19.

For overprint see No. 348.

Sinking of Eidsvold and Nissa Maru, 50th Anniv. A66

Designs: 45c, Eidsvold hit by torpedo. 80c, Eidsvold sinking. $1.05, Nissa Maru hit by torpedo. $1.20, Nissa Maru sinking.

1992, June 17 Litho. *Perf. 14x13½*

343 A66	45c multicolored	2.25	2.25
344 A66	80c multicolored	3.00	3.00
345 A66	$1.05 multicolored	3.50	3.50
346 A66	$1.20 multicolored	3.75	3.75
	Nos. 343-346 (4)	12.50	12.50

Christmas — A67

Coastline, booby birds: a, 40c, Plants on shore, birds. b, 40c, Birds, rocks offshore. c, 45c, Birds on shore. d, $1.05, Birds in flight, coastline. e, $1.20, Forest, rocky coastline.

1992, Oct. 7 Litho. *Perf. 14½*

347 A67	Strip of 5, #a.-e.	7.00	9.00

No. 341 Ovptd. in Red Violet

1992, Sept. 1 Litho. *Perf. 15x14½*

348 A65	$5 on #342	11.00	8.75

Kuala Lumpur Philatelic Exhibition.

Starting with No. 349, Christmas Island stamps are valid for postage on items mailed in Australia and Australian stamps are valid on items posted on Christmas Island.

Seabirds — A68

Designs: a, Abbott's booby. b, Christmas Island frigatebird. c, Common noddy. d, Golden bosunbird. e, Brown booby.

1993, Mar. 4 Litho. *Perf. 14½x14*

349 A68	45c Strip of 5, #a.-e.	3.75	4.25
f.	Souvenir sheet of 5, #a.-e.	4.00	4.50
g.	As "f," overprinted	9.00	9.00
h.	As "f," overprinted	7.00	7.00

No. 349g Ovptd. in Gold in sheet margin with Taipei '93 emblem and: "ASIAN INTERNATIONAL INVITATION STAMP EXHIBITION / TAIPEI '93" in Chinese and English.

No. 349h Ovptd. in Gold in Sheet Margin with "INDOPEX '93 / 6TH ASIAN INTERNATIONAL PHILATELIC EXHIBITION 1993 / PAMERAN INTERNASIONAL PENGUMPULAN / KEENAM DI ASIA TAHUN 1993" and show emblem.

Issued: No. 349g, 4/93; No. 349h, 5/29/93.

Scenic Views — A69

1993, June 1 *Perf. 14x14½*

350 A69	85c Dolly Beach	1.75	1.75
351 A69	95c Blow holes	2.10	2.10
352 A69	$1.05 Merrial Beach	2.25	2.25
353 A69	$1.20 Rain forest	2.50	2.50
	Nos. 350-353 (4)	8.60	8.60

Christmas — A70

1993, Sept. 2 Litho. *Perf. 14½x14*

354 A70	40c Turtle on beach	1.25	1.25
355 A70	45c Crabs, wave	1.25	1.25
356 A70	$1 Frigatebird, rainforest	2.50	2.50
	Nos. 354-356 (3)	5.00	5.00

Naming of Christmas Island, 350th Anniv. — A71

1993, Dec. 1 Litho. *Perf. 14x14½*

357 A71	$2 multicolored	3.75	3.75

New Year 1994 (Year of the Dog) — A72

1994, Jan. 20 Litho. *Perf. 14x14½*

358 A72	45c shown	1.25	*1.50*
359 A72	45c Pekingese	1.25	*1.50*
a.	Pair, #358-359	3.00	*4.00*
b.	Souvenir sheet of 1, #359a	4.00	*4.00*
c.	As "b," overprinted	*4.75*	*4.75*
d.	As "b," overprinted	*7.75*	*7.75*
e.	As "b," overprinted	*8.00*	*8.00*
f.	As "b," overprinted	*15.50*	*15.50*

No. 359c Ovptd. in gold in sheet margin with dog and "Melbourne / STAMP & COIN SHOW / 11-13 February 1994;" No. 359d with "HONG KONG '94 STAMP EXHIBITION" and show emblem; No. 359e with "Canberra /Stamp Show '94 / 19-21 March / 1994" and show emblem; No. 359f with "QUEENSLAND STAMP & COIN SHOW 1994 / JUNE 11, 12, 13."

Issued: No. 359c, 2/11/94; No. 359d, 2/18/94; No. 359e, 3/19/94; No. 359f, 1995.

Christmas Island Railway Steam Locomotives A73

85c, Locomotive No. 4. 95c, Locomotive No. 9. $1.20, Locomotive No. 1.

1994, May 19 Litho. *Perf. 14x14½*

360 A73	85c multicolored	2.00	2.00
361 A73	95c multicolored	2.25	2.25
362 A73	$1.20 multicolored	2.60	2.60
	Nos. 360-362 (3)	6.85	6.85

Orchids — A74

a, Brachypeza archytas. b, Thelasis capitata. c, Corymborkis veratrifolia. d, Flickingeria nativitatis. e, Dendrobium crumenatum.

1994, Aug. 16 Litho. *Perf. 14½x14*

363 A74	45c Strip of 5, #a.-e.	7.00	7.00

Christmas A75

1994, Sept. 8 Litho. *Perf. 14x14½*

364 A75	40c Angel	.70	.60
365 A75	45c Wise man	.90	.60
366 A75	80c Bethlehem	1.50	1.50
	Nos. 364-366 (3)	3.10	2.70

New Year 1995 (Year of the Boar) — A76

Design: 85c, Stylized boar, diff.

1995, Jan. 12 Litho. *Perf. 14x14½*

367 A76	45c shown	.80	.80
368 A76	85c multicolored	1.40	1.40
a.	Souvenir sheet, #367-368	3.00	3.00
b.	As "a," overprinted	*7.00*	*7.00*
c.	As "a," overprinted	*15.00*	*15.00*

No. 368b ovptd. in gold in sheet margin with outline of boar and: "STAMP & COIN FAIR / ROYAL EXHIBITION BUILDING / MELBOURNE VIC. 3000 . 10-12 FEB 1995."

No. 368c ovptd. in sheet margin with Taiwan flag and map of Australia with flag, and also

Chinese characters, dates and "STAMP TAIWAN, SYDNEY, / AUSTRALIA MAY 20-28 1995."

Christmas Island Golf Course, 40th Anniv. — A77

1995, May 11 Litho. *Perf. 14*
369 A77 $2.50 multicolored 6.00 6.00

Christmas A78

Santa Claus riding great frigatebird: 40c, Reading map. 45c, Dropping presents. 80c, Waving.

1995, Sept. 14 Litho. *Perf. 14x14½*
370 A78 40c multicolored .90 .75
371 A78 45c multicolored 1.00 .75
372 A78 80c multicolored 1.50 1.50
Nos. 370-372 (3) 3.40 3.00

End of World War II, 50th Anniv. — A79

No. 373a, RAAF reconnaissance flight, 1945. No. 373b, Arrival of HMS Rother, 1945.

Litho. & Engr.
1995, Oct. 12 *Perf. 14x14½*
373 Pair 2.75 2.75
a.-b. A79 45c any single 1.00 1.00

Angelfish A80

1995, Oct. 12 Litho.
374 A80 75c Lemonpeel 1.25 *1.75*
375 A80 $1 Emperor 1.90 *2.50*

See also Nos. 381-387.

New Year 1996 (Year of the Rat) A81

Litho. with Foil Application
1996, Jan. 9 *Perf. 14x14½*
376 A81 45c Facing right 1.25 1.25
377 A81 45c Facing left 1.25 1.25
a. Pair, #376-377 3.00 3.00
b. Souvenir sheet, #377a 3.75 3.75
c. As "b," overprinted *10.00 10.00*

No. 377c overprinted in gold in sheet margin "STAMP AND COIN FAIR / MELBOURNE / 23-25 February 1996."

Fish — A82

20c, Pinktail triggerfish. 30c, Longnose filefish. 45c, Princess anthias. 85c, Green moon wrasse. 90c, Spotted boxfish. 95c, Moorish idol. $1.20, Glass bigeye.

1996-97 Litho. *Perf. 14x14½*
381 A82 20c multicolored .40 .40
382 A82 30c multicolored .60 .50
383 A82 45c multicolored .90 .50
384 A82 85c multicolored 1.75 *2.00*
385 A82 90c multicolored 1.00 1.00
386 A82 95c multicolored 1.75 1.75
387 A82 $1.20 multicolored 2.25 *3.25*
Nos. 381-387 (7) 8.65 9.40

Issued: 20c, 30c, 45c, 90c, 4/18/96; 85c, 95c, $1.20, 7/17/97.

Birds — A83

1996, July 11 Litho. *Perf. 14½x14*
399 A83 45c White-eye 1.25 1.25
400 A83 85c Hawk-owl 2.00 2.00

Christmas A84

Sailing ships, words from Christmas carol: 40c, "I Saw Three Ships." 45c, "Come sailing in." 80c, "On Christmas day in the morning."

1996, Sept. 12 Litho. *Perf. 14*
401 A84 40c multicolored 1.00 .75
402 A84 45c multicolored 1.10 .90
403 A84 80c multicolored 1.60 1.60
Nos. 401-403 (3) 3.70 3.25

Exploration of Australian Coast & Christmas Island by Willem de Vlamingh, 300th Anniv. — A85

"Portrait of a Dutch Navigator," by Jan Verkolje.

1996, Oct. 27 Litho. *Perf. 14*
404 A85 45c multicolored 1.25 1.25

No. 404 was issued se-tenant with Australia No. 1571 (No. 1571a). Value, pair $4.

New Year 1997 (Year of the Ox) — A86

Constellation and: No. 405, Ox facing right. No. 406, Ox facing left.

Litho. with Foil Application
1997, Jan. 6 *Perf. 14x14½*
405 A86 45c multicolored 1.00 1.00
406 A86 45c multicolored 1.00 1.00
a. Pair, #405-406 2.75 2.75
b. Souvenir sheet, #405-406 3.00 3.00

Christmas A87

Santa on Christmas Island: 40c, Reading letters. 45c, Making toys. 80c, In sleigh.

1997, Sept. 11 Litho. *Perf. 14x14½*
407 A87 40c multicolored .65 .65
408 A87 45c multicolored .75 .75
409 A87 80c multicolored 1.75 1.75
Nos. 407-409 (3) 3.15 3.15

New Year 1998 (Year of the Tiger) — A88

Litho. with Foil Application
1998, Jan. 5 *Perf. 14x14½*
410 A88 45c shown 1.25 1.25
411 A88 45c Looking backward 1.25 1.25
a. Pair, #410-411 3.00 3.00
b. Souvenir sheet of 2, #410-411 3.50 3.50

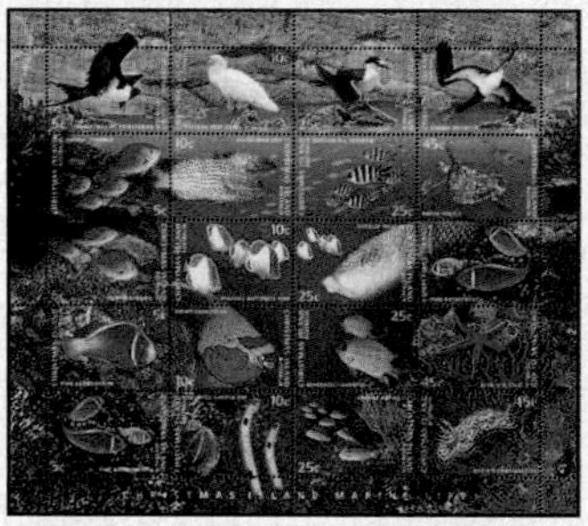

Marine Life — A89

Designs: a, 5c, Frigatebird. b, 5c, Ambon chromis, denomination LR. c, 5c, Ambon chromis, denomination LL. d, 5c, Pink anemonefish, denomination, UR. e, 5c, Pink anemonefish, denomination LL. f, 10c, Eastern reef egret. g, 10c, Whitelined cod. h, 10c, Pyramid butterfly fish. i, 10c, Dusky parrotfish. j, 10c, Spotted garden eel. k, 25c, Sooty tern. l, 25c, Scissortail sergeant. m, 25c, Thicklip wrasse. n, 25c, Blackaxil chromis. o, 25c, Orange anthias. p, 45c, Brown booby. q, 45c, Green turtle. r, 45c, Pink anemonefish. s, 45c, Blue sea star. t, 45c, Kunie's chromodoris.

1998, Mar. 12 Litho. *Perf. 14*
412 A89 Sheet of 20, #a.-t. 10.00 10.00

Tree Flowers of Christmas — A90

1998, Sept. 3 Litho. *Perf. 14½x14*
413 A90 40c Orchid tree .80 .80
414 A90 80c Flame tree 1.60 1.60
415 A90 95c Sea hibiscus 1.60 1.60
Nos. 413-415 (3) 4.00 4.00

New Year 1999 (Year of the Rabbit) A91

Litho. with Foil Application
1999, Jan. 14 *Perf. 14x14½*
416 A91 45c shown 1.00 1.00
417 A91 45c Rabbit looking left 1.00 1.00
a. Pair, #416-417 2.75 2.75
b. Souvenir sheet, #417a 3.25 3.25

Festivals on Christmas Island — A92

Children's drawings: No. 418, Carrying balloons in parade, by Fong Jason. No. 419, Giant crab, by Siti Zanariah Zainal. 85c, Children at night, by Tan Diana, vert. $1.20, Green mosque, tree, by Anwar Ramian, vert.

1999, July 15 Litho. *Perf. 14x14½*
418 A92 45c multicolored .75 .75
419 A92 45c multicolored .75 .75
a. Pair, #418-419 1.75 1.75

Perf. 14½x14
420 A92 85c multicolored 1.00 1.00
421 A92 $1.20 multicolored 1.75 1.75
Nos. 418-421 (4) 4.25 4.25

Christmas A93

Designs: 40c, Santa Claus in hammock. 45c, Santa, birds, crab, lizard, cake. 95c, Santa, booby-drawn sleigh.

1999, Sept. 9 Litho. *Perf. 14x14½*
422 A93 40c multicolored .95 .80
423 A93 45c multicolored 1.10 .95
424 A93 95c multicolored 1.75 1.75
Nos. 422-424 (3) 3.80 3.50

New Year 2000 (Year of the Dragon) A94

Litho. with Foil Application
2000, Jan. 13 *Perf. 14x14½*
425 A94 45c shown 1.10 1.10
426 A94 45c Dragon facing left 1.10 1.10
a. Pair, #425-426 3.00 3.00
b. Souvenir sheet, #426a 3.50 3.50

Faces of Christmas Island — A95

Ordinary people: a, Yeow Jian Min, without shirt. b, Ida Chin, with blue shirt. c, Ho Tak Wah, old man. d, Thomas Faul and James Neill. e, Siti Sanniah Kawi, with striped blouse.

2000, Apr. 13 Litho. *Perf. 14½x14*
427 A95 45c Strip of 5, #a.-e. 4.75 4.75

Christmas — A96

No. 428: a, We three kings of Orient are. b, Bearing gifts we traverse afar. 45c, Star of wonder, star of night.

2000, Sept. 5 Litho. *Perf. 14½x14*
428 Pair 1.90 1.90
a.-b. A96 40c Any single .60 .60
429 A96 45c multi .60 .60

New Year 2001 (Year of the Snake) A97

Snake color: 45c, Green. $1.35, Silver.

Litho. with Foil Application

2001, Jan. 8 *Perf. 14x14½*

430-431 A97 Set of 2 3.00 3.00
a. Souvenir sheet, #430-431 4.00 *4.00*

Fungi — A98

Designs: $1, Chaetocalathus semisupinus. $1.50, Pycnoporus sanguineus.

2001, Oct. 25 **Litho.** *Perf. 14x14½*

432-433 A98 Set of 2 4.00 *4.00*

New Year 2002 (Year of the Horse) — A99

Zodiac Animals and Their Chinese Characters A100

Designs: 45c, Purple horse. $1.35, Gold horse.

No. 436: a, Rat. b, Ox. c, Tiger. d, Rabbit. e, Dragon. f, Snake. g, Horse. h, Sheep. i, Monkey. j, Cock. k, Dog. l, Boar.

Litho. With Gold Foil Application

2002, Jan. 8 *Perf. 14x14½*

434-435 A99 Set of 2 3.00 3.00
a. Souvenir sheet, #434-435 4.00 4.00
436 Sheet of 14, #a-l, #435a 12.00 12.00
a.-d. A100 5c Any single .55 .55
e.-h. A100 15c Any single, orange background .60 .60
i.-l. A100 25c Any single, orange background .65 .65

See Nos. 442, 447, 451, 456, 462-463.

Worldwide Fund for Nature (WWF) — A101

Christmas Island birds — No. 437: a, Imperial pigeon. b, Hawk owl.
$1, Goshawk. $1.50, Thrush.

2002, May 1 **Litho.** *Perf. 14½x14*

437 A101 45c Horiz. pair, #a-b 1.60 1.60
438 A101 $1 multi 1.60 1.60
439 A101 $1.50 multi 2.75 2.75
Nos. 437-439 (3) 5.95 5.95

Zodiac Animals Type of 2002 and

New Year 2003 (Year of the Ram) A102

Designs: 50c, Yellow and orange ram. $1.50, Blue ram.

No. 442: a, Rat. b, Ox. c, Tiger. d, Rabbit. e, Dragon. f, Snake. g, Horse. h, Sheep. i, Monkey. j, Cock. k, Dog. l, Boar.

Litho. With Gold Foil Application

2003, Jan. 7 *Perf. 14x14½*

440-441 A102 Set of 2 3.50 3.50
a. Souvenir sheet, #440-441 4.00 4.00
442 Sheet of 14, #a-l, #441a 12.00 12.00
a.-d. A100 10c Any single, red violet background .50 .50
e.-h. A100 15c Any single, red violet background .60 .60
i.-l. A100 25c Any single, red violet background .70 .70

See No. 463.

Christmas — A103

Designs: 45c, Arrival of Santa Claus on whale shark. 50c, Santa giving gifts to red crabs.

2003, Oct. 31 **Litho.** *Perf. 14½x14*

443-444 A103 Set of 2 3.00 3.00

Zodiac Animals Type of 2002 and

New Year 2004 (Year of the Monkey) A104

Designs: 50c, Yellow and orange monkey. $1.45, Red orange monkey, lotus flower.

No. 447: a, Rat. b, Ox. c, Tiger. d, Rabbit. e, Dragon. f, Snake. g, Horse. h, Sheep. i, Monkey. j, Cock. k, Dog. l, Boar.

Litho. With Gold Foil Application

2004, Jan. 6 *Perf. 14x14½*

445-446 A104 Set of 2 4.50 4.50
446a Souvenir sheet, #445-446 5.50 5.50
447 Sheet of 14, #a-l, #446a 12.00 12.00
a.-d. A100 10c Any single, light and dark blue background .50 .50
e.-h. A100 15c Any single, light and dark blue background .60 .60
i.-l. A100 25c Any single, light and dark blue background .70 .70

No. 446a exists with a 2004 Hong Kong Stamp Expo overprint in sheet margin in red. This sheet was sold at the show and was sold at some post offices in Australia, but not on Christmas Island. Value: *$15.*

See No. 463.

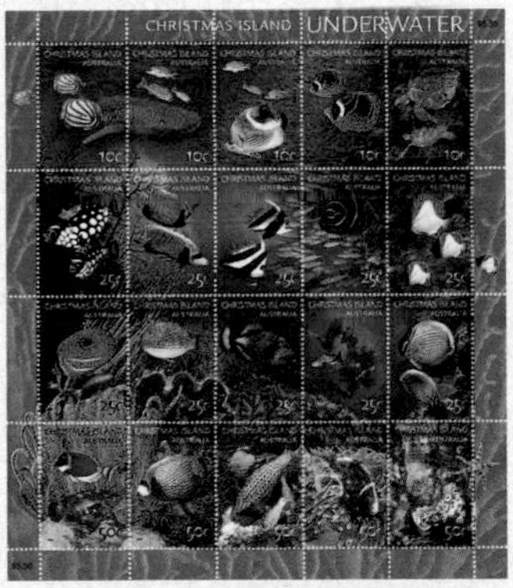

Marine Life — A105

No. 448: a, Two butterflyfish, rear of whale shark. b, Three striped fish, front of whale shark. c, Four fish. d, Two fish. e, Two green turtles. f, Two triggerfish (polka dots), red coral at LL. g, Two fish with thin horizontal stripes with yellow tails. h, Two fish with thick vertical stripes. i, Black and white fish. j, Three fish. k, Yellow fish with black spot, blue fish, red coral, yellow coral. l, Striped fish, clam. m, Black fish, small red fish. n Red fish, divers. o, Two striped fish, red coral under denomination. p, Blue and yellow fish, red and white spotted fish, yellow coral. q, Blue and yellow fish, yellow coral, sea anemones. r, Three blue fish with orange spots. s, Sea anemone and two anemonefish. t, Nudibranch, red coral and starfish.

2004, July 13 **Litho.** *Perf. 14½x14*

448 A105 Sheet of 20 11.00 11.00
a.-e. 10c Any single .25 .25
f.-o. 25c Any single .45 .45
p.-t. 50c Any single .95 .95

Zodiac Animals Type of 2002 and

New Year 2005 (Year of the Cock) A106

Designs: 50c, Cock, spirals at right. $1.45, Cock, spirals at right.

No. 451: a, Rat. b, Ox. c, Tiger. d, Rabbit. e, Dragon. f, Snake. g, Horse. h, Sheep. i, Monkey. j, Cock. k, Dog. l, Boar.

Litho. With Gold Foil Application

2005, Jan. 4 *Perf. 14x14½*

449-450 A106 Set of 2 4.50 4.50
450a Souvenir sheet, #449-450 4.50 4.50
450b As "a," with Taipei 2005 emblem overprinted in margin 5.00 5.00
451 Sheet of 14, #a-l, #450a 14.00 14.00
a.-d. A100 10c Any single, red and yellow background .45 .45
e.-h. A100 15c Any single, red and yellow background .45 .45
i.-l. A100 25c Any single, red and yellow background .65 .65

See No. 463.

Christmas A107

Santa Claus, birds and: 45c, Palm tree, presents. 90c, Sleigh, crabs.

2005, Nov. 1 **Litho.** *Perf. 14¼x14*

452 A107 45c multi 1.25 1.25
a. Booklet pane of 4 5.00 —
453 A107 90c multi 2.25 2.25

No. 452a exists with two different margins. These two panes were issued in a booklet that also contained three examples of Australia No. 2423a. The entire booklet sold for $9.95.

Zodiac Animals Type of 2002 and

New Year 2006 (Year of the Dog) A108

Designs: 50c, Purple dog. $1.45, Copper dog.

No. 456: a, Rat. b, Ox. c, Tiger. d, Rabbit. e, Dragon. f, Snake. g, Horse. h, Sheep. i, Monkey. j, Cock. k, Dog. l, Boar.

Litho. With Copper Foil Application

2006, Jan. 5 *Perf. 14x14½*

454-455 A108 Set of 2 3.25 3.25
455a Souvenir sheet, #454-455 3.25 3.25
456 Sheet of 14, #a-l, #455a 9.00 9.00
a.-d. A100 10c Any single, brown and yellow background .30 .30
e.-h. A100 15c Any single, brown and yellow background .35 .35
i.-l. A100 25c Any single, brown and yellow background .50 .50

See No. 463.

Buildings — A109

Designs: 50c, Mosque. $1.45, Tai Jin House.

No. 458: a, Tai Pak Kong Temple. b, Soon Tian Temple.

2006, June 13 **Litho.** *Perf. 14½x14*

457 A109 50c multi 1.25 1.25
458 A109 $1 Horiz. pair, #a-b 4.50 4.50
459 A109 $1.45 multi 3.25 3.25
Nos. 457-459 (3) 9.00 9.00

Zodiac Animals Types of 1996-2006 and

New Year 2007 (Year of the Boar) A110

Zodiac Animals A111

Designs: Nos. 460, 463l, 50c, Boar facing right. $1.45, Boar facing left.

No. 462: a, Rat. b, Ox. c, Tiger. d, Rabbit. e, Dragon. f, Snake. g, Horse. h, Sheep. i, Monkey. j, Cock. k, Dog. l, Boar.

Litho. With Copper Foil Application

2007, Jan. 9 *Perf. 14x14½*

460-461 A110 Set of 2 4.25 4.25
461a Souvenir sheet, #460-461 4.25 4.25
462 Sheet of 14, #a-l, #461a 10.00 10.00
a.-d. A100 10c Any single, multicolored background .25 .25
e.-h. A100 15c Any single, multicolored background .30 .25
i.-l. A100 25c Any single, multicolored background .50 .50

Self-Adhesive

Serpentine Die Cut 12¼ Syncopated (#463a-463l), Serpentine Die Cut (#463m)

463 Sheet of 13 19.00
a. A81 50c Like #376 1.10 1.10
b. A86 50c Like #405 1.10 1.10
c. A88 50c Like #410 1.10 1.10
d. A91 50c Like #416 1.10 1.10
e. A94 50c Like #425 1.10 1.10
f. A97 50c Like #430 1.10 1.10
g. A99 50c Like #434 1.10 1.10
h. A102 50c Like #440 1.10 1.10
i. A104 50c Like #445 1.10 1.10
j. A106 50c Like #449 1.10 1.10
k. A108 50c Like #454 1.10 1.10
l. A110 50c Like #460 1.10 1.10
m. A111 $1 multi 3.00 3.00
n. Booklet pane, 2 each #463a-463b 4.00
o. Booklet pane, 2 each #463c-463d 4.00
p. Booklet pane, 2 each #463e-463f 4.00
q. Booklet pane, 2 each #463g-463h 4.00
r. Booklet pane, 2 each #463i-463j 4.00
s. Booklet pane, 2 each #463k-463l 4.00
Complete booklet, #463n-463s 25.00

Complete booklet sold for $12.95.

Christmas A112

Santa Claus: 45c, In boat. 50c, Hoisted by crane. $1.10, On beach.

2007, Nov. 1 **Litho.** *Perf. 14x14½*

464-466 A112 Set of 3 4.00 4.00

New Year 2008 (Year of the Rat) — A113

Designs: 50c, Rat. $1.45, Chinese character for "rat."

No. 469: a, Rat, diff. b, Ox. c, Dragon. d, Snake. e, Tiger. f, Rabbit. g, Horse. h, Pig. i, Goat. j, Monkey. k, Rooster. l, Dog.

Litho. With Foil Application

2008, Jan. 8 *Perf. 14*

467 A113 50c multi 1.00 1.00
a. Perf. 14¾x14 *7.00 7.00*

Perf. 14¾x14

468 A113 $1.45 multi 2.75 2.75
a. Souvenir sheet, #467a, 468 3.75 3.75
b. As "a," with Olympex emblem in margin 3.75 3.75
469 Sheet of 14, #467a, 468, 469a-469l 11.00 11.00
a.-d. A113 10c Any single .25 .25
e.-h. A113 15c Any single .35 .35
i.-l. A113 25c Any single .50 .50
m. Booklet pane of 4, #469a, 469b, 2 #468 6.75 —
n. Booklet pane of 4, #469e, 469f, 2 #467a 2.75 —
o. Booklet pane of 4, #469c, 469d, 2 #467a 2.75 —
p. Booklet pane of 4, #469g, 469i, 2 #467a 3.00 —
q. Booklet pane of 4, #469j, 469k, 2 #467a 3.25 —
r. Booklet pane of 4, #469h, 469l, 2 #467a 3.00 —
Complete booklet, #469m-469r 22.00

Complete booklet sold for $10.95. Issued: No. 468b, 8/8.

Territorial Status of Christmas Island, 50th Anniv. A114

No. 470: a, Gecarcoidea natalis. b, Papasula abbotti. c, Asplenium listeri.
$1.45, Seal of Union of Christmas Island Workers. $2.45, Christmas Island flag.

2008, June 10 **Litho.** *Perf. 14¼*

470 Horiz. strip of 3 3.75 3.75
a.-c. A114 50c Any single 1.00 1.00
471 A114 $1.45 multi 3.50 3.50
472 A114 $2.45 multi 5.50 5.50
Nos. 470-472 (3) 12.75 12.75

Christmas — A115

Designs: Nos. 473, 475, 50c, Christmas tree, bird, crabs and shells. Nos. 474, 476, $1.20, Crabs with gifts and Christmas lights.

2008, Oct. 31 **Litho.** *Perf. 14½x14*

473-474 A115 Set of 2 3.00 3.00

Serpentine Die Cut 11¼ Syncopated

Self-Adhesive

475 A115 50c multi 1.00 1.00
a. Booklet pane of 10 10.00

Booklet Stamp

476 A115 $1.20 multi 2.00 2.00
a. Booklet pane of 5 10.00

No. 475 was also printed in sheets of 10.

Christmas With Personalized Picture — A116

Designs as before.

Serpentine Die Cut 11½x11¼ Syncopated

2008, Oct. 31 **Litho.**

Self-Adhesive

477 A116 50c multi *4.00 4.00*
478 A116 $1.20 multi *7.00 7.00*

Nos. 477-478 each were sold in sheets of 20 and have personalized pictures and a straight edge at right, and lack separations between the stamp and the personalized photo. Sheets of 20 of No. 477 sold for $23, and No. 478 sold for $37.

New Year 2009 (Year of the Ox) — A117

Designs: 55c, Rat. $1.65, Chinese character for "ox."
No. 481: a, Rat. b, Ox, diff. c, Dragon. d, Snake. e, Tiger. f, Rabbit. g, Horse. h, Pig. i, Goat. j, Monkey. k, Rooster. l, Dog.

Litho. With Foil Application

2009, Jan. 8 *Perf. 14¾x14*

479 A117 55c multi .90 .90
480 A117 $1.65 multi 2.75 2.75
a. Souvenir sheet, #479-480 4.00 4.00
481 Sheet of 14, #479-480, 481a-481l 13.00 13.00
a.-d. A117 10c Any single .30 .30
e.-h. A117 20c Any single .35 .35
i.-l. A117 25c Any single .50 .50
m. Booklet pane of 4, #481b, 481e, 2 #480 6.50 —
n. Booklet pane of 4, #481c, 481f, 2 #479 2.75 —
o. Booklet pane of 4, #481d, 481g, 2 #479 2.75 —
p. Booklet pane of 4, #481i, 481j, 2 #479 3.00 —
q. Booklet pane of 4, #481k, 481l, 2 #479 3.00 —
r. Booklet pane of 4, #481a, 481h, 2 #479 2.75 —
Complete booklet, #481m-481r 21.00

No. 479 was issued in a sheet of 9 + 9 labels that could be personalized and removed. The sheet sold for $15.95. Gutter strips of 10 of No. 484 exist with five labels forming a picture featuring the 12 Zodiac animals.
Complete booklet sold for $12.95.

Christmas — A118

2009, Nov. 2 **Litho.** *Perf. 14¾x14*

482 A118 $1.25 multi 3.25 3.25

Booklet Stamp

Self-Adhesive

Serpentine Die Cut 11¼ Syncopated

483 A118 $1.25 multi 3.25 3.25
a. Booklet pane of 5 16.50

New Year 2010 (Year of the Tiger) — A119

Designs: 55c, Tiger. $1.65, Chinese character for "tiger."
No. 486: a, Rat. b, Ox. c, Dragon. d, Snake. e, Tiger, diff. f, Rabbit. g, Horse. h, Pigs. i, Goat. j, Monkey. k, Rooster. l, Dog.

Litho. With Foil Application

2010, Jan. 12 *Perf. 14¾x14*

484 A119 55c multi 1.25 1.25
485 A119 $1.65 multi 3.25 3.25
a. Souvenir sheet, #484-485 5.50 5.50
486 Sheet of 14, #484-485, 486a-486l 14.50 14.50
a.-d. A119 10c Any single .30 .30
e.-h. A119 20c Any single .40 .40
i.-l. A119 25c Any single .55 .55
m. Booklet pane of 4, #486e, 486f, 2 #485 8.00 —
n. Booklet pane of 4, #486c, 486d, 2 #484 3.25 —
o. Booklet pane of 4, #486g, 486i, 2 #484 4.00 —
p. Booklet pane of 4, #486j, 486k, 2 #484 4.00 —
q. Booklet pane of 4, #486h, 486l, 2 #484 4.00 —
r. Booklet pane of 4, #486a, 486b, 2 #484 3.25 —
Complete booklet, #486m-486r 23.00

Complete booklet sold for $12.95. A sheet of 13 self-adhesive stamps containing a round $1 stamp depicting a flower and stamps similar to Nos. 467, 479, 484, 486c, 486d, 486f, 486g, 486h, 486i, 486j, 486k, 486l, sold for $9.95.
No. 484 was issued in a sheet of 9 + 9 labels that could be personalized and removed. The sheet sold for $15.95. Gutter strips of 10 of No. 484 exist with five labels forming a picture featuring the 12 Zodiac animals.
A sheet containing lithographed versions of Nos. 486a-486l and 12 labels that could not be personalized sold for $10.

Worldwide Fund for Nature (WWF) A120

No. 487 — Christmas Island frigatebird: a, Adult on nest. b, Adults and chick at nest.
No. 488 — Christmas Island frigatebird: a, Chick and adult at nest. b, Adult in flight.

2010, Aug. 17 **Litho.** *Perf. 14¼*

487 Horiz. pair 4.25 4.25
a.-b. A120 60c Either single 1.60 1.25
488 Horiz. pair 9.75 9.75
a.-b. A120 $1.80 Either single 4.25 2.75
c. Souvenir sheet, #487a-487b, 488a-488b 14.00 14.00

Christmas — A121

Golden bosunbird: 60c, Carrying gift. $1.30, Flying away from gift on beach.

2010, Nov. 1 **Litho.** *Perf. 14¾x14*

489 A121 60c multi 2.25 2.25
490 A121 $1.30 multi 4.50 4.50

Booklet Stamp

Self-Adhesive

Serpentine Die Cut 11¼ Syncopated

491 A121 60c multi 2.25 2.25
a. Booklet pane of 10 22.50
491B A121 $1.30 multi 4.50 4.25
c. Booklet pane of 5 22.50

New Year 2011 (Year of the Rabbit) — A122

Designs: 60c, Rabbit. $1.80, Chinese character for "rabbit."
No. 494: a, Rat. b, Ox. c, Dragon. d, Snake. e, Tiger. f, Rabbit, diff. g, Horse. h, Pig. i, Goat. j, Monkey. k, Rooster. l, Dog.

Litho. With Foil Application

2011, Jan. 11 *Perf. 14¾x14*

492 A122 60c multi 1.25 1.25
493 A122 $1.80 multi 3.75 3.75
a. Souvenir sheetof 2, #492-493 5.50 5.50
494 Sheet of 14, #492-493, 494a-494l 13.00 13.00
a.-d. A122 15c Any single .30 .30
e.-h. A122 20c Any single .40 .40
i.-l. A122 25c Any single .50 .50
m. Booklet pane of 4, #494a, 494b, 2 #492 3.75 —
n. Booklet pane of 4, #494e, 494f, 2 #492 4.00 —
o. Booklet pane of 4, #494g, 494i, 2 #492 4.25 —
p. Booklet pane of 4, #494h, 494l, 2 #492 4.25 —
q. Booklet pane of 4, #494j, 494k, 2 #492 4.25 —
r. Booklet pane of 4, #494c, 494d, 2 #493 9.75 —
Complete booklet, #494m-494r 31.00

Complete booklet sold for $14.95. A sheet of 12 containing Nos. 494a-494l + 12 labels that could not be personalized sold for $15.95.

Crabs — A123

No. 495: a, Red crab. b, Robber crab.
No. 496: a, Jackson's crab. b, Blue crab.

2011, June 7 **Litho.** *Perf. 14¾x14*

495 A123 60c Horiz. pair, #a-b 4.00 4.00
496 A123 $1.20 Horiz. pair, #a-b 7.50 7.50

Christmas A124

Santa Claus: 55c, Giving cracker to crab. $1.50, In water holding flippers.

2011, Oct. 31 *Perf. 14x14¾*

497 A124 55c multi 1.75 1.75
498 A124 $1.50 multi 4.00 4.00

Booklet Stamps
Self-Adhesive

Serpentine Die Cut 11¼ Syncopated

499 A124 55c multi 1.75 1.75
a. Booklet pane of 10 17.50
500 A124 $1.50 multi 4.00 4.00
a. Booklet pane of 5 20.00

New Year 2012 (Year of the Dragon) — A125

Designs: 60c, Dragon. $1.80, Chinese character for "dragon."
No. 503: a, Rat. b, Ox. c, "Dragon" in circle. d, Snake. e, Tiger. f, Rabbit. g, Horse. h, Pig. i, Goat. j, Monkey. k, Rooster. l, Dog.

Litho. with Foil Application

2012, Jan. 10 *Perf. 14¾x14*

501 A125 60c multi 1.40 1.40
502 A125 $1.80 multi 4.00 4.00
a. Souvenir sheet of 2, #501-502 5.50 5.50
b. As "a," with 2012 Beijing Intl. Stamp & Coin Expo overprint in sheet margin in gold 5.00 5.00
503 Sheet of 14, #501-502, 503a-503l 11.00 11.00
a.-d. A125 15c Any single .35 .35
e.-h. A125 20c Any single .45 .45
i.-l. A125 25c Any single .55 .55
m. Booklet pane of 4, #503c, 503d, 2 #502 8.75 —
n. Booklet pane of 4, #503g, 503i, 2 #501 4.00 —
o. Booklet pane of 4, #503j, 503k, 2 #501 4.00 —
p. Booklet pane of 4, #503h, 503l, 2 #501 4.00 —
q. Booklet pane of 4, #503a, 503b, 2 #501 3.50 —
r. Booklet pane of 4, #503e, 503f, 2 #501 3.75 —
Complete booklet, #503m-503r 28.00

Complete booklet sold for $12.95. Issued: No. 502b, 11/2.

Ferns
A126

No. 504: a, Tectaria devexa. b, Asplenium listeri.
No. 505: a, Bolbitis heteroclita. b, Pteris tripartita.

2012, May 1 Litho. *Perf. 14x14¾*

504	Horiz. pair	3.00	3.00
a.-b.	A126 60c Either single	1.25	1.25
505	Horiz. pair	6.00	6.00
a.-b.	A126 $1.20 Either single	2.50	2.50

Christmas — A127

Designs: 55c, Sand sculpture of Santa Claus, frigatebirds, turtle and crabs. $1.60, Santa Claus decorating sand sculpture of Christmas tree, starfish, crabs, bird.

2012, Nov. 1 *Perf. 14¾x14*

506	A127 55c multi	1.50	1.50
507	A127 $1.60 multi	3.75	3.75
a.	Souvenir sheet of 2, #506-507	5.25	5.25

Booklet Stamp
Self-Adhesive

Serpentine Die Cut 11¼ Syncopated

508	A127 $1.60 multi	3.75	3.75
a.	Booklet pane of 5	19.00	

New Year Types of 2008-12 and

New Year 2013 (Year of the Snake) — A128

Rat and Apples — A129

Flower
A130

Designs: No. 509, 60c, Snake. $1.80, Chinese character for "snake."
No. 511: a, Rat and apples. b, Ox and cherries. c, Dragon and tomatoes. d, Snake amd eggs. e, Tiger and fish. f, Rabbit and oranges. g, Horse and bananas. h, Boar and spinach. i, Goat and onions. j, Monkey and grapes. k, Rooster and pumpkins. l, Dog and milk bottles.
No. 512: a, Like No 511g. b, Like No. 511h. c, Like No. 511i. d, Like No. 511j. e, Like No. 511k. f, Like No. 511l. g, Rat with purple foil. h, Ox with purple foil. i, Tiger with purple foil. j, Rabbit with purple foil. k, Dragon with purple foil. l, Like No. 509.

Litho. With Foil Application

2013, Jan. 13 *Perf. 14¾x14*

509	A128 60c multi	1.25	1.25
510	A128 $1.80 multi	3.75	3.75
a.	Souvenir sheet of 2, #509-510	5.25	5.25
b.	As "a," with emblem overprinted in gold in sheet margin	4.75	4.75
511	Sheet of 14, #509-510, 511a-511l	10.00	10.00
a.-d.	A129 15c Any single	.30	.30
e.-h.	A129 20c Any single	.40	.40
i.-l.	A129 25c multi	.55	.55
m.	Booklet pane of 4, #511d, 511g, 2 #510	9.00	—
n.	Booklet pane of 4, #511i, 511j, 2 #509	4.00	—
o.	Booklet pane of 4, #511k, 511l, 2 #509	4.00	—
p.	Booklet pane of 4, #511a, 511h, 2 #509	3.50	—
q.	Booklet pane of 4, #511b, 511e, 2 #509	3.50	—
r.	Booklet pane of 4, #511c, 511f, 2 #509	3.50	—
	Complete booklet, #511m-511r	27.50	

Issued: No. 510b, 9/26. China International Collection Expo (No. 510b).

Self-Adhesive

Serpentine Die Cut 12¼, Serpentine Die Cut (#512m)

512	Sheet of 13	25.00	
a.-b.	A129 20c Either single	.70	.70
c.-f.	A129 25c Any single	.90	.90
g.	A113 50c pur & multi	1.75	1.75
h.	A117 55c pur & multi	2.00	2.00
i.	A119 55c pur & multi	2.00	2.00
j.	A122 60c pur & multi	2.10	2.10
k.	A125 60c pur & multi	2.10	2.10
l.	A128 60c pur & multi	2.10	2.10
m.	A130 $1 pur & multi	3.75	3.75

Complete booklet sold for $12.95. No. 512 sold for $9.95.

Fish — A131

No. 513: a, Cocos angelfish. b, Ladder wrasse.
$1.20, Redtooth triggerfish. $1.80, Red-striped pigfish.

2013, May 21 Litho. *Perf. 14x14¾*

513	Horiz. pair	2.50	2.50
a.-b.	A131 60c Either single	1.25	1.25
514	A131 $1.20 multi	2.50	2.50
515	A131 $1.80 multi	3.50	3.50
	Nos. 513-515 (3)	8.60	8.50

Flowering Shrubs — A132

No. 516: a, Colubrina pedunculata. b, Abutilon listeri.
No. 517: a, Urena lobata var. sinuata. b, Indigofera hirsuta.
No. 518, Like No. 516a. No. 519, Like No. 516b.

2013, June 18 *Perf. 14¾x14*

516	A132 60c Horiz. pair, #a-b	2.40	2.40
517	A132 $1.20 Horiz. pair, #a-b	4.50	4.50

Booklet Stamps
Self-Adhesive

Serpentine Die Cut 11¼ Syncopated

518	A132 60c multi	1.25	1.25
519	A132 60c multi	1.25	1.25
a.	Booklet pane of 10, 5 each #518-519	16.00	

Christmas
A133

Designs: 55c, Santa Claus riding on frigatebird. $1.80, Frigatebird and crab in balloon gondola.

2013, Nov. 1 Litho. *Perf. 14x14¾*

520	A133 55c multi	1.10	1.10
521	A133 $1.80 multi	3.50	3.50
a.	Souvenir sheet of 2, #520-521	5.00	5.00

Booklet Stamps
Self-Adhesive

Serpentine Die Cut 11¼ Syncopated

522	A133 $1.80 multi	3.50	3.50
a.	Booklet pane of 5	20.00	

Litho. With Foil Application

523	A133 $1.80 multi	3.50	3.50
a.	Booklet pane of 10	40.00	

New Year 2014 (Year of the Horse) — A134

Designs: 60c, Horse. $1.80, Chinese character for "horse."
No. 526: a, Rat. b, Ox. c, Dragon. d, Snake. e, Tiger. f, Rabbit. g, Horse, diff. h, Pig. i, Goat. j, Monkey. k, Rooster. l, Dog.

Litho. With Foil Application

2014, Jan. 7 *Perf. 14¾x14*

524	A134 60c multi	1.10	1.10
525	A134 $1.80 multi	3.25	3.25
a.	Souvenir sheet of 2, #524-525	4.50	4.50
526	Sheet of 14, #524-525, 526a-526l	8.75	8.75
a.-d.	A134 15c Any single	.25	.25
e.-h.	A134 20c Any single	.35	.35
i.-l.	A134 25c Any single	.45	.45
m.	Booklet pane of 4, #526g, 526i, 2 #525	7.75	—
n.	Booklet pane of 4, #526j, 526k, 2 #524	3.25	—
o.	Booklet pane of 4, #526h, 526l, 2 #524	3.25	—
p.	Booklet pane of 4, #526a, 526b, 2 #524	3.00	—
q.	Booklet pane of 4, #526e, 526f, 2 #524	3.25	
r.	Booklet pane of 4, #526c, 526d, 2 #524	3.00	—
	Complete booklet, #526m-526r	23.50	

Complete booklet sold for $12.95.

Christmas Island National Park — A135

Designs: No. 527a, Forest. No. 527b, Beach. $1.40, Sea cliffs. $2.10, Wetlands.

2014, June 17 Litho. *Perf. 14x14¾*

527	Horiz. pair	3.00	3.00
a.-b.	A135 70c Either single	1.40	1.40
528	A135 $1.40 multi	2.75	2.75
529	A135 $2.10 multi	4.00	4.00
	Nos. 527-529 (3)	9.75	9.75

Red Crab Migration
A136

Designs: 70c, Red crab. $2.10, Red crabs migrating.

2014, Aug. 12 Litho. *Perf. 14x14¾*

530-531	A136 Set of 2	5.25	5.25

Christmas — A137

Designs: 65c, Crab offering gift to Santa Claus. $1.80, Crab holding gift-wrapped coconut.

2014, Oct. 31 Litho. *Perf. 14¾x14*

532	A137 65c multi	1.25	1.25
533	A137 $1.80 multi	3.25	3.25
a.	Souvenir sheet of 2, #532-533	4.50	4.50

Booklet Stamps
Self-Adhesive

Serpentine Die Cut 11¼ Syncopated

534	A137 65c multi	1.25	1.25
a.	Booklet pane of 10 + 10 etiquettes	12.50	
535	A137 $1.80 multi	3.25	3.25
a.	Booklet pane of 5	16.50	

New Year 2015 (Year of the Goat) — A138

Designs: 70c, Goat. $2.10, Chinese character for "goat."
No. 538: a, Rat. b, Ox. c, Dragon. d, Snake. e, Goat, diff. f, Monkey. g, Rooster. h, Dog. i, Tiger. j, Rabbit. k, Horse. l, Pig.

Litho. With Foil Application

2015, Jan. 8 *Perf. 14¾x14*

536	A138 70c multi	1.10	1.10
537	A138 $2.10 multi	3.25	3.25
a.	Souvenir sheet of 2, #536-537	4.50	4.50
538	Sheet of 14, #536-537, 538a-538l	9.00	9.00
a.-d.	A138 15c Any single	.25	.25
e.-h.	A138 25c Any single	.40	.40
i.-l.	A138 30c Any single	.50	.50
m.	Booklet pane of 4, #538e, 538f, 2 #537	8.00	—
n.	Booklet pane of 4, #538g, 538h, 2 #536	3.25	—
o.	Booklet pane of 4, #538a, 538l, 2 #536	3.25	—
p.	Booklet pane of 4, #538b, 538i, 2 #536	3.25	—
q.	Booklet pane of 4, #538c, 538j, 2 #536	3.25	
r.	Booklet pane of 4, #538d, 538k, 2 #536	3.25	—
	Complete booklet, #538m-538r	24.50	

Complete booklet sold for $14.95.

Christmas — A139

Designs: 65c, Waterfall, Christmas tree made of red crabs. $1.80, Red crabs, snowman made of turtle and coconut.

2015, Oct. 30 Litho. *Perf. 14¾x14*

539	A139 65c multi	.95	.95
540	A139 $1.80 multi	2.60	2.60
a.	Souvenir sheet of 2, #539-540	3.75	3.75

Booklet Stamps
Self-Adhesive

Serpentine Die Cut 11¼ Syncopated

541	A139 $1.80 multi	2.60	2.60
a.	Booklet pane of 5	13.00	

Litho. With Foil Application

542	A139 65c multi	.95	.95
a.	Booklet pane of 10	9.50	

CILICIA

sə-'li-sh͵ē-͵ə

LOCATION — A territory of Turkey, in Southeastern Asia Minor
GOVT. — Former French occupation
AREA — 6,238 sq. mi.
POP. — 383,645
CAPITAL — Adana

British and French forces occupied Cilicia in 1918 and in 1919 its control was transferred to the French. Eventually part of Cilicia was assigned to the French Mandated Territory of Syria but by the Lausanne Treaty of 1923 which fixed the boundary between Syria and Turkey, Cilicia reverted to Turkey.

40 Paras = 1 Piaster

Issued under French Occupation

Numbers in parentheses are those of basic Turkish or French stamps.

Turkish Stamps of 1913-19 Handstamped

Perf. 11½, 12, 12½, 13½

1919 **Unwmk.**

On Pictorial Issue of 1913

2 A24 2pa red lilac (254) 9.00 9.00
a. Inverted overprint 17.50 17.50
b. Double overprint 27.50 27.50
3 A25 4pa dk brown (255) 7.25 7.25
a. Inverted overprint 17.50 17.50
b. Double overprint 20.00 20.00
4 A27 6pa dk blue (257) 27.50 20.00
a. Inverted overprint 32.50 32.50
b. Double overprint 50.00 50.00
5 A32 1¾pi slate & red brown (262) 8.75 8.75
a. Inverted overprint 17.50 17.50
b. Double overprint 20.00 20.00

On Issue of 1915

6 A17 1pi blue (300) 3.75 3.75
a. Inverted overprint 8.00 8.00
b. Double overprint 10.00 10.000
c. In pair with unovptd. stamp 20.00 20.00
7 A21 20pa carmine rose (318) 13.50 12.00
a. Inverted overprint 20.00 20.00
b. Double overprint 35.00 35.00
9 A22 20pa carmine rose (330) 35.00 32.50
a. Inverted overprint 40.00 40.00
b. Double overprint 40.00 40.00

On Commemorative Issue of 1916

9A A41 5pa green (345) 130.00 92.50
10 A41 20pa ultra (347) 7.25 7.25
a. Double overprint 12.00 12.00
11 A41 1pi violet & black (348) 9.50 9.50
a. Double overprint 27.50 27.50
b. Perf 12½ 9.50 9.50
c. In pair with unovptd. stamp 16.00 16.00
12 A41 5pi yel brown & black (349) 4.00 4.00
a. Double overprint 6.50 6.50

On Issue of 1916-18

13 A44 10pa grn (424) 8.75 8.75
a. Perf 11½ (424a) 8.75 8.75
b. Double overprint 24.00 24.00
14 A47 50pa ultra (428) 45.00 35.00
a. Perf 11½ (428a) 45.00 35.00
b. Double overprint 90.00 90.00
15 A51 25pi carmine, *straw* (434) 8.75 8.75
16 A52 50pi car (437) 8.75 8.75
17 A52 50pi ind (438) 32.50 32.50

On Issue of 1917

18 A53 5pi on 2pa Prus blue (547) 15.00 15.00
a. Perf 11½ (547c) 15.00 15.00

On Issue of 1919

19 A47 50pa ultra (555) 40.00 32.50
a. Perf 11½ (555a) 40.00 32.50
b. Double overprint 80.00 80.00
20 A48 2pi org brn & indigo (556) 40.00 32.50
21 A49 5pi pale blue & black (557a) 40.00 32.50
a. Perf 11½ (557) 40.00 32.50
b. Perf 11½x12½ (557b) 40.00 32.50
c. Double overprint 90.00 90.00

On Newspaper Stamp of 1916

22 A10 5pa on 10pa gray green (P137) 4.75 4.75
d. Inverted overprint 11.00 11.00
e. Double overprint 14.00 14.00

On Semi-Postal Stamps of 1915

22A A21 20pa car rose (B8) 92.50 80.00
22B A21 1pi ultra (B9) 2,250. 1,700.
22C A21 1pi ultra (B13) 1,900. 1,200.

On Semi-Postal Stamps of 1916

23 A17 1pi bl (B19) 10.50 10.50
a. Inverted overprint 16.00 16.00
b. Double overprint 16.00 16.00
c. Perf 13¼ 25.00 25.00
24 A21 20pa car rose (B28) 3.75 3.75
a. Inverted overprint 7.50 7.50
b. Double overprint 10.00 10.00
25 A21 1pi ultra (B29) 8.75 8.75
a. Inverted overprint 15.00 15.00
b. Double overprint 25.00 25.00

Turkish Stamps of 1913-18 Handstamped

1919

On Pictorial Issue of 1913

31 A24 2pa red lil (254) 4.00 4.00
a. Inverted overprint 6.50 6.50
b. Double overprint 12.00 12.00
c. In pair with unovptd. stamp 16.00 16.00
32 A25 4pa dk brn (255) 15.00 15.00
a. Inverted overprint 22.00 22.00
b. Double overprint 40.00 40.00

On Issue of 1915

33 A17 1pi blue (300) 13.50 13.50
a. Inverted overprint 20.00 20.00
b. Double overprint 35.00 35.00
34 A22 20pa car rose (330) 5.00 5.00
a. Inverted overprint 9.50 9.50
b. Double overprint 15.00 15.00
c. In pair with unovptd. stamp 20.00 20.00

On Commemorative Issue of 1916

35 A41 20pa ultra (347) 15.00 15.00
a. Inverted overprint 30.00 30.00
b. Perf 12½ (347a) 15.00 15.00
36 A41 1pi vio & blk (348) 3.25 3.25
a. Inverted overprint 6.50 6.50
b. Perf 12½ (348a) 3.25 3.25

On Issue of 1917

40 A53 5pi on 2pa Prus bl (547) 13.50 13.50
a. Perf 11½ (547c) 13.50 13.50

On Newspaper Stamp of 1916

41 A10 5pa on 10pa gray grn (P137) 27.50 27.50
a. Inverted overprint 50.00 50.00
b. In pair with unovptd. stamp 60.00 60.00

On Semi-Postal Stamp of 1915

41A A21 20pa car rose (B8) 210.00 150.00

On Semi-Postal Stamps of 1916

42 A17 1pi blue (B19) 6.50 6.50
a. Inverted overprint 12.00 12.00
b. Double overprint 13.00 13.00
c. Perf 12 (B19a) 8.00 8.00
d. Perf 12x13¼ (B19b) 8.00 8.00
43 A21 20pa car rose (B28) 3.25 3.25
a. Inverted overprint 8.00 *8.00*
b. Double overprint 9.00 *9.00*
Nos. 31-43 (11) 316.50 256.50

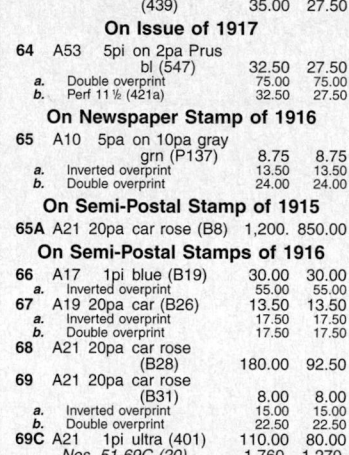

Turkish Stamps of 1913-19 Handstamped

1919

On Pictorial Issue of 1913

51 A24 2pa red lil (254) 11.00 11.00
a. Inverted overprint 16.00 16.00
b. Double overprint 25.00 25.00
c. In pair with unovptd. stamp 40.00 40.00
52 A25 4pa dk brn (255) 3.75 3.75
a. Inverted overprint 7.50 7.50
b. Double overprint 10.00 10.00

On Issue of 1915

53 A17 1pi blue (300) 5.50 5.50
a. Inverted overprint 11.00 11.00
b. Double overprint 15.00 15.00
55 A22 5pa ocher (328) 40.00 35.00
a. Double overprint 80.00 80.00
56 A22 20pa car rose (330) 4.00 4.00
a. Inverted overprint 8.00 8.00
b. Double overprint 12.00 12.00
c. In pair with unovptd. stamp 17.50 17.50

On Commemorative Issue of 1916

57 A41 20pa ultra (347) 4.00 4.00
a. Inverted overprint 8.00 8.00
b. Double overprint 12.00 12.00
c. Double overprint, one inverted 9.50 9.50
d. In pair with unovptd. stamp 17.50 17.50
58 A41 1pi vio & blk (348) 3.75 3.75
a. Inverted overprint 6.50 6.50
b. Double overprint 10.00 10.00
59 A41 5pi yel brn & blk (349) 12.00 12.00
a. Inverted overprint 16.00 16.00
b. Double overprint 16.00 16.00

On Issue of 1916

59A A17 1pi blue (372) — —

On Issue of 1916-18

60 A43 5pa org (421) 45.00 40.00
a. Inverted overprint 70.00 70.00
b. Perf 11½ (421a) 45.00 40.00
61 A46 1pi dl vio (426) 13.50 13.50
a. Inverted overprint 21.00 21.00
b. Double overprint 35.00 35.00
63 A52 50pi green, *straw* (439) 35.00 27.50

On Issue of 1917

64 A53 5pi on 2pa Prus bl (547) 32.50 27.50
a. Double overprint 75.00 75.00
b. Perf 11½ (421a) 32.50 27.50

On Newspaper Stamp of 1916

65 A10 5pa on 10pa gray grn (P137) 8.75 8.75
a. Inverted overprint 13.50 13.50
b. Double overprint 24.00 24.00

On Semi-Postal Stamp of 1915

65A A21 20pa car rose (B8) 1,200. 850.00

On Semi-Postal Stamps of 1916

66 A17 1pi blue (B19) 30.00 30.00
a. Inverted overprint 55.00 55.00
67 A19 20pa car (B26) 13.50 13.50
a. Inverted overprint 17.50 17.50
b. Double overprint 17.50 17.50
68 A21 20pa car rose (B28) 180.00 92.50
69 A21 20pa car rose (B31) 8.00 8.00
a. Inverted overprint 15.00 15.00
b. Double overprint 22.50 22.50
69C A21 1pi ultra (401) 110.00 80.00
Nos. 51-69C (20) 1,760. 1,270.

Turkey No. 424 Handstamped

1919

71 A44 10pa green (420) 9.50 9.50
a. Inverted overprint 17.50 17.50
b. Double overprint 25.00 25.00
c. Perf 11½ (420a) 11.00 11.00

"T.E.O." stands for "Territoires Ennemis Occupés."

Turkish Stamps of 1913-19 Overprinted in Black, Red or Blue

In this setting there are various broken and wrong font letters and the letter "i" is sometimes replaced by a "t."

1919

On Pictorial Issue of 1913

75 A30 1pi blue (R) (260) 4.75 4.75
a. Inverted overprint 11.00 11.00
b. Double overprint 11.00 11.00
c. Double overprint, one inverted 20.00 20.00

On Issue of 1915

76 A21 20pa car rose (318) 8.75 8.75

On Commemorative Issue of 1916

76A A41 5pa grn (345) 200.00 110.00
77 A41 20pa ultra (347) 13.50 13.50
a. Inverted overprint 20.00 20.00
b. Double overprint 30.00 30.00
c. Perf 12½ (347a) 13.50 13.50
78 A41 1pi vio & blk (348) 24.00 24.00
a. Inverted overprint 35.00 35.00
b. Double overprint 60.00 60.00
c. Double overprint, one inverted 65.00 65.00

On Issue of 1916-18

79 A43 5pa org (Bl) (421) 4.75 4.75
a. Inverted overprint 9.50 9.50
b. Double overprint 13.00 13.00
c. Double overprint, one inverted 11.00 11.00
d. Perf 11½ (421a) 4.75 4.75
80 A44 10pa grn (424) 8.75 8.75
a. Inverted overprint 16.00 16.00
b. Double overprint 22.50 22.50
c. Double overprint, one inverted 20.00 20.00
d. Perf 11½ (424a) 8.75 8.75
81 A45 20pa dp rose (Bk) (425) 27.50 27.50
a. Double overprint 60.00 60.00
82 A45 20pa dp rose (Bl) (425) 1.00 1.00
a. Inverted overprint 5.50 5.50
b. Double overprint 8.00 8.00
c. Double overprint, one inverted 10.00 10.00
83 A48 2pi org brn & indigo (429) 1.60 1.60
a. Double overprint 5.50 5.50
b. Perf 11½ (429a) 1.60 1.60
83C A49 5pi pale blue & black (R) (430) 1.60 1.60
a. Inverted overprint 9.50 9.50
b. Double overprint 9.50 9.50
c. Double overprint, one inverted 12.00 12.00
d. Perf 11½ (430a) 1.60 1.60
84 A51 25pi car, *straw* (434) 5.50 5.50
a. Inverted overprint 15.00 15.00
b. Double overprint 20.00 20.00
c. Double overprint, one inverted 13.50 13.50
85 A52 50pi grn, *straw* (439) 92.50 87.50
a. Inverted overprint 150.00 150.00
b. Double overprint 130.00 130.00
c. Double overprint, one inverted 160.00 160.00

On Issue of 1917

85A A53 5pi on 2pa Prus bl (547) —
86 A53 5pi on 2pa Prus bl (548) 13.50 13.50
a. Perf 11½ (548c) 13.50 13.50

On Newspaper Stamps of 1916-19

87 A10 5pa on 10p gray green (P137) 2.25 2.25
a. Inverted overprint 5.50 5.50
b. Double overprint 7.00 7.00
c. Double overprint, one inverted 13.50 13.50
88 A21 5pa on 2pa ol green (P173) 1.00 1.00
a. Inverted overprint 5.50 5.50
b. Double overprint 7.00 7.00
c. Double overprint, one inverted 6.50 6.50

On Semi-Postal Stamps of 1915-17

90 A21 20pa car rose (B28) 8.75 8.75
a. Double overprint 16.00 16.00
91 A41 10pa car (B42) 3.25 3.25
a. Inverted overprint 7.25 7.25
b. Double overprint 9.00 9.00
c. Double overprint, one inverted 12.00 12.00
d. Perf 12½ (B42b) 3.25 3.25
92 A11 10pa on 20pa vio brn (B38) 3.25 3.25
a. Inverted overprint 9.50 9.50
b. Double overprint 10.00 10.00

c. Double overprint, one inverted 13.50 13.50
93 SP1 10pa red vio (B46) 2.50 2.50
a. Overprint sideways 8.00 8.00

It is understood that the newspaper and semi-postal stamps overprinted "Cilicie" were used as ordinary postage stamps.

A1

1920 Blue Surcharge *Perf. 11½*

98 A1 70pa on 5pa red 2.40 2.40
a. Double surcharge 40.00 40.00
b. Triple surcharge 240.00
c. Inverted surcharge 35.00 35.00
d. Double overprint, one inverted 45.00 45.00
e. In pair with unovptd. stamp 110.00
99 A1 3½pi on 5pa red 3.00 2.75
a. Se-tenant with No. 98, horiz. pair 120.00 120.00
b. As "a," inverted surcharge 240.00 240.00
c. Double surcharge 40.00 40.00
d. Inverted surcharge 35.00 35.00
e. Double surcharge, one inverted 45.00 45.00

Nos. 98-99 exist with a variety of surcharge misspellings. For detailed listings, see the *Scott Classic Specialized Catalogue.*

French Offices in Turkey No. 26 Surcharged

1920 *Perf. 14x13½*

100 A3 20pa on 10c rose red (I) 2.00 2.00
a. "PARAS" omitted 72.50 72.50

Three types of "20" exist on No. 100: I, "2" bold; II "2" faint; III, "0" distinctly taller than "2." See the *Scott Classic Specialized Catalogue of Stamps and Covers* for detailed listings.

Stamps of France, 1900-17, Surcharged

1920

101 A16 5pa on 2c vio brn 1.60 1.60
102 A22 10pa on 5c green 2.00 2.00
103 A22 20pa on 10c red 4.00 4.00
104 A22 1pi on 25c blue 2.75 2.25
105 A20 2pi on 15c gray green 12.00 12.00
106 A18 5pi on 40c red & gray bl 26.00 26.00
107 A18 10pi on 50c bis brn & lav 32.50 32.50
108 A18 50pi on 1fr claret & ol grn 180.00 180.00
109 A18 100pi on 5fr dk bl & buff 900.00 900.00
Nos. 101-109 (9) 1,160. 1,160.

Nos. 106 to 109 surcharged in four lines.
"O.M.F." stands for "Occupation Militaire Francaise."

Stamps of France, 1917, Surcharged

1920

110 A16 5pa on 2c vio brn (109b) 13.00
111 A22 10pa on 5c grn (110b) 13.00
b. Double surcharge 75.00
c. On ordinary paper (110) 19.00
112 A22 20pa on 10c red (162) 9.75
a. Inverted surcharge 75.00
b. Double surcharge 67.50
113 A22 1pi on 25c bl (168d) 6.00
114 A20 2pi on 15c gray grn (139c) 27.00
115 A18 5pi on 40c red & gray bl (121) 50.00
116 A18 20pi on 1fr claret & ol grn (125) 190.00
a. "O.M.F. Cilicie" omitted 625.00
b. Double surcharge 625.00
Nos. 110-116 (7) 308.75

On Nos. 115 and 116 "SAND. EST" is placed vertically. "Sand. Est" is an abbreviation of Sandjak de l'Est (Eastern County).
Nos. 110-116 were prepared for use, but never issued.

Stamps of France, 1900-17, Surcharged

First Setting: 1.75-2mm spacing between "Cilicie" and figures of value

1920

117 A16 5pa on 2c vio brn 1.25 1.25
a. Inverted surcharge 32.50 27.50
b. "Cililie" 35.00 35.00
c. Surcharge 5pi (error) 60.00 60.00
h. Double surcharge 35.00 35.00
119 A22 10pa on 5c green 1.50 1.50
a. Inverted surcharge 30.00 26.00
b. Surch. 5pa (error), upright 55.00 55.00
c. Surch. 5pa (error), invtd. 75.00 67.50
121 A22 20pa on 10c red 1.75 1.75
a. Inverted surcharge 32.50 27.50
b. Surch. 10pa (error), upright 60.00 60.00
c. Surch. 10pa (error), invtd. 80.00 72.50
f. Double surcharge 35.00 35.00
g. Double surcharge, one inverted 47.50 47.50
122 A22 1pi on 25c blue 2.00 2.00
a. Double surcharge 72.50 72.50
b. Inverted surcharge 55.00 52.50
123 A20 2pi on 15c gray green 2.25 2.25
a. Double surcharge 45.00 45.00
b. Inverted surcharge 35.00 32.50
c. Double surcharge, one inverted 55.00 55.00
124 A18 5pi on 40c red & gray blue 4.00 4.00
a. Double surcharge 65.00 65.00
b. Inverted surcharge 40.00 40.00
e. "PIASRTES" 72.50 72.50
125 A18 10pi on 50c bis brn & lav 12.50 12.50
a. Double surcharge 60.00 60.00
b. Inverted surcharge 55.00 47.50
c. First "S" in "PIASTRES" inverted 110.00 110.00
e. "PIASRTES" 72.50 72.50
126 A18 50pi on 1fr claret & ol grn 17.50 17.50
a. Inverted surcharge 130.00
b. Double surcharge 180.00
e. "PIASRTES" 87.50
127 A18 100pi on 5fr dk bl & buff 45.00 45.00
a. Inverted surcharge 180.00
d. "PIASRTES" *925.00*
Nos. 117-127 (9) 87.75 87.75

This surcharge has "O.M.F." in thicker letters than the preceding issues.
There were two printings of this surcharge, which may be distinguished by the spacing between "Cilicie" and figures of value. See the *Scott Classic Specialized Catalogue of Stamps and Covers* for detailed listings.
For overprints see Nos. C1-C2.

AIR POST STAMPS

Nos. 123 and 124 Handstamped

Perf. 14x13½
1920, July 15 **Unwmk.**

C1 A20 2pi on 15c gray grn *9,250.* 9,250.
C2 A18 5pi on 40c red & gray blue 9,500. 9,500.
a. "PIASRTES"

A very limited number of Nos. C1 and C2 were used on two air mail flights between Adana and Aleppo. At a later date impressions from a new handstamp were struck "to oblige" on stamps of the regular issue of 1920 (Nos. 123, 124, 125 and 126) that were in stock at the Adana Post Office.

Counterfeits exist.

POSTAGE DUE STAMPS

Turkish Postage Due Stamps of 1914 Handstamped

Handstamped

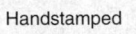

1919 **Unwmk.** *Perf. 12*

J1 D1 5pa claret 22.00 22.00
a. Inverted overprint 35.00 35.00
b. Double surcharge 50.00 50.00
J2 D2 20pa red 22.50 22.50
a. Inverted overprint 35.00 35.00
b. Double surcharge 50.00 50.00
J3 D3 1pi dark blue 35.00 35.00
a. Inverted overprint 50.00 50.00
J4 D4 2pi slate 45.00 45.00
a. Inverted overprint 65.00 65.00
Nos. J1-J4 (4) 124.50 124.50

Handstamped

J5 D1 5pa claret 26.00 26.00
a. Inverted overprint 40.00 40.00
b. Double overprint 55.00 55.00
J6 D2 20pa red 30.00 30.00
a. Inverted overprint 45.00 45.00
b. Double overprint 60.00 60.00
J7 D3 1pi dark blue 35.00 35.00
a. Inverted overprint 47.50 47.50
J8 D4 2pi slate 35.00 35.00
a. Inverted overprint 47.50 47.50
Nos. J5-J8 (4) 126.00 126.00

Handstamped

J9 D1 5pa claret 22.00 22.00
a. Inverted overprint 32.50 32.50
b. Double overprint 32.50 32.50
J10 D2 20pa red 22.50 22.50
a. Inverted overprint 32.50 32.50
b. Double overprint 35.00 35.00
J11 D3 1pi dark blue 35.00 35.00
a. Inverted overprint 47.50 47.50
J12 D4 2pi slate 22.00 22.00
a. Inverted overprint 32.50 32.50
Nos. J9-J12 (4) 101.50 101.50

Postage Due Stamps of France Surcharged

1921

J13 D2 1pi on 10c choc 11.00 11.00
a. Inverted overprint 130.00
J14 D2 2pi on 20c olive grn 11.00 11.00
a. Inverted overprint 130.00
J15 D2 3pi on 30c red 11.00 11.00
a. Inverted overprint 92.50
J16 D2 4pi on 50c vio brn 10.50 10.50
a. Inverted overprint 92.50
Nos. J13-J16 (4) 43.50 43.50

COCHIN CHINA

'kō-chən 'chī-nə

LOCATION — The southernmost state of French Indo-China in the Cambodian Peninsula.
GOVT. — French Colony
AREA — 26,476 sq. mi.
POP. — 4,615,968
CAPITAL — Saigon

100 Centimes = 1 Franc

Surcharged in Black on Stamps of French Colonies

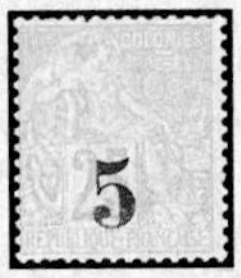

a

b

c

1886-87 **Unwmk.** *Perf. 14x13½*

1 A9(a) 5c on 25c yel, *straw* 225.00 120.00
2 A9(b) 5c on 2c brn, *buff* 40.00 *32.50*
3 A9(b) 5c on 25c yel, *straw* 32.50 27.50
a. Inverted surcharge *275.00* *275.00*
4 A9(c) 5c on 25c blk, *rose* ('87) 60.00 47.50
a. Double surch., one of type b *3,750.* *2,750.*
b. Triple surch., two of type b — —
c. Inverted surcharge 375.00 375.00
d. Double surch., both type "a" *2,750.* *3,250.*
e. Triple surch., types "a," "b" and "c" *8,750.*
Nos. 1-4 (4) 357.50 227.50

1888

5 A9 15c on half of 30c brn, *bis* 100.00

No. 5 was prepared but not issued.
The so-called Postage Due stamps were never issued.
Stamps of Cochin China were superseded by those of Indo-China in 1892.

COCOS ISLANDS

ˈkō-kəs ˈī-ləndz

(Keeling Islands)

LOCATION — Indian Ocean, 1,330 miles northwest of Australia, 580 miles southwest of Java
GOVT. — A territory of Australia
AREA — 6 sq. mi.
POP. — 670 (1994)

Of 27 small coral islands making up two atolls, two islands are inhabited. Cocos Islands stamps are also valid within Australia.

12 Pence = 1 Shilling
100 Cents = 1 Dollar (1969)

Catalogue values for all unused stamps in this country are for Never Hinged items.

Copra Industry — A1

Super Constellation A2

Map of Islands — A3

Designs: 1sh, Coco palms. 2sh, Sailboat (dukong). 2sh3p, Fairy tern.

Perf. 14½

1963, June 11 Unwmk. Engr.

1	A1	3p dk red brown		1.50	1.40
2	A2	5p vio blue		1.75	1.00
3	A3	8p red		2.00	1.75
4	A1	1sh green		2.00	1.00
5	A3	2sh dull purple		8.00	3.00
6	A2	2sh3p green		15.00	5.00
		Nos. 1-6 (6)		30.25	13.15
		Set, hinged		17.50	

"Simpson and His Donkey" by Wallace Anderson — A3a

1965, Apr. 14 Photo. *Perf. 13½x13*

7	A3a	5p brt grn, sepia & blk	.85	.85

ANZAC issue. See note after Australia No. 387.

Nos. 8-31 are valid for postage in Australia.

Turbo Lajonkairii — A4

Blenny — A5

Designs: 2c, Tridacna crocea (shell). 3c, Tridacna derasa (shell). 5c, Porites cocosensis (coral). 6c, Flyingfish. 10c, Banded rail (bird). 15c, Java sparrow. 20c, Red-tailed tropic bird. 30c, Sooty tern. 50c, Eastern reef heron. $1, Great frigate bird.

Perf. 13½

1969, July 9 Unwmk. Photo.

Size: 21½x27mm, 26½x22mm

8	A4	1c multicolored	.30	*.55*
9	A4	2c multicolored	1.00	.70
10	A5	3c multicolored	.40	.25
11	A5	4c multicolored	.30	*.45*
a.		Salmon omitted	2,000.	
12	A5	5c multicolored	.35	.30
13	A5	6c multicolored	.80	.75
14	A5	10c multicolored	.90	.80
15	A5	15c multicolored	.90	.60
16	A5	20c multicolored	.90	.45
17	A5	30c multicolored	.90	.50
18	A4	50c multicolored	.90	.50

Size: 21½x34mm

19	A4	$1 multicolored	2.75	1.50
		Nos. 8-19 (12)	10.40	7.35

"Dragon" — A6

"Juno" — A7

Perf. 13½x13, 13x13½

1976, Mar. 29 Photo.

20	A6	1c shown	.35	.35
21	A7	2c shown	.35	.35
22	A7	5c "Beagle"	.35	.35
23	A7	10c "Sydney"	.40	.40
24	A7	15c "Emden"	.65	.65
25	A7	20c "Ayesha"	.65	.65
26	A6	25c "Islander"	.65	.65
27	A6	30c "Cheshire"	.65	.65
28	A7	35c "Jukung"	.65	.65
29	A7	40c "Scotia"	.65	.65
30	A6	50c "Orontes"	.70	.70
31	A6	$1 Royal Yacht "Gothic"	.90	.90
		Nos. 20-31 (12)	6.95	6.95

Historic ships.

Flag, Southern Cross, Islands' Map — A8

Council Emblem, Sailboat A9

1979, Sept. 3 Litho. *Perf. 15½*

32	A8	20c multicolored	.40	*.35*
33	A9	50c multicolored	.60	*.75*

Inauguration of Cocos Islands' postal service (20c), and establishment of Cocos Islands Council (50c).

Forcipiger Flavissimus A10

Fish: 2c, Chaetodon ornatissimus. 5c, Anthias. 10c, Meyer's coralfish. 15c, Halichoeres. 20c, Amphiprion clarkii. 22c, Balistapus undulatus. 25c, Maori wrasse. 28c, Macropharyngodon meleagris. 30c, Chaetodon madagascariensis. 35c, Centropyge colini. 40c, Bodianus axillaris. 50c, Coris-gaimardi. 55c, Spotted wrasse. 60c, Epinepnelus tauvina. $1, Paracanthurus hepatus. $2, Striped butterflyfish.

1979-80 Litho. *Perf. 15½*

34	A10	1c multicolored	.25	*1.00*
35	A10	2c multicolored	.25	*.35*
36	A10	5c multicolored	.40	*1.05*
37	A10	10c multi ('80)	.25	*1.00*
38	A10	15c multicolored	.35	.35
39	A10	20c multicolored	.45	.35
40	A10	22c multi ('80)	.40	.35
41	A10	25c multi ('80)	.45	*1.00*
42	A10	28c multi ('80)	.40	.35
43	A10	30c multicolored	.55	.45
44	A10	35c multicolored	.65	*1.50*
45	A10	40c multicolored	.70	.55
46	A10	50c multicolored	1.00	.75
47	A10	55c multi ('80)	.85	*1.25*
48	A10	60c multi ('80)	.75	.75
49	A10	$1 multicolored	1.15	*3.00*
50	A10	$2 multi ('80)	2.25	*3.25*
		Nos. 34-50 (17)	11.10	*17.30*

Sailboats in Lagoon A11

Christmas: 25c, Yachts and seagulls, vert.

1979, Oct. 22 Litho. *Perf. 15½*

51	A11	25c multicolored	.40	.30
52	A11	55c multicolored	.60	*.70*

Star of Bethlehem, Map of Cocos Islands A12

Christmas (Map of Cocos Islands and): 28c, Three kings. 60c, Nativity.

1980, Oct. 22 Litho. *Perf. 13½x13*

53	A12	15c multicolored	.25	.25
54	A12	28c multicolored	.30	.30
55	A12	60c multicolored	.70	.70
		Nos. 53-55 (3)	1.25	1.25

Flag and Arms of Great Britain — A13

Australian Territory Status, 25th Anniv. (British Flag and Arms of Past Administrators): No. 57, Ceylon, 1878, 1942-1946. No. 58, Straits Settlements, 1886. No. 59, Singapore, 1946. No. 60, Australia (flag), 1955.

1980, Nov. 24 Litho. *Perf. 13½x13*

56	A13	22c multicolored	.25	.25
57	A13	22c multicolored	.25	.25
58	A13	22c multicolored	.25	.25
59	A13	22c multicolored	.25	.25
60	A13	22c multicolored	.25	.25
a.		Strip of 5, Nos. 56-60	1.75	1.75

Eye of the Wind, Map of Cocos Islands — A14

28c, Expedition routes, horiz. 35c, Francis Drake, Golden Hinde. 60c, Prince Charles, Eye of the Wind.

1980, Dec. 18 *Perf. 13x13½, 13½x13*

61	A14	22c shown	.40	.40
62	A14	28c multicolored	.40	.40
63	A14	35c multicolored	.40	.40
64	A14	60c multicolored	.65	.65
		Nos. 61-64 (4)	1.85	1.85

Operation Drake circumnavigation.

Livestock in Quarantine A15

1981, May 12 Litho. *Perf. 13½x13*

65	A15	22c Aerial view of station	.30	.30
66	A15	45c shown	.40	.40
67	A15	60c Livestock, diff.	.70	.70
		Nos. 65-67 (3)	1.40	1.40

West Island Quarantine Station opening.

Catalina Guba II A16

Inauguration of Air Service to Indian Ocean: No. 69, Avro Lancastrian. No. 70, Douglas DC4 Skymaster, Lockheed Constellation. No. 71, Lockheed Electra. No. 72, Boeing 727.

1981, June 23 Litho. *Perf. 13½x13*

68	A16	22c multicolored	.35	.35
69	A16	22c multicolored	.35	.35
70	A16	22c multicolored	.35	.35
71	A16	22c multicolored	.35	.35
72	A16	22c multicolored	.35	.35
a.		Strip of 5, #68-72	1.75	1.75

Prince Charles and Lady Diana — A17

1981, July 29 Litho. *Perf. 13½x13*

73	A17	24c multicolored	.30	.30
74	A17	60c multicolored	.75	.75

Royal Wedding.

Angels We Have Heard on High — A18

Christmas: Carols: 30c, Shepherds Why this Jubilee. 60c,

1981, Oct. 22 Photo. *Perf. 13½x13*

75	A18	18c shown	.30	.30
76	A18	30c multicolored	.40	.40
77	A18	60c multicolored	.50	.50
		Nos. 75-77 (3)	1.20	1.20

Sesquicentennial of Charles Darwin's Visit — A19

1981, Dec. 28 Litho. *Perf. 13½x13*

78	A19	24c Coral	.35	.35
79	A19	45c Darwin, coral	.45	.45
80	A19	60c Beagle, coral	.65	.65
		Nos. 78-80 (3)	1.45	1.45

Souvenir Sheet

81	Sheet of 2	1.15	1.15
a.	A19 24c Atoll	.55	.55
b.	A19 24c Atoll, diff.	.55	.55

125th Anniv. of Annexation to the British Dominions A20

1982, Mar. 31 Litho. *Perf. 13½x14*

82	A20	24c Queen Victoria	.30	.30
83	A20	45c British flag	.55	.55
84	A20	60c Capt. Fremantle	.65	.65
		Nos. 82-84 (3)	1.50	1.50

Scouting Year — A21

Perf. 13½x14, 14x13½

1982, July 21 Litho.

85	A21	27c Baden-Powell	.45	.45
86	A21	75c Emblem, map, vert.	1.00	1.00

Macroglossum Corythus — A22

1c, Presic villida, vert. 2c, Cephonodes picus. 10c, Chasmina candida, vert. 20c, Nagia linteola. 25c, Eublemma rivula, vert. 30c, Eurrhyparodes tricoloralis, vert. 35c, Hippotion boerhaviae. 40c, Euploea core corinna, vert. 45c, Psara hipponalis. 50c, Danaus chrysippus. 55c, Hypolimas misippus, vert. 60c, Spodoptera litura, vert. $1, Achaea janata, vert. $2, Hippotion velox. $3, Utetheisa pulchelloides.

1982, Sept. 6

87	A22	1c multicolored	1.10	.75
88	A22	2c multicolored	.40	*.50*
89	A22	5c shown	1.60	.90
90	A22	10c multicolored	.40	*.50*
91	A22	20c multicolored	.40	*.60*
92	A22	25c multicolored	.40	*.70*
93	A22	30c multicolored	.40	*.60*
94	A22	35c multicolored	1.75	.90
95	A22	40c multicolored	.40	*.75*
96	A22	45c multicolored	.55	*.75*
97	A22	50c multicolored	.60	*1.40*
98	A22	55c multicolored	.60	*.90*
99	A22	60c multicolored	.65	*1.90*
100	A22	$1 multicolored	2.75	3.25
101	A22	$2 multicolored	2.10	*3.50*
102	A22	$3 multicolored	3.00	3.50
		Nos. 87-102 (16)	17.10	21.40

Christmas A23

1982, Oct. 25 *Perf. 13x13½*

104	A23	21c Holy Family	.25	.25
105	A23	35c Angel	.35	.35
106	A23	75c Flight into Egypt	1.00	1.00
		Nos. 104-106 (3)	1.60	1.60

Christmas — A24

The Birth of Christ: a, God Will Look After Us; b, Our Baby King Jesus; c, Your Saviour is Born; d, Wise Men Followed the Star; e, And Worship the Lord.

1983, Oct. 31 Litho. *Perf. 14x13½*

107	A24	Strip of 5	1.60	1.60
a.-e.		24c any single	.30	.30

Cocos-Malay Culture — A25

Festive Occasions: 45c, Hari Raya. 75c, Melenggok dance. 85c, Wedding.

1984, Jan. 27 Litho. *Perf. 14x13½*

108	A25	45c multicolored	.55	.50
109	A25	75c multicolored	.85	.70
110	A25	85c multicolored	1.10	.80
		Nos. 108-110 (3)	2.50	2.00

75th Anniv. of Barrel Mail (1909-1955) A26

Designs: 35c, Mail distribution, Direction Isld. 55c, Jukongs retrieving barrels from ocean liner. 70c, Morea receiving outgoing barrel mail, 1909. $1, Barrel mail recovery.

1984, Apr. 20 Litho. *Perf. 13½x14*

111	A26	35c multicolored	.55	.55
112	A26	55c multicolored	.95	.95
113	A26	70c multicolored	1.10	1.10
		Nos. 111-113 (3)	2.60	2.60

Souvenir Sheet

114	A26	$1 multicolored	2.25	*2.25*

375th Anniv. of Islands' Discovery — A27

1984, July 10 Litho. *Perf. 14x13½*

115	A27	30c Capt. William Keeling	.70	.55
116	A27	65c The Hector	1.40	1.25
117	A27	95c Astrolabe	1.75	1.60
118	A27	$1.10 Map, 1666	2.00	1.90
		Nos. 115-118 (4)	5.85	5.30

AUSIPEX '84 — A28

45c, Malay Settlement, Home Island. 55c, West Island Air Strip, settlement. $2, Jukong ships racing, Melbourne Exhibition Center.

1984, Sept. 21 Litho. *Perf. 13½*

119	A28	45c multicolored	.65	.55
120	A28	55c multicolored	.70	.70

Souvenir Sheet

121	A28	$2 multicolored	3.00	3.00

Christmas A29

1984, Oct. 31 Litho. *Perf. 13½*

122	A29	24c Fish	.40	.40
123	A29	35c Butterfly	.60	.60
124	A29	55c Bird	1.00	1.00
		Nos. 122-124 (3)	2.00	2.00

Souvenir Sheet

Act of Self-Determination — A30

Integration with Australia: a, Australians welcoming Cocos islanders. b, Australian flag over the islands.

1984, Nov. 30 Litho. *Perf. 13½x14*

125	A30	Sheet of 2	2.50	2.50
a.-b.		30c any single	1.10	1.10

Crafts — A31

1985, Jan. 30 *Perf. 14x13½*

126	A31	30c Boat building	.55	.35
127	A31	45c Blacksmith	.80	.50
128	A31	55c Woodcarving	1.15	.80
		Nos. 126-128 (3)	2.50	1.65

Cable-laying Ships — A32

1985, Apr. 24 *Perf. 13½x14*

129	A32	33c Scotia	1.45	1.00
130	A32	65c Anglia	2.25	1.60
131	A32	80c Patrol	2.25	*2.75*
		Nos. 129-131 (3)	5.95	5.35

Birds A33

33c, Redfooted booby, vert. 60c, Nankeen night heron. $1, Buff-banded rail.

1985, July 17 *Perf. 13½*

132	A33	33c multicolored	2.50	2.50
133	A33	60c multicolored	2.75	2.75
134	A33	$1 multicolored	3.00	3.00
a.		"Block" of 3, #132-134	9.00	9.00

Nos. 132-134 printed in a continuous design.

Seashells A34

1c, Trochus maculatus. 2c, Smaragdia rangiana. 3c, Chama. 4c, Cypraea moneta. 5c, Drupa morum. 10c, Conus miles. 15c, Terebra maculata. 20c, Fragum fragum. 30c, Turbo lajonkairii. 33c, Mitra fissurata. 40c, Lambis lambis. 50c, Tridacna squamosa. 60c, Cypraea histrio. $1, Phillidia varicosa. $2, Halgerda tessellata. $3, Harminoea cymbalum.

1985-86 Litho. *Perf. 13½x14*

135	A34	1c multicolored	.65	*1.10*
136	A34	2c multicolored	.65	*1.10*
137	A34	3c multicolored	.65	*1.10*
138	A34	4c multicolored	1.10	*1.10*
139	A34	5c multicolored	.65	*1.10*
140	A34	10c multicolored	.75	*1.75*
141	A34	15c multicolored	2.25	1.50
142	A34	20c multicolored	2.25	1.75
143	A34	30c multicolored	2.25	1.75
144	A34	33c multicolored	2.25	1.75
145	A34	40c multicolored	2.25	1.75
146	A34	50c multicolored	2.25	*2.25*
147	A34	60c multicolored	2.25	*2.75*
148	A34	$1 multicolored	3.25	*3.25*
149	A34	$2 multicolored	3.25	*3.25*
150	A34	$3 multicolored	3.75	*3.75*
		Nos. 135-150 (16)	30.45	31.00

Issue dates: 1c, 5c, 33c, $1, Sept. 18. 2c, 3c, 10c, $3, Jan. 29, 1986. 15c-30c, 40c, Apr. 30, 1986. 4c, 50c, 60c, $2, July 30, 1986.

For surcharges see Nos. 225, 228-229, 231-233.

Souvenir Sheet

Christmas — A35

a, Star LR. b, Star LL. c, Star UR. d, Star UL.

1985, Oct. 30 *Perf. 13½x14*

151	A35	Sheet of 4	3.00	3.00
a.-d.		27c any single	.75	.75

Darwin's Visit to the Islands — A36

1986, Apr. 1 Litho. *Perf. 14x13½*

152	A36	33c Charles Darwin	.75	.75
153	A36	60c Map of voyage	1.40	*2.00*
154	A36	$1 HMS Beagle	2.00	*2.75*
		Nos. 152-154 (3)	4.15	*5.50*

Christmas A37

1986, Oct. 20 Litho. *Perf. 13½x14*

155	A37	30c Coconut palm, holly	.70	.70
156	A37	90c Shell, ornament	2.50	2.50
157	A37	$1 Tropical fish, bell	2.50	2.50
		Nos. 155-157 (3)	5.70	5.70

Sailboats A38

a, Jukong. b, Ocean racers. c, Sarimanok. d, Ayesha. No. 158 has a continuous design.

1987, Jan. 28

158		Strip of 4	6.00	6.00
a.-d.	A38	36c any single	1.15	1.15

Island Views — A39

1987, Apr. 8

159	A39	70c Direction Is.	2.00	1.75
160	A39	90c West Is.	2.75	*3.00*
161	A39	$1 Golf course, Cocos	3.25	*3.50*
		Nos. 159-161 (3)	8.00	*8.25*

Communications — A40

1987, July 29 Litho. *Perf. 13½x14*

162	A40	70c	Radio	1.50	1.50
163	A40	75c	Air service	1.60	1.60
164	A40	90c	Satellite	1.90	1.90
165	A40	$1	Airmail	2.25	2.25
			Nos. 162-165 (4)	7.25	7.25

Industries A41

1987, Sept. 16

166	A41	45c	Batik printing	1.40	1.40
167	A41	65c	Boat building	1.90	1.90
168	A41	75c	Copra production	2.25	2.25
			Nos. 166-168 (3)	5.55	5.55

Industrial activities of the Cocos Malay people.

Christmas — A42

1987, Oct. 28 *Perf. 14x13½*

169	A42	30c	Peace on Earth	.45	.45
170	A42	90c	Unity	1.25	1.25
171	A42	$1	Goodwill Towards All	1.75	1.75
			Nos. 169-171 (3)	3.45	3.45

Australia Bicentennial A43

Arrival of the First Fleet, Sydney Cove, Jan. 1788: a, Five aboriginals on shore. b, Four aboriginals on shore, one in canoe. c, Ships entering bay, kangaroos. d, Europeans land, white cranes. e, Flag raising.

1988, Jan. 26 Litho. *Perf. 13*

172		Strip of 5	10.00	10.00
a.-e.	A43	37c any single	1.25	1.25

No. 172 has a continuous design. See Christmas Is. No. 213.

Life Cycle of the Coconut — A44

1988, Apr. 13 Litho. *Perf. 14x13½*

173	A44	37c	Flower	.65	.65
174	A44	65c	Small nut stage	1.25	1.25
175	A44	90c	Mature nuts	1.45	*1.45*
176	A44	$1	Seedlings	1.90	*1.90*
a.			Souvenir sheet of 4, #173-176	7.50	7.50
			Nos. 173-176 (4)	5.25	5.25

For surcharge see No. O1.

Cocos Postage Stamps, 25th Anniv. A45

Litho. & Engr.

1988, June 15 *Perf. 15x14*

177	A45	37c	No. 1	1.25	.85
178	A45	55c	No. 4	1.50	1.25
179	A45	65c	No. 2	1.75	1.75
180	A45	70c	No. 3	2.00	2.00
181	A45	90c	No. 5	2.25	*2.75*
182	A45	$1	No. 6	2.50	*3.00*
			Nos. 177-182 (6)	11.25	11.60

For overprint and surcharge see Nos. 216, 236.

Flowering Plants — A46

1c, Pisonia grandis. 2c, Cocos nucifera. 5c, Morinda citrifolia. 10c, Cordia subcordata. 30c, Argusia argentea. 37c, Calophyllum inophyllum. 40c, Barringtonia asiatica. 50c, Caesalpinia bonduc. 90c, Terminalia catappa. $1, Pemphis acidula. $2, Scaevola sericea. $3, Hibiscus tiliaceus.

1988-89 Litho. *Perf. 14x13½*

183	A46	1c	multicolored	.55	*1.00*
184	A46	2c	multicolored	.55	*1.00*
185	A46	5c	multicolored	1.10	1.10
186	A46	10c	multicolored	.75	*1.10*
189	A46	30c	multicolored	1.10	*1.60*
190	A46	37c	multicolored	1.60	1.40
191	A46	40c	multicolored	1.10	*1.60*
192	A46	50c	multicolored	1.40	*3.25*
194	A46	90c	multicolored	2.00	*5.00*
195	A46	$1	multicolored	2.00	*2.75*
197	A46	$2	multicolored	2.50	*3.00*
198	A46	$3	multicolored	3.75	*4.50*
			Nos. 183-198 (12)	18.40	*27.30*

Issued: 1c, 5c, 37c, $3, 7/29; 2c, 10c, 30c, $2, 1/18/89; 40c, 50c, 90c, $1, 4/19/89.

For self-adhesive sheet of 3 see No. 217.

Souvenir Sheet

1988, July 30

199	A46	$3	like No. 198	*9.00*	*9.00*

SYDPEX '88.

Christmas A47

1988, Oct. 12 Litho. *Perf. 13½x14*

200	A47	32c	multicolored	.90	.90
201	A47	90c	multicolored	2.10	2.10
202	A47	$1	multicolored	2.50	2.50
			Nos. 200-202 (3)	5.50	5.50

1st Aerial Survey of the Indian Ocean Air Route, 50th Anniv. — A48

40c, P.G. Taylor, pilot. 70c, *Guba II* seaplane and crew. $1, *Guba II* landing off Direction Island. $1.10, Unissued 5sh stamp of Australia, 1939.

1989, July 19 Litho. *Perf. 14x13½*

203	A48	40c	multicolored	1.00	1.00
204	A48	70c	multicolored	1.60	1.60
205	A48	$1	multicolored	2.25	2.25
206	A48	$1.10	multicolored	2.50	2.50
			Nos. 203-206 (4)	7.35	7.35

Jukong, Traditional Sailing Vessel of the Cocos Malay People — A49

1989, Oct. 18 Litho. *Perf. 14x13½*

207	A49	35c	multicolored	1.10	1.10
208	A49	80c	multicolored	2.50	2.50
209	A49	$1.10	multicolored	3.50	3.50
			Nos. 207-209 (3)	7.10	7.10

Christmas.

Naval Engagement of the HMAS *Sydney* and the German Raider SMS *Emden*, 75th Anniv. — A50

Designs: 40c, HMAS *Sydney*. 70c, SMS *Emden*. $1, Steam launch belonging to the *Emden*. $1.10, HMAS *Sydney* and naval crest.

1989, Nov. 9 Litho. *Perf. 13½x14*

210		Strip of 4 + label	7.25	*7.50*
a.	A50	40c multicolored	.65	.65
b.	A50	70c multicolored	1.25	1.25
c.	A50	$1 multicolored	1.75	1.75
d.	A50	$1.10 multicolored	1.90	1.90
e.		Souvenir sheet of 4, #210a-210d	10.00	10.00

Crabs — A52

1990, May 31 Litho. *Perf. 14½*

212	A52	45c	Xanthid	1.40	1.40
213	A52	75c	Ghost	2.50	2.50
214	A52	$1	Red-backed mud crab	2.75	2.75
215	A52	$1.30	Coconut, vert.	3.50	3.50
			Nos. 212-215 (4)	10.15	10.15

No. 180 Ovptd. in Red

Litho. & Engr.

1990, Aug. 24 *Perf. 15x14*

216	A45	70c	gray, black & red	12.00	12.00

Flowering Plants Type of 1988

1990, Aug. 24 Photo. *Rouletted 9½*

Self-Adhesive

217		Sheet of 3	12.00	12.00
a.	A46	10c like No. 186	.40	.40
b.	A46	90c like No. 194	2.75	2.75
c.	A46	$2 like No. 197	6.00	6.00

World Stamp Exhibition, New Zealand 1990. Nos. 217a-217c inscribed 1990.

Explorers and Their Ships A54

45c, Capt. Keeling, Hector, 1609. 75c, Capt. Fitzroy, Beagle, 1836. $1, Capt. Belcher, Samarang, 1846. $1.30, Capt. Fremantle, Juno, 1857.

1990, Aug. 24 Litho. *Perf. 14½*

218	A54	45c	violet brown	1.60	*1.75*
219	A54	75c	pale bl & vio brn	2.75	*3.75*
220	A54	$1	pale yel & vio brn	3.25	*5.00*
221	A54	$1.30	buff & vio brn	5.25	*7.50*
a.			Souv. sheet of 4, #218-221, imperf.	11.00	11.00
			Nos. 218-221 (4)	12.85	*18.00*

Christmas — A55

1990, Dec. 12 Litho. *Rouletted 5*

222	A55	40c	Star at left	1.40	1.40
a.			Bklt. pane of 10 + 2 labels	27.50	
223	A55	70c	Star in center	2.50	2.50
a.			Bklt. pane, 4 #222, 2 #223 + 6 labels	35.00	
224	A55	$1.30	Star at right	5.00	5.00
			Nos. 222-224 (3)	8.90	8.90

Nos. 140, 141, 143, 146-147, 179 Surcharged in Blue or Black

No. 225

No. 228

No. 229

No. 231

No. 232

No. 233

No. 236

Litho., Litho. & Engr.

1990-91 *Perf. 13½x14, 15x14*

225	A34	(1c) on 30c #143	*6.50*	*6.50*
228	A34	(43c) on 10c #140	*47.50*	*47.50*
229	A34	(43c) on 10c #140	*19.00*	*19.00*
231	A34	70c on 60c #147 (bk)	*10.00*	*10.00*
232	A34	80c on 50c #146 (bk)	*10.00*	*10.00*
233	A34	$1.20 on 15c #141 (bk)	*10.00*	*10.00*
236	A45	$5 on 65c #179	*45.00*	*45.00*
		Nos. 225-236 (7)	*148.00*	*148.00*

Issued: No. 236, 11/11; No. 228, 12/18; Nos. 225, 229, 231-233, 1/1991.

Beaded Sea Star — A56

75c, Feather star. $1, Slate pencil urchin. $1.30, Globose sea urchin.

1991, Feb. 28 **Litho.** *Perf. 14½*

237	A56	45c shown	1.25	1.25
238	A56	75c multicolored	1.75	1.75
239	A56	$1 multicolored	2.50	2.50
240	A56	$1.30 multicolored	3.00	3.00
		Nos. 237-240 (4)	8.50	8.50

Hari Raya — A57

1991, Mar. **Litho.** *Perf. 14½*

241	A57	45c multicolored	1.25	1.25
242	A57	75c multi, diff.	1.90	1.90
243	A57	$1.30 multi, diff.	3.50	3.50
		Nos. 241-243 (3)	6.65	6.65

Christmas — A58

1991, Nov. 6 **Litho.** *Perf. 15½*

244	A58	38c Child praying	1.00	1.00
245	A58	43c Child sleeping	1.25	1.25
246	A58	$1 Child singing	2.50	2.50
247	A58	$1.20 Child in wonder	3.25	3.25
		Nos. 244-247 (4)	8.00	8.00

Souvenir Sheet

248	Sheet of 4	8.50	8.50
a.	A58 38c Two children	.95	.95
b.	A58 43c Three girls	1.05	1.05
c.	A58 $1 Boy, two girls	2.50	2.50
d.	A58 $1.20 Boy, girl	2.75	2.75

Nos. 248a-248d are in a continuous design depicting a children's choir.

Crustaceans A59

Designs: 5c, Lybia tessellata. 10c, Pilodius areolatus. 20c, Trizopagurus strigatus. 30c, Lophozozymus pulchellus. 40c, Thalamitoides quadridens. 45c, Calcinus elegans, vert. 50c, Clibarius humilis. 60c, Trapezia rufopunctata, vert. 80c, Pylopaguropsis magnimanus, vert. $1, Trapezia ferruginea, vert. $2, Trapezia guttata, vert. $3, Trapezia cymodoce, vert.

1992 **Litho.** *Perf. 14½*

249	A59	5c multicolored	1.20	*1.75*
250	A59	10c multicolored	1.20	*1.75*
251	A59	20c multicolored	1.20	*1.75*
252	A59	30c multicolored	1.25	*3.00*
253	A59	40c multicolored	1.40	*3.00*
254	A59	45c multicolored	1.50	*3.00*
255	A59	50c multicolored	1.50	*4.00*
256	A59	60c multicolored	1.75	*4.00*
257	A59	80c multicolored	2.10	*4.00*
258	A59	$1 multicolored	2.75	*4.00*
259	A59	$2 multicolored	5.50	5.50
260	A59	$3 multicolored	8.50	8.50
		Nos. 249-260 (12)	29.85	*44.25*

Issued: 10c, 30c, 50c, 80c, $1, $2, 8/11; others, 2/28.

Discovery of America, 500th Anniv. — A60

1992, May 22 **Litho.** *Perf. 14½*

261	A60	$1.05 multicolored	4.00	4.00

Buff-banded Rail — A61

No. 262: a, 10c, Bird looking for food. b, 15c, Adult with chick. c, 30c, Two adults eating. d, 45c, Adult with eggs, hatchling.

No. 263: a, 45c, Two birds, one in water. b, 85c, Chick in nest. c, $1.20, Bird's head.

1992, June 18 **Litho.** *Perf. 14*

262	A61	Strip of 4, #a.-d.	6.00	6.00

Souvenir Sheet

263	A61	Sheet of 3, #a.-c.	7.50	7.50

World Wildlife Fund (No. 262).

World War II, 50th Anniv. — A62

45c, Royal Air Force Spitfire fighters. 85c, Japanese bombing of Kampong. $1.20, Sunderland reconnaissance flying boat.

1992, Oct. 13 **Litho.** *Perf. 14½*

264	A62	45c multicolored	1.90	1.90
265	A62	85c multicolored	3.50	3.50
266	A62	$1.20 multicolored	4.75	4.75
		Nos. 264-266 (3)	10.15	10.15

Festive Season — A63

40c, Storm waves on reef edge. 80c, Direction Island. $1, Moorish idols among coral.

1992, Nov. 10 **Litho.** *Perf. 15x14½*

267	A63	40c multicolored	1.50	1.50
268	A63	80c multicolored	2.75	2.75
269	A63	$1 multicolored	3.50	3.50
		Nos. 267-269 (3)	7.75	7.75

Corals — A64

45c, Lobophyllia hemprichii. 85c, Pocillopora eydouxi. $1.05, Fungia scutaria. $1.20, Sarcophyton sp.

1993, Jan. 28 **Litho.** *Perf. 14½*

270	A64	45c multicolored	.90	.90
271	A64	85c multicolored	1.60	1.60
272	A64	$1.05 multicolored	2.25	2.25
273	A64	$1.20 multicolored	2.75	2.75
		Nos. 270-273 (4)	7.50	7.50

A65

Island Currency Tokens: 45c, 5r token, 1968. 85c, Island scene token, 1968. $1.05, 150r token, 1977. $1.20, Token, 1910.

1993, Mar. 30 **Litho.** *Perf. 15x14½*

274	A65	45c multicolored	1.40	1.40
275	A65	85c multicolored	2.25	2.25
276	A65	$1.05 multicolored	3.00	3.00
277	A65	$1.20 multicolored	3.75	3.75
		Nos. 274-277 (4)	10.40	10.40

A66

Education: 5c, Primary classroom activities. 45c, Secondary studies. 85c, Crafts, traditional basket weaving. $1.05, Office staff, higher education. $1.20, Marine officers, coxswain's training.

1993, June 1 **Litho.** *Perf. 14½*

278	A66	5c multicolored	.95	.95
279	A66	45c multicolored	1.50	1.50
280	A66	85c multicolored	2.50	2.50
281	A66	$1.05 multicolored	2.75	2.75
282	A66	$1.20 multicolored	3.25	3.25
		Nos. 278-282 (5)	10.95	10.95

Air-Sea Rescue Service A67

45c, Men in lifeboat. 85c, Westwind Seascan. $1.05, R.J. Hawke inter-island ferry.

1993, Aug. 17 **Litho.** *Perf. 14½*

283	A67	45c multicolored	2.00	2.00
284	A67	85c multicolored	3.00	3.00
285	A67	$1.05 multicolored	4.00	4.00
a.		Souvenir sheet of 3, #283-285	12.00	12.00
		Nos. 283-285 (3)	9.00	9.00

A limited printing exists of No. 285a with Taipei '95 overprint. Value, $110.

Festive Season — A68

1993, Oct. 24 **Litho.** *Perf. 14½*

286	A68	40c pink & multi	1.50	1.50
287	A68	80c blue & multi	3.00	3.00
288	A68	$1 yellow & multi	4.00	4.00
		Nos. 286-288 (3)	8.50	8.50

From No. 289 on, Cocos Island stamps are valid for postage in Australia.

Map and Reef Life — A69

Reef triggerfish — No. 289: a, Two fish, purple coral (b). b, Three fish. c, Two fish. d, Two fish, red coral (e). e, One fish.

Green turtles — No. 290: a, Eggs, turtles. b, Two turtles (c). c, Group of baby turtles. d, Baby turtle. e, Fish, large turtle.

Pyramid butterflyfish — No. 291: a, Three fish. b, Two small, one large fish, coral (c). c, One small, one large fish, coral (d). d, Three fish, coral (e). e, Coral, one fish.

Junkongs sailing craft — No. 292: a, One boat, red sail. b, Two boats, one blue & white sail, one red sail. c, One boat, yellow sail. d, Two boats sailing away. e, Two boats, one red sail, one white & blue sail.

1994, Feb. 17 **Litho.** *Perf. 14½x14*

289	A69	5c Strip of 5, #a.-e.	1.40	*1.75*
290	A69	10c Strip of 5, #a.-e.	1.75	*2.25*
291	A69	20c Strip of 5, #a.-e.	2.25	*3.00*
292	A69	45c Strip of 5, #a.-e.	5.25	*5.75*
f.		Sheet of 20, #289-292	11.00	*14.50*

No. 292 also produced in sheets of 20.

Puppets — A70

1994, June 16 **Litho.** *Perf. 14½x14*

293	A70	45c Prabu Abjasa	.95	.95
294	A70	90c Prabu Pandu	1.75	1.75
295	A70	$1 Judistra	1.90	1.90
296	A70	$1.35 Abimanju	2.50	2.50
		Nos. 293-296 (4)	7.10	7.10

Christmas A71

1994, Oct. 31 **Litho.** *Perf. 14x14½*

297	A71	40c Angel	.80	.80
298	A71	45c Wise man	1.00	1.00
299	A71	80c Bethlehem	1.60	1.60
		Nos. 297-299 (3)	3.40	3.40

Seabirds A72

45c, White-tailed tropicbird, masked booby. 85c, Great frigatebird, white tern.

1995, Mar. 16 **Litho.** *Perf. 14x14½*

300	A72	45c multicolored	.80	.80
301	A72	85c multicolored	1.60	1.60
a.		Souvenir sheet of 2, #300-301	3.00	3.00
b.		As "a," overprinted	7.75	7.75

No. 301b ovptd. in gold in sheet margin with Jakarta '95 exhibition emblem and: "8th Asian International Philatelic Exhibition / PAMERAN FILATELI INTERNASIONAL ASIA VIII."

No. 301b issued 8/19/95.

Insects — A73

No. 302: a, Yellow crazy ant. b, Aedes mosquito. c, Hawk moth. d, Scarab beetle. e, Lauxaniid fly.
$1.20, Common eggfly butterfly.

1995, July 13 Litho. *Perf. 14½x14*
302 A73 45c Strip of 5, #a.-e. 6.00 6.00
303 A73 $1.20 multicolored 2.75 2.75

Fish — A74

Designs: 5c, Redspot wrasse. 30c, Gilded triggerfish. 40c, Saddled butterflyfish. 45c, Ringeyed hawkfish. 75c, Orangespine unicornfish. 80c, Blue tang. 85c, Humpback wrasse. 90c, Threadfin butterflyfish. $1, Bluestripe snapper. $1.05, Longnosed butterflyfish. $1.20, Freckled hawkfish. $2, Powder blue surgeonfish.

1995-97 Litho. *Perf. 14x14½*
304 A74 5c multicolored .40 .40
305 A74 30c multicolored .60 .60
306 A74 40c multicolored .95 .95
307 A74 45c multicolored 1.10 1.10
308 A74 75c multicolored 1.60 1.60
309 A74 80c multicolored 1.75 1.75
310 A74 85c multicolored 1.75 1.75
311 A74 90c multicolored 2.00 2.00
312 A74 $1 multicolored 2.25 2.25
313 A74 $1.05 multicolored 2.25 2.25
314 A74 $1.20 multicolored 3.00 3.00
315 A74 $2 multicolored 5.25 5.25
Nos. 304-315 (12) 22.90 22.90

Issued: 40c, 80c, $1.05, 11/1/95; 30c, 45c, 85c, $2, 8/8/96; 5c, 75c, 90c, $1, $1.20, 8/14/97.
See Nos. 327-329, 335.

Festive Season — A75

Designs: 45c, Greeting others, asking forgiveness. 75c, Drum beaters celebrate Hari Raya Puasa. 85c, Sharing food with friends.

1996, Feb. 19 Litho. *Perf. 14*
316 A75 45c multicolored .80 .80
317 A75 75c multicolored 1.90 1.90
318 A75 85c multicolored 2.25 2.25
Nos. 316-318 (3) 4.95 4.95

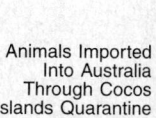

Animals Imported Into Australia Through Cocos Islands Quarantine Station — A76

1996, June 13 Litho. *Perf. 14½x14*
319 A76 45c Black rhinoceros 1.40 1.40
320 A76 50c Alpacas 1.60 1.60
321 A76 $1.05 Boran cattle 2.75 2.75
322 A76 $1.20 Ostrich 3.75 3.75
Nos. 319-322 (4) 9.50 9.50

A77

Festive Season: 45c, Tambourine, dancing on shore, bird. 75c, Woman clapping, sailboats racing. 85c, Fish, night scene on beach.

1997, Jan. 6 Litho. *Perf. 14x14½*
323 A77 45c multicolored .95 .95
324 A77 75c multicolored 1.50 1.50
325 A77 85c multicolored 1.90 1.90
Nos. 323-325 (3) 4.35 4.35

A78

Children's drawings: a, Gift package. b, Mosque. c, Cocos Malay woman. d, Island scene. e, Two dancers.

1998, Jan. 22 Litho. *Perf. 14*
326 A78 45c Strip of 5, #a.-e. 4.75 4.75
Festive Season.

Fish Type of 1995

Designs: 70c, Crowned squirrelfish. 95c, Sixstripe wrasse. $5, Goldback anthias.

1998, Aug. 13 Litho. *Perf. 14x14½*
327 A74 70c multicolored 1.25 1.25
328 A74 95c multicolored 1.50 1.50
329 A74 $5 multicolored 8.25 8.25
Nos. 327-329 (3) 11.00 11.00

Jukong Boats, Hari Raya Festival — A79

a, Women placing items in leaves, people along beach. b, Two women, boats along beach. c, Flowers, man in boat. d, Palm trees, two men, man in boat. e, Two people in boat.

1999, Feb. 11 Litho. *Perf. 14½x14*
330 A79 45c Strip of 5, #a.-e. 4.75 4.75

Flora and Fauna — A80

a, 45c, Two birds on tree branch. b, 25c, Bird in flight. c, 10c, Sailboat with sail down. d, 5c, Sailboat with red sails. e, 45c, Two birds in flight. f, 25c, Butterflies. g, 10c, School of fish. h, 5c, School of fish swimming left, coral. i, 45c, Red hibiscus flower. j, 25c, Three birds in flight. k, 10c, Two moorish idols. l, 5c, Turtles. m, 45c, Butterfly, flowers. n, 25c, Moth with wings folded, flowers. o, 10c, Two gold fish. p, 5c, Various fish swimming right. q, 45c, Yellow hibiscus. r, 25c, Butterfly on flowers. s, 10c, Two birds in flight. t, 5c, Large fish, coral.

1999, June 17 Litho. *Perf. 14x14½*
331 A80 Sheet of 20, #a.-t. 17.00 17.00

Faces of Cocos Islands A81

Ordinary people: a, Ratma Anthoney, with white shirt. b, Nakia Haji Dolman, with multicolored head covering. c, Muller Eymin, with white head covering. d, Courtney Press, with flowered outfit. e, Mhd Abu-Yazid, with blue shirt with stripes.

2000, Apr. 13 Litho. *Perf. 14x14½*
332 A81 45c Strip of 5, #a.-e. 5.00 5.00

Worldwide Fund for Nature — A82

No. 333: a, Purple crab. b, Little nipper crab.
No. 334: a, Horn-eyed ghost crab. b, Smooth-banded ghost crab.

2000, June 20 Litho. *Perf. 14x14¾*
333 A82 5c Pair, #a-b 1.10 1.10
334 A82 45c Pair, #a-b 2.25 2.25

Fish Type of 1995

No. 335: a, Wideband fusilier. b, Striped surgeonfish. c, Orangeband surgeonfish. d, Indo-Pacific sergeant.

2001, Feb. 8 Litho. *Perf. 14x14½*
335 Block of 4 5.00 5.00
a.-d. A74 45c Any single .90 .90

Turtles — A83

No. 336: a, Loggerhead. b, Hawksbill. c, Leatherback. d, Green.

2002, Oct. 1 Litho. *Perf. 14x14½*
336 A83 Block of 4 5.50 5.50
a.-d. 45c Any single 1.00 1.00

Shore Birds — A84

No. 337: a, Eastern reef egret. b, Sooty tern. c, Ruddy turnstone. d, Whimbrel.

2003, June 17
337 Horiz. strip of 4 7.50 7.50
a.-d. A84 50c Any single 1.45 1.45

Royal Visit, 50th Anniv. — A85

Queen Elizabeth II and: No. 338a, Cocos Malay musicians. No. 338b, Royal Yacht Gothic. $1, Clunies Ross (Oceania) House. $1.45, Dignitary presenting model of Malay jukong.

2004, Mar. 16
338 A85 50c Horiz. pair, #a-b 2.75 2.75
339 A85 $1 multi 2.75 2.75
340 A85 $1.45 multi 4.00 4.00
a. Souvenir sheet, #338a, 338b, 339, 340 10.00 10.00
b. As "a," with 2004 World Stamp Championship emblem ovptd. in gold in margin 10.00 10.00
Nos. 338-340 (3) 9.50 9.50

No. 340b issued 8/28.

Worldwide Fund for Nature (WWF) A86

Designs: No. 341a, Blacktip reef shark. No. 341b, Gray reef sharks. $1, Blacktip reef sharks. $1.45, Gray reef shark.

2005, Jun 21 *Perf. 14½x14*
341 A86 50c Horiz. pair, #a-b 3.50 3.50
342 A86 $1 multi 3.50 3.50
343 A86 $1.45 multi 5.00 5.00
Nos. 341-343 (3) 12.00 12.00

Wildlife — A87

No. 344: a-e, Various birds. f-t, Various fish and marine life.

2006, June 13 *Perf. 14¾x14*
344 A87 Sheet of 20 21.00 21.00
a.-e. 10c Any single .50 .50
f.-o. 25c Any single .80 .80
p.-t. 50c Any single 1.75 1.75

Mollusks A88

Designs: No. 345a, Oriental moonsnail. No. 345b, Perly nautilus. $1, Partridge tun. $1.45, Giant clam.

2007, Mar. 20 *Perf. 14x14½*
345 A88 50c Horiz. pair, #a-b 3.50 3.50
346 A88 $1 multi 3.50 3.50
347 A88 $1.45 multi 5.50 5.50
Nos. 345-347 (3) 12.50 12.50

Birds — A89

No. 345, vert: a, Black-winged stilt. b, Chinese pond heron.
$1, White-breasted waterhen. $1.45, Saunders' tern.

2008, Feb. 26 *Perf. 14*
348 A89 50c Horiz. pair, #a-b 3.50 3.50
349 A89 $1 multi 3.50 3.50
350 A89 $1.45 multi 5.00 5.00
Nos. 348-350 (3) 12.00 12.00

History of Cocos Islands — A90

No. 351: a, Sighting of islands by Captain William Keeling, 1609. b, Visit of Charles Darwin, 1836.
$1.10, Control of islands by Clunies Ross family, 1827-1978. $1.65, Australian territory, 1955.

2009, Apr. 21 *Perf. 14¼*
351 A90 55c Horiz. pair, #a-b 3.50 3.50
352 A90 $1.10 multi 3.50 3.50
353 A90 $1.65 multi 5.50 5.50
Nos. 351-353 (3) 12.50 12.50

Flowers — A91

No. 354: a, Ipomoea pes-caprae. b, Hibiscus tiliaceus.
No. 355: a, Suriana maritima. b, Morinda citrifolia.

2010, Sept. 15 Litho. *Perf. 14¾x14*

354 A91	60c Horiz. pair, #a-b	2.40	2.40
355 A91	$1.20 Horiz. pair, #a-b	4.75	4.75

Boats — A92

Designs: 60c, Jukongs. $1.20, Small boat. $1.80, Glass-bottom boat, horiz. $3, Yacht, horiz.

Perf. 14¾x14, 14x14¾

2011, Jan. 18 Litho.

356 A92	60c multi	1.25	1.25
357 A92	$1.20 multi	2.40	2.40
358 A92	$1.80 multi	3.75	3.75
359 A92	$3 multi	6.00	6.00
	Nos. 356-359 (4)	13.40	13.40

Miniature Sheet

Marine Life — A93

No. 360: a, Sea cucumbers with red coloring. b, Fan coral with breaks at right. c, Sea cucumbers with purple coloring. d, Pink anemonefish in sea anemone. e, Christmas tree worm, tip at upper left. f, Mushroom coral. g, Giant clam. h, Fin of Spotted lionfish. i, Eye of Scribbled filefish (brown and blue fish). j, School of Neon fusiliers. k, Fan coral (intact). l, Nudibranch. m, Pink anemonefish in sea anemone, close-up. n, Christmas tree worms. o, Eye of Foster's hawkfish (pink and red fish). p, Foliaceous coral. q, Durban dancing shrimp. r, Magnificent sea anemone. s, Brain coral. t, Crown of thorns sea star.

2011, Sept. 6 *Perf. 14¼*

360 A93	Sheet of 20	25.00	25.00
a.-t.	60c Any single	1.25	1.25

A sheet of 9 stamps containing stamps similar to Nos. 360a, 360b, 360d, 360e, 360j, 360l, 360m, 360n, and 360t but with glossy varnish was sold only with a set of nine gift cards for $9.99.

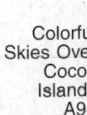

Colorful Skies Over Cocos Islands A94

Skies over: 60c, Pier. $1.20, Rocks in water. $1.80, Beach. $3, Palm trees.

2012, May 22 *Perf. 14x14¾*

361-364 A94	Set of 4	13.00	13.00

Butterflies — A95

No. 365: a, Meadow argus. b, Common crow.
No. 366: a, Australian painted lady. b, Varied eggfly.

2012, Aug. 2

365 A95	Horiz. pair	2.50	2.50
a.-b.	60c Either single	1.25	1.25
366 A95	Horiz. pair	5.25	5.25
a.-b.	$1.20 Either single	2.60	2.60

Cocos Islands Postage Stamps, 50th Anniv. — A96

Designs: 5c, Sea turtle and underwater photographer. 60c, Man in outrigger canoe. $1, Sailboarder. $1.20, Coconut. $2, Egret.

2013, June 4 *Perf. 14¾x14*

367-371 A96	Set of 5	9.25	9.25
371a	Souvenir sheet of 5, #367-371	9.25	9.25

A booklet containing five of No. 368 was produced locally and in very limited quantities.

Barrel Mail — A97

Designs: 60c, Men and barrels in ocean, cover franked with Australia #213. $3, Men on shore signaling ship, cover franked with Australia #166 and 236.

2013, Aug. 6 Litho. *Perf. 14¼*

372-373 A97	Set of 2	6.50	6.50

Historical Cocos Islands Maps — A98

Designs: No. 374a, 17th cent. map with natives at right. No. 374b, Map from 18th cent. with French inscriptions. $1.40, Map from 19th cent. $2.10, Map from 20th cent.

2014, June 24 Litho. *Perf. 14¼*

374	Horiz. pair	2.80	2.80
a.-b.	A98 70c Either single	1.40	1.40
375 A98	$1.40 multi	2.75	2.75
376 A98	$2.10 multi	4.00	4.00
	Nos. 374-376 (3)	9.55	9.55

Battle of the Cocos Islands, Cent. — A99

Warships: 70c, HMAS Sydney. $3.50, SMS Emden.

2014, Oct. 14 Litho. *Perf. 14¼*

377-378 A99	Set of 2	7.25	7.25

Worldwide Fund for Nature (WWF) A100

Birds: No. 379, 70c, Herald petrels. No. 380, 70c, Oriental pratincoles. No. 381, 70c, Little curlews. No. 382, 70c, Indian yellow-nosed albatrosses.

2015, Apr. 22 Litho. *Perf. 14¼*

379-382 A100	Set of 4	4.50	4.50

A101

Uninhabited Islands — A102

No. 383: a, Pulu Klapa Satu (green water in foreground). b, Pulu Maraya (white beach in foreground).
No. 384: a, Pulu Blan Madar (at twilight). b, Pulu Beras (at midday).

2015, Aug. 25 Litho. *Perf. 14¾x14*

383 A101	Horiz. pair	2.00	2.00
a.-b.	70c Either single	1.00	1.00
384 A102	Horiz. pair	4.00	4.00
a.-b.	$1.40 Either single	2.00	2.00

OFFICIAL STAMP

No. 175 Ovptd. and Srchd. in Dark Blue

1991, Jan. 25 Litho. *Perf. 14x13½*

O1 A44 (43c) on 90c multi			*110.00*

No. O1 was not sold to the public unused. Used value is for a canceled-to-order example. Mint examples exist in the marketplace. Value, $250.

COLOMBIA

kə-'ləm-bē-ə

LOCATION — On the northwest coast of South America, bordering on the Caribbean Sea and the Pacific Ocean
GOVT. — Republic
AREA — 456,535 sq. mi.
POP. — 39,309,422 (1999 est.)
CAPITAL — Bogota

In 1810 the Spanish Viceroyalty of New Granada gained its independence and with Venezuela and Ecuador formed the State of Greater Colombia. In 1832 this state split into three independent units as Venezuela, Ecuador and the Republic of New Granada. The name of the country has been, successively, Granadine Confederation (1858-61), United States of New Granada (1861), United States of Colombia (1861-65), and the Republic of Colombia (1885 to date).

100 Centavos = 1 Peso

Catalogue values for unused stamps in this country are for Never Hinged items, beginning with Scott 594 in the regular postage section, Scott B1 in the semi-postal section, Scott C200 in the airpost section, Scott CE1 in the airpost special delivery section, Scott E2 in the special delivery section, and Scott RA33 in the postal tax section.

In the earlier days many towns did not have handstamps for canceling and stamps were canceled with pen and ink. Pen cancellations, therefore, do not indicate fiscal use. (Postage stamps were not used for revenue purposes.) Used values for Nos. 1-128 are for stamps with illegible manuscript cancels or handstamp cancels of Bogota or Medellin. Stamps with legible manuscript or other handstamped town-name cancels sell for more.

Fractions of many Colombian stamps of both early and late issues are found canceled, their use to pay postage having been tolerated even though forbidden by the postal laws and regulations. Many are known to have been made for philatelic purposes.

Watermarks

Wmk. 116 — Crosses and Circles

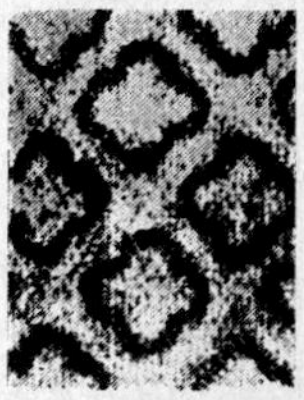

Wmk. 127 — Quatrefoils

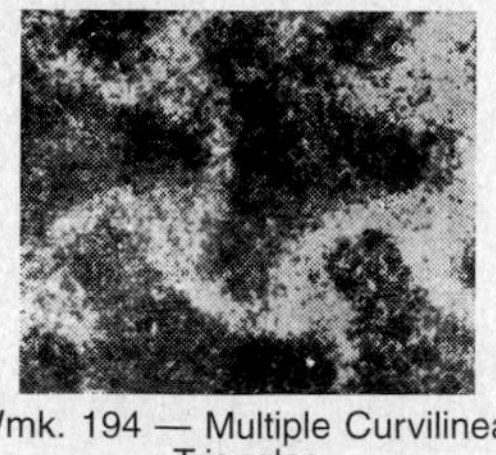

Wmk. 194 — Multiple Curvilinear Triangles

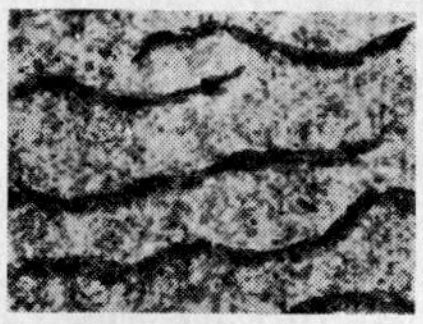

Wmk. 229 — Wavy Lines

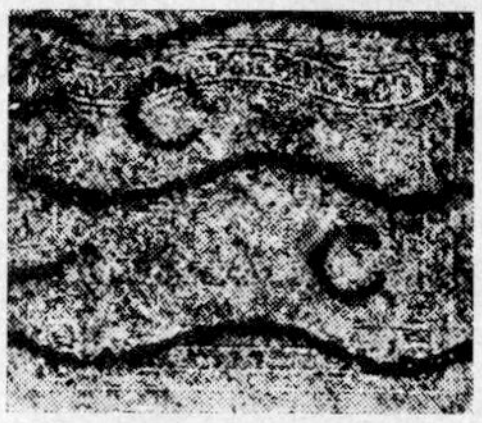

Wmk. 255 — Wavy Lines and C Multiple

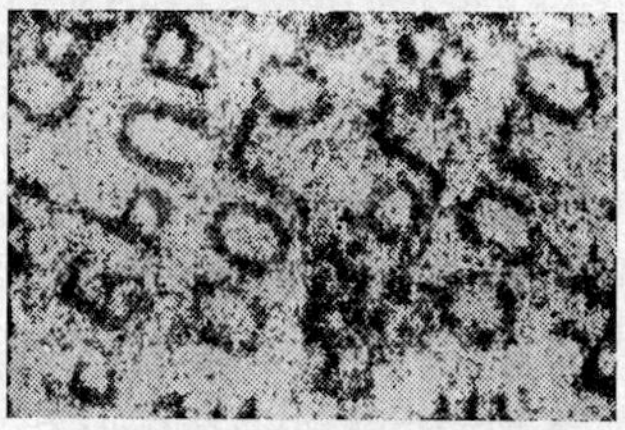

Wmk. 331 — REPUBLICA DE COLOMBIA

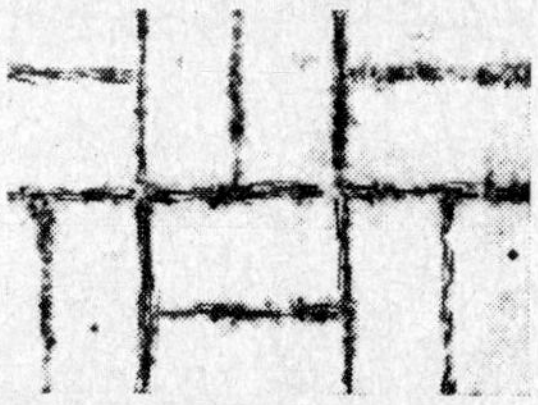

Wmk. 334 — Rectangles

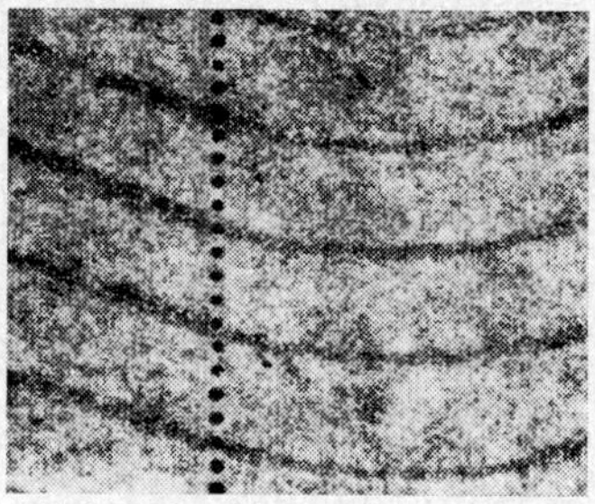

Wmk. 346 — Parallel Curved Lines

Stamps inscribed "Colombia" that show the Panama Canal area were used in Panama and can be found in Vol. 5.

Granadine Confederation

Coat of Arms — A1

Type A1 — Asterisks in frame. Wavy lines in background.

Type A2 — Diamond-shaped ornaments in frame. Straight lines in background. Numerals larger.

1859 Unwmk. Litho. *Imperf.*
Wove Paper

1	A1	2½c green	120.00	120.00
a.		2½c yellow green	120.00	120.00
2	A1	5c blue	140.00	87.50
a.		Tête bêche pair	*4,500.*	*7,250.*
b.		"50" instead of "5"		*7,500.*
3	A1	5c violet	375.00	120.00
a.		Tête bêche pair	*6,000.*	*6,000.*
b.		"50" instead of "5"		*15,000.*
4	A1	10c red brown	140.00	80.00
a.		10c buff	140.00	80.00
6	A1	20c blue	120.00	67.50
a.		20c gray blue	120.00	67.50
b.		Se-tenant with 5c	—	—
c.		Tête bêche pair	*40,000.*	*32,500.*
7	A1	1p carmine	72.50	*120.00*
a.		1p rose	110.00	150.00
8	A1	1p rose, *bluish*	350.00	

The 10c green is an essay.

Reprints of No. 7 are in brown rose or brown red. Wavy lines of background are much broken; no dividing lines between stamps.

Coat of Arms — A2

1860 Laid Paper

9	A2	5c lilac	325.00	210.00

Wove Paper

10	A2	5c gray lilac	85.00	65.00
a.		5c lilac	85.00	65.00
11	A2	10c yellow buff	85.00	55.00
a.		Tête bêche pair	*7,000.*	*7,000.*
12	A2	20c blue	210.00	140.00

United States of New Granada

Arms of New Granada — A3

1861

13	A3	2½c black	1,450.	400.00
14	A3	5c yellow	400.00	175.00
a.		5c buff	400.00	175.00
16	A3	10c blue	1,250.	175.00
17	A3	20c red	500.00	475.00
18	A3	1p pink	1,250.	375.00

There are 54 varieties of the 5c, 20c, and 1 peso.

Forgeries exist of Nos. 13-18.

United States of Colombia

Coat of Arms — A4

1862

19	A4	10c blue	250.00	125.00
20	A4	20c red	*4,500.*	725.00
21	A4	50c green	250.00	175.00
22	A4	1p red lilac	600.00	175.00
23	A4	1p red lil, *bluish*	*5,500.*	*1,750.*

No. 23 is on a thinner, coarser wove paper than Nos. 19-22.

Coat of Arms — A5

1863

24	A5	5c orange	100.00	65.00
a.		Star after "Cent"	110.00	72.50
25	A5	10c blue	175.00	24.00
a.		Period after "10"	200.00	30.00
26	A5	20c red	225.00	75.00
a.		Star after "Cent"	250.00	82.50
b.		Transfer of 50c in stone of 20c	*18,500*	*5,500.*

Bluish Paper

28	A5	10c blue	175.00	32.50
a.		Period after "10"	190.00	35.00
29	A5	50c green	210.00	75.00
a.		Star after "Cent"	210.00	77.50

Ten varieties of each.

Coat of Arms — A6

1864 Wove Paper

30	A6	5c orange	60.00	37.50
a.		Tête bêche pair	475.00	400.00
31	A6	10c blue	55.00	15.00
a.		Period after 10	55.00	15.00
32	A6	20c scarlet	100.00	55.00
33	A6	50c green	85.00	55.00
34	A6	1p red violet	350.00	175.00

Two varieties of each.

Arms of Colombia
A7 A9

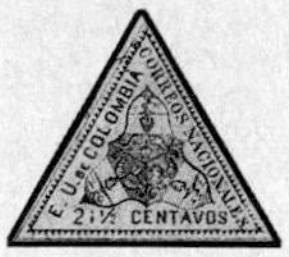

A8

1865

35	A7	1c rose	10.00	10.00
a.		bluish pelure paper	30.00	21.00
36	A8	2½c black, *lilac*	21.00	14.00
37	A9	5c yellow	47.50	20.00
a.		5c orange	47.50	20.00
38	A9	10c violet	67.50	4.50
39	A9	20c blue	67.50	20.00
40	A9	50c green	120.00	52.50
41	A9	50c grn (small figures)	120.00	52.50
42	A9	1p vermilion	125.00	18.00
a.		1p rose red	125.00	18.00
b.		Period after "PESO"	150.00	20.00

Ten varieties of each of the 5c, 10c, 20c, and 50c, and six varieties of the 1 peso. No. 36 was used as a carrier stamp.

A10

A11

A12

A13

A14

A15

A16

1866 White Wove Paper

45	A10	5c orange	72.50	27.50
46	A11	10c lilac	17.00	5.25
a.		Pelure paper	21.00	11.50
47	A12	20c light blue	42.50	21.00
a.		Pelure paper	67.50	52.50
48	A13	50c green	17.00	13.00
49	A14	1p rose red, *bluish*	92.50	32.50
a.		1p vermilion	92.50	32.50
51	A15	5p blk, *green*	500.00	210.00
52	A16	10p blk, *vermilion*	350.00	200.00

There are several varieties of the 1 peso having the letters "U," "N," "S" and "O" smaller.

A17

A18

A19

A20

A21

TEN CENTAVOS:
Type I — "B" of "COLOMBIA" over "V" of "CENTAVOS".
Type II — "B" of "COLOMBIA" over "VO" of "CENTAVOS."
ONE PESO:
Type I — Long thin spear heads. Diagonal lines in lower part of shield.
Type II — Short thick spear heads. Horizontal and a few diagonal lines in lower part of shield.
Type III — Short thick spear heads. Crossed lines in lower part of shield. Ornaments at each side of circle are broken. (See No. 97.)

1868

53	A17	5c orange	67.50	52.50
54	A18	10c lilac (I)	4.25	1.10
a.		10c red violet (I)	4.25	1.10
b.		10c lilac (II)	4.25	1.10
c.		10c red violet (II)	4.25	1.10
d.		Printed on both sides	7.50	2.50
55	A19	20c blue	3.00	1.25
56	A20	50c yellow green	3.50	2.40
57	A21	1p ver (II)	4.25	2.10
a.		Tête bêche pair	140.00	100.00
b.		1p rose red (I)	60.00	27.50
c.		1p rose red (II)	4.00	2.10
		Nos. 53-57 (5)	82.50	59.35

See Nos. 83-84, 96-97.

Counterfeits or reprints.

10c — There is a large white dot at the upper left between the circle enclosing the "X" and the ornament below.

50c — There is a shading of dots instead of dashes below the ribbon with motto. There are crossed lines in the lowest section of the shield instead of diagonal or horizontal ones.

1p — The ornaments in the lettered circle are broken. There are crossed lines in the lowest section of the shield. These counterfeits, or reprints, are on white paper, wove and laid, on colored wove paper and in fancy colors.

A22

Two varieties

1869-70 **Wove Paper**

59	A22	2½c black, *violet*	4.75	2.50
a.		Laid paper ('70)	325.00	250.00
b.		Laid batonné paper ('70)	30.00	24.00

Nos. 59, 59a, 59b were used as carrier stamps.

Counterfeits, or reprints, are on magenta paper wove or ribbed.

A23

A24

1870 **Wove Paper**

62	A23	5c orange	2.00	1.25
a.		5c yellow	2.00	1.25
63	A24	25c black, *blue*	16.00	13.00

See No. 89.

In the counterfeits, or reprints, of No. 63, the top of the "2" of "25" does not touch the down stroke. The counterfeits are on paper of various colors.

A25

A26

5 pesos — The ornament at the left of the "C" of "Cinco" cuts into the "C," and the shading of the flag is formed of diagonal lines.

10 pesos — The stars have extra rays between the points, and the central part of the shield has some horizontal lines of shading at each end.

Surface Colored, Chalky Paper

1870

64	A25	5p blk, *green*	100.00	67.50
65	A26	10p blk, *vermilion*	120.00	67.50

See Nos. 77-79, 125-126.

A27

A28

A29

TEN CENTAVOS:
Type I — "S" of "CORREOS" 2½mm high. First "N" of "NACIONALES" small.
Type II — "S" of "CORREOS" 2mm high. First "N" of "NACIONALES" wide.

1871-74 **Thin Porous Paper**

66	A27	1c green ('72)	3.50	3.50
67	A27	1c rose ('73)	3.50	3.50
a.		1c carmine ('73)	3.50	3.50
68	A28	2c brown	1.60	1.60
a.		2c red brown	1.60	1.60
69	A29	10c vio (I) ('74)	2.50	2.50
a.		10c lilac (I) ('74)	2.50	2.50
b.		10c violet (II) ('74)	2.50	2.50
c.		10c lilac (II) ('74)	2.50	2.50
d.		As #69, laid paper ('72)	140.00	140.00
e.		As "b," laid paper ('72)	140.00	140.00
		Nos. 66-69 (4)	11.10	11.10

Counterfeits or reprints.

1c — The outer frame of the shield is broken near the upper left corner and the "A" of "Colombia" has no cross-bar.

2c — There are scratches across "DOS" and many white marks around the letters on the large "2." The counterfeits, or reprints, are on white wove and bluish white laid paper.

Condor — A30

Liberty Head
A31 A32

5 pesos, redrawn — The ornament at the left of the "C" only touches the "C," and the shading of the flag is formed of vertical and diagonal lines.

10 pesos, redrawn — The stars are distinctly five pointed, and there is no shading in the central part of the shield.

1877 **Wove Paper**

73	A30	5c purple	7.25	2.10
a.		5c lilac	7.25	2.10
74	A31	10c bister brown	3.50	.90
a.		10c red brown	3.50	.90
b.		10c violet brown	3.50	.90
75	A32	20c blue	4.25	1.40
a.		20c violet blue	25.00	3.50
77	A26	10p blk, *rose*	120.00	67.50
78	A25	5p blk, *lt grn,* redrawn	42.50	32.50
79	A26	10p blk, *rose,* redrawn	17.00	2.75
a.		10p blk, *dark rose,* redrawn	17.00	2.75
		Nos. 73-79 (6)	194.50	107.15

Stamps of the issues of 1871-77 are known with private perforations of various gauges, also with sewing machine perforation.

In the counterfeits, or reprints, of the 5 pesos the ornament at the left of the "C" of "Cinco" is separated from the "C" by a black line.

In the counterfeits, or reprints, of the 10 pesos the outer line of the double circle containing "10" is broken at the top, below "OS" of "Unidos," and the vertical lines of shading contained in the double circle are very indistinct. There is a colorless dash below the loop of the "P" of "Pesos."

1876-79 **Laid Paper**

80	A30	5c lilac	85.00	65.00
81	A31	10c brown	47.50	2.75
82	A32	20c blue	100.00	67.50
83	A20	50c green ('79)	97.50	65.00
84	A21	1p pale red (II) ('79)	62.50	15.00
		Nos. 80-84 (5)	392.50	215.25

1879 **Wove Paper**

89	A24	25c green	32.50	32.50

1881 **Blue Wove Paper**

93	A30	5c violet	20.00	13.00
a.		5c lilac	20.00	13.00
94	A31	10c brown	12.00	2.50
95	A32	20c blue	12.00	3.75
96	A20	50c yellow green	12.50	7.50
97	A21	1p ver (III)	17.00	7.50
		Nos. 93-97 (5)	73.50	34.25

For types of 1p, see note over No. 53.

Reprints of the 10c and 20c are much worn. On the 10c the letters "TAVOS" of "CENTAVOS" often touch. On the 20c the letters "NT" of "VEINTE" touch and the left arm of the "T" is too long. Reprints of the 25c, 50c and 1p have the characteristics previously described. The reprints are on white wove or laid paper, on colored papers, and in fancy colors. Stamps on green paper exist only as reprints.

A34

A35

A36

1 centavo — The period before "UNION" is round and there are rays between the stars and the condors.

2 centavos — The "2's" and "C's" in the corners are placed upright.

5 centavos — The last star at the right almost touches the frame.

10 centavos — The letters of the inscription are thin; there are rays between the stars and the condor.

1881 **White Wove Paper** ***Imperf.***

103	A34	1c green	5.00	4.00
104	A35	2c vermilion	2.10	1.60
a.		2c rose	2.50	1.60
106	A34	5c blue	5.00	1.60
a.		Printed on both sides		
107	A36	10c violet	4.25	1.25
108	A34	20c black	4.75	2.00
		Nos. 103-108 (5)	21.10	10.45

The stamps of this issue are found with perforations of various gauges, also sewing machine perforation, all of which are unofficial.

See Nos. 112, 114-115.

Liberty Head — A37

1881 ***Imperf.***

109	A37	1c blk, *green*	3.50	*5.00*
110	A37	2c blk, *lilac rose*	3.50	*5.00*
111	A37	5c blk, *lilac*	8.50	1.75
		Nos. 109-111 (3)	15.50	*11.75*

Nos. 109 to 111 are found with regular or sewing machine perforation, unofficial.

Reprints:

1c — The top line of the stamp and the top frame extend to the left. 2c — There is a curved line over the scroll below the "AV" of "CENTAVOS."

5c — There are scratches across the "5" in the upper left corner. All three values were reprinted on the three colors of paper of the originals.

A37a

Redrawn

1 centavo — The period before "UNION" is square and the rays between the stars and the condor have been wholly or partly erased.

2 centavos — The "2's" and "C's" in the corners are placed diagonally.

5 centavos — The last star at the right touches the wing of the condor.

10 centavos — The letters of the inscription are thick; there are no rays under the stars; the last star at the right touches the wing of the condor and this wing touches the frame.

1883 ***Imperf.***

112	A34	1c green	4.75	4.25
113	A37a	2c rose	2.10	1.75
114	A34	5c blue	4.00	1.00
a.		5c ultramarine	4.00	1.00
b.		Printed on both sides, reverse ultra	25.00	20.00
115	A36	10c violet	5.00	1.40
		Nos. 112-115 (4)	15.85	8.40

The stamps of this issue are found with regular or sewing machine perforation, privately applied.

A38

A39

1883 *Perf. 10½, 12, 13½*

116	A38	1c gray grn, *grn*	1.00	1.00
a.		Imperf., pair	5.00	5.00
117	A39	2c red, *rose*	1.00	*1.25*
a.		2c org red, *rose*	1.00	*1.25*
b.		2c red, *buff*	12.00	12.00
c.		Imperf., pair (#117 or 117a)	7.75	7.75
d.		"DE LOS" in very small caps	15.00	15.00
118	A38	5c blue, *bluish*	2.50	1.50
a.		5c dk bl, *bluish*	2.50	1.00
b.		5c blue	3.25	2.50
c.		Imperf., pair (#118 or 118a)	7.75	7.75
d.		As "b," imperf., pair	12.00	12.00
119	A39	10c org, *yel*	1.25	*1.40*
a.		"DE LOS" in large caps	60.00	26.00
b.		Imperf., pair	16.00	16.00
120	A39	20c vio, *lilac*	1.40	1.40
a.		Imperf., pair	16.00	16.00
122	A38	50c brn, *buff*	3.00	3.25
a.		Perf. 12	3.00	3.25
123	A38	1p claret, *bluish*	5.50	1.90
a.		Imperf., pair	16.00	16.00
		Nos. 116-123 (7)	15.65	11.70

Redrawn Types of 1877

1883 (?) *Perf. 10½, 12*

125	A25	5p orange brown	10.00	6.00
126	A26	10p black, *gray*	10.00	7.25

1886 *Perf. 10½, 11½, 12*

127	A38	5p brown, *straw*	10.00	5.50
a.		Imperf., pair	32.50	32.50
128	A38	10p black, *rose*	10.00	5.50
a.		Imperf., pair	32.50	32.50

Republic of Colombia

A40

Simón Bolívar — A41

Pres. Rafael Núñez — A42

1886 *Perf. 10½ and 13½*

129	A40	1c grn, *grn*	1.75	.70
a.		Imperf., pair	6.75	6.75
130	A41	5c blue, *bl*	1.75	.40
a.		5c ultra, *blue*	1.75	.40
b.		Imperf., pair (#130)	6.75	6.75
131	A42	10c orange	3.50	.70
a.		Imperf., pair	9.25	9.25
b.		Pelure paper	4.50	1.00
		Nos. 129-131 (3)	7.00	1.80

Gen. Antonio Jose de Sucre y Alcala — A43

Gen. Antonio Nariño — A44

1887

133	A43	2c org red, *rose*	2.25	1.00
a.		2c orange red, *yellowish*	6.00	6.00
b.		2c orange red	7.25	7.25
c.		Imperf., pair (#133)	10.00	10.00
134	A44	20c pur, *grysh*	3.00	1.10
a.		Imperf., pair	8.50	8.50
b.		Pelure paper	3.50	2.25

Impressions of No. 134 on white, blue or greenish blue paper were not regularly issued.

Arms — A45

1888

135	A45	50c brn, *buff*	1.75	*1.90*
a.		Imperf., pair	6.00	6.00
136	A45	1p claret, *bluish*	8.00	2.10
137	A45	1p claret	3.50	1.60
138	A45	5p org brn	8.50	6.50
139	A45	5p black	14.50	9.50
140	A45	10p black, *rose*	21.00	6.75
		Nos. 135-140 (6)	57.25	28.35

See Nos. 155, 158-159.

Nariño — A46

1889

141	A46	20c pur, *grayish*	1.90	1.25
a.		Imperf., pair	9.25	9.25

Impressions on white, blue or greenish blue paper were not regularly issued.

A47

A48

A49

A50

A51

1890-91 *Perf. 10½, 13½, 11*

142	A47	1c grn, *grn*	1.90	1.60
143	A48	2c org red, *rose*	.95	.95
144	A49	5c bl, *grnsh bl*	1.40	.40
a.		5c deep blue, *blue*	1.40	.40
b.		Imperf., pair	5.50	5.50
146	A50	10c brn, *yel*	1.00	.40
a.		10c brown, *buff*	1.00	.40
147	A51	20c vio, pelure paper	3.50	*3.50*
		Nos. 142-147 (5)	8.75	*6.85*

A52

A52a

A53

A53a

A54

Perf. 10½, 12, 13½, 14 to 15½

1892-99 **Ordinary Paper**

148	A47	1c red, *yel*	.85	.40
149	A52	2c red, *rose*	42.50	42.50
150	A52	2c green	.50	.30
a.		2c yellow green	.50	.30
151	A49	5c blk, *buff*	13.00	.35
152	A52a	5c org brn, *pale buff*	1.00	.30
a.		5c red brown, *salmon* ('97)	1.00	.30
153	A50	10c bis brn, *rose*	.75	.40
a.		10c brown, *brownish*	2.00	1.60
154	A53	20c brn, *bl*	.75	.40
a.		20c red brown, *blue*	.75	.40
b.		20c yel brn, *grnsh bl* ('97)	5.50	*13.00*
c.		20c brown, *buff* ('97)	19.00	13.00
155	A45	50c vio, *vio*	1.25	.75
156	A53a	50c red vio, *vio* ('99)	1.75	
157	A54	1p bl, *grnsh*	2.10	.90
a.		1p blue, *buff*	2.10	.90
158	A45	5p red, *pale rose*	8.50	3.25
159	A45	10p blue	16.00	3.25
a.		Thin, pale rose paper	27.50	7.25
		Nos. 148-159 (12)	88.95	
		Nos. 148-155,157-159 (11)		52.80

Type A53a is a redrawing of type A45. The letters of the inscriptions are slightly larger and the numerals "50" slightly smaller than in type A45.

The 20c brown on white paper is believed to be a chemical changeling.

Nos. 148, 150-152a, 153-155, 157, 159 exist imperf. Value per pair, $6-9.

A56

1899

162	A56	1c red, *yellow*	.70	.35
163	A56	5c red brn, *sal*	.70	.35
164	A56	10c brn, *lil rose*	2.00	.95
165	A56	50c blue, *lilac*	1.40	1.25
		Nos. 162-165 (4)	4.80	2.90

Cartagena Issues

A57

1899 **Blue Overprint** ***Imperf.***

167	A57	5c red, *buff*	30.00	30.00
a.		Sewing machine perf.	30.00	30.00
168	A57	10c ultra, *buff*	30.00	30.00
a.		Sewing machine perf.	30.00	30.00

Nos. 167 and 167a differ slightly from the illustration.

Bolivar No. 55 Overprinted with 7 Parallel Wavy Lines and

A58

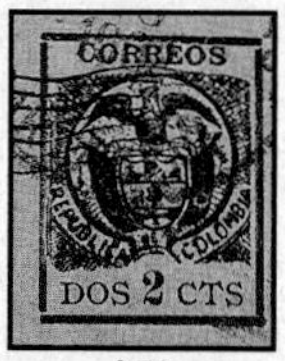

A59

A60

A61

Perf. 14 (#169), Sewing Machine Perf.

1899 **Purple Overprint**

169	A18	1c black	60.00	60.00
170	A58	1c brn, *buff*	20.00	20.00
a.		Altered from 10c	30.00	30.00
171	A59	2c blk, *buff*	20.00	20.00
a.		Altered from 10c	30.00	30.00
172	A60	5c mar, *grnsh bl*	18.00	18.00
a.		Perf. 12	18.00	18.00
b.		Without overprint	10.50	10.50
173	A61	10c red, *sal*	18.00	18.00
a.		Perf. 12	18.00	18.00
		Nos. 169-173 (5)	136.00	136.00

Types A58 and A59 illustrate Nos. 170a and 171a, which were made from altered plates of the 10c (No. 168). Nos. 170 and 171 were made from altered plate of the 5c denomination (No. 167), show part of the top flag of the "5" and differ slightly from the illustrations.

Nos. 170-173 exist imperf. Values about same as perf.

A62

1900 **Purple Overprint** ***Imperf.***

174	A62	5c red	25.00	25.00
a.		Perf. 12	35.00	35.00

A63

A64

"Gobierno Provisorio" at Top

1900 **Litho.** ***Perf. 12 Vertically***

175	A63	1c (ctvo) blk, *bl grn*	47.50	8.00
a.		"cvo."	120.00	14.50
b.		"cvos."	47.50	8.00
c.		"centavo"	55.00	47.50
176	A63	2c black	26.00	6.00
177	A63	5c blk, *pink*	26.00	6.00
a.		Name at side (V)	62.50	9.00
178	A63	10c blk, *pink*	26.00	6.00
a.		Name at side (V)	62.50	9.00
179	A63	20c blk, *yellow*	47.50	8.00
a.		Name at side (G)	92.50	12.00
		Nos. 175-179 (5)	173.00	34.00

"Gobierno Provisional" at Top
Name at Side in Black or Green

180	A64	1c (ctvo.) blk, *bl grn*	47.50	8.00
a.		"centavo"	125.00	47.50
181	A64	2c blk, *bl grn*	30.00	5.00
182	A64	5c blk (G)	30.00	5.00
a.		"ctvos." smaller	47.50	9.00
183	A64	10c blk, *pink*	30.00	5.00
184	A64	20c blk, *yel* (G)	47.50	8.00
		Nos. 180-184 (5)	185.00	31.00

Issues of the rebel provisional government in Cucuta.

A65

A66

Purple Overprint

1901 ***Sewing Machine Perf.***

185	A65	1c black	1.00	1.00
a.		Without overprint	2.25	2.25
b.		Double overprint	2.50	2.50
c.		Imperf., pair	2.50	2.50
d.		Inverted overprint	1.25	1.25
186	A66	2c blk, *rose*	1.00	1.00
a.		Imperf., pair	2.50	2.50
b.		Without overprint	2.25	2.25
c.		Double overprint	2.50	2.50

A67

A68

1901 **Rose Overprint**

187	A67	1c blue	1.00	1.00
a.		Imperf., pair	4.00	4.00
188	A68	2c brown	1.00	1.00
a.		Imperf., pair	4.00	4.00
b.		Without overprint	1.00	1.00

A69

A70

Sewing Machine or Regular Perf. 12, 12½

1902 **Magenta Overprint**

No.	Type	Description	Unused	Used
189	A69	5c violet	2.25	2.25
a.		Without overprint	2.25	2.25
b.		Double overprint	2.25	2.25
c.		Imperf., pair	4.75	4.75
190	A70	10c yel brn	2.25	2.25
a.		Double overprint	2.25	2.25
b.		Imperf., pair	4.75	4.75
c.		Without overprint	2.25	2.25
d.		Printed on both sides	3.25	3.25

A71

A72

1902 **Magenta Overprint**

No.	Type	Description	Unused	Used
191	A71	5c yel brn	2.25	2.25
a.		Without overprint	2.10	2.10
b.		Imperf., pair	6.00	6.00
192	A71	10c black	1.75	1.75
a.		Without overprint	1.50	1.50
b.		Imperf., pair	9.00	9.00
193	A72	20c maroon	5.50	4.50
b.		Imperf., pair	15.00	15.00
		Nos. 191-193 (3)	9.50	8.50

Nos. 191-193 exist tête bêche. Value of 10c and 20c, each $15.

Washed examples of Nos. 167-174, 185-193 are offered as "without overprint."

Barranquilla Issues

Magdalena River — A75

Iron Quay at Sabanilla — A76

La Popa Hill — A77

1902-03 ***Imperf.***

No.	Type	Description	Unused	Used
194	A75	2c green	1.60	1.60
195	A75	2c dk bl	1.60	1.60
196	A75	2c rose	22.50	22.50
197	A76	10c scarlet	1.10	1.10
198	A76	10c orange	13.00	13.00
199	A76	10c rose	1.75	1.75
200	A76	10c maroon	1.90	1.90
201	A76	10c claret	1.90	1.90
202	A77	20c violet	3.50	3.50
a.		Laid paper		9.50
203	A77	20c dl bl	9.50	9.50
204	A77	20c dl bl, *pink*	*125.00*	*125.00*
205	A77	20c car rose	20.00	20.00
		Nos. 194-205 (12)	*203.35*	*203.35*

Sewing Machine Perf. and Perf. 12

No.	Type	Description	Unused	Used
194a	A75	2c green	9.50	9.50
195a	A75	2c dark blue	9.50	9.50
196a	A75	2c carmine	*47.50*	*47.50*
197a	A76	10c scarlet	4.75	4.75
198a	A76	10c orange	*35.00*	*35.00*
199a	A76	10c rose	6.50	6.50
200a	A76	10c maroon	6.50	6.50
201a	A76	10c claret	6.00	6.00
202b	A77	20c purple	.70	.70
c.		20c lilac	.70	.70
203a	A77	20c dull blue	9.50	9.50
204a	A77	20c dull blue, *rose*	*150.00*	*150.00*
205b	A77	20c carmine rose	*72.50*	*72.50*
		Nos. 194a-205b (12)	*357.95*	*357.95*

See Nos. 240-245.

Cruiser "Cartagena" — A78

Bolívar — A79

General Próspero Pinzón — A80

A81

A82

1903-04 ***Imperf.***

No.	Type	Description	Unused	Used
209	A78	5c blue	2.75	2.75
210	A78	5c bister	4.50	4.50
211	A79	50c yellow	3.75	3.75
212	A79	50c green	4.50	4.50
213	A79	50c scarlet	4.50	4.50
214	A79	50c carmine	4.50	4.50
a.		50c rose	4.50	4.50
215	A79	50c pale brown	4.50	4.50
216	A80	1p yellow brn	1.60	1.60
217	A80	1p rose	2.50	2.50
218	A80	1p blue	2.50	2.50
219	A80	1p violet	25.00	25.00
220	A81	5p claret	5.50	5.50
221	A81	5p pale brown	8.00	8.00
222	A81	5p blue green	7.50	7.50
223	A82	10p pale green	7.75	7.75
224	A82	10p claret	25.00	25.00
		Nos. 209-224 (16)	114.35	114.35

Nos. 216 and 217 measure 20½x26½mm and No. 218, 18x24mm. Stamps of this issue exist with forged perforations.

Perf. 12

No.	Type	Description	Unused	Used
209a	A78	5c blue	9.50	9.50
210a	A78	5c bister	9.50	9.50
211a	A79	50c yellow	9.50	9.50
b.		50c orange	25.00	25.00
212a	A79	50c green	25.00	25.00
213a	A79	50c scarlet	11.50	11.50
214b	A79	50c rose	11.50	11.50
215a	A79	50c pale brown	11.50	11.50
216a	A80	1p yellow brown	5.25	5.25
217a	A80	1p rose	7.50	7.50
218a	A80	1p blue	9.50	7.50
219a	A80	1p violet	62.50	62.50
220a	A81	5p claret	20.00	20.00
221a	A81	5p pale brown	22.50	22.50
222a	A81	5p blue green	22.50	22.50
223a	A82	10p pale green	30.00	30.00
224a	A82	10p claret	77.50	77.50
		Nos. 209a-224a (16)	345.25	343.25

Laid Paper ***Imperf.***

No.	Type	Description	Unused	Used
240	A76	10c dk bl, *lil*	6.25	6.25
241	A76	10c dk bl, *bluish*	3.75	3.75
242	A76	10c dk bl, *brn*	3.75	3.75
243	A76	10c dk bl, *sal*	9.25	9.25
244	A76	10c dk bl, *grnsh bl*	5.00	5.00
245	A76	10c dk bl, *dp rose*	3.75	3.75
		Nos. 240-245 (6)	31.75	31.75

Perf. 12

No.	Type	Description	Unused	Used
240a	A76	10c dk bl, *lilac*	13.50	13.50
241a	A76	10c dk bl, *bluish*	9.25	9.25
242a	A76	10c dk bl, *brn*	9.25	9.25
243a	A76	10c dk bl, *salmon*	72.50	72.50
244a	A76	10c dk bl, *grnsh bl*	20.00	20.00
245a	A76	10c dk bl, *deep rose*	9.25	9.25
		Nos. 240a-245a (6)	133.75	133.75

A82a

Imperf., Sewing Machine Perf.

1902 **Typeset**

No.	Type	Description	Unused	Used
255	A82a	10c black, *rose*	3.50	3.50
256	A82a	20c blk, *orange*	2.50	2.50

This issue was printed in either Cali or Popayan.

Medellin Issue

A83

1902

No.	Type	Description	Unused	Used
257	A83	1c grn, *straw*	.35	*.50*
258	A83	2c salmon, *rose*	.35	*.50*
259	A83	5c dp bl, *grnsh*	.35	*.50*
260	A83	10c pale brn, *straw*	.35	*.50*
261	A83	20c pur, *rose*	.45	*.50*
262	A83	50c dl rose, *grnsh*	2.25	*3.00*
263	A83	1p blk, *yellow*	4.50	*6.75*
264	A83	5p slate, *blue*	35.00	35.00
265	A83	10p dk brn, *rose*	22.50	22.50
		Nos. 257-265 (9)	66.10	69.75

For overprint see No. L8.

Imperf., Pairs

No.	Type	Description	Unused	Used
257a	A83	1c	11.00	11.00
258a	A83	2c	11.00	11.00
259a	A83	5c	11.00	11.00
260a	A83	10c	11.00	11.00
261a	A83	20c	11.00	11.00
262a	A83	50c	11.00	11.00
263a	A83	1p	27.50	27.50
264a	A83	5p	80.00	80.00
265a	A83	10p	50.00	50.00

Regular Issue

A84

A85

A86

A87

A88

A89

A90

A91

A92

1902 ***Imperf.***

No.	Type	Description	Unused	Used
266	A84	2c blk, *rose*	.25	.25
267	A85	4c red, *grn*	.25	.25
268	A86	5c grn, *grn*	.25	.25
269	A87	10c blk, *pink*	.25	.25
c.		10c blk, *rose*	1.10	1.10
270	A88	20c brn, *buff*	.25	.25
271	A89	50c dk grn, *rose*	1.40	1.40
272	A90	1p pur, *buff*	.60	.60
273	A91	5p grn, *bl*	4.25	4.25
274	A92	10p grn, *pale grn*	13.00	6.50
		Nos. 266-274 (9)	20.50	14.00

For overprint see No. H4.

Sewing Machine Perf.

No.	Type	Description	Unused	Used
266a	A84	2c blk, *rose*	1.90	1.90
267a	A85	4c red, *grn*	1.60	1.60
268a	A86	5c grn, *blue*	1.90	1.90
269a	A87	10c blk, *pink*	1.90	1.90
270a	A88	20c brn, *buff*	3.25	2.50
271a	A89	50c dk grn, *rose*	6.50	5.25
272a	A90	1p pur, *buff*	7.75	6.50
273a	A91	5p grn, *blue*	35.00	35.00
274a	A92	10p grn, *pale grn*	65.00	65.00
		Nos. 266a-274a (9)	124.80	121.55

1903 ***Perf. 12***

No.	Type	Description	Unused	Used
266b	A84	2c blk, *rose*	1.40	1.40
269b	A87	10c blk, *pink*	1.60	1.60
270b	A88	20c brn, *buff*	1.60	1.60
272b	A90	1p pur, *buff*	3.25	3.25
273b	A91	5p grn, *blue*	27.50	27.50
274b	A92	10p grn, *pale grn*	52.50	45.00
		Nos. 266b-274b (6)	87.85	80.35

1903 ***Imperf.***

No.	Type	Description	Unused	Used
284	A85	4c blue, *grn*	.35	.35
285	A86	5c blue, *blue*	.35	.35
286	A88	20c blue,*buff*	.35	.35
288	A89	50c blue, *rose*	1.75	1.75
		Nos. 284-288 (4)	2.80	2.80

Sewing Machine Perf.

No.	Type	Description	Unused	Used
284a	A85	4c blue, *grn*	2.25	1.75
285a	A86	5c blue, *blue*	2.25	1.75
286a	A88	20c blue, *buff*	3.25	2.50
288a	A89	50c blue, *rose*	6.50	5.75
		Nos. 284a-288a (4)	14.25	11.75

Perf. 12

No.	Type	Description	Unused	Used
284b	A85	4c blue, *grn*	2.50	2.50
285b	A86	5c blue, *blue*	2.50	2.50
286b	A88	20c blue, *buff*	3.50	3.50
288b	A89	50c blue, *rose*	9.75	9.75
		Nos. 284b-288b (4)	18.25	18.25

A93

1904 **Pelure Paper** ***Imperf.***

No.	Type	Description	Unused	Used
303	A93	½c yellow brn	1.10	1.10
304	A90	1c blue green	1.10	1.10
a.		1c yellow green	1.10	1.10
306	A84	2c blue	.90	.65
307	A86	5c carmine	1.00	1.00
308	A87	10c violet	1.10	.90
		Nos. 303-308 (5)	5.20	4.75

For overprint see No. H13.

1904 ***Perf. 13***

No.	Type	Description	Unused	Used
303a	A93	½c yellow brown	4.25	4.25
304b	A90	1c blue green	5.50	5.00
c.		1c yellow green	7.50	7.00
306a	A84	2c blue	2.50	2.50

Perf. 12

No.	Type	Description	Unused	Used
307a	A86	5c carmine	2.25	2.25
308a	A87	10c violet	2.25	2.25
		Nos. 303a-308a (5)	16.75	16.25

A94

A95

Pres. José Manuel Marroquín — A96

Imprint: "Lit. J.L.Arango Medellin, Col."

1904 **Wove Paper** ***Perf. 12***

No.	Type	Description	Unused	Used
314	A94	½c yellow	.85	.25
315	A94	1c green	.85	.25
316	A94	2c rose	.85	.25
317	A94	5c blue	1.40	.25
318	A94	10c violet	1.75	.25
319	A94	20c black	1.75	.25
320	A95	1p brown	19.00	3.00
321	A96	5p red & blk, *yel*	60.00	60.00
322	A96	10p bl & blk, *grnsh*	60.00	60.00
		Nos. 314-322 (9)	146.45	124.50

Redrawn

No.	Type	Description	Unused	Used
314a	A94	½c	.85	.25
315a	A94	1c	.85	.25
316a	A94	2c	.85	.25
317a	A94	5c	1.40	.25
319a	A94	20c	1.75	.25
		Nos. 314a-319a (5)	5.70	1.25

Imperf., Pairs

No.	Type	Description	Unused	Used
314b	A94	½c	3.25	3.25
315b	A94	1c	2.50	2.50
316b	A94	2c	3.25	3.25
317b	A94	5c	3.25	3.25
318a	A94	10c	4.25	4.25

319b	A94	20c	7.75	7.75
320a	A95	1p	65.00	65.00
		Nos. 314b-320a (7)	89.25	89.25

On the redrawn types, the imprint is close to the base of the design instead of being spaced from it. On the redrawn 2c and 5c, the lower end of the vertical white line below "OR" of "CORREOS" forms a hook which turns to the right instead of to the left as in the originals.

See Nos. 325-330. For surcharges see Nos. 351-354, L1-L7, L9-L13, L15-L25.

A97

100p has different frame.

1903 ***Imperf.***

323	A97	50p org yel, *pale pink*	92.50	92.50
324	A97	100p dk bl, *dk rose*	77.50	77.50

Imprint: "Lit. Nacional"

Perf. 10, 13, 13½ and Compound

1908

325	A94	½c orange	.85	.25
a.		½c yellow	.85	.25
b.		Imperf., pair	2.50	1.90
c.		Without imprint	5.25	5.25
326	A94	1c yel grn	.75	.25
a.		Without imprint	.75	.25
d.		Imperf., pair	4.00	3.25
327	A94	2c red	.75	.25
a.		2c carmine	.75	.25
b.		Imperf., pair	4.00	3.25
328	A94	5c blue	.60	.25
a.		Imperf., pair	4.25	5.25
329	A94	10c violet	*50.00*	1.00
330	A94	20c gray blk	*50.00*	1.00
		Nos. 325-330 (6)	*102.95*	3.00

The above stamps may be easily distinguished from those of 1904 by the perforation, by the height of the design, 24mm instead of 23mm, and by the "Lit. Nacional" imprint.

Camilo Torres
A99

Policarpa Salavarrieta
A100

Bolívar Demanding Liberation of Slaves — A105

Designs: 2c, Nariño. 5c, Bolívar. 10c, Francisco José de Caldas. 20c, Francisco de Paula Santander. 10p, Bolívar Resigning.

1910, Aug. **Engr.** ***Perf. 12***

331	A99	½c violet & blk	.50	.30
a.		Center inverted	425.00	425.00
332	A100	1c deep green	.40	.25
333	A100	2c scarlet	.40	.25
334	A100	5c deep blue	1.25	.45
335	A100	10c plum	10.00	5.00
336	A100	20c black brn	15.00	5.50
337	A105	1p dk violet	85.00	25.00
338	A105	10p claret	325.00	250.00
		Nos. 331-338 (8)	437.55	286.75

Colombian independence centenary.

Caldas
A107

Monument to Battle of Boyacá
A113

View of Cartagena
A114

Coat of Arms
A118

Designs: 1c, Torres. 2c, Narino. 4c, Santander. 5c, Bolivar. 10c, Jose Maria Cordoba. 1p, Sucre. 2p, Rufino Cuervo. 5p, Antonio Ricaurte y Lozano.

1917 **Engr.** ***Perf. 14***

339	A107	½c bister	.35	.25
340	A107	1c green	.30	.25
341	A107	2c car rose	.30	.25
342	A107	4c violet	.90	.30
343	A107	5c dull blue	3.00	.25
344	A107	10c gray	3.00	.25
345	A113	20c red	1.50	.25
346	A114	50c carmine	1.75	.25
347	A107	1p brt blue	12.00	.40
348	A107	2p orange	13.50	.45
349	A107	5p gray	40.00	11.00
350	A118	10p dk brown	47.50	11.50
		Nos. 339-350 (12)	124.10	25.40

The 1c, 5c, 10c, 50c, 2p, 5p and 10p also exist perf. 11½ and 11½ compounded with 14.

Litho. varieties of Nos. 343, 345 and 346 are counterfeits made to defraud the government.

Imperforate examples of Nos. 339-350 are not known to have been regularly issued.

See Nos. 373-374, 400-405. For overprints and surcharges see Nos. 369-370, 377, 409-410, 440, C1, O3, O5-O9.

Nos. 318-319, 329-330 Surcharged in Red

1918 **On Issue of 1904**

351	A94	½c on 20c black	1.25	.35
352	A94	3c on 10c violet	3.00	.60

On Issue of 1908

353	A94	½c on 20c gray blk	10.00	6.25
354	A94	3c on 10c violet	15.00	5.00
		Nos. 351-354 (4)	29.25	12.20

Nos. 351-354 inclusive exist with surcharge reading up or down. On one stamp in each sheet the letter "S" in "Especie" is omitted. All denominations exist with a small zero before the decimal in the surcharge.

A119

1918 **Litho.** ***Perf. 13½***

358	A119	3c red	.95	.25
a.		Imperf., pair	5.00	5.00

A120

1920 **Engr.** ***Perf. 14***

359	A120	3c red, *org*	.40	.25
a.		Imperf., pair	3.75	3.75

See No. 371-372. For surcharge see No. 453.

A121

A122

A123

Perf. 10, 13½ and Compound

1920-21 **Litho.**

360	A121	½c yellow	1.40	.50
361	A121	1c green	.85	.25
362	A121	2c red	.65	.25
363	A122	3c green	.65	.25
a.		3c yellow green	.65	.25
364	A121	5c blue	1.25	.25
365	A121	10c violet	6.00	1.50
366	A121	20c deep green	6.75	4.00
367	A123	50c dark red	8.50	4.00
		Nos. 360-367 (8)	26.05	11.00

The tablet with "PROVISIONAL" was added separately to each design on the various lithographic stones and its position varies slightly on different stamps in the sheet. For some values there were two or more stones, on which the tablet was placed at various angles.

Nos. 360-366 exist imperf.

See No. 375.

No. 342 Surcharged in Red

a

(15mm wide) — b

1921

369	A107 (a)	3c on 4c violet	.95	.25
a.		Double surcharge	15.00	
370	A107 (b)	3c on 4c violet	3.75	2.00

See No. 377.

Types of 1917-21

1923-24 **Engr.** ***Perf. 13½***

371	A120	1½c chocolate	1.25	.60
372	A120	3c blue	.50	.25
373	A107	5c claret ('24)	3.00	.25
374	A107	10c blue	9.25	.50

Litho.

375	A121	10c dark blue	12.50	7.25
		Nos. 371-375 (5)	26.50	8.85

No. 342 Surcharged in Red

(18mm wide)

1924

377	A107	3c on 4c vio	3.75	1.50
a.		Double surcharge	15.00	
b.		Double surch., one invtd.	15.00	
c.		With added surch. "3cs." in red		

A124

1924-25 **Litho.** ***Perf. 10, 10x13½***

379	A124	1c red	.85	.25
380	A124	3c dp blue ('25)	.85	.25

Exist imperf. Value, each pair $6.25.

A125

A126

Black, Red or Green Srch. & Ovpt.

Imprint of Waterlow & Sons

1925 ***Perf. 14, 14½***

382	A125	1c on 3c bis brn	.70	.25
383	A126	4c violet (R)	.50	.25
a.		Inverted surcharge	8.75	8.75

Imprint of American Bank Note Co.

Perf. 12

384	A125	1c on 3c bis brn	7.50	6.25
a.		Inverted surcharge	19.00	19.00
385	A126	4c violet (G)	.50	.30
a.		Inverted overprint	9.50	9.50
		Nos. 382-385 (4)	9.20	7.05

Correos

Provisional

Revenue stamps of basic types A125 and A126 were handstamped as above in violet or blue by the Cali post office in 1925, but were not authorized by the government. Denominations so overprinted are 1c, 2c, 3c, 4c and 5c.

A127

A128

Perf. 10, 13½x10

1926 **Litho.** **Wmk. 194**

395	A127	1c gray green	.50	.25
396	A128	4c deep blue	.55	.25

Exist imperf. Value, each pair $5.

Types of 1917 and

Sabana Station — A129

1926-29 **Unwmk.** **Engr.** ***Perf. 14***

400	A107	4c deep blue	.50	.25
401	A118	8c dark blue	.60	.25
402	A107	30c olive bister	6.00	.70
403	A129	40c brn & yel brn	9.25	1.25
404	A107	5p violet	9.25	.90
a.		Perf. 11 ('29)	12.00	1.00
405	A118	10p green	15.00	2.50
a.		Perf. 11 ('29)	30.00	4.75
		Nos. 400-405 (6)	40.60	5.85

For surcharges & overprint see Nos. 409-410, O4.

Death of Bolívar
A130

1930, Dec. 17 ***Perf. 12½***

408	A130	4c dk blue & blk	.60	.35

Cent. of the death of Simón Bolívar. See Nos. C80-C82.

Nos. 400 and 402 Surcharged in Red or Dark Blue

1932, Jan. 20 *Perf. 14*

409 A107 1c on 4c dp bl (R) .30 .25
a. Inverted surcharge 5.25 5.25
410 A107 20c on 30c ol bis 10.00 .70
a. Inverted surcharge 21.00
b. Double surcharge 21.00

Emerald Mine — A131

Oil Wells — A132

Coffee Cultivation A133

Platinum Mine — A134

Gold Mining — A135

Christopher Columbus — A136

Imprint: "Waterlow & Sons Ltd. Londres"

1932 Wmk. 229 *Perf. 12½*

411 A131 1c green .60 .25
412 A132 2c red .60 .25
413 A133 5c brown .70 .25
414 A134 8c blue blk 4.75 .60
415 A135 10c yellow 3.50 .25
416 A136 20c dk blue 10.00 .40
Nos. 411-416 (6) 20.15 2.00

See Nos. 441-442, 464-466a, 517. For surcharges see Nos. 455, 527, O1, O10-O11, O13, RA30.

Pedro de Heredia — A137

Perf. 11½

1934, Jan. 10 Unwmk. Litho.

417 A137 1c dark green 3.00 .80
418 A137 5c chocolate 3.75 .65
419 A137 8c dark blue 3.00 .80
Nos. 417-419 (3) 9.75 2.25

Cartagena, 400th anniv. See Nos. C111-C114.

Coffee Picking — A138

1934, Dec. Engr. *Perf. 12*

420 A138 5c brown 3.00 .25

Soccer — A139

Condor — A145

Allegory of Olympic Games at Barranquilla — A140

Foot Race A141

Tennis A142

Pier at Puerto Colombia A143

View of the Bay A144

Designs: 4c, Discus Thrower. 10c, Hurdling. 15c, Athlete in stadium. 18c, Baseball. 24c, Swimming. 50c, View of Barranquilla. 1p, Post and Telegraph Building. 2p, Monument to Flag. 5p, Coat of Arms.

1935, Jan. 26 Litho. *Perf. 11½*

421 A139 2c bluish grn & buff 1.60 .50
422 A139 4c deep green 1.60 .50
423 A140 5c dk brn & yel 1.60 .50
a. Horiz. pair, imperf. btwn. 240.00
424 A141 7c dk carmine 3.00 1.75
425 A142 8c blk & pink 2.50 2.50
426 A141 10c brown & bl 3.50 1.75
427 A143 12c indigo 4.25 3.00
428 A141 15c bl & red brn 7.25 5.50
429 A141 18c dk vio & buff 10.00 8.25
430 A144 20c purple & grn 8.50 7.00
431 A144 24c bluish grn & ultra 8.50 6.75
432 A144 50c ultra & buff 13.00 10.00
433 A145 1p drab & blue 120.00 62.50
434 A145 2p dull grn & gray 140.00 110.00
435 A145 5p pur blk & bl 475.00 500.00
436 A145 10p black & gray 550.00 575.00
Nos. 421-436 (16) 1,350. 1,295.

3rd Natl. Olympic Games, Barranquilla. Counterfeits of 10p exist.

Oil Wells — A155

Gold Mining — A157

Imprint: "American Bank Note Co."

1935, Mar. Unwmk. Engr. *Perf. 12*

437 A155 2c carmine rose .45 .25
439 A157 10c deep orange 25.00 .25

See Nos. 468, 470, 498, 516. For surcharge and overprints see Nos. 496, 596, O2.

No. 347 Surcharged in Black

1935, Aug. *Perf. 14*

440 A107 12c on 1p brt bl 4.75 1.50

Types of 1932
Imprint: "Lit. Nacional Bogotá"

1935-36 Litho. *Perf. 11, 11½, 12½*

441 A131 1c lt green .25 .25
a. Imperf., pair 4.25
442 A133 5c brown ('36) .70 .25
a. Imperf., pair 4.75 4.00

For overprints and surcharges, see Nos. 527, O1.

Bolívar A159

Tequendama Falls A160

Wmk. Wavy Lines. (229)

1937 Engr. *Perf. 12½*

443 A159 1c deep green .25 .25
a. Perf. 14 .25 .25
444 A160 12c deep blue 3.25 1.10

See No. 570. For surcharges and overprints see Nos. 454, 456, C231, C326, O12.

Soccer Player A161

Discus Thrower A162

Runner — A163

1937, Jan. 4 Photo. Unwmk.

445 A161 3c lt green 1.40 .85
446 A162 10c carmine rose 3.75 1.75
447 A163 1p black 35.00 26.00
Nos. 445-447 (3) 40.15 28.60

National Olympic Games, Manizales. For surcharge see No. 452.

Exposition Palace — A164

Stadium at Barranquilla A165

Monument to the Colors A166

1937, Jan. 4

448 A164 5c violet brown 2.75 .40
449 A165 15c blue 6.75 4.50
450 A166 50c orange brn 19.00 9.75
Nos. 448-450 (3) 28.50 14.65

Barranquilla National Exposition.

Stamps of 1926-37 Surcharged in Black

1937-38 Unwmk. *Perf. 12½*

452 A161 1c on 3c lt grn 1.00 1.00
a. Inverted surcharge 2.25 2.25
453 A118 5c on 8c dk bl .50 .45
a. Inverted surcharge 2.25 2.25

Wmk. 229

454 A160 2c on 12c dp bl .50 .40
455 A134 5c on 8c bl blk .60 *.65*
a. Invtd. surcharge 2.00 2.00
456 A160 10c on 12c dp bl ('38) 5.50 1.00
a. Dbl. surcharge 11.00 11.00
Nos. 452-456 (5) 8.10 3.50

Calle del Arco — A168

Entrance to Church of the Rosary — A169

Arms of Bogotá A170

Gonzálo Jiménez de Quesada A171

Bochica A172

Santo Domingo Convent A173

Mass of the Conquistadors — A174

1938, July 27 Unwmk. *Perf. 12½*

457	A168	1c yellow green	.25	.25
458	A169	2c scarlet	.25	.25
459	A170	5c brown blk	.35	.25
460	A171	10c brown	.75	.40
461	A172	15c brt blue	3.75	1.60
462	A173	20c brt red vio	3.75	1.60
463	A174	1p red brown	50.00	29.00
		Nos. 457-463 (7)	59.10	33.35

Bogotá, 400th anniversary.

Types of 1932
Imprint: "Litografia Nacional Bogotá"

1938, Dec. 5 Litho. *Perf. 10½, 11*

464	A132	2c rose	1.00	.35
465	A135	10c yellow	2.50	.35
466	A136	20c dull blue	10.00	1.25
a.		20c dark blue, perf. 12½ ('44)	62.50	6.25
		Nos. 464-466 (3)	13.50	1.95

Types of 1935 and

Bolívar
A175

Coffee Picking
A176

Arms of
Colombia
A177

Christopher
Columbus
A178

Caldas
A179

Sabana Station
A180

Imprint: "American Bank Note Co."

Wmk. 255

1939, Mar. 3 Engr. *Perf. 12*

467	A175	1c green	.25	.25
468	A155	2c car rose	.25	.25
469	A176	5c dull brown	.25	.25
470	A157	10c deep orange	.50	.25
471	A177	15c dull blue	1.75	.25
472	A178	20c violet blk	19.00	.25
473	A179	30c olive bister	5.50	.35
474	A180	40c bister brn	17.00	3.75
		Nos. 467-474 (8)	44.50	5.60

See Nos. 497-499, 515, 518, 574. For surcharges and overprints see Nos. 506-507, 520-522, 596, RA26, RA47.

Gen.
Santander
A181

Allegory
A182

Gen.
Santander
A183

Statue at
Cúcuta
A184

Birthplace of
Santander
A185

Church at
Rosario
A186

Paya — A187

Bridge at
Boyacá — A188

Death of General
Santander
A189

Invasion of the
Liberators
A190

Perf. 13x13½, 13½x13

1940, May 6 Engr. Wmk. 229

475	A181	1c olive green	.25	.25
476	A182	2c dk carmine	.50	.35
477	A183	5c sepia	.25	.25
478	A184	8c carmine	1.75	1.75
479	A185	10c orange yel	.80	.60
480	A186	15c dark blue	2.10	1.40
481	A187	20c green	2.75	2.10
482	A188	50c violet	6.50	6.00
483	A189	1p deep rose	20.00	20.00
484	A190	2p orange	65.00	65.00
		Nos. 475-484 (10)	99.90	97.70

Death of General Francisco Santander, cent.

Tobacco Plant
A194

Gen.
Santander
A195

Garcia
Rovira — A196

R.
Galan — A197

Antonio Sucre — A198

1940-43 Engr. Wmk. 255 *Perf. 12*

488	A194	8c rose car & grn	1.25	.65
489	A195	15c dp blue ('43)	1.25	.25
490	A196	20c gray blk ('41)	4.75	.50
491	A197	40c brown bis ('41)	2.75	.50
492	A198	1p black	5.00	1.25
		Nos. 488-492 (5)	15.00	3.15

See Nos. 500, 554. For overprint see No. RA28.

Arms of
Palmira — A199

Unwmk.

1942, July 4 Litho. *Perf. 11*

493	A199	30c claret	5.50	.65

8th Natl. Agricultural Exposition, held at Palmira.

Paradise of
Isaacs,
Palmira — A200

1942, July 4

494	A200	50c lt blue grn	5.50	.85

Issued in honor of the writer, Jorge Isaacs.

Signing Treaty of
the Wisconsin
A201

1942, Nov. 21 *Perf. 10½*

495	A201	10c dull orange	3.75	.50
a.		"2. XI.1902" instead of "21. XI. 1902"	22.50	*25.00*
b.		Perf. 12	6.00	6.00

40th anniv. of the signing of the Treaty of the Wisconsin, Nov. 21, 1902.

No. 470 Surcharged
in Black

1944 Wmk. 255 *Perf. 12*

496	A157	5c on 10c dp org	.25	.25

Counterfeits exist of No. 496 with inverted or double surcharge.

Types of 1935-41 and

National
Shrine — A202

San Pedro
Alejandrino
A203

Imprint: "Columbian Bank Note Co."

1944-45 Unwmk. Engr. *Perf. 11*

497	A175	1c green	.25	.25
498	A155	2c rose	.25	.25
499	A176	5c dull brown	.25	.25
500	A196	20c gray black	3.75	.75
501	A202	30c dl ol grn ('45)	2.25	1.25
502	A203	50c rose	2.25	1.25
		Nos. 497-502 (6)	9.00	4.00

No. 499
Surcharged in
Black

1944, Oct.

506	A176	1c on 5c dull brn	.25	.25
507	A176	2c on 5c dull brn	.25	.25

Nos. 506 and 507 exist with inverted or double surcharge, created by favor.

Flag — A204

Arms — A205

Murillo Toro — A206

Hospital of
St. John of
God
A207

Virrey Solis
A208

1944, Oct. 10 Litho.

508	A204	2c ultra & bis	.25	.25
a.		Sheet of 18	15.00	
b.		Imperf., pair	15.00	
509	A205	5c ultra & bis	.25	.25
a.		Sheet of 22	18.00	
b.		Imperf., pair	15.00	
510	A206	20c blk & bluish grn	.80	.80
a.		Sheet of 8	16.00	
b.		Imperf., pair	22.50	
511	A207	40c blk & red	3.50	3.50
a.		Sheet of 4	26.00	
512	A208	1p blk & red	9.50	9.50
a.		Sheet of 2	30.00	
		Nos. 508-512 (5)	14.30	14.30

Souvenir Sheet

Perf. 11x11½ All Around, Stamps Imperf.

513	Sheet of 5, #508-512	25.00	*40.00*
	Never hinged	40.00	

75th anniv. of Gen. Benevolent Assoc. of Cundinamarca.

Nos. 508-513 were printed in composite sheets containing one each of Nos. 508a, 509a, 510a, 511a and 512a, and two of 513. Fifty of these were presented to government officials.

Murillo
Toro — A210

1944, Nov. 10 *Perf. 11*

514	A210	5c lt brown	.30	.25

Types of 1932-39 and

San Pedro Alejandrino A211

Imprint: "Litografia Nacional Bogota"

1944 Litho. *Perf. 12½*

515	A175 1c dp green		.25	.25
	a.	1c olive green	.35	.25
	b.	Imperf., pair	1.75	1.75
516	A155 2c dk carmine		.25	.25
	a.	Imperf., pair	1.75	1.75
517	A135 10c yellow org		3.50	.45
518	A179 30c gray olive		12.00	1.75
	a.	Imperf., pair	35.00	
519	A211 50c rose		12.00	5.25
	Nos. 515-519 (5)		28.00	7.95

No. 469 Overprinted in Green, Blue or Red

Wmk. 255

1945, July 19 Engr. *Perf. 12*

520	A176 5c dull brn (G)	.40	.25
521	A176 5c dull brn (R)	.40	.25
522	A176 5c dull brn (Bl)	.40	.25
	Nos. 520-522 (3)	1.20	.75

Portraits are Joseph Stalin, Franklin D. Roosevelt and Winston Churchill.

Nos. 520-522 exist with overprint inverted. Value, $20 each.

Clock Tower, Cartagena — A212

1945, Nov. 15

523	A212 50c olive black	4.25	1.60

For overprints see Nos. 543-544.

Sierra Nevada of Santa Marta A213

Designs: 30c, Seaplane Tolima. 50c, San Sebastian Fort, Cartagena.

Unwmk.

1945, Dec. 14 Litho. *Perf. 11*

524	A213 20c light green	2.00	1.40
525	A213 30c pale blue	2.00	1.40
526	A213 50c salmon pink	2.00	1.40
	Nos. 524-526 (3)	6.00	4.20

25th anniv. of the 1st airmail service in America, according to the inscription, but earlier services are known to have existed.

No. 442 Surcharged in Black

1946, Mar. 8 *Perf. 11x11½, 12½*

527	A133 1c on 5c brown	.25	.25
	a. Inverted surcharge	.90	

Gen. Antonio Jose de Sucre — A216

Wmk. 255

1946, Apr. 16 Engr. *Perf. 12*

Size: 19x26½mm

528	A216 1c brn & turq grn	.25	.25
529	A216 2c vio & rose car	.25	.25

Size: 23x31mm

530	A216 5c sepia & blue	.25	.25
531	A216 9c dk grn & red	.50	*1.60*
532	A216 10c ultra & org	.40	.50
533	A216 20c blk & dp org	.40	.50
534	A216 30c brn red & grn	.55	.35
535	A216 40c ol blk & red vio	.55	.40
536	A216 50c dp brn & vio	.55	.40
	Nos. 528-536 (9)	3.70	4.50

Map of South America — A217

Unwmk.

1946, June 7 Litho. *Perf. 11*

537	A217 15c ultra	.50	.50
	a. Imperf., pair	4.00	

National Observatory — A218

1946, Aug.

538	A218 5c fawn	.25	.25
	a. Imperf., pair	6.00	

See No. 565.

Andrés Bello — A219

Wmk. 255

1946, Sept. 3 Engr. *Perf. 12*

539	A219 3c sepia	.25	.25
540	A219 10c orange	.40	.35
541	A219 15c slate black	.45	.35
	Nos. 539-541,C145 (4)	1.35	1.20

Bello (1781-1865), poet and educator.

Joaquín de Cayzedo y Cuero — A220

1946, Sept. 20 Wmk. 229 *Perf. 12½*

542	A220 2p bluish green	3.50	1.25

See No. 568. For surcharge see No. 613.

Type of 1945, Overprinted in Black or Green

1946, Dec. 6 Wmk. 255 *Perf. 12*

543	A212 50c red (Bk)	1.50	2.75
	a. Double overprint	25.00	
544	A212 50c red (G)	1.50	2.75
	a. Double overprint	25.00	

5th Central American and Caribbean Championship Games.

Coffee — A221

Engraved and Lithographed

1947, Jan. 10 Wmk. 229 *Perf. 12½*

545	A221 5c multicolored	.30	.25

Colombian Orchid: Masdevallia Nycterina A222

Designs (Orchids): 2c, Miltonia vexillaria. No. 548, Cattleya chocoensis. No. 549, Odontoglossum crispum. No. 550, Cattleya dowiana aurea. 10c, Cattleya labiata trianae.

1947, Feb. 7 Wmk. 255 *Perf. 12*

546	A222 1c multicolored	.25	.25
547	A222 2c multicolored	.25	.25
548	A222 5c multicolored	.60	.25
549	A222 5c multicolored	.60	.25
550	A222 5c multicolored	.60	.25
551	A222 10c multicolored	.90	.35
	Nos. 546-551 (6)	3.20	1.60

Antonio Nariño — A228

Alberto Urdaneta y Urdaneta — A229

Perf. 12½

1947, May 9 Litho. Unwmk.

552	A228 5c blue, *grnsh*	.25	.25
553	A229 10c red brn, *grnsh*	.30	.25
	Nos. 552-553,C146-C147 (4)	1.40	1.20

4th Pan-American Press Congress, 1946.

Sucre Type of 1940

1947 Wmk. 255 Engr. *Perf. 12*

554	A198 1p violet	2.75	1.25

José Celestino Mutis and José Jerónimo Triana A230

Miguel A. Caro and Rufino J. Cuervo — A231

1947 Wmk. 229 *Perf. 12½*

555	A230 25c olive green	.50	.40
556	A231 3p dark purple	4.00	3.75

See Nos. 567, 569. For surcharge see No. 610.

Metropolitan Cathedral, Plaza Bolívar, Bogotá — A232

National Capitol A233

Ministry of Foreign Affairs A234

A235

1948, Apr. 2

557	A232 5c black brown	.25	.25
558	A233 10c orange	.40	.55
559	A234 15c dark blue	.40	.55
	Nos. 557-559,C148-C149 (5)	2.20	2.50

Miniature Sheet

Imperf

560	A235 50c slate	2.00	1.60

9th Pan-American Conf., Bogotá.

No. RA5A Overprinted in Black

1948 Unwmk. *Perf. 12½*

Without Gum

561	PT3 1c yellow orange	.25	.25

The letter "C" is the initial of "CORREOS."

Nos. RA33, RA24 and RA25 Overprinted in Black

1948 Wmk. 255 *Perf. 12.*

562	PT6 1c olive	.25	.25
563	PT6 2c green	.25	.25
564	PT6 20c brown	.25	.25
	Nos. 562-564 (3)	.75	.75

Nos. 561-564 exist with inverted and double overprints.

Observatory Type of 1946

Unwmk.

1948, June 30 Litho. *Perf. 11*

565	A218 5c blue	.25	.25

Simón Bolívar — A236

Wmk. 255

1948, May 29 Engr. *Perf. 12*

566 A236 15c green		.40	.25

Types of 1946-47

1948 Unwmk. *Perf. 12½*

567 A230 25c green		.25	.25
568 A220 2p dp green		.55	.25
569 A231 3p dp red violet		.55	.35
	Nos. 567-569 (3)	1.35	.85

Falls Type of 1937

1948 Wmk. 229

570 A160 10c red		.25	.25

For overprints see Nos. C231, C326.

Carlos Martinez Silva — A237

Perf. 13½

1948, Dec. 21 Unwmk. Litho.

571 A237 40c carmine		.40	.25

Juan de Dios Carrasquilla A238

1949, May 20 Wmk. 229 *Perf. 12½*

572 A238 5c bister		.25	.25

75th anniv. of the foundation of the Colombian Soc. of Agriculture.

Julio Garavito Armero — A239

Wmk. 229

1949, Apr. 24 Engr. *Perf. 12*

573 A239 4c green		.35	.25

Issued to honor Julio Garavito Armero (1865-1920), mathematician.

Coffee Type of 1939

Imprint: "American Bank Note Co."

1949, Aug. 4 Wmk. 255

574 A176 5c blue		.25	.25

Arms of Colombia — A240

1949, Oct. 7 Unwmk. *Perf. 13*

575 A240 15c blue		.25	.25

Issued to honor the new Constitution. See Nos. C164-C165.

Shield and Tree — A241

1949, Oct. 13 Wmk. 229 *Perf. 12½*

576 A241 5c olive		.25	.25

4th anniv. of Colombia's 1st Forestry Cong. and propaganda for the government's reforestation program.

Francisco Javier Cisneros — A242

1949, Dec. 15 Photo. Unwmk.

577 A242 50c red vio & yel		.75	.60
578 A242 50c green & vio		.75	.60
579 A242 50c brown & lt bl		.75	.60
	Nos. 577-579 (3)	2.25	1.80

50th anniv. (in 1948) of the death of Francisco Javier Cisneros.

Masdevallia Chimaera A243

Odontoglossum Crispum — A244

Eastern Hemisphere — A245

Designs: 3c, Cattleya labiata trianae. 4c, Masdevallia nycterina. 5c, Cattleya dowiana aurea. 11c, Miltonia vexillaria. 18c, Santo Domingo post office.

1950, Aug. 22 Photo. *Perf. 13*

580 A243 1c brown		.25	.25
581 A244 2c violet		.25	.25
582 A243 3c rose lilac		.25	.25
583 A243 4c emerald		.30	.25
584 A243 5c red orange		.50	.25
585 A244 11c red		1.50	1.50
586 A244 18c ultra		2.50	.50
	Nos. 580-586 (7)	5.55	3.25

Miniature Sheet

Imperf

587 A245 50c orange yel		3.50	3.50

75th anniv. (in 1949) of the UPU. See No. C199. For surcharge see No. C232.

Antonio Baraya — A246

Perf. 12½

1950, Nov. 27 Unwmk. Engr.

588 A246 2c red		.25	.25

Colombian Farm A247

1950, Dec. 28 Photo. *Perf. 11½*

589 A247 5c dp car & buff		.25	.25
590 A247 5c bl grn & gray		.25	.25
591 A247 5c vio bl & gray		.25	.25
	Nos. 589-591 (3)	.75	.75

Issued to publicize rural life.

Arms of Bogotá A248

Arms of Colombia A249

Perf. 12x12½

1950, Dec. 28 Engr. Wmk. 255

592 A248 5p deep green		2.00	1.50
593 A249 10p red orange		6.00	2.00

Catalogue values for unused stamps in this section, from this point to the end of the section, are for Never Hinged items.

Map and Badge — A250

Perf. 12½x13

1951, Jan. 30 Photo. Unwmk.

594 A250 20c red, yel & bl		.60	.25

60th anniversary (in 1947) of the formation of the Colombian Society of Engineers.

Guillermo Valencia — A251

1951, Oct. 20 Engr. *Perf. 13x13½*

595 A251 25c black		1.20	.25

Issued to honor Guillermo Valencia (1873-1943), newspaper founder, governor of Cauca, presidential candidate, author.

No. 468 Overprinted in Black

1951, Dec. 11 Wmk. 255 *Perf. 12*

596 A155 2c carmine rose		.30	.25

Issued to publicize the reversion of the Mares oil concession to Colombia.

Nicolas Osorio — A252

No. 598, Pompilio Martinez. No. 599, Ezequiel Uricoechea. No. 600, Jose M. Lombana.

Perf. 11½

1952, Aug. 6 Unwmk. Engr.

Various Frames

597 A252 1c deep blue		.25	.25
598 A252 1c deep blue		.25	.25
599 A252 1c deep blue		.25	.25
600 A252 1c deep blue		.25	.25
	Nos. 597-600 (4)	1.00	1.00

Nos. 597-600 were printed in a single sheet containing four panes of twenty-five each, separated by double rows of ornamental tabs. Although inscribed "sobretasa," the stamps were for ordinary postage.

Types of Postal Tax Stamps of 1945-50 and

Communications Building
A253 A253a

1952 *Perf. 12*

601 A253 5c ultra		.35	.25

Wmk. 255

602 PT10 20c brown		10.00	4.50
603 PT6 25c dk gray		*42.50*	*42.50*
604 PT10 25c blue green		1.00	.25
605 A253a 50c orange yel		25.00	13.00
606 A253a 1p rose carmine		2.50	.30
607 A253a 2p lilac rose		25.00	9.75
608 A253a 2p violet		3.00	.65
	Nos. 601-608 (8)	109.35	71.20

Although inscribed "sobretasa," Nos. 601-608 were issued for ordinary postage.

For surcharges see Nos. 612, RA48.

Cathedral of Manizales — A254

Perf. 11½

1952, Oct. 10 Photo. Unwmk.

609 A254 23c blue & gray blk		.50	.25

Centenary of city of Manizales.
For surcharge see No. 619.

No. 555 Surcharged in Blue

1952, Oct. 30 Wmk. 229 *Perf. 12½*

610 A230 15c on 25c olive green		.45	.25

Latin American Siderurgical Conf., 1952. See No. C226.

Queen Isabella I and Monument A255

Perf. 12½

1953, Mar. 10 Unwmk. Engr.

611 A255 23c blue & black .95 .70

5th cent. of the birth of Queen Isabella I of Spain.

For surcharge see No. 693.

Nos. 606 and 568 Surcharged with New Values in Dark Blue

1953, Oct. 19 Wmk. 255

612 A253a 40c on 1p rose car 1.60 .25
613 A220 50c on 2p dp green 1.60 .25

Manuel Ancizar A256

Portraits: 23c, José Jeronimo Triana. 30c, Manuel Ponce de Leon. 1p, Agustin Codazzi.

Perf. 12½x13

1953, Nov. Engr. Unwmk.

Frames in Black

614 A256 14c rose red .70 .65
615 A256 23c ultra .60 .25
616 A256 30c chocolate .45 .25
617 A256 1p emerald .45 .25
Nos. 614-617 (4) 2.20 1.40

Cent. (in 1950) of the establishment of the Chorographic Commission. For surcharges and overprint see Nos. 620, 687, 690, 692, C284.

Murillo Toro and Map — A257

Black Surcharge

Engraved and Lithographed

1953, Dec. 12 Wmk. 255 *Perf. 12*

618 A257 5c on 5p multi .40 .25

2nd Natl. Phil. Exhib., Bogotá, Dec. 1953. See No. C237.

Nos. 609 and 614 Surcharged with New Value or New Value and Ornaments

1953 Unwmk. *Perf. 11½, 12½x13*

619 A254 5c on 23c (C) .40 .25
620 A256 5c on 14c (Bk) .40 .25

No. 614 surcharged "CINCO" in blue is listed as No. 687.

Symbolical of St. Francis Receiving Christ's Wounds — A258

1954, Apr. 23 Photo. *Perf. 11½*

621 A258 5c sepia & green .40 .25

400th anniversary of the establishment of Colombia's first Franciscan community.

Soldier, Map and Arms A259

1954, June 13 Engr. *Perf. 13*

622 A259 5c dull blue .25 .25

1st anniv. of the assumption of the presidency by Gen. Gustavo Rojas Pinilla. See Nos. C255, 637a.

Sports Emblem — A260

Design: 10c, Stadium and athlete holding arms of Colombia.

1954, July 18 Unwmk.

623 A260 5c deep blue .50 .25
624 A260 10c red .85 .25
Nos. 623-624,C256-C257 (4) 3.65 1.10

7th Natl. Athletic Games, Cali, July 1954.

History Academy Seal — A261

1954, July 24

625 A261 5c ultra & green .30 .25

50th anniversary (in 1952) of the Colombian Academy of History.

Convent and Cell of St. Peter Claver — A262

1954, Sept. 9

627 A262 5c dark green .25 .25
a. Souvenir sheet 8.00 *12.00*

300th anniv. of the death of St. Peter Claver.

No. 627a contains one stamp similar to No. 627, but printed in greenish black. Sheet size: 121x129½mm. See Nos. C258-C258a.

Mercury — A263

1954, Oct. 29

628 A263 5c orange .55 .25
Nos. 628,C259-C260 (3) 1.65 .75

1st Intl. Fair and Exhibition, Bogota, 1954.

Tapestry Madonna A264

College Cloister A265

Designs: 10c, Brother Cristobal de Torres. 20c, College chapel and arms.

Perf. 12½x11½, 11½x12½

1954, Dec. 6

629 A264 5c orange & blk .40 .25
630 A264 10c blue .40 .25
631 A265 15c violet brn .40 .25
632 A265 20c black & brn 1.00 .35
a. Souvenir sheet 12.00 *16.00*
Nos. 629-632,C263-C266 (8) 6.80 2.80

Founding of the Senior College of Our Lady of the Rosary, Bogota, 300th anniv. (in 1953).

No. 632a contains four stamps similar to Nos. 629-632, but printed in different colors: 5c yellow and black, 10c green, 15c dull violet, 20c black and light-blue.

Steel Mill — A266

1954, Dec. 12 *Perf. 12½x13*

633 A266 5c ultra & blk .25 .25

Issued to mark the opening of the Paz del Rio steel mill, October 1954. See No. C267.

José Marti — A267

1955, Jan. 28 *Perf. 13½x13*

634 A267 5c deep carmine .25 .25

Centenary of the birth of José Marti (1853-1895), Cuban patriot. See No. C268.

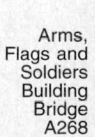

Arms, Flags and Soldiers Building Bridge A268

1955, Mar. 23 *Perf. 12½*

635 A268 10c claret .30 .25

Issued to honor Colombian soldiers who served in Korea, 1951-53. See Nos. 637a, C269.

Fleet Emblem — A269

M. S. City of Manizales and New York Skyline A270

1955, Apr. 12 Unwmk.

636 A269 15c deep green .25 .25
637 A270 20c violet .45 .25
a. Souvenir sheet 9.50 *12.00*
Nos. 636-637,C270-C271 (4) 2.00 1.15

Grand-Colombian Merchant Fleet.

No. 637a contains four stamps similar to Nos. 622, 635-637, but printed in different colors: 5c blue, 10c dark carmine, 15c green, 20c purple.

Hotel Tequendama and Church of San Diego — A271

1955, May 16 Photo. *Perf. 11½x12*

638 A271 5c blue .25 .25

See No. C273.

Bolivar's Country Estate, Bogotá A272

1955, Sept. 28 Engr. *Perf. 12½*

639 A272 5c deep ultra .25 .25

50th anniv. of Rotary Intl. See No. C274.

Belalcazar, Jiménez de Quesada and Balboa A273

Caravels and Columbus A274

5c, San Martin, Bolivar and Washington.

Engraved and Photogravure

1955, Oct. 29 *Perf. 13x12½*

640 A273 2c yel grn & brn .50 .25
641 A273 5c brt bl & brn .50 .25
642 A274 23c lt ultra & blk .55 .25
a. Souvenir sheet 24.00 24.00
Nos. 640-642,C275-C280 (9) 29.85 15.00

7th Cong. of the Postal Union of the Americas and Spain, Bogota, Oct. 12-Nov. 9, 1955.

No. 642a contains one each of Nos. 640-642, printed in slightly different shades.

José Eusebio Caro — A275

1955, Nov. 29 Engr. *Perf. 13½x13*

643	A275	5c brown	.25	.25

José Eusebio Caro (1817-53), poet. See No. C281.

Departmental Issue

Map — A276

View of San Andres Harbor — A277

Cattle at Waterhole A278

Designs: 2c, Docks, Atlantico. 3c, "Industry," Antioquia. 4c, Cartagena Harbor, Bolivar. No. 647, Steel Mill, Boyaca. No. 648, Cattle, Cordoba. No. 649, Map. No. 650, San Andres Harbor. No. 651, Cacao picker, Cauca. 10c, Coffee picker, Caldas. 15c, Salt Mine Chapel, Zipaquira, Cundinamarca. 20c, Tropical plants and map, Choco. 23c, Harvester, Huila. 25c, Banana plantation, Magdalena. 30c, Gold mining, Nariño. 40c, Tobacco plantation, Santander. 50c, Oil wells, North Santander. 60c, Cotton plantation, Tolima. 1p, Sugar industry, Cauca. 3p, Amazon river at Leticia, Amazonas. 5p, Windmills and panoramic view, La Guajira. 10p, Rubber plantation, Vaupes.

Perf. 13½x13, 13x13½, 13

Engr.; Engr. & Litho.

1956 Unwmk.

Various Frames

644	A277	2c car & grn	.25	.25
645	A276	3c brn vio & blk	.25	.25
646	A277	4c grn & blk	.25	.25
647	A276	5c dk brn & bl	.25	.25
648	A277	5c ol & dk vio brn	.30	.25
649	A276	5c bl & blk	.25	.25
650	A277	5c car & grnsh bl	.25	.25
651	A277	5c ol grn & red brn	.25	.25
652	A276	10c org & blk	.40	.25
653	A276	15c ultra & blk	.25	.25
654	A276	20c dk brn & bl	.25	.25
655	A277	23c ultra & ver	.30	.25
656	A277	25c ol grn & blk	.30	.25
657	A277	30c ultra & brn	.25	.25
658	A277	40c dl pur & red brn	.25	.25
659	A277	50c dk grn & blk	.25	.25
660	A277	60c pale brn & grn	.25	.25
661	A278	1p mag & grnsh bl	1.90	.25
662	A278	2p grn & red brn	2.75	.25
663	A278	3p car & blk	4.25	.50
664	A278	5p brn & lt ultra	7.50	1.00
665	A276	10p red brn & grn	20.00	6.00
		Nos. 644-665 (22)	40.95	12.25

Nos. 645, 647, 649, 652-654 measure 27x32mm, No. 665 27x37mm. See Nos. 681-684, 685, 688-689. For surcharges and overprints see Nos. 685, 688-689, C289, C312.

Columbus and Proposed Lighthouse A279

1956, Oct. 12 Photo. *Perf. 12*

666	A279	3c gray black	.50	.25

Issued in honor of Christopher Columbus. See Nos. C285, C306.

Altar of St. Elizabeth and Tomb of Jimenez de Quesada A280

1956, Nov. 19 Unwmk.

667	A280	5c red lilac	.25	.25

7th cent. of St. Elizabeth of Hungary, patron saint of Sante Fé de Bogotá. See No. C286.

St. Ignatius of Loyola — A281

1956, Nov. 26 Engr. *Perf. 12½x13*

668	A281	5c blue	.25	.25

400th anniv. of the death of St. Ignatius of Loyola. See No. C287. For overprint see No. C324.

Javier Pereira — A282

1956, Dec. 28 Unwmk. *Perf. 12*

669	A282	5c blue	.25	.25

Issued to honor 167-year-old Javier Pereira. See No. C288.

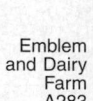

Emblem and Dairy Farm A283

Designs: 2c, Emblem and tractor. 5c, Emblem, coffee and corn.

1957, Mar. 5 Photo. *Perf. 14x13½*

670	A283	1c lt ol grn	.25	.25
671	A283	2c lt brn	.25	.25
672	A283	5c lt bl	.25	.25
		Nos. 670-672,C292-C296 (8)	3.35	2.60

Agrarian Savings Bank of Colombia, 25th anniv.

For overprint see No. C322.

Arms of Military Academy and Gen. Rafael Reyes A284

Design: 10c, Arms and Academy.

1957, July 20 Engr. *Perf. 12½*

673	A284	5c blue	.25	.25
674	A284	10c orange	.40	.25
a.		Souv. sheet of 2	22.50	22.50
		Nos. 673-674,C299-C300 (4)	1.40	1.00

50th anniv. of the Colombian Military Academy.

No. 674a contains one each of Nos. 673-674 in slightly different shades.

For overprints see Nos. C328, C312.

Statue of José Matias Delgado — A285

1957, Sept. 16 Photo. *Perf. 12*

675	A285	2c rose brn	.25	.25

Issued in honor of Jose Matias Delgado, liberator of El Salvador. See No. C301.

Santo Michelena, Marcos y Crespo, P. Alcantara Herran and UPU Monument A286

1957, Oct. 10 Unwmk.

676	A286	5c green	.25	.25
677	A286	10c gray	.30	.25
		Nos. 676-677,C302-C303 (4)	1.25	1.00

Intl. Letter Writing Week and 14th UPU Cong.

St. Vincent de Paul and Children — A287

1957, Oct. 18

678	A287	1c dark olive green	.25	.25

Colombian Society of St. Vincent de Paul, cent. See No. C304. For overprint see No. C323.

Fencer A288

1957, Nov. 22 Photo. *Perf. 12*

679	A288	4c lilac	.25	.25

3rd South American Fencing Championship. See No. C305. For overprint see No. C332.

Francisco José de Caldas and Hypsometer — A289

1958, May 12 Unwmk. *Perf. 12*

680	A289	10c black	.25	.25
		Nos. 680,C309-C310 (3)	1.40	.75

International Geophysical Year, 1957-58.

Departmental Issue Type of 1956

Designs as before.

1958 Engr. *Perf. 13*

681	A276	3c ultra & brn	.25	.25
682	A276	3c ol grn & pur	.25	.25
683	A276	10c grn & brn	.25	.25
684	A276	10c dk bl & brn	.25	.25
		Nos. 681-684 (4)	1.00	1.00

Nos. 646, C291, 614, 653, 655, 616, C308, 615 and 611 Surcharged with New Value, and Old Value Obliterated, or Overprinted in Dark Blue or Green

Perf. 12½, 12½x13, 13

1958-59 Unwmk.

685	A277	2c on 4c grn & blk	.25	.25
686	AP48	5c dp plum & multi ('59)	.25	.25
687	A256	5c on 14c blk & rose red ("CINCO") ('59)	.30	.30
688	A276	5c on 15c ultra & blk	.25	.25
689	A277	5c on 23c ultra & ver (G)	.25	.25
690	A256	5c on 30c blk & choc ("CINCO")	.25	.25
691	AP40	10c on 25c rose vio	.25	.25
692	A256	20c on 23c blk & ultra (G) ("VEINTE") ('59)	.30	.25
693	A255	20c on 23c bl & blk ('59)	.30	.25
		Nos. 685-693 (9)	2.40	2.30

On No. 686 the words "Correo Extra Rapido" are obliterated in dark blue.

Father Rafael Almanza and Church of San Diego, Bogota A290

1958, Oct. 23 Photo. *Perf. 14x13*

695	A290	10c purple	.25	.25
		Nos. 695,C313-C314 (3)	.80	.75

For overprint see No. C336.

Msgr. R. M. Carrasquilla and Church A291

1959, Jan. 22 *Perf. 14x13*

696	A291	10c dk red brn	.25	.25
		Nos. 696,C315-C316 (3)	1.30	.75

Cent. of the birth of Msgr. R. M. Carrasquilla (1857-1930), rector of Our Lady of the Rosary Seminary, Bogotá. For overprints see Nos. C335, C341.

Miss Universe 1959 — A292

1959, June 26 Photo. *Perf. 11½*

697	A292	10c multi	.80	.25
		Nos. 697,C317-C318 (3)	50.05	49.15

Luz Marina Zuluaga, Miss Universe, 1959.

For overprint see No. C342.

Jorge Eliecer Gaitan — A293

1959, July 28 Engr. *Perf. 12x13½*

698 A293 10c on 3c gray bl (Bl) .25 .25
699 A293 30c rose vio .45 .25
Nos. 698-699,C319-C320 (4) 4.20 3.50

Issued in honor of Jorge Eliecer Gaitan (1898-1948), lawyer and politician.

No. 698 exists without blue surcharge.

Gen. Francisco de Paula Santander — A294

Designs: Nos. 701, 703, Simon Bolivar.

1959 Litho. Wmk. 331 *Perf. 12½*

700 A294 5c brown & yel .25 .25
701 A294 5c ultra & bl .25 .25
702 A294 10c gray & grn .25 .25
703 A294 10c gray & red .25 .25
Nos. 700-703,C389 (5) 4.50 1.45

Capitol, Bogota A295

1959

704 A295 2c dk bl & red brn .25 .25
705 A295 3c blk brn & lilac .25 .25

Stamp of 1859 and Mail Transport by Mule — A296

Designs (various stamps of 1859 and): 10c, Mail boat on the Magdalena river. 15c, as 5c. 25c, Train.

Unwmk.

1959, Dec. 1 Photo. *Perf. 12*

709 A296 5c org & grn .25 .25
710 A296 10c rose cl & bl .25 .25
711 A296 15c car rose & grn .40 .40
712 A296 25c bl & red brn .50 .50
Nos. 709-712,C351-C354 (8) 5.90 4.15

Centenary of Colombian postage stamps.

Two-Toed Sloth — A297

Designs: 10c, Alexander von Humboldt. 20c, Spider monkey.

1960, Feb. 12 *Perf. 12*

713 A297 5c grnsh bl & brn .25 .25
714 A297 10c blk & dp car .25 .25
715 A297 20c cit & gray brn .25 .25
Nos. 713-715,C357-C359 (6) 8.10 5.40

Cent. of the death of Alexander von Humboldt (1769-1859), German naturalist and geographer.

For overprint and surcharge see Nos. C411, C413.

Anthurium Andreanum A298

Flower: 20c, Espeletia grandiflora.

1960, May 10

716 A298 5c multi .85 .25
717 A298 20c brn, yel & gray ol .85 .25
Nos. 716-717,C360-C370 (13) 17.85 18.30

See Nos. C420-C425. For overprint see No. C412.

Lincoln Statue, Washington A299

Wmk. 331

1960, June 10 Litho. *Perf. 10½*

718 A299 20c rose lil & blk .35 .25
Nos. 718,C375-C376 (3) 2.15 1.50

Florero House, Cradle of the Republic A300

Arms of Santa Cruz de Mompox — A301

Design: 5c, First coins of Republic.

Unwmk.

1960, July 19 Photo. *Perf. 12*

719 A301 5c grn & ocher .25 .25
720 A300 20c ol bis & mar .25 .25
721 A301 20c multi .25 .25
Nos. 719-721,C377-C385 (12) 7.90 6.05

Colombia's independence, 150th anniv.

St. Isidore and Farm Animals — A302

Design: 20c, Nativity by Gregorio de Arce Vasquez y Ceballos.

1960, Sept. 26 *Perf. 12*

722 A302 10c multi .25 .25
723 A302 20c multi .25 .25
Nos. 722-723,C387 (3) .75 .75

St. Isidore the Farmer, patron saint of the rural people.

See Nos. 747, C388, C439-C440.

UN Headquarters and Emblem A303

Wmk. 331

1960, Oct. 24 Litho. *Perf. 11*

724 A303 20c blk & pink .25 .25

Souvenir Sheet

Imperf

725 A303 50c dk brn, brt grn & blk 4.00 4.00

15th anniversary of the United Nations.

Pan-American Highway through Colombia — A304

1961, Mar. 7 Unwmk. *Perf. 10½x11*

726 A304 20c brn & grnsh bl .75 .70
Nos. 726,C390-C393 (5) 3.75 3.50

8th Pan-American Highway Congress, Bogota, May 20-29, 1960.

Alfonso Lopez — A305

1961, Mar. 22 Photo. *Perf. 12½*

727 A305 10c brt rose & brn .25 .25
728 A305 20c vio & brn .25 .25
Nos. 727-728,C394-C395 (4) 1.35 1.00

Alfonso Lopez (1886-1959), President of Colombia. See No. C396.

Cauca River Bridge, Cali A306

Page from Resolutions of Confederated Cities — A307

1961-62 *Perf. 12½x13, 13½x13*

729 A306 10c red brn, bl, grn & red ('62) .25 .25
730 A307 20c pale brn & blk .25 .25
Nos. 729-730,C397-C401 (7) 3.75 2.45

50th anniversary (in 1960) of the Department of Valle del Cauca.

View of Cucuta and Arms A308

No. 732, Arms of Ocana and Pamplona.

1961, Aug. 29 *Perf. 13x13½*

731 A308 20c bl, blk, yel & red .25 .25
732 A308 20c ocher, ultra & red .25 .25
Nos. 731-732,C402-C403 (4) 1.45 1.00

50th anniv. (in 1960) of the Department of North Santander.

Arms of Popayan — A309

Designs: No. 734, Arms of Barranquilla. No. 735, Arms of Bucaramanga.

Perf. 12½x13

1961, Oct. 10 Unwmk.

Arms in Multicolor

733 A309 10c blue & silver .25 .25
734 A309 20c blue & yellow .25 .25
735 A309 20c blue & gold .25 .25
Nos. 733-735,C404-C408 (8) 3.20 2.00

Issued to honor Atlantico Department.

Basketball A310

1961, Dec. 16 Litho. *Perf. 13½x14*

736 A310 20c shown .25 .25
737 A310 20c Runners .25 .25
738 A310 20c Boxers .50 .25
739 A310 25c Soccer .25 .25
Nos. 736-739,C414-C418 (9) 4.35 2.65

4th Bolivarian Games, Barranquilla, 1961.

Colombian Anti-Malaria Emblem — A311

Design: 50c, Malaria eradication emblem and mosquito in swamp.

1962, Apr. 12 Unwmk. *Perf. 12*

740 A311 20c lt bis & red .25 .25
741 A311 50c bis & ultra .30 .25
Nos. 740-741,C426-C428 (5) 6.45 6.15

Engineers Society Emblem — A312

1962, June 12 Photo. *Perf. 11½x12*

742 A312 10c multi .25 .25
Nos. 742,C429-C432 (5) 3.70 3.55

Colombian Society of Engineers, 75th anniv.

Flags of American Nations — A313

1962, June 28 *Perf. 13*

Flags in National Colors

743 A313 25c blk & org ver .25 .25

Souvenir Sheet

744 A313 2.50p blk & yel 5.75 5.75

70th anniv. of the founding of the Organization of American States.
See No. C433.

Woman Casting Ballot and Statue of Policarpa Salavarrieta — A314

Perf. 12x12½

1962, July 20 **Litho.** **Wmk. 229**

745 A314 10c lt bl, gray & blk .25 .25

Issued to publicize women's political rights. See Nos. 752, C434, C448-C450.

Scouts at Campfire and Tents — A315

Perf. 11½x12

1962, July 28 **Photo.** **Unwmk.**

746 A315 10c brt grnsh bl & brn .30 .30
Nos. 746,C435-C438 (5) 9.30 7.40

Colombian Boy Scouts, 30th anniv.

St. Isidore Type of 1960 Redrawn

1962, Aug. 28 *Perf. 12*

747 A302 10c pink & multi .25 .25
Nos. 747,C439-C440 (3) 5.00 5.00

The frame on No. 747 is solid color with white inscription similar to type AP82.

Railroad Map of Colombia — A316

1962, Sept. 28 *Perf. 12½*

748 A316 10c blk, gray, grn & red .25 .25
Nos. 748,C441-C444 (5) 7.75 5.50

Progress of Colombian railroads and the completion of the Atlantic Line from Santa Marta to Bogota.

Post Horn — A317

Perf. 13½x14

1962, Oct. 18 **Litho.** **Wmk. 346**

749 A317 20c gold, dl gray vio & blk .25 .25
Nos. 749,C445-C446 (3) .90 .75

50th anniv. of the founding of the Postal Union of the Americas and Spain, UPAE.

"Virgin of the Rock" — A318

1963, Mar. 11 **Wmk. 346**

750 A318 60c multi .25 .25

Vatican II, the 21st Ecumenical Council of the Roman Catholic Church. See No. C447.

Red Cross Centenary Emblem — A319

1963, May 1 *Perf. 12x12½*

751 A319 5c olive bister & red .25 .25

Centenary of International Red Cross.

Women's Rights Type of 1962

1963, July 11 **Wmk. 346**

752 A314 5c org, gray & blk .25 .25
Nos. 752,C448-C450 (4) 1.30 1.00

Manuel Mejia J. and Flag of National Coffee Growers Assn. A320

Perf. 12½x13

1965, Feb. 10 **Engr.** **Unwmk.**

753 A320 25c rose & blk .25 .25
Nos. 753,C464-C466 (4) 6.50 1.15

Manuel Mejia J. (1887-1958), banker and manager of the National Coffee Growers Association.

Julio Arboleda (1817-62), Writer, Soldier and Statesman A321

1966, Mar. 9 **Litho.** *Perf. 14x13½*

754 A321 5c lt brn, lt yel grn & blk .30 .25

Spanish Galleon, 16th Century A322

History of Maritime Mail: 15c, Rio Hacha brigantine, 1850. 20c, Uraba canoe. 40c, Magdalena River steamship and barge, 1900. 50c, Modern motor ship and sea gull.

1966, June 16 **Photo.** **Unwmk.**

755 A322 5c org & multi .40 .25
756 A322 15c car rose, blk & brn .40 .25
757 A322 20c brt grn, org & blk .40 .25
758 A322 40c dp bl & multi .50 .25
759 A322 50c pale bl & multi 1.25 .60
Nos. 755-759 (5) 2.95 1.60

Plumed Hogfish A323

Design: 10p, Bat ray and brittle starfish.

1966, Aug. 25 **Photo.** *Perf. 12½x13*

760 A323 80c multi .25 .25
761 A323 10p multi 8.25 5.25
Nos. 760-761,C481-C483 (5) 27.75 20.15

Arms of Venezuela, Colombia and Chile A324

1966, Oct. 11 **Litho.** *Perf. 14x13½*

762 A324 40c yel & multi .25 .25
Nos. 762,C484-C485 (3) .95 .75

Visits of Eduardo Frei and Raul Leoni, presidents of Chile and Venezuela.

Camilo Torres, 1766-1816, Lawyer — A325

Portraits: 60c, Jorge Tadeo Lozano (1771-1816), naturalist. 1p, Francisco Antonio Zea (1776-1822), naturalist and politician.

Perf. 13½x14

1967, Jan. 18 **Litho.** **Unwmk.**

763 A325 25c vio & bis .30 .25
764 A325 60c dk red brn & bis .30 .25
765 A325 1p grn & bis .50 .25
Nos. 763-765,C486-C487 (5) 1.90 1.25

Issued to honor famous men of Colombia.

Map of South America and Arms A326

1967, Feb. 2 **Litho.** *Perf. 14x13½*

766 A326 40c multi .30 .25
767 A326 60c multi .30 .25
Nos. 766-767,C488 (3) 1.10 .75

Declaration of Bogota for cooperation and world peace, signed by Colombia, Chile, Ecuador, Peru and Venezuela.

Monochaetum Orchid and Bee — A327

Orchid: 2p, Passiflora vitifolia and butterfly.

1967, May 23 **Litho.** *Perf. 14*

768 A327 25c multi .35 .25
769 A327 2p multi 2.50 1.50
Nos. 768-769,C489-C491 (5) 9.60 3.15

1st Natl. Orchid Exhib. and the Topical Phil. Flora and Fauna Exhib., Medellin, Apr. 1967.

Lions Emblem — A328

1967, July 12 **Litho.** *Perf. 13½x14*

770 A328 10p multi 3.50 2.00

50th anniv. of Lions Intl. See No. C492.

SENA Emblem — A329

Lithographed and Embossed

1967, Sept. 20 **Unwmk.**

771 A329 5p gold, brt grn & blk 1.50 .25

10th anniv. of Natl. Apprenticeship Service, SENA. See No. C494.

Gold Diadem in Calima Style — A330

Pre-Columbian Art: 3p, Gold statuette, ornamental globe and bird, horiz.

Perf. 13½x14, 14x13½

1967, Oct. 13 **Photo.**

772 A330 1.60p brt rose lil, gold & brn .95 .25
773 A330 3p dk bl, gold & brn 1.25 .40
Nos. 772-773,C495-C497 (5) 20.85 11.40

Meeting of the UPU Committee of Postal Studies, Bogota, Oct., 1967.

Radar Installation A331

1p, Map of communications network.

1968, May 14 Litho. *Perf. 13½x14*

774 A331 50c brt yel grn, blk & org brn .25 .25
775 A331 1p multi .35 .25
Nos. 774-775,C498-C499 (4) 1.15 1.00

20th anniv. of the National Telecommunications Service (TELECOM).

The Eucharist — A332

1968, June 6 Litho. *Perf. 13½x14*

776 A332 60c multi .25 .25
Nos. 776,C500-C501 (3) .80 .75

39th Eucharistic Cong., Bogotá, 8/18-25.

St. Augustin, by Gregorio Vasquez — A333

Designs: 60c, The Gathering of Manna, by Gregorio Vasquez. 1p, The Marriage of the Virgin, by Baltazar de Figueroa. 5p, Jeweled monstrance, c. 1700. 10p, Pope Paul VI, painting by Roman Franciscan nuns.

1968, Aug. 13 Photo. *Perf. 13*

777 A333 25c multicolored .25 .25
778 A333 60c multicolored .25 .25
779 A333 1p multicolored .25 .25
780 A333 5p multicolored .80 .25
781 A333 10p multicolored 1.60 .45
a. Souvenir sheet of 2 4.00 4.00
Nos. 777-781,C502-C506 (10) 10.70 5.20

39th Eucharistic Congress. Bogotá, Aug. 18-25. No. 781a contains two imperf. stamps similar to Nos. 780-781.

Pope Paul VI — A334

1968, Aug. 22 Litho. *Perf. 13½x14*

782 A334 25c multi .30 .25
Nos. 782,C507-C509 (4) 1.30 1.00

Visit of Pope Paul VI to Colombia, 8/22-24.

Arms of National University — A335

1968, Oct. 29 Litho. *Perf. 13½x14*

783 A335 80c multi .40 .25

Centenary of the founding of the National University. See No. C510.

Stamp of Antioquia, 1868 — A336

1968, Nov. 20 Litho. *Perf. 12x12½*

784 A336 30c emer & bl .30 .25

Souvenir Sheet

785 A336 5p lt olive & blue 3.75 3.75

Cent. of the 1st postage stamps of Antioquia and the 7th Natl. Phil. Exhib., Medellin, Nov. 20-29.

Institute Emblem — A337

1969, Mar. 5 Litho. *Perf. 13½x14*

786 A337 20c multi .35 .25

25th anniv. (in 1967) of the Inter-American Agricultural Sciences Institute. See No. C511.

Battle of Boyaca (Detail), by José Maria Espinosa — A338

Design: 30c, Army of liberation crossing Pisba Pass, by Francisco Antonio Caro.

1969, July 24 Litho. *Perf. 13½x14*

787 A338 20c gold & multi .35 .25
788 A338 30c gold & multi .35 .25
Nos. 787-788,C517 (3) 1.70 .85

Fight for independence, sesquicentennial.

"Poverty" A339

1970, Mar. 1 Litho. *Perf. 14*

789 A339 30c bl & multi .35 .25

Colombian Institute for Family Welfare and 10th anniv. of the Children's Rights Law.

Greek Mask and Pre-Columbian Symbol of Literary Contest — A340

1970, Sept. 12 Litho. *Perf. 14x13½*

790 A340 30c dk brn, red org & ocher .25 .25

3rd Latin American Theatrical Festival of the Universities, Manizales, Sept. 12-20.

Colombian Stamps, Envelope and Emblem A341

1970, Sept. 24 Litho. *Perf. 14x13½*

791 A341 2p brt bl & multi .30 .25

Issued to publicize Philatelic Week.

Arms of Ibague and Discobolus A342

1970, Oct. 13

792 A342 80c buff, emer & sepia .25 .25

9th National Games in Ibague.

St. Theresa, by Baltazar de Figueroa — A343

1970, Oct. 28 Litho. *Perf. 13½x14*

793 A343 2p multi .50 .25

Elevation of St. Theresa (1515-1582), to Doctor of the Church. See No. C568. For overprint see No. C568.

Casa Cural A344

1971, May 20 Litho. *Perf. 14x13½*

794 A344 1.10p multi .30 .25

Fourth centenary (in 1970) of the founding of Guacari, Valle. See No. 809.

Dancers and Music, Currulao — A345

1p, Chicha Maya dancers and music.

1971 Litho. *Perf. 13½x14*

795 A345 1p pink & multi .35 .25
796 A345 1.10p lt bl & multi .35 .25

Souvenir Sheets

Imperf

797 Sheet of 3 6.00 6.00
a. A345 2.50p Napanga .65 .65
b. A345 2.50p Joropo .65 .65
c. A345 5p Guabina 1.25 1.25
798 Sheet of 3 6.00 6.00
a. A345 4p Bambuco 1.00 1.00
b. A345 4p Cumbia 1.00 1.00
c. A345 4p Currulao 1.00 1.00

Issued: No. 795, 12/20; No. 796, 8/5; Nos. 797-798, 8/10.

Constitutional Assembly, by Delgado A346

1971, Oct. 2 *Perf. 14*

801 A346 80c multi .25 .25

Sequicentennial of Gran Colombian Constitutional Assembly in Rosario del Cucuta.
See No. C589. For overprint see No. C589.

Arrows Emblem — A347

1972, Feb. 24 *Perf. 13½x14*

802 A347 60c blk & gray .30 .25

Inter-Governmental Committee on European Migration, 20th anniversary.

Student and World Map A348

1972, Mar. 15 *Perf. 14x13½*

803 A348 1.10p lt grn & brn .25 .25

20th anniv. of ICETEX, an organization which furnishes financial help for educational purposes and for technical studies abroad.

UN Emblem, Soldier and Frigate A349

1972, Apr. 7

804 A349 1.20p lt bl & multi .25 .25

Colombian Battalion in Korea, 20th anniv.

Mother Francisca Josefa del Castillo — A350

1972, Apr. 6 *Perf. 13½x14*

805 A350 1.20p brn & multi .25 .25

Tercentenary (in 1971) of the birth of Mother Francisca Josefa del Castillo, Poor Clare abbess and writer.

Handicraft A351

1972, Apr. 11

806 A351 1.10p multi .35 .25

Nos. 806,C569-C571 (4) 1.55 1.00

Colombian artisans.

Maxillaria Triloris — A352

1972, Apr. 20

807 A352 20p green & multi 7.25 .75

10th Natl. Phil. Exhib., Medellin.

Emeralds — A353

1972, June 16 Litho. ***Perf. 13½x14***

808 A353 1.10p multi 1.25 .25

Type of 1971

Design: Antonio Nariño House.

1972, June 17 ***Perf. 14x13½***

809 A344 1.10p multi .60 .25

4th centenary, town of Leyva.

San Andres and Providencia Islands — A354

1972, June 24 ***Perf. 13½x14***

810 A354 60c bl & multi .25 .25

Sesquicentennial of annexation by Colombia of San Andres and Providencia Islands.

Postal Service Emblem A355

1972, Nov. 15 Litho. ***Perf. 12½x12***

811 A355 1.10p emerald .25 .25

Family A356

1972, Nov. 23

812 A356 60c orange .25 .25

Social progress.

Radio League Emblem — A357

1973, Apr. 6 Litho. ***Perf. 12x12½***

813 A357 60c lt bl, ultra & red .25 .25

40th anniversary of the Colombian Radio Amateurs' League.

Human Figure, Tamalameque A358

Excavated Ceramic Artifacts: 1p, Winged urn, Tairona. 1.10p, Jug, Muisca.

1973, June 15 Litho. ***Perf. 13½x14***

814 A358 60c lt bl & multi .40 .25

815 A358 1p org & multi .80 .25

816 A358 1.10p vio bl & multi .50 .25

Nos. 814-816,C583-C586 (7) 7.25 2.75

Antonio Nariño, by José M. Espinosa — A359

1973, Dec. 13 Litho. ***Perf. 13½x14***

817 A359 60c multi .25 .25

Sesquicentennial of the death of General Antonio Nariño (1765-1823).

Child — A360

1973, Dec. 17

818 A360 1.10p multi .25 .25

National Campaign for Children's Welfare.

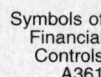

Symbols of Financial Controls A361

1973, Dec. 20 Litho. ***Perf. 14x13½***

819 A361 80c ultra, ocher & blk .25 .25

50th anniv. of Comptroller-general's Office.

Mother Laura Montoya — A362

1974, June 18 Litho. ***Perf. 13½x14***

820 A362 1p multi .25 .25

Mother Laura Montoya (1874-1949), founder and Mother Superior of the Missionaries of Mary Immaculata and St. Catherine of Siena.

Runner and Games' Emblem A363

1974, July 18 Litho. ***Perf. 14x13½***

821 A363 2p ver, yel & brn .35 .25

10th National Games, Pereira.

José Rivera A364

1974, Aug. 3 Litho. ***Perf. 14x13½***

822 A364 10p grn & multi 1.40 .25

50th anniv. of the publication of "La Voragine" (The Whirlpool) by José Eustasio Rivera.

Abstract Pattern — A365

1974, Oct. 24 Litho. ***Perf. 13½x14***

823 A365 1.10p multi .25 .25

Cent. of Natl. Insurance Co. See No. C610.

Train Emerging from Tunnel — A366

1974, Nov. 27 Litho. ***Perf. 13½x14***

824 A366 1.10p multi .25 .25

Centenary of the Antioquia railroad.

Boy, Puppy and Soccer Ball — A367

Christmas: 1p, Girl with racket and kitten.

1974, Dec. 9

825 A367 80c multi .25 .25

826 A367 1p multi .25 .25

A368

1975, Apr. 11 Litho. ***Perf. 14x13½***

827 A368 80c Gold Animal .45 .25

828 A368 1.10p Gold necklace .45 .25

Nos. 827-828,C621-C622 (4) 6.65 1.35

Pre-Columbian Sinu culture artifacts.

For surcharge see No. 840.

Guglielmo Marconi — A369

1975, June 2 Litho. ***Perf. 13½x14***

829 A369 3p multi .30 .25

Birth centenary of Guglielmo Marconi (1874-1937), Italian electrical engineer and inventor.

Santa Marta Cathedral — A370

1975, July 26

830 A370 80c multi .30 .25

400th anniv. of Santa Marta City. See No. C623.

Rafael Nuñez — A371

1975, Sept. 28 Litho. ***Perf. 13½x14***

831 A371 1.10p multi .30 .25

Rafael Nunez (1825-1894), philosopher, poet, political leader, birth sesquicentenary.

For surcharge see No. 848.

Arms of Medellin — A372

1975-79 ***Perf. 13½x14, 12 (1.20p)***

832	A372	1p	shown	.40	.25
833	A372	1.20p	Ibagué	.35	.25
834	A372	1.20p	Tunja	.25	.25
835	A372	1.50p	Cucuta	.55	.25
836	A372	1.50p	Cartagena	.25	.25
836A	A372	4p	Sogamoso	1.00	.25
837	A372	5p	Popayan	.50	.25
838	A372	5p	Barranquilla	.55	.25
839	A372	10p	San Gil	1.00	.25
839A	A372	10p	Socorro	1.00	.25
			Nos. 832-839A (10)	5.85	2.50

1p for the tercentenary of Medellin; No. 835, the cent. of Cucuta's reconstruction.

Issued: 1p, 11/4; No. 835, 11/29; No. 836, 2/10/76; No. 833, 7/30/76; No. 834, 12/2076; No. 837, 8/30/77; No. 838, 9/20/77; 10p, 8/9/79; 4p, 9/14/79.

See Nos. 905-913, C818. For surcharge see No. 849.

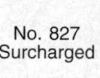

No. 827 Surcharged

1975 ***Perf. 14x13½***

840	A368	1.20p on 80c multi		.35	.25

Purace Indians, Cauca — A373

1976, Nov. 10 **Litho.** ***Perf. 13½x14***

841	A373	1.50p	multi	.25	.25

Callicore A374

5p, Morpho (butterfly). 20p, Anthurium.

1976, Nov. 17 ***Perf. 12***

842	A374	3p	multicolored	.90	.25
843	A374	5p	multicolored	1.50	.25
844	A374	20p	multicolored	4.25	1.00
			Nos. 842-844 (3)	6.65	1.50

Rotary Emblem — A375

1976, Dec. 3 **Litho.** ***Perf. 12***

845	A375	1p	multicolored	.25	.25

Rotary Club of Colombia, 50th anniversary.

Declaration of Independence, by John Trumbull — A376

1976, Dec. 21 **Litho.** ***Perf. 12***

846	A376 Strip of 3		10.00	*11.50*
a.-c.	30p any single		2.75	2.00

American Bicentennial. No. 846 printed in sheets of 4 triptychs.

Policeman with Dog — A377

1976, Dec. 29 ***Perf. 13½x14***

847	A377	1.50p multicolored	.25	.25

Honoring the National Police.
For surcharge see No. 850.

Nos. 831, 834, 847 Surcharged in Light Brown

1977, June **Litho.** ***Perf. 13½x14, 12***

848	A371	2p on 1.10p multi	.40	.25
849	A372	2p on 1.20p multi	.25	.25
850	A377	2p on 1.50p multi	.25	.25
		Nos. 848-850 (3)	.90	.75

Souvenir Sheet

Postal Museum, Bogota — A378

1977, July 27 **Litho.** ***Perf. 14***

855	A378	25p multi	3.50	3.50

Postal Museum, Bogota.

Mother and Child — A379

1977-78 **Litho.** ***Perf. 12***

856	A379	2p multi	.25	.25
857	A379	2.50p multi ('78)	1.75	.25

National good nutrition plan.
Issue dates: 2p, Aug. 30; 2.50p, Jan. 26.

Jacana and Eichhornia A380

20p, Mayan cotinga and pyrostegia venusta.

1977, Sept. 6 **Litho.** ***Perf. 14***

858	A380	10p multicolored	2.50	.25
859	A380	20p multicolored	4.00	.50
		Nos. 858-859,C644-C647 (6)	10.20	1.75

Fidel Cano, by Francisco Cano — A381

1977, Sept. 16 ***Perf. 14***

860	A381	4p multicolored	.25	.25

90th anniversary of El Espectador, newspaper founded by Fidel Cano.

Abacus and Alphabet — A382

1977, Sept. 16 ***Perf. 13½x14***

861	A382	3p multicolored	.25	.25

Popular education.

Cattleya Triannae — A383

1978-79 **Litho.** ***Perf. 12***

862	A383	2.50p multi	.75	.25
863	A383	3p multi ('79)	.75	.25

Issue dates: 2.50p, Apr. 18. 3p, May 10.

Sprinting and Games Emblem A384

Sports: a, sprinting. b, basketball. c, baseball. d, boxing. e. bicycling. f, fencing. g, soccer. h, gymnastics. i, judo. j, weight lifting. k, wrestling. l, swimming. m, tennis. n, target shooting. o, volleyball. p, water polo.

1978, June 27 **Litho.** ***Perf. 14***

868	Sheet of 16	29.00	29.00
a.-p.	A384 10p, any single	1.25	.25

13th Central American and Caribbean Games, Medellin.

"Sigma 2" by Alvaro Herrán A385

1978, June 30

869	A385	8p multicolored	.55	.25

Chamber of Commerce, Bogota, centenary.

Gen. Tomás Cipriano de Mosquera (1778-1878), Statesman A386

1978, Oct. 6 **Litho.** ***Perf. 12***

870	A386	6p multicolored	.45	.25

Anthurium Narinenses — A387

1979, July 23 ***Perf. 12***

871	A387	3p red & multi	.30	.25
872	A387	3p purple & multi	.30	.25
873	A387	3p rose & purple	.30	.25
874	A387	3p white & multi	.30	.25
a.		Block of 4, #871-874	2.50	2.50

Gen. Rafael Uribe, by Acevedo Bernal — A388

1979, Oct. 31 **Litho.** ***Perf. 12***

875	A388	8p multicolored	.50	.25

Gen. Uribe, statesman, 60th death anniv.

Village, by Leonor Alarcon — A389

1979, Nov. 22 ***Perf. 14***

876	A389	15p multicolored	1.60	.60

Community Work Boards, 20th anniversary.

Introduction of Color Television A390

1980, Mar. 4 **Litho.** ***Perf. 14***

877	A390	5p multicolored	.60	.25

Bullfight, Arms of Cali A391

1980, Mar. 25

878	A391	5p multicolored	.70	.25

Cali Tourist Festival, 12/25/79-1/2/80.

"Learn to Write" — A392

a, shown. b, "a." c, "b." d, "c." e, "ch." f, "d." g, "e." h, "f." i, "g." j, "h." k, "i." l, "j." m, "k." n, "l." o, "ll." p, "m." q, "n." r, "ñ." s, "o." t, "p." u, "q." v, "r." w, "s." x, "t." y, "u." z, "v." aa, "w." ab, "x." ac, "y." ad, "z."

1980, Apr. 25 Litho. *Perf. 12½*
879 Block of 30 27.50 27.50
a.-ad. A392 4p any single .75 .25

Each stamp shows letter of alphabet and corresponding animal or subject. Issued in sheets of 90 (10x9).

Villavicencio Festival — A393

Design: 9p, Vallenato festival.

1980 Litho. *Perf. 14*
880 A393 5p multicolored .55 .25
881 A393 9p multicolored .55 .25

Issue dates: 5p, July 15; 9p, June 17.

Gustavo Uribe Ramirez and Tree A394

1980, Aug. 5 Litho. *Perf. 12*
882 A394 10p multicolored 1.10 .25

Gustavo Uribe Ramirez (1893-1968), ecologist.

Narino Palace (Former Presidential Residence) — A395

1980, Sept. 19 Litho. *Perf. 14*
883 A395 5p multicolored .70 .25

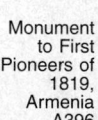

Monument to First Pioneers of 1819, Armenia A396

1980, Oct. 14
884 A396 5p multicolored .60 .25

11th National Games, Neiva — A397

1980, Nov. 28 *Perf. 13½x14*
885 A397 5p multicolored .60 .25

Fight against Cancer — A398

1980, Dec. 9
886 A398 10p multicolored .50 .25

Xavier University Law Faculty, 50th Anniversary A399

1980, Dec. 16 Litho. *Perf. 14½*
887 A399 20p multicolored .85 .30

Death of Bolivar — A400

1980, Dec. 17 *Perf. 12*
888 A400 25p multicolored 1.25 .60

Simon Bolivar, death sesquicentennial. See No. C696.

José Maria Obando, President of Colombia A401

115th Anniv. of Constitution (Former Presidents): b, Jose Hilario Lopez. c, Manuel Murillo Toro. d, Santiago Perez. e, Rafael Reyes. f, Carlos E. Restrepo. g, Jose Vicente Concha. h, Miguel Abadia Mendez. i, Eduardo Santos. j, Mariano Ospina Perez.

1981, June 9 Litho. *Perf. 12*
889 Strip of 10 *6.00*
a.-j. A401 5p multicolored .50 .25

1981, Sept. 23 Litho. *Perf. 12*

Designs: a, Rafael Nunez (1825-94). b, Marco Fidel Suarez (1855-1927). c, Pedro Nel Ospina (1858-1927). d, Enrique Olaya Herrera (1880-1937). e, Alfonso Lopez Pumarejo (1886-1959). f, Aquileo Parra (1825-1900). g, Santos Gutierrez (1820-72). h, Tomas Cipriano de Mosquera (1789-1878). i, Mariano Ospina Rodriguez. j, Pedro Alcantara Herran (1800-72).

890 Strip of 10 *50.00*
a.-j. A401 7p multicolored 3.50 .50

1981, Aug. 11 Litho. *Perf. 12*

Designs like No. 889.

891 Strip of 10 *55.00*
a.-j. A401 7p multicolored 4.00 1.00

1981, Nov. 11 Litho. *Perf. 12*

Designs: a, Manuel Maria Mallarino. b, Santos Acosta. c, Eustorgio Salgar. d, Julian Trujillo. e, Francisco Javier Zaldua. f, Guillermo Leon Valencia. g, Laureano Gomez. h, Manuel A. Sanclemente. i, Miguel Antonio Caro. j, Jose Eusebio Otalora.

892 Strip of 10 *32.50*
a.-j. A401 7p multicolored 2.50 .40

1981, Dec. 15 Litho. *Perf. 12*

Designs: a, Ruben Piedrahita Arango. b, Jorge Holguin. c, Ramon Gonzalez Valencia. d, Jose Manuel Marroquin. e, Carlos Holguin. f, Bartolome Calvo. g, Sergio Camargo. h, Jose Maria Rojas Garrido. i, J.M. Campo Serrano. j, Eliseo Payan.

893 Strip of 10 25.00
a.-j. A401 7p multicolored 1.75 .30

1982, May 3 *Perf. 12*

Designs: a, Simon Bolivar. b, Francisco de Paula Santander. c, Joaquin Mosquera. d, Domingo Caicedo. e, Jose Ignacio de Marquez. f, Roberto Urdaneta Arbelaez. g, Carlos Lozano y Lozano. h, Guillermo Quintero Calderon. i, Jose de Obaldia. j, Juan de Dios Aranzazu.

894 Strip of 10 14.50
a.-j. A401 7p multicolored 1.40 .25

See No. 1110, 1329.

Jose Maria Villa and West Bridge over Cauca River A404

1981, Nov. 25 Litho. *Perf. 14x13½*
895 A404 60p multicolored 1.50 .30

Agrarian, Mineral and Industrial Credit Bank, 50th Anniv. — A405

1981, Dec. 9 Litho. *Perf. 14*
896 A405 15p multicolored .50 .25

Los Nevados Park — A406

1981, Dec. 10 Litho. *Perf. 13½x14*
897 A406 20p multicolored .70 .25

Girl Sitting on Fence — A407

1982, Feb. 22 Litho. *Perf. 12½x12*
898 Strip of 3 5.00 5.00
a. A407 30p shown 1.10 .40
b. A407 30p Girl, basket 1.10 .40
c. A407 30p Boy, wheelbarrow 1.10 .40

Floral Bouquet — A408

Various floral arrangements (background): a, Flowers in vase (gray). b, Roses (red). c, Daisies (green). d, Roses (blue). e, Assorted (red). f, Yellow & orange flowers (green). g, Assorted (lilac). h, Roses (gray). i, Pink flowers (green). j, Flowers in basket (gray).

1982, July 28
900 Strip or block of 10 17.00 17.00
a.-j. A408 7p, any single 1.75 .30

Hipotecario Bank, 50th Anniv. — A409

1982, July 29 *Perf. 14*
901 A409 9p black & green .50 .25

St. Thomas Aquinas (1225-1274) A410

Paintings by Zurbaran.

1982 Litho. *Perf. 12*
902 A410 5p multicolored .40 .25
903 A410 5p St. Teresa of Avila .40 .25
904 A410 5p St. Francis of Assisi .40 .25
Nos. 902-904 (3) 1.20 .75

Issued: No. 902, 8/6; No. 903, 9/28; No. 904, 10/4.

Arms Type of 1975

1982-90 Litho. *Perf. 14, 12 (50p)*
905 A372 10p Buga .40 .25
906 A372 10p San Juan de Pasto 1.25 .25
907 A372 16p Rionegro .70 .25
908 A372 20p Santa Fe de Bogota 1.00 .25
909 A372 20p Santiago de Cali .30 .25
910 A372 23p Honda .75 .25
911 A372 50p Cartago .70 .25
912 A372 55p Antioquia ('86) 1.00 .25
Nos. 905-912 (8) 6.10 2.00

Issued: 16p, 23p, No. 905, 12/7; No. 908, 3/1/83; No. 906, 4/12/83; No. 909, 7/25/86; 55p, 8/5/86; 50p, 5/30/90.
See No. C818.

Gabriel Marquez, 1982 Nobel Prize, Literature — A412

1982, Dec. 10 *Perf. 13½x14*
917 A412 7p gray & green .25 .25

See Nos. C731-C732.

Public Education Bicentenary (Society of Mary for Education)
A413

1983, May 6
918 A413 9p gold & blk .40 .25

José Maria Espinosa Prieto, Painter — A414

1983, June 3 ***Perf. 12***
919 A414 9p Self-portrait, 1860 .40 .25

250th Anniv. of City of Cucuta — A415

1983, June 23 Litho. ***Perf. 12***
920 A415 9p multicolored .35 .25

Porfirio Barba-Jacob (1883-1942), Poet — A416

1983, July 29 Litho. ***Perf. 13½x14***
921 A416 9p Portrait .35 .25

Simon Bolivar, 200th Birth Anniv. A417

1983, July 24 ***Perf. 12***
922 A417 9p multicolored .30 .25

See Nos. C736-C737.

Royal Spanish Botanical Expedition, 200th Anniv. — A418

No. 923, Cinchona lancefolia. No. 924, Passiflora laurifolia. No. 925, Cinchona cordiflora.

1983, Aug. 18 ***Perf. 14***
923 A418 9p multicolored .25 .25
924 A418 9p multicolored .25 .25
925 A418 60p multicolored 1.75 .50
Nos. 923-925,C738-C740 (6) 6.25 1.90

Dawn in the Andes, by Alejandro Obregon A420

1983, Oct. 5 Litho. ***Perf. 12***
928 A420 20p multicolored .50 .25

See No. C741.

Francisco de Paula Santander (1792-1840), General — A421

1984, Mar. 6 Litho. ***Perf. 14½x14***
929 A421 12p light olive green .30 .25
930 A421 12p pale carmine .30 .25
931 A421 12p light ultra .30 .25
Nos. 929-931 (3) .90 .75

Admiral Jose Prudencio Padilla (1784-1831) — A423

1984, May 17 Litho. ***Perf. 12***
933 A423 10p multicolored .40 .25

Luis Antonio Calvo (1882-1945) Composer — A424

1984, July 26
934 A424 18p multicolored .40 .25

Diego Fallon (1834-1905), Educator, Musician, Poet — A425

1984, Aug. 31 ***Perf. 12***
935 A425 20p multicolored .45 .25

Candelario Obeso (1849-1884), Writer — A426

1984, Sept. 4 ***Perf. 14x13½***
936 A426 20p multicolored .45 .25

Site of Marandua, Future City A427

1984, Sept. 28 ***Perf. 12***
937 A427 15p multicolored .35 .25

See No. C744.

Christmas 1984 A428

Nativity and Children Playing, by Jose Uriel Sierra, Age 7.

1984, Dec. 14
938 A428 12p multicolored .35 .25

See No. C746.

Dr. Luis Eduardo Lopez, Education Minister A429

1984, Dec. 21
939 A429 22p multicolored .45 .25

Maria Concepcion Loperena de Fernandez de Castro, Independence War Heroine — A430

1985, Jan. 6
940 A430 12p multicolored .35 .25

Gonzalo Mejia (1885-1956) — A431

1985, Feb. 25
941 A431 12p Portrait, biplane, camera .45 .25

Aviation, motion picture and meat exporting industrialist.

Self-portrait with Wife — A432

1985, Feb. 25
942 A432 37p multicolored .80 .30

Pedro Nel Gomez (1899-1984), painter. See No. C748.

Fauna A433

No. 943, Hydrochaeris hydrochaeris. No. 944, Felis pardalis. No. 945, Tremarctos ornatus, vert. No. 946, Tapirus pinchaque.

1985 ***Perf. 14***
943 A433 12p multicolored .50 .30

Perf. 13
944 A433 15p multicolored .50 .25
945 A433 15p multicolored .50 .25
946 A433 20p multicolored .85 .30
Nos. 943-946,C758 (5) 3.85 1.35

Carlos Gardel (1890-1935), Entertainer A434

1985, June 23 ***Perf. 14***
947 A434 15p Portrait, Fokker F-31 Trimotor .30 .25

Camina Literacy Program — A435

1985, Nov. 25 ***Perf. 13½x14***
948 A435 15p Tree, alphabet .30 .25

Christmas 1985 A436

1985, Dec. 4 Litho. ***Perf. 13***
949 A436 15p multicolored .40 .25

Rafael Pombo Children's Foundation. See No. C755.

Eduardo Carranza (b. 1913), Poet — A437

1986, Feb. 13
950 A437 18p multicolored .30 .25

Colombian Free University, Cent. — A438

1986, Feb. 14
951 A438 18p multicolored .30 .25

Gen. Antonio Ricaurte (b. 1786), Liberator
A439

1986, May 7 Litho. *Perf. 13*
952 A439 18p Leiva birthplace .30 .25

Jose Asuncion Silva (1865-1896), Poet, and Scene from Nocturno — A440

1986, May 30 Litho. *Perf. 12*
953 A440 18p multicolored .30 .25

Fernando Gomez Martinez (1897-1985), Journalist — A441

1986, June 19
954 A441 24p multicolored .30 .25

Santiago de Cali, 450th Anniv.
A442

1986, July 25 Litho. *Perf. 13*
955 A442 25p La Merced .30 .25

A443

Monsignor Jose Vicente Castro Silva (1885-1968), rector of the Mayor del Rosario School: portrait by Ricardo Gomez.

1986, Aug. 4 Litho. *Perf. 12*
956 A443 20p multicolored .35 .25

A444

1986, Oct. 14 Litho. *Perf. 12*
957 A444 40p Natl. University .60 .40

Faculties: Fine Arts, cent., and Architecture, 50th anniv.

Rafael Maya (1897-1980), Poet, and Salamanca University Entrance — A445

1986, Oct. 15
958 A445 25p multicolored .35 .25

See No. C772.

Condor in Flight — A446

Inia goefrenis A446a

No. 962, Inia goeffrensis. No. 963, Procyon cancrivorus. No. 964, Monachus tropicalis. No. 965, Pteronura brasiliensis. No. 966, Trichechus manatus. No. 967, Odocoileus virginianus. No. 968, Trogon personatus personatus. Nos. 962-968 horiz.

1986-89 Litho. *Perf. 12*
959 A446 20p ultra .35 .25
960 A446 25p ultra ('87) .50 .25

Perf. 14½x14, 14x14½
961 A446a 30p grn ('87) .50 .25
962 A446a 30p dull vio ('87) .50 .25

Engr.
Wmk. 334
963 A446a 35p chest brn ('88) .75 .25
964 A446a 35p dark grn ('88) .75 .25
965 A446a 40p deep org ('88) .75 .25
966 A446a 40p gray ('88) .85 .25
967 A446a 40p tan ('89) .85 .25
968 A446a 45p dark vio ('88) .85 .25
Nos. 959-968 (10) 6.65 2.50

Issued: 20p, 11/6; 25p, 5/25; No. 961, 6/8; No. 962, 12/24; No. 963, 8/6; No. 964, 9/20; No. 965, 9/20; No. 966, 11/29; No. 967, 4/29; No. 968, 12/16.

See Nos. 996-1001, C778-C781.

A447

1987, Jan. 29 Unwmk. *Perf. 12*
969 A447 25p multicolored .50 .25

Pedro Uribe Mejia (1886-1972), pioneer of Colombian coffee industry.

A448

1987, May 3 *Perf. 13½x13*
970 A448 500p Santa Barbara Church 5.50 1.75

Mompox, 450th anniv.

Writers
A449

Portraits and scenes from works: 70p, Jorge Isaacs (1837-1895), novelist, and scene from *Maria.* 90p, Aurelio Martinez Mutis (1884-1954), poet, and scene from *La Epopeya del Condor.*

1987 *Perf. 12*
971 A449 70p multicolored .90 .25
972 A449 90p multicolored 1.25 .40

Issue dates: 70p, July 28. 90p, Sept. 2.

A450

Social Security & Communications.

1987 Litho. *Perf. 13½x13*
973 A450 35p multicolored .40 .25

A451

Natl. Anthem, Cent.: Score, lyricist Rafael Nunez and composer Oreste Sindici. Dated 1987.

1988, May 25 Litho. *Perf. 12*
974 A451 70p multicolored .80 .25

Human Rights — A452

Perf. 14½x14, 14x14½
1988-89 Engr.
975 A452 30p Life .35 .25
976 A452 35p Suffrage .35 .25
977 A452 40p Association, horiz. .45 .25
978 A452 45p Culture, horiz. .35 .25
Nos. 975-978 (4) 1.50 1.00

Issued: 30p, 35p, 5/12; 40p, 7/1; 45p, 10/27/89.

See Nos. C797, C807.

Pasto, 450th Anniv.
A453

1988, May 20 Litho. *Perf. 12*
979 A453 60p Cathedral, Pasto .70 .35

Dated 1987.

Bogota Aqueduct and Sewage System, Cent. — A454

1988, May 20
980 A454 100p Waterfall 1.25 .35

Maria Currea de Aya (1888-1985), Women's Rights Activist — A455

1988, May 27
981 A455 80p multicolored .95 .25

A456

Sailfish, Istiaophorus Americanus.

Perf. 14x13½
1988, July 19 Engr. Wmk. 334
982 A456 (A) dark blue 4.25 2.25
983 A456 (B) Prus blue 1.25 .40

At the time of issue, No. 982 was sold for 400p and No. 983 for 100p. See type A486.

A457

Unwmk.
1988, Aug. 10 Litho. *Perf. 12*
984 A457 120p multicolored 1.25 .35

San Bartolome College, founded in 1604.

Jorge Alvarez Lleras (1885-1952), Engineer and Director of the Natl. Astronomical Observatory — A458

1988, Aug. 17
985 A458 90p multicolored 1.00 .45

Pres. Eduardo Santos (1888-1974)
A459

1988, Aug. 30
986 A459 80p multicolored .85 .25

Andres Bello Seminary
A460

Unwmk.

1988, Dec. 27 Litho. *Perf. 12*

987	A460	115p multicolored	1.25	.25

Adpostal, 25th Anniv.
A461

1989, May 3

988	A461	45p multicolored	.40	.25

Military Leaders — A462

Bolivar and Santander at the Los Llanos Campaign — A463

1989 Litho. *Perf. 12*

989	A462	40p Santander	.60	.25
990	A462	40p Bolivar	.60	.25
991	A463	45p multicolored	.60	.25
		Nos. 989-991 (3)	1.80	.75

Liberation campaign, 170th anniv.

Issued: No. 989, 8/25; No. 990, 7/25; 45p, 8/7.

From Boyaca to Santa Fe — A464

1989, Aug. 7 Litho. *Perf. 12*

992	45p multicolored	1.50	.45
993	45p multicolored	1.50	.45
a.	A464 Pair, #992-993	4.00	2.00

Liberation campaign, 170th anniv.

Liberation Campaign Triptych — A466

Designs: a, Gen. Santander, liberation force. b, Simon Bolivar riding mount. c, Insurgent cavalry.

Unwmk.

1989, Aug. 7 Litho. *Perf. 13*

994	A466	Strip of 3	4.50	1.75
a.-c.		45p any single	1.25	.55

Liberation Campaign, 170th anniv.

Tunja, 450th Anniv.
A467

1989, Aug. 8 *Perf. 12*

995	A467	45p multicolored	.40	.25

Fauna Type of 1988

Designs: No. 996, Harpia harpyja, horiz. No. 997, Urocyon cinereoargenteus. No. 998, Dendrobates histrionicus. No. 1000, Phenacosaurus indenenae. No. 1001, Cebuella pygmaea. No. 1002, Eurypyga helias, horiz.

Perf. 14½x14, 14x14½

1989-90 Engr. Wmk. 334

996	A446a	45p black	1.00	.25
997	A446a	50p blue gray	.60	.25
998	A446a	50p deep claret	.40	.25
999	A446a	55p red brown	.85	.25
1000	A446a	60p brown	.60	.25
1001	A446a	60p org brown	.60	.25
		Nos. 996-1001 (6)	4.05	1.50

Issued: 45p, 9/7; Nos. 997, 1000, 3/1/90; No. 998, 4/25; 55p, 8/18; No. 1001, 8/6.

A468

1989, Aug. 30 Unwmk. *Perf. 12*

1011	A468	135p multicolored	1.25	.80

City of Armenia, cent.

Espeletia Hartwegiana
A469

1990, Mar. 28 Litho. *Perf. 12*

1012	A469	60p multicolored	.35	.25

Gen. Francisco De Paula Santander (1792-1840) — A470

1990, May 6 *Perf. 14x13½*

1013	A470	50p multicolored	.40	.25
		Nos. 1013,C823-C827 (6)	3.80	2.75

See Nos. 1046-1047.

General Santander Police Academy, 50th Anniv. — A471

1990, May 16 *Perf. 12*

1014	A471	60p multicolored	.40	.25

Department of La Guajira
A473

1990, July 1 *Perf. 12*

1016	A473	60p multicolored	.60	.25

Celba Pentandra
A474

1990, July 15 Litho. *Perf. 12*

1017	A474	60p multicolored	.50	.25

Tibouchina lepidota — A475

1990, Aug. 8 Litho. *Perf. 12*

1018	A475	70p multicolored	.90	.25

Ceroxylon quindiuense
A476

Unwmk.

1990, Aug. 28 Litho. *Perf. 14*

1019	A476	70p multicolored	.50	.25

St. John Bosco — A477

1990, Sept. 28 *Perf. 12*

1020	A477	60p multicolored	.60	.25

Salesian Order in Colombia, cent.

A478

1991, Mar. 28 Litho. *Perf. 12*

1021	A478	70p multicolored	.50	.25

Miraculous Christ, Pilgrimage Church of Buga.

Moths and Butterflies
A479

No. 1022, Callithea philotima. No. 1023, Anaea syene, vert. No. 1024, Thecla coronata, vert. No. 1025, Agrias amydon. No. 1026, Morpho rhetenor. No. 1027, Heliconius longarenus.

1991, Apr. 18 Litho. *Perf. 14*

1022	A479	70p multicolored	.90	.25
1023	A479	70p multicolored	.90	.25
1024	A479	80p multicolored	1.10	.25
1025	A479	80p multicolored	1.20	.25
1026	A479	170p multicolored	2.50	.35
1027	A479	190p multicolored	2.50	.35
		Nos. 1022-1027 (6)	9.10	1.70

Nos. 1025-1027 are airmail.

New Constitution
A480

1991, July 4 Litho. *Perf. 14*

1028	A480	70p multicolored	.40	.25

A481

1991, July 19 *Perf. 12*

1029	A481	80p multicolored	.40	.30

Pres. Dario Echandia Olaya (1897-1989). See No. 1042.

A482

1991, Aug. 7

1030	A482	70p multicolored	.35	.25

Col. Antanasio Girardot (1791-1813).

A483

1991, Aug. 15 Litho. *Perf. 14*

1031 A483 80p multicolored .50 .25

Luis Carlos Galan Sarmiento (1943-1989), political reformer.

A484

Pre-Columbian Artifacts: 80p, Statue of cat god. No. 1033, Pitcher from tomb of high official. No. 1034, Statue with two heads. 210p, Flying fish, horiz.

1991, Aug. 24 *Perf. 12*

1032 A484	80p multicolored	.75	.25
1033 A484	90p multicolored	.90	.25
1034 A484	90p multicolored	.90	.25
1035 A484	210p multicolored	2.00	.30
	Nos. 1032-1035 (4)	4.55	1.05

Nos. 1034-1035 are airmail.

Colonial Architecture A485

80p, Cloister of St. Augustine, Tunja. No. 1037, Community Bridge, Chia. No. 1038, Roadside Chapel, Pamplona. 190p, Church of Immaculate Conception, Bogota.

1991 Litho. *Perf. 12*

1036 A485	80p multi	.75	.25
1037 A485	90p multi	1.25	.25
1038 A485	90p multi, vert.	1.00	.30
1039 A485	190p multi, vert.	2.00	.35
	Nos. 1036-1039 (4)	5.00	1.15

Issue dates: No. 1037, Sept. 9; others, Sept. 27. Nos. 1038-1039 are airmail.

Istiaphorus Americanus A486

1991, Sept. 3 *Perf. 14*

1040 A486 830p multicolored 6.50 1.50

Colombian Police Force, Cent. A487

1991, Oct. 12 *Perf. 12*

1041 A487 80p multicolored .60 .25

President Type of 1991

Pres. Alberto Lleras Camargo (1906-1990)

1991, Nov. 5

1042 A481 80p multicolored .45 .25

Sogamoso City Hall — A489

1991, Dec. 17 Litho. *Perf. 12*

1043 A489 80p multicolored .50 .25

A490

Designs: No. 1044, Diana Turbay Quintero (1950-91), journalist. No. 1045, Indalecio Lievano Aguirre (1917-82), diplomat.

1992 Litho. *Perf. 14*

1044 A490 80p multicolored .45 .25
1045 A490 80p multicolored .45 .25

Issued: No. 1044, Jan. 24; No. 1045, Apr. 21.

Santander Type of 1990 and

Battle of Boyaca — A491a

1992, Apr. 2 *Perf. 14*

Size: 26x37mm

1046 A470 80p Monument .50 .30
1047 A470 190p Portrait 1.25 .70

Souvenir Sheet

Perf. 13½x14

1047A A491a 950p multicolored 6.50 6.50

Nos. 1047-1047A are airmail. Gen. Francisco de Paula Santander, bicent. of birth.

A492

Ministers of Justice: 100p, Enrique Low Murtra (1939-91). 110p, Rodrigo Lara Bonilla (1946-84).

1992, Apr. 30 Litho. *Perf. 12*

1048 A492 100p multicolored .70 .30
1049 A492 110p multicolored .80 .30

A493

1992, May 18 *Perf. 14*

1050 A493 110p multicolored .75 .40

15th natl. games, Barranquilla.

Wildlife — A494

No. 1051, Oroaetus icidori. No. 1052, Tremarctos ornatus.

1992, Apr. 14 Litho. *Perf. 12*

1051 A494 (B) multicolored 1.90 .80
1052 A494 (A) multicolored 9.00 3.50

Nos. 1051-1052 had face values of 200p and 950p respectively on date of issue.

Endangered Species A495

No. 1053, Crocodylus acatus. No. 1054, Vultur gryphus, vert.

1992, Aug. 4

1053 A495 100p multicolored 1.25 .40
1054 A495 100p multicolored 1.25 .40

A496

1992, Aug. 24 Litho. *Perf. 14*

1055 A496 100p multicolored .60 .30
1056 A496 110p multicolored .60 .30

Maria Lopez de Escobar, founder of the House of the Mother and Child. No. 1056 is airmail.

A497

1992, Sept. 23 Litho. *Perf. 12*

1057 A497 100p multicolored .50 .30

Conference of First Ladies of the Americas and Caribbean, Cartagena.

Recycling — A498

1992, Oct. 9 Litho. *Perf. 12*

1058 A498 100p multicolored .50 .30

Discovery of America, 500th Anniv. — A499

Paintings: 100p, Zenaida, by Ana Mercedes Hoyos. No. 1060, Estudio Para 1/500, by Beatriz Gonzalez. No. 1061, Blue Eagle, by Alejandro Obregon. 230p, Cantileo, by Luis Luna. 260p, Corn, by Antonio Caro. 400p, Grand Curtain, by Luis Caballero. 440p, Homage to Guatavita, by Alejandro Obregon.

1992, Oct. 5 Litho. *Perf. 13½x14*

1059 A499	100p multicolored	.50	.30
1060 A499	110p multicolored	.50	.30
1061 A499	110p multicolored	.50	.30
1062 A499	230p multicolored	1.25	.70
1063 A499	260p multicolored	1.50	.80
	Nos. 1059-1063 (5)	4.25	2.40

Souvenir Sheets

Perf. 12

1064 A499 400p multicolored 3.00 3.00
1065 A499 440p multicolored 3.00 3.00

Nos. 1061-1063 are airmail.

World Post Day — A500

1992, Oct. 19 Litho. *Perf. 12*

1066 A500 (B) multicolored 1.20 .65

No. 1066 had face value of 200p on day of issue.

Christmas — A501

Children's paintings of: 100p, Nativity scene. 110p, Adoration of the Magi.

1992, Nov. 20 Litho. *Perf. 12*

1067 A501 100p multicolored .60 .30
1068 A501 110p multicolored .60 .30

No. 1068 is airmail.

Three Musicians, by Fernando Botero
A502

1993, Feb. 5 **Litho.** ***Perf. 12***
1069 A502 (B) multicolored 1.25 .80

No. 1069 had a face value of 250p on day of issue.

Lions Intl. Campaign Against Amblyopia
A503

1993, Mar. 26 ***Perf. 14***
1070 A503 100p multicolored .50 .30

Holy Week in Popayan
A504

1993, Apr. 5 ***Perf. 14x13½***
1071 A504 (B) multicolored 1.25 .80

No. 1071 had a face value of 250p on day of issue.

A505

1993, Apr. 7 ***Perf. 12***
1072 A505 (B) multicolored 1.25 .80

Pan American Health Org., 90th anniv.
No. 1072 had a face value of 250p on day of issue.

A506

1993, Apr. 14
1073 A506 (B) multicolored 1.25 .80

Franciscans of Mary Immaculate, cent. No. 1073 had a face value of 250p on day of issue.

A507

1993, Apr. 22 **Litho.** ***Perf. 14***
1074 A507 (B) multicolored 1.25 .80

EXFILBO '93, 18th Natl. Philatelic Exhibition. No. 1074 had a face value of 250p on day issue.

Guillermo Cano, writer — A508

1993, July 2 **Litho.** ***Perf. 12***
1075 A508 250p multicolored 1.50 .75

Human Rights
A509

Rights: a, 150p, Of prisoners. b, 150p, Of the elderly. c, 200p, Of the infirm. d, 200p, Of children. e, 220p, Of women. f, 220p, Of the poor. g, 460p, To clean environment. h, 520p, Of indigenous people.
Painting: 800p, Peace, Rights, and Freedom, by Alfredo Vivero, vert.

1993, June 10 ***Perf. 14***
1076 A509 Block of 8, #a.-h. 12.00 7.50

Souvenir Sheet

1077 A509 800p multicolored 5.50 5.50

Nos. 1076e-1076h are airmail.

Amazon Region of Colombia — A510

No. 1078a, Parrot. No. 1078b, Anaconda. No. 1079a, Victoria regia. No. 1079b, Flor Ipecacuana. 880p, Map, native, horiz.

1993 **Litho.** ***Perf. 12***
1078 A510 150p Pair, #a.-b. 1.75 1.25
1079 A510 220p Pair, #a.-b. 2.50 1.50

Souvenir Sheet

1080 A510 880p multicolored 5.00 5.00

Nos. 1079-1080 are airmail.

Famous People — A511

Designs: a, 150p, Alberto Pumarejo (1893-1970). b, 150p, Lorencita Villegas de Santos (1892-1960). c, 200p, Meliton Rodriguez (1875-1942). d, 200p, Tomas Carrasquilla (1858-1940).

1993 **Litho.** ***Perf. 14x13½***
1081 A511 Block of 4, #a.-d. 4.00 2.75

Christmas — A512

1993, Nov. 30 ***Perf. 12***
1082 A512 200p Holy Family .95 .60
1083 A512 220p Shepherd 1.60 1.10

No. 1083 is airmail.

Tourism
A513

Designs: No. 1084a, San Andres Providence. b, Cocuy Natl. Park. c, Lake Cocha. d, Waterfalls, Serrania de la Macarena. 250p, Lake Otun. No. 1086a, Chicamocha River. b, Sierra Nevada de Santa Marta mountains. 520p, Penol Reservoir.

1993, Dec. 1 **Litho.** ***Perf. 12***
1084 A513 220p Block of 4, #a.-d. 4.50 3.00
1085 A513 250p multicolored 1.25 .75
1086 A513 460p Pair, #a.-b. 4.75 3.00
1087 A513 520p multicolored 2.75 1.50
Nos. 1084-1087 (4) 13.25 8.25

Nos. 1084, 1086-87 are airmail.

A514

1993, Dec. 21 **Litho.** ***Perf. 14***
1088 A514 150p multicolored .60 .40

Natl. Museum, 170th anniv.

A515

1994, Jan. 25 **Litho.** ***Perf. 14***
1089 A515 300p Marie Poussepin 1.50 .80

A516

Birds: 180p, Ognorhynchus icterotis. 240p, Rallus semiplumbeus. 270p, Semnornis ramphastinus. 560p, Anas cyanoptera.

1994, Mar. 4
1090 A516 180p multi 1.40 .40
1091 A516 240p multi 1.60 .55
1092 A516 270p multi, horiz. 2.00 .70
1093 A516 560p multi, horiz. 4.00 1.40
Nos. 1090-1093 (4) 9.00 3.05

Nos. 1092-1093 are airmail.

A517

1994, Apr. 11 **Litho.** ***Perf. 14***
1094 A517 300p multicolored 1.25 .80

Air Force, 75th anniv.

Latin American Presidential Summit, Cartagena
A518

1994, June 14 **Litho.** ***Perf. 14***
1095 A518 300p shown 1.00 .65
1096 A518 630p Flags 2.10 1.60

No. 1096 is airmail.

1994 World Cup Soccer Championships, US — A519

World Cup Trophy and: 180p, Soccer player, Colombian flag. 270p, Two players with ball. 560p, Soccer ball, Colombian flag, vert.
1110p, Soccer player offering hand to another.

1994, May 26 *Perf. 12*

1097	A519	180p multicolored	.80	.40
1098	A519	270p multicolored	1.20	.55
1099	A519	560p multicolored	2.50	1.40
		Nos. 1097-1099 (3)	4.50	2.35

Souvenir Sheet

1100	A519	1110p multicolored	7.00	7.00

Nos. 1098-1099 are airmail.

Ricardo Rendon (1894-1931), Artist — A520

1994, June 30 **Litho.** *Perf. 12*

1101	A520	240p black	1.40	.65

1993 Census — A521

1994, Aug. 12 *Perf. 14*

1102	A521	240p multicolored	1.10	.45

Ministry of Communications Inravision, 30th Anniv.— A522

1994, Aug. 3

1103	A522	180p multicolored	1.00	.50

Intl. Year of the Family A523

1994, Sept. 1 **Litho.** *Perf. 14*

1104	A523	300p multicolored	1.25	.65

America Issue — A524

Methods of mail delivery: 270p, Horse, bicycle. 300p, Men holding stamps showing truck, ship, plane.

1994, Oct. 18 **Litho.** *Perf. 13*

1105	A524	270p multicolored	1.60	.65
1106	A524	300p multicolored	2.40	.70

No. 1105 is airmail.

Colombian Society of Engineers, Cent. A525

1994, Oct. 20 **Litho.** *Perf. 12*

1107	A525	180p multicolored	.75	.40

Christmas A526

1994, Nov. 22 **Litho.** *Perf. 13½x13*

1108	A526	270p Magi	.95	.65
1109	A526	300p Holy family	1.10	.70

No. 1108 is airmail.

Former President Type of 1981

Miniature Sheet of 20

Designs: a, Jose Miguel Pey. b, Jorge Tadeo Lozano. c, Antonio Narino. d, Camilo Torres. e, Jose Fernandez Madrid. f, Jose Maria del Castillo y Rada. g, Custodio Garcia Rovira. h, Antonio Villavicencio. i, Liborio Mejia. j, Rafael Urdaneta. k, Juan Garcia del Rio. l, Jose Maria Melo. m, Tomas Herrera. n, Froilan Largacha. o, Salvador Camacho Roldan. p, Ezequiel Hurtado. q, Dario Echandia Olaya. r, Alberto Lleras Camargo. s, Gustavo Rojas Pinilla. t, Carlos Lleras Restrepo.

1995, Apr. 4 **Litho.** *Perf. 12*

1110	A401	270p #a.-t.	35.00	35.00

World Offroad Bicycle Championships, Melgar — A527

1995, Mar. 30 *Perf. 14*

1111	A527	400p multicolored	1.60	.90

A528

1995, Oct. 12 **Litho.** *Perf. 12*

1112	A528	220p multicolored	1.00	.45

Gen. Jose Maria Obando (1795-1861), President.

A529

1995, Nov. 28 *Perf. 14*

1113	A529	400p Clean air	1.50	.75
1114	A529	400p Clean water	1.50	.75

Preserve the environment. America issue.

Christmas A530

Stained glass windows: 220p, Flight into Egypt. 330p, Nativity.

1995, Dec. 18 *Perf. 12*

1115	A530	220p multicolored	.75	.40
1116	A530	330p multicolored	1.10	.65

No. 1116 is airmail.

Bogotá to Boyacá World Cycling Championship — A531

1995, Oct. 4 **Litho.** *Perf. 12*

1117	A531	400p multicolored	1.75	.75

León De Greiff (1895-1976), Poet — A532

1996, May 2 **Litho.** *Perf. 12*

1118	A532	400p black	1.40	.60

Mosquera Courtyard, Natl. Capitol A533

1996, July 18 **Litho.** *Perf. 14*

1119	A533	400p multicolored	1.50	.60

Medellin Rapid Transit System A534

1996, July 2 *Perf. 12*

1120	A534	500p multicolored	2.00	.90

A535

1996, June 20

1121	A535	500p multicolored	1.60	.75

Community of St. John of God in Colombia, 400th anniv.

A536

Arms: a, Santa Maria la Antigua del Darien. b, San Sebastian de Mariquita. c, Villa de la Marinilla. d, Villa of Santa Cruz of Mompox.

1996, June 25

1122	A536	400p Block of 4, #a.-d.	5.00	5.00
e.		As "d," inscribed AEREO	15.00	15.00
f.		Block of 4, #1122a-1122c, 1122e	20.00	20.00

Issued in sheets of 16 stamps.

1996 Summer Olympic Games, Atlanta — A537

1996, July 16

1123	A537	500p multicolored	2.00	.75

SAYCO (Colombian Authors and Composers Society), 50th Anniv. — A538

1996, Aug. 17 **Litho.** *Perf. 12*

1124	A538	400p multicolored	1.50	.60

Exfilbo '96, 20th Natl. Philatelic Exhibition A539

Jewelry from Gold Museum, Bogotá.

1996, Oct. 19 **Litho.** *Perf. 12*

1125	A539	400p multicolored	1.50	.60

Souvenir Sheet

Founders Theater, Manizales, 30th Anniv. — A540

Drop curtain: a, Eagle, people watching man drawing on ground, vert. b, People, animals on hillside.

1996, Oct. 28 *Perf. 14*
1126 A540 4000p #a.-b. 30.00 30.00

Christmas A541

Designs: No. 1127, Mailman handing woman letter. No. 1128, Woman reading letter, mailman holding bundle of mail.

1996, Nov. 22
1127 A541 400p multicolored 1.75 .40
1128 A541 400p multicolored 1.75 .40

No. 1128 is airmail.

America Issue — A542

1996, Nov. 29 *Perf. 12*
1129 A542 500p Men's costume 1.75 .60
1130 A542 500p Women's costume 1.75 .60

Historical Landmarks — A543

a, Cemetery, Santa Cruz of Mompox. b, Carved face, San Agustin Archaelogical Park. c, Entrance, Palace of the Inquisition, Cartagena de Indias. d, Inside ruins, Tierradentro Archaelogical Park.

1996, Dec. 6 *Perf. 14*
1131 A543 400p Block of 4, #a.-d. 10.00 10.00

Alvaro Gomez Hurtado (1919-95), Politician, Writer — A544

1997, Mar. 18 **Litho.** *Perf. 12*
1132 A544 400p multicolored 1.50 .75

Bogotá Journalists Assoc., 50th Anniv. A545

1997, July 10 **Litho.** *Perf. 12*
1133 A545 400p multicolored 1.50 .40

Natl. Festival of Porro — A546

1997, June 26 *Perf. 13½x14*
1134 A546 400p multicolored 1.50 .40

Pres. Virgilio Barco (1921-97) — A547

1997, Nov. 27 **Litho.** *Perf. 14*
1135 A547 500p multicolored 1.75 .40

Colombia in Peace A548

500p, Children playing. 1100p, Children dancing.

1997, Dec. 30 **Litho.** *Perf. 12*
1136 A548 500p multicolored 1.40 .40
1137 A548 1100p multicolored 3.00 .90

No. 1137 is airmail.

America Issue A549

500p, Postman by day. 1100p, Postman by night.

1997, Dec. 30
1138 A549 500p multicolored 2.00 .50
1139 A549 1100p multicolored 4.00 1.25

No. 1139 is airmail.

Jorge Eliecer Gaitan (1903-48), Politician — A550

1998, Apr. 24 **Litho.** *Perf. 14*
1140 A550 500p multicolored 1.75 .80

Free University, 75th Anniv. A551

1998, July 1 **Litho.** *Perf. 14*
1141 A551 500p black & red 2.75 .75

Santander Industrial University, 50th Anniv. — A552

1998, May 14 *Perf. 12*
1142 A552 500p multicolored 1.75 .80

City of Manizales, 150th Anniv. — A553

1998, July 24 **Litho.** *Perf. 12*
1143 A553 500p multicolored 2.75 .75

A554

Pre-Columbian art, agency: a, Tairona, Bank of the Republic. b, Malagana, Controller General. c, Quimbaya, Bank Superintendent.

1998, July 24
1144 A554 500p Strip of 3, #a.-c. 7.50 7.50

Natl. financial agencies, 70th anniv.

A555

1998, Aug. 21 *Perf. 14*
1145 A555 500p multicolored 2.75 .80

Pres. Misael Pastrana Borrero (1923-97).

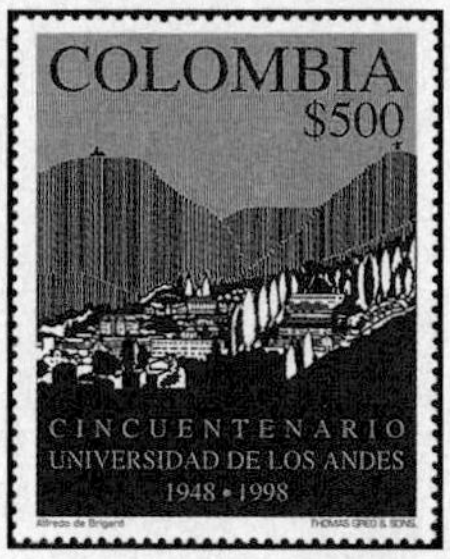

University of the Andes, 50th Anniv. A556

1998, Sept. 28
1146 A556 500p multicolored 2.25 .80

Christmas A557

Designs: 500p, Woman kneeling down to get water with bowl, cherubs in sky. No. 1148a, Magi. No. 1148b, Nativity scene.

1998, Nov. 19 **Litho.** *Perf. 14*
1147 A557 500p multicolored 1.25 .75
1148 A557 1000p Pair, #a.-b. 4.75 3.25

No. 1148 is airmail.

A558

Emblems of Colombian Academies: a, Language. b, Medicine. c, Law. d, History. e, Science. f, Ecomonics. g, Religion.

1998, Dec. 15 *Perf. 12*
Sheet of 7 + Label
1149 A558 500p #a.-g. 14.00 14.00

A559

1999, Apr. 16 *Perf. 14*
1150 A559 1000p multicolored 2.25 1.00

Gen. José Hilario López.

Famous Women — A559a

America Issue: 600p, Soledad Román de Nuñez. 1200p, Bertha Herández de Ospina.

1999, Mar. 25 **Litho.** *Perf. 12*
1151 A559a 600p multicolored 1.50 .50
1152 A559a 1200p multicolored 3.00 1.00

No. 1152 is airmail.

Turtles — A560

a, Chelonia mydas. b, Dermochelys coriacea. c, Eretmochelys imbricata.

1999, Apr. 16 ***Perf. 14***
1153 A560 1300p Strip of 3, #a.-c. 13.00 13.00

Dr. Eduardo Zuleta Angel, Diplomat (b. 1899) — A561

1999, Sept. 9 **Litho.** ***Perf. 12***
1154 A561 600p multicolored 1.40 .45

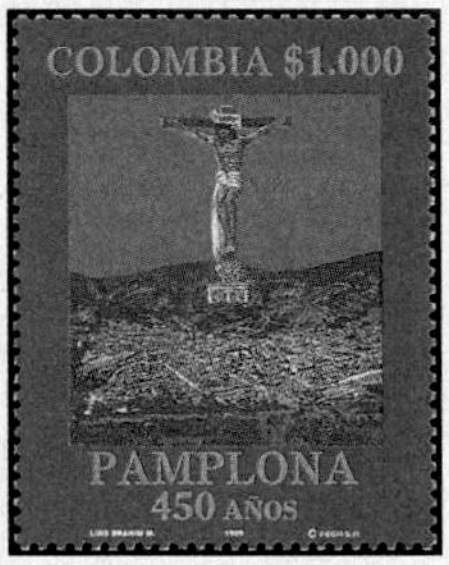

Pamplona, 450th Anniv. A562

1999 **Litho.** ***Perf. 12***
1155 A562 1000p multicolored 2.75 .75

Sovereign Military Order of Malta, 900th Anniv. — A563

1999, June 24 ***Perf. 14***
1156 A563 1200p multicolored 4.00 1.25

Japanese Immigration to Colombia — A564

Designs: a, Red at right. b, Red at left.

1999, May 12 ***Perf. 13½x14***
1157 A564 1300p Pair, #a.-b. 6.00 6.00

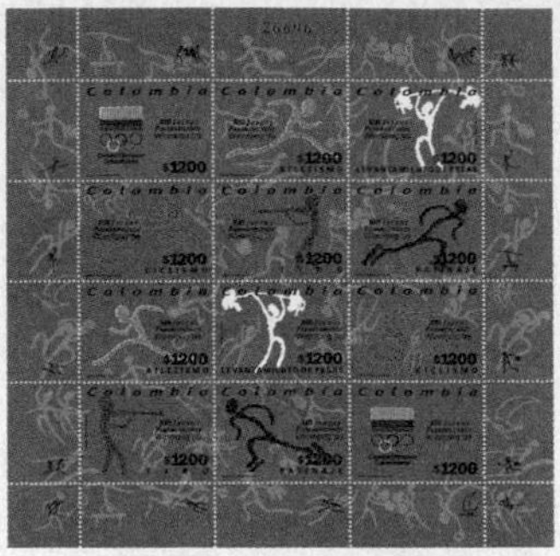

Pan American Games, Winnipeg, Manitoba — A565

Designs: a, Flag, Olympic rings. b, Runner facing right. c, Weight lifter facing left. d, Cyclist facing right. e, Shooter facing left. f, Roller skater facing right. g, Runner facing left. h, Weight lifter facing right. i, Cyclist facing left. j, Shooter facing right. k, Roller skater facing left. l, Like "a," with lilac vertical line under "12."

1999, July 23 **Litho.** ***Perf. 14***
1158 A565 1200p Sheet of 12, #a.-l. 30.00 30.00

Luis A. Robles (b. 1849) — A566

1999, Oct. 27
1159 A566 600p multi 1.10 .40

Manufacture of Aspirin, Cent. A567

1999, Dec. 1 ***Perf. 12¾***
1160 A567 600p multi 1.10 .40

Value is for stamp with surrounding selvage.

UPU, 125th Anniv. A568

1999, Oct. 29 ***Perf. 14¼***
1161 A568 1000p "125" 1.75 .75
1162 A568 1300p "1874-1999" 2.75 1.00

Inter-American Development Bank, 40th Anniv. — A569

Abstract art: a, "Colombia" in yellow. b, "Colombia" in red.

1999, Nov. 19 ***Perf. 14x14¼***
1163 A569 1000p Pair, #a.-b. 3.50 1.40

America Issue, A New Millennium Without Arms — A570

a, Stylized hands. b, Large flower at LR.

1999, Nov. 9 ***Perf. 14***
1164 A570 1200p Pair, #a.-b. 4.25 1.90

Christmas — A571

a, Holy Family, animals. b, Angel, Magi.

1999, Nov. 29 ***Perf. 13½x14***
1165 A571 600p Pair, #a.-b. 2.25 .90

Millennium — A572

Designs: a, Nude man, flag, dove. b, Globe, rainbow, "2000."

2000, Jan. 3 ***Perf. 14***
1166 A572 1000p Pair, #a.-b. 4.00 4.00

University of Medellin, 50th Anniv. A573

2000, Feb. 1 **Litho.** ***Perf. 14***
1167 A573 1000p multi 1.50 .65

Father José Rafael Faría Bermúdez (1896-1979) A574

2000, Mar. 6 **Litho.** ***Perf. 14***
1168 A574 1300p multi 1.75 .90

2000 Summer Olympics, Sydney A575

2000, Apr. 21
1169 A575 1000p multi 1.75 .75

Popayán Religious Music Festival A576

2000, July 7
1170 A576 1000p multi 1.90 .65

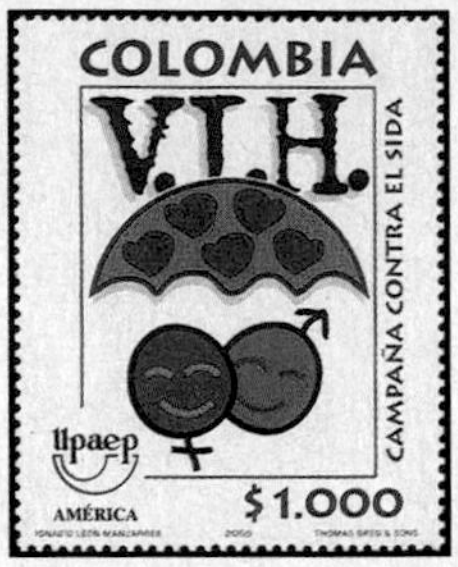

America Issue, Campaign Against AIDS A577

2000, Sept. 19 **Litho.** ***Perf. 14x13½***
1171 A577 1000p multi 4.00 1.60

Radio Station HJCK, 50th Anniv. — A578

2000, Sept. 28 **Litho.** ***Perf. 14***
1172 A578 1000p multi 1.50 .65

Birth Registration A579

2000, Nov. 14 **Litho.** ***Perf. 14¼***
1173 A579 1000p multi 1.50 .60

Paintings A580

No. 1174: a, Archangel, by Fernando Botero. b, Gypsy Woman With Tamourine, by Jean-Baptiste-Camille Corot. c, Vera Sergine Renoir, by Renoir. d, Man on Horse, by Botero. e, Mother Superior, by Botero. f, A Town, by Botero. g, Flowers, by Botero. h, Cézanne, by Botero. i, Patio, by Botero. j, Absinthe Drinker in Grenelle, by Toulouse-Lautrec. k, A Little Valley, by Corot. l, The Studio, by Botero.

2001, Jan. 31 ***Perf. 12***
1174 Sheet of 12 15.00 15.00
a.-l. A580 650p Any single .95 .45

Children's Day — A581

2001, Mar. 15 **Litho.** ***Perf. 14***
1175 A581 1100p multi 3.75 1.40

Abolition of Slavery, 150th Anniv. — A582

2001, May 21 **Litho.** ***Perf. 14¼x14***
1176 A582 1100p multi 3.75 1.40

Discovery of Magdalena River, 500th Anniv. — A583

2001, June 13 **Litho.** ***Perf. 14***
1177 A583 1100p multi 3.75 1.40

Copa America Soccer Tournament A584

2001, July 18 **Litho.** ***Perf. 12¾***
1178 A584 1900p multi 5.25 1.75

Values are for examples with surrounding selvage.

America Issue — Los Katios Natl. Park, UNESCO World Heritage Site — A585

2001, Aug. 17 ***Perf. 13¾x14***
1179 A585 2100p multi 7.50 3.00

Year of Dialogue Among Civilizations A586

2001, Oct. 9 ***Perf. 14***
1180 A586 650p multi 2.50 .80

Reclining Woman, by Fernando Botero — A587

2001, Oct. 23 ***Perf. 14¼***
1181 A587 1100p multi 4.00 1.40

Christmas A588

2001, Nov. 19 ***Perf. 14***
1182 A588 1100p multi 4.00 1.40

National Beauty Pageant — A589

Flag, Miss Colombia Vanesa A. Mendoza Bustos and: a, Cartagena de Indias. b, St. Francis of Assisi Cathedral, Quibdo.

2002, Jan. 22 ***Perf. 14x14¼***
1183 A589 800p Horiz. pair, #a-b 3.00 1.00

Natural Riches of Colombia — A590

Parts of map of Colombia, various wildlife and/or natives and: a, Bird and clouds at left. b, Turtle at upper left. c, Fish and whales at left. d, Man on horse at center. e, Volcano at upper left. f, Red and blue parrots at right. g, Flamingos at left. h, Snake at upper left.

2002, Feb. 1 ***Perf. 14¼x14***
1184 A590 2300p Sheet of 8, #a-h 45.00 45.00

Children's Day — A591

2002, Feb. 18 ***Perf. 12***
1185 A591 1400p multi 2.50 1.10

New Emblem of Adpostal — A592

2002, Mar. 7 ***Perf. 14***
1186 A592 800p multi 1.60 .60

7th South American Games A593

2002, Jan. 7
1187 A593 2100p multi 3.00 1.25

Oxyura Jamaicensis A594

2002, Apr. 30 **Litho.** ***Perf. 12***
1188 A594 3900p multi 6.50 3.00

Souvenir Sheet

Frogs — A595

No. 1189: a, 7200p, Hyla crepitans. b, 7600p, Dendrobates histrionicus.

2002, Apr. 30 ***Perf. 13¾x14***
1189 A595 Sheet of 2, #a-b 21.00 21.00

Souvenir Sheet

Butterflies — A596

No. 1190: a, Dryas iulia. b, Dryadula phaetusa, vert.

2002, Apr. 30 ***Perf. 12***
1190 A596 13,700p Sheet of 2, #a-b 37.50 37.50

Foundation for Reconstructive Surgery, 25th Anniv. — A597

2002, May 24 ***Perf. 14***
1191 A597 1000p multi 1.60 .60

Pre-Columbian Art — A598

No. 1192, 800p: a, Nariño pectoral. b, Nariño disc.
No. 1193, 1400p: a, Calima diadem. b, Calima pectoral.
No. 1194, 2100p: a, Anthropomorphic Tairona pectoral. b, Round Tairona pectoral.

2002, June 7 ***Perf. 13½x14***
Horiz. Pairs, #a-b
1192-1194 A598 Set of 3 15.00 15.00

Surgical Society of Bogota San José Hospital, Cent. — A599

No. 1195: a, Early doctors and nurse. b, Hospital.

2002, July 22 ***Perf. 14***
1195 A599 800p Horiz. pair, #a-b 2.75 2.75

Consuelo Araújo Noguera (1940-2001), Assassinated Former Minister of Culture — A600

2002, Aug. 1
1196 A600 1400p multi 2.50 1.00

Union Network International A601

2002, Aug. 12
1197 A601 1000p multi 1.60 .65

America Issue — Youth, Education and Literacy — A602

No. 1198: a, Person reading book. b, Letters amd words.

2002, Oct. 9
1198 A602 2500p Horiz. pair, #a-b 7.00 6.00

Christmas
A603

2002, Nov. 6 Litho. *Perf. 14x13¾*
1199 A603 800p multi 2.00 .65

Colombian History Academy, Cent. — A604

No. 1200: a, Mural scene with Simon Bolivar at UR. b, Mural scene with horsemen at top. c, Mural scene with man with outstretched arms at UL. d, Cafetal, 1956. e, Batalla de Palonegro, 1905. f, Tigre Cazando Sabanera, 1963. g, El Barqueo, 1936. h, Colombia Asesinada, 1902. i, Dos Mujeres, 1951. j, Bearded man at left, Plaza de Santander. k, Carriage, Plaza de Santander. l, Horse, man and woman, Plaza de Santander.

2002, Nov. 19 *Perf. 13¾x14*
1200 A604 800p Sheet of 12, #a-l 22.50 22.50

Peace Treaty Ending War of 1,000 Days, Cent. A605

2002, Nov. 21 *Perf. 14x13¾*
1201 A605 1600p multi 3.50 1.10

Carnival
A606

No. 1202: a, shown. b, Participants holding masks on sticks. c, Participants on float.

2003, Jan. 4 *Perf. 14*
1202 Horiz. strip of 3 6.50 6.50
a.-b. A606 1000p Either single 1.25 1.25
c. A606 1200p multi 1.60 1.60

Printed in sheets of 3 horizontal strips and 2 horiz. strips of 3 labels.

Articulated Bus, Bogota
A607

2003, Mar. 13 *Perf. 12*
1203 A607 1000p multi 1.60 .70

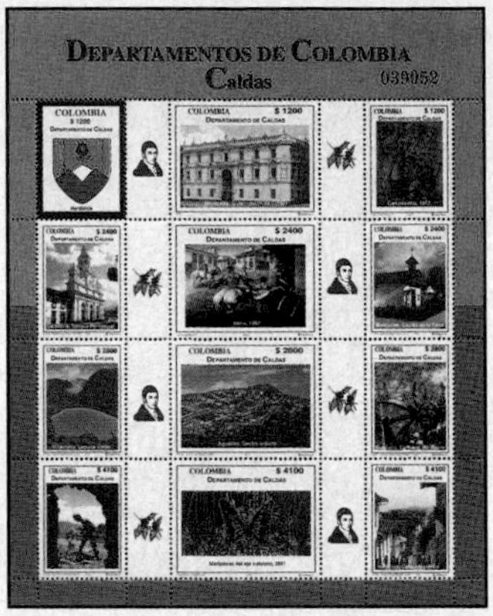

Departments — A608

No. 1204 — Caldas Department: a, 1200p, Arms. b, 1200p, Government office building, Manizales, horiz. c, 1200p, Campesinos, 1957. d, 2400p, Church, Salamina. e, 2400p, Neira, 1997, horiz. f, 2400p, Enea Chapel, Manizales. g, 2800p, Laguna Verde, Villamaria. h, 2800p, Aguadas, horiz. i, 2800p, Devil's carnival, Riosucio. j, 4100p, Miner, Marmato. k, 4100p, Mariposas del Eje Cafetero, 2001, horiz. l, 4100p, Pacora.

No. 1205, 1000p — Huila Department: a, Arms. b, Government office building, Neiva, horiz. c, La Gaitana. d, Bordones Waterfall, Isnos. e, San Agustín World Heritage Archaeological Park, horiz. f, Lavapatas Spring, San Agustín. g, La Tatacoa Desert, Villavieja. h, Liberty tree, Gigante, horiz. i, Sombrero maker, Suaza. j, Nuestra Señora de los Dolores Church, Aipe. k, Paisaje, horiz. l, Dancers.

No. 1206 — 2400p: a, Historic center of Barichara. b, Ophthalmologic Foundation of Santander, Bucaramanga, horiz. c, Girón. d, Santander Industrial University Intl. Piano Festival, 20th anniv. emblem. e, Petroleum Christ Statue, refinery, Barrancabermeja, horiz. f, Church, San Andrés. g, Gustavo Cote Uribe (1918-94), writer. h, Chamber of Commerce, Bucaramanga, horiz. i, Carnival of Eastern Colombia, Bucaramanga. j, Historic center of Albania. k, Chicamocha River Canyon, Cepitá, horiz. l, Entreguerras.

Sheets of 12, #a-l, + 8 labels

2003 *Perf. 12*
1204 A608 Caldas 42.50 42.50
1205 A608 Huila 17.50 17.50
1206 A608 Santander 35.00 35.00

Issued: No. 1204, Apr. 11. No. 1205, June 29. No. 1206, July 22. Size of horiz. stamps: 46x37mm.

See Nos. 1224-1226, 1246, 1265-1267, 1273, 1288-1289, 1316, 1335-1336, 1359, 1377, 1393.

Fish and Coral of the Rosario Islands — A609

2003, Jan. 16 Litho. *Perf. 12*
1207 A609 1000p multi 3.25 .85

Hapalopsittaca Fuertesi — A610

2003, June 13
1208 A610 1000p multi 3.25 .85

Souvenir Sheets

Orchids — A611

No. 1209 — 2400p: a, Masdevallia ignea. b, Miltoniopsis vexillaria, horiz.
No. 1210 — 2800p: a, Odontoglossum crispum, horiz. b, Masdevallia macrura.
No. 1211 — 5000p: a, Cimbidium. b, Oncidium obryzatum.
No. 1212 — 7000p: a, Cattleya dowiana. b, Cattleya trianaei (49x49mm).

Sheets of 2, #a-b

Perf. 14¼, 13¾x14 (#1212b)
2003, June 13
1209-1212 A611 Set of 4 50.00 50.00

Tejo, National Sport
A612

No. 1213: a, Players, tree in foreground (49x39mm). b, Players, light poles (49x39mm). c, Cacique Turmeque.

2003, July 25 *Perf. 12*
1213 Horiz. strip of 3 10.00 10.00
a.-c. A612 2400p Any single 2.25 1.40

America Issue — A613

Flora and fauna: a, Denomination at UR. b, Denomination at LR.

2003, Oct. 9 Litho. *Perf. 12*
1214 A613 1600p Vert. pair, #a-b 5.00 5.00

Printed in sheets of four pairs and four labels.

Souvenir Sheet

Colombia Libraries National Reading Plan — A614

No. 1215: a, 1200p, Building. b, 4100p, Building, diff.

2003, Oct. 30 Litho. *Perf. 12*
1215 A614 Sheet of 2, #a-b 8.00 8.00

General Ramón Arturo Rincón Quiñones (1922-75) — A615

2003, Oct. 31
1216 A615 1000p multi 1.75 .50

Souvenir Sheet

Administrative Security Deparment, 50th Anniv. — A616

2003, Oct. 31
1217 A616 4100p multi 6.00 6.00

Armed Forces A617

No. 1218 — Arms and mottos: a, General Command of Military Forces. b, National Army. c, National Navy. d, Air Force. e, Colombian Forces in Korea, 50th anniv.

2003, Nov. 7

1218	Vert. strip of 5	8.00	8.00
a.-e.	A617 1200p Any single	1.10	.60

Christmas — A618

No. 1219: a, Good Shepherd, sheep. b, Tree, comet, airplane, rabbit. c, Rabbits, dog. d, Automobile, angel, reindeer, horse. e, Sheep, woman with basket, swan, house. f, Branch with leaves, horse and rider, duck, Indian with bow and arrow.

2003, Dec. 2 Litho. *Perf. 12*

1219	Block of 6	9.00	9.00
a.-f.	A618 1000p Any single	1.10	.65

Colombia and the Eldorado Legend — A619

No. 1220: a, Print of Eldorado ceremony, by Teodoro De Bry, 1595. b, Watercolor painting of Lake Guatavita, by M. María Paz, 1855. c, Watercolor painting of Lake Guatavita, by Gonzalo Ariza, 1984. d, Print of Lake Guatavita, by A. Humboldt Thibault and F. Schoell, 1813. e, Photo of Lake Guatavita, by Fernando Urbina Rangel, 1983. f, Print of Lake Guatavita, by Eustacio Barreto, 1883.

No. 1221 — Muisca raft: a, 1700p, Front. b, 2000p, Back, vert.

2004, Mar. 10

1220	A619 2800p Sheet of 6, #a-f, + 3 labels	13.00	13.00

Souvenir Sheet

1221	A619 Sheet of 2, #a-b	3.00	3.00

Locomotives — A620

No. 1222, 1100p: a, 2-8-2. b, 4-8-0.
No. 1223, 1300p: a, 2-6-2. b, 4-6-2.

2004, Mar. 19 Horiz. Pairs, #a-b

1222-1223	A620 Set of 2	13.50	13.50

Nos. 1222-1223 each printed in sheets of four pairs and two pairs of labels.

Departments Type of 2003

No. 1224, 1100p — Nariño Department: a, Galeras Volcano, San Juan de Pasto, horiz. b, Statue of Gen. Antonio Nariño. c, Nariño Government Building, San Juan de Pasto, horiz. d, Farm, Catambuco, horiz. e, Nuestra Señora de las Lajas Sanctuary, Ipiales. f, Sandoná city center, horiz. g, Gallery of Mirrors, horiz. h, Barnizadores de Pasto Chorography Commission. i, Golden palms, horiz. j, El Morro, Tumaco, horiz. k, Virgen de la Playa Sanctuary, San Pablo. l, Festival of Whites and Blacks, horiz.

No. 1225, 2000p — Tolima Department: a, Nevado del Tolima, horiz. b, Tolima arms. c, Ambalema, horiz. d, Bowls, La Chamba, horiz. e, Natural Bridge, Icononzo. f, Hermitage, Mariquita, horiz. g, Matachos, horiz. h, Prison, Ibagué. i, Alberto Castilla Conservatory Room, horiz. j, Fishermen, Magdalena River, horiz. k, Cacique Calarcá. l, Tolima Art Museum, Ibagué.

No. 1226, 3000p — Chocó Department: a, Coat of Arms. b, Quibdó skyline, horiz. c, Indian girls. d, San Pacho Fiesta. e, Carrasquilla College, Quibdó, horiz. f, Houses, Nóvita. g, Canoe on San Juan River. h, Women grinding corn meal, horiz. i, Nuestra Senora del Rosario Church, Condoto. j, Utría Bay. k, Bellavista Church, Bojayá, horiz. l, Goldsmith, Acandi.

Horiz. stamps are 46x37mm.

Sheets of 12, #a-l, +8 labels

2004 Litho. *Perf. 13¾x14*

1224	A608	Nariño	10.50	10.50
1225	A608	Tolima	18.00	18.00
1226	A608	Chocó	30.00	30.00
	Nos. 1224-1226 (3)		58.50	58.50

Issued: No. 1224, 8/5; No. 1225, 4/16. No. 1226, 11/17

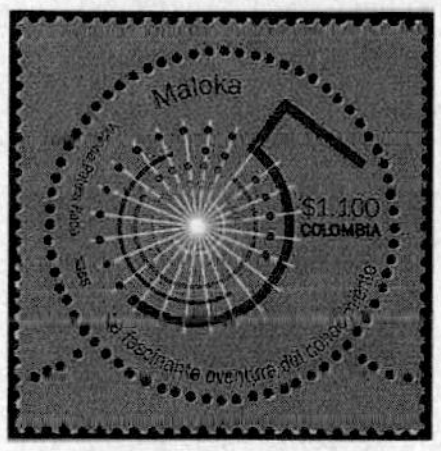

Maloka Science and Technology Center A621

2004, July 6 Litho. *Perf. 12¾*

1227	A621 1100p multi	1.25	1.25

Values are for stamps with surrounding selvage.

2004 Summer Olympics, Athens — A622

2004, Aug. 5 *Perf. 13¾x14*

1228	A622 4400p multi	3.75	3.75

Natl. Association of Contractors, 60th Anniv. A623

No. 1229: a, Denomination in white. b, Denomination in black.

2004, Aug. 5 *Perf. 14x13¾*

1229	Pair	4.50	4.50
a.-b.	A623 2800p Either single	2.25	2.25

Printed in sheets containing 6 pairs and one large central label.

FIFA (Fédération Internationale de Football Association), Cent. — A624

2004, Aug. 25 *Perf. 13¼x14*

1230	A624 3500p multi	3.00	3.00

Women's Citizenship, 50th Anniv. — A625

2004, Sept. 24 *Perf. 14*

1231	A625 15,000p multi	13.00	13.00

Fair and Expositions Corporation, 50th Anniv. — A626

2004, Oct. 14 *Perf. 13½x13*

1232	A626 1300p multi	1.25	1.25

Colombian Radio Announcers Association, 50th Anniv. — A627

2004, Oct. 21 *Perf. 14*

1233	A627 1700p multi	1.60	1.60

17th National Games — A628

2004, Dec. 10 Litho. *Perf. 12¾*

1234	A628 7000p multi + label	6.25	6.25

Printed in sheets of 4 + 5 labels.

America Issue — Environmental Conservation — A629

Designs: No. 1235, 5000p, Whale, Gorgona National Nature Park. No. 1236, 5000p, Hammerhead sharks, Malpelo Flora and Fauna Sanctuary.

2004, Dec. 14 *Perf. 14*

1235-1236	A629 Set of 2	9.00	9.00

Miniature Sheet

Christmas — A630

No. 1237 — Inscriptions: a, Jesús en la mansion de su padre. b, Eterna sumision a Dios. c, Jesús desciende al seno de su madre. d, Aceptacion de milagro divino. e, La ilusion de Maria. f, Voluntad divina en manos del emperador. g, Paciencia, expectativa y anhelo. h, Belén: Humilde hospedaje. i, Nacimiento, la faz de Dios encarnado.

2004, Dec. 15

1237	A630 2800p Sheet of 9, #a-i	32.50	32.50

Pre-Columbian Gold Artifacts From Gold Museum — A631

No. 1238, 1200p: a, Tumaco ear covering. b, Zenú nose ring.

No. 1239, 1800p: a, Cauma nose ring. b, Tierradentro bracelet.

Pairs, #a-b

2005, Jan. 21 *Perf. 12x12½*

1238-1239	A631 Set of 2	5.25	5.25

Issued: No. 1238, 1/21; No. 1239, 3/28.

Rotary International, Cent. — A632

2005, Feb. 23 *Perf. 13½x14*

1240	A632 3100p multi	2.75	2.75

Souvenir Sheet

Butterflies — A633

No. 1241: a, Protographium tyastes panamensis. b, Dismorphia zaela laura. c, Actinote ozomene.

2005, June 7 Litho. *Perf. 14¼*

1241	A633 4600p Sheet of 3, #a-c	13.00	13.00

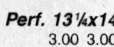

FENALCO (Natl. Federation of Retailers), 60th Anniv. A634

2005, June 10 *Perf. 14*
1242 A634 1200p multi 1.10 1.10

Souvenir Sheets

Department Centenaries — A635

No. 1243, 3100p: a, Map of Caldas Department. b, Map of Colombia highlighting Caldas.
No. 1244, 3700p: a, Map of Huila Department. b, Map of Colombia highlighting Huila.
No. 1245, 4200p: a, Map of Atlantico Department. b, Map of Colombia highlighting Atlantico.

Sheets of 2, #a-b

2005, June *Perf. 14x13½*
1243-1245 A635 Set of 3 25.00 25.00

Departments Type of 2003

No. 1246 — San Andrés y Providencia Department: a, Aerial view of San Andrés, horiz. b, Arms. c, Aerial view of Johnny Cay, horiz. d, Cayo Cangrejo, horiz. e, Artisan. f, Culture House, San Andrés, horiz. g, Morgan Head, Santa Catalina Island, horiz. h, Island view. i, Ensenada, San Andrés, horiz. j, Island architecture, horiz. k, Baptist Church, San Andrés. l, Aerial view of Providencia and Santa Catalina Islands.
Horiz. stamps are 46x37mm.

2005, July 20 *Perf. 13¾x14*
1246 A608 1200p Sheet of 12, #a-l 13.00 13.00

Bogota Botanical Gardens — A636

2005, Aug. 5 *Perf. 14*
1247 A636 1400p multi 1.25 1.25

15th Bolivarian Games — A637

2005, Aug. 11 *Perf. 13¾x14*
1248 A637 3500p multi 3.25 3.25

Association of Graduates of the University of the Andes, 50th Anniv. A638

2005, Sept. 14 *Perf. 14*
1249 A638 2000p multi 1.75 1.75

Intl. Day of Ozone Layer Protection A639

2005, Sept. 16
1250 A639 2000p multi 1.75 1.75

Souvenir Sheet

Publication of Don Quixote, 400th Anniv. — A640

No. 1251 — Paintings of Miguel de Cervantes by: a, Ricardo Rendón Bravo. b, Eduardo Ramírez Villamizar, vert. c, Santiago Martínez Delgado, vert.

Perf. 13½x14 (#1251a), 14x13½
2005, Oct. 25
1251 A640 1300p Sheet of 3, #a-c 3.50 3.50

Colpatria Bank, 50th Anniv. A641

2005, Nov. 2 *Perf. 14x13½*
1252 A641 1200p multi 1.10 1.10

Arms of City of Facatativá A642

2005, Oct. 30 **Litho.** *Perf. 14*
1253 A642 1800p multi 1.75 1.75

Latin Union, 50th Anniv. — A643

2005, Dec. 1 *Perf. 13½x14*
1254 A643 5000p multi 4.75 4.75

Printed in sheets of 4.

Souvenir Sheet

America Issue, Fight Against Poverty — A644

2005, Nov. 30 *Perf. 14x13½*
1255 A644 Sheet of 2 #1255a 9.50 9.50
a. 5000p Single stamp 4.75 4.75

Souvenir Sheet

Escuela de Lanceros (Military School), 50th Anniv. — A645

2005, Nov. 30 *Perf. 14*
1256 A645 Sheet of 2 #1256a 19.00 19.00
a. 10,000p Single stamp 9.50 9.50

Christmas A646

2005, Dec. 9 *Perf. 14*
1257 A646 3100p multi 3.00 3.00

Printed in sheets of 7.

Colombian Journalism A647

2006, Feb. 9 **Litho.**
1258 A647 2000p multi 1.90 1.90

St. Francis Xavier (1506-52) A648

2006, Apr. 7
1259 A648 4500p multi 3.75 3.75

Pope John Paul II (1920-2005) A649

2006, Apr. 4
1260 A649 4800p multi 3.75 3.75

Souvenir Sheet

Frederic Chopin (1810-49), Composer — A650

2006, May 25 *Perf. 13½x13*
1261 A650 5300p multi 5.00 5.00

Printed in sheets of 4.

Gold Artifacts Type of 2005

No. 1262: a, Quimbaya striated lime receptacle with handles. b, Quimbaya thin lime receptacle.

2006, Jan. 26 *Perf. 12x12½*
1262 A631 1500p Pair, #a-b 3.50 3.50

Italian Cultural Institute of Bogota, 50th Anniv. — A651

No. 1263: a, Lute at lower left. b, Violin at lower right.

2006, Feb. 23 *Perf. 14*
1263 A651 1300p Horiz. pair, #a-b 2.25 2.25

Souvenir Sheet

Rayo Museum, 25th Anniv. — A652

No. 1264: a, Artwork in blue, white, red, yellow and black. b, Artwork in white, blue, tan and black.

2006, Jan. 21 *Perf. 13½x13*

1264 A652 Sheet, 2 each #a-b 4.50 4.50
a.-b. 1300p Either single 1.10 1.10

Departments Type of 2003

No. 1265 — Valle del Cauca Department: a, Mapping Commission drawing of Cali, horiz. b, Arms of Valle del Cauca. c, Arms and panoramic view of Sevilla, horiz. d, Calima Lake, El Darién, horiz. e, La Ermita, Santiago de Cali. f, Port of Buenaventura, horiz. g, Railroad station, Palmira, horiz. h, Sugar cane. i, Salsa dancers, Cali, horiz. j, El Paraiso Museum, El Cerrito, horiz. k, Basilica, Buga. l, Aerial view of Valle del Cauca, horiz.

No. 1266 — Boyacá Department: a, Plaza de Bolivar, Tunja, horiz. b, Arms of Boyacá. c, Mapping Commission drawing of Campo de Boyacá, horiz. d, Bolivar Monument, Campo de Boyacá, horiz. e, Altar of the Virgin of Chiquinquirá. f, Panoramic view of Garagoa, horiz. g, Plaza de los Libertadores, Duitama, horiz. h, Emeralds. i, Plaza Mayor, Villa de Leyva, horiz. j, Sierra Nevada del Cocuy, horiz. k, Temple of the Sun, Sogamoso. l, El Salitre Farm, Paipa, horiz.

No. 1267 — Quindío Department: a, Quindío Pass, 1836, horiz. b, Quimbaya culture sculpture. c, Coffee plantation house, Quimbaya, horiz. d, Coffee bean picker, Pijao, horiz. e, Valle de Cocora, Salento. f, Botanical Gardens, Calarca, horiz. g, La Estación Metropolitan Cultural Center, Armenia, horiz. h, Monument and government building, Armenia. i, Free Cemetery, Circasia, horiz. j, Aerial view of Buenavista, horiz. k, San José Temple, Génova. l, Founding of Armenia, horiz.

Horizontal stamps are 46x37mm.

Sheets of 12, #a-l, + 8 labels

2006 *Perf. 13½x14*

1265 A608 1300p Valle del Cauca 13.00 13.00
1266 A608 2000p Boyacá 20.00 20.00
1267 A608 3300p Quindío 32.50 32.50
Nos. 1265-1267 (3) 65.50 65.50

20th Central American and Caribbean Games A653

2006, July 15 **Litho.** *Perf. 14*

1268 A653 2000p multi 1.75 1.75

Pres. Alberto Lleras Camargo (1906-90) — A654

Denominations: a, 1300p. b, 3300p.

2006, Dec. 6 **Litho.** *Perf. 14x13¾*

1269 A654 Horiz. pair, #a-b + alternating labels 4.25 4.25

Souvenir Sheet

America Issue, Energy Conservation — A655

No. 1270: a, Left hand. b, Right hand.

2006, Dec. 28 *Perf. 12*

1270 A655 5000p Sheet of 2, #a-b 9.50 9.50

Christmas — A656

Denominations: a, 1300p. b, 3300p.

2006, Dec. 13 *Perf. 13¾x14*

1271 A656 Vert. pair, #a-b 4.25 4.25

General José Maria Cordova Military School, Cent. — A657

2007, May 30 *Perf. 14*

1272 A657 10,000p multi 11.00 11.00

Departments Type of 2003

No. 1273 — Sucre Department: a, Coat of arms. b, St. Francis of Assisi Cathedral, Sincelejo, horiz. c, Palm trees, Tolú. d, Cattle, Sucre. e, Bull ring, Sincelejo, horiz. f, Church, Corozal. g, Musical score of "Fiesta en Corraleja." h, Painting of fandango dancers, horiz. i, Fisherman, Caimito. j, Palm trees, Sincelejo. k, Cane weaver, Sampués, horiz. l, Hammocks, Morroa.

Horizontal stamps are 46x37mm.

Sheet of 12, #a-l, + 8 Labels

2007, May 30 *Perf. 12*

1273 A608 3300p Sucre 42.50 42.50

Miniature Sheet

Scouting, Cent. — A658

No. 1274: a, International and Colombian Scouting emblems, Scouts with Lord Robert Baden-Powell. b, Emblem of 21st World Scout Jamboree, Colombian Scouting emblem, children's drawing of Colombian scout. c, Scouting emblem, Lord Robert Baden-Powell. d, International and Colombian Scouting emblems, animal track.

2007, June 26 *Perf. 14*

1274 A658 1500p Sheet of 8, 2 each #a-d, + central label 12.50 12.50

Souvenir Sheet

El Espectador Newspaper, 120th Anniv. — A659

No. 1275: a, Newspaper from 1887. b, Paperboy, horiz.

2007, June 28 *Perf. 12*

1275 A659 4500p Sheet of 2, #a-b 9.25 9.25

Pan American Games, Rio de Janeiro — A660

2007, July 9 *Perf. 14*

1276 A660 3700p multi 3.75 3.75

Fourth Spanish Language Intl. Congress — A661

2007, June 25

1277 A661 5300p multi + label 5.25 5.25

Caja de Compensación Familiar, 50th Anniv. — A662

2007, Oct. 10 **Litho.** *Perf. 14*

1278 A662 3500p multi 3.75 3.75

Colombian Association of Engineers, 50th Anniv. A663

2007, Oct. 17

1279 A663 1400p multi 1.40 1.40

Bogota Honors and Awards — A664

No. 1280: a, 2007 UNESCO World Book Capital. b, Venice Biennale Golden Lion Award for Architecture. c, 2007 Latin American Cultural Capital.

2007, Oct. 23

1280 A664 3700p Horiz. strip of 3, #a-c 11.00 11.00

Minuto de Dios, 50th Anniv. A665

2007, Nov. 22

1281 A665 1600p multi 1.60 1.60

Christmas A666

2007, Nov. 27

1282 A666 3300p multi 3.25 3.25

America Issue, Education For All — A667

2007, Dec. 13

1283 A667 3500p multi 3.50 3.50

Pres. Carlos Lleras Restrepo (1908-94)
A668

2008, Apr. 8 **Litho.** *Perf. 12*
1284 A668 1400p multi 1.60 1.60

Colombian Friendship With Japan, Cent.
A669

2008, May 22 *Perf. 14*
1285 A669 5200p multi 6.25 6.25

New Emblem of Postal Network of Colombia
A670

2008, May 28
1286 A670 2100p multi 2.50 2.50

Compare with Type A685.

National Institute for the Blind, 50th Anniv.
A671

Litho. & Embossed

2008, June 10
1287 A671 1400p multi 1.75 1.75

Departments Type of 2003

No. 1288 — Antioquia Department: a, Medellín skyline, horiz. b, Arms of Antioquia. c, Necoclí, horiz. d, Silleteros Parade, horiz. e, Purse. f, Rafael Uribe Uribe Palace of Culture, horiz. g, Molas, horiz. h, Lipaugus weberi. i, Waterfall, Támesis, horiz. j, Coffee cups, horiz. k, Santa Fé de Antioquia Church. l, Orquideorama, Medellín Botanical Gardens, horiz.

No. 1289 — Amazonas Department: a, Departmental emblem. b, Monkey, Isla de los Micos, horiz. c, Victoria Regia water lily. d, Butterfly, Puerto Nariño. e, Indigenous child, horiz. f, Caiman. g, Beaded mask. h, Dolphin, horiz. i, Amazonas landscape. j, Flower. k, Fisherman casting net, horiz. l, Fruits at Plaza de Mercado, Puerto Leticia.

Horizontal stamps are 50x40mm.

Sheets of 12, #a-l, + 8 labels

2008 **Litho.** *Perf. 13¾x14*
1288 A608 1500p Antioquia 15.00 15.00

Perf. 12

1289 A608 1600p Amazonas 22.00 22.00

Issued: No. 1288, 10/22; No. 1289, 7/18.

Battle of Maracaibo Lake, 185th Anniv. — A672

2008, July 30 *Perf. 12*
1290 A672 3900p multi 4.50 4.50

Treaty of Amity and Commerce Between Colombia and Switzerland, Cent. — A673

2008, July 31 *Perf. 14*
1291 A673 5200p multi 6.00 6.00

2008 Summer Olympics, Beijing — A674

2008, Aug. 1
1292 A674 5000p multi 5.75 5.75

Souvenir Sheet

1293 A674 10,000p multi 11.50 11.50

Aguadas, Bicent. — A675

2008, Aug. 15
1294 A675 3500p multi 3.75 3.75

Accordion Festival, Villanueva
A676

2008, Sept. 25
1295 A676 5600p multi 6.00 6.00

Pres. Alfonso López Michelsen (1913-2007)
A677

2008, Oct. 8
1296 A677 5100p multi 4.50 4.50

Miniature Sheet

Ministry of Communications, 85th Anniv. — A678

No. 1297 — Arms of Colombia and: a, Stylized person, emblem for Government Online program. b, Children, emblem for Computers for Education progam, vert. c, Girl with "@" balloon, campaign for clean Internet. d, Emblem for Compartel, vert.

2008, Oct. 29
1297 A678 1500p Sheet of 4, #a-d 5.00 5.00

Episcopal Conference of Colombia, Cent. — A679

2008, Nov. 6
1298 A679 1500p multi 1.40 1.40

18th Carlos Lleras Restrepo National Games
A680

2008, Nov. 21
1299 A680 1500p multi 1.40 1.40

Natl. Department of Planning, 50th Anniv.
A681

2008, Dec. 9
1300 A681 1500p multi 1.40 1.40

Christmas
A682

Adoration of the Shepherds, by Gregorio Vásquez de Arce y Ceballos: a, 1400p. b, 3500p.

2008, Dec. 12
1301 A682 Vert. pair, #a-b 4.50 4.50

Miniature Sheet

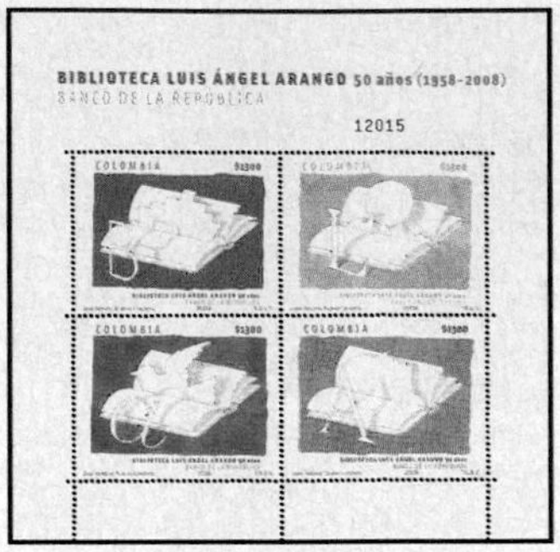

Luis Angel Arango Library, 50th Anniv. — A683

No. 1302 — Open book with: a, Ship page and "B." b, Sun page and "L." c, Dove page and "a." d, Face page and "A."

2008, Dec. 16 *Perf. 13¾x14*
1302 A683 1300p Sheet of 4, #a-d 4.75 4.75

America Issue, National Festivals — A684

Paintings: No. 1303, 1400p, November 11, 1811, Absolute Independence of Cartagena, by Cecilia Porras. No. 1304, 1400p, Liberty Indian, by unknown artist, vert.

2008, Dec. 29 *Perf. 13¾x14, 14x13¾*
1303-1304 A684 Set of 2 2.50 2.50

4-72 Colombia Postal Network Emblem — A685

Designs: 200p, Emblem on blue background with red frame. 400p, Emblem against blue background, and three arrows against red, blue and yellow backgrounds. 500p, Emblem against white background with blue frame. 600p, Emblem and map of Colombia.

2009, Mar. 1 **Litho.** *Perf. 14*
1305-1308 A685 Set of 4 1.40 1.40

Souvenir Sheet

Cali Philatelic Club, 70th Anniv. — A686

No. 1309: a, Necklace with flower-shaped pendant. b, Miltoniopsis roezlii, vert.

2009, Mar. 12 *Perf. 12*
1309 A686 2000p Sheet of 2, #a-b 7.50 7.50

Inter-America Development Bank, 50th Anniv. — A687

2009, Mar. 27
1310 A687 3700p multi 3.25 3.25

President Julio César Turbay (1916-2005) — A688

2009, Apr. 1 ***Perf. 14x13½***
1311 A688 1700p multi 1.40 1.40

Printed in sheets of 9 + 6 labels.

Naval School for Non-Commissioned Officers, Barranquilla, 75th Anniv. — A689

2009, Apr. 17 ***Perf. 14***
1312 A689 4000p multi 3.50 3.50

Colombian War School, Cent. A690

2009, May 8 ***Perf. 12***
1313 A690 5500p multi 5.50 5.50

President Guillermo León Valencia (1909-71) A691

2009, May 27
1314 A691 4200p multi 4.25 4.25

Fight of July 20, 1810, by Julián Rubiano Chávez A692

2009, June 25 ***Perf. 12***
1315 A692 1700p multi 1.75 1.75

Departments Type of 2003
Miniature Sheet

No. 1316 — La Guajira Department: a, Arms of La Guajira. b, Francisco el Hombre, mural in La Guajira Cultural Center, horiz. c, Waterfall, Montes de Oca. d, Phoenicopterus ruber. e, Domingueka, Kogui village, horiz. f, Cape of La Vela. g, Majayuts (Wayuu women). h, Riohacha Cathedral, horiz. i, Cardinalis phoeniceus. j, Aloe vulgaris. k, Caesalpinia coriaria, horiz. l, Wayuu mochilas (bags).
Horizontal stamps are 50x40mm.

Sheet of 12, #a-l, + 8 Labels

2009, July 24 **Litho.** ***Perf. 12***
1316 A608 1700p La Guajira 21.00 21.00

Miniature Sheet

Heliconia Varieties — A693

No. 1317: a, Heliconia stricta. b, Heliconia rostrata. c, Heliconia wagneriana. d, Heliconia orthotricha. e, Heliconia psittacorum.

2009, Aug. 14 **Litho.** ***Perf. 12***
1317 A693 2000p Sheet of 5, #a-e, + 5 labels 10.00 10.00

Miniature Sheet

First Colombian Postage Stamps, 150th Anniv. — A694

No. 1318: a, Colombia #1. b, Colombia #6. c, Colombia #4. d, Colombia #3. e, Colombia #7. f, Map of Colombia and text on gray background.
10,000p, Like No. 1318f with blue background.

2009, Aug. 25 ***Perf. 12***
1318 A694 4000p Sheet of 6, #a-f 24.00 24.00

Souvenir Sheet

1319 A694 10,000p multi 10.00 10.00

America Issue, Traditional Games — A695

No. 1320 — Chaza player: a, Bare-handed. b, Holding racquet.

2009, Oct. 13 **Litho.** ***Perf. 14***
1320 A695 5000p Horiz. pair, #a-b 10.00 10.00

Rafael Uribe Uribe (1859-1914), General — A696

2009, Oct. 20
1321 A696 1500p multi 1.50 1.50

Madrid Town Hall A697

2009, Nov. 13
1322 A697 10,000p multi 10.50 10.50

Madrid, Cundinamarca Department, 450th anniv.

Miniature Sheet

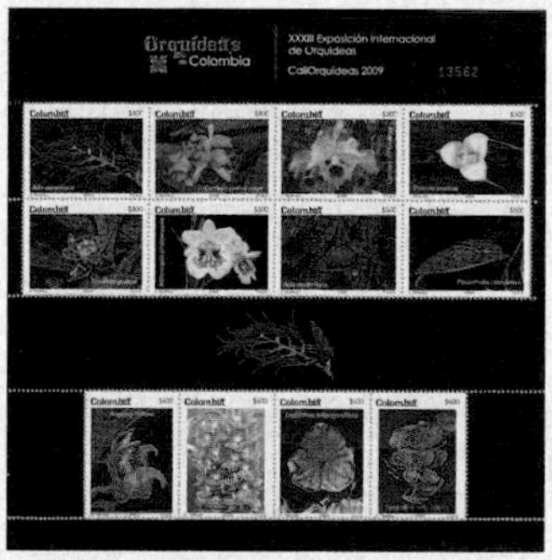

Orchids — A698

No. 1323: a, 500p, Ada aurantiaca (many flowers). b, 500p, Cattleya patinii cogn. c, 500p, Cattleya schroderae. d, 500p, Dracula amaliae. e, 500p, Huntleya gustavi. f, 500p, Miltoniopsis phalaenopsis. g, 500p, Ada aurantiaca (one flower). h, 500p, Pleurothallis casapensis. i, 600p, Anguloa cliftonii, vert. j, 600p, Cycnoche barthriorum, vert. k, 600p, Lepanthes telipogoniflora, vert. l, 600p, Lepanthes calodictyon, vert.

2009, Nov. 20
1323 A698 Sheet of 12, #a-l 6.50 6.50

33rd Intl. Orchid Exposition, Cali.

Miniature Sheet

Independence, Bicent. — A699

No. 1324: a, Bishop Andrés Rosillo y Meruelo (1758-1835). b, José Félix de Restrepo (1760-1832), statesman. c, Camilo Torres Tenorio (1766-1816), President of the Congress. d, Bishop Juan Fernández de Sotomayor (1777-1849). e, Antonio Villavicencio y Berástegui (1775-1816), President of the United Provinces of New Granada. f, Juan de Dios Morales (1767-1810), governmental minister and revolutionary. g, José María Carbonel (1778-1816), revolutionary agitator. h, Antonio Morales Galavís (1784-1852), military commander. i, José Ramón de Leyva (1747-1816), military commander. j, Nicolás Mauricio de Omaña, priest, lawyer.

2009, Nov. 24
1324 A699 6000p Sheet of 10, #a-j 65.00 65.00

Christmas A700

2009, Nov. 27 ***Perf. 12***
1325 A700 5000p multi 6.50 6.50

Souvenir Sheet

Campaign for a Mine-free World — A701

2009, Dec. 3 ***Perf. 14***
1326 A701 20,000p multi 22.50 22.50

Winning Designs in Stamp Design Contest — A702

No. 1327: a, Abstract face, by Vito. b, Collage, by Caracha. c, People holding hands, by D. Bueno.

2009, Dec. 15
1327 A702 1800p Horiz. strip of 3, #a-c 7.50 7.50

Miniature Sheet

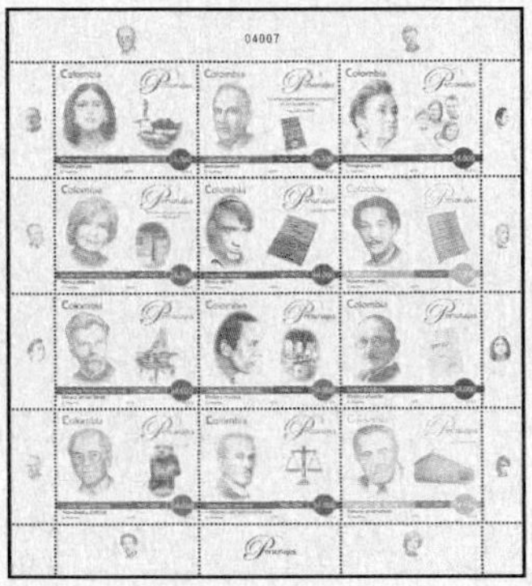

Famous People — A703

No. 1328: a, Mercedes Abrego (1770-1813), spy. b, Gerardo Molina R. (1906-91), politician. c, Virginia Gutiérrez (1922-99), social anthropologist. d, María Mercedes Carranza (1945-2003), poet. e, Gonzalo Arango (1931-76), poet. f, Adolfo Mejía (1905-76), composer. g, General Benjamin Herrera (1853-1924). h, César Uribe Piedrahita (1896-1951), medical writer. i, Emilio Robledo (1875-1962), medical educator. j, Luis Duque Gómez (1916-2000), archaeologist. k, Enrique A. Becerra (1883-1954), jurist. l, Hugo Escobar Sierra (1927-2003), politician.

2010, Jan. 28 *Perf. 13½x14*
1328 A703 4000p Sheet of 12, #a-l 60.00 60.00

Presidents Type of 1981

Miniature Sheet

No. 1329 — Presidents, coup leaders and other leaders of Colombia: a, Virgilio Barco Vargas. b, Julio César Turbay Ayala. c, Alfonso López Michelsen. d, Misael Pastrana Borrero. e, Carlos Lemos Simmonds. f, Victor Mosquera Chaux. g, Indalecio Liévano Aguirre. h, Rafael Azuero Manchola. i, Gabriel París Gordillo. j, Deogracias Fonseca. k, Rafael Navas Pardo. l, Luis Ernesto Ordóñez. m, Diego Euclides de Angulo. n, Clímaco Calderón Reyes. o, Andrés Cerón Serrano. p, Ignacio Gutiérrez Vergara. q, Juan José Nieto Gil. r, Rufino Cuervo. s, Manuel Rodríguez Torices. t, José Joaquín Camacho.

2010, Jan. 28 *Perf. 14*
1329 Sheet of 20 47.50 47.50
a.-t. A401 1900p Any single 2.00 2.00

Ninth South American Games, Medellin — A704

2010, Feb. 18
1330 A704 5800p multi 8.00 8.00

Pope John Paul II (1920-2005) — A705

2010, Feb. 19 *Perf. 13x13¼*
1331 A705 4400p multi 5.50 5.50

Miniature Sheet

Endangered Birds — A706

No. 1332: a, Crax alberti. b, Ognorhynchus icterotis. c, Hapalopsittaca fuertesi. d, Amazilia castaneiventris. e, Rallus semiplumbeus. f, Coeligena prunellei. g, Grallaria gigantea. h, Bangsia aureocincta. i, Hypopyrrhus pyrohypogaster.

2010, Apr. 6 *Perf. 13¼x13*
1332 A706 1900p Sheet of 9, #a-i 22.50 22.50

Souvenir Sheet

Expo 2010, Shanghai — A707

2010, May 7 *Perf. 13¾x14*
1333 A707 5000p multi 6.00 6.00

Miniature Sheet

Discovery of San Andrés, Providencia and Santa Catalina Archipelago, 500th Anniv. — A708

No. 1334: a, San Andrés Island. b, Providencia and Santa Catalina Islands. c, Quitasueño Keys. d, Bolivar Key. e, Roncador Keys. f, Bajo Nuevo Keys. g, Serranilla Keys. h, Serrana Keys. i, Alburquerque Keys.

2010, June 12 **Litho.** *Perf. 14*
1334 A708 5900p Sheet of 9, #a-i, + 3 labels 85.00 85.00

Departments Type of 2003

No. 1335 — Guainía Department: a, Arms of Guainía. b, Princess Inírida Monument, horiz. c, Egretta alba. d, Cerro Mavicure. e, Canoe on Inírida River, horiz. f, Curripaco baskets. g, Guacamaya superba. h, Confluence of the Guaviare and Inírida Rivers, horiz. i, Remanso. j, Cualé Rapids. k, Children from Paujil, horiz. l, Coco Petroglyphs.

No. 1336 — Atlántico Department: a, Arms of Atlántico. b, Palacio de la Cultura, Barranquilla, horiz. c, Tubará rock paintings. d, Fluvicola pica. e, Julio Flórez Museum, Usiacurí, horiz. f, Tocagua Marsh, Luruaco. g, Bull's head carnival mask. h, San Antonio de Padua Church, Soledad, horiz. i, Tabebuya rosea. j, Iraca Palm handicrafts. k, Pier at Puerto Colombia, horiz. l, Customs House, Barranquilla.

Horiz. stamps are 50x40mm.

Sheets of 12, #a-l, + 8 labels

2010 *Perf. 12x12½*
1335 A608 600p Guainía 15.00 15.00
1336 A608 2000p Atlántico 35.00 35.00

Issued: No. 1335, 7/24; No. 1336, 6/15.

Gonzalo Jiménez de Quesada Police Academy — A709

2010, June 24 *Perf. 14*
1337 A709 2000p multi 2.50 2.50

Bambuco National Pageant and Folklore Festival, Neiva, 50th Anniv. — A710

2010, June 22 *Perf. 13¼x13*
1338 A710 4200p multi 5.50 5.50

Admiral Padilla Naval Academy — A711

2010, July 3 *Perf. 14*
1339 A711 500p multi 4.00 4.00

Miniature Sheet

Norte de Santander Department, Cent. — A712

No. 1340: a, Map of Norte de Santander Department. b, Government building. c, Estoraques Nature Area. d, Catatumbo River. e, Santa Ana de Ocaña Cathedral. f, Santa Clara de Pamplona Cathedral.

2010, July 14 **Litho.**
1340 A712 6000p Sheet of 6, #a-f 47.50 47.50

Teresa Pizarro de Angulo (c. 1930-2000), National Beauty Pageant Director — A713

2010, Aug. 3
1341 A713 5900p multi 8.00 8.00

Pinillos National College, Bicent. (in 2009) A714

2010, Aug. 27 **Litho.** *Perf. 14*
1342 A714 4000p multi 5.25 5.25

America Issue, National Symbols — A715

No. 1343: a, Colombian flag. b, Colombian coat of arms.

2010, Oct. 12 *Perf. 13½x14*
1343 A715 2100p Horiz. pair, #a-b 6.50 6.50

Medellin Institute of Fine Arts, Cent. A716

2010, Oct. 19 *Perf. 14x13¾*
1344 A716 4400p multi 5.50 5.50

Miniature Sheet

Valle del Cauca Department, Cent. — A717

No. 1345: a, Map of Valle del Cauca Department. b, Sula granti. c, Overo Chapel. d, Pance River, Farallones Park. e, llama Culture vessel. f, Sonso Lake, Buga.

2010, Nov. 18 *Perf. 14*
1345 A717 4000p Sheet of 6, #a-f 32.50 32.50

Colombia National Ballet, 50th Anniv. — A718

2010, Nov. 22
1346 A718 1200p multi 6.00 6.00

Christmas A719

2010, Nov. 23 ***Perf. 13x13¼***
1347 A719 5000p multi 6.50 6.50

Eduardo Caballero Calderón (1910-93), Writer A720

2010, Dec. 1 ***Perf. 14***
1348 A720 3000p multi 4.00 4.00

Miniature Sheet

Independence, Bicent. — A721

No. 1349 — Various paintings depicting scenes from towns declaring independence in 1810: a, Caratgena. b, Mompox. c, Pamplona. d, Socorro. e, Santa Marta. f, Chocó. g, Popayán. h, Cali. i, Tunja. j, Santa Fé de Bogotá. k, Santa Fé de Antioquia. l, Pore.

2010, Oct. 22 ***Perf. 13½x14***
1349 A721 2000p Sheet of 12, #a-l 32.50 32.50

Radio Station HJCK, Bogota A722

2011, Feb. 10 ***Perf. 14***
1350 A722 600p multi 1.50 1.50

4-72 Colombia Postal Network Emblem and "Es Tu Correo!" — A723

Frame Color
Serpentine Die Cut 12½
2011, Mar. 22 **Self-Adhesive**
1351 A723 10,000p blue 13.50 13.50
1352 A723 20,000p red 27.50 27.50

El Catolicismo Newspaper, 162nd Anniv. — A724

2011, Mar. 30 ***Perf. 13x13¼***
1353 A724 1700p multi 2.75 2.75

Souvenir Sheet

Biological Diversity — A725

2011, Apr. 11 ***Perf. 13***
1354 A725 6100p multi 10.00 10.00

Office of the Attorney General — A726

2011, May 10 ***Perf. 14***
1355 A726 1600p multi 3.00 3.00

Under-20 World Cup Soccer Championships, Colombia A727

2011, July 21 **Litho.** ***Perf. 13¼x13***
1356 A727 2000p multi 3.25 3.25

Rufino José Cuervo (1844-1911), Writer — A728

2011, July 27 ***Perf. 14***
1357 A728 5000p multi 8.00 8.00

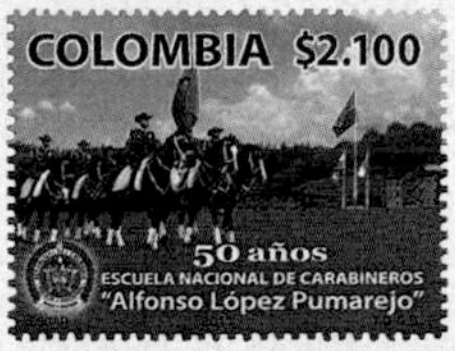

Alfonso López Pumarejo National Carabiniers School, 50th Anniv. — A729

2011, Aug. 9 ***Perf. 14***
1358 A729 2100p multi 3.25 3.25

Departments Type of 2003
Miniature Sheet

No. 1359 — Norte de Santander Department: a, Arms of Norte de Santander. b, Virgin of Torcoroma and church, horiz. c, Locomotive. d, Sculpture of Barí Indian. e, Laguna Brava and Sisavita Complex, horiz. f, Southern tamandua, El Bojoso Reserve. g, Clock Tower, Cucuta. h, Street in La Play de Belén, horiz. i, Historic church, Rosario. j, Piedras Negras National Park. k, Pamplona University, horiz. l, Páramo de Guerrero.
Horiz. stamps are 46x37mm.

Sheet of 12, #a-l, + 8 labels

2011, Aug. 25 ***Perf. 13¼x13***
1359 A608 3000p Norte de Santander *55.00 55.00*

Souvenir Sheet

Intl. Year of Forests — A730

2011, Aug. 30 ***Perf. 14***
1360 A730 6200p multi 10.00 10.00

Miniature Sheet

Heroines of Independence — A731

No. 1361: a, Manuela Beltrán Archila. b, Manuela Cañizares. c, Manuela Sanz de Santamaría. d, Policarpa Salvarrieta. e, Matilde Anaray. f, Juana Velasco de Gallo. g, Simona Amaya. h, Antonia Santos. i, Simona Duque de Alzate. j, Manuela Sáenz de Thorne.

2011, Sept. 12 ***Perf. 13x13¼***
1361 A731 1500p Sheet of 10, #a-j 24.00 24.00

Intl. Year of People of African Descent — A732

2011, Oct. 12 ***Perf. 13¼x13***
1362 A732 5000p multi 8.00 8.00

2011 Pan American Games, Guadalajara, Mexico — A733

2011, Oct. 19 ***Perf. 14***
1363 A733 600p multi 1.00 1.00

Souvenir Sheet

Postal Union of the Americas, Spain and Portugal (UPAEP), Cent. — A734

2011, Nov. 11
1364 A734 1800p multi 3.00 3.00

Bolívar House, Bucaramanga — A735

2011, Nov. 15 ***Perf. 13x13¼***
1365 A735 1200p multi 2.00 2.00

Declaration of Independence of Cartagena, 200th Anniv. — A736

2011, Nov. 26 ***Perf. 14***
1366 A736 6000p multi 9.00 9.00

Emblem of United Nations AIDS Program A737

2011, Dec. 1
1367 A737 1900p multi 3.25 3.25

Mailbox — A738

2011, Dec. 2 **Litho.**
1368 A738 500p multi 1.25 1.25

America issue.

Christmas A739

2011, Dec. 2
1369 A739 1600p multi 2.75 2.75

Souvenir Sheet

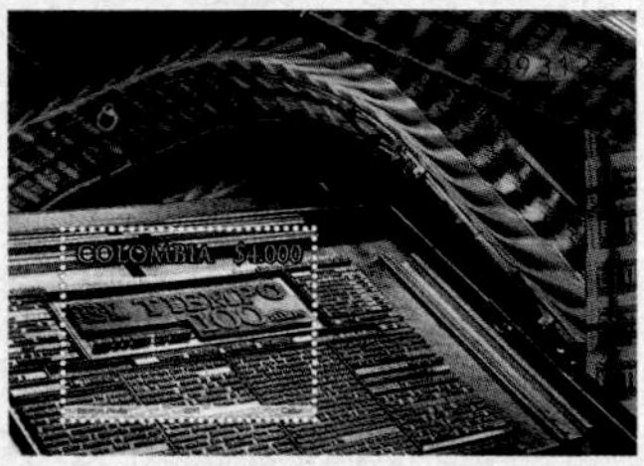

El Tiempo Newspaper, Cent. — A740

2011, Dec. 13 ***Perf. 13x13¼***
1370 A740 4000p multi 6.50 6.50

2012 Summer Olympics, London — A741

No. 1371: a, Swimming, fencing, wrestling. b, Equestrian, running, cycling. c, Judo, boxing, weight lifting. d, Shot put, soccer, tennis.

2012, Mar. 6 ***Perf. 14x14¼***
1371 Horiz. strip of 4 20.00 20.00
a.-d. A741 3000p Any single 4.00 4.00

Nos. 1371a-1371d were printed in sheets of 8 containing two of each stamp.

National Police Magazine, Cent. — A742

2012, Mar. 23 ***Perf. 14***
1372 A742 2000p multi 3.50 3.50

National Police Symphony, Cent. — A743

2012, Mar. 23
1373 A743 6400p multi 11.00 11.00

Diplomatic Relations Between Colombia and South Korea, 50th Anniv. — A744

No. 1374: a, Ginseng flowers and root. b, Coffee bush and beans.

2012, May 1 ***Perf. 13x13¼***
1374 A744 600p Horiz. pair, #a-b 2.50 2.50

See South Korea No. 2379.

Souvenir Sheet

Neiva, 400th Anniv. — A745

2012, May 4 ***Perf. 14***
1375 A745 4000p multi 6.50 6.50

Souvenir Sheet

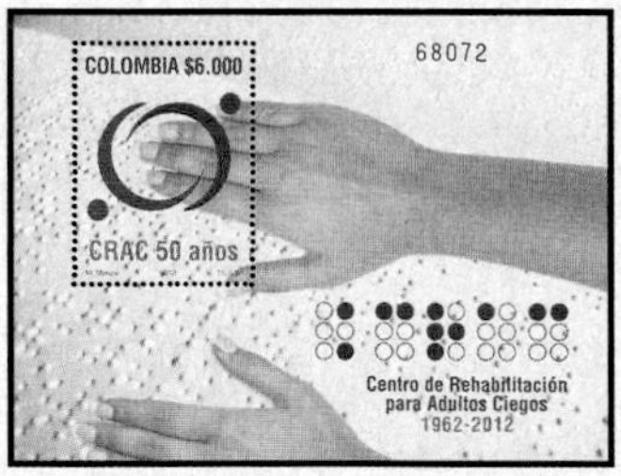

Rehabilitation Center for Blind Adults, 50th Anniv. — A746

2012, June 3 **Litho. & Embossed**
1376 A746 6000p multi 10.00 10.00

Departments Type of 2003
Miniature Sheet

No. 1377 — Cauca Department: a, Arms of Cauca. b, Puracé National Park, horiz. c, Gorgona National Park. d, Samanea saman. e, Laguna Grande de la Magdalena, horiz. f, Niña Maria de Caloto icon. g, Street in San Sebastian. h, Nuestra Senñora de la Asuncion Cathedral, Popayán, horiz. i, Battle of Bajo Palacé. j, Tierradentro National Archaeological Park. k, San Andrés Church, Pisimbalá, horiz. l, Megaptera novaeangliae.
Horiz. stamps are 46x37mm.

Sheet of 12, #a-l, + 8 labels

2012, July 24 **Litho.** ***Perf. 12x12½***
1377 A608 1200p Cauca 24.00 24.00

Miniature Sheet

Famous Men — A747

No. 1378: a, Diego de Torres y Moyachoque (1549-90), Turmequé cacique. b, Pantaléon Germán Ribón (1774-1816), military leader. c, Cayetano Betancur (1910-82), philosopher. d, Luis Bermúdez (1912-94), composer.

2012, Aug. 16 ***Perf. 13¼***
1378 A747 4600p Sheet of 4, #a-d 30.00 30.00

Rafael Pombo (1833-1912), Writer of Children's Literature — A748

2012, Aug. 23 ***Perf. 13x13¼***
1379 A748 2100p multi + label 3.50 3.50

Voceadores de Prensa, Painting by Débora Arango Pérez (1907-2005) A749

2012, Aug. 28 ***Perf. 14***
1380 A749 2400p multi 4.00 4.00

19th National Games and 3rd Paranational Games — A750

2012, Sept. 5
1381 A750 1500p multi 2.75 2.75

Art by Omar Rayo A751

No. 1382 — Art with stripes of: a, White, black and red. b, White, black and yellow. c, White, green, yellow, red and blue.

2012, Sept. 20 ***Perf. 13x13¼***
1382 Horiz. strip of 3 5.00 5.00
a.-c. A751 1000p Any single 1.50 1.50

Jorge Palacios Preciado (1940-2003), Historian — A752

2012, Sept. 29
1383 A752 500p multi .85 .85

Plaza Mayor, Leyva A753

2012, Oct. 4
1384 A753 4500p multi 8.50 8.50

First Congress of the United Provinces of New Granada, Bicent.

Souvenir Sheet

America Issue, Myths and Legends — A754

No. 1385: a, El Hojarasquin. b, El Ribiel and El Tesoro de Morgan.

2012, Oct. 9
1385 A754 4000p Sheet of 2, #a-b 13.00 13.00

Fedepalma (National Federation of Oil Palm Growers), 50th Anniv. — A755

2012, Oct. 24 ***Perf. 14***
1386 A755 6000p multi 9.50 9.50

Gen. Francisco de Paula Santander (1792-1840) — A756

2012, Nov. 16 ***Perf. 13¼***
1387 A756 1000p multi 1.75 1.75

Christmas A757

2012, Dec. 14 ***Perf. 14***
1388 A757 2500p multi 4.25 4.25

Medals Won at 2012 Summer Olympics, London A758

2012, Dec. 18 ***Perf. 13***
1389 A758 1800p multi 4.00 4.00

A souvenir sheet containing one 30,000p stamp depicting medals won at the 2012 Summer Olympics was produced in limited quantities.

Miniature Sheet

Proclamation of State Constitutions, 200th Anniv. — A759

No. 1391 — Seals of state of: a, Socorro. b, Cundinamarca. c, Tunja. d, Antioquia. e, Cartagena de Indias. f, Neiva.

Litho. & Embossed
2012, Dec. 19 ***Perf. 13¼x13***
1391 A759 500p Sheet of 6, #a-f 5.00 5.00

Renaming of Los Hermanos National Park After Gloria Valencia de Castaño (1927-2011), Television Personality — A760

2013, Apr. 29 **Litho.**
1392 A760 1800p multi + label 2.00 2.00

Departments Type of 2003
Miniature Sheet

No. 1393 — Cundinamarca Department: a, Arms of Cundinamarca. b, Tequendama Falls, Soacha, horiz. c, Poster commemorating bicentennial of Cundinamarca's independence. d, Basilica del Santo Cristo, Ubaté. e, Salt Cathedral, Zipaquirá, horiz. f, Ironworks, Pacho. g, Lagunas del Cerro, Machetá. h, Cliffs, Suesca, horiz. i, St. John the Baptist Parish Church, San Juan de Rioseco. j, Chapel, Siecha. k, Bridge of the Commoners, Chía, horiz. l, Versalles Falls, Guaduas.
Horiz. stamps are 46x37mm.

2013, July 16 ***Perf. 13¼x13***
Sheet of 12, #a-l, + 8 labels
1393 A608 2100p Cundinamarca 27.00 27.00

2013 World Games, Cali — A761

2013, July 26 **Litho.** ***Perf. 14***
1394 A761 2200p multi + label 2.40 2.40

Deportivo Independiente Medellín Soccer Team, Cent. — A762

2013, July 28 ***Perf. 14x13½***
1395 A762 4500p multi 4.75 4.75

Town of Río de Oro, 355th Anniv. — A763

2013, Aug. 1 ***Perf. 13½x14***
1396 A763 800p multi .85 .85

Alfonso Palacio Rudas (1912-96), Politician — A764

2013, Aug. 9 **Litho.**
1397 A764 7000p multi 7.50 7.50

Soledad Acosta de Samper (1833-1913), Writer — A765

2013, Sept. 3 ***Perf. 13¼x13***
1398 A765 2500p multi 2.60 2.60

Campaign Against Crime A766

2013, July 19 **Litho.** ***Perf. 14x13½***
1399 A766 2000p multi 2.25 2.25

Aspects of Life of Coffee Pickers — A767

2013, July 30 **Litho.** ***Perf. 14½x14¼***
1400 A767 2000p multi 2.25 2.25

Discovery of the Pacific Ocean by Vasco Núñez de Balboa, 500th Anniv. — A768

2013, Sept. 9 **Litho.** ***Perf. 13½x14***
1401 A768 1400p multi 1.50 1.50

Pres. Alfonso López Michelsen (1913-2007) A769

2013, Sept. 9 **Litho.** ***Perf. 13½x14***
1402 A769 2500p multi 2.60 2.60

Christmas A770

2013, Nov. 26 **Litho.** ***Perf. 14x13½***
1403 A770 3500p multi 3.75 3.75

Pereira, 150th Anniv. (in 2013) A771

2014, Mar. 13 **Litho.** ***Perf. 13x13¼***
1404 A771 2500p multi 2.60 2.60

Gimnasio Moderno, Bogota, Cent. A772

2014, Mar. 18 **Litho.** ***Perf. 13x13¼***
1405 A772 800p multi .85 .85

Jaguar Mask — A773

2014, May 13 **Litho.** ***Perf. 13½***
1406 A773 7200p multi + label 7.75 7.75

Artisans of Colombia, 50th anniv. No. 1406 was printed in sheets of 4 + 4 labels.

Souvenir Sheet

2014 World Cup Soccer Championships, Brazil — A774

No. 1407: a, Soccer ball. b, Emblem of the Colombian Soccer Federation, vert.

2014, May 23 **Litho.** ***Perf. 13¾***
1407 A774 2600p Sheet of 2, #a-b 5.50 5.50
c. Booklet pane of 2, #1407a-1407b *10.00* —
Complete booklet, 5 #1407c *50.00*

Issued: No. 1407c, 7/8. Each example of No. 1407c in the complete booklet has a different pane margin. These pane margins differ from the sheet margin on No. 1407.

Official Journal, 150th Anniv. A775

2014, Oct. 9 **Litho.** ***Perf. 13x13¼***
1408 A775 1300p multi 1.25 1.25

4-72 Colombia Postal Network Emblem and Text — A776

Serpentine Die Cut 12¼x12¾
2014, Aug. 25 **Litho.**
Self-Adhesive
Frame Color
1409 A776 10,000p blue 10.50 10.50
1410 A776 20,000p red 21.00 21.00

Scouting in Colombia, Cent. (in 2013) — A777

2014, Nov. 22 **Litho.** ***Perf. 13¼x13***
1411 A777 3000p multi 2.60 2.60

Fanny Mikey (c. 1930-2008), Founder of Bogota Ibero-American Theater Festival — A778

2014, Dec. 2 Litho. ***Perf. 13¼x13***

1412	A778	500p multi	.45	.45

Christmas — A779

Perf. 13½x13¼

2014, Dec. 10 Litho.

1413	A779	100p multi	.25	.25

Augusto Ramirez Ocampo (c. 1934-2011), Politician — A780

2014, Dec. 23 Litho. ***Perf. 13¼x13***

1414	A780	1000p multi	.85	.85

Gabriel García Márquez (1927-2014), 1982 Nobel Literature Laureate — A781

2015, July 14 Litho. ***Perf. 13¼x13***

1415	A781	200p multi	.25	.25

Souvenir Sheet

Imperf

1416	A781	10,000p multi	7.00	7.00

No. 1416 contains one 45x56mm stamp.

Fauna — A782

Designs: 200p, Allobates juanii. 500p, Eriocnemis mirabilis. 1000p, Diglosa gloriosissima. 2000p, Crocodylus intermedius. 5000p, Ateles hybridus. 10,000p, Phyllobates terribilis. 20,000p, Batrachemys dahli.

Serpentine Die Cut 12¾

2015, July 14 Litho.

Self-Adhesive

1417	A782	200p multi	.25	.25
1418	A782	500p multi	.35	.35
1419	A782	1000p multi	.70	.70
1420	A782	2000p multi	1.40	1.40
1421	A782	5000p multi	3.50	3.50
1422	A782	10,000p multi	7.00	7.00
1423	A782	20,000p multi	14.00	14.00
		Nos. 1417-1423 (7)	27.20	27.20

SEMI-POSTAL STAMP

Catalogue values for unused stamps in this section are for Never Hinged items.

Girl Giving First Aid — SP1

Perf. 13½x14

1966, Apr. 26 Litho. Unwmk.

B1	SP1	5c + 5c multicolored	.25	.25

Issued for the Red Cross.

AIR POST STAMPS

No. 341 Overprinted

1919 Unwmk. ***Perf. 14***

C1	A107	2c car rose	3,500.	1,700.
a.		Numerals "1" with serifs	*7,250.*	*4,250.*

Used for the first experimental flight from Barranquilla to Puerto Colombia, 6/18/19. Values are for faulty stamps.

Issued by Compania Colombiana de Navegacion Aerea

From 1920 to 1932 the internal airmail service of Colombia was handled by the Compania Colombiana de Navegacion Aerea (1920) and the Sociedad Colombo-Alemana de Transportes Aéreos, known familiarly as "SCADTA" (1920-1932).

These organizations, under government contracts, operated and maintained their own post offices and issued stamps which were the only legal franking for airmail service during this period, both in the internal and international mails. All letters had to bear government stamps as well.

Woman and Boy Watching Plane — AP1

Designs: No. C3, Clouds and small biplane at top. No. C4, Tilted plane viewed close-up from above. No. C5, Flier in plane watching biplane. No. C6, Lighthouse. No. C7, Fuselage and tail of biplane. No. C8, Condor on cliff. No. C9, Plane at rest; pilot foreground. No. C10, Ocean liner.

1920, Feb. Unwmk. Litho. ***Imperf.***

Without Gum

C2	AP1	10c multi	3,000.	1,875.
C3	AP1	10c multi	3,800.	1,875.
C4	AP1	10c multi	4,600.	1,875.
C5	AP1	10c multi	3,500.	1,875.
C6	AP1	10c multi	3,000.	1,875.
C7	AP1	10c multi	11,000.	3,800.
C8	AP1	10c multi	6,000.	3,000.
C9	AP1	10c multi	3,500.	1,875.
C10	AP1	10c multi	4,600.	2,750.

Nos. C2-C10 were overprinted on the nine lighter-colored varieties of a set of 18 publicity labels produced by the Curtiss Co. for inclusion with packs of cigarettes. These labels were printed setenant, in panes of 18 (3x6). Value for the set of 18 values without overprint: $4,000.

Flier in Plane Watching Biplane — AP2

1920, Mar.

C11	AP2	10c green	60.00	*92.50*

Four other 10c stamps, similar to No. C11, have two designs showing plane, mountains and water. They are printed in deep green or light brown red. Some authorities state that these four were not used regularly.

Issued by Sociedad Colombo-Alemana de Transportes Aereos (SCADTA)

Seaplane over Magdalena River — AP3

1920-21 Litho. ***Perf. 12***

C12	AP3	10c yellow ('21)	60.00	47.50
C13	AP3	15c blue ('21)	65.00	52.50
C14	AP3	30c blk, *rose*	30.00	16.00
C15	AP3	30c rose ('21)	60.00	45.00
C16	AP3	50c pale green	60.00	47.50
		Nos. C12-C16 (5)	275.00	208.50

For surcharges see Nos. C17-C24, C36-C37.

No. C16 Handstamp Surcharged in Violet or Black

a

b

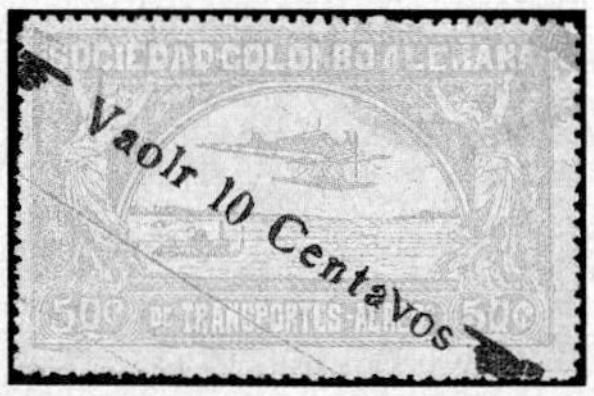

c

d

e

f

g

1921

C17	AP3 (a)	10c on 50c	1,250.	1,200.
C18	AP3 (b)	10c on 50c	1,250.	1,200.
C19	AP3 (c)	10c on 50c	1,250.	1,200.
C20	AP3 (b)	30c on 50c	925.	625.
C21	AP3 (d)	30c on 50c	925.	625.
C22	AP3 (e)	30c on 50c	1,850.	1,450.
C23	AP3 (f)	30c on 50c	1,850.	1,450.
C24	AP3 (g)	30c on 50c	1,850.	1,450.

No. C16 with Typwritten Surcharge in Red

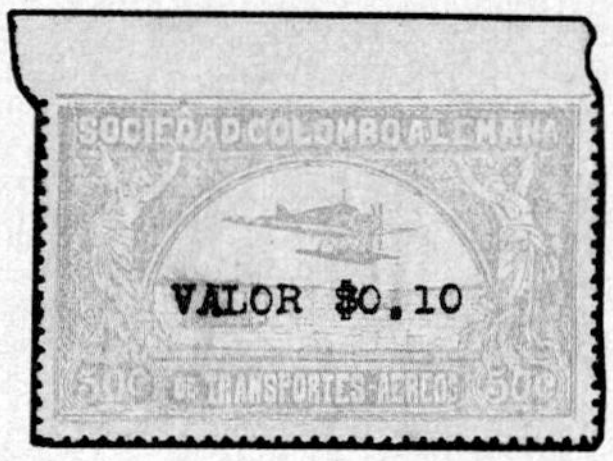

1921

C24A	AP3	10c on 50c	—	*1,500.*
C24B	AP3	30c on 50c		—

Plane over Magdalena River — AP4

Plane over Bogota Cathedral AP5

1921 ***Perf. 11½***

C25	AP4	5c orange yellow	4.50	4.00
C26	AP4	10c slate green	2.10	1.50
C27	AP4	15c orange brown	2.10	1.60
C28	AP4	20c red brown	4.50	2.10
a.		Horiz. pair, imperf. vert.	*210.00*	
C29	AP4	30c green	2.10	1.10
C30	AP4	50c blue	3.25	1.25
C31	AP4	60c vermilion	85.00	32.50
C32	AP5	1p gray black	22.50	5.00
C33	AP5	2p rose	42.50	20.00
C34	AP5	3p violet	125.00	72.50
C35	AP5	5p olive green	325.00	300.00
		Nos. C25-C35 (11)	618.55	441.55

Exist imperf.

For surcharge see No. C52.

Nos. C16 and C12 Handstamp Surcharged

h

i

1921-22 *Perf. 12*

C36 AP3 (h) 20c on 50c 3,750. 2,500.
C37 AP3 (i) 30c on 10c 850. 575.

Seaplane over Magdalena River — AP6

Plane over Bogota Cathedral AP7

1923-28 Wmk. 116 *Perf. 14x14½*

C38	AP6	5c	orange yellow	1.75	.25
C39	AP6	10c	green	1.75	.25
C40	AP6	15c	carmine	1.75	.25
C41	AP6	20c	gray	1.75	.25
C42	AP6	30c	blue	1.75	.25
C43	AP6	40c	purple ('28)	12.50	8.00
C44	AP6	50c	green	2.10	.25
C45	AP6	60c	brown	3.25	.25
C46	AP6	80c	olive grn ('28)	32.50	30.00
C47	AP7	1p	black	14.50	3.25
C48	AP7	2p	red orange	21.00	6.00
C49	AP7	3p	violet	37.50	25.00
C50	AP7	5p	olive green	67.50	32.50
			Nos. C38-C50 (13)	199.60	106.50

For surcharges and overprints see Nos. C51, C53-C54, CF1.

Nos. C41 and C31 Surcharged in Carmine and Dark Blue

No. C51

No. C52

1923

C51 AP6 30c on 20c gray (C) 92.50 57.50
C52 AP4 30c on 60c ver 85.00 37.50

Nos. C41-C42 Overprinted in Black

1928 Wmk. 116 *Perf. 14x14½*

C53 AP6 20c gray 80.00 62.50
C54 AP6 30c blue 80.00 62.50

Goodwill flight of Lt. Benjamin Mendez from New York to Bogota.

Magdalena River and Tolíma Volcano AP8

Columbus' Ship and Plane AP9

1929, June 1 Wmk. 127 *Perf. 14*

C55	AP8	5c	yellow org	1.25	.25
C56	AP8	10c	red brown	1.25	.25
C57	AP8	15c	deep green	1.25	.25
C58	AP8	20c	carmine	1.25	.25
C59	AP8	30c	gray blue	1.25	.25
C60	AP8	40c	dull violet	1.25	.25
C61	AP8	50c	dk olive grn	2.50	.25
C62	AP8	60c	orange brown	3.75	.25
C63	AP8	80c	green	11.00	3.25
C64	AP9	1p	blue	12.00	2.50
C65	AP9	2p	brown orange	18.00	5.75
C66	AP9	3p	pale rose vio	42.50	18.00
C67	AP9	5p	olive green	100.00	37.50
			Nos. C55-C67 (13)	197.25	69.00

For surcharges and overprints see Nos. C80-C95, CF2, CF4.

For International Airmail

AP10

AP11

1929, June 1 Wmk. 127 *Perf. 14*

C68	AP10	5c	yellow org	6.25	*7.25*
C69	AP10	10c	red brown	1.25	*3.00*
C70	AP10	15c	deep green	1.25	*3.00*
C71	AP10	20c	carmine	1.25	*3.75*
C72	AP10	25c	violet blue	1.25	.85
C73	AP10	30c	gray blue	1.25	.95
C74	AP10	50c	dk olive grn	1.25	*1.90*
C75	AP10	60c	brown	2.50	*3.00*
C76	AP11	1p	blue	5.50	*7.25*
C77	AP11	2p	red orange	8.50	*10.00*
C78	AP11	3p	violet	100.00	100.00
C79	AP11	5p	olive green	125.00	*140.00*
			Nos. C68-C79 (12)	255.25	*280.95*

This issue was sold abroad for use on correspondence to be flown from coastal to interior points of Colombia. Cancellations are those of the country of origin rather than Colombia.

For overprint see No. CF3.

Nos. C63, C66 and C64 Surcharged in Black

m

n

1930, Dec. 15

C80 AP8(m) 10c on 80c 7.25 7.25
C81 AP9(n) 20c on 3p 13.50 13.50
C82 AP9(n) 30c on 1p 17.00 13.50
Nos. C80-C82 (3) 37.75 *34.25*

Simon Bolivar (1783-1830).

Colombian Government Issues

Nos. C55-C67 Overprinted in Black

o

p

Wmk. 127

1932, Jan. 1 Typo. *Perf. 14*

C83	AP8(o)	5c	yellow org	10.00	10.00
C84	AP8(o)	10c	red brown	2.25	.60
C85	AP8(o)	15c	deep green	3.75	3.75
C86	AP8(o)	20c	carmine	1.90	.35
C87	AP8(o)	30c	gray blue	1.90	.60
C88	AP8(o)	40c	dull violet	2.50	1.25
C89	AP8(o)	50c	dk ol grn	5.00	3.75
C90	AP8(o)	60c	orange brn	4.25	3.75
C91	AP8(o)	80c	green	17.00	17.00
C92	AP9(p)	1p	blue	14.50	12.00
C93	AP9(p)	2p	brown org	37.50	35.00
C94	AP9(p)	3p	pale rose vio	77.50	65.00
C95	AP9(p)	5p	olive green	125.00	*140.00*
			Nos. C83-C95 (13)	303.05	293.05

Coffee AP12

Gold AP16

Designs: 10c, 50c, Cattle. 15c, 60c, Petroleum. 20c, 40c, Bananas. 3p, 5p, Emerald.

1932-39 Wmk. 127 Photo. *Perf. 14*

C96	AP12	5c	org & blk brn	.90	.25
C97	AP12	10c	lake & blk	1.00	.25
C98	AP12	15c	bl grn & vio blk	.50	.25
C99	AP12	15c	ver & vio blk ('39)	4.00	.25
C100	AP12	20c	car & ol blk	.85	.25
C101	AP12	20c	turq grn & ol blk ('39)	4.25	.35
C102	AP12	30c	dk bl & blk brn	2.40	.25
C103	AP12	40c	dk vio & ol bis	1.10	.25
C104	AP12	50c	dk grn & brnsh blk	6.75	1.50
C105	AP12	60c	dk brn & blk vio	1.40	.25
C106	AP12	80c	grn & blk brn	9.50	2.00
C107	AP16	1p	dk bl & ol bis	10.00	1.25
C108	AP16	2p	org brn & ol bis	16.00	2.75
C109	AP16	3p	dk vio & emer	26.00	7.25
C110	AP16	5p	gray blk & emer	57.50	21.00
			Nos. C96-C110 (15)	142.15	38.10

For overprint see No. CF5.

Nos. C104, C106-C108 Surcharged

a

b

1934, Jan. 5

C111 AP12(a) 10c on 50c 4.50 4.50
C112 AP12(a) 15c on 80c 6.25 6.25
C113 AP16(b) 20c on 1p 6.50 6.50
C114 AP16(b) 30c on 2p 7.25 7.25
Nos. C111-C114 (4) 24.50 24.50

400th anniversary of Cartagena.

Nos. C100 and C103 Surcharged in Black or Carmine

1939, Jan. 15

C115 AP12 5c on 20c (Bk) .35 .35
C116 AP12 5c on 40c (C) .35 .25
C117 AP12 15c on 20c (Bk) 1.50 .50
a. Double surcharge 12.00
b. Pair, one with dbl. surch. 14.00
c. Inverted surcharge 12.00 12.00

No. CF5 Surcharged in Black

C118 AP12 5c on 20c .70 .70
Nos. C115-C118 (4) 2.90 1.80

Nos. C102-C103 Surcharged in Black or Red

1940, Oct. 20

C119 AP12 15c on 30c 1.25 .50
a. Inverted surcharge 12.00
C120 AP12 15c on 40c (R) 2.00 .75
a. Double surcharge 12.00

Pre-Columbian Monument — AP18

Proclamation of Independence — AP22

Designs: 10c, 40c, Symbol of Legend of El Dorado. 15c, 50c, Spanish Fortifications, Cartagena. 20c, 60c, Colonial Bogotá. 2p, 5p, National Library, Bogota.

Unwmk.

1941, Jan. 28 Engr. *Perf. 12*

C121	AP18	5c	gray black	.25	.25
C122	AP18	10c	yellow org	.25	.25
C123	AP18	15c	carmine rose	.25	.25
C124	AP18	20c	yellow grn	.35	.25
a.			Horiz. pair, imperf. vert.	87.50	
C125	AP18	30c	deep blue	.35	.25
C126	AP18	40c	rose lake	1.40	.25
C127	AP18	50c	turq green	1.40	.25
C128	AP18	60c	sepia	1.40	.25
C129	AP18	80c	olive blk	3.25	.40
C130	AP22	1p	blue & blk	4.00	.50
C131	AP22	2p	red org & blk	8.00	2.00
C132	AP22	3p	violet & blk	16.00	6.50
C133	AP22	5p	lt green & blk	40.00	20.00
			Nos. C121-C133 (13)	76.90	31.40

See Nos. C151-C163, C217-C225. For overprints see Nos. C175-C198, C200-C216, C226, C290.

San Sebastian Fort, Cartagena — AP24

National Capitol, Bogotá
AP27

Designs: 5c, 20c, 50c, San Sebastian Fort, Cartagena. 10c, 30c, 60c, Tequendama Waterfall. 15c, 40c, 80c, Bay of Santa Maria.

Unwmk.

1945, Nov. 3 Litho. *Perf. 11*

C134	AP24	5c blue gray	.25	.25
C135	AP24	10c yellow org	.25	.25
C136	AP24	15c rose	.25	.25
C137	AP24	20c lt yel grn	.30	.25
C138	AP24	30c ultra	.30	.25
C139	AP24	40c claret	.50	.25
C140	AP24	50c bluish grn	.55	.25
C141	AP24	60c lt vio brn	2.25	.80
C142	AP24	80c dk slate grn	3.50	.80
C143	AP27	1p dk blue	5.00	.75
C144	AP27	2p red orange	7.00	2.50
		Nos. C134-C144 (11)	20.15	6.60

Part-perforate varieties exist for all denominations except 80c.

Imperf., Pairs

C134a	AP24	5c	8.50
C135a	AP24	10c	8.50
C136a	AP24	15c	8.50
C137a	AP24	20c	8.50
C138a	AP24	30c	8.50
C139a	AP24	40c	8.50
C140a	AP24	50c	8.50
C141a	AP24	60c	8.50
C142a	AP24	80c	10.50
C143a	AP27	1p	17.50
C144a	AP27	2p	60.00

Bello Type of Regular Issue, 1946

Wmk. 255

1946, Sept. 3 Engr. *Perf. 12*

C145	A219	5c deep blue	.25	.25

Francisco José de Caldas
AP29

Manuel del Socorro Rodriguez
AP30

Perf. 12½

1947, May 9 Litho. Unwmk.

C146	AP29	5c dp bl, *grnsh*	.35	.25
C147	AP30	10c red org, *grnsh*	.50	.45

4th Pan-American Press Congress (1946).

Chancellery Patio — AP31

Capitol, Patio Rafael Nunez
AP32

AP33

1948, Apr. 2 Engr. Wmk. 229

C148	AP31	5c dark brown	.25	.25
C149	AP32	15c deep blue	.90	.90

Miniature Sheet

Imperf

C150	AP33	50c brown	1.90	1.90

9th Pan-American Conference, Bogotá.

Types of 1941

1948, July 21 Unwmk. *Perf. 12*

C151	AP18	5c orange yel	.25	.25
C152	AP18	10c scarlet	.25	.25
C153	AP18	15c deep blue	.25	.25
C154	AP18	20c violet	.25	.25
C155	AP18	30c yellow grn	.35	.25
C156	AP18	40c gray	.40	.25
C157	AP18	50c rose lake	.40	.25
C158	AP18	60c olive gray	.70	.25
C159	AP18	80c red brn	.85	.25
C160	AP22	1p ol grn & vio brn	1.50	.30
C161	AP22	2p dp grn & brt bl	2.50	.65
C162	AP22	3p rose car & blk	5.50	3.75
C163	AP22	5p lt brn & turq grn	14.00	7.00
		Nos. C151-C163 (13)	27.20	13.95

"Air Week" 5c Blue

The War and Air Department issued a 5c blue stamp in May, 1949, to publicize Air Week (Semana de Aviacion). This stamp had no franking value and its use was optional during May 16-23.

Justice and Liberty — AP34

Design: 10c, Liberty holding tablet of laws.

1949, Oct. 7 Unwmk. *Perf. 13*

C164	AP34	5c blue green	.25	.25
C165	AP34	10c orange	.25	.25

Issued to honor the new Constitution.

Wing — AP35

For Domestic Postage

1950, June 22 Litho. *Perf. 12*

C166	AP35	5c orange yellow	.25	.30
C167	AP35	10c brown red	.35	.30
C168	AP35	15c lt blue	.40	.40
C169	AP35	20c lt green	.60	*.95*
C170	AP35	30c lilac gray	1.50	*2.40*
C171	AP35	60c chocolate	1.90	*3.50*

With Network as in Parenthesis

C172	AP35	1p gray (buff)	14.00	*16.00*
C173	AP35	2p bl (pale grn)	14.00	*20.00*
C174	AP35	5p red brn (red brn)	40.00	*60.00*
		Nos. C166-C174 (9)	73.00	103.85

No. C172 was issued both with and without network.

Nos. C151-C157 and C160-C163 Overprinted in Black

1950, July 18

C175	AP18	5c orange yel	.25	.25
C176	AP18	10c scarlet	.25	.25
C177	AP18	15c deep blue	.25	.25
C178	AP18	20c violet	.25	.25
C179	AP18	30c yellow green	.30	.25
C180	AP18	40c gray	2.50	.80
C181	AP18	50c rose lake	.75	.40
C182	AP22	1p ol grn & vio brn	4.00	4.50
C183	AP22	2p dp grn & brt bl	7.50	6.00
C184	AP22	3p rose car & blk	10.00	16.00
C185	AP22	5p lt brn & turq grn	35.00	52.50
		Nos. C175-C185 (11)	61.05	81.45

Nos. C151-C163 Overprinted in Black

1950, July 12

C186	AP18	5c orange yel	.25	.25
C187	AP18	10c scarlet	.25	.25
C188	AP18	15c deep blue	.25	.25
C189	AP18	20c violet	.25	.25
C190	AP18	30c yellow green	.25	.25
C191	AP18	40c gray	.55	.25
C192	AP18	50c rose lake	.55	.25
C193	AP18	60c olive gray	.85	.25
C194	AP18	80c red brown	1.25	.50
C195	AP22	1p ol grn & vio brn	1.50	.70
C196	AP22	2p dp grn & brt bl	4.50	2.40
C197	AP22	3p rose car & blk	10.00	12.00
C198	AP22	5p lt brn & turq grn	30.00	35.00
		Nos. C186-C198 (13)	50.45	52.60

On Nos. C175-C198, "L" stands for LANSA, "A" for AVIANCA.

UPU Type

Miniature Sheet

Unwmk.

1950, Aug. 22 Photo. *Imperf.*

C199	A245	50c gray	3.50	3.50

75th anniv. (in 1949) of the UPU.

Catalogue values for unused stamps in this section, from this point to the end of the section, are for Never Hinged items.

Types of 1941 Overprinted at Lower Right in Black

Unwmk.

1951, Sept. 15 Engr. *Perf. 12*

C200	AP18	40c orange yel	1.60	1.00
C201	AP18	50c ultra	2.10	1.40
C202	AP18	60c gray	1.60	1.00
C203	AP18	80c car rose	1.50	1.00
C204	AP22	1p red org & red brn	6.00	6.00
C205	AP22	2p rose car & bl	7.25	7.25
C206	AP22	3p choc & emer	18.00	20.00
C207	AP22	5p org & gray	47.50	52.50
		Nos. C200-C207 (8)	85.55	90.15

Types of 1941 Overprinted at Lower Right in Black

1951-54

C208	AP18	40c orange yel	5.50	.55
C209	AP18	50c ultra	16.00	.65
C210	AP18	60c gray	4.50	.55
a.		Overprint centered	4.50	.55
C211	AP18	80c car rose	1.00	.35
C212	AP22	1p red org & red brn	4.75	.50
C213	AP22	1p ol grn & vio brn ('54)	7.00	.95
C214	AP22	2p rose car & bl	4.75	.70
C215	AP22	3p choc & emer	8.75	2.10
C216	AP22	5p org & gray	16.00	2.25
		Nos. C208-C216 (9)	68.25	8.60

All values except the 2p and 3p exist without overprint.

Types of 1941

1952, May 10 Engr.

C217	AP18	5c ultra	.50	.25
C218	AP18	10c ultra	.50	.25
C219	AP18	15c ultra	.50	.25
C220	AP18	20c ultra	.90	.40
C221	AP18	30c ultra	2.50	.95

Color Change

C222	AP18	5c car rose	.50	.25
C223	AP18	10c car rose	.50	.25
C224	AP18	20c car rose	.95	.25
C225	AP18	30c car rose	2.00	.55
		Nos. C217-C225 (9)	8.85	3.40

Type of 1941 Surcharged in Blue

1952, Oct. 30

C226	AP18	70c on 80c car rose	1.75	.80

Latin American Siderurgical Conf., 1952.

Type of Postal Tax Stamps, 1948-50, Nos. 602 and 604 Surcharged or Overprinted in Black

1953 Wmk. 255 *Perf. 12*

C227	PT10	5c on 8c blue	.25	.25
C228	PT10	15c on 20c brown	.30	.25
C229	PT10	15c on 25c bl grn	1.60	.25
C230	PT10	25c blue green	.90	.25
		Nos. C227-C230 (4)	3.05	1.00

Many varieties of overprint or surcharge exist on Nos. C227-C231.

No. 570 Overprinted in Blue

1953, Aug. Wmk. 229 *Perf. 12½*
C231 A160 10c red .25 .25

"Extra Rapido"

Stamps inscribed "Extra Rapido" are for use on domestic airmail carried by airlines other than AVIANCA.

No. 585 Surcharged and Overprinted in Dark Blue

1953 Unwmk. *Perf. 13*
C232 A244 5c on 11c red .50 .35

Capitol and Arms — AP37

Revenue Stamps Overprinted "Correo Extra-Rapido"

Gray Security Paper

1953 Wmk. 255 Engr. *Perf. 12*
C233 AP37 1c on 2c green .25 .25
C234 AP37 50c red orange .25 .25

AP38

Real Estate Tax Stamps Ovptd. "Correo Extra-Rapido" in Black or Carmine

1953
C235 AP38 5c red orange .25 .25
C236 AP38 20c brown (C) .30 .25

On 20c, overprint is at bottom of stamp and two lines of ornaments cover real estate tax inscription at top.

Castillo y Rada and Map — AP39

Real Estate Tax Stamp Surcharged "Correo Aereo, II Exposicion Filatelica Nacional, Bogota Dicbre 1953, 15 Centavos"

1953, Dec. 12 Engr. & Litho.
C237 AP39 15c on 10p multi .50 .35

2nd Natl. Philatelic Exhib., Bogota, Dec. 1953.

No. RA45 Overprinted in Black

1953
C238 PT10 10c purple .25 .25

Galeras Volcano — AP40

Retreat of San Diego — AP41

Designs: No. C241, Las Lajas Shrine, Narino. No. C242, 50c, Bolivar monument. 20c, 80c, Ruiz mountain, Manizales. 40c, George Isaacs monument, Cali. 60c, Mono Fountain, Tunja. 1p, Stadium, Medellin. 2p, Pastelillo Fort, Cartagena. 3p, Santo Domingo University gate. 5p, Las Lajas Shrine. 10p, Map of Colombia.

Perf. 13½x13, 13

1954, Jan. 15 Engr. Unwmk.
C239 AP40 5c dp red vio .25 .25
C240 AP41 10c black .25 .25
C241 AP40 15c red orange .25 .25
C242 AP40 15c car rose .25 .25
C243 AP40 20c brown .25 .25
C244 AP40 30c brown org .25 .25
C245 AP40 40c blue .25 .25
C246 AP40 50c dk violet brn .35 .25
C247 AP40 60c dk brown .40 .25
C248 AP40 80c red brown .55 .25

Size: 37x27mm

Center in Black

C249 AP41 1p deep blue 3.25 .25
C250 AP41 2p dark green 4.75 .40
C251 AP41 3p carmine rose 11.00 1.40

Size: 38x32mm, 32x38mm

C252 AP41 5p dk grn & red brn 14.50 3.50
C253 AP40 10p gray grn & red org 20.00 7.50
Nos. C239-C253 (15) 56.55 15.55

See Nos. C307-C308. For surcharges and overprints see Nos. 691, C321, C325, C330, C333-C334, C343-C346.

Condor Carrying Shield AP42

Inscribed: "Correo Extra-Rapido"

1954, Apr. 23 Litho. *Perf. 12½*
C254 AP42 5c lilac rose .95 .40

For overprint see No. RA53.

Soldier-Map-Arms Type

1954, June 13 Engr. *Perf. 13*
C255 A259 15c carmine .40 .25

See No. C271a.

Games Type

Design: 20c, Stadium and Athlete holding arms of Colombia.

1954, July 18
C256 A260 15c chocolate .70 .25
C257 A260 20c deep blue green 1.60 .35

Church of St. Peter Claver, Cartagena AP45

1954, Sept. 9
C258 AP45 15c brown .40 .25
a. Souvenir sheet 8.00 *12.00*

St. Peter Claver, 300th death anniv.

No. C258a contains one stamp similar to No. C258, but printed in red brown.

Mercury Type

1954, Oct. 29
C259 A263 15c deep blue .55 .25

Inscribed "Extra Rapido"

C260 A263 50c scarlet .55 .25

Archbishop Manuel José Mosquera, Death Cent. — AP47

Inscribed: "Correo Extra Rapido"

1954, Nov. 17
C261 AP47 2c yellow green .25 .25

Virgin of Chiquinquira — AP48

Inscribed: "Correo Extra Rapido"

1954, Dec. 4 Engr. & Litho.
C262 AP48 5c org brn & multi .25 .25

See No. C291. For overprint see No. 686.

College Types

Designs: 20c, Brother Cristobal de Torres. 50c, College chapel and arms.

Perf. 12½x11½, 11½x12½

1954, Dec. 6 Engr. Unwmk.
C263 A264 15c orange & blk .50 .25
C264 A264 20c ultra .85 .25
C265 A265 25c dark brown .85 .25
C266 A265 50c black & car 2.40 .95
a. Souvenir sheet 12.00 *16.00*
Nos. C263-C266 (4) 4.45 1.40

No. C266a contains four stamps similar to Nos. C263-C266, but printed in different colors: 15c red and black, 20c pale purple, 25c brown, 50c black and olive green.

Steel Mill Type

1954, Dec. 12 *Perf. 12½x13*
C267 A266 20c green & blk 1.75 .60

Marti Type

1955, Jan. 28 *Perf. 13½x13*
C268 A267 15c deep green .30 .25

Korean Veterans Type

1955, Mar. 23 *Perf. 12½*
C269 A268 20c dark green .55 .25

Merchant Fleet Types

1955, Apr. 12 *Perf. 12½*
C270 A269 25c black .40 .25
C271 A270 50c dark green .90 .40
a. Souvenir sheet 9.50 *12.00*

No. C271a contains 4 stamps similar to Nos. C255, C269-C271, but printed in different colors; 15c lilac red, 20c olive, 25c bluish black, 50c bluish green.

Marco Fidel Suarez (1855-1927), Pres. 1918-21 — AP56

Inscribed: "Correo Extra Rapido"

1955, April 23 *Perf. 13*
C272 AP56 10c deep blue .25 .25

Hotel-Church Type

1955, May 16 Photo. *Perf. 11½x12*
C273 A271 15c rose brown .40 .25

Rotary Type

Unwmk.

1955, Oct. 17 Engr. *Perf. 13*
C274 A272 15c dk carmine rose .40 .25

Atahualpa, Tisquesuza and Montezuma AP59

Ferdinand the Catholic and Queen Isabella I AP60

Designs: 15c, O'Higgins, Santander and Sucre. 20c, Marti, Hidalgo and Petion. 1p, Artigas, Solano Lopez and Murillo. 2p, Abdon Calderon, Baron de Rio Branco and José de La Mar.

1955, Oct. 12 Engr. & Photo.

Inscribed: "Extra Rapido"

C275 AP59 2c dull brn & blk .45 .25
C276 AP60 5c dk brn & yel .45 .25

Regular Air Post

C277 AP59 15c rose car & blk .55 .25
C278 AP59 20c pale brn & blk .85 .25
a. Souvenir sheet of 2 30.00 30.00

Inscribed: "Extra Rapido"

C279 AP60 1p ol gray & brn 15.00 7.50
C280 AP60 2p violet & blk 11.00 5.75
Nos. C275-C280 (6) 27.90 14.15

7th Cong. of the Postal Union of the Americas and Spain, Bogota, Oct. 12-Nov. 9, 1955.

No. C278a contains one each of Nos. C277-C278 printed in different shades.

Caro Type

1955, Nov. 29 Engr. *Perf. 13½x13*
C281 A275 15c gray green .40 .25

University of Salamanca AP62

Inscribed: "Extra Rapido"

1955, Nov. 29 Unwmk. *Perf. 13*
C282 AP62 20c dark brown .25 .25

University of Salamanca, 7th centenary.

Type of Postal Tax Stamp of 1948-50 Surcharged

1956 Wmk. 255 Engr. *Perf. 12*
C283 PT10 2c on 8c blue .25 .25

No. 617 Overprinted in Black

1956 Unwmk. *Perf. 12½x13*
C284 A256 1p black & emerald .40 .25

Columbus Type

1956, Oct. 11 Photo. *Perf. 12*
C285 A279 15c intense blue .65 .25

See No. C306.

St. Elizabeth Type

1956, Nov. 19

C286 A280 15c red brown .50 .25

St. Ignatius Type

1956, Nov. 26 Engr. *Perf. 12½x13*

C287 A281 5c brown .25 .25

Javier Pereira — AP63

1956, Dec. 28 Unwmk. *Perf. 12*

C288 AP63 20c rose carmine .25 .25

Issued to honor 167-year-old Javier Pereira.

No. 649 and Type of 1941 Overprinted in Red

1957 *Perf. 13½x13*

C289 A276 5c blue & black 7.50 3.25

Perf. 12

C290 AP22 5p orange & gray 11.00 7.50

The overprint measures 14mm.

Virgin Type of 1954
Engraved and Lithographed

1957, May 23 Unwmk. *Perf. 13*

C291 AP48 5c dp plum & multi .25 .25

Bank Type

No. C292, 20c, Emblem, cow, horse & herd. 10c, Emblem & tractor. 15c, Emblem, coffee & corn. No. C293, Emblem & dairy farm.

1957 Photo. *Perf. 14x13½*

C292 A283 5c chocolate .25 .25
C293 A283 5c orange .25 .25
C294 A283 10c green .70 .45
C295 A283 15c black .40 .25
C296 A283 20c dull red 1.00 .65
Nos. C292-C296 (5) 2.10 1.20

No. C292 is inscribed "Extra Rapido." Issued: No. C292, 3/5; others 5/23.

Cyclist AP64

1957, July 6 Unwmk. *Perf. 12*

C297 AP64 2c brown .25 .25
C298 AP64 5c ultra .25 .25

Seventh Bicycle Tour of Colombia.

Academy Type

Designs: 15c, Coat of arms and Gen. Rafael Reyes. 20c, Coat of arms and Academy.

1957, July 20 Engr. *Perf. 12½*

C299 A284 15c rose carmine .30 .25
C300 A284 20c brown .45 .25

Delgado Type

1957, Sept. 15 Photo. *Perf. 12*

C301 A285 10c slate blue .25 .25

UPU Type

1957, Oct. 10

C302 A286 15c dark red brown .30 .25
C303 A286 25c dark blue .40 .25

St. Vincent de Paul Type

1957, Oct. 18

C304 A287 5c rose brown .25 .25

Fencing Type

1957, Nov. 23 *Perf. 12*

C305 A288 20c dark red brown .40 .30

Columbus Type Inscribed "Extra Rapido"

1958, Jan. 8 Unwmk. *Perf. 12*

C306 A279 3c dark green .25 .25

Scenic Type

Design: 25c, Las Lajas Shrine.

1958, June 20 Engr. *Perf. 13*

C307 AP40 25c dark blue .30 .25
C308 AP40 25c rose violet .30 .25

IGY Type

1958, May 12 Photo. *Perf. 12*

C309 A289 25c green .50 .25

Inscribed "Extra Rapido"

C310 A289 1p purple .65 .25

No. 659 Ovptd. in Carmine

1958, Oct. 16 Engr. *Perf. 13*

C312 A277 50c dk green & blk .50 .25

Almanza Type

1958, Oct. 23 Photo. *Perf. 14x13*

C313 A290 25c dark gray .30 .25

Inscribed "Extra Rapido"

C314 A290 10c olive green .25 .25

Carrasquilla Type

1959, Jan. 22 Photo. *Perf. 14x13*

C315 A291 25c carmine rose .25 .25
C316 A291 1p dark blue .80 .25

Miss Universe Type

1959, June 26 Unwmk. *Perf. 11½*

C317 A292 1.20p multicolored 1.75 1.40
C318 A292 5p multicolored 47.50 47.50

Gaitan Type Inscribed and Surcharged in Black or Blue

1959, July 28 Engr. *Perf. 12x13½*

C319 A293 2p on 1p black 1.75 1.50
C320 A293 2p on 1p black (Bl) 1.75 1.50

The 1p black, type A293, exists without surcharge.

No. C247 Surcharged in Dark Blue

1959, Aug. 24 Unwmk. *Perf. 13*

C321 AP40 50c on 60c dk brown 1.75 .40

Regular and Air Post Issues of 1948-59 Ovptd. in Black or Red

1959-60

C322 A283 5c orange .35 .25
C323 A287 5c rose brn ('60) .50 .50
C324 A281 5c brown (R) .40 .30
C325 AP41 10c black .25 .25
a. Double overprint 2.50 2.50
C326 A160 10c red, #C231 .40 .25
a. Double overprint 1.40 1.40
C328 A284 15c rose car .25 .25
a. Inverted overprint 3.00 3.00
C330 AP40 20c brown .25 .25
a. Double overprint 1.40 1.40
C331 A284 20c brown .25 .25
C332 A288 20c dk red brn ('60) .25 .25
C333 AP40 25c rose vio ('60) .25 .25
C334 AP40 25c dark blue .25 .25
C335 A291 25c car rose .25 .25
C336 A290 25c dark gray .25 .25
C338 AP40 30c brown org .25 .25
C340 AP40 50c on 60c dk brn .40 .25
C341 A291 1p dark blue .95 .25
a. Double overprint 2.50 2.50
C342 A292 1.20p brn, ultra, car & ol 1.50 .80
C343 AP41 2p dk grn & blk 2.00 .25
C344 AP41 3p car rose & blk 6.00 .50
a. Double overprint 10.00 10.00
C345 AP41 5p dk grn & red brn 8.00 1.10
a. Double overprint 10.00 10.00
b. Inverted overprint 10.00 10.00
C346 AP40 10p gray grn & red org 10.00 2.25
Nos. C322-C346 (21) 33.00 9.20

Issued following agreement between the Colombian government and AVIANCA to unify the air postage used on all mail carried by AVIANCA.

Vertical overprint on Nos. C342 and C346.

Airmail Stamp of 1919 and Planes AP66

60c, Nos. C349a, C350a, Planes of 1919 and 1959. Nos. C349b, C350b, Stamp of 1919 and Planes.

Unwmk.

1959, Dec. 5 Photo. *Perf. 12*

C347 AP66 35c lt bl, blk & red .65 .25
C348 AP66 60c yel grn & gray 1.10 .75

Souvenir Sheets

C349 Sheet of 2 12.00 12.00
a. AP66 1p orange & gray 2.00 1.50
b. AP66 1p lilac, gray & red 2.00 1.50

Inscribed "Extra Rapido"

1960, May 17

C350 Sheet of 2 12.00 12.00
a. AP66 1.50p red orange & gray 2.00 1.50
b. AP66 1.50p olive, gray & rose 2.00 1.50

Nos. C347-C350 for the 40th anniv. of air post service and of the AVIANCA company.

Type of Regular Issue and

1859 Stamp and Seaplane AP67

Designs (various stamps of 1859 and): 10c, Map of Colombia. 25c, Pres. Mariano Ospina. 1.20p, Plane over mountains.

1959, Dec. 1 Photo. *Perf. 12*

C351 A296 25c choc & red .50 .35
C352 AP67 50c ver & ultra 1.25 .65
C353 AP67 1.20p yel grn & car 2.50 1.50

Inscribed "Extra Rapido"

C354 A296 10c lemon & vio .25 .25
Nos. C351-C354 (4) 4.50 2.75

Souvenir Sheet

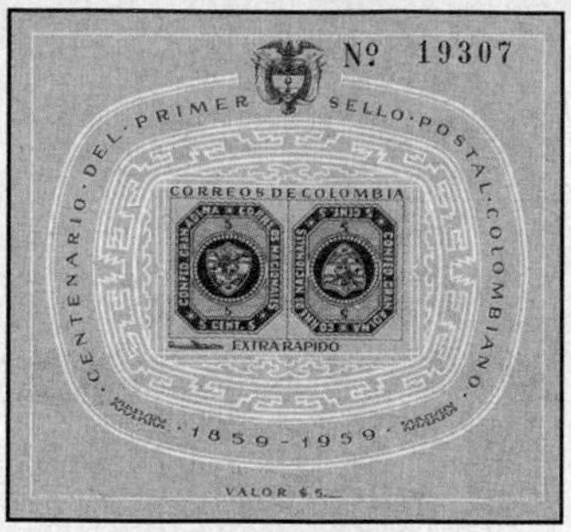

Tête Bêche 5c Stamps of 1859 — AP68

Wmk. 331

1959, Dec. 23 Litho. *Imperf.*

C355 AP68 5p blue, *pink* 19.00 19.00

Cent. of Colombian postage stamps.

No. C355 exists with inscription "VALOR $5.10" instead of "VALOR $5."

Eldorado Airport, Bogota AP69

1960, Jan. 5 Wmk. 331 *Perf. 12½*

C356 AP69 35c black & ocher .65 .25
C356A AP69 60c ver & gray .75 .45

Inscribed "Extra Rapido"

C356B AP69 1p Prus bl & gray 1.25 .70
Nos. C356-C356B (3) 2.65 1.40

Ant Bear AP70

1.30p, Armadillo. 1.45p, Parrot fish.

Unwmk.

1960, Feb. 12 Photo. *Perf. 12*

C357 AP70 35c sepia 1.60 .25
C358 AP70 1.30p rose car & dk brn 3.00 2.40
C359 AP70 1.45p lt bl, bl & yel 2.75 2.00
Nos. C357-C359 (3) 7.35 4.65

Alexander von Humboldt, German naturalist and geographer (1769-1859).

Flower Type

Nos. C360, C362, C366, Passiflora mollissima. Nos. C361, C364, C367, Odontoglossum luteo purpureum. Nos. C363, C369, Anthurium andreanum. Nos. C365, C370, Stanhopea tigrina. No. C368, Espeletia grandiflora.

1960, May 10 Photo. *Perf. 12*

Flowers in Natural Colors

C360 A298 5c dark blue .25 .25
C361 A298 35c maroon .55 .25
C362 A298 60c dark blue 1.10 .70
C363 A298 1.45p dark brown 1.25 1.10

Inscribed "Extra Rapido"

C364 A298 5c maroon .25 .25
C365 A298 10c brown .25 .25
C366 A298 1p dark blue 2.50 *3.00*
C367 A298 1p maroon 2.50 *3.00*
C368 A298 1p brown 2.50 *3.00*
C369 A298 1p brown 2.50 *3.00*
C370 A298 1p brown 2.50 *3.00*
Nos. C360-C370 (11) 16.15 *17.80*

See Nos. C420-C425.

Fleeing Family and Uprooted Oak Emblem AP71

Perf. 10, 11

1960, May 24 Litho. Wmk. 331

C371 AP71 60c bl grn & gray .40 .25

World Refugee Year, 7/1/59-6/30/60.

Souvenir Sheet

Pan-American Highway Through Colombia — AP72

1960, May 28 Litho. *Imperf.*

C372 AP72 2.50p brn & aqua 7.50 7.50

8th Pan-American Highway Congress, Bogota, May 20-29.

Lincoln Type

1960, June 6 *Perf. 10½*

C375 A299 40c dl red brn & blk 1.40 1.00
C376 A299 60c rose red & blk .40 .25

Type of Regular Issue and

Joaquin Camacho, Jorge Tadeo Lozano and Jose Miguel Pey AP73

Flag, Coins and Arms of Mompox and Cartagena — AP74

No. C378, Arms of Cartagena. 35c, 1.45p, Colombian flag. 60c, Andres Rosillo, Antonio Villavicencio and Joaquin Caicedo. 1p, Manuel de Bernardo Alvarez and Joaquin Gutierrez. 1.20p, Jose Antonio Galan statue. 1.30p, Front page of newspaper La Bagatela, 1811. 1.65p, Antonia Santos, Jose Acevedo y Gomez and Liborio Mejia.

Unwmk.

1960, July 20 Photo. *Perf. 12*

C377 AP73 5c lilac & brn .25 .25
C378 A301 5c dp bl grn & multi .25 .25
C379 AP73 35c multicolored .25 .25
C380 AP73 60c red brn & grn .45 .25
C381 AP73 1p ver & sl grn 1.10 .70
C382 A301 1.20p ultra & ind 1.10 .70
C383 AP73 1.30p orange & blk 1.10 .70
C384 AP73 1.45p multicolored 1.40 1.10
C385 AP73 1.65p green & brn 1.25 1.10
Nos. C377-C385 (9) 7.15 5.30

Souvenir Sheet

Stamps Inscribed "Extra Rapido"

C386 AP74 Sheet of 4 7.50 7.50
a. 50c deep claret & multi 1.00 1.00
b. 50c green & multi 1.00 1.00
c. 1p brown olive, yel, blue & car 1.00 1.00
d. 1p lilac & gray 1.00 1.00

150th anniv. of Colombia's independence.

St. Isidore Type

Designs: 35c, No. C388a, St. Isidore and farm animals. No. C388b, Nativity.

Unwmk.

1960, Sept. 26 Photo. *Perf. 12*

C387 A302 35c multicolored .25 .25

Souvenir Sheet

Stamps Inscribed "Extra Rapido"

C388 A302 Sheet of 2 10.00 10.00
a. 1.50p multicolored 3.00 3.00
b. 1.50p multicolored 3.00 3.00

See Nos. C439-C440.

Type of Regular Issue, 1959

Wmk. 331

1960, Nov. 23 Litho. *Perf. 12½*

C389 A294 35c Bolivar 3.50 .45

Pan-American Highway Type

1961, Mar. 7 Unwmk. *Perf. 10½x11*

C390 A304 10c rose lil & emer .75 *.70*
C391 A304 20c ver & lt bl .75 *.70*
C392 A304 30c black & emer .75 *.70*

Inscribed "Extra Rapido"

C393 A304 10c dk blue & emer .75 *.70*
Nos. C390-C393 (4) 3.00 *2.80*

8th Pan-American Highway Congress, Bogota, May 20-29, 1960.

Lopez Type

1961, Mar. 22 Photo. *Perf. 12½*

C394 A305 35c blue & brown .60 .25

Inscribed "Extra Rapido"

C395 A305 10c emerald & brn .25 .25

Souvenir Sheet

C396 A305 1p lilac & brn 6.00 6.00

Brother Damian and San Francisco Church, Cali AP75

Designs: 10c, View of Cali, vert. No. 398, Emblem of University del Valle, vert. 1.30p, Fine Arts School, Cali. 1.45p, Agricultural College, Palmira.

Perf. 13x13½, 13½x13

1961, Aug. 17 Photo. Unwmk.

C397 AP75 35c vio brn & ol .40 .25
C398 AP75 35c olive & grn .40 .25
C399 AP75 1.30p sepia & pink 1.10 .50
C400 AP75 1.45p multicolored 1.10 .70

Inscribed: "Extra Rapido"

C401 AP75 10c brn & yel grn .25 .25
Nos. C397-C401 (5) 3.25 1.95

50th anniv. (in 1960) of the department of Valle del Cauca.

View of Cucuta AP76

10c, Church of the Rosary, Cucuta, vert.

1961, Aug. 29

C402 AP76 35c brn ol & grn .70 .25

Inscribed: "Extra Rapido"

C403 AP76 10c dk brn & gray grn .25 .25

50th anniv. (in 1960) of the department of North Santander.

Old and New Ships of Barranquilla AP77

Arms and View of San Gil — AP78

Hotel, Popayan AP79

Statue of Christ in Procession AP80

Design: 1.45p, View of Velez.

Perf. 12½x13, 13x12½

1961, Oct. 10 Photo. Unwmk.

C404 AP77 35c gold & bl .55 .25
C405 AP78 35c bl grn, yel & red .55 .25
C406 AP79 35c car & brn .55 .25
C407 AP78 1.45p brown & grn .55 .25

Inscribed: "Extra Rapido"

C408 AP80 10c brown & yel .25 .25
Nos. C404-C408 (5) 2.45 1.25

Types of Regular and Air Post

Souvenir Sheets

Designs, No. C409: 35c, Barranquilla arms. 40c, Popayan arms. c, Arms and view of San Gil. d, Holy Week in Popayan.

No. C410: a, Old and new ships at Barranquilla. b, Hotel, Popayan. c, Bucaramanga arms. d, Holy Week in Popayan.

C409 Sheet of 4 12.00 12.00
a. A309 35c gold & multi 1.00 1.00
b. A309 40c gold & multi 1.00 1.00
c. AP78 1p blue, yellow & red 2.00 2.00
d. AP80 1p car rose & yellow 2.00 2.00

Stamps Inscribed: "Extra Rapido"

C410 Sheet of 4 12.00 12.00
a. AP77 50c gold & car rose 1.50 1.50
b. AP79 50c gold & blue 1.50 1.50
c. A309 50c pink & multi 1.50 1.50
d. AP80 50c blue & yellow 1.50 1.50

Nos. C404-C408 are in honor of the Atlantico Department. Nos. C409-C410 are in honor of the Departments of Atlantico, Cauca and Santander.

Nos. 713, 716 and 715 Overprinted and Surcharged

1961, Sept. *Perf. 12*

C411 A297 5c grnsh bl & brn .25 .25
C412 A298 5c multicolored .25 .25
C413 A297 10c on 20c cit & gray brn .25 .25
Nos. C411-C413 (3) .75 .75

"Aereo" in script on No. C412.

See Nos. C420-C425.

Sports Type

Designs: No. C414, Women divers. No. C415, Tennis, mixed doubles. 1.45p, No. C419b, Baseball. No. C417, Torch bearer. Nos. C418, C419a, Bolivar statue and flags of six participating nations. No. C419c, Soccer. No. C419d, Basketball.

1961, Dec. 16 Litho. *Perf. 13½x14*

C414 A310 35c ultra, yel & brn .75 .25
C415 A310 35c car, yel & brn .75 .25
C416 A310 1.45p Prus grn, yel & brn 1.10 .65

Inscribed: "Extra Rapido"

C417 A310 10c car lake, yel & brn .25 .25
C418 A310 10c ol, yel, bl & red .25 .25
Nos. C414-C418 (5) 3.10 1.65

Souvenir Sheet

Stamps Inscribed: "Extra Rapido"

Imperf

C419 Sheet of 4 8.00 8.00
a. A310 50c multi .60 .60
b. A310 50c multi .60 .60
c. A310 1p multi 1.25 1.25
d. A310 1p multi 1.25 1.25

Flower Type of 1960

5c, Passiflora mollissima. 10c, Espeletia grandiflora. 20c, 2p, Odontoglossum luteo purpureum. 25c, Stanhopea tigrina. 60c, Anthurium Andreanum.

Unwmk.

1962, Jan. 30 Photo. *Perf. 12*

Flowers in Natural Colors

C420 A298 5c gray .25 .25
C421 A298 10c gray blue .25 .25
C422 A298 20c rose lilac .25 .25
C423 A298 25c citron .30 .25
C424 A298 60c light brown .30 .25

Inscribed "Extra Rapido"

C425 A298 2p salmon pink 2.75 1.25
Nos. C420-C425 (6) 4.10 2.50

Anti-Malaria Type

Designs: 40c, Colombian anti-malaria emblem. 1p, 1.45p, Malaria eradication emblem and mosquito in swamp.

1962, Apr. 12 Litho. *Perf. 12*

C426 A311 40c yellow & red .25 .25
C427 A311 1.45p gray & ultra .65 .40

Inscribed "Extra Rapido"

C428 A311 1p yel grn & ultra 5.00 5.00
Nos. C426-C428 (3) 5.90 5.65

WHO drive to eradicate malaria.

Type of Regular Issue, 1962 and

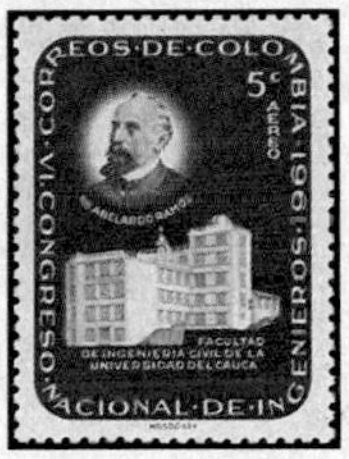

Abelardo Ramos and Engineering School, Cauca — AP81

Designs: 10c, Miguel Triana, Andres A. Arroyo and Monserrate shrine with cable cars. 15c, Diodoro Sanchez and first meeting place of Engineers Society. 2p, Engineers Society emblem.

1962, June 12 Photo. *Perf. 11½x12*

C429 AP81 5c blue & dp rose .25 .25
C430 AP81 10c green & sepia .25 .25
C431 AP81 15c lilac & sepia .45 .30

Inscribed: "Extra Rapido"

C432 A312 2p blk, yel, red & bl 2.50 2.50
Nos. C429-C432 (4) 3.45 3.30

75th anniv. of the founding of the Colombian Soc. of Engineers and 6th Natl. Cong. of Engineers.

American States Type

1962, June 28 Photo. *Perf. 13*

Flags in National Colors

C433 A313 35c black & blue .35 .25

Women's Rights Type

Perf. 12x12½

1962, July 20 Litho. Wmk. 229

C434 A314 35c buff, gray & blk .25 .25

See Nos. C448-C450.

Scout Type

Designs: 15c, No. C438, Scouts at campfire and tents. 40c and No. C437, Girl Scouts.

Perf. 11½x12

1962, July 26 Photo. Unwmk.

C435 A315 15c brown & rose .30 .25
C436 A315 40c dp cl & pink .40 .30
C437 A315 1p blue & buff .80 .55

Inscribed "Extra Rapido"

C438 A315 1p purple & yel 7.50 6.00
Nos. C435-C438 (4) 9.00 7.10

Nos. C435 and C438 for 30th anniv. of the Colombian Boy Scouts. Nos. C436 and C437 for the 25th anniv. of the Girl Scouts.

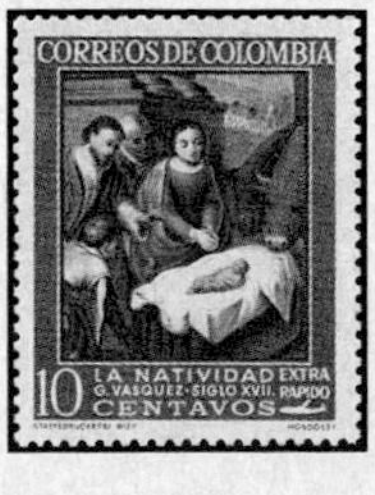

Nativity by Gregorio Vasquez AP82

Design: 2p, St. Isidore, similar to type A302.

Inscribed "Extra Rapido"
Unwmk.

1962, Aug. 28 Photo. *Perf. 12*
C439 AP82 10c gray & multi .25 .25
C440 AP82 2p gray & multi 4.50 4.50

See Nos. C387-C388.

Type of Regular Issue, 1962 and

Pres. Aquileo Parra and Magdalena River Bridge AP83

Design: 5c, Locomotives of 1854 and 1961. 10c, Railroad map of Colombia.

1962, Sept. 28 Photo. *Perf. 12½*
C441 AP83 5c sep & slate grn .25 .25
C442 A316 10c multicolored .25 .25

Engr.
C443 AP83 1p dull pur & brn 2.00 .25

Inscribed: "Extra Rapido."
C444 AP83 5p bl, brn & dl grn 5.00 4.50
Nos. C441-C444 (4) 7.50 5.25

Progress of Colombian railroads and completion of the Atlantic Line from Santa Maria to Bogota.

UPAE Type

Designs: 50c, Map of Americas and carrier pigeon. 60c, Post horn.

Perf. 13½x14
1962, Oct. 18 Litho. Wmk. 346
C445 A317 50c slate grn & gold .40 .25
C446 A317 60c gold & plum .25 .25

Pope John XXIII AP84

1963, Mar. 11
C447 AP84 60c gold, red brn, buff & red .40 .25

Vatican II, the 21st Ecumenical Council of the Roman Catholic Church.

Women's Rights Type of 1962

1963-64 *Perf. 12x12½*
C448 A314 5c sal, gray & blk ('64) .25 .25
C449 A314 45c pale grn, gray & blk .40 .25
C450 A314 45c brt pink, gray & blk .40 .25
Nos. C448-C450 (3) 1.05 .75

Games Emblem — AP85

1963, Aug. 12 *Perf. 13x14*
C451 AP85 20c gray & multi .25 .25
C452 AP85 80c buff & multi .25 .25

South American Athletic Championships (22nd for men, 12th for women), Cali, June 30-July 7.

Bolivar Statue by Arenas-Betancourt — AP86

Perf. 14x13½
1963, Aug. 30 Unwmk.
C453 AP86 1.90p olive bis & blue .25 .25

Centenary of the city of Pereira.
For surcharge see No. C574.

Tennis Player — AP87

1963, Oct. 11 *Perf. 13½x14*
C454 AP87 55c multicolored .25 .25

30th South American Tennis Championships, Medellin, Oct. 3-13.

Pres. John F. Kennedy and Alliance for Progress Emblem AP88

1963, Dec. 17 Litho. *Perf. 14x13½*
C455 AP88 10c multicolored .25 .25

President John F. Kennedy (1917-1963).

Church of the True Cross, National Pantheon, Bogota — AP89

2p, Christ of the Martyrs, bell and tomb.

Perf. 13½x14
1964, Mar. 10 Photo. Unwmk.
C459 AP89 1p multicolored .25 .25
C460 AP89 2p multicolored .35 .25

View of Cartagena AP90

1964, Mar. 18 Litho. *Perf. 14x13½*
C461 AP90 3p vio, bl, ocher & brn 1.40 .60

Cartagena's independence in 1811, Simon Bolivar's visit in 1812 and the siege of 1815.

Eleanor Roosevelt AP91

1964, Nov. 10 Photo. *Perf. 12*
C462 AP91 20c ol & dl red brn .25 .25

Eleanor Roosevelt (1884-1962).

Alberto Castilla and Score of "El Bunde" AP92

1964, Nov. 10 Unwmk.
C463 AP92 30c ol bis & Prus grn .25 .25

Department of Tolima and Maestro Alberto Castilla (1878-1937) who in 1906 founded the Tolima Conservatory of Music in Ibague.

Mejia Type

Mejia portrait and: 45c, Women picking coffee. 5p, Mules carrying coffee bags. 10p, Loading coffee on freighter "Manuel Mejia."

1965, Feb. 10 Engr. *Perf. 12½x13*
C464 A320 45c brown & blk .25 .25
C465 A320 5p gray grn & blk 2.50 .25
C466 A320 10p ultra & blk 3.50 .40
Nos. C464-C466 (3) 6.25 .90

ITU Emblem AP93

1965, Oct. 25 Photo. *Perf. 12*
C467 AP93 80c Prus bl, lt bl & red .25 .25

Cent. of the ITU.

Cattleya Truanae — AP94

1965, Oct. 3 Litho. *Perf. 13½x14*
C468 AP94 20c yellow & multi 1.00 .40

Fifth Philatelic Exhibition.

Cent. of the Telegraph in Colombia — AP95

No. C469, Pres. Manuel Murillo Toro statue, telegraph and orbits. No. C470, Telegraph and satellites over South America, horiz.

1965, Nov. 1 *Perf. 13½x14, 14x13½*
C469 AP95 60c multicolored .25 .25
C470 AP95 60c multicolored .25 .25

Junkers F-13 Seaplane, 1920 AP96

History of Colombian Aviation: 10c, Dornier Wal, 1924. 20c, Dornier Mercur, 1926. 50c, Trimotor Ford, 1932. 60c, De Havilland biplane, 1930. 1p, Douglas DC-4, 1947. 1.40p, Douglas DC-3, 1944. 2.80p, Superconstellation 1049, 1951. 3p, Boeing 720B jet, 1961.

Perf. 14x13½
1965-66 Photo. Unwmk.
C471 AP96 5c multicolored .25 .25
C472 AP96 10c multicolored .25 .25
C473 AP96 20c multicolored .25 .25
C474 AP96 50c multicolored .25 .25
C475 AP96 60c multicolored .40 .25
C476 AP96 1p multicolored .75 .25
C477 AP96 1.40p multicolored .90 .25
C478 AP96 2.80p multicolored 1.60 .60
C479 AP96 3p multicolored 2.40 .85
Nos. C471-C479 (9) 7.05 3.20
Nos. C471-C479,CE4 (10) 7.60 3.45

Issued: 5c, 60c, 3p, 12/13/65; 10c, 1p, 1.40p, 7/15/66; 20c, 50c, 2.80p, 12/14/66.

Automobile Club Emblem and Car on Road AP97

1966, Feb. 16 Litho. *Perf. 14x13½*
C480 AP97 20c multicolored .25 .25

25th anniv. (in 1965) of the Automobile Club of Colombia.

Fish Type

Fish: 2p, Flying fish. 2.80p, Queen angelfish. 20p, King mackerel.

1966, Aug. 25 Photo. *Perf. 12½x13*
C481 A323 2p multicolored .50 .25
C482 A323 2.80p multicolored 1.25 .90
C483 A323 20p multicolored 17.50 13.50
Nos. C481-C483 (3) 19.25 14.65

Coat of Arms Type

1966, Oct. 11 Litho. *Perf. 14x13½*
C484 A324 1p ultra & multi .40 .25
C485 A324 1.40p red & multi .30 .25

Portrait Type

80c, Father Felix Restrepo Mejia, S.J. (1887-1965), theologian, scholar. 1.70p, José Joaquin Casas (1866-1951), educator, diplomat.

Perf. 13½x14
1967, Jan. 18 Litho. Unwmk.
C486 A325 80c dk bl & bis .30 .25
C487 A325 1.70p blk & bis .50 .25

Declaration of Bogota Type

1967, Feb. 2 Litho. *Perf. 14x13½*
C488 A326 3p multicolored .50 .25

See note after No. 767.

Orchid Type

Orchids: 1p, Cattleya dowiana aurea, vert. 1.20p, Masdevallia coccinea, vert. 5p, Catasetum macrocarpum and bee.

1967, May 23 Litho. *Perf. 14*
C489 A327 1p multicolored 1.00 .25
C490 A327 1.20p multicolored .75 .25
C491 A327 5p multicolored 5.00 .90
a. Souv. sheet of 3, #C489-C491 17.50 17.50
Nos. C489-C491 (3) 6.75 1.40

Lions Type

1967, July 12 Litho. *Perf. 13½x14*
C492 A328 25c multicolored .25 .25

"First Caesarean Section" by Grau AP98

Perf. 14x13½
1967, Sept. 7 Litho. Unwmk.
C493 AP98 80c multicolored .25 .25

Issued to publicize the 6th Congress of Colombian Surgeons, Bogota, Sept. 25.

SENA Type
Lithographed and Embossed

1967, Sept. 20 *Perf. 13½x14*
C494 A329 2p gold, ver & blk .50 .25

Pre-Columbian Art Type

Designs: 30c, Bird pectoral. 5p Ornamental pectoral. 20p, Pitcher.

1967, Oct. 13 Photo. *Perf. 13½x14*

C495	A330	30c ver, gold & brn	.40	.25
C496	A330	5p red, gold & brn	3.25	.50
a.		Souvenir sheet of 2	12.00	12.00
C497	A330	20p vio, gold & brn	15.00	10.00
		Nos. C495-C497 (3)	18.65	10.75

No. C496a also commemorates the 6th Natl. Phil. Exhib. No. C496a contains 2 imperf. stamps in changed colors similar to Nos. C495-C496 (30c has green background and 5p maroon background).

Telecommunications Type

Designs: 50c, Signal lights. 1p, Early Bird satellite, Southern Cross and radar.

Perf. 13½x14

1968, May 14 Litho. Unwmk.

C498	A331	50c blk, ver & emer	.25	.25
C499	A331	1p ultra, yel & gray	.30	.25

Eucharist Type

1968, June 6 Litho. *Perf. 13½x14*

C500	A332	80c rose lil, red, yel & blk	.25	.25
C501	A332	3p bl, red, yel & blk	.30	.25

Eucharistic Congress Type

Designs: 80c, The Last Supper, by Gregorio Vasquez, horiz. 1p, St. Francis Xavier Preaching, by Gregorio Vasquez. 2p, The Dream of the Prophet Elias, by Gregorio Vasquez. 3p, Monstrance, c. 1700. 20p, Pope Paul VI, painting by Roman Franciscan nuns.

1968, Aug. 13 Photo. *Perf. 13*

C502	A333	80c multicolored	.25	.25
C503	A333	1p multicolored	.40	.25
C504	A333	2p multicolored	.45	.25
C505	A333	3p lil & multi	.95	.25
C506	A333	20p gold & multi	5.50	2.75
		Nos. C502-C506 (5)	7.55	3.75

Shrine of the Eucharist, Bogotá AP99

1.20p, Pope Paul VI giving blessing and Papal arms. 1.80p, Cathedral of Bogotá.

Perf. 14x13½, 13½x14

1968, Aug. 22 Litho.

C507	AP99	80c multi	.30	.25
C508	AP99	1.20p multi, vert.	.30	.25
C509	AP99	1.80p multi, vert.	.40	.25
		Nos. C507-C509 (3)	1.00	.75

Visit of Pope Paul VI to Colombia.

Computer Symbols — AP100

1968, Oct. 29 Litho. *Perf. 13½x14*

C510	AP100	20c buff, car & grn	.25	.25

Cent. of the Natl. University and the 1st Data Processing Cong. in 1967 at the University.

Agriculture Institute Type

1968, Mar. 5 Litho. *Perf. 13½x14*

C511	A337	1p gray & multi	.25	.25

Microscope and Pen — AP101

1969, Mar. 24 Litho. *Perf. 14*

C512	AP101	5p blk, yel, ver & pur	2.40	.35

20th anniv. (in 1968) of the University of the Andes.

Alexander von Humboldt and Andes AP102

1969, May 3 Litho. *Perf. 14x13½*

C513	AP102	1p grn & brn	.65	.35

Alexander von Humboldt (1769-1859), German naturalist and traveler.

Map of Colombia, Amphibian Plane and Letter AP103

Design: 1.50p, No. C516b, Globe, letter, and jet of Avianca airlines.

1969, June 18 Litho. *Perf. 14x13½*

C514	AP103	1p multi	.45	.25
C515	AP103	1.50p multi	.65	.25

Souvenir Sheet

Imperf

C516	Sheet of 2	7.50	7.50
a.	AP103 5p green & multi	1.00	1.00
b.	AP103 5p violet & multi	1.00	1.00

50th anniv. of the 1st air post flight in Colombia. No. C516 also for 8th Natl. Philatelic Exhibition, EXFILBA 69, Barranquilla, June 18-22. No. C516 contains 2 stamps in the designs of the 1p and 1.50p.

Independence Type

2.30p, Simon Bolivar, José Antonio Anzoategui, Francisco de Paula Santander and victorious army entering Bogotá, 9/18/1819; painting by Ignacio Castillo Cervantes.

1969, July 24 Litho. *Perf. 13½x14*

C517	A338	2.30p gold & multi	1.00	.35

Social Security Emblem — AP104

1969, Oct. 29 Litho. *Perf. 13½x14*

C518	AP104	20c emer & blk	.25	.25

20th anniv. of the Colombian Institute of Social Security.

Neurosurgeons' Congress Emblem — AP105

1969, Oct. 29

C519	AP105	70c vio, red & yel	.50	.30

Issued to publicize the 13th Congress of Latin-American Neurosurgeons, Bogotá.

Junkers F-13 AP106

Nos. C521, C522b, Globe with airlines from Bogota & Boeing jet. No. C522a, like No. C520.

1969, Nov. 28 Litho. *Perf. 14x13½*

C520	AP106	2p grn & multi	.75	.25
C521	AP106	3.50p ultra & multi	1.40	.50

Souvenir Sheet

Imperf

C522	Sheet of 2	7.50	7.50
a.	AP106 3.50p lt grn & multi	.75	.75
b.	AP106 5p ultra & multi	1.00	1.00

50th anniv. of AVIANCA; No. C522 also publicizes the 1st Interamerican Phil. Exhib., Bogota, Nov. 28-Dec. 7.

No. C522 contains 2 imperf. stamps.

Child Mailing Letter — AP107

Christmas: 1.50p, Praying child and gifts.

1969, Dec. 16 Litho. *Perf. 13½x14*

C523	AP107	60c ocher & multi	.80	.25
C524	AP107	1p multicolored	.85	.25
C525	AP107	1.50p multicolored	1.10	.25
		Nos. C523-C525 (3)	2.75	.75

Radar Station and Pre-Columbian Head — AP108

1970, Mar. 25 Litho. *Perf. 14x13½*

C526	AP108	1p dl grn, blk & brick red	.30	.25

Issued to publicize the opening of the communications satellite earth station at Chocontá in Cundinamarca Province.

Emblem of Colombian Youth Sports Institute — AP109

2.30p, Games' emblem (dove and 3 rings).

1970, Apr. 6 Litho. *Perf. 13½x14*

C527	AP109	1.50p dk ol grn, yel & blk	.30	.25
C528	AP109	2.30p red & multi	.40	.25

9th Natl. Youth Games, Ibague, July 10-20.

Art Exhibition Emblem — AP110

1970, Apr. 30 Litho. *Perf. 13½x14*

C529	AP110	30c multicolored	.25	.25

2nd Biennial Art Exhib., Medellin, 6/1-7/14.

Eduardo Santos, Rural and Urban Buildings AP111

1970, June 18 Litho. *Perf. 14x13½*

C530	AP111	1p grn, yel & blk	.25	.25

Issued to commemorate the founding (in 1939) of the Territorial Credit Institute.

UN Emblem, Scales and Dove — AP112

1970, June 26 *Perf. 13½x14*

C531	AP112	1.50p dk bl, lt bl & yel	.25	.25

25th anniversary of United Nations.

EXFILCA Emblem — AP113

1970, Nov. Litho. *Perf. 13½x14*

C532	AP113	10p bl, gold & blk	5.00	.25

EXFILCA 70, 2nd Interamerican Philatelic Exhib., Caracas, Venezuela, Nov. 27-Dec. 6.

Mother Juana Ruperta in Napanga Costume and Music by Efrain Orozco — AP114

Designs: 1p, Dancers from Eastern Plains and music by Alejandro Wills. No. C535, Guabina man, woman and folk song. No. C536, Bambuco man and woman, and music. No. C537, Man and woman dancing the Cumbia, and music.

1970-71 Litho. *Perf. 13½x14*

C533	AP114	60c dp lil rose & multi	.70	.25
C534	AP114	1p ultra & multi	.65	.25
C535	AP114	1.30p bl & multi	.75	.25

C536 AP114 1.30p emer & multi ('71) .90 .25
C537 AP114 1.30p lil & multi ('71) .65 .25
Nos. C533-C537 (5) 3.65 1.25

Athlete and Games Emblem — AP115

Design: 2p, Games emblem.

1971, Mar. 11

C542 AP115 1.50p multicolored .90 .90
C543 AP115 2p blk, org & grn .80 .55

6th Pan-American Games, Cali, 7/30-8/13.

Gilberto Alzate Avendano AP116

1971, Apr. 29 Litho. *Perf. 14x13½*

C544 AP116 1p bl & multi .60 .25

Avendano (1910-60), journalist, popular leader.

Commemorative Medal — AP117

Lithographed and Embossed

1971, June 21 *Perf. 14x13½*

C545 AP117 1p slate grn & gold .60 .30

Centenary (in 1970) of the Bank of Bogota.

Olympic Center — AP118

Soccer — AP119

Designs (Games Emblem and): Nos. C546-C546C, Olympic Center. No. 547, Soccer. No. C548, Wrestling. No. C549, Bicycling. No. C550, Volleyball. No. C551, Diving (women). No. C552, Fencing. No. C553, Sailing. No. C554, Equestrian. No. C555, Jumping. No. C556, Rowing. No. C557, Cali emblem. No. C558, Basketball (women). No. C559, Stadium. No. C560, Baseball. No. C561, Hockey. No. C562, Weight lifting. No. C563, Medals. No. C564, Boxing. No. C565, Gymnastics (women). No. C566, Sharpshooting.

1971, July 16 Litho. *Perf. 13½x14*

Multicolored and Emblem Color:

C546 AP118 1.30p yellow 1.50 .30
C546A AP118 1.30p green 1.50 .30
C546B AP118 1.30p blue 1.50 .30
C546C AP118 1.30p carmine 1.50 .30
C547 AP119 1.30p emerald 1.50 .30
C548 AP119 1.30p lilac 1.50 .30
C549 AP119 1.30p blue 1.50 .30
C550 AP119 1.30p carmine 1.50 .30
C551 AP119 1.30p blue 1.50 .30
C552 AP119 1.30p carmine 1.50 .30
C553 AP119 1.30p blue 1.50 .30
C554 AP119 1.30p gray 1.50 .30
C555 AP119 1.30p green 1.50 .30
C556 AP119 1.30p blue 1.50 .30
C557 AP118 1.30p orange 1.50 .30
C558 AP119 1.30p carmine 1.50 .30
C559 AP118 1.30p light blue 1.50 .30
C560 AP119 1.30p plum 1.50 .30
C561 AP119 1.30p yel grn 1.50 .30
C562 AP119 1.30p pink 1.50 .30
C563 AP118 1.30p deep org 1.50 .30
C564 AP119 1.30p plum 1.50 .30
C565 AP119 1.30p lilac rose 1.50 .30
C566 AP119 1.30p green 1.50 .30
a. Sheet of 25, #C546-C566 60.00 60.00

6th Pan American Athletic Games, Cali. No. C546B appears twice in sheet.

Battle of Carabobo, by Martin Tovar y Tovar — AP120

1971, Nov. 25 Litho. *Perf. 13½x14*

C567 AP120 1.50p multicolored 1.25 .25

Sesquicentennial of the Battle of Carabobo.

St. Theresa Type Overprinted

1972 Litho. *Perf. 13½x14*

C568 A343 2p multicolored .30 .25

See note after No. 793.

Vendor — AP121

Designs: 50c, Woman wearing shawl, and woven shawl. 3p, Fruit vendor (puppet).

1972, Apr. 11 Litho. *Perf. 13½x14*

C569 AP121 50c multicolored .35 .25
C570 AP121 1p multicolored .35 .25
C571 AP121 3p multicolored .50 .25
Nos. C569-C571 (3) 1.20 .65

Colombian artisans.

Mormodes Rolfeanum AP122

1972, Apr. 20 *Perf. 14x13½*

C572 AP122 1.30p multicolored .75 .25

7th World Orchidology Congress, Medellin.

Congo Grande Dancer — AP123

1972, June 21 Litho. *Perf. 13½x14*

C573 AP123 1.30p multicolored .60 .25

International Carnival of Barranquilla.

No. C453 Surcharged in Brown

1972, Oct. 5 Litho. *Perf. 14x13½*

C574 AP86 1.30p on 1.90p .75 .25

Laureano Gomez, by Ridriguez Cubillos — AP124

No. C576, Guillermo Leòn Valencia Muñoz.

1972 *Perf. 13½x14*

C575 AP124 1.30p multicolored .25 .25
C576 AP124 1.30p multicolored .25 .25

Laureano Gomez (1898-1966), Guillermo Leon Valencia Munoz (1909-71), Presidents of Colombia.

Issued: No. C575, 10/17; No. C576, 11/28.

Benito Juarez — AP125

1972, Dec. 12 *Perf. 13½x14*

C577 AP125 1.50p multicolored .25 .25

Benito Juarez (1806-1872), revolutionary leader and president of Mexico.

Rebecca Fountain AP126

1972, Dec. 19 Litho.

C578 AP126 80c multicolored .70 .45
C579 AP126 1p multicolored .65 .25

"Bucaramanga" — AP127

1972, Dec. 22 *Perf. 14x13½*

C580 AP127 5p multicolored 1.00 .25

Founding of Bucaramanga, 350th anniv.

Xavier University AP128

1973, May 8 Litho. *Perf. 14x13½*

C581 AP128 1.30p lt grn & sep .30 .25
C582 AP128 1.50p lt bl & sep .30 .25

350th anniversary of the founding of Xavier University in Bogotá.

Ceramic Type

Excavated Ceramic Artifacts: 1p, Winged urn, Tairona. 1.30p, Woman and child, Sinu. 1.70p, Two-headed figure, Quimbaya. 3.50p, Man, Tumaco.

1973 Litho. *Perf. 13½x14*

C583 A358 1p multicolored 1.75 1.20
C584 A358 1.30p multicolored .90 .25
C585 A358 1.70p multicolored 1.00 .25
C586 A358 3.50p multicolored 1.90 .30
Nos. C583-C586 (4) 3.15 1.75

Issue dates: 1p, Oct. 11; others, June 15.

Battle of Maracaibo, by Manuel F. Rincon AP129

1973, July 24 Litho. *Perf. 14x13½*

C587 AP129 10p bl & multi 2.50 .25

Battle of Maracaibo, sesquicentennial.

Bank Emblem AP130

1973, Oct. 1 Litho. *Perf. 14x13½*

C588 AP130 2p multicolored .30 .25

50th anniv. of the Bank of the Republic.

No. 801 Overprinted "AEREO"

1973, Oct. 11 *Perf. 14*

C589 A346 80c multicolored .30 .25

Pres. Pedro Nel Ospina, by Coroleano Leudo — AP131

1973, Nov. 9 *Perf. 13½x14*

C590 AP131 1.50p multicolored .25 .25

50th anniversary of the Ministry of Communications founded under Pres. Ospina.

Arms of Toro — AP132

1973, Dec. 1
C591 AP132 1p multicolored .25 .25

Founding of Toro, Valle del Cauca, 4th cent.

Bolivar, Battle of Bombona AP133

1973, Dec. 7 Litho. *Perf. 14x13½*
C592 AP133 1.30p multicolored .25 .25

Sesquicentennial (in 1972) of the Battle of Bombona.

Nicolaus Copernicus AP134

1974, Feb. 19 Litho. *Perf. 13½x14*
C593 AP134 2.50p multicolored .70 .25

500th anniversary of the birth of Nicolaus Copernicus (1473-1543), Polish astronomer.

Andes, Map of South America AP135

1974, May 11 Litho. *Perf. 14*
C594 AP135 2p multicolored .50 .25

Meeting of Communications Ministers of Members of the Andean Group, Cali, May 7-11, 1974.

Television Set AP136

1974, July 16 Litho. *Perf. 14x13½*
C595 AP136 1.30p org, blk & brn .25 .25

20th anniversary of Colombian television and 10th anniversary of INRAVISION, the National Institute of Radio and Television.

Championship Emblem — AP137

1974, Aug. 5 Litho. *Perf. 14x13½*
C596 AP137 4.50p multicolored .40 .25

2nd World Swimming Championships, Cali.

Condor — AP138

1974, Aug. 28 *Perf. 14*
C597 AP138 1.50p multicolored .25 .25

Bank of Colombia centenary.

UPU Envelope AP139

1974, Sept. 9 Litho. *Perf. 14*
C598 AP139 20p multicolored 3.00 .30

Centenary of Universal Postal Union.

Symbol of Flight — AP140

1974, Sept. *Perf. 12x12½*
C599 AP140 20c olive .25 .25

Gen. José Maria Cordoba — AP141

1974, Oct. 14 Litho. *Perf. 13½x14*
C609 AP141 1.30p multicolored .25 .25

Sesquicentennial of the Battles of Junin and Ayacucho.

Insurance Type

Design: 3p, Abstract pattern.

1974, Oct. 24 Litho. *Perf. 13½x14*
C610 A365 3p multicolored .30 .25

White-tailed Trogon, Letter — AP142

Designs (UPU Letter and): 1.30p, Keelbilled Toucan, horiz. 2p, Peruvian cock-of-the-rock, horiz. 2.50p, Scarlet macaw.

Perf. 13½x14, 14x13½

1974, Nov. 14
C611 AP142 1p multicolored 1.10 .25
C612 AP142 1.30p multicolored 1.10 .25
C613 AP142 2p multicolored 1.75 .25
C614 AP142 2.50p multicolored 1.75 .25
Nos. C611-C614 (4) 5.70 1.00

Centenary of Universal Postal Union.
For surcharge see No. C656.

Forest No. 1, by Roman Roncancio — AP143

Boy with Thorn in Finger, by Gregorio Vazquez AP144

Paintings: 3p, Women Fruit Vendors, by Miguel Diaz Vargas (1886-1956). 5p, Annunciation, Santafereña School, 17th-18th cent.

Perf. 13½x14, 14x13½

1975, Mar. 12 Litho.
C615 AP143 2p multicolored .75 .25
C616 AP144 3p multicolored .60 .25
C617 AP144 4p multicolored .65 .25
C618 AP144 5p multicolored 1.10 .25
Nos. C615-C618 (4) 3.00 1.00

Modern and Colonial Colombian paintings.

Trees and Lake AP145

Design: 6p, Victoria regia, Amazon River.

1975, Mar. 12 *Perf. 14x13½*
C619 AP145 1p yellow & multi .25 .25
C620 AP145 6p yellow & multi .60 .25

Nature conservation of trees and Amazon Region.

Gold Treasure Type

Designs: 2p, Nose pendant. 10p, Alligator-shaped staff ornament.

1975, Apr. 11 Litho. *Perf. 14x13½*
C621 A368 2p grn, gold & brn 1.00 .25
C622 A368 10p multicolored 4.75 .60

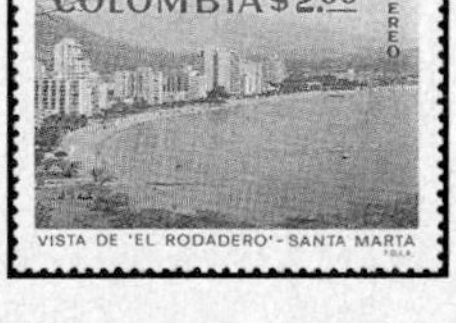

El Rodadero, Santa Maria AP146

1975, July 26 Litho. *Perf. 14x13½*
C623 AP146 2p multicolored .25 .25

400th anniversary of Santa Marta City.

AP147

1975, Aug. 31 Litho. *Perf. 13½x14*
C624 AP147 4p multicolored .25 .25

Intl. Women's Year 1975. Maria de Jesus Paramo de Collazos founded 1st normal school for women in Bucaramanga in 1875.

AP148

1976, Mar. 12 Litho. *Perf. 13½x14*
C625 AP148 5p "Sugar Cane" 1.25 .25

4th Congress of Latin-American and Caribbean sugar-exporting countries, Cali, 3/8-12.

View of Bogota — AP149

1976, July 2 Litho. *Perf. 12*
C626 AP149 10p shown 1.25 .90
C627 AP149 10p Barranquilla 1.25 .90
C628 AP149 10p Cali 1.25 .90
C629 AP149 10p Medellin 1.25 .90
a. Block of 4, #C626-C629 6.00 6.00

Habitat, UN Conf. on Human Settlements, Vancouver, Canada, May 31-June 11.

University Emblem and "90" — AP150

1976, Aug. 6 Litho. *Perf. 13½x14*
C630 AP150 5p lt blue & multi .50 .25

Univ. of Colombia day school, 90th anniv.

Miguel Samper — AP151

1976, Oct. 29 Litho. *Perf. 13½x14*
C631 AP151 2p multicolored .25 .25

Samper (1825-99), economist and writer.

Telephone, 1895 — AP152

1976, Nov. 2
C632 AP152 3p multicolored .25 .25

Centenary of first telephone call by Alexander Graham Bell, Mar. 10, 1876.

747 Jumbo Jet AP153

1976, Dec. 3 Litho. ***Perf. 12***
C633 AP153 2p multicolored .25 .25

Inauguration of 747 jumbo jet service by Avianca.
For surcharge see No. C636.

Convent, Church and Plaza de San Francisco — AP154

1976, Dec. 29 Litho. ***Perf. 14***
C634 AP154 6p multicolored .50 .25

150th anniv. of the Congress of Panama.

Souvenir Sheet

Bank of the Republic Emblem — AP155

1977, June 6 Litho. ***Perf. 14***
C635 AP155 25p multicolored 13.00 13.00

Opening of Philatelic Museum of Medellin under auspices of Banco de la Republica.

No. C633 Surcharged in Light Brown

1977, June Litho. ***Perf. 12***
C636 AP153 3p on 2p multi .25 .25

Coffee — AP156

1977-78 Litho. ***Perf. 12½***
C640 AP156 3p multi .50 .25
C641 AP156 3.50p multi ('78) .50 .25

Colombian coffee.

Coffee Grower, Pack Mule — AP157

1977, Aug. 9 Litho. ***Perf. 13½x14***
C642 AP157 10p multicolored .50 .25

National Federation of Coffee Growers, 50th anniversary.

Beethoven and 9th Symphony AP158

1977, Aug. 17
C643 AP158 8p multicolored 1.25 .25

Sesquicentennial of the death of Ludwig van Beethoven (1770-1827).

Bird Type

Tropical Birds and Plants: No. C644, Woodpecker and Meriania. C645, Purple gallinule and water lilies. No. C646, Xipholaena punicea and Cochlospermum orinocense. No. C647, Crowned flycatcher and Jacaranda copaia.

1977, Sept. 6 Litho. ***Perf. 14***
C644 A380 5p multicolored .75 .25
C645 A380 5p multicolored .75 .25
C646 A380 10p multicolored 1.10 .25
C647 A380 10p multicolored 1.10 .25
Nos. C644-C647 (4) 3.70 .80

Games' Emblem — AP159

1977, Sept. 9 ***Perf. 12x12½***
C648 AP159 6p multicolored .25 .25

13th Central American and Caribbean Games, Medellin, 1978.

La Cayetana, by Enrique Grau AP160

No. C650, Water Nymphs, by Beatriz Gonzalez.

1977, Sept. 13 ***Perf. 14x13½***
C649 AP160 8p multicolored .80 .25
C650 AP160 8p multicolored .80 .25

Women's suffrage, 20th anniversary.

Judge Francisco Antonio Moreno, by Joaquin Gutierrez AP161

Design: 25p, Viceroy Manuel de Guirior.

1977, Sept. 13 ***Perf. 12***
C651 AP161 20p multicolored 1.60 .75
C652 AP161 25p multicolored 2.40 1.10

Bicentenary of National Library.

Federico Lleras Acosta — AP162

1977, Sept. 27 Litho. ***Perf. 14***
C653 AP162 5p multicolored .30 .25

Dr. Federico Lleras Acosta, veterinarian and bacteriologist; birth centenary.

Cauca University Arms — AP163

1977, Oct. 14
C654 AP163 5p multicolored .30 .25

Sesquicentennial of the University of Cauca.

CUDECOM Building, Bogota AP164

1977, Oct. 14
C655 AP164 1.50p multicolored .25 .25

Colombian Society of Engineers, 90th anniv.

No. C612 Surcharged with New Value and Bars in Brown

1977, Dec. 3 Litho. ***Perf. 14x13½***
C656 AP142 2p on 1.30p multi .30 .25

Lost City, Tayrona Culture — AP165

1978, Apr. 18 Litho. ***Perf. 12½***
C657 AP165 3.50p multicolored .25 .25

Creator of Energy, by Arenas Betancourt AP166

1978, Apr. 25 ***Perf. 12***
C658 AP166 4p blue & multi .25 .25

Sesquicentennial of Antioquia University Law School.

Column of the Slaves — AP167

1978, May 9
C659 AP167 2.50p multicolored .25 .25

Sesquicentennial of Ocana Convention (meeting of various political groups).

Statue of Catalina, Cartagena AP168

1978, May 30 Litho. ***Perf. 12***
C660 AP168 4p blk & lt bl .25 .25

Sesquicentennial of University of Cartagena.

Gold Pendant, Tolima — AP169

1978, July 11 Litho. ***Perf. 12x12½***
C661 AP169 3.50p multicolored .25 .25

Apotheosis of Spanish Language, by Luis Alberto Acuña — AP170

1978, Aug. 9 ***Perf. 14***
C662 AP170 Strip of 3 4.75 4.75
a.-c. 11p, any single 1.10 1.10

Millennium of Spanish language.

Presidential Guard — AP171

1978, Aug. 16 ***Perf. 13½x14***
C663 AP171 9p multicolored .45 .45

Presidential Guard Battalion, 50th anniv.

Figure, Muisca Culture — AP172

1978, Sept. 12 **Litho.** ***Perf. 12½***
C664 AP172 3.50p multicolored .30 .25

Apse of Carmelite Church — AP173

1978, Oct. 12 ***Perf. 13***
C665 AP173 30p multicolored 2.75 .40

Souvenir Sheet

Perf. 13½x14

C666 AP173 50p multicolored 8.75 8.75

ESPAMER '78 Philatelic Exhibition, Bogota, Oct. 12-21.

Owl, Gold Ornament, Calima — AP174

No. C669, Gold frog, Quimbaya culture. No. C670, Gold nose pendant, Tairona, horiz.

1978-80 **Litho.** ***Perf. 12½***
C667 AP174 3.50p multi .40 .25
C668 AP174 4p multi ('79) .25 .25
C669 AP174 4p multi ('79) .40 .25
C670 AP174 5p multi ('80) .60 .25
Nos. C667-C670 (4) 1.65 1.00

Virgin and Child, by Gregorio Vasquez — AP175

1978, Nov. 28 ***Perf. 13½x14***
C671 AP175 2.50p multicolored .25 .25

Christmas 1978.

Bull Ring, Cathedral, Manizales AP176

1979, Jan. 6 **Litho.** ***Perf. 14***
C672 AP176 7p multicolored .80 .25

Manizales Fair.

Children Playing Hopscotch, and IYC Emblem — AP177

No. C674, Child at blackboard and UNESCO emblem. No. C675, The Paper Collector, by Omar Gordillo, and UN emblem.

1979, July 19 ***Perf. 13½x14, 14x13½***
C673 AP177 8p multi .40 .30
C674 AP177 12p multi, horiz. .55 .45
C675 AP177 12p multi .55 .45
Nos. C673-C675 (3) 1.50 1.20

International Year of the Child.

Rio Prado Hydroelectric Station — AP178

1979, Aug. 24 ***Perf. 13½x14***
C676 AP178 5p multicolored .80 .25

Tomb, 6th Century — AP179

1979, Sept. 25 **Litho.** ***Perf. 14***
C677 AP179 8p multicolored .80 .35

San Augustin Archaeological Park.

Gonzalo Jimenez de Quesada, by C. Leudo AP180

1979, Oct. 11 ***Perf. 12***
C678 AP180 20p multicolored 3.50 1.50

Gonzalo Jimenez de Quesada (1500-1579), Spanish conquistador.

Hill, Penny Black, Colombia No. 1 — AP181

1979, Oct. 23 ***Perf. 13½x14***
C679 AP181 15p multicolored .90 .25

Sir Rowland Hill (1795-1879), originator of penny postage.

Amazon Region — AP182

Tourism: 14p, San Fernando Fortress.

1979 **Litho.** ***Perf. 13½x14***
C680 AP182 7p multicolored .60 .25
C681 AP182 14p multicolored 1.60 .75

Issue dates: 7p, Nov. 16; 14p, Nov. 9.
See Nos. C717-C719.

AP183

Creche Sculptures: No. C682, Three Kings and soldiers. No. C683, Nativity. No. C684, Shepherds.

1979, Nov. 30 ***Perf. 12***
C682 AP183 3p multicolored 1.50 1.10
C683 AP183 3p multicolored 1.50 1.10
C684 AP183 3p multicolored 1.50 1.10
a. Strip of 3, #C682-C684 4.50 3.50

Christmas 1979.

AP184

Magdalena Bridge, Avianca emblem.

1979, Dec. 5 ***Perf. 14***
C685 AP184 15p multicolored .70 .25

Barranquilla, 350th anniversary; Avianca National Airline, 60th anniversary.

AP185

Boy Playing Flute, by Judith Leyster.

1980, Feb. 15 ***Perf. 13½x14***
C686 AP185 6p multicolored .60 .25

2nd Intl. Music Competition, Ibague, Dec. 1979.

Gen. Antonio José de Sucre, 150th Death Anniversary AP186

1980, Feb. 15 **Litho.** ***Perf. 12½x12***
C687 AP186 12p multicolored .60 .25

The Watchman, by Edgar Negret AP187

1980, Feb. 26 ***Perf. 12x12½***
C688 AP187 25p multicolored 2.50 1.40

Virgin Mary, by Real del Sarte, 1929 AP188

1980, May 23 **Litho.** ***Perf. 14x13½***
C689 AP188 12p multicolored .60 .25

Apparition of the Virgin Mary to Sister Catalina Labouri Gontard, 150th anniv.

San Gil Produce Market, by Luis Roncancio — AP189

1980, May 27 ***Perf. 13½x14***
C690 AP189 12p multicolored .70 .25

Pres. Enrique Olaya Herrera, by Miguel Diaz Vargas — AP190

1980, Oct. 28 **Litho.** ***Perf. 12***
C691 AP190 20p multicolored 1.25 .40

Enrique Olaya Herrera (1880-1936), president, 1930-1934.

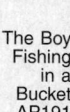

The Boy Fishing in a Bucket
AP191

Christmas (Christmas Stories by Rafael Pombo): No. C693, The Frog and the Mouse. No. C694, The Seven Lives of the Cat.

1980, Nov. 21 Litho. *Perf. 14½*

C692	AP191	4p	multicolored	.25	.25
C693	AP191	4p	multicolored	.25	.25
C694	AP191	4p	multicolored	.25	.25
			Nos. C692-C694 (3)	.75	.75

28th World Golf Cup, Cajica — AP192

1980, Dec. 9 Litho. *Perf. 13½x14*

C695	AP192	30p	multicolored	4.50	3.00

Bolivar Type

Simon Bolivar Death Sesquicentennial: 6p, Portrait, last words to Colombia, vert.

1980, Dec. 17 *Perf. 12*

C696	A400	6p	multicolored	.80	.45

St. Peter Claver Holding Cross
AP193

1981, Jan. 13 *Perf. 14½*

C697	AP193	15p	multicolored	.70	.30

St. Peter Claver (1580-1654), helped American Indians.

Sculptured Bird, San Augustin
AP194

Archaeological Finds: No. C699, Funeral chamber, Tierradentro. No. C700, Chamber hallway, Tierradentro. No. C701, Statue of man, San Augustin.

1981, May 12 Litho. *Perf. 14*

C698	AP194	7p	multicolored	1.00	.25
C699	AP194	7p	multicolored	1.00	.25
C700	AP194	7p	multicolored	1.00	.25
C701	AP194	7p	multicolored	1.00	.25
a.			Block of 4, #C698-C701	5.00	5.00

See Nos. C707-C710D.

Child with Hobby Horse, by Fernando Botero — AP195

4th Biennial Arts show, Medellin: 20p, Square Abstract, by Omar Rayo. 25p, Flowers, by Alejandro Obregon.

1981, May 15 *Perf. 12*

C702	AP195	20p	multicolored	1.25	.25
C703	AP195	25p	multicolored	1.40	.40
C704	AP195	50p	multicolored	2.50	.75
			Nos. C702-C704 (3)	5.15	1.40

8th South American Swimming Championships, Medellin — AP196

1981, June 5

C705	AP196	15p	multicolored	.60	.25

Santamaria Bull Ring, 50th Anniv. — AP197

1981, June 9 Litho. *Perf. 12*

C706	AP197	30p	multicolored	3.25	1.75

Quimbaya Culture — AP197a

1981, Sept. 23 Litho. *Perf. 14*
Yellow Background

C707	9p	Man	1.00	.25
C708	9p	Seated man	1.00	.25
C709	9p	Seal, print	1.00	.25
C710	9p	Jug	1.00	.25
e.		AP197a Block of 4, #C707-C710	5.00	3.50

Calima Culture — AP197b

1981, Dec. 17 White Background

C710A	9p	Anthropomorphic container	1.50	.25
C710B	9p	Jar	1.50	.25
C710C	9p	Anthropomorphic jar	1.50	.25
C710D	9p	Urn	1.50	.25
f.		AP197b Block of 4, #C710A-C710D	9.00	9.00

Fruit
AP198

1981, Nov. 3 Litho. *Perf. 14*

C711	Block of 6	24.00	20.00
a.-f.	AP198 25p, any single	3.50	1.50

Revolt of the Comuneros, 200th Anniv. — AP199

1981, Nov. 21 Litho. *Perf. 12*

C712	AP199	20p	multicolored	.90	.40

Jose Manuel Restrepo, Historian, 1775?-1860?
AP200

1981, Dec. 1 Litho. *Perf. 12*

C713	AP200	35p	multicolored	1.40	.75

Andres Bello, 1780?-1865
AP201

1981, Dec. 11 Litho. *Perf. 12*

C714	AP201	18p	multicolored	.70	.25

Colombia's Admission to UPU, 100th Anniv.
AP202

30p, No. 103. 50p, Hemispheres, Nos. 104-108.

1981 Litho. *Perf. 12*

C715	AP202	30p	multicolored	1.25	.35

Size: 100x70mm
Imperf

C716	AP202	50p	multicolored	4.75	4.75

Issued: No. C715, Dec. 18. No. C716, Dec. 28.

Tourism Type of 1979

1982 Litho. *Perf. 12*

C717	AP182	20p	Solano Bay	.60	.25
C718	AP182	20p	Tota Lake, Boyaca	.60	.25
C719	AP182	20p	Corrales, Boyaca	.60	.25
			Nos. C717-C719 (3)	1.80	.75

Issued: No. C717, 6/2; others, 6/16.

1982 World Cup — AP202a

Players and team emblems: a, "America." b, "A. B." c, "Cali." d, "C." e, "C/D." f, "Junior F.B.C." g, "D/M." h, Stadium. i, "M." j, "Club Atletico Nacional." k, "D/P." l, "Quindio." m, "Santa Fe." n, "T." o, "Santa Marta."

1982, June 21 *Perf. 14*

C720	Sheet of 15	10.00	6.75
a.-o.	AP202a 9p, any single	.70	.30

Bogota Gun Club Centenary
AP202b

1982, July 16 *Perf. 12*

C721	AP202b	20p	multicolored	.70	.25

Gold Crocodile Figure, Tairona Culture
AP202c

Tairona Culture Exhibit, Gold Museum: Various figures. Nos. C723-C727 vert.

1982, July 28
Gold, Black and

C722	AP202c	25p	light brown	2.75	.95
C723	AP202c	25p	bright pink	2.75	.95
C724	AP202c	25p	green	2.75	.95
C725	AP202c	25p	dark blue	2.75	.95
C726	AP202c	25p	violet	2.75	.95
C727	AP202c	25p	red	2.75	.95
			Nos. C722-C727 (6)	16.50	5.70

Government Buildings, Pereira — AP203

1982, Aug. 4 Litho. *Perf. 12*

C728 AP203 35p multicolored 1.25 .40

Biplane in Flight, by Edgar Antonio Bustos AP204

1982, Aug. 5 *Perf. 14*

C729 AP204 18p multicolored .60 .25

American Air Forces Cooperation System.

Magdalena River AP205

1982, Oct. 21 Litho. *Perf. 12*

C730 AP205 30p multicolored 1.40 .75

Marquez Type

1982, Dec. 10 *Perf. 13½x14*

C731 A412 25p gray & blue .70 .25
C732 A412 30p gray & brown 1.00 .25

San Andres Archipelago — AP206

1983, Apr. 9 Litho. *Perf. 12*

C733 AP206 25p Liberty Fort .60 .25

Opening of Las Gaviotas (The Seagulls) Ecological Center, Bogota — AP207

1983, June 1 Litho.

C734 AP207 12p multicolored .40 .25

50th Anniv. of Radio Amateurs League AP208

1983, June 11 *Perf. 14x13½*

C735 AP208 12p multicolored .30 .25

Bolivar Type

1983, July 24 *Perf. 12*

C736 A417 30p multicolored .80 .25
C737 A417 100p multicolored 2.50 1.75

Botanical Exhibition Type

No. C738, Begonia guaduensis. No. C739, Chinchona ovaliflora. No. C740, Begonia urticae.

1983, Aug. 18 *Perf. 14*

C738 A418 12p multicolored .55 .25
C739 A418 12p multicolored .55 .25
C740 A418 40p multicolored 2.90 .40
Nos. C738-C740 (3) 4.00 .80

Cartagena, 450th Anniv. — AP208a

12p, Customs Square. 35p, Historic sites, Cartagena.

1983, Sept. 9 Litho. *Perf. 12*

C740A AP208a 12p multi .50 .25
C740B AP208a 35p multi 1.25 .30

Painting Type

1983, Oct. 5 Litho. *Perf. 12*

C741 A420 30p multicolored 2.00 .50

Scouting Year — AP209

1983, Oct. 24

C742 AP209 12p multicolored .25 .25

Coffee Beans — AP210

1984, Mar. 28 Litho. *Perf. 14½x14*

C743 AP210 14p multicolored .25 .25

Marandua City Type

1984, Sept. 28 *Perf. 12*

C744 A427 30p multicolored .75 .25

AP211

1984, Nov. 2

C745 AP211 45p multicolored .90 .25

45th Cong. of Americanists, Bogota, 1985.

Christmas Type

1984, Dec. 14

C746 A428 14p multicolored .35 .25

AP212

Design: Dove, map and flags of Colombia, Mexico, Costa Rica and Venezuela.

1985, Feb. 15

C747 AP212 40p multicolored .90 .30

Contadora Group of Latin American countries.

Gomez Type

1985, Feb. 25

C748 A432 40p multicolored .95 .30

Birds — AP213

14p, Dryocopus lineatus nuperus. 20p, Xiphorhynchus picus. 50p, Eriocnemis cupreoventris. 55p, Momotus momota.

1985

C749 AP213 14p multicolored .80 .30
C750 AP213 20p multicolored 1.50 .30
C751 AP213 50p multicolored 3.50 1.00
C752 AP213 55p multicolored 4.50 1.25
Nos. C749-C752 (4) 10.30 2.85

Issued: 14p, 4/12; 20p, 50p, 8/6; 55p, 8/29.

AP214

1985, July 15

C753 AP214 20p multicolored .30 .25

Admiral Padilla Naval School, 50th anniv.

1985 Census AP215

1985, Oct. 15 *Perf. 12*

C754 AP215 20p multicolored .40 .25

Christmas Type

1985, Dec. 4 Litho. *Perf. 13*

C755 A436 20p Girl, Christmas tree .40 .25

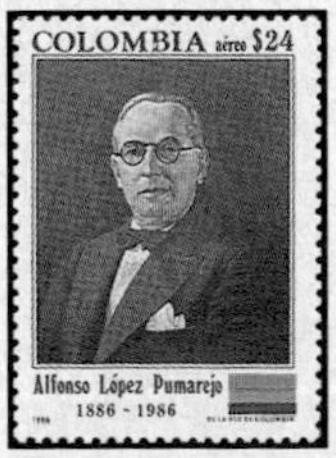

Alfonso Lopez Pumarejo (1886-1959), President, 1934-38, 1942-45 — AP216

1986, Jan. 31

C756 AP216 24p multicolored .35 .25

Coffee Berries, Natl. Cycling Team AP217

1986, Feb. 4

C757 AP217 60p multicolored 1.25 .75

Natl. Coffee Producers Assoc. sponsorship of natl. cycling team, 25th anniv.

Fauna Type of 1985

1986, Feb. 18

C758 A433 50p Pudu mephistophiles 1.50 .25

World Communications Day — AP218

1986, May 17 Litho. *Perf. 13*

C759 AP218 50p multicolored .65 .25

Intl. Peace Year — AP219

1986, June 13 Litho. *Perf. 13*

C760 AP219 55p multicolored 1.00 .45

AP220

24p, Portrait, papal arms. 55p, Portrait, Medellin cathedral, horiz. 60p, Blessing crowd, horiz.

200p, Praying, Madonna of Bogota.

1986, July 1 Litho. *Perf. 13*

C761 AP220 24p multicolored 1.00 .25
C762 AP220 55p multicolored 1.00 .25
C763 AP220 60p multicolored 1.00 .25
Nos. C761-C763 (3) 3.00 .75

Souvenir Sheet

C764 AP220 200p multicolored 4.50 3.50

Visit of Pope John Paul II.

Nos. C762-C763 each printed in sheets of 20 with se-tenant labels picturing religious symbols.

AP221

1986, July 15 *Perf. 12*

C765 AP221 25p multicolored .30 .25

Enrique Santos Montejo (1886-1971), journalist.

Bach, Handel and Schutz, Composers
AP222

1986, July 17 *Perf. 13*

C766 AP222 70p Bach 1.50 .40
C767 AP222 100p Text, music 2.00 .55

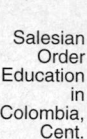

Salesian Order Education in Colombia, Cent.
AP223

1986, July 23 *Perf. 12*

C768 AP223 25p De La Salle, founder .35 .25

Completion of Coal Mining Complex, El Cerrejon
AP224

1986, July 29 **Litho.** *Perf. 12*

C769 AP224 55p multi 1.25 .75

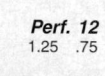

AP225

Natl. Constitution, Cent. — AP226

25p, The Five Signators, by R. Vasquez, detail, & Bogota Cathedral. 200p, Pres. Nunez & Miguel Antonio Caro, Natl. Council of Delegates chairman, & Presidential Palace, constitution.

1986, Aug. 5 **Litho.** *Perf. 14*

C770 AP225 25p multi .35 .25

Souvenir Sheet

Perf. 12

C771 AP226 200p multi 3.00 3.00

Poet Type

Federico Garcia Lorca (1898-1936), poet, and birthplace, Fuentevaqueros, Granada, Spain.

1986, Sept. 26 **Litho.** *Perf. 12*

C772 A445 60p multi .90 .50

Gratitude for Intl. Aid after the Armero Mudslide Disaster
AP227

1986, Nov. 13

C773 AP227 50p multi 1.00 .75

Christmas
AP228

Wood sculpture: Virgin Mestiza, Nerina.

1986, Dec. 19 **Litho.** *Perf. 12*

C774 AP228 25p multi .35 .25

The Apotheosis of Popayan, by Ephrain Martinez Zambrano (1898-1956) — AP229

1987, Jan. 13

C775 100p Popayan riding horse 2.50 1.25
C776 100p Onlookers 2.50 1.25
a. AP229 Pair, #C775-C776 5.00 3.50

AP230

1987, Mar. 16 **Litho.** *Perf. 12*

C777 AP230 30p multi .50 .25

The Conversion of St. Augustine of Hippo, 1600th anniv.

Type of 1987

30p, Phoenicopterus ruber. 35p, Pseudemys scripta, horiz. No. C780, Crax alberti. No. C781, Symphysodon aequifasciatum, horiz.

Perf. 14½x14, 14x14½

1987-89 **Wmk. 334**

C778 A446a 30p lake .35 .25
C779 A446a 35p dark red brn .40 .25
C780 A446a 45p dark blue gray .30 .25
C781 A446a 45p blue .30 .25
Nos. C778-C781 (4) 1.35 1.00

Issue dates: 30p, June 8. 35p, Dec. 24. No. C780, Dec. 6, 1988. No. C781, June 23, 1989.

AP231

Perf. 13½x13

1987, Apr. 10 **Unwmk.**

C783 AP231 25p multi .30 .25

Natl. University School of Mining, Medellin, cent.

Purebred Horses
AP232

1987, June 17 *Perf. 12*

C784 AP232 60p White horse 1.25 .30
C785 AP232 70p Black horse 1.25 .30

El Espectador Newspaper, Cent.
AP233

Design: Frontispieces from 1887, 1915, 1948, 1974 and portraits of founder Don Fidel Cano, editors Don Luis Cano, Luis Gabriel Cano Isaza and Alfonso Cano Isaza.

1987, July 24 *Perf. 12½x12*

C786 AP233 60p multi .85 .25

Intl. Year of Shelter for the Homeless
AP234

1987, Sept. 21 *Perf. 14*

C787 AP234 60p multi .50 .25

Flags
AP235

1987, Nov. 27 **Litho.** *Perf. 13x13½*

C788 AP235 80p multi 1.00 .30

Ist Meeting of the eight Latin-American Presidents, Acapulco, Nov.

Christmas
AP236

1987, Dec. 8 **Litho.** *Perf. 14*

C789 AP236 30p multi .45 .25

Rural Telephone System
AP237

1988, Feb. 4 **Litho.** *Perf. 14*

C790 AP237 70p multi .80 .30

Founding of Bogota, 450th Anniv. — AP238

1988, Apr. 11 **Litho.** *Perf. 12*

C791 AP238 70p multi .90 .25

Bogota, 450th Anniv.
AP238a

Unwmk.

1988, July 1 **Litho.** *Perf. 12*

C792 AP238a 80p Modern district, vert. .75 .25
C793 AP238a 90p Colonial district .85 .30

Gold Artifacts
AP239

Artifacts in the Gold Museum: 70p, Mask. 80p, Two-headed human figure inside a circle, Muisca tribe. 90p, Ritual figure of the Quimbaya.

1988 *Perf. 12*

C794 AP239 70p multi .90 .50
C795 AP239 80p multi 1.00 .60
C796 AP239 90p multi 1.40 .75
Nos. C794-C796 (3) 3.30 1.85

Issue dates: 70p, May 13; 80p, 90p, Oct. 7.

Human Rights Type

Perf. 14x14½

1988, July 1 **Engr.** **Wmk. 334**

C797 A452 40p Communication, horiz. .40 .25

AP240

1988, Sept. 28 Litho. *Perf. 12*
C798 AP240 80p multi .90 .25

Zipa Tisquesusa (d. 1538), Chibcha Indian leader during revolt against Spanish Conquistadors.

AP241

1988, Nov. 23 Litho. *Perf. 12*
C799 AP241 40p multi .60 .25

Christmas.

Agustin Nieto Caballero (1889-1975), Educator — AP242

Unwmk.

1989, Mar. 18 Litho. *Perf. 12*
C800 AP242 100p multi .90 .50

Pres. Laureano Gomez (1889-1965) AP243

1989, Mar. 29
C801 AP243 45p multi .45 .25

Intl. Coffee Organization — AP244

1989, Apr. 3
C802 AP244 110p multi 1.00 .50

12th Session of the UN Commission on Human Rights — AP245

1989, Apr. 28
C803 AP245 100p multi 1.00 .40

French Revolution, Bicent. AP246

1989, June 29 Litho. *Perf. 12*
C804 AP246 100p multi .90 .40

PHILEXFRANCE '89 — AP247

a, Bananas, tropical fruits. b, Fruits, flowers. c, Birds, animals. d, Precious gems, metals and mineral resources. e, View of fields, Colombian carrying produce basket. f, Waterfall. g, Fish, coast.

1989 Litho. *Perf. 14*
C805 AP247 Pane of 7 17.50 17.50
a.-g. 110p any single 1.75 .40

No. C805 printed in sheets containing panes of 7, rouletted between.

Souvenir Sheet

Los Lanceros, by R. Arenas Betancur — AP248

1989 Litho. *Perf. 12*
C806 AP248 250p multicolored 2.25 1.25

Human Rights Type

Perf. 14½x14

1989, Aug. 18 Engr. Wmk. 334
C807 A452 55p Family .40 .25

Natl. Anti-Drugs Campaign AP249

Unwmk.

1989, Aug. 23 Litho. *Perf. 12*
C808 AP249 115p multicolored .90 .25

America Issue AP250

UPAE emblem and artifacts or customs of pre-Columbian peoples: 115p, Quimbaya, Calima or Tolima gold smiths. 130p, Potter and Sinu ceramic figurine.

1989 *Perf. 12*
C809 AP250 115p multicolored 1.25 .40
C810 AP250 130p multicolored 1.25 .60

Issue dates: 115p, Oct. 12; 130p, Aug. 23.

Joaquin Quijano Mantilla (1878-1944), Journalist — AP251

1989, Sept. 29 *Perf. 12*
C811 AP251 170p multicolored 1.50 .50

Arts and Crafts in Barro-Raquira AP252

1989 Litho. *Perf. 12*
C812 AP252 55p multicolored .40 .25

Christmas.

Boeing 767 AP253

1989, Dec. 5 Litho. *Perf. 12*
C813 AP253 130p multicolored 1.25 .30

Bolivar Installed at the Congress of Angostura, by Tito Salas — AP254

1989, Dec. 12
C814 AP254 130p multicolored 1.10 .50

Creation of the Republic, 1819.

Fathers of the Nation Leaving the Constitutional Convention AP255

1989, Dec. 12
C815 AP255 130p shown 1.10 .50
C816 AP255 130p Arms 1.10 .50
C817 AP255 130p Temple of the Rosary 1.10 .50
Nos. C815-C817 (3) 3.30 1.50

Constitution of the Republic, 1821.

Arms Type of Regular Issue, 1982

1990, Mar. 1 Litho. *Perf. 12*
C818 A372 60p Velez .30 .25

Presidential Summit, Cartagena AP256

1990, Feb. 15 Litho. *Perf. 12*
C819 AP256 130p Plaza de la Aduana .55 .25

Colombian National Radio, 50th Anniv. — AP257

1990, Feb. 16 Litho. *Perf. 12*
C820 AP257 150p multicolored 1.00 .25

Teresa Cuervo Borda (1889-1976), Art Historian — AP258

1990, Mar. 28 Litho. *Perf. 12*
C821 AP258 60p multicolored .35 .25

Second Latin American Theater Festival, Bogota — AP259

1990, Apr. 10
C822 AP259 150p buff, tan & gold 1.00 .25

Santander Type

No. C823, Santander holding the Constitution. No. C824, Central Cemetery, Bogota and National Pantheon. No. C825, Santander, as organizer of public education. No. C826, "Postman of New Granada" (Man and burro) by Joseph Brown and Jose Maria del Castillo, horiz. 500p, Santander on death bed.

1990, May 6 *Perf. 14x13½*
C823 A470 60p multicolored .30 .25
C824 A470 60p multicolored .30 .25
C825 A470 70p multicolored .40 .25
C826 A470 70p multicolored .40 .25
Nos. C823-C826 (4) 1.40 .80

Souvenir Sheet

Perf. 12

C827 A470 500p multi 2.00 1.50

No. C827 contains one 54x40mm stamp.

First Postage Stamp, 150th Anniv. AP260

1990, May 6 *Perf. 14*
C828 AP260 150p multicolored .80 .40

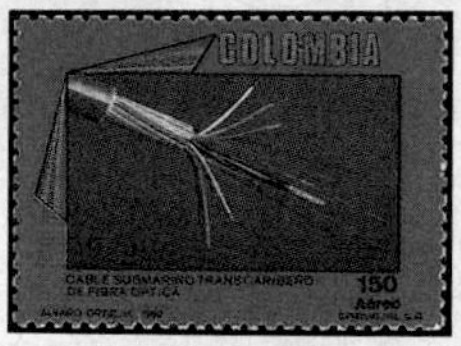

Trans-Caribbean Fiber Optic Cable — AP261

1990, May 19 *Perf. 12*
C829 AP261 150p multicolored 1.25 .40

Institute of Industrial Development, 25th Anniv. — AP262

1990, May 22
C830 AP262 60p multicolored .40 .25

Souvenir Sheet

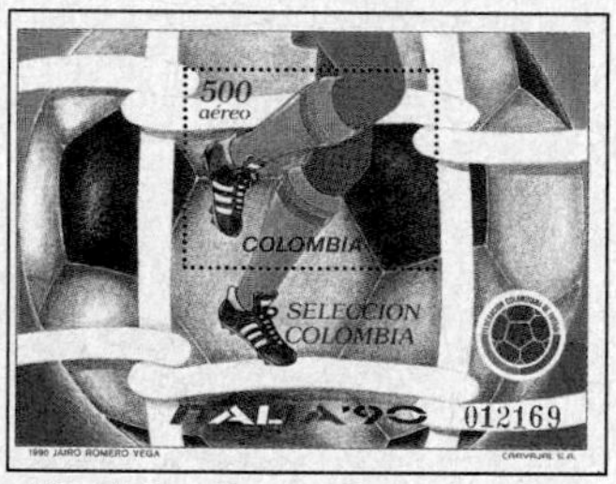

World Cup Soccer Championships, Italy — AP263

1990, June 8
C831 AP263 500p multicolored 4.50 3.50

AP264

1990, June 27
C832 AP264 130p multicolored .80 .25

Organization of American States, cent.

AP265

1990, July 26
C833 AP265 170p multicolored 1.25 .50

Museum of Gold, 50th Anniv.

Dolphins, Marine Birds
AP266

1990, Oct. 12 **Litho.** *Perf. 12*
C834 AP266 150p shown 2.50 .25
C835 AP266 170p Jungle fauna, vert. 2.50 .25

AP267

1990, Nov. 16 **Litho.** *Perf. 12*
C836 AP267 70p multicolored .50 .25

Monastery of Our Lady of Las Lajas.

AP268

1991, Feb. 8 **Litho.** *Perf. 12*
C837 AP268 170p multicolored 1.00 .50

Newspaper Publishing, 200th Anniv.

AP269

1990, Nov. 1 **Litho.** *Perf. 12*
C838 AP269 70p multicolored .60 .25

Christmas.

AP270

Whales and Dolphins: 80p, Megaptera novaeangliae, breaching. 170p, Megaptera novaeangliae, diving. 190p, Inia geoffrensis, Sotalia fluviatilis, horiz.

1991, May 31 **Litho.** *Perf. 14*
C839 AP270 80p multicolored 1.25 .25
C840 AP270 170p multicolored 2.75 .30
C841 AP270 190p multicoloed 3.25 .30
Nos. C839-C841 (3) 7.25 .85

America Issue
AP271

1991, Oct. 11 **Litho.** *Perf. 14*
C842 AP271 90p shown .60 .30
C843 AP271 190p Ship arriving in New World 1.25 .50

Adoration of the Magi — AP272

1991, Dec. 20 **Litho.** *Perf. 14*
C844 AP272 90p multicolored .60 .30

Christmas.

AP273

1991, Dec. 2
C845 AP273 190p Country flags 1.10 .50

Fifth summit of Latin American presidents.

AP274

1992, Feb. 8 **Litho.** *Perf. 12*
C846 AP274 210p multicolored 1.25 .60

8th UNCTAD Conference, Cartagena.

Proclamation of New Constitution, July 4, 1991 — AP275

1991, Nov. 27 **Litho.** *Perf. 14*
C847 AP275 90p multicolored .40 .25

Export Products
AP276

1992, Mar. 11 *Perf. 12*
C848 AP276 90p Flowers .60 .30
C849 AP276 210p Fruits, vegetables, horiz. 1.40 .65

Copyright Protection
AP277

1992, Apr. 13 **Litho.** *Perf. 12*
C850 AP277 190p multicolored 1.50 .60

1992 Summer Olympics
AP278

1992, June 4 **Litho.** *Perf. 14*
C851 AP278 110p multicolored .75 .30

Earth Summit '92 — AP279

a, Tree, mountain landscape. b, Birds in tree.

1992, June 2 **Litho.** *Perf. 14*
C852 A279 230p Pair, #a.-b. 2.75 2.00

America Issue
AP280

Paintings: 230p, Discovery of America by Christopher Columbus, by Salvador Dali. 260p, Magical America, Myth and Legend, by Alfredo Vivero.

1992, July 22 *Perf. 14x13½*
C853 AP280 230p multicolored 1.75 .70
C854 AP280 260p multicolored 2.00 .75

McDonnell Douglas MD83
AP281

1992, Sept. 22 **Litho.** *Perf. 12*
C855 AP281 110p multicolored .50 .30

Curtain of Colon Theatre
AP282

1992, Oct. 12 **Litho.** *Perf. 12*
C856 AP282 230p multicolored 1.25 .65

Gloria Lara, 1938-82 — AP283

1992, Nov. 27 **Litho.** ***Perf. 12***

C857 AP283 230p multicolored 1.25 .65

AP284

1993, June 7 **Litho.** ***Perf. 12***

C858 AP284 220p multicolored 1.25 .60

1993 American Soccer Cup, Ecuador.

Intl. Year of Indigenous People — AP285

1993, July 1 ***Perf. 14***

C859 AP285 460p multicolored 2.50 1.25

South American Eliminations for 1994 World Cup Soccer Championships, US — AP286

1993, July 31 **Litho.** ***Perf. 12***

C860 AP286 220p multicolored 1.75 .60

AP287

America Issue (Endangered species): a, 220p, Saguinus oedipus. b, 220p, Porphyrula martinica. c, 460p, Rupicola peruviana. d, 520p, Trichecus manatus.

1993, Oct. 19 **Litho.** ***Perf. 12***

C861 AP287 Block of 4, #a.-d. 7.50 7.50

AP288

1994, Mar. 21 **Litho.** ***Perf. 12***

C862 AP288 630p multicolored 3.25 1.75

Intl. Decade for Natural Disaster Reduction.

Beatification of Josemaria Escriva de Balaguer — AP289

1994, May 17 **Litho.** ***Perf. 13½x14***

C863 AP289 560p multicolored 2.50 1.40

First Airmail Delivery, 75th Anniv. AP290

Design: 270p, William Knox Martin, airplane over Port Colombia, 1919.

1994, July 29 **Litho.** ***Perf. 14***

C864 AP290 270p multicolored 1.25 .55

Natl. Institute of Medical Law & Forensic Sciences, 80th Anniv. AP291

1994, Oct. 27 **Litho.** ***Perf. 12***

C865 AP291 560p multicolored 2.25 1.25

Sociedad Colombo-Alemana de Transportes Aereos (SCADTA), 75th Anniv. — AP292

1995, Jan. 2 **Litho.** ***Perf. 12***

C866 AP292 330p No. C15 1.10 .50

Flora and Fauna — AP293

Iguana iguana: No. C867a, Facing right. b, Facing left.

Rain forest: No. C868a, Nuts on branch, flowers. b, Waterfall, hanging red flower.

1995, Jan. 17

C867 AP293 650p Pair, #a.-b. 6.50 6.50

C868 AP293 750p Pair, #a.-b. 6.50 6.50

Nos. C867-C868 are continuous designs.

SCADTA, 75th Anniv. AP294

1995, Mar. 30 **Litho.** ***Perf. 14***

C869 AP294 330p No. C9 1.50 .75

FAO, 50th Anniv. AP295

1995, Apr. 25 **Litho.** ***Perf. 13x13½***

C870 AP295 750p multicolored 3.50 1.75

Andres Bello Organization, 25th Anniv. — AP296

1995, Apr. 27 ***Perf. 13½x13***

C871 AP296 650p multicolored 2.50 1.25

Colombian Firefighters, Cent. — AP297

1995, May 5 ***Perf. 12***

C872 AP297 330p multicolored 1.50 .75

Fenalco, 50th Anniv. — AP298

1995, May 25 ***Perf. 13½***

C873 AP298 330p multicolored 1.25 .65

UN, 50th Anniv. — AP299

1995, June 21 ***Perf. 12***

C874 AP299 750p multicolored 3.00 1.50

First Pacific Ocean Games — AP300

1995, June 23

C875 AP300 750p multicolored 3.00 1.50

11th Summit of Non-Aligned Countries, Cartagena — AP302

1995, Oct. 13 **Litho.** ***Perf. 12***

C877 AP302 650p multicolored 2.75 1.25

Motion Pictures, Cent. AP303

Design: 330p, Charlie Chaplin and Jackie Coogan in "The Kid," Estela López Pomareda in "María," first Colombian feature length film.

1995, Oct. 19 ***Perf. 14***

C878 AP303 330p black & sepia 1.50 .75

AP304

1995, Nov. 23 ***Perf. 12***

C879 AP304 650p multicolored 2.10 1.00

Andes Development Corporation (CAF), 25th Anniv.

AP305

Fight against illegal drug trafficking: No. C880, Locating illegally grown plants. No. C881, Hands in handcuffs, horiz.

1995, Nov. 21 ***Perf. 14***

C880 AP305 330p multicolored .70 .45

C881 AP305 330p multicolored .70 .45

Miniature Sheet of 16

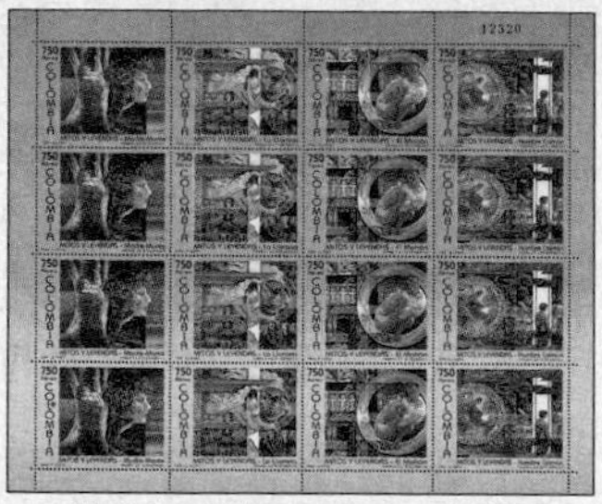

Myths and Legends — AP306

Madre-Monte: a.-d.
La Llorona: e.-h.
El Mohán: i.-l.
Hombre Caimán: m.-p.
Background color changes from top to bottom rows. Top row is blue. Row 2 is blue green. Row 3 is green. Row 4 is lilac. Each design comes in all four colors.

1995, Dec. 6
C882 AP306 750p #a.-p. 40.00 40.00

See No. C886.

José Asunción Silva (1865-96), Poet AP307

1996, Apr. 23 Litho. *Perf. 12*
C883 AP307 400p multicolored 1.25 .75

Isla de Providencia AP308

1996, Apr. 25 *Perf. 14*
C884 AP308 800p multicolored 2.75 1.40

Policarpa Salavarrieta (1796-1817), Patriot — AP309

1996, Apr. 26
C885 AP309 900p multicolored 3.00 1.50

Myths and Legends Type

Designs: a, Kogui Creation. b, Yonna Wayu. c, Jaguar Man. d, Master of the Animals.

1996, Aug. 12 Litho. *Perf. 13½x14*
C886 AP306 900p Block of 4, #a.-d. 13.00 13.00

Metropolitan Basilica, Medellin AP310

1996, July 12
C887 AP310 400p multicolored 1.10 .55

National Archives Building AP311

1996, July 30 Litho. *Perf. 14*
C888 AP311 400p multicolored 1.25 .60

CERLALC, 25th Anniv. AP312

1996, Aug. 16 Litho. *Perf. 12*
C889 AP312 800p multicolored 2.75 1.25

UNESCO.

Pioneers in Petroleum Industry — AP313

a, Jorge Isaacs, pumping oil. b, Francisco Burgos Rubio, refinery at night. c, Diego Martínez Camargo, derrick. d, Prisciliano Cabrales Lora, off-shore drilling. e, Manuel María Palacio, oil tanker loading offshore. f, Roberto De Mares, refinery, lake. g, General Virgilio Barco Maldonado, men positioning equipment. h, Roustabout, "ECOPETROL" emblem.

1996, Sept. 5 Litho. *Perf. 13½x14*
C890 AP313 800p Block of 8, #a.-h. 20.00 20.00

Colombian Golf Federation, 50th Anniv. AP314

1996, Sept. 19 Litho. *Perf. 12*
C891 AP314 400p multicolored 2.25 .60

Covenant for the Children AP315

1997, Feb. 28 Litho. *Perf. 14*
C892 AP315 400p multicolored 2.00 .75

AP316

1997, Apr. 25 *Perf. 12*
C893 AP316 800p multicolored 4.00 1.75

Motion pictures in Colombia, cent.

AP317

1997, May 13 Litho. *Perf. 12*
C894 AP317 400p multicolored 2.00 .75

Social Security Institute, 50th anniv.

Ericsson in Colombia, Cent. — AP318

1997, May 22 *Perf. 13½x14*
C895 AP318 900p multicolored 4.50 2.00

Bogotá Colonial Bldg., Home of Natl. Mint and Numismatic Museum — AP319

1997, July 10 *Perf. 12*
C896 AP319 800p multicolored 3.00 1.40

Phytelephas Seemannii — AP320

1997, July 23 *Perf. 13½x14*
C897 AP320 900p multicolored 3.00 .90

Cordoba Cattle Fair AP321

1997, June 21 *Perf. 14*
C898 AP321 400p multicolored 1.50 .45

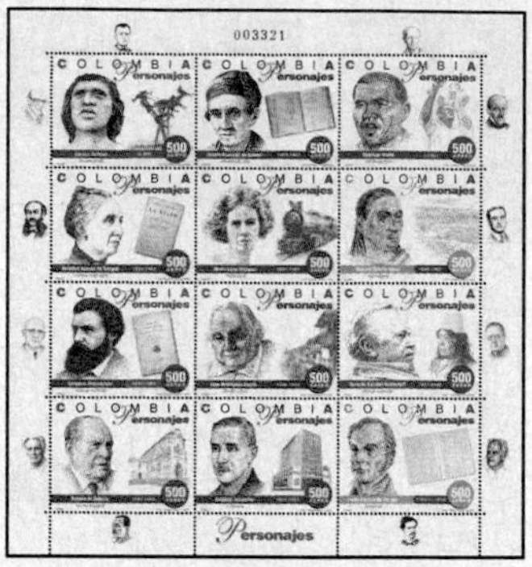

Personalities — AP322

No. C899: a, Cacique Gaitana, 16th cent., Indian resistance leader. b, Josefa Acevedo de Gómez (1803-61), writer. c, Domingo Bioho (d. 1621), black leader. d, Soledad Acosta de Samper (1831-1913), historian. e, Maria Cano Márquez (1897-1967), popular leader. f, Manuel Quintín Lame (1880-1967), native leader. g, Ezequiel Uricoechea (1834-80), linguist, naturalist. h, Juan Rodríguez Freyle (1566-1642), colonial reporter. i, Gerardo Reichel-Dolmatoff (1912-94), archaeologist. j, Ramón de Zubiría (1922-95), writer, educator. k, Esteban Jaramillo (1874-1947), economist. l, Pedro Fermín de Vargas (1762-c. 1810), economist.

No. C900: a, Luis Carlos "el tuerto" López (1879-1950), poet. b, Aurelio Arturo (1906-74), poet. c, Enrique Pérez Arbeláez (1896-1972), botanist. d, José Maria González Benito (1843-1903), mathematician, astronomer. e, José Manuel Rivas Sacconi (1917-91), diplomat. f, Eduardo Lemaitre Román (1914-94), historian. g, Diójenes Arrieta (1848-93), politician. h, Gabriel Turbay Abunader (1901-47), politician, diplomat. i, Guillermo Echavarría Misas (1888-1985), aviation pioneer. j, Juan Friede Alter (1901-90), historian. k, Fabio Lozano Torrijos (1865-1947), diplomat. l, Lino de Pombo (1797-1862), engineer, diplomat.

Sheets of 12

1997, Dec. 19 Litho. *Perf. 13½x14*
C899 AP322 500p #a.-l. 22.50 22.50
C900 AP322 500p #a.-l. 22.50 22.50

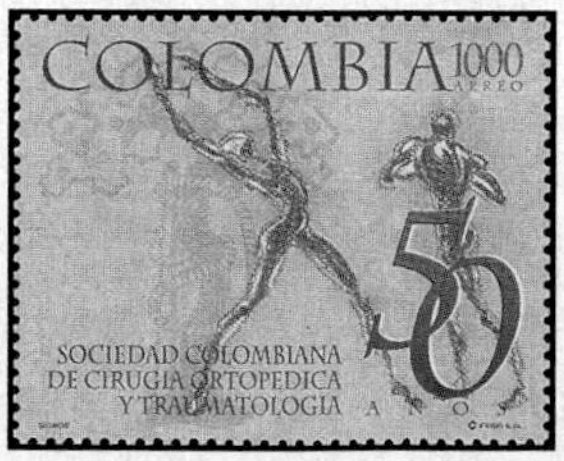

Colombian Society of Orthopedic Surgery and Traumatology, 50th Anniv. — AP323

1997 *Perf. 12*
C901 AP323 1000p multicolored 3.00 1.00

AP324

1998, Apr. 30 Litho. *Perf. 14*
C902 AP324 1000p multicolored 3.00 .80

Organization of American States, 50th anniv.

AP325

1998, May 22
C903 AP325 1000p bl & org 3.00 .80

4th Bolivar Philatelic Exhibition, Santa Fe de Bogota.

World Health Organization, 50th Anniv. — AP326

1998, Apr. 7 *Perf. 12*
C904 AP326 1100p multicolored 3.00 1.00

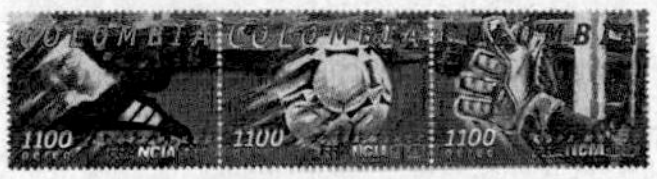

1998 World Cup Soccer Championships, France — AP327

Stylized designs: a, Foot. b. Soccer ball. c, Hand.

1998, June 9 Litho. *Perf. 14*
C905 AP327 1100p Strip of 3, #a.-c. 12.00 12.00

Intl. Year of the Ocean — AP328

1998, May 22 *Perf. 12*
C906 AP328 1100p ARC Gloria 3.50 .95

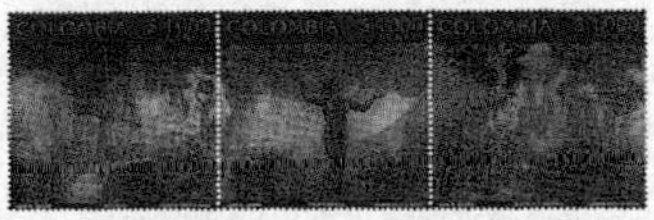

Myths and Legends — AP329

Designs: a, Bochica. b, Chimingagua. c, Bachue and Huitica.

Perf. 13¼x12¾
1998, Nov. 27 Litho.
C907 AP329 1000p Strip of 3, #a.-c. 15.00 15.00

AIR POST SPECIAL DELIVERY STAMPS

Catalogue values for unused stamps in this section are for Never Hinged items.

Post Horn and Wings APSD1

Unwmk.
1958, May 19 Litho. *Perf. 12*
CE1 APSD1 25c dk bl & red .55 .25

No. CE1 Ovptd. in Red

1959
CE2 APSD1 25c dk bl & red .50 .25

Jet Plane and Envelope — APSD2

1963, Oct. 4 *Perf. 14*
CE3 APSD2 50c red & blk .25 .25

Aviation Type

80c, Boeing 727 jet, 1966.

Perf. 14x13½
1966, Dec. 14 Photo. Unwmk.
CE4 AP96 80c crim & multi .55 .25

AIR POST REGISTRATION STAMPS

Issued by Sociedad Colombo-Alemana de Transportes Aereos (SCADTA)

No. C41 Overprinted in Red

1923 Wmk. 116 *Perf. 14x14½*
CF1 AP6 20c gray 4.75 1.10

No. C58 Overprinted in Black

1929 Wmk. 127 *Perf. 14*
CF2 AP8 20c carmine 8.00 7.00

Same Overprint on No. C71

CF3 AP10 20c carmine 6.50 6.00

Colombian Government Issues

No. C86 Overprinted in Black

1932
CF4 AP8 20c carmine 6.50 6.00

No. C100 Overprinted

CF5 AP12 20c car & ol blk 6.00 1.25

For surcharge see No. C118.

SPECIAL DELIVERY STAMPS

Special Delivery Messenger — SD1

1917 Unwmk. Engr. *Perf. 14*
E1 SD1 5c dark green *60.00 150.00*

Catalogue values for unused stamps in this section, from this point to the end of the section, are for Never Hinged items.

SD2

1987, July 31 Litho. *Perf. 14*
E2 SD2 25p emerald & ver .30 .30
E3 SD2 30p emerald & ver .35 .35

REGISTRATION STAMPS

R1

R2

1865 Unwmk. Litho. *Imperf.*
F1 R1 5c black 87.50 47.50
F2 R2 5c black 110.00 50.00

R3

R4

Vertical Lines in Background

1870 White Paper
F3 R3 5c black 3.00 2.50
F4 R4 5c black 3.00 2.50

Horizontal Lines in Background

F5 R3 5c black 10.00 8.50
F6 R4 5c black 3.00 2.50
Nos. F3-F6 (4) 19.00 16.00

Reprints of Nos. F3 to F6 show either crossed lines or traces of lines in background.

R5

1881 *Imperf.*
F7 R5 10c violet 60.00 52.50
a. Sewing machine perf. 67.50 60.00
b. Perf. 11 75.00 62.50

R6

1883 *Perf. 12, 13½*
F8 R6 10c red, *orange* 2.00 *2.50*

R7

1889-95 *Perf. 12, 13½*
F9 R7 10c red, *grysh* 9.50 4.50
F10 R7 10c red, *yelsh* 9.50 4.50
F11 R7 10c dp brn, *rose buff* ('95) 2.00 1.60
F12 R7 10c yel brn, *lt buff* ('92) 2.00 1.60
Nos. F9-F12 (4) 23.00 12.20

Nos. F9-F12 exist imperf.

R9

1902 *Imperf.*
F13 R9 20c red brown, *blue* 1.60 1.60
a. Sewing machine perf. 4.75 4.75
b. Perf. 12 4.75 4.75

Medellin Issue

R10

1902 Laid Paper *Perf. 12*
F16 R10 10c blk vio 15.00 15.00
a. Wove paper 21.00 21.00

Regular Issue
Imperf

1903
F17 R9 20c blue, *blue* 1.60 1.60
a. Sewing machine perf. 4.75 4.75
b. Perf. 12 4.75 4.75

R11

1904 Pelure Paper *Imperf.*
F19 R11 10c purple 3.75 3.75
a. Sewing machine perf. 5.00 3.75
b. Perf. 12 6.25 5.00

R12

Imprint: "J. L. Arango"

1904 Wove Paper *Perf. 12*
F20 R12 10c purple 2.50 .60
a. Imperf., pair 7.75 7.75

Imprint: "Lit. Nacional"

1909 *Perf. 10, 14, 10x14, 14x10*
F21 R12 10c purple 2.75 .85
a. Imperf., pair 6.25 6.25

For overprints see Nos. LF1-LF4.

Execution at Cartagena in 1816 — R13

1910, July 20 Engr. *Perf. 12*

F22	R13 10c red & black	21.00	*90.00*

Centenary of National Independence.

Pier at Puerto Colombia — R14

Tequendama Falls — R15

Perf. 11, 11½, 14, 11½x14

1917, Aug. 25

F23	R14 4c green & ultra	.55	*3.50*
a.	Center inverted	575.00	575.00
F24	R15 10c deep blue	8.00	.60

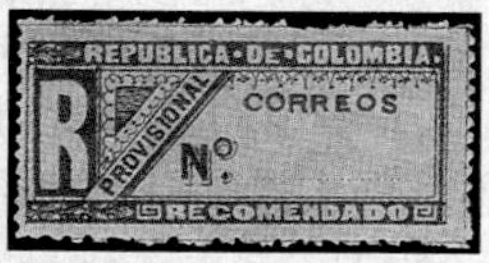

R16

1925 Litho. *Perf. 10x13½*

F25	R16 (10c) blue	4.25	1.90
a.	Imperf., pair	15.00	12.50
b.	Perf. 13½x10	7.50	5.00

ACKNOWLEDGMENT OF RECEIPT STAMPS

AR1

1893 Unwmk. Litho. *Perf. 13½*

H1	AR1 5c ver, *blue*	4.75	4.75

1894 *Perf. 12*

H2	AR1 5c vermilion	4.50	*5.00*

AR2

1902-03 *Imperf.*

H3	AR2 10c blue, *blue*	3.50	5.00
a.	10c, blue, *greenish blue*	3.50	5.00
b.	Sewing machine perf.	3.50	5.00
c.	Perf. 12	3.50	5.00

The handstamp "AR" in circle is believed to be a postmark.

AR2a

Purple Handstamp

1903 *Imperf.*

H4	AR2a 10c black, *pink*	25.00	25.00

AR3

1904 Pelure Paper *Imperf.*

H12	AR3 5c pale blue	10.50	10.50
a.	Perf. 12	10.50	10.50

No. 307 Overprinted in Black, Green or Violet

H13	A86 5c carmine	17.50	17.50

AR4

1904 *Perf. 12*

H16	AR4 5c blue	3.25	2.75
a.	Imperf., pair	8.75	8.75

For overprints see Nos. LH1-LH2.

General José Acevedo y Gómez — AR5

1910, July 20 Engr.

H17	AR5 5c orange & green	7.00	*17.50*

Centenary of National Independence.

Sabana Station AR6

Map of Colombia AR7

1917 *Perf. 14*

H18	AR6 4c bister brown	5.50	*6.00*
H19	AR7 5c orange brown	5.50	*4.50*
a.	Imperf., pair	14.00	

LATE FEE STAMPS

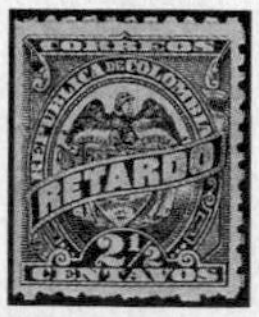

LF1

1886 Unwmk. Litho. *Perf. 10½*

I1	LF1 2½c blk, *lilac*	4.00	3.25
a.	Imperf., pair	15.00	15.00

LF2

1892 *Perf. 12, 13½*

I2	LF2 2½c dk bl, *rose*	3.50	2.50
a.	Imperf., pair	15.00	
I3	LF2 2½c ultra, *pink*	3.50	2.50

LF3

1902 *Imperf.*

I4	LF3 5c purple, *rose*	1.00	1.00
a.	Perf. 12	2.10	2.10

LF4

1914 *Perf. 10, 13½*

I6	LF4 2c vio brown	5.00	5.00
I7	LF4 5c blue green	5.00	4.25

Overprints illustrated above are unauthorized and of private origin.

POSTAGE DUE STAMPS

These are not, strictly speaking, postage due stamps but were issued to cover an additional fee, "Sobreporte," charged on mail to foreign countries with which Colombia had no postal conventions.

D1

D2

D3

1866 Unwmk. Litho. *Imperf.*

J1	D1 25c black, *blue*	80.00	55.00
J2	D2 50c black, *yellow*	55.00	*80.00*
J3	D3 1p black, *rose*	160.00	*125.00*
	Nos. J1-J3 (3)	295.00	260.00

DEPARTMENT STAMPS

These stamps are said to be for interior postage, to supersede the separate issues for the various departments.

Regular Issues Handstamped in Black, Violet, Blue or Green — a

On Stamps of 1904

1909 Unwmk. *Perf. 12*

L1	A94 ½c yellow	2.50	2.50
a.	Imperf., pair	7.50	7.50
L2	A94 1c yel grn	3.75	2.50
L3	A94 2c red	5.50	3.75
a.	Imperf., pair	15.00	15.00
L4	A94 5c blue	6.25	4.00
L5	A94 10c violet	8.75	8.75
L6	A94 20c black	14.00	14.00
L7	A95 1p brown	22.50	21.00

On Stamp of 1902

L8	A83 10p dk brn, *rose*	25.00	25.00
	Nos. L1-L8 (8)	88.25	81.50

On Stamps of 1908

Perf. 10, 13, 13½ and Compound

L9	A94 ½c orange	2.90	2.90
a.	Imperf., pair	7.50	7.50
L10	A94 1c green	5.00	5.00
a.	Without imprint	6.25	6.25
L11	A94 2c red	5.50	5.50
a.	Imperf., pair		
L12	A94 5c blue	5.50	5.50
a.	Imperf., pair	15.00	15.00
L13	A94 10c violet	8.75	8.75

On Tolima Stamp of 1888

Perf. 10½

L14	A23 1p red brn	27.50	27.50
	Nos. L9-L14 (6)	55.15	55.15

Regular Issues Handstamped — b

On Stamps of 1904

Perf. 12

L15	A94 ½c yellow	2.50	2.50
L16	A94 1c yellow grn	4.25	4.25
L17	A94 2c red	7.50	7.50
L18	A94 5c blue	7.50	7.50
L19	A94 10c violet	10.00	10.00
L20	A94 20c black	14.00	14.00
L21	A94 1p brown	25.00	25.00
	Nos. L15-L21 (7)	70.75	70.75

On Stamps of 1908

Perf. 10, 13, 13½

L22	A94 ½c orange	2.75	2.75
L23	A94 1c yellow grn	7.75	7.75
L24	A94 2c red	6.25	6.25
a.	Imperf., pair	15.00	15.00
L25	A94 5c light blue	7.50	7.50
	Nos. L22-L25 (4)	24.25	24.25

The handstamps on Nos. L1-L25 are, as usual, found inverted and double.

DEPARTMENT REGISTRATION STAMPS

Registration Stamps of 1904 Handstamped like Nos. L1-L25

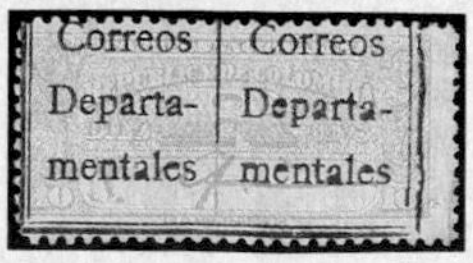

1909 Unwmk. *Perf. 12*

LF1	R12 (a) 10c purple	30.00	30.00
LF2	R12 (b) 10c purple	30.00	30.00

On Registration Stamp of 1909

Perf. 10, 13

LF3	R12 (a)	10c purple	30.00	30.00
LF4	R12 (b)	10c purple	30.00	30.00
		Nos. LF1-LF4 (4)	120.00	120.00

Nos. LF1-LF4 exist imperf. Value per pair, $125.

DEPARTMENT ACKNOWLEDGMENT OF RECEIPT STAMPS

Acknowledgment of Receipt Stamp of 1904 Hstmpd.

1909 Unwmk. *Perf. 12*

LH1	AR4 (a)	5c blue	30.00	30.00
a.		Imperf., pair	125.00	
LH2	AR4 (b)	5c blue	30.00	30.00
a.		Imperf., pair	125.00	

LOCAL STAMPS FOR THE CITY OF BOGOTA

A1

Pelure Paper

1889 Unwmk. Litho. *Perf. 12*

LX1	A1	½c black	1.10	1.10
a.		Imperf., pair	7.25	7.25

Impressions on bright blue and blue-gray paper were not regularly issued.

A2

White Wove Paper

1896 *Perf. 12, 13½*

LX2	A2	½c black	1.10	1.10

A3

1903 *Imperf.*

LX3	A3	10c black, *pink*	7.25	1.40
a.		Perf. 12	7.25	1.40

OFFICIAL STAMPS

Stamps of 1917-1937 Overprinted in Black or Red

a

b

1937 Unwmk. *Perf. 11, 12, 13½*

O1	A131 (a)	1c green	.25	.25
O2	A157 (a)	10c dp org	.25	.25
O3	A107 (b)	30c olive bis	2.10	1.00
O4	A129 (b)	40c brn & yel brn	1.60	.80
O5	A114 (b)	50c car	1.60	.80
O6	A107 (b)	1p lt bl	13.00	5.50
O7	A107 (b)	2p org	15.00	6.50
O8	A107 (b)	5p gray	47.50	*52.50*
O9	A118 (b)	10p dk brn	110.00	*125.00*

Wmk. 229

Perf. 12½

O10	A132 (a)	2c red	.25	.25
O11	A133 (a)	5c brn	.25	.25
O12	A160 (a)	12c dp bl (R)	1.00	.50
O13	A136 (b)	20c dk bl (R)	1.60	.80
		Nos. O1-O13 (13)	194.40	194.40

Tall, wrong font "I's" in OFICIAL exist on all stamps with "a" overprint.

POSTAL TAX STAMPS

"Greatest Mother" PT1

Perf. 11½

1935, May 27 Unwmk. Litho.

RA1	PT1	5c olive blk & scar	4.00	1.25

Required on all mail during Red Cross Week in 1935 (May 27-June 3) and in 1936.

Mother and Child — PT2

Perf. 10½, 10½x11

1937, May 24 Unwmk.

RA2	PT2	5c red	2.75	.90

Required on all mail during Red Cross Week. The tax was for the Red Cross.

Ministry of Posts and Telegraphs Building — PT3

1939-45 Litho. *Perf. 10½, 12½*

RA3	PT3	¼c dp bl	.25	.25
RA3A	PT3	¼c dk vio brn ('45)	.25	.25
RA4	PT3	½c pink	.25	.25
RA5	PT3	1c violet	.30	.25
RA5A	PT3	1c yel org ('45)	1.75	.70
RA6	PT3	2c pck grn	.55	.25
RA7	PT3	20c lt brn	4.50	1.50
		Nos. RA3-RA7 (7)	7.85	3.45

Obligatory on all mail. The tax was for the construction of the new Communications Building.

The 25c of type PT3 and PT4 were not usable on postal matter.

For overprint see No. 561.

Ministry of Posts and Telegraphs Building — PT4

Perf. 12½x13

1940, Jan. 20 Engr. Wmk. 229

RA8	PT4	¼c ultra	.25	.25
RA9	PT4	½c carmine	.25	.25
RA10	PT4	1c violet	.25	.25
RA11	PT4	2c bl grn	.30	.25
RA12	PT4	20c brown	1.25	.25
		Nos. RA8-RA12 (5)	2.30	1.25

See note after No. RA7. See No. RA18.

"Protection" — PT5

1940, Apr. 25 Wmk. 255 *Perf. 12*

RA13	PT5	5c rose carmine	.30	.25

See No. RA17.

Postal Tax Stamps of 1939 Surcharged in Black

1943 Unwmk. *Perf. 10½*

RA14	PT3	½c on 1c violet	.25	.25
a.		Inverted surcharge	2.00	
RA15	PT3	½c on 2c pck grn	.25	.25
RA16	PT3	½c on 20c lt brn	.25	.25
		Nos. RA14-RA16 (3)	.75	.75

Types of 1940

Imprint: "Litografia Colombia Bogota S.A."

1944 Litho. *Perf. 11*

RA17	PT5	5c dark rose	.40	.25

Imprint: "Lito-Colombia Bogota-Colombia"

RA18	PT4	¼c ultra	.25	.25

Ministry of Posts and Telegraphs Building — PT6

1945-48 Wmk. 255 Engr. *Perf. 12*

RA19	PT6	¼c ultra	.25	.25
RA20	PT6	¼c sepia ('46)	.25	.25
RA21	PT6	½c car rose	.25	.25
RA22	PT6	½c dp mag ('46)	.25	.25
RA23	PT6	1c vio ('46)	.25	.25
RA23A	PT6	1c red org ('46)	.25	.25
RA24	PT6	2c grn ('46)	.25	.25
RA25	PT6	20c brn ('47)	7.50	.30
a.		20c red brown ('48)	.70	.25
		Nos. RA19-RA25 (8)	9.25	2.05

These stamps were obligatory on all mail. The surtax was for the construction of the new Communications Building. See Nos. 603, RA33. For overprints see Nos. 562-564.

No. 469 Overprinted in Carmine

1946, May 25

RA26	A176	5c dull brown	.45	.25

The surtax was for the Red Cross.

Ministry of Posts and Telegraphs Building — PT7

1946 Unwmk. Litho. *Perf. 11*

RA27	PT7	3c blue	.25	.25

No. 490 Overprinted in Carmine

1947 Wmk. 255 *Perf. 12*

RA28	A196	20c gray black	5.25	2.90

Arms of Colombia and Red Cross — PT8

Perf. 12½

1947, Sept. Unwmk. Engr.

RA29	PT8	5c car lake	.25	.25

The surtax of Nos. RA29 and RA40 was for the Red Cross. See No. RA40.

No. 466 Overprinted in Carmine

RA30	A136	20c dark blue	32.50	20.00

Catalogue values for unused stamps in this section, from this point to the end of the section, are for Never Hinged items.

Type of 1945

1947 Wmk. 255 Engr. *Perf. 12*

RA33	PT6	1c olive bister	.30	.25

Black Surcharge — PT9

1948 Unwmk. Litho. *Perf. 11*

RA36	PT9	1c on 5c lt brn	.30	.25
RA37	PT9	1c on 10c lt vio	.30	.25
RA38	PT9	1c on 25c red	.30	.25
RA39	PT9	1c on 50c ultra	.30	.25
		Nos. RA36-RA39 (4)	1.20	1.00

Type of 1947

1948 *Perf. 10½*

RA40	PT8	5c vermilion	.25	.25

Ministry of Posts and Telegraphs Building — PT10

1948-50 Wmk. 255 Engr. *Perf. 12*

RA41	PT10	1c rose car ('49)	.30	.25
RA42	PT10	2c green ('50)	.30	.25
RA43	PT10	3c blue	.30	.25
RA44	PT10	5c gray	.30	.25
RA45	PT10	10c purple	.30	.25
		Nos. RA41-RA45 (5)	1.50	1.25

A 25c stamp of type PT10 was for use on telegrams, later for regular postage. See Nos. 602, 604. For overprints and surcharge see Nos. C227-C230, C238, C283, RA51.

Mother and Child — PT11

Dark Blue Surcharge

Unwmk.

1950, May 25 Litho. *Perf. 11*

RA46 PT11 5c on 2c gray, red, blk & yel 1.25 .40
a. "195" instead of "1950" 2.50 2.50
b. Top bar and "19" of "1950" omitted 2.50 2.50

Marginal perforations omitted, creating 26 straight-edged stamps in each sheet of 44. Surtax for Red Cross.

No. 574 Overprinted in Black

1950, May 26 Wmk. 255 *Perf. 12*

RA47 A176 5c blue .25 .25
a. Inverted overprint 8.00

Telegraph Stamp Surcharged in Black

RA48 A253a 8c on 50c org yel .25 .25

Fiscal stamps of type A253a were available for postal use after May 9, 1952. See Nos. 605-608.

Arms and Cross — PT12

Bartolome de Las Casas Aiding Youth — PT13

Perf. 12½

1951, May Unwmk. Engr.

RA49 PT12 5c red .25 .25
RA50 PT13 5c carmine .25 .25

The surtax was for the Red Cross.

No. RA43 Surcharged in Black

1951 Wmk. 255 *Perf. 12*

RA51 PT10 1c on 3c blue .25 .25

Type of 1951

Engraved; Cross Lithographed

1953 Unwmk. *Perf. 12½*

RA52 PT13 5c grn & car .35 .25

Surtax of Nos. RA52-RA60 for the Red Cross.

No. C254 Overprinted in Carmine

1954

RA53 AP42 5c lilac rose 2.00 .90

St. Peter Claver Offering Gifts to Slaves — PT14

Engraved; Cross Typographed

1955, May 2 Unwmk. *Perf. 13*

RA54 PT14 5c dp plum & red .30 .25

Death of St. Peter Claver, 300th anniv.

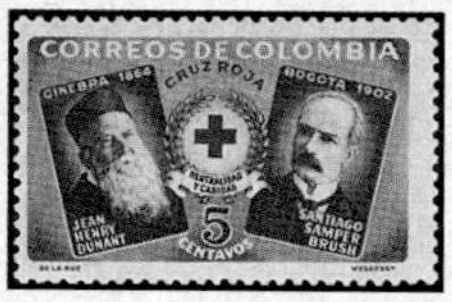

Jean Henri Dunant and Santiago Samper Brush PT15

Photo.; Red Cross & "Cruz Roja" Engr.

1956, June 1 Unwmk. *Perf. 13*

RA55 PT15 5c brown & red .45 .25

Nurses and Ambulances PT16

1958, June 2 Photo. *Perf. 12*

RA56 PT16 5c gray & red .25 .25

St. Louisa de Marillac and Church PT17

No. RA58, Henri Dunant and battle scene.

1960, Sept. 1 Litho. *Perf. 11*

RA57 PT17 5c brown & rose .30 .25
RA58 PT17 5c vio blue & rose .30 .25

No. RA57 for 3rd cent. of the Sisters of Charity. No. RA58 for cent. (in 1959) of the Red Cross idea.

Manuelita de la Cruz — PT18

1961, Nov. 2 Engr. *Perf. 13*

RA59 PT18 5c dull pur & red .25 .25
RA60 PT18 5c brown & red .25 .25

Issued in memory of Red Cross Nurse Manuelita de la Cruz, who died in the line of duty during the floods of 1955. Obligatory on domestic mail for a month.

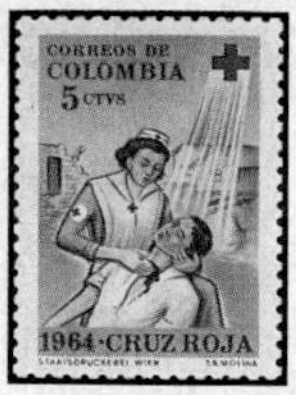

Red Cross Worker, Patient — PT19

1965, Apr. 30 Photo. *Perf. 12*

RA61 PT19 5c blue gray & red .25 .25

Obligatory on domestic mail during May.

Nurse's Cap — PT20

1967, June 1 Litho. *Perf. 12*

RA62 PT20 5c brt bl & red .25 .25

Red Cross — PT21

1969, July 1 Litho. *Perf. 12x12½*

RA63 PT21 5c vio bl & red .25 .25

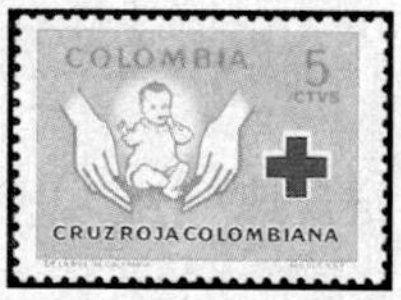

Child Care — PT22

1970, July 1 Litho. *Perf. 12½x12*

RA64 PT22 5c light bl & red .25 .25

ANTIOQUIA

ant-ē-'ō-kē-ə

Originally a State, now a Department of the Republic of Colombia. Until the revolution of 1885, the separate states making up the United States of Colombia were sovereign governments in their own right. On August 4, 1886, the National Council of Bogotá, composed of two delegates from each state, adopted a new constitution which abolished the sovereign rights of states, which then became departments with governors appointed by the President of the Republic. The nine original states represented at the Bogotá Convention retained some of their previous rights, as management of their own finances, and all issued postage stamps until as late as 1904. For Panama's issues, see Panama Nos. 1-30.

Coat of Arms
A1 A2

A3

A4

Wove Paper

1868 Unwmk. Litho. *Imperf.*

1 A1 2½c blue 1,000. 750.
2 A2 5c green 750. 575.
3 A3 10c lilac 3,000. 1,000.
4 A4 1p red 675. 750.

Reprints of Nos. 1, 3 and 4 are on a bluish white paper and all but No. 3 have scratches across the design.

A5

A6

A7

A8

A9

A10

1869

5 A5 2½c blue 3.75 3.25
6 A6 5c green 5.50 5.00
7 A7 5c green 5.50 5.00
8 A8 10c lilac 7.25 3.50
9 A9 20c brown 7.25 3.50
10 A10 1p rose red 14.50 13.00
a. 1p vermilion 27.50 25.00
Nos. 5-10 (6) 43.75 33.25

Reprints of Nos. 7, 8 and 10 are on a bluish white paper; reprints of Nos. 5 and 10a on white paper. The 10c blue is believed to be a reprint.

A11

A12

A13

A14

A15

A16

A17

A18

1873

12 A11 1c yellow grn 5.25 4.00
a. 1c green 5.25 4.00
13 A12 5c green 8.75 6.50
14 A13 10c lilac 25.00 21.00
15 A14 20c yellow brn 8.75 7.50
a. 20c dark brown 8.75 7.50

16	A15	50c blue	2.00	1.75
17	A16	1p vermilion	3.75	3.00
18	A17	2p black, *yellow*	8.75	8.00
19	A18	5p black, *rose*	65.00	55.00

A19

A20

Liberty Head
A21 A22

Pedro Justo Berrio — A23

1875-85

20	A19	1c blk, *grn*, unglazed ('76)	1.60	2.40
a.		Glazed paper	2.60	3.25
b.		1c blk, *lt grn*, laid paper ('85)	3.75	3.50
21	A19	1c black ('76)	1.10	1.00
a.		Laid paper	160.00	110.00
22	A19	1c bl grn ('85)	2.50	4.00
23	A19	1c red lil, laid paper ('85)	2.50	4.00
24	A20	2½c blue	2.50	1.90
a.		Pelure paper ('78)	*1,500.*	*1,100.*
25	A21	5c green	16.00	14.50
a.		Laid paper	160.00	87.50
26	A22	5c green	16.00	14.50
a.		Laid paper	160.00	87.50
27	A23	10c lilac	25.00	21.00
a.		Laid paper	160.00	125.00
28	A20	10c vio, pelure paper ('78)	*900.00*	675.00

Arms — A24

Liberty — A25

A26

A27

1878-85

29	A24	2½c blue, pelure paper	2.75	2.50
30	A24	2½c green ('83)	2.50	2.10
a.		Laid paper ('83)	80.00	55.00
31	A24	2½c blk, *buff* ('85)	7.25	6.50
32	A25	5c green ('83)	4.50	4.00
a.		Pelure paper	32.50	27.50
b.		Laid paper ('82)	40.00	13.00
33	A25	5c violet ('83)	9.50	7.50
a.		5c blue violet ('83)	9.50	7.50
34	A26	10c vio, laid paper ('82)	190.00	65.00
35	A26	10c scar ('83)	2.50	2.10
a.		Tete beche pair	110.00	110.00
36	A27	20c brown ('83)	4.50	4.00
a.		Laid paper ('82)	6.00	5.50

A28

A29

Liberty — A30

Coat of Arms — A31

1883-85

37	A28	5c brown	5.25	3.50
a.		Laid paper	225.00	87.50
38	A28	5c green ('85)	140.00	45.00
a.		Laid paper ('85)	160.00	75.00
39	A28	5c yel, laid paper ('85)	5.50	4.50
40	A29	10c bl grn, laid paper	5.50	4.75
41	A29	10c bl, *bl* ('85)	5.50	4.50
42	A29	10c lil, laid paper ('85)	12.00	7.50
a.		Wove paper ('85)	125.00	80.00
43	A30	20c bl, laid paper ('85)	4.50	4.00

1886 **Wove Paper**

55	A31	1c grn, *pink*	.65	.55
56	A31	2½c blk, *orange*	.65	.55
57	A31	5c ultra, *buff*	2.00	1.75
a.		5c blue, *buff*	3.75	3.25
58	A31	10c rose, *buff*	1.75	1.60
a.		Transfer of 50c in stone of 10c	140.00	140.00
59	A31	20c dk vio, *buff*	1.75	1.60
61	A31	50c yel brn, *buff*	3.25	2.75
62	A31	1p yel, *grn*	5.25	4.50
63	A31	2p green, *vio*	5.25	4.50
		Nos. 55-63 (8)	20.55	17.80

1887-88

64	A31	1c red, *vio*	.50	.45
65	A31	2½c lil, *pale lil*	.50	*.60*
66	A31	5c car, *buff*	.65	.65
67	A31	5c red, *grn*	3.75	1.75
68	A31	10c brn, *grn*	.85	*.80*
		Nos. 64-68 (5)	6.05	4.25

Medellin Issue

A32

A33

A34

1888 **Typeset**

69	A32	2½c blk, *yellow*	16.00	14.50
70	A33	5c blk, *yellow*	8.75	7.50
71	A34	5c red, *yellow*	5.25	4.50
		Nos. 69-71 (3)	30.00	26.50

Two varieties of No. 69, six of No. 70 and ten of No. 71.

A35

1889

72	A35	2½c red	8.00	6.75

Ten varieties including "eentavos."

Regular Issue

Coat of Arms — A36

1889 **Litho.** ***Perf. 13½***

73	A36	1c blk, *rose*	.25	.25
74	A36	2½c blk, *blue*	.25	.25
75	A36	5c blk, *yellow*	.30	.30
76	A36	10c blk, *green*	.30	.30
		Nos. 73-76 (4)	1.10	1.10

A37

A38

A39

A40

Coat of Arms — A41

1890

78	A37	20c blue	1.40	1.40
79	A38	50c vio brn	2.50	2.50
a.		Transfer of 20c in stone of 50c	95.00	95.00
80	A38	50c green	2.25	2.25
81	A39	1p red	2.00	2.00
82	A40	2p blk, *mag*	14.50	14.50
83	A41	5p blk, *org red*	22.50	22.50
		Nos. 78-83 (6)	45.15	45.15

Nos. 73-76, 82-83 exist imperf.

The so-called "errors" of Nos. 73 to 76, printed on paper of wrong colors, are essays or, possibly, reprints. They exist perforated and imperforate.

See No. 96.

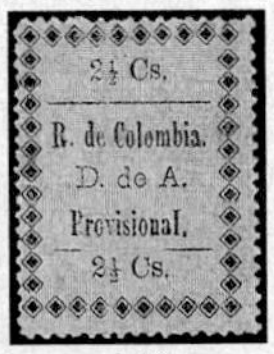
A42

A43

A44

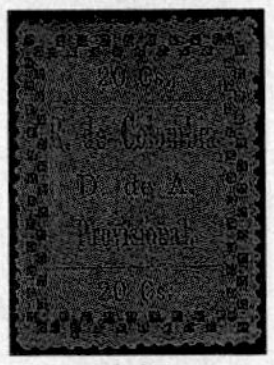
A45

1890 **Typeset** ***Perf. 14***

84	A42	2½c blk, *buff*	2.25	2.25
85	A43	5c blk, *orange*	2.25	2.25
86	A44	10c blk, *buff*	7.00	7.00
87	A44	10c blk, *rose*	9.00	9.00
88	A45	20c blk, *orange*	9.00	9.00
		Nos. 84-88 (5)	29.50	29.50

20 varieties of the 5c, 10 each of the other values.

A46

1892 **Litho.** ***Perf. 13½***

89	A46	1c brn, *brnsh*	.40	.40
90	A46	2½c pur, *lil*	.40	.40
92	A46	5c blk, *gray*	1.10	.55
a.		Transfer of 2½c in stone of 5c	200.00	
		Nos. 89-92 (3)	1.90	1.35

1893

93	A46	1c blue	.25	.25
94	A46	2½c green	.40	.40
95	A46	5c vermilion	.25	.25
96	A36	10c pale brown	.25	.25
		Nos. 93-96 (4)	1.15	1.15

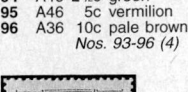

A47

1896 ***Perf. 14***

97	A47	2c gray	.25	.25
98	A47	2c lilac rose	.25	.25
99	A47	2½c brown	.25	.25
100	A47	2½c steel blue	.25	.25
101	A47	3c orange	.25	.25
102	A47	3c olive grn	.25	.25
103	A47	5c green	.25	.25
104	A47	5c yellow buff	.30	.30
105	A47	10c brown vio	.55	.55
106	A47	10c violet	.55	.55
107	A47	20c brown org	1.40	1.40
108	A47	20c blue	1.40	1.40
109	A47	50c gray brn	1.40	1.40
110	A47	50c rose	1.40	1.40
111	A47	1p blue & blk	17.50	17.50
112	A47	1p rose red & blk	17.50	17.50
113	A47	2p orange & blk	55.00	55.00
114	A47	2p dk grn & blk	55.00	55.00
115	A47	5p red vio & blk	95.00	95.00
116	A47	5p purple & blk	95.00	95.00
		Nos. 97-116 (20)	343.75	343.75

#115-116 with centers omitted are proofs.

General José María Córdoba — A48

1899 ***Perf. 11***

117	A48	½c grnsh bl	.25	.25
118	A48	1c slate blue	.25	.25
119	A48	2c slate brown	.25	.25
120	A48	3c red	.25	.25
121	A48	4c bister brown	.25	.25
122	A48	5c green	.25	.25
123	A48	10c scarlet	.25	.25
124	A48	20c gray violet	.25	.25
125	A48	50c olive bister	.25	.25
126	A48	1p greenish blk	.25	.25
127	A48	2p olive gray	.25	.25
		Nos. 117-127 (11)	2.75	2.75

Numerous part-perf. and imperf. varieties of Nos. 117-127 exist.

Used values for Nos. 117-127 are for favor-canceled stamps with oval cancels in violet. Postally used examples are valued at $1.75 each.

A49

A50

A50a

1901 **Typeset** ***Perf. 12***

128	A49	1c red	.25	.25
129	A50	1c ultra	.65	.65
130	A50	1c bister	.65	.65
130A	A50a	1c dull red	.65	.65
130B	A50a	1c ultra	4.50	4.50
		Nos. 128-130B (5)	6.70	6.70

Eight varieties of No. 128, four varieties of Nos. 129-130B.

A51

A52

Atanasio Girardot
A53

Dr. José Félix Restrepo
A54

1902 Litho. Wove Paper

131	A51 1c brt rose	.25	.25
a.	Laid paper	.65	.65
b.	Imperf., pair	2.75	
132	A51 2c blue	.25	.25
a.	Transfer of 3c in stone of 2c	6.00	6.00
133	A51 3c green	.25	.25
a.	Imperf., pair	5.00	
134	A51 4c dull violet	.25	.25
135	A52 5c rose red	.25	.25
136	A53 10c rose lilac	.25	.25
a.	Small head	5.75	5.75
b.	10c rose	.25	.25
137	A53 20c gray green	.25	.25
138	A53 30c brt rose	.25	.25
139	A53 40c blue	.25	.25
140	A53 50c brn, *yel*	.25	.25

Laid Paper

141	A54 1p purple & blk	.80	.80
142	A54 2p rose & blk	.80	.80
143	A54 5p sl bl & blk	1.50	1.50
	Nos. 131-143 (13)	5.60	5.60

1903 Wove Paper

143A	A51 1c blue	.25	.25
144	A51 2c violet	.25	.25
a.	Imperf.	3.00	

A55

A56

A57

Designs: 1p, Francisco Antonio Zea. 2p, Custodio Garcia Rovira. 3p, La Pola (Policarpa Salavarrieta). 4p, J. M. Restrepo. 5p, José Fernández Madrid. 10p, Juan del Corral.

1903-04

145	A55 4c yellow brn	.35	.30
146	A55 5c blue	.35	.30
147	A56 10c yellow	.35	.30
148	A56 20c purple	.35	.30
149	A56 30c brown	.90	.85
150	A56 40c green	.90	.85
151	A56 50c rose	.35	.30
152	A57 1p olive gray	.90	.85
153	A57 2p purple	.90	.85
154	A57 3p dark blue	.90	.85
155	A57 4p dull red	1.50	1.50
156	A57 5p red brown	4.50	2.10
157	A57 10p scarlet	9.25	5.25
	Nos. 145-157 (13)	21.50	14.60

Nos. 145-146, 151, 153-157 exist imperf. Value of pairs, $4 to $5.

Manizales Issue

Stamps of these designs are local private post issues.

OFFICIAL STAMPS Stamps of 1903-04 with overprint "OFICIAL" were never issued.

REGISTRATION STAMPS

R1

1896 Unwmk. Litho. *Perf. 14*

F1	R1 2½c rose	1.25	1.25
F2	R1 2½c dull blue	1.25	1.25

Córdoba
R2

R3

1899 *Perf. 11*

F3	R2 2½c dull blue	.25	.25
F4	R3 10c red lilac	.25	.25

R4

1902 *Perf. 12*

F5	R4 10c purple, *blue*	.30	.30
a.	Imperf.	—	

ACKNOWLEDGMENT OF RECEIPT STAMPS

AR1

1902-03 Unwmk. Litho. *Perf. 12*

H1	AR1 5c black, *rose*	1.10	1.10
H2	AR1 5c slate ('03)	.35	.35

LATE FEE STAMPS

Córdoba — LF1

1899 Unwmk. Litho. *Perf. 11*

I1	LF1 2½c dark green	.30	.30
a.	Imperf., pair	3.00	

LF2

1901 Typeset *Perf. 12*

I2	LF2 2½c red violet	.80	.80
a.	2½c purple	.80	.80

LF3

1902 Litho.

I3	LF3 2½c violet	.25	.25

City of Medellin

Stamps of the designs shown were not issued by any governmental agency but by the Sociedad de Mejoras Publicas.

BOLIVAR

bə-'lē-,vär

Originally a State, now a Department of the Republic of Colombia. (See Antioquia.)

A1

1863-66 Unwmk. Litho. *Imperf.*

1	A1 10c green	*1,200.*	*600.00*
a.	Five stars below shield	*2,500.*	*2,400.*
2	A1 10c red ('66)	27.50	*30.00*
a.	Diagonal half used as 5c on cover		120.00
b.	Five stars below shield	80.00	72.50
3	A1 1p red	6.75	*7.75*

Fourteen varieties of each. Counterfeits of Nos. 1 and 1a exist.

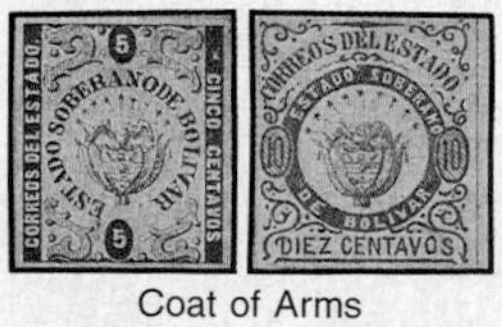
Coat of Arms
A2 A3

A4

A5

1873

4	A2 5c blue	7.25	7.25
5	A3 10c violet	7.25	7.25
6	A4 20c yellow green	32.50	32.50
7	A5 80c vermilion	65.00	65.00
	Nos. 4-7 (4)	112.00	112.00

A6

A7

A8

1874-78

8	A6 5c blue	27.50	14.00
9	A7 5c blue ('78)	8.00	7.25
10	A8 10c violet ('77)	4.00	3.75
	Nos. 8-10 (3)	39.50	25.00

Bolívar — A9

Dated "1879"

1879 White Wove Paper *Perf. 12½*

11	A9 5c blue	.30	.30
a.	Imperf., pair	.90	
12	A9 10c violet	.25	.25
13	A9 20c red	.30	.30
a.	20c green (error)	11.00	11.00

Bluish Laid Paper

15	A9 5c blue	.30	.30
a.	Imperf., pair	2.25	
16	A9 10c violet	1.60	1.60
a.	Imperf., pair	4.50	
17	A9 20c red	.40	.40
a.	Imperf., pair	2.00	
	Nos. 11-17 (6)	3.15	3.15

Stamps of 80c and 1p on white wove paper and 1p on bluish laid paper were prepared but not placed in use.

Dated "1880"

1880 White Wove Paper *Perf. 12½*

19	A9 5c blue	.30	.30
a.	Imperf., pair	1.60	
20	A9 10c violet	.40	.40
a.	Imperf., pair	1.60	
21	A9 20c red	.40	.40
a.	20c green (error)	14.00	14.00
23	A9 80c green	2.50	2.50
24	A9 1p orange	2.75	2.75
a.	Imperf., pair	5.50	
	Nos. 19-24 (5)	6.35	6.35

Bluish Laid Paper

25	A9 5c blue	.30	.30
a.	Imperf., pair	1.40	
26	A9 10c violet	2.50	2.50
27	A9 20c red	.40	.40
a.	Imperf., pair	3.00	
28	A9 1p orange	450.00	
a.	Imperf.	*475.00*	

A11

A12

A13

A15

A16

Dated "1882"
White Wove Paper

1882	Perf. 12, 16x12		
29	A11 5c blue	.35	.35
30	A12 10c lilac	.25	.25
31	A13 20c red	.35	.35
33	A15 80c green	.65	.65
34	A16 1p orange	.65	.65
	Nos. 29-34 (5)	2.25	2.25

Nos. 29, 30 and 34 are known imperforate. They are printer's waste and were not issued through post offices.

A17

1882	Engr. Perf. 12		
35	A17 5p blue & rose red	.65	.65
a.	Imperf., pair	5.25	
b.	Perf. 16	8.00	6.75
c.	Perf. 14	6.75	6.75
36	A17 10p brown & blue	1.75	1.75
a.	Imperf., pair	8.75	
b.	Perf. 16	7.25	6.00
c.	Rouletted	8.75	8.75

Dated "1883"

1883	Litho. Perf. 12, 16x12		
37	A11 5c blue	.25	.25
a.	Imperf., pair	1.00	
b.	Perf. 12	12.00	2.40
38	A12 10c lilac	.30	.30
39	A13 20c red	.30	.30
41	A15 80c green	.30	.30
42	A16 1p orange	1.60	1.60
a.	Perf. 16x12	2.25	2.25
	Nos. 37-42 (5)	2.75	2.75

1884	Dated "1884"		
43	A11 5c blue	.30	.30
a.	Perf. 12	16.00	16.00
44	A12 10c lilac	.25	.25
45	A13 20c red	.25	.25
a.	Perf. 12	8.00	8.00
47	A15 80c green	.30	.35
a.	Perf. 12	4.00	4.00
48	A16 1p orange	.30	.30
	Nos. 43-48 (5)	1.40	1.45

1885	Dated "1885"		
49	A11 5c blue	.25	.25
50	A12 10c lilac	.25	.25
51	A13 20c red	.25	.25
53	A15 80c green	.25	.25
54	A16 1p orange	.30	.30
	Nos. 49-54 (5)	1.30	1.30

The note after No. 34 will also apply to imperforate stamps of the 1884-85 issues.

A18

1891	Perf. 14		
55	A18 1c black	.30	.30
56	A18 5c orange	.30	.30
a.	Imperf., pair	.90	
57	A18 10c carmine	.30	.30
58	A18 20c blue	.65	.65
59	A18 50c green	.95	.95
60	A18 1p purple	.95	.95
	Nos. 55-60 (6)	3.45	3.45

For overprint see Colombia No. 169.

Bolívar A19

José Fernández Madrid A20

Manuel Rodriguez Torices A21

José María García de Toledo A22

1903	Laid Paper Imperf.		
62	A19 50c dk bl, *pink*	.65	.65
a.	Bluish paper	.65	.65
63	A19 50c sl grn, *pink*	.65	.65
a.	Rose paper	2.25	2.25
b.	Greenish blue paper	3.25	3.25
c.	Yellow paper	4.50	4.50
d.	Brown paper	4.50	4.50
e.	Salmon paper	8.00	8.00
64	A19 50c pur, *pink*	2.25	2.25
a.	White paper	4.50	4.50
b.	Brown paper	4.50	4.50
c.	Greenish blue paper	4.50	4.50
d.	Lilac paper	4.50	4.50
e.	Rose paper	4.00	4.00
f.	Yellow paper	4.50	4.50
g.	Salmon paper	6.50	6.50
h.	As "a," wove paper	9.75	9.75
65	A20 1p org, *sal*	.65	.65
a.	Yellow paper	5.00	5.00
b.	Greenish blue paper	16.00	16.00
66	A20 1p gray grn, *lil*	1.60	1.60
a.	Yellow paper	7.00	7.00
b.	Salmon paper	8.00	8.00
c.	Green paper	8.00	8.00
d.	White wove paper	12.00	
67	A21 5p car rose, *lil*	.65	.65
a.	Brown paper	1.25	1.25
b.	Yellow paper	1.25	1.25
c.	Greenish blue paper	5.00	5.00
d.	Bluish paper	6.50	6.50
e.	Salmon paper	8.00	8.00
f.	Rose paper	9.75	9.75
68	A22 10p dk bl, *bluish*	1.40	1.40
a.	Greenish blue paper	1.40	1.40
b.	Rose paper	8.00	8.00
c.	Salmon paper	8.00	8.00
d.	Yellow paper	8.00	8.00
e.	Brown paper	9.00	9.00
f.	Lilac paper	12.00	12.00
g.	White paper	9.75	9.75
69	A22 10p pur, *grnsh bl*	3.75	3.75
a.	Bluish paper	8.00	8.00
b.	Rose paper	7.25	7.25
c.	Yellow paper	8.00	8.00
d.	Brown paper	8.00	8.00
	Nos. 62-69 (8)	11.60	11.60

Sewing Machine Perf.
Laid Paper

70	A19 50c dk bl, *pink*	1.10	1.10
a.	Bluish paper	1.10	1.10
71	A19 50c sl grn, *pink*	2.25	2.25
72	A19 50c pur, *grnsh bl*	4.50	4.50
a.	White paper	4.50	4.50
b.	White wove paper	8.00	
73	A20 1p org, *sal*	2.25	2.25
74	A20 1p gray grn, *lil*	9.75	9.75
a.	Yellow paper	9.75	9.75
75	A21 5p car rose, *yel*	1.75	1.75
a.	Lilac paper	4.50	4.50
b.	Brown paper	4.50	4.50
c.	Bluish paper	6.00	6.00
d.	White wove paper	9.75	
76	A22 10p dk bl, *grnsh bl*	5.00	5.00
a.	Bluish paper	7.50	7.50
b.	Yellow paper	9.75	9.75
c.	As "b," wove paper	12.00	
77	A22 10p pur, *grnsh bl*	7.50	7.50
a.	Bluish paper	13.00	13.00
b.	Rose paper	8.50	8.50
c.	Yellow paper	13.00	13.00
	Nos. 70-77 (8)	34.10	34.10

José María del Castillo y Rada — A23

Manuel Anguiano — A24

Pantaleón C. Ribón — A25

1904	Sewing Machine Perf.		
89	A23 5c black	.25	.25
90	A24 10c brown	.25	.25
91	A25 20c red	.30	.30
92	A25 20c red brown	.65	.65
	Nos. 89-92 (4)	1.45	1.45

Imperf., pairs

89a	A23 5c black	4.00	4.00
90a	A24 10c brown	3.00	3.00
91a	A25 20c red	7.25	7.25
92a	A25 20c red brown	7.25	7.25

A26

A27

A28

1904	Imperf.		
93	A26 ½c black	.65	.65
a.	Tête bêche pair	3.75	3.75
94	A27 1c blue	1.25	1.25
95	A28 2c purple	1.40	1.40
	Nos. 93-95 (3)	3.30	3.30

REGISTRATION STAMPS

Simón Bolívar — R1

White Wove Paper
Perf. 12½, 16x12

1879	Unwmk. Litho.		
F1	R1 40c brown	.75	.75

Bluish Laid Paper

F2	R1 40c brown	.75	.75
a.	Imperf., pair	3.50	

Dated "1880"

1880	White Wove Paper		
F3	R1 40c brown	.35	.35

Bluish Laid Paper

F4	R1 40c brown	.75	.75
a.	Imperf., pair	3.50	

Simón Bolívar — R2

Dated "1882" to "1885"
White Wove Paper

1882-85	Perf. 16x12		
F5	R2 40c brown (1882)	.35	.35
F6	R2 40c brown (1883)	.30	.30
F7	R2 40c brown (1884)	.30	.30
F8	R2 40c brown (1885)	.30	.30
	Nos. F5-F8 (4)	1.25	1.25

Perf. 12

F5a	R2 40c	19.00	
F6a	R2 40c	16.00	
F7a	R2 40c	16.00	
F8a	R2 40c	16.00	
	Nos. F5a-F8a (4)	67.00	

R3

1903	Laid Paper Imperf.		
F9	R3 20c orange, *rose*	.65	.65
a.	Salmon paper	1.25	1.25
b.	Greenish blue paper	6.50	6.50

Sewing Machine Perf.

F10	R3 20c orange, *rose*	2.75	2.75
a.	Salmon paper	2.75	2.75
b.	Greenish blue paper	6.50	6.50

R4

1904	Wove Paper		
F11	R4 5c black	3.25	3.25

ACKNOWLEDGMENT OF RECEIPT STAMPS

AR1

1903	Unwmk. Litho. Imperf. Laid Paper		
H1	AR1 20c org, *rose*	2.75	2.75
a.	Yellow paper	1.40	1.40
b.	Greenish blue paper	5.50	5.50
H2	AR1 20c dk bl, *yel*	2.25	2.25
a.	Brown paper	3.75	3.75
b.	Rose paper	2.75	2.75
c.	Salmon paper	7.50	7.50
d.	Greenish blue paper	7.50	7.50

Sewing Machine Perf.

H3	AR1 20c org, *grnsh bl*	6.75	6.75
a.	Yellow paper	7.75	7.75
H4	AR1 20c dk bl, *yel*	7.75	7.75
a.	Lilac paper	7.75	7.75
	Nos. H1-H4 (4)	19.50	19.50

AR2

1904	Wove Paper		
H5	AR2 2c red	1.25	1.25

LATE FEE STAMPS

LF1

1903 Unwmk. Litho. *Imperf.*

Laid Paper

I1	LF1	20c car rose, *bluish*	.65	.65
I2	LF1	20c pur, *bluish*	.65	.65
a.		Rose paper	2.25	2.25
b.		Brown paper	2.25	2.25
c.		Lilac paper	2.25	2.25
d.		Yellow paper	7.00	7.00

Sewing Machine Perf.

I3	LF1	20c car rose, *bluish*	3.75	3.75
I4	LF1	20c pur, *bluish*	3.75	3.75
a.		Rose paper	6.50	6.50
b.		Lilac paper	6.50	6.50
c.		Yellow paper	12.00	12.00
		Nos. I1-I4 (4)	8.80	8.80

BOYACA

bō-yä-cä

Originally a State, now a Department of the Republic of Colombia. (See Antioquia.)

Diego Mendoza Pérez — A1

1902 Unwmk. Litho. *Perf. 13½*

Wove Paper

1	A1	5c blue green	.80	.80
a.		Bluish paper	95.00	95.00
b.		Imperf., pair	16.00	16.00

Laid Paper

Perf. 12

2	A1	5c green	110.00	110.00

Coat of Arms
A2 A3

Gen. Próspero Pinzón — A4

A5

Monument of Battle of Boyacá — A6

President José Manuel Marroquin — A7

1903 Litho. *Imperf.*

4	A2	10c dark gray	.30	.30
5	A3	20c red brown	.35	.35
6	A5	1p red	3.25	3.25
a.		1p claret	3.75	3.75
8	A6	5p black, *rose*	1.25	1.25
a.		5p black, *buff*	12.00	12.00
9	A7	10p black, *buff*	1.25	1.25
a.		10p black, *rose*	12.00	12.00
b.		As "a,"tête bêche pair	24.00	
		Nos. 4-9 (5)	6.40	6.40

Perf. 12

10	A2	10c dark gray	.35	.35
11	A3	20c red brown	.40	.40
12	A4	50c green	.35	.35
13	A4	50c dull blue	2.50	2.50
14	A5	1p red	.35	.35
a.		1p claret	3.00	3.00
16	A6	5p black, *rose*	11.00	11.00
a.		5p black, *buff*	9.50	9.50
17	A7	10p black, *buff*	1.10	1.10
a.		10p black, *rose*	11.00	11.00
b.		Tête bêche pair	12.00	12.00
		Nos. 10-17 (7)	16.05	16.05

Statue of Bolívar — A8

1904

18	A8	10c orange	.25	.25
a.		Imperf., pair	3.75	3.75

CAUCA

Stamps of these designs were issued by a provincial post between 1879(?) and 1890.

Stamps of this design are believed to be of private origin and without official sanction.

Items inscribed "No hay estampillas" (No stamps available) and others inscribed "Manuel E. Jiménez" are considered by specialists to be receipt labels, not postage stamps.

CUNDINAMARCA

kün-di-nə-'mär-kə

Originally a State, now a Department of the Republic of Colombia.

(See Antioquia.)

Coat of Arms
A1 A2

1870 Unwmk. Litho. *Imperf.*

1	A1	5c blue	5.25	5.25
2	A2	10c red	16.00	16.00

The counterfeits, or reprints, show traces of the cuts made to deface the dies.

A3

A4

A5

A6

1877-82

3	A3	10c red ('82)	3.50	3.50
a.		Laid paper ('77)	4.50	4.50
4	A4	20c green ('82)	7.50	7.50
a.		Laid paper ('77)	12.00	12.00
7	A5	50c purple ('82)	8.25	8.25
8	A6	1p brown ('82)	12.00	12.00
		Nos. 3-8 (4)	31.25	31.25

A7

Redrawn

1884

10	A7	5c blue	.80	.80
11	A7	5c blue (redrawn)	.80	.80
a.		Tête bêche pair	80.00	80.00

The redrawn stamp has no period after "COLOMBIA."

A8

A9

A10

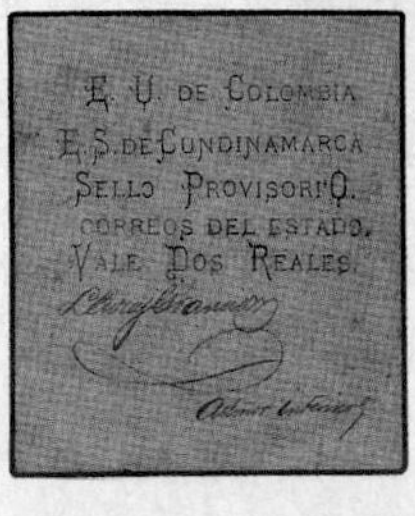

A11

1883 Typeset

13	A8	10c black, *yellow*	14.00	14.00
14	A9	50c black, *rose*	14.00	14.00
15	A10	1p black, *brown*	37.50	37.50
16	A11	2r black, *green*	*2,200.*	

Typeset varieties exist: 4 of the 10c, 2 each of 50c and 1p.

Some experts doubt that No. 16 was issued. The variety without signature and watermarked "flowers" is believed to be a proof. Forgeries exist.

A12

1886 Litho.

17	A12	5c blue	.80	.80
18	A12	10c red	5.00	5.00
19	A12	10c red, *lilac*	2.75	2.75
20	A12	20c green	4.25	4.25
a.		20c yellow green	5.00	5.00
21	A12	50c purple	5.50	5.50
22	A12	1p orange brown	5.75	5.75
		Nos. 17-22 (6)	24.05	24.05

Nos. 17 to 22 have been reprinted. The colors are aniline and differ from those of the original stamps. The impression is coarse and blurred.

A13

A14

A15

A16

A17

A18

A19

A20

A21

1904 *Perf. 10½, 12*

23	A13	1c orange	.25	.25
24	A14	2c gray blue	.25	.25
25	A15	3c rose	.35	.35
26	A15	5c olive grn	.35	.35
27	A16	10c pale brn	.35	.35
28	A17	15c pink	.35	.35
29	A18	20c blue, *grn*	.35	.35
30	A18	20c blue	.60	.60
31	A19	40c blue	.60	.60
32	A19	40c blue, *buff*	21.00	21.00
33	A20	50c red vio	.60	.60
34	A21	1p gray grn	.60	.60
		Nos. 23-34 (12)	25.65	25.65

Imperf

23a	A13	1c	orange	.75	.75
24a	A14	2c	blue	.75	.75
b.		2c	slate	6.50	6.50
25a	A15	3c	rose	.90	.90
26a	A15	5c	olive green	1.60	1.60
27a	A16	10c	pale brown	2.00	2.00
28a	A17	15c	pink	.50	.50
29a	A18	20c	blue, *green*	2.00	2.00
30a	A18	20c	blue	2.00	2.00
31a	A19	40c	blue	.70	.70
32a	A19	40c	blue, *buff*	21.00	21.00
33a	A20	50c	red violet	.70	.70
34a	A21	1p	gray green	.70	.70
			Nos. 23a-34a (12)	33.60	33.60

REGISTRATION STAMPS

R1

1883 Unwmk. *Imperf.*

F1	R1	black, *orange*	17.00	17.00

R2

1904 *Perf. 12*

F2	R2 10c	bister	.85	.85
a.		Imperf.	3.75	3.75

INSURED LETTER STAMP

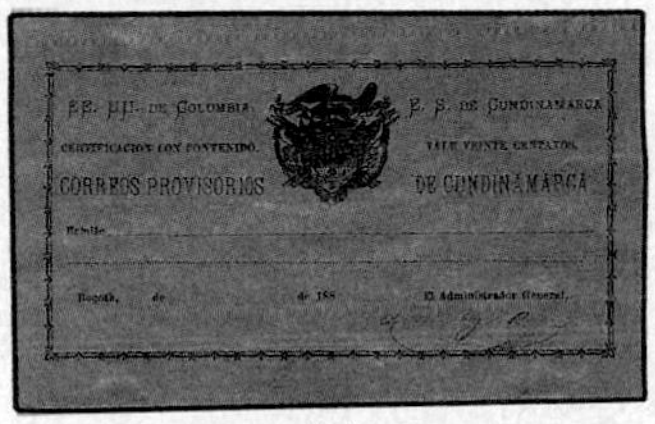

IL1

1883 *Imperf.*

Thin Paper with Vertical Mesh

G1	IL1	20c blk, *emerald grn*	80.00	120.00

Magdalena

Items inscribed "No hay estampillas" (No stamps available) are considered by specialists to be not postage stamps but receipt labels.

Panama

Issues of Panama as a state and later Department of Colombia are listed with the Republic of Panama issues (Nos. 1-30).

SANTANDER

săn-ˌtăn-ˈde̜ə̜r

Originally a State, now a Department of the Republic of Colombia.
(See Antioquia.)

Coat of Arms
A1 A2

1884 Unwmk. Litho. *Imperf.*

1	A1 1c blue		.30	.30
a.	1c gray blue		.50	.50
2	A2 5c red		.50	.50
3	A2 10c bluish purple		1.90	1.90
a.	Tête bêche pair		—	
	Nos. 1-3 (3)		2.70	2.70

No. 2 exists unofficially perforated 14.

A3

1886 *Imperf.*

4	A3	1c blue	.90	.90
5	A3	5c red	.30	.30
6	A3	10c red violet	.50	.50
a.		10c deep violet	.50	.50
b.		Inscribed "CINCO CENTAVOS"	26.00	26.00
		Nos. 4-6 (3)	1.70	1.70

The numerals in the upper corners are omitted on No. 5, while on No. 6 there are no numerals in the side panels. No. 6 exists unofficially perforated 12.

A4

1887

7	A4	1c blue	.25	.25
a.		1c ultramarine	1.75	1.75
8	A4	5c red	1.75	1.75
9	A4	10c violet	5.50	5.50
		Nos. 7-9 (3)	7.50	7.50

A5 A6

A7

1889 *Perf. 11½ and 13½*

10	A5	1c blue	.35	.35
11	A6	5c red	1.25	1.25
12	A7	10c purple	.45	.45
a.		Imperf., pair	16.00	*20.00*
		Nos. 10-12 (3)	2.05	2.05

A8

1892 *Perf. 13½*

13	A8	5c red, *rose buff*	1.00	1.00

A9

1895-96

14	A9	5c brown	.70	.70
15	A9	5c yel grn ('96)	.70	.70

A10 A11

A12

1899 *Perf. 10*

16	A10	1c black, *green*	.35	.35
17	A11	5c black, *pink*	.35	.35

Perf. 13½

18	A12	10c blue	.70	.70
a.		Perf. 12	1.00	1.00
		Nos. 16-18 (3)	1.40	1.40

A13

1903 *Imperf.*

19	A13	50c red	.60	.60
a.		50c rose	.60	.60
b.		"SANTENDER"	2.50	2.50
c.		"Corrcos"	2.50	2.50
d.		"Corceos"	2.50	2.50
e.		Tête bêche pair	4.75	4.75
f.		Pair, one without overprint	2.75	2.75

The overprint "Correos de Departmento Bucaramanga" on the 50c red revenue stamp has been proved to be a cancellation.

A14 A15

Arms
A16

Locomotive
A17

A18 A19

A20

1904 *Imperf.*

22	A14	5c dark green	.25	.25
a.		5c yellow green	.40	.40
24	A15	10c rose	.25	.25
25	A16	20c brown violet	.25	.25
26	A17	50c yellow	.25	.25
27	A18	1p black	.25	.25
28	A19	5p dark blue	.35	.35
29	A20	10p carmine	.40	.40
		Nos. 22-29 (7)	2.00	2.00

1905

30	A14	5c pale blue	.45	.45
31	A15	10c red brown	.45	.45
32	A16	20c yellow green	.45	.45
33	A17	50c red violet	.60	.60
34	A18	1p dark blue	.60	.60
35	A19	5p pink	.60	.60
36	A20	10p red	1.60	1.60
		Nos. 30-36 (7)	4.75	4.75

A21

1907 *Imperf.*

37	A21	½c on 50c rose	.80	*1.60*

City of Cucuta

Stamps of these and similar designs on white and yellow paper, with and without surcharges of ½c, 1c or 2c, are believed to have been produced without government authorization.

TOLIMA

tə-lē-mə

Originally a State, now a Department of the Republic of Colombia.
(See Antioquia.)

A1

1870 Unwmk. Typeset *Imperf.*

White Wove Paper

1	A1	5c black	62.50	62.50
2	A1	10c black	75.00	75.00
a.		Vert. se-tenant pair	1,500.	1,500.

Printed from two settings. Setting I, ten types of 5c. Setting II, six types of 5c and four types of 10c.

Blue Laid Batonné Paper

3	A1	5c black	*950.00*	

Buff Laid Batonné Paper

4	A1	5c black	150.00	100.00

Blue Wove Paper

5	A1	5c black	70.00	45.00

Blue Vertically Laid Paper

6	A1	5c black	110.00	70.00
a.		Paper with ruled blue vertical lines		

Blue Horizontally Laid Paper

7	A1	5c black	100.00	75.00

Blue Quadrille Paper

8	A1	5c black	150.00	80.00

Ten varieties each of Nos. 3-5 and 7; 20 varieties each of Nos. 6 and 8.

Official imitations were made in 1886 from new settings of the type. There are only 2 varieties of each value. They are printed on blue and white paper, wove, batonné, laid, etc.

A2 A3

A4 A5

Yellowish White Wove Paper

1871 Litho. *Imperf.*

9	A2	5c deep brown	2.25	2.25
a.		5c red brown	2.25	2.25
b.		Value reads "CINGO"	40.00	40.00

10 A3 10c blue 6.25 6.25
11 A4 50c green 8.00 8.00
12 A5 1p carmine 13.00 13.00
Nos. 9-12 (4) 29.50 29.50

The 5p stamps, type A2, are bogus varieties made from an altered die of the 5c.

The 10c, 50c and 1 peso stamps have been reprinted on bluish white wove paper. They are from new plates and most copies show traces of fine lines with which the dies had been defaced. Reprints of the 5c have a large cross at the top. The 10c on laid batonné paper is known only as a reprint.

A6

A7

A8

A9

1879

Grayish or White Wove Paper

14 A6 5c yellow brown .45 .45
a. 5c purple brown .45 .45
15 A7 10c blue .50 .50
16 A8 50c green, *bluish* .50 .50
a. White paper 1.60 1.60
17 A9 1p vermilion 2.25 2.25
a. 1p carmine rose 9.00 9.00
Nos. 14-17 (4) 3.70 3.70

A10

1883 ***Imperf.***

18 A6 5c orange .45 .45
19 A7 10c vermilion .95 .95
20 A10 20c violet 1.50 1.50
Nos. 18-20 (3) 2.90 2.90

Coat of Arms — A12

1884 ***Imperf.***

23 A12 1c gray .25 .25
24 A12 2c rose lilac .25 .25
a. 2c slate .25 .25
25 A12 2½c dull orange .25 .25
26 A12 5c brown .25 .25
27 A12 10c blue .35 .35
a. 10c slate .25 .25
28 A12 20c lemon .35 .35
a. Laid paper 5.00 5.00
29 A12 25c black .30 .30
30 A12 50c green .30 .30
31 A12 1p vermilion .40 .40
32 A12 2p violet .60 .60
a. Value omitted 30.00 30.00
33 A12 5p yellow .40 .40
34 A12 10p lilac rose 1.10 1.10
a. Laid paper 30.00 30.00
b. 10p gray *175.00*
Nos. 23-34 (12) 4.80 4.80

A13

A14

Condor with Long Wings Touching Flagstaffs
A15 A16

1886 **Litho.** ***Perf. 10½, 11***

White Paper

36 A13 5c brown 1.40 1.40
a. 5c yellow brown 1.40 1.40
b. Imperf., pair 17.50
37 A14 10c blue 3.75 3.75
a. Imperf., pair 17.50
38 A15 50c green 3.25 3.25
a. Imperf., pair 17.50
39 A16 1p vermilion 2.75 2.75
a. Imperf., pair 26.00
Nos. 36-39 (4) 11.15 11.15

No. 38 has been reprinted in pale gray green, perforated 10½, and No. 39 in bright vermilion, perforated 11½. The impressions show many signs of wear.

Lilac Tinted Paper

36c A13 5c orange brown 12.50 12.50
37b A14 10c blue 12.50 12.50
38b A15 50c green 9.25 9.25
39b A16 1p vermilion 8.25 8.25
Nos. 36c-39b (4) 42.50 42.50

Items similar to A15 and A16 but with condor with long wings and upper flagstaffs omitted are forgeries.

A17

A18

Condor with Short Wings
A19 A20

1886 **White Paper** ***Perf. 12***

44 A19 1c gray 6.25 6.25
45 A17 2c rose lilac 6.50 6.50
46 A18 2½c dull org 19.00 19.00
47 A19 5c brown 8.50 8.00
48 A20 10c blue 8.00 8.00
49 A20 20c lemon 6.50 6.50
a. Tête bêche pair 275.00 275.00
50 A20 25c black 6.25 6.25
51 A20 50c green 3.75 3.75
52 A20 1p vermilion 5.00 4.25
53 A20 2p violet 7.25 7.25
b. Tête bêche pair 190.00 190.00
54 A20 5p orange 13.00 13.00
55 A20 10p lilac rose 7.50 7.50
Nos. 44-55 (12) 97.50 96.25

Imperf., Pairs

44a A19 1c 17.00
47a A19 5c 29.00
48a A20 10c 29.00
52a A20 1p 21.00
53a A20 2p 26.00
54a A20 5p 40.00
55a A20 10p 17.00

A23

1888 ***Perf. 10½***

62 A23 5c red .25 .25
63 A23 10c green .30 .30
64 A23 50c blue .75 .75
65 A23 1p red brown 1.90 1.90
Nos. 62-65 (4) 3.20 3.20

For overprint see Colombia No. L14.

1895 ***Perf. 12, 13½***

66 A23 1c blue, *rose* .25 .25
67 A23 2c grn, *lt grn* .25 .25
68 A23 5c red .25 .25
69 A23 10c green .50 .50
70 A23 20c blue, *yellow* .30 .30
71 A23 1p brown 2.10 2.10
Nos. 66-71 (6) 3.65 3.65

Imperf., Pairs

62a A23 5c 8.75
63a A23 10c 12.00
64a A23 50c 14.50 14.50
65a A23 1p 21.00
66a A23 1c 21.00
67a A23 2c 21.00
70a A23 20c 24.00

"No Hay Estampillas"

Items inscribed "No hay estampillas" (No stamps available) are considered by specialists to be not postage stamps but receipt labels.

"Honda Issue"

This item seems to be of private origin.

A24

A25

A26

A27

A28

A29

A30

A31

Sewing Machine or Regular Perf. 12

1903-04 **Litho.**

79 A24 4c black, *green* .25 .25
80 A25 10c dull blue .25 .25
81 A26 20c orange .50 .50
82 A27 50c black, *rose* .25 .25
a. 50c black, *buff* .25 .25
84 A28 1p brown .25 .25
85 A29 2p gray .25 .25
86 A30 5p red .25 .25
a. Tête bêche pair 8.00 *12.00*
87 A31 10p black, *blue* .25 .25
a. 10p black, *light green* .25 .25
b. 10p black, *grn, glazed* 3.75 3.75
Nos. 79-87 (8) 2.25 2.25

Imperf

79a A24 4c black, *green* .25 .25
80a A25 10c dull blue .25 .25
81a A26 20c orange 1.25 1.25
82b A27 50c black, *rose* 1.75 1.75
c. 50c black, *buff* 1.75 1.75
84a A28 1p brown .25 .25
85a A29 2p gray .25 .25
86b A30 5p red .25 .25
c. Tête bêche pair 12.00 *16.00*
87c A31 10p black, *blue* 2.50 2.50
d. Tête bêche pair
e. 10p black, *light green* 3.75 3.75
f. 10p black, *green,* glazed 19.00 19.00
Nos. 79a-87c (8) 6.75 6.75

COMORO ISLANDS

ˈkä-mə-ˌrō ˈī-ləndz

LOCATION — In Mozambique Channel between Madagascar and Mozambique
GOVT. — Republic
AREA — 838 sq. mi.
POP. — 562,723 (1999 est.)
CAPITAL — Moroni

The Comoro Archipelago consists of the islands of Mayotte, Anjouan, Grand Comoro (Grande Comore) and Moheli, which issued their own stamps as French protectorates or colonies from 1887-1914. The archipelago was attached to Madagascar from 1914 to 1946, when it became a separate French territory. In July 1975, Anjouan, Grand Comoro and Moheli united to declare independence as the State of Comoro. Mayotte remained French.

100 Centimes = 1 Franc

Catalogue values for all unused stamps in this country are for Never Hinged items.

Anjouan Bay — A2

Comoro Woman Grinding Grain — A3

Moroni Mosque on Grand Comoro A4

1950 Unwmk. Engr. *Perf. 13*

30	A2	10c blue	.30	.50
31	A2	50c green	.30	.50
32	A2	1fr dk ol brn	.40	.50
33	A3	2fr brt grn	.75	.50
34	A3	5fr purple	1.10	.75
35	A3	6fr vio brn	1.25	1.10
36	A4	7fr red	1.10	.75
37	A4	10fr dk grn	1.25	1.00
38	A4	11fr dp ultra	1.50	1.25
		Nos. 30-38 (9)	7.95	6.85

Imperforates

Most Comoro Islands stamps exist imperforate in issued and trial colors, and also in small presentation sheets in issued colors.

Common Design Types pictured following the introduction.

Military Medal Issue
Common Design Type

1952 Engraved and Typographed

39	CD101	15fr multi	50.00	40.00

Mosque of Ouani, Anjouan — A5

Coelacanth A6

1952-54 Engr.

40	A5	15fr dark brown	2.00	1.75
41	A5	20fr red brown	4.00	3.50
42	A6	40fr aqua & indigo ('54)	25.00	18.00
		Nos. 40-42 (3)	31.00	23.25

FIDES Issue
Common Design Type

Design: 9fr, Women at water pump.

1956 Unwmk. *Perf. 13x12½*

43	CD103	9fr dp vio	2.25	1.60

Human Rights Issue
Common Design Type

1958 Engr. *Perf. 13*

44	CD105	20fr ol grn & dk bl	11.00	11.00

Flower Issue
Common Design Type

1959 Photo. *Perf. 12½x12*

45	CD104	10fr Colvillea	5.50	4.50

View of Dzaoudzi and Radio Symbol A8

Comoro radio station: 25fr, Radio tower and radio waves over Islands.

1960, Dec. 23 Engr. *Perf. 13*

46	A8	20fr maroon, vio bl & grn	1.75	1.25
47	A8	25fr ultra, brn & grn	2.00	1.00

Harpa Conoidalis — A9

Sea Shells: 50c, Cypraecassis rufa. 2fr, Murex ramosus. 5fr, Turbo marmoratus. 20fr, Pterocera scorpio. 25fr, Charonia tritonis.

1962, Jan. 13 Photo.
Shells in Natural Colors

48	A9	50c lilac & brn	1.25	1.25
49	A9	1fr yel & red	1.25	1.25
50	A9	2fr pale grn & pink	2.75	2.75
51	A9	5fr yel & grn	3.25	3.25
52	A9	20fr salmon & brn	11.50	11.50
53	A9	25fr bister & pink	16.00	16.00
		Nos. 48-53,C5-C6 (8)	81.00	71.00

Wheat Emblem and Globe A10

1963, Mar. 21 Engr. *Perf. 13*

54	A10	20fr choc & dk grn	5.50	4.50

FAO "Freedom from Hunger" campaign.

Red Cross Centenary Issue
Common Design Type

1963, Sept. 2 Unwmk. *Perf. 13*

55	CD113	50fr emer, gray & car	9.50	7.00

Human Rights Issue
Common Design Type

1963, Dec. 10 Engr.

56	CD117	15fr dk red & yel grn	9.50	7.50

Tobacco Pouch — A13

Designs: 4fr, Censer. 10fr, Carved lamp.

1963, Dec. 27 *Perf. 13*
Size: 22x36mm

57	A13	3fr multi	.80	.80
58	A13	4fr org, dp cl & sl grn	1.10	1.10
59	A13	10fr org brn, dk red brn & grn	2.00	2.00
		Nos. 57-59,C8-C9 (5)	18.90	12.65

Philatec Issue
Common Design Type

1964, Mar. 31

60	CD118	50fr dk bl, red & grn	4.50	4.00

Grand Comoro Canoe — A14

Design: 30fr, Boutre felucca.

Size: 22x37mm

1964, Aug. 7 Photo. *Perf. 13x12½*

61	A14	15fr multi	3.00	2.50
62	A14	30fr lt grn & multi	5.50	4.50
		Nos. 61-62,C10-C11 (4)	20.00	11.25

Spiny Lobster — A15

Designs: 12fr, Hammerhead shark, horiz. 20fr, Turtle, horiz. 25fr, Merou fish.

1965, Dec. 20 Engr. *Perf. 13*

63	A15	1fr grn, lil & ocher	1.25	.75
64	A15	12fr org red, slate & gray	2.75	1.60
65	A15	20fr org, red & bl grn	4.00	1.75
66	A15	25fr bl grn, dk brn & red	7.00	3.25
		Nos. 63-66 (4)	15.00	7.35

Hotel Itsandra, Moroni A16

Design: 15fr, Lake Salé, Grand Comoro.

1966, Dec. 19 Photo. *Perf. 12½x13*

67	A16	15fr multi	1.10	.70
68	A16	25fr multi	1.25	.70
		Nos. 67-68,C18-C19 (4)	16.35	9.65

Comoro Sunbird A17

Birds: 10fr, Malachite kingfisher. 15fr, Rothschild's fody. 30fr, Cuckoo-roller.

1967, June 20 Photo. *Perf. 12½x13*
Size: 36x23mm

69	A17	2fr ocher & multi	2.75	1.50
70	A17	10fr lil & multi	4.50	2.00
71	A17	15fr yel grn & multi	6.50	3.00
72	A17	30fr pink & multi	13.50	6.50
		Nos. 69-72,C20-C21 (6)	50.75	27.50

For surcharge see No. 133.

WHO Anniversary Issue
Common Design Type

1968, May 4 Engr. *Perf. 13*

73	CD126	40fr grn, vio & dp car	2.75	2.00

Surgeonfish A19

Design: 25fr, Imperial angelfish.

1968, Aug. 1 Engr. *Perf. 13*
Size: 36x22mm

74	A19	20fr vio bl, yel & red brn	3.50	3.50
75	A19	25fr Prus bl, dk bl & org	4.25	4.25
		Nos. 74-75,C23-C24 (4)	25.75	17.00

For surcharge & overprint see Nos. C52, C74.

Human Rights Year Issue
Common Design Type

1968, Aug. 10 Engr. *Perf. 13*

76	CD127	60fr brn, grn & org	3.50	3.50

Msoila Prayer Rug and Praying Man — A20

Each stamp shows a different prayer position.

1969, Feb. 27 Engr. *Perf. 13*

77	A20	20fr bl grn, rose red & pur	1.40	.95
78	A20	30fr pur, rose red & bl grn	1.60	1.40
79	A20	45fr rose red, pur & bl grn	3.00	1.75
		Nos. 77-79 (3)	6.00	4.10

Vanilla Flower A21

Design: 15fr, Flower of ylang-ylang tree. 25fr, Poinsettia (country name at upper left).

1969-70 Photo. *Perf. 12½x13*
Size: 36x23mm

80	A21	10fr multi	1.25	.60
81	A21	15fr multi	1.75	.80
82	A21	25fr multi ('70)	4.25	1.50
		Nos. 80-82,C26-C28 (6)	28.50	16.90

Issued: Nos. 80-81, 3/20. No. 82, 3/5.

ILO Issue
Common Design Type

1969, Nov. 24 Engr. *Perf. 13*

83	CD131	5fr org, emerald & gray	1.25	.75

UPU Headquarters Issue

Common Design Type

1970, May 20 Engr. *Perf. 13*

84	CD133	65fr pur, bl grn & red brn	5.50	2.00

Chiromani Costume, Anjouan — A22

25fr, Bouiboui costume, Grand Comoro.

1970, Oct. 30 Photo. *Perf. 12½x13*

85	A22	20fr grn, yel & red	1.60	.80
86	A22	25fr brn, yel & dk bl	1.90	1.10

Friday Mosque — A23

1970, Dec. 18 Engr. *Perf. 13*

87	A23	5fr rose car, grn & grnsh bl	.75	.75
88	A23	10fr dp lil, grn & vio	1.00	.75
89	A23	40fr cop red, grn & dp brn	1.75	1.40
		Nos. 87-89 (3)	3.50	2.90

Great White Egret — A24

Birds: 10fr, Comoro pigeon. 15fr, Green-backed heron. 25fr, Comoro blue pigeon. 35fr, Humbolt's flycatcher. 40fr, Allen's gallinule.

1971, Mar. 12 Photo. *Perf. 12½x13*

90	A24	5fr multi	1.50	.80
91	A24	10fr yel & multi	2.00	.80
92	A24	15fr bl & multi	3.25	1.75
93	A24	25fr org & multi	4.75	2.00
94	A24	35fr yel grn & multi	6.50	2.50
95	A24	40fr gray & multi	8.00	3.25
		Nos. 90-95 (6)	26.00	11.10

For overprint see No. 145.

Pyrostegia Venusta — A25

Flowers: 3fr, Dogbane, horiz. 20fr, Frangipani.

Size: 22x36mm, 36x22mm

1971, July 19 Photo. *Perf. 13*

96	A25	1fr ver & grn	.95	.85
97	A25	3fr yel, grn & red	1.40	1.00
98	A25	20fr ver & grn	3.50	2.50
		Nos. 96-98,C37-C38 (5)	17.35	11.50

For surcharges see Nos. 131-132, C75, C83.

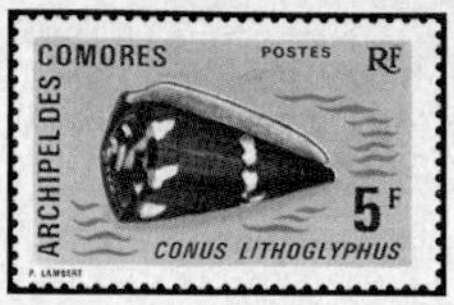

Lithograph Cone A26

Sea Shells: 10fr, Pacific lettered cone. 20fr, Aulicus cone. 35fr, Polita nerita. 60fr, Snake-head cowrie.

1971, Oct. 4

99	A26	5fr lt ultra & multi	1.25	1.00
100	A26	10fr multi	1.75	1.40
101	A26	20fr vio & multi	3.75	2.25
102	A26	35fr lt bl & multi	7.25	2.75
103	A26	60fr lt vio & multi	9.50	3.50
		Nos. 99-103 (5)	23.50	10.90

For surcharge see No. 150.

De Gaulle Issue

Common Design Type

Designs: 20fr, Gen. de Gaulle, 1940. 35fr, Pres. de Gaulle, 1970.

1971, Nov. 9 Engr. *Perf. 13*

104	CD134	20fr dk car & blk	4.00	2.50
105	CD134	35fr dk car & blk	5.00	3.25

Louis Pasteur, Slides, Microscope A27

1972, Aug. 2

106	A27	65fr indigo, org, & ol brn	5.50	4.75

Sesquicentennial of the birth of Louis Pasteur (1822-1895), chemist.

Type of Air Post Issue 1971

Designs: 10fr, View of Goulaivoini. 20fr, Bay, Mitsamiouli. 35fr, Gate and fountain, Foumbouni. 50fr, View of Moroni.

1973, June 28 Photo. *Perf. 13*

107	AP10	10fr bl & multi	1.00	.30
108	AP10	20fr grn & multi	1.50	.75
109	AP10	35fr bl & multi	2.50	1.25
110	AP10	50fr bl & multi	2.75	1.75
		Nos. 107-110,C53 (5)	17.25	10.55

For overprint see No. 143.

Bank of Madagascar and Comoros — A28

Buildings in Moroni: 15fr, Post and Telecommunications Administration. 20fr, Prefecture.

1973, July 10 Photo. *Perf. 13x12½*

111	A28	5fr multi	.65	.55
112	A28	15fr multi	.90	.80
113	A28	20fr multi	1.25	1.00
		Nos. 111-113 (3)	2.80	2.35

For surcharge see No. 134.

Salimata Hamissi Mosque A29

20fr, Zaouiyat Chaduli Mosque, vert.

Perf. 12½x13, 13x12½

1973, Oct. 20 Photo.

114	A29	20fr multi	1.25	.95
115	A29	35fr multi	2.10	1.25

For surcharges see Nos. 135, 138.

Cheikh Mausoleum A30

Design: 50fr, Mausoleum of President Said Mohamed Cheikh (different view).

1974, Mar. 16 Engr. *Perf. 13*

116	A30	35fr grn, ol brn & blk	1.60	1.10
117	A30	50fr grn, ol brn & blk	2.50	1.25

For surcharge see No. 140.

Koran Stand, Anjouan A31

Designs: 15fr, Carved combs, vert. 20fr, 3-legged table, vert. 75fr, Sugar press.

1974, May 10 Photo. *Perf. 12½x13*

118	A31	15fr emer & multi	1.25	.60
119	A31	20fr grn & multi	1.40	.65
120	A31	35fr multi	2.25	1.10
121	A31	75fr multi	4.50	2.00
		Nos. 118-121 (4)	9.40	4.35

For overprints and surcharge see Nos. 137, 141, 149.

UPU Emblem, Symbolic Postmark A32

1974, Oct. 9 Engr. *Perf. 13x12½*

122	A32	30fr multi	2.00	1.75

Centenary of Universal Postal Union.
For surcharge see No. 155.

Bracelet A33

1975, Feb. 28 Engr. *Perf. 13*

123	A33	20fr shown	1.10	.95
124	A33	35fr Diadem	1.90	1.25
125	A33	120fr Saber	5.00	3.25
126	A33	135fr Dagger	7.00	4.00
		Nos. 123-126 (4)	15.00	9.45

For surcharges see Nos. 136, 142, 151, 154.

Mohani Village, Moheli — A34

50fr, Djoezi Village, Moheli. 55fr, Chirazi tombs.

1975, May 26 Photo. *Perf. 13*

127	A34	30fr vio bl & multi	2.00	1.00
128	A34	50fr Prus bl & multi	3.25	1.50
129	A34	55fr grn & multi	3.50	2.50
		Nos. 127-129 (3)	8.75	5.00

For overprints and surcharge see Nos. 139, 146, 148.

Scuba Diver Photographing Coelacanth — A35

1975, June 27 Engr. *Perf. 13*

130	A35	50fr multi	8.25	5.75

1975 coelacanth expedition.
For overprint see No. 147.

STATE OF COMORO

In 1978 the islands' name became the Federal and Islamic Republic of the Comoros.

Issues of 1971-75 Srchd. and Ovptd. with Bars and: "ETAT COMORIEN" in Black, Silver or Red

Tambourine Player — A36

No. 153, Women dancers & tambourine players.

Printing & Perforations as Before, Photogravure (A36)

1975 *Perf. 13 (A36)*

131	A25	5fr on 1fr	*.40*	*.25*
132	A25	5fr on 3fr	*.40*	*.25*
133	A17	10fr on 2fr	*1.25*	*.50*
134	A28	15fr on 20fr (R)	*.80*	*.25*
135	A29	15fr on 20fr (S)	*.80*	*.25*
136	A33	15fr on 20fr	*.80*	*.25*
137	A31	20fr	*1.00*	*.25*
138	A29	25fr on 35fr	*1.00*	*.25*
139	A34	30fr	*1.00*	*.60*
140	A30	30fr on 35fr	*1.00*	*.30*
141	A31	30fr on 35fr	*1.00*	*.30*
142	A33	30fr on 35fr	*1.00*	*.60*
143	AP10	35fr	*1.25*	*.75*
144	SP2	35fr on 35fr + 10fr	*1.25*	*.75*
145	A24	40fr	*2.75*	*1.50*
146	A34	50fr	*1.90*	*1.90*
147	A35	50fr	*2.50*	*1.25*
148	A34	50fr on 55fr (S)	*1.90*	*.95*
149	A31	75fr	*2.00*	*.55*
150	A26	75fr on 60fr (S)	*4.00*	*2.00*
151	A33	100fr on 120fr	*2.50*	*.90*
152	A36	100fr bl & multi	*3.25*	*1.75*
153	A36	100fr on 150fr (S)	*2.50*	*.90*
154	A33	200fr on 135fr	*6.00*	*2.40*
155	A32	500fr on 30fr	*12.00*	*6.75*
		Nos. 131-155 (25)	*54.25*	*26.40*

Nos. 152-153 exist without overprint or surcharge. Value, each $90.

No. 155 exists with red surcharge. Value $12.

Litho. & Embossed "Gold Foil" Stamps

These stamps generally are of a different design format than the rest of the issue. Since there is a commemorative inscription tieing them to the issue a separate illustration is not being shown.

Apollo-Soyuz — A37

Spacecraft and astronauts: 10fr, Soyuz lift-off, Alexei A. Leonov and Valeri N. Kubasov, vert. 30fr, Apollo lift-off, Thomas P. Stafford, Vance D. Brand, Donald K. Slayton, vert. 50fr, Meeting in space. 100fr, Chairman Brezhnev, President Ford talking with astronauts and cosmonauts. 200fr, Spacecraft preparing to dock. 400f, Return to Earth. 500fr, Spacecraft, mission emblems. 1500fr, Apollo-Soyuz crew. No. 164, Preparing to dock, diff.

1975, Dec. 15 Litho. *Perf. 13½*

156 A37	10fr multicolored	.40	.25
157 A37	30fr multicolored	.50	.25
158 A37	50fr multicolored	.70	.55
159 A37	100fr multicolored	1.00	.60
160 A37	200fr multicolored	2.00	1.25
161 A37	400fr multicolored	4.00	2.50
	Nos. 156-161 (6)	8.60	5.40

Litho. & Embossed

Size: 45x45mm

162 A37 1500fr gold & multi 17.50 —

Souvenir Sheets

Litho.

163 A37 500fr multicolored 4.50 1.75

Litho. & Embossed

164 A37 1500fr gold & multi 17.50 —

Nos. 159-164 are airmail. No. 163 contains one 64x44mm stamp. No. 164 contains one 45x45mm stamp.

No. 162 exists in a souvenir sheet of 1. Value $50.

For overprints see Nos. 477-478.

A38

American Revolution, Bicent. — A39

Designs: 15fr, Lewis and Clark, Blackfoot Indian. 25fr, John C. Fremont, Kit Carson, Indian dancer. 35fr, Daniel Boone, Buffalo Bill Cody, wagon train. 40fr, Richard E. Egan, Johnny Frey, Pony Express. 75fr, Henry Wells, William G. Fargo, stagecoach. 400fr, Frontiersman, Indian. 500fr, Leland Stanford, Thomas C. Dunant, transcontinental railroad. 1000fr, George Washington, winter at Valley Forge. 1500fr, John Paul Jones, ship.

1976, Jan. 15 Litho.

165 A38	15fr multicolored	.25	.25
166 A38	25fr multicolored	.45	.25
167 A38	35fr multicolored	.75	.35
168 A38	40fr multicolored	.85	.45
169 A38	75fr multicolored	1.50	.60
170 A38	500fr multicolored	6.25	2.50
	Nos. 165-170 (6)	10.05	4.40

Litho. & Embossed

171 A39 1000fr gold & multi 13.50 —

Souvenir Sheets

Litho.

172 A38 400fr multicolored 5.50 1.75

Litho. & Embossed

173 A39 1500fr gold & multi 16.50 —

Nos. 170-173 are airmail. See Nos. 230, 232 and note after No. 479.

No. 171 exists in a souvenir sheet of 1. Value $55.

1976 Winter Olympics, Innsbruck — A40

1976, Mar. 30 Litho.

174 A40	5fr Women's figure skating	.25	.25
175 A40	30fr Slalom skiing	.25	.25
176 A40	35fr Speed skating	.50	.25
177 A40	50fr Downhill skiing	.65	.50
178 A40	200fr Ski jumping	2.10	1.00
179 A40	400fr Cross country skiing	4.50	1.25
	Nos. 174-179 (6)	8.25	3.50

Litho. & Embossed

Size: 56x35mm

180 A40 1000fr Downhill skier, hockey *13.00* —

Souvenir Sheets

Litho.

181 A40 500fr Hockey 8.00 1.75

Litho. & Embossed

182 A40 1000fr Olympic Rings *11.00* —

Nos. 178-182 are airmail. Nos. 181-182 contain one 58x35mm stamp. For overprint see No. 471.

No. 162 exists in a souvenir sheet of 1. Value $45.

1976 Summer Olympics, Montreal — A41

20fr, Runner, Athens, 1896. 25fr, Sprints. 40fr, High jump, Paris, 1900. 75fr, High jump. 100fr, Women stretching, St. Louis, 1904. 500fr, Uneven parallel bars.

400fr, Olympic Stadium, Montreal.

1976, Mar. 30 Litho.

183 A41	20fr multicolored	.25	.25
184 A41	25fr multicolored	.35	.25
185 A41	40fr multicolored	.50	.25
186 A41	75fr multicolored	1.00	.45
187 A41	100fr multicolored	1.10	.50
188 A41	500fr multicolored	6.00	1.75
	Nos. 183-188 (6)	9.20	3.45

Souvenir Sheet

189 A41 400fr multicolored 4.50 1.25

Nos. 187-189 are airmail.

For overprint see No. 476.

Fairy Tales — A42

15fr, Hansel & Gretel. 30fr, Alice in Wonderland. 35fr, Pinocchio. 40fr, Good Little Henry. 50fr, Peter and the Wolf. 400fr, Thousand and One Nights.

1976, June 28

190 A42	15fr multicolored	.25	.25
191 A42	30fr multicolored	.50	.25
192 A42	35fr multicolored	.65	.25
193 A42	40fr multicolored	.65	.25
194 A42	50fr multicolored	1.00	.25
195 A42	400fr multicolored	6.50	2.00
	Nos. 190-195 (6)	9.55	3.25

No. 195 is airmail. Nos. 190-191, 193, 195 are vert.

Invention of Telephone, Cent. — A43

Designs: 10fr, A. G. Bell, 1st telephone. 25fr, Charles Bourseul, Paris-London phone service, 1891. 75fr, Philipp Reis, telephone operators. 100fr, Earth to Moon to Earth communications. 200fr, Satellite. 400fr, Ship-to-Satellite communications. No. 201, Satellite in orbit, antenna. No. 203, Global communications.

1976, July 1

196 A43	10fr multicolored	.25	.25
197 A43	25fr multicolored	.35	.25
198 A43	75fr multicolored	1.00	.30
199 A43	100fr multicolored	1.40	.50
200 A43	200fr multicolored	2.25	.90
201 A43	500fr multicolored	5.50	1.75
	Nos. 196-201 (6)	10.75	3.95

Souvenir Sheets

202 A43	400fr multicolored	7.00	1.75
203 A43	500fr multicolored	7.00	1.75

Nos. 199-203 are airmail. Nos. 202-203 contain a 73x44mm stamp. For overprint see No. 472.

Comoro Flag, Map and Government Buildings — A44

1976, Nov. 18 Litho. *Perf. 13½*

204 A44	30fr multi	.75	.30
205 A44	50fr multi	1.50	.30

1st anniversary of independence.

For overprints and surcharges see Nos. 353-372.

Viking Probe to Mars — A45

Designs: 5fr, Nicolaus Copernicus, rocket launch. 10fr, Albert Einstein, Carl Sagan, Thomas Young, horiz. 25fr, Viking probe orbiting Mars. 35fr, Discovery of America by Vikings, horiz. 100fr, Flag, Viking landing on Mars. 500fr, Viking emblem, surface of Mars, horiz. 400fr, Viking probe. No. 212, Wagon train, frontiersman, rocket launch. No. 214, Viking on Martian surface, robotic shovel.

1976, Nov. 23

206 A45	5fr multicolored	.25	.25
207 A45	10fr multicolored	.25	.25
208 A45	25fr multicolored	.35	.25
209 A45	35fr multicolored	.35	.25
210 A45	100fr multicolored	1.25	.40
211 A45	500fr multicolored	7.00	1.50
	Nos. 206-211 (6)	9.45	2.90

Litho. & Embossed

Size: 57x39mm

212 A45 1500fr gold & multi *14.00* —

Souvenir Sheets

Litho.

213 A45 400fr multicolored *5.00* 1.50

Litho. & Embossed

214 A45 1500fr gold & multi *15.00* —

American Revolution, bicentennial. Nos. 211-214 are airmail. No. 213 contains one 60x42mm stamp.

No. 212 exists in a souvenir sheet of 1. Value $50.

UN Postal Administration, 25th Anniv. — A46

Designs: 15fr, UN #24, irrigating field. 30fr, UN #43, doctor, nurse. 50fr, UN #162, mother holding child. 75fr, UN #42, communications satellite in orbit. 200fr, UN #32, Concorde, Zeppelin. 400fr, UN #18, cargo plane. 500fr, People passing letters around globe.

1976, Nov. 25 Litho.

215 A46	15fr multicolored	.25	.25
216 A46	30fr multicolored	.30	.25
217 A46	50fr multicolored	.60	.30
218 A46	75fr multicolored	.80	.30
219 A46	200fr multicolored	2.50	1.00
220 A46	400fr multicolored	5.00	2.00
	Nos. 215-220 (6)	9.45	4.10

Souvenir Sheet

221 A46 500fr multicolored *5.00* 2.00

Nos. 219-221 are airmail. No. 221 contains one 57x40mm stamp. For overprints see Nos. 282-284, 473.

Comoro Flag, UN Headquarters and Emblem — A47

1976, Nov. 25

222 A47	40fr multicolored	1.40	.30
223 A47	50fr multicolored	1.90	.40

1st anniv. of UN membership.

Type of 1976 and

US Bicentennial — A48

Civil War Battles: 10fr, Fort Sumter, Lincoln. 30fr, Bull Run, Gen. P.G.T. Beauregard, vert. 50fr, Antietam, Gen. Joseph E. Johnston. 100fr, Gettysburg, Gen. Meade. 200fr, Chattanooga, Gen. Sherman, vert. 400fr, Appomattox, Gen. Pickett. 500fr, Surrender at Appomattox, Generals Lee and Grant. 1000fr, Lincoln, battlefield. No. 230, Pres. Kennedy, lunar lander.

1976, Dec. 30 Litho.

224 A48	10fr multicolored	.25	.25
225 A48	30fr multicolored	.30	.25
226 A48	50fr multicolored	.65	.25
227 A48	100fr multicolored	1.10	.45
228 A48	200fr multicolored	2.50	.80
229 A48	400fr multicolored	5.00	1.50
	Nos. 224-229 (6)	9.80	3.50

Litho. & Embossed

Size: 61x51mm

230 A39 1500fr gold & multi *17.00* —

Souvenir Sheets

Litho.

231 A48 500fr multicolored *6.50* 1.75

Litho. & Embossed

232 A39 1000fr gold & multi *9.50* —

American Revolution bicentennial. Nos. 227-232 are airmail. No. 231 contains one 60x42mm stamp.

No. 230 exists in a souvenir sheet of 1. Value $50.

Endangered Species — A49

15fr, Andean condor, vert. 20fr, Australian tiger cat. 35fr, Leopard, vert. 40fr, White rhinoceros. 75fr, Nyala, vert. 400fr, Orangutan.

500fr, Lemur, vert.

1976, Dec. 30 **Litho.**

233	A49	15fr multicolored	.30	.25
234	A49	20fr multicolored	.65	.25
235	A49	35fr multicolored	1.00	.25
236	A49	40fr multicolored	1.25	.45
237	A49	75fr multicolored	3.00	.55
238	A49	400fr multicolored	8.00	1.50
		Nos. 233-238 (6)	14.20	3.25

Souvenir Sheet

239	A49	500fr multicolored	7.00	1.75

Nos. 238-239 airmail. No. 239 contains one 40x58mm stamp.
See note after No. 479.

Endangered Species — A50

1977, Apr. 14

240	A50	10fr Wolf	.25	.25
241	A50	30fr Aye-aye	.45	.25
242	A50	40fr Cephalopus zebra	.90	.30
243	A50	50fr Giant tortoise	1.00	.30
244	A50	200fr Ocelot	3.00	.75
245	A50	400fr Penguin	6.50	1.50
		Nos. 240-245 (6)	12.10	3.35

Souvenir Sheet

246	A50	500fr Sumatran tiger	8.00	1.50

Nos. 244-246 airmail. No. 246 contains one 58x40mm stamp.

Giffard Airship, 1851 and Paris-St. Germain Train, 1837, France — A51

Airships & Locomotives: 25fr, Santos-Dumont's airship, 1906, Brazilian Tander 120FIN, Brazil. 50fr, Astra, 1914, Trans-Siberian Express, 1905, Russia. 75fr, R.34, 1919, Southern Belle, 1910, Great Britain. 200fr, Navy airship, Pacific Class locomotive, 1930, US. No. 252, Hindenburg, Rheingold Express, 1933, Germany. No. 253, Graf-Zeppelin, 1928, Nord-Express Type 231, 1925, Germany.

1977, Apr. 14

247	A51	20fr multicolored	.30	.25
248	A51	25fr multicolored	.30	.25
249	A51	50fr multicolored	.75	.25
250	A51	75fr multicolored	1.10	.25
251	A51	200fr multicolored	2.75	.60
252	A51	500fr multicolored	6.25	1.60
		Nos. 247-252 (6)	11.45	3.20

Souvenir Sheet

253	A51	500fr multi, horiz.	6.00	2.00

Nos. 251-253 are airmail. No. 253 contains one 58x39mm stamp.

Nobel Prize, 75th Anniv. — A52

Nobel Prize winners: 30fr, Medicine. 40fr, Physics. 50fr, Literature. 100fr, Physics. 200fr, Chemistry. 400fr, Peace.

1977, July 7

254	A52	30fr multicolored	.75	.25
255	A52	40fr multicolored	.75	.25
256	A52	50fr multicolored	1.25	.25
257	A52	100fr multicolored	3.25	.25
258	A52	200fr multicolored	5.50	.75
259	A52	400fr multicolored	12.50	1.25
		Nos. 254-259 (6)	24.00	3.00

Souvenir Sheet

260	A52	500fr Nobel medal	5.50	1.75

Nos. 258-260 are airmail.
See note after No. 479.

Peter Paul Rubens, 400th Birth Anniv. — A53

Portraits: 20fr, Portrait of the Artist's Daughter, Clara. 25fr, Suzanne Fourment. 50fr, Toilet of Venus, (detail). 75fr, Ceres (detail). 200fr, Young Woman with Blonde Braided Hair. No. 266, Helene Fourment in her Wedding Dress. No. 267, Self-portrait.

1977, July 7

261	A53	20fr multicolored	.25	.25
262	A53	25fr multicolored	.30	.25
263	A53	50fr multicolored	.65	.25
264	A53	75fr multicolored	1.10	.30
265	A53	200fr multicolored	2.50	.60
266	A53	500fr multicolored	6.25	1.50
		Nos. 261-266 (6)	11.05	3.15

Souvenir Sheet

267	A53	500fr multicolored	5.50	1.75

Nos. 265-267 are airmail.
See note after No. 479.

Fish A54

1977, Nov. 21

268	A54	30fr Swordfish	.50	.25
269	A54	40fr Gaterin	1.00	.25
270	A54	50fr Sea scorpion	1.75	.25
271	A54	100fr Chaetodon lunula	3.25	.45
272	A54	200fr Amphiprion	4.00	.75
273	A54	400fr Tetrodon	7.50	1.50
		Nos. 268-273 (6)	18.00	3.45

Souvenir Sheet

274	A54	500fr Coelacanth	8.00	2.00

Nos. 272-274 airmail. No. 274 contains one 52x47mm stamp.

Space Exploration — A55

30fr, Jupiter lander. 50fr, Voyager probe, Uranus, vert. 75fr, Pioneer probe, Venus. 100fr, Space shuttle, vert. 200fr, Viking III, Mars. 400fr, Apollo-Soyuz, vert.
500fr, Allegory of the Sun.

1977, Nov. 21

275	A55	30fr multicolored	.30	.25
276	A55	50fr multicolored	.60	.25
277	A55	75fr multicolored	1.00	.25
278	A55	100fr multicolored	1.10	.40
279	A55	200fr multicolored	2.50	.60
280	A55	400fr multicolored	5.00	1.25
		Nos. 275-280 (6)	10.50	3.00

Souvenir Sheet

281	A55	500fr multicolored	5.00	1.75

Nos. 279-281 airmail. No. 281 contains one 52x42mm stamp.

No. 219 Overprinted in One Line in Gold, Silver or Red "Paris-New-York - 22 Nov. 1977"

1977, Nov. 22

282	A46	200fr multicolored	5.00	2.75
283	A46	200fr multicolored (S)	30.00	—
284	A46	200fr multicolored (R)	10.00	—
		Nos. 282-284 (3)	45.00	2.75

Birds — A56

15fr, Porphyrula alleni. 20fr, M. superciliosus. 35fr, Alcedo vintsioides johannae. 40fr, Terpsiphone. 75fr, Nectarinia comorensis. 400fr, Egretta alba.
500fr, Foudia eminentissima, horiz.

1978, Feb. 6

285	A56	15fr multicolored	.35	.25
286	A56	20fr multicolored	.50	.25
287	A56	35fr multicolored	.70	.30
288	A56	40fr multicolored	1.00	.40
289	A56	75fr multicolored	2.00	.50
290	A56	400fr multicolored	8.00	2.25
		Nos. 285-290 (6)	12.55	3.95

Souvenir Sheet

291	A56	500fr multicolored	7.50	1.75

Nos. 290-291 are airmail. For overprint and surcharges see Nos. 444-448.

World Cup Soccer Championships, Argentina — A57

Designs: 30fr, Greece, 5th. cent. B.C. 50fr, Brittany, 19th cent. 75fr, London, 14th cent. 100fr, Italy, 18th cent. 200fr, England, 19th cent. 400fr, English Cup match, 1891. 500fr, English Cup final, 1962. No. 298, Player, satellite. No. 300, Players.

1978, Feb. 6

292	A57	30fr multicolored	.30	.25
293	A57	50fr multicolored	.60	.25
294	A57	75fr multicolored	.75	.30
295	A57	100fr multicolored	1.10	.40
296	A57	200fr multicolored	2.50	.60
297	A57	400fr multicolored	5.00	1.25
		Nos. 292-297 (6)	10.25	3.05

Litho. & Embossed

Size: 60x42mm

298	A57	1000fr gold & multi	11.00	—

Souvenir Sheets

Litho.

299	A57	500fr multicolored	6.00	1.75

Litho. & Embossed

300	A57	1000fr gold & multi	10.00	4.00

Nos. 296-300 are airmail. No. 300 contains one 60x42mm stamp.
No. 298 exists in a souvenir sheet of 1. Value $50.
For overprints and surcharges see Nos. 402-408, 449-453.

Composers — A58

1978, Apr. 5 **Litho.**

301	A58	30fr J.S. Bach	.90	.25
302	A58	40fr W.A. Mozart	1.10	.25
303	A58	50fr Berlioz	1.50	.30
304	A58	100fr Verdi	3.00	.30
305	A58	200fr Tchaikovsky	4.50	.60
306	A58	400fr George Gershwin	9.00	1.25
		Nos. 301-306 (6)	20.00	2.95

Souvenir Sheet

307	A58	500fr Beethoven	9.00	1.75

Nos. 305-307 are airmail. For overprints and surcharges see Nos. 454-458.

Albrecht Durer, 450th Death Anniv. — A59

Portraits: 20fr, Oswolt Krel. 25fr, Elspeth Tucher. 50fr, Hieronymus Holzschuher. 75fr, Young Woman. 200fr, Emperor Maximilian I. No. 313, Young Woman, (detail). No. 314, Self-portrait.

1978, Apr. 5

308	A59	20fr multicolored	.25	.25
309	A59	25fr multicolored	.30	.25
310	A59	50fr multicolored	.65	.30
311	A59	75fr multicolored	1.00	.30
312	A59	200fr multicolored	2.50	.60
313	A59	500fr multicolored	6.00	1.60
		Nos. 308-313 (6)	10.70	3.30

Souvenir Sheet

314	A59	500fr multicolored	5.50	1.75

Nos. 312-314 airmail. No. 314 contains one 42x52mm stamp. See note after No. 479.

Issues Not Valid for Postage

The government changed in May 1978. A number of sets that had not been issued seem to have been invalid for postage until they were overprinted with the new country name. These are a set of 9 for the 25th anniv. of Elizabeth's coronation, a set of 7 for butterflies, a set of 6 for the 10th Intl. Communications Year, a set of 7 for the history of aviation, a set of 9 for Rubens, and a set of 9 for Durer.

These sets, unoverprinted, exist both mint and cancelled to order. They are no scarcer than the previous listed issues.

See note after No. 479.

Islamic Republic

Nos. 204-205 Surcharged and Overprinted with 3 Lines and: "République / Fédérale / et Islamique / des Comores"

1978, July 24 **Litho.** ***Perf. 13½***

353	A44	30fr multi	1.75	—
354	A44	40fr on 30fr multi	1.75	—
355	A44	50fr multi	1.75	—
356	A44	100fr on 50fr multi	1.75	—
		Nos. 353-356 (3)	1.50	

Nos. 353 and 355 were also overprinted to commemorate World Cup Soccer winner; Albrecht Dürer; Railroad anniversary; Voyager I and II; 1980 Olympic Games; World Cup Soccer, Espana '82.

Nos. 353, 355 Overprinted

1978, July 25 **Litho.** ***Perf. 13½***

357	A44	30fr multi	*8.50*	—
358	A44	50fr multi	*12.50*	—

Coronation of Queen Elizabeth II, 25th anniv.

Nos. 353, 355 Overprinted

1978, July 26 Litho. Perf. 13½

359	A44	30fr multi	*6.00*	—
360	A44	50fr multi	*9.00*	—

Birth of Capt. James Cook, 250th anniv.

Nos. 353, 355 Overprinted

1978, July 31 Litho. Perf. 13½

365	A44	30fr multi	*6.00*	—
366	A44	50fr multi	*10.00*	—

Intl. Civil Aviation Organization.

Nos. 353, 355 Overprinted

1978, Aug. 3 Litho. Perf. 13½

371	A44	30fr multi	*7.00*	—
372	A44	50fr multi	*8.00*	—

Intl. Year of the Child (in 1979).

Europe-Africa A66

Various satellites or spacecraft.

1978, Dec. 16

386	A66	10fr multicolored	.25	.25
387	A66	25fr multicolored	.25	.25
388	A66	35fr multicolored	.40	.25
389	A66	50fr multicolored	.65	.25
390	A66	100fr multicolored	1.10	.60
391	A66	500fr multicolored	5.50	1.25
		Nos. 386-391 (6)	8.15	2.85

Souvenir Sheet

392	A66	500fr multicolored	5.50	1.75

Nos. 390-392 airmail. No. 392 contains one 61x40mm stamp.

Sir Rowland Hill — A67

20fr, Saxony #1. 30fr, Netherlands #1. 40fr, Great Britain #2. 75fr, US #2. 200fr, France #33. 400fr, Basel #3L1. 1500fr, British Guiana #13.

500fr, Moheli, Mayotte, Anjouan, Grand Comoro #1. No. 401, 1500fr, Hill, Mauritius #3.

1978, Dec. 16

393	A67	20fr multi	.25	.25
394	A67	30fr multi	.30	.25
395	A67	40fr multi	.60	.25
396	A67	75fr multi	.75	.30
397	A67	200fr multi	2.10	.60
398	A67	400fr multi	4.50	1.25
		Nos. 393-398 (6)	8.50	2.90

Litho. & Embossed

Size: 39x58mm

399	A67	1500fr multi	13.00	—

Souvenir Sheets

Litho.

400	A67	500fr multi	5.50	1.75

Litho. & Embossed

401	A67	1500fr multi	13.00	—

Nos. 397-401 are airmail. No. 400 contains one 57x49mm stamp. No. 401 contains one 58x39mm stamp.

No. 399 exists in a souvenir sheet of 1. Value $40.

Nos. 292-297, 299 Ovptd. in Black & Silver

1978, Dec. 16

402	A57	30fr multicolored	.30	.25
403	A57	50fr multicolored	.60	.25
404	A57	75fr multicolored	.90	.25
405	A57	100fr multicolored	1.10	.45
406	A57	200fr multicolored	2.25	.60
407	A57	400fr multicolored	4.75	1.25
		Nos. 402-407 (6)	9.90	3.05

Souvenir Sheet

408	A57	500fr multicolored	5.50	1.25

Nos. 406-407 are airmail.

Exists with Country name in red on silver. Value approx. triple those of overprints in black.

Galileo and Voyager I — A68

Exploration of Solar System: 30fr, Kepler and Voyager II. 40fr, Copernicus and Voyager I, 100fr, Huygens and Voyager II. 200fr, William Herschel and Voyager II. 400fr, Urbain Leverrier and Voyager II. 500fr, Voyagers I and II, symbolic solar system.

1979, Feb. 19 Litho. Perf. 13

409	A68	20fr multi	.25	.25
410	A68	30fr multi	.30	.25
411	A68	40fr multi	.50	.25
412	A68	100fr multi	1.10	.25
413	A68	200fr multi	1.90	.50
414	A68	400fr multi	4.00	1.00
		Nos. 409-414 (6)	8.05	2.50

Souvenir Sheet

415	A68	500fr multi	5.00	1.50

Nos. 413-415 airmail.

Philidor, Anderssen, Steinitz and King — A69

100fr, Chess pieces and board, Venetian chess player. 500fr, Chess Grand Masters Alekhine, Spassky, Fischer, and bishop.

1979, Feb. 19

416	A69	40fr multi	.50	.25
417	A69	100fr multi	1.00	.25
418	A69	500fr multi	5.00	1.50
		Nos. 416-418 (3)	6.50	2.00

Chess Grand Masters. No. 418 airmail.

Nos. 419-425 are reserved for Summer Olympics set of 6 with one souvenir sheet, released Mar. 28, 1979. Values: set, unused $7; set, used $3; souvenir sheet, unused $6; souvenir sheet, used $3.

Charaxes Defulvata — A71

Fauna: 50fr, Leptosomus discolor. 75fr, Bee eater.

1979, Apr. 10 Litho. Perf. 12½

426	A71	30fr multi	1.75	.30
427	A71	50fr multi	4.50	1.00
428	A71	75fr multi	6.50	2.00
		Nos. 426-428 (3)	12.75	3.30

Otto Lilienthal and Glider — A72

History of Aviation: No. 430, Wright brothers and Flyer A. No. 431, Louis Bleriot and Bleriot XI. 100fr, Claude Dornier and Dornier-Wal hydrofoil. 200fr, Charles Lindbergh and Spirit of St. Louis.

1979, May 2 Perf. 13

Black Overprint and Surcharge

429	A72	30fr multi	.50	.50
430	A72	50fr multi	.80	.80
431	A72	50fr on 75fr multi	.80	.80
432	A72	100fr multi	1.60	1.60
433	A72	200fr multi	2.50	2.50
		Nos. 429-433 (5)	6.20	6.20

No. 433 airmail.

For unoverprinted stamps see note after No. 314.

Papilio Dardanus Cenea A73

Butterflies: 15fr, Papilio dardanus. 30fr, Chrysiridia croesus. 50fr, Precis octavia. 75fr, Bunaea alcinoe.

1979, May 2

Black Overprint and Surcharge

434	A73	5fr on 20fr multi	.25	.25
435	A73	15fr multi	.35	.25
436	A73	30fr multi	.70	.45
437	A73	50fr multi	1.40	.95
438	A73	75fr multi	2.25	1.50
		Nos. 434-438 (5)	4.95	3.40

For unoverprinted stamps see note after No. 314.

Man Reading Proclamation — A74

1979, May 2 Litho. Perf. 13½

Black Surcharge and Overprint

439	A74	5fr on 25fr coronation coach	.25	.25
440	A74	10fr Drummer	.30	.30
441	A74	50fr on 40fr with crown, orb, scepter	.70	.70
442	A74	50fr on 200fr shown	1.10	1.10
443	A74	100fr St. Edward's Crown	1.40	1.40
		Nos. 439-443 (5)	3.75	3.75

No. 442 is airmail.

For unoverprinted stamps see note after No. 314.

Nos. 285-289 (Birds) Overprinted or Surcharged like A72-A74

1979, May 2 Litho. Perf. 13

444	A56	15fr multi	.30	.30
445	A56	30fr on 35fr multi	.70	.70
446	A56	50fr on 20fr multi	1.25	1.25
447	A56	50fr on 40fr multi	1.25	1.25
448	A56	200fr on 75fr multi	4.00	4.00
		Nos. 444-448 (5)	7.50	7.50

Nos. 292-296 (Soccer) Overprinted or Surcharged like A72-A74

1979, May 2 Litho. Perf. 13

449	A57	1fr on 100fr multi	.25	.25
450	A57	2fr on 75fr multi	.25	.25
451	A57	3fr on 30fr multi	.25	.25
452	A57	50fr multi	.90	.55
453	A57	200fr multi	2.25	2.25
		Nos. 449-453 (5)	3.90	3.55

No. 453 airmail.

Nos. 301-305 (Composers) Overprinted or Surcharged like A72-A74

1979, May 2 Perf. 13½

454	A58	5fr on 100fr multi	.25	.25
455	A58	30fr multi	1.25	1.25
456	A58	40fr multi	1.75	1.75
457	A58	50fr multi	2.25	2.25
458	A58	50fr on 200fr multi	3.50	3.50
		Nos. 454-458 (5)	9.00	9.00

No. 458 airmail.

Intl. Year of the Child — A75

Intl. Year of the Child emblem and: 20fr, Astronaut on moon, child in astronaut costume. 30fr, Luger, child with snowboard. 40fr, Woman from Dürer painting, child practicing Chinese calligraphy. 100fr, Steam locomotive, child with toy train. 200fr, Adults and children playing soccer. 400fr, Olympic rower, child in rowboat.

500fr, Karl Benz, boy in toy car, horiz.

No. 465A, Louis Blériot, child with remote-control airplane, horiz.

No. 465B, Capt. James Cook, child with teddy bear and toy gun, horiz.

1979, May 30 Litho. Perf. 13½

459	A75	20fr multi	.25	.25
460	A75	30fr multi	.30	.25
461	A75	40fr multi	.40	.25
462	A75	100fr multi	1.00	.35

463	A75	200fr multi	2.00	.50
464	A75	400fr multi	4.00	1.10
		Nos. 459-464 (6)	7.95	2.70

Souvenir Sheet

465	A75	500fr multi	5.75	2.75

Litho. & Embossed

Size: 51x42mm

465A	A75	1500fr gold & multi	13.50	—

Souvenir Sheet

Perf. 13¼

465B	A75	1500fr gold & multi	13.50	—

Nos. 463-465A are airmail. Nos. 465 and 465B each contain one 51x42mm stamp.

Litchi Nuts — A76

1979, June 15 Litho. *Perf. 12½*

466	A76	60fr shown	1.00	.30
467	A76	70fr Papayas	1.25	.45
468	A76	100fr Avocados	1.40	.55
469	A76	125fr Bananas	1.90	.90
		Nos. 466-469 (4)	5.55	2.20

For surcharges see Nos. 515, 533.

Basketball Players — A77

1979, Aug. 28 Litho. *Perf. 13*

470	A77	200fr multi	2.50	1.40

Indian Ocean Olympics.

Nos. 176, 198, 218, 187, 159-160 and Type A78 Overprinted in Black

Nimbus Weather Satellite — A78

No. 475, Apollo-Soyuz. No. 479, Molniya.

Printing & Perfs. as Before, Litho. (A78)

1979, Sept. 15 *Perf. 13 (A78)*

471	A40	35fr multi	.70	.70
472	A43	75fr multi	1.50	1.50
473	A46	75fr multi	1.50	1.50
474	A78	75fr multi	1.50	1.50
475	A78	100fr multi	2.10	2.10
476	A41	100fr multi	2.10	2.10
477	A37	100fr multi	2.10	2.10
478	A37	200fr multi	4.25	4.25
479	A78	200fr multi	4.25	4.25
		Nos. 471-479 (9)	20.00	20.00

Nos. 476-479 airmail.
For type A78 see note after No. 314.

Nos. 166-167, 169, 235-236, 257, 262, 309, 311, the unissued Rubens set (4 values) and Durer set (5 values) exist with this overprint, supposedly also issued Sept. 15. Value, set of 18 $12.

Dugout on Beach A80

Anjouan Puppet — A81

1980, Jan. 4 Litho. *Perf. 13*

498	A80	60fr multi	1.00	.25
499	A81	100fr multi	1.50	.45

For surcharge see No. 534.

Sultan Said Ali — A82

1980, Feb. 20 *Perf. 12½x13*

500	A82	40fr shown	.75	.25
501	A82	60fr Sultan Ahmed	1.00	.25

Sherlock Holmes, Doyle — A83

1980, Feb. 25 *Perf. 12½*

502	A83	200fr multi	4.75	1.75

Sir Arthur Conan Doyle (1859-1930), writer.
For surcharge see No. 513.

Grand Mosque, Holy Ka'aba, Mecca — A84

1980, Mar. 12 *Perf. 13x12½*

503	A84	75fr multi	1.00	.40

Hegira, 1350th anniv.
For surcharge see No. 514.

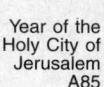

Year of the Holy City of Jerusalem A85

1980, Mar. 12 *Perf. 13x13½*

504	A85	60fr multi	1.00	.40

Kepler, Copernicus and Pluto — A86

1980, Apr. 30 Litho. *Perf. 12½*

505	A86	400fr multi	4.50	2.25

Discovery of Pluto, 50th anniversary.
For surcharge see No. 531.

Muscle System, Avicenna — A87

1980, Apr. 30 Engr. *Perf. 13*

506	A87	60fr multi	1.00	.40

Avicenna, Arab physician, birth millennium.

Soccer Players — A88

World Cup Soccer 1982; Various soccer scenes. 60fr, 150fr, 500fr, vert.

1981, Feb. 20 Litho. *Perf. 12½*

507	A88	60fr multi	.65	.25
508	A88	75fr multi	.75	.25
509	A88	90fr multi	1.25	.25
510	A88	100fr multi	1.10	.45
511	A88	150fr multi	1.90	.60
		Nos. 507-511 (5)	5.65	1.80

Souvenir Sheet

512	A88	500fr multi	5.00	1.50

For overprints & surcharge see Nos. 532, 555-560.

Nos. 502-503, 469 Surcharged

and

Merops Superciliosus A89

Red, Black or Blue Surcharge

Perf. 12½, 13x12½ (No. 514)

1981, Feb. Litho.

513	A83	15fr on 200fr multi	.50	.50
514	A84	20fr on 75fr multi	.50	.50
515	A76	40fr on 125fr multi (Bk)	1.50	1.50
516	A89	60fr on 75fr multi (Bl)	3.00	3.00
		Nos. 513-516 (4)	5.50	5.50

A90

Space Exploration: 50fr, Apollo program, vert. 75fr, 100fr, 500fr, Columbia space shuttle.

1981, July 13 Litho. *Perf. 14*

517	A90	50fr multi	.60	.25
518	A90	75fr multi	.75	.25
519	A90	100fr multi	1.25	.30
520	A90	450fr multi	6.00	1.50
		Nos. 517-520 (4)	8.60	2.30

Souvenir Sheet

521	A90	500fr multi	5.00	1.50

For overprints and surcharges see Nos. 599, 804F.

Prince Charles and Lady Diana, Buckingham Palace — A91

1981, Sept. 1 Litho. *Perf. 14½*

522	A91	125fr shown	1.00	.30
523	A91	200fr Highwood House	1.50	.60
524	A91	450fr Carnarvon Castle	3.50	1.25
a.		Souvenir sheet of 3	6.50	2.00
		Nos. 522-524 (3)	6.00	2.15

Royal wedding. No. 524a contains Nos. 522-524 in changed colors.
For overprints see Nos. 551-553.

Official Stamp Flag Type

1981, Oct. Litho. *Perf. 13*

526	O1	5fr multi	.25	.25
527	O1	15fr multi	.25	.25
528	O1	25fr multi	.30	.25
529	O1	35fr multi	.40	.25
530	O1	75fr multi	.75	.35
		Nos. 526-530 (5)	1.95	1.35

Nos. 505, 509, 468, 499 Surcharged

1981, Nov. Litho. *Perf. 12½*

531	A86	5fr on 400fr multi	.40	.40
532	A88	20fr on 90fr multi	.80	.80
533	A76	45fr on 100fr multi	2.00	.25
534	A81	45fr on 100fr multi	2.00	.25
		Nos. 531-534 (4)	5.20	1.70

75th Anniv. of Grand Prix — A92

Winners and their Cars: 20fr, Mercedes, 1914. 50fr, Delage, 1925. 75fr, Rudi Caracciola, 1926. 90fr, Stirling Moss, 1955. 150fr, Maserati, 1957.
500fr, Changing wheels, vert.

1981, Dec. 28 Litho. *Perf. 12½*

535	A92	20fr multicolored	.30	.25
536	A92	50fr multicolored	.65	.25
537	A92	75fr multicolored	.90	.25
538	A92	90fr multicolored	1.10	.35
539	A92	150fr multicolored	1.60	.45
		Nos. 535-539 (5)	4.55	1.55

Souvenir Sheet

Perf. 13

540	A92	500fr multicolored	6.00	1.75

For overprint see No. 600.

Scouting Year — A93

1982, Jan. 5 *Perf. 12½*

541	A93	50fr Climbing rocks	.60	.25
542	A93	75fr Boating	.85	.25
543	A93	250fr Sailing	3.00	.90
544	A93	350fr Sailing, diff.	3.75	1.10
		Nos. 541-544 (4)	8.20	2.50

Souvenir Sheet

Perf. 13

545	A93	500fr Baden-Powell	6.50	1.75

For overprint see No. 601.

21st Birthday of Princess of Wales — A94

Various portraits of Princess Diana.

1982, July 1 Litho. *Perf. 14*

546	A94	200fr multi	2.00	.60
547	A94	300fr multi	3.25	.90

Souvenir Sheet

548	A94	500fr multi	5.00	1.50

Johannes von Goethe (1749-1832) A95

1982, July

549	A95	75fr multi	.75	.25
550	A95	350fr multi	3.75	.90

Nos. 522-524a Overprinted in Blue

1982, July 31 *Perf. 14½*

551	A91	125fr multi	1.50	.60
552	A91	200fr multi	2.50	.90
553	A91	450fr multi	4.50	2.00
a.		Souvenir sheet of 3	7.50	7.50
		Nos. 551-553 (3)	8.50	3.50

Birth of Prince William of Wales, June 21.

Nos. 507-512 Overprinted with Finalists and Score in Red

1982, Sept. 20 Litho. *Perf. 12½*

555	A88	60fr multi	.65	.25
556	A88	75fr multi	.75	.35
557	A88	90fr multi	1.00	.45
558	A88	100fr multi	1.10	.45
559	A88	150fr multi	1.40	.60
		Nos. 555-559 (5)	4.90	2.10

Souvenir Sheet

560	A88	500fr multi	5.00	1.50

Italy's victory in 1982 World Cup.

Paintings by Norman Rockwell A96

1982, Oct. 11 Litho. *Perf. 14*

561	A96	60fr 1931	.65	.25
562	A96	75fr 1925	.70	.25
563	A96	100fr 1922	1.25	.25
564	A96	150fr 1919	1.40	.55
565	A96	200fr 1924	2.00	.60
566	A96	300fr 1918	3.50	1.00
		Nos. 561-566 (6)	9.50	2.90

Sultans of Anjouan — A97

30fr, Said Mohamed Sidi, vert. 60fr, Ahmed Abdallah, vert. 75fr, Salim. 300fr, Sidi, Abdallah.

1982, Dec. *Perf. 12½x13, 13x12½*

567	A97	30fr multicolored	.40	.25
568	A97	60fr multicolored	.75	.25
569	A97	75fr multicolored	1.00	.25
570	A97	300fr multicolored	3.50	1.40
		Nos. 567-570 (4)	5.65	2.15

Landscapes — A98

1983, Sept. 30 Litho. *Perf. 13*

571	A98	60fr D'Ziani Lake	.75	.30
572	A98	100fr Sunset	1.25	.45
573	A98	175fr Anjouan, vert.	2.00	.75
574	A98	360fr Itsandra	4.00	1.25
575	A98	400fr Anjouan, diff.	5.00	1.60
		Nos. 571-575 (5)	13.00	4.35

For surcharge see No. 815S.

Woman from Moheli A99

1983, Oct. 17 Litho. *Perf. 12½x13*

576	A99	30fr shown	.45	.25
577	A99	45fr Woman, diff.	.65	.25
578	A99	50fr Man from Mayotte	.70	.25
		Nos. 576-578 (3)	1.80	.75

Horses — A100

1983, Nov. 30 Litho. *Perf. 13*

579	A100	75fr Arabian	.70	.25
580	A100	100fr Anglo-Arabian	1.00	.30
581	A100	125fr Lippizaner	1.20	.40
582	A100	150fr Tennessee	1.50	.50
583	A100	200fr Appaloosa	2.00	.70
584	A100	300fr Pure English	3.00	1.00
585	A100	400fr Clydesdale	4.00	1.25
586	A100	500fr Andalusian	5.00	1.50
		Nos. 579-586 (8)	18.40	5.90

Double Portrait, by Raphael A101

200fr, Girl, fresco detail. 300fr, St. George Killing Dragon. 400fr, Balthazar Castiglione.

1983, Dec. 30 Litho. *Perf. 13*

587	A101	100fr shown	1.25	.45
588	A101	200fr multicolored	2.50	.80
589	A101	300fr multicolored	3.25	.90
590	A101	400fr multicolored	5.50	1.25
		Nos. 587-590 (4)	12.50	3.40

For surcharges see Nos. 703, 800E, 815M.

Ships and Automobiles — A102

1984, Oct. 9 Litho. *Perf. 12½*

591	A102	100fr William Fawcett	1.25	.30
592	A102	100fr De Dion, 1885	1.50	.30
593	A102	150fr Lightning	1.90	.45
594	A102	150fr Benz Victoria, 1893	2.25	.60
595	A102	200fr Rapido	2.50	.75
596	A102	200fr Columbia Electric, 1901	3.00	.75
597	A102	350fr Sindia	4.50	1.00
598	A102	350fr Fiat, 1902	5.00	1.10
		Nos. 591-598 (8)	21.90	5.25

For surcharge see No. 812Q.

Nos. 521, 540, 545, C126, C131 Ovptd. in Black, Blue, Red or Gold

No. 599

No. 600

No. 601

No. 603

No. 599, '85 / HAMBOURG (Bk). No. 600, TSUKUBA EXPO '85 (Bl). No. 601, ARGENTINA '85/BUENOS AIRES (R). No. 602, Rome, ITALIA '85 emblem (R). No. 603, OLYMPHILEX/ '85 / LAUSANNE (G).

1985, Mar. 11 *Perf. 14, 13*

Souvenir Sheets

599	A90	500fr multi	5.00	5.00
600	A92	500fr multi	5.00	5.00
601	A93	500fr multi	5.00	5.00
602	AP31	500fr multi	5.00	5.00
603	AP32	500fr multi	5.00	5.00
		Nos. 599-603 (5)	25.00	25.00

Nos. 602-603 airmail.

Victor Hugo (1802-1885), Author, Pantheon, Paris — A103

Anniversaries and events: 200fr, IYY, Jules Verne (1828-1905), author. 300fr, IYY, Mark Twain (1835-1910), author. 450fr, Queen Mother, 85th birthday, vert. 500fr, Statue of Liberty, cent., vert.

1985, May 27 Litho. *Perf. 13*

604	A103	100fr multi	1.25	.30
605	A103	200fr multi	2.25	.60
606	A103	300fr multi	3.50	.90
607	A103	450fr multi	5.00	1.25
608	A103	500fr multi	6.00	1.50
		Nos. 604-608 (5)	18.00	4.55

For surcharges see Nos. 704, 800A.

Sea Shells — A104

75fr, Lambis chiragra. 125fr, Strombe lentifinosum. 200fr, Tonna gala. 300fr, Cymbium glans. 450fr, Lambis crocata.

1985, Oct. 23 *Perf. 14*

609	A104	75fr multicolored	1.00	.25
610	A104	125fr multicolored	1.40	.35
611	A104	200fr multicolored	2.25	.60
612	A104	300fr multicolored	3.50	.90
613	A104	450fr multicolored	5.50	1.40
		Nos. 609-613 (5)	13.65	3.50

Comoros Admission to UN, 10th Anniv. — A105

1985, Nov. 12 Litho. *Perf. 13x12½*

614	A105	5fr multi	.25	.25
615	A105	30fr multi	.30	.25
616	A105	75fr multi	.90	.25
617	A105	125fr multi	1.40	.50
618	A105	400fr multi	4.50	1.50
		Nos. 614-618 (5)	7.35	2.75

For surcharge see No. 800F.

Moroni Rotary Club, 20th Anniv. — A106

1985, Nov. 30 *Perf. 13*

619	A106	25fr multi	.40	.25
620	A106	75fr multi	.90	.40
621	A106	125fr multi	1.10	.45
622	A106	500fr multi	4.00	2.00
		Nos. 619-622 (4)	6.40	3.10

Mushrooms — A107

75fr, Boletus edulis. 125fr, Sarcoscypha coccinea. 200fr, Hypholoma fasciculare. 350fr, Astraeus hygrometricus. 500fr, Armillariella mellea.

1985, Dec. 24 *Perf. 13½*

623	A107	75fr multicolored	1.00	.30
624	A107	125fr multicolored	1.20	.45
625	A107	200fr multicolored	2.25	.60
626	A107	350fr multicolored	4.00	.90
627	A107	500fr multicolored	5.50	1.50
		Nos. 623-627 (5)	13.95	3.75

For surcharge see No. 815R.

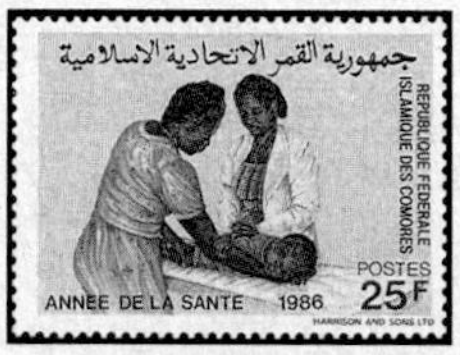

Health Year A108

25fr, Pediatric examination. 100fr, Weighing child. 200fr, Immunization.

1986, Oct. 2 Litho. *Perf. 15x14½*

628	A108	25fr multicolored	.35	.25
629	A108	100fr multicolored	1.50	.60
630	A108	200fr multicolored	2.75	1.25
		Nos. 628-630 (3)	4.60	2.10

For surcharge see No. 705.

Musical Instruments A109

1986, Dec. 24 Litho. *Perf. 13*

631	A109	75fr Ndzoumara	.90	.40
632	A109	125fr Ndzedze	1.25	.60
633	A109	210fr Gaboussi	2.10	.90
634	A109	500fr Ngoma	6.00	1.75
		Nos. 631-634 (4)	10.25	3.65

For surcharges see Nos. 796P, 796T, 800L, 815A.

Role of Women in National Development — A110

1987, Mar. 7 Litho. *Perf. 13*

635	A110	75fr Working fields	.55	.30
636	A110	125fr Harvesting crops, vert.	1.10	.50
637	A110	1000fr Basketweaving	10.00	3.50
		Nos. 635-637 (3)	11.65	4.30

Service Organizations — A111

Emblems and activities: 75fr, Nos. 642, Kiwanis or 643c, Rotary Intl. for child survival. 125fr, Nos. 641, Kiwanis or 643b, Lions Intl. for aid to the handicapped. 210fr, No. 643a, Kiwanis helping poor and homeless children.

1988 Litho. *Perf. 13½*

638	A111	75fr dk bl, lt bl & multi	.75	.30
639	A111	125fr dk brn, lt brn & multi	1.40	.45
640	A111	210fr org, yel & multi	2.25	.75
641	A111	425fr red, pink & multi	4.50	1.75
642	A111	500fr bl, yel & multi	6.00	2.00
643		Strip of 3	13.00	6.00
a.	A111	210fr grn, lt grn & multi	2.10	.75
b.	A111	425fr pur, pink & multi	4.50	1.75
c.	A111	500fr red, orange & multi	6.00	2.00
		Nos. 638-643 (6)	27.90	11.25

For surcharges see Nos. 654-656, 815B, 815W.

A112

1988 Olympics, Calgary and Seoul — A113

75fr, Women's figure skating. 100fr, Running. 125fr, Women's speed skating. 150fr, Equestrian. 350fr, Two-man luge. 400fr, Biathlon. 500fr, Pole vault. 600fr, Soccer.

No. 652, Women's downhill skiing, satellite. No. 653, Track, satellite.

1988 Litho. *Perf. 13½*

644	A112	75fr multicolored	.65	.25
645	A112	100fr multicolored	1.00	.30
646	A112	125fr multicolored	1.00	.40
647	A112	150fr multicolored	1.50	.50
648	A112	350fr multicolored	3.25	.90
649	A112	400fr multicolored	4.00	1.40
650	A112	500fr multicolored	4.00	1.25
651	A112	600fr multicolored	6.00	1.50
		Nos. 644-651 (8)	21.40	6.50

Souvenir Sheets

652	A113	750fr multicolored	7.75	1.50
653	A113	750fr multicolored	7.75	1.50

Nos. 649 and 651-653 are airmail.

For surcharges see Nos. 800C, 800M, 815V.

No. 643 and Service Organization Types Surcharged

No. 655, like #643b. No. 656, like #643c.

1988, July 18 Litho. *Perf. 13½*

654		Strip of 3	5.50	5.00
a.	A111	75fr on 210fr #643a	.65	.45
b.	A111	200fr on 425fr #643b	1.75	.90
c.	A111	300fr on 500fr #643c	2.75	1.25
655	A111	125fr on 425fr pur, lt pur & multi, blk letters	1.10	.60
656	A111	400fr on 500fr car, pink & multi	3.75	2.00
		Nos. 654-656 (3)	10.35	7.60

Nos. 655-656 not issued without surcharge.

Discovery of America, 500th Anniv. (in 1992) — A114

Designs: 75fr, Christopher Columbus, *Santa Maria*. 125fr, Martin Alonzo Pinzon (c. 1441-1493), *Pinta*. 150fr, Vicente Yanez Pinzon (c. 1460-1523), *Nina*. 250fr, Search for Cipango, legendary rich islands off the coast of Asia. 375fr, *Santa Maria* shipwrecked. 450fr, Preparing for 4th voyage. 750fr, Samana Cay landing.

1988, Apr. 18 Litho. *Perf. 13½*

657	A114	75fr multi	.65	.25
658	A114	125fr multi	1.10	.30
659	A114	150fr multi	1.50	.45
660	A114	250fr multi	2.10	.75
661	A114	375fr multi	3.75	1.00
662	A114	450fr multi	4.50	1.25
		Nos. 657-662 (6)	13.60	4.00

Souvenir Sheet

663	A114	750fr multi, horiz.	7.75	1.50

Nos. 661-663 airmail. No. 663 contains one 42x30mm stamp.

For surcharges see Nos. 702, 815D.

1992 Summer Olympics, Barcelona A115

1988, Apr. 18

664	A115	75fr Discus, vert.	.60	.25
665	A115	100fr shown	.90	.30
666	A115	125fr Cycling	1.25	.35
667	A115	150fr Wrestling	1.50	.50
668	A115	375fr Basketball, vert.	3.75	1.00
669	A115	600fr Tennis, vert.	6.00	1.25
		Nos. 664-669 (6)	14.00	3.65

Souvenir Sheet

670	A115	750fr Marathon, vert.	7.75	1.50

Nos. 668-670 are airmail.

Famous Men — A116

Rotary Intl. — A117

150fr, Yuri Gagarin (1934-68), USSR, cosmonaut. 300fr, Jean-Henri Dunant, Red Cross founder. 400fr, Roger Clemens, baseball player. 500fr, Garry Kasparov, USSR, 1985 world chess champion. 600fr, Paul Harris, US, Rotary founder. 750fr, Neil Armstrong walking on the Moon, John F. Kennedy. No. 678, The Thinker by Rodin, Rotary Intl. emblem.

1988, Dec. 6 Litho. *Perf. 13½*

671	A116	150fr multi	1.75	.50
672	A116	300fr multi	1.75	.50
673	A116	400fr multi	1.75	.50
674	A116	500fr multi	1.75	.50
675	A116	600fr multi	1.75	.50
a.		Souv. sheet of 5, #671-675 + label	10.00	—
		Nos. 665-669 (5)	18.40	3.50

Litho. & Embossed

676	A117	1500fr gold & multi	15.00	—

Souvenir Sheets

Litho.

677	A116	750fr multi	7.75	1.50

Litho. & Embossed

678	A117	1500fr gold & multi	15.00	—

Intl. Red Cross, 125th anniv. (300fr), Rotary Intl. (600fr, Nos. 676, 678). Nos. 674-678 are airmail.

Nos. 672-673 exist in souv. sheets of 1.

No. 676 exists in a souvenir sheet of 1. Value $42.50.

Inventors and Sportsmen A118

Portraits and modes of transportation: Designs: 75fr, Alain Prost, F-1 MacLaren-Honda. 125fr, George Stephenson and locomotive *Borsig of 1935.* 500fr, Ettore Bugatti (1881-1947), 1939 Bugatti Aravis Type 57. 600fr, Rudolf Diesel (1858-1913) and V200 BB diesel-electric locomotive. 750fr, Dennis Conner, captain of the *Stars and Stripes,* winner of the 1987 America's Cup. No. 684, Michael Fay, patron of the *New Zealand,* an entry in the America's Cup. No. 685, Enzo Ferrari and 1989 Ferrari Formula 1, horiz.

1988, Dec. 27 Litho. *Perf. 13½*

679	A118	75fr multi	.75	.45
680	A118	125fr multi	1.25	.25
681	A118	500fr multi	5.00	1.25
682	A118	600fr multi	6.00	1.25
683	A118	750fr multi	7.00	1.25
684	A118	1000fr multi	10.00	1.25
		Nos. 679-684 (6)	30.00	5.70

Souvenir Sheet

685	A118	1000fr multi	10.00	1.50

Nos. 683-685 are airmail.
Nos. 679-684 exist in souv. sheets of 1.

Scouts, Butterflies and Birds — A119

Scouts involved in various activities and species: 50fr, Gathering specimens, *Papilio nireus aristophontes oberthur* female. 75fr, Studying specimen and male. 150fr, Cooking out, *Charaxes fulvescens separanus poulton.* 375fr, Picking mushrooms, *Lonchura cucullatus.* 450fr, Examining specimen, *Charaxes castor comoranus rothschild.* 500fr, Identifying specimen, *Zosterops maderaspatana.* 750fr, Studying specimens, *Foudia omissa* and *Charaxes paradoxa lathy* female. No. 692, Photographing specimen, *Junonia rhadama.* No. 694, Examining specimen, *Agapornis cana cana.*

1989 Litho.

686	A119	50fr multi	.50	.25
687	A119	75fr multi	.60	.25
688	A119	150fr multi	1.40	.30
689	A119	375fr multi	4.00	.75
690	A119	450fr multi	4.75	1.00
691	A119	500fr multi	5.75	1.25
		Nos. 686-691 (6)	17.00	3.80

Litho. & Embossed

692	A119	1500fr gold & multi	16.00	—

Souvenir Sheets

Litho.

693	A119	750fr multi	10.00	1.50

Litho. & Embossed

694	A119	1500fr gold & multi	13.00	—

Nos. 690-694 are airmail. Issue dates: Nos. 692, 694, May 15; others, Mar. 15.
No. 692 exists in a souvenir sheet of 1. Value $42.50.
For surcharges see Nos. 800D, 815T.

Gold Medalists of the 1988 Summer Olympics A120

Communication satellites, various equestrians and their mounts: 75fr, Nicole Uphoff, West Germany, individual dressage, and Aussat K3. 150fr, Pierre Durand, France, individual jumping, and Brazilsat. 375fr, Janos Martinek, Hungary, individual modern pentathlon, and ECS 4. 600fr, Mark Todd, New Zealand, individual three-day event, and Olympus. 750fr, Team jumping, West Germany, and satellite. No. 699, Pierre Durand, France, individual show jumping. No. 701, Nicole Uphoff, West Germany, individual dressage.

1989, Apr. 10 Litho. *Perf. 13½*

695	A120	75fr multi	.65	.25
696	A120	150fr multi	1.25	.35
697	A120	375fr multi	3.00	.75
698	A120	600fr multi	5.00	1.25
		Nos. 695-698 (4)	9.90	2.60

Litho. & Embossed

699	A120	1500fr gold & multi	16.00	—

Souvenir Sheets

Litho.

700	A120	750fr multi	6.75	1.50

Litho. & Embossed

701	A120	1500fr gold & multi	13.00	—

No. 701 contains one 39x38mm stamp. Nos. 698-701 are airmail.
No. 699 exists in a souvenir sheet of 1. Value $45.
For surcharges see Nos. 796Q, 804I.

Nos. 660, 588, 605 and 630 Surcharged

1989 Litho. *Perfs. as Before*

702	A114	25fr on 250fr #660	.40	.25
703	A101	150fr on 200fr #588	1.50	.50
704	A103	150fr on 200fr #605	1.50	.50
705	A108	150fr on 200fr #630	1.50	.50
		Nos. 702-705 (4)	4.90	1.75

1992 Summer Olympics, Barcelona A121

1989, Apr. 26 Litho. *Perf. 13½*

706	A121	75fr Running	.65	.25
707	A121	150fr Soccer	1.25	.40
708	A121	300fr Tennis	2.50	.60
709	A121	375fr Baseball	3.25	.80
710	A121	500fr Pommel horse	4.00	1.00
711	A121	600fr Table tennis	5.00	1.25
		Nos. 706-711 (6)	16.65	4.30

Souvenir Sheet

712	A121	750fr Equestrian	6.75	1.50

Nos. 710-712 are airmail.
For surcharges see Nos. 796J, 796K, 800J, 812R.

Dr. Joseph-Ignace Guillotin (1738-1814) — A122

French Revolution, Bicent.: 150fr, French artillery, Gen. Francois-Christophe Kellermann (1735-1820). 375fr, Royalist insurgents & leader, Jean Cottereau (1757-94). 600fr, King Louis XVI (1774-92), troops. 1000fr, Storming of the Bastille & Jacques Necker, statesman (1732-1804). No. 717, Lafayette, Mounier, Sieyes & Declaration of the Rights of Man and Citizen. No. 719, Robespierre & St. Just before the Convention on 9 Thermidor.

1989, Oct. 25 Litho. *Perf. 13½*

713	A122	75fr multicolored	.70	.25
714	A122	150fr multicolored	1.25	.35
715	A122	375fr multicolored	3.00	.60
716	A122	600fr multicolored	5.00	1.25
		Nos. 713-716 (4)	9.95	2.45

Litho. & Embossed

717	A122	1500fr gold & multi	13.00	—

Souvenir Sheets

Litho.

718	A122	1000fr multicolored	8.50	1.75

Litho. & Embossed

719	A122	1500fr gold & multi	13.00	

Philexfrance 1989. No. 716-719 are airmail.
No. 714 incorrectly inscribed "Francois-Etienne."
Nos. 713-716 exist in souvenir sheets of 1.
No. 717 exists in a souvenir sheet of 1. Value $22.
For surcharges see Nos. 796B, 800W, 804J.

Airport Pavilion A124

Designs: 10fr, 25fr, Airport pavilion. 50fr, 75fr, 150fr, Federal Assembly.

1990, Apr. 1 Litho. *Perf. 13*

722	A124	5fr brn, org & brt red	.25	.25
723	A124	10fr brn, org & brt bl	.25	.25
724	A124	25fr brn, org & brt grn	.25	.25
725	A124	50fr blk & brt red	.45	.25
726	A124	75fr blk & brt bl	.75	.30
727	A124	150fr blk & grn	1.40	.60
		Nos. 722-727 (6)	3.35	1.90

World Cup Soccer Championships, Italy — A125

Players from: 50fr, Brazil. 75fr, England. 100fr, Federal Republic of Germany. 150fr, Belgium. 375fr, Italy. 600fr, Argentina. 750fr, Argentina and Italy.

1990 Litho. *Perf. 13½*

728	A125	50fr multicolored	.45	.25
729	A125	75fr multicolored	.65	.30
730	A125	100fr multicolored	.80	.35
731	A125	150fr multicolored	1.10	.45
732	A125	375fr multicolored	3.00	1.00
733	A125	600fr multicolored	5.00	1.25
		Nos. 728-733 (6)	11.00	3.60

Litho. & Embossed

734	A125	1500fr gold & multi	13.00	5.00

Souvenir Sheets

Litho.

735	A125	750fr multicolored	6.75	1.50

Litho. & Embossed

736	A125	1500fr gold & multi	13.00	—

Nos. 732-736 are airmail.
No. 734 exists in a souvenir sheet of 1. Value $22.50.
For surcharges see Nos. 796L, 796O, 804K.

Telecom '91 A125a

1990, Oct. 29 Litho. *Perf. 13½*

736A	A125a	75fr Emblem, vert.	1.00	.60
736B	A125a	150fr shown	2.00	1.25

Nos. 736A-736B exist imperf.

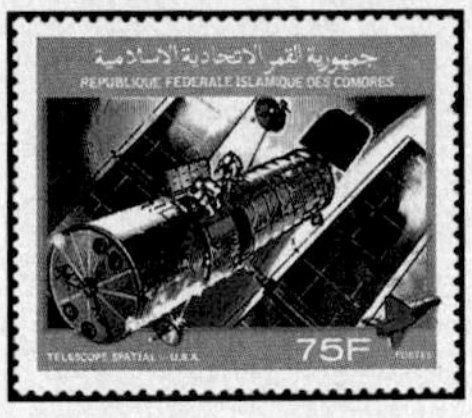

A126

Designs: 75fr, Hubble Space Telescope placed in orbit. 150fr, Pope John Paul II, Pres. Gorbachev meet Dec. 3, 1989. 200fr, Kevin Mitchell, San Francisco Giants, Natl. League Most Valuable Player, 1989. 250fr, De Gaulle, France, and Adenauer, West Germany, meet in Sept. 1962. 300fr, Cassini probe to Titan, 2002. 375fr, Bullet train and Concorde, France. 450fr, Garry Kasparov, World Chess Champion. 500fr, Paul Harris (1868-1947), founder of Rotary Intl.

1990, Nov. 26 Litho. *Perf. 13½*

737	A126	75fr sil & multi	.75	.25
738	A126	150fr sil & multi	1.50	.40
739	A126	200fr sil & multi	2.00	.40
740	A126	250fr sil & multi	2.50	.40
741	A126	300fr sil & multi	3.00	.50
742	A126	375fr sil & multi	3.75	.65
743	A126	450fr sil & multi	4.50	1.00
744	A126	500fr sil & multi	5.25	.75
		Nos. 737-744 (8)	23.25	4.35

Nos. 743-744 are airmail.
No. 737-744 exist in souv. sheets of 1. Value, set of 8 $50.
For surcharges see Nos. 796A, 796R, 800I, 804A, 804L, 815E, 815U.

A127

Winter Olympics participants: 75fr, Edi Reinalter, Switzerland, slalom, 1948. 100fr, Canadian hockey team, 1924. 375fr, Gratia Van der Oye, women's slalom, Holland, 1936. 600fr, Heikki Hasu, Finland, combined cross country and ski jumping, 1948. 750fr, Helene Engelman & Alfred Berger, Austria, pairs figure skating, 1924. No. 751, Speed skater, horiz. No. 751A, Luge, horiz.

1990, Dec. 10

746	A127	75fr multicolored	.60	.25
747	A127	100fr multicolored	.75	.30
748	A127	375fr multicolored	3.50	1.00
749	A127	600fr multicolored	6.00	1.25
		Nos. 746-749 (4)	10.85	2.80

Souvenir Sheet

750	A127	750fr multicolored	7.00	1.50

Litho. & Embossed

751	A127	1500fr gold & multi	16.00	—

Souvenir Sheet

751A	A127	1500fr gold & multi	15.00	—

1992 Winter Olympics, Albertville. Nos. 748-751A are airmail. No. 750 contains one 36x41mm stamp.
No. 751 exists in a souvenir sheet of 1, Value $22.
For surcharges see Nos. 796M, 800K, 804M, 812S.

A128

Ground station, Moroni Volo-Volo.

1991, May 17 Litho. *Perf. 13½*

752	A128	75fr multicolored	1.00	.25
753	A128	150fr multicolored	1.60	.45
754	A128	225fr multicolored	2.40	.75
755	A128	300fr multicolored	3.50	1.00
756	A128	500fr multicolored	5.50	1.25
		Nos. 752-756 (5)	14.00	3.70

For surcharge see 815N.

Indian Ocean Conference — A129

1991, June 17

757	A129	75fr multicolored	.50	.25
758	A129	150fr multicolored	1.40	.75
759	A129	225fr multicolored	2.00	1.00
		Nos. 757-759 (3)	3.90	2.00

World War II, 50th Anniv. A130

Actors, Films: 150fr, Errol Flynn, Objective Burma. 300fr, Henry Fonda, The Longest Day. 450fr, Humphrey Bogart, Sahara.

1991, Aug. 5

760	A130	150fr sil & multi	1.75	.45
761	A130	300fr sil & multi	3.25	.75
762	A130	450fr sil & multi	5.00	.90
		Nos. 760-762 (3)	10.00	2.10

No. 762 is airmail. Nos. 760-762 exist in souvenir sheets of 1. Value, set of 3 $15.

For surcharges see Nos. 796D, 800H, 804B, 804G.

A131

Charles de Gaulle A132

De Gaulle and: 125fr, Battle of Koufra. 375fr, Battle of Britain. 500fr, Battle of Monte Cassino. 1000fr, Airplanes. 1500fr, De Gaulle at podium.

1991, Aug. 5 Litho. *Perf. 13½*

763	A131	125fr multi	1.50	.30
764	A131	375fr multi	3.00	.75
765	A131	500fr multi	5.00	.90
		Nos. 763-765 (3)	9.50	1.95

Souvenir Sheet

766	A131	1000fr multi	12.00	2.00

Litho. & Embossed

767	A132	1500fr gold & multi	16.00	—

Nos. 765-767 are airmail. No. 767 exists in souvenir sheet of 1. Value $20.

For surcharges see Nos. 796G, 804N, 816I.

Anniversaries and Events — A133

Designs: 100fr, Satellite Columbus in polar orbit. 150fr, Gandhi. 250fr, Jean-Henri Dunant. 300fr, Wolfgang Amadeus Mozart. 375fr, Brandenburg Gate. 400fr, Konrad Adenauer. 450fr, Elvis Presley. 500fr, Ferdinand von Zeppelin.

1991, Nov. 18 Litho. *Perf. 13½*

768	A133	100fr multicolored	1.25	.30
769	A133	150fr multicolored	1.60	.35
770	A133	250fr multicolored	2.50	.60
771	A133	300fr multicolored	3.00	.60
772	A133	375fr multicolored	4.25	.90
773	A133	400fr multicolored	5.00	.90
774	A133	450fr multicolored	5.50	1.00
a.		Souv. sheet, #771, 774	—	—
775	A133	500fr multicolored	5.50	1.00
a.		Souv. sheet, #772-773, 775	—	—
		Nos. 768-775 (8)	28.60	5.65

Nobel Peace Prize, 90th anniv. (No. 770). Mozart, bicent. of death (No. 771). Brandenburg Gate, bicent. (No. 772). Konrad Adenauer, 25th anniv. of death (No. 773). Elvis Presley, 15th anniv. of death (in 1992) (No. 774). Count Zeppelin, 75th anniv. of death (in 1992) (No. 775).

Nos. 774-775 are airmail. Nos. 768-775 exist in souvenir sheets of 1. Value, set $50.

For surcharges see Nos. 796F, 796H, 800G, 804C, 804O, 815F, 815O, 816J.

Mushrooms — A134

75fr, Cepe comestible. 150fr, Geastre en etoile. 600fr, Pezize ecarlate.

1992, Mar. 23 Litho. *Perf. 13½*

776	A134	75fr multicolored	.80	.40
777	A134	150fr multicolored	1.50	.60
778	A134	600fr multicolored	6.00	1.50
		Nos. 776-778 (3)	8.30	2.50

No. 778 is airmail. Nos. 776-778 exist imperf. and in souvenir sheets of one. Values, imperf set $12; set of souvenir sheets $10.

Shells A135

125fr, Conus textile. 150fr, Cypraecassis rufa. 500fr, Leporicypraea mappa. 750fr, Nautilus pompilius.

1992, Mar. 23

779	A135	125fr multicolored	1.60	.50
780	A135	150fr multicolored	1.75	.65
781	A135	500fr multicolored	6.00	1.90
		Nos. 779-781 (3)	9.35	3.05

Souvenir Sheet

782	A135	750fr multicolored	10.50	2.00

Nos. 781-782 are airmail. Nos. 779-781 exist imperf. and in souvenir sheets of one. Values, imperf set $15; set of souvenir sheets $12. No. 782 exists imperf. Value, $12.

For surcharges see Nos. 800N, 816K.

Space Programs A136

Designs: 75fr, Mercury rocket, chimpanzee Ham, US. 125fr, Mars Observer, US. No. 785, Veronica rocket, cat Felix, France. No. 786, Mars rover, US, Mars car, USSR. 500fr, Phobos project, USSR. 600fr, Sputnik II, dog Laika, USSR. 1000fr, Viking, US, vert.

1992, Mar. 30 Litho. *Perf. 13½*

783	A136	75fr multicolored	1.25	.25
784	A136	125fr multicolored	1.75	.30
785	A136	150fr multicolored	2.25	.70
786	A136	150fr multicolored	2.10	.70
787	A136	500fr multicolored	6.50	1.25
a.		Souv. sheet, #784, 786-787	—	—
788	A136	600fr multicolored	7.75	1.40
a.		Souv. sheet, #783, 785, 788	—	—
		Nos. 783-788 (6)	21.60	4.60

Souvenir Sheet

789	A136	1000fr multicolored	13.00	2.25

Nos. 787-789 are airmail. Nos. 783-788 exist imperf. and in souvenir sheets of one. Values: imperf set, $32.50; set of souvenir sheets, $25. No. 789 contains one 30x42mm stamp.

For surcharges see Nos. 800O, 804Q.

Voyages of Discovery A137

Designs: 75fr, Space shuttle Endeavour, sailing ship Endeavour, Capt. Cook. 100fr, Satellite, sailing ship Golden Hinde, Sir Francis Drake. 150fr, ISO observation satellite, sailing ship Susan Constant, John Smith. 225fr, Probe B, sailing ship Discovery, Robert F. Scott. 375fr, Magellan probe over Venus, sailing ship, Ferdinand Magellan. 500fr, Newton probe, sailing ship Sao Gabriel, Vasco da Gama.

1000fr, Hermes-Columbus space shuttle, Columbus and his fleet.

1992, May 28 Litho. *Perf. 13½*

790	A137	75fr multicolored	1.25	.25
791	A137	100fr multicolored	1.40	.30
792	A137	150fr multicolored	2.25	.45
793	A137	225fr multicolored	2.75	.75
794	A137	375fr multicolored	5.25	1.00
795	A137	500fr multicolored	6.00	1.25
a.		Souvenir sheet of 6, #790-795	15.00	7.00
		Nos. 790-795 (6)	18.90	4.00

Souvenir Sheet

796	A137	1000fr multicolored	13.00	2.25

Nos. 794-796 are airmail. Nos. 790-795 exist imperf. in souvenir sheets of one. Values: imperf sets $35; set of souvenir sheets $45.

For surcharges see Nos. 796E, 800P, 804P.

Various Stamps Surcharged

a — (Obliterator of dots)

Methods and Perfs as Before

1992-95

796A	A126	10fr on 300fr #741	—	
796B	A122	15fr on 375fr #715	—	
796C	AP41	25fr on 210fr #C164	—	
796D	A130	25fr on 300fr #761	—	
796E	A137	25fr on 375fr #794	—	
796F	A133	35fr on 400fr #773	—	
796G	A131	50fr on 375fr #764	—	
796H	A133	50fr on 375fr #772	—	
796I	AP34	50fr on 475fr #C138	—	
796J	A121	75fr on 300fr #708	—	—
796K	A121	75fr on 375fr #709	—	
796L	A125	75fr on 375fr #732	—	
796M	A127	75fr on 375fr #748	—	
796N	AP42	75fr on 600fr #C170	—	
796O	A125	100fr on 375fr #732	—	
796P	A109	150fr on 210fr #633	—	
796Q	A120	150fr on 375fr #697	—	—
796R	A126	150fr on 375fr #742	—	
796S	AP40	150fr on 450fr #C162	—	
796T	A109	150fr on 500fr #634	—	
796U	AP42	150fr on 500fr #C169	—	

No. 796J exists with quadruple surcharge.

No. 796Q exists with inverted surcharge and with double surcharge, one inverted.

Organization of African Unity, 30th Anniv. — A138

1993, Feb. 15 Litho. *Perf. 13½x13*

797	A138	25fr blue & multi	.25	.25
798	A138	50fr pink & multi	.50	.25

Perf. 12

799	A138	75fr green & multi	1.40	.45
800	A138	150fr vermilion & multi	2.25	1.00
		Nos. 797-800 (4)	4.40	1.95

Various Stamps Surcharged

b — (Bar obliterator)

Methods and Perfs as Before

1992-95

800A	A103	50fr on 450fr #607	—	
x.		Zero in surcharge thin at top and bottom	—	
800B	AP47	75fr on 800fr #C192	—	
800C	A112	100fr on 350fr #648	—	—
800D	A119	100fr on 375fr #689	—	
g.		Zero in surcharge thin at top and bottom	—	
y.		150fr on 375fr #689 (error)	—	
800E	A101	100fr on 400fr #590	—	—
800F	A105	100fr on 400fr #618	—	
h.		Zero in surcharge thin at top and bottom	—	
800G	A133	100fr on 400fr #773	—	
i.		Zero in surcharge thin at top and bottom	—	
800H	A130	125fr on 450fr #762	—	
800I	A126	150fr on 250fr #740	—	—
800J	A121	150fr on 375fr #709	—	
z.		Zero in surcharge thin at top and bottom	—	
800K	A127	150fr on 375fr #748	—	
a.		Zero in surcharge thin at top and bottom	—	
800L	A109	150fr on 500fr #634	—	—
k.		Zero in surcharge thin at top and bottom	—	
800M	A112	150fr on 500fr #650	—	
b.		Zero in surcharge thin at top and bottom	—	
800N	A135	150fr on 500fr #781	—	—
800O	A136	150fr on 500fr #787	—	
800P	A137	150fr on 500fr #795	—	
c.		Zero in surcharge thin at top and bottom	—	

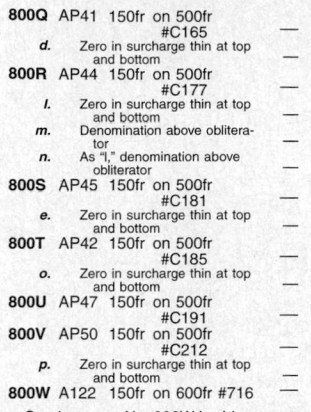

800Q AP41 150fr on 500fr #C165 —
d. Zero in surcharge thin at top and bottom —
800R AP44 150fr on 500fr #C177 —
l. Zero in surcharge thin at top and bottom —
m. Denomination above obliterator —
n. As "l," denomination above obliterator —
800S AP45 150fr on 500fr #C181 —
e. Zero in surcharge thin at top and bottom —
800T AP42 150fr on 500fr #C185 —
o. Zero in surcharge thin at top and bottom —
800U AP47 150fr on 500fr #C191 —
800V AP50 150fr on 500fr #C212 —
p. Zero in surcharge thin at top and bottom —
800W A122 150fr on 600fr #716 —

Surcharge on No. 800W is sideways reading top to bottom. Nos. 800B and 800F exist with inverted surcharge, Nos. 800F, 800R, 800W, and perhaps other values exist with misplaced surcharge.

No. 800F exists with zeros in surcharge in different sizes.

1994 World Cup Soccer Championships, U.S. — A139

1993, May 12 Litho. *Perf. 13x12½*

801 A139 25fr red & multi .25 .25
802 A139 75fr brown & multi .65 .30
803 A139 100fr blue & multi 1.40 .40
804 A139 150fr green & multi 1.60 .60
Nos. 801-804 (4) 3.90 1.55

Various Stamps Surcharged Type "b" in Black or Red

Methods and Perfs as Before

1992-95

804A A126 200fr on 300fr #741 —
s. Zero in surcharge thin at top and bottom —
804B A130 200fr on 300fr #761 —
804C A133 200fr on 300fr #771 —
w. Zero in surcharge thin at top and bottom — —
804D AP45 200fr on 300fr #C180 —
x. Zero in surcharge thin at top and bottom —
804E AP47 200fr on 300fr #C190 —
t. Zero in surcharge thin at top and bottom —
804F A90 200fr on 450fr #520 —
u. Overprint right side up —
y. Overprint right side up, zero in surcharge thin at top and bottom —
804G A130 200fr on 450fr #762 —
a. Zero in surcharge thin at top and bottom —
b. As "a," two obliterators —
804H AP40 200fr on 450fr #C162 —
c. Zero in surcharge thin at top and bottom —
804I A120 225fr on 375fr #697 —
804J A122 225fr on 375fr #715 —
804K A125 225fr on 375fr #732 —
804L A126 225fr on 375fr #742 —
804M A127 225fr on 375fr #748 —
v. "f" in surcharge omitted —
804N A127 225fr on 375fr #764 —
804O A133 225fr on 375fr #772 —
804P A137 225fr on 375fr #794 —
804Q A136 225fr on 500fr #787 —

Red Surcharge

804R AP40 200fr on 300fr #C161 —

Surcharge on No. 804F is inverted.

No. 804D exists with "020fr" surcharge. Nos. 804D and 804F exist with zeroes in surcharge in different sizes.

Intl. Telecommunications Day — A140

1993, May 17

805 A140 50fr red & multi .40 .25
806 A140 75fr blue & multi .65 .30
807 A140 100fr green & multi 1.10 .40
808 A140 150fr black & multi 1.60 .60
Nos. 805-808 (4) 3.75 1.55

Miniature Sheet

Prehistoric Animals — A141

Designs: a, 75fr, Edaphosaurus. b, 75fr, Moschops. c, 75fr, Sauroctonus. d, 75fr, Ornitholestes. e, 75fr, Kentrosaurus. f, 75fr, Compsognathus. g, 75fr, Styracosaurus. h, 75fr, Acanthopholis. i, 150fr, Edmontonia. j, 150fr, Struthiomimus. k, 450fr, Dromiceiomimus. l, 450fr, Iguanodon. m, 150fr, Diatryma. n, 150fr, Uintatherium. o, 525fr, Synthetoceras. p, 525fr, Euryapteryx.

1200fr, Tyrannosaurus rex.

1994, Apr. 5 Litho. *Perf. 13½*

809 A141 Sheet of 16, #a.-p. 22.50 9.00

Souvenir Sheet

810 A141 1200fr multicolored 13.00 3.00

No. 810 is airmail and contains one 42x60mm stamp.

Miniature Sheets

Flora — A142

No. 811a: 75fr, Hibiscus syriacus. b, 75fr, Anacardier. c, 75fr, Suillus lutens. d, 150fr, Pyrostegia venusta. e, 150fr, Manioc. f, 150fr, Lycogala epidendron. g, 525fr, Allamanda cathartica. h, 525fr, Cacao. i, 525fr, Clathrus ruber.

Butterflies, insects: No. 812a, 75fr, Colotis zoe. b, 150fr, Acherontia atropos. c, 450fr, Danaus chrysippus. d, 75fr, Charaxes comoranus. e, 150fr, Euchloron megaera. f, 450fr, Papilio phorbanta. g, 75fr, Hypurgus ova. h, 150fr, Onthophagus catta. i, 450fr, Echinosoma bolivari.

1994, May 24 Litho. *Perf. 13½*

811 A142 Sheet of 9 16.00 5.50
j. Souvenir sheet of 3, #811a, 811d, 811g *16.00 5.00*
k. Souvenir sheet of 3, #811b, 811e, 811h *16.00 5.00*
l. Souvenir sheet of 3, #811c, 811f, 811i *16.00 5.00*
812 A142 Sheet of 9, #a.-i. 15.00 5.00
j. Souv. sheet of 3, #812a-812c *16.00 5.00*
k. Souv. sheet of 3, #812d-812f *16.00 5.00*
l. Souv. sheet of 3, #812g-812i *16.00 5.00*

For surcharges see No. 826F.

Independence, 20th Anniv. — A142a

Designs: 100fr, 200fr, 300fr, Maps of Grand Comoro, Moheli, Mayotte and Anjouan.

1995 (?) Litho. *Perf. 13x12¾*

812M A142a 100fr multi
812N A142a 200fr multi — —
812O A142a 300fr multi

For surcharge see No. 826M.

Various Stamps Surcharged in Gold

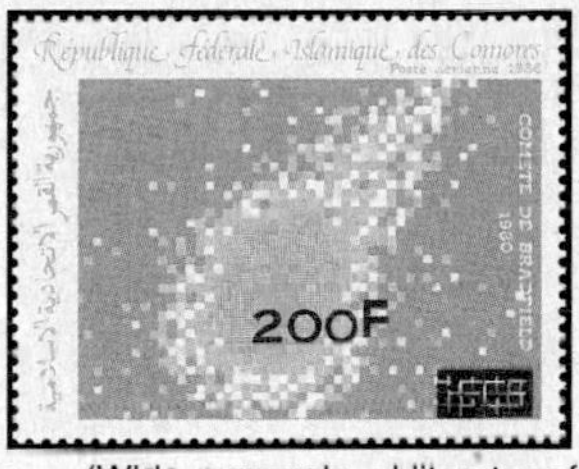

c — (Wide numerals, obliterator of small sqares in grid)

Methods and Perfs as Before

1996, Dec.

812P AP40 200fr on 300fr #C161 —
812Q A102 200fr on 350fr #598 —
812R A121 200fr on 375fr #709 —
v. "2" same size as "0" —
812S A127 200fr on 375fr #748 —
812T AP31 200fr on 400fr #C125 — —
812U AP44 200fr on 500fr #C177 —

Size of numerals and obliteration grids varies.

A143

Diana, Princess of Wales (1961-97): Various portraits.

1997, Dec. 15 Litho. *Perf. 14*

813 A143 150fr Sheet of 12, #a.-l. 10.00 4.00
814 A143 375fr Sheet of 6, #a.-f. 12.00 5.00

Souvenir Sheet

815 A143 1000fr multicolored 5.50 2.25

Various Stamps Surcharged Type "c" in Black

Methods and Perfs as Before

1996, Dec.

815A A109 200fr on 210fr #633 —
815B A111 200fr on 210fr #640 —
815C AP41 200fr on 210fr #C164 — —
815D A114 200fr on 250fr #660 —
815E A126 200fr on 250fr #740 —
815F A133 200fr on 250fr #770 —
815G AP30 200fr on 250fr #C116 — —
815H AP38 200fr on 250fr #C151 —
815I AP38 200fr on 250fr #C152 —
x. Pair, #815H-815I + label —
815J AP42 200fr on 250fr #C168 —
815K AP42 200fr on 250fr #C184 —
815L AP28 200fr on 260fr #C110 — —
815M A101 200fr on 300fr #589 —
y. With gold obliterator over old value — —
815N A128 200fr on 300fr #755 —
815O A133 200fr on 300fr #771 —
815P AP31 200fr on 300fr #C124 —
815Q AP37 200fr on 300fr #C150 —
815R A107 200fr on 350fr #626 —
815S A98 200fr on 360fr #574 —
815T A119 200fr on 375fr #689 —
815U A126 200fr on 375fr #742 —
815V A112 200fr on 400fr #649 —
815W A111 200fr on 425fr #641 —

Size of surcharge numerals and obliteration grid varies. Black surcharge on No. 815My is misplaced. No. 815Q exists with misplaced surcharge that is faintly tripled, a surcharge with thinner zeroes, and a pair containing No. C150 next to No. 815Q with misplaced surcharge that is faintly tripled and has thinner zeroes. No. 815W exists with an inverted surcharge and with a double surcharge, one inverted.

A144

1997, Dec. 15 Litho. *Perf. 14*

816 A144 200fr Mother Teresa (1910-97) 1.50 1.00

No. 816 was issued in sheets of 9.

Aromatic Plants — A144a

Designs: 25fr, 50fr, 1000fr, Piper nigrum. 100fr, 125fr, 200fr, Cinnamomum ceylanicum. 300fr, Syzigium aromaticum. 500fr, Myristica fragrans.

1997, Dec. 15 Litho. *Perf. 14*

816A A144a 25fr multi —
816B A144a 50fr multi —
816C A144a 100fr multi —
816D A144a 125fr multi —
816E A144a 200fr multi —
816F A144a 300fr multi —
816G A144a 500fr multi —
816H A144a 1000fr multi —

Various Stamps Surcharged Type "c" in Black

Methods and Perfs as Before

1996, Dec.

816I A131 200fr on 500fr #765 — —
816J A133 200fr on 500fr #775 — —
816K A135 200fr on 500fr #781 — —
816L AP42 200fr on 500fr #C169 — —
816M AP42 200fr on 500fr #C185 — —
816N AP42 200fr on 600fr #C170 — —
816O AP42 200fr on 600fr #C186 — —

Size of surcharge and obliteration grid varies.

Vertical Pairs from No. B4 Surcharged with Silver Bar to Obliterate Surtax

Methods and Perfs as before.

1996, Dec.

816P Surcharged pair of #B4a, B4e —
t. SP3 200fr on 200fr+10fr Galileo —
u. SP3 200fr on 200fr+10fr Planet A & 3 stars —
816Q Surcharged pair of #B4b, B4f —
v. SP3 200fr on 200fr+10fr Copernicus —
w. SP3 200fr on 200fr+10fr ICE —
816R Surcharged pair of #B4c, B4g —
x. SP3 200fr on 200fr+10fr Kepler —
y. SP3 200fr on 200fr+10fr Planet A & 5 stars —
816S Surcharged pair of #B4d, B4h —
z. SP3 200fr on 200fr+10fr Halley —
aa. SP3 200fr on 200fr+10fr Vega —

A full sheet of Nos. 816P-816S is not known to exist.

Cats A145

Designs, vert: 75fr, Silver banded. 150fr, Lac de Van. No. 819, 200fr, European short hair. No. 820, 200fr, Somali. No. 821, 375fr, Japanese bobtail. No. 822, 375fr, Egyptian mau.

No. 823, each 375fr: a, Poupée de chiffon. b, Maine coon. c, Norwegian forest cat. d, Persian. e, Droop-eared. f, Marbled American short hair.

No. 824, each 375fr: a, Manx. b, Cashmere. c, British shorthair. d, Cornish rex. e, American curl. f, Ocicat.

No. 825, 1500fr, Silver-chocolate Somali. No. 826, 1500fr, Chocolate Persian, vert.

1998, June 3 Litho. *Perf. 14*
817-822 A145 Set of 6 7.50 7.50

Sheets of 6
823-824 A145 Set of 2 24.00 24.00

Souvenir Sheets
825-826 A145 Set of 2 17.50 6.00

No. C215D Surcharged Type "c" in Red or Black

Methods and Perfs as Before

1997 (?)

826A AP52a 100fr on 225fr — —
826B AP52a 200fr on 225fr — —
826C AP52a 200fr on 225fr (Bk) —
826D AP52a 500fr on 225fr —
826E AP52a 600fr on 225fr —

Size of surcharge numerals varies. No. 826B exists with inverted surcharge, No. 826C exists with double surcharge.

No. 811 Surcharged on Six Stamps

d — (Obliterator of Triangles and Wavy Lines)

Methods and Perfs as Before

1998 (?)

826F Sheet of 9 —
g. A142 200fr on 150fr Pyrostegia venusta —
h. A142 200fr on 150fr Manioc —
i. A142 200fr on 150fr Lycogala epidendron —
j. A142 200fr on 525fr Allamanda cathartica —
k. A142 200fr on 525fr Cacao —
l. A142 200fr on 525fr Clathrus ruber —

The three 75fr stamps on the sheet received no surcharge.

No. 812O Surcharged

e — (Obliterator of Bars, Dots, and Semicircles)

Methods and Perfs as Before

1998 (?)

826M A142a 100fr on 300fr —

Size of surcharge numerals varies.

Marine Life A146

No. 827, each 150fr: a, Pomacanthus imperator. b, Cephalopholis miniatus. c, Diver. d, Nautilus pompilius. e, Sphyraena barracuda. f, Manta birostris. g, Lutjanus sebae. h, Chaetodonplus duboulayi. i, Amphiprion bicinctus.

No. 828, vert , each 150fr: a, Istiophorus platypterus. b, Sterna fuscata. c, Larus pipixcan. d, Hippocampus kuda. e, Amphiprion ocellaris (2 fish). f, Octopus vulgaris. g, Chaetodon striatus. h, Actini aquina. i, Acanthurus leucosternon.

No. 829: a, Diomedea exulans. b, Delphinus delphis. c, Sailboat. d, Sphyrna zygaena. e, Loligo forbesi. f, Galeocerdo cuvieri. g, Pomacanthus imperator, diff. h, Amphiprion ocellaris (1 fish). i, Forcipiger flavissimus. j, Electrophorus electricus. k, Dermochelys coriaoea. l, Asterias rubens.

No. 830, 1500fr, Mastigias papua, vert. No. 831, 1500fr, Sepia officinalis. No. 832, 1500fr, Zancius canescens.

1998, Aug. 10 Litho. *Perf. 14*

Sheets of 9 or 12
827-828 A146 Set of 2 13.00 13.00
829 A146 200fr #a.-l. 12.00 12.00

Souvenir Sheets
830-832 A146 Set of 3 22.50 22.50

Nos. 830-832 each contain one 51x38mm or 38x51mm stamp.

Betty Boop — A146a

No. 832A: b, Wearing hula skirt, dancing. c, With dog, wearing blue dress, in pink heart. d, Wearing polka dot dress. e, In bathtub. f, Face in red heart. g, Holding top hat. h, With flamingos. i, With dog, Wearing red dress, blue ribbon. j, Wearing hula skirt, on surf board.

1125fr, With fishing pole.

1998 Litho. *Perf. 13¼*
832A A146a 300fr Sheet of 9, #b-j 16.00 16.00

Souvenir Sheet
832K A146a 1125fr multi 7.00 7.00

No. 832A contains nine 35x41mm stamps.

Popeye — A146b

No. 832L: m, Wimpy. n, Popeye, Olive Oyl, ship's wheel. o, Swee'Pea. p, Head of Popeye. q, Popeye. r, Head of Olive Oyl. s, Jeep. t, Olive Oyl. u, Brutus.

No. 832V, 1125fr, Popeye with spinach can. No. 832W, 1125fr, Like #832Ln, horiz.

1998
832L A146b 450fr Sheet of 9, #m-u 24.00 24.00

Souvenir Sheets
832V-832W A146b Set of 2 14.00 14.00

No. 832L contains nine 35x51mm stamps, No. 832W contains one 60x50mm stamp.

Coelacanth — A147

World Wildlife Fund: a, Swimming right, colored background. b, Swimming right, white background. c, In net. d, Swimming left.

No. 833E: f, Like #833a. g, Like #833d. h, Like #833c. i, Like #833b.

1998
833 A147 200fr Strip of 4, #a-d 6.00 6.00
833E A147 375fr Sheet of 4, #f-i 37.50

No. 833 was issued in sheets of 3 vertical strips.

No. 833E exists imperf. Value $45.

I Love Lucy — A147a

No. 833F, vert. — Lucy: g, With black ribbon in hair. h, Wearing burlap sack. i, With trapeze in mouth. j, With one arm raised. k, On telephone. l, Wearing red and white apron. m, Wearing bright green dress. n, Wearing blue dress. o, With fishing gear.

1125fr, With Ricky, with fishing gear.

1998 Litho. *Perf. 13¼*
833F A147a 250fr Sheet of 9, #g-o 13.00 13.00

Souvenir Sheet
833P A147a 1125fr multi 7.00 7.00

No. 833F contains nine 35x51mm stamps.

Diana, Princess of Wales (1961-97) A148

Nos. 834-835, 835J, Various portraits.

No. 836, 1125fr, Wearing scarf, green dress. No. 837, 1125fr, Wearing black and white hat and outfit.

1998 Litho. *Perf. 13½*

Sheets of 9
834 A148 250fr #a.-i. 13.00 13.00
835 A148 350fr #a.-i. 18.00 18.00
835J A148 450fr #k.-s. 24.00 24.00

Souvenir Sheets
836-837 A148 Set of 2 13.00 13.00

Nos. 835, 835J contain 42x51mm stamps. Nos. 836-837 each contain one 42x60mm stamp.

Entertainers A149

No. 838: Various portraits of Grace Kelly (Princess Grace of Monaco) (1929-92).

No. 839: Various portraits of Frank Sinatra (1915-98).

1998 Sheets of 9
838 A149 300fr #a.-i. 16.00 16.00
839 A149 500fr #a.-i. 26.50 26.50

Classic Automobiles — A150

No. 840, each 150fr: a, 1936 Jaguar SS. b, 1939 Lincoln Continental. c, 1903 Mercedes. d, 1936 MG-TA. e, 1946 Oldsmobile Custom Cruiser 98. f, 1933 Pontiac. g, 1940 Rolls-Royce Silver Ghost 40/50. h, 1950 Studebaker Starlight Coupe. i, 1932 Ford V8.

No. 841, each 150fr: a, 1927 Alfa Romeo RLSS. b, 1933 DuPont Model G. c, Bentley Speed Six. d, 1932 Cadillac 355. e, 1955 Corvette. f, 1934 Chrysler Airflow. g, Buick Coupe deVille. h, Model T Ford. i, 1920 Duesenberg Model A.

No. 842, 1500fr, Rolls-Royce Phantom II Continental. No. 843, 1500fr, 1927 Daimler Double Six.

1998, Oct. 29 Litho. *Perf. 14*

Sheets of 9
840-841 A150 Set of 2 13.00 13.00

Souvenir Sheets
842-843 A150 Set of 2 17.00 17.00

Birds — A151

No. 844, 75fr, Macareux moine. No. 845, 75fr, Calliste à tête verte. No. 846, 150fr, Soutmanga de la reine Christine. No. 847, 150fr, Rale d'eau. No. 848, 200fr, Lophophore replendissant. No. 849, 200fr, Francolin noir. No. 850, 375fr, Mesia à oreillonis argentes. No. 851, 375fr, Mérion splendide.

No. 852: a, Canard plongeur austral. b, Garrot a ceil d'or. c, Harle huppé. d, Canard colvert. e, Canard branchu. f, Sarcelle elegante.

No. 853: a, Emérillon. b, Nyctale de tengmalm. c, Aigle royal d, Kétoupa malais. e, Caracara. f, Chouette à lunettes

No. 854, Jacana du mexique. No. 855, Toucan de cuvier.

1999, Jan. 23 **Litho.** ***Perf. 14***

844-851 A151 Set of 8 8.50 8.50

Sheets of 6, #a-f

852-853 A151 375fr Set of 2 22.50 22.50

Souvenir Sheets

854-855 A151 1500fr Set of 2 16.00 16.00

Fauna A152

No. 856, vert, each 150fr: a, Giraffa camaloprdalis. b, Macaca fusata. c, Loxodonta africana. d, Ovis dalli. e, Phoenicopterus ruber. f, Orcinus orca. g, Ursus horribilis. h, Lemur catta.

No. 857, vert, each 150fr: a, Pongo pygmaeus. b, Ceratotherium simum. c, Ailuropoda melanoleuca. d, Tursiops truncartus. e, Felis caracel. g, Eudyptes chrysocome. h, Bison bison. i, Panthera uncia.

No. 858, vert, each 150fr: a, Phascolarctos cinereus. b, Ammotragus levia. c, Hippopatamus amphibius. d, Saimiri bollviensis. e, Acinonyx jubatus. f, Gorilla gorilla. g, Branta sandvicensis. h, Thalarctos maritimus.

No. 859, each 150fr: a, Panthera tigris. b, Phoca groenlandica. c, Acipenser sturio. d, Lepidochelys kempii. e, Ailuropoda melanoleuca. f, Isurus oxyrinchus. g, Chelydra serpentina. h, Eretmochelys imbricata.

Each 1500fr: No. 860: Pan troglodytes, vert. No. 861, Panthera tigris altaica, vert. No. 862, Oryx gazella, vert. No. 863, Hippotigris zebra. No. 864, Diceros bicornis. No. 865, Panthera leo. No. 866, Amazona viridgenalis. No. 867, Pygoscelis papua, vert.

1999, Jan. 25 **Sheets of 8**

856-859 A152 Set of 4 25.00 25.00

Souvenir Sheets

860-867 A152 Set of 8 65.00 65.00

Fish A153

No. 868, 75fr, Pomacantus imperator. No. 869, 75fr, Heniochus intermedium. No. 870, 150fr, Mirolaprichthys. No. 871, 150fr, Pomacanthus paru. No. 872, 375fr, Ostzacion tuberculatus. No. 873, 375fr, Colisa calia.

No. 874, each 150fr: a, Coris aygula. b, Chromis caeruleys. c, Euxiphipops navarchus. d, Pseudobalistes fuscus. e, Zebrasoma flavescens. f, Mycteroperca urba. g, Epinephelus flavocaeruleus. h, Equetus lanceolatus. i, Acanthurus leucostemon.

No. 875, each 150fr: a, Chaetodon tinkeri. b, Ostzaciidae. c, Seatophagus argus. d, Adioryx coruscus. e, Pygoplites diacanthus. f, Paracanthurus hepatus. g, Chaetodon plebius. h, Lythrypnus dalli. i, Myrichthys oculatus.

Each 1500fr: No. 876, Amphipzion percula. No. 877, Cymnothorne undulatus.

1998, Oct.-Nov. **Litho.** ***Perf. 14***

868-873 A153 Set of 6 7.00 7.00

Sheets of 9

874-875 A153 Set of 2 14.00 14.00

Souvenir Sheets

876-877 A153 Set of 2 16.00 16.00

Marine Life — A154

No. 878, 75fr, Tubastrea aurea. No. 879, 75fr, Condylachtis gigantea. No. 880, 150fr, Paracanthurus hepatus. No. 881, 150fr, Balistoides conspicillum. No. 882, 200fr, Diodon holocanthus. No. 883, 200fr, Sebastes rubrivintus. No. 884, 375fr, Trygonorhina fasciata. No. 885, 375fr, Phocoenoides dalli.

No. 886, each 150fr: a, Epinephelus guttatus. b, Diademichthys lineatus. c, Plotosus lineatus. d, Rhinomuraena quaesita. e, Zanclus cornutus. f, Persephona punctata. g, Murex pecten. h, Tetrosomus gibbosus.

No. 887, each 150fr: a, Lythrypnus dalli. b, Premnas biaculeatus. c, Pseudanthias tuka. d, Capros aper. e, Balistoides conspicillum. f, Oreaster reticulatus. g, Octopus joubini. h, Fasciolaris tulipa.

Each 1500fr: No. 888, S. picturatus. No. 889, Megaptera novaeangliae.

1999

878-885 A154 Set of 8 8.50 8.50

Sheets of 8

886-887 A154 Set of 2 17.00 17.00

Souvenir Sheets

888-889 A154 Set of 2 19.00 19.00

Prehistoric Animals — A155

No. 890, each 150fr: a, Meganeura. b, Archaeopteryx. c, Peteinosaurus. d, Eudimorphodon. e, Brachiosaurus. f, Gallimimus. g, Tarbosaurus. h, Parasaurolophus. i, Sauropelta. j, Herrarasaurus. k, Stegosaurus. l, Lambeosaurus.

No. 891, each 150fr: a, Ramphorhinchus. b, Quetzalcoatlus. c, Pterodactylus. d, Pteranodon. e, Dimorphodon. f. Camarasaurus. g, Tenontosaurus. h, Protoceratops. i, Coelurosaurus. j, Mixosaurus. k, Ceresiosaurus. l, Sharovipteryx.

Each 1500fr: No. 892, Ceratosaurus. No. 893, Mesosaurus. No. 894, Megazostrodon. No. 895, Diatryma.

1999 **Sheets of 12**

890-891 A155 Set of 2 19.00 19.00

Souvenir Sheets

892-895 A155 Set of 4 32.50 32.50

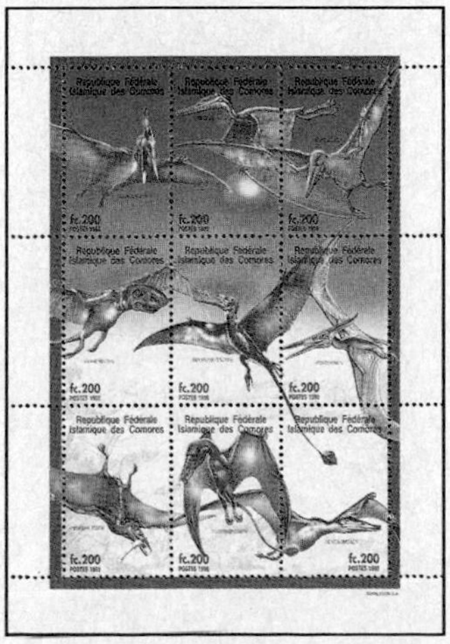
Prehistoric Animals, Lemurs and Butterflies — A156

Prehistoric animals — No. 895A — Prehistoric sea creatures: b, Eurhinodelphis. c, Stenopterygius. d, Ichthyosaurus. e, Pakicetus. f, Xenacanthus. g, Zygorhiza. h, Basilosaurus. i, Mesosaurus. j, Cetotherium. No. 896: a, Elasmosaurus (b). b, Quetzalcoatl (c). c, Mesadactylus (b). d, Dimorphodon (e). e, Rhamphorhynchus (c, d, f, i). f, Pteranodon (c, i). g, Pterodactylus (h). h, Eudimorphodon (i). i, Ornithodesmus (g, h).

Lemurs — No. 897: a, Haplorhinien primitif. b, Aye aye (c, e, f). c, Lemur vari. d, Indri. e, Makis varis (f, i). f, Potto. g, Lemur catta. h, Lemur macaos. i, Microcebe souris.

Butterflies — No. 898: a, Charaxes nobilis. b, Charaxes eupale. c, Charaxes brutus. d, Lobobunea turlini. e, Papilio nobilis. f, Athletes gigas. g, Papilio antimachus. h, Epiphora albida. i, Papilio zalmoxis.

1998 **Sheets of 9** ***Perf. 13¼x13½***

895A A156 150fr #b-j 6.50 6.50
896 A156 200fr #a.-i. 9.75 9.75
897 A156 250fr #a.-i. 12.00 12.00
898 A156 300fr #a.-i. 14.50 14.50

See Nos. 928-933.

A157

Endangered Species — A157a

Designs: 75fr, Galago crassicaudatus. 150fr, Vulpes vulpes. 200fr, Anomalurus pusillus. 375fr, Loxodonta africana, vert.

Primates, vert: Nos. 903a-903c, Various views of Pan troglodytes. Nos. 903d-903f, Various views of gorilla gorilla. Nos. 903g-903i, Various views of pongo pygmaeus.

No. 904, each 375fr: a, Tragelaphus strepsiceros. b, Capra hircus. c, Egretta alba. d, Tockus flavirostris.

No. 905, each 375fr: a, Ursus maritimus. b, Megaptera novaeangliae. c, Phoca vitulina. d, Aptenodytes forsteri.

No. 906, each 375fr: a, Pelecanus occidentalis. b, Orcinus orca. c, Delphinus delphis. d, Iguana iguana.

No. 907: a, Panthera tigris altaica. b, Camelus bactrianus. c, Canus lupus. d, Cuon alpinus. e, Rangifer tarandus dawsoni. f, Gulo gulo.

Each 1500fr: No. 908, Loxodonta africana, vert. No. 909, Ursus thibetanus.

Perf. 14, 14½x14 (#904-906)

1999, Jan. 25 **Litho.**

899-902 A157 Set of 4 4.50 4.50
903 A157 150fr Sheet of 9, #a.-i. 8.00 8.00

Sheets of 4

904-906 A157a Set of 3 24.00 24.00

Sheet of 6

907 A157 375fr #a.-f. 12.00 12.00

Souvenir Sheets

908-909 A157 Set of 2 16.00 16.00

Mushrooms
A158 A159

No. 910, 75fr, Russula xerampelina. No. 911, 75fr, Catathelasma imperiale. No. 912, 150fr, Cortinarius violaceus. No. 913, 150fr, Cortinarius camphoratus. No. 914, 200fr, Rozites caperata. No. 915, 200fr, Coprinus picaceus. No. 916, 375fr, Coprinus cromatus. No. 917, 375fr, Russula cavipes.

No. 918, each 150fr: a, Boletus edulis. b, Suillus grevillei. c, Boletinus cavipes. d, Morchella esculenta. e, Morchella conica. f, Clitocybe dealbata. g, Hygrocybe nigrescens. h, Clitocybe geotropa. i, Lepiota cristata.

No. 919, each 150fr: a, Amanita citrina. b, Amanita phalloides. c, Cortinarius praestans. d, Phallus impudicus. e, Cortinarius bicolor. f, Cortinarius renidens. g, Lactarius torminosus. h, Boletus satanas. i, Cystolepiota bucknalii.

No. 920, each 375fr: a, Amanita muscaria. b, Coprinus comatus. c, Clitocybe odora. d, Cantharellus cibarius. e, Mycena epipterygia. f, Marasmius oreades.

No. 921, each 375fr: a, Boletus edulis. b, Laccaria laccata. c, Agaricus campestris. d, Hypholoma fasciculare. e, Leplota procera. f, Russula aurata.

Each 1500fr: No. 922, Ramaria aurea, horiz. No. 923, Panellus serotinus. No. 924, Macrolepiota procera. No. 925, Amanita muscaria. No. 926, Hebeloma crustuliniforme. No. 927, Lepiota molybdites.

1999 **Litho.** ***Perf. 14***

910-917 A158 Set of 8 8.50 8.50

Sheets of 9

918-919 A158 Set of 2 14.00 14.00

Sheets of 6

920-921 A159 Set of 2 24.00 24.00

Souvenir Sheets

922-925 A158 Set of 4 32.50 32.50
926-927 A159 Set of 2 16.00 16.00

Raptors — A160

No. 927A — Birds: b, Souimanga royal. c, Martin-pecheur huppe. d, Pie-grieche. e, Barbican a tete roughe. f, Beau-marquet. g, Rollier a poitrine lilas. h, Pintade vulturine. i, Grenadier. j, Outarde korhaon.

No. 928: a, Sparrow hawk. b, Red-tailed buzzard. c, Dark kite. d, African fish eagle. e, Bald eagle. f, Fawn-colored vulture. g, Peregrine falcon. h, Osprey. i, Harpie eagle.

Dinosaurs — No. 929: a, Dilophosaurus. b, Megalosaurus. c, Ceratosaurus. d, Coelophysls. e, Tyrannosaurus. f, Deinonychus. g, Allosaurus. h, Stegosaurus. i, Albertosaurus.

Gems — No. 930: a, Ruby. b, Liroconite. c, Emerald. d, Euclase. e, Diamond. f, Chrysoberyl. g, Plancheite. h, Kasolite. i, Indigolite.

Meteorites — No. 931: a, Martian. b, Antarctic. c, C2 Chondrite. d, Archondrite. e, Octaedrite moyenne. f, Iron. g, Tektite. h, Chondrite olivine. i, Iron, diff.

Mushrooms — No. 932: a, Paxillus atrotomentosus. b, Craterellus cornucopioides. c, Boletus satanas. d, Clavaria truncata. e, Phallus impudicus. f, Scleroderma aurantiacum. g, Amanita citrina. h, Catathe lasma. i, Inocybe fastigiata.

1125fr, Wulfenite.

1998 **Sheets of 9** ***Perf. 13¼x13½***

927A A160 175fr #b-j 8.00 8.00
928 A160 200fr #a.-i. 9.75 9.75
929 A160 250fr #a.-i. 11.50 11.50
930 A160 375fr #a.-i. 17.50 17.50
931 A160 400fr #a.-i. 19.00 19.00
932 A160 400fr #a.-i. 19.00 19.00

Souvenir Sheet

933 A160 1125fr multicolored 5.75 5.75

No. 933 contains one 36x51mm stamp.

Captions on Nos. 928e and 928h are transposed.

See Nos. 896-898.

"Illegal" Stamps

Comoro Islands postal officials have declared as "illegal" the following items:

Muhammad Ali, sheet of nine 300fr stamps (previously No. 934);

Muhammad Ali, 1125fr souvenir sheet (previously No. 935);

Babe Ruth, sheet of nine 375fr stamps;

Babe Ruth, two 1125fr souvenir sheets;

Ocean Life, sheet of nine stamps with values of 100, 150, 250, 300, 350, 400, 450, and 500fr;

Horses, sheet of nine stamps with values of 100, 150, 250, 300, 350, 400, 450, and 500fr;

Pandas, sheet of nine stamps with values of 100, 150, 250, 300, 350, 400, 450, and 500fr;

Flora and Fauna: 25fr Harpe costata, 25fr Hibiscus, 50fr Volute lapponica, 50fr Tournesol de Comoros, 100fr Ghetonia mydas, 125fr Octopus vulgaris, 150fr Ylang ylang, 300fr Coelacanth, 300fr Tellina variegata.

Famous People: 250fr, Willy Messerschmitt, Messerschmitt BF-109G-6/R6. 300fr, Louis Pasteur, rabies vaccine administered to Joseph Meister. 350fr, Dr. Albert Schweitzer. 400fr, Ferdinand von Zeppelin, flying Zeppelin. 475fr, Henri Dunant, Nobel Prize. 500fr, Albert Einstein, Gravity Probe B. 550fr, Ayrton Senna, race car. 600fr, Pope John Paul II. 750fr, Iranian Pres. Mohammad Khatami, Pope John Paul II. 800fr, Crew of Apollo 11. 1125fr souvenir sheet, Lindbergh, Spirit of St. Louis.

Submarines — A161

No. 934: a, USS Salt Lake City, US. b, Le Terrible, France. c, Amethyste, France.

1999 **Litho.** ***Perf. 13¼***

934 A161 150fr Sheet of 3, #a-c 3.00 3.00

Automobiles — A161a

No. 935: a, Cadillac Eldorado, Cadillac Series 62, US. b, Aston Martin DB2 IV Mark III, Austin Healey. c, Alfa Romeo Superlegera, Alfa Romeo Giuletta.

1125fr, Aston Martin DB5.

1999

935 A161a 200fr Sheet of 3, #a-c 3.50 3.50

Souvenir Sheet

935D A161a 1125fr multi 7.00 7.00

No. 935D contains one 51x30mm stamp.

Motorcycles — A162

No. 935E: f, Honda NR. g, Christian Leliard and motorcycle. h, Joe S. Wright and motorcycle.

1999

935E A162 250fr Sheet of 3, #f-h 4.50 4.50

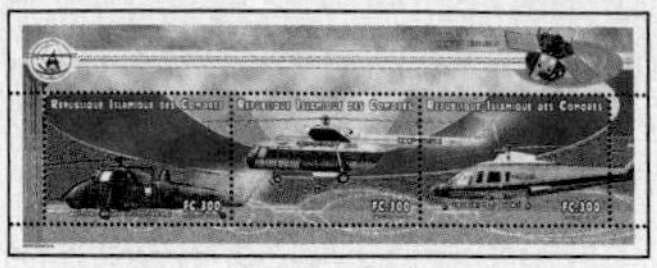

Helicopters — A162a

No. 936: a, Westland Wessex. b, MIL MI-8. c, Sikorsky 5-76 Spirit.

1999

936 A162a 300fr Sheet of 3, #a-c 5.50 5.50

Dogs and Sleds — A163

No. 937: a, Alaskan malamute, US. b, Greenlandic. c, Siberian husky.

1999

937 A163 400fr Sheet of 3, #a-c 7.00 7.00

Airplanes A164

No. 938: a, Tupolev Tu-160. b, Lockheed F-117A. c, Rafale C.01.

No. 939: a, Ilyshin Il-76. b, Boeing E-3. c, Concorde.

1125fr, Concorde, diff.

1999 **Litho.** ***Perf. 13¼***

Sheets of 3

938 A164 375fr #a.-c. 6.50 6.50
939 A164 450fr #a.-c. 8.00 8.00

Souvenir Sheet

940 A164 1125fr mulicolored 7.00 7.00

No. 940 contains one 50x30mm stamp.

Trains A165

No. 941: a, Series E. b, Series 9100. c, Kitson-Still I-C-I.

No. 942: a, HST 125. b, TGV. c, RTG.

1125fr, Sereis DD40AX.

1999 **Litho.** ***Perf. 13¼***

Sheets of 3

941 A165 400fr #a.-c. 7.25 7.25
942 A165 500fr #a.-c. 9.00 9.00

Souvenir Sheet

943 A165 1125fr mulicolored 7.00 7.00

No. 943 contains one 50x30mm stamp.

Space Achievements — A166

No. 944: a, Shuttles Discovery, Buran. b, Ariane V. c, John Glenn, Saturn V.

No. 945: a, Valentina Tereshkova, Soyuz 4. b, Dogs Laika, Bielka. c, Yuri Gagarin, Vostok 1.

1125fr, Space Shuttle Discovery, John Glenn.

1999 **Litho.** ***Perf. 13¼***

Sheets of 3

944 A166 500fr #a.-c. 9.00 9.00
945 A166 600fr #a.-c. 11.00 11.00

Souvenir Sheet

946 A166 1125fr multi 7.00 7.00

No. 946 contains one 51x30mm stamp.

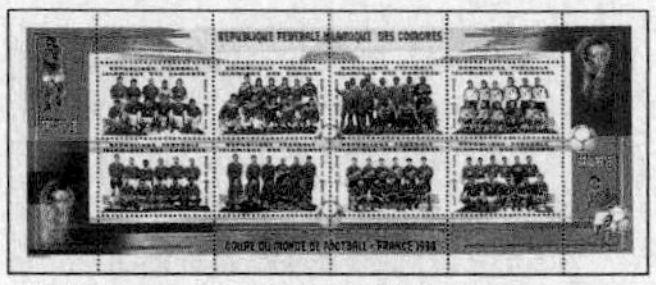

Teams in 1998 World Cup Soccer Tournament — A167

Players in 1998 World Cup Soccer Tournament — A168

No. 947, 150fr: a, Italy. b, Chile, c, Cameroun. d, Austria. e, Netherlands. f, Belgium. g, South Korea. h, Mexico.

No. 948, 250fr: a, Brazil. b, Scotland. c, Morocco. d, Norway. e, Spain. f, Nigeria. g, Paraguay. h, Bulgaria.

No. 949, 300fr: a, France. b, South Africa. c, Saudi Arabia. d, Denmark. e, Germany. f, United States. g, Yugoslavia. h, Iran.

No. 950, 500fr: a, England. b, Colombia. c, Romania. d, Tunisia. e, Argentina. f, Croatia. g, Jamaica. h, Japan.

No. 951, 350fr: a, Desailly, French flag. b, Ronaldo, Brazilian flag. c, Suker, Croatian flag. d, Kluivert, Netherlands flag. e, French players, World Cup trophy. f, Brazilian player (yellow and green shirt). g, Croatian player (checked shirt). h, Netherlands player (orange shirt).

1998 **Litho.** ***Perf. 13x13½***

Sheets of 8, #a-h

947-950 A167 Set of 4 50.00 50.00
951 A168 multi 14.50 14.50

Trucks — A169

No. 952: a, Truck with ornamentation over cab. b, Blue truck. c, Green truck. d, Yellow truck.

1999 **Litho.** ***Perf. 13¼***

952 A169 350fr Sheet of 4, #a-d — —

Automobile Racing, Chess, Tennis and Table Tennis, Fishing and Diving — A170

No. 953, 250fr — Automobile racing: a, Giuseppe Farina and Alfa 1500. b, Juan Fangio and Mercedes 2.5L. c, Jack Brabham and Cooper Climax 2.5L. d, Jim Clark and Lotus Climax 1.5L.

No. 954, 300fr — Chess players: a, Garry Kasparov. b, Akiba Rubinstein. c, Max Euwe. d, Mikhail Botvinnik.

No. 955, 375fr — Fishing and diving: a, Shark fishing. b, Sport fishing. c, Diver, back half of shark. d, Diver, front half of shark.

No. 956, 500fr — Chess players: a, Bent Larsen. b, José Raúl Capablanca. c, Boris Spassky. d, Bobby Fischer.

No. 957, 600fr — Tennis and table tennis: a, Female tennis player. b, Male table tennis player. c, Female table tennis player. d, Male tennis player.

No. 958, 1125fr — Chess players: a, Samuel Reshevsky. b, Vassili Smyslov.

No. 959, 1125fr — Fishing and diving: a, Sport fishing, diff. b, Divers and marine life.

No. 960, 1125fr — Tennis and table tennis: a, Male table tennis player, diff. b, Women tennis players.

1999 ***Perf. 13¼***

Sheets of 4, #a-d

953-957 A170 Set of 5 47.50 47.50

Souvenir Sheets of 2, #a-b

958-960 A170 Set of 3 21.00 21.00

Nos. 816E, 816G Surcharged

Methods and Perfs. As Before

2001, June 16

963 A144a 100fr on 500fr multi — —
964 A144a 125fr on 200fr multi — —

Traditional Costumes A171

Designs: 125fr, Woman. No. 966, 150fr, No. 969, 300fr, Woman, diff. No. 967, 150fr, No. 968, 300fr, Man.

2002, Apr. 8 **Litho.** ***Perf. 13¼x13***

965-969 A171 Set of 5 *8.50 8.50*

Flowers — A172

Designs: 50fr, Cananga odorata. 600fr, Vanilla planifolia.

2003, Oct. 9

970-971 A172 Set of 2 *5.25 5.25*

Marine Mammals A173

Designs: 75fr, Peponocephala electra. 1000fr, Megaptera novaeangliae.

2003, Oct. 9 ***Perf. 13x13¼***

972-973 A173 Set of 2 *9.00 9.00*

Wood Handicrafts A174

Designs: 100fr, Carved door. 300fr, Candleholder.

2003, Oct. 9 *Perf. 13¼x13*
974-975 A174 Set of 2 *3.25 3.25*

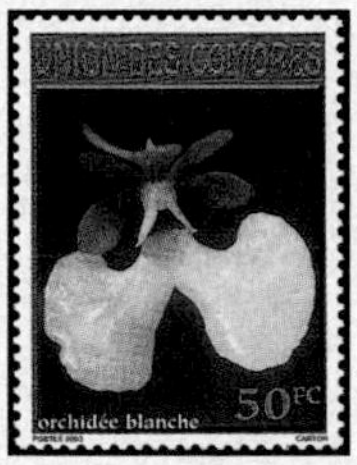

Orchids — A175

Orchid color: 50fr, White. 75fr, Yellow. 100fr, Mauve. 600fr, Red.

2003, Oct. 9
976-979 A175 Set of 4 *6.50 6.50*

Diplomatic Relations Between Comoro Islands and People's Republic of China, 30th Anniv. — A176

No. 980: a, 125fr, Chinese President Hu Jintao and Comoro Islands President Azali Assoumani, country flags. b, 125fr, Coelacanth, Worldwide Fund for Nature emblem, country arms. c, 300fr, Comoros Islands Broadcasting Center, country arms. d, 600fr, Comoros Islands People's Palace, country flags.

2006, Jan. 1 **Litho.** *Perf. 12*
980 A176 Block of 4, #a-d 5.75 5.75

Comoro Islands postal officials have declared as "illegal" the following items:

Impressionist Paintings, sheet of five 500fr stamps.

Paintings in the Louvre, six different sheets of two 500fr stamps.

American Actors and Actresses, four different sheets of four 350fr stamps.

European Astronauts, three souvenir sheets of one 500fr stamp.

Disneyland, 50th anniv., souvenir sheet of one 500fr stamp.

Léopold Sédar Senghor (1906-2001), First President of Senegal — A177

Perf. 13x13¼, 13¼x13

2007, June 1 **Litho.**

980E	A177	125fr pur & blk		—
981	A177	125fr grn & multi	.70	.70
982	A177	125fr yel & multi, vert.	.70	.70
983	A177	300fr grn & blk	1.75	1.75
983A	A177	300fr blue & multi		—
984	A177	300fr red vio & blk, vert.	1.75	1.75
985	A177	350fr pur & multi, vert.	2.00	2.00
986	A177	500fr brn & blk, vert.	2.75	2.75
		Nos. 981-983, 984-986 (7)	9.65	9.65

Dated 2006.

Medicinal Plants — A178

Designs: 75fr, Cymbopogon citratus. 125fr, Ocimum suave. 150fr, Aloe molucaca. 250fr, Like 75fr. 300fr, Like 150fr. 500fr, Like 125fr.

2007, June 1 *Perf. 13¼x13*
987-992 A178 Set of 6 7.75 7.75

A179

Transportation and Space — A180

No. 993 — Military aircraft and flags: a, 125fr, B-24 Liberator, U.S. flag. b, 150fr, Mitsubishi G4-M3, Japanese flag. c, 225fr, Petlyakov Pe-2, Russian flag. d, 300fr, Savoia-Marchetti SM-79, Italian flag. e, 400fr, Nakajima Ki84, Japanese flag. f, 1000fr, Dornier Do-335, German flag.

3000fr, Mitsubishi A6M5, Japanese flag.

2008, Oct. 1 *Perf. 13x13¼*
993 A179 Sheet of 6, #a-f 12.50 12.50

Souvenir Sheet

Perf. 13¼ Syncopated

994 A180 3000fr multi 17.00 17.00

Medical Vehicles

No. 995 — Red Cross flag and: a, 125fr, English ambulance. b, 150fr, ASLAV-A, Australia. c, 225fr, Red Cross vehicle, U.S. d, 300fr, Devon Air Ambulance helicopter, United Kingdom. e, 400fr, USNS Mercy. f, 1000fr, Medical worker on motorcycle, Hong Kong.

3000fr, M1133 Medical evacuation vehicle, U.S.

2008, Oct. 1 *Perf. 13x13¼*
995 A179 Sheet of 6, #a-f 12.50 12.50

Souvenir Sheet

Perf. 13¼ Syncopated

996 A180 3000fr multi 17.00 17.00

Submarines

No. 997: a, 125fr, Nautilus, 1800. b, 150fr, Brandtaucher, 1850. c, 225fr, Pioneer, 1861. d, 300fr, Flach, 1866. e, 400fr, Ictineo I 1858. f, 1000fr, Resurgam, 1878.

3000fr, Turtle, 1776.

2008, Oct. 1 *Perf. 13x13¼*
997 A179 Sheet of 6, #a-f 12.50 12.50

Souvenir Sheet

Perf. 13¼ Syncopated

998 A180 3000fr multi 17.00 17.00

U.S. High Speed Trains

No. 999 — Acela Express and U.S. landmarks: a, 125fr, Hollywood sign. b, 150fr, Golden Gate Bridge. c, 225fr, World Trade Center. d, 300fr, Statue of Liberty. e, 400fr, San Francisco skyline. f, 1000fr, White House.

3000fr, U.S. Capitol.

2008, Oct. 1 *Perf. 13x13¼*
999 A179 Sheet of 6, #a-f 12.50 12.50

Souvenir Sheet

Perf. 13¼ Syncopated

1000 A180 3000fr multi 17.00 17.00

Chinese High Speed Trains

No. 1001 — Maglev, flag of People's Republic of China, and Chinese landmarks: a, 200fr, Xian. b, 250fr, Tea house. c, 350fr, Pudong. d, 450fr, Great Wall of China. e, 500fr, Potala Palace. f, 1000fr, Gate of Heavenly Peace.

3000fr, Great Wall of China, diff.

2008, Oct. 1 *Perf. 13x13¼*
1001 A179 Sheet of 6, #a-f 15.50 15.50

Souvenir Sheet

Perf. 13¼ Syncopated

1002 A180 3000fr multi 17.00 17.00

Japanese High Speed Trains

No. 1003 — Shinkansen, Japanese flag, and Japanese landmarks: a, 200fr, Amanohashidate. b, 250fr, Itsukushima Shrine. c, 350fr, Umeda Sky Building, Osaka. d, 450fr, Buildings in Shiodome. e, 500fr, Temple in Kyoto. f, 1000fr, Himeji Castle.

3000fr, Minato Mirai 21.

2008, Oct. 1 *Perf. 13x13¼*
1003 A179 Sheet of 6, #a-f 15.50 15.50

Souvenir Sheet

Perf. 13¼ Syncopated

1004 A180 3000fr multi 17.00 17.00

Automobiles

No. 1005: a, 200fr, 1886 Daimler. b, 250fr,1906 Renault GP. c, 350fr, 1923 Ford Model T. d, 450fr, 1954 Mercedes Benz 300 SL. e, 500fr, 1988 Ferrari Testarossa. f, 1000fr, 2007 Bugatti Veyron.

3000fr, 2007 Lamborghini Murcielago LP640 Versace.

2008, Oct. 1 *Perf. 13x13¼*
1005 A179 Sheet of 6, #a-f 15.50 15.50

Souvenir Sheet

Perf. 13¼ Syncopated

1006 A180 3000fr multi 17.00 17.00

Airplanes and Airports

No. 1007 — Airplane at airport and flag: a, 200fr, Changri Airport, Singapore flag. b, 250fr, John F. Kennedy Airport, New York, and U.S. flag. c, 350fr, Frankfort Airport, German flag. d, 450fr, Narita Airport, Tokyo, Japanese flag. e, 500fr, Beijing Airport, flag of People's Republic of China. f, 1000fr, Schiphol Airport, Amsterdam, Netherlands flag.

3000fr, 2007 Heathrow Airport, London, British flag.

2008, Oct. 1 *Perf. 13x13¼*
1007 A179 Sheet of 6, #a-f 15.50 15.50

Souvenir Sheet

Perf. 13¼ Syncopated

1008 A180 3000fr multi 17.00 17.00

Mars Probes

No. 1009 — Mars and: a, 200fr, Spirit. b, 250fr, Mars Polar. c, 350fr, Viking. d, 450fr, Mars Climate. e, 500fr, Phoenix. f, 1000fr, Sojourner.

3000fr, Mariner 3.

2008, Oct. 1 *Perf. 13x13¼*
1009 A179 Sheet of 6, #a-f 15.50 15.50

Souvenir Sheet

Perf. 13¼ Syncopated

1010 A180 3000fr multi 17.00 17.00

Ocean Liners

No. 1011: a, 200fr, Titanic. b, 250fr, Golden Princess. c, 350fr, Mauretania. d, 450fr, MS Queen Victoria. e, 500fr, Queen Elizabeth 2. f, 1000fr, Queen Mary 2.

3000fr, Pacific Princess.

2008, Oct. 1 *Perf. 13x13¼*
1011 A179 Sheet of 6, #a-f 15.50 15.50

Souvenir Sheet

Perf. 13¼ Syncopated

1012 A180 3000fr multi 17.00 17.00

Postal Vehicles

No. 1013: a, 125fr, English postal van, carrier pigeon with letter, British flag. b, 150fr, Swiss postal bus, Horn, Swiss flag. c, 225fr, Spanish postal truck, posthorn, Spanish flag. d, 300fr, Swedish postal truck, carrier pigeon with letter, Swedish flag. e, 400fr, Israeli postal van, carrier pigeon with letter, Israeli flag. f, 1000fr, German postal buses, post horn, German flag.

3000fr, Hungarian postal van, posthorn, Hungarian flag.

2009, Jan. 5 *Perf. 13x13¼*
1013 A179 Sheet of 6, #a-f 12.50 12.50

Souvenir Sheet

Perf. 13¼ Syncopated

1014 A180 3000fr multi 16.50 16.50

Dated 2008.

Subway Trains

No. 1015: a, 125fr, Beijing train and system map, Forbidden City, flag of People's Republic of China. b, 150fr, London train and system map, Big Ben, British flag. c, 225fr, Paris train and system map, Eiffel Tower, French flag. d, 300fr, Tokyo train and system map, Tokyo Tower, Japanese flag. e, 400fr, New York train and system map, Statue of Liberty, U.S. flag. f, 1000fr, Moscow train and system map, Red Square, Russian flag.

3000fr, Madrid train and system map, Statue of Bear and Tree, Spanish flag.

2009, Jan. 5 *Perf. 13x13¼*
1015 A179 Sheet of 6, #a-f 12.50 12.50

Souvenir Sheet

Perf. 13¼ Syncopated

1016 A180 3000fr multi 16.50 16.50

Dated 2008.

German High Speed Trains

No. 1017 — ICE, flag of Germany and: a, 125fr, Cologne Cathedral. b, 150fr, Neuschwanstein Castle. c, 225fr, Göltsch Viaduct. d, 300fr, Kaiser Wilhelm Memorial Church, Berlin. e, 400fr, Brandenburg Gate. f, 1000fr, Eltz Castle.

3000fr, Brandenburg Gate, diff.

2009, Jan. 5 *Perf. 13x13¼*
1017 A179 Sheet of 6, #a-f 12.50 12.50

Souvenir Sheet

Perf. 13¼ Syncopated

1018 A180 3000fr multi 16.50 16.50

Dated 2008.

French High Speed Trains

No. 1019 — TGV, flag of France and: a, 125fr, Notre Dame Cathedral, Paris. b, 150fr, Louvre Museum. c, 225fr, Hôtel de Ville, Paris. d, 300fr, Eiffel Tower. e, 400fr, Moulin Rouge. f, 1000fr, Arc de Triomphe.

3000fr, Eiffel Tower, diff.

2009, Jan. 5 *Perf. 13x13¼*
1019 A179 Sheet of 6, #a-f 12.50 12.50

Souvenir Sheet

Perf. 13¼ Syncopated

1020 A180 3000fr multi 16.50 16.50

Dated 2008.

Fire Trucks

No. 1021: a, 125fr, Zuk, Poland. b, 150fr, Isuzu Forward, Japan. c, 225fr, Pegaso 7217, Spain. d, 300fr, A LF 16/12, Germany. e, 400fr, WPFD Engine 3, U.S. f, 1000fr, Scientific Support Truck, United Kingdom.

3000fr, Palm Beach fire truck, U.S.

2009, Jan. 5 *Perf. 13x13¼*
1021 A179 Sheet of 6, #a-f 12.50 12.50

Souvenir Sheet

Perf. 13¼ Syncopated

1022 A180 3000fr multi 16.50 16.50

Dated 2008.

Sailing Ships and Lighthouses

No. 1023 — Various lighthouses and: a, 125fr, Lettie G, 1893. b, 150fr, Maple Leaf, 1904. c, 225fr, Etoile, 1930. d, 300fr, Brigantine St. Lawrence, 1952. e, 400fr, Cuauhtemoc, 1982. f, 1000fr, Royal clipper, 2001.

3000fr, Belle Poule, 1834.

2009, Jan. 5 *Perf. 13x13¼*
1023 A179 Sheet of 6, #a-f 12.50 12.50

Souvenir Sheet

Perf. 13¼ Syncopated

1024 A180 3000fr multi 16.50 16.50

Dated 2008.

Airplanes

No. 1025: a, 125fr, Airbus A380. b, 150fr, Concorde F-BTSD. c, 225fr, Concorde G-

BOAC. d, 300fr, Airbus A380, diff. e, 400fr, Airbus A380, diff. f, 1000fr, Concorde F-BVFC.
3000fr, Concorde F-BTSD, diff.

2009, Jan. 5 ***Perf. 13x13¼***
1025 A179 Sheet of 6, #a-f 12.50 12.50

Souvenir Sheet

Perf. 13¼ Syncopated

1026 A180 3000fr multi 16.50 16.50

Dated 2008.

Antique Automobiles

No. 1027: a, 200fr, 1893 Duryea. b, 250fr, 1897 Oldsmobile. c, 350fr, 1896 Ford. d, 450fr, 1903 Vauxhall. e, 500fr, 1886 Daimler Maybach. f, 1000fr, 1906 Haynes.
3000fr, 1904 Mercedes Simplex.

2009, Jan. 5 ***Perf. 13x13¼***
1027 A179 Sheet of 6, #a-f 15.00 15.00

Souvenir Sheet

Perf. 13¼ Syncopated

1028 A180 3000fr multi 16.50 16.50

Dated 2008.

Combat Vehicles

No. 1029: a, 200fr, Jino Motors truck, South Korea. b, 250fr, PTU, Singapore. c, 350fr, BRDM, Russia. d, 450fr, KRAZ AVC-30, Ukraine. e, 500fr, Avalanche truck, Russia. f, 1000fr, Fahd 240/30, Egypt.
3000fr, 1904 Humber Flying Pig MK2, FV1611, Great Britain.

2009, Jan. 5 ***Perf. 13x13¼***
1029 A179 Sheet of 6, #a-f 15.00 15.00

Souvenir Sheet

Perf. 13¼ Syncopated

1030 A180 3000fr multi 16.50 16.50

Dated 2008.

Motorcycles and Their Inventors

No. 1031: a, 200fr, 1885 Daimler, Karl Benz. b, 250fr, 1901 NSU, Christian Schmidt. c, 350fr, 1920 Excelsior 20R, William G. Henderson. d, 450fr, 1914 Indian V-Twin, Oscar Hedstrom. e, 500fr, 1927 Böhmerland, Albin Hugo Liebisch. f, 1000fr, 1923 BMW R32, Max Friz.
3000fr, 1905 Scott, Alfred Angus Scott.

2009, Jan. 5 ***Perf. 13x13¼***
1031 A179 Sheet of 6, #a-f 15.00 15.00

Souvenir Sheet

Perf. 13¼ Syncopated

1032 A180 3000fr multi 16.50 16.50

Dated 2008.

A181

Birds and Lighthouses, Famous People — A182

No. 1033: a, 125fr, Alopochen aegyptiacus, El Montaza Lighthouse, Egypt. b, 150fr, Larus dominicanus, Agulhas Lighthouse, South Africa. c, 225fr, Gavia stellata, Europa Point Lighthouse, Gibraltar. d, 300fr, Oceanites oceanicus, Ilha do Goa Lighthouse, Mozambique. e, 400fr, Thalassarche cauta, Walvis Bay Lighthouse, Namibia. f, 1000fr, Pelecanus rufescens, Bwene Lighhouse, Tanzania.
3000fr, Phaethon aethereus, Lagos Lighthouse, Nigeria.

2009, Jan. 7 ***Perf. 13x13¼***
1033 A181 Sheet of 6, #a-f 12.50 12.50

Souvenir Sheet

Perf. 13¼ Syncopated

1034 A182 3000fr multi 16.50 16.50

Dated 2008.

Scouting Centenary (in 2007)

No. 1035 — Robert Baden-Powell, Scouting emblem and: a, 125fr, Two Scouts saluting. b, 150fr, Two Scouts reading map. c, 225fr, Two Scouts standing with book. d, 300fr, Three Scouts looking at plant. e, 400fr, Two Scouts standing. f, 1000fr, Scouts and tent.
3000fr, Scouts practicing first aid.

2009, Jan. 7 ***Perf. 13x13¼***
1035 A181 Sheet of 6, #a-f 12.50 12.50

Souvenir Sheet

Perf. 13¼ Syncopated

1036 A182 3000fr multi 16.50 16.50

Dated 2008.

Medical Pioneers

No. 1037: a, 125fr, Sir Humphry Davy. b, 150fr, Robert Koch. c, 225fr, Emil Adolf von Behring. d, 300fr, Louis Pasteur. e, 400fr, Sir Frederick Banting. f, 1000fr, Sir Alexander Fleming.
3000fr, Jean Henri Dunant.

2009, Jan. 7 ***Perf. 13x13¼***
1037 A181 Sheet of 6, #a-f 12.50 12.50

Souvenir Sheet

Perf. 13¼ Syncopated

1038 A182 3000fr multi 16.50 16.50

Dated 2008.

Classical Composers

No. 1039: a, 125fr, Joseph Haydn. b, 150fr, Louis Hector Berlioz. c, 225fr, Franz Schubert. d, 300fr, Ludwig van Beethoven. e, 400fr, Franz Liszt. f, 1000fr, Johannes Brahms.
3000fr, Wolfgang Amadeus Mozart.

2009, Jan. 7 ***Perf. 13x13¼***
1039 A181 Sheet of 6, #a-f 12.50 12.50

Souvenir Sheet

Perf. 13¼ Syncopated

1040 A182 3000fr multi 16.50 16.50

Dated 2008.

Ornithologists

No. 1041: a, 125fr, John James Audubon and Corvus cristatus. b, 150fr, John Gould and Trogon ambiguus. c, 225fr, Audubon and Columba migratoria. d, 300fr, Gould and Tanager darwinii. e, 400fr, Audubon and Corvus corax. f, 1000fr, Gould and Astrapia nigra.
3000fr, Gould, Audubon, two birds.

2009, Jan. 7 ***Perf. 13x13¼***
1041 A181 Sheet of 6, #a-f 12.50 12.50

Souvenir Sheet

Perf. 13¼ Syncopated

1042 A182 3000fr multi 16.50 16.50

Dated 2008.

Paleontologists

No. 1043: a, 125fr, Barnum Brown and Archaeopteryx. b, 150fr, Thomas Condon and Gallimimus. c, 225fr, Robert Broom and Irritator. d, 300fr, William Buckland and Dimorphodon. e, 400fr, Edward Drinker Cope and Parasaurolophus. f, 1000fr, Edwin H. Colbert and Allosaurus.
3000fr, Roy Chapman Andrews and fossil dinosaur egg.

2009, Jan. 7 ***Perf. 13x13¼***
1043 A181 Sheet of 6, #a-f 12.50 12.50

Souvenir Sheet

Perf. 13¼ Syncopated

1044 A182 3000fr multi 16.50 16.50

Dated 2008.

Humanists

No. 1045: a, 125fr, Miriam Makeba and Nelson Mandela. b, 150fr, Mahatma Gandhi. c, 225fr, Mother Teresa. d, 300fr, Yassir Arafat. e, 400fr, Shirin Ebadi. f, 1000fr, Mohammed El-Baradei.
3000fr, Dr. Martin Luther King, Jr.

2009, Jan. 7 ***Perf. 13x13¼***
1045 A181 Sheet of 6, #a-f 12.50 12.50

Souvenir Sheet

Perf. 13¼ Syncopated

1046 A182 3000fr multi 16.50 16.50

Dated 2008.

Aviators

No. 1047: a, 125fr, Edward Rickenbacker. b, 150fr, Jimmy Doolittle. c, 225fr, Beryl Markham. d, 300fr, Elinor Smith. e, 400fr, Antoine de Saint-Exupéry. f, 1000fr, Charles Lindbergh.
3000fr, Wiley Post.

2009, Jan. 7 ***Perf. 13x13¼***
1047 A181 Sheet of 6, #a-f 12.50 12.50

Souvenir Sheet

Perf. 13¼ Syncopated

1048 A182 3000fr multi 16.50 16.50

Dated 2008.

Astronauts and Cosmonauts

No. 1049: a, 125fr, Yuri Gagarin and Vostok 1. b, 150fr, Neil Armstrong and Apollo 11. c, 225fr, Alan Shepard, Jr. and Apollo 14. d, 300fr, Valentina Tereshkova and Vostok 6. e, 400fr, Pavel Popovich and Soyuz 14. f, 1000fr, John Glenn and Mercury 6.
3000fr, Yang Liwei and Shenzhou 5.

2009, Jan. 7 ***Perf. 13x13¼***
1049 A181 Sheet of 6, #a-f 12.50 12.50

Souvenir Sheet

Perf. 13¼ Syncopated

1050 A182 3000fr multi 16.50 16.50

Dated 2008.

Mineralogists

No. 1051: a, 200fr, Ignacy Domeyko and sulfur. b, 250fr, James Dwight Dana and barite. c, 350fr, William Niven and rhodochrosite. d, 450fr, George Kunz and legrandite. e, 500fr, Waldemar Brogger and pyrite. f, 1000fr, Otto von Abich and rutile.
3000fr, Max von Laue and calcite.

2009, Jan. 7 ***Perf. 13x13¼***
1051 A181 Sheet of 6, #a-f 15.00 15.00

Souvenir Sheet

Perf. 13¼ Syncopated

1052 A182 3000fr multi 16.50 16.50

Dated 2008.

Entomologists

No. 1053: a, 200fr, Nathan Banks and Nymphalis antiopa. b, 250fr, Louis Agassiz and Apatura ilia. c, 350fr, Henry Walter Bates and Gonepterix rhamni. d, 450fr, Per Olof Christopher Aurivillius and Biston betularius. e, 500fr, John Henry Comstock and Parnassius apollo. f, 1000fr, Jean Henri Fabre and Acronicta aceris.
3000fr, William Kirby and Acherontia atropos.

2009, Jan. 7 ***Perf. 13x13¼***
1053 A181 Sheet of 6, #a-f 15.00 15.00

Souvenir Sheet

Perf. 13¼ Syncopated

1054 A182 3000fr multi 16.50 16.50

Dated 2008.

Mycologists

No. 1055: a, 200fr, Charles Horton Peck and Chroogomphus vinicolor. b, 250fr, Michel Adanson and Macrolepiota procera. c, 350fr, Miles Joseph Berkeley and Paxillus involutus. d, 450fr, Andrea Cesalpino and Tricholoma flavovirens. e, 500fr, Eduard Fischer and Phallus impudicus. f, 1000fr, Charles Edwin Bessey and Armillariella mellea.
3000fr, Peter Adolph Karsten and Marasmius oreades.

2009, Jan. 7 ***Perf. 13x13¼***
1055 A181 Sheet of 6, #a-f 15.00 15.00

Souvenir Sheet

Perf. 13¼ Syncopated

1056 A182 3000fr multi 16.50 16.50

Dated 2008.

Explorers

No. 1057: a, 200fr, Ferdinand Magellan. b, 250fr, Vasco da Gama. c, 350fr, Christopher Columbus. d, 450fr, James Cook. e, 500fr, Marco Polo. f, 1000fr, Amerigo Vespucci.
3000fr, Columbus, diff.

2009, Jan. 7 ***Perf. 13x13¼***
1057 A181 Sheet of 6, #a-f 15.00 15.00

Souvenir Sheet

Perf. 13¼ Syncopated

1058 A182 3000fr multi 16.50 16.50

Dated 2008.

David Livingstone

No. 1059 — Livingstone, map of Africa, and: a, 200fr, Livingstone with compass. b, 250fr, Lion attacking man. c, 350fr, Livingstone with rifle. d, 450fr, Men reading newspapers, African man and boy. e, 500fr, Livingstone with daughter. f, 1000fr, Livingstone reading book to Africans.
3000fr, Meeting Henry M. Stanley.

2009, Jan. 7 ***Perf. 13x13¼***
1059 A181 Sheet of 6, #a-f 15.00 15.00

Souvenir Sheet

Perf. 13¼ Syncopated

1060 A182 3000fr multi 16.50 16.50

Dated 2008.

Nobel Peace Prize Recipients

No. 1061: a, 200fr, Jane Addams, 1931, and peace marchers. b, 250fr, Nelson Mandela, 1993, and globe. c, 350fr, Kofi Annan, 2001, United Nations emblem and dove. d, 450fr, Mother Teresa, 1979, and children. e, 500fr, Aung San Suu Kyi, 1991, Burmese children. f, 1000fr, Wangari Muta Maathai, 2004, globe and dove.
3000fr, Dr. Albert Schweitzer, 1952, map of Africa, Red Cross, hands.

2009, Jan. 7 ***Perf. 13x13¼***
1061 A181 Sheet of 6, #a-f 15.00 15.00

Souvenir Sheet

Perf. 13¼ Syncopated

1062 A182 3000fr multi 16.50 16.50

Dated 2008.

World Chess Champions

No. 1063: a, 200fr, Boris Spassky. b, 250fr, Bobby Fischer. c, 350fr, Anatoly Karpov. d, 450fr, Garry Kasparaov. e, 500fr, Vladimir Kramnik. f, 1000fr, Viswanathan Anand.
3000fr, Tigran Petrosian.

2009, Jan. 7 ***Perf. 13x13¼***
1063 A181 Sheet of 6, #a-f 15.00 15.00

Souvenir Sheet

Perf. 13¼ Syncopated

1064 A182 3000fr multi 16.50 16.50

Dated 2008.

Vincent Van Gogh

No. 1065 — Self-portraits and: a, 200fr, Vincent's Bedroom in Arles. b, 250fr, Olive Trees and the Alpilles in the Background. c, 350fr, Wheat Field with Cypresses. d, 450fr, The Night Café in the Place Lamartine in Arles. e, 500fr, The Red Vineyard. f, 1000fr, Starry Night.
3000fr, Starry Night over the Rhone.

2009, Jan. 7 ***Perf. 13x13¼***
1065 A181 Sheet of 6, #a-f 15.00 15.00

Souvenir Sheet

Perf. 13¼ Syncopated

1066 A182 3000fr multi 16.50 16.50

Dated 2008.

70th Birthday of Romy Schneider

No. 1067 — Schneider and scenes from her films: a, 200fr, Le Trio Infernal, 1974. b, 250fr, Adorable Sinner, 1959. c, 350fr, Ludwig, 1972. d, 450fr, Sissi: The Young Empress, 1956. e, 500fr, César and Rosalie, 1972. f, 1000fr, Max and the Junkmen, 1971.
3000fr, Christine, 1958.

2009, Jan. 7 ***Perf. 13x13¼***
1067 A181 Sheet of 6, #a-f 15.00 15.00

Souvenir Sheet

Perf. 13¼ Syncopated

1068 A182 3000fr multi 16.50 16.50

Dated 2008.

A183

Mushrooms and Fauna — A184

No. 1069 — Mushrooms: a, 125fr, Amanita caesarea. b, 150fr, Amanita pantherina. c, 225fr, Pleurotus eryngii. d, 300fr, Amanita rubescens. e, 400fr, Boletus edulis. f, 1000fr, Pluteus leoninus.
3000fr, Amanita phalloides.

2009, Mar. 2 ***Perf. 13x13¼***
1069 A183 Sheet of 6, #a-f 11.50 11.50

Souvenir Sheet
Perf. 13¼ Syncopated
1070 A184 3000fr multi 15.50 15.50

Camels

No. 1071: a, 125fr, Camelus dromedarius. b, 150fr, Camelus bactrianus. c, 225fr, Camelus bactrianus, diff. d, 300fr, Camelus dromedarius, diff. e, 400fr, Camelus dromedarius, diff. f, 1000fr, Camelus bactrianus, diff.
3000fr, Two Camelus bactrianus.

2009, Mar. 2 ***Perf. 13x13¼***
1071 A183 Sheet of 6, #a-f 11.50 11.50

Souvenir Sheet
Perf. 13¼ Syncopated
1072 A184 3000fr multi 15.50 15.50

Gorillas

No. 1073: a, 125fr, Gorilla gorilla gorilla. b, 150fr, Gorilla gorilla. c, 225fr, Gorilla beringei graueri. d, 300fr, Gorilla beringei beringei. e, 400fr, Gorilla beringei. f, 1000fr, Gorilla gorilla diehli.
3000fr, Gorilla gorilla, diff.

2009, Mar. 2 ***Perf. 13x13¼***
1073 A183 Sheet of 6, #a-f 11.50 11.50

Souvenir Sheet
Perf. 13¼ Syncopated
1074 A184 3000fr multi 15.50 15.50

Dogs

No. 1075: a, 125fr, Aidi. b, 150fr, Africanis. c, 225fr, Sloughi. d, 300fr, Basenji. e, 400fr, Boerboel. f, 1000fr, Azawakh.
3000fr, Rhodesian ridgeback.

2009, Mar. 2 ***Perf. 13x13¼***
1075 A183 Sheet of 6, #a-f 11.50 11.50

Souvenir Sheet
Perf. 13¼ Syncopated
1076 A184 3000fr multi 15.50 15.50

Beetles

No. 1077: a, 125fr, Trachelophorus giraffa. b, 150fr, Cicindela campestris. c, 225fr, Leptinotarsa decemlineata (light blue frame). d, 300fr, Gelastorcoris oculatus (light blue frame). e, 400fr, Scarites guineensis. f, 1000fr, Goliathus albosignatus.
3000fr, Staphylinus olens.

2009, Mar. 2 ***Perf. 13x13¼***
1077 A183 Sheet of 6, #a-f 11.50 11.50

Souvenir Sheet
Perf. 13¼ Syncopated
1078 A184 3000fr multi 15.50 15.50

Bees and Wasps

No. 1079: a, 125fr, Chrysis ignita. b, 150fr, Megarhyssa macrurus. c, 225fr, Leptinotarsa decemlineata (yellowish green frame). d, 300fr, Gelastorcoris oculatus (yellowish green frame). e, 400fr, Parazumia symmorpha. f, 1000fr, Pteromalus puparum.
3000fr, Sphex ichneumoneus.

2009, Mar. 2 ***Perf. 13x13¼***
1079 A183 Sheet of 6, #a-f 11.50 11.50

Souvenir Sheet
Perf. 13¼ Syncopated
1080 A184 3000fr multi 15.50 15.50

Fish

No. 1081: a, 125fr, Latimeria chalumnae. b, 150fr, Synanceia verrucosa. c, 225fr, Scorpaena scrofa. d, 300fr, Periophthalmus argentilineatus. e, 400fr, Lophius americanus. f, 1000fr, Pristis microdon.
3000fr, Narcine brasiliensis.

2009, Mar. 2 ***Perf. 13x13¼***
1081 A183 Sheet of 6, #a-f 11.50 11.50

Souvenir Sheet
Perf. 13¼ Syncopated
1082 A184 3000fr multi 15.50 15.50

Shells and Lighthouses

No. 1083: a, 125fr, Pleurotomaria fricana and Hood Point Lighthouse. b, 150fr, Patella ferruginea and Swakopmund Lighthouse. c, 225fr, Tectus pyramis and Cape Columbine Lighthouse. d, 300fr, Monodonta turbinata and Seal Point Lighthouse. e, 400fr, Mesalia opalina and Moroni Lighthouse. f, 1000fr, Cypraea diliculum and Cape Agulhas Lighthouse.
3000fr, Ranella olearia and Umhlanga Rocks Lighthouse.

2009, Mar. 2 ***Perf. 13x13¼***
1083 A183 Sheet of 6, #a-f 11.50 11.50

Souvenir Sheet
Perf. 13¼ Syncopated
1084 A184 3000fr multi 15.50 15.50

Cats

No. 1085: a, 200fr, Sokoke. b, 250fr, Abyssinian. c, 350fr, Egyptian Mau. d, 450fr, Sokoke, diff. e, 500fr, Abyssinian, diff. f, 1000fr, Egyptian Mau, diff.
3000fr, Felis nigripes.

2009, Mar. 2 ***Perf. 13x13¼***
1085 A183 Sheet of 6, #a-f 14.50 14.50

Souvenir Sheet
Perf. 13¼ Syncopated
1086 A184 3000fr multi 15.50 15.50

Owls

No. 1087: a, 200fr, Otus pembaensis. b, 250fr, Ptilopsis granti. c, 350fr, Tyto alba. d, 450fr, Asio otus. e, 500fr, Strix woodfordii. f, 1000fr, Tyto soumagnei.
3000fr, Bubo africanus.

2009, Mar. 2 ***Perf. 13x13¼***
1087 A183 Sheet of 6, #a-f 14.50 14.50

Souvenir Sheet
Perf. 13¼ Syncopated
1088 A184 3000fr multi 15.50 15.50

Kingfishers

No. 1089: a, 200fr, Megaceryle maxima. b, 250fr, Alcedo atthis. c, 350fr, Halcyon senegalensis. d, 450fr, Ipsidina picta. e, 500fr, Todiramphus chloris. f, 1000fr, Alcedo cristata.
3000fr, Halcyon malimbica.

2009, Mar. 2 ***Perf. 13x13¼***
1089 A183 Sheet of 6, #a-f 14.50 14.50

Souvenir Sheet
Perf. 13¼ Syncopated
1090 A184 3000fr multi 15.50 15.50

Butterflies

No. 1091: a, 200fr, Crenis pechuelli. b, 250fr, Charaxes zingha. c, 350fr, Taenaris catops turdula. d, 450fr, Danaus chrysippus alcippus. e, 500fr, Anaea cyanae. f, 1000fr, Epiphile orea negrina.
3000fr, Cithaeria aurora.

2009, Mar. 2 ***Perf. 13x13¼***
1091 A183 Sheet of 6, #a-f 14.50 14.50

Souvenir Sheet
Perf. 13¼ Syncopated
1092 A184 3000fr multi 15.50 15.50

Dolphins

No. 1093: a, 200fr, Stenella coeruleoalba. b, 250fr, Stenella attenuata. c, 350fr, Sousa plumbea. d, 450fr, Stenella longirostris. e, 500fr, Tursiops truncatus. f, 1000fr, Lissodelphis peronii.
3000fr, Lagenorhynchus cruciger.

2009, Mar. 2 ***Perf. 13x13¼***
1093 A183 Sheet of 6, #a-f 14.50 14.50

Souvenir Sheet
Perf. 13¼ Syncopated
1094 A184 3000fr multi 15.50 15.50

Frogs

No. 1095: a, 200fr, Xenopos laevis. b, 250fr, Astyloternus robustus. c, 350fr, Mantella aurantiaca. d, 450fr, Rana goliath. e, 500fr, Pyxicephalus adspersus. f, 1000fr, Breviceps mossambicus.
3000fr, Phrynomantis bifasciatus.

2009, Mar. 2 ***Perf. 13x13¼***
1095 A183 Sheet of 6, #a-f 14.50 14.50

Souvenir Sheet
Perf. 13¼ Syncopated
1096 A184 3000fr multi 15.50 15.50

Prehistoric Animals

No. 1097: a, 200fr, Heterodontosaurus. b, 250fr, Malawisaurus. c, 350fr, Carnotaurus. d, 450fr, Rhamphorhynchus. e, 500fr, Ouranosaurus. f, 1000fr, Herrerasaurus.
3000fr, Abrictosaurus.

2009, Mar. 2 ***Perf. 13x13¼***
1097 A183 Sheet of 6, #a-f 14.50 14.50

Souvenir Sheet
Perf. 13¼ Syncopated
1098 A184 3000fr multi 15.50 15.50

SEMI-POSTAL STAMPS

Anti-Malaria Issue
Common Design Type
Perf. 12½x12

1962, Apr. 7 **Engr.** **Unwmk.**
B1 CD108 25fr + 5fr brt pink 4.00 4.00

WHO drive to eradicate malaria.

Nurse Feeding Infant — SP1

1967, July 3 **Engr.** ***Perf. 13***
B2 SP1 25fr + 5fr multi 3.25 3.25

For the Red Cross.

Mother and Child — SP2

1974, Aug. 10 **Engr.** ***Perf. 13***
B3 SP2 35fr + 10fr red & dk brn 2.75 2.75

For the Red Cross.
For surcharge see No. 144.

Space Achievements SP3

World Philatelic Programs emblems (stamp collecting or Halley's Comet) and astronomer or satellite: a, Galileo. b, Copernicus. c, Kepler. d, Halley. e, *Planet A*, Japan, and 3 stars. f, *ICE*, US. g, *Planet A*, 5 stars. h, *Vega*, USSR.

Miniature Sheet

1988 **Litho.** ***Perf. 13½***
B4 Sheet of 8 15.00 15.00
a.-h. SP3 200fr +10fr multi 1.50 1.50

See No. C193.
For surcharges see Nos. 816P-816S.

AIR POST STAMPS

Comoro Village — AP1

Comoro Men and Moroni Mosque — AP2

Design: 200fr, Mosque of Ouani, Anjouan.

1950-54 **Unwmk.** **Engr.** ***Perf. 13***
C1 AP1 50fr grn & red brn 4.50 1.40
C2 AP2 100fr dk brn & red 6.75 1.75
C3 AP1 200fr dk grn, rose brn & pur ('54) 26.00 9.50
Nos. C1-C3 (3) 37.25 12.65

Liberation Issue
Common Design Type

1954, June 6
C4 CD102 15fr sepia & red 35.00 20.00

Madrepora Fructicosa AP3

100fr, Coral, shells and sea anemones.

1962, Jan. 13 **Photo.** ***Perf. 12½x13***
C5 AP3 100fr multi 15.00 15.00
C6 AP3 500fr multi 30.00 20.00

Telstar Issue
Common Design Type

1962, Dec. 5 **Engr.** ***Perf. 13***
C7 CD111 25fr dp vio, dl pur & red lil 5.00 3.00

Type of Regular Issue
Unwmk.

1963, Dec. 27 **Engr.** ***Perf. 13***
Size: 26½x48mm
C8 A13 65fr Baskets 5.00 3.50
C9 A13 200fr Pendant 10.00 5.25

Boat Type of Regular Issue

1964, Aug. 7 **Photo.** ***Perf. 13***
Size: 27x48mm
C10 A14 50fr Mayotte pirogue 4.50 1.75
C11 A14 85fr Schooner 7.00 2.50

Olympic Torch and Boxers — AP4

1964, Oct. 10 Engr. *Perf. 13*
C12 AP4 100fr red brn, dk brn & gray grn 7.50 7.50

18th Olympic Games, Tokyo, Oct. 10-25.

Order of Star of Grand Comoro — AP5

1964, Dec. 10 Photo. *Perf. 13*
C13 AP5 500fr multi 17.50 15.00

ITU Issue
Common Design Type

1965, May 17 Engr. *Perf. 13*
C14 CD120 50fr gray, grnsh bl & ol 20.00 10.00

French Satellite A-1 Issue
Common Design Type

Designs: 25fr, Diamant rocket and launching installations. 30fr, A-1 satellite.

1966, Jan. 17 Engr. *Perf. 13*
C15 CD121 25fr dk pur & ultra 4.50 4.50
C16 CD121 30fr dk pur & ultra 6.00 6.00
a. Strip of 2, #C15-C16 + label 11.00 11.00

French Satellite D-1 Issue
Common Design Type

1966, May 16 Engr. *Perf. 13*
C17 CD122 30fr dk grn, org & brn 4.00 4.00

Old Gun Battery, Dzaoudzi — AP6

200fr, Ksar Castle, Mutsamudu, vert.

1966, Dec. 19 Photo. *Perf. 13*
C18 AP6 50fr multi 5.00 2.50
C19 AP6 200fr multi 9.00 5.75

Bird Type of Regular Issue

Birds: 75fr, Madagascar paradise flycatchers. 100fr, Blue-cheeked bee eaters.

1967, June 20 Photo. *Perf. 13*
Size: 27x48mm
C20 A17 75fr yel grn & multi 10.50 6.50
C21 A17 100fr lt bl & multi 13.00 8.00

Woman Skier — AP7

1968, Apr. 29 Engr. *Perf. 13*
C22 AP7 70fr brt grn, lt bl & choc 6.50 4.75

10th Winter Olympic Games, Grenoble, France, Feb. 6-18, 1968.

Fish Type of Regular Issue

50fr, Moorish idol. 90fr, Diagramma lineatus.

1968, Aug. 1 Engr. *Perf. 13*
Size: 47½x27mm
C23 A19 50fr plum blk & yel 8.00 4.00
C24 A19 90fr brt grn, yel & gray grn 10.00 5.25

For surcharge & overprint see Nos. C52, C74.

Swimmer, Butterfly Stroke — AP8

1969, Jan. 27 Photo. *Perf. 12½*
C25 AP8 65fr ver, grnsh bl & blk 5.25 3.50

19th Olympic Games, Mexico City, 10/12-27.

Flower Type of Regular Issue

50fr, Heliconia sp. 85fr, Tuberose. 200fr, Orchid (angraecum eburneum).

1969, Mar. 20 Photo. *Perf. 13*
Size: 27x48mm
C26 A21 50fr multi, vert. 4.75 3.50
C27 A21 85fr multi, vert. 5.50 4.50
C28 A21 200fr multi, vert. 11.00 6.00
Nos. C26-C28 (3) 21.25 14.00

Concorde Issue
Common Design Type

1969, Apr. 17 Engr.
C29 CD129 100fr pur & brn org 24.00 16.00

View of EXPO, Globe and Moon — AP9

90fr, Geisha, map of Japan & EXPO emblem.

1970, Sept. 13 Photo. *Perf. 13*
C30 AP9 60fr slate & multi 4.50 2.40
C31 AP9 90fr multi 5.50 3.25

EXPO '70 International Exposition, Osaka, Japan, Mar. 15-Sept. 13.

Sunset over Mutsamudu — AP10

Map of Archipelago — AP11

Designs: 20fr, Sada Village, Mayotte. 65fr, Old Iconi Palace, Grand Comoro. 85fr, Nioumatchoua Island, Moheli.

1971, May 3 Photo. *Perf. 13*
C32 AP10 15fr dk bl & multi 1.20 .65
C33 AP10 20fr multi 1.75 .80
C34 AP10 65fr grn & multi 3.75 1.60
C35 AP10 85fr bl & multi 5.50 2.50

Engr.
C36 AP11 100fr brn red, grn & vio bl 7.50 5.50
Nos. C32-C36 (5) 19.70 11.05

See Nos. 107-110, C45-C49, C53, C62-C64. For overprints & surcharges see Nos. 143, C69, C71, C73, C76-C77, C79-C80, C82, C84.

Flower Type of Regular Issue

Flowers: 60fr, Hibiscus schizopetalus. 85fr, Acalypha sanderii.

1971, July 19 Photo. *Perf. 13*
Size: 27x48mm
C37 A25 60fr grn, ver & yel 5.00 2.40
C38 A25 85fr grn, red & yel 6.50 4.75

For surcharge see No. C75.

Mural, Moroni Airport — AP12

Designs: 85fr, Mural in Arrival Hall, Moroni Airport. 100fr, View of Moroni Airport.

1972, Mar. 30 Photo. *Perf. 13*
C39 AP12 65fr gray & multi 2.00 .85
C40 AP12 85fr gray & multi 2.25 1.20

Engr.
C41 AP12 100fr brn, bl & slate grn 4.00 2.10
Nos. C39-C41 (3) 8.25 4.15

New airport in Moroni.

Eiffel Tower and Moroni Telephone Exchange — AP13

75fr, Frenchman and Comoro Islander talking on telephone, radio tower and beacons.

1972, Apr. 24
C42 AP13 35fr dl red & gray 1.25 .85
C43 AP13 75fr dk car, vio & bl 2.25 .95

First radio-telephone connection between France and Comoro Islands.

Underwater Spear-fishing — AP14

1972, July 5 Engr. *Perf. 13*
C44 AP14 70fr vio bl, brt grn & mar 8.75 5.50

For surcharge see No. C78.

Types of 1971

Designs: 20fr, Cape Sima. 35fr, Bambao Palace. 40fr, Domoni Palace. 60fr, Gomajou Peninsula. 100fr, Map of Anjouan Island.

1972, Nov. 15 Photo.
C45 AP10 20fr brn & multi .90 .65
C46 AP10 35fr dk grn & multi 1.20 .80
C47 AP10 40fr bl & multi 1.75 .95
C48 AP10 60fr grnsh blk & multi 2.50 1.60

Engr.
C49 AP11 100fr mar, bl & sl grn 13.50 7.25
Nos. C45-C49 (5) 19.85 11.25

Pres. Said Mohamed Cheikh (1904-70) AP15

1973, Mar. 16 Photo. *Perf. 13*
C50 AP15 20fr multi 1.25 .80
C51 AP15 35fr multi 1.60 1.00

For overprints see Nos. C70, C72.

No. C24 Surcharged

1973, Apr. 30 Engr. *Perf. 13*
C52 A19 120fr on 90fr multi 13.00 7.25

Intl. Commission for Coelacanth Studies.

Map of Grand Comoro AP16

1973, June 28 Engr. *Perf. 13*
C53 AP16 135fr vio, bl & dk brn 9.50 6.50

See Nos. C65, C68. For surcharges see Nos. C90-C92.

Karthala Volcano AP17

1973, July 16 Photo. *Perf. 13x12½*
C54 AP17 120fr multi 7.50 5.50

Eruption of Karthala, Sept. 1972.
For surcharge see No. C89.

Armauer G. Hansen — AP18

Design: 150fr, Nicolaus Copernicus (1473-1543), Polish astronomer.

1973, Sept. 5 Engr. *Perf. 13*
C55 AP18 100fr brn, dk bl & sl grn 7.00 3.50
C56 AP18 150fr grnsh bl, vio bl & choc 8.00 5.25

Cent. of the discovery of the Hansen bacillus, the cause of leprosy.
For overprint & surcharge see Nos. C81, C93.

Pablo Picasso (1881-1973) — AP19

1973, Sept. 30 Photo.
C57 AP19 200fr blk & multi 12.00 9.75

Souvenir Sheet

C58 AP19 100fr blk & multi 16.00 14.50

For overprint see No. C87.

Order of the Star of Anjouan — AP20

1974, Jan. 7 Photo. *Perf. 13*
C59 AP20 500fr brn, bl & gold 13.00 9.50

For overprint see No. C95.

Said Omar ben Soumeth — AP21

135fr, Grand Mufti Said Omar, horiz.

1974, Jan. 31 *Perf. 13x13½, 13½x13*
C60 AP21 135fr blk & multi 4.50 2.75
C61 AP21 200fr blk & multi 5.50 3.50

For overprint & surcharge see Nos. C85, C88.

Types of 1971-73

Designs (Views on Mayotte): 20fr, Moya Beach. 35fr, Chiconi. 90fr, Port Mamutzu. 120fr, Map of Mayotte.

1974, Aug. 31 Photo. *Perf. 13*
C62 AP10 20fr bl & multi 1.20 .95
C63 AP10 35fr grn & multi 2.50 2.00
C64 AP10 90fr multi 6.25 3.50

Engr.

C65 AP16 120fr ultra & grn 9.00 5.50
Nos. C62-C65 (4) 18.95 11.95

Jet Take-off — AP22

1975, Jan. 10 Engr. *Perf. 13*
C66 AP22 135fr multi 7.25 4.75

First direct route Moroni-Hahaya-Paris.
For surcharge see No. C86.

Rotary Emblem, Meeting House, Map — AP23

1975, Feb. 23 Photo. *Perf. 13*
C67 AP23 250fr multi 10.50 7.25

Rotary Intl., 70th anniv., Moroni Rotary Club, 10th anniv.
For surcharge see No. C94.

Map Type of 1973

Design: 230fr, Map of Moheli, horiz.

1975, May 26 Engr. *Perf. 13*
C68 AP16 230fr ocher, ol grn & bl 11.00 8.00

STATE OF COMORO

Issues of 1968-75 Surcharged and Overprinted in Black, Silver, Red or Orange

1975 Printing & Perfs. as Before
C69 AP10 10fr on 20fr #C62 .60 .25
C70 AP15 20fr (S) 1.00 .25
C71 AP10 30fr on 35fr (R) #C63 1.00 .25
C72 AP15 35fr (S) 1.25 .75
C73 AP10 40fr (O) 1.50 .75
C74 A19 50fr 2.50 1.25
C75 A25 75fr on 60fr 2.00 1.10
C76 AP10 75fr on 60fr 2.00 1.10
C77 AP10 75fr on 65fr (O) 2.00 1.10
C78 AP14 75fr on 70fr 2.50 1.25
C79 AP11 100fr #C36 4.00 2.00
C80 AP11 100fr #C49 4.00 2.00
C81 AP18 100fr 4.00 2.00
C82 AP10 100fr on 85fr (O) 2.50 1.50
C83 A25 100fr on 85fr 2.50 1.50
C84 AP10 100fr on 90fr 2.50 1.50
C85 AP21 100fr on 135fr (S) 2.50 1.50
C86 AP22 100fr on 135fr 3.00 2.00
C87 AP19 200fr (S) 8.00 4.00
C88 AP21 200fr (S) 6.00 3.50
C89 AP17 200fr on 120fr 8.00 4.00
C90 AP16 200fr on 120fr 6.00 3.50
C91 AP16 200fr on 135fr 6.00 3.50
C92 AP16 200fr on 230fr 6.00 3.50
C93 AP18 400fr on 150fr 10.00 5.25
C94 AP23 400fr on 250fr 10.00 5.25
C95 AP20 500fr 12.00 7.25
Nos. C69-C95 (27) 113.35 61.80

See postage section for airmail stamps that are part of joint postage/airmail sets.

Rotary Emblem, Landscape AP26

1979, July 31 Litho. *Perf. 13x12½*
C107 AP26 400fr multi 7.00 3.00

Rotary International.

IYC Emblem, Mother and Child — AP27

1979, July 31 *Perf. 13x13½*
C108 AP27 250fr multi 3.50 3.50

Intl. Year of the Child. See No. CB1. For surcharges see Nos. C121, C202.

Dimadjou Dispensary, Map of Southern Africa, Emblem AP28

260fr, Globe, Concorde, emblem.

1980, Feb. 23 Litho. *Perf. 12½*
C109 AP28 100fr shown 1.25 .40
C110 AP28 260fr multicolored 3.00 1.00

Rotary International, 75th anniv. and Moroni Rotary Club, 15th anniv. (100fr).
For surcharges see Nos. 815L, C119-C120.

First Transatlantic Flight, 50th Anniversary — AP29

1980, May 30 Litho. *Perf. 13*
C111 AP29 200fr multi 3.50 1.75

No. C111 Surcharged in Blue

1981, Feb. Litho. *Perf. 13*
C112 AP29 30fr on 200fr multi 1.00 .35

The Dove and the Rainbow, by Picasso — AP30

Picasso Birth Centenary: 70fr, Still Life on a Sideboard. 150fr, Studio with Plaster Head. 250fr, Bowl and Pot, vert. 500fr, The Red Tablecloth.

1981, June 30 Litho. *Perf. 12½*
C113 AP30 40fr multi .55 .25
C114 AP30 70fr multi .95 .25
C115 AP30 150fr multi 1.90 .50
C116 AP30 250fr multi 3.25 .70
C117 AP30 500fr multi 6.25 1.50
Nos. C113-C117 (5) 12.90 3.20

For surcharges see Nos. 815G, C118.

Nos. C114, C109-C110, CB1 Srchd.

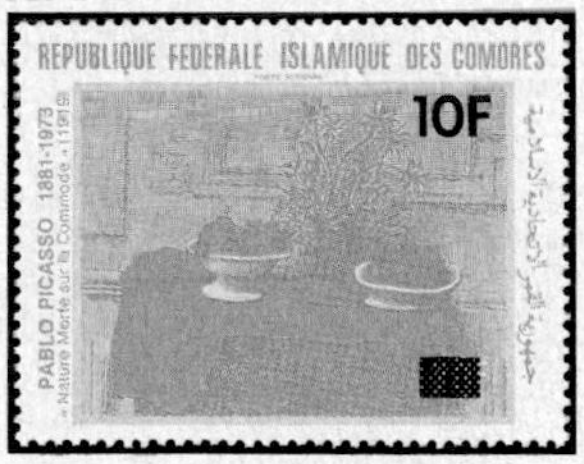

1981, Nov. Litho. *Perf. 12½, 13*
C118 AP30 10fr on 70fr multi .40 .40
C119 AP28 10fr on 100fr multi .80 .80
C120 AP28 50fr on 260fr multi 2.00 .25
C121 AP27 50fr on 200fr+30fr multi 2.00 .25
Nos. C118-C121 (4) 5.20 1.70

Manned Flight Bicentenary — AP31

Balloons: 100fr, Montgolfiere, 1783. 200fr, Lunardi, 1784. 300fr, Blanchard and Jeffries, 1785. 400fr, Giffard, 1852, horiz.
500fr, Paris Siege. 1870.

1983, Apr. 20 Litho. *Perf. 13*
C122 AP31 100fr multicolored 1.00 .30
C123 AP31 200fr multicolored 1.90 .50
C124 AP31 300fr multicolored 3.25 .90
C125 AP31 400fr multicolored 4.50 1.25
Nos. C122-C125 (4) 10.65 2.95

Souvenir Sheet

C126 AP31 500fr multicolored 5.50 1.50

For overprints and surcharges see Nos. 602, 812T, 815P.

Pre-Olympic Year Sailing — AP32

1983, June 30 Litho. *Perf. 13*

C127	AP32 150fr Type 470	1.50	.40
C128	AP32 200fr Flying Dutch-man	2.25	.50
C129	AP32 300fr Type 470, diff.	3.25	.90
C130	AP32 400fr Finn	4.75	1.00
	Nos. C127-C130 (4)	11.75	2.80

Souvenir Sheet

C131	AP32 500fr Soling	5.50	1.50

For overprint and surcharge see Nos. 603, C206.

1984 Summer Olympics — AP33

1984, July 10 Litho. *Perf. 13*

C132	AP33 60fr Basketball	.50	.25
C133	AP33 100fr Basketball, diff.	.90	.40
C134	AP33 165fr Basketball, diff.	1.50	.65
C135	AP33 175fr Baseball, horiz.	1.60	.65
C136	AP33 200fr Baseball, horiz.	1.90	.80
	Nos. C132-C136 (5)	6.40	2.75

Souvenir Sheet

C137	AP33 500fr Basketball, diff.	8.00	1.50

Nos. C132-C134 vert.

Development Conference AP34

1984, July 2 Litho. *Perf. 13*

C138	AP34 475fr Tools for devel-opment	5.50	2.00

For surcharge see No. 796I.

Audubon Bicentenary — AP35

100fr, Hirundo rustica, vert.. 125fr, Icterus galbula, vert. 150fr, Buteo lineatus. 500fr, Sphyropicus varius.

1985, Jan. 15 Litho. *Perf. 13*

C139	AP35 100fr multicolored	1.25	.40
C140	AP35 125fr multicolored	1.50	.50
C141	AP35 150fr multicolored	2.00	.60
C142	AP35 500fr multicolored	5.25	2.00
	Nos. C139-C142 (4)	10.00	3.50

Moroni Port Missile Defense — AP36

No. C146, Ngome Ntsoudjini Scout troop.

1985, May 20 Litho. *Perf. 13x12½*

C145	AP36 200fr multi	3.00	1.25
C146	AP36 200fr multi	3.00	1.25
a.	Pair, #C145-C146 + label	6.00	6.00

PHILEXAFRICA '85, Lome.
For surcharges see Nos. C207-C208.

Natl. Flag, Sun, Outline Map of Islands — AP37

1985, July 6

C147	AP37 10fr multi	.30	.25
C148	AP37 15fr multi	.30	.25
C149	AP37 125fr multi	2.25	.60
C150	AP37 300fr multi	5.50	1.50
	Nos. C147-C150 (4)	8.35	2.60

Natl. independence, 10th anniv.
For surcharge see No. 815Q.

Runners — AP38

1985, Nov. 12

C151	AP38 250fr shown	2.75	1.75
C152	AP38 250fr Mining	2.75	1.75
a.	Pair, #C151-C152 + label	6.00	6.00

PHILEXAFRICA '85, Lome, Togo, 11/16-24.
For surcharges see Nos. 815H-815I, C204-C205.

Air Transport Union, UTA, 50th Anniv. — AP39

25fr, F-AOUL seaplane. 75fr, Camel driver, DC-8. 100fr, Noratlas and Heron DC-4s. 125fr, UTA cargo plane. 1000fr, Aircraft, 1935-1985.

1985, Dec. 30 Litho. *Perf. 13*

C153	AP39 25fr multi	.25	.25
C154	AP39 75fr multi	.75	.30
C155	AP39 100fr multi	1.10	.40
a.	Souv. sheet of 3, #C153-C155, perf. 12½	3.50	2.25
C156	AP39 125fr multi	1.40	.60

Size: 40x52mm

Perf. 12½x13

C157	AP39 1000fr multi	12.00	6.00
a.	Souv. sheet of 2, #C156-C157, perf. 12½	13.00	8.00
	Nos. C153-C157 (5)	15.50	7.55

Halley's Comet — AP40

Comets, astronomers and probes: 125fr, Edmond Halley, Giotto probe. 150fr, Giacobini-Zinner, 1959. 225fr, Encke, 1961. 300fr, Bradfield, 1980. 450fr, Planet A probe.

1986, Mar. 7 *Perf. 13*

C158	AP40 125fr multi	1.25	.45
C159	AP40 150fr multi	1.50	.50
C160	AP40 225fr multi	2.50	.90
C161	AP40 300fr multi	3.00	1.25
C162	AP40 450fr multi	5.00	1.75
	Nos. C158-C162 (5)	13.25	4.85

For surcharges see Nos. 796S, 804H, 804R, 812P.

1986 World Cup Soccer Championships, Mexico — AP41

Various soccer plays.

1986, June 11 Litho. *Perf. 13*

C163	AP41 125fr multi	1.25	.45
C164	AP41 210fr multi	2.25	.80
C165	AP41 500fr multi	5.50	2.00
C166	AP41 600fr multi	6.00	2.25
	Nos. C163-C166 (4)	15.00	5.50

For surcharges see Nos. 796C, 800Q, 815C.

Tennis at the 1988 Summer Olympics — AP42

Various players.

1987, Jan. 28 Litho. *Perf. 13½*

C167	AP42 150fr multi	1.75	.45
C168	AP42 250fr multi	3.00	.75
C169	AP42 500fr multi	5.50	1.50
C170	AP42 600fr multi	6.75	1.75
	Nos. C167-C170 (4)	17.00	4.45

For overprints and surcharges see Nos. 796N, 796U, 815J, 816L, 816N, C183-C186, C203.

World Wildlife Fund — AP43

Various pictures of the mongoose lemur.

1987, Feb. 18 *Perf. 13*

C171	AP43 75fr multi, vert.	2.50	.50
C172	AP43 100fr multi	3.50	.75
C173	AP43 125fr multi	5.50	1.00
C174	AP43 150fr multi	6.50	1.25
	Nos. C171-C174 (4)	18.00	3.50

1988 Winter Olympics, Calgary AP44

1987, Apr. 10 Litho. *Perf. 13½*

C175	AP44 150fr Slalom	1.25	.45
C176	AP44 225fr Ski jumping	2.25	.75
C177	AP44 500fr Women's gi-ant slalom	5.50	1.60
C178	AP44 600fr Luge	6.00	2.25
	Nos. C175-C178 (4)	15.00	5.05

For surcharges see Nos. 800R, 812U.

AP45

Aviation History AP46

Designs: 200fr, Inventors Didier Daurat and Raymond Vanier with 1935 Air Blue F-ANR1. 300fr, Farman biplane, 1st scheduled airmail delivery, Paris-LeMans-St. Nazaire, Aug. 17, 1918. 500fr, Bleriot aircraft, 1st scheduled air-mail delivery, Villacoublay-Vendome-Poitiers-Pauillac, Oct. 15, 1913. 1000fr, Henri Pequet and his aircraft, Feb. 18, 1911.

1987, Dec. 29 Litho. *Perf. 13*

C179	AP45 200fr multi	2.25	.65
C180	AP45 300fr multi	3.25	1.00
C181	AP45 500fr multi	5.50	1.60

Perf. 12½x13

C182	AP46 1000fr multi	11.00	2.25
	Nos. C179-C182 (4)	22.00	5.50

Airmail history exposition, Allahabad.
For surcharges see Nos. 800S, 804D.

Nos. C167-C170 Ovptd. in Red for 1988 Olympic Tennis Champions

Overprint includes name of athlete and "Medaille d'or / Seoul" or "Medaille / d'argent / Seoul."

1988, Nov. Litho. *Perf. 13½*

C183	AP42 150fr "Miloslav Mecir / (Tchec.)"	1.25	.75
C184	AP42 250fr "Tim Mayotte / (U.S.A.)"	1.90	1.40
C185	AP42 500fr "Steffi Graf / (R.F.A.)"	5.00	2.75
C186	AP42 600fr "Gabriela Sabatini / (Argentine)"	6.00	3.75
	Nos. C183-C186 (4)	14.15	8.65

For surcharges see Nos. 800T, 815K, 816M, 816O.

Early Aviators and Aircraft — AP47

100fr, Alberto Santos-Dumont (1873-1932), & *Bagatelle,* 1st documented power flight in Europe, Oct. 23, 1906. 150fr, Wright Brothers & *Flyer A.* 200fr, Louis Bleriot (1872-1936) & *Bleriot XI,* 1st crossing of the English Channel in a heavier-than-air craft, July 25, 1909. 300fr, Henri Farman (1874-1958) & Voisin biplane, 1st fixed-route 1-kilometer circular flight, Jan. 13, 1908. 500fr, Gabriel (1880-1973) & Charles (1882-1912) Voisin, established 1st biplane factory (1908), & Voisin biplane. 800fr, Roland Garros (1888-1918), 1st trans-Mediterranean flight, Sept. 23, 1913.

1988, Dec. 7 Litho. *Perf. 13*

C187	AP47	100fr pur	.90	.45
C188	AP47	150fr brt lil rose	1.60	.60
C189	AP47	200fr blk	2.00	.90
C190	AP47	300fr dark yel org	3.00	.90
C191	AP47	500fr dark blue	5.00	1.50
C192	AP47	800fr lt olive grn	7.50	3.00
		Nos. C187-C192 (6)	20.00	7.35

For surcharges see Nos. 800B, 800U, 804E, C209.

Souvenir Sheet

Space Achievements — AP48

Design: World Philatelic Programs stamp collecting emblem, Soviet satellite and Edmond Halley.

1988 Litho. *Perf. 13½*

C193	AP48	750fr multi	8.00	1.50

Nos. C108, C168, C151-C152, C128, C145-C146 and C189 Surcharged

1989 Litho. *Perfs. as Before*

C202	AP27	5fr on 250fr #C108	.25	.25
C203	AP42	25fr on 250fr #C168	.25	.25
C204	AP38	50fr on 250fr #C151	.50	.25
C205	AP38	50fr on 250fr #C152	.50	.25
a.		Pair, #C204-C205 + label	1.25	1.25
C206	AP32	150fr on 200fr #C128	1.40	.60
C207	AP36	150fr on 200fr #C145	1.40	.60
C208	AP36	150fr on 200fr #C146	1.40	.60
a.		Pair, #C207-C208 + label	6.00	6.00
C209	AP47	150fr on 200fr #C189	1.40	.60
		Nos. C202-C209 (8)	7.10	3.40

World Cup Soccer, Championships, Italy — AP50

Various soccer plays and map of Italy.

1990, June Litho. *Perf. 13*

C210	AP50	75fr multicolored	.60	.30
C211	AP50	150fr multicolored	1.40	.60
C212	AP50	500fr multicolored	4.25	1.90
C213	AP50	1000fr multicolored	8.75	4.00
		Nos. C210-C213 (4)	15.00	6.80

For surcharge see No. 800V.

Souvenir Sheet

Garry Kasparov, Anatoly Karpov, Russian Chess Champions — AP51

Litho. & Embossed

1991, Aug. 5 *Perf. 13½*

C214	AP51	1500fr gold & multi	12.00	—

World Chess Championships.

1992 Summer Olympics, Barcelona AP52

Litho. & Embossed

1992, July 28 *Perf. 13½*

C215	AP52	1500fr gold & multi	26.50	12.00

Sculpted Table — AP52a

1994 (?) Litho. *Perf. 13¼x13½*

Background Color

C215A	AP52a	15fr blue	—	—
C215B	AP52a	75fr green	—	—
C215C	AP52a	100fr pink	—	—
C215D	AP52a	225fr orange	—	—

For surcharges see Nos. 826A-826E.

Sea Turtles AP53

1995 Litho. *Perf. 13½x13¼*

Frame Color

C216	AP53	10fr blue	25.00	25.00
C217	AP53	25fr pink	—	—
C218	AP53	30fr green	25.00	25.00
C219	AP53	50fr lilac	50.00	50.00

No. C215A Surcharged in Blue Violet

Perf. 13¼x13½

2001, June 16 Litho.

C220	AP52a	300fr on 15fr	—	—

AIR POST SEMI-POSTAL STAMP

Type of Air Post 1979

Design: IYC emblem, mother and son.

1979, July 31 Photo. *Perf. 13½x13*

CB1	AP27	200fr + 30fr multi	3.50	3.50

International Year of the Child.
For surcharge see No. C121.

POSTAGE DUE STAMPS

Anjouan Mosque — D1

1950 Unwmk. Engr. *Perf. 14x13*

J1	D1	50c deep green	1.20	.95
J2	D1	1fr black brown	1.20	1.00

Coelacanth — D2

1954

J3	D2	5fr dk brown & green	1.10	1.00
J4	D2	10fr gray & red brown	1.50	1.50
J5	D2	20fr indigo & blue	2.75	2.50
		Nos. J3-J5 (3)	5.35	5.00

Hibiscus D3

2fr, 15fr, 40fr, 50fr, vertical.

1977, Nov. 19 Litho. *Perf. 13½*

J6	D3	1fr shown	.35	.25
J7	D3	2fr Pineapple	.35	.25
J8	D3	5fr White butterfly	.35	.25
J9	D3	10fr Chameleon	.35	.25
J10	D3	15fr Blooming banana	.35	.25
J11	D3	20fr Orchids	.35	.25
J12	D3	30fr Allamanda cathartica	.50	.25
J13	D3	40fr Cashews	.95	.25
J14	D3	50fr Custard apple	1.10	.25
J15	D3	100fr Breadfruit	2.10	.75
J16	D3	200fr Vanilla	4.50	.95
J17	D3	500fr Ylang ylang	10.75	1.50
		Nos. J6-J17 (12)	22.00	5.45

OFFICIAL STAMPS

Comoro Flag — O1

Perf. 13x12½

1979-85 Litho. Unwmk.

O1	O1	5fr multi	.25	.25
O2	O1	10fr multi	.25	.25
O3	O1	20fr multi	.25	.25
O4	O1	30fr multi	.50	.25
O5	O1	40fr multi	.65	.25
O6	O1	60fr multi ('80)	.60	.25
O7	O1	75fr multi ('85)	.40	.25
O8	O1	100fr multi	1.25	.60
		Nos. O1-O8 (8)	4.15	2.35

See Nos. 526-530.

Pres. Said Mohamed Cheikh (1904-1970) — O2

1980-85

O9	O2	100fr multi	1.00	.40
O10	O2	125fr multi ('85)	2.00	1.50
O11	O2	400fr multi	3.00	1.25
		Nos. O9-O11 (3)	6.00	3.15

CONGO, DEMOCRATIC REPUBLIC

ˌde-mə-ˈkra-tik ri-ˈpə-blik of ˈkäŋ-ˌgō

LOCATION — Central Africa
GOVT. — Republic
AREA — 895,348 sq. mi. (estimated)
POP. — 22,480,000 (est. 1971)
CAPITAL — Kinshasa (Leopoldville)

Congo was an independent state, founded by Leopold II of Belgium, until 1908 when it was annexed to Belgium as a colony. Congo became an independent republic in 1960. The name was changed to Republic of Zaire, Oct. 28, 1971. In 1998 some issues again used the name Congo Democratic Republic. See Zaire in Vol. 6 for later issues.

100 Centimes = 1 Franc
100 Sengi = 1 Li-Kuta,
100 Ma-Kuta = 1 Zaire (1967)

Catalogue values for all unused stamps in this country are for Never Hinged items.

Belgian Congo Flower Issue of 1952-53 Overprinted or Surcharged

Perf. 11½

1960, June 30 Photo. Unwmk.

Flowers in Natural Colors

Size: 21x25½mm

Granite Paper

323	A86	10c dp plum & ocher	.25	.25
324	A86	10c on 15c red & yel grn	.25	.25
325	A86	20c grn & gray	.25	.25
326	A86	40c grn & sal	.25	.25
327	A86	50c on 60c bl grn & pink	.25	.25
328	A86	50c on 75c dp plum & gray	.25	.25
329	A86	1fr car & yel	.30	.25
330	A86	1.50fr vio & ap grn	.30	.25
331	A86	2fr ol grn & buff	.30	.25
332	A86	3fr ol grn & pink	.45	.25
333	A86	4fr choc & lil	1.50	1.00
334	A86	5fr dp plum & lt bl grn	.55	.25
335	A86	6.50fr dk car & lil	.70	.25
336	A86	8fr grn & lt yel	.80	.30
337	A86	10fr dp plum & pale ol	1.50	.30
338	A86	20fr vio bl & dl sal	3.50	.80

Nos. 324, 327-328 exist without "CONGO" overprint but with surcharge, also without surcharge but with "CONGO." Inverted and double overprints exist. Values from $10 to $50 each.

Belgian Congo Flower Issue of 1952-53 Overprinted or Surcharged

Size: 22x32mm

339	A86	50fr dp plum & gray bl	19.00	6.00
340	A86	100fr grn & buff	45.00	10.00
		Nos. 323-340 (18)	75.40	21.40

Belgian Congo Nos. 306-317, Ovptd. or Srchd. in Red, Blue, Black or Brown

341	A92	10c bl & brn (R)	.25	.25
342	A93	20c red org & sl (Bl)	.25	.25
343	A92	40c brn & bl (Bk)	.25	.25
344	A93	50c brt ultra, red & sep (R)	.25	.25
345	A92	1fr brn, grn & blk (Br)	.25	.25
346	A93	1.50fr blk & org yel (R)	.25	.25
347	A92	2fr crim, blk & brn (Bl)	.45	.25
348	A93	3.50fr on 3fr blk, gray & lil rose (Bk)	.65	.25
349	A92	5fr brn, dk brn & brt grn (Br)	.85	.25
350	A93	6.50fr bl, brn & org yel (R)	1.00	.25
a.		Black overprint	1.75	.60
351	A92	8fr org brn, ol bis & lil (Br)	1.25	.40
352	A93	10fr multi (R)	1.60	.60
		Nos. 341-352 (12)	7.30	3.50

Inverted and double overprints exist. Values from $15 to $20 each.

Same Overprint on Belgian Congo No. 318

1960

353	A94	50c gldn brn, ocher & red brn	1.00	1.00

Same Overprint and Surcharge of New Value on Belgian Congo Nos. 321-322

Inscription in French

354	A95	3.50fr on 3fr gray & red	1.00	.70

Inscription in Flemish

355	A95	3.50fr on 3fr gray & red	1.00	.70
		Nos. 353-355 (3)	3.00	2.40

Nos. 353-355 are known with inverted overprints. Value, each $10.

Map of Congo A93a

1960 Photo. *Perf. 11½*

356	A93a	20c brown	.25	.25
357	A93a	50c rose red	.25	.25
358	A93a	1fr green	.25	.25
359	A93a	1.50fr red brn	.25	.25
360	A93a	2fr rose car	.25	.25
361	A93a	3.50fr lilac	.25	.25
362	A93a	5fr brt bl	.25	.25
363	A93a	6.50fr gray	.25	.25
364	A93a	10fr orange	.50	.25
365	A93a	20fr ultra	.90	.25
		Nos. 356-365 (10)	3.40	2.50

Congo's Independence.

Nos. 356-365 exist imperf. Value, set unused $25.

For overprints see Nos. 371-380.

Flag, People and Broken Chain — A94

1961, Jan. 4 Unwmk. *Perf. 11½*

Flag in Blue and Yellow

366	A94	2fr rose vio	.25	.25
367	A94	3.50fr vermilion	.25	.25
368	A94	6.50fr yel brn	.25	.25
369	A94	10fr brt grn	.35	.25
370	A94	20fr car rose	.50	.30
		Nos. 366-370 (5)	1.60	1.30

Signing of the Independence Agreement by Belgium, Jan. 4, 1959.

Nos. 356-365 Overprinted in Blue, Black or Red: "Conference Coquilhatville Avril Mai 1961"

1961

371	A93a	20c brn (Bl)	1.75	1.75
372	A93a	50c rose red (Bk)	1.75	1.75
373	A93a	1fr grn (R)	1.75	1.75
374	A93a	1.50fr red brn (Bl)	1.75	1.75
375	A93a	2fr rose car (Bk)	1.75	1.75
376	A93a	3.50fr lil (Bl)	1.75	1.75
377	A93a	5fr brt bl (R)	1.75	1.75
378	A93a	6.50fr gray (R)	1.75	1.75
379	A93a	10fr org (Bk)	1.75	1.75
380	A93a	20fr ultra (R)	1.75	1.75
		Nos. 371-380 (10)	17.50	17.50

Coquilhatville Conf., Apr.-May, 1961.

Nos. 371-380 exist with inverted overprints. Value $15 each.

Pres. Joseph Kasavubu — A95

Kasavubu and Map of Congo — A96

10fr-100fr, Kasavubu in uniform and map.

Perf. 11½

1961, June 30 Unwmk. Photo.

Portrait and Inscription in Dark Brown

381	A95	10c yellow	.25	.25
382	A95	20c dp rose	.25	.25
383	A95	40c bl grn	.25	.25
384	A95	50c salmon	.25	.25
385	A95	1fr lilac	.25	.25
386	A95	1.50fr lt brn	.25	.25
387	A95	2fr brt grn	.25	.25
388	A96	3.50fr rose pink	.25	.25
389	A96	5fr gray	*6.50*	.25
390	A96	6.50fr ultra	1.00	.25
391	A96	8fr olive	1.00	.25
392	A95	10fr lt vio	2.25	.80
393	A95	20fr orange	2.25	.25
394	A95	50fr lt bl	3.75	.35
395	A95	100fr apple green	6.25	.55
		Nos. 381-395 (15)	25.00	4.70

First anniversary of independence.

Exists imperf. Value, set $70.

Nos. 381-387, 389 and 392 Overprinted: "REOUVERTURE du PARLEMENT JUILLET 1961"

1961

Portrait and Inscription in Dark Brown

396	A95	10c yellow	.25	.25
397	A95	20c dp rose	.25	.25
398	A95	40c bl grn	.25	.25
399	A95	50c salmon	.55	.35
400	A95	1fr lilac	.55	.35
401	A95	1.50fr lt brn	1.50	1.00
402	A95	2fr brt grn	1.50	1.00
403	A96	5fr gray	1.50	1.00
404	A95	10fr lt vio	1.50	1.00
		Nos. 396-404 (9)	7.85	5.45

Congolese parliament re-opening, 7/1961.

Nos. 396-404 exist with inverted overprints. Value $9 each.

Dag Hammarskjold and Map of Africa with Congo — A97

1962, Jan. 20 Photo. *Perf. 11½*

Gray Background

405	A97	10c dk brn	.25	.25
406	A97	20c Prus bl	.25	.25
407	A97	30c brown	.25	.25
408	A97	40c dk bl	.25	.25
409	A97	50c brn red	.25	.25
410	A97	3fr ol grn	*5.00*	*2.00*
411	A97	6.50fr dk vio	1.50	.35
412	A97	8fr red brn	1.75	.50
		Nos. 405-412 (8)	9.50	4.10

Souvenir Sheets

Imperf

413	A97	25fr blk brn	10.00	10.00
a.		Overprint in green	4.50	4.50

Dag Hammarskjold, Sec. Gen. of the UN, 1953-61.

Nos. 405-412 exist imperf. Value, set unused $20.

No 413a is overprinted "30 Juin 1962" on stamp and "2eme Anniversaire de l'Independance" on sheet margin. Issued June 30, 1962.

For overprints see Nos. 417-424.

Malaria Eradication Emblem and Mosquito — A98

1962, June 15 Granite Paper

414	A98	1.50fr yel, blk & dk red	.25	.25
415	A98	2fr yel grn, brn & bl grn	.30	.25
416	A98	6.50fr ultra, blk & mar	.40	.25
		Nos. 414-416 (3)	.95	.75

WHO drive to eradicate malaria.

Nos. 414-416 exist imperf. Value, set unused $2.

Nos. 405-412 Overprinted in Blue, Purple, Black or Carmine

1962, Oct. 15 Gray Background

417	A97	10c dk brn (Bl)	.25	.25
418	A97	20c Prus bl (P)	.25	.25
419	A97	30c brn (Bk)	.25	.25
420	A97	40c dk bl (C)	.25	.25
421	A97	50c brn red (Bl)	*2.50*	*1.00*
422	A97	3fr ol grn (P)	.25	.25
423	A97	6.50fr dk vio (Bk)	.25	.25
424	A97	8fr red brn (C)	.40	.25
		Nos. 417-424 (8)	4.40	2.75

Reorganization of Adoula administration.

Inverted overprints exist. Value, $8.00 each.

Canceled to Order

Starting in 1963, values in the used column are for "canceled to order" stamps. Postally used examples sell for much more.

A99

1963, Jan. 28 Engr. *Perf. 10½x13*

425	A99	2fr dull purple	*1.50*	*1.00*
426	A99	4fr red	.25	.25
427	A99	7fr dark blue	.25	.25
428	A99	20fr slate green	.50	.25
		Nos. 425-428 (4)	2.50	*1.75*

Congo's 1st participation at the UPU Cong., New Delhi, Mar. 1963.

Nos. 425-428 exist imperf. Value, set unused $20.

An imperf sheet containing No. 428 in brown exists. Value $30.

For overprints see Nos. 468-471.

Shoebill — A100

Birds: 10c, Pelicans. 20c, Crested guinea fowl, horiz. 30c, Openbill. 40c, White-bellied storks, horiz. 2fr, Marabou. 3fr, Greater flamingos, horiz. 4fr, Congolese peacock. 5fr, Hartlaub ducks, horiz. 6fr, Secretary bird. 7fr,

Black-casqued hornbill, horiz. 8fr, Sacred ibis and nest. 10fr, Crowned crane, horiz. 20fr, Saddle-bill stork, horiz.

1963 Unwmk. Photo. *Perf. 11½*

429	A100	10c pink, ultra & ocher	.25	.25
430	A100	20c rose red, bl & blk	.25	.25
431	A100	30c grn, ocher & blk	.25	.25
432	A100	40c gray, org & blk	.25	.25
433	A100	1fr brn, emer & gray	.25	.25
434	A100	2fr gray, red & ind	*3.25*	.60
435	A100	3fr ol grn, blk & rose	.25	.25
436	A100	4fr car rose, vio bl & grn	.25	.25
437	A100	5fr lake, lt bl & blk	.45	.25
438	A100	6fr pur, yel & blk	*3.50*	.60
439	A100	7fr bl grn, blk & ind	.55	.25
440	A100	8fr yel, org & blk	.65	.25
441	A100	10fr bl, blk & rose	.65	.25
442	A100	20fr cit, red & blk	1.20	.25
		Nos. 429-442 (14)	12.00	4.20

Nos. 429-442 exist imperf. Value, set unused $50.

Nos. 436 and 438 exist in imperf sheets of one. Value, each $40.

Cinchona Ledgeriana — A101

Red Cross Nurse — A102

10c, 30c, 5fr, Strophanthus sarmentosus.

Perf. 12½x13½, 13½x12½

1963, May 25 Engr. Unwmk.

Cross in Red

443	A101	10c vio & dl grn	.25	.25
444	A101	20c magenta & bl	.25	.25
445	A101	30c grn & org	.25	.25
446	A101	40c bl & vio	.25	.25
447	A101	5fr ol & rose claret	.25	.25
448	A101	7fr org & blk	.25	.25
449	A102	9fr gray olive & red	.25	.25
450	A102	20fr purple & red	*2.50*	1.00
		Nos. 443-450 (8)	4.25	2.75

International Red Cross centenary.

Nos. 443-450 exist imperf. Value, set unused $15.

A souvenir sheet of three contains imperf. 5fr, 7fr, and 20fr stamps similar to Nos. 447, 448 and 450, but in changed colors. Size: 109x75mm. Value $30.

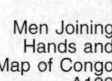

Men Joining Hands and Map of Congo A103

1963, June 29 Photo. *Perf. 11½*

451	A103	4fr multi	1.25	.50
452	A103	5fr multi	.25	.25
453	A103	9fr multi	.25	.25
454	A103	12fr multi	.35	.25
		Nos. 451-454 (4)	2.10	1.25

Issued to celebrate national reconciliation.

Nos. 451-454 exist imperf. Value, set unused $10.

Bulldozer and Kabambare Sewer, Leopoldville — A104

Designs: 30c, 5fr, 12fr, Excavator and blueprint. 50c, 9fr, Building Ituri road.

1963, July 1 Engr. Unwmk.

455	A104	20c multi	.25	.25
456	A104	30c multi	.25	.25
457	A104	50c multi	.25	.25
458	A104	3fr multi	1.50	.60
459	A104	5fr multi	.25	.25
460	A104	9fr multi	.25	.25
461	A104	12fr multi	.25	.25
		Nos. 455-461 (7)	3.00	2.10

Issued to publicize aid to Congo by the European Economic Community.

Nos. 455-461 exist imperf. Value, set unused $20.

Leopoldville Airport N'Djili — A105

5fr, 7fr, 50fr, Tail assembly and airport.

1963, Nov. 30 Photo. *Perf. 11½*

462	A105	2fr gray, yel & red brn	.25	.25
463	A105	5fr mag, vio & yel	.25	.25
464	A105	6fr bl, yel & dk brn	1.75	.60
465	A105	7fr multi	.25	.25
466	A105	30fr lil, yel & ol	.40	.25
467	A105	50fr multi	.65	.30
		Nos. 462-467 (6)	3.55	1.90

Issued to publicize Air Congo.

Nos. 462-467 exist imperf. Value, set unused $15.

For surcharge see No. 606.

Nos. 425-428 Overprinted with Silver Frame on Three Sides and Black Inscription: "15e anniversaire / 10 DECEMBRE 1948 / DROITS DE L'HOMME / 10 DECEMBRE 1963"

Engraved and Typographed

1963, Dec. 10 *Perf. 10½x13*

468	A99	2fr dull purple	.25	.25
469	A99	4fr red	.25	.25
470	A99	7fr dark blue	.25	.25
471	A99	20fr slate green	.35	.25
		Nos. 468-471 (4)	1.10	1.00

Universal Declaration of Human Rights, 15th anniv.

Nos. 468-471 exist with side date panels transposed ("1963" at left, "1948" at right). Value, each $15.

Laboratory Technician and Atomic Emblem A106

1.50fr, 60fr, University. 8fr, 75fr, First African nuclear reactor. 25fr, 100fr, University and crest.

1964, Feb. 1 Photo. *Perf. 14x12½*

472	A106	50c multi	.25	.25
473	A106	1.50fr multi	.25	.25
474	A106	8fr multi	*3.00*	*2.75*
475	A106	25fr multi	.25	.25
476	A106	30fr multi	.35	.25
477	A106	60fr multi	.60	.35
478	A106	75fr multi	.70	.60
479	A106	100fr multi	1.25	1.00
a.		Souv. sheet of 3	7.00	7.00
		Nos. 472-479 (8)	6.65	5.70

Lovanium University, Leopoldville, 10th anniv.

No. 479a contains 3 imperf. multicolored stamps: 20fr, design as 50c; 30fr, as 8fr; 100fr.

Nos. 472-479 exist imperf. Value, set unused $25.

Belgian Congo Issues of 1952-59 Overprinted "REPUBLIQUE DU CONGO" and Surcharged in Black on Overprinted Metallic Panels

1964 *Perf. 11½*

480	A93	1fr on 20c red org & sl (#307)	.25	.25
481	A86	2fr on 1.50fr (#273)	*11.00*	*3.75*
482	A93	5fr on 6.50fr (#315)	.80	.25
483	A86	8fr on 6.50fr (#278)	1.10	.35

Republic Issues of 1960-61 Surcharged in Black on Overprinted Metallic Rectangles or Ovals

484	A86	1fr on 6.50fr (#335)	.25	.25
485	A93	1fr on 20c (#342)	.25	.25
486	A86	2fr on 1.50fr (#330)	.25	.25
487	A95	3fr on 20c (#382)	.55	.25
488	A95	4fr on 40c (#383)	.55	.25
489	A93	5fr on 6.50fr ("Congo" red) (#350)	.80	.25
a.		"Congo" black	.80	.25
490	A93a	6fr on 6.50fr (#363)	.80	.25
491	A93a	7fr on 20c (#356)	.80	.25
		Nos. 480-491 (12)	17.40	6.60

Pole Vault A107

7fr, 20fr, Javelin, vert. 8fr, 100fr, Hurdling.

Perf. 11½

1964, July 13 Unwmk. Photo.

Granite Paper

492	A107	5fr gray, dk brn & car	.25	.25
493	A107	7fr rose, vio & emer	.95	.35
494	A107	8fr org, yel, red brn & vio bl	.25	.25
495	A107	10fr bl, vio brn & mag	.25	.25
496	A107	20fr gray grn, red brn & ver	.25	.25
497	A107	100fr lil, dk brn & grn	.95	.25
a.		Souv. sheet of 3	10.00	10.00
		Nos. 492-497 (6)	2.90	1.60

18th Olympic Games, Tokyo, Oct. 10-25.

No. 497a contains 3 imperf. stamps (20fr orange & dark brown, pole vault; 30fr citron and dark brown, hurdling; 100fr dull green and dark brown, javelin). Sheet issued Sept. 10.

Nos. 492-497 exist imperf. Value, set unused $40.

National Palace, Leopoldville — A108

1964, Sept. 15 Granite Paper

498	A108	50c lil rose & bl	.25	.25
499	A108	1fr bl & lil rose	.25	.25
500	A108	2fr brn red & vio	.25	.25
501	A108	3fr emer & red	.25	.25
502	A108	4fr org & vio bl	.25	.25
503	A108	5fr gray vio & emer	.25	.25
504	A108	6fr sep & org	.25	.25
505	A108	7fr gray ol & red brn	.25	.25
506	A108	8fr rose red & vio bl	*2.00*	.30
507	A108	9fr vio bl & rose red	.25	.25
508	A108	10fr brn ol & grn	.25	.25
509	A108	20fr bl & brn org	.25	.25
510	A108	30fr dk car rose & grn	.25	.25
511	A108	40fr ultra & dk car rose	.35	.25
512	A108	50fr brn org & grn	.40	.25
513	A108	100fr slate & ver	.85	.25
		Nos. 498-513 (16)	6.60	4.05

Nos. 498-513 exist imperf. Value, set unused $25.

For overprints and surcharges see Nos. 574-577, 593-598, 609-615, 670-671, 673-674, 676-677, 680, 684-687.

Pres. John F. Kennedy (1917-63) A109

1964, Dec. 8 Photo. *Perf. 13½*

514	A109	5fr dk bl & blk	.25	.25
515	A109	6fr rose claret & blk	.25	.25
516	A109	9fr brn & blk	.25	.25
517	A109	30fr pur & blk	.55	.25
518	A109	40fr dl grn & blk	*3.50*	1.00
519	A109	60fr red brn & blk	1.20	.35
		Nos. 514-519 (6)	6.00	2.35

Souvenir Sheet

520	A109	150fr blk & mar	6.50	6.50

Nos. 514-519 exist imperf. Value, set unused $60. No. 520 exists imperf. Value, unused $60.

Rocket and Unisphere — A110

Engraved and Typographed

1965, Mar. 1 Unwmk. *Perf. 12*

521	A110	50c lil & blk	.25	.25
522	A110	1.50fr bl & lil	.25	.25
523	A110	2fr red brn & brt grn	.25	.25
524	A110	10fr brt grn & dk red	1.00	.55
525	A110	18fr vio bl & brn	.25	.25
526	A110	27fr rose red & grn	.35	.25
527	A110	40fr gray & org	.45	.25
		Nos. 521-527 (7)	2.80	2.05

New York World's Fair, 1964-65.

Nos. 521-527 exist imperf. Value, set unused $20.

Basketball A111

6fr, 40fr, Soccer, horiz. 15fr, 60fr, Volleyball.

1965, Apr. Photo. *Perf. 13½*

528	A111	5fr blk, grnsh bl & ocher	.25	.25
529	A111	6fr blk, bl gray & crim	.25	.25
530	A111	15fr blk, org & yel grn	.25	.25
531	A111	24fr blk, rose lil & brt grn	.40	.25
532	A111	40fr blk, brt grn & ultra	*2.00*	.70
533	A111	60fr blk, bl & red lil	.70	.25
		Nos. 528-533 (6)	3.85	1.95

First African Games, Leopoldville, Mar. 31-Apr. 7, 1965.

Nos. 528-533 exist imperf. Value, set unused $15.

For surcharges see Nos. 604-605.

Earth and Satellites A112

Designs: 9fr, 15fr, 20fr, 40fr, Satellites at left, globe at right.

Perf. 14x14½

1965, June 28 Photo. Unwmk.

534	A112	6fr blk, sal & vio	.25	.25
535	A112	9fr blk, lt grn & gray	.25	.25
536	A112	12fr org, gray & blk	.25	.25
537	A112	15fr grn, ultra & blk	.25	.25
538	A112	18fr blk, lt grn & gray	1.50	.40
539	A112	20fr blk, sal & vio	.25	.25
540	A112	30fr grn, ultra & blk	.25	.25
541	A112	40fr org, gray & blk	.35	.25
		Nos. 534-541 (8)	3.35	2.15

Cent. of the ITU.

Nos. 534-541 exist imperf. Value, set unused $30.

Congolese Paratrooper and Parachutes A113

1965, July 5 *Perf. 13x14*

542	A113	5fr brt bl & brn	.25	.25
543	A113	6fr org & brn	.25	.25
544	A113	7fr br grn & brn	.40	.25
545	A113	9fr brt pink & brn	.25	.25
546	A113	18fr lem & brn	.25	.25
		Nos. 542-546 (5)	1.40	1.25

Fifth anniversary of independence.

Nos. 542-546 exist imperf. Value, set unused $15.

Matadi Harbor and ICY Emblem — A114

ICY Emblem and: 8fr, 25fr, Katanga mines. 9fr, 60fr, Tshopo Dam, Stanleyville.

1965, Oct. 25 Photo. *Perf. 13x14*

547 A114 6fr ultra, blk & yel .25 .25
548 A114 8fr org red, blk & bl .25 .25
549 A114 9fr bl grn, blk & brn org .25 .25
550 A114 12fr car rose, blk & gray 1.00 .35
551 A114 25fr ol, blk & rose red .25 .25
552 A114 60fr gray, blk & org .65 .25
Nos. 547-552 (6) 2.65 1.60

International Cooperation Year, 1965.
Nos. 547-552 exist imperf. Value, set unused $20.
For overprints and surcharges see Nos. 559-560, 607-608.

Soldiers Giving First Aid — A115

The Army Serving the Country: 7fr, Bridge building. 9fr, Feeding child. 19fr, Maintenance of telegraph lines. 20fr, House building. 30fr, Soldier and flag. (19fr, 20fr, 30fr, vert.)

Perf. 12½x13, 13x12½

1965, Nov. 17

553 A115 5fr sal, brn & red .25 .25
554 A115 7fr yel & grn .25 .25
555 A115 9fr ol & brn .25 .25
556 A115 19fr brt grn & brn 1.10 .60
557 A115 20fr lt bl & brn .30 .25
558 A115 30fr multi .50 .25
Nos. 553-558 (6) 2.65 1.85

See Nos. 582-586.
Nos. 553-558 exist imperf. Value, set unused $15.
For surcharges see Nos. 602, 678-679, 683.

Nos. 551-552 Overprinted with UN Emblem and "6e Journée Météorologique Mondiale / 23.3.66." on Metallic Strip

1966, Mar. 23 Photo. *Perf. 13x14*

559 A114 25fr ol & blk 1.40 .55
560 A114 60fr gray & blk 1.40 .65

6th World Meteorological Day.
Nos. 559-560 exist imperf. Value, set unused $10.

Woman's Head and Goat — A116

10fr, Sculptured heads. 12fr, Sitting figure and two heads, vert. 53fr, Figure with earrings and kneeling woman with bowl, vert.

Perf. 11½x13, 13x11½

1966, Apr. 23 Litho. Unwmk.

561 A116 10fr red, blk & gray .25 .25
562 A116 12fr grn, blk & bl .25 .25
563 A116 15fr dp bl, blk & lil .30 .25
564 A116 53fr dp rose, blk & vio bl 1.50 1.10
Nos. 561-564 (4) 2.30 1.85

Intl. Negro Arts Festival, Dakar, Senegal, Apr. 1-24.
Nos. 561-564 exist imperf. Value, set unused $15.

Pres. Joseph Desiré Mobutu and Fishing Industry
A117

Pres. Mobutu and: 4fr, Pyrethrum harvest. 6fr, Building industry. 8fr, Winnowing rice. 10fr, Cotton harvest. 12fr, Banana harvest. 15fr, Coffee harvest. 24fr, Pineapple harvest. No. 573a, Pres. Mobutu without cap, and men rolling up sleeves.

1966, May 1 Photo. *Perf. 11½*

565 A117 2fr dk brn & dk bl .25 .25
566 A117 4fr dk brn & org .25 .25
567 A117 6fr dk brn & ol .75 .60
568 A117 8fr dk brn & brt grnsh bl .25 .25
569 A117 10fr dk brn & brn red .25 .25
570 A117 12fr dk brn & vio .25 .25
571 A117 15fr dk brn & lt ol grn .25 .25
572 A117 24fr dk brn & lil rose .25 .25
Nos. 565-572 (8) 2.50 2.35

Souvenir Sheet

Perf. 11x11½

573 Sheet of 4 2.25 2.25
a. A117 15fr red, black & ultra .50 .50

Lt. Gen. Joseph Desiré Mobutu, Pres. of Congo, and publicizing the "Back to Work" campaign.
Nos. 565-572 exist imperf. Value, set unused $15. No. 573 exists imperf. Value, unused $10.
For surcharges see Nos. 601, 603, 616, 619-624, 672, 675, 681-682.

Nos. 510-513 Overprinted

1966, June 13 *Perf. 11½*

574 A108 30fr dk car rose & grn 1.10 1.10
575 A108 40fr ultra & dk car rose 1.20 1.20
576 A108 50fr brn org & grn 1.40 1.40
577 A108 100fr slate & ver 1.40 1.40
Nos. 574-577 (4) 5.10 5.10

Inauguration of WHO Headquarters, Geneva.

Soccer Player — A118

30fr, 2 soccer players. 50fr, 3 soccer players. 60fr, Jules Rimet Cup, soccer ball & globe.

1966, July 25 Photo. *Perf. 14*

578 A118 10fr ocher, vio & brt grn .25 .25
579 A118 30fr brt rose lil, vio & ap grn .45 .25
580 A118 50fr ap grn, Prus bl & tan 1.50 1.00
581 A118 60fr brt grn, dk brn & gold 1.50 .50
Nos. 578-581 (4) 3.70 2.00

World Cup Soccer Championship, Wembley, England, July 11-30.
Nos. 578-581 exist imperf. Value, set unused $15.
For overprints see Nos. 587-590.

Army Type of 1965

The Army Serving the Country: 2fr, Soldiers giving first aid. 6fr, Feeding child. 10fr, House building, vert. 18fr, Bridge building. 24fr, Soldier and flag, vert.

1966, Aug. 8 *Perf. 12½x13, 13x12½*

582 A115 2fr ver, ind & red .25 .25
583 A115 6fr ultra red brn .25 .25
584 A115 10fr yel grn & red brn .75 .50
585 A115 18fr car rose & vio .25 .25
586 A115 24fr multi .25 .25
Nos. 582-586 (5) 1.75 1.50

Nos. 582-586 exist imperf. Value, set unused $10.

#578-581 Overprinted in Black ("a"), Carmine or Green ("b"): "FINALE / ANGLETERRE-ALLEMAGNE / 4-2"

1966, Nov. 14 Photo. *Perf. 14*

587 A118 10fr pair, B and C .60 .60
588 A118 30fr pair, B and G 2.25 2.00
589 A118 50fr pair, B and C 3.50 2.50
590 A118 60fr pair, B and C 4.50 3.75
Nos. 587-590 (4) 10.85 8.85

England's victory in the World Soccer Cup Championship. The two colors of the overprint alternate in the sheets.

Souvenir Sheets

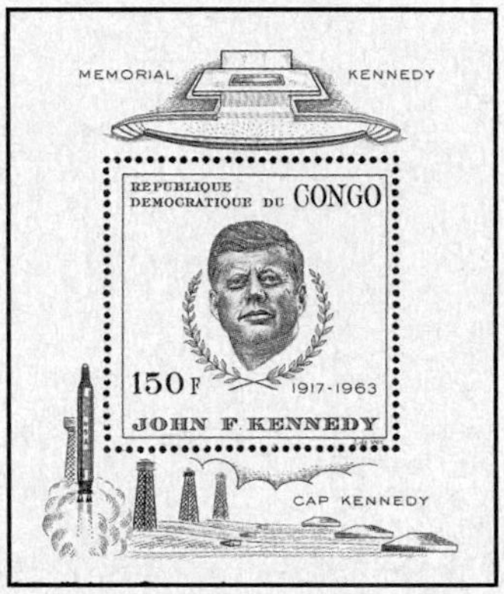

Pres. John F. Kennedy — A119

1966, Dec. 28 Engr. *Perf. 13*

591 A119 150fr brown 22.50 17.50
592 A119 150fr slate 22.50 17.50

Issued in memory of Pres. John F. Kennedy. No. 591 has slate green, No. 592 deep orange marginal design. Two imperf. sheets exist: 150fr brown with violet blue margin and 150fr slate with lilac margin. Size: 65x76mm. Values, $20 each.

Nos. 498-503 Surcharged in Black, Red or Maroon and

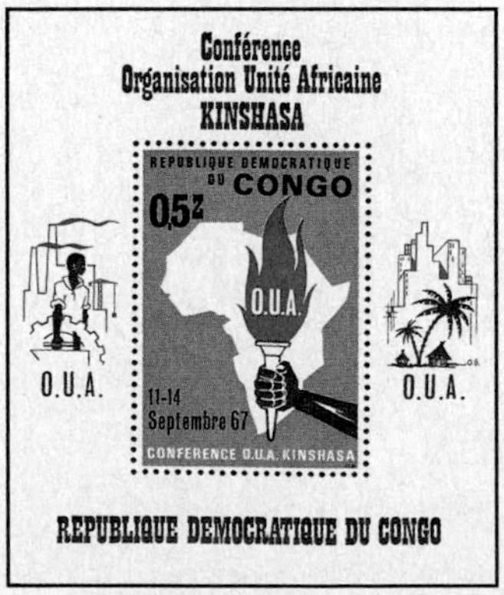

Map of Africa, Torch — A120

1967, Sept. 11 Photo. *Perf. 11½*

593 A108 1k on 2fr .25 .25
a. Inverted overprint 5.00
594 A108 3k on 5fr .25 .25
595 A108 5k on 4fr .35 .25
596 A108 6.60k on 1fr (R) .50 .25
a. Inverted overprint 5.00
597 A108 9.60k on 50c .70 .30
a. Inverted overprint 5.00
598 A108 9.80k on 3fr (M) .75 .50
Nos. 593-598 (6) 2.80 1.80

Souvenir Sheet

599 A120 50k grnsh bl, blk & red 2.50 2.50

4th meeting of the Org. for African Unity, Kinshasa (Leopoldville), Sept. 9-11.
No. 599 exists imperf. Value, unused $15.
No. 599 in other colors was not a postal issue.

Souvenir Sheet

Horn Blower and EXPO Emblem — A121

1967, Sept. 28 Engr. *Perf. 11½*

600 A121 50k dk brn 3.50 3.50

EXPO '67, International Exhibition, Montreal, Apr. 28-Oct. 27, 1967.
No. 600 exists imperf. Value, unused $15.

Nos. 565-566 and 582 Overprinted: "NOUVELLE CONSTITUTION 1967" and Surcharged with New Value on Metallic Panel in Magenta or Brown

Perf. 11½, 12½x13

1967, Oct. 9 Photo.

601 A117 4k on 2fr (M) .25 .25
602 A115 5k on 2fr (B) .45 .25
603 A117 21k on 4fr (M) 1.50 .90
Nos. 601-603 (3) 2.20 1.40

Promulgation of the Constitution, June 4, 1967.

Nos. 528 and 530 Surcharged with New Value and Overprinted: "1ers Jeux Congolais / 25/6 au 2/7/1967 / Kinshasa"

1967, Oct. 16 Photo. *Perf. 13½*

604 A111 1k on 5fr multi .35 .25
605 A111 9.60k on 15fr multi .75 .65

First Congolese Games, Kinshasa, June 25-July 2, 1967.

No. 465 Surcharged with New Value and Overprinted: "1er VOL BAC / ONE ELEVEN / 14/5/67"

1967, Oct. 16 *Perf. 11½*

606 A105 9.60k on 7fr multi 1.20 .25

1st flight of the BAC 111 in the service of Air Congo, May 14, 1967.

Nos. 547 and 549 Surcharged in Red or Black: "JOURNÉE MONDIALE / DE L'ENFANCE / 8-10-67"

1968, Feb. 10 Photo. *Perf. 13x14*

607 A114 1k on 6fr (R) .35 .25
608 A114 9k on 9fr (B) 1.00 .70

Intl. Children's Day. The surcharge is on a rectangle printed in metallic ink.

Nos. 498, 504 and 501 Surcharged in Blue or Red: "Année Internationale / du Tourisme 24-10-1967"

1968, Feb. 10 *Perf. 11½*

609 A108 5k on 50c lil rose & bl (Bl) .45 .25
610 A108 10k on 6fr sepia & org (R) .65 .55
611 A108 15k on 3fr emer & red (R) 1.00 1.00
Nos. 609-611 (3) 2.10 1.80

International Tourist Year. The surcharge is on a rectangle printed in metallic ink.

Nos. 500, 498 and 502 Surcharged in Black, Violet Blue or Gold

1968, July Photo. *Perf. 11½*

612	A108	1k on 2fr	.30	.25
613	A108	2k on 50c (VBl)	.45	.25
614	A108	2k on 50c (G)	.45	.25
615	A108	9.60k on 4fr	2.00	1.10
		Nos. 612-615 (4)	3.20	1.85

The surcharge on No. 612 consists of a black rectangle and new denomination in upper right corner; the surcharge on No. 613 has a violet blue rectangle with denomination printed in white on it; on No. 614 the rectangle is gold and the denomination black; on No. 615 the rectangle is black and the denomination white.

No. 565 Surcharged in White on Black Rectangle

1968, Oct. Photo. *Perf. 11½*

616	A117	10k on 2fr dk brn & dk bl	.70	.25

Leopard
A122

1968, Nov. 5 Litho. *Perf. 10½*

617	A122	2k brt grnsh bl & blk	.30	.25
618	A122	9.60k red & blk	1.50	.25

Nos. 617-618 exist imperf. Value, set unused $10.

Mobutu Type of 1966 Surcharged

1968, Dec. 20 Photo. *Perf. 11½*

619	A117	15s on 2fr sep & brt bl	.25	.25
620	A117	1k on 6fr sep & brn	.25	.25
621	A117	3k on 10fr sep & emer	.25	.25
622	A117	5k on 12fr sep & org	.35	.25
623	A117	20k on 15fr sep & brt grn	1.25	.50
624	A117	50k on 24fr sep & brt lil	3.25	1.50
		Nos. 619-624 (6)	5.60	3.00

Human Rights Flame — A123

1968, Dec. 30 *Perf. 12½x13*

625	A123	2k lt ultra & brt grn	.25	.25
626	A123	9.60k grn & dp car	.75	.30
627	A123	10k brt lil & brn	.75	.35
628	A123	40k org brn & pur	2.50	1.25
		Nos. 625-628 (4)	4.25	2.15

International Human Rights Year.

Nos. 625-628 exist imperf. Value, set unused $15.

Type of 1968 Overprinted in Gold

1969, Jan. 27 Photo. *Perf. 12½x13*

629	A123	2k ap grn & red brn	.25	.25
630	A123	9.60k rose & emer	.75	.30
631	A123	10k gray & ultra	.75	.35
632	A123	40k grnsh bl & pur	2.50	1.25
		Nos. 629-632 (4)	4.25	2.15

4th summit meeting of OCAM (Organisation Communitee Afrique et Malgache), Kinshasa, Jan. 27.

Nos. 629-632 exist imperf. Value, set unused $15.

Kinshasa Fair Emblem and Cotton Boll — A124

Fair Emblem and: 6k, Copper. 9.60k, Coffee. 9.80k, Diamond. 11.60k, Oil palm fruits.

1969, May 2 Photo. *Perf. 12½x13*

633	A124	2k brt pur, gold & red lil	.25	.25
634	A124	6k grn, gold & bl grn	.95	.50
635	A124	9.60k brn, gold & lt brn	1.25	.40
636	A124	9.80k ultra & gold	1.40	.60
637	A124	11.60k hn brn, gold & brn	1.60	.90
		Nos. 633-637 (5)	5.45	2.65

Kinshasa Fair, Limete, June 30-July 21.

Nos. 633-637 exist imperf. Value, set unused $25.

Fair Entrance, Emblem — A125

Fair Emblem and: 3k, Gecomin Mining Co. Pavilion. 10k, Administration Building. 25k, Pavilion of the Organization for African Unity.

1969, June 30 Photo. *Perf. 11½*

Granite Paper

638	A125	2k brt rose lil & gold	.25	.25
639	A125	3k blue & gold	.25	.25
640	A125	10k lt ol grn & gold	.80	.40
641	A125	25k copper red & gold	1.80	1.00
		Nos. 638-641 (4)	3.10	1.90

Kinshasa Fair, Limete, June 30-July 21.

Nos. 638-641 exist imperf. Value, set unused $15.

Congo Arms — A126

Pres. Mobutu — A127

1969, July-Sept. Litho. *Perf. 14*

642	A126	10s org & blk	.25	.25
643	A126	15s ultra & blk	.25	.25
644	A126	30s brt grn & blk	.25	.25
645	A126	60s brt rose lil & blk	.25	.25
646	A126	90s dp bister & blk	.25	.25

Perf. 13

647	A127	1k sky bl & multi	.25	.25
648	A127	2k org & multi	.25	.25
649	A127	3k multi	.30	.25
650	A127	5k brt rose & multi	.40	.25
651	A127	6k ultra & multi	.40	.25
652	A127	9.60k multi	.75	.40
653	A127	10k lt lil & multi	1.00	.50
654	A127	20k yel & multi	1.75	1.00
655	A127	50k multi	5.00	2.50
656	A127	100k fawn & multi	10.00	6.00
		Nos. 642-656 (15)	21.35	12.90

Nos. 642-656 exist imperf. Value, set unused $25.

Well Driller, by Oscar Bonnevalle — A128

Paintings: 4k, Preparation of cocoa, by Jean Van Noten. 8k, Dock workers, by Constantin Meunier. 10k, Poultry shop, by Henri Evenepoel. 15k, Steel industry, by Constantin Meunier.

Perf. 13x14, 14x13 (8k)

1969, Dec. 15 Litho.

Size: 41x41mm

657	A128	3k multi	.25	.25
658	A128	4k multi	.25	.25

Size: 28x41mm

659	A128	8k multi	.50	.30

Size: 41x41mm

660	A128	10k multi	.75	.40
661	A128	15k multi	1.50	.70
		Nos. 657-661 (5)	3.25	1.90

50th anniv. of the ILO.

Nos. 657-661 exist imperf. Value, set unused $15.

Souvenir Sheet

Adoration of the Kings, by Rubens — A129

1969, Dec. Engr. *Perf. 13*

662	A129	50k red lilac	5.50	5.50

Issued for Christmas 1969.

No. 662 exists imperf. Value, unused $9.

Pres. Mobutu, Map and Flag of Congo A130

1970, June 30 Litho. *Perf. 13½x13*

663	A130	10s multi	.25	.25
664	A130	90s pur & multi	.25	.25
665	A130	1k brn & multi	.25	.25
666	A130	2k multi	.25	.25
667	A130	7k multi	.35	.25
668	A130	10k multi	.55	.25
669	A130	20k multi	1.25	.60
		Nos. 663-669 (7)	3.15	2.10

10th anniversary of independence.

Nos. 663-669 exist imperf. Value, set unused $12.

Issues of 1964-1966 Surcharged

Perf. 11½, 12½x13, 13x12½

1970, Sept. 24 Photo.

670	A108	10s on 1fr (#499)	.25	.25
671	A108	20s on 2fr (#500)	.25	.25
672	A117	20s on 2fr (#565)	1.00	.50
673	A108	30s on 3fr (#501)	.25	.25
674	A108	40s on 4fr (#502)	.25	.25
675	A117	40s on 4fr (#566)	1.00	.50
676	A108	60s on 7fr (#505)	3.00	1.75
677	A108	90s on 9fr (#507)	3.00	1.75
678	A115	90s on 9fr (#555)	.60	.40
679	A115	1k on 7fr (#554)	.60	.40
680	A108	1k on 6fr (#504)	.50	.25
681	A117	1k on 12fr (#570)	2.75	1.75
682	A117	2k on 24fr (#572)	1.25	.50
683	A115	2k on 24fr (#586)	1.25	.50
684	A108	3k on 30fr (#510)	2.25	1.25
685	A108	4k on 40fr (#511)	.50	.25
686	A108	5k on 50fr (#512)	9.00	5.00
687	A108	10k on 100fr (#513)	2.25	1.25
		Nos. 670-687 (18)	29.95	17.05

Telecommunications Building, Geneva — A131

Designs: 2k, 6.60k, UPU Headquarters, Bern. 9.80k, 10k, 11k, UN Headquarters, NY.

1970, Oct. 24 Photo. *Perf. 11½*

688	A131	1k pink & grn	.25	.25
689	A131	2k org & grn	.25	.25
690	A131	6.60k grnsh bl & rose car	.40	.25
691	A131	9.60k yel & vio bl	.50	.35
692	A131	9.80k lt ultra & brn	.50	.35
693	A131	10k lt pur & brn	.50	.35
694	A131	11k rose & brn	.70	.45
		Nos. 688-694 (7)	3.10	2.25

ITU; new UPU Headquarters, Bern; 25th anniv. of the UN.

Nos. 688-694 exist imperf. Value, set unused $35.

Pres. Mobutu, Congolese Flag and Arch — A132

1970, Nov. 24 Litho. *Perf. 13*

695	A132	2k yel & multi	.25	.25
696	A132	10k bl & multi	1.00	.50
697	A132	20k red & multi	2.50	1.50
		Nos. 695-697 (3)	3.75	2.25

Fifth anniversary of new government.

Nos. 695-697 exist imperf. Value, set unused $6.

Apollo 11 in Flight A133

Designs: 2k, Astronaut and spacecraft on moon. 7k, Pres. Mobutu decorating astronauts' wives. 10k, Pres. Mobutu with Neil A. Armstrong, Col. Edwin E. Aldrin, Jr. and Lt. Col. Michael Collins. 30k, Armstrong, Aldrin and Collins in space suits.

1970, Dec. 24 *Perf. 13x13½*

698	A133	1k bl & blk	.30	.25
699	A133	2k brt pur & blk	.50	.25
700	A133	7k dl org & blk	1.50	.85
701	A133	10k rose red & blk	2.00	1.25
702	A133	30k grn & blk	5.50	3.50
		Nos. 698-702 (5)	9.80	6.10

Visit of US Apollo 11 astronauts and their wives to Kinshasa.

Nos. 698-702 exist imperf. Value, set unused $25.

Metopodontus Savagei — A134

Designs: Various insects of Congo.

1971, Jan. 25 Photo. *Perf. 11½*

703	A134	10s dl rose & multi	.75	.30
704	A134	50s gray & multi	.75	.30
705	A134	90s multi	.75	.30
706	A134	1k citron & multi	.75	.30
707	A134	2k gray grn & multi	.75	.30
708	A134	3k lt vio & multi	1.75	.60
709	A134	5k bl & multi	5.00	2.00
710	A134	10k multi	7.00	2.50
711	A134	30k grn & multi	16.00	6.75
712	A134	40k ocher & multi	25.00	10.00
		Nos. 703-712 (10)	58.50	23.35

Colotis Protomedia — A135

Various butterflies and moths of Congo.

1971, Feb. 24

713	A135	10s lt ultra & multi	.75	.35
714	A135	20s choc & multi	.75	.35
715	A135	70s dp org & multi	.75	.35
716	A135	1k vio bl & multi	.75	.35
717	A135	3k multi	1.75	.60
718	A135	5k dk grn & multi	4.75	1.50
719	A135	10k multi	6.25	2.00
720	A135	15k emer & multi	11.00	3.50
721	A135	25k yel & multi	17.50	4.50
722	A135	40k multi	24.00	11.00
		Nos. 713-722 (10)	68.25	24.50

Nos. 713-722 exist imperf. Value, set unused $75.

UN Emblem, Racial Unity — A136

1971, Mar. 21 Photo. *Perf. 11½*

723	A136	1k lt grn & multi	.25	.25
724	A136	4k gray & multi	.25	.25
725	A136	5k lt lil & multi	.40	.25
726	A136	10k lt bl & multi	.90	.35
		Nos. 723-726 (4)	1.80	1.10

Intl. year against racial discrimination.

Nos. 723-726 exist imperf. Value, set unused $12.

Hypericum Bequaertii A137

Flowers: 4k, Dissotis brazzae. 20k, Begonia wollastonii. 25k, Cassia alata.

1971, May 24 Litho. *Perf. 14*

727	A137	1k multi	1.00	.25
728	A137	4k multi	1.75	.45
729	A137	20k multi	9.25	2.50
730	A137	25k multi	12.00	3.25
		Nos. 727-730 (4)	24.00	6.45

Nos. 727-730 exist imperf. Value, set unused $30.

Obelisk at N'sele, Pres. Mobutu A138

1971, May 20 Photo. *Perf. 11½*

731	A138	4k gold & multi	.55	.25

4th anniversary of the People's Revolutionary Movement.

No. 731 exists imperf. Value, unused $6.

Radar Station A139

Designs: 1k, Waves. 6k, Map of Africa with telecommunications network.

1971, June 25 Photo. *Perf. 11½*

732	A139	1k rose & multi	.25	.25
733	A139	3k yel & multi	.55	.35
734	A139	6k lt bl & multi	1.40	1.00
		Nos. 732-734 (3)	2.20	1.60

3rd World Telecommunications Day, May 17 (1k); opening of satellite telecommunications ground station, Kinshasa, June 30 (3k); Pan-African telecommunication system (6k).

Nos. 732-734 exist imperf. Value, set unused $15.

Grass Monkeys A140

Designs: 20s, Moustached monkeys, vert. 70s, De Brazza's monkeys. 1k, Yellow baboons. 3k, Pygmy chimpanzee, vert. 5k, Mangabeys, vert. 10k, Owlfaced monkeys. 15k, Diana monkeys. 25k, Black-and-white colobus, vert. 40k, L'Hoest's monkeys, vert.

1971, Aug.

735	A140	10s vio & multi	.75	.35
736	A140	20s lt bl & multi	.75	.35
737	A140	70s ocher & multi	1.25	.45
738	A140	1k gray & multi	1.25	.45
739	A140	3k rose & multi	2.00	1.00
740	A140	5k brn & multi	4.50	2.50
741	A140	10k multi	8.75	4.75
742	A140	15k multi	14.00	6.50
743	A140	25k brt bl & multi	23.50	11.00
744	A140	40k red & multi	32.50	16.00
		Nos. 735-744 (10)	89.25	43.35

Nos. 735-744 exist imperf. Value, set unused $120.

Hotel Inter-Continental, Kinshasa — A141

1971, Oct. 2 Photo. *Perf. 13*

745	A141	2k silver & multi	.25	.25
746	A141	12k gold & multi	.55	.25

Nos. 745-746 exist imperf. Value, set unused $6.

Man Reading A142

Designs: 2.50k, Open book and abacus. 7k, Five letters surrounding symbolic head.

1971, Oct. 24

747	A142	50s multi	.25	.25
748	A142	2.50k multi	.25	.25
749	A142	7k multi	1.40	1.00
		Nos. 747-749 (3)	1.90	1.50

Fight against illiteracy.

Nos. 747-749 exist imperf. Value, set unused $10.

Succeeding issues are listed in Vol. 6 under Zaire. Beginning in 1998, Zaire reverted to using the Congo name, at least temporarily. Until the situation is resolved, the current stamps inscribed "Congo" will be listed under Zaire.

SEMI-POSTAL STAMPS

Women Carrying Food, Wheat Emblem, and Tractor SP22

1963, Mar. 21 Photo. *Perf. 14x13*

B48	SP22	5fr + 2fr multi	.25	.25
B49	SP22	9fr + 4fr multi	.45	.25
B50	SP22	12fr+ 6fr multi	.50	.25
B51	SP22	20fr+ 10fr multi	2.25	1.75
		Nos. B48-B51 (4)	3.45	2.50

FAO "Freedom from Hunger" campaign.

Nos. B48-B51 exist imperf. Value, set unused $30.

No. B51 exists in an imperf sheet of one, in light and dark violet. Value $30.

CONGO, PEOPLE'S REPUBLIC

'pē-pəls ri-'pə-blik of 'käŋ-ˌgō

(ex-French)

LOCATION — West Africa at equator
GOVT. — Republic
AREA — 132,046 sq. mi.
POP. — 2,716,814 (1999 est.)
CAPITAL — Brazzaville

The former French colony of Middle Congo became a member state of the French Community on November 28, 1958, and achieved independence on August 15, 1960. For some years before 1958, the colony was joined with three other French territories to form French Equatorial Africa. Issues of Middle Congo (1907-1933) are listed under that heading.

100 Centimes = 1 Franc

Catalogue values for all unused stamps in this country are for Never Hinged items.

Allegory of New Republic
A7

1959 Unwmk. Engr. *Perf. 13*

89	A7	25fr brn, dp claret, org & ol	.75	.25

1st anniv. of the proclamation of the Republic.

Imperforates

Most stamps of the Republic of the Congo exist imperforate in issued and trial colors, and also in small presentation sheets in issued colors.

Common Design Types pictured following the introduction.

C.C.T.A. Issue
Common Design Type

1960 Unwmk. *Perf. 13*

90	CD106	50fr dl grn & plum	1.00	1.00

President Fulbert Youlou — A8

1960

91	A8	15fr grn, blk & car	.35	.35
92	A8	85fr indigo & car	2.00	.45

Flag, Map and UN Emblem — A9

1961, Mar. 11 *Perf. 13*
Flag in Green, Yellow & Red

93	A9	5fr vio brn & dk bl	.25	.25
94	A9	20fr org & dk bl	.45	.25
95	A9	100fr grn & dk bl	2.00	.80
		Nos. 93-95 (3)	2.70	1.30

Congo's admission to United Nations.

Rainbow Runner
A10

Fish: 50c, 3fr, Rainbow runner. 1fr, 2fr, Sloan's viperfish. 5fr, Hatchet fish. 10fr, A deep-sea fish.

1961, Nov. 28 Engr.

96	A10	50c brn, ol grn & sal	.30	.25
97	A10	1fr bl grn & sepia	.30	.25
98	A10	2fr ultra, sep & dk grn	.30	.25
99	A10	3fr dk bl, grn & salmon	.45	.30
100	A10	5fr red brn, grn & blk	.70	.30
101	A10	10fr blue & red brn	1.40	.45
		Nos. 96-101 (6)	3.45	1.80

Brazzaville Market — A11

1962, Mar. 23 Unwmk. *Perf. 13*

102	A11	20fr blk, red & grn	.80	.25

Abidjan Games Issue
Common Design Type

20fr, Boxing. 50fr, Running, finish line.

1962, July 21 Photo. *Perf. 12½x12*

103	CD109	20fr car, brt pink, brn & blk	.45	.25
104	CD109	50fr car, brt pink, brn & blk	.90	.30
		Nos. 103-104,C7 (3)	3.85	1.80

African-Malgache Union Issue
Common Design Type

1962, Sept. 8

105	CD110	30fr multicolored	1.50	.50

Waves Around Globe
A11a

Design: 100fr, Orbit patterns around globe.

1963, Sept. 19 *Perf. 12½*

106	A11a	25fr org, grn & ultra	.75	.30
107	A11a	100fr lt red brn, bl & plum	1.75	.90

Issued to publicize space communications.

King Makoko's Collar — A12

Unwmk.
1963, Oct. 21 Engr. *Perf. 13*

108	A12	10fr shown	.45	.25
109	A12	15fr Kebekebe mask	.60	.25

UNESCO Emblem, Scales and Tree
A12a

1963, Dec. 10 Unwmk. *Perf. 13*

110	A12a	25fr grn, dk bl & brn	.80	.30

15th anniv. of the Universal Declaration of Human Rights.

Barograph and WMO Emblem
A12b

1964, Mar. 23 Engr.

111	A12b	50fr grn, red brn & ultra	1.50	.60

Fourth World Meteorological Day.

Mechanic with Machine — A13

1964, Apr. 8

112	A13	20fr grnsh bl, mag & dk brn	.80	.30

Training of technicians.

Corn and Tools
A14

1964, Apr. 24 Unwmk. *Perf. 13*

113	A14	80fr brn, grn & brn car	1.60	.60

Importance of manual labor.

Diaboua Ballet
A15

Kébékébé Dance — A16

1964, May 8 Engr.

114	A15	30fr multicolored	1.25	.30
115	A16	60fr multicolored	2.25	.65

Carved Figure — A17

1964, May 22

116	A17	50fr brn red & sepia	1.50	.55

Classroom
A18

1964, May 26

117	A18	25fr dk brn, red & blue	.80	.30

Issued to publicize education.

Type of Air Post Issue, 1963, Inscribed

1964, Aug. 15 Photo. *Perf. 13x12*

118	AP5	20fr lt bl, red, ocher, dk brn & grn	.80	.25

1st anniv. of the revolution and Natl. Feast Day, Aug. 15.

Fire Squid
A19

15fr, Johnson's deep-sea angler (fish).

1964, Oct. 20 Engr. *Perf. 13*

119	A19	2fr ver, lt grn & brn	.80	.50
120	A19	15fr vio, lt ol grn & dp cl	2.75	1.50

Cooperation Issue
Common Design Type

1964, Nov. 7 Unwmk. *Perf. 13*

121	CD119	25fr car, brt grn & dk brn	.80	.35

Communications Emblems — A20

1965, Jan. 1 Litho. *Perf. 12½x13*

122	A20	25fr ol, red brn & blk	.80	.25

Issued to commemorate the establishment of the national postal administration.

Sitatunga — A21

Dancer on Stilts — A22

Design: 20fr, Elephant, horiz.

1965, Mar. 15 Engr. *Perf. 13*

123	A21	15fr redsh brn, dl grn & bl	1.00	.40
124	A21	20fr blk, dp bl & sl grn	1.00	.40
125	A22	85fr lil & multi	3.50	1.50
		Nos. 123-125 (3)	5.50	2.30

Pres. Alphonse Massamba-Debat A23

1965-66 Photo. *Perf. 12x12½*

126 A23 20fr dk brn, grn & yel .40 .25
127 A23 25fr brn, bl grn, emer & blk ('66) .40 .25
128 A23 30fr brn, bl grn, org & blk ('66) .70 .25
Nos. 126-128 (3) 1.50 .75

Soccer Player A24

Designs: 25fr, Games' emblem (map of Africa and runners). 50fr, Field ball player. 85fr, Runner. 100fr, Bicyclist.

1965, July 17 Photo. *Perf. 12½*

Size: 28x28mm

129 A24 25fr blk, red, yel & grn .50 .30

Size: 34x34mm

130 A24 40fr yel grn & multi .70 .45
131 A24 50fr red & multi .70 .45
132 A24 85fr blk & multi 1.25 .65
133 A24 100fr yel & multi 1.75 .75
a. Min. sheet of 5, #129-133 7.50 7.50
Nos. 129-133 (5) 4.90 2.60

1st African Games, Brazzaville, July 18-25.

Arms of Congo — A25

1965, Nov. 15 Litho. *Perf. 12½x13*

134 A25 20fr multicolored .80 .25

Cooperative Village A26

30fr, Gymnastic drill team with streamers.

1966, Feb. 18 *Perf. 12½x13*

135 A26 25fr multicolored .80 .25
136 A26 30fr multicolored .80 .30

Sculptured Mask — A27

Designs: 30fr, Weaver, painting. 85fr, String instrument, painting, horiz.

Perf. 13x12½, 12½x13

1966, Apr. 9 Photo.

137 A27 30fr multicolored .70 .30
138 A27 85fr multicolored 1.90 .70
139 A27 90fr multicolored 2.25 1.00
Nos. 137-139 (3) 4.85 2.00

Intl. Negro Arts Festival, Dakar, Senegal, 4/1-24.

Men and Clocks A28

1966, Apr. 15 *Perf. 12½x12*

140 A28 70fr pale brn, ocher & dk brn 1.60 .50

Introduction of the shorter work day (less lunch time, earlier quitting time).

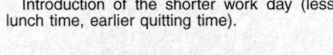

WHO Headquarters, Geneva — A29

1966, May 3 Photo. *Perf. 12½x13*

141 A29 50fr org yel, vio & bl 1.50 .50

Inauguration of the WHO Headquarters, Geneva.

Church of St. Peter Claver — A30

1966, June 15 Photo. *Perf. 13x12½*

142 A30 70fr multicolored 1.50 .40

Women's Basketball — A31

Sport: 1fr, Women's volleyball, horiz. 3fr, Women's field ball, horiz. 5fr, Athletes of various races. 10fr, Torch bearer. 15fr, Soccer and gold medal of First African Games.

1966, July 15 Engr. *Perf. 13*

143 A31 1fr ultra, choc & ol .25 .25
144 A31 2fr choc, grn & bl .25 .25
145 A31 3fr dk grn, dk car & choc .25 .25
146 A31 5fr slate, emer & choc .30 .25
147 A31 10fr dl bl, dk grn & vio .55 .25
148 A31 15fr vio, car & choc .75 .30
Nos. 143-148 (6) 2.35 1.55

Jules Rimet Cup and Globe A32

1966, July 15 Photo. *Perf. 12½x12*

149 A32 30fr brt red, gold, blk & bl 1.25 .45

8th World Soccer Cup Championship, Wembley, England, July 11-30.

Savorgnan de Brazza School A33

1966, Sept. 15 Photo. *Perf. 12½x12*

150 A33 30fr dk pur, grn, yel & blk .80 .25

Pointe-Noire Railroad Station — A34

1966, Oct. 15 Engr. *Perf. 13*

151 A34 60fr grn, red & brn 1.50 .60

Student with Microscope — A35

1966, Nov. 28 Engr. *Perf. 13*

152 A35 90fr brn, grn & ind 1.50 .70

20th anniv. of UNESCO.

Balumbu Mask — A36

Masks: 10fr, Kuyu. 15fr, Bakwélé. 20fr, Batéké.

1966, Dec. 12 Engr. *Perf. 13*

153 A36 5fr car rose & dk brn .45 .25
154 A36 10fr Prus bl & brn .50 .25
155 A36 15fr sep, dl org & dk bl .60 .25
156 A36 20fr dp bl & multi .80 .25
Nos. 153-156 (4) 2.35 1.00

Order of the Revolution and Map — A37

Learning the Alphabet A38

Design: 45fr, Harvesting and loading sugar cane, and sugar mill.

Perf. 12x12½, 12½x12

1967, Mar. 15 Photo.

157 A37 20fr org & multi .80 .30
158 A38 25fr blk, ocher & dk car .80 .35
159 A38 45fr blk, yel grn & lt bl 1.50 .30
Nos. 157-159 (3) 3.10 .95

Issued to honor the members of the Order of the Revolution (20fr); to publicize the literacy campaign (25fr); to publicize, sugar production (45fr).

Mahatma Gandhi — A39

1967, Apr. 21 Engr. *Perf. 13*

160 A39 90fr bl & blk 2.25 .75

Issued in memory of Mohandas K. Gandhi (1869-1948), Hindu nationalist leader.

"Elegant Lady" — A40

Dolls: 10fr, Fruit vendor 25fr, Woman pounding saka-saka. 30fr, Mother and child.

1967, June Photo. *Perf. 13x12½*

161 A40 5fr gold & multi .25 .25
162 A40 10fr yel grn & multi .45 .25
163 A40 25fr lt ultra & multi .50 .25
164 A40 30fr multicolored .60 .25
Nos. 161-164 (4) 1.80 1.00

ITY Emblem, Village and Waterfall A41

1967, July 5 Engr. *Perf. 13*

165 A41 60fr rose cl, org & ol grn .90 .40

Issued for International Tourist Year, 1967.

Europafrica Issue

Symbols of Cooperation — A42

1967, July 20 Photo. *Perf. 12x12½*

166 A42 50fr multicolored .90 .30

Arms of Brazzaville — A43

1967, Aug. 15 Litho. *Perf. 12½x13*

167 A43 30fr yel & multi .80 .35

Fourth anniversary of the revolution.

UN Emblem, Dove and People — A44

1967, Oct. 24 Photo. *Perf. 13x12½*

168	A44	90fr bl, dk brn, red brn & yel	1.75	.60

Issued for United Nations Day, Oct. 24.

Boy and UNICEF Emblem — A45

1967, Dec. 11 Engr. *Perf. 13*

169	A45	90fr mar, blk & ultra	1.75	.60

21st anniv. of UNICEF.

Albert Luthuli, Dove and Globe A46

1968, Jan. 29 Engr. *Perf. 13*

170	A46	30fr brt grn & ol bis	.80	.35

Albert Luthuli (1899-1967) of South Africa, winner of 1960 Nobel Peace Prize.

Arms of Pointe Noire — A47

1968, Feb. 20 Litho. *Perf. 12½x13*

171	A47	10fr brt pink & multi	.80	.30

Motherhood — A48

1968, May 25 Engr. *Perf. 13*

172	A48	15fr dk car rose, sky bl & blk	.80	.30

Issued for Mother's Day.

Mayombe Viaduct — A49

1968, June 24

173	A49	45fr maroon, slate grn & bl	2.00	.45

A50

1968, July 29 Photo. *Perf. 13x12½*

174	A50	5fr Daimler, 1889	.45	.25
175	A50	20fr Berliet, 1897	.90	.30
176	A50	60fr Peugeot, 1898	1.75	.40
177	A50	80fr Renault, 1900	2.75	.70
178	A50	85fr Fiat, 1902	3.25	.90
		Nos. 174-178,C67-C68 (7)	17.85	6.05

Tanker, Refinery and Map of Area Served — A50a

1968, July 30 *Perf. 12½*

179	A50a	30fr multicolored	.80	.30

Issued to commemorate the opening of the Port Gentil (Gabon) Refinery, June 12, 1968.

WHO Emblem and Tree of Life — A51

1968, Nov. 28 Engr. *Perf. 13*

180	A51	25fr dk grn, red & dp lil	.80	.30

20th anniv. of WHO.

Development Bank Issue

Common Design Type

1969, Sept. 10 Engr. *Perf. 13*

181	CD130	25fr car rose, grn & ocher	.40	.25
182	CD130	30fr bl, grn & ocher	.40	.25

Bicycle A52

Bicycles & Motorcycles: 75fr, Hirondelle. 80fr, Folding bicycle. 85fr, Peugeot. 100fr, Excelsior Manxman. 150fr, Norton. 200fr, Brough Superior "Old Bill." 300fr, Matchless and N.L.G.-J.A.P.S.

1969, Oct. 6 Engr. *Perf. 13*

183	A52	50fr multicolored	1.25	.30
184	A52	75fr multicolored	1.50	.30
185	A52	80fr multicolored	1.75	.40
186	A52	85fr multicolored	2.00	.50
187	A52	100fr multicolored	3.00	.85
188	A52	150fr multicolored	4.00	1.00
189	A52	200fr multicolored	5.25	1.75
190	A52	300fr multicolored	9.50	2.75
		Nos. 183-190 (8)	28.25	7.85

Mayombe Train and Tourist Year Emblem A53

40fr, Train and Mbamba Tunnel, vert.

Perf. 13x12½, 12½x13

1969, Oct. 20 Photo.

191	A53	40fr multicolored	2.40	.40
192	A53	60fr multicolored	4.00	.65

Issued for African Tourist Year.

Loutete Cement Works A54

Loutete Cement Works: 15fr, Mixing tower, vert. 25fr, Cable transport, vert. 30fr, General view of plant.

1969, Dec. 10 Engr. *Perf. 13*

193	A54	10fr dk gray, rose cl & dk ol	.25	.25
194	A54	15fr Prus bl, red brn & pur	.50	.25
195	A54	25fr mar, brn & Prus bl	.60	.25
196	A54	30fr vio brn, ultra & blk	.70	.25
a.		Min. sheet of 4, #193-196	2.75	2.75
		Nos. 193-196 (4)	2.05	1.00

ASECNA Issue

Common Design Type

1969, Dec. 12

197	CD132	100fr dull brown	2.00	.40
		Nos. 197 (1)	2.00	.40

Pineapple Harvest and ILO Emblem A55

30fr, Worker at lathe and ILO emblem.

1969, Dec. 20 Engr. *Perf. 13*

198	A55	25fr bl, olive & brn	.60	.25
199	A55	30fr rose red, choc & slate	.85	.35

50th anniv. of the ILO.

SOTEXCO Textile Plant, Kinsoundi A56

20fr, Women in spinnery. 25fr, Hand-printing textiles. 30fr, Checking woven cloth.

1970, Jan. 20

200	A56	15fr grn, blk & lil	.45	.25
201	A56	20fr plum, car & sl grn	.45	.25
202	A56	25fr bl, slate & brn	.60	.25
203	A56	30fr gray, car rose & brn	.60	.25
		Nos. 200-203 (4)	2.10	1.00

Hotel Cosmos, Brazzaville A57

1970, Jan. 30

204	A57	90fr slate grn, bl & red brn	1.40	.50

The status of the three sets for Kennedy, etc., Summer Olympics, and Baroque paintings is not certain.

Linzolo Church — A58

Diosso Gorge A59

Design: 90fr, Foulakari waterfall.

1970 Engr. *Perf. 13*

205	A58	25fr multicolored	.80	.25
206	A59	70fr multicolored	1.50	.30
207	A59	90fr multicolored	2.25	.40
		Nos. 205-207 (3)	4.55	.95

Issue dates: 25fr, Feb. 10; others, Feb. 25.

Volvaria Esculenta — A60

Mushrooms: 10fr, Termitomyces entoloмoides. 15fr, Termitomyces microcarpus. 25fr, Termitomyces aurantiacus. 30fr, Termitomyces mammiformis. 50fr, Tremella fuciformis.

1970, Mar. 31 Photo. *Perf. 13*

208	A60	5fr multicolored	6.75	1.00
209	A60	10fr multicolored	9.00	1.40
210	A60	15fr multicolored	13.50	2.00
211	A60	25fr multicolored	22.50	4.00
212	A60	30fr multicolored	32.50	5.75
213	A60	50fr multicolored	70.00	10.00
		Nos. 208-213 (6)	154.25	24.15

Laying Coaxial Cable A61

Design: 30fr, Full view of rail car; 3 cable layers on railway roadbed.

1970, Apr. 30 Engr. *Perf. 13*

214	A61	25fr dk brn & multi	1.00	.30
215	A61	30fr brn & multi	1.25	.60

Issued to publicize the laying of the coaxial cable linking Brazzaville and Pointe Noire.

For surcharges see Nos. 263-264.

UPU Headquarters Issue

Common Design Type

1970, May 20

216	CD133	30fr dk pur, gray & mag	.80	.25

Mother Feeding Child — A62

Design: 90fr, Mother nursing infant.

1970, May 30 Photo.

217	A62	85fr vio bl & multi	1.00	.30
218	A62	90fr lil & multi	1.10	.40

Issued for Mother's Day.

Dag Hammarskjold, UN Emblem — A63

UN Emblem and: No. 220, Trygve Lie, horiz. No. 221, U Thant, horiz.

1970, June 20 Engr. *Perf. 13*

219	A63	100fr scar, dk red & dk pur	1.40	.80
220	A63	100fr dk red, ultra & ind	1.40	.80
221	A63	100fr grn, emer & dk red	1.40	.80
a.		Souv. sheet of 3, #219-221	5.50	5.50
		Nos. 219-221 (3)	4.20	2.40

25th anniv. of the UN and to honor its Secretaries General.

Brillantaisia Vogeliana A64

Sternotomis Variabilis — A65

Plants and Beetles: 2fr, Plectranthus decurrens. 3fr, Myrianthemum mirabile. 5fr, Connarus griffonianus. 15fr, Chelorrhina polyphemus. 20fr, Metopodontus savagei.

Perf. 12½x12, 12x12½

1970, June 30 **Photo.**

222	A64	1fr dk grn & multi	.70	.25
223	A64	2fr multicolored	.70	.25
224	A64	3fr indigo & multi	.70	.25
225	A64	5fr lemon & multi	1.40	.25
226	A65	10fr lilac & multi	2.25	.40
227	A65	15fr orange & multi	3.25	.40
228	A65	20fr multicolored	3.25	.60
		Nos. 222-228 (7)	12.25	2.40

For surcharge see No. 288.

Stegosaurus — A66

Prehistoric Fauna: 20fr, Dinotherium, vert. 60fr, Brachiosaurus, vert. 80fr, Arsinoitherium.

1970, July 20

229	A66	15fr dl grn, ocher & red brn	1.75	.30
230	A66	20fr lt bl & multi	3.50	.65
231	A66	60fr lt bl & multi	6.25	.95
232	A66	80fr lt bl & multi	8.00	1.75
		Nos. 229-232 (4)	19.50	3.65

Mikado 141, 1932 A67

Locomotives: 60fr, Steam locomotive 130+032, 1947. 75fr, Alsthom BB 1100, 1962. 85fr, Diesel BB BB 302, 1969.

1970, Aug. 20 **Engr.** *Perf. 13*

233	A67	40fr mag, bl grn & blk	2.75	.80
234	A67	60fr blk, bl & grn	3.25	.90
235	A67	75fr red, bl & blk	4.50	1.25
236	A67	85fr car, sl grn & ocher	7.50	1.75
		Nos. 233-236 (4)	18.00	4.70

Cogniauxia Padolaena — A68

Tropical Flowers: 2fr, Celosia cristata. 5fr, Plumeria acutifolia. 10fr, Bauhinia variegata. 15fr, Poinsettia. 20fr, Thunbergia grandiflora.

1971, Feb. 10 **Photo.** *Perf. 12x12½*

237	A68	1fr lil & multi	.25	.25
238	A68	2fr yel & multi	.25	.25
239	A68	5fr ultra & multi	.25	.25
240	A68	10fr yel & multi	1.10	.25
241	A68	15fr multicolored	1.60	.30
242	A68	20fr dk red & multi	2.75	.40
		Nos. 237-242 (6)	6.20	1.70

Green Night Adder — A69

Reptiles: 10fr, African Egg-eating snake, horiz. 15fr, Flap-necked chameleon. 20fr, Nile crocodile, horiz. 25fr, Rock python, horiz. 30fr, Gaboon viper. 40fr, Brown house snake, horiz. 45fr, Jameson's mamba.

Perf. 12x12½, 12½x12

1971, June 26 **Photo.**

243	A69	5fr multicolored	.40	.25
244	A69	10fr multicolored	.40	.25
245	A69	15fr multicolored	1.40	.25
246	A69	20fr red & multi	2.25	.25
247	A69	25fr grn & multi	3.00	.35
248	A69	30fr multicolored	3.75	.75
249	A69	40fr bis & multi	4.25	.95
250	A69	45fr multicolored	5.75	1.00
		Nos. 243-250 (8)	21.20	4.05

Pseudimbrasia Deyrollei — A70

Caterpillars: 15fr, Bunaea alcinoe, vert. 20fr, Epiphora vacuna ploetzi. 25fr, Imbrasia eblis. 30fr, Imbrasia dione, vert. 40fr, Holocera angulata.

1971, July 3 *Perf. 13*

251	A70	10fr ver, blk & grn	1.00	.25
252	A70	15fr multicolored	1.50	.30
253	A70	20fr yel grn, blk & ocher	2.25	.40
254	A70	25fr multicolored	3.50	.60
255	A70	30fr red, blk & yel	5.00	.90
256	A70	40fr bl, blk & org	6.75	1.25
		Nos. 251-256 (6)	20.00	3.70

Boy Scout — A70a

Scouts, Lord Baden-Powell — A70b

Designs: c, Scout facing left. d, Scout facing forward. e, Lord Baden-Powell.

Embossed on Metallic Foil

1971, July 14 *Die Cut Perf. 10½*

256A	A70a	90fr Block of 4, #b.-e, silver	*12.00*	*12.00*
256F	A70b	1000fr gold	*30.00*	*30.00*

No. 256F is airmail.

Cymothoe Sangaris A71

Butterflies and Moths: 40fr, Papilio dardanus, vert. 75fr, Iolaus timon. 90fr, Papilio phorcas, vert. 100fr, Euchloron megaera.

1971, Oct. 15 *Perf. 12½x12, 12x12½*

257	A71	30fr yel & multi	1.75	.40
258	A71	40fr grn & multi	3.25	.65
259	A71	75fr multicolored	5.25	1.25
260	A71	90fr multicolored	7.00	1.90
261	A71	100fr ultra & multi	9.50	2.50
		Nos. 257-261 (5)	26.75	6.70

Black and White Men Working Together — A72

1971, Oct. 30 *Perf. 13x12½*

262	A72	50fr org & multi	1.60	.50

Intl. Year Against Racial Discrimination.

Nos. 214-215 Surcharged

1971, Nov. 18 **Engr.** *Perf. 13*

263	A61	30fr on 25fr multicolored	.65	.30
264	A61	40fr on 30fr multicolored	.95	.35

Inauguration of cable service between Brazzaville and Pointe Noire. Words of surcharge arranged differently on No. 264.

Map of Congo — A73

1971, Dec. 31 **Photo.** *Perf. 12½x13*

265	A73	30fr bl & multi	.35	.25
266	A73	40fr yel grn & multi	.45	.25
267	A73	100fr gray & multi	1.10	.40
		Nos. 265-267 (3)	1.90	.90

"Labor, Democracy, Peace."

Lion — A74

2fr, African elephants. 3fr, Leopard. 4fr, Hippopotamus. 5fr, Gorilla, vert. 20fr, Potto. 30fr, De Brazza's monkey. 40fr, Pygmy chimpanzee, vert.

1972, Jan. 31 **Engr.** *Perf. 13*

268	A74	1fr grn & multi	.35	.25
269	A74	2fr dk red & multi	.50	.25
270	A74	3fr red brn & multi	.80	.25
271	A74	4fr vio & multi	1.00	.25
272	A74	5fr brn & multi	1.10	.25
273	A74	20fr org & multi	2.75	.35
274	A74	30fr ocher & multi	3.50	.45
275	A74	40fr Prus bl & multi	5.25	.75
		Nos. 268-275 (8)	15.25	2.80

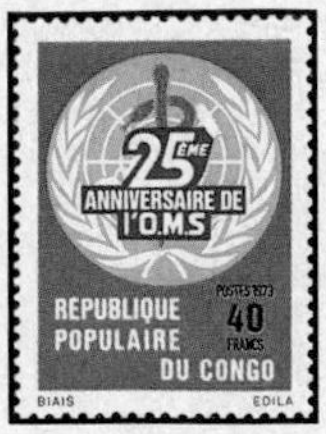

WHO, 25th Anniv. — A75

Perf. 12½x13, 13x12½

1973, June 30 **Typo.**

276	A75	40fr WHO Emblem	.65	.25
277	A75	50fr WHO emblem, horiz.	.95	.25

Kronenbourg Brewery — A76

Brewery Trademark and: 40fr, Laboratory. 75fr, Vats and controls. 85fr, Automatic control room. 100fr, Pressure room. 250fr, Bottling plant.

1973, July 15 **Engr.** *Perf. 13*

278	A76	30fr red & multi	.50	.25
279	A76	40fr red & multi	.60	.25
280	A76	75fr red & multi	1.20	.30
281	A76	85fr red & multi	1.75	.40
282	A76	100fr red & multi	1.90	.55
283	A76	250fr red & multi	3.75	1.00
		Nos. 278-283 (6)	9.70	2.75

Kronenbourg Brewery, Brazzaville.

Golwe Locomotive, 1935 — A77

Locomotives: 40fr, Diesel, 1935. 75fr, Diesel Whithcomb, 1946. 85fr, Diesel CC200.

1973, Aug. 1 **Engr.** *Perf. 13*

284	A77	30fr indigo & multi	2.00	.50
285	A77	40fr vio bl & multi	3.00	.85
286	A77	75fr multicolored	4.25	1.50
287	A77	85fr multicolored	5.50	2.75
		Nos. 284-287 (4)	14.75	5.60

No. 225 Srchd. and Ovptd. in Ultramarine

1973, Aug. 16 **Photo.** *Perf. 12½x12*

288	A64	100fr on 5fr multicolored	1.75	.60

African solidarity in drought emergency.

African Postal Union Issue

Common Design Type

1973, Sept. 12 **Engr.** *Perf. 13*

289	CD137	100fr bl grn, vio & brn	1.60	.50

Bees, Beehive, Honeycomb A78

1973, Dec. 10 **Engr.** *Perf. 13*

290	A78	30fr sl grn, dk red & bl	1.10	.25
291	A78	40fr sl bl, sl grn & lt grn	1.50	.25

"Work and economy."

Family, UN and FAO Emblems A79

40fr, Grain, emblems. 100fr, Grain, emblems, vert.

1973, Dec. 10

292 A79	30fr dk car & dk brn	.50	.25
293 A79	40fr dk grn, yel & ind	.60	.25
294 A79	100fr grn, brn & org	1.40	.40
	Nos. 292-294 (3)	2.50	.90

World Food Program, 10th anniversary.

Amilcar Cabral, Cattle and Child — A80

1974, July 15 **Engr.** ***Perf. 13***

295 A80	100fr multicolored	1.60	.60

First death anniversary of Amilcar Cabral (1924-1973), leader of anti-Portuguese guerrilla activity in Portuguese Guinea.

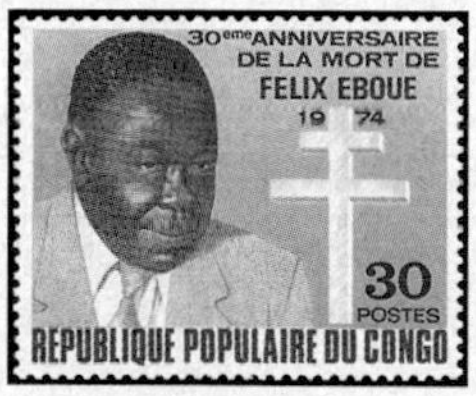

Félix Eboué, Cross of Lorraine A81

1974, Aug. 31 **Litho.** ***Perf. 13***

296 A81	30fr bl & multi	.80	.30
297 A81	40fr brt pink & multi	1.60	.60

Félix A. Eboué (1884-1944), Governor of Chad, first colonial governor to join Free French in WWII, 30th death anniversary.

Pineapples A82

1974, Nov. 12

298 A82	30fr shown	.60	.30
299 A82	30fr Bananas	.70	.30
300 A82	30fr Safous	.70	.30
301 A82	40fr Avocados	1.25	.30
302 A82	40fr Mangos	1.25	.30
303 A82	40fr Papaya	1.25	.30
304 A82	40fr Orange	1.25	.30
	Nos. 298-304 (7)	7.00	2.10

Charles de Gaulle and Conference Building — A83

1974, Nov. 25 **Engr.** ***Perf. 13***

305 A83	100fr multicolored	5.00	1.90

Brazzaville Conference, 25th anniversary.

George Stephenson and Various Locomotives — A84

1974, Dec. 15

306 A84	75fr slate green & olive	4.00	1.00

George Stephenson (1781-1848), English inventor and railroad founder.

UDEAC Issue

Presidents and Flags of Cameroun, CAR, Congo, Gabon and Meeting Center — A84a

1974, Dec. 8 **Photo.** ***Perf. 13***

307 A84a	40fr gold & multi	.65	.25

See note after Cameroun No. 595.
See No. C195.

Irish Setter A85

1974, Dec. 15 **Photo.** ***Perf. 13x13½***

308 A85	30fr shown	1.25	.30
309 A85	40fr Borzoi	1.50	.30
310 A85	75fr Pointer	3.25	.75
311 A85	100fr Great Dane	4.50	.80
	Nos. 308-311 (4)	10.50	2.15

1974, Dec. 15

Designs: Cats.

312 A85	30fr Havana chestnut	1.25	.30
313 A85	40fr Red Persian	1.50	.30
314 A85	75fr Blue British	3.50	.75
315 A85	100fr African serval	5.00	.80
	Nos. 312-315 (4)	11.25	2.15

Labor Party Flags and People A86

40fr, Hands holding flowers and tools.

1974, Dec. 31 **Engr.** ***Perf. 13x12½***

316 A86	30fr red & multi	.65	.25
317 A86	40fr red & multi	.95	.25

5th anniversary of Congolese Labor Party and of introduction of red flag.

Symbols of Development — A87

U Thant and UN Headquarters — A88

Paul G. Hoffman and UN Emblem A89

Perf. 13x12½, 12½x13

1975, Feb. 28 **Litho.**

318 A87	40fr multicolored	.80	.35
319 A88	50fr light blue & multi	.80	.35
320 A89	50fr yellow & multi	.80	.35
	Nos. 318-320 (3)	2.40	1.05

National economic development.

Map of China and Mao Tse-tung — A90

1975, Mar. 9 **Engr.** ***Perf. 13***

321 A90	75fr multicolored	5.50	1.50

25th anniv. of the PRC.

Woman Breaking Bonds, Women's Activities, Map of Congo A91

1975, June 20 **Litho.** ***Perf. 12½***

322 A91	40fr gold & multi	.80	.35

Revolutionary Union of Congolese Women, URFC, 10th anniversary.

CARA Soccer Team — A92

Design: 40fr, Team captain and manager receiving trophy, vert.

1975, July 15 **Litho.** ***Perf. 12½***

323 A92	30fr multicolored	.65	.25
324 A92	40fr multicolored	.95	.25

CARA team, winners of African Soccer Cup 1974.

Citroen, 1935 — A93

Designs: Early autombiles.

1975, July 17 ***Perf. 12***

325 A93	30fr shown	1.10	.40
326 A93	40fr Alfa Romeo, 1911	1.35	.40
327 A93	50fr Rolls Royce, 1926	1.75	.55
328 A93	75fr Duryea, 1893	3.50	.70
	Nos. 325-328 (4)	7.70	2.05

Tipoye Transport — A94

1975, Aug. 5

329 A94	30fr shown	.90	.40
330 A94	40fr Dugout canoe	1.00	.65

Traditional means of transportation.

Raising Red Flag — A95

1975, Aug. 15

331 A95	30fr shown	.80	.25
332 A95	40fr National Conference	.80	.25

2nd anniv. of installation of popular power (30fr) and 3rd anniv. of Natl. Conf. (40fr).

Line Fishing — A96

Traditional Fishing: 30fr, Trap fishing, horiz. 60fr, Spear fishing. 90fr, Net fishing, horiz.

1975, Aug. 31 Litho. *Perf. 12*

333	A96	30fr multicolored	.80	.25
334	A96	40fr multicolored	.80	.30
335	A96	60fr multicolored	1.25	.50
336	A96	90fr multicolored	2.50	1.00
		Nos. 333-336 (4)	5.35	2.05

Woman Pounding "Foufou" — A97

Household Tasks: No. 338, Woman chopping wood. 40fr, Woman preparing manioc, horiz.

1975, Sept. 5

337	A97	30fr multicolored	.60	.25
338	A97	30fr multicolored	.60	.25
339	A97	40fr multicolored	.90	.25
		Nos. 337-339 (3)	2.10	.75

Musical Instruments A98

1975, Sept. 20 *Perf. 12½*

340	A98	30fr Esanga	.75	.25
341	A98	40fr Kalakwa	1.25	.25
342	A98	60fr Likembe	1.50	.30
343	A98	75fr Ngongui	2.00	.40
		Nos. 340-343 (4)	5.50	1.20

Dzeke (Congolese) Shell Money — A99

Ancient Money: No. 346, like No. 344. Nos. 345, 347, Okengo, Congolese, iron bar. 40fr, Gallic coin, c. 60 B.C. 50fr, Roman denarius, 37 B.C. 60fr, Danubian coin, 2nd cent. B.C. 85fr, Greek stater, 4th cent. B.C.

1975-76 Engr. *Perf. 13*

344	A99	30fr red & multi	.60	.25
345	A99	30fr vio & multi	.60	.25
346	A99	35fr ol & multi	.90	.25
347	A99	35fr dk car rose & multi	.90	.25
348	A99	40fr Prus bl & brn	.90	.25
349	A99	50fr Prus bl & ol	1.00	.30
350	A99	60fr dk grn & brn	1.25	.35
351	A99	85fr mag & sl grn	2.10	.45
		Nos. 344-351 (8)	8.25	2.35

Nos. 346-347 inscribed "1976" and issued Mar. 1976; others issued Oct. 5, 1975.

Moschops — A100

Pre-historic Animals: 70fr, Tyrannosaurus. 95fr, Cryptocleidus. 100fr, Stegosaurus.

1975, Oct. 15 Litho. *Perf. 13*

352	A100	55fr multicolored	2.25	.30
353	A100	75fr multicolored	3.25	.35
354	A100	95fr multicolored	5.75	.75
355	A100	100fr multicolored	8.00	1.25
		Nos. 352-355 (4)	19.25	2.65

Albert Schweitzer (1875-1965), Medical Missionary — A101

1975, Oct. 15 Engr.

356	A101	75fr ol, brn & red	1.50	.40

Alexander Fleming A102

Designs: No. 358, André Marie Ampère. No. 359, Clement Ader.

1975, Nov. 15 Engr. *Perf. 13*

357	A102	60fr brn, grn & blk	1.60	.45
358	A102	95fr blk, red & grn	2.50	.65
359	A102	95fr red, blue & indigo	2.50	.65
		Nos. 357-359 (3)	6.60	1.75

Fleming (1881-1955), developer of penicillin; Ampère (1775-1836), physicist; Ader (1841-1925), aviation pioneer.

UN Emblem "ONU" and "30" — A103

1975, Dec. 20 Engr. *Perf. 13*

360	A103	95fr car, ultra & grn	1.60	.50

United Nations, 30th anniversary.

Women's Broken Chain — A104

Design: 60fr, Equality between man and woman, globe, IWY emblem.

1975, Dec. 20 Litho. *Perf. 12½*

361	A104	35fr mag, ocher & gray	.90	.25
362	A104	60fr ultra, brn & blk	1.75	.50

International Women's Year, 1975.

Pres. Marien Ngouabi, Flag and Workers — A105

Echo of the P.C.T. A106

1975, Dec. 31 *Perf. 12½x12, 13x12½*

363	A105	30fr multicolored	.55	.25
364	A106	35fr multicolored	.65	.25

6th anniversary of the Congolese Labor Party (P.C.T.). See No. C215.

A.G. Bell and 1876 Telephone A107

1976, Apr. 25 Litho. *Perf. 12½x13*

365	A107	35fr yel, brn & org brn	.65	.25

Cent. of 1st telephone call by Alexander Graham Bell, Mar. 10, 1876. See No. C229.

Women Selling Fruit and Vegetables A108

1976, Sept. 19 Litho. *Perf. 12½x13*

366	A108	35fr shown	.50	.25
367	A108	60fr Market scene	1.20	.30

Congolese Coiffure — A109

Designs: Various women's hair styles.

1976, Oct. 10 Litho. *Perf. 13*

368	A109	35fr multicolored	.55	.25
369	A109	60fr multicolored	.90	.25
370	A109	95fr multicolored	1.40	.35
371	A109	100fr multicolored	1.60	.40
		Nos. 368-371 (4)	4.45	1.25

Pole Vault, Map of Central Africa A110

95fr, Long jump and map of Central Africa.

1976, Oct. 25 *Perf. 12½*

372	A110	60fr yel & multi	.70	.25
373	A110	95fr yel & multi	1.25	.40
		Nos. 372-373,C230-C231 (4)	6.45	2.50

Gold medalists, 1st Central African Games, Yaoundé, July 27-30, 1975.

Antelope A111

1976, Oct. 27 Litho. *Perf. 12½*
Size: 36x36mm

374	A111	5fr shown	.55	.25
375	A111	10fr Buffalos	.65	.25
376	A111	15fr Hippopotamus	1.00	.30
377	A111	20fr Wart hog	2.00	.35
378	A111	25fr Elephants	2.25	.40
		Nos. 374-378 (5)	6.45	1.55

1976, Dec. 8 Size: 26x36mm

Designs: Birds.

379	A111	5fr Saddle-bill storks	1.00	.25

Size: 36x36mm

380	A111	10fr Malachite kingfisher	1.25	.25
381	A111	20fr Crowned cranes	2.00	.60
		Nos. 379-381 (3)	4.25	1.10

Bicycling, Map of Participants A112

1976, Dec. 21 Photo. *Perf. 12½x13*

382	A112	35fr shown	.35	.25
383	A112	60fr Fieldball	.60	.25
384	A112	80fr Running	1.00	.35
385	A112	95fr Soccer	1.25	.40
		Nos. 382-385 (4)	3.20	1.25

First Central African Games, Libreville, Gabon, June-July 1976.

Heliotrope A113

Flowers: 5fr, Water lilies. 15fr, Bird-of-paradise flower.

1976, Dec. 23 Photo. *Perf. 12½x13*

386	A113	5fr multicolored	.25	.25
387	A113	10fr multicolored	.35	.25
388	A113	15fr multicolored	.60	.25
		Nos. 386-388 (3)	1.20	.75

Torch and Olive Branches A114

1976, Dec. 25 Litho. *Perf. 12½x13*

389	A114	35fr multicolored	.80	.25

National Pioneer Movement.

The Spirit of '76 — A115

125fr, Pulling down George III statue. 150fr, Battle of Princeton. 175fr, Generals of Revolutionary War. 200fr, Burgoyne's surrender at Saratoga. 500fr, Battle of Lexington.

1976, Dec. 29 Litho. *Perf. 14*

390 A115 100fr multicolored 1.00 .25
391 A115 125fr multicolored 1.10 .35
392 A115 150fr multicolored 1.60 .40
393 A115 175fr multicolored 2.00 .50
394 A115 200fr multicolored 2.25 .60
Nos. 390-394 (5) 7.95 2.10

Souvenir Sheet

395 A115 500fr multicolored 5.75 1.50

American Bicentennial.

Dugout Canoe Race A116

Design: 60fr, 2-man dugout canoes.

1977, Mar. 27 Litho. *Perf. 13x13½*

396 A116 35fr multicolored .60 .25
397 A116 60fr multicolored 1.00 .35

Dugout canoe races on Congo River.

Lilan Goua A117

Fresh-water Fish: 15fr, Liko ko. 25fr, Liyan ga. 35fr, Mbessi. 60fr, Mongandza.

1977, June 15 Litho. *Perf. 12½*

398 A117 10fr multicolored .75 .25
399 A117 15fr multicolored .90 .25
400 A117 25fr multicolored 1.25 .25
401 A117 35fr multicolored 2.00 .30
402 A117 60fr multicolored 3.50 .45
Nos. 398-402 (5) 8.40 1.50

Traditional Headdress — A118

1977, June 30 Litho. *Perf. 12½*

403 A118 35fr shown .45 .30
404 A118 60fr Leopard cap .90 .35

See Nos. C234-C235.

Bondjo Wrestling A119

40fr, 50fr, Bondjo wrestling, diff. 40fr, horiz.

1977, July 15

405 A119 25fr multicolored .50 .25
406 A119 40fr multicolored .60 .25
407 A119 50fr multicolored .70 .30
Nos. 405-407 (3) 1.80 .80

"Schwaben" LZ 10, 1911 — A120

Zeppelins: 60fr, "Viktoria Luise." LZ 11, 1913. 100fr, LZ 120. 200fr, LZ 127. 300fr, "Graf Zeppelin II" LZ 130.

1977, Aug. 5 Litho. *Perf. 11*

408 A120 40fr multicolored .50 .25
409 A120 60fr multicolored .75 .25
410 A120 100fr multicolored 1.25 .30
411 A120 200fr multicolored 2.50 .60
412 A120 300fr multicolored 4.00 .95
Nos. 408-412 (5) 9.00 2.35

History of the Zeppelin. Exist imperf. See No. C236.

Coat of Arms and Rising Sun A121

1977, Aug. 15

413 A121 40fr multicolored .80 .25

14th anniversary of the revolution.

Victor Hugo and The Hunchback of Notre Dame — A122

Designs (Hugo and): 60fr, Les Miserables. 100fr, Les Travailleurs de la Mer (octopus).

1977, Aug. 20 Engr. *Perf. 13*

414 A122 35fr multicolored .75 .30
415 A122 60fr multicolored 1.00 .30
416 A122 100fr multicolored 1.90 .45
Nos. 414-416 (3) 3.65 1.05

Victor Hugo (1802-1885), French novelist.

Mao Tse-tung A123

Lithographed; Gold Embossed

1977, Sept. 9 *Perf. 12x12½*

417 A123 400fr red & gold 16.00 8.00

Chairman Mao Tse-tung (1893-1976), Chinese Communist leader, 1st death anniv.

Peter Paul Rubens A124

1977, Sept. 20 Gold Embossed

418 A124 600fr gold & lt bl 10.00 6.00

Peter Paul Rubens (1577-1640), painter.

Child Leading Blind Woman Across Street A125

1977, Oct. 22 Litho. *Perf. 12½x13*

419 A125 35fr multicolored .80 .25

World Health Day: To see is life.

Paul Kamba and Records A126

1977, Oct. 29

420 A126 100fr multicolored 1.60 .50

Paul Kamba (1912-1950), musician.

Trajan Vuia and Flying Machine — A127

Designs: 75fr, Louis Bleriot and plane. 100fr, Roland Garros and plane. 200fr, Charles Lindbergh and Spirit of St. Louis. 300fr, Tupolev Tu-144. 500fr, Lindbergh and Spirit of St. Louis over ship in Atlantic.

1977, Nov. 18 Litho. *Perf. 14*

421 A127 60fr multicolored .60 .25
422 A127 75fr multicolored .90 .25
423 A127 100fr multicolored 1.10 .30
424 A127 200fr multicolored 2.25 .50
425 A127 300fr multicolored 3.25 .70
Nos. 421-425 (5) 8.10 2.00

Souvenir Sheet

426 A127 500fr multicolored 5.75 1.25

History of aviation.

Elizabeth II and Prince Philip A128

Design: 300fr, Elizabeth II wearing Crown.

1977, Dec. 21

427 A128 250fr multicolored 2.25 .65
428 A128 300fr multicolored 2.75 .70

Reign of Queen Elizabeth II, 25th anniv.

See No. C239. For overprints see Nos. 468-469, C244.

King Baudouin A129

Design: No. 430, Charles de Gaulle.

1977, Dec. 21

429 A129 200fr multicolored 2.25 .65
430 A129 200fr multicolored 2.25 .65

King Baudouin of Belgium and Charles de Gaulle, president of France.

Ambete Sculpture A130

Congolese art: 85fr, Babembe sculpture.

1978, Feb. 18 Engr. *Perf. 13*

431 A130 35fr lt brn & multi .65 .25
432 A130 85fr lt grn & multi 1.50 .45

St. Simon, by Rubens A131

Rubens Paintings: 140fr, Duke of Lerma. 200fr, Madonna and Saints. 300fr, Rubens and his Wife Helena Fourment. 500fr, Farm at Laeken.

1978, Mar. 7 Litho. *Perf. 13½x14*

433 A131 60fr gold & multi .60 .25
434 A131 140fr gold & multi 1.50 .30
435 A131 200fr gold & multi 2.25 .45
436 A131 300fr gold & multi 3.50 .65
Nos. 433-436 (4) 7.85 1.65

Souvenir Sheet

437 A131 500fr gold & multi 6.00 1.40

Peter Paul Rubens, 400th birth anniv.

Pres. Ngouabi and Microphones — A132

60fr, Ngouabi at his desk, horiz. 100fr, Portrait.

Perf. 12½x13, 13x12½

1978, Mar. 18 **Litho.**

438 A132 35fr multicolored .45 .25
439 A132 60fr multicolored .50 .25
440 A132 100fr multicolored .90 .40
Nos. 438-440 (3) 1.85 .90

Pres. Marien Ngouabi, 1st death anniv.

Ferenc Puskas and Argentina '78 Emblem — A133

Players and Emblem: 75fr, Giacinto Facchetti. 100fr, Bobby Moore. 200fr, Raymond Kopa. 300fr, Pele. 500fr, Franz Beckenbauer.

1978, Apr. 4 ***Perf. 14x13½***

441 A133 60fr multicolored .60 .25
442 A133 75fr multicolored .70 .25
443 A133 100fr multicolored 1.10 .25
444 A133 200fr multicolored 2.25 .55
445 A133 300fr multicolored 3.25 .75
Nos. 441-445 (5) 7.90 2.05

Souvenir Sheet

446 A133 500fr multicolored 6.25 1.25

11th World Cup Soccer Championship, Argentina, June 1-25.
For overprints see Nos. 481-486.

Pearl S. Buck and Chinese Women — A134

Nobel Prize winners: 75fr, Fridtjof Nansen, refugees and Nansen passport. 100fr, Henri Bergson, book and flame. 200fr, Alexander Fleming and Petri dish. 300fr, Gerhart Hauptmann and book. 500fr, Henri Dunant and Red Cross Station.

1978, Apr. 29

447 A134 60fr multicolored .60 .25
448 A134 75fr multicolored .70 .25
449 A134 100fr multicolored 1.10 .30
450 A134 200fr multicolored 2.00 .50
451 A134 300fr multicolored 2.75 .60
Nos. 447-451 (5) 7.15 1.90

Souvenir Sheet

452 A134 500fr multicolored 6.00 1.40

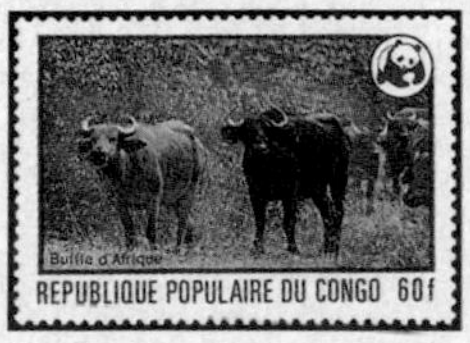

African Buffalos A135

Endangered animals and Wildlife Fund Emblem: 35fr, Okapi, vert. 85fr, Rhinoceros. 150fr, Chimpanzee, vert. 200fr, Hippopotamus. 300fr, Buffon's kob, vert.

1978 ***Perf. 14½***

453 A135 35fr multicolored 1.25 .45
454 A135 60fr multicolored 1.75 .55
455 A135 85fr multicolored 4.25 .85
456 A135 150fr multicolored 6.00 1.25
457 A135 200fr multicolored 8.00 1.75
458 A135 300fr multicolored 15.00 2.50
Nos. 453-458 (6) 36.25 7.35

Issue dates: 35fr, Aug. 11; others, July 11.

Emblem, Young People, Gun and Fist — A136

1978, July 28 ***Perf. 12½***

459 A136 35fr multicolored .80 .30

11th World Youth Festival, Havana, 7/28-8/5.

Pyramids and Camels — A137

Seven Wonders of the Ancient World: 50fr, Hanging Gardens of Babylon. 60fr, Statue of Zeus, Olympia. 95fr, Colossus of Rhodes. 125fr, Mausoleum of Halicarnassus. 150fr, Temple of Artemis, Ephesus. 200fr, Lighthouse, Alexandria. 300fr, Map of Eastern Mediterranean showing locations. 50fr, 60fr, 95fr, 125fr, 200fr, vertical.

1978, Aug. 12 **Litho.** ***Perf. 14***

460 A137 35fr multicolored .50 .25
461 A137 50fr multicolored .60 .25
462 A137 60fr multicolored .75 .25
463 A137 95fr multicolored 1.00 .30
464 A137 125fr multicolored 1.25 .45
465 A137 150fr multicolored 1.75 .55
466 A137 200fr multicolored 2.25 .75
467 A137 300fr multicolored 3.25 1.00
Nos. 460-467 (8) 11.35 3.80

Nos. 427-428 Overprinted in Silver

No. 468

No. 469

1978, Sept. **Litho.** ***Perf. 14***

468 A128 250fr multicolored 2.25 .90
469 A128 300fr multicolored 2.75 1.25

25th anniversary of coronation of Queen Elizabeth II. See No. C244.

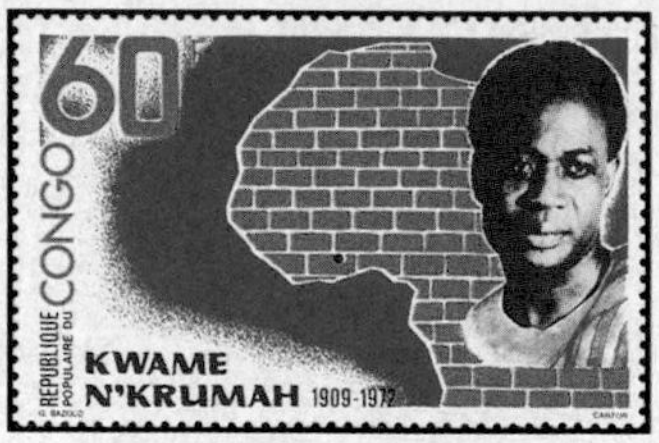

Kwame Nkrumah and Map of Africa — A138

1978, Sept. 23 **Litho.** ***Perf. 13x12½***

470 A138 60fr multicolored .80 .40

Nkrumah (1909-72), Pres. of Ghana.

Wild Boar Hunt — A139

Local hunting and fishing: 50fr, Fish smoking. 60fr, Hunter with spears and dog, vert.

1978 **Litho.** ***Perf. 12***

471 A139 35fr multicolored 2.00 .25
472 A139 50fr multicolored .80 .25
473 A139 60fr multicolored 2.75 .25
Nos. 471-473 (3) 5.55 .75

Issue dates: 35fr, 60fr, Oct. 5; 50fr, Oct. 10.

View of Kalchreut, by Dürer — A140

Paintings by Dürer: 150fr, Elspeth Tucher, vert. 250fr, "The Great Piece of Turf," vert. 350fr, Self-portrait, vert.

1978, Nov. 23 **Litho.** ***Perf. 14***

474 A140 65fr multicolored .60 .25
475 A140 150fr multicolored 1.40 .35
476 A140 250fr multicolored 2.25 .65
477 A140 350fr multicolored 3.50 .90
Nos. 474-477 (4) 7.75 2.15

Albrecht Dürer (1471-1528), German painter.

Basketmaker A141

Productive Labor: 90fr, Woodcarver. 140fr, Women hoeing field.

1978, Nov. 18 **Litho.** ***Perf. 12½***

Size: 25x36mm

478 A141 85fr multicolored .90 .40
479 A141 90fr multicolored 1.00 .40

Size: 27x48mm

Perf. 12

480 A141 140fr multicolored 1.50 .65
Nos. 478-480 (3) 3.40 1.45

Nos. 441-446 Overprinted in Silver

a

b

c

d

e

f

1978, Nov. ***Perf. 14x13½***

481 A133 (a) 60fr multicolored .65 .25
482 A133 (b) 75fr multicolored .75 .35
483 A133 (c) 100fr multicolored 1.05 .45
484 A133 (d) 200fr multicolored 2.10 .65
485 A133 (e) 300fr multicolored 3.00 1.00
Nos. 481-485 (5) 7.55 2.70

Souvenir Sheet

486 A133 (f) 500fr multicolored 6.00 2.40

Winners, World Soccer Cup Championships 1962-1978.

Heart and Charts A142

1978, Dec. 16 Engr. *Perf. 13*

487 A142 100fr multicolored 1.60 .50

Fight against hypertension.

Party Emblem and Road — A143

1978, Dec. 31 Litho. *Perf. 12½x12*

488 A143 60fr multicolored .65 .25

Congolese Labor Party, 9th anniversary.

Capt. Cook, Polynesians and House — A144

Capt. James Cook (1728-1779): 150fr, Island scene. 250fr, Polynesian longboats. 350fr, Capt. Cook's ships off Hawaii.

1979, Jan. 16 *Perf. 14½*

489 A144 65fr multicolored .70 .25
490 A144 150fr multicolored 1.75 .35
491 A144 250fr multicolored 2.75 .60
492 A144 350fr multicolored 3.50 1.00
Nos. 489-492 (4) 8.70 2.20

Pres. Marien Ngouabi — A145

1979, Mar. 18 Litho. *Perf. 12*

493 A145 35fr multicolored .35 .25
494 A145 60fr multicolored .50 .25

Assassination of President Ngouabi, 2nd anniv.

"1979," IYC Emblem, Child A146

A146a

1979, Apr. 30 Litho. *Perf. 12½x13*

495 A146 45fr multicolored .45 .25
496 A146 75fr multicolored .90 .35

Souvenir Sheet

Perf. 14½

496A A146a 250fr multicolored 2.75 1.00

International Year of the Child.
Issued: 45fr, 75fr, Apr. 30; 250fr, Sept. 5.

Pottery Vases and Solanum — A147

Design: 150fr, Mail runner, Concorde, train, UPU emblem, envelope.

1979, June 8 Litho. *Perf. 13*

497 A147 60fr multicolored 1.75 .60

Engr.

498 A147 150fr multicolored 3.50 1.25

Philexafrique II, Libreville, Gabon, June 8-17. Nos. 497, 498 each printed in sheets of 10 with 5 labels showing exhibition emblem.

Rowland Hill, Diesel Locomotive, Germany No. 78 — A148

Designs (Rowland Hill and): 100fr, Old steam locomotive and France No. B10. 200fr, Diesel locomotive and US No. 245. 300fr, Steam locomotive and England-Australia First Aerialpost vignette, 1919. 500fr, Electric train, Concorde and Middle Congo No. 75.

1979, June 30 *Perf. 14*

499 A148 65fr multicolored .60 .25
500 A148 100fr multicolored 1.00 .25
501 A148 200fr multicolored 2.25 .50
502 A148 300fr multicolored 3.00 .75
Nos. 499-502 (4) 6.85 1.75

Souvenir Sheet

503 A148 500fr multicolored 5.75 1.25

Sir Rowland Hill (1795-1879), originator of penny postage.

Salvador Allende, Flags, Demonstrators — A149

1979, July 21 Litho. *Perf. 12½*

504 A149 100fr multicolored 1.60 .50

Salvador Allende, president of Chile.

Old Man Telling Stories — A150

1979, July 28

505 A150 45fr multicolored .80 .25

Story telling as education.

Handball Players A151

75fr, Players and ball. 250fr, Pres. Ngouabi, cup on map of Africa, player.

1979, July 31 Litho. *Perf. 12½*

Size: 40x30mm, 30x40mm

506 A151 45fr multi .60 .25
507 A151 75fr multi, vert. 1.00 .25

Size: 22x40mm

Perf. 12x12½

508 A151 250fr multicolored 2.75 1.00

Marien Ngouabi Handball Cup.

Map and Flag of Congo — A152

1979, Aug. 15

509 A152 50fr multicolored .80 .25

16th anniversary of revolution.

Souvenir Sheet

Virgin and Child, by Dürer — A153

1979, Aug. 13 *Perf. 13½*

510 A153 500fr red brn & lt grn 6.50 2.50

Albrecht Dürer (1471-1528), German engraver and painter.

Bach and Contemporary Instruments — A155

No. 512, Albert Einstein, astronauts on moon.

1979, Sept. 10 *Perf. 13½*

511 A155 200fr multicolored 2.25 .75
512 A155 200fr multicolored 2.25 .75

Yoro Fishing Port A156

1979, Sept. 26 Litho. *Perf. 12½*

513 A156 45fr shown .65 .25
514 A156 75fr Port at night .95 .35

Mukukulu Dam — A157

1979, Oct. 5 *Perf. 12½x12*

515 A157 20fr multicolored .60 .25
516 A157 45fr multicolored 1.10 .30

Emblem, Control Tower, Jets A158

1979, Dec. 12 Litho. *Perf. 12½*

517 A158 100fr multicolored 1.60 .50

ASECNA (Air Safety Board), 20th anniv.

Congolese Labor Party, 10th Anniversary A159

1979, Dec. 31

518 A159 45fr multicolored .80 .25

A160

1980, Mar. 30 Litho. *Perf. 12½*

519 A160 45fr multicolored .60 .25
520 A160 95fr multicolored 1.10 .30

Post Office, 15th Anniversary.

A161

1980, May 5

521 A161 100fr multicolored 3.50 1.00

Visit of Pope John Paul II.

Rotary International, 75th Anniversary — A162

1980, May 10 Litho. *Perf. 12½*

522 A162 150fr multicolored 1.50 .50

Pointe Noire Foundry A163

1980, June 18 Litho. *Perf. 12½*

523 A163 30fr shown .30 .25
524 A163 35fr Different view .50 .25

Claude Chappe, Tower — A164

1980, June 21 Litho. *Perf. 12½*

525 A164 200fr multicolored 2.50 1.00

Claude Chappe (1763-1805), French engineer.

Mossaka Harbor — A165

1980, June 23

532 A165 45fr shown .60 .25
533 A165 90fr Different view 1.10 .25

Papilio Dardanus (Front and Back) — A167

15fr, Kalima aethiops. 20fr, Papilio demodocus. 60fr, Euphaedra. 90fr, Hypolimnas misippus.
300fr, Charaxes smaragdalis.

1980, July 12 Litho. *Perf. 12½*

534 A167 5fr shown .60 .30
a. Perf. 12½x13 1.60 1.60
535 A167 15fr multicolored 1.40 .30
a. Perf. 12½x13 2.00 2.00
536 A167 20fr multicolored 1.40 .40
a. Perf. 12½x13 2.40 2.40
537 A167 60fr multicolored 3.25 .75
538 A167 90fr multicolored 6.50 1.00
Nos. 534-538 (5) 13.15 2.75

Souvenir Sheet

539 A167 300fr multicolored 10.00 17.00

July 31st Hospital — A168

1980, July 31

540 A168 45fr multicolored .80 .25

Human Rights Emblem, People — A169

1980, Aug. 2

541 A169 350fr shown 2.75 1.00
542 A169 500fr Man breaking chain 4.50 1.50

Human Rights Convention, 32nd anniv.

Citizens and Congolese Arms A170

95fr, Dove on flag, fists, vert. 150fr, Dove holding Congolese arms.

1980, Aug. 15 *Perf. 12½*

543 A170 75fr shown .70 .30
544 A170 95fr multicolored .90 .30
545 A170 150fr multicolored 1.50 .60
Nos. 543-545 (3) 3.10 1.20

August 13-15th Revolution, 17th anniv.

Coffee and Cocoa Trees on Map of Congo — A171

Coffee and Cocoa Day: 95fr, Branches, map of Congo.

1980, Aug. 18 *Perf. 13½x13*

546 A171 45fr multicolored .60 .25
547 A171 95fr multicolored 1.10 .40

Logging A172

1980, Aug. 28

548 A172 70fr shown .80 .30
549 A172 75fr Wood transport .80 .30

Pres. Neto of Angola, 1st Death Anniv. — A173

1980, Sept. 11

550 A173 100fr multicolored .90 .30

Lark — A174

Designs: Birds.

1980, Sept. 17

551 A174 45fr multi, horiz. .90 .30
552 A174 75fr multi, horiz. 1.10 .30
553 A174 90fr multi, horiz. 1.40 .35
554 A174 150fr multicolored 2.25 .50
555 A174 200fr multicolored 3.00 1.00
556 A174 250fr multicolored 3.50 1.25
a Souv. sheet of 6, #551-556 22.50 17.50
Nos. 551-556 (6) 12.15 3.70

World Tourism Conference, Manila, Sept. 27 — A175

1980, Sept. 27 Litho. *Perf. 13½x13*

557 A175 100fr multicolored .90 .35

First Day of School Term — A176

1980, Oct. 2 Photo. *Perf. 13*

558 A176 50fr multicolored .70 .25

First House in Brazzaville — A177

Brazzaville Centenary: 65fr, First native village. 75fr, Old Town Hall, 1912. 150fr, View from bank of Bacongo, 1912. 200fr, Meeting of explorer Savorgnan de Brazza and chief Makoko, 1880.

1980, Oct. 3 Litho. *Perf. 12½*

559 A177 45fr multicolored .50 .25
560 A177 65fr multicolored .70 .30
561 A177 75fr multicolored 1.00 .40
562 A177 150fr multicolored 1.75 .65
563 A177 200fr multicolored 2.25 1.00
Nos. 559-563 (5) 6.20 2.60

Boys on Bank of Congo River — A178

1980, Oct. 30

564 A178 80fr shown .85 .25
565 A178 150fr Djoue Bridge 1.90 .40

Revolutionary Stadium and Athletes — A179

1980, Nov. 20 *Perf. 13x12½*

566 A179 60fr multicolored .80 .25

Rebuilt Railroad Bridge over Congo River A180

1980, Nov. 29 *Perf. 13x13½*

567 A180 75fr multicolored .90 .30

Mangoes, Loudima Fruit Packing Station A181

1980, Dec. 2 *Perf. 13*

568 A181 10fr shown .25 .25
569 A181 25fr Oranges .50 .25
570 A181 40fr Citrons .60 .25
571 A181 85fr Mandarins 1.10 .30
Nos. 568-571 (4) 2.45 1.05

African Postal Union, 5th Anniversary A182

1980, Dec. 24 *Perf. 13½*

572 A182 100fr multicolored .90 .30

Moungouni Earth Satellite Station A183

1980, Dec. 30 *Perf. 12½*

573 A183 75fr multicolored .80 .25

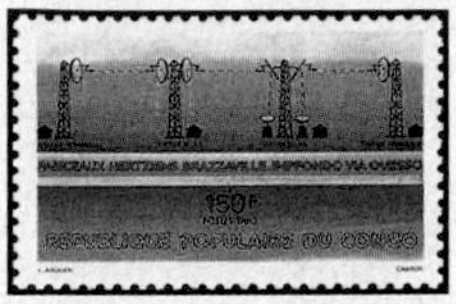

Hertzian Wave Communication, Brazzaville — A184

1980, Dec. 30 ***Perf. 12½x12***

574 A184 150fr multicolored 1.60 .40

1980 African Handball Champion Team — A185

Perf. 12½x13, 13x12½

1981, Jan. 26 **Litho.**

575 A185 100fr Receiving cup, vert. 1.25 .35
576 A185 150fr shown 1.50 .60

Pres. Denis Sassou-Nguesso — A186

1981, Feb. 5 **Litho.** ***Perf. 12½***

577 A186 45fr multicolored .45 .25
578 A186 75fr multicolored .60 .25
579 A186 100fr multicolored .90 .25
Nos. 577-579 (3) 1.95 .75

Luna 17, 1970. — A187

Space Conquest: 150fr, Space shuttle in orbit. 200fr, Shuttle, space station. 300fr, Shuttle, landing field. 500fr, Shuttle lift-off.

1981, May 4 **Litho.** ***Perf. 14x13½***

580 A187 100fr multicolored 1.00 .25
581 A187 150fr multicolored 1.40 .40
582 A187 200fr multicolored 2.00 .55
583 A187 300fr multicolored 2.75 .80
Nos. 580-583 (4) 7.15 2.00

Souvenir Sheet

584 A187 500fr multicolored 5.00 1.40

For overprint see No. 725.

Fight Against Apartheid — A188

1981, May 5 **Litho.** ***Perf. 12½***

585 A188 100fr deep blue .90 .25

Twin Palm Tree of Louingui — A189

1981, May 22 ***Perf. 12x12½***

586 A189 75fr multicolored 1.00 .25

13th World Telecommunications Day — A190

1981, June 6 ***Perf. 12½***

587 A190 120fr multicolored 1.50 .50

Rubber Extraction — A191

1981, June 27 ***Perf. 13***

588 A191 50fr shown .60 .25
589 A191 70fr Sap draining .90 .30

Intl. Year of the Disabled A192

1981, June 29 **Engr.**

590 A192 45fr multicolored .60 .25

See No. B7.

Bird Trap — A194

Designs: Animal traps. 10fr vert.

1981, July

596 A194 5fr multicolored .90 .25
597 A194 10fr multicolored .90 .25
598 A194 15fr multicolored 1.40 .25
599 A194 20fr multicolored 1.40 .25
600 A194 30fr multicolored 2.00 .25
601 A194 35fr multicolored 2.00 .30
Nos. 596-601 (6) 8.60 1.55

Mausoleum of King Maloango — A195

1981, July 4 **Litho.** ***Perf. 12½***

602 A195 75fr shown .70 .25
603 A195 150fr Mausoleum, portrait 1.25 .40

Prince Charles and Lady Diana, Coach A196

Royal wedding: Couple and coaches.

1981, Sept. 1 **Litho.** ***Perf. 14½***

604 A196 100fr multicolored 1.00 .25
605 A196 200fr multicolored 2.00 .55
606 A196 300fr multicolored 3.25 .80
Nos. 604-606 (3) 6.25 1.60

Souvenir Sheet

607 A196 400fr multicolored 4.00 1.10

World Food Day — A197

1981, Oct. 16 **Litho.** ***Perf. 13½x13***

608 A197 150fr multicolored 1.75 .55

12th World UPU Day A198

1981, Oct. 24 **Engr.** ***Perf. 13x12½***

609 A198 90fr multicolored .90 .25

Royal Guard A199

1981, Oct. 31 **Litho.** ***Perf. 12½x13***

610 A199 45fr multicolored .90 .25

Eradication of Manioc Beetle — A200

1981, Nov. 18 **Litho.** ***Perf. 12½***

611 A200 75fr multicolored 1.20 .25

Natl. Red Cross — A201

1981, Nov. 18 ***Perf. 13***

612 A201 10fr Bandaging patient .30 .25
613 A201 35fr Treating child .50 .25
614 A201 60fr Drawing well water .80 .25
Nos. 612-614 (3) 1.60 .75

Giant Baobab ("Tree of Savorgnan de Brazza") A202

1981, Dec. 19 **Litho.** ***Perf. 13***

615 A202 45fr multicolored .90 .25
616 A202 75fr multicolored 1.25 .30

Fetish Figure — A203

Designs: Various carved figures.

1981, Dec. 19 ***Perf. 12½***

617 A203 15fr multicolored .30 .25
a. Perf. 12½x13 .30 .25
618 A203 25fr multicolored .40 .25
a. Perf. 12½x13 .40 .25
619 A203 45fr multicolored .50 .25
620 A203 50fr multicolored .60 .25
a. Perf. 12½x13 .60 .35
621 A203 60fr multicolored .70 .25
Nos. 617-621 (5) 2.50 1.25

Caves of Bangou A204

1981, Dec. 29 ***Perf. 13x13½***

622 A204 20fr multicolored .45 .25
623 A204 25fr multicolored .45 .25

King Makoko and His Queen, Ivory Sculptures by R. Engongodzo — A205

Perf. 13½x13, 13x13½

1982, Feb. 27 **Litho.**

624 A205 25fr Woman, vert. .35 .25
625 A205 35fr Woman, diff., vert. .45 .25
626 A205 100fr shown 1.00 .30
Nos. 624-626 (3) 1.80 .80

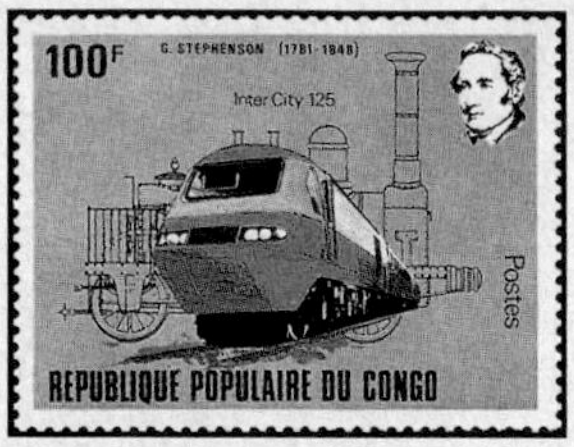

George Stephenson (1781-1848) and Inter City 125, Gt. Britain — A206

Locomotives: 150fr, Sinkansen Bullet Train, Japan. 200fr, Advanced Passenger Train, Gt. Britain. 300fr, TGV-001, France.

1982, Mar. 2 Litho. *Perf. 12½*

627 A206 100fr multicolored 1.00 .25
628 A206 150fr multicolored 1.60 .40
629 A206 200fr multicolored 2.25 .55
630 A206 300fr multicolored 3.25 .80
Nos. 627-630 (4) 8.10 2.00

Scouting Year A207

1982, Apr. 13 Litho. *Perf. 13*

631 A207 100fr Looking through binoculars 1.25 .25
632 A207 150fr Reading map 1.50 .40
633 A207 200fr Helping woman 2.25 .55
634 A207 300fr Crossing rope bridge 3.25 .80
Nos. 631-634 (4) 8.25 2.00

Souvenir Sheet

635 A207 500fr Hiking, horiz. 5.00 1.75

For overprint see No. 726.

Franklin Roosevelt A208

1982, June 12 Litho. *Perf. 13*

636 A208 150fr shown 1.75 .60
637 A208 250fr Washington 2.75 .85
638 A208 350fr Goethe 3.75 1.10
Nos. 636-638 (3) 8.25 2.55

21st Birthday of Princess Diana, July 1 — A209

1982, June 12 *Perf. 14*

639 A209 200fr Candles 2.00 .55
640 A209 300fr "21" 2.75 .80

Souvenir Sheet

641 A209 500fr Diana 5.00 1.40

5-Year Plan, 1982-1986 A210

60fr, Road construction. 100fr, Communications, vert. 125fr, Operating room equipment, vert. 150fr, Hydroelectric power, vert.

Perf. 13x12½, 12½x13

1982, June 19

642 A210 60fr multicolored .80 .25
643 A210 100fr multicolored 1.25 .30
644 A210 125fr multicolored 1.60 .35
645 A210 150fr multicolored 1.75 .40
Nos. 642-645 (4) 5.40 1.30

ITU Plenipotentiary Conference, Nairobi — A211

1982, June 26 *Perf. 13*

646 A211 300fr multicolored 3.00 .90

Nos. 604-607 Overprinted in Blue

1982, July 30 *Perf. 14½*

647 A196 100fr multicolored .90 .30
648 A196 200fr multicolored 1.75 .60
649 A196 300fr multicolored 2.75 1.00
Nos. 647-649 (3) 5.40 1.90

Souvenir Sheet

650 A196 400fr multicolored 3.50 2.50

Birth of Prince William of Wales, June 21.

Nutrition Campaign A212

1982, July 24 Litho. *Perf. 12½*

651 A212 100fr multicolored 1.40 .25

WHO African Headquarters, Brazzaville — A213

1982, July 24 Litho. *Perf. 12½*

652 A213 125fr multicolored 1.60 .45

TB Bacillus Centenary — A214

1982, Aug. 7 *Perf. 12½x12*

653 A214 250fr Koch, bacillus 3.25 1.10

Pres. Sassou-Nguesso and 1980 Simba Prize — A215

1982, Oct. 20 Litho. *Perf. 13*

654 A215 100fr multicolored .90 .30

Turtles — A216

Various turtles and tortoises.

1982, Dec. 1

655 A216 30fr multicolored .90 .25
656 A216 45fr multicolored 1.50 .30
657 A216 55fr multicolored 1.60 .40
Nos. 655-657 (3) 4.00 .95

Boy Gathering Coconuts — A217

1982, Dec. 11

658 A217 100fr multicolored 1.40 .30

Nest in Tree Trunk — A218

1982, Dec. 29 *Perf. 12½*

659 A218 40fr shown 1.00 .25
660 A218 75fr Nests in palm tree 1.60 .25
661 A218 100fr Woven nest on thorn branch 2.50 .40
Nos. 659-661 (3) 5.10 .90

Hertzian Wave Communication Network — A219

1982, Dec. 30 *Perf. 13x12½*

662 A219 45fr multicolored .45 .25
663 A219 60fr multicolored .50 .25
664 A219 95fr multicolored .90 .30
Nos. 662-664 (3) 1.85 .80

30th Anniv. of Customs Cooperation Council — A220

1983, Jan. 26 Litho. *Perf. 12½x13*

665 A220 100fr Headquarters .90 .30

Mausoleum of Pres. Marien Ngouabi — A221

1983, Feb. 8 *Perf. 13*

666 A221 60fr multicolored .50 .25
667 A221 80fr multicolored .80 .25

Ironsmiths — A222

1983 *Perf. 12½*

668 A222 45fr shown .80 .25
669 A222 150fr Weaver, vert. 1.50 .50

Issue dates: 45fr, Mar. 5; 150fr, Feb. 24.

Carved Chess Pieces, by R. Engongonzo — A223

Various pieces.

1983, Feb. 26 *Perf. 13*

670 A223 40fr multicolored .40 .25
671 A223 60fr multicolored 1.00 .25
672 A223 95fr multicolored 2.00 .50
Nos. 670-672 (3) 3.40 1.00

Easter 1983 A224

Raphael drawings: 200fr, Transfiguration study. 300fr, Deposition from Cross, horiz. 400fr, Christ in Glory.

1983, Apr. 20 **Litho.** ***Perf. 13***
673 A224 200fr multicolored 2.00 .50
674 A224 300fr multicolored 3.25 .65
675 A224 400fr multicolored 4.50 .85
Nos. 673-675 (3) 9.75 2.00

Seashells A225

1983 **Litho.** ***Perf. 15x14***
675A A225 25fr multicolored *150.00 65.00*
676 A225 35fr multicolored 1.25 .30
677 A225 65fr multicolored 1.60 .35
Dated 1982.

A226

Various traditional combs.

1983, May ***Perf. 14***
678 A226 30fr multicolored .35 .25
679 A226 70fr multicolored .90 .25
680 A226 85fr multicolored 1.00 .25
Nos. 678-680 (3) 2.25 .75

A227

Litho & Engr.
1983, Aug. 10 ***Perf. 12½x13***
681 A227 60fr multicolored .65 .25
682 A227 100fr multicolored .95 .30
20th anniv. of revolution.

Centenary of the Arrival of Christian Missionaries — A228

Churches and Clergymen: 150fr, A. Carrie, Church of the Sacred Heart, Loango, vert, 250fr, Msgr. Augouard; St. Louis, Liranga; St. Joseph, Linzolo.

1983, Aug. 23 ***Perf. 12½***
683 A228 150fr multicolored 1.60 .40
684 A228 250fr multicolored 2.75 .70

Local Flowers — A229

1984, Jan. 20 **Litho.** ***Perf. 12½***
685 A229 5fr Liana thunderaie, vert. .25 .25
686 A229 15fr Bougainvillea .35 .25
687 A229 20fr Anthurium, vert. .50 .25
688 A229 45fr Allamanda 1.00 .25
689 A229 75fr Hibiscus, vert. 1.40 .30
Nos. 685-689 (5) 3.50 1.30

35th Anniv. of World Peace Council A230

1984, Mar. 31 **Litho.** ***Perf. 13x12½***
690 A230 50fr multicolored .45 .25
691 A230 100fr multicolored .90 .30

Anti-Nuclear Arms Campaign A231

1984, May 31 **Litho.** ***Perf. 12x12½***
692 A231 200fr Explosion, victims 1.75 .50

Agriculture Day A232

Perf. 13x13½, 13½x13
1984, June 30 **Litho.**
693 A232 10fr Rice .25 .25
694 A232 15fr Pineapples .25 .25
695 A232 60fr Manioc, vert. .60 .25
696 A232 100fr Palm tree, map, vert. 1.10 .35
Nos. 693-696 (4) 2.20 1.10

Congress Palace — A233

1984, July 27 ***Perf. 13***
697 A233 60fr multicolored .60 .25
698 A233 100fr multicolored 1.00 .30
Chinese-Congolese cooperation.

CFCO-Congo Railways, 50th Anniv. — A234

10fr, Loulombo Station. 25fr, Les Bandas Chinese Labor Camp. 125fr, "50". 200fr, Administration building.

1984, July 30 ***Perf. 13½***
699 A234 10fr multicolored .35 .25
700 A234 25fr multicolored .60 .25
701 A234 125fr multicolored 2.75 .70
702 A234 200fr multicolored 6.25 1.00
Nos. 699-702 (4) 9.95 2.20

Locomotives — A235

Ships on the Congo River — A236

1984, Aug. 24 ***Perf. 12½***
703 A235 100fr CC 203 1.10 .35
704 A236 100fr Tugboat 1.10 .35
705 A235 150fr BB 103 1.60 .50
706 A236 150fr Pusher tugboat 1.60 .50
707 A235 300fr BB-BB 301 3.25 1.10
708 A236 300fr Dredger 3.25 1.10
709 A235 500fr BB 420 L'Eclair 5.25 1.75
710 A236 500fr Cargo ship 5.25 1.75
Nos. 703-710 (8) 22.40 7.40

World Fisheries Year A237

1984, Oct. 16 ***Perf. 13½***
711 A237 5fr Basket of fish .50 .25
712 A237 20fr Net fishermen in boat .80 .25
713 A237 25fr School of fish .80 .25
714 A237 40fr Net fisherman 1.25 .30
715 A237 55fr Trawler 2.25 .35
Nos. 711-715 (5) 5.60 1.40

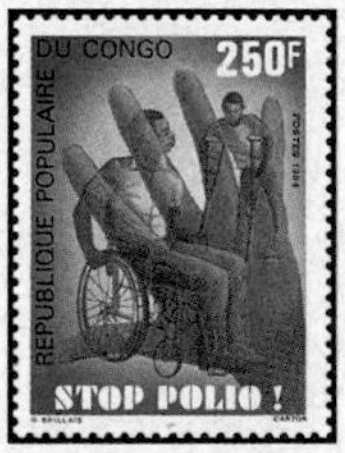

Anti-polio Campaign A238

250fr, Disabled men, hand. 300fr, Target, disabled women, horiz.

1984, Oct. 30
716 A238 250fr multicolored 2.75 .90
717 A238 300fr multicolored 3.25 1.00

M'Bamou Palace Hotel, Brazzaville A239

1984, Dec. 15 ***Perf. 14½***
718 A239 60fr multicolored .50 .25
719 A239 100fr multicolored 1.00 .30

Fauna A240

1984, Dec. ***Perf. 15x14½***
720 A240 30fr Pangolin 2.50 .75
721 A240 70fr Bat 5.50 1.50
722 A240 85fr Civet cat 6.75 2.00
Nos. 720-722 (3) 14.75 4.25

Congo River Logging A241

1984, Dec. ***Perf. 13½x13***
723 A241 60fr Log raft, crew hut .60 .25
724 A241 100fr Tugboat pushing logs 1.25 .35

Nos. 584, 635 Ovptd. in Black or Green
Souvenir Sheets

1985, Mar. 8 ***Perf. 14x13½, 13***
725 A187 500fr TSUKUBA EXPO '85 5.75 4.50
726 A207 500fr ITALIA '85 emblem, ROME (G) 5.75 4.50
See Nos. C336-C337.

Zonocerus Variegatus — A242

1985, Mar. 15 ***Perf. 13***
727 A242 125fr multicolored 1.75 .35

Burial of a Teke Chief — A243

1985, Apr. 30 *Perf. 12½*

728 A243 225fr multicolored 2.25 .75

Edible Fruit A244

5fr, Trichoscypha acuminata, vert. 10fr, Aframomum africanum. 125fr, Gambeya lacuurtiana. 150fr, Landolphia jumelei.

Perf. 13½, 13 (#732A), 13½x13¼ (#732B)

1985, June 15

729	A244	5fr	multicolored	.25	.25
730	A244	10fr	multicolored	.25	.25
730A	A244	90fr	like #730		
731	A244	125fr	multicolored	1.40	.40
732	A244	150fr	multicolored	1.75	.55
732A	A244	205fr	like #731		
732B	A244	300fr	Like #732	—	—

Sizes: No. 729, 22x36mm, Nos. 731, 732A, 36x22mm.

Nos. 730A, 732A, 732B inscribed "Congo" only.

For overprints, see Nos. 1155, 1170, 1183-1185.

Compare type A244 with type A352.

Lions Club Intl., 30th Anniv. — A245

1985, June 25 *Perf. 12½*

733 A245 250fr Flag, District 403B 2.75 .70

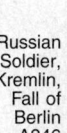

Russian Soldier, Kremlin, Fall of Berlin A246

1985, July 27 *Perf. 12*

734 A246 60fr multicolored .80 .25

Defeat of Nazi Germany, end of World War II, 40th anniv.

Lady Olave Baden-Powell, Girl Guides Founder — A247

Anniversaries and events: 150fr, Girl Guides, 75th anniv. 250fr, Jacob Grimm, fabulist; Sleeping Beauty. 350fr, Johann Sebastian Bach, composer; European Music Year, St. Thomas Church organ, Leipzig. 450fr, Queen Mother, 85th birthday, vert. 500fr, Statue of Liberty, cent., vert.

1985, Aug. 26 *Perf. 13*

735	A247	150fr	multicolored	1.60	.50
736	A247	250fr	multicolored	2.25	.90
737	A247	350fr	multicolored	3.00	1.25
738	A247	450fr	multicolored	3.75	1.60
739	A247	500fr	multicolored	5.00	2.00
			Nos. 735-739 (5)	15.60	6.25

PHILEXAFRICA '85, Lome, Togo, Nov. 16-24 — A248

1985, Oct. 10 *Perf. 13x12½*

740	A248	250fr	shown	2.75	1.00
741	A248	250fr	Airport, postal van	2.75	1.00
a.			Pair, #740-741 + label	6.50	6.50

Mushrooms — A249

100fr, Coprinus, vert. 150fr, Cortinarius. 200fr, Armillariella mellea. 300fr, Dictyophora. 400fr, Crucibulum vulgare.

1985, Dec. 14 **Litho.** *Perf. 13*

742	A249	100fr	multicolored	1.50	.35
743	A249	150fr	multicolored	2.25	.50
744	A249	200fr	multicolored	3.00	.85
745	A249	300fr	multicolored	4.00	1.25
746	A249	400fr	multicolored	6.00	1.50
			Nos. 742-746 (5)	16.75	4.45

Arbor Day — A250

1986, Mar. 6 *Perf. 13½*

747	A250	60fr	Planting sapling	.45	.25
748	A250	200fr	Map, lifecycle diagram	1.90	.90

Children's Hoop Races — A251

1986, Apr. 30 *Perf. 12½*

749	A251	5fr	Two boys	.30	.25
750	A251	10fr	One boy	.30	.25
751	A251	60fr	Three boys, horiz.	.80	.25
a.			Souvenir sheet of 3, #749-751	2.00	1.75
			Nos. 749-751 (3)	1.40	.75

A252

1986, June 5 **Litho.** *Perf. 13½*

752	A252	60fr	Garbage disposal	.60	.25
753	A252	125fr	Dumping garbage	1.20	.45

Intl. Environment Day.

A253

Traditional Modes of Transporting Goods: 5fr, Basket on head, child in sling carrier. 10fr, Child in carrier on hip, large basket strapped to forehead. 60fr, Man carrying load on shoulder.

1986, July 15 **Litho.** *Perf. 13x12½*

754	A253	5fr	multicolored	.30	.25
755	A253	10fr	multicolored	.30	.25
756	A253	60fr	multicolored	.80	.40
			Nos. 754-756 (3)	1.40	.90

Mission of the Sisters of St. Joseph of Cluny, Cent. A254

1986, Aug. 19 **Litho.** *Perf. 12½x13*

757 A254 230fr multicolored 2.75 1.25

A255

1986, Aug. 30 **Litho.** *Perf. 13½*

758	A255	40fr	multicolored	.45	.25
759	A255	60fr	multicolored	.55	.25
760	A255	100fr	multicolored	1.00	.35
			Nos. 758-760 (3)	2.00	.85

UNESCO intl. communications development program.

A256

1986, Sept. 15 **Litho.** *Perf. 13½*

761 A256 100fr multicolored .90 .30

Intl. Peace Year.

World Food Day A257

1986, Oct. 16

762	A257	75fr	Food staples	.80	.25
763	A257	120fr	Mother feeding child	1.25	.40

UN Child Survival Campaign A258

Mothers, children and pinwheels in various designs.

1986, Oct. 27

764	A258	15fr	multi, vert.	.25	.25
765	A258	30fr	multicolored	.25	.25
766	A258	70fr	multi, vert.	.70	.30
			Nos. 764-766 (3)	1.20	.80

A258a

1986, Dec. 5 **Litho.** *Perf. 12x12½*

766A A258a 100fr multicolored 1.50 .35

27th Soviet Communist Party congress.

A259

1987, Feb. 10 **Litho.** *Perf. 13½*

767	A259	30fr	multicolored	.25	.25
768	A259	45fr	multicolored	.45	.25
769	A259	75fr	multicolored	.70	.25
770	A259	120fr	multicolored	1.10	.35
			Nos. 767-770 (4)	2.50	1.10

Election of President Sassou-Nguesso, head of the Organization of African States.

Traditional Wedding A260

1987, Feb. 18 **Litho.** *Perf. 12½x13*

771	A260	5fr	multicolored	.25	.25
772	A260	15fr	multicolored	.25	.25
773	A260	20fr	multicolored	.25	.25
			Nos. 771-773 (3)	.75	.75

The Blue Lake — A261

1987, July 16 *Perf. 12½*
774 A261 5fr multicolored .25 .25
775 A261 15fr multicolored .25 .25
776 A261 75fr multicolored 1.00 .30
777 A261 120fr multicolored 1.25 .40
Nos. 774-777 (4) 2.75 1.20

Pres. Marien Ngouabi — A262

1987, July 16 *Perf. 13*
778 A262 75fr multicolored .75 .30
779 A262 120fr multicolored 1.25 .40

Tenth death anniv.

Congress of African Scientists — A263

1987, Sept. 10 *Perf. 13x12½*
780 A263 15fr multicolored .25 .25
781 A263 90fr multicolored .70 .30
782 A263 230fr multicolored 2.00 .80
Nos. 780-782 (3) 2.95 1.35

4th African Games, Nairobi — A264

1987, Oct. 30 *Perf. 12½*
783 A264 75fr multicolored .75 .40
784 A264 120fr multicolored 1.25 .60

Raoul Follereau (1903-1977), Philanthropist — A265

1987, Oct. 20 *Perf. 13½*
785 A265 120fr multicolored 1.50 .60

Cure leprosy.

FAO, 40th Anniv. — A266

1987, Nov. 17 *Perf. 12½*
786 A266 300fr multicolored 2.75 1.10

Anti-Apartheid Campaign A267

Nelson Mandela A268

Perf. 13½x15, 14½x15
1987, Sept. 21 **Litho.**
787 A267 60fr multicolored .60 .25
788 A268 240fr multicolored 2.40 .75

Natl. UNICEF Vaccination Campaign A269

30fr, Inoculating adults, horiz. 500fr, Inoculating children, horiz.

Perf. 13½x14½, 14½x13½
1987, Sept. 28
789 A269 30fr multicolored .25 .25
790 A269 45fr shown .50 .25
791 A269 500fr multicolored 5.25 2.00
Nos. 789-791 (3) 6.00 2.50

No. 791 is airmail.

Africa Fund — A270

1987, Sept. 28 *Perf. 13½x15*
792 A270 25fr multicolored .30 .25
793 A270 50fr multicolored .65 .25
794 A270 70fr multicolored .80 .25
Nos. 792-794 (3) 1.75 .75

Self-sufficiency in Food Production by the Year 2000 — A271

1987, Nov. 20 **Litho.** *Perf. 13½*
795 A271 20fr multicolored .25 .25
796 A271 55fr multicolored .60 .25
797 A271 100fr multicolored 1.10 .35
Nos. 795-797 (3) 1.95 .85

Simon Kimbangu (b. 1887), Founder of the Church of Christ on Earth — A272

75fr, Kimbangu, vert. 120fr, Kimbangu, parrot, vert. 240fr, Kimbanguist Church, Nkamba.

1987, Nov. 28 *Perf. 12½*
798 A272 75fr multicolored .70 .30
799 A272 120fr multicolored 1.10 .40
800 A272 240fr multicolored 2.75 1.00
a. Souvenir sheet of 3, #798-800 5.75 5.00
Nos. 798-800 (3) 4.55 1.70

October Revolution, Russia, 70th Anniv. — A273

Lenin inspecting revolutionary troops, Red Square, from an unspecified painting.

1988, Feb. 19 **Litho.** *Perf. 12½x12*
801 A273 75fr multicolored 2.10 .60
802 A273 120fr multicolored 3.00 1.00

African Writers Opposing Apartheid — A274

1988, Apr. 6 **Litho.** *Perf. 13½*
803 A274 15fr multicolored .25 .25
804 A274 60fr multicolored .50 .25
805 A274 75fr multicolored .80 .30
Nos. 803-805 (3) 1.55 .80

For overprint see No. 1157.

Intl. Fund for Agricultural Development (IFAD), 10th Anniv. — A275

1988, Apr. 30
806 A275 240fr multicolored 2.25 .85

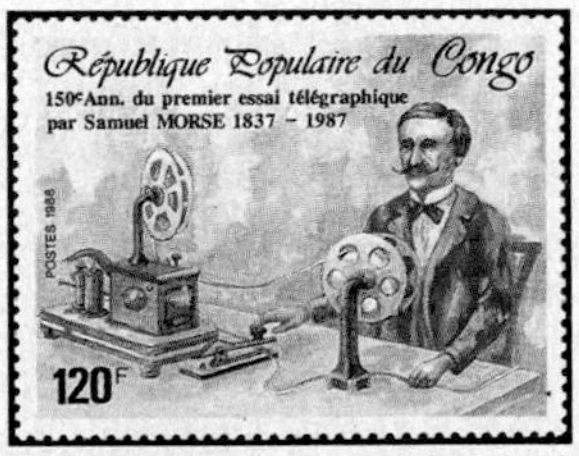

Invention of the Telegraph by Samuel Morse, 150th Anniv. (in 1987) — A276

1988, Apr. 28
807 A276 90fr Morse, vert. .90 .30
808 A276 120fr shown 1.10 .40

A277

5fr, Eucalyptus trees, Brazzaville. 10fr, Stop cutting down trees.

1988, Sept. 20 **Litho.** *Perf. 13½*
809 A277 5fr multicolored .30 .25
810 A277 10fr multicolored .50 .25

Fight against desertification.

A278

Campaigns: No. 812, Return to the Land Campaign (farming). 120fr, Self-sufficiency in food production.

1988, Aug. 12 **Litho.** *Perf. 13½*
811 A278 75fr shown .75 .30
812 A278 75fr multicolored .75 .30
813 A278 120fr multicolored .90 .40
Nos. 811-813 (3) 2.40 1.00

Congo Revolution, 25th anniv.

Yoro Fishing Village A279

1988, Sept. 1
814 A279 35fr shown .45 .25
815 A279 40fr Liberty Place .45 .25

Intl. Day for the Fight Against AIDS A280

75fr, Emblem. 180fr, Modified UN emblem, campaign emblem.

1988, Dec. 1 **Litho.** *Perf. 13½*
816 A280 60fr shown .45 .25
817 A280 75fr multicolored .70 .25
818 A280 180fr multicolored 1.75 .60
Nos. 816-818 (3) 2.90 1.10

Natl. Committee for the Fight Against AIDS and Evangelical Anglican Church of Congo anti-AIDS campaign.

February 5 Movement, 10th Anniv. A281

75fr, Rally. 120fr, Pres. Sassou-Nguesso, natl. achievements.

1989, Apr. 21 **Litho.** *Perf. 13½*
819 A281 75fr multicolored .75 .30
820 A281 120fr multicolored 1.00 .40

UN Declaration of Human Rights, 40th Anniv. (in 1988) A282

1989, May 19 *Perf. 13*
821 A282 120fr multicolored .90 .40
822 A282 350fr multicolored 2.75 1.20

Marien Nguabi, Founder of Congo Labor Party A282a

1989, July 31 Litho. *Perf. 12½x13*

822A A282a 240fr red & yellow 2.25 .75

Red Cross and Red Crescent Societies, 125th Annivs. A283

120fr, Dunant, emblem, Congo Red Cross.

1989, Sept. 19 Litho. *Perf. 13*

823 A283 75fr shown 1.20 .40
824 A283 120fr multicolored 1.40 .65

No. 824 is airmail.

Organization of African Unity, 25th Anniv. — A284

1989, Oct. 19 Litho. *Perf. 12½*

825 A284 120fr multicolored 1.10 .40

African Development Bank, 25th Anniv. — A285

1989, Dec. 22 Litho. *Perf. 12½x13*

826 A285 75fr multicolored .80 .35
827 A285 120fr multicolored 1.10 .40

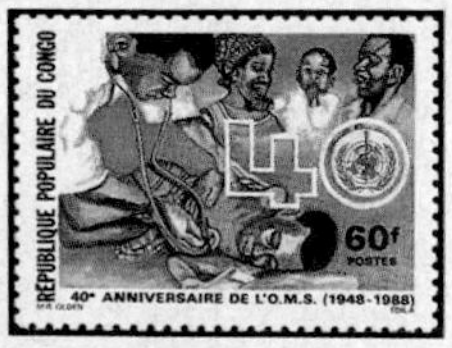

WHO, 40th Anniv. (in 1988) A286

1989, Dec. 28 Litho. *Perf. 12½*

828 A286 60fr shown .75 .35
829 A286 75fr Blood donation, vert. .90 .50

See Nos. 846-847 for overprints.

Congo Labor Party (PCT), 20th Anniv. — A287

1989, Dec. 22 Litho. *Perf. 13x12½*

830 A287 75fr multicolored .75 .35
831 A287 120fr multicolored 1.10 .40

Cacti A288

35fr, Opuntia phaeacantha discata. 40fr, Opuntia ficus indica. 60fr, Opuntia erinacea. 75fr, Opuntia rufida. 120fr, Opuntia leptocaulis.

220fr, Opuntia compresa.

Perf. 12½x13, 13x12½

1989, Nov. 22

832 A288 35fr multicolored .35 .25
833 A288 40fr multicolored .50 .25
834 A288 60fr multicolored .90 .25
835 A288 75fr multicolored 1.25 .30
836 A288 120fr multicolored 1.75 .45
Nos. 832-836 (5) 4.75 1.50

Souvenir Sheet

Perf. 12½

837 A288 220fr multicolored 5.00 2.10

Nos. 832-833, 835 and 837 vert. No. 837 contains one 32x40mm stamp.

1992 Winter Olympics, Albertville A289

1989, Dec. 22 *Perf. 12½*

838 A289 75fr Ice dancing .60 .25
839 A289 80fr Nordic skiiing .60 .30
840 A289 100fr Speed skating .90 .35
841 A289 120fr Luge 1.10 .45
842 A289 200fr Alpine skiing 1.75 .70
843 A289 240fr Ice hockey 2.25 .85
844 A289 400fr Ski jumping 3.25 1.40
Nos. 838-844 (7) 10.45 4.30

Souvenir Sheet

Perf. 13

845 A289 500fr Bobsled 4.50 2.40

No. 845 contains one 32x40mm stamp.

Nos. 828-829 Ovptd. in 3 or 5 Lines

1989, Dec. 28 *Perf. 12½*

846 A286 60fr multicolored .75 .45
847 A286 75fr multicolored .90 .60

Health care for everyone.

Intl. Literacy Year — A290

1990, June 26 Litho. *Perf. 13½*

848 A290 75fr bl, blk & yel .80 .35

Birds A291

Designs: 25fr, Tourterelle des bois. 50fr, Fauvette pitchou, vert. 70fr, Faucon crecerelle, vert. 150fr, Perroquet gris, vert.

1990, July 10

849 A291 25fr multicolored .35 .25
850 A291 50fr multicolored .70 .30
851 A291 70fr multicolored 1.10 .55
852 A291 150fr multicolored 2.10 1.25
Nos. 849-852 (4) 4.25 2.35

Dance Masks — A292

1990, July 24 *Perf. 13*

853 A292 120fr Mondo 1.10 .40
854 A292 360fr Bapunu 3.50 1.25
855 A292 400fr Kwele 4.00 1.50
Nos. 853-855 (3) 8.60 3.15

For overprints see Nos. 1172, 1173.

Flowering Plants — A293

30fr, Tournesol (sunflower). 45fr, Cassia alata, horiz. 75fr, Oeillette (opium poppy). 90fr, Acalypha sanderil.

1990, Sept. 15 Litho. *Perf. 12½*

856 A293 30fr multicolored .25 .25
857 A293 45fr multicolored .45 .25
858 A293 75fr multicolored .70 .25
859 A293 90fr multicolored 1.00 .35
Nos. 856-859 (4) 2.40 1.10

1992 Summer Olympics, Barcelona — A294

100fr, Street scene, vert. 200fr, Sailing, diff. 240fr, Marketplace. 350fr, Harbor. 500fr, Monument, vert.

750fr, Cathedral, vert.

1990, June 28 Litho. *Perf. 13½*

860 A294 100fr multicolored .70 .30
861 A294 150fr shown .95 .35
862 A294 200fr multicolored 1.20 .40
863 A294 240fr multicolored 1.50 .55
864 A294 350fr multicolored 2.40 .75
865 A294 500fr multicolored 3.25 .90
Nos. 860-865 (6) 10.00 3.25

Souvenir Sheet

866 A294 750fr multicolored 5.50 3.50

Nos. 864-865 airmail. Nos. 860-865 exist in miniature sheets of 1.

Royal Necklaces A295

1990, Aug. 18 Litho. *Perf. 13½*

867 A295 75fr shown .75 .35
868 A295 100fr Necklace, diff. 1.00 .60

Boy Scouts Observing Nature A296

Scout: 35fr, Photographing butterfly, Euphaedra eusimoides. 40fr, Picking mushrooms, Armillaria mellea. 75fr, Drawing butterfly, Palla decius. 80fr, Using magnifying glass, Kallima ansorgei. 500fr, Using microscope, Cortinarius speciosissimus. 600fr, Feeding butterfly, Graphium illyris. No. 874B, Photographing butterfly, Berberia plistonax, horiz. 750fr, Photographing mushrooms, Volvariella bombycina. No. 875A, Examining mushrooms, Coprinus domesticus.

1991, June 8 Litho. *Perf. 13½*

869 A296 35fr multicolored .50 .25
870 A296 40fr multicolored .60 .25
871 A296 75fr multicolored .80 .25
872 A296 80fr multicolored 1.00 .25
873 A296 500fr multicolored 4.50 1.25
874 A296 600fr multicolored 4.50 1.25
a. Min. sheet of 4, #869, 871-872, 874 8.50 3.75
Nos. 869-874 (6) 11.90 3.50

Litho. & Embossed

874B A296 1500fr gold & multi *32.50* —

Souvenir Sheets

Litho.

875 A296 750fr multicolored 5.25 2.25

Litho. & Embossed

875A A296 1500fr gold & multi 14.00 —

Nos. 869-874 exist in souvenir sheets of 1. Nos. 873-875 are airmail.

Medicinal Plants — A297

Designs: 15fr, Ocimum viride. 20fr, Kalanchoe pinnata, vert. 30fr, Euphorbia hirta. 60fr, Catharanthus roseus, vert. 75fr, Bidens pilosa, vert. 100fr, Brillantaisia patula, vert. 120fr, Cassia occidentalis, vert.

1991, Jan. 30 Litho. *Perf. 11½*

876	A297	15fr multicolored	.30	.25
877	A297	20fr multicolored	.30	.25
878	A297	30fr multicolored	.30	.25
879	A297	60fr multicolored	.60	.25
880	A297	75fr multicolored	.80	.35
881	A297	100fr multicolored	1.20	.55
882	A297	120fr multicolored	1.25	.75
		Nos. 876-882 (7)	4.75	2.65

Mushrooms A298

30fr, Amanita rubescens. 45fr, Catathelasma imperiale. 75fr, Amanita caesarea. 90fr, Boletus regius. 120fr, Pluteus cervinus. 150fr, Boletus chrysenteron. 200fr, Agaricus arvensis.
350fr, Boletus versipellis, horiz.

1991, Mar. 25 Litho. *Perf. 13*

883	A298	30fr multi	.35	.25
883A	A298	45fr multi	.50	.25
883B	A298	75fr multi	.90	.25
883C	A298	90fr multi	1.10	.25
883D	A298	120fr multi	1.35	.40
883E	A298	150fr multi	1.75	.60
883F	A298	200fr multi	2.50	.75
		Nos. 883-883F (7)	8.45	2.75

Souvenir Sheet

Perf. 12½

883G	A298	350fr multi	8.00	3.00

No. 883G contains one 40x32mm stamp.

Trains — A298a

Designs: 60fr, Dr-16, Finland. 75fr, TGV, France. 120fr, S350, Italy. 200fr, DE24000, Turkey. 250fr, DE1024, Germany.

1991, Apr. 10 Litho. *Perf. 12½x12¼*

883H	A298a	60fr multi	.65	.25
883I	A298a	75fr multi	.70	.30
883J	A298a	120fr multi	1.25	.45
883K	A298a	200fr multi	2.25	.75
883L	A298a	250fr multi	3.25	1.00

Dated 1990.

African Tourism Year — A299

1991, Apr. 15 Litho. *Perf. 13½*

884	A299	75fr shown	.80	.35
885	A299	120fr Zebra, map	1.20	.60

Allegory of New Republic — A300

1991, May 13 Litho. *Perf. 13*

888	A300	15fr blue	.25	.25
889	A300	30fr brt grn	.25	.25
890	A300	60fr org yel	.40	.25
891	A300	75fr brt pink	.55	.30
892	A300	120fr dk brown	1.00	.45
		Nos. 888-892 (5)	2.45	1.50

Trans-Siberian Railroad, Cent. — A301

1991, June 6 Litho. *Perf. 13*

899	A301	120fr Map	1.50	.50
900	A301	240fr Map, train	3.00	1.20

Telecom 91 — A302

1991, June 29 Litho. *Perf. 13*

901	A302	75fr multicolored	.75	.30
902	A302	120fr multi, vert.	1.25	.60

6th World Forum and Exposition on Telecommunications, Geneva, Switzerland.

Insects — A303

1991, July 2 *Perf. 12½*

903	A303	75fr Peanut beetle	1.00	.25
904	A303	120fr Centaur, horiz.	1.40	.45
905	A303	200fr Coffee beetle	2.25	.75
906	A303	300fr Goliath beetle	3.50	1.50
		Nos. 903-906 (4)	8.15	2.95

Water conservation A304

1991, July 16 Litho. *Perf. 12½*

907	A304	75fr multicolored	.80	.35

Amnesty Intl., 30th Anniv. A305

Designs: 40fr, Candle, sun, vert. 75fr, "30," broken chains, vert.

1991, Aug. 13 *Perf. 13½*

908	A305	40fr multicolored	.35	.25
909	A305	75fr multicolored	.60	.25
910	A305	80fr multicolored	.70	.35
		Nos. 908-910 (3)	1.65	.85

Congo Postage Stamps, Cent. — A306

75fr, Similar to French Congo #1. 120fr, Similar to French Congo #35. 240fr, Similar to Congo Republic #89. 500fr, Similar to French Congo #1, 35 and Congo Republic #89.

Litho. & Engr.

1991, Aug. *Perf. 13x13½*

911	A306	75fr beige & dk grn	.80	.30
912	A306	120fr beige, dk grn & brn	1.10	.45
913	A306	240fr multicolored	2.25	1.10
914	A306	500fr multicolored	4.50	2.00
a.		Strip of 4, #911-914	10.00	9.00

Ducks A307

75fr, Anas acuta. 120fr, Somateria mollissima, vert. 200fr, Anas clypeata, vert. 240fr, Anas platyrhynchos.

1991, Aug. 8 Litho. *Perf. 12½*

915	A307	75fr multicolored	1.25	.30
916	A307	120fr multicolored	1.50	.45
917	A307	200fr multicolored	2.00	.75
918	A307	240fr multicolored	3.50	1.00
		Nos. 915-918 (4)	8.25	2.50

Automobiles and Space — A308

Designs: 35fr, Ferrari 512S by Pininfarina. 40fr, Vincenzo Lancia, Lancia Stratos by Bertone. 75fr, Maybach Zeppelin type 12, Wilhelm Maybach. 80fr, Mars Observer, 1992. 500fr, Magellan probe surveying Venus. 600fr, Magnification of Sun, Ulysses probe. 750fr, Crew of Apollo 11.

1991, Aug. 23 Litho. *Perf. 13½*

919	A308	35fr multicolored	.30	.25
920	A308	40fr multicolored	.30	.25
921	A308	75fr multicolored	.60	.30
922	A308	80fr multicolored	.65	.30
923	A308	500fr multicolored	4.25	2.25
924	A308	600fr multicolored	5.00	2.50
		Nos. 919-924 (6)	11.10	5.85

Souvenir Sheet

925	A308	750fr multicolored	6.50	3.50

Nos. 923-925 are airmail. No. 925 contains one 60x42mm stamp. Nos. 919-921 exist in souvenir sheets of 1.

Butterflies A309

75fr, Petit bleu. 120fr, Charaxe. 240fr, Papillon feuille, vert. 300fr, Papillon de l'oranger, vert.

1991, Aug. 31 *Perf. 11½*

926	A309	75fr multi	1.20	.30
927	A309	120fr multi	1.50	.50
928	A309	240fr multi	2.10	.80
929	A309	300fr multi	3.75	1.00
		Nos. 926-929 (4)	8.55	2.60

For overprints see Nos. 1156, 1165.

Celebrities and Organizations — A310

Designs: 100fr, Bo Jackson, baseball and football player. 150fr, Nick Faldo, golfer. 200fr, Rickey Henderson, Barry Bonds, baseball players. 240fr, Garry Kasparov, World Chess Champion. 300fr, Starving child, Lions and Rotary Clubs emblems. 350fr, Wolfgang Amadeus Mozart. 400fr, De Gaulle, Churchill. 500fr, Jean-Henri Dunant, founder of Red Cross. 750fr, De Gaulle, vert.

1991, Sept. 2 *Perf. 13½*

930	A310	100fr multicolored	1.00	.40
931	A310	150fr multicolored	1.40	.60
932	A310	200fr multicolored	2.00	.80
933	A310	240fr multicolored	2.75	.95
934	A310	300fr multicolored	3.00	1.25
935	A310	350fr multicolored	3.75	1.40
936	A310	400fr multicolored	4.50	1.60
937	A310	500fr multicolored	5.00	2.00
		Nos. 930-937 (8)	23.40	9.00

Souvenir Sheet

938	A310	750fr multicolored	8.00	3.50

Nos. 936-938 are airmail. No. 938 contains one 35x50mm stamp.
For overprint, see No. 1199.

Gen. Charles de Gaulle in Africa — A311

120fr, De Gaulle, Free French flag, vert. 240fr, De Gaulle, Appeal of Brazzaville, 1940.

1991, Sept. 2 *Perf. 13½x13, 13x13½*

939	A311	75fr multicolored	.90	.40
940	A311	120fr multicolored	1.25	.60
941	A311	240fr multicolored	2.40	1.20
		Nos. 939-941 (3)	4.55	2.20

A312

Paintings — A313

1991, Oct. 12 *Perf. 11½*

942	A312	75fr multicolored	.75	.35
943	A313	120fr multicolored	1.10	.45

Discovery of America, 500th Anniv. (in 1992) — A314

20fr, Portrait of Christopher Columbus by Sebastian Del Pombo. 35fr, Portrait of Columbus. 40fr, Portrait of Columbus facing right. 55fr, Santa Maria. 75fr, Nina. 150fr, Pinta. 200fr, Arms & signature of Columbus.

1991, May 30 ***Perf. 13***

944	A314	20fr multicolored	.40	.25
945	A314	35fr multicolored	.40	.25
946	A314	40fr multicolored	.50	.35
947	A314	55fr multicolored	.65	.35
948	A314	75fr multicolored	.95	.35
949	A314	150fr multicolored	1.75	.85
950	A314	200fr multicolored	2.25	1.00
		Nos. 944-950 (7)	6.90	3.40

Primates A315

30fr, Cercopithecus diana. 45fr, Pan troglodytes. 60fr, Theropithecus gelada. 75fr, Papio hamadryas. 90fr, Macaca nemestrina. 120fr, Gorilla gorilla. 240fr, Mandrillus sphinx.
250fr, Gorilla gorilla.

1991, Dec. 13 **Litho.** ***Perf. 13***

951	A315	30fr multicolored	.35	.25
952	A315	45fr multicolored	.45	.25
953	A315	60fr multicolored	.85	.25
954	A315	75fr multicolored	1.00	.35
955	A315	90fr multicolored	1.20	.50
956	A315	120fr multicolored	1.60	.50
957	A315	240fr multicolored	3.50	.75
		Nos. 951-957 (7)	8.95	2.85

Souvenir Sheet

958	A315	250fr multicolored	4.25	1.50

Nos. 953-958 are vert.

Anniversaries and Events A316

Designs: 50fr, Launching of Sputnik II with dog, Laika, 1957. 75fr, Mahatma Gandhi and Martin Luther King, Jr. 1964. 120fr, Launching of Meteosat and ERS-1 over Europe and Africa. 240fr, Maybach Zeppelin automobile and Ferdinand von Zeppelin, 75th death anniversary. 300fr, Konrad Adenauer, 25th death anniversary and opening of the Brandenburg Gate, 1989. 500fr, Pope John Paul II's visit to Africa. 600fr, Elvis Presley, American entertainer.

1992, Feb. 4 **Litho.** ***Perf. 13½***

959	A316	50fr multicolored	.75	.25
960	A316	75fr multicolored	.75	.25
961	A316	120fr multicolored	1.25	.45
962	A316	240fr multicolored	2.75	.85
963	A316	300fr multicolored	2.50	.80
964	A316	500fr multicolored	5.25	1.40
a.		Souvenir sheet of 3, #960, 963-964	11.50	5.75
		Nos. 959-964 (6)	13.25	4.00

Souvenir Sheet

965	A316	600fr multicolored	6.00	2.40

Nos. 959-964 exist in souvenir sheets of 1.
Nos. 962, 964-965 are airmail.
For Overprint, see No. 1166.

Explorers A317

Genoa '92: 75fr, Juan de la Cosa, nautical chart. 95fr, Martin Alonso Pinzon, astrolabe. 120fr, Alonso de Ojeda, hour glass. 200fr, Vicente Yanez Pinzon, sun dial. 250fr, Bartholomew Columbus, quadrant.
400fr, Columbus, flag, horiz.

1992, Oct. 21 **Litho.** ***Perf. 13***

966	A317	75fr multicolored	1.00	.30
967	A317	95fr multicolored	1.20	.30
968	A317	120fr multicolored	1.90	.30
969	A317	200fr multicolored	2.75	.40
970	A317	250fr multicolored	3.75	.50
		Nos. 966-970 (5)	10.60	1.80

Souvenir Sheet

971	A317	400fr multi	14.00	14.00

Birds — A318

Designs: 60fr, Sagittarius serpentarius. 75fr, Ephippiorhynchus senegalensis. 120fr, Bugeranus carunculatus. 200fr, Ardea melanocephala. 250fr, Phoenicopterus ruber roseus.
400fr, Balearica regulorum.

1992, Oct. 21

972	A318	60fr multicolored	.70	.25
973	A318	75fr multicolored	.80	.25
974	A318	120fr multicolored	1.10	.30
975	A318	200fr multicolored	2.00	.40
976	A318	250fr multicolored	2.75	.50
		Nos. 972-976 (5)	7.35	1.70

Souvenir Sheet

977	A318	400fr multicolored	4.00	1.00

For overprint, see No. 1191.

Wild Cats — A319

1992, Nov. 21 **Litho.** ***Perf. 13***

978	A319	45fr Panthera leo	.50	.50
979	A319	60fr Panthera tigris	.60	.60
980	A319	75fr Lynx lynx	.70	.70
981	A319	95fr Caracal caracal	.80	.80
982	A319	250fr Leopardus pardalis	2.25	2.25
		Nos. 978-982 (5)	4.85	4.85

Souvenir Sheet

983	A319	400fr Acinonyx jubatus	4.50	1.75

No. 983 contains one 32x40mm stamp.

1992 Winter Olympics, Albertville — A320

Gold medalists: 150fr, N. Mishkutyonok, A. Dmitriev, pairs figure skating, Unified team. 200fr, I. Appelt, H. Winkler, G. Haldacher, T. Schroll, 4-man bobsled, Austria. 500fr, Gunda Niemann, speed skating, Germany. 600fr, Bjorn Daehlie, cross-country skiing, Norway. 750fr, Alberto Tomba, giant slalom, Italy.

1992, Dec. 21 **Litho.** ***Perf. 13½***

984	A320	150fr multicolored	1.25	.40
985	A320	200fr multicolored	1.75	.50
986	A320	500fr multicolored	4.00	1.10
987	A320	600fr multicolored	6.00	1.00
		Nos. 984-987 (4)	13.00	3.00

Souvenir Sheet

988	A320	750fr multicolored	7.00	2.00

Nos. 986-988 are airmail. No. 988 contains one 35x50mm stamp. Name on No. 987 spelled incorrectly.

1992 Summer Olympics, Barcelona A321

Barcelona landmarks, Olympic event: 75fr, Steeple of La Sagrada Familia, baseball. 100fr, The Muse, Palace of Music, running. 150fr, Cupola interior, long jump. 200fr, St. Paul Hospital, pole vault. 400fr, Sculpture, by Miro, shot put. 500fr, Galley, Maritime Museum, table tennis. 750fr, La Sagrada Familia, tennis.

1992, Dec. 21

989	A321	75fr multicolored	.80	.25
990	A321	100fr multicolored	1.00	.30
991	A321	150fr multicolored	1.25	.40
992	A321	200fr multicolored	2.00	.65
993	A321	400fr multicolored	3.50	.65
994	A321	500fr multicolored	4.50	1.00
		Nos. 989-994 (6)	13.05	3.25

Souvenir Sheet

995	A321	750fr multicolored	7.00	1.50

Nos. 993-995 are airmail.

Christmas A321a

Paintings: 95fr, The Madonna of the Grand Duke, by Raphael. 120fr, Virgin and Child, by Francesco Mazzo. 200fr, The Madonna with a Book, by Botticelli. 250fr, The Madonna Carondelet, by Fra Bartolommeo. 400fr, Madonna and Child, by Raphael.

1992, Dec. 20 **Litho.** ***Perf. 12½***

995A	A321a	95fr multicolored	1.25	.30
995B	A321a	120fr multicolored	—	—
995C	A321a	200fr multicolored	2.75	.75
995D	A321a	250fr multicolored	3.25	1.25
		Nos. 995A-995D (4)	7.25	2.30

Souvenir Sheet

995E	A321a	400fr multicolored	4.50	1.90

Nos. 995A-995E were not available until late 1993.
For overprint, see No. 1192.

Birds of Prey — A322

1993, Jan. 15 **Litho.** ***Perf. 12½x13***

996	A322	45fr Charognard	.65	.25
997	A322	75fr Vulture	2.00	.30
998	A322	120fr Eagle	2.50	.65
		Nos. 996-998 (3)	5.15	1.20

A323

Traditional ceramics.

1993, Dec. 21 **Litho.** ***Perf. 13½***

999	A323	45fr Liloko	.60	.30
1000	A323	75fr Mbeya	1.20	.50
1001	A323	120fr Jug with ladles, Mbeya	1.75	.85
		Nos. 999-1001 (3)	3.55	1.65

1994 World Cup Soccer Championships, United States — A324

Design: 75fr, Player stretching to kick ball. 95fr, Goalie diving to stop ball. 120fr, Player stretching to kick ball. 200fr, Player kicking. 250fr, Goalie catching ball. 400fr, Players competing for ball.

1993, Jan. 15 **Litho.** ***Perf. 12¾***

1002	A324	75fr multi	1.40	.80
1003	A324	95fr multi	1.45	1.10
1004	A324	120fr multi	2.40	1.40
1005	A324	200fr multi	3.50	2.10
1006	A324	250fr multi	4.00	2.75
		Nos. 1002-1006 (5)	12.75	8.15

Souvenir Sheet

Perf. 12½

1007	A324	400fr multi	6.00	4.00

No. 1007 contains one 40x32mm stamp.

Wild Animals A325

Designs: 60fr, Damaliscus lunatus. 75fr, Gazella granti. 95fr, Equus quagga. 120fr, Panthera pardus. 200fr, Syncerus caffer. 250fr, Hippopotamus ampibius. 300fr, Necrosyrtes monachu. 350fr, Panthera leo.

1993, Feb. 20 **Litho.** ***Perf. 13***

1008	A325	60fr multicolored	.75	.25
1009	A325	75fr multicolored	1.25	.25
1010	A325	95fr multicolored	1.40	.30
1011	A325	120fr multicolored	1.90	.30
1012	A325	200fr multicolored	3.25	.40
1013	A325	250fr multicolored	4.00	.40
1014	A325	300fr multicolored	4.75	.40
1015	A325	350fr multicolored	5.50	.75
a.		Sheet of 8, #1008-1015	20.00	20.00
		Nos. 1008-1015 (8)	22.80	3.05

No. 1015a is a continuous design.

Wild Flowers — A326

Designs: 75fr, Hibiscus schizopetalus. 95fr, Pentas lanceolata. 120fr, Ricinus communis. 200fr, Delonix regia. 250fr, Stapelia gigantea.

1993, May 20 Litho. *Perf. 12½*

1016	A326	75fr multicolored	.85	.30
1017	A326	95fr multicolored	1.10	.40
1018	A326	120fr multicolored	2.25	.50
1019	A326	200fr multicolored	3.75	1.00
1020	A326	250fr multicolored	4.50	1.60
		Nos. 1016-1020 (5)	12.45	3.80

Deep Sea Submersibles A327

1993, June 25

1021	A327	75fr Transport PC-1202	1.25	.50
1022	A327	95fr J. Sea Link 1	1.60	.75
1023	A327	120fr Nemo	2.00	1.00
1024	A327	200fr Robot	3.00	1.50
1025	A327	250fr Alvin	3.75	2.00
		Nos. 1021-1025 (5)	11.60	5.75

Souvenir Sheet

1026	A327	400fr Star III	8.00	4.00

No. 1026 contains one 32x40mm stamp.

1996 Summer Olympic Games, Atlanta A329

Designs: 50fr, Equestrian. 75fr, Cycling. 120fr, Sailing. 240fr, shown. 300fr, Hurdles. 500fr, Women's basketball. 750fr, Running.

1993, Apr. 26 Litho. *Perf. 13½*

1030-1035	A329	Set of 6	15.00	4.00
1035a		Sheet of 6, #1030-1035	17.50	6.00

Souvenir Sheet

1036	A329	750fr multicolored	6.50	1.50

Nos. 1030-1036 exist imperf. Nos. 1030-1035 exist in souvenir sheets of 1.

Brasiliana '93 — A330

Birds: 75fr, Vidua whydah. 95fr, Vidua regia. 120fr, Steganura paradisea. 200fr, Vidua macroura. 250fr, Anthreptes platura.
400fr, Coliuspasser macrourus, horiz.

1993, July 15 Litho. *Perf. 12x12½*

1037-1041	A330	Set of 5	11.00	11.00

Souvenir Sheet

1042	A330	400fr multicolored	11.00	11.00

Prehistoric Animals — A331

75fr, Ichthyostega. 95fr, Archaeopteryx. 120fr, Brachiosaurus. 200fr, Tyrannosaurus. 250fr, Pteranodon, vert.
400fr, Brontosaurus.

1993, Aug. 20 Litho. *Perf. 13*

1043	A331	75fr multicolored	1.00	1.00
1044	A331	95fr multicolored	1.25	1.25
1045	A331	120fr multicolored	1.60	1.60
1046	A331	200fr multicolored	2.50	2.50
1047	A331	250fr multicolored	3.50	3.50
		Nos. 1043-1047 (5)	9.85	9.85

Souvenir Sheet

1048	A331	400fr multicolored	6.50	6.50

No. 1048 contains one 32x40mm stamp.

Powered Flight, 90th Anniv. — A332

Designs: 75fr, Wilbur Wright, Model B airplane, vert. 95fr, Orville Wright and Model B biplane, vert. 120fr, First flight by Orville Wright. 200fr, Flight at Kitty Hawk. 250fr, Wright Brothers and airplane.

Perf. 12¼x12½, 12½x12¼

1993, Dec. 17 Litho.

1049	A332	75fr multi	.65	.65
1050	A332	95fr multi	.85	.85
1051	A332	120fr multi	.95	.95
1052	A332	200fr multi	1.75	1.75
1053	A332	250fr multi	2.25	2.25
		Nos. 1049-1053 (5)	6.45	6.45

Evolution of the Elephant A333

1994, June 20 Litho. *Perf. 12½*

1054	A333	25fr Palaeomastodon	.75	.30
1055	A333	45fr Mammut	1.25	.50
1056	A333	50fr Amebelodon	1.45	.50
1057	A333	75fr Platybelodon	2.25	.80
1058	A333	120fr Mammuthus	3.50	1.40
		Nos. 1054-1058 (5)	9.20	3.50

Protection of Nature — A335

Designs: 50fr, Choeropsis liberiensis. 90fr, Hyemoschus aquaticus. 205fr, Taurotragus euryceros, vert. 300fr, Redunca redunca, vert.

1994, Aug. 27 Litho. *Perf. 12½*

1063	A335	50fr multicolored	.50	.35
1064	A335	90fr multicolored	.80	.35
1065	A335	205fr multicolored	1.90	1.10
1066	A335	300fr multicolored	2.75	1.60
		Nos. 1063-1066 (4)	5.95	3.40

For overprint see No. 1167.

Seaplanes — A336

Designs: 30fr, Cant Z-505, Italy. 45fr, Martin Mariner PBM-3, US. No. 1069, E-59, Russia. No. 1070, Short Sunderland, Great Britain. No. 1071, Martin Mars XPB2M-1, US.
400fr, Boeing 314, US.

1994, Sept. 2 Litho. *Perf. 12½*

1067	A336	30fr multicolored	.40	.25
1068	A336	45fr multicolored	.50	.25
1069	A336	90fr multicolored	1.00	.40
1070	A336	90fr multicolored	1.00	.40
1071	A336	90fr multicolored	1.00	.40
		Nos. 1067-1071 (5)	3.90	1.70

Souvenir Sheet

1071A	A336	400fr multicolored	5.00	2.50

No. 1071A contains one 40x32mm stamp.

Intl. Year of the Family — A337

205fr, African map, child. 300fr, Family, native huts.

1995, Jan. 28 Litho. *Perf. 12½*

1072	A337	90fr shown	.75	.40
1073	A337	205fr multicolored	1.60	1.00
1074	A337	300fr multicolored	2.50	1.50
		Nos. 1072-1074 (3)	4.85	2.90

For overprint see No. 1168.

Insects — A338

1994, July 24 Litho. *Perf. 12½*

1075	A338	90fr Tarantula	1.90	.40
1076	A338	205fr Spider	4.50	1.10
1077	A338	240fr Ladybug	5.00	1.25
		Nos. 1075-1077 (3)	11.40	2.75

Souvenir Sheet

1078	A338	400fr Bee	4.75	2.00

Costumes — A338a

1995 Litho. *Perf. 12¾x12½*

1078A	A338a	90fr M'Bochi	.90	.60
1078B	A338a	205fr Téké	1.50	.90
1078C	A338a	500fr Loango	3.50	1.50
		Nos. 1078A-1078C (3)	5.90	3.00

Rotary Intl., 90th Anniv. A339

Designs: 90fr, Polio victim. No. 1080, Playing ball with children. No. 1081, Children with food. 300fr, Delivering polio vaccine.
1500fr, Paul Harris, Rotary emblem.

1996, Feb. 6 Litho. *Perf. 14*

1079	A339	90fr multicolored	.60	.25
1080	A339	205fr multicolored	1.25	.50
1081	A339	205fr multicolored	1.25	.50
1082	A339	300fr multicolored	1.60	.60
		Nos. 1079-1082 (4)	4.70	1.85

Souvenir Sheet

1083	A339	1500fr multicolored	5.00	3.25

For overprint, see Mo. 1201.

18th World Scout Jamboree, The Netherlands — A340

Designs: No. 1084, Handshake. No. 1085, Scout helping another with arm sling. 205fr, Saving life in water. 300fr, Lord Baden-Powell.
1000fr, Scout salute.

1996, Feb. 6 Litho. *Perf. 14*

1084	A340	90fr multicolored	.60	.25
1085	A340	90fr multicolored	.60	.25
1086	A340	205fr multicolored	1.25	.40
1087	A340	300fr multicolored	1.75	.50
		Nos. 1084-1087 (4)	4.20	1.40

Souvenir Sheet

1088	A340	1000fr multicolored	4.50	2.10

1998 World Cup Soccer Tournament A340a

Various players. Denominations: 90fr, 150fr, 205fr, 300fr, 400fr, 500fr.

1996 Litho. *Perf. 12¾*

1088A-1088F	A340a	Set of 6	5.00	5.00

Souvenir Sheet

Perf. 13¼x13

1088G	A340a	1000fr Player's legs	3.00	3.00

No. 1088G contains one 40x31mm stamp.

Antique Automobiles — A341

90fr, 1936 Armstrong Siddeley Twelve. 150fr, 1935 Aston Martin Mark II. 205fr, 1938 Morris 8. 300fr, 1955-62 MG Series MGA. 400fr, 1932 SS1. 500fr, 1938 Alvis 25 SB.

1996, Apr. 30 Litho. *Perf. 12½x12*

1089	A341	90fr multicolored	.40	.25
1090	A341	150fr multicolored	.65	.40
1091	A341	205fr multicolored	.85	.50
1092	A341	300fr multicolored	1.25	.75
1093	A341	400fr multicolored	1.75	1.00
1094	A341	500fr multicolored	2.10	1.25
		Nos. 1089-1094 (6)	7.00	4.15

Domestic Cats — A342

90fr, Persian. 150fr, Siamese. 205fr, Norwegian forest. 300fr, Exotic shorthair. 400fr, Maine coon. 500fr, Red abyssinian.
1000fr, Turkish Angora.

1996, Mar. 10 *Perf. 13x12½*

1095	A342	90fr multicolored	.40	.25
1096	A342	150fr multicolored	.65	.40
1097	A342	205fr multicolored	.90	.50
1098	A342	300fr multicolored	1.35	.75
1099	A342	400fr multicolored	1.75	1.00
1100	A342	500fr multicolored	2.25	1.25
		Nos. 1095-1100 (6)	7.30	4.15

Souvenir Sheet

1101	A342	1000fr multicolored	3.00	2.50

No. 1101 contains one 32x40mm stamp.

1996 Summer Olympic Games, Atlanta A343

1996 *Perf. 13x12½, 12½x13*

1102	A343	90fr Fencing, vert.	.50	.25
1103	A343	150fr Archery, vert.	.80	.40
1104	A343	205fr Basketball, vert.	1.10	.55
1105	A343	300fr Baseball, vert.	1.60	.80
1106	A343	400fr Volleyball	2.25	1.10
1107	A343	500fr 2-man kayak	2.50	1.25
		Nos. 1102-1107 (6)	8.75	4.35

Souvenir Sheet

1108	A343	1000fr Judo, vert.	5.25	2.50

No. 1108 contains one 32x40mm stamp.

Flowers — A344

Designs: 90fr, Nerium oleander. 150fr, Eucaliptus globulus. 205fr, Centaurea cyanus. 300fr, Coffea arabica. 400fr, Hibiscus sabdariffa. 500fr, Cassia angustifolia.

1996, May 10 *Perf. 12½*

1109	A344	90fr multicolored	.40	.25
1110	A344	150fr multicolored	.65	.40
1111	A344	205fr multicolored	.90	.55
1112	A344	300fr multicolored	1.25	.80
1113	A344	400fr multicolored	1.75	1.10
1114	A344	500fr multicolored	2.00	1.25
		Nos. 1109-1114 (6)	6.95	4.35

Mother Carrying Baby — A345

1996 **Litho.** *Perf. 13*

1115	A345	40fr blue	*4.00*	*2.00*
1116	A345	50fr violet brown	*5.00*	*2.50*
1117	A345	90fr orange	*9.00*	*4.50*
1118	A345	100fr green blue	*10.00*	*5.00*
1119	A345	115fr gray	*11.00*	*5.50*
1120	A345	205fr brown	*20.00*	*10.00*
		Nos. 1115-1120 (6)	*59.00*	*29.50*

It has been stated that this set was not issued.
See Nos. 1145-1150.
For overprints, see Nos. 1159, 1185A.

A346

1996, Aug. 31 **Litho.** *Perf. 13½*

1121	A346	90fr orange & multi	.50	.30
1122	A346	205fr green & multi	1.25	.75

Investiture of Pres. Pascal Lissouba, 4th anniv.

Owls — A347

1996, Mar. 29 *Perf. 14½*

1123	A347	90fr Tyto alba	.70	.25
1124	A347	205fr Bubo poensis	1.50	.50
1125	A347	300fr Scotopelia peli	2.40	.90
1126	A347	500fr Asio capensis	3.50	1.50
		Nos. 1123-1126 (4)	8.10	3.15

Military Aircraft — A348

Designs: 90fr, Vought-Sikorsky Vindicator SB2U-1. 150fr, Grumman Wildcat F4F-3. 205fr, North American SNJ-2. 300fr, Brewster Bermuda. 400fr, Blackburn Skua 1. 500fr, Mitsubishi Type 98-1.
1000fr, P-40 Warhawk (Flying Tigers).

1996, June 24 **Litho.** *Perf. 12½x12*

1127	A348	90fr multicolored	.35	.25
1128	A348	150fr multicolored	.60	.30
1129	A348	205fr multicolored	.80	.50
1130	A348	300fr multicolored	1.20	.75
1131	A348	400fr multicolored	1.60	1.00
1132	A348	500fr multicolored	2.00	1.25
		Nos. 1127-1132 (6)	6.55	4.05

Souvenir Sheet

Perf. 13

1133	A348	1000fr multicolored	4.00	2.50

No. 1133 contains one 32x40mm stamp.

Aquatic Flowers — A348a

Design: 90fr, Cyrtosperma senegalense.

1996, July 3 **Litho.** *Perf. 14x14¼*

1133A	A348a	90fr multi	.70	.50

An additional stamp was issued in this set. The editors would like to examine it.

Crocodilians A348b

1996, July 16 **Litho.** *Perf. 14*

1133C	A348b	205fr Nile crocodile	1.25	.90
1133D	A348b	255fr Gavial	1.60	1.00
1133E	A348b	300fr Caiman	1.90	1.00
		Nos. 1133C-1133E (3)	4.75	2.90

United Nations, 50th Anniv. — A348c

1996 **Litho.** *Perf. 12½*

1133F	A348c	300fr multi	—	—

Arctocebus Calabarensis A349

a, 90fr, With young. b, 205fr, Touching leaf. c, 300fr, Climbing to left. d, 255fr, Walking on branch.

1998, June 3 **Litho.** *Perf. 14*

1134	A349	Strip of 4, #a.-d.	5.00	5.00

No. 1134 issued in sheets of 12 stamps. World Wildlife Fund.

Endangered Species — A350

No. 1135, Kabus defassa, vert. No. 1136, Caphalophus sylvicutor. 205fr, Potamochoerus porcus. 300fr, Tragelaplus spekei.

1996 **Litho.** *Perf. 14*

1135	A350	90fr multi	.55	.25
1136	A350	90fr multi, vert.	.55	.25
1137	A350	205fr multi, vert.	1.10	.45
1138	A350	300fr multi	1.60	.65
		Nos. 1135-1138 (4)	3.80	1.60

Diana, Princess of Wales (1961-97) — A351

Nos. 1139-1141: Various portraits with white rose.
Diana, rose, famous people in sheet margin: 750fr, Henry Kissinger, vert. No. 1143, Mother Teresa, vert. No. 1144, Hillary Clinton, vert.

1998, Aug. 31 **Litho.** *Perf. 14*

Sheets of 6

1139	A351	205fr #a.-f.	5.50	2.00
1140	A351	255fr #a.-f., vert.	7.00	2.75
1141	A351	300fr #a.-f., vert.	8.00	3.00

Souvenir Sheets

1142	A351	750fr multicolored	3.00	3.00
1143-1144	A351	1000fr each	5.00	5.00

Stamps of Type A345 inscribed only "Congo" ovptd.

1998 **Litho.** *Perf. 13*

1145	A345	40fr blue		*8.00*
1146	A345	50fr violet brown		*8.00*
1147	A345	90fr orange		*8.00*
1148	A345	100fr green blue	—	*8.00*
1149	A345	115fr gray		*8.00*
1150	A345	205fr brown		*8.00*
		Nos. 1145-1150 (6)		*48.00*

A352

Designs: 90fr, Aframomum africanum. 205fr, Gambeya lacuurtiana (37x24mm). 300fr, Landolphia jumeli.

Perf. 13½x13¼, 13 (#1152)

1998 **Litho.**

1151	A352	90fr multi		*10.00*
1152	A352	205fr multi	—	*10.00*
1153	A352	300fr multi		*10.00*
		Nos. 1151-1153 (3)		*30.00*

No. 1153 has denomination in yellow.

No. 732A Overprinted

No. 929 Overprinted

1998 **Litho.** *Perf. 13*

1155	A244	205fr multi	—	—
1156	A309	300fr multi	—	—

An additional stamp was issued in this set. The editors would like to examine them.

Nos. 732B, 804, 854, 855, 929, 963, 1066, 1074, 1118, 1133D Ovptd. Like

and

A355

Perfs. as before, Perf. 14 (#1164), Perf. 13½x13¼ (#1170)
Methods as before, Litho. (#1164, 1170)

1998

1157	A274	60fr multi (#804)		
1159	A345	100fr green blue (#1118)		
1164	A348b	255fr multi (#1133D)		
1165	A309	300fr multi (#929)		
1166	A316	300fr multi (#963)		—

1167 A335 300fr multi (#1066)
a. Overprint reading horizontally
1168 A337 300fr multi (#1074)
1169 A355 300fr multi — —
1170 A244 300fr multi (#732B)
a. Overprint reading horizontally — —
1172 A292 360fr multi (#854)
a. Inverted overprint — —
1173 A292 400fr multi (#855) — —

Numbers have been reserved for additional overprinted stamps. Overprint reads horizontally on Nos. 1157, 1159, 1166, 1169, 1172 and 1173, vertically reading down on Nos. 1164, 1167, 1168 and 1170, and vertically reading up on No. 1165. No. 1170 has white denomination.

The editors would like to see examples of No. 1169 without the overprint.

1998 World Cup Soccer Championships, France — A358

Designs: 90fr, Netherlands, 4th place. 205fr, Croatia, bronze medal. 300fr, Brazil, silver medal. 500fr, France, gold medal.

1998, Nov. 16 Litho. *Perf. 13x13¼*
1175-1178 A358 Set of 4 12.00 5.00

Masks — A359

90fr, Kwele wood mask. 150fr, Kwele wood mask. No. 1181, Teke/Tsangui wood mask. No. 1182, Kuyu wood mask.

Perf. 13¼x13½
1998, Nov. 20 Litho.
1179 A359 90fr multicolored .90 .40
1180 A359 150fr multicolored 1.20 .70
1181 A359 205fr multicolored 1.20 1.00
1182 A359 205fr multicolored 1.20 1.00
Nos. 1179-1182 (4) 4.50 3.10

No. 732B Overprinted

Type I — Unserifed Upper and Lower Case Letters, 7x3mm

Type II — Serifed Upper and Lower Case Letters, 12x3mm

Type III — Upper Case Letters, 9x2mm

Methods and Perfs as Before

1999 ?
1183 A244 300fr multi (I) — —
1184 A244 300fr multi (II) — —
1185 A244 300fr multi (III) — —

No. 1119 Overprinted Like No. 1149 But With Wider "G" In Overprint

Method and Perf. As Before

1999 ?
1185A A345 115fr gray —

Nos. 934, 975, 995B, 1082, C342-C343 Overprinted Like No. 1157 and

A359a

Methods as Before, Litho. (#1204)

1999 ? *Perf. as Before, 12½ (#1204)*
1187 AP120 200fr multi (#C342) — —
1188 AP120 200fr multi (#C343) — —
a. Horiz. pair, #1187-1188, + central label — —
1191 A318 200fr multi (#975) — —
1192 A321a 200fr multi (#995B) — —
1199 A310 300fr multi (#934) — —
1201 A339 300fr multi (#1082) — —
1204 A359a 300fr multi — —

The editors would like to see examples of No. 1204 without the overprint. Overprint reads horizontally on No. 1204, horizontally and inverted on Nos. 1187-1188, vertically reading down on Nos. 1191 and 1199, and vertically reading up on Nos. 1192 and 1201.

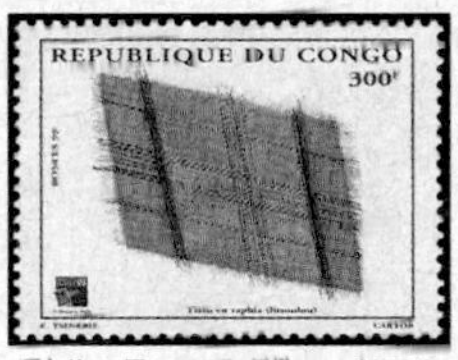

PhilexFrance 99 — A360

Design: 205fr, Raffia cloth with tassels. 300fr, Woven raffia cloth.

1999, July 2 Litho. *Perf. 13x13¼*
1211 A360 205fr multi 2.00 1.00
1212 A360 300fr multi 2.50 1.50

First French Postage Stamp, 150th Anniv. A361

Litho. With Hologram

1999 *Perf. 13x13¼*
1213 A361 300fr multi 2.50 2.50

Central African Economic and Monetary Community Week — A363

Designs: 90fr, Map and flags. 205fr, Map and circle of flags.

1999 Litho. *Perf. 14½*
1227 A363 90fr multi — 5.00
1228 A363 205fr multi — —

Additional stamps may exist in this set. The editors would like to examine any examples.

Third Pan-African Music Festival — A364

Designs: 120fr, Emblem. 270fr, Map of Africa with drummers.

2001, Aug. 4 Litho. *Perf. 13½x13*
1229-1230 A364 Set of 2 3.25 3.25

Independence, 40th Anniv. — A365

Designs: 90fr, Dove, vine, map, hands, people. 205fr, Tools, clasped and opened hands, map.

2001, Nov. 15 Litho. *Perf. 13¼x13*
1231-1232 A365 Set of 2 *30.00* —

Birds — A366

Designs: 90fr, Egretta garzetta. 120fr, Ardea cenerea. 205fr, Ardea purpurea. 270fr, Ciconia nigra.

2001 *Perf. 13¼*
1233 A366 90fr multi — —
1234 A366 120fr multi — —
1234B A366 205fr multi —
1235 A366 270fr multi — —

Two additional stamps were issued in this set. The editors would like to examine any examples.

Type of A345 Inscribed "REPUBLIQUE DU CONGO" Overprinted "LEGAL" Like No. 1145

2001 ? Litho. *Perf. 13*
1236 A345 90fr blue — —

Fruit — A367

Designs: 40fr, Mbila esobe. 50fr, Ikami. 70fr, Tsia, vert. 80fr, Bamou. 120fr, Malombo. 270fr, Ntondolo, vert.

2002, June 25 Litho. *Perf. 13½*
1237-1242 A367 Set of 6 — —

Birds — A368

Designs: 40fr, Calao (hornbill). 80fr, Cigogne blanche (white stork). 120fr, Grue cendrée (gray crane). 270fr, Marabout.

2002, July 23 *Perf. 13½x13*
1243-1246 A368 Set of 4 — —

Elephants A369

Designs; 120fr, Mammoth. 270fr, Elephant on savannah, horiz. 350fr, Elephant, horiz. 500fr, Forest elephant near lake.

Perf. 13¼x13, 13x13¼
2003, June 20
1247-1250 A369 Set of 4 — —

Flowers — A370

Designs: 120fr, Muflier (antirrhinum). 270fr, Pivoine (peony). 400fr, Petunia. 600fr, Mauve (mallow), horiz.

2003, July 6
1251-1254 A370 Set of 4 6.50 6.50

Moringa Olifera — A371

Highlighted portion: 30fr, Bark. 70fr, Root. 90fr, Leaves. 115fr, Seeds and open pod. 120fr, Flowers. 360fr, Pod.

2005, Feb. 3 Litho. *Perf. 13¼x13*
1255-1260 A371 Set of 6 5.00 5.00

Dated 2004.

Fruits — A372

Designs: 120fr, Custard apple. 200fr, Tangerine. 270fr, Guava. 360fr, Grapefruit.

2005, July 13 Litho. *Perf. 13½*
1261-1264 A372 Set of 4 7.25 7.25

Albert Einstein (1879-1955), Physicist — A373

2005, Aug. 17 Litho. *Perf. 13¼x13*
1265 A373 400fr multi 4.25 4.25

A374

Brazzaville, 125th Anniv. — A375

2005, Oct. 3 ***Perf. 13¼x13***
1266 A374 120fr multi 1.10 1.10
Perf. 13½x13¼
1267 A375 360fr multi 3.25 3.25

Pope Benedict XVI — A376

Pope Benedict XVI: 360fr, Waving. 500fr, Holding crucifix.

2005, Nov. 28 ***Perf. 13¼x13½***
1268-1269 A376 Set of 2 4.25 3.75

Coat of Arms — A377

Colors: 30fr, Dark brown. 40fr, Red. 50fr, Bister brown. 60fr, Dark green.

2006, Jan. 4 **Litho.** ***Perf. 13½***
1270-1273 A377 Set of 4 — —

Denis Sassou-Nguesso, President of African Union — A378

2006, Mar. 14 **Litho.** ***Perf. 13x13¼***
1274 A378 500fr multi 2.40 2.40

Léopold Sédar Senghor (1906-2001), First President of Senegal — A379

2006, May 15
1275 A379 360fr multi 1.75 1.75

Animals — A380

Designs: 40fr, Crocodile. 50fr, Pangolin, horiz. 60fr, Lizard, horiz. 120fr, Cat, horiz.

2006 **Litho.** ***Perf. 13¼x13, 13x13¼***
1276-1279 A380 Set of 4 5.00 2.50

World Religion Day — A381

2007 ***Perf. 13½x13***
1280 A381 120fr multi 1.20 1.00

Opening of Pierre Savorgnan de Brazza Memorial, Brazzaville — A382

Memorial and: 120fr, Statue. 500fr, Photo of Savorgnan de Brazza. 1000fr, Statue, diff.

2008 ***Perf. 13¼***
1281-1283 A382 Set of 3 7.00 7.00

Pan-African Postal Union, 30th Anniv. — A383

2010 **Litho.** ***Perf. 13½x13¼***
1284 A383 120fr multi 1.00 1.00

Pan-African Postal Union, 30th Anniv. — A384

2010 **Litho.** ***Perf. 13½x13¼***
1285 A384 360fr multi 3.00 3.00

SEMI-POSTAL STAMPS

Anti-Malaria Issue
Common Design Type

1962, Apr. 7 **Engr.** ***Perf. 12½x12***
B3 CD108 25fr + 5fr bister 1.40 1.00

Freedom from Hunger Issue
Common Design Type

1963, Mar. 21 **Unwmk.** ***Perf. 13***
B4 CD112 25fr + 5fr vio bl, bl grn & brn 1.40 1.00

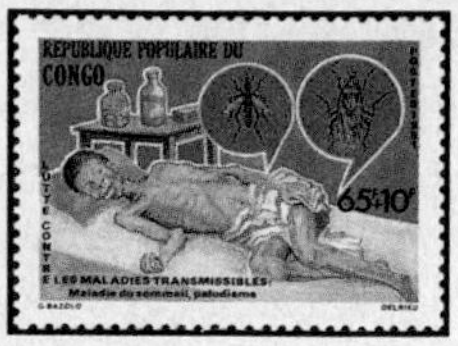

Boy Suffering from Sleeping Sickness — SP1

Fight Against Communicable Diseases; 40fr+5fr, Examination, treatment, vert.

1981, June 6 **Litho.** ***Perf. 13***
B5 SP1 40fr + 5fr multi .60 .25
B6 SP1 65fr + 10fr multi 1.00 .30

IYD Type of 1981

1981, June 29 ***Perf. 12½***
B7 A192 75fr + 5fr multi .90 .35

AIR POST STAMPS

Olympic Games Issue
French Equatorial Africa No. C37 Surcharged in Red Like Chad No. C1

1960 **Unwmk.** **Engr.** ***Perf. 13***
C1 AP8 250fr on 500fr grnsh blk, blk & sl 8.00 8.00

17th Olympic Games, Rome, 8/25-9/11.

Helicrysum Mechowiam — AP1

Flowers: 200fr, Cogniauxia podolaena. 500fr, Thesium tencio.

1961, Sept. 28 **Engr.** ***Perf. 13***
C2 AP1 100fr grn, lil & yel 2.90 1.60
C3 AP1 200fr bl grn, yel & brn 4.75 2.40
C4 AP1 500fr brn red, yel & sl grn 14.50 6.00
Nos. C2-C4 (3) 22.15 10.00

Air Afrique Issue
Common Design Type

1961, Nov. 25 **Unwmk.** ***Perf. 13***
C5 CD107 50fr lil rose, sl grn & grn 1.75 .90

Loading Timber, Pointe-Noire Harbor — AP2

1962, June 8 **Photo.** ***Perf. 12½x12***
C6 AP2 50fr multicolored 1.50 .90

Opening of the Intl. Fair and Exhib., Pointe-Noire, June 8-11.

Abidjan Games — AP3

1962, July 21 ***Perf. 12x12½***
C7 AP3 100fr Basketball 2.50 1.25

Costus Spectabilis — AP4

Design: 250fr, Mountain acanthus.

1963 **Unwmk.** ***Perf. 13***
C8 AP4 100fr multicolored 4.00 1.75
C9 AP4 250fr multicolored 8.00 3.25

Issued: 100fr, 8/9; 250fr, 11/4.

Brazzaville City Hall and Pres. Fulbert Youlou — AP4a

1963, Aug. **Photo.** ***Perf. 13x12***
C10 AP4a 100fr multicolored 150.00 125.00

African Postal Union Issue
Common Design Type

1963, Sept. 8 ***Perf. 12½***
C13 CD114 85fr pur, ocher & red 1.40 .75

Air Afrique Issue, 1963
Common Design Type
Perf. 13x12

1963, Nov. 19 **Unwmk.** **Photo.**
C14 CD115 50fr multicolored 1.60 .60

Liberty Place, Brazzaville — AP5

1963, Nov. 28
C15 AP5 25fr multicolored 1.00 .40

See No. 118.

Europafrica Issue
Common Design Type

1963, Nov. 30 ***Perf. 12x13***
C16 CD116 50fr gray, yel & dk brn 1.60 1.00

Timber Industry — AP6

1964, May 12 **Engr.** ***Perf. 13***
C17 AP6 100fr grn, brn red & blk 2.50 1.10

Chiefs of State Issue

Map and Presidents of Chad, Congo, Gabon and CAR AP6a

1964, June 23 **Photo.** ***Perf. 12½***
C18 AP6a 100fr multicolored 1.60 1.00

See note after Central African Republic No. C19.

Europafrica Issue

Sunburst, Wheat, Cogwheel and Globe — AP7

1964, July 20 ***Perf. 12x13***
C19 AP7 50fr yel, Prus bl & mar 1.60 .75

See note after Cameroun No. 402.

Hammer Thrower, Olympic Flame and Stadium — AP8

50fr, 100fr, vert.

1964, July 30 **Engr.** ***Perf. 13***

C20	AP8 25fr shown	.40	.30
C21	AP8 50fr Weight lifter	.75	.60
C22	AP8 100fr Volleyball	1.60	1.10
C23	AP8 200fr High jump	3.00	2.25
a.	Min. sheet of 4, #C20-C23	7.25	7.25
	Nos. C20-C23 (4)	5.75	4.25

18th Olympic Games, Tokyo, 10/10-25/64.

Communications Symbols — AP8a

1964, Nov. 2 **Litho.** ***Perf. 12½x13***
C24 AP8a 25fr dl rose & dk brn .80 .45

See note after Chad No. C19.

Town Hall, Brazzaville — AP9

1965, Jan. 30 **Photo.** ***Perf. 12½***
C25 AP9 100fr multicolored 1.10 .75

Coupling Hooks — AP10

1965, Feb. 27 **Photo.** ***Perf. 13x12***
C26 AP10 50fr multicolored 1.40 .75

Economic Europe-Africa Association.

Breguet Dial Telegraph, ITU Emblem and Telstar — AP11

1965, May 17 **Engr.** ***Perf. 13***
C27 AP11 100fr dk bl, ocher & brn 2.25 .75

Cent. of the ITU.

Pope John XXIII (1881-1963), St. Peter's Cathedral — AP12

Perf. 12½x13

1965, June 26 **Photo.** **Unwmk.**
C28 AP12 100fr gldn brn & multi 1.50 .75

Pres. John F. Kennedy — AP13

Portraits: 25fr on 50fr, Patrice Lumumba, premier of Congo Republic (ex-Belgian). 50fr, Sir Winston Churchill. 80fr, Barthélémy Boganda, premier of Central African Republic.

1965, June ***Perf. 12½***

C29	AP13 25fr on 50fr dk brn & red	.50	.40
a.	Surcharge omitted	35.00	35.00
C30	AP13 50fr dk brn & yel grn	1.00	1.00
C31	AP13 80fr dk brn & bl	1.75	1.50
C32	AP13 100fr dk brn & org yel	2.60	2.25
a.	Min. sheet of 4, #C29-C32	6.25	6.25
	Nos. C29-C32 (4)	5.85	5.15

A second miniature sheet contains one each of Nos. C29a, C30-C32. Value, $50.

Issued: 25fr, 80fr, 6/25; 50fr, 100fr, No. C32a, 6/26.

Log Rolling — AP14

1965, Aug. 14 **Engr.** ***Perf. 13***
C33 AP14 50fr grn, brn & red brn 1.60 .75

Issued to publicize national unity.

World Map and Symbols of Agriculture and Industry — AP15

1965, Oct. 18 **Engr.** ***Perf. 13***
C34 AP15 50fr dk bl, blk, brn & org 1.40 .90

International Cooperation Year, 1965.

Abraham Lincoln — AP16

1965, Dec. 15 **Photo.** ***Perf. 13***
C35 AP16 90fr pink & multi 1.40 .60

Centenary of death of Abraham Lincoln.

Charles de Gaulle, Torch and Map of Africa — AP17

1966, Feb. 28 **Engr.** ***Perf. 13***
C36 AP17 500fr dk red, dk grn & dk red brn 30.00 26.00

22nd anniv. of the Brazzaville Conf.

D-1 Satellite over Brazzaville Space Tracking Station — AP18

1966, May 15 **Engr.** ***Perf. 13***
C37 AP18 150fr blk, dl red & bl grn 2.25 1.25

Grain, Atom Symbol and Map of Africa and Europe — AP19

1966, July 20 **Photo.** ***Perf. 12x13***
C38 AP19 50fr multicolored .90 .75

See note after Gabon No. C46.

Pres. Massamba-Debat and President's Palace — AP20

3rd anniv. of the Revolution: 30fr, Robespierre and storming of the Bastille. 50fr, Lenin and storming of the Winter Palace.

1966, Aug. 15 **Photo.** ***Perf. 12x12½***

C39	AP20 25fr multicolored	.45	.30
C40	AP20 30fr multicolored	.65	.30
C41	AP20 50fr multicolored	1.60	.50
a.	Souv. sheet of 3, #C39-C41	2.25	2.25
	Nos. C39-C41 (3)	2.70	1.10

Air Afrique Issue, 1966

Common Design Type

1966, Aug. 31 **Photo.** ***Perf. 13***
C42 CD123 30fr lilac, lemon & blk 1.00 .25

Dr. Albert Schweitzer — AP21

1966, Sept. 4 **Photo.** ***Perf. 12½***
C43 AP21 100fr red, blk, bl & lilac 2.25 1.25

Issued to honor Dr. Albert Schweitzer (1875-1965), medical missionary.

Crab, Microscope and Pagoda — AP22

1966, Dec. 26 **Photo.** ***Perf. 13***
C44 AP22 100fr multicolored 1.75 1.00

9th Intl. Anticancer Cong., Tokyo. 10/23-29.

AP23

Birds: 50fr, Social Weaver. 75fr, European Bee-eater. 100fr, Lilac-breasted roller. 150fr, Regal sunbird. 200fr, Crowned cranes. 250fr, Secretary bird. 300fr, Knysna touraco.

1967 Photo. *Perf. 13*

C45 AP23 50fr multicolored 1.60 .75
C46 AP23 75fr multicolored 3.25 1.00
C47 AP23 100fr multicolored 3.25 1.00
C48 AP23 150fr multicolored 4.25 2.25
C49 AP23 200fr multicolored 7.50 2.50
C50 AP23 250fr multicolored 9.50 3.00
C51 AP23 300fr multicolored 13.50 5.00
Nos. C45-C51 (7) 42.85 15.50

Issued: Nos. C45-C47, 2/13; others, 6/20.

Shackled Hands AP24

1967, May 24 Photo. *Perf. 12½x13*

C52 AP24 500fr multicolored 8.00 3.00

Issued for African Liberation Day.

Sputnik 1, Explorer 6 and Earth — AP25

Space Craft: 75fr, Ranger 6, Lunik 2 and moon. 100fr, Mars 1, Mariner 4 and Mars. 200fr, Gemini, Vostok and earth.

1967, Aug. 1 Engr. *Perf. 13*

C53 AP25 50fr multicolored .60 .30
C54 AP25 75fr multicolored 1.10 .35
C55 AP25 100fr multicolored 1.60 .60
C56 AP25 200fr multicolored 2.75 1.50
Nos. C53-C56 (4) 6.05 2.75

Space explorations.

African Postal Union Issue, 1967
Common Design Type

1967, Sept. 9 Engr. *Perf. 13*

C57 CD124 100fr ver, ol & emer 1.60 .60

Boy Scouts, Tents and Jamboree Emblem — AP26

Design: 70c, Borah Peak, Idaho; tents, Scout sign and Jamboree emblem.

1967, Sept. 29

C58 AP26 50fr multicolored .80 .30
C59 AP26 70fr multicolored 1.20 .50

12th Boy Scout World Jamboree, Farragut State Park, ID, Aug. 1-9.

Sikorsky S-43 and Map of Africa — AP27

1967, Oct. 2 Photo. *Perf. 13*

C60 AP27 30fr multicolored .75 .30

30th anniv. of the 1st airmail connection by Aeromaritime Lines from Casablanca to Pointe-Noire.

Men of Four Races Dancing on Globe — AP28

1968, Feb 8 Engr. *Perf. 13*

C61 AP28 70fr dk brn, ultra & emer 1.50 .60

Friendship among peoples.

The Oath of the Horatii, by Jacques Louis David — AP29

Paintings: 25fr, On the Barricades, by Delacroix. No. C63, Grandfather and Grandson, by Ghirlandajo, vert. No. C64, The Demolition of the Bastille, by Hubert Robert. 200fr, Negro Woman Arranging Peonies, by Jean F. Bazille.

1968 Photo. *Perf. 12x12½, 12½x12*

C62 AP29 25fr multicolored 1.75 .35
C63 AP29 30fr multicolored .90 .30
C64 AP29 30fr multicolored 1.75 .50
C65 AP29 100fr multicolored 2.25 .90
C66 AP29 200fr multicolored 5.00 1.75
Nos. C62-C66 (5) 11.65 3.80

Issue dates: Nos. C62, C64, Aug. 15. Nos. C63, C65-C66, Mar. 20.
See Nos. C78-C81, C111-C115.

Early Automobile Type

1968, July 29 Photo. *Perf. 13x12½*

C67 A50 150fr Ford, 1915 3.50 1.75
C68 A50 200fr Citroen, 1922 5.25 1.75

Europafrica Issue

Square Knot — AP30

1968, July 20 Photo. *Perf. 13*

C69 AP30 50fr multicolored 1.50 .50

5th anniv. of the economic agreement between the European Economic Community and the African and Malgache Union.

Martin Luther King, Jr. — AP31

1968, Aug. 5 *Perf. 12½*

C70 AP31 50fr lt grn, Prus grn & blk 1.60 .40

Robert F. Kennedy — AP32

1968, Sept. 30 Photo. *Perf. 13x12½*

C71 AP32 50fr dp car, ap grn & blk .85 .40

Running — AP33

Olympic Rings and: 20fr, Soccer, vert. 60fr, Boxing, vert. 85fr, High jump.

1968, Dec. 27 Engr. *Perf. 13*

C72 AP33 5fr emer, brt bl & choc .25 .25
C73 AP33 20fr dk bl, brn & dk grn .45 .25
C74 AP33 60fr mar, brt grn & choc .90 .60
C75 AP33 85fr blk, car rose & choc 1.75 .85
Nos. C72-C75 (4) 3.35 1.95

19th Olympic Games, Mexico City, 10/12-27.

PHILEXAFRIQUE Issue

G. De Gueidan, by Nicolas de Largillière AP34

1968, Dec. 30 Photo. *Perf. 12½*

C76 AP34 100fr pink & multi 2.75 1.75

Issued to publicize PHILEXAFRIQUE, Philatelic Exhibition, in Abidjan, Feb. 14-23. Printed with alternating pink label.
See Nos. C89-C93.

2nd PHILEXAFRIQUE Issue
Common Design Type

Design: 50fr, Middle Congo No. 72 and Pointe-Noire harbor.

1969, Feb. 14 Engr. *Perf. 13*

C77 CD128 50fr car rose, sl grn & bis brn 2.00 1.75

Painting Type of 1968

Paintings: 25fr, Battle of Rivoli, by Carle Vernet. 50fr, Battle of Marengo, by Jacques Augustin Pajou. 75fr, Battle of Friedland, by Horace Vernet. 100fr, Battle of Jena, by Charles Thevenin.

1969, May 20 Photo. *Perf. 12x12½*

C78 AP29 25fr vio bl & multi 1.25 .45
C79 AP29 50fr cop red & multi 1.75 .80
C80 AP29 75fr grn & multi 3.00 1.10
C81 AP29 100fr brn & multi 5.00 1.40
Nos. C78-C81 (4) 11.00 3.75

Bicentenary of birth of Napoleon I.

Ernesto Ché Guevara — AP35

1969, June 10 Photo. *Perf. 12½*

C82 AP35 90fr brn, org & blk 1.60 .50

Issued in memory of Ernesto Ché Guevara (1928-1967), Cuban revolutionist.

Doll, Train and Space Toy — AP36

1969, June 20 Engr. *Perf. 13*

C83 AP36 100fr mag, org & gray 1.75 .75

International Toy Fair, Nuremberg, Germany.

Europafrica Issue

Ribbon Tied Around Bar — AP37

1969, Aug. 5 Photo. *Perf. 13x12*

C84 AP37 50fr bl grn, lil & blk .90 .35

See note after Chad No. C11.

Souvenir Sheet

Armstrong, Aldrin and Collins — AP38

Design: No. C85b, Blast-off from Moon.

Embossed on Gold Foil

1969, Sept. 15 *Imperf.*

C85 AP38 1000fr #a-b 40.00 37.50

See note after Algeria No. 427. No. C85 contains one each of Nos. C85a and C85b with simulated perforations.

Painter, Poto-Poto School — AP39

150fr, Sculpture lesson (man, infant and sculpture). 200fr, Potter working on vase.

1970, Feb. 20 **Engr.** ***Perf. 13***

C86	AP39	100fr multicolored	2.25	.60
C87	AP39	150fr multicolored	3.00	.95
C88	AP39	200fr multicolored	3.75	1.75
		Nos. C86-C88 (3)	9.00	3.30

Painting Type (Philexafrique)

Paintings: 150fr, Child with Cherries, by John Russell. 200fr, Erasmus, by Hans Holbein the Younger. 250fr, "Silence" (head), by Bernardino Luini. 300fr, Scene from the Massacre of Scio, by Delacroix. 500fr, The Capture of Constantinople by the Crusaders, by Delacroix.

1970 **Photo.** ***Perf. 12½***

C89	AP34	150fr lil & multi	4.50	1.50
C90	AP34	200fr multicolored	5.75	1.75
C91	AP34	250fr brn & multi	6.25	2.25
C92	AP34	300fr multicolored	8.00	3.25
C93	AP34	500fr brn & multi	13.50	4.50
		Nos. C89-C93 (5)	38.00	13.25

Aurichalcite — AP40

1970, Mar. 20

C94	AP40	100fr shown	5.25	1.75
C95	AP40	150fr Dioptase	8.00	2.50

Lenin — AP41

1970, June 25 **Photo.** ***Perf. 12½***

C96	AP41	45fr shown	1.00	.35
C97	AP41	75fr Lenin, seated	1.75	.50

Centenary of the birth of Lenin (1870-1924), Russian communist leader.

Karl Marx — AP42

Design: No. C99, Friedrich Engels.

1970, July 10 **Engr.** ***Perf. 13***

C98	AP42	50fr emer, dk brn & dk red	1.40	.35
C99	AP42	50fr ultra, dk brn & dk red	1.40	.35

Karl Marx (1818-1883) and Friedrich Engels (1820-1895), German socialist writers.

Otto Lilienthal's Glider, 1891 — AP43

Designs: 50fr, "Spirit of St. Louis," Lindbergh's first transatlantic solo flight, 1927. 70fr, Sputnik 1, first satellite in space. 90fr, First man on the moon, Apollo 11, 1969.

1970, Sept. 5 **Engr.** ***Perf. 13***

C100	AP43	45fr dp car, bl & ol bis	1.00	.30
C101	AP43	50fr emer, sl grn & brn	1.00	.35
C102	AP43	70fr brt bl, ol bis & dp car	1.25	.50
C103	AP43	90fr brn, bl & ol gray	1.90	.75
		Nos. C100-C103 (4)	5.15	1.90

Forerunners of space exploration.

Saint on Horseback AP44

Designs from Stained Glass Windows, Brazzaville Cathedral: 150fr, Saint with staff. 250fr, The Elevation of the Host, from rose window.

1970, Dec. 10 **Photo.** ***Perf. 12½***

C104	AP44	100fr multicolored	1.25	.50
C105	AP44	150fr multicolored	1.75	.85
C106	AP44	250fr multicolored	3.00	1.75
a.		Souv. sheet of 3, #C104-C106	6.75	6.75
		Nos. C104-C106 (3)	6.00	3.10

Christmas 1970.

Marilyn Monroe and NYC — AP45

Portraits: 150fr, Martine Carol and Paris. 200fr, Erich von Stroheim and Vienna. 250fr, Sergei Eisenstein and Moscow.

1971, Mar. 16 **Engr.** ***Perf. 13***

C107	AP45	100fr brt grn, red brn & ultra	7.00	.50
C108	AP45	150fr brn, brt lil & ultra	7.00	.75
C109	AP45	200fr choc & ultra	7.00	1.10
C110	AP45	250fr brt grn, brn vio & ultra	7.00	1.25
		Nos. C107-C110 (4)	28.00	3.60

History of motion pictures.

Painting Type of 1968

Paintings: 100fr, Christ Carrying Cross, by Paolo Veronese. 150fr, Christ on the Cross, Burgundian School, 1500, vert. 200fr, Descent from the Cross, by Rogier van der Weyden. 250fr, Christ Laid in the Tomb, Flemish School, 1500, vert. 500fr, Resurrection, by Hans Memling, vert.

1971, Apr. 26 **Photo.** ***Perf. 13***

C111	AP29	100fr green & multi	1.75	.75
C112	AP29	150fr green & multi	2.75	.90
C113	AP29	200fr green & multi	4.00	1.10
C114	AP29	250fr green & multi	4.50	1.60
C115	AP29	500fr green & multi	10.00	3.00
		Nos. C111-C115 (5)	23.00	7.35

Easter 1971.

Map of Africa and Telecommunications System — AP46

1971, June 18 **Photo.** ***Perf. 12½***

C116	AP46	70fr bl, gray & dk brn	.80	.30
C117	AP46	85fr bl, lil rose & dk brn	1.25	.35
C118	AP46	90fr grn, yel & dk brn	1.60	.70
		Nos. C116-C118 (3)	3.65	1.35

Pan-African telecommunications system.

Globe and Waves — AP47

1971, June 19

C119	AP47	65fr lt bl & multi	.80	.30

3rd World Telecommunications Day.

Japanese Mask and Play — AP48

Design: 150fr, Japanese and African women, symbolic leaves.

1971, June 28 **Engr.** ***Perf. 13***

C120	AP48	75fr lil, blk & mag	1.00	.70
C121	AP48	150fr dk brn, brn red & red lil	1.60	1.10

PHILATOKYO '71 International Stamp Exhibition, Tokyo, Apr. 20-30.

13th World Boy Scout Jamboree, Japan, gold foil 1000fr airmail and silver foil souv. sheet of four 90fr, issued July 14. Values: 1000fr single, $30; sheet of four, $13.

Olympic Torch and Rings — AP49

350fr, Olympic rings and various sports.

1971, July 20 **Engr.** ***Perf. 13***

C122	AP49	150fr multi	1.90	.95
C123	AP49	350fr multi, horiz.	4.50	2.50

Pre-Olympic Year, 1971.

Scout Emblem, Japanese Dragon and African Carved Canoe — AP50

Designs (Boy Scout Emblem and): 90fr, Japanese mask and African boy, vert. 100fr, Japanese woman and African drummer, vert. 250fr, Congolese mask.

1971, Aug. 25

C124	AP50	85fr multicolored	1.10	.30
C125	AP50	90fr multicolored	1.25	.35
C126	AP50	100fr multicolored	1.60	.45
C127	AP50	250fr multicolored	3.25	.90
		Nos. C124-C127 (4)	7.20	2.00

13th Boy Scout World Jamboree, Asagiri Plain, Japan, Aug. 2-10.

Olympic Rings and Running — AP51

Designs (Olympic Rings and): 85fr, Hurdles. 90fr, Weight lifting, boxing, discus, running, javelin. 100fr, Wrestling. 150fr, Boxing.

1971, Sept. 30

C128	AP51	75fr plum, bl & dk brn	.75	.35
C129	AP51	85fr scar, sl & dk brn	.85	.35
C130	AP51	90fr vio bl & dk brn	1.10	.60
C131	AP51	100fr brn & slate	1.40	.60
C132	AP51	150fr grn, red & dk brn	2.40	1.00
		Nos. C128-C132 (5)	6.50	2.90

75th anniv. of the 1st modern Olympic Games.

Congo No. C36 and de Gaulle — AP52

Design: No. C135, Charles de Gaulle.

1971, Nov. 9

C133	AP52	500fr slate grn & multi	18.00	15.00

Pres. Marien Ngouabi's Tribute to de Gaulle — AP53

Lithographed; Gold Embossed

Perf. 12½

C134	AP53	1000fr gold, grn & red	27.50	20.00
C135	AP53	1000fr gold, grn & red	27.50	20.00
a.		Pair, #C134-C135	55.00	55.00

Charles de Gaulle (1890-1970), president of France.

African Postal Union Issue, 1971
Common Design Type

Design: 100fr, Allegory of Congo Republic (woman) and UAMPT Building, Brazzaville.

1971, Nov. 13 Photo. *Perf. 13x13½*
C136 CD135 100fr bl & multi 1.60 .75

Flag of Congo Republic and "Revolution" — AP54

1971, Nov. 30
C137 AP54 100fr red & multi 1.75 .60

8th anniversary of revolution.

Workers and Flag — AP55

40fr, Flag of Congo Republic and sun.

1971, Dec. 31 Photo. *Perf. 13x12½*
C138 AP55 30fr multicolored .75 .30
C139 AP55 40fr red & multi 1.50 .50

2nd anniv. of founding of Congolese Labor Party (No. C138), and adoption of red flag (No. C139).

Book Year Emblem — AP56

1972, June 3 Litho. *Perf. 12½*
C140 AP56 50fr red, grn & yel 1.00 .40

International Book Year 1972.

Congolese Soccer Team — AP57

No. C142, Captain of winning team and cup, vert.

1973, Feb. 22 Photo. *Perf. 13*
C141 AP57 100fr ultra, red & blk 1.50 .75
C142 AP57 100fr red, yel & blk 1.50 .75

Girl Holding Bird, Environment Emblem — AP58

1973, Mar. 5 Engr.
C143 AP58 85fr org, slate grn & bl 1.75 .90

UN Conference on Human Environment, Stockholm, Sweden, June 5-16, 1972.

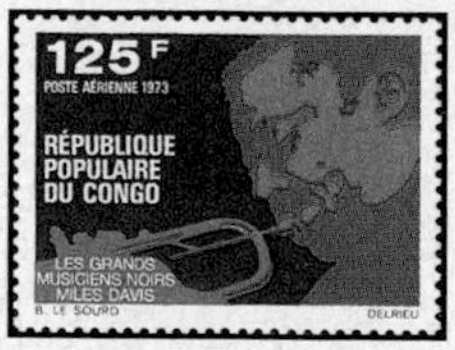

Miles Davis AP59

Designs: 140fr, Ella Fitzgerald. 160fr, Count Basie. 175fr, John Coltrane.

1973, Mar. 5 Photo. *Perf. 13x13½*
C144 AP59 125fr multicolored 3.50 .95
C145 AP59 140fr multicolored 3.50 1.00
C146 AP59 160fr multicolored 4.50 1.50
C147 AP59 175fr multicolored 4.50 1.50
Nos. C144-C147 (4) 16.00 4.95

Black American jazz musicians.

Olympic Rings, Hurdling — AP60

1973, Mar. 15 Engr. *Perf. 13*
C148 AP60 100fr shown 1.10 .60
C149 AP60 150fr Pole vault, vert. 1.75 .90
C150 AP60 250fr Wrestling 2.75 1.50
Nos. C148-C150 (3) 5.60 3.00

20th Olympic Games, Munich, 8/26-9/11/72.

Refinery and Storage Tanks, Djéno — AP61

Designs: 230fr, Off-shore drilling platform, vert. 240fr, Workers assembling drill, vert. 260fr, Off-shore drilling installation.

1973, Mar. 20
C151 AP61 180fr red, bl & indigo 3.25 1.50
C152 AP61 230fr red, bl & blk 4.00 1.50
C153 AP61 240fr red, ind & brn 4.50 1.60
C154 AP61 260fr red, bl & blk 7.25 2.25
Nos. C151-C154 (4) 19.00 6.85

Oil installations, Pointe-Noire.

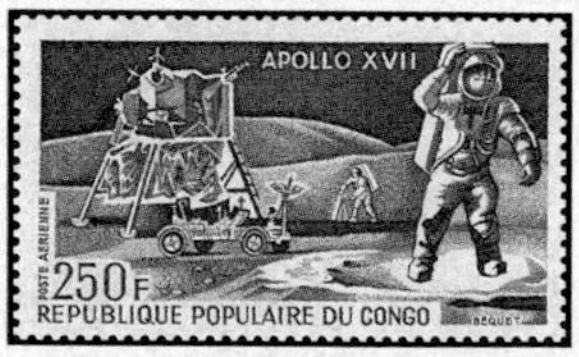

Astronauts, Landing Module and Lunar Rover on Moon — AP62

1973, Mar. 31
C155 AP62 250fr multicolored 4.00 1.75

Apollo 17 US moon mission, 12/7-19/72.

ITU Emblem, Symbols of Communications AP63

1973, May 24 Engr. *Perf. 13*
C156 AP63 120fr multicolored 2.25 .90

5th International Telecommunications Day.

White Horse, by Delacroix — AP64

Designs: Paintings by Eugene Delacroix.

1973, June 30 Photo. *Perf. 13*
C157 AP64 150fr shown 2.25 1.50
C158 AP64 250fr Lion sleeping 5.00 2.40
C159 AP64 300fr Lion and tiger 5.25 2.50
Nos. C157-C159 (3) 12.50 6.40

See Nos. C169-C171.

Copernicus and Heliocentric System — AP65

1973, June 30 Engr.
C160 AP65 50fr multicolored 1.00 .45

500th anniversary of the birth of Nicolaus Copernicus (1473-1543), Polish astronomer.

Plane, Ship, Rocket, Village, Sun and Clouds — AP66

1973, July
C161 AP66 50fr red & multi 1.60 .60

Cent. of intl. meteorological cooperation.

Pres. Marien Ngouabi — AP67

1973, Aug. 12 Photo. *Perf. 13*
C162 AP67 30fr multicolored .35 .25
C163 AP67 40fr aqua & multi .45 .25
C164 AP67 75fr red & multi 1.00 .35
Nos. C162-C164 (3) 1.80 .85

10th anniversary of independence.

Stamps, Album, African Woman AP68

40fr, No. C167, Stamps in shape of map of Congo, album, globe. No. C168, Like 30fr.

1973, Aug. 12
C165 AP68 30fr pur & multi 1.90 .30
C166 AP68 40fr multicolored .25 .25
C167 AP68 100fr dk brn & multi 3.75 .80
C168 AP68 100fr ocher & multi .90 .40
Nos. C165-C168 (4) 6.80 1.75

Nos. C165, C168 for the 10th anniv. of the revolution, Nos. C166-C167 the Intl. Philatelic Exhib., Brazzaville.

Painting Type of 1973 Inscribed "EUROPAFRIQUE"

Designs: Details from "Earth and Paradise," by Jan Brueghel, the Elder.

1973, Oct. 10 Photo. *Perf. 13*
C169 AP64 100fr Spotted hyena 3.00 1.50
C170 AP64 100fr Leopard and lion 3.00 1.50
C171 AP64 100fr Elephant and creatures 3.00 1.50
Nos. C169-C171 (3) 9.00 4.50

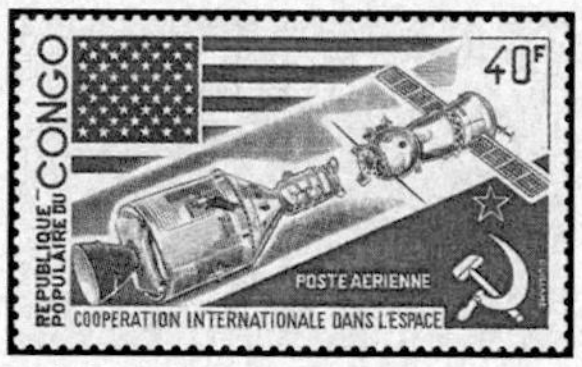

US and Russian Spacecraft Docking — AP69

Design: 80fr, US and USSR spacecraft docked in space and emblems of 1975 joint space mission.

1973, Oct. 15 Engr. *Perf. 13*
C172 AP69 40fr bl, red & brn .50 .35
C173 AP69 80fr red, grn & bl 1.10 .50

Planned joint US and Soviet space missions.
For overprint see No. C251.

UPU Monument, Satellites, Big Dipper — AP70

1973, Nov. 20 Engr. *Perf. 13*
C174 AP70 80fr vio bl & lt bl 1.60 .50

Universal Postal Union Day.

Astronauts Working in Space — AP71

40fr, Spacecraft & Skylab docking in space.

1973, Nov. 30

C175 AP71 30fr ultra, sl grn & choc .65 .25
C176 AP71 40fr mag, org & sl grn .95 .25

Skylab, first space laboratory.

Goalkeeper, Soccer — AP72

Design: 100fr, Soccer player kicking ball.

1973, Dec. 20

C177 AP72 40fr sl grn, sepia & brn .75 .25
C178 AP72 100fr pur, red & slate grn 1.90 .75

World Soccer Cup, Munich, 1974.

John F. Kennedy (1917-1963) AP73

1973, Dec. 20 Photo. *Perf. 12½*

C179 AP73 150fr ultra, gold & blk 1.75 .90

Runners — AP74

1973, Dec. 20 Engr. *Perf. 13*

C180 AP74 40fr sl grn, red & brn .60 .25
C181 AP74 100fr red, sl grn, & brn 1.75 .75

2nd African Games, Lagos, Nigeria.

Flag over Map of Congo — AP75

1973, Dec. 31 Photo.

C182 AP75 40fr dp grn & multi .80 .25

4th anniversary of Congolese Labor Party and of the Congo Red Flag.

Soccer and Games Emblem — AP76

1974, June 20 Photo. *Perf. 13*

C183 AP76 250fr multicolored 3.75 1.90

World Cup Soccer Championship, Munich, June 13-July 7.

Astronauts Yuri A. Gagarin and Alan B. Shepard — AP77

Designs: 30fr, Space, globe, Russian and American flags with names of astronauts who perished in space. 100fr, Alexei Leonov and Neil A. Armstrong in space and on moon.

1974, June 30 Engr. *Perf. 13*

C184 AP77 30fr red, ultra & brn .45 .25
C185 AP77 40fr red, bl & brn .70 .25
C186 AP77 100fr car, grn & brn 1.60 .90
Nos. C184-C186 (3) 2.75 1.40

For overprint see No. C254.

Soccer Game Superimposed on Ball — AP78

1974, July 31 Photo. *Perf. 13*

C187 AP78 250fr multicolored 3.50 1.75

Germany's victory in World Cup Soccer Championship.

Link-up Emblem, Stages of Link-up — AP79

300fr, Spacecraft docking over globe.

1974, Aug. 8 Engr. *Perf. 13*

C188 AP79 200fr pur, bl & red 2.25 1.10
C189 AP79 300fr multi, horiz. 3.50 1.50

Russo-American space cooperation.
For overprint see No. C255.

Symbols of Communications, UPU Emblem — AP80

1974, Aug. 10

C190 AP80 500fr blk & red 6.75 3.00

Centenary of Universal Postal Union.
For surcharge see No. C194.

Lenin and Pendulum Trace Pattern — AP81

1974, Sept. 16 Engr. *Perf. 13*

C191 AP81 150fr multicolored 2.10 1.10

Lenin (1870-1924).

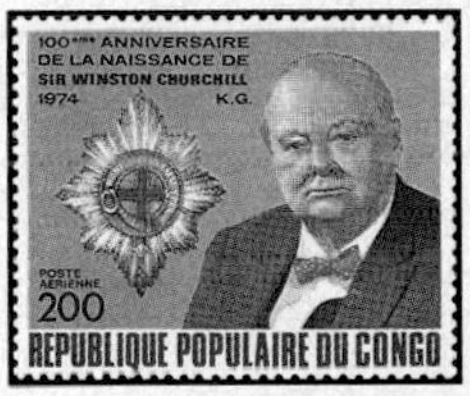

Churchill and Order of the Garter AP82

Marconi and Wireless Telegraph AP83

1974, Oct. 1 Litho. *Perf. 13*

C192 AP82 200fr lt grn & multi 2.50 1.25
C193 AP83 200fr lt ultra & multi 2.50 1.25

No. C190 Srchd. in Violet Blue with New Value, 2 Bars and "9 OCTOBER 1974"

1974, Oct. 9

C194 AP80 300fr on 500fr multi 4.25 2.75

Universal Postal Union Day.

UDEAC Issue

Presidents and Flags of Cameroun, CAR, Gabon and Congo — AP83a

1974, Dec. 8 Photo. *Perf. 13*

C195 AP83a 100fr gold & multi 1.60 .50

See note after Cameroun No. 595.

Regatta at Argenteuil, by Monet — AP84

Impressionist Paintings: 40fr, Seated Dancer, by Degas. 50fr, Girl on Swing, by Renoir. 75fr, Girl with Straw Hat, by Renoir. All vertical.

1974, Dec. 15

C196 AP84 30fr gold & multi 1.50 .35
C197 AP84 40fr gold & multi 2.00 .35
C198 AP84 50fr gold & multi 2.75 .50
C199 AP84 75fr gold & multi 3.25 .80
Nos. C196-C199 (4) 9.50 2.00

National Fair AP85

1974, Dec. 20

C200 AP85 30fr multicolored .95 .35

National Fair, Aug. 24-Sept. 8.

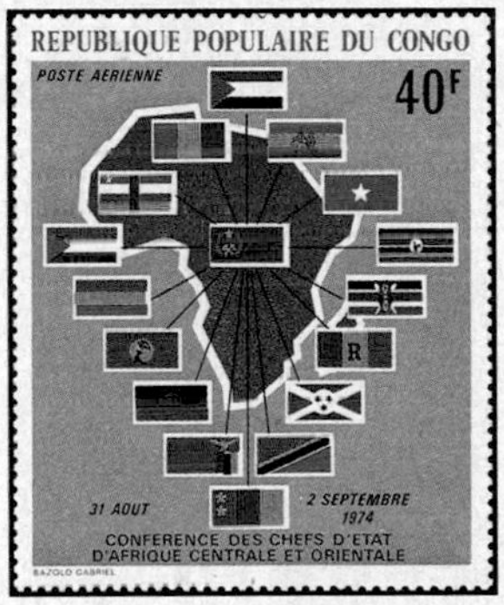

Flags of Participating Nations, Map of Africa — AP86

1974, Dec. 20 *Perf. 13*

C201 AP86 40fr ultra & multi .80 .45

Conference of Chiefs of State of Central and East Africa, Brazzaville, Aug. 31-Sept. 2.

"Five Weeks in a Balloon," by Jules Verne AP87

Design: 50fr, "Around the World in 80 Days," by Jules Verne.

1975, June 30 Litho. *Perf. 12½*

C202 AP87 40fr multicolored 1.40 .50
C203 AP87 50fr multicolored 1.75 1.00

Jules Verne (1828-1905), French science fiction writer, 70th death anniversary.

Paris-Brussels Train, 1890 — AP88

Design: 75fr, Santa Fe, 1880.

1975, June 30

C204 AP88 50fr ocher & multi 2.00 .75
C205 AP88 75fr lt bl & multi 4.25 .90

Soyuz and Apollo-Soyuz Emblem — AP89

Design: 100fr, Apollo and emblem.

1975, July 20 Litho. *Perf. 12½*

C206 AP89 95fr org, blk & mag 1.25 .50
C207 AP89 100fr vio, bl & blk 1.40 .60

Apollo Soyuz space test project (Russo-American space cooperation), launching July 15; link-up, July 17.

For overprints see Nos. C252-C253.

Bicycling and Montreal Olympic Emblem — AP90

Designs (Montreal Olympic Emblem and): 40fr, Boxing, vert. 50fr, Basketball, vert. 95fr, High jump. 100fr, Javelin. 150fr, Running.

Perf. 12½x13, 13x12½

1975, Oct. 30 Photo.

C208 AP90 40fr multicolored .50 .25
C209 AP90 50fr red & multi .60 .25
C210 AP90 85fr bl & multi 1.00 .35
C211 AP90 95fr org & multi 1.10 .45
C212 AP90 100fr multicolored 1.40 .50
C213 AP90 150fr multicolored 1.75 .80
Nos. C208-C213 (6) 6.35 2.60

Pre-Olympic Year 1975.

Map of Africa, Sports and Flags — AP91

1975, Dec. 20 Litho. *Perf. 12½*

C214 AP91 30fr multicolored .80 .35

1st African Games, Brazzaville, 10th anniv.

Workers and Flag — AP92

1975, Dec. 31 Litho. *Perf. 12½*

C215 AP92 60fr multicolored 1.10 .25

Congolese Labor Party (P.C.T.), 6th anniv.

Alphonse Fondere — AP93

Historic Ships: 5fr, like 30fr. 10fr, 40fr, Hamburg, 1839. 15fr, 50fr, Gomer, 1831. 20fr, 60fr, Great Eastern, 1858. 95fr, J.M. White II, 1878.

1976 Engr. *Perf. 13*

C216 AP93 5fr multicolored .25 .25
C217 AP93 10fr multicolored .25 .25
C218 AP93 15fr multicolored .30 .25
C219 AP93 20fr multicolored .50 .25
C220 AP93 30fr multicolored .75 .25
C221 AP93 40fr multicolored 1.00 .35
C222 AP93 50fr multicolored 1.25 .50
C223 AP93 60fr multicolored 1.75 .60
C224 AP93 95fr multicolored 2.50 1.00
Nos. C216-C224 (9) 8.55 3.70

Issued: Nos. C216-C219, May; Nos. C220-C224, Mar. 7.

Europafrica Issue

Peasant Family, by Louis Le Nain — AP94

Paintings: 80fr, Boy with Top, by Jean B. Chardin. 95fr, Venus and Aeneas, by Nicolas Poussin. 100fr, The Rape of the Sabine Women, by Jacques Louis David.

1976, Mar. 20 Litho. *Perf. 12½*

C225 AP94 60fr gold & multi 1.25 .45
C226 AP94 80fr gold & multi 1.40 .70
C227 AP94 95fr gold & multi 1.90 .70
C228 AP94 100fr gold & multi 2.10 .85
Nos. C225-C228 (4) 6.65 2.70

Nos. C225-C228 printed in sheets of 8 stamps and horizontal gutter with commemorative inscription.

Telephone Type of 1976

1976, Apr. 25 Litho. *Perf. 12½x13*

C229 A107 60fr pink, mar & crim .90 .30

Sports Type of 1976

Designs: 150fr, Runner and map of Central Africa. 200fr, Discus and map.

1976, Oct. 25 *Perf. 12½*

C230 A110 150fr multicolored 1.75 .75
C231 A110 200fr multicolored 2.75 1.10

Map of Africa, Flag and OAU Headquarters AP95

1976, Dec. 16 Typo. *Perf. 13x14*

C232 AP95 60fr multicolored .80 .35

13th anniv. of the Organization for African Unity.

Europafrica Issue

Map of Europe and Africa — AP96

1977, June 28 Litho. *Perf. 13*

C233 AP96 75fr multicolored .90 .45

Headdress Type of 1977

1977, June 30 *Perf. 12½*

250fr, Two straw caps. 300fr, Beaded cap.

C234 A118 250fr multicolored 2.75 1.50
C235 A118 300fr multicolored 3.00 1.75

Zeppelin Type of 1977

Souvenir Sheet

Design: 500fr, LZ 127 over US Capitol.

1977, Aug. 5 Litho. *Perf. 11*

C236 A120 500fr multicolored 6.75 2.00

No. C236 exists imperf.

Checkerboard AP97

1977, Aug. 20 Engr. *Perf. 13*

C237 AP97 60fr red & blk .90 .35

Lomé Convention on General Agreement on Tariffs and Trade (GATT).

Newton, Intelsat Satellite and Classical "Planets" — AP98

1977, Aug. 25

C238 AP98 140fr multicolored 2.00 .90

Isaac Newton (1642-1727), natural philosopher and mathematician.

Elizabeth II Type of 1977

Souvenir Sheet

Design: 500fr, Royal family on balcony.

1977, Dec. 21 Litho. *Perf. 14*

C239 A128 500fr multicolored 5.75 1.75

For overprint see No. C244.

Mallard AP99

Birds: 75fr, Purple heron, vert. 150fr, Reed warbler, vert. 240fr, Hoopoe, vert.

1978, May 22 *Perf. 13x12½, 12½x13*

C240 AP99 65fr multicolored 1.40 .50
C241 AP99 75fr multicolored 1.40 .50
C242 AP99 150fr multicolored 3.50 1.00
C243 AP99 240fr multicolored 5.50 1.75
Nos. C240-C243 (4) 11.80 3.75

No. C239 Overprinted in Silver: "ANNIVERSAIRE DU / COURONNEMENT / 1953-1978"

1978, Sept. Litho. *Perf. 14*

Souvenir Sheet

C244 A128 500fr multicolored 4.50 3.00

25th anniv. of coronation of Elizabeth II.

Philexafrique II-Essen Issue

Common Design Types

No. C245, Leopard and Congo No. C243. No. C246, Eagle and Wurttemberg No. 1.

1978, Nov. 1 Litho. *Perf. 12½*

C245 CD138 100fr multicolored 2.00 1.10
C246 CD139 100fr multicolored 2.00 1.10
a. Pair, #C245-C246 7.00 7.00

Map of Africa, Satellites AP100

1978, Nov. 25 Engr. *Perf. 13*

C247 AP100 100fr multicolored 1.60 .50

Pan-African Telecommunications Network, PANAFTEL.

Map of Africa and People — AP101

1979, Aug. 2 Litho. *Perf. 12½*

C248 AP101 45fr multicolored .50 .25
C249 AP101 75fr multicolored .85 .40

5th Conference of Panafrican Youth Movement, Brazzaville, Aug. 2-7.

Abala Peasant Woman AP102

1979, Aug. 20

C250 AP102 150fr multicolored 1.75 .90

Nos. C173, C206-C207, C186, C189 Overprinted

No. C251

No. C252

Perf. 13, 12½

1979, Nov. 5 **Engr., Litho.**

C251	AP69 80fr multicolored	1.00	.90
C252	AP89 95fr multicolored	1.10	1.00
C253	AP89 100fr multicolored	1.10	1.00
C254	AP77 100fr multicolored	1.10	1.00
C255	AP79 300fr multicolored	3.00	2.75
	Nos. C251-C255 (5)	7.30	6.65

Apollo 11 moon landing, 10th anniversary.

Runner, Olympic Rings — AP103

Pre-Olympic Year: 100fr, Boxing. 200fr, Fencing. 300fr, Soccer. 500fr, Moscow '80 emblem.

1979 **Litho.** *Perf. 13½*

C256	AP103 65fr multi	.60	.25
C257	AP103 100fr multi	.95	.25
C258	AP103 200fr multi, vert.	1.90	.50
C259	AP103 300fr multi	2.75	.75
C260	AP103 500fr multi, vert.	4.75	1.25
	Nos. C256-C260 (5)	10.95	3.00

Cross-Country Skiing — AP104

Lake Placid '80 Emblem and: 60fr, Slalom. 200fr, Ski jump, 350fr, Downhill skiing, horiz. 500fr, Woman skier.

1979, Dec *Perf. 14½*

Size: 24x42mm, 42x24mm

C261	AP104 40fr multicolored	.45	.25
C262	AP104 60fr multicolored	.60	.25
C263	AP104 200fr multicolored	1.90	.45
C264	AP104 350fr multicolored	3.50	.90

Size: 31½x46½mm

Perf. 14

C265	AP104 500fr multicolored	4.50	1.40
	Nos. C261-C265 (5)	10.95	3.25

13th Winter Olympic Games, Lake Placid, NY, Feb. 12-24, 1980.

Nos. C261-C265 Overprinted in Black

1980, Apr. 28

C266	AP104 40fr Zimiatov	.45	.25
C267	AP104 60fr Moser-Proell	.60	.25
C268	AP104 200fr Tomanen	1.90	.75
C269	AP104 350fr Stock	3.50	1.25
C270	AP104 500fr Stenmark-Wenzel	4.75	1.90
	Nos. C266-C270 (5)	11.20	4.40

Long Jump, Olympic Rings — AP105

1980, May 2 **Litho.** *Perf. 14½*

C271	AP105 75fr multi, vert.	.90	.25
C272	AP105 150fr multi	1.40	.30
C273	AP105 250fr multi, vert.	2.25	.50
C274	AP105 350fr multi, vert.	3.25	.70
	Nos. C271-C274 (4)	7.80	1.75

Souvenir Sheet

C275	AP105 500fr multi	5.00	1.60

22nd Summer Olympic Games, Moscow, July 19-Aug. 3.

For overprints see Nos. C292-C296.

Stadium, Mascot, Madrid Club Emblem — AP106

Stadium, Mascot and Club Emblem: 75fr, Zaragoza. 100fr, Madrid Athletic Club. 150fr, Valencia. 175fr, Spain. 250fr, Barcelona.

1980, June 23 **Litho.** *Perf. 14x13½*

C276	AP106 60fr multicolored	.60	.25
C277	AP106 75fr multicolored	.60	.25
C278	AP106 100fr multicolored	1.00	.25
C279	AP106 150fr multicolored	1.40	.35
C280	AP106 175fr multicolored	1.60	.50
	Nos. C276-C280 (5)	5.20	1.60

Souvenir Sheet

C281	AP106 250fr multicolored	2.75	1.25

World Soccer Cup 1982.

For overprints see Nos. C298-C303.

Adoration of the Shepherds — AP107

Rembrandt Paintings: 100fr, The Burial. 200fr, Christ at Emmaus. 300fr, Annunciation, vert. 500fr, Crucifixion, vert.

1980, July 4 *Perf. 12½*

C282	AP107 65fr multicolored	.55	.30
C283	AP107 100fr multicolored	.85	.50
C284	AP107 200fr multicolored	1.75	.60
C285	AP107 300fr multicolored	2.50	.85
C286	AP107 500fr multicolored	4.50	1.50
	Nos. C282-C286 (5)	10.15	3.75

Albert Camus (1913-1960), Writer — AP108

Design: 150fr, Jacques Offenbach (1819-1880), composer, vert.

1980, July 5 **Engr.** *Perf. 13*

C287	AP108 100fr multicolored	1.25	.50
C288	AP108 150fr multicolored	2.25	1.25

Raffia Dancing Skirts — AP109

Traditional Dancing Costumes: 300fr, Tam-tam dancers, vert. 350fr, Masks.

1980, Aug. 6 **Litho.** *Perf. 13½*

C289	AP109 250fr multicolored	2.75	.95
C290	AP109 300fr multicolored	3.25	1.50
C291	AP109 350fr multicolored	4.00	1.90
	Nos. C289-C291 (3)	10.00	4.35

Nos. C271-C275 Overprinted

75fr, Dombrowki (RDA), 150fr, Saneiev (URSS), 250fr, Simeoni (IT), 350fr, Thompson (GB)

1980, Nov. 14 **Litho.** *Perf. 14½*

C292	AP105 75fr multicolored	.70	.30
C293	AP105 150fr multicolored	1.40	.60
C294	AP105 250fr multicolored	2.25	.90
C295	AP105 350fr multicolored	3.25	1.50
	Nos. C292-C295 (4)	7.60	3.30

Souvenir Sheet

C296	AP105 500fr multicolored	5.00	4.00

The Studio by Picasso — AP109a

150fr, Landscape. 200fr, Cannes Studio. 300fr, Still Life. 500fr, Still Life, diff.

1981, July 4 *Perf. 12½*

C296A	AP109a 100fr shown	1.10	.50
C296B	AP109a 150fr multi	1.60	.75
C296C	AP109a 200fr multi	2.10	1.00
C296D	AP109a 300fr multi	3.75	1.50
C296E	AP109a 500fr multi	6.25	2.50
	Nos. C296A-C296E (5)	14.80	6.25

1st Seminar on Petroleum, Gas and Energy Alternatives, Brazzaville AP109b

45fr, Emblem, oil platform, other energy sources. 100fr, Emblem, map, oil platforms. 150fr, Map, other energy sources. 200fr, Maps of Africa, Congo, oil worker.

1981 **Litho.** *Perf. 12½*

C296F	AP109b 45fr multi	20.00	13.00
C296G	AP109b 75fr multi	32.50	19.00
C296H	AP109b 100fr multi	45.00	27.50
C296I	AP109b 150fr multi	65.00	40.00
C296J	AP109b 200fr multi	90.00	50.00
	Nos. C296F-C296J (5)	252.50	149.50

1350th Anniv. of Mohamed's Death at Medina — AP110

400fr, Medina Mosque minaret.

1982, July 17 **Litho.** *Perf. 13*

C297	AP110 400fr multi	3.75	1.75

Nos. C276-C281 Overprinted in Black on Silver

No. C298

No. C299

No. C300

No. C301

No. C302

1982, Oct. 7 **Litho.** *Perf. 14x13½*

C298	AP106 60fr multicolored	.55	.25
C299	AP106 75fr multicolored	.65	.30
C300	AP106 100fr multicolored	1.00	.45
C301	AP106 150fr multicolored	1.60	.60
C302	AP106 175fr multicolored	1.75	.60
	Nos. C298-C302 (5)	5.55	2.20

Souvenir Sheet

C303	AP106 250fr multicolored	2.50	1.90

50th Anniv. of Amelia Earhart's Transatlantic Flight — AP111

1982, Dec. 4 **Engr.** *Perf. 13*

C304	AP111 150fr multicolored	1.75	.75

Wind Surfing
AP112

Various wind surfing scenes, 1984 Olympic Games, 100fr, 300fr, 400fr vert.

1983, June 4 Litho. *Perf. 13*

C305	AP112	100fr multicolored	.90	.25
C306	AP112	200fr multicolored	1.75	.50
C307	AP112	300fr multicolored	2.75	.70
C308	AP112	400fr multicolored	3.50	1.00
		Nos. C305-C308 (4)	8.90	2.45

Souvenir Sheet

C309	AP112	500fr multicolored	5.00	2.50

For overprint see No. C336.

Manned Flight Bicentenary
AP113

Various balloons: 100fr, Montgolfiere, 1783. 200fr, Flesselles, 1784. 300fr, Auguste Piccard, 1931. 400fr, Don Piccard.
500fr, Mail transport balloon, 1870.

1983, June 7

C310	AP113	100fr multicolored	1.10	.25
C311	AP113	200fr multicolored	2.10	.40
C312	AP113	300fr multicolored	3.00	.60
C313	AP113	400fr multicolored	4.50	.90
		Nos. C310-C313 (4)	10.70	2.15

Souvenir Sheet

C314	AP113	500fr multicolored	5.75	1.60

For overprint see No. C337.

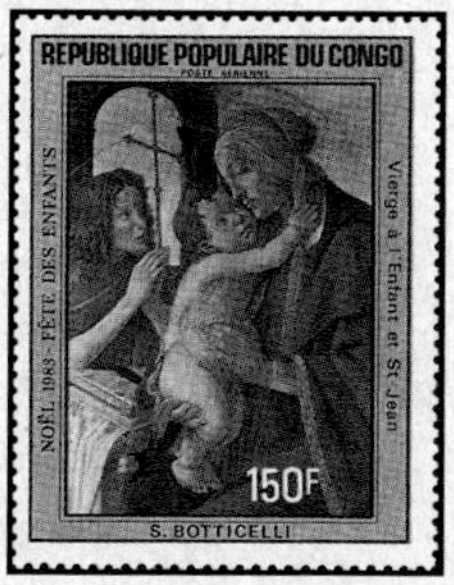

Christmas 1983
AP114

Various Virgin and Child Paintings by Botticelli.

1984, Jan. 21 Litho. *Perf. 13*

C315	AP114	150fr multicolored	1.25	.50
C316	AP114	350fr multicolored	3.00	1.10
C317	AP114	500fr multicolored	4.50	1.50
		Nos. C315-C317 (3)	8.75	3.10

Vase of Flowers, by Manet (1832-83)
AP115

Paintings: 200fr, Small Holy Family, by Raphael. 300fr, La Belle Jardiniere, by Raphael. 400fr, Virgin of Loretto, by Raphael. 500fr, Portrait of Richard Wagner (1813-83), by Giuseppe Tivoli.

1984, Feb. 24 Litho. *Perf. 13*

C318	AP115	100fr multicolored	.90	.30
C319	AP115	200fr multicolored	1.90	.70
C320	AP115	300fr multicolored	2.75	1.00
C321	AP115	400fr multicolored	3.75	1.40
C322	AP115	500fr multicolored	5.00	1.50
		Nos. C318-C322 (5)	14.30	4.90

1984 Summer Olympics — AP116

1984, Mar. 31 *Perf. 13*

C323	AP116	45fr Judo, vert.	.45	.25
C324	AP116	75fr Judo, diff.	.70	.25
C325	AP116	150fr Wrestling	1.40	.50
C326	AP116	175fr Fencing	1.60	.60
C327	AP116	350fr Fencing, diff.	3.25	1.10
		Nos. C323-C327 (5)	7.40	2.70

Souvenir Sheet

C328	AP116	500fr Boxing	5.00	2.50

1984 Summer Olympic Gold Medalists — AP117

Sailing/yachting: 100fr, Stephan Van Den Berg, Netherlands, Windglider Class. 150fr, US, Soling Class. 200fr, Spain, 470 Class. 500fr, US, Flying Dutchman Class.

1984, Dec. 18 Litho. *Perf. 13*

C329	AP117	100fr multi, vert.	1.00	.45
C330	AP117	150fr multi	1.40	.65
C331	AP117	200fr multi	2.00	.90
C332	AP117	500fr multi, vert.	4.50	2.25
		Nos. C329-C332 (4)	8.90	4.25

Virgin and Child, by Giovanni Bellini (c. 1430-1516) — AP118

Religious paintings: 100fr, Holy Family, by Andrea del Sarto (1486-1530). 400fr, Virgin with Angels, by Cimabue (c. 1240-1302).

1985, Feb. 12 Litho. *Perf. 13*

C333	AP118	100fr multi, vert.	.80	.45
C334	AP118	200fr multi	1.60	.90
C335	AP118	400fr multi, vert.	3.00	1.75
		Nos. C333-C335 (3)	5.40	3.10

Christmas 1984.

Nos. C309, C314 Ovptd. with Exhibition in Blue or Green

Overprint's are: No. C336, OLYMPHILEX '85 / LAUSANNE (B). No. C337, MOPHILA '85 / HAM - BURG (G).

1985, Mar. 8 *Perf. 13*

Souvenir Sheets

C336	AP112	500fr multicolored	5.00	4.00
C337	AP113	500fr multicolored	5.00	4.00

Audubon Birth Bicentenary — AP119

Illustrations of North American bird species by Audubon: 100fr, Passiformes fringillidae, vert. 150fr, Eudocimus ruber, vert. 200fr, Buteo jamaicensis. 350fr, Camptorhynchus labradorius.

1985, Apr. 11 *Perf. 13½*

C338	AP119	100fr multicolored	1.00	.45
C339	AP119	150fr multicolored	1.50	.65
C340	AP119	200fr multicolored	1.90	.90
C341	AP119	350fr multicolored	3.75	1.50
		Nos. C338-C341 (4)	8.15	3.50

PHILEXAFRICA '85, Lome — AP120

Youths in public service activities: No. C342, Community health care. No. C343, Agriculture.

1985, May 20 *Perf. 13*

C342	AP120	200fr multicolored	2.50	1.50
C343	AP120	200fr multicolored	2.50	1.50
a.		Pair, #C342-C343 + label	6.00	6.00

For overprints see Nos. 1187-1188.

Admission to UN, 25th Anniv. — AP121

1985, Aug. 13

C344	AP121	190fr multicolored	1.75	.75

Rainbow, emblem
AP122

1985, Oct. 25 *Perf. 12½*

C345	AP122	180fr multicolored	1.60	.65

UN, 40th Anniv.

Christmas — AP123

Paintings: 100fr, The Virgin and the Infant Jesus, by David. 200fr, Adoration of the Magi, by Hieronymus Bosch (1450-1516). 400fr, Virgin and Child, by Van Dyck.

1985, Dec. 20 Litho. *Perf. 13*

C346	AP123	100fr multicolored	.90	.35
C347	AP123	200fr multicolored	1.90	.75
C348	AP123	400fr multicolored	3.50	1.75
		Nos. C346-C348 (3)	6.30	2.85

Nos. C346-C347 vert.

Halley's Comet — AP124

125fr, Halley, comet. 150fr, West's Comet, 1976. 225fr, Ikeya Seki's Comet, 1965. 300fr, Trajectory diagram. 350fr, Comet, Vega probe.

1986, Feb. 17

C349	AP124	125fr multicolored	1.00	.50
C350	AP124	150fr multicolored	1.25	.60
C351	AP124	225fr multicolored	1.75	.90
C352	AP124	300fr multicolored	2.25	1.25
C353	AP124	350fr multicolored	2.75	1.50
		Nos. C349-C353 (5)	9.00	4.75

Nos. C350-C351 vert.

Cosmos-Frantel Hotel — AP125

1986, May 1 *Perf. 13½*

C354	AP125	250fr multicolored	2.50	.90

1986 World Cup Soccer Championships, Mexico — AP126

Various soccer plays.

1986, July 22 Litho. *Perf. 13*

C355	AP126	150fr multicolored	1.25	.60
C356	AP126	250fr multicolored	2.00	1.00
C357	AP126	440fr multicolored	3.75	1.75
C358	AP126	600fr multicolored	6.50	2.50
		Nos. C355-C358 (4)	13.50	5.85

Air Africa, 25th Anniv. — AP127

1986, Nov. 29 Litho. *Perf. 13½*
C359 AP127 200fr multicolored 2.00 .75

1988 Winter Pre-Olympics, Calgary — AP128

150fr, Downhill skiing. 250fr, Bobsled. 440fr, Women's cross-country skiing. 600fr, Ski jumping.

1986, Dec. 15 *Perf. 13*
C360 AP128 150fr multicolored 1.25 .60
C361 AP128 250fr multicolored 2.25 .95
C362 AP128 440fr multicolored 4.00 1.50
C363 AP128 600fr multicolored 5.75 2.40
Nos. C360-C363 (4) 13.25 5.45

Nos. C361-C362 vert.

Christmas AP129

Paintings by Rogier van der Weyden (c.1399-1464): 250fr, Virgin and Child. 440fr, The Nativity. 500fr, Virgin with Carnation.

1986, Dec. 23 *Perf. 13½*
C364 AP129 250fr multicolored 2.25 1.00
C365 AP129 440fr multicolored 4.25 1.75
C366 AP129 500fr multicolored 4.50 2.10
Nos. C364-C366 (3) 11.00 4.85

Crocodiles, World Wildlife Fund — AP130

75fr, Osteolaemus tetraspis. 100fr, Crocodylus cataphractus. 125fr, Osteolaemus tetraspis, diff. 150fr, Crocodylus cataphractus, diff.

1987, Jan. 22 *Perf. 13*
C367 AP130 75fr multicolored 2.25 1.10
C368 AP130 100fr multicolored 2.75 1.25
C369 AP130 125fr multicolored 3.50 1.75
C370 AP130 150fr multicolored 4.00 3.00
Nos. C367-C370 (4) 12.50 7.10

1988 Summer Olympics, Seoul — AP131

1987, July 11 Litho. *Perf. 13*
C371 AP131 100fr Backstroke .90 .35
C372 AP131 200fr Freestyle 1.75 .75
C373 AP131 300fr Breaststroke 2.75 1.10
C374 AP131 400fr Butterfly 3.50 1.40
Nos. C371-C374 (4) 8.90 3.60

Souvenir Sheet

C375 AP131 750fr Start of event 6.75 3.50

Launch of Sputnik, First Artificial Satellite, 30th Anniv. — AP132

1987, June 5 *Perf. 12½x12*
C376 AP132 60fr multicolored .50 .25
C377 AP132 240fr multicolored 2.25 1.10

Butterflies — AP133

75fr, Precis epicleli. 120fr, Deilephila nerii. 450fr, Euryphene senegalensis. 550fr, Precis almanta.

1987, Sept. 4 *Perf. 12½*
C378 AP133 75fr multicolored 1.20 .30
C379 AP133 120fr multicolored 2.00 .45
C380 AP133 450fr multicolored 6.00 1.75
C381 AP133 550fr multicolored 8.00 2.40
Nos. C378-C381 (4) 17.20 4.90

Coubertin, Eternal Flame and Greece No. 125 — AP134

Cameo portrait, athletes and stamps: 120fr, Runners, France No. 198. 350fr, Congo Republic No. C22, hurdler. 600fr, High jump, Congo Republic No. C75.

1987, Nov. 4
C382 AP134 75fr shown .80 .30
C383 AP134 120fr multicolored 1.10 .45
C384 AP134 350fr multicolored 3.50 1.25
C385 AP134 600fr multicolored 5.25 2.10
Nos. C382-C385 (4) 10.65 4.10

Pierre de Coubertin (1863-1937), promulgator of the modern Olympics.

Arrival of Schweitzer in Lambarene, 75th Anniv. — AP135

1988, Apr. 17 Litho. *Perf. 12½*
C386 AP135 240fr multicolored 2.75 1.25

Dr. Albert Schweitzer (1875-1965), Nobel Peace Prize winner of 1952, founded Lambarene Hospital, Gabon, in 1913.

1988 Summer Olympics, Seoul — AP136

Pentathlon: 75fr, Swimming. 170fr, Cross-country running, vert. 200fr, Shooting. 600fr, Equestrian. 700fr, Fencing.

1988, June 10 Litho. *Perf. 13*
C387 AP136 75fr multicolored .70 .25
C388 AP136 170fr multicolored 1.60 .60
C389 AP136 200fr multicolored 1.75 .70
C390 AP136 600fr multicolored 5.00 2.00
Nos. C387-C390 (4) 9.05 3.55

Souvenir Sheet

C391 AP136 750fr multicolored 6.75 3.75

Elimination Matches, 1990 World Cup Soccer Championships — AP137

Various athletes and cities in Italy.

1989, June 15 Litho. *Perf. 13*
C392 AP137 75fr Bari .60 .30
C393 AP137 120fr Rome 1.00 .45
C394 AP137 500fr Florence 4.75 1.90
C395 AP137 550fr Naples 5.25 2.00
Nos. C392-C395 (4) 11.60 4.65

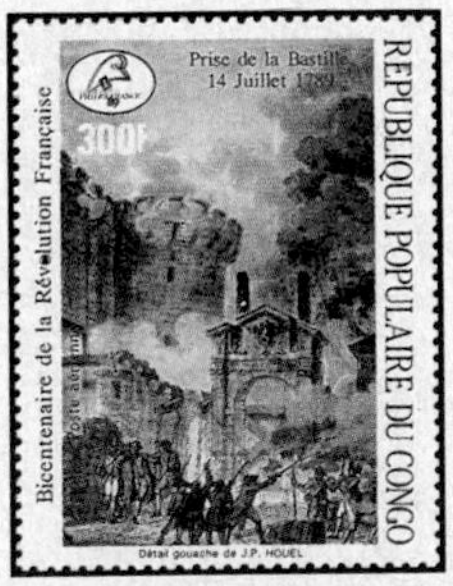

PHILEXFRANCE '89 — AP138

Paintings: 300fr, Storming of the Bastille, July 14, 1789, from a gouache by J.P. Houel. 400fr, Eiffel Tower, by G. Seurat.

1989, June 22
C396 AP138 300fr multicolored 2.75 1.10
C397 AP138 400fr multicolored 3.75 1.50

French revolution, bicent. (300fr); Eiffel Tower, cent. (400fr).

First Moon Landing, 20th Anniv. AP139

Man's first step on the Moon: No. C398, Astronaut on ladder. No. C399, Conducting experiments on the Moon's surface.

1989, June 22
C398 AP139 400fr multicolored 3.75 1.50
C399 AP139 400fr multicolored 3.75 1.50

World Cup Soccer Championships, Italy — AP140

Various soccer plays and architecture.

1990, June 8 Litho. *Perf. 13*
C400 AP140 120fr multicolored 1.00 .50
C401 AP140 240fr multicolored 2.10 .95
C402 AP140 500fr multicolored 4.25 2.00
C403 AP140 600fr multicolored 5.25 2.40
Nos. C400-C403 (4) 12.60 5.85

Pan African Postal Union, 10th Anniv. AP141

1991, Jan. 10 Litho. *Perf. 13½*
C404 AP141 60fr shown .55 .25
C405 AP141 120fr Emblem 1.00 .50

1992 Winter Olympics, Albertville AP142

120fr, Ice hockey. 300fr, Speed skating. 1500fr, Slalom skiing.

1991, June 8 Litho. *Perf. 13½*
C406 AP142 120fr multi 1.40 .60
C407 AP142 300fr multi 3.00 1.50

Litho. & Embossed

C408 AP142 1500fr multi 15.00 15.00

Numbers have been reserved for souvenir sheets in this set.

1992 Summer Olympics, Barcelona
AP143

No. C411, Equestrian. No. C412, Long jump.

Litho. & Embossed

1992, Dec. 21		*Perf. 13½*	
C411 AP143 1500fr gold & multi		16.00	16.00

Souvenir Sheet

C412 AP143 1500fr gold & multi	21.00	21.00

Anniversaries
AP144

Designs: 90fr, Victor Schoelcher, missionary, death cent. 205fr, Martin Luther King, civil rights reformer, 25th death anniv. 300fr, Claude Chappe (1763-1805), bicent. of visual telegraph.

1993	Litho.	*Perf. 14*	
C413 AP144	90fr multicolored	*1.00*	*.50*
C414 AP144	205fr multicolored	*2.50*	*1.25*
C415 AP144	300fr multicolored	*3.50*	*1.75*
	Nos. C413-C415 (3)	*7.00*	*3.50*

1994 Winter Olympics, Lillehammer
AP145

1993, Apr. 26	Litho.	*Perf. 13*	
C416 AP145	400fr Ice dancing	*4.00*	*1.40*
C417 AP145	600fr Ice hockey	*7.50*	*1.75*

Souvenir Sheet

C418 AP145 750fr Downhill skiing	*8.00*	*4.00*

Nos. C416-C417 exist in imperf. souvenir sheets of 1. Nos. C416-C418 exist imperf.

AIR POST SEMI-POSTAL STAMPS

Hathor Pillar — SPAP1

Unwmk.

1964, Mar. 9	Engr.	*Perf. 13*	
CB1 SPAP1	10fr + 5fr vio & chnt	.90	.50
CB2 SPAP1	25fr + 5fr org brn & slate grn	1.10	.70
CB3 SPAP1	50fr + 5fr slate grn & brn red	2.25	1.60
	Nos. CB1-CB3 (3)	4.25	2.80

UNESCO world campaign to save historic monuments in Nubia.

POSTAGE DUE STAMPS

Messenger — D6

MH. 1521 Broussard Plane — D7

Early Transportation: 1fr, Litter. 2fr, Canoe. 5fr, Bicyclist. 10fr, Steam locomotive. 25fr, Seaplane.

Unwmk.

1961, Dec. 4	Engr.	*Perf. 11*	
J34 D6	50c ultra, ol bis & red	.25	.25
a.	Pair, #J34, J40	.25	
J35 D6	1fr red brn, red & grn	.25	.25
a.	Pair, #J35, J41	.30	
J36 D6	2fr grn, ultra & brn	.25	.25
a.	Pair, #J36, J42	.40	
J37 D6	5fr pur & gray brn	.25	.25
a.	Pair, #J37, J43	.50	
J38 D6	10fr bl, grn & chocolate	.70	.70
a.	Pair, #J38, J44	1.40	1.40
J39 D6	25fr bl, dk grn & dk brn	1.60	1.60
a.	Pair, #J39, J45	3.25	

Modern transportation: 1fr, Land Rover. 2fr, River boat transporting barge. 5fr, Trailer-truck. 10fr, Diesel locomotive. 25fr, Boeing 707 jet plane.

J40 D7	50c ultra, olive bis & red	.25	.25
J41 D7	1fr red & grn	.25	.25
J42 D7	2fr ultra, grn & brn	.25	.25
J43 D7	5fr pur & gray brn	.25	.25
J44 D7	10fr dk grn & chocolate	.70	.70
J45 D7	25fr bl, dk grn & sepia	1.60	1.60
	Nos. J34-J45 (12)	6.60	6.60

Pairs printed tête bêche, se-tenant at the base.

Flowers — D8

Flowers: 2fr, Phaeomeria magnifica. 5fr, Millettia laurentii. 10fr, Tuberose. 15fr, Pyrostegia venusta. 20fr, Hibiscus.

1971, Mar. 25	Photo.	*Perf. 12x12½*	
J46 D8	1fr multi	.35	.35
J47 D8	2fr multi	.45	.45
J48 D8	5fr pink & multi	.55	.55
J49 D8	10fr dk grn & multi	.70	.70
J50 D8	15fr multi	1.10	1.10
J51 D8	20fr multi	1.40	1.40
	Nos. J46-J51 (6)	4.55	4.55

Flowers and Fruit — D9

5fr, Passiflora quadrangulares. 10fr, Cannaceae, vert. 15fr, Ananas comosus, vert.

1986, June 5	Litho.	*Perf. 13*	
J52 D9	5fr multicolored	.25	.25
J53 D9	10fr multicolored	.45	.45
J54 D9	15fr multicolored	.55	.55
	Nos. J52-J54 (3)	1.25	1.25

OFFICIAL STAMPS

Coat of Arms — O1

Perf. 14x13

1968-70	Unwmk.	Typo.	
O1 O1	1fr multi ('70)	.25	.25
O2 O1	2fr multi ('70)	.25	.25
O3 O1	5fr multi ('70)	.25	.25
O4 O1	10fr multi ('70)	.25	.25
O5 O1	25fr emer & multi	.45	.25
O6 O1	30fr red & multi	.60	.25
O7 O1	50fr multi ('70)	1.10	.50
O8 O1	85fr multi ('70)	2.25	.90
O9 O1	100fr multi ('70)	2.75	1.10
O10 O1	200fr multi ('70)	3.75	2.00
	Nos. O1-O10 (10)	11.90	6.00

COOK ISLANDS

'kuk 'ī-ləndz

(Rarotonga)

LOCATION — South Pacific Ocean, northeast of New Zealand
GOVT. — Internal self-government, linked to New Zealand
AREA — 91 sq. mi.
POP. — 19,103 (1996)
CAPITAL — Avarua

Fifteen islands in Northern and Southern groups extend over 850,000 square miles of ocean.

Separate stamp issues used by Aitutaki (1903-32 and 1972 onward) and Penrhyn Islands (1902-32 and 1973 onward). Niue is included geographically, but administered separately. It continues to issue separate stamps.

12 Pence = 1 Shilling
20 Shillings = 1 Pound
100 Cents = 1 Dollar (1967)

Catalogue values for unused stamps in this country are for Never Hinged items, beginning with Scott 127 in the regular postage section, Scott B1 in the semi-postal section, Scott C1 in the air post section, Scott CB1 in the air post semi-postal section and Scott O16 in the official section.

Watermarks

Wmk. 61 — Single-lined N Z and Star Close Together

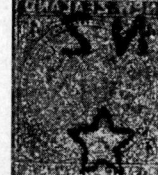

Wmk. 62 — Single-lined N Z and Star Wide Apart

Wmk. 253 — Multiple N Z and Star

A1

1892	Unwmk.	Typo.	*Perf. 12½*	
	Toned Paper			
1	A1	1p black	35.00	30.00
2	A1	1½p violet	47.50	45.00
a.		Imperf, pair	*19,000.*	
3	A1	2½p blue	47.50	45.00
4	A1	10p carmine	160.00	150.00
		Nos. 1-4 (4)	290.00	270.00
	White Paper			
5	A1	1p black	35.00	30.00
a.		Vert. pair, imperf. between	*11,000.*	
6	A1	1½p violet	47.50	45.00
7	A1	2½p blue	47.50	45.00
8	A1	10p carmine	160.00	150.00
		Nos. 5-8 (4)	290.00	270.00

Nos. 1-8 were printed in sheets of 60 (6x10), from a setting of six slightly different cliches.

Queen Makea Takau — A2

1893-94		Wmk. 62	*Perf. 12x11½*	
9	A2	1p brown	50.00	*55.00*
10	A2	1p blue ('94)	13.00	2.50
11	A2	1½p brt violet	17.50	8.50
12	A2	2½p rose	55.00	27.50
13	A2	5p olive gray	22.50	16.00
14	A2	10p green	85.00	57.50
		Nos. 9-14 (6)	243.00	*167.00*

Perf. 12½ examples of Nos. 10, 12 are from a part of the normal perf. 12x11½ sheets. They were caused by a partial deviation of the original perforating.

Wrybill (Torea) — A3

1898-1900			*Perf. 11*	
15	A3	½p blue ('00)	6.50	*15.00*
a.		"d" omitted at upper right	*1,750.*	
16	A2	1p brown	29.00	21.00
17	A2	1p blue	6.00	5.50
18	A2	1½p violet	13.00	7.50
19	A3	2p chocolate	15.00	8.50
20	A2	2½p car rose	25.00	13.00
21	A2	5p olive gray	27.50	21.00
22	A3	6p red violet	22.50	*29.00*
23	A2	10p green	26.00	*57.50*
24	A3	1sh car rose	57.50	57.50
		Nos. 15-24 (10)	228.00	*235.50*

No. 17 Surcharged in Black

1899				
25	A2	½p on 1p blue	40.00	*50.00*
a.		Double surcharge	1,000.	*1,200.*
b.		Inverted surcharge	1,200.	1,100.

No. 16 Overprinted in Black

1901

26 A2 1p brown 210.00 160.00
 a. Inverted overprint 2,400. 1,900.
 c. Double overprint 1,900. 1,900.

Some single stamps were overprinted by favor. Other varieties could exist.
Forgeries exist.

Types of 1893-98

1902 **Unwmk.**

27 A3 ½p green 9.50 9.00
 a. Vert. pair, imperf. horiz. *1,400.*
28 A2 1p rose 14.00 *21.00*
29 A2 2½p dull blue 15.00 *25.00*
 Nos. 27-29 (3) 38.50 *55.00*

1902 **Wmk. 61** ***Perf. 11***

30 A3 ½p green 4.25 *3.75*
31 A2 1p rose 4.75 *3.50*
32 A2 1½p brt violet 4.75 *10.00*
33 A3 2p chocolate 9.50 *12.00*
 a. Figures of value omitted *2,750.* *3,600.*
 b. Perf. 11x14 *2,250.*
34 A2 2½p dull blue 4.50 *8.25*
35 A2 5p olive gray 42.50 *57.50*
36 A3 6p purple 37.50 *32.50*
37 A2 10p blue green 55.00 *120.00*
38 A3 1sh car rose 55.00 *82.50*
 a. Perf. 11x14 *3,000.*
 Nos. 30-38 (9) 217.75 *330.00*

1909-19 ***Perf. 14, 14x14½, 14½x14***

39 A3 ½p green, perf 14½x14 ('11) 11.00 *9.50*
 a. ½p dp grn, perf 14 ('15) 9.50 *17.50*
 b. As "a," wmk upright 14.00 *22.50*
40 A2 1p red, wmk. sideways ('09) 15.00 5.00
41 A2 1½p purple, perf 14x15 ('16) 19.00 4.75
42 A3 2p dp brown ('19) 6.00 *57.50*
43 A2 10p dp green ('18) 37.50 *110.00*
44 A3 1sh car rose ('19) 32.50 *110.00*
 Nos. 39-44 (6) 121.00*296.75*

Nos. 39-40 are on both ordinary and chalky paper; Nos. 41-44 on chalky paper.

New Zealand Stamps of 1909-19 Surcharged in Dark Blue or Red

1919 **Typo.** ***Perf. 14x15***

48 A43 ½p yel green (R) .45 *1.25*
 a. Pair, one without surcharge
49 A42 1p carmine 1.25 *4.50*
50 A47 1½p brown org (R) .60 *.90*
51 A43 2p yellow (R) 1.75 *2.00*
52 A43 3p chocolate 3.25 *15.00*

Engr. ***Perf. 14x14½***

53 A44 2½p dull blue (R) 2.75 2.50
54 A45 3p violet brown 3.00 2.00
55 A45 4p purple 2.25 *4.25*
56 A44 4½p dark green 2.25 *9.50*
57 A45 6p car rose 2.00 *5.50*
58 A44 7½p red brown, perf 14x13½ 2.10 *6.50*
59 A45 9p ol green (R) 3.75 *17.50*
60 A45 1sh vermilion 2.75 *27.50*
 Nos. 48-60 (13) 28.15 *98.90*

The Polynesian surcharge restates the denomination of the basic stamp.

Landing of Capt. Cook
A4

Avarua Waterfront
A5

Capt. James Cook — A6

Palm — A7

Houses at Arorangi — A8

Avarua Harbor — A9

1920 **Unwmk.** **Engr.** ***Perf. 14***

61 A4 ½p green & black 4.75 *25.00*
62 A5 1p car & black 5.50 *25.00*
 a. Center inverted *700.00*
63 A6 1½p blue & black 10.00 10.00
64 A7 3p red brn & blk 2.50 *6.50*
65 A8 6p org & red brn 4.25 *10.00*
66 A9 1sh vio & black 8.00 *20.00*
 Nos. 61-66 (6) 35.00 *96.50*

The stamps overprinted or inscribed "Rarotonga" were used throughout the Cook Islands.
For surcharges see Nos. 78, 79.

New Zealand Postal-Fiscal Stamps of 1906-13 Overprinted in Red or Dark Blue — a

Perf. 14, 14½, 14x14½

1921 **Typo.** **Wmk. 61**

67 PF1 2sh blue (R) 32.50 *65.00*
68 PF1 2sh6p brown 22.50 *60.00*
69 PF1 5sh green (R) 32.50 *77.50*
70 PF1 10sh claret 90.00 *140.00*
71 PF2 £1 rose 140.00 *250.00*
 Nos. 67-71 (5) 317.50 *592.50*

Types of 1920 Issue

1924-26 **Engr.** ***Perf. 14***

72 A4 ½p yel grn & black 5.25 10.00
73 A5 1p carmine & black 7.00 2.50

Issued: ½p, May 13, 1926; 1p, Nov. 10, 1924.

New Zealand Stamps of 1926 Overprinted in Red

1926-28 **Typo.** ***Perf. 14, 14½x14***

74 A56 2sh blue ('27) 17.50 *47.50*
 a. 2sh dark blue 12.00 *47.50*
75 A56 3sh violet ('28) 19.00 *50.00*

Rarotongan Chief (Te Po) — A10

Avarua Harbor — A11

1927, Oct. 15 **Engr.** ***Perf. 14***

76 A10 2½p dk bl & red brn 8.00 *29.00*
77 A11 4p dull vio & bl grn 13.00 *20.00*

No. 63 Surcharged in Red

1931 **Unwmk.**

78 A6 2p on 1½p blue & blk 11.00 3.25

Same Surcharge on Type of 1920

Wmk. 61

79 A6 2p on 1½p blue & blk 5.50 *13.00*

No. 79 was not issued without surcharge.

New Zealand Postal-Fiscal Stamps of 1931-32 Overprinted Type "a" in Blue or Red

1931, Nov. 12 **Typo.**

80 PF5 2sh6p dp brown (Bl) 12.00 *26.00*
81 PF5 5sh green (R) 21.00 *65.00*
82 PF5 10sh dk car (Bl) 45.00 *110.00*
83 PF5 £1 pink (Bl) ('32) 105.00 *190.00*
 Nos. 80-83 (4) 183.00 *391.00*

See Nos. 103-108, 124A-126C.

Landing of Capt. Cook — A12

Capt. James Cook — A13

Double Canoe — A14

Islanders Unloading Ship — A15

View of Avarua Harbor — A16

R.M.S. Monowai — A17

King George V — A18

Unwmk.

1932, Mar. 16 **Engr.** ***Perf. 13***

Center in Black

84 A12 ½p deep green 4.00 *19.00*
 a. Perf. 14 32.50 *105.00*
85 A13 1p brown lake 7.75 5.25
 a. Center inverted *9,500.* *9,500.*
 b. Perf. 14 17.50 *28.00*
86 A14 2p brown 3.50 *6.50*
 b. Perf. 14 10.00 *24.00*
87 A15 2½p dark ultra 24.00 *70.00*
 b. Perf. 14 19.00 *65.00*

Perf. 14

88 A16 4p ultra 12.00 *65.00*
 a. Perf. 13 25.00 *75.00*
 b. Perf. 14x13 35.00 *130.00*
89 A17 6p orange 5.00 *17.50*
 a. Perf. 13 30.00 *57.50*
90 A18 1sh deep violet 22.00 *26.00*
 Nos. 84-90 (7) 78.25 *209.25*

Nos. 84 to 90 were available for postage in Aitutaki, Penrhyn and Rarotonga and replaced the special issues for those islands.
Inverted centers of the 1p and 2p are from printers waste.

1933-36 **Wmk. 61** ***Perf. 14***

91 A12 ½p dp grn & blk 1.20 *5.25*
92 A13 1p dk car & black ('35) 1.50 *2.40*
93 A14 2p brn & blk ('36) 1.75 .60
94 A15 2½p dk ultra & blk 1.75 *2.50*
95 A16 4p blue & black 1.75 .60
96 A17 6p org & blk ('36) 2.00 *2.50*
97 A18 1sh dp vio & black ('36) 27.50 *42.50*
 Nos. 91-97 (7) 37.45 *56.35*

See Nos. 116-121.

Silver Jubilee Issue

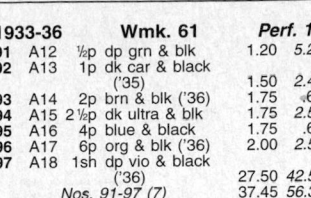

Types of 1932 Overprinted in Black or Red

1935, May 7

98 A13 1p dk car & brn red .65 *2.00*
99 A15 2½p dk ultra & bl (R) 2.00 *3.50*
100 A17 6p dull org & green 7.25 *8.50*
 Nos. 98-100 (3) 9.90 *14.00*
Set, never hinged 16.00

The vertical spacing of the overprint is wider on No. 100.

New Zealand Stamps of 1926 Overprinted in Black — b

1936, July 15 **Typo.** ***Perf. 14***

101 A56 2sh blue 15.00 *50.00*
102 A56 3sh violet 15.00 *80.00*

1931-35 New Zealand Postal-Fiscal Stamps Ovptd. Type "b" in Black or Red

1932-36

103 PF5 2sh6p brown ('36) 35.00 *95.00*
104 PF5 5sh grn (R) ('36) 40.00 *130.00*
105 PF5 10sh dk car ('36) 85.00 *250.00*
106 PF5 £1 pink ('36) 110.00 *275.00*
107 PF5 £3 lt grn (R) 500.00 *900.00*
108 PF5 £5 dk blue (R) 250.00 *400.00*
 Nos. 103-108 (6) 1,020. *2,050.*

Issue dates: Mar. 1932, July 15, 1936.

New Zealand Stamps of 1937 Overprinted in Black

Perf. 14x13½

1937, June 1 **Engr.** **Wmk. 253**

109 A78 1p rose carmine .25 .25
110 A78 2½p dark blue .25 .25
111 A78 6p vermilion .35 .30
 Nos. 109-111 (3) .85 .80
Set, never hinged 2.50

King George VI
A19

Village and Palms
A20

Coastal Scene with Canoe — A21

1938, May 2 Wmk. 61 *Perf. 14*

112 A19 1sh dp violet & blk 7.00 *15.00*
113 A20 2sh dk red brn & blk 14.00 19.00
114 A21 3sh yel green & blue 35.00 *42.50*
Nos. 112-114 (3) 56.00 76.50
Set, never hinged 100.00

See Nos. 122-124.

Mt. Ikurangi behind Avarua — A22

Perf. 13½x14

1940, Sept. 2 Engr. Wmk. 253

115 A22 3p on 1½p violet & blk .80 .80

Issued only with surcharge. Stamps without surcharge are from the printer's archives.

Types of 1932-38

1944-46 Engr. *Perf. 14*

116 A12 ½p dk ol grn & blk ('45) 1.00 *4.50*
117 A13 1p dk car & blk ('45) 1.50 1.25
118 A14 2p brn & blk ('46) .90 *7.00*
119 A15 2½p dk bl & blk ('45) .60 *2.00*
120 A16 4p blue & black 2.50 *15.00*
121 A17 6p org & black 1.00 *2.50*
122 A19 1sh dp vio & blk 1.00 *3.50*
123 A20 2sh dk red brn & blk 27.50 *50.00*
124 A21 3sh yel green & blue ('45) 25.00 *40.00*
Nos. 116-124 (9) 61.00 125.75
Set, never hinged 100.00

New Zealand Nos. AR76, AR78, AR86 and Type of 1931 Postal-Fiscal Stamps Overprinted Type "b" in Black or Red

1943-50 Wmk. 253 Typo. *Perf. 14*

124A PF5 2sh6p brn ('46) 11.50 *22.50*
125 PF5 5sh green (R) 7.75 *22.50*
126 PF5 10sh dp pink ('48) 35.00 *90.00*
126A PF5 £1 pink ('47) 40.00 *97.50*
126B PF5 £3 lt grn (R) ('46) 47.50 *190.00*
126C PF5 £5 dk bl (R) ('50) 175.00 *425.00*
Nos. 124A-126C (6) 316.75 *847.50*
Set, never hinged 550.00

For surcharges see Nos. 192-194.

Catalogue values for unused stamps in this section, from this point to the end of the section, are for Never Hinged items.

Peace Issue

New Zealand Nos. 248, 250, 254 and 255 Overprinted in Black or Blue

c

d

Perf. 13x13½, 13½x13

1946, June 1 Engr.

127 A94 (c) 1p emerald .40 .25
128 A96 (d) 2p rose vio (Bl) .40 .40
129 A100(c) 6p org red & red brn .75 .70
130 A101(c) 8p brn lake & blk (Bl) .65 .65
Nos. 127-130 (4) 2.20 2.00

Ngatangiia Channel, Rarotonga A23

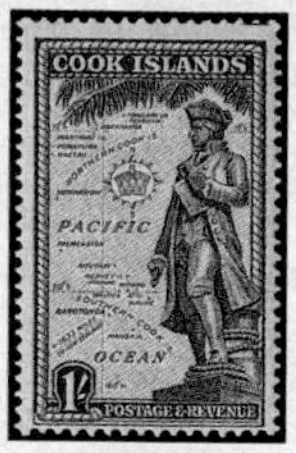

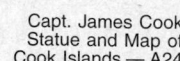

Capt. James Cook Statue and Map of Cook Islands — A24

Designs: 1p, Cook and map of Hervey Isls. 2p, Rev. John Williams, his ship Messenger of Peace, and map of Rarotonga. 3p, Aitutaki map and palms. 5p, Mail plane landing at Rarotonga airport. 6p, Tongareva (Penrhyn) scene. 8p, Islander's house, Rarotonga. 2sh, Thatched house, mat weaver. 3sh, Steamer Matua offshore.

Perf. 13½x13, 13x13½

1949, Aug.1 Engr. Wmk. 253

131 A23 ½p brown & violet .25 *1.25*
132 A23 1p green & orange 4.00 2.50
133 A23 2p carmine & brn 2.50 2.50
134 A23 3p ultra & green 2.25 *2.50*
135 A23 5p purple & grn 7.00 2.00
136 A23 6p car rose & blk 7.00 3.25
137 A23 8p orange & olive .75 *4.75*
138 A24 1sh chocolate & bl 6.50 4.75
139 A24 2sh rose car & brn 4.75 *16.00*
140 A24 3sh bl grn & lt ultra 12.50 *29.00*
Nos. 131-140 (10) 47.50 *68.50*

For surcharge see No. 147.

Coronation Issue

Type of New Zealand

1953, May 25 Photo. *Perf. 14x14½*

145 A113 3p brown 1.00 1.00
146 A114 6p slate black 1.90 1.90

No. 135 Surcharged with New Value and Two Dots

1960, Apr. 1 Engr. *Perf. 13½x13*

147 A23 1sh6p on 5p purple & grn .55 .55

Tiare Maori — A25

Fishing God — A26

Queen Elizabeth II — A27

Island Scene A28

3sh, Administration building, Mangaia. 5sh, Ship in Rarotonga harbor. 3p, 5p, 6p, 1sh, horiz.

Perf. 13½x13, 13x13½

Litho.; Engr.; (1sh6p)

1963, June 4

148 A25 1p shown .60 *.70*
149 A26 2p shown .25 *.50*
150 A25 3p Frangipani .55 *.70*
151 A26 5p Fairy tern 6.75 2.10
152 A25 6p Hibiscus .90 .75
153 A26 8p Bonito 3.75 1.60
154 A25 1sh Oranges .80 .75
155 A27 1sh6p shown 2.25 2.10
156 A28 2sh gray & brown 1.60 1.25
157 A28 3sh emer & black 1.60 1.90
158 A28 5sh ultra & brown 13.00 5.25
Nos. 148-158 (11) 32.05 17.60

For overprints and surcharges see Nos. 167-169, 179-181, 183-184, 186-190.

Solar Eclipse and Palm Tree — A29

1965, May 31 Litho. *Perf. 13x13½*

159 A29 6p black, lt blue & yel .30 .30

Observation of the solar eclipse on Manuae Island, May 30, 1965. Exists imperf.

For surcharge see No. 185.

Flag of New Zealand and Map of Cook Islands A30

Designs: 10p, London Missionary Society Church and graveyard. 1sh, Reading of Proclamation of Cession, Oct. 8, 1900, and Queen Elizabeth II. 1sh9p, Nikao School and flag of New Zealand.

Perf. 13½x13

1965, Sept. 16 Litho. Wmk. 253

160 A30 4p blue & red .25 .25
161 A30 10p multicolored .25 .25
162 A30 1sh multicolored .25 .25
163 A30 1sh9p multicolored .45 .45
Nos. 160-163 (4) 1.20 1.20

Establishment of internal self-government.

For surcharges see Nos. 182, 191.

Nos. 160-162 and 156-158 Overprinted in Red: "In Memoriam / Sir Winston Churchill / 1874-1965"

1966, Jan. 24 Litho. Wmk. 253

164 A30 4p blue & red .75 .30
165 A30 10p multicolored 2.25 .60
a. Inverted overprint *275.00*
166 A30 1sh multicolored 2.25 .90
167 A28 2sh gray & brown 2.25 1.60
168 A28 3sh emer & black 2.25 1.60
169 A28 5sh ultra & brown 2.75 2.25
Nos. 164-169 (6) 12.50 7.25

Statesman and WWII leader.

Adoration of the Wise Men, by Fra Angelico — A31

Paintings: 2p, Nativity, by Hans Memling, vert. 4p, Adoration of the Wise Men, by Velazquez. 10p, Adoration of the Wise Men, by Hieronymus Bosch. 1sh6p, Adoration of the Shepherds, by Jose Ribera, vert.

Perf. 13x14½, 14½x13

1966, Nov. 28 Photo. Unwmk.

170 A31 1p multicolored .25 .25
171 A31 2p multicolored .25 .25
172 A31 4p multicolored .25 .25
173 A31 10p multicolored .40 .40
174 A31 1sh6p multicolored .50 .50
Nos. 170-174 (5) 1.65 1.65

Christmas. Issued in sheets of 6 with ornamental gold border.

Perf. 13x12, 12x13

170a A31 1p .50 *.55*
171a A31 2p 15.00 *11.50*
172a A31 4p 1.20 *1.00*
173a A31 10p 2.60 *4.50*
174a A31 1sh6p 32.50 6.75
Nos. 170a-174a (5) 51.80 *24.30*

Tennis and Queen Elizabeth A32

Sport: 1p, Women's basketball and Games' emblem. 4p, Boxing and team emblem. 7p, Soccer and Queen Elizabeth II.

1967, Jan. 12 *Perf. 13½*

175 A32 ½p brt olive & multi .25 .25
176 A32 1p brt blue & multi .25 .25
177 A32 4p purple & multi .25 .25
178 A32 7p red & multi .25 .25
Nos. 175-178,C10-C11 (6) 1.50 1.50

Second South Pacific Games, Noumea, New Caledonia, Dec. 8-18, 1966.

Nos. 148-155, 157-161 Surcharged with New Value or Black or Red

Pair (#181b), with Type I on left (#181) and Type II on right (#181a)

1967

179 A25 1c on 1p .35 *1.75*
180 A26 2c on 2p .25 .25
181 A25 2½c on 3p (I) .25 .25
a. Type II .25 .25
b. Pair, #181 and #181a .35 .45
182 A30 3c on 4p .25 .25
183 A26 4c on 5p 7.25 .40
184 A25 5c on 6p .25 .25
185 A29 5c on 6p 4.00 1.25
186 A26 7c on 8p .25 .25
187 A25 10c on 1sh .25 .25
188 A27 15c on 1sh6p (R) 1.60 1.10
189 A28 30c on 3sh (R) 18.00 5.50
190 A28 50c on 5sh (R) 3.25 2.00
191 A30 $1 on 10p (R) 13.50 8.00
Nos. 179-191 (13) 49.45 21.50

Issued: 2c, 2½c, 3c, 5c, 7c, 10c, 4/3; others 5/4.

No. 191 is surcharged "10/ $1.00" and 3 bars over old value.

Numerous varieties of surcharge include wrong-font "c," thin numerals, etc.

Nos. 126A, 126B and 126C Surcharged in Red

Wmk. 253

1967, June 6 Typo. *Perf. 14*

192 PF5 $2 on £1 pink 72.50 *200.00*
193 PF5 $6 on £3 lt green 125.00 *225.00*
194 PF5 $10 on £5 dk blue 225.00 *375.00*
Nos. 192-194 (3) 422.50 800.00

Frequently found with stained gum.

Stamp of 1892, Village and Queen Victoria A33

Designs: 3c (4p), PO, Rarotonga, and Elizabeth II. 8c (10p), View of Avarua, Rarotonga, and 10p stamp of 1892. 18c (1sh9p), Map of Cook Islands, DC-3, S.S. Moana Roa and Capt. Cook.

Perf. 13½

1967, July 3 Photo. Unwmk.

195 A33 1c (1p) multi .25 .25
196 A33 3c (4p) multi .25 .25
197 A33 8c (10p) multi .30 .30
198 A33 18c (1sh9p) multi 1.10 .80
a. Souvenir sheet of 4, #195-198 3.00 3.00
Nos. 195-198 (4) 1.90 1.60

75th anniv. of the 1st Cook Islands stamps. Issued in sheets of 8 stamps and 1 label with inscription in yellow margin.

Hibiscus — A34

Elizabeth II A35

Elizabeth II and Flowers — A36

Flowers: 1c, Rose of Sharon. 2c, 15c, Frangipani. 2½c, Butterfly pea. 3c, Suva queen and Queen Elizabeth II. 4c, Water lily. 5c, Bauhania. 6c, Yellow hibiscus. 8c, Alamanda and Queen Elizabeth II. 9c, Stephanotis. 10c, Flaymboyant poinciana. 20c, Thunbergia. 25c, Canna lily and Queen Elizabeth II. 30c, Poinsettia. 50c, Gardenia.

The $4 exists with "FOUR DOLLARS" in two widths: type 1, 32½mm; type 2, 33½mm.

1967-69 Photo. *Perf. 14x13½*

199	A34	½c gold & multi	.30	.25
200	A34	1c gold & multi	.30	.25
201	A34	2c gold & multi	.30	.25
202	A34	2½c gold & multi	.40	.25
203	A34	3c gold & multi	.80	.25
204	A34	4c *Walter Lily*	1.10	*1.75*
205	A34	4c *Water Lily*	3.00	1.50
206	A34	5c gold & multi	.60	.25
207	A34	6c gold & multi	.65	.25
208	A34	8c gold & multi	.65	.25
209	A34	9c gold & multi	.65	.25
210	A34	10c gold & multi	.65	.25
211	A34	15c gold & multi	.65	.25
212	A34	20c gold & multi	7.00	.50
213	A34	25c gold & multi	1.20	.60
214	A34	30c gold & multi	1.00	.70
215	A34	50c gold & multi	1.60	1.00
216	A35	$1 gold & multi	3.25	2.25
217	A35	$2 gold & multi	7.25	3.50
218	A36	$4 multi, type 2 ('68)	4.75	*9.00*
a.		Type 1	40.00	*55.00*
219	A36	$6 multi ('68)	3.00	*7.50*
219A	A36	$8 multi ('69)	9.00	*11.00*
220	A36	$10 multi ('68)	5.75	*12.00*
		Nos. 199-220 (23)	53.85	54.05

Nos. 199-220 (except No. 204) were reprinted in 1970/71 with the fluorescent printing described below. Value, set: unused $60; used $35.

For surcharges see Nos. 290-291, 305-309, B1-B13, B17-B18, B20. For overprints see Nos. 277-283, 302-304, 315, 351-356, O1-O15.

Fluorescence

Since 1968 a number of stamps have been issued with a "fluorescent security underprinting" in a multiple coat of arms pattern. Some issues have this underprint, some do not.

Stamps issued both with and without the underprint are Nos. 199-203, 205-220, 283, 290-291.

From Nos. 292-296 onward, all stamps have this underprint unless otherwise noted.

Ia Orana Maria, by Gauguin A37

Gauguin Paintings: 3c, Riders on the Beach. 5c, Still Life with Flowers. 8c, Whispered Words. 15c, Maternity. 22c, Why Are You Angry?

1967, Oct. 23 Photo. *Perf. 13½*

221	A37	1c gold & multi	.25	.25
222	A37	3c gold & multi	.25	.25
223	A37	5c gold & multi	.25	.25
224	A37	8c gold & multi	.25	.25
225	A37	15c gold & multi	.30	.25
226	A37	22c gold & multi	.50	.50
a.		Souvenir sheet of 6, #221-226	3.75	3.75
		Nos. 221-226 (6)	1.80	1.75

Nos. 221-226 are printed in sheets of 6 (3x2).

Holy Family by Rubens — A38

Paintings: 3c, Adoration of the Magi, by Albrecht Durer. 4c, The Lucca Madonna, by Jan Van Eyck. 8c, Adoration of the Shepherds, by Jacopo da Bassano. 15c, Nativity, by El Greco. 25c, Madonna and Child, by Antonio Allegri da Correggio.

1967, Dec. 4 *Perf. 12x13*

227	A38	1c gold & multi	.25	.25
228	A38	3c gold & multi	.25	.25
229	A38	4c gold & multi	.25	.25
230	A38	8c gold & multi	.25	.25
231	A38	15c gold & multi	.25	.25
232	A38	25c gold & multi	.30	.30
		Nos. 227-232 (6)	1.55	1.55

Christmas.

Capt. Cook and Matavai Bay, Tahiti, by Sydney Parkinson A39

1c, Ships off Huahine Island, Tahiti, by John & James Clevely. 2c, town & harbor of Kamchatka, by John Webber, & Queen Elizabeth II. 4c, "The Ice Islands" (Antarctica), by William Hodges.

1968, Sept. 12 Photo. *Perf. 13*

233	A39	½c gold & multi	.25	.25
234	A39	1c gold & multi	.25	.25
235	A39	2c gold & multi	.25	.25
236	A39	4c gold & multi	.25	.25
		Nos. 233-236,C12-C15 (8)	4.30	4.30

Bicent. of Capt. Cook's 1st voyage of discovery. Printed in sheets of 10 stamps and 2 labels (3x4). Labels show portraits of Elizabeth II and Cook.

Gymnast A40

1968, Oct. 21

237	A40	1c Sailing	.25	.25
238	A40	5c shown	.25	.25
239	A40	15c High jump	.25	.25
240	A40	20c Woman diver	.30	.25
241	A40	30c Bicyclist	.55	.25
242	A40	50c Woman hurdler	.45	.30
		Nos. 237-242 (6)	2.05	1.55

19th Olympic Games, Mexico City, Oct. 12-27. Printed in sheets of 10 stamps and 2 labels (3x4).

Virgin and Child, by Titian — A41

Paintings: 4c, Holy Family, by Raphael. 10c, Madonna of the Rosary, by Murillo. 20c, Adoration of the Magi, by Memling. 30c, Adoration of the Magi, by Ghirlandajo.

1968, Dec. 2 Photo. *Perf. 13*

243	A41	1c gold & multi	.25	.25
244	A41	4c gold & multi	.25	.25
245	A41	10c gold & multi	.25	.25
246	A41	20c gold & multi	.30	.30
247	A41	30c gold & multi	.45	.45
a.		Souv. sheet, #243-247 + label	2.00	2.00
		Nos. 243-247 (5)	1.50	1.50

Issued in sheets of 6 (2x3).

Training on Ropeway A42

Designs: ½c, Boy Scouts cooking over campfire. 5c, Training with signal flags, and Queen Elizabeth II. 10c, Planting a tree. 20c, Erecting a hut. 30c, Lord Baden-Powell, lake and mountains (visit to Rarotonga in 1935).

1969, Feb. 6 Photo. *Perf. 13½*

248	A42	½c multicolored	.25	.25
249	A42	1c multicolored	.25	.25
250	A42	5c multicolored	.25	.25
251	A42	10c multicolored	.25	.25
252	A42	20c multicolored	.30	.30
253	A42	30c multicolored	.40	.40
		Nos. 248-253 (6)	1.70	1.70

5th Natl. Boy Scout Jamboree, Christchurch, New Zealand, Jan. 2-12.

Issued in sheets of 10 stamps and 2 labels (4x3).

Soccer — A43

No. 254b, Pole vault. No. 255a, Weight lifting. No. 255b, Basketball, Elizabeth II. No. 256a, Long jump. No. 256b, Tennis. No. 257a, Running. No. 257b, Javelin, Elizabeth II. No. 258a, Boxing. No. 258b, Golf.

Perf. 13½x13

1969, July 7 Photo. Unwmk.

254	A43	½c Pair, #a.-b.	.60	.60
255	A43	1c Pair, #a.-b.	.60	.60
256	A43	4c Pair, #a.-b.	1.30	1.30
257	A43	10c Pair, #a.-b.	1.75	1.75
258	A43	15c Pair, #a.-b.	3.00	3.00
c.		Souv. sheet, #254-258 + 2 labels	9.00	9.00
		Nos. 254-258 (5)	7.25	7.25

3rd South Pacifc Games, Port Moresby, Papua and New Guinea, Aug. 13-23.

Issued in sheets of 10.

Map of Cook Islands and Capt. Cook — A44

Map of Cook Islands and: 5c, Premier Albert Henry of Cook Islands. 25c, Coat of arms of New Zealand. 30c, Queen Elizabeth II.

1969, Oct. 8 Photo. *Perf. 13*

264	A44	5c red & multi	.40	.40
265	A44	10c lemon & multi	1.20	1.20
266	A44	25c green & multi	.60	.60
267	A44	30c blue & multi	.60	.60
		Nos. 264-267 (4)	2.80	2.80

South Pacific Conf., Noumea, Oct. 1969.

Madonna and Child, by Filippo Lippi A45

Paintings: 4c, Holy Family, by Baccio della Porta. 10c, Madonna and Child, by Anton Raphael Mengs. 20c, Madonna and Child, by Le Maître de Flemalle. 30c, Madonna and Child by Correggio.

1969, Nov. 21 Photo. *Perf. 13½*

268	A45	1c buff & multi	.25	.25
269	A45	4c buff & multi	.25	.25
270	A45	10c buff & multi	.25	.25
271	A45	20c buff & multi	.25	.25
272	A45	30c buff & multi	.25	.25
a.		Souv. sheet, #268-272 + label	1.60	1.60
		Nos. 268-272 (5)	1.25	1.25

Issued in sheets of 8 stamps, one label with portrait of Queen Elizabeth II.

Resurrection of Christ, by Raphael — A46

The Resurrection of Christ by: 8c, Dirk Bouts. 20c, Albert Altdorfer. 25c, Murillo.

1970, Mar. 12 Photo. *Perf. 13½*

Size: 25½x56mm

273	A46	4c gold & multi	.25	.25
274	A46	8c gold & multi	.25	.25
275	A46	20c gold & multi	.25	.25
276	A46	25c gold & multi	.25	.25
a.		Souv. sheet, #273-276 + 2 labels	1.60	1.60
		Nos. 273-276 (4)	1.00	1.00

Easter 1970.

Printed in sheets of 8 stamps and a label (3x3) showing portrait of Queen Elizabeth II and name of painting and painter.

See Nos. 316-318.

Nos. 205, 208, 211-212, 214, 217 Overprinted: "KIA ORANA / APOLLO 13 /ASTRONAUTS / Te Atua to / Tatou Irinakianga"

1970, Apr. Perf. 14x13½

277	A34	4c gold & multi	.30	.30
278	A34	8c gold & multi	.30	.30
279	A34	15c gold & multi	.30	.30
280	A34	20c gold & multi	.35	.35
281	A34	30c gold & multi	.45	.45
282	A35	$2 gold & multi	1.50	1.50

No. 218 Overprinted: "KIA ORANA / APOLLO 13 /ASTRONAUTS"

283	A36	$4 gold & multi	3.00	3.00
		Nos. 277-283 (7)	6.20	6.20

Splashdown of Apollo 13 west of Rarotonga, Apr. 17, 1970.

Issued: Nos. 277-282, 4/17; $4, 4/30.

Values for Nos. 283, 290-291 are for stamps with fluorescence. Stamps without fluorescence sell for more.

Queen Elizabeth II, Prince Philip, Princess Anne and Prince Charles — A47

Design: 30c, Wedgwood bust of Capt. Cook and "Endeavour." $1, Royal visit commemorative coin, obverse and reverse.

1970, June 12 Photo. Perf. 13½

284	A47	5c gold & multi	.45	.30
285	A47	30c gold & multi	1.60	1.50
286	A47	$1 gold & multi	4.50	4.50
a.		Souv. sheet, #284-286 + label	10.50	10.50
		Nos. 284-286 (3)	6.55	6.30

Visit of the British royal family.

Nos. 284-286 Overprinted in Silver or Black: "Fifth Anniversary Self-Government August 1970"

1970, Aug. 27 Photo. Perf. 13½

287	A47	5c gold & multi (S)	.50	.25
288	A47	30c gold & multi	1.40	1.00
289	A47	$1 gold & multi	2.10	1.40
		Nos. 287-289 (3)	4.00	2.65

5th anniv. of self-government. The overprint on No. 287 is arranged in one line around 3 sides of the design; the overprint on Nos. 288-289 is in 3 horizontal lines.

Nos. 219A-220 Surcharged

1970, Nov. 11 Photo. Perf. 14x13½

290	A36	$4 on $8 multi	*3.75*	*3.75*
291	A36	$4 on $10 multi	*2.75*	*2.75*

In each sheet of 15, 3 stamps have 2 surcharged bars instead of one. See second note after No. 283.

Nativity A48

Illuminations from 14th Century Robert de Lisle Psalter: 4c, Angel and shepherds. 10c, The Circumcision. 20c, The Adoration of the Kings. 30c, The Presentation at the Temple.

1970, Nov. 30 Photo. Perf. 13½

292	A48	1c gold & multi	.25	.25
293	A48	4c gold & multi	.25	.25
294	A48	10c gold & multi	.25	.25
295	A48	20c gold & multi	.25	.25
296	A48	30c gold & multi	.30	.30
a.		Souv. sheet, #292-296 + label	1.75	1.75
		Nos. 292-296 (5)	1.30	1.30

Christmas.

Issued in sheets of 5 stamps and a label (3x2) showing portrait of Queen Elizabeth II and source of design.

Nos. 214-215 Overprinted "PLUS 20c // UNITED // KINGDOM // SPECIAL // MAIL SERVICE"

1971

296B	A34	30c +20c multi	.40	.60
296C	A34	50c +20c multi	1.25	2.25

Issued: 30c, 2/25; 50c, 3/8.

Nos. 296B-296C were issued to prepay regular postage plus the fee of a private carrier who had contracted to deliver mail within the United Kingdom during a postal strike. The strike ended on March 8, and these stamps were withdrawn March 12.

Queen Elizabeth II and Prince Philip — A49

Designs: 4c, Royal family at Balmoral. 10c, Prince Philip sailing. 15c, Prince Philip as polo player. 25c, Prince Philip and royal yacht.

1971, Mar. 11 Litho. Perf. 13½

297	A49	1c brt blue & multi	.25	.25
298	A49	4c brt blue & multi	.30	.30
299	A49	10c brt blue & multi	.70	.70
300	A49	15c brt blue & multi	1.00	1.00
301	A49	25c brt blue & multi	1.75	1.75
a.		Souv. sheet, #297-301 + 2 labels	6.00	6.00
		Nos. 297-301 (5)	4.00	4.00

Visit of Prince Philip, Duke of Edinburgh to Rarotonga, Feb. 27, 1971. Printed in sheets of 10 stamps and 2 labels showing Queen Elizabeth II commemorative coin and a portrait of Prince Philip.

Nos. 210, 213-214 Overprinted

1971, Sept. 8 Photo. Perf. 14x13½

302	A34	10c gold & multi	.60	.60
303	A34	25c gold & multi	.60	.60
304	A34	30c gold & multi	.60	.60
		Nos. 302-304 (3)	1.80	1.80

4th South Pacific Games, Papeete, French Polynesia, Sept. 8-19.

Nos. 202, 205, 208-209 and 211 Surcharged with New Value and Three Bars

1971, Oct. 20

305	A34	10c on 2½c multi	.25	.25
306	A34	10c on 4c multi	.25	.25
307	A34	10c on 8c multi	.25	.25
308	A34	10c on 9c multi	.25	.25
309	A34	10c on 15c multi	.25	.25
		Nos. 305-309 (5)	1.25	1.25

Madonna and Child, by Bellini — A50

Christmas: Paintings of the Madonna and Child, by Giovanni Bellini.

1971, Nov. 30 Perf. 13½

310	A50	1c gold & multi	.25	.25
311	A50	4c gold & multi	.25	.25
312	A50	10c gold & multi	.30	.30
313	A50	20c gold & multi	.60	.60
314	A50	30c gold & multi	.90	.90
a.		Souv. sheet, #310-314 + label	2.75	2.75
		Nos. 310-314 (5)	2.30	2.30

See No. B14.

No. 216 Overprinted: "SOUTH PACIFIC / COMMISSION / FEB. 1947-1972"

1972, Feb. 17 Photo. Perf. 14x13½

315	A35	$1 gold & multi	.80	.80

South Pacific Commission, 25th anniv.

Easter Type of 1970

Illuminations from 14th century Robert de Lisle Psalter: 5c, St. John. 10c, Christ crucified. 30c, Virgin Mary.

1972, Mar. 6 Photo. Perf. 13½

Size: 21x68mm

316	A46	5c gold & multi	.25	.25
317	A46	10c gold & multi	.25	.25
318	A46	30c gold & multi	.40	.40
a.		Souvenir sheet of 3, #316-318	1.25	1.25
		Nos. 316-318 (3)	.90	.90

Printed in sheets of 12.

For surcharges see Nos. B15-B16, B19.

Rocket over Moon — A51

No. 319a, Shown. No. 319b, Earth over moon. No. 320a, Landing module and astronaut. No. 320b, Astronaut collecting moon rocks. No. 321a, Earth and rocket over moon. No. 321b, Lunar rover and astronaut. No. 322a, Helicopter over raft in Pacific. No. 322b, Capsule and parachutes.

1972, Apr. 17

319	A51	5c Pair, #a.-b.	.25	.25
320	A51	10c Pair, #a.-b.	.50	.50
321	A51	25c Pair, #a.-b.	1.40	1.40
322	A51	30c Pair, #a.-b.	1.90	1.90
c.		Souvenir sheet of 8	6.50	6.50
		Nos. 319-322 (4)	4.05	4.05

Apollo moon explorations.

No. 322c contains Nos. 319-322 arranged in 2 blocks of 4 divided by a map showing splashdown area of Apollo X, XII and XIII.

For surcharges see Nos. B21-B24.

High Jump, Olympic Rings — A52

1972, June 26

327	A52	10c shown	.30	.30
328	A52	25c Running	.65	.65
329	A52	30c Boxing	.65	.65
a.		Souv. sheet, #327-329 + label	2.25	2.25
		Nos. 327-329 (3)	1.60	1.60

20th Olympic Games, Munich, Aug. 26-Sept. 10. Sheets of 8 stamps and label.

See No. B29.

Rest on Flight to Egypt, by Caravaggio — A53

Paintings: 5c, Virgin of the Swallows, by Guercino. 10c, Virgin with Green Cushion, by Andrea Solario. 20c, Virgin and Child, by Lorenzo di Credi. 30c, Virgin and Child, by Giovanni Bellini.

1972, Oct. 11 Photo. Perf. 13½

330	A53	1c gold & multi	.30	.30
331	A53	5c gold & multi	.30	.30
332	A53	10c gold & multi	.40	.40
333	A53	20c gold & multi	.60	.60
334	A53	30c gold & multi	1.10	1.10
a.		Souv. sheet, #330-334 + label	4.00	4.00
		Nos. 330-334 (5)	2.70	2.70

Christmas. See No. B30.

Princess Elizabeth and Prince Philip — A54

Designs: 5c, Wedding ceremony, Westminster Abbey. 15c, Bridal portrait. 30c, Official wedding picture of royal family.

1972, Nov. 20 Size: 29x40mm

335	A54	5c silver & multi	.30	.30
336	A54	10c silver & multi	.40	.40

Size: 40x40mm

337	A54	15c silver & multi	.50	.50

Size: 66x40mm

338	A54	30c silver & multi	.60	.60
		Nos. 335-338 (4)	1.80	1.80

25th anniversary of the marriage of Queen Elizabeth II and Prince Philip.

Nos. 335-337 printed in sheets of 8 stamps and one label; No. 338 in sheets of 6.

1c Coin with Queen Elizabeth II and Taro Leaf A55

Queen Elizabeth II Coins: 2c, Pineapples. 5c, Hibiscus. 10c, Oranges. 20c, Fairy terns. 50c, Bonito. $1, Tangaroa, Polynesian god of creation, vert.

1973, Mar. 15 Photo. Perf. 13x13½

Size: 37x24mm

339	A55	1c dp car, blk & gold	.25	.25
340	A55	2c blue, blk & gold	.25	.25
341	A55	5c green, blk & gold	.25	.25

Size: 46x30mm

342	A55	10c vio, blue, blk & sil	.25	.25
343	A55	20c dk green, blk & sil	.40	.40
344	A55	50c dp car, black & sil	.60	.60

Size: 32x54½mm

345	A55	$1 blue, blk & silver	.90	.90
		Nos. 339-345 (7)	2.90	2.90

Coinage commemorating silver wedding anniversary of Queen Elizabeth II.

Printed in sheets of 20 stamps and label showing Westminster Abbey.

"Noli me Tangere," by Titian — A56

Paintings: 10c, Descent from the Cross, by Rubens. 30c, The Lamentation of Christ, by Dürer.

1973, Apr. 9

346	A56	5c gold & multi	.25	.25
347	A56	10c gold & multi	.35	.35
348	A56	30c gold & multi	.40	.40
a.		Souvenir sheet of 3, #346-348	1.10	1.10
		Nos. 346-348 (3)	1.00	1.00

Easter. Printed in sheets of 15 stamps and one label.

See Nos. 378-380, B31-B33, B39-B41.

Queen Elizabeth II in Coronation Regalia — A57

1973, June 1 Photo. ***Perf. 14x13½***

349	A57	10c gold & multi	.75	.75

Souvenir Sheet

Perf. 13½x14½

350	A57	50c gold & multi	3.25	3.25

20th anniv. of the coronation of Queen Elizabeth II. No. 349 printed in sheets of 5 stamps and one label.

Nos. 206, 208, 210, 212-214 Overprinted: "TENTH ANNIVERSARY / CESSATION OF / NUCLEAR TESTING / TREATY"

1973, July 25 Photo. ***Perf. 14x13½***

351	A34	5c gold & multi	.25	.25
352	A34	8c gold & multi	.25	.25
353	A34	10c gold & multi	.25	.25
354	A34	20c gold & multi	.25	.25
355	A34	25c gold & multi	.40	.40
356	A34	30c gold & multi	.40	.40
		Nos. 351-356 (6)	1.80	1.80

Nuclear Test Ban Treaty, 10th anniv. and as protest against French nuclear testing on Mururoa atoll.

Tipairua — A58

Historic South Pacific sailing vessels.

1973, Sept. 17 Photo. ***Perf. 13½x13***

357	A58	½c shown	.25	.25
358	A58	1c Wa'a Kaulua	.25	.25
359	A58	1½c Tainui	.25	.25
360	A58	5c War canoe	.70	.70
361	A58	10c Pahi	.80	.80
362	A58	15c Amatasi	1.00	1.00
363	A58	25c Vaka	1.40	1.40
		Nos. 357-363 (7)	4.65	4.65

Annunciation A59

Designs from 15th Century Prayer Book: 5c, The Visitation. 10c, Adoration of the Shepherds. 20c, Adoration of the Kings. 30c, Slaughter of the Innocents.

1973, Oct. 30 Photo. ***Perf. 13x13½***

364	A59	1c multicolored	.25	.25
365	A59	5c multicolored	.25	.25
366	A59	10c multicolored	.25	.25
367	A59	20c multicolored	.25	.25
368	A59	30c multicolored	.25	.25
a.		Souv. sheet, #364-368 + label	1.00	1.00
		Nos. 364-368 (5)	1.25	1.25

Christmas. See Nos. B34-B38.

Princess Anne — A60

1973, Nov. 14 Photo. ***Perf. 14***

369	A60	25c shown	.30	.30
370	A60	30c Mark Phillips	.35	.35
371	A60	50c Princess and Mark Phillips	.50	.50
a.		Souv. sheet, #369-371 + label	1.10	1.10
		Nos. 369-371 (3)	1.15	1.15

Wedding of Princess Anne and Capt. Mark Phillips.

Running and Games Emblem A61

1c, Diving. 3c, Boxing. 10c, Weight lifting. 30c, Bicycling. 50c, Discobolus.

1974, Jan. 24 Photo. ***Perf. 14***

372	A61	1c multi, vert.	.25	.25
373	A61	3c multi, vert.	.25	.25
374	A61	5c multi	.25	.25
375	A61	10c multi	.25	.25
376	A61	30c multi	.75	.75
		Nos. 372-376 (5)	1.75	1.75

Souvenir Sheet

377	A61	50c multi, vert.	2.00	2.00

10th British Commonwealth Games, Christchurch, New Zealand, Jan. 24-Feb. 2. No. 377 contains one stamp 35x45mm.

Easter Type of 1973 Dated "1974"

Paintings: 5c, Jesus Carrying Cross, by Raphael. 10c, Jesus in the Arms of God, by El Greco. 30c, Descent from the Cross, by Caravaggio.

1974, Mar. 25 ***Perf. 13½x13***

378	A56	5c gold & multi	.25	.25
379	A56	10c gold & multi	.25	.25
380	A56	30c gold & multi	.45	.45
a.		Souvenir sheet of 3, #378-380	1.40	1.40
		Nos. 378-380 (3)	.95	.95

Easter. See Nos. B39-B41.

Phallicium Glaucum A62

Queen Elizabeth II — A63

Queen and Shells — A64

Cook Islands sea shells: 1c, Vasum turbinellus. 1 ½c, Corculum cardissa. 2c, Terebellum terebellum. 3c, Aulica vespertilio. 4c, Strombus gibberulus. 5c, Cymatium pileare. 6c, Cyprae caputserpentis. 8c, Bursa granularis. 10c, Tenebra muscaria. 15c, Mitra mitra. 20c, Natica alapillonis roding. 25c, Gloripallium pallium. 30c, Conus miles. 50c, Conus textile. 60c, Oliva sericea roding.

The designs of the 2c, 5c, 10c, 30c include portrait of Queen Elizabeth II.

1974-75 Photo. ***Perf. 13½***

381	A62	½c shown	.25	.25
382	A62	1c multicolored	.25	.25
383	A62	1½c multicolored	.25	.25
384	A62	2c multicolored	.25	.25
385	A62	3c multicolored	.25	.25
386	A62	4c multicolored	.25	.25
387	A62	5c multicolored	.25	.25
388	A62	6c multicolored	.25	.25
389	A62	8c multicolored	.25	.25
390	A62	10c multicolored	.25	.25
391	A62	15c multicolored	.30	.30
392	A62	20c multicolored	.50	.50
393	A62	25c multicolored	.60	.60
394	A62	30c multicolored	.70	.70
395	A62	50c multicolored	1.10	1.10
396	A62	60c multicolored	1.75	1.10
397	A63	$1 shown	2.75	2.00
398	A63	$2 multi ('75)	5.75	4.00

Perf. 14x13½

399	A64	$4 multi ('75)	8.50	6.00
400	A64	$6 multi ('75)	13.50	9.50
401	A64	$8 multi ('75)	17.00	11.50
402	A64	$10 multi ('75)	21.00	16.00
		Nos. 381-402 (22)	75.95	55.80

Issued: 50c, 60c, $1, 8/26; $2, 1/27; $4, 3/17; $6, 4/29; $8, 5/30; $10, 6/30; others, 5/17.

For surcharges & overprints see Nos. 488-498, 526-528, 991, O16-O26, O30-O31.

Soccer Player and Map of Oceania A65

50c, Munich stadium & map of Oceania. $1, Soccer player, Munich stadium & World Cup.

1974, July 5 Photo. ***Perf. 13½***

Size: 31x29mm

403	A65	25c multicolored	.30	.30
404	A65	50c multicolored	.55	.55

Size: 68x28½mm

405	A65	$1 multicolored	.90	.90
a.		Souvenir sheet of 3, #403-405	2.00	2.00
		Nos. 403-405 (3)	1.75	1.75

World Cup Soccer Championship, Munich, June 13-July 7. Nos. 403-405 printed in sheets of 8 and commemorative label.

$2.50 Capt. Cook Silver Coin — A66

Commemorative Silver Coins: $7.50, $7.50 coin with Queen Elizabeth II on obverse; Capt. Cook, map of Islands and "Resolution" on reverse. $2.50 coin shows "Resolution," "Adventure" and globe on reverse.

1974, July 22 Photo. ***Perf. 14***

406	A66	$2.50 sil, vio & blk	11.00	7.25
407	A66	$7.50 grn, sil & blk	22.00	15.00
a.		Souvenir sheet of 2, #406-407	40.00	40.00

Bicentenary of Capt. Cook's 2nd voyage of discovery. Nos. 406-407 printed in sheets of 5 and commemorative label.

Cook Islands Nos. 1, 49, 62, 66, 77 — A67

Stamps of Cook Islands: 25c, DC-3 over old Rarotonga landing strip, and No. 19. 30c, Rarotonga Post Office, UPU emblem and No. 65. 50c, UPU emblem and Nos. 1, 19, 49, 62, 65-66 and 77.

1974, Sept. 16 Photo. ***Perf. 13½x14***

408	A67	10c gold & multi	.25	.25
409	A67	25c gold & multi	.40	.40
410	A67	30c gold & multi	.50	.50
411	A67	50c gold & multi	.95	.95
a.		Souv. sheet, #408-411, perf. 13½	2.00	2.00
		Nos. 408-411 (4)	2.10	2.10

Cent. of UPU. Nos. 408-411 printed in sheets of 8 and commemorative label.

Virgin and Child, with St. John, by Raphael — A68

Paintings: 5c, Holy Family, by Andrea del Sarto. 10c, Nativity, by Correggio. 20c, Holy Family, by Rembrandt. 30c, Nativity, by Van der Weyden.

1974, Oct. 15 Photo. ***Perf. 13½***

412	A68	1c multicolored	.25	.25
413	A68	5c multicolored	.25	.25
414	A68	10c multicolored	.25	.25
415	A68	20c multicolored	.50	.50
416	A68	30c multicolored	.75	.75
a.		Souv. sheet, #412-416 + label	2.25	2.25
		Nos. 412-416 (5)	2.00	2.00

Christmas 1974. Nos. 412-416 printed in sheets of 15 and one label showing Queen Elizabeth II.

See Nos. B42-B46.

Churchill and Blenheim Palace A69

Sir Winston Churchill (1874-1965) and: 10c, Parliament. 25c, Chartwell. 30c, Buckingham Palace. 50c, St. Paul's Cathedral.

1974, Nov. 20 Photo. *Perf. 14*

417 A69 5c violet & multi .25 .25
418 A69 10c maroon & multi .25 .25
419 A69 25c dk blue & multi .35 .35
420 A69 30c brown & multi .45 .45
421 A69 50c multicolored .85 .85
a. Souv. sheet, #417-421 + label 3.00 3.00
Nos. 417-421 (5) 2.15 2.15

Nos. 417-421 printed in sheets of 5 stamps and one label showing $100 commemorative gold coin.

Vasco Nunez de Balboa — A70

5c, Ferdinand Magellan & route around South America. 10c, Juan Sebastian de Elcano & ship. 25c, Andres de Urdaneta & ship. 25c, Miguel Lopez de Legaspi & ship.

1975, Feb. 3 *Perf. 13½*

422 A70 1c multicolored .30 .25
423 A70 5c multicolored .30 .25
424 A70 10c multicolored 1.10 .35
425 A70 25c multicolored 2.60 1.10
426 A70 30c multicolored 3.00 1.25
Nos. 422-426 (5) 7.30 3.20

16th century explorers of the Pacific Ocean.

Apollo and Apollo-Soyuz Emblem — A71

Apollo-Soyuz Emblem &: No. 427b, Soyuz. No. 428a, Aleksei A. Leonov & Valery N. Kubasov. No. 428b, Donald K. Slayton, Vance D. Brand & Thomas P. Stafford. No. 429a, Cosmonaut inside Soyuz capsule. No. 429b, American astronauts inside Apollo capsule.

1975, July 15 Photo. *Perf. 13½*

427 A71 25c Pair, #a.-b. .90 .90
428 A71 30c Pair, #a.-b. 1.00 1.00
429 A71 50c Pair, #a.-b. 1.60 1.60
c. Souvenir sheet of 6, #427-429 3.25 3.25
Nos. 427-429 (3) 3.50 3.50

Apollo Soyuz space test project (Russo-American space cooperation), launching July 15; link-up, July 17. Printed sheets of 18 stamps and 2 labels showing flags.

$100 Gold Commemorative Coin — A72

1975, Aug. 8 Photo. *Perf. 13½x13*

433 A72 $2 gold & dp violet 4.00 3.75

Bicentenary of the completion of Capt. Cook's second voyage of discovery.

Cook Islands' Flag, Map of Islands and New Zealand A73

Prime Minister Sir Albert Henry — A74

Design: 25c, View of Rarotonga and flag.

1975, Aug. 8 *Perf. 13½x13, 13x13½*

434 A73 5c gold & multi .50 .25
435 A74 10c gold & multi .65 .25
436 A73 25c gold & multi 1.60 .55
Nos. 434-436 (3) 2.75 1.05

Tenth anniversary of self-government.

Virgin and Child, 15th Century, Flemish — A75

Paintings: 10c, Madonna in the Field, by Raphael. 15c, Holy Family, by Raphael. 20c, Adoration of the Shepherds, by J. B. Mayno. 35c, Annunciation, by Murillo.

1975, Dec. 1 Photo. *Perf. 13½*

437 A75 6c gold & multi .25 .25
438 A75 10c gold & multi .25 .25
439 A75 15c gold & multi .30 .30
440 A75 20c gold & multi .35 .35
441 A75 35c gold & multi .55 .55
a. Souv. sheet, #437-441 + label 1.75 1.75
Nos. 437-441 (5) 1.70 1.70

Christmas. See Nos. B47-B51.

Descent from the Cross, by Raphael A76

Paintings: 15c, Pieta, by Veronese. 35c, Pieta, by El Greco.

1976, Mar. 29 Photo. *Perf. 13½*

442 A76 7c gold & multi .25 .25
443 A76 15c gold & multi .55 .55
444 A76 35c gold & multi 1.20 1.20
a. Souvenir sheet of 3, #442-444 2.00 2.00
Nos. 442-444 (3) 2.00 2.00

Easter. Nos. 442-444 printed in sheets of 20 with label showing Queen Elizabeth II.
See Nos. B52-B54.

Benjamin Franklin and "Resolution" — A77

Designs: $2, Capt. James Cook and "Resolution." $3, Cook, "Resolution" and Franklin.

1976, May 29 Photo. *Perf. 13½*

445 A77 $1 gold & multi 4.50 3.00
446 A77 $2 gold & multi 9.50 6.25

Souvenir Sheet

Perf. 13

447 A77 $3 gold & multi 13.50 8.50

American Bicentennial. No. 447 contains one stamp 73x31mm. Nos. 445-446 printed in sheets of 5 and corner label with Franklin's request to assist Capt. Cook.
For overprint see No. O29.

Nos. 445-447 Overprinted "Royal Visit July 1976"

1976, July 6 Photo. *Perf. 13½*

448 A77 $1 gold & multi 2.50 2.00
449 A77 $2 gold & multi 6.25 5.75

Souvenir Sheet

Perf. 13

450 A77 $3 gold & multi 8.25 7.00

Visit of Queen Elizabeth II and Prince Philip to the United States.

High Hurdles — A78

15c, Field hockey. 30c, Fencing. 35c, Soccer.

1976, July 22 *Perf. 13½*

451 A78 7c Pair, #a.-b. .25 .25
452 A78 15c Pair, #a.-b. .40 .40
453 A78 30c Pair, #a.-b. 1.10 1.10
454 A78 35c Pair, #a.-b. 1.25 1.25
c. Souvenir sheet of 8, #451-454 4.50 4.50
Nos. 451-454 (4) 3.00 3.00

21st Olympic Games, Montreal, Canada, 7/17-8/1. Printed in sheets of 10 stamps + 2 labels.

The Visitation — A80

Designs: 10c, Virgin and Child. 15c, Adoration of the Shepherds. 20c, Adoration of the Kings. 35c, Holy Family. After painted Renaissance altar sculptures.

1976, Oct. 12 Photo. *Perf. 14x13½*

459 A80 6c gold & multi .25 .25
460 A80 10c gold & multi .25 .25
461 A80 15c gold & multi .25 .25
462 A80 20c gold & multi .25 .25
463 A80 35c gold & multi .25 .25
a. Souv. sheet, #459-463 + label 1.25 1.25
Nos. 459-463 (5) 1.25 1.25

Christmas. Nos. 459-463 printed in sheets of 20 with label showing Queen Elizabeth II.
See Nos. B55-B59.

$5 Silver Coin, 1976 — A81

1976, Nov. 15 Photo. *Perf. 13½*

464 A81 $1 multicolored 2.00 1.50

National Wildlife and Conservation Day. Issued in sheets of 5 stamps and commemorative label.
See Nos. 502, 536.

A82

No. 465a, Crown. No. 465b, Elizabeth II in Coronation Vestments. No. 466a, Westminster Abbey. No. 466b, Coach in procession. No. 467a, Queen and Prince Philip after coronation. No. 467b, Investiture of Sir Albert Henry, Premier of Cook Islands, 1974.

1977, Feb. 7 Photo. *Perf. 13½x13*

465 A82 25c Pair, #a.-b. .35 .35
466 A82 50c Pair, #a.-b. 1.00 1.00
467 A82 $1 Pair, #a.-b. 2.00 2.00
c. Souv. sheet, #465-467, perf. 13 3.25 3.25
Nos. 465-467 (3) 3.35 3.35

Reign of Queen Elizabeth II, 25th anniv. Printed in sheets of 8.
For overprints see No. O27.

Crucifixion, by Rubens — A83

Paintings by Rubens: 15c, Christ Between the Thieves. 35c, Descent from the Cross.

1977, Mar. 28 Photo. *Perf. 14x13½*

471 A83 7c gold & multi .40 .40
472 A83 15c gold & multi .40 .40
473 A83 35c gold & multi 1.20 1.20
a. Souv. sheet, #471-473, perf 13 2.25 2.25
Nos. 471-473 (3) 2.00 2.00

Easter 1977, and 400th birth anniv. of Peter Paul Rubens (1577-1640), Flemish painter. Nos. 471-473 printed in sheets of 24 stamps and corner label with portrait of Queen Elizabeth II and description.
See Nos. B60-B62.

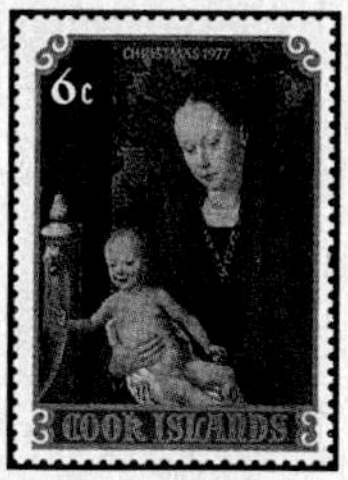

Virgin and Child, by Memling — A84

Virgin and Child by: 10c, Hans Memling. 15c, Geertgen Tot Sin Jans. 20c, Carlo Crivelli. 35c, School of Henry Blex.

1977, Oct. 3 Photo. *Perf. 13½*

474 A84 6c gold & multi .25 .25
475 A84 10c gold & multi .25 .25
476 A84 15c gold & multi .25 .25
477 A84 20c gold & multi .40 .40
478 A84 35c gold & multi .70 .70
a. Souv. sheet, #474-478 + label 2.00 2.00
Nos. 474-478 (5) 1.85 1.85

Christmas. Nos. 474-478 printed in sheets of 24 and label. See Nos. B63-B67.

$5-silver Coin, 1977 — A85

1977, Nov. 15 Photo. *Perf. 13½*
479 A85 $1 silver & multi 2.00 .95

National Wildlife Conservation Day. No. 479 issued in sheets of 5 and one label.

Capt. Cook, by Nathaniel Dance and "Resolution" — A86

$1, "Capt. Cook Landing at Owyhee" and Capt. Cook. $2, Cook Islands $200 commemorative coin, 1978, and Cook Monument, Hawaii, 1825.

1978, Jan. 20 Litho. *Perf. 13½*
480 A86 50c gold & multi .85 .85
481 A86 $1 gold & multi 1.40 1.40
482 A86 $2 gold & multi 2.75 2.75
a. Souvenir sheet of 3, #480-482 5.25 5.25
Nos. 480-482 (3) 5.00 5.00

Bicentennial of Capt. Cook's arrival in Hawaii.
Nos. 480-482 issued in sheets of 5 with corner label showing ship off Hawaiian coast.
For overprints see Nos. 499-501a.

Pieta, by Rogier van der Weyden A87

Paintings, National Gallery, London: 35c, Burial of Jesus, by Michelangelo. 75c, Jesus at Emmaus, by Caravaggio.

1978, Mar. 20 Photo. *Perf. 13½x13*
483 A87 15c gold & multi .25 .25
484 A87 35c gold & multi .50 .50
485 A87 75c gold & multi 1.00 1.00
a. Souv. sheet, #483-485 + label 1.40 1.40
Nos. 483-485 (3) 1.75 1.75

Easter. Nos. 483-485 printed in sheets of 5 and corner label showing National Gallery.
See Nos. B68-B70.

Souvenir Sheets

Coronation of Queen Elizabeth II, 25th anniv. — A88

1978, June 6 Photo. *Perf. 13*
486 A88 Sheet of 4 + 2 labels 1.20 1.20
a. 50c Queen Elizabeth II .30 .30
b. 50c Lion of England .30 .30
c. 50c Imperial State Crown .30 .30
d. 50c Tangaroa figure .30 .30
487 A88 Sheet of 4 + label 1.20 1.20
a. 70c like 486a .30 .30
b. 70c Scepter with Cross .30 .30
c. 70c St. Edward's Crown .30 .30
d. 70c Rarotongan staff god .30 .30
e. Souv. sheet of 8, #486a-487d + label 2.50 2.50

Coronation of Queen Elizabeth II, 25th anniv.

Nos. 381, 383, 388-389, 393-396 Srchd. in Silver, Black or Gold

1978, Nov. 10 Photo. *Perf. 13½*
488 A62 5c on 1½c multi (S) .25 .25
489 A62 7c on ½c multi .30 .30
490 A62 10c on 6c multi (G) .45 .45
491 A62 10c on 8c multi (G) .45 .45
492 A62 15c on ½c multi .70 .70
493 A62 15c on 25c multi (S) .70 .70
494 A62 15c on 30c multi .70 .70
495 A62 15c on 50c multi (S) .70 .70
496 A62 15c on 60c multi (G) .70 .70
497 A62 17c on ½c multi .85 .85
498 A62 17c on 50c multi (S) .85 .85
Nos. 488-498 (11) 6.65 6.65

See Nos. 526-528.

Nos. 480-482a Overprinted in Black on Silver Panel

1978, Nov. 13 Litho. *Perf. 13½*
499 A86 50c gold & multi .90 .90
500 A86 $1 gold & multi 1.75 1.75
501 A86 $2 gold & multi 3.50 3.50
a. Souvenir sheet of 3, #499-501 16.00 16.00
Nos. 499-501 (3) 6.15 6.15

250th anniv. of Capt. Cook's birth. Similar overprint in 4 lines was applied to labels. Label of No. 501a overprinted only with dates 1728, 1978.

Coin Type of 1976

$1, $5 Silver coin, 1978 (Polynesian warbler).

1978, Nov. 15 Photo. *Perf. 13½*
502 A81 $1 multicolored 1.60 1.60

National Wildlife and Conservation Day. Sheets of 24 containing 4 panes of 6.

A89

Virgin and Child by: 15c, Rogier van der Weyden. 17c, Carlo Crivelli. 35c, Murillo.

1978, Dec. 8 Photo. *Perf. 13*
503 A89 15c multicolored .40 .40
504 A89 17c multicolored .70 .70
505 A89 35c multicolored .85 .85
a. Souvenir sheet of 3, #503-505 2.00 2.00
Nos. 503-505 (3) 1.95 1.95

Christmas. See Nos. B71-B73.

A90

Descent from the Cross, by Gaspar de Crayer (Details): 10c, Pieta. 12c, St. John. 15c, Mary Magdalene. 20c, Cherubs.

1979, Apr. 5 Photo. *Perf. 13*
506 A90 10c multicolored .25 .25
507 A90 12c multicolored .25 .25
508 A90 15c multicolored .30 .30
509 A90 20c multicolored .70 .70
Nos. 506-509 (4) 1.50 1.50

Easter. See No. B74.

A91

20c, Capt. Cook, by John Weber. 30c, Resolution, by Henry Roberts. 35c, Endeavour. 50c, Death of Capt. Cook, by George Carter.

1979, July 23 Photo. *Perf. 14x13½*
510 A91 20c multicolored .45 .45
511 A91 30c multicolored .65 .65
512 A91 35c multicolored .75 .75
513 A91 50c multicolored .90 .90
a. Souvenir sheet of 4 3.00 3.00
Nos. 510-513 (4) 2.75 2.75

Capt. Cook (1728-1779), explorer. No. 513a contains 4 stamps similar to Nos. 510-513 with black frames.

Sir Rowland Hill, Originator of Penny Postage — A92

No. 514a, Postrider. No. 514b, Stagecoach. No. 514c, Automobile. No. 514d, Streamlined train. No. 515a, Cap-Horniers, sailing ship. No. 515b, River steamer. No. 515c, Liner Deutschland. No. 515d, Liner United States. No. 516a, Balloon Neptune. No. 516b, Junkers F13. No. 516c, Graf Zeppelin. No. 516d, Concorde.

1979, Sept. 10 *Perf. 14½*
514 A92 30c Block of 4, #a.-d. 1.10 1.10
515 A92 35c Block of 4, #a.-d. 1.20 1.20
516 A92 50c Block of 4, #a.-d. 1.90 1.90
e. Souv. sheet of 12, #514-516 4.50 4.50
Nos. 514-516 (3) 4.20 4.20

Nos. 381, 383, 396 Srchd. in Gold or Silver

1979, Sept. 12 Photo. *Perf. 13½*
526 A62 6c on ½c multi .25 .25
527 A62 10c on 1½c multi (S) .25 .25
528 A62 15c on 60c multi .25 .25
Nos. 526-528 (3) .75 .75

Nos. 526-528 have 3 thick bars of equal length over old value.

Girl and Baby, IYC Emblem — A93

IYC Emblem and: 50c, Boy playing tree drum. 65c, Children dancing.

1979, Oct. 10 *Perf. 13*
529 A93 30c multicolored .25 .25
530 A93 50c multicolored .40 .40
531 A93 65c multicolored .55 .55
Nos. 529-531 (3) 1.20 1.20

See No. B75.

Apollo 11 Emblem — A94

50c, Apollo 11 crew, lunar map. 60c, Astronaut walking on moon. 65c, Splashdown.

1979, Nov. 7 *Perf. 14*
532 A94 30c multicolored .35 .35
533 A94 50c multicolored .55 .55
534 A94 60c multicolored .65 .65
535 A94 65c multicolored .75 .75
a. Souv. sheet, #532-535, perf. 13 2.75 2.75
Nos. 532-535 (4) 2.30 2.30

Apollo 11 moon landing, 10th anniv.

Coin Type of 1976

$1, $5 Silver coin, 1979 (Rarotonga fruit dove).

Perf. 13½x14½
1979, Nov. 15 Photo.
536 A81 $1 multicolored 1.75 1.75

National Wildlife and Conservation Day.

Christmas Tree Ornaments — A95

Christmas (Flowers and): 10c, Star. 12c, Bells and candle. 15c, Ancestral statue.

1979, Dec. 14 *Perf. 14*
537 A95 6c multicolored .25 .25
538 A95 10c multicolored .25 .25
539 A95 12c multicolored .25 .25
540 A95 15c multicolored .25 .25
Nos. 537-540,B76-B79 (8) 2.10 2.10

See also Nos. C16-C19, CB1-CB4.

A96

Bible illustrations by Gustave Dore, 1833-1883: No. 541a, Flagellation. No. 541b, Jesus Wearing Crown of Thorns. No. 542a, Jesus Mocked. No. 542b, Jesus Falls. No. 543a, The Crucifixion. No. 543b, Descent from the Cross.

1980, Mar. 31 Photo. *Perf. 13*
541 A96 20c Pair, #a.-b. .55 .55
542 A96 30c Pair, #a.-b. .80 .80
543 A96 35c Pair, #a.-b. .90 .90
Nos. 541-543 (3) 2.25 2.25

Easter. See Nos. 553, B80-B83.

Doves with Olive Branch, Rotary Emblem A97

1980, May 27 Photo. *Perf. 14*

547	A97 30c shown		.40	.40
548	A97 35c Flowers		.45	.45
549	A97 50c Flags, globe		.65	.65
	Nos. 547-549 (3)		1.50	1.50

Rotary Intl., 75th anniv. See No. B87

Easter Type of 1980 and

New Zealand No. 1 — A98

No. 550a, Postrider. No. 550b, Coach. No. 550c, Automobile. No. 550d, Train.

New Zealand #2 and: No. 551a, Sailing ship. No. 551b, River steamer. No. 551c, Transatlantic liner (facing left). No. 551d, Transatlantic liner (facing right).

New Zealand #3 and: No. 552a, 1870-71 mail balloon. No. 552b, 1919 plane. No. 552c, Graf Zeppelin. No. 552d, Concorde.

1980, Aug. 22 Photo. *Perf. 14*

550	A98 30c Block of 4, #a.-d.	1.40	1.10
551	A98 35c Block of 4, #a.-d.	1.75	1.50
552	A98 50c Block of 4, #a.-d.	2.60	2.00
e.	Souvenir sheet of 12	7.00	6.00
	Nos. 550-552 (3)	5.75	4.60

Souvenir Sheet

Perf. 13

553	A96 Sheet of 6, #541-543	3.00	1.75

ZEAPEX '80, New Zealand Intl. Stamp Exhib., Auckland, Aug. 23-31. No. 552e contains four each of Nos. 550-552 arranged horizontally (4x3). No. 553 has black on gold overprint: "ZEAPEX / '80 / Auckland / +10c" in margin.

Queen Mother Elizabeth, 80th Birthday — A99

1980, Sept. 22 Photo. *Perf. 13*

554	A99 50c multicolored	.80	.80

Souvenir Sheet

555	A99 $2 multicolored	1.60	1.60

No. 554 issued in sheets of 9 (3x3).

Johannes Kepler, Spacecraft — A100

Designs: Nos. 556a, 559a, Kepler, spacecraft (diff.). No. 556b, Kepler, Apollo Command Module, moon. No. 559b, Kepler, lunar rover, astronaut on moon. Nos. 557a-558b, Jules Verne, various scenes from From Earth to Moon, vert.

1980, Nov. 7 Photo. *Perf. 13*

556	A100 12c Pair, #a-b	.50	.50
557	A100 20c Pair, #a-b	.50	.50
558	A100 30c Pair, #a-b	1.25	1.25
c.	Souvenir sheet, #557-558	2.50	2.50
559	A100 50c Pair, #a-b	2.75	2.75
c.	Souv. sheet, #556, 559	3.50	3.50
	Nos. 556-559 (4)	5.00	5.00

Death anniversaries of Johannes Kepler, German astronomer and Jules Verne, French science fiction writer.

Burning Bush Coral — A101

Daisy Coral — A102

Nos. 564a, 570a, 576a, Siphonogorgia. Nos. 564b, 570b, 576b, Pavona practorta. Nos. 564c, 570c, 576c, Stylaster echinatus. Nos. 564d, 570d, 576d, Tubastraea. Nos. 565a, 571a, 577a, Millepora alcicornis. Nos. 565b, 571b, 577b, Junceella gemmaea. Nos. 565c, 571c, 577c, Fungia fungites. Nos. 565d, 571d, 577d, Heliofungia actiniformis. Nos. 566a, 572a, 578a, Distichopora violacea. Nos. 566b, 572b, 578b, Stylaster. Nos. 566c, 572c, 578c, Gonipora. Nos. 566d, 572d, 578d, Caulastraea echinulata. Nos. 567a, 573a, 579a, Ptilosarcus gurneyi. Nos. 567b, 573b, 579b, Stylophora pistillata. Nos. 567c, 573c, 579c, Melithaea squamata. Nos. 567d, 573d, 579d, Porites andrewsi. Nos. 568a, 574a, 580a, Lobophyllia bemprichii. Nos. 568b, 574b, 580b, Palauastrea ramosa. Nos. 568c, 574c, 580c, Bellonella indica. Nos. 568d, 574d, 580d, Pectinia alcicornis. Nos. 569a, 575a, 581a, Sarcophyton digitatum. Nos. 569b, 575b, 581b, Melithaea albitincta. Nos. 569c, 575c, 581c, Plerogyra sinuosa. Nos. 569d, 575d, 581d, Dendrophyllia gracilis.

1980-82 *Perf. 13½x13*

Strips of 4 (#564-575) or Blocks of 4 (#576-581)

564	A101	1c #a.-d.	.25	.25
565	A101	3c #a.-d.	.30	.30
566	A101	4c #a.-d.	.35	.35
567	A101	5c #a.-d.	.45	.45
568	A101	6c #a.-d.	.55	.55
569	A101	8c #a.-d.	.65	.65
570	A101	10c #a.-d.	.80	.80
571	A101	12c #a.-d.	1.00	1.00
572	A101	15c #a.-d.	1.25	1.25
573	A101	20c #a.-d.	1.40	1.40
574	A101	25c #a.-d.	2.00	2.00
575	A101	30c #a.-d.	2.25	2.25
576	A101	35c #a.-d.	2.75	2.75
577	A101	50c #a.-d.	3.50	3.50
578	A101	60c #a.-d.	4.75	4.75
579	A101	70c #a.-d.	5.25	5.25
580	A101	80c #a.-d.	5.50	5.50
581	A101	$1 #a.-d.	6.25	6.25

Perf. 14x13½

582	A102	$2 like #566c	5.00	5.00
583	A102	$3 like #565d	7.00	7.00
584	A102	$4 like #567b	9.00	9.00
585	A102	$6 like #564c	13.50	13.50
586	A102	$10 like #569b	20.00	20.00
		Nos. 564-586 (23)	93.75	93.75

Issued: 1-8c, 11/21/80; 10-30c, 12/19/80; 35-60c, 3/16/81; 70c, 80c, 4/13/81; $1, 5/20/81; $2, $3, 11/27/81; $4, $6, 1/11/82; $10, 3/5/82.

For surcharges see Nos. 710-714, 716, 738, 740, 811-815, 953-954, 956-957, 959, 961-962, 964, 978-979, 984-986, B109-B111, O50-O53. For overprints see Nos. 992, 1049.

Annunciation, 13th Century Prayerbook Illustration — A102a

1980, Dec. 1 Photo. *Perf. 14*

652	A102a 15c shown	.25	.25
653	A102a 30c Visitation	.35	.35
654	A102a 40c Nativity	.45	.45
655	A102a 50c Epiphany	.60	.60
a.	Souvenir sheet of 4, #652-655	1.50	1.50
	Nos. 652-655 (4)	1.65	1.65

Christmas. See Nos. B88-B91.

Crucifixion, 12th Cent. Prayerbook Illustration — A103

1981, Apr. 10 *Perf. 14*

656	A103 15c shown	.25	.25
657	A103 25c Placing in Tomb	.35	.35
658	A103 40c Marys at the Tomb	.55	.55
	Nos. 656-658 (3)	1.15	1.15

Easter. See Nos. B92-B95.

Prince Charles and Lady Diana — A104

1981, July 29 Photo. *Perf. 14*

659	A104 $1 Charles	.60	.60
660	A104 $2 shown	1.50	1.50
a.	Souv. sheet of 2, #659-660	2.25	2.25

Royal Wedding. Issued in sheets of 4.

For overprints and surcharges see Nos. 679-680, 715, 835, 980-981, B97-B98.

Soccer Players — A105

Designs: Various soccer players.

1981, Oct 20 Photo. *Perf. 14*

661	A105 20c Pair, #a.-b.	.85	.85
662	A105 30c Pair, #a.-b.	1.50	1.50
663	A105 35c Pair, #a.-b.	2.00	2.00
664	A105 50c Pair, #a.-b.	2.60	2.60
	Nos. 661-664 (4)	6.95	6.95

ESPANA '82 World Cup Soccer Championships. See No. B96.

Virgin and Child, by Rubens — A107

Christmas: Rubens Paintings: 15c, Coronation of St. Catherine. 40c, Adoration of the Shepherds. 50c, Adoration of the Kings.

1981, Dec. 14 Photo. *Perf. 14x13½*

669	A107 8c shown	.45	.45
670	A107 15c multicolored	.45	.45
671	A107 40c multicolored	1.40	1.40
672	A107 50c multicolored	1.60	1.60
	Nos. 669-672 (4)	3.90	3.90

Souvenir Sheets

1982, Jan. 18

673	A107 75c +5c like #669	1.00	1.00
674	A107 75c +5c like #670	1.00	1.00
675	A107 75c +5c like #671	1.00	1.00
676	A107 75c +5c like #672	1.00	1.00

Surtax was for school children. See No. B99.

21st Birthday of Princess Diana A108

No. 677a, 21st Birthday. No. 677b, 1 July 1982. No. 678a, Wedding portrait. No. 678b, 1 July 1982. No. 678d, $1.25, No. 678e, $2.50, both inscribed "21st Birthday / 1 July 1982."

1982, June 21 Photo. *Perf. 14*

677	A108 $1.25 Pair, #a.-b.	4.00	4.00
678	A108 $2.50 Pair, #a.-b.	9.00	9.00
c.	Souv. sheet of 2, #d.-e.	7.25	7.25

Issued in sheets of 4.

See Nos. 681-682. For surcharges and overprints see Nos. 739-740, 833-834, 982.

Nos. 659-660a Overprinted

No. 680d, $1; No. 680e, $2, both inscribed "21 JUNE 1982 ROYAL BIRTH."

1982, July 12

679	A104 $1 Pair, #a.-b.	2.00	2.00
680	A104 $2 Pair, #a.-b.	4.25	4.25
c.	Souv. sheet of 2, #d.-e.	4.50	4.50

Issued in sheets of 4.

For surcharges see Nos. 987-988.

Design A108 Inscribed

No. 682d, $1.25; No. 682e, $2.50, both inscribed "Royal Birth / June 1982."

1982, Aug. 3

681	A108 $1.25 Pair, #a.-b.	3.00	3.00
682	A108 $2.50 Pair, #a.-b.	6.00	6.00
c.	Souv. sheet of 2, #d.-e.	6.00	6.00

Issued in sheets of 4.

Serenade, by Norman Rockwell (1894-1978) A109

1982, Sept. 10 Photo. *Perf. 14*

683	A109	5c shown	.25	.25
684	A109	10c The Hikers	.25	.25
685	A109	20c The Doctor and the Doll	.25	.25
686	A109	30c Home From Camp	.25	.25
		Nos. 683-686 (4)	1.00	1.00

Christmas A110

Princess Diana Holding Prince William. Various Details from Virgin with Garlands, by Rubens.

1982, Nov. 30 Photo. *Perf. 14*

687	A110	35c multicolored	1.20	.90
688	A110	48c multicolored	1.60	1.20
689	A110	60c multicolored	1.75	1.40
690	A110	$1.70 multicolored	5.50	5.50
		Nos. 687-690 (4)	10.05	9.00

Souvenir Sheets

Perf. 13½

691		Sheet of 4	7.00	7.00
a.		A110 60c like 35c	1.60	1.60
b.		A110 60c like 48c	1.60	1.60
c.		A110 60c like #689	1.60	1.60
d.		A110 60c like $1.70	1.60	1.60
692	A110	75c + 5c like 35c	2.50	2.50
693	A110	75c + 5c like 48c	2.50	2.50
694	A110	75c + 5c like 60c	2.50	2.50
695	A110	75c + 5c like $1.70	2.50	2.50

No. 691 contains 4 stamps (27x32mm., showing only painting details) plus 2 labels showing Diana and William. Nos. 692-695 show Diana and William (27x39mm), multicolored margins show painting details. Surtax was for child welfare.

Commonwealth Day — A111

No. 696a, Tangaroa statue. No. 696b, Rarotonga oranges. No. 696c, Rarotonga Airport. No. 696d, Prime Minister Thomas Davis.

1983, Mar. 14 Photo. *Perf. 14*

696 A111 60c Block of 4, #a.-d. 2.75 2.75

For overprints see No. O46.

Scouting Year — A112

36c, Camping. 48c, Rope swing. 60c, Tree planting.

1983, Apr. 5 Photo. *Perf. 13x13½*

700	A112	12c Pair, #a.-b.	.65	.65
701	A112	36c Pair, #a.-b.	2.00	2.00
702	A112	48c Pair, #a.-b.	2.40	2.40
703	A112	60c Pair, #a.-b.	3.00	3.00
		Nos. 700-703 (4)	8.05	8.05

Souvenir Sheet of 8

704 #a.-d. 7.25 7.25

No. 704 contains one each of Nos. 700-703 with 2c surtax.

Nos. 700-704 Overprinted

1983, July 4 Photo. *Perf. 13x13½*

705	A112	12c Pair, #a.-b.	.50	.50
706	A112	36c Pair, #a.-b.	2.25	2.25
707	A112	48c Pair, #a.-b.	2.75	2.75
708	A112	60c Pair, #a.-b.	3.50	3.50
		Nos. 705-708 (4)	9.00	9.00

Souvenir Sheet of 8

709 A112 #a.-d. 7.00 7.00

Nos. 569, 572, 574-575, 579, 587, 660 Surcharged in Black or Gold

No. 710a

No. 712a

No. 715

No. 716

Perf. 13½x13, 14x13½, 14

1983, Aug. 12 Photo.

Strips of 4, #a.-d. (#710-713) or Block of 4, #a.-d. (#714)

710	A101	18c on 8c #569	3.00	3.00
711	A101	36c on 15c #572	4.75	4.75
712	A101	36c on 30c #575	4.75	4.75
713	A101	48c on 25c #574	7.25	7.25
714	A101	72c on 70c #579	12.00	12.00
715	A104	96c on $2 #660 (G)	3.75	3.75
716	A102	$5.60 on $6 #585 (G)	24.00	24.00
		Nos. 710-716 (7)	59.50	59.50

A114

A115

1983, Sept. 9 *Perf. 14*

732	Pair	.70	.70
a.	A114 6c Gt. Britain	.35	.35
b.	A115 6c Cook Islds. Group Federal flag	.35	.35
733	Pair	.90	.90
a.	A114 12c Raratonga ensign	.45	.45
b.	A115 12c New Zealand	.45	.45
734	Pair	1.00	1.00
a.	A114 15c Cook Islds, 1973-79	.50	.50
b.	A115 15c Cook Islds, 1983	.50	.50
c.	Souvenir sheet of 6, #732-734	2.00	2.00
735	Pair	1.60	1.60
a.	A114 20c like #732a	.80	.80
b.	A115 20c like #732b	.80	.80
736	Pair	2.00	2.00
a.	A114 30c like #733a	1.00	1.00
b.	A115 30c like #733b	1.00	1.00
737	Pair	2.40	2.40
a.	A114 35c like #734a	1.20	1.20
b.	A115 35c like #734b	1.20	1.20
c.	Souvenir sheet of 6, #735-737	3.75	3.75
	Nos. 732-737 (6)	8.60	8.60

Nos. 732-737 have different background landscapes; Nos. 735-737 airmail with silver background. Nos. 734c, 737c perf. 13½.

Nos. 576, 586, 678 Surcharged in Black or Gold

Perf. 13½x13, 14x13½, 14

1983, Aug. 30 Photo.

Block of 4, #a.-d.

738 A101 36c on 35c #576 4.75 4.75

Pair, #a.-b. (#739)

739	A108	96c on $2.50 #678 (G)	7.75	7.75
740	A102	$5.60 on $10 #586 (G)	19.00	19.00
		Nos. 738-740 (3)	31.50	31.50

Satellite Earth Station — A116

Designs: Various satellites in orbit.

1983, Oct. 10 Litho. *Perf. 13½*

744	A116	36c multicolored	.80	.80
745	A116	48c multicolored	1.25	1.25
746	A116	60c multicolored	1.40	1.40
747	A116	96c multicolored	2.25	2.25
		Nos. 744-747 (4)	5.70	5.70

Souvenir Sheet

748 A116 $2 multicolored 4.00 4.00

World Communications Year.

Christmas A117

Raphael Paintings: 12c, La Belle Jardiniere. 18c, Madonna and Child with Five Saints. 36c, Madonna and Child with Saint John. 48c, Madonna of the Fish. 60c, Madonna of the Baldacchino.

1983 Photo. *Perf. 14*

749	A117	12c multicolored	.90	.90
750	A117	18c multicolored	.90	.90
751	A117	36c multicolored	1.60	1.60
752	A117	48c multicolored	2.00	2.00
753	A117	60c multicolored	3.00	3.00
		Nos. 749-753 (5)	8.40	8.40

Souvenir Sheets

Perf. 13½

754		Sheet of 5	3.25	3.25
a.		A117 12c + 3c like #749	.25	.25
b.		A117 18c + 3c like #750	.30	.20
c.		A117 36c + 3c like #751	.55	.55
d.		A117 48c + 3c like #752	.70	.70
e.		A117 60c + 3c like #753	.90	.90
755	A117	85c + 5c like #749	1.30	1.30
756	A117	85c + 5c like #750	1.30	1.30
757	A117	85c + 5c like #751	1.30	1.30
758	A117	85c + 5c like #752	1.30	1.30
759	A117	85c + 5c like #753	1.30	1.30

Nos. 749-753 issued in sheets of 5 + label. Surtax was for children's charities.

Issued: Nos. 749-754, Nov. 14; others, Dec. 9.

Manned Flight Bicent. — A118

Various balloons: 36c, 1st manned flight, 1783. 48c, Ascent of Adorne, Strasbourg, 1784. 60c, 1785. 72c, Man on horse, 1785. 96c, Godard's aerial acrobatics, 1850.

$2.50, Blanchard & Jefferies, 1785.

1984, Jan. 16 Photo. *Perf. 13*

760	A118	36c multicolored	.65	.65
761	A118	48c multicolored	.80	.80
762	A118	60c multicolored	.90	.90
763	A118	72c multicolored	1.25	1.25
764	A118	96c multicolored	1.40	1.40
		Nos. 760-764 (5)	5.00	5.00

Souvenir Sheets

765	A118	$2.50 multicolored	3.50	3.50
766		Sheet of 5	5.50	5.50
a.		A118 36c + 5c like 36c	.65	.65
b.		A118 48c + 5c like 48c	.75	.75
c.		A118 60c + 5c like 60c	1.05	1.05
d.		A118 72c + 5c like 72c	1.25	1.25
e.		A118 96c + 5c like 96c	1.60	1.60

No. 765 contains 1 stamp 30x48mm, perf. 13½.

Save the Whales Campaign A119

10c, Cuvier's beaked whale. 18c, Risso's dolphin. 20c, True's beaked whale. 24c, Long-finned pilot whale. 30c, Narwhal. 36c, Beluga whale. 42c, Common dolphin. 48c, Commerson's dolphin. 60c, Bottle-nosed dolphin. 72c, Sowerby's whale. 96c, Common porpoise. $2, Boutu.

1984, Feb. 10 Photo. *Perf. 13*

767	A119	10c multicolored	.35	.35
768	A119	18c multicolored	.55	.50
769	A119	20c multicolored	.60	.60
770	A119	24c multicolored	.80	.80

771	A119	30c	multicolored	.95	.95
772	A119	36c	multicolored	1.10	1.10
773	A119	42c	multicolored	1.40	1.40
774	A119	48c	multicolored	1.50	1.50
775	A119	60c	multicolored	2.00	2.00
776	A119	72c	multicolored	2.40	2.40
777	A119	96c	multicolored	2.75	2.75
778	A119	$2	multicolored	6.75	6.75
			Nos. 767-778 (12)	21.15	21.10

1984 Summer Olympics A120

Posters of Various Summer Olympics: 18c, Athens, 1896. 24c, Paris, 1900. 36c, St. Louis, 1904. 48c, London, 1948. 60c, Tokyo, 1964. 72c, Berlin, 1936. 96c, Rome, 1960. $1.20, Los Angeles, 1932.

72c, 96c, $1.20 airmail.

1984, Mar. 8 Photo. *Perf. 13½*

779	A120	18c	multicolored	.30	.30
780	A120	24c	multicolored	.35	.35
781	A120	36c	multicolored	.50	.50
782	A120	48c	multicolored	.65	.65
783	A120	60c	multicolored	.75	.75
784	A120	72c	multicolored	.95	.95
785	A120	96c	multicolored	1.30	1.30
786	A120	$1.20	multicolored	1.75	1.75
			Nos. 779-786 (8)	6.55	6.55

For overprints see Nos. 826-828.

Coral — A121

and

Nos. 582-586 Surcharged

1c, Siphonogorgia. 2c, Millepora alcicornis. 3c, Distichopora violacea. 5c, Ptilosarcus gurneyi. 10c, Lobophyllia bemprichii. 12c, Sarcophyton digitatum. 14c, Pavona praetorta. 18c, Junceela gemmacea. 20c, Stylaster. 24c, Stylophora pistillata. 30c, Palauastrea ramosa. 36c, Melithaea albitincta. 40c, Stylaster echinatus. 42c, Fungia fungites. 48c, Goniopora. 50c, Melithaea squamata. 52c, Bellonella indica. 55c, Plerogyra sinuosa. 60c, Tubastraea. 70c, Heliofungia actinformis. 85c, Caulastraea echinulata. 96c, Porites andrewsi. $1.10, Pectinia alcicornis. $1.20, Dendrophyllia gracilis.

1984 *Perf. 13½x13*

787	A121	1c	multi	.25	.25
788	A121	2c	multi	.25	.25
789	A121	3c	multi	.25	.25
790	A121	5c	multi	.25	.25
791	A121	10c	multi	.25	.25
792	A121	12c	multi	.25	.25
793	A121	14c	multi	.25	.25
794	A121	18c	multi	.35	.35
795	A121	20c	multi	.35	.35
796	A121	24c	multi	.40	.40
797	A121	30c	multi	.50	.50
798	A121	36c	multi	.60	.60
799	A121	40c	multi	.65	.65
800	A121	42c	multi	.75	.75
801	A121	48c	multi	.80	.80
802	A121	50c	multi	.85	.85
803	A121	52c	multi	.85	.85
804	A121	55c	multi	1.20	1.20
805	A121	60c	multi	1.30	1.30
806	A121	70c	multi	1.40	1.40
807	A121	85c	multi	1.60	1.60
808	A121	96c	multi	1.90	1.90
809	A121	$1.10	multi	2.50	2.50
810	A121	$1.20	multi	2.75	2.75

Perf. 14x13½

Size: 59½x38½mm

811	A102	$3.60	on $2 #582	6.50	6.50
812	A102	$4.20	on $3 #583	7.25	7.25
813	A102	$5	on $4 #584	8.75	8.75
814	A102	$7.20	on $6 #585	12.50	12.50
815	A102	$9.60	on $10 #586	14.00	14.00
			Nos. 787-815 (29)	69.50	69.50

Issued: Nos. 787-801, 3/23; Nos. 802-810, 5/15; Nos. 811-813, 6/28; No. 814, 7/20; No. 815, 8/10.

For surcharges & overprints see Nos. 948-952, 955, 958, 960, 963, 965-967, B105-B108, O32-O45.

Nos. 784-786 Overprinted With Winners

No. 826

No. 827

No. 828

1984, Aug. 24 Photo. *Perf. 13½*

826	A120	72c	multicolored	1.00	1.00
827	A120	96c	multicolored	1.50	1.50
828	A120	$1.20	multicolored	1.90	1.90
			Nos. 826-828 (3)	4.40	4.40

1984 Summer Olympics. Nos. 826-828 airmail.

AUSIPEX '84 — A123

36c, Captain Cook's cottage. 48c, The Endeavour. 60c, Cook's landing. $2, Portrait, by John Webber.

1984, Sept. 20

829	A123	36c	multicolored	1.30	1.30
830	A123	48c	multicolored	1.75	1.75
831	A123	60c	multicolored	2.00	2.00
832	A123	$2	multicolored	6.75	6.75
a.			Souv. sheet, #829-832, 90c ea	9.50	9.50
b.			Sheet of 4, STAMPEX '86 emblem	9.00	9.00
			Nos. 829-832 (4)	11.80	11.80

No. 832b issued Aug. 4, 1986, for STAMPEX '86, Adelaide, Aug. 4-10; margin ovptd. with exhibition emblem, stamp picturing James Cook ovptd. with gold circle and black "Stampex 86 / Adelaide."

Nos. 677-678 Ovptd. & Surcharged in Gold

No. 659 Ovptd. & Surcharged in Silver

1984, Oct. 15 Photo. *Perf. 14*

833	A108	$1.25	Pair, #a.-b.	2.00	2.00
834	A108	$2.50	Pair, #a.-b.	5.50	5.50
835	A104	$3	on $1 No. 659	3.75	3.75
			Nos. 833-835 (3)	11.25	11.25

Nos. 833-835 printed in sheets of 4 stamps.

A124

Christmas (Paintings): 36c, Virgin on Throne with Child, by Giovanni Bellini (c. 1430-1516). 48c, Virgin and Child, 15th century, artistunknown. 60c, Virgin and Child with Saints, by Alvise Vivarini (c. 1446-1505). 96c, Virgin and Child with Angels, by Hans Memling (c. 1435-1494). $1.20, Adoration of the Magi, by Giovanni Tiepolo (1696-1770).

1984

838	A124	36c	multicolored	.65	.65
839	A124	48c	multicolored	.85	.85
840	A124	60c	multicolored	1.10	1.10
841	A124	96c	multicolored	1.75	1.75
842	A124	$1.20	multicolored	2.10	2.10
			Nos. 838-842 (5)	6.45	6.45

Souvenir Sheets

Perf. 13½

843			Sheet of 5	4.50	4.50
a.	A124	36c +5c	like #838	.55	.55
b.	A124	48c +5c	like #839	.70	.70
c.	A124	60c +5c	like #840	.80	.80
d.	A124	96c +5c	like #841	1.20	1.20
e.	A124	$1.20 +5c	like #842	1.40	1.40
844	A124	95c + 5c	like #838	1.40	1.40
845	A124	95c + 5c	like #839	1.40	1.40
846	A124	95c + 5c	like #840	1.40	1.40
847	A124	95c + 5c	like #841	1.40	1.40
848	A124	95c + 5c	like #842	1.40	1.40

Surtax of No. 843 for children's organizations, of Nos. 844-848 for youth education.

Issued: Nos. 838-843, 11/21; Nos. 844-848, 12/10.

A125

Illustrations of North American bird species by artist, naturalist John J. Audubon: 30c, Downy woodpecker. 55c, Black-throated blue warbler. 65c, Yellow-throated warbler. 75c, Chestnut-sided warbler. 95c, Dickcissel. $1.15, White-crowned sparrow. $1.30, Red-cockaded woodpecker. $2.80, Seaside sparrow. $5.30, Zenaida dove.

1985, Apr. 23 *Perf. 13x13½*

849	A125	30c	multicolored	1.20	1.20
850	A125	55c	multicolored	2.25	2.25
851	A125	65c	multicolored	2.40	2.40
852	A125	75c	multicolored	3.00	3.00
853	A125	95c	multicolored	3.75	3.75
854	A125	$1.15	multicolored	3.75	3.75
			Nos. 849-854 (6)	16.35	16.35

Souvenir Sheets

855	A125	$1.30	multicolored	2.10	2.10
856	A125	$2.80	multicolored	3.75	3.75
857	A125	$5.30	multicolored	7.50	7.50

Audubon birth bicentenary.

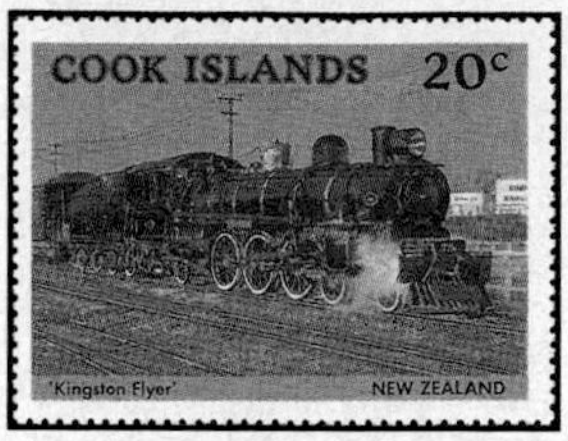

Locomotives — A126

20c, Kingston Flyer, New Zealand. 55c, Class 640, Italy. 65c, Gotthard, Switzerland. 75c, Union Pacific 6900, US. 95c, Super Continental, Canada. $1.15, TGV, France. $2.20, Flying Scotsman, U.K. $3.40, Orient Express, Europe.

1985, May 14 Litho. *Perf. 14x13½*

858	A126	20c	multicolored	.25	.25
859	A126	55c	multicolored	.35	.35
860	A126	65c	multicolored	.45	.45
861	A126	75c	multicolored	.50	.50
862	A126	95c	multicolored	.65	.65
863	A126	$1.15	multicolored	.70	.70
864	A126	$2.20	multicolored	1.40	1.40
865	A126	$3.40	multicolored	2.00	2.00
			Nos. 858-865 (8)	6.30	6.30

Intl. Youth Year — A127

Paintings: 55c, Helena Fourment, by Rubens. 65c, Vigee-Lebrun and Daughter, by Elizabeth Vigee-Lebrun (1755-1842). 75c, On the Terrace, by Renoir. $1.30, Young Mother Sewing, by Mary Cassatt (1845-1926).

1985, June 6 Photo. *Perf. 13x13½*

866	A127	55c	multicolored	2.75	2.75
867	A127	65c	multicolored	3.25	3.25
868	A127	75c	multicolored	3.75	3.75
869	A127	$1.30	multicolored	6.00	6.00
			Nos. 866-869 (4)	15.75	15.75

Souvenir Sheet

870			Sheet of 4	10.00	10.00
a.	A127	55c + 10c	like #866	1.75	1.75
b.	A127	65c + 10c	like #867	2.10	2.10
c.	A127	75c + 10c	like #868	2.40	2.40
d.	A127	$1.30 + 10c	like #869	3.75	3.75

Surtax for youth organizations.

Queen Mother, 85th Birthday A128

Portraits: 65c, Lady Elizabeth, 1908, by Mable Hankey. 75c, Duchess of York, 1923, by Savely Sorine. $1.15, Duchess of York, 1925, by Philip De Laszlo. $2.80, $5.30, Queen Elizabeth, 1938, by Sir Gerald Kelly.

1985, June 28

871	A128	65c multi	.65	.65
872	A128	75c multi	.75	.75
873	A128	$1.15 multi	1.20	1.20
874	A128	$2.80 multi	2.60	2.60
874A		Sheet of 4 ('86)	4.75	4.75
b.-e.		A128 55c, like #871-874	1.20	1.20
		Nos. 871-874A (5)	9.95	9.95

Souvenir Sheet

875	A128	$5.30 multi	5.00	5.00

Nos. 871-874 printed in sheets of four.
No. 874A issued 8/4/86, for 86th birthday.
For surcharges see Nos. B114, B116, B122, B134, B140.

A129

Portraits of prime ministers: 30c, Albert Henry, 1965-78. 50c, Sir Thomas Davis, 1978-83. 65c, Geoffrey Henry, 1983.

1985, July 29

876	A129	30c multicolored	1.00	1.00
877	A129	50c multicolored	2.00	2.00
878	A129	65c multicolored	2.40	2.40
		Nos. 876-878 (3)	5.40	5.40

Souvenir Sheet

879		Sheet of 3	4.50	4.50
a.		A129 55c like #876	1.40	1.40
b.		A129 55c like #877	1.40	1.40
c.		A129 55c like #878	1.40	1.40

Self-government, 20th anniv.

A130

1985, July 29 *Perf. 14*

880	A130	55c Golf	4.25	4.25
881	A130	65c Rugby	4.75	4.75
882	A130	75c Tennis	5.50	5.50
		Nos. 880-882 (3)	14.50	14.50

Souvenir Sheet

883		Sheet of 3	13.00	13.00
a.		A130 55c + 10c like #880	3.75	3.75
b.		A130 65c + 10c like #881	3.75	3.75
c.		A130 75c + 10c like #882	3.75	3.75

South Pacific Mini Games, Rarotonga, July 31-Aug. 10. Surtax for the benefit of the Mini Games.

A131

Seahorse & conf. emblems: 55c, South Pacific Bureau for Economic Cooperation. 65c, No. 887b, South Pacific Forum. 75c, No. 887c, Pacific Islands Conf.

1985, July 29 *Perf. 14*

884	A131	55c blk, scar & gold	1.40	1.40
885	A131	65c blk, vio & gold	1.60	1.60
886	A131	75c blk, brt grn & gold	1.75	1.75
		Nos. 884-886 (3)	4.75	4.75

Souvenir Sheet

887		50c Sheet of 3, #a.-c.	3.00	3.00

Pacific islands conf., Rarotonga, 7/30-8/10.

A132

Virgin and Child paintings by Botticelli: 55c, Madonna of the Magnificent. 65c, Madonna with Pomegranate. 75c, Madonna with Child & Six Angels. 95c, Madonna & Child with St. John.

1985

888	A132	55c multicolored	1.75	1.75
889	A132	65c multicolored	2.25	2.25
890	A132	75c multicolored	2.75	2.75
891	A132	95c multicolored	3.50	3.50
		Nos. 888-891 (4)	10.25	10.25

Souvenir Sheets

Perf. 13½

892	A132	$2.75 Sheet of 4	6.50	6.50
a.		A132 50c like #888	1.40	1.40
b.		A132 50c like #889	1.40	1.40
c.		A132 50c like #890	1.40	1.40
d.		A132 50c like #891	1.40	1.40

Imperf

893	A132	$1.20 like #888	2.00	2.00
894	A132	$1.45 like #889	2.25	2.25
895	A132	$2.20 like #890	3.50	3.50
896	A132	$2.75 like #891	4.25	4.25

Christmas. Issue dates: Nos. 888-892, Nov. 18; Nos. 893-896, Dec. 9.

Halley's Comet — A133

Paintings: 55c, No. 902a, The Eve of the Deluge, by John Martin (1789-1854). 65c, No. 902b, Lot and His Daughters, by Lucas van Leyden (1494-1533). 75c, No. 902c, Auspicious Comet, 1587, anonymous. $1.25, No. 902d, Events Following Charles I, by Herman Saftleven (1609-1658). $2, No. 902e, Ossian Receiving Napoleonic Officers, by Anne Louis Girodet-Trioson (1764-1824). $4, Halley's Comet over the Thames, 1759, by Samuel Scott (1702-1772).

1986, Mar. 13 **Photo.** *Perf. 14*

897	A133	55c multicolored	1.10	1.10
898	A133	65c multicolored	1.40	1.40
899	A133	75c multicolored	1.60	1.60
900	A133	$1.25 multicolored	3.25	3.25
901	A133	$2 multicolored	4.75	4.75
		Nos. 897-901 (5)	12.10	12.10

Souvenir Sheets

Perf. 13½

902		Sheet of 5 + label	6.50	6.50
a.-e.		A133 70c, each single	1.25	1.25
903	A133	$4 multicolored	7.50	7.50

For surcharges see Nos. B113, B115, B117, B123, B129.

Elizabeth II, 60th Birthday — A134

Various portraits.

1986, Apr. 21 *Perf. 13x13½*

904	A134	95c multi	1.40	1.40
905	A134	$1.25 multi	1.60	1.60
906	A134	$1.50 multi	1.90	1.90
		Nos. 904-906 (3)	4.90	4.90

Souvenir Sheets

907	A134	$1.10 like #904	2.25	2.25
908	A134	$1.95 like #905	4.00	4.00
909	A134	$2.45 like #906	5.75	5.75

For surcharges see Nos. 972-974, B118, B124, B127, B136-B137, B139.

AMERIPEX '86 — A135

Designs: $1, US No. 1, The Resolution, Rarotonga. $1.50, Downtown Chicago. $2, No. 398, Benjamin Franklin, The Resolution.

1986, May 21 **Photo.** *Perf. 14*

910	A135	$1 multi	3.50	3.50
911	A135	$1.50 multi	5.25	5.25
912	A135	$2 multi	6.75	6.75
		Nos. 910-912 (3)	15.50	15.50

For surcharges see Nos. B119, B128, B130.

Statue of Liberty, Cent. — A136

1986, July 4

913	A136	$1 Head	1.00	1.00
914	A136	$1.25 Torch	1.25	1.25
915	A136	$2.75 Liberty Is.	2.75	2.75
		Nos. 913-915 (3)	5.00	5.00

For surcharges see Nos. B120, B125, B132.

Wedding of Prince Andrew and Sarah Ferguson — A137

1986, July 23

916	A137	$1 Sarah Ferguson	.80	.80
917	A137	$2 Prince Andrew	1.60	1.60

Size: 60x33½mm

Perf. 13½x13

918	A137	$3 Couple	2.40	2.40
		Nos. 916-918 (3)	4.80	4.80

Nos. 916-918 each printed in sheets of 4.
For surch. see Nos. 975-977, B121, B131, B135.

Christmas A138

Paintings by Rubens: 55c, No. 922a, The Holy Family. $1.30, $6.40, No. 922b, Virgin with Garland. $2.75, No. 922c, Adoration of Magi.

1986, Nov. 17 **Litho.** *Perf. 13½*

919	A138	55c multi	1.40	1.40
920	A138	$1.30 multi	3.25	3.25
921	A138	$2.75 multi	6.50	6.50
		Nos. 919-921 (3)	11.15	11.15

Souvenir Sheets

922		Sheet of 3	14.00	14.00
a.-c.		A138 $2.40, any single	4.50	4.50
923	A138	$6.40 multi	15.00	15.00

No. 922 contains 3 stamps 38½x49mm.
For surcharges see Nos. B100-B104, B112, B126, B133, B138, B141.

Stamps of 1980-84 Surcharged in Black

Strips of 4, #a.-d. (#953, 954, 956, 957) or

Blocks of 4, #a.-d. (#959, 961, 962, 964)

1987, Feb. **Litho.** *Perfs. as before*

948	A121	5c on 1c #787	.25	.25
949	A121	5c on 2c #788	.25	.25
950	A121	5c on 3c #789	.25	.25
951	A121	5c on 12c #792	.25	.25
952	A121	5c on 14c #793	.25	.25
953	A101	10c on 15c #572	.55	.55
954	A101	10c on 25c #574	.55	.55
955	A121	18c on 24c #796	.25	.25
956	A101	18c on 12c #571	1.10	1.10
957	A101	18c on 20c #573	1.10	1.10
958	A121	55c on 52c #803	.90	.90
959	A101	55c on 35c #576	3.25	3.25
960	A121	65c on 42c #800	1.00	1.00
961	A101	65c on 50c #577	4.50	4.50
962	A101	65c on 60c #578	4.50	4.50
963	A121	75c on 48c #801	1.25	1.25
964	A101	75c on 70c #579	4.50	4.50
965	A121	95c on 96c #808	1.50	1.50
966	A121	95c on $1.10 #809	1.50	1.50
967	A121	95c on $1.20 #810	1.50	1.50

Stamps of 1981-86 Surcharged in Black (A102), Black and Gold (#968-970, A137) or Gold (#971, A134, A104, A108)

968	A123	$1.30 on 36c #829	1.90	1.90
969	A123	$1.30 on 48c #830	1.90	1.90
970	A123	$1.30 on 60c #831	1.90	1.90
971	A123	$1.30 on $2 #832	1.90	1.90
972	A134	$2.80 on 95c #904	4.25	4.25
973	A134	$2.80 on $1.25 #905	4.25	4.25
974	A134	$2.80 on $1.50 #906	4.25	4.25
975	A137	$2.80 on $1 #916	4.25	4.25
976	A137	$2.80 on $2 #917	4.25	4.25
977	A137	$2.80 on $3 #918	4.25	4.25
978	A102	$6.40 on $4 #584	7.50	7.50
979	A102	$7.20 on $6 #585	8.50	8.50
980	A104	$9.40 on $1 #659	11.00	11.00
981	A104	$9.40 on $2 #660	11.00	11.00

Pair, #a.-b.

982	A108	$9.40 on $2.50 #678	22.00	22.00
		Nos. 948-982 (35)	122.30	122.30

Issued: 5c, Nos. 955, 958, 960, 963, 95c, $6.40, $7.20, 2/10; 10c, Nos. 956-957, 959, 961-962, 964, 2/11; $12.30, $2.80, $9.40, 2/12.
For surcharge see No. B111.

Stamps of 1980-82 Surcharged in Black (A102) or Gold (A104)

No. 984

No. 989

Perfs. as before

1987, June 17 **Photo.**

984	A102	$2.80 on $2 #582	2.75	2.75
985	A102	$5 on $3 #583	4.75	4.75
986	A102	$9.40 on $10 #586	8.50	8.50

Pairs, #a.-b.

987	A104	$9.40 on $1 #679	17.00	17.00
988	A104	$9.40 on $2 #680	17.00	17.00
		Nos. 984-988 (5)	50.00	50.00

Souvenir Sheet

989	A104	$9.20 on #680c	15.00	15.00

Nos. 399 and 584 Ovptd. in Black on Gold Bar

1987, Nov. 20 **Photo.** ***Perf. 14x13½***

991	A64	$4 on #399	4.00	4.00
992	A102	$4 on #584	4.00	4.00

Christmas — A139

The Holy Family, religious paintings by Rembrandt in European museums: $1.25, No. 996a, The Louvre, Paris. $1.50, No. 996b, $6, The Holy Family with Angels, The Hermitage, Leningrad. $1.95, No. 996c, The Alte Pinakothek, Munich.

1987, Dec. 7 **Photo.** ***Perf. 13½***

993	A139	$1.25 multi	2.50	2.50
994	A139	$1.50 multi	3.50	3.50
995	A139	$1.95 multi	4.50	4.50
		Nos. 993-995 (3)	10.50	10.50

Souvenir Sheets

996		Sheet of 3	8.50	8.50
a.-c.	A139	$1.15 any single	2.50	2.50

Perf. 13x13½

997	A139	$6 multi	11.00	11.00

Size of Nos. 996a-996c: 49½x38½mm. No. 997 contains 1 stamp 39½x31½mm.

1988 Summer Olympics, Seoul A140

Designs: a, Cook Islands commemorative silver coin (obverse and reverse) issued on Aug. 20, 1987, for the '88 Summer Games. b, Seoul Olympic Park, torch and emblem. c, Steffi Graf, women's tennis champion, and '88 gold medal.

1988, Apr. 26 **Photo.** ***Perf. 13½x14***

998		Strip of 3	15.00	15.00
a.-c.	A140	$1.50 multicolored	5.00	5.00

Souvenir Sheet

Perf. 13½

999	A140	$10 multi	15.00	15.00

Participation of national athletes in the Olympics for the first time, introduction of tennis as an Olympic gold-medal event.

No. 999 contains one stamp 114x47mm combining the designs of Nos. 998a-998c.

Nos. 998-999 Overprinted

a-c

d

1988, Oct. 12 **Photo.** ***Perf. 13½x14***

1000		Strip of 3	12.00	12.00
a.-c.	A140	$1.50 multicolored	4.00	4.00

Souvenir Sheet

Perf. 13½

1001	A140(d)	$10 on No. 999	16.00	16.00

Christmas A141

Paintings by Albrecht Durer: 70c, Virgin and Child. 85c, Virgin and Child, diff. 95c, Virgin and Child, diff. $1.25, Virgin and Child, diff. $6.40, The Nativity.

1988, Nov. 11 ***Perf. 13½***

1002	A141	70c multi	2.75	2.75
1003	A141	85c multi	3.25	3.25
1004	A141	95c multi	3.75	3.75
1005	A141	$1.25 multi	5.00	5.00
		Nos. 1002-1005 (4)	14.75	14.75

Souvenir Sheet

1006	A141	$6.40 multi	12.00	12.00

No. 1006 contains one stamp 45x60mm.

Scene and Left Half of Mission Emblem A142

1st Moon Landing, 20th Anniv. — A144

No. 1007a, Launch vehicle in space. No. 1007b, *Eagle* landing on Moon. No. 1008a, Astronaut descending ladder. No. 1008b, Astronaut on Moon. No. 1009a, Seismic experiment. No. 1009b, Solar wind experiment. No. 1010a, Liftoff from Moon. No. 1010b, Splashdown and recovery.

The "b" stamps have the right half of the emblem.

1989, July 14 **Photo.** ***Perf. 13***

1007	A142	40c Pair, #a.-b.	3.00	3.00
1008	A142	55c Pair, #a.-b.	4.50	4.50
1009	A142	65c Pair, #a.-b.	5.00	5.00
1010	A142	75c Pair, #a.-b.	5.50	5.50
		Nos. 1007-1010 (4)	18.00	18.00

Souvenir Sheet

1011	A144	$4.20 Armstrong and Aldrin	8.75	8.75

Printed with continuous designs.

World Wildlife Fund A145

Endangered bird species: 15c, $1, Pomarea dimidiata. 20c, $1.25, Pomarea dimidiata (two). 65c, $1.50, Ptilinopus rarotongensis (two). 70c, $1.75, Ptilinopus rarotongensis.

1989, Oct. 4 **Photo.** ***Perf. 13½x13***

1016	A145	15c multicolored	1.40	1.40
1017	A145	20c multicolored	2.00	2.00
1018	A145	65c multicolored	5.50	5.50
1019	A145	70c multicolored	6.25	6.25
		Nos. 1016-1019 (4)	15.15	15.15

Souvenir Sheets Without WWF Emblem

Perf. 13½

1020	A145	$1 like 15c	2.75	2.75
1021	A145	$1.25 like 20c	3.25	3.25
1022	A145	$1.50 like 65c	3.75	3.75
1023	A145	$1.75 like 70c	4.25	4.25

World Wildlife Fund. Nos. 1020-1023 are airmail and contain one 52x34mm stamp; decorative margins continue the designs.

For overprints see Nos. C24-C27.

Christmas — A146

Details of *Adoration of the Magi,* by Rubens: 70c, Witnesses. 85c, Madonna. 95c, Christ child. $1.50, Attendant. $6.40, Entire painting.

1989, Nov. 24 **Photo.** ***Perf. 13½x13***

1024	A146	70c multicolored	1.60	1.60
1025	A146	85c multicolored	1.75	1.75
1026	A146	95c multicolored	2.10	2.10
1027	A146	$1.50 multicolored	3.25	3.25
		Nos. 1024-1027 (4)	8.70	8.70

Souvenir Sheet

Perf. 13½

1028	A146	$6.40 multicolored	15.00	15.00

No. 1028 contains one 45x60mm stamp.

Religious History A147

70c, John Williams, LMS Mission Church. 85c, Bernardine Castanie, Roman Catholic Church. 95c, Osborne J.P. Widstoe, Church of Jesus Christ of Latter Day Saints. $1.60, J.E. Caldwell, Seventh Day Adventist Church.

1990, Feb. 19 **Photo.** ***Perf. 13½x13***

1029	A147	70c multicolored	1.00	1.00
1030	A147	85c multicolored	1.20	1.20
1031	A147	95c multicolored	1.40	1.40
1032	A147	$1.60 multicolored	2.40	2.40
		Nos. 1029-1032 (4)	6.00	6.00

Souvenir Sheet

Perf. 13½

1033		Sheet of 4	7.00	7.00
a.	A147	90c like 70c	1.50	1.50
b.	A147	90c like 85c	1.50	1.50
c.	A147	90c like 95c	1.50	1.50
d.	A147	90c like $1.60	1.50	1.50

No. 1033 contains 4 36x36mm stamps.

Penny Black, 150th Anniv. — A148

Paintings: 85c, No. 1038a, *Woman Writing a Letter,* by Gerard Terborch (1617-1681). $1.15, No. 1038b, *Portrait of George Gisze,* by Hans Holbein the Younger. $1.55, No. 1038c, *Portrait of Mrs. John Douglas,* by Thomas Gainsborough. $1.85, No. 1038d, *Portrait of a Gentleman,* by Albrecht Durer.

1990, May 2 **Photo.** ***Perf. 13½***

1034	A148	85c multicolored	1.40	1.40
1035	A148	$1.15 multicolored	2.00	2.00
1036	A148	$1.55 multicolored	2.60	2.60
1037	A148	$1.85 multicolored	3.25	3.25
		Nos. 1034-1037 (4)	9.25	9.25

Souvenir Sheet

1038		Sheet of 4	13.00	13.00
a.-d.	A148	$1.05 any single	3.00	3.00

The margin of No. 1038 pictures the Stamp World '90 emblem and Great Britain #1-2.

1992 Olympics A149

Designs: a. Summer Games, Barcelona (runners). b. Eternal flame, commemorative coin obverse (Queen Elizabeth II) and reverse (athletes). c. Winter Games, Albertville (skier).

1990, June 15 **Photo.** ***Perf. 14***

1039		Strip of 3	18.00	18.00
a.-c.	A149	$1.85 any single	6.00	6.00

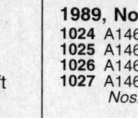

Queen Mother, 90th Birthday A150

1990, July 20 Photo. *Perf. 13½*

1040	A150 $1.85 multicolored		6.50	6.50

Souvenir Sheet

1041	A150 $6.40 multicolored	13.00	13.00

Christmas A151

Paintings: 70c, Adoration of the Magi by Memling. 85c, The Holy Family by Lotto. 95c, Madonna and Child with Saints John and Catherine by Titian. $1.50, The Holy Family by Titian. $6.40, Madonna and Child Enthroned, Surrounded by Saints by Vivarini.

1990, Nov. 29 Litho. *Perf. 14*

1042	A151	70c multicolored	1.75	1.75
1043	A151	85c multicolored	2.40	2.40
1044	A151	95c multicolored	2.50	2.50
1045	A151	$1.50 multicolored	3.75	3.75
		Nos. 1042-1045 (4)	10.40	10.40

Souvenir Sheet

1046	A151 $6.40 multicolored	15.00	15.00

For overprints and surcharges see Nos. 1251, 1254, 1257-1258.

Souvenir Sheet

1992 Olympic Games — A152

1991, Feb. 12 *Perf. 13½*

1047	A152 $6.40 multicolored	15.00	15.00

Discovery of America 500th Anniv. (in 1992) — A153

1991, Feb. 14 Photo. *Perf. 13½x13*

1048	A153 $1 multicolored	4.25	4.25

No. 586 Ovptd. "65th BIRTHDAY" in Gold

1991, Apr. 22 Litho. *Perf. 14x13½*

1049	A102 $10 multicolored	18.00	18.00

Christmas A154

Paintings: 70c, Adoration of the Child, by Delle Notti (Gerrit van Honthorst). 85c, Birth of the Virgin, by Murillo. $1.15, Adoration of the Shepherds, by Rembrandt. $1.50, Adoration of the Shepherds, by Le Nain. $6.40, Madonna and Child, by Fra Filippo Lippi, vert.

1991, Nov. 12 Litho. *Perf. 14*

1050	A154	70c multicolored	1.00	1.00
1051	A154	85c multicolored	3.00	3.00
1052	A154	$1.15 multicolored	4.25	4.25
1053	A154	$1.50 multicolored	5.75	5.75
		Nos. 1050-1053 (4)	14.00	14.00

Souvenir Sheet

1054	A154 $6.40 multicolored	15.00	15.00

For overprints and surcharges see Nos. 1252-1253, 1255-1256.

Marine Life — A155

A155a

5c, Red-breasted maori wrasse. 10c, Blue sea star. 15c, Black & gold angelfish. 20c, Spotted pebble crab. 25c, Black-tipped cod. 30c, Spanish dancer. 50c, Royal angelfish. 80c, Squirrel fish. 85c, Red pencil sea urchin. 90c, Red-spot rainbow fish. $1, Black-lined maori wrasse. $2, Longnose butterflyfish. $3, Red-spot rainbow fish. $5, Blue sea star. $7, Royal angelfish. $10, Spotted pebble crab. $15, Red pencil sea urchin.

1992-94 Litho. *Perf. 14½x13½*

1058	A155	5c multi	.40	.40
1059	A155	10c multi	.40	.40
1062	A155	15c multi	.40	.40
1064	A155	20c multi	.50	.50
1065	A155	25c multi	.55	.55
1066	A155	30c multi	.65	.65
1071	A155	50c multi	1.10	1.10
1076	A155	80c multi	1.75	1.75
1077	A155	85c multi	1.75	1.75
1078	A155	90c multi	1.75	1.75
1080	A155	$1 multi	2.00	2.00
1081	A155	$2 multi	3.75	3.75
1082	A155a	$3 multi	4.50	4.50
1083	A155a	$5 multi	8.00	8.00
1085	A155a	$7 multi	12.00	12.00
1087	A155a	$10 multi	17.00	17.00
1089	A155a	$15 multi	25.00	25.00
	Nos. 1058-1089 (17)		81.50	81.50

Issued: 85c, 90c, $1, $2, 3/23/92; $3, $5, 10/25/93; $7, 12/6/93; $10, 1/31/94; $15, 9/9/94; others, 1/22/92.

See Nos. 1154-1176 for stamps with buff border. For overprints see Nos. O54-O68.

Endangered Wildlife — A156

No. 1095, Tiger. No. 1096, Asiatic elephant. No. 1097, Grizzly bear. No. 1098, Black rhinoceros. No. 1099, Chimpanzee. No. 1100, Asian bighorn. No. 1101, Heavisides dolphin. No. 1102, Eagle owl. No. 1103, Bee hummingbird. No. 1104, Felisconcolor cougar. No. 1105, European otter. No. 1106, Red kangaroo.

1992 Litho. *Perf. 14*

1095-1106	$1.15 Set of 12	20.00	20.00

Issued: No. 1095, 4/6; No. 1096, 4/7; No. 1097, 4/8; No. 1098, 4/9; No. 1099, 4/10; No. 1100, 4/11; No. 1101, 7/13; No. 1102, 7/14; No. 1103, 7/15; No. 1104, 7/16; No. 1105, 7/17; No. 1106, 7/18.

See Nos. 1119-1124, 1134-1138.

For surcharges see Nos. 1239-1250.

Discovery of America, 500th Anniv. — A157

1992, May 22 Litho. *Perf. 14x14½*

1107	A157 $6 multicolored	9.00	9.00

Souvenir Sheet

Perf. 15x14

1107A	A157 $10 Coming ashore	10.50	10.50

Issued: No. 1107, 5/22. No. 1107A, 9/21. No. 1107A contains one 40x30mm stamp.

1992 Summer Olympics, Barcelona — A158

Designs: No. 1108a, $50 coin, soccer players. b, Flags of Spain, Cook Islands, Barcelona medal. c, $10 coin, basketball players. No. 1109a, Runners. b, $10, $50 coins. c, Cyclists. $6.40, Javelin.

1992, July 24 Litho. *Perf. 13*

1108	A158 $1.75 Strip of 3, #a.-c.	9.00	9.00
1109	A158 $2.25 Strip of 3, #a.-c.	11.00	11.00

Souvenir Sheet

1110	A158 $6.40 multicolored	19.00	19.00

6th Festival of Pacific Arts, Rarotonga A159

80c, UNESCO poster. 85c, $1, $1.75, Different carvings of Rarotongan fertility god, Tangaroa.

1992, Oct. 16 Litho. *Perf. 15x14*

1111	A159	80c multicolored	1.75	1.75
1112	A159	85c multicolored	2.00	2.00
1113	A159	$1 multicolored	2.40	2.40
1114	A159	$1.75 multicolored	3.75	3.75
		Nos. 1111-1114 (4)	9.90	9.90

For overprints see Nos. 1231-1234.

Overprinted in Black

1992, Oct. 16

1115	A159	80c on #1111	2.10	2.10
1116	A159	85c on #1112	2.50	2.50
1117	A159	$1 on #1113	2.50	2.50
1118	A159	$1.75 on #1114	4.75	4.75
		Nos. 1115-1118 (4)	11.85	11.85

Endangered Wildlife Type of 1992

No. 1119, Jackass penguin. No. 1120, Asian lion. No. 1121, Peregrine falcon. No. 1122, Persian fallow deer. No. 1123, Key deer. No. 1124, Alpine ibex.

1992 Litho. *Perf. 14*

1119	A156	$1.15 multicolored	1.75	1.75
1120	A156	$1.15 multicolored	1.75	1.75
1121	A156	$1.15 multicolored	1.75	1.75
1122	A156	$1.15 multicolored	1.75	1.75
1123	A156	$1.15 multicolored	1.75	1.75
1124	A156	$1.15 multicolored	1.75	1.75
		Nos. 1119-1124 (6)	10.50	10.50

Issued: No. 1119, 11/2; No. 1120, 11/3; No. 1121, 11/4; No. 1122, 11/5; No. 1123, 11/6; No. 1124, 11/7.

Christmas A160

Paintings by El Parmigianino: 70c, Worship of Shepherds. 85c, $6.40, Virgin with Long Neck. $1.15, Virgin with Rose. $1.90, St. Margaret's Virgin.

1992, Nov. 20 Litho. *Perf. 13½*

1125	A160	70c multicolored	1.00	1.00
1126	A160	85c multicolored	1.60	1.60
1127	A160	$1.15 multicolored	2.10	2.10
1128	A160	$1.90 multicolored	3.75	3.75
		Nos. 1125-1128 (4)	8.45	8.45

Souvenir Sheet

1129	A160 $6.40 multicolored	12.50	12.50

No. 1129 contains one 36x47mm stamp.

Queen Elizabeth II's Accession to the Throne, 40th Anniv. — A161

Various portraits of Queen Elizabeth II.

1992, Dec. 10 Litho. *Perf. 14*

1130	A161	80c multicolored	1.25	1.25
1131	A161	$1.15 multicolored	2.00	2.00
1132	A161	$1.50 multicolored	3.25	3.25
1133	A161	$1.95 multicolored	4.50	4.50
		Nos. 1130-1133 (4)	11.00	11.00

Endangered Wildlife Type of 1992

No. 1134, English mandrill. No. 1135, Gorilla. No. 1136, Vanessa atlanta. No. 1137, Sichuan takin. No. 1138, Ring tailed lemur.

1993 Litho. *Perf. 14*

1134	A156	$1.15 multicolored	2.00	2.00
1135	A156	$1.15 multicolored	2.00	2.00
1136	A156	$1.15 multicolored	2.00	2.00
1137	A156	$1.15 multicolored	2.00	2.00
1138	A156	$1.15 multicolored	2.00	2.00
		Nos. 1134-1138 (5)	10.00	10.00

Issued: No. 1134, 2/1; No. 1135, 2/2; No. 1136, 2/3; No. 1137, 2/4; No. 1138, 2/5.

Coronation of Queen Elizabeth II, 40th Anniv. — A162

Designs: $1, Coronation ceremony. $2, Coronation portrait. $3, Queen, family on balcony, Buckingham Palace.

1993, June 2 Litho. *Perf. 14*

1139 A162 $1 multicolored 2.25 2.25
1140 A162 $2 multicolored 4.75 4.75
1141 A162 $3 multicolored 7.00 7.00
Nos. 1139-1141 (3) 14.00 14.00

Christmas A163

Paintings: 70c, Virgin with Child, by Filippo Lippi. 85c, Bargellini Madonna, by Lodovico Carracci. $1.15, Virgin of the Curtain, by Raphael. $2.50, Holy Family, by Il Bronzino. $4, Saint Zachary Virgin, by Il Parmigianino.

1993, Nov. 8 Litho. *Perf. 14*

1142 A163 70c multicolored 1.00 1.00
1143 A163 85c multicolored 1.40 1.40
1144 A163 $1.15 multicolored 1.75 1.75
1145 A163 $2.50 multicolored 3.50 3.50

Size: 32x47mm

Perf. 13½

1146 A163 $4.00 multicolored 6.25 6.25
Nos. 1142-1146 (5) 13.90 13.90

1994 Winter Olympics, Lillehammer — A164

1994, Feb. 11 Litho. *Perf. 13½x14*

1147 A164 $5 multicolored 10.00 10.00

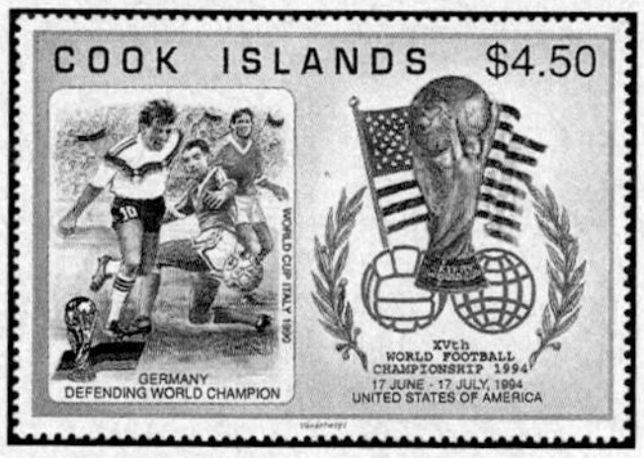

1994 World Cup Soccer Championships, US — A165

1994, June 17 Litho. *Perf. 14*

1148 A165 $4.50 multicolored 8.00 8.00

First Manned Moon Landing, 25th Anniv. — A166

Apollo 11 emblem and: No. 1149a, First step onto Moon, US flag. No. 1149b, Astronaut carrying experiment packs on Moon. No. 1150a, Astronaut, US flag. No. 1150b, Flag, reflection shown in astronaut's visor.

1994, July 20

1149 A166 $2.25 Pair, #a.-b. + label 9.00 9.00
1150 A166 $2.25 Pair, #a.-b. + label 9.00 9.00

Living Reef Type of 1992

1994, Oct. 24 Litho. *Perf. 14½x13½*

Size: 41x31mm

Buff & Multicolored

1154 A155 5c like #1058 .50 .50
1158 A155 15c like #1062 .50 .50
1160 A155 20c like #1064 .60 .60
1161 A155 25c like #1065 .65 .65
1162 A155 30c like #1066 .75 .75
1167 A155 50c like #1071 1.40 1.40
1172 A155 80c like #1076 2.25 2.25
1173 A155 85c like #1077 2.40 2.40
1174 A155 90c like #1078 2.50 2.50
1176 A155 $1 like #1080 2.75 2.75
Nos. 1154-1176 (10) 14.30 14.30

Miniature Sheet

The Return of Tommy Tricker — A167

Scenes from film: a, Three people in canoe. b, Traditional dancers. c, Couple walking on beach. d, Aerial view of island. e, Girls performing hand gestures. f, Girls walking along sand bar.

1994, Nov. 23 Litho. *Perf. 14*

1191 A167 85c Sheet of 6, #a.-f. 9.50 9.50

See No. 1213.

Christmas — A168

Paintings: No. 1192a, The Virgin and Child, by Morales. b, Adoration of Kings, by Gerard David. c, Adoration of Kings, by Vinc Foppa. d, The Madonna & Child with St. Joseph & Infant Baptist, by Baroccio.

No. 1193a, Madonna with Iris, in style of Durer. b, Adoration of Shepherds, by Le Nain. c, The Virgin and Child, by follower of Leonardo. d, The Mystic Nativity, by Botticelli.

1994, Nov. 30 Litho. *Perf. 14*

1192 A168 85c Block of 4, #a.-d. 6.75 6.75
1193 A168 $1 Block of 4, #a.-d. 7.75 7.75

Robert Louis Stevenson (1850-94), Writer — A169

Adventure scenes from books: a, "Treasure Island." b, "David Balfour." c, "Dr. Jekyll and Mr. Hyde." d, "Kidnapped."

1994, Dec. 12 *Perf. 14x15*

1194 A169 $1.50 Block of 4, #a.-d. 14.00 14.00

UN, 50th Anniv. — A170

$4.50, FAO, 50th anniv.

1995 Litho. *Perf. 13x13½*

1195 A170 $4.75 multicolored 6.25 6.25

Perf. 13½

1196 A170 $4.50 multicolored 6.75 6.75

Each issued in sheets of 4.

Issued: $4.75, 7/17; $4.50, 10/12.

Queen Mother, 95th Birthday — A172

1995, Aug. 31

1197 A172 $5 multicolored 12.00 12.00

End of World War II, 50th Anniv. — A173

Designs: a, German surrender, Rheims. b, Japanese surrender, Tokyo Bay.

1995, Sept. 4 *Perf. 13*

1198 A173 $3.50 Pair, #a.-b. 22.00 22.00

No. 1198 was issued in sheets of 4 stamps.

Year of the Sea Turtle A174

Designs: 85c, Green turtle in water. $1, Hawksbill turtle in water. $1.75, Green turtle nesting. $2.25, Hawksbill turtle hatchlings leaving nest.

1995, Nov. 20 Litho. *Perf. 14*

1199 A174 85c multicolored 2.00 2.00
1200 A174 $1 multicolored 2.75 2.75
1201 A174 $1.75 multicolored 4.25 4.25
1202 A174 $2.25 multicolored 5.75 5.75
Nos. 1199-1202 (4) 14.75 14.75

1996 Summer Olympics, Atlanta A175

1996, Jan. 12 Litho. *Perf. 14*

1203 A175 85c Discus 1.40 1.40
1204 A175 $1 Torch bearer 1.75 1.75
1205 A175 $1.50 Sprinting 2.60 2.60
1206 A175 $1.85 Gymnastics 3.50 3.50
1207 A175 $2.10 Archery 4.00 4.00
1208 A175 $2.50 Javelin 4.50 4.50
Nos. 1203-1208 (6) 17.75 17.75

Queen Elizabeth II, 70th Birthday — A176

Designs: $1.90, No. 1212a, In blue hat, coat. $2.25, No. 1212b, Wearing tiara. $2.75, No. 1212c, In robes of Order of the Garter.

1996, June 21 Litho. *Perf. 14*

1209 A176 $1.90 multicolored 3.00 3.00
1210 A176 $2.25 multicolored 4.00 4.00
1211 A176 $2.75 multicolored 4.50 4.50
Nos. 1209-1211 (3) 11.50 11.50

Sheet of 3

1212 A176 $2.50 #a.-c. + label 14.00 14.00

Nos. 1209-1211 were issued in sheets of 4.

"The Return of Tommy Tricker" Type of 1994

No. 1213a-1213f, like #1191a-1191f.

1997, Aug. 28 Litho. *Perf. 14*

1213 A167 90c Sheet of 6, #a.-f. 9.50 9.50

Nos. 1213a-1213f Overprinted in Silver

a

b

1997, Sept. 12 Litho. *Perf. 14*

1214 A167 90c Sheet 6, #a.-f. 9.00 9.00

Nos. 1214a, 1214d-1214e are overprinted type "a"; Nos. 1214b-1214c, 1214f type "b."

Butterflies A177

5c, Lampides boeticus (female). 10c, Vanessa atalanta. 15c, Lampides boeticus (male). 20c, Papilio godeffroyi. 25c, Danaus hamata. 30c, Xois sesara. 50c, Vagrans egista. 70c, Parthenos sylvia. 80c, Hyblaea sanguinea. 85c, Melanitis leda. 90c, Ascalapha odorata. $1, Precis villida. $1.50, Parthenos sylvia. $2, Lampides boeticus. $3, Precis villida. $4, Melanitis leda. $5, Vagrans egista. $7, Hyblaea sanguinea. $10, Vanessa atalanta. $15, Papilio godeffroyi.

1997-98 Litho. *Perf. 13*

1215 A177 5c multi .25 .25
1216 A177 10c multi .25 .25
1217 A177 15c multi .25 .25
1218 A177 20c multi .30 .30
1219 A177 25c multi .35 .35
1220 A177 30c multi .35 .35
1221 A177 50c multi .55 .55
1222 A177 70c multi .80 .80
1223 A177 80c multi .95 .95
1224 A177 85c multi .95 .95
1225 A177 90c multi 1.00 1.00
1226 A177 $1 multi 1.10 1.10

Perf. 13½

Size: 41x25mm

1226A A177 $1.50 multi 1.60 1.60
1226B A177 $2 multi 2.25 2.25
1226C A177 $3 multi 3.25 3.25
1226D A177 $4 multi 4.75 4.75
1226E A177 $5 multi 5.50 5.50
1226F A177 $7 multi 8.50 8.50
1226G A177 $10 multi 11.50 11.50
1226H A177 $15 multi 15.00 15.00
Nos. 1215-1226H (20) 59.45 59.45

Issued: 5c, 10c, 15c, 20c, 25c, 30c, 50c, 70c, 10/22/97; 80c, 85c, 90c, $1, 11/12/97; $1.50, $2, $3, 3/11/98; $4, $5, 6/19/98; $7, $10, 9/18/98; $15, 11/13/98.

For surcharges, see Nos. 1259-1264.

Queen Elizabeth II and Prince Philip, 50th Wedding Anniv.
A178

1997, Nov. 20 *Perf. 14*

1227	A178 $2 multicolored	3.00	3.00

Souvenir Sheet

1228	A178 $5 like #1227, close-up	9.00	9.00

No. 1228 is a continuous design.

Diana, Princess of Wales (1961-97) — A179

1998, Mar. 18 **Litho.** *Perf. 14*

1229	A179 $1.15 shown	1.50	1.50

Souvenir Sheet

1230	A179 $3.50 like #1229	5.25	5.25

No. 1229 was issued in sheets of 5 + label. See No. B142.

Nos. 1111-1114 Ovptd.

Printing Methods and Perfs as before

1999, Dec. 31

1231	A159	80c on #1111	1.25	1.25
1232	A159	85c on #1112	1.25	1.25
1233	A159	$1 on #1113	1.50	1.50
1234	A159	$1.75 on #1114	2.50	2.50
		Nos. 1231-1234 (4)	6.50	6.50

Queen Mother, 100th Birthday — A180

No. 1235: a, As child. b, As young woman. c, Wearing green hat. d, Wearing tiara.

2000, Oct. 20 **Litho.** *Perf. 14*

1235	A180 $4.50 Sheet of 4, #a-d	18.00	18.00

Souvenir Sheet

1236	A180 $6 Wearing blue hat	5.50	5.50

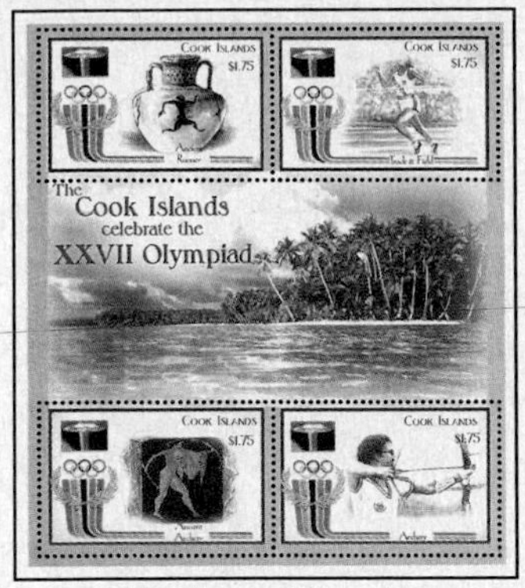

2000 Summer Olympics, Sydney — A181

No. 1237: a, Ancient runner. b, Track and field. c, Ancient archery. d, Archery.

2000, Nov. 14

1237	A181 $1.75 Sheet of 4, #a-d	9.00	9.00

Souvenir Sheet

1238	A181 $3.90 Torch bearer	4.50	4.50

Nos. 1095-1106 Surcharged in Gold

2001, Apr. 30 **Litho.** *Perf. 14*

1239	A156	80c on $1.15 #1101	1.25	1.25
1240	A156	80c on $1.15 #1102	1.25	1.25
1241	A156	80c on $1.15 #1103	1.25	1.25
1242	A156	80c on $1.15 #1104	1.25	1.25
1243	A156	80c on $1.15 #1105	1.25	1.25
1244	A156	80c on $1.15 #1106	1.25	1.25
1245	A156	90c on $1.15 #1095	1.25	1.25
1246	A156	90c on $1.15 #1096	1.25	1.25
1247	A156	90c on $1.15 #1097	1.25	1.25
1248	A156	90c on $1.15 #1098	1.25	1.25
1249	A156	90c on $1.15 #1099	1.25	1.25
1250	A156	90c on $1.15 #1100	1.25	1.25
		Nos. 1239-1250 (12)	15.00	15.00

Nos. 1042-1045, 1050-1053 Surcharged or Overprinted in Black or Gold

2002, Nov. 11 **Litho.** *Perf. 14*

1251	A151	20c on 70c #1042	.25	.25
1252	A154	20c on 70c #1050	.25	.25
1253	A154	80c on $1.15 #1052 (G)	1.50	1.50
1254	A151	85c #1043	1.60	1.60
1255	A154	85c #1051	1.60	1.60
1256	A154	90c on $1.50 #1053	1.75	1.75
1257	A151	95c #1044	1.90	1.90
1258	A151	$1 on $1.50 #1045	2.25	2.25
		Nos. 1251-1258 (8)	11.10	11.10

Nos. 1226A-1226F Surcharged

Methods and Perfs As Before

2003, June 30

1259	A177	20c on $1.50 #1226A	.30	.30
1260	A177	80c on $2 #1226B	1.00	1.00
1261	A177	85c on $3 #1226C	1.25	1.25
1262	A177	85c on $4 #1226D	1.25	1.25
1263	A177	90c on $5 #1226E	1.50	1.50
1264	A177	90c on $7 #1226F	1.50	1.50
		Nos. 1259-1264 (6)	6.80	6.80

Obliterator on Nos. 1260-1264 is a Moai head.

United We Stand — A182

2003, Sept. 30 **Litho.** *Perf. 14*

1265	A182 90c multi	3.00	3.00

Printed in sheets of 4.

2004 Summer Olympics, Athens
A183

Designs: 40c, Poster for 1992 Barcelona Olympics. 60c, Pancration, horiz. $1, Cycling, horiz. $2, Gold medal, 1936 Berlin Olympics.

2004, Sept. 29 **Litho.** *Perf. 14¼*

1266-1269	A183 Set of 4	6.50	6.50

Worldwide Fund for Nature (WWF) — A184

Birds of Suwarrow National Park: 80c, Cook Islands reed warblers. 90c, Mangaia kingfishers. $1.15, Rarotonga starlings. $1.95, Atiu swiftlets.

2005, June 13 **Litho.** *Perf. 14*

1270-1273	A184 Set of 4	6.50	6.50

Each stamp printed in sheets of 4.

Pope John Paul II (1920-2005)
A185

2005, Nov. 11

1274	A185 $1.35 multi	2.75	2.75

Printed in sheets of 5 + label.

A186

A187

A188

Designs: 5c, Black-lined Maori wrasse. 10c, Blue lorikeets. 20c, Daisy coral. 30c, Ocean sunfish. 40c, Female Lampides boeticus butterfly. 50c, Rarotonga starlings.

No. 1285: a, Mangaia kingfishers. b, Cook Islands reef warblers. c, Rarotonga starlings, diff. d, Matiu swiftlets.

No. 1286: a, Male Lampides boeticus. b, Vagrans egista. c, Melantis leda. d, Female Lampides boeticus, diff.

No. 1287: a, Daisy coral, diff. b, Hydroid coral. c, Sea star. d, Smooth sea star.

No. 1288: a, Black-tipped cod. b, Red spot rainbow fish. c, Black-lined Maori wrasse, diff. d, Fish (incorrectly identified as Smooth sea star).

No. 1289: a, Three Ocean sunfish, Latin name at LL. b, Three Ocean sunfish, large clump of seaweed, Latin name at LR. c, Two Ocean sunfish, diver. d, Three Ocean sunfish, small clump of seaweed at top, Latin name at LR.

No. 1290: a, Blue lorikeets on palm branch. b, Blue lorikeets in tree hollow. c, Blue lorikeets and white flowers. d, Blue lorikeets and pink flowers.

No. 1291 — Queen Elizabeth II and: a, Hawksbill turtle. b, Leatherback turtle. c, Green turtle. d, Olive ridley turtle.

No. 1292 — Queen Elizabeth II and: a, Sowerby's whales. b, Cuvier's beaked whales. c, Bottle-nosed dolphin. d, Commerson's dolphins.

$7.50, Queen Elizabeth II, fish and marine life. $10, Queen Elizabeth II, butterflies and flowers. $15, Queen Elizabeth II and birds.

Illustrations A187 and A188 reduced.

2007 **Litho.** *Perf. 13¼*

1279	A186	5c multi	.25	.25
1280	A186	10c multi	.25	.25
1281	A186	20c multi	.30	.30
1282	A186	30c multi	.45	.45
1283	A186	40c multi	.60	.60
1284	A186	50c multi	.75	.75

Size: 48x27mm

Perf. 14x14¾

1285	Block of 4	4.75	4.75
a.-d.	A186 80c Any single	1.10	1.10
1286	Block of 4	5.25	5.25
a.-d.	A186 90c Any single	1.25	1.25
1287	Block of 4	5.75	5.75
a.-d.	A186 $1 Any single	1.40	1.40
1288	Block of 4	6.50	6.50
a.-d.	A186 $1.10 Any single	1.60	1.60
1289	Block of 4	7.00	7.00
a.-d.	A186 $1.20 Any single	1.75	1.75

1290	Block of 4	11.50	11.50
a.-d.	A186 $2 Any single	2.75	2.75

Perf. 13¾

1291	Block of 4	19.00	19.00
a.-d.	A187 $3 Any single	4.75	4.75
1292	Block of 4	31.00	31.00
a.-d.	A187 $5 Any single	7.75	7.75

Perf. 13¼

1293	A188 $7.50 multi	12.00	12.00
1294	A188 $10 multi	15.50	15.50
1295	A188 $15 multi	24.00	24.00
	Nos. 1279-1295 (17)	144.85	144.85

Issued: Nos. 1279-1290, 3/20; No. 1291, 10/10; No. 1292, 11/13; Nos. 1293-1295, 12/10.

Miniature Sheet

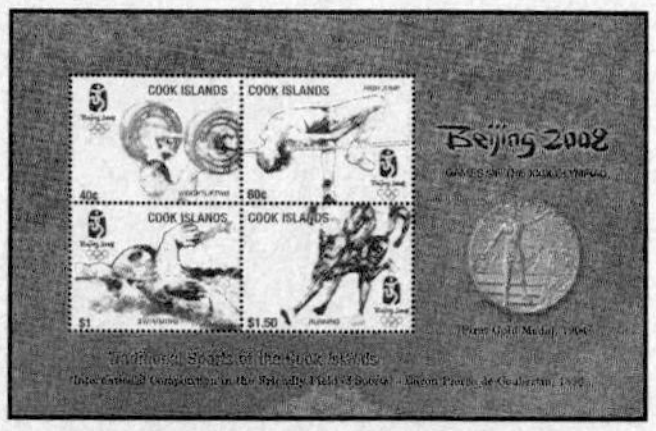

2008 Summer Olympics, Beijing — A189

No. 1296: a, 40c, Weight lifting. b, 60c, High jump. c, $1, Swimming. d, $1.50, Running.

2008, July 28 Litho. *Perf. 14¾x14*

1296	A189 Sheet of 4, #a-d	5.25	5.25

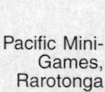

Pacific Mini-Games, Rarotonga A190

Designs: 20c, Shot put and discus. 80c, High jump. 90c, Weight lifting. $3, Running.

2009, Sept. 21 Litho. *Perf. 13¾*

1297-1300	A190 Set of 4	7.25	7.25
1300a	Souvenir sheet, #1297-1300	7.25	7.25

Nos. 1297-1300 Ovptd. in Gold with Names of Winners

Overprint text: 20c, Daniel Kilama / New Caledonia / Men's Discus Throw / 27th Sept. 2009. 80c, Johanna Sui / Tahiti / Women's High Jump / 24th Sept. 2009. 90c, Yukio Peter / Nauru / 84kg Clean & Jerk / 1st Oct. 2009. $3, Niko Verekauta / Fiji / Men's 100 metres / 24th Sept. 2009.

2009, Oct. 21 Litho. *Perf. 13¾*

1301-1304	A190 Set of 4	7.25	7.25
1304a	Souvenir sheet, #1301-1304	7.25	7.25

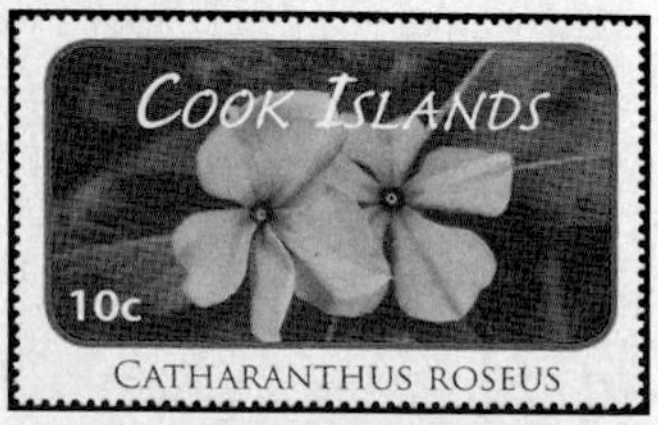

Flowers — A191

Designs: 10c, Catharanthus roseus. 20c, Ixora casei. 30c, Hibiscus rosa-sinensis cultivar. 40c, Heliconia psittacorum. 50c, Hibiscus schizopetalus, vert. 70c, Alpinia purpurata, vert. 80c, Bougainvillea spectabilis. 90c, Hibiscus rosa-sinensis. $1, Nymphaea capensis. $1.10, Euphorbia pulcherrima. $1.20, Impatiens walleriana. $2, Anthurium andraeanum. $3, Chrysanthemum cultivar. $4, Acalypha pendula, vert. $5, Heliconia rostrata, vert. $7.50, Tagetes patular cultivar. $10, Phalaenopsis cultivar. $20, Catharanthus roseus, diff.

2010, Sept. 10 Litho. *Perf. 13¾*

Sizes: 60x37mm, 37x60mm

1305	A191	10c multi	.25	.25
1306	A191	20c multi	.30	.30
1307	A191	30c multi	.45	.45
1308	A191	40c multi	.60	.60
1309	A191	50c multi	.75	.75
1310	A191	70c multi	1.00	1.00
1311	A191	80c multi	1.25	1.25
1312	A191	90c multi	1.40	1.40
1313	A191	$1 multi	1.50	1.50
1314	A191	$1.10 multi	1.60	1.60
1315	A191	$1.20 multi	1.75	1.75
1316	A191	$2 multi	3.00	3.00
1317	A191	$3 multi	4.50	4.50
1318	A191	$4 multi	5.75	5.75
1319	A191	$5 multi	7.25	7.25
1320	A191	$7.50 multi	11.00	11.00
1321	A191	$10 multi	14.50	14.50
1322	A191	$20 multi	29.00	29.00
		Nos. 1305-1322 (18)	85.85	85.85

See Nos. 1328-1337, 1388-1389.
For overprints see Nos. O70-O117.

ANZAC Day A192

Designs: 80c, Girl Guides in parade. 90c, Boy Scouts in parade. $1.10, Monument, vert. $1.20, Cook Islands flag, vert.

No. 1327: a, Church interior. b, Church exterior.

Perf. 14¾x14¼, 14¼x14¾

2010, Sept. 14

1323-1326	A192 Set of 4	6.00	6.00

Souvenir Sheet

1327	A192 $3 Sheet of 2, #a-b	9.00	9.00

For overprints, see Nos. 1391-1400.

Flower Type of 2010 in Smaller Sizes

Designs as before.

2010, Oct. 27 Litho. *Perf. 14*

Sizes: 42x28mm, 28x42mm

1328	A191	10c multi	.25	.25
1329	A191	20c multi	.30	.30
1330	A191	30c multi	.50	.50
1331	A191	50c multi	.80	.80
1332	A191	80c multi	1.25	1.25
1333	A191	90c multi	1.50	1.50
1334	A191	$1 multi	1.60	1.60
1335	A191	$1.10 multi	1.75	1.75
1336	A191	$1.20 multi	1.90	1.90
1337	A191	$2 multi	3.25	3.25
		Nos. 1328-1337 (10)	13.10	13.10

For surcharges, see Nos. 1437-1445.

Expo 2010, Shanghai A193

Designs: 80c, Anthurium flower. 90c, Angelfish. $1.10, Fish near ocean floor. $1.20, Coconuts.

$6, Palm tree and ocean, vert.

2010, Oct. 27 *Perf. 14¾x14¼*

1338-1341	A193 Set of 4	6.50	6.50

Souvenir Sheet

Perf. 14¼

1342	A193 $6 multi	9.75	9.75

No. 1342 contains one 38x50mm stamp.

Miniature Sheet

Aerial Views of Islands — A194

No. 1343: a, 10c, Aitutaki. b, 10c, Penrhyn. c, 20c, Palmerston. d, 20c, Mitiaro. e, 30c, Rarotonga. f, 30c, Takutea. g, 50c, Atiu. h, 70c, Suwarrow. i, 80c, Pukapuka. j, 80c, Nassau. k, 90c, Mangaia. l, 90c, Manihiki. m, 90c, Manuae. n, $1.10, Rakahanga. o, $1.20, Mauke.

2010, Nov. 8 *Perf. 14*

1343	A194 Sheet of 15, #a-o	14.00	14.00

Service of Queen Elizabeth II and Prince Philip — A195

Designs: 80c, Queen Elizabeth II. 90c, Queen and Prince Philip. $1, Queen and Prince Philip, diff. $1.10, Queen and Prince Philip, diff. $1.20, Queen and Prince Philip, diff. $1.50, Prince Philip.

$6.60, Queen and Prince Philip, diff.

2010, Dec. 6 Litho. *Perf. 13¼*

1344-1349	A195 Set of 6	9.75	9.75
1349a	Sheet of 6, #1344-1349, + 3 labels	9.75	9.75

Souvenir Sheet

1350	A195 $6.60 multi	10.00	10.00

Worldwide Fund for Nature (WWF) — A196

Rimatara lorikeet: 80c, Pair on flower. 90c, In flight. $2.40, On branch. $3.60, Trio at nest.

2010, Dec. 9 Litho. *Perf. 14*

1351-1354	A196 Set of 4	11.50	11.50

A197

Engagement of Prince William and Catherine Middleton — A198

Designs: Nos. 1355, 1358a, 1360, Middleton. Nos. 1356, 1358b, 1361, Prince in military uniform.

No. 1357: a, Prince in military uniform. b, Prince playing polo. c, Middleton, fence. d, Prince, man and woman in background. e, Middleton, woman in background. f, Couple, Prince at left. g, Middleton with black hat. h, Prince. i, Couple, Middleton at left. j, Hands of couple, engagement ring.

$8.10, Couple, Prince in uniform at left.

2011, Jan. 14 *Perf. 14*

1355	A197 $2.40 multi	3.75	3.75
1356	A197 $3.60 multi	5.50	5.50

Miniature Sheets

1357	A198 10c Sheet of 10, #a-j	1.60	1.60

Perf. 13¾x13½

1358	A197 Sheet of 2, #a-b	9.25	9.25

Souvenir Sheets

Perf. 14¼

1359	A197 $8.10 multi	12.50	12.50
1360	A197 $11 multi	17.00	17.00
1361	A197 $11 multi	17.00	17.00
	Nos. 1359-1361 (3)	46.50	46.50

No. 1358 contains two 28x44mm stamps. Nos. 1359-1361 each contain one 38x50mm stamp.

Peonies — A199

No. 1362: a, 80c, Pink peonies (30x40mm). b, 90c, Purple peony (30x30mm). c, $1.10, Peach peonies (30x30mm). d, $1.20, Pink peony (30x30mm).

$8.10, Red peony.

2011, Apr. 8 Litho. *Perf. 14¾*

1362	A199 Sheet of 4, #a-d	6.25	6.25

Souvenir Sheet

1363	A199 $8.10 multi	13.00	13.00

No. 1363 contains one 70x60mm stamp.

Wedding of Prince William and Catherine Middleton A200

Designs: 20c, Couple, Prince at right. 30c, Westminster Abbey. 80c, Couple, Prince at left.

2011, Apr. 29 *Perf. 13¼*

1364-1366 A200	Set of 3	2.10	2.10
1366a	Souvenir sheet of 3, #1364-1366	2.10	2.10

Rarotonga Tourism — A201

Designs: 10c, Whale breaching ocean's surface near boat. 20c, Palm trees, boat. 30c, Starfish. 50c, Palm trees near ocean. 70c, Crab. 80c, Cook Islands flag on boat. 90c, Airplane, windsurfer. $1, Trees near beach. $1.10, Cliffs, airplane. $1.20, Palm trees near beach. $1.50, Goat. $2, Chicken. $3, Island and beach. $4, Fish. $5, Aerial view of Rarotonga. cruise ship.

2011, July 22 **Litho.** *Perf. 14*

1367 A201	10c	multi	.25	.25
1368 A201	20c	multi	.35	.35
1369 A201	30c	multi	.50	.50
1370 A201	50c	multi	.85	.85
1371 A201	70c	multi	1.25	1.25
1372 A201	80c	multi	1.40	1.40
1373 A201	90c	multi	1.50	1.50
1374 A201	$1	multi	1.75	1.75
1375 A201	$1.10	multi	1.90	1.90
1376 A201	$1.20	multi	2.00	2.00
1377 A201	$1.50	multi	2.50	2.50
1378 A201	$2	multi	3.50	3.50
1379 A201	$3	multi	5.00	5.00
1380 A201	$4	multi	6.75	6.75
1381 A201	$5	multi	8.50	8.50
a.	Sheet of 15, #1367-1381		38.00	38.00
	Nos. 1367-1381 (15)		38.00	38.00

National Environment Service A202

Designs: 80c, Bristle-thighed curlew. 90c, Fiddler crab. $1.10, Taro plant and flower. $1.20, Wetlands flora.

2011, Oct. 21 *Perf. 13¾*

1382-1385 A202	Set of 4	6.50	6.50

Nos. 1382-1385 each were printed in sheets of 4.

Souvenir Sheets

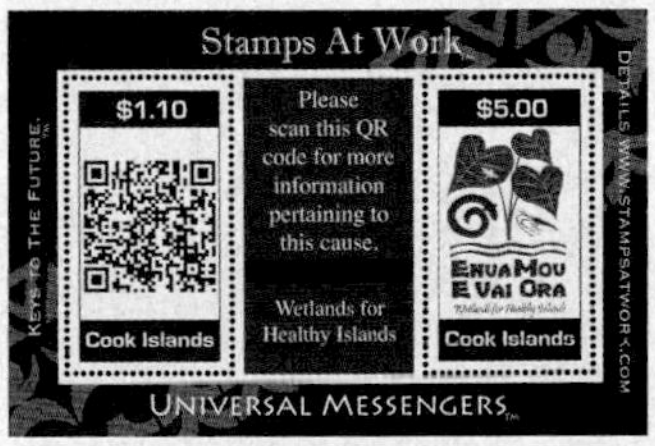

Stamps at Work — A203

No. 1386: a, $1.10, Quick response code. b, $5, Emblem for Wetlands for Healthy Islands.
No. 1387: a, $1.10, Quick response code, text and website address. b, $5, Damage from 2011 Japan tsunami.

2011, Oct. 21 *Perf. 15x14¼*

Sheets of 2, #a-b

1386-1387 A203	Set of 2	19.50	19.50

Twenty percent of the sales of No. 1387 were donated to Japan tsunami relief efforts.

Flowers Type of 2010 With Head of Queen Elizabeth II Added at Lower Right

Designs: $26.90, Plumeria rubra. $31.10, Hypolimnas bolina.

2011, Oct. 25 *Perf. 14¼x15*

Size: 44x29mm

1388 A191	$26.90	multi	42.50	42.50
1389 A191	$31.10	multi	50.00	50.00

Christmas A204

No. 1390: a, Five gold rings. b, Six geese a laying. c, Seven swans a swimming. d, Eight maids a milking.

2011, Dec. 23 **Litho.** *Perf. 13¼*

1390	Horiz. strip of 4	13.00	13.00
a.	A204 $1.10 multi	1.75	1.75
b.	A204 $1.20 multi	1.90	1.90
c.	A204 $2.10 multi	3.50	3.50
d.	A204 $3.60 multi	5.75	5.75
e.	Souvenir sheet of 4, #1390a-1390d	13.00	13.00

Nos. 1323-1327 Overprinted in Gold or Silver

Methods and Perfs As Before

2012, Jan. 10

1391 A192	80c	On No. 1323 (G)	1.40	1.40
1392 A192	80c	On No. 1323 (S)	1.40	1.40
1393 A192	90c	On No. 1324 (G)	1.50	1.50
1394 A192	90c	On No. 1324 (S)	1.50	1.50
1395 A192	$1.10	On No. 1325 (G)	1.90	1.90
1396 A192	$1.10	On No. 1325 (S)	1.90	1.90
1397 A192	$1.20	On No. 1326 (G)	2.00	2.00
1398 A192	$1.20	On No. 1326 (S)	2.00	2.00
		Nos. 1391-1398 (8)	13.60	13.60

Souvenir Sheets of 2, #a-b

1399 A192	$3	On No. 1327 (G)	10.00	10.00
1400 A192	$3	On No. 1327 (S)	10.00	10.00

Overprint reads up on Nos. 1395-1398.

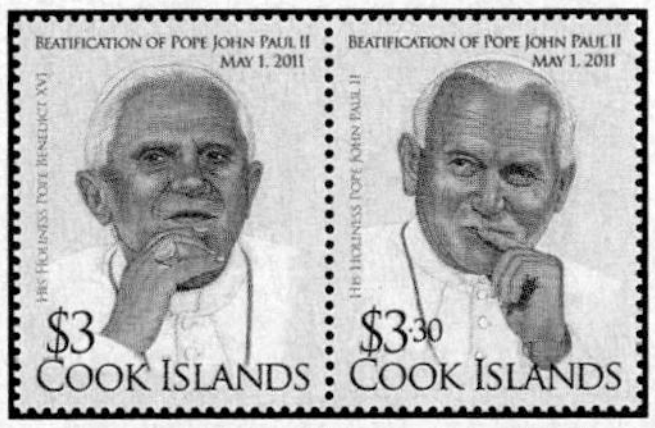

Beatification of Pope John Paul II — A205

No. 1401: a, $3, Pope Benedict XVI. b, $3.30, Pope John Paul II.

2012, Jan. 10 **Litho.** *Perf. 13¾*

1401 A205	Horiz. pair, #a-b	10.50	10.50

No. 1401 was printed in sheets containing two pairs.

Reign of Queen Elizabeth II, 60th Anniv. — A206

Queen Elizabeth II: 80c, Wearing tiara. 90c, Wearing red hat. $1, Wearing tiara, diff. $1.10, Wearing gray hat. $1.20, With dog. $1.50, Wearing aquamarine dress.
$6.60, Wearing aquamarine dress, diff.

2012, Feb. 6 *Perf. 13¼*

1402-1407 A206	Set of 6	11.00	11.00
1407a	Souvenir sheet of 6, #1402-1407, + 3 labels	11.00	11.00

Souvenir Sheet

1408 A206	$6.60	multi	11.00	11.00

Worldwide Fund for Nature (WWF) — A207

Designs: 90c, Partula assimilis. $1.20, Libera fratercula. $1.50, Lamprocystis globosa. $2.70, Sinployea peasei.

2012, Apr. 11 *Perf. 14*

1409-1412 A207	Set of 4	10.00	10.00
1412a	Sheet of 16, 4 each #1409-1412	40.00	40.00

2012 Summer Olympics, London — A208

Designs: 80c, Swimming. 90c, Map of South Pacific, Great Britain and Ireland. $2, Sailing.

2012, June 22 *Perf. 13¾*

1413-1415 A208	Set of 3	6.00	6.00
1415a	Souvenir sheet of 3, #1413-1415	6.00	6.00
1415b	Souvenir sheet of 6, 2 each #1413-1415	12.00	12.00

Miniature Sheets

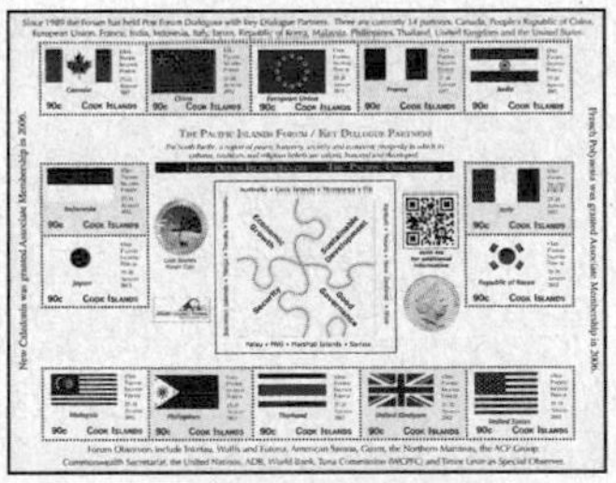

43rd Pacific Islands Forum, Rarotonga — A209

No. 1416 — Flag of: a, Canada. b, People's Republic of China. c, European Union. d, France. e, India. f, Indonesia. g, Italy. h, Japan. i, Republic of Korea. j, Malaysia. k, Philippines, l, Thailand. m, United Kingdom. n, United States.
No. 1417 — Flag of: a, Australia. b, Cook Islands. c, Fiji. d, Kiribati. e, Micronesia. f, Nauru. g, New Zealand. h, Niue. i, Palau. j, Papua New Guinea. k, Marshall Islands. l, Samoa. m, Solomon Islands. n, Tonga. o, Tuvalu. p, Vanuatu.

2012, Aug. 22 *Perf. 14*

1416 A209	90c	Sheet of 14, #a-n	21.00	21.00
1417 A209	90c	Sheet of 16, #a-p	24.00	24.00

Adoration of the Magi, by Giotto di Bondone A210

Entry into Jerusalem, by Giotto A211

Lamentation, by Giotto — A212

Kiss of Judas, by Giotto A213

Life of Mary Magdalene - Raising of Lazarus, by Giotto A214

Death of Mary, by Giotto A215

Perf. 14¾x14¼

2012, Nov. 16 **Litho.**

Stamps With White Frames

1418	Horiz. pair	2.80	2.80
a.	A210 80c multi	1.40	1.40
b.	A211 80c multi	1.40	1.40
1419	Horiz. pair	3.00	3.00
a.	A212 90c multi	1.50	1.50
b.	A213 90c multi	1.50	1.50
1420	Horiz. pair	10.00	10.00
a.	A214 $3 multi	5.00	5.00
b.	A215 $3 multi	5.00	5.00
	Nos. 1418-1420 (3)	15.80	15.80

Miniature Sheet

Stamps Without White Frame

1421	Sheet of 6	16.00	16.00
a.	A210 80c multi	1.40	1.40
b.	A211 80c multi	1.40	1.40
c.	A212 90c multi	1.50	1.50
d.	A213 90c multi	1.50	1.50
e.	A214 $3 multi	5.00	5.00
f.	A215 $3 multi	5.00	5.00

Christmas.

Miniature Sheets

A215a

43rd Pacific Islands Forum, Rarotonga — A215b

No. 1422G: i, Woman with Cook Islands sash with Minister of Education Teina Bishop, New Zealand Prime Minister John Key and John Carter, New Zealand High Commissioner to the Cook Islands. j, Canoe with sails. k, Women from Aitutaki holding a quilted bedspread. l, Leaders of Pacific islands seated in row. m, President of French Polynesia Oscar Temaru and Cook Islands Prime Minister Henry Puna in front of airplane. n, Australian Prime Minister Julia Gillard. o, Canoe on shore.

No. 1422H: p, Pres. Temaru, Prime Minister Puna, Cook Islands Deputy Prime Minister Tom Marsters and entourage walking away from airplane. q, Prime Minister Puna departing airplane, two women. r, U.S. airplane. s, People leaving Royal New Zealand Air Force airplane. t, Crowds near entrance to Aitutaki Airport. u, U.S. Secretary of State Hillary Clinton with Cook Island Minister of Finance Mark Brown. v, Aitutaki dancers performing for leaders.

2012, Nov. 30 Litho. *Perf. 14*

1421G	A215a 80c	Sheet of 7, #i-o, + label	9.50	9.50
1421H	A215b 90c	Sheet of 7, #p-v, + label	10.50	10.50

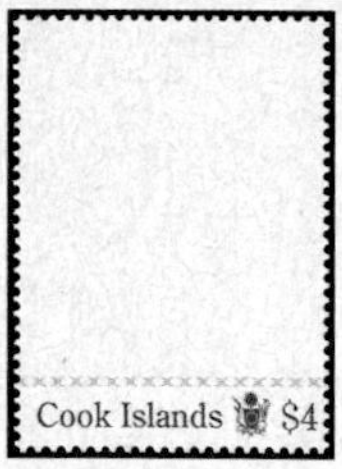

A216

Personalizable Stamps — A217

2012, Dec. 21 Litho. *Perf. 14x14¾*

1422	A216 $4 multi		6.75	6.75
1423	A217 $4 multi		6.75	6.75

Items Commemorating British Coronations — A218

Coronation of Queen Elizabeth II, 60th Anniv. — A219

Various items commemorating the coronation of: 80c, Queen Victoria. 90c, King Edward VII. $1.10, King George V. $1.20, Seed packet for Coronation mixture of sweet pea seeds. $3.60, Illustration from *The Coronation Cut-Out Story Book*.
$3.90, Queen Elizabeth II.

2013, Feb. 6 Litho. *Perf. 14*

1424-1428	A218	Set of 5	12.50	12.50

Souvenir Sheet

Perf. 15x14

1429	A219 $3.90 multi		6.50	6.50

Nos. 1424-1428 each were printed isn sheets of 8 + central label.

A220

A221

A222

A223

A224

Cook Islands Marine Park A225

2013, Feb. 20 Litho. *Perf. 14*

1430	A220 80c multi		1.40	1.40
1431	A221 80c multi		1.40	1.40
1432	A222 80c multi		1.40	1.40
1433	A223 90c multi		1.50	1.50
1434	A224 90c multi		1.50	1.50
1435	A225 90c multi		1.50	1.50
	Nos. 1430-1435 (6)		8.70	8.70

New Year 2013 (Year of the Snake) A226

No. 1436 — Snake with background color of: a, Green. b, Red.

Perf. 14¾x14¼

2013, Feb. 21 Litho.

1436	A226 $1.20 pair, #a-b		4.00	4.00

Printed in sheets containing 2 each of Nos. 1436a-1436b.

Nos. 1328, 1330-1337 Surcharged in Gold

Methods and Perfs. As Before

2013, Apr. 9

1437	A191 20c on 10c #1328		.35	.35
1438	A191 20c on 30c #1330		.35	.35
1439	A191 20c on 50c #1331		.35	.35
1440	A191 20c on 80c #1332		.35	.35
1441	A191 20c on 90c #1333		.35	.35
1442	A191 20c on $1 #1334		.35	.35
1443	A191 20c on $1.10 #1335		.35	.35
1444	A191 20c on $1.20 #1336		.35	.35
1445	A191 20c on $2 #1337		.35	.35
	Nos. 1437-1445 (9)		3.15	3.15

Ships — A227

No. 1446, 20c: a, Ndrua. b, Hamatafua.
No. 1447, 50c: a, Single-masted Vaa Kalua. b, Double-masted Vaa Kalua.
No. 1448, 60c: a, Vaka Motu. b, Toniaki.
No. 1449, 80c: a, Vaka. b, Pahi.
No. 1450, 90c: a, Vaka, diff. b, Pahi, diff.
No. 1451, $2.30: a, Vaka Motu, diff. b, Tipaerua.
No. 1452, $4.50: a, Pahi, diff. b, Waka Tou. c, Tipaerua, diff.

2013, May 24 Litho. *Perf. 14¾x14¼*

Horiz. Pairs, #a-b

1446-1451	A227	Set of 6	17.00	17.00

Souvenir Sheet

1452	A227 $4.50	Sheet of 3, #a-c	22.00	22.00

Animals — A228

Designs: No. 1453, $1.50, American bison. No. 1454, $1.50, Gazella dama. No. 1455, $1.50, Phascolarctos cinereus. No. 1456, $1.50, Eurasian lynx. No. 1457, $1.50, Loxodonta africana. No. 1458, $1.50, Grus americana.

2013, May 31 Litho. *Perf. 14x14¾*

1453-1458	A228	Set of 6	14.50	14.50

Miniature Sheet

Duchess of Cambridge — A229

No. 1459 — Duchess of Cambridge: a, Wearing pink dress (40x52mm). b, Wearing dark blue jacket and black hat (40x26mm). c, Wearing yellow jacket and hat, meeting with group of dignitaries (40x26mm). d, Wearing white dress and hat, reviewing Scout troop (40x26mm). e, Wearing light blue dress (40x52mm). f, Wearing polka dot dress (40x52mm). g, Wearing wedding gown, kissing Duke of Cambridge (40x26mm).

2013, Aug. 1 Litho. *Perf. 13¼*

1459	A229 $1	Sheet of 7, #a-g	11.50	11.50

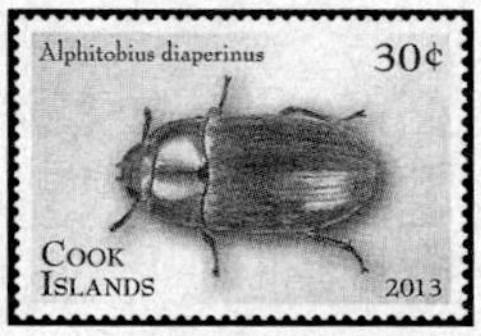

Insects and Spiders A230

Designs: 30c, Alphitobius diaperinus. 50c, Leptocoris rufomarginatus. 70c, Nabis capsiformis. $1, Polistes jokahamae. $1.30, Agrius convulvi. $1.50, Harmonia octomaculata. $1.70, Cosmopolites sordidus. $3.80, Graeffea crouanii. $4.10, Leptoglossus australis. $5.30, Nezara viridula. $6.50, Neoscona theisi. $8.50, Tholumis tillarga.

2013, Sept. 2 Litho. *Perf. 14*

Stamps With White Frames

1460	A230	30c multi	.50	.50
1461	A230	50c multi	.85	.85
1462	A230	70c multi	1.25	1.25
1463	A230	$1 multi	1.60	1.60
1464	A230	$1.30 multi	2.10	2.10
1465	A230	$1.50 multi	2.50	2.50
1466	A230	$1.70 multi	2.75	2.75
1467	A230	$3.80 multi	6.25	6.25
1468	A230	$4.10 multi	6.75	6.75
1469	A230	$5.30 multi	8.75	8.75
1470	A230	$6.50 multi	10.50	10.50
1471	A230	$8.50 multi	14.00	14.00
	Nos. 1460-1471 (12)		57.80	57.80

Miniature Sheet

Stamp Without White Frame

1472	Sheet of 12	58.00	58.00
a.	A230 30c multi	.50	.50
b.	A230 50c multi	.85	.85
c.	A230 70c multi	1.25	1.25
d.	A230 $1 multi	1.60	1.60
e.	A230 $1.30 multi	2.10	2.10
f.	A230 $1.50 multi	2.50	2.50
g.	A230 $1.70 multi	2.75	2.75
h.	A230 $3.80 multi	6.25	6.25
i.	A230 $4.10 multi	6.75	6.75
j.	A230 $5.30 multi	8.75	8.75
k.	A230 $6.50 multi	10.50	10.50
l.	A230 $8.50 multi	14.00	14.00

See Nos. 1491-1503.

Great Britain No. 1 — A231

Litho. & Embossed With Foil Application

2013, Sept. 18 *Perf. 13x13¼*

1473	A231	$8 blk & gold	13.50	13.50

Souvenir Sheets

2013 China International Collection Exposition, Beijing — A232

No. 1474 — Stamps inscribed "Cook Islands": a, $1, Painting by Paul Gauguin. b, $3, Beijing Exhibition Center.

No. 1475 — Stamps inscribed "Rarotonga / Cook Islands": a, $1, Painting by Paul Gauguin, diff. b, $3, Beijing Exhibition Center.

2013, Sept. 26 **Litho.** *Perf. 12*

1474	A232	Sheet of 2, #a-b	6.75	6.75
1475	A232	Sheet of 2, #a-b	6.75	6.75

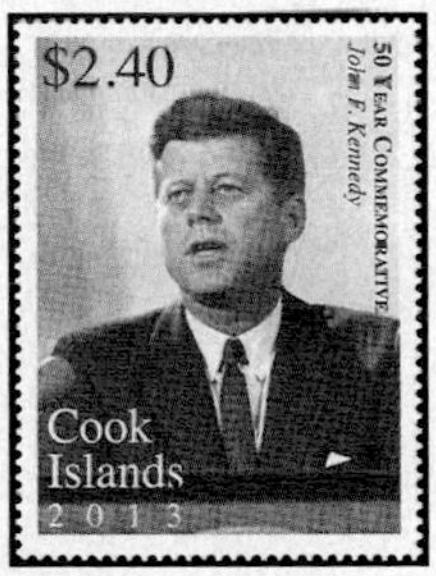

Pres. John F. Kennedy (1917-63) A233

Designs: $2.40, Pres. Kennedy. $3.10, Pres. Kennedy and quote.

2013, Nov. 8 **Litho.** *Perf. 14¼*

1476-1477	A233	Set of 2	9.00	9.00

Christmas — A234

Paintings by: $1, Gerard van Honthorst. $1.30, Michelangelo Merisi da Caravaggio. No. 1480, $1.50, Rembrandt.

No. 1481: a, $1.50, Bernardo Daddi. b, $1.70, Pieter Aertsen. c, $4.50, Lorenzo Lotto.

2013, Nov. 18 **Litho.** *Perf. 13¼*

1478-1480	A234	Set of 3	6.25	6.25

Souvenir Sheet

1481	A234	Sheet of 3, #a-c	13.00	13.00

Highland Paradise Scenes — A235

Various scenes from Highland Paradise tourist educational show.

2014, Jan. 3 **Litho.** *Perf. 13¼*

1482	A235	10c multi	.25	.25
1483	A235	20c multi	.35	.35
1484	A235	30c multi	.50	.50
1485	A235	50c multi	.85	.85
1486	A235	60c multi	1.00	1.00
1487	A235	$1 multi	1.60	1.60
1488	A235	$1.30 multi	2.10	2.10
1489	A235	$1.50 multi	2.50	2.50
1490	A235	$1.70 multi	2.75	2.75
		Nos. 1482-1490 (9)	11.90	11.90

Dated "2013."

Insects and Spiders Type of 2013

Designs: 10c, Teleogryllus oceanicus. 40c, Euconocephalus roberti. $1, Apis mellifera. $2.10, Crocidolomia pavonana. $2.50, Junonia villida. $3, Aedes polynesiensis. $3.50, Homalodisca coagulata. $4.50, Lygus flavoscutellatus. $5.50, Euploea lewinii perryi. $6.70, Hypolimnas bolina. $7, Porcellio laevis. $10.10, Vagrans egista bodenia.

2014, Jan. 6 **Litho.** *Perf. 14*

Stamps With White Frames

1491	A230	10c multi	.25	.25
1492	A230	40c multi	.65	.65
1493	A230	$1 multi	1.60	1.60
1494	A230	$2.10 multi	3.50	3.50
1495	A230	$2.50 multi	4.00	4.00
1496	A230	$3 multi	5.00	5.00
1497	A230	$3.50 multi	5.75	5.75
1498	A230	$4.50 multi	7.25	7.25
1499	A230	$5.50 multi	9.00	9.00
1500	A230	$6.70 multi	11.00	11.00
1501	A230	$7 multi	11.50	11.50
1502	A230	$10.10 multi	16.50	16.50
		Nos. 1491-1502 (12)	76.00	76.00

Miniature Sheet

Stamp Without White Frame

1503		Sheet of 12	76.00	76.00
a.	A230	10c multi	.25	.25
b.	A230	40c multi	.65	.65
c.	A230	$1 multi	1.60	1.60
d.	A230	$2.10 multi	3.50	3.50
e.	A230	$2.50 multi	4.00	4.00
f.	A230	$3 multi	5.00	5.00
g.	A230	$3.50 multi	5.75	5.75
h.	A230	$4.50 multi	7.25	7.25
i.	A230	$5.50 multi	9.00	9.00
j.	A230	$6.70 multi	11.00	11.00
k.	A230	$7 multi	11.50	11.50
l.	A230	$10.10 multi	16.50	16.50

Souvenir Sheet

New Year 2014 (Year of the Horse) — A236

No. 1504 — Horse, with denomination color of: a, Red. b, White.

2014, Jan. 8 **Litho.** *Perf. 13¼*

1504	A236	$3 Sheet of 2, #a-b	9.75	9.75

Souvenir Sheet

Christening of Prince George of Cambridge — A237

No. 1505 — Prince George being held by: a, $4, Duchess of Cambridge. b, $5, Duke of Cambridge.

2014, Jan. 14 **Litho.** *Perf. 14*

1505	A237	Sheet of 2, #a-b	14.50	14.50

Easter — A238

No. 1506 — Religious painting by: a, 50c, Il Moro. b, $1, Tintoretto. c, $1.30, Giovanni Bellini. d, $1.50, Raphael (Sanzio). e, $1.70, William Blake.

$9.50, Painting by Hans Memling.

2014, Apr. 9 **Litho.** *Perf. 13¼*

1506	A238	Sheet of 5, #a-e, + label	10.50	10.50

Souvenir Sheet

1507	A238	$9.50 multi	16.50	16.50

Small Island Developing States — A239

No. 1508: a, Tropical cyclone. b, Rising sea levels at Rarotonga. c, Pacific Small Island Developing States emblem. d, Map of Cook Islands. e, "Island Voices Global Choices" emblem. f, Fishing boats. g, Sailboat. h, Cruise liner. i, Kayak. j, Wind surfing. k, Nurse shark. l, Barracuda. m, Triggerfish. n, Pilot whale. o, Manta ray. p, Flag of Cook Islands.

No. 1509: a, Like #1508a. b, Like #1508p. c, Like #1508b. d, Like #1508c. e, Like #1508d. f, Like #1508e.

No. 1510: a, Like #1508f. b, Like #1508p. c, Like #1508g. d, Like #1508h. e, Like #1508i. f, Like #1508j.

No. 1511: a, Like #1508k. b, Like #1508p. c, Like #1508l. d, Like #1508m. e, Like #1508n. f, Like #1508o.

2014, May 9 **Litho.** *Perf. 13¼*

1508		Block of 18, #1508a-1508o, 3 #1508p	15.50	15.50
a.-p.	A239	50c Any single	.85	.85

Miniature Sheets

1509		Sheet of 6	21.00	21.00
a.-f.	A239	$2 Any single	3.50	3.50
1510		Sheet of 6	25.50	25.50
a.-f.	A239	$2.40 Any single	4.25	4.25
1511		Sheet of 6	27.00	27.00
a.-f.	A239	$2.60 Any single	4.50	4.50
		Nos. 1509-1511 (3)	73.50	73.50

No. 1508 was printed in sheets containing 3 blocks of 18. The frame on each stramp in the sheet, depicting a map of the Pacific Ocean, differs.

Souvenir Sheet

Nelson Mandela (1918-2013), President of South Africa — A240

No. 1512 — Mandela with: a, $2.50, Child. b, $4.50, U. S. Pres. Bill Clinton.

2014, May 13 **Litho.** *Perf. 14*

1512	A240	Sheet of 2, #a-b	12.00	12.00

Tourism — A241

No. 1513, 30c: a, Relaxing. b, Shopping. c, Dancing. d, Dining.

No. 1514, 50c: a, Church service. b, Scootering. c, Hiking. d, Snorkeling.

No. 1515, $1: a, Kayaking. b, Swimming. c, Scuba diving. d, Fishing.

No. 1516, $1.70: a, Vaka sailing. b, Windsurfing. c, Kitesurfing. d, Paddleboarding.

No. 1517, $3.80: a, Whale watching, b, Sightseeing. c, Glass bottom boat. d, Birdwatching.

No. 1518, $4.10: a, Rugby. b, Beach volleyball. c, Golfing. d, Bike riding.

2014, June 23 **Litho.** *Perf. 14¼x14*

Blocks of 4, #a-d

1513-1518	A241	Set of 6	80.00	80.00

Insects — A242

No. 1519: a, $4, Western honey bee. b, $11.50, Castor semi-looper moth. c, $13.60, Spotted ladybird.

2014, Sept. 12 **Litho.** *Perf. 13¼*

1519	A242	Horiz. strip of 3, #a-c, + 3 labels	46.00	46.00

Worldwide Fund for Nature (WWF) A243

Various depictions of spotless crake: Nos. 1520, 1524a, $1. Nos. 1521, 1524b, $1.30. Nos. 1522, 1524c, $1.50. Nos. 1523, 1524d, $1.70

$7.50, Spotless crake, diff.

Perf. 14¾x14¼

2014, Nov. 28 **Litho.**

Stamps With White Frame

1520-1523	A243	Set of 4	8.75	8.75

Stamps Without White Frame

1524	A243	Strip of 4, #a-d	8.75	8.75

Souvenir Sheet

1525	A243	$7.50 multi	12.00	12.00

Souvenir Sheet

Christmas — A244

No. 1526 — Religious paintings by: a, Giotto di Bondone. b, Jan Gossaert. c, Caravaggio.

Perf. 14¾x14¼

2014, Dec. 12 **Litho.**

1526 A244 $1.50 Sheet of 3, #a-c 7.00 7.00

Souvenir Sheet

New Year 2015 (Year of the Sheep) — A245

No. 1527: a, $3.80, Red ram. b, $4.10, Blue ram.

2015, Jan. 5 **Litho.** ***Perf. 13¼***

1527 A245 Sheet of 2, #a-b 11.50 11.50

Miniature Sheet

Easter — A246

No. 1528 — Religious paintings by: a, Matthias Grünewald. b, Peter Paul Rubens. c, Jean Jouvenet. d, Giampietrino.

2015, Mar. 31 **Litho.** ***Perf. 14***

1528 A246 $2 Sheet of 4, #a-d 12.50 12.50

Souvenir Sheet

Birth of Princess Charlotte of Cambridge — A247

No. 1529: a, Duchess of Cambridge holding Princess Charlotte. b, Duke of Cambridge holding Prince George.

Perf. 14¾x14¼

2015, June 23 **Litho.**

1529 A247 $4.50 Sheet of 2, #a-b 12.00 12.00

Magna Carta, 800th Anniv. A248

Quotations starting with: $1, "To no one will we deny or delay. . ." $1.30, "No free man shall be seized. . ." $1.50, "Given by our hand in the meadow. . ." $1.70, "To no one will we deny or delay. . .," diff.

2015, July 15 **Litho.** ***Perf. 14¼x14¾***

1530-1533 A248 Set of 4 7.25 7.25

A249

Self-Government, 50th Anniv. — A250

No. 1535 — Cook Islands stamps: a, #162. b, #164. c, #195. d, #233. e, #253. f, #288. g, #301. h, #322. i, #357. j, #409.

No. 1536 — Cook Islands stamps: a, #435. b, #464. c, #479. d, #502. e, #531. f, #549. g, #660. h, #685. i, #696a. j, #760. k, #877. l, #919. m, #B113. n, #998a. o, #1010b.

No. 1537 — Cook Islands stamps: a, #1029. b, #1048. c, #1111. d, #1140. e, #1191b. f, #1198b. g, #1204. h, #1214a. i, #O68. j, #1234. k, #1238. l, #1241. m, #1258. n, #1265. o, #1269.

No. 1538 — Cook Islands stamps: a, #1271. b, #1291a. c, #1296c. d, #1299. e, #1343a. f, #1383. g, #1422Hq. h, #1434. i, #1482. j, #1534.

2015, Aug. 5 **Litho.** ***Perf. 14***

1534 A249 $1 multi 1.25 1.25

Miniature Sheets

Perf. 13¾

1535	Sheet of 10	1.25	1.25
a.-j.	A250 10c Any single	.25	.25
1536	Sheet of 15	6.00	6.00
a.-o.	A250 30c Any single	.40	.40
1537	Sheet of 15	7.50	7.50
a.-o.	A250 40c Any single	.50	.50
1538	Sheet of 10	6.50	6.50
a.-j.	A250 50c Any single	.65	.65
	Nos. 1535-1538 (4)	21.25	21.25

New Year 2016 (Year of the Monkey) A251

Designs: $2.60: Adult and juvenile monkeys, leaves. $3, Juvenile monkey on back of adult.

No. 1541: a, $3.80, Like $2.60. b, $4.10, Like $3.

2015, Sept. 25 **Litho.** ***Perf. 13¼***

1539-1540 A251 Set of 2 7.25 7.25

Self-Adhesive

1541 A251 Sheet of 2, #a-b 10.50 10.50

No. 1541 contains two 51x51mm diamond-shaped stamps.

Miniature Sheet

Queen Elizabeth II, Longest-Reigning British Monarch — A252

No. 1542 — Various photographs of Queen Elizabeth II: a, $1.30. b, $1.50. c, $1.70. d, $2.

2015, Nov. 20 **Litho.** ***Perf. 14***

1542 A252 Sheet of 4, #a-d 8.75 8.75

Souvenir Sheet

Christmas — A253

No. 1543 — Details from Nativity, by Antoniazzo Romano: a, Joseph and saint. b, Infant Jesus and animals. c, Virgin Mary and saint.

2015, Dec. 9 **Litho.** ***Perf. 13¼***

1543 A253 $1 Sheet of 3, #a-c 4.00 4.00

SEMI-POSTAL STAMPS

Catalogue values for unused stamps in this section are for Never Hinged items.

Nos. 203-204, 223, 210, 213, 215-216 Surcharged

Perf. 14x13½, 13½

1968, Feb. 12 **Photo.**

B1	A34	3c + 1c multi	.25	.25
B2	A34	4c + 1c multi	.25	.25
B3	A37	5c + 2c multi	.25	.25
B4	A34	10c + 2c multi	.25	.25
B5	A34	25c + 5c multi	.30	.30
B6	A34	50c + 10c multi	.60	.60
B7	A35	$1 + 10c multi	1.00	1.00
		Nos. B1-B7 (7)	2.90	2.90

Surtax for the victims of hurricane of Dec. 15-18, 1967. The surcharge on No. B3 is printed on a silver rectangle. The surcharge on No. B7 is in smaller type with serifs, measuring 7½mm in depth.

Nos. 210, 213-214 Surcharged in Ultramarine

1971, Sept. 8 **Photo.** ***Perf. 14x13½***

B8	A34	10c + 1c multi	.25	.25
B9	A34	10c + 3c multi	.25	.25
B10	A34	25c + 1c multi	.40	.40
B11	A34	25c + 3c multi	.40	.40
B12	A34	30c + 1c multi	.50	.50
B13	A34	30c + 3c multi	.50	.50
		Nos. B8-B13 (6)	2.30	2.30

4th South Pacific Games, Papeete, French Polynesia, Sept. 8-19.

Christmas Type of Regular Issue

Souvenir Sheet

50c+5c, Holy Family in a Garland of Flowers, by Jan Brueghel and Pieter van Avont.

1971, Nov. 30 **Photo.** ***Perf. 13½***

B14 A50 50c + 5c gold & multi 1.25 1.25

No. B14 contains one stamp 45x40mm.

Nos. 316-318, 211, 213 and 215 Surcharged in Red or Black

a

b

1972, Mar. 30 **Photo.** ***Perf. 13½***
B15 A46(a) 5c + 2c multi (R) .25 .25
B16 A46(a) 10c + 2c multi (R) .25 .25
B17 A34(b) 15c + 5c multi .25 .25
B18 A34(b) 25c + 5c multi .45 .45
B19 A46(a) 30c + 5c multi (R) .55 .55
B20 A34(b) 50c + 10c multi 1.00 1.00
Nos. B15-B20 (6) 2.75 2.75

Surtax for victims of hurricane of Mar. 22-26.

Nos. 319-322c with Surcharge Similar to Type "a"

1972, May 24 **Photo.** ***Perf. 13½***
B21 A51 5c + 2c, pair, #a.-b. .25 .25
B22 A51 10c + 2c, pair, #a.-b. .35 .35
B23 A51 25c + 2c, pair, #a.-b. .75 .75
B24 A51 30c + 2c, pair, #a.-b. 1.10 1.10
c. Souvenir sheet of 8 4.25 4.25
Nos. B21-B24 (4) 2.45 2.45

Surtax for victims of hurricane of Mar. 22-26. Stamps of No. B24c each surcharged 3c.

Olympic Type of Regular Issue
Souvenir Sheet

50c+5c, Pierre de Coubertin, Olympic rings.

1972, June 26
B29 A52 50c + 5c multi 2.10 2.10

Christmas Type of Regular Issue
Souvenir Sheet

Design: 50c+5c, Nativity, by Correggio.

1972, Oct. 11 **Photo.** ***Perf. 13½***
B30 A53 50c + 5c multi 1.50 1.25

No. B30 contains one stamp 30x40mm.

Easter Type of Regular Issue
Souvenir Sheets

1973, Apr. 30 **Photo.** ***Perf. 13½x14***
B31 A56 50c + 5c like #346 .65 .65
B32 A56 50c + 5c like #347 .65 .65
B33 A56 50c + 5c like #348 .65 .65
Nos. B31-B33 (3) 1.95 1.95

Surtax was for school children.

Christmas Type of Regular Issue
Souvenir Sheets

1973, Dec. 3 **Photo.** ***Perf. 13x13½***
B34 A59 50c + 5c like #364 .40 .40
B35 A59 50c + 5c like #365 .40 .40
B36 A59 50c + 5c like #366 .40 .40
B37 A59 50c + 5c like #367 .40 .40
B38 A59 50c + 5c like #368 .40 .40
Nos. B34-B38 (5) 2.00 2.00

Surtax was for school children.

Easter Type of 1973
Dated "1974"
Souvenir Sheets

1974, Apr. 22 ***Perf. 13½x14***
B39 A56 50c + 5c like #378 .50 .50
B40 A56 50c + 5c like #379 .50 .50
B41 A56 50c + 5c like #380 .50 .50
Nos. B39-B41 (3) 1.50 1.50

Christmas Type of 1974
Souvenir Sheets

1974 **Photo.** ***Perf. 13½x13***
B42 A68 50c + 5c like #412 .40 .40
B43 A68 50c + 5c like #413 .40 .40
B44 A68 50c + 5c like #414 .40 .40
B45 A68 50c + 5c like #415 .40 .40
B46 A68 50c + 5c like #416 .40 .40
Nos. B42-B46 (5) 2.00 2.00

Christmas Type of 1975
Souvenir Sheets

1975, Dec. 1 ***Perf. 13½***
B47 A75 75c + 5c like #437 .55 .55
B48 A75 75c + 5c like #438 .55 .55
B49 A75 75c + 5c like #439 .55 .55
B50 A75 75c + 5c like #440 .55 .55
B51 A75 75c + 5c like #441 .55 .55
Nos. B47-B51 (5) 2.75 2.75

Size of stamps: 23x40mm.

Easter Type of 1976
Souvenir Sheets

1976, May 3 **Photo.** ***Perf. 13½***
B52 A76 60c + 5c like #442 .60 .60
B53 A76 60c + 5c like #443 .60 .60
B54 A76 60c + 5c like #444 .60 .60
Nos. B52-B54 (3) 1.80 1.80

Size of stamps: 36x36mm.

Christmas Type of 1976
Souvenir Sheets

1976, Nov. 2 **Photo.** ***Perf. 14x13½***
B55 A80 75c + 5c like #459 .60 .60
B56 A80 75c + 5c like #460 .60 .60
B57 A80 75c + 5c like #461 .60 .60
B58 A80 75c + 5c like #462 .60 .60
B59 A80 75c + 5c like #463 .60 .60
Nos. B55-B59 (5) 3.00 3.00

Easter Type of 1977
Souvenir Sheets

1977, Apr. 18 **Photo.** ***Perf. 13½x14***
B60 A83 60c + 5c like #471 .60 .60
B61 A83 60c + 5c like #472 .60 .60
B62 A83 60c + 5c like #473 .60 .60
Nos. B60-B62 (3) 1.80 1.80

Size of stamps: 30x42mm.

Christmas Type of 1977
Souvenir Sheets

1977, Oct. 31 **Photo.** ***Perf. 14x13½***
B63 A84 75c + 5c like #474 .60 .60
B64 A84 75c + 5c like #475 .60 .60
B65 A84 75c + 5c like #476 .60 .60
B66 A84 75c + 5c like #477 .60 .60
B67 A84 75c + 5c like #478 .60 .60
Nos. B63-B67 (5) 3.00 3.00

Easter Type of 1978
Souvenir Sheets

1978, Apr. 10 **Photo.** ***Perf. 14x13½***
B68 A87 60c + 5c like #483 .50 .50
B69 A87 60c + 5c like #484 .50 .50
B70 A87 60c + 5c like #485 .50 .50
Nos. B68-B70 (3) 1.50 1.50

Christmas Type of 1978
Souvenir Sheets

1979, Jan. 12 **Photo.** ***Perf. 13***
B71 A89 75c + 5c like #503 .50 .50
B72 A89 75c + 5c like #504 .50 .50
B73 A89 75c + 5c like #505 .50 .50
Nos. B71-B73 (3) 1.50 1.50

Easter Type of 1979
Souvenir Sheet

1979, Apr. 5 **Photo.** ***Perf. 13***
B74 Sheet of 4 1.00 1.00
a. A90 10c + 2c like #506 .25 .25
b. A90 12c + 2c like #507 .25 .25
c. A90 15c + 2c like #508 .25 .25
d. A90 20c + 2c like #509 .35 .35

IYC Type of 1979
Souvenir Sheet

1979, Oct. 10
B75 Sheet of 3 1.40 1.40
a. A93 30c + 5c like #529 .30 .30
b. A93 50c + 5c like #530 .45 .45
c. A93 65c + 5c like #531 .55 .55

Christmas Type of 1979

1980, Jan. 15 **Photo.** ***Perf. 14***
B76 A95 6c + 2c like #537 .25 .25
B77 A95 10c + 2c like #538 .25 .25
B78 A95 12c + 2c like #539 .25 .25
B79 A95 15c + 2c like #540 .35 .35
Nos. B76-B79 (4) 1.00 1.00

Easter Type of 1980
Souvenir Sheets

1980, Mar. 31 **Photo.** ***Perf. 13***
B80 A96 Sheet of 6, #a.-f. 1.40 1.40

No. B80 contains Nos. 541-543, each stamp with 2c surcharge.

1980, Apr. 23 **Souvenir Sheets**
B81 A96 75c + 5c like #541a .55 .55
B82 A96 75c + 5c like #541b .55 .55
B83 A96 75c + 5c like #542a .55 .55
B84 A96 75c + 5c like #542b .55 .55
B85 A96 75c + 5c like #543a .75 .55
B86 A96 75c + 5c like #543b .55 .55
Nos. B81-B86 (6) 3.50 3.30

Surtax was for school children.

Rotary Type of 1980
Souvenir Sheet

1980, May 27 **Photo.** ***Perf. 14***
B87 Sheet of 3 1.60 1.60
a. A97 30c + 3c like #547 .40 .40
b. A97 35c + 3c like #548 .50 .50
c. A97 50c + 3c like #549 .70 .70

Christmas Type of 1980
Souvenir Sheets

1981, Jan. 9 **Photo.** ***Imperf.***
B88 A102a 75c + 5c like #652 .55 .55
B89 A102a 75c + 5c like #653 .55 .55
B90 A102a 75c + 5c like #654 .55 .55
B91 A102a 75c + 5c like #655 .55 .55
Nos. B88-B91 (4) 2.20 2.20

Easter Type of 1981
Souvenir Sheets

1981, Apr. 10 **Photo.** ***Perf. 13½***
B92 Sheet of 3 1.20 1.20
a. A103 15c + 2c like #656 .25 .25
b. A103 25c + 2c like #657 .35 .35
c. A103 40c + 2c like #658 .60 .60

1981, Apr. 28 ***Imperf.***
B93 A103 75c + 5c like #656 .80 .80
B94 A103 75c + 5c like #657 .80 .80
B95 A103 75c + 5c like #658 .80 .80
Nos. B93-B95 (3) 2.40 2.40

Surtax was for school children.

Espana '82 Soccer Type
Souvenir Sheet

1981 **Photo.** ***Perf. 13½***
B96 A105 Sheet of 8, #a.-h. 6.50 6.50

No. B96 contains Nos. 661-664, each stamp with 3c surcharge.

Royal Wedding Type of 1981
Nos. 659-660a Surcharged in Black

1981, Nov. 10 **Photo.** ***Perf. 14***
B97 A104 $1 + 5c multi 1.00 1.00
B98 A104 $2 + 5c multi 2.00 2.00
a. Souvenir sheet of 2 4.00 4.00

Intl. Year of the Disabled. No. B98a contains Nos. B97-B98 each with 10c surtax, which was for benefit of the disabled; black overprint in margin.

Christmas Type of 1981
Souvenir Sheet

1981, Dec. 14 **Photo.** ***Perf. 13½***
B99 Sheet of 4 3.25 3.25
a. A107 8c + 3c like #669 .25 .25
b. A107 15c + 3c like #670 .40 .40
c. A107 40c + 3c like #671 1.00 1.00
d. A107 50c + 3c like #672 1.25 1.25

Surtax was for school children.

Nos. 919-923 Surcharged in Silver

No. B100

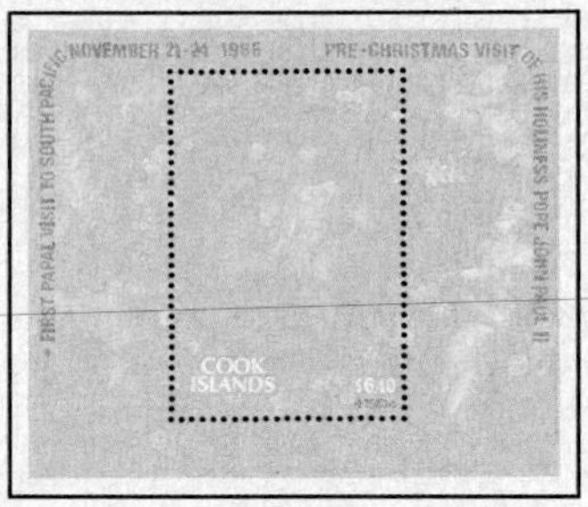

No. B104

1986, Nov. 21 **Litho.** ***Perf. 13½***
B100 A138 55c + 10c multi 2.50 2.50
B101 A138 $1.30 + 10c multi 5.25 5.25
B102 A138 $2.75 + 10c multi 10.00 10.00
Nos. B100-B102 (3) 17.75 17.75

Souvenir Sheets

B103 Sheet of 3 16.00 16.00
a.-c. A138 $2.40 + 10c on Nos. 922a-922c, any single 5.25 5.25
B104 A138 $6.40 + 50c multi 16.00 16.00

No. B103 ovptd. in margin "VISIT TO SOUTH PACIFIC / OF POPE JOHN PAUL II" and "FIRST PAPAL VISIT / NOVEMBER 21-24 1986."

For surcharge see No. B112.

Stamps of 1982 and 1987 Surcharged in Sans-serif Capitals

No. B109

Perfs. as before

1987, June 30 **Photo.**

Surcharged +25c

B105 A121 55c on #958 1.10 1.10
B106 A121 65c on #960 1.25 1.25
B107 A121 75c on #963 1.40 1.40
B108 A121 95c on #965 1.60 1.60

Surcharged +50c

B109 A101 $2.80 on #582 4.50 4.50
B110 A101 $5 on #583 7.75 7.75
B111 A102 $6.40 on #978 9.50 9.50
Nos. B105-B111 (7) 27.10 27.10

Stamps of 1985-86 Surcharged in Silver or Black

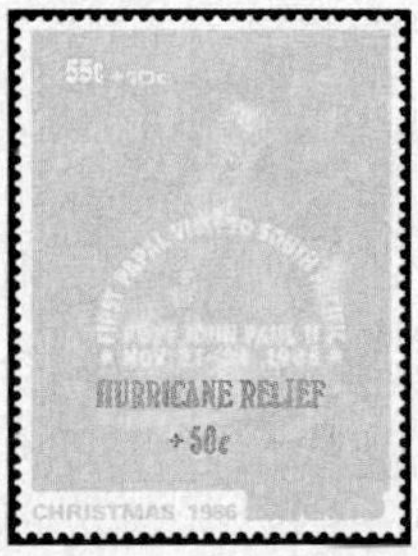

1987 ***Perfs. as before***

Surcharged +50c

B112 A138 55c on #B100 1.40 1.40
B113 A133 55c on #897 (B) 1.40 1.40
B114 A128 65c on #871 1.50 1.50
B115 A133 65c on #898 1.50 1.50
B116 A128 75c on #872 1.60 1.60
B117 A133 75c on #899 1.60 1.60
B118 A134 95c on #908 (B) 1.90 1.90
B119 A135 $1 on #910 2.10 2.10
B120 A136 $1 on #913 2.10 2.10
B121 A137 $1 on #916 2.10 2.10
B122 A128 $1.15 on #873 2.25 2.25
B123 A133 $1.25 on #900 2.25 2.25
B124 A134 $1.25 on #905 2.25 2.25
B125 A136 $1.25 on #914 (B) 2.25 2.25
B126 A138 $1.30 on #920 2.50 2.50

B127	A134	$1.50 on #906 (B)	2.50	2.50
B128	A135	$1.50 on #911 (B)	2.50	2.50
B129	A133	$2 on #901 (B)	3.25	3.25
B130	A135	$2 on #912 (B)	3.25	3.25
B131	A137	$2 on #917	3.25	3.25
B132	A136	$2.75 on #915	4.50	4.50
B133	A138	$2.75 on #921	4.50	4.50
B134	A128	$2.80 on #874	4.50	4.50
B135	A137	$3 on #918	4.75	4.75
		Nos. B112-B135 (24)	61.70	61.70

Souvenir Sheets

B136	A134	$1.10 on #907 (B)	2.00	2.00
B137	A134	$1.95 on #908	3.00	3.00
B138		on #922, #a.-c.	11.00	11.00
B139	A134	$2.45 on #909 (B)	3.75	3.75
B140	A128	$5.30 on #875	7.25	7.25
B141	A138	$6.40 on #B104	8.50	8.50
		Nos. B136-B141 (6)	35.50	35.50

Issued: Nos. B118, B121, B124, B127, B131, B135-B137, B139-B140, 7/31; others 6/30.

No. 1230 Surcharged in Silver
Souvenir Sheet

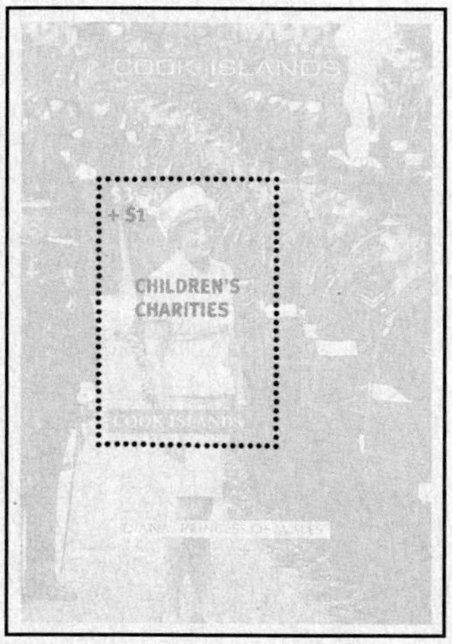

1998, Nov. 20 Litho. *Perf. 14*

B142	A179	$3.50 +$1 multi	4.75	4.75

AIR POST STAMPS

Catalogue values for unused stamps in this section are for Never Hinged items.

Stamps of 1936-63 Overprinted and Surcharged

Perf. 13x13½, 13½x13
Litho., Engr.

1966, Apr. 22 Wmk. 253

C1	A25	6p on #152	.70	.25
C2	A26	7p on 8p #153	1.00	.25
C3	A25	10p on 3p #150	.65	.35
C4	A25	1sh on #154	.70	.45
C5	A27	1sh6p on #155	1.25	1.25
C6	A28	2sh3p on 3sh #157	1.00	1.00
C7	A28	5sh on #158	1.60	1.75
C8	A28	10sh on 2sh #156	2.00	*8.00*

No. 106 Overprinted

Perf. 14
Typo.

C9	PF5	£1 pink	12.00	*16.00*
a.		Airplane missing	*37.50*	*50.00*
		Nos. C1-C9 (9)	20.90	29.30

#C9a occurs on all stamps from the right vertical column of the sheet due to a lack of airplane symbols. The size and position of the airplane symbol varies in relation to "Airmail" on the other stamps. The surcharges are printed on silver ovals.

2nd So. Pacific Games' Type

Sport: 10p, Women runners and Games' emblem. 2sh3p, Runner and team emblem.

Perf. 13½

1967, Jan. 12 Unwmk. Photo.

C10	A32	10p org & multi	.25	.25
C11	A32	2sh3p multi	.25	.25

Capt. Cook Type of Regular Issue

6c, The "Resolution" and "Discovery" Beating Through the Ice, by Webber. 10c, The Island of Otaheite, by Hodges, and Queen Elizabeth II. 15c, View of Karakakooa (Kealakekua), Hawaii, by Webber. 25c, The Landing at Middleburg, Tonga, by Hodges, & Captain Cook. (All horiz.)

1968, Sept. 12 Photo. *Perf. 13*

C12	A39	6c gold & multi	.35	.35
C13	A39	10c gold & multi	.60	.60
C14	A39	15c gold & multi	.75	.75
C15	A39	25c gold & multi	1.60	1.60
		Nos. C12-C15 (4)	5.65	5.65

See note after No. 236.

Christmas Type of 1979

1979, Dec. 14 Photo. *Perf. 14*

C16	A95	20c like #537	.25	.25
C17	A95	25c like #538	.30	.30
C18	A95	30c like #539	.35	.35
C19	A95	35c like #540	.45	.45
		Nos. C16-C19 (4)	1.35	1.35

Franklin D. Roosevelt — AP1

80c, Benjamin Franklin. $1.40, George Washington, by Gilbert Stuart.

1982, Sept. 30 Photo. *Perf. 14*

C20	AP1	60c multicolored	.90	.90
C21	AP1	80c multicolored	1.10	1.10
C22	AP1	$1.40 multicolored	2.00	2.00
a.		Souvenir sheet of 3	4.25	4.25
		Nos. C20-C22 (3)	4.00	4.00

No. C22a contains Nos. C20-C22, perf. 13½ with portraits in square frames.

No. C22 Overprinted in Gold and Black

1983, Aug. 12 Photo. *Perf. 14*

C23	AP1	96c on $1.40 multi	1.60	1.60

Endangered Bird Species Type
Souvenir Sheets

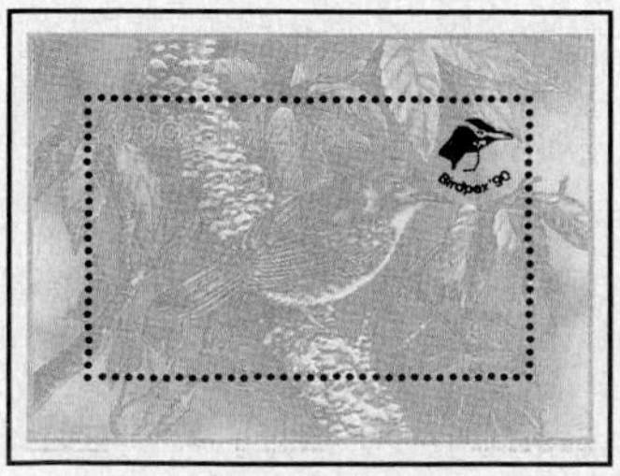

Nos. 1020-1023 Overprinted

1990, Dec. 5 Litho. *Perf. 13½*

C24	A145	$1 Flycatcher	3.50	3.50
C25	A145	$1.25 Flycatchers	4.25	4.25
C26	A145	$1.50 Fruit dove	5.50	5.50
C27	A145	$1.75 Fruit doves	6.25	6.25
		Nos. C24-C27 (4)	19.50	19.50

Birdpex '90, 20th Intl. Ornithological Cong., New Zealand.

AIR POST SEMI-POSTAL STAMPS

Catalogue values for unused stamps in this section are for Never Hinged items.

Christmas Type of 1979

1980, Jan. 15 Photo. *Perf. 14*

CB1	A95	20c + 4c like #C16	.30	.30
CB2	A95	25c + 4c like #C17	.35	.35
CB3	A95	30c + 4c like #C18	.40	.40
CB4	A95	35c + 4c like #C19	.55	.55
		Nos. CB1-CB4 (4)	1.60	1.60

OFFICIAL STAMPS

Flower Issue of 1967-69 Overprinted or Surcharged in Black on Silver

1975 Photo. Unwmk. *Perf. 14x13½*

O1	A34	1c multi (#200)	.25
O2	A34	2c multi (#201)	.25
O3	A34	3c multi (#203)	.25
O4	A34	4c multi (#205)	.25
O5	A34	5c on 2½c multi (#202)	.25
O6	A34	8c multi (#208)	.30
O7	A34	10c on 6c multi (#207)	.30
O8	A34	18c on 20c multi (#212)	.35
O9	A34	25c on 9c multi (#209)	.55
O10	A34	30c on 15c multi (#211)	.65
O11	A34	50c multi (#215)	.70
O12	A35	$1 multi (#216)	1.30
O13	A35	$2 multi (#217)	2.00
O14	A36	$4 multi (#218)	3.75
O15	A36	$6 multi (#219)	4.50
		Nos. O1-O15 (15)	15.65

No. O1-O15 were not sold to the public unused. Arrangement of surcharge varies on different denominations.

Silver panel on Nos. O14-O15 measures 26½x6mm and is rounded at both ends.

Issue dates: 1c-$2, Mar. 17, $4-$6, May 19.

Catalogue values for unused stamps in this section, from this point to the end of the section, are for Never Hinged items.

Nos. 381-382, 389, 393-396, 467, 446 Ovptd. or Srchd. in Silver or Black

Photo., Litho.

1978, Oct. 19 *Perf. 13½*

O16	A62	1c multi (S)	.85	.25
O17	A62	2c on ½c multi	.85	.25
O18	A62	5c on ½c multi	.95	.25
O19	A62	10c on 8c multi (S)	1.10	.25
O20	A62	15c on 50c multi (S)	1.25	.25
O21	A62	18c on 60c multi (S)	1.25	.25
O22	A62	25c multicolored	1.60	.25
O23	A62	30c multi (S)	1.60	.30
O24	A62	35c on 60c multi (S)	1.60	.35
O25	A62	50c multi (S)	2.10	.50
O26	A62	60c multi (S)	2.40	.60
O27	A82	$1 Pair, #a.-b. (S)	10.00	2.00
O29	A77	$2 multicolored	7.25	2.25
O30	A64	$4 multi ('79)	13.50	3.50
O31	A64	$6 multi ('79)	13.50	5.50
		Nos. O16-O31 (15)	59.80	16.75

Diagonal overprints on No. O27. Overprint on No. O29-O31: 19x4mm.

Nos. 790-791, 795, 797, 799, 805, 807, 809-810 Ovptd. or Srchd. in Silver

1985, July 10 Photo. *Perf. 13½x13*

O32	A121	5c multi	.55	.55
O33	A121	10c multi	.55	.55
O34	A121	20c multi	.65	.65
O35	A121	30c multi	.65	.65
O36	A121	40c multi	.65	.65
O37	A121	55c on 85c multi	.80	.80
O38	A121	60c multi	.80	.80
O39	A121	$1.10 multi	1.60	1.25
O40	A121	$2 on $1.20 multi	3.25	2.50
		Nos. O32-O40 (9)	9.50	8.40

Nos. 792-794, 802, 806, 696 and 583-586 Ovptd. or Srchd. in Silver, Gold (75c) or Black and Silver ($5, $18)

1986-90 Photo. *Perfs. as Before*

O41	A121	12c multi	5.00	5.00
O42	A121	14c multi	5.00	5.00
O43	A121	18c multi	5.00	5.00
O44	A121	50c multi	6.25	6.25
O45	A121	70c multi	6.75	6.75
O46	A111	75c on 60c, #a.-d.	13.50	13.50
O50	A102	$5 on $3 multi	17.00	17.00
O51	A102	$9 on $4 multi	9.00	9.00
O52	A102	$14 on $6 multi	14.00	14.00
O53	A102	$18 on $10 multi	20.00	20.00
		Nos. O41-O53 (10)	101.50	101.50

Issued: $9, 5/30/89; $14, 7/12/89; $18, 6/4/90; others 5/5/86.

Nos. 1058-1059, 1062, 1064-1066, 1071, 1076-1078, 1080-1083, 1085, 1087 Ovptd. in Silver

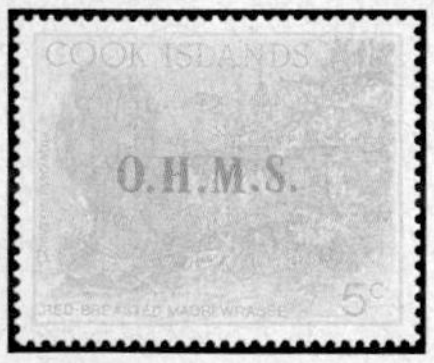

1995-98 Litho. *Perf. 14½x13½*

O54	A155	5c multicolored	.40	.40
O55	A155	10c multicolored	.40	.40
O56	A155	15c multicolored	.50	.50
O57	A155	20c multicolored	.55	.55
O58	A155	25c multicolored	.60	.60
O59	A155	30c multicolored	.65	.65
O60	A155	50c multicolored	.80	.80
O61	A155	80c multicolored	1.30	1.30
O62	A155	85c multicolored	1.30	1.30
O63	A155	90c multicolored	1.30	1.30
O64	A155	$1 multicolored	1.50	1.50
O65	A155	$2 multicolored	2.40	2.40
O66	A155a	$3 multicolored	3.75	3.75
O67	A155a	$5 multicolored	4.75	4.75
O68	A155a	$7 multicolored	6.75	6.75
O69	A155a	$10 multi	8.50	8.50
		Nos. O54-O69 (16)	35.45	35.45

Overprint on Nos. O66-O69 has larger, sans serif letters.

Nos. O66-O69 were not sold unused to local customers.

Issued: 5c-90c, 2/24/95; $1-$2, 5/15/95; $3-$7, 7/17/98, $10, 11/12/98.

Nos. 1305-1322 Overprinted in Gold

2010, Oct. 12 Litho. *Perf. 13¾*
Sizes: 60x37mm, 37x60mm

O70	A191	10c multi	.25	.25
O71	A191	20c multi	.30	.30
O72	A191	30c multi	.50	.50

O73	A191	40c multi	.65	.65
O74	A191	50c multi	.80	.80
O75	A191	70c multi	1.10	1.10
O76	A191	80c multi	1.25	1.25
O77	A191	90c multi	1.50	1.50
O78	A191	$1 multi	1.60	1.60
O79	A191	$1.10 multi	1.75	1.75
O80	A191	$1.20 multi	1.90	1.90
O81	A191	$2 multi	3.25	3.25
O82	A191	$3 multi	4.75	4.75
O83	A191	$4 multi	6.50	6.50
O84	A191	$5 multi	8.00	8.00

Size: 60x37mm

O85	A191	$7.50 multi	12.00	12.00
O86	A191	$10 multi	16.00	16.00
O87	A191	$20 multi	32.00	32.00
		Nos. O70-O87 (18)	94.10	94.10

Overprint reads up on vertical stamps.

Nos. 1305-1309 Overprinted in Metallic Green Like No. O70

2010, Oct. 12 Litho. *Perf. 13¾*

Sizes: 60x37mm, 37x60mm

O88	A191	10c multi	.25	.25
O89	A191	20c multi	.30	.30
O90	A191	30c multi	.50	.50
O91	A191	40c multi	.65	.65
O92	A191	50c multi	.80	.80
O93	A191	70c multi	1.10	1.10
O94	A191	80c multi	1.25	1.25
O95	A191	90c multi	1.50	1.50
O96	A191	$1 multi	1.60	1.60
O97	A191	$1.10 multi	1.75	1.75
O98	A191	$1.20 multi	1.90	1.90
O99	A191	$2 multi	3.25	3.25
O100	A191	$3 multi	4.75	4.75
O101	A191	$4 multi	6.50	6.50
O102	A191	$5 multi	8.00	8.00
		Nos. O88-O102 (15)	34.10	34.10

Overprint reads up on vertical stamps.

Nos. 1305-1309 Overprinted in Metallic Red Like No. O70

2010, Oct. 12 Litho. *Perf. 13¾*

Sizes: 60x37mm, 37x60mm

O103	A191	10c multi	.25	.25
O104	A191	20c multi	.30	.30
O105	A191	30c multi	.50	.50
O106	A191	40c multi	.65	.65
O107	A191	50c multi	.80	.80
O108	A191	70c multi	1.10	1.10
O109	A191	80c multi	1.25	1.25
O110	A191	90c multi	1.50	1.50
O111	A191	$1 multi	1.60	1.60
O112	A191	$1.10 multi	1.75	1.75
O113	A191	$1.20 multi	1.90	1.90
O114	A191	$2 multi	3.25	3.25
O115	A191	$3 multi	4.75	4.75
O116	A191	$4 multi	6.50	6.50
O117	A191	$5 multi	8.00	8.00
		Nos. O103-O117 (15)	34.10	34.10

Overprint reads up on vertical stamps.

CORFU

kor-ˈfü

LOCATION — An island in the Ionian Sea opposite the Greek-Albanian border
GOVT. — A department of Greece
AREA — 245 sq. mi.
POP. — 114,620 (1938)
CAPITAL — Corfu

In 1922 Italy occupied Corfu (Kerkyra) during a controversy with Greece over the assassination of an Italian official in Epirus. Italy again occupied Corfu in 1941-43.

100 Centesimi = 1 Lira
100 Lepta = 1 Drachma

Watermark

Wmk. 140 — Crown

Wmk. 252 — Crowns

ISSUED UNDER ITALIAN OCCUPATION

Italian Stamps of 1901-23 Overprinted

1923, Sept. 20 Wmk. 140 *Perf. 14*

N1	A48	5c green	6.75	*11.50*
N2	A48	10c claret	6.75	*11.50*
N3	A48	15c slate	6.75	*11.50*
N4	A50	20c brown orange	6.75	*11.50*
N5	A49	30c orange brown	6.75	*11.50*
N6	A49	50c violet	6.75	*11.50*
N7	A49	60c blue	6.75	*11.50*
a.		Vert. pair, one without overprint	*1,600.*	
N8	A46	1 l brown & green	6.75	*11.50*
		Nos. N1-N8 (8)	54.00	*92.00*
		Set, never hinged	125.00	

Italian Stamps of 1901-23 Surcharged

1923, Sept. 24

N9	A48	25 l on 10c claret	65.00	45.00
N10	A49	60 l on 25c blue	10.00	
N11	A49	70 l on 30c org brn	10.00	
N12	A49	1.20d on 50c violet	27.50	*45.00*
N13	A46	2.40d on 1 l brn & grn	27.50	*45.00*
N14	A46	4.75d on 2 l grn & org	15.00	
		Nos. N9-N14 (6)	155.00	
		Set, never hinged	275.00	

Nos. N10, N11, N14 were not placed in use.

Issue for Corfu and Paxos

Nos. N15-N34, NC1-NC12, NJ1-NJ11 and NRA1-NRA3 have been extensively counterfeited, some with forged cancellations.

Stamps of Greece, 1937-38, Overprinted in Black

Perf. 12x13½, 12½x12, 13½x12

1941, June 5 Wmk. 252

N15	A69	5 l brn red & blue	6.00	4.00
a.		Inverted overprint	*65.00*	*47.50*
b.		Double overprint	*85.00*	*110.00*
N16	A70	10 l bl & brn red (On 397)	2.00	*3.00*
N17	A70	10 l bl & brn red (On 413)	1,600.	1,300.
N18	A71	20 l black & grn	3.00	*4.00*
a.		Inverted overprint	*85.00*	*47.50*
N19	A72	40 l green & blk	3.50	*4.50*
a.		Inverted overprint	*85.00*	*47.50*
b.		Double overprint	*85.00*	*110.00*
N20	A73	50 l brown & blk	2.00	*3.00*
a.		Inverted overprint	*55.00*	*47.50*
N21	A74	80 l ind & yel brn	4.00	*5.00*
N22	A67	1d green	15.00	15.00
N23	A84	1.50d green	15.00	15.00
N24	A75	2d ultra	8.00	*11.00*
N25	A67	3d red brown	8.00	11.00
N26	A76	5d red	8.00	*11.00*
N27	A77	6d olive brown	8.00	*11.00*
N28	A78	7d dark brown	12.00	*12.00*
N29	A67	8d deep blue	25.00	25.00
N30	A79	10d red brown	725.00	400.00
N31	A80	15d green	30.00	30.00
N32	A81	25d dark blue	30.00	30.00
N33	A84	30d org brn	120.00	100.00
N34	A67	100d carmine lake	375.00	350.00
		Nos. N15-N34 (20)	2,999.	2,344.
		Set, never hinged	4,000.	

AIR POST STAMPS

Greece Nos. C37 and C26-C35, Overprinted Like Nos. N15-N34

Perf. 12½x13, 13x12½, 13½x12½

1941, June 5 Unwmk.

NC1	D3	50 l dk brown	11.50	8.00
NC2	AP16	1d red	750.00	275.00
NC3	AP17	2d gray blue	11.50	8.00
NC4	AP18	5d violet	13.50	13.00
NC5	AP19	7d deep ultra	17.50	13.00
NC6	AP20	10d bister brn (On C26)	950.00	400.00
NC7	AP20	10d brown org (On C35)	65.00	50.00
NC8	AP21	25d rose	135.00	60.00
NC9	AP22	30d dk grn	145.00	90.00
NC10	AP23	50d violet	145.00	90.00
a.		Double overprint		*550.00*
NC11	AP24	100d brown	*1,300.*	*650.00*

On No. C36

Serrate Roulette 13½

NC12	D3	50 l vio brn	90.00	25.00
a.		On No. C36a	*350.00*	
		Nos. NC1-NC12 (12)	*3,634.*	*1,682.*
		Set, never hinged	6,000.	

POSTAGE DUE STAMPS

Postage Due Stamps of Greece, 1913-35 Overprinted Like #N15-N34

1941, June 5 Unwmk.

Serrate Roulette 13½

NJ1	D3	10 l carmine	5.00	5.00
NJ2	D3	25 l ultra	5.00	5.00
NJ3	D3	80 l lilac brown	1,150.	450.00

Perf. 12½x13, 13½x12½

NJ4	D3	1d lt bl (On J80)	*1,600.*	*800.00*
NJ5	D3	2d light red	8.50	*13.50*
NJ6	D3	5d gray	22.50	22.50
NJ7	D3	10d gray green	22.50	22.50
NJ8	D3	15d red brown	22.50	22.50
NJ9	D3	25d light red	22.50	25.00
NJ10	D3	50d orange	22.50	25.00
NJ11	D3	100d slate green	600.00	450.00
		Nos. NJ1-NJ11 (11)	*3,481.*	*1,841.*
		Set, never hinged	5,000.	

POSTAL TAX STAMPS

Greece Nos. RA61-RA63 Overprinted Like Nos. N15-N34 Wmk., Unwmk.

1941, June 5 *Perf. 13½*

NRA1	PT7	10 l brt rose, *pale rose*	3.00	*4.00*
NRA2	PT7	50 l gray grn, *pale green*	5.00	*6.00*
NRA3	PT7	1d dull blue, *lt blue*	37.50	40.00
		Nos. NRA1-NRA3 (3)	45.50	50.00
		Set, never hinged	65.00	

Stamps overprinted "CORFU" were replaced by Italian stamps overprinted "Isole Jonie." See Ionian Islands.

COSTA RICA

ˌkōs-tə-ˈrē-kə

LOCATION — Central America between Nicaragua and Panama
GOVT. — Republic
AREA — 19,730 sq. mi.
POP. — 3,674,490 (1999 est.)
CAPITAL — San Jose

8 Reales = 100 Centavos = 1 Peso
100 Centimos = 1 Colon (1900)

Catalogue values for unused stamps in this country are for Never Hinged items, beginning with Scott 238 in the regular postage section, Scott C117 in the air post section, Scott CE1 in the air post special delivery section, Scott E1 in the special delivery section, and Scott RA1 in the postal tax section.

Watermarks

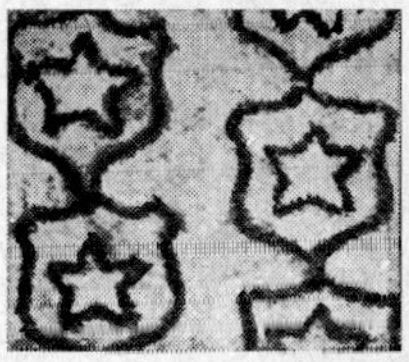

Wmk. 215 — Small Star in Shield, Multiple

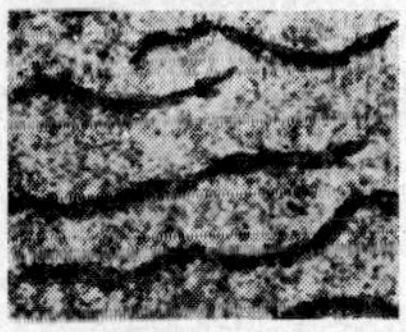

Wmk. 229 — Wavy Lines

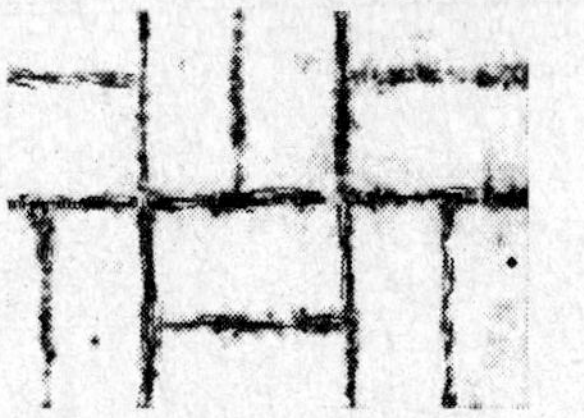

Wmk. 334 — Rectangles

Values for unused stamps are for examples with original gum as defined in the catalogue introduction. Very fine examples of Nos. 1-22 will have perforations just clear of the design on one or more sides due to the placement of the stamps on the plates and to imperfect perforating methods.

Coat of Arms — A1

1863 Unwmk. Engr. *Perf. 12*

1	A1	½r blue	.40	*1.10*
a.		½r light blue	.40	*1.10*
b.		Pair, imperf. horiz.	*6,000.*	
2	A1	2r scarlet	1.75	*2.25*
3	A1	4r green	16.00	*16.00*
4	A1	1p orange	42.50	*42.50*
		Nos. 1-4 (4)	60.65	61.85

The ½r was printed from two plates. The second is in light blue with little or no sky over the mountains.

Imperforate stamps of Nos. 1-2 are corner stamps from poorly perforated sheets.

Nos. 1-3 Surcharged in Red or Black

a

b

c

d

e

1881-82 Red or Black Surcharge

7	A1(a) 1c on ½r ('82)	3.00	*6.00*
a.	On No. 1a	15.00	—
8	A1(b) 1c on ½r ('82)	18.00	*30.00*
9	A1(c) 2c on ½r, #1a	3.00	2.75
a.	On No. 1	8.00	—
12	A1(c) 5c on ½r	15.00	
13	A1(d) 5c on ½r ('82)	65.00	
14	A1(d) 10c on 2r (Bk) ('82)	72.50	—
15	A1(e) 20c on 4r ('82)	300.00	—

Overprints with different fonts and "OFICIAL" were never placed in use, and are said to have been surcharged to a dealer's order. The ½r surcharged "DOS CTS" is not a postage stamp. It probably is an essay.

Postally used examples of Nos. 7-15 are rare. Nos. 13-15 exist with a favor cancel having a hyphen between "San" and "Jose." Values same as unused. Fake cancellations exist.

Counterfeits exist of surcharges on Nos. 7-15.

Gen. Prospero Fernández — A6

1883, Jan. 1

16	A6 1c green	3.00	1.50
17	A6 2c carmine	3.25	1.50
18	A6 5c blue violet	32.50	2.00
19	A6 10c orange	150.00	12.00
20	A6 40c blue	3.00	*3.00*
	Nos. 16-20 (5)	191.75	20.00

Unused examples of 40c usually lack gum.

For overprints see Nos. O1-O20, O24, Guanacaste 1-38, 44.

President Bernardo Soto Alfaro — A7

1887

21	A7 5c blue violet	7.00	.50
22	A7 10c orange	4.00	3.00

Unused examples of 5c usually lack gum.

For overprints see Nos. O22-O23, Guanacaste 42-43, 45.

A8

A9

1889 Black Overprint

23	A8 1c rose	5.00	3.00
24	A9 5c brown	7.00	3.00

Vertical and inverted overprints are fakes.

For overprints see Guanacaste Nos. 47-54.

President Soto Alfaro
A10 A11

A12

A13

A14

A15

A16

A17

A18

A19

1889 *Perf. 14-16 & Compound*

25	A10 1c brown	.35	*.45*
a.	Horiz. pair, imperf. vert	*150.00*	
b.	Imperf. pair	*100.00*	
c.	Horiz. or vert. pair, imperf. btwn.	*150.00*	
26	A11 2c dark green	.35	*.45*
a.	Imperf., pair	50.00	
b.	Vert. pair, imperf. horiz.	125.00	
c.	Horiz. pair, imperf. btwn.	125.00	
27	A12 5c orange	.45	.35
a.	Imperf., pair		*250.00*
b.	Horiz. pair, imperf. btwn.	*150.00*	
28	A13 10c red brown	.40	.35
a.	Vert. or horiz. pair, imperf. btwn.	*150.00*	
29	A14 20c yellow green	.30	*.35*
a.	Vert. pair, imperf. horiz.	200.00	
b.	Horizontal pair, imperf. btwn.	*150.00*	
30	A15 50c rose red	1.00	
	Telegram cancel		.75
31	A16 1p blue	1.25	
	Telegram cancel		.75
32	A17 2p dull violet	6.00	
a.	2p slate	6.00	
	Telegram cancel		4.00
33	A18 5p olive green	25.00	
	Telegram cancel		10.00
34	A19 10p black	100.00	
	Telegram cancel		45.00
	Nos. 25-34 (10)	135.10	1.95

Nos. 30-34 normally were used on telegrams and most examples were removed from the forms and sold by the government.

Most unused examples of No. 34 have no gum or only part gum. These sell for somewhat less.

For overprints see Nos. O25-O30, Guanacaste 55-67.

Arms of Costa Rica
A20 A21

A22

A23

A24

A25

A26

A27

A28

A29

1892 *Perf. 12-15 & Compound*

35	A20 1c grnsh blue	.30	*.40*
36	A21 2c yellow	.30	*.40*
37	A22 5c red lilac	.30	.25
a.	5c violet	60.00	.30
38	A23 10c lt green	.80	.35
a.	Horiz. pair, imperf. btwn.	—	*100.00*
39	A24 20c scarlet	12.00	.25
a.	Horiz. pair, imperf. btwn.	—	*100.00*
40	A25 50c gray blue	4.00	*4.25*
41	A26 1p green, *yel*	1.25	1.00
42	A27 2p brown red, *lilac*	3.00	1.00
a.	2p rose red, *pale lil*	12.00	1.00
43	A28 5p dk blue, *blue*	2.00	1.00
44	A29 10p brown, *pale buff*	35.00	5.00
a.	10p brown, *yellow*	8.00	
	Nos. 35-44 (10)	58.95	13.90

Imperfs. of Nos. 35-44 are proofs.

Nos. 42-43 unused are normally without gum and are valued thus.

For overprints see Nos. O31-O36.

Statue of Juan Santamaría
A30

Juan Mora Fernández
A31

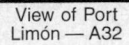

View of Port Limón — A32

Braulio Carrillo ("Branlio" on stamp) — A33

National Theater — A34

José M. Castro — A35

Birris Bridge — A36

Juan Rafael Mora — A37

Jesús Jiménez — A38

Coat of Arms — A39

1901, Jan. *Perf. 12-15½*

45	A30 1c green & blk	3.25	.30
a.	Horiz. pair, imperf. btwn.	*150.00*	
46	A31 2c ver & blk	1.25	.30
47	A32 5c gray blue & blk	3.25	.30
a.	Vert. pair, imperf. btwn.	—	*300.00*
48	A33 10c ocher & blk	3.25	.35
49	A34 20c lake & blk	22.50	.25
a.	Vert. pair, imperf. btwn.	*1,000.*	
50	A35 50c dull lil & dk bl	5.50	1.00
51	A36 1col ol bis & blk	110.00	3.50
52	A37 2col car rose & dk grn	16.00	3.00
53	A38 5col brown & blk	75.00	3.50
54	A39 10col yel grn & brn red	29.00	3.00
	Nos. 45-54 (10)	269.00	15.50

The 2c exists with center inverted. Value $77,500.

Nos. 45-57 in other colors are private reprints made in 1948. They have little value.

For surcharge and overprints see Nos. 58, 78, O37-O44.

Remainders

In 1914 the government sold a large quantity of stamps at very much less than face value. The lot included most regular issues from 1901 to 1911 inclusive, postage due stamps of 1903 and Official stamps of 1901-03. These stamps were canceled with groups of thin parallel bars. The higher valued used stamps, such as Nos. 64, 65-68a, sell for much less than the values quoted, which are for stamps with regular postal cancellations. A few sell for much higher prices.

José M. Cañas — A40

Julián Volio — A41

Eusebio Figueroa Oreamuno — A42

1903 *Perf. 13½, 14, 15*

55	A40 4c red vio & blk	2.00	.70
56	A41 6c olive grn & blk	7.25	4.00
57	A42 25c gray lil & brn	16.00	.30
	Nos. 55-57 (3)	25.25	5.00

See note on private reprints following No. 54.

For overprints see Nos. 81, O45-O47.

No. 49 Surcharged in Black:

1905

58	A34 1c on 20c lake & blk	.60	.60
a.	Inverted surcharge	10.00	10.00
b.	Diagonal surcharge	.60	.60

Examples surcharged in other colors are proofs.

Statue of Juan Santamaria A43

Juan Mora Fernández A44

José M. Cañas A45

Mauro Fernández A46

Braulio Carrillo — A47

Julián Volio — A48

Eusebio Figueroa Oreamuno A49

José M. Castro A50

Jesús Jiménez — A51

Juan Rafael Mora — A52

Perf. 11x14, 14 (1c, 5c, 10c, 25c)

1907 **Unwmk.**

59	A43 1c red brn & ind	8.00	.40
a.	Perf. 11x14	60.00	3.00
b.	Imperf pair	15.00	—
60	A44 2c yel grn & blk	3.00	.30
a.	Perf. 14	3.00	.30
b.	Imperf pair	15.00	—
61	A45 4c car & indigo	12.00	2.50
a.	Perf. 14	500.00	45.00
b.	Imperf pair	15.00	—
62	A46 5c yel & dull bl	3.00	.30
a.	Perf. 11x14	60.00	1.00
b.	Imperf pair	15.00	—
63	A47 10c blue & blk	10.00	.50
a.	Perf. 11x14	20.00	1.00
b.	Imperf pair	30.00	—
64	A48 20c olive grn & blk	25.00	6.00
a.	Perf. 14	25.00	6.00
	Remainder cancel		2.00
b.	Imperf pair	—	
65	A49 25c gray lil & blk	3.00	3.00
	Remainder cancel		1.00
a.	Perf. 11x14	150.00	50.00
b.	Imperf pair	—	
66	A50 50c red lil & blue	75.00	25.00
	Remainder cancel		2.00
a.	Perf. 14	175.00	50.00
b.	Imperf pair	100.00	
67	A51 1col brown & blk	25.00	20.00
a.	Perf. 14	25.00	20.00
	Remainder cancel		2.00
b.	Imperf pair	—	
68	A52 2col claret & grn	160.00	100.00
	Remainder cancel		3.00
a.	Perf. 14	300.00	150.00
b.	Imperf pair	200.00	
	Nos. 59-68 (10)	324.00	158.00

The remainder cancel value applies to both perforations.

The imperforate varieties of the above set are valued without gum. Ungummed stamps were probably placed on the market in London, while gummed stamps appear to have been sent to Costa Rica and accepted for postal use. There is a small premium for gummed stamps.

The 1c, 2c, 5c, 20c, 50c, 1 col and 2 col exist with center inverted. Value, set $62,500.

Nos. 59-68 exist with papermaker's watermark.

No. 65b with brown vignette is a proof. Value, pair $40. The actual No. 65b (black vignette) is worth much more.

For overprints see Nos. 77, 79-80, 82-84, O48-O55, O60-O64.

Statue of Juan Santamaria A53

Juan Mora Fernández A54

José M. Cañas A55

Mauro Fernández A56

Braulio Carrillo — A57

Julián Volio — A58

Eusebio Figueroa Oreamuno A59

Jesús Jiménez A60

1910 ***Perf. 12***

69	A53 1c brown	.25	.25
70	A54 2c dp green	.30	.25
71	A55 4c scarlet	.35	.35
72	A56 5c orange	1.00	.25
73	A57 10c deep blue	.40	.25
74	A58 20c olive grn	.50	.35
75	A59 25c dp violet	17.00	1.50
76	A60 1col dk brown	.50	.50
	Nos. 69-76 (8)	20.30	3.70

For overprints and surcharge see Nos. 111C-111J, B1, C2, O56-O59.

No. 60a Overprinted in Red

1911 ***Perf. 14***

77	A44 2c yel grn & blk	3.00	1.10
a.	Inverted overprint	6.00	5.00
b.	Double overprint, both inverted	45.00	

Stamps of 1901-07 Overprinted in Red or Black

78	A30 1c grn & blk (R)	3.00	1.00
a.	Black overprint	32.50	18.00
b.	Inverted overprint		
79	A43 1c red brn & ind (Bk)	1.25	.40
a.	Inverted overprint	4.50	3.50
b.	Double overprint	5.50	5.00
80	A44 2c yel grn & blk (Bk)	1.00	.40
a.	Inverted overprint	3.75	3.50
b.	Dbl. ovpt., one as on No. 77	40.00	27.50
c.	Double overprint, one inverted	15.00	15.00
d.	Pair, one stamp No. 77	25.00	18.00
e.	Perf. 11x14	30.00	*1.00*

No. 55 Overprinted in Black

81	A40 4c red vio & blk	1.50	.65

Stamps of 1907 Overprinted in Blue, Black or Rose

Perf. 14, 11x14 (#83, 84)

82	A46 5c yel & bl (Bl)	2.00	.25
a.	"Habilitada"	3.25	2.50
b.	"2911"	5.50	3.25
c.	Roman "I" in "1911"	4.00	2.50
d.	Double overprint	5.50	5.00
e.	Inverted overprint	6.00	3.75
f.	Black overprint	—	2.00
g.	Triple overprint	6.00	
h.	Vert. pair, imperf. horiz.	*100.00*	
83	A47 10c blue & blk (Bk)	5.00	1.40
a.	As #83, Roman "I" in "1911"	7.00	5.00
c.	As #83, double overprint	20.00	11.50
d.	Perf. 14	45.00	5.25
84	A47 10c blue & blk (R)	15.00	13.50
a.	Roman "I" in "1911"	*100.00*	*100.00*
c.	Perf. 14	*100.00*	*100.00*
	Nos. 77-84 (8)	31.75	18.70

Many counterfeits of overprint exist.

Telegraph Stamps Surcharged in Rose, Blue or Black

A61

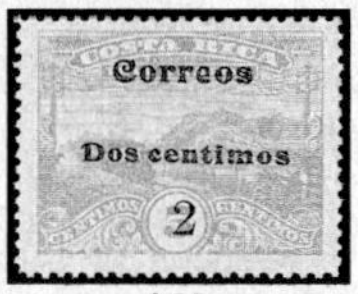

A62

A63

1911 ***Perf. 12***

86	A61 1c on 10c bl (R)	.50	.25
a.	"Coereos"	7.75	6.00
b.	Inverted surcharge		
87	A61 1c on 10c bl (Bk)	*210.00*	*87.50*
88	A61 1c on 25c vio (Bk)	.50	.25
a.	"Coereos"	8.75	6.00
b.	Pair, one without surcharge	20.00	
c.	Double surcharge	9.00	
e.	Double surch., one inverted	12.50	
89	A61 1c on 50c red brn (Bl)	.55	.40
a.	Inverted surcharge	5.50	5.00
b.	Double surcharge	4.50	
90	A61 1c on 1col brn (R)	.55	.40
91	A61 1c on 5col red (Bl)	1.00	.55
92	A61 1c on 10col dk brn (R)	1.50	.70

Perf. 14

93	A62 2c on 5c brn org (Bk)	3.50	1.90
a.	Inverted surcharge	*9.00*	*3.75*
b.	"Correos" inverted	*17.50*	
c.	Double surcharge	9.00	

Perf. 14x11

94	A62 2c on 10c bl (R)	100.00	100.00
a.	Perf. 14	*350.00*	*350.00*
b.	"Correos" inverted	2,000.	
c.	As "b," perf. 14	—	
95	A62 2c on 50c cl (Bk)	1.00	.55
a.	Inverted surcharge	4.50	3.25
b.	Double surcharge	12.50	
c.	Perf. 14	45.00	20.00
96	A62 2c on 1col brn (Bk)	1.25	.70
a.	Inverted surcharge	12.50	
b.	Double surcharge	16.00	
c.	Perf. 14	2.00	.80
97	A62 2c on 2col car (Bk)	1.25	.60
a.	Inverted surcharge	8.00	5.00
b.	"Correos" inverted	10.00	5.50
c.	Double surcharge		
d.	Perf. 14	27.50	16.00
98	A62 2c on 5col grn (Bk)	1.00	.70
a.	Inverted surcharge	10.00	7.00
b.	"Correos" inverted	*16.00*	*4.25*
c.	Perf. 14	6.00	3.00
99	A62 2c on 10col mar (Bk)	1.50	.70
a.	"Correos" inverted	*400.00*	
b.	Perf. 14	6.00	3.00

Perf. 12

100	A63 5c on 5c org (Bl)	.40	.25
a.	Double surcharge	27.50	16.00
b.	Inverted surcharge	27.50	9.50
c.	Pair, one without surcharge	16.00	

Counterfeits exist of Nos. 87, 94 and all minor varieties. Genuine used examples of No. 94 are rare and have a cancel only used on registered mail. Genuine "Coereos" errors do not exist on No. 87. Used examples of No. 94 with target cancels are counterfeits. No. 94c is unique. All examples of Nos. 94b and 94c have stains and are valued thus.

Nos. 93-99 exist with papermaker's watermark.

Coffee Plantation — A64

1921, June 17 **Litho.** ***Perf. 11½***

103	A64 5c bl & blk	3.00	3.00
a.	Tête bêche pair	15.00	6.50
b.	Imperf., pair	*40.00*	
c.	As "a," imperf.	*150.00*	

Centenary of coffee raising in Costa Rica.

Liberty with Torch of Freedom — A65

1921 **Typo.** ***Perf. 11***

104	A65 5c violet	1.00	.40
a.	Imperf, pair	*100.00*	

Cent. of Central American independence.

Beware of trimmed singles that look like No. 104a.

For overprint see No. 111.

Juan Mora and Julio Acosta — A66

1921, Sept. 15 ***Perf. 11½***

105	A66 2c orange & blk	1.75	1.75
106	A66 3c green & blk	1.75	1.75
107	A66 6c scarlet & blk	3.00	3.00
108	A66 15c dk blue & blk	5.00	5.00
109	A66 30c orange brn & blk	6.50	6.50
	Nos. 105-109 (5)	18.00	18.00

Centenary of Central American independence. Issue requested by Costa Rican Philatelic Society. Authorized by decree calling for 2,000 of 30c and 5,000 each of other values. Nos. 105-109 imperf were not regularly issued. Inverted centers exist of both perf and imperf. They are rare. Used values are for Independence commemorative cancel.

Each sheet of 20 (4x5) contains 5 tête-bêche pairs. Value, set of 5 pairs $40.

Simón Bolívar — A67

1921 Engr. *Perf. 12*

110	A67 15c deep violet	.75	.25

For overprint see No. 111H. For surcharge see No. 148.

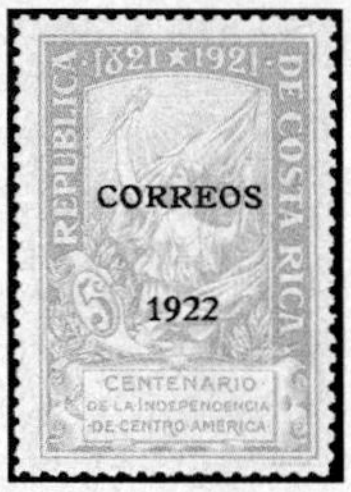

No. 104 Overprinted

1922 *Perf. 11*

111	A65 5c violet	.75	.40
a.	Inverted overprint	10.00	
b.	Double overprint	15.00	

Stamps of 1910-1921 Overprinted in Blue, Red, Black or Gold

1922 *Perf. 12*

111C	A53 1c brown (Bl)	.30	.25
111D	A54 2c deep green (R)	.40	.25
111E	A55 4c scarlet	.30	.25
111F	A56 5c orange	2.00	.40
111G	A57 10c deep blue (R)	.75	.40
111H	A67 15c deep violet (G)	4.00	2.00
	Nos. 111C-111H (6)	7.75	3.55

Inverted overprints occur on all values. Value, set $20. Counterfeits predominate.

No. 72 Overprinted

1923

111J	A56 5c orange	3.00	.75
k.	"VD." for "UD."	*75.00*	*75.00*

Jesús Jiménez — A68

1923, June 18 Litho. *Perf. 11½*

112	A68 2c brown	.40	.40
113	A68 4c green	.40	.40
114	A68 5c blue	.60	.40
115	A68 20c carmine	.85	.50
116	A68 1col violet	1.10	1.25
	Nos. 112-116 (5)	3.35	2.95

Pres. Jesús Jiménez (1823-98).
Nos. 112-116, imperf, were not regularly issued. Value, set $5.
For overprints see Nos. O65-O69.

National Monument A70

Harvesting Coffee — A71

Banana Growing — A73

General Post Office A74

Columbus Soliciting Aid of Isabella A75

Christopher Columbus A76

Columbus at Cariari A77

Map of Costa Rica — A78

Manuel M. Gutiérrez — A79

1923-26 Engr. *Perf. 12*

117	A70 1c violet	.25	.25
118	A71 2c yellow	.50	.25
119	A73 4c deep green	.75	.30
120	A74 5c light blue	1.50	.25
121	A74 5c yellow grn ('26)	.50	.25
122	A75 10c red brown	3.00	.25
123	A75 10c car rose ('26)	.50	.25
124	A76 12c carmine rose	10.00	3.00
125	A77 20c deep blue	10.00	.65
126	A78 40c orange	11.00	3.00
127	A79 1col olive green	2.40	.80
	Nos. 117-127 (11)	40.40	9.25

See Nos. 151-156. For surcharges & overprints see Nos. 136-140, 147, 189, 218, C2.

Rodrigo Arias Maldonado — A80

1924 *Perf. 12½*

128	A80 2c dark green	.25	.25
a.	Perf. 14	.50	.25

See No. 162.

Map of Guanacaste A81

Mission at Nicoya A82

1924 Litho. *Perf. 12*

129	A81 1c carmine rose	.30	.25
130	A81 2c violet	.40	.25
131	A81 5c green	.40	.25
132	A81 10c orange	2.25	.50
133	A82 15c light blue	1.00	.50
134	A82 20c gray black	2.00	1.00
135	A82 25c light brown	3.00	1.50
	Nos. 129-135 (7)	9.35	4.25

Centenary of annexation of Province of Guanacaste to Costa Rica.
Exist imperf. Value, set, $50.

Stamps of 1923 Surcharged

a

b

1925

136	A74(a) 3c on 5c lt blue	.30	.25
137	A75(a) 6c on 10c red brn	.40	.25
138	A78(a) 30c on 40c orange	1.50	.40
139	A79(b) 45c on 1col ol grn	1.75	.50
a.	Double surcharge	*250.00*	
	Nos. 136-139 (4)	3.95	1.40

No. 124 Surcharged

1926

140	A76 10c on 12c car rose	1.50	.30

College of San Luis, Cartago A83

Chapui Asylum, San José — A84

Normal School, Heredia A85

Ruins of Ujarrás A86

1926 Unwmk. Engr. *Perf. 12½*

143	A83 3c ultra	.55	.25
144	A84 6c dark brown	.55	.25
145	A85 30c deep orange	2.00	.40
146	A86 45c black violet	4.00	1.60
	Nos. 143-146 (4)	7.10	2.50

For surcharges see Nos. 190-190D, 217.

No. 124 Surcharged in Black

1928, Jan. 7 *Perf. 12*

147	A76 10c on 12c car rose	4.75	4.75

Issued in honor of Col. Charles A. Lindbergh during his Good Will Tour of Central America.
The surcharge was privately reprinted using an original die. Reprints can be distinguished by distinct dots under the "10s." All errors and inverted surcharges are reprints.

No. 110 Surcharged

1928

148	A67 5(c) on 15c dp violet	.25	.25
a.	Inverted surcharge	35.00	

Type I — A88

Type II

Type III

Type IV

Type V

Surcharge Typo. (I-V) & Litho. (V)

1929 *Perf. 12½*

149	A88 5c on 2col car (I)	.50	.25
a.-d.	Types II-V	.60	.25
e.	Type V (litho.)	3.00	3.00

Telegraph Stamp Surcharged for Postage as in 1929, Surcharge Lithographed

1929

150	A88 13c on 40c deep grn	.35	.25
a.	Inverted surcharge	1.00	1.00

Excellent counterfeits exist of No. 150a.

Types of 1923-26 Issues Dated "1929"
Imprint of Waterlow & Sons

1930 Size: 26x21½mm ***Perf. 12½***

151	A70	1c dark violet	.70	.25
155	A74	5c green	.70	.25
156	A75	10c carmine rose	.70	.25
		Nos. 151-156 (3)	2.10	.75

Juan Rafael Mora — A89

1931, Jan. 29

157	A89	13c carmine rose	.60	.25

For surcharge see No. 209.

Seal of Costa Rica Philatelic Society ("Octubre 12 de 1932") — A90

1932, Oct. 12 ***Perf. 12***

158	A90	3c orange	.25	.25
159	A90	5c dark green	.40	.25
160	A90	10c carmine rose	.50	.25
161	A90	20c dark blue	.85	.40
		Nos. 158-161 (4)	2.00	1.15

Phil. Exhib., Oct. 12, 1932. See Nos. 179-183.

Maldonado Type of 1924

1934, Aug. 11 ***Perf. 12½***

162	A80	3c dark green	.25	.25

Red Cross Nurse — A91

1935, May 31 ***Perf. 12***

163	A91	10c rose carmine	7.50	.25

50th anniv. of the founding of the Costa Rican Red Cross Society.

Air View of Cartago A92

Miraculous Statuette and View of Cathedral A93

Vision of 1635 — A94

1935, Aug. 1 ***Perf. 12½***

164	A92	5c green	.25	.25
165	A93	10c carmine	.25	.25
166	A92	30c orange	.25	.25
167	A94	45c dark violet	1.00	.55
168	A93	50c blue black	1.00	1.00
		Nos. 164-168 (5)	2.75	2.30

Tercentenary of the Patron Saint, Our Lady of the Angels, of Costa Rica.

Map of Cocos Island A95

1936, Jan. 29 ***Perf. 14, 11½ (25c)***

169	A95	4c ocher	.50	.25
170	A95	8c dark violet	.65	.25
171	A95	25c orange	.80	.25
172	A95	35c brown vio	.95	.25
173	A95	40c brown	1.25	.40
174	A95	50c yellow	1.50	.60
175	A95	2col yellow grn	11.00	10.00
176	A95	5col green	30.00	25.00
		Nos. 169-176 (8)	46.65	37.00

Exist imperf. Value, set, $50.

For surcharges see Nos. 196-200, C55-C56.

Map of Cocos Island and Ships of Columbus A96

1936, Dec. 5 ***Perf. 12***

177	A96	5c green	.40	.25
178	A96	10c carmine rose	.55	.25

For overprints see Nos. 247, O80-O81.

Seal of Costa Rica Philatelic Society ("Diciembre 1937") — A97

1937, Dec. 15

179	A97	2c dark brown	.45	.25
180	A97	3c black	.45	.25
181	A97	5c green	.45	.25
182	A97	10c orange red	.45	.25
		Nos. 179-182 (4)	1.80	1.00

Souvenir Sheet
Imperf

183		Sheet of 4	6.50	4.00
a.	A97	2c dark brown	.25	.25
b.	A97	3c black	.25	.25
c.	A97	5c green	.25	.25
d.	A97	10c orange red	.25	.25

Phil. Exhib., Dec. 1937.

Purple Guaria Orchid, National Flower — A98

Tuna — A99

Native with Donkey Carrying Bananas A101

3c, Cacao pod. 10c, Coffee harvesting.

1937-38 Wmk. 229 ***Perf. 12½***

184	A98	1c green & vio ('38)	.55	.25
185	A98	3c chocolate ('38)	.55	.25

Unwmk. ***Perf. 12***

186	A99	2c olive gray	.40	.25
187	A101	5c dark green	.55	.25
188	A101	10c carmine rose	.90	.25
		Nos. 184-188 (5)	2.95	1.25

National Exposition.

No. 125 Overprinted in Black

1938, Sept. 23 Unwmk. ***Perf. 12***

189	A77	20c deep blue	1.50	.30

No. 146 Surcharged in Red

a

b

c

d

e

1940 ***Perf. 12½***

190	A86(a)	15c on 45c blk vio	.60	.30
190A	A86(b)	15c on 45c blk vio	.60	.30
190B	A86(c)	15c on 45c blk vio	.60	.30
190C	A86(d)	15c on 45c blk vio	.60	.30
190D	A86(e)	15c on 45c blk vio	.60	.30
		Nos. 190-190D (5)	3.00	1.50

No. 190D exists with inverted surcharge. Value, $5.

Allegory A103

Black Overprint

1940, Dec. 2 Engr. ***Perf. 12***

191	A103	5c green	.25	.25
192	A103	10c rose carmine	.50	.25
193	A103	20c deep blue	1.50	1.00
194	A103	40c brown	4.50	2.75
195	A103	55c orange yellow	11.00	7.50
		Nos. 191-195 (5)	17.75	11.75

Pan-American Health Day. See Nos. C46-C54.

Exist without overprint.

Stamps of 1936 Srchd. in Black

1941 ***Perf. 14, 11½***

196	A95	15c on 25c orange	.50	.50
197	A95	15c on 35c brn vio	.50	.50
198	A95	15c on 40c brown	.50	.50
199	A95	15c on 2col yel grn	.50	.50
200	A95	15c on 5col green	1.00	1.00
		Nos. 196-200 (5)	3.00	3.00

Nos. 196-200 exist with surcharge inverted. Value, set of 5, $20.

National Stadium A104

Engr.; Flags Typo. in Natl. Colors

1941, May 8 ***Perf. 12½***

201	A104	5c green	.70	.25
a.		Flags omitted	*200.00*	
202	A104	10c orange	.55	.30
203	A104	15c car rose	.80	.40
204	A104	25c dk blue	.85	.55
205	A104	40c chestnut	3.25	1.40
206	A104	50c purple	4.25	2.00
207	A104	75c red orange	6.75	5.75
208	A104	1col dk carmine	13.00	10.50
		Nos. 201-208 (8)	30.15	21.15

Caribbean and Central American Soccer Championship. See Nos. C57-C66, C121-C123.

No. 157 Surcharged in Black

1941, July 26 ***Perf. 12***

209	A89	5c on 13c car rose	.25	.25

Cleto González Viquez — A105

Design: 5c, José Rodriguez.

1941-45 Engr. ***Perf. 12½***

210	A105	3c dp orange	.25	.25
210A	A105	3c dp plum ('43)	.25	.25
210B	A105	3c carmine ('45)	.25	.25
211	A105	5c dp violet	.25	.25
211A	A105	5c brown blk ('43)	.25	.25
		Nos. 210-211A (5)	1.25	1.25

See No. 256.

Old University of Costa Rica A106

New National University A107

1941, Aug. 26 ***Perf. 12***

212	A106	5c green	.40	.25
213	A107	10c yellow org	.40	.25
214	A106	15c lilac rose	.75	.25
215	A107	25c dull blue	1.00	.35
216	A106	50c fawn	7.50	2.25
		Nos. 212-216 (5)	10.05	3.35

National University, founded in 1940. See Nos. C74-C80.

Nos. 144, 189 Srchd. in Black or Red

1942, April *Perf. 12½, 12*
217 A84 5c on 6c dk brn .35 .25
218 A77 15c on 20c dp bl (R) .65 .25

Nos. 217-218 exist with inverted surcharge. Value, each $10.

Torch of Freedom, "Victory" and Flags of American Nations — A108

1942, Sept. 25 *Perf. 12*
219 A108 5c rose .30 .25
220 A108 5c yellow grn .30 .25
221 A108 5c purple .30 .25
222 A108 5c dp blue .30 .25
223 A108 5c red orange .30 .25
Nos. 219-223 (5) 1.50 1.25

For overprints see Nos. 238-241.

Juan Mora Fernández — A109

Designs: 2c, Bruno Carranza. 3c, Tomas Guardia. 5c, Manuel Aguilar. 15c, Francisco Morazan. 25c, Jose M. Alfaro. 50c, Francisco M. Oreamuno. 1col, Jose M. Castro. 2col, Juan Rafael Mora.

1943-47 **Engr.**
224 A109 1c red lilac .25 .25
225 A109 2c black .25 .25
226 A109 3c deep blue .25 .25
227 A109 5c brt blue grn .25 .25
a. 5c bright green ('47) .25 .25
228 A109 15c scarlet .25 .25
229 A109 25c brt ultra 1.00 .25
230 A109 50c dp violet 3.00 .45
231 A109 1col black brown 4.00 2.00
232 A109 2col deep orange 5.00 3.00
Nos. 224-232 (9) 14.25 6.95

See Nos. 344-368, C81-C91A, C124-C127, C154-C158, C179-C181, C768-C772, C790-C794, C854-C858. For surcharges see Nos. C154-C158, C182, C184-C185.

View of San Ramón A118

1944, Jan. 19
233 A118 5c dark green .25 .25
234 A118 10c orange .25 .25
235 A118 15c rose pink .30 .25
236 A118 40c gray black 1.25 .80
237 A118 50c deep blue 2.40 1.60
Nos. 233-237 (5) 4.45 3.15

100th anniv. of the founding of the City of San Ramón. See Nos. C94-C102.

Catalogue values for unused stamps in this section, from this point to the end of the section, are for Never Hinged items.

Nos. 220-223 Overprinted in Red or Black

1944, Sept. 18
238 A108 5c yel green .30 .25
239 A108 5c purple (R) .30 .25
240 A108 5c dp blue (R) .30 .25
241 A108 5c red orange .30 .25
Nos. 238-241 (4) 1.20 1.00

Amicable settlement of a boundary dispute with Panama. This overprint also exists on No. 219.

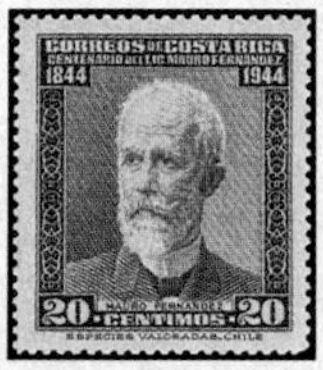

Mauro Fernández (1844-1905), Statesman — A119

Unwmk.
1945, July 21 **Engr.** *Perf. 14*
242 A119 20c deep green .30 .25

For surcharge see No. 246.

Coffee Harvesting — A120

1945, Oct. 9 *Perf. 12*
243 A120 5c dk green & blk .30 .25
244 A120 10c orange & blk .30 .25
245 A120 20c car rose & blk .50 .25
Nos. 243-245 (3) 1.10 .75

No. 242 Surcharged in Red Brown

1946 **Unwmk.** *Perf. 14*
246 A119 15c on 20c dp green .30 .25

Exists with inverted surcharge. Value, $6.

No. O80 Overprinted in Red

1947, Mar. 19 *Perf. 12*
247 A96 5c green .30 .25

Exist with inverted overprint. Value, $6.

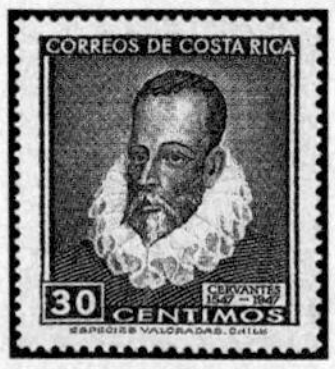

Cervantes — A121

Wmk. 215
1947, Nov. 10 **Engr.** *Perf. 14*
249 A121 30c deep blue .45 .25
250 A121 55c deep carmine .80 .40

Miguel de Cervantes Saavedra, novelist, playwright & poet, 400th birth anniv.

A122

1947, Aug. 26 **Unwmk.** *Perf. 12*
251 A122 5c brt green .25 .25
252 A122 10c car rose .25 .25
253 A122 15c ultra .25 .25
254 A122 25c orange red .35 .25
255 A122 50c lilac .55 .30
Nos. 251-255,C160-C167 (13) 7.35 6.30

Franklin D. Roosevelt. For surcharges see Nos. C224-C226.

Small Portrait Type of 1941

Design: 3c, Bishop Bernardo A. Thiel.

1948 *Perf. 12½*
256 A105 3c deep ultra .25 .25

Old University of Costa Rica A123

Black Surcharge

1953, June 25 **Litho.** *Perf. 12*
257 A123 5c on 10c green .35 .25

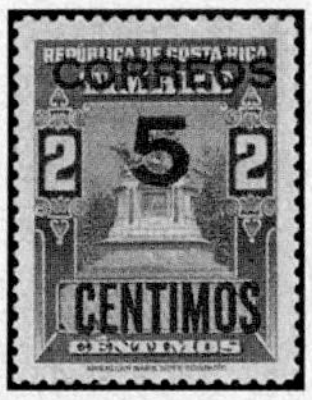

Revenue Stamp Surcharged in Red or Blue — A124

1955-56 **Unwmk.** **Engr.** *Perf. 12*
258 A124 5c on 2c emerald .25 .25
259 A124 15c on 2c emer (Bl) .25 .25
260 A124 15c on 2c emer ('56) .25 .25
Nos. 258-260,C341-C344 (7) 2.35 2.10

For surcharges see Nos. C341-C344, C431-C433.

Justo A. Facio — A125

1960, Apr. 20 **Photo.** *Perf. 13½*
261 A125 10c brown red .40 .25

Centenary of the birth (in 1859) of Prof. Justo A. Facio. Exists imperf. Value, $35.

Nos. RA12-RA15 Surcharged in Red

1963, Mar.
262 PT3 10c on 5c dk car .40 .25
263 PT3 10c on 5c sepia .40 .25
264 PT3 10c on 5c dull grn .40 .25
265 PT3 10c on 5c blue .40 .25
Nos. 262-265 (4) 1.60 1.00

Anglo-Costa Rican Bank — A126

1963 **Unwmk.** *Perf. 13½*
266 A126 10c gray .35 .25

Centenary of the Anglo-Costa Rican Bank.

Arms of San José — A127

Coats of Arms: 35c, Cartago. 50c, Heredia. 55c, Alajuela. 65c, Guanacaste. 1col, Puntarenas. 2col, Limon.

1969, Sept. 14 **Litho.** *Perf. 14x13½*
267 A127 15c multicolored .30 .25
268 A127 35c multicolored .30 .25
269 A127 50c gray & multi .30 .25
270 A127 55c buff & multi .30 .25
271 A127 65c multicolored .75 .25
272 A127 1col pink & multi 2.75 .40
273 A127 2col multicolored 3.75 .60
Nos. 267-273 (7) 8.45 2.25

Alberto M. Brenes Mora — A128

1976, Mar. 1 **Litho.** *Perf. 10½*
274 A128 1col violet blue .65 .25
Nos. 274,C653-C657 (6) 9.15 4.40

Prof. Alberto Manuel Brenes Mora, botanist, birth centenary.

Map of Costa Rica, Reader with Book — A129

1978, July 17 **Litho.** *Perf. 13½*
275 A129 50c multicolored .40 .25

National five-year literacy plan.

A130

1983, May 17 **Litho.** *Perf. 13x13½*
276 A130 10c multicolored .40 .25
277 A130 50c multicolored .35 .25
278 A130 10col multicolored 1.40 .30
Nos. 276-278 (3) 2.15 .80

World Communications Year.

A131

1983, May 30 **Litho.** *Perf. 10½*
279 A131 20col black 2.40 .55

1st World Cong. of Human Rights, 1982.

UPU Membership Centenary — A132

1983, June 30 Litho. *Perf. 16*

280 A132 3col #17, monument 1.25 .25
281 A132 10col #20, San Jose post office 2.40 .50

French Alliance Centenary — A133

Scene in San Jose, by Christina Fournier.

1983, July 21 Litho. *Perf. 11*

282 A133 12col multicolored 2.00 .55

Christmas 1983 — A134

Nativity tableau in continuous design.

1983, Dec. 5 Litho. *Perf. 13½*

283 1.50col multi .25 .25
284 1.50col multi .25 .25
285 1.50col multi .25 .25
a. A134 Strip of 3, #283-285 1.60 1.60

Costa Rican Gardens Association.

Fishery Development Administration A135

1983, Dec. 19 Litho. *Perf. 13½*

286 A135 8.50col multi .80 .30

Local Birds — A136

10c, Quetzal. 50c, Cyanerpes cyaneus. 1col, Turdus grayi. 1.50col, Momotus momota. 3col, Colibri thalassinus. 10col, Notiochelindon cyanoleuca.

1984, Jan. 9 Litho. *Perf. 13½*

287 A136 10c multicolored .55 .25
288 A136 50c multicolored .65 .25
289 A136 1col multicolored .65 .25
290 A136 1.50col multicolored .65 .25
291 A136 3col multicolored 1.50 .25
292 A136 10col multicolored 4.75 .30
Nos. 287-292 (6) 8.75 1.55

Dated 1983. 10c, 1.50col, 3col vert.

José Joaquin Mora, Hero of 1856 Independence Campaign — A137

Paintings, Juan Santamaria Museum, San José: 1.50col, Pancha Carrasco. 3 col, Death of Juan Santamaria, horiz. 8.50col, Juan Rafael Mora Porras.

1984, Apr. 10 Litho. *Perf. 10½*

293 A137 50c multi .25 .25
294 A137 1.50col multi .25 .25
295 A137 3col multi .25 .25
296 A137 8.50col multi .80 .55
Nos. 293-296 (4) 1.55 1.30

For surcharge see No. 440.

Jesus Bonilla Chavarria, Composer A138

Musicians and Composers: 5col, Benjamin Gutierrez (b. 1937). 12col, Pilar Jimenez (1835-1922). 13col, Jose Daniel Zuniga Zeledon (1889-1981).

1984, May 30 Litho. *Perf. 13½*

297 A138 3.50col black & lil .30 .25
298 A138 5col black & pink .40 .25
299 A138 12col black & grn 1.00 .80
300 A138 13col black & yel 1.25 .90
Nos. 297-300 (4) 2.95 2.20

Figurines, Jade Museum — A139

1984, June 27 Litho. *Perf. 13½*

301 A139 4col Man (pendant) .80 .25
302 A139 7col Seated man 1.60 .40
303 A139 10col Dish, horiz. 2.10 .50
Nos. 301-303 (3) 4.50 1.15

1984 Summer Olympics A140

1984, July 27

304 A140 1col Basketball .25 .25
305 A140 8col Swimming .65 .25
306 A140 11col Bicycling .90 .40
307 A140 14col Running 1.25 .65
308 A140 20col Boxing 1.60 1.25
309 A140 30col Soccer 2.50 1.40
Nos. 304-309 (6) 7.15 4.20

Public Street Lighting Centenary A141

1984, Aug. 9 Litho. *Perf. 10½*

310 A141 6col Street scene by Luis Chacon .55 .40

10th Natl. Stamp Exhibition, Sept. 10-16 — A142

No. 311, Natl. monument. No. 312, Juan Mora Fernandez monument.

1984, Sept. 10 Litho. *Perf. 10½*

311 A142 10col multicolored .90 .55
312 A142 10col multicolored .90 .55
a. Min. sheet, 2 each #311-312 15.00 10.00

Natl. Arms — A143

1984, Oct. 29 Engr. *Perf. 14x13½*

313 A143 100col dk green 8.00 3.75
314 A143 100col yel org 8.00 3.75

Detail from Sistine Virgin by Raphael — A144

1984, Dec. 7 Litho. *Perf. 10½*

315 3col multicolored .25 .25
316 3col multicolored .25 .25
a. A144 Pair, #315-316 2.00 2.00

20th Intl. Bicycle Race, Costa Rica — A146

1984, Dec. 19 Litho. *Perf. 13½*

317 A146 6col multi .65 .30

Intl. Youth Year A147

1985, Jan. 31 *Perf. 10½*

322 A147 11col IYY emblem, #C476 1.60 .55

Scouting Movement, 75th anniv.

Labor Monument, San Jose — A148

Natl. values: 11col, Freedom of speech-wooden hand printing press. 13col, Neutrality-dove, natl. flag, outline map.

1985, Feb. 28

323 A148 6col shown .80 .30
324 A148 11col bl, blk & yel 1.25 .50
325 A148 13col multi 1.40 .55

Size: 68x38mm

326 A148 30col Nos. 323-325 4.00 1.10
Nos. 323-326 (4) 7.45 2.45

Natl. Red Cross Cent., UN 40th Anniv. A149

1985, May 3 *Perf. 10½*

327 A149 3col No. 163, horiz. 2.00 .25
328 A149 5col No. C120 3.00 .25

Club Emblem A150

1st Club Pres., Ricardo Saprissa Ayma A151

Design: No. 330, Hands holding soccer ball.

1985, July 16 *Perf. 10½*

329 A150 3col multi .50 .25
330 A150 3col multi .50 .25
a. Pair, #329-330 1.50 1.00
331 A151 6col multi 1.00 .30
Nos. 329-331 (3) 2.00 .80

Saprissa Soccer Club, 50th Anniv.

Orchids — A152

No. 332, Brassia arcuigera. No. 333, Encyclia peraltensis. No. 334, Maxillaria especie. No. 335, Oncidium turialbae. No. 336, Trichopilia marginata. No. 337, Stanhopea ecornuta.

1985, Dec. 3

332 A152 6col multicolored 3.50 .80
333 A152 6col multicolored 3.50 .80
334 A152 6col multicolored 3.50 .80
a. Strip of 3, #332-334 14.50 5.00
335 A152 13col multicolored 4.00 1.40
336 A152 13col multicolored 4.00 1.40
337 A152 13col multicolored 4.00 1.40
a. Strip of 3, #335-337 16.50 5.50
Nos. 332-337 (6) 22.50 6.60

11th Natl. Philatelic Exposition A153

1985, Dec. 3 Litho. *Perf. 13½*

338	A153	20col No. C41	1.25	.55

Christmas 1985 — A153a

1985, Dec. 12 Litho. *Perf. 10½*

338A	A153a	3col multi	.40	.25

Compulsory Education, Cent. A154

Designs: 3col, Primary school, horiz. 30col, Mauro Fernandez Acuna, founder.

1986, Feb. 28 *Perf. 13½*

339	A154	3col pale yel & brn	.25	.25
340	A154	30col pale pink & brn	1.60	.80

Agriculture Students — A155

1986, Mar. 21 *Perf. 10½*

341		10col Students on farm	.50	.25
342		10col IDB emblem	.50	.25
343		10col Capo Bianco fisherman	.50	.25
a.		A155 Strip of 3, #341-343	3.00	3.00
		Nos. 341-343 (3)	1.50	.75

Inter-American Development Bank Annual Governors' Assembly, San Jose.

Presidents Type of 1943

Designs: Nos. 344, 349, 354, 359, 364, Francisco J. Orlich Bolmarcich, 1962-66.

Nos. 345, 350, 355, 360, 365, Jose Joaquin Trejos Fernandez, 1966-70.

Nos. 346, 351, 356, 361, 366, Daniel Oduber Quiros, 1974-78.

Nos. 347, 352, 357, 362, 367, Rodrigo Carazo Odio, 1978-82.

Nos. 348, 353, 358, 363, 368, Luis Alberto Monge Alvarez, 1982-86.

1986, May 12 Litho. *Perf. 10½*

344	A109	3col turq blue	.40	.25
345	A109	3col turq blue	.40	.25
346	A109	3col turq blue	.40	.25
347	A109	3col turq blue	.40	.25
348	A109	3col turq blue	.40	.25
a.		Strip of 5, #344-348	*2.25*	*1.90*
349	A109	6col yel brn	.65	.25
350	A109	6col yel brn	.65	.25
351	A109	6col yel brn	.65	.25
352	A109	6col yel brn	.65	.25
353	A109	6col yel brn	.65	.25
a.		Strip of 5, #349-353	5.00	4.50
354	A109	10col brn org	.95	.30
355	A109	10col brn org	.95	.30
356	A109	10col brn org	.95	.30
357	A109	10col brn org	.95	.30
358	A109	10col brn org	.95	.30
a.		Strip of 5, #354-358	8.25	8.00
359	A109	11col slate gray	1.25	.40
360	A109	11col slate gray	1.25	.40
361	A109	11col slate gray	1.25	.40
362	A109	11col slate gray	1.25	.40
363	A109	11col slate gray	1.25	.40
a.		Strip of 5, #359-363	10.00	9.00
364	A109	13col olive	1.60	.45
365	A109	13col olive	1.60	.45
366	A109	13col olive	1.60	.45
367	A109	13col olive	1.60	.45
368	A109	13col olive	1.60	.45
a.		Strip of 5, #364-368	13.50	10.50
		Nos. 344-368 (25)	24.25	8.25
		Nos. 348a-368a (5)	39.00	

1986 World Cup Soccer Championships, Mexico — A156

1986, May 30 Litho. *Perf. 13½*

369	A156	1col Players	.30	.25
370	A156	1col Character trademark, vert.	.30	.25
371	A156	4col as No. 370	1.40	.25
372	A156	6col as No. 369	2.00	.25
373	A156	11col Players, diff.	4.00	.40
		Nos. 369-373 (5)	8.00	1.40

A second printing of No. 370 differs in paper and shade from the first printing, but the most obvious difference is in the absence of the initials "LIL" by the left foot of the soccer player. Unused stamps are rare. Value for used, $3.

Intl. Peace Year — A157

Peace in many languages: a, "Hoa binh," etc. b, "Vrede," etc. c, "Pace," etc.

1986, July 31 Litho. *Perf. 10½*

374		Strip of 3	4.50	1.25
a.-c.		A157 5col, any single	.55	.25

A158

Gold Museum, Central Bank of Costa Rica — A158a

Designs: Various undescribed works of Pre-Columbian art.

1986, Sept. 19 *Perf. 10½*

375	A158	Strip of 5	6.00	1.00
a.-e.		6col any single	.40	.25
376	A158a	Strip of 5	10.50	2.00
a.-e.		13col any single	.80	.40

Exist perf 13½, value $11.50 for the two strips of 5 unused

A159

Fauna and Flora — A160

2col, Centurio senex. 3col, Glossophaga soricina. 4col, Ectophylla alba. 5col, Ectophylla alba, diff. 6col, Agalychnis callidryas. 10col, Dendrobates pumilio. 11col, Hyla ebraccata. 20col, Phyllobates lugubris. 50col, Agalychnis callidryas, diff.

1986, Dec. 16 Litho. *Perf. 13x13½*

377	A159	2col multicolored	.25	.25
378	A159	3col multicolored	.45	.25
379	A159	4col multicolored	.60	.25
380	A159	5col multicolored	.85	.25
381	A159	6col multicolored	1.00	.25
382	A159	10col multicolored	1.40	.25
383	A159	11col multicolored	1.60	.40
384	A159	20col multicolored	2.40	.65
		Nos. 377-384 (8)	8.55	2.55

Souvenir Sheet

Perf. 12½x12

385	A160	50col multicolored	*60.00*	*40.00*

Natl. Science and Technology Day — A161

Mural (detail), by Francisco Amighetti, Clorito Picado Social Security Clinic.

1987, July 31 Litho. *Perf. 10½*

386	A161	8col multi	*4.00*	.25

Natl. Museum, Cent. A162

Artifacts: No. 387a, Dowel-shaped figure of a man. No. 387b, Ape-like carved stone figurine. No. 387c, Polished stone ritual figure. No. 387d, Carved granite capital. No. 387e, Two-legged pot. No. 388a, Bowl. No. 388b, Sculpture. No. 388c, Water jar.

1987, Aug. 7

387		Strip of 5	5.00	2.40
a.-e.		A162 8col any single, vert.	.40	.25
388		Strip of 3	5.00	2.75
a.-c.		A162 15col any single	.65	.25
		Nos. 387-388 (2)	10.00	5.15

Horse-drawn Wagon — A163

No. 390, Street in old San Jose. No. 391, Provincial coat of arms.

1987, Oct. 26

389	A163	20col shown	.95	.50
390	A163	20col multicolored	.95	.50
a.		Pair, #389-390	2.00	2.00
391	A163	20col multicolored	.95	.50
		Nos. 389-391 (3)	2.85	1.50

City of San Jose, 250th anniv. Rotary Club, 60th anniv.

Columbus Day A164

1987, Oct. 26 *Perf. 10½*

392	A164	30col Map, 16th cent.	2.25	.65

Day of the Race; 495th anniv. of Columbus's departure from Palos, Spain, on first journey to the New World.

Discovery of America, 500th Anniv. (in 1992) — A165

Maps of Honduras, Nicaragua, Costa Rica and Panama, believed to be Asia by Columbus: No. 393, Costa Rica, 16th cent. No. 394, Map of "Asia" by Bartholomeu Columbus (1461-1514).

1987, Nov. 20 Litho. *Perf. 13½*

393	A165	4col yel & dk red brn	.25	.25
394	A165	4col yel & dk red brn	.25	.25
a.		Pair, #393-394	2.00	2.00

Pres. Oscar Arias, 1987 Nobel Peace Prize Winner — A166

1987, Dec. 2 *Perf. 10½*

395	A166	10col multi	*2.50*	.30

Two Houses, a Watercolor by Fausto Pacheco (1899-1966) A167

1987, Dec. 22 Litho. *Perf. 10½*

396	A167	1col multi	.55	.30

Intl. Year of Shelter for the Homeless.

17th General Conference for the Preservation of Natural Resources A168

1988, Feb. 1 Litho. *Perf. 13½*

397	A168	5col Green turtle	.80	.25
398	A168	5col Emblem, golden toad	.80	.25
399	A168	5col Blue butterfly	.80	.25
a.		A168 Strip of 3, #397-399	2.50	2.50

Intl. Red Cross and Red Crescent Organizations, 125th Annivs. — A169

1988, Apr. 18 Litho. *Perf. 10½*

400 A169 30col lt blue & dark red 1.40 .65

North and South Campaign A170

1988, June 6 Photo. *Perf. 11½*

Granite Paper

401 A170 18col Adult education 2.40 .25
402 A170 20col Cultural radio programs 2.40 .25

Cultural cooperation with Liechtenstein. See Liechtenstein Nos. 886-887. For overprint see No. C921.

A171

1988, June 27 Litho. *Perf. 10½*

403 A171 3col dk blue, dark red & yel .40 .25

Anglo-Costa Rican Bank, 125th anniv.

A172

No. 404, Character trademark. No. 405, Games emblem.

1988, Sept. 16 Litho. *Perf. 13½*

404 A172 25col multicolored .95 .50
405 A172 25col multicolored .95 .50
a. Pair, #404-405 5.00 5.00

1988 Summer Olympics, Seoul.

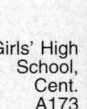

Girls' High School, Cent. A173

1988, Oct. 17 Litho. *Perf. 10½*

406 A173 10col Student, courtyard .50 .25

A174

1988, Nov. 18

407 A174 10col gray, greenish bl & red brn .40 .25

Educator Omar Dengo (1888-1928) and the Teachers' College, Heredia.

A175

Indian glass-bead and lion-tooth necklace.

1988, Nov. 28 *Perf. 13½*

408 A175 4col multi .25 .25

Discovery of America, 500th anniv. (in 1992).

A176

1988, Dec. 26 Litho. *Perf. 10½*

409 A176 2col Observation tower .65 .30

Natl. Meteorological Institute, cent. For surcharge see No. 439.

A177

Indigenous flora: 5col, Eschweilera costarricensis. 10col, Heliconia wagneriana. 15col, Heliconia lophocarpa. 20col, Aechmea magdalenae. 25col, Psammisia ramiflora. 30col, Passiflora vitifolia.

1989, Feb. 28

410 A177 5col multicolored .50 .25
411 A177 10col multicolored .95 .25
412 A177 15col multicolored 1.25 .25
413 A177 20col multicolored 1.50 .25
414 A177 25col multicolored 1.75 .25
415 A177 30col multicolored 2.25 .25
Nos. 410-415 (6) 8.20 1.50

A178

1989, July 1 Litho. *Perf. 10½*

416 A178 30col Nation at Arms 1.40 .50

French Revolution, bicent.

A179

1989, Aug. 28 Litho. *Perf. 13½*

417 A179 10col Sugar mill .65 .25

Grecia County, 151st anniv.
For overprints see Nos. RA106-RA109.

America Issue — A180

UPAE emblem and pre-Columbian stone carvings: 50col, Three-footed bench for grinding corn. 100col, Sphere.

Litho. & Engr.

Perf. 12½x12

1989, Oct. 12 Wmk. 334

418 A180 50col multi 2.50 1.10
419 A180 100col multi 5.50 1.75

For overprint see No. C916.

A181

Perf. 10½

1989, Oct. 23 Litho. Unwmk.

420 A181 10col Orchid *2.00* .25

"100 Years of Democracy" summit of Presidents.

A182

Perf. 13½

1989, Nov. 27 Litho. Unwmk.

421 A182 18col Map, H.F. Pittier, emblem .80 .25

Natl. Geographic Institute, cent.
For surcharge see No. 452.

America Issue — A183

Pre-Columbian gold frog figurine and facing portraits of Ferdinand V and Isabella I on gold coin struck by Spain from 1476 to 1516.

1989, Dec. 4 *Perf. 10½*

422 A183 4col multicolored .25 .25

Discovery of America, 500th anniv. (in 1992).

Natl. Theater, Cent. A184

Perf. 10½

1990, Feb. 27 Litho. Unwmk.

423 A184 5col *Coffee Allegory* .65 .30

World Cup Soccer Championships, Italy — A185

1990, June 1 Litho. *Perf. 10½*

424 A185 5col multicolored .25 .25

Univ. of Costa Rica, 50th Anniv. A187

1990, Aug. 24 Litho. *Perf. 10½*

426 A187 18col multicolored .75 .25

Education, Democracy, Peace — A188

Litho. & Engr.

1990, Oct. 31 *Perf. 12½*

427 A188 100col shown 2.25 1.10
428 A188 200col Flag as map 4.50 1.75
429 A188 500col National arms 12.00 4.50
Nos. 427-429 (3) 18.75 7.35

"Invisible" security printing is sometimes visible.

For overprints see Nos. 448, C920. For surcharges see Nos. 546-548, 553.

Hospitals — A190

No. 431, St. Vincent de Paul Hospital, Heredia. No. 432, Natl. Psychiatric hospital.

1990, Dec. 18 Engr. *Perf. 13x12½*

431 A190 50col multicolored 1.90 .60
432 A190 100col multicolored 3.25 .80

America Issue — A191

1990, Dec. 21 Litho. *Perf. 10½*

433 A191 18col Ara macao 1.00 .40
434 A191 18col Ara ambigua 1.00 .40
a. Pair, #433-434 8.00 8.00

435 A191 24col Cassia grandis 1.90 1.90
436 A191 24col Tabebuia ochracea 1.90 1.90
a. Pair, #435-436 8.00 8.00
Nos. 433-436 (4) 5.80 4.60

Costa Rica-Panama Border Treaty, 50th Anniv. — A192

Designs: a, Flags, national arms. b, Presidents. c, Map.

1991, May 24 Litho. *Perf. 10½*
437 Strip of 3 4.00 2.50
a.-c. A192 10col Any single 1.00 .60

Discovery of America, 500th Anniv. (in 1992) — A193

1991, Oct. 11 Litho. *Perf. 13½*
438 A193 4col multicolored .70 .25

No. 409 Surcharged

No. 296 Surcharged

1991, Oct. 21 Litho. *Perf. 10½*
439 A176 1col on 2col #409 .30 .25
440 A137 3col on 8.50col #296 .30 .25

Former Presidents, Supreme Court of Justice — A194

Designs: a, Benito Serrano Jimenez. b, Luis Davila Solera. c, Fernando Baudrit Solera. d, Alejandro Alvarado Garcia.

Perf. 14½x13½
1992, Feb. 28 Litho.
441 A194 5col Strip of 4, #a.-d. 3.50 2.00

A sheet exists containing an unissued 5th stamp. Value, sheet $500.

DINADECO, Natl. Directorate of Community Development, 25th Anniv. A195

1992, Apr. 28 Litho. *Perf. 10½*
442 A195 15col multicolored 3.00 .60

Compare with No. C505.

A196

1992, May 26 Litho. *Perf. 13½*
443 A196 15col lake & black 1.25 .35

Dr. Solon Nunez Frutos, public health pioneer.

A197

Solar Eclipse: a, Total eclipse. b, Post Office Bldg. during eclipse. c, Partial eclipse.

1992, July 17 Litho. *Perf. 13*
444 A197 45col Strip of 3, #a.-c. 10.00 6.00

A198

1992, Aug. 14 Litho. *Perf. 13½*
445 A198 35col multicolored 2.00 .60

Interamerican Institute for Agricultural Cooperation, 50th anniv.

A199

1992, Nov. 5 Litho. *Perf. 10½*
446 A199 2col Waterfall .70 .30
447 A199 15col Coastline 1.00 .40

Cocos Island, 450th anniv. of discovery.

No. 427 Overprinted

Litho. & Engr.
1992, Nov. 27 *Perf. 12½*
448 A188 100col black & blue 5.00 2.50

America Issue A200

1992, Dec. 15 Litho. *Perf. 10½*
449 A200 15col Anolis townsendi *3.50* .30
450 A200 35col Pinaroloxias inornata *5.50* .50

Natl. Theater A201

Detail from painting "Allegory of Fine Arts," by Roberto Fontana.

1993, Jan. 29 Litho. *Perf. 10½*
451 A201 20col multicolored .80 .25

No. 421 Surcharged

1993, Mar. 26 Litho. *Perf. 13½*
452 A182 5col on 18col multi .50 .25

50,000 stamps originally were overprinted with a tiny block and four thin bars over the value, but this was considered unacceptable. So these stamps plus 1,550,000 unoverprinted stamps were overprinted with the large black square and surcharge, as shown.

Protection of the Dolphin A202

10col, Delphinus delphis. 20col, Stenella coeruleoalbus.

1993, May 17 Litho. *Perf. 10½*
453 A202 10col multicolored 2.50 .50
454 A202 20col multicolored 4.50 .50

Costa Rican Civil Service, 40th Anniv. — A203

1993, May 28 Litho. *Perf. 13½*
455 A203 5col multicolored .45 .25

Costa Rican Chamber of Industries, 50th Anniv. A204

1993, July 15 *Perf. 10½*
456 A204 45col multicolored 1.40 .90

School of Communication Sciences, University of Costa Rica, 25th Anniv. — A205

1993, Aug. 19 Litho. *Perf. 13½*
457 A205 20col black, blue & red 1.00 .50

Protection of the Tropical Rain Forest — A206

1993, Aug. 27 *Perf. 10½*
458 A206 2col Passiflora vitifolia 1.40 .40
459 A206 35col Gurania megistantha 2.50 .80

Social Guarantees and Labor Code, 50th Anniv. A207

1993, Sept. 14 Litho. *Perf. 10½*
460 A207 20col multicolored .50 .30

A208

1993, Oct. 25 Litho. *Perf. 13½*
461 A208 45col multicolored 1.00 .70

Intl. Assoc. of Professional Custom-House Agents, 15th Congress.

A209

1993, Nov. 26 *Perf. 10½*
462 A209 20col multicolored .65 .30

Miguel Angel Castro Carazo (1893-1960), educator and humanitarian.

For surcharge see No. 481.

A211

1993, Dec. 23 Litho. *Perf. 10½*
464 A211 20col multicolored .55 .30

Law School of Costa Rica, 150th anniv.

A212

1994, Mar. 18 Litho. *Perf. 13*

465	A212	20col Natl. Theater	.55	.30

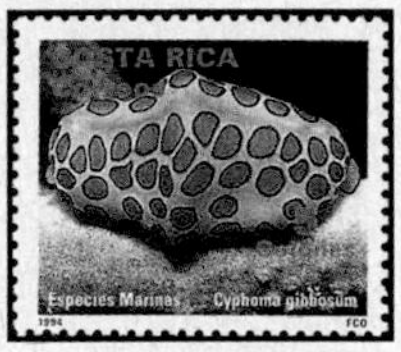

Marine Life — A213

5col, Cyphoma gibbosum. 10col, Ophioderma rubicundum. 15col, Myripristis jacobus. 20col, Holocanthus passer. 35col, Paranthias furcifer. 45col, Tubastraea coccinea. 50col, Acanthaster plancl. 55col, Ocypode. 70col, Arothron meleagris. 100col, Thalassoma lucasanum.

Litho. & Embossed

1994, Apr. 29 *Perf. 12½x12*

466	A213	5col multicolored	.40	.25
467	A213	10col multicolored	.80	.25
468	A213	15col multicolored	1.25	.30
469	A213	20col multicolored	1.60	.35
470	A213	35col multicolored	2.75	.55
471	A213	45col multicolored	3.50	.75
472	A213	50col multicolored	4.00	.85
473	A213	55col multicolored	4.50	.95
474	A213	70col multicolored	5.50	1.25
		Nos. 466-474 (9)	24.30	5.50

Souvenir Sheet

Perf. 13

475	A213	100col multicolored	11.00	8.00

America Issue A214

Illustrations from 19th century Book of Figueroa: a, Man on horseback. b, Back of ox carrying bundles.

1994, Dec. 19 Litho. *Perf. 10½*

476	A214	20col Pair, #a.-b. + label	1.75	1.40

No. 476 is a continuous design.

Rotary Intl., 90th Anniv. — A215

1995, Mar. Litho. *Perf. 13½*

477	A215	20col multicolored	.90	.40

Antonio Jose de Sucre (1795-1830) — A216

Design: 30col, Jose Marti (1853-95).

1995, June Litho. *Perf. 10½*

478	A216	10col multicolored	.25	.25
479	A216	30col multicolored	.65	.65

Guanacaste Institute, 50th Anniv. — A217

1995, July 24 *Perf. 13½*

480	A217	50col grn, blk & bis	1.00	1.00

No. 462 Surcharged in Blue or Black

1995, Sept. 11 Litho. *Perf. 10½*

481	A209	5col on 20col multi	.30	.25

UN, 50th Anniv. — A218

1995, Oct. 24 Litho. *Perf. 10½*

482	A218	5col multicolored	.40	.25

13th Natl. Philatelic Expo — A219

Paintings by Lola Fernández: No. 483, Noviembre. No. 484, Enero.

1995, Dec. 1

483	A219	50col multicolored	1.00	1.00
484	A219	50col multicolored	1.00	1.00
a.		Pair, Nos. 483-484	3.00	3.00

America Issue A220

30col, Jabiru mycteria. No. 486, View of coast. No. 487, River, trees. 50col, Atta cephalotes.

1995, Dec. 25 Litho. *Rouletted 13½*

485	A220	30col multicolored	1.50	.80
486	A220	40col multicolored	1.50	1.25
487	A220	40col multicolored	1.50	1.25
a.		Pair, #486-487	3.50	3.00
488	A220	50col multicolored	2.00	1.50
a.		Souvenir sheet, #485-488	12.00	8.00
		Nos. 485-488 (4)	6.50	4.80

Seaport City of Limón A221

Designs: a, Early picture of steam train. b, Photo of ship in port, 1922. c, Aerial view of seaport, 1995. d, Painting of fruit seller, by Diego Villalobos. e, Drawing of Calipso singers, by Jorge Esquivel.

1996, Jan. 31 Litho. *Perf. 10½*

489		Strip of 5	6.00	5.00
a.-e.	A221	30col Any single	1.00	.60

Jerusalem, 3000th Anniv. — A222

1996, May 17 Litho. *Perf. 13½*

490	A222	30col multicolored	.80	.65

1996 Summer Olympic Games, Atlanta A223

Olympic swimmers, coaches from Costa Rica: a, F. Rivas, M.M. Paris. b, S. Poll, R. Yglesias. c, C. Poll, A. Cruz.

1996, July 18 Litho. *Perf. 10½*

491		Strip of 3	3.00	3.00
a.-c.	A223	5col Any single	1.00	.50

No. 491 is a continuous design.

A224

First lady, presidents: a, Juana del Castillo. b, Juan Mora Fernández. c, J.M. Castro Madriz. d, Pacífica Fernández.

1996, Sept. 13 Litho. *Perf. 10½*

492		Block of 4, #a.-d.	3.00	3.00
a.-d.	A224	30col Any single	1.00	.60

Independence, 175th anniv. No. 492 was issued in sheets of 16 stamps.

A225

1996, Oct. 4 Litho. *Perf. 13½*

493	A225	15col multicolored	.40	.25

Aqueducts and sewage systems, 35th anniv. Exists imperf.

A226

America issue (Paintings): No. 494, Black from Lemon, by Manuel da la Cruz González. No. 495, Peasant Women, by Gonzalo Morales Alvarado, vert.

1996, Dec. 16 *Perf. 10½*

494	A226	45col multicolored	2.50	1.00
495	A226	45col multicolored	2.50	1.00

A227

Entrance of the Saints at San Ramón, parade of people: a, Building with palm trees on top. b, Church on hill. c, Tree, holy family.

1997, Aug. 14 Litho. *Perf. 13½*

496	A227	30col Strip of 3, #a.-c.	4.00	2.50

Costa Rican traditions.

School of Fine Arts, Cent. A228

1997, Sept. 24 *Perf. 10½*

497	A228	50col multicolored	1.40	.70

Radio Netherlands, 50th Anniv. — A229

1997, Sept. 26 *Perf. 13½*

498	A229	45col multicolored	1.10	.65

Exists imperf.

14th Natl. Philatelic Exhibition A230

1997, Oct. 9 *Perf. 10½*

499	A230	30col Postmen	1.00	.50

America Issue.

Church of the Immaculate Conception, Heredia, Bicent. — A231

1997, Nov. 10 Litho. *Perf. 10½*

502	A231	50col multicolored	1.25	1.00

Second Republic, 50th Anniv. — A232

Former Pres. José Figueres demolishing wall of Fort Bellavista: 10col, 45col, Complete photo. 30col, Detail of Figueres' head. 50col, Hammer head hitting wall.

Litho. & Engr.

1998, Mar. 30 *Perf. 12½*

503	A232	10col multicolored	.60	.30
504	A232	30col multicolored	.90	.30
505	A232	45col multicolored	1.40	.30
506	A232	50col multicolored	1.50	.40
a.		Souvenir sheet of 2, #504, 506	4.50	3.25

Natl. University, 25th Anniv. — A233

1998, July 27 Litho. *Perf. 10½*
507 A233 50col multicolored 2.50 1.25

Butterflies A234

10col, Caligo memnon. 15col, Morpho peleides. 20col, Papilio thoas. 30col, Siproeta stelenes. 35col, Ascia monuste. 40col, Parides iphidamas. 45col, Smyrna blonfildia. 50col, Callicore pitheas. 55col, Historis odius. 60col, Danaus plexippus.

1998, July 16

508	A234	10col multicolored	.80	.30
509	A234	15col multicolored	1.25	.40
510	A234	20col multicolored	1.75	.60
511	A234	30col multicolored	2.50	.90
512	A234	35col multicolored	3.00	1.10
513	A234	40col multicolored	3.25	1.25
514	A234	45col multicolored	3.50	1.40
515	A234	50col multicolored	4.00	1.50
516	A234	55col multicolored	4.50	1.75
517	A234	60col multicolored	5.50	1.90
		Nos. 508-517 (10)	30.05	11.10

1998 World Cup Soccer Championships, France — A235

1998, Feb. 27 Litho. *Perf. 10½*
518 A235 50col multicolored 1.25 1.00

A236

1998, Nov. 30 Litho. *Perf. 13½*
519 A236 50col brn, yel brn & lt yel 2.00 .80

Carmen Lyra (1888-1949), author.

A237

1998, Dec. 11 Litho. *Perf. 13½*
520 A237 50col multicolored 2.50 1.40

Gandhi (1869-1948).

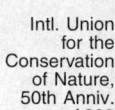

Intl. Union for the Conservation of Nature, 50th Anniv. A238

Turtles: a, Rhinociemmys pulcherrima. b, Trachemys scripta. c, Chelydra serpentina.

1998, Dec. 1

521	A238 Strip of 3		10.00	10.00
a.	A238 70col multi		3.50	3.50
b.	A238 60col multi		3.00	3.00
c.	A238 70col multi		3.50	3.50

Mushrooms A239

No. 522: a, Morchella esculenta. b, Boletus edulis.

1999, July 2 Litho. *Perf. 10½*
522 Pair 4.50 4.50
a.-b. A239 50col Either single 2.25 2.25

SOS Children's Villages, 50th Anniv. — A240

1999, June Litho. *Perf. 10½*
523 A240 50col multicolored 2.50 .90

Costa Rican Institute of Electricity, 50th Anniv. A241

1999, Sept. 21 Litho. *Perf. 13¼*
524 A241 75col multi .80 .60

A242

1999, Oct. 7 Engr. *Perf. 13¾x14*
525 A242 300col violet 3.00 3.00

Archbishop Víctor M. Sanabria (1899-1952). See No. 538.

A243

1999, Oct. 29 Litho. *Perf. 13¼*
526 A243 50col multi .80 .50

Intl. Year of Older Persons.

Supreme Election Tribunal, 50th Anniv. A244

1999, Nov. 5 *Perf. 10½*
527 A244 70col multi 1.80 .80

UPU, 125th Anniv. — A245

1999, Dec. 1 *Perf. 13¼*
528 A245 75col multi .90 .70

Carmen Granados (1915-99), Humorist — A246

1999, Dec. 1
529 A246 50col multi .90 .60

America Issue, A New Millennium Without Arms — A247

1999, Dec. 1
530 A247 50col shown .75 .50
531 A247 70col Face, hands, diff. 1.00 .70

PhilexFrance '99 — A248

1999, Dec. 1
532 A248 300col shown 5.00 3.50
533 A248 300col Flower, Eiffel Tower 5.00 3.50

Natl. Bank, 50th Anniv. — A249

No. 534 — Pre-Columbian artifacts: a, Jaguar. b, Scorpion. c, Bat. d, Crab. e, Beast with horns.

No. 535 — Obverse and reverse of coins: a, Gold, from 1825. b, Gold, from 1850. c, Silver one-eighth peso. d, Gold 20-peso. e, 1935 1-colon.

2000, Jan. 28 Litho. *Perf. 13¼*
534 Vert. strip of 5 9.50 7.00
a.-e. A249 60col Any single 1.25 1.00
535 Vert. strip of 5 22.50 12.50
a.-e. A249 90col Any single 3.00 1.50

2000 Summer Olympics, Sydney — A250

No. 536, 60col: a, Taekwando. b, Cycling. c, Swimming. d, Soccer.

No. 537, 70col: a, Running. b, Boxing. c, Men's rings. d, Tennis.

2000, Aug. 31 Blocks of 4, #a-d
536-537 A250 Set of 2 10.00 10.00

There were two printings of Nos. 536-537. In the first printing, colors are paler, and the green Olympic ring is misregistered on Nos. 536a-536d. In the second, colors are more intense, and the green ring is properly registered. Values the same.

Famous Person Type of 1999

Pres. Rafael A. Calderón Guardia (1900-70).

2000, Sept. 14 Engr. *Perf. 12½*
538 A242 100col deep blue 1.10 .50
a. Perf 13¾x14 3.25 1.50

Paintings by Max Jiménez — A251

No. 539: a, Fishermen in Cojimar. b, Adamant.

2000, Nov. Litho. *Perf. 10½*
539 Horiz. pair 4.00 2.50
a.-b. A251 50col Either single 1.00 .50

America Issue, Fight Against AIDS — A252

Designs: 60col, Stylized people. 90col, Stylized person.

2000, Dec. *Perf. 13¼*
540-541 A252 Set of 2 2.50 2.00

Christmas — A253

2000, Dec.
542 A253 100col multi 1.60 1.25

America Issue — UNESCO World Heritage A254

Birds form Cocos Island Natl. Park: 95col, Coccyzus ferrugineus. 115col, Pinaroloxias inornata.

2001, Apr. 5 Litho. *Perf. 10½*
543-544 A254 Set of 2 6.00 4.00

Costa Rica — Netherlands Diplomatic Relations, 150th Anniv. — A255

2001, July 20
545 A255 65col multi 1.00 .75

No. 429 Surcharged

2001 Method and Perf. As Before
546 A188 65col on 500col multi 1.00 .75
547 A188 80col on 500col multi 1.25 1.00
548 A188 95col on 500col multi 1.50 1.10
Nos. 546-548 (3) 3.75 2.85

Issued: No. 846, 8/24. Nos. 547-548, 9/7.

Third Hispanic-Costa Rican Exposition — A256

Orchids: a, Guaria turrialba. b, Tricopilia.

2001, Oct. 5 Litho. *Perf. 13¼*
549 A256 65col Horiz. pair, #a-b 2.50 2.50

Campaign Against Child Labor — A257

2001, Nov. 15 *Perf. 13¼*
550 A257 100col multi 1.60 1.25

Pres. Tomás Guardia (1832-82) and Locomotive — A258

2001, Nov. 21
551 A258 65col multi 2.00 .80

A second printing of No. 551 was issued in 2002. It features a lighter beige and has yellow gum. This printing of 500 sheets of 15 stamps was made to complete the contract. Value, unused $25.

Costa Rican Team for 2002 World Cup Soccer Championships, Japan and Korea — A259

2002, Mar. 15 *Perf. 10½*
552 A259 65col multi 1.50 .80

No. 428 Surcharged in Red

Litho. & Engr.
2002, Jan. 24 *Perf. 12½*
553 A188 65col on 200col multi 1.00 .75

America Issue — Youth, Education and Literacy — A260

Designs: 65col, Children and globe. 100col, Blind person reading Braille.

Litho. & Embossed
2002, Mar. *Perf. 10½*
554-555 A260 Set of 2 2.50 2.00

Taiwan Friendship Bridge A261

2002, Apr. 3 Litho.
556 A261 95col multi 1.25 1.00

16th Rio Group Congress A262

2002, Apr. 10
557 A262 65col blue & green 1.00 .75

Pan-American Health Organization, Cent. — A263

No. 558: a, People (red denomination at UR). b, Emblem. c, Mother and child (black denomination at LR). d, Child and man (red denomination at LR).
50col, Emblem.

2002, July 5
558 A263 10col Block of 4, #a-d .65 .65
559 A263 50col multi .70 .70

In Remembrance of Sept. 11, 2001 Terrorist Attacks — A264

Litho. & Embossed
2002, Sept. 11
560 A264 110col multi 4.00 2.00

Marine Life of Uvita Island A265

Designs: No. 561, 75col, Gorgona flabellum. No. 562, 75col, Ulva lactuca. No. 563, 75col, Cittarium pica. No. 564, 75col, Liriope tetraphyla.

Litho & Embossed
2002, Sept. 25
561-564 A265 Set of 4 6.00 6.00

Space Exploration — A266

No. 565: a, Dr. Franklin Chang-Diaz, astronaut, and space shuttle. b, Phanaeus changdiazi and satellite.

Litho. & Embossed
2003, June 15 *Perf. 10½*
565 A266 115col Horiz. pair, #a-b 4.00 4.00

Coco Island National Park — A267

No. 566: a, Denomination at UR. b, Denomination at UL.

2003, Aug. 1
566 A267 75col Horiz. pair, #a-b 3.00 3.00

America Issue - Fish — A268

No. 567: a, Archocentrus sajica. b, Astatheros diquis.

2003
567 A268 110col Horiz. pair, #a-b 5.00 5.00

Scenes from Cocorí, by Joaquín Gutiérrez — A269

No. 568: a, Boy, turtle, monkey and bird. b, Boy looking at reflection in water. c, Toucan in tree, boy and monkey on ground. d, Sailor, girl and boy. e, Boy, bird on branch. f, Jaguar, turtle armadillo, monkey, boy and father. g, Boy and monkey pushing turtle. h, Monkey with open arms, turtle, boy. i, Mother and boy. j, Mother, boy, rose bush. k, Boy, father playing musical instrument (80x150mm).

Litho. & Embossed
2003, Sept. 3 *Perf. 10½*
568 A269 Sheet of 11 14.00 14.00
a.-j. 25col Any single .80 .60
k. 225col multi 5.00 5.00

National Anthem, Cent. — A270

No. 569: a, Lyricist José María Zeledón (24x35mm). b, Flag, text of anthem (49x35mm).

2003, Sept. 10 Litho.
569 A270 75col Horiz. pair, #a-b 4.00 4.00

Election of Pope John Paul II, 25th Anniv. — A271

2003, Oct. 16 Litho. *Perf. 13¼x13½*
570 A271 130col multi 3.00 3.00

Charles Lindbergh's Flight to Costa Rica, 75th Anniv. — A272

Litho. & Embossed
2003, Dec. 16 *Perf. 13½x13¼*
571 A272 110col multi 2.00 2.00

Guayabo de Turrialba Archaeological Monument — A273

2003, Dec. 18
572 A273 110col multi 2.00 2.00

America Issue A274

Flora: No. 573, 75col, Ceiba pentandra. No. 574, 75col, Tetranema floribundum. 90col, Ceiba pentandra, diff. 110col, Tetranema gamboanum.

2004, Mar. 23 Litho. *Perf. 10½*
573-576 A274 Set of 4 6.00 6.00

Volcanoes A275

Designs: 85col, Arenal. 120col, Irazú. 140col, Poás.

2004-05 *Perf. 10½*
577-579 A275 Set of 3 6.00 6.00
577a Perf. 13¼ ('05) 1.50 1.50
578a Perf. 13¼ ('05) 2.00 2.00
579a Perf. 13¼ ('05) 2.50 2.50

Issued: Nos. 577-579, 6/24/04; 577a, 578a, 579a, 2005.

Nos. 577a, 578a and 579a have printer's inscription "LIL S.A."

2004 Summer Olympics, Athens A276

No. 580 — Various athletes in: a, Blue. b, Yellow orange. c, Green. d, Red.

2004, July 15

580 Horiz. strip of 4 8.00 8.00
a.-d. A276 120col Any single 2.00 2.00

Dr. Miguel Angel Rodríguez, Organization of American States President A277

2004, Sept. 15

581 A277 120col multi 2.00 2.00

FIFA (Fédération Internationale de Football Association), Cent. — A278

No. 582: a, Emblem (34x34mm). b, Soccer player and field (39x34mm).

2004, Feb. 15 Litho. ***Perf. 10½***

582 A278 140col Horiz. pair, #a-b 5.00 5.00

Rotary International, Cent. — A279

No. 583: a, Emblem and frog. b, Centenary emblem. c, Emblem and butterfly.

2005, Feb. 23

583 Horiz. strip of 3 7.50 7.50
a.-c. A279 140col Any single 2.50 2.50

Souvenir Sheet

Popes — A280

No. 584: a, Pope John Paul II (1920-2005). b, Pope Benedict XVI.

2005, Aug. 22

584 A280 140col Sheet of 4, 2 each #a-b 10.00 10.00

An imperf. sheet lacking postal validity exists. Value, $150.

Intl. Year of Physics — A281

No. 585: a, Albert Einstein (1879-1955). b, Max Planck (1858-1947).

2005, June 7

585 Horiz. pair 3.50 3.50
a.-b. A281 95col Either single 1.75 1.75

Flora and Fauna in National Parks — A282

No. 586: a, Passiflora vitifolia. b, Dryas iulia moderata. c, Potos flavus.

2005, Oct. 11 Litho. ***Perf. 10½***

586 Strip of 3 4.50 4.50
a.-c. A282 85col Any single 1.40 1.40

America Issue, Fight Against Poverty — A283

No. 587: a, Child at computer. b, Man sawing wood. c, Medical worker.

2005, Oct. 19

587 Strip of 3 6.50 6.50
a.-c. A283 120col Any single 2.10 2.10

Intl. Year of Sports and Physical Education A284

2005, Dec. 6

588 A284 85col multi 1.50 1.50

Cartago Sport Club, Cent. — A285

2006, Mar. 20

589 A285 85col multi 1.75 1.75

Miniature Sheet

National Campaign Against Nicaraguan Pres. William Walker, 150th Anniv. — A286

No. 590: a, Juan Rafael Mora, National Monument. b, Juan Santamaría Monument, barracks. c, Map (50x40mm). d, Gen. José María Cañas, Santa Rosa House. e, Luis Molina, Joaquín Bernardo Calvo.

2006, Apr. 7

590 A286 85col Sheet of 5, #a-e 8.50 8.50

2006 World Cup Soccer Championships, Germany — A287

2006, May 15

591 A287 120col multi 2.40 2.40

America Issue, Energy Conservation — A288

2006, July 31 Litho. ***Perf. 10½***

592 A288 155col multi + label 3.00 3.00

Miniature Sheet

Birds and Marine Life of Cocos Island — A289

No. 593: a, Sula sula. b, Mycteroperca olfax. c, Zanclus cornutis. d, Eretmochely imbricaas. e, Tursiops truncatus. f, Myripristis berndti. g, Dendroica petechia aureola. h, Carcharhinus limbatus. i, Anous stolidus. j, Acarus rubroviolaceus.

2006, Aug. 25 Litho. ***Perf. 10½***

593 A289 180col Sheet of 10, #a-j 35.00 35.00

Pres. José Figueres Ferrer (1906-90) — A290

2006, Sept. 25 ***Perf. 10½***

594 A290 115col gray & multi 3.00 3.00

Souvenir Sheet

Imperf

595 A290 1000col tan & multi 30.00 30.00

No. 594 was printed in sheets of 6 + 3 labels. Value, $20.

Fruits A291

No. 596: a, Hymenaea courbaril. b, Bixa orellana. c, Garcinia intermedia.

2006, Oct. 12 ***Perf. 10½***

596 Strip of 3 9.00 9.00
a.-c. A291 155col Any single 3.00 3.00

National Symbols — A292

No. 597: a, Flag. b, Coat of arms.

2006, Nov. 27

597 A292 155col Pair, #a-b 6.00 6.00

Printed in sheets containing two pairs.

Pres. Francisco J. Orlich (1907-69) — A293

2007, Mar. 7
598 A293 115col multi 2.25 2.25

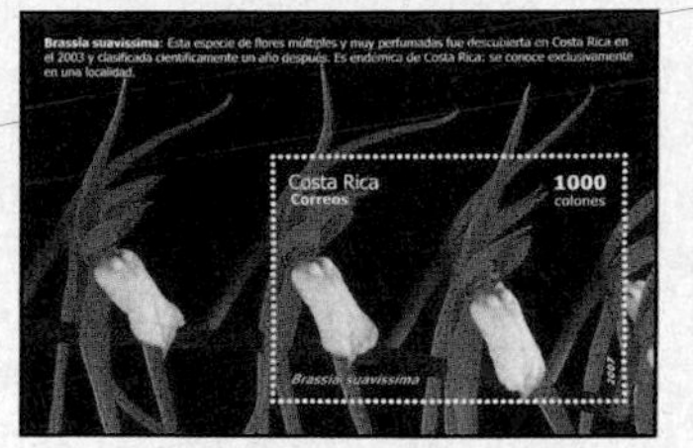

Orchids — A294

No. 599: a, Guarianthe skinneri (pink flowers). b, Galeandra arundinis. c, Encyclia ossenbachiana. d, Dracula inexperata. e, Guarianthe skinneri (white flowers). f, Kefersteinia retanae. g, Coryanthes kaiseriana. h, Psychopsis krameriana. i, Chondroscaphe yamilethae. j, Cattleya dowiana.
1000col, Brassia suavissima.

2007, Mar. 19 Litho. *Perf. 10½*
599 A294 180col Sheet of 10, #a-j 18.00 18.00

Souvenir Sheet
Imperf
600 A294 1000col multi 40.00 40.00

No. 599 contains ten 45x37mm stamps. No. 600 has simulated perforations.

Salesian Order in Costa Rica, Cent. — A295

2007, Apr. 30 *Perf. 10½*
601 A295 110col multi 2.25 2.25

Miniature Sheet

Pre-Columbian Art — A296

No. 602: a, Frog-shaped gold pendant (25x45mm). b, Bird-shaped jadeite pendant (25x45mm). c, Stone metate, horiz. (50x30mm). d, Ceramic censer with alligator (25x45mm). e, Stone figure of warrior (25x45mm).

2007, May 4
602 A296 155col Sheet of 5, #a-e 15.00 15.00

America Issue, Education For All — A297

No. 603: a, 115col, Teacher and students. b, 155col, Family around fire.

2007, June 8
603 A297 Horiz. pair, #a-b 6.00 6.00

Plasma Technology — A298

No. 604: a, Astronaut and spacecraft's robot arm. b, Plasma containment vessel.

2007, July 6
604 A298 240col Horiz. pair, #a-b 9.50 9.50

Guanacaste Musical Instruments — A299

Designs: No. 605, 115col, Marimba. No. 606, 115col, Quijongo, vert. (30x50mm).

2007, July 25
605-606 A299 Set of 2 4.50 4.50

Nos. 605-606 were printed in sheets containing two of each stamp + label.

Virgin of the Angels Icon, 225th Anniv. as Patron of Cartago — A300

No. 607 — Icon with denomination at: a, LR. b, LL.
1000col, Interior of Cartago Basilica, vert.

2007, July 27
607 A300 115col Horiz. pair, #a-b 4.50 4.50

Souvenir Sheet
608 A300 1000col multi 30.00 30.00

No. 608 contains one 75x115mm stamp.

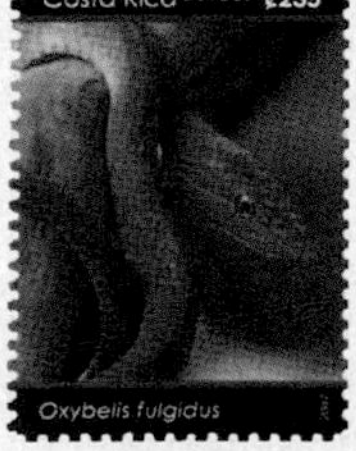

Fauna of National Parks — A301

No. 609: a, Oxybelis fulgidus. b, Stagmomantis sp. c, Heliodoxa jacula. d, Pulsatrix perspicillata.

2007, Aug. 17 Litho. *Perf. 10½*
609 Horiz. strip of 4 18.00 18.00
a.-d. A301 235col Any single 4.50 4.50

2007 Special Olympics, Shanghai — A302

No. 610: a, Cycling. b, Swimming. c, Running.

2007, Sept. 10
610 Horiz. strip of 3 14.00 14.00
a.-c. A302 240col Any single 3.50 3.50

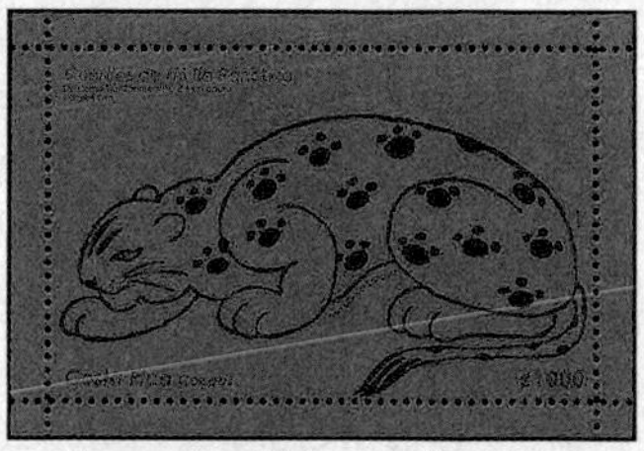

Accounts of My Aunt Panchita, Children's Book by Carmen Lyra — A303

No. 611, vert. — Text: a, Por qué Tío Conejo tiene las orejas tan largas. b, La Mica. c, Uvieta. d, Tío Conejo y los caites de su abuela.
1000col, De como Tío Conejo salió de un apuro.

2007, Oct. 18
611 A303 100col Sheet of 4, #a-d 8.00 8.00

Souvenir Sheet
612 A303 1000col multi 30.00 30.00

No. 611 contains four 37x50mm stamps.

Ox Cart Heritage — A304

No. 613: a, Man with oxen. b, Decorated wheel.

2007, Nov. 23
613 A304 180col Vert. pair, #a-b, + central label 7.00 7.00

Esquipulas II Central American Peace Accords, 20th Anniv. — A305

No. 614 — Nobel Peace medal of Pres. Oscar Arias Sánchez: a, Reverse (three men). b, Obverse (Alfred Nobel).

2007, Dec. 10
614 A305 135col Horiz. pair, #a-b 5.25 5.25

Dr. Fernando Centeno Güell (1907-93), Poet and Educator — A306

2008, Feb. 14
615 A306 115col multi 2.25 2.25

Churches — A307

No. 616: a, Our Lord of Agony Chapel, Guanacaste. b, San Francisco Church, San José. c, Our Lady of Sorrow Church, San José. d, Santa Ana Church, San José. e, Our Lady of Carmel Cathedral, Puntarenas. f, San Bartolomé Apóstol Church, Heredia.
1000col, Our Lady of Mercy Parish Church, San José.

2008, Mar. 17
616 A307 230col Sheet of 6, #a-f 27.50 27.50

Souvenir Sheet
617 A307 1000col multi 50.00 30.00

No. 616 contains six 40x40mm stamps.

Souvenir Sheet

Women's Superior College, 120th Anniv. — A308

2008, Mar. 31
618 A308 1000col multi 30.00 30.00

Miniature Sheet

Marine Mammals — A309

No. 619: a, Megaptera novaengliae, side view. b, Sotalia guianensis. c, Stenella attenuata. d, Megaptera novaengliae flukes.

2008, June 16 Litho. *Perf. 10½*
619 A309 240col Sheet of 4, #a-d 19.00 19.00

Intl. Year of Planet Earth — A310

No. 620: a, San Vicente Cataracts. b, Santa Elena Peninsula.

2008, July 1
620 Pair 7.00 7.00
a.-b. A310 175col Either single 3.50 3.50

Miniature Sheet

Art — A311

No. 621: a, La Ultima Escena, by Rudy Espinoza. b, Mujer que Avanza, sculpture by Crisanto Badilla. c, Transitoriedad del Hombre, by Miguel Hernández. d, Arquetipo, by Lola Fernández.

2008, July 3
621 A311 240col Sheet of 4, #a-d 19.00 19.00

Miniature Sheet

Ministry of Labor and Social Security, 80th Anniv. — A312

No. 622 — Details from mural "The Second Republic," by Luccio Ranucci: a, Man with hat, striped pole. b, Woman with basket of fruit. c, Man and woman embracing. d, Man carrying sack on head.

2008, Aug. 28 Litho. *Perf. 10½*
622 A312 240col Sheet of 4, #a-d 19.00 19.00

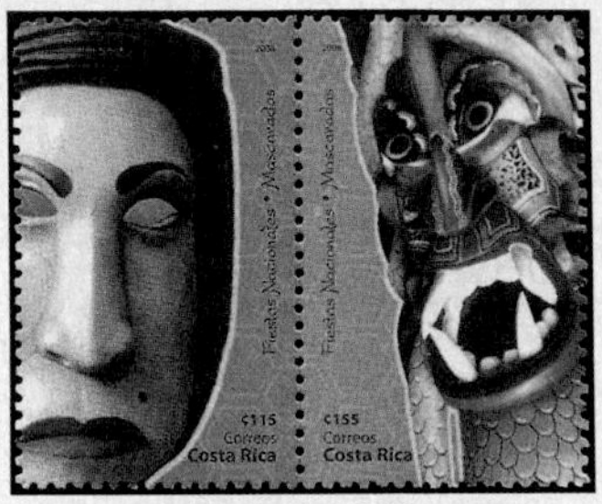

Masks — A313

No. 623 — Masks with background colors of: a, 115col, Brown orange. b, 155col, Green.

2008, Oct. 31
623 A313 Horiz. pair, #a-b 5.50 5.50

Hogar Crea Drug Rehabilitation Centers in Costa Rica, 25th Anniv. — A314

2009, Feb. 25 Litho. *Perf. 10½*
624 A314 160col multi 3.20 3.20

Carlos Luis Fallas (1906-66), Author — A315

2009, Apr. 30 Litho. *Perf. 10½*
625 A315 150col multi 2.00 2.00

Miniature Sheet

Children's Literature — A316

No. 626: a, Tolo, the Giant North Wind (kite), by Adela Ferreto de Saénz. b, The Ship of the Stars (ship and boy), by Alfredo Cardona Peña. c, Old Stories (rabbit and gourds), by María Leal de Noguera. d, Paul's Music (boy holding box), by Lara Ríos.

2009, May 27
626 A316 65col Sheet of 4, #a-d 5.00 5.00

Alberto Martén, Economist, Solidarity Movement Founder — A317

2009, June 19
627 A317 135col multi 2.50 2.50

Miniature Sheet

Costa Rican Electrical Institute (ICE), 60th Anniv. — A318

No. 628: a, People and ICE building. b, Construction workers in tunnel. c, Lineman on ladder. d, Computers and satellite dishes. e, Houses and windmills. f, Hand planting seedling, girl.

2009, June 30
628 A318 340col Sheet of 6, #a-f 10.00 10.00

Diplomatic Relations Between Costa Rica and Switzerland — A319

2009, July 8
629 A319 225col multi 4.00 4.00

Miniature Sheet

National Parks — A320

No. 630: a, Arenal Volcano. b, Celeste River. c, Cerro Chirripó. d, Cocos Island. e, Monteverde. f, Poás Volcano. g, Tortuguero.

2009, Aug. 24
630 A320 240col Sheet of 7, #a-g 8.25 8.25

America Issue, Traditional Games — A321

No. 631: a, Marbles. b, Kite flying.

2009, Sept. 9 Litho. *Perf. 10½*
631 Horiz. pair 2.00 2.00
a.-b. A321 135col Either single .75 .75

Intl. Holocaust Remembrance Day — A322

2010, Jan. 27 *Perf. 13¼*
632 A322 500col gray & black 4.00 4.00

No. 632 was printed in sheets of four with labels at left, bottom and right. Value, $27.50.

Miniature Sheet

Locomotives — A323

No. 633: a, Steam locomotive, 1889. b, Electric Series AEG locomotive, 1926. c, Yellow and white Apolo Series Diesel-electric locomotive, 1990. d, Blue, white and red Diesel-electric locomotive, 1979-80.

2010, May 4 Litho. *Perf. 10½*

633 A323 200col Sheet of 4, #a-d 3.25 3.25

America Issue, National Symbols — A324

2010, June 24

634 Horiz. pair 4.00 4.00
a. A324 280col Turdus grayi 1.25 1.25
b. A324 340col Odocoileus virginianus 1.50 1.50

No. 634 was printed in sheets containing two pairs.

Miniature Sheet

Endangered Birds — A325

No. 635: a, 400col, Platalea ajaja. b, 400col, Icterus mesomelas. c, 1000col, Morphnus guianensis. d, 1000col, Harpia harpyja.

2010, June 24 Litho. *Perf. 10½*

635 A325 Sheet of 4, #a-d 15.00 15.00

University Anniversaries — A326

No. 636: a, Mural by Eduardo Torijano at University of Costa Rica. b, Monument to Disarmament, Work and Peace by Thelvia Marin at Univeristy for Peace.

2010, Aug. 26

636 A326 500col Pair, #a-b 4.00 4.00

University of Costa Rica, 70th anniv., University for Peace, 30th anniv.

Miniature Sheet

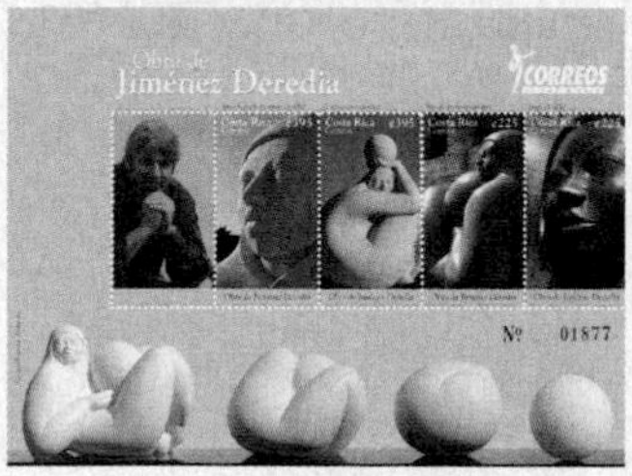

Details of Sculptures by Jiménez Deredia — A327

No. 637: a, 225col, Pareja. b, 225col, Ricordo Profondo. c, 395col, Continuación. d, 395col, Génesi Ricordo Profondo. Names of sculptures are in sheet margin above stamps.

Perf. 10½ on 2 or 3 Sides

2011, Feb. 23

637 A327 Sheet of 4, #a-d, + label 5.00 5.00

Souvenir Sheet

Opening of New National Stadium — A328

No. 638 — National Stadium built in: a, 1924. b, 2011.

2011, Mar. 26 *Perf. 10½*

638 A328 1000col Sheet of 2, #a-b 8.00 8.00

Pres. Laura Chinchilla A329

2011, May 9 *Perf. 10½ Vert.*

639 A329 340col multi 2.00 2.00

Souvenir Sheet

Cartoons by Costa Rican Artists — A330

No. 640 — Cartoons by: a, 500col, Francisco "Paco" Hernández (1885-1961) and Noé Solano (1889-1971). b, 1000col, Hugo Diaz "Lalo" (1930-2001) and Jorge Chavarria "Kokin" (1932-94).

2011, June 15 *Perf. 10½*

640 A330 Sheet of 2, #a-b 6.00 6.00

Miniature Sheet

Athletes — A331

No. 641: a, 200col, Hanna Gabriel, boxer. b, 200col, Nery Brenes, sprinter. c, 330col, Bryan Ruiz, soccer player. d, 330col, Andrey Amador, cyclist.

2011, July 14

641 A331 Sheet of 4, #a-d 4.25 4.25

Rights of the Child — A332

No. 642 — Banner inscribed: a, Participación. b, No Discriminación. c, Educación.

2011, Aug. 12

642 Horiz. strip of 3 4.75 4.75
a. A332 225col multi .90 .90
b. A332 340col multi 1.40 1.40
c. A332 600col multi 2.40 2.40

Miniature Sheet

Flora and Fauna of Monteverde Children's Forest — A333

No. 643: a, 500col, Forest and lake. b, 500col, Lithobates vibicarius. c, 1000col, Lepanthes ciliisepala. d, 1000col, Leopardus wiedii.

2011, Aug. 24 *Perf. 10½ on 3 Sides*

643 A333 Sheet of 4, #a-d, + 2 labels 15.00 15.00

Tricolín, Comic Strip by Carlos Figueroa — A334

No. 644: a, Tricolín, Tricolína and Costa Rican flag. b, Tricolín and Tricolína donating money for Red Cross. c, Tricolín and Pepín planting flower. d, Tricolín, Tricolína, and Pepín.

2011, Sept. 9 *Die Cut Perf. 12x11½*
Self-Adhesive

644 Block or horiz. strip of 4 5.50
a. A334 300col multi 1.25 1.25
b. A334 320col multi 1.25 1.25
c. A334 350col multi 1.40 1.40
d. A334 395col multi 1.60 1.60

Mailboxes — A335

No. 645: a, Black mailbox. b, Blue mailbox.

2011, Oct. 10 *Perf. 10½*

645 A335 400col Pair, #a-b 3.25 3.25

America issue. No. 645 was printed in sheets containing two pairs.

Souvenir Sheet

Scouting in Costa Rica, Cent. — A336

No. 646 — Boy Scouts and Girl Guides: a, Near tents. b, Around campfire.

2011, Oct. 28

646 A336 340col Sheet of 2, #a-b 2.75 2.75

Souvenir Sheet

National Museum, 125th Anniv. — A337

No. 647: a, Grinding stone, butterfly at right. b, Butterfly at left, Pre-Columbian stone sphere.

2012, May 4

647 A337 395col Sheet of 2, #a-b 3.25 3.25

Bank of Costa Rica, 135th Anniv. A338

2012, June 7

648 A338 275col multi 1.50 1.50

No. 648 was printed in sheets of 2. Value, $3.50.

Souvenir Sheet

2012 Summer Olympics, London — A339

No. 649: a, 365col, Runner. b. 435col, Taekwondo.

2012, June 25
649 A339 Sheet of 2, #a-b 3.25 3.25

Souvenir Sheet

Intl. Year of Cooperatives — A340

No. 650: a, 275col, People holding rainbow and trees. b, 395col, People wrapping ribbons around sphere.

2012, July 6
650 A340 Sheet of 2, #a-b 2.75 2.75

Manuel Antonio National Park — A341

2012, Aug. 24 ***Perf. 10½ Horiz.***
Booklet Stamp
651 A341 545col multi 3.00 3.00
a. Booklet pane of 3 15.00 —
Complete booklet, #651a 15.00

Souvenir Sheet

America Issue — A342

No. 652: a, 385col, Legend of La Segua. b, 485col, Legend of the Cart Without Oxen.

2012, Oct. 9 ***Perf. 10½***
652 A342 Sheet of 2, #a-b 3.50 3.50

Souvenir Sheet

First Costa Rican Postage Stamps, 150th Anniv. — A343

No. 653: a, Costa Rica #1. b, Costa Rica #2.

Litho. & Embossed With Foil Application

2013, Apr. 17
653 A343 1000col Sheet of 2, #a-b 8.00 8.00

Souvenir Sheet

Bancrédito Commercial Bank, 95th Anniv. — A344

2013, May 15 **Litho.**
654 A344 400col multi 1.60 1.60

"Costa Rica, Land of Immigrants" A345

2013, June 20
655 A345 500col multi 2.00 2.00

No. 655 was printed in sheets of 2.

Souvenir Sheet

Braulio Carrillo National Park — A346

2013, Aug. 23 **Litho.** ***Perf.***
656 A346 1500col multi 6.00 6.00

Jorge Manuel Dengo (1918-2012), Vice-President — A347

2013, Sept. 18 **Litho.** ***Perf. 10½***
657 A347 500col multi 2.00 2.00

No. 657 was printed in sheets of 2.

Campaign Against Discrimination A348

2013, Oct. 9 **Litho.** ***Perf. 10½***
658 A348 300col multi 1.25 1.25

America issue. No. 658 was printed in sheets of 2 + central label.

Souvenir Sheet

Pres. Juan Rafael Mora Porras (1814-60) — A349

2014, Feb. 7 **Litho.** ***Perf. 10½***
659 A349 360col multi 1.40 1.40

America issue.

Souvenir Sheet

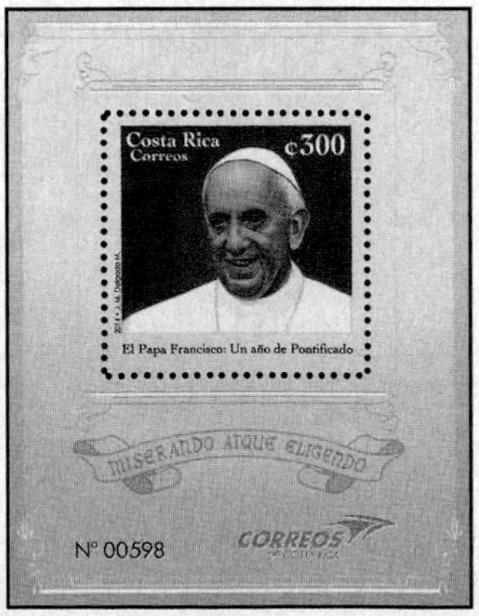

Election of Pope Francis, 1st Anniv. — A350

2014, Mar. 19 **Litho.** ***Perf. 10½***
660 A350 300col multi 2.00 2.00

Souvenir Sheet

2014 World Cup Soccer Championships, Brazil — A351

No. 661: a, 500col, 2014 World Cup mascot. b, 710col, World Cup.

2014, Apr. 24 **Litho.** ***Perf. 10½***
661 A351 Sheet of 2, #a-b 6.00 6.00

Souvenir Sheet

Endangered Cats in Corcovado National Park — A352

No. 662: a, 690col, Puma yagouaroundi. 1220col, Panthera onca.

2014, Aug. 22 **Litho.** ***Perf. 13***
662 A352 Sheet of 2, #a-b 9.00 9.00

Souvenir Sheet

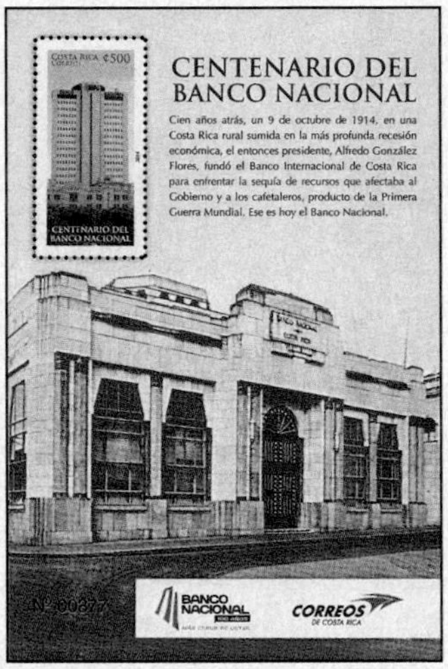

National Bank, Cent. — A353

2014, Nov. 3 **Litho.** ***Perf. 10½***
663 A353 500col multi 1.90 1.90

Vuelta de Costa Rica Bicycle Race, 50th Anniv. A354

2014, Dec. 11 **Litho.** ***Perf. 13¼***
664 A354 500col multi 1.90 1.90

No. 664 was printed in sheets of 2.

Souvenir Sheet

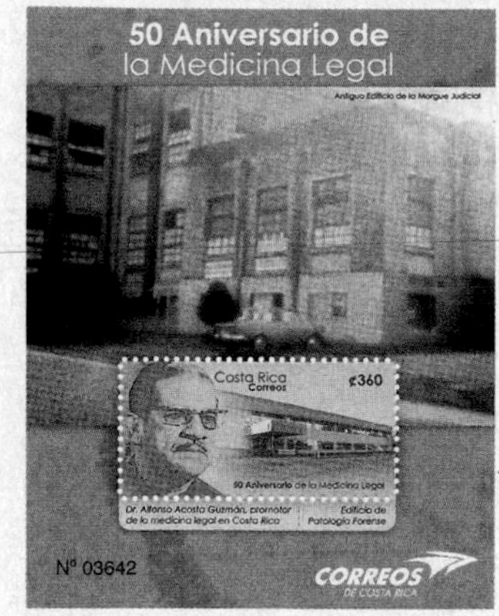

Forensic Medicine in Costa Rica, 50th Anniv. — A355

2015, Jan. 30 Litho. *Perf. 10½*
665 A355 360col multi 1.40 1.40

Costa Rica Chamber of Commerce, Cent. — A356

2015, Mar. 4 Litho. *Perf. 10½*
666 A356 500col multi 1.90 1.90

No. 666 was printed in sheets of 2.

Souvenir Sheet

El Buen Pastor Episcopal Church, San José, 150th Anniv. — A357

2015, Apr. 23 Litho. *Imperf.*
667 A357 1000col multi 3.75 3.75

No. 667 has simulated perforations.

Souvenir Sheet

Education and Training For All — A358

No. 668 — Adult students with denomination in: a, Orange yellow. b, Blue.

2015, May 7 Litho. *Perf. 10½*
668 A358 690col Sheet of 2, #a-b 5.25 5.25

National Apprentice Institute, 50th anniv.; Normal School, cent.

Fire Departments in Costa Rica, 150th Anniv. — A359

No. 669: a, Fire fighters spraying water on fire. b, Fire fighters, truck and children.

2015, July 16 Litho. *Perf. 14*
669 A359 1500col Sheet of 2, #a-b 11.50 11.50

Nelson Mandela (1918-2013), President of South Africa — A360

2015, July 18 Litho. *Perf. 10½*
Booklet Stamp
670 A360 1220col multi 4.75 4.75
a. Booklet pane of 3 14.50 —
Complete booklet, #670a 14.50

Coral Reefs of Cahuita National Park — A361

No. 671: a, Coral and sea urchin. b, Coral. 1000col, Coral, diff.

2015, Aug. 24 Litho. *Perf. 13x13¼*
671 A361 500col Sheet of 2, #a-b 3.75 3.75

Souvenir Sheet

672 A361 1000col multi 3.75 3.75

Campaign Against Human Trafficking A362

2015, Oct. 9 Litho. *Perf. 10½*
673 A362 500col black & blue .90 1.90

America Issue. No. 673 was printed in sheets of 2.

POSTAL-FISCAL STAMPS

From April 1884 through September 1889 revenue stamps were permitted for postal use, when post offices exhausted supplies of regular postage stamps.

Used values are for stamps with postal cancels.

PF1

1884 Engr. *Perf. 12*
AR1 PF1 1c rose .50 *5.00*
AR2 PF1 2c light blue *20.00* 5.00

PF2

1888
AR3 PF2 5c brown .50 *3.00*
AR4 PF2 10c blue *.25* 3.00

Nos. AR2-AR4 are normally found without gum.

SEMI-POSTAL STAMPS

No. 72 Surcharged in Red

1922 Unwmk. *Perf. 12*
B1 A56 5c + 5c orange 1.00 .40

Issued for the benefit of the Costa Rican Red Cross Society. In 1928, owing to a temporary shortage of the ordinary 5c stamp, No. B1 was placed on sale as a regular 5c stamp, the surtax being disregarded.

Discus Thrower SP1

Trophy SP2

Parthenon SP3

1924 Litho. *Imperf.*

B2	SP1	5c dark green	1.60	*2.00*
B3	SP2	10c carmine	1.60	*2.00*
B4	SP3	20c dark blue	20.00	*20.00*
a.		Tête bêche pair	60.00	*60.00*

Perf. 12

B5	SP1	5c dark green	1.60	*2.25*
B6	SP2	10c carmine	1.60	*2.25*
B7	SP3	20c dark blue	3.50	*4.00*
a.		Tête bêche pair	16.00	*20.00*
		Nos. B2-B7 (6)	29.90	*32.50*

These stamps were sold at a premium of 10c each, to help defray the expenses of athletic games held at San José in Dec. 1924.

AIR POST STAMPS

Airplane AP1

Perf. 12½

1926, June 4 Unwmk. Engr.
C1 AP1 20c ultramarine 3.00 .65

No. 123 Overprinted

1930, Mar. 14 *Perf. 12*
C2 A75 10c carmine rose 2.00 .25

Inverted or double overprints are fakes.

AP3

1930-32 *Perf. 12½*

C3	AP3	5c on 10c dk brn ('32)	.40	.25
C4	AP3	20c on 50c ultra	.50	.25
C5	AP3	40c on 50c ultra	.60	.25
		Nos. C3-C5 (3)	1.50	.75

The existence of genuine inverted or double surcharges of Nos. C3-C5 is in doubt.

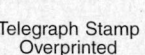

Telegraph Stamp Overprinted

1930, Mar. 19

C6	AP3	1col orange	2.00	.50

No. O79 Surcharged in Red

1930, Mar. 11

C7	O7	8c on 1col lilac & blk	.80	.65
C8	O7	20c on 1col lilac & blk	1.25	.70
C9	O7	40c on 1col lilac & blk	2.40	1.50
C10	O7	1col on 1col lilac & blk	3.50	2.00
		Nos. C7-C10 (4)	7.95	4.85

AP6

Red Surcharge on Revenue Stamps

1931-32 *Perf. 12*

C11	AP6	2col on 2col gray grn	35.00	35.00
C12	AP6	3col on 5col lil brn	35.00	35.00
C13	AP6	5col on 10col gray blk	35.00	35.00
		Nos. C11-C13 (3)	105.00	105.00

There were two printings of this issue which were practically identical in the colors of the stamps and the surcharges.

Nos. C11 and C13 have the date "1929" on the stamp, No. C12 has "1930."

AP7

Black Overprint on Telegraph Stamp

1932, Mar. 8 *Perf. 12½*

C14	AP7	40c green	3.00	.30
a.		Inverted overprint	32.50	27.50

Unofficial "proofs," inverts and double overprints were made from a defaced plate.

Mail Plane about to Land AP8

Allegory of Flight AP9

1934, Mar. 14 *Perf. 12*

C15	AP8	5c green	.25	.25
C16	AP8	10c carmine rose	.25	.25
C17	AP8	15c chocolate	.40	.25
C18	AP8	20c deep blue	.40	.25
C19	AP8	25c deep orange	.55	.25
C20	AP8	40c olive blk	1.75	.25
C21	AP8	50c gray blk	.85	.25
C22	AP8	60c orange yel	1.50	.25
C23	AP8	75c dull violet	2.75	.50
C24	AP9	1col deep rose	1.50	.25
C25	AP9	2col lt blue	7.50	.95
C26	AP9	5col black	7.50	4.75
C27	AP9	10col red brown	10.00	8.00
		Nos. C15-C27 (13)	35.20	16.45

Nos. C15-C27 with holes punched through were for use of government officials.

See Nos. C216-C219. For overprints see Nos. C67-C73, C92-C93, C103-C116, CO1-CO13.

Airplane over Poás Volcano — AP10

1937, Feb. 10

C28	AP10	1c black	.45	.35
C29	AP10	2c brown	.45	.35
C30	AP10	3c dk violet	.45	.35
		Nos. C28-C30 (3)	1.35	1.05

First Fair of Costa Rica.

Puntarenas — AP11

Perf. 12, 12½

1937, Dec. 15 **Unwmk.**

C31	AP11	2c black gray	.25	.25
C32	AP11	5c green	.30	.25
C33	AP11	20c deep blue	.30	.25
C34	AP11	1.40col olive brn	2.50	2.50
		Nos. C31-C34 (4)	3.35	3.25

National Bank AP12

1938, Jan. 11 **Wmk. 229** *Perf. 12½*

C35	AP12	1c purple	.25	.25
C36	AP12	3c red orange	.25	.25
C37	AP12	10c carmine rose	.30	.25
C38	AP12	75c brown	2.50	2.00
		Nos. C35-C38 (4)	3.30	2.75

Nos. C31-C38 for the Natl. Products Exposition held at San José, Dec. 1937.

Airport Administration Building, La Sabana — AP13

1940, May 2 **Engr.** **Unwmk.**

C39	AP13	5c green	.30	.25
C40	AP13	10c rose pink	.30	.25
C41	AP13	25c lt blue	.40	.25
C42	AP13	35c red brown	.40	.25
C43	AP13	60c red org	.55	.40
C44	AP13	85c violet	1.40	1.00
C45	AP13	2.35col turq grn	6.50	5.50
		Nos. C39-C45 (7)	9.85	7.90

Opening of the Intl. Airport at La Sabana.

Duran Sanatorium AP14

Overprinted in Black

1940, Dec. 2 *Perf. 12*

C46	AP14	10c scarlet	.25	.25
C47	AP14	15c purple	.25	.25
C48	AP14	25c lt blue	.50	.40
C49	AP14	35c bister brn	.70	.65
C50	AP14	60c pck green	1.00	.95
C51	AP14	75c olive	2.75	2.50
C52	AP14	1.35col red org	8.75	8.00
C53	AP14	5col sepia	45.00	40.00
C54	AP14	10col red lilac	140.00	100.00
		Nos. C46-C54 (9)	199.20	153.00

Pan-American Health Day. Nos. C46-C54 exist without overprint. Value, set $5,000.

No. 174 Surcharged in Black or Blue

1940, Dec. 17 *Perf. 14*

C55	A95	15c on 50c yel (Bk)	1.00	1.00
C56	A95	30c on 50c yel (Bl)	1.00	1.00

Pan-American Aviation Day, proclaimed by President F. D. Roosevelt.

The 15c surcharge exists normal and inverted on No. 171, Value, normal $30. Inverted surcharge is worth more.

International Soccer Game at National Stadium — AP15

1941, May 8 *Perf. 12*

C57	AP15	15c red	.80	.25
C58	AP15	30c dp ultra	.90	.25
C59	AP15	40c red brn	.95	.35
C60	AP15	50c purple	1.40	.80
C61	AP15	60c brt green	1.60	.90
C62	AP15	75c yel org	2.75	1.40
C63	AP15	1col dull vio	4.75	4.50
C64	AP15	1.40col rose	9.50	8.75
C65	AP15	2col blue grn	20.00	17.50
C66	AP15	5col black	52.50	37.50
		Nos. C57-C66 (10)	95.15	72.20

Caribbean and Central American Soccer Championship. See Nos. C121-C123. For surcharges see Nos. C145-C147.

Air Post Stamps of 1934 Overprinted or Surcharged in Black

1941, June 2

C67	AP8	5c on 20c dp bl	.25	.25
C68	AP8	15c on 20c dp bl	.25	.25
C69	AP8	40c on 75c dl vio	.35	.25
C70	AP9	65c on 1col dp rose	.65	.50
C71	AP9	1.40col on 2col lt bl	3.25	3.25
C72	AP9	5col black	12.00	12.00
C73	AP9	10col red brn	14.50	12.50
		Nos. C67-C73 (7)	31.25	29.00

Issued in commemoration of the settlement of the Costa Rica-Panama border dispute.

Nos. C67-C73 are found with hyphen omitted in overprint.

Nos. C67-C69 exist with inverted overprint. Value, each, $35.

University Types of 1941

1941, Aug. 26 *Perf. 12*

C74	A107	15c salmon	.25	.25
C75	A106	30c lt blue	.30	.25
C76	A107	40c orange	.40	.30
C77	A106	60c turq green	.50	.40
C78	A107	1col violet	1.90	1.90
C79	A106	2col black	4.75	4.75
C80	A107	5col sepia	16.00	16.00
		Nos. C74-C80 (7)	24.10	23.85

Portrait Type of 1943-47

Designs: 40c, Manuel Aguilar. No. C83, Francisco Morazan. No. C83A, Jose R. De Gallegos. 50c, Jose M. Alfaro. 60c, Francisco M. Oreamuno. 65c, Jose M. Castro. 85c, Juan Rafael Mora. 1col, Jose M. Montealegre. 1.05col, Braulio Carrillo. 1.15col, Jesus Jimenez. 1.40col, Bruno Carranza. 2col, Tomas Guardia.

1943-45 **Engr.**

C81	A109	10c rose pink	.25	.25
C82	A109	40c blue	.30	.25
C82A	A109	40c car rose	.30	.25
C83	A109	45c magenta	.50	.30
C83A	A109	45c black	.25	.25
C84	A109	50c turq grn	1.75	.25
C84A	A109	50c red org	.40	.25
C85	A109	60c brt ultra	.65	.25
C85A	A109	60c brt green	.25	.25
C86	A109	65c scarlet	.95	.30
C86A	A109	65c brt ultra	.30	.25
C87	A109	85c dp org	1.25	.50
C87A	A109	85c dull pur	1.60	.65
C88	A109	1col black	1.60	.50
C88A	A109	1col scarlet	.65	.40
C88B	A109	1.05col bis brn	.90	.55
C89	A109	1.15col red brn	2.10	1.75
C89A	A109	1.15col green	3.00	1.25
C90	A109	1.40col dp vio	3.25	2.40
C90A	A109	1.40col org yel	1.75	1.60
C91	A109	2col black	5.25	1.25
C91A	A109	2col olive grn	1.60	.50
		Nos. C81-C91A (22)	28.85	14.20

Issued: Nos. C82A, C83A, C84A, C85A, C86A, C87A, C88A, C88B, C89A, C90A, C91A, 1945.

See Nos. C124-C127, C179-C181. For surcharges see Nos. C154-C158, C182, C184-C185.

Nos. C26-C27 Ovptd. in Red or Blue

1943, Sept. 16

C92	AP9	5col black (R)	4.50	3.00
C93	AP9	10col red brown (Bl)	5.25	3.25

Mercury and Plane AP31

1944, Jan. 19

C94	AP31	10c red org	.25	.25
C95	AP31	15c dk car	.25	.25
C96	AP31	40c brt ultra	.40	.25
C97	AP31	45c dp red lil	.40	.30
C98	AP31	60c turq grn	.55	.40
C99	AP31	1col dk red brn	1.60	.80
C100	AP31	1.40col gray blk	8.75	5.25
C101	AP31	5col violet	24.00	16.00
C102	AP31	10col black	70.00	62.50
		Nos. C94-C102 (9)	106.20	86.00

City of San Ramón founding, 100th anniv.

No. CO10 With Additional Overprint in Black

1944, Nov. 22

C103	AP9	1col deep rose	2.00	.95
a.		Blue overprint	100.00	100.00

Nos. CO1-CO13 Overprinted in Carmine or Black

1945, Jan. 12 **Unwmk.** *Perf. 12*

C104	AP8	5c green	.60	.50
C105	AP8	10c car rose (Bk)	.60	.55
C106	AP8	15c chocolate	.60	.55
C107	AP8	20c deep blue	.50	.40
C108	AP8	25c dp org (Bk)	.60	.60
C109	AP8	40c olive blk	.35	.35

C110	AP8	50c gray blk	.60	.60
C111	AP8	60c org yel (Bk)	.90	.35
C112	AP8	75c dull violet	.75	.50
C113	AP9	1col dp rose (Bk)	.75	.35
C114	AP9	2col light blue	8.00	4.50
C115	AP9	5col black	8.00	5.50
C116	AP9	10col red brn (Bk)	11.00	8.25
		Nos. C104-C116 (13)	33.25	23.00

No. C104 exists inverted & overprinted in black. This is probably a trial color. Value, $50.

Catalogue values for unused stamps in this section, from this point to the end of the section, are for Never Hinged items.

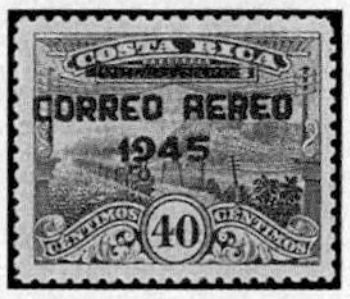

AP32

Telegraph Stamps Overprinted in Black or Carmine

1945, Feb. 28 Unwmk. *Perf. 12½*

C117	AP32	40c green (C)	.30	.25
C118	AP32	50c ultra (C)	.30	.25
C119	AP32	1col orange (Bk)	1.00	.40
		Nos. C117-C119 (3)	1.60	.90

No. C117 exists with inverted overprint. Value, $10.

Florence Nightingale and Edith Cavell AP33

1945 Engr.

C120	AP33	1col black & car	1.00	.50

Costa Rican Red Cross Soc., 60th anniv
For surcharge see No. C183.

Soccer Type of 1941 Inscribed: "Febrero 1946"

1946, May 13 *Perf. 12*

C121	AP15	25c green	1.60	.65
C122	AP15	30c dull yellow	2.00	.65
C123	AP15	55c deep blue	2.40	.65
		Nos. C121-C123 (3)	6.00	1.95

Portrait Type of 1943-47

Designs: 25c, Aniceto Esquivel. 30c, Vicente Herrera. 55c, Prospero Fernandez. 75c, Bernardo Soto.

1946, May 12

C124	A109	25c blue	.25	.25
C125	A109	30c red brown	.25	.25
C126	A109	55c plum	.40	.30
C127	A109	75c blue green	.60	.40
		Nos. C124-C127 (4)	1.50	1.20

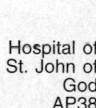

Hospital of St. John of God AP38

1946, June 24 Unwmk. *Perf. 12½*
Center in Black

C128	AP38	5c yellow grn	.40	.25
C129	AP38	10c dk brown	.50	.25
C130	AP38	15c carmine	.50	.25
C131	AP38	25c dk blue	.50	.25
C132	AP38	30c dp orange	.95	.25
C133	AP38	40c olive grn	.50	.25
C134	AP38	50c violet	.95	.25
C135	AP38	60c dk sl grn	1.90	.55
C136	AP38	75c brown	1.40	.40
a.		Horiz. pair, imperf. btwn.	100.00	
C137	AP38	1col blue	1.90	.35
C138	AP38	2col brn org	2.40	.80
C139	AP38	3col dk vio brn	4.75	2.00
C140	AP38	5col yellow	6.50	2.40
		Nos. C128-C140 (13)	23.15	8.25

Nos. C128, C129, C132 and C135 exist imperf.

Rafael Iglesias — AP39

3col, Ascensión Esquivel. 5col, Cleto González Viquez. 10col, Ricardo Jiménez Oreamuno.

1947, Jan. 15 Wmk. 215 *Perf. 14*
Center in Black

C141	AP39	2col blue	2.00	1.25
C142	AP39	3col dp car	2.75	1.60
C143	AP39	5col dk green	4.75	2.00
C144	AP39	10col orange	7.25	5.25
		Nos. C141-C144 (4)	16.75	10.10

Nos. C141-C144 also exist in a souvenir sheet of 4. Value, $600. The sheet in sepia is a proof and worth less.

Nos. C121-C123 Surcharged in Black

1947, May 5 Unwmk. *Perf. 12*

C145	AP15	15c on 25c green	.95	.80
C146	AP15	15c on 30c dull yel	.95	.80
C147	AP15	15c on 55c dp blue	.95	.80
		Nos. C145-C147 (3)	2.85	2.40

Nos. C145-C147 exist with inverted surcharge.

Columbus in Cariari AP43

1947, May 18 Engr. *Perf. 12½*
Center in Black

C148	AP43	25c green	.30	.25
C149	AP43	30c dp ultra	.40	.25
C150	AP43	40c red orange	.50	.25
C151	AP43	45c violet	.65	.30
C152	AP43	50c brt carmine	.70	.25
C153	AP43	65c brown org	2.00	.95
		Nos. C148-C153 (6)	4.55	2.25

For surcharges see Nos. C178, C220-C223.

Nos. C84A, C85A, C127, C88A, and C88B Surcharged with New Value in Black or Red

1947, June 3 *Perf. 12*

C154	A109	15c on 50c red org	.40	.30
C155	A109	15c on 60c brt grn (R)	.40	.30
C156	A109	15c on 75c bl grn (R)	.40	.30
C157	A109	15c on 1col scar	.55	.50
C158	A109	15c on 1.05col bis brn	.40	.30
		Nos. C154-C158 (5)	2.15	1.70

No. C155 is known with black surcharge. Value, $10. No. C156 with inverted surcharge. Value, $10.

Early Steam Locomotive — AP44

1947, Nov. 10 *Perf. 12½*

C159	AP44	35c bl grn & blk	2.40	.55

Electric railroad to the Pacific coast, 50th anniv.

Roosevelt Type of Regular Issue

1947, Aug. 26 *Perf. 12*

C160	A122	15c green	.25	.25
C161	A122	30c car rose	.25	.25
C162	A122	45c red brown	.25	.25
C163	A122	65c orange yel	.25	.25
C164	A122	75c blue	.30	.25
C165	A122	1col olive grn	.50	.35
C166	A122	2col black	1.40	1.00
C167	A122	5col scarlet	2.50	2.40
		Nos. C160-C167 (8)	5.55	4.60

For surcharges see Nos. C224-C226.

National Theater AP46

Rafael Iglesias AP47

1948, Jan. 26 *Perf. 12½*
Center in Black

C168	AP46	15c brt ultra	.25	.25
C169	AP46	20c red	.25	.25
C170	AP47	35c dk green	.40	.25
C171	AP46	45c purple	.50	.25
C172	AP46	50c carmine	.50	.25
C173	AP46	75c red violet	1.10	.80
C174	AP46	1col olive	2.00	1.10
C175	AP46	2col red brn	3.25	1.60
C176	AP47	5col org yel	5.25	4.00
C177	AP47	10col brt blue	12.00	8.00
		Nos. C168-C177 (10)	25.50	16.75

50th anniversary of National Theater.

No. C150 Surcharged in Carmine

1948, Apr. 21

C178	AP43	35c on 40c	1.10	.50

Exists with surcharge inverted.

Portrait Type of 1943-47

5c, Salvador Lara. 15c, Carlos Duran.

1948 Engr. *Perf. 12*

C179	A109	5c sepia	.25	.25
C180	A109	10c olive brown	.25	.25
C181	A109	15c violet	.25	.25
		Nos. C179-C181 (3)	.75	.75

Nos. C88B, C120, C89A and C90A Surcharged in Carmine or Black

Perf. 12½, 12

1949, Aug. 28 Unwmk.

C182	A109	35c on 1.05col bis brn	.35	.25
C183	AP33	50c on 1col blk & car	.60	.45
a.		2nd & 3rd lines both read "125 Aniversario"	5.00	3.00
C184	A109	55c on 1.15col grn	.85	.70
C185	A109	55c on 1.40col org yel (Bk)	.90	.60
		Nos. C182-C185 (4)	2.70	2.00

125th anniv. of the annexation of the province of Guanacaste.
Overprint differs on No. C183, with "Guanacaste" in capitals, and lower case "a" in "Anexión."
The variety "l" for "i" in "Anexion" is found on Nos. C182, C184 and C185.

Symbols of UPU AP48

1950, Jan. 11 Photo. *Perf. 11½*

C186	AP48	15c lilac rose	.25	.25
C187	AP48	25c chalky blue	.40	.40
C188	AP48	1col gray green	.55	.55
		Nos. C186-C188 (3)	1.20	1.20

75th anniv. of the UPU.

Battle of El Tejar, Cartago AP49

Occupation of Limón — AP50

25c, Lucha ranch. 35c, Trenches of San Isidro Battalion. 55c, 75c, Observation post. 80c, 1col, Dr. Carlos Luis Valverde.

Inscribed: "Guerra de Liberacion Nacional 1948"

Engraved; Center Photogravure

1950, July 20 *Perf. 12½*
Center in Black

C189	AP49	15c brt car	.25	.25
C190	AP50	20c dull green	.25	.25
C191	AP49	25c dull blue	.30	.25
C192	AP49	35c chestnut	.40	.25
C193	AP49	55c lilac	.70	.25
C194	AP49	75c red org	1.10	.30
C195	AP50	80c gray	1.10	.50
C196	AP50	1col org yel	1.50	.55
		Nos. C189-C196 (8)	5.60	2.60

2nd anniv. of the War for Natl. Liberation.

Bull (Cattle Raising) — AP51

1c, 10c, 2col, Bull. 2c, 30c, 3col, Tuna fishing. 3c, 65c, Pineapple. 5c, 50c, 5col, Bananas. 45c, 80c, 10col, Coffee picker.

Inscribed: "Feria Nacional Agricola Ganadera e Industrial Cartago 1950"

1950, July 27 Center in Black

C197	AP51	1c brt green	.55	.25
C198	AP51	2c brt blue	.55	.25
C199	AP51	3c chocolate	.65	.25
C200	AP51	5c dp ultra	.65	.25
C201	AP51	10c green	.65	.25
C202	AP51	30c purple	.65	.25
C203	AP51	45c vermilion	.70	.25
C204	AP51	50c blue gray	.80	.25
C205	AP51	65c dk blue	.80	.25
C206	AP51	80c dp rose	2.00	.65
C207	AP51	2col org yel	4.00	1.60
C208	AP51	3col blue	7.25	4.00
C209	AP51	5col carmine	10.50	6.50
C210	AP51	10col dp claret	10.50	6.50
		Nos. C197-C210 (14)	40.25	21.50

National Agricultural, Livestock and Industrial Fair, Cartago, 1950.
For surcharge see No. RA1.

Queen Isabella I and Caravels of Columbus AP52

Unwmk.

1952, Mar. 4 Engr. *Perf. 13*

C211	AP52	15c carmine	.30	.25
C212	AP52	20c orange	.55	.25
C213	AP52	25c ultra	.80	.25
C214	AP52	55c dp green	2.75	.25
C215	AP52	2col violet	5.25	.50
		Nos. C211-C215 (5)	9.65	1.50

Birth of Queen Isabella I of Spain, 500th anniv.

Mail Plane Type of 1934

1952-53 *Perf. 12*

C216	AP8	5c blue	.40	.25
C217	AP8	10c green	.40	.25
C218	AP8	15c car rose ('53)	.55	.25
C219	AP8	35c purple	1.40	.25
		Nos. C216-C219 (4)	2.75	1.00

Nos. C216-C217 were reprinted in 1953 in different shades. Values the same.

Nos. C149-C151, C153 Surcharged in Red: "HABILITADO PARA CINCO CENTIMOS 1953"

1953, Apr. 24 *Perf. 12½*

Center in Black

C220	AP43	5c on 30c dp ultra	2.00	1.50
C221	AP43	5c on 40c red org	.40	.30
C222	AP43	5c on 45c vio	.40	.30
C223	AP43	5c on 65c brn org	.40	.30
		Nos. C220-C223 (4)	3.20	2.40

Nos. C161-C163 Surcharged in Black

1953, Apr. 11 *Perf. 12*

C224	A122	15c on 30c car rose	.30	.25
C225	A122	15c on 45c red brn	.30	.25
C226	A122	15c on 65c org yel	.30	.25
		Nos. C224-C226 (3)	.90	.75

Refinery of Vegetable Oils and Fats — AP53

Industries: 10c, Pottery. 15c, Sugar. 20c, Soap. 25c, Lumber. 30c, Matches. 35c, Textiles. 40c, Leather. 45c, Tobacco. 50c, Preserving. 55c, Canning. 60c, General. 65c, Metals. 75c, Pharmaceuticals. 80c, Pharmaceuticals. 1col, Paper. 2col, Rubber. 3col, Airplane maintenance. 5col, Marble. 10col, Beer.

Engraved; Center Photogravure

1954-59 Unwmk. *Perf. 13x12½*

Center in Black

C227	AP53	5c red	.25	.25
C228	AP53	10c dk blue	.25	.25
C229	AP53	15c green	.25	.25
C230	AP53	20c violet	.25	.25
C231	AP53	25c magenta	.30	.25
C232	AP53	30c purple	.65	.40
C233	AP53	35c red vio	.40	.25
C234	AP53	40c black	.65	.30
C235	AP53	45c dk green	1.25	.40
C236	AP53	50c vio brown	.80	.25
C237	AP53	55c yellow	.65	.25
C238	AP53	60c brown	1.50	.65
C239	AP53	65c carmine	1.75	.95
C240	AP53	75c violet	2.40	.80
C240A	AP53	80c pur & gray	1.25	.80
C241	AP53	1col blue	.80	.40
a.		Imperf., pair	100.00	
C242	AP53	2col rose pink	2.40	1.25
C243	AP53	3col ol grn	3.25	2.00
C244	AP53	5col black	5.25	1.60
C245	AP53	10col yellow	14.50	9.50
		Nos. C227-C245 (20)	38.80	21.05

Issued: 30c, 35c, 60c, 65c, 75c, 2col, 3col, Oct. 20; 80c, Oct. 2, 1959; others, Sept. 1.

See Nos. C252-C255. For surcharges and overprint, see Nos. C314-C315, C334-C336, RA2, RA11.

Globe, Rotary Emblem — AP54

25c, Hand protecting boy. 40c, 2col, Hospital. 45c, Globe & palm leaves. 60c, Lighthouse.

1956, Feb. 7 Engr. *Perf. 12*

C246	AP54	10c green	.25	.25
C247	AP54	25c dk blue	.25	.25
C248	AP54	40c dk brown	.50	.40
C249	AP54	45c brt red	.30	.25
C250	AP54	60c dk red vio	.50	.30
C251	AP54	2col yel org	1.25	.65
		Nos. C246-C251 (6)	3.05	2.10

50th anniv. of Rotary Intl. (in 1955).

Industries Type of 1954

Designs as in 1954.

Engraved; Center Photogravure

1956, Feb. 17 *Perf. 12*

Center in Black

C252	AP53	5c ultra	.30	.25
C253	AP53	10c violet blue	.40	.25
C254	AP53	15c orange yel	.50	.25
C255	AP53	75c red orange	.80	.30
		Nos. C252-C255 (4)	2.00	1.05

Map of Costa Rica — AP55

10c, Map of Guanacaste. 15c, Inn. 20c, House of Santa Rosa. 25c, Gen. Jose Manuel Quiros. 30c, Old Presidential Palace. 35c, Joaquin Bernardo Calvo. 40c, Luis Molina. 45c, Gen. Jose Joaquin Mora. 50c, Gen. Jose Maria Canas. 55c, Juan Santamaria monument. 60c, National monument. 65c, Antonio Vallerriestra. 70c, Ramon Castilla y Marquesado. 75c, San Carlos fortress. 80c, Francisco Maria Oreamuno. 1col, Pres. Juan Rafael Mora.

1957, June 21 Engr. *Perf. 13½x13*

C256	AP55	5c lt blue	.25	.25
C257	AP55	10c green	.30	.25
C258	AP55	15c dp orange	.30	.25
C259	AP55	20c lt brown	.30	.25
C260	AP55	25c vio blue	.40	.25
C261	AP55	30c violet	.50	.25
C262	AP55	35c car rose	.55	.25
C263	AP55	40c slate	.55	.25
C264	AP55	45c rose red	.65	.25
C265	AP55	50c ultra	.70	.25
C266	AP55	55c ocher	1.10	.25
C267	AP55	60c brt car	.95	.30
C268	AP55	65c carmine	1.10	.30
C269	AP55	70c orange yel	1.25	.30
C270	AP55	75c emerald	1.25	.30
C271	AP55	80c dk brown	1.60	.40
C272	AP55	1col black	1.75	.40
		Nos. C256-C272 (17)	13.50	4.75

Centenary of War of 1856-57.

Cleto Gonzalez Viquez — AP56

Highway and Gonzalez Viquez AP57

Designs: 10c, Ricardo Jimenez Oreamuno. 20c, Puntarenas wharf and Jimenez. 35c, Post and Telegraph Bldg. and Jimenez. 55c, Pipeline and Gonzalez Viquez. 80c, National Library and Gonzalez Viquez. 1col, Electric train and Jimenez. 2col, Gonzales and Jimenez.

1959, Nov. 23 Engr. *Perf. 13½*

C274	AP56	5c car & ultra	.25	.25
C275	AP56	10c red & gray	.25	.25

Perf. 13½x13

C276	AP57	15c dk bl grn & blk	.25	.25
C277	AP57	20c car & brn	.50	.25
C278	AP57	35c rose lil & bl	.25	.25
C279	AP57	55c olive & vio	.50	.25
C280	AP57	80c ultra	.60	.35
C281	AP57	1col orange & mar	.85	.50
C282	AP57	2col gray & mar	2.00	1.60
		Nos. C274-C282 (9)	5.45	3.95

For surcharge and overprint see Nos. C337, C339.

Soccer AP58

Designs: Various soccer scenes.

Perf. 13½

1960, Mar. 7 Unwmk. Photo.

C283	AP58	10c black	.30	.30
C284	AP58	25c ultra	.30	.30
C285	AP58	35c red orange	.30	.30
C286	AP58	50c red brown	.40	.30
C287	AP58	85c Prus green	1.10	.90
C288	AP58	5col dp claret	2.50	2.50
		Nos. C283-C288 (6)	4.90	4.60

Souvenir Sheet

Imperf

C289	AP58	2col blue	6.50	6.50

3rd Pan-American Soccer Games, San José, Mar. 1960.

Nos. C283-C288 exist imperf. Value, pair $150.

WRY Uprooted Oak Emblem — AP59

1960, Apr. 7 Unwmk. *Perf. 11½*

Granite Paper

C290	AP59	35c vio bl, blk & yel	.30	.25
C291	AP59	85c black & brt pink	.65	.55

Refugee Year, July 1, 1959-June 30, 1960.

Banner and "OEA" — AP60

35c, "OEA" in oval. 55c, Clasped hands. 2col, "OEA" & map of Americas. 5col, Flags forming bird. 10col, Map of Costa Rica, flags & "OEA."

1960, Aug. 15 Litho. *Perf. 10*

C292	AP60	25c black & multi	.25	.25
a.		Multi, impression sideways	60.00	
C293	AP60	35c multicolored	.30	.30
a.		Pair, imperf. between	60.00	
C294	AP60	55c multicolored	.50	.40
C295	AP60	5col multicolored	3.00	2.75
C296	AP60	10col black & multi	5.00	4.50
		Nos. C292-C296 (5)	9.05	8.20

Souvenir Sheet

Imperf

C297	AP60	2col multicolored	2.75	2.75

Pan-American Conf., San Jose, Aug. 15.

St. Louisa de Marillac and Orphanage — AP61

St. Vincent de Paul — AP62

25c, St. Vincent & old seminary. 50c, St. Louisa & sickroom. 1col, St. Vincent & new seminary.

1960, Oct. 26 Engr. *Perf. 14x13½*

C298	AP61	10c green	.25	.25
C299	AP61	25c carmine	.25	.25
C300	AP61	50c dk blue	.25	.25
C301	AP61	1col brown org	.40	.30
C302	AP62	5col brown	2.10	1.75
		Nos. C298-C302 (5)	3.25	2.80

St. Vincent (1581?-1660) and St. Louisa (1591-1660). Nos. C298-C302 exist imperf.

Runner AP63

Sports: 2c, Woman swimmer. 3c, Bicyclist. 4c, Weight lifter. 5c, Woman tennis player. 10c, Boxers. 25c, Soccer player. 85c, Basketball player. 1col, Baseball batter. 5col, Romulus and Remus statue. 10col, Pistol marksman.

Perf. 13½x14

1960, Dec. 14 Photo. Unwmk.

Designs in Black

C303	AP63	1c brt yellow	.25	.25
C304	AP63	2c lt ultra	.25	.25
C305	AP63	3c dp rose	.25	.25
C306	AP63	4c yellow	.25	.25
C307	AP63	5c brt yel grn	.25	.25
C308	AP63	10c pink	.25	.25
C309	AP63	25c lt bl grn	.25	.25
C310	AP63	85c lilac	1.25	.80
C311	AP63	1col gray	1.40	1.00
C312	AP63	10col lt violet	10.50	8.00
		Nos. C303-C312 (10)	14.90	11.55

Souvenir Sheets

Perf. 14x13½

C313	AP63	5col multi	6.00	6.00

17th Olympic Games, Rome, 8/25-9/11.

Nos. C303-C313 exist imperf.

No. C255 Srchd. and Ovptd. in Blue or Ultramarine

Engraved and Photogravure

1961, Apr. 21 *Perf. 12*

Center in Black

C314	AP53	25c on 75c red org (Bl)	.25	.25
C315	AP53	75c red orange (U)	.55	.25

15th Amateur Baseball Championships.

Alberto Brenes C. — AP64

No. C317, Manuel Aguilar. No. C318, Agustin Gutierrez L. No. C319, Vicente Herrera.

1961, June 12 Photo. *Perf. 12*

C316 AP64 10c deep claret .25 .25
C317 AP64 10c blue .25 .25
C318 AP64 25c bright violet .25 .25
C319 AP64 25c gray .25 .25
Nos. C316-C319 (4) 1.00 1.00

First Continental Congress of Lawyers, San José, June 11-15. Exist imperf.
See Nos. C330-C333.

Miguel Obregon — AP65

1961, July 19 Litho. *Perf. 13½*

C320 AP65 10c Prussian green .40 .25

Birth centenary of Prof. Miguel Obregon L. Exists imperf. Value $50.

UN Food and Agriculture Organization AP66

UN day (UN Organizations): 20c, WHO. 25c, ILO. 30, ITU. 35c, World Meteorological Organization. 45c, UNESCO. 85c, ICAO. 5col, "United Nations" holding the world. 10col, Int. Bank for Reconstruction and Development.

Perf. 11½

1961, Oct. 24 Unwmk. Engr.

C321 AP66 10c lt green .25 .25
C322 AP66 20c orange .25 .25
C323 AP66 25c Prus grn .25 .25
C324 AP66 30c dk blue .25 .25
C325 AP66 35c carmine rose .90 .25
C326 AP66 45c violet .30 .25
C327 AP66 85c blue .65 .55
C328 AP66 10col dk sl grn 5.25 4.50
Nos. C321-C328 (8) 8.10 6.55

Souvenir Sheet

Imperf

C329 AP66 5col ultra 4.50 4.50

For overprint see No. C338.

Portrait Type of 1961

No. C330, Dr. José Maria Soto Alfaro. No. C331, Dr. Elias Rojas Roman. No. C332, Dr. Andres Saenz Llorente. No. C333, Dr. Juan José Ulloa Giralt.

1961 Photo. *Perf. 13½*

C330 AP64 10c blue green .25 .25
C331 AP64 10c violet .25 .25
C332 AP64 25c dark gray .30 .25
C333 AP64 25c deep claret .30 .25
Nos. C330-C333 (4) 1.10 1.00

9th Congress of Physicians of Central America and Panama.

Nos. C229, C236 and C280 Surcharged in Black, Orange or Red

No. C334

No. C334A

Engraved; Center Photogravure

1962 *Perf. 13x12½, 13½x13*

C334 AP53 10c ("10") on 15c .25 .25
C334A AP53 10c ("c0.10") on 15c (R) .25 .25
C335 AP53 25c on 15c .25 .25
C336 AP53 35c on 50c (O) .30 .25

Engr.

C337 AP57 85c on 80c (R) .95 .80
Nos. C334-C337 (5) 2.00 1.80

No. C336 exists with double surcharge. Value, $35.

Nos. C324 and C282 Overprinted in Red

1962, Sept. 12 *Perf. 11½, 13½x13*

C338 AP66 30c dark blue .55 .40
C339 AP57 2col gray & mar 1.60 1.25

2nd Central American Phil. Convention.

Revenue Stamp Surcharged in Red

1962 Engr. *Perf. 12*

C341 A124 25c on 2c emer .25 .25
C342 A124 35c on 2c emer .25 .25
C343 A124 45c on 2c emer .40 .30
C344 A124 85c on 2c emer .70 .55
Nos. C341-C344 (4) 1.40 1.20

Arms and Malaria Eradication Emblem AP67

1963, Feb. 14 Photo. *Perf. 11½*

C345 AP67 25c brt rose .25 .25
C346 AP67 35c brown org .25 .25
C347 AP67 45c ultra .30 .25
C348 AP67 85c blue grn .65 .50
C349 AP67 1col dk blue 1.10 .65
Nos. C345-C349 (5) 2.55 1.90

WHO drive to eradicate malaria.

Central American Tapir — AP68

Designs: 5c, Paca. 25c, Jaguar. 30c, Ocelot. 35c, Whitetail deer. 40c, Manatee. 85c, White-throated capuchin monkey. 5col, White-lipped peccary.

Perf. 13½

1963, May Unwmk. Photo.

C354 AP68 5c yel ol & brn .25 .25
C355 AP68 10c orange & sl .30 .25
C356 AP68 25c blue & yel .50 .35
C357 AP68 30c lt yel grn & brn .70 .40
C358 AP68 35c bis & red brn 1.00 .40
C359 AP68 40c emer & sl bl 1.25 .55
C360 AP68 85c green & blk 4.00 .55
C361 AP68 5col gray grn & choc 12.00 4.00
Nos. C354-C361 (8) 20.00 6.75

See Nos. C367-C370.

Stamp of 1863 and Packet "Monarch" — AP69

Issue of 1863 and: 2col, Recaredo Bonilla Carrillo, Postmaster, 1862-63. 3col, Burros, overland mail transport, 1839. 10col, Burro railway car.

1963, June 26 Litho.

C362 AP69 25c dl rose & chlky bl .25 .25
C363 AP69 2col gray bl & org 1.75 1.25
C364 AP69 3col bister & emer 3.00 2.00
C365 AP69 10col dl grn & ocher 10.50 6.00
Nos. C362-C365 (4) 15.50 9.50

Centenary of Costa Rica's stamps.
No. C362 is inscribed "William Le Lacheur," the builder and captain of the "Monarch."

Souvenir Sheets

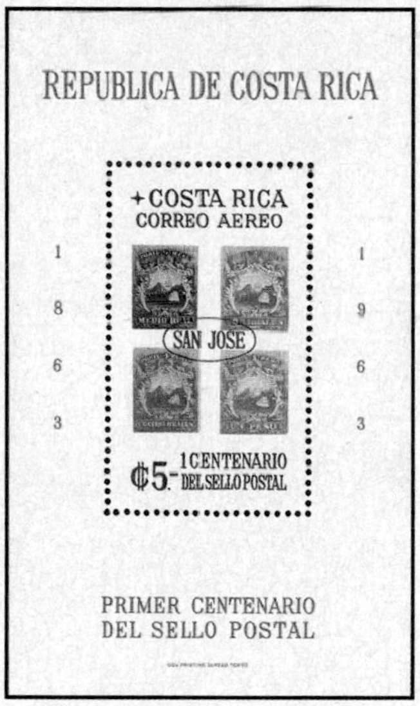

Stamps of 1863 and San José Postmark — AP70

Perf. 13½, Imperf.

1963, June 26 Unwmk.

C366 AP70 5col bl, red, grn & org 5.50 5.50

Cent. of Costa Rica's stamps.
In 1968 examples of No. C366 were overprinted "2-4 Agosto 1968" and "III Exposicion Filatelioa Nacional / 'Costa Rica 68'". Value, $10.50.

Animal Type of 1963 Surcharged in Red

No. C367, Little anteater. No. C368, Gray fox. No. C369, Armadillo. No. C370, Great anteater.

1963, Sept. 14 Photo. *Perf. 13½*

C367 AP68 10c on 1c brt grn & org brn 1.10 .30
C368 AP68 25c on 2c org yel & ol grn 1.10 .30
C369 AP68 35c on 3c bluish grn & brn 1.50 .30
C370 AP68 85c on 4c dp rose & dk brn 2.75 .65
Nos. C367-C370 (4) 6.45 1.55

Examples of No. C370 exist without surcharge.

Pres. Kennedy — AP71

Portraits — Presidents: 25c, Francisco J. Orlich, Costa Rica. 30c, Julio A. Rivera, El Salvador. 35c, Miguel Ydigoras F., Guatemala. 85c, Dr. Ramon Villeda M., Honduras. 1col, Luis A. Somoza, Nicaragua. 3col, Roberto F. Chiari, Panama.

1963, Dec. 7 Unwmk. *Perf. 14*

Portraits in Black Brown

C371 AP71 25c violet brn .30 .25
C372 AP71 30c brt lil rose .30 .25
C373 AP71 35c ocher .30 .25
C374 AP71 85c gray blue .50 .25
C375 AP71 1col orange brn .55 .30
C376 AP71 3col lt ol grn 2.50 1.60
C377 AP71 5col gray 3.25 2.25
Nos. C371-C377 (7) 7.70 5.15

Meeting of Central American Presidents with Pres. John F. Kennedy, San José, Mar. 18-20, 1963.

Ancestral Figure — AP72

Ancient Art: 5c, Dog, horiz. 10c, Ornamental stool, horiz. 25c, Male figure. 30c, Ceremonial dancer. 35c, Ceramic vase. 50c, Frog. 55c, Bell. 75c, Six-limbed figure. 85c, Seated man. 90c, Bird-shaped jug. 1col, Twin human beaker, horiz. 2col, Alligator, horiz. 3col, Twin-tailed lizard. 5col, Figure under arch. 10col, Polished stone figure.

1963-64 Photo. *Perf. 12*

C378 AP72 5c lt yel grn & Prus grn .25 .25
C379 AP72 10c buff & dk grn .25 .25
C380 AP72 25c rose & dk brn .25 .25
C381 AP72 30c ocher & Prus grn ('64) .25 .25
C382 AP72 35c sal & sl grn .25 .25
C383 AP72 45c lt bl & dk brn .25 .25
C384 AP72 50c dl bl & dk brn .40 .25
C385 AP72 55c yel grn & dk brn .55 .25
C386 AP72 75c ocher & dk red brn .55 .25
C387 AP72 85c yel & red brn 1.40 1.40
C388 AP72 90c cit & red brn ('64) 1.75 1.75
C389 AP72 1col lt bl & dk brn ('64) 1.00 .30
C390 AP72 2col buff & dk grn ('64) 1.60 .65
C391 AP72 3col yel grn & dk brn ('64) 5.25 .95
C392 AP72 5col cit & sep ('64) 5.25 5.25
C393 AP72 10col rose lil & sl grn 8.75 8.75
Nos. C378-C393 (16) 28.00 21.30

For surcharges and overprint see Nos. C395, C397-C398, C400, C426-C428.

Flags of Central American States — AP73

1964, Mar. 11 *Perf. 14*

C394 AP73 30c bl, gray, red & blk 1.00 .35

Central American Independence issue. For surcharge see No. C396.

Nos. C381, C394 and C387 Surcharged

1964, Oct. *Perf. 12, 14*

C395 AP72 5c on 30c .55 .25
C396 AP73 15c on 30c .55 .25
C397 AP72 15c on 85c .55 .25
Nos. C395-C397 (3) 1.65 .75

No. C388 Surcharged in Black

1964, Nov. 22 *Perf. 12*

C398 AP72 15c on 90c cit & red brn .50 .25

Paris Postal Conference.

Alfredo Gonzalez F. — AP74

1965, June Photo. *Perf. 12*

C399 AP74 35c dk blue green 3.25 .25

50th anniv. of the National Bank and honoring Alfredo Gonzalez Flores (1877-1962), 1st governor of the bank.

No. C390 Overprinted in Black

1965, Aug. 14 Unwmk. *Perf. 12*

C400 AP72 2col buff & dk grn 1.40 .80

75th anniv. of Chapui Asylum, San José.

Girl, FAO Emblem and Hands Holding Grain — AP75

FAO Emblem and: 15c, Map of Costa Rica and silos, horiz. 50c, World population chart and children. 1col, Plane over map of Costa Rica, horiz.

1965, Oct. 25 Litho. *Perf. 14*

C401 AP75 15c lt brn & blk .25 .25
C402 AP75 35c black & yel .25 .25
C403 AP75 50c ultra & dk grn .25 .25
C404 AP75 1col grn, blk & sil .40 .25
Nos. C401-C404 (4) 1.15 1.00

FAO "Freedom from Hunger" campaign.

Church of Nicoya — AP76

5c, Leonidas Briceno B. 15c, Scroll dated "25 de Julio de 1964." 35c, Map of Guanacaste and Nicoya peninsula. 50c, Dancing couple. 1col, Map showing local products.

1965, Dec. 20 *Perf. 13½x14*

C405 AP76 5c red brn & blk .40 .25
C406 AP76 10c blue & gray .40 .25
C407 AP76 15c bis & slate .40 .25
C408 AP76 35c blue & slate .40 .25
C409 AP76 50c gray & vio bl .55 .25
C410 AP76 1col buff & slate 1.10 .40
Nos. C405-C410 (6) 3.25 1.65

Acquisition of the Nicoya territory.

Runner and Olympic Rings — AP77

Olympic Rings and Emblem: 10c, Bicyclists. 40c, Judo. 65c, Basketball. 80c, Soccer. 1col, Hands holding torches, and Mt. Fuji.

1965, Dec. 23 *Perf. 13x13½*

C411 AP77 5c bister & multi .25 .25
C412 AP77 10c lt lil & multi .25 .25
C413 AP77 40c multicolored .25 .25
C414 AP77 65c lemon & multi .25 .25
C415 AP77 80c tan & multi .40 .25
C416 AP77 1col multicolored .50 .30
a. Souvenir sheet of 2 6.00 3.00
Nos. C411-C416 (6) 1.90 1.55

18th Olympic Games, Tokyo, Oct. 10-25, 1964. No. C416a contains two 1col stamps, one like No. C416, the other with gray background replacing yellow orange.

No. C416a was issued both perf and imperf. Same values.

Nos. C411-C416 exist imperf.

Pres. Kennedy Speaking in San José Cathedral — AP78

Designs: 45c, Friendship 7 capsule circling globe, and Kennedy, horiz. 85c, Kennedy and John, Jr. 1col, Curtis-Lee Mansion and flame from Kennedy grave, Arlington, Va.

Perf. 13½x13, 13x13½

1965, Dec. 23 Litho. Unwmk.

C417 AP78 45c brt bl & lil .25 .25
C418 AP78 55c org & brt bl .30 .25
C419 AP78 85c gray, dk brn & red brn .55 .40
C420 AP78 1col multicolored .65 .50
a. Souvenir sheet of 2 1.25 1.25
Nos. C417-C420 (4) 1.75 1.40

President John F. Kennedy (1917-63). No. C420a contains two 1col stamps, one like No. C420, the other with green background replacing dark blue. Exists with light blue background instead of green; value $150.

No. C420a was issued both perf and imperf. Same values.

Nos. C417-C420 exist imperf.

For surcharges see Nos. C429-C430.

Firemen with Hoses — AP79

Designs: 5c, Fire engine "Knox," horiz. 10c, 1866 fire pump. 35c, Fireman's badge. 50c, Emblem and flags of Confederation of Central American Fire Brigades.

1966, Mar. 12 Litho. *Perf. 11*

C421 AP79 5c black & red .30 .25
C422 AP79 10c bister & red .40 .25
C423 AP79 15c blk, red brn & red .55 .25
C424 AP79 35c black & yel .95 .25
C425 AP79 50c dk blue & red 2.00 .50
Nos. C421-C425 (5) 4.20 1.50

Centenary of San José Fire Brigade.

Nos. C381, C383, C386 and C418-C419 Surcharged

a

b

1966, Dec. Photo. *Perf. 12*

C426 AP72(a) 15c on 30c .25 .25
C427 AP72(a) 15c on 45c .25 .25
C428 AP72(a) 35c on 75c .25 .25

Litho. *Perf. 13x13½*

C429 AP78(a) 35c on 55c .25 .25
C430 AP78(b) 50c on 85c .45 .25
Nos. C426-C430 (5) 1.45 1.25

Revenue Stamps (Basic Type of A124) Surcharged

1967, Jan. Engr. *Perf. 12*

C431 A124 15c on 5c blue .25 .25
C432 A124 35c on 10c claret .30 .25
C433 A124 50c on 20c rose red .50 .25
Nos. C431-C433 (3) 1.05 .75

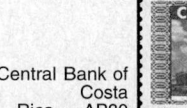

Central Bank of Costa Rica — AP80

1967, Mar. 1 Litho. *Perf. 11*

C434 AP80 5c brt green .35 .25
C435 AP80 15c brown .35 .25
C436 AP80 35c scarlet .35 .25
Nos. C434-C436 (3) 1.05 .75

Power Lines — AP81

Telecommunications Building, San Pedro — AP82

Electrification Program: 15c, Telephone Central. 25c, La Garita Dam. 35c, Rio Mache Reservoir. 50c, Cachi Dam.

1967, Apr. 24 Litho. *Perf. 11*

C437 AP81 5c dark gray .25 .25
C438 AP82 10c brt rose .25 .25
C439 AP81 15c brown org .25 .25
C440 AP82 25c brt ultra .25 .25
C441 AP82 35c brt green .30 .25
C442 AP82 50c red brown .40 .30
Nos. C437-C442 (6) 1.70 1.55

Chondrorhyncha Aromatica — AP83

Orchids: 10c, Miltonia endresii. 15c, Stanhopea cirrhata. 25c, Trichopilia suavis. 35c, Odontoglossum schlieperianum. 50c, Cattleya skinneri. 1col, Cattleya dowiana. 2col, Odontoglossum chiriquense.

1967, June 15 Engr. *Perf. 13x13½*

Orchids in Natural Colors

C443 AP83 5c multicolored .25 .25
C444 AP83 10c olive & multi .40 .30
C445 AP83 15c multicolored .55 .30
C446 AP83 25c multicolored .95 .30
C447 AP83 35c dull vio & multi 1.25 .30
C448 AP83 50c brown & multi 1.60 .30
C449 AP83 1col vio & multi 3.50 .80
C450 AP83 2col dk ol bis & multi 6.00 1.50
Nos. C443-C450 (8) 14.50 4.05

Issued for the University Library.

Institute Emblem — AP84

1967, Oct. 6 Litho. *Perf. 13x13½*

C451 AP84 50c vio bl, lt bl & bl .40 .25

Inter-American Agriculture Institute, 25th anniv.

Church of Solitude — AP85

Costa Rican Churches: 10c, Basilica of Santo Domingo, Heredia. 15c, Cathedral of Tilaran. 25c, Cathedral of Alajuela. 30c, Mercy Church. 35c, Basilica of Our Lady of Angels. 40c, Church of St. Raphael, Heredia. 45c, Ujarras ruins. 50c, Ruins of parish church, Cartago. 55c, Cathedral of San José. 65c, Parish church, Puntarenas. 75c, Church of Orosi. 80c, Cathedral of St. Isidro, the General. 85c, St. Ramon Church. 90c, Church of the Abandoned. 1col, Coronado Church. 2col, Church of St. Teresita. 3col, Parish Church, Heredia. 5col, Carmelite Church. 10col, Limon Cathedral.

1967, Dec. 15 Engr. *Perf. 12½*

C452 AP85 5c green .25 .25
C453 AP85 10c blue .25 .25
C454 AP85 15c lilac .25 .25
C455 AP85 25c dull yel .25 .25
C456 AP85 30c orange brn .25 .25
C457 AP85 35c lt blue .25 .25
C458 AP85 40c dp orange .30 .25

C459	AP85	45c dl bl grn	.30	.25
C460	AP85	50c olive	.40	.25
C461	AP85	55c brown	.40	.25
C462	AP85	65c car rose	.65	.25
C463	AP85	75c sepia	.70	.30
C464	AP85	80c yellow	1.40	.45
C465	AP85	85c violet blk	1.60	.45
C466	AP85	90c emerald	1.60	.65
C467	AP85	1col slate	1.25	.35
C468	AP85	2col brt green	5.50	1.75
C469	AP85	3col orange	7.25	3.00
C470	AP85	5col vio blue	8.00	3.00
C471	AP85	10col carmine	9.75	4.50
		Nos. C452-C471 (20)	40.60	17.20

Nos. C452 and C454 exist imperf; Nos. C455 and C470 exist imperf horiz.

See Nos. C561-C576.

LACSA Emblem — AP86

45c, LACSA emblem, jet, horiz. 50c, Decorated wheel, anniversary emblem.

Perf. 13x13½, 13½x13

1967, Dec. 12 Litho. & Engr.

C472	AP86	40c ultra, grnsh bl & gold	.25	.25
C473	AP86	45c blk, pale grn, ultra & gold	.30	.25
C474	AP86	50c blue & multi	.40	.25
		Nos. C472-C474 (3)	.95	.75

20th anniv. (in 1966) of Lineas Aereas Costaricenses, LACSA, Costa Rican Airlines.

Scout Directing Traffic — AP87

Designs: 25c, Campfire under tree. 35c, Flag of Costa Rica, Scout flag and emblem. 50c, Encampment, horiz. 65c, Photograph of first Scout troop, horiz.

1968, Mar. 15 ***Perf. 13***

C475	AP87	15c lt bl, blk & lt brn	.25	.25
C476	AP87	25c lt ultra, vio bl & org	.25	.25
C477	AP87	35c blue & multi	.40	.25
C478	AP87	50c multicolored	.65	.30
C479	AP87	65c sal, dk bl & brn	.80	.40
		Nos. C475-C479 (5)	2.35	1.45

Costa Rican Boy Scouts, 50th anniversary.

Runner — AP88

Sports: 40c, Women's running. 55c, Boxing. 65c, Bicycling. 75c, Weight lifting. 1col, High diving. 3col, Rifle shooting.

1969, Jan. 17 Litho. ***Perf. 10x11***

C481	AP88	30c multi	.25	.25
C482	AP88	40c multi	.25	.25
C483	AP88	55c multi	.25	.25
C484	AP88	65c lil & multi	.30	.25
C485	AP88	75c multi	.30	.25
C486	AP88	1col multi	.40	.25
C487	AP88	3col multi	1.60	.95
		Nos. C481-C487 (7)	3.35	2.45

19th Olympic Games, Mexico City, 10/12-27.

Philatelic Exhibition Emblem — AP89

1969, June 5 Litho. ***Perf. 11x10***

C488	AP89	35c multicolored	.25	.25
C489	AP89	40c pink & multi	.25	.25
C490	AP89	50c lt blue & multi	.25	.25
C491	AP89	2col multicolored	.95	.55
		Nos. C488-C491 (4)	1.70	1.30

4th Natl. Philatelic Exhib., San José, 6/5-8.

ILO Emblem AP90

1969, Oct. 29 Litho. ***Perf. 10***

C492	AP90	35c bl grn & blk	.25	.25
C493	AP90	50c scarlet & blk	.25	.25

50th anniv. of the ILO.

Soccer — AP91

Designs: 65c, Soccer ball, map of North and Central America. 85c, Soccer player. 1col, Two players in action.

1969, Nov. 23 Litho. ***Perf. 11x10***

C494	AP91	65c gray & multi	.30	.25
C495	AP91	75c multicolored	.30	.25
C496	AP91	85c multicolored	.40	.30
C497	AP91	1col pink & multi	.55	.40
		Nos. C494-C497 (4)	1.55	1.20

Issued to publicize the 4th Soccer Championships (CONCACAF), Nov. 23-Dec. 7.

Stylized Crab — AP92

1970, May 14 Litho. ***Perf. 12½***

C498	AP92	10c blk & lil rose	.25	.25
C499	AP92	15c blk & yel	.25	.25
C500	AP92	50c blk & brn org	.25	.25
C501	AP92	1.10col blk & emer	.55	.25
		Nos. C498-C501 (4)	1.30	1.00

10th Inter-American Cancer Cong., 5/22-29.

Costa Rica No. 124, Magnifying Glass and Stamps — AP93

2col, Father, son with stamps, album.

1970, Sept. 14 Litho. ***Perf. 11***

C502	AP93	1col ultra, brn & car rose	1.00	.25
C503	AP93	2col blk, pink & ultra	1.25	.55

The 5th National Philatelic Exhibition.

EXPO Emblem and Costa Rican Cart — AP94

EXPO Emblem and: 10c, Japanese floral arrangement, vert. 35c, Pavilion and Tower of the Sun. 40c, Japanese tea ceremony. 45c, Woman picking coffee, vert. 55c, Earth seen from moon, vert.

1970, Oct. 22 Litho. ***Perf. 13x13½***

C504	AP94	10c multicolored	.25	.25
C505	AP94	15c green & multi	.25	.25
C506	AP94	35c blue & multi	.55	.25
C507	AP94	40c gray & multi	.65	.25
C508	AP94	45c multicolored	.70	.25
C509	AP94	55c black & multi	1.90	.30
		Nos. C504-C509 (6)	4.30	1.55

EXPO '70 International Exhibition, Osaka, Japan, Mar. 15-Sept. 13.

Escazu Valley, by Margarita Bertheau — AP95

Paintings: 25c, "Irazu," by Rafael A. Garcia, vert. 80c, Shore landscape, by Teodorico Quiros. 1col, "The Other Face," by Cesar Valverde. 2.50col, Mother and Child, by Luis Daell, vert.

1970, Nov. 4 Litho. ***Perf. 12½***

C510	AP95	25c multi	.80	.30
C511	AP95	45c multi	.80	.30
C512	AP95	80c multi	1.25	.55
C513	AP95	1col multi	1.25	.65
C514	AP95	2.50col multi	2.50	2.00
		Nos. C510-C514 (5)	6.60	3.80

Arms of Costa Rica, 1964 — AP96

Various Coats of Arms, dated: 10c, Nov. 27, 1906. 15c, Sept. 29, 1848. 25c, Apr. 21, 1840. 35c, Nov. 22, 1824. 50c, Nov. 2, 1824. 1col, Mar. 6, 1824. 2col, May 10, 1823.

1971, Feb. 10 Litho. ***Perf. 14x13½***

C515	AP96	5c buff & multi	.40	.25
C516	AP96	10c multi	.40	.25
C517	AP96	15c yel & multi	.50	.25
C518	AP96	25c pink & multi	.50	.25
C519	AP96	35c multi	.65	.25
C520	AP96	50c rose & multi	.70	.25
C521	AP96	1col beige & multi	.80	.40
C522	AP96	2col multi	1.60	.80
		Nos. C515-C522 (8)	5.55	2.70

National Theater AP97

1971, Apr. 14 Litho. ***Perf. 11***

C523	AP97	2col plum	.40	.30

Organization of American States meeting.

José Matias Delgado, Manuel José Arce AP98

Flag of Costa Rica — AP99

Independence Leaders: 10c, Miguel Larreinaga and Manuel Antonio de la Cerda, Nicaragua. 15c, José Cecilio del Valle, Dionisio de Herrera, Honduras. 35c, Pablo Alvarado and Florencio del Castillo, Costa Rica. 50c, Antonio Larrazabal and Pedro Molina, Guatemala. 2col, Costa Rica coat of arms.

1971, Sept. 14 ***Perf. 13***

C524	AP98	5c multi	.25	.25
C525	AP98	10c multi	.25	.25
C526	AP98	15c gray, brn & blk	.25	.25
C527	AP98	35c multi	.25	.25
C528	AP98	50c multi	.25	.25
C529	AP99	1col multi	.25	.25
C530	AP99	2col multi	.40	.40
		Nos. C524-C530 (7)	1.90	1.90

Central American Independence, sesqui.

Soccer Federation Emblem — AP100

1971, Dec. 6

C531	AP100	50c multi	.30	.25
C532	AP100	60c multi	.30	.25

50th anniv. of Soccer Federation of Costa Rica.

Children of the World — AP101

1972, Jan. 11 ***Perf. 12½***

C533	AP101	50c multi	.25	.25
C534	AP101	1.10col red & multi	.40	.25

25th anniv. (in 1971) of UNICEF.

Tree of Guanacaste AP102

Designs: 40c, Hermitage, Liberia. 55c, Petroglyphs, Rincón Brujo. 60c, Painted head, sculpture from Curubandé, vert.

1972, Feb. 28 ***Perf. 11***

C535	AP102	20c brn, ol & brt grn	.40	.25
C536	AP102	40c brn & ol	.40	.25
C537	AP102	55c blk & brn	.40	.25
C538	AP102	60c blk, buff & ver	.40	.25
		Nos. C535-C538 (4)	1.60	1.00

Bicentenary of the founding of the city of Liberia, Guanacaste.

Farm and Family — AP103

Designs: 45c, Cattle, dairy products and meat, horiz. 50c, Kneeling figure with plant. 10col, Farmer and map of Americas.

1972, June 30 Litho. *Perf. 12½*

C539 AP103 20c multi .30 .25
C540 AP103 45c multi .30 .25
C541 AP103 50c dp yel, grn & blk .30 .25
C542 AP103 10col brn, org & blk 2.50 1.75
Nos. C539-C542 (4) 3.40 2.50

30th anniversary of the Inter-American Institute of Agricultural Sciences.

Inter-American Exhibitions AP104

1972, Aug. 26 Litho. *Perf. 13*

C543 AP104 50c orange & brn .25 .25
C544 AP104 2col blue & vio .40 .30

4th Interamerican Philatelic Exhibition, EXFILBRA, Rio de Janeiro, Aug. 26-Sept. 2.

First Book Printed in Costa Rica — AP105

Intl. Book Year: 50c, 5col, Natl. Library, horiz.

1972, Dec. 7 Litho. *Perf. 12½*

C545 AP105 20c brt blue .40 .25
C546 AP105 50c gold & multi .40 .25
C547 AP105 75c multicolored .40 .25
C548 AP105 5col multicolored 1.90 .95
Nos. C545-C548 (4) 3.10 1.70

No. C545 exists on thin dull paper with shiny gum. Values: unused $20, used $10.

Road to Irazú Volcano AP106

1972-73 *Perf. 11x11½, 11½x11*

C549 AP106 5c like 20c .30 .25
C550 AP106 15c Coco-Culebra Bay .30 .25
C551 AP106 20c shown .30 .25
C552 AP106 25c like 15c .30 .25
C553 AP106 40c Manuel Antonio Beach .30 .25
C554 AP106 45c Tourist Office emblem .30 .25
C555 AP106 50c Lindora Lake .30 .25
C556 AP106 60c San Jose P.O., vert. .30 .25
C557 AP106 80c like 40c .40 .25
C558 AP106 90c like 45c .40 .25
C559 AP106 1col like 50c .40 .25
C560 AP106 2col like 60c .70 .50
Nos. C549-C560 (12) 4.30 3.25

Tourism year of the Americas.

Issued: 20c, 25c, 80c, 90c, 1col, 2col, 12/26; others, 3/21/73.

No. C555 exists with inverted center, used only. Value $10,000.

Church Type of 1967

Designs as before.

1973, July 16 Engr. *Perf. 12½*

C561 AP85 5c slate grn .25 .25
C562 AP85 10c olive .25 .25
C563 AP85 15c orange .25 .25
C564 AP85 25c brown .25 .25
C565 AP85 30c rose claret .25 .25
C566 AP85 35c violet .25 .25
C567 AP85 40c brt green .25 .25
C568 AP85 45c dull yellow .25 .25
C569 AP85 50c rose magenta .25 .25
C570 AP85 55c blue .25 .25
C571 AP85 65c black .30 .25
C572 AP85 75c rose red .40 .25
C573 AP85 80c yellow grn .45 .25
C574 AP85 85c lilac .50 .25
C575 AP85 90c brt pink .55 .25
C576 AP85 1col dark blue .65 .25
Nos. C561-C576 (16) 5.35 4.00

Human Rights Flame — AP107

1973, Dec. 10 Photo. *Perf. 10½*

C577 AP107 50c black & red .40 .25

25th anniversary of the Universal Declaration of Human Rights.

OAS Emblem — AP108

1973, Dec. 17 Litho. *Perf. 10½*

C578 AP108 20c dk bl & dp car .40 .25

25th anniv. of the OAS.

Joaquin Vargas Calvo — AP109

No. C580, Alejandro Monestel. No. C581, Julio Mata. No. C582, Julio Fonseca. No. C583, Rafael A. Chaves. No. C584, Manuel M. Gutierrez.

1974, Jan. 14

C579 AP109 20c shown .40 .25
C580 AP109 20c multicolored .40 .25
C581 AP109 20c multicolored .40 .25
C582 AP109 60c multicolored .40 .25
C583 AP109 2col multicolored .90 .30
C584 AP109 5col multicolored 2.10 1.25
Nos. C579-C584 (6) 4.60 2.55

Costa Rican composers honored by the National Symphony Orchestra.

Revenue Stamps Overprinted in Black — AP110

1974, Apr. 5 Engr. *Perf. 12*

C585 AP110 50c brown .25 .25
C586 AP110 1col violet .30 .25
C587 AP110 2col orange .70 .40
C588 AP110 5col olive 1.75 1.75
Nos. C585-C588 (4) 3.00 2.65

Telephone Building, San Pedro — AP111

Designs: 65c, Rio Macho Control, horiz. 85c, Turbines, Rio Macho Center. 1.25col, Cachi Dam and reservoir, horiz. 2col, I.C.E. Headquarters.

1974, July 30 Litho. *Perf. 10½*

C589 AP111 50c gold & multi .25 .25
C590 AP111 65c gold & multi .25 .25
C591 AP111 85c gold & multi .30 .25
C592 AP111 1.25col gold & multi .40 .25
C593 AP111 2col gold & multi .80 .40
Nos. C589-C593 (5) 2.00 1.40

25th anniversary of Costa Rican Electrical Institute (I.C.E.).

EXFILMEX 74 Emblem AP112

1974, Aug. 22 *Perf. 13*

C594 AP112 65c green .25 .25
C595 AP112 3col lilac rose .65 .40

5th Inter-American Philatelic Exhibition, EXFILMEX-74 UPU, Mexico City, Oct. 26-Nov. 3.

Map of Costa Rica, 4-S Emblem AP113

50c, Young harvesters and 4-S emblem.

1974, Oct. 7 Litho. *Perf. 12x11*

C596 AP113 20c brt green .40 .25
C597 AP113 50c multicolored .40 .25

25th anniversary of 4-S Clubs of Costa Rica (similar to US 4-H Clubs).

Roberto Brenes Mesen — AP114

Designs: 85c, "Love and Death," manuscript. 5col, Hands of writer, horiz.

1974, Oct. 14 Litho. *Perf. 10½*

C598 AP114 20c black & brn .25 .25
C599 AP114 85c black & red .25 .25
C600 AP114 5col black & red brn 1.60 .90
Nos. C598-C600 (3) 2.10 1.40

Mesen, educator & writer, birth centenary.

"Life Insurance" AP115

Designs: 20c, Ricardo Jiménez Oreamuno and Tomás Soley Güell, horiz. 50c, Harvest Insurance (hand holding shovel), horiz. 85c, Maritime insurance (hand holding paper boat). 1.25col, INS emblem. 2col, Workers rehabilitation (arm with crutch). 2.50col, Workers' Compensation (hand holding wrench). 20col, Fire insurance (hands protecting house).

1974, Oct. 30 *Perf. 14*

C601 AP115 20c multi .25 .25
C602 AP115 50c multi .25 .25
C603 AP115 65c multi .25 .25
C604 AP115 85c multi .25 .25
C605 AP115 1.25col multi .30 .25
C606 AP115 2col multi .55 .25
C607 AP115 2.50col multi .65 .40
C608 AP115 20col multi 4.50 4.50
Nos. C601-C608 (8) 7.00 6.40

Costa Rican Insurance Institute (Instituto Nacional de Seguros, INS), 50th anniversary.

For surcharges see Nos. C721-C722.

WPY Emblem — AP116

1974, Nov. 13 Litho. *Perf. 11x11½*

C609 AP116 2col vio bl & red .50 .25

World Population Year.

Oscar J. Pinto F. — AP117

Designs: 50c, Alberto Montes de Oca D., champion sharpshooter. 1col, Eduardo Garnier, sports promoter. O. J. Pinto, introducer of soccer.

1974, Dec. 2 *Perf. 13*

C610 AP117 20c gray & dk bl .25 .25
C611 AP117 50c gray & dk bl .25 .25
C612 AP117 1col gray & dk bl .50 .25
Nos. C610-C612 (3) 1.00 .75

First Central American Olympic Games, held in Guatemala, 1973.

Mormodes Buccinator AP118

Masdevallia Ephippium AP119

Orchids: No. C614, Gongora claviodora. No. C616, Encyclia spondiadum. No. C617, Lycaste skinneri alba. No. C618, Peristeria elata. No. C619, Miltonia roezelii. No. C620, Brassavola digbyana. No. C621, Epidendrum mirabile. No. C622, Barkeria lindleyana. No. C623, Cattleya skinneri. No. C624, Sobralia macrantha. No. C625, Lycaste cruenta. No. C626, Oncidium obryzatum. No. C627, Gongora armeniaca. No. C628, Sievekingia suavis. No. C629, Hexisea imbricata. No. C630, Warcewiczella discolor. No. C631, Oncidium kramerianum. No. C632, Cattleya dowiana.

1975, Mar. 7 Litho. *Perf. 10½, 13½*

C613 AP118 25c shown .65 .25
C614 AP118 25c multi .65 .25
C615 AP119 25c shown .65 .25

C616 AP119 25c multi .65 .25
a. Block of 4, #C613-C616 2.60 1.25
b. As "a," perf. 10½ 1.60 1.25
C617 AP118 65c multi 1.60 .25
C618 AP118 65c multi 1.60 .25
C619 AP119 65c multi 1.60 .25
C620 AP119 65c multi 1.60 .25
a. Block of 4, #C617-C620, perf. 13½ 6.50 2.25
b. As "a," perf. 10½ 16.00 2.25
C621 AP118 80c multi 2.25 .30
C622 AP118 80c multi 2.25 .30
C623 AP119 80c multi 2.25 .30
C624 AP119 80c multi 2.25 .30
a. Block of 4, #C621-C624 9.00 2.50
b. As "a," perf. 10½ 16.00 2.50
C625 AP118 1.40col multi 2.75 .40
C626 AP118 1.40col multi 2.75 .40
C627 AP119 1.40col multi 2.75 .40
C628 AP119 1.40col multi 2.75 .40
a. Block of 4, #C625-C628 11.00 4.50
b. As "a," perf. 10½ 9.75 4.50

Perf. 13½

C629 AP118 1.75col multi 1.60 .40
C630 AP118 2.15col multi 1.60 .55
C631 AP119 2.50col multi 2.75 1.10
C632 AP119 3.25col multi 3.25 1.40
Nos. C613-C632 (20) 38.20 8.25

5th National Orchid Exhibition.

Nos. C613-C628 were printed in both perforations on two different papers: dull finish and shiny. Nos. C629-C632 were printed on shiny paper.

Most examples of Nos. C617-C620, perf 10½, were surcharged.

For overprints and surcharges see Nos. C715-C720, C723-C728.

Radio Club Emblem AP120

Members' Flags and Emblem — AP121

Design: 2col, Federation emblem.

1975, Apr. 16 Litho. *Perf. 13½*

C633 AP120 1col blk & red lil .50 .25
C634 AP121 1.10col multi .55 .25
C635 AP120 2col black & bl .95 .25
Nos. C633-C635 (3) 2.00 .75

16th Central American Radio Amateurs' Convention, San José, May 2-4.

Nicoya Beach AP122

Designs: 75c, Driving cattle. 1col, Colonial Church, Nicoya. 3col, Savannah riders, vert.

1975, Aug. 1 Litho. *Perf. 13½*

C636 AP122 25c gray & multi .25 .25
C637 AP122 75c gray & multi .25 .25
C638 AP122 1col gray & multi .30 .25
C639 AP122 3col gray & multi 1.00 .85
Nos. C636-C639 (4) 1.80 1.60

Sesqui. of annexation of Nicoya District.

Costa Rica #158 AP123

Designs (Type A90 of 1932): No. C641, #159. No. C642, #160. No. C643, #161.

1975, Aug. 14 Litho. *Perf. 12*

C640 AP123 2.20col blk & org .40 .35
C641 AP123 2.20col blk & dk grn .40 .35
C642 AP123 2.20col blk & car rose .40 .35
C643 AP123 2.20col blk & dk bl .40 .35
a. Block of 4, #C640-C643 4.00 4.00

6th Natl. Phil. Exhib., San José, Aug. 14-17.
For surcharges see Nos. C885-C892.

IWY Emblem AP124

1975, Oct. 9 Litho. *Perf. 10½*

C644 AP124 40c vio bl & red .25 .25
C645 AP124 1.25col blk & ultra .40 .25

International Women's Year 1975.

UN Emblem AP125

UN, 30th Anniv.: 60c, UN General Assembly, horiz. 1.20col, UN Headquarters, NY.

1975, Oct. 24 *Perf. 12*

C646 AP125 10c bl & blk .25 .25
C647 AP125 60c multi .25 .25
C648 AP125 1.20col multi .40 .25
Nos. C646-C648 (3) .90 .75

The Visitation, by Jorge Gallardo AP126

Paintings by Jorge Gallardo: 1col, Nativity and Star. 5col, St. Joseph in his Workshop, Virgin and Child.

1975, Nov. 3 *Perf. 10½*

C649 AP126 50c multi .30 .25
C650 AP126 1col multi .50 .25
C651 AP126 5col multi 1.75 .70
Nos. C649-C651 (3) 2.55 1.20

Christmas 1975.

"20-30" Club Emblem — AP127

1976, Jan. 16 Litho. *Perf. 12*

C652 AP127 1col multi .40 .25

"20-30" Club of Costa Rica, 20th anniv.

Quercus Brenessi Trel — AP128

Plants: 30c, Maxillaria albertii schecht. 55c, Calathea brenesii standl. 2col, Brenesia costaricensis schlecht. 10col, Philodendron brenesii standl.

1976, Mar. 1 *Perf. 10½*

C653 AP128 5c multi .50 .25
C654 AP128 30c multi .50 .25
C655 AP128 55c multi .75 .25
C656 AP128 2col tan & multi 1.25 .40
C657 AP128 10col multi 5.50 3.00
Nos. C653-C657 (5) 8.50 4.15

Prof. Alberto Manuel Brenes Mora, botanist, birth centenary.

"Literary Development" AP129

Designs: 1.10col, Man holding book, stylized. 5col, Costa Rican flag emanating from book, horiz.

1976, Apr. 9 Litho. *Perf. 16*

C658 AP129 15c multi .25 .25
C659 AP129 1.10col multi .25 .25
C660 AP129 5col multi .95 .80
Nos. C658-C660 (3) 1.45 1.30

Publishing in Costa Rica.
Nos. C658-C660 exist imperf.

Postrider, 1839 — AP130

Costa Rica No. 13, Post Office AP131

Designs: 65c, Costa Rica No. 14 and Post Office. 85c, Costa Rica No. 15 and Post Office. 2col, UPU Monument, Bern, vert.

1976, May 24 *Perf. 10½*

C661 AP130 20c apple grn & blk .30 .25
C662 AP131 50c bister & multi .30 .25
C663 AP131 65c multi .30 .25
C664 AP131 85c multi .30 .25
C665 AP130 2col blk & lt bl .80 .50
Nos. C661-C665 (5) 2.00 1.50

Cent. of UPU (in 1974).

Nos. C662-C664 exist without the surcharges on reproductions of Nos. 13-15.

Telephones, 1876 and 1976 — AP132

Designs: 2col, Wall telephone. 5col, Alexander Graham Bell.

1976, June 28

C666 AP132 1.60col lt bl & blk .40 .25
C667 AP132 2col multicolored .50 .25
C668 AP132 5col yellow & blk 1.25 .95
Nos. C666-C668 (3) 2.15 1.45

Centenary of first telephone call by Alexander Graham Bell, Mar. 10, 1876.

Inverted Center Stamp of 1901 and Association Emblems — AP133

Design: 5col, 1901 stamp between Costa Rican Philatelic Society and Interamerican Philatelic Federation emblems.

1976, Nov. 11 Litho. *Perf. 10½*

C669 AP133 50c multi .25 .25
C670 AP133 1col multi .25 .25
C671 AP133 2col multi .40 .25
Nos. C669-C671 (3) .90 .75

Souvenir Sheet

Perf. 12

C672 AP133 5col multi 5.25 2.50

7th Natl. Phil. Exhib. and 9th Plenary Assembly of the Interamerican Phil. Fed. (FIAF), San José, Nov. 1976.

No. C670 exists in colors of No. C671.

No. C671 exists on thin dull paper, with bright gum. Value, mint, $25.

No. C672 was issued both perf and imperf. Same values.

"Seeing Eye" and Map of Costa Rica AP134

Amadeo Quiros Blanco — AP135

1976, Nov. 22 *Perf. 16*

C673 AP134 35c black & blue .25 .25
C674 AP135 2col multicolored .55 .40

General Audit Office, 25th anniversary.

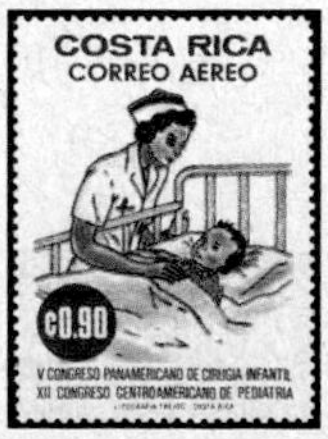

Nurse Attending Child — AP136

1.10col, National Children's Hospital, horiz.

1976, Nov. 29

C675 AP136 90c multi .25 .25
C676 AP136 1.10col multi .40 .25

5th Panamerican Congress of Pediatric Surgery and 12th Congress of Pediatrics.

LACSA Circling Globe — AP137

Designs: 1.20col, Route map. 3col, LACSA emblem and Costa Rican flag.

1976, Dec. 1 *Perf. 10½*

C677 AP137 1col multi .25 .25
C678 AP137 1.20col multi .40 .25
C679 AP137 3col multi 1.10 .70
Nos. C677-C679 (3) 1.75 1.20

Costa Rican Air Lines (LACSA), 30th anniversary.

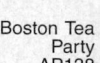

Boston Tea Party AP138

US Bicent.: 5col, Declaration of Independence. 10col, Ringing Liberty Bell to announce Independence, vert.

1976, Dec. 24

C680 AP138 2.20col multi .40 .30
C681 AP138 5col multi 1.00 .70
C682 AP138 10col multi 1.75 1.40
Nos. C680-C682 (3) 3.15 2.40

Tree of Guanacaste AP139

Felipe J. Alvarado AP140

Designs (Rotary Emblem and): 60c, Dr. Paul Blanco Cervantes Hospital, horiz. 3col, Map of Costa Rica, horiz. 10col, Paul Harris.

1977, Mar. 31 Litho. *Perf. 16*

C683 AP139 40c multi .25 .25
C684 AP140 50c multi .25 .25
C685 AP139 60c multi .25 .25
C686 AP139 3col multi .95 .65
C687 AP140 10col multi 3.25 2.50
Nos. C683-C687 (5) 4.95 3.90

Rotary Club of San José, 50th anniversary.

Boruca Cloth AP141

Design: 1.50col, Painted wood ornament.

1977, Feb. 22

C688 AP141 75c multi .25 .25
C689 AP141 1.50col multi .30 .25

Natl. Artisan & Small Industry Program.

Juana Pereira — AP142

Designs: 1col, First Church of Our Lady of the Angels, horiz. 1.10col, Our Lady of the Angels (gold sculpture). 1.25col, Crown of Our Lady of the Angels.

1977, June 6 Litho. *Perf. 10½*

C690 AP142 50c multi .25 .25
C691 AP142 1col multi .25 .25
C692 AP142 1.10col multi .25 .25
C693 AP142 1.25col multi .40 .25
Nos. C690-C693 (4) 1.15 1.00

50th anniv. of the coronation of Our Lady of the Angels, patron saint of Costa Rica.

Alonso de Anguciana de Gamboa — AP143

Designs: 75c, Church of Esparza. 1col, Statue of Our Lady of Candlemas. 2col, Statue of Diego de Artieda y Chirino.

1977, July 4 Litho. *Perf. 10½*

C694 AP143 35c multi .25 .25
C695 AP143 75c multi .25 .25
C696 AP143 1col multi .30 .25
C697 AP143 2col multi .65 .40
Nos. C694-C697 (4) 1.45 1.15

400th anniv. of the founding of Esparza. For surcharge see No. C883.

CARE Emblem and Child — AP144

1col, CARE emblem and soybeans, horiz.

1977, Sept. 14 Litho. *Perf. 16*

C698 AP144 80c multi .25 .25
C699 AP144 1col multi .40 .25

20th anniversary of CARE (relief organization) in Costa Rica.

Institute's Emblem — AP145

First Map of Americas, 1540 — AP146

1977, Oct. 21 Litho. *Perf. 16*

C700 AP145 50c blk & multi .50 .25
C701 AP146 1.40col blk & multi .95 .40

Hispanic Cultural Institute of Costa Rica, 25th anniversary.

Mercy Church, by Ricardo Ulloa B. — AP147

Paintings: 1col, Christ, by Floria Pinto de Herrero. 5col, St. Francis and the Birds, by Louisa Gonzalez Y Saenz.

1977, Nov. 9 Litho. *Perf. 10½*

C702 AP147 50c multi .40 .25
C703 AP147 1col multi .40 .25
C704 AP147 5col multi 1.75 .70
Nos. C702-C704 (3) 2.55 1.20

Health Ministry Emblem — AP148

1977, Nov. 16 *Perf. 16*

C705 AP148 1.40col multi .40 .25

Creation of Ministry of Health.

Picnic — AP149

Designs: 50c, Weaver. 2col, Beach scene. 5col, Fruit and vegetable market. 10col, Swans on lake.

1978, Mar. 21 Litho. *Perf. 10½*

C706 AP149 50c blk & multi .25 .25
C707 AP149 1col blk & multi .40 .25
C708 AP149 2col blk & multi 1.00 .25
C709 AP149 5col blk & multi 1.90 .85
C710 AP149 10col blk & multi 2.50 1.90
Nos. C706-C710 (5) 6.05 3.50

Conf. of Latin American Tourist Organizations.

San Martin — AP150

1978, Aug. 7 Litho. *Perf. 10½*

C711 AP150 5col multi 1.25 .80

Gen. José de San Martin (1778-1850), soldier and statesman, fought for South American independence.

Geographical Institute Emblem — AP151

1978, Aug. 28 Litho. *Perf. 12½*

C712 AP151 5col multi 1.25 .65

Pan-American Geography and History Institute, 50th anniversary. Exists imperf.

University Federation Emblem — AP152

1978, Sept. 18 *Perf. 11*

C713 AP152 80c ultra .40 .25

Central American University Federation, 30th anniversary.

Emblems — AP153

1978, Oct. 24 *Perf. 16*

C714 AP153 2col aqua, blk & gold .55 .40

6th Interamerican Philatelic Exhibition, Argentina 78, Buenos Aires, Oct. 1978.

Nos. C629-C631 Overprinted

1978, Nov. 1 Litho. *Perf. 13½*

C715 AP118 1.75col multi .55 .30
C716 AP118 2.15col multi .70 .40
C717 AP119 2.50col multi .95 .55
Nos. C715-C717 (3) 2.20 1.25

1st Pan Am flight in Costa Rica, 50th anniv.

Nos. C629-C631 Overprinted: "50 Aniversario de la / visita de Lindbergh a / Costa Rica 1928-1978"

1978, Nov. 1

C718 AP118 1.75col multi 1.40 .30
C719 AP118 2.15col multi 1.60 .40
C720 AP119 2.50col multi 2.10 .50
Nos. C718-C720 (3) 5.10 1.20

50th anniversary of Lindbergh's visit.

Nos. C603 and C607 Surcharged

1978, Nov. 8 *Perf. 14*

C721 AP115 50c on 65c multi .25 .25
C722 AP115 2col on 2.50col multi .55 .25

Asilo Carlos Maria Ulloa, birth centenary.

No. C617-C620, C630-C631 Surcharged

Perf. 10½, 13½

1978, Nov. 13 Litho.

C723 AP118 50c on 65c .65 .60
C724 AP118 50c on 65c .65 .60
C725 AP119 50c on 65c .65 .60
C726 AP119 50c on 65c .65 .60
a. Block of 4, #C723-C726 2.75 2.75
C727 AP118 1.20col on 2.15col 1.25 .55
C728 AP119 2col on 2.50col 1.25 .55
Nos. C723-C728 (6) 5.10 3.50

Nos. C723-C726, perf. 13½, value *$20*, unused, *$10*, used, each. No. C726a, unused, *$400*.

Star over Map of Costa Rica — AP154

1978, Nov. 13 *Perf. 10½*

C729 AP154 50c blue & blk .25 .25
C730 AP154 1col rose lil & blk .25 .25
C731 AP154 5col orange & blk 1.40 .65
a. Strip of 3, #C729-C731 2.00 2.00

Christmas 1978. Nos. C729-C731 printed in sheets of 100 and se-tenant in sheet of 15 (3x5). Value, se-tenant sheet, $20.

"Flying Men," Chorotega AP155

Designs: 1.20col, Oviedo giving his History of Indies to Duke of Calabria, horiz. 10col, Lord of Oviedo's coat of arms.

1978, Nov. 20 *Perf. 11½*

C732 AP155 85c multi .25 .25
C733 AP155 1.20col blk & lt bl .25 .25
C734 AP155 10col multi 2.00 2.00
Nos. C732-C734 (3) 2.50 2.50

500th birth anniv. of Gonzalo Fernandez de Oviedo, 1st chronicler of Spanish Indies.

Msgr. Domingo Rivas AP156

San José Cathedral AP157

1978, Dec. 6 *Perf. 16, 13½ (20col)*

C735 AP156 1col black & indigo .25 .25
C736 AP157 20col multicolored 3.75 3.50

Centenary of the Cathedral of San José.

View of Coco Island AP158

Designs: 2.10, 3, 5 col, various views of Coco Island. 10col, Installation of memorial plaque, people and flag. 5, 10col vert.

1979, Apr. 30 **Litho.** *Perf. 10½*

C737 AP158 90c multi .40 .25
C738 AP158 2.10col multi .80 .40
C739 AP158 3col multi 1.25 .55
C740 AP158 5col multi 1.90 1.00
C741 AP158 10col multi 3.75 2.25
a. Souv. sheet, #C737-C741 12.00 12.00
Nos. C737-C741 (5) 8.10 4.45

Visit of Pres. Rodrigo Carazo Odio to Coco Island, June 24, 1978, in the interest of national defense.
No. C741a exists imperf. Value $750.

Shrimp AP159

Designs: 85c, Mahogany snapper. 1.80col, Corvina. 3col, Crayfish. 10col, Tuna.

1979, May 14 **Litho.** *Perf. 13½*

C742 AP159 60c multi .50 .25
C743 AP159 85c multi .50 .25
C744 AP159 1.80col multi .95 .25
C745 AP159 3col multi 1.40 .55
C746 AP159 10col multi 5.00 3.50
Nos. C742-C746 (5) 8.35 4.80

Marine life protection.

Hungry Nestlings, IYC Emblem — AP160

1979, May 24 *Perf. 11*

C747 AP160 1col multi .80 .25
C748 AP160 2col multi 1.60 .50
C749 AP160 20col multi 10.50 5.50
Nos. C747-C749 (3) 12.90 6.25

International Year of the Child.

Microwave Transmitters, Mt. Irazu — AP161

Design: 1col, Arenal Dam, horiz.

1979, June 28 **Litho.** *Perf. 14*

C750 AP161 1col multi .25 .25
C751 AP161 5col multi 1.10 .70

Costa Rican Electricity Institute, 30th anniversary.

Costa Rica No. 1 and Rowland Hill AP162

Design: 10col, Penny Black and Hill.

1979, July 16 *Perf. 13*

C752 AP162 5col lil rose & bl gray 1.25 .55
C753 AP162 10col dl bl & blk 2.40 1.25

Sir Rowland Hill (1795-1879), originator of penny postage.

Poverty, by Juan Ramon Bonilla AP163

National Sculpture Contest: 60c, Hope, by Hernan Gonzalez. 2.10col, Cattle, by Victor M. Bermudez, horiz. 5col, Bust of Clorito Picado, by Juan Rafael Chacon. 20col, Mother and Child, by Francisco Zuniga.

1979, July 16 **Litho.** *Perf. 12*

C754 AP163 60c multi .25 .25
C755 AP163 1col multi .30 .25
C756 AP163 2.10col multi .65 .25
C757 AP163 5col multi 1.60 1.10
C758 AP163 20col multi 5.25 2.50
Nos. C754-C758 (5) 8.05 4.35

Danaus Plexippus — AP164

Butterflies: 1col, Phoebis philea. 1.80col, Rothschildia. 2.10col, Prepona omphale. 2.60col, Marpesia marcella. 4.05col, Morpho cypris.

1979, Aug. 31 **Litho.** *Perf. 13½*

C759 AP164 60c multi *3.00* .40
C760 AP164 1col multi *5.00* .40
C761 AP164 1.80col multi *7.00* .65
C762 AP164 2.10col multi *10.00* 1.25
C763 AP164 2.60col multi *10.00* 2.50
C764 AP164 4.05col multi *18.00* 3.50
Nos. C759-C764 (6) *53.00* 8.70

SOS Emblem, Houses AP165

Children's Drawings: 5col, 5.50col, Landscapes, diff.

1979, Sept. 18

C765 AP165 2.50col multi .95 .40
C766 AP165 5col multi 2.00 .60
C767 AP165 5.50col multi 2.40 .90
Nos. C765-C767 (3) 5.35 1.90

SOS Children's Villages, 30th anniversary.

President Type of 1943

Presidents of Costa Rica: 60c, Rafael Yglesias C. 85c, Ascension Esquivel Ibarra. 1col, Cleto Gonzalez Viquez. 2col, Ricardo Jimenez Oreamuno.

1979, Oct. 8 **Litho.** *Perf. 13½*

C768 A109 10c dk blue .25 .25
C769 A109 60c dull purple .25 .25
C770 A109 85c red orange .25 .25
C771 A109 1col red orange .30 .25
C772 A109 2col brown .65 .40
a. Strip of 5, #C768-C772 1.75 1.40
Nos. C768-C772 (5) 1.70 1.40

Printed in sheets of 100 and se-tenant in sheets of 25 (5x5).
See Nos. C790-C794.

Holy Family, Creche — AP167

1979, Nov. 16 **Litho.** *Perf. 12½*

C773 AP167 1col multi .25 .25
C774 AP167 1.60col multi .65 .25

Christmas 1979.

Reforestation AP168

1980, Jan. 14 **Litho.** *Perf. 11*

C775 AP168 1col multi .25 .25
C776 AP168 3.40col multi .65 .50

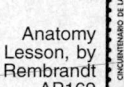

Anatomy Lesson, by Rembrandt AP169

1980, Feb. 7 **Litho.** *Perf. 10½*

C777 AP169 10col multi 4.00 1.75

Legal medicine teaching in Costa Rica, 50th anniversary.

Rotary Intl., 75th Anniv. — AP170

1980, Feb. 26 *Perf. 16*

C778 AP170 2.10col multi .35 .25
C779 AP170 5col multi 1.00 .65

14th Intl. Symposium on Remote Sensing of the Environment, San José, Apr. 23-30 — AP171

Designs: 5col, Gulf of Nicoya, satellite photo.

1980, Mar. 10 **Litho.** *Perf. 12½*

C780 AP171 2.10col Puerto Limon .35 .25
C781 AP171 5col multicolored 1.00 .65

Exist imperf.

Soccer, Moscow '80 Emblem — AP172

1980, Apr. 16 **Litho.** *Perf. 10½*

C782 AP172 1col shown *.50* .25
C783 AP172 3col Bicycling *8.00* .75
C784 AP172 4.05col Baseball *8.00* 1.00
C785 AP172 20col Swimming *8.00* 5.00
Nos. C782-C785 (4) *24.50* 7.00

22nd Summer Olympic Games, Moscow, July 19-Aug. 3.

Poas Volcano AP173

1980, May 14 **Litho.** *Perf. 10½*

C786 AP173 1col shown .25 .25
C787 AP173 2.50col Cahuita Beach .55 .40

National Parks Service, 10th anniversary.

José Maria Zeledon Brenes, Score — AP174

Design: 10col, Manuel Maria Gutierrez.

1980, June 25 Litho. *Perf. 12½*

C788	AP174	1col multi	.25	.25
C789	AP174	10col multi	1.60	1.40

National anthem composed by Brenes (words) and Gutierrez (music). Nos. C788-C789 exist imperf.

President Type of 1943

1col, Alfredo Gonzalez F. 1.60col, Federico Tinoco G. 1.80col, Francisco Aguilar B. 2.10col, Julio Acosta G. 3col, Leon Cortes C.

1980, Aug. 14 Litho. *Perf. 11*

C790	A109	1col dk red	.25	.25
C791	A109	1.60col slate bl	.40	.25
C792	A109	1.80col brown	.40	.25
C793	A109	2.10col dull green	.50	.25
C794	A109	3col dark purple	.80	.50
		Nos. C790-C794 (5)	2.35	1.50

8th Natl. Phil. Exhib. — AP175

1980, Sept. 11 *Perf. 13½*

C795	AP175	5col multi	.80	.60
C796	AP175	20col multi	3.25	2.75

Fruits — AP176

1980, Sept. 24 *Perf. 10½*

C797	AP176	10c shown	.25	.25
C798	AP176	60c Cacao	.50	.25
C799	AP176	1col Coffee	.80	.25
C800	AP176	2.10col Bananas	1.60	.25
C801	AP176	3.40col Flowers	2.00	.50
C802	AP176	5col Sugar cane	2.40	.95
		Nos. C797-C802 (6)	7.55	2.45

Giant Tree, by Jorge Carvajal — AP177

Paintings: 2.10col, Secret Look, by Rolando Cubero. 2.45col, Consuelo, by Fernando Carballo. 3col, Volcano, by Lola Fernandez. 4.05col, attending Mass, by Francisco Amighetti.

1980, Oct. 22 Litho. *Perf. 10½*

C803	AP177	1col multi	.40	.25
C804	AP177	2.10col multi	.55	.25

Size: 28x30mm

C805	AP177	2.45col multi	.70	.30

Size: 22x36mm

C806	AP177	3col multi	.80	.40
C807	AP177	4.05col multi	1.25	.50
		Nos. C803-C807 (5)	3.70	1.70

Virgin and Child, by Raphael AP178

Christmas 1980: 10col, Virgin and Child and St. John, by Raphael.

1980, Nov. 11 *Perf. 13½*

C808	AP178	1col multi	.40	.30
C809	AP178	10col multi	2.40	1.75

Juan Santamaria International Airport AP179

1col, Caldera Harbor. 2.10col, Rio Frio Railroad Bridge. 2.60col, Highway to Colon. 5col, Huetar post office.

1980, Dec. 11 Litho. *Perf. 10½*

Sizes: 30x30mm, 31x25mm (1.30col), 25x32mm (2.60col)

C810	AP179	1col multi	.25	.25
C811	AP179	1.30col shown	.40	.25
C812	AP179	2.10col multi	.80	.40
C813	AP179	2.60col multi	.80	.40
C814	AP179	5col multi	1.25	.80
		Nos. C810-C814 (5)	3.50	2.10

Paying your taxes means progress. For surcharge see No. C884.

Repertorio Americano Cover, J. Garcia Monge and Signature — AP180

1981, Jan. 2 Litho. *Perf. 10½*

C815	AP180	1.60col multi	.30	.25
C816	AP180	3col multi	.60	.40

Birth centenary of J. Garcia Monge, founder of Repertorio Americano journal.

Arms of Aserri (Site of Cornea Bank) — AP181

1981, Jan. 28 Litho. *Perf. 13½*

C817	AP181	1col shown	.25	.25
C818	AP181	1.80col Eye	.55	.25
C819	AP181	5col Rojas	1.60	.80
		Nos. C817-C819 (3)	2.40	1.30

Establishment of human cornea bank, founded by Abelardo Rojas.

Harpia Harpyja — AP182

2.50col, Ara macao. 3col, Felis concolor. 5.50col, Ateles geoffrovi.

1980, Dec. 23 *Perf. 11*

C820	AP182	2.10col shown	1.60	.40
C821	AP182	2.50col multi	2.10	.55
C822	AP182	3col multi	2.75	.65
C823	AP182	5.50col multi	5.50	1.10
		Nos. C820-C823 (4)	11.95	2.70

Medical and Surgical Clinic AP183

1981, Apr. 8 Litho. *Perf. 10½*

C824	AP183	5c multi	.25	.25
C825	AP183	10c multi	.25	.25
C826	AP183	50c multi	.25	.25
C827	AP183	1.30col multi	.40	.25
C828	AP183	3.40col multi	.55	.50
C829	AP183	4.05col multi, vert.	.80	.55
		Nos. C824-C829 (6)	2.50	2.05

University of Costa Rica, 40th anniversary.

Mail Transport by Horse — AP184

1981, May 6 Litho. *Perf. 10½*

C830	AP184	1col shown	.25	.25
C831	AP184	2.10col Train, 1857	.55	.25
C832	AP184	10col Mail carriers, 1858	2.40	1.60
		Nos. C830-C832 (3)	3.20	2.10

Heinrich von Stephan (1831-97), UPU founder.

13th World Telecommunications Day — AP185

1981, May 18 *Perf. 11*

C833	AP185	5col multi	3.00	.60
C834	AP185	25col multi	7.50	4.00

Bishop Bernardo Thiel — AP186

1981, June 8 Litho. *Perf. 10½*

C835		Strip of 5, stained glass windows	2.75	2.75
a.		AP186 1col Sts. Peter & Paul	.25	.25
b.		AP186 1col St. Vincent de Paul	.25	.25
c.		AP186 1col Death of St. Joseph	.25	.25
d.		AP186 1col Archangel Michael	.25	.25
e.		AP186 1col Holy Family	.25	.25
C836	AP186	2col shown	.65	.40

Consecration of Bernardo Augusto Thiel as Bishop of San Jose.

Juan Santamaria AP187

2.40col, Alajuela Cathedral, horiz.

1981, June 26 *Perf. 13½*

C837	AP187	1col shown	.25	.25
C838	AP187	2.45col multi	.50	.40

Alajuela province.

Potters — AP188

1.60col, Bricklayers. 1.80col, Farmers. 2.50col, Fishermen. 3col, Nurse, patient. 5col, Children, traffic policeman.

1981, July 10 Litho. *Perf. 10½*

C839	AP188	15c shown	.25	.25
C840	AP188	1.60col multi	.25	.25
C841	AP188	1.80col multi	.25	.25
C842	AP188	2.50col multi	.25	.25
C843	AP188	3col multi	.40	.25
C844	AP188	5col multi	.70	.25
		Nos. C839-C844 (6)	2.10	1.50

Model of New Natl. Archives AP189

Natl. Archives Centenary: 1.40col, Leon Fernandez Bonilla, founder, vert. 2col, Arms, vert. 3col, St. Thomas University, former headquarters.

1981, Aug. 24 Litho. *Perf. 13½*

C845	AP189	1.40col multi	.30	.25
C846	AP189	2col multi	.50	.25
C847	AP189	3col multi	.65	.50
C848	AP189	3.50col multi	.70	.60
		Nos. C845-C848 (4)	2.15	1.60

Men Reaching for Sun, Map AP190

1col, Man in wheelchair, stairs, vert. 2.60col, Man reaching for scale, vert.

1981, Sept. 9 Litho. *Perf. 11*

C849	AP190	1col multi	.30	.25
C850	AP190	2.60col multi	.80	.25
C851	AP190	10col shown	3.50	.80
		Nos. C849-C851 (3)	4.60	1.30

Intl. Year of the Disabled.

World Food Day — AP191

1981, Oct. 16 Litho. *Perf. 10½*

C852	AP191	5col multi	.40	.25
C853	AP191	10col multi	.80	.55

President Type of 1943

1col, Rafael A. Calderon Guardia, 1940. 2col, Teodoro Picado Michalski, 1944. 3col, José Figueres Ferrer, 1953. 5col, Otilio Ulate Blanco, 1949. 10col, Mario Echandi Jimenez, 1958.

1981, Dec. 7 Litho. *Perf. 13½*

C854	A109	1col pink	.55	.55
C855	A109	2col orange	.55	.55
C856	A109	3col green	.70	.55
C857	A109	5col dk bl	1.25	.90
C858	A109	10col blue	2.50	2.00
		Nos. C854-C858 (5)	5.55	4.55

Bar Assoc. of Costa Rica Centenary (1981) AP192

1col, Emblem, horiz. 2col, E. Figueroa, 1st president. 20col, Bar building, horiz.

1982, Mar. 22 Litho. *Perf. 13½*

C859	AP192 1col multi		.25	.25
C860	AP192 2col multi		.25	.25
C861	AP192 20col multi		2.50	1.40
	Nos. C859-C861 (3)		3.00	1.90

National Progress AP193

95c, Housing. 1.15col, Agricultural fair. 1.45col, Education. 1.65col, Drinkable water. 1.80col, Rural medical care. 2.10col, Recreational areas. 2.35col, Natl. Theater Square. 2.60col, Communications. 3col, Electric railroad. 4.05col, Irrigation.

1982 *Perf. 10½*

C862	AP193 95c multi	.25	.25
C863	AP193 1.15col multi	.25	.25
C864	AP193 1.45col multi	.25	.25
C865	AP193 1.65col multi	.25	.25
C866	AP193 1.80col multi	.25	.25
C867	AP193 2.10col multi	.25	.25
C868	AP193 2.35col multi	.40	.25
C869	AP193 2.60col multi	.40	.25
C870	AP193 3col multi	.55	.25
C871	AP193 4.05col multi	.55	.45
	Nos. C862-C871 (10)	3.40	2.70

Issue dates: 1.80col, 2.10col, 2.60col, 3col, 4.05col, May 5; others, June 16.

City of Alajuela Bicentenary AP194

Designs: 5col, Central Park Fountain. 10col, Juan Santamaria Historical and Cultural Museum, horiz. 15col, Church of Christ of Esquipulas. 20col, Monsignor Esteban Lorenzo de Tristan, 25col, Father Juan Manuel Lopez del Corral.

1982, Aug. 9

C872	AP194 5col multi	.55	.30
C873	AP194 10col multi	1.25	.55
C874	AP194 15col multi	1.75	1.25
C875	AP194 20col multi	2.40	1.25
C876	AP194 25col multi	3.00	1.60
	Nos, C872-C876 (5)	8.95	4.95

Perez Zeledon County, 50th Anniv. (1981) — AP195

Designs: 10c, Saint's Stone. 50c, Monument to Mothers. 1col, Pedro Perez Zeledon, 1.25col, St. Isidore Labrador Church. 3.50col, Municipal Building, horiz. 4.25col, Arms.

1982, Aug. 30

C877	AP195 10c multi	.25	.25
C878	AP195 50c multi	.25	.25
C879	AP195 1col multi	.25	.25
C880	AP195 1.25col multi	.25	.25
C881	AP195 3.50col multi	.40	.25
C882	AP195 4.25col multi	.55	.25
	Nos. C877-C882 (6)	1.95	1.50

Nos. C695 and C813 Surcharged

No. C883

No. C884

1982, Oct. 28 Litho. *Perf. 10½*

C883	AP143 3col on 75c multi	.40	.25
C884	AP179 5col on 2.60col multi	.55	.25

Nos. C640-C643 Surcharged and Overprinted

1982, Oct. 28 *Perf. 12*

C885	AP123 8.40col on #C640	.55	.40
C886	AP123 8.40col on #C641	.55	.40
C887	AP123 8.40col on #C642	.55	.40
C888	AP123 8.40col on #C643	.55	.40
C889	AP123 9.70col on #C640	.65	.55
C890	AP123 9.70col on #C641	.65	.55
C891	AP123 9.70col on #C642	.65	.55
C892	AP123 9.70col on #C643	.65	.55
	Nos. C885-C892 (8)	4.80	3.80

9th Natl. Stamp Exhibition.

TB Bacillus Centenary AP196

1982, Nov. 19 *Perf. 13½*

C893	AP196 1.50col Koch	.25	.25
C894	AP196 3col Koch, slide	.40	.25
C895	AP196 3.30col Health Ministry	.40	.25
	Nos. C893-C895 (3)	1.05	.75

Pan-American Blood Donors' Society, 7th Cong. — AP197

30col, Natl. Blood Assoc. emblem. 50col, Cong. emblem.

1982, Nov. 25 *Perf. 11*

C896	AP197 30col multi	2.00	1.40
C897	AP197 50col multi	3.25	2.00

AP198

8.40col, Emblem, horiz. 9.70col, Emblem, diff. 11.70col, Handshake, horiz. 13.05col, Emblem, diff., horiz.

1982, Dec. 13 Litho. *Perf. 10½*

C898	AP198 8.40col multi	.55	.25
C899	AP198 9.70col multi	.80	.40
C900	AP198 11.70col multi	.80	.40
C901	AP198 13.05col multi	.95	.50
	Nos. C898-C901 (4)	3.10	1.55

Inter-Governmental Migration Committee, 30th anniv.

AP199

4.80col, St. Francis of Assisi, by El Greco. 7.40col, Portrait, diff.

1983, Jan. 3 *Perf. 16*

C902	AP199 4.80col multi	.55	.25
C903	AP199 7.40col multi	.80	.25

For surcharges see Nos. C908-C911.

Visit of Pope John Paul II — AP200

1983, Mar. 1 Litho. *Perf. 10½*

C904	AP200 5col multi	*2.75*	.25
C905	AP200 10col multi	*2.75*	.50
C906	AP200 15col multi	*6.00*	.75
	Nos. C904-C906 (3)	*11.50*	1.50

Bolivar, by Francisco Zuniga Chavarria — AP201

1983, July 22 Litho. *Perf. 16*

C907	AP201 10col multi	1.10	.25

Nos. C902-C903 Surcharged

1983, Sept. 23 Litho. *Perf. 16*

C908	AP199 10c on 4.80col	.25	.25
C909	AP199 50c on 4.80col	.25	.25
C910	AP199 1.50col on 7.40col	.25	.25
C911	AP199 3col on 7.40col	.25	.25
	Nos. C908-C911 (4)	1.00	1.00

LACSA Costa Rica Airlines, 40th Anniv. — AP202

Various childrens' drawings: 1col, Adriana E. Hidalgo. 7col, Osvaldo A.G. Vega. 16col, David V. Rodriguez.

1986, Dec. 12 Litho. *Perf. 13½*

C912	AP202 1col multi	*.55*	.25
C913	AP202 7col multi	*3.50*	.30
C914	AP202 16col multi	*8.00*	.75
	Nos. C912-C914 (3)	*12.05*	1.30

Nos. C912-C913 exist perf 11. Unused examples are rare. Value used, $5 each.

Roman Macaya Lahmann, Aviation Pioneer AP203

1988, Sept. 26 Litho. *Perf. 10½*

C915	AP203 10col multi	.50	.25

No. 418 Overprinted

1990, Nov. 5

C916	A180 50col multicolored	4.00	1.50

Bagging Coffee Beans — AP204

Perf. 10½

1990, Nov. 16 Litho. Unwmk.

C917	AP204 50col multicolored	3.00	.80

AP205

1990, Dec. 6

C918	AP205 50col blue & black	3.50	.80

First postage stamps, 150th anniv.

AP206

Banana Picker, 1897, by Alleardo Villa.

1991, Mar. 25 Litho. *Perf. 10½*
C919 AP206 30col multicolored 2.00 .40

National Theater.

No. 428 Overprinted

Litho. & Engr.
1991, Sept. 13 *Perf. 12½*
C920 A188 200col 8.00 2.00

12th Natl. Philatelic Exposition.

No. 402 Overprinted

1991, Oct. 11 Litho. *Perf. 11½*
Granite Paper
C921 A170 20col multicolored 4.00 1.50

Basketball, cent.

Social Security Administration, 50th Anniv. AP207

1991, Nov. 1 Litho. *Perf. 13½*
C922 AP207 15col multicolored 3.00 .50

La Poesia by Vespasiano Bignami — AP208

1992, Jan. 24 Litho. *Perf. 10½*
C923 AP208 35col multicolored 5.00 1.50

National Theater.

Discovery of America, 500th Anniv. AP209

No. C924 — Columbus' ships: a, Nina. b, Santa Maria. c, Pinta.

1992, Oct. 8 Litho. *Perf. 13½*
C924 Strip of 3 5.00 3.00
a.-c. A209 45col Any single 1.50 .90

Intl. Arts Festival — AP210

1993, Mar. 15 Litho. *Perf. 13½*
C925 AP210 45col multicolored 1.40 .50

Telecommunications Institute, 30th Anniv. — AP211

1993, Nov. 25 Litho. *Perf. 13½*
C926 AP211 45col multicolored 1.00 .70

Ministry of the Interior, 150th Anniv. AP212

1994, Mar. 8 Litho. *Perf. 10½*
C927 AP212 45col multicolored 1.00 .70

Intl. Year of the Family — AP213

1994, May 5 Litho. *Perf. 10½*
C928 AP213 45col multicolored 2.50 1.30

LACSA, 50th Anniv. AP214

1996, Mar. 29 Litho. *Perf. 10½*

C929	AP214	5col Douglas DC-3	.25	.25
C930	AP214	10col Curtiss C-46	.25	.25
C931	AP214	20col Beechcraft	.40	.40
C932	AP214	30col DC-6B	.65	.65
C933	AP214	35col BAC 1-11	.70	.70
C934	AP214	40col Convair CV 440	.90	.90
C935	AP214	45col Electra L-188	.95	.95
C936	AP214	50col Boeing 727-200	1.00	1.00
C937	AP214	55col Douglas DC-8	1.25	1.25
C938	AP214	60col Airbus A320	1.40	1.40
		Nos. C929-C938 (10)	7.75	7.75

No. C932 Surcharged

2001, Oct. 5 Litho. *Perf. 10½*
C939 AP214 5col on 30col multi .40 .25

10th Intl. Art Festival — AP215

2006, Mar. 17 Litho. *Perf. 10½*
C940 AP215 120col multi 2.00 2.00

AIR POST SPECIAL DELIVERY STAMPS

Catalogue values for unused stamps in this section are for Never Hinged items.

UPU Headquarters and Monument, Bern — APSD1

Perf. 10x11
1970, May 20 Litho. Unwmk.
CE1 APSD1 35c multi .75 .25
CE2 APSD1 60c multi .75 .25

Opening of the UPU Headquarters in Bern. The red and black label attached to the 60c is inscribed "EXPRES." Values are for stamps with label attached.

Stamps with labels removed were used for regular airmail.

AIR POST OFFICIAL STAMPS

Air Post Stamps of 1934 Ovptd. in Red

1934 Unwmk. *Perf. 12*

CO1	AP8	5c green	.25	.25
CO2	AP8	10c car rose	.25	.25
CO3	AP8	15c chocolate	.50	.50
CO4	AP8	20c deep blue	.80	.80
CO5	AP8	25c deep org	.80	.80
CO6	AP8	40c olive blk	.80	.80
CO7	AP8	50c gray blk	.80	.80
CO8	AP8	60c org yel	.95	.95
CO9	AP8	75c dull vio	.95	.95
CO10	AP9	1col deep rose	1.60	1.60
CO11	AP9	2col light blue	4.75	4.75
CO12	AP9	5col black	8.00	8.00
CO13	AP9	10col red brown	12.00	12.00
		Nos. CO1-CO13 (13)	32.45	32.45

For overprints see Nos. C103-C116.

SPECIAL DELIVERY STAMPS

Catalogue values for unused stamps in this section are for Never Hinged items.

Winged Letter SD1

Unwmk.
1972, Mar. 20 Litho. *Perf. 11*
E1 SD1 75c brown & red .30 .30
E2 SD1 1.50col blue & red .50 .40

1973 *Perf. 11x12*
E3 SD1 75c green & red .30 .30

1973, Nov. 5 Litho. *Perf. 12*
E4 SD1 75c lilac & orange 1.50 .75

Exists perf 11x11½.

Concorde SD2

1976, May 17 Litho. *Perf. 16*
E5 SD2 1col vermilion & multi .75 .75

SD3

1979, June 15 Litho. *Perf. 12½*
E6 SD3 2col multi .90 .50

SD4

1980, Dec. 18 Litho. *Perf. 12½*
E7 SD4 2col multi .80 .50

1982, Dec. 20 Litho. *Perf. 11*
E8 SD4 4col multi .65 .40

POSTAGE DUE STAMPS

D1

1903 Unwmk. Engr. *Perf. 14*
Numerals in Black

J1	D1	5c slate blue	6.75	1.25
J2	D1	10c brown orange	6.75	1.25
J3	D1	15c yellow green	3.50	1.75
J4	D1	20c carmine	4.75	1.75
J5	D1	25c slate gray	4.75	2.40
J6	D1	30c brown	6.00	2.50
J7	D1	40c olive bister	6.75	2.50
J8	D1	50c red violet	6.75	2.50
		Nos. J1-J8 (8)	46.00	15.90

D2

1915 Litho. *Perf. 12*

J9	D2	2c orange	1.25	.55
J10	D2	4c dark blue	1.25	.55
J11	D2	8c gray green	1.25	.55
J12	D2	10c violet	1.25	.55
J13	D2	20c brown	1.25	.55
		Nos. J9-J13 (5)	6.25	2.75

OFFICIAL STAMPS

Values for unused stamps are for examples with original gum as defined in the catalogue introduction. Examples without gum have probably been used and are so regarded.

Very fine examples of Nos. O1-O24 will have perforations just clear of the design on one or more sides.

Nos. O1-O55, to about 1915, normally were not canceled when affixed to official mail. Occasionally they were canceled in a foreign country of destination. Used values are for favor-canceled stamps or for stamps without gum.

Regular Issues Overprinted

Overprinted in Red, Black, Blue or Green

1883-85 Unwmk. *Perf. 12*

O1	A6	1c green (R)	2.00	1.10
O2	A6	1c green (Bk)	4.00	1.10
O3	A6	2c carmine (Bk)	4.00	1.40
O4	A6	2c carmine (Bl)	2.40	1.60
O5	A6	5c blue vio (R)	7.00	3.00
O6	A6	10c orange (G)	10.00	4.00
O7	A6	40c blue (R)	10.00	4.00
		Nos. O1-O7 (7)	39.40	16.20

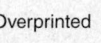

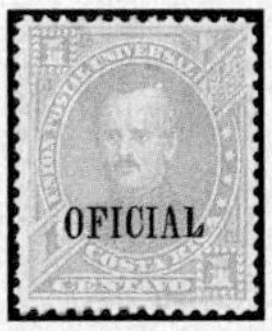

Overprinted

1886

O8	A6	1c green (Bk)	3.50	1.10
O9	A6	2c carmine (Bk)	3.50	1.60
O10	A6	5c blue vio (R)	24.00	11.00
O11	A6	10c orange (Bk)	24.00	11.00
		Nos. O8-O11 (4)	55.00	24.70

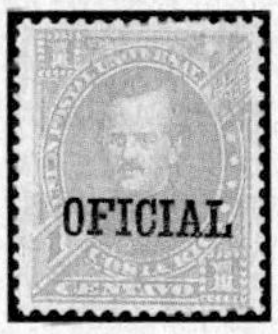

Overprinted

O12	A6	1c green (Bk)	3.50	1.00
O13	A6	2c carmine (Bk)	3.50	1.40
O14	A6	5c blue vio (R)	24.00	11.00
O15	A6	10c orange (Bk)	24.00	11.00
		Nos. O12-O15 (4)	55.00	24.40

Nos. O8-O11 and O12-O15 exist se-tenant in vertical pairs.

Overprinted in Black

O16	A6	5c blue vio	60.00	35.00
O17	A6	10c orange	—	275.00

Overprinted

1887

O18	A6	1c green	1.25	.55
O19	A6	2c carmine	1.25	.50
O21	A6	10c orange	37.50	24.00
c.		Double overprint	42.50	
O22	A7	5c blue vio	12.00	3.50
O23	A7	10c orange	.90	.50
c.		Double overprint	27.50	
O24	A6	40c blue	1.25	.50
		Nos. O18-O24 (6)	54.15	29.55

Overprinted "OFICAL"

O18a	A6	1c green		
O19a	A6	2c carmine	*14.50*	*14.50*
O22a	A7	5c blue violet	*14.50*	
O23a	A7	10c orange	*14.50*	*3.50*
O24a	A6	40c blue	*17.00*	*17.00*
		Nos. O18a-O24a (5)	*60.50*	

Dangerous counterfeits exist of Nos. O18a-O24a.

Without Period

O18b	A6	1c green	14.50	10.00
O19b	A6	2c carmine	14.50	10.00
O22b	A7	5c blue violet	14.50	10.00
O23b	A7	10c orange	14.50	10.00
		Nos. O18b-O23b (4)	58.00	40.00

Nos. O18b-O23b are from a separate plate without periods. No. O23 exists without period (position 32). These must be collected in pairs.

Issues of 1889-1901 Overprinted

1889 *Perf. 14, 15*

O25	A10	1c brown	.25	.25
O26	A11	2c dk green	.25	.25
O27	A12	5c orange	.25	.25
O28	A13	10c red brown	.25	.25
O29	A14	20c yellow grn	.40	.25
O30	A15	50c rose red	1.40	1.40
		Nos. O25-O30 (6)	2.80	2.65

1892

O31	A20	1c grnsh blue	.25	.25
O32	A21	2c yellow	.25	.25
O33	A22	5c violet	.25	.25
O34	A23	10c lt green	3.50	1.60
O35	A24	20c scarlet	.25	.25
O36	A25	50c gray blue	.65	.55
		Nos. O31-O36 (6)	5.15	3.15

1901-02

O37	A30	1c green & blk	.40	.40
O38	A31	2c ver & blk	.40	.40
O39	A32	5c gray bl & blk	.40	.40
O40	A33	10c ocher & blk	.80	.80
O41	A34	20c lake & blk	1.25	1.25
O42	A35	50c lilac & dk bl	10.00	4.00
O43	A36	1col ol bis & blk	17.50	10.00
		Nos. O37-O43 (7)	30.75	17.25

No. 46 Overprinted in Green

1903

O44	A31	2c ver & blk	3.00	3.00
b.		"PROVISIORO"	10.00	10.00
d.		Inverted overprint	10.00	10.00
f.		As "b," inverted	13.00	10.00

Counterfeit overprints exist.

Regular Issue of 1903 Overprinted Like Nos. O25-O43

1903 *Perf. 14, 12½x14*

O45	A40	4c red vio & blk	1.40	1.40
O46	A41	6c ol grn & blk	1.75	1.75
O47	A42	25c gray lil & brn	9.50	6.00
		Nos. O45-O47 (3)	12.65	9.15

Counterfeit overprints exist.

Regular Issue of 1907 Overprinted

1908 *Perf. 14*

O48	A43	1c red brn & ind	.25	.25
O49	A44	2c yel grn & blk	.25	.25
O50	A45	4c car & ind	.25	.25
O51	A46	5c yel & dull bl	.25	.25
O52	A47	10c blue & blk	.80	.80
O53	A49	25c gray lil & blk	.30	.25
O54	A50	50c red lil & bl	.55	.55
O55	A51	1col brown & blk	1.25	1.25
		Nos. O48-O55 (8)	3.90	3.85

Various varieties of the overprint and basic stamps exist.

Imperf examples of Nos. O48, O49, O53 were found in 1970.

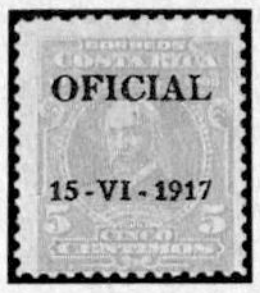

Regular Issue of 1910 Overprinted in Black

1917

O56	A56	5c orange	.40	.40
a.		Inverted overprint	6.00	3.50
O57	A57	10c deep blue	.25	.25
a.		Inverted overprint	3.50	3.50

No. 74 Surcharged

1920 Red Surcharge *Perf. 12*

O58	A58	15c on 20c olive grn	.55	.55

Nos. 72, 61, 59, 65-67 Surcharged or Overprinted

1921 Black Surcharge *Perf. 12*

O59	A56	10c on 5c orange	.50	.50
a.		"10 CTS." inverted	17.50	

Perf. 14

O60	A45	4c car & indigo	.40	.40
a.		"1291" for "1921"	12.00	
O61	A43	6c on 1c red brn & ind	.55	.55
O62	A49	20c on 25c gray lil & blk	.55	.55

Overprinted like No. O60

O63	A50	50c red lil & bl	2.50	1.75
O64	A51	1col brown & blk	5.00	3.00
		Nos. O59-O64 (6)	9.50	6.75

Nos. O60 to O64 exist with date and new values inverted. These may be printer's waste but probably were deliberately made.

Regular Issue of 1923 Overprinted

1923 *Perf. 11½*

O65	A68	2c brown	.25	.25
O66	A68	4c green	.25	.25
O67	A68	5c blue	.40	.40
O68	A68	20c carmine	.25	.25
O69	A68	1col violet	.50	.50
		Nos. O65-O69 (5)	1.65	1.65

Nos. O65 to O69 exist imperforate but were not regularly issued in that condition.

O7

1926 Unwmk. Engr. *Perf. 12½*

O70	O7	2c ultra & blk	.25	.25
O71	O7	3c mag & blk	.25	.25
O72	O7	4c lt bl & blk	.25	.25
O73	O7	5c grn & blk	.25	.25
O74	O7	6c ocher & blk	.25	.25
O75	O7	10c rose red & blk	.25	.25
O76	O7	20c ol grn & blk	.25	.25
O77	O7	30c red org & blk	.25	.25
O78	O7	45c brown & blk	.25	.25
O79	O7	1col lilac & blk	.50	.50
		Nos. O70-O79 (10)	2.75	2.75

See Nos. O82-O94. For surcharges see Nos. C7-C10.

Regular Issue of 1936 Overprinted in Black

1936 Unwmk. *Perf. 12*

O80	A96	5c green	.25	.25
O81	A96	10c carmine rose	.25	.25

Type of 1926

1937 *Perf. 12½*

O82	O7	2c vio & blk	.25	.25
O83	O7	3c bis brn & blk	.25	.25
O84	O7	4c rose car & blk	.25	.25
O85	O7	5c ol grn & blk	.25	
O86	O7	8c blk brn & blk	.25	
O87	O7	10c rose lake & blk	.25	
O88	O7	20c ind & blk	.25	.25
O89	O7	40c red org & blk	.25	.25
O90	O7	55c dk vio & blk	.25	
O91	O7	1col brn vio & blk	.30	.30
O92	O7	2col gray bl & blk	.70	.70
O93	O7	5col dl yel & blk	3.00	3.00
O94	O7	10col blue & blk	45.00	20.00
		Nos. O82-O94 (13)	51.25	

Nine stamps of this series exist with perforated star (2c, 3c, 4c, 20c, 40c, 1col, 2col, 5col, 10col). These were issued to officials for postal purposes. Unpunched stamps were sold to collectors but had no franking power. Values for unused are for unpunched.

POSTAL TAX STAMPS

The 1927 postal tax stamps covered the 10c per book charge for books sent by mail. The stamps were sold at the post office and applied to any package containing books.

Regular Stamps and Revenue Stamps Overprinted in Black

Nos. RA1B-RA1D Overprinted

1927, Mar. 17

RA1A	A75	10c red brown	25.00	5.00
RA1B		50c brown (overprinted on revenue stamp)	25.00	10.00
RA1C	A79	1col olive green	25.00	10.00
RA1D		2col blue green (overprinted on revenue stamp)	300.00	200.00
		Nos. RA1A-RA1D (4)	375.00	225.00

No. 124 Surcharged in Black

1927, Dec. 23

RA1E A76 10c on 12c carmine rose 25.00 5.00

Catalogue values for unused stamps in this section are for Never Hinged items.

Most postal tax issues were to benefit the Children's Village and were obligatory on all mail during Dec.

No. C198 Surcharged in Red

Engraved; Center Photogravure

1958 Unwmk. *Perf. 12½*

RA1 AP51 5c on 2c brt bl & blk .30 .25

Type of 1954 Surcharged in Green

Design: Like No. C228, pottery.

RA2 AP53 5c on 10c dk bl & blk .50 .25

a. Inverted surcharge 8.50

Father Edward J. Flanagan — PT1

Paintings: No. RA4, Boy by El Greco. No. RA5, Boy by Jose Ribera. No. RA6, Girl by Amadeo Modigliani.

Perf. 13½

1959, Nov. 25 Unwmk. Photo.

RA3 PT1 5c green .65 .25
RA4 PT1 5c dl gray vio .65 .25
RA5 PT1 5c olive .65 .25
RA6 PT1 5c lilac rose .65 .25
Nos. RA3-RA6 (4) 2.60 1.00

Nos. RA3-RA6 exist imperf.

Father Peralta — PT2

Designs: No. RA8, Girl by Renoir. No. RA9, Boys with cups by Velazquez. No. RA10, Singing children, sculpture by F. Zuñiga.

1960 Litho. *Perf. 14*

RA7 PT2 5c chocolate .65 .25
RA8 PT2 5c dp org .65 .25
RA9 PT2 5c plum .65 .25
RA10 PT2 5c grysh bl .65 .25
Nos. RA7-RA10 (4) 2.60 1.00

Nos. RA7-RA10 exist imperf.

No. C229 Surcharged in Black

Engraved; Center Photogravure

1961 *Perf. 13x12½*

RA11 AP53 5c on 15c grn & blk .40 .25

Nicolas, Son of Rubens — PT3

Designs: No. RA13, Madonna by Bellini. RA14, Angel playing stringed instrument by Melozzo. RA15, Msgr. Rubén Odio H.

1962 Photo. *Perf. 13½*

RA12 PT3 5c dark carmine .70 .25
RA13 PT3 5c sepia .70 .25
RA14 PT3 5c dull green .70 .25
RA15 PT3 5c blue .70 .25
Nos. RA12-RA15 (4) 2.80 1.00

For surcharges see Nos. 262-265.

Type of 1962, Inscribed "1963"

Designs as before.

1963 Photo. *Perf. 13½*

RA16 PT3 5c sepia (RA12) .45 .25
RA17 PT3 5c ultra (RA13) .45 .25
RA18 PT3 5c dk car (RA14) .45 .25
RA19 PT3 5c black (RA15) .45 .25
Nos. RA16-RA19 (4) 1.80 1.00

Boys in Workshop — PT4

Designs: No. RA21, Two playing boys. No. RA22, Teacher and children. No. RA23, Priest with boys.

1964 Litho. *Perf. 12½*

RA20 PT4 5c bright green .40 .25
RA21 PT4 5c rose lilac .40 .25
RA22 PT4 5c blue .40 .25
RA23 PT4 5c brown .40 .25
Nos. RA20-RA23 (4) 1.60 1.00

Brother Casiano de Madrid — PT5

Designs: No. RA25, National Children's Hospital. No. RA26, Poinsettia. No. RA27, Santa Claus with children (diamond).

1965, Dec. 10 Litho. *Perf. 10*

RA24 PT5 5c red brown .25 .25
RA25 PT5 5c green .25 .25
RA26 PT5 5c red .25 .25
RA27 PT5 5c ultra .25 .25
Nos. RA24-RA27 (4) 1.00 1.00

Christmas Ornaments — PT6

1966 Litho. *Perf. 11*

RA28 PT6 5c shown .25 .25
RA29 PT6 5c Angel .25 .25
RA30 PT6 5c Church .25 .25
RA31 PT6 5c Reindeer .25 .25
Nos. RA28-RA31 (4) 1.00 1.00

General Post Office, San José — PT7

1967, Mar. Litho. *Perf. 11*

RA32 PT7 10c blue .40 .25

No. RA32 was issued as a postal tax stamp to be used by organizations normally allowed free postage. On Dec. 15, 1972, it was authorized for use as an ordinary postage stamp.

Madonna and Child — PT8

1967 Litho. *Perf. 11*

RA33 PT8 5c olive green .25 .25
RA34 PT8 5c dp lil rose .25 .25
RA35 PT8 5c brt blue .25 .25
RA36 PT8 5c grnsh blue .25 .25
Nos. RA33-RA36 (4) 1.00 1.00

Star of Bethlehem, Mother and Child — PT9

1968, Dec. Litho. *Perf. 12½*

RA37 PT9 5c gray .25 .25
RA38 PT9 5c rose red .25 .25
RA39 PT9 5c dk rose brn .25 .25
RA40 PT9 5c bister brn .25 .25
Nos. RA37-RA40 (4) 1.00 1.00

Madonna and Child — PT10

1969, Dec. Litho. *Perf. 12½*

RA41 PT10 5c dk blue .25 .25
RA42 PT10 5c orange .25 .25
RA43 PT10 5c brown red .25 .25
RA44 PT10 5c blue green .25 .25
Nos. RA41-RA44 (4) 1.00 1.00

Christ Child, Star — PT11

1970, Dec. Litho. *Perf. 12½*

RA45 PT11 5c brt purple .35 .25
RA46 PT11 5c lilac rose .35 .25
RA47 PT11 5c olive .35 .25
RA48 PT11 5c ocher .35 .25
Nos. RA45-RA48 (4) 1.40 1.00

Christ Child and "PAX" — PT12

1971, Nov. 29

RA49 PT12 10c dk blue .25 .25
RA50 PT12 10c orange .25 .25
RA51 PT12 10c brown .25 .25
RA52 PT12 10c green .25 .25
Nos. RA49-RA52 (4) 1.00 1.00

Madonna and Child — PT13

1972, Nov. 30 *Perf. 11x11½*

RA53 PT13 10c dk blue .25 .25
RA54 PT13 10c brt red .25 .25
RA55 PT13 10c lilac .25 .25
RA56 PT13 10c green .25 .25
Nos. RA53-RA56 (4) 1.00 1.00

Madonna and Child — PT14

1973, Nov. 30 Litho. *Perf. 12½*

RA57 PT14 10c purple .25 .25
RA58 PT14 10c car rose .25 .25
RA59 PT14 10c gray .25 .25
RA60 PT14 10c orange brn .25 .25
Nos. RA57-RA60 (4) 1.00 1.00

Boys Eating Cake, by Murillo — PT15

Paintings: No. RA62, Virgin and Child, with St. John, by Raphael. No. RA63, Maternity, by Juan R. Bonilla. No. RA64, Praying Child, by Reynolds.

1974, Nov. 25 *Perf. 13*

RA61 PT15 10c brt pink .30 .25
RA62 PT15 10c rose lilac .30 .25
RA63 PT15 10c dk gray .30 .25
RA64 PT15 10c violet bl .30 .25
Nos. RA61-RA64 (4) 1.20 1.00

See No. RA110.

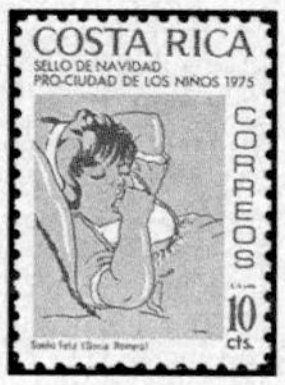

"Happy Dreams," by Sonia Romero — PT16

Paintings: No. RA66, Virgin with Carnation, by Leonardo da Vinci. No. RA67, Children with Tortoise, by Francisco Amighetti. No. RA68, Boy with Pigeon, by Picasso.

1975, Nov. 25 Litho. *Perf. 10½*

RA65 PT16 10c gray .30 .25
RA66 PT16 10c red lilac .30 .25
RA67 PT16 10c orange brown .30 .25
RA68 PT16 10c brt blue .30 .25
Nos. RA65-RA68 (4) 1.20 1.00

Virgin and Child, by Hans Memling — PT17

Paintings: No. RA70, Girl with Sombrero, by Auguste Renoir. No. RA71, Meditation (boy), by Floria Pinto de Herrero. No. RA72, Gaston de Mezerville (boy), by Lolita Zeller de Peralta.

1976, Nov. 24 Litho. *Perf. 10½*

RA69 PT17 10c rose lilac .30 .25
RA70 PT17 10c rose carmine .30 .25
RA71 PT17 10c gray .30 .25
RA72 PT17 10c violet blue .30 .25
Nos. RA69-RA72 (4) 1.20 1.00

Boy's Head, by Amparo Cruz — PT18

Paintings: No. RA74, Girl's head, by Rubens. No. RA75, Girl and infant, by Cristina Fournier. No. RA76, Mariano Goya, by Goya.

1977, Nov. Litho. *Perf. 10½*

RA73 PT18 10c gray olive	.30	.25
RA74 PT18 10c rose red	.30	.25
RA75 PT18 10c brt ultra	.30	.25
RA76 PT18 10c brt rose lil	.30	.25
Nos. RA73-RA76 (4)	1.20	1.00

Boy with Kite — PT19

Designs: Nos. RA78-RA79, Girl flying kite.

1978, Nov. 20 Litho. *Perf. 12½*

RA77 PT19 10c magenta	.30	.25
RA78 PT19 10c slate	.30	.25
RA79 PT19 10c lilac	.30	.25
RA80 PT19 10c violet blue	.30	.25
Nos. RA77-RA80 (4)	1.20	1.00

Boy Leaning on Tree — PT20

1979, Nov. 19 Litho. *Perf. 12½*

RA81 PT20 10c blue	.25	.25
RA82 PT20 10c orange	.25	.25
RA83 PT20 10c magenta	.25	.25
RA84 PT20 10c green	.25	.25
Nos. RA81-RA84 (4)	1.00	1.00

Boy on Swing — PT21

1980, Nov. 18 Litho. *Perf. 12½*

RA85 PT21 10c brt blue	.25	.25
RA86 PT21 10c brt yellow	.25	.25
RA87 PT21 10c crimson rose	.25	.25
RA88 PT21 10c brt green	.25	.25
Nos. RA85-RA88 (4)	1.00	1.00

Boy Riding Toy Car — PT22

1981, Nov. 19 Litho. *Perf. 11*

RA89 PT22 10c blue	.25	.25
RA90 PT22 10c green	.25	.25
RA91 PT22 10c red	.25	.25
RA92 PT22 10c orange	.25	.25
Nos. RA89-RA92 (4)	1.00	1.00

Youth Running Machine — PT23

1982, Nov. 19 Litho. *Perf. 10½*

RA93 PT23 10c red	.25	.25
RA94 PT23 10c gray	.25	.25
RA95 PT23 10c purple	.25	.25
RA96 PT23 10c grnsh blue	.25	.25
Nos. RA93-RA96 (4)	1.00	1.00

Youths Working on Wheelchair — PT24

1983, Nov. 24 Litho. *Perf. 16*

RA97 PT24 10c red	.25	.25
RA98 PT24 10c orange	.25	.25
RA99 PT24 10c ultra	.25	.25
RA100 PT24 10c green	.25	.25
Nos. RA97-RA100 (4)	1.00	1.00

Christmas 1983.

Girl on Bicycle — PT25

1984, Nov. 20 Litho. *Perf. 10½*

RA101 PT25 10c violet	.70	.30

Christmas 1984.

Taking a Child in Out of the Cold — PT26

1985, Dec. 1 Litho. *Perf. 13*

RA102 PT26 10c dull brown	.70	.30

Christmas 1985.

Depressed Child — PT27

1986, Dec. 1 Litho. *Perf. 10½*

RA103 PT27 10c lemon	.70	.30

Christmas stamps, 25th anniv.; Christmas 1986.

Christmas — PT28

1987, Dec. 1 Litho. *Perf. 10½*

RA104 PT28 10c dk ol bis & brt bl	.60	.30

No postal tax stamp was issued for 1988.

Teaching Children — PT29

1989, Dec. 1 Litho. *Perf. 13½*

RA105 PT29 1col blue, blk & brt apple grn	.60	.30

Christmas 1989.

No. 417 Ovptd. in Red, Blue, Green, or Orange

1990, Nov. 16 Litho. *Perf. 13½*

RA106 A179 10col multi (R)	.90	.25
RA107 A179 10col multi (Bl)	.90	.25
RA108 A179 10col multi (G)	.90	.25
RA109 A179 10col multi (O)	.90	.25
Nos. RA106-RA109 (4)	3.60	1.00

No. RA109 exists with a silver overprint.

Art Type of 1974

Design: 10col, Praying Child, by Reynolds.

1991, Nov. 18 Litho. *Perf. 10½*

RA110 PT15 10col dark ultra	1.20	.35

PT30

Boy in workshop.

1992, Dec. 1 Litho. *Perf. 10½*

RA111 PT30 10col red	.60	.30

Christmas.

PT31

1993, Nov. 17

RA112 PT31 10col multicolored	.50	.30

Christmas.

PT32

1994, Nov. 23 Litho. *Perf. 10½*

RA113 PT32 11col lilac & slate	.70	.30

Christmas.

No. RA113 exists imperf.

PT33

Painting of mother and child, by Claudio Carazo.

1995, Dec. 1 *Perf. 13½*

RA114 PT33 12col multicolored	.70	.30
a. Miniature sheet, #RA114 + 5 labels	3.25	3.25

Christmas.

No. RA114a contains 4 progressive proofs of No. RA114 + one label of text and sold for 112col.

PT34

1996, Dec. 1 Litho. *Perf. 10½*

RA115 PT34 14col Sculpture	.60	.30

PT35

Bust of Antonio Obando Chan, by Olger Villegas Cruz.

1997, Dec. 1

RA116 PT35 15col multicolored	.50	.30

Christmas.

PT36

No. RA117: a, Flower. b, Flower up close, one in background. c, Berries on branch.

1998 Litho. *Perf. 13½*

RA117 Strip of 3	1.75	1.30
a.-c. PT36 16col Any single	.50	.30

Christmas.

Children's Village PT37

1999, Dec. 1 Litho. *Perf. 13¼*

RA118 PT37 17col multi	.50	.30

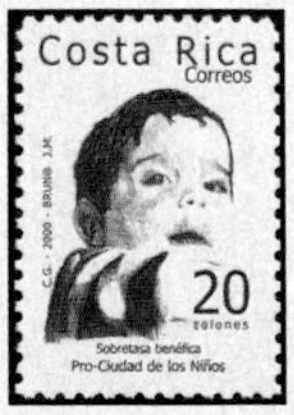

Child — PT38

Color: a, Green. b, Red. c, Blue. d, Brown.

2000, Dec. 1 Litho. *Perf. 10½*

RA119 Horiz. strip of 4	4.50	2.50
a.-d. PT38 20col Any single	.80	.40

Child Examining Stamp — PT39

Panel color: a, Purple. b, Green. c, Red. d, Orange.

2001, Dec. 1 Litho. *Perf. 10½*

RA120 Horiz. strip of 4	2.00	1.40
a.-d. PT39 21col Any single	.40	.30

Child — PT40

Panel color: a, Purple. b, Blue. c, Orange. d, Green.

2002 Litho. *Perf. 10½*
RA121 Horiz strip of 4 1.85 1.50
a.-d. PT40 22col Any single .40 .30

Child Pointing at Star — PT41

No. RA122 — Background color: a, Purple. b, Green. c, Red. d, Yellow orange.

2003, Dec. 1 Litho. *Perf. 13½x13¼*
RA122 Horiz. strip of 4 1.80 1.50
a.-d. PT41 23col Any single .40 .30

Three Magi — PT42

No. RA123 — Magi in: a, Lemon. b, Green. c, Purple. d, Red violet.

2004 Litho. *Perf. 13¼*
RA123 Horiz. strip of 4 2.50 2.00
a.-d. PT42 25col Any single .50 .40

Children — PT43

No. RA124 — Denomination color: a, White. b, Buff. c, Dull orange. d, Red.

2005, Dec. 1 Litho. *Perf. 10½*
RA124 Horiz. strip of 4 2.50 2.00
a.-d. PT43 28col Any single .50 .40

Surtax for Children's Village.

Child Reading PT44

No. RA125 — Frame color: a, Yellow bister. b, Dull brown. c, Olive green. d, Orange brown.

2006, Dec. 1 Litho. *Perf. 10½*
RA125 Horiz. strip of 4 2.60 2.25
a.-d. PT44 32col Any single .60 .55

Children's Art — PT45

No. RA126: a, Family and hearts. b, Children at school. c, Children on playground equipment. d, Boy on skateboard.

2007, Dec. 1 Litho. *Perf. 10½*
RA126 Horiz. strip of 4 2.60 2.60
a.-d. PT45 35col Any single .60 .60

Surtax for Children's Village.

Children's Art — PT46

No. RA127: a, Child flying kite, by Luis Paulino Murillo Méndez. b, Boy and jaguar, by David Malavassi Zúñiga. c, Bird and sailboat, by Valeria Vargas Arias. d, Child in water, by Dannia María Berrocal Fonseca.

2008, Dec. 1 Litho. *Perf. 13½*
RA127 Horiz. strip of 4 2.80 2.80
a.-d. PT46 40col Any single .65 .65

Surtax for Children's Village.

Miniature Sheet

Masquerade Costumes — PT47

No. RA128: a, Devil and man in purple hat. b, Bull and clown. c, Grim reaper. d, Stilt walker and tall woman.

2009, Dec. 1 Litho. *Perf. 10½*
RA128 PT47 45col Sheet of 4, #a-d 2.50 2.50

Surtax for Children's Village.

Children's Art — PT48

No. RA129: a, School, tree and sun (gray panels). b, Child in workshop (blue panels). c, Sun, hills, flora and fauna (pink panels). d, Sun, house on hill (yellow panels).

2010, Dec. 1
RA129 Horiz. strip of 4 2.00 2.00
a.-d. PT48 45col Any single .40 .30

Surtax for Children's Village.

Children's Art — PT49

No. RA130: a, Head (orange yellow panel). b, Children with banner (blue panel). c, Children in playground (yellow green panel). d, Various children (bright rose panel).

2011, Dec. 1
RA130 PT49 55col Block of 4, #a-d 2.00 2.00

Surtax for Children's Village.

Boy Holding Sun — PT50

No. RA131 — Background color: a, Light blue. b, Blue. c, Brown orange. d, Yellow bister.

2012, Dec. 1 Litho. *Perf. 10½*
RA131 Horiz. strip of 4 1.50 1.50
a.-d. PT50 60col Any single .30 .30

Surtax for Children's Village.

PT51

No. RA132: a, Forest (denomination in olive green). b, Arches in wall (denomination in orange). c, Rock formation (denomination in lilac). d, Toucan (denomination in blue).

2013, Dec. 2 Litho. *Perf. 10½*
RA132 PT51 60col Block of 4, #a-d 2.00 2.00

No. RA132 was printed in sheets of 20 (5 of each stamp) + 4 labels. Surtax for Children's Village.

Traditional Dishes — PT52

No. RA133: a, Gallo pinto. b, Olla de carne. c, Casado con pollo. d, Picadillo de Vainica.

2014, Dec. 1 Litho. *Perf. 13½x13*
RA133 Strip of 4 1.00 1.00
a.-d. PT52 65col Any single .25 .25

Surtax for Children's Village.

GUANACASTE

ˌgwä-nə-ˈkästā

(A province of Costa Rica)

LOCATION — Northwestern coast of Central America
AREA — 4,000 sq. mi. (approx.)
POP. — 69,531 (estimated)
CAPITAL — Liberia

Residents of Guanacaste were allowed to buy Costa Rican stamps, overprinted "Guanacaste," at a discount from face value because of the province's isolation and climate, which make it difficult to keep mint stamps. Use was restricted to the province.

Counterfeits of most Guanacaste overprints are plentiful.

For 5c stamps between Nos. 5-43, unused examples without gum sell for slightly more than the used value.

Very fine examples of Nos. 1-54 will have perforations just clear of the design on one or more sides.

Dangerous counterfeits exist of Nos. 1-63.

On Issue of 1883

16mm

1885 Unwmk. *Perf. 12*

Overprinted Horizontally in Black

1	A6	1c green	4.00	3.25
2	A6	2c carmine	4.00	3.25
a.		"Gnanacaste"	*250.00*	
3	A6	10c orange	35.00	21.00
a.		"Gnanacaste"	*500.00*	

Same Overprint in Red

4	A6	1c green	4.00	3.25
a.		"Gnanacaste"	*200.00*	
b.		Overprinted in black & red	*300.00*	
5	A6	5c blue violet	30.00	4.00
a.		"Gnanacaste"	*350.00*	
6	A6	40c blue	25.00	21.00

17½mm

Overprinted Horizontally in Black

7	A6	1c green	10.00	7.00
8	A6	2c carmine	10.00	7.00
9	A6	5c blue violet	45.00	15.00
10	A6	10c orange	60.00	35.00
11	A6	40c blue	60.00	60.00

Same Overprint in Red

12	A6	5c blue violet	*1,000.*	200.00
13	A6	40c blue	*2,000.*	

18½mm — c

Overprinted Horizontally in Black

14	A6	2c carmine	10.00	7.00
15	A6	10c orange	100.00	75.00

Same Overprint in Red

16	A6	1c green	7.00	7.00
a.		Double ovpt., one in blk	250.00	
17	A6	5c blue violet	45.00	15.00
18	A6	40c blue	75.00	75.00

Same Overprint, Vertically in Black

19	A6	1c green	*5,000.*	
20	A6	2c carmine	*4,250.*	
21	A6	5c blue violet	700.00	175.00
22	A6	10c orange	150.00	120.00

e

f

g

h

i

Overprinted Type e, Vertically

23	A6	1c green	3,000.	2,000.
24	A6	2c carmine	1,000.	300.00
25	A6	5c blue violet	400.00	75.00

26	A6	10c orange	75.00	75.00

Overprinted Type f, Vertically

27	A6	1c green	2,000.	2,000.
28	A6	2c carmine	1,000.	400.00
29	A6	5c blue violet	400.00	125.00
30	A6	10c orange	100.00	100.00

Overprinted Type g, Vertically

31	A6	1c green	2,500.	2,500.
32	A6	2c carmine	1,000.	1,000.
33	A6	5c blue violet	600.00	200.00
34	A6	10c orange	150.00	150.00

Overprinted Type h, Vertically

35	A6	1c green	3,000.	1,500.
36	A6	2c carmine	1,000.	300.00
37	A6	5c blue violet	400.00	75.00
38	A6	10c orange	60.00	60.00

Overprinted Type i, Vertically

39	A6	1c green		—
39A	A6	2c carmine		*275.00*
40	A6	5c blue violet		20.00
41	A6	10c orange		*200.00*

On Issues of 1883-87

Overprinted Horizontally in Black

1888-89

42	A7	5c blue violet	15.00	3.00

Overprinted Horizontally in Black

43	A7	5c blue violet	15.00	3.00

Overprinted Horizontally in Black

44	A6	2c carmine	3.00
45	A7	10c orange	3.00

Inverted overprints are fakes.

On Issue of 1889

Overprinted Like Nos. 7-13

1889 **Horizontally**

47	A8	2c blue	20.00

Vertically

48	A8	2c blue (c)	250.00
49	A8	2c blue (e)	75.00
51	A8	2c blue (f)	75.00
52	A8	2c blue (g)	250.00
54	A8	2c blue (h)	75.00

Nos. 47-54 are overprinted "Correos." Stamps without "Correos" are known postally used. Unused examples are valued the same as Nos. 47-54, unused. The 1c without "Correos" is known postally used. The 1c with "Correos" is counterfeit.

On Nos. 25-33 Overprinted Horizontally in Black

1889 *Perf. 14 and 15*

55	A10	1c brown	10.00	3.50
56	A11	2c dark green	4.50	1.50
57	A12	5c orange	6.75	2.10
58	A13	10c red brown	6.75	2.10
59	A14	20c yellow green	1.00	.70
60	A15	50c rose red	1.75	1.50
61	A16	1p blue	4.50	4.50
62	A17	2p violet	6.75	6.75
63	A18	5p olive green	37.50	37.50
		Nos. 55-63 (9)	79.50	60.15

Nos. 61-63 with remainder cancels sell for about half the used values shown.

Overprinted "GUAGACASTE"

60a	A15	50c rose red	*325.00*	*325.00*
61a	A16	1p blue	*325.00*	*325.00*
62a	A17	2p violet	*400.00*	*400.00*
63a	A18	5p olive green	*600.00*	*600.00*

Values for Nos. 60a-63a used are for examples with remainder cancels.

Overprinted Horizontally in Black

64	A10	1c brown	2.25	1.50
a.		Vert. pair, imperf. between		
65	A11	2c dark green	2.25	1.50
66	A12	5c orange	2.25	1.50
67	A13	10c red brown	2.25	1.50
		Nos. 64-67 (4)	9.00	6.00

CRETE

'krēt

LOCATION — An island in the Mediterranean Sea south of Greece
GOVT. — A department of Greece
AREA — 3,235 sq. mi.
POP. — 336,150 (1913)
CAPITAL — Canea

Formerly Crete was a province of Turkey. After an extended period of civil wars, France, Great Britain, Italy and Russia intervened and declaring Crete an autonomy, placed it under the administration of Prince George of Greece as High Commissioner. In October, 1908, the Cretan Assembly voted for union with Greece and in 1913 the union was formally effected.

40 Paras = 1 Piaster
4 Metallik = 1 Grosion (1899)
100 Lepta = 1 Drachma (1900)

Issued Under Joint Administration of France, Great Britain, Italy and Russia

British Sphere of Administration District of Heraklion (Candia)

A1

Handstamped

1898 **Unwmk.** *Imperf.*

1	A1	20pa violet	400.00	225.00

A2

1898 **Litho.** *Perf. 11½*

2	A2	10pa blue	6.50	2.00
a.		Horiz. pair, imperf. btwn.	200.00	
b.		Imperf., pair	225.00	
c.		Horiz. pair, imperf. vert.		—
3	A2	20pa green	6.50	2.00
a.		Imperf., pair	225.00	

1899

4	A2	10pa brown	6.50	2.00
a.		Horiz. pair, imperf. btwn.	225.00	
b.		Imperf., pair	225.00	
5	A2	20pa rose	8.00	2.00
a.		Imperf., pair	225.00	

Used values for Nos. 2-5 are for stamps canceled by the straight-line "Heraklion" town postmark. Stamps canceled with any other postmark used for postal duty are scarce and worth much more. Other cancellations, values from: Ag. Thomas, $65; Ag. Myron, $70; Arkanais, $90; Episkopi, $170; Kastelli, $175; Moirais, $175; Xarakas, $190; Chersonissos, $235; and Moxos.

Counterfeits exist of Nos. 1-5.

Russian Sphere of Administration District of Rethymnon

Coat of Arms
A3 A4

1899 **Handstamped** *Imperf.*

Laid paper

No Gum

10	A3	1m green	13.00	5.00
11	A3	2m black	10.00	4.00
12	A3	2m rose	300.00	225.00
13	A4	1m blue	85.00	75.00

Wove paper

10E	A3	1m green	13.00	5.00
11E	A3	2m black	13.00	5.00
13E	A4	1m blue	100.00	50.00

Quadrille paper

10J	A3	1m green	350.00	—
11J	A3	2m black	350.00	80.00

Nos. 10-13 normally have a circular control mark applied in violet or blue on blocks of four stamps. They also are known without this control mark (errors) and occasionally with the small round control marks of the next issue, in blue or violet (probably proofs). They are sometimes found with pin-perforations. Other varieties exist.

Counterfeits exist.

Poseidon's Trident — A5a
A5

1899 **Litho.** *Perf. 11½*

With Control Mark Overprinted in Violet

Without Stars at Sides

14	A5	1m orange	175.00	115.00
15	A5	2m orange	175.00	115.00
16	A5	1gr orange	175.00	115.00
17	A5	1m green	175.00	115.00
18	A5	2m green	175.00	115.00
19	A5	1gr green	175.00	115.00
20	A5	1m yellow	175.00	115.00
21	A5	2m yellow	175.00	115.00
22	A5	1gr yellow	175.00	115.00
23	A5	1m rose	175.00	115.00
24	A5	2m rose	175.00	115.00
25	A5	1gr rose	175.00	115.00
26	A5	1m violet	175.00	115.00
27	A5	2m violet	175.00	115.00
28	A5	1gr violet	175.00	115.00
29	A5	1m blue	175.00	115.00
30	A5	2m blue	175.00	115.00
31	A5	1gr blue	175.00	115.00
32	A5	1m black	1,250.	1,150.
33	A5	2m black	1,250.	1,150.
34	A5	1gr black	1,250.	1,150.

With Stars at Sides

35	A5a	1m blue	37.50	32.50
36	A5a	2m blue	15.00	12.50
37	A5a	1gr blue	13.50	9.00
38	A5a	1m rose	160.00	75.00
39	A5a	2m rose	15.00	12.50
40	A5a	1gr rose	12.50	9.00
41	A5a	1m green	37.50	32.50
42	A5a	2m green	15.00	12.50
43	A5a	1gr green	12.50	9.00
44	A5a	1m violet	37.50	32.50
45	A5a	2m violet	15.00	12.50
46	A5a	1gr violet	12.50	10.00
a.		Horiz. pair, imperf. btwn.	250.00	
b.		Vert. pair, imperf. horiz.	190.00	
		Nos. 35-46 (12)	383.50	259.50

Almost all of Nos. 14 to 46 may be found without control mark, with double control marks and in various colors.

Used values for Nos. 10-46 are for stamps with postmarks of Rethymnon. Thirteen other post offices existed, and stamps with postmarks other than Rethymnon are scarce and command significant premiums: Ag. Galini, $125; Amari, $90; Anogeia, $525; Garazo, $160; Damasta, $550; Kastelli, $125; Margaritais, $550; Melampes, $375; Pigi, $125; Roystika, $70; Xenia, $105; Spili, $105; Fodede, $550.

Counterfeits exist of Nos. 14-46.

Nos. 14-31 exist imperf. Value, unused pair each $900.

Issued by the Cretan Government

Hermes — A6

Hera — A7

Prince George of Greece — A8

Talos — A9

Minos — A10

St. George and the Dragon — A11

1900, Mar. 1 **Engr.** *Perf. 14*

50	A6	1 l violet brown	.45	.35
51	A7	5 l green	1.90	.35
52	A8	10 l red	1.50	.40
53	A7	20 l carmine rose	5.75	1.25
		Nos. 50-53 (4)	9.60	2.35

See #64-71. For overprints and surcharges see #54-63, 72-73, 85, 88, 93, 97-99, 108, 111.

Overprinted

Red Overprint

54	A8	25 l blue	1.15	.90
55	A6	50 l lilac	2.40	1.30
56	A9	1d gray violet	12.00	13.50
57	A10	2d brown	37.50	32.50
58	A11	5d green & blk	200.00	200.00
		Nos. 54-58 (5)	253.05	248.20

Black Overprint

59	A8	25 l blue	2.00	.90
60	A6	50 l lilac	2.25	1.60
61	A9	1d gray violet	9.75	6.75
a.		Inverted overprint	*350.00*	*350.00*
62	A10	2d brown	25.00	18.00
63	A11	5d green & blk	110.00	110.00
		Nos. 59-63 (5)	149.00	137.25

1901 **Without Overprint**

64	A6	1 l bister	1.00	1.15
65	A7	20 l orange	3.50	1.15
66	A8	25 l blue	8.75	.85
67	A6	50 l lilac	37.50	29.00
68	A6	50 l ultra	13.00	13.00
69	A9	1d gray violet	42.50	27.50
70	A10	2d brown	13.50	11.50
71	A11	5d green & blk	17.00	13.00
		Nos. 64-71 (8)	136.75	97.15

No. 64 is a revenue stamp that was used for postage for short periods in 1901 and 1904.

Types A6 to A8 in olive yellow, and types A9 to A11 in olive yellow and black are revenue stamps.

See note following No. 53.

Surcharges with the year "1922" on designs A6, A8, A9, A11, A13, A15-A23 and D1 are listed under Greece.

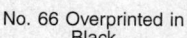

No. 66 Overprinted in Black

1901

72	A8	25 l blue	25.00	1.00
a.		First letter of ovpt. invtd.	475.00	300.00
b.		Inverted overprint	700.00	350.00
c.		"S" of "PROSORINON" omitted	200.00	80.00

No. 65 Surcharged in Black

1904, Dec.

73	A7	5 l on 20 l orange	2.75	1.00
a.		Without "5" at right	*150.00*	*150.00*

Mycenaean Seal — A12

Britomartis (Cortyna Coin) — A13

Prince George — A14

Kydon and Dog (Cydonia Coin) — A15

Triton (Itanos Coin) — A16

Ariadne (Knossos Coin) — A17

Zeus as Bull Abducting Europa (Cortyna Coin) A18

Palace of Minos Ruins, Knossos A19

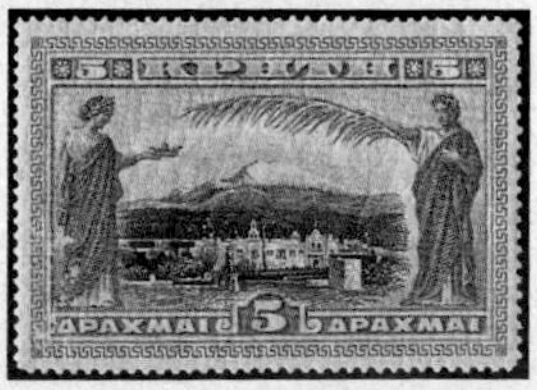

Arkadi Monastery and Mt. Ida — A20

1905, Feb. 15

74	A12	2 l dull violet	1.60	.40
75	A13	5 l yellow grn	2.00	.40
76	A14	10 l red	2.00	1.00
77	A15	20 l blue grn	5.50	1.00
78	A16	25 l ultra	7.00	1.00
79	A17	50 l yellow brn	7.50	3.25
80	A18	1d rose car & dp brn	72.50	62.50
81	A19	3d orange & blk	50.00	40.00
82	A20	5d ol grn & blk	25.00	25.00
		Nos. 74-82 (9)	173.10	134.55

For overprints see Nos. 86-87, 89, 91-92, 94-95, 104, 106, 109-110, 112-113, 115-120.

The so-called revolutionary stamps of 1905 were issued for sale to collectors and, so far as can be ascertained, were of no postal value.

A. T. A. Zaimis A21

Prince George Landing at Suda A22

1907, Aug. 28

83	A21	25 l blue & blk	37.50	1.00
84	A22	1d green & blk	10.00	7.00

Administration under a High Commissioner.
For overprints see Nos. 90, 105, 107.

Stamps of 1900-1907 Overprinted in Black

1908, Sept. 21

85	A6	1 l violet brn	.55	.40
a.		Inverted overprint	—	
86	A12	2 l dull violet	.55	.40
a.		Pair, one without ovpt.	—	
87	A13	5 l yellow grn	.55	.40
88	A8	10 l red	1.15	.80
a.		Pair, one without ovpt.	—	
89	A15	20 l blue grn	3.00	1.00
90	A21	25 l blue & blk	8.50	2.50
91	A17	50 l yellow brn	11.50	4.25
a.		Inverted overprint	—	
92	A18	1d rose car & dp brn	95.00	67.50
93	A10	2d brown	10.00	8.00
94	A19	3d orange & blk	45.00	37.50
95	A20	5d ol grn & blk	35.00	30.00
		Nos. 85-95 (11)	210.80	152.75

This overprint exists inverted and double, as well as with incorrect, reversed, misplaced and omitted letters. Similar errors are found on the Postage Due and Official stamps with this overprint.

Hermes by Praxiteles — A23

1908

96	A23	10 l brown red	3.00	.80
a.		Pair, one without overprint	150.00	150.00
b.		Inverted overprint	—	
c.		Double overprint	—	

Nos. 96 and 114 were not regularly issued without overprint.
For overprints see Nos. 103, 114.

No. 53 Surcharged

1909

97	A7	5 l on 20 l car rose	210.00	*225.00*

Forgeries exist of No. 97.

On No. 65

98	A7	5 l on 20 l orange	1.50	1.25
a.		Inverted surcharge	150.00	150.00
b.		Double surcharge	120.00	120.00

Overprinted on Nos. 64, J1

99	A6	1 l bister	4.00	4.00
100	D1	1 l red	1.50	1.50

No. J4 Surcharged

101	D1	2 l on 20 l red	1.50	1.50
b.		Inverted surcharge	75.00	
c.		Second letter of surcharge "D" instead of "P"	50.00	50.00

No. J4 Surcharged

102	D1	2 l on 20 l red	1.45	1.30
a.		Double overprint	*125.00*	*125.00*

Overprinted in Black

a

b

c

103	A23(a)	10 l brown red	3.50	1.00
a.		Inverted overprint	110.00	
104	A15(a)	20 l blue grn	5.00	1.00
105	A21(c)	25 l blue & blk	5.25	2.00
106	A17(a)	50 l yellow brn	8.00	4.00
107	A22(b)	1d green & blk	12.00	7.00
108	A10(a)	2d brown	12.00	10.00
109	A19(b)	3d org & blk	125.00	115.00
110	A20(b)	5d ol grn & blk	52.50	52.50
		Nos. 103-110 (8)	223.25	192.50

Stamps of 1900-08 Overprinted in Red or Black

1909-10

111	A6	1 l violet brown	.40	.25
112	A12	2 l dull violet	.40	.25
113	A13	5 l yellow green	.40	.25
114	A23	10 l brown red (Bk)	.60	.60
115	A15	20 l blue green	2.00	.70
116	A16	25 l ultra	2.75	.75
117	A17	50 l yellow brn	7.00	2.00
118	A18	1d rose car & dp brn (Bk)	100.00	100.00
119	A19	3d orange & blk	85.00	85.00
120	A20	5d ol grn & blk	55.00	55.00
		Nos. 111-120 (10)	253.55	244.80

POSTAGE DUE STAMPS

D1

1901 Unwmk. Litho. *Perf. 14*

J1	D1	1 l red	.30	.30
J2	D1	5 l red	.50	.30
J3	D1	10 l red	.75	.40
J4	D1	20 l red	1.00	*.50*
J5	D1	40 l red	11.50	11.50
J6	D1	50 l red	11.50	11.50
J7	D1	1d red	22.50	22.50
J8	D1	2d red	14.00	12.50
		Nos. J1-J8 (8)	62.05	59.50

For overprints and surcharges see Nos. 100-102, J9-J26.

Surcharged in Black

1901

J9	D1	1d on 1d red	11.00	10.00

Overprinted in Black

1908

J10	D1	1 l red	.35	.35
J11	D1	5 l red	.60	.60
J12	D1	10 l red	.60	.60
J13	D1	20 l red	2.00	2.00
J14	D1	40 l red	8.25	7.50
J15	D1	50 l red	10.50	9.00
J16	D1	1d red	475.00	475.00
a.		Pair, one without ovpt.		—
J17	D1	1d on 1d red	11.50	10.00
J18	D1	2d red	19.00	10.00
		Nos. J10-J18 (9)	527.80	515.05

Nos. J10-J18 exist with inverted overprint. See note after No. 95.
Counterfeits of No. J16 exist.

Overprinted in Black

1910

J19	D1	1 l red	.45	.30
J20	D1	5 l red	1.00	.35
J21	D1	10 l red	1.00	.35
J22	D1	20 l red	3.25	1.75
J23	D1	40 l red	11.00	6.00
J24	D1	50 l red	16.50	12.00
J25	D1	1d red	27.50	27.50
J26	D1	2d red	27.50	27.50
		Nos. J19-J26 (8)	88.20	75.75

OFFICIAL STAMPS

O1

O2

Unwmk.

1908, Jan. 14 Litho. *Perf. 14*

O1 O1 10 l dull claret 18.00 1.50
O2 O2 30 l blue 37.50 1.50

Nos. O1-O2 exist imperf.

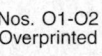

Nos. O1-O2 Overprinted

O3 O1 10 l dull claret 13.00 1.50
a. Inverted overprint 100.00 100.00
O4 O2 30 l blue 27.50 1.50
a. Inverted overprint 200.00 200.00

See note after No. 95.

Nos. O1-O2 Overprinted

1910

O5 O1 10 l dull claret 2.25 1.40
O6 O2 30 l blue 2.25 1.40

Nos. O5-O6 remained in use until 1922, nine years after union with Greece.

CROATIA

krō-'ā-sh,ē,-ə

LOCATION — Southeastern Europe
GOVT. — Independent state
AREA — 44,453 sq. mi.
POP. — 7,000,000 (approx.)
CAPITAL — Zagreb

The Independent Croatian State of 1941-45 became part of the Yugoslav Federation in 1945.

Croatia declared its independence in 1991.

100 Paras = 1 Dinar
100 Banica = 1 Kuna

Catalogue values for unused stamps in this country are for Never Hinged items, beginning with Scott 1 in the regular postage section, Scott B1 in the semi-postal section, Scott C1 in the airmail section and Scott RA1 in the postal tax section.

Watermark

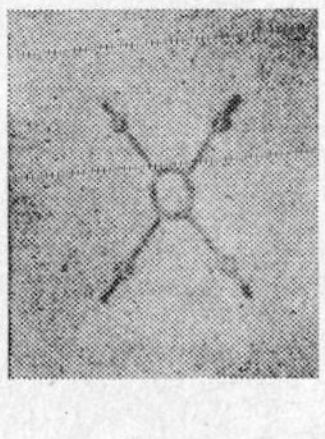
Wmk. 278 — Network Connecting Circles

Yugoslavia Nos. 143 to 148B Overprinted in Black

Perf. 12½

1941, Apr. 12 Unwmk. Typo.

1 A16 50p orange 4.50 3.75
a. Inverted overprint 225.00
2 A16 1d yellow grn 5.25 3.75
a. Double overprint 110.00
3 A16 1.50d red 6.00 2.25
a. Double overprint 110.00
4 A16 2d deep magenta 6.75 3.75
5 A16 3d dull red brn 11.00 6.75
a. Double overprint 110.00
6 A16 4d ultra 15.00 7.50
7 A16 5d dark blue 18.50 8.25
8 A16 5.50d dk violet brn 22.50 9.00
a. Double overprint 110.00
Nos. 1-8 (8) 89.50 45.00

Counterfeit overprints exist of Nos. 1-8, especially the inverted and double overprint varieties.

Yugoslavia Nos. 142 to 154 Overprinted in Black

1941, Apr. 21

9 A16 25p black .75 .50
a. Inverted overprint 75.00
b. Double overprint 75.00
10 A16 50p orange .75 .50
a. Inverted overprint 75.00
11 A16 1d yellow grn .75 .50
a. Inverted overprint —
12 A16 1.50d red .80 .50
a. Double overprint 150.00
13 A16 2d deep magenta .80 .50
14 A16 3d dull red brn 1.10 .95
15 A16 4d ultra 1.50 1.40
16 A16 5d dark blue 1.90 1.40
a. Double overprint 200.00
17 A16 5.50d dk violet brn 2.25 1.40
a. Inverted overprint 375.00
b. Double overprint 200.00
18 A16 6d slate blue 3.00 2.25
19 A16 8d sepia 3.75 2.25
20 A16 12d brt violet 4.50 3.00
a. Inverted overprint 375.00
21 A16 16d dull violet 5.25 4.50
a. Double overprint 200.00
22 A16 20d blue 6.75 5.25
23 A16 30d bright pink 12.00 10.00
Nos. 9-23 (15) 45.85 34.90

The overprint exists double, both inverted, on Nos. 16, 18 and 19.

Yugoslavia Nos. 147, 148 Surcharged in Black

1941, May 16

24 A16 1d on 3d dull red brn .40 .40
a. Inverted overprint 75.00
b. Double overprint 75.00
25 A16 2d on 4d ultra .40 .40
a. Inverted overprint 75.00
b. Double overprint 75.00

Postage Due Stamps of Yugoslavia, Nos. J28, J30 to J32, Overprinted in Black

1941, May 17

26 D4 50p violet .50 .45
27 D4 2d deep blue 1.35 1.25
28 D4 5d orange 1.90 1.40
29 D4 10d chocolate 2.25 1.60
Nos. 26-29 (4) 6.00 4.70

Counterfeit cancellations exist for Nos. 1-29 on cover.

Imperforates

Nearly all Croatian stamps, from No. 30 through 80, B3 through B76, J6 through J25, O1 through O24 and RA1 through RA7 exist imperforate, imperforate vertically, and imperforate horizontally. These are primarily from the special Ministerial Albums issued by the State Printing Office.

Ozalj Castle — A1

Designs: 50b, City of Jajce. 75b, Old Waradin. 1k, Velebit Mountains. 1.50k, Zelanjak. 2k, Zagreb Cathedral. 3k, Osjek Cathedral. 4k, Drina River. No. 38, Konjic. No. 39, Zemun. 6k, Dubrovnik. 7k, Save River. 8k, Sarajevo. 10k, Plitvice. 12k, Klis Fortress, Split. 20k, Hvar. 30k, Syrmia. 50k, Senj. 100k, Banjaluka (without "F.I.").

Perf. 11¼.

1941-43 Unwmk. Photo.

Ordinary Paper

30 A1 25b henna .25 .25
31 A1 50b slate blue .25 .25
32 A1 75b dk olive grn .25 .25
33 A1 1k Prussian green .25 .25
34 A1 1.50k deep green .25 .25
35 A1 2k carmine lake .25 .25
36 A1 3k brown red .25 .25
37 A1 4k deep ultra .25 .25
38 A1 5k black 2.00 1.15
39 A1 5k blue .25 .25
40 A1 6k lt olive brn .25 .25
41 A1 7k orange red .30 .25
42 A1 8k chestnut .40 .30
43 A1 10k dark plum .90 .45
44 A1 12k olive brown 1.50 .50
45 A1 20k golden brown 1.10 .40
46 A1 30k black brown 1.50 .50
47 A1 50k dk slate green 3.75 1.60
48 A1 100k violet 5.25 3.50
Nos. 30-48 (19) 19.20 *11.05*

Nos. 30-48 exist with a variety of perforations, including 11¼x10¾ and 12. Examples of Nos. 30, 36 and 48 exist with a special printer's mark in the design. Two varieties of printer's mark are known for No. 30, one for the first printing, and one for the second. Usually one stamp per pane has the printer's mark.

Nos. 31, 35 and 43 exist on thin to pelure paper, as does No. 32, though the latter was not issued to the public. Shades of all values exist.

For overprints and surcharge see Nos. 49-51, 53.

Tête bêche Pairs

30a A1 25b 1.75 *2.75*
31a A1 50b 2.00 *3.50*
33a A1 1k 2.50 *4.00*
34a A1 1.50k 2.75 *5.00*
35a A1 2k 3.00 *6.00*
37a A1 4k 3.95 *6.50*
38a A1 5k 7.00 *7.50*
40a A1 6k 4.00 *7.00*
41a A1 7k 4.50 *7.25*
42a A1 8k 5.00 *8.00*
43a A1 10k 5.50 *9.50*
45a A1 20k 6.50 *10.00*
46a A1 30k 7.25 *11.00*
47a A1 50k 13.00 *13.00*
Nos. 30a-47a (14) 68.70 *101.00*

Types of 1941 Overprinted in Brown or Green

1942, Apr. 9

49 A1 2k dark brown .60 .40
50 A1 5k dark carmine .90 .85
51 A1 10k dark blue green (G) 1.50 1.25
Nos. 49-51 (3) 3.00 *2.50*

First anniversary of Croatian independence.

The overprint exists double on No. 50.

Tête bêche pairs of Nos. 49-51 are from Ministerial Albums.

Banjaluka ("F.I." at upper right) — A20

1942, June 13

52 A20 100k violet 4.25 4.25

Banjaluka Philatelic Exhibition.

No. 52 exists in se-tenant pair with No. 48. Value unused, $300.

No. 52 exists with a special printer's mark in the design. The mark typically appears on one stamp in a given pane.

No. 35 Surcharged in Red Brown with New Value and Bar

1942, June 23

53 A1 25b on 2k carmine lake .55 .55
a. Tête bêche pair 3.25 3.25

No. 53 exists with double surcharge. It is not scarce.

Trakoscan Castle — A21

Design: 12.50k, Citadel of Veliki Tabor.

1943, Mar. 28 Pelure Paper

54 A21 3.50k brown carmine .75 .55
55 A21 12.50k violet black 1.00 .85

Nos. 54 was reissued in 1944 on ordinary paper, perf 12. Value the same for both varieties. No. 55 also exists on ordinary paper. It is scarce.

Catherine Zrinski — A23

2k, Fran Krsto Frankopan. 3.50k, Peter Zrinski.

Various Frames

1943, June 7 Engr. *Perf. 12¼x12½*

56 A23 1k dark blue .40 .40
57 A23 2k dark olive green .40 .40
58 A23 3.50k dark red .50 *.55*
Nos. 56-58 (3) 1.30 *1.35*

Many perforation varieties of this issue exist, including 12x12½, 12½x13, 12½, 13, 12½x14, 13x12½, and 14x12½.

Rudjer Boscovich — A26

1943, Dec. 13 *Perf. 11*

59 A26 3.50k copper red .50 .40
60 A26 12.50k dk violet brn .65 .50

Rugjer Boscovich (1711-1787). Mathematician and physicist.

No. 60 exists with a special printer's mark in the design. The mark typically appears on one stamp in a given pane.

Ante Pavelich — A27

1943-44 Litho. *Perf. 12½, 14*

61	A27	25b	orange ver	.30	.25
62	A27	50b	Prus blue	.30	.25
63	A27	75b	olive green	.30	.25
64	A27	1k	lt green	.30	.25
65	A27	1.50k	dull gray vio	.30	.25
66	A27	2k	rose lake	.30	.25
67	A27	3k	rose brown	.30	.25
68	A27	3.50k	bright blue	.30	.25
a.			3.50k dark blue, perf. 11½	4.00	*4.75*
69	A27	4k	brt red violet	.30	.25
70	A27	5k	ultra	.30	.25
71	A27	8k	orange brn	.35	.25
72	A27	9k	rose pink	.35	.25
73	A27	10k	violet brn	.40	.25
74	A27	12k	dk olive bis	.45	.25
75	A27	12.50k	gray black	.55	.25
76	A27	18k	dull brown	.70	.30
77	A27	32k	dark brown	.75	.30
78	A27	50k	grnsh blue	1.50	.50
79	A27	70k	orange	1.90	.90
80	A27	100k	violet	3.00	1.50
			Nos. 61-80 (20)	12.95	7.25

Nos. 61 and 63 measure 20½x26mm. Nos. 62 and 64-80 measure 22x27½mm.

Nos. 61, 63, 67, 70, 71 and 72 are perf 12½. Nos. 62, 64-66, 68, 69, 73 and 75-80 are perf 14. No. 74 exists either perf 12½ or 14.

No. 80 exists with a special printer's mark in the design. The mark typically appears on one stamp in a given pane.

Issue dates: 2k, 1943; No. 68a, June 13, 1943, Pavelich's Saint's Day; others, 1944.

"Labor Day 1945" — A28

1945 Photo. *Perf. 11½*

81	A28 3.50k red brown	.85	*1.60*

No. 81 exists imperforate. Value, never hinged $900.

From 1951 to 1972 44 labels were circulated by a Croatian Government in Exile. These had no postal value.

GOVT. — Independent state
AREA — 21,823 sq. mi.
POP. — 4,676,865 (1999 est.)
CAPITAL — Zagreb

Croatia declared its independence from Yugoslavia in 1991.

100 Paras = 1 Dinar (1991)
100 Lipa = 1 Kuna (1994)

Nos. RA20, RA20a Srchd. in Black and Gold

1991, Nov. 21 Litho. *Perf. 14*

100	PT10 4d on 1.20d #RA20	.70	.70
a.	Perf. 11x10½	.50	.50
b.	Perf. 11	7.50	7.50

A35

1991, Dec. 10 *Perf. 12*

101	A35 30d multicolored	2.00	2.00

Declaration of independence, 10/8/91.

A36

Christmas: Creche figures of the Holy Family from Kosljun Monastery.

1991, Dec. 11 *Perf. 12*

102	A36 4d multicolored	.80	.80

No. RA21 Surcharged in Black and Gold

1992, Jan. 3 *Perf. 10½x11*

103	PT11 20d on 1.70d #RA21	5.75	5.75

Croatian Arms — A37

1992, Jan. 15 *Perf. 11x10½*

104	A37 10d multicolored	.60	.60
a.	Perf. 14	.40	.40

See No. RA22.

1992 Winter Olympics, Albertville A38

1992, Feb. 4 *Perf. 11x10½*

105	A38 30d multicolored	*1.50*	*1.50*

Croatian Cities and Landmarks A39

A39a

Designs: 6d, Knin. 7d, Eltz Castle, Vukovar. 20d, Church, Ilok. 30d, Starcevic Street, Gospic. 45d, Rector's Palace, Dubrovnik. 50d, St. Jakov's Cathedral, Sibenik. 100d, Vinkovci. 200d, Pazin, vert. No. 115, Beli Manastir. 500d, Slavonski Brod. 1000d, Varazdin. 2000d, Karlovac. 5000d, Zadar, vert. 10,000d, Vis.

1992-94 *Perf. 14*

107	A39	6d	multi	*.25*	*.25*
108	A39	7d	multi	*.25*	*.25*
109	A39	20d	multi	*.35*	*.35*
a.			Perf. 11x10½	*1.00*	*1.00*
110	A39	30d	multi	*.90*	*.90*
111	A39	45d	multi	*.90*	*.90*
112	A39	50d	multi	*.90*	*.90*
113	A39a	100d	multi	*.65*	*.65*
114	A39a	200d	multi	*.35*	*.35*
115	A39	300d	multi	*2.00*	*2.00*
117	A39a	500d	multi	*1.90*	*1.90*
118	A39a	1000d	multi	*1.00*	*.70*
119	A39a	2000d	multi	*2.00*	*1.50*
120	A39a	5000d	multi	*3.00*	*2.50*
121	A39a	10,000d	multi	*5.50*	*5.00*
			Nos. 107-121 (14)	*19.95*	*18.15*

Issued: 6d, 4/18; 7d, 4/8; No. 109, 2/28; No. 109a, 9/9; 30d, 5/21; 45d, 4/14; 50d, 4/28; 115, 6/26; 100d, 12/14; 500d, 2/9/93; 1000d, 3/16/93; 200d, 4/9/93; 2000d, 5/20/93; 5000d, 9/24/93; 10,000d, 2/22/94.

See Nos. 355-356, 437A, 456.

Statue of King Tomislav — A40

1992, May 5 Engr. *Perf. 12½ Horiz.*
Coil Stamp

124	A40 10d dark green	.40	.40

Railroad Station, Zagreb, Cent. — A41

1992, June 30 Litho. *Perf. 14*

125	A41 30d multicolored	.40	.30

Matica, Society of Knowledge and Literacy, 150th Anniv. — A42

1992, July 8

126	A42 20d red, gold & black	.35	.30

Bishop Josip Juraj Strossmayer, Founder — A43

1992, July 9

127	A43 30d multicolored	.40	.40

Croatian Academy of Arts and Sciences, 125th anniv., in 1991.

1992 Summer Olympics, Barcelona A44

Design: 105d, Abstract design.

1992, July 25

128	A44 40d shown	.30	.30
129	A44 105d multicolored	1.25	1.25

Flowers A45

Designs: 30d, Edraianthus pumilio. 85d, Degenia velebitica, vert.

1992, July 28

130	A45 30d multicolored	.35	.35
131	A45 85d multicolored	.90	.90

Wildlife — A46

40d, Monticola solitarius. 75d, Elaphe situla.

1992, July 31

132	A46 40d multicolored	.45	.45
133	A46 75d multicolored	.85	.85

Discovery of America, 500th Anniv. — A47

Europa: 30d, 60d, Sailing ship. 75d, 130d, Indian in Chicago, by Ivan Mestrovic (1883-1962).

1992, Sep. 4 Litho. *Perf. 14*

134	A47 30d multicolored	*.55*	*.55*
135	A47 60d multicolored	*1.15*	*1.15*
136	A47 75d red & black	*1.30*	*1.30*
137	A47 130d red, blk & gold	*2.00*	*2.00*
	Nos. 134-137 (4)	*5.00*	*5.00*

Issued: 30d, 75d, July 31; others, Sept. 4.

A48

1992, Oct. 2

138	A48 40d multicolored	.35	.35
139	A48 130d multi, diff.	1.00	1.00

Declaration of Croatian Literary Language, 25th Anniv. (No. 138). Spelling reform by Dr. Ivan Broz, cent. (No. 139).

A49

1992, Oct. 16

140	A49 90d multicolored	.65	.40

City of Samobor, 750th Anniv.

Gift of the St. Juraj Church by Archbishop Mucimir, 1100th Anniv. — A50

1992, Oct. 30

141	A50 60d multicolored	.40	.30

Reign of King Bela IV, 750th Anniv. — A51

1992, Nov. 16 Litho. *Perf. 14*
142 A51 180d multicolored .85 .85

Christmas A52

1992, Dec. 7
143 A52 80d multicolored .40 .35

Blaz Lorkovic (1839-1892), Scientist — A53

1992, Dec. 21
144 A53 250d multicolored .90 .90

Kolo Literature Review, 150th Anniv. — A54

1992, Dec. 22
145 A54 300d multicolored 1.10 1.10

Ivan Bunic-Vucic (1592-1658) A55

1992, Dec. 29
146 A55 350d multicolored 1.10 1.10

800th Anniv. of Krapina — A55a

1993, Jan. 15
146A A55a 300d multicolored .70 .70

Nikola Tesla (1856-1943), Physicist A56

1993, Jan. 30
147 A56 250d multicolored .70 .70

Self-Portrait, by Ferdo Quiquerez (1845-1893) A57

1993, Feb. 10
148 A57 100d multicolored .40 .40

Wildlife — A58

1993, Feb. 23 Litho. *Perf. 14*
149 A58 500d Cervus elaphus 1.00 1.00
150 A58 550d Haliaeetus albicilla 1.00 1.00

Self-Portrait, by Zlatko Sulentic (1893-1971) A59

1993, Mar. 17
151 A59 350d multicolored .55 .55

Lipik Health and Convalescent Home, Cent. — A60

1993, Apr. 22 Litho. *Perf. 14*
152 A60 400d multicolored .55 .55

Ivan Goran Kovacic (1913-1943), Author — A61

1993, Apr. 24
153 A61 200d multicolored .35 .35

59th PEN Congress, Dubrovnik A62

1993, Apr. 24
154 A62 800d multicolored 1.25 1.25

Ivan Kukuljevic (1816-89), Politician, Historian, Writer — A63

1993, May 2 Litho. *Perf. 14*
155 A63 500d multicolored .65 .65

Croatian Natl. Theatre, Split, Cent. — A64

1993, May 6 Litho. *Perf. 14*
156 A64 600d multicolored .75 .75

Pag, 500th Anniv. — A65

1993, May 18
157 A65 800d multicolored .75 .75

Croatian Membership in United Nations, 1st Anniv. — A66

1993, May 22
158 A66 500d multicolored .60 .60

Europa A67

Contemporary paintings by: 700d, Ivo Dulcic (1916-75). 1000d, Miljenko Stancic (1926-77). 1100d, Ljubo Ivancic (b. 1925).

1993, June 5
159 A67 700d multicolored .75 .75
160 A67 1000d multicolored 1.50 1.50
161 A67 1100d multicolored 2.25 2.25
a. Min. sheet, 2 each #159-161 9.00 9.00
Nos. 159-161 (3) 4.50 4.50

Intl. Art Biennial, Venice — A68

Works of art by: 250d, Milivoj Bijelic. 600d, Ivo Dekovic. 1000d, Zeljko Kipke.

1993, June 10 Litho. *Perf. 14*
162 A68 250d multicolored .30 .30
a. Souvenir sheet of 4 1.00 1.00
163 A68 600d multicolored .85 .85
a. Souvenir sheet of 4 3.00 3.00
164 A68 1000d multicolored 1.20 1.20
a. Souvenir sheet of 4 4.00 4.00
Nos. 162-164 (3) 2.35 2.35

1993 Mediterranean Games — A69

1993, June 15 Litho. *Perf. 14*
165 A69 700d multicolored .65 .65

Adolf Waldinger (1843-1904), Painter — A70

1993, June 16
166 A70 300d multicolored .35 .35

Famous Croatian Battles A71

1993, July 6 Litho. *Perf. 14*
167 A71 800d Krbavskom, 1493 .65 .65
168 A71 1300d Sisak, 1593 1.10 1.10

Miroslav Krleza (1893-1981), Writer — A72

1993, July 7
169 A72 400d multicolored .40 .40

Croatian Membership in UPU, 1st Anniv. — A73

1993, July 20 Litho. *Perf. 14*
170 A73 1800d multicolored 1.25 .80

Vlaho Paljetak (1893-1944), Composer A74

1993, Aug. 7
171 A74 500d multicolored .45 .45

Stamp Day — A75

1993, Sept. 9 Litho. *Perf. 14*
172 A75 600d multicolored .50 .50

Map of Istria, 1620 — A76

1993, Sept. 20
173 A76 2200d multicolored 1.20 1.20

Incorporation of Istria, Rijeka and Zadar into Croatia, 50th anniv.

Tadija Smiciklas (1843-1914), Historian — A77

1993, Oct. 1
174 A77 800d black, gold & red .60 .60

Archaelogical Museum, Split, Cent. — A78

1993, Oct. 27
175 A78 1000d multicolored .60 .60

A79

1993, Nov. 17 Litho. *Perf. 14*
176 A79 3000d multicolored 1.50 1.50

Uprising of 13th Pioneer Battalion, Villefranche-de-Rouergue, France, 50th anniv.

A80

Josip Eugen Tomic (1843-1906), writer.

1993, Nov. 18
177 A80 900d multicolored .50 .50

Publication of De Esscentiis, by Hermana Dalmatin, 850th Anniv. — A81

1993, Nov. 30
178 A81 1000d multicolored .50 .50

Christmas A82

Paintings: 1000d, Christmas at the Front, by Miroslav Sutej. 4000d, Birth of Christ, 15th cent. fresco, Marienkirch of Dvigrad.

1993, Dec. 3
179 A82 1000d multicolored 1.00 1.00
180 A82 4000d multicolored 2.00 2.00

Organized Skiing in Croatia, Cent. — A83

1993, Dec. 15
181 A83 1000d multicolored .80 .80

Croatian Natl. Guard, 125th Anniv. A84

1993, Dec. 22
182 A84 1100d multicolored .80 .80

Printers of Senj, 500th Anniv. — A85

1994, Jan. 29
183 A85 2200d multicolored 1.10 .80

1994 Winter Olympics, Lillehammer A86

1994, Feb. 12
184 A86 4000d multicolored 1.90 1.60

Dinosaurs from Western Istria — A87

a, 2400d, Iguanodons. b, 4000d, Map, skeleton.

1994, Mar. 7
185 A87 Pair, #a.-b. 3.25 3.25

Nos. 185a-185b are a continuous design.

Zora Dalmatinska Magazine, 150th Anniv. — A88

1994, Mar. 15
186 A88 800d multicolored .50 .35

Croatian University, Zagreb, 325th Anniv. — A89

Design: 2200d, University building, Emperor Leopold I's seal, vice-chancellor's chain.

1994, Apr. 19 Litho. *Perf. 14*
187 A89 2200d multicolored 1.10 .75

Protect the Environment A90

1994, Apr. 22 Litho. *Perf. 14*
188 A90 3800d Canis lupus 2.00 1.75

ILO, 75th Anniv. — A91

1994, May 2
189 A91 1000d multicolored .60 .40

A92

Europa — A93

European inventions, discoveries: 3800d, Faust Vrancic (1551-1617), parachute. 4000d, Slavoljub Penkala (1871-1922), fountain pen.

1994, May 16
190 A92 3800d multicolored *2.25 2.00*
191 A93 4000d multicolored *2.75 2.00*

A94

1994, June 3
192 A94 2.40k Iris croatica 1.00 .60
193 A94 4k Colchicum visianii 1.60 1.25

A95

Drazen Petrovic (1964-93), basketball player.

1994, June 7
194 A95 1k multicolored .75 .75

Tourism in Croatia, 150th Anniv. — A96

Designs: 80 l, Plitvice Lakes Natl. Park. 1k, Waterfalls, Krka River. 1.10k, Kornati Islands Natl. Park. 2.20k, Kopacki Trscak nature reserve. 2.40k Sailboats, Opatijska Riviera resort. 3.80k, Brijuni islands. 4k, Trakoscan castle, Zagorje.

1994, June 15 Litho. *Perf. 14*
196 A96 80 l multicolored .45 .25
197 A96 1k multicolored .50 .30
198 A96 1.10k multicolored .55 .35
199 A96 2.20k multicolored 1.25 .40
200 A96 2.40k multicolored 1.40 .60
201 A96 3.80k multicolored 2.10 .75
202 A96 4k multicolored 2.40 1.00
a. Min. sheet of 7, #196-202 + 2 labels 8.50 8.00
Nos. 196-202 (7) 8.65 3.65

Croatian Musicians A97

Designs: 1k, Kresimir Baranovic (1894-1975), composer, vert. 2.20k, Vatroslav Lisinski (1819-54), composer, vert. 2.40k, Pauline song-book (1644), harpist.

1994, June 20
211 A97 1k multicolored .50 .35
212 A97 2.20k multicolored 1.10 .75
213 A97 2.40k multicolored 1.25 .85
Nos. 211-213 (3) 2.85 1.95

Croatian Fraternal Union, Cent. — A98

1994, Aug. 15 Litho. *Perf. 14*
214 A98 2.20k multicolored 1.25 1.25

A99

1994, Aug. 31
215 A99 80 l multicolored .50 .50

Intl. Year of the Family.

A100

1994, Sept. 10
216 A100 1k multicolored .60 .60

Intl. Olympic Committee, cent.

Visit of Pope John Paul II — A101

1994, Sept. 10
217 A101 1k multicolored .75 .75

No. 217 printed with se-tenant label.

Antoine de Saint-Exupery (1900-44), Aviator, Author A102

1994, Sept. 20
218 A102 3.80k multicolored 1.90 1.40

13th Intl. Congress on Early Christian Archeology A103

1994, Sept. 23
219 A103 4k multicolored 2.00 1.40

No. 219 printed with se-tenant label.

Modern Croatian Paintings A104

Designs: 2.40k, Still Life with Fruits and Basket, by Marino Tartaglia, 1926. 3.80k, In the Park, by Milan Steiner, c. 1918. 4k, Self-portrait, by Vilko Gecan, 1929.

1994, Oct. 12
220 A104 2.40k multicolored 1.00 .75
221 A104 3.80k multicolored 1.60 1.25
222 A104 4k multicolored 1.75 1.25
Nos. 220-222 (3) 4.35 3.25

Ivan Belostenec (1594-1675), Writer & Lexicographer A105

1994, Nov. 9
223 A105 2.20k multicolored 1.10 .90

City of Zagreb, Zagreb Bishopric, 900th Anniv. — A106

Designs: No. 224a, 1k, Zagreb exchange building, designed by V. Kovacic, S. Penkala's airplane, Cibona office tower, designed by Hrzic, Pitesa and Serbetic. b, 1k, Maxi Cat, by Zlatko Grgic, Zagreb School of Animated Film. c, 1k, St. Mark's Church, Gradec; photo of gas lantern, by Toso Dabac. d, 4k, Late Gothic bishop's staff, Valvasor's view of Zagreb.
13.50k, Zagreb street scene, Penkala's airplane, vert.

1994, Nov. 16
224 A106 Strip of 4, #a.-d. 3.00 3.00

Souvenir Sheet

225 A106 13.50k multicolored 5.00 5.00

No. 224 is a continuous design. No. 225 contains one 24x48mm stamp.

Christmas A107

Design: 1k, Epiphany, by unknown sculptor.

1994, Dec. 1 Litho. *Perf. 14*
226 A107 1k multicolored .60 .50

Virgin Mary's Sanctuary, Loreto, 700th Anniv. — A108

Design: 4k, The Moving of the Holy House, by Giovanni Battista Tiepolo.

1994, Dec. 10
227 A108 4k multicolored 2.00 1.50

Necktie in Croatia — A109

Tie designs: 1.10k, Businessman's, 1995. 3.80k, English Dandy, 1810. 4k, Croatian soldier, 1630.

1995, Jan. 19 Litho. *Perf. 14*
228 A109 1.10k multicolored .60 .45
229 A109 3.80k multicolored 1.90 1.50
230 A109 4k multicolored 2.00 1.90
a. Souvenir sheet of 3, #228-230 4.75 4.75
Nos. 228-230 (3) 4.50 3.85

Croatian Monasteries — A110

1k, Jesuit Monastery, Zagreb, 350th anniv. 2.40k, Franciscan Monastery, Visovac, 550th anniv.

1995, Feb. 16
231 A110 1k multicolored .50 .30
232 A110 2.40k multicolored 1.25 .95

Hunting Dogs — A111

Designs: 2.20k, Istrian short-haired. 2.40k, Posavinian. 3.80k, Istrian wire-haired.

1995, Mar. 9 Litho. *Perf. 14*
233 A111 2.20k multicolored 1.00 .75
234 A111 2.40k multicolored 1.25 .80
235 A111 3.80k multicolored 1.75 1.40
Nos. 233-235 (3) 4.00 2.95

Town of Split, 1700th Anniv. — A112

No. 236: a, 1k, Drawing of reconstruction of Diocletian's Palace. b, 2.20k, "Split Harbour," by Emanuel Vidovic, 1937. c, 4k, Modern view of town, bust of Marko Marulic by Ivan Mestrovic.
13.40k, Buildings, vert.

1995, Apr. 20 Litho. *Perf. 14*
236 A112 Strip of 3, #a.-c. 4.00 4.00

Souvenir Sheet

237 A112 13.40k multicolored 6.25 6.25

No. 237 contains one 24x48mm stamp.

World Team Handball Championships, Iceland — A113

1995, May 4
238 A113 4k multicolored 2.00 1.25

Peace & Freedom A114

Europa: 2.40k, Clearing storm clouds. 4k, Hands of angel, by Francisco Robba.

1995, May 9
239 A114 2.40k multicolored *1.75 1.25*
240 A114 4k multicolored *2.25 1.60*

Anti-Austria Demonstrations, 150th Anniv. — A115

1995, May 15
241 A115 1.10k multicolored .65 .45
242 A115 3.80k multicolored 1.25 1.10

Croatian surrender to British forces at Bleiburg, 50th anniv. (No. 242).

Independence Day — A116

1995, May 30 Litho. *Perf. 14*
243 A116 1.10k multicolored .75 .40

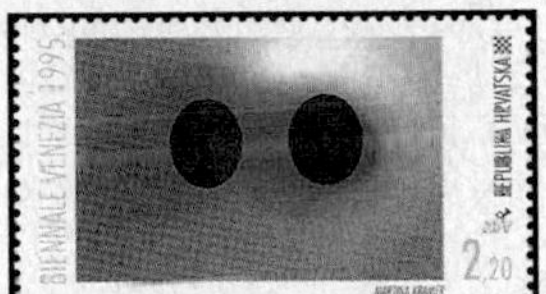

Croatian Sculptures at Venice Biennial, 1995 — A117

2.20k, Installation (a part), by Martina Kramer. 2.40k, Paracelsus Paraduchamps, by Mirko Zrinscak, vert. 4k, Shadows, by Goran Petercol.

1995, June 8 Litho. *Perf. 14*
244 A117 2.20k multicolored 1.00 .65
245 A117 2.40k multicolored 1.10 .75
246 A117 4k multicolored 1.90 1.75
Nos. 244-246 (3) 4.00 3.15

St. Anthony of Padua (1195-1231) — A118

1995, June 13
247 A118 1k multicolored .45 .30

Marine Life — A119

1995, June 29 Litho. *Perf. 14*
248 A119 2.40k Caretta caretta 1.00 .90
249 A119 4k Tursiops truncatus 1.75 1.50

Liberation of the City of Knin — A120

1995, Aug. 5 Litho. *Perf. 14*
250 A120 1.30k multicolored .75 .60

Krka River Hydroelectric Power Plant, Cent. — A121

1995, Aug. 28

251 A121 3.60k multicolored 1.45 1.00

Stamp Day — A122

1995, Sept. 9 Litho. *Perf. 14*

252 A122 1.30k multicolored .70 .70

Franz von Suppe (1819-95), Composer A123

1995, Sept. 15

253 A123 6.50k multicolored 3.00 2.00

See Austria Nos. 1686-1687.

Liberation of Petrinja from Turkish Rule, 400th Anniv. — A124

1995, Sept. 21

254 A124 2.20k multicolored 1.10 .90

Croatian Music — A125

Composers, conductors: 1.20k, Ivo Tijardovic (1895-1976). 1.40k, Lovro Von Matacic (1899-1985). 6.50k, Jakov Gotovac (1895-1982).

1995, Sept. 23

255 A125 1.20k multicolored .55 .55
256 A125 1.40k multicolored .65 .60
257 A125 6.50k multicolored 3.25 2.50
Nos. 255-257 (3) 4.45 3.65

Herman Bollé (1845-1926), Architect — A126

2.40k, Izidor Krsnjavi (1845-1927), painter. 3.60k, Croatian National Theatre, cent.

1995, Oct. 14 Litho. *Perf. 14*

258 A126 1.80k multicolored .80 .50
259 A126 2.40k multicolored 1.00 .70
260 A126 3.60k multicolored 1.75 1.25
Nos. 258-260 (3) 3.55 2.45

Croatian Towns — A127

1995, Oct. 20

261 A127 1k Bjelovar .45 .45
262 A127 1.30k Osijek, vert. .55 .55
263 A127 1.40k Cakovec, vert. .60 .60
264 A127 2.20k Rovinj 1.10 1.10
265 A127 2.40k Korcula 1.25 1.25
266 A127 3.60k Zupanja 1.60 1.60
Nos. 261-266 (6) 5.55 5.55

See No. 448.

UN, FAO, 50th Anniv. — A128

No. 268, "5, 0" in form of cracker, FAO.

1995, Oct. 24

267 A128 3.60k multicolored 1.40 1.00
268 A128 3.60k multicolored 1.60 1.00
a. Pair, #267-268 3.25 3.25

Croatian Scientists — A129

1k, Spiro Brusina (1845-1908). 2.20k, Bogoslav Sulek (1816-95). 6.50k, Front of European language dictionary, published by Faust Vrancic (1551-1617).

1995, Oct. 30

269 A129 1k multicolored .65 .30
270 A129 2.20k multicolored 1.00 .65
271 A129 6.50k multicolored 3.00 2.25
Nos. 269-271 (3) 4.65 3.20

Institute for Blind Children, Cent. — A130

1995, Nov. 23 Litho. *Perf. 14*

272 A130 1.20k multicolored 1.00 1.00

Christmas A131

1995, Dec. 1

273 A131 1.30k multicolored .65 .45

Maroc Polo's Return from China, 700th Anniv. A132

1995, Dec. 7

274 A132 3.60k multicolored 1.75 1.50

Liberated Towns A133

1995, Dec. 16

275 A133 20 l Hrvatska Kostajnica .25 .25
276 A133 30 l Slunj .25 .25
277 A133 50 l Gracac .35 .35
278 A133 1.20k Drnis, vert. .70 .70
279 A133 6.50k Glina 3.25 3.25
280 A133 10k Obrovac, vert. 4.50 4.50
Nos. 275-280 (6) 9.30 9.30

Incunabula A134

Designs: 1.40k, Lectionary of Bernardin of Split. 3.60k, Spovid Opcena (General Confession).

1995, Dec. 28

281 A134 1.40k multicolored .75 .40
282 A134 3.60k multicolored 1.75 1.25

Spirituality of the Croats — A135

Designs: No. 283, Mosaic of St. Marko Krizevcanin (1589-1619), Catholic martyr. No. 284, Veneration of Miraculous Crucifix, St. Guido's Church, Rijeka, 700th anniv. No. 285, Ivan Merz (1896-1928), Catholic educator.

1996, Jan. 18 Litho. *Perf. 14*

283 A135 1.30k multicolored .60 .50
284 A135 1.30k multicolored .60 .50
285 A135 1.30k multicolored .60 .50
a. Strip of 3, Nos. 283-285 2.00 2.00

Political Anniversaries A136

1.20k, Rakovica Uprising by Eugen Kvaternik, 125th anniv., horiz. 1.40k, Ante Starcevic (1823-96). 2.20k, Constitution of Neutral Peasant Republic of Croatia, 75th anniv., Stjepan Radic (1871-1928). 3.60k, Labin Republic, 75th anniv.

1996, Feb. 28

286 A136 1.20k multicolored .60 .50
287 A136 1.40k multicolored .70 .60
288 A136 2.20k multicolored .95 .80
289 A136 3.60k multicolored 1.75 1.40
Nos. 286-289 (4) 4.00 3.30

Institute for Pharmacognosy, University of Zagreb, Cent. — A137

1996, Mar. 23 Litho. *Perf. 14*

290 A137 6.50k multicolored 3.00 2.00

Croatian Music — A138

a, Vinko Jelíc (1596-1636), composer. b, First performance of opera "Love and Music." c, Josip Stolcer Slavenski (1896-1955), composer. d, "Lijepa Nasa," Croatian national anthem, 150th anniv.

1996, Mar. 28

291 A138 2.20k Strip of 4, #a.-d. 3.75 3.75

A139

Famous Women Writers (Europa): 2.20k, Cvijeta Zuzoric (b. 1551 or 1552). 3.60k, Ivana Brlic Mazuranic (1874-1938).

1996, Apr. 11 Litho. *Perf. 14*

292 A139 2.20k multicolored 1.60 1.60
293 A139 3.60k multicolored 2.25 2.25

A140

The Zrinskis and The Frankopans: 1.30k, Nikola Subic Zrinski of Sziget (1508-56). 1.40k, Nikola Zrinski (1620-64). 2.20k, Petar Zrinski (1621-71). 2.40k, Katarina Zrinski (1625-73). 3.60k, Fran Krsto Frankopan (1643-71).

1996, Apr. 30

294 A140 1.30k multicolored .55 .55
295 A140 1.40k multicolored .60 .60
296 A140 2.20k multicolored 1.00 1.00
297 A140 2.40k multicolored 1.10 1.10
298 A140 3.60k multicolored 1.40 1.40
a. Sheet of 5, #294-298 5.00 5.00
Nos. 294-298 (5) 4.65 4.65

Natl. Guard, 5th Anniv. — A141

1996, May 28 Litho. *Perf. 14*

299 A141 1.30k multicolored .65 .65

Flowers — A142

Designs: 2.40k, Campanula istriaca. 3.60k, Centaurea ragusina.

1996, June 5

300 A142 2.40k multicolored 1.00 1.00
301 A142 3.60k multicolored 1.60 1.60

England '96, European Soccer Championship A143

1996, June 8

302 A143 2.20k red & black 1.10 .90

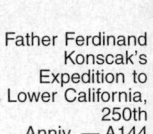

Father Ferdinand Konscak's Expedition to Lower California, 250th Anniv. — A144

1996, June 10

303 A144 2.40k multicolored 1.10 1.00

1996 Summer Olympics, Atlanta A145

1996, July 4

304 A145 3.60k multicolored 1.75 1.25

A146

1996, July 4

305 A146 1.40k multicolored .65 .60

Josip Fon, founder of Croatian Sokol Gymnastics Society, 150th birth anniv.

A147

1996, Sept. 9 Litho. *Perf. 14*

306 A147 1.30k multicolored .65 .40

Croatian postage stamps, 5th anniv.

1st Written Reference, Zumberak Region, 700th Anniv. — A148

1996, Sept. 14

307 A148 2.20k multicolored 1.00 1.00

A149

1996, Sept. 19

308 A149 1.30k multicolored .60 .60

First written record of fishing in Croatia, 1000th anniv.

A150

Events of the early Middle Ages: 1.20k, Vekenega's Book of Gospels, 900th anniv. 1.40k, Visit by Saxon Benedictine abbot Gottschalk (805-870), to Duke Trpimir's court, 1150th anniv.

1996, Sept. 19

309 A150 1.20k multicolored .55 .50
310 A150 1.40k multicolored .65 .55

Scientists A151

Designs: a, Gjuro Pilar (1846-93), geologist. b, Frane Bulic (1846-1934), archeologist. c, Ante Sercer (1896-1968), otolaryngologist.

1996, Oct. 4 Litho. *Perf. 14*

311 A151 2.40k Strip of 3, #a.-c. 3.25 3.25

Beginning of Higher Education in Croatia, 600th Anniv. — A152

Oldest preserved Croatian text written in Latin script, "Order and Law" of Dominican nuns, Zadar.

1996, Oct. 16 *Perf. 13½*

312 A152 1.40k multicolored .70 .50

Paintings — A153

Designs: 1.30k, Rain, by Menci Clement Crncic (1865-1930). 1.40k, The Peljesac-Korcula Channel, by Mato Celestin Medovic (1857-1919). 3.60k, Pink Dream, by Vlaho Bukovac (1855-1922).

1996, Nov. 7 Litho. *Perf. 14*

313 A153 1.30k multicolored .60 .60
314 A153 1.40k multicolored .70 .70
315 A153 3.60k multicolored 1.75 1.75
Nos. 313-315 (3) 3.05 3.05

UNICEF, 50th Anniv. — A154

1996, Nov. 15

316 A154 3.60k multicolored 1.60 1.25

City of Osijek, 800th Anniv. — A155

Views of city: No. 317, River bank, church, coat of arms. No. 318, Boats in water, view looking down covered walkway through building.

1996, Dec. 2 Litho. *Perf. 14*

317 A155 2.20k multicolored 1.00 .75
318 A155 2.20k multicolored 1.00 .75
a. Pair, #317-318 2.25 2.25

Christmas — A156

1996, Dec. 3

319 A156 1.30k multicolored .70 .50

First Croatian Savings Bank, Zagreb, 150th Anniv. — A157

Design: 3.60k, Publishing of "The Bases of Corn Trade," by Josip Sipus, bicent.

1996, Dec. 14

320 A157 2.40k multicolored 1.00 .80
321 A157 3.60k multicolored 1.75 1.25

Motion Pictures, Cent. — A158

Designs: a, Shooting of film, "Vatroslav Lisinski," Oktavijan Miletic, cameraman, director. b, Characters from animated series, "Professor Baltazar." c, Mirjana Bohanec, Relja Basic in "Who Sings Means No Harm."

1997, Jan. 16 Litho. *Perf. 14*

322 A158 1.40k Strip of 3, #a.-c. 2.00 2.00

Great Europeans A159

Designs: 2.20k, Miguel de Cervantes (1547-1676), author. 3.60k, Johannes Gutenberg (1397-1468), printer, horiz.

1997, Feb. 7

323 A159 2.20k multicolored .90 .65
324 A159 3.60k multicolored 1.50 1.10

Legends A160

Europa: 1.30k, Home Genies, from story, "Stribor's Forest." 3.60k, "Vili Joze," by Vladimir Nazor, vert.

1997, Mar. 6 Litho. *Perf. 14*

325 A160 1.30k multicolored *1.10 1.10*
326 A160 3.60k multicolored *2.75 2.75*

Fauna of Croatia — A161

1997, Apr. 22 Litho. *Perf. 14*

327 A161 1.40k Pinna nobilis .60 .60
328 A161 2.40k Radziella styx 1.00 1.00
329 A161 3.60k Tonna galea 1.60 1.60
Nos. 327-329 (3) 3.20 3.20

Admission of Croatia to UN, 5th Anniv. A162

1997, May 22 Litho. *Perf. 14*

330 A162 6.50k Pres. Franjo Tudjman 3.00 3.00

First Croatian Esperantist Conference, 90th Anniv. A163

Ludwig Lazarus Zamenhof, conf. logo.

1997, May 31

331 A163 1.20k multicolored .70 .70

Congress of Intl. Amateur Rugby Federation, Dubrovnik A164

1997, June 6

332 A164 2.20k multicolored 1.10 .80

Siege of Vukovar, Serbo-Croatian War, 1991 — A165

Painting by Zlatko Kauzlaric Atac.

1997, June 8 Litho. *Perf. 14*

333 A165 6.50k multicolored 3.00 3.00

Croatian Kings — A166

1.30k, King Peter Svacic, 900th death anniv. 2.40k, King Stephen Drzislav, 1000th death anniv.

1997, July 3

334	A166	1.30k multicolored	.60	.60
335	A166	2.40k multicolored	1.25	1.25

16th Century Courier from Dubrovnik A167

1997, Sept. 9 **Litho.** ***Perf. 14***

336	A167	2.30k multicolored	1.10	.90

Stamp Day.

Croatian Olympic Medals — A168

Designs: 1k, Tennis, bronze, Barcelona, 1992. 1.20k, Basketball, silver, Barcelona 1992. 1.40k, Water polo, silver, Atlanta, 1996. 2.20k, Handball, gold, Atlanta, 1996.

1997, Sept. 10

337	A168	1k multicolored	.40	.40
338	A168	1.20k multicolored	.50	.50

Size: 27x31mm

339	A168	1.40k multicolored	.75	.75
340	A168	2.20k multicolored	1.00	1.00
		Nos. 337-340 (4)	2.65	2.65

Defense of Sibenik — A169

Designs: No. 341, Fort, airplanes. No. 342, Turkish cavalry, fort.

1997, Sept. 18

341	A169	1.30k multicolored	.50	.50
342	A169	1.30k multicolored	.50	.50
a.		Pair, #341-342	1.25	1.25

Serbo-Croatian War, 1991 (No. 341). War with the Turks, 350th anniv. (No. 342).

Anniversaries A170

No. 343: a, Frane Petríc (1529-97), philosopher. b, Vicko Lovrin, 16th century painter. c, Frano Krsiníc (1897-1982), sculptor. d, Dubravko Dujsin (1894-1947), actor.

1997, Oct. 17 **Litho.** ***Perf. 14***

343	A170	1.40k Strip of 4, #a.-d.	2.75	2.75

A171

A172

1997, Oct. 23

344	A171	2.20k multicolored	1.00	.70
345	A172	3.60k multicolored	1.50	1.00

Use of Croatian language in parliament, 150th anniv. (No. 344).

Croatian Grammar School, Zadar, cent. (No. 345).

Palaeontological Finds in Croatia — A173

Designs: 1.40k, Gomphotherium angustidens. 2.40k, Viviparus novskaensis.

1997, Nov. 6

346	A173	1.40k multicolored	.60	.60
347	A173	2.40k multicolored	1.10	1.10

Modern Art A174

Paintings: 1.30k, Painter in the Pond, by Nikola Masic (1852-1902). 2.20k, Angelus, by Emanuel Vidovic (1870-1953). 3.60k, Tree in the Snow, by Slava Raskaj (1877-1906).

1997, Nov. 14

348	A174	1.30k multicolored	.60	.45
349	A174	2.20k multicolored	.90	.55
350	A174	3.60k multicolored	1.75	1.25
		Nos. 348-350 (3)	3.25	2.25

Contemporary Christmas Painting, by Ivan Antolcic — A175

"Birth of Jesus," by Isidor Krsnjavi A176

1997, Nov. 28 **Litho.** ***Perf. 13½***

351	A175	1.30k multicolored	.50	.40

Perf. 14

352	A176	3.60k multicolored	1.60	1.10

Croatian Literature — A177

1997, Dec. 18 ***Perf. 14***

353	A177	1k shown	.55	.40
354	A177	1.20k Book, words	.60	.40

Printing of the translation of "Electra," by Dominko Zlataric, 400th anniv. (No. 353). Publication of "The Best of Folk Speech and the Illyric or Croatian Language," by Filip Grabovac, 250th anniv. (No. 354).

Cities and Landmarks Type of 1992

1997 **Litho.** ***Perf. 14***

355	A39	5 l Ilok	.25	.25
356	A39	10 l Dubrovnik	.25	.25

Events and Festivals — A178

Europa: 1.45k, Varazdin Baroque Evenings, musical notes. 4k, Dubrovnik Summer Festival.

1998, Jan. 23 ***Perf. 13½***

357	A178	1.45k multicolored	*1.00*	*1.00*
358	A178	4k multicolored	*2.50*	*2.50*

1998 Winter Olympic Games, Nagano — A179

1998, Feb. 7 ***Perf. 14***

359	A179	2.45k multicolored	1.10	.75

Croatian Events of 1848 — A180

a, 1.60k, Flag, battle near Moor. b, 4k, Portrait of Ban Josip Jelacic. c, 1.60k, Croatian Assembly.

1998, Mar. 25 **Litho.** ***Perf. 14***

360	A180	Strip of 3, #a.-c.	3.25	3.25

No. 360b is 21x32mm.

Ante Topic Mimara (1898-1987), Art Collector, Painter A181

1998, Apr. 7 **Litho.** ***Perf. 14***

361	A181	2.65k multicolored	1.25	.90

A182

Mushrooms: a, 1.30k, Amanita caesarea. b, 7.20k, Morchella conica. c, 1.30k, Lactarius deliciosus.

1998, Apr. 22

362	A182	Strip of 3, #a.-c.	4.50	4.50

A183

1998, May 8

363	A183	1.50k multicolored	.65	.65

Archbishop Alojzije Stepinac (1898-1960).

27th European Regional Conference of Interpol, Dubrovnik A184

1998, May 13

364	A184	2.45k multicolored	1.10	.90

Souvenir Sheet

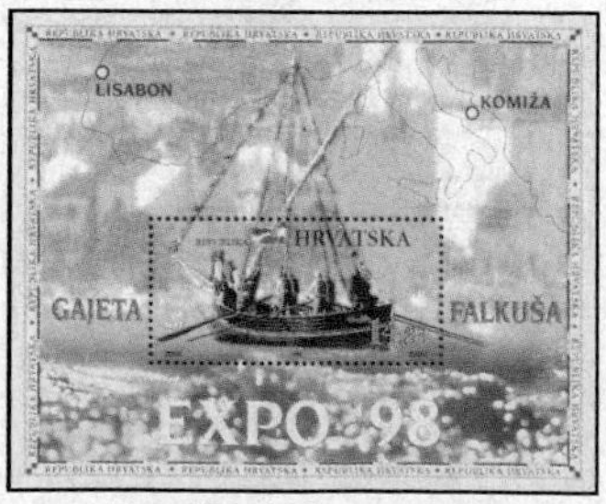

Expo '98, Lisbon — A185

1998, June 3 **Litho.** ***Perf. 14***

365	A185	14.85k Fishing boat, Falkusa	6.25	6.25

1998 World Cup Soccer Championships, France — A186

1998, June 10

366	A186	4k multicolored		2.00	1.50

Writers A187

1.20k, Juraj Barakovic (1548-1628). 1.50k, Milan Begovic (1876-1948). 1.60k, Mate Balota (Mijo Mirkovic, 1898-1963). 2.45k, Antun Gustav Matos (1873-1914). 2.65k, Matija Antun Relkovic (1732-98). 4.00k, Antun Branko Simic (1898-1925).

1998, June 13 Litho. *Perf. 14*

367	A187	1.20k	multicolored	.60	.50
368	A187	1.50k	multicolored	.70	.60
369	A187	1.60k	multicolored	.75	.70
370	A187	2.45k	multicolored	1.00	.90
371	A187	2.65k	multicolored	1.10	1.00
372	A187	4k	multicolored	1.75	1.60
			Nos. 367-372 (6)	5.90	5.30

19th Conference of the Countries of the Danube Region, Osijek — A188

1998, June 15

373	A188	1.80k multicolored		.75	.65

Stjepan Betlheim (1898-1970), Psychiatrist A189

1998, July 22

374	A189	1.50k multicolored		.65	.50

Souvenir Sheet

Croatian Soccer Team, Bronze Medalists at 1998 World Cup Soccer Championships, France — A190

Portions of team picture, denomination: a, red, LL. b, yellow, CR (player in yellow & blue shirt). c, yellow, CL. d, yellow, LR.

1998, July 24

375	A190	4k Sheet of 4, #a.-d.		7.25	7.25

Croatian Ships — A191

1.20k, Serilia Liburnica. 1.50k, Condura Croatica. 1.60k, Dubrovnik carrack. 1.80k, Bracera. 2.45k, Ship from the Neretva. 2.65k, Bark. 4k, Training ship, "Villa Velebita." 7.20k, Passenger ship, "Amorella." 20k, Missile gun boat, "Kralj Petar Kresimir IV."

1998, Aug. 27 Litho. *Perf. 14*

376	A191	1.20k	multi	.70	.70
376A	A191	1.50k	multi	.80	.80
376B	A191	1.60k	multi	.85	.85
376C	A191	1.80k	multi	.90	.90
376D	A191	2.45k	multi	1.30	1.30
376E	A191	2.65k	multi	1.50	1.50
376F	A191	4k	multi	2.00	2.00
376G	A191	7.20k	multi	3.50	3.50
376H	A191	20k	multi	9.25	9.25
i.	Sheet of 9, #376-376H + 3 labels			20.00	20.00
	Nos. 376-376H (9)			20.80	20.80

Stamp Day — A192

1998, Sept. 9

377	A192	1.50k multicolored		.65	.50

Bishopric of Sibenik, 700th Anniv. — A193

1998, Sept. 29 Litho. *Perf. 14*

378	A193	4k multicolored		1.60	1.60

Pope John Paul II, Second Visit to Croatia A194

1998, Oct. 2

379	A194	1.50k multicolored		.90	.90

History of Public Transportation A195

Designs: a, 1.50k, Horse tram. b, 1.50k, First automobile in Zagreb, 1901. c, 7.20k, Zagreb funicular. d, 1.50k, Karlovac-Rijeka Railway Line, 1873. e, 1.50k, New Highway, Zagreb-Rijeka.

1998, Oct. 23 Litho. *Perf. 14*

380	A195	Strip of 5, #a.-e.		6.00	6.00

No. 380c is 20x24mm.

Christmas — A196

Adoration of the Shepherds, by Juraj Julije Klovic (1498-1578).

1998, Nov. 21 *Perf. 14x13*

381	A196	1.50k multicolored		.80	.75

See Vatican City No. 1088.

Father Luka Ibrisimovic (1620-98) A197

1998, Nov. 30 Litho. *Perf. 14*

382	A197	1.90k multicolored		.90	.75

Universal Declaration of Human Rights, 50th Anniv. — A198

1998, Dec. 10

383	A198	5k multicolored		2.00	2.00

Modern Art A199

Paintings: 1.90k, Paromlin Road, by Josip Vanista. 2.20k, Cypresses, by Frano Simunovic, vert. 5k, Koma, by Dalibor Martinis, vert.

1998, Dec. 15

384	A199	1.90k	multicolored	.90	.90
385	A199	2.20k	multicolored	1.00	1.00
386	A199	5k	multicolored	2.10	2.10
			Nos. 384-386 (3)	4.00	4.00

Zagreb Intl. Trade Fair — A200

1999, Jan. 21 Litho. *Perf. 14*

387	A200	1.80k multicolored		.90	.80

Cardinal Juraj Haulik (1788-1869), Archbishop of Zagreb — A201

Photo. & Engr.

1999, Jan. 28 *Perf. 11½*

388	A201	5k multicolored		2.10	2.10

See Slovakia 321.

National Parks — A202

Europa: 1.80k, Mljet Island. 5k, Lonja Field.

1999, Mar. 12 Litho. *Perf. 14*

389	A202	1.80k multicolored		*2.00*	*2.00*
390	A202	5k multicolored		*3.50*	*3.50*

Vipera Ursinii — A203

World Wildlife Fund: a, One coiled in grass and rock. b, Two. c, Head. d, One coiled on rock.

1999, Apr. 27 Litho. *Perf. 14*

391	A203	2.20k Strip of 4, #a.-d.		4.25	4.25

Council of Europe, 50th Anniv. — A204

1999, May 5

392	A204	2.80k multicolored		1.25	1.25

19th Convention of the Foundation of European Carnival Cities, Dubrovnik — A205

1999, May 8

393	A205	2.30k multicolored		1.10	1.10

Croatian Coins — A206

Designs: a, 2.30k, Obv., rev. of 1849 kreutzer. b, 5k, One kuna.

1999, May 30 Litho. *Perf. 14*

394	A206	Pair, #a.-b.		3.25	3.25

Minting of Jelacic kreutzer, 150th anniv. (No. 394a). Croatian kuna, 5th anniv. (No. 394b).

Famous Croats — A207

1.80k, Vladimir Nazor (1876-1949), poet. 2.30k, Ferdo Livadic (1799-1879), composer. 2.50k, Ivan Rendic (1849-1932), sculptor. 2.80k, Milan Lenuci (1849-1924), architect. 3.50k, Vjekoslav Klaic (1849-1929), historian, muscician. 4k, Emilij Laszowski (1868-1949), historian. 5k, Antun Kanizlic (1699-1777), poet, missionary.

1999, June 18

395	A207	1.80k	multicolored	.65	.65
396	A207	2.30k	multicolored	.95	.90
397	A207	2.50k	multicolored	1.25	1.10
398	A207	2.80k	multicolored	1.30	1.30
399	A207	3.50k	multicolored	1.40	1.40
400	A207	4k	multicolored	1.60	1.60
401	A207	5k	multicolored	2.10	2.10
			Nos. 395-401 (7)	9.25	9.05

Euphrasian Basilica, Porec — A208

1999, June 25
402 A208 4k multicolored 1.75 1.75

2nd World Military Games, Zagreb A209

1999, Aug. 7 Litho. *Perf. 14*
403 A209 2.30k multicolored 1.10 .90

Discovery of Early Krapina Man, Cent. — A210

Designs: a, 1.80k, Bones, rendition of Krapina man. b, 4k, Ancient bones, paleontologist Dragutin Gorjanovic-Kramberger.

1999, Aug. 23
404 A210 Pair, #a.-b. 3.00 3.00

Stamp Day and UPU, 125th Anniv. — A211

1999, Sept. 9 Litho. *Perf. 14*
405 A211 2.30k multicolored 1.10 1.00

Paulist Order in Lepoglava, 600th Anniv. — A212

a, Lace, Jesus Expelling the Money Changers from Temple, by Ivan Ranger, altar angel from St. Mary's Church, Lepoglava. b, St. Mary's Church facade, altar angel. c, St. Elizabeth, lace.

1999, Sept. 11 Litho.
406 A212 5k Strip of 3, #a.-c. 6.50 6.50

150th Anniv. of "Jelacic March" by Johann Strauss the Elder — A213

1999, Sept. 16 Litho.
407 A213 3.50k multicolored 1.75 1.75

World Ozone Layer Protection Day A214

1999, Sept. 16 Litho.
408 A214 5k multicolored 2.10 2.10

Grammar School Anniversaries A215

1999, Oct. 15 Litho. *Perf. 14*
409 A215 2.30k Pazin, cent. 1.00 .90
410 A215 3.50k Pozega, 300th anniv. 1.50 1.25

Andrija Hebrang (1899-1949), Politician — A216

1999, Oct. 21
411 A216 1.80k multicolored .80 .80

Our Lady of the Rose Garden, by Blaz Jurjev Trogiranin A217

1999, Oct. 28
412 A217 5k multicolored 2.00 2.00

Christmas, opening of exhibition of Croatian religious art and artifacts, Vatican City.

Christmas — A218

1999, Nov. 24 Litho. *Perf. 14*
413 A218 2.30k multicolored 1.10 1.10

Modern Art A219

Designs: 2.30k, Winter Landscape, by Gabrijel Jurkic (1886-1974). 3.50k, Klek, by Oton Postruznik (1900-78). 5k, Stone Table, by Ignjat Job (1895-1936), vert.

1999, Dec. 15
414 A219 2.30k multicolored 1.10 1.10
415 A219 3.50k multicolored 1.40 1.40
416 A219 5k multicolored 2.00 2.00
Nos. 414-416 (3) 4.50 4.50

Pres. Franjo Tudjman (1922-99) — A220

1999, Dec. 16 Vignette Color
417 A220 2.30k black 1.10 1.00
418 A220 5k blue 2.50 2.00

Millennium A221

2000, Jan. 1 Litho. *Perf. 14*
419 A221 2.30k multi 2.75 2.25

Valentine's Day — A222

2000, Feb. 1
420 A222 2.30k multi 2.00 1.60

Split Grammar School, 300th Anniv. — A223

2000, Mar. 25 Litho. *Perf. 14*
421 A223 2.80k multi 1.25 1.10

Croatian Writers' Assoc., 100th Anniv. — A224

2000, Apr. 22 Litho. *Perf. 14*
422 A224 2.30k black & red 2.75 2.75

A225

A226

A227

A228

A229

(1.80k) Lo Schiavone (Andrija Medulic, c. 1500-63), painter; (2.30k) Matija Petar Katancic (1750-1825), writer; (2.80k) Marija Ruzicka-Strozzi (1850-1937), actress; (3.50k) Marko Marulic (1450-1524), writer; (5k) Blaz Jurjev Trogiranin (c. 1390-1450), painter.

2000, Apr. 22
423 A225 1.80k multi .65 .65
424 A226 2.30k multi .95 .95
425 A227 2.80k multi 1.10 1.10
426 A228 3.50k multi 1.40 1.40
427 A229 5k multi 1.90 1.90
Nos. 423-427 (5) 6.00 6.00

Europa, 2000

Common Design Type and

A230

2000, May 9
428 A230 2.30k multi *2.00 2.00*
429 CD17 5k multi *4.25 4.25*

Independence Day — A231

2000, May 30 Litho. *Perf. 14*
430 A231 2.30k multi 1.50 1.50

Souvenir Sheet

Expo 2000, Hanover — A232

2000, June 1
431 A232 14.40k multi 6.25 6.25

Flora — A233

No. 432: a, 3.50k, Micromeria croatica. b, 5k, Geranium dalmaticum.

2000, June 5
432 A233 Pair, #a-b 4.00 4.00
c. Booklet pane of 10 #432a 15.00
Booklet, #432c 16.00
d. Booklet pane of 10 #432b 20.00
Booklet, #432d 21.00

Kastav Statute, 600th Anniv. — A234

2000, June 6
433 A234 1.80k multi .85 .85

World Mathematics Year — A235

2000, June 15
434 A235 3.50k multi 1.60 1.60

Ivan Ranger (1700-53), Artist — A236

2000, June 19
435 A236 1.80k multi .85 .85

Souvenir Sheet

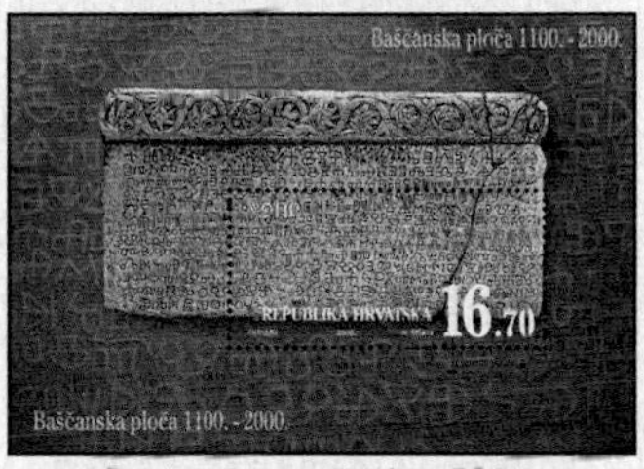

Baska Stone Tablet, 900th Anniv. — A237

2000, June 24
436 A237 16.70k multi 7.25 7.25

Archdeacon Toma of Split (1200-68) A238

2000, July 10
437 A238 3.50k multi 1.60 1.60

Type of 1992-94 Redrawn

2000, Aug. 1 Litho. *Perf. 14*
437A A39a 3.50k Vis 1.60 1.60

No. 437A has "HP" and post horn in LR corner.

Stamp Day — A239

No. 438: a, 2.30k, Austria #5. b, 2.30k, Automatic mail sorting equipment.

2000, Sept. 9 Litho. *Perf. 14*
438 A239 Pair, #a-b 2.25 2.25

First stamps used in Croatia, 150th anniv. (No. 438a).

2000 Summer Olympics, Sydney A240

2000, Sept. 15
439 A240 5k multicolored 3.00 3.00

Altarpiece, Church of the Blessed Virgin Mary, Ostarije A241

2000, Nov. 23
440 A241 2.30k multi 1.10 1.10
a. Booklet pane of 10 11.00
Booklet, #440a 11.50

Modern Art A242

Designs: 1.80k, Korcula, by Vladimir Varlaj. 2.30k, Brusnik, by Duro Tiljak. 5k, Boats, by Ante Kastelacic.

2000, Dec. 1
441-443 A242 Set of 3 4.00 4.00

See Nos. 471-473, 505-507.

Start of New Millennium A243

2001, Jan. 1 Litho. *Perf. 14*
444 A243 2.30k multi 1.75 1.75

Souvenir Sheet

Equestrian Statue of Charlemagne — A244

2001, Jan. 19
445 A244 14.40k multi 6.25 6.25

Crowning of Charlemagne as Emperor of the Romans, 1200th anniv. (in 2000).

Dzore Drzic (1461-1501), Writer — A245

2001, Mar. 15 Litho. *Perf. 14*
446 A245 2.80k multi 1.40 1.40

Comic Strip "Black Rider," by Andrija Maurovic (1901-81) A246

2001, Mar. 29
447 A246 5k multi 2.25 2.25

Makarska A247

2001, Mar. 30
448 A247 2.30k multi 1.00 1.00
a. Perf. 14 syncopated 1.00 1.00

Issued: No. 448a, 6/2/06.

Janica Kostelic, Skier — A248

2001, Apr. 19 Litho. *Perf. 14*
449 A248 2.80k multi 2.40 2.00

Kastel Stafilic Olive Trees, 1500th Anniv. — A249

2001, Apr. 20
450 A249 1.80k multi .85 .85

Europa — A250

No. 451: a, 3.50k, Denomination at R. b, 5k, Denomination at L.

2001, May 9
451 A250 Horiz. pair, #a-b 3.50 3.50

World No Smoking Day — A251

2001, May 31
452 A251 2.50k multi 1.10 1.10

Butterflies A252

Designs: 2.50k, Parnassius apollo. 2.80k, Maculinea teleius. 5k, Coenonympha oedippus.

2001, June 5
453-455 A252 Set of 3 4.75 4.75

Type of 1992 Redrawn

2001, June 21 Litho. *Perf. 14*
456 A39 2.80k Eltz Castle, Vukovar 1.25 1.25
a. Perf. 14 syncopated 1.10 1.10

No. 456 has "1991-2001" inscription, and "HP" and post horn at LL.
Issued: No. 456a, 6/19/06.

Souvenir Sheet

Trsteno Arboretum — A253

2001, July 12 Litho. *Perf. 14*
457 A253 14.40k multi 6.50 6.50

World Esperanto Congress, Zagreb — A254

2001, July 21
458 A254 5k multi 2.40 2.40

Refugee Organizations, 50th Annivs. A255

Designs: 1.80k, UN High Commissioner for Refugees. 5k, Intl. Organization for Migration.

2001, July 28
459-460 A255 Set of 2 3.25 3.25

Victory of Goran Ivanisevic at Wimbledon A256

2001, Aug. 31
461 A256 2.50k multi 2.50 2.25

Printed in sheets of 9 + label.

Stamp Day — A257

2001, Sept. 9
462 A257 2.50k multi .90 .90

Printed in sheets of 16 + 4 labels.

Native Dog Breeds A258

Designs: 1.80k, Croatian sheepdog. 5k, Dalmatian.

2001, Oct. 4
463-464 A258 Set of 2 3.25 3.25

Independence, 10th Anniv. — A259

2001, Oct. 8
465 A259 2.30k multi 1.10 1.10

Printed in sheets of 25 + 5 labels.

Year of Dialogue Among Civilizations — A260

2001, Oct. 9
466 A260 5k multi 4.00 4.00

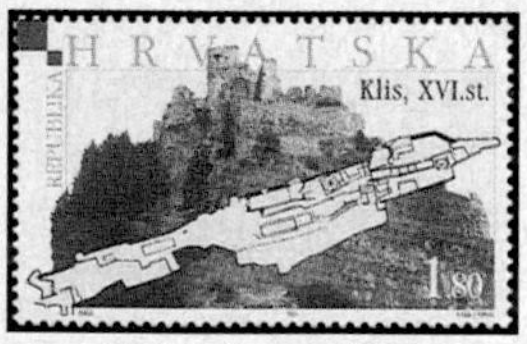

Fortresses — A261

Designs: 1.80k, Klis, 16th cent. 2.50k, Ston, 14th-15th cents. 3.50k, Sisak, 16th cent.

2001, Oct. 26 **Litho.** ***Perf. 14***
467-469 A261 Set of 3 3.50 3.50

See Nos. 499-501, 525-527, 565-567, 594-596, 630-632.

Adoration of the Magi Altarpeice, Church of the Visitation of Mary, Cucerje — A262

2001, Nov. 22 **Litho.** ***Perf. 14***
470 A262 2.30k multi 1.10 1.00
a. Booklet pane of 10 11.00 11.00
Complete booklet, #470a 11.00

Modern Art Type of 2000

Designs: No. 471, 2.50k, Maternité du Port-Royal, by Leo Junek. No. 472, 2.50k, Amphitheater Ruins, by Vjekoslav Parac. 5k, Nude with a Baroque Figure, by Slavko Sohaj, vert.

2001, Dec. 1
471-473 A242 Set of 3 4.75 4.75

Croatian Nobel Laureates — A263

Laureates: 2.80k, Lavoslav (Leopold) Ruzicka, Chemistry, 1939. 3.50k, Vladimir Prelog, Chemistry, 1975. 5k, Ivo Andric, Literature, 1961.

2001, Dec. 5
474-476 A263 Set of 3 5.50 5.50

Famous Croats and Events — A264

Designs: 1.80k, Ivan Gucetic (1451-1502), writer. 2.30k, Dobrisa Cesaric (1902-80), writer. 2.50k, Publishing of Juraj Rattkay's *History of Croatian Rulers,* 350th anniv. 2.80k, Franjo Vranjanin Laurana (c. 1420-1502), sculptor. 3.50k, Beatification of Bishop Augustin Kazotic (c. 1260-1323), 300th anniv. 5k, Matko Laginja (1852-1930), politician and writer.

2002, Jan. 24 **Litho.** ***Perf. 14***
477-482 A264 Set of 6 8.00 8.00

2002 Winter Olympics, Salt Lake City — A265

2002, Feb. 8
483 A265 5k multi 2.40 2.40

Croatian Chamber of Economy, 150th Anniv. — A266

2002, Feb. 16
484 A266 2.50k multi 1.25 1.25

Souvenir Sheet

Trpimir's Deed of Gift, 1150th Anniv. — A267

2002, Mar. 4
485 A267 14.40k multi 6.50 6.50

Franjo Cardinal Kuharic (1919-2002) A268

2002, Mar. 25
486 A268 2.30k multi .90 .90

Divan, by Vlaho Bukovac — A269

Litho. & Engr.

2002, Apr. 23 ***Perf. 11¾***
487 A269 5k multi 2.40 2.40

See Czech Republic No. 3169.

Royal Borough of Krizevci, 750th Anniv. — A270

2002, Apr. 24 **Litho.** ***Perf. 14***
488 A270 1.80k multi .85 .85

Varazdin Post Office, Cent. — A271

2002, Apr. 26
489 A271 2.30k multi 1.10 1.10

Europa — A272

Clown color: a, 3.50k, Orange. b, 5k, Blue.

2002, May 9 **Litho.** ***Perf. 14***
490 A272 Horiz. pair, #a-b *4.25 4.25*

2002 World Cup Soccer Championships, Japan and Korea — A273

Stylized players facing: a, 3.50k, Left. b, 5k, Right.

2002, May 15
491 A273 Horiz. pair, #a-b 4.00 4.00

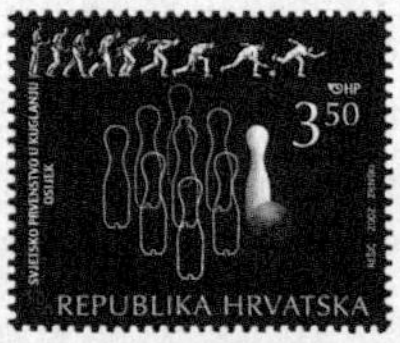

World Bowling Championships, Osijek — A274

2002, May 18
492 A274 3.50k multi 1.60 1.60

Oak Trees — A275

Designs: 1.80k, Quercus rober. 2.50k, Quercus petraea. 2.80k, Quercus ilex.

2002, June 5
493-495 A275 Set of 3 3.25 3.25
493a Booklet pane of 10 6.00 —
Complete booklet, #493a 6.25
494a Booklet pane of 10 12.00 —
Complete booklet, #494a 12.50
495a Booklet pane of 10 14.75 —
Complete booklet, #495a 15.25

15th World Animated Films Festival, Zagreb — A276

2002, June 18
496 A276 5k multi 2.40 2.40

Lace — A277

Lace from: 3.50k, Pag Island, Croatia. 5k, Liedekerke, Belgium.

2002, July 13 **Photo.** ***Perf. 11½***
497-498 A277 Set of 2 4.00 4.00

See Belgium Nos. 1927-1928.

Fortresses Type of 2001

Designs: No. 499, 2.50k, Nehaj, 16th cent. No. 500, 2.50k, Skocibuha, 16th cent. 5k, Veliki Tabor, 16th cent.

2002, Sept. 20 **Litho.** ***Perf. 14***
499-501 A261 Set of 3 4.50 4.50

Old Slavonic Academy, Krk, Cent. — A278

2002, Oct. 3 **Litho. & Embossed**
502 A278 4k red & black 1.75 1.75

Children's Help Line 48 26 051, 5th Anniv. — A279

2002, Oct. 15 **Litho.**
503 A279 2.30k multi 1.10 1.10

Christmas A280

2002, Nov. 21
504 A280 2.30k multi 1.25 1.25
a. Booklet pane of 10 12.50 —
Complete booklet, #504a 13.00

Modern Art Type of 2002

Designs: No. 505, 2.50k, Flowers on the Window, by Antun Motika (1902-92), vert. No. 506, 2.50k, The Girl in the Boat, by Milivoj Uzelac (1897-1977), vert. 5k, On the Drava River, by Krsto Hegedusic (1901-75).

2002, Dec. 2 **Litho.** ***Perf. 14***
505-507 A242 Set of 3 4.75 4.75

Zagreb Bishopric, 150th Anniv. — A281

2002, Dec. 11
508 A281 2.80k multi 1.40 1.40

Printed in sheets of 19 + label.

Pavao Ritter Vitezovic (1652-1713), Writer — A282

2002, Dec. 13
509 A282 2.30k multi 1.10 1.10

Pacta Conventa, 900th Anniv. — A283

2002, Dec. 14
510 A283 3.50k multi 1.60 1.60

Fairies From Stories by Ivana Brlic Mazuranic — A284

No. 511: a, 2.30k, Kosjenka, fairy character from *Regoc.* b, 2.80k, Tintilinic, fairy character from *Suma Striborova.*

2003, Jan. 15
511 A284 Horiz. pair, #a-b 2.40 2.40

St. Valentine's Day — A285

Litho. With Foil Application

2003, Feb. 1
512 A285 2.30k multi 1.10 1.10

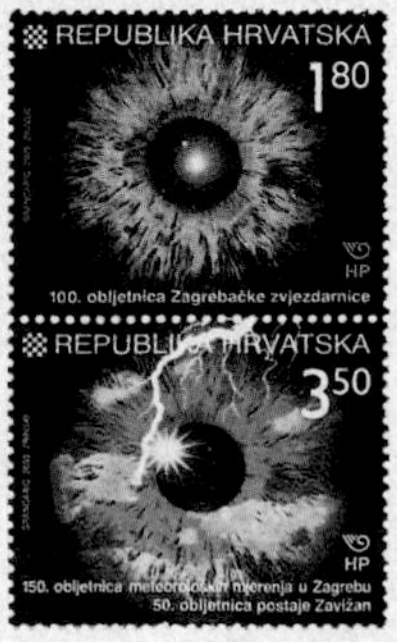

Astronomy and Meteorology A286

No. 513: a, 1.80k, Zagreb Astronomical Observatory, cent. b, 3.50k, Meteorological measurements in Zagreb, 150th anniv.; Meteorological station on Zavizan, 50th anniv.

2003, Feb. 17 **Litho.**
513 A286 Pair, #a-b 2.25 2.25

Souvenir Sheet

Croatia, 2003 World Handball Champions — A287

No. 514: a, Five team members, one wearing red shirt. b, Eight team members, one with arm extended. c, Six team members. d, Four team members, one wearing blue shirt.

2003, Feb. 20
514 A287 4k Sheet of 4, #a-d 7.00 7.00

Paulist High School, Lepoglava, 500th Anniv. — A288

2003, Mar. 1
515 A288 5k multi 2.40 2.40

Missal of Hrvoje Vukcic Hrvatinic, 600th Anniv. — A289

2003, Mar. 25
516 A289 5k multi 2.40 2.40

Land Mine Danger A290

2003, Apr. 8
517 A290 2.30k multi 1.10 1.10

Alpine Skiing World Cup Victories of Janica and Ivica Kostelic A291

No. 518: a, Janica. b, Ivica.

2003, Apr. 16
518 A291 3.50k Pair, #a-b 5.00 5.00

Printed in sheets containing 4 vertical pairs and 2 labels.

Christian Institutions in Rome Founded by Croatian Roman Brotherhood of St. Jerome, 550th Anniv. — A292

2003, Apr. 22
519 A292 2.80k multi 1.25 1.25

Famous Croatians A293

Designs: 1.80k, Antun Soljan (1932-93), writer. 2.30k, Hanibal Lucic (1485-1553), writer. 5k, Federiko Benkovic (1667-1753), painter.

2003, Apr. 22
520-522 A293 Set of 3 4.25 4.25

Poster for Performance of Marya Delvard, by Tomislav Krizman, 1907 — A294

Poster for Performance of "The Firebird," by Boris Bucan, 1983 — A295

2003, May 9 **Litho.** ***Perf. 14***
523 A294 3.50k multi *1.50 1.50*
524 A295 5k multi *2.25 2.25*

Europa.

Fortresses Type of 2001

Designs; 1.80k, Kostajnica, 15th-18th cent. 2.80k, Slavonski Brod, 18th cent. 5k, Minceta Tower, 15th cent., vert.

2003, May 13
525-527 A261 Set of 3 4.25 4.25

Visit of Pope John Paul II — A296

2003, June 2
528 A296 2.30k multi 1.75 1.75

Rodents A297

Designs: 2.30k, Sciuris vulgaris. 2.80k, Glis glis. 3.50k, Castor fiber.

2003, June 5
529-531 A297 Set of 3 4.00 4.00
531a Booklet pane, 6 #529, 2 each #530-531 13.00 —
Complete booklet, #531a 13.00

Souvenir Sheet

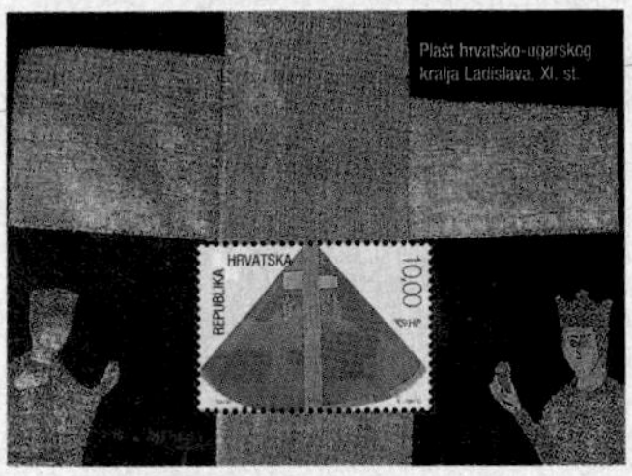

Robe of King Ladislaus, 11th Cent. — A298

2003, June 13
532 A298 10k multi 4.25 4.25

Stamp Day — A299

2003, Sept. 9 **Litho.** ***Perf. 14***
533 A299 2.30k multi 1.10 1.10

Souvenir Sheet

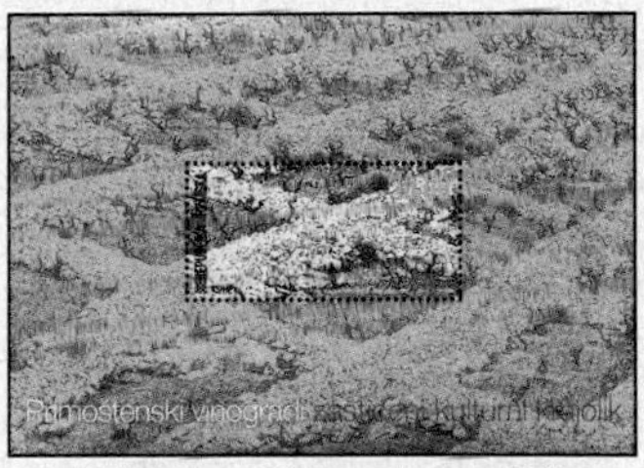
Primosten Vineyards — A300

Litho. with Foil Application

2003, Sept. 19
534 A300 10k multi 4.75 4.75

Ursuline Sisters in Croatia, 300th Anniv. — A301

2003, Oct. 20 **Litho.**
535 A301 2.50k multi 1.10 1.10

Christmas A302

2003, Nov. 20 **Litho.** ***Perf. 14***
536 A302 2.30k multi 1.00 1.00

Self-Adhesive

Serpentine Die Cut 5¼

537 A302 2.30k multi 1.00 1.00

Modern Art A304

Designs: 1.80k, Flower Girl II, by Slavko Kopac, vert. No. 539, 3.50k, Dry Stone Wall 5-71, by Oton Gliha. No. 540, 3.50k, Pont des Arts, by Josip Racic.

2003, Nov. 21 *Perf. 14*
538-540 A304 Set of 3 4.00 4.00

See Nos. 568-570, 604-606, 636-638, 668-670, 712-714, 749-751.

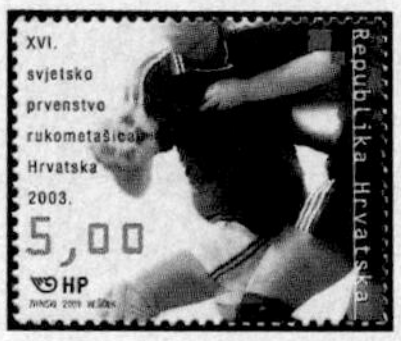

18th World Women's Handball Championships — A305

2003, Dec. 1
541 A305 5k multi 2.25 2.25

Musicians — A306

No. 542: a, Josip Hatze (1879-1959), composer. b, Zagreb Soloists, 50th anniv.

2004, Jan. 5 **Litho.** *Perf. 14*
542 A306 5k Horiz. pair, #a-b 4.50 4.50

Hval's Manuscript, 600th Anniv. — A307

2004, Jan. 22
543 A307 2.30k multi 1.40 1.40

European Boxing Championships, Pula — A308

2004, Feb. 19 **Litho.** *Perf. 14*
544 A308 2.80k multi 1.25 1.25

Worldwide Fund for Nature (WWF) — A309

Ardea purpurea: a, In grass. b, Standing with head extended. c, With young. d, In flight.

2004, Mar. 22
545 Strip or block of 4 8.50 8.50
a.-d. A309 5k Any single 1.75 1.75

Famous Croats — A310

Designs: 2.30k, Ivan Lucic (1604-79), historian. No. 547, 3.50k, Antun Vrancic (1504-75), archbishop, writer. No. 548, 3.50k, St. Jerome, sculpture by Andrija Alesi (c. 1425-1504). 10k, Printing of Croatian grammar book, by Bartol Kasic (1575-1650), 400th anniv.

2004, Apr. 22
546-549 A310 Set of 4 8.25 8.25

Souvenir Sheet

Risnjak National Park — A311

2004, Apr. 22
550 A311 10k multi 5.25 5.25

Martyrdom of St. Domnio, 1700th Anniv. — A312

2004, May 7
551 A312 3.50k multi 1.75 1.75

Europa A313

Designs: No. 552, 3.50k, Summer vacation items. No. 553, 3.50k, Winter vacation items.

2004, May 9
552-553 A313 Set of 2 *3.00 3.00*

FIFA (Fédération Internationale de Football Association), Cent. A314

2004, May 21 **Litho.** *Perf. 14*
554 A314 2.50k multi 1.25 1.25

Medicinal Herbs — A315

Designs: 2.30k, Rosa canina. 2.80k, Viola odorata. 3.50k, Mentha piperita.

2004, June 5

555-557	A315 Set of 3	4.00	4.00
555a	Booklet pane of 10	10.00	—
	Complete booklet, #555a	10.50	
556a	Booklet pane of 10	12.50	—
	Complete booklet, #556a	13.00	
557a	Booklet pane of 10	16.50	—
	Complete booklet, #557a	17.50	

Nos. 555-557 are impregnated with a floral scent.

Intl. Marionette Union Congress, Intl. Puppetry Art Festival, Rijeka A316

2004, June 6
558 A316 3.50k multi 1.75 1.75

European Soccer Championships, Portugal — A317

2004, June 12
559 A317 3.50k multi 1.75 1.75

Values are for stamps with surrounding selvage.

Restoration of Old Bridge, Mostar, Bosnia & Herzegovina A318

2004, July 23 **Litho.** *Perf. 14*
560 A318 3.50k multi 1.75 1.75

2004 Summer Olympics, Athens — A319

2004, Aug. 13
561 A319 3.50k multi 1.75 1.75

Virovitica A320

2004, Aug. 16
562 A320 5k multi 2.40 2.40
a. Perf. 14 syncopated — —

Issued: No. 562a, 12/7/07. For surcharge see No. 779.

Zagreb Post Office, Cent. A321

2004, Sept. 9
563 A321 2.30k multi 1.00 1.00

Printed in sheets of 16 + 4 labels.

Father Andrija Kacic Miosic (1704-60), Poet — A322

2004, Sept. 15
564 A322 2.80k multi 1.25 1.25

Fortresses Type of 2001

Designs: No. 565, 3.50k, Dubovac, 15th-19th cent. No. 566, 3.50k, Gripe, 17th cent. No. 567, 3.50k, Valpovo, 15th-18th cent.

2004, Sept. 29
565-567 A261 Set of 3 4.75 4.75

Modern Art Type of 2003

Designs: No. 568, 2.30k, Self-portrait, by Miroslav Kraljevic, vert. No. 569, 2.30k, Noon in Supetar, by Jerolim Mise, vert. No. 570, 2.30k, Stari Grad, by Juraj Plancic, vert.

2004, Nov. 15 **Litho.** *Perf. 14*
568-570 A304 Set of 3 3.25 3.25

Christmas A323

2004, Nov. 25
571 A323 2.30k multi 1.10 1.10

Antun and Stjepan Radic and Plowman — A324

2004, Dec. 22 **Litho.** *Perf. 14*
572 A324 7.20k multi 3.25 3.25

Croatian People's Peasant Party, Cent.

Fairy Tale Characters — A325

No. 573: a, Mermaid Halugica. b, Dwarf Pedalj Muza Lakat Brade.

2005, Jan. 14
573 A325 5k Horiz. pair, #a-b 4.50 4.50

World Conference on the Information Society, Tunis — A326

2005, Feb. 10
574 A326 2.80k multi 1.40 1.40

Values are for stamps with surrounding selvage.

Souvenir Sheet

Bust of Livia Drusilla — A327

2005, Feb. 24
575 A327 10k multi 5.00 5.00

Souvenir Sheet

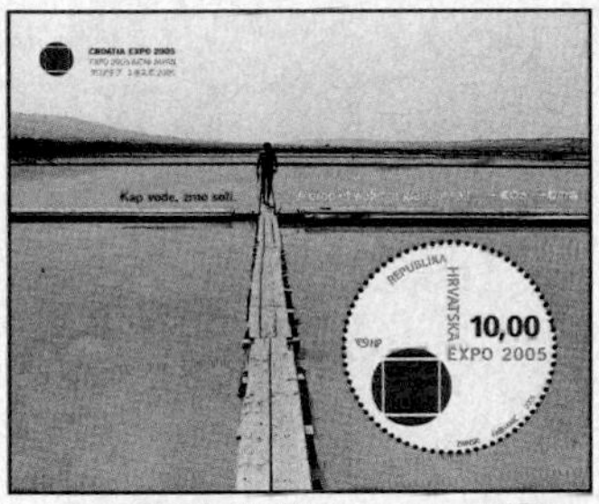

Expo 2005, Aichi, Japan — A328

2005, Mar. 25 ***Perf.***
576 A328 10k multi 5.00 5.00

Pope John Paul II (1920-2005) A329

2005, Apr. 8 ***Perf. 14***
577 A329 2.30k multi 1.25 1.25

World Music Days, Zagreb A330

Stjepan Sulek (1914-86), Composer A331

2005, Apr. 15
578 A330 2.30k multi 1.10 1.10
579 A331 2.30k multi 1.10 1.10

Insects — A332

Designs: 1.80k, Coccinella septempunctata. 2.30k, Rosalia alpina. 3.50k, Lucanus cervus.

2005, Apr. 22
580-582 A332 Set of 3 3.75 3.75

Liberation of Western Slavonia, 10th Anniv. A333

2005, May 1
583 A333 1.80k multi .95 .95

Dr. Josip Buturac (1905-93), Historian — A334

2005, May 6
584 A334 2.80k multi 1.25 1.25

Europa — A335

No. 585: a, Loaf of bread. b, Glass of wine.

2005, May 9
585 A335 3.50k Horiz. pair, #a-b *3.50 3.50*

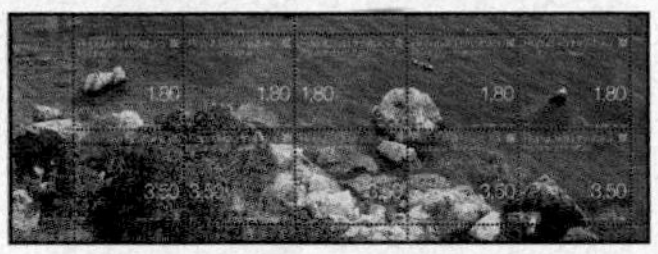

Coast of Hvar Island — A336

No. 586: a, Rock at L, tree tops at bottom. b, Tree tops at LL. c, Rock at R. d, Canoe, rock at R. e, Small rock in center. f, Rocks at UL, trees. g, Rocks at R, trees. h, Tree tops at LL corner, rock at UR corner. i, Rocks at UL and LL corners. j, Rocks at LL.

2005, May 24 **Litho.** ***Perf. 14***
586 A336 Booklet pane of 10 13.00 —
a.-e. 1.80k Any single .90 .90
f.-j. 3.50k Any single 1.40 1.40
Complete booklet, #586 14.00

Kresimir Cosic (1948-95), Basketball Player — A337

2005, May 25
587 A337 3.50k multi 1.50 1.50

Printed In sheets of 9 + 1 label.

Krapanj Island Sponge and Coral Diving — A338

2005, June 2 **Litho.**
588 A338 3.50k multi 1.75 1.75

Portions of the design were applied by a thermographic process producing a shiny, raised effect.

Emperor Constantine's Bath, Varazdinske Toplice A339

2005, June 20 ***Perf. 14***
589 A339 1.80k multi 1.00 1.00

Intl. Fire Brigade Olympics, Varazdin A340

2005, July 15
590 A340 2.30k multi 1.25 1.25

Printed in sheets of 8 + 2 labels.

European Philatelic Cooperation, 50th Anniv. (in 2006) A341

Designs: 7.20k, Vignette of #134. 8k, Stylized gull.

2005, Sept. 8
591-592 A341 Set of 2 *7.00 7.00*
592a Souvenir sheet, #591-592 *60.00 60.00*

Europa stamps, 50th anniv. (in 2006).

Telegraph A342

2005, Sept. 9
593 A342 2.30k multi 1.25 1.25

First overhead telegraph lines in Croatia, 155th anniv., Stamp Day.

Fortresses Type of 2001

Designs: 1k, Ilok, 14th-15th cents. 2.30k, Motovun, 13th-15th cents., vert. 3.50k, St. Nicholas, 16th cent.

2005, Sept. 15
594-596 A261 Set of 3 3.50 3.50

Famous People — A343

Designs: 1k, Adam Baltazar Krcelic (1715-78), historian. No. 598, 2.30k, Dragutin Tadijanovic (b. 1905), poet. No. 599, 2.30k, Tin Ujevic (1891-1955), poet. 2.80k, Madonna and Child, by Juraj Culinovic (c.1433-1504).

2005, Nov. 4
597-600 A343 Set of 4 4.00 4.00

Clock Tower, Rijeka — A344

2005, Nov. 10 **Litho.** ***Perf. 14***
601 A344 3.50k multi 1.75 1.75
a. Perf. 14 syncopated 1.75 1.75

Issued: No. 601a, 6/12/06. For surcharge see No. 778.

Christmas A345

2005, Nov. 22 ***Perf. 14***
602 A345 2.30k multi 1.25 1.25

Booklet Stamp
Self-Adhesive
Serpentine Die Cut 5¼

603 A345 2.30k multi 1.25 1.25
a. Booklet pane of 10 12.50 12.50
Complete booklet, #603a 12.50 12.50

Modern Art Type of 2003

Designs: 1.80k, Zadar, by Edo Murtic. 5k, Meander, by Julije Knifer. 10k, Drawing, by Miroslav Sutej, vert.

2005, Dec. 1 ***Perf. 14***
604-606 A304 Set of 3 8.75 8.75

Davis Cup and Members of Croatian Tennis Team — A346

2005, Dec. 22 **Litho.** ***Perf. 14***
607 A346 5k multi 2.75 2.75

Croatia, winners of 2005 Davis Cup. Printed in sheets of 9 + label.

Composers A347

Designs: 1.80k, Boris Papandopulo (1906-91). 2.30k, Milo Cipra (1906-85). 2.80k, Ivan Brkanovic (1906-87).

2006, Jan. 17
608-610 A347 Set of 3 3.50 3.50

2006 Winter Olympics, Turin — A348

2006, Feb. 10
611 A348 3.50k multi 1.90 1.90

Rembrandt (1606-69), Painter A349

2006, Mar. 7

612 A349 5k multi 2.75 2.75

Famous Men — A350

Designs: No. 613, 1k, Andrija Ljudevit Adamic (1766-1828), merchant. No. 614, 1k, Josip Kozarac (1858-1906), writer. 5k, Vanja Radaus (1906-75), sculptor. 7.20k, Ljubo Karaman (1886-1971), art historian.

2006, Mar. 21 ***Perf. 14 Syncopated***

613-616 A350 Set of 4 7.25 7.25

European Track and Field Championships, Göteborg, Sweden — A351

2006, Apr. 4

617 A351 2.30k multi 1.25 1.25

2006 World Cup Soccer Championships, Germany A352

2006, Apr. 4

618 A352 2.80k multi 1.25 1.25

Flag and Crowd — A353

No. 619 — Location and placement of denomination: a, At left, with denomination above crowd. b, At right, with top of numerals over red in flag. c, At left, with top of "8" and "0" above white in flag. d, At left, with serif of "1" above red in flag. e, At left, with entire denomination above red in flag. f, At right, with parts of "5" and "0" above red in flag. g, At right, with entire denomination above red in flag. h, At right, with entire denomination above white in flag. i, At left, with entire denomination above red in flag. j, At right, with denomination above crowd.

2006, Apr. 25

619 A353 Booklet pane of 10 16.00 —
a.-e. 1.80k Any single 1.00 1.00
f.-j. 3.50k Any single 2.10 2.10
Complete booklet, #619 17.00

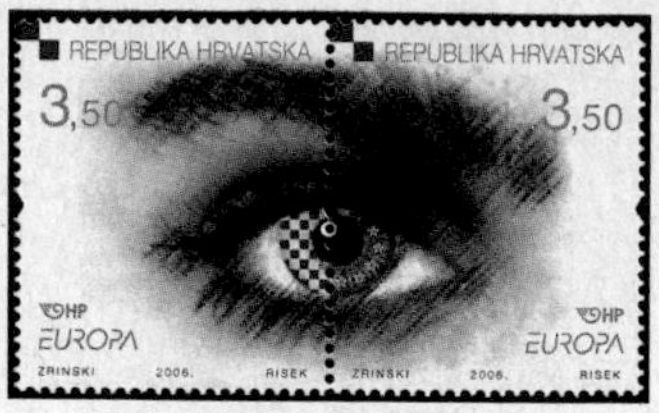

Europa — A354

No. 620: a, Denomination at left. b, Denomination at right.

2006, May 9

620 A354 3.50k Horiz. pair, #a-b 3.50 3.50

Worldwide Fund for Nature (WWF) A355

No. 621 — Various views of Sterna albifrons with denomination in: a, Gray. b, Dull green. c, Yellow orange. d, Red.

2006, May 23

621 Strip of 4 10.00 10.00
a.-d. A355 5k Any single 2.40 2.40

Croatian Automobile Club, Cent. — A356

Perf. 13¾x14 Syncopated

2006, June 4

622 A356 5k multi 2.75 2.75

Aquatic Flowers A357

Designs: 2.30k, Nymphaea alba. 2.80k, Nuphar lutea. 3.50k, Menyanthes trifoliata.

2006, June 5 ***Perf. 14 Syncopated***

623-625 A357 Set of 3 4.50 4.50
623a Booklet pane of 10 12.50 12.50
Complete booklet, #623a 12.50
624a Booklet pane of 10 14.00 14.00
Complete booklet, #624a 14.00
625a Booklet pane of 10 18.00 18.00
Complete booklet, #625a 18.00

Nikola Tesla (1856-1943), Inventor — A358

Perf. 14x13½ Syncopated

2006, July 10 **Litho.**

626 A358 3.50k multi 1.75 1.75

Bjelovar, 250th Anniv. A359

Perf. 14 Syncopated

2006, Aug. 22 **Litho.**

627 A359 2.80k multi 1.50 1.50

Stamp Day — A360

2006, Sept. 9 **Litho. & Embossed**

628 A360 2.30k multi 1.25 1.25

Jewish Community of Zagreb, 200th Anniv. — A361

Perf. 14¼x13¾ Syncopated

2006, Sept. 15 **Litho.**

629 A361 5k multi 2.75 2.75

Fortresses Type of 2001

Designs: No. 630, 1k, St. Mary of Mercy Church, Vrboska, 16th cent. No. 631, 1k, Church of the Holy Spirit, Sudurad, 16th cent. 7.20k, Frankapan Citadel, Ogulin, 16th cent.

Perf. 13¾x14¼ Syncopated

2006, Sept. 21

630-632 A261 Set of 3 4.75 4.75

White Cane Safety Day — A362

Perf. 14 Syncopated

2006, Oct. 15 **Litho. & Embossed**

633 A362 1.80k black & red 1.00 1.00

Christmas A363

Perf. 14¼ Syncopated

2006, Nov. 27 **Litho.**

634 A363 2.30k multi 1.25 1.25

Booklet Stamp
Self-Adhesive
Serpentine Die Cut 5¼

635 A363 2.30k multi 1.25 1.25
a. Booklet pane of 10 12.50
Complete booklet, #635a 12.50

Modern Art Type of 2003

Designs: 1k, Still Life, by Vladimir Becic. 1.80k, Composition Tyma 3, by Ivan Picelj. 10k, Self-portrait as Hunter, by Nasta Rojc, vert.

2006, Dec. 1 ***Perf. 14 Syncopated***

636-638 A304 Set of 3 6.00 6.00

Classical Gymnasium, Zagreb, 400th Anniv. — A364

Perf. 14 Syncopated

2007, Jan. 9 **Litho.**

639 A364 5k multi 2.40 2.40

Fairy Tale Characters — A365

No. 640: a, Monster Orko. b, Devil Macic.

2007, Jan. 18

640 A365 2.30k Horiz. pair, #a-b 2.50 2.50

National and University Library, Zagreb, 400th Anniv. A366

2007, Feb. 22

641 A366 5k multi 2.50 2.50

Crustaceans A367

Designs: 1.80k, Palinurus elephas. 2.30k, Nephrops norvegicus. 2.80k, Astacus astacus.

2007, Mar. 15

642 A367 1.80k multi .85 .85
a. Booklet pane of 10 8.50 —
Complete booklet, #642a 8.50
643 A367 2.30k multi 1.05 1.05
a. Booklet pane of 10 10.50 —
Complete booklet, #643a 10.50
644 A367 2.80k multi 1.35 1.35
a. Booklet pane of 10 13.50 —
Complete booklet, #644a 13.50
Nos. 642-644 (3) 3.25 3.25

Native Breeds of Farm Animals A368

Designs: 2.80k, Istrian ox. 3.50k, Posavina horse. 5k, Dalmatian donkey.

2007, Mar. 20

645-647 A368 Set of 3 5.75 5.75

Europa — A369

No. 648: a, Scouting emblem and dove. b, Scout neckerchief.

2007, Apr. 16
648 A369 3.50k Horiz. pair, #a-b 3.25 3.25

Scouting, cent.

Scientists — A370

Designs: 5k, Andrija Mohorovicic (1857-1936), seismologist. 7.20k, Duro Baglivi (1668-1707), physician.

Perf. 14x13½ Syncopated
2007, Apr. 23
649-650 A370 Set of 2 6.00 6.00

Souvenir Sheet

World Championship Victory of Croatian Water Polo Team — A371

No. 651: a, Man with red shirt at right, denomination at UL. b, Man with red shirt at LR, denomination at UR. c, Man with red shirt at left, denomination at UR.

Litho. With Foil Application
2007, May 3 ***Perf. 14¼ Syncopated***
651 A371 5k Sheet of 3, #a-c 7.75 7.75

World Table Tennis Championships, Zagreb — A372

Perf. 14 Syncopated
2007, May 21 Litho. & Embossed
652 A372 3.50k multi 1.75 1.75

Starting with No. 652 some stamps have an imprinted wing-shaped tagging design that looks like a watermark.

Diplomatic Relations Between Croatia and People's Republic of China, 15th Anniv. — A373

No. 653: a, "China" in Glagolithic letters. b, "Croatia" in Chinese characters.

2007, May 30 Litho. *Perf. 12*
653 A373 5k Horiz. pair, #a-b 5.00 5.00

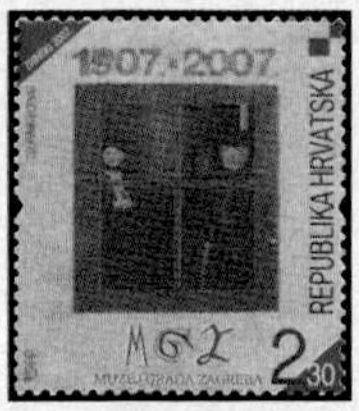

Zagreb City Museum, Cent. — A374

2007, May 31 ***Perf. 14 Syncopated***
654 A374 2.30k multi 1.10 1.10

Souvenir Sheet

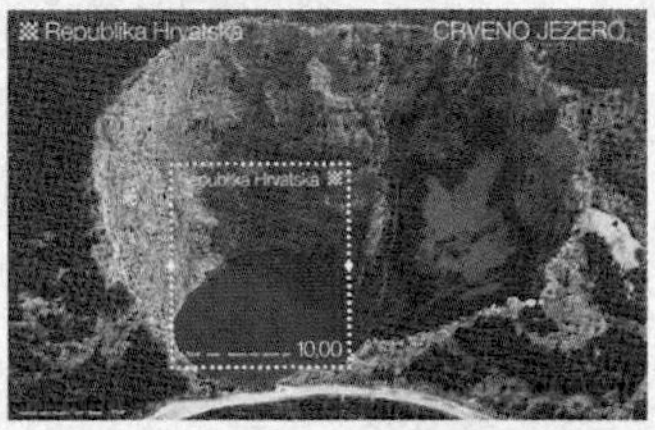

Red Lake — A375

2007, June 8
655 A375 10k multi 4.50 4.50

First Croatian Philatelic Exhibition, Cent. — A376

Perf. 14 Syncopated
2007, Sept. 9 Litho. & Embossed
656 A376 2.80k multi 1.25 1.25

Stamp Day.

Lighthouses — A377

Designs: No. 657, 5k, St. John on the Sea Lighthouse. No. 658, 5k, Porer Lighthouse. No. 659, 5k, Savudrija Lighthouse.

Perf. 13¾x14¼ Syncopated
2007, Sept. 14 Litho.
657-659 A377 Set of 3 7.00 7.00

Veprinac Statute, 500th Anniv. — A378

Perf. 14¼x13¾ Syncopated
2007, Oct. 2
660 A378 2.70k multi 1.25 1.25

City Views — A379

Designs: 1.80k, Omis. 2.30k, Koprivnica, horiz. 2.80k, Krk.

2007, Oct. 30 ***Perf. 14 Syncopated***
661 A379 1.80k multi .85 .85
a. Perf. 14 ('10) .70 .70
662 A379 2.30k multi 1.00 1.00
663 A379 2.80k multi 1.30 1.30
Nos. 661-663 (3) 3.15 3.15

For surcharge see No. 777.

Blanka Vlasic, 2007 World Women's High Jump Champion A380

2007, Nov. 8
664 A380 2.30k multi 1.25 1.25

Christmas A381

Perf. 14¼ Syncopated
2007, Nov. 15 Litho.
665 A381 2.30k multi 1.25 1.25

Booklet Stamp
Self-Adhesive
Serpentine Die Cut 5¼
666 A381 2.30k multi 1.25 1.25
a. Booklet pane of 10 12.50
Complete booklet, #666a 12.50

Marija Juric Zagorka (1873-1957), Writer — A382

Perf. 14¼x13¾ Syncopated
2007, Nov. 16
667 A382 7.20k multi 3.25 3.25

Modern Art Type of 2003

Designs: 2.80k, Area by the Sava River, by Branko Senoa. No. 669, 5k, Pegasus's Garden, by Ferdinand Kulmer. No. 670, 5k, Bridgeport, by Ivan Benkovic.

Perf. 14 Syncopated
2007, Dec. 1 Litho.
668-670 A304 Set of 3 5.75 5.75

New Year 2008 — A383

2007, Dec. 5
671 A383 1.80k multi .80 .80

Composers A384

Designs: No. 672, 2.30k, Igor Kuljeric (1938-2006). No. 673, 2.30k, Krsto Odak (1888-1965).

2008, Jan. 22
672-673 A384 Set of 2 2.25 2.25

Publication of *Arithmetika Horvatszka*, by Mijo Silobod Bolsic, 250th Anniv. — A385

Perf. 13¾x14 Syncopated
2008, Jan. 25
674 A385 3.50k multi 1.75 1.75

Steam Locomotives — A386

Designs: No. 675, 5k, MAV 601/JZ 32. No. 676, 5k, MAV 651/JZ 31.

2008, Feb. 15
675-676 A386 Set of 2 4.50 4.50

Nos. 675-676 were printed in sheets of 6 containing three of each stamp.

St. Nicholas Church, Cavtat A387

Perf. 14 Syncopated
2008, Mar. 8 Litho.
677 A387 7.20k multi 3.25 3.25

For surcharge see No. 780.

2008 Summer Olympics, Beijing A388

2008, Mar. 11
678 A388 5k multi 2.00 2.00

Printed in sheets of 9 + label.

Flowers — A389

Designs: 1.80k, Helleborus niger. 2.80k, Onosma stellulata. 3.50k, Lonicera glutinosa.

2008, Mar. 20
679 A389 1.80k multi .95 .95
a. Booklet pane of 10 9.50 —
Complete booklet, #679a 9.50
680 A389 2.80k multi 1.50 1.50
a. Booklet pane of 10 15.00 —
Complete booklet, #680a 15.00
681 A389 3.50k multi 1.75 1.75
a. Booklet pane of 10 17.50 —
Complete booklet, #681a 17.50
Nos. 679-681 (3) 4.20 4.20

Famous Writers — A390

Designs: 2.30k, Petar Zoranic (1508-c. 1569), novelist. 2.80k, Silvije Strahimir Kranjcevic (1865-1908), poet. 7.20k, Marin Drzic (1508-67), dramatist.

Perf. 14 Syncopated

2008, Apr. 22 **Litho.**

682-684 A390 Set of 3 5.75 5.75

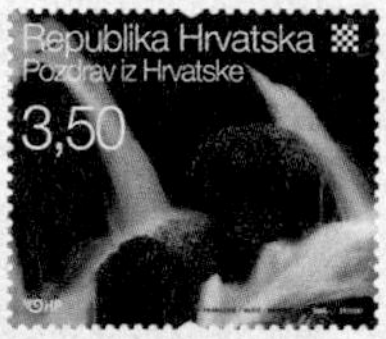

Waterfall, Plitvice Lakes National Park — A391

No. 685 — Part of waterfall with: a, Country name in white, denomination at UL, "HP" symbol in white at LL. b, Country name in white, denomination at UR, "HP" symbol in white at LL, green foliage at UL. c, Country name in black, denomination at UR. d, Country name in white, denomination at UR, "HP" symbol in black at LL. e, Country name in white, denomination at UR, "HP" symbol in white at LL, green foliage at UR. f, Country name in white, denomination in black at LR, "HP" symbol in black at LL, rock with foliage in center. g, Country name in white, denomination in black at LR, "HP" symbol in black at LL, all rocks covered by spray. h, Country name in black, denomination at LR. i, Country name in white, denomination in white at LR. j, Country name in white, denomination in black at LR, "HP" symbol in white at LL.

Perf. 14 Syncopated

2008, Apr. 25 **Litho.**

685	Booklet pane of 10	17.50	—	
a.-j.	A391 3.50k Any single	1.75	1.75	
	Complete booklet, #685	17.50		

2008 Volkswagen Beetle — A392

2008, May 8

686 A392 2.30k multi + label 1.10 1.10

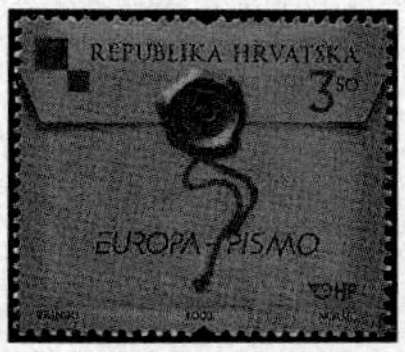

Europa A393

Designs: 3.50k, Insured envelope with wax seal. 5k, Airmail envelope.

2008, May 9 **Litho.**

687 A393 3.50k multi 1.60 1.60

Litho. & Embossed

688 A393 5k multi 2.40 2.40

Portions of the design of No. 687 were applied using a thermographic process producing a shiny raised effect.

UEFA Euro 2008 Soccer Championships, Austria and Switzerland — A394

2008, May 14 **Litho.** ***Perf. 14x13½***

689 A394 3.50k multi 1.50 1.50

Values are for stamps with surrounding selvage. Printed in sheets of 9 + label.

Adris Group — A395

2008, May 16 ***Perf. 14 Syncopated***

690 A395 2.30k multi + label 1.10 1.10

Souvenir Sheet

Ivan Vucetic (1858-1925), Fingerprint Classifier — A396

2008, Apr. 20

691 A396 10k multi 5.00 5.00

Souvenir Sheet

Expo Zaragoza 2008 — A397

Litho. With Foil Application

2008, June 16

692 A397 10k multi 4.50 4.50

Souvenir Sheet

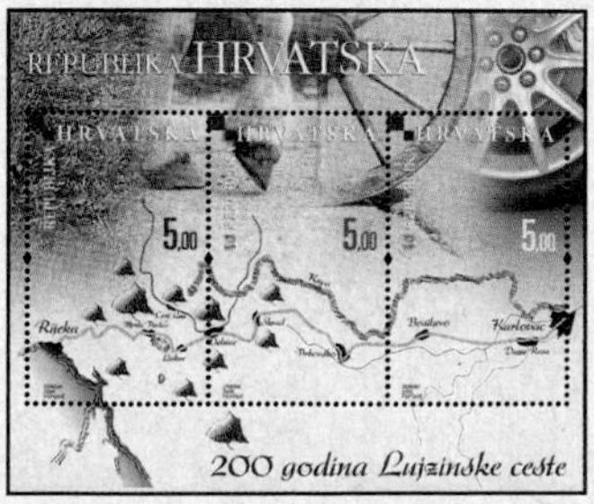

Lujzinske Road, 200th Anniv. — A398

No. 693 — Parts of map of Lujzinske Road with denomination in: a, Red. b, Green. c, White.

Perf. 14x13½ Syncopated

2008, June 17 **Litho.**

693 A398 5k Sheet of 3, #a-c 7.00 7.00

Western Union — A399

2008, July 11 ***Perf. 14 Syncopated***

694 A399 3.50k multi + label 1.50 1.50

Postal Workers' Games — A400

Litho. With Foil Application

2008, Sept. 9 ***Perf. 14 Syncopated***

695 A400 2.80k multi 1.30 1.30

Stamp Day.

Lighthouses A401

Designs: No. 696, 5k, Pinida Lighthouse. No. 697, 5k, Vnetak Lighthouse. No. 698, 5k, Zaglav Lighthouse.

Perf. 14¼x13¾ Syncopated

2008, Sept. 12 **Litho.**

696-698 A401 Set of 3 7.00 7.00

Order of St. Clare, Split, 700th Anniv. — A402

2008, Sept. 16

699 A402 2.80k multi 1.25 1.25

Details From Native Costumes A403

Costume from: 10 l, Sunja. 20 l, Bistra. 50 l, Bizovac. 1k, Ravni Kotari. 10k, Pag.

2008, Sept. 30 ***Perf. 14 Syncopated***

700-704	A403	Set of 5	6.00	6.00
701a		Perf. 14 ('10)	.25	.25
703a		Perf. 14 ('10)	.35	.35
704a		Sheet of 5, #700-704 + label	6.00	6.00

European Healthy Cities Movement, 20th Anniv. — A404

2008, Oct. 17 ***Perf. 14¼ Syncopated***

705 A404 2.80k multi + label 1.25 1.25

Collegium Ragusinum, Dubrovnik, 350th Anniv. — A405

Perf. 14¼x13¾ Syncopated

2008, Nov. 7 **Litho. & Embossed**

706 A405 7.20k multi 3.00 3.00

Intl. Amateur Radio Union Region 1 Conference, Cavtat — A406

Perf. 13¾x14¼ Syncopated

2008, Nov. 14 **Litho.**

707 A406 3.50k multi 1.50 1.50

The Book on the Art of Trading, by Benedikt Kotruljevic, 550th Anniv. of Publication A407

Perf. 14¼x13¾ Syncopated

2008, Oct. 22 **Litho.**

708 A407 2.80k multi 1.25 1.25

New Year's Day — A408

Perf. 14 Syncopated

2008, Nov. 21 **Litho.**

709 A408 1.80k multi .75 .75

Christmas A409

2008, Nov. 27 ***Perf. 14 Syncopated***

710 A409 2.80k multi 1.50 1.50

Booklet Stamp
Self-Adhesive

711 A409 2.80k multi 1.00 1.00
a. Booklet pane of 10 10.00
Complete booklet, #711a 10.00

Modern Art Type of 2003

Designs: 1.65k, Two Trees at the Foot of a Hill, by Oskar Herman. 1.80k, Carousel, by Nevenka Djordjevic. 6.50k, Still Life, by Ivo Rezek.

Perf. 14 Syncopated

2008, Dec. 1 **Litho.**
712-714 A304 Set of 3 4.50 4.50

Zora Choral Society, 150th Anniv. — A410

Perf. 14x13¾ Syncopated

2008, Dec. 5
715 A410 1.65k multi .75 .75

Ivan Mestrovic (1883-1962), Sculptor — A411

Perf. 14 Syncopated

2008, Dec. 15 **Litho.**
716 A411 5k multi 2.10 2.10

21st Men's World Handball Championships — A412

Perf. 13¾x14¼ Syncopated

2009, Jan. 16 **Litho. & Embossed**
717 A412 3.50k multi 1.50 1.50

Printed in sheets of 9 + label

Bruno Bjelinski (1909-92), Composer A413

Josip Andreis (1909-82), Musicologist A414

Perf. 14¼x13¾ Syncopated

2009, Jan. 21 **Litho.**
718 A413 1.80k multi .75 .75
719 A414 3.50k multi 1.50 1.50

Street and Bridge, Sisak — A415

2009, Jan. 22 ***Perf. 14 Syncopated***
720 A415 8k multi 3.50 3.50

Remains of St. Tryphon in Kotor, 1200th Anniv. — A416

No. 721 — St. Tryphon: a, Drawing. b, Sculpture from altarpiece, Kotor Cathedral.

2009, Feb. 3 ***Perf. 14¼ Syncopated***
721 A416 3.50k Horiz. pair, #a-b 2.75 2.75

Fairy Tale Characters — A417

No. 722: a, Svarozic. b, Bjesomar.

2009, Feb. 27
722 A417 1.65k Horiz. pair, #a-b 1.50 1.50

Souvenir Sheet

Protection of Polar Regions and Glaciers — A418

No. 723: a, Sun over glacier. b, Intl. Polar Year emblem and glacier.

2009, Mar. 27 **Litho. & Embossed**
723 A418 5k Sheet of 2, #a-b 3.75 3.75

Easter A419

Perf. 14 Syncopated

2009, Mar. 30 **Litho.**
724 A419 3.50k multi 1.60 1.60

Entry Into NATO A420

2009, Apr. 4
725 A420 8k multi 3.00 3.00

Juraj Sizgoric (1445-c. 1509), Poet — A421

Juraj Habdelic (1609-78), Writer — A422

Ljudevit Gaj (1809-72), Writer, Illyrian Movement Leader — A423

Petar Segedin (1909-98), Writer — A424

Perf. 14¼x13¾ Syncopated

2009, Apr. 22

726	A421	3.50k multi	1.25	1.25
727	A422	3.50k multi	1.25	1.25
728	A423	5k multi	1.90	1.90
729	A424	5k multi	1.90	1.90
		Nos. 726-729 (4)	6.30	6.30

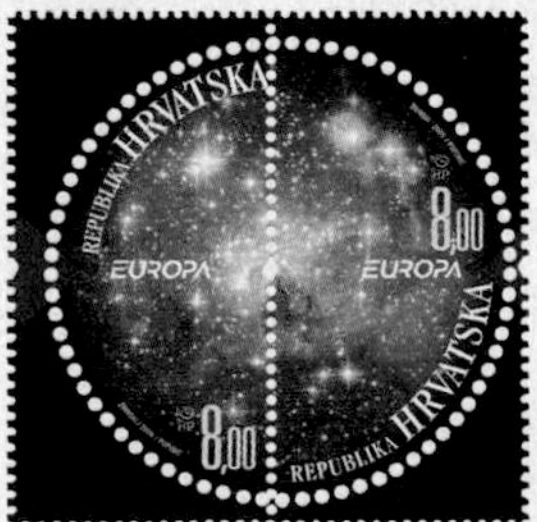

Europa — A425

No. 730 — Image of space from Hubble Space Telescope with red diamond at: a, Left. b, Right.

Perf. 14x13½ Syncopated

2009, May 9 **Litho.**
730 A425 8k Horiz. pair, #a-b 6.00 6.00

Intl. Year of Astronomy. Values are for stamps with surrounding selvage.

Franciscans in Cakovec, 350th Anniv. — A426

2009, May 20 ***Perf. 14 Syncopated***
731 A426 3.50k multi 1.40 1.40

Souvenir Sheet

King Andrew's Charter Proclaiming Varazdin as Free Royal Borough, 800th Anniv. — A427

Perf. 14 Syncopated

2009, June 9 **Litho.**
732 A427 15k multi 6.00 6.00

Souvenir Sheet

St. John, Sculpture by Ivan Duknovic (c. 1440-1509) — A428

2009, June 23 ***Perf. 14***
733 A428 10k multi 4.75 4.75

Zagreb Jazz Quartet, 50th Anniv. A429

2009, June 29
734 A429 10.70k multi 5.00 5.00

Fish — A430

Designs: 3.50k, Acipenser naccarii. No. 736, 5k, Knipowitschia mrakovcici. No. 737, 5k, Ballerus sapa.

2009, Sept. 1 Litho. *Perf. 14*

735 A430 3.50k multi 1.75 1.75
a. Booklet pane of 10 17.50 —
Complete booklet, #735a 17.50
736 A430 5k multi 2.50 2.50
a. Booklet pane of 10 25.00 —
Complete booklet, #736a 25.00
737 A430 5k multi 2.50 2.50
a. Booklet pane of 10 25.00 —
Complete booklet, #737a 25.00
Nos. 735-737 (3) 6.75 6.75

Stamp Day — A431

2009, Sept. 9

738 A431 3.50k multi 1.50 1.50

Croatian Post Inc., 10th Anniv.

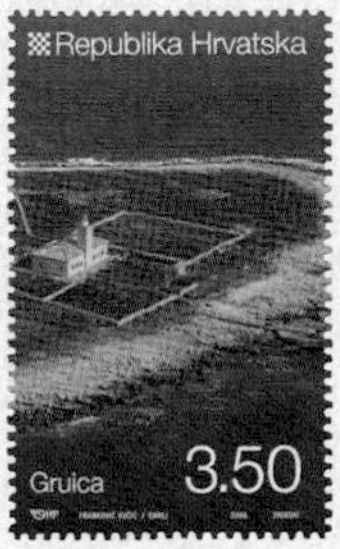

Lighthouses A432

Designs: No. 739, 3.50k, Gruica Lighthouse. No. 740, 3.50k, Strazica Lighthouse. 8k, Voscica Lighthouse.

2009, Sept. 11

739-741 A432 Set of 3 5.75 5.75

Franciscan Order, 800th Anniv. — A433

2009, Sept. 17 Litho. *Perf. 14*

742 A433 3.50k multi 1.60 1.60

Souvenir Sheet

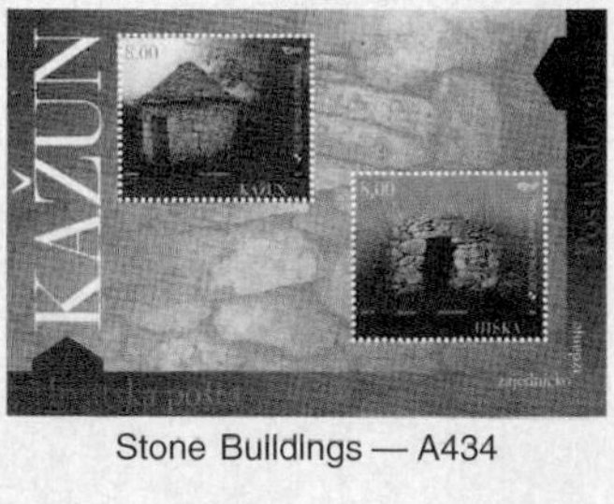

Stone Buildings — A434

No. 743 — Stone building in: a, Pazin, Croatia. b, Kopriva na Krasu, Slovenia.

2009, Sept. 25

743 A434 8k Sheet of 2, #a-b 7.50 7.50

See Slovenia No. 812.

St. Martin's Hermit Chapel, Podsused, 800th Anniv. A435

2009, Oct. 29

744 A435 3.50k multi 1.60 1.60

National Folk Dance Ensemble, 60th Anniv. A436

2009, Nov. 11

745 A436 3.50k multi 1.60 1.60

Rights of the Child A437

2009, Nov. 20

746 A437 3.50k multi 1.30 1.30

Declaration of the Rights of the Child, 50th anniv.; UN Convention on the Rights of the Child, 20th anniv.

New Year's Day — A438

2009, Nov. 24 Litho. *Perf. 14*

747 A438 3.50k multi 1.50 1.50

Serpentine Die Cut 5¼
Booklet Stamp
Self-Adhesive

748 A438 3.50k multi 1.50 1.50
a. Booklet pane of 10 15.00
Complete booklet, #748a 15.00

Modern Art Type of 2003

Designs: No. 749, 1.80k, Gray Sail, by Zlatko Prica. No. 750, 1.80k, A Bosom Full of Wind, by Nives Kavuric Kurtovic, vert. No. 751, 1.80k, Flora, by Ordan Petlevski.

2009, Dec. 1 Litho. *Perf. 14*

749-751 A304 Set of 3 2.00 2.00

A439

Christmas A440

2009, Dec. 4 Litho. *Perf. 14*

752 A439 3.50k multi 1.50 1.50
753 A440 8k multi 3.25 3.25

Serpentine Die Cut 5¼
Booklet Stamp
Self-Adhesive

754 A439 3.50k multi 1.50 1.50
a. Booklet pane of 10 15.00
Complete booklet, #754a 15.00

Statute of Lastovo, 700th Anniv. — A441

2010, Jan. 8 Litho. *Perf. 14*

755 A441 3.50k multi 1.60 1.60

2010 Winter Olympics, Vancouver A442

2010, Feb. 12 *Perf. 14¼x14*

756 A442 3.50k multi 1.60 1.60

Souvenir Sheet

Peonies — A443

No. 757: a, Paeonia mascula. b, Paeonia officinalis.

2010, Mar. 8 Litho. *Perf. 14*

757 A443 3k Sheet of 2, #a-b 3.00 3.00

Embroidery A444

Embroidery from: 1.60k, Primorje. 3.10k, Medimurje. 4.60k, Posavina. 7.10k, Draganic.

2010, Mar. 15

758-761 A444 Set of 4 7.75 7.75
761a Sheet of 4, #758-761 7.75 7.75

Fruit A445

Designs: 1k, Fragaria vesca. No. 763, Vitis vinifera. No. 764, Ribes uva-crispa.

2010, Mar. 16 Litho. & Embossed

762 A445 1k multi .45 .45
a. Booklet pane of 10 4.50 —
Complete booklet, #762a 4.50
763 A445 4k multi 1.75 1.75
a. Booklet pane of 10 17.50 —
Complete booklet, #763a 17.50
764 A445 4k multi 1.75 1.75
a. Booklet pane of 10 17.50 —
Complete booklet, #764a 17.50
Nos. 762-764 (3) 3.95 3.95

Easter A446

2010, Mar. 19 Litho. *Perf. 14*

765 A446 3.10k multi 1.40 1.40

Establishment of Bjelovar-Krizevci Diocese — A447

2010, Mar. 19

766 A447 6.50k multi 2.75 2.75

Printed in sheets of 8 + 2 labels.

Steam Locomotives — A448

No. 767: a, Series MAV 326/JZ 125. b, Series SüdB 18.

2010, Mar. 29

767 Vert. pair + central label 6.75 6.75
a.-b. A448 7.10k Either single 3.25 3.25

Capuchin Order in Croatia, 400th Anniv. — A449

2010, Apr. 15

768 A449 6.10k multi 2.75 2.75

Famous Men — A450

Designs: 1.60k, Grgo Gamulin (1910-97), art historian. 3.10k, Janko Polic Kamov (1886-1910), writer. 4.50k, Ivan Matetic Ronjgov (1880-1960), composer. 6.10k, Marko Antun de Dominis (1560-1624), archbishop and physicist.

2010, Apr. 22
769-772 A450 Set of 4 7.00 7.00

Souvenir Sheet

Expo 2010, Shanghai — A451

2010, Apr. 29
773 A451 10k multi 4.50 4.50

Europa — A452

No. 774 — Children's book and: a, Fairy on branch, fairy with horn. b, Fairy looking at butterfly, fairy on flower.

Litho. With Foil Application
2010, May 7 ***Perf. 14***
774 A452 7.10k Horiz. pair, #a-b 6.25 6.25

Souvenir Sheet

Lubenice — A453

2010, May 21 **Litho.**
775 A453 10k multi 4.75 4.75

2010 World Cup Soccer Championships, South Africa — A454

2010, June 11
776 A454 4.50k multi 2.25 2.25

Printed in sheets of 9 + label.

Nos. 562a, 601, 661a and 677 Surcharged

Methods and Perfs. As Before
2010

777	A379 1.60k on 1.80k #661a	.65	.65
778	A344 3.10k on 3.50k #601	1.25	1.25
779	A320 4.50k on 5k #562a	2.10	2.10
780	A367 7.10k on 7.20k #677	3.25	3.25
	Nos. 777-780 (4)	7.25	7.25

Issued: Nos. 777-778, 5/17; Nos. 779-780, 7/19.

Lighthouses A455

Designs: No. 781, 3.10k, Vir Lighthouse. No. 782, 3.10k, Veli Rat Lighthouse. No. 783, 3.10k, Tajer Lighthouse.

2010, Sept. 7 **Litho.** ***Perf. 14***
781-783 A455 Set of 3 4.50 4.50

Souvenir Sheet

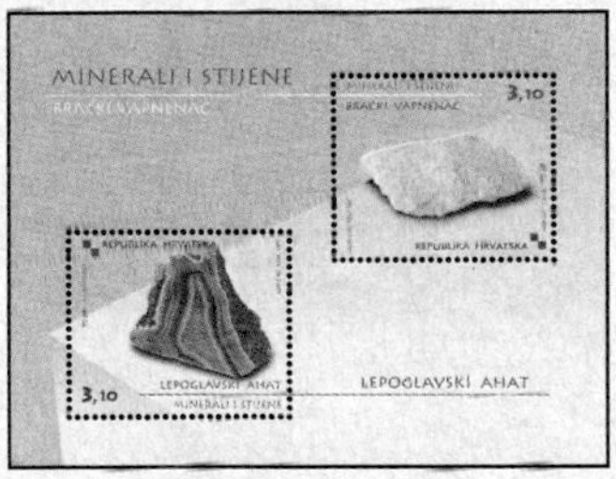

Minerals — A456

No. 784: a, Calcite from Brac. b, Agate from Lepoglava.

Litho. & Embossed (#784a), Litho.
2010, Oct. 15
784 A456 3.10k Sheet of 2, #a-b 3.00 3.00

Souvenir Sheet

Dubrovnik Tramway, Cent. — A457

2010, Nov. 22 **Litho.** ***Perf. 14***
785 A457 15k multi 7.00 7.00

Adoration of the Shepherds, by Josip Biffel — A458

2010, Nov. 25
786 A458 3.10k multi 1.50 1.50

Booklet Stamp
Self-Adhesive
Serpentine Die Cut 5¼

787 A458 3.10k multi 1.50 1.50
a. Booklet pane of 10 15.00
Complete booklet, #787a 15.00

Christmas.

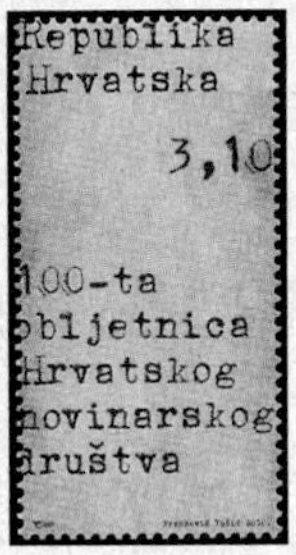

A459

2010, Dec. 1 **Litho.** ***Perf. 14***
788 A459 3.10k multi 1.40 1.40

Croatian Journalist Society, cent.

A460

2010, Dec. 6
789 A460 1.60k multi .75 .75

New Year 2011.

Intl. Children's Festival, Sibenik — A461

2011, Feb. 14 **Litho.** ***Perf. 14***
790 A461 1.60k multi .85 .85

Fauna — A462

Designs: 1.60k, Ursus arctos. 3.10k, Falco eleonorae. 4.60k, Monachus monachus.

2011, Mar. 15

791	A462 1.60k multi	.80	.80
a.	Booklet pane of 10	8.00	—
	Complete booklet, #791a	8.00	
792	A462 3.10k multi	1.60	1.60
a.	Booklet pane of 10	16.00	—
	Complete booklet, #792a	16.00	
793	A462 4.60k multi	2.40	2.40
a.	Booklet pane of 10	24.00	—
	Complete booklet, #793a	24.00	
	Nos. 791-793 (3)	4.80	4.80

Stations of the Cross — A463

No. 794 — Station: a, 1. b, 2. c, 3. d, 4. e, 5. f, 6. g, 7. h, 8. i, 9. j, 10. k, 11. l, 12. m, 13. n, 14.

2011, Mar. 23
794 Booklet pane of 14 24.50 —
a.-n. A463 3.10k Any single 1.75 1.75
Complete booklet, #794 24.50

Visit to Croatia of Pope Benedict XVI — A464

2011, Apr. 4 **Litho.**
795 A464 3.10k multi 1.75 1.75

Souvenir Sheet

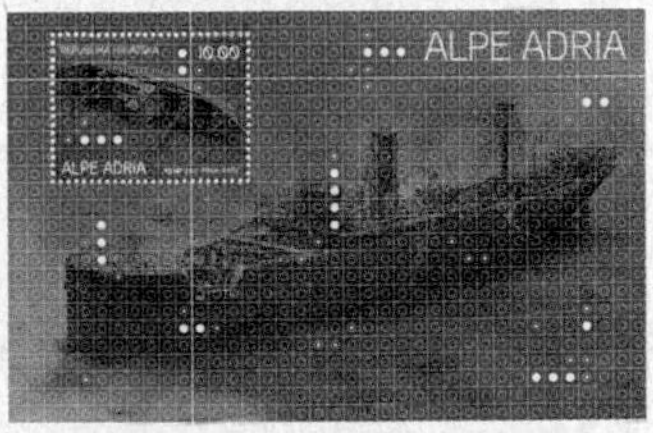

Wreck of the Elhawl Star, Rijeka Harbor — A465

2011, Apr. 14 ***Perf. 14***
796 A465 10k multi 5.00 5.00

Souvenir Sheet

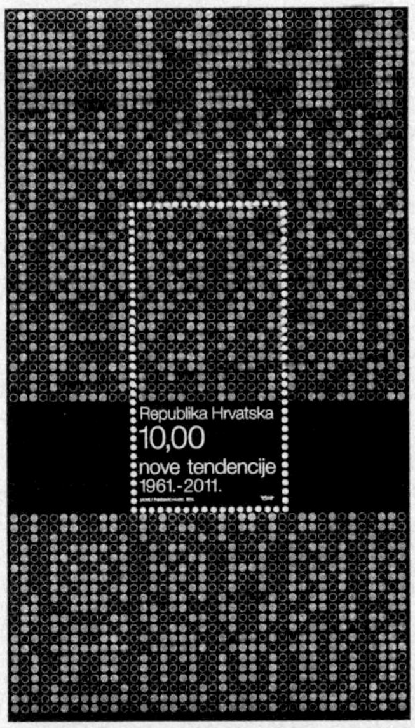

New Tendencies Art Exhibit, 50th Anniv. — A466

2011, Apr. 15
797 A466 10k black & silver 5.00 5.00

Famous People — A467

Designs: No. 798, 1.60k, Jagoda Truhelka (1864-1957), writer. No. 799, 1.60k, August Harambasic (1861-1911), poet and politician. No. 800, 1.60k, Grigor Vitez (1911-66), writer.

2011, Apr. 22
798-800 A467 Set of 3 2.25 2.25

Croatian Academy of Sciences and Arts, 150th Anniv. — A468

2011, Apr. 29
801 A468 9.50k multi 4.50 4.50

Europa — A469

No. 802 — Paintings: a, Beech, by Josip Zanki. b, Forest Scene with Spider's Web, by Lovro Artukovic.

2011, May 5
802 A469 7.10k Horiz. pair, #a-b 6.25 6.25

Intl. Year of Forests.

Castles and Palaces A470

Arms and: No. 803, 3.10k, Pejacevic Castle, Nasice. No. 804, 3.10k, Hilleprand-Mailáth Castle, Donji Miholjac. No. 805, 4.60k, Hilleprand-Prandau Normann-Ehrenfels Castle, Valpovo. No. 806, 4.60k, Palace of Prince Eugene of Savoy, Bilje.

2011, June 16 **Litho.** ***Perf. 14***
803-806 A470 Set of 4 7.00 7.00
806a Sheet of 8, 2 each #803-806, + 8 labels 15.00 15.00

Nos. 803-806 each were printed in sheets of 9 + label. See Nos. 876-879, 956-959.

Independence, 20th Anniv. — A471

2011, June 24
807 A471 3.10k multi 1.50 1.50

Printed in sheets of 25 + 5 labels.

Eucharistic Miracle of Ludbreg, 600th Anniv. — A472

2011, Sept. 1
808 A472 5k multi 2.50 2.50

Quick Response Code — A473

2011, Sept. 9
809 A473 3.10k brown & black 1.60 1.60

Stamp Day.

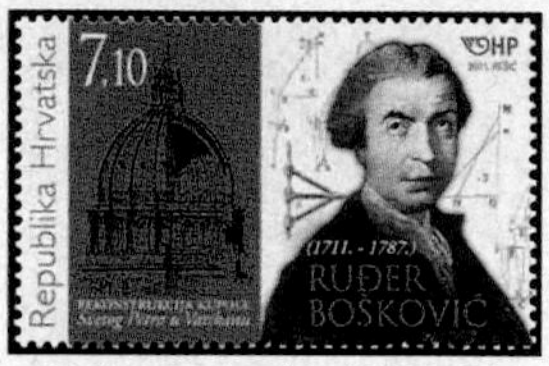

Rudjer Boskovich (1711-87), Astronomer, and Dome of St. Peter's Basilica — A474

2011, Sept. 13
810 A474 7.10k multi 3.75 3.75

See Vatican City No. 1482.

Lighthouses — A475

Designs: No. 811, 3.10k, Prisnjak Lighthouse. No. 812, 3.10k, Mulo Lighthouse. 7.10k, Blitvenica Lighthouse.

2011, Oct. 18
811-813 A475 Set of 3 6.50 6.50

Institute of Art History, Zagreb, 50th Anniv. — A476

2011, Oct. 28
814 A476 4.60k multi 2.50 2.50

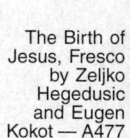

The Birth of Jesus, Fresco by Zeljko Hegedusic and Eugen Kokot — A477

2011, Nov. 3
815 A477 3.10k multi 1.75 1.75

Serpentine Die Cut 5¼
Booklet Stamp
Self-Adhesive

816 A477 3.10k multi 1.75 1.75
a. Booklet pane of 10 17.50
Complete booklet, #816a 17.50

Christmas.

Siege of Vukovar, 20th Anniv. A478

2011, Nov. 18 ***Perf. 14***
817 A478 3.10k multi 1.75 1.75

Ivica Kostelic, 2011 World Cup Skiing Overall Champion A479

2011, Nov. 23
818 A479 7.10k multi 3.50 3.50

Printed in sheets of 9 + label.

New Year 2012 A480

Litho. With Foil Application
2011, Nov. 24
819 A480 3.10k multi 1.60 1.60

Art A481

Designs: 3.10k, Space-B, by Ante Kuduz. 4.50k, Woman with Cat, by Marijan Trepse, vert. 9.50k, Lovers, by Anka Krizmanic.

2011, Dec. 1 **Litho.** ***Perf. 14***
820-822 A481 Set of 3 8.00 8.00

Vasa Posta Foundation A482

2011, Dec. 5
823 A482 3.10k multi 1.60 1.60

Printed in sheets of 8 + label.

New Year 2012 (Year of the Dragon) A483

2012, Jan. 4
824 A483 1.60k ol brn & blk .90 .90

St. Valentine's Day — A484

2012, Feb. 1 ***Perf. 14x13¾***
825 A484 3.10k multi + 2 labels 2.25 2.25
a. Booklet pane of 4 + 8 labels 9.00 —
Complete booklet, #825a 9.00

No. 825 was printed in sheets of 4 stamps + 8 labels. These sheets were affixed inside booklet covers, and booklet panes have folds along the left margin and throuch the center row of perforations.

Cats — A485

No. 826: a, 1.60k, Ragdoll cat and bird. b, 1.60k, Domestic cat and ball. c, 3.10k, Siamese cat and sock. d, 3.10k, Persian cat and mouse.

2012, Feb. 21 ***Perf. 14***
826 A485 Block of 4, #a-d 4.50 4.50

Flowers A486

Designs: 1.60k, Galanthus nivalis. 3.10k, Primula vulgaris. 4.60k, Crocus vernus.

2012, Mar. 15
827 A486 1.60k multi .80 .80
a. Booklet pane of 10 8.00 —
Complete booklet, #827a 8.00
828 A486 3.10k multi 1.50 1.50
a. Booklet pane of 10 15.00 —
Complete booklet, #828a 15.00
829 A486 4.60k multi 2.25 2.25
a. Booklet pane of 10 22.50 —
Complete booklet, #829a 22.50
Nos. 827-829 (3) 4.55 4.55

Easter A487

2012, Mar. 16
830 A487 3.10k multi 1.50 1.50
a. Booklet pane of 4 6.00 —
Complete booklet, #830a 6.00

Famous People A488

Designs: No. 831, 1.60k, Bishop Juraj Dobrila (1812-82). No. 832, 1.60k, Vesna Parun (1922-2010), poet. No. 833, 1.60k, Dragojla Jarnevic (1812-75), poet.

2012, Apr. 19
831-833 A488 Set of 3 2.25 2.25

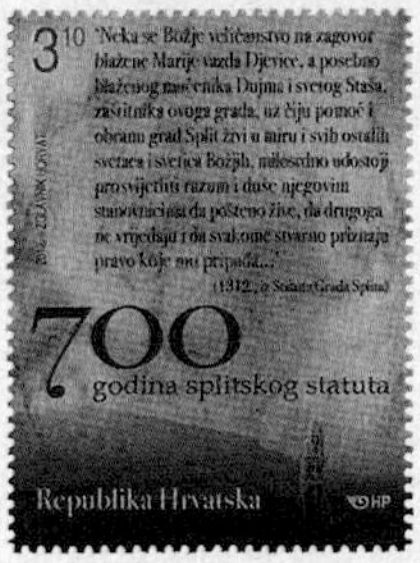

Statute of Split, 700th Anniv. A489

2012, Apr. 25

834 A489 3.10k multi 1.50 1.50

No. 834 was printed in sheets of 10 + 2 labels.

Paklenica National Park — A490

Apoxyomenos Statue Found in the Adriatic Sea — A491

2012, May 9

835 A490 7.10k multi 3.50 3.50

836 A491 7.10k multi 3.50 3.50

Europa.

Croatian Chess Federation, Cent. A492

2012, May 12

837 A492 4.60k multi 2.25 2.25

No. 837 was printed in sheets of 9 + label.

Lighthouses — A493

Designs: 3.10k, St. Peter's Lighthouse. No. 839, 7.10k, St. Nicholas's Lighthouse. No. 840, 7.10k, Pokonji Dol Lighthouse.

2012, May 31

838-840 A493 Set of 3 8.25 8.25

Croatian Soccer Team's Participation in 2012 European Soccer Championships A494

2012, June 8

841 A494 4.60k multi 2.00 2.00

Printed in sheets of 9 + label.

UNESCO Intangible Cultural Heritage of Croatia A495

Designs: 1.60k, Festival of St. Blaise (Festa Sv. Vlaha). 3.10k, Lacemaking, Hvar. 4.60k, Gingerbread heart, butterfly and cross. 7.10k, Carved wooden bird toy.

2012, June 12

842-845 A495 Set of 4 6.50 6.50

845a Souvenir sheet of 4, #842-845 + 5 labels 6.50 6.50

Miniature Sheet

Seafood Dishes — A496

No. 846: a, Rakovica (spider crab). b, Kamenice (oysters). c, Hobotnica (octopi). d, Orada (gilthead sea bream).

2012, July 2 ***Serpentine Die Cut 5¼***

Self-Adhesive

846 A496 4.60k Sheet of 4, #a-d, + 4 etiquettes 7.50 7.50

2012 Summer Olympics, London — A497

2012, July 23 ***Perf. 14***

847 A497 3.10k multi 1.25 1.25

Printed in sheets of 9 + label.

A498

A499

A500

Hemaris Croatica — A501

2012, Sept. 18

848 Strip of 4 7.00 7.00

a. A498 4.60k multi 1.75 1.75

b. A499 4.60k multi 1.75 1.75

c. A500 4.60k multi 1.75 1.75

d. A501 4.60k multi 1.75 1.75

Worldwide Fund for Nature (WWF).

Theater in Hvar, 400th Anniv. — A502

2012, Sept. 25

849 A502 1.60k multi .65 .65

Locomotives — A503

No. 850: a, MAV 424/JDZ/JZ 11. b, SüdB 29/JDZ 124.

2012, Oct. 1

850 Vert. pair + 2 central labels 5.50 5.50

a.-b. A503 7.10k Either single 2.75 2.75

First locomotives on Zidani Most-Sisak line, 150th anniv.

Souvenir Sheet

Diplomatic Relations Between Croatia and San Marino, 20th Anniv. — A504

No. 851 —Traditional costumes with denomination at: a, LR. b, LL.

2012, Oct. 16

851 A504 7.10k Sheet of 2, #a-b 5.50 5.50

See San Marino No. 1874.

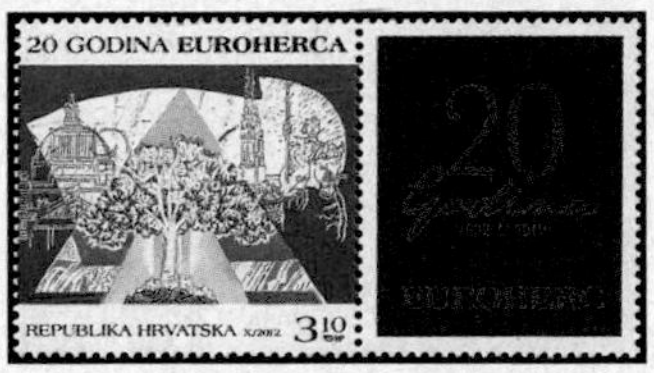

Euroherc Insurance Company, 20th Anniv. — A505

2012, Oct. 19

852 A505 3.10k multi + label 1.25 1.25

Souvenir Sheet

Rocks and Minerals — A506

No. 853: a, Roselite. b, Zebrato granite.

Litho. & Embossed With Foil Application

2012, Oct. 24 ***Perf.***

853 A506 5k Sheet of 2, #a-b 4.00 4.00

Intl. Day of the Romani Language — A507

2012, Nov. 5 **Litho.** ***Perf. 14***

854 A507 3.10k multi 1.25 1.25

Krapina Neanderthal Man Museum A508

Designs: 1.60k. Timeline and statues of hominids. 3.10k, Diorama of Neanderthals in cave.

2012, Nov. 7

855-856 A508 Set of 2 1.90 1.90

Christmas A509

Litho. With Foil Application

2012, Nov. 15 ***Perf. 14***

857 A509 3.10k multi 1.25 1.25

Booklet Stamp

Self-Adhesive

Serpentine Die Cut 5¼

858 A509 3.10k multi 1.25 1.25

a. Booklet pane of 10 12.50

Complete booklet, #858a 12.50

Greek Catholic Church in Croatia, 400th Anniv. — A510

2012, Nov. 27 Litho. *Perf. 14*

859 A510 3.10k multi 1.25 1.25

New Year 2013 — A511

Litho. With Foil Application

2012, Dec. 4

860 A511 3.10k multi 1.25 1.25

Dogs — A512

No. 861: a, German shepherd with bone. b, Yorkshire terrier with sausages. c, Golden retriever with newspaper. d, Bichon frisé in basket.

2013, Feb. 21 Litho.

861 A512 3.10k Block or vert. strip of 4, #a-d 4.25 4.25

Easter A513

2013, Mar. 11

862 A513 3.10k multi 1.10 1.10

Amphibians A514

Designs: 1.60k, Bombina bombina. 3.10k, Salamandra salamandra. 4.60k, Proteus anguinus.

2013, Apr. 8

863 A514 1.60k multi .55 .55
a. Booklet pane of 10 5.50 —
Complete booklet, #863a 5.50
864 A514 3.10k multi 1.10 1.10
a. Booklet pane of 10 11.00 —
Complete booklet, #864a 11.00
865 A514 4.60k multi 1.60 1.60
a. Booklet pane of 10 16.00 —
Complete booklet, #865a 16.00
Nos. 863-865 (3) 3.25 3.25

Famous People A515

Designs: No. 866, 1.20k, Stjepan Gradic (1613-83), diplomat. No. 867, 1.20k, Antonija Krasnik (1874-1956), decorative artist. No. 868, 5.80k, Ranko Marinkovic (1913-2001), writer. No. 869, 5.80k, Milka Trnina (1863-1941), opera singer.

2013, Apr. 16

866-869 A515 Set of 4 5.00 5.00

Souvenir Sheet

Bridges — A516

No. 870: a, Railway Bridge, Zagreb (49x24mm). b, Old Bridge, Tounj (36x30mm).

2013, Apr. 29

870 A516 7.10k Sheet of 2, #a-b 5.00 5.00

Europa — A517

Postal vehicles: No. 871, 7.10k, Moped. No. 872, 7.10k, Van.

2013, May 9

871-872 A517 Set of 2 5.25 5.25

A518

Admission of Croatia to European Union — A519

2013, July 1

873 A518 3.10k multi 1.10 1.10

Souvenir Sheet

874 A519 20k multi 7.00 7.00

No. 873 was printed in sheets of 25 stamps + 5 labels.

Pula Film Festival, 60th Anniv. A520

2013, July 2

875 A520 3.10k multi 1.10 1.10

Castles and Palaces Type of 2011

Arms and: No. 876, 1.60k, Odescalchi Castle, Ilok. No. 877, 1.60k, Eltz Castle, Vukovar. No. 878, 1.60k, Pejacevic Castle, Virovitica. No. 879, 1.60k, Turkovic Castle, Kutjevo.

2013, July 18

876-879 A470 Set of 4 2.25 2.25
879a Souvenir sheet of 8, 2 each #876-879, + 8 labels 4.50 4.50

Mushrooms A521

No. 880: a, Macrolepiota procera. b, Boletus regius. c, Tuber magnatum, Tuber melanosporum.

2013, Sept. 3 *Perf. 14*

880 Horiz. strip of 3 5.25 5.25
a.-c. A521 4.60k Any single 1.75 1.75

Lapitch, the Little Shoemaker A522

2013, Sept. 4

881 A522 3.10k multi 1.10 1.10

Publishing of Lapitch, the Little Shoemaker, children's book by Ivana Brlic Mazuranic, cent.

Souvenir Sheet

Portrait of Count Teodor Pejacevic (1855-1928), by Vlaho Bukovac — A523

2013, Sept. 18

882 A523 11k multi 4.00 4.00

Diplomatic relations between Croatia and the Sovereign Military Order of Malta, 20th anniv.

Lighthouses — A524

Designs: 4.60k, Plocica Lighthouse. 5.80k, Stoncica Lighthouse. 7.60k, Sucuraj Lighthouse.

2013, Sept. 26 *Perf. 14*

883-885 A524 Set of 3 6.50 6.50

Salesians in Croatia, Cent. — A525

2013, Oct. 1 Litho. *Perf. 14*

886 A525 1.20k multi .45 .45

Gas Lighting System in Zagreb, 150th Anniv. — A526

2013, Oct. 3 Litho. *Perf. 14*

887 A526 7.60k multi 2.75 2.75

No. 887 was printed in sheets of 8 + label.

Souvenir Sheet

Peasant's Revolt, 440th Anniv. — A527

2013, Oct. 11 Litho. *Perf. 14*

888 A527 11k multi 4.00 4.00

Mirko (1871-1913) and Stevo (1875-1936) Seljan, Explorers, Map of Guayra Falls, South America — A528

2013, Oct. 15 Litho. *Perf. 14*

889 A528 7.60k multi 2.75 2.75

Faros Swimming Marathon — A529

2013, Nov. 5 Litho. *Perf. 14*

890 A529 7.60k multi 2.75 2.75

No. 890 was printed in sheets of 9 + label.

Christmas A530

Litho. With Foil Application

2013, Nov. 27 *Perf. 14*
891 A530 3.10k multi 1.10 1.10

Litho.

Booklet Stamp
Self-Adhesive

Serpentine Die Cut 5¼

892 A530 3.10k multi 1.10 1.10
a. Booklet pane of 10 11.00
Complete booklet, #892a 11.00

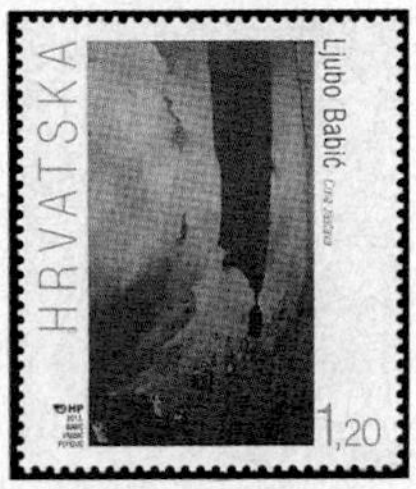

Art — A531

Designs: 1.20k, Black Flag, by Ljubo Babic. 3.10k, Sappho, by Bela Cikos Sesija. 5.80k, PAFAMA, by Josip Seissel.

2013, Dec. 3 **Litho.** *Perf. 14*
893-895 A531 Set of 3 3.75 3.75

New Year 2014 A532

Litho. With Foil Application

2013, Dec. 5 *Perf. 14*
896 A532 3.10k multi 1.10 1.10

2014 Winter Olympics, Sochi, Russia A533

2014, Feb. 7 **Litho.** *Perf. 14*
897 A533 3.10k multi 1.10 1.10

No. 897 was printed in sheets of 9 + label.

Pets — A534

No. 898: a, Chinchilla eating apple slice. b, Guinea pig eating biscuit. c, Rabbit in top hat. d, Hamster with carrot.

2014, Feb. 21 **Litho.** *Perf. 14*
898 A534 3.10k Block of 4, #a.-d. 4.50 4.50

Temple of Augustus, Pula — A535

2014, Mar. 3 **Litho.** *Perf. 14*
899 A535 2.80k multi 1.00 1.00

Souvenir Sheet

University of Zagreb Faculty of Science Botanical Garden, 125th Anniv. — A536

2014, Apr. 1 **Litho.** *Perf. 14*
900 A536 11k multi 4.00 4.00

Dalmatian Braided Bread — A537

2014, Apr. 2 **Litho.** *Perf. 14*
901 A537 3.10k multi 1.10 1.10

Easter.

Miniature Sheet

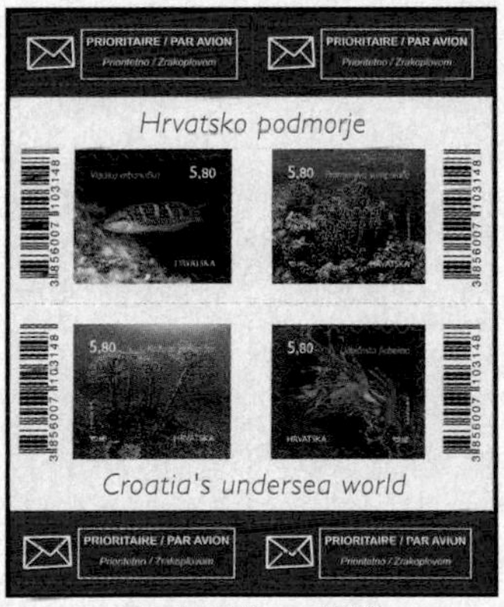

Marine Life — A538

No. 902: a, Ornate wrasse (Vladika arbanaska), b, Golden sponge (Promjenjiva sumporaca). c, European fan worm (Kozasti perjaničar). d, mediterranean violet aeolid (Ljubicasta flabelina).

Serpentine Die Cut 5¼

2014, Apr. 9 **Litho.**

Self-Adhesive

902 A538 Sheet of 4 + 4 etiquettes 8.50
a.-d. 5.80k Any single 2.10 2.10

Orchids A539

Designs: No. 903, Ophrys dinarica. No. 904, Serapias istriaca. 3.10k, Ophrys libunica.

2014, Apr. 11 **Litho.** *Perf. 14*
903 A539 2.80k multi 1.00 1.00
a. Booklet pane of 10 10.00
Complete booklet, #903a 10.00
904 A539 2.80k multi 1.00 1.00
a. Booklet pane of 10 10.00
Complete booklet, #904a 10.00
905 A539 3.10 multi 1.10 1.10
a. Booklet pane of 10 11.00
Complete booklet, #905a 11.00

Famous People A540

Designs: 1.20k, Ivan Bjelovucic (1889-1949), first man to fly over Alps. 2.80k, Ivan Gundulic (1589-1638), writer. 3.10k, Ivan Mazuranic (1814-90), poet. 7.60k, Dora Pejacevic (1885-1923), composer.

2014, Apr. 18 **Litho.** *Perf. 14*
906-909 A540 Set of 4 5.50 5.50

Canonization of Popes John Paul II and John XXIII — A541

No. 910—Arms and portrait of: a, Pope John Paul II. b, Pope John XXIII.

2014, Apr. 25 **Litho.** *Perf. 14*
910 A541 7.60k Pair, #a.-b. 5.75 5.75

Europa A542

Musical instruments:3.10k, Lijerica. 7.60k, Sopile.

2014, May 9 **Litho.** *Perf. 14*
911-912 A542 Set of 2 4.00 4.00

Lighthouses — A543

Designs: 2.80k, Palagruza Lighthouse. No. 914, 5.80k, Struga Lighthouse. No. 915, 5.80k, Susac Lighthouse.

2014, May 30 **Litho.** *Perf. 14*
913-915 A543 Set of 3 5.25 5.25

Villa Angiolina, Opatija, 170th Anniv. A544

2014, June 11 **Litho.** *Perf. 14*
916 A544 2.80k multi 1.00 1.00

No. 916 was printed in sheets of 8 + central label.

2014 World Cup Soccer Championships, Brazil — A545

2014, June 12 **Litho.** *Perf. 14*
917 A545 7.60k multi 2.75 2.75

No. 917 was printed in sheets of 9 + label.

Volunteer Fire Departments in Croatia, 150th Anniv. — A546

2014, June 17 **Litho.** *Perf. 14*
918 A546 5k multi 1.90 1.90

No. 918 was printed in sheets of 8 + 2 labels.

Prelog, 750th Anniv. — A547

2014, Sept. 23 **Litho.** *Perf. 14*
919 A547 3.10k multi 1.10 1.10

Souvenir Sheet

Carved Wooden Doorway of Split Cathedral, 800th Anniv. — A548

2014, Sept. 23 **Litho.** *Perf. 14*
920 A548 11k multi 3.75 3.75

Statute of the Town and Island of Korcula, 800th Anniv. — A549

2014, Sept. 26 **Litho.** *Perf. 14*
921 A549 2.80k multi .95 .95

St. Nicholas Benedictine Monastery, Trogir, 950th Anniv. — A550

2014, Sept. 30 Litho. *Perf. 14*
922 A550 2.80k multi .95 .95

Locomotives — A551

No. 923: a, KkStB 229/JDZ/JZ 116. b, MAV 375/JDZ/HDZ/JZ 51.

2014, Oct. 1 Litho. *Perf. 14*
923 Vert. pair + 2 central labels 3.50 3.50
a.-b. A551 5k Either single 1.75 1.75

Monument in Mirogoj Cemetery, Zagreb A552

2014, Oct. 14 Litho. *Perf. 14*
924 A552 7.60k multi 2.50 2.50

World War I, cent.

Details from Traditional Costumes — A553

Detail from costume from: 3.10k, Slavonia. 5.80k, Vrlika. 7.60k, Gorski Kotar. 11k, Lovas.

2014, Oct. 20 Litho. *Perf. 14*
925 A553 3.10k multi 1.00 1.00
926 A553 5.80k multi 1.90 1.90
927 A553 7.60k multi 2.50 2.50
928 A553 11k multi 3.75 3.75
a. Souvenir sheet of 4, #925-928 9.25 9.25
Nos. 925-928 (4) 9.15 9.15

Souvenir Sheet

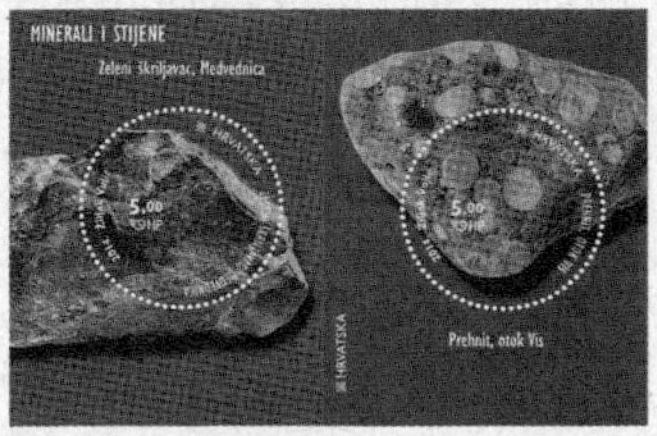

Rocks and Minerals — A554

No. 929: a, Green schist (green background). b, Prehnite (blue background).

Litho. & Embossed

2014, Oct. 24 *Perf.*
929 A554 5k Sheet of 2, #a-b 3.25 3.25

Souvenir Sheet

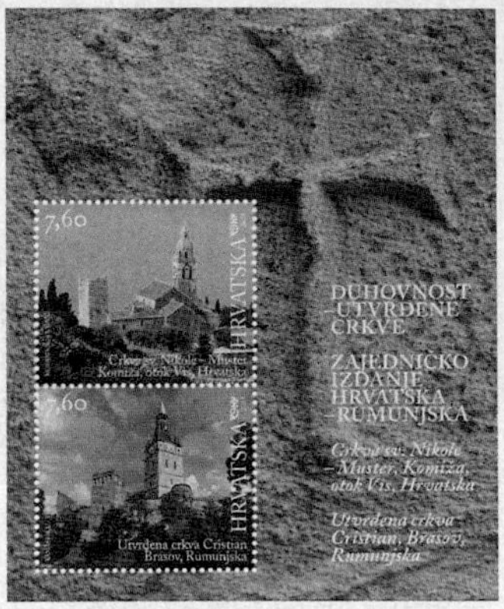

Fortified Churches — A555

No. 930: a, St. Nicholas Church, Muster. b, Evangelical Church, Cristian, Romania.

2014, Nov. 14 Litho. *Perf. 14*
930 A555 7.60k Sheet of 2, #a-b 5.00 5.00

See Romania No.

Requisition, by Ivan Generalic (1914-92) — A556

2014, Nov. 17 Litho. *Perf. 14*
931 A556 3.10k multi 1.00 1.00

Christmas — A557

Litho. With Foil Application

2014, Nov. 27 *Perf. 14*
932 A557 3.10k multi 1.00 1.00

Booklet Stamp
Self-Adhesive

Serpentine Die Cut 5¼
933 A557 3.10k multi 1.00 1.00
a. Booklet pane of 10 10.00
Complete booklet, #933a 10.00

Royal University Library and Land Archives A558

Designs: No. 934, 4.60k, Building exterior. No. 935, 4.60k, Reading room. No. 936, 4.60k, Table lamps, vert.

2014, Dec. 1 Litho. *Perf. 14*
934-936 A558 Set of 3 4.50 4.50

New Year 2015 — A559

2014, Dec. 4 Litho. *Perf. 14*
937 A559 3.10k multi 1.00 1.00

St. Valentine's Day — A560

2015, Feb. 4 Litho. *Perf. 14*
938 A560 6.50k multi 1.90 1.90

Values are for stamps with surrounding selvage.

112 Emergency Services Day — A561

2015, Feb. 11 Litho. *Perf. 14*
939 A561 6.50k brt orange & blk 1.90 1.90

Pet Birds — A562

No. 940: a, Canary wearing horned helmet. b, Budgerigar wearing captain's hat. c, Zebra finch with didgeridoo. d, Sulphur-crested cockatoo wearing leather jacket.

2015, Feb. 19 Litho. *Perf. 14*
940 A562 3.10k Block of 4, #a-d 3.75 3.75

Rotary International District 1913, 110th Anniv. — A563

2015, Feb. 23 Litho. *Perf. 14*
941 A563 3.10k multi .90 .90

Easter — A564

Litho. With Foil Application

2015, Mar. 16 *Perf. 14*
942 A564 3.10k multi .90 .90

Croatian Paralympic Committee, 50th Anniv. — A565

2015, Mar. 23 Litho. *Perf. 14*
943 A565 5k multi 1.50 1.50

No. 943 was printed in sheets of 9 + label.

Lace — A566

No. 944: a, Colors of Croatian flag, lace from Lepoglav. b, Colors of Spanish flag, lace from Seville.

2015, Mar. 31 Litho. *Perf. 14*
944 A566 7.60k Pair, #a-b 4.50 4.50

See Spain No. 4037.

Wildlife — A567

Designs: 2.80k, Capreolus capreolus. 4.60k, Vulpes vulpes. 6.50k, Sus scrofa.

2015, Apr. 15 Litho. *Perf. 14*
945 A567 2.80k multi .85 .85
a. Booklet pane of 10 8.50 —
Complete booklet, #945a 8.50
946 A567 4.60k multi 1.40 1.40
a. Booklet pane of 10 14.00 —
Complete booklet, #946a 14.00
947 A567 6.50k multi 2.00 2.00
a. Booklet pane of 10 20.00 —
Complete booklet, #947a 20.00
Nos. 945-947 (3) 4.25 4.25

Famous People — A568

Designs: No. 948, 3.10k, Ivan Supek (1915-2007), scientist and writer. No. 949, 3.10k, Luka Sorkocevic (1734-89), composer. No. 950, 3.10k, Josip Juraj Strossmayer (1815-1905), bishop and politician.

2015, Apr. 21 Litho. *Perf. 14*
948-950 A568 Set of 3 2.75 2.75

1000th Stamp Design of Croatia Post — A569

2015, Apr. 27 Litho. *Perf. 14*
951 A569 3.10k multi .95 .95

Souvenir Sheet

Bridges — A570

No. 952: a, Modrus 1 Bridge. b, Krka River Bridge.

2015, Apr. 29 Litho. *Perf. 14*
952 A570 7.60k Sheet of 2, #a-b 4.50 4.50

Europa A571

Toys: 4.60k, To Tak wood pieces and connectors. 7.60k, Porcelain doll.

2015, May 7 Litho. *Perf. 14*
953-954 A571 Set of 2 3.75 3.75

International Telecommunications Union, 150th Anniv. — A572

2015, May 15 Litho. *Perf. 14*
955 A572 10k multi 3.00 3.00

Castles and Palaces Type of 2011

Designs: No. 956, 4.60k, Jankovic Castle, Daruvar. No. 957, 4.60k, Markovic-Kulmer Castle, Cernik. No. 958, 4.60k, Erdödy-Rubido Castle, Gornja Rijeka. No. 959, 4.60k, Old Town, Durdevac.

2015, May 20 Litho. *Perf. 14*
956-959 A470 Set of 4 5.50 5.50
959a Souvenir sheet of 8, 2 each #956-959, + 8 labels 11.00 11.00

Lighthouses — A573

Designs: 2.80k, Daksa Lighthouse. 3.10k, Glavat Lighthouse. 4.60k, Grebeni Lighthouse. 6.50k, Sveti Andrija Lighthouse.

2015, June 10 Litho. *Perf. 14*
960-963 A573 Set of 4 5.00 5.00

Bracera — A574

2015, July 9 Litho. *Perf. 14*
964 A574 5.80k multi 1.75 1.75

A575

UNESCO Intangible Cultural Heritage — A576

Designs: No. 965, 3.10k, Zvoncari (carnival procession of bell ringers from Kastav). No. 966, 3.10k, Becarac (musician with stringed instrument). No. 967, 3.10k, Klapsko Pjevanje (a capella singers). No. 968, 3.10k, Sinjska Alka (horseman at Alka Chivalric Tournament, Sinj).

11k, Alka Chivalric Tournament, 300th anniv.

2015, July 27 Litho. *Perf. 14*
965-968 A575 Set of 4 3.75 3.75
968a Souvenir sheet of 4, #965-968, + 5 labels 3.75 3.75

Souvenir Sheet

Litho., Sheet Margin Litho. With Foil Application

969 A576 11k multi 3.25 3.25

Victory and Homeland Thanksgiving Day — A577

2015, Aug. 3 Litho. *Perf. 14*
970 A577 3.10k multi .90 .90

2015 Men's European Basketball Cahmpionships, Zagreb — A578

2015, Sept. 4 Litho. *Perf. 14*
971 A578 5k multi 1.50 1.50

No. 971 was printed in sheets of 8 + label.

Traffic Safety — A579

2015, Sept. 7 Litho. *Perf. 14*
972 A579 3.10k multi .95 .95

Christmas A580

2015, Nov. 25 Litho. *Perf. 14*
973 A580 3.10k multi .90 .90

Booklet Stamp Self-Adhesive

Serpentine Die Cut 5¼

974 A580 3.10k multi .90 .90
a. Booklet pane of 10 9.00
Complete booklet, #974a 9.00

Sculpture A581

Designs: 1.20k, Metal Sculpture XX, by Dusan Dzamonja. 3.10k, Dunja I, by Kosta Angeli Radovani. 4.60k, The Bull, by Vojin Bakic.

2015, Dec. 1 Litho. *Perf. 14*
975-977 A581 Set of 3 2.50 2.50

SEMI-POSTAL STAMPS

Catalogue values for unused stamps in this section are for Never Hinged items.

Types of Yugoslavia, 1941, Overprinted in Gold "NEZAVISNA / DRZAVA / HRVATSKA"

Perf. 11½

1941, May 10 Unwmk. Engr.
B1 SP80 1.50d + 1.50d bl blk 22.50 22.50
B2 SP81 4d + 3d choc 22.50 22.50

Panes of 16 stamps and 9 labels.
This overprint exists on Yugoslavia No. B124. Value $2,500.

In 1941, 5,000 sets of Yugoslavia Nos. 142-154 were overprinted "NEZAVISNA DRZAVA HRVATSKA 10. IV. 1941" and with a small shield in red or blue. Sold for double face value. Value: set, $550.

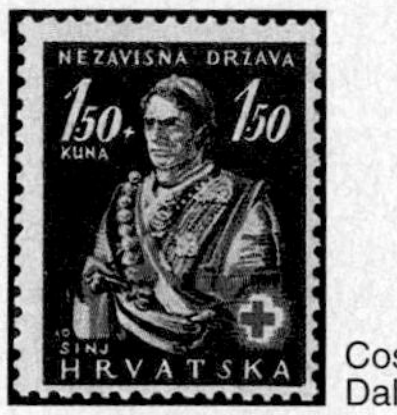

Costume of Sinj, Dalmatia — SP1

Designs (Costumes): 2k+2k, Travnik, Bosnia. 4k+4k, Turopolje, Croatia.

1941, Oct. 12 Photo. *Perf. 10½x10*
B3 SP1 1.50k + 1.50k Prus bl & red 1.00 1.00
B4 SP1 2k + 2k ol brn & red 1.25 1.25
B5 SP1 4k + 4k brn lake & red 2.25 2.25
Nos. B3-B5 (3) 4.50 4.50

The surtax aided the Croatian Red Cross.
Nos. B3-B5 were issued in panes of 20 stamps and 5 labels.
Nos. B3-B5 exist with a special printer's mark in the design. The printer's mark appears on one stamp in one pane of the four in the printed sheet. Value, $35 each.

Soldiers with Arms of the Axis States — SP4

1941, Dec. 3 *Perf. 11*
B6 SP4 4k + 2k blue 3.75 *4.00*

The surtax was used for Croatian Volunteers in the East.
Issued in panes of 100 stamps.

Model Plane — SP5

Model Plane — SP6

Designs: 3k+3k, Boy with model plane. 4k+4k, Model seaplane in flight.

1942, Mar. 25
B7 SP5 2k + 2k sepia 1.90 1.90
B8 SP6 2.50k + 2.50k dl grn 1.90 1.90
B9 SP5 3k + 3k brn car 1.90 1.90
B10 SP6 4k + 4k dp bl 1.90 1.90
Nos. B7-B10 (4) 7.60 7.60

Nos. B7-B10 were issued both in panes of 25 and in panes of 24 plus label.
Nos. B7-B10 exist with a special printer's mark in the design. The mark appears on one stamp in every pane. Value, $10

Values for used souvenir sheets are for those with special philatelic cancels. Faked postal cancellations on souvenir sheets are common, especially using cancellers stolen after WWII. Genuine postal cancellations are the exception and sell for much more. Expertization is recommended.

Souvenir Sheets

Perf. 11

B11 Sheet of 2 45.00 45.00
a. SP5 2k+8k brown carmine 15.00 15.00
b. SP5 3k+12k deep blue 15.00 15.00

Imperf

B12 Sheet of 2 45.00 45.00
a. SP5 2k+8k deep blue 15.00 15.00
b. SP5 3k+12k brown carmine 15.00 15.00

The sheets measure 125x110mm.
Aviation Exposition of Zagreb. The surtax aided society of Croatian Wings (Hrvatska Krila).
Nos. B11-B12 exist with colors of stamps and inscriptions transposed, with missing colors and with one stamp missing.
Nos. B11-B12 exist with a special printer's mark in the design. The mark typically appears on one stamp in a given pane.

Boy Trumpeters SP10

Triumphal Arch — SP11

Mother and Child — SP12

1942, July 5 *Perf. 11½*

B13 SP10 3k + 1k lake 1.50 1.50
B14 SP11 4k + 2k dk brn 1.60 1.60
B15 SP12 5k + 5k dp bl grn 2.40 2.40
Nos. B13-B15 (3) 5.50 5.50

The surtax was for national welfare. Issued in panes of 25.

Nos. B13-B15 exist with a special printer's mark in the design. The printer's mark appears on one stamp in one pane of the four in the printed sheet. Value, $40 each.

Matthew Gubec SP13

Ante Starcevich SP14

SP15

1942, Nov. 22 *Perf. 14½*

B16 SP13 3k + 6k dark red 1.00 1.00
B17 SP14 4k + 7k sepia 1.00 1.00

Souvenir Sheets

Perf. 12, Imperf.

B18 SP15 5k + 20k dull blue 24.00 24.00

Heroes of Senj, May 9, 1937. Nos. B16-B17 were printed in panes of 16 + 9 labels, each bearing a hero's name. The surtax aided the Natl. Youth Soc.

Sestine Peasant — SP16

Designs: 3k+1k, Slavonian peasant. 4k+2k, Bosnian peasant. 10k+5k, Dalmatian peasant. 13k+6k, Sestine peasant.

1942, Oct. 4 *Perf. 11½*

B20 SP16 1.50k + 50b org brn & red 1.40 1.40
B21 SP16 3k + 1k dl pur & red 1.40 1.40
B22 SP16 4k + 2k dp bl & red 2.10 2.10
B23 SP16 10k + 5k dk ol bis & red 3.00 3.00
B24 SP16 13k + 6k rose lake & red 5.50 5.50
Nos. B20-B24 (5) 13.40 13.40

The surtax aided the Croatian Red Cross. Issued in panes of 24 stamps plus label.

Croatian Labor Corpsman — SP20

Designs: 3k+3k, Corpsman with wheelbarrow. 7k+4k, Corpsman plowing.

1943, Jan. 17 **Wmk. 278** *Perf. 11*

B25 SP20 2k + 1k ol gray & sepia 4.75 *5.00*
B26 SP20 3k + 3k brn & sepia 4.75 *5.00*
B27 SP20 7k + 4k gray bl & sepia 4.75 *5.00*
Nos. B25-B27 (3) 14.25 *15.00*

The surtax aided the State Labor Service (Drzavna Radna Sluzba). Issued in panes of 9.

Arms of Zagreb and "Golden Bull" — SP23

1943, Mar. 21 **Unwmk.**

B28 SP23 3.50k (+ 6.50k) ultra 4.50 *4.75*

700th anniversary of Zagreb's "Golden Bull," a Magna Carta of civic rights and privileges granted to the city in 1242 by King Bela because the Croats annihilated Tartar hordes at Grobnik.

Issued in panes of 8 with marginal inscriptions.

Ante Pavelich — SP24

1943, Apr. 10 *Perf. 13¾x14*

B29 SP24 5k + 3k copper red .60 .60
a. Sheetlet of 16 #B29 + 9 labels 12.00 12.00
B30 SP24 7k + 5k dark green .60 .60
a. Sheetlet of 16 #B30 + 9 labels 12.00 12.00

Surtax aided the National Youth Society.

Nos. B29-B30 were issued in panes of 100 stamps. Nos. B29a and B30a were issued Apr. 12 and are perf 14½.

Souvenir Sheets

1943, May 17 *Perf. 12, Imperf.*

B31 SP24 12k + 8k dp ultra 30.00 30.00

Sailor at Sea of Azov — SP26

Designs: 2k+1k, Flier at Sevastopol and Rzhev. 3.50k+1.50k, Infantrymen at Stalingrad. 9k+4.50k, Panzer Division at Don River.

1943, July 1 *Perf. 11*

B33 SP26 1k + 50b grn .40 .25
B34 SP26 2k + 1k dk red .40 .25
B35 SP26 3.50k + 1.50k dk bl .40 .25
B36 SP26 9k + 4.50k chestnut .40 .25
Nos. B33-B36 (4) 1.60 1.00

Souvenir Sheets

Perf. 11, Imperf.

B37 Sheet of 4 7.50 7.50
a. SP26 1k+50b dark blue 1.40 *1.40*
b. SP26 2k+1k green 1.40 *1.40*
c. SP26 3.50k+1.50k dk red brown 1.40 *1.40*
d. SP26 9k+4.50k bluish black 1.40 *1.40*

Surtax aided the National Youth Society. Issued to honor the Croatian Legion which fought with the Germans in Russia. The surtax aided the Legion.

Issued in panes of 100.

St. Mary's Church and Cistercian Cloister, Zagreb, in 1650 SP31

1943, Sept. 12 **Engr.** *Perf. 14½*

B39 SP31 18k + 9k dl gray vio 5.25 5.25

Souvenir Sheet

Perf. 12½

B40 SP31 18k + 9k blk brn 13.00 13.00

Croatian Phil. Soc. Exhibition at Zagreb. No. B39 issued in pane of 40.

Nos. B39-B40 exist with a special printer's mark in the design. The printer's mark appears on one stamp in the pane for No. 39, value $30; the mark appears on one souvenir sheet of the six in the printed sheet for No. B40, value $52.50.

No. B39 Ovptd. in Red

1943, Sept. 12

B41 SP31 18k + 9k dl gray vio 12.00 *14.00*

Return to Croatia of the Dalmatian and Croatian coasts.

The overprint exists inverted, double, and double, one inverted.

No. B41 exists with a special printer's mark in the design. The mark typically appears on one stamp in a given pane.

Mother and Children — SP33

Nurse and Patient — SP34

1943, Oct. 3 **Litho.** *Perf. 11*

Cross in Red

B42 SP33 1k + 50b bl grn .75 .75
B43 SP33 2k + 1k bril car .75 .75
B44 SP33 3.50k + 1.50k brt bl .75 .75
B45 SP34 8k + 3k red brn .90 .90
B46 SP34 9k + 4k yel grn 1.00 1.00
B47 SP33 10k + 5k dp vio 1.00 1.00
B48 SP34 12k + 6k brt ultra 1.25 1.25
B49 SP33 12.50k + 6k dk brn 1.75 1.75
B50 SP34 18k + 8k brn org 2.00 2.00
B51 SP34 32k + 12k dk gray 3.25 3.25
Nos. B42-B51 (10) 13.40 13.40

The surtax aided the Croatian Red Cross. Issued in panes of 100.

Post Horn and Arms — SP35

Carrier Pigeon and Plane — SP36

Mercury — SP37

Winged Wheel — SP38

1944, Feb. 3

B52 SP35 7k + 3.50k ol bis & red .90 .90
a. Double impression of red —
B53 SP36 16k + 8k bl & dk bl .90 .90
B54 SP37 24k + 12k red & rose red .90 .90
B55 SP38 32k + 16k gray & red .90 .90
Nos. B52-B55 (4) 3.60 3.60

The surtax benefited communications and railway employees. Panes of 9.

St. Sebastian — SP39

War Invalids SP40

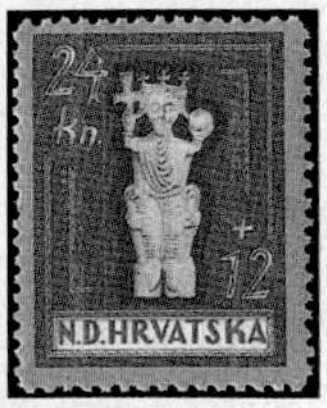

Statue of Ancient Croatian King — SP41

Death of King Peter Svacic, 1097 — SP42

1944, Feb. 15

B56 SP39 7k + 3.50k org red & rose car 1.00 1.00
B57 SP40 16k + 8k yel grn & dk grn 1.00 1.00
B58 SP41 24k + 12k yel brn & red 1.00 1.00
B59 SP42 32k + 16k bl & dk bl 1.00 1.00
Nos. B56-B59 (4) 4.00 4.00

The surtax aided wounded war victims.

Issued in panes of eight stamps, with marginal inscriptions and a central label picturing St. Sebastian.

Black Legion in Combat — SP43

Guarding the Drina — SP44

Jure Francetic — SP45

1944, May 22 Photo. *Imperf.*

B60	SP43	3.50k + 1.50k brn red	.25	.25
B61	SP44	12.50k + 6.50k slate bl	.25	.25
B62	SP45	18k + 9k olive brn	.25	.25
		Nos. B60-B62 (3)	.75	.75

Third anniversary of Croatian independence.
The surtax aided the National Youth Society. Panes of 20.

Perf. 14½

B63	SP45	12.50k + 287.50k int blk	12.00	*14.50*

Issued to commemorate Jure Francetic.
Issued in pane of 30.

Labor Corpsmen Marching SP46 — Corpsman Digging SP47

Designs: 18k+9k, Officer instructing corpsman. 32k+16k, Pavelich reviewing Labor Corps. Panes of 8 plus label.

Perf. 11½, 12½, 14½

1944, Aug. 20 Engr.

B65	SP46	3.50k + 1k dk red	.50	.50
B66	SP47	12.50k + 6k sepia	.50	.50
B67	SP47	18k + 9k dk bl	.50	.50
B68	SP47	32k + 16k gray grn	.50	.50
		Nos. B65-B68 (4)	2.00	2.00

Nos. B68 exists only perf 12½, while B65-B67 exist perf 11½, 12½ or 14½. Values are for copies perf 11½ or 12½. Values Nos. B65-B67 perf 14½, $5 each unused or used.

Souvenir Sheet
Perf. 12½

B69	SP47	32k + 16k dk brn, *cr*	4.50	*5.00*

The surtax aided the State Labor Service (Drzavna Radna Sluzba).

Palm Leaf — SP51

1944, Nov. 12 Litho. *Perf. 11*

B70	SP51	2k + 1k dl grn & red	.45	.45
B71	SP51	3.50k + 1.50k car lake & red	.45	.45
B72	SP51	12.50k + 6k ind & red	.45	.45
		Nos. B70-B72 (3)	1.35	1.35

The surtax aided the Croatian Red Cross. Panes of 16.

Men of Storm Division — SP52

70k+70k, Soldiers of Storm Division in action. 100k+100k, Storm Division emblem.

1944 Unwmk. Litho. *Perf. 11*

B73	SP52	50k + 50k brick red	175.00	*190.00*
B74	SP52	70k + 70k sepia	175.00	*190.00*
B75	SP52	100k + 100k chlky, pale & dp bl	175.00	*190.00*
		Nos. B73-B75 (3)	525.00	*570.00*

Nos. B73-B75 issued in panes of 20.

Souvenir Sheet

B76		Sheet of 3	1,650.	1,650.
a.	SP52	50k + 50k brick red	400.	400.
b.	SP52	70k + 70k sepia	400.	400.
c.	SP52	100k + 100k chalky, pale & deep blue	400.	400.

Nos. B76a to B76c are inscribed "O. A." in brick red at right below design. The sheet measures 216x132mm. The surtax aided the First Croatian Storm Division. Counterfeits are plentiful.

Postman SP55 — Telephone Line Repairman SP56

24k+12k, Switchboard operator. 50k+25k, 100k+50k, Postman delivering parcel.

1945 Photo.

B77	SP55	3.50k + 1.50k sl gray	.40	.40
B78	SP56	12.50k + 6k brn car	.40	.40
B79	SP56	24k + 12k dk grn	.40	.40
B80	SP56	50k + 25k brn vio	.40	.40
		Nos. B77-B80 (4)	1.60	1.60

Souvenir Sheet

B81	SP56	100k + 50k dp brn	11.00	11.00

The surtax on #B77-B81 aided employees of the P.T.T. Panes of 8.

Famous Croatians SP60

No. B100, Ban Josip Jelacic (1801-59). No. B101, Dr. Ante Starcevic (1823-96). 7d + 3d, Stjepan Radic (1871-1928).

1992 Litho. *Perf. 11x10½*

B100	SP60	4d +2d multi	.65	.65
B101	SP60	4d +2d multi	.65	.65

Perf. 14

B102	SP60	7d +3d multi	.65	.65
		Nos. B100-B102 (3)	1.95	1.95

Issued: No. B100, 2/1; No. B101, 3/4; No. B102, 4/2.
The surcharge on Nos. B100-B102 was initially an obligatory tax on all internal and overseas mail. From May 15, 1992, these stamps were valid for postage at their 6d or 10d face values.

AIR POST STAMPS

Catalogue values for unused stamps in this section are for Never Hinged items.

Airplane, Zagreb Cathedral and Port of Dubrovnik AP1

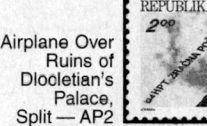

Airplane Over Ruins of Diocletian's Palace, Split — AP2

Coat of Arms, Airplane, Zagreb Cathedral and Pula Amphitheatre AP3

Paper Airplane Made From Picture of Osijek Cathedral AP4

1991-92 Litho. *Perf. 11x10½*

C1	AP1	1d multicolored	*.50*	.50
a.		Perf. 14	.50	.50
C2	AP2	2d multicolored	*1.50*	.50
a.		Perf. 14	.50	.50
C3	AP3	3d multicolored	*.50*	.50
C4	AP4	4d multicolored	*.50*	.50
		Nos. C1-C4 (4)	*3.00*	2.00

Issued: No. C1, 9/9/91; No. C1a, 6/24/92; No. C2, 10/9/91; No. C2a, 1992; No. C3, 11/20/91; No. C4, 2/14/92.

Miniature Sheet

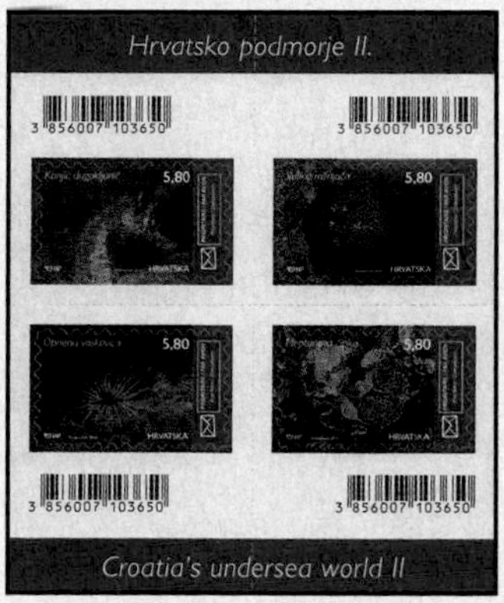

Marine Life — AP5

No. C5: a, Long-snouted seahorse (konjic dugokljunic). b, Violescent sea-whip (velika roznjaca). c, Cylinder anemone (opnena voskovica). d, Neptune's lace (neptunova cipka).

Serpentine Die Cut 5½x5¼

2015, June 15 Litho.

Self-Adhesive

C5	AP5	Sheet of 4	7.00	
a.-d.		5.80k Any single	1.75	1.75

POSTAGE DUE STAMPS

Yugoslavia Nos. J28-J32 Overprinted in Black

1941, Apr. 26 Unwmk. *Perf. 12½*

J1	D4	50p violet	.40	*.65*
a.		Double overprint	150.00	
b.		50p rose violet	9.00	*18.00*
c.		As "b," double overprint	200.00	
J2	D4	1d deep magenta	.40	*.65*
a.		Inverted overprint	200.00	
b.		Double overprint		*300.00*
J3	D4	2d deep blue	10.00	*20.00*
a.		Double overprint	300.00	
J4	D4	5d orange	1.25	*2.00*
a.		Double overprint	300.00	
J5	D4	10d chocolate	6.00	*12.00*
		Nos. J1-J5 (5)	18.05	*35.30*
		Set, never hinged	40.00	

Counterfeit overprints exist, particularly of Nos. J3 and J5.

D1

1941, Sept. 12 Litho. *Perf. 11*

J6	D1	50b carmine lake	.25	*.50*
J7	D1	1k carmine lake	.25	*.50*
J8	D1	2k carmine lake	.30	*.70*
J9	D1	5k carmine lake	.50	*1.00*
J10	D1	10k carmine lake	.75	*1.40*
		Nos. J6-J10 (5)	2.05	*4.10*
		Set, never hinged	5.00	

D2

1943 *Perf. 11½, 12x12½, 12½*

Size: 24x24mm

J11	D2	50b lt blue & gray	.25	*.25*
J12	D2	1k lt blue & gray	.25	*.25*
J13	D2	2k lt blue & gray	.25	*.25*
J14	D2	4k lt blue & gray	.25	*.35*
J15	D2	5k lt blue & gray	.25	*.40*
J16	D2	6k lt blue & gray	.25	*.45*
J17	D2	10k blue & indigo	.25	*.40*
J18	D2	15k blue & indigo	.25	*1.10*
J19	D2	20k blue & indigo	.65	*1.60*
		Nos. J11-J19 (9)	2.65	*5.05*
		Set, never hinged	5.00	

1942, July 30 *Perf. 10½, 11½*

Size: 25x24¼mm

J20	D2	50b lt blue & gray	.25	*.40*
J21	D2	1k lt blue & gray	.25	*.50*
J22	D2	2k lt blue & gray	.25	*.50*
J23	D2	5k lt blue & gray	.25	*.50*
J24	D2	10k lt blue & blue	.65	*1.10*
J25	D2	20k lt blue & blue	.90	*1.60*
		Nos. J20-J25 (6)	2.55	*4.60*
		Set, never hinged	6.00	

Nos. J21-J25 exist both perf 10½ and 11½. No. J20 exists only perf 11½.

OFFICIAL STAMPS

Croatian Coat of Arms
O1 O2

1942-43 **Unwmk.** **Litho.**

Ordinary Paper

Perf. 11½

O1	O1	25b	rose lake	.25	.25
O2	O1	50b	slate blk	.25	.25
O3	O1	75b	gray grn	.25	.25
O4	O1	1k	orange brn	.25	.25
O5	O1	2k	turq blue	1.10	*1.10*
O6	O1	3k	vermilion	.25	.25
O7	O1	4k	brown vio	.25	.25
O8	O1	5k	ultra, *thin paper*	.25	*.40*
O9	O1	6k	brt violet	.25	.25
O10	O1	10k	lt green	.25	*.30*
O11	O1	12k	brown rose	.25	*.35*
O12	O1	20k	dark blue	.25	*.40*
O13	O2	30k	brn vio & gray	.25	*.40*
O14	O2	40k	vio blk & gray	.30	*.50*
O15	O2	50k	brn lake & gray	.65	*1.00*
O16	O2	100k	black & pink	.65	*1.00*
			Nos. O1-O16 (16)	5.70	*7.20*
			Set, never hinged	8.00	

Perf. 10½

O1a	O1	25b	rose lake	.25	.25
O2a	O1	50b	slate blk	.25	.25
O3a	O1	75b	gray grn	.25	.25
O4a	O1	1k	orange brn	.25	.25
O5a	O1	2k	turq blue	1.10	*2.00*
O6a	O1	3k	vermilion	.25	.25
O7a	O1	4k	brown vio	.25	.25
O8a	O1	5k	ultra	.95	*1.75*
O9a	O1	6k	brt violet	1.40	*2.50*
O10a	O1	10k	lt green	.25	.25
O11a	O1	12k	brown rose	1.25	*2.25*
O12a	O1	20k	dark blue	1.25	*2.25*
O13a	O2	30k	brn vio & gray	.25	*.40*
O14a	O2	40k	vio blk & gray	.30	*.50*
O15a	O2	50k	brn lake & gray	.65	*1.00*
O16a	O2	100k	black & pink	.65	*1.00*
			Nos. O1a-O16a (16)	9.55	*15.40*
			Set, never hinged	15.00	

1943-44 **Thin Paper** ***Perf. 11½***

O17	O1	25b	claret	.25	.25
O18	O1	50b	gray	.25	.25
O19	O1	75b	dull green	.25	.25
O20	O1	1k	orange brn	.25	.25
O21	O1	2k	slate blue	.25	.25
O22	O1	3.50k	car rose	.25	.25
a.			Ordinary paper	3.00	*3.00*
O23	O1	6k	brt red vio	.25	.25
O24	O1	12.50k	deep orange	.25	.25
a.			Ordinary paper	2.00	*2.00*
			Set, never hinged	1.50	

POSTAL TAX STAMPS

Catalogue values for unused stamps in this section are for Never Hinged items.

Nurse and Soldier — PT1

Unwmk.

1942, Oct. 4 **Litho.** ***Perf. 11***

RA1 PT1 1k olive grn & red .85 .80

The tax aided the Croatian Red Cross. Issued in sheets of 24 plus label.

No. RA1 can be found with a red cross printed on the nurse's hat. The original design included this element, but it was removed from the final approved design. Early printings of No. RA1, probably trial printings, included the red cross.

Wounded Soldier — PT2

1943, Oct. 3

RA2 PT2 2k blue & red .70 .70

The tax aided the Croatian Red Cross.

Ruins — PT3

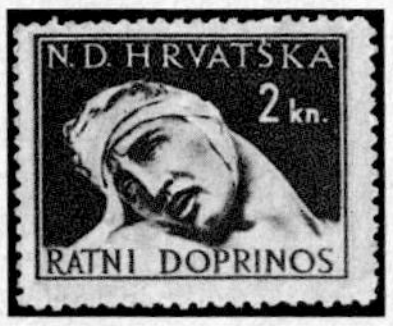

Wounded Soldier — PT4

1944, Jan. 1 **Photo.** ***Perf. 12***

RA3	PT3	1k	dk slate green	.25	.25
RA4	PT4	2k	carmine lake	.30	.30
RA5	PT4	5k	black	.35	.35
RA6	PT4	10k	deep blue	.55	.40
RA7	PT4	20k	brown	1.10	.90
			Nos. RA3-RA7 (5)	2.55	2.20

Interior of Zagreb Cathedral PT10

1991, Apr. 1 **Litho.** ***Perf. 14***

RA20	PT10 1.20d black & gold	.65	.55
a.	Perf. 11x10½	.85	.80
b.	Perf. 11	15.00	12.00
c.	Imperf	.90	.90

Worker's Fund. Required on mail during April 1991.

For surcharges see Nos. 100, 100a.

Shrine of the Virgin, 700th Anniv. PT11

1991, May 16 ***Perf. 10½x11***

RA21	PT11 1.70d multicolored	.80	.65
a.	Imperf	1.25	1.10

Workers' Fund. Required on mail May 16-31.

Croatian Arms Type of 1992

1991, July 1 ***Perf. 11x10½***

RA22	A37 2.20d multicolored	.80	.70
a.	Imperf	1.25	1.00

Required on mail during July.

Members of Parliament PT12

1991, Aug. 1 ***Perf. 11x10½***

RA23	PT12 2.20d multicolored	.80	.70
a.	Imperf	1.25	1.00

Worker's Fund. Required on mail during Aug.

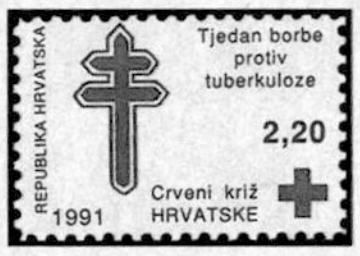

Red Cross and Tuberculosis PT13

1991, Sept 14 ***Perf. 11***

RA24 PT13 2.20d blue & red .50 .45

Required on mail Sept. 14-21.

Re-erection of Ban Josip Jelacic Equestrian Statue, Zagreb PT14

1991, Nov. 1 ***Perf. 11x10½***

RA25	PT14 2.20d multicolored	.80	.70
a.	Imperf.	1.25	1.00

Worker's Fund. Required on mail during Nov.

New Constitution PT15

1991, Dec. 2 **Litho.** ***Perf. 10¾x10½***

Language of Inscription

RA26	PT15 2.20d English	*3.25*	*3.00*
RA27	PT15 2.20d Croatian	*1.15*	*1.00*
RA28	PT15 2.20d French	*3.25*	*3.00*
RA29	PT15 2.20d German	*3.25*	*3.00*
RA30	PT15 2.20d Russian	*3.25*	*3.00*
RA31	PT15 2.20d Spanish	*3.25*	*3.00*
a.	Vert. strip, #RA26-RA31	*35.00*	*35.00*
	Nos. RA26-RA31 (6)	17.40	16.00

Nos RA26-RA31 were printed in sheet containing 15 of No. RA27, 2 each of the other stamps and five labels. Obligatory on mail Dec. 2-31.

Sheet exists imperf. Value $225.

"VUKOVAR" with Barbed Wire — PT16

1992, Jan. 1 **Litho.** ***Perf. 11x10½***

RA32	PT16 2.20d black & brown	1.15	.90
a.	Imperf.	1.60	1.40

Vukovar Refugee's Fund. Required on mail during Jan.

Red Cross PT17

Red Cross and Solidarity PT18

1992 ***Perf. 11***

RA33	PT17 3d red & black	.50	.50
RA34	PT18 3d red & black	.30	.30

Issued: No. RA33, May 8. No. RA34, June 1.

No. RA33 was required on mail May 8-15; No. RA34, June 1-7.

Madonna of Bistrica — PT19

1992, Aug. 1 **Litho.** ***Perf. 14***

RA35 PT19 5d blue & gold .45 .40

Required on mail, Aug. 1-8.

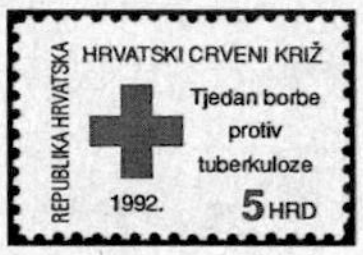

Red Cross — PT20

1992, Sept. 21 **Litho.** ***Perf. 11***

RA36 PT20 5d black & red .50 .30

Required on mail Sept. 14-21.

St. George Slaying Dragon PT21

1992, Nov. 4 ***Perf. 14***

RA37 PT21 15d multicolored .50 .30

Cancer Research League. Required on mail Nov. 4-11.

See No. RA43.

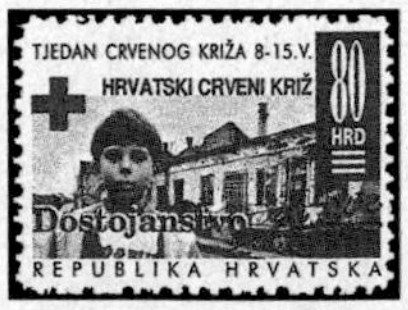

Red Cross — PT22

1993, May 8 **Litho.** ***Rough Perf. 11***

RA38 PT22 80d black & red .50 .30

Required on mail May 8-15.

Red Cross and Solidarity PT23

1993, June 1

RA39 PT23 100d black & red .50 .30

Required on mail June 1-7.

Cardinal Stepinac (1898-1960) PT24

1993, July 15 Litho. *Perf. 14*
RA40 PT24 150d multicolored .50 .30

Required on mail July 15-22.

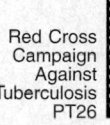

Zrinski-Frankopan Foundation — PT25

Design: 200d, Gen. Peter Zrinski (1621-1671), Politician and Fran Krsto Frankopan, Count of Tersat (1643-1671), Poet.

1993, Aug. 12 Litho. *Perf. 14*
RA41 PT25 200d gray & blue .50 .30

Required on mail Aug. 12-19.

Red Cross Campaign Against Tuberculosis PT26

1993, Sept. 14 Litho. *Perf. 11*
RA42 PT26 300d gray, red & black .50 .45

Required on mail Sept. 14-21.

St. George Slaying Dragon Type of 1992

1993, Oct. 11 Litho. *Perf. 14*
RA43 PT21 400d multicolored .45 .40

Cancer Research League. Required on mail Oct. 11-31.

Save the Children of Croatia PT27

1993, Nov. 1 *Perf. 13½x14*
RA44 PT27 400d multicolored .50 .45

Required on mail Nov. 1-30.

Croatian Red Cross — PT28

1994, May 5 Litho. *Perf. 11*
RA45 PT28 500d multicolored .50 .45

Required on mail May 8-15.

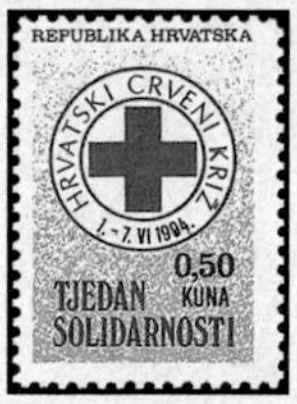

Red Cross Solidarity — PT29

1994, May 5 Litho. *Perf. 11*
RA46 PT29 50 l multicolored .50 .45

Required on mail June 1-7.

Ludberg Church — PT30

1994, July 15 *Perf. 14*
RA47 PT30 50 l multicolored .50 .30

Required on mail July 15-22.

Save the Children of Croatia — PT31

1994, Aug. 16 Litho. *Perf. 14*
RA48 PT31 50 l multicolored .50 .30

Required on mail Aug. 16-29.

St. George Slaying Dragon — PT32

1994, Sept. 1
RA49 PT32 50 l multicolored .50 .30

Cancer Research League. Required on mail Sept. 1-8.

PT33

1994, Sept. 14 *Perf. 11*
RA50 PT33 50 l blk, grn & red .50 .30

Red Cross Campaign against Tuberculosis. Required on mail Sept. 14-21.

PT34

1994, Oct. 15 Litho. *Perf. 14*
RA51 PT34 50 l multicolored .50 .35

Town of Slavonski Brod, 750th anniv.

Homage to Olympia, by Ivan Lackovic PT35

Intl. Olympic Committee, Cent. — PT36

Designs: a, Tennis. b, Soccer. c, Basketball. d, Team handball. e, Canoeing, kayaking. f, Water polo. g, Track and field. h, Gymnastics.

1994, Nov. 2 Litho. *Perf. 14*
RA52 PT35 50 l Pair, #a.-b. 1.40 1.25
RA53 PT36 50 l Sheet of 8, #a.-h. 5.75 5.75
RA54 PT36 50 l Sheet of 8, #a.-h. 5.75 5.75

Nos. RA52b, RA53a, RA53d-RA53e, RA53h, RA54b-RA54c, RA54f-RA54g have IOC centennial emblem. Others have emblem of Croatian Olympic Committee.
Required on mail Nov. 2-15.

Natl. Olympic Committee PT37

Designs: a, Rowing. b, Pétanque. c, Monument to Drazen Petrovic, Olympic Park, Lausanne. d, Tennis. e, Basketball.

1995, Apr. 17 Litho. *Perf. 14*
RA55 PT37 50 l Strip of 5, #a.-e. 2.00 2.00

Required on mail Apr. 17-30.

Red Cross Stamps — PT38

1995, May 8 *Perf. 11*
RA56 PT38 50 l multicolored .50 .30

Required on mail May 8-15.

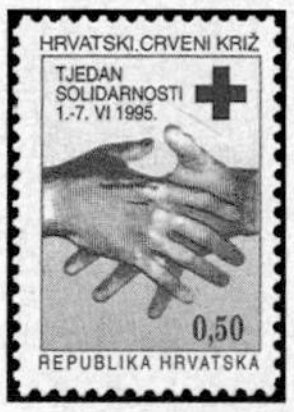

Red Cross Stamps — PT39

1995, June 1
RA57 PT39 50 l multicolored .50 .30

Required on mail June 1-7.

Sts. Peter and Paul Cathedral, Osijek — PT40

1995, July 17 *Perf. 14*
RA58 PT40 65 l multicolored .50 .40

Required on mail July 17-30.

Holy Mother of Freedom PT41

Design: No. RA59, Like No. RA60, but with black surcharge on white panel. #RA60, Croatian Pieta, by Ivan Lackovic. #RA61, Gedenkstatte Church Project.

1995, Aug. 14 Litho. *Perf. 14*
RA59 PT41 65 l on 50 l multi 2.50 2.50
RA60 PT41 65 l multicolored .55 .50
RA61 PT41 65 l multicolored .55 .50
Nos. RA59-RA61 (3) 3.60 3.50

No. RA59 not issued without surcharge. Examples without surcharge are printer's waste. Required on mail Aug. 14-27.

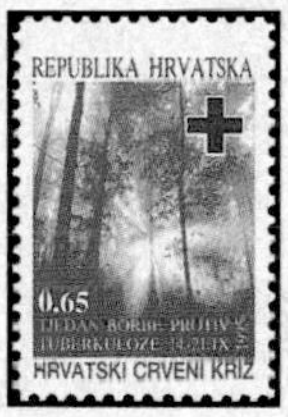

Red Cross and Tuberculosis — PT42

1995, Sept. 14 Litho. *Perf. 11*
RA62 PT42 65 l multicolored .50 .40

Required on mail Sept. 14-21.

Save the Croatian Children — PT43

1995, Oct. 16 *Perf. 14*
RA63 PT43 65 l multicolored .50 .40

Required on mail Oct. 16-29.

PT44

Performance scene: a, Woman seated at top of steps. b, Gathering of people. c, People, large statue in background.

1995, Oct. 16
RA64 PT44 65 l Strip of 3, #a.-c. 1.50 1.50

Croatian Natl. Theater, Zagreb, cent. No. RA64 has continuous design. Required on mail 10/16-29.

PT45

1995, Nov. 6 Litho. *Perf. 14*
RA65 PT45 65 l multicolored .50 .35

Fight against drugs. Required on mail Nov. 20-30.

PT46

1995, Nov. 20 Litho. *Perf. 14x13¾*
RA66 PT46 65 l multicolored .50 .35

Croatian Anti-Cancer League. Required on mail Nov. 20-30.

PT47

1996, Feb. 15 Litho. *Perf. 14x13½*
RA67 PT47 65 l multicolored .50 .35

Croatian Anti-Cancer League. Required on mail Feb. 15-28.

PT48

1996, Mar. 18 Litho. *Perf. 14*
RA68 PT48 65 l multicolored .50 .35

Sanctuary of the Virgin Mary of Bistrica. Required on mail Mar. 18-31.

Croatian Olympic Committee PT49

1996, Apr. 17 Litho. *Perf. 14*
RA69 PT49 65 l multi .60 .35

No. RA69 exists imperf. and in booklets, which were not placed on sale. Required on mail Apr. 17-30.

PT50

1996, May 8 Litho. *Perf. 11*
RA70 PT50 65 l multicolored .50 .35

Red Cross. Required on mail May 8-15.

PT51

1996, June 6 Litho. *Perf. 11*
RA71 PT51 65 l multicolored .50 .35

Red Cross Solidarity Week. Required on mail June 1-7.

PT52

1996, June 14 Litho. *Perf. 14x13½*
RA72 PT52 65 l multicolored .50 .35

For Croatian children. Required on mail 6/14-27.

PT53

1996, July 3 Litho. *Perf. 14*
RA73 PT53 65 l multicolored .50 .35

Osijek, 800th anniv. Required on mail July 3-16.

PT54

1996, July 17 Litho. *Perf. 14*
RA74 PT54 65 l multicolored .50 .35

Renovation of Dakovo Cathedral. Required on mail July 17-30.

PT55

1996, Aug. 1 Litho. *Perf. 14*
RA75 PT55 65 l multicolored .50 .35

Split, 1700th anniv. Required on mail Aug. 1-14.

PT56

1996, Aug. 16 Litho. *Perf. 14x13½*
RA76 PT56 65 l multicolored .50 .35

Aid to Vukovar. Required on mail 8/16-29.

PT57

1996, Sept. 1 Litho. *Perf. 14*
RA77 PT57 65 l multicolored .55 .35

Fight against drugs. Required on mail Sept. 1-12.

PT58

1996, Sept. 14 Litho. *Perf. 11*
RA78 PT58 65 l multicolored .50 .35

Red Cross Tuberculosis Week. Required on mail Sept. 14-21.

PT59

1996, Oct. 10 Litho. *Perf. 14*
RA79 PT59 65 l multicolored .55 .35

Isolation of insulin, 75th anniv. Required on mail Oct. 10-17.

PT60

1996, Nov. 11 Litho. *Perf. 14*
RA80 PT60 65 l multicolored .50 .35

Remete pilgrimage. Required on mail Nov. 11-24.

PT61

1997, Jan. 6 Litho. *Perf. 14*
RA81 PT61 65 l multicolored .50 .35

Antun Mihanovic (1796-1861), natl. anthem lyricist. Required on mail Jan. 6-26.

House of Dr. Ante Starcevic PT62

1997, Jan. 27 Litho. *Perf. 14*
RA82 PT62 65 l multicolored .50 .35

Required on mail Jan. 27-Feb. 14.

PT63

1997, Feb. 15 Litho. *Perf. 14*
RA83 PT63 65 l multicolored .50 .35

Croatian Anti-Cancer League. Required on mail Feb. 15-28.

PT64

1997, May 8 Litho. *Perf. 10½x11*
RA84 PT64 65 l multicolored .50 .35
a. Perf 10½ .50 .35
b. Perf 11 *35.00*

Red Cross. Required on mail May 8-15.

Numerous charity stamps were issued between 1997 and 2001, but their use on mail was not obligatory.

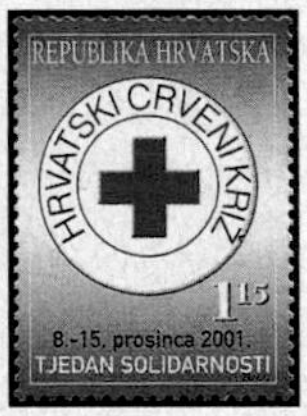

Red Cross Solidarity Week — PT65

2001, Dec. 8 Litho. *Perf. 14*
RA85 PT65 1.15k red & black 1.25 1.00

Obligatory on mail Dec. 8-15.

Red Cross Week — PT66

2002, May 8
RA86 PT66 1.15k multi 1.25 1.10

Obligatory on mail May 8-15.

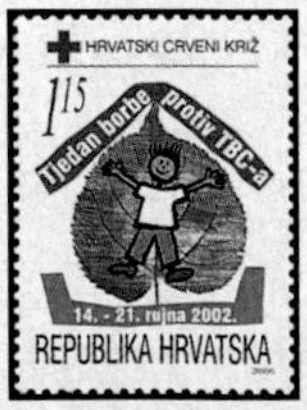

Red Cross Anti-Tuberculosis Week — PT67

2002, Sept. 14
RA87 PT67 1.15k multi 1.25 1.00

Obligatory on mail Sept. 14-21.

Red Cross Solidarity Week — PT68

2002, Dec. 8

RA88 PT68 1.15k multi 1.25 1.00

Obligatory on mail Dec. 8-15.

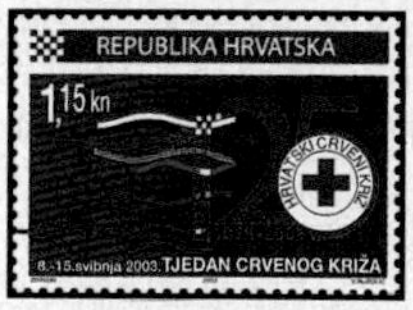

Red Cross Week — PT69

2003, May 8

RA89 PT69 1.15k multi 1.25 1.10

Obligatory on mail May 8-15.

Red Cross Anti-Tuberculosis Week — PT70

2003, Sept. 14

RA90 PT70 1.15k multi 1.25 1.10

Obligatory on mail Sept. 14-21.

Red Cross Solidarity Week — PT71

2003, Dec. 8

RA91 PT71 1.15k multi 1.25 1.10

Obligatory on mail Dec. 8-15.

Red Cross Week — PT72

2004, May 8

RA92 PT72 1.15k multi 1.25 1.10

Obligatory on mail May 8-15.

Red Cross Anti-Tuberculosis Week — PT73

2004, Sept. 14

RA93 PT73 1.15k multi .50 .50

Obligatory on mail Sept. 14-21.

Red Cross Solidarity Week — PT74

2004, Dec. 8

RA94 PT74 1.15k multi .50 .50

Obligatory on mail Dec. 8-15.

Red Cross Week — PT75

2005, May 8 **Litho.** ***Perf. 14***

RA95 PT75 1.15k multi .60 .60

Obligatory on mail May 8-15.

Red Cross Anti-Tuberculosis Week — PT76

2005, Sept. 14

RA96 PT76 1.15k multi .50 .50

Obligatory on mail Sept. 14-21.

Red Cross Solidarity Week — PT77

2005, Dec. 8

RA97 PT77 1.15k multi .50 .50

Obligatory on mail Dec. 8-15.

Red Cross Week — PT78

2006, May 8 **Litho.** ***Perf. 14***

RA98 PT78 1.15k multi 1.25 1.25

Obligatory on mail May 8-15.

Red Cross Anti-Tuberculosis Week — PT79

2006, Sept. 14

RA99 PT79 1.15k multi 1.25 1.25

Obligatory on mail Sept. 14-21.

Red Cross Solidarity Week — PT80

2006, Dec. 8

RA100 PT80 1.15k multi 1.25 1.25

Obligatory on mail Dec. 8-15.

Red Cross Week — PT81

2007, May 8 **Litho.** ***Perf. 14¼***

RA101 PT81 1.15k multi — —

Obligatory on mail May 8-15.

Red Cross Anti-Tuberculosis Week — PT82

2007, Sept. 14 **Litho.** ***Perf. 14¼***

RA102 PT82 1.15k multi — —

Obligatory on mail Sept. 14-21.

Red Cross Solidarity Week — PT83

2007, Dec. 8 **Litho.** ***Perf. 14¼***

RA103 PT83 1.15k multi — —

Obligatory on mail Dec. 8-15.

Red Cross Week — PT84

2008, May 8 **Litho.** ***Perf. 14¼***

RA104 PT84 1.15k multi — —

Obligatory on mail May 8-15.

Red Cross Anti-Tuberculosis Week — PT85

2008, Sept. 14 **Litho.** ***Perf. 14¼***

RA105 PT85 1.15k multi .45 .45

Obligatory on mail Sept. 14-21.

Red Cross Solidarity Week — PT86

2008, Dec. 8 **Litho.** ***Perf. 14¼***

RA106 PT86 1.15k multi — —

Obligatory on mail Dec. 8-15.

Red Cross Week — PT87

2009, May 8 **Litho.** ***Perf. 14¼***

RA107 PT87 1.75k multi — —

Obligatory on mail May 8-15.

Red Cross Anti-Tuberculosis Week — PT88

2009, Sept. 14 **Litho.** ***Perf. 14¼***

RA108 PT88 1.75k multi — —

Obligatory on mail Sept. 14-21.

Red Cross Solidarity Week — PT89

2009, Dec. 8 **Litho.** ***Perf. 14¼***

RA109 PT89 1.75k multi — —

Obligatory on mail Dec. 8-15.

Red Cross Week — PT90

2010, May 8 **Litho.** ***Perf. 14¼***

RA110 PT90 1.55k on 1.75k multi — —

Obligatory on mail May 8-15. No. RA110 was not issued without surcharge.

Red Cross Anti-Tuberculosis Week — PT91

2010, Sept. 14 **Litho.** ***Perf. 14¼***

RA111 PT91 1.55k multi — —

Obligatory on mail Sept. 14-21.

Red Cross Solidarity Week — PT92

2010, Dec. 8 Litho. ***Perf. 14¼***
RA112 PT92 1.55k multi — —
Obligatory on mail Dec. 8-15.

Red Cross Week — PT93

2011, May 8 Litho. ***Perf. 14¼***
RA113 PT93 1.55k multi — —
Obligatory on mail May 8-15.

Red Cross Anti-Tuberculosis Week — PT94

2011, Sept. 14 Litho. ***Perf. 14¼***
RA114 PT94 1.55k multi — —
Obligatory on mail Sept. 14-21.

Red Cross Solidarity Week — PT95

2011, Dec. 8 Litho. ***Perf. 14¼***
RA115 PT95 1.55k multi — —
Obligatory on mail Dec. 8-15.

Red Cross Week — PT96

2012, May 8 Litho. ***Perf. 14¼***
RA116 PT96 1.55k multi — —
Obligatory on mail May 8-15.

Red Cross Anti-Tuberculosis Week — PT97

2012, Sept. 14 Litho. ***Perf. 14¼***
RA117 PT97 1.55k multi — —
Obligatory on mail Sept. 14-21.

Red Cross Solidarity Week — PT98

2012, Dec. 8 Litho. ***Perf. 14¼***
RA118 PT98 1.55k multi — —
Obligatory on mail Dec. 8-15.

Red Cross Week — PT99

2013, May 8 Litho. ***Perf. 14¼***
RA119 PT99 1.55k multi — —
Obligatory on mail May 8-15.

Red Cross Anti-Tuberculosis Week — PT100

2013, Sept. 14 Litho. ***Perf. 14¼***
RA120 PT100 1.55k multi — —
Obligatory on mail Sept. 14-21.

Red Cross Solidarity Week PT101

2013, Dec. 8 Litho. ***Perf. 14¼***
RA121 PT101 1.55k multi — —
Obligatory on mail Dec. 8-15.

CUBA

'kyü-bə

LOCATION — The largest island of the West Indies; south of Florida
GOVT. — Former Spanish possession
AREA — 44,206 sq. mi.
POP. — 11,096,395 (1999 est.)
CAPITAL — Havana

Formerly a Spanish possession, Cuba made several unsuccessful attempts to gain her freedom, which finally led to the intervention of the US in 1898. In that year under the Treaty of Paris, Spain relinquished the island to the US in trust for its inhabitants.

In 1902 a republic was established and the Cuban Congress took over the government from the military authorities.

8 Reales Plata = 1 Peso
100 Centesimos = 1 Escudo or Peseta (1867)
1000 Milesimas = 100 Centavos = 1 Peso

Catalogue values for unused stamps in this country are for Never Hinged items, beginning with Scott 402 in the regular postage section, Scott B3 in the semi-postal section, Scott C38 in the airpost section, Scott CB1 in the airpost semi-postal section, Scott E13 in the special delivery section, and Scott RA1 in the postal tax section.

Pen cancellations are common on the earlier stamps of Cuba. Stamps so canceled sell for very much less than those with postmark cancellations.

Watermarks

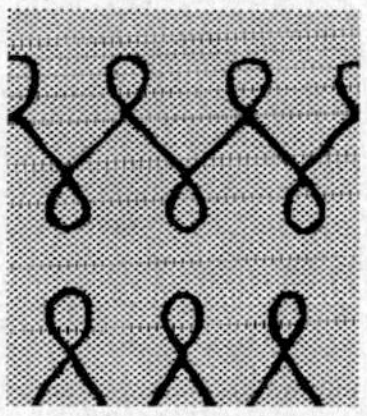

Wmk. 104 — Loops

Loops from different rows may or may not be directly opposite each other.

Wmk. 105 — Crossed Lines

Wmk. 106 — Star

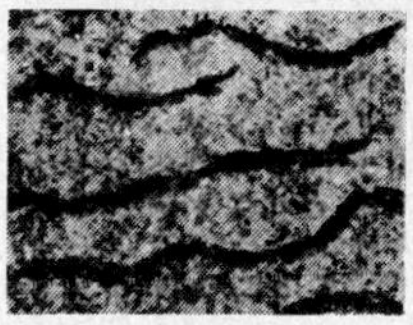

Wmk. 229 — Wavy Lines

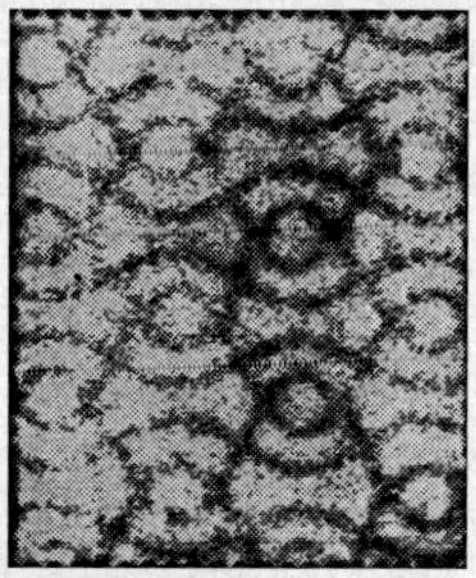

Wmk. 320

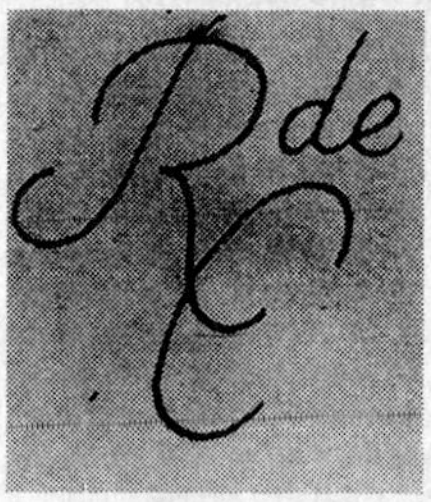

Wmk. 321 — "R de C"

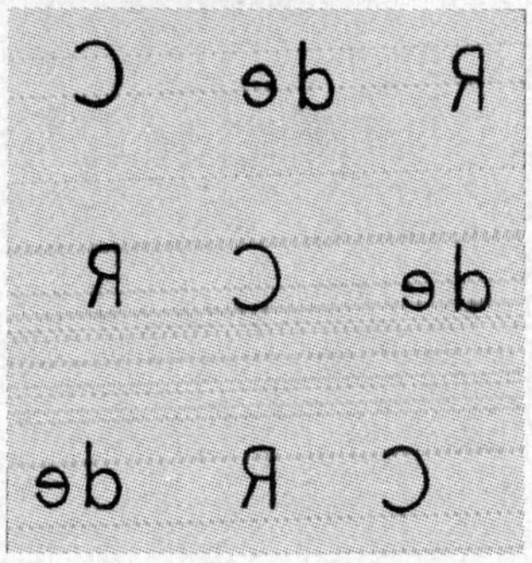

Wmk. 376 — "R de C"

Issued under Spanish Dominion

Used also in Puerto Rico: Nos. 1-3, 9-14, 17-21, 32-34, 35A-37, 39-41, 43-45, 47-49, 51-53, 55-57.

Used also in the Philippines: Nos. 2-3.

Identifiable cancellations of those countries will increase the value of the stamps.

Queen Isabella II — A1

Blue Paper

1855 Typo. Wmk. 104 *Imperf.*

1	A1	½r p blue green	125.00	7.25
a.		½r p blackish green	300.00	30.00
2	A1	1r p gray green	125.00	6.00
3	A1	2r p carmine	1,000.	15.00
4	A1	2r p orange red	1,500.	20.00
a.		2r p vermilion	1,600.	22.00
		Nos. 1-4 (4)	2,750.	48.25

See Nos. 9-14. For surcharges see Nos. 5-8, 15.

Counterfeit surcharges are plentiful.

Nos. 3-4 Surcharged

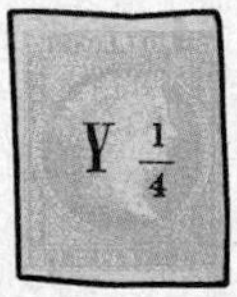

1855-56

5	A1	¼r p on 2r p car	1,500.	400.00
a.		Without fraction bar	*3,000.*	2,000.
6	A1	¼r p on 2r p org red	*4,000.*	800.00
a.		Without fraction bar	—	*3,000.*

Surcharged

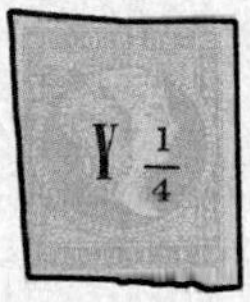

7	A1	¼r p on 2r p car	1,250.	300.00
a.		Without fraction bar	*2,500.*	1,500
8	A1	¼r p on 2r p org red	1,800.	600.00
a.		Without fraction bar	—	—

The "Y ¼" surcharge met the "Ynterior" rate for delivery within the city of Havana.

Rough Yellowish Paper

1856 Wmk. 105

9	A1	½r p yellow grn	10.00	2.00
10	A1	1r p green	1,250.	30.00
a.		1r p emerald	*1,750.*	100.00
11	A1	2r p orange red	800.00	40.00

White Smooth Paper

1857 Unwmk.

12	A1	½r p blue	5.00	1.00
13	A1	1r p gray green	5.00	1.00
a.		1r p pale yellow green	5.00	3.25
14	A1	2r p dull rose	25.00	5.00
		Nos. 12-14 (3)	35.00	7.00

Surcharged

1860

15	A1	¼r p on 2r p dl rose	250.00	100.00
a.		1 of ¼ inverted	500.00	200.00
		On cover		1,500.
b.		"Y ½" instead of "1 ¼"		—

Queen Isabella II
A2 A3

1862-64 *Imperf.*

16	A2	¼r p black	30.00	*60.00*
17	A3	¼r p blk, *buff* ('64)	30.00	*60.00*
18	A3	½r p green ('64)	5.00	1.00
19	A3	½r p grn, *pale rose* ('64)	15.00	3.00
20	A3	1r p bl, *sal* ('64)	6.00	2.00
a.		Diagonal half used as ½r p on cover		300.00
21	A3	2r p ver, *buff* ('64)	30.00	8.00
a.		2r p red, *buff*	35.00	15.00
		Nos. 16-21 (6)	116.00	134.00

No. 17 Overprinted in Black

1866

22	A3	¼r p black, *buff*	85.00	*120.00*

Exists with handstamped "1866."

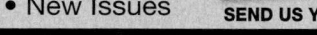

A5

1866

23	A5	5c dull violet	50.00	60.00
24	A5	10c blue	6.00	1.00
25	A5	20c green	4.00	1.00
a.		Diag. half used as 10c on cover		—
26	A5	40c rose	50.00	60.00
		Nos. 23-26 (4)	110.00	122.00

For the Type A5 20c in dull lilac, see Spain No. 87.

Stamps Dated "1867"

1867 *Perf. 14*

27	A5	5c dull violet	40.00	35.00
28	A5	10c blue	35.00	4.00
a.		Imperf., pair	110.00	*6.50*
b.		Diagonal half used as 5c on cover		300.00
29	A5	20c green	30.00	5.00
a.		Imperf., pair	110.00	75.00
b.		Diag. half used as 10c on cover		325.00
30	A5	40c rose	20.00	30.00
		Nos. 27-30 (4)	125.00	74.00

A6

1868 **Stamps Dated "1868"**

31	A6	5c dull violet	30.00	20.00
32	A6	10c blue	5.00	2.00
a.		Diagonal half used as 5c on cover		250.00
33	A6	20c green	10.00	4.00
a.		Diag. half used as 10c on cover		275.00
34	A6	40c rose	25.00	15.00
a.		Diag. half used as 20c on cover		175.00
		Nos. 31-34 (4)	70.00	41.00

Nos. 31-34 Overprinted in Black

1868

35	A6	5c dull violet	75.00	32.50
35A	A6	10c blue	75.00	32.50
36	A6	20c green	75.00	32.50
37	A6	40c rose	75.00	32.50
		Nos. 35-37 (4)	300.00	130.00

1869 **Stamps Dated "1869"**

38	A6	5c rose	50.00	40.00
39	A6	10c red brown	5.00	2.00
a.		Diagonal half used as 5c on cover		140.00
40	A6	20c orange	10.00	3.00
41	A6	40c dull violet	40.00	30.00
		Nos. 38-41 (4)	105.00	75.00

Nos. 38-41 Ovptd. Like Nos. 35-37

42	A6	5c rose	100.00	40.00
43	A6	10c red brown	100.00	40.00
44	A6	20c orange	100.00	40.00
45	A6	40c dull violet	100.00	40.00
		Nos. 42-45 (4)	400.00	160.00

"Espana" — A8

1870 *Perf. 14*

46	A8	5c blue	300.00	125.00
47	A8	10c green	5.00	2.00
a.		Diagonal half used as 5c on cover		250.00
48	A8	20c red brown	4.00	3.00
a.		Diag. half used as 10c on cover		300.00
49	A8	40c rose	300.00	100.00

"Espana" — A9

1871

50	A9	12c red lilac	25.00	12.00
a.		Imperf., pair	100.00	—
51	A9	25c ultra	3.00	1.00
a.		Imperf., pair	50.00	—
b.		Diagonal half used as 12c on cover		125.00
52	A9	50c gray green	4.00	2.00
a.		Imperf., pair	75.00	—
b.		Diagonal half used as 25c on cover		250.00
53	A9	1p yel brown	40.00	15.00
a.		Imperf., pair	125.00	—
		Nos. 50-53 (4)	72.00	30.00

King Amadeo — A10

1873 *Perf. 14*

54	A10	12½c dark green	40.00	30.00
55	A10	25c gray	3.00	1.00
a.		Diagonal half used as 12½c on cover		120.00
b.		25c lilac	10.00	4.00
c.		As "b," half used as 12½c on cover		150.00
d.		As "b," imperf., pair	50.00	—
56	A10	50c brown	3.00	1.00
a.		Imperf., pair	75.00	—
b.		Half used as 25c on cover		200.00
57	A10	1p red brown	450.00	75.00
a.		Diagonal half used as 50c on cover		750.00

"España" — A11

1874

58	A11	12½c brown	30.00	25.00
a.		Half used as 5c on cover		500.00
59	A11	25c ultra	1.00	.60
a.		Diagonal half used as 12½c on cover		100.00
60	A11	50c dp violet	2.00	5.00
a.		Diagonal half used as 25c on cover		200.00
b.		"1374" instead of "1874"	—	—
61	A11	50c gray	5.00	2.00
a.		Diagonal half used as 25c on cover		175.00
62	A11	1p carmine	350.00	400.00
a.		Imperf., pair	600.00	*210.00*
		Nos. 58-62 (5)	388.00	432.60

Examples of Nos. 61, 63-65, 67-87 with fine impressions in slightly different colors are proofs.

Coat of Arms — A12

1875

63	A12	12½c lt violet	1.50	2.00
a.		Imperf., pair	100.00	
64	A12	25c ultra	1.00	1.50
a.		Imperf., pair	100.00	—
b.		Diagonal half used as 12½c on cover		100.00
65	A12	50c blue green	1.00	2.00
a.		Imperf., pair	100.00	
b.		Diag. half used as 25c on cover		*80.00*
66	A12	1p brown	15.00	10.00
b.		Diag. half used as 50c on cover		135.00
		Nos. 63-66 (4)	18.50	15.50

King Alfonso XII — A13

1876

67	A13	12½c green	3.00	6.00
a.		12½c emerald green	8.75	6.00
68	A13	25c gray	4.00	3.00
a.		Diagonal half used as 12½c on cover		100.00
b.		25c pale violet	4.50	3.25
d.		25c bluish gray	4.50	3.25
69	A13	50c ultra	3.00	6.00
a.		Imperf., pair	75.00	*16.00*
b.		Diag. half used as 25c on cover		100.00
70	A13	1p black	15.00	25.00
a.		Imperf., pair	40.00	*40.00*
b.		Diag. half used as 50c on cover		125.00
		Nos. 67-70 (4)	25.00	40.00

King Alfonso XII — A14

1877

71	A14	10c lt green	40.00	—
72	A14	12½c gray	6.00	12.00
a.		Imperf., pair	100.00	—
b.		Diagonal half used on cover		300.00
73	A14	25c dk green	1.00	.50
a.		Imperf., pair	100.00	—
b.		Diagonal half used as 12½c on cover		75.00
74	A14	50c black	1.00	1.50
a.		Imperf., pair	100.00	—
b.		Half used as 25c on cover		100.00
75	A14	1p brown	30.00	25.00
		Nos. 71-75 (5)	78.00	

No. 71 was not placed in use.

1878 **Stamps Dated "1878"**

76	A14	5c blue	1.00	2.00
77	A14	10c black	100.00	
78	A14	12½c brown bis	6.00	10.00
a.		12½c olive brown	6.00	10.00
c.		Diagonal half used on cover		200.00
d.		As "a," diagonal half used on cover		200.00
79	A14	25c yel green	1.00	2.00
b.		No. 79, diagonal half used as 12½c on cover		100.00
c.		25c deep green	1.00	2.00
80	A14	50c dk blue grn	1.00	2.00
b.		Diagonal half used as 25c on cover		100.00
81	A14	1p carmine	25.00	15.00
b.		1p rose	16.00	*500.00*
c.		Diagonal half used as 50c on cover		*900.00*
		Nos. 76-81 (6)	134.00	31.00

No. 77 was not placed in use.

Imperf., Pairs

76a	A14	5c blue	100.00
77a	A14	10c black	400.00
78b	A14	12½c brown bister	100.00
79a	A14	25c deep green	100.00
80a	A14	50c dk blue green	200.00
81a	A14	1p carmine	150.00

1879 **Stamps Dated "1879"**

82	A14	5c slate black	1.00	3.00
83	A14	10c orange	200.00	*75.00*
84	A14	12½c rose	1.00	3.00
85	A14	25c ultra	1.00	2.00
a.		Diagonal half used as 12½c on cover		100.00
b.		Imperf., pair	75.00	
86	A14	50c gray	1.00	1.00
a.		Diag. half used as 25c on cover		100.00
87	A14	1p olive bister	25.00	30.00
		Nos. 82-87 (6)	229.00	114.00

A15

1880

88	A15	5c green	1.00	2.00
89	A15	10c lake	125.00	—
a.		Double impression of frame and lettering	200.00	
90	A15	12½c gray	1.00	.50
91	A15	25c gray blue	1.00	.50
a.		Diagonal half used as 12½c on cover		100.00
92	A15	50c brown	1.00	.50
a.		Diagonal half used as 25c on cover		100.00
93	A15	1p yellow brn	8.00	5.00
a.		Diagonal half used as 50c on cover		400.00
		Nos. 88-93 (6)	137.00	8.50

No. 89 was not placed in use.

A16

1881

94	A16	1c green	1.00	.50
95	A16	2c lake	50.00	
96	A16	2½c olive bister	1.00	.50
97	A16	5c gray blue	.50	.25
98	A16	10c yellow brown	.50	.25
a.		Diagonal half used as 5c on cover		100.00
99	A16	20c dark brown	6.00	10.00
		Nos. 94-99 (6)	59.00	11.50

No. 95 was not placed in use.

A17

1882

100	A17	1c green	.75	.50
a.		Diag. half used as ½c on cover		150.00
101	A17	2c lake	5.00	3.00
a.		Diag. half used as 1c on cover		100.00
102	A17	2½c dk brown	10.00	5.00
103	A17	5c gray blue	8.00	.50
a.		Diag. half used as 2½c on cover		100.00
104	A17	10c olive bister	.75	.50
a.		Diag. half used as 5c on cover		100.00
105	A17	20c red brown	130.00	50.00
a.		Diag. half used as 10c on cover		500.00
		Nos. 100-105 (6)	154.50	59.50

See Nos. 121-131. For surcharges see Nos. 106-120.

Issue of 1882 Surcharged or Overprinted in Black, Blue or Red

a

b

c

d

e

1883 **Type "a"**

106	A17	5 on 5c (R)	3.00	2.00
a.		Triple surcharge		
b.		Double surcharge	25.00	25.00
c.		Inverted surcharge	30.00	30.00
d.		Without "5" in surcharge	20.00	20.00
e.		Dbl. surch., types "a" & "d"	75.00	—
107	A17	10 on 10c (Bl)	3.50	2.50
a.		Inverted surcharge	75.00	
b.		Double surcharge	30.00	30.00
108	A17	20 on 20c	45.00	75.00
a.		"10" instead of "20"	75.00	*75.00*
b.		Double surcharge	75.00	
c.		As "a," inverted surcharge	*90.00*	*90.00*
109	A17	5 on 5c (R)	3.00	2.00
a.		Inverted surcharge	30.00	30.00
b.		Double surcharge	25.00	25.00
110	A17	10 on 10c (Bl)	10.00	12.00
a.		Inverted surcharge	35.00	35.00
b.		Double surcharge	35.00	35.00
111	A17	20 on 20c	120.00	150.00
a.		Double surcharge		
b.		Dbl. surch., types "b" & "c"		

Type "c"

112	A17	5 on 5c (R)	2.50	2.00
a.		Inverted surcharge	35.00	35.00
b.		Dbl. surch., types "c" & "d"		—
c.		Dbl. surch., types "c" & "a"		
113	A17	10 on 10c (Bl)	10.00	12.00
a.		Inverted surcharge	40.00	40.00
b.		Double surcharge	40.00	40.00

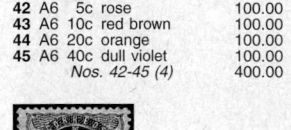

114 A17 20 on 20c 60.00 100.00
- *a.* "10" instead of "20" 100.00 120.00
- *b.* Double surcharge 100.00 120.00
- *c.* Dbl. surch., types "a" & "c" 100.00 120.00

Type "d"

115 A17 5 on 5c (R) 3.00 2.00
- *a.* Inverted surcharge 35.00 35.00
- *b.* Double surcharge 30.00 30.00

116 A17 10 on 10c (Bl) 4.00 3.00
- *a.* Inverted surcharge 40.00 40.00
- *b.* Double surcharge 40.00 40.00
- *c.* Dbl. surch., types "d" & "c" — —

117 A17 20 on 20c 85.00 100.00
- *a.* Dbl. surch., types "a" & "d" — —

Type "e"

118 A17 5c gray blue (R) 4.00 3.00
- *a.* Double overprint 40.00 40.00

119 A17 10c olive bis (Bl) 12.00 15.00
- *a.* Double overprint 40.00 40.00

120 A17 20c red brown 250.00 300.00
- *a.* Double overprint 300.00 300.00

Nos. 106-120 (15) 615.00 780.50

Handstamped overprints and surcharges are counterfeits.

Numerous other varieties exist.

Type of 1882

Original 1st retouch 2nd retouch

The differences between the stamps of 1882 and the various retouches are as follows:

Original state: The medallion is surrounded by a heavy line of color of nearly even thickness, touching the horizontal line below the word "Cuba" (or "Filipinas," "Puerto Rico," as the case may be); the opening in the hair above the temple is narrow and pointed.

1st retouch: The line around the medallion is thin, except at the upper right, and does not touch the horizontal line above it; the opening in the hair is slightly wider and a trifle rounded; the lock of hair above the forehead is shaped like a broad "V" and ends in a point; there is a faint white line below it, which is not found on the stamps in the original state. Owing to wear of the plate the shape of the lock of hair and the width of the white line below it vary.

2nd retouch: The opening in the hair forms a semi-circle; the lock above the forehead is nearly straight, having only a slight wave, and the white line is much broader than before.

1883-86

121 A17 1c grn, 2nd retouch 150.00 40.00

122 A17 2½c olive bister .50 .30

124 A17 2½c violet 1.00 .40
- *a.* 2½c red lilac ('85) 1.00 .40
- *b.* 2½c ultramarine 125.00 150.00

125 A17 5c gray bl, 1st retouch 100.00 .50
- *a.* Diag. half used as 2½c on cover 75.00

126 A17 5c gray bl, 2nd retouch 120.00 2.00
- *a.* Diag. half used as 2½c on cover 125.00

127 A17 10c brn, 1st retouch 3.00 1.00
- *a.* Diagonal half used as 5c on cover 75.00
- *c.* Imperf, pair 300.00 —

128 A17 20c olive bister 15.00 10.00

Nos. 121-128 (7) 389.50 54.20

1888

129 A17 2½c red brown 1.75 .85

130 A17 10c blue 1.50 1.00
- *a.* Diagonal half used as 5c on cover 175.00

131 A17 20c brnsh gray 15.00 10.00

Nos. 129-131 (3) 18.25 11.85

King Alfonso XIII — A18

1890-97

132	A18	1c gray brown	20.00	6.50
133	A18	1c ol gray ('91)	10.00	4.00
134	A18	1c ultra ('94)	5.00	.50
135	A18	1c dk vio ('96)	1.50	.40
136	A18	2c slate blue	10.00	3.00
137	A18	2c lilac brn ('91)	2.00	.75
138	A18	2c rose ('94)	35.00	5.00
139	A18	2c claret ('96)	9.00	5.00
140	A18	2½c emerald	12.50	5.00
141	A18	2½c salmon ('91)	60.00	5.00
142	A18	2½c lilac ('94)	4.00	3.00
143	A18	2½c rose ('96)	4.00	6.00

144 A18 5c olive gray 1.00 .75
- *b.* Diagonal half used as 2½c on cover 500.00

145 A18 5c emerald ('91) 1.00 .50
- *b.* Diagonal half used as 2½c on cover 500.00

146 A18 5c sl blue ('96) .75 1.00
- *b.* Diagonal half used as 2½c on cover 600.00

147 A18 10c brown violet 6.00 1.00
- *b.* Diagonal half used as 5c on cover 500.00

148 A18 10c claret ('91) 2.50 .50
- *b.* Diagonal half used as 5c on cover 400.00

149	A18	10c emerald ('96)	1.00	1.50
150	A18	20c dk violet	2.00	1.00
151	A18	20c ultra ('91)	25.00	8.00
152	A18	20c red brn ('94)	20.00	30.00
153	A18	20c violet ('96)	15.00	10.00

- *b.* Diagonal half used as 10c on cover 600.00

154 A18 40c orange brn ('97) 40.00 35.00

155 A18 80c lilac brn ('97) 80.00 70.00

Nos. 132-155 (24) 367.25 203.40

Imperf., Pairs

134a	A18	1c ultramarine	90.00
135a	A18	1c dark violet	90.00
138a	A18	2c rose	90.00
139a	A18	2c claret	90.00
142a	A18	2½c lilac	90.00
143a	A18	2½c rose	90.00
145a	A18	5c emerald	90.00
146a	A18	5c slate blue	90.00
148a	A18	10c claret	90.00
149a	A18	10c emerald	90.00
152a	A18	20c red brown	135.00
153a	A18	20c violet	125.00
154a	A18	40c orange brown	115.00
155a	A18	80c red brown	175.00

King Alfonso XIII — A19

1898

156	A19	1m orange brn	.75	1.00
157	A19	2m orange brn	.30	1.00
158	A19	3m orange brn	.30	1.00
159	A19	4m orange brn	6.00	12.00
160	A19	5m orange brn	.30	1.00
161	A19	1c black vio	.30	1.00
162	A19	2c dk blue grn	.30	1.00
163	A19	3c dk brown	.30	1.00
164	A19	4c orange	16.00	12.00
165	A19	5c car rose	1.25	.50
166	A19	6c dk blue	.50	1.50
167	A19	8c gray brown	2.00	4.00
168	A19	10c vermilion	1.30	.75
169	A19	15c slate green	6.00	10.00
170	A19	20c maroon	4.00	1.00
171	A19	40c dark lilac	5.00	8.00
172	A19	60c black	10.00	20.00
173	A19	80c red brown	20.00	25.00
174	A19	1p yel green	20.00	25.00
175	A19	2p slate blue	35.00	40.00
		Nos. 156-175 (20)	129.60	166.75

Nos. 156-160 were issued for use on newspapers.

Nos. 156-175 exist imperf. Value, unused pairs, $7,500. Only one set of pairs is currently known.

For surcharges see Nos. 176-189C, 196-200.

Issued under Administration of the United States
Puerto Principe Issue

Issues of Cuba of 1898 and 1896 Surcharged

a

b

Black Surcharge on Nos. 156-158, 160

1898-99

Types a, c, d, e, f, g and h are 17½mm high, the others are 19½mm high.

176 A19 (a) 1c on 1m org brn 50.00 30.00

177 A19 (b) 1c on 1m org brn 45.00 35.00
- *a.* Broken figure "1" 75.00 65.00
- *b.* Inverted surcharge 200.00
- *d.* As "a," inverted *250.00*

c

d

178 A19 (c) 2c on 2m org brn 24.00 20.00
- *a.* Inverted surcharge 250.00 50.00

179 A19 (d) 2c on 2m org brn 40.00 35.00
- *a.* Inverted surcharge 350.00 100.00

k

l

179B A19 (k) 3c on 1m org brn 300. 175.
- *c.* Double surcharge 1,500. 750.

An unused example is known with "cents" omitted.

179D A19 (l) 3c on 1m org brn *1,500.* *750.*
- *e.* Double surcharge — —

e

f

179F A19 (e) 3c on 2m org brn *1,500.*

Value is for examples with minor faults.

179G A19 (f) 3c on 2m org brn — *2,000.*

Value is for examples with minor faults.

180 A19 (e) 3c on 3m org brn 30. *30.*
- *a.* Inverted surcharge 110.

181 A19 (f) 3c on 3m org brn 75. 75.
- *a.* Inverted surcharge *200.*

g

h

i

j

182 A19 (g) 5c on 1m org brn 700. 200.
- *a.* Inverted surcharge *500.*

183 A19 (h) 5c on 1m org brn *1,300.* *500.*
- *a.* Inverted surcharge *700.*

184 A19 (g) 5c on 2m org brn 750. 275.

185 A19 (h) 5c on 2m org brn 1,500. 500.

186 A19 (g) 5c on 3m org brn 650. 175.
- *a.* Inverted surcharge 1,200. 700.

187 A19 (h) 5c on 3m org brn 400.
- *a.* Inverted surcharge 1,000.

188 A19 (g) 5c on 5m org brn 100. 75.
- *a.* Inverted surcharge 400. 200.
- *b.* Double surcharge — —

189 A19 (h) 5c on 5m org brn 350. 250.
- *a.* Inverted surcharge 425.
- *b.* Double surcharge — —

The 2nd printing of Nos. 188-189 has shiny ink. Values are for the 1st printing.

189C A19 (i) 5c on 5m org brn *7,500.*

No. 191

Black Surcharge on No. P25

190 N2 (g) 5c on ½m bl grn 250. 75.
- *a.* Inverted surcharge 500. 150.
- *b.* Pair, one without surcharge 500.

Value for 190b is for pair with unsurcharged stamp at right. Also exists with unsurcharged stamp at left.

191 N2 (h) 5c on ½m bl grn 300. 90.
- *a.* Inverted surcharge 200.

192 N2 (i) 5c on ½m bl grn 550. 200.
- *a.* Dbl. surch., one diagonal *11,500.*

193 N2 (j) 5c on ½m bl grn 800. 300.

Red Surcharge on No. 161

196 A19 (k) 3c on 1c blk vio 65. 35.
- *a.* Inverted surcharge 325.

197 A19 (l) 3c on 1c blk vio 125. 55.
- *a.* Inverted surcharge 400.

198 A19 (i) 5c on 1c blk vio 25. 30.
- *a.* Inverted surcharge 125.
- *b.* Surcharge vert. reading up *3,500.*
- *c.* Double surcharge *400.* *600.*
- *d.* Double invtd. surch. —

Value for No. 198b is for surcharge reading up. One example is known with surcharge reading down.

199 A19 (j) 5c on 1c blk vio 55. 55.
- *a.* Inverted surcharge 250.
- *b.* Vertical surcharge *2,000.*
- *c.* Double surcharge 1,000. 700.

m

200 A19 10c on 1c blk vio (m) 20. *50.*
a. Broken figure "1" 40. *100.*

Black Surcharge on Nos. P26-P30

201 N2 (k) 3c on 1m bl grn 350. 350.
a. Inverted surcharge 450.
b. "EENTS" 550. 450.
c. As "b", inverted 850.
202 N2 (l) 3c on 1m bl grn 550. 400.
a. Inverted surcharge 850.
203 N2 (k) 3c on 2m bl grn 900. 400.
a. "EENTS" 1,250. 500.
b. Inverted surcharge 1,150.
c. As "a," inverted 950.
204 N2 (l) 3c on 2m bl grn 1,250. 875.
a. Inverted surcharge 950.
205 N2 (k) 3c on 3m bl grn 900. 400.
a. Inverted surcharge 750.
b. "EENTS" 1,250. 450.
c. As "b," inverted 700.
206 N2 (l) 3c on 3m bl grn 1,200. 550.
a. Inverted surcharge 700.
211 N2 (i) 5c on 1m bl grn 1,800.
a. "EENTS" — 2,500.
212 N2 (j) 5c on 1m bl grn 2,250.
213 N2 (i) 5c on 2m bl grn 1,800.
a. "EENTS" — 1,900.
214 N2 (j) 5c on 2m bl grn 2,300.
215 N2 (i) 5c on 3m bl grn 550.
a. "EENTS" 1,000.
216 N2 (j) 5c on 3m bl grn — 1,000.
217 N2 (i) 5c on 4m bl grn *2,500.* 900.
a. "EENTS" *3,000.* 1,500.
b. Inverted surcharge *2,500.*
c. As "a," inverted 2,000.
218 N2 (j) 5c on 4m bl grn *1,500.*
a. Inverted surcharge *2,000.*
219 N2 (i) 5c on 8m bl grn *2,500.* 1,250.
a. Inverted surcharge 1,500.
b. "EENTS" — 1,800.
c. As "b," inverted 2,500.
220 N2 (j) 5c on 8m bl grn 2,000.
a. Inverted surcharge 2,500.

Beware of forgeries of the Puerto Principe issue. Obtaining expert opinions is recommended.

United States Stamps Nos. 279, 267, 267b, 279Bf, 279Bh, 268, 281, 282C and 283 Surcharged in Black

1899 Wmk. 191 *Perf. 12*

221 A87 1c on 1c yel grn 4.50 .40
Never hinged 11.50
222 A88 2c on 2c reddish car, III 10.00 .75
Never hinged 25.00
b. 2c on 2c vermilion, type III 10.00 .75
222A A88 2c on 2c reddish car, IV 6.00 .40
Never hinged 15.00
c. 2c on 2c vermilion, IV 6.00 .40
d. As No. 222A, inverted surcharge *5,500.* *4,000.*
223 A88 2½c on 2c reddish car, III 5.00 .80
Never hinged 12.50
b. 2½c on 2c vermilion, III 5.00 .80
223A A88 2½c on 2c reddish car, IV 3.50 .50
Never hinged 8.75
c. 2½c on 2c vermilion, IV 3.50 .50
224 A89 3c on 3c purple 12.00 1.75
Never hinged 30.00
a. Period between "B" and "A" 40.00 35.00
225 A91 5c on 5c blue 12.50 2.00
Never hinged 30.00
226 A94 10c on 10c brn, I 25.00 6.00
Never hinged 70.00
b. "CUBA" omitted *7,000.* *4,000.*
226A A94 10c on 10c brn, II *6,000.*
Nos. 221-226 (8) 78.50 12.60

The 2½c was sold and used as a 2c stamp. Excellent counterfeits of this and the preceding issue exist, especially inverted and double surcharges.

Issues of the Republic under US Military Rule

Statue of Columbus A20

Royal Palms A21

"Cuba" — A22

Ocean Liner — A23

Cane Field — A24

1899 Wmk. US-C (191C) *Perf. 12*

227 A20 1c yellow green 3.50 .25
Never hinged 8.75
228 A21 2c carmine 3.50 .25
Never hinged 8.75
a. scarlet 3.50 .25
b. Booklet pane of 6 *5,500.*
229 A22 3c purple 3.50 .30
Never hinged 8.75
230 A23 5c blue 4.50 .30
Never hinged 11.00
231 A24 10c brown 11.00 .80
Never hinged 27.50
Nos. 227-231 (5) 26.00 1.90

No. 228b was issued by the Republic.
See Nos. 233-237 in Scott Standard Catalogue Vol 2. For surcharge see No. 232.

Issues of the Republic

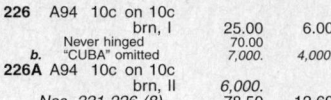

No. 229 Surcharged in Carmine

1902, Sept. 30

232 A22 1c on 3c purple 2.75 .50
a. Inverted surcharge 150.00 150.00
b. Surcharge sideways (numeral horizontal) 200.00 200.00
c. Double surcharge 200.00 200.00

Counterfeits of the errors are plentiful.

Re-engraved

The re-engraved stamps of 1905-07 may be distinguished from the issue of 1899 as follows:

ORIGINAL RE-ENGRAVED

1c — The ends of the label inscribed "Centavo" are rounded instead of square.
2c — The foliate ornaments, inside the oval disks bearing the numerals of value, have been removed.
5c — Two lines forming a right angle have been added in the upper corners of the label bearing the word "Cuba."
10c — A small ball has been added to each of the square ends of the label bearing the word "Cuba."

1905 Unwmk. *Perf. 12*

233 A20 1c green 1.75 .25
234 A21 2c rose 1.20 .25
a. Booklet pane of 6 150.00
236 A23 5c blue 42.50 1.00
237 A24 10c brown 3.50 .50
Nos. 233-237 (4) 48.95 2.00

Maj. Gen. Antonio Maceo — A26

1907

238 A26 50c gray bl & blk 1.75 .80

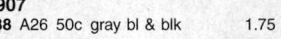

Bartolomé Masó A27

Máximo Gómez A28

Julio Sanguily A29

Ignacio Agramonte A30

Calixto García A31

José M. Rodriquez y Rodriquez (Mayia) A32

Carlos Roloff — A33

1910, Feb. 1

239 A27 1c grn & vio 1.00 .25
a. Center inverted 260.00 260.00
240 A28 2c car & grn 1.90 .25
a. Center inverted 575.00 575.00
241 A29 3c vio & bl 1.35 .25
242 A30 5c bl & grn 20.00 .80
243 A31 8c ol & vio 1.35 .30
244 A32 10c brn & bl 8.00 .65
a. Center inverted 850.00
245 A26 50c vio & blk 1.90 .50
246 A33 1p slate & blk 9.25 4.00
Nos. 239-246 (8) 44.75 7.00
Set, never hinged 72.50

1911-13

247 A27 1c green 1.00 .25
248 A28 2c car rose 1.35 .25
a. Booklet pane of 6 ('13) 82.50
250 A30 5c ultra 3.75 .25
251 A31 8c ol grn & blk 2.00 .60
252 A33 1p black 9.50 2.00
Nos. 247-252 (5) 17.60 3.35
Set, never hinged 25.00

Map of Cuba — A34

1914-15

253 A34 1c green .80 .25
a. Booklet pane of 6 100.00
254 A34 2c car rose .95 .25
a. Booklet pane of 6 100.00
255 A34 2c red ('15) 1.50 .25
a. Booklet pane of 6 100.00
256 A34 3c violet 4.75 .35
257 A34 5c blue 6.50 .25
258 A34 8c ol grn 5.25 .70
259 A34 10c brown 9.50 .35
260 A34 10c ol grn ('15) 11.50 .55
261 A34 50c orange 75.00 10.00
262 A34 1p gray 110.00 24.00
Nos. 253-262 (10) 225.75 36.95
Set, never hinged 400.00

Complete set of eight 1914 stamps, imperf. pairs, value $1,500.
Nos. 253, 254, 256 and E5 exist with "1917 GOB./CONSTITUCIONAL/CAMAGUEY" overprint. These were not authorized.

Gertrudis Gómez de Avellaneda, Cuban Poetess (1814-73) A34a

1914

263 A34a 5c blue 18.00 5.00
Never hinged 27.50

José Martí A35

Máximo Gómez A36

José de la Luz Caballero A37

Calixto García A38

Ignacio Agramonte A39

Tomás Estrada Palma A40

José A. Saco — A41

Antonio Maceo — A42

Carlos Manuel de Céspedes — A43

1917-18 Unwmk. *Perf. 12*

264	A35	1c bl grn	1.00	.25
a.		Booklet pane of 6	40.00	
b.		Booklet pane of 30	250.00	
265	A36	2c rose	1.05	.25
a.		Booklet pane of 6	50.00	
b.		Booklet pane of 30	210.00	
266	A36	2c lt red ('18)	.85	.25
a.		Booklet pane of 6	50.00	
267	A37	3c violet	1.10	.25
a.		Imperf. pair	275.00	
b.		Booklet pane of 6	50.00	
268	A38	5c dp bl	1.05	.25
269	A39	8c red brn	5.50	.25
270	A40	10c yel brn	3.25	.25
271	A41	20c gray grn	18.50	1.60
272	A42	50c dl rose	18.50	.70
273	A43	1p black	19.00	.70
		Nos. 264-273 (10)	69.80	4.75
		Set, never hinged	110.00	

1925-28 Wmk. 106 *Perf. 12*

274	A35	1c bl grn	1.10	.25
a.		Booklet pane of 6	350.00	
275	A36	2c brt rose	1.20	.25
a.		Booklet pane of 6	75.00	
b.		Booklet pane of 30	350.00	
276	A38	5c dp bl	2.50	.25
277	A39	8c red brn ('28)	5.75	.65
278	A40	10c yel brn ('27)	7.00	.70
279	A41	20c olive grn	11.00	1.10
		Nos. 274-279 (6)	28.55	3.20
		Set, never hinged	50.00	

1926 *Imperf.*

280	A35	1c blue green	2.75	2.00
281	A36	2c brt rose	2.75	2.00
282	A38	5c deep blue	3.50	2.75
		Nos. 280-282 (3)	9.00	6.75
		Set, never hinged	10.00	

See Nos. 304-310. For overprint and surcharge see Nos. 317-318, 644.

Arms of Republic A44

1927, May 20 Unwmk. *Perf. 12*

283	A44	25c violet	18.00	3.50
		Never hinged	27.50	

25th anniversary of the Republic.

For surcharges see Nos. 355, C3.

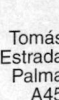

Tomás Estrada Palma A45

Designs: 2c, Gen. Gerardo Machado. 5c, Morro Castle. 8c, Havana Railway Station. 10c, Presidential Palace. 13c, Tobacco Plantation. 20c, Treasury Building. 30c, Sugar Mill. 50c, Havana Cathedral. 1p, Galician Clubhouse, Havana.

1928, Jan. 2 Wmk. 106

284	A45	1c deep green	.60	.30
285	A45	2c brt rose	.60	.30
286	A45	5c deep blue	1.75	.50
287	A45	8c lt red brn	3.75	1.10
288	A45	10c bister brn	1.50	.80
289	A45	13c orange	2.10	.80
290	A45	20c olive grn	2.50	.95
291	A45	30c dk violet	5.25	.75
292	A45	50c carmine rose	8.00	2.75
293	A45	1p gray black	16.00	6.25
		Nos. 284-293 (10)	42.05	14.50
		Set, never hinged	67.50	

Sixth Pan-American Conference.

Capitol, Havana A55

1929, May 18

294	A55	1c green	.50	.35
295	A55	2c carmine rose	.50	.30
296	A55	5c blue	.65	.40
297	A55	10c bister brn	1.35	.50
298	A55	20c violet	4.50	2.75
		Nos. 294-298 (5)	7.50	4.30
		Set, never hinged	12.00	

Opening of the Capitol, Havana.

Hurdler — A56

1930, Mar. 15 Engr.

299	A56	1c green	.95	.45
300	A56	2c carmine	.95	.50
301	A56	5c deep blue	1.25	.50
302	A56	10c bister brn	2.50	.95
303	A56	20c violet	15.00	3.25
		Nos. 299-303 (5)	20.65	5.65
		Set, never hinged	32.50	

2nd Central American Athletic Games.

Types of 1917 Portrait Issue
Flat Plate Printing

1930-45 Wmk. 106 Engr. *Perf. 10*

304	A35	1c blue green	.80	.25
a.		Booklet pane of 6	50.00	
b.		Booklet pane of 30	—	
305	A36	2c brt rose	75.00	—
a.		Booklet pane of 6	1,200.	
305B	A37	3c dk rose vio ('42)	4.00	.75
c.		Booklet pane of 6	42.50	
306	A38	5c dk blue	2.75	.25
306A	A39	8c red brn ('45)	2.75	.25
307	A40	10c brown	2.75	.25
a.		10c yellow brown ('35)	3.50	.75
307B	A41	20c olive grn ('41)	4.75	.75
		Nos. 304-307B (7)	92.80	2.50

Nos. 305 and 305B were printed for booklet panes and all examples have straight edges.

For surcharge see No. 644.

Rotary Press Printing

308	A35	1c blue grn	1.10	.25
309	A36	2c brt rose	1.10	.25
a.		Booklet pane of 50		
310	A37	3c violet	1.50	.25
a.		3c dull violet ('38)	1.10	.25
b.		3c rose violet ('41)	1.10	.25
c.		Booklet pane of 50		
		Nos. 308-310 (3)	3.70	.75

Flat plate stamps measure 18½x21½mm; rotary press, 19x22mm.

The Mangos of Baragua — A57

War Memorial — A61

Battle of Mal Tiempo A58

Battle of Coliseo A59

Maceo, Gómez and Zayas A60

Wmk. 229

1933, Apr. 23 Photo. *Perf. 12½*

312	A57	3c dk brown	2.00	.30
313	A58	5c dk blue	1.75	.40
314	A59	10c emerald	3.50	.40
315	A60	13c red	4.00	1.10
316	A61	20c black	7.75	3.00
		Nos. 312-316 (5)	19.00	5.20
		Set, never hinged	29.00	

War of Independence and dedication of the "Soldado Invasor" (the American Army that came to the aid of the revolution against Spain) monument.

Types of 1917 Issues with Carmine or Black Overprint Reading Up or Down

Rotary Press Printing

Wmk. 106

1933, Dec. 23 Engr. *Perf. 10*

317	A35	1c blue green (C)	1.50	.25

With Additional Surcharge of New Value and Bars

318	A37	2c on 3c vio (Bk)	1.50	.25

Establishment of a revolutionary junta.

Catalogue values for Nos. 317-318 unused are for examples with overprint reading up. Values for overprint reading down, $4.

Dr. Carlos J. Finlay — A62

1934, Dec. 3 Engr. *Perf. 10*

319	A62	2c dark carmine	1.35	.50
320	A62	5c dark blue	3.75	1.50
		Set, never hinged	8.00	

Cent. of the birth of Dr. Carlos J. Finlay (1833-1915), physician-biologist who found that a mosquito transmitted yellow fever.

Pres. José Miguel Gómez — A63

Gómez Monument A64

1936, May *Perf. 10*

322	A63	1c green	2.25	.40
323	A64	2c carmine	3.25	.50
		Set, never hinged	8.00	

Unveiling of a monument to Gen. José Miguel Gómez, ex-president.

Matanzas Issue

Map of Cuba A65

2c, Map of Free Zone. 4c, S. S. "Rex" in Matanzas Bay. 5c, Ships in Matanzas Bay. 8c, Caves of Bellamar. 10c, Valley of Yumuri. 20c, Yumuri River. 50c, Ships Leaving Port.

Wmk. 229

1936, May 5 Photo. *Perf. 12½*

324	A65	1c blue green	.45	.25
325	A65	2c red	.70	.25
326	A65	4c claret	1.20	.25
327	A65	5c ultra	1.75	.25
328	A65	8c orange brn	3.00	.70
329	A65	10c emerald	3.25	.70
330	A65	20c brown	6.25	2.50
331	A65	50c slate	11.50	3.50
		Nos. 324-331,C18-C21,CE1,E8 (14)	55.70	21.85
		Set, never hinged	92.50	

Exist imperf. Value 20% more.

"Peace and Work" A73

Máximo Gómez Monument — A74

Torch — A75

"Independence" — A76

"Messenger of Peace" — A77

1936, Nov. 18 ***Perf. 12½***

332	A73	1c emerald	.75	.25
333	A74	2c crimson	.90	.30
334	A75	4c maroon	1.05	.30
335	A76	5c ultra	4.00	.55
336	A77	8c dk green	6.00	1.20
		Nos. 332-336,C22-C23,E9 (8)	26.55	7.20
		Set, never hinged	48.00	

Maj. Gen. Máximo Gómez, birth centenary.
Issued both perf and imperf. Values for imperfs are approx. 400% higher.

Sugar Cane — A78

Primitive Sugar Mill — A79

Modern Sugar Mill — A80

Wmk. 106

1937, Oct. 2 **Engr.** ***Perf. 10***

337	A78	1c yellow green	1.75	.40
338	A79	2c red	1.00	.25
339	A80	5c bright blue	2.25	.40
		Nos. 337-339 (3)	5.00	1.05
		Set, never hinged	8.50	

Cuban sugar cane industry, 400th anniv.

Argentine Emblem — A81

Mountain Scene (Bolivia) — A82

Arms of Brazil — A83

Canadian Scene — A84

Camilo Henriquez (Chile) A85

Gen, Francisco de Paula Santander (Colombia) A86

Natl. Monument (Costa Rica) — A87

Autograph of José Marti (Cuba) — A88

Columbus Lighthouse (Dominican Rep.) — A89

Juan Montalvo (Ecuador) — A90

Abraham Lincoln (US) A91

Quetzal and Scroll (Guatemala) A92

Arms of Haiti A93

Francisco Morazán (Honduras) A94

Fleet of Columbus — A95

Wmk. 106

1937, Oct. 13 **Engr.** ***Perf. 10***

340	A81	1c deep green	.75	.75
341	A82	1c green	.75	.75
342	A83	2c carmine	.75	.75
343	A84	2c carmine	.75	.75
344	A85	3c violet	1.75	1.75
345	A86	3c violet	1.75	1.75
346	A87	4c bister brown	2.10	2.10
347	A88	4c bister brown	3.75	3.75
348	A89	5c blue	1.90	1.90
349	A90	5c blue	1.90	1.90
350	A91	8c citron	7.00	7.00
351	A92	8c citron	3.25	3.25
352	A93	10c maroon	3.25	3.25
353	A94	10c maroon	3.25	3.25
354	A95	25c rose lilac	35.00	35.00
		Nos. 340-354,C24-C29,E10-E11 (23)	132.90	132.90
		Set, never hinged	170.00	

Nos. 340-354 were sold by the Cuban PO for 3 days, Oct. 13-15, during which no other stamps were sold. They were postally valid for the full face value. Proceeds from their three-day sale above 30,000 pesos were paid by the Cuban POD to the Assoc. of American Writers and Artists. Remainders were overprinted "SVP" (Without Postal Value).

No. 283 Surcharged in Green

1937, Nov. 19 **Unwmk.** ***Perf. 12***

355	A44	10c on 25c violet	16.00	4.00
		Never hinged	22.50	

Centenary of Cuban railroads.

Ciboney Indian and Cigar — A96

Cigar and Globe — A97

Tobacco Plant and Cigars — A98

1939, Aug. 28 **Wmk. 106** ***Perf. 10***

356	A96	1c yellow green	.75	.25
357	A97	2c red	1.00	.25
358	A98	5c brt ultra	1.75	.30
		Nos. 356-358 (3)	3.50	.80
		Set, never hinged	5.25	

General Calixto García
A99 A100

1939, Nov. 6 ***Perf. 10, Imperf.***

359	A99	2c dark red	.95	.25
360	A100	5c deep blue	1.25	.40
		Set, never hinged	3.50	

Birth centenary of General Garcia.
Values are for perf examples. Value of imperfs approx. 20% higher.

Gonzalo de Quesada — A101

1940, Apr. 30 **Engr.** ***Perf. 10***

361	A101	2c rose red	1.75	.50
		Never hinged	2.75	

Pan American Union, 50th anniversary.

Rotary Club Emblem, Cuban Flag and Tobacco Plant — A102

1940, May 18 **Wmk. 106** ***Perf. 10***

362	A102	2c rose red	2.75	.75
		Never hinged	4.00	

Rotary Intl. Convention held at Havana.

Lions Emblem, Cuban Flag and Royal Palms — A103

1940, July 23

363	A103	2c orange vermilion	2.75	.75
		Never hinged	4.00	

Lions International Convention, Havana.

Dr. Nicolás J. Gutiérrez A104

1940, Oct. 28

364	A104	2c orange ver	1.90	.30
365	A104	5c blue	2.50	.30
a.		Sheet of four, imperf., unwmkd.	8.50	3.00
		Never hinged	12.00	
b.		As "a," black overprint ('51)	11.00	4.75
		Never hinged	17.00	
		Set, never hinged	5.50	

100th anniv. of the publication of the 1st Cuban Medical Review, "El Repertorio Medico Habanero."
No. 365a contains 2 each of Nos. 364-365 imperf. and sold for 25c.
For overprint see No. C43A.
In 1951 No. 365a was overprinted in black: "50 Aniversario Descubrimiento Agente Transmisor de la Flebre Amarilla por el Dr. Carlos J. Finlay Honor a los Martires de la Ciencia 1901 1951." The overprint is illustrated over No. C43A, but does not include the plane and "Correo Aereo."

Major General Guillermo Moncada — A105

Moncada Riding into Battle A106

1941, June 25

366	A105	3c dk brown, *buff*	1.75	.50
367	A106	5c bright blue	1.75	.50
		Set, never hinged	5.50	

Maj. Gen. Guillermo Moncada (1841-96).

Globe Showing Western Hemisphere A107

Maceo, Bolívar, Juárez, Lincoln and Arms of Cuba A108

"Labor: Wealth of America" — A109

Tree of Fraternity, Havana A110

Statue of Liberty — A111

Perf. 10, Imperf.

1942, Feb. 23 **Wmk. 106**

368	A107	1c emerald	.45	.25
369	A108	3c orange brown	.70	.25
370	A109	5c blue	1.20	.25
371	A110	10c red violet	3.00	1.00
372	A111	13c red	2.10	.65
		Nos. 368-372 (5)	7.45	2.40
		Set, never hinged	11.00	

Spirit of Democracy in the Americas.

The imperforate varieties are without gum. Value, set mint $10, used $5.

Ignacio Agramonte Loynaz — A112

Rescue of Sanguily by Agramonte A113

1942, Apr. 10 ***Perf. 10***

373	A112	3c bister brn	1.35	.50
374	A113	5c brt blue, *bluish*	2.75	1.00
		Set, never hinged	6.25	

100th anniv. of the birth of Ignacio Agramonte Loynaz, patriot.

"Unmask the Fifth Columnists" — A114

"Be Careful, The Fifth Column is Spying on You" — A115

"Destroy it. The Fifth Column is like a Serpent" — A116

"Fulfill your Patriotic Duty by Destroying the Fifth Column" — A117

"Don't be Afraid of the Fifth Column. Attack It" — A118

1943, July 5

375	A114	1c dk blue grn	.50	.25
376	A115	3c red	.85	.25
377	A116	5c brt blue	.85	.25
378	A117	10c dull brown	3.00	.70
379	A118	13c dull rose vio	4.25	1.50
		Nos. 375-379 (5)	9.45	2.95
		Set, never hinged	13.50	

General Eloy Alfaro and Flags of Cuba and Ecuador A119

1943, Sept. 20

380	A119	3c green	2.50	.30
		Never hinged	3.00	

General Eloy Alfaro of Ecuador, 100th birth anniv.

Retirement Security A120

1943, Nov. 8 **Wmk. 106** ***Perf. 10***

381	A120	1c yellow green	.65	.30
382	A120	3c vermilion	.65	.30
383	A120	5c bright blue	1.00	.40

1944, Mar. 18

384	A120	1c bright yel grn	1.40	.40
385	A120	3c salmon	1.40	.40
386	A120	5c light blue	3.00	1.10
		Nos. 381-386 (6)	8.10	2.90
		Set, never hinged	12.00	

Half the proceeds from the sale of Nos. 381-386 were used for the Communications Ministry Employees' Retirement Fund.

Portrait of Columbus — A121

Bartolomé de Las Casas — A122

First Statue of Columbus at Cárdenas — A123

Discovery of Tobacco A124

Columbus Sights Land A125

1944, May 19

387	A121	1c dk yellow grn	.35	.25
a.		Pair, imperf horiz.		150.00
388	A122	3c brown	.55	.25
389	A123	5c brt blue	1.00	.25
390	A124	10c dark violet	3.00	.75
391	A125	13c dark red	5.00	1.75
		Nos. 387-391,C36-C37 (7)	13.50	4.40
		Set, never hinged	27.50	

450th anniv. of the discovery of America.

Major General Carlos Roloff — A126

1944, Aug. 21

392	A126	3c violet	1.35	.30
		Never hinged	2.25	

Maj. Gen. Carlos Roloff, 100th birth anniv.

Americas Map and 1st Brazilian Postage Stamps — A127

1944, Dec. 20 **Engr.**

393	A127	3c brown orange	3.00	.75
		Never hinged	4.50	

Cent. of the 1st postage stamps of the Americas, issued by Brazil in 1843.

Seal of the Society — A128

Luis de las Casas and Luis Maria Penalyer A129

1945, Oct. 5 **Wmk. 106** ***Perf. 10***

394	A128	1c yellow green	.50	.25
395	A129	2c scarlet	1.25	.25
		Set, never hinged	2.75	

Sesquicentenary of the founding of the Economic Society of Friends of the Country.

Aged Couple A130

1945, Dec. 27

396	A130	1c dk yellow grn	.25	.25
397	A130	2c scarlet	.40	.25
398	A130	5c cobalt blue	.90	.25

1946, Mar. 26

399	A130	1c brt yellow grn	.75	.25
400	A130	2c salmon pink	.45	.25
401	A130	5c light blue	.75	.25
		Nos. 396-401 (6)	3.50	1.50
		Set, never hinged	5.00	

See note after No. 386.

Catalogue values for unused stamps in this section, from this point to the end of the section, are for Never Hinged items.

Gabriel de la Concepcion Valdés Plácido A131

1946, Feb. 5

402	A131	2c scarlet	1.00	.30

Cent. of the death of the poet Gabriel de la Concepcion Valdés.

Manuel Marquez Sterling — A132

1946, Apr. 30

403 A132 2c scarlet 3.50 .30

Founding of the Manuel Marquez Sterling Professional School of Journalism, 3th anniv.

Globe and Cross — A133

1946, July 4 **Engr.**

404 A133 2c scarlet, *pink* 1.25 .25

80th anniv. of the Intl. Red Cross.

Cow and Milkmaid — A134

1947, Feb. 20 **Wmk. 106** ***Perf. 10***

405 A134 2c scarlet 3.50 .40

1947 National Livestock Exposition.

Franklin D. Roosevelt — A135

1947, Apr. 12

406 A135 2c vermilion 3.00 .40

2nd anniv. of the death of Franklin D. Roosevelt.

Antonio Oms Sarret and Aged Couple A136

1947, Oct. 20

407 A136 1c dp yellow grn .50 .30
408 A136 2c scarlet .50 .30
409 A136 5c lt blue 1.00 .55
Nos. 407-409 (3) 2.00 1.15

See note after No. 386.

Marta Abreu Arenabio de Estevez — A137

"Charity" — A138

Marta Abreu Monument, Santa Clara A139

"Patriotism" A140

1947, Nov. 29

410 A137 1c dp yellow grn .70 .30
411 A138 2c scarlet 1.25 .30
412 A139 5c brt blue 2.50 .40
413 A140 10c dk violet 4.50 1.00
Nos. 410-413 (4) 8.95 2.00

Birth cent. of Marta Abreu Arenabio de Estevez, philanthropist and humanitarian.

Armauer Hansen A141

1948, Apr. 9

414 A141 2c rose carmine 2.50 .40

International Leprosy Congress, Havana.

Mother and Child A142

1948, Oct. 15 **Engr.**

415 A142 1c yellow grn .40 .25
416 A142 2c scarlet .50 .25
417 A142 5c brt blue 1.20 .40
Nos. 415-417 (3) 2.10 .90

See note after No. 386.

Death of José Martí — A143

Martí Rowing to Shore — A144

1948, Nov. 10 **Wmk. 106** ***Perf. 10***

418 A143 2c scarlet .85 .25
419 A144 5c brt blue 2.50 .45

50th anniversary of the death of José Martí, patriot (in 1945).

Tobacco Picking — A145

Liberty Carrying Flag and Cigars — A146

Cigar and Arms of Cuba — A147

1948, Dec. 6 **Size: 22½x26mm**

420 A145 1c green .35 .25
421 A146 2c rose car .50 .30
422 A147 5c brt blue 1.00 .30
Nos. 420-422 (3) 1.85 .85

Cuba's tobacco industry. See Nos. 445-447. For overprints and surcharge see Nos. 448-451, 512.

Equestrian Statue of Gen. Antonio Maceo — A148

Sword Salute to Maceo A149

Designs: 2c, Portrait of Maceo. 5c, Mausoleum, El Cacahual. 10c, East to West invasion. 20c, Battle of Peralejo. 50c, Declaration of Baragua. 1p, Death of Maceo at San Pedro.

1948, Dec. 15 **Wmk. 229** ***Perf. 12½***

423 A148 1c blue green .40 .25
424 A148 2c red .45 .25
425 A148 5c blue .60 .25
426 A149 8c black & brown 1.10 .40
427 A149 10c brown & bl grn 1.10 .25
428 A149 20c blue & car 4.50 1.10
429 A149 50c car & ultra 7.25 2.75
430 A149 1p black & violet 16.00 4.25
Nos. 423-430 (8) 31.40 9.50

Birth cent. (in 1945) of Maceo.

Symbol of Pharmacy A150

1948, Dec. 28 ***Perf. 10***

431 A150 2c rose carmine 1.75 .40

1st Pan-American Congress of Pharmacy, Havana, Dec. 1948.

Morro Lighthouse — A151

1949, Jan. 17 **Wmk. 229** ***Perf. 12½***

432 A151 2c carmine 2.50 .40

Centenary (in 1944) of the erection of the Morro Lighthouse.

Jagua Castle, Cienfuegos A152

1949, Jan. 27 **Wmk. 106** ***Perf. 10***

433 A152 1c yellow green 1.00 .30
434 A152 2c rose red 2.00 .30

200th anniv. of the construction of Jagua Castle and the cent. of the publication of the 1st newspaper in Cienfuegos.

Manuel Sanguily y Garritt — A153

1949, Mar. 31

435 A153 2c rose red 1.00 .30
436 A153 5c blue 2.50 .30

Manuel Sanguily y Garritt (1848-1925), cabinet member, editor, author.

Map of Isle of Pines — A154

1949, Apr. 26

437 A154 5c blue 3.00 .75

20th anniv. of the recognition of Cuban ownership of the Isle of Pines.

Ismael Cespedes — A155

1949, Sept. 28

438 A155 1c yellow green .60 .30
439 A155 2c scarlet .60 .30
440 A155 5c brt blue 1.25 .30
Nos. 438-440 (3) 2.45 .90

See note after No. 386.

Gen. Enrique Collazo — A156

1950, Feb. 28 **Engr.** ***Perf. 10***

441	A156	2c scarlet	.90	.25
442	A156	5c brt blue	2.50	.45

Centenary (in 1948) of the birth of General Enrique Collazo.

Enrique José Varona — A157

1950, Feb. 28

443	A157	2c scarlet	.90	.25
444	A157	5c brt blue	2.50	.25

Centenary of the birth of Enrique José Varona, writer and patriot.

Tobacco Types of 1948

1950, June 20 **Re-engraved**

Size: 21x25mm

445	A145	1c green	1.25	.30
446	A146	2c rose red	1.25	.30
447	A147	5c blue	2.00	.30
		Nos. 445-447 (3)	4.50	.90

The re-engraved stamps show slight differences in many minor details.

For overprints and surcharge see Nos. 448-451, 512.

No. 446 Overprinted in Black

1950, Apr. 27

448	A146	2c rose red	2.25	.30

Natl. Bank of Cuba opening, Apr. 27, 1950.

Re-engraved Tobacco Types of 1950 Overprinted in Carmine

1950, May 18

449	A145	1c yellow green	.50	.30
450	A146	2c lilac rose	.75	.30
451	A147	5c light blue	2.25	.30
		Nos. 449-451 (3)	3.50	.90

75th anniv. (in 1949) of the UPU.
No. 451 exists with surcharge inverted.

Manuel Balanzategui, Antonio L. Pausa and Train Wreck A158

1950, Sept. 21 **Engr.**

452	A158	1c yellow grn	1.50	.75
453	A158	2c scarlet	1.50	.75
454	A158	5c brt blue	4.25	1.25
		Nos. 452-454 (3)	7.25	2.75

Fernando Figueredo — A159

1951, Mar. 17 **Wmk. 106** ***Perf. 10***

455	A159	1c green	1.40	.25
456	A159	2c scarlet	1.40	.25
457	A159	5c brt blue	2.25	.25
		Nos. 455-457 (3)	5.05	.75

Three-fourths of the proceeds from the sale of these stamps were used for the Communication Ministry Employees' Retirement Fund.

See Nos. 474, C51-C56, E15. For surcharges see Nos. 474, C51-C56, E15.

Miguel Teurbe Tolón and Flag — A160

Narciso Lopez — A161

Emilia Teurbe Tolón Sewing Flag — A162

Cuban Flag — A163

Engraved and Lithographed

1951, July 3 **Wmk. 229** ***Perf. 13***

458	A160	1c Prus grn, ultra & red	.75	.30
459	A161	2c red & gray blk	1.00	.30
460	A162	5c ultra & red	3.00	.45
461	A163	10c rose vio, bl & red	5.00	.60
		Nos. 458-461,C41-C43,E13 (8)	31.25	5.40

Centenary of adoption of Cuba's flag.

Clara Louise Maass and Hospitals A164

Hospitals: Lutheran Memorial, Newark, N.J. and Las Animas, Havana.

Wmk. 106

1951, Aug. 24 **Engr.** ***Perf. 10***

462	A164	2c scarlet	3.00	.50

75th anniv. of the birth of Clara Louise Maass, (1876-1901), American nurse and martyr in yellow fever fight.

Airmail Type and

José Raul Capablanca — A165

Capablanca Club, Havana A166

Wmk. 229

1951, Nov. 1 **Photo.** ***Perf. 13***

463	A165	1c blue grn & org	6.25	.65
464	AP27	2c rose car & dk brn	8.00	1.25
465	A166	5c black & dp ultra	16.00	1.90
		Nos. 463-465,C44-C46,E14 (7)	95.25	13.60

Jose Raul Capablanca, World Chess titlist (1921). Value imperf., set of 7 pairs, $1,500.

Antonio Guiteras Holmes — A167

Guiteras Preparing Social Legislation A168

Fort of the Morrillo A169

Wmk. 106

1951, Oct. 22 **Engr.** ***Perf. 10***

466	A167	1c yellow green	.45	.25
467	A168	2c rose carmine	.75	.25
468	A169	5c deep blue	1.50	.40
		Nos. 466-468,C47-C49 (6)	19.20	4.60

16th anniv. of the Action of the Morrillo and to honor Antonio Guiteras Holmes, who was killed there.

Souvenir sheets containing stamps similar to Nos. 466-468, but in different colors, are listed as Nos. C49a-C49b.

Poinsettia — A170

1951, Dec. 1 **Engr. and Typo.**

469	A170	1c green & car	5.00	.25
470	A170	2c rose car & grn	5.50	.50

See Nos. 498-499.

Maj. Gen. José Maceo — A171

1952, Feb. 6 **Engr.**

471	A171	2c yellow brown	.75	.25
472	A171	5c indigo	1.50	.25

Birth centenary of Maceo.

Isabella I — A172

1952, Feb. 22

473	A172	2c bright red	2.25	.50

500th anniv. of the birth of Queen Isabella I of Spain.

Souvenir sheets containing 2c stamps of type A172 are listed as Nos. C50a-C50b.

Type of 1951 Surcharged in Green

1952, Mar. 18

474	A159	10c on 2c yel brn	2.75	.40

Receipt of Autonomy A173

Designs: 2c, Tomas Estrada Palma and Luis Estevez Romero. 5c, Barnet, Finlay, Guiteras and Nuñez. 8c, Capitol. 20c, Map, Central Highway. 50c, Sugar Mill.

Centers in Black

Wmk. 106

1952, May 27 **Engr.** ***Perf. 12½***

475	A173	1c dk green	.35	.25
476	A173	2c dk carmine	.40	.25
477	A173	5c dk blue	.60	.25
478	A173	8c dk brown car	.95	.25
479	A173	20c dk olive grn	2.40	.40
480	A173	50c dp orange	4.75	.80
		Nos. 475-480,C57-C60,E16 (11)	21.65	4.75

50th anniv. of the Republic of Cuba.

Hands Holding Coffee Beans A174

Designs: 2c, Map and man picking coffee beans. 5c, Farmer with pan of beans.

1952, Aug. 22 **Wmk. 229** ***Perf. 13½***

481	A174	1c green	.70	.25
482	A174	2c rose red	1.70	.30
483	A174	5c dk vio bl & aqua	2.50	.40
		Nos. 481-483 (3)	4.90	.95

Bicentenary of coffee cultivation.

Col. Charles Hernandez y Sandrino — A175

1952, Oct. 7 **Wmk. 106** ***Perf. 10***

484	A175	1c yellow grn	.30	.30
485	A175	2c scarlet	.55	.30
486	A175	5c blue	.65	.30
487	A175	8c black	1.90	.45
488	A175	10c brown red	1.90	.45
489	A175	20c brown	9.00	3.75
		Nos. 484-489,C63-C72,E17 (17)	63.95	25.15

See note after No. 457.

Alonso Alvarez de la Campa — A176

Portraits: 2c, Carlos A. Latorre. 3c, Anacleto Bermudez. 5c, Eladio G. Toledo. 8c, Angel Laborde. 10c, Jose M. Medina. 13c, Pascual Rodriguez. 20c, Carlos Verdugo.

Frame Engraved; Center in Black

1952, Nov. 27

490	A176	1c green	.40	.25
491	A176	2c carmine	.75	.25
492	A176	3c purple	.90	.25
493	A176	5c blue	.90	.60
494	A176	8c bister brn	2.00	.50
495	A176	10c orange brn	1.50	.50
496	A176	13c lilac rose	3.00	.75
497	A176	20c olive grn	4.50	1.25
		Nos. 490-497,C73-C74 (10)	22.95	6.15

Execution of 8 medical students, 81st anniv.

Christmas Type of 1951

Centers: Tree.

Frame Engr.; Center Typo.

1952, Dec. 1 Dated "1952-1953"

498	A170	1c yel grn & car	7.25	1.75
499	A170	3c vio & dk grn	7.25	1.75

Birthplace of José Martí — A177

Marti at St. Lazarus Quarry — A178

No. 501, Court martial. No. 502, Martiano house, Havana. No. 504, El Abra ranch, Isle of Pines. No. 505, Symbols, "Marti the Poet." No. 506, Marti and Bolivar statue, Caracas. No. 507, At desk in New York. No. 508, House where revolutionary party was formed. No. 509, 1st issue of "Patria."

1953 Engr. *Perf. 10*

500	A177	1c dk grn & red brn	.50	.25
501	A177	1c dk grn & red brn	.50	.25
502	A177	3c purple & brn	.55	.25
503	A178	3c purple & brn	.55	.25
504	A177	5c dp bl & dk brn	1.00	.25
505	A178	5c ultra & brn	1.00	.25
506	A178	10c red brn & blk	2.00	.40
507	A178	10c dk brn & blk	2.00	.40
508	A178	13c dk ol grn & dk brn	3.25	.80
509	A177	13c dk ol grn & brn	3.25	1.00
		Nos. 500-509,C79-C89 (21)	38.75	13.40

Centenary of birth of José Marti.

Rafael Montoro Valdez — A179

1953, Mar. 5

510	A179	3c dark violet	2.10	.30

Rafael Montoro Valdez, statesman, birth cent.

Francisco Carrera Justiz — A180

1953, Mar. 9

511	A180	3c rose red	2.10	.30

Francisco Carrera Justiz, educator, statesman.

No. 446 Surcharged with New Value

1953, June 16

512	A146	3c on 2c rose red	1.50	.25

Board of Accounts Bldg., Havana — A181

1953, Nov. 3 Engr.

513	A181	3c blue	1.35	.45
		Nos. 513,C90-C91 (3)	7.60	2.25

1st Intl. Cong. of Boards of Accounts, Havana, Nov. 2-9.

Miguel Coyula Llaguno — A182

Communications Assoc. Flag — A183

Designs: 3c, 8c, Enrique Calleja Hensell. 10c, Antonio Ginard Rojas.

1954 Dated 1953

514	A182	1c green	.30	.25
515	A182	3c rose red	.30	.25
516	A183	5c blue	1.40	.25
517	A182	8c brn car	2.25	.40
518	A182	10c brown	3.50	.65
		Nos. 514-518,C92-C95,E19 (10)	25.35	8.25

Nos. 515 and 517 show the same portrait, but inscriptions are arranged differently.

See note after No. 457.

Carlos J. Finlay — A184

Maximo Gomez — A184a

Portraits: 1c, José Marti. 3c, José de la Luz Caballero. 4c, Miguel Aldama. 5c, Calixto Garcia. 8c, Ignacio Agramonte. 10c, Tomas Estrada Palma. 14, Serafin Sanchez. 20c, José Antonio Saco. 50c, Antonio Maceo. 1p, Carlos Manuel de Cespedes.

1954-56 Wmk. 106 *Perf. 10*

519	A184	1c green	.45	.25
520	A184a	2c rose car	.45	.25
521	A184	3c violet	.45	.25
521A	A184	4c red lil ('56)	.50	.25
522	A184a	5c slate bl	.60	.25
523	A184a	8c car lake	.90	.25
524	A184	10c sepia	.90	.25
525	A184	13c org red	.75	.25
525A	A184a	14c gray ('56)	1.25	.25
526	A184	20c olive	2.50	.25
527	A184a	50c org yel	3.50	.45
528	A184a	1p orange	7.00	.45
		Nos. 519-528 (12)	19.25	3.40

See Nos. 674-680. For surcharges see Nos. 636, 641-643.

Maj. Gen. José M. Rodriguez — A185

Design: 5c, Gen. Rodriguez on horseback.

1954, June 8 Engr. *Perf. 12½*

Center in Dark Brown

529	A185	2c dark carmine	.90	.25
530	A185	5c deep blue	2.40	.40

Cent. of the birth of Maj. Gen. José Maria Rodriguez (in 1851).

Gen. Batísta Sanatorium — A186

1954, Sept. 21 Wmk. 106 *Perf. 10*

531	A186	3c deep blue	1.50	.25

See No. C107.

Santa Claus — A187

1954, Dec. 15

532	A187	2c dk grn & car	7.25	1.25
533	A187	4c car & dk grn	7.25	1.25

Christmas 1954.

Maria Luisa Dolz — A188

1954, Dec. 23

534	A188	4c deep blue	1.75	.30

Cent. of the birth of Maria Luisa Dolz, educator and defender of women's rights. See No. C108.

Cuban Flag and Scouts Saluting A189

1954, Dec. 27 *Perf. 12½*

535	A189	4c dark green	2.25	.30

Issued to publicize the national patrol encampment of the Boy Scouts of Cuba.

Rotary Emblem and Paul P. Harris — A190

1955, Feb. 23 Engr. Wmk. 106

536	A190	4c blue	2.75	.25

Rotary International, 50th anniversary.

See No. C109.

Maj. Gen. Francisco Carrillo — A191

Portrait: 5c, Gen. Carrillo standing.

1955, Mar. 8 *Perf. 10*

537	A191	2c brt red & dk bl	.75	.25
538	A191	5c dk bl & dk brn	1.50	.30

Cent. of the birth of Maj. Gen. Francisco Carrillo (1851-1926).

Stamp of 1885 and Convent of San Francisco — A192

Designs (including 1855 stamp): 4c, Volanta carriage. 10c, Havana, 19th century. 14c, Captain general's residence.

1955, Apr. *Perf. 12½*

539	A192	2c lil rose & dk grnsh bl	.95	.25
540	A192	4c ocher & dk grn	1.25	.30
541	A192	10c ultra & dk red	3.00	.85
542	A192	14c grn & dp org	7.00	2.00
		Nos. 539-542,C110-C113 (8)	20.55	6.65

Cent. of Cuba's 1st postage stamps.

Maj. Gen. Mario G. Menocal A193

Gen. Emilio Nuñez A194

Portraits: 10c, J. G. Gomez. 14c, A. Sanchez de Bustamente.

1955, June 22

543	A193	2c dark green	.65	.25
544	A194	4c lilac rose	.80	.25
545	A193	10c deep blue	1.50	.40
546	A194	14c gray violet	3.00	.90
		Nos. 543-546,C114-C116,E20 (8)	18.95	6.05

See note after No. 457.

Turkey — A195

Gen. Emilio Nuñez — A196

1955, Dec. 15 Engr.

547	A195	2c slate grn & dk car	6.75	1.50
548	A195	4c rose lake & brt grn	6.75	1.50

Christmas 1955.

1955, Dec. 27

549	A196	4c claret	1.75	.45
		Nos. 549,C127-C128 (3)	7.00	1.90

Cent. of the birth of Gen. Emilio Nunez, Cuban revolutionary hero.

Francisco Cajigal de la Vega (1695-1777) A197

1956, Mar. 27 *Perf. 12½*

552	A197	4c rose brn & slate bl	1.75	.55

Cuban post bicent. See No. C129.

Julian del Casal — A198

Portraits: 4c, Luisa Perez de Zambrana. 10c, Juan Clemente Zenea. 14c, José Joaquin Palma.

1956, May 2 Portraits in Black

553	A198	2c green	.50	.25
554	A198	4c rose lilac	.50	.25
555	A198	10c blue	1.75	.25
556	A198	14c violet	3.25	.25
		Nos. 553-556,C131-C133,E21 (8)	16.75	3.75

See note after No. 457.

Victor Muñoz — A199

1956, May 13
557 A199 4c brown & green 1.25 .55

Victor Munoz (1873-1922), founder of Mother's Day in Cuba. See No. C134.

Masonic Temple, Havana — A200

1956, June 5
558 A200 4c blue 1.50 .55

See No. C135.

Virgin of Charity, El Cobre — A201

1956, Sept. 8 *Perf. 12½*
559 A201 4c brt blue & yel 1.25 .30

Issued in honor of Our Lady of Charity of Cobre, patroness of Cuba. See No. C149.

"The Cry of Yara" — A202

1956, Oct. 10
560 A202 4c dk grn & brn 1.40 .30

Cuba's Independence from Spain.

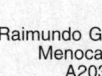

Raimundo G. Menocal A203

1956, Dec. 3 Wmk. 106 *Perf. 12½*
561 A203 4c dark brown 1.25 .30

Cent. of the birth of Prof. Raimundo G. Menocal, physician.

The Three Wise Men — A204

1956, Dec. 1
562 A204 2c red & slate grn 6.50 1.25
563 A204 4c slate grn & red 6.50 1.25

Christmas 1956.

Martin Morua Delgado — A205

1957, Jan. 30
564 A205 4c dark green 1.00 .30

Delgado, patriot, birth cent.

Boy Scouts at Campfire — A206

1957, Feb. 22 Wmk. 106 *Perf. 12½*
565 A206 4c slate grn & red 1.50 .40

Cent. of the birth of Lord Baden-Powell, founder of the Boy Scouts. See No. C152.

"The Blind," by M. Vega A207

Paintings: 4c, "The Art Critics" by M. Melero. 10c, "Volanta in Storm" by A. Menocal. 14c, "The Convalescent" by L. Romañach.

1957, Mar. Engr. *Perf. 12½*

Side and Lower Inscriptions in Dark Brown

566 A207 2c olive green .50 .25
567 A207 4c orange red .90 .30
568 A207 10c olive green 1.25 .50
569 A207 14c ultra 1.50 .55
Nos. 566-569,C153-C155,E22 (8) 14.40 4.30

See note after No. 457.

Emblem of Philatelic Club of Cuba — A208

1957, Apr. 24
570 A208 4c ocher, blue & red 2.00 .30

Issued for Stamp Day, Apr. 24, and the National Philatelic Exhibition. See No. C156.

Juan F. Steegers — A209

1957, Apr. 30
571 A209 4c blue 1.40 .30

Juan Francisco Steegers y Perera (1856-1921), dactyloscopy pioneer. See No. C157.

Victoria Bru Sanchez — A210

1957, June 3 Wmk. 106 *Perf. 12½*
572 A210 4c indigo 1.75 .30

Joaquin de Aguero in Battle of Jucaral — A211

1957, July 4
573 A211 4c dark green 1.60 .30

Issued to honor Joaquin de Aguero, Cuban freedom fighter and patriot. See No. C162.

Boy, Dogs and Cat — A212

1957, July 17
574 A212 4c Prus green 2.00 .55

Mrs. Jeanette Ryder, founder of the Humane Society of Cuba. See Nos. C163-C163a.

Col. Rafael Manduley del Rio — A213

1957, July 31
575 A213 4c Prus green 2.75 1.50

Issued to honor Col. Manduley del Rio, patriot, on the cent. of his birth (in 1856).

Palace of Justice A214

1957, Sept. 2 Engr. *Perf. 12½*
576 A214 4c blue gray 1.25 .40

Opening of the new Palace of Justice in Havana. See No. C165.

Generals of the Liberation — A215

1957, Sept. 26
577 A215 4c dl grn & red brn 1.00 .30
578 A215 4c dl bl & red brn 1.00 .30
579 A215 4c rose & brown 1.00 .30
580 A215 4c org yel & brn 1.00 .30
581 A215 4c lt violet & brn 1.00 .30
Nos. 577-581 (5) 5.00 1.50

Generals of the army of liberation.

1st Publication Printed in Cuba — A216

1957, Oct. 18 Wmk. 106 *Perf. 12½*
582 A216 4c slate blue 1.00 .40
Nos. 582,C167-C168 (3) 3.75 1.15

José Marti National Library.

Patio — A217

1957, Nov. 19
583 A217 4c red brn & grn 1.00 .40
Nos. 583,C173-C174 (3) 6.00 1.40

Cent. of the 1st Cuban Normal School.

Trinidad, Founded 1514 — A218

Fortifications, Havana, 1611 — A219

Views: 10c, Padre Pico street, Santiago de Cuba. 14c, Church of Our Lady, Camaguey.

1957, Dec. 17 Engr. *Perf. 12½*
584 A218 2c brown & indigo .30 .25
585 A219 4c slate grn & brn .70 .25
586 A219 10c sepia & red 1.60 .30
587 A219 14c green & dk red 2.40 .25
Nos. 584-587,C175-C177,E23 (8) 13.80 3.50

See note after No. 457.

Nativity — A220

1957, Dec. 20
588 A220 2c multicolored 4.50 .90
589 A220 4c multicolored 4.50 .90

Christmas 1957.

Dayton Hedges and Ariguanabo Textile Factory A221

1958, Jan. 30 Wmk. 106 *Perf. 12½*
590 A221 4c blue .65 .75

Issued to honor Dayton Hedges, founder of Cuba's textile industry. See No. C178.

Dr. Francisco Dominguez Roldan — A222

1958, Feb. 21
591 A222 4c green 1.25 .30

Roldan (1864-1942), who introduced radiotherapy and physiotherapy to Cuba.

José Ignacio Rivero y Alonso — A223

1958, Apr. 1

592	A223	4c lt olive green	1.25	.70

José Ignacio Rivero y Alonso, editor of Diario de la Marina, 1919-44. See No. C179.

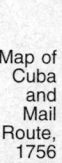

Map of Cuba and Mail Route, 1756 A224

1958, Apr. 24 *Perf. 12½*

593	A224	4c dk grn, aqua & buff	1.00	.30

Issued for Stamp Day, Apr. 24 and the National Philatelic Exhibition. See No. C180.

Maj. Gen. José Miguel Gomez — A225

1958, June 6 Wmk. 106 *Perf. 12½*

594	A225	4c slate	1.00	.40

Maj. Gen. José Miguel Gomez, President of Cuba, 1909-13. See No. C181.

Nicolas Ruiz Espadero — A226

Musicians: 4c, Ignacio Cervantes. 10c, José White. 14c, Brindis de Salas.

1958, June 27 *Perf. 12½*

Indigo Emblem

595	A226	2c brown	.60	.25
596	A226	4c dark gray	.60	.25
597	A226	10c olive green	.80	.25
598	A226	14c red	1.10	.25

Green Emblem

Physicians: 2c, Tomas Romay Chacon. 4c, Angel Arturo Aballi. 10c, Fernando Gonzalez del Valle. 14c, Vicente Antonio de Castro.

599	A226	2c brown	.70	.25
600	A226	4c gray	1.10	.25
601	A226	10c dark carmine	.80	.25
602	A226	14c dark blue	1.10	.25

Red Emblem

Lawyers: 2c, Jose Maria Garcia Montes. 4c, Jose A. Gonzalez Lanuza. 10c, Juan B. Hernandez Barreiro. 14c, Pedro Gonzalez Llorente.

603	A226	2c sepia	.50	.25
604	A226	4c gray	.80	.25
605	A226	10c olive grn	1.00	.25
606	A226	14c slate blue	1.10	.25
		Nos. 595-606 (12)	10.20	3.00

For surcharges see Nos. 629-631.

Carlos de la Torre — A227

1958, Aug. 29 Engr. Wmk. 321

607	A227	4c violet blue	1.50	.40
		Nos. 607,C182-C184 (4)	26.00	5.50

Dr. Carlos de la Torre y Huerta (1858-1950), naturalist. For surcharge see No. 632.

Poey's "Memorias" Title Page — A228

Felipe Poey — A229

1958, Sept. 26 Wmk. 106

608	A228	2c black & lt violet	.80	.25
609	A229	4c brown black	.95	.25
		Nos. 608-609,C185-C191,E26-E27 (11)	91.00	22.60

Felipe Poey (1799-1891), naturalist.

Theodore Roosevelt — A230

1958, Oct. 27 *Perf. 12½*

610	A230	4c gray green	1.25	.40

Theodore Roosevelt, birth cent. See No. C192.

Cattleyopsis Lindenii Orchid — A231

4c, Oncidium Guibertianum Orchid.

Engraved and Photogravure

1958, Dec. 16 Wmk. 321 *Perf. 12½*

611	A231	2c multicolored	5.50	1.25
612	A231	4c multicolored	5.50	1.25

Christmas. For surcharge see No. 633.

Flag and Revolutionary A232

Engr. & Typo.

1959, Jan. 28 Wmk. 321

613	A232	2c car rose & gray	.75	.30

Day of Liberation, Jan. 1, 1959.

Gen. Adolfo Flor Crombet (1848-95) — A233

1959, Mar. 18 Engr. Wmk. 106

614	A233	4c slate green	1.10	.40

For surcharge see No. 634.

Maria Teresa Garcia Montes — A234

1959, Nov. 11 *Perf. 12½*

615	A234	4c brown	1.10	.40

Maria Teresa Garcia Montes (1880-1930), founder of the Musical Arts Society. See No. C198. For surcharge see No. 635.

Carlos Manuel de Cespedes — A235

Presidents: No. 617, Salvador Cisneros Betancourt. No. 618, Manuel de Jesus Calvar. No. 619, Bartolomé Maso. No. 620, Juan B. Spotorno. No. 621, Tomas Estrada Palma. No. 622, Francisco Javier de Céspedes. No. 623, Vicente Garcia.

1959, Oct. 10 Wmk. 106 *Perf. 12½*

616	A235	2c slate blue	.55	.25
617	A235	2c green	.55	.25
618	A235	2c deep violet	.55	.25
619	A235	2c orange brown	.55	.25
620	A235	4c dark carmine	.70	.25
621	A235	4c deep brown	.70	.25
622	A235	4c dark gray	.70	.25
623	A235	4c dark violet	.70	.25
		Nos. 616-623 (8)	5.00	2.00

Issued to honor former Cuban presidents.

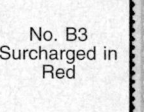

No. B3 Surcharged in Red

1960

624	SP2	2c on 2c + 1c car & ultra	1.00	.25

See No. C199.

Rebel Attack on Moncada Barracks A236

Designs: 2c, Rebels disembarking from "Granma." 10c, Battle of the Uvero. 12c, Map of Cuba and rebel ("The Invasion").

1960, Jan. 28 Wmk. 320

625	A236	1c gray ol, bl & ver	.25	.25
626	A236	2c bl, gray ol & brn	.70	.25
627	A236	10c bl, gray ol & red	1.75	.65
628	A236	12c brt bl, brn & grn	2.40	.30
		Nos. 625-628,C200-C202 (7)	17.10	3.85

First anniversary of revolution.

Stamps of 1956-59 Surcharged with New Value in Carmine or Silver

1960, Feb. 3

629	A226	1c on 4c dk gray & ind	.50	.25
630	A226	1c on 4c gray & grn	.50	.25
631	A226	1c on 4c gray & red	.50	.25
632	A227	1c on 4c violet bl	.50	.25
633	A231	1c on 4c multi (S)	.60	.50
634	A233	1c on 4c slate grn	.50	.25
635	A234	1c on 4c brown	.50	.25
636	A184a	2c on 14c gray	.90	.25
		Nos. 629-636,C203-C204 (10)	8.00	3.55

Tomas Estrada Palma Statue, Havana — A237

Statues: 2c, Mambi Victorioso (Battle of San Juan Hill), Santiago de Cuba. 10c, Marta Abreo de Estevez. 12c, Ignacio Agramonte, Camaguey.

Wmk. 321

1960, Mar. 28 Engr. *Perf. 12½*

637	A237	1c brn & dk bl	.25	.25
638	A237	2c green & red	.30	.25
639	A237	10c choc & red	.90	.25
640	A237	12c gray ol & vio	1.25	.45
		Nos. 637-640,C206-C208 (7)	7.40	2.95

See note after No. 386.

Nos. 521A, 522 and 525 Surcharged in Violet Blue, Red or Black

1960 Wmk. 106 *Perf. 10*

641	A184	2c on 4c red lil (VB)	.80	.40
642	A184a	2c on 5c sl bl (R)	1.25	.40
643	A184	2c on 13c org red	1.25	.40

No. 307B Surcharged in Black

644	A41	10c on 20c ol grn	1.25	.50
		Nos. 641-644 (4)	4.55	1.70

17th Olympic Games, Rome, Aug. 25-Sept. 11 — A238

Wmk. 321

1960, Sept. 22 Engr. *Perf. 12½*

645	A238	1c Sailboats	.45	.25
646	A238	2c Marksman	.55	.25
		Nos. 645-646,C212-C213 (4)	3.30	1.25

For souvenir sheet see No. C213a.

Camilo Cienfuegos and View of Escolar A239

1960, Oct. 27 Litho. Unwmk.

647	A239	2c brn, bl, grn & red	1.25	.25

1st anniv. of the death of Camilo Cienfuegos, revolutionary hero.

Morning Glory A240

Tobacco and Christmas Hymn A241

1960 Litho. *Perf. 12½*

648	A240	1c red	.75	.75
649	A241	1c Tobacco	1.50	1.50
650	A241	1c Mariposa	1.50	1.50
651	A241	1c Guaiacum	1.50	1.50
652	A241	1c Coffee	1.50	1.50
a.		Block of 4, #649-652	7.00	
653	A240	2c ultra	1.00	1.00
654	A241	2c Tobacco	3.00	3.00
655	A241	2c Mariposa	3.00	3.00
656	A241	2c Guaiacum	3.00	3.00
657	A241	2c Coffee	3.00	3.00
a.		Block of 4, #654-657	14.00	
658	A240	10c ocher	3.00	2.50
659	A241	10c Tobacco	10.00	6.00
660	A241	10c Mariposa	10.00	6.00
661	A241	10c Guaiacum	10.00	6.00
662	A241	10c Coffee	10.00	6.00
a.		Block of 4, #659-662	47.50	
		Nos. 648-662 (15)	62.75	46.25

Issued for Christmas 1960.

Nos. 648-662 were printed in three sheets of 25. Nine stamps of type A240 form a center cross, stamps of type A241 form a block of four in each corner with the musical bars joined in an oval around the floral designs.

"Public Capital for Economic Benefit" — A242

Designs: 2c, Chart and symbols of agriculture and industry. 6c, Cogwheels.

Perf. 11½

1961, Jan. 10 Unwmk. Photo.

663	A242	1c yel, blk & org	.40	.25
664	A242	2c bl, blk & red	.40	.25
665	A242	6c yel, red org & blk	1.00	.25
		Nos. 663-665,C215-C218 (7)	9.90	2.90

Issued to publicize the conference of underdeveloped countries, Havana.

Jesus Menéndez and Sugar Cane — A243

1961, Jan. 22 Litho. *Perf. 12½*

666	A243	2c dk grn & brn	.60	.25

Jesus Menéndez, leader in sugar industry.

Overprinted in Red

1961, May 2

667	A243	2c dk grn & brn	1.50	.25

Issued for May Day, 1961.

Dove and UN Emblem — A244

1961, Apr. 12 Litho. *Perf. 12½*

668	A244	2c red brn & yel grn	.60	.25
669	A244	10c emer & rose lil	1.25	.45
a.		Souv. sheet, #668-669, imperf.	5.00	
		Nos. 668-669,C222-C223 (4)	3.95	1.45

15th anniv. (in 1960) of the UN.

Stamp Day A245

Stamp Day: 1c, Revolutionary 10c stamp of 1874, 1868 "cancel." 2c, #238, 1902 "cancel." 10c, #613, 1959 "cancel."

1961, Apr. 24 Unwmk.

670	A245	1c dull rose & dk grn	.35	.25
671	A245	2c salmon & dk grn	.40	.25
672	A245	10c pale grn, car rose & blk	2.00	.40
		Nos. 670-672 (3)	2.75	.90

For overprint see No. 681.

Hand Releasing Dove — A246

1961, July 26 *Perf. 12½*

673	A246	2c blk, red, yel & gray	1.50	.25

26th of July (1953) movement, Castro's revolt against Fulgencio Batista.

Burelage on back consisting of wavy lines and diagonal rows of "CUBA CORREOS" in pale salmon.

Portrait Type of 1954

Designs: Same as before. On the 2c, "1833" is replaced by "?."

Wmk. 321 (Nos. 674, 676); Unwmkd. *Perf. 12½ (Nos. 674, 676); Rouletted*

1961-69 Engr.

674	A184	1c brown red	.50	.25
675	A184	1c lt blue ('69)	.30	.25
676	A184a	2c slate green	.50	.25
677	A184a	2c yel grn ('69)	.30	.25
678	A184	3c org ('64)	1.50	.25
679	A184	13c brn ('64)	1.50	.30
680	A184	20c lilac ('69)	1.75	.25
		Nos. 674-680 (7)	6.35	1.80

Issued: Nos. 674, 676, 8/1; Nos. 678-679, 12/764; others, 9/69.

For Nos. 675, 677-680, see embargo note following No. 702.

No. 672 Ovptd. in Red

Perf. 12½

1961, Oct. 7 Litho. Unwmk.

681	A245	10c pale grn, car rose & blk	2.00	.45

1st Official Phil. Exhib., Havana, Oct. 7-17.

Education Year — A247

Designs: One letter (per stamp) of "CUBA," book and various quotations by Jose Marti about the virtues of literacy.

1961, Nov. 22

682	A247	1c pale grn, red & blk	.25	.25
683	A247	2c blue, red & blk	.25	.25
684	A247	10c vio, red & blk	.90	.25
685	A247	12c org, red & blk	1.75	.60
		Nos. 682-685 (4)	3.15	1.35

A248

Christmas A249

No. 686, Polymita flammulata. No. 687, Polymita fulminata. No. 688, Polymita nigrofasciata. No. 689, Polymita fuscolimbata. No. 690, Polymita roseolimbata. No. 691, Tiaris canorus. No. 692, Ara tricolor. No. 693, Priotelus temnurus. No. 694, Mellisuga helenae. No. 695, Campephilus principalis. No. 696, Othreis toddi. No. 697, Uranidia boisduvalii. No. 698, Phoebis avellaneda. No. 699, Phaloe cubana. No. 700, Papilio gundlachianus.

1c, Snails. 2c, Birds, vert. 10c, Butterflies.

1961, Dec. 1

686	A248	1c multicolored	.50	.25
687	A249	1c multicolored	.50	.25
688	A249	1c multicolored	.50	.25
689	A249	1c multicolored	.50	.25
690	A249	1c multicolored	.50	.25
a.		Block of 5 + label, Nos. 686-690	2.50	1.50
691	A248	2c multicolored	2.00	.50
692	A249	2c multicolored	2.00	.50
693	A249	2c multicolored	2.00	.50
694	A249	2c multicolored	2.00	.50
695	A249	2c multicolored	2.00	.50
a.		Block of 5 + label, Nos. 691-695	12.50	4.00
696	A248	10c multicolored	3.00	1.00
697	A249	10c multicolored	3.00	1.00
698	A249	10c multicolored	3.00	1.00
699	A249	10c multicolored	3.00	1.00
700	A249	10c multicolored	3.00	1.00
a.		Block of 5 + label, Nos. 696-700	15.00	7.50
		Nos. 686-700 (15)	27.50	8.75

Stamps of the same denomination printed se-tenant in sheets of 20 stamps plus 5 labels picturing bells and star. Stamps of Type A249 are arranged in blocks of 4; Type A248 stamps and labels form a cross in sheet.

See Nos. 760-774, 912-926, 1025-1039, 1179-1193, 1303-1317, 1464-1478, 1572-1586.

3rd Anniv. of the Revolution A250

1962, Jan. 3

701	A250	1c multi	.85	.35
702	A250	2c multi	1.75	.45

See Nos. C226-C228.

Cuban goods have been embargoed by the United States since a Feb. 7, 1962 proclamation by President Kennedy, but according to the Office of Foreign Assets Control of the Treasury Department, used Cuban stamps can be imported and sold without limitation, and unused stamps may be imported for personal use, but not resold.

Natl. Militia A251

Silhouettes of militiamen and women and their peace-time occupations: 1c, Farmer. 2c, Welder. 3c, Seamstress.

1962, Feb. 26

703	A251	1c blue grn & blk	.30	.25
704	A251	2c deep blue & blk	.60	.25
705	A251	10c brt org & blk	2.10	.55
		Nos. 703-705 (3)	3.00	1.05

Bay of Pigs Invasion, 1st Anniv. — A252

1962, Apr. 17

706	A252	2c multi	.45	.25
707	A252	3c multi	.45	.25
708	A252	10c multi	3.00	.65
		Nos. 706-708 (3)	3.90	1.15

1st West Indies Packet A253

1962, Apr. 24

709	A253	10c red & gray	3.25	.90

Stamp Day. See No. E32.

Intl. Labor Day — A254

1962, May 1

710	A254	2c ocher & blk	.35	.25
711	A254	3c ver & blk	.75	.25
712	A254	10c greenish blue & blk	2.50	.70
		Nos. 710-712 (3)	3.60	1.20

Natl. Sports Institute (INDER) Emblem and Athletes — A255

1962, July 25 Wmk. 321

713	A255	1c Judo	.35	.25
714	A255	1c Discus	.35	.25
715	A255	1c Gymnastics	.35	.25
716	A255	1c Wrestling	.35	.25
717	A255	1c Weight lifting	.35	.25
718	A255	2c Roller skating	.35	.25
719	A255	2c Equestrian	.35	.25
720	A255	2c Archery	.35	.25
721	A255	2c Bicycling	.35	.25
722	A255	2c Bowling	.35	.25
723	A255	3c Power boating	1.00	.25
724	A255	3c One-man kayak	1.00	.25
725	A255	3c Swimming	1.00	.25
726	A255	3c Sculling	1.00	.25
727	A255	3c Yachting	1.00	.25
728	A255	9c Soccer	.90	.35
729	A255	9c Volleyball	.90	.35
730	A255	9c Baseball	.90	.35
731	A255	9c Basketball	.90	.35
732	A255	9c Tennis	.90	.35
733	A255	10c Boxing	.90	.35
734	A255	10c Underwater fishing	.90	.35
735	A255	10c Model-plane flying	.90	.35
736	A255	10c Pistol shooting	.90	.35
737	A255	10c Water polo	.90	.35
738	A255	13c Paddleball	1.00	.50
739	A255	13c Fencing	1.00	.50
740	A255	13c Sports Palace	1.00	.50

741 A255 13c Chess 1.00 .50
742 A255 13c Jai alai 1.00 .50
Nos. 713-742 (30) 22.50 9.75

Stamps of the same denomination printed se-tenant in sheets of 25. Various combinations possible.

9th Anniv. of the Revolution A256

Attack on Moncada Barracks: Abel Santamaria and: 2c, Barracks under siege. 3c, Children at Moncada School.

1962, July 26

743 A256 2c brn car & dark ultra .65 .35
744 A256 3c dark ultra & brn car 1.10 .55

8th World Youth Festival for Peace and Friendship, Helsinki, July 28-Aug. 6 — A257

1962, July 28

745 A257 2c Dove, emblem 1.00 .25
746 A257 3c Hand grip, emblem 1.75 .55
a. Min. sheet of 2, Nos. 745-746, imperf. 6.50 6.50

9th Central American and Caribbean Games, Kingston, Jamaica, Aug. 11-25 A258

1962, Aug. 27

747 A258 1c Boxing .25 .25
748 A258 2c Tennis .25 .25
749 A258 3c Baseball .25 .25
750 A258 13c Fencing 2.40 .80
Nos. 747-750 (4) 3.15 1.55

A259

First Natl. Congress of the Federation of Cuban Women — A260

1962, Oct. 1

751 A259 9c rose, blk & grn 1.10 .25
752 A260 13c blk, grn & lt blue 2.40 .65

Latin American University Games — A261

1962, Oct. 13 **Wmk. 106**

753 A261 1c Running .40 .25
754 A261 2c Baseball .85 .25
755 A261 3c Basketball 1.25 .25
756 A261 13c World map 2.50 .55
Nos. 753-756 (4) 5.00 1.30

World Health Organization Campaign to Eradicate Malaria — A262

Designs: 1c, Magnified specimen of the parasitic protozoa, microscope. 2c, Swamp and mosquito. 3c, Chemist's structural formulas for quinine, cinchona plant.

1962, Dec. 14

757 A262 1c multi .50 .25
758 A262 2c multi .50 .25
759 A262 3c multi 1.75 .45
Nos. 757-759 (3) 2.75 .95

Christmas Type of 1961

No. 760, Epicrates angulifer. No. 761, Cricosaurus typica. No. 762, Anolis equestris. No. 763, Tropidophis wrighti. No. 764, Cyclura macleayi. No. 765, Cubispa turquino. No. 766, Chrysis superba. No. 767, Essostruta roberto. No. 768, Hortensia conciliata. No. 769, Lachnopus argus. No. 770, Monophyllus cubanus. No. 771, Capromys pilorides. No. 772, Capromys pre-hensilis. No. 773, Solenodon cubensis. No. 774, Capromys pilorides (Blanca).

2c, Reptiles. 3c, Insects, vert. 10c, Rodents.

1962, Dec. 21 **Unwmk.**

760 A248 2c multi .65 .25
761 A249 2c multi .65 .25
762 A249 2c multi .65 .25
763 A249 2c multi .65 .25
764 A249 2c multi .65 .25
a. Block of 5 + label, Nos. 760-764 3.50 1.50
765 A248 3c multi 1.00 .60
766 A249 3c multi 1.00 .60
767 A249 3c multi 1.00 .60
768 A249 3c multi 1.00 .60
769 A249 3c multi 1.00 .60
a. Block of 5 + label, Nos. 765-769 5.50 4.50
770 A248 10c multi 4.00 1.25
771 A249 10c multi 4.00 1.25
772 A249 10c multi 4.00 1.25
773 A249 10c multi 4.00 1.25
774 A249 10c multi 4.00 1.25
a. Block of 5 + label, Nos. 770-774 21.00 9.00
Nos. 760-774 (15) 28.25 10.50

Christmas 1962. See note after No. 700.

Around 1962 a 1ctv. label picturing Fidel Castro was used as a voluntary contribution stamp. It is not inscribed "Correos" and was not valid for postage.

Soviet Space Flights — A263

Spacecraft and cosmonauts: 1c, Vostok 1, Yuri A. Gagarin, Apr. 12, 1961. 2c, Vostok 2, Gherman S. Titov, Aug. 6-7, 1961. 3c, Vostok 3, Andrian G. Nikolaev, Aug. 11-15, 1962, and Vostok 4, Pavel R. Popovich, Aug. 12-15, 1962. 9c, Vostok 5, Valery F. Bykovsky, June 14-19, 1963. 13c, Vostok 6, Valentina V. Tereshkova, June 16-19, 1963.

1963-64 **Wmk. 321**

775 A263 1c ultra, red & yel .35 .25
776 A263 2c grn, yel & rose lake .65 .25
777 A263 3c yel, vio & ver .65 .25
778 A263 9c red, dark vio & yel 1.25 .45
779 A263 13c dark blue green, dull red brown & yel 3.25 .70
Nos. 775-779 (5) 6.15 1.90

Issued: 1c, 2c, 3c, 2/26/63; others, 8/15/64.

Attack of the Presidential Palace, 6th Anniv. — A264

9c, Guerillas attacking palace. 13c, Four student leaders. 30c, Jose A. Echeverria, Menelao Mora.

1963, Mar. 13

780 A264 9c dark red & blk 1.10 .25
781 A264 13c chalky blue & sep 1.40 .45
782 A264 30c org & grn 3.50 1.00
Nos. 780-782 (3) 6.00 1.70

4th Pan American Games, Sao Paulo, Brazil, Apr. 20-May 5 — A265

1963, Apr. 20

783 A265 1c Baseball 1.25 .35
784 A265 13c Boxing 3.25 .65

Stamp Day A266

3c, Mask mailbox, 19th cent. 10c, Mask mailbox at the Plaza de la Catedral, Havana.

1963, Apr. 25

785 A266 3c black & dark org 1.00 .25
786 A266 10c black & pur 2.50 .50

See Nos. 828-829, 956-957 and 1102-1103.

Labor Day — A267

1963, May 1

787 A267 3c shown .50 .25
788 A267 13c Four workers 1.75 .60

Intl. Children's Week, June 1-7 — A268

1963, June 1

789 A268 3c blue blk & bister brn .50 .25
790 A268 30c blue blk & red 2.75 .80

Ritual Effigy — A269

Taino Civilization artifacts: 3c, Wood-carved throne, horiz. 9c, Stone-carved figurine.

1963, June 29

791 A269 2c org & red brn .75 .25
792 A269 3c ultra & red brn .90 .25
793 A269 9c rose & gray 1.60 .45
Nos. 791-793 (3) 3.25 .95

Montane Anthropology Museum, 60th anniv.

Broken Chains at Moncada A270

2c, Attack on the Presidential Palace. 3c, The insurrection. 7c, Strike of April 9. 9c, Triumph of the revolution. 10c, Agricultural reform and nationalization of industry. 13c, Bay of Pigs victory.

1963, July 26

794 A270 1c pink & blk .25 .25
795 A270 2c lt blue & vio brn .25 .25
796 A270 3c lt vio & brn .25 .25
797 A270 7c apple green & rose .25 .25
798 A270 9c olive bister & rose vio .50 .30
799 A270 10c beige & sage grn 1.50 .50
800 A270 13c pale org & slate blue 2.25 .90
Nos. 794-800 (7) 5.25 2.70

Indigenous Fruit — A271

1963, Aug. 19

801 A271 1c Star apple .25 .25
802 A271 2c Cherimoya .25 .25
803 A271 3c Cashew nut .35 .25
804 A271 10c Custard apple 2.00 .45
805 A271 13c Mangoes 2.50 1.40
Nos. 801-805 (5) 5.35 2.60

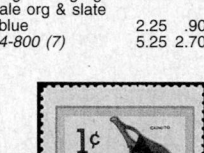

Geometric Shapes A272

View of a Town — A273

Designs: No. 806, Circle, triangle, square, vert. No. 807, Roof, window, vert. No. 808, View of a town. No. 809, View of a town in blue. No. 810, View of a town in olive bister and red. No. 811, Circle, triangle, vert. No. 812, House, roof and doorway, vert. No. 813, House, girders.

1963, Sept. 29 **Unwmk.**

806 A272 3c multi .50 .25
807 A272 3c multi .50 .25
808 A273 3c multi .50 .25
809 A273 3c multi .50 .25
810 A273 13c multi 1.50 .55
811 A272 13c multi 1.50 .55
812 A272 13c multi 1.50 .55
813 A272 13c multi 1.50 .55
Nos. 806-813 (8) 8.00 3.20

7th Intl. Congress of the Intl. Union of Architects.

Ernest Hemingway (1899-1961), American Author — A274

Hemingway and: 3c, The Old Man and the Sea. 9c, For Whom the Bell Tolls. 13c, Hemingway Museum (former residence), San Francisco de Paula, near Havana.

1963, Dec. 5 **Wmk. 321**

814 A274 3c brn & lt blue .75 .25
815 A274 9c sage grn & pink 1.75 .25
816 A274 13c blk & yel grn 3.00 .60
Nos. 814-816 (3) 5.50 1.10

Natl. Museum, 50th Anniv. — A275

Works of art: 2c, El Zapateo (Dance), by Victor P. Landaluze. 3c, Abduction of the Mulatto Women, by Carlos Enriquez, vert. 9c, Greek Panathean amphora, vert. 13c, My Beloved (bust of a young woman), by Jean Antoine Houdon, vert.

1964, Mar. 19 **Unwmk.**

817 A275 2c multi .25 .25
818 A275 3c multi .80 .25
819 A275 9c multi 1.10 .40
820 A275 13c multi 2.40 .65
Nos. 817-820 (4) 4.55 1.55

General Strike on Apr. 9, 6th Anniv. — A276

Rebel leaders: 2c, Bernardo Juan Borrell. 3c, Marcelo Salado. 10c, Oscar Lucero. 13c, Sergio Gonzalez.

1964, Apr. 9

821 A276 2c blk, yel grn & dull org .40 .25
822 A276 3c blk, red & dull org .70 .25
823 A276 10c blk, pur & beige 1.25 .30
824 A276 13c blk, brt blue & beige 2.50 .60
Nos. 821-824 (4) 4.85 1.40

Bay of Pigs Invasion, 3rd Anniv. A277

Designs: 3c, Fish in net. 10c, Victory Monument. 13c, Fallen eagle, vert.

1964, Apr. 17

825 A277 3c multi .30 .25
826 A277 10c multi .70 .35
827 A277 13c multi 2.00 .70
Nos. 825-827 (3) 3.00 1.30

Stamp Day Type of 1963

3c, Vicente Mora Pera, 1st postal director. 13c, Unissued provisional stamp, 1871.

1964, Apr. 24

828 A266 3c ocher & dull lil .50 .25
829 A266 13c dull vio & lt olive grn 2.50 .50

Labor Day — A278

1964, May 1

830 A278 3c Industry .40 .25
831 A278 13c Agriculture 1.60 .55

Diplomatic Relations with China — A279

Designs: 1c, China Monument, Havana. 2c, Cuban and Chinese farmers. 3c, Natl. flags.

1964, May 15

832 A279 1c multi .35 .25
833 A279 2c org brn, blk & apple grn .70 .25
834 A279 3c multi 1.40 .25
Nos. 832-834 (3) 2.45 .75

15th UPU Congress, Vienna, May-June A280

13c, Hemispheres on world map. 30c, Heinrich von Stephan. 50c, UPU Monument, Bern.

1964, May 29

835 A280 13c multicolored .85 .30
836 A280 30c multicolored 1.90 .80
837 A280 50c multicolored 4.00 1.40
Nos. 835-837 (3) 6.75 2.50

Development of Natl. Industry A281

1964, June 16

838 A281 1c Fish .40 .25
839 A281 2c Cow .60 .25
840 A281 13c Chickens 2.50 .60
Nos. 838-840 (3) 3.50 1.10

Merchant Fleet — A282

1964, June 30

841 A282 1c Rio Jibacoa .25 .25
842 A282 2c Camilo Cienfuegos .40 .25
843 A282 3c Sierra Maestra .60 .25
844 A282 9c Bahia de Siguanea 1.25 .50
845 A282 10c Oriente 3.50 .90
Nos. 841-845 (5) 6.00 2.15

Unification of Viet Nam — A283

Designs: 2c, Vietnamese guerrilla, American soldier. 3c, Northerner and southerner shaking hands over map of united Viet Nam. 10c, Ox-drawn plow, machinised harvester. 13c, Natl. flags and profiles of Cuban and Vietnamese farmers.

1964, July 20

846 A283 2c multi .30 .25
847 A283 3c multi .45 .25
848 A283 10c multi 1.00 .25
849 A283 13c multi 2.75 .60
Nos. 846-849 (4) 4.50 1.35

11th Anniv. of the Revolution — A284

Designs: 3c, Raul Gomez Garcia and poem. 13c, Cover of La Historia Me Absolvera, by Fidel Castro.

1964, July 25

850 A284 3c red, tan & blk .50 .25
851 A284 13c multi 3.00 .40

1964 Summer Olympics, Tokyo, Oct. 10-25 — A285

1964, Oct. 10 **Wmk. 376** ***Perf. 10***

852 A285 1c Gymnastics .30 .25
853 A285 2c Rowing .30 .25
854 A285 3c Boxing .30 .25
855 A285 7c Running, horiz. .70 .25
856 A285 10c Fencing, horiz. 1.50 .55
857 A285 13c Foil, cleats, oar, boxing glove, sun, horiz. 2.50 .85
Nos. 852-857 (6) 5.60 2.40

Satellite and Globe A286

Satellite and Partial Globe A287

No. C31 and Partial Globe A288

Various satellites and rockets.

1964, Oct. 15

858 A286 1c shown .25 .25
859 A287 1c shown .25 .25
860 A287 1c Globe LL .25 .25
861 A287 1c Globe UR .25 .25
862 A287 1c Globe UL .25 .25
a. Block of 5 + label, Nos. 858-862 1.00 1.00
863 A286 2c Spacecraft and globe .55 .25
864 A287 2c Globe LR .55 .25
865 A287 2c Globe LL .55 .25
866 A287 2c Globe UR .55 .25
867 A287 2c Globe UL .55 .25
a. Block of 5 + label, Nos. 863-867 3.00 1.50
868 A286 3c Satellite and globe .75 .35
869 A287 3c Globe LR .75 .35
870 A287 3c Globe LL .75 .35
871 A287 3c Globe UR .75 .35
872 A287 3c Globe UL .75 .35
a. Block of 5 + label, Nos. 868-872 4.00 2.50
873 A286 9c Satellite and globe, diff 1.75 .70
874 A287 9c Globe LR 1.75 .70
875 A287 9c Globe LL 1.75 .70
876 A287 9c Globe UR 1.75 .70
877 A287 9c Globe UL 1.75 .70
a. Block of 5 + label, Nos. 873-877 11.00 5.00
878 A286 13c Satellite and globe, diff. 2.40 1.75
879 A287 13c Globe LR 2.40 1.75
880 A287 13c Globe LL 2.40 1.75
881 A287 13c Globe UR 2.40 1.75
882 A287 13c Globe UL 2.40 1.75
a. Block of 5 + label, Nos. 878-882 16.00 10.00
883 A288 50c blk & lt grn 4.00 2.50
a. Souvenir sheet of one, Wmk. 321 15.00 12.50
Nos. 858-883 (26) 32.50 19.00

Experimental Cuban postal rocket flight, 25th anniv. Stamps of the same denomination printed se-tenant in sheets of 20 stamps and 5 inscribed labels. Stamps of Type A287 arranged in blocks of 4 with a complete globe in center of block; Type A286 stamps and labels form a cross in center of sheet. Inscribed "1939-Cohete Postal Cubano-1964."

No. 883a contains one 46x28mm stamp.

Type of A288 Ovptd. in Silver

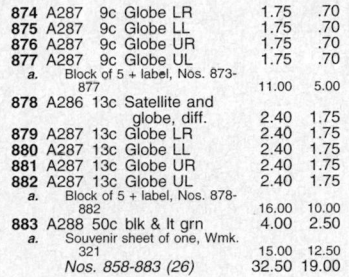

1964, Oct. 17 **Unwmk.**

884 A288 50c dark red brown & lt grn 5.00 1.50

No. 884 not issued without overprint.

40th Death Anniv. of Lenin — A289

Designs: 13c, Lenin Mausoleum, horiz. 30c, Lenin, star, hammer and sickle.

1964, Nov. 7 **Wmk. 376**

885 A289 3c org & blk .40 .25
886 A289 13c pur, pink & blk 1.10 .35
887 A289 30c blue & blk 2.25 .80
Nos. 885-887 (3) 3.75 1.40

Havana Zoo — A290

1964, Nov. 25

888 A290 1c Leopard, horiz. .30 .25
889 A290 2c Elephant .30 .25
890 A290 3c Fallow deer .30 .25
891 A290 4c Kangaroo, horiz. .30 .25
892 A290 5c Lions, horiz. .40 .25
893 A290 6c Eland, horiz. .50 .25
894 A290 7c Zebra, horiz. .50 .25
895 A290 8c Hyena, horiz. .75 .25
896 A290 9c Tiger, horiz. .75 .25
897 A290 10c Guanaco, horiz. .80 .25
898 A290 13c Chimpanzees, horiz. .90 .25
899 A290 20c Peccary, horiz. 1.10 .25
900 A290 30c Raccoon 1.60 .60
901 A290 40c Hippopotamus, horiz. 2.75 1.00
902 A290 50c Tapir, horiz. 3.00 1.40
903 A290 60c Dromedary 4.50 1.90
904 A290 70c Bison, horiz. 4.75 1.90
905 A290 80c Black bear 5.00 2.40
906 A290 90c Water buffalo, horiz. 5.50 3.00

Size: 47x32mm

907 A290 1p Deer in nature park, horiz. 9.25 3.00
Nos. 888-907 (20) 43.25 18.20

Heroes of the 1895 War of Independence — A291

1964, Dec. 7

908 A291 1c Jose Marti .25 .25
909 A291 2c Antonio Maceo .40 .25
910 A291 3c Maximo Gomez .75 .35
911 A291 13c Calixto Garcia 1.90 .70
Nos. 908-911 (4) 3.30 1.55

Christmas Type of 1961

No. 912, Dwarf cup coral. No. 913, Eusmilia fastigiata. No. 914, Acropora palmata. No. 915, Acropora profilera. No. 916, Diploria labyrinthiformis. No. 917, Condylactis gigantea. No. 918, Physalia physalis. No. 919, Aurelia aurita. No. 920, Linuche unguiculata. No. 921, Cassiopea frondosa. No. 922, Neocrinus blakei. No. 923, Eucidaris tribuloidas. No. 924, Tripneutes. No. 925, Ophiocoma echinata. No. 926, Oreaster celiculatus.

2c, Coral. 3c, Jellyfish. 10c, Starfish, sea-urchins.

1964, Dec. 18

912 A248 2c multi .80 .30
913 A249 2c multi .80 .30
914 A249 2c multi .80 .30
915 A249 2c multi .80 .30
916 A249 2c multi .80 .30
a. Block of 5 + label, Nos. 912-916 4.50 2.00
917 A248 3c multi 1.25 .50
918 A249 3c multi 1.25 .50
919 A249 3c multi 1.25 .50
920 A249 3c multi 1.25 .50
921 A249 3c multi 1.25 .50
a. Block of 5 + label, Nos. 917-921 7.50 3.00
922 A248 10c multi 2.25 1.00
923 A249 10c multi 2.25 1.00
924 A249 10c multi 2.25 1.00
925 A249 10c multi 2.25 1.00
926 A249 10c multi 2.25 1.00
a. Block of 5 + label, Nos. 922-926 12.50 7.00
Nos. 912-926 (15) 21.50 9.00

Christmas 1964. See note after No. 700.

Dr. Tomas Romay (1764-1849), Physician and Scientist — A292

Romay Monument — A293

Designs: 2c, First vaccination against smallpox. 3c, Portrait and treatise on vaccination.

1964, Dec. 21

927 A292 1c blk & olive brn .50 .25
928 A292 2c blk & tan .50 .25
929 A293 3c olive & dark red brown .60 .25
930 A293 10c bister & blk 2.40 .40
Nos. 927-930 (4) 4.00 1.15

Second Declaration of Havana A294

Map of Latin America and ripples or map of Cuba and peasant breaking shackles under text from the Declaration of Havana: No. 931a, 932a "Visperas de su muerte..." No. 931b, 932b, "Un continente, que juntos suponen representos..." No. 931c, 932c, "Y no se ocultaran ni el gobierna..." No. 931d, 932d, "Millones de mulatos latinamericanos que saben..." No. 931e, "A labran la tierra en condiciones..."

1964, Dec. 23

931 Strip of 5 5.00 3.50
a.-e. A294 3c any single .75 .40
932 Strip of 5 15.00 12.50
a.-e. A294 13c any single 1.75 1.50

Nos. 931-932 printed in sheets of 25 (5x5).

Dioramas in New Cuban Postal Museum — A295

1965, Jan. 4

Yellow & Black Border

933 A295 13c Maritime Post 3.25 .85
934 A295 30c Insurrection Post 2.50 1.25

Souvenir Sheet

Imperf

935 Sheet of 2 8.50 7.50
a. A295 13c like #933, blue & blk border 1.00 1.00
b. A295 30c like #934, blue & blk border 3.00 3.00
Nos. 933-935 (3) 14.25 9.60

Stamps in No. 935 have simulated perforations; buff margin is inscribed "PRECIO 50c" LR.

Fishing Fleet — A296

1965, May 1

936 A296 1c Schooner .25 .25
937 A296 2c Omicron .30 .25
938 A296 3c Victoria .45 .25
939 A296 9c Cardenas .70 .30
940 A296 10c Sigma 2.75 .60
941 A296 13c Lambda 4.25 1.00
Nos. 936-941 (6) 8.70 2.65

Intl. Women's Day — A297

1965, Mar. 8

942 A297 3c Lidia Doce 1.10 .30
943 A297 13c Clara Zetkin 1.60 .60

Technical Revolution — A298

Designs: 3c, Jose Antonio Echeverria University School. 13c, Stylized symbols of science and research, molecular structure and satellite dish.

1965, Mar. 31

944 A298 3c tan, blk & dark red brn .50 .25
945 A298 13c multi 2.50 .70

Cosmonauts, Rocket — A299

30c, Cosmonauts Pavel I. Balyayev, Aleksei A. Leonov taking first space walk.

1965, Apr. 2

946 A299 30c dark blue, blk & brn 2.50 .70
947 A299 50c brt pink & blue blk 4.50 1.40

Flight of Voskhod 2, the first man to walk in space, Mar. 17.

Abstract Wood Carving by Eugenio Rodriguez A300

Paintings in the Natl. Museum, Havana: 3c, Garden with Sunflowers, by Victor Manuel. 10c, Abstract, by Wilfredo Lam, horiz. 13c, Children, by Enrique Ponce, horiz.

1965, Apr. 12

948 A300 2c multi .35 .25

Size: 35x46mm

949 A300 3c multi .55 .25

Size: 46x35mm

950 A300 10c multi 1.50 .45

Size: 43x37mm

951 A300 13c multi 2.50 .80
Nos. 948-951 (4) 4.90 1.75

Abraham Lincoln — A301

Designs: 1c, Log cabin, birth site, horiz. 2c, Memorial, Washington, DC, horiz. 3c, Monument, Washington, DC. 13c, Portrait, quote.

1965, Apr. 15

952 A301 1c yel bister, red brn & gray .25 .25
953 A301 2c lt blue & dark blue .45 .25
954 A301 3c red org, blk & blue blk 1.25 .35
955 A301 13c org, blk & blue blk 2.50 .60
Nos. 952-955 (4) 4.45 1.45

Stamp Day Type of 1963

Stamp Day 1965: 3c, 18th Cent. postmarks and packet. 13c, No. C16 and airplanes over capital.

1965, Apr. 24

956 A266 3c sep & dark org 3.00 .25
957 A266 13c brt blue, sal rose & blk 2.75 .60

Intl. Quiet Sun Year — A302

1c, Sun, Earth's magnetic pole, horiz. 2c, Sun Year emblem. 3c, Earth's magnetic field, horiz. 6c, Atmospheric currents, horiz. 30c, Solar rays on planet surface. 50c, Effect on satellite orbits, horiz.

1965, May 10

958 A302 1c multicolored .25 .25
959 A302 2c multicolored .25 .25
960 A302 3c multicolored .55 .25
961 A302 6c multicolored .60 .25
962 A302 30c multicolored 2.10 .55
963 A302 50c multicolored 2.75 1.40
a. Souv. sheet of one, imperf. 8.00 8.00
b. As "a," changed colors 14.00 14.00
Nos. 958-963 (6) 6.50 2.95

Stamps in Nos. 963a-963b have simulated perforations.

Stamp in No. 963b is blue blk, Prus blue, org yel & red. Issued Oct. 10 for the Philatelic Space Exhibition, Havana, Oct. 10-17.

Intl. Telecommunications Union, Cent. — A303

1965, May 17

964 A303 1c Station, horiz. .25 .25
965 A303 2c Satellite .25 .25
966 A303 3c Telstar, horiz. .30 .25
967 A303 10c Telstar, receiving station 1.10 .25
968 A303 30c ITU emblem, horiz. 3.00 .90
Nos. 964-968 (5) 4.90 1.90

9th Communist World Youth and Students Congress — A304

1965, June 10

969 A304 13c Flags of Cuba and Algeria, emblem 1.50 .30
970 A304 30c Flags, guerrillas 2.50 .50

Matias Perez, Cuban Aeronautics Pioneer — A305

1965, June 23

971 A305 3c pink & blk 1.75 .95
972 A305 13c dull vio & blk, diff. 2.75 .95

Flowers and Maps of Their Locations
A306

1c, Rosa canina, Europe. 2c, Chrysanthemum hortorum, Asia. 3c, Strelitzia reginae, Africa. 4c, Dahlia pinnata, No. America. 5c, Cattleya labiata, So. America. 13c, Grevillea banksii, Oceania. 30c, Brunfelsia nitida, Cuba.

1965, July 20

973	A306	1c multicolored	.25	.25
974	A306	2c multicolored	.30	.25
975	A306	3c multicolored	.30	.30
976	A306	4c multicolored	.30	.25
977	A306	5c multicolored	1.60	.25
978	A306	13c multicolored	3.25	.95
979	A306	30c multicolored	4.75	1.60
		Nos. 973-979 (7)	10.75	3.85

1st Natl. Games — A307

1965, July 25

980	A307	1c Swimming	.25	.25
981	A307	2c Basketball	.35	.25
982	A307	3c Gymnastics	.70	.25
983	A307	30c Hurdling	2.75	.70
		Nos. 980-983 (4)	4.05	1.45

Revolution Museum Opening
A308

1965, July 26

984	A308	1c Anti-tank guns	.25	.25
985	A308	2c Tanks	.25	.25
986	A308	3c Bazookas	.25	.25
987	A308	10c Uniform, guerillas	.75	.25
988	A308	13c Compass, yacht Granma	2.10	.45
		Nos. 984-988 (5)	3.60	1.45

A309

1c, Finlay's signature. 2c, Anopheles mosquito. 3c, Portrait. 7c, Microscope. 9c, Dr. Claudio Delgado. 10c, Monument. 13c, Discussing theory with doctors.

1965, Aug. 20

989	A309	1c multicolored	.25	.25
990	A309	2c multicolored	.25	.25
991	A309	3c multicolored	.35	.25
992	A309	7c multicolored	.45	.25
993	A309	9c multicolored	.75	.25
994	A309	10c multicolored	1.90	.30
995	A309	13c multicolored	3.00	.65
		Nos. 989-995 (7)	6.95	2.20

Carlos J. Finlay (1833-1915), discovered transmission of yellow fever via aedes aegypti (not anopheles) mosquito. Nos. 990-995 vert.

Butterflies
A310

No. 996, Dismorphia cubana. No. 997, Anetia numidia briarea. No. 998, Carathis gortynoides. No. 999, Hymenitis cubana. No. 1000, Eubaphe heros. No. 1001, Lycorea ceres demeter. No. 1002, Eubaphe disparitis. No. 1003, Siderone nemesis. No. 1004, Syntomidopsis variegata. No. 1005, Ctenuchidia virgo. No. 1006, Prepona antimache crossina. No. 1007, Sylepta reginalis. No. 1008, Chlosyne perezi perezi. No. 1009, Anaea clytemnestra iphigenia. No. 1010, Anetia cubana.

1965, Sept. 22 **Unwmk.**

996	A310	2c multicolored	.50	.25
997	A310	2c multicolored	.50	.25
998	A310	2c multicolored	.50	.25
999	A310	2c multicolored	.50	.25
1000	A310	2c multicolored	.50	.25
a.		Strip of 5, Nos. 996-1000	3.75	2.50
1001	A310	3c multicolored	.75	.25
1002	A310	3c multicolored	.75	.25
1003	A310	3c multicolored	.75	.25
1004	A310	3c multicolored	.75	.25
1005	A310	3c multicolored	.75	.25
a.		Strip of 5, Nos. 1001-1005	5.00	3.25
1006	A310	13c multicolored	3.00	.80
1007	A310	13c multicolored	3.00	.80
1008	A310	13c multicolored	3.00	.80
1009	A310	13c multicolored	3.00	.80
1010	A310	13c multicolored	3.00	.80
a.		Strip of 5, Nos. 1006-1010	17.00	8.25
		Nos. 996-1010 (15)	21.25	6.50

Cuban Mint, 50th Anniv.
A311

Coins (obverse and reverse).

1965, Oct. 13

1011	A311	1c 20 centavos, 1962	.30	.25
1012	A311	2c 1 peso, 1934	.30	.25
1013	A311	3c 40 centavos, 1962	.30	.25
1014	A311	8c 1 peso, 1915	.80	.25
1015	A311	10c Marti peso, 1953	1.90	.40
1016	A311	13c 20 pesos, 1915	2.75	.50
		Nos. 1011-1016 (6)	6.35	1.90

Tropical Fruit — A312

1965, Nov. 15 ***Perf. 12½***

1017	A312	1c Oranges	.25	.25
1018	A312	2c Custard apples	.25	.25
1019	A312	3c Papayas	.25	.25
1020	A312	4c Bananas	.35	.25
1021	A312	10c Avocado	.60	.25
1022	A312	13c Pineapple	.95	.70
1023	A312	20c Guavas	2.50	.70
1024	A312	50c Marmalade plums	5.50	1.25
		Nos. 1017-1024 (8)	10.65	3.90

Christmas Type of 1961

Birds: No. 1025, Icterus galbula. No. 1026, Passerina ciris. No. 1027, Setophaga ruticillar. No. 1028, Dendroica tusca. No. 1029, Pheucticus ludovicianus. No. 1030, Pyranga olivacea. No. 1031, Dendroica dominica. No. 1032, Vermivora pinus. No. 1033, Protonotaria citrea. No. 1034, Wilsonia citrina. No. 1035, Passerina cyanea. No. 1036, Anas discors. No. 1037, Aix sponsa. No. 1038, Spatula clypeata. No. 1039, Nycticorax hoactli.

1965, Dec. 1

1025	A248	3c multicolored	1.60	1.25
1026	A249	3c multicolored	1.60	1.25
1027	A249	3c multicolored	1.60	1.25
1028	A249	3c multicolored	1.60	1.25
1029	A249	3c multicolored	1.60	1.25
a.		Block of 5 + label, Nos. 1025-1029	9.00	7.25
1030	A248	5c multicolored	1.75	1.75
1031	A249	5c multicolored	1.75	1.75
1032	A249	5c multicolored	1.75	1.75
1033	A249	5c multicolored	1.75	1.75
1034	A249	5c multicolored	1.75	1.75
a.		Block of 5 + label, Nos. 1030-1034	10.00	10.00
1035	A248	13c multicolored	4.00	3.00
1036	A249	13c multicolored	4.00	3.00
1037	A249	13c multicolored	4.00	3.00
1038	A249	13c multicolored	4.00	3.00
1039	A249	13c multicolored	4.00	3.00
a.		Block of 5 + label, Nos. 1035-1039	21.00	20.00
		Nos. 1025-1039 (15)	36.75	30.00

Christmas 1965. See note after No. 700.

Intl. Athletic Competition, Havana, 7th Anniv. — A313

1965, Dec. 11 **Wmk. 376** ***Perf. 10***

1040	A313	1c Hurdling	.25	.25
1041	A313	2c Discus	.25	.25
1042	A313	3c Shot put	.55	.25
1043	A313	7c Javelin	.55	.25
1044	A313	9c High jump	.70	.35
1045	A313	10c Hammer throw	1.40	.60
1046	A313	13c Running	2.00	.90
		Nos. 1040-1046 (7)	5.70	2.85

Fish in the Natl. Aquarium — A314

1c, Echeneis naucrates. 2c, Katsuwonus pelamis. 3c, Abudefduf saxatilis. 4c, Istiophorus. 5c, Epinephelus striatus. 10c, Lutianus analis. 13c, Ocyurus chrysurus. 30c, Holocentrus ascensionis.

1965, Dec. 5 **Unwmk.** ***Perf. 12½***

1047	A314	1c multicolored	.25	.25
1048	A314	2c multicolored	.25	.25
1049	A314	3c multicolored	.55	.25
1050	A314	4c multicolored	.65	.25
1051	A314	5c multicolored	.65	.25
1052	A314	10c multicolored	.80	.30
1053	A314	13c multicolored	2.75	.80
1054	A314	30c multicolored	4.50	1.25
		Nos. 1047-1054 (8)	10.40	3.60

Andre Voisin (d. 1964), French Naturalist — A315

13c, Portrait, flags, microscope, plant.

1965, Dec. 21 **Wmk. 376**

1055	A315	3c shown	1.00	.25
1056	A315	13c multicolored	2.50	.55

Transportation — A316

1c, Skoda bus, Czechoslovakia. 2c, Ikarus bus, Hungary. 3c, Leyland bus, G.B. 4c, TEM-4 locomotive, USSR. 7c, BB-69.000 locomotive, France. 10c, Remolcador tugboat, DDR. 13c, 15 de Marzo freighter, Spain. 20c, Ilyushin 18 jet, USSR.

1965, Dec. 30

1057	A316	1c multicolored	.25	.25
1058	A316	2c multicolored	.25	.25
1059	A316	3c multicolored	.25	.25
1060	A316	4c multicolored	3.00	.70
1061	A316	7c multicolored	3.00	.70
1062	A316	10c multicolored	1.25	.35
1063	A316	13c multicolored	2.00	.60
1064	A316	20c multicolored	2.50	1.00
		Nos. 1057-1064 (8)	12.50	4.10

A317

7th Anniv. of the Revolution
A318

1966, Jan. 2

1065	A317	1c Guerrillas	.25	.25
1066	A317	2c Commander and tank	.25	.25
1067	A317	3c Sailor, patrol boat	.90	.25
1068	A318	10c Jet aircraft	1.90	.45
1069	A318	13c Rocket	2.25	.70
		Nos. 1065-1069 (5)	5.55	1.90

Conference of Asian, African and South American Countries, Havana — A319

1966, Jan. 3

1070	A319	2c Emblem at R	.25	.25
1071	A319	3c Emblem at L	.40	.25
1072	A319	13c Emblem at center	2.10	.55
		Nos. 1070-1072 (3)	2.75	1.05

Guardalabarca Beach — A320

1966, Feb. 10

1073	A320	1c shown	.30	.25
1074	A320	2c Gran Piedra mountain	.30	.25
1075	A320	3c Guama Village	.90	.25
1076	A320	13c Soroa waterfall, vert.	2.50	.60
		Nos. 1073-1076 (4)	4.00	1.35

11th Medical and 7th Natl. Dental Congresses — A321

1966, Feb. 28 **Wmk. 376**

1077	A321	3c multi	.30	.25
1078	A321	13c multi, diff.	1.50	.55

Folk Art A322

1c, Afro-cuban ritual puppet. 2c, Sombreros. 3c, Ceramic vase. 7c, Lanterns, lamp. 9c, Table lamp. 10c, Shark, wood sculpture. 13c, Snail-shell necklace, earrings.

1966, Feb. 28 **Unwmk.**

1079	A322	1c multicolored	.25	.25
1080	A322	2c multicolored	.25	.25
1081	A322	3c multicolored	.25	.25
1082	A322	7c multicolored	.25	.25
1083	A322	9c multicolored	.80	.25
1084	A322	10c multicolored	1.25	.30
1085	A322	13c multicolored	2.50	.60
		Nos. 1079-1085 (7)	5.55	2.15

Nos. 1079-1083 vert.

Chelsea College, by Canaletto — A323

Ceramics and paintings in the National Museum: 1c, Ming vase. 3c, Portrait of a Lady, by Goya. 13c, Portrait of Fayum, encaustic painting. Nos. 1086, 1088-1089 vert.

1966, Mar. 31 **Wmk. 376**

1086	A323	1c multi	.25	.25
1087	A323	2c multi	.85	.25
1088	A323	3c multi	.75	.25
1089	A323	13c multi	3.00	.70
		Nos. 1086-1089 (4)	4.85	1.45

First Man in Space, 5th Anniv. A324

Designs: 1c, Konstantin Eduardovich Tsiolkovsky (1857-1935), Soviet rocket and space sciences pioneer. 2c, Cosmonauts in training, vert. 3c, Yuri Gagarin, rocket, Earth. 7c, Cosmonauts Nikolaev and Popovich, vert. 9c, Tereshkova and Bykovsky. 10c, Komarov, Feoktistov and Yegorov. 13c, Leonov taking first space walk.

1966, Apr. 12

1090	A324	1c multi	.25	.25
1091	A324	2c multi	.25	.25
1092	A324	3c multi	.35	.25
1093	A324	7c multi	.60	.25
1094	A324	9c multi	.85	.25
1095	A324	10c multi	1.10	.30
1096	A324	13c multi	2.25	.55
		Nos. 1090-1096 (7)	5.65	2.10

Bay of Pigs Invasion, 5th Anniv. A325

1966, Apr. 17

1097	A325	2c Tank	.25	.25
1098	A325	3c Burning ship, plane crash	.95	.25
1099	A325	9c Tank in ditch	.40	.25
1100	A325	10c Soldier, gunners	1.75	.25
1101	A325	13c Operations map	3.00	.70
		Nos. 1097-1101 (5)	6.35	1.70

Stamp Day Type of 1963

Designs: 3c, Cuban Postal Museum interior. 13c, No. 613 and stamp collector.

1966, Apr. 24

1102	A266	3c sage grn & sal rose	1.25	.25
1103	A266	13c brn, sal rose & blk	3.50	.80

Stamp Day 1966. 1st Anniv. of the Cuban Postal Museum (No. 1102); 1st anniv. of the Cuban Philatelic Federation (No. 1103).

Flowers and Symbols of Industry — A326

1966, May 1

1104	A326	2c Anvil	.25	.25
1105	A326	3c Machete	.30	.25
1106	A326	10c Hammer	.70	.25
1107	A326	13c Hemisphere, gearwheel	1.75	.90
		Nos. 1104-1107 (4)	3.00	1.65

Labor Day.

Opening of the World Health Organization Headquarters, Geneva — A327

Views of WHO headquarters and emblem or emblem on flag.

1966, May 3

1108	A327	2c blk & yel org	.25	.25
1109	A327	3c blk, lt blue & yel org	.70	.25
1110	A327	13c blk, lt blue & yel org	2.10	.55
		Nos. 1108-1110 (3)	3.05	1.05

10th Central American and Caribbean Games, Puerto Rico, June 11-25 A328

1966, June 11

1111	A328	1c Running, vert.	.25	.25
1112	A328	2c Rifle shooting	.30	.25
1113	A328	3c Baseball, vert.	.45	.25
1114	A328	7c Volleyball, vert.	.45	.25
1115	A328	9c Soccer, vert.	.80	.25
1116	A328	10c Boxing, vert.	1.40	.25
1117	A328	13c Basketball, vert.	3.50	.55
		Nos. 1111-1117 (7)	7.15	2.05

Progress in Education A329

Designs: 1c, Makarenko School, Playa de Tarara. 2c, Natl. Literacy Campaign Museum. 3c, Lantern, literacy campaign emblem for 1961. 10c, Frank Pais education team in the mountains. 13c, Farmer, factory worker.

1966, June 15

1118	A329	1c grn & blk	.25	.25
1119	A329	2c yel, olive bister & blk	.25	.25
1120	A329	3c brt blue, lt blue & blk	.30	.25
1121	A329	10c golden brn, brn & blk	.90	.25
1122	A329	13c multi	2.40	.45
		Nos. 1118-1122 (5)	4.10	1.45

1st Graduating class of Makarenko School (1c), 5th anniv. of the Natl. Literacy Campaign (3c), 4th anniv. of agricultural and industrial trade education (13c).

12th Congress of the Cuban Labor Organization — A330

1966, Aug. 12

1123	A330	3c multi	.75	.25

Sea Shells — A331

1c, Liguus flammellus. 2c, Cypraea zebra. 3c, Strombus pugilis. 7c, Aequipecten muscosu. 9c, Liguus fasciatus crenatus. 10c, Charonia variegata. 13c, Liguus fasciatus archeri.

1966, Aug. 25 **Unwmk.**

1124	A331	1c multicolored	.35	.25
1125	A331	2c multicolored	.45	.25
1126	A331	3c multicolored	.70	.25
1127	A331	7c multicolored	.80	.25
1128	A331	9c multicolored	.90	.25
1129	A331	10c multicolored	1.75	.40
1130	A331	13c multicolored	3.50	.80
		Nos. 1124-1130 (7)	8.45	2.45

Breeding Messenger Pigeons — A332

2c, Timer. 3c, Coops. 7c, Breeder tending coops. 9c, Pigeons in yard. 10c, Two men, message. 13c, Baracoa to Havana championship flight, July 26, 1959.

1966, Sept. 18 **Wmk. 376**

1131	A332	1c shown	.40	.25
1132	A332	2c multicolored	.40	.25
1133	A332	3c multicolored	.40	.25
1134	A332	7c multicolored	.80	.25
1135	A332	9c multicolored	.80	.35
1136	A332	10c multicolored	2.50	.50

Size: 47x32mm

1137	A332	13c multicolored	3.75	.90
		Nos. 1131-1137 (7)	9.05	2.75

Provincial and Natl. Coats of Arms, Map of Cuba — A333

1966, Oct. 10

1138	A333	1c Pinar del Rio	.25	.25
1139	A333	2c Havana	.30	.25
1140	A333	3c Matanzas	.30	.25
1141	A333	4c Las Villas	.40	.25
1142	A333	5c Camaguey	.60	.25
1143	A333	9c Oriente	1.00	.45

Size: 30x48mm

1144	A333	13c National arms	2.25	.55
		Nos. 1138-1144 (7)	5.10	2.25

17th World Chess Olympiad, Havana — A334

1c, Pawn. 2c, Rook. 3c, Knight. 9c, Bishop. 10c, Queen, games, horiz. 13c, King and emblem, horiz.

30c, Capablanca Vs. Lasker, 1914, horiz.

1966, Oct. 18

1145	A334	1c multicolored	.30	.25
1146	A334	2c multicolored	.30	.25
1147	A334	3c multicolored	.50	.25
1148	A334	9c multicolored	1.00	.25
1149	A334	10c multicolored	2.40	.25
1150	A334	13c multicolored	3.25	.60
		Nos. 1145-1150 (6)	7.75	1.85

Souvenir Sheet

Imperf

1151	A334	30c multicolored	12.00	12.00

No. 1151 contains one 49½x31mm stamp.

Cuban-Soviet Diplomatic Relations — A335

2c, Lenin Hospital. 3c, Oil tanker, world map. 10c, Workers, gearwheels. 13c, Agriculture.

1966, Nov. 7

1152	A335	2c multicolored	.25	.25
1153	A335	3c multicolored	.35	.25
1154	A335	10c multicolored	1.10	.25
1155	A335	13c multicolored	2.25	.70
		Nos. 1152-1155 (4)	3.95	1.45

2nd Song Festival A336

Cuban composers and their compositions: 1c, Amadeo Roldan. 2c, Eduardo Sanchez de Fuentes. 3c, Moises Simons. 7c, Jorge Anckermann. 9c, Alejandro G. Caturla. 10c, Eliseo Grenet. 13c, Ernesto Lecuona.

1966, Nov. 18

1156	A336	1c multicolored	.25	.25
1157	A336	2c multicolored	.30	.25
1158	A336	3c multicolored	.30	.25
1159	A336	7c multicolored	.80	.25
1160	A336	9c multicolored	.80	.25
1161	A336	10c multicolored	3.00	.45
1162	A336	13c multicolored	4.00	.90
		Nos. 1156-1162 (7)	9.45	2.60

Viet Nam War — A337

Flag of Viet Nam and: 2c, US aircraft discharging bombs, dead cattle. 3c, Gas mask and victims. 13c, US bombs, women and children.

1966, Nov. 23

1163	A337	2c multi	.40	.25
1164	A337	3c multi	.60	.25
1165	A337	13c multi	2.00	.60
		Nos. 1163-1165 (3)	3.00	1.10

10th Anniv. of Successful Revolution Campaigns — A338

Revolution leaders, scenes of the insurrection: 1c, Antonio Fernandez. 2c, Candido Gonzalez. 3c, Jose Tey. 7c, Tony Aloma. 9c, Otto Parellada. 10c, Juan Manuel Marquez. 13c, Frank Pais.

1966, Nov. 30

1166	A338	1c multicolored	.25	.25
1167	A338	2c multicolored	.25	.25
1168	A338	3c multicolored	.25	.25
1169	A338	7c multicolored	.30	.25
1170	A338	9c multicolored	.60	.25
1171	A338	10c multicolored	2.00	.50
1172	A338	13c multicolored	1.90	.80
		Nos. 1166-1172 (7)	5.55	2.55

Intl. Leisure Time and Recreation Seminar — A339

9c, World map, stopwatch, eye. 13c, Earth, clock, emblem.

1966, Dec. 2

1173	A339	3c shown	.25	.25
1174	A339	9c multicolored	1.40	.25
1175	A339	13c multicolored	1.75	.60
		Nos. 1173-1175 (3)	3.40	1.10

1st Natl. Telecommunications Forum — A340

1966, Dec. 12

1176	A340	3c shown	.75	.25
1177	A340	10c Satellite in orbit	3.75	.25
1178	A340	13c Shell, satellite	5.50	.70
a.		Souv. sheet of 3, #1176-1178, imperf	15.00	15.00
		Nos. 1176-1178 (3)	10.00	1.20

No. 1178a sold for 30c.

Christmas Type of 1961

No. 1179, Cypripedium eurylochus. No. 1180, Cattleya speciosissima. No. 1181, Cattleya mendelii majestica. No. 1182, Cattleya trianae amesiana. No. 1183, Cattleya labiata macfarlanei. No. 1184, Cypripedium morganiae burfordense. No. 1185, Cattleya Countess of Derby. No. 1186, Cypripedium hookerae volunteanum. No. 1187, Cattleya warscewiczii reginae burfordense. No. 1188, Cypripedium stonei cannartae. No. 1189, Cattleya mendelii Duchess of Montrose. No. 1190, Oncidium macranthum. No. 1191, Cypripedium stonei platytoenium. No. 1192, Cattleya dowiana aurea. No. 1193, Laelia anceps.

1966, Dec. 20 **Unwmk.**

1179	A248	1c multicolored	.90	.25
1180	A249	1c multicolored	.90	.25
1181	A249	1c multicolored	.90	.25
1182	A249	1c multicolored	.90	.25
1183	A249	1c multicolored	.90	.25
a.		Block of 5 + label, #1179-1183	5.00	1.00
1184	A248	3c multicolored	1.40	.25
1185	A249	3c multicolored	1.40	.25
1186	A249	3c multicolored	1.40	.25
1187	A249	3c multicolored	1.40	.25
1188	A249	3c multicolored	1.40	.25
a.		Block of 5 + label, #1184-1188	8.00	1.00
1189	A248	13c multicolored	5.00	.50
1190	A249	13c multicolored	5.00	.50
1191	A249	13c multicolored	5.00	.50
1192	A249	13c multicolored	5.00	.50
1193	A249	13c multicolored	5.00	.50
a.		Block of 5 + label, #1189-1193	27.50	2.75
		Nos. 1179-1193 (15)	36.50	5.00

Christmas 1966. See note after No. 700.

8th Anniv. of the Revolution — A341

No. 1194, Liberation, 1959. No. 1195, Agrarian Reform, 1960. No. 1196, Education, 1961. No. 1197, Agriculture, 1965. No. 1198, Rodin's Thinker, Planning, 1962. No. 1199, Organization, 1963. No. 1200, Economy, 1964. No. 1201, Solidarity, 1966.

1967, Jan. 2

1194	A341	3c multicolored	.30	.25
1195	A341	3c multicolored	.30	.25
1196	A341	3c multicolored	.30	.25
1197	A341	3c multicolored	.30	.25
a.		Strip of 4, Nos. 1194-1197	1.25	.90
1198	A341	13c multicolored	1.90	.45
1199	A341	13c multicolored	1.90	.45
1200	A341	13c multicolored	1.90	.45
1201	A341	13c multicolored	1.90	.45
a.		Strip of 4, Nos. 1198-1201	7.75	4.25
		Nos. 1194-1201 (8)	8.80	2.80

Nos. 1198-1201 vert.

Spring, by Jorge Arche — A342

Paintings in the Natl. Museum: 1c, Coffee Machine, by Angel Acosta Leon, vert. 2c, Country People, by Eduardo Abela, vert. 13c, Still-life, by Amelia Pelaez, vert. 30c, Landscape, by Gonzalo Escalante.

1967, Feb. 27

1202	A342	1c multi	.30	.25
1203	A342	2c multi	.50	.25
1204	A342	3c multi	.70	.25
1205	A342	13c multi	2.00	.80
1206	A342	30c multi	5.50	1.50
		Nos. 1202-1206 (5)	9.00	3.05

Natl. Events, Mar. 13, 1957 A343

3c, Attack on Presidential Palace. 13c, Landing of Corynthia. 30c, Cienfuegos revolt.

1967, Mar. 13 **Wmk. 376**

1207	A343	3c multicolored	.25	.25

Size: 41x28mm

1208	A343	13c multicolored	2.50	.70
1209	A343	30c multicolored	2.40	.80
		Nos. 1207-1209 (3)	5.15	1.75

Evolution of Man — A344

Prehistoric men: 2c, Australopithecus. 3c, Pithecanthropus erectus. 4c, Sinanthropus pekinensis. 5c, Neanderthal man. 13c, Cro-magnon man carving tusk. 20c, Cro-magnon man painting petroglyph.

1967, Mar. 31 **Unwmk.**

1210	A344	1c multi	.30	.25
1211	A344	2c multi	.50	.25
1212	A344	3c multi	.50	.25
1213	A344	4c multi	.75	.25
1214	A344	5c multi	1.10	.25
1215	A344	13c multi	3.75	.50
1216	A344	20c multi	7.50	.90
		Nos. 1210-1216 (7)	14.40	2.65

Stamp Day A345

Carriages.

1967, Apr. 24

1217	A345	3c Victoria	.35	.25
1218	A345	9c Volante	2.00	.45
1219	A345	13c Quitrin	3.00	.80
		Nos. 1217-1219 (3)	5.35	1.50

EXPO '67, Montreal, Apr. 28-Oct. 27 — A346

1c, Cuban pavilion. 2c, Space exploration. 3c, Petroglyph, hieroglyph. 13c, Agriculture, computer technology. 20c, Athletes.

1967, Apr. 28

1220	A346	1c multicolored	.40	.25
1221	A346	2c multicolored	.40	.25
1222	A346	3c multicolored	.55	.25
1223	A346	13c multicolored	3.00	.70
1224	A346	20c multicolored	3.50	.80
		Nos. 1220-1224 (5)	7.85	2.25

Botanical Gardens, Sequicentennial A347

Flowering plants: 1c, Eugenia malaccencis. 2c, Jacaranda filicifolia. 3c, Coroupita guianensis. 4c, Spathodea campanulata. 5c, Cassia fistula. 13c, Plumieria alba. 20c, Erythrina poeppigiana.

1967, May 30

1225	A347	1c multicolored	.25	.25
1226	A347	2c multicolored	.25	.25
1227	A347	3c multicolored	.45	.25
1228	A347	4c multicolored	.45	.25
1229	A347	5c multicolored	.90	.25
1230	A347	13c multicolored	2.75	.55
1231	A347	20c multicolored	4.75	.65
		Nos. 1225-1231 (7)	9.80	2.45

Natl. Ballet — A348

1967, June 15

1232	A348	1c Giselle	.35	.25
1233	A348	2c Swan Lake	.35	.25
1234	A348	3c Don Quixote	.50	.25
1235	A348	4c Calaucan	1.00	.25
1236	A348	13c Swan Lake	2.75	.70
1237	A348	20c Nutcracker	4.00	1.25
		Nos. 1232-1237 (6)	8.95	2.95

Intl. Ballet Festival, Havana.

5th Pan American Games, Winnipeg, Canada, July 22-Aug. 7 — A349

1967, July 22

1238	A349	1c Baseball, horiz.	.25	.25
1239	A349	2c Swimming, horiz.	.35	.25
1240	A349	3c Basketball	.50	.25
1241	A349	4c Gymnastic rings	.85	.25
1242	A349	5c Water polo	1.00	.25
1243	A349	13c Weight lifting, horiz.	3.00	.45
1244	A349	20c Javelin	4.75	.80
		Nos. 1238-1244 (7)	10.70	2.50

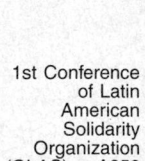

1st Conference of Latin American Solidarity Organization (OLAS) — A350

Portrait of representative, map of South American homeland: No. 1245, Camilo Torres, Colombia. No. 1246, Luis de la Puente Uceda, Peru. No. 1247, Luis A. Turcios Lima, Guatemala. No. 1248, Fabricio Ojeda, Venezuela.

1967, July 28 **Wmk. 376**

1245	A350	13c pale grn, blk & red	2.00	.50
1246	A350	13c lil, blk & red	2.00	.50
1247	A350	13c dark chalky blue, blk & red	2.00	.50
1248	A350	13c golden brn, blk & red	2.00	.50
		Nos. 1245-1248 (4)	8.00	2.00

Portrait of Sonny Rollins, by Alan Davie — A351

Bathers, by Gustave Singier A352

Modern Art: No. 1250, Twelve Selenites, by Felix Labisse. No. 1251, Night of the Drinker, by Friedensreich Hundertwasser. No. 1252, Figure, by Mariano. No. 1253, All-Souls, by Wilfredo Lam. No. 1254, Darkness and Cracks, by Antonio Tapies. No. 1256, Torso of a Muse, by Jean Arp. No. 1257, Figure, by M.W. Svanberg. No. 1258, Oppenheimer's Information, by Erro. No. 1259, Where Cardinals Are Born, by Max Ernst. No. 1260, Havana Landscape, by Portocarrero. No. 1261, EG 12, by Victor Vasarely. No. 1262, Frisco, by Alexander Calder. No. 1263, The Man with the Pipe, by Picasso. No. 1264, Abstract Composition, by Sergei Poliakoff. No. 1265, Painting, by Bram van Velde. No. 1266, Sower of Fires, by R. Matta. No. 1267, The Art of Living, by Rene Magritte. No. 1268, Poem, by Joan Miro. No. 1269, Young Tigers, by Jean Messagier. No. 1270, Painting, by M. Vieira da Silva. No. 1271, Live Cobra, by Pierre Alechinsky. No. 1272, Stalingrad, by Asger Jorn. 30c, Warriors, by Edouard Pignon. 50c, Cloister, a mural at the exhibition representing the Salon de Mayo pictures.

1967, July 29 **Unwmk.**

1249	A351	1c shown	.80	.25
1250	A351	1c multi	.80	.25
1251	A351	1c multi	.80	.25
1252	A351	1c multi	.80	.25
1253	A351	1c multi	.80	.25
a.		Strip of 5, Nos. 1249-1253	4.50	1.50

Sizes: 36½x54mm, 36½x53mm, 36½x45mm, 36½x41mm

1254	A352	2c multi	.80	.25
1255	A352	2c shown	.80	.25
1256	A352	2c multi	.80	.25
1257	A352	2c multi	.80	.25
1258	A352	2c multi	.80	.25
a.		Strip of 5, Nos. 1254-1258	4.50	2.50

Sizes: 36½x54mm, 36½x40mm, 36½x42mm, 36½x49mm

1259	A352	3c multi	1.50	.25
1260	A352	3c multi	1.50	.25
1261	A352	3c multi	1.50	.25
1262	A352	3c multi	1.50	.25
1263	A352	3c multi	1.50	.25
a.		Strip of 5, Nos. 1259-1263	7.50	3.50

Sizes: 35x15mm, 35x67mm, 35x46½mm, 35x55mm

1264	A352	4c multi	1.75	.80
1265	A352	4c multi	1.75	.80
1266	A352	4c multi	1.75	.80
1267	A352	4c multi	1.75	.80
1268	A352	4c multi	1.75	.80
a.		Strip of 5, Nos. 1264-1268	9.00	4.00

Sizes: 49x32mm, 49x35mm, 49x46mm

1269	A351	13c multi	4.50	2.75
1270	A351	13c multi	4.50	2.75
1271	A351	13c multi	4.50	2.75
1272	A351	13c multi	4.50	2.75
a.		Strip of 4, Nos. 1269-1272	19.00	11.00

Size: 54x32mm

1273	A351	30c multi	17.50	11.00
		Nos. 1249-1273 (25)	59.75	29.75

Souvenir Sheet

Imperf

1274	A351	50c multi	25.00	12.50

Salon de Mayo Art Exhibition, Havana. No. 1274 contains one 88x45mm stamp with simulated perforations. Issued Oct. 7.

World Underwater Fishing Championships — A353

1967, Sept. 5

1275	A353	1c Green moray	.25	.25
1276	A353	2c Octopus	.25	.25
1277	A353	3c Great barracuda	.25	.25
1278	A353	4c Blue shark	.75	.25
1279	A353	5c Spotted jewfish	1.60	.25
1280	A353	13c Sting ray	3.25	.70
1281	A353	20c Green turtle	6.50	.85
		Nos. 1275-1281 (7)	12.85	2.80

Soviet Space Program A354

1967, Oct. 4 **Wmk. 376**

1282	A354	1c Sputnik 1	.25	.25
1283	A354	2c Lunik 3	.25	.25
1284	A354	3c Venusik	.25	.25
1285	A354	4c Cosmos	.40	.25
1286	A354	5c Mars 1	.65	.25
1287	A354	9c Electron 1 & 2	.75	.25
1288	A354	10c Luna 9	1.10	.45
1289	A354	13c Luna 10	2.50	.60
a.		Souv. sheet of 8, #1282-1289, imperf.	15.00	15.00
		Nos. 1282-1289 (8)	6.15	2.55

Stamps in No. 1289a have simulated perfs.

50th Anniv. of the October Revolution, Russia A355

Paintings: 1c, Storming the Winter Palace, by Sokolov-Skalia and Miasnikov. 2c, Lenin Addressing Congress, by W.A. Serov. 3c, Lenin, by H.D. Nalbandian. 4c, Lenin Explaining Electrification Map, by L.A. Schmatko. 5c, Dawn of the Five-Year Plan, by J.D. Romas. 13c, Kusnetzkroi Steel Furnace No. 1, by P. Kotov. 30c, Victory, by A. Krivonogov.

1967, Nov. 7 **Unwmk.**

1290	A355	1c 64x36mm	.25	.25
1291	A355	2c 48x36mm	.25	.25
1292	A355	3c 35x37mm	.45	.25
1293	A355	4c 48x36mm	.45	.25
1294	A355	5c 50x36mm	3.75	.50
1295	A355	13c 36x50mm	3.00	.50
1296	A355	30c 50x36mm	4.00	.85
		Nos. 1290-1296 (7)	12.15	2.85

Castle of the Royal Forces, Havana — A356

Historic architecture: 2c, Iznaga Tower, Trinidad, vert. 3c, Castle of Our Lady of the Angels, Cienfuegos. 4c, St. Francis de Paula Church, Havana. 13c, St. Francis Convent, Havana. 30c, Castle del Morro, Santiago de Cuba.

1967, Nov. 7 **Wmk. 376**

Sizes: 26x47mm (1c), 41x29mm (3c, 4c), 38½x31mm (13c)

1297	A356	1c multi	.25	.25
1298	A356	2c multi	.25	.25
1299	A356	3c multi	.65	.25
1300	A356	4c multi	.65	.25
1301	A356	13c multi	3.25	.50
1302	A356	30c multi	5.00	1.00
		Nos. 1297-1302 (6)	10.05	2.50

Christmas Type of 1961

Birds: No. 1303, Struthia camelus australis. No. 1304, Chysolophus pictus. No. 1305, Ciconia ciconia ciconia. No. 1306, Balearica pavonina. No. 1307, Dromiceius novaehollandiae. No. 1308, Anodorhynchus hyacinthus. No. 1309, Psittacus erithacus. No. 1310, Domicella garrula. No. 1311, Ramphastos sulfuratus. No. 1312, Kakatoe galerita galerita. No. 1313, Phoenicopterus ruber. No. 1314, Pelecanus erythrorhynchos. No. 1315, Alopochen aegyptiacus. No. 1316, Dendronessa galericulata. No. 1317, Chenopsis atrata.

1967, Dec. 20

1303	A248	1c multicolored	1.75	.60
1304	A249	1c multicolored	1.75	.60
1305	A249	1c multicolored	1.75	.60
1306	A249	1c multicolored	1.75	.60
1307	A249	1c multicolored	1.75	.60
a.		Block of 5 + label, Nos. 1303-1307	10.00	3.25
1308	A248	3c multicolored	2.40	1.00
1309	A249	3c multicolored	2.40	1.00
1310	A249	3c multicolored	2.40	1.00
1311	A249	3c multicolored	2.40	1.00
1312	A249	3c multicolored	2.40	1.00
a.		Block of 5 + label, Nos. 1308-1312	14.00	5.50
1313	A248	13c multicolored	4.50	1.75
1314	A249	13c multicolored	4.50	1.75
1315	A249	13c multicolored	4.50	1.75
1316	A249	13c multicolored	4.50	1.75
1317	A249	13c multicolored	4.50	1.75
a.		Block of 5 + label, Nos. 1313-1317	25.00	9.00
		Nos. 1303-1317 (15)	43.25	16.75

Christmas 1967. See note after No. 700.

Ernesto "Che" Guevara (1928-1967), Revolution Leader — A356a

1968, Jan. 3

1318	A356a	13c blk, dark red & buff	2.50	.55

Cultural Congress, Havana — A357

Abstract designs: No. 1319, Independence fostering culture. No. 1320, Integral formation of man. No. 1321, Responsibility of intellectuals. No. 1322, Relationship between culture and the mass media. No. 1323, The arts versus science and technology.

1968, Jan. 4

1319	A357	3c multi, vert.	.25	.25
1320	A357	3c multi, vert.	.25	.25
1321	A357	13c multi, vert.	1.50	.40
1322	A357	13c multi, vert.	1.75	.50
1323	A357	30c multi	2.40	.85
		Nos. 1319-1323 (5)	6.15	2.25

Canaries and Breeding Cycles A358

1968, Apr. 13

1324	A358	1c F.C.C. 4016	.25	.25
1325	A358	2c A.C.C. 774	.25	.25
1326	A358	3c A.C.C. 122	.40	.25
1327	A358	4c F.C.C. 4477	.40	.25
1328	A358	5c A.C.C 117	.75	.25
1329	A358	13c A.N.R. 1175	4.00	.55
1330	A358	20c A.C.C. 777	5.50	.70
		Nos. 1324-1330 (7)	11.55	2.50

Stamp Day A359

Paintings: 13c, The Village Postman, by J. Harris. 30c, The Philatelist, by G. Sciltian.

1968, Apr. 24 **Unwmk.**

1331	A359	13c multi	2.00	.50
1332	A359	30c multi	3.00	.70

World Health Organization, 20th Anniv. — A360

1968, May 10 **Wmk. 376**

1333	A360	13c Nurse, mother, child	1.60	.55
1334	A360	30c Surgeons	2.10	.80

Intl. Children's Day — A361

1968, June 1

1335	A361	3c multi	1.25	.25

Seville Camaguey Flight, 35th Anniv. — A362

1968, June 20

1336	A362	13c Plane Four Winds	2.25	.45
1337	A362	30c Capt. Barberan, Lt. Collar, pilots	2.75	.60

Natl. Food Production — A363

1968, June 29

1338	A363	1c Yellow tuna, can	.25	.25
1339	A363	2c Cow, dairy products	.25	.25
1340	A363	3c Rooster, eggs	.50	.25
1341	A363	13c Rum, sugar cane	3.00	.50
1342	A363	20c Crayfish, box	3.50	.70
		Nos. 1338-1342 (5)	7.50	1.95

Attack of Moncada Barracks, 15th Anniv. A364

1968, July 26

Size: 43x29mm (13c)

1343 A364	3c Siboney farm-house	.25	.25
1344 A364	13c Assault route, Santiago de Cuba	1.75	.55
1345 A364	30c Students, school	3.00	.80
	Nos. 1343-1345 (3)	5.00	1.60

Committee for the Defense of the Revolution, 8th Anniv. — A365

1968, Sept. 28

1346 A365	3c multi	2.00	.25

Guerilla Day A366

Che Guevara and: 1c, Rifleman and "En Cualquier Lugar..." 3c, Machine gunners and "Crear tres muchos Viet Nam." 9c, Silhouette of battalion and "Este Tipo De Lucha..." 10c, Guerillas cheering and "Hoy aquilatamos..." 13c, Map of Caribbean, So. America and "Hasta La Victoria Siempre."

1968, Oct. 8

1347 A366	1c gold, brt blue grn & blk	.25	.25
1348 A366	3c gold, org brn blk	.25	.25
1349 A366	9c multi	.60	.25
1350 A366	10c gold, lt olive grn & blk	1.40	.25
1351 A366	13c gold, red org & blk	2.50	.70
	Nos. 1347-1351 (5)	5.00	1.70

Cuban War of Independence, Cent. — A367

Independence fighters and scenes: No. 1352, C.M. de Cespedes, broken wheel. No. 1353, E. Betances, horsemen, flag. No. 1354, I. Agramonte, Clavellinas Monument. No. 1355, A. Maceo, Baragua Protest. No. 1356, J. Marti, horsemen. No. 1357, M. Gomez, The Invasion. No. 1358, J.A. Mella, declaration. No. 1359, A. Guiteras, El Morrillo monument. No. 1360, A. Santamaria, attack on Moncada Barracks. No. 1361, F. Pais memorial. No. 1362, J. Echeverria, student protest. No. 1363, C. Cienfuegos, insurrection. No. 1364, Che Guevara, 1st Declaration of Havana.

1968, Oct. 10 **Unwmk.**

1352 A367	1c multicolored	.25	.25
1353 A367	1c multicolored	.25	.25
1354 A367	1c multicolored	.25	.25
1355 A367	1c multicolored	.25	.25
1356 A367	1c multicolored	.25	.25
a.	Strip of 5, Nos. 1352-1356	1.00	1.00
1357 A367	3c multicolored	.25	.25
1358 A367	3c multicolored	.25	.25
1359 A367	3c multicolored	.25	.25
1360 A367	3c multicolored	.25	.25
1361 A367	3c multicolored	.25	.25
a.	Strip of 5, Nos. 1357-1361	1.75	1.00
1362 A367	9c multicolored	1.25	.25
1363 A367	13c multicolored	3.00	.70
1364 A367	30c multicolored	3.50	1.10
	Nos. 1352-1364 (13)	10.25	4.55

Souvenir Sheet

The Burning of Bayamo, by J.E. Hernandez Giro — A368

1968, Oct. 18 ***Imperf.***

1365 A368	50c multi	9.00	9.00

Natl. Philatelic Exhibition, independence cent. Stamp in No. 1365 has simulated perforations.

19th Summer Olympics, Mexico City, Oct. 12-27 — A369

1c, Parade of athletes. 2c, Women's basketball, vert. 3c, Hammer throw, vert. 4c, Boxing. 5c, Water polo. 13c, Pistol shooting. 30c, Mexican flag, calendar stone.
50c, Running.

1968, Oct. 21 ***Perf. 12½***

1366 A369	1c multicolored	.25	.25
1367 A369	2c multicolored	.25	.25
1368 A369	3c multicolored	.25	.25
1369 A369	4c multicolored	.25	.25
1370 A369	5c multicolored	.45	.25
1371 A369	13c multicolored	3.00	.55

Size: 32x50mm

1372 A369	30c multicolored	4.50	.80
	Nos. 1366-1372 (7)	8.95	2.60

Souvenir Sheet

Imperf

1373 A369	50c multicolored	15.00	4.00

Stamp in No. 1373 has simulated perforations.

Civilian Activities of the Armed Forces A370

3c, Crop dusting. 9c, Che Guevara's Brigade. 10c, Road building. 13c, Plowing, harvesting.

1968, Dec. 2 **Wmk. 376** ***Perf. 12½***

1374 A370	3c multicolored	.25	.25
1375 A370	9c multicolored	.60	.25
1376 A370	10c multicolored	1.00	.25
1377 A370	13c multicolored	2.10	.70
	Nos. 1374-1377 (4)	3.95	1.45

San Alejandro School of Painting, Sesquicentennial — A371

Paintings: 1c, Manrique de Lara's Family, by Jean Baptiste Vermay, vert. 2c, Seascape, by Leopoldo Romanach. 3c, Wild Cane, by Antonio Rodriguez, vert. 4c, Self-portrait, by Miguel Melero, vert. 5c, The Lottery List, by Jose Joaquin Tejada. 13c, Portrait of Nina, by Armando B. Menocal, vert. 30c, Landscape, by Esteban B. Chartrand. 50c, Siesta, by Guillermo Collazo.

1968, Dec. 30 **Unwmk.**

Sizes: 38x48mm (1c, 3c), 39x50mm (4c, 13c), 53x36mm (30c)

1378 A371	1c multi	.25	.25
1379 A371	2c multi	.25	.25
1380 A371	3c multi	.30	.25
1381 A371	4c multi	.30	.25
1382 A371	5c multi	1.40	.40
1383 A371	13c multi	4.00	.70
1384 A371	30c multi	6.25	1.10
	Nos. 1378-1384 (7)	12.75	3.20

Souvenir Sheet

Imperf

1385 A371	50c multi	9.00	3.50

No. 1385 contains one 52x41½mm stamp that has simulated perforations.

10th Anniv. of the Revolution A372

1969, Jan. 3 **Wmk. 376** ***Perf. 12½***

1386 A372	13c multi	2.00	.60

Villaclarenos Rebellion, Cent. — A373

1969, Feb. 6

1387 A373	3c Gutierrez and Sanchez	1.00	.25

Women's Day — A374

Design: Mariana Grajales, rose and statue.

1969, Mar. 8

1388 A374	3c multi	1.25	.25

Cuban Pioneers and Young Communists Unions — A375

1969, Apr. 4

1389 A375	3c Pioneers	.40	.25
1390 A375	13c Young Communists	2.25	.80

Guaimaro Assembly, Cent. — A376

1969, Apr. 10

1391 A376	3c dark brn	1.00	.25

The Postman, by Jean C. Cazin A377

Paintings: 30c, Portrait of a Young Man, by George Romney.

1969, Apr. 24 **Unwmk.**

1392 A377	13c multi	2.50	.60

Size: 35½x43½mm

1393 A377	30c multi	4.00	.90

Stamp Day.

Agrarian Reform, 10th Anniv. A378

1969, May 17 **Wmk. 376**

1394 A378	13c multi	2.25	.70

Marine Life A379

1c, Petrochirus bahamensis. 2c, Stenopus hispidus. 3c, Panulirus argus. 4c, Callinectes sapidus. 5c, Gecarcinus ruricola. 13c, Macrobrachium carcinus. 30c, Carpilius coralinus.

1969, May 20 **Unwmk.**

1395 A379	1c multicolored	.25	.25
1396 A379	2c multicolored	.40	.25
1397 A379	3c multicolored	.40	.25
1398 A379	4c multicolored	.50	.25
1399 A379	5c multicolored	.50	.25
1400 A379	13c multicolored	3.50	.45
1401 A379	30c multicolored	5.25	.80
	Nos. 1395-1401 (7)	10.80	2.50

Intl. Labor Organization, 50th Anniv. — A380

1969, June 6 **Wmk. 376**

1402 A380	3c shown	.45	.25
1403 A380	13c Blacksmith breaking chains	2.25	.70

Paintings in the Natl. Museum — A381

Designs: 1c, Flowers, by Raul Milian, vert. 2c, Annunciation, by Antonia Eiriz. 3c, Factory, by Marcelo Pogolotti, vert. 4c, Territorial Waters, by Luis Martinez Pedro, vert. 5c, Miss Sarah Gale, by John Hoppner, vert. 13c, Two Women Wearing Mantilla, by Ignacio Zuloaga. 30c, Virgin and Child, by Francisco de Zurbaran.

1969, June 15 **Unwmk.**

1404	A381	1c 39x59mm	.25	.25
1405	A381	2c	.25	.25
1406	A381	3c 39½x49mm	1.10	.25
1407	A381	4c 39½x43mm	.30	.25
1408	A381	5c 39½x45½mm	.30	.25
1409	A381	13c 38x41½mm	2.10	.70
1410	A381	30c 39x45mm	3.25	.90
		Nos. 1404-1410 (7)	7.55	2.85

Broadcasting Institute — A382

13c, Hemispheres, tower. 1p, Waves on graph.

1969, July 5 **Wmk. 376**

1411	A382	3c shown	.40	.25
1412	A382	13c multicolored	2.10	.80
1413	A382	1p multicolored	5.00	1.75
		Nos. 1411-1413 (3)	7.50	2.80

Fish A383

1c, Apogon maculatus. 2c, Bodianus rufus. 3c, Microspathodon chrysurus. 4c, Gramma loreto. 5c, Chromis marginatus. 13c, Myripristis jacobus. 30c, Nomeus gronovii, vert.

1969, July 20 **Unwmk.**

1414	A383	1c multicolored	.25	.25
1415	A383	2c multicolored	.25	.25
1416	A383	3c multicolored	.40	.25
1417	A383	4c multicolored	.40	.25
1418	A383	5c multicolored	.60	.25
1419	A383	13c multicolored	3.75	.55
1420	A383	30c multicolored	5.25	.90
		Nos. 1414-1420 (7)	10.90	2.70

Natl. Film Industry, 10th Anniv. — A384

1969, Aug. 5 **Wmk. 376**

1421	A384	1c Poster	.25	.25
1422	A384	3c Documentaries	.25	.25
1423	A384	13c Cartoons	3.00	.60
1424	A384	30c Entertainers	3.50	.70
		Nos. 1421-1424 (4)	7.00	1.80

Napoleon in Milan, by Andrea Appiani — A385

Paintings in the Napoleon Museum, Havana: 2c, Hortensia de Beauharnais, by Francois Gerard. 3c, Napoleon as First Consul, by J.B. Regnault. 4c, Elisa Bonaparte, by Robert Lefevre. 5c, Napoleon Planning Coronation Ceremony, by J.G. Vibert, horiz. 13c, Napoleon as Cuirassier Corporal, by Jean Meissonier. 30c, Napoleon Bonaparte, by LeFevre.

1969, Aug. 20 **Unwmk.**

1425	A385	1c	.25	.25
1426	A385	2c 41½x55mm	.25	.25
1427	A385	3c 45½x56mm	.25	.25
1428	A385	4c 43x62½mm	.45	.25
1429	A385	5c 63x47½mm	.70	.30
1430	A385	13c 43x62½mm	3.25	.70
1431	A385	30c 45x59½mm	4.25	.90
		Nos. 1425-1431 (7)	9.40	2.90

See Nos. 2448-2453.

Cuba's Victory at the 17th World Amateur Baseball Championships, Santo Domingo — A386

1969, Sept. 11

1432	A386	13c multi	2.75	.60

No. 1432 printed se-tenant with inscribed label listing finalists.

Alexander von Humboldt (1769-1859), German Naturalist — A387

1969, Sept. 14

1433	A387	3c Surinam eel	.25	.25
1434	A387	13c Night ape	2.50	1.00
1435	A387	30c Condors	4.00	.85
		Nos. 1433-1435 (3)	6.75	2.10

World Fencing Championships, Havana — A388

Designs: 1c, Ancient Egyptians in combat. 2c, Roman gladiators. 2c, Viking and Norman. 4c, Medieval tournament. 5c, French musketeers. 13c, Japanese samurai. 30c, Mounted Cubans, War of Independence. 50c, Modern fencers.

1969, Oct. 2

1436	A388	1c multi	.25	.25
1437	A388	2c multi	.25	.25
1438	A388	3c multi	.25	.25
1439	A388	4c multi	.40	.25
1440	A388	5c multi	.65	.25
1441	A388	13c multi	3.00	.45
1442	A388	30c multi	4.75	.80
		Nos. 1436-1442 (7)	9.55	2.50

Souvenir Sheet

Imperf

1443	A388	50c multi	12.00	5.00

Stamp in No. 1443 has simulated perforations.

Natl. Revolutionary Militia, 10th Anniv. — A389

1969, Oct. 26 **Wmk. 376**

1444	A389	3c multi	1.25	.25

Disappearance of Maj. Camilo Cienfuegos, 10th Anniv. — A390

1969, Oct. 28

1445	A390	13c multi	2.50	.60

Agriculture — A391

No. 1446, Strawberries, grapes. No. 1447, Onions, asparagus. No. 1448, Rice. No. 1449, Banana. No. 1450, Pineapple, vert. No. 1451, Tobacco, vert. No. 1452, Citrus fruits, vert. No. 1453, Coffee, vert. No. 1454, Rabbits, vert. No. 1455, Pigs, vert. No. 1456, Sugar cane. No. 1457, Bull.

1969, Nov. 2 **Unwmk.**

1446	A391	1c multicolored	.25	.25
1447	A391	1c multicolored	.25	.25
1448	A391	1c multicolored	.25	.25
1449	A391	1c multicolored	.25	.25
a.		Strip of 4, #1446-1449	1.00	.80
1450	A391	3c multicolored	.50	.50
1451	A391	3c multicolored	.50	.50
1452	A391	3c multicolored	.50	.50
1453	A391	3c multicolored	.50	.50
1454	A391	3c multicolored	.50	.50
a.		Strip of 5, #1450-1454	2.75	2.50
1455	A391	10c multicolored	.50	.25
1456	A391	13c multicolored	2.75	.60
1457	A391	30c multicolored	4.00	.85
		Nos. 1446-1457 (12)	10.75	5.20

Sporting Events — A392

1c, 2nd Natl. Games. 2c, 11th Anniv. Games. 3c, Barrientos Commemorative, vert. 10c, 2nd Olympic Trials, vert. 13c, 6th Socialist Bicycle Race, vert. 30c, 6th Capablanca Memorial Chess Championships, vert.

1969, Nov. 15

1458	A392	1c multicolored	.25	.25
1459	A392	2c multicolored	.25	.25
1460	A392	3c multicolored	.25	.25
1461	A392	10c multicolored	.40	.25
1462	A392	13c multicolored	2.75	.80
1463	A392	30c multicolored	4.00	1.25
		Nos. 1458-1463 (6)	7.90	3.05

Christmas Type of 1961

Flowering plants: No. 1464, Plumbago capensis. No. 1465, Petrea volubilis. No. 1466, Clitoria ternatea. No. 1467, Duranta repens. No. 1468, Ruellia tuberosa. No. 1469, Turnera ulmifolia. No. 1470, Thevetia peruviana. No. 1471, Hibiscus elatus. No. 1472, Allamanda cathartica. No. 1473, Cosmos sulphureus. No. 1474, Delonix regia. No. 1475, Neriun oleander. No. 1476, Cordia sebestena. No. 1477, Lochnera rosea. No. 1478, Jatropha integerrima.

1969, Dec. 1

1464	A248	1c multicolored	.40	.25
1465	A249	1c multicolored	.40	.25
1466	A249	1c multicolored	.40	.25
1467	A249	1c multicolored	.40	.25
1468	A249	1c multicolored	.40	.25
a.		Block of 5 + label, Nos. 1464-1468	3.00	1.00
1469	A248	3c multicolored	1.00	.25
1470	A249	3c multicolored	1.00	.25
1471	A249	3c multicolored	1.00	.25
1472	A249	3c multicolored	1.00	.25
1473	A249	3c multicolored	1.00	.25
a.		Block of 5 + label, Nos. 1469-1473	6.00	1.25
1474	A248	13c multicolored	2.25	1.00
1475	A249	13c multicolored	2.25	1.00
1476	A249	13c multicolored	2.25	1.00
1477	A249	13c multicolored	2.25	1.00
1478	A249	13c multicolored	2.25	1.00
a.		Block of 5 + label, Nos. 1474-1478	11.00	5.00
		Nos. 1464-1478 (15)	18.25	7.50

Christmas 1969. See note after No. 700.

Zapata Swamp Fauna — A393

1c, Trelanorhynus variabilis. 2c, Hyla insulsa. 3c, Atractosteus tristoechus. 4c, Capromys nana. 5c, Crocodylus rhombifer. 13c, Amazona leucocephala. 30c, Agelaius phoeniceus assimilis.

1969, Dec. 15

1479	A393	1c multicolored	.25	.25
1480	A393	2c multicolored	.25	.25
1481	A393	3c multicolored	.25	.25
1482	A393	4c multicolored	.25	.25
1483	A393	5c multicolored	.25	.25
1484	A393	13c multicolored	4.50	.55
1485	A393	30c multicolored	5.00	1.00
		Nos. 1479-1485 (7)	10.75	2.80

Nos. 1482, 1484-1485 vert.

Tourism A394

1970, Jan. 25 **Wmk. 376**

1486	A394	1c Jibacoa Beach	.25	.25
1487	A394	3c Trinidad City	.25	.25
1488	A394	13c Santiago de Cuba	1.90	.80
1489	A394	30c Vinales Valley	2.75	1.00
		Nos. 1486-1489 (4)	5.15	2.30

Medicinal Plants — A395

1970, Feb. 10 **Unwmk.**

1490	A395	1c	Guarea guara	.25	.25
1491	A395	3c	Ocimum sanctum	.25	.25
1492	A395	10c	Canella winterana	.45	.25
1493	A395	13c	Bidens pilosa	2.25	.70
1494	A395	30c	Turnera ulmifolia	2.75	.85
1495	A395	50c	Picramnia pentandra	4.00	1.00
			Nos. 1490-1495 (6)	9.95	3.30

11th Central American and Caribbean Games, Panama, Feb. 28-Mar. 14 — A396

1970, Feb. 28 **Wmk. 376**

1496	A396	1c	Weight lifting	.25	.25
1497	A396	3c	Boxing	.25	.25
1498	A396	10c	Gymnastics	.25	.25
1499	A396	13c	Running	2.40	.65
1500	A396	30c	Fencing	3.50	.90
			Nos. 1496-1500 (5)	6.65	2.30

Souvenir Sheet

Imperf

1501	A396	50c	Baseball	12.00	6.00

No. 1501 contains one 50x37mm stamp that has simulated perforations.

EXPO '70, Osaka, Japan, Mar. 15-Sept. 13 — A397

1c, Enjoying life. 2c, Improving on nature, vert. 3c, Better living standard. 13c, Intl. cooperation, vert. 30c, Cuban pavilion.

1970, Mar. 15

1502	A397	1c	multicolored	.25	.25
1503	A397	2c	multicolored	.40	.25
1504	A397	3c	multicolored	.40	.25
1505	A397	13c	multicolored	2.75	.55
1506	A397	30c	multicolored	4.00	.80
			Nos. 1502-1506 (5)	7.80	2.10

Speleological Soc., 30th Anniv. — A398

Petroglyphs in Cuban caves: 1c, Ambrosio Cave, Varadero Matanzas. 2c, Cave No. 1, Punta del Este, Isle of Pines. 3c, Pichardo Cave, Cubitas Camaguey Mountains. 4c, Ambrosio Cave, diff. 5c, Cave No. 1, diff. 13c, Garcia Ribiou Cave, Havana. 30c, Cave No. 2, Punta del Este.

1970, Mar. 28 **Unwmk.**

Sizes: 29x45mm (1c, 3c, 4c, 13c)

1507	A398	1c	multi	.25	.25
1508	A398	2c	shown	.25	.25
1509	A398	3c	multi	.25	.25
1510	A398	4c	multi	.25	.25
1511	A398	5c	multi	.25	.25
1512	A398	13c	multi	2.25	.70
1513	A398	30c	multi	4.75	.80
			Nos. 1507-1513 (7)	8.25	2.75

Aviation Pioneers — A399

1970, Apr. 10

1514	A399	3c	Jose D. Blino	1.00	.25
1515	A399	13c	Adolfo Teodore	3.50	.70

Lenin Birth Centenary — A400

Paintings and quotes: 1c, Lenin in Kazan, by O. Vishniakov. 2c, Young Lenin, by V. Prager. 3c, Second Socialist Party Congress, by Y. Vinogradov. 4c, First Manifesto, by F. Golubkov. 5c, First Day of Soviet Power, by N. Babasiuk. 13c, Lenin in Smolny, by M. Sokolov. 30c, Autumn in Gorky, by A. Varlamov. 50c, Lenin at Gorky, by N. Baskakov.

1970, Apr. 22

Sizes: 67½x46mm (1c, 4c, 5c)

1516	A400	1c	multi	.25	.25
1517	A400	2c	shown	.25	.25
1518	A400	3c	multi	.25	.25
1519	A400	4c	multi	.25	.25
1520	A400	5c	multi	.25	.25
1521	A400	13c	multi	2.75	.55
1522	A400	30c	multi	3.25	.70
			Nos. 1516-1522 (7)	7.25	2.50

Souvenir Sheet

Imperf

1523	A400	50c	multi	13.00	6.50

No. 1523 contains one 48x46mm stamp that has simulated perforations.

Stamp Day — A401

13c, The Letter, by J. Arche. 30c, Portrait of A Cadet, Anonymous.

1970, Apr. 24

1524	A401	13c	multicolored	3.00	.60

Size: 30x44mm

1525	A401	30c	multicolored	3.75	.80

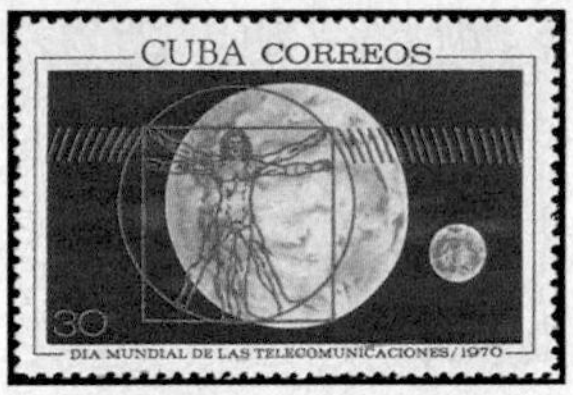

Da Vinci's Anatomical Drawing, Earth, Moon — A402

1970, May 17 **Wmk. 376**

1526	A402	30c	multi	3.50	.60

World Telecommunications Day.

Ho Chi Minh (1890-1969), President of North Viet Nam — A403

No. 1527, Vietnamese fisherman. No. 1528, Two women. No. 1529, Plowing field. No. 1530, Teacher, students in air-raid shelter. No. 1531, Nine women in paddy. No. 1532, Camouflaged machine shop.

1970, May 19 **Unwmk.**

1527	A403	1c	multicolored	.25	.25

Size: 32x44mm

1528	A403	3c	multicolored	.50	.25
1529	A403	3c	multicolored	.50	.25

Size: 33x45mm

1530	A403	3c	multicolored	.50	.25
1531	A403	3c	multicolored	.70	.25

Size: 34x41½mm

1532	A403	3c	multicolored	.70	.25

Size: 34x39mm

1533	A403	13c	shown	3.25	.70
			Nos. 1527-1533 (7)	6.40	2.20

Cuban Cigar Industry A404

3c, Plantation, Eden cigar band. 13c, Factory, El Mambi band. 30c, Packing cigars, Lopez Hermanos band.

1970, July 5

1534	A404	3c	multicolored	.25	.25
1535	A404	13c	multicolored	2.25	.70
1536	A404	30c	multicolored	3.25	1.00
			Nos. 1534-1536 (3)	5.75	1.95

Projected Sugar Production: Over 10 Million Tons — A405

1c, Cane-crushing. 2c, Sowing and crop dusting. 3c, Cutting sugar cane. 10c, Transporting cane. 13c, Modern cutting machine. 30c, Intl. Brigade, cane cutters, vert. 1p, Sugar warehouse.

1970, July 26

1537	A405	1c	multicolored	.25	.25
1538	A405	2c	multicolored	.25	.25
1539	A405	3c	multicolored	.25	.25
1540	A405	10c	multicolored	5.00	.45
1541	A405	13c	multicolored	1.50	.25
1542	A405	30c	multicolored	2.25	.70
1543	A405	1p	multicolored	4.00	2.00
			Nos. 1537-1543 (7)	13.50	4.15

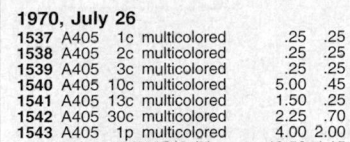

Pedro Figueredo (d. 1870), Composer — A406

Versions of the Natl. Anthem.

1970, Aug. 17

1544	A406	3c	1868 Version	.30	.25
1545	A406	20c	1898 Version	2.75	.60

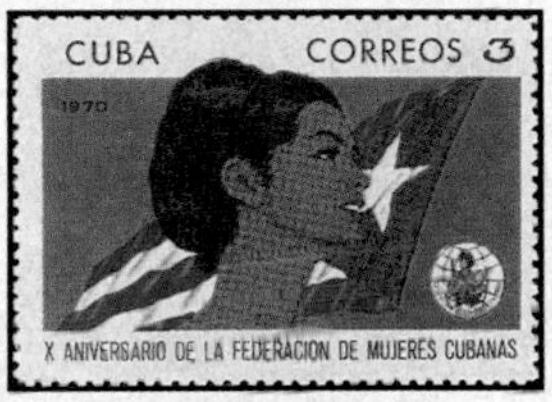

Women's Federation, 10th Anniv. — A407

1970, Aug. 23

1546	A407	3c	multi	1.00	.50

Militia, by Servando C. Moreno — A408

Paintings in the Natl. Museum: 2c, Washerwomen, by Aristides Fernandez. 3c, Puerta del Sol, Madrid, by L. Paret Y Alcazar. 4c, Fishermen's Wives, by Joaquin Sorolla. 5c, Portrait of a Woman, by Thomas de Keyser. 13c, Mrs. Edward Foster, by Sir Thomas Lawrence. 30c, Tropical Gypsy, by Victor M. Garcia.

1970, Aug. 31

1547	A408	1c	shown	.25	.25

Size: 45x41mm

1548	A408	2c	multi	.25	.25
1549	A408	3c	multi	.25	.25

Size: 40x41mm

1550	A408	4c	multi	.25	.25

Size: 38x45½mm

1551	A408	5c	multi	.25	.25
1552	A408	13c	multi	2.50	.50
1553	A408	30c	multi	4.00	.80
			Nos. 1547-1553 (7)	7.75	2.55

See Nos. 1640-1646, 1669-1675, 1773-1779.

Havana Declaration, 10th Anniv. — A409

1970, Sept. 2

1554	A409	3c	Jose Marti Square	.75	.25

Committee for the Defense of the Revolution, 10th Anniv. A410

1970, Sept. 28

1555 A410 3c multi .55 .25

39th Sugar Technician's Assoc. (ATAC) Conference — A411

1970, Oct. 11

1556 A411 30c multi 3.25 .70

Wildlife — A412

1c, Numida meleagris galeata. 2c, Dendrocygna arborea. 3c, Phasianus colchicus torquatus. 4c, Zenaida macroura macroura. 5c, Colinus virginianus cubanensis. 13c, Sus scrofa. 30c, Odocoileus virginianus.

1970, Oct. 20

1557	A412	1c multicolored	.70	.25
1558	A412	2c multicolored	.80	.25
1559	A412	3c multicolored	.95	.25
1560	A412	4c multicolored	1.10	.25
1561	A412	5c multicolored	1.25	.25
1562	A412	13c multicolored	2.00	1.00
1563	A412	30c multicolored	3.25	1.50
		Nos. 1557-1563 (7)	10.05	3.75

Black-magic Feast, by M. Puente — A413

Afro-Cuban folk paintings: 3c, Hat Dance, by V.P. Landaluze. 10c, Los Hoyos Conga Dance, by Domingo Ravenet. 13c, Climax of the Rumba, by Eduardo Abela.

1970, Nov. 5

Sizes: 36x48½mm (3c, 13c), 44½x44mm (10c)

1564	A413	1c shown	.25	.25
1565	A413	3c multi	.35	.25
1566	A413	10c multi	.90	.45
1567	A413	13c multi	2.50	.70
		Nos. 1564-1567 (4)	4.00	1.65

Road Safety Week A414

1970, Nov. 15

1568	A414	3c Zebra, road signs	1.10	.25
1569	A414	9c Prudence the Bear	1.60	.25

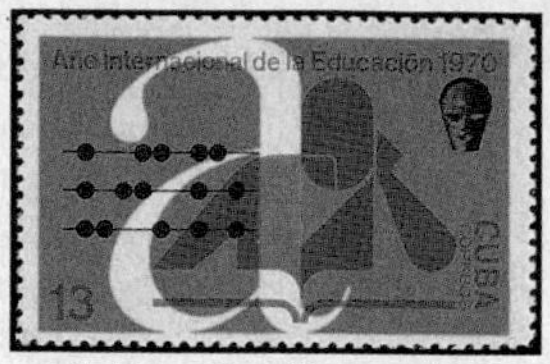

Intl. Education Year — A415

1970, Nov. 20

1570	A415	13c Abacus, "a"	2.50	.25
1571	A415	30c Cow, microscope	3.25	.70

Christmas Type of 1961

Birds: No. 1572, Dives atroviolaceus. No. 1573, Glaucidium siju siju. No. 1574, Todus multicolor. No. 1575, Xiphidiopicus percussus percussus. No. 1576, Ferminia cerverai. No. 1577, Teretistris fornsi. No. 1578, Myadestes elisabeth elisabeth. No. 1579, Polioptila lembeyei. No. 1580, Vireo gundlachii gundlachii. No. 1581, Teretistris fernandinae. No. 1582, Torreornis inexpectata inexpectata. No. 1583, Chondrohierax wilsonii. No. 1584, Accipiter gundlachi. No. 1585, Starnoenas cyanocephala. No. 1586, Aratinga euops.

1970, Dec. 1

1572	A248	1c multicolored	.80	.25
1573	A249	1c multicolored	.80	.25
1574	A249	1c multicolored	.80	.25
1575	A249	1c multicolored	.80	.25
1576	A249	1c multicolored	.80	.25
a.		Block of 5 + label, Nos. 1572-1576	5.00	1.00
1577	A248	3c multicolored	1.75	.35
1578	A249	3c multicolored	1.75	.35
1579	A249	3c multicolored	1.75	.35
1580	A249	3c multicolored	1.75	.35
1581	A249	3c multicolored	1.75	.35
a.		Block of 5 + label, Nos. 1577-1581	10.00	2.00
1582	A248	13c multicolored	2.50	.90
1583	A249	13c multicolored	2.50	.90
1584	A249	13c multicolored	2.50	.90
1585	A249	13c multicolored	2.50	.90
1586	A249	13c multicolored	2.50	.90
a.		Block of 5 + label, Nos. 1582-1586	15.00	5.00
		Nos. 1572-1586 (15)	25.25	7.50

Christmas 1970. See note after No. 700.

Camilo Cienfuegos Military Academy — A416

1970, Dec. 2

1587 A416 3c multi 1.25 .25

7th Congress of the Intl. Organization of Journalists — A417

1971, Jan. 4

1588 A417 13c multi 2.25 .50

World Meteorology Day — A418

1971, Feb. 16

Size: 39½x35½mm (3c)

1589	A418	1c Class, weather chart, computer, vert.	.25	.25
1590	A418	3c Weather map	.25	.25
1591	A418	8c Equipment, vert.	1.00	.25
1592	A418	30c shown	4.75	1.25
		Nos. 1589-1592 (4)	6.25	2.00

6th Pan American Games, Cali, Colombia — A419

1971, Feb. 20

1593	A419	1c Emblem, vert.	.25	.25
1594	A419	2c Women's running, vert.	.25	.25
1595	A419	3c Rifle shooting	.25	.25
1596	A419	4c Gymnastics, vert.	.25	.25
1597	A419	5c Boxing, vert.	.25	.25
1598	A419	13c Water polo	2.40	.30
1599	A419	30c Baseball	3.00	.55
		Nos. 1593-1599 (7)	6.65	2.10

Porcelain and Mosaics in the Metropolitan Museum, Havana — A420

Designs: 1c, Parisian vase, 19th cent. 3c, Mexican bowl, 17th cent. 10c, Parisian vase, diff. 13c, Colosseum, Italian mosaic, 19th cent. 20c, Mexican bowl, 17th cent. 30c, St. Peter's Square, Italian mosaic, 19th cent.

1971, Mar. 11

Sizes: 34½x53mm (1c, 10c), 46x53mm (3c), 42x48mm (20c)

1600	A420	1c multi	.25	.25
1601	A420	3c multi	.25	.25
1602	A420	10c multi	.40	.25
1603	A420	13c shown	2.25	.25
1604	A420	20c multi	2.25	.55
1605	A420	30c multi	2.75	.65
		Nos. 1600-1605 (6)	8.15	2.20

See Nos. 1699-1705.

Natl. Child Centers, 10th Anniv. — A421

1971, Apr. 10

1606 A421 3c multi .75 .25

Manned Space Flight 10th Anniv. — A422

Cosmonauts in training.

1971, Apr. 12

1607	A422	1c multi	.25	.25
1608	A422	2c multi, diff.	.25	.25
1609	A422	3c multi, diff.	.25	.25
1610	A422	4c multi, diff.	.25	.25
1611	A422	5c multi, diff.	.25	.25
1612	A422	13c multi, diff.	2.25	.30
1613	A422	30c multi, diff.	3.25	.65
		Nos. 1607-1613 (7)	6.75	2.20

Souvenir Sheet

Imperf

1614 A422 50c multi 10.00 10.00

Stamp in No. 1614 has simulated perf.

Bay of Pigs Invasion, 10th Anniv. A423

1971, Apr. 17

1615 A423 13c multi 2.00 .60

Stamp Day — A424

Packets: 13c, Jeune Richard attacking the Windsor Castle, 1807. 30c, Orinoco.

1971, Apr. 24

1616	A424	13c multi	2.40	.80
1617	A424	30c multi	3.50	1.00

Cuban Intl. Broadcast Service, 10th Anniv. — A425

1971, May 1 **Wmk. 376**

1618	A425	3c multi	.40	.25
1619	A425	50c multi	4.50	.90

Orchids A426

1c, Cattleya skinnerii. 2c, Vanda hibrida. 3c, Cypripedium collossum. 4c, Cypripedium gloucophyllum. 5c, Vanda tricolor. 13c, Cypripedium mowgh. 30c, Cypripedium solum.

1971, May 15

1620	A426	1c multicolored	.25	.25
1621	A426	2c multicolored	.25	.25
1622	A426	3c multicolored	.25	.25
1623	A426	4c multicolored	.25	.25
1624	A426	5c multicolored	.25	.25
1625	A426	13c multicolored	2.40	.45
1626	A426	30c multicolored	4.75	.85
		Nos. 1620-1626 (7)	8.40	2.55

See Nos. 1677-1683 and 1780-1786.

Enrique Loynaz del Castillo (b. 1861), Composer — A427

1971, June 5 **Wmk. 376**

1627	A427	3c Portrait, Invasion Hymn	.90	.25

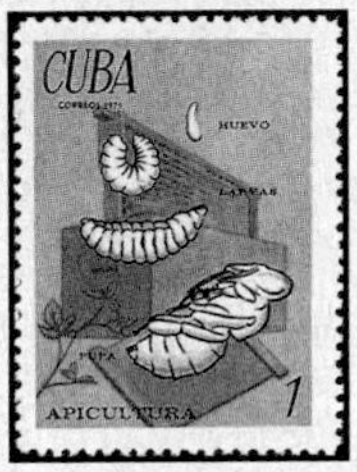

Bee Keeping — A428

1971, June 20 **Unwmk.**

1628	A428	1c Egg, larvae, pupa	.25	.25
1629	A428	3c Worker	.25	.25
1630	A428	9c Drone	.45	.25
1631	A428	13c Defense of hive	2.25	.30
1632	A428	30c Queen	3.50	.80
		Nos. 1628-1632 (5)	6.70	1.85

Children's Drawings — A429

1971, Aug. 30 **Size: 45x39mm**

1633	A429	1c Sailboat	.25	.25
1634	A429	3c The Little Train	.85	.25

Sizes: 45½x35½mm (9c, 13c), 47x37½mm (10c)

1635	A429	9c Sugar Cane Cutter	.25	.25
1636	A429	10c Return of the Fishermen	.40	.25
1637	A429	13c The Zoo	1.60	.30

Size: 47x42mm

1638	A429	20c House and Garden	2.50	.55

Size: 31½x50mm

1639	A429	30c Landscape	2.75	.85
		Nos. 1633-1639 (7)	8.60	2.70

Art Type of 1970

Paintings in the Natl. Museum: 1c, St. Catherine of Alexandria, by F. Zurburan. 2c, The Cart, by Federico Americo. 3c, St. Christopher and Child, by J. Bassano. 4c, Little Devil, by Rene Portocarrero. 5c, Portrait of a Woman, by Nicolas Maes. 13c, Phoenix, by Raul Martinez. 30c, Sir William Pitt, by Thomas Gainsborough.

1971, Sept. 20

1640	A408	1c 31x55mm	.25	.25
1641	A408	2c 48x37mm	.25	.25
1642	A408	3c 31x55mm	.25	.25
1643	A408	4c 37x48mm	.25	.25
1644	A408	5c 37x48mm	.40	.25
1645	A408	13c 39x48½mm	2.25	.45
1646	A408	30c 39x48½mm	3.25	.75
		Nos. 1640-1646 (7)	6.90	2.45

Sport Fishing — A431

1c, Albula vulpes. 2c, Seriola species. 3c, Micropterus salmoides. 4c, Coryphaena hippurus. 5c, Megalops atlantica. 13c, Acanthocybium solandri. 30c, Makaira ampla.

1971, Oct. 30

1647	A431	1c multicolored	.25	.25
1648	A431	2c multicolored	.25	.25
1649	A431	3c multicolored	.25	.25
1650	A431	4c multicolored	.25	.25
1651	A431	5c multicolored	.30	.25
1652	A431	13c multicolored	2.00	.55
1653	A431	30c multicolored	3.25	.95
		Nos. 1647-1653 (7)	6.55	2.75

19th World Amateur Baseball Championships — A432

1971, Nov. 22 **Wmk. 376**

1654	A432	3c shown	.25	.25
1655	A432	1p Globe as baseball	6.25	1.40

Execution of Medical Students, Cent. A433

Paintings: 3c, Dr. Fermin Valdez Dominguez, anonymous. 13c, Execution of the Medical Students, by M. Mesa. 30c, Capt. Federico Capdevila, anonymous.

1971, Nov. 27 **Unwmk.**

Size: 61½x46mm (13c)

1656	A433	3c multi	.35	.25
1657	A433	13c multi	1.90	.40
1658	A433	30c multi	3.00	.55
		Nos. 1656-1658 (3)	5.25	1.20

Spindalis Zena Pretrei — A434

Birds: 1c, Falco sparverius sparverioides vigors. 2c, Glaucidium siju siju. 3c, Priotelus temnurus temnurus. 4c, Saurothera merlini merlini. 5c, Nesoceleus fernandinae. 30c, Mimocichla plumbea rubripes. 50c, Chlorostilbon ricordii ricordii and Archilochus colubris. Nos. 1659-1663 vert.

1971, Dec. 10

1659	A434	1c multi	.40	.25
1660	A434	2c multi	.40	.25
1661	A434	3c multi	.65	.25
1662	A434	4c multi	.70	.25
1663	A434	5c multi	.90	.25
1664	A434	13c shown	1.60	.55
1665	A434	30c multi	3.25	1.75
		Nos. 1659-1665 (7)	7.90	3.55

Size: 55½x29mm

1666	A434	50c multi	6.00	1.75

Death centenary of Ramon de la Sagra, naturalist.

Cuba's Victory at the World Amateur Baseball Championships — A435

1971, Dec. 8 **Wmk. 376**

1667	A435	13c multi	2.00	.60

UNICEF, 25th Anniv. A436

1971, Dec. 11

1668	A436	13c multi	2.50	.70

Art Type of 1970

Paintings in the Natl. Museum: 1c, Arrival of an Ambassador, by Vittore Carpaccio. 2c, Senora Malpica, by G. Collazo. 3c, La Chorrera Tower, by Esteban Chartrand. 4c, Creole Landscape, by Carlos Enriquez. 5c, Sir William Lemon, by George Romney. 13c, Landscape, by Henry Cleenewerk. 30c, Valencia Beach, by Joaquin Sorolla y Bastida.

1972, Jan. 25 **Unwmk.**

1669	A408	1c 50x33mm	.25	.25
1670	A408	2c 27½x52mm	.25	.25
1671	A408	3c 50x33mm	.25	.25
1672	A408	4c 35x43mm	.25	.25
1673	A408	5c 35x43mm	.25	.25
1674	A408	13c 43x33mm	2.00	.40
1675	A408	30c 43x33mm	3.50	.95
		Nos. 1669-1675 (7)	6.75	2.60

Academy of Sciences, 10th Anniv. — A437

1972, Feb. 20 **Wmk. 376**

1676	A437	13c Capitol Type of 1929	2.00	.50

Orchid Type of 1971

1c, Brasso cattleya sindorossiana. 2c, Cypripedium doraeus. 3c, Cypripedium exul. 4c, Cypripedium rosy dawn. 5c, Cypripedium champolliom. 13c, Cypripedium bucolique. 30c, Cypripedium sullanum.

1972, Feb. 25 **Unwmk.**

1677	A426	1c multicolored	.25	.25
1678	A426	2c multicolored	.25	.25
1679	A426	3c multicolored	.25	.25
1680	A426	4c multicolored	.25	.25
1681	A426	5c multicolored	.25	.25
1682	A426	13c multicolored	2.75	.65
1683	A426	30c multicolored	3.50	.80
		Nos. 1677-1683 (7)	7.50	2.70

Eduardo Agramonte (1849-1872), Revolutionary, Physician — A438

1972, Mar. 8

1684	A438	3c Portrait by F. Martinez	.60	.25

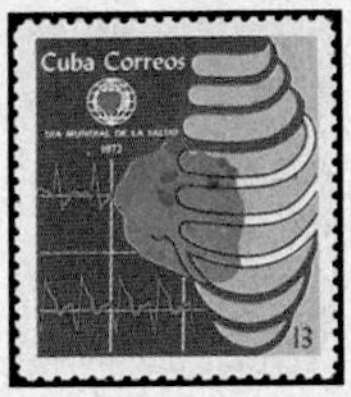

World Health Day — A439

1972, Apr. 7 **Wmk. 376**

1685	A439	13c multi	2.00	.50

Soviet Space Program — A440

1c, Sputnik 1. 2c, Vostok 1. 3c, Valentina Tereshkova. 4c, Alexei Leonov. 5c, Lunokhod 1, moon vehicle. 13c, Linking Soyuz capsules. 30c, Victims of Soyuz 11 accident.

1972, Apr. 12 **Unwmk.**

1686	A440	1c multicolored	.25	.25
1687	A440	2c multicolored	.25	.25
1688	A440	3c multicolored	.25	.25
1689	A440	4c multicolored	.25	.25
1690	A440	5c multicolored	.25	.25
1691	A440	13c multicolored	2.10	.40
1692	A440	30c multicolored	2.50	.70
		Nos. 1686-1692 (7)	5.85	2.35

Stamp Day — A441

Designs: 13c, Postmaster-Gen. Vicente Mora Pera, by Ramon Loy. 30c, Soldier's Letter, Cuba to Venezuela, 1897.

1972, Apr. 24

1693	A441	13c shown	1.75	.50

Size: 48x39mm

1694	A441	30c multi	2.75	.55

Labor Day — A442

1972, May 1 **Wmk. 376**

1695	A442	3c multi	.90	.25

Jose Marti, Ho Chi Minh — A443

3rd Conference Against War in Indo-China, May 19 — A444

30c, Roses, conference emblem.

1972, May 19

1696 A443 3c shown .40 .25
1697 A444 13c shown 1.60 .40
1698 A443 30c multicolored 2.00 .55
Nos. 1696-1698 (3) 4.00 1.20

Metropolitan Museum Type of 1971

Portraits: 1c, Salvador del Muro, by J. Del Rio. 2c, Luis de las Casas, by Del Rio. 3c, Cristopher Columbus, anonymous. 4c, Tomas Gamba, by V. Escobar. 5c, Maria Galarraga, by Escobar. 13c, Isabel II, by Federico Madrazo. 30c, Carlos III, by Miguel Melero.

1972, May 25 **Unwmk.**

Size: 34x43½mm

1699 A420 1c multi .25 .25
1700 A420 2c multi .25 .25
1701 A420 3c multi .25 .25
1702 A420 4c multi .40 .25
1703 A420 5c multi .40 .25

Size: 34x51½mm

1704 A420 13c multi 2.00 .40
1705 A420 30c multi 2.50 .70
Nos. 1699-1705 (7) 6.05 2.35

Children's Songs Competition, Natl. Library A445

1972, June 5 **Wmk. 376**

1706 A445 3c multi .80 .25

Thoroughbred Horses — A446

1972, June 30 **Unwmk.**

1707 A446 1c Tarpan .25 .25
1708 A446 2c Kertag .25 .25
1709 A446 3c Creole .25 .25
1710 A446 4c Andalusian .25 .25
1711 A446 5c Arabian .25 .25
1712 A446 13c Quarter horse 3.00 .55
1713 A446 30c Pursang 3.50 .80
Nos. 1707-1713 (7) 7.75 2.60

Frank Pais (d. 1957), Educator, Revolutionary — A447

1972, July 26 **Wmk. 376**

1714 A447 13c blk & red 1.75 .50

1972 Summer Olympics, Munich, Aug. 26-Sept. 10 — A448

1c, Athlete, emblems, vert. 2c, "M," boxing. 3c, "U," weight lifting. 4c, "N," fencing. 5c, "I," rifle shooting. 13c, "C," running. 30c, "H," basketball.
50c, Gymnastics.

1972, Aug. 26 **Unwmk.**

1715 A448 1c multicolored .25 .25
1716 A448 2c multicolored .25 .25
1717 A448 3c multicolored .25 .25
1718 A448 4c multicolored .25 .25
1719 A448 5c multicolored .25 .25
1720 A448 13c multicolored 2.00 .35
1721 A448 30c multicolored 2.50 .65
Nos. 1715-1721 (7) 5.75 2.25

Souvenir Sheet

Imperf

1722 A448 50c multicolored 6.00 1.90

Stamp in No. 1722 has simulated perforations.

Intl. Hydrological Decade — A449

Landscapes: 1c, Tree Trunks, by Domingo Ramos. 3c, Cyclone, by Tiburcio Lorenzo. 8c, Vinales, by Ramos. 30c, Forest and Brook, by Antonio R. Morey, vert.

1972, Sept. 20

1723 A449 1c multi .25 .25
1724 A449 3c multi .25 .25
1725 A449 8c multi .80 .25
1726 A449 30c multi 2.50 .55
Nos. 1723-1726 (4) 3.80 1.30

Butterflies from the Gundlach Collection — A450

1c, Papilio thoas oviedo. 2c, Papilio devilliers. 3c, Papilio polixenes polixenes. 4c, Papilio androgeus epidaurus. 5c, Papilio cayguanabus. 13c, Papilio andraemon hernandezi. 30c, Papilio celadon.

1972, Sept. 25

1727 A450 1c multicolored .25 .25
1728 A450 2c multicolored .25 .25
1729 A450 3c multicolored .25 .25
1730 A450 4c multicolored .25 .25
1731 A450 5c multicolored .30 .25
1732 A450 13c multicolored 3.50 .85
1733 A450 30c multicolored 4.75 1.10
Nos. 1727-1733 (7) 9.55 3.20

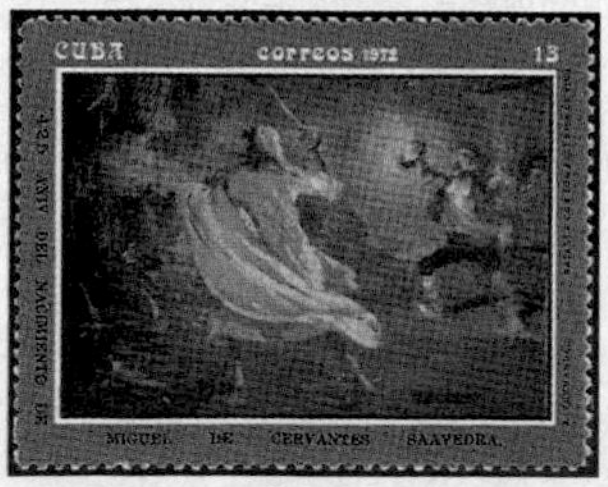

A451

Miguel de Cervantes Saavedra (1547-1616), Spanish Author — A452

Paintings by A. Fernandez: 3c, In La Mancha, vert. 13c, Battle with Wine Skins. 30c, Don Quixote de La Mancha, vert. 50c, Scene from Don Quixote, by Jose Moreno Carbonero.

1972, Sept. 29

Size: 34½x46mm (3c, 30c)

1734 A451 3c multi .25 .25
1735 A451 13c shown 2.10 .50
1736 A451 30c multi 2.25 .55
Nos. 1734-1736 (3) 4.60 1.30

Souvenir Sheet

Perf. 12½ on 3 Sides

1737 A452 50c shown 5.00 2.25

Guerrilla Day, 5th Anniv. — A453

3c, Ernesto "Che" Guevara. 13c, Tamara "Tania" Bunke. 30c, Guido "Inti" Peredo.

1972, Oct. 8

1738 A453 3c multicolored .25 .25
1739 A453 13c multicolored 2.25 .50
1740 A453 30c multicolored 2.50 .60
Nos. 1738-1740 (3) 5.00 1.35

Traditional Musical Instruments A454

1972, Oct. 25

1741 A454 3c Abwe (rattles) .25 .25
1742 A454 13c Bonko enchemiya (drum) 2.25 .45
1743 A454 30c Iya (drum) 2.50 .55
Nos. 1741-1743 (3) 5.00 1.25

MATEX '72, 3rd Natl. Philatelic Exhibition, Matanzas — A455

1972, Nov. 18 **Wmk. 376**

1744 A455 13c No. 467 2.50 .45
1745 A455 30c No. C49 3.00 .55

Nos. 1744-1745 printed se-tenant with insribed labels picturing Type A232, emblem of the Cuban Philatelic Federation.

Historic Ships A456

1c, Viking long boat, 6th-9th cent. 2c, Caravel, 15th cent., vert. 3c, Galleass, 16th cent. 4c, Galleon, 17th cent., vert. 5c, Clipper, 19th cent. 13c, Steam packet, 19th cent. 30c, Atomic icebreaker Lenin.

1972, Nov. 30 **Unwmk.**

1746 A456 1c multicolored .25 .25
1747 A456 2c multicolored .25 .25
1748 A456 3c multicolored .25 .25
1749 A456 4c multicolored .30 .25
1750 A456 5c multicolored .35 .25
1751 A456 13c multicolored 2.10 .75

Size: 52½x29mm.

1752 A456 30c multicolored 6.00 1.25
Nos. 1746-1752 (7) 9.50 3.25

UNESCO Save Venice Campaign — A457

3c, Lion of St. Mark. 13c, Bridge of Sighs, vert. 30c, St. Mark's Cathedral.

1972, Dec. 8

1753 A457 3c multicolored .25 .25
1754 A457 13c multicolored 1.75 .45
1755 A457 30c multicolored 2.25 .85
Nos. 1753-1755 (3) 4.25 1.55

Cuba, World Amateur Baseball Champion in 1972 — A458

1972, Dec. 15

1756 A458 3c Umpire 1.25 .30

Sport Events, 1972 — A459

1972, Dec. 22

1757 A459 1c shown .25 .25
1758 A458 2c Pole vault .25 .25
1759 A458 3c like No. 1756 .25 .25
1760 A458 4c Wrestling .25 .25
1761 A458 5c Fencing .25 .25
1762 A458 13c Boxing 1.75 .55
1763 A458 30c Marlin 2.50 .80
Nos. 1757-1763 (7) 5.50 2.60

Barrientos Memorial Athletics Championships, 11th Amateur Baseball Championships, Cerro Pelado Intl. Tournament, Central American and Caribbean Fencing Tournament, Giraldo Cordova Tournament, Ernest Hemingway Natl. Fishing Contest.

No. 1759 inscribed "XI serie nacional de beisbol aficionado."

Medals Won by Cubans at the 1972 Summer Olympics, Munich A460

1c, Bronze, Women's 100-meter. 2c, Bronze, women's relay. 3c, Gold, 54kg boxing. 4c, Silver, 81kg boxing. 5c, Bronze, 51kg boxing. 13c, Gold, 87kg boxing. 30c, Gold, silver cup, heavyweight boxing. 50c, Bronze, basketball.

1973, Jan. 28

1764	A460	1c multi	.25	.25
1765	A460	2c multi	.25	.25
1766	A460	3c multi	.25	.25
1767	A460	4c multi	.25	.25
1768	A460	5c multi	.25	.25
1769	A460	13c multi	1.75	.60
1770	A460	30c multi	2.25	.90
		Nos. 1764-1770 (7)	5.25	2.75

Souvenir Sheet
Imperf

1771	A460	50c multi	6.00	2.25

Stamp in No. 1771 has simulated perforations.

A461

Portrait by A.M. Esquivel.

1973, Feb. 10

1772	A461	13c multi	2.25	.45

Gertrudis Gomez de Avellaneda (1814-1873), poet.

Art Type of 1970

Paintings in the Natl. Museum: 1c, Bathers in the Lagoon, by C. Enriquez. 2c, Still-life, by W.C. Heda. 3c, Gallantry, by P. Landaluze. 4c, Return in the Late Afternoon, by C. Troyon. 5c, Elizabetta Mascagni, by F.X. Fabre. 13c, The Picador, by De Lucas Padilla, horiz. 30c, In the Garden, by Arburu Morell.

1973, Feb. 28
Sizes: 36x46mm, 46x36mm

1773	A408	1c multi	.25	.25
1774	A408	2c multi	.25	.25
1775	A408	3c multi	.25	.25
1776	A408	4c multi	.25	.25
1777	A408	5c multi	.25	.25
1778	A408	13c multi	1.60	.55
1779	A408	30c multi	2.25	.80
		Nos. 1773-1779 (7)	5.10	2.60

Orchid Type of 1971

1c, Dendrobium hybrid. 2c, Cypripedium exul. 3c, Vanda miss. joaquin rose marie. 4c, Phalaenopsis schilleriana. 5c, Vanda gilbert tribulet. 13c, Dendrobium hybrid, diff. 30c, Arachnis catherine.

1973, Mar. 26

1780	A426	1c multicolored	.25	.25
1781	A426	2c multicolored	.25	.25
1782	A426	3c multicolored	.25	.25
1783	A426	4c multicolored	.25	.25
1784	A426	5c multicolored	.40	.25
1785	A426	13c multicolored	3.00	.55
1786	A426	30c multicolored	3.50	.80
		Nos. 1780-1786 (7)	7.90	2.60

A462

1973, Apr. 7 **Wmk. 376**

1787	A462	10c multi, *buff*	1.25	.30

World Health Day. World Health Organization, 25th anniv.

Anti-Polio Campaign — A463

1973, Apr. 9 **Unwmk.**

1788	A463	3c multi	.70	.25

Soviet Space Program — A464

1c, Soyuz rocket launch, vert. 2c, Luna 1, Moon. 3c, Luna 16 taking-off from Moon, vert. 4c, Venera 7. 5c, Molniya 1, vert. 13c, Mars 3. 30c, Radar observation ship, Yuri Gagarin.

1973, Apr. 12

1789	A464	1c multicolored	.25	.25
1790	A464	2c multicolored	.25	.25
1791	A464	3c multicolored	.25	.25
1792	A464	4c multicolored	.25	.25
1793	A464	5c multicolored	.25	.25
1794	A464	13c multicolored	1.25	.70
1795	A464	30c multicolored	3.50	.85
		Nos. 1789-1795 (7)	6.00	2.80

Stamp Day A465

Postmarks: 13c, Santiago de Cuba, 1760. 30c, Havana, 1760.

1973, Apr. 24

1796	A465	13c multi	1.90	.50
1797	A465	30c multi	2.10	.60

See Nos. 1888-1891.

Portrait by A. Espinosa A466

1973, May 11

1798	A466	13c multi	1.50	.45

Maj.-Gen. Ignacio Agramonte (1841-1873).

Birthplace, Torun, and Inventions — A467

Copernicus Monument, Warsaw — A468

13c, Copernicus, spacecraft. 30c, Manuscript, Frombork Tower.

1973, May 25

1799	A467	3c shown	.25	.25
1800	A467	13c multicolored	1.60	.45
1801	A467	30c multicolored	3.00	.60
		Nos. 1799-1801 (3)	4.85	1.30

Souvenir Sheet
Perf. 12½ on 3 Sides

1802	A468	50c shown	6.50	2.25

500th anniversary of the birth of Nicolaus Copernicus (1473-1543), Polish astronomer.

Improvement of School Education — A469

1973, June 12 **Wmk. 376**

1803	A469	13c multi	1.50	.25

Cattle — A470

1973, June 28 **Unwmk.**

1804	A470	1c Jersey	.25	.25
1805	A470	2c Charolaise	.25	.25
1806	A470	3c Creole	.25	.25
1807	A470	4c Swiss	.25	.25
1808	A470	5c Holstein	.25	.25
1809	A470	13c Santa Gertrudis	1.60	.40
1810	A470	30c Brahman	3.25	.75
		Nos. 1804-1810 (7)	6.10	2.40

A471

1973, July 10 **Wmk. 376**

1811	A471	13c multi	1.50	.30

10th Communist Festival of Youths and Students, East Berlin.

A472

3c, Siboney Farm, Santiago de Cuba. 13c, Moncada Barracks. 30c, Revolution Plaza, Havana.

1973, July 26 **Unwmk.**

1812	A472	3c multicolored	.35	.25
1813	A472	13c multicolored	1.50	.30
1814	A472	30c multicolored	2.25	.45
		Nos. 1812-1814 (3)	4.10	1.00

20th anniv. of the Revolution.

10th Anniv. of the Revolutionary Navy — A473

3c, Midshipman, missile frigate.

1973, Aug. 3 **Wmk. 376**

1815	A473	3c multicolored	.85	.30

Interior, by Manuel Vicens A474

Paintings in the Natl. Museum: 1c, Amalia of Saxony, by J.K. Rossler. 3c, Margarita of Austria, by J. Pantoja de la Cruz. 4c, City Hall Official, anonymous. 5c, View of Santiago de Cuba, by Hernandez Giro. 13c, The Catalan, by J.J. Tejada. 30c, Alley in Guayo, by Tejada.

1973, Aug. 30 **Unwmk.**
Sizes: 26½x41mm (1c, 3c), 28½x39mm (4c, 13c, 30c)

1816	A474	1c multi	.25	.25
1817	A474	2c multi	.25	.25
1818	A474	3c multi	.25	.25
1819	A474	4c multi	.25	.25
1820	A474	5c multi	.25	.25
1821	A474	13c multi	1.90	.60
1822	A474	30c multi	2.50	.70
		Nos. 1816-1822 (7)	5.65	2.55

WMO Emblem, Paintings by J. Madrazo A475

1973, Sept. 4

1823	A475	8c Spring	.75	.25
1824	A475	8c Summer	.75	.25
1825	A475	8c Fall	.75	.25
1826	A475	8c Winter	.75	.25
		Nos. 1823-1826 (4)	3.00	1.00

World Meteorogogical Organization, cent. Nos. 1823-1826 printed se-tenant in strips of 4; frame reversed on 2nd and 4th stamp in strip.

A476

27th World and 1st Pan American Weight Lifting Championships: Various weightlifting positions.

1973, Sept. 12

1827	A476	1c multi, diff.	.25	.25
1828	A476	2c shown	.25	.25
1829	A476	3c multi, diff.	.25	.25
1830	A476	4c multi, diff.	.25	.25
1831	A476	5c multi, diff.	.25	.25
1832	A476	13c multi, diff.	1.60	.45
1833	A476	30c multi, diff.	2.75	.90
		Nos. 1827-1833 (7)	5.60	2.60

A477

Flowering plants: 1c, Erythrina standleyana. 2c, Lantana camara. 3c, Canavalia maritima. 4c, Dichromena colorata. 5c, Borrichia arborescens. 13c, Anguria pedata. 30c, Cordia sebestena.

1973, Sept. 28

1834	A477	1c multicolored	.25	.25
1835	A477	2c multicolored	.25	.25
1836	A477	3c multicolored	.25	.25
1837	A477	4c multicolored	.25	.25
1838	A477	5c multicolored	.25	.25
1839	A477	13c multicolored	2.10	.65
1840	A477	30c multicolored	3.25	.90
		Nos. 1835-1840 (6)	6.35	2.55

8th World Trade Union Congress, Varna, Bulgaria — A478

1973, Oct. 5 **Wmk. 376**

1841	A478	13c multi	1.50	.35

Cuban Natl. Ballet, 25th Anniv. — A479

1973, Oct. 28 **Unwmk.**

1842	A479	13c gold & brt ultra	2.00	.40

Sea Shells — A480

1c, Liguus fasciatus fasciatus. 2c, Liguus fasciatus guitarti. 3c, Liguus fasciatus whartoni. 4c, Liguus fasciatus angelae. 5c, Liguus fasciatus trinidadense. 13c, Liguus blainianus. 30c, Liguus vittatus.

1973, Oct. 29

1843	A480	1c multicolored	.25	.25
1844	A480	2c multicolored	.25	.25
1845	A480	3c multicolored	.25	.25
1846	A480	4c multicolored	.25	.25
1847	A480	5c multicolored	.25	.25
1848	A480	13c multicolored	2.75	.70
1849	A480	30c multicolored	3.75	.85
		Nos. 1843-1849 (7)	7.75	2.80

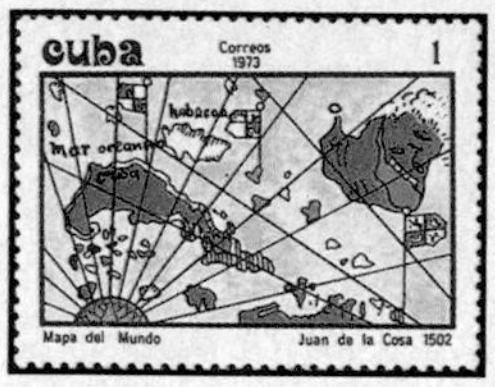

Maps of Cuba A481

1973, Oct. 29

1850	A481	1c Juan de la Cosa, 1502	.25	.25
1851	A481	3c Ortelius, 1572	.25	.25
1852	A481	13c Bellini, 1762	1.75	.25
1853	A481	40c 1973	2.10	.80
		Nos. 1850-1853 (4)	4.35	1.55

15th Anniversary of the Revolution — A482

1974, Jan. 2

1854	A482	1c No. 625	.25	.25
1855	A482	3c No. 626	.25	.25
1856	A482	13c No. C200	4.00	.55
1857	A482	40c No. C201	1.60	.80
		Nos. 1854-1857 (4)	6.10	1.85

Woman, by F. Ponce de Leon — A483

Portraits in the Camaguey Museum: 3c, Mexican Girls, by J. Arche. 8c, Young Woman, by A. Menocal. 10c, Mulatto Woman Drinking from Coconut, by L. Romanach. 13c, Head of an Old Man, by J. Arburu.

1974, Jan. 10

1858	A483	1c multi	.25	.25
1859	A483	3c multi	.25	.25
1860	A483	8c multi	.35	.25
1861	A483	10c multi	1.10	.25
1862	A483	13c multi	1.60	.40
		Nos. 1858-1862 (5)	3.55	1.40

Amilcar Cabral — A484

1974, Jan. 20

1863	A484	13c multi	1.40	.25

Amilcar Cabral, Guinea-Bissau freedom fighter, 1st death anniv.

Lenin, by I.V. Kosmin — A485

1974, Jan. 21

1864	A485	30c multi	3.00	.55

50th death anniv. of Lenin.

12th Central American and Caribbean Games, Santo Domingo — A486

1974, Feb. 8

1865	A486	1c Emblem	.25	.25
1866	A486	2c Javelin	.25	.25
1867	A486	3c Boxing	.25	.25
1868	A486	4c Baseball, horiz.	.25	.25
1869	A486	13c Basketball, horiz.	1.60	.25
1870	A486	30c Volleyball, horiz.	2.40	.70
		Nos. 1865-1870 (6)	5.00	1.95

Portrait by F. Martinez — A487

1974, Feb. 27

1871	A487	13c multi	1.40	.25

Carlos M. de Cespedes (d. 1874), patriot.

Portrait of a Man, by J.B. Vermay — A488

Paintings in the Natl. Museum: 2c, The Wet Nurse, by C.A. Van Loo. 3c, Cattle in River, by R. Morey. 4c, Village, by Morey. 13c, Faun and Bacchus, by Rubens. 30c, Young Woman Playing Cards, by R. Madrazo.

1974, Mar. 7

1872	A488	1c shown	.25	.25
1873	A488	2c multi	.25	.25
1874	A488	3c multi	.25	.25
1875	A488	4c multi	.25	.25
1876	A488	13c multi	1.40	.25
1877	A488	30c multi	2.50	.55
		Nos. 1872-1877 (6)	4.90	1.80

Council for Mutual Economic Assistance (COMECON), 25th Anniv. — A489

30c, Comecon building, Moscow.

1974, Mar. 15

1878	A489	30c multicolored	2.00	.70

Visit of Leonid I. Brezhnev to Cuba, Jan. 28-Feb. 3 — A490

13c, Jose Marti, Lenin, flags. 30c, Brezhnev, Fidel Castro.

1974, Mar. 28

1879	A490	13c multicolored	2.00	.30
1880	A490	30c multicolored	2.10	.55
		Nos. 1879-1880 (2)	4.10	.85

Science Fiction A491

Paintings by A. Sokolov.

1974, Apr. 12

1881	A491	1c Martian Crater	.25	.25
1882	A491	2c Fiery Labyrinth	.25	.25
1883	A491	3c Amber Wave	.25	.25
1884	A491	4c Flight Through Space	.25	.25
1885	A491	13c Planet in Nebula	2.00	.25
1886	A491	30c World of Two Suns	3.25	.60
		Nos. 1881-1886 (6)	6.25	1.85

Cosmonauts Day.

UPU, Cent. A492

1974, Apr. 15

1887	A492	30c Letter, 1874	2.50	.60

Stamp Day Type of 1973

Postmarks.

1974, Apr. 24

1888	A465	1c Havana	.25	.25
1889	A465	3c Matanzas	.40	.25
1890	A465	13c Trinidad	1.50	.25
1891	A465	20c Guana Vacoa	2.25	.35
		Nos. 1888-1891 (4)	4.40	1.10

18th Sports Congress of Friendly Armies — A493

1974, May 5 **Wmk. 376**

1892	A493	3c multi	.80	.25

Felipe Poey (1799-1891), Naturalist — A494

1c, Eumaeus atala atala. 2c, Pineria terebra. 3c, Chaetodon sedentarius. 4c, Eurema dina dina. 13c, Hemitrochus fuscolabiata. 30c, Eupomacentrus partitus. 50c, Apogon binotatus.

1c, 4c, Butterflies. 2c, 13c, Sea shells. 3c, 30c, 50c, Fish.

1974, May 26 ***Perf. 12½x12***

1893	A494	1c multicolored	.25	.25
1894	A494	2c multicolored	.25	.25
1895	A494	3c multicolored	.25	.25
1896	A494	4c multicolored	.80	.25
1897	A494	13c multicolored	2.75	.45
1898	A494	30c multicolored	3.50	.55
		Nos. 1893-1898 (6)	7.80	2.00

Souvenir Sheet

Imperf

1899	A494	50c multicolored	7.00	2.50

Stamp in No. 1899 has simulated perforations.

Havana Philharmonic Orchestra, 50th Anniv. — A495

1c, Antonio Mompo, cello. 3c, Cesar Perez Sentenat, piano. 5c, Pedro Mercado, trumpet. 10c, Pedro Sanjuan, Havana Philharmonic emblem. 13c, Roberto Ondina, flute.

1974, June 8 ***Perf. 12½***

1900	A495	1c multi	.25	.25
1901	A495	3c multi	.25	.25
1902	A495	5c multi	.25	.25
1903	A495	10c multi	1.40	.25
1904	A495	13c multi	1.75	.25
		Nos. 1900-1904 (5)	3.90	1.25

Garden Flowers — A496

1c, Heliconia humilis. 2c, Anthurium andraeanum. 3c, Canna generalis. 4c, Alpinia purpurata. 13c, Gladiolus grandiflorus. 30c, Amomum capitatum.

1974, June 12

1905	A496	1c multicolored	.25	.25
1906	A496	2c multicolored	.25	.25
1907	A496	3c multicolored	.25	.25
1908	A496	4c multicolored	.25	.25
1909	A496	13c multicolored	1.75	.25
1910	A496	30c multicolored	4.50	.60
		Nos. 1905-1910 (6)	7.25	1.85

A497

World Amateur Boxing Championships: Emblem and various boxers.

Perf. 12x12½

1974, Aug. 24 **Litho.** **Unwmk.**

1911	A497	1c multi	.25	.25
1912	A497	3c multi	.35	.25
1913	A497	13c multi	1.60	.25
		Nos. 1911-1913 (3)	2.20	.75

A498

Extinct birds.

1974, Aug. 28 ***Perf. 13***

1914	A498	1c Dodo	.40	.25
1915	A498	3c Ara de Cuba (parrot)	.40	.25
1916	A498	8c Passenger pigeon	.85	.25
1917	A498	10c Moa	2.75	.55
1918	A498	13c Great auk	3.50	.80
		Nos. 1914-1918 (5)	7.90	2.10

Pres. Salvador Allende of Chile (d. 1973) A499

1974, Sept. 11

1919	A499	13c multi	1.25	.45

Wildflowers A500

1974, Sept. 14 ***Perf. 13x12½***

1920	A500	1c Suriana maritima	.25	.25
1921	A500	3c Cassia ligustrina	.25	.25
1922	A500	8c Flaveria linearis	.30	.25
1923	A500	10c Stachytarpheta jamaicensis	2.10	.25
1924	A500	13c Bacopa monnieri	3.50	.85
		Nos. 1920-1924 (5)	6.40	1.85

Model Aircraft — A501

1974, Sept. 22 ***Perf. 12½***

1925	A501	1c shown	.25	.25
1926	A501	3c Sky diving	.25	.25
1927	A501	8c Glider	.45	.25
1928	A501	10c Crop dusting	1.25	.25
1929	A501	13c Commercial aviation	2.00	.25
		Nos. 1925-1929 (5)	4.20	1.25

Civil Aeronautic Institute, 10th anniv. Nos. 1927-1929 horiz.

History of Cuban Baseball — A502

1c, Indians playing ball. 3c, 1st Official game, 1874. 8c, Emilio Sabourin. 10c, Umpire, players, 1974. 13c, Latin-American Stadium, Havana.

1974, Oct. 3 ***Perf. 13***

1930	A502	1c multicolored	.25	.25
1931	A502	3c multicolored	.25	.25
1932	A502	8c multicolored	.40	.25
1933	A502	10c multicolored	1.25	.25
1934	A502	13c multicolored	2.10	.25
		Nos. 1930-1934 (5)	4.25	1.25

Nos. 1930-1932 vert.

Mambi 10c Stamp (Revolutionary Junta Issue), Cent. — A503

1974, Oct. 10

1935	A503	13c multi	1.50	.25

16th Conference of Customs Organizations of Socialist Countries — A504

1974, Oct. 15

1936	A504	30c Comecon Building, Moscow	2.00	.55

Disappearance of Major Camilo Cienfuegos, 15th Anniv. — A505

Wmk. 376

1974, Oct. 28 **Litho.** ***Perf. 13***

1937	A505	3c multi	.75	.25

8th World Mining Conference — A506

1974, Nov. 3

1938	A506	13c multi	1.50	.25

Petroleum Institute, 15th Anniv. — A507

1974, Nov. 20

1939	A507	3c multi	.70	.25

Intersputnik Earth Station Opening — A508

1974, Nov. 30 **Unwmk.**

1940	A508	3c shown	.25	.25
1941	A508	13c Satellite, satellite dish	1.25	.25
1942	A508	1p Satellite, flags	3.25	1.10
		Nos. 1940-1942 (3)	4.75	1.60

Philatelic Federation, 10th Anniv. — A509

1974, Nov. 30 ***Perf. 12½x13***

1943	A509	30c multi	2.40	.45

Souvenir Sheet

Mercury — A510

1974, Dec. 6 ***Imperf.***

1944	A510	50c multi	6.00	1.25

4th Natl. Phil. Exhib., Havana.

1st World Peace Congress, 25th Anniv. — A511

1974, Dec. 16 **Wmk. 376** ***Perf. 13***

1945	A511	30c *F. Joliot-Curie,* by Picasso	3.00	.45

Ruben Martinez Villena (b. 1899), Revolutionary — A512

1974, Dec. 20 **Unwmk.**

1946	A512	3c red org & yel	.75	.25

Souvenir Sheet

Cuban Victories, 1st Amateur Boxing Championships — A513

1975, Jan. 6 **Litho.** ***Imperf.***

1947	A513	50c Trophy	6.00	1.25

The Word, by Marcelo Pogolotti A514

Paintings in the Natl. Museum: 2c, *The Silk-Cotton Tree*, by Henry Cleenewerk. 3c, *Landscape*, by Guillermo Collazo. 5c, *Still-life*, by Francisco Peralta. 13c, *Maria Wilson*, by Federico Martinez, vert. 30c, *The Couple*, by Mariano Fortuny.

1975, Jan. 20 ***Perf. 13***

1948	A514	1c multi	.25	.25
1949	A514	2c multi	.25	.25
1950	A514	3c multi	.25	.25
1951	A514	5c multi	.25	.25
1952	A514	13c multi	1.50	.25
1953	A514	30c multi	2.75	.45
		Nos. 1948-1953 (6)	5.25	1.70

Intl. Women's Year A515

1975, Feb. 6

1954	A515	13c multi	1.25	.25

Fishing Industry A516

Various fish and fishing vessels.

1975, Feb. 22

1955	A516	1c Long-finned tuna	.25	.25
1956	A516	2c Tuna	.25	.25
1957	A516	3c Mediterranean grouper	.25	.25
1958	A516	8c Hake	.25	.25
1959	A516	13c Prawn	1.10	.70
1960	A516	30c Lobster	3.25	.70
		Nos. 1955-1960 (6)	5.35	2.40

Minerals — A517

1975, Mar. 15 **Litho.** ***Perf. 13x12½***

1961	A517	3c Nickel	.40	.25
1962	A517	13c Copper	1.60	.25
1963	A517	30c Chromium	2.75	.45
		Nos. 1961-1963 (3)	4.75	.95

Cosmonaut's Day — A518

1c, Cosmodrome. 2c, Probe, vert. 3c, Eclipse. 5c, Threshold to Space. 13c, Midday on Mars. 30c, Cosmonaut's view of Earth.

1975, Apr. 12 ***Perf. 13x12½, 12½x13***

1964	A518	1c multicolored	.25	.25
1965	A518	2c multicolored	.25	.25
1966	A518	3c multicolored	.25	.25
1967	A518	5c multicolored	.40	.25
1968	A518	13c multicolored	1.50	.25
1969	A518	30c multicolored	2.50	.45
		Nos. 1964-1969 (6)	5.15	1.70

The future of space.

Stamp Day A519

Various covers.

1975, Apr. 24 ***Perf. 13***

1970	A519	3c multi	.25	.25
1971	A519	13c multi	1.40	.25
1972	A519	30c multi	2.10	.40
		Nos. 1970-1972 (3)	3.75	.90

Victory Over Fascism, 30th Anniv. — A520

Design: Raising red flag over Reichstag, Berlin.

1975, May 9 ***Perf. 13x12½***

1973	A520	30c multi	2.00	.40

A521

Works in the Decorative Art Museum — A522

1c, Sevres porcelain vase, vert. 2c, Meissen porcelain statue *Shepherdess and Dancers*, vert. 3c, Chinese porcelain dish *Lady with Parasol*. 5c, Chinese screen detail *The Phoenix*, vert. 13c, *Allegory of Music*, by Francois Boucher (1703-70), vert. 30c, *Portrait of a Lady*, by L. Tocque, vert. 50c, *The Swing*, by Hubert Robert (1733-1808).

1975, May 10 ***Perf. 12½x13, 13x12½***

1974	A521	1c multi	.25	.25
1975	A521	2c multi	.25	.25
1976	A521	3c shown	.25	.25
1977	A521	5c multi	.40	.25
1978	A521	13c multi	1.50	.25
1979	A521	30c multi	2.00	.40
		Nos. 1974-1979 (6)	4.65	1.65

Souvenir Sheet

Perf. 13x12½ on 3 Sides

1980	A522	50c shown	5.50	1.25

No. 1980 contains one 25x39mm stamp.

Intl. Children's Day — A523

Wmk. 376

1975, May 31 **Litho.** ***Perf. 13***

1981	A523	3c multi	.50	.25

Indigenous Birds — A524

Designs: 1c, Vireo gundlachi. 2c, Gymnoglaux lawrenci. 3c, Aratingo eoups. 5c, Staroenas cyanocephala. 13c, Chondrohierax wilsoni. 30c, Cyanolimnas cerverai.

1975, June 18 **Unwmk.**

1982	A524	1c multicolored	.25	.25
1983	A524	2c multicolored	.25	.25
1984	A524	3c multicolored	.25	.25
1985	A524	5c multicolored	.40	.25
1986	A524	13c multicolored	1.75	.40
1987	A524	30c multicolored	2.50	.70
		Nos. 1982-1987 (6)	5.40	2.10

See Nos. 2121-2125, 2180-2182, C276-C276.

Scientific Investigation Center, 10th Anniv. — A525

1975, July 1 ***Perf. 12½***

1988	A525	13c multi	1.40	.25

Irrigation and Drainage Commission, 25th Anniv. — A526

1975, Aug. 2 ***Perf. 13***

1989	A526	13c multi	1.40	.25

Afforestation A527

Designs: 1c, Cedrela mexicana. 3c, Swietenia mahagoni. 5c, Calophyllum brasiliense. 13c, Hibiscus tiliaceus. 30c, Pinus caribaea.

1975, Aug. 20

1990	A527	1c multicolored	.25	.25
1991	A527	3c multicolored	.40	.25
1992	A527	5c multicolored	.40	.25
1993	A527	13c multicolored	1.10	.25
1994	A527	30c multicolored	1.75	.40
		Nos. 1990-1994 (5)	3.90	1.40

Cuban Women's Federation, 15th Anniv. — A528

1975, Aug. 23

1995	A528	3c multi	.50	.25

Intl. Conference on the Independence of Puerto Rico — A529

1975, Sept. 5 **Litho.**

1996	A529	13c multi	1.00	.25

A530

7th Pan American Games, Mexico: Aztec calendar stone and various athletes.

1975, Sept. 20 *Perf. 12½x13*

1997 A530 1c Baseball .25 .25
1998 A530 3c Boxing .25 .25
1999 A530 5c Basketball .25 .25
2000 A530 13c High jump 1.50 .30
2001 A530 30c Weight lifting 2.10 .30
Nos. 1997-2001 (5) 4.35 1.35

Souvenir Sheet

Imperf

2002 A530 50c Stone, emblem 4.00 1.25

A531

1975, Sept. 28 *Perf. 12½x13*

2003 A531 3c multi .50 .25

Revolutionary Defense Committees (CDR), 15th anniv.

Friendship Among the Peoples Institute, 15th Anniv. A532

1975, Oct. 8 *Perf. 12½x13*

2004 A532 3c multi .30 .25

Natl. Bank, 25th Anniv. A533

Designs: 1-peso coins and banknotes identified by serial numbers.

1975, Oct. 13 *Perf. 13x12½*

2005 A533 13c Coin, 1915 1.10 .25
2006 A533 13c C882736A, 1934 1.10 .25
2007 A533 13c A000387A, 1946 1.10 .25
2008 A533 13c 933906, 1964 1.10 .25
2009 A533 13c K000000, 1976 1.10 .25
a. Strip of 5, Nos. 2005-2009 6.00 1.50
Nos. 2005-2009 (5) 5.50 1.25

Locomotives — A534

1c, La Junta, 1837. 3c, Steam engine 2-8-0 No. 12. 5c, Diesel TEM 4 No. 51010. 13c, Diesel DVM 9I-7 55. 30c, Diesel M 62K No. 61601.

1975, Oct. 28 **Unwmk.** *Perf. 12½*

2010 A534 1c multicolored .25 .25
2011 A534 3c multicolored .30 .25
2012 A534 5c multicolored .30 .25
2013 A534 13c multicolored 2.50 .25
2014 A534 30c multicolored 3.00 .45
Nos. 2010-2014 (5) 6.35 1.45

Railway history.

Development of the Textile Industry — A535

1975, Nov. 10 *Perf. 13x12½*

2015 A535 13c Bobbins, flag, loom operator 1.25 .25

Veterinary Medicine — A536

Parasites and host species: 1c, Haemonchus, lamb. 2c, Ancylostoma caninum, dog. 3c, Dispharynx nasuta, rooster. 5c, Gasterophilus intestinalis, horse. 13c, Ascaris lumbricoides, pig. 30c, Boophilus microplus, bull.

1975, Nov. 25 **Litho.** *Perf. 13*

2016 A536 1c multicolored .25 .25
2017 A536 2c multicolored .25 .25
2018 A536 3c multicolored .25 .25
2019 A536 5c multicolored .25 .25
2020 A536 13c multicolored 1.40 .25
2021 A536 30c multicolored 2.50 .40
Nos. 2016-2021 (6) 4.90 1.65

Manuel Ascunce Domenech Educational Detachment A537

1975, Nov. 27 **Litho.**

2022 A537 3c multi .40 .25

Development of Agriculture and Irrigation — A538

1975, Dec. 15 **Litho.** *Perf. 13x12½*

2023 A538 13c Irrigation 1.25 .25

1st Communist Party Congress — A539

1975, Dec. 17 *Perf. 12½x13, 13x12½*

2024 A539 3c "1," revolutionaries, vert. .25 .25
2025 A539 13c shown 1.10 .25
2026 A539 30c Party leaders 1.50 .30
Nos. 2024-2026 (3) 2.85 .80

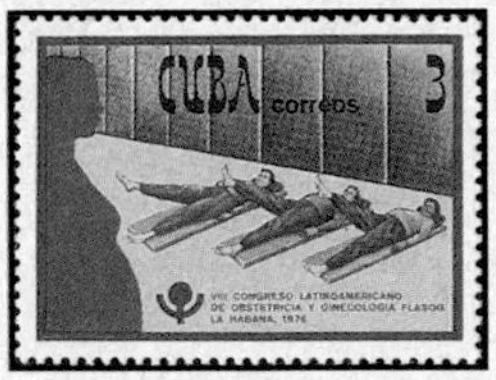

8th Latin-American Obstetrics and Gynecology Congress — A540

1976, Jan. 24 *Perf. 13*

2027 A540 3c multi .60 .25

Paintings in Natl. Museums — A541

Designs: 1c, *Seated Woman,* by Victor Manuel, vert. 2c, *Garden,* by Santiago Rusinol. 3c, *Guadalquivir River,* by Manuel Barron y Carrillo. 5c, *Self-portrait,* by Jan Havicksz Steen, vert. 13c, *Portrait of a Woman,* by Louis Michel Van Loo, vert. 30c, *La Chula,* by Jose Arburu Morell, vert.

Sizes: 29x40mm (1c, 5c, 13c), 40x29mm (2c), 44x27mm (3c), 27x44mm (30c)

Perf. 13, 12½ (3c, 30c)

1976, Jan. 30

2028 A541 1c multi .25 .25
2029 A541 2c multi .25 .25
2030 A541 3c multi .25 .25
2031 A541 5c multi .25 .25
2032 A541 13c multi 1.40 .25
2033 A541 30c multi 2.25 .50
Nos. 2028-2033 (6) 4.65 1.75

10th Cong. of Ministers from Socialist Communications Organizations, Feb. 12, Havana — A542

1976, Feb. 12 **Litho.** *Perf. 13*

2034 A542 13c multi 1.40 .25

Hunting Dogs A543

1976, Feb. 20

2035 A543 1c American foxhound .25 .25
2036 A543 2c Labrador retriever .25 .25
2037 A543 3c Borzoi .25 .25
2038 A543 5c Irish setter .25 .25
2039 A543 13c Pointer 2.40 .30
2040 A543 30c Cocker spaniel 3.25 .40
Nos. 2035-2040 (6) 6.65 1.70

Socialist Constitution — A544

1976, Feb. 24 *Perf. 12½*

2041 A544 13c Natl. flag, arms, anthem 1.40 .25

Chess Champions — A545

Designs: 1c, Ruy Lopez Segura and chessboard. 2c, Francois Philidor and frontispiece of his book, *Analysis of the Game of Chess.* 3c, Wilhelm Steinitz and knight. 13c, Emanuel Lasker and king. 30c, Jose Raul Capablanca learning to play chess as a small boy.

1976, Mar. 15 *Perf. 13x12½*

2042 A545 1c multi .25 .25
2043 A545 2c multi .25 .25
2044 A545 3c multi .25 .25
2045 A545 13c multi 1.75 .25
2046 A545 30c multi 1.90 .55
Nos. 2042-2046 (5) 4.40 1.55

Havana Radio Intl. Broadcasts, 15th Anniv. — A546

1976, Mar. 26

2047 A546 50c multi 2.00 .70

World Health Day — A547

1976, Apr. 7

2048 A547 30c multi 1.50 .45

Child Care Centers, 15th Anniv. — A548

1976, Apr. 10 *Perf. 12½x13*

2049 A548 3c multi .60 .25

1st Manned Space Flight, 15th Anniv. A549

1c, Gagarin, lift-off. 2c, V. Tesreshkova, rockets. 3c, A. Leonov's space walk, vert. 5c, Spacecraft, vert. 13c, Spacecraft, diff., vert. 30c, Space link-up.

1976, Apr. 12 ***Perf. 13***

2050 A549 1c multicolored .25 .25
2051 A549 2c multicolored .25 .25
2052 A549 3c multicolored .25 .25
2053 A549 5c multicolored .40 .25
2054 A549 13c multicolored 1.10 .25
2055 A549 30c multicolored 1.75 .35
Nos. 2050-2055 (6) 4.00 1.60

Bay of Pigs Invasion, 15th Anniv. — A550

1976, Apr. 17 ***Perf. 13x12½, 12½x13***

2056 A550 3c shown .25 .25
2057 A550 13c Bomber, pilot .95 .25
2058 A550 30c Soldiers exulting, vert. 1.75 .45
Nos. 2056-2058 (3) 2.95 .95

Natl. Militia, 17th anniv. (3c); Air Force, 15th anniv. (13c); proclamation of the socialist revolution, 15th anniv. (30c).

Nat. Assoc. of Small Farmers (ANAP), 15th Anniv. — A551

1976, May 17 ***Perf. 13x12½***

2059 A551 3c multi .60 .25

1976 Summer Olympics, Montreal — A552

1976, May 25 ***Perf. 12½x13***

2060 A552 1c Volleyball .25 .25
2061 A552 2c Basketball .25 .25
2062 A552 3c Long jump .25 .25
2063 A552 4c Boxing .25 .25
2064 A552 5c Weight lifting .25 .25
2065 A552 13c Judo 1.10 .25
2066 A552 30c Swimming 1.75 .45
Nos. 2060-2066 (7) 4.10 1.95

Souvenir Sheet

Imperf

2067 A552 50c Character trade-mark (beaver) 4.00 1.25

See Nos. 2106, 2112.

Modern Secondary Schools — A553

1976, June 12 **Litho.** ***Perf. 13***

2068 A553 3c red, pale grn & blk .60 .25

Indigenous Birds — A554

Designs: 1c, Teretistris fornsi. 2c, Glaucidium siju. 3c, Nesoceleus fernandinae. 5c, Todus mutlicolor. 13c, Accipiter gundlachi. 30c, Priotelus temnurus.

1976, June 15 ***Perf. 13x12½***

2069 A554 1c multicolored .30 .25
2070 A554 2c multicolored .30 .25
2071 A554 3c multicolored .40 .25
2072 A554 5c multicolored .70 .25
2073 A554 13c multicolored 1.40 .25
2074 A554 30c multicolored 3.25 .80
Nos. 2069-2074 (6) 6.35 2.05

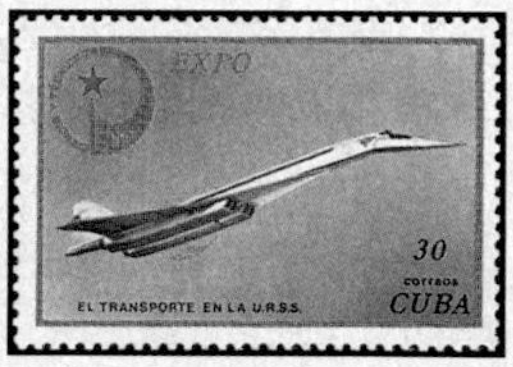

EXPO '76, USSR A555

1976, July 5 ***Perf. 12½x13, 13x12½***

2075 A555 1c Anatomical scanning device .25 .25
2076 A555 3c Child, doe .25 .25
2077 A555 10c Cosmonauts .50 .25
2078 A555 30c Tupolev supersonic jet 2.50 .55
Nos. 2075-2078 (4) 3.50 1.30

Public health and industrial safety (1c), environmental protection (3c), space exploration (10c) and modern transportation (30c). Nos. 2075-2077 vert.

Death Cent. of "El Inglesito" A556

1976, Aug. 4 ***Perf. 13***

2079 A556 13c Henry M. Reeve .70 .25

Portrait of G. Collazo, by Jean Dabour — A557

Paintings by Collazo: 2c, *The Art Lovers,* horiz. 3c, *The Patio.* 5c, *Coconut Tree.* 13c, *New York Studio,* horiz. 30c, *R. Emelina Collazo.*

Sizes: 33x44mm, 44x33mm (2c), 31x46mm (5c, 30c), 46x31mm (13c)

Perf. 13, 12½x13 (5c, 30c), 13x12½ (13c)

1976, Sept. 2

2080 A557 1c multi .25 .25
2081 A557 2c multi .25 .25
2082 A557 3c multi .25 .25
2083 A557 5c multi .25 .25
2084 A557 13c multi .65 .25
2085 A557 30c multi 2.10 .50
Nos. 2080-2085 (6) 3.75 1.75

Camilo Cienfuegos Military Schools, 10th Anniv. — A558

1976, Sept. 23 ***Perf. 13***

2086 A558 3c multi .40 .25

Development of the Merchant Marine — A559

Various cargo and passenger ships.

1976, Oct. 2 ***Perf. 12½***

2087 A559 1c multi .30 .25
2088 A559 2c multi .30 .25
2089 A559 3c multi .30 .25
2090 A559 5c multi .45 .25
2091 A559 13c multi 1.40 .45
2092 A559 30c multi 2.75 .80
Nos. 2087-2092 (6) 5.50 2.25

8th Intl. Health Film Festival of Socialist Countries, Havana — A560

1976, Oct. 4 ***Perf. 13x12½***

2093 A560 3c multi .40 .25

5th Intl. Ballet Festival, Havana A561

Scenes from ballets. 2c, 5c, 13c, 30c vert.

1976, Nov. 6 ***Perf. 13***

2094 A561 1c *Apollo* .25 .25
2095 A561 2c *The River and the Forest* .25 .25
2096 A561 3c *Giselle* .25 .25
2097 A561 5c *Oedipus Rex* .25 .25
2098 A561 13c *Carmen* 1.10 .25
2099 A561 30c *Vital Song* 2.10 .35
Nos. 2094-2099 (6) 4.20 1.60

3rd Military Games A562

1976, Nov. 25 ***Perf. 13***

2100 A562 3c multi .50 .25

Granma Landings, 20th Anniv. — A563

1976, Dec. 2 ***Perf. 13x12½***

2101 A563 1c Landing craft .25 .25
2102 A563 3c Landing force .25 .25
2103 A563 13c Castro, soldiers 1.00 .25
2104 A563 30c Globe, rifles 1.60 .55
Nos. 2101-2104 (4) 3.10 1.30

Souvenir Sheet

Cuban Landscape, by F. Cadava — A564

1976, Dec. 8 ***Perf. 13x13½***

2105 A564 50c multi 5.25 2.00

CIENFUEGOS '76, 5th natl. phil. exhib.

Summer Olympics Type of 1976 and

Victory of Cuban Athletes at the Montreal Games — A565

1976, Dec. 10 ***Perf. 12½x13***

2106 A565 1c Volleyball .25 .25
2107 A565 2c Hurdles .25 .25
2108 A565 3c Running (starting blocks) .25 .25
2109 A565 8c Boxing .25 .25
2110 A565 13c Running (finish line) .85 .25
2111 A565 30c Judo 1.75 .45
Nos. 2106-2111 (6) 3.60 1.70

Souvenir Sheet

Imperf

2112 A552 50c like No. 2063 5.00 1.25

Paintings in the Natl. Museum A566

1c, *Golden Cross Inn,* by S. Scott. 3c, *Portrait of a Man,* by J.C. Verspronck, vert. 5c, *Venetian Landscape,* by Francesco Guardi. 10c, *Valley Corner,* by H. Cleenewerck, vert. 13c, *F. Xaviera Paula,* anonymous, vert. 30c, *F. de Medici,* by C. Allori, vert.

Perf. 13, 12½x13 (3c, 10c, 30c), 12½ (13c)

1977, Jan. 18

Sizes: 40x29mm, 27x42mm (3c, 10c, 30c), 27x43½mm (13c)

2113 A566 1c multi .25 .25
2114 A566 3c multi .25 .25
2115 A566 5c multi .25 .25
2116 A566 10c multi .55 .25
2117 A566 13c multi .85 .40
2118 A566 30c multi 2.10 .40
Nos. 2113-2118 (6) 4.25 1.65

Rural Transport A567

1977, Feb. 15 *Perf. 13*

2119	A567 3c multi	.80	.25

Constitution of Popular Government — A568

1976, Dec. 1 *Perf. 13x12½*

2120	A568 13c multi	.70	.25

Bird Type of 1975

Designs: 1c, Xiphidiopicus percussus. 4c, Tiaris canora. 10c, Dives atroviolaceus. 13c, Ferminia cerverai. 30c, Mellisuga helenae.

1977, Feb. 25 *Perf. 13*

2121	A524 1c multicolored	.40	.25
2122	A524 4c multicolored	.45	.25
2123	A524 10c multicolored	.95	.25
2124	A524 13c multicolored	1.40	.25
2125	A524 30c multicolored	2.75	.65
	Nos. 2121-2125 (5)	5.95	1.65

Lenin Park Aquarium, Havana — A569

Designs: 1c, Chichlasoma meeki. 3c, Barbus tetrazona tetrazona. 5c, Cyprinus carpio. 10c, Betta splendens. 13c, Pterophyllum scalare, vert. 30c, Hemigrammus caudovittatus.

1977, Mar. 15

2126	A569 1c multicolored	.25	.25
2127	A569 3c multicolored	.25	.25
2128	A569 5c multicolored	.25	.25
2129	A569 10c multicolored	.30	.25
2130	A569 13c multicolored	1.25	.25
2131	A569 30c multicolored	2.50	.50
	Nos. 2126-2131 (6)	4.80	1.75

Sputnik (1st Artificial Satellite), 20th Anniv. — A570

1c, DDR #370, *Sputnik.* 3c, Hungary #1216, *Luna 16.* 5c, North Korea #134, *Cosmos.* 10c, Poland #822, *Sputnik 3.* 13c, Yugoslavia #870, Earth, Moon. 30c, Cuba #866, Earth, Moon. 50c, Russia #2021, *Sputnik.*

1977, Apr. 12 *Perf. 13x12½*

2132	A570 1c multi	.25	.25
2133	A570 3c multi	.25	.25
2134	A570 5c multi	.25	.25
2135	A570 10c multi	.35	.25
2136	A570 13c multi	1.10	.25
2137	A570 30c multi	1.90	.40
	Nos. 2132-2137 (6)	4.10	1.65

Souvenir Sheet

Imperf

2138	A570 50c multi	4.25	1.25

No. 2138 has simulated perfs.

Antonio Maria Romeu (1876-1955), Composer — A571

1977, May 10 **Litho.** *Perf. 13*

2139	A571 3c multi	.35	.25

See No. C251.

Flowering Plants — A572

Designs: 1c, Hibiscus rosa sinensis. 2c, Nerium oleander. 5c, Allamanda cathartica. 10c, Pelargonium zonale.

1977, May 31

2140	A572 1c multicolored	.25	.25
2141	A572 2c multicolored	.25	.25
2142	A572 5c multicolored	.25	.25
2143	A572 10c multicolored	.40	.25
	Nos. 2140-2143 (4)	1.15	1.00

Dr. Juan Tomas Roig (b. 1877), botanist. See Nos. C252-C254.

Fire Prevention Week — A573

2c, Horse-drawn fire pump, diff. 6c, Early motorized vehicle. 10c, Modern truck. 13c, Turntable-ladder truck. 30c, Crane vehicle.

1977, June 20

2144	A573 1c shown	.25	.25
2145	A573 2c multicolored	.25	.25
2146	A573 6c multicolored	.25	.25
2147	A573 10c multicolored	.50	.25
2148	A573 13c multicolored	.90	.25
2149	A573 30c multicolored	1.90	.40
	Nos. 2144-2149 (6)	4.05	1.65

Natl. Decorations (Ribbons and Medals of Honor) — A574

1977, July 26 *Perf. 12x12½*

2150	A574 1c shown	.25	.25
2151	A574 3c multi, diff.	.25	.25

See Nos. C255-C256.

Paintings by Jorge Arche — A575

Perf. 13x12½, 12½x13 (10c), 13 (5c)

1977, Aug. 25

Sizes: 26x38mm, 29x40mm (5c), 38x26mm (10c)

2152	A575 1c *Portrait of Mary*	.25	.25
2153	A575 3c *Jose Marti*	.25	.25
2154	A575 5c *Portrait of Aristides*	.25	.25
2155	A575 10c *Bathers*	.50	.25
	Nos. 2152-2155 (4)	1.25	1.00

Nos. 2152-2154 vert. See Nos. C257-C259.

4th Military Spartakiad (Summer Sports) — A576

1977, Sept. 10 *Perf. 13*

2156	A576 1c Boxing	.25	.25
2157	A576 3c Volleyball	.25	.25
2158	A576 5c Parachuting	.25	.25
2159	A576 10c Running	.35	.25
	Nos. 2156-2159 (4)	1.10	1.00

See Nos. C260-C261.

Intl. Airmail Service, 50th Anniv. A577

Designs: 1c, Biplane and No. C62. 2c, Three-engine plane and Cuba-Key West 1st flight cancel, Oct. 28, 1927. 5c, Flying boat and intl. airmail service 1st flight cachet. 10c, Jet aircraft and Havana-Madrid cachet, Apr. 26, 1948.

1977, Oct. 27 **Litho.** *Perf. 12x12½*

2160	A577 1c multi	.25	.25
2161	A577 2c multi	.25	.25
2162	A577 5c multi	.25	.25
2163	A577 10c multi	.50	.25
	Nos. 2160-2163 (4)	1.25	1.00

See Nos. C263-C264.

October Revolution, Russia, 60th Anniv. — A578

3c, Cruiser *Aurora.* 13c, Lenin, Flags. 30c, Hammer, sickle, symbols of agriculture, technology.

1977, Nov. 7 *Perf. 13x12½*

2164	A578 3c multicolored	.25	.25
2165	A578 13c multicolored	.40	.25
2166	A578 30c multicolored	1.40	.40
	Nos. 2164-2166 (3)	2.05	.90

Felines, Havana Zoo — A579

1977, Nov. 24 **Litho.** *Perf. 13*

2167	A579 1c Cat	.25	.25
2168	A579 2c Black panther	.25	.25
2169	A579 8c Puma	.25	.25
2170	A579 10c Leopard	1.10	.25
	Nos. 2167-2170 (4)	1.85	1.00

See Nos. C266-C267.

Martyrs of the Revolution, 20th Death Annivs. — A580

3c, Cienfuegos Uprising. 20c, Siege on the Presidential Palace.

1977, Dec. 2 *Perf. 12½x12*

2171	A580 3c multicolored	.25	.25
2172	A580 20c multicolored	1.00	.25

See No. C268.

Intl. Measurement System — A581

1977, Dec. 9

2173	A581 3c multi	.40	.25

Havana University, 250th Anniv. — A582

1978, Jan. 5 *Perf. 13x12½*

2174	A582 3c multi	.25	.25

See Nos. C270-C271.

Landscape with Figures, by J. Pilliment — A583

Paintings in the Natl. Museum of Art: 1c, *Seated Woman,* by R. Madrazo, vert. 4c, *Girl,* by J. Sorolla, vert. 10c, *The Cow,* by E. Abela.

Perf. 12x12½, 13 (4c, 6c, 10c)

1978, Feb. 20

Sizes: 27x42mm, 29x40mm (4c), 40x29mm (6c, 10c)

2175	A583 1c multi	.25	.25
2176	A583 4c multi	.25	.25
2177	A583 6c shown	.25	.25
2178	A583 10c multi	.60	.25
	Nos. 2175-2178 (4)	1.35	1.00

See Nos. C273-C274.

Frontier Troops, 15th Anniv. — A584

1978, Mar. 5 *Perf. 13*

2179	A584 13c multi		1.50	.25

Bird Type of 1975

Birds: 1c, Myadestes elisabeth. 4c, Paliop-tila lembeyei. 10c, Teretistris fernandinae.

Perf. 13, 12½x12 (4c)

1978, Mar. 10 **Size: 42x27mm**

2180	A524	1c multicolored	.45	.25
2181	A524	4c multicolored	.55	.25
2182	A524	10c multicolored	1.40	.25
		Nos. 2180-2182 (3)	2.40	.75

Name of bird inscribed below vignette. See Nos. C275-C276.

Cosmonaut's Day — A585

1978, Apr. 12 *Perf. 13*

2183	A585	1c Intercosmos, vert.	.25	.25
2184	A585	2c Luna 24	.25	.25
2185	A585	5c Venera 9, vert.	.35	.25
2186	A585	10c Cosmos	.35	.25
		Nos. 2183-2186 (4)	1.20	1.00

See Nos. C278-C279.

9th World Trade Unions Congress, Prague — A586

1978, Apr. 16

2187	A586	30c ver, deep brn & blk	1.00	.45

Cactus Flowers — A587

Designs: 1c, Melocactus guitarti. 4c, Leptocereus wrightii. 6c, Opuntia militaris. 10c, Cylindropuntia hystrix.

1978, May 15 ***Perf. 12½x13 (1c), 13***

2188	A587	1c multicolored	.25	.25
2189	A587	4c multicolored	.25	.25
2190	A587	6c multicolored	.25	.25
2191	A587	10c multicolored	.65	.25
		Nos. 2188-2191 (4)	1.40	1.00

Natl. Botanical Gardens. See Nos. C281-C282.

Lenin Park Aquarium, Havana — A588

Designs: 1c, Barbus arulios. 4c, Hiphes-sobrycon flammeus. 6c, Poecilia reticulata. 10c, Colis lalia.

1978, June 15 *Perf. 13*

2192	A588	1c multicolored	.25	.25
2193	A588	4c multicolored	.25	.25
2194	A588	6c multicolored	.30	.25
2195	A588	10c multicolored	.65	.25
		Nos. 2192-2195 (4)	1.45	1.00

See Nos. C286-C287.

MEDELLIN '78, 13th Central American and Caribbean Games — A589

1978, July 1

2196	A589	1c Basketball	.25	.25
2197	A589	3c Boxing	.25	.25
2198	A589	5c Weight lifting	.25	.25
2199	A589	10c Fencing, horiz.	.45	.25
		Nos. 2196-2199 (4)	1.20	1.00

See Nos. C288-C289.

Attack on Moncada Barracks, 25th Anniv. — A590

1978, July 26

2200	A590	3c multi	.25	.25

See Nos. C290-C291.

World Youth and Students Festival, Havana A591

Natl. flags and views of host cities.

1978, July 28

2201	A591	3c Prague, 1947	.25	.25
2202	A591	3c Budapest, 1949	.25	.25
2203	A591	3c Berlin, 1951	.25	.25
2204	A591	3c Bucharest, 1953	.25	.25
2205	A591	3c Warsaw, 1955	.25	.25
a.		Strip of 5, Nos. 2201-2205	1.40	1.40
		Nos. 2201-2205 (5)	1.25	1.25

See Nos. C292-C297.

Young Workers' Army, 5th Anniv. — A592

1978, Aug. 3

2206	A592	3c multi	.30	.25

Tuna Industry A593

1978, Aug. 30 ***Perf. 12½x12***

2207	A593	1c Tuna boat	.25	.25
2208	A593	2c Processing ship	.25	.25
2209	A593	5c Shrimp boat	.25	.25
2210	A593	10c Inshore stern trawler	.40	.25
		Nos. 2207-2210 (4)	1.15	1.00

See Nos. C298-C299.

Paintings by Amelia Pelaez del Casal (1896-1968) — A594

1c, *The White Mantle.* 3c, *Still-life with Flowers*, vert. 6c, *Women*, vert. 10c, *Fish*, vert.

Perf. 13x12½, 13 (3c, 6c), 12½x13

1978, Sept. 15

2211	A594	1c multicolored	.25	.25
2212	A594	3c multicolored	.25	.25
2213	A594	6c multicolored	.25	.25
2214	A594	10c multicolored	.45	.25
		Nos. 2211-2214 (4)	1.20	1.00

See Nos. C301-C303.

African Fauna, Havana Zoo A595

1978, Oct. 20 *Perf. 13*

2215	A595	1c Rhinoceros	.25	.25
2216	A595	4c Okapi, vert.	.25	.25
2217	A595	6c Mandrill	.25	.25
2218	A595	10c Giraffe, vert.	.65	.25
		Nos. 2215-2218 (4)	1.40	1.00

See Nos. C307-C308.

Natl. Ballet, 30th Anniv. — A596

3c, *Grande Pas de Quatre.*

1978, Oct. 28 ***Perf. 13x12½***

2219	A596	3c multicolored	.25	.25

See Nos. C309-C310.

A597

Flowers of the Pacific: Various species.

1978, Nov. 30 **Litho.** *Perf. 13*

2220	A597	1c multi	.25	.25
2221	A597	4c multi	.25	.25
2222	A597	6c multi	.25	.25
2223	A597	10c multi	.50	.25
		Nos. 2220-2223 (4)	1.25	1.00

See Nos. C311-C312.

A598

1979, Jan. 1 ***Perf. 12½x13 (3c), 13***

2224	A598	3c Castro, soldier	.25	.25
2225	A598	13c Industry	.50	.25
2226	A598	1p Flag, globe, flame	3.25	1.25
		Nos. 2224-2226 (3)	4.00	1.75

Triumph of the Revolution, 20th anniv.

Doves and Pigeons A599

Designs: 1c, Starnoenas cyanocephala. 3c, Geotrygon chysia. 7c, Geotrygon caniceps. 8c, Geotrygon montana. 13c, Columba leucocephala. 30c, Columba inornata.

1979, Jan. 30 *Perf. 13*

2227	A599	1c multicolored	.35	.25
2228	A599	3c multicolored	.40	.25
2229	A599	7c multicolored	.40	.25
2230	A599	8c multicolored	.50	.25
2231	A599	13c multicolored	.90	.25
2232	A599	30c multicolored	1.90	.80
		Nos. 2227-2232 (6)	4.45	2.05

Paintings in the Natl. Museum of Art A600

Designs: 1c, *Genre Scene*, by David Teniers. 3c, *Arrival of Spanish Troops*, by J. Louis Meissonier. 6c, *A Joyful Gathering*, by Sir David Wilkie. 10c, *A Robbery*, by E. De Lucas Padilla. 13c, *Tea Time*, by R. Madrazo, vert. 30c, *Peasants in Front of a Tavern*, by Adriaen van Ostade.

1979, Feb. 20

2233	A600	1c multi	.25	.25
2234	A600	3c multi	.25	.25
2235	A600	6c multi	.30	.25
2236	A600	10c multi	.45	.25
2237	A600	13c multi	.80	.25
2238	A600	30c multi	1.75	.30
		Nos. 2233-2238 (6)	3.80	1.55

See Nos. 2262-2267, C317.

Marine Flora — A601

Designs: 3c, Nymphaea capensis. 10c, Nymphaea ampla. 13c, Nymphaea coerulea. 30c, Nymphaea rubra.

1979, Mar. 20

2239	A601	3c	multicolored	.25	.25
2240	A601	10c	multicolored	.40	.25
2241	A601	13c	multicolored	.65	.25
2242	A601	30c	multicolored	1.50	.40
			Nos. 2239-2242 (4)	2.80	1.15

All are incorrectly inscribed "Nymphaca."

A602

1979, Mar. 24

2243	A602	3c	multi	.25	.25

Cuban film industry, 20th anniv.

A603

1979, Apr. 12

2244	A603	1c	Rocket launch	.25	.25
2245	A603	4c	Soyuz	.25	.25
2246	A603	6c	Salyut	.35	.25
2247	A603	10c	Link-up	.50	.25
2248	A603	13c	Soyuz, Salyut	.85	.25
2249	A603	30c	Parachute landing	1.90	.25
			Nos. 2244-2249 (6)	4.10	1.50

Cosmonaut's Day. See No. C315.

6th Summit Meeting of Non-Aligned Countries — A604

1979, Apr. 17

2250	A604	3c	Understanding, cooperation	.25	.25
2251	A604	13c	Fight colonialism	.50	.25
2252	A604	30c	New world economic order	1.40	.40
			Nos. 2250-2252 (3)	2.15	.90

House of the Americas Museum, 20th Anniv. — A605

1979, Apr. 28 *Perf. 13x12½*

2253	A605	13c	Cuna Indian tapestry	.40	.25

Agrarian Reform, 20th Anniv. — A606

1979, May 17 *Perf. 12½x12*

2254	A606	3c	multi	.40	.25

Souvenir Sheet

The Party, by Jules Pascin — A607

1979, May 18 *Perf. 13*

2255	A607	50c	multi	3.50	1.25

PHILASERDICA '79 phil. exhib., Sofia.

Nocturnal Butterflies — A608

Designs: 1c, Eulepidotis rectimargo. 4c, Othreis materna. 6c, Noropsis hieroglyphica. 10c, Heterochroma. 13c, Melanchroia regnatrix. 30c, Attera gemmata.

1979, May 25

2256	A608	1c	multicolored	.25	.25
2257	A608	4c	multicolored	.25	.25
2258	A608	6c	multicolored	.40	.25
2259	A608	10c	multicolored	.40	.25
2260	A608	13c	multicolored	.80	.25
2261	A608	30c	multicolored	2.00	.45
			Nos. 2256-2261 (6)	4.10	1.70

Art Type of 1979

Paintings by Victor Manuel Garcia (d. 1969): 1c, *Main Avenue, Paris.* 3c, *Portrait of Enmita.* 6c, *San Juan River, Matanzas.* 10c, *Woman Carrying Hay.* 13c, *Still-life with Vase.* 30c, *Street at Night.* Nos. 2262-2267 vert.

1979, June 15

2262	A600	1c	multi	.25	.25
2263	A600	3c	multi	.25	.25
2264	A600	6c	multi	.25	.25
2265	A600	10c	multi	.30	.25
2266	A600	13c	multi	.45	.25
2267	A600	30c	multi	1.60	.45
			Nos. 2262-2267 (6)	3.10	1.70

See No. C317.

World Peace Council, 30th Anniv. A609

1979, June 29 *Perf. 12½x13*

2268	A609	30c	multi	1.00	.35

1980 Summer Olympics, Moscow — A610

1979, July 30 *Perf. 13x12½*

2269	A610	1c	Wrestling	.30	.25
2270	A610	4c	Boxing	.30	.25
2271	A610	6c	Women's volleyball	.30	.25
2272	A610	10c	Shooting	.40	.25
2273	A610	13c	Weight lifting	.65	.25
2274	A610	30c	High jump	2.10	.30
			Nos. 2269-2274 (6)	4.05	1.55

Roses — A611

Designs: 1c, Rosa eglanteria. 2c, Rosa centifolia anemonoides. 3c, Rosa indica vulgaris. 5c, Rosa eglanteria punicea. 10c, Rosa sulfurea. 13c, Rosa muscosa alba. 20c, Rosa gallica purpurea velutina.

1979, Aug. 20 *Perf. 13*

2275	A611	1c	multicolored	.25	.25
2276	A611	2c	multicolored	.25	.25
2277	A611	3c	multicolored	.25	.25
2278	A611	5c	multicolored	.25	.25
2279	A611	10c	multicolored	.30	.25
2280	A611	13c	multicolored	.50	.25
2281	A611	20c	multicolored	1.00	.25
			Nos. 2275-2281 (7)	2.80	1.75

A612

1979, Aug. 30

2282	A612	13c	multi	.50	.25

Council for Mutual Economic Assistance, 30th anniv.

Cubana Airlines, 50th Anniv. A613

Various aircraft.

1979, Oct. 8

2283	A613	1c	Ford trimotor	.25	.25
2284	A613	2c	Sikorsky S-38	.25	.25
2285	A613	3c	Douglas DC-3	.35	.25
2286	A613	4c	Brittania	.35	.25
2287	A613	13c	Ilyushin IL-14	.90	.25
2288	A613	40c	Tupolev TU-104	2.50	.40
			Nos. 2283-2288 (6)	4.60	1.65

Disappearance of Camilo Cienfuegos, 20th Anniv. — A614

1979, Oct. 28

2289	A614	3c	multi	.30	.25

Reinoso, Sugar Cane and Blossom A615

1979, Nov. 12

2290	A615	13c	multi	.75	.25

Sugar Cane Research Institute, 15th anniv., and sesquicentennial of the birth of Alvaro Reinoso.

Zoo Animals A616

1979, Nov. 15

2291	A616	1c	Chimpanzees	.25	.25
2292	A616	2c	Leopards	.25	.25
2293	A616	3c	Deer	.25	.25
2294	A616	4c	Lion cubs	.25	.25
2295	A616	5c	Bear cubs	.25	.25
2296	A616	13c	Squirrels	.30	.25
2297	A616	30c	Pandas	.70	.30
2298	A616	50c	Tiger cubs	1.40	.60
			Nos. 2291-2298 (8)	3.65	2.40

Insects A617

Designs: 1c, Rhina oblita. 5c, Odontocera josemartii, vert. 6c, Pinthocoelium columbinum. 10c, Calasoma splendida, vert. 13c, Homophileurus cubanus, vert. 30c, Heterops dimidiata, vert.

1980, Jan. 25

2299	A617	1c	multicolored	.25	.25
2300	A617	5c	multicolored	.25	.25
2301	A617	6c	multicolored	.25	.25
2302	A617	10c	multicolored	.50	.25
2303	A617	13c	multicolored	.95	.25
2304	A617	30c	multicolored	2.10	.70
			Nos. 2299-2304 (6)	4.30	1.95

1980 Summer Olympics, Moscow — A618

1980, Feb. 20 *Perf. 12½*

2305 A618 1c Weight lifting .25 .25
2306 A618 2c Shooting .25 .25
2307 A618 5c Javelin .30 .25
2308 A618 6c Wrestling .30 .25
2309 A618 8c Judo .30 .25
2310 A618 10c Running .30 .25
2311 A618 13c Boxing .65 .25
2312 A618 30c Women's volley-ball 1.60 .60
Nos. 2305-2312 (8) 3.95 2.35

Souvenir Sheet

Imperf

2313 A618 50c Mischa character 3.00 1.60

No. 2313 contains one 32x40mm stamp.

Paintings in the Natl. Museum A619

Designs: 1c, *The Oak Trees,* by Henry Joseph Harpignies, vert. 4c, *Family Reunion,* by Willem van Mieris. 6c, *Domestic Fowl,* by Melchior De Hondecoeter, vert. 9c, *Innocence,* by William A. Bougereau, vert. 13c, *Venetian Scene II,* by Michele Marieschi. 30c, *Spanish Peasant Woman,* by Joaquin Dominguez Bequer, vert.

Sizes: 29x40mm, 40x29mm (4c), 28x42mm (9c, 30c), 38x26mm (13c)

Perf. 12½, 13 (9c, 30c), 12½x13 (13c)

1980, Mar. 11

2314 A619 1c multi .25 .25
2315 A619 4c multi .25 .25
2316 A619 6c multi .25 .25
2317 A619 9c multi .65 .25
2318 A619 13c multi .85 .25
2319 A619 30c multi 1.90 .65
Nos. 2314-2319 (6) 4.15 1.90

Souvenir Sheet

LONDON '80 — A620

1980, Apr. 1 *Perf. 13*

2320 A620 50c *Malvern Hall,* by John Constable 3.50 1.60

Intercosmos Program — A621

1c, Emblem, flags. 4c, Astrophysics. 6c, Satellite communications. 10c, Meteorology. 13c, Biology and medicine. 30c, Surveying satellite.

1980, Apr. 12

2321 A621 1c multicolored .25 .25
2322 A621 4c multicolored .25 .25
2323 A621 6c multicolored .25 .25
2324 A621 10c multicolored .45 .25
2325 A621 13c multicolored .60 .25
2326 A621 30c multicolored 1.90 .65
Nos. 2321-2326 (6) 3.70 1.90

Cuban Postage Stamps, 125th Anniv. — A622

1980, Apr. 24 *Perf. 12½*

2327 A622 30c Nos. 1, 7 and 613 1.25 .45

Orchids — A623

Designs: 1c, Bletia purpurea. 4c, Oncidium leiboldii. 6c, Epidendrum cochieatum. 10c, Cattleyopsis lindenii. 13c, Encyclia fucata. 30c, Encyclia phoenicea.

1980, May 20 *Perf. 13*

2328 A623 1c multicolored .25 .25
2329 A623 4c multicolored .25 .25
2330 A623 6c multicolored .25 .25
2331 A623 10c multicolored .50 .25
2332 A623 13c multicolored .90 .25
2333 A623 30c multicolored 1.90 .60
Nos. 2328-2333 (6) 4.05 1.85

Marine Mammals — A624

Designs: 1c, Tursiops truncatus. 3c, Megaptera novaeangliae, vert. 13c, Ziphius cavirostris. 30c, Monachus tropicalis.

1980, June 20

2334 A624 1c multicolored .50 .25
2335 A624 3c multicolored .50 .25
2336 A624 13c multicolored 1.50 .25
2337 A624 30c multicolored 3.50 .50
Nos. 2334-2337 (4) 6.00 1.25

Urban Reform Campaign, 20th Anniv. — A625

Nationalization of Foreign Industry, 20th Anniv. — A626

1980, July 26 *Perf. 13x12½, 12½x13*

2338 A625 3c multi .25 .25
2339 A626 13c multi .35 .25

Moncada Program.

Colonial Copperware A627

3c, Wine pitcher, 19th cent. 13c, Oil jar, 18th cent. 30c, Lidded pitcher, 19th cent.

Perf. 12½, 12½x13 (13c)

1980, July 29

Sizes: 27x43½mm, 38x26mm (13c)

2340 A627 3c multicolored .25 .25
2341 A627 13c multicolored .70 .25
2342 A627 30c multicolored 1.40 .30
Nos. 2340-2342 (3) 2.35 .80

Cuban Women's Federation, 20th Anniv. — A628

1980, Aug. 23 *Perf. 13*

2343 A628 3c multi .40 .25

Souvenir Sheet

ESPAMER '80, Madrid — A629

Design: *Clotilde Passing Through the Country Garden,* by Joaquin Sorolla y Bastida.

1980, Aug. 29

2344 A629 50c multi 3.50 1.60

Postage stamps of Spain, 130th anniv.

1st Havana Declaration, 20th Anniv. — A630

1980, Sept. 2

2345 A630 13c multi .50 .25

Construction of Naval Vessels in Cuba, 360th Anniv. — A631

Ships under construction: 1c, *Our Lady of Atocha,* galleon, 1620. 3c, *El Rayo,* warship, 1749. 7c, *Santisima Trinidad,* 1769. 10c, *Santisima Trinidad,* diff., 1805, vert. 13c, Steamships *Congreso* and *Colon,* 1851. 30c, Cardenas and Chullima shipyards.

1980, Sept. 15

2346 A631 1c multi .25 .25
2347 A631 3c multi .25 .25
2348 A631 7c multi .25 .25
2349 A631 10c multi .50 .25
2350 A631 13c multi .95 .25
2351 A631 30c multi 1.60 .60
Nos. 2346-2351 (6) 3.80 1.85

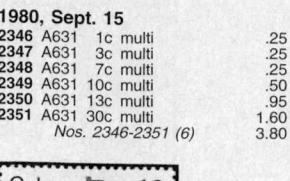

A633

1980, Sept. 26 *Perf. 13*

2354 A633 13c multi .60 .25

Fidel Castro's 1st speech before the UN General Assembly, 20th anniv.

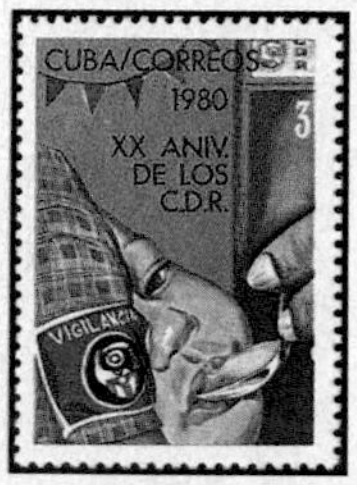

A634

1980, Sept. 28 *Perf. 13x12½*

2355 A634 3c multi .30 .25

Revolutionary defense committees, 20th anniv.

Souvenir Sheet

ESSEN '80, 49th Intl. Philatelic Federation Congress — A635

Painting: *Portrait of a Lady,* by Ludger Tom Ring The Younger.

1980, Oct. 2 **Litho.** *Perf. 13*

2356 A635 50c multi 3.75 1.25

Early Locomotives — A636

1c, Josefa. 2c, Chaparra Sugar Co. No. 22. 7c, Steam storage locomotive. 10c, 2-4-2 locomotive. 13c, 2-4-0 locomotive. 30c, Oil combustion engine, 1909.

1980, Oct. 15

2357 A636 1c multicolored .25 .25
2358 A636 2c multicolored .25 .25
2359 A636 7c multicolored .25 .25
2360 A636 10c multicolored .40 .25
2361 A636 13c multicolored .65 .25
2362 A636 30c multicolored 1.60 .60
Nos. 2357-2362 (6) 3.40 1.85

Lighthouses A637

3c, Roncali, San Antonio. 13c, Jagua, Cienfuegos. 30c, Maisi Point, Guantanamo.

1980, Oct. 30

2363	A637	3c multicolored	.25	.25
2364	A637	13c multicolored	.70	.25
2365	A637	30c multicolored	1.60	.25
		Nos. 2363-2365 (3)	2.55	.75

See Nos. 2440-2442, 2553-2555, 2614-2616.

Victory of Cuban Athletes at the 1980 Summer Olympics, Moscow — A638

1980, Nov. 10 Litho. *Perf. 12½x12*

2366	A638	13c Bronze medals	.50	.25
2367	A638	30c Silver medals	1.10	.25
2368	A638	50c Gold medals	2.25	.55
		Nos. 2366-2368 (3)	3.85	1.05

Nos. 2366-2368 each printed se-tenant with label containing statistical data.

Wildflowers A639

Designs: 1c, Pancratium arenicolum. 4c, Urechites lutea. 6c, Solanum elaegnifolium. 10c, Hamelia patens. 13c, Morinda royoc. 30c, Centrosema virginianum.

1980, Nov. 20 *Perf. 13*

2369	A639	1c multicolored	.25	.25
2370	A639	4c multicolored	.25	.25
2371	A639	6c multicolored	.30	.25
2372	A639	10c multicolored	.50	.25
2373	A639	13c multicolored	.95	.25
2374	A639	30c multicolored	2.25	.40
		Nos. 2369-2374 (6)	4.50	1.65

Souvenir Sheet

7th Natl. Stamp Exhibition — A640

1980, Nov. 22

2375	A640	50c Mail train	3.00	1.25

2nd Communist Party Congress A641

13c, Industry, communication. 30c, Athletics, elderly, education.

1980, Dec. 17

2376	A641	3c shown	.25	.25
2377	A641	13c multicolored	.40	.25
2378	A641	30c multicolored	1.10	.25
		Nos. 2376-2378 (3)	1.75	.75

Paintings in the Natl. Museum of Art A642

Designs: 1c, *Lady Mayo,* by Anton Van Dyck, vert. 6c, *The Spinner,* by Giovanni Battista Piazzetta, vert. 10c, *Daniel Collyer,* by Francis Cotes, vert. 13c, *Gardens, Palma de Mallorca,* by Santiago Rusinol Prats. 20c, *Landscape with Roadway and Houses,* by Frederick Waters Watts. 50c, *Landscape with Sheep,* by Jean-Francois Millet.

1981, Jan. 20

2379	A642	1c multi	.25	.25
2380	A642	6c multi	.25	.25
2381	A642	10c multi	.50	.25
2382	A642	13c multi	.60	.25
2383	A642	20c multi	1.00	.30
2384	A642	50c multi	2.10	.60
		Nos. 2379-2384 (6)	4.70	1.90

See Nos. 2510-2515.

Pelagic Fish A643

Designs: 1c, Isurus oxyrhynchus. 3c, Lampris reglus. 10c, Istiophorus platypterus. 13c, Mola mola, vert. 30c, Coruphaena hippurus. 50c, Tetrapturus albidus.

1981, Feb. 25

2385	A643	1c multicolored	.25	.25
2386	A643	3c multicolored	.25	.25
2387	A643	10c multicolored	.45	.25
2388	A643	13c multicolored	1.75	.25
2389	A643	30c multicolored	1.10	.40
2390	A643	50c multicolored	2.00	.95
		Nos. 2385-2390 (6)	5.80	2.35

1982 World Cup Soccer Championships, Spain — A644

Globe and various soccer players.

1981, Mar. 20 *Perf. 12½*

2391	A644	1c multi	.25	.25
2392	A644	2c multi	.25	.25
2393	A644	3c multi	.25	.25
2394	A644	10c multi, vert.	.45	.25
2395	A644	13c multi, vert.	.45	.25
2396	A644	50c multi	1.75	.65
		Nos. 2391-2396 (6)	3.40	1.90

Souvenir Sheet

Perf. 13

2397	A644	1p Soccer ball, flag	4.75	2.00

No. 2397 contains one 40x32mm stamp.

Opening of the 1st Kindergarten, 20th Anniv. — A645

1981, Apr. 10 *Perf. 13*

2398	A645	3c multi	.65	.25

1st Man in Space, 20th Anniv. A646

Designs: 1c, Jules Verne, Russian scientist Konstantin E. Tsiolkovski, and Sergei P. Korolev, designer of the 1st Soviet spacecraft, vert. 2c, Yuri Gagarin, 1st man in space. 3c, Valentina Tereshkova, 1st woman in space, and *Vostok 6.* 5c, Aleksei A. Leonov, 1st man to walk in space. 13c, Konstantin Feoktistov, Boris Yegorov and Vladimir Komarov, *Voskhod 1* crew, 1st 3-man orbital flight. 30c, Valeri Ryumin and Leonid Popov, set a space endurance record. 50c, Arnaldo Tamayo Mendez, 1st Cuban cosmonaut, and Soviet cosmonaut Yuri Romanenko on joint space flight, vert.

1981, Apr. 12 *Perf. 12½*

2399	A646	1c multi	.25	.25
2400	A646	2c multi	.25	.25
2401	A646	3c multi	.25	.25
2402	A646	5c multi	.25	.25
2403	A646	13c multi	.45	.25
2404	A646	30c multi	1.00	.35
2405	A646	50c multi	2.25	.60
		Nos. 2399-2405 (7)	4.70	2.20

A647

Designs: 3c, Rocket, aircraft. 13c, Hand raising gun.

1981, Apr. 19 Litho. *Perf. 13*

2406	A647	3c multi, vert.	.25	.25
2407	A647	13c multi, vert.	.40	.25
2408	A647	30c multi	.95	.60
		Nos. 2406-2408 (3)	1.60	1.10

Creation of armed forces (DAAFAR) (3c), Bay of Pigs Invasion, 20th Anniv. (13c), Proclamation of the socialist revolution (30c).

Attack on Goicuria Barracks, 25th Anniv. — A648

1981, Apr. 29

2409	A648	3c multi	.30	.25

Natl. Assoc. of Small Farmers (ANAP), 20th Anniv. A649

1981, May 17

2410	A649	3c multi	.50	.25

Souvenir Sheet

WIPA '81 — A650

1981, May 22 Litho.

2411	A650	50c Austria No. 643	4.00	1.50

Fighting Cocks A651

1981, May 25 *Perf. 12½x13, 13x12½*

2412	A651	1c Canelo, vert.	.25	.25
2413	A651	3c Cenizo	.25	.25
2414	A651	7c Blanco, vert.	.25	.25
2415	A651	13c Pinto, vert.	.50	.25
2416	A651	30c Giro	1.60	.35
2417	A651	50c Jabao, vert.	2.40	.60
		Nos. 2412-2417 (6)	5.25	1.95

Ministry of the Interior, 20th Anniv. — A652

1981, June 6 *Perf. 13*

2418	A652	13c multi	.40	.25

Souvenir Sheet

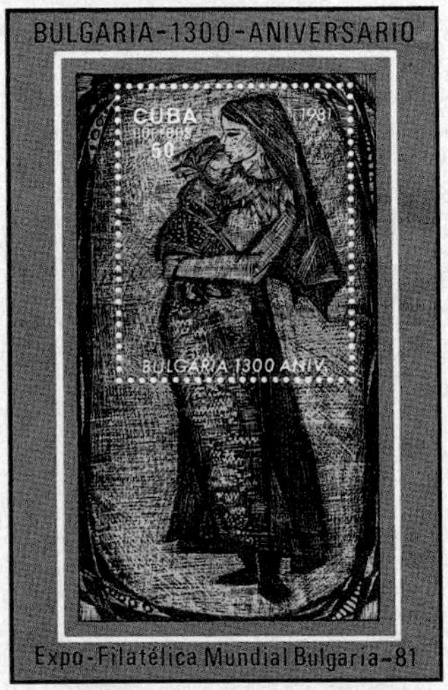

Mother and Child, by Zlatka Dabova — A653

1981, June 14

2419	A653	50c gold, sil & blk	2.25	1.10

Bulgaria, 1300th anniv. BULGARIA '81 phil. exhib.

Horse-drawn Carriages — A654

1981, June 25

2420 A654 1c Streetcar .25 .25
2421 A654 4c Bus .25 .25
2422 A654 9c Breake .25 .25
2423 A654 13c Landau .40 .25
2424 A654 30c Phaeton 1.40 .45
2425 A654 50c Funeral coach 2.50 .75
Nos. 2420-2425 (6) 5.05 2.20

House in the Country, by Mario Caridad — A655

1981, July 15 ***Perf. 12½***

2426 A655 30c multi 1.25 .30

Intl. Year of the Disabled.

Sandinistas, 25th Anniv. — A656

1981, July 23 ***Perf. 13***

2427 A656 13c multi .50 .25

State Institutions, 20th Annivs. — A657

1981, July 26 ***Perf. 12½***

2428 A657 3c multi .25 .25
2429 A657 13c multi, diff. .45 .25
2430 A657 30c multi, diff. 1.25 .25
Nos. 2428-2430 (3) 1.95 .75

Institute for Sports, Physical Education and Recreation (3c); Radio Havana (13c); and Ministry of Foreign Trade (MINCEX) (30c).

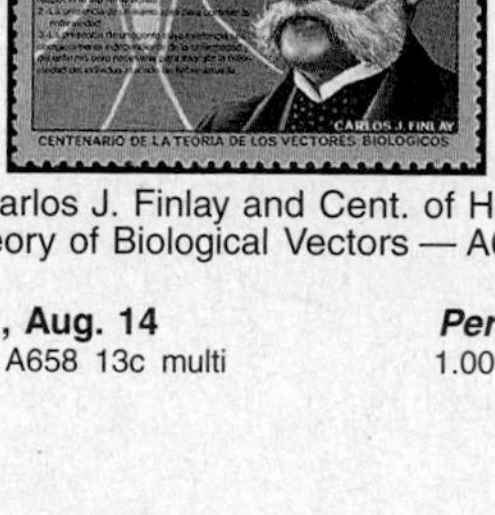

Carlos J. Finlay and Cent. of His Theory of Biological Vectors — A658

1981, Aug. 14 ***Perf. 13***

2431 A658 13c multi 1.00 .25

Nonaligned Countries Movement, 20th Anniv. — A659

1981, Sept. 1

2432 A659 50c multi 1.50 .80

Horses — A660

Nos. 2433-2437 vert.

1981, Sept. 15 ***Perf. 13***

Size: 29x40mm

2433 A660 1c multi .25 .25
2434 A660 3c multi, diff. .25 .25
2435 A660 8c multi, diff. .25 .25
2436 A660 13c multi, diff. .35 .25
2437 A660 30c multi, diff. 1.10 .45

Size: 68x27mm

Perf. 12½

2438 A660 50c Herd 1.75 .75
Nos. 2433-2438 (6) 3.95 2.20

Souvenir Sheet

Idyll in a Tea House, by Kitagawa Utamaro — A661

1981, Oct. 9 ***Perf. 13***

2439 A661 50c multi 2.75 1.25

PHILATOKYO '81.

Lighthouse Type of 1980

1981, Oct. 15 **Litho.**

2440 A637 3c North Rock .25 .25
2441 A637 13c Lucrecia Point .50 .25
2442 A637 40c East Guano 2.10 .50
Nos. 2440-2442 (3) 2.85 1.00

Jose Marti Natl. Library, 80th Anniv. — A662

Sugar mills, lithographs from *Los Ingenios,* by Eduardo Laplante (b. 1818): 3c, Flor de Cuba, 1838. 13c, El Progreso, 1845. 30c, Santa Teresa, 1847.

1981, Oct. 18 ***Perf. 12½x12***

2443 A662 3c multi .25 .25
2444 A662 13c multi .35 .25
2445 A662 30c multi 1.25 .55
Nos. 2443-2445 (3) 1.85 1.05

Pablo Picasso (b. 1881) and No. 1263 A663

1981, Oct. 25 ***Perf. 12½x13***

2446 A663 30c multi 1.25 .40

Souvenir Sheet

ESPAMER '81, Buenos Aires — A664

1981, Nov. 13 ***Perf. 13***

2447 A664 1p Packet 4.00 2.00

Art Type of 1969

Paintings in the Napoleon Museum: 1c, *Napoleon in Coronation Costume,* anonymous. 3c, *Napoleon with Landscape in the Background,* by Jean Horace Vernet. 10c, *Bonaparte in Egypt,* by Edouard Detaille. 13c, *Napoleon on Horseback,* by Hippolyte Bellange. 30c, *Napoleon in Normandy,* by Bellange. 50c, *Death of Napoleon,* anonymous.

1981, Dec. 1 ***Perf. 12½***

Sizes: 42x58mm, 58x42mm (3c, 13c, 30c, 50c)

2448 A385 1c multi .25 .25
2449 A385 3c multi, horiz. .25 .25
2450 A385 10c multi .40 .25
2451 A385 13c multi, horiz. .40 .25
2452 A385 30c multi, horiz. 1.25 .40
2453 A385 50c multi, horiz. 2.10 .70
Nos. 2448-2453 (6) 4.65 2.10

Napoleon Museum, 20th anniv.

25th Annivs. A665

1981, Dec. 2 ***Perf. 13***

2454 A665 3c Revolutionaries, vert. .25 .25
2455 A665 20c Marksman .45 .25
2456 A665 1p Yacht *Granma* 5.25 1.40
Nos. 2454-2456 (3) 5.95 1.90

November 30th insurrection (3c); creation of the revolutionary armed forces (20c); and disembarking of revolutionary forces (1p).

Fauna — A666

1981, Dec. 14 **Litho.** ***Perf. 12½x12***

2457 A666 1c Hummingbird .60 .25
2458 A666 2c Parakeet .95 .25
2459 A666 5c Hutia .25 .25
2460 A666 20c Almiqui .65 .25
2461 A666 35c Manatee 1.25 .25
2462 A666 40c Crocodile 1.00 .55
Nos. 2457-2462 (6) 4.70 1.80

Fernando Ortiz, Folklorist, Birth Cent. A667

1981, Dec. 20 ***Perf. 12½x13***

2463 A667 3c Portrait by Jorge Arche y Silva .25 .25
2464 A667 10c Hanging idol .40 .25
2465 A667 30c Arara drum 1.50 .45
2466 A667 50c Chango statue 2.25 .70
Nos. 2463-2466 (4) 4.40 1.65

Literacy Campaign, 20th Anniv. — A668

1981, Dec. 25 ***Perf. 12½x12***

2467 A668 5c Conrado Benitez .30 .25
2468 A668 5c Manuel Asunce .30 .25
a. Pair, #2467-2468 .75 .25
Nos. 2467-2468 (2) .60 .50

A669

1982 World Cup Soccer Championships, Spain — A670

Various athletes.

1982, Jan. 15 ***Perf. 13***

2469 A669 1c multi, vert. .25 .25
2470 A669 2c multi, vert. .25 .25
2471 A669 5c multi, vert. .25 .25
2472 A669 10c multi, vert. .30 .25
2473 A669 20c shown .70 .25
2474 A669 40c multi 1.25 .50
2475 A669 50c multi, vert. 1.60 .70
Nos. 2469-2475 (7) 4.60 2.45

Souvenir Sheet

2476 A670 1p shown 5.00 2.50

No. 2476 contains one 32x40mm stamp.

10th World Trade Unions Congress, Havana — A671

1982, Feb. 10 **Litho.**
2477 A671 30c Lazaro Pena, delegate 1.00 .40

Butterflies — A672

Designs: 1c, Euptoieta hegesia. 4c, Metamorpha stelenes insularis. 5c, Heliconius charithonius ramsdeni. 20c, Phoebis avellaneda. 30c, Hamadryas ferox diasia. 60c, Marpesia eleuchea.

1982, Feb. 25 ***Perf. 12½***
2478 A672 1c multicolored .25 .25
2479 A672 4c multicolored .25 .25
2480 A672 5c multicolored .25 .25
2481 A672 20c multicolored 1.40 .30
2482 A672 30c multicolored 2.25 .55
2483 A672 50c multicolored 4.00 .95
Nos. 2478-2483 (6) 8.40 2.55

Exports — A673

3c, Sugar (processing plant). 4c, Lobster (fishing boat). 6c, Canned fruits. 7c, Agricultural machinery. 8c, Nickel (passenger jet, industrial complex, car). 9c, Rum. 10c, Coffee. 30c, Fresh fruit. 50c, Tobacco. 1p, Cement. Nos. 2489-2493 vert.

1982, Feb. 26 ***Perf. 12x12½, 12½x12***
2484 A673 3c lt grn .25 .25
2485 A673 4c car rose .25 .25
2486 A673 6c dull blue .25 .25
2487 A673 7c brt org .40 .25
2488 A673 8c brt vio .40 .25
2489 A673 9c slate .40 .25
2490 A673 10c dull red brn .50 .25
2491 A673 30c bister .75 .25
2492 A673 50c orange 2.10 .40
2493 A673 1p olive bister 4.00 1.25
Nos. 2484-2493 (10) 9.30 3.65

Tulips A674

1982, Mar. 30 ***Perf. 12½x13***
2494 A674 1c Greenland .25 .25
2495 A674 3c Mariette .25 .25
2496 A674 8c Ringo .25 .25
2497 A674 20c La Tulipe Noire .80 .25
2498 A674 30c Jewel of Spring 1.40 .25
2499 A674 50c Orange Parrot 1.90 .60
Nos. 2494-2499 (6) 4.85 1.85

Communist Youth Organization, 20th Anniv. — A675

1982, Apr. 4 ***Perf. 13***
2500 A675 5c multi .30 .25

2nd UN Congress on the Peaceful Use of Outer Space — A676

1c, Gorizont. 3c, Meteor. 6c, Salyut-Soyuz link-up. 20c, Lunokhod moon vehicle. 30c, Venera with heat shield. 50c, Intelsat-4a.

1982, Apr. 12
2501 A676 1c multicolored .25 .25
2502 A676 3c multicolored .25 .25
2503 A676 6c multicolored .25 .25
2504 A676 20c multicolored .50 .25
2505 A676 30c multicolored 1.40 .30
2506 A676 50c multicolored 2.00 .60
Nos. 2501-2506 (6) 4.65 1.90

Cover A677

1982, Apr. 24 ***Perf. 12½x12***
2507 A677 20c Havana-Veracruz .75 .25
2508 A677 30c Havana-Tampico 1.25 .25

Stamp Day. English post office, 1842-1877 (20c); and French post office, 1862-1877 (30c).

Broadcasting and Television Institute (ICRT), 20th Anniv. — A678

1982, May 24 ***Perf. 12x12½***
2509 A678 30c multi 1.00 .25

Art Type of 1981 With Larger Type

Paintings in the Natl. Museum of Art: 1c, *Portrait of a Youth* (girl), by Jean B. Greuze, vert. 3c, *Procession in Brittany*, by Jules Breton. 9c, *Landscape*, by Jean Piliment. 20c, *Late Afternoon*, by William A. Bouguereau, vert. 30c, *Tiger*, by Ferdinand V.E. Delacroix. 40c, *The Chair*, by Wilfredo Lam, vert.

Perf. 13, 13x12½ (3c), 12x12½ (20c, 40c), 12½x12 (30c)

1982, May 31 **Litho.**
2510 A642 1c 29x40mm .25 .25
2511 A642 3c 46x36mm .25 .25
2512 A642 9c 40x29mm .25 .25
2513 A642 20c 27x42mm .65 .25
2514 A642 30c 42x27mm 1.25 .40
2515 A642 40c 27x42mm 2.00 .40
Nos. 2510-2515 (6) 4.65 1.80

Souvenir Sheet

PHILEXFRANCE '82 — A679

1p, Steamship Louisiana at St. Nazaire.

1982, June 7 ***Perf. 13***
2516 A679 1p multicolored 5.00 2.50

DEPORFILEX '82 — A680

1982, June 10 ***Perf. 13x12½***
2517 A680 20c Hurdler, No. 300 1.50 .25

Reptiles A681

Designs: 1c, Pseudemys decussata. 2c, Tropidophis pardalis. 3c, Crocodylus rhombifer. 20c, Cyclura nubila. 30c, Anolis allisonis. 50c, Alsophis cantherigerus.

1982, June 15 ***Perf. 13***
2518 A681 1c multicolored .25 .25
2519 A681 2c multicolored .25 .25
2520 A681 3c multicolored .25 .25
2521 A681 20c multicolored .85 .25
2522 A681 30c multicolored 1.25 .30
2523 A681 50c multicolored 2.40 .50
Nos. 2518-2523 (6) 5.25 1.80

George Dimitrov (1882-1949), Bulgarian Prime Minister — A682

1982, June 18
2524 A682 30c multi 1.00 .25

Koch, Bacillus A683

1982, July 18
2525 A683 20c multi 1.25 .25

Discovery of the tubercle bacillus by Dr. Robert Koch, cent.

14th Central American and Caribbean Games — A684

1982, Aug. 1
2526 A684 1c Baseball .25 .25
2527 A684 2c Boxing .25 .25
2528 A684 10c Water polo .35 .25
2529 A684 20c Javelin .80 .30
2530 A684 35c Weight lifting 1.25 .50
2531 A684 50c Volleyball 2.00 .55
Nos. 2526-2531 (6) 4.90 2.10

Hydraulic Development Plan, 20th Anniv. — A685

5c, Fruit, *Elchornia crassipes,* ship. 20c, Arid soil, *Nymphaea alba,* irrigation & reservoir systems.

1982, Aug. 9
2532 A685 5c multi .40 .25
2533 A685 20c multi 1.25 .25

Souvenir Sheet

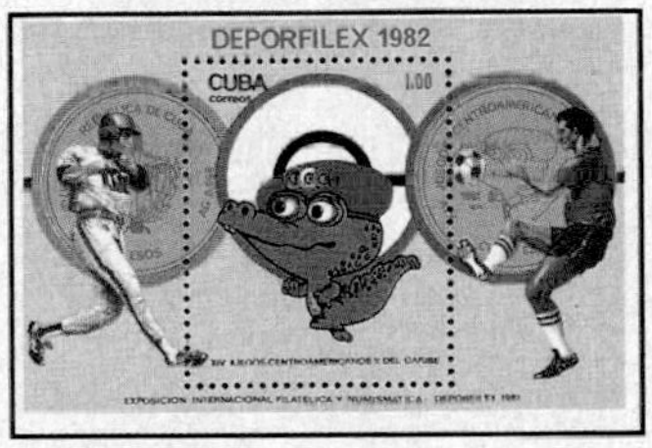

DEPORFILEX '82, Intl. Stamp and Coin Exhibition — A686

1982, Aug. 10 **Litho.**
2534 A686 1p Cuco, character trademark 4.75 2.25

14th Central American and Caribbean Games.

Namibia Day — A687

1982, Aug. 26
2535 A687 50c multi 1.75 .75

1982 World Cup Soccer Championships, Spain — A688

Various athletes.

1982, Aug. 30

2536	A688	5c multi	.25	.25
2537	A688	20c multi	.75	.30
2538	A688	30c multi	1.10	.40
2539	A688	50c multi	1.90	.80
		Nos. 2536-2539 (4)	4.00	1.75

Also exist in miniature sheets of 16 + 9 labels containing 4 each Nos. 2536-2539 in blocks of 4.

Natl. Folklore Ensemble, 20th Anniv. — A689

Paintings by V.P. Landaluze.

1982, Sept. 10

2540	A689	20c *Little Devil*, vert.	.80	.25
2541	A689	30c *Day of Kings*	1.10	.45

Prehistoric Fauna — A690

Designs: 1c, Ornimegalonyx oteroi, vert. 5c, Crocodylus rhombifer. 7c, Aquila borrasi, vert. 20c, Geocapromys colombianus. 35c, Megalocnus rodens, vert. 50c, Nesophontes micrus.

1982, Sept. 15 **Litho.**

2542	A690	1c multicolored	.65	.25
2543	A690	5c multicolored	.25	.25
2544	A690	7c multicolored	2.75	.40
2545	A690	20c multicolored	.65	.25
2546	A690	35c multicolored	1.00	.50
2547	A690	50c multicolored	1.40	.65
		Nos. 2542-2547 (6)	6.70	2.30

15th Death Anniv. of Che Guevara — A691

1982, Oct. 8 ***Perf. 13x12½***

2548	A691	20c multi	.70	.25

Discovery of America, 490th Anniv. — A692

1982, Oct. 12 ***Perf. 13***

2549	A692	5c shown	1.10	.25
2550	A692	20c *Santa Maria*, vert.	1.25	.40
2551	A692	35c *Pinta*, vert.	1.90	.90
2552	A692	50c *Nina*, vert.	2.40	1.10
		Nos. 2549-2552 (4)	6.65	2.65

Lighthouse Type of 1980

5c, Jutías Caye. 20c, Paredon Grande Caye. 30c, Morro Santiago de Cuba.

1982, Oct. 25

2553	A637	5c multicolored	1.00	.25
2554	A637	20c multicolored	2.75	.25
2555	A637	30c multicolored	3.75	.45
		Nos. 2553-2555 (3)	7.50	.95

George Washington, 250th Birth Anniv. — A693

Designs: Quotations and anonymous oil paintings, 18th-19th cent.

1982, Oct. 29 ***Perf. 12x12½***

2556	A693	5c multi	.25	.25
2557	A693	20c multi, diff.	.75	.25

Souvenir Sheet

8th Natl. Philatelic Exposition, Ciego de Avila — A694

1982, Nov. 13

2558	A694	1p Paddle steamer *Almendares*	5.00	2.50

8th Congress of the Cuban Philatelic Federation, Nov. 13-22.

Lenin Park, 10th Anniv. A695

1982, Dec. 28

2559	A695	5c multi	.65	.25

Chess Champion Jose Raul Capablanca and King — A696

1982, Dec. 29

2560	A696	5c shown	.25	.25
2561	A696	20c Rook	1.10	.25
2562	A696	30c Knight	1.40	.50
2563	A696	50c Queen	2.25	.80
a.		Bklt. pane of 4, Nos. 2560-2563	20.00	10.00
		Nos. 2560-2563 (4)	5.00	1.80

Exist in sheets of 4+2 labels picturing chessmen.

USSR, 60th Anniv. — A697

1982, Dec. 30 ***Perf. 13x12½***

2564	A697	30c multi	1.25	.25

World Communications Year — A698

1983, Jan. 24 **Litho.** ***Perf. 13***

2565	A698	20c multi	.75	.25

No. 507 and Birthplace — A699

1983, Jan. 28 ***Perf. 13x12½***

2566	A699	5c multi	.30	.25

Jose Marti (b. 1853), writer, revolution leader.

1984 Summer Olympics, Los Angeles A700

1983, Jan. 31 ***Perf. 13***

2567	A700	1c Javelin	.25	.25
2568	A700	5c Volleyball	.25	.25
2569	A700	6c Basketball	.25	.25
2570	A700	20c Weight lifting	.80	.25
2571	A700	30c Wrestling	1.10	.40
2572	A700	50c Boxing	1.75	.60
a.		Block of 6, #2567-2572	4.50	2.00
		Nos. 2567-2572 (6)	4.40	2.00

Souvenir Sheet

Perf. 13½x13

2573	A700	1p Judo	5.00	2.50

No. 2573 contains one 32x40mm stamp.

Radio Rebelde, 25th Anniv. — A701

1983, Feb. 24 ***Perf. 13***

2574	A701	20c multi	.70	.25

Karl Marx, Death Cent. A702

1983, Mar. 14

2575	A702	30c multi	1.00	.40

1st Manned Balloon Flight, Bicent. — A703

Various balloons.

1983, Mar. 30

2576	A703	1c multi	.25	.25
2577	A703	3c multi	.25	.25
2578	A703	5c multi	.25	.25
2579	A703	7c multi	.35	.25
2580	A703	30c multi	2.10	.70
2581	A703	50c multi	2.10	.70
		Nos. 2576-2581 (6)	5.30	2.40

Souvenir Sheet

2582	A703	1p Jose D. Blino	4.00	2.00

No. 2582 contains one 32x40mm stamp.

Cosmonauts' Day — A704

1983, Apr. 12 **Litho.**

2583	A704	1c *Vostok 1*	.25	.25
2584	A704	4c Satellite *Frances D1*	.25	.25
2585	A704	5c *Mars 2*	.25	.25
2586	A704	20c *Soyuz*	.75	.25
2587	A704	30c Meteorological satellite	1.10	.50
2588	A704	50c Intercosmos satellite	1.75	.70
		Nos. 2583-2588 (6)	4.35	2.20

Stamp Day A705

1983, Apr. 24

2589	A705	20c Havana-Key West cover	.75	.30
2590	A705	30c Spain-Havana cover	1.25	.30

1st Intl. airmail services.

Souvenir Sheet

TEMBAL '83, Basel — A706

1983, May 21 ***Perf. 13½x13***

2591	A706	1p Weasel	5.00	2.50

Simon Bolivar, Liberator of South America A707

1983, July 24 *Perf. 12½x13*

2592	A707	5c	Jose Rafael de las Heras	.25	.25
2593	A707	20c	Bolivar	.60	.25

Attack of Moncada Barracks, 30th Anniv. — A708

Designs: 5c, Jose Marti, Moncada barracks. 20c, Abel Santamaria, Jose Luis Tasende and Boris Luis Santa Coloma, martyrs, vert. 30c, *History Will Absolve Me*, declaration of Fidel Castro, vert.

1983, July 26 *Perf. 13*

2594	A708	5c	multi	.25	.25
2595	A708	20c	multi	.70	.25
2596	A708	30c	multi	.90	.50
			Nos. 2594-2596 (3)	1.85	1.00

Souvenir Sheet

Alberto Santos-Dumont (1873-1932) — A709

1983, July 29 *Perf. 13x13½*

2597	A709	1p	Dumont's aircraft	5.00	2.50

BRASILIANA '83, Rio; 140th anniv. of 1st stamp issued in the Americas.

9th Pan American Games, Caracas — A710

1983, Aug. 14 *Perf. 13x12½*

2598	A710	1c	Weight lifting	.25	.25
2599	A710	2c	Volleyball	.25	.25
2600	A710	3c	Baseball	.25	.25
2601	A710	20c	High jump	.75	.25
2602	A710	30c	Basketball	1.10	.50
2603	A710	50c	Boxing	1.75	.70
			Nos. 2598-2603 (6)	4.35	2.20

Port, by Claude Joseph Vernet — A711

1983, Sept. 5

2604	A711	30c	multi	1.75	.55

French alliance, cent.

Pres. Salvador Allende of Chile (d. 1973) — A712

1983, Sept. 12

2605	A712	20c	multi	.70	.25

1st Congress of Farmers at Arms, 25th Anniv. — A713

1983, Sept. 21 *Perf. 12½x12*

2606	A713	5c	multi	.25	.25

Raphael, 500th Birth Anniv. — A714

1983, Sept. 30 **Litho.** *Perf. 13*

2607	A714	1c	*Girl with Veil*	.25	.25
2608	A714	2c	*The Cardinal*	.25	.25
2609	A714	5c	*Francesco M. Della Rovere*	.25	.25
2610	A714	20c	*Portrait of a Youth*	.75	.25
2611	A714	30c	*Magdalena Doni*	1.10	.40
2612	A714	50c	*La Fornarina*	1.75	.65
			Nos. 2607-2612 (6)	4.35	2.05

State Quality Seal A715

1983, Oct. 14

2613	A715	5c	multi	.40	.25

Lighthouse Type of 1980

1983, Oct. 20

2614	A637	5c	Carapachibey	.25	.25
2615	A637	20c	Cadiz Bay	.80	.30
2616	A637	30c	Gobernadora Point	2.00	.80
			Nos. 2614-2616 (3)	3.05	1.35

Turtles A716

Designs: 1c, Eretmochelys imbricata. 2c, Lepidochelys kempi. 5c, Chrysemys decussata. 20c, Caretta caretta. 30c, Chelonia mydas. 50c, Dermochelys coriacea.

1983, Nov. 15

2617	A716	1c	multicolored	.25	.25
2618	A716	2c	multicolored	.25	.25
2619	A716	5c	multicolored	.25	.25
2620	A716	20c	multicolored	.80	.25
2621	A716	30c	multicolored	1.40	.25
2622	A716	50c	multicolored	2.75	.75
			Nos. 2617-2622 (6)	5.70	2.00

World Communications Year — A717

1983, Nov. 23

2623	A717	1c	Bell's Gallow Frame, telephone	.25	.25
2624	A717	5c	Telegram, airmail	.25	.25
2625	A717	10c	Satellite, satellite dish	.45	.25
2626	A717	20c	Television, radio	.75	.25
2627	A717	30c	24th Communications conf.	1.10	.40
			Nos. 2623-2627 (5)	2.80	1.40

Nos. 319 and 990 A718

1983, Dec. 3 *Perf. 13x12½*

2628	A718	20c	multi	.70	.25

See note after No. 320.

Flowers, Birds — A719

Designs: No. 2629, Opuntia dillenii. No. 2630, Euphorbia podocarpifolia. No. 2631, Dinema cubincola. No. 2632, Guaiacum officinale. No. 2633, Magnolia cubensis. No. 2634, Jatropha angustifolia. No. 2635, Cochlospermum vitifolium. No. 2636, Tabebuia lepidota. No. 2637, Kalmiella ericoides. No. 2638, Jatropha integerrima. No. 2639, Melocactus actinacanthus. No. 2640, Cordia sebestana. No. 2641, Tabernae - montana apoda. No. 2642, Lantana camara. No. 2643, Cordia gerascanthus. No. 2644, Tiaris canora. No. 2645, Phaethon lepturus. No. 2646, Myadestes elisabeth. No. 2647, Saurothera merlini. No. 2648, Polioptila lembeyei. No. 2649, Mellisuga helenae. No. 2650, Mimus polyglottos. No. 2651, Todus multicolor. No. 2652, Amazona leucocephala. No. 2653, Ferminia cerverai. No. 2654, Pelecanus occidentalis. No. 2655, Melanerpes superciliaris. No. 2656, Mimocichla plumbea. No. 2657, Aratinga euops. No. 2658, Sturnella magna. No. 2658B, Hedychium coronarium. No. 2658C, Priotelus temnurus.

1983, Dec. 20 *Perf. 13*

2629	A719	5c	multicolored	.55	.25
2630	A719	5c	multicolored	.55	.25
2631	A719	5c	multicolored	.55	.25
2632	A719	5c	multicolored	.55	.25
2633	A719	5c	multicolored	.55	.25
a.			Strip of 5, Nos. 2629-2633	4.00	2.00
2634	A719	5c	multicolored	.55	.25
2635	A719	5c	multicolored	.55	.25
2636	A719	5c	multicolored	.55	.25
2637	A719	5c	multicolored	.55	.25
2638	A719	5c	multicolored	.55	.25
2639	A719	5c	multicolored	.55	.25
2640	A719	5c	multicolored	.55	.25
2641	A719	5c	multicolored	.55	.25
2642	A719	5c	multicolored	.55	.25
2643	A719	5c	multicolored	.55	.25
a.			Block of 10, Nos. 2634-2643	6.50	4.00
2644	A719	5c	multicolored	.55	.25
2645	A719	5c	multicolored	.55	.25
2646	A719	5c	multicolored	.55	.25
2647	A719	5c	multicolored	.55	.25
2648	A719	5c	multicolored	.55	.25
a.			Strip of 5, Nos. 2644-2648	4.00	2.00
2649	A719	5c	multicolored	.55	.25
2650	A719	5c	multicolored	.55	.25
2651	A719	5c	multicolored	.55	.25
2652	A719	5c	multicolored	.55	.25
2653	A719	5c	multicolored	.55	.25
2654	A719	5c	multicolored	.55	.25
2655	A719	5c	multicolored	.55	.25
2656	A719	5c	multicolored	.55	.25
2657	A719	5c	multicolored	.55	.25
2658	A719	5c	multicolored	.55	.25
a.			Block of 10, Nos. 2649-2658	6.50	4.00
			Nos. 2629-2658 (30)	16.50	7.50

Souvenir Sheets

2658B	A719	100c	multicolored	5.00	4.50
2658C	A719	100c	multicolored	5.00	4.50

Flowers — A720

1983, Dec. 30 *Perf. 12½*

2659	A720	60c	Tobacco	1.75	.55
2660	A720	70c	Lily	2.25	.60
2661	A720	80c	Mariposa	2.50	.70
2662	A720	90c	Orchid	3.50	1.00
			Nos. 2659-2662 (4)	10.00	2.85

25th Anniv. of the Revolution — A721

1983, Dec. 31 **Litho.** *Perf. 13*

2663	A721	5c	shown	.25	.25
2664	A721	20c	Flags, Santa Clara Rlwy. tracks	3.50	1.00

25th Anniv. of the Revolution — A722

1984, Jan. 8

2665	A722	20c	Guevara, Castro	.70	.25
2666	A722	20c	Star	.70	.25
2667	A722	20c	PCC emblem, workers	1.75	.80
a.			Strip of 3, #2665-2667	3.25	1.50
			Nos. 2665-2667 (3)	3.15	1.30

Lenin, 60th Death Anniv. A723

1984, Jan. 21 *Perf. 12½x12*

2668	A723	30p	Spasski Tower, Russia Nos. 295, 265	1.25	.25

Cuban Labor Union, 45th Anniv. A724

1984, Jan. 28 *Perf. 13*

2669	A724	5c	multi	.25	.25

Butterflies — A725

Designs: 1c, Ixias balice. 2c, Phoebis avellaneda. 3c, Anthocaris sara. 5c, Victorina. 20c, Heliconius cydno cydnides. 30c, Parides gundlachianus calzadillae. 50c, Catagramma sorana.

1984, Jan. 31 *Perf. 13x12½*

2670	A725	1c	multicolored	.25	.25
2671	A725	2c	multicolored	.25	.25
2672	A725	3c	multicolored	.25	.25
2673	A725	5c	multicolored	.25	.25
2674	A725	20c	multicolored	.80	.25
2675	A725	30c	multicolored	1.40	.65
2676	A725	50c	multicolored	2.40	.95
			Nos. 2670-2676 (7)	5.60	2.85

Marine Mammals — A726

Designs: 1c, Grampus griseus, vert. 2c, Delphinus delphis, vert. 5c, Physeter catodon. 6c, Stenella plagiodon, vert. 10c, Pseudorca crassidens. 30c, Tursiops truncatus, vert. 50, Megaptera novaeangliae.

1984, Feb. 15 *Perf. 12x12½, 12½x12*

2677	A726	1c	multicolored	.25	.25
2678	A726	2c	multicolored	.25	.25
2679	A726	5c	multicolored	.25	.25
2680	A726	6c	multicolored	.25	.25
2681	A726	10c	multicolored	.70	.25
2682	A726	30c	multicolored	1.60	.40
2683	A726	50c	multicolored	2.75	.70
			Nos. 2677-2683 (7)	6.05	2.35

Augusto C. Sandino (1893-1934), Nicaraguan Revolutionary — A727

1984, Feb. 21 *Perf. 13*

2684	A727	20c	multi	.70	.25

Red Cross in Cuba, 75th Anniv. — A728

1984, Mar. 10

2685	A728	30c	Flag, No. 404	1.25	.35

Cuban Film Industry, 25th Anniv. A729

1984, Mar. 24

2686	A729	20c	multi	.80	.30

Caribbean Flowers — A730

Designs: 1c, Brownea grandiceps. 2c, Couroupita guianensis. 5c, Triplaris surinamensis. 20c, Amherstia nobilis. 30c, Plumieria alba. 50c, Delonix regia.

1984, Mar. 29

2687	A730	1c	multicolored	.25	.25
2688	A730	2c	multicolored	.25	.25
2689	A730	5c	multicolored	.25	.25
2690	A730	20c	multicolored	.80	.30
2691	A730	30c	multicolored	1.10	.50
2692	A730	50c	multicolored	2.00	.90
			Nos. 2687-2692 (6)	4.65	2.45

Cosmonauts' Day — A731

1984, Apr. 12

2693	A731	2c	*Electron 1,* 1964	.25	.25
2694	A731	3c	*Electron 2,* 1964	.25	.25
2695	A731	5c	*Intercosmos 1,* 1969	.25	.25
2696	A731	10c	*Mars 5,* 1974	.40	.25
2697	A731	30c	*Soyuz,* 1969	1.10	.50
2698	A731	50c	USSR-Bulgaria space flight, 1979	2.00	.90
			Nos. 2693-2698 (6)	4.25	2.40

Souvenir Sheet

Perf. 12½

2699	A731	1p	*Luna 1,* 1959	4.00	2.00

No. 2699 contains one 32x40mm stamp.

Mothers' Day — A732

1984, Apr. 19 *Perf. 13*

2700	A732	20c	Red roses	.80	.30
2701	A732	20c	Pink roses	.80	.30

Stamp Day — A733

Designs: Mural, by R. Rodriguez Radillo (details).

1984, Apr. 24 *Perf. 13x12½*

2702	A733	20c	Mexican runner	.80	.30
2703	A733	30c	Egyptian boatman	1.10	.50

See Nos. 2787-2788, 2860-2861, 3025-3026, 3122-3123, 3213-3214.

Souvenir Sheet

ESPANA '84, Madrid — A734

1984, Apr. 27 *Perf. 13x13½*

2704	A734	1p	Clipper ship	4.75	2.25

Women's Basketball, 1984 Summer Olympics A735

1984, May 5 *Perf. 13*

2705	A735	20c	multi	1.25	.35

Agrarian Reform Act, 25th Anniv. — A736

1984, May 17 *Perf. 13½x13*

2706	A736	5c	multi	.40	.25

Banco Popular de Ahorro, 1st Anniv. — A737

1984, May 18 *Perf. 13*

2707	A737	5c	multi	.40	.25

Early Locomotives — A738

1984, June 11 *Perf. 12½x12*

2708	A738	1c	multi	.25	.25
2709	A738	4c	multi, diff.	.25	.25
2710	A738	5c	multi, diff.	.25	.25
2711	A738	10c	multi, diff.	.40	.25
2712	A738	30c	multi, diff.	1.25	.40
2713	A738	50c	multi, diff.	2.10	.80
			Nos. 2708-2713 (6)	4.50	2.20

Souvenir Sheet

19th UPU Congress, HAMBURG '84 — A739

1984, June 19 *Perf. 13x13½*

2714	A739	1p	Nos. 73, 232	4.50	2.25

Intl. Olympic Committee, 90th Anniv. — A740

1984, June 23 *Perf. 13*

2715	A740	30c	Coubertin, torch-bearer	1.40	.50

Children's Day A741

1984, July 15 *Perf. 12½x13*

2716	A741	5c	multi	.25	.25

1984 Summer Olympics, Los Angeles A742

1984, July 28 *Perf. 13*

2717	A742	1c	Wrestling	.25	.25
2718	A742	3c	Discus	.25	.25
2719	A742	5c	Volleyball	.25	.25
2720	A742	20c	Boxing	.80	.30
2721	A742	30c	Basketball	1.10	.50
2722	A742	50c	Weight lifting	2.00	.90
			Nos. 2717-2722 (6)	4.65	2.45

Souvenir Sheet

Perf. 12½

2723 A742 1p Baseball 4.50 2.25

No. 2723 contains one 32x40mm stamp.

Emilio Roig de Leuchsenring (1889-1964), Historian A743

1984, Aug. 8 ***Perf. 13***

2724 A743 5c multi .25 .25

Friendship Games, Aug. 18-26, Havana — A744

1984, Aug. 18

2725	A744	3c	Volleyball	.25	.25
2726	A744	5c	Women's volley-ball	.35	.25
2727	A744	8c	Water polo	.35	.25
2728	A744	30c	Boxing	1.25	.35
			Nos. 2725-2728 (4)	2.20	1.10

Cattle Breeding A745

1984, Sept. 20

2729	A745	2c	Artificial pastures	.25	.25
2730	A745	3c	Cuban carib	.25	.25
2731	A745	5c	Charolaise, vert.	.25	.25
2732	A745	30c	Cuban cebu, vert.	1.25	.40
2733	A745	50c	White-udder	2.25	.75
			Nos. 2729-2733 (5)	4.25	1.90

Souvenir Sheet

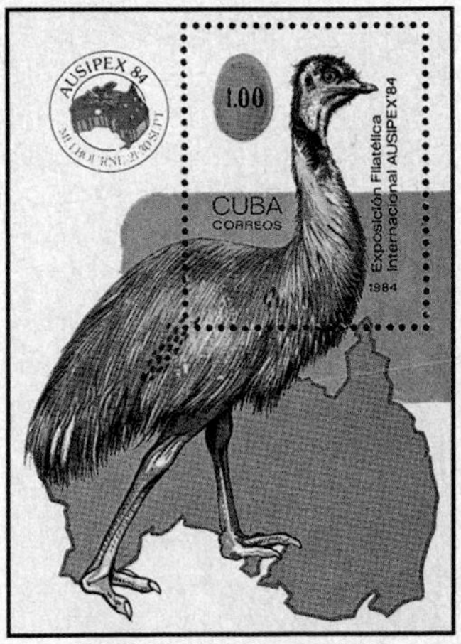

AUSIPEX '84, Sept. 21-30, Melbourne — A746

1984, Sept. 21 ***Perf. 12½***

2734 A746 1p Emu 5.00 2.75

Fauna — A747

Designs: 1c, Polymita. 2c, Solenodon cubanus. 3c, Alsophis cantherigerus. 4c, Osteopilus septentrionalis. 5c, Mellisuga helenae. 10c, Capromys melanurus. 30c, Todus multicolor. 50c, Parrots (cotorra).

1984, Oct. 10 ***Perf. 13***

2735	A747	1c	multicolored	.25	.25
2736	A747	2c	multicolored	.25	.25
2737	A747	3c	multicolored	.25	.25
2738	A747	4c	multicolored	.25	.25
2739	A747	5c	multicolored	.55	.25
2740	A747	10c	multicolored	.30	.25
2741	A747	30c	multicolored	2.40	.95
2742	A747	50c	multicolored	3.75	1.25
			Nos. 2735-2742 (8)	8.00	3.70

ESPAMER '85, Havana — A748

1984, Oct. 12

2743		Sheet of 4 + 2 labels	5.00	2.50
	a.	A748 5c Ferdinand, Isabella	.25	.25
	b.	A748 20c Departure from Palos	1.50	.70
	c.	A748 30c *Nina, Pinta, Santa Maria*	2.25	1.10
	d.	A748 50c Landing in America	1.00	.50

Columbus Day.

Souvenir Sheet

9th Natl. Phil. Exhibition, Oct. 20-28, Santiago de Cuba — A749

1984, Oct. 20 ***Perf. 12½***

2744 A749 1p multicolored 4.50 2.25

Natl. Revolutionary Militia, 25th Anniv. — A750

1984, Oct. 26 ***Perf. 12½x13***

2745 A750 5c multi .30 .25

Disappearance of Camilo Cienfuegos, 25th Anniv. — A751

1984, Oct. 28 ***Perf. 13x12½***

2746 A751 5c multi .40 .25

UN Child Survival Campaign A752

1984, Nov. 11 ***Perf. 13***

2747 A752 5c Breast-feeding .40 .25

Classic Automobiles — A753

1984, Nov. 25

2748	A753	1c	1909 Morgan	.25	.25
2749	A753	2c	1922 Austin	.25	.25
2750	A753	5c	1903 De Dion-Bouton	.25	.25
2751	A753	20c	1908 Ford Model T	.95	.25
2752	A753	30c	1885 Benz	1.50	.35
2753	A753	50c	1910 Benz	2.75	.70
			Nos. 2748-2753 (6)	5.95	2.05

Postal Museum, 20th Anniv. — A754

1985, Jan. 2 ***Perf. 13x12½***

2754 A754 20c multi .75 .25

Portrait of Celia Sanchez, by E. Escobedo A755

1985, Jan. 11 ***Perf. 13***

2755 A755 5c multi .40 .25

Celia Sanchez (1920-1980), party leader.

PORTO '85, Intl. Pigeon Exhibition — A756

1985, Jan. 23

2756 A756 20c multi 1.25 .25

1986 World Cup Soccer Championships, Mexico — A757

Athletes and Flags of previous host nations.

1985, Jan. 25

2757	A757	1c	Chile, 1962	.25	.25
2758	A757	2c	Great Britain, 1966	.25	.25
2759	A757	3c	Mexico, 1970	.25	.25
2760	A757	4c	Federal Republic of Germany, 1974	.25	.25
2761	A757	5c	Argentina, 1978	.25	.25
2762	A757	30c	Spain, 1982	1.40	.50
2763	A757	50c	Sweden, 1958	2.25	.65
			Nos. 2757-2763 (7)	4.90	2.40

Souvenir Sheet

Perf. 12½

2764 A757 1p Mexico, 1986 4.00 2.00

No. 2764 contains one 40x32mm stamp.

Baconao Natl. Park — A758

Dinosaurs.

1985, Feb. 14 ***Perf. 13x12½***

2765	A758	1c	Pteranodon	.30	.25
2766	A758	2c	Brontosaurus	.30	.25
2767	A758	4c	Iguanodontus	.30	.25
2768	A758	5c	Estegosaurus	.30	.25
2769	A758	8c	Monoclonius	.50	.25
2770	A758	30c	Corythosaurus	1.50	.50
2771	A758	50c	Tyrannosaurus	2.75	.70
			Nos. 2765-2771 (7)	5.95	2.45

13th Congress of the Postal Unions of the Americas, Havana — A759

Design: Uruguay #196, congress emblem and Argentina #287.

1985, Mar. 11 ***Perf. 12½x12***

2772 A759 20c multi 2.50 .70

ESPAMER '85 — A760

Indian activities: 1c, Playing ball. 2c, Medicine man preparing calumet and other ritual items. 5c, Net and spear fishing. 20c, Potter. 30c, Hunting. 50c, Hollowing-out canoe, decorating paddle. 1p, Cooking.

1985, Mar. 19 *Perf. 12½x13*

2773	A760	1c	multi	.25	.25
2774	A760	2c	multi	.25	.25
2775	A760	5c	multi	.40	.25
2776	A760	20c	multi	.40	.25
2777	A760	30c	multi	.65	.40
2778	A760	50c	multi	2.75	.80
			Nos. 2773-2778 (6)	4.70	2.20

Souvenir Sheet

Perf. 12½

2779	A760	1p	multi	5.00	2.50

No. 2779 contains one 32x40mm stamp.
An imperf. souvenir sheet exists containing Nos. 2773-2779.

Cosmonauts' Day — A761

Designs: 2c, Spacecraft orbiting Moon. 3c, Two spacecraft. 10c, Space walkers linked. 13c, Space walkers welding. 20c, *Vostok 2.* 50c, *Lunokhod 1* moon vehicle.

1985, Apr. 12 *Perf. 13x12½*

2780	A761	2c	multi	.25	.25
2781	A761	3c	multi	.25	.25
2782	A761	10c	multi	.45	.25
2783	A761	13c	multi	.65	.25
2784	A761	20c	multi	.75	.25
2785	A761	50c	multi	2.50	.70
			Nos. 2780-2785 (6)	4.85	1.95

12th Youth and Students Festival, Moscow A762

1985, Apr. 19 *Perf. 13*

2786	A762	30c	Lenin Mausoleum	.65	.50

Stamp Day Type of 1984

Mural, by R. Rodriguez Radillo (1967), details: 20c, Roman charioteer (courier of *Cursus Publicus*). 35c, Medieval nobleman, monks (monastic messenger mail).

1985, Apr. 24 *Perf. 13x12½*

2787	A733	20c	multi	.80	.25
2788	A733	35c	multi	1.10	.40

Mothers' Day — A763

1985, May 2 *Perf. 13*

2789	A763	1c	Peonies	.25	.25
2790	A763	4c	Carnations	.25	.25
2791	A763	5c	Dahlias	.25	.25
2792	A763	13c	Roses	.45	.25
2793	A763	20c	Roses, diff.	.75	.25
2794	A763	50c	Tulips	2.00	.55
			Nos. 2789-2794 (6)	3.95	1.80

50th Death Anniv. of Antonio Guiteras and Carlos Aponte, Revolutionaries — A764

1985, May 9 *Perf. 12½x12*

2795	A764	5c	multi	.25	.25

End of WWII, 40th Anniv. A765

1985, May 10

2796	A765	5c	shown	.25	.25
2797	A765	20c	Soviet memorial, Berlin-Treptow	.65	.30
2798	A765	30c	Dove	1.10	.55
			Nos. 2796-2798 (3)	2.00	1.10

Souvenir Sheet

ARGENTINA '85, Buenos Aires — A766

1985, June 5 *Perf. 13½x13*

2799	A766	1p	*Vulture gryphus*	4.50	2.25

Motorcycle, Cent. — A767

1985, June 28 *Perf. 13*

2800	A767	2c	1885 Daimler	.25	.25
2801	A767	5c	1910 Kaiser Tricycle	.25	.25
2802	A767	10c	1925 Fanomobile	.55	.25
2803	A767	30c	1926 Mars A20	1.50	.30
2804	A767	50c	1936 Simson BSW	2.75	.70
			Nos. 2800-2804 (5)	5.30	1.75

Development of Health Care Since the Revolution — A768

1985, July 18 *Perf. 12½x12*

2805	A768	5c	Hospitals	.25	.25

Federation of Cuban Women (FMC), 25th Anniv. — A769

1985, Aug. 23

2806	A769	5c	multi	.25	.25

No. 2806 printed se-tenant with label picturing federation emblem.

Universiade Games, Japan — A770

1985, Aug. 27 *Perf. 13*

2807	A770	50c	multi	1.75	.55

1st Havana Declaration, 25th Anniv. — A771

1985, Sept. 2

2808	A771	5c	Jose Marti statue, revolutionaries	.40	.25

Souvenir Sheet

ITALIA '85 — A772

1985, Sept. 25 *Perf. 12½*

2809	A772	1p	Roman galley	5.00	2.50

Revolutionary Defense Committees (CDR), 25th Anniv. — A773

1985, Sept. 28 *Perf. 13*

2810	A773	5c	multi	.25	.25

Aquarium Fish — A774

Designs: 1c, Centropyge argi. 3c, Holacanthus tricolor. 5c, Chaetodon capistratus. 10c, Chaetodon sedentarius. 20c, Chaetodon ocellatus. 50c, Holacanthus ciliaris.

1985, Sept. 30 **Litho.**

2811	A774	1c	multicolored	.25	.25
2812	A774	3c	multicolored	.25	.25
2813	A774	5c	multicolored	.25	.25
2814	A774	10c	multicolored	.40	.25
2815	A774	20c	multicolored	.95	.50
2816	A774	50c	multicolored	2.40	1.60
			Nos. 2811-2816 (6)	4.50	3.10

Communist Party Central Committee, 20th Anniv. — A775

1985, Oct. 1

2817	A775	5c	multi	.40	.25

Souvenir Sheet

EXFILNA '85 — A776

1985, Oct. 18

2818	A776	1p	Spain No. C45, Cuba No. 387	5.00	2.50

UN, 40th Anniv. — A777

1985, Oct. 24

2819	A777	20c	multi	.90	.25

Sites on the UNESCO World Heritage List — A778

Designs: 2c, Plaza Vieja, 16th cent. 5c, Royal Army Castle, c. 1558. 20c, Havana Cathedral, c. 1748. 30c, Captains-General Palace (Havana City Museum), 1776. 50c, The Temple, 1827.

1985, Nov. 25

2820 A778 2c multi .25 .25
2821 A778 5c multi .25 .25
2822 A778 20c multi .95 .25
2823 A778 30c multi 1.50 .45
2824 A778 50c multi 2.40 .60
Nos. 2820-2824 (5) 5.35 1.80

1986 World Cup Soccer Championships, Mexico — A779

Various athletes.

1986, Jan. 20

2825 A779 1c multi .25 .25
2826 A779 4c multi .25 .25
2827 A779 5c multi .25 .25
2828 A779 10c multi .30 .25
2829 A779 30c multi 1.10 .30
2830 A779 50c multi 1.60 .55
Nos. 2825-2830 (6) 3.75 1.85

Souvenir Sheet

Perf. 13½x13

2831 A779 1p multi 4.50 2.25

No. 2831 contains one 32x40mm stamp.

3rd Communist Party Congress, Havana — A780

1986, Feb. 4 ***Perf. 13***

2832 A780 5c shown .25 .25
2833 A780 20c Party and natl. flags, emblem 1.25 .25

Natl. Sports Institute (INDER), 25th Anniv. A781

1986, Feb. 23

2834 A781 5c multi .30 .25

A782

1986, Feb. 23

2835 A782 5c multi .30 .25

Ministry of Domestic Trade, 25th anniv.

A783

Exotic flowers in the Botanical Gardens: 1c, Tecomaria capensis. 3c, Michelia champaca. 5c, Thunbergia grandiflora. 8c, Dendrobium phalaenopsis. 30c, Allamanda violacea. 50c, Rhodactus bleo.

1986, Feb. 25 ***Perf. 12½x12***

2836 A783 1c multicolored .25 .25
2837 A783 3c multicolored .25 .25
2838 A783 5c multicolored .25 .25
2839 A783 8c multicolored .30 .25
2840 A783 30c multicolored 1.25 .25
2841 A783 50c multicolored 1.90 .40
Nos. 2836-2841 (6) 4.20 1.65

Gundlach and Birds — A784

Designs: 1c, Agelaius assimilis. 3c, Dendroica pityophila. 7c, Myiarchus sagrae. 9c, Dendroica petechia gundlachi. 30c, Geotrygon caniceps. 50c, Colaptes auratus chrysocaulosus.

1986, Mar. 14 Litho. ***Perf. 13½x13***

2842 A784 1c multicolored .30 .25
2843 A784 3c multicolored .30 .25
2844 A784 7c multicolored .55 .40
2845 A784 9c multicolored .70 .50
2846 A784 30c multicolored 3.00 2.00
2847 A784 50c multicolored 4.75 3.25
Nos. 2842-2847 (6) 9.60 6.65

Juan Cristobal Gundlach (d. 1896), ornithologist.

Pioneers Youth Organization, 25th Anniv. — A785

1986, Apr. 3 ***Perf. 13***

2848 A785 5c Induction .30 .25

150th Birth Anniv. of Maximo Gomez — A786

1986, Apr. 4

2849 A786 20c multi .90 .25

A787

1986, Apr. 10 ***Perf. 12½***

2850 A787 5c multi .40 .25

Kindergartens, 25th anniv.

A788

1st Man In Space, 25th Anniv.: 1c, *Vostok* and rocket designer Sergei Korolev. 2c, Yuri Gagarin, *Vostok 1.* 5c, Valentina Tereshkova, *Vostok 6.* 20c, *Salyut-Soyuz* space link. 30c, Capsule landing. 50c, *Soyuz* rocket launch. 1p, Konstantin Tsiolkovski (1857-1935), rocket scientist.

1986, Apr. 12 ***Perf. 13x13½***

2851 A788 1c multi .25 .25
2852 A788 2c multi .25 .25
2853 A788 5c multi .25 .25
2854 A788 20c multi .60 .25
2855 A788 30c multi .80 .25
2856 A788 50c multi 1.75 .55
Nos. 2851-2856 (6) 3.90 1.80

Souvenir Sheet

Perf. 12½

2857 A788 1p multi 4.50 2.25

No. 2857 contains one 32x40mm stamp.

Natl. Flag and No. 2407 A789

1986, Apr. 19 ***Perf. 13***

2858 A789 5c shown .25 .25
2859 A789 20c Banners, natl. crest 1.10 .25

Bay of Pigs invasion, 25th anniv. (5c); Proclamation of Socialist Revolution, 25th anniv. (20c).

Stamp Day Type of 1984

Mural, by R. Rodriguez Radillo (1967), details.

1986, Apr. 24 ***Perf. 13x12½***

2860 A733 20c Mail coach, 18th-19th cent. .75 .25
2861 A733 30c Pony Express 1.00 .25

Radio Havana, 25th Anniv. — A790

1986, May 1

2862 A790 5c multi .40 .25

EXPO '86, Vancouver — A791

Locomotives: 1c, *Stourbridge Lion,* 1829, US. 4c, Stephenson's *Rocket,* 1829, GB. 5c, 1st Russian locomotive, 1845. 8c, Seguin's locomotive, 1830, France. 30c, 1st Canadian locomotive, 1836. 50c, Urban locomotive, Belgian Grand Central Rlwy., 1872. 1p, US locomotive pulling Cuban sugar train, 1837.

1986, May 2 Litho. ***Perf. 12½x12***

2863 A791 1c multi .25 .25
2864 A791 4c multi .25 .25
2865 A791 5c multi .25 .25
2866 A791 8c multi .25 .25
2867 A791 30c multi .80 .30
2868 A791 50c multi 2.10 .55
Nos. 2863-2868 (6) 3.90 1.85

Souvenir Sheet

Perf. 13x13½

2869 A791 1p multi 5.00 2.50

No. 2869 contains one 40x32mm stamp.

Assoc. of Small Farmers, (ANAP), 25th Anniv. — A792

1986, May 17 ***Perf. 13***

2870 A792 5c multi .40 .25

Intl. Peace Year A793

1986, June 2

2871 A793 30c multi 1.00 .25

Ministry of the Interior (MININT), 25th Anniv. — A794

1986, June 6

2872 A794 5c multi .40 .25

Martin Luther King, Jr. A795

1986, June 27 *Perf. 13½x13*

2873 A795 20c multi 1.00 .25

Bonifacio Byrne (d. 1936), Poet A796

1986, July 5 *Perf. 13*

2874 A796 5c multi .30 .25

Cuban Union of Writers and Artists (UNEAC), 25th Anniv. — A797

Sandinista Movement in Nicaragua (FSLN), 25th Anniv. — A798

1986, July 10 *Perf. 13x12½*

2875 A797 5c multi .30 .25

1986, July 23 *Perf. 13x12*

Augusto Cesar Sandino and Carlos Fonseca.

2876 A798 20c multi .75 .25

Ministry of Transportation, 25th Anniv. — A799

1986, Aug. 1 *Perf. 13*

2877 A799 5c multi .50 .25

7th University Games of Central America and the Caribbean A800

1986, Aug. 9

2878 A800 20c multi 1.00 .25

Souvenir Sheet

STOCKHOLMIA '86 — A801

Designs: a, 2c Mambi Revolutionary stamp of 1897. b, Sweden Type A7, cancellation.

1986, Aug. 28 *Perf. 12½*

2879 A801 Sheet of 2 4.50 2.25

a.-b. 50c multi

Nonaligned Countries Movement, 25th Anniv. — A802

1986, Sept. 1 *Perf. 13½x13*

2880 A802 50c multi 2.00 .45

Orchids — A803

Designs: 1c, Cattleya hardyana. 4c, Brassolaelio cattleya. 5c, Phalaenopsis marget moses. 10c, Laelio cattleya prism palette. 30c, Phalaenopsis violacea. 50c, Disa uniflora.

1986, Sept. 15 *Perf. 12½*

2881 A803 1c multicolored .25 .25
2882 A803 4c multicolored .25 .25
2883 A803 5c multicolored .25 .25
2884 A803 10c multicolored .30 .25
2885 A803 30c multicolored 1.25 .30
2886 A803 50c multicolored 1.90 .50
Nos. 2881-2886 (6) 4.20 1.80

Latin American History — A804

Pre-Columbian artifacts: No. 2887, Mayan dwelling and votive jade sculpture. No. 2888, Inca vase and Tiahuanacu sun gate (Bolivia). No. 2889, Spain No. C47, discovery of America 500th anniv. emblem, scroll. No. 2890, Diaguitan duck-shaped pitcher and Pucara de Quitor ruins (Chile). No. 2891, San Agustin Archaeological Park megaliths and Quimbayan sculpture (Colombia). No. 2892, Moler grinding stone and Chorotega ceramic figurine. No. 2893, Tabaco idol and Indian dwelling (Cuba). No. 2894, Spain No. C38. No. 2895, Taino dwelling and chair (Dominica). No. 2896, Tolita statue and Ingapirca Castle ruins. No. 2897, Maya vase and Tikal Temple (Guatemala). No. 2898, Copan ruins and Maya idol. No. 2899, Spain No. C37. No. 2900, Chichen Itza Temple and Zapotecan urn (Mexico). No. 2901, Punta de Zapote megaliths and Ometepe ceramic figurine. No. 2902, Tonosi lidded ceramic bowl and Barriles monoliths. No. 2903, Ruins at Machu-Picchu and Inca statue (Peru). No. 2904, Spain No. C49. No. 2905, Teepees and triangular sculpture (Puerto Rico). No. 2906, Fertility statue from Santa Ana and Santo Domingo Cave.

1986, Oct. 12 *Perf. 13*

2887 A804 1c multi .25 .25
2888 A804 1c multi .25 .25
2889 A804 1c multi .25 .25
2890 A804 1c multi .25 .25
2891 A804 1c multi .25 .25
a. Strip of 5, Nos. 2887-2891 1.00 1.00
2892 A804 5c multi .25 .25
2893 A804 5c multi .25 .25
2894 A804 5c multi .25 .25
2895 A804 5c multi .25 .25
2896 A804 5c multi .25 .25
a. Strip of 5, Nos. 2892-2896 1.00 1.00
2897 A804 10c multi .30 .25
2898 A804 10c multi .30 .25
2899 A804 10c multi .30 .25
2900 A804 10c multi .30 .25
2901 A804 10c multi .30 .25
a. Strip of 5, Nos. 2897-2901 1.50 1.00
2902 A804 20c multi .70 .30
2903 A804 20c multi .70 .30
2904 A804 20c multi .70 .30
2905 A804 20c multi .70 .30
2906 A804 20c multi .70 .30
a. Strip of 5, Nos. 2902-2906 3.50 1.50
Nos. 2887-2906 (20) 7.50 5.25

Discovery of America, 500th anniv. (in 1992). See Nos. 2966-2985, 3065-3084, 3253-3272, 3463-3466.

Intl. Brigades, Spain, 50th Anniv. — A805

1986, Oct. 14 *Perf. 12½x12*

2907 A805 30c multi .75 .35

Paintings in the Natl. Museum A806

Designs: 2c, *Two Children,* by Gutierrez de la Vega, vert. 4c, *Sed,* by Jean-Georges Vibert. 6c, *Virgin and Child,* by Niccolo Abbate, vert. 10c, *Bullfight,* by Eugenio de Lucas Velazquez. 30c, *The Five Senses,* anonymous. 50c, *Arrival at Thomops Castle,* by Jean Louis Ernest.

1986, Nov. 5 *Perf. 13*

2908 A806 2c multi .25 .25
2909 A806 4c multi .25 .25
2910 A806 6c multi .25 .25
2911 A806 10c multi .40 .25
2912 A806 30c multi 1.10 .30
2913 A806 50c multi 1.90 .55
Nos. 2908-2913 (6) 4.15 1.85

Anniversaries — A807

1986, Dec. 2 **Litho.** *Perf. 12½*

2914 A807 5c *Granma* .45 .25

Size: 26x38mm

2915 A807 20c Soldier, rifle, flag 1.50 .25

Granma Landings, 30th anniv. (5c); Revolutionary Armed Forces, 30th anniv. (20c).

Scholarship Program, 25th Anniv. — A808

1986, Dec. 22 *Perf. 13*

2916 A808 5c Guevara, students .30 .25

Natl. Literacy Campaign, 25th Anniv. — A809

1986, Dec. 25 *Perf. 13x12½*

2917 A809 5c Marti, man learning to write .30 .25

Siege of La Plata, 30th Anniv. A810

1987, Jan. 17 *Perf. 12½x12*

2918 A810 5c Map, revolutionaries .30 .25

Paintings in the Natl. Museum A811

3c, *Gypsy,* by Joaquin Sorolla. 5c, *Sir Walter Scott,* by Sir John W. Gordon. 10c, *Farm Meadows,* by Alfred de Breanski. 20c, *Still-life,* by Isaac van Duynen. 30c, *Landscape with Figures,* by Francesco Zuccarelli. 40c, *The Failure* (defeated bullfighter), by Ignacio Zuloaga.

1987, Feb. 5 *Perf. 13*

2919 A811 3c multi, vert. .25 .25
2920 A811 5c multi, vert. .25 .25
2921 A811 10c multi .40 .25
2922 A811 20c multi 1.00 .25
2923 A811 30c multi 1.10 .30
2924 A811 40c multi, vert. 1.60 .50
Nos. 2919-2924 (6) 4.60 1.80

Siege of the Presidential Palace, 30th Anniv. — A812

1987, Mar. 13 *Perf. 12½x12*

2925 A812 5c Palace, van, Echeverra .30 .25

Lazarus Ludwig Zamenhof and Russia Type A77 — A813

1987, Mar. 16 *Perf. 13½x13*

2926 A813 30c multi 1.00 .30

Esperanto, cent.

Souvenir Sheet

EXFILNA '87, 10th Natl. Stamp Exposition, Holguin — A814

1987, Mar. 28 *Perf. 13x13½*
2927 A814 1p Nos. 552, C129 4.50 2.25

25th Anniv. and 5th Cong. of the Youth Communist League (U.J.C.) — A815

1987, Apr. 4 *Perf. 13*
2928 A815 5c multi .30 .25

Intercosmos, 20th Anniv. — A816

1987, Apr. 12 Litho. *Perf. 12½x12*
2929 A816 3c *Intercosmos 1* .25 .25
2930 A816 5c *Intercosmos 2* .25 .25
2931 A816 10c *TD* .30 .25
2932 A816 20c *Cosmos 93* .75 .25
2933 A816 30c *Prognoz* 1.00 .30
2934 A816 50c *Vostok 3* 1.60 .55
Nos. 2929-2934 (6) 4.15 1.85

Souvenir Sheet
Perf. 13½x13

2935 A816 1p Rocket, *Vostok 3* 4.50 2.25

No. 2935 contains one 32x40mm stamp.

Stamp Day A817

Stamped covers and canceled stamps.

1987, Apr. 24 *Perf. 13*
2936 A817 30c Havana, 1890 1.25 .30
2937 A817 50c Santiago de Cuba, 1869 2.10 .60

Mothers' Day — A818

Various dahlias and roses.

1987, May 2
2938 A818 3c multi .25 .25
2939 A818 5c multi .25 .25
2940 A818 10c multi .25 .25
2941 A818 13c multi .30 .25
2942 A818 30c multi .70 .25
2943 A818 50c multi 1.25 .50
Nos. 2938-2943 (6) 3.00 1.75

Bone-lengthening Procedure (Femur in Frame) — A819

1987, May 4
2944 A819 5c multi .30 .25

ORTOPEDIA '87, medical congress for orthopedists from Spanish and Portuguese-speaking countries, Havana.

Cuban Broadcasting and Television Institute, 25th Anniv. — A820

1987, May 24 *Perf. 13*
2945 A820 5c multi .30 .25

Battle of Uvero, 30th Anniv. A821

Views of monument, Sierra Maestra Mts.

1987, May 28 *Perf. 13½x13*
2946 A821 5c multicolored .30 .25

CAPEX '87 — A822

Natl. flags, stamps and 19th cent. mail carriers pictured on cigarette cards: 3c, Messenger, llamas and Bolivia Type A9. 5c, Early p.o., automobile and France Type A17. 10c, Messengers riding elephants and Thailand Type A2. 20c, Messenger riding camel and stamp of Egypt, 1879. 30c, Mail troika and stamp of Russia. 50c, Post rider and stamp of Indo-China. 1p, Post rider and Mambi Revolutionary stamp.

1987, June 15 *Perf. 12½x13*
2947 A822 3c multi .25 .25
2948 A822 5c multi .25 .25
2949 A822 10c multi .25 .25
2950 A822 20c multi .50 .25
2951 A822 30c multi .70 .25
2952 A822 50c multi 1.25 .50
Nos. 2947-2952 (6) 3.20 1.75

Souvenir Sheet
Perf. 13½x13

2953 A822 1p multi 4.50 2.25

No. 2953 contains one 32x40mm stamp.

Dinosaur Exhibits, Bacanao Natl. Park A823

1987, June 25 *Perf. 13*
2954 A823 3c multi .25 .25
2955 A823 5c multi .25 .25
2956 A823 10c multi .40 .25
2957 A823 20c multi .90 .25
2958 A823 35c multi 1.40 .30
2959 A823 40c multi 1.60 .40
Nos. 2954-2959 (6) 4.80 1.70

Frank Pais (d. 1957), Teacher and Student Leader — A824

1987, July 30 *Perf. 12½x12*
2960 A824 5c Pais, Rafael Maria Mendive University .30 .25

10th Pan American Games, Indianapolis — A825

1987, Aug. 8
2961 A825 50c multi 1.75 .45

Printed se-tenant with inscribed label picturing the 1991 Havana Games character trademark.

Siege of Cienfuegos, 30th Anniv. — A826

1987, Sept. 5 *Perf. 13*
2962 A826 5c Memorial .30 .25

Souvenir Sheet

HAFNIA '87, Denmark — A827

1987, Sept. 16 *Perf. 13½x13*
2963 A827 1p Danish mailman, 1887, Type A6 4.50 2.25

Souvenir Sheet

ESPAMER '87, La Coruna, Oct. 2-12 — A828

1987, Oct. 2
2964 A828 1p La Coruna Port, 1525 4.50 2.25

20th Heroic Guerrillas Day — A829

1987, Oct. 8 *Perf. 12½x12*
2965 A829 50c Coins, #1364 1.25 .55

Latin American History Type of 1986

Indians and birds: No. 2966, Tehuelche Indian of Argentina, *Habia rubica.* No. 2967, *Ramphastos cuvieri,* Tibirica Indian of Brazil. No. 2968, Spain #C31 & discovery of America 500th anniv. emblem. No. 2969, *Vultur gryphus,* Lautaro Indian of Chile. No. 2970, Calarca Indian of Colombia, *Opisthocomus hoazin.* No. 2971, *Priotelus temnurus,* Hatuey Indian of Cuba. No. 2972, *Columbigallina passerina,* Enriquillo Indian of the Dominican Republic. No. 2973, Spain #427. #2974, *Semnornis ramphastinus,* Ruminahui Indian of Ecuador. No. 2975, *Pharomachrus mocinno,* Tecum Uman Indian of Guatemala. No. 2976, Anacaona Indian of Haiti, *Aramus guarauna.* No. 2977, Lempira Indian of Honduras, *Diglossa baritula.* #2978, Spain #C42. No. 2979, *Onychorhinchus mexicanus,* Cuauhtemoc Indian of Mexico. No. 2980, *Setofaga picta,* Nicarao Indian of Nicaragua. No. 2981, *Rupicola peruviana,* Atahualpa Indian of Peru. No. 2982, Atlacatl Indian of El Salvador, *Bluteo jamaicensis.* #2983, Spain #432. No. 2984, Abayuba Indian of Uruguay, *Phytotoma rutila.* No. 2985, Guaycaypuro Indian of Venezuela, *Ara arauna.*

1987, Oct. 12 *Perf. 13*
2966 A804 1c multi .25 .25
2967 A804 1c multi .25 .25
2968 A804 1c multi .25 .25
2969 A804 1c multi .25 .25
2970 A804 1c multi .25 .25
a. Strip of 5, Nos. 2966-2970 1.00 1.00
2971 A804 5c multi .40 .25
2972 A804 5c multi .40 .25
2973 A804 5c multi .40 .25
2974 A804 5c multi .40 .25
2975 A804 5c multi .40 .25
a. Strip of 5, Nos. 2971-2975 2.00 1.00
2976 A804 10c multi .65 .25
2977 A804 10c multi .65 .25
2978 A804 10c multi .65 .25
2979 A804 10c multi .65 .25
2980 A804 10c multi .65 .25
a. Strip of 5, Nos. 2976-2980 3.25 1.00
2981 A804 20c multi 1.00 .40
2982 A804 20c multi 1.00 .40
2983 A804 20c multi 1.00 .40
2984 A804 20c multi 1.00 .40
2985 A804 20c multi 1.00 .40
a. Strip of 5, Nos. 2981-2985 5.00 2.00
Nos. 2966-2985 (20) 11.50 5.75

Discovery of America, 500th anniv. (in 1992). *Vultur* is spelled incorrectly on No. 2969.

October Revolution, Russia, 70th Anniv. — A830

1987, Nov. 7 *Perf. 12½x12*
2986 A830 30c Soviet spacecraft, Russia No. 379 1.00 .25

Cuban Railway, 150th Anniv. — A831

Stamps on stamps.

1987, Nov. 19 *Perf. 13x12½*

2987 A831 3c No. 453 .25 .25
2988 A831 5c No. 1061 .25 .25
2989 A831 10c No. 2010 .25 .25
2990 A831 20c No. 2011 .55 .25
2991 A831 35c No. 2360 1.00 .30
2992 A831 40c No. 2361 1.25 .40
Nos. 2987-2992 (6) 3.55 1.70

Souvenir Sheet

Perf. 13x13½

2993 A831 1p No. 355 4.75 2.25

No. 2993 contains 40x32mm one stamp.

An imperf. sheet containing Nos. 2987-2992 exists, inscribed to promote the 17th Pan American Railway Congress. Value, $7.

San Alejandro Art School, 170th Anniv. — A832

Paintings: 1c, *Landscape,* by Domingo Ramos. 2c, *Portrait of Rodriguez Morey,* by Eugenio Gonzalez Olivera. 3c, *Landscape with Malangas and Palm Trees,* by Valentin Sanz Carta. 5c, *Wagons,* by Eduardo Morales. 10c, *Portrait of Elena Herrera,* by Armando Menocal, vert. 30c, *Rape of Dejanira,* by Miguel Melero, vert. 50c, *The Card Player,* by Leopoldo Romanach.

1988, Jan. 12 *Perf. 13x12½, 12½x13*

2994 A832 1c multi .25 .25
2995 A832 2c multi .25 .25
2995A A832 3c multi .25 .25
2996 A832 5c multi .25 .25
2997 A832 10c multi .30 .25
2998 A832 30c multi .85 .25
2999 A832 50c multi 1.50 .50
Nos. 2994-2999 (7) 3.65 2.00

Poisonous Mushrooms A833

Designs: 1c, Boletus satanas. 2c, Amanita citrina. 3c, Tylopilus felleus. 5c, Paxillus involutus. 10c, Inocybe patouillardii. 30c, Amanita muscaria. 50c, Hypholoma fasciculare.

1988, Feb. 15 *Perf. 13*

3000 A833 1c multicolored .25 .25
3001 A833 2c multicolored .25 .25
3002 A833 3c multicolored .25 .25
3003 A833 5c multicolored .25 .25
3004 A833 10c multicolored .55 .25
3005 A833 30c multicolored 1.50 .55
3006 A833 50c multicolored 2.40 1.00
Nos. 3000-3006 (7) 5.45 2.80

Radio Rebelde, 30th Anniv. — A834

1988, Feb. 24 *Perf. 12½x12*

3007 A834 5c multi .30 .25

Monuments A835

1988 **Litho.** *Perf. 13*

3008 A835 5c Mario Munoz, Santiago de Cuba .45 .25
3009 A835 5c Frank Pais Memorial, eternal flame .45 .25

Battle fronts, 30th annivs. Issue dates: No. 3008, Mar. 5. No. 3009, Mar. 11.

Mothers' Day — A836

1988, Mar. 30

3010 A836 1c Red roses .25 .25
3011 A836 2c Pale pink peonies .25 .25
3012 A836 3c Daisies .25 .25
3013 A836 5c Dahlias .25 .25
3014 A836 13c White roses .30 .25
3015 A836 35c Carnations .90 .25
3016 A836 40c Pink roses 1.10 .30
Nos. 3010-3016 (7) 3.30 1.80

Cosmonauts' Day — A837

1988, Apr. 12

3017 A837 2c *Gorizont* .25 .25
3018 A837 3c *Mir-Kvant* space link .25 .25
3019 A837 4c *Signo 3* .25 .25
3020 A837 5c Mars, space probe .25 .25
3021 A837 10c *Phobos* .30 .25
3022 A837 30c *Vega* .85 .25
3023 A837 50c Spacecraft 1.50 .50
Nos. 3017-3023 (7) 3.65 2.00

Souvenir Sheet

Perf. 13½x13

3024 A837 1p Spacecraft, diff. 4.25 2.00

No. 3024 contains one 32x40mm stamp.

Stamp Day Type of 1984

Mural, by R. Rodriguez Radillo (1967) details: 30c, Mail coach, telegraph operator. 50c, Passenger pigeon.

1988, Apr. 24 *Perf. 13x12½*

3025 A733 30c multi 1.10 .40
3026 A733 50c multi 1.90 .50

Institute for Research on Sugar Cane and Byproducts (ICIDCA), 25th Anniv. — A838

1988, May 23 *Perf. 12½x12*

3027 A838 5c multi .40 .25

Cubana Airlines Transatlantic Flights — A839

1988, May 25

3028 A839 2c Madrid, 1948 .25 .25
3029 A839 4c Prague, 1961 .25 .25
3030 A839 5c Berlin, 1972 .25 .25
3031 A839 10c Luanda, 1975 .30 .25
3032 A839 30c Paris, 1983 1.00 .25
3033 A839 50c Moscow, 1987 1.60 .50
Nos. 3028-3033 (6) 3.65 1.75

Souvenir Sheet

FINLANDIA '88 — A840

1988, June 1 *Perf. 12½*

3034 A840 1p Steam packet *Furst Menschikoff* 4.00 2.00

Postal Union of the Americas and Spain (UPAE) Conference on Stamps of the Americas, Havana — A841

1988, June 20 *Perf. 12½x12*

3035 A841 20c multi 1.25 .35

Beetles A842

Designs: 1c, Megasoma elephas fabricus. 3c, Platycoelia flavoscutellata ohaus, vert.. 4c, Plusiotis argenteola bates. 5c, Heterosternus oberthuri ohaus. 10c, Odontotaenius zodiacus truqui. 35c, Chrysophora chrysochlora latreille, vert.. 40c, Phanaeus leander waterhouse.

1988, June 30 *Perf. 13*

3036 A842 1c multicolored .25 .25
3037 A842 3c multicolored .25 .25
3038 A842 4c multicolored .25 .25
3039 A842 5c multicolored .25 .25
3040 A842 10c multicolored .40 .25
3041 A842 35c multicolored 1.25 .30
3042 A842 40c multicolored 1.60 .50
Nos. 3036-3042 (7) 4.25 2.05

Jose Raul Capablanca (1888-1942), Chess Champion — A843

1988, July 15 *Perf. 12½x13, 13x12½*

3043 A843 30c Chessmen, vert. .65 .30
3044 A843 40c J. Corzo, Capablanca .90 .30
3045 A843 50c Lasker, Capablanca .95 .40
3046 A843 1p Winning configuration, 1921, vert. 2.40 .90
3047 A843 3p Portrait by E. Valderrama, vert. 7.25 2.40
3048 A843 5p Chessmen, Capablanca 13.00 4.50
Nos. 3043-3048 (6) 25.15 8.80

Souvenir Sheets

3049 Sheet of 2 1.60 .80
a. A843 30c No. 464, vert. .60 .40
b. like No. 3043, size: 32x40mm .60 .40
3050 Sheet of 2 2.10 1.05
a. A843 40c No. 465 .70 .40
b. like No. 3044, size: 40x32mm .70 .40
3051 Sheet of 2 3.00 1.50
a. A843 50c No. C44 .75 .50
b. like No. 3045, size: 40x32mm .75 .50
3052 Sheet of 2 5.50 2.75
a. A843 1p No. 464, vert. 2.10 1.00
b. like No. 3046, size: 32x40mm 2.10 1.00
3053 Sheet of 2 16.00 8.00
a. A843 3p No. C46, vert. 6.25 3.00
b. like No. 3047, size: 32x40mm 6.25 3.00
3054 Sheet of 2 27.50 13.50
a. A843 5p No. C45, vert. 10.50 5.00
b. like No. 3048, size: 32x40mm 10.50 5.00
Nos. 3049-3054 (6) 55.70 27.60

Attack on Moncada Barracks, 35th Anniv. A844

1988, July 26 *Perf. 13*

3055 A844 5c blk, yel ocher & red .30 .25

Souvenir Sheet

PRAGA '88 — A845

1988, Aug. 26 *Perf. 12½*

3056 A845 1p Czechoslovakia #45 4.00 2.00

Czechoslovakian postage stamps, 70th anniv.

Revolutionary Invasion Force, 30th Anniv. — A846

1988, Aug. 31 *Perf. 12½x12*

3057 A846 5c multi .30 .25

World Marxist Review, 30th Anniv. A847

1988, Sept. 1 *Perf. 13*
3058 A847 30c multi 1.25 .35

Locomotives — A848

1988, Sept. 19 *Perf. 12½x13*
3059 A848 20c Stephenson's *Rocket*, 1837 .50 .25
3060 A848 30c Miller, US, 1839 .95 .45
3061 A848 50c *La Junta* 2.00 .90
3062 A848 1p J.G. Brill trolley, US, 1922 3.50 1.25
3063 A848 2p TEM 4K, USSR, c. 1960 6.75 3.00
3064 A848 5p CAP 9 electric, c. 1988 15.00 8.00
Nos. 3059-3064 (6) 28.70 13.85

Latin American History Type of 1986

Natl. arms & patriots: No. 3065, San Martin, Argentina. No. 3066, M.A. Padilla, Bolivia. No. 3067, #390 & discovery of America 500th anniv. emblem. No. 3068, Tiradentes, Brazil. No. 3069, O'Higgins, Chile. No. 3070, A. Narino, Colombia. No. 3071, Marti, Cuba. No. 3072, #391 & emblem. No. 3073, Duarte, Dominican Republic. No. 3074, Sucre, Ecuador. No. 3075, M.J. Arce, El Salvador. No. 3076, Dessalines, Haiti. No. 3077, #C36 & emblem. No. 3078, Hidalgo, Mexico. No. 3079, J.D. Estrada, Nicaragua. No. 3080, Diaz, Paraguay. No. 3081, F. Bolognesi, Peru. No. 3082, #C37 & emblem. No. 3083, Artigas, Uruguay. No. 3084, Bolivar, Venezuela.

1988, Oct. 12 *Perf. 13*
3065 A804 1c multi .25 .25
3066 A804 1c multi .25 .25
3067 A804 1c multi .25 .25
3068 A804 1c multi .25 .25
3069 A804 1c multi .25 .25
a. Strip of 5, Nos. 3065-3069 1.00 .50
3070 A804 5c multi .25 .25
3071 A804 5c multi .25 .25
3072 A804 5c multi .25 .25
3073 A804 5c multi .25 .25
3074 A804 5c multi .25 .25
a. Strip of 5, Nos. 3070-3074 1.00 .50
3075 A804 10c multi .25 .25
3076 A804 10c multi .25 .25
3077 A804 10c multi .25 .25
3078 A804 10c multi .25 .25
3079 A804 10c multi .25 .25
a. Strip of 5, Nos. 3075-3079 1.50 .75
3080 A804 20c multi .45 .25
3081 A804 20c multi .45 .25
3082 A804 20c multi .45 .25
3083 A804 20c multi .45 .25
3084 A804 20c multi .45 .25
a. Strip of 5, Nos. 3080-3084 2.50 1.25
b. Sheet of 20, Nos. 3065-3084 7.50 7.50
Nos. 3065-3084 (20) 6.00 5.00

Discovery of America, 500th anniv. (in 1992).

Havana Museum, 20th Anniv. — A849

Design: Captain-General's Palace and Maces of Municipal Havana.

1988, Oct. 16 Litho. *Perf. 12½x12*
3085 A849 5c multi + label .40 .25

Anniversaries — A850

1988, Oct. 28 *Perf. 13*
3086 A850 5c *Swan Lake* .60 .25
3087 A850 5c Theater in 1838 and 1988 .60 .25
a. Pair, Nos. 3086-3087 1.25 .40

Natl. Ballet, 40th anniv. (No. 3086); Grand Theater of Havana, 150th anniv. (No. 3087).

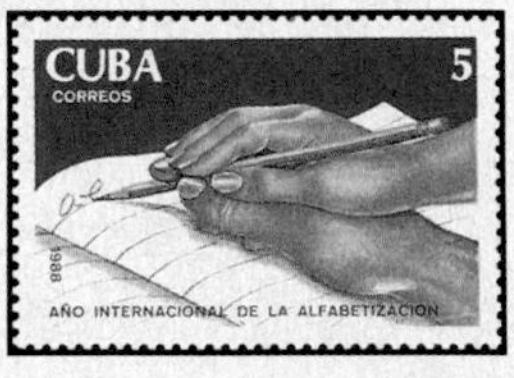

Intl. Literacy Year A851

1988, Dec. 5
3088 A851 5c multi .30 .25

UN Declaration of Human Rights, 40th Anniv. — A851a

1988, Dec. 10
3088A A851a 30c multi 1.25 .35

Battle of Santa Clara, 30th Anniv. — A852

1988, Dec. 28 *Perf. 13x12½*
3089 A852 30c Monument, Che Guevara Plaza 1.25 .35

30th Anniv. of the Revolution — A853

1989, Jan. 1 *Perf. 13*
3090 A853 5c multi .25 .25
3091 A853 20c multi .65 .25
3092 A853 30c multi .85 .25
3093 A853 50c multi 1.75 .50
Nos. 3090-3093 (4) 3.50 1.25

Edible Mushrooms — A854

Designs: 2c, Pleurotus levis. 3c, Pleurotus floridanus. 5c, Amanita caesarea. 10c, Lentinus cubensis. 40c, Pleurotus ostreatus (brown). 50c, Pleurotus ostreatus (yellow)

1989, Jan. 10
3094 A854 2c multicolored .25 .25
3095 A854 3c multicolored .25 .25
3096 A854 5c multicolored .25 .25
3097 A854 10c multicolored .45 .25
3098 A854 40c multicolored 1.60 .40
3099 A854 50c multicolored 1.75 .50
Nos. 3094-3099 (6) 4.55 1.90

2c, 3c, 5c, 40c, 50c, vert.

Souvenir Sheet

INDIA '89 — A855

1989, Jan. 20
3100 A855 1p Indian River Post, 1858 4.00 2.00

Central Organization of Cuban Trade Unions (CTC), 50th Anniv. — A856

1989, Jan. 28 *Perf. 12½*
3101 A856 5c No. 2477, CTC emblem .30 .25

Butterflies A857

Designs: 1c, Metamorpho dido. 3c, Callithea saphhira. 5c, Papilio zagreus. 10c, Mynes sestia. 30c, Papilio dardanus. 50c, Catagranma sorana.

1989, Feb. 15
3102 A857 1c multicolored .25 .25
3103 A857 3c multicolored .25 .25
3104 A857 5c multicolored .25 .25
3105 A857 10c multicolored .30 .25
3106 A857 30c multicolored 1.40 .30
3107 A857 50c multicolored 2.50 .65
Nos. 3102-3107 (6) 4.95 1.95

1990 World Cup Soccer Championships, Italy — A858

Various athletes.

1989, Mar. 15 *Perf. 13*
3108 A858 1c multi .25 .25
3109 A858 3c multi, diff. .25 .25
3110 A858 5c multi, diff. .25 .25
3111 A858 10c multi, diff. .25 .25
3112 A858 30c multi, diff. 1.25 .25
3113 A858 50c multi, diff. 2.10 .40
Nos. 3108-3113 (6) 4.35 1.65

Souvenir Sheet

Perf. 12½

3114 A858 1p multi, diff., horiz. 4.00 2.00

No. 3114 contains one 40x32mm stamp.

Natl. Revolutionary Police (PNR), 30th Anniv. — A859

1989, Mar. 23 *Perf. 13*
3115 A859 5c multi .30 .25

Cosmonauts' Day — A860

Spacecraft and rocket mail covers: 1c, *Zodiac* and cover, Australia 1934. 3c, Lighthouse and cover, India, 1934. 5c, Cover, England, 1934. 10c, *Icarus* and cover, The Netherlands, 1935. 40c, *La Douce France* and cover, France, 1935. 50c, Rocket mail cover, Cuba, 1939.

1989, Apr. 12
3116 A860 1c multi .25 .25
3117 A860 3c multi .25 .25
3118 A860 5c multi .25 .25
3119 A860 10c multi .25 .25
3120 A860 40c multi 1.10 .40
3121 A860 50c multi 1.40 .55
Nos. 3116-3121 (6) 3.50 1.95

Stamp Day Type of 1984

Details of mural by R. Rodriguez Radillo (1967): 30c, Mail coach, Satellite dish. 50c, Galleon, longboats, train, passenger pigeon, horses.

1989, Apr. 24 Litho. *Perf. 13x12½*
3122 A733 30c multi .65 .30
3123 A733 50c multi 4.75 2.00

Casa de Las Americas, 30th Anniv. A861

1989, Apr. 28 *Perf. 12½x13*
3124 A861 5c multi .30 .25

Souvenir Sheet

BULGARIA '89 — A862

1989, May 1 *Perf. 12½*
3125 A862 1p Bulgaria No. 346 4.50 2.25

58th FIP Congress and 101st anniv. of Bulgarian Railways.

Cuban Postal Code A863

1989, May 5 ***Perf. 13***

3126	A863	5c multi	.30	.25

Mothers' Day — A864

Perfume bottles and flowers.

1989, May 10

3127	A864	1c Habano, tobacco	.25	.25
3128	A864	3c Violeta, violets	.25	.25
3129	A864	5c Mariposa, mariposa	.25	.25
3130	A864	13c Coral Negro, roses	.35	.25
3131	A864	30c Ala Alonso, jasmine	1.00	.30
3132	A864	50c D'Man, lemon blossoms	1.75	.70
		Nos. 3127-3132 (6)	3.85	2.00

Agrarian Reform Law, 30th Anniv. — A865

1989, May 17 ***Perf. 12x12½***

3133	A865	5c multi	.30	.25

Council for Mutual Economic Assistance (CAME), 40th Anniv. A866

1989, June 1 **Litho.** ***Perf. 12½x13***

3134	A866	30c multi	1.25	.25

13th World Communist Youth and Student Festival, Pyongyang — A867

1989, July 1 **Litho.** ***Perf. 12½***

3135	A867	30c multi	1.25	.25

Souvenir Sheet

Rouget de Lisle Singing La Marseillaise, by Pils — A868

1989, July 7 ***Perf. 13***

3136	A868	1p multi	4.00	2.00

PHILEXFRANCE '89, French revolution bicent. and Cuban revolution 30th anniv.

BRASILIANA '89 — A869

Exotic birds: 1c, Ramphastos toco. 3c, Agamia agami. 5c, Eudocimus ruber. 10c, Psophia leucoptera. 35c, Harpia harpyja. 50c, Cephalopterus ornatus.

1989, July 28 **Litho.** ***Perf. 12½***

3137	A869	1c multicolored	.25	.25
3138	A869	3c multicolored	.25	.25
3139	A869	5c multicolored	.25	.25
3140	A869	10c multicolored	.40	.25
3141	A869	35c multicolored	1.50	.50
3142	A869	50c multicolored	2.00	.70
		Nos. 3137-3142 (6)	4.65	2.20

Warships A870

1989, Sept. 29 **Litho.** ***Perf. 12½***

3143	A870	1c *El Fenix*	.25	.25
3144	A870	3c *Triunfo*	.25	.25
3145	A870	5c *El Rayo*	.25	.25
3146	A870	10c *San Carlos*	.30	.25
3147	A870	30c *San Jose*	1.25	.40
3148	A870	50c *San Genaro*	1.90	.70
		Nos. 3143-3148 (6)	4.20	2.10

America Issue — A871

UPAE emblem and pre-Columbian art: 5p, Stone carving, Indians in dugout canoe. 20p, Petroglyph, Indian drawing on stone wall.

1989, Oct. 12 ***Perf. 12½x12***

3149	A871	5c multi	.25	.25
3150	A871	20c multi	.80	.40

Latin American History — A872

Writers and orchids: No. 3151, Domingo Sarmiento (1811-1888), Argentine educator, and *Govenia utriculata.* No. 3152, Joaquim Maria Machado de Assis (1839-1908), Brazilian novelist, and *Laelia grandis.* No. 3153, Salvador No. 69 and discovery of America anniv. emblem. No. 3154, Jorge Isaacs (1837-1895), Colombian novelist, and *Cattleya trianae.* No. 3155, Alejo Carpentier, Cuban writer, and *Cochleanthes discolor.* No. 3156, Pablo Neruda (1904-1973), Chilean poet, and *Oxalis adenophylla.* No. 3157, Pedro Urena, Dominican writer, and *Epidendrum fragrans.* No. 3158, Salvador No. 86 and anniv. emblem. No. 3159, Juan Montalvo (1832-1889), Ecuadorian satirist, and *Miltonia vexillaria.* No. 3160, Miguel Asturias (1899-1974), Guatemalan writer awarded the 1966 Lenin Peace Prize and 1967 Nobel Prize for literature, and *Odontoglossum rossii.* No. 3161, Jose C. del Valle, Honduran writer, and *Laelia anceps.* No. 3162, Alfonso Reyes (1889-1959), Mexican poet, and *Laelia anceps alba.* No. 3163, Salvador No. 87 and anniv. emblem. No. 3164, Ruben Dario (1867-1917), Nicaraguan poet, and *Brassavola acaulis.* No. 3165, Belisario Porras (1856-1942), president of Panama, and *Pescatorea celina.* No. 3166, Ricardo Palma (1833-1919), Peruvian writer, and *Coryanthes leucocorys.* No. 3167, Eugenio Maria de Hostos (1839-1903), Puerto Rican writer, and *Guzmania berteroniana.* No. 3168, Salvador No. 88 and anniv. emblem. No. 3169, Jose E. Rodo (1872-1917), Uruguayan philosopher, essayist, and *Cypella hebertii.* No. 3170, Romulo Gallegos, Venezuelan writer, and *Cattleya mossiae.*

1989, Oct. 27 **Litho.** ***Perf. 13***

3151	A872	1c multicolored	.25	.25
3152	A872	1c multicolored	.25	.25
3153	A872	1c multicolored	.25	.25
3154	A872	1c multicolored	.25	.25
3155	A872	1c multicolored	.25	.25
a.		Strip of 5, Nos. 3151-3155	1.00	.50
3156	A872	5c multicolored	.25	.25
3157	A872	5c multicolored	.25	.25
3158	A872	5c multicolored	.25	.25
3159	A872	5c multicolored	.25	.25
3160	A872	5c multicolored	.25	.25
a.		Strip of 5, Nos. 3156-3160	1.00	.50
3161	A872	10c multicolored	.35	.25
3162	A872	10c multicolored	.35	.25
3163	A872	10c multicolored	.35	.25
3164	A872	10c multicolored	.35	.25
3165	A872	10c multicolored	.35	.25
a.		Strip of 5, Nos. 3161-3165	2.00	1.00
3166	A872	20c multicolored	.55	.25
3167	A872	20c multicolored	.55	.25
3168	A872	20c multicolored	.55	.25
3169	A872	20c multicolored	.55	.25
3170	A872	20c multicolored	.55	.25
a.		Strip of 5, Nos. 3166-3170	3.00	1.50
b.		Sheet of 20, #3151-3170	8.00	8.00
		Nos. 3151-3170 (20)	7.00	5.00

Discovery of America 500th anniv. (in 1992).

Disappearance of Camilo Cienfuegos, 30th Anniv. — A873

1989, Oct. 28

3171	A873	5c multicolored	.30	.25

Founding of the City of Trinidad, 475th Anniv. A874

1989, Nov. 6 ***Perf. 12½x13***

3172	A874	5c multicolored	.30	.25

Paintings in the Natl. Museum — A875

Designs: 1c, *Familiar Scene,* by Antoine Faivre. 2c, *Flowers,* by Emile Jean Horace Vernet (1789-1863). 5c, *The Judgement of Paris,* by Charles Le Brun (1619-1690). 20c, *Outskirts of Nice,* by Eugene Louis Boudin (1824-1898). 30c, *Portrait of Sarah Bernhardt,* by G.J.V. Clairin. 50c, *Fishermen in Port,* by C.J. Vernet.

Perf. 12½, 12½x13 (30p)

1989, Nov. 20 **Litho.**

Size of 30p: 36x46mm

3173	A875	1c multicolored	.25	.25
3174	A875	2c multicolored	.25	.25
3175	A875	5c multicolored	.25	.25
3176	A875	20c multicolored	.85	.25
3177	A875	30c multicolored	1.10	.25
3178	A875	50c multicolored	2.25	.55
		Nos. 3173-3178 (6)	4.95	1.80

11th Pan-American Games, Havana, 1991 — A876

1989, Dec. 15 **Litho.** ***Perf. 12½***

3179	A876	5c Cycling	.25	.25
3180	A876	5c Fencing	.25	.25
3181	A876	5c Water polo	.25	.25
3182	A876	5c Shooting	.25	.25
3183	A876	5c Archery	.25	.25
3184	A876	20c Tennis, vert.	.65	.25
3185	A876	30c Swimming, vert.	1.10	.25
3186	A876	35c Diving, vert.	1.40	.30
3187	A876	40c Field hockey	1.50	.30
3188	A876	50c Basketball, vert.	2.25	.65
		Nos. 3179-3188 (10)	8.15	3.00

Jose Marti's *Golden Age,* Cent. — A877

1989, Dec. 20 ***Perf. 13***

3189	A877	5c scar, light blue & blk	.40	.25

Cuban Postal Museum, 25th Anniv. — A878

1990, Jan. 2 ***Perf. 13x12½***

3190 A878 5c *Almendares* .25 .25
3191 A878 30c Mail train 2.50 .80

Speleological Soc., 50th Anniv. — A879

1990, Jan. 15 ***Perf. 12½***

3192 A879 30c multicolored 2.00 .35

1990 World Cup Soccer Championships, Italy — A880

Various Italian architecture and athletes: No. 3193a, Dribbling (in red and blue). No. 3193b, Heading (in red and green). No. 3193c, Kicking (in green). 10c, Goalie catching ball. 30c, Dribbling, diff. 50c, Kicking, diff. 1p, Goalie catching ball, diff.

1990, Jan. 30 **Litho.** ***Perf. 12½***

3193 Strip of 3 .50 .25
a.-c. A880 5c any single .25 .25
3194 A880 10c multicolored .25 .25
3195 A880 30c multicolored 1.25 .30
3196 A880 50c multicolored 2.10 .55
a. Sheet of 6, #3193a-3193c, 3194-3196 + 3 labels 4.25 2.10
Nos. 3193-3196 (4) 4.10 1.35

Souvenir Sheet

3197 A880 1p multicolored 3.50 1.75

No. 3193 has a continuous design picturing The Colosseum.

1992 Summer Olympics, Barcelona — A881

1990, Feb. 20 **Litho.** ***Perf. 12½***

3198 A881 1c Baseball .25 .25
3199 A881 4c Running .25 .25
3200 A881 5c Basketball .25 .25
3201 A881 10c Women's volleyball .45 .25
3202 A881 30c Wrestling 1.10 .30
3203 A881 50c Boxing 2.00 .65
Nos. 3198-3203 (6) 4.30 1.95

Souvenir Sheet

3204 A881 1p High jump 4.00 2.00

Nos. 3198-3201 and 3203 are vert. No. 3204 contains one 40x32mm stamp.

75th Universal Esperanto Congress — A882

1990, Mar. 7

3205 A882 30c Tower of Babel 1.25 .35

No. 3205 printed se-tenant with inscribed label publicizing the congress.

Souvenir Sheet

1992 Winter Olympics, Albertville — A883

1990, Mar. 30 **Litho.** ***Perf. 13***

3206 A883 1p multicolored 4.50 2.25

Cosmonauts' Day — A884

Spacecraft and rocket mail covers: 1c, Austria, 1932. 2c, Germany, 1933. 3c, Netherlands, 1934. 10c, Belgium, 1935. 30c, Yugoslavia, 1935. 50c, United States, 1936.

1990, Apr. 12 ***Perf. 12½***

3207 A884 1c multicolored .25 .25
3208 A884 2c multicolored .25 .25
3209 A884 3c multicolored .25 .25
3210 A884 10c multicolored .25 .25
3211 A884 30c multicolored 1.10 .25
3212 A884 50c multicolored 2.00 .55
Nos. 3207-3212 (6) 4.10 1.80

Stamp Day Type of 1984

Details of mural by R. Rodriguez Radillo (1967): 30c, Train station. 50c, Jet aircraft in flight.

1990, Apr. 24 ***Perf. 13x12½***

3213 A733 30c multicolored 2.40 .75
3214 A733 50c multicolored 1.40 .45

Labor Day, Cent. A885

1990, Apr. 30 ***Perf. 13***

3215 A885 5c multicolored .40 .25

Souvenir Sheet

Great Britain No. 1 on Cover — A886

1990, May 3

3216 A886 1p multicolored 4.00 2.00

Stamp World London '90, Penny Black 150th anniv.

Penny Black, 150th Anniv. A887

Portraits of Sir Rowland Hill and stamps of Great Britain.

1990, May 6 **Litho.** ***Perf. 12½x12***

3217 A887 2c No. 1 .25 .25
3218 A887 3c No. 2 .25 .25
3219 A887 5c Type A5 .25 .25
3220 A887 10c No. 5 .25 .25
3221 A887 30c First day postmark 1.25 .25
3222 A887 50c 5 #1 on Mulready envelope 2.25 .60
Nos. 3217-3222 (6) 4.50 1.85

Celia Sanchez Manduley (1920-1980) — A888

1990, May 9 ***Perf. 12½x13***

3223 A888 5c multicolored .50 .25

Ho Chi Minh (1890-1969), Vietnamese Communist Party Leader — A889

1990, May 19 ***Perf. 12½***

3224 A889 50c multicolored 1.40 .45

Oceanography Institute, 25th Anniv. — A890

Designs: 5c, Specimen analysis and *Lachnolaimus maximus*. 30c, Research ship, fish, coral reef. 50c, Specimen collection and *Panulirus argus*.

1990, June 18 **Litho.** ***Perf. 12½***

3225 A890 5c multicolored .25 .25
3226 A890 30c multicolored 1.00 .25
3227 A890 50c multicolored 1.60 .40
Nos. 3225-3227 (3) 2.85 .90

5th Latin American Botanical Conference A891

Designs: 3c, Banara minutiflora. 5c, Oplonia nannophylla. 10c, Jacquinia brunnescens. 30c, Rondeletia brachycarpa. 50c, Rondeletia odorata.

1990, June 25 **Litho.** ***Perf. 12½***

3228 A891 3c multicolored .25 .25
3229 A891 5c multicolored .25 .25
3230 A891 10c multicolored .50 .25
3231 A891 30c multicolored 1.60 .25
3232 A891 50c multicolored 2.40 .60
Nos. 3228-3232 (5) 5.00 1.60

Tourism A892

1990, June 30

3233 A892 5c Wind surfing .25 .25
3234 A892 10c Spear fishing .35 .25
3235 A892 30c Deep sea fishing 1.00 .25
3236 A892 40c Hunting 1.60 .55
Nos. 3233-3236 (4) 3.20 1.30

Nos. 3233, 3236 vert.

Art Treasures A893

5c, "La Flauta Del Dios Pan." 20c, "Un Pastor." 50c, "Ganimedes." 1p, "Venus Anadiomena."

1990, July 20

3237 A893 5c multicolored .25 .25
3238 A893 20c multicolored .60 .25
3239 A893 50c multicolored 1.60 .40
3240 A893 1p multicolored 2.50 .85
a. Sheet of 4, #3237-3240 5.00 5.00
Nos. 3237-3240 (4) 4.95 1.75

Birds A894

Designs: 2c, Podiceps cristatus. 3c, Gallirallus australis. 5c, Nestor notabilis. 10c, Xenicus longipes. 30c, Cracticus torquatus. 50c, Prosthemadera novaeseelandiae.
1p, Kiwi.

1990, Aug. 24 **Litho.** ***Perf. 13***

3241 A894 2c multicolored .25 .25
3242 A894 3c multicolored .25 .25
3243 A894 5c multicolored .25 .25
3244 A894 10c multicolored .50 .25
3245 A894 30c multicolored 1.50 .35
3246 A894 50c multicolored 2.40 .65
Nos. 3241-3246 (6) 5.15 2.00

Souvenir Sheet

3247 A894 1p multicolored 4.50 2.25

New Zealand '90. No. 3247 contains one 39x31mm stamp.

8th UN Congress on Crime Prevention A895

1990, Aug. 27 **Litho.** ***Perf. 12½***

3248 A895 50c blue, silver & red 1.75 .45

Discovery of America, 500th Anniv. (in 1992) — A896

1990, Oct. 12 Litho. *Perf. 12½*

3249	A896	5c	Ship, shore	.25	.25
3250	A896	20c	Columbus, village	1.00	.35

Cuban Television, 40th Anniv. — A897

1990, Oct. 12 Litho. *Perf. 13*

3251	A897	5c	multicolored	.35	.25

Nationalization of Railroads, 30th Anniv. — A898

1990, Oct. 13 *Perf. 13x12½*

3252	A898	50c	multicolored	2.40	.75

Latin American History Type of 1986

Latin American stamps or flags and costumes: No. 3253, Argentina. No. 3254, Bolivia. No. 3255, Argentina No. 91. No. 3256, Colombia. No. 3257, Costa Rica. No. 3258, Cuba. No. 3259, Chile. No. 3260, Dominican Republic No. 110. No. 3261, Ecuador. No. 3262, El Salvador. No. 3263, Guatemala. No. 3264, Mexico. No. 3265, Puerto Rico No. 133. No. 3266, Nicaragua. No. 3267, Panama. No. 3268, Paraguay. No. 3269, Peru. No. 3270, El Salvador No. 103. No. 3271, Puerto Rico. No. 3272, Venezuela.

1990, Oct. 27 *Perf. 12½*

3253	A804	1c	multicolored	.25	.25
3254	A804	1c	multicolored	.25	.25
3255	A804	1c	multicolored	.25	.25
3256	A804	1c	multicolored	.25	.25
3257	A804	1c	multicolored	.25	.25
a.			Strip of 5, Nos. 3253-3257	1.00	.50
3258	A804	5c	multicolored	.25	.25
3259	A804	5c	multicolored	.25	.25
3260	A804	5c	multicolored	.25	.25
3261	A804	5c	multicolored	.25	.25
3262	A804	5c	multicolored	.25	.25
a.			Strip of 5, Nos. 3258-3262	1.00	.50
3263	A804	10c	multicolored	.30	.25
3264	A804	10c	multicolored	.30	.25
3265	A804	10c	multicolored	.30	.25
3266	A804	10c	multicolored	.30	.25
3267	A804	10c	multicolored	.30	.25
a.			Strip of 5, Nos. 3263-3267	1.50	.75
3268	A804	20c	multicolored	.85	.25
3269	A804	20c	multicolored	.85	.25
3270	A804	20c	multicolored	.85	.25
3271	A804	20c	multicolored	.85	.25
3272	A804	20c	multicolored	.85	.25
a.			Strip of 5, Nos. 3268-3272	4.50	2.25
b.			Sheet of 20, #3253-3272	5.00	5.00
			Nos. 3253-3272 (20)	8.25	5.00

Discovery of America, 500th anniv. (in 1992).

11th Jai Alai World Championships A899

1990, Nov. 14 Litho. *Perf. 12½*

3273	A899	30c	multicolored	1.25	.40

No. 3273 printed with se-tenant label.

11th Pan American Games, Havana — A900

1990, Nov. 15 Litho. *Perf. 12½*

3274	A900	5c	Judo	.25	.25
3275	A900	5c	Sailing	.25	.25
3276	A900	5c	Kayak	.25	.25
3277	A900	5c	Rowing	.25	.25
3278	A900	5c	Equestrian	.25	.25
3279	A900	10c	Table tennis	.30	.25
3280	A900	20c	Men's gymnastics, vert.	.60	.25
3281	A900	30c	Baseball, vert.	.90	.25
3282	A900	35c	Team handball, vert.	1.10	.35
3283	A900	50c	Soccer, vert.	1.60	.70
			Nos. 3274-3283 (10)	5.75	3.05

See Nos. 3311-3320.

A901

1990, Nov. 20 Litho. *Perf. 13*

3284	A901	5c	Boxing	.25	.25
3285	A901	30c	Baseball	1.10	.25
3286	A901	50c	Volleyball	1.90	.50
			Nos. 3284-3286 (3)	3.25	1.00

16th Central American and Caribbean Games, Mexico.

Butterflies A902

Designs: 2c, Chioides marmorosa. 3c, Composia fidelissima. 5c, Danaus plexippus. 10c, Hypolimnas misippus. 30c, Hypna iphigenia. 50c, Hemiargus ammon

1991, Jan. 25 Litho. *Perf. 12½*

3287	A902	2c	multicolored	.25	.25
3288	A902	3c	multicolored	.25	.25
3289	A902	5c	multicolored	.35	.25
3290	A902	10c	multicolored	.50	.25
3291	A902	30c	multicolored	1.40	.25
3292	A902	50c	multicolored	2.25	.50
			Nos. 3287-3292 (6)	5.00	1.75

Jose Luis Guerra Aguiar (1914-1990), Director of Postal Museum — A903

1991, Feb. 17 Litho. *Perf. 12½*

3293	A903	5c	multicolored	.45	.25

A904

1991, Feb. 20

3294	A904	1c	Long jump	.25	.25
3295	A904	2c	Javelin	.25	.25
3296	A904	3c	Field hockey	.25	.25
3297	A904	5c	Weight lifting	.25	.25
3298	A904	40c	Cycling	1.25	.35
3299	A904	50c	Gymnastics	1.75	.50
			Nos. 3294-3299 (6)	4.00	1.85

Souvenir Sheet

3300	A904	1p	Torchbearer	3.50	1.75

1992 Summer Olympics, Barcelona.

A905

1st Man in Space, 30th anniv.: 5c, Yuri Gagarin. No. 3302, Cosmonaut Y. Romanenko. No. 3303, Cosmonaut A. Tamayo Mendez. No. 3304, Mir space station. No. 3305, Mir space station, docked Soyuz, earth. 50c, Soviet space shuttle Buran.

1991, Apr. 12 Litho. *Perf. 13*

3301	A905	5c	multicolored	.25	.25
3302	A905	10c	multicolored	.25	.25
3303	A905	10c	multicolored	.25	.25
a.			Pair, #3302-3303	.40	.25
3304	A905	30c	multicolored	1.00	.25
3305	A905	30c	multicolored	1.00	.25
a.			Pair, #3304-3305	2.00	1.00
3306	A905	50c	multicolored	1.60	.50
a.			Sheet of 6, #3301-3306	4.50	—
			Nos. 3301-3306 (6)	4.35	1.75

Proclamation of the Socialist Revolution, 30th Anniv. — A906

Design: 50c, Ship, jet on fire.

1991, Apr. 19 *Perf. 12½*

3307	A906	5c	multicolored	.25	.25
3308	A906	50c	multicolored	1.60	.80

Bay of Pigs invasion, 30th anniv., No. 3308.

Stamp Day A907

Details from mural by R. Rodriguez Radillo: 30c, Rocket lift-off. 50c, Dish antenna, horiz.

1991, Apr. 24 *Perf. 12½x13, 13x12½*

3309	A907	30c	multicolored	1.00	.30
3310	A907	50c	multicolored	1.75	.40

11th Pan American Games Type of 1990

1991, May 15 Litho. *Perf. 12½*

3311	A900	5c	Volleyball	.25	.25
3312	A900	5c	Rhythmic gymnastics	.25	.25
3313	A900	5c	Synchronized swimming	.25	.25
3314	A900	5c	Weight lifting	.25	.25
3315	A900	5c	Baseball	.25	.25
3316	A900	10c	Bowling	.25	.25
3317	A900	20c	Boxing	.55	.25
3318	A900	30c	Running	.85	.25
3319	A900	35c	Wrestling	1.10	.30
3320	A900	50c	Karate	1.50	.50
			Nos. 3311-3320 (10)	5.50	2.80

Nos. 3311-3315 & 3317 are vert.

Airships A908

Designs: 5c, First ellipsoidal, 1784, J.B.M. Meusnier. 10c, First with steam engine, 1852, H. Giffard. 20c, First with gas engine, 1872, P. Haenlein. 30c, First with gasoline engine, 1896, H. Wolfert. 50c, First rigid aluminum, 1897, D. Schwarz. 1p, LZ-129 Hindenburg, 1936, F. von Zeppelin.

1991, July 1 Litho. *Perf. 13*

3321	A908	5c	multicolored	.25	.25
3322	A908	10c	multicolored	.35	.25
3323	A908	20c	multicolored	.70	.30
3324	A908	30c	multicolored	.90	.50
3325	A908	50c	multicolored	1.60	.95
3326	A908	1p	multicolored	3.25	1.60
			Nos. 3321-3326 (6)	7.05	3.85

Espamer '91, Buenos Aires, Argentina.

Simon Bolivar A909

1991, June 22 Litho. *Perf. 12½x13*

3327	A909	50c	multicolored	2.00	.60

Amphictyonic Cong. of Panama, 165th anniv.

Birds
A910

Designs: 45c, Melanerpes superciliaris. 50c, Myadestes elisabeth. 2p, Priotelus temnurus. 4p, Tiaris canora. 5p, Campephilus principalis. 10p, Amazona leucocephala, horiz. 16.45p, Mellisuga helenae, horiz.

1991, July 15 *Perf. 12½x13, 13x12½*

3328	A910	45c multicolored	1.25	.40
3329	A910	50c multicolored	1.50	.50
3330	A910	2p multicolored	5.25	2.00
3331	A910	4p multicolored	10.00	3.50
3332	A910	5p multicolored	12.50	4.25
3333	A910	10p multicolored	25.00	6.50
3334	A910	16.45p multicolored	40.00	13.00
		Nos. 3328-3334 (7)	95.50	30.15

Tourism — A911

Designs: No. 3335, Varadero Beach, vert. No. 3336, Cayo Largo, vert. No. 3337, Artillerymen at fortress San Carlos de la Cabana. No. 3338, Tres Reyes del Morro Castle.

1991, July 30

3335	A911	20c multicolored	.60	.25
3336	A911	20c multicolored	.60	.25
3337	A911	30c multicolored	1.00	.30
3338	A911	30c multicolored	1.00	.30
		Nos. 3335-3338 (4)	3.20	1.10

Panamfilex '91 — A912

11th Pan American Games venues: 5c, Pan American Stadium. 20c, Swimming venue. 30c, Multisports center. 50c, Velodrome. 1p, Havana City Coliseum and Sports Center.

1991, Aug. 4 **Litho.** *Perf. 12½*

3339	A912	5c multicolored	.25	.25
3340	A912	20c multicolored	.60	.30
3341	A912	30c multicolored	.80	.50
3342	A912	50c multicolored	1.50	.90
		Nos. 3339-3342 (4)	3.15	1.95

Souvenir Sheet

3343	A912	1p multicolored	3.50	1.75

No. 3343 contains one 40x32mm stamp.

Paintings
A913

5c, Kataoka Dengoemon Takafusa, by Utagawa Kuniyoshi. 10c, Evening Walk, by Hosoda Eishi. 20c, Courtesans, by Torii Kiyonaga. 30c, Conversation, by Utamaro. 50c, Bridge at Inari-bashi, by Hiroshige. 1p, On the Terrace, by Kiyonaga.

1991, Sept. 9 **Litho.** *Perf. 12½x13*

3344	A913	5c multicolored	.25	.25
3345	A913	10c multicolored	.35	.25
3346	A913	20c multicolored	.70	.30
3347	A913	30c multicolored	.90	.40
3348	A913	50c multicolored	1.60	.75
3349	A913	1p multicolored	3.25	1.75
		Nos. 3344-3349 (6)	7.05	3.70

Phila Nippon '91, Tokyo.

Souvenir Sheet

1992 Winter Olympics, Albertville — A914

1991, Sept. 25 **Litho.** *Perf. 12½*

3350	A914	1p multicolored	3.50	1.75

Cuban Communist Party, 4th Congress
A915

1991, Oct. 10

3351	A915	5c shown	.25	.25
3352	A915	50c Congress symbol	1.75	.50

Discovery of America, 500th Anniv. (in 1992) — A916

Designs: 5c, Columbus, Vicente and Martin Pinzon. 20c, Santa Maria, Nina and Pinta.

1991, Oct. 12

3353	A916	5c multicolored	.25	.25
3354	A916	20c multicolored	1.25	.25

Jose Marti
A917

1991, Oct. 15 *Perf. 13x12½*

3355	A917	50c multicolored	2.00	.40

Publication of "Simple Verses," cent.

Latin American History
A918

Stamps or musicians and instruments: No. 3356, Julian Aguirre, Argentina, charango. No. 3357, Eduardo Caba, Bolivia, antara. No. 3358, Chile #2. No. 3359, Heitor Villalobos, Brazil, resonator trumpet. No. 3360, Guillermo Uribe-Holguin, Colombia, drum. No. 3361, Miguel Failde, Cuba, claves. No. 3362, Enrique Soro, Chile, drum. No. 3363, Chile #57. No. 3364, Segundo L. Moreno, Ecuador, xylophone. No. 3365, Ricardo Castillo, Guatemala, marimba. No. 3366, Carlos Chavez, Mexico, guitar. No. 3367, Luis A. Delgadillo, Nicaragua, maracas. No. 3368, Chile #69. No. 3369, Alfredo De Saint-Malo, Panama, mejorana. No. 3370, Jose Asuncion Flores, Paraguay, harp. No. 3371, Daniel Alomia, Peru, flute. No. 3372, Juan Morell y Campos, Puerto Rico, cuatro. No. 3373, Chile #72. No. 3374, Eduardo Farini, Uruguay, drums. No. 3375, Juan V. Lecuna, Venezuela, cuatro, diff.

1991, Oct. 27 *Perf. 13*

3356	A918	1c multicolored	.25	.25
3357	A918	1c multicolored	.25	.25
3358	A918	1c multicolored	.25	.25
3359	A918	1c multicolored	.25	.25
3360	A918	1c multicolored	.25	.25
a.		Strip of 5, #3356-3360	1.00	.50
3361	A918	5c multicolored	.25	.25
3362	A918	5c multicolored	.25	.25
3363	A918	5c multicolored	.25	.25
3364	A918	5c multicolored	.25	.25
3365	A918	5c multicolored	.25	.25
a.		Strip of 5, #3361-3365	1.00	.50
3366	A918	10c multicolored	.40	.25
3367	A918	10c multicolored	.40	.25
3368	A918	10c multicolored	.40	.25
3369	A918	10c multicolored	.40	.25
3370	A918	10c multicolored	.40	.25
a.		Strip of 5, #3366-3370	2.00	1.00
3371	A918	20c multicolored	.80	.25
3372	A918	20c multicolored	.80	.25
3373	A918	20c multicolored	.80	.25
3374	A918	20c multicolored	.80	.25
3375	A918	20c multicolored	.80	.25
a.		Strip of 5, #3371-3375	4.00	2.00
b.		Sheet of 20, #3356-3375	8.00	—
		Nos. 3356-3375 (20)	8.50	5.00

Discovery of America, 500th anniv. in 1992 (Nos. 3358, 3363, 3368, 3373).

Jose Marti Pioneers Organization, 1st Congress
A919

1991, Oct. 29

3376	A919	5c multicolored	.35	.25

Toussaint L'Ouverture (1743-1803) — A920

1991, Nov. 20 *Perf. 12½x13*

3377	A920	50c multicolored	2.00	.40

Haitian Revolution, Bicent.

Cuban Revolutionary Armed Forces, 35th Anniv. — A921

Design: 50c, Landing of the Granma expedition, 35th anniv., vert.

Perf. 12½x12, 12x12½

1991, Dec. 2 **Litho.**

3378	A921	5c multicolored	.25	.25
3379	A921	50c multicolored	1.75	.40

Gen. Ignacio Agramonte (1841-1873), Revolutionary Hero — A922

1991, Dec. 23 **Litho.** *Perf. 12½x13*

3380	A922	5c multicolored	.30	.25

Souvenir Sheet

1992 Winter Olympics, Albertville — A923

1992, Jan. 15 *Perf. 13*

3381	A923	1p multicolored	3.50	1.75

1992 Summer Olympics, Barcelona — A924

1992, Jan. 20 **Litho.** *Perf. 13x12½*

3382	A924	3c Table tennis	.25	.25
3383	A924	5c Handball	.25	.25
3384	A924	10c Shooting	.30	.25
3385	A924	20c Long jump, vert.	.60	.25
3386	A924	35c Judo	1.25	.40
3387	A924	50c Fencing	1.60	.40
		Nos. 3382-3387 (6)	4.25	1.80

Souvenir Sheet

Perf. 12½

3388	A924	100c Rhythmic gymnastics, vert.	3.50	1.75

No. 3388 contains one 32x40mm stamp.

Environmental Protection A925

1992, Feb. 10 ***Perf. 13***

3389	A925	5c	Terraced hillsides	.25	.25
3390	A925	20c	Save the whales	.60	.25
3391	A925	35c	Ozone hole over Antarctica	1.25	.40
3392	A925	40c	Nuclear disarmament	1.40	.40
			Nos. 3389-3392 (4)	3.50	1.30

Dogs A926

1992, Mar. 10 **Litho.** ***Perf. 13x12½***

3393	A926	5c	Boxer	.25	.25
3394	A926	10c	Great dane	.25	.25
3395	A926	20c	German shepherd	.65	.25
3396	A926	30c	Various breeds	1.10	.25
3397	A926	35c	Doberman pinscher	1.10	.30
3398	A926	40c	Fox terrier	1.40	.40
3399	A926	50c	Poodle	1.75	.50
			Nos. 3393-3399 (7)	6.50	2.20

Souvenir Sheet

Perf. 12½

3400	A926	1p	Bichon frise, vert.	4.00	2.00

No. 3400 contains one 32x40mm stamp.

Nos. 3401-3404 will not be assigned.

Union of Young Communists, 30th Anniv. — A928

1992, Apr. 4 **Litho.** ***Perf. 13***

3405	A928	5c	multicolored	.35	.25

Cuban Revolutionary Party, Cent. — A929

1992, Apr. 10 ***Perf. 13x12½***

3406	A929	5c	multicolored	.25	.25
3407	A929	50c	multicolored	1.75	.50

Discovery of America, 500th Anniv. — A930

1992, Apr. 14 ***Perf. 12½***

3408	A930	5c	Landing at Bariay	.25	.25
3409	A930	20c	Landing at San Salvador	.70	.25

Granada '92 Philatelic Exhibition — A931

Views of the Alhambra, Granada: 5c, With Sierra Nevada mountains beyond. 10c, Arches at sunset. 20c, Interior architecture. 30c, Patio, fountain of lions. 35c, Bedroom. 50c, View of Albaicin.

1992, Apr. 17 ***Perf. 13***

3410	A931	5c	multicolored	.25	.25
3411	A931	10c	multicolored	.25	.25
3412	A931	20c	multicolored	.75	.25
3413	A931	30c	multicolored	1.25	.25
3414	A931	35c	multicolored	1.50	.40
3415	A931	50c	multicolored	2.10	.50
			Nos. 3410-3415 (6)	6.10	1.90

La Bodeguita Del Medio Restaurant, 50th Anniv. — A932

1992, Apr. 26

3416	A932	50c	multicolored	1.75	.50

Fish A933

Designs: 5c, Holacanthus isabelita. 10c, Equetus lanceolatus. 20c, Acanthurus coeruleus. 30c, Abudefduf saxatilis. 50c, Microspathodon chrysurus.

1992, May 15 **Litho.** ***Perf. 12½***

3417	A933	5c	multicolored	.25	.25
3418	A933	10c	multicolored	.25	.25
3419	A933	20c	multicolored	.65	.25
3420	A933	30c	multicolored	1.10	.25
3421	A933	50c	multicolored	1.90	.50
			Nos. 3417-3421 (5)	4.15	1.50

Orchids — A934

1992, June 20 **Litho.** ***Perf. 12½***

3422	A934	3c	Cattleya hibrida	.25	.25
3423	A934	5c	Phalaenopsis	.25	.25
3424	A934	10c	Cattleyopsis lindenii	.25	.25
3425	A934	30c	Bletia purpurea	1.00	.25
3426	A934	35c	Oncidium luridum	1.10	.30
3427	A934	40c	Vanda hibrida	1.40	.40
			Nos. 3422-3427 (6)	4.25	1.70

Soroa Orchid Garden, 40th anniv.

Mellisuga Helenae — A935

1992, July 7 ***Perf. 13***

3428	A935	5c	Sitting on nest	.40	.25
3429	A935	10c	Wings extended	.60	.30
3430	A935	20c	Sitting on branch	1.25	.40
3431	A935	30c	In flight	2.00	1.00
			Nos. 3428-3431 (4)	4.25	1.95

World Wildlife Fund.

Tourism A936

1992, July 15 **Litho.** ***Perf. 12½***

3432	A936	10c	Guardalavaca Beach	.35	.25
3433	A936	20c	Bucanero Hotel	.60	.25
3434	A936	30c	Sailing ship, Havana	1.10	.40
3435	A936	50c	Varadero Beach	1.50	.50
			Nos. 3432-3435 (4)	3.55	1.40

Souvenir Sheet

Expo '92, Seville — A937

1992, July 27 **Litho.** ***Perf. 13***

3436	A937	1.50p	multicolored	4.50	2.25

1992 Summer Olympics, Barcelona A938

Athlete, sport: 5c, Eligio (Kid Chocolate) Sardinas, boxing. 35c, Ramon Fonst, fencing. 40c, Sergio Martinez, cycling. 50c, Martin Dihigo, baseball.

1992, July 20 **Litho.** ***Perf. 12½x13***

3437	A938	5c	multicolored	.25	.25
3438	A938	35c	multicolored	1.10	.30
3439	A938	40c	multicolored	1.25	.40
3440	A938	50c	multicolored	1.75	.60
			Nos. 3437-3440 (4)	4.35	1.55

Olymphilex '92.

Discovery of America, 500th Anniv. — A939

5c, Alvarez Cabral. 10c, Alonso Pinzon. 20c, Alonso de Ojeda. 30c, Amerigo Vespucci. 35c, Prince Henry the Navigator. 40c, Bartolomeu Dias. 1p, Columbus' fleet.

1992, Sept. 18 **Litho.** ***Perf. 12½***

3441	A939	5c	multicolored	.25	.25
3442	A939	10c	multicolored	.30	.25
3443	A939	20c	multicolored	.70	.25
3444	A939	30c	multicolored	1.10	.30
3445	A939	35c	multicolored	1.25	.30
3446	A939	40c	multicolored	1.50	.40
			Nos. 3441-3446 (6)	5.10	1.75

Souvenir Sheet

Perf. 13

3447	A939	1p	multi, vert.	3.25	1.60

Genoa '92. No. 3447 contains one 32x40mm stamp.

1992 Summer Olympics Medal Winners, Barcelona — A940

Medals and participants in events: No. 3448, Bronze, 4x100-meter relay, women's high jump, and women's 800-meter. No. 3449, Gold, high jump, women's discus. No. 3450, Silver, 4x400-meter relay, bronze, discus. No. 3451, Gold and silver, boxing. No. 3452, Gold, baseball. No. 3453, Gold, women's volleyball. No. 3454, Gold, silver, and bronze, judo. No. 3455, Gold and bronze, Greco-Roman and freestyle wrestling. No. 3456, Silver and bronze, fencing, silver, weight lifting.

1992, Sept. 24 **Litho.** ***Perf. 13***

3448	A940	5c	multicolored	.25	.25
3449	A940	5c	multicolored	.25	.25
3450	A940	5c	multicolored	.25	.25
3451	A940	20c	multicolored	.65	.25
3452	A940	20c	multicolored	.65	.25
3453	A940	20c	multicolored	.65	.25
3454	A940	50c	multicolored	1.75	.50
3455	A940	50c	multicolored	1.75	.50
3456	A940	50c	multicolored	1.75	.50
			Nos. 3448-3456 (9)	7.95	3.00

6th World Track and Field Cup, Havana A941

1992, Sept. 24 **Litho.** ***Perf. 13***

3457	A941	5c	High jump	.25	.25
3458	A941	20c	Javelin	.65	.25
3459	A941	30c	Hammer throw	1.00	.25
3460	A941	40c	Long jump, vert.	1.40	.40
3461	A941	50c	Hurdles, vert.	1.75	.50
			Nos. 3457-3461 (5)	5.05	1.65

Souvenir Sheet

3462	A941	1p	Women's relay	3.50	1.75

No. 3462 contains one 40x32mm stamp.

Latin American History Type of 1986

Discovery of America: No. 3463a, Columbus, Queen Isabella. b, Columbus at Rabida Monastery. c, Columbus, pointing up, outlining his plan. d, Columbus, with scroll, before Salamanca Council. e, Departure of Columbus' fleet from Palos.

No. 3464a, Three ships stopping at Canary Islands. b, Columbus speaking to crew. c, Land sighted, Oct. 12, 1492. d, Columbus landing in New World. e, Meeting natives.

No. 3465a, Grounding of Santa Maria at Hispanola. b, Arrival of Nina at Palos. c, Columbus welcomed in Barcelona. d, Columbus describes his voyage to Ferdinand and Isabella. e, Departure of fleet from Cadiz on second voyage.

No. 3466a, King and Queen welcome Columbus. b, Fleet on Columbus' third voyage. c, Columbus deported from Hispanola to Spain as prisoner. d, Columbus on ship, fourth voyage. e, Death of Columbus, May 20, 1506 in Valladolid.

1992, Oct. 3 *Perf. 13*

3463 A804 1c Strip of 5, #a.-e. .65 .30
3464 A804 5c Strip of 5, #a.-e. .65 .30
3465 A804 10c Strip of 5, #a.-e. 1.25 .75
3466 A804 20c Strip of 5, #a.-e. 4.00 1.50
Nos. 3463-3466 (4) 6.55 2.85

Jose Maria Chacon y Calvo (1892-1969), Historian A942

1992, Oct. 29 *Perf. 13*

3467 A942 30c multicolored 1.00 .40

Churches A943

Designs: 5c, Basilica of Nuestra Senora de la Caridad del Cobre. 20c, Santa Maria del Rosario Church. 30c, Espiritu Santo Church. 50c, Santo Angel Custodio Church.

1992, Nov. 10 **Litho.** *Perf. 12½*

3468 A943 5c multicolored .25 .25
3469 A943 20c multicolored .75 .25
3470 A943 30c multicolored 1.00 .25
3471 A943 50c multicolored 2.00 .30
Nos. 3468-3471 (4) 4.00 1.05

Development of the Diesel Engine — A944

1993, Jan. 20 **Litho.** *Perf. 12½*

3472 A944 5c Truck .25 .25
3473 A944 10c Automobile .25 .25
3474 A944 30c Tugboat .55 .40
3475 A944 40c Locomotive 2.50 1.25
3476 A944 50c Tractor 1.00 .65
Nos. 3472-3476 (5) 4.55 2.80

Souvenir Sheet

3477 A944 1p Rudolf Diesel 3.50 1.75

No. 3477 contains one 40x32mm stamp. Rudolf Diesel, 80th anniv. of death (No. 3477).

Davis Cup Tennis Competition — A945

Various tennis players in action.

Perf. 12x12½, 12½x12

1993, Feb. 10 **Litho.**

3478 A945 5c multi, vert. .25 .25
3479 A945 20c multi, vert. .60 .25
3480 A945 30c multi, vert. .90 .40
3481 A945 35c multicolored 1.00 .50
3482 A945 40c multicolored 1.25 .60
Nos. 3478-3482 (5) 4.00 2.00

Souvenir Sheet

Perf. 12½

3483 A945 1p multicolored 2.50 1.25

No. 3483 contains one 40x32mm stamp.

Scientists A946

Designs: 3c, Pierre-Paul-Emile Roux (1853-1933), bacteriologist. 5c, Carlos J. Finlay (1833-1915), suggested mosquito as carrier of yellow fever. 10c, Ivan Petrovich Pavlov (1849-1936), physiologist, investigated conditioned reflexes. 20c, Louis Pasteur, chemist, developer of pasteurization. 30c, Santiago Ramon y Cajal (1852-1934), histologist, isolated the neuron. 35c, Sigmund Freud, psychoanalyst. 40c, Wilhelm Conrad Roentgen, physicist, discoverer of x-ray. 50c, Joseph Lister, surgeon, introduced principle of antisepsis. 1p, Robert Koch, bacteriologist, developer of tuberculin, vert.

1993, Mar. 3 **Litho.** *Perf. 12½*

3484 A946 3c multicolored .25 .25
3485 A946 5c multicolored .25 .25
3486 A946 10c multicolored .25 .25
3487 A946 20c multicolored .55 .25
3488 A946 30c multicolored .80 .40
3489 A946 35c multicolored .90 .50
3490 A946 40c multicolored 1.10 .60
3491 A946 50c multicolored 1.25 .65
Nos. 3484-3491 (8) 5.35 3.15

Souvenir Sheet

3492 A946 1p multicolored 2.75 1.40

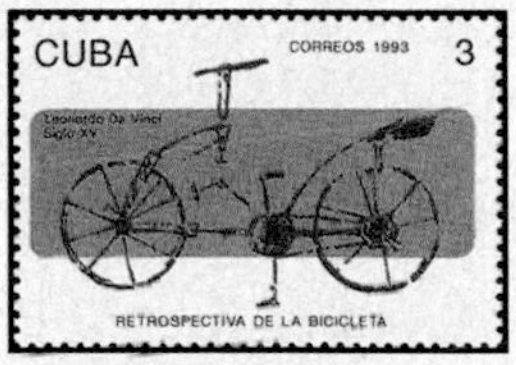

Bicycles — A947

Bicycles designed by: 3c, Leonardo da Vinci, 15th cent. 5c, Karl Von Drais de Sauerbrun, 1813. 10c, Ernest Michaux, 1856. 20c, James Starley, 1869. 30c, Harry Lawson, 1879. 35c, Guaso (Cuba), 1992.

1993, Apr. 14 *Perf. 13*

3493 A947 3c multicolored .25 .25
3494 A947 5c multicolored .25 .25
3495 A947 10c multicolored .45 .25
3496 A947 20c multicolored .90 .25
3497 A947 30c multicolored 1.40 .40
3498 A947 35c multicolored 1.50 .50
Nos. 3493-3498 (6) 4.75 1.90

Cuban Natl. Museum, 80th Anniv. A948

Paintings by Joaquin Sorolla y Bastida (1863-1923): 3c, Child Eating Watermelon, 1920, vert. 5c, Valencian Fisherwomen, 1909. 10c, Regattas. 20c, Contadina, 1889. 40c, Summer, 1904. 50c, Boats on the Ocean, 1908.

1993, May 29 **Litho.** *Perf. 13x12½*

3499 A948 3c multicolored .25 .25

Perf. 12½x13

3500 A948 5c multicolored .30 .25
3501 A948 10c multicolored .35 .25
3502 A948 20c multicolored .65 .25
3503 A948 40c multicolored 1.25 .60
3504 A948 50c multicolored 1.75 .65
Nos. 3499-3504 (6) 4.55 2.25

Water Birds A949

Designs: 3c, Jacana spinosa. 5c, Ardea herodias, vert. 10c, Himantopus mexicanus. 20c, Nycticorax nycticorax. 30c, Grus canadensis, vert. 50c, Aramus guarauna.

Perf. 12½, 13x12½ (5, 30c)

1993, June 15

3505 A949 3c multicolored .25 .25
3506 A949 5c multicolored .25 .25
3507 A949 10c multicolored .40 .25
3508 A949 20c multicolored .80 .25
3509 A949 30c multicolored 1.10 .40
3510 A949 50c multicolored 2.25 .65
Nos. 3505-3510 (6) 5.05 2.05

Brasiliana '93. Nos. 3506, 3510 are 27x44mm.

Anniversaries — A950

No. 3511, Jose Marti, Moncada Barracks. No. 3512, "History Will Absolve Me," declaration of Fidel Castro, Marti. No. 3513, Jose Marti, Rafael M. Mendive, vert. No. 3514, Carlos Manuel de Cespedes, gear wheels.

1993, July 26 **Litho.** *Perf. 13*

3511 A950 5c multicolored .25 .25
3512 A950 5c multicolored .25 .25
3513 A950 5c multicolored .25 .25
3514 A950 5c multicolored .25 .25
Nos. 3511-3514 (4) 1.00 1.00

Attack on Moncada Barracks, 40th anniv. (No. 3511). Declaration of Fidel Castro, 40th anniv. (No. 3512). Birth of Jose Marti, 140th anniv. (No. 3513). Declaration of the Ten Years' War, 125th anniv. (No. 3514).

Flowers from Cienfuegos Botanical Gardens A951

Designs: 3c, Sedum allantoides. 5c, Heliconia caribaea. 10c, Anthurium andraeanum. 20c, Pseudobombax ellipticum. 35c, Ixora coccinea. 50c, Callistemon speciosus.

1993, Aug. 20

3515 A951 3c multicolored .25 .25
3516 A951 5c multicolored .25 .25
3517 A951 10c multicolored .35 .25
3518 A951 20c multicolored .70 .25
3519 A951 35c multicolored 1.10 .50
3520 A951 50c multicolored 1.90 .65
Nos. 3515-3520 (6) 4.55 2.15

Bangkok '93, Intl. Philatelic Exhibition A952

Butterflies: 3c, Battus devillievs. 5c, Anteos maerula. 20c, Ascia monuste evonima. 30c, Junonia coenia. 35c, Anartia jatrophae guantanamo. 50c, Hypolimnas misippus.

1993, Sept. 10 **Litho.** *Perf. 13*

3521 A952 3c multicolored .25 .25
3522 A952 5c multicolored .25 .25
3523 A952 20c multicolored .70 .25
3524 A952 30c multicolored 1.00 .40
3525 A952 35c multicolored 1.10 .40
3526 A952 50c multicolored 1.60 .65
Nos. 3521-3526 (6) 4.90 2.20

Endangered Species A953

1993, Oct. 12 **Litho.** *Perf. 13*

3527 A953 5c Phoenicopterus ruber .25 .25
3528 A953 50c Ajaia ajaja 1.75 .65

Latin American Revolutionaries A954

Flags, map and: No. 3529, Simon Bolivar. No. 3530, Jose Marti. No. 3531, Benito Juarez, Mexican President. No. 3532, Ernesto "Che" Guevara.

1993, Oct. 27 **Litho.** *Perf. 13*

3529 A954 50c multicolored 1.40 .65
3530 A954 50c multicolored 1.40 .65
3531 A954 50c multicolored 1.40 .65
3532 A954 50c multicolored 1.40 .65
a. Block of 4, #3529-3532 7.25 3.50
Nos. 3529-3532 (4) 5.60 2.60

17th Central American and Caribbean Games, Ponce, Puerto Rico — A955

1993, Nov. 10 **Litho.** *Perf. 12½*

3533 A955 5c Swimming .25 .25
3534 A955 10c Pole vault .25 .25
3535 A955 20c Boxing .70 .25
3536 A955 35c Gymnastics, vert. 1.10 .40
3537 A955 50c Baseball, vert. 1.60 .65
Nos. 3533-3537 (5) 3.90 1.80

Souvenir Sheet

3538 A955 1p Basketball 3.75 1.75

No. 3538 contains one 40x32mm stamp.

Mariana Grajales (1808-93), Patriot — A956

1993, Nov. 27 *Perf. 13*

3539 A956 5p multicolored .30 .25

Peter I. Tchaikovsky (1840-93), Composer A957

1993, Nov. 30

3540 A957 5c Portrait .25 .25
3541 A957 20c Swan Lake Ballet .65 .25
3542 A957 30c Statue .90 .40
3543 A957 50c Museum, horiz. 1.25 .65
Nos. 3540-3543 (4) 3.05 1.55

A958

1994, Jan. 1 Litho. *Perf. 13*

3544 A958 5c multicolored .30 .25

35th anniv. of the Revolution.

A959

Various soccer players.

1994, Jan. 1

3545 A959 5c multicolored .25 .25
3546 A959 20c multicolored .60 .25
3547 A959 30c multicolored .85 .40
3548 A959 35c multicolored .95 .40
3549 A959 40c multicolored 1.25 .50
3550 A959 50c multicolored 1.40 .65
Nos. 3545-3550 (6) 5.30 2.45

Souvenir Sheet

3551 A959 1p multicolored 3.00 1.50

1994 World Cup Soccer Championships, US. No. 3551 contains one 40x31mm stamp.

Cats A960

1994, Feb. 15 Litho. *Perf. 12½*

3552 A960 5c Blue Persian .25 .25
3553 A960 10c Havana .25 .25
3554 A960 20c Maine coon .70 .25
3555 A960 30c Blue British shorthair 1.00 .40
3556 A960 35c Bicolor Persian 1.10 .40
3557 A960 50c Gold chinchilla 1.60 .65
Nos. 3552-3557 (6) 4.90 2.20

Souvenir Sheet
Perf. 13

3558 A960 1p Abyssinian, vert. 4.00 2.00

No. 3558 contains one 30x38mm stamp.

Medicinal Plants — A961

Designs: 5c, Salvia officinalis. 10c, Aloe barbadensis. 20c, Helianthus annuus. 30c, Matricaria chamomilla. 40c, Calendula officinalis. 50c, Tilia platyphyllos.

1994, Mar. 30 Litho. *Perf. 12½*

3559 A961 5c multicolored .25 .25
3560 A961 10c multicolored .25 .25
3561 A961 20c multicolored .65 .25
3562 A961 30c multicolored .90 .40
3563 A961 40c multicolored 1.25 .50
3564 A961 50c multicolored 1.50 .65
Nos. 3559-3564 (6) 4.80 2.30

Carriages — A962

Designs: 5c, Public coach, 1860. 10c, Coach of Ferdinand VII, Maria Louisa. 30c, Louis XV-style coach. 35c, Elizabeth II gala day's coach. 40c, Catalina II's summer coach. 50c, Volanta habanera.

1994, Apr. 20 *Perf. 12½x12*

3565 A962 5c multicolored .25 .25
3566 A962 10c multicolored .25 .25
3567 A962 30c multicolored 1.00 .40
3568 A962 35c multicolored 1.10 .40
3569 A962 40c multicolored 1.40 .50
3570 A962 50c multicolored 1.60 .65
Nos. 3565-3570 (6) 5.60 2.45

No. 3570 is 68x37mm.

Aquaculture — A963

Designs: 5c, Crassostrea rhizophorae. 20c, Cardisoma guanhumi. 30c, Tilapia melanopleura. 35c, Hippospongia lachne. 40c, Panulirus argus. 50c, Cyprinus carpio.

1994, May 10 Litho. *Perf. 12½*

3571 A963 5c multicolored .35 .25
3572 A963 20c multicolored .60 .25
3573 A963 30c multicolored .85 .40
3574 A963 35c multicolored 1.00 .40
3575 A963 40c multicolored 1.25 .50
3576 A963 50c multicolored 1.50 .65
Nos. 3571-3576 (6) 5.55 2.45

Intl. Olympic Committee, Cent. — A964

1994, June 23 Litho. *Perf. 12½*

3577 A964 5c Flag, runners .25 .25
3578 A964 30c Flag, world map .85 .40
3579 A964 50c Flag, Olympic flame 1.50 .65
Nos. 3577-3579 (3) 2.60 1.30

Scientists A965

Designs: 5c, Michael Faraday (1791-1867), physicist. 10c, Marie Curie (1867-1934), physical chemist. 20c, Pierre Curie (1859-1906), chemist. 30c, Albert Einstein (1879-1955), physicist, mathematician. 40c, Max Planck (1858-1947), theoretical physicist. 50c, Otto Hahn (1879-1968), physical chemist.

1994, July 20 Litho. *Perf. 12½*

3580 A965 5c multicolored .25 .25
3581 A965 10c multicolored .25 .25
3582 A965 20c multicolored .70 .25
3583 A965 30c multicolored 1.00 .40
3584 A965 40c multicolored 1.40 .50
3585 A965 50c multicolored 1.75 .65
Nos. 3580-3585 (6) 5.35 2.30

Cactus Flowers A966

Designs: 5c, Opuntia dillenii. 10c, Opuntia millspaughii, vert. 30c, Leptocereus santamarinae. 35c, Pereskia marcanoi. 40c, Dendrocereus nudiflorus, vert. 50c, Pilocereus robinii.

1994, Aug. 15 Litho. *Perf. 12½*

3586 A966 5c multicolored .25 .25
3587 A966 10c multicolored .30 .25
3588 A966 30c multicolored 1.00 .40
3589 A966 35c multicolored 1.10 .40
3590 A966 40c multicolored 1.50 .50
3591 A966 50c multicolored 1.75 .65
Nos. 3586-3591 (6) 5.90 2.45

Souvenir Sheet

2nd Spanish-Cuban Philatelic Exhibition, Havana — A967

Design: 1p, Cuban postal rocket, #C31.

1994, Sept. 18

3592 A967 1p multicolored 3.00 1.50

Experimental postal rocket flight, 55th anniv.

Dogs A968

1994, Sept. 20

3593 A968 5c Rough collie .25 .25
3594 A968 20c American cocker spaniel .70 .25
3595 A968 30c Dalmatian .95 .40
3596 A968 40c Afghan hound 1.40 .50
3597 A968 50c English cocker spaniel 1.60 .65
Nos. 3593-3597 (5) 4.90 2.05

Cayo Largo Island A969

Fauna: 15c, Carpilius corallinus. 65c, Cyclura nubila, vert. 75c, Pelecanus occidentalis. 1p, Chelonia mydas.

1994, Sept. 30 Litho. *Perf. 12½*

3598 A969 15c multicolored .30 .25
3599 A969 65c multicolored 1.50 .90
3600 A969 75c multicolored 1.75 1.00
3601 A969 1p multicolored 2.50 1.25
Nos. 3598-3601 (4) 6.05 3.40

A970

1994, Oct. 28

3602 A970 15c multicolored .50 .25

Camilo Cienfuegos Gorriaran, revolutionary, 35th anniv. of disappearance.

A971

Fauna of the Caribbean: 10c, Epinephelus flavolimbatus, horiz. No. 3604, Phoenicopterus ruber. No. 3605, Aetobatus narinari. No. 3606, Istiophorus platypterus, horiz. No. 3607, Tursiops truncatus, horiz. No. 3608, Pelecanus occidentalis.

1994, Oct. 30

3603 A971 10c multicolored .30 .25
3604 A971 15c multicolored .30 .25
3605 A971 15c multicolored .30 .25
3606 A971 15c multicolored .30 .25
3607 A971 65c multicolored 1.75 .90
3608 A971 65c multicolored 1.75 .90
Nos. 3603-3608 (6) 4.70 2.80

ICAO, 50th Anniv. A972

1994, Nov. 9

3609 A972 65c multicolored 1.75 .90

Zoological Garden, Havana, 55th Anniv. — A973

1994, Nov. 14 Litho. *Perf. 13*

3610 A973 15c Bronze monument .25 .25
3611 A973 65c Ara chloroptera 1.40 .90
3612 A973 75c Carduelis carduelis 1.60 1.00
Nos. 3610-3612 (3) 3.25 2.15

Cuban Philatelic Federation, 30th Anniv. — A974

1994, Nov. 20

3613 A974 15c multicolored .50 .25

America Issue — A975

Postal transportation: 15c, 18th Cent. Spanish galleon, maritime postal service, vert. 65c, 19th Cent. postal rider, insurgent postal service.

1994, Dec. 12

3614 A975 15c multicolored .25 .25
3615 A975 65c multicolored 1.75 .90

Postal Museum, 30th Anniv. — A976

1995, Jan. 2

3616 A976 15c multicolored .50 .25

Lizards — A977

Designs: 15c, Anolis baracoae. 65c, Sphaerodactylus ramsdeni. 75c, Leiocephalus raviceps. 85c, Sphaerodactylus ruibali. 90c, Anolis ophiolepis. 1p, Sphaerodactylus armasi.

1994, Nov. 30 Litho. ***Perf. 12½***

3617 A977 15c multicolored .30 .25
3618 A977 65c multicolored 1.60 .90
3619 A977 75c multicolored 1.75 1.00
3620 A977 85c multicolored 2.00 1.25
3621 A977 90c multicolored 2.25 1.25
3622 A977 1p multicolored 2.50 1.40
Nos. 3617-3622 (6) 10.40 6.05

Cuban War of Independence, Cent. — A978

1995, Feb. 24 Litho. ***Perf. 12½***

3623 A978 15c Jose Marti, flag .50 .25

Pan American Games, Mar del Plata, Argentina — A979

1995, Mar. 11 Litho. ***Perf. 13***

3624 A979 10c Boxing, vert. .25 .25
3625 A979 15c Weight lifting, vert. .25 .25
3626 A979 65c Volleyball, vert. 1.10 .80
3627 A979 75c Wrestling 1.25 1.00
3628 A979 85c Baseball 1.50 1.00
3629 A979 90c High jump 1.60 1.10
Nos. 3624-3629 (6) 5.95 4.40

National Aquarium, 35th Anniv. — A980

Fish: 10c, Holacanthus cillaris. 15c, Hypoplectrus guttavarius. 65c, Anisotremus virginicus. 75c, Amblycirrhitus pinos. 85c, Pomaacanthus paru. 90c, Acanthurus coeruleus.

1995, Apr. 28 Litho. ***Perf. 13***

3630 A980 10c multicolored .25 .25
3631 A980 15c multicolored .30 .25
3632 A980 65c multicolored 1.40 .70
3633 A980 75c multicolored 1.50 .80
3634 A980 85c multicolored 2.00 1.10
3635 A980 90c multicolored 2.00 1.10
Nos. 3630-3635 (6) 7.45 4.20

FAO, 50th Anniv. A981

1995, Apr. 7 Litho. ***Perf. 13***

3636 A981 75c multicolored 1.40 1.00

First Cuban Postage Stamp, 140th Anniv. — A982

65c, Ornamental letter drop, envelope.

1995. Apr. 24 Litho. ***Perf. 12½***

3637 A982 15c black & blue green .30 .25
3638 A982 65c multicolored 1.40 .75

Jose Marti, Death Cent. A983

Designs: 15c, Marti killed in combat, signature, portrait. 65c, Landing of Marti, Cuban patriots on Playitas beach. 75c, Montecristi Manifesto signed in Domincan Republic, Marti. 85c, Meeting of Marti, Maceo, Gomez at La Mejorana Farm. 90c, Marti's mausoleum, Santiago, Cuba, vert.

1995, May 19 ***Perf. 12½x13, 13x12½***

3639 A983 15c multicolored .25 .25
3640 A983 65c multicolored 1.25 .80
3641 A983 75c multicolored 1.40 1.00
3642 A983 85c multicolored 1.75 1.00
3643 A983 90c multicolored 1.75 1.10
Nos. 3639-3643 (5) 6.40 4.15

Antonio Maceo (1845-96), Revolutionary — A984

1995, June 14 Litho. ***Perf. 12½***

3644 A984 15c multicolored .60 .25

Butterflies — A985

Designs: 10c, Dione vanillae. 15c, Eunica tatila. 65c, Melete salacia. 75c, Greta cubana. 85c, Eurema daira. 90c, Phoebis sennae.

1995, June 20 ***Perf. 12½x13***

3645 A985 10c multicolored .25 .25
3646 A985 15c multicolored .25 .25
3647 A985 65c multicolored 1.25 .80
3648 A985 75c multicolored 1.40 1.00
3649 A985 85c multicolored 1.75 1.00
3650 A985 90c multicolored 1.75 1.10
Nos. 3645-3650 (6) 6.65 4.40

World War II Combat Planes — A986

Designs: 10c, Supermarine "Spitfire," Great Britain. 15c, IL-2, Russia. 65c, Curtiss P-40, US. 75c, Messerschmitt Bf-109, Germany. 85c, Morane-Sauinier 406, France.

1995, July 30 Litho. ***Perf. 12½***

3651 A986 10c multicolored .30 .25
3652 A986 15c multicolored .30 .25
3653 A986 65c multicolored 1.40 .80
3654 A986 75c multicolored 1.60 1.00
3655 A986 85c multicolored 1.90 1.00
Nos. 3651-3655 (5) 5.50 3.30

A987

1995, Aug. 6 Litho. ***Perf. 12½***

3656 A987 15c multicolored .50 .25

Ernesto Lecuona, composer, pianist, birth cent.

A988

Color of Horse or Horses

1995, Aug. 10

3657 A988 10c golden brown, white .40 .25
3658 A988 15c white, horiz. .40 .25
3659 A988 65c dark brown, white 1.75 .80
3660 A988 75c red brown 2.10 1.00
3661 A988 85c tan 2.50 1.00
3662 A988 90c white 2.50 1.10
Nos. 3657-3662 (6) 9.65 4.40

Singapore '95.

Souvenir Sheet

Beijing Intl. Stamp & Coin Expo '95 — A989

1995, Aug. 28 ***Perf. 13***

3663 A989 50c multicolored 1.25 .75

1996 Summer Olympics, Atlanta — A990

1995, Sept. 25 Litho. ***Perf. 13***

3664 A990 10c Wrestling .25 .25
3665 A990 15c Weight lifting .25 .25
3666 A990 65c Women's volleyball 1.10 .80
3667 A990 75c Women's athletics 1.25 1.00
3668 A990 85c Baseball 1.50 1.00
3669 A990 90c Women's judo 1.60 1.10
Nos. 3664-3669 (6) 5.95 4.40

Souvenir Sheet

3670 A990 1p Boxing 3.00 1.50

No. 3670 contains one 30x36mm stamp.

Cuban Sugar Industry, 400th Anniv. A991

Paintings from "Los Ingenios," by Edouard Laplante, 1852: 15c, Steam train, sugar factory. 65c, Sugar factory, tower, bridge.

1995, Oct. 3

3671 A991 15c multicolored 1.75 .35
3672 A991 65c multicolored 1.00 .70

UN, 50th Anniv. A992

1995, Oct. 24 Litho. *Perf. 13*

3673 A992 65c multicolored 1.10 .80

Zoological Gardens, Havana — A993

Designs: 10c, Panthera leo, vert. 15c, Equus grevyi. 65c, Pongo pygmaeus, vert. 75c, Elephas maximus. 85c, Sciurus vulgaris. 90c, Procyon lotor.

1995, Oct. 30 Litho. *Perf. 13*

3674 A993 10c multicolored .25 .25
3675 A993 15c multicolored .30 .25
3676 A993 65c multicolored 1.25 .80
3677 A993 75c multicolored 1.50 1.00
3678 A993 85c multicolored 1.90 1.00
3679 A993 90c multicolored 2.10 1.10
Nos. 3674-3679 (6) 7.30 4.40

UNESCO, 50th Anniv. — A994

UNESCO World Culture and National Heritage sites: 65c, Santa Clara de Asis Convent. 75c, San Francisco de Asis Minor Basilica.

1995, Nov. 4

3680 A994 65c multicolored 1.10 .80
3681 A994 75c multicolored 1.25 1.00

Orchids — A995

Designs: 5c, Epidendrum porpax. 10c, Cyrtopodium punctatum. 15c, Polyrrhiza lindeni. 40c, Bletia patula. 45c, Galeandra beyrichii. 50c, Vanilla dilloniana. 65c, Macradenia lutescens. 75c, Oncidium luridum. 85c, Ionopsis utricularioides.

1995, Nov. 10 *Perf. 12½*

3681A A995 5c multicolored .30 .25
3681B A995 10c multicolored .50 .25
3681C A995 15c multicolored .65 .25
3682 A995 40c multicolored .80 .55
3683 A995 45c multicolored .90 .55
3684 A995 50c multicolored 1.00 .65
3685 A995 65c multicolored 1.25 .80
3686 A995 75c multicolored 1.40 1.00
3687 A995 85c multicolored 1.75 1.00
Nos. 3681A-3687 (9) 8.55 5.30

Issued: 40c-85c, 11/10/95; 5c-15c, 6/28/96.

Motion Pictures, Cent. — A996

1995, Dec. 7 *Perf. 13*

3688 A996 15c Lumiere Brothers .30 .25
3689 A996 15c Marilyn Monroe .30 .25
3690 A996 15c Marlene Dietrich .30 .25
3691 A996 15c Vittorio DeSica .30 .25
3692 A996 15c Charlie Chaplin .30 .25
3693 A996 15c Greta Garbo .30 .25
3694 A996 65c Humphrey Bogart 1.40 .80
3695 A996 75c Montaner 1.60 1.00
3696 A996 85c Cantinflas 1.90 1.00
Nos. 3688-3696 (9) 6.70 4.30

Souvenir Sheet

4th Cuban-Spanish Philatelic Exhibition, Havana — A997

1995, Dec. 11 Litho. *Perf. 13*

3697 A997 1p multicolored 3.00 1.50

America Issue — A998

1995, Dec. 12

3698 A998 15c Centurus superciliaris .35 .25
3699 A998 65c Todus multicolor 1.60 .80

Generals Who Died in 1895 War — A999

Designs: No. 3700, Alfonso Goulet Goulet, Francisco Adolfo Crombet Ballon. No. 3701, Jesus Calvar O, Jose Guillermo Moncada, Tomas Jordan. No. 3702, Francisco Borrero Lavadi, Francisco Inchaustegui Cabrera.

1995, Dec. 20 *Perf. 12½*

3700 A999 15c multicolored .35 .25
3701 A999 15c multicolored .35 .25
3702 A999 15c multicolored .35 .25
a. Strip of 3, #3700-3702 1.10 .90
Nos. 3700-3702 (3) 1.05 .75

See Nos. 3758-3760.

Island of Coco Cay, Jardines del Rey A1000

Bird, scenic view: 10c, Sterna antillarum, aerial view of island. 15c, Eudocimus albus, people on beach. 45c, Spindalis zena, couple on steps of resort complex. 50c, Turdus plumbeus, resort. 65c, Mimus polyglottos, resort. 75c, Phoenicopterus ruber, couple in pool at resort.

1995, Dec. 23

3703 A1000 10c multicolored .25 .25
3704 A1000 15c multicolored .30 .25
3705 A1000 45c multicolored 1.00 .55
3706 A1000 50c multicolored 1.10 .60
3707 A1000 65c multicolored 1.40 .80
3708 A1000 75c multicolored 1.60 1.00
Nos. 3703-3708 (6) 5.65 3.45

Patriots — A1001

Designs: 15c, Carlos M. de Céspedes (1819-74). 65c, José Marti (1853-95). 75c, Antonio Maceo (1845-96). 1.05p, Ignacio Agramonte (1841-73). 2.05p, Máximo Gómez (1836-1905). 3p, Calixto Garcia (1839-98).

1996, Jan. 10

3709 A1001 15c green .25 .25
3710 A1001 65c blue 1.10 .80
3711 A1001 75c carmine 1.25 1.00
3712 A1001 1.05p lilac 1.90 1.40
3713 A1001 2.05p brown 3.75 2.50
3714 A1001 3p light brown 5.25 3.75
Nos. 3709-3714 (6) 13.50 9.70

See Nos. 3755-3757.

Organization of Solidarity of the Peoples of Africa, Asia and Latin America (OSPAAAL), 30th Anniv. — A1002

1996, Jan. 14

3715 A1002 65c multicolored 1.50 .75

Scientists — A1003

10c, Leonardo da Vinci (1452-1519). 15c, Mikhail V. Lomonosov (1711-65), atmospheric scientist. 65c, James Watt (1736-1819), engineer, inventor. 75c, Guglielmo Marconi (1874-1937), physicist. 85c, Charles R. Darwin (1809-82), naturalist.

1996, Jan. 30 Litho. *Perf. 12½*

3716 A1003 10c multicolored .35 .25
3717 A1003 15c multicolored .35 .25
3718 A1003 65c multicolored 1.75 .80
3719 A1003 75c multicolored 2.00 1.00
3720 A1003 85c multicolored 2.25 1.00
Nos. 3716-3720 (5) 6.70 3.30

1996 Summer Olympics, Atlanta — A1004

1996, Feb. 15 Litho. *Perf. 12½*

3721 A1004 10c Athletics, vert. .30 .25
3722 A1004 15c Weight lifting, vert. .30 .25
3723 A1004 65c Judo, vert. 1.40 .80
3724 A1004 75c Wrestling 1.60 1.00
3725 A1004 85c Boxing 1.90 1.00
Nos. 3721-3725 (5) 5.50 3.30

Souvenir Sheet

3726 A1004 1p Baseball, vert. 3.00 1.50

No. 3726 contains one 40x32mm stamp.

Espamer '96, Aviation and Space, Philatelic Exhibition, Seville — A1005

1996, Mar. 4

3727 A1005 15c C-4 Autogiro .25 .25
3728 A1005 65c CASA C-352 1.25 .80
3729 A1005 75c Alcotan C-201 1.60 1.00
3730 A1005 85c CASA C-212 1.75 1.00
Nos. 3727-3730 (4) 4.85 3.05

Juan C. Gundlach (1810-1896), Ornithologist — A1006

Birds: 10c, Ceryle alcyon. 15c, Setophaga ruticilla. 65c, Geothlypis trichas. 75c, Passerina ciris. 85c, Bombycilla cedrorum.
1p, Vireo gundlachi.

1996, Mar. 15 *Perf. 12½*

3731 A1006 10c multicolored .30 .25
3732 A1006 15c multicolored .30 .25
3733 A1006 65c multicolored 1.40 .80
3734 A1006 75c multicolored 1.60 1.00
3735 A1006 85c multicolored 1.90 1.00
Nos. 3731-3735 (5) 5.50 3.30

Souvenir Sheet

3736 A1006 1p multicolored 3.75 1.90

No. 3736 contains one 40x32mm stamp.

Souvenir Sheet

ESPAMER '96, Stamp Exhibition of America and Europe, Seville — A1007

1996, Mar. 14 Litho. *Perf. 12½*

3737 A1007 1p multicolored 3.00 1.50

First Man in Space, 35th Anniv. — A1008

Designs: 15c, Yuri A. Gagarin (1934-68). 65c, Spaceship, map showing orbital route.

1996, Apr. 12 Litho. *Perf. 12½*

3738 A1008 15c multi .25 .25
3739 A1008 65c multi, horiz. 1.10 .80

Bay of Pigs Invasion, 35th Anniv. — A1009

1996, Apr. 19

3740 A1009 15c shown .35 .25
3741 A1009 65c Natl. flags 1.60 .80

Cuban Sailing Ships A1010

Designs: 10c, Bahama. 15c, Santísima Trinidad. 65c, Principe de Asturias. 75c, San Pedro de Alcántara. 85c, Santa Ana.
1p, San Genaro.

1996, May 8 Litho. *Perf. 12½*

3742 A1010 10c multicolored .25 .25
3743 A1010 15c multicolored .30 .25
3744 A1010 65c multicolored 1.40 .80
3745 A1010 75c multicolored 1.60 1.00
3746 A1010 85c multicolored 1.75 1.00
Nos. 3742-3746 (5) 5.30 3.30

Souvenir Sheet

3747 A1010 1p multicolored 2.00 1.00

CAPEX '96. No. 3747 contains one 40x32mm stamp.

Fauna of the Caribbean A1011

Designs: 10c, Todus multicolor. No. 3749, Eulampis jugularis. No. 3750, Aix sponsa. No. 3751, Chaetodon ocellatus. No. 3752, Papilio cresphontes. No. 3753, Hypoplectrus indigo.

1996, June 18 Litho. *Perf. 12½*

3748 A1011 10c multicolored .30 .25
3749 A1011 15c multicolored .30 .25
3750 A1011 15c multicolored .30 .25
3751 A1011 15c multicolored .30 .25
3752 A1011 65c multicolored 1.40 .80
3753 A1011 65c multicolored 1.40 .80
Nos. 3748-3753 (6) 4.00 2.60

Jose M. Maceo Grajales (1849-96), Revolutionary War Leader — A1012

1996, July 5

3754 A1012 15c multicolored .50 .25

Patriot Type of 1996

Designs: 10c. Serafin Sánchez. 85c, Juan Gualberto Gomez. 90c, Quintin Bandera.

1996, July 10

3755 A1001 10c orange .25 .25
3756 A1001 85c olive 1.75 1.00
3757 A1001 90c olive brown 2.00 1.10
Nos. 3755-3757 (3) 4.00 2.35

Generals Who Died in 1895 War Type of 1995

No. 3758, Esteban Tamayo (1843-96), Angel Guerra (1842-96). No. 3759, Juan Fernández Ruz (1821-96), José Maria Aguirre (1843-96), Serafin Sánchez (1846-96). No. 3760, Juan Bruno Zayas (1867-96), Pedro Vargas Sotomayor (1868-96).

1996, July 30

3758 A999 15c multicolored .35 .25
3759 A999 15c multicolored .35 .25
3760 A999 15c multicolored .35 .25
a. Strip of 3, #3758-3760 1.70 .90
Nos. 3758-3760 (3) 1.05 .75

Santiago de Cuba — A1013

Flower, scenic view: 15c, Jacaranda arborea, beach. 65c, Begonia bissei, Fort San Pedro de la Roca. 75c, Byrsonima crassifolia, palm trees, mountains, vert. 85c, Pereskia zinniiflora, church, vert.

Perf. 13x12½, 12½x13

1996, Sept. 27 Litho.

3761 A1013 15c multicolored .30 .25
3762 A1013 65c multicolored 1.40 .80
3763 A1013 75c multicolored 1.60 1.00
3764 A1013 85c multicolored 1.75 1.00
Nos. 3761-3764 (4) 5.05 3.05

Steam Locomotives — A1014

Designs: 10c, Baldwin 0-4-2, 1878. 15c, American 2-6-0, 1904. 65c, Baldwin 4-6-0, 1906. 75c, Rogers 2-4-4, 1914. 90c, Baldwin 2-8-0, 1920.

1996, Sept. 30 *Perf. 12½*

3765 A1014 10c multicolored .30 .25
3766 A1014 15c multicolored .30 .25
3767 A1014 65c multicolored 1.40 .80
3768 A1014 75c multicolored 1.60 .90
3769 A1014 90c multicolored 1.75 1.00
Nos. 3765-3769 (5) 5.35 3.20

Traditional Costumes A1015

America Issue: 15c, Free black couple, 19th cent. 65c, Guayabera couple, 20th cent.

1996, Oct. 12 Litho. *Perf. 12½*

3770 A1015 15c multicolored .35 .25
3771 A1015 65c multicolored 1.60 .80

UNICEF, 50th Anniv. — A1016

1996, Nov. 8 Litho. *Perf. 12½*

3772 A1016 15c multicolored .50 .25

World Chess Championship Won by José Raúl Capablanca, 75th Anniv. — A1017

Designs: 15c, Portrait, chess board. 65c, Portrait, seated at chess board. 75c, Rook with top shaped as world, portrait. 85c, Playing chess as a child. 90c, In championship match, 1921.

1996, Nov. 30 Litho. *Perf. 12½*

3773 A1017 15c multicolored .25 .25
3774 A1017 65c multicolored 1.25 .80
3775 A1017 75c multicolored 1.40 1.00
3776 A1017 85c multicolored 1.60 1.00
3777 A1017 90c multicolored 1.75 1.10
Nos. 3773-3777 (5) 6.25 4.15

Revolutionary Armed Forces and Return of Castro from Mexico, 40th Anniv. — A1018

1996, Dec. 2

3778 A1018 15c Yacht Granma .25 .25
3779 A1018 65c Armed forces 1.60 1.00

Maj. Gen. Antonio Maceo (1845-96) — A1019

Designs: 10c, Monument, Santiago, vert. No. 3781, Portrait, vert. No. 3782, Monument, Duaba. 65c, Detail of painting showing Maceo dying from combat wounds. 75c, Maceo, young man and monument, San Pedro.

1996, Dec. 7

3780 A1019 10c multicolored .25 .25
3781 A1019 15c multicolored .30 .25
3782 A1019 15c multicolored .30 .25
3783 A1019 65c multicolored 1.60 1.10
3784 A1019 75c multicolored 1.90 1.40
Nos. 3780-3784 (5) 4.35 3.25

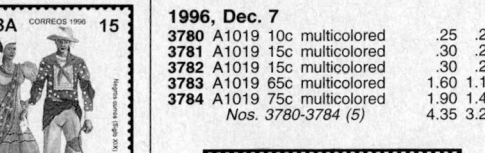

Medals Won at 1996 Summer Olympic Games, Atlanta — A1020

Medal, sport: No. 3785a, Gold, judo. b, Bronze, wrestling.
No. 3786: a, Gold, weight lifting. b, Gold, wrestling. c, Silver, fencing. d, Silver, swimming.
No. 3787: a, Gold, women's volleyball. b, Gold, boxing. c, Silver, women's running. d, Gold, baseball.

1996, Dec. 10

3785 A1020 10c Pair, #a-b + 4 labels .50 .25
3786 A1020 15c Block, #a-d + 2 labels 1.25 .65
3787 A1020 65c Block, #a-d + 2 labels 5.00 2.50
Nos. 3785-3787 (3) 6.75 3.40

New Year 1996 (Year of the Rat) — A1021

1996, Dec. 28 Litho. *Perf. 12½*

3788 A1021 15c multicolored .50 .25

Espamer '98 — A1022

Locomotives: 15c, Minho Douro 0-6-0, Portugal. No. 3790, Vulcan Iron Works 0-4-0, Brazil. No. 3791, Baldwin 2-6-0, Dominican Republic. No. 3792, American Locomotive Co. 2-6-4, Panama. No. 3793, Baldwin 0-4-0, Puerto Rico. No. 3794, Slaughter, Gruning Co. 0-4-0, Spain. No. 3795, Yorkshire Engine Co. 4-4-0, Argentina. No. 3796, 2-6-0 Paraguay. No. 3797, H.K. Porter Co. 2-8-2, Chile. No. 3798, 2-6-0, Mexico.
1p, Baldwin 0-4-2 (1884), Cuba.

1996, Dec. 30

3789 A1022 15c multicolored .30 .25
3790 A1022 65c multicolored 1.50 .85
3791 A1022 65c multicolored 1.50 .85
3792 A1022 65c multicolored 1.50 .85
3793 A1022 65c multicolored 1.50 .85
3794 A1022 65c multicolored 1.50 .85
3795 A1022 75c multicolored 1.75 1.00
3796 A1022 75c multicolored 1.75 1.00
3797 A1022 75c multicolored 1.75 1.00
3798 A1022 75c multicolored 1.75 1.00
Nos. 3789-3798 (10) 14.80 8.50

Souvenir Sheet

3799 A1022 1p multicolored 3.50 1.75

No. 3799 contains one 36x28mm.

Hong Kong '97, Intl. Philatelic Exhibition — A1023

Cats: 10c, Brown-point Siamese, vert. No. 3801, Japanese bobtail. No. 3802, Burmese, vert. No. 3803, Singapore. No. 3804, Korat. 1p, Blue-point Siamese.

1997, Jan. 15 Litho. *Perf. 12½*

3800	A1023	10c	multicolored	.25	.25
3801	A1023	15c	multicolored	.30	.25
3802	A1023	15c	multicolored	.30	.25
3803	A1023	65c	multicolored	1.75	1.00
3804	A1023	75c	multicolored	2.10	1.10
			Nos. 3800-3804 (5)	4.70	2.85

Souvenir Sheet

3805	A1023	1p	multicolored	4.00	2.00

No. 3805 contains one 40x31mm stamp.

Motion Pictures, Cent. A1024

Film scenes from: 15c, "El Romance del Palmar," directed by Ramón Peón. 65c, "Memorias del Subdesarrollo," directed by Tomás Gutiérrez Alea, vert.

1997, Jan. 24 Litho. *Perf. 13*

3806	A1024	15c	multicolored	.30	.25
3807	A1024	65c	multicolored	1.60	1.00

Zoo Animals A1025

Designs: 10c, Camelus dromedarius. No. 3809, Ailuropada melanoleuca. No. 3810, Cerothoterium simun. 75c, Pongo pygmaeus. 90c, Bison bonasus.

1997, Feb. 20 Litho. *Perf. 12½*

3808	A1025	10c	multicolored	.25	.25
3809	A1025	15c	multicolored	.30	.25
3810	A1025	15c	multicolored	.30	.25
3811	A1025	75c	multicolored	1.75	1.00
3812	A1025	90c	multicolored	2.00	1.10
			Nos. 3808-3812 (5)	4.60	2.85

New Year 1997 (Year of the Ox) — A1026

1997, Feb. 22

3813	A1026	15c	multicolored	.50	.25

Attack on the Presidential Palace, 40th Anniv. — A1027

1997, Mar. 13 Litho. *Perf. 12½*

3814	A1027	15c	Menelao Mora Morales	.60	.25

1998 World Cup Soccer Championships, France — A1028

Action scenes: 10c, Three players. No. 3816, Player in green, player in blue & yellow. No. 3817, Player in yellow & black, player in green. 65c, Player in yellow & blue, player in blue and red. 75c, Player in red & blue, player in yellow & black.
1p, Player down.

1997, Mar. 25

3815	A1028	10c	multicolored	.25	.25
3816	A1028	15c	multicolored	.30	.25
3817	A1028	15c	multicolored	.30	.25
3818	A1028	65c	multicolored	1.75	1.00
3819	A1028	75c	multicolored	2.00	1.25
			Nos. 3815-3819 (5)	4.60	3.00

Souvenir Sheet

3820	A1028	1p	multicolored	2.40	1.25

No. 3820 contains one 40x31mm stamp.

Young Communist League (UJC), 35th Anniv. — A1029

1997, Apr. 4

3821	A1029	15c	multicolored	.75	.25

Paddle Steamer Caledonia — A1030

Stamp Day: 15c, Maritime Postal Service, 170th anniv. 65c, Air Postal Service, 70th anniv.

1997, Apr. 24 Litho. *Perf. 12½*

3822	A1030	15c	multicolored	.40	.25
3823	A1030	65c	multicolored	1.60	.95

Death of Generals in War of 1895, 102nd Anniv. — A1031

No. 3824, Adolfo de Castillo, Enrique del Junco Cruz-Muñoz. No. 3825, Alberto Rodríguez Acosta, Mariano Sánchez Vaillant.

1997, May 18 Litho. *Perf. 12½*

3824	A1031	15c	multicolored	.30	.25
3825	A1031	15c	multicolored	.30	.25
a.			Pair, #3824-3825	.65	.30

Gen. Gregorio Luperon, Death Cent. — A1032

1997, May 20

3826	A1032	65c	multicolored	1.60	1.00

Butterflies — A1033

Designs: 10c, Eurema nicippe. No. 3828, Eurema dina. No. 3829, Colobura dirce clementi. 65c, Vanesa atalanta. 85c, Kricogonia castalia.

1997, May 20

3827	A1033	10c	multicolored	.25	.25
3828	A1033	15c	multicolored	.30	.25
3829	A1033	15c	multicolored	.30	.25
3830	A1033	65c	multicolored	1.60	.90
3831	A1033	85c	multicolored	1.90	1.00
			Nos. 3827-3831 (5)	4.35	2.65

Cuban Assoc. of the UN, 50th Anniv. A1034

1997, May 31

3832	A1034	65c	multicolored	1.60	.95

Chinese In Cuba, 150th Anniv. — A1035

1997, May 29 *Perf. 13*

3833	A1035	15c	multicolored	.90	.50

14th World Festival of Youth and Students A1036

Designs: 10c, Dove holding olive twig, rainbow. No. 3835, Children playing on playground equipment, vert. No. 3836, Monument with arms extended. 65c, Maj. Ernesto "Che" Guevara, revolutionary hero. 75c, Monument, diff.

1997, July 28 Litho. *Perf. 12½*

3834	A1036	10c	multicolored	.25	.25
3835	A1036	15c	multicolored	.30	.25
3836	A1036	15c	multicolored	.30	.25
3837	A1036	65c	multicolored	1.60	.95
3838	A1036	75c	multicolored	1.90	1.00
			Nos. 3834-3838 (5)	4.35	2.70

Frank País (1934-57), Revolutionary Hero — A1037

1997, July 30

3839	A1037	15c	multicolored	.50	.25

Seven Wonders of the Ancient World A1038

Designs: 10c, Lighthouse of Alexandria. No. 3841, Pyramids of Egypt. No. 3842, Gardens of Semiramis at Babylon. No. 3843, Colossus at Rhodes. No. 3844, Mausoleum of Halicarnassus. No. 3845, Statue of Zeus at Olympia. 75c, Temple of Artemis at Ephesus.

1997, July 30

3840	A1038	10c	multicolored	.25	.25
3841	A1038	15c	multicolored	.30	.25
3842	A1038	15c	multicolored	.30	.25
3843	A1038	15c	multicolored	.30	.25
3844	A1038	65c	multicolored	1.60	.95
3845	A1038	65c	multicolored	1.60	.95
3846	A1038	75c	multicolored	1.75	1.00
			Nos. 3840-3846 (7)	6.10	3.90

Independence of India, 50th Anniv. — A1039

1997, Aug. 15

3847	A1039	15c	Mahatma Gandhi	.50	.25

Caribbean Birds — A1040

No. 3848, Sicalis flaveola. No. 3849, Eubucco bourcierii. No. 3850, Trogon curucui. No. 3851, Amazona leucocephala. No. 3852, Amazona ochrocephala. No. 3853, Hylocharis eliciae. No. 3854, Carduelis carduelis.

1997, Aug. 15

3848	A1040	15c	multicolored	.30	.25
3849	A1040	15c	multicolored	.30	.25
3850	A1040	15c	multicolored	.30	.25
3851	A1040	15c	multicolored	.30	.25
3852	A1040	65c	multicolored	1.60	1.00
3853	A1040	65c	multicolored	1.60	1.00
3854	A1040	75c	multicolored	1.90	1.10
			Nos. 3848-3854 (7)	6.30	4.10

Famous Composers — A1041

10c, Liszt. No. 3856, Chopin. No. 3857, Bach. No. 3858, Beethoven. 65c, Ignacio Cervantes (1847-1905). 75c, Mozart.

1997, Sept. 15 Litho. *Perf. 12½*

3855 A1041 10c multicolored .50 .25
3856 A1041 15c multicolored .50 .25
3857 A1041 15c multicolored .50 .25
3858 A1041 15c multicolored .50 .25
3859 A1041 65c multicolored 1.75 .95
3860 A1041 75c multicolored 1.90 1.00
Nos. 3855-3860 (6) 5.65 2.95

Tourism in Pinar del Rio — A1042

Bird, scene: 10c, Myadestes elisabeth, Viñales Valley. 15c, Corvus nasicus, Jutia Key. 65c, Dendroica pityophila, Soroa Falls. 75c, Tyrannus cubensis, San Juan River.

1997, Sept. 27 Litho.

3861 A1042 10c multi .40 .25
3862 A1042 15c multi .40 .25
3863 A1042 65c multi, vert. 1.60 .95
3864 A1042 75c multi, vert. 1.75 1.00
Nos. 3861-3864 (4) 4.15 2.45

Caribbean Flowers — A1043

Designs: No. 3865, Hibiscus elatus (majagua). No. 3866, Cordia sebestena (vomitel). No. 3867, Bidens pilosa (romerillo). No. 3868, Catharanthus roseus (vicaria). 65c, Reullia tuberosa (salta perico). 75c, Turnera ulmifolia (marilope).

1997, Sept. 30

3865 A1043 15c multicolored .40 .25
3866 A1043 15c multicolored .40 .25
3867 A1043 15c multicolored .40 .25
3868 A1043 15c multicolored .40 .25
3869 A1043 65c multicolored 1.60 .95
3870 A1043 75c multicolored 1.75 .95
Nos. 3865-3870 (6) 4.95 2.90

Eastern University, 50th Anniv. — A1044

1997, Oct. 1 *Perf. 13*

3871 A1044 15c multicolored .50 .25

Che Guevara (1928-67), 5th Cuban Communist Party Congress A1045

1997, Oct. 8

3872 A1045 15c Flags .40 .25
3873 A1045 15c Text, Guevara 1.60 .95
3874 A1045 75c Portrait of Guevara 1.75 .95
Nos. 3872-3874 (3) 3.75 2.15

America Issue — A1046

1997, Oct. 12 Litho. *Perf. 13*

3875 A1046 15c 19th cent. postman .50 .25
3876 A1046 65c 20th cent. postman 1.60 .85

Hominids — A1047

Designs: 10c, Australopithecus. No. 3878, Pithecanthropus (Java man). No. 3879, Sinanthropus (Peking man). No. 3880, Neanderthal. 65c, Cro-magnon man. 75c, Oberkassel man.

1997, Oct. 30 *Perf. 12½*

3877 A1047 10c multicolored .30 .25
3878 A1047 15c multicolored .50 .25
3879 A1047 15c multicolored .50 .25
3880 A1047 15c multicolored .50 .25
3881 A1047 65c multicolored 1.75 .95
3882 A1047 75c multicolored 1.90 .95
Nos. 3877-3882 (6) 5.45 2.90

October Revolution, 80th Anniv. — A1048

1997, Nov. 7 *Perf. 12½*

3884 A1048 75c multicolored 1.75 1.00

Cuban Railroad, 160th Anniv. — A1049

10c, John Bull, 1830, UK. No. 3886, Old Ironsides, Baldwin, 1832, US. No. 3887, Baldwin Pacific Type 4-6-2, 1910-13, US. 65c, TE.M4:1 diesel electric, 1970, USSR. 75c, TE.114-K, diesel electric, 1975, USSR.

1997, Nov. 19 Litho. *Perf. 12½*

3885 A1049 10c multicolored .25 .25
3886 A1049 15c multicolored .30 .25
3887 A1049 15c multicolored .30 .25
3888 A1049 65c multicolored 1.60 .95
3889 A1049 75c multicolored 1.75 .95
Nos. 3885-3889 (5) 4.20 2.65

UN Conference on Commerce and Employment, Havana, 50th Anniv. — A1050

1997, Nov. 21

3890 A1050 65c multicolored 1.50 .95

Victor Manuel Garcia, Painter, Birth Cent. A1051

1997, Dec. 29 Litho. *Perf. 12½*

3891 A1051 15c #1553, Garcia .50 .25

Visit of Pope John Paul II A1052

Pope John Paul II, different coats of arms, and: 65c, Havana Cathedral. 75c, Basilica of Our Lady of Charity, Cobre, vert.

No. 3894, vert: a, Pope John Paul II greeting Fidel Castro. b, Pope waving.

1998, Jan. 18 Litho. *Perf. 12½*

3892 A1052 65c multicolored 1.50 .95
3893 A1052 75c multicolored 1.75 .95

Souvenir Sheet of 2

3894 A1052 50c #a.-b. 3.00 1.50

Nos. 3894a-3894b are 32x40mm.

Assassination of Jesus Menendez, 50th Anniv. — A1053

1998, Jan. 22

3895 A1053 15c multicolored .55 .25

1998 World Cup Soccer Championships, France — A1054

Various soccer plays: 10c, 2 players. No. 3897, Player in black & yellow. No. 3898, Player on ground, 1 in striped shirt. No. 3899, 3 players, 2 in striped shirts. No. 3900, 3 players, 2 in blue shirts.

1p, Player with #11 on sleeve.

1998, Feb. 10 Litho. *Perf. 12½*

3896 A1054 10c multi, vert. .50 .25
3897 A1054 15c multi, vert. .60 .25
3898 A1054 15c multi, vert. .60 .25
3899 A1054 65c multi 2.10 1.00
3900 A1054 65c multi 2.10 1.00
Nos. 3896-3900 (5) 5.90 2.75

Souvenir Sheet

Perf. 13

3901 A1054 1p multicolored 3.00 1.50

No. 3901 contains one 40x32mm stamp.

Capt. Isabel Rubio Diaz, Medical Aide During Revolution, Death Cent. — A1055

1998, Feb. 15 *Perf. 13*

3902 A1055 15c multicolored .65 .25

Brig. Gen. Vidal Ducasse Reeve (1852-98) A1056

1998, Feb. 19 *Perf. 12½*

3903 A1056 15c multicolored .65 .25

No. 3903 inscribed "Revee."

"Radio Rebelde," 40th Anniv. — A1057

1998, Feb. 23

3904 A1057 15c multicolored .65 .25

Fire Engines A1058

Designs: 10c, 1901 Shand Mason & Co., London. No. 3906, 1905 Horse-drawn municipal fire wagon, Havana. No. 3907, 1921 American-La France Fire Engine Co. 65c, 1952 Chevrolet 6400, US. 75c, 1956 American-La France Foamite Co., US.

1998, Mar. 10

3905 A1058 10c multicolored .40 .25
3906 A1058 15c multicolored .45 .25
3907 A1058 15c multicolored .45 .25
3908 A1058 65c multicolored 1.50 .90
3909 A1058 75c multicolored 1.75 .90
Nos. 3905-3909 (5) 4.55 2.55

Protest of Baragua, 120th Anniv. — A1059

1998, Mar. 15

3910 A1059 15c multicolored .65 .25

Victory at Cuito Cuanavale, Angola, 10th Anniv. — A1060

1998, Mar. 23 **Litho.** ***Perf. 12½***

3911	A1060 15c multicolored	.65	.25

New Year 1998 (Year of the Tiger) — A1061

1998, Mar. 30

3912	A1061 15c multicolored	.65	.25

Dogs — A1062

1998, Apr. 15 **Litho.** ***Perf. 12½***

3913	A1062 10c Chihuahua	.40	.25
3914	A1062 15c Beagle	.45	.25
3915	A1062 15c Xoloitzcuintle	.45	.25
3916	A1062 65c German pointer	1.60	1.00
3917	A1062 75c Chow chow	1.90	1.25
	Nos. 3913-3917 (5)	4.80	3.00

Evolution of the Chimpanzee A1063

Pan troglodytes and: 10c, Proconsul. No. 3919, Cranium. No. 3920, Right hand and foot. 65c, New-born chimpanzee. 75c, Map of Africa showing chimpanzee's range.

1998, May 15 **Litho.** ***Perf. 12½***

3918	A1063 10c multicolored	.40	.25
3919	A1063 15c multicolored	.40	.25
3920	A1063 15c multicolored	.40	.25
3921	A1063 65c multicolored	1.60	1.25
3922	A1063 75c multicolored	1.75	1.25
	Nos. 3918-3922 (5)	4.55	3.25

Lisbon '98, World Stamp Exhibition — A1064

Deep sea fish: No. 3923, Raja batis. No. 3924, Eurypharynx pelecanoides. 65c, Caulophryne. 75c, Chauliodus sloanl.

1998, May 22 **Litho.** ***Perf. 12½***

3923	A1064 15c multicolored	.40	.25
3924	A1064 15c multicolored	.40	.25
3925	A1064 65c multicolored	1.60	1.10
3926	A1064 75c multicolored	1.80	1.25
	Nos. 3923-3926 (4)	4.20	2.85

Souvenir Sheet

Juvalux '98, World Stamp Exhibition for Youth Philately and Postal History, Luxembourg — A1065

1998, May 20 **Litho.** ***Perf. 12½***

3927	A1065 1p Postman on bicycle	3.00	1.50

Federico Garcia Lorca (1898-1936), Poet — A1066

1998, June 2

3928	A1066 75c multicolored	2.25	1.25

Intl. Year of the Oceans A1067

No. 3929, Canarreos flower coral, coral crab, small fish. No. 3030, French angel fish, brain coral, gorgonia.

1998, June 5

3929	A1067 65c multicolored	1.50	1.00
3930	A1067 65c multicolored	1.50	1.00
a.	Pair, #3929-3930	3.50	1.75

Diana, Princess of Wales (1961-97) A1068

Various portraits, color of clothes: No. 3931, Pale yellow and pink. No. 3932, Black and white. No. 3933, Multicolored print. No. 3934, Red. No. 3935, Pink and black plaid. 65c, White. 75c, Blue.

1998, June 30 **Litho.** ***Perf. 13***

3931	A1068 10c multicolored	.30	.25
3932	A1068 10c multicolored	.30	.25
3933	A1068 10c multicolored	.30	.25
3934	A1068 15c multicolored	.40	.25
3935	A1068 15c multicolored	.40	.25
3936	A1068 65c multicolored	1.90	1.10
3937	A1068 75c multicolored	2.10	1.25
	Nos. 3931-3937 (7)	5.70	3.60

Expo 2000, Hanover A1069

No. 3938, Mascot, "Twipsy." No. 3939, Mascot in London, 1851. No. 3940, Mascot in Brussels, 1958. No. 3941, German flag, map of Germany. 65c, Mascot in Paris, 1889. 75c, Mascot on top of world, fireworks.

1998, July 31 ***Perf. 12½***

3938	A1069 15c multi, vert.	.40	.25
3939	A1069 15c multi	.40	.25
3940	A1069 15c multi	.40	.25
3941	A1069 15c multi	.40	.25
3942	A1069 65c multi, vert.	1.90	1.00
3943	A1069 75c multi	2.10	1.25
	Nos. 3938-3943 (6)	5.60	3.25

Maracaibo '98, 18th Central America and Caribbean Games — A1070

1998, Aug. 8

3944	A1070 15c multicolored	.50	.25

Attack on Moncada Barracks, 45th Anniv. — A1071

Designs: 15c, Siboney farmhouse, Abel Santamaría. 65c, Barracks, José Marti.

1998, July 26 **Litho.** ***Perf. 13***

3945	A1071 15c multicolored	.40	.25
3946	A1071 65c multicolored	1.90	.95

Democratic Republic of Korea, 50th Anniv. — A1072

1998, Sept. 8 **Litho.** ***Perf. 13***

3947	A1072 75c Kim Il Sung (1912-94)	2.25	1.10

Japanese Immigration to Cuba, Cent. — A1073

1998, Sept. 9 **Litho.** ***Perf. 13***

3948	A1073 75c multicolored	2.25	1.10

Orchids A1074

10c, Coelogyne flaccida. No. 3950, Dendrobium fimbriatum. No. 3951, Arunding graminifolia. No. 3952, Bletia patula. No. 3953, Phaius tankervilliaea.

1998, Sept. 10

3949	A1074 10c multicolored	.30	.25
3950	A1074 15c multicolored	.50	.25
3951	A1074 15c multicolored	.50	.25
3952	A1074 65c multicolored	1.90	1.00
3953	A1074 65c multicolored	1.90	1.00
	Nos. 3949-3953 (5)	5.10	2.75

5th Congress of the Revolution Defense Committees A1075

1998, Sept. 25 **Litho.** ***Perf. 13***

3954	A1075 15c multicolored	.45	.25

World Tourism Day — A1076

Holguin Province, reptiles: 10c, Looking through gateway, city of Gibara, anolis equestris, vert. 15c, Mayabe Valley, anolis vermiculatus, vert. 65c, Guardalavaca Beach, anolis allisoni. 75c, Mayari pine forest, anolis mestrei.

1998, Sept. 27

3955	A1076 10c multicolored	.30	.25
3956	A1076 15c multicolored	.50	.25
3957	A1076 65c multicolored	1.90	.95
3958	A1076 75c multicolored	2.10	1.25
	Nos. 3955-3958 (4)	4.80	2.70

Women Who Aided Cuban Revolutionary Movements A1077

America Issue: 65c, Bernarda Toro Pelegrin (1852-1911). 75c, Maria Magdalena Cabrales Isaac (1842-1905).

1998, Oct. 12

3959	A1077 65c multicolored	1.90	.95
3960	A1077 75c multicolored	2.10	1.25

World Wildlife Fund Protected Fauna — A1078

Arantinga Euops: 10c, Two on tree branch. 15c, One looking out of nest. 65c, One on tree branch. 75c, One up close.

1998, Oct. 21

3961 A1078 10c multicolored .45 .30
3962 A1078 15c multicolored .65 .50
3963 A1078 65c multicolored 2.75 .95
3964 A1078 75c multicolored 3.25 1.25
Nos. 3961-3964 (4) 7.10 3.00

Cuban Natl. Ballet, 50th Anniv. — A1079

1998, Oct. 28

3965 A1079 15c Swan Lake .50 .25
3966 A1079 65c Giselle 1.90 .95

Massacre of O'Farrill and Goicuria, 40th Anniv. — A1080

Rogelio Perea, Angel Ameijeiras, Pedro Gutiérrez.

1998, Nov. 8

3967 A1080 15c multicolored .45 .25

Battle of Guisa, 40th Anniv. A1081

Design: Capt. Braulio Coroneaux, tank.

1998, Nov. 30 Litho. *Perf. 12½*

3968 A1081 15c multicolored .45 .25

A1082

1998, Dec. 10 Litho. *Perf. 12½*

3969 A1082 65c multicolored 1.90 .95

Universal Declaration of Human Rights, 50th anniv.

A1083

Calixto Garcia Iñiguez (1839-98), revolutionary Major General.

1998, Dec. 11 *Perf. 13*

3970 A1083 65c multicolored 1.90 .95

Padre Félix Varela (1788-1853) — A1084

1998, Dec. 16

3971 A1084 75c multicolored 2.25 1.10

War for Independence, Cent. — A1085

War heroes, historical scene; No. 3972, Carlos Manuel de Céspedes. No. 3973, Ignacio Agramonte. No. 3974, Máximo Gómez. No. 3975, José Maceo. No. 3976, Salvador Cisneros. No. 3977, Calixto Garcia. No. 3978, Adolfo Flor. No. 3979, Serafin Sánchez. 65c, José Martí. 75c, Antonio Maceo.

1998, Dec. 25 Litho. *Perf. 12½*

3972 A1085 15c multicolored .45 .25
3973 A1085 15c multicolored .45 .25
3974 A1085 15c multicolored .45 .25
3975 A1085 15c multicolored .45 .25
3976 A1085 15c multicolored .45 .25
3977 A1085 15c multicolored .45 .25
3978 A1085 15c multicolored .45 .25
3979 A1085 15c multicolored .45 .25
3980 A1085 65c multicolored 1.90 .95
3981 A1085 75c multicolored 2.10 1.10
a. Sheet of 10, #3972-3981 + 3 labels 8.00 8.00
Nos. 3972-3981 (10) 7.60 4.05

Battle for Palma Soriano, 40th Anniv. A1086

1998, Dec. 27 Litho. *Perf. 13*

3982 A1086 15c multicolored .45 .25

Cuban Revolution, 40th Anniv. — A1087

a, Boat, soldiers in water. b, Fidel Castro with soldier. c, Castro giving speech, pigeons.

1999, Jan. 1

3983 A1087 65c Strip of 3, #a.-c. 4.75 2.40

Natl. Revolutionary Police, 40th Anniv. — A1088

1999, Jan. 5

3984 A1088 15c multicolored .50 .25

Cuban Workers' Trade Union Organization, 60th Anniv. — A1089

1999, Jan. 28 Litho. *Perf. 12½*

3985 A1089 15c multicolored .45 .25

New Year 1999 (Year of the Rabbit) — A1090

1999, Feb. 5 *Perf. 13*

3986 A1090 75c multicolored 1.60 1.10

Lenin (1870-1924) — A1091

1999, Feb. 21 Litho. *Perf. 12½*

3987 A1091 75c multicolored 1.60 1.10

Dinosaurs — A1092

1999, Mar. 10

3988 A1092 10c Ornithosuchus .30 .25
3989 A1092 15c Saltopus .50 .25
3990 A1092 15c Bactrosaurus .50 .25
3991 A1092 65c Protosuchus 1.90 .95
3992 A1092 75c Mussaurus 2.10 1.10
Nos. 3988-3992 (5) 5.30 2.80

Cuban Musicians — A1093

1999, Mar. 22 *Perf. 13*

3993 A1093 5c Dámaso Pérez Prado .25 .25
3994 A1093 15c Benny Moré .50 .25
3995 A1093 15c Chano Pozo .50 .25
3996 A1093 35c Miguelito Valdés 1.25 .50
3997 A1093 65c Bola de Nieve 1.90 .95
3998 A1093 75c Rita Montaner 2.10 1.10
Nos. 3993-3998 (6) 6.50 3.30

Simón Bolivar's Visit to Cuba, Bicent. A1094

1999, Mar. 25

3999 A1094 65c Portrait 1.90 .95
4000 A1094 65c Monument 1.90 .95
a. Pair, #3999-4000 4.25 2.00

State Security Organization, 40th Anniv. — A1095

1999, Mar. 26 Litho. *Perf. 12½*

4001 A1095 65c multicolored 1.90 .95

Souvenir Sheet

China '99 World Philatelic Exhibition — A1096

1999, Apr. 10 Litho. *Perf. 12½*

4002 A1096 1p Giant panda 3.00 1.50

Stamp Day A1097

1999, Apr. 24

4003 A1097 15c Postal rocket .50 .25
4004 A1097 65c Post rider 1.90 .80

Test of Cuban Postal Rocket, 60th anniv. Insurgent Postal Service, 130th anniv.

Casa de las Américas, 40th Anniv. — A1098

1999, Apr. 24

4005 A1098 65c multicolored 1.90 .80

Souvenir Sheet

IBRA '99, World Philatelic Exhibition, Nuremberg — A1099

1999, Apr. 27

4006 A1099 1p Train	3.00	1.50

Agrarian Reform Law, 40th Anniv. A1100

1999, May 17

4007 A1100 65c multicolored	1.60	.80

Felipe Poey, Scientist, Birth Bicent. A1101

Fish: 5c, Gramma loreto Poey. 15c, Liopropoma rubre Poey. No. 4010, Hypoplectrus gummigutta. No. 4011, Stegastes dorsopunicans.

1p, Portrait of Poey, hypoplectrus guttavarius.

1999, May 26 Litho. *Perf. 12½*

4008 A1101 5c multicolored	.25	.25
4009 A1101 15c multicolored	.40	.25
4010 A1101 65c multicolored	1.90	.80
4011 A1101 65c multicolored	1.90	.80
Nos. 4008-4011 (4)	4.45	2.10

Souvenir Sheet

Perf. 13¼x13

4012 A1101 1p multicolored	3.00	1.00

No. 4012 contains one 32x40mm stamp.

Souvenir Sheet

Philexfrance '99, World Philatelic Exhibition — A1102

Sculpture in sheet margin: "1814," by Jean Louis Meissonier (1815-1891).

1999, June 2 *Perf. 13*

4013 A1102 1p multicolored	3.00	1.50

1999 Pan-American Games, Winnipeg — A1103

1999, June 25 Litho. *Perf. 13*

4014 A1103 15c Baseball	.40	.25
4015 A1103 65c Volleyball, vert	1.90	.80
4016 A1103 75c Boxing	2.10	.90
Nos. 4014-4016 (3)	4.40	1.95

People's Republic of China, 50th Anniv. A1104

5c, Victory at Wioming, by Gao Hong. 15c, Nanchang Insurrection, by Cai Lang. 40c, Red Army Crossing a Swamp, by Gao Quan. 65c, Occupation of the Presidential Palace, by Cheng Yifei and Wei Jingshan. 75c, Proclamation of the People's Republic of China, by Dong Xiwen.

1999, Aug. 21 Litho. *Perf. 12¾*

4017 A1104 5c multicolored	.25	.25
4018 A1104 15c multicolored	.40	.25
4019 A1104 40c multicolored	1.10	.70
4020 A1104 65c multicolored	1.75	1.10
4021 A1104 75c multicolored	2.00	1.40
Nos. 4017-4021 (5)	5.50	3.70

China 1999 World Philatelic Exhibition, Beijing — A1105

No. 4022, Morning Glories, by Qi Baishi. No. 4023, Three Galloping Horses, by Xu Beihong. No. 4024, Hunan Woman, by Fu Baoshi. No. 4025, Birthplace of Luxun, by Wu Guanzhong. No. 4026, Horse Riders, by Huangzhou. 40c, Pine Tree, by He Xiangning. 65c, Sleep, by Jin Shangyi. 75c, Poetic Scene in Xun Yang, by Chen Yifei.

1999, Aug. 22 Litho. *Perf. 13*

4022 A1105 5c multicolored	.25	.25
4023 A1105 5c multicolored	.25	.25
4024 A1105 15c multicolored	.40	.25
4025 A1105 15c multicolored	.40	.25
4026 A1105 15c multicolored	.40	.25
4027 A1105 40c multicolored	1.10	.70
4028 A1105 65c multicolored	1.75	1.10
4029 A1105 75c multicolored	2.00	1.25
a. Sheet of 8, #4022-4029 + label	8.00	8.00
Nos. 4022-4029 (8)	6.55	4.30

UPU, 125th Anniv. A1106

1999, Sept. 16 Litho. *Perf. 12¾*

4030 A1106 75c multicolored	1.50	1.00

World Tourism Day A1107

Butterflies and Havana tourist sites: 10c, Antia numidia, Morro Castle. 15c, Papilio polyxenes, Havana Cathedral. 65c, Dryas julia, Convent of San Francisco. 75c, Eueides cleobaea, Capitol.

1999, Sept. 27 *Perf. 12½x12¾*

4031 A1107 10c multicolored	.25	.25
4032 A1107 15c multicolored	.40	.25
4033 A1107 65c multicolored	1.75	1.00
4034 A1107 75c multicolored	2.00	1.10
Nos. 4031-4034 (4)	4.40	2.60

Expo 2000, Hanover, Germany A1108

5c, World map, Expo 2000 emblem. No. 4036, "Twipsy" mascot, vert. No. 4037, "Twipsy" and 1876 Philadelphia Exposition. No. 4038, "Twipsy" and 1970 Osaka Exposition. 65c, "Twipsy" and 2000 Exposition. 75c, "Twipsy" and 1967 Montreal Exposition.

1999, Oct. 1 *Perf. 12¾*

4035 A1108 5c multicolored	.25	.25
4036 A1108 15c multicolored	.35	.25
4037 A1108 15c multicolored	.35	.25
4038 A1108 15c multicolored	.35	.25
4039 A1108 65c multicolored	1.60	1.00
4040 A1108 75c multicolored	2.00	1.10
Nos. 4035-4040 (6)	4.90	3.10

Cubana Airlines, 70th Anniv. — A1109

1999, Oct. 8 *Perf. 12½x12¼*

4041 A1109 15c Fokker	.35	.25
4042 A1109 15c DC-10	.35	.25
4043 A1109 65c A-320	1.60	1.00
4044 A1109 75c DC-3	2.00	1.10
Nos. 4041-4044 (4)	4.30	2.60

America Issue, A New Millennium Without Arms — A1110

1999, Oct. 12 *Perf. 12¾*

4045 A1110 15c Pigeon, mushroom cloud	.40	.25
4046 A1110 65c Dove, globe	1.60	1.10

National Instiutions, 40th Anniv. — A1111

1999, Oct. 16 *Perf. 12¾*

4047 A1111 15c MINFAR	.35	.25
4048 A1111 65c Natl. Revolutionary Militia	1.50	1.00

Disappearance of Camilo Cienfuegos, 40th Anniv. — A1112

1999, Oct. 28 Litho. *Perf. 12¾*

4049 A1112 15c multicolored	1.40	.25

Souvenir Sheet

12th Congress of Cuban Philatelic Federation — A1113

1999, Dec. 11 *Perf. 13*

4050 A1113 1p multicolored	2.50	1.25

Ernest Hemingway (1899-1961), Writer — A1114

1999, Dec. 15 *Perf. 12½x12¼*

4051 A1114 65c multicolored	1.50	1.00

9th Summit of Ibero-American Heads of State and Government, Havana — A1115

Designs: 65c, Plaza Vieja. 75c, Plaza of St. Francis of Assisi.

1p, Plaza de Armas.

1999, Nov. 5 Litho. *Perf. 12¾x12½*

4052 A1115 65c multi	1.50	1.00
4053 A1115 75c multi	1.60	1.10

Souvenir Sheet

Perf. 13

4054 A1115 1p multi	2.50	1.25

No. 4054 contains one 40x31mm stamp.

Rubén Martínez Villena (1899-1934), Revolutionary — A1116

1999, Dec. 20 *Perf. 12½x12¾*

4055 A1116 15c multi .40 .25

Dr. Tomás Romay Chacón (1764-1849) A1117

1999, Dec. 21 *Perf. 13*

4056 A1117 65c multi 1.40 .90

New Year 2000 (Year of the Dragon) — A1118

2000, Jan. 10 *Perf. 12½*

4057 A1118 15c multi .40 .25

Folklore A1119

Paintings depicting Cuban folklore by Concepción Ferrant (1882-1968): 10c, Rumba Caliente. 15c, Cachumba. 65c, En Casa de un Babalao. 75c, Tata Cuñengue.

2000, Jan. 26 *Perf. 12½x12¾*

4058	A1119 10c multi		.25	.25
4059	A1119 15c multi		.35	.30
4060	A1119 65c multi		1.40	1.00
4061	A1119 75c multi		1.60	1.10
	Nos. 4058-4061 (4)		3.60	2.65

Butterflies — A1120

10c, Helcyra superba. No. 4063, Pantaporia punctata. No. 4064, Neptis themis. 65c, Curetis acuta. 75c, Chrysozephyrus ataxus.

2000, Feb. 25 *Perf. 12¾*

4062	A1120 10c multi	.30	.25
4063	A1120 15c multi	.40	.30
4064	A1120 15c multi	.40	.30
4065	A1120 65c multi	1.60	1.25
4066	A1120 75c multi	1.90	1.40
	Nos. 4062-4066 (5)	4.60	3.50

Bangkok 2000 Stamp Exhibition.

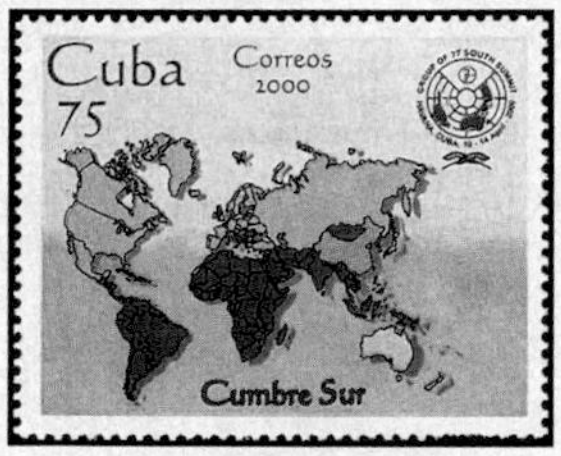

Group of 77 South Summit, Havana — A1121

2000, Apr. 7 **Litho.** *Perf. 13x12½*

4067 A1121 75c multi 2.00 1.25

Lenin, 130th Anniv. of Birth — A1122

2000, Apr. 22 *Perf. 12¾*

4068 A1122 75c multi 2.00 1.25

Che Guevara in Congo, 35th Anniv. A1123

2000, Apr. 24

4069 A1123 65c multi 1.75 1.10

Stamp Day — A1124

Designs: 65c, Cuba #2, building. 90c, Airplane, cover, Jaime González, pilot of first experimental airmail flight in Cuba.

2000, Apr. 24

4070	A1124 65c multi	1.75	1.10
4071	A1124 90c multi	2.25	1.50

Capt. San Luis (Eliseo Reyes), Military Hero (1940-67) A1125

2000, Apr. 27

4072 A1125 65c multi 1.75 1.10

The Stamp Show 2000, London A1126

Locomotives: 5c, 1882 Baldwin 0-6-0. 10c, 1895 Baldwin 2-8-0. 15c, 1912 Baldwin 2-8-0. 65c, 1919 Alco 2-8-0. 75c, 1925 Alco 2-8-2. 1p, 1920 Henschel 2-6-0.

2000, May 5 *Perf. 12¾*

4073	A1126 5c multi	.25	.25
4074	A1126 10c multi	.30	.25
4075	A1126 15c multi	.40	.30
4076	A1126 65c multi	1.60	1.10
4077	A1126 75c multi	1.90	1.25
	Nos. 4073-4077 (5)	4.45	3.15

Souvenir Sheet

Perf. 13

4078 A1126 1p multi 3.00 1.50

No. 4078 contains one 40x32mm stamp.

WIPA 2000 Philatelic Exhibition, Vienna — A1127

Airships of: 10c, Henri Giffard, 1852. 15c, Albert and Gaston Tissandier, 1883, vert. 50c, Charles Renard and Arthur Krebs, 1884. 65c, Pierre and Paul Lebaudy, 1903. 75c, August von Perseval, 1906.
1p, Ferdinand von Zeppelin.

Perf. 12½x12¼, 12¼x12½

2000, May 18

4079	A1127 10c multi	.35	.25
4080	A1127 15c multi	.50	.30
4081	A1127 50c multi	1.40	.90
4082	A1127 65c multi	1.90	1.10
4083	A1127 75c multi	2.10	1.25
	Nos. 4079-4083 (5)	6.25	3.80

Souvenir Sheet

Perf. 12½

4084 A1127 1p multi 3.00 1.50

No. 4084 contains one 40x32mm stamp.

Second World Meeting of Friendship and Solidarity With Cuba — A1128

2000, June 23 **Litho.** *Perf. 12¾*

4085 A1128 65c multi 1.50 1.10

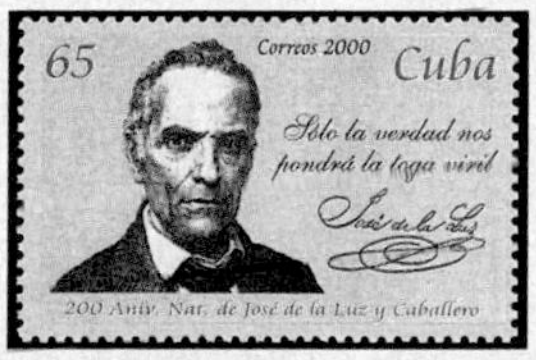

José de la Luz y Caballero (1800-62), Educator — A1129

2000, July 11 *Perf. 12½x12¼*

4086 A1129 65c multi 1.50 1.10

Amadeo Roldan (1900-39), Violinist — A1130

2000, July 12 *Perf. 12¾*

4087 A1130 65c multi 1.50 1.10

La Edad de Oro, by José Marti — A1131

5c, Bebé y El Señor Don Pomposo. 10c, La Muñeca Negra. 15c, Nene Traviesa. 50c, Los Dos Ruiseñores. 65c, Frontispiece of La Edad de Oro. 75c, El Camarón Encantado.

2000, July 20

4088-4093	A1131 Set of 6	6.00	4.25
4093a	Sheet of 6, #4088-4093	6.00	6.00

Latin American Association for Integration — A1132

2000, Aug. 12

4094 A1132 65c multi 1.75 1.25

Souvenir Sheet

Olymphilex 2000, Sydney — A1133

2000, Aug. 17 *Perf. 13*

4095 A1133 1p multi 2.25 1.10

2000 Summer Olympics, Sydney A1134

Designs: 5c, Runners. 15c, Soccer. 65c, Baseball. 75c, Cycling.

2000, Aug. 20 *Perf. 12¾*

4096-4099 A1134 Set of 4 4.50 4.00

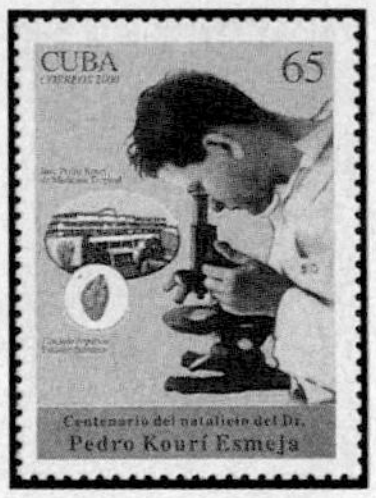

Dr. Pedro Kouri Esmeja (1900-64) A1135

2000, Aug. 21 **Litho.**
4100 A1135 65c multi 1.75 1.25

Federation of Cuban Women, 40th Anniv. — A1136

2000, Aug. 23
4101 A1136 15c multi .40 .30

España 2000 Intl. Philatelic Exhibition — A1137

Designs: 10c, 1851 Havana-Bilbao stampless cover, ship. No. 4103, 15c, Spain #1, Cibeles Fountain, Madrid. No. 4104, 15c, 1850 Zaragoza-Cadiz cover, Palacio de Cristal, Madrid. 65c, Spain #1-5, Palacio de Comunicaciones, Madrid. 75c, Cuba #1, Centro Gallego, Havana.

2000, Sept. 7 ***Perf. 12¾x12½***
4102-4106 A1137 Set of 5 4.75 3.00
4106a Sheet of 5, #4102-4106 + label 4.75 4.75

Souvenir Sheet

Perf. 12½

4107 A1137 100c Queen Isabella II, vert. 3.00 2.25

No. 4107 contains one 32x40mm stamp.

Beaches — A1138

No. 4108, Coconuts Bay, PRC. No. 4109, Varadero Beach, Cuba.

2000, Sept. 26 ***Perf. 12½x12¼***
4108-4109 A1138 15c Set of 2 .80 .80
4109a Pair, #4108-4109 .80 .80

See People's Republic of China No. 3052.

World Tourism Day — A1139

Marine life: 10c, Eretmochelys imbricata, vert. 15c, Epinephelus striatus, vert. 65c, Pomacanthus paru. 75c, Anisotremus surinamensis.

Perf. 12½x12¾, 12¾x12½
2000, Sept. 27
4110-4113 A1139 Set of 4 4.00 2.00

Committees of Defense of the Revolution, 40th Anniv. — A1140

2000, Sept. 28 ***Perf. 12¾***
4114 A1140 15c multi .40 .30

America Issue — AIDS Prevention A1141

Ribbon, heart-shaped map and: 15c, Family. 65c, Couple.

2000, Oct. 12
4115-4116 A1141 Set of 2 2.75 1.25

Cuban Military in Angola, 25th Anniv. — A1142

2000, Nov. 7
4117 A1142 75c multi 2.00 1.40

Visit by Alexander von Humboldt, Bicent. — A1143

Humboldt and: 15c, House in Trinidad. 65c, House in Havana, Political Essay on the Island of Cuba.

2000, Dec. 19 **Litho.** ***Perf. 12¾***
4118-4119 A1143 Set of 2 2.50 1.25

20th Pan-American Railway Congress A1144

2000, Sept. 18 **Litho.** ***Perf. 12¾***
4120 A1144 65c multi 1.75 1.25

Millennium — A1145

Snails: a, Polymita versicolor. b, Polymita picta iolimbata. c, Polymita picta roseolimbata. d, Polymita picta picta. e, Polymita picta nigrolimbata.

2000, Dec. 20
4121 A1145 65c Block of 5, #a-e, + label 8.00 4.00

New Year 2001 (Year of the Snake) — A1146

2001, Jan. 10
4122 A1146 15c multi .50 .25

Hong Kong 2001 Stamp Exhibition — A1147

Birds: 5c, Aix galericulata. 10c, Chrysolophus pictus. 15c, Ardea cinerea. 65c, Gallus gallus. 75c, Streptotelia decaocto.

2001, Jan. 25 ***Perf. 12¾***
4123-4127 A1147 Set of 5 4.50 3.25

Souvenir Sheet

Perf. 12½

4128 A1147 1p Grus grus 3.00 1.25

No. 4128 contains one 32x40mm stamp.

National Institute for Sport Physical Education and Recreation, 40th Anniv. — A1148

2001, Feb. 23 ***Perf. 12½x12¼***
4129 A1148 65c multi 1.60 .80

UN High Commissioner for Refugees, 50th Anniv. — A1149

2001, Mar. 15 ***Perf. 12¾x12½***
4130 A1149 65c multi 1.50 .75

Antique Locomotives — A1150

Locomotives from, 10c, 1863. 15c, 1876. 40c, 1885. 65c, 1914. 75c, 1932.

2001, Mar. 20 ***Perf. 12½x12¼***
4131-4135 A1150 Set of 5 4.75 2.40

105th Interparliamentary Union Congress, Havana — A1151

2001, Mar. 30 ***Perf. 12¾***
4136 A1151 65c multi 1.75 .80

Bay of Pigs Invasion, 40th Anniv. — A1152

2001, Apr. 19 ***Perf. 12¾x12½***
4137 A1152 65c multi 1.50 .75

Cats and Dogs A1153

Designs: 10c, Cats, emblem of Cat Aficionados Association. No. 4139, 15c, Dogs, Cats, emblem of Aniplant. No. 4140, 15c, Dogs, emblem of Cynological Federation of Cuba. 65c, Dogs, emblem of Sporting Dog Federation of Cuba. 75c, Dogs, cats.

2001, Apr. 25 ***Perf. 12½x12¾***
4138-4142 A1153 Set of 5 4.00 2.00

Radio Havana, 40th Anniv. — A1154

2001, May 1 ***Perf. 12½x12¼***
4143 A1154 65c multi 1.50 .75

Tourism Convention — A1155

2001, May 7 ***Perf. 12¾x12½***
4144 A1155 65c multi 1.50 .75

Belgica 2001 Intl. Stamp Exhibition, Brussels A1156

Designs: 5c, St. Michel Cathedral. 10c, Sablon Church, horiz. 15c, Royal Residence, horiz. 65c, Sacred Heart Basilica, horiz. 75c, Atomium.
1p, Royal Palace.

2001, May 10 ***Perf. 12¾***
4145-4149 A1156 Set of 5 4.00 2.00

Souvenir Sheet
Perf. 12½

4150 A1156 100c multi 2.40 1.25

No. 4150 contains one 32x40mm stamp.

Interior Ministry, 40th Anniv. A1157

2001, June 6 ***Perf. 12¾***
4151 A1157 65c multi 1.75 .80

Phila Nippon '01, Japan A1158

Japanese trains: 5c., JR 500. 10c, JR 700. 15c, MAX 1. 65c, MAX 2. 75c, 300.

2001, June 20 **Litho.** ***Perf. 12¾***
4152-4156 A1158 Set of 5 3.75 1.50

Souvenir Sheet
Perf. 12½

4157 A1158 100c Zero 2.40 1.25

No. 4157 contains one 40x32mm stamp.

Republic of San Marino, 1700th Anniv. — A1159

2001, July 20 **Litho.** ***Perf. 12½x12¼***
4158 A1159 75c multi 1.75 .75

Aquaculture — A1160

Designs: 5c, Tinca tinca. 10c, Rana temporaria. 15c, Cardisoma guanhumi. 65c, Mytilus edulis. 75c, Tilapia mariae.
1p, Potamobius pallipes.

2001, Sept. 17 ***Perf. 12¾***
4159-4163 A1160 Set of 5 3.75 1.50

Souvenir Sheet
Perf. 12½

4164 A1160 1p multi 2.40 1.25

No. 4164 contains one 40x32mm stamp.

Recovery of Raw Materials, 40th Anniv. — A1161

2001, Sept. 21 ***Perf. 12¾x12½***
4165 A1161 65c multi 1.60 .75

Tourism — A1162

Designs: 10c, Valle de Viñales. 15c, Trinidad. 65c, Sirena Beach, Cayo Largo del Sur. 75c, Morro Castle, Havana.

2001, Sept. 27
4166-4169 A1162 Set of 4 3.75 1.75

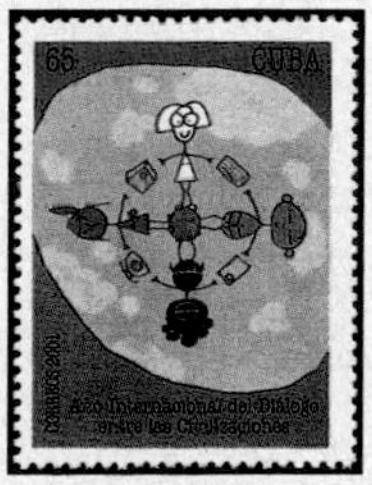

Year of Dialogue Among Civilizations A1163

2001, Oct. 9 ***Perf. 12¾***
4170 A1163 65c multi 1.50 .75

America Issue — UNESCO World Heritage A1164

Flora and fauna from Desembarco del Granma Natl. Park: 15c, Tetramicra malpighiarum. 65c, Liggus vittatus.

2001, Oct. 12 ***Perf. 12½x12¾***
4171-4172 A1164 Set of 2 1.75 .85

José Marti National Library, Cent. A1165

2001, Oct. 18 ***Perf. 12¾***
4173 A1165 15c multi .35 .25

Cuban Airliner Explosion Near Barbados, 25th Anniv. — A1166

Various details of painting.

2001, Oct. 22
4174 Horiz. strip of 5 3.25 1.60
a. A1166 5c shown .25 .25
b. A1166 10c multi .25 .25
c. A1166 15c multi .35 .25
d. A1166 50c multi 1.10 .55
e. A1166 65c multi 1.40 .90

Eduardo R. Chibas, Communist Leader, Cent. of Birth — A1167

2001, Nov. 27 **Litho.** ***Perf. 13***
4175 A1167 65c multi 1.60 .80

Napoleonic Museum, 40th Anniv. — A1168

Equestrian statues of Napoleon and map of battle of: No. 4176, 10c, Eylau. No. 4177, 10c, Marengo. 65c, Waterloo. 75c, Aboukir.

2001, Dec. 1 ***Perf. 12¾x12½***
4176-4179 A1168 Set of 4 3.75 1.75

Pablo de la Torriente Brau (1901-36), Writer — A1169

2001, Dec. 12 ***Perf. 12¾***
4180 A1169 75c multi 1.75 .80

Cuban Federation of Pigeon Fanciers, 4th Congress A1170

Pigeons: No. 4181, 65c, Empedrado oscura 2021-61-ME. No. 4182, 65c, Empedrado claro 2241-55-ME. No. 4183, 65c, Mosaico 1561-66-HM. No. 4184, 65c, Mosaico, 3013-67-HM. No. 4185, 65c Bronceado, 338-59-HE.

2001, Dec. 14 ***Perf. 12½***
4181-4185 A1170 Set of 5 7.00 3.50

Film Stars Who Never Won Academy Awards A1171

Designs: 5c, Tyrone Power. No. 4187, 10c, Ava Gardner. No. 4188, 10c, Steve McQueen. No. 4189, 15c, Rita Hayworth. No. 4190, 15c, Marilyn Monroe. No. 4191, 15c, James Dean. No. 4192, 65c, Rock Hudson. No. 4193, 65c, Natalie Wood. 75c, Richard Burton.

2001, Dec. 20
4186-4194 A1171 Set of 9 8.00 3.50
a. Sheet of 9, #4186-4194 8.00 3.50

New Year 2002 (Year of the Horse) — A1172

2002, Jan. 21 **Litho.** ***Perf. 12½x12¾***
4195 A1172 15c multi .45 .30

Cigar Production — A1173

Cigars and: 5c, Hat, Cuba No. 358, tobacco leaf. 10c, Clock, cigar cylinder. 15c, Map of Cuba, Simon Bolivar. 65c, Cuba Nos. 356, 357, map, cigar smoker. 75c, Flag, tobacco field, man.
1p, Fidel Castro, map, star.

2002, Feb. 15 *Perf. 12¾*
4196-4200 A1173 Set of 5 4.00 2.00

Souvenir Sheet

Perf. 13 13¼

4201 A1173 1p multi 2.50 1.25

Fourth Havana Festival, Cohiba brand, 36th anniv. No. 4201 contains one 40x32mm stamp.

Second UPAEP Information Workshop — A1174

2002, Feb. 21 *Perf. 12½x12¼*
4202 A1174 65c multi 1.50 .75

Explorers A1175

Explorers: 5c, Reading map. 15c, Tying knots. 50c, Starting campfire for cooking. 65c, Starting fire. 75c, Using orientation techniques.

2002, Mar. 20 *Perf. 12½*
4203-4207 A1175 Set of 5 5.00 2.50
a. Sheet of 5, #4203-4207, + label 7.00 3.50

Union of Young Communists, 40th Anniv. — A1176

2002, Apr. 4 *Perf. 12½x12¼*
4208 A1176 15c multi .30 .25

ExpoVid 2002 Wine Event — A1177

Designs: 15c, Cigar smokers, wine bottles and glasses, map of wine producing areas. 65c, Wine glass and barrels. 75c, Wine glass and vineyard.

2002, June 5 *Perf. 12¾x12½*
4209-4211 A1177 Set of 3 3.50 1.75

2002 World Cup Soccer Championships, Japan and Korea — A1178

Player and flag from: No. 4212, 15c, South Korea. No. 4213, 15c, France. No. 4214, 15c, Germany. No. 4215, 15c, Brazil. No. 4216, 15c, Spain. 65c, Argentina. 75c, Italy. 85c, Japan.

2002, Apr. 21 **Litho.** *Perf. 12½*
4212-4219 A1178 Set of 8 6.50 3.25
4219a Sheet, #4212-4219 8.50 4.25

Souvenir Sheet

Hispano-Cubano Philatelic Exposition — A1179

2002, Apr. 27 *Perf. 13*
4220 A1179 1p multi 2.25 1.10

Juan Tomas Roig, Botanist, 125th Anniv. of Birth A1180

Designs: 5c, Bust of Roig, experimental agronomic station, Santiago de las Vegas. 10c, Bust and house of Roig. 15c, Roig, laboratory glassware and Nicotiana tabacum. 50c, Building, Allophyllum roiggi, and sculpture of Roig. 65c, Roig, laboratory glassware and botanical dictionary.

2002, May 10 *Perf. 12½x12¾*
4221-4225 A1180 Set of 5 3.25 1.50
4225a Sheet, #4221-4225, + label 5.00 2.40

Medi Cuba Suiza — A1181

2002, June 18 *Perf. 12¾x12½*
4226 A1181 75c multi 1.60 .80

Mushrooms A1182

Designs: 5c, Amanita junquillea. 15c, Lepiota puellaris. 45c, Cortinarius cumatilis. 65c, Pholliota adiposa. 75c, Coprinus comatus.

2002, June 20 *Perf. 12¾*
4227-4231 A1182 Set of 5 4.50 2.25
4231a Sheet, #4227-4231, + label 8.00 4.00

Nicolás Guillén (1902-89), Poet — A1183

2002, July 10 *Perf. 12¾x12½*
4232 A1183 65c multi 1.75 .90

Dockers, By Marcelo Pogolotti (1902-88) A1184

2002, July 12 *Perf. 12¾*
4233 A1184 15c multi .50 .30

Agostinho Neto (1922-79), Pres. of Angola — A1185

2002, Sept. 17 *Perf. 12¾x12½*
4234 A1185 65c multi 1.75 .90

España 2002 Youth Philatelic Exposition, Salamanca — A1186

Birds: 5c, Calidris minutilla. 10c, Tringa melanoleucas. 15c, Charadius semipalmatus. 65c, Plurialis squatarola. 75c, Arenaria interpres.
1p, Porzana carolina.

2002, Sept. 20 *Perf. 12½x12¼*
4235-4239 A1186 Set of 5 4.75 2.25
4239a Sheet, #4235-4239, + label 8.00 4.00

Souvenir Sheet

Perf. 13

4240 A1186 1p multi 2.50 1.25

No. 4240 contains one 40x31mm stamp.

Third Intl. Meeting of War Correspondents — A1187

2002, Oct. 7 *Perf. 12¾*
4241 A1187 65c multi 1.75 .90

Ernesto "Che" Guevara (1928-67), Revolutionary Leader — A1188

Various depictions of Guevara: 5c, 10c, 15c, 50c, 65c, 75c.

2002, Oct. 8 **Litho.**
4242-4247 A1188 Set of 6 5.25 2.75
4247a Sheet, #4242-4247 30.00 6.00

America Issue — Youth, Education and Literacy — A1189

Designs: 15c, Emblem of Literacy Army, man with book, teacher with student. 65c, Building, flag, children at computer.

2002, Oct. 12 *Perf. 12½x12¼*
4248-4249 A1189 Set of 2 2.00 1.00

Old Automobiles — A1190

Designs: No. 4250, 5c, 1956 Pontiac Catalina. No. 4251, 5c, 1957 Mercury Monterrey. 15c, 1959 Cadillac Fleetwood. 65c, Hudson Hornet. 75c, 1957 Chevrolet Bel Air. 85c, 1957 Mercedes-Benz 190SL.

2002, Oct. 19 *Perf. 12¾*
4250-4255 A1190 Set of 6 6.00 3.50
a. Sheet, #4250-4255, + 6 labels 16.00 4.00

15th Intercontinental Baseball Cup — A1191

Baseball players: 5c, G. Mesa. 15c, A. Pacheco. 50c, O. Linares. 65c, O. Kindelan. 75c, L. Ulacia.

2002, Nov. 1
4256-4260 A1191 Set of 5 5.00 3.00
4260a Sheet of 5, #4256-4260 + 4 labels 15.00 4.75

20th Havana Intl. Fair — A1192

2002, Nov. 3
4261 A1192 65c multi 1.75 .90

Railroads, 165th Anniv. — A1193

Designs: 5c, Rocket. 15c, Miller. 50c, Vulcan. 65c, Consolidation. 75c, Mikado.

2002, Nov. 12 *Perf. 12½x12¼*
4262-4266 A1193 Set of 5 5.00 3.00
4266a Sheet, #4262-4266, + label 15.00 3.75

Camagüey Ballet, 35th Anniv. — A1194

Designs: 65c, Twelve dancers. 75c, Two dancers.

2002, Dec. 1 *Perf. 12¾*
4267-4268 A1194 Set of 2 3.50 2.00

Pan-American Health Organization, Cent. — A1195

2002, Dec. 2
4269 A1195 65c multi 1.50 .90

Paintings of Wilfredo Lam (1902-82) A1196

Designs: 15c, Emi Cosinca, 1950. 45c, Yo Soy, 1949. 65c, Retrado de H.H., 1941-42. 75c, Mujer Sentada, 1951.

2002, Dec. 8 *Perf. 12¾*
4270-4273 A1196 Set of 4 5.00 3.00
4273a Sheet, #4270-4273, + 4 labels 14.00 3.00

Dulce M. Loynaz (1902-97), Writer A1197

Perf. 12½x12¾

2002, Dec. 19 **Litho.**
4274 A1197 65c multi 1.50 .90

Souvenir Sheet

Tursiops Truncatus — A1198

2002, Dec. 20 *Perf. 12½*
4275 A1198 1p multi 3.00 1.50

Fifth National Philatelic Competition.

Prehistoric and Modern-Day Animals — A1199

Designs: 5c, Megaloceros, Cervus elaphus. 10c, Theropithecus, Papio anubis. 15c, Coelodonta, Diceros bicornis. 45c, Canis dirus, Canis lupus. 65c, Ursus spelaeus, Ursus arctos. 75c, Smilodon, Panthera leo. 1p, Mammuthus primigenius.

2002, Dec. 27 *Perf. 12½x12¼*
4276-4281 A1199 Set of 6 5.00 2.00

Souvenir Sheet

Perf. 13

4282 A1199 1p multi 2.75 1.10

No. 4282 contains one 40x32mm stamp.

New Year 2003 (Year of the Ram) A1200

Ram with background in: No. 4283, 15c, Green. No. 4284, 15c, Red.

2003, Jan. 6 *Perf. 12½*
4283-4284 A1200 Set of 2 .80 .40

San Alejandro Academy for Arts, 185th Anniv. — A1201

Paintings by: 5c, Amelia Pelaez. 15c, René Portocarrero. 65c, Mario Carreña, horiz. 75c, Servando Cabrera.

2003, Jan. 12 *Perf. 12¾*
4285-4288 A1201 Set of 4 4.00 2.00

José Martí (1853-95), Patriot — A1202

Designs: 15c, Birthplace. No. 4290, 65c, Martí and text. No. 4291, 65c, Martí, sky and text, horiz. 75c, Portrait.
1p, Martí, horiz.

2003, Jan. 28 *Perf. 12¾*
4289-4292 A1202 Set of 4 5.00 2.50

Souvenir Sheet

Perf. 12½

4293 A1202 1p multi 2.75 1.40

No. 4293 contains one 40x32mm stamp.

Arrival of Europeans at Havana, 510th Anniv. — A1203

Various Cuban stamps and: No. 4294, 15c, Woman with Cigar boxes, map of Cuba (diamond-shaped). No. 4295, 15c, Men at table holding cigars and drinks (diamond-shaped). 50c, Tobacco farmer, field, hands rolling cigar. 65c, Building, Trinidad. 75c, Cigar, building, palm tree, people in room.
1p, Indian lighting cigar, vert.

2003, Feb. 6 *Perf. 12½*
4294-4298 A1203 Set of 5 5.00 2.50

Souvenir Sheet

4299 A1203 1p multi 2.75 1.40

No. 4299 contains one 32x40mm stamp.

Radio Rebelde, 45th Anniv. A1204

2003, Feb. 13 *Perf. 12¾*
4300 A1204 65c multi 1.50 .85

Félix Varela (1788-1853), Priest — A1205

2003, Feb. 25 *Perf. 12½*
4301 A1205 65c multi 1.50 .85

Military Units, 45th Anniv. — A1206

Designs: No. 4302, 15c, 2nd Frank Pais Front. No. 4303, 15c, 3rd Mario Muñoz Front.

2003 *Perf. 12¾*
4302-4303 A1206 Set of 2 1.10 .55

Issued: No. 4302, 3/5; No. 4303, 3/11.

16th World Sexology Congress A1207

2003, Mar. 11
4304 A1207 65c multi 1.50 .85

Transportation and Shipping — A1208

Designs: 5c, Container ship. 10c, Truck. 15c, Train. 65c, Airplane and delivery van. 75c, Airplane and delivery van, diff.

2003, Apr. 10 *Perf. 12½*
4305-4309 A1208 Set of 5 4.00 2.00

Flora & Fauna — A1209

Designs: 5c, Nymphaea ampla, Lepisosteus tristoechus. 10c, Magnolia grandiflora, Spindalis zena pretrei. 15c, Lillium candidum, Polymita picta. 65c, Strelitzia regiae, Solenodon cubanus. 75c, Hibiscus rosasinensis, Mellisuga helenae.

2003, May 15
4310-4314 A1209 Set of 5 4.00 2.00

Pan American Games, Santo Domingo, Dominican Republic A1210

Designs: 5c, Kayaking. 15c, Judo. 50c, Track. 65c, Volleyball.

2003, June 27 *Perf. 12½x12¾*
4315-4318 A1210 Set of 4 3.00 1.50

Attack on Moncada Barracks, 50th Anniv. — A1211

Designs: 15c, Men and barracks. 65c, Fidel Castro, text.

2003, July 26 *Perf. 12¾*
4319-4320 A1211 Set of 2 1.75 .75

Railroads A1212

Designs: 5c, Three-wheeled handcar, 1930-35. 10c, Crane, 1920. 15c, B-B 120/120 E locomotive, 1925. 65c, DVM-9 Ganz Mavag locomotive, 1969. 75c, 2-6-0 locomotive, 1905.

2003, Aug. 7
4321-4325 A1212 Set of 5 4.00 2.00

UN Conference to Combat Desertification — A1213

2003, Aug. 25 *Perf. 12½x12¼*
4326 A1213 65c multi 1.50 .85

Expo Bangkok A1214

Wildlife: 5c, Nyctea scandiaca. 10c, Fratercula arctica. 15c, Sula bassana. 65c, Ursus maritimus. 75c, Alopex lagopus.
1p, Pagolphilus groenlandicus.

2003, Aug. 28 *Perf. 12¾*
4327-4331 A1214 Set of 5 4.00 2.00

Souvenir Sheet
Perf. 12½

4332 A1214 1p multi 2.75 1.40

No. 4332 contains one 32x40mm stamp.

Butterflies and Flowers — A1215

Designs: 5c, Dione juno, Gardenia jasminoides. 15c, Apatura ilia, Chrysanthemus sinence. 65c, Inachis io, Hibiscus rosasinensis. 75c, Marpesia iole, Althaea rosea.
1p, Danaus plexippus, Zantedeschia aethiopica, vert.

2003, Sept. 11 **Litho.** *Perf. 12½*
4333-4336 A1215 Set of 4 4.00 2.00

Souvenir Sheet

4337 A1215 1p multi 2.75 1.40

No. 4337 contains one 32x40mm stamp.

Ecotourism — A1216

Bird and location: 10c, Aratinga eops, Baracoa. 15c, Xiphidiopicus percussus, Valle de los Ingenios. 65c, Tiaris canora, Sierra Maestra. 75c, Priotelus temnurus, Granma.

2003, Sept. 27 *Perf. 12¾x12½*
4338-4341 A1216 Set of 4 4.00 2.00

Worldwide Fund for Nature (WWF) — A1217

Crocodylus rhombifer: No. 4342, 15c, Eggs and hatchling. No. 4343, 15c, Adult at water's edge. 65c, Capturing prey. 75c, With open mouth.

2003, Sept. 30 **Litho.** *Perf. 12¾*
4342-4345 A1217 Set of 4 5.00 2.50
4345a Sheet, 4 each #4342-4345 20.00 12.50

America Issue — Flora and Fauna — A1218

Designs: 15c, Xiphidiopicus percussus. 65c, Encyclia phoenicea.

2003, Oct. 12
4346-4347 A1218 Set of 2 1.75 .85

35th Baseball World Cup — A1219

Cuban players: 5c, Antonio Muñoz. 10c, Lourdes Gourriel. No. 4350, 15c, Jorge L. Valdes. No. 4351, 15c, Lazaro Vargas. 65c, Lazaro Valle. 75c, Javier Mendez.
1p, Players celebrating, vert.

2003, Oct. 17 *Perf. 12½x12¼*
4348-4353 A1219 Set of 6 4.50 2.25

Souvenir Sheet
Perf. 12½

4354 A1219 1p multi 2.75 1.40

No. 4354 contains one 32x40mm stamp.

Ballet — A1220

Designs: No. 4355, 65c, National Ballet of Cuba, 55th anniv. No. 4356, 65c, Alicia Alonso as Giselle, 60th anniv., vert.

Perf. 12¾x12½, 12½x12¾
2003, Oct. 28
4355-4356 A1220 Set of 2 3.00 1.50

Powered Flight, Cent. — A1221

Emblem and: 5c, Wright Brothers. 15c, Pitcairn PA-5. 65c, Stearman C-3MB. 75c, Douglas M-2.

2003, Dec. 17 *Perf. 12½x12¼*
4357-4360 A1221 Set of 4 4.00 2.00

Cuban Revolution, 45th Anniv. — A1222

2004, Jan. 1 *Perf. 12¾*
4361 A1222 65c multi 1.50 .85

Expocuba, 15th Anniv. — A1223

2004, Jan. 4 *Perf. 12½x12¼*
4362 A1223 65c multi 1.50 .85

2004 Summer Olympics, Athens — A1224

Sports: 10c, Baseball. 15c (No. 4363A), Track. 65c, Boxing. 75c, Equestrian.

2004, Jan. 6 **Litho.**
4363-4365 A1224 Set of 4 3.75 1.90

New Year 2004 (Year of the Monkey) A1225

Monkey with denomination in: No. 4366, 15c, Blue. No. 4367, 15c, Orange.

2004, Jan. 9 *Perf. 12¾*
4366-4367 A1225 Set of 2 1.00 .50

Julio A. Mella (1903-29), Communist Leader A1226

2004, Jan. 10
4368 A1226 65c multi 1.50 1.10

José Martí (1853-95) — A1227

Designs: No. 4369, 5c, Martí in 1862, Colegio San Pablo, Prado No. 88. No. 4370, 5c, Martí's father, Mariano, Tapineria No. 16, Valencia. No. 4371, 5c, Martí's mother, Leonor Pérez, birthplace, Paula No. 41. No. 4372, 10c, Martí's high school, 1862, Martí, Fermín Valdés Domínguez, 1869. No. 4373, 10c, Martí in 1869, Havana Royal Jail. No. 4374, 15c, Martí in 1870, El Abra farm, Isle of Pines. No. 4375, 15c, Martí in 1870, Martí Forge. No. 4376, 15c, Martí and son, José Francisco, 1879, Guanabacoa Lyceum. 65c, Martí and son, 1879, Mercaderes Law Offices. 75c, Martí in 1895, La Jatía farm, Oriente.

2004, Jan. 28 *Perf. 12½x12¼*
4369-4378 A1227 Set of 10 4.75 2.75

See Nos. 4525-4535, 4570-4578, 4691-4700, 4800-4807.

Town of Santa María de Puerto del Principe, 490th Anniv. — A1228

2004, Feb. 2 *Perf. 12¾x12½*
4379 A1228 15c multi .50 .25

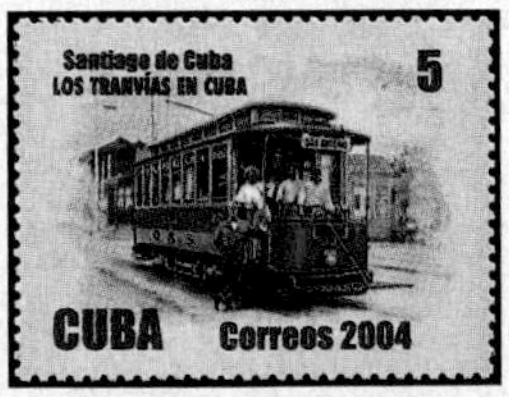

Trolleys A1229

Designs: 5c, Santiago. 10c, Havana. 15c, Camagüey. 65c, Matanzas. 75c, Camagüey, diff.
1p, Havana, diff.

2004, Feb. 20 *Perf. 12¾*
4380-4384 A1229 Set of 5 3.75 1.90

Souvenir Sheet
Perf. 12½

4385 A1229 1p multi 2.50 1.25

No. 4385 contains one 40x32mm stamp.

Souvenir Sheet

Cuba — Mexico Binational Philatelic Exhibition — A1230

2004, Feb. 25 ***Perf. 12½***
4386 A1230 1p multi 2.50 1.25

EGREM Recording Co., 40th Anniv. — A1231

Recording artists: 10c, Cascarita, Julio Cuevas. 15c, Carlos Puebla. 65c, Benny Moré. 75c, Compay Segundo.

2004, Mar. 24 ***Perf. 12¾***
4387-4390 A1231 Set of 4 3.50 1.75

España 2004 Intl. Philatelic Exhibition — A1232

Dogs: 5c, Spanish pointer. 10c, Spanish hound. 15c, Mallorquin bulldog. 65c, Catalan sheepdog. 75c, Pyrenean mastiff.
1p, Spanish mastiff.

2004, Mar. 24 ***Perf. 12½x12¼***
4391-4395 A1232 Set of 5 3.75 1.90

Souvenir Sheet
Perf. 12½
4396 A1232 1p multi 2.50 1.25

No. 4396 contains one 40x32mm stamp.

National Police, 45th Anniv. — A1233

2004, Mar. 26 ***Perf. 12½x12¼***
4397 A1233 15c multi + label .35 .25

Souvenir Sheet

Second Cuban Sports Olympiad — A1234

2004, Apr. 18 ***Perf. 12½***
4398 A1234 1p multi 2.50 1.25

Nature and Man Foundation, 10th Anniv. — A1235

2004, May 16 Litho. ***Perf. 12¼x12½***
4399 A1235 65c multi 1.50 .75

FIFA (Fédération Internationale de Football Association), Cent. — A1236

FIFA emblem and various players: 10c, 15c, 65c, 75c.

2004, May 21 ***Perf. 12¾***
4400-4403 A1236 Set of 4 3.50 1.75

Pets
A1237

Designs: 5c, Parakeets. 10c, Fish. 15c, Dogs. 65c, Cats. 75c, Finches.
1p, Horse, horiz.

2004, June 25 ***Perf. 12½x12¾***
4404-4408 A1237 Set of 5 3.75 1.90

Souvenir Sheet
Perf. 12½
4409 A1237 1p multi 2.50 1.25

No. 4409 contains one 40x32mm stamp.

Intl. Chess Federation, 80th Anniv. — A1238

Chess players: 15c, Maria Teresa Mora. 65c, José Raúl Capablanca, horiz. 75c, Ernesto "Che" Guevara.

2004, July 20 ***Perf. 12¾***
4410-4412 A1238 Set of 3 3.50 1.75

Minerals — A1239

Designs: 5c, Corundum. 10c, Thenardite. 15c, Uraninite. 65c, Realgar. 75c, Fluorite.
1p, Copper.

2004, July 30 ***Perf. 13***
4413-4417 A1239 Set of 5 3.50 1.75

Souvenir Sheet
Perf. 12½
4418 A1239 1p multi 2.50 1.25

No. 4418 contains one 40x32mm stamp.

Convention Hall, 25th Anniv. — A1240

2004, Sept. 3 ***Perf. 12¾***
4419 A1240 65c multi 1.50 1.25

Cuban Aviation, 75th Anniv. — A1241

Designs: 15c, Lockheed Constellation. 65c, IL-62M. 75c, Airbus 330.

2004, Oct. 8 ***Perf. 12½x12¼***
4420-4422 A1241 Set of 3 3.50 1.75

America Issue — A1242

Map of Cuba and: 15c, Bird over islands. 65c, Fish and marine life.

2004, Oct. 12
4423-4424 A1242 Set of 2 1.75 .90

Marine Mammals — A1243

Designs: 5c, Delphinus delphis. 10c, Lagenorhynchus obliquidens. 15c, Stenella attenuata. 65c, Grampus griseus. 75c, Tursiops truncatus.
1p, Orcinus orca.

2004, Oct. 20 ***Perf. 12½x12¼***
4425-4429 A1243 Set of 5 3.50 1.75

Souvenir Sheet
Perf. 13
4430 A1243 1p multi 2.50 1.25

No. 4430 contains one 40x32mm stamp.

Disappearance of Camilo Cienfuegos, 45th Anniv. A1244

2004, Oct. 28 ***Perf. 12¾***
4431 A1244 65c multi 1.50 .75

Railroad Stations, Cent. — A1245

Designs: 15c, Agramonte Station, 1906 ALCO No. 48 4-6-0. 65c, Aguacate Station, 1907 BLW No. 57 4-6-0. 75c, Guira de Melina Station, 1903 ALCO No. 7 4-4-0.

2004, Nov. 10 ***Perf. 13***
4432-4434 A1245 Set of 3 3.50 1.75

Souvenir Sheet

13th Philatelic Congress, Havana — A1245a

2004, Nov. 20 Litho. ***Perf. 12½***
4434A A1245a 1p multi 2.25 2.25

Founding of San Cristóbal de la Habana, 485th Anniv. A1246

Designs: 15c, Temple. 65c, Painting showing priest in red vestments at base of tree. 75c, Paintig showing group of men at base of tree.

Perf. 12½x12¾
2004, Nov. 30 **Litho.**
4435-4437 A1246 Set of 3 3.00 1.50

Latin American Parliament Foundation, 40th Anniv. — A1246a

2004, Nov. 30 Litho. *Perf. 12¾*
4437A A1246a 65c multi 1.40 .70

Ministry of Foreign Affairs, 45th Anniv. — A1247

2004, Dec. 23 *Perf. 12½x12¼*
4438 A1247 65c multi 1.40 .70

Alejo Carpentier (1904-80), Writer — A1248

2004, Dec. 26 *Perf. 12¾*
4439 A1248 65c multi 1.40 .70

First Baseball Game in Cuba, 130th Anniv. — A1249

Baseball players: 5c, Rey Vicente Anglada. 10c, Braudilio Vinent. 15c, Rogelio Garcia. 65c, Luis G. Casanova. 75c, Victor Mesa.
1p, Martin Dihigo, vert.

2004, Dec. 27 *Perf. 12½x12¼*
4440-4444 A1249 Set of 5 5.25 2.50

Souvenir Sheet
Perf. 12½
4445 A1249 1p multi 2.25 1.10
No. 4445 contains one 32x40mm stamp.

Jose L. Guerra Aguiar Cuban Postal Museum, 40th Anniv. — A1250

Designs: 15c, Plaza Mayor, Trinidad and 1855 Trinidad to Barcelona cover. 65c, Charity Sanctuary, El Cobre and 1861 El Cobre to Santiago de Cuba cover. 85c, Matanzas Cathedral, Matanzas and 1848 Mantanzas to Havana cover.

2005, Jan. 2 *Perf. 12¾x12½*
4446-4448 A1250 Set of 3 3.50 1.75

New Year 2005 (Year of the Rooster) A1251

Designs: No. 4449, 15c, Rooster in air. No. 4450, 15c, Rooster on ground.

2005, Jan. 4 *Perf. 12¼x12½*
4449-4450 A1251 Set of 2 .60 .30

Ministry of Information Technology and Communications, 5th Anniv. — A1252

2005, Jan. 12 *Perf. 12½x12¼*
4451 A1252 65c multi 1.40 .70

Dinosaurs — A1253

Designs: 5c, Carnotaurus. 10c, Oviraptor. 30c, Parasaurolophus. 65c, Sauropelta. 90c, Iguanodon.
1p, Velociraptor.

2005, Jan. 20 Litho. *Perf. 12½x12¼*
4452-4456 A1253 Set of 5 4.25 2.10

Souvenir Sheet
Perf. 13
4457 A1253 1p multi 2.25 1.10
No. 4457 contains one 40x32mm stamp.

Miguel de Cervantes and Title Page of *Don Quixote* — A1254

2005, Jan. 24 *Perf. 12¾x12½*
4458 A1254 65c multi 1.40 .70
Publication of *Don Quixote*, 400th anniv.

Bridges A1255

Designs: 10c, Bacunayagua Bridge. 15c, La Concordia Bridge. 50c, El Triunfo Bridge. 65c, Yayabo Bridge. 75c, Canimar Bridge.
1p, Plaza Bridge.

2005, Feb. 5 *Perf. 13x12¾*
4459-4463 A1255 Set of 5 4.75 2.40

Souvenir Sheet
Perf. 13
4464 A1255 1p multi 2.25 1.10
No. 4464 contains one 40x32mm stamp.

Cuban Telecommunications Enterprise, 10th Anniv. — A1256

2005, Feb. 24 *Perf. 12½x12¾*
4465 A1256 90c multi 1.90 .95

Parrots — A1257

Designs: 5c, Amazona ochrocephala, Amazona leucocephala. 10c, Agapornis personata, Agapornis fischeri. 15c, Cacatua galerita, Cacatua leadbeateri. 65c, Psittacula krameri, Psittacula himalayana, vert. 1.05p, Aratinga guarouba, Aratinga euops.
1p, Ara macao, Ara araruana, Anodorhynchus hyacythus.

Perf. 12½x12¼, 12¼x12½
2005, Feb. 23 Litho.
4466-4470 A1257 Set of 5 4.25 2.10

Souvenir Sheet
Perf. 13
4471 A1257 1p multi 2.25 1.10
No. 4471 contain one 32x40mm stamp.

Cats A1258

Various cats: 5c, 10c, 40c, 65c, 75c. 10c is vert.

2005, Mar. 15 *Perf. 12¾*
4472-4476 A1258 Set of 5 4.25 2.10

Perf. 13
4477 A1258 1p Two cats, vert. 2.25 1.10
No. 4477 contains one 32x40mm stamp.

Cuba — Canada Diplomatic Relations, 60th Anniv. — A1259

2005, Mar. 20 *Perf. 12¾x12½*
4478 A1259 65c multi 1.40 .70

Wildlife — A1260

2005, Mar. 21 *Perf. 12½x12¼*
4479 A1260 15c Manatee .30 .25
4480 A1260 65c Parrot 1.40 .70
4481 A1260 75c Crocodile 1.50 .75
4482 A1260 90c Hummingbird 1.90 .95
Nos. 4479-4482 (4) 5.10 2.65

World Water Day — A1261

2005, Mar. 22 *Perf. 13*
4483 A1261 90c multi 1.90 .95

Boats — A1262

Designs: 10c, Fishing boat, fish. 20c, Schooner, fish. 30c, Bonito boat, bonito. 45c, Shrimp boat, shrimp. 90c, Lobster boat, lobster.
1p, Cargo ship, horiz.

2005, Apr. 15 *Perf. 12½*
4484-4488 A1262 Set of 5 4.25 2.10

Souvenir Sheet
4489 A1262 1p multi 2.25 1.10

First Cuban Postage Stamps, 150th Anniv. — A1263

Designs: 15c, St. Francis of Assisi Convent, Cuba #1. 65c, Morro Lighthouse, Cuba #2. 75c, Colonial Post Office, Cuba #3.

2005, Apr. 24 *Perf. 12¾x12½*
4490-4492 A1263 Set of 3 3.50 1.75

Social Security For All — A1264

2005, May 5 Litho.
4493 A1264 65c multi 1.40 .70

Major General Máximo Gómez (1836-1905) — A1265

2005, June 17 *Perf. 12½*
4494 A1265 1.05p multi 2.25 1.10

Souvenir Sheet

Santiago de Cuba, 490th Anniv. — A1266

2005, July 4 *Perf. 13*
4495 A1266 1p multi 2.25 1.10

16th World Youth and Student Festival, Venezuela — A1267

2005, July 29 *Perf. 12¾x12½*
4496 A1267 65c multi 1.40 .70

Dances A1268

Parrot and: No. 4497, 65c, Samba dancers and Brazilian flag. No. 4498, 65c, Son dancers, Cuban flag.

2005, Aug. 15 *Perf. 12¾*
4497-4498 A1268 Set of 2 2.75 1.50

See Brazil Nos. 2967-2968.

Cuban — Soviet Space Flight, 25th Anniv. — A1269

No. 4499: a, Cosmonaut Arnaldo Tamayo Mendez. b, Cosmonaut Yuri Romanenko.

2005, Sept. 18 *Perf. 12½*
4499 A1269 90c Horiz. pair, #a-b 4.00 2.00

Albert Einstein's Visit to Cuba, 75th Anniv. — A1270

Designs: 65c, Caricature of Einstein. 75c, Equation for energy, Einstein writing.

2005, Sept. 21
4500-4501 A1270 Set of 2 4.00 2.00

Locomotives — A1271

Designs: 5c, DSB B40, 1869. 10c, Great Northern, 1902. No. 4504, 15c, Minaret, 1929. No. 4505, 15c, C. F. White, 1885. 2.05p, Western Pacific FP7A 805D.
1p, 14th No. 4 Krauss & Co., 1884.

2005, May 10 **Litho.** *Perf. 12¾*
4502-4506 A1271 Set of 5 5.50 2.75

Souvenir Sheet

Perf. 13

4507 A1271 1p multi 2.25 1.10

No. 4507 contains one 40x32mm stamp.

Zoo Animals A1272

Designs: 10c, Loxodonta africana. 15c, Acunonyx jubatus, horiz. 50c, Synceros caffer, horiz. 65c, Giraffa camelopardalis. 75c, Panthera leo.
1p, Equus burchelli, horiz.

2005, July 21 *Perf. 12¾*
4508-4512 A1272 Set of 5 4.75 2.40

Souvenir Sheet

Perf. 13

4513 A1272 1p multi 2.25 1.10

No. 4513 contains one 40x32mm stamp.

Santiago de Cuba, 490th Anniv. — A1273

2005, Sept. 22 *Perf. 12¾x12½*
4514 A1273 75c multi 1.60 .80

Revolutionary Defense Committees, 45th Anniv. — A1274

2005, Sept. 28 *Perf. 12½x12¼*
4515 A1274 50c multi 1.10 .55

Diplomatic Relations Between Cuba and People's Republic of China, 45th Anniv. — A1275

No. 4516: a, Chinese General Secretary Hu Jintao and Cuban Pres. Fidel Castro. b, Great Wall of China and Morro Castle, Havana.

2005, Sept. 28 *Perf. 13x13¼*
4516 A1275 15c Horiz. pair, #a-b 1.00 .50

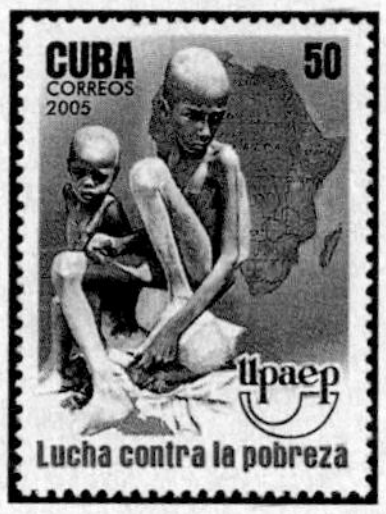

America Issue, Fight Against Poverty A1276

Designs: 50c, Starving children, map of Africa. 75c, Woman and child, map of South America.

2005, Oct. 12 *Perf. 12¾*
4517-4518 A1276 Set of 2 2.75 1.40

Horses A1277

Breeds: 10c, Gelderlander. 20c, Arabian. 30c, Quarterhorse. 65c, Wild horses. 75c, Lipizzaner.
100c, Holsteiner, vert.

2005, Oct. 21 *Perf. 12¾*
4519-4523 A1277 Set of 5 4.25 2.10

Souvenir Sheet

Perf. 12¾x12½

4524 A1277 100c multi 2.25 1.10

No. 4524 contains one 32x40mm stamp.

José Martí Type of 2004

Martí and: No. 4525, 5c, Central University, Madrid, 1871. No. 4526, 5c, Zaragoza University, 1871. No. 4527, 5c, F. Valdés Dominguez, Teatro Principal, Zaragoza, 1872. No. 4528, 10c, Victor Hugo House, Paris, 1872. No. 4529, 10c, Moneda No. 12, Mexico City, 1875. No. 4530, 15c, Normal School, Guatemala City, 1876. No. 4531, 15c, San Ildefonso No. 40, Mexico City, 1894. No. 4532, 15c, Plaza de Guardiola, Mexico City, 1894. 65c, Plaza Bolívar, Caracas, 1885. 75c, Santa María College, Caracas, 1893.
1p, Martínez Ibor Tobacco Factory, Tampa, 1892.

2005, Oct. 20 *Perf. 12½x12¼*
4525-4534 A1227 Set of 10 4.75 2.40

Souvenir Sheet

Perf. 13

4535 A1227 1p multi 2.25 1.10

No. 4535 contains one 40x32mm stamp.

World Summit on the Information Society, Tunis — A1278

2005, Nov. 16 *Perf. 12½x12¼*
4536 A1278 75c multi 1.60 .80

Establishment of Local Delivery of Mail in Havana, 150th Anniv. — A1279

Designs 15c, Cuba #7, cover to Havana. 65c, Cuba #16, Colonial Havana mailbox.

2005, Nov. 19 *Perf. 12¾x12½*
4537-4538 A1279 Set of 2 1.60 .80

Cuban Men Convicted of Terrorism Imprisoned In the United States A1280

2005, Nov. 25 *Perf. 12½x12¾*
4539 A1280 65c multi 2.00 1.00

Europa Stamps, 50th Anniv. (in 2006) A1281

Designs: 1.30p, Spain #1126, Castilla de la Fuerza, Havana. 2.05p, Spain #1010, Santisima Church, Trinidad, Cuba. 2.55p, Spain #1526, Morro Castle, Santiago de Cuba. 3.90p, Spain #1263, San Cristóbal Cathedral, Havana.

2005, Nov. 30 *Perf. 12½*
4540-4543 A1281 Set of 4 20.00 10.00
4543a Souvenir sheet, #4540-4543 20.00 10.00

Nos. 4540-4543, 4543a exist imperf. Values, same.

Jewelry A1282

Jewelry by: 5c, Antonio Barcala. 10c, Raúl Valladares. 45c, Carlos de la Torre. 65c, J. Carlo Rafart. 75c, Osvaldo Castilla.
1p, 19th cent. jewelry in Gold Museum.

2005, Dec. 1 *Perf. 12¾*
4544-4548 A1282 Set of 5 4.25 2.10

Souvenir Sheet

Perf. 12½

4549 A1282 1p multi 2.25 1.10

No. 4549 contains one 32x40mm stamp.

Friendship Among the Peoples Institute, 45th Anniv. — A1283

2005, Dec. 14 *Perf. 12¾x12½*

4550 A1283 1.05p multi 2.25 1.10

Snails and Mushrooms A1284

Designs: 10c, Clathrus cancellatus. 20c, Polymita genus picta. 30c, Lepiota puellaris. 65c, Polymita genus muscarum. 75c, Clitocybe infundibuliformis.

1p, Polymita genus versicolor, horiz.

2005, Dec. 15 *Perf. 12¾*

4551-4555 A1284 Set of 5 4.25 2.10

Souvenir Sheet

Perf. 13

4556 A1284 1p multi 2.25 1.10

No. 4556 contains one 40x32mm stamp.

Hotel Inglaterra, 130th Anniv. — A1285

2005, Dec. 23 *Perf. 12¾x12½*

4557 A1285 65c multi 1.40 .70

New Year 2006 (Year of the Dog) — A1286

Designs: No. 4558, 15c, Shih tzu. No. 4559, 15c, Pug.

2006, Jan. 4 *Perf. 12¼x12½*

4558-4559 A1286 Set of 2 .60 .30

Organization of Solidarity of the People of Asia, Africa and Latin America, 40th Anniv. A1287

2006, Jan. 16 *Perf. 12¾*

4560 A1287 65c multi 1.40 .70

Establishment of Cuban Postal Service, 250th Anniv. — A1288

Stampless cover and: 75c, Horse and rider. 2.05p, Ship.

2006, Mar. 1 *Perf. 12½x12¼*

4561-4562 A1288 Set of 2 6.00 3.00

OPEC Intl. Development Fund, 30th Anniv. — A1289

2006, Mar. 23 **Litho.**

4563 A1289 75c multi 1.60 .80

Souvenir Sheet

Havana '06 Intl. Philatelic Exhibition — A1290

2006, Mar. 25 *Perf. 12½*

4564 A1290 1p multi 2.25 1.10

Pope John Paul II (1920-2005) — A1291

Designs: 65c, Pope, Mass in Santa Clara. 75c, Mass in Camagüey (44x27mm). 90c, Mass in Santiago de Cuba (44x27mm). 1.05p, Pope, Mass in Havana.

2006, Apr. 2 *Perf. 12½x12¼*

4565-4568 A1291 Set of 4 7.25 3.75

Bay of Pigs Invasion, 45th Anniv. — A1292

2006, Apr. 17 *Perf. 12¼x12½*

4569 A1292 65c multi 1.40 .70

José Martí Type of 2004

Martí and: No. 4570, Madame Griffou's Hotel, New York, 1890. No. 4571, Gonzalo de Quesada, 116 West 64th Street, New York, 1893. No. 4572, Son, José Francisco, 324 Classon Ave., New York, 1885. No. 4573, Masonic Temple, New York, 1888.

No. 4574: a, Cajobabo beach, Gomez monument. b, Martí monument, monument at Dos Ríos.

Martí and: 75c, Hardman Hall, New York, 1891. 85c, Office, 120 Front Street, New York, 1891. 90c, María Mantilla, Bath Beach, Long Island.

1p, Home of Teodoro Pérez, Cayo Hueso, 1893.

2006, May 19 **Litho.** *Perf. 12½x12¼*

4570	A1227	5c	multi	.25	.25
4571	A1227	5c	multi	.25	.25
4572	A1227	10c	multi	.25	.25
4573	A1227	10c	multi	.25	.25
4574	A1227	15c	Horiz. pair, #a-b	.65	.65
4575	A1227	75c	multi	1.60	1.60
4576	A1227	85c	multi	1.90	1.90
4577	A1227	90c	multi	1.90	1.90
			Nos. 4570-4577 (8)	7.05	7.05

Souvenir Sheet

Perf. 13

4578 A1227 1p multi 2.25 2.25

No. 4578 contains one 40x32mm stamp.

Prehistoric Animals — A1293

Designs: 5c, Dsungaripetrus, Yangchuanosaurus. 10c, Pterodactylus, Sprinosaurus. 30c, Pteranodon, Pachycephalosaurus. 35c, Scaphognathus, Muttaburrasaurus. 65c, Quetzalcoatlus, Stegosaurus. 1.05p, Sordes, Saichania.

1p, Stenonychosaurus, vert.

2006, May 24 *Perf. 12½x12¼*

4579-4584 A1293 Set of 6 5.50 5.50

Souvenir Sheet

Perf. 12½

4585 A1293 1p multi 2.25 2.25

No. 4585 contains one 32x40mm stamp.

Ministry of the Interior, 45th Anniv. — A1294

2006, June 6 *Perf. 12½x12¼*

4586 A1294 75c multi 1.60 1.60

Fowl — A1295

Designs: 5c, Chickens. No. 4588, 15c, Turkeys. No. 4589, 15c, Guinea fowl. 45c, Geese. 50c, Pheasants. 75c, Peafowl.

1p, Ducks.

2006, June 15 *Perf. 12½x12¼*

4587-4592 A1295 Set of 6 4.50 4.50

Souvenir Sheet

Perf. 13

4593 A1295 1p multi 2.25 2.25

No. 4593 contains one 40x32mm stamp.

Cerro Pelado Declaration, 40th Anniv. — A1296

Designs: 65c, Ship, man and crowd. 75c, People in cargo hoist. 85c, Men assisting woman down ship's stairs, flags of Cuba and Puerto Rico.

2006, June 25 *Perf. 12½x12¾*

4594-4596 A1296 Set of 3 4.75 4.75

2006 World Cup Soccer Championships, Germany — A1296a

Various Cuban soccer players: 15c, 45c, 65c, 75c.

2006, June **Litho.** *Perf. 12¾*

4596A-4596D A1296a Set of 4 4.00 4.00

Genetic Engineering and Biotechnology Center, 20th Anniv. — A1297

2006, July 1 *Perf. 12½x12¼*

4597 A1297 65c multi 1.40 1.40

Comic Strips by Virgilio Martinez — A1298

Designs: 15c, Pucho y Sus Perrerias. 65c, Cucho.

2006, July 16 *Perf. 12¾x12¼*

4598-4599 A1298 Set of 2 1.75 1.75

Airplanes — A1299

Designs: 10c, Granville GeeBee R2. No. 4601, 15c, Bücker Jungmann. No. 4602, 15c, Comte AC-4 Gentleman. 50c, Mustang TF-51. 75c, Supermarine Spitfire. 85c, Lavochkin La-9.
1p, Bücker Jungmeister.

2006, July 20 *Perf. 12¾*
4600-4605 A1299 Set of 6 5.50 5.50

Souvenir Sheet
Imperf

4606 A1299 1p multi 2.25 2.25
No. 4606 contains one 36x28mm stamp.

Dogs — A1300

Designs: 5c, Bulldog. 10c, American cocker spaniel. 15c, Shar-pei. 20c, Airedale terrier. 35c, Pomeranian. 2.05p, Dalmatian.
1p, Whippet, vert.

2006, Aug. 18 *Perf. 12½x12¼*
4607-4612 A1300 Set of 6 6.25 6.25

Souvenir Sheet
Perf. 13

4613 A1300 1p multi 2.25 2.25

Recovery of Raw Materials, 45th Anniv. — A1301

Designs: 15c, Ernesto "Che" Guevara. 65c, Cuban and recovery program flags.

2006, Aug. 24 *Perf. 12¾*
4614-4615 A1301 Set of 2 1.75 1.75

14th Congress of Non-Aligned Countries, Havana A1302

2006, Sept. 10
4616 A1302 65c multi 1.40 1.40

Pedro Santacilia, Benito Juárez and Mexico House, Havana — A1303

2006, Sept. 15 *Perf. 12½x12¼*
4617 A1303 65c multi 1.40 1.40

Benito Juárez (1806-72), President of Mexico.

Souvenir Sheet

7th Hispano-Cuban Philatelic Exposition — A1304

No. 4618: a, Statue, arms of Cuba, denomination at LR. b, Statue, arms of Spain, denomination at LL.

2006, Sept. 20 *Imperf.*
4618 A1304 50c Sheet of 2, #a-b 2.25 2.25

España 06 World Philatelic Exposition, Malaga, Spain — A1305

Designs: 5c, Rio Hanabanilla. 10c, Laguna Bacanao. 15c, Sierra de la Gran Piedra. 20c, Valle de los Ingenios. 50c, Laguna del Tesoro. 75c, Sierra Maestra.
1p, Valle de Viñales.

2006, Sept. 20 *Perf. 12¾*
4619-4624 A1305 Set of 6 3.75 3.75

Souvenir Sheet
Perf. 13

4625 A1305 1p multi 2.25 2.25
No. 4625 contains one 40x32mm stamp.

America Issue, Energy Conservation — A1306

Equipment for harnessing energy source: No. 4626, 65c, Petroleum. No. 4627, 65c, Water. No. 4628, 65c, Solar. No. 4629, 65c, Wind.

2006, Oct. 12 *Perf. 12¾*
4626-4629 A1306 Set of 4 5.50 5.50

Saiz Brothers Association, 20th Anniv. A1307

2006, Oct. 18
4630 A1307 75c multi 1.60 1.60

20th Intl. Ballet Festival, Havana A1308

Dancers: 75c, Alicia Alonso and Igor Youskévitch. 85c, Alonso.

2006, Oct. 28 *Perf. 12¼x12½*
4631-4632 A1308 Set of 2 3.50 3.50

A1309

Belgica '06 Intl. Youth Philately Exposition, Belgium — A1310

Trains: 5c, Rocket and Intercity Diesel-electric. 10c, Turbine locomotive, Diesel-electric locomotive. 15c, Shinkasen and City of Los Angeles. 65c, Steam locomotive, Diesel locomotive. 75c, TEE Diesel-electric, TGV electric. 85c, Brisbane electric monorail, Wuppertal monorail.
No. 4639: a, Steam locomotive. b, Diesel locomotive.

2006, Nov. 2 *Perf. 12¾*
4633-4638 A1309 Set of 6 5.50 5.50

Souvenir Sheet
Perf. 12½

4639 A1310 50c Sheet of 2, #a-b 2.25 2.25

TeleFood Emblem — A1311

2006, Nov. 11 *Perf. 12¾*
4640 A1311 75c multi 1.60 1.60

Animals Serving Man — A1312

Designs: 5c, Equus caballus, Greek horse-drawn chariot. 15c, Camelus dromedarius, Ibn Battuta on camel. 30c, Capra aegagrus, Roman musician. 40c, Lama lama, Peruvian pre-Columbian ceramic llama. 50c, Felis catus, painting by Kuniyoshi Utagawa. 1.05p, Elephas maximus, elephant with Indian caparison.
1p, Canis familiaris, Grecian with dog.

2006, Oct. 1 **Litho.** *Perf. 12½x12¼*
4641-4646 A1312 Set of 6 5.50 5.50

Souvenir Sheet
Perf. 12½

4647 A1312 1p multi 2.25 2.25
No. 4647 contains one 40x32mm stamp.

Fire Fighting and Rescue Equipment — A1313

Designs: 5c, 1899 Horse-drawn ambulance, Brazil, and megaphone. 10c, Fireman's hat, and 1898 Merryweather fire truck, England. 20c, 1910 Laurin & Klement fire truck, Bohemia, and fire hydrant. 30c, 1939 American La France ladder truck, US, and badge. 45c, 1925 Leyland Motors pumper motorcycle, United Kingdom, and portable hose and tank. 90c, Brussels fire badge and 1930 Magirus ladder truck, Germany.
1p, Fireman spraying water, vert.

2006, Nov. 13 *Perf. 12¾*
4648-4653 A1313 Set of 6 4.50 4.50

Souvenir Sheet
Perf. 12½

4654 A1313 1p multi 2.25 2.25
No. 4654 contains one 32x40mm stamp.

Santiago Rebellion, 50th Anniv. — A1314

2006, Nov. 30 *Perf. 12½x12¼*
4655 A1314 65c multi 1.40 1.40

Governmental Reorganization, 30th Anniv. — A1315

2006, Dec. 2
4656 A1315 75c multi 1.60 1.60

Granma Landings, 50th Anniv. — A1316

Revolutionary Armed Forces, 50th Anniv. — A1317

2006, Dec. 2 *Perf. 13*
4657 A1316 65c multi 1.40 1.40
4658 A1317 65c multi 1.40 1.40

General Antonio Maceo Grajales (1845-96) — A1317a

2006, Dec. 7 Litho. *Perf. 12½x12¼*
4658A A1317a 1.05p multi 2.10 2.10

Intl. Film and Television School, 20th Anniv. — A1318

2006, Dec. 15 *Perf. 12¾*
4659 A1318 75c multi 1.60 1.60

Martí Forge Museum, 55th Anniv. — A1319

2006, Dec. 15 *Perf. 12½x12¼*
4660 A1319 90c multi 1.90 1.90

Literacy Campaign, 45th Anniv. A1320

2006, Dec. 19 *Perf. 12¾*
4661 A1320 65c multi 1.40 1.40

Major General Ignacio Agramonte y Loinaz (1841-73) — A1321

2006, Dec. 23 *Perf. 12½x12¼*
4662 A1321 65c multi 1.40 1.40

Special Education, 45th Anniv. — A1322

2007, Jan. 4 *Perf. 12¾*
4663 A1322 85c multi 1.75 1.75

Francesa Pharmacy, 125th Anniv. A1323

2007, Jan. 18 Litho.
4664 A1323 65c multi 1.40 1.40

Electric Trains A1324

Designs: 5c, First American electric locomotive, 1895. 10c, Locomotive, Netherlands. 15c, Interurban train, Australia. 65c, High-speed train, Italy. 85c, Helensburgh-Bridgeton train, Great Britain. 1.05p, Lyon-St. Etienne interurban train, France.
1p, High-speed train, Germany.

2007, Jan. 18 *Perf. 12¾*
4665-4670 A1324 Set of 6 6.00 6.00

Souvenir Sheet

Imperf

4671 A1324 1p multi 2.25 2.25

No. 4671 contains one 40x32mm stamp with simulated perforations.

12th Intl. Information Fair and Convention — A1325

2007, Feb. 12 *Perf. 12½x12¼*
4672 A1325 75c multi 1.60 1.60

Cats A1326

Designs: 10c, Two cats. No. 4674, 15c, Kitten with paw raised. No. 4675, 15c, Cat. 50c, Cat and telephone. 75c, Cat with ball. 90c, Cat, diff.
1p, Cat, diff.

2007, Feb. 14 *Perf. 12¾*
4673-4678 A1326 Set of 6 5.50 5.50

Souvenir Sheet

Imperf

4679 A1326 1p multi 2.25 2.25

No. 4679 contains one 40x32mm stamp with simulated perforations.

Fifth Congress of Cuban Pigeon Fanciers Federation — A1327

2007, Feb. 24 *Perf. 12¾*
4680 A1327 75c multi 1.60 1.60

Souvenir Sheet

Patria Newspaper, 115th Anniv. — A1328

Imperf. With Simulated Perforations

2007, Mar. 14
4681 A1328 1p multi 2.25 2.25

Animals in National Zoo — A1329

Designs: 5c, Ara ararauana. 10c, Tsetudo elephantopus. 15c, Balearica regulorum. 20c, Procyon lotor. 45c, Panthera pardus. 2.05p, Pongo pygmaeus.
1p, Giraffa camelopardalis, vert.

2007, Mar. 31 *Perf. 12½x12¼*
4682-4687 A1329 Set of 6 6.50 6.50

Souvenir Sheet

Imperf

4688 A1329 1p multi 2.25 2.25

No. 4688 contains one 32x40mm stamp with simulated perforations.

Raúl Roa García (1907-82), Foreign Minister A1330

2007, Apr. 18 *Perf. 12¾*
4689 A1330 65c multi 1.40 1.40

Union of Young Communists, 45th Anniv. — A1331

2007, Apr. 4 *Perf. 12½x12¼*
4690 A1331 75c multi 1.60 1.60

José Martí Type of 2004

Martí and: No. 4691, 5c, Cuban High School, Tampa, 1892. No. 4692, 5c, Casa de los Pedrosa, Tampa, 1892. No. 4693, 10c, Hotel Duval, Cayo Hueso, 1891. No. 4694, 10c, Hotel Cherokee, Tampa, 1891. No. 4695, 15c, Cayo Hueso Committee, 1891 (68x28mm). No. 4696, 15c, F. Valdés Domínguez, Gato Brothers Cigar Factory, Cayo Hueso, 1894. 35c, Club San Carlos, Cayo Hueso, 1893. 40c, Hotel Myrtle Bank, Kingston, 1892. 50c, Gen. Francisco Gómez Toro, Friends of the Country Society Building, Santo Domingo, 1894. 65c, Máximo Gómez, Gómez's house, Montecristi.

2007, Apr. 10 *Perf. 12½x12¼*
4691-4700 A1227 Set of 10 5.50 5.50

World Food Program Children's Art Exhibition, 10th Anniv. — A1332

2007, May 3 Litho. *Perf. 12¾*
4701 A1332 65c multi 1.40 1.40

Folklore Union — A1333

2007, May 7 *Perf. 12¼x12½*
4702 A1333 75c multi 1.60 1.60

Islands and Wildlife — A1334

Designs: 5c, Cayo Guillermo, pelican. No. 4704, 15c, Cayo Las Brujas, sea gull. No. 4705, 15c, Cayo Levisa, conches. 20c, Cayo Santa Maria, iguana. 50c, Cayo Ensenachos, plover. 85c, Cayo Largo, Carey turtle.
1p, Cayo Coco, flamingos.

2007, May 8 *Perf. 12½x12¼*
4703-4708 A1334 Set of 6 4.25 4.25

Souvenir Sheet

Imperf

4709 A1334 1p multi 2.25 2.25

No. 4709 contains one 40x32mm stamp.

Singers and Songwriters A1335

Designs: 5c, Benny Moré. 10c, Ignacio Piñeiro. 30c, Arsenio Rodríguez. 35c, Miguelito Cuní. 65c, Pio Leyva. 75c, Ibrahim Ferrer.
1p, Miguel Matamoros.

2007, May 10 *Perf. 12¾*
4710-4715 A1335 Set of 6 4.75 4.75

Souvenir Sheet

Imperf

4716 A1335 1p multi 2.25 2.25

No. 4716 contains one 32x40mm stamp with simulated perforations.

Souvenir Sheet

Martí Studies Youth Seminary, 35th Anniv. — A1336

2007, May 19 ***Imperf.***
4717 A1336 1p multi 2.25 2.25

Cuban Radio and Television Institute, 45th Anniv. — A1337

2007, May 24 ***Perf. 12½x12¼***
4718 A1337 3p multi 6.50 6.50

Integral Development Group of the Capital, 20th Anniv. — A1338

2007, May 26 **Litho.**
4719 A1338 65c multi 1.40 1.40

Cuban Admission to the United Nations, 60th Anniv. A1339

2007, May 29 ***Perf. 12¾***
4720 A1339 65c multi 1.40 1.40

2007 Pan American Games, Rio de Janeiro — A1340

Designs: No. 4721, 15c, Fencing. No. 4722, 15c, Boxing. 20c, Wrestling. 45c, Running. 65c, Gymnastics. 75c, Cycling.
1p, Games emblem, vert.

2007, June 20 ***Perf. 12¾***
4721-4726 A1340 Set of 6 5.00 5.00

Souvenir Sheet

Imperf

4727 A1340 1p multi 2.25 2.25

No. 4727 contains one 32x40mm stamp.

Third Technological Transfer and Intl. Trade Workshop — A1341

2007, July 3 ***Perf. 12½x12¼***
4728 A1341 65c multi 1.40 1.40

Frank País (1934-57), Revolutionary Hero — A1342

2007, July 30 ***Perf. 12¾***
4729 A1342 65c multi 1.40 1.40

Radio Cubana, 85th Anniv. A1343

2007, Aug. 22 ***Perf. 12¾***
4730 A1343 65c multi 1.40 1.40

Seven Wonders of the Modern World A1344

Designs: 10c, Great Wall of China. 15c, Petra, Jordan. 20c, Christ the Redeemer Statue, Brazil. 40c, Machu Picchu, Peru. 65c, Chichén Itzá Pyramids, Mexico. 75c, Roman Colosseum. 85c, Taj Mahal, India.

2007, Aug. 16 **Litho.** ***Perf. 12¾***
4731-4737 A1344 Set of 7 6.25 6.25

Transportation — A1345

Designs: 10c, Cocotaxis (40x29mm). 15c, Lada 2105 taxi (40x29mm). 30c, Girón VI bus (40x29mm). 40c, Bus trailer on truck (44x27mm). 75c, DAF articulated bus (44x27mm). 85c, Yutong bus (44x27mm).
1p, La Gaviota train.

Perf. 12¾, 12½x12¼ (#4741-4743)

2007, Sept. 3
4738-4743 A1345 Set of 6 5.25 5.25

Souvenir Sheet

Imperf

4744 A1345 1p multi 2.00 2.00

No. 4744 contains one 40x32mm stamp with simulated perforations.

Central Youth Club, 20th Anniv. — A1346

2007, Sept. 8 ***Perf. 12¼x12½***
4745 A1346 65c multi 1.40 1.40

Cubans Convicted of Espionage by United States A1347

Designs: No. 4746, 65c, Raised hand with "Cuban Five" emblem. No. 4747, 65c, Fernando González Liort. No. 4748, 65c, Gerardo Hernández Nordelo. No. 4749, 65c, Antonio Guerrero Rodriguez. No. 4750, 65c, Ramón Labañino Salazar. No. 4751, 65c, René González Schwerert.

2007, Sept. 12 ***Perf. 12¾***
4746-4751 A1347 Set of 6 8.00 8.00

Tree Planting Campaign — A1348

2007, Oct. 24 ***Perf. 12½x12¼***
4752 A1348 65c multi 1.40 1.40

Rose Varieties A1349

Designs: 5c, Pink Parfait. No. 4754, 15c, Alison Wheatcroft. No. 4755, 15c, Prima Ballerina. 45c, Fragrant Cloud. 50c, Blue Moon. 75c, Grandmère Jenny.
1p, Rosa highdownensis.

2007, Oct. 25 ***Perf. 12¾***
4753-4758 A1349 Set of 6 4.25 4.25

Souvenir Sheet

Imperf

4759 A1349 1p multi 2.00 2.00

No. 4759 contains one 40x32mm stamp with simulated perforations.

International Design Conference — A1350

Designs: 75c, Electronic machine. 85c, Caricatures.

2007, Oct. 26 ***Perf. 12½x12¼***
4760-4761 A1350 Set of 2 3.25 3.25

Souvenir Sheet

International Air Mail Service From Cuba, 80th Anniv. — A1351

2007, Oct. 27 ***Imperf.***
4762 A1351 1p multi 2.00 2.00

Seventh Natl. Philatelic Championship. No. 4762 has simulated perforations.

Protected Animals — A1352

Designs: 5c, Eretmochelys imbricata. 10c, Trichechus manatus. 20c, Mesocapromys sanfelipensis. 30c, Mesocapromys nanus. 45c, Epinephelus itajara. 85c, Balistes vetula.
1p, Chelonia mydas.

2007, Nov. 15 ***Perf. 12½x12¼***
4763-4768 A1352 Set of 6 4.00 4.00

Souvenir Sheet

Imperf

4769 A1352 1p multi 2.00 2.00

No. 4769 contains one 40x32mm stamp with simulated perforations.

Cuban UNESCO Commission, 60th Anniv. — A1353

2007, Nov. 17 ***Perf. 12½x12¼***
4770 A1353 65c multi 1.40 1.40

Cuban Railroads, 170th Anniv. — A1354

2007, Nov. 19 ***Perf. 12¾***
4771 A1354 3p multi 6.00 6.00

Camagüey Ballet, 40th Anniv. — A1355

2007, Dec. 1 **Litho.**
4772 A1355 75c multi 1.50 1.50

Infomed Health Network, 15th Anniv. — A1356

2007, Dec. 15

4773 A1356 65c green & black 1.40 1.40

Federation of University Students, 85th Anniv. — A1357

2007, Dec. 20

4774 A1357 65c multi 1.40 1.40

Seven Marvels of Cuban Civil Engineering — A1358

Designs: 5c, White Aqueduct, Havana. 10c, Sewer system, Havana. 20c, Central Highway, Santiago. 30c La Bahia Tunnel, Havana. 85c, Bacunayagua Bridge, Matanzas. 90c, La Farola Viaduct, Guantánamo.
1p, FOSCA Building, Havana.

2007, Dec. 31 *Perf. 12¾*

4775-4780 A1358 Set of 6 5.00 5.00

Souvenir Sheet

Imperf

4781 A1358 1p multi 2.00 2.00

No. 4781 contains one 40x32mm stamp with simulated perforations.

World Ozone Layer Protection Day, 20th Anniv. — A1359

2007 *Perf. 12¾*

4782 A1359 65c multi 1.40 1.40

Tourism — A1360

No. 4783, 75c — El Yunque, Baracoa and: a, Atlantea perezi. b, Polymita picta.
No. 4784, 75c — Alexander von Humboldt National Park and: a, Eleutherodactylus iberia. b, Solenodon cubanus.

2007 Litho. Horiz. Pairs, #a-b

4783-4784 A1360 Set of 2 6.00 6.00

Miniature Sheet

America Issue, Education For All — A1361

No. 4785: a, Teacher and children, children in uniforms, girl at computer. b, Students at table. c, Students, flag, marchers. d, Artist, people sitting in front of building, man at computer.

2007

4785 A1361 75c Sheet of 4, #a-d 6.00 6.00

Ernesto "Che" Guevara (1928-67) — A1362

Designs: 65c, Guevara sitting with other men. 75c, Monument to Guevara, La Higuera, Bolivia. 85c, Guevara and text. 90c, Guevara and marchers.

2007 *Perf. 12½x12¼*

4786-4789 A1362 Set of 4 6.50 6.50
4789a Miniature sheet, #4786-4789 6.50 6.50

Historic Central City of Cienfuegos — A1363

Buildings: 15c, City Hall. 65c, San Lorenzo and Santo Tomás College. 75c, Tomás Terry Theater. 85c, Ferrer Palace.
1p, Gazebo, José Martí Park.

2007 Litho. *Perf. 12¾*

4790-4793 A1363 Set of 4 5.00 5.00

Souvenir Sheet

Imperf

4794 A1363 1p multi 2.00 2.00

No. 4794 contains one 40x32mm stamp with simulated perforations.

University of Havana, 280th Anniv. — A1364

2008, Jan. 5 Litho. *Perf. 12½x12¼*

4795 A1364 65c multi 1.40 1.40

2008 Summer Olympics, Beijing — A1365

Designs: 15c, Baseball. 45c, Swimming. 65c, Discus. 75c, Volleyball.

2008, Jan. 18 *Perf. 12¾*

4796-4799 A1365 Set of 4 4.00 4.00

José Martí Type of 2004

Designs: No. 4800, 15c, Martí at Twilight Park, New York, 1892, vert. No. 4801, 15c, Martí with members of Cuban Revolutionary Party, 1892, vert. 30c, Martí, and family of Carmen Miyares, Sandy Hill, New York, 1893, vert. 40c, Mausoleum, Santa Ifigenia, vert. 45c, Martí, tomb of Félix Varela, San Agustín. 50c, Martí, Dellundé House, Cabo Haitiano. 65c, Hanábana Memorial, Matanzas. 85c, Cover from 1889 in Postal Museum.

2008, Jan. 28

4800-4807 A1227 Set of 8 7.00 7.00

Subway Trains and Stations — A1366

Trains and stations in: No. 4808, 15c, New York. No. 4809, 15c, Paris. 30c, Caracas. 65c, Madrid. 75c, Mexico City. 1.05p, Tokyo.
No. 4814: a, 1866 London Underground train. b, Modern London Underground train, Westminster station emblem.

2008, Feb. 15 *Perf. 12½x12¼*

4808-4813 A1366 Set of 6 6.25 6.25

Souvenir Sheet

Imperf

4814 A1366 50c Sheet of 2, #a-b 2.00 2.00

No. 4814 contains two 39x24mm stamps with simulated perforations.

Radio Rebelde, 50th Anniv. A1367

2008, Feb. 24 *Perf. 12¾*

4815 A1367 75c multi 1.50 1.50

Frontier Guards, 45th Anniv. A1368

2008, Mar. 3

4816 A1368 65c multi 1.40 1.40

Dr. Mario Muñoz Monroy Third Guerrilla Front, 50th Anniv. — A1369

2008, Mar. 6 Litho. *Perf. 12¾*

4817 A1369 75c multi 1.50 1.50

Aquaculture — A1370

Designs: No. 4817A, Cyprinus carpio. No. 4817B, Hypophthalmicthys molitrix. 45c, Aristychthys nobilis. 65c, Penaeus vannamei. 75c, Ctenopharyngodon idella. 85c, Clarias gariepinus.
1p, Oreochromis aurea.

2008, Apr. 8 *Perf. 12½x12¼*

4817A	A1370	15c multi	.30	.30
4817B	A1370	15c multi	.30	.30
4817C	A1370	45c multi	.90	.90
4818	A1370	65c multi	1.30	1.30
4819	A1370	75c multi	1.50	1.50
4820	A1370	85c multi	1.75	1.75
	Nos. 4817A-4820 (6)		6.05	6.05

Souvenir Sheet

Imperf

4821 A1370 1p multi 2.00 2.00

No. 4821 contains one 31x28mm stamp.

Souvenir Sheet

Cuban Postal Stationery, 130th Anniv. — A1371

2008, Apr. 24 *Imperf.*

4822 A1371 1p multi 2.00 2.00

Bohemia Magazine, Cent. — A1372

2008, May 10 *Perf. 12¾*

4823 A1372 65c multi 1.40 1.40

Second Frank Pais Front, 50th Anniv. — A1373

2008, Mar. 11 Litho. *Perf. 12¾*
4824 A1373 65c multi 1.40 1.40

Birds — A1374

Designs: 5c, Cartacuba (Cuban tody). 10c, Ruiseñor (nightingale). 15c, Carpintero verde (green woodpecker). 50c, Tocororo (Cuban trogon). 65c, Catey (parakeet), horiz. 75c, Cabrerito de la Ciénaga (Zapata sparrow), horiz. 90c, Zunzuncito (hummingbird), horiz. 1.05p, Juan Chiví (Cuban vireo), horiz.

2008, May 22
4825-4832 A1374 Set of 8 8.50 8.50

"Wings of Liberty" Symposium, Cuban National Museum of Natural History.

Visit of Indonesian Pres. Sukarno, 48th Anniv. — A1375

Sukarno and: No. 4833, 65c, Fidel Castro (shown). No. 4834, 65c, Ernesto "Che" Guevara.

2008 Litho. *Perf. 12½x12¼*
4833-4834 A1375 Set of 2 2.60 2.60

Flora and Fauna at Ramsar Sites in Cuba and Iran — A1376

No. 4835: a, Cyanolimnas cerverai and Nymphaea ampla, Ciénaga de Zapata, Cuba. b, Nelumbo nucifera and Porphyrio porphyrio, Anzali, Iran.

2008, Oct. 16 Litho. *Perf. 12½x12¼*
4835 Horiz. pair with central label 3.00 3.00
a.-b. A1376 75c Either single 1.50 1.50

See Iran No. 3003.

Cuban Literature, 400th Anniv. — A1377

Designs: 15c, Emblem written backward on torn page. 75c, Snails. 2.05p, White star in red triangle.

2008, Oct. 20 *Perf. 12¼x12½*
4836-4838 A1377 Set of 3 6.00 6.00

National Ballet, 60th Anniv. A1378

Designs: 10c, Dancers in Swan Lake (El Lago de los Cisnes). 15c, Dancers in Giselle. 50c, Dancers in Coppélia, horiz. 65c, Dancer in Romeo and Juliet, horiz. 75c, Dancers in The Nutcracker (Cascanueces), horiz. 85c, Scenery for Sleeping Beauty (La Bella Durmiente del Bosque), horiz.
1p, Ballerina at Intl. Ballet Festival, Havana.

2008, Oct. 28 *Perf. 12¾*
4839-4844 A1378 Set of 6 6.00 6.00

Souvenir Sheet
Imperf

4845 A1378 1p multi 2.00 2.00

No. 4845 has simulated perforations.

Vilma Espín Guillois (1930-2007), Wife of Pres. Raúl Castro — A1379

2008 *Perf. 12¾*
4846 A1379 65c multi 1.40 1.40

Joséito Fernández (1908-79), Singer A1380

2008
4847 A1380 65c multi 1.40 1.40

Dr. Carlos J. Finlay (1833-1915), Yellow Fever Researcher A1381

2008
4848 A1381 65c multi 1.40 1.40

José Raúl Capablanca (1888-1942), World Chess Champion — A1382

Designs: 1.05p, Capablanca playing chess. 2.05p, Capablanca seated, vert.

2008 *Perf. 12½x12¼, 12¼x12½*
4849-4850 A1382 Set of 2 6.25 6.25

Dogs — A1383

Designs: 10c, Neapolitan mastiff. 15c, Golden retriever. 40c, Rottweiler. 65c, Shetland sheepdog. 85c, Chow chow. 90c, Boxer.
1p, Chihuahua.

2008 *Perf. 12¾*
4851-4856 A1383 Set of 6 6.25 6.25

Souvenir Sheet
Imperf

4857 A1383 1p multi 2.00 2.00

Owls and Butterflies A1384

Designs: No. 4858, 15c, Tyto alba, Lycaena dispar. No. 4859, 15c, Bubo bubo, Lolana iolas. 45c, Strix nebulosa, Vanessa cardui. 65c, Strix aluco, Colias erate. 75c, Asio otus, Aporia crataegi. 85c, Strix uralensis, Colias hecla.
1p, Anthocharis damone butterfly, horiz.

2008 *Perf. 12¾*
4858-4863 A1384 Set of 6 6.00 6.00

Souvenir Sheet
Imperf

4864 A1384 1p multi 2.00 2.00

No. 4864 contains one 40x32mm stamp. EFIRO 2008 Intl. Philatelic Exhibition, Romania (No. 4864).

Animals in National Zoo — A1385

Designs: 5c, Panthera leo. 10c, Ailurus fulgens. 15c, Cacatua galerita. 30c, Crocodylus rhombifer. 40c, Phoenicopterus ruber. 2.05p, Equus burchelli.
1p, Loxodonta africana.

2008 *Perf. 12½x12¼*
4865-4870 A1385 Set of 6 6.25 6.25

Souvenir Sheet
Imperf

4871 A1385 1p multi 2.00 2.00

No. 4871 contains one 40x32mm stamp with simulated perforations.

Ernesto "Che" Guevara (1928-67), Revolutionary Leader — A1386

Designs: 65c, Guevara as infant with mother, birthplace in Rosario, Argentina. 75c, Guevara as boy, childhood home, Villa Nydia. 85c, Guevara as young man, Guevara on bicycle. 1.05p, Guevara on raft, Guevara with cigar.

2008 *Perf. 12¾*
4872-4875 A1386 Set of 4 6.75 6.75
4875a Souvenir sheet, #4872-4875 6.75 6.75

America Issue, National Holidays — A1387

Designs: 15c, Starting Day of the War of Independence. 65c, Liberation Day. 75c, Labor Day. 2.05p, National Rebellion Day.

2008 Litho. *Perf. 12½x12¼*
4876-4879 A1387 Set of 4 7.25 7.25
4879a Souvenir sheet of 4, #4876-4879 7.25 7.25

Tourism A1388

Buildings in: No. 4880, 15c, Havana. No. 4881, 15c, Trinidad. 30c, Sancti Spiritus. 65c, Camagüey. 75c, Bayamo. 85c, Santiago de Cuba.
1p, Baracoa.

2008 *Perf. 12¼x12½*
4880-4885 A1388 Set of 6 5.75 5.75

Souvenir Sheet
Imperf

4886 A1388 1p multi 2.00 2.00

No. 4886 contains one 32x40mm stamp with simulated perforations.

Gran Caribe Hotels, 50th Anniv. A1389

Designs: 5c, Hotel Habana Riviera. 10c, Hotel Habana Libre, vert. 15c, Hotel Deauville, vert. 50c, Hotel Victoria, vert. 65c, Hotel Presidente.
1p, Hotel Sevilla, vert.

2008 *Perf. 12¾*
4887-4891 A1389 Set of 5 3.00 3.00

Souvenir Sheet
Imperf

4892 A1389 1p multi 2.00 2.00

No. 4892 contains one 32x40mm stamp with simulated perforations.

Carlos de la Torre y la Huerta (1858-1950), Naturalist — A1390

De la Torre y la Huerta and: 5c, Hand holding shells. 15c, Polymita picta nigrolimbata, light blue background. 50c, Polymita picta nigrolimbata, pink background. 65c, Polymita picta iolimbata. 75c, Polymita picta nigrolimbata, light green background. 90c, Polymita picta fuscolimbata.
1p, Liguus fasciatus.

2008 ***Perf. 12½x12¼***
4893-4898 A1390 Set of 6 6.00 6.00

Souvenir Sheet
Imperf

4899 A1390 1p multi 2.00 2.00

No. 4899 contains one 40x32mm stamp with simulated perforations.

Paleolithic Man and Animals — A1391

Designs: 10c, Australopithecus afarensis and Megatherium. 15c, Australopithecus africanus and Toxodon. 50c, Australopithecus robustus and Bison. 65c, Homo habilis and Hippidion. 75c, Homo erectus and Meganteron. 90c, Neanderthal man and Mammoths.
1p, Coelodonts.

2008 ***Perf. 12¾***
4900-4905 A1391 Set of 6 6.25 6.25

Souvenir Sheet
Imperf

4906 A1391 1p multi 2.00 2.00

No. 4906 contains one 45x34mm stamp with simulated perforations.

A1392

Transportation — A1392a

Designs: 15c, 1802 steam carriage of Richard Trevithick. 30c, 1829 steam carriage of Sir Goldsworthy Gurney. 40c, 1832 steam carriage of William Church. 65c, 1858 steam carriage of Thomas Rickett. 75c, 1890 Motorwagen of Karl Benz. 85c, 1836 steam omnibus of Walter Hancock.
1p, 1958 Panhard-Levassor automobile.

2008 ***Perf. 12½x12¼***
4907-4912 A1392 Set of 6 6.25 6.25

Souvenir Sheet
Imperf

4913 A1392a 1p multi 2.00 2.00

No. 4913 has simulated perforations.

Matanzas, 315th Anniv. — A1393

Designs: 15c, Building arches, Plaza de la Vigía. 40c, Palacio Junco Provincial Museum. 50c, Fire house. 75c, Palace of Justice. 85c, Sauto Theater. 90c, Palace of Government.
1p, Unknown Soldier's Monument, vert.

2008 ***Perf. 12½x12¼***
4914-4919 A1393 Set of 6 7.25 7.25

Souvenir Sheet
Imperf

4920 A1393 1p multi 2.00 2.00

No. 4920 has simulated perforations.

Triumph of the Cuban Revolution, 50th Anniv. — A1394

No. 4921, 15c: a, Liberation Day (man with wide-brimmed hat at left). b, Liberation Day (tank at left). c, Arrival of Fidel Castro in Havana. d, First march. e, Fidel Castro, Revolutionary Government Prime Minister, addressing crowd. f, Camilo Cienfuegos dissolves Bureau for the Repression of Communist Activities. g, Granting of Cuban citizenship to Ernesto "Che" Guevara. h, Fidel Castro's first visit to Venezuela. i, Creation of the P.N.R. (National Revolutionary Police). j, Creation of State Security organizations. k, Creation of T.G.F. (Border Guard). l, Agrarian Reform Law. m, Takeover of Cuban telephone system. n, Creation of the F.M.C. (Federation of Cuban Women). o, Creation of the C.D.R. (Committees for the Defense of the Revolution). p, Start of literacy campaign. q, Creation of I.N.D.E.R. (Institute of Sports, Physical Education and Recreation). r, Radio across Cuba. s, Designation of Guevara as Industry Minister. t, Creation of Union of Young Communists. u, Creation of the Civil Defense. v, Creation of the National Civil Defense Committee. w, First sugar harvest. x, Guevara speaks at the United Nations.

No. 4922, 15c: a, Constitution of the Central Committee of the Cuban Communist Party. b, Day of the Heroic Guerrilla. c, Free distribution of Guevara's diary. d, First National Education and Cultural Congress. e, First Congress of the P.C.C. (Cuban Communist Party). f, First Rural Education Congress. g, Establishment in Cuba of Intl. Children's Day. h, Vaccinations in Cuba, 205th anniv. i, Creation of M.I.N.A.Z. (Cuban Ministry of Sugar). j, Creation of I.N.P. (National Fishing Institute). k, Development of fishing industry. l, 11th World Youth and Student Festival. m, Cuban cosmonaut. n, Day of Cuban Science (building at right). o, Day of Cuban Science (building at left). p, Family doctors and nurses. q, Elimination of apartheid, 15th anniv. r, Beginning of Battle of Ideas. s, Social security. t, Creation of the E.I.E.D. u, National culture (ballet dancer at left). v, National culture (guitarists at right). w, Batlle of Ideas program (classroom at right). x, Battle of Ideas program (people waving flags at right).

No. 4923, 1p, Cuban flags. No. 4924, 1p, Revolution Plaza, Havana.

2009, Jan. 1 **Litho.** ***Perf. 12¾***

Sheets of 24, #a-x

4921-4922 A1394 Set of 2 14.50 14.50

Souvenir Sheets
Imperf

4923-4924 A1394 Set of 2 4.00 4.00

Nos. 4923-4924 have simulated perforations.

Ernesto "Che" Guevara and Cuban Flag — A1394a

2009 **Litho.** ***Perf. 12¾***
4924A A1394a 75c multi 1.50 1.50

Cuban Revolution, 50th anniv. See Russia No. 7124.

Second World Baseball Classic A1395

Designs: 5c, Batter swinging at ball. 10c, Play at home plate. 15c, Fielder stretching to catch ball. 45c, Pitcher in wind-up. 65c, Runner sliding into base. 75c, Runner and fielder watching ball.
1p, Cuban team.

2009, Jan. 27 ***Perf. 12¾***
4925-4930 A1395 Set of 6 4.50 4.50

Souvenir Sheet
Imperf

4931 A1395 1p multi 2.00 2.00

No. 4931 has simulated perforations.

Souvenir Sheet

Cuban Workers' Union, 70th Anniv. — A1396

2009, Jan. 29 ***Imperf.***
4932 A1396 1p multi 2.00 2.00

No. 4932 has simulated perforations.

Santa María del Puerto de Príncipe, 495th Anniv. A1397

2009, Feb. 2 ***Perf. 12¾***
4933 A1397 90c multi 1.90 1.90

Souvenir Sheet

13th Intl. Information Fair and Convention, Havana — A1398

2009, Feb. 9 ***Imperf.***
4934 A1398 1p multi 2.00 2.00

No. 4934 has simulated perforations.

Charles Darwin (1809-92), Naturalist A1398a

Designs: 10c, Darwin and his birthplace, Shrewsbury, England. 65c, HMS Beagle and map of its expedition. 75c, Publication of *On the Origin of Species.* 85c, Darwin and his notes.

Perf. 12½x12¼

2009, Feb. 12 **Litho.**
4934A-4934D A1398a Set of 4 4.75 4.75

Art — A1399

Designs: 15c, Coloritmo, by Alejandro Otero. 30c, Atmósfera Cromoplástica IV, by Luis Tomasello. 40c, Autopista del Sur, by León Ferrari. 65c, Tridim-L, by Victor Vasarely. 75c, Untitled work, by Jesús Soto. 85c, Untitled work, by Julio Le Parc.
1p, Physicromie 105, by Carlos Cruz Diez, horiz.

2009, Feb. 25 ***Perf. 12¾***
4935-4940 A1399 Set of 6 6.25 6.25

Souvenir Sheet
Imperf

4941 A1399 1p multi 2.00 2.00

No. 4941 has simulated perforations.

High Speed Trains A1400

Designs: No. 4942, 15c, Acela Express, US. No. 4943, 15c, AVE, Spain. 30c, ATP Eurostar, Great Britain. 65c, ICE, Germany. 75c, ICN, Switzerland. 1.05p, TGV, France.
No. 4948: a, Shinkansen Model 500, Japan. b, Shinkansen Model 700, Japan.

2009, Feb. 27 ***Perf. 12½x12¼***
4942-4947 A1400 Set of 6 6.25 6.25

Souvenir Sheet
Imperf

4948 A1400 50c Sheet of 2, #a-b 2.00 2.00

No. 4948 has simulated perforations.

Cuban Arts and Cinematographic Industry Institute, 50th Anniv. — A1401

Designs: No. 4949, 10c, Actress from *La Bella del Alhambra.* No. 4950, 10c, Actress from *Reina y Rey.* No. 4951, 15c, Character from animated film *Elpidio Valdés.* No. 4952, 15c, Actresses from *Lucía.* 45c, Actor from *Primera Carga al Machete.* 65c, Actor from *El Hombre de Maisinicú.* 75c, Actor and actress from *Clandestinos.* 90c, Actress from *Retrato de Teresa.* 1.05p, Santiago Alvarez, ICAIC reporter.
1p, Scene from *Fresa y Chocolate.*

2009, Mar. 24 ***Perf. 12½x12¼***
4949-4957 A1401 Set of 9 8.75 8.75

Souvenir Sheet
Imperf

4958 A1401 1p multi 2.00 2.00

No. 4958 has simulated perforations.

State Security Organizations, 50th Anniv. — A1402

2009, Mar. 26 ***Perf. 12¼x12½***
4959 A1402 65c multi 1.40 1.40

Motorcycles — A1403

Designs: 10c, Cagiva Mito N1. 15c, Honda CBR 900. 50c, Hyosung-GT 8. 65c, Kawasaki ZX-7R 750cc. 75c, Gussi MGS. 90c, Ducati Monster 900.
1p, Hyosung-GT 125-R-LD, vert.

2009, Apr. 8 ***Perf. 12¾***
4960-4965 A1403 Set of 6 6.25 6.25

Souvenir Sheet
Imperf
4966 A1403 1p multi 2.00 2.00

China 2009 World Philatelic Exhibition, Luoyang. No. 4966 has simulated perforations.

Cats A1404

Designs: 10c, Cat and kittens. 15c, Kittens and baseball. 40c, Two cats clawing fabric. 65c, Two cats on tile floor. 75c, Cat. 1.05p, Cat eating food.
1p, Two cats on roof, vert.

2009, Apr. 12 ***Perf. 12¾***
4967-4972 A1404 Set of 6 6.25 6.25

Souvenir Sheet
Imperf
4973 A1404 1p multi 2.00 2.00

No. 4973 has simulated perforations.

Tourism A1405

Art from hotels and restaurants: No. 4974, 10c, Stained-glass window, by René Portocarrero, Bodeguita del Medio Restaurant. No. 4975, Detail from mural, by Amelia Peláez, Hotel Habana Libre Tryp. 45c, Painting by Domingo Ramos, Hotel Nacional de Cuba, horiz. 65c, Detail from mural, by Mariano Rodríguez, Hotel Bello Caribe, horiz. 75c, Detail from mural, by Raúl Martínez, Hotel Bella Caribe, horiz. 85c, Mural, by Manuel A. Sosabravo, Hotel Habana Libre Tryp, horiz.
1p, Mural by various artists, Hotel Inglaterra, horiz.

2009, Apr. 21 ***Perf. 12¾***
4974-4979 A1405 Set of 6 6.00 6.00

Souvenir Sheet
Imperf
4980 A1405 1p multi 2.00 2.00

No. 4980 has simulated perforations.

Haydee Santamaría Cuadrado (1922-80), Founder of Casa de las Americas — A1406

2009, Apr. 28 ***Perf. 12¾***
4981 A1406 3p multi 6.00 6.00

World Heritage Sites A1407

Designs: 15c, Havana. 45c, Cienfuegos. 50c, Trinidad. 1.05p, Camagüey.

2009, May 8 **Litho.**
4982-4985 A1407 Set of 4 4.50 4.50
4985a Souvenir sheet, #4982-4985 4.50 4.50

Parrots A1408

Designs: 5c, Guacamayo sereno. 10c, Guacamayo azul-dorado. 15c, Guacamayo de hombro rojo. No. 4989, 20c, Guacamayo cuellodorado. No. 4990, Guacamayo de Jacinto. 65c, Guacamayo escarlata. 75c, Guacamayo frente rojo. 90c, Guacamayo militar.

2009, May 16
4986-4993 A1408 Set of 8 6.00 6.00

Institute of Design, 25th Anniv. — A1409

2009, May 28 ***Perf. 12½x12¼***
4994 A1409 65c multi 1.40 1.40

Souvenir Sheet

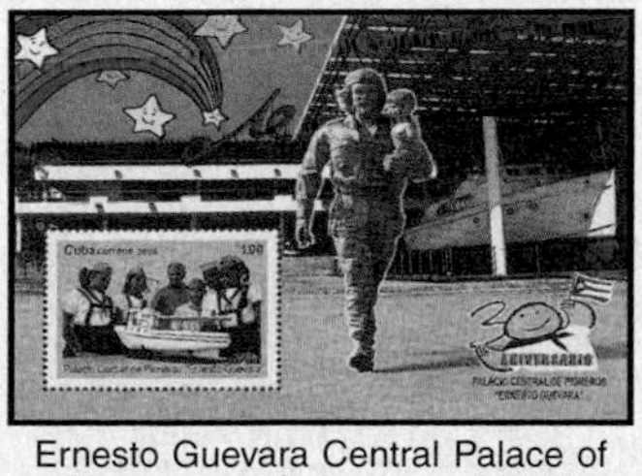

Ernesto Guevara Central Palace of Pioneers, 30th Anniv. — A1410

2009, June 1 ***Imperf.***
4995 A1410 1p multi 2.00 2.00

No. 4995 has simulated perforations.

National Revolutionary Police, 50th Anniv. — A1411

2009, June 6 ***Perf. 12½x12¼***
4996 A1411 1.05p multi 2.10 2.10

FORDES Gallery, 5th Anniv. — A1412

2009, June 14
4997 A1412 75c multi 1.50 1.50

Zoo Animals A1413

Designs: 5c, Ceratotherium simum. 10c, Syncerus caffer caffer. 15c, Acinonyx jubatus, vert. 30c, Papio hamadryas, vert. 40c, Struthio camelus, vert. 2.05p, Lycaon pictus, vert.
1p, Hippopotamus amphibius.

2009, June 20 ***Perf. 12¾***
4998-5003 A1413 Set of 6 6.25 6.25

Souvenir Sheet
Imperf
5004 A1413 1p multi 2.00 2.00

No. 5004 contains one 47x30mm stamp with simulated perforations.

Cuban Cuisine — A1414

Designs: 40c, Arroz con pollo a la chorrera (chicken with rice). 45c, Plátano maduro frito (fried plantains). 50c, Frijoles negros dormidos (black beans with onion).

2009, June 29 ***Perf. 12½x12¼***
5005-5007 A1414 Set of 3 2.75 2.75

Diplomatic Relations Between Cuba and Sri Lanka, 50th Anniv. — A1415

2009, July 29 ***Perf. 12¼x12½***
5008 A1415 1.05p multi 2.10 2.10

Peace and National Sovereignty Movement, 60th Anniv. — A1416

2009, Aug. 4 ***Perf. 12¾***
5009 A1416 65c multi 1.40 1.40

Los Malagones Peasant Militia, 50th Anniv. — A1417

2009, Aug. 31 ***Perf. 12¼x12½***
5010 A1417 90c multi 1.90 1.90

Havana Convention Center, 30th Anniv. — A1418

2009, Sept. 3 ***Perf. 12¾***
5011 A1418 50c multi 1.00 1.00

Tourism A1419

Birds: 15c, Coloptes fernandinae. 40c, Torreonis inexpectata. 50c, Ferminia cerverai. 65c, Agelaius assimilis. 75c, Mellisuga helenae. 90c, todus multicolor.
1p, Aratinga euops.

2009, Sept. 14 ***Perf. 12¾***
5012-5017 A1419 Set of 6 6.75 6.75

Souvenir Sheet
Imperf
5018 A1419 1p multi 2.00 2.00

No. 5018 has simulated perforations.

People's Republic of China, 60th Anniv. A1420

2009, Sept. 28 **Litho.** ***Perf. 12¾***
5019 A1420 85c multi 1.75 1.75

Cubana Airlines, 80th Anniv. — A1421

Designs: 5c, Ford Trimotor. 15c, Sikorsky S-38B. 45c, DC-3. 50c, DC-4. 65c, IL-62M. 75c, IL-96 300.
1p, Tu-204.

2009, Oct. 8 ***Perf. 12½x12¼***
5020-5025 A1421 Set of 6 5.25 5.25

Souvenir Sheet

Imperf

5026 A1421 1p multi 2.00 2.00

No. 5026 has simulated perforations.

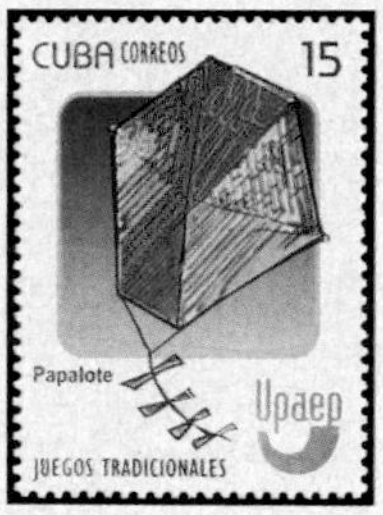

America Issue, Traditional Games A1422

Designs: 15c, Kite. 65c, Top. 75c, Dominos. 2.05p, Jacks.

2009, Oct. 12 ***Perf. 12¾***
5027-5030 A1422 Set of 4 7.25 7.25
5030a Souvenir sheet, #5027-5030 7.25 7.25

Souvenir Sheet

First Rocket Mail Flight in Cuba, 70th Anniv. — A1423

2009, Oct. 15 ***Imperf.***
5031 A1423 1p multi 2.00 2.00

Ministry of the Revolutionary Armed Forces, 50th Anniv. — A1424

2009, Oct. 16 ***Perf. 12¾***
5032 A1424 75c multi 1.50 1.50

Disappearance of Camilo Cienfuegos, 50th Anniv. — A1425

2009, Oct. 28 ***Perf. 12½x12¼***
5033 A1425 65c multi 1.40 1.40

Rights of the Child Convention, 20th Anniv. A1426

2009, Nov. 20 ***Perf. 12¾***
5034 A1426 1.05p multi 2.10 2.10

Cuban Federation of Sport Fishing, 30th Anniv. — A1427

Designs: 15c, Fisherman pulling fish into boat. 30c, Fisherman in water holding rod and fish. 45c, Sailfish and boat. No. 5038, 65c, Fisherman in water holding rod and fish, horiz. 75c, Fish on line, two fishermen in boat, horiz. 85c, Fishermen on sea wall, horiz.
No,. 5041, 65c, Tilapia, horiz

Perf. 12¼x12½, 12½x12¼

2009, Nov. 21
5035-5040 A1427 Set of 6 6.50 6.50

Souvenir Sheet

Imperf

5041 A1427 65c multi 1.40 1.40

No. 5041 has simulated perforations.

Ministry of Foreign Relations, 50th Anniv. — A1428

2009, Dec. 23 ***Perf. 12½x12¼***
5042 A1428 1.05p multi 2.10 2.10

Peony A1429

2009 ***Perf. 13¼x13½***
5043 A1429 30c multi .60 .60

Printed in sheets of 4.

José L. Guerra Aguiar Cuban Postal Museum, 45th Anniv. — A1430

2010, Jan. 2 ***Perf. 12½x12¼***
5044 A1430 65c multi 1.40 1.40

A1431

A1432

A1433

New Year 2010 (Year of the Tiger) A1434

2010, Jan. 5 ***Perf. 12¾***
5045 A1431 15c multi .30 .30
5046 A1432 15c multi .30 .30
5047 A1433 15c multi .30 .30
5048 A1434 15c multi .30 .30
a. Souvenir sheet, #5045-5048 1.25 1.25
Nos. 5045-5048 (4) 1.20 1.20

January 1960 Speech of Fidel Castro, 50th Anniv. — A1435

2010, Jan. 15 ***Perf. 12½x12¼***
5049 A1435 65c multi 1.40 1.40

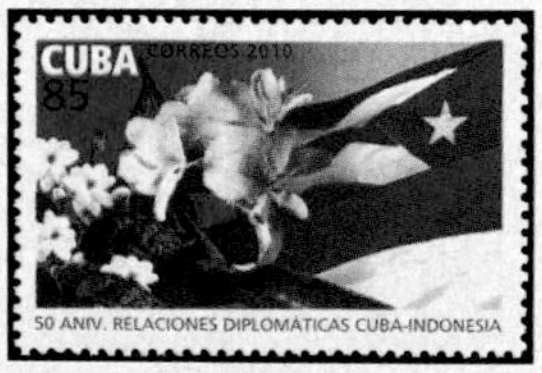

Diplomatic Relations Between Cuba and Indonesia, 50th Anniv. — A1436

2010, Jan. 22
5050 A1436 85c multi 1.75 1.75

Association of Rebel Youth, 50th Anniv. — A1437

2010, Jan. 28
5051 A1437 3p multi 6.00 6.00

Trains A1438

Designs: 5c, Fidel Castro leaving train. 10c, DF7G-C locomotive. 15c, Tank car. 65c, Flat car carrying shipping containers. 75c, Box cars. 1.05p, DF7K-C locomotive.
1p, Locomotive at end of track, vert.

2010, Jan. 29 ***Perf. 12¾***
5052-5057 A1438 Set of 6 5.50 5.50

Souvenir Sheet

Imperf

5058 A1438 1p multi 2.00 2.00

Diplomatic Relations Between Cuba and India, 50th Anniv. — A1439

2010, Feb. 10 ***Perf. 12¾***
5059 A1439 85c multi 1.75 1.75

National Aquarium, 50th Anniv. — A1440

Designs: 10c, Bispira brunnea. No. 5061, 15c, Hypoplectrus gummigutta. No. 5062, 15c, Holocanthus ciliaris. 50c, Seal. 75c, Epinephelus guttatus. 85c, Tursiops truncatus.
1p, Acanthurus coeruleus.

2010, Feb. 12 ***Perf. 12¾***
5060-5065 A1440 Set of 6 5.00 5.00

Souvenir Sheet

Imperf

5066 A1440 1p multi 2.00 2.00

No. 5066 has simulated perforations.

A1441

La Colmenita Youth Theater Company, 20th Anniv. — A1442

2010, Feb. 14 ***Perf. 12¾***
5067 A1441 50c multi 1.00 1.00
5068 A1442 50c multi 1.00 1.00

Underwater Photography — A1443

Designs: 10c, Fish and coral. 15c, Coral and starfish. 45c, Crab and sea anemone. 50c, Sponges and feather duster worms. 75c, Sea cucumber and coral. 85c, Sea horse and diver photographing tube worm.
1p, Fish and diver.

2010, Feb. 20 ***Perf. 12½x12¼***
5069-5074 A1443 Set of 6 5.75 5.75

Souvenir Sheet
Imperf
5075 A1443 1p multi 2.00 2.00

Central Planning, 50th Anniv. — A1444

2010, Mar. 11 ***Perf. 12½x12¼***
5076 A1444 75c multi 1.50 1.50

Dogs and Art — A1445

Designs: 10c, Peruvian hairless dog, Mochica figurine of dog, Peru. 15c, Bichon Frise, pitcher depicting hunter and dogs. 40c, Neapolitan mastiff, Roman mosaic of hunter and dog. 65c, Chihuahua, figurine of dog, map of Colima, Mexico. 75c, Pug, Chinese painting of hunters and dog. 90c, King Charles spaniel, The Birth of Louis XIII, by Peter Paul Rubens.
1p, Pharaoh hound, Egyptian painting from tomb of Ipy.

2010, Mar. 12 ***Perf. 12¾***
5077-5082 A1445 Set of 6 6.00 6.00

Souvenir Sheet
Imperf
5083 A1445 1p multi 2.00 2.00

No. 5083 has simulated perforations.

Diplomatic Relations Between Cuba and Canada, 65th Anniv. — A1446

2010, Mar. 16 ***Perf. 12¾***
5084 A1446 65c multi 1.40 1.40

Bilateral Relations Between Cuba and Namibia, 20th Anniv. A1447

2010, Mar. 24 **Litho.**
5085 A1447 85c multi 1.75 1.75

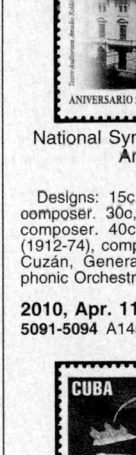

2010 World Cup Soccer Championships, South Africa — A1448

Flags of competing nations, various soccer players and list of teams in: 15c, Groups A and B. 45c, Groups C and D. 65c, Groups E and F. 75c, Groups G and H.

2010, Mar. 24
5086-5089 A1448 Set of 4 4.00 4.00

Congress of the Young Communist's League — A1449

2010, Apr. 2
5090 A1449 65c multi 1.40 1.40

National Symphonic Orchestra, 50th Anniv. — A1450

Designs: 15c, Amadeo Roldán (1900-39), composer. 30c, Gonzalo Roig (1890-1970), composer. 40c, Enrique González Mántici (1912-74), composer. 75c, Manuel Duchesne Cuzán, General director of National Symphonic Orchestra.

2010, Apr. 11 ***Perf. 12½x12¼***
5091-5094 A1450 Set of 4 3.25 3.25

Diplomatic Relations Between Cuba and Cambodia, 50th Anniv. — A1451

2010, Apr. 15
5095 A1451 85c multi 1.75 1.75

Cuban National Chorus, 50th Anniv. — A1452

2010, Apr. 17 **Litho.**
5096 A1452 90c multi 1.90 1.90

First Cuban Computer, 40th Anniv. — A1453

2010, Apr. 18 ***Perf. 12¾***
5097 A1453 75c multi 1.50 1.50

First Cuban Stamps, 155th Anniv. — A1454

Designs: 75c, Matanzas mail box, 1859, bicyclist in front of building. 85c, Cuba #147, account book of first postal administrator, 1765.

2010, Apr. 24 ***Perf. 12½x12¼***
5098-5099 A1454 Set of 2 3.25 3.25

Tourism A1455

Designs: 15c, Santiago de Cuba. 20c, Guantánamo. 35c, Holguín. 65c, Camagüey. 75c, Granma. 90c, Las Tunas.
1p, Santiago de Cuba, diff.

2010, May 4 ***Perf. 12¼x12½***
5100-5105 A1455 Set of 6 6.00 6.00

Souvenir Sheet
Imperf
5106 A1455 1p multi 2.00 2.00

ICAIC Latin American Newsreels, 50th Anniv. — A1456

2010, June 1 ***Perf. 12¾***
5107 A1456 75c multi 1.50 1.50

Flora and Fauna A1457

Designs: 15c, Dellia sp. 35c, Bietia purpurea. 40c, Anolis equestris. 65c, Broughtonia orgiesiana. 75c, Priotrochatella stellata. 85c, Todus multicolor, vert.
1p, Pinus caribaea.

Perf. 12½x12¼, 12¼x12½
2010, June 11
5108-5113 A1457 Set of 6 6.50 6.50

Souvenir Sheet
Imperf
5114 A1457 1p multi 2.00 2.00

Expo 2010, Shanghai — A1458

Map of China, aviation posters and aircraft: 5c, Savoia-Marchetti 55X. 10c, Farman 60 Goliath. 15c, Fokker VII. 45c, Koolhoven F.K. 50. 65c, Junkers 52/3M. 85c, Latécoère 28.
1p, Handley Page 42E.

2010, Apr. 26 **Litho.** ***Perf. 12½x12¼***
5115-5120 A1458 Set of 6 4.50 4.50

Souvenir Sheet
Imperf
5121 A1458 1p multi 2.00 2.00

No. 5121 has simulated perforations.

Writings of José Martí — A1459

Designs: No. 5122, 15c, *La Patria Libre,* white warbler, flag similar to Chile's. No. 5123, 15c, *La Nacion,* great antshrike, flag of Argentina. No. 5124, 15c, *Revista Universal,* king vulture, flag of Mexico. No. 5125, 15c, Proclamation of President of Paraguay, plantcutter, flag of Paraguay. No. 5126, 15c, *Patria,* hummingbird, flag of Cuba. No. 5127, 15c, Montecristi Manifesto, woodpecker, flag similar to Dominican Republic's. No. 5128, 15c, *La República Española y la Revolucion Cubana,* house sparrow and flag similar to Spain's, vert. No. 5129, 15c, *Mis Hijos* (translation of Victor Hugo's *Mes Fils*), long-tailed tit, flag of France, vert. No. 5130, 15c, *Guatemala,* quetzal, flag of Guatemala, vert. 65c, Pamphlet for International Monetary Conference, crested gallito, flag of Uruguay, vert. 75c, *Revista Venezolana,* troupial, flag of Venezuela, vert. 90c, Books of poetry, quill pen and inkwell, vert.

Perf. 12½x12¼, 12¼x12½
2010, May 19
5122-5133 A1459 Set of 12 7.50 7.50

Birds Endemic to Various Countries — A1460

Designs: 5c, Eumomota superciliosa, Nicaragua. 10c, Priotelus temnurus, Cuba. 15c, Amazona imperialis, Dominica. No. 5137, 20c, Amazona guildingii, St. Vincent and the Grenadines. No. 5138, 20c, Fregata magnificens, Antigua and Barbuda. 65c, Vultur gryphus, Bolivia. 75c, Icterus icterus, Venezuela, vert. 90c, Turdus rufiventris, Brazil, vert.

2010, May 26 ***Perf. 12¾***
5134-5141 A1460 Set of 8 6.00 6.00

Ernest Hemingway Intl. Fishing Tournament, 60th Anniv. — A1461

Emblem and: No. 5142, 65c, Fishing boat, rod and reel. No. 5143, 65c, Ernest Hemingway. No. 5144, 65c, Swordfish. No. 5145, 65c Trophy.

2010, May 29 *Perf. 12¼x12½*
5142-5145 A1461 Set of 4 5.25 5.25

Dr. Enrique Hart Ramírez (1900-89), Judge — A1462

2010, June 1 *Perf. 12¾*
5146 A1462 65c multi 1.40 1.40

Diplomatic Relations Between Cuba and North Korea, 50th Anniv. — A1463

2010, Aug. 29 **Litho.**
5147 A1463 85c multi 1.75 1.75

La Caridad Theater, Santa Clara, 125th Anniv. A1464

Designs: 15c, Theater in 1885. 30c, Theater in 2010. 75c, Theater interior. 90c, Marta Abreu de Estévez (1845-1909), philanthropist, vert.

2010, Sept. 8
5148-5151 A1464 Set of 4 4.25 4.25

Architectural Arches of Havana — A1465

Designs: 15c, Elliptical arch. 65c, Mixtilinear arch. 75c, Polylobular arch.

2010, Sept. 9 *Perf. 12½x12¼*
5152-5154 A1465 Set of 3 3.25 3.25

Lighthouses A1466

Maps and: No. 5155, 15c, Cayo Jutía Lighthouse, Pinar del Rio. No. 5156, 15c, Cayo Cruz del Padre Lighthouse, Matanzas. No. 5157, 15c, Cayo Lucrecia Lighthouse, Holguin. 2.05p, Morro Lighthouse, Santiago de Cuba.

2010, Sept. 15 *Perf. 12¼x12½*
5155-5158 A1466 Set of 4 5.00 5.00
5158a Souvenir sheet, #5155-5158 5.00 5.00

Electric Automobiles — A1467

Designs: 5c, 1893 Jeantaud and Raffard. 10c, 1903 American Pope-Tribune. 15c, 1903 STAE. 20c, Matra Zoom. 45c, Zilent. 75c, Jeep Treo.
1p, Aptera, vert.

2010, Sept. 20 *Perf. 12¾*
5159-5164 A1467 Set of 6 3.50 3.50

Souvenir Sheet

Imperf

5165 A1467 1p multi 2.00 2.00

Portugal 2010 Intl. Philatelic Exhibition. No. 5165 has simulated perforations.

Tourism — A1468

Designs: 20c, Papilio androgeus epidaurus, Viñales National Park. 50c, Mesocapromys nanus, Ciénaga de Zapata National Park. 75c, Trichechus manatus manatus, Alejandro de Humboldt National Park. 90c, Amazona leucocephala, Desembarco del Granma National Park.

2010, Sept. 27 *Perf. 12½x12¼*
5166-5169 A1468 Set of 4 4.75 4.75

Diplomatic Relations Between Cuba and People's Republic of China, 50th Anniv. — A1469

Designs: No. 5170, 15c, Chinese Army, flag of People's Republic of China. No. 5171, 15c, Chinese landscape, arms of People's Republic of China. No. 5172, 85c, Cuban soldiers, horses and boat, flag of Cuba. No. 5173, 85c, Cuban landscape, arms of Cuba.

2010, Sept. 28
5170-5173 A1469 Set of 4 4.00 4.00

America Issue, National Symbols A1470

Designs: No. 5174, 65c, School children, Cuban flag and coat of arms, bust of José Marti. No. 5175, 65c, Cuban coat of arms. No. 5176, 65c, Cuban flag. No. 5177, 65c, Cuban national anthem.

2010, Oct. 12 **Litho.** *Perf. 12¾*
5174-5177 A1470 Set of 4 5.25 5.25

World Statistics Day — A1471

2010 *Perf. 12½x12¼*
5178 A1471 65c multi 1.40 1.40

Cuban Television, 60th Anniv. A1472

2010, Oct. 24 *Perf. 12¾*
5179 A1472 1.05p multi 2.10 2.10

22nd Intl. Ballet Festival, Havana — A1473

2010, Oct. 28 *Perf. 12¼x12½*
5180 A1473 65c multi 1.40 1.40

Souvenir Sheet

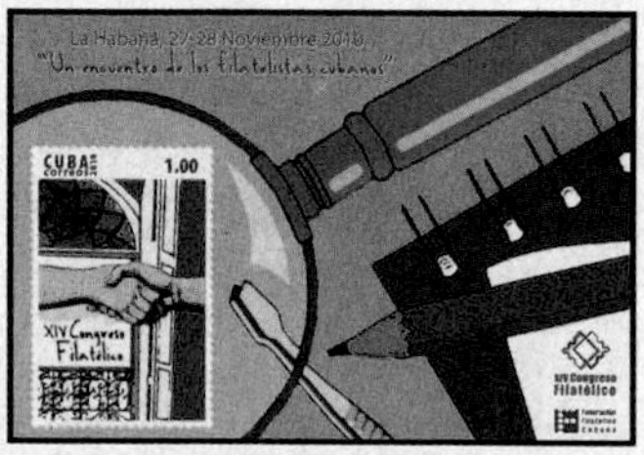

14th Philatelic Congress, Havana — A1474

2010 *Imperf.*
5181 A1474 1p multi 2.00 2.00

Diplomatic Relations Between Cuba and Viet Nam. 50th Anniv. — A1475

2010, Dec. 2 *Perf. 12¼x12½*
5182 A1475 85c multi 1.75 1.75

Diplomatic Relations Between Cuba and Russia, 50th Anniv. — A1476

2010, Dec. 2 *Perf. 12¾*
5183 A1476 75c multi 1.50 1.50

Diplomatic Relations Between Cuba and Bulgaria, 50th Anniv. — A1477

No. 5184: a, Alexander Nevsky Cathedral, Sofia, Bulgaria, flag of Bulgaria. b, Flag of Cuba, Havana Cathedral.

2010, Dec. 10 *Perf. 12½x12¼*
5184 A1477 75c Horiz. pair, #a-b 3.00 3.00

Dora Alonso (1910-2001), Writer — A1478

2010, Dec. 22 *Perf. 12¾*
5185 A1478 75c multi 1.50 1.50

Diplomatic Relations Between Cuba and Mongolia, 50th Anniv. — A1479

2010 *Perf. 12¼x12½*
5186 A1479 85c multi 1.75 1.75

Souvenir Sheet

14th Intl. Information Convention and Fair, Havana — A1481

2011, Feb. 7 **Litho.** ***Imperf.***
5188 A1481 1p multi 2.00 2.00

Airplanes and Female Aviators — A1482

Designs: 10c, Bleriot, Matilde Moisant (1878-1964). 15c, Stinson "American Girl," Ruth Elder (1902-77). 20c, Lockheed Vega, Ruth Rowland (1901-80). 50c, Golden Eagle, Bobbi Trout (1906-2003). 65c, Seversky Executive, Jacqueline Cochran (1906-80). 90c, Lockheed Electra, Amelia Earhart (1897-1937).

1p, Curtiss Robin, Berta Moraleda, first Cuban aviatrix.

2011, Feb. 12 ***Perf. 12½x12¼***
5189-5194 A1482 Set of 6 5.00 5.00

Souvenir Sheet

Imperf

5195 A1482 1p multi 2.00 2.00

Indipex 2011 Intl. Philatelic Exhibition, New Delhi.

New Year 2011 (Year of the Rabbit) A1483

Rabbit and background color of: No. 5196, 15c, Green. No. 5197, 15c, Red.

2011, Feb. 15 ***Perf. 12¾***
5196-5197 A1483 Set of 2 .60 .60

Postal Union of the Americas, Spain and Portugal (UPAEP), Cent. — A1484

2011, Feb. 17
5198 A1484 65c multi 1.40 1.40

Eastern Army, 50th Anniv. — A1486

2011, Apr. 21 **Litho.** ***Perf. 12½x12¼***
5200 A1486 65c multi 1.40 1.40

Earth Day A1487

Designs: 65c, Cart. 90c, Fountain.

2011, Apr. 22 ***Perf. 12¾***
5201-5202 A1487 Set of 2 3.25 3.25

Radio Havana, 50th Anniv. — A1488

2011, May 1 ***Perf. 12½x12¼***
5203 A1488 2.05p multi 4.25 4.25

Flora and Fauna A1489

Designs: 15c, Anolis vermiculata, Nymphaea. 35c, Apis mellifera, Bidens alba. 40c, Lycorea ceres demeter, Euphorbia helenae. 65c, Osteopilus septentrionalis, Plumeria obtusa. 75c, Ardea alba, Avicennia germinanas. 85c, Liguus fasciatus, Catopsis sp.

1p, Crocodylus rhombifer, Coccoloba uvifera, vert.

2011, June 6 ***Perf. 12¾***
5204-5209 A1489 Set of 6 6.50 6.50

Souvenir Sheet

Imperf

5210 A1489 1p multi 2.00 2.00

Ministry of the Interior, 50th Anniv. — A1490

2011, June 8 ***Perf. 12½x12¼***
5211 A1490 90c multi 1.90 1.90

Western Army, 50th Anniv. A1491

2011, June 14 ***Perf. 12¾***
5212 A1491 75c multi 1.50 1.50

Dances A1492

Designs: No. 5213, 10c, Danzón. No. 5214, 10c, Mambo. 45c, Son. 65c, Rumba. 75c, Cha cha cha. 85c, Salsa.

No. 5219: a, Female Carnaval dancer. b, Male Carnaval dancer.

2011, June 29 ***Perf. 12¼x12½***
5213-5218 A1492 Set of 6 6.00 6.00

Souvenir Sheet

Imperf

5219 A1492 50c Sheet of 2, #a-b 2.00 2.00

Diplomatic Relations Between Cuba and the Philippines, 65th Anniv. A1493

2011, July 1 ***Perf. 12¾***
5220 A1493 85c multi 1.75 1.75

Locomotives — A1494

Designs: 5c, Best Friend of Charleston, 1830. 10c, Lafayette, 1837. 15c, Robert Stephenson Patentee, 1830. 65c, Thomas Ellis St. David, 1848. 75c, Stephenson long-boiler, 1848. 90c, 4-2-2 Stirling single-wheeler No. 1, 1870.

1p, Shinkansen, 1964.

2011, July 28 ***Perf. 12½x12¼***
5221-5226 A1494 Set of 6 5.25 5.25

Souvenir Sheet

Imperf

5227 A1494 1p multi 2.00 2.00

Japan 2011 Intl. Philatelic Exhibition, Yokohama.

Baracoa, 500th Anniv. — A1495

2011, Aug. 15 ***Perf. 12½x12¼***
5228 A1495 3p multi 6.00 6.00

Non-Aligned Countries Movement, 50th Anniv. — A1496

2011, Sept. 6 ***Perf. 12¾***
5229 A1496 65c multi 1.40 1.40

Birds Endemic to Various Countries — A1497

Designs: 5c, Ramphastos sulfuratus, Belize. 10c, Melanerpes portoricensis, Puerto Rico. 15c, Icterus nigrogularis, Curaçao. 30c, Eumomota superciliosa, El Salvador. 50c, Vanellus chilensis lampronotus, Uruguay, vert. 65c, Pharomachrus mocinno, Guatemala, vert. 75c, Pelecanus occidentalis, St. Kitts and Nevis, vert. 85c, Orthorhycus cristatus, St. Eustatius, Caribbenan Netherlands, vert.

Perf. 12½x12¼, 12¼x12½

2011, Sept. 19
5230-5237 A1497 Set of 8 6.75 6.75

America Issue — A1498

Designs: No. 5238, 65c, Blue mailbox, denomination in pale orange. No. 5239, 65c, Blue green mailbox, denomination in pale rose. No. 5240, 65c, Three mailboxes, denomination in light blue. No. 5241, 65c, Blue green mailbox, denomination in lilac.

2011, Oct. 12 ***Perf. 12¾***
5238-5241 A1498 Set of 4 5.25 5.25

Animals — A1499

Designs: 5c, Ursus maritimus, map of Arctic region. 10c, Cervus elaphus canadensis, map of North America. 15c, Lama glama, map of South America. 50c, Canis lupus, map of Europe. 65c, Pongo pygmaeus, map of East Asia. 85c, Phascolarctos cinereus, map of Australia.

1p, Panthera leo, map of Africa.

2011, Oct. 18 ***Perf. 12½x12¼***
5242-5247 A1499 Set of 6 4.75 4.75

Souvenir Sheet

Imperf

5248 A1499 1p multi 2.00 2.00

Coral and Fish — A1500

Corals: 10c, Scolymia cubensis. 15c, Mussa angulosa. 20c, Manicina areolata. 30c, Mycetophyllia lamarckiana. 50c, Acropora prolifera. 65c, Tubastraea coccinea.
1p, Stylaster roseus.

2011, Oct. 18 ***Perf. 12½x12¼***
5249-5254 A1500 Set of 6 4.00 4.00

Souvenir Sheet
Imperf

5255 A1500 1p multi 2.00 2.00

Revista Pionero, 50th Anniv. — A1501

2011, Nov. 25 ***Perf. 12½x12¼***
5256 A1501 1.05p multi 2.10 2.10

Havana Tourist Attractions A1502

Designs: 5c, La Giraldilla, Castillo de la Fuerza. 10c, El Templete Monument. 15c, Plaza de la Catedra. 20c, Bacardi Building. 65c, Grand Theater of Havana. 75c, National Capitol (now Cuban Academy of Sciences).
1p, Morro Castle.

2011, Dec. 12 ***Perf. 12¼x12½***
5257-5262 A1502 Set of 6 4.00 4.00

Souvenir Sheet
Imperf

5263 A1502 1p multi 2.00 2.00

Birds and Protected Habitats A1503

Designs: 5c, Contopus caribaeus, Hanabanilla Nature Preserve. 10c, Saurothera merlini, Caguanes National Park. 20c, Spindalis zena, Topes de Collantes Nature Preserve. 45c, Otus lawrencii, Jobo Rosado Protected Area. 65c, Teretistris fernandinae, Alturas de Banao Ecological Reserve. 85c, Priotelus temnurus, El Nicho Nature Preserve.
1p, Grus canadensis, Caguanes National Park.

2011, Dec. 13 ***Perf. 12¼x12½***
5264-5269 A1503 Set of 6 4.75 4.75

Souvenir Sheet
Imperf

5270 A1503 1p multi 2.00 2.00

Stage Debut of Ballerina Alicia Alonso, 80th Anniv. — A1504

No. 5271 — Alonso with feet: a, Not visible. b, Visible.

2011, Dec. 29 ***Perf. 12¼x12½***
5271 A1504 65c Horiz. pair, #a-b 2.60 2.60

African National Congress, Cent. — A1505

2012, Jan. 8 ***Perf. 12¾***
5272 A1505 85c multi 1.75 1.75

Artemisa Province, 1st Anniv. A1506

2012, Jan. 9
5273 A1506 65c multi 1.40 1.40

Electrical Workers Day A1507

2012, Jan. 14
5274 A1507 75c multi 1.50 1.50

Communication Workers Day — A1508

2012, Feb. 24 ***Perf. 12½x12¼***
5275 A1508 65c multi 1.40 1.40

Woman at a Window, by René Portocarrero (1912-85) A1509

2012, Feb. 24 ***Perf. 12¾***
5276 A1509 1.05p multi 2.10 2.10

Diplomatic Relations Between Ukraine and Cuba, 20th Anniv. — A1510

2012, Mar. 12 ***Perf. 12½x12¼***
5277 A1510 75c multi 1.50 1.50

Alejandro Robaina and His Automobile — A1511

No. 5278 — Tobacco field and: a, Robaina (1919-2010), farmer of cigar tobacco. b, Automobile.

2012, Mar. 20 ***Perf. 12¾***
5278 A1511 65c Horiz. pair, #a-b 2.60 2.60

Diplomatic Relations Between Azerbaijan and Cuba, 20th Anniv. — A1512

2012, Apr. 16 **Litho.**
5279 A1512 75c multi 1.50 1.50

Diplomatic Relations Between Belarus and Cuba, 20th Anniv. — A1513

2012, Apr. 16 ***Perf. 12½x12¼***
5280 A1513 75c multi 1.50 1.50

Capt. Orlando Pantoja Tamayo (1933-67), Capt. Eliseo Reyes Rodriguez (1940-67), First Lt. Antonio Briones Montoto (1939-67), Guerrillas in Intl. Conflicts — A1514

2012, Apr. 25 **Litho.** ***Perf. 12½x12¼***
5281 A1514 65c multi 1.40 1.40

Afro-Cuban Dances — A1515

Designs: 15c, Elegbá. 20c, Ogún. 30c, Shangó. 50c, Oyá. 65c, Yemayá. 75c, Obatalá.
1p, Oghún.

2012, May 7 **Litho.** ***Perf. 12¼x12½***
5282-5287 A1515 Set of 6 5.25 5.25

Souvenir Sheet
Imperf

5288 A1515 1p multi 2.00 2.00

No. 5288 has simulated perforations.

Butterflies — A1516

Designs: 5c, Phoebis avellaneda. 10c, Parides gundiachianus. 15c, Greta cubana. 35c, Eurytides celadon. 40c, Anartia chrysopelea. 65c, Dismorphia cubana. 75c, Calisto israel. 85c, Libytheana motya.

2012, May 22 **Litho.** ***Perf. 12¾***
5289-5296 A1516 Set of 8 6.75 6.75

Cuban Institute of Radio and Television, 50th Anniv. — A1517

2012, May 24 **Litho.** ***Perf. 12¾***
5297 A1517 90c multi 1.90 1.90

Visit of Pope Benedict XVI to Cuba — A1518

2012, June 6 **Litho.** ***Perf. 12¼x12½***
5298 A1518 75c multi 1.50 1.50

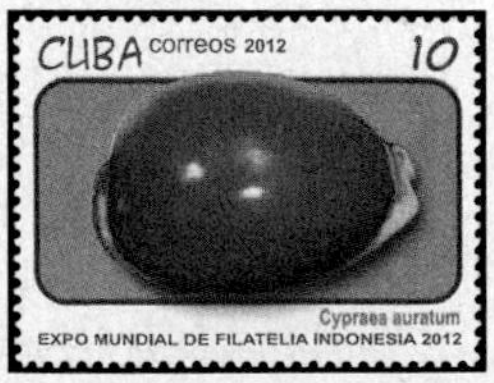

Shells A1519

Designs: 10c, Cypraea auratum. 30c, Strombus pugilis. 45c, Voluta fulgetrum. 65c, Architectonica maximum. 75c, Murex beaui. 85c, Spondylus aurantium.
1p, Epitonium pretiosum, vert.

2012, June 6 **Litho.** ***Perf. 12¾***
5299-5304 A1519 Set of 6 6.25 6.25

Souvenir Sheet
Imperf

5305 A1519 1p multi 2.00 2.00

No. 5305 has simulated perforations.

Paulina Alvarez (1912-65), Singer — A1520

2012, June 13 Litho. *Perf. 12¾*
5306 A1520 1.05p multi 2.10 2.10

2012 Summer Olympics, London A1521

Cuban Olympic gold medal winning athletes: 10c, Orlando Martinez. 15c, Téofilo Stevenson. 20c, Alberto Juantorena. 50c, María Caridad Colón. 65c, Driulys González. 90c, Mireya Luis.
1p, Javier Sotomayor, horiz.

2012, July 5 Litho. *Perf. 12¾*
5307-5312 A1521 Set of 6 5.00 5.00

Souvenir Sheet
Imperf

5313 A1521 1p multi 2.00 2.00
No. 5313 has simulated perforations.

Diplomatic Relations Between Cuba and Timor, 10th Anniv. — A1522

2012, July 18 Litho. *Perf. 12½x12¼*
5314 A1522 75c multi 1.50 1.50

Civil Defense, 50th Anniv. — A1523

2012, July 20 Litho. *Perf. 12½x12¼*
5315 A1523 65c multi 1.40 1.40

Cienfuegos Military Insurrection, 55th Anniv. — A1524

2012, Sept. 5 Litho. *Perf. 12¼x12½*
5316 A1524 65c multi 1.40 1.40

2012 National Census — A1525

2012, Sept. 6 Litho. *Perf. 12½x12¼*
5317 A1525 65c multi 1.40 1.40

National Lyric Theater, 50th Anniv. — A1526

Perf. 12¼x12½
2012, Sept. 14 Litho.
5318 A1526 65c multi 1.40 1.40

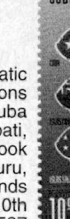

Diplomatic Relations Between Cuba and Kiribati, Tonga, Cook Islands, Nauru, Solomon Islands and Fiji, 10th Anniv. — A1527

Perf. 12¼x12½
2012, Sept. 26 Litho.
5319 A1527 75c multi 1.50 1.50

Diplomatic Relations Between Cuba and France, 110th Anniv. — A1528

2012, Oct. 3 Litho. *Perf. 12¼x12½*
5320 A1528 75c multi 1.50 1.50

Diplomatic Relations Between Cuba and Switzerland, 110th Anniv. — A1529

2012, Oct. 3 Litho. *Perf. 12¼x12½*
5321 A1529 75c multi 1.50 1.50

Myths and Legends A1530

Designs: No. 5322, 65c, La Gaviota del Rio San Juan (The Gull of San Juan River). No. 5323, 65c, El Güije. No. 5324, 65c, La Giraldilla statue, La Macorina driving car. No. 5325, 65c, La Tatgua y las Matas de Guao.

2012, Oct. 12 Litho. *Perf. 12¾*
5322-5325 A1530 Set of 4 5.25 5.25
America Issue.

Miner's Day — A1531

2012, Oct. 24 Litho. *Perf. 12½x12¼*
5326 A1531 65c multi 1.40 1.40

Cirilo Villaverde (1812-94), Writer — A1532

2012, Oct. 27 Litho. *Perf. 12½x12¼*
5327 A1532 75c multi 1.50 1.50

First Cuban Expedition to Antarctica, 30th Anniv. — A1533

2012, Nov. 7 Litho. *Perf. 12¾*
5328 A1533 75c multi 1.50 1.50

Road Safety Campaign — A1534

Designs: 65c, Children's drawing of girl and traffic light. 90c, Children, car, traffic signs.

2012, Nov. 20 Litho. *Perf. 12¾*
5329-5330 A1534 Set of 2 3.25 3.25

Ameijeiras Brothers Hospital, Havana, 30th Anniv. — A1535

2012, Nov. 26 Litho. *Perf. 12¾*
5331 A1535 65c multi 1.40 1.40

Flora and Fauna A1536

Designs: 5c, Ardilla (squirrel). 10c, Bala de Cañón (cannonball tree flower). 15c, Flor de loto (lotus flower). 65c, Pavo real (peacock), vert. 75c, Polimita (snail), vert. 90c, Orquídea (orchid), vert.
1p, Zorzal real (red-legged thrush), vert.

Perf. 12½x12¼, 12¼x12½
2012, Nov. 29 Litho.
5332-5337 A1536 Set of 6 5.25 5.25

Souvenir Sheet
Imperf

5338 A1536 1p multi 2.00 2.00
Second Cuban Philatelic Cup.

Camagüey Ballet, 50th Anniv. — A1537

Designs: 75c, Fernando Alonso (1914-2013), ballet director, and dancers. 85c, Dancers in *Don Quixote*.

2012, Dec. 1 Litho. *Perf. 12¾*
5339-5340 A1537 Set of 2 3.25 3.25

Diplomatic Relations Between Cuba and Jamaica, Trinidad & Tobago, Barbados and Guyana, 40th Anniv. — A1538

2012, Dec. 6 Litho. *Perf. 12¾*
5341 A1538 65c multi 1.40 1.40

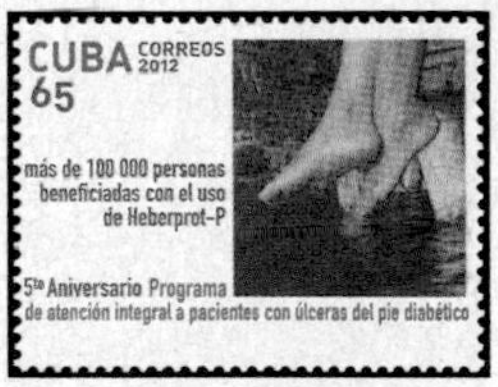

Program For Combatting Diabetic Foot Ulcers, 5th Anniv. — A1539

Designs: 65c, Person's feet. 75c, Boxes and vial of Heberprot-P.

2012, Dec. 14 Litho. *Perf. 12¾*
5342-5343 A1539 Set of 2 3.00 3.00

Orchids A1540

Various orchids: 5c, 10c, 15c, 65c, 75c, 90c.
1p, Orchid, diff.

2013, Jan. 15 Litho. *Perf. 12¾*
5344-5349 A1540 Set of 6 5.25 5.25

Souvenir Sheet
Imperf

5350 A1540 1p multi 2.00 2.00
No. 5350 has simulated perforations.

Finland-Cuba Friendship Association, 50th Anniv. — A1541

2013, Jan. 17 Litho. *Perf. 12¾*

5351 A1541 75c multi 1.50 1.50

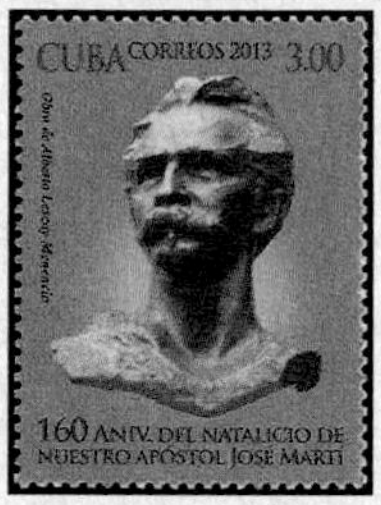

Bust of José Martí, by Alberto Lescay Menencio A1542

2013, Jan. 19 Litho. *Perf. 12¾*

5352 A1542 3p multi 6.00 6.00

Martí (1853-95), national hero.

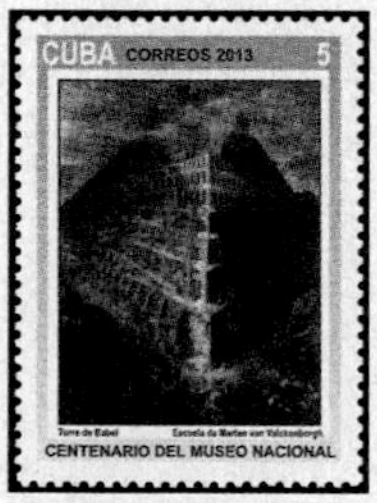

National Museum, Cent. — A1543

Paintings: 5c, Torre de Babel (Tower of Babel), by School of Marten van Valckenborgh. 10c, Paisaje (Landscape), by Thomas Creswick. 50c, Saludos al Mar Caribe (Salute to the Caribbean Sea), by Mario Carreño. 65c, Jarrón con Flores (Vase with Flowers), by Amelia Peláez. 75c, Gallo Amarillo (Yellow Rooster), by Mariano Rodríguez. 85c, La Alicantina (Woman from Alicante), by Hermenegildo Anglada.
1p, Homenaje a la Soledad (Homage to Solitude), by Servando Cabrera Moreno.

2013, Jan. 25 Litho. *Perf. 12¾*

5353-5358 A1543 Set of 6 6.00 6.00

Souvenir Sheet

Imperf

5359 A1543 1p multi 2.00 2.00

No. 5359 has simulated perforations.

Items Connected to José Martí (1853-95), National Hero — A1544

Designs: 10c, Braid of Martí's hair from childhood, drawing of woman sewing. 15c, Shackle, drawing of men trying to remove leg shackles. 20c, Rostrum from San Carlos Club, Tampa, Florida. 30c, Mambisa badge with flag design. 35c, Colt revolvers. 40c, Pen, drawing of Martí writing.

2013, Jan. 28 Litho. *Perf. 12¾*

5360-5365 A1544 Set of 6 3.00 3.00

Chamber of Commerce, 50th Anniv. — A1545

2013, Feb. 1 Litho. *Perf. 12¾*

5366 A1545 90c multi 1.90 1.90

Customs Department, 50th Anniv. — A1546

2013, Feb. 5 Litho. *Perf. 12¾*

5367 A1546 1.05p multi 2.10 2.10

Third World Baseball Classic — A1547

No. 5368, 15c — Baseball and: a, Cuban uniform shirt., flags of Japan, People's Republic of China, Cuba and Brazil. b, Pitcher for Cuban team, trophy.
No. 5369, 65c — Baseball and: a, Player with glove, trophy. b, Flags of United States, Mexico, Italy and Canada, baseball glove.
No. 5370, 75c — Baseball and: a, Batter, trophy. b, Flags of Venezuela, Puerto Rico, Dominican Republic and Spain, batting helmet.
No. 5371, 85c — Baseball and: a, Catcher's mask, flags of South Korea, Netherlands, Australia and Republic of China. b, Catcher, trophy.

2013, Mar. 2 Litho. *Perf. 12½x12¼*

Horiz. Pairs, #a-b

5368-5371 A1547 Set of 4 9.75 9.75

José Raúl Capablanca (1888-1942), World Chess Champion — A1548

Capablanca and chess position in match between Capablanca and: 15c, Ossip Bernstein, 1911. 65c, Rudolf Spielmann, 1927. 75c, Mikhail Botvinnik, 1936. 85c, Jens Enevoldsen, 1939.

2013, Mar. 8 Litho. *Perf. 12½x12¼*

5372-5375 A1548 Set of 4 5.00 5.00

Pets A1549

Designs: 5c, Pigeon. 15c, Parrot, vert. 50c, Dog. 65c, Turtle. 75c, Cat. 85c, Rabbit.
1p, Horse.

Perf. 12½x12¼, 12¼x12½

2013, Mar. 12 Litho.

5376-5381 A1549 Set of 6 6.00 6.00

Souvenir Sheet

Imperf

5382 A1549 1p multi 2.00 2.00

No. 5382 has simulated perforations.

Souvenir Sheet

Informática 2013 International Convention and Fair — A1550

2013, Mar. 18 Litho. *Imperf.*

5383 A1550 1p multi 2.00 2.00

Prehistoric Animals — A1551

Designs: 5c, Cricosaurus. 15c, Pterosaurus, vert. 50c, Caribemys. 65c, Gallardosaurus. 75c, Camarasaurus. 85c, Ichthyosaurus.
1p, Vinialesaurus.

Perf. 12½x12¼, 12¼x12½

2013, Apr. 3 Litho.

5384-5389 A1551 Set of 6 6.00 6.00

Souvenir Sheet

Imperf

5390 A1551 1p multi 2.00 2.00

No. 5390 has simulated perforations.

Sauto Theater, 150th Anniv. A1552

2013, Apr. 6 Litho. *Perf. 12¾*

5391 A1552 65c multi 1.40 1.40

Australia 2013 Intl. Philatelic Exhibition, Melbourne — A1553

No. 5392, 15c: a, Parrot. b, Lyrebird.
No. 5393, 45c: a, Garfish. b, Platypus.
No. 5394, 85c: a, Hutia. b, Koala.
1p, Kangaroo and crocodile, horiz.

2013, Apr. 10 Litho. *Perf. 12¼x12½*

Horiz. Pairs, #a-b

5392-5394 A1553 Set of 3 6.00 6.00

Souvenir Sheet

Imperf

5395 A1553 1p multi 2.00 2.00

No. 5392 has simulated perforations.

Labor Day — A1554

2013, May 1 Litho. *Perf. 12¾*

5396 A1554 65c multi 1.40 1.40

Visit of Dr. Alexander Fleming to Cuba, 60th Anniv. — A1555

2013, May 12 Litho. *Perf. 12½x12¼*

5397 A1555 65c multi 1.40 1.40

First Flight From Key West to Havana, by Domingo Rosillo del Toro, Cent. — A1556

2013, May 17 Litho. *Perf. 12½x12¼*

5398 A1556 2.05p multi 4.25 4.25

Souvenir Sheet

National Ballet of Cubaa, 65th Anniv. — A1557

2013, May 20 Litho. *Imperf.*

5399 A1557 1p multi 2.00 2.00

No. 5399 has simulated perforations.

Butterflies — A1558

Designs: 5c, Papilio caiguanabus. 10c, Proteides maysi. 15c, Allosmaitia coelebs. 40c, Anetia cubana. 65c, Kricogonia cabrerai. 75c, Papilio oxynius. 85c, Atlantea perezi. 90c, Eurema lucina.

2013, May 22 Litho. *Perf. 12¾*

5400-5407 A1558 Set of 8 7.75 7.75

Compare with Type A1608.

Ministry of Construction, 50th Anniv. — A1559

2013, May 23 Litho. *Perf. 12¾*
5408 A1559 90c multi 1.90 1.90

Debut of Alicia Alonso in Ballet *Giselle,* 70th Anniv. — A1560

Paintings of Alonso by: 5c, Servando Cabrera Moreno. 15c, Lorenzo Homar. 20c, Carlos Guzmán. 65c, Alicia Leal. 75c, Francisco Rodón (48x31mm). 90c, Agostino Brotto (48x31mm).
1p, Photograph of Alonso and other dancers, vert.

Perf. 12¾, 12½x12¾ (75p, 90p)
2013, June 5 Litho.
5409-5414 A1560 Set of 6 5.50 5.50

Souvenir Sheet
Imperf

5415 A1560 1p multi 2.00 2.00

No. 5415 contains one 31x48mm stamp with simulated perforations.

Eighth Federation of University Students Congress — A1561

2013, June 12 Litho. *Perf. 12¾*
5416 A1561 65c multi 1.40 1.40

Souvenir Sheet

Seventh International Forum on Industrial Design, Havana — A1562

2013, June 18 Litho. *Imperf.*
5417 A1562 1p multi 2.00 2.00

No. 5417 has simulated perforations.

Ernesto "Che" Guevara (1928-67), Guerrilla Leader A1563

2013, June 28 Litho. *Perf. 12¾*
5418 A1563 65c multi 1.40 1.40

Birds A1564

Designs: 10c, Lophura diardi. 35c, Polyplectron bicalcaratum. 40c, Grus japonensis, vert. 50c, Pica sericea. 65c, Phasianus versicolor. 75c, Falco cherrug, vert.
1p, Pavo cristatus, vert.

Perf. 12½x12¼, 12¼x12½
2013, July 17 Litho.
5419-5424 A1564 Set of 6 5.50 5.50

Souvenir Sheet
Imperf

5425 A1564 1p multi 2.00 2.00

Thailand 2013 International Philatelic Exhibition, Bangkok. No. 5425 has simulated perforations.

Simón Bolívar (1783-1830), Liberator of South America — A1565

Designs: No. 5426, 65c, Paintings of Bolívar. No. 5427, 65c, Bolívar House, Havana, vert.

Perf. 12½x12¼, 12¼x12½
2013, July 24 Litho.
5426-5427 A1565 Set of 2 2.60 2.60

Bolívar House, 20th anniv. as museum.

Dr. Mario Muñoz Monroy (1912-53), Revolutionist A1566

2013, July 26 Litho. *Perf. 12¾*
5428 A1566 75c multi 1.50 1.50

Assault on the Moncada and Carlos M. De Céspedes Barracks, 60th Anniv. — A1567

Designs: 45c, Moncada Barracks. 75c, Barracks, diff.

2013, July 26 Litho. *Perf. 12¾*
5429-5430 A1567 Set of 2 2.40 2.40

Angerona Coffee Plantation, 200th Anniv. — A1568

2013, Aug. 12 Litho. *Perf. 12¾*
5431 A1568 1.05p multi 2.10 2.10

El Brinco Cave A1569

2013, Sept. 6 Litho. *Perf. 12½x12¼*
5432 A1569 75c multi 1.50 1.50

22nd Congress of the Postal Union of Spain, Portugal and the Americas, Havana — A1570

Designs: 65p, Quill pen writing on computer screen. 1p, UPAEP emblem.

2013, Sept. 9 Litho. *Perf. 12¾*
5433 A1570 65c multi 1.40 1.40

Souvenir Sheet
Imperf

5434 A1570 1p multi 2.00 2.00

No. 5434 contains one 40x32mm stamp.

Armed Peasants Congress, 55th Anniv. — A1571

2013, Sept. 21 Litho. *Perf. 12¾*
5435 A1571 85c multi 1.75 1.75

8th Congress of the Committee for the Defense of the Revolution — A1572

2013, Sept. 28 Litho. *Perf. 12¾*
5436 A1572 65c multi 1.40 1.40

Mantanzas, 320th Anniv. — A1573

2013, Oct. 12 Litho. *Perf. 12¾*
5437 A1573 65c multi 1.40 1.40

Campaign Against Discrimination — A1574

Campaign against: No. 5438, 65c, Child abuse. No. 5439, 65c, Homophobia. No. 5440, 65c, Racial discrimination. No. 5441, 65c, Disability discrimination.

2013, Oct. 12 Litho. *Perf. 12¾*
5438-5441 A1574 Set of 4 5.25 5.25

America Issue.

North Korean National Holiday, 65th Anniv. — A1575

2013, Oct. 16 Litho. *Perf. 12¼x12½*
5442 A1575 85c multi 1.75 1.75

Brasiliana 2013 International Philatelic Exhibition, Rio de Janeiro — A1576

No. 5443, 15c: a, Cuica player. b, Tres player.
No. 5444, 40c: a, Woman of Candomblé religion. b, Woman of Cuban Santería religion.
No. 5445, 90c: a, Samba dancer. b, Rumba dancer.
1p, Statue of Jesus Christ, Havana.

2013, Oct. 16 Litho. *Perf. 12¼x12½*
Horiz. Pairs, #a-b
5443-5445 A1576 Set of 3 6.00 6.00

Souvenir Sheet
Imperf

5446 A1576 1p multi 2.00 2.00

No. 5446 has simulated perforations.

Tenth National Championship of Philately — A1577

Famous people: 15c, Mario Benedetti (1920-2009), writer. 20c, Alexander von Humboldt (1769-1859), geographer and naturalist. 45c, Nat King Cole (1919-65), singer. 65c, Juan Manuel Fangio (1911-95), race car driver. 75c, Antonio Gades (1936-2004), flamenco dancer. 85c, María Félix (1914-2002), actress.
1p, Ernest Hemingway (1899-1961), writer.

2013, Oct. 22 Litho. *Perf. 12½x12¼*
5447-5452 A1577 Set of 6 6.25 6.25

Souvenir Sheet
Imperf

5453 A1577 1p multi 2.00 2.00

No. 5453 has simulated perforations.

Bayamo, 500th Anniv. — A1578

Designs: 50c, Church steeple. 65c, Carlos M. Céspedes Barracks and flagpole, horiz.

2013, Nov. 5 Litho. *Perf. 12¾*
5454-5455 A1578 Set of 2 2.40 2.40

Arab House, Havana, 30th Anniv. — A1579

Designs: 75c, Bottle from Syria, 19th cent. 85c, Doorway.

2013, Nov. 13 Litho. *Perf. 12¾*
5456-5457 A1579 Set of 2 3.25 3.25

National Museum of Dance, Havana — A1580

Perf. 12¼x12½
2013, Nov. 25 Litho.
5458 A1580 75c multi 1.50 1.50

Cuban Revolutionary Fighters Association, 20th Anniv. — A1581

2013, Dec. 6 Litho. *Perf. 12¾*
5459 A1581 1.05p multi 2.10 2.10

General Prosecutor's Office, 40th Anniv. — A1582

2013, Dec. 23 Litho. *Perf. 12¾*
5460 A1582 65c multi 1.40 1.40

Colonel Juan Delgado González (1868-98) — A1583

Perf. 12½x12¼
2013, Dec. 27 Litho.
5461 A1583 90c multi 1.90 1.90

Triumph of Cuban Revolutionists, 55th Anniv. — A1584

2013, Dec. 30 Litho. *Perf. 12¾*
5462 A1584 65c multi 1.40 1.40

Santísima Trinidad, 500th Anniv. — A1585

Designs: 40c, Trinidad Church. 85c, Manaca-Iznaga Tower, locomotive.

2014, Jan. 12 Litho. *Perf. 12¼x12½*
5463-5464 A1585 Set of 2 2.50 2.50

Consecration of the Greek Orthodox Cathedral of St. Nicholas, 10th Anniv. — A1586

Designs: 90c, Cathedral, Archbishop Bartholomew of Constantinople, Fidel Castro. 1p, St. Nicholas, vert.

2014, Jan. 25 Litho. *Perf. 12½x12¼*
5465 A1586 90c multi 1.90 1.90

Souvenir Sheet
Imperf

5466 A1586 1p multi 2.00 2.00

No. 5466 has simulated perforations.

2014 World Cup Soccer Championships, Brazil — A1587

Designs: 35c, Soccer player. 65c, Maracana Stadium, Rio de Janeiro. 75c, Mascot. 85c, Player making bicycle kick.

2014, Feb. 1 Litho. *Perf. 12¼x12½*
5467-5470 A1587 Set of 4 5.25 5.25

Santa María del Puerto Príncipe (Camagüey), 500th Anniv. — A1588

Famous people from Camagüey: 5c, Enrique José Varona (1848-1933), writer. 10c, Gertrudis Gómez de Avellaneda (1814-73), writer. 15c, Vicentina de la Torre (1926-95), dancer. 65c, Fidelio Ponce de León (1895-1949), painter. 75c, Rafael Fortún (1919-82), sprinter. 85c, Jorge González Allué (1910-2001), composer.
1p, Plaza del Carmen, vert.

2014, Feb. 2 Litho. *Perf. 12¾*
5471-5476 A1588 Set of 6 5.25 5.25

Souvenir Sheet
Imperf

5477 A1588 1p multi 2.00 2.00

No. 5477 has simulated perforations.

Diplomatic Relations Between Cuba and Haiti, 110th Anniv. — A1589

2014, Feb. 3 Litho. *Perf. 12¾*
5478 A1589 3p multi 6.00 6.00

Fans A1590

Woman holding fan and fan from: 5c, 1860. 10c, 1860, diff. 15c, 1920. 45c, 1795-1800. 65c, 1850. 75c, 1717.

Perf. 12½x12¼
2014, Feb. 14 Litho.
5479-5484 A1590 Set of 6 4.50 4.50

20th Congress of Worker's Central Union — A1591

Perf. 12½x12¼
2014, Feb. 21 Litho.
5485 A1591 75c multi 1.50 1.50

Community of Latin American States Summit, Havana — A1592

Perf. 12¼x12½
2014, Feb. 24 Litho.
5486 A1592 75c multi 1.50 1.50

9th Congress of Federation of Cuban Women — A1593

2014, Mar. 5 Litho. *Perf. 12¼x12½*
5487 A1593 65c multi 1.40 1.40

Hugo Chávez (1954-2013), President of Venezuela — A1594

Chávez: 65c, Saluting. 75c, With hand over heart. 85c, With arm raised.

2014, Mar. 5 Litho. *Perf. 12½x12¼*
5488-5490 A1594 Set of 3 4.50 4.50

Alejandro Robaina Pereda (1919-2010), Tobacco Grower — A1595

Cigar box and: 10c, Hand holding tobacco seedling, classification of tobacco leaves. 15c, Tobacco growers in field. 30c, Tobacco leaves and equipment for cigar making. 65c, Cigars with Robaina band. 75c, Cigar humidor, lit match. 85c, Cigar box art for Vegas Robaina cigars.
1p, Robaina, vert.

Perf. 12½x12¼
2014, Mar. 20 Litho.
5491-5496 A1595 Set of 6 5.75 5.75

Souvenir Sheet
Imperf

5497 A1595 1p multi 2.00 2.00

No. 5497 has simulated perforations.

Gertrudis Gomez de Avellaneda (1814-73), Writer — A1596

Perf. 12¼x12½

2014, Mar. 22 **Litho.**
5498 A1596 1.05p multi 2.10 2.10

Operation Transbordo, 50th Anniv. — A1597

Designs: 45c, Alberto Delgado Delgado (1932-64), undercover agent. 65c, Boat.

2014, Mar. 26 **Litho.** ***Perf. 12¾***
5499-5500 A1597 Set of 2 2.25 2.25

Diplomatic Relations Between Antigua and Barbuda and Cuba, 20th Anniv. — A1598

2014, Apr. 4 **Litho.** ***Perf. 12¾***
5501 A1598 65c multi 1.40 1.40

National Revolutionary Police, 55th Anniv. — A1599

2014, Apr. 19 **Litho.** ***Perf. 12¾***
5502 A1599 90c multi 1.90 1.90

Ministry of Science, Technology and the Environment, 20th Anniv. — A1600

2014, Apr. 21 **Litho.** ***Perf. 12½x12¼***
5503 A1600 90c multi 1.90 1.90

Flags of South Africa and Cuba, Nelson Mandela (1918-2013), President of South Africa — A1601

2014, Apr. 28 **Litho.** ***Perf. 12¾***
5504 A1601 85c multi 1.75 1.75

Diplomatic relations between South Africa and Cuba, end of apartheid in South Africa, 20th anniv.

Labor Day — A1602

2014, May 1 **Litho.** ***Perf. 12¼x12½***
5505 A1602 65c multi 1.40 1.40

Ernesto "Che" Guevara (1928-67), Minister of Industry, and Metallurgical Industries — A1603

Guevara, photographs of industry, plants or finished products and emblem of: 10c, Planta Mecanica. 45c, Profix. 75c, CIME. 85c, Inpud. 90c, Taino.

2014, May 2 **Litho.** ***Perf. 12½x12¼***
5506-5510 A1603 Set of 5 6.25 6.25

State Council Historical Affairs Office, 50th Anniv. — A1604

2014, May 9 **Litho.** ***Perf. 12½x12¼***
5511 A1604 75c multi 1.50 1.50

Bejucal, 300th Anniv. — A1605

2014, May 10 **Litho.** ***Perf. 12¼x12½***
5512 A1605 65c multi 1.40 1.40

St. Francis of Assisi Basilica and Convent Museum, 20th Anniv. — A1606

2014, May 16 **Litho.** ***Perf. 12½x12¼***
5513 A1606 90c multi 1.90 1.90

First Agrarian Reform Law, 55th Anniv. — A1607

2014, May 17 **Litho.** ***Perf. 12½x12¼***
5514 A1607 65c multi 1.40 1.40

Butterflies — A1608

Designs: 5c, Eurema amelia. 10c, Astraptes cassander. 15c, Panoquina corrupta. 20c, Chioldes marmorosa. 40c, Eunica heraclitus. 50c, Parachoranthus magdalia. 65c, Holguinia holguin. 75c, Eantis munroei. 90c, Oarisma nanus.

2014, May 22 **Litho.** ***Perf. 12¾***
5515-5523 A1608 Set of 9 7.50 7.50

Compare with Type A1558.

Diplomatic Relations Between Cuba and Congo Republic, 50th Anniv. — A1609

2014, May 23 **Litho.** ***Perf. 12¼x12½***
5524 A1609 85c multi 1.75 1.75

National Museum of Natural History, 50th Anniv. — A1610

2014, May 26 **Litho.** ***Perf. 12½x12¼***
5525 A1610 75c multi 1.50 1.50

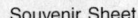

Souvenir Sheet

Hotel Cubanacan Comodoro — A1611

2014, May 31 **Litho.** ***Imperf.***
5526 A1611 1p multi 2.00 2.00

Third Cuba Philately Cup.

Sancti Spiritus, 500th Anniv. — A1612

Designs: 65c, Rio Yayabo Bridge. 75c, Parroquial Mayor Church, vert.

Perf. 12½x12¼, 12¼x12½

2014, June 4 **Litho.**
5527-5528 A1612 Set of 2 3.00 3.00

Diplomatic Relations Between Nigeria and Cuba, 40th Anniv. — A1613

2014, July 1 **Litho.** ***Perf. 12¼x12½***
5529 A1613 85c multi 1.75 1.75

Office of the Comptroller General, 5th Anniv. — A1614

2014, Aug. 1 **Litho.** ***Perf. 12½x12¼***
5530 A1614 90c multi 1.90 1.90

Spanish Heritage Festival, 25th Anniv. — A1615

2014, Aug. 5 **Litho.** ***Perf. 12½x12¼***
5531 A1615 65c multi 1.40 1.40

Show Jumping Horses — A1616

Designs: 15c, Golden Horse. 20c, Captain VZ. 30c, Fairmont R.E. 65c, Gigaa VDP. 75c, Google. 85c, Goldmann Jr.
1p, Fumuto and rider.

Perf. 12½x12¼

2014, Aug. 16 **Litho.**
5532-5537 A1616 Set of 6 6.00 6.00

Size: 83x83mm

Imperf

5538 A1616 1p multi 2.00 2.00

No. 5538 has simulated perforations.

African Animals and Map of Africa — A1617

2014, Sept. 2 Litho. ***Perf. 12½x12¼***
5539 A1617 85c multi 1.75 1.75

Diplomatic relations between Cuba and Burundi, Cameroun, Gabon, Senegal, Uganda, Liberia and Madagascar, 40th anniv.

Latin American Parliament, 50th Anniv. — A1618

2014, Sept. 5 Litho. ***Perf. 12½x12¼***
5540 A1618 65c multi 1.40 1.40

Diplomatic Relations Between Benin and Cuba, 40th Anniv. — A1619

2014, Sept. 12 Litho. ***Perf. 12¾***
5541 A1619 85c multi 1.75 1.75

Guitars — A1620

Perf. 12¼x12½

2014, Sept. 25 **Litho.**
5542 A1620 65c multi 1.40 1.40

75th birthday of Leo Brouwer, guitarist and composer.

People's Republic of China, 65th Anniv. — A1621

Perf. 12½x12¼

2014, Sept. 29 **Litho.**
5543 A1621 85c multi 1.75 1.75

Lighthouses A1622

Designs: 15c, Morro Castle Lighthouse, Havana. 35c, Cayo Jutías Lighthouse, Pinar del Rio. 75c, Cayo Cruz del Padre Lighthouse, Matanzas. 85c, Morro Lighthouse, Santiago.

2014, Oct. 5 Litho. ***Perf. 12¼x12½***
5544-5547 A1622 Set of 4 4.25 4.25

Philakorea 2014 Intl. Stamp Exhibition, Seoul — A1623

Dogs: 10c, Poodle (caniche). 20c, Yorkshire terrier. 30c, Schnauzer. 40c, Beagle. 65c, German shepherd (pastor aleman). 75c, Golden retriever.
1p, Collie (pastor escocés de pelo largo).

Perf. 12½x12¼

2014, June 15 **Litho.**
5548-5553 A1623 Set of 6 5.00 5.00

Souvenir Sheet

Imperf

5554 A1623 1p multi 2.00 2.00

No. 5554 contains one 43x33mm stamp with simulated perforations.

Malaysia 2014 Intl. Stamp Exhibition, Kuala Lumpur — A1624

Cats: 10c, Shorthaired cat (pelos cortos). 20c, Persian cat (Persas). 40c, Balinese cat (Balineses). 65c. Bengal cat (Bengalies). 75c, Siamese cat (Siameses), horiz. 85c, Semi-longhaired cat (pelos semi-largos).
1p, Cuban blue cat (azules cubanos).

Perf. 12¼x12½, 12½x12¼

2014, July 30 **Litho.**
5555-5560 A1624 Set of 6 6.00 6.00

Souvenir Sheet

Imperf

5561 A1624 1p multi 2.00 2.00

No. 5554 has simulated perforations.

Trains A1625

Designs: 5c, Talgo AVE series 100. 15c, Alstom FGC series 113. 50c, Siemens AVE series 103. 65c, Talgo AVE series 130. 75c, CRH380A. 85c, JR-Maglev MLX01.
1p, Cabina AVE series 102.

Perf. 12½x12¼

2014, Sept. 15 **Litho.**
5562-5567 A1625 Set of 6 6.00 6.00

Souvenir Sheet

Imperf

5568 A1625 1p multi 2.00 2.00

No. 5568 contains one 61x26mm trapezoidal stamp with simulated perforations.

Marine Life A1626

Designs: 5c, Volvarina moresi. 10c, Sepia officinalis. 30c, Amblyrhynchus cristatus. 65c, Physeter macrocephalus, vert. 75c, Aptenodytes patagonicus, vert. 85c, Eretmochelys imbricata, vert.
1p, Pomacanthus arcuatus, vert.

2014, Oct. 4 **Litho.** ***Perf. 12¾***
5569-5574 A1626 Set of 6 5.50 5.50

Souvenir Sheet

Imperf

5575 A1626 1p multi 2.00 2.00

No. 5575 has simulated perforations.

Famous Men — A1626a

Designs: No. 5575A, 65c, José Martí (1853-95), writer. No. 5575B, 65c, Antonio Maceo Grajales (1845-96), military leader. No. 5575C, 65c, Ignacio Agramonte y Loynaz (1841-73), revolutionist. No. 5575D, 65c, Carlos Manuel de Céspedes (1819-74), declarer of Cuban independence.

2014, Oct. 12 **Litho.** ***Perf. 12¾***
5575A-5575D A1626a Set of 4 5.25 5.25

America Issue.

Airplanes of Cubana Arilines — A1627

Designs: 15c, Curtiss Robin. 20c, Bristol Britannia. 45c, Lockheed 10 Electra. 75c, Antonov 158.

2014, Oct. 22 Litho. ***Perf. 12½x12¼***
5576-5579 A1627 Set of 4 3.25 3.25

Independence of Malawi, Tanzania and Zambia, 50th Anniv. — A1628

2014, Oct. 24 Litho. ***Perf. 12¼x12½***
5580 A1628 85c multi 1.75 1.75

National Road Safety Day A1629

Children's drawings: 15c, Taxi and signs. 20c, Children in crosswalk. 40c, Tractor and cow on road. 50c, Car, sign and traffic light. 65c, Child chasing ball in street. 75c, Railroad crossing.
1p, Policeman, crosswalk, traffic light.

2014, Nov. 17 **Litho.** ***Perf. 12¾***
5581-5586 A1629 Set of 6 5.50 5.50

Souvenir Sheet

Imperf

5587 A1629 1p multi 2.00 2.00

No. 5587 has simulated perforations.

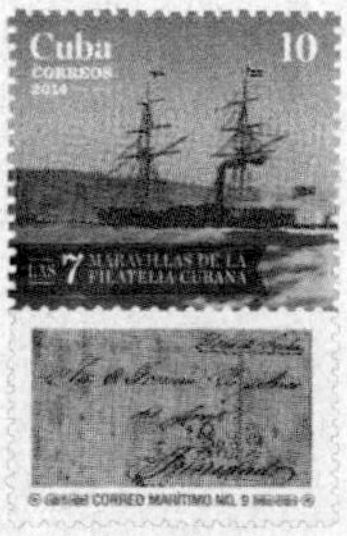

Cuban Philatelic Treasures A1630

Designs: 10c, Stampless cover, ship. 20c, Cover with three stamps, mask. 30c, Havana local post cover with two stamps, watchtower, horiz. 65c, Cover with Mambí insurrection stamps, mounted soldier with Cuban flag. 75c, Cover with Puerto Principe surcharges, tower. 85c, Experimental rocket mail cover, rocket.
1p, Statue and birds, horiz.

Perf. 12¼x12½, 12½x12¼

2014, Nov. 20 **Litho.**
5588-5593 A1630 Set of 6 5.75 5.75

Souvenir Sheet

Imperf

5594 A1630 1p multi 2.00 2.00

No. 5554 contains one 44x31mm stamp with simulated perforations.

Diplomatic Relations Between Cuba and the Bahamas, 40th Anniv. — A1631

Perf. 12½x12¼

2014, Nov. 28 **Litho.**
5595 A1631 3p multi 6.00 6.00

José Antonio Echeverria City University, 50th Anniv. — A1632

2014, Dec. 2 Litho. ***Perf. 12½x12¼***
5596 A1632 65c multi 1.40 1.40

2014 Diabetes Congress, Varadero Beach — A1633

Designs: 65c, Infected foot, bottle of medicine and surgeon's saw. 75c, People pulling on fabric covering over feet.

Perf. 12½x12¼

2014, Dec. 10 **Litho.**
5597-5598 A1633 Set of 2 3.00 3.00

Protected Flora and Fauna — A1634

Designs: 5c, Todus multicolor. 10c, Peireskia cubensis. 15c, Eretmochelys imbricata. 75c, Tetramicra eulophiae. 85c, Starnoenas cyanocephala. 90c, Bonnetia cubensis.
1p, Colaptes fernandinae, vert.

2014, Dec. 15 **Litho.** ***Perf. 12¾***
5599-5604 A1634 Set of 6 5.75 5.75

Souvenir Sheet

Imperf

5605 A1634 1p multi 2.00 2.00

No. 5605 has simulated perforations.

Tomás Romay Chacón (1764-1849), Physician — A1635

Perf. 12½x12¼

2014, Dec. 21 **Litho.**
5606 A1635 65c multi 1.40 1.40

José Luis Guerra Aguiar Postal Museum, 50th Anniv. — A1636

Designs: 5c, 1826 stampless cover from Santiago de Cuba to Puerto Principe. 10c, 1883 cover with stamps depicting King Alfonso XII. 15c, Handstamp and free frank covers of General Máximo Gómez Báez. 20c, Cuba #238, printing stone for stamp similar to #238. 65c, Handstamp, cover with Cuba #C324-C325. 75c, Children looking at museum exhibit, magnifying glass and album pages.
1p, Cover with Cuba #935a-935b.

2015 Jan. 9 **Litho.** ***Perf. 12½x12¼***
5607-5612 A1636 Set of 6 4.00 4.00

Souvenir Sheet

Imperf

5613 A1636 1p multi 2.00 2.00

No. 5613 contains one 44x33mm stamp with simulated perforations.

National Organization of Collective Law Offices, 50th Anniv. — A1637

2015, Jan. 22 **Litho.** ***Perf. 12½x12¼***
5614 A1637 65c multi 1.40 1.40

Faustino Pérez Hernández (1920-92), Central Committee Member, Zaza Dam — A1640

Perf. 12½x12¼

2015, Feb. 15 **Litho.**
5629 A1640 1.05p multi 2.10 2.10

Ballet "Dioné," 75th Anniv. — A1641

Designs: 75c, Composer Eduardo Sánchez de Fuentes (1874-1944) and scene from ballet. 90c, Dancers Alicia and Fernando Alonso.

2015, Mar. 4 **Litho.** ***Perf. 12½x12¼***
5630-5631 A1641 Set of 2 3.50 3.50

Ballet Performances of Anna Pavlova in Cuba, Cent. — A1642

Perf. 12¼x12½

2015, Mar. 18 **Litho.**
5632 A1642 65c multi 1.40 1.40

Explosion of Ship "La Coubre" in Havana Harbor, 55th Anniv. — A1644

2015, Apr. 1 **Litho.** ***Perf. 12½x12¼***
5634 A1644 3p multi 6.00 6.00

Landing of José Martí and General Máximo Gómez Báez at Playita, 120th Anniv. — A1647

No. 5649 — Playita and: a, 65c, Martí. b, 75c, Gómez.

2015, Apr. 11 **Litho.** ***Perf. 12¼x12½***
5649 A1647 Horiz. pair, #a-b 3.00 3.00

Use of First Stamps in Cuba, 160th Anniv. — A1649

No. 5651: a, 10c, Havana postal badge, mailman and mailboxes. b, 30c, Padlock and key, horse-drawn postal wagons. c, 65c, Post office scale, postal workers sorting mail. d, 75c, Title of Postal Administration, post office.

2015, Apr. 24 **Litho.** ***Perf. 12½x12¼***
5651 A1649 Block of 4, #a-d 3.75 3.75

Labor Day — A1650

2015, May 1 **Litho.** ***Perf. 12¼x12½***
5652 A1650 75c multi 1.50 1.50

Diplomatic Relations Between Cuba and Russia, 55th Anniv. — A1651

2015, May 8 **Litho.** ***Perf. 12¼x12½***
5653 A1651 85c multi 1.75 1.75

Havana Explosion and Fire of 1890, 125th Anniv. — A1652

Firefighter killed in explosion and horse-drawn: 5c, Cervantes pumper. 10c, Colón pumper. 15c, Fire wagon. 40c, Ambulance. 65c, Gámiz pumper. 75c, Cuba pumper.
1p, Megaphone and monument plaque listing the victims, vert.

2015, May 15 **Litho.** ***Perf. 12¾***
5654-5659 A1652 Set of 6 4.25 4.25

Souvenir Sheet

Imperf

5660 A1652 1p multi 2.00 2.00

No. 5660 has simulated perforations.

Ferry "Pinero" — A1653

2015, May 16 **Litho.** ***Perf. 12½x12¼***
5661 A1653 75c multi 1.50 1.50

Arrival of Fidel Castro and other Moncada Barracks attackers at Batabanó, 60th anniv.

International Telecommunication Union, 150th Anniv. — A1654

2015, May 17 **Litho.** ***Perf. 12¼x12½***
5662 A1654 65c multi 1.40 1.40

Elisio Reyes (1940-67), Guerrilla Fighter — A1655

2015, May 23 **Litho.** ***Perf. 12½x12¼***
5663 A1655 65c multi 1.40 1.40

SEMI-POSTAL STAMPS

Common Design Types pictured following the introduction.

Curie Issue

Common Design Type

Wmk. 106

1938, Nov. 23 **Engr.** ***Perf. 10***
B1 CD80 2c + 1c salmon 4.25 1.00
B2 CD80 5c + 1c deep ultra 4.25 1.40
Set, never hinged 12.00

40th anniv. of the discovery of radium by Pierre and Marie Curie. Surtax for the benefit of the Intl. Union for the Control of Cancer.

Catalogue values for unused stamps in this section, from this point to the end of the section, are for Never Hinged items.

"Agriculture" Supporting "Industry" SP2

Engr., Center Typo.

1959, May 7 Wmk. 321 *Perf. 12½*

B3	SP2	2c + 1c car & ultra	.70	.25

Agricultural reforms. See No. CB1. For surcharges see Nos. 624, C199.

Nurse — SP3

Wmk. 229

1959, Sept. 22 Photo. *Perf. 12½*

B4	SP3	2c + 1c crimson rose	.40	.25

Exists imperf, value about double.

AIR POST STAMPS

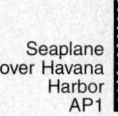

Seaplane over Havana Harbor AP1

Wmk. 106

1927, Nov. 1 Engr. *Perf. 12*

C1	AP1	5c dark blue	8.00	1.00
		Never hinged	13.50	

For overprint see No. C30.

Type of 1927 Issue Overprinted

1928, Feb. 8

C2	AP1	5c carmine rose	6.25	1.60
		Never hinged	9.00	

No. 283 Surcharged in Red

1930, Oct. 27 Unwmk.

C3	A44	10c on 25c violet	5.75	1.60
		Never hinged	8.50	

Airplane and Coast of Cuba — AP3

For Foreign Postage

1931, Feb. 26 Wmk. 106 *Perf. 10*

C4	AP3	5c green	.45	.25
C5	AP3	10c dk blue	.45	.25
C6	AP3	15c rose	.90	.30
C7	AP3	20c brown	.90	.25
C8	AP3	30c dk violet	1.25	.25
C9	AP3	40c dp orange	4.00	.35
C10	AP3	50c olive grn	6.75	.35
C11	AP3	1p black	10.00	.90
		Nos. C4-C11 (8)	24.70	2.90
		Set, never hinged	37.50	

See No. C40. For surcharges see Nos. C16-C17, C203, C225.

Airplane AP4

For Domestic Postage

1931-46

C12	AP4	5c rose vio ('32)	.40	.25
a.		5c brown violet ('36)	.40	.25
C13	AP4	10c gray blk	.40	.25
C14	AP4	20c car rose	3.25	.90
C14A	AP4	20c rose pink ('46)	1.40	.25
C15	AP4	50c dark blue	5.25	.90
		Nos. C12-C15 (5)	10.70	2.55
		Set, never hinged	17.00	

See #C130. For overprints see #C31, E29-E30.

Type of 1931 Surcharged in Black

1935, Apr. 24 *Perf. 10*

C16	AP3	10c + 10c red	15.00	9.50
		Never hinged	20.00	
a.		Double surcharge	110.00	

Imperf

C17	AP3	10c + 10c red	40.00	40.00
		Never hinged	55.00	55.00

Matanzas Issue

Air View of Matanzas AP5

10c, Airship "Macon." 20c, Airplane "The Four Winds." 50c, Air View of Fort San Severino.

Wmk. 229

1936, May 5 Photo. *Perf. 12½*

C18	AP5	5c violet	.85	.30
C19	AP5	10c yellow orange	1.00	.50
C20	AP5	20c green	3.75	1.90
C21	AP5	50c greenish slate	9.00	3.75
		Nos. C18-C21 (4)	14.60	6.45
		Set, never hinged	22.50	

Exist imperf. Value 20% more.

"Lightning" AP9

Allegory of Flight AP10

1936, Nov. 18

C22	AP9	5c violet	2.10	1.10
C23	AP10	10c orange brown	2.75	1.50
		Set, never hinged	6.00	

Major Gen. Maximo Gomez, birth cent.

Flat Arch (Panama) — AP11

Carlos Antonio López (Paraguay) — AP12

Inca Gate, Cuzco (Peru) — AP13

Atlacatl (Salvador) AP14

José Enrique Rodó (Uruguay) AP15

Simón Bolívar (Venezuela) AP16

Wmk. 106

1937, Oct. 13 Engr. *Perf. 10*

C24	AP11	5c red	7.75	7.75
C25	AP12	5c red	7.75	7.75
C26	AP13	10c blue	7.75	7.75
C27	AP14	10c blue	7.75	7.75
C28	AP15	20c green	10.00	10.00
C29	AP16	20c green	10.00	10.00
		Nos. C24-C29 (6)	51.00	51.00
		Set, never hinged	67.50	

See note after No. 354.

Type of 1927 Ovptd. in Black

1938, May Wmk. 106

C30	AP1	5c dark orange	7.25	1.60
		Never hinged	10.00	

1st airplane flight from Key West to Havana, made by Domingo Rosillo, 1913.

Type of 1931-32 Overprinted

1939, Oct. 15

C31	AP4	10c emerald	32.50	6.50
		Never hinged	55.00	

Issued in connection with an experimental postal rocket flight held at Havana.

Sir Rowland Hill, Map of Cuba and First Stamps of Britain, Spanish Cuba and Republic of Cuba — AP17

1940, Nov. 28 Engr. Wmk. 106

C32	AP17	10c brown	6.75	2.00
		Never hinged	11.00	

Souvenir Sheet

Unwmk. *Imperf.*

C33		Sheet of 4	22.50	22.50
		Never hinged	35.00	
a.		AP17 10c light brown	5.50	3.50
		Never hinged	8.00	

Cent. of the 1st postage stamp.

Sheet sold for 60c.

No. C33 exists with each of the four stamps overprinted in black: "Exposicion de la ACNU/24 de Octubre de 1951/Dia de las Naciones" and "Historia de la Aviacion" in lower margin. Value, $80.

For overprints see Nos. C39, C211.

Poet José Heredia and Palms AP18

Heredia and Niagara Falls — AP19

1940, Dec. 30 Wmk. 106

C34	AP18	5c emerald	3.25	1.00
C35	AP19	10c greenish slate	4.00	1.60
		Set, never hinged	11.00	

Death cent. of José Maria Heredia y Campuzano (1803-39), poet and patriot.

First Cuban Land Sighted by Columbus AP20

Columbus Lighthouse AP21

1944, May 19

C36	AP20	5c olive green	1.10	.40
C37	AP21	10c slate black	2.50	.75

450th anniv. of the discovery of America.

Catalogue values for unused stamps in this section, from this point to the end of the section, are for Never Hinged items.

Conference of La Mejorana (Maceo, Gomez and Marti) AP22

1948, May 21 Wmk. 229 *Perf. 12½*

C38	AP22	8c org yel & blk	4.50	.80

50th anniv. of the start of the War of 1895.

Souvenir Sheet

No. C33 Overprinted in Ultramarine

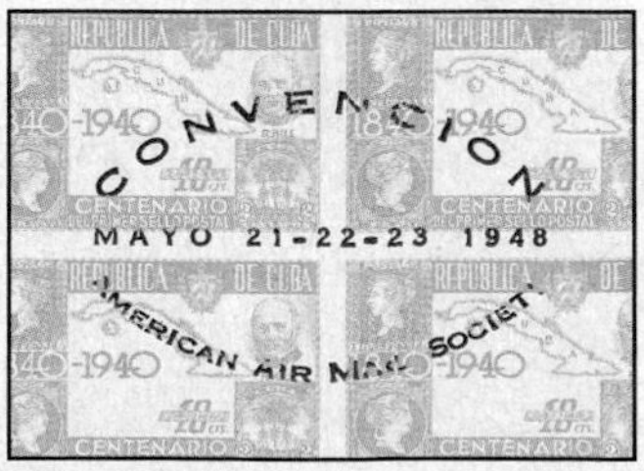

1948, May 21 Unwmk. *Imperf.*

C39	AP17	Sheet of 4	22.50	9.50

The overprint is applied in the center of the sheet, so that a part of the overprint falls on each stamp.

American Air Mail Soc. Convention, Havana, May 21 to 23, 1948. The sheets sold for 60c each.

Type of 1931

1948, June 15 Wmk. 106 *Perf. 10*

C40	AP3	8c orange brown	2.75	.80

Narciso Lopez Landing at Cárdenas AP23

Flag on Cuban Fort — AP24

Flag on Morro Castle, Havana — AP25

Engraved and Lithographed

1951, July 3 Wmk. 229 *Perf. 13*

C41 AP23 5c ol grn, ultra & red 2.75 .30
C42 AP24 8c red brn, bl & red 4.25 .30
C43 AP25 25c gray blk, bl & red 6.00 1.90
Nos. C41-C43 (3) 13.00 2.50

Centenary of adoption of Cuba's flag.

Souvenir Sheet

No. 365a Overprinted in Green

1951, Aug. 24 Unwmk. *Imperf.*

C43A Sheet of 4 18.00 9.00

50th anniv. of the discovery of the cause of yellow fever by Dr. Carlos J. Finlay, and to honor the martyrs of science.

Postage Type and

Resignation Play of Dr. Lasker AP26

Capablanca Making "The Exact Play" — AP27

Wmk. 229

1951, Nov. 1 Photo. *Perf. 13*

C44 AP26 5c shown 8.00 .80
C45 AP27 8c shown 12.00 1.25
C46 A165 25c Capablanca 22.50 3.25
Nos. C44-C46 (3) 42.50 5.30

30th anniv. of the winning of the World Chess title by José Raul Capablanca.

Morrillo Types of Regular Issue

Wmk. 106

1951, Nov. 22 Engr. *Perf. 10*

C47 A167 5c violet 3.25 .70
C48 A168 8c deep green 4.50 1.00
C49 A169 25c dark brown 8.75 2.00
a. Souv. sheet of 6, black brown, perf. 13 72.50 35.00
b. Souv. sheet of 6, green, imperf. 225.00 125.00
Nos. C47-C49 (3) 16.50 3.70

Nos. C49a and C49b contain one each of the 1c, 2c and 5c of types A167-A169 and of the 5c, 8c and 25c airmail stamps of types A167-A169. Sheets are unwatermarked and measure 124x133mm.

Isabella Type of Regular Issue, 1952

1952, Feb. 22

C50 A172 25c purple 5.75 1.25
a. Souv. sheet of 2, perf. 11 35.00 35.00
b. Souv. sheet of 2, imperf. 35.00 35.00

Nos. C50a and C50b contain one each of a 2c of type A172 and a 25c air-mail stamp of type A172. In No. C50a, the 2c and marginal inscriptions are brown carmine; the 25c, dark blue. In No. C50b, the 2c and marginal inscriptions are dark blue; the 25c, brown carmine. Sheets measure 108x18mm.

Type of Regular Issue of 1951 Surcharged in Various Colors

1952, Mar. 18

Color: Yellow Brown

C51 A159 5c on 2c .90 .30
C52 A159 8c on 2c (C) 1.75 .30
C53 A159 10c on 2c (Bl) 1.75 .30
C54 A159 25c on 2c (V) 3.25 1.50
C55 A159 50c on 2c (C) 13.50 3.00
C56 A159 1p on 2c (Bl) 20.00 12.00
Nos. C51-C56 (6) 41.15 17.40

Country School AP32

Entrance, University of Havana — AP33

10c, Presidential Mansion. 25c, Banknote.

Wmk. 106

1952, May 27 Engr. *Perf. 12½*

Centers Various Shades of Green

C57 AP32 5c dark purple .60 .25
C58 AP33 8c dark red .95 .25
C59 AP32 10c deep blue 1.90 .25
C60 AP32 25c dark violet brn 3.25 1.00
Nos. C57-C60 (4) 6.70 1.75

Foundation of the Republic of Cuba, 50th anniv.

Plane and Map — AP34

Agustín Parlá — AP35

1952, July 22 Engr. *Perf. 10*

C61 AP34 8c black 2.00 .55
a. Souv. sheet, 8c deep blue 18.00 10.00
b. Souv. sheet, 8c deep green 18.00 10.00
C62 AP35 25c ultra 5.50 1.60
a. Souv. sheet, 25c deep blue 18.00 10.00
b. Souv. sheet, 25c deep green 18.00 10.00

30th anniv. of the Key West-Mariel flight of Agustin Parla.

The four souvenir sheets are perf. 11.

Col. Charles Hernandez y Sandrino — AP36

1952, Oct. 7

C63 AP36 5c orange .80 .30
C64 AP36 8c brt yel grn .80 .30
C65 AP36 10c dk brown 1.00 .30
C66 AP36 15c dk Prus grn 1.90 .80
C67 AP36 20c aqua 2.50 1.00
C68 AP36 25c crimson 1.90 1.00
C69 AP36 30c dk vio bl 5.25 2.50
C70 AP36 45c rose lilac 8.00 3.50
C71 AP36 50c indigo 6.50 2.50
C72 AP36 1p bister 16.00 5.00
Nos. C63-C72 (10) 44.65 17.20

Three-fourths of the proceeds from the sale were used for the Communications Ministry Employees' Retirement Fund.

Entrance, University of Havana — AP37

F. V. Dominguez, M. Estebanez and F. Capdevila — AP38

Engr.; Center Typo.

1952, Nov. 27

C73 AP37 5c indigo & dk blue 2.25 .40
C74 AP38 25c org & dk grn 6.75 1.40

Execution of 8 medical students, 81st anniv.

AP39

Lockheed Constellation Airliners — AP40

1953, May 22 Engr.

C75 AP39 8c orange brn 1.75 .25
C76 AP39 15c scarlet 3.25 .70

Typographed and Engraved

C77 AP40 2p dp green & dk brn 42.50 10.00
C78 AP40 5p blue & dk brn 82.50 17.50
Nos. C75-C78 (4) 130.00 28.45

See Nos. C120-C121. For surcharge, see No. C224.

Page of Manifesto of Montecristi — AP42

House of Maximo Gomez AP43

No. C79, Marti in Kingston, Jamaica, No. C80, With Workers in Tampa, Florida. No. C83, Marti addressing liberating army. No. C84, Portrait. No. C85, Dos Rios obelisk. No. C86, Marti's first tomb. No. C87, Present tomb. No. C88, Monument in Havana. No. C89, Martian forge.

1953 Engr. *Perf. 10*

C79 AP42 5c dk car & blk .30 .25
C80 AP42 5c dk car & blk .30 .25
C81 AP43 8c dk green & blk .65 .25
C82 AP42 8c dk green & blk .65 .25
C83 AP43 10c dk blue & dk car 1.75 .75
C84 AP42 10c dk blue & dk car 1.75 .75
C85 AP42 15c violet & gray 1.50 .90
C86 AP43 15c violet & gray 1.50 .90
C87 AP42 25c brown & car 4.75 1.25
C88 AP42 25c brown & car 4.75 1.25
C89 AP43 50c yellow & bl 6.25 2.50
Nos. C79-C89 (11) 24.15 9.30

Cent. of the birth of José Marti.

Board of Accounts Building — AP44

25c, Plane above Board of Accounts Bldg.

1953, Nov. 3

C90 AP44 8c rose carmine 2.25 .70
C91 AP44 25c dk gray grn 4.00 1.10

1st Intl. Cong. of Boards of Account, Havana, Nov. 2-9, 1953.

Miguel Coyula Llaguno AP45

Antonio Ginard Rojas AP46

Designs: 10c, Gregorio Hernandez Saez. 1p, Communications Association Flag.

1954

C92 AP45 5c dark blue .65 .25
C93 AP46 8c red violet .80 .25
C94 AP46 10c orange 1.40 .35
C95 AP45 1p black 9.50 4.50
Nos. C92-C95 (4) 12.35 5.35

See note after No. C72.

Alvaro Reinoso — AP47

Plane and Harvesters Cutting Cane AP48

Designs in Lower Triangle: 5c, Four-engine Plane and Cane Field. 10c, Tractor pulling loaded wagons. 15c, Train of sugar cane. 20c, Modern mill. 25c, Evaporators. 30, Sacks of sugar. 40c, Loading sugar on ship. 45c, Ox cart. 50c, Primitive sugar mill.

1954, Apr. 27 Engr.

C96 AP47 5c yellow green .55 .25
C97 AP48 8c brown 1.50 .50
C98 AP48 10c dark green 1.50 .50
C99 AP48 15c henna brn 3.75 .50
C100 AP48 20c blue 1.50 .25

C101 AP48 25c scarlet 1.15 .25
C102 AP48 30c lilac rose 3.00 .95
C103 AP48 40c deep blue 6.25 1.25
C104 AP48 45c violet 5.00 2.50
C105 AP48 50c brt blue 5.00 1.60
C106 AP47 1p dk gray blue 13.50 3.25
Nos. C96-C106 (11) 42.70 11.80

For surcharges see Nos. C204.

Sanatorium Type of Regular Issue

1954, Sept. 21 Wmk. 106 *Perf. 10*
C107 A186 9c deep green 2.50 .65

Dolz Type of Regular Issue, 1954

1954, Dec. 23
C108 A188 12c carmine 3.50 .70

Rotary Type of Regular Issue, 1955

1955, Feb. 23
C109 A190 12c carmine 2.50 .65

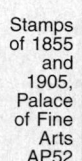

Stamps of 1855 and 1905, Palace of Fine Arts AP52

Designs (including 2 stamps): 12c, Plaza de la Fraternidad. 24c, View of Havana. 30c, Plaza de la Republica.

1955, Apr. 24 *Perf. 12½*
C110 AP52 8c dk grnsh bl & grn 1.00 .35
C111 AP52 12c dk ol grn & red 1.10 .35
C112 AP52 24c dk red & ultra 2.00 .95
C113 AP52 30c dp org & brn 4.25 1.60
Nos. C110-C113 (4) 8.35 3.25

Cent. of Cuba's 1st postage stamps.

Mariel Bay — AP53

Views: 12c, Varadero beach. 1p, Vinales valley.

1955, June 22 Wmk. 106
C114 AP53 8c dk car & dk grn .75 .25
C115 AP53 12c dk ocher & brt bl 1.75 .55
C116 AP53 1p dk grn & ocher 7.50 2.50
Nos. C114-C116 (3) 10.00 3.30

See note after No. C72.

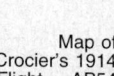

Map of Crocier's 1914 Flight — AP54

Design: 30c, Crocier in plane.

1955, July 4 *Perf. 10*
C117 AP54 12c red & dk grn 1.00 .25
C118 AP54 30c dk grn & mag 3.00 .80

35th anniv. of the death of Jaime Gonzalez Crocier, aviation pioneer.

Cuban Museum, Tampa, Fla. — AP55

1955, July 1 Engr. *Perf. 12½*
C119 AP55 12c red & dk brn 3.25 .65

Cent. of Tampa's incorporation as a town.

Lockheed Type of 1953
Typographed and Engraved

1955, Sept. 21 Wmk. 106
C120 AP40 2p bl & ol grn 29.00 6.50
C121 AP40 5p dp rose & ol grn 62.50 15.00

Wright Brothers' Plane and Stamps AP56

Designs: 12c, Spirit of St. Louis. 24c, Graf Zeppelin. 30c, Constellation passenger plane. 50c, Convair jet fighter.

Engraved and Photogravure

1955, Nov. 12 Wmk. 106 *Perf. 12½*
Inscription and Plane in Black
C122 AP56 8c car & bl 1.10 .35
C123 AP56 12c yel grn & car 2.50 .70
C124 AP56 24c vio & car 7.50 2.50
C125 AP56 30c bl & red org 6.50 3.25
C126 AP56 50c ol grn & red org 8.50 4.00
a. Souvenir sheet of 5 57.50 26.00
Nos. C122-C126 (5) 26.10 10.80

International Centenary Philatelic Exhibition in Havana, Nov. 12-19, 1955.

No. C126a is printed on thick paper and measures 140x178mm. It contains one each of Nos. C122-C126 with the background of each stamp printed in a different color from the perforated stamps.

"Three Friends" and Gen. Emilio Nuñez AP57

Design: 12c, Landing on the Cuban Coast.

1955, Dec. 27 Engr. Unwmk.
C127 AP57 8c ultra & dk car 2.00 .55
C128 AP57 12c grn & dk red brn 3.25 .90

Gen. Emilio Nuñez, Cuban revolutionary hero, birth cent.

Post Type of Regular Issue, 1956

Bishop P. A. Morell de Santa Cruz (1694-1768).

1956, Mar. 27 Wmk. 106
C129 A197 12c dk brn & grn 3.25 .55

Plane Type of 1931-46

1956 Engr. *Perf. 10*
C130 AP4 50c greenish blue 5.00 1.00

Portrait Type of Regular Issue, 1956

Portraits: 8c, Gen. Julio Sanguily. 12c, Gen. José Maria Aguirre. 30c, Col. Ernesto Fonts Sterling.

1956, May 2 *Perf. 12½*
Portraits in Black
C131 A198 8c brown 1.25 .25
C132 A198 12c dull yellow 2.00 .25
C133 A198 30c indigo 3.00 1.50
Nos. C131-C133 (3) 6.25 2.00

See note after No. C72.

Mother and Child — AP60

Masonic Temple Havana — AP61

1956, May 13 Wmk. 106 *Perf. 12½*
C134 AP60 12c ultra & red 3.00 .40

Issued in honor of Mother's Day 1956.

1956, June 5
C135 AP61 12c olive green 3.25 .55

Pigeon AP62

Gundlach Hawk — AP63

Birds: 8c, Wood duck. 19c, Herring gulls. 24c, White pelicans. 29c, Common merganser. 30c, Quail. 50c, Herons (great white, great blue and Wurdemann's). 1p, Northern caracara. 2p, Middle American jacana. 5p, Ivory-billed woodpecker.

1956
C136 AP62 8c blue .50 .25
C137 AP62 12c gray blue 10.00 .25
C138 AP63 14c green 2.25 .25
C139 AP63 19c redsh brn 1.50 .55
C140 AP63 24c lilac rose 1.60 .55
C141 AP62 29c green 2.50 .55
C142 AP62 30c dk olive bis 3.00 .80
C143 AP63 50c slate blk 5.75 1.10
C144 AP63 1p dk car rose 8.75 2.25
C145 AP62 2p rose violet 17.50 4.25
C146 AP63 5p brt red 47.50 8.75
Nos. C136-C146 (11) 100.85 19.55

See Nos. C205, C235-C237. For surcharges and overprints, see Nos. C147, C151, C197, C209-C210

Type of 1956 Surcharged

Design: 24c, White pelicans.

1956, July 13
C147 AP63 8c on 24c deep org 2.50 .75

Opening of the new building of the Cuba Philatelic Club, Havana, July 14, 1956.

Hubert de Blanck — AP64

1956, July 6
C148 AP64 12c ultra 2.75 .40

Hubert de Blanck (1856-1932), composer.

Church of Our Lady of Charity — AP65

1956, Sept. 8
C149 AP65 12c green & carmine 3.25 .55
a. Souvenir sheet of 2, imperf. 18.00 9.50

Issued in honor of Our Lady of Charity of Cobre, patroness of Cuba.

No. C149a contains one each of Nos. 559 and C149. No. C149a exists with yellow of No. 559 omitted.

Benjamin Franklin AP66

1956, Oct. 5 Engr. *Perf. 12½*
C150 AP66 12c red brown 3.25 .55

Type of 1956 Surcharged in Blue

Design: 2p, Middle American jacana.

1956, Oct. 26 Wmk. 106
C151 AP62 12c on 2p dark gray 3.25 .95

Issued in honor of the 12th Inter-American Press Association Conference, Havana.

Lord Baden-Powell AP67

1957, Feb. 22
C152 AP67 12c slate 3.25 .70

Centenary of the birth of Lord Baden-Powell, founder of the Boy Scouts.

Hanabanilla Waterfall AP68

12c, Sierra de Cubitas. 30c, Puerto Boniato.

1957, Mar. 29
C153 AP68 8c blue & red .75 .25
C154 AP68 12c green & red 2.75 .50
C155 AP68 30c ol grn & dk pur 3.25 .70
Nos. C153-C155 (3) 6.75 1.45

See note after No. 457.

Philatelic Club, Havana — AP69

1957, Apr. 24 Wmk. 106 *Perf. 12½*
C156 AP69 12c yel, grn & brn 2.75 .40

Stamp Day, and the Natl. Phil. Exhib.

Fingerprint — AP70

1957, Apr. 30
C157 AP70 12c claret brown 2.40 .40

Birth cent. (in 1856) of Juan Francisco Steegers y Perera, dactyloscopy pioneer.

Baseball Player — AP71

1957, May 17 Wmk. 106 *Perf. 12½*

C158 AP71 8c shown 1.25 .40
C159 AP71 12c Ballerina 2.50 .50
C160 AP71 24c Girl diver 3.50 1.25
C161 AP71 30c Boxers 5.25 1.60
Nos. C158-C161 (4) 12.50 3.75

Issued to honor young Cuban athletes.

Joaquin de Aguero — AP72

1957, July 4

C162 AP72 12c indigo 1.75 .40

Issued to honor Joaquin de Aguero, Cuban freedom fighter and patriot.

Jeanette Ryder — AP73

1957, July 17

C163 AP73 12c dk red brn 2.50 .55
a. Pair, #574, C163 7.00 3.50

Mrs. Jeanette Ryder, founder of the Humane Society of Cuba.

José M. de Heredia y Girard — AP74

1957, Aug. 16 Engr. Wmk. 106

C164 AP74 8c dk blue vio 1.50 .30

José Maria de Heredia y Girard (1842-1905), Cuban born French poet.

Justice Type of Regular Issue, 1957

1957, Sept. 2 *Perf. 12½*

C165 A214 12c green 2.75 .50

John Robert Gregg — AP75

1957, Oct. 1

C166 AP75 12c dark green 2.50 .70

90th anniv. of the birth of John Robert Gregg, inventor of the Gregg shorthand system.

D. Figarola Caneda — AP76

José Marti National Library AP77

1957, Oct. 18 Wmk. 106 *Perf. 12½*

C167 AP76 8c ultra .75 .25
C168 AP77 12c chocolate 2.00 .50

José Marti National Library.

Map of Cuba and UN Emblem AP78

1957, Oct. 24

C169 AP78 8c dk green & brn 1.15 .25
C170 AP78 12c car rose & grn 1.75 .55
C171 AP78 30c ind & brt pink 4.00 1.25
Nos. C169-C171 (3) 6.90 2.05

Issued for United Nations Day, 1957.

Map of Cuba and Florida AP79

1957, Oct. 28

C172 AP79 12c dk red brn & bl 2.40 .80

30th anniv. of airmail service from Key West to Havana.

Type of Regular Issue, 1957 and

Stairway and Bell Tower AP80

Design: 12c, Facade of Normal School.

1957, Nov. 19 Engr. *Perf. 12½*

C173 A217 12c indigo & ocher 1.75 .40
C174 AP80 30c dk car & gray 3.25 .60

View Types of Regular Issue, 1957

Views: 8c, El Viso Fort, El Caney. 12c, Sancti Spiritus Church. 30c, Concordia Bridge, Matanzas.

1957, Dec. 17 *Perf. 12½*

C175 A218 8c dk gray & red .80 .30
C176 A219 12c brown & gray 1.50 .40
C177 A218 30c red brn & bl gray 3.50 .75
Nos. C175-C177 (3) 5.80 1.45

See note after No. C72.

Hedges Types of Regular Issue, 1958

8c, Dayton Hedges & Matanzas rayon factory.

1958, Jan. 30 Wmk. 106 *Perf. 12½*

C178 A221 8c green 1.15 .80

Diario de la Marina Building — AP81

1958, Apr. 1

C179 AP81 29c black 4.25 1.10

Jose Ignacio Rivero y Alonso, editor of the newspaper, Diario de la Marina.

Map Showing Sea Mail Route, 1765 AP82

1958, Apr. 24 Wmk. 106 *Perf. 12½*

C180 AP82 29c dk bl aqua & buff 4.75 1.25

Issued for Stamp Day, Apr. 24, and the National Philatelic Exhibition.

Gen. Gomez in Battle — AP83

1958, June 6 Engr.

C181 AP83 12c slate green 2.00 .55

Issued in honor of Maj. Gen. José Miguel Gomez, President of Cuba, 1909-13.

Snail (Polymita Picta) — AP84

12c, Megalocnus Rodens. 30c, Ammonite.

1958, Aug. 29 Wmk. 321 *Perf. 12½*

C182 AP84 8c gray, red & yel 5.00 1.25
C183 AP84 12c brn, *yel grn* 7.50 1.75
C184 AP84 30c grn, *pink* 12.00 2.10
Nos. C182-C184 (3) 24.50 5.10

Centenary of the birth of Dr. Carlos de la Torre, naturalist.

Papilio Caiguanabus AP85

Cuban Sea Bass — AP86

12c, Teria gundlachia. 14c, Teria ebriola. 19c, Nathalis felicia. 29c, Butter Hamlet. 30c, Tattler.

1958, Sept. 26 Wmk. 106 *Perf. 12½*

C185 AP85 8c multicolored 3.00 .65
C186 AP85 12c emer, blk & org 3.50 .65
C187 AP85 14c multicolored 5.25 .95
C188 AP85 19c blk, blk & yel 6.75 1.25
C189 AP86 24c multicolored 7.50 1.25
C190 AP86 29c blk, brn & ultra 11.00 1.60
C191 AP86 30c blk, yel grn & sep 16.00 2.25
Nos. C185-C191 (7) 53.00 8.60

Felipe Poey (1799-1891), naturalist.

Battle of San Juan Hill, 1898 — AP87

Wmk. 106

1958, Oct. 27 Engr. *Perf. 12½*

C192 AP87 12c black brown 2.75 .50

Birth centenary of Theodore Roosevelt.

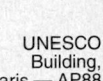

UNESCO Building, Paris — AP88

Design: 30c, "UNESCO" and map of Cuba.

1958, Nov. 7

C193 AP88 12c dk slate grn 2.25 .50
C194 AP88 30c dp ultra 4.25 1.60

UNESCO Headquarters in Paris opening, Nov. 3.

Postal Notice of 1765 — AP89

Design: 30c, Administrative postal book of St. Cristobal, Havana, 1765.

1959, Apr. 24 Wmk. 321 *Perf. 12½*

C195 AP89 12c Prus blue & sep 1.50 .40
C196 AP89 30c sepia & Prus bl 2.50 1.40

Issued for Stamp Day, Apr. 24, and the National Philatelic Exhibition.

Type of 1956 Surcharged in Dark Blue

1959, Oct. 17 Wmk. 321 *Perf. 12½*

C197 AP63 12c on 1p emerald 2.40 1.25

Issued to publicize the meeting of the American Soc. of Travel Agents, Oct. 17-23.

Musical Arts Building — AP90

Wmk. 106

1959, Nov. 11 Engr. *Perf. 12½*

C198 AP90 12c yellow green 3.00 .70

40th anniversary of the Musical Arts Society.

No. CB1 Surcharged in Red

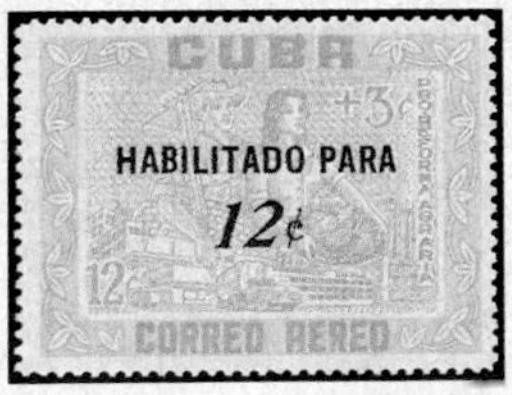

Engr. & Typo.

1960 Wmk. 321 *Perf. 12½*

C199 SPAP1 12c on 12 + 3c car & grn 2.25 .75

Type of Regular Issue, 1960

8c, Battle of Santa Clara. 12c, Rebel forces entering Havana. 29c, Bank-note changing hands ("Clandestine activities in the cities").

Wmk. 320

1960, Jan. 28 Engr. *Perf. 12½*

C200 A236 8c bl, gray ol & sal 2.25 .50
C201 A236 12c gray ol & ocher 3.25 .40
C202 A236 29c gray & car 6.50 1.50
Nos. C200-C202 (3) 12.00 2.40

Nos. C9 and C104 Srchd. in Red

1960, Feb. 3 **Wmk. 106**

C203 AP3 12c on 40c dp org 1.75 .65
C204 AP48 12c on 45c vio 1.75 .65

Pigeon Type of 1956

1960, Feb. 12 **Wmk. 321**

C205 AP62 12c brt blue grn 2.00 .55

Statue Type of Regular Issue, 1960.

Statues: 8c, José Marti, Matanzas. 12c, Heroes of the Cacarajicara, Pinar del Rio. 30c, Cosme de la Torriente, Isle of Pines, horiz.

1960, Mar. 28 ***Perf. 12½***

C206 A237 8c gray & car .70 .25
C207 A237 12c blue & car 1.25 .25
C208 A237 30c violet & brn 2.75 1.25
Nos. C206-C208 (3) 4.70 1.75

See note after No. 386.

Type of 1956 and No. C33 Overprinted in Dark Blue

1960, Apr. 24 **Wmk. 321** ***Perf. 12½***

C209 AP62 8c orange yel .65 .40
C210 AP62 12c cerise 1.75 .65

Souvenir Sheet

C211 AP17 Sheet of 4 35.00 35.00

Stamp Day, 4/24/60, and Natl. Phil. Exhib.
No. C211 has added marginal inscription in dark blue for cent. of the ¼r on 2r (No. 15).

Type of Olympic Games Issue, 1960
Wmk. 321

1960, Sept. 22 **Engr.** ***Perf. 12½***

C212 A238 8c Boxer .80 .25
C213 A238 12c Runner 1.50 .50
a. Souvenir sheet of 4 5.50 5.50

17th Olympic Games, Rome, Aug. 25-Sept. 11. No. C213a contains one each imperf. of types of Nos. 645-646 and Nos. C212-C213 in dark blue.

No. C3 and Flight Symbols of 1930, 1960 — AP91

1960, Oct. 30 **Litho.** **Unwmk.**

C214 AP91 8c multicolored 3.50 2.00

30th anniv. of national air mail service.

Sword of Sheaf of Wheat — AP92

12c, Two workers, horiz. 30c, Three maps, horiz. 50c, Hand inscribed "Peace" in 5 languages.

1961, Jan. 10 **Photo.** ***Perf. 11½***
Granite Paper

C215 AP92 8c multicolored .60 .25
C216 AP92 12c multicolored 2.00 .25
C217 AP92 30c black & red 2.50 .65
C218 AP92 50c blk, bl & red 3.00 1.00
Nos. C215-C218 (4) 8.10 2.15

Conf. of Underdeveloped Countries, Havana.

José Marti and "Declaration of Havana" — AP93

Background in Spanish, English or French.

1961, Jan. 28 **Litho.** ***Perf. 12½***

C219 AP93 8c pale grn, blk & red 1.25 .85
C220 AP93 12c org yel, blk & pale vio 1.75 1.00
C221 AP93 30c pale bl, blk & pale brn 4.00 3.50
a. Souvenir sheet of 3 15.00 15.00
Nos. C219-C221 (3) 7.00 5.35

Declaration of Havana, Sept. 1, 1960.
Sheets of 25 are imprinted in margin "E" for Spanish, "I" for English or "F" for French.
No. C221a contains one each of Nos. C219-C221, imperf. The 8c has background in Spanish, the 12c in English and the 30e in French.

UN Type of 1961

1961, Apr. 12 **Unwmk.** ***Perf. 12½***

C222 A244 8c dp car & yel .60 .25
C223 A244 12c brt ultra & org 1.50 .50
a. Souv. sheet of 2, #C222-C223, imperf. 10.00 10.00

Nos. C76 and C7 Surcharged

Wmk. 106

1961, Oct. 1 **Engr.** ***Perf. 10***

C224 AP39 8c on 15c No. C76 1.00 .40
C225 AP3 8c on 20c No. C7 1.00 .40

Revolution Anniv. Type of 1962
Perf. 12½

1962, Jan. 3 **Litho.** **Unwmk.**

C226 A250 8c multi .85 .30
C227 A250 12c multi 1.90 .55
C228 A250 30c multi 2.50 .90
Nos. C226-C228 (3) 5.25 1.75

1st Sugarcane Harvest in Socialist Cuba, 1st Anniv. — AP94

1962, Jan. 16

C229 AP94 8c salmon pink & dark brn 1.00 .25
C230 AP94 12c bluish lil & blk 2.50 .45

Cuban goods have been embargoed by the United States since a Feb. 7, 1962 proclamation by President Kennedy, but according to the Office of Foreign Assets Control of the Treasury Department, used Cuban stamps can be imported and sold without limitation, and unused stamps may be imported for personal use, but not resold.

Intl. Radio Service AP95

1962, Mar. 26 **Wmk. 321**

C231 AP95 8c multi 1.10 .25
C232 AP95 12c multi 2.25 .55
C233 AP95 30c multi 3.25 1.25
C234 AP95 1p multi 7.00 3.25
Nos. C231-C234 (4) 13.60 5.30

Bird Type of 1956

1962, July 20 **Engr.** **Wmk. 321**

C235 AP63 1p like #C144, royal blue 5.75 5.75
C236 AP62 2p like #C145, dark red 17.00 15.00
C237 AP63 5p like #C146, rose lake 37.50 32.50
Nos. C235-C237 (3) 60.25 53.25

PRAGA '62 — AP96

1962, Aug. 18 **Litho.**

C238 AP96 31c Czechoslovakia No. 1080 3.50 1.50

Souvenir Sheet
Imperf

C239 AP96 31c like No. C238 17.50 12.00

No. C239 contains one 60x35½mm stamp.

Achievements of the Revolution — AP97

1966, July 26 **Wmk. 376** ***Perf. 12½***

C240 AP97 1c Agrarian reform .25 .25
C241 AP97 2c Industrialization .25 .25
C242 AP97 3c Urban reform .50 .25
C243 AP97 7c Eradication of unemployment .50 .25
C244 AP97 9c Education .95 .25
C245 AP97 10c Public health 2.10 .25
C246 AP97 13c Excerpt from *La Historia Me Absolvera,* by Castro 2.75 .45
Nos. C240-C246 (7) 7.30 1.95

Camaguey-Seville Flight, 35th Anniv. — AP98

1971, Jan. 12 **Unwmk.**

C247 AP98 13c Aircraft 2.75 .25
C248 AP98 30c Map, Lieut. Menendez Palaez 3.25 .70

Havana-Santiago de Chile Direct Air Service, 1st Anniv. — AP99

1972, June 26 **Wmk. 376**

C249 AP99 25c multi 3.00 .75

6th Congress of Latin American and Caribbean Exporters of Sugar, Havana — AP100

Perf. 12½x12

1977, Feb. 28 **Unwmk.**

C250 AP100 13c multi .75 .25

Composer Type of 1977

1977, May 10 ***Perf. 13***

C251 A571 13c Jorge Ankerman and score 1.00 .25

Flower Type of 1977

Designs: 13c, Caesalpinia pulcherrima. 30c, .Catharanthus roseus.

1977, May 31

C252 A572 13c multicolored .85 .25
C253 A572 30c multicolored 1.75 .50

Souvenir Sheet
Perf. 13½x13

C254 A572 50c Juan Tomas Roig 4.00 .90

No. C254 contains one 32x40mm stamp.

Natl. Decorations Type of 1977

1977, July 26 ***Perf. 12x12½***

C255 A574 13c multi, diff. .80 .25
C256 A574 30c multi, diff. 1.50 .45

Art Type of 1977

Paintings by Jorge Arche: 13c, *My Wife and I*, vert. 30c, *Domino Players.* 50c, *Self-portrait*, vert.

1977, Aug. 25 ***Perf. 13x12½***
Size: 26x38mm

C257 A575 13c multi .65 .25

Size: 40x29mm
Perf. 13

C258 A575 30c multi 1.60 .40

Souvenir Sheet
Perf. 13½x13

C259 A575 50c multi 4.00 4.00

No. C259 contains one 32x40mm stamp.

Spartakiad Type of 1977

1977, Sept. 10 ***Perf. 13***

C260 A576 13c Grenade-throwing .60 .25
C261 A576 30c Rifle-shooting, horiz. 1.50 .40

10th Heroic Guerrilla's Day AP101

1977, Oct. 8 ***Perf. 12½x13***

C262 AP101 13c Guerrilla fighters 1.00 .25

Airmail Service Type of 1977

1977, Oct. 27 *Perf. 12x12½*

C263 A577 13c Havana-Mexico cachet .85 .25
C264 A577 30c Havana-Prague cachet 1.75 .55

Souvenir Sheet

Adoration of the Magi, by Rubens — AP102

1977, Nov. 18 *Perf. 13*

C265 AP102 50c multi 4.00 4.00

Rubens' 400th birth anniv.

Havana Zoo Type of 1977

1977, Nov. 24

C266 A579 13c Tiger 1.25 .25
C267 A579 30c Lion 1.90 .55

Revolution Martyrs Type of 1977

1977, Dec. 2 *Perf. 12½x12*

C268 A580 13c *Corynthia* landing .75 .25

Pan American Health Organization (OPS), 75th Anniv. — AP103

1977, Dec. 2

C269 AP103 13c multi .75 .25

Havana University Type of 1978

1978, Jan. 5 *Perf. 13x12½*

C270 A582 13c Crossed sabres, university .75 .25
C271 A582 30c University, statue, crowd 1.10 .50

Portrait of Jose Marti (b. 1853), by A. Menocal AP104

1978, Jan. 28

C272 AP104 13c multi .80 .25

Art Type of 1978

Paintings in the Nat. Museum of Art: 13c, *El Guadalquivir*, by M. Barron. 30c, *Portrait of H.E. Ridley*, by J.J. Masqueries, vert.

1978, Feb. 20 *Perf. 12½x12, 13*

Sizes: 42x27mm, 29x40mm

C273 A583 13c multi 1.00 .25
C274 A583 30c multi 1.10 .40

Bird Type of 1975

Designs: 13c, Torreornis inexpectata, horiz. 30c, Ara tricolor.

1978, Mar. 10 *Perf. 12½x12, 13*

Size: 42x27mm, 27x42mm

C275 A524 13c multicolored 1.60 .50
C276 A524 30c multicolored 2.40 1.10

Baragua Protest, Cent. — AP105

1978, Mar. 15 *Perf. 13x13½*

C277 AP105 13c *Antonio Maceo*, by A. Melero .70 .25

Cosmonaut's Day Type of 1978

1978, Apr. 12 *Perf. 13*

C278 A585 13c Venera 10 .70 .25

Size: 36x46mm

Perf. 12½x13

C279 A585 30c Lunokhod 2, vert. 1.25 .50

SOCFILEX '78, Budapest — AP106

1978, May 7 *Perf. 13x12½*

C280 AP106 30c Parliament, Hungary No. 217 1.75 .55

Cactus Type of 1978

Designs: 13c, Rhodocactus cubensis. 30c, Harrisia taetra.

1978, May 15 *Perf. 13*

C281 A587 13c multicolored .90 .25
C282 A587 30c multicolored 1.90 .35

World Telecommunications Day — AP107

1978, May 17

C283 AP107 30c multi 1.25 .45

Organization of African Unity, 15th Anniv. — AP108

1978, May 25 *Perf. 13x12½*

C284 AP108 30c multi 1.00 .45

Souvenir Sheet

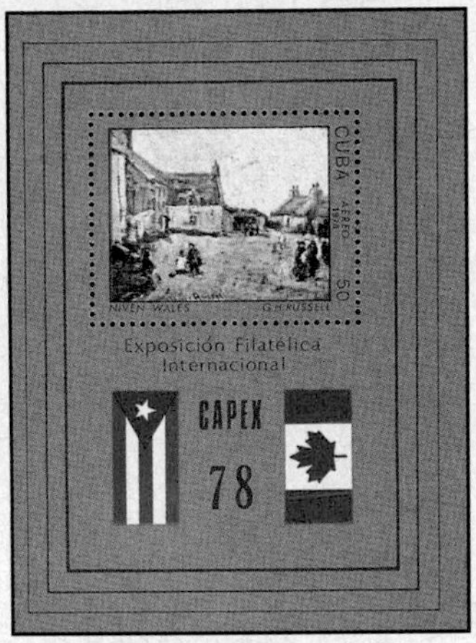

CAPEX '78, Toronto — AP109

1978, June 9 *Perf. 13x13½*

C285 AP109 50c *Niven, Wales*, by G.H. Russell 3.50 2.25

Aquarium Type of 1978

Designs: 13c, Carassias auratus, vert. 30c, Symphysodon aequifasciata axelrodi.

1978, June 15 *Perf. 13*

C286 A588 13c multicolored 1.90 .25
C287 A588 30c multicolored 3.00 .50

MEDELLIN Games Type of 1978

1978, July 1

C288 A589 13c Volleyball .60 .25
C289 A589 30c Running 1.25 .45

Attack on Moncada Type of 1978

1978, July 26

C290 A590 13c Soldiers bearing rifles .45 .25
C291 A590 30c Stylized dove, banners 1.10 .35

Youth Festival Type of 1978

Natl. flags and views of host cities.

1978, July 28

C292 A591 13c Moscow, 1957 .70 .25
C293 A591 13c Vienna, 1959 .70 .25
C294 A591 13c Helsinki, 1962 .70 .25
C295 A591 13c Sofia, 1968 .70 .25
C296 A591 13c Berlin, 1973 .70 .25
a. Strip of 5, Nos. C292-C296 3.75 1.75
Nos. C292-C296 (5) 3.50 1.25

Size: 46x36mm

Perf. 13x12½

C297 A591 30c Havana, 1978 1.50 .35

Tuna Industry Type of 1978

1978, Aug. 30 *Perf. 12½x12*

C298 A593 13c Stern trawler .90 .25
C299 A593 30c Refrigerator ship 1.60 .60

Souvenir Sheet

PRAGA '78 — AP110

1978, Sept. 8 *Perf. 13*

C300 AP110 50c *Marina*, by A. Brandeis 3.75 2.00

Art Type of 1978

Paintings by Amelia Pelaez del Casal (1896-1968).

1978, Sept. 15 *Perf. 12x12½, 13*

C301 A594 13c *Yellow Flowers*, vert. .55 .25
C302 A594 30c *Still-life in Blue*, vert. 1.25 .45

Souvenir Sheet

Perf. 13½x13

C303 A594 50c *Portrait of Amelia*, by L. Romanach, vert. 4.00 .90

No. C303 contains one 32x40mm stamp.

Socialist Communication Organizations Congress (OSS), 20th Anniv. — AP111

1978, Sept. 25 *Perf. 13*

C304 AP111 30c multi 1.25 .25

Souvenir Sheet

EXFILNA '78, 6th Natl. Philatelic Exposition — AP112

1978, Oct. 10 *Imperf.*

C305 AP112 50c 1st Postal Card, issued in 1878 3.25 2.00

No. C305 has simulated perfs.

Intl. Anti-Apartheid Year — AP113

1978, Oct. 16 *Perf. 12½*

C306 AP113 13c multi 1.60 1.00

Zoo Type of 1978

Designs: 13c, Acinonyx jubatos. 30c, Loxodonta africana, vert.

1978, Oct. 20 *Perf. 13*

C307 A595 13c multicolored 1.00 .25
C308 A595 30c multicolored 2.40 .65

Natl. Ballet Type of 1978

1978, Oct. 28 *Perf. 12½x13*

C309 A596 13c *Giselle*, vert. .85 .25
C310 A596 30c *Genesis*, vert. 1.60 .30

Pacific Flora Type of 1978

1978, Nov. 30 *Perf. 13*

C311 A597 13c multi, diff. .80 .25
C312 A597 30c multi, diff. 1.60 .30

25th Death Anniv. of Julius and Ethel Rosenberg, American Communists Executed for Espionage — AP114

1978, Dec. 20
C313 AP114 13c multi .60 .25

Julio A. Mella (d. 1929) AP115

1979, Jan. 10
C314 AP115 13c multi .60 .25

Cosmonaut's Day Type of 1979

1979, Apr. 12 ***Perf. 13½x13***

Souvenir Sheet

C315 A603 50c Orbital complex 3.75 2.00

No. C315 contains one 32x40mm stamp.

Intl. Year of the Child — AP116

1979, June 1 ***Perf. 13x12½***
C316 AP116 13c multi 1.00 .25

Art Type of 1979

50c, Portrait of Victor Emmanuel Garcia, by J. Arche, vert.

1979, June 15 ***Perf. 13½x13***
C317 A600 50c multicolored 3.50 1.75

No. C317 contains one 32x40mm stamp.

CARIFESTA '79, Festival of Caribbean Peoples, Havana AP117

1979, July 16 ***Perf. 12½x13***
C318 AP117 13c multi .75 .25

10th World Universiade Games, Mexico City — AP118

1979, Sept. 1 ***Perf. 13x12½***
C319 AP118 13c grn, pale grn & gold .75 .25

6th Conference of Nonaligned Countries — AP119

1979, Sept. 3
C320 AP119 50c Convention Palace 1.75 .90

Sir Rowland Hill (d. 1879), Originator of Penny Postage — AP120

1979, Sept. 4 ***Perf. 13½x13***
C321 AP120 30c Hill, casket 1.50 .25

SOCFILEX '79, Bucharest — AP121

1979, Oct. 25 ***Perf. 12½***
C322 AP121 30c Romania No. 683, flags 1.40 .40

Intl. Radio Consultative Committee (CCIR), 50th Anniv. — AP122

1979, Nov. 30 ***Perf. 12½x12***
C323 AP122 30c Ground receiving station 1.40 .40

1st Soviet-Cuban Joint Space Flight — AP123

1980, Sept. 23 ***Perf. 12½***
C324 AP123 13c multi .50 .25
C325 AP123 30c multi 1.50 .35

Capt. Mariano Barberan, Lt. Joaquin Collar, and Their Airplane Cuatro Vientos. — AP124

1993, June 11 **Litho.** ***Perf. 13***
C326 AP124 30c multicolored 1.00 .45

1st Flight Seville-Camaguey, 60th anniv.

AIR POST SEMI-POSTAL STAMP

Catalogue values for unused stamps in this section are for Never Hinged items.

Farm Couple and Factory SPAP1

Engr. & Typo.

1959, May 7 **Wmk. 321** ***Perf. 12½***
CB1 SPAP1 12c + 3c car & grn 2.00 .80

Agricultural reforms. See No. C199.

AIR POST SPECIAL DELIVERY STAMPS

Matanzas Issue

Matanzas Harbor APSD1

Wmk. 229

1936, May 5 **Photo.** ***Perf. 12½***
CE1 ASPD1 15c light blue 5.00 3.50
Never hinged 8.00

Exists imperf. Value $6.50 unused, $4.50 used.

SPECIAL DELIVERY STAMPS

Issued under Administration of the United States

US No. E5 Surcharged in Red

1899 **Wmk. 191** ***Perf. 12***
E1 SD3 10c blue 130. 100.
Never hinged 300.
a. No period after "CUBA" 575. 400.

Issue of the Republic under US Military Rule

Special Delivery Messenger SD2

Printed by the US Bureau of Engraving and Printing

1899 **Wmk. US-C (191C)**

Inscribed: "Immediata"

E2 SD2 10c orange 52.50 15.00
Never hinged 120.00

Issues of the Republic
Inscribed: "Inmediata"

1902 ***Perf. 12***
E3 SD2 10c orange 3.00 1.00

J. B. Zayas SD3

1910 **Unwmk.**
E4 SD3 10c orange & blue 20.00 3.25
Never hinged 30.00
a. Center inverted 1,250.

Airplane and Morro Castle SD4

1914, Feb. 24 ***Perf. 12***
E5 SD4 10c dark blue 15.00 1.25

Exists imperf. Value, pair $500.

1927 **Wmk. Star (106)**
E6 SD4 10c deep blue 12.00 .50
Never hinged 18.00

1935 ***Perf. 10***
E7 SD4 10c blue 12.00 .40
Never hinged 15.00

Matanzas Issue

Mercury SD5

Wmk. Wavy Lines (229)

1936, May 5 **Photo.** ***Perf. 12½***
E8 SD5 10c deep claret 8.00 3.50
Never hinged 9.50

Exists imperf. Value $7.50 unused, $5 used.

"Triumph of the Revolution" — SD6

1936, Nov. 18
E9 SD6 10c red orange 9.00 2.00
Never hinged 11.00

Maj. Gen. Máximo Gómez (1836-1905).

Temple of Quetzalcoatl (Mexico) SD7

Ruben Dario (Nicaragua) SD8

Wmk. 106

1937, Oct. 13 Engr. *Perf. 10*

E10 SD7 10c deep orange 7.00 7.00
E11 SD8 10c deep orange 7.00 7.00
Set, never hinged 18.00

Issued for the benefit of the Association of American Writers and Artists. See note after No. 354.

Letter and Symbols of Transportation — SD9

1945, Oct. 30

E12 SD9 10c olive brown 2.75 .40
Never hinged 3.75

Catalogue values for unused stamps in this section, from this point to the end of the section, are for Never Hinged items.

Governor's Building, Cárdenas SD10

Engraved and Lithographed

1951, July 3 Wmk. 229 *Perf. 13*

E13 SD10 10c henna brn, ultra & red 8.50 1.25

Cent. of the adoption of Cuba's flag.

Chess Type of Regular Issue, 1951

1951, Nov. 1 Photo.

E14 A166 10c dk grn & rose brn 22.50 4.50

Type of Regular Issue of 1951 Surcharged in Red Violet

Wmk. 106

1952, Mar. 18 Engr. *Perf. 10*

E15 A159 10c on 2c yel brn 5.50 1.40

Arms and Bars from National Hymn — SD12

1952, May 27 *Perf. 12½*

E16 SD12 10c dp org & bl 5.50 .80

Republic of Cuba founding, 50th anniv.

Type of Air Post Stamps of 1952 Inscribed: "Entrega Especial"

1952, Oct. 7 *Perf. 10*

E17 AP36 10c pale olive grn 5.00 2.40

Three-fourths of the proceeds from the sale of No. E17 were used for the Communications Ministry Employees' Retirement Fund.

Roseate Tern — SD13

1953, July 28

E18 SD13 10c blue 5.75 1.60

Gregorio Hernandez Saez — SD14

1954, Feb. 23

E19 SD14 10c olive green 5.25 1.10

Felix Varela — SD15

1955, June 22 *Perf. 12½*

E20 SD15 10c brown car 3.00 .95

See note after No. E17.

Portrait Type of Regular Issue, 1956 Inscribed: "Entrega Especial"

Portrait: 10c, Jose Jacinto Milanes.

1956, May 2 Wmk. 106

E21 A198 10c dk car rose & blk 4.50 .75

See note after No. E17.

Painting Type of Regular Issue, 1957 Inscribed: "Entrega Especial"

10c, "Yesterday" by E. Garcia Cabrera.

1957, Mar. 15 Engr. *Perf. 12½*

E22 A207 10c dk brn & turq bl 3.50 1.25

See note after No. E17.

View Type of Regular Issue, 1957 Inscribed: "Entrega Especial"

10c, Independence square, Pino del Rio.

1957, Dec. 17

E23 A218 10c dk pur & brn 3.00 1.00

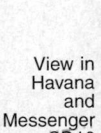

See note after No. E17.

View in Havana and Messenger SD16

1958, Jan. 10 Engr.

E24 SD16 10c blue 2.75 .80
E25 SD16 20c green 3.50 .80

See Nos. E28, E31.

Fish Type of Regular Issue, 1958 Inscribed: "Entrega Especial"

Fish: 10c, Blackfish snapper. 20c, Mosquitofish.

1958, Sept. 26 Wmk. 106 *Perf. 12½*

E26 AP86 10c blk, bl, pink & yel 8.75 2.50
E27 AP86 20c blk, ultra & pink 27.50 11.00

See note after No. C191.

Messenger Type of 1958

1960 Wmk. 321 *Perf. 12½*

E28 SD16 10c brt vio 3.50 .80

Plane Type of Air Post Issue, of 1931-46, Srchd. in Black or Red

1960 Wmk. 106 *Perf. 10*

E29 AP4 10c on 20c car rose 3.00 .50
E30 AP4 10c on 50c grnsh bl (R) 3.00 .50

Messenger Type of 1958

1961, June 28 Wmk. 321 *Perf. 12½*

E31 SD16 10c orange 3.50 .80

West Indies Packet Type of 1962

Perf. 12½

1962, Apr. 24 Litho. Unwmk.

E32 A253 10c buff, dull ultra & brn 7.50 1.75

POSTAGE DUE STAMPS

Issued under Administration of the United States

Postage Due Stamps of the United States Nos. J38, J39, J41 and J42 Surcharged in Black Like Nos. 221-226A

D2

1899 Wmk. 191 *Perf. 12*

J1 D2 1c dp claret 45.00 5.25
Never hinged 110.00
J2 D2 2c dp claret 45.00 5.25
Never hinged 110.00
a. Inverted surcharge *3,500.*
J3 D2 5c dp claret 42.50 5.25
Never hinged 105.00
J4 D2 10c dp claret 25.00 2.50
Never hinged 60.00
Nos. J1-J4 (4) 157.50 18.25

Issues of the Republic

D1

1914 Unwmk. Engr. *Perf. 12*

J5 D1 1c carmine rose 8.00 1.25
J6 D1 2c carmine rose 10.00 1.25
J7 D1 5c carmine rose 15.00 2.50
Nos. J5-J7 (3) 33.00 5.00

1927-28

J8 D1 1c rose red 5.50 .90
J9 D1 2c rose red 8.50 .90
J10 D1 5c rose red 10.00 1.25
Nos. J8-J10 (3) 24.00 3.05

NEWSPAPER STAMPS

Issued under Spanish Dominion

N1

1888 Unwmk. Typo. *Perf. 14*

P1 N1 ½m black .25 *.25*
P2 N1 1m black .25 *.30*
P3 N1 2m black .25 *.30*
P4 N1 3m black 1.60 1.00
P5 N1 4m black 2.10 *2.00*
P6 N1 8m black 8.00 *8.50*
Nos. P1-P6 (6) 12.45 12.35

N2

1890

P7 N2 ½m red brown .55 *.65*
P8 N2 1m red brown .55 *.65*
P9 N2 2m red brown .90 *.95*
P10 N2 3m red brown 1.10 *1.10*
P11 N2 4m red brown 8.25 5.50
P12 N2 8m red brown 8.25 5.50
Nos. P7-P12 (6) 19.60 14.35

1892

P13 N2 ½m violet .25 *.30*
P14 N2 1m violet .25 *.30*
P15 N2 2m violet .25 *.30*
P16 N2 3m violet 1.10 .35
P17 N2 4m violet 4.25 1.90
P18 N2 8m violet 8.75 3.00
Nos. P13-P18 (6) 14.85 6.15

1894

P19 N2 ½m rose .25 *.30*
a. Imperf. pair 40.00 40.00
P20 N2 1m rose .50 .35
P21 N2 2m rose .55 .35
P22 N2 3m rose 2.10 1.40
P23 N2 4m rose 3.50 1.60
P24 N2 8m rose 6.00 4.00
Nos. P19-P24 (6) 12.90 8.00

1896

P25 N2 ⅛m blue green .25 *.30*
P26 N2 1m blue green .25 *.30*
P27 N2 2m blue green .25 *.30*
P28 N2 3m blue green 2.75 1.50
P29 N2 4m blue green 5.75 *7.00*
P30 N2 8m blue green 10.50 *10.00*
Nos. P25-P30 (6) 19.75 19.40

For surcharges see Nos. 190-193, 201-220.

POSTAL TAX STAMPS

Catalogue values for unused stamps in this section are for Never Hinged items.

Mother and Child — PT1

Wmk. Star. (106)

1938, Dec. 1 Engr. *Perf. 10*

RA1 PT1 1c bright green .90 .25

The tax benefited the National Council of Tuberculosis fund for children's hospitals. Obligatory on all mail during December and January. This note applies also to Nos. RA2-RA4, RA7-RA10, RA12-RA15, RA17-RA21.

Nurse with Child — PT2

1939, Dec. 1

RA2 PT2 1c orange vermilion .90 .25

"Health" Protecting Children — PT3

1940, Dec. 1

RA3 PT3 1c deep blue .90 .25

Mother and Child — PT4

1941, Dec. 1

RA4 PT4 1c olive bister	.95	.25

Victory — PT5

1942-44

RA5 PT5 ½c orange	.65	.25
RA6 PT5 ½c gray ('44)	.95	.25

Issued: No. RA5, 7/1/42; No. RA6, 10/3/44.

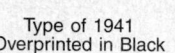

Type of 1941 Overprinted in Black

1942, Dec. 1

RA7 PT4 1c salmon	.90	.30
a. Inverted overprint	75.00	65.00

As PT3 — PT6

1943, Dec. 1

RA8 PT6 1c brown	.95	.25

As PT4 — PT7

1949, Dec. 9

RA9 PT7 1c blue	.75	.25

Type of 1949 Inscribed: "1950"

1950, Dec. 1 **Engr.**

RA10 PT7 1c rose red	.75	.25

Proposed Communications Building — PT8

1951, June 5 **Wmk. 106** ***Perf. 10***

RA11 PT8 1c violet	.95	.25

The tax was to help build a new Communications Building. This note applies also to Nos. RA16, RA34, RA43.

Woman Holding Child Aloft — PT9

1951, Dec. 1

RA12 PT9 1c violet blue	.55	.25
RA13 PT9 1c brown carmine	.55	.25
RA14 PT9 1c olive bister	.55	.25
RA15 PT9 1c deep green	.55	.25
Nos. RA12-RA15 (4)	2.20	1.00

Proposed Communications Building — PT10

1952, Feb. 8

RA16 PT10 1c slate blue	.40	.25

See Nos. RA34, RA43.

Child — PT11

1952, Dec. 1

RA17 PT11 1c rose carmine	.75	.25
RA18 PT11 1c yellow green	.75	.25
RA19 PT11 1c blue	.75	.25
RA20 PT11 1c orange	.75	.25
Nos. RA17-RA20 (4)	3.00	1.00

Hands Reaching for Lorraine Cross — PT12

1953, Dec. 1 ***Perf. 9½***

RA21 PT12 1c rose carmine	.65	.30

Child's Head, Lorraine Cross — PT13

1954, Nov. 1 ***Perf. 9½x10***

RA22 PT13 1c rose red	.75	.30
RA23 PT13 1c violet	.75	.30
RA24 PT13 1c bright blue	.75	.30
RA25 PT13 1c emerald	.75	.30
Nos. RA22-RA25 (4)	3.00	1.20

The tax benefited the Natl. Council of Tuberculosis fund for children's hospitals. Obligatory on all mail during Nov., Dec., Jan. & Feb. This note also applies to Nos. RA26-RA33, RA35-RA42.

Rose and Watering Can — PT14

1955, Nov. 1

RA26 PT14 1c red orange	.75	.30
RA27 PT14 1c red lilac	.75	.30
RA28 PT14 1c bright blue	.75	.30
RA29 PT14 1c orange yellow	.75	.30
Nos. RA26-RA29 (4)	3.00	1.20

Child and Protective Hands — PT15

1956, Nov. 1

RA30 PT15 1c rose red	.75	.30
RA31 PT15 1c yellow brown	.75	.30
RA32 PT15 1c bright blue	.75	.30
RA33 PT15 1c emerald	.75	.30
Nos. RA30-RA33 (4)	3.00	1.20

Building Type of 1952

1957, Jan. 18 ***Perf. 10***

RA34 PT10 1c rose red	.50	.30

Mother and Child by Silvia Arrojo Fernandez — PT16

Wmk. 321

1957, Nov. 1 **Engr.** ***Perf. 10***

RA35 PT16 1c dull rose	.75	.30
RA36 PT16 1c bright blue	.75	.30
RA37 PT16 1c gray	.75	.30
RA38 PT16 1c emerald	.75	.30
Nos. RA35-RA38 (4)	3.00	1.20

National Council of Tuberculosis — PT17

1958

RA39 PT17 1c rose red	.50	.30
RA40 PT17 1c red brown	.50	.30
RA41 PT17 1c gray	.50	.30
RA42 PT17 1c emerald	.50	.30
Nos. RA39-RA42 (4)	2.00	1.20

Building Type of 1952

1958 **Wmk. 321**

RA43 PT10 1c rose red	.50	.30

CURACAO

ˈcər-ə-sau

LOCATION — North of Venezuela, east of Aruba in Caribbean Sea
AREA — 171 sq. mi.
POP. — 135,822 (2005)
CAPITAL — Willemstad

On Oct. 10, 2010, Curaçao, formerly part of Netherlands Antilles, became a constituent state within the Kingdom of the Netherlands. Stamps issued from 1873 to 1949 inscribed "Curaçao" were valid in all islands that comprised the Netherlands Antilles. These stamps are listed under "Netherlands Antilles."

100 Cents = 1 Gulden

Catalogue values for all unused stamps in this country are for Never Hinged items.

Map of Curaçao and West Indies, Arms and Flag A1

Perf. 13¾

2010, Oct. 10 **Litho.** **Unwmk.**

1 A1 111c multi	1.25	1.25

Souvenir Sheet

Touit Purpurata — A2

2010, Oct. 25 **Litho.** ***Perf. 13¾***

2 A2 1500c multi	17.00	17.00

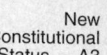

New Constitutional Status — A3

Designs: 1c, Sphere with colors of Curaçao flag, Diploria labyrinthiformis. 3c, Yellowtail snapper. 5c, Yellow goatfish. 30c, Blue hamlet. 63c, Rock beauty angelfish. 81c, Palometa jack. 112c, Spotfin butterflyfish. 166c, Cherubfish. 285c, Cocoa damselfish. 405c, Jewel damselfish. 630c, Schoolmaster snapper. Fish have colors of Curaçao flag.

2011, Jan. 11 ***Perf. 13¼x12¾***

3 A3 1c multi	.25	.25
4 A3 3c multi	.25	.25
5 A3 5c multi	.25	.25
6 A3 30c multi	.35	.35
7 A3 63c multi	.70	.70
8 A3 81c multi	.90	.90
9 A3 112c multi	1.25	1.25
10 A3 166c multi	1.90	1.90
11 A3 285c multi	3.25	3.25
12 A3 405c multi	4.50	4.50
13 A3 630c multi	7.00	7.00
Nos. 3-13 (11)	20.60	20.60

See Nos. 13A-13C, 215-216.

New Constitutional Status Type of 2011

Designs: 8c, Schoolmaster snapper. 115c, Spotfin butterflyfish. 171c, Cherubfish.

2012 **Litho.** ***Perf. 13¼x12¾***

13A A3 8c multi	—	—
13B A3 115c multi	—	—
13C A3 171c multi	—	—

A4

Rabbit and: 112c, Big Wild Goose Pagoda, Xian, China. 145c, Great Wall of China, horiz. 166c, Temple of Heaven. 285c, Mountains near Li River, horiz. 405c, Paper lanterns.

Perf. 12¾x13¼, 13¼x12¾

2011, Feb. 11 **Litho.**

14-18 A4 Set of 5	12.50	12.50

New Year 2011 (Year of the Rabbit).

A5

Musical instruments: 49c, Double bass. 63c, Steel pan drums. 82c, Accordion. 145c, Saxophone. 166c, Djembe. 236c, Piano. 285c, Trombone. 405c, Pan flute. 700c, Cymbals.

2011, Mar. 11 ***Perf. 12¾x13¼***

19-27 A5 Set of 9	24.00	24.00

Banknotes A6

Designs: 63c, 1947 Curaçao 1-gulden note. 75c, 1970 Netherlands Antilles 2½-gulden note. 112c, 1958 Curaçao 5-gulden note. 175c, 1948 Curaçao 10-gulden note. 200c, 1970 Netherlands Antilles 1-gulden note. 250c, 1967 Netherlands Antilles 5-gulden note. 300c, 1979 Netherlands Antilles 25-gulden note. 350c, 1972 Netherlands Antilles 50-gulden note. 475c, 1967 Netherlands Antilles

250-gulden note. 500c, 1962 Netherlands Antilles 500-gulden note.

2011, Apr. 11 ***Perf. 14***
28-37 A6 Set of 10 28.00 28.00

2011 Paper Money Fair, Maastricht, Netherlands.

Souvenir Sheet

Prehistoric Animals — A7

No. 38: a, 700c, Ankylosaurus. b, 800c, Spinosaurus. c, 1000c, Saurolophus.

2011, June 11 ***Perf. 13¼x12¾***
38 A7 Sheet of 3, #a-c 28.00 28.00

New Technologies A8

Designs: 275c, Social media. 375c, Fiber optics. 475c Blackberry PIN messaging. 625c, Cloud computing.

2011, July 11
39-42 A8 Set of 4 19.50 19.50

Souvenir Sheet

Preservation of Polar Regions and Glaciers — A9

No. 43 — Iceberg and: a, 112c, Emblem. b, 405c, Map of Antarctica.

2011, Aug. 11 ***Perf. 13½***
43 A9 Sheet of 2, #a-b 5.75 5.75

Foods — A10

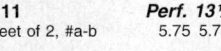

Designs: 63c, Almond cake. 81c, Apple pie. 112c, Blueberry pancakes. 145c, Broken glass cake. 166c, Lemon cake. 172c, Funchi (polenta cake). 195c, Chocolate cake. 285c, Fruit cake. 405c, Cherry cheesecake. 630c, Pumpkin cake

2011, Sept. 11 ***Perf. 13¼x12¾***
44-53 A10 Set of 10 25.00 25.00

Christmas — A11

Evergreen branches, candle and: 63c, Christmas cake (Bolo di Pasku), candy cane and hard candies. 112c, Ayaka. 145c, New Year's cake (Pan dushi) and hard candies. 166c, Christmas ham (Ham di Pasku). 172c, Salmon (Salmou di bari). 250c, Nuts (Nechi). 405c, Pickled pork (Sult).

2011, Nov. 11 ***Perf. 12¾x13¼***
54-60 A11 Set of 7 17.00 17.00

Miniature Sheet

Vegetables — A12

No. 61: a, 150c, Pumpkin and squashes. b, 200c, Okra. c, 225c, Onions. d, 325c, Bell peppers. e, 500c, Corn. f, 750c, Tomatoes.

2011, Dec. 11
61 A12 Sheet of 6, #a-f 24.00 24.00

Fish — A13

Designs: 25c, Myripristis botche. 150c, Neoniphon opercularis. 225c, Sargocentron spiniferum. 325c, Anyperodon leucogrammicus. 475c, Cephalopholis sonnerati. 500c, Epinephelus caeruleopunctatus. 700c, Abudefduf vaigiensis.

2012, Jan. 12 ***Perf. 14***
62-68 A13 Set of 7 27.00 27.00

Nos. 62-68 were printed in sheets of 14 containing two of each stamp and a central label.

New Year 2012 (Year of the Dragon) A14

Designs: No. 69, 500c, Dragon. No. 70, 500c, Dragon facing left, horiz.
No. 71, 500c, Yin-yang, dragon, Chinese character.

Perf. 13½x14, 14x13½
2012, Feb. 13 **Litho. & Embossed**
69-70 A14 Set of 2 11.50 11.50

Souvenir Sheet

71 A14 500c multi 5.75 5.75

Miniature Sheet

Birds — A15

No. 72: a, 75c, Laughing gulls (24x27mm). b, 150c, Dunlins (36x27mm). c, 200c, Gannets (24x27mm). d, 225c, Frigatebirds (36x27mm). e, 300c, Snowy egret (24x27mm). f, 350c, Flamingos (36x27mm). g, 500c, Great blue heron (24x27mm). h, 700c, Pelican (36x27mm).

Perf. 13¼x13¾
2012, Mar. 12 **Litho.**
72 A15 Sheet of 8, #a-h 28.00 28.00

Miniature Sheet

Railways in Curaçao — A16

No. 73: a, 200c, Dumping cars (40x21mm). b, 250c, Horse tram (30x39mm). c, 300c, Plymouth locomotive (30x42mm). d, 350c, Motor tram (40x18mm).

2012, Apr. 12 ***Perf. 14x13½***
73 A16 Sheet of 4, #a-d, + central label 12.50 12.50

Souvenir Sheet

June 6, 2012 Transit of Venus — A17

2012, May 21 ***Perf. 13¼***
74 A17 2500c multi 32.50 32.50

A18

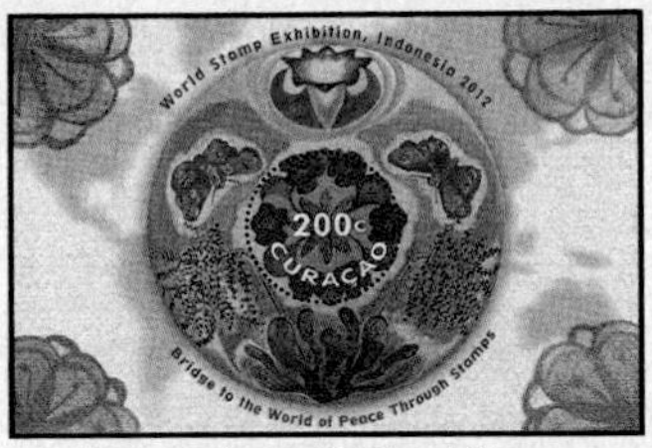

Indonesia 2012 World Stamp Exhibition, Jakarta — A19

2012, June 18 ***Perf. 13½x13***
75 A18 10c multi .25 .25

Souvenir Sheet
Perf.

76 A19 200c multi 2.25 2.25

Fruit — A20

Designs: 275c, Watermelons. 375c, Pineapples. 475c, Bananas. 625c, Mangos.

2012, June 12 ***Perf. 13x13½***
77-80 A20 Set of 4 19.50 19.50

Miniature Sheet

Sports — A21

No. 81: a, 25c, Cycling. b, 50c, Swimming. c, 75c, Sailboarding. d, 100c, Soccer. e, 125c, Handball. f, 150c, Judo. g, 175c, Track. h, 200c, Baseball.

2012, July 12 ***Perf. 13¾***
81 A21 Sheet of 8, #a-h 10.00 10.00

Flora — A22

Designs: 75c, Datura metel. 100c, Opuntia wentiana. 150c, Caesalpina pulcherrima. 200c, Melocactus macracanthus. 250c, Crescentia cujete, horiz. 300c, Ritterocereus griseus, horiz. 350c, Calutropis procera, horiz. 450c, Zizyphus spina-cristi, horiz.

Perf. 13x13½, 13½x13
2012, Aug. 13
82-89 A22 Set of 8 21.00 21.00

Miniature Sheet

Tourist Attractions — A23

No. 90: a, Tafelberg. b, Penha. c, Brug di Ponton Koningin Emmabrug (Queen Emma Pontoon Bridge), Willemstad. d, Bark'i Fruta (fruit market). e, Kenepa Grandi Beach. f, Landhuis Zeelandia. g, Koningin Julianabrug (Queen Juliana Bridge). h, Houses along Berg Altena. i, Handelskade, Willemstad. j, Statuut-monument (Statute of Autonomy Monument).

2012, Sept. 27 ***Perf. 13½x13***
90 A23 171c Sheet of 10, #a-j 19.50 19.50

Christmas — A24

Designs: 64c, Angel. 115c, Madonna and Child. 171c, Shepherd and donkey. 190c, Star of Bethlehem. 293c, Three Kings.

2012, Nov. 12 ***Perf. 13x13¼***
91-95 A24 Set of 5 9.50 9.50

Souvenir Sheet

End of Mayan Calendar Cycle — A25

No. 96: a, 200c, Pyramid at Chichen Itza, Mexico. b, 400c, Mayan Calendar. c, 600c, Date of end of Mayan Calendar cycle (Dec. 21, 2012).

2012, Dec. 21 ***Perf.***
96 A25 Sheet of 3, #a-c 13.50 13.50

Faith — A26

Designs: 118c, Names of various deities. 175c, Words for "faith" in various languages. 200c, Candles. 250c, Statue of Buddha and prayer wheel. 300c, Cross and stained-glass window depicting saint. 350c, Star of David and Torah.

2013, Jan. 21 ***Perf. 13¼x12¾***

97	A26 118c multi	1.40	1.40
a.	Tete-beche pair	2.80	2.80
98	A26 175c multi	2.00	2.00
a.	Tete-beche pair	4.00	4.00
99	A26 200c multi	2.25	2.25
a.	Tete-beche pair	4.50	4.50
100	A26 250c multi	2.75	2.75
a.	Tete-beche pair	5.50	5.50
101	A26 300c multi	3.50	3.50
a.	Tete-beche pair	7.00	7.00
102	A26 350c multi	4.00	4.00
a.	Tete-beche pair	8.00	8.00
	Nos. 97-102 (6)	15.90	15.90

New Year 2013 (Year of the Snake) A27

Various snakes and flowers: 175c, 301c, 428c.
500c, Snake in tree.

2013, Feb. 22 ***Perf. 13¼x12¾***
103-105 A27 Set of 3 10.50 10.50

Souvenir Sheet

Perf. 14x13¼

106 A27 500c multi 5.75 5.75

No. 106 contains one 50x40mm stamp.

Abstract Art — A28

Various works of abstract art and silhouettes of people: 118c, 175c, 200c, 250c, 301c, 450c.
250c, 301c, 450c are vert.

Perf. 13¼x12¾, 12¾x13¼

2013, Mar. 13
107-112 A28 Set of 6 17.00 17.00

Suggestions for Environmentally Friendly Living — A29

Inscriptions: 65c, Saving energy using LED lights. 118c, Drive Green. 175c, Solar energy. 181c, Recycle. 301c, Wind energy. 350c, Rainwater. 428c, Plant trees and protect wetlands.

2013, Apr. 15 ***Perf. 13¼x12¾***
113-119 A29 Set of 7 18.00 18.00

Souvenir Sheet

Royal Transition in the Netherlands — A30

No. 120 — Silhouette of: a, New King Willem-Alexander. b, Abdicating Queen Beatrix.

Litho. with Foil Application

2013, Apr. 30 ***Perf. 13¾***
120 A30 1000c Sheet of 2, #a-b 22.50 22.50

Baseball A31

Designs: 65c, Batter hitting ball. 118c, Catcher. 175c, Pitcher. 181c, Team celebrating victory. 301c, Outfielder. 350c, Fielder tagging runner out at base. 428c, Baseball field.

2013, May 13 **Litho.** ***Perf. 13¼x12¾***
121-127 A31 Set of 7 18.00 18.00

Ocean Liner Freewinds A32

Freewinds and: 118c, Palm fronds. 175c, Birds.
250c, Bow of Freewinds, vert.

2013, June 1 **Litho.** ***Perf. 13½x13***
128-129 A32 Set of 2 3.25 3.25

Souvenir Sheet

Perf. 13x13½

130 A32 250c multi 3.00 3.00

Virtues — A33

Designs: 118c, Respect. 175c, Love. 250c, Hope. 301c, Forgiveness. 350c, Mercy. 428c, Peace.

2013, July 22 **Litho.** ***Perf. 12¾x13¼***
131-136 A33 Set of 6 18.00 18.00

Souvenir Sheet

Schottegat, Curaçao — A34

2013, Aug. 20 **Litho.** ***Perf. 13¾***
137 A34 1000c multi 11.50 11.50

Miniature Sheet

Tourist Attractions — A35

No. 138: a, Den Dunki Bridge. b, Spaanse (Spanish) Water. c, Blue Room. d, Veeris Hill. e, Boca Tabla Natural Bridge. f, Playa Kanoa. g, Noordkant. h, Blow hole near Watamula. i, Hato Caves. j, Natural Swimming Pool.

Perf. 13¼x12¾

2013, Sept. 27 **Litho.**
138 A35 175c Sheet of 10, #a-j 19.50 19.50

Fairy Tales — A36

Designs: 100c, The Wolf and the Seven Goats. 145c, The Frog Prince. 190c, Little Red Riding Hood. 293c, Pinocchio, vert. 301c, Puss in Boots, vert. 428c, Jack and the Beanstalk, vert.

Perf. 13¼x12¾, 12¾x13¼

2013, Oct. 21 **Litho.**
139-144 A36 Set of 6 16.50 16.50

Christmas A37

Fireworks and: 65c, Building with wreath and decorations in fence. 118c, Building with wreaths on gate. 175c, Shop, other buildings, street lights, Christmas tree. 190c, Church tower, vert. 301c, Clock tower with bells, street light, vert.

Perf. 13¼x12¾, 12¾x13¼

2013, Nov. 13 **Litho.**
145-149 A37 Set of 5 9.50 9.50

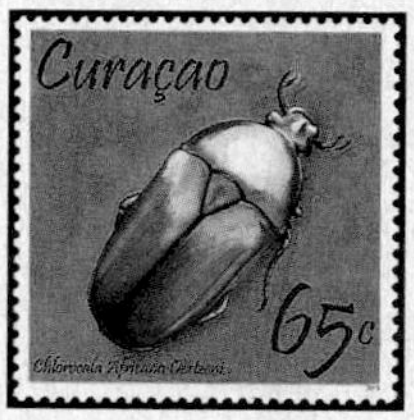

Beetles A38

Designs: 65c, Chlorocala africana oertzeni. 118c, Stephanorrhina julia. 175c, Amaurodes passerinii nyanzanus. 181c, Cetonischema speciosa jouselini protaetia. 250c, Goliathus orientalis. 301c, Eudicella aethiopica. 428c, Ranzania bertoloni. 500c, Dicronorrhina layardi.

Perf. 13¾x12¾

2013, Dec. 13 **Litho.**
150-157 A38 Set of 8 22.50 22.50

A39

A40

A41

Emancipation of Slaves in Kingdom of the Netherlands, 150th Anniv. — A42

2013 **Litho.**

158 Souvenir booklet 28.50
a. A39 500c multi, perf. 13¼ 5.75 5.75
b. A40 500c multi, perf. 5.75 5.75
c. A41 750c multi, perf. 13¼ 8.50 8.50
d. A42 750c multi, perf. 13¼x14 8.50 8.50

Nos. 158a-158d were each printed in booklet panes of 1.

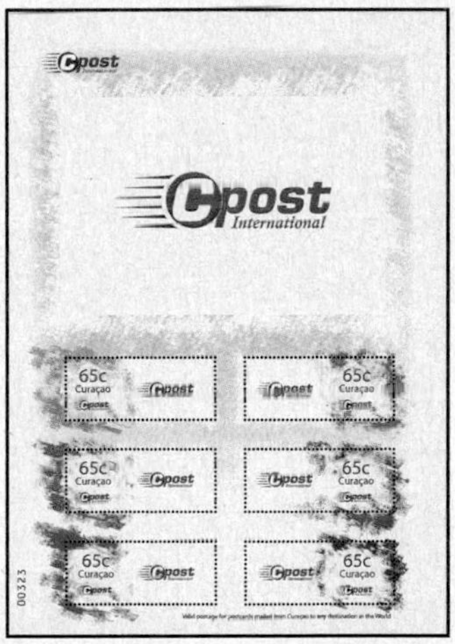

In 2014 Curacao began issuing personalizable stamps. Stamps were made available in sheets of 6 stamps. Numerous different frame designs, inscriptions, emblems and denominations have been reported.

Kingdom of the Netherlands, 200th Anniv. — A43

Designs: 150c, Crown and heraldic lion. 200c, Crown. 250c, Coat of arms. 300c, Post horn and motto, horiz. 350c, Heraldic lion and motto, horiz.

Perf. 12¾x13¼, 13¼x12¼

2014, Jan. 14 **Litho.**

159-163 A43 Set of 5 14.00 14.00

Miniature Sheet

New Year 2014 (Year of the Horse) — A44

No. 164 — Horse and: a, Men on boat (40x21mm). b, Building (30x42mm). c, Lanterns (30x39mm). d, Man carrying buckets (40x18mm).

2014, Jan. 31 **Litho.** ***Perf. 14x13¼***

164 A44 300c Sheet of 4, #a-d, + central label 13.50 13.50

Friendship — A45

Quote and heart with: 65c, Cake. 119c, Roses. 177c, Chocolate candies. 183c, Tedddy bear. 305c, Gemstone. 434c, Drink with fruit garnishes.

Perf. 12¾x13¼

2014, Feb. 14 **Litho.**

165-170 A45 Set of 6 14.50 14.50

Birds of Prey — A46

Designs: 100c, Haliaeetus leucocephalus. 200c, Spizaetus ornatus. 250c, Aquila chrysaetos. 300c, Geranoaetus melanoleucus. 350c, Falconidae polyborinae. 400c, Pandion haliaetus.

2014, Mar. 14 **Litho.** ***Perf. 13¼***

171-176 A46 Set of 6 18.00 18.00

Miniature Sheet

William Shakespeare (1564-1616), Writer — A47

No. 177 — Shakespeare, with denomination at: a, Lower right. b, Upper right. c, Bottom center above name. d, Lower left, next to country name.

2014, Apr. 23 **Litho.** ***Perf. 12¾x13¼***

177 A47 400c Sheet of 4, #a-d 18.00 18.00

Automobiles A48

Designs: 65c, 1964 Ford Mustang. 119c, 1965 Ford Mustang Fastback. 177c, 2014 Ford Mustang. 183c, 1958 Porsche 356A Speedster. 430c, 1964 Porsche 356C. 676c, 2014 Porsche 911 Targa.

2014, May 14 **Litho.** ***Perf. 13¼x12¾***

178-183 A48 Set of 6 18.50 18.50

Miniature Sheet

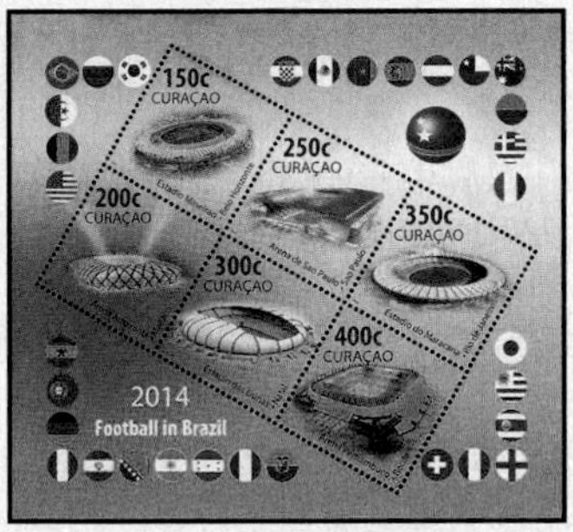

Stadiums of the 2014 World Cup Soccer Championships, Brazil — A49

No. 184: a, 150c, Estadio Mineirao, Belo Horizonte. b, 200c, Arena Amazonia, Manaus. c, 250c, Arena de Sao Paulo, Sao Paulo. d, 300c, Estadio das Dunas, Natal. e, 350c, Esttadio do Maracana, Rio de Janeiro. f, 400c, Arena Pernambuco, Recife.

2014, June 12 **Litho.** ***Perf. 14x13¼***

184 A49 Sheet of 6, #a-f 18.50 18.50

Peace — A50

Designs: 65c, Dove and "Peace." 119c, Hebrew, Dutch, French and Latin words for "peace." 177c, Hindi, German, Danish and Italian words for "peace." 183c, Family, Papiamento word for "peace," Papiamento, English, Spanish and French words for "family." 305c, Arabic, Farsi, Russian and Spanish words for "peace." 434c, Chinese, Icelandic, Greek and Finnish words for "peace."

2014, July 28 **Litho.** ***Perf. 13¼x12¾***

185-190 A50 Set of 6 14.50 14.50

Miniature Sheet

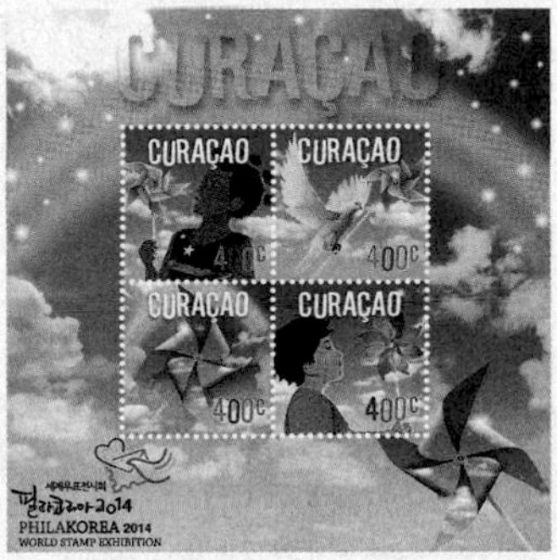

PhilaKorea 2014 World Stamp Exhibition, Seoul — A51

No. 191 — Pinwheel and: a, Girl facing left. b, Dove. c, Rainbow. d, Boy facing right.

2014, Aug. 7 **Litho.** ***Perf. 12¾x13¼***

191 A51 400c Sheet of 4, #a-d 18.00 18.00

Fight Against Cancer — A52

Ribbons and various silhouettes of people: 86c, 119c, 177c, 183c, 285c, 750c.

Perf. 12¾x13¼

2014, Aug. 22 **Litho.**

192-197 A52 Set of 6 18.00 18.00

World Orchid Conference, South Africa — A53

Orchids: 119c, Angraecum stella-africae. 177c, Disa longicornu. 183c, Stenoglottis fimbriata. 305c, Ansellia africana. 382c, Calanthe sylvatica. 434c, Disa uniflora.

Perf. 12¾x13¼

2014, Sept. 10 **Litho.**

198-203 A53 Set of 6 18.00 18.00

Miniature Sheet

XCOR Space Expeditions — A54

No. 204: a, Space plane at space port. b, Space plane control panel. c, Space port. d, Stars, wing of space plane. e, Nose of space plane. f, XCOR Space Expeditions emblem. g, Earth's horizon as seen from space. h, Burning exhaust of test engine. i, Burning exhaust of space plane in flight. j, Earth, wing of space plane.

2014, Sept. 26 **Litho.** ***Perf. 14***

204 A54 177c Sheet of 10, #a-j 20.00 20.00

Caricatures of Marine Life — A55

Designs: 100c, Turtle, starfish, shell. 119c, Fish, oyster with pearl. 177c, Octopus, snail. 305c, Dolphin. 500c, Crab, sea urchin, shells, starfish.

2014, Oct. 14 **Litho.** ***Perf. 13x13½***

205-209 A55 Set of 5 13.50 13.50

Christmas A56

Christmas gifts and various children: 65c, 119c, 117c, 183c, 305c.

2014, Nov. 14 **Litho.** ***Perf. 13¼***

210-214 A56 Set of 5 9.50 9.50

New Constitutional Status Type of 2011

Designs: 2c, Cocoa damselfish. 4c, Jewel damselfish.

2014 **Litho.** ***Perf. 13¼x12¾***

215 A3 2c multi .25 .25
216 A3 4c multi .25 .25

Miniature Sheet

Fish — A57

No. 217: a, Bladefin bass. b, Yellowbar basslet. c, Spanish flag. d, Spottail golden bass. e, Rough-tongue bass. f, Dragonette. g, Saber goby. h, Longfin-scorpionfish. i, Deep sea toad. j, Banded basslet.

2014, Nov. 30 Litho. *Perf. 14x13¾*
217 A57 177c Sheet of 10, #a-j 20.00 20.00

Curaçao Carnaval, 45th Anniv. — A58

Various costumed participants: 65c, 119c, 177c, 183c, 305c, 434c.

2015, Jan. 19 Litho. *Perf. 13¼x13¾*
218-223 A58 Set of 6 14.50 14.50

New Year 2015 (Year of the Goat) — A59

Various goats: 177c, 183c, 305c, 535c.

2015, Feb. 19 Litho. *Perf. 13½x14*
224-227 A59 Set of 4 13.50 13.50

Miniature Sheet

Zeppelins — A60

No. 228 — Various zeppelins with color of: a, 343c, Purple. b, 350c, Red. c, 425c, Green. d, 500c, Yellow.

2015, Mar. 19 Litho. *Perf. 13x12¾*
228 A60 Sheet of 4, #a-d 18.00 18.00

Miniature Sheet

Travels of Pope Francis — A61

No. 229: a, Pope Francis, two women. b, Dove, Pope Francis, hands and camera. c, Back of head of Pope Francis. d, Pope Francis kissing child.

2015, Apr. 20 Litho. *Perf. 13¼*
229 A61 400c Sheet of 4, #a-d 18.00 18.00

SEMI-POSTAL STAMPS

Youth Care — SP1

Rabbit: 63c+26c, Writing molecular diagram on blackboard, molecular model. 112c+45c, With chemicals in test tubes and flasks. 166c+75c, Conducting experiment with plants and chemicals. 285c+125c, In rocket ship.

2011, Oct. 11 Litho. *Perf. 12¾x13¼*
B1-B4 SP1 Set of 4 10.00 10.00

Intl. Year of Chemistry.

Intl. Year of Cooperatives SP2

Stylized people and: 64c+26c, Construction tools, bird. 190c+75c, Rowboat, fish. 293c+125c, Rowboat, house, flower, bird, fish.

2012, Oct. 9 *Perf. 13¼x12¾*
B5-B7 SP2 Set of 3 8.75 8.75

SP3

SP4

SP5

Abolition of Slavery, 150th Anniv. — SP6

2013, July 1 Litho. *Perf. 13¼x12¾*
B8 SP3 65c +25c multi 1.00 1.00
B9 SP4 118c +45c multi 1.90 1.90
B10 SP5 175c +75c multi 2.75 2.75
B11 SP6 301c +125c multi 4.75 4.75
Nos. B8-B11 (4) 10.40 10.40

Wladimir "Coco" Balantien, Holder of New Record for Home Runs in a Japanese Baseball Season — SP7

2013, Dec. 2 Litho. *Perf. 12¾x13¼*
B12 SP7 118c +100c multi 2.50 2.50

CYPRUS

'sī-prəs

LOCATION — An island in the Mediterranean Sea off the coast of Turkey
GOVT. — Republic
AREA — 3,572 sq. mi.
POP. — 754,064 (1999 est.)
CAPITAL — Nicosia

The British Crown Colony of Cyprus became a republic in 1960.

Turkey invaded Cyprus in 1974 resulting in the the northern 40% of the island becoming the Turkish Republic of Northern Cyprus. No other country recognizes this division of the island.

See Turkey in Volume 6.

12 Pence = 1 Shilling
40 Paras = 1 Piaster
9 Piasters = 1 Shilling
20 Shillings = 1 Pound
1000 Milliemes = 1 Pound (1955)
100 Cents = 1 Cyprus Pound (1983)
100 Cents = 1 Euro (2008)

Catalogue values for unused stamps in this country are for Never Hinged items, beginning with Scott 156 in the regular postage section and Scott RA1 in the postal tax section.

Values for unused stamps are for examples with original gum as defined in the catalogue introduction. Very fine examples of Nos. 1, 2 and 7-10 will have perforations touching the design on at least one or more sides due to the narrow spacing of the stamps on the plates and to imperfect perforation methods. Stamps with perfs clear on all four sides are scarce and will command higher prices.

Watermark

Wmk. 344 — Map of Cyprus and KC/K Delta

Queen Victoria — A1

A2

A3

A4

A5

A6

A7

Various Watermarks as in Great Britain (#20, 23, 25, 27 & 29)

1880 Typo. *Perf. 14*
1 A1 ½p rose (P 15) 125.00 115.00
Plate 12 240.00 *300.00*
Plate 19 5,750. 950.00
b. Double overprint (P 15) *45,000.*
2 A2 1p red (P 216) 19.00 *55.00*
Plate 217 18.00 *60.00*
Plate 174 1,500. 1,500.
Plate 181 525.00 210.00
Plate 184 22,000. 3,250.
Plate 193 840.00
Plate 196 725.00
Plate 201 22.50 *57.50*
Plate 205 90.00 57.50
Plate 208 135.00 65.00
Plate 215 18.00 *57.50*
Plate 218 26.00 *65.00*
Plate 220 550.00 475.00
b. Double overprint (P 218) 5,400.
Double overprint (P 208) *27,500.*
c. Pair, one without ovpt. (P 208) *27,500.*
3 A3 2½p claret (P 14) 4.50 *13.50*
Plate 15 6.00 *37.50*
4 A4 4p lt ol grn (P 16) 150.00 *240.00*
5 A5 6p ol gray (P 16) 575.00 *750.00*
6 A6 1sh green (P 13) 900.00 525.00

Black Surcharge

7 A7 30 paras on 1p red (P 216) 150.00 *95.00*
Plate 201 180.00 110.00
Plate 217 210.00 210.00
Plate 220 175.00 *190.00*
b. Dbl. surch., one invtd. (P 220) 2,000. *1,500.*
Dbl. surch., one invtd. (P 216) 7,750.

No. 2 Surcharged

18mm Long

1881
8 A2 ½p on 1p (205, 216) 82.50 *100.00*
Plate 174 225.00 *400.00*
Plate 181 210.00 *260.00*
Plate 201 115.00 *140.00*
Plate 205 85.00 *100.00*
Plate 208 225.00 *375.00*
Plate 215 840.00 *1,000.*
Plate 217 1,000. 900.00
Plate 218 550.00 *675.00*
Plate 220 325.00 *450.00*

16mm Long

9 A2 ½p on 1p (P 201) 140.00 *190.00*
Plate 216 400.00 *460.00*
Plate 218 *17,500.*
a. Double surcharge (P 201, 216) 3,750. 3,000.

13mm Long

10 A2 ½p on 1p red (P 215) 52.50 *75.00*
Plate 205 425.00
Plate 217 175.00 105.00
Plate 218 90.00 *125.00*
c. Double surcharge (P 215) 550.00 *700.00*
Double surcharge (P 205) 875.00
e. Triple surcharge (P 215) 875.00
Triple surcharge (P 205) *4,750.*
Triple surcharge (P 217) —
Triple surcharge (P 218) *4,750.*
h. Quadruple surch. (P 205, 215) *7,500.*
j. "CYPRUS" double (P 218) *6,000.*

A8

1881, July Typo. Wmk. 1
11 A8 ½pi emerald green 210.00 52.50
12 A8 1pi rose 425.00 37.50
13 A8 2pi ultramarine 525.00 37.50
14 A8 4pi olive green 1,050. 325.00
15 A8 6pi olive gray 1,900. 500.00

Postage and revenue stamps of Cyprus with "J.A.B." (the initials of Postmaster J.A. Bulmer) in manuscript, or with "POSTAL SURCHARGE" (with or without "J. A. B."), were not Postage Due stamps but were employed for accounting purposes between the chief PO at Larnaca and the sub-offices.

See Nos. 19-25, 28-37. For surcharges see Nos. 16-18, 26-27.

A9

A10

1882 Black Surcharge Wmk. 1

16 A9 ½pi on ½pi grn 750.00 92.50
17 A10 30pa on 1pi rose 1,750. 140.00
a. Double surcharge, one inverted *1,400.* *850.00*

1884 Wmk. 2

18 A9 ½pi on ½pi green 190.00 10.00
a. Double surcharge *3,200.*

See Nos. 26, 27.

1882-94 Die B

For description of Dies A and B see "Dies of British Colonial Stamps" in Table of Contents.

19 A8 ½pi green 14.00 2.50
20 A8 30pa violet 11.00 *14.00*
21 A8 1pi rose 15.50 8.50
22 A8 2pi blue 17.50 2.10
23 A8 4pi pale ol grn 20.00 *40.00*
24a A8 6pi 275.00 *800.00*
25a A8 12pi 190.00 *450.00*
Nos. 19-25a (7) 543.00 *1,317.*

Die A

19a A8 ½pi 22.50 3.25
b. ½pi emerald *6,000.* 525.00
20a A8 30pa lilac 85.00 27.50
21a A8 1pi 110.00 4.00
22a A8 2pi 170.00 4.00
23a A8 4pi 375.00 35.00
24 A8 6pi olive gray 75.00 21.00
25 A8 12pi brown org 225.00 45.00
Nos. 19a-25 (7) 1,062. 139.75

A11

Type I — Figures "½" 8mm apart.
Type II — Figures "½" 6mm apart.
The space between the fraction bars varies from 5½ to 8½mm but is usually 6 or 8mm.

Black Surcharge Type I

1886 Wmk. 2

26 A11 ½pi on ½pl grn 525.00 16.00
a. Type II 325.00 100.00
b. Double surcharge, type II

Wmk. 1

27 A11 ½pi on ½pi grn *8,750.* 500.00
a. Type II *24,000.*

No. 27a probably is a proof.

1894-96 Wmk. 2

28 A8 ½pi grn & car rose 5.25 1.75
29 A8 30pa violet & green 3.00 3.25
30 A8 1pi rose & ultra 8.50 1.75
31 A8 2pi ultra & mar 11.50 1.75
32 A8 4pi ol green & vio 21.00 11.50
33 A8 6pi ol gray & grn 19.00 *35.00*
34 A8 9pi brown & rose 27.50 *27.50*
35 A8 12pi brn org & blk 24.00 *67.50*
36 A8 18pi slate & brown 60.00 57.50
37 A8 45pi dk vio & ultra 125.00 *165.00*
Nos. 28-37 (10) 304.75 *372.50*

King Edward VII — A12

1903 Typo.

38 A12 ½pi grn & car rose 11.00 1.40
39 A12 30pa violet & green 22.50 4.25
40 A12 1pi carmine rose & ultra 30.00 5.00
41 A12 2pi ultra & mar 90.00 18.00
42 A12 4pi ol green & vio 50.00 22.50
43 A12 6pi ol brown & grn 52.50 *145.00*
44 A12 9pi brn & car rose 125.00 *260.00*
45 A12 12pi org brn & blk 37.50 *80.00*
46 A12 18pi black & brown 100.00 *175.00*
47 A12 45pi dk vio & ultra 250.00 *600.00*
Nos. 38-47 (10) 768.50 *1,311.*

1904-07 Wmk. 3

48 A12 5pa bis & blk ('07) 1.25 2.00
49 A12 10pa org & grn ('07) 6.00 1.90
50 A12 ½pi grn & car rose 10.00 1.60
51 A12 30pa reddish violet & green 20.00 2.75
52 A12 1pi car rose & ultra 12.00 1.10
53 A12 2pi ultra & maroon 16.00 2.00
54 A12 4pi ol grn & red vio 22.00 13.50
55 A12 6pi ol brn & green 24.00 17.00
56 A12 9pi brn & car rose 52.50 9.75
57 A12 12pi org brn & blk 37.50 *57.50*
58 A12 18pi black & brown 55.00 15.00
59 A12 45pi dk vio & ultra 120.00 *175.00*
Nos. 48-59 (12) 376.25 *299.10*

King George V — A13

1912

61a A13 10pa org yel & br grn ('15) 2.75 1.60
62 A13 ½pi grn & car rose 2.90 .35
63 A13 30pa violet & green 3.25 2.40
64 A13 1pi car & ultra 5.75 1.90
65 A13 2pi ultra & maroon 8.50 2.25
66 A13 4pi ol grn & red vio 5.50 *5.25*
67 A13 6pi ol brn & green 6.00 *11.50*
68 A13 9pi brn & car rose 42.50 28.00
69 A13 12pi org brn & blk 25.00 *57.50*
70 A13 18pi black & brown 50.00 *50.00*
71 A13 45pi dl vio & ultra 130.00 *170.00*
Nos. 61a-71 (11) 282.15 330.75

1921-23 Wmk. 4

72 A13 10pa orange & grn 16.00 13.50
73 A13 10pa gray & yellow 16.00 9.50
74 A13 30pa violet & grn 3.75 2.00
75 A13 30pa green 9.00 1.75
76 A13 1pi rose & ultra 26.00 *45.00*
77 A13 1pi violet & car 4.00 5.00
78 A13 1½pi orange & blk 12.50 7.25
79 A13 2pi ultra & red vio 35.00 25.00
80 A13 2pi rose & ultra 16.00 *27.50*
81 A13 2¾pi ultra & red vio 11.00 *12.00*
82 A13 4pi ol grn & red vio 19.00 *26.00*
83 A13 6pi ol brn & green 37.50 *80.00*
84 A13 9pi brn & carmine 47.50 *95.00*
85 A13 18pi black & brn 90.00 *175.00*
86 A13 45pi dl vio & ultra 275.00 *325.00*
Nos. 72-86 (15) 618.25 *849.50*

Wmk. 3

87 A13 10sh grn & red, *yel* 425.00 *900.00*
88 A13 £1 vio & black, *red* 1,400. *3,250.*

Years of issue: Nos. 73, 75, 77-78, 80-81, 87-88, 1923; others, 1921.

A14

1924-28 Chalky Paper Wmk. 4

89 A14 ¼pi gray & brn org 2.10 .55
90 A14 ½pi gray blk & blk 6.25 *14.50*
91 A14 ½pi grn & dp grn ('25) 2.50 1.10
92 A14 ¾pi grn & dp grn 4.25 1.10
93 A14 ¾pi gray blk & blk ('25) 4.50 1.10
94 A14 1pi brn vio & org brown 2.40 2.10
95 A14 1½pi org & black 3.50 *14.50*
96 A14 1½pi carmine ('25) 5.25 1.60
97 A14 2pi car & green 4.25 *21.00*
98 A14 2pi org & black ('25) 15.00 4.25
99 A14 2½pi ultra ('25) 9.00 1.90
100 A14 2¾pi ultra & dull vio 3.75 5.00
101 A14 4pi ap grn & vio 5.25 5.25
102 A14 4½pi black & yel, *emer* 4.00 5.25
103 A14 6pi grn ol & grn 5.25 *9.00*
104 A14 9pi brn & dk vio 9.00 5.75
105 A14 12pi org brn & blk 14.50 *65.00*
106 A14 18pi blk & org 29.00 5.75
Revenue cancel 1.00
107 A14 45pi gray vio & ultra 65.00 45.00
Revenue cancel 1.50
108 A14 90pi grn & red, *yel* 125.00 *270.00*
Revenue cancel 3.75
109 A14 £5 blk, *yel* ('28) 3,750. *8,000.*
On cover (overfranked) 275.00
Revenue cancel 275.00

Wmk. 3

110 A14 £1 vio & black, *red* 350.00 *900.00*
Revenue cancel 12.50
Nos. 89-108 (20) 319.75 *479.70*

Nos. 96 and 99 are on ordinary paper.

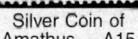

Silver Coin of Amathus — A15

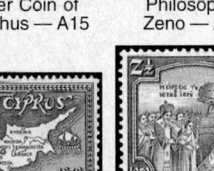

Philosopher Zeno — A16

Map of Cyprus — A17

Discovery of Body of St. Barnabas — A18

Cloisters of Bella Paise Monastery — A19

Badge of the Colony — A20

Hospice of Umm Haram at Larnaca — A21

Statue of Richard Coeur de Lion, London — A22

St. Nicholas Cathedral, Famagusta — A23

King George V — A24

Perf. 12

1928, Feb. 1 Engr. Wmk. 4

114 A15 ¾pi dark violet 3.75 1.60
115 A16 1pi Prus bl & blk 4.00 2.00
116 A17 1½pi red 7.50 2.25
117 A18 2½pi ultramarine 4.75 2.75
118 A19 4pi dp red brown 9.50 9.50
119 A20 6pi dark blue 14.00 *32.50*
120 A21 9pi violet brown 11.00 *17.50*
121 A22 18pi dk brn & blk 30.00 *35.00*
122 A23 45pi dp blue & vio 52.50 *62.50*
123 A24 £1 ol brn & deep blue 275.00 *400.00*
Nos. 114-123 (10) 412.00 *565.60*

50th year of Cyprus as a British colony.

Ruins of Vouni Palace — A25

Columns at Salamis — A26

Peristerona Church — A27

Soli Theater — A28

Kyrenia Castle and Harbor — A29

Kolossi Castle — A30

St. Sophia Cathedral — A31

Bairakdar Mosque — A32

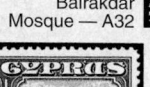

Queen's Window, St. Hilarion Castle — A33

Buyuk Khan, Nicosia — A34

Forest Scene — A35

1934, Dec. 1 Engr. *Perf. 12½*

125 A25 ¼pi yel brn & ultra 1.40 1.10
Never hinged 2.10
a. Vert. pair, imperf. between *52,500. 35,000.*
126 A26 ½pi green 1.90 1.25
Never hinged 2.10
a. Vert. pair, imperf. between *18,000. 20,000.*
127 A27 ¾pi violet & blk 3.50 .45
Never hinged 4.50
a. Vert. pair, imperf. between *52,500.*
128 A28 1pi brown & blk 3.00 2.50
Never hinged 4.50
a. Vert. pair, imperf. between *26,000. 26,000.*
b. Horiz. pair, imperf. btwn. *19,000.*
129 A29 1½pi rose red 4.00 2.10
Never hinged 6.00
130 A30 2½pi dark ultra 5.25 2.40
Never hinged 7.75
131 A31 4½pi dk car & blk 5.25 5.00
Never hinged 14.00
132 A32 6pi blue & black 12.50 *20.00*
Never hinged 26.00
133 A33 9pi dl vio & blk brown 20.00 8.50
Never hinged 32.50
134 A34 18pi ol grn & black 55.00 50.00
Never hinged 120.00
135 A35 45pi blk & emer 120.00 85.00
Never hinged 225.00
Nos. 125-135 (11) 231.80 *178.30*
Set, never hinged 405.00

Common Design Types pictured following the introduction.

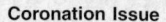

Silver Jubilee Issue
Common Design Type

1935, May 6 *Perf. 11x12*

136 CD301 ¾pi gray blk & ultra 4.25 1.50
137 CD301 1½pi car & dk bl 6.25 3.00
138 CD301 2½pi ultra & brn 5.25 1.90
139 CD301 9pi brn vio & ind 24.00 *28.00*
Nos. 136-139 (4) 39.75 *34.40*
Set, never hinged 60.00

Coronation Issue
Common Design Type

1937, May 12 *Perf. 11x11½*

140 CD302 ¾pi dark gray 1.00 1.00
141 CD302 1½pi dark carmine 1.25 *2.50*
142 CD302 2½pi deep ultra 1.50 *3.00*
Nos. 140-142 (3) 3.75 6.50
Set, never hinged 7.75

Ruins of Vouni Palace — A36

Columns at Salamis — A37

Peristerona Church — A38

Soli Theater — A39

Kyrenia Castle and Harbor — A40

Kolossi Castle — A41

Map of Cyprus — A42

Bairakdar Mosque — A43

Citadel, Famagusta — A44

Buyuk Khan — A45

Forest Scene A46

King George VI A47

1938-44 Wmk. 4 *Perf. 12½*

143 A36 ¼pi yel brn & ultra .60 .60
144 A37 ½pi green .80 .50
145 A38 ¾pi violet & blk 7.25 1.75
146 A39 1pi orange .90 .40
a. Perf. 13½x12½ ('44) 375.00 30.00
Never hinged 575.00
147 A40 1½pi rose car 3.25 2.00
147A A40 1½pi lt vio ('43) .90 .75
147B A38 2pi carmine & blk ('42) .90 .45
c. Perf. 12½x13½ ('44) 2.00 *12.50*
Never hinged 3.25
148 A41 2½pi ultramarine 15.00 4.50
148A A41 3pi dp ultra ('42) 1.25 .60
149 A42 4½pi gray .90 .40
150 A43 6pi blue & black 1.25 *1.10*
151 A44 9pi dk vio & blk 1.00 .80
152 A45 18pi ol grn & blk 5.00 1.75
153 A46 45pi blk & emer 16.00 5.00
154 A47 90pi blk & brt vio 21.00 8.00
155 A47 £1 ind & dl red 45.00 32.50
Nos. 143-155 (16) 121.00 61.10
Set, never hinged 275.00

See Nos. 164-166.

Catalogue values for unused stamps in this section, from this point to the end of the section, are for Never Hinged items.

Peace Issue
Common Design Type

1946, Oct. 21 Engr. *Perf. 13½x14*

156 CD303 1½pi purple .50 .25
157 CD303 3pi deep blue .50 .45

Silver Wedding Issue
Common Design Types

1948, Dec. 20 Photo. *Perf. 14x14½*

158 CD304 1½pi purple 1.00 .55

Engr.; Name Typo.
Perf. 11½x11

159 CD305 £1 dark blue 57.50 *77.50*

UPU Issue
Common Design Types
Perf. 13½, 11x11½

1949, Oct. 10 Engr. Wmk. 4

160 CD306 1½pi violet .65 *1.60*
161 CD307 2pi deep carmine 1.75 1.60
162 CD308 3pi indigo 1.10 1.10
163 CD309 9pi rose violet 1.10 4.00
Nos. 160-163 (4) 4.60 8.30

Types of 1938-43

1951, July 2 Engr. *Perf. 12½*

164 A37 ½pi purple 3.25 .75
165 A40 1½pi deep green 6.25 1.25
166 A41 4pi deep ultra 4.75 1.40
Nos. 164-166 (3) 14.25 3.40

Coronation Issue
Common Design Type

1953, June 2 *Perf. 13½x13*

167 CD312 1½pi brt grn & black 1.50 1.00

Carobs A48

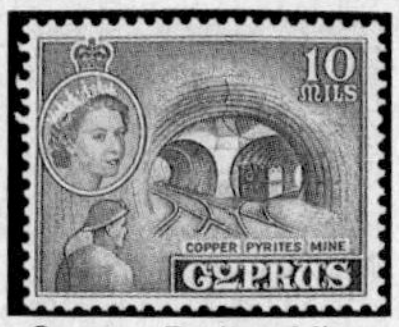

Copper Pyrites Mine A49

St. Hilarion Castle A50

Queen Elizabeth II and Cyprian Coin Devices — A51

Designs: 3m, Grapes. 5m, Oranges. 15m, Troodos forest. 20m, Aphrodite beach. 25m, Coin of Paphos. 30m, Kyrenia. 35m, Harvest in Mesaoria. 40m, Famagusta harbor. 100m, Hala Sultan Tekke. 250m, Kanakaria church. £1, Queen Elizabeth II and devices of Byzantium, Lusignan, Ottoman Empire and Venice.

Perf. 11½

1955, Aug. 1 Engr. Wmk. 4

168 A48 2m chocolate .25 .50
169 A48 3m violet blue .25 .25
170 A48 5m orange 1.00 .25
171 A49 10m gray grn & chocolate 1.25 .25
172 A49 15m indigo & olive 3.50 .50
173 A49 20m ultra & brown 1.25 .25
174 A49 25m aquamarine 3.25 .70
175 A49 30m carmine & blk 3.00 .25
176 A49 35m aqua & orange 1.25 .50
177 A49 40m choc & dk grn 2.00 .75

Perf. 13½

178 A50 50m red brn & aqua 2.10 .30
179 A50 100m bl green & mag 13.00 .60
180 A50 250m vio brn & dk blue gray 14.00 12.00

Perf. 11x11½

181 A51 500m lilac rose & grnsh gray 32.50 14.00
182 A51 £1 grnsh gray & brn red 29.00 *47.50*
Revenue cancel 1.00
Nos. 168-182 (15) 107.60 78.60

Republic

Nos. 168-182 Overprinted in Dark Blue

1960, Aug. 16 Ovpt. 10x6½mm

183 A48 2m chocolate .25 *.50*
184 A48 3m violet blue .25 .25
185 A48 5m orange .25 .25

Overprint 12½x11mm

186 A49 10m gray grn & choc .25 .25
187 A49 15m indigo & ol .45 .30
188 A49 20m ultra & brn .50 *.50*
a. Double overprint *11,000.*
189 A49 25m aquamarine .60 .60
190 A49 30m car & black .75 .30
a. Double overprint *40,000.*
191 A49 35m aqua & org 1.00 .70
192 A49 40m choc & dk grn 1.10 1.25

2-line overprint 2½mm apart

193 A50 50m red brown & aqua 1.25 .75
194 A50 100m bl grn & mag 3.00 1.75
195 A50 250m vio brn & dk blue gray 10.00 5.25

2-line overprint 22mm apart

196 A51 500m lil rose & grnsh gray 45.00 22.00
197 A51 £1 grnsh gray & brn red 82.50 45.00
Nos. 183-197 (15) 147.15 79.65

The overprint, in Greek and Turkish, reads "Republic of Cyprus."

Map of Cyprus — A52

Wmk. 314

1960, Aug. 16 Engr. ***Perf. 11½***
198 A52 10m brown & green .25 .25
199 A52 30m blue & brown .75 .70
200 A52 100m purple & black 2.25 2.25
Nos. 198-200 (3) 3.25 3.20

Independence of Republic of Cyprus.

Europa Issue

Nineteen Doves Flying as One CD4

Perf. 14x13½
1962, Mar. 19 Litho. Unwmk.
201 CD4 10m lilac *.30 .25*
202 CD4 40m deep ultra *.90 .35*
203 CD4 100m emerald *.90 .60*
Nos. 201-203 (3) *2.10 1.20*

Admission of Cyprus to Council of Europe.

Malaria Eradication Emblem A54

1962, May 14 ***Perf. 14x13½***
204 A54 10m gray green & black .25 .25
205 A54 30m red brown & black .45 .45

WHO drive to eradicate malaria.

Iron Age Jug — A55

St. Barnabas Church, Salamis A56

Designs: 5m, Grapes. 10m, Head of Apollo. 15m, St. Sophia Church, Nicosia. 30m, Temple of Apollo. 35m, Head of Aphrodite. 40m, Skiing on Mt. Troodos. 50m, Ruins of Gymnasium, Salamis. 100m, Hala Sultan Tekke (sheep, Salt Lake Larnaca and tomb). 250m, Bella Paise Monastery. 500m, Cyprus mouflon. £1, St. Hilarion Castle.

Perf. 13½x14, 14x13½
1962, Sept. 17 Wmk. 344
206 A55 3m dk brn & sal .25 .30
207 A55 5m dull green & red lilac .25 .25
208 A55 10m dk slate grn & yel green .25 .25
209 A55 15m dk brn & rose vio .40 .25
210 A56 25m salmon & brn .45 .25
211 A56 30m lt bl & dk bl .25 .25
212 A55 35m dk bl & pale grn .45 .25
213 A56 40m vio bl & dk bl 1.50 1.75
214 A56 50m olive bis & dk grn .60 .25
215 A55 100m brn & yel brn 4.25 .30
216 A56 250m tan & black 11.00 2.40
217 A55 500m brown & olive 21.00 9.00
218 A56 £1 gray & green 22.50 *30.00*
Nos. 206-218 (13) 63.15 45.50

Wmk. 344 is found in two positions: normal or inverted on vertical stamps, and reading up or down on horizontal stamps.

For overprints see Nos. 232-236, 265-268. For surcharge see No. 273.

Europa Issue, 1962
Common Design Type
Perf. 14x13½
1963, Jan. 28 Wmk. 344
Size: 36x20mm
219 CD5 10m ultra & black *3.75 .25*
220 CD5 40m red & black *15.00 1.40*
221 CD5 150m green & black *57.50 2.75*
Nos. 219-221 (3) *76.25 4.40*

Cypriot Farm Girl — A57

Cub Scout and Tents — A58

75m, Statue of Demeter, goddess of agriculture.

1963, Mar. 21 ***Perf. 13½x14***
222 A57 25m blk, ultra & ocher .50 .45
223 A57 75m dk car, gray & blk 3.25 1.75

FAO "Freedom from Hunger" campaign.

1963, Aug. 21 Wmk. 344

20m, Sea Scout. 150m, Boy Scout & mouflon.

224 A58 3m multicolored .25 .25
225 A58 20m multicolored .40 .25
226 A58 150m multicolored 2.00 2.50
a. Souvenir sheet of 3 130.00 130.00
Nos. 224-226 (3) 2.65 3.00

Boy Scout movement in Cyprus, 50th anniv. No. 226a contains 3 imperf. stamps similar to Nos. 224-226 with simulated perforations. Sold for 250m.

Red Cross Nurse — A59

Children's Home, Kyrenia A60

Perf. 13½x14, 14x13½
1963, Sept. 9 Litho. Wmk. 344
227 A59 10m multicolored .75 .25
228 A60 100m multicolored 3.50 4.00

Intl. Red Cross, cent.

Europa Issue

Stylized Links, Symbolizing Unity — CD6

1963, Nov. 4 ***Perf. 14x13½***
229 CD6 20m multicolored *5.75 .70*
230 CD6 30m multicolored *6.50 .70*
231 CD6 150m multicolored *42.50 3.75*
Nos. 229-231 (3) *54.75 5.15*

Nos. 208, 211, 213-215 Overprinted in Ultramarine

1964, May 5 ***Perf. 13½x14, 14x13½***
232 A55 10m dk sl grn & yel grn .25 .25
233 A55 30m lt blue & dk blue .25 .25
234 A55 40m vio bl & dull bl .50 .30
235 A55 50m ol bis & dk grn .35 .35
236 A55 100m brn & yel brown .50 .75
Nos. 232-236 (5) 1.85 1.90

Decision by the UN and its Security Council to help restore the country to normality and to seek a solution of its problems.

Clay Mask and Soli Theater A62

Designs: 35m, Curium theater. 50m, Salamis theater. 100m, Performance of "Othello" in front of Othello Tower.

1964, June 15 ***Perf. 13½x14***
237 A62 15m multicolored .45 .25
238 A62 35m multicolored .45 .25
239 A62 50m multicolored .45 .25
240 A62 100m multicolored 1.75 2.25
Nos. 237-240 (4) 3.10 3.00

400th anniversary of Shakespeare's birth.

Boxers A63

14th century B.C. art: 10m, Runners, vert. 75m, Chariot.

1964, July 6 ***Perf. 13½x14, 14x13½***
241 A63 10m brn, bis & blk .25 .25
242 A63 25m gray bl, bl & brn .30 .25
243 A63 75m brick red, blk & brn .65 .80
a. Souvenir sheet of 3 9.00 *13.50*
Nos. 241-243 (3) 1.20 1.30

18th Olympic Games, Tokyo, Oct. 10-25, 1964. No. 243a contains three imperf. stamps similar to Nos. 241-243 with gray marginal inscription. Sheet sold for 250m; the difference between face value and selling price went for the promotion of classical athletics in Cyprus.

Europa Issue

Symbolic Daisy — CD7

Perf. 13½x14
1964, Sept. 14 Litho. Wmk. 344
244 CD7 20m bis brn & red brn *2.50 .35*
245 CD7 30m lt blue & dk blue *3.25 .35*
246 CD7 150m grn & ol grn *30.00 2.75*
Nos. 244-246 (3) *35.75 3.45*

CEPT, 5th anniv. The 22 petals of the flower symbolize the 22 members of the organization.

Satyr Drinking Wine, 5th Century B.C. Statuette — A65

Modern Winery A66

Cypriot Wine Industry: 10m, Dionysus and Acme drinking wine, 3rd century mosaic. 50m, Commandaria wine, Knight Templar and Kolossi Castle.

Perf. 14x13½, 13½x14
1964, Oct. 26 Wmk. 344
247 A66 10m multicolored .45 .25
248 A65 40m multicolored .80 1.25
249 A65 50m multicolored .80 .30
250 A66 100m multicolored 2.00 2.00
Nos. 247-250 (4) 4.05 3.80

Pres. John F. Kennedy (1917-1963) — A67

Perf. 14x13½
1965, Feb. 15 Litho. Wmk. 344
251 A67 10m violet blue .25 .25
252 A67 40m green .45 .45
253 A67 100m rose claret .55 .45
a. Souvenir sheet of 3 4.00 7.00
Nos. 251-253 (3) 1.25 1.15

No. 253a contains 3 imperf. stamps similar to Nos. 251-253 with simulated perforations. Sold for 250m, 100m going to charitable organizations in Cyprus.

Old Couple — A68

Mother and Children by A. Diamantis — A69

45m, Man with broken leg (accident insurance).

1965, Apr. 12 *Perf. 13½x14*

254	A68	30m dull green & tan	.25	.25
255	A68	45m dk vio bl, bl & gray	.40	.30

Perf. 13½x12½

256	A69	75m buff & red brown	1.25	2.00
		Nos. 254-256 (3)	1.90	2.55

Introduction of Social Insurance Law.

ITU Emblem, Old and New Communication Equipment — A70

1965, May 17 **Litho.** *Perf. 14x13½*

257	A70	15m brn, yel & black	.65	.25
258	A70	60m grn, lt grn & black	7.50	3.25
259	A70	75m dk & lt bl & black	8.50	4.50
		Nos. 257-259 (3)	16.65	8.00

ITU, cent.

ICY Emblem A71

1965, May 17 **Wmk. 344**

260	A71	50m multicolored	1.00	.25
261	A71	100m multicolored	1.75	.90

International Cooperation Year.

Europa Issue

Leaves and Fruit CD8

Perf. 14x13½

1965, Sept. 27 **Litho.** **Wmk. 344**

262	CD8	5m org, org brn & black	1.10	*.25*
263	CD8	45m lt grn, org brn & black	*5.25*	*.80*
264	CD8	150m gray, org brn & black	*19.00*	*2.75*
		Nos. 262-264 (3)	*25.35*	*3.80*

Nos. 206, 208, 211 and 216 Overprinted in Dark Blue

1966, Jan. 31 *Perf. 13½x14, 14x13½*

265	A55	3m dk brn & salmon	.35	.40
266	A55	10m dk sl grn & yel green	.40	.25
267	A56	30m lt bl & dk blue	.40	.25
268	A56	250m tan & black	1.35	*2.40*
		Nos. 265-268 (4)	2.50	3.30

UN General Assembly's resolution to mediate the dispute between Greeks and Turks on Cyprus, Dec. 18, 1965.

St. Barnabas, Ancient Icon — A73

Chapel over Tomb of St. Barnabas A74

Bishop Anthemios of Constantine Dreaming of St. Barnabas, Discovering Tomb, etc. — A75

Design: 15m, Discovery of body of St. Barnabas (scene as in type A18).

Perf. 13x14, 14x13

1966, Apr. 25 **Litho.** **Wmk. 344**

269	A73	15m multicolored	.25	.25
270	A74	25m multicolored	.25	.25
271	A73	100m multicolored	.75	*1.75*

Size: 110x91mm

Imperf

272	A75	250m multicolored	5.50	*12.00*
		Nos. 269-272 (4)	6.75	14.25

1900th anniv. of the death of St. Barnabas.

No. 206 Surcharged with New Value and Three Bars

Perf. 13½x14

1966, May 30 **Litho.** **Wmk. 344**

273	A55	5m on 3m dk brn & sal	.45	.25

Gen. K. S. Thimayya A76

1966, June 6 *Perf. 14x13½*

274	A76	50m tan & black	.35	.25

In memory of Gen. Kodendera Subayya Thimayya (1906-1965), commander of the UN Peace-keeping Force on Cyprus.

Europa Issue

Symbolic Sailboat — CD9

Perf. 13½x14

1966, Sept. 26 **Litho.** **Wmk. 344**

275	CD9	20m multicolored	*.50*	*.25*
276	CD9	30m multicolored	*.50*	*.25*
277	CD9	150m multicolored	*3.75*	*1.40*
		Nos. 275-277 (3)	*4.75*	*1.90*

Stavrovouni Monastery A78

St. Nicholas Cathedral, Famagusta A79

Ingot Bearer, Bronze Age — A80

Designs: 5m, St. James' Church, Tricomo, vert. 10m, Zeno of Citium, marble bust, vert. 15m, Ship from 7th cent. BC vase, horiz. 20m, Silver coin, 4th cent. BC (head of Hercules with lion skin). 25m, Sleeping Eros (1st cent. marble statue; horiz.). 35m, Hawks on 11th cent. gold and enamel scepter from Curium. 40m, Marriage of David (7th cent. silver disc). 50m, Silver coin of Alexander the Great showing Hercules and Zeus, horiz. 100m, Bird catching fish on 7th cent. BC jug. 500m, The Rape of Ganymede (3rd cent. mosaic). £1, Aphrodite (1st cent. marble statue).

Perf. 12x12½, 12½x12

1966, Nov. 21 **Litho.** **Wmk. 344**

278	A78	3m bl, dl yel, grn & black	.50	.25
279	A78	5m dk bl, ol & blk	.25	.25
280	A78	10m olive & black	.25	.25

Perf. 14x13½, 13½x14

281	A79	15m org brn, blk & red brn	.25	.25
282	A79	20m red brn & blk	1.50	1.40
283	A79	25m red brn, gray & black	.50	.25
284	A79	30m aqua, tan & blk	.70	.30
285	A79	35m dk car, yel & blk	.70	.45
286	A79	40m brt bl, gray & blk	.85	.45
287	A79	50m org brn, gray & blk	1.25	.25
288	A79	100m gray, buff, blk & red	4.50	.25

Perf. 13x14

289	A80	250m dull yel, grn & blk	1.25	.50
290	A80	500m multicolored	3.25	1.00
291	A80	£1 gray, lt gray & black	2.75	*7.00*
		Nos. 278-291 (14)	18.50	12.85

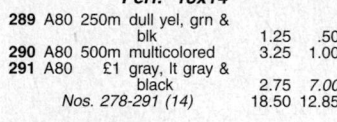

Electric Power Station, Limassol — A81

Arghaka-Maghounda Dam — A82

Designs: 35m, Troodos Highway. 50m, Cyprus Hilton Hotel. 100m, Ships in Famagusta Harbor.

Perf. 14x13½, 13½x14

1967, Apr. 10 **Litho.** **Wmk. 344**

292	A81	10m lt brn, dark brn & yellow	.25	.25
293	A82	15m lt bl, bl & grn	.25	.25
294	A82	35m dark gray, indigo & dark grn	.30	.30
295	A82	50m gray, olive & blue	.30	.30
296	A82	100m gray, ind & bl	.30	.30
		Nos. 292-296 (5)	1.40	1.40

1st development program, 1962-66, completion.

Europa Issue, 1967

Common Design Type

1967, May 2 *Perf. 13x14*

Size: 21x37mm

297	CD10	20m yel grn & olive	*.50*	*.25*
298	CD10	30m rose vio & pur	*.50*	*.25*
299	CD10	150m pale brn & brn	*3.25*	*1.25*
		Nos. 297-299 (3)	*4.25*	*1.75*

Javelin Thrower, Map of Eastern Mediterranean and "Victory" — A83

Map of Eastern Mediterranean, Victory Statue and: 35m, Runner. 100m, High jumper. 250m, Amphora, map of Eastern Mediterranean and Victory statue.

Perf. 13½x13

1967, Sept. 4 **Litho.** **Wmk. 344**

300	A83	15m multicolored	.25	.25
301	A83	35m multicolored	.25	.30
302	A83	100m multicolored	.60	*1.00*

Size: 97x77mm

Imperf

303	A83	250m multicolored	2.50	*6.50*
		Nos. 300-303 (4)	3.60	8.05

Cyprus-Crete-Salonika Athletic Games.

Marble Forum at Salamis, Church of St. Barnabas and Bellapais Abbey A84

ITY Emblem and: 40m, Famagusta Beach. 50m, Plane and Nicosia International Airport. 100m, Youth Hostel and skiing on Mt. Troodos.

Perf. 13½x13

1967, Oct. 16 **Litho.** **Wmk. 344**

304	A84	10m multicolored	.25	.25
305	A84	40m multicolored	.25	*1.00*
306	A84	50m multicolored	.25	.25
307	A84	100m multicolored	.25	*1.00*
		Nos. 304-307 (4)	1.00	2.50

Intl. Tourist Year, 1967.

St. Andrew, 6th Century Mosaic — A85

Crucifixion, 15th Century — A86

The Three Kings, 15th Century Fresco — A87

1967, Nov. 8 *Perf. 13x13½*

308 A85 25m multicolored .25 .25
309 A86 50m multicolored .25 .25
310 A87 75m multicolored .25 .25
Nos. 308-310 (3) .75 .75

St. Andrew's Monastery, cent. (25m); Exhibition of Art of Cyprus, Paris, Nov. 7, 1967-Jan. 3, 1968 (50m); 20th anniv. of UNESCO (75m).

Human Rights Flame and Stars — A88

Designs: 90m, Human Rights flame and UN emblem. 250m, Scroll showing Article One of the Declaration of Human Rights.

Perf. 13½x14

1968, Mar. 18 **Litho.** **Wmk. 344**

311 A88 50m multicolored .25 .25
312 A88 90m multicolored .25 .70

Size: 110x90mm

Imperf

313 A88 250m multicolored 1.25 *4.75*
Nos. 311-313 (3) 1.75 5.70

Intl. Human Rights Year.

Europa Issue, 1968

Common Design Type

1968, Apr. 29 *Perf. 14x13½*

314 CD11 20m multicolored *.40* *.25*
315 CD11 30m dk car rose, gray brn & blk *.50* *.25*
316 CD11 150m multicolored *2.00* *1.25*
Nos. 314-316 (3) *2.90* *1.75*

Boy Holding Milk, UNICEF Emblem A89

Aesculapius and WHO Emblem — A90

Perf. 14x13½, 13½x14

1968, Sept. 2 **Wmk. 344**

317 A89 35m dk red, lt brn & blk .25 .25
318 A90 50m gray ol, blk & grn .25 .25

21st anniv. of UNICEF (No. 317), 20th anniv. of the WHO (No. 318).

Discus Thrower — A91

ILO Emblem — A92

25m, Runners. 100m, Stadium, Mexico City.

Perf. 13½x14, 14x13½

1968, Oct. 24 **Litho.**

319 A91 10m multicolored .25 .25
320 A91 25m vio blue & multi .25 .25
321 A91 100m blue & multi, horiz. .25 *1.25*
Nos. 319-321 (3) .75 1.75

19th Olympic Games, Mexico City, 10/12-27.

Perf. 12x13½

1969, Mar. 3 **Wmk. 344**

322 A92 50m bl, vio bl & org brn .25 .25
323 A92 90m gray, blk & org brn .25 .55

ILO, 50th anniv.

Ancient Map of Cyprus A93

Design: 50m, Medieval map of Cyprus.

Perf. 13½x13

1969, Apr. 7 **Wmk. 344**

324 A93 35m multicolored .25 .30
325 A93 50m olive & multi .25 .30

1st Intl. Congress of Cypriot Studies.

Europa Issue

"EUROPA" and "CEPT" CD12

1969, Apr. 28 **Litho.** *Perf. 14x13½*

326 CD12 20m bl, blk & gray *.55* *.25*
327 CD12 30m cop red, blk & ocher *.55* *.25*
328 CD12 150m grn, blk & yel *1.90* *.85*
Nos. 326-328 (3) *3.00* *1.35*

CEPT, 10th anniv.

European Roller — A95

Birds: 15m, Audouin's gull. 20m, Cyprus warbler. 30m, Eurasian jay, vert. 40m, Hoopoe, vert. 90m, Eleonora's falcon, vert.

Perf. 13½x12, 12x13½

1969, July 7 **Wmk. 344**

329 A95 5m multicolored .45 .25
330 A95 15m multicolored .60 .25
331 A95 20m multicolored .60 .25
332 A95 30m multicolored .65 .25
333 A95 40m multicolored .75 .30
334 A95 90m multicolored 1.90 4.50
Nos. 329-334 (6) 4.95 5.80

Nativity, Mural, 1192 A96

Christmas: 45m, Nativity, mural in Church of Ayios Nicolaos tis Steghis, 14th century. 250m, Virgin and Child between Archangels Michael and Gabriel, mosaic in Church of Panayia Angeloktistos, 6th-7th centuries. Design of 20m is a mural in Church of Panayia tou Arakos, Lagoudhera.

1969, Nov. 24 **Litho.** *Perf. 13½x13*

335 A96 20m multicolored .25 .25
336 A96 45m multicolored .25 .25

Size: 109x89mm

Imperf

337 A96 250m dk blue & multi 5.00 *12.00*
Nos. 335-337 (3) 5.50 12.50

Mahatma Gandhi A97

1970, Jan. 26 *Perf. 14x13½*

338 A97 25m multicolored .35 .35
339 A97 75m multicolored 1.40 1.50

Birth cent. of Mohandas K. Gandhi (1869-1948), leader in India's struggle for independence.

Europa Issue

Interwoven Threads CD13

1970, May 4 **Litho.** **Wmk. 344**

340 CD13 20m brn, yel & org *.40* *.25*
341 CD13 30m brt bl, yel & org *.40* *.25*
342 CD13 150m brt rose lil, yel & orange *1.90* *1.40*
Nos. 340-342 (3) *2.70* *1.90*

Landscape with Flowers — A99

Designs: Various landscapes with flowers.

Perf. 13x14

1970, Aug. 3 **Litho.** **Wmk. 344**

343 A99 10m multicolored .25 .25
344 A99 50m multicolored .25 .25
345 A99 90m multicolored .60 *1.40*
Nos. 343-345 (3) 1.10 1.90

European Nature Conservation Year.

Education Year Emblem — A100

Grapes and Partridge (Mosaic) A101

UN Emblem, Dove, Globe and Wheat A102

Perf. 13x14, 14x13

1970, Sept. 7 **Litho.** **Wmk. 344**

346 A100 5m tan, blk & brn .25 .25
347 A101 15m multicolored .25 .25
348 A102 75m multicolored .25 .75
Nos. 346-348 (3) .75 1.25

Intl. Education Year (No. 346); 50th General Assembly of the Intl. Vine and Wine Office (No. 347); 25th anniv. of the UN (No. 348).

Virgin and Child, Mural from Podhithou Church, 16th Century — A103

Perf. 14x14½

1970, Nov. 23 **Photo.** **Unwmk.**

349 A103 Strip of three .45 .45
a. 25m Left angel .25 .25
b. 25m Virgin and Child .25 .25
c. 25m Right angel .25 .25
350 A103 75m multicolored .35 .35

Christmas.

Design of No. 349 is same as No. 350, but divided by perforation into 3 stamps with 25m denomination each. Size of No. 349: 71x46mm; size of No. 350: 42x31mm.

Cotton Napkin — A104

Festive Costume — A105

Drinking Cup, 7th Cent. B.C. A106

Mouflon from Mosaic Pavement, 3rd Century — A107

Cypriot Art: 5m, St. George, bas-relief on pine board, 19th cent. 20m, kneeling donors, painting, Church of St. Mamas, 1465. 25m, Mosaic head, 5th cent. A.D. 30m, Athena mounting horse-drawn chariot, terracotta figurine, 5th cent. B.C. 40m, Shepherd playing pipe, 14th cent. fresco. 50m, Woman's head, limestone, 3rd cent. B.C. 75m, Angel, mosaic, 6th cent. 90m, Mycenaean silver bowl, 14th cent. B.C. 500m, Woman and tree, decoration from amphora, 7th-6th cent. B.C. £1, God statue (horned helmet), from Enkomi, 12th cent. B.C., vert.

Perf. 12½x13½ (A104), 13x14 (A105), 14x13 (A106), 13½x13, 13x13½ (A107)

1971, Feb. 22 Litho. Wmk. 344

351 A104 3m blk, red & brn .35 .50
352 A104 5m citron, red brn & black .25 .25
353 A105 10m multicolored .25 .30
354 A106 15m bister brn, blk & slate .25 .25
355 A105 20m slate, red brn & black .40 .50
356 A105 25m multicolored .30 .25
357 A106 30m multicolored .30 .25
358 A105 40m gray & multi 1.10 1.10
359 A105 50m bl, bis & blk .90 .25
360 A105 75m cit & multi 2.00 1.25
361 A106 90m multicolored 2.25 2.50
362 A107 250m lt red brn, brn & black 1.75 .40
363 A107 500m tan & multi .90 .50
364 A107 £1 multicolored 1.75 .75
Nos. 351-364 (14) 12.75 9.05

For surcharges & overprints see Nos. 403, 424-427, 444, RA1.

Europa Issue

"Fraternity, Co-operation, Common Effort" — CD14

1971, May 3 Litho. *Perf. 14x13½*
Size: 36½x23½mm

365 CD14 20m lt bl, vio bl & blk *.30 .25*
366 CD14 30m brt yel grn, grn & blk *.30 .25*
367 CD14 150m yel, grn & blk *2.00 1.25*
Nos. 365-367 (3) 2.60 1.75

Archbishop Kyprianos, 1821 — A109

Paintings: 30m, Young Greek Taking Oath, horiz. 100m, Bishop Germanòs of Patras Declaring Greek Independence.

Perf. 13x13½, 13½x13

1971, July 9 Wmk. 344

368 A109 15m multicolored .25 .25
369 A109 30m multicolored .25 .25
370 A109 100m multicolored .25 .50
Nos. 368-370 (3) .75 1.00

150th anniversary of Greek independence.

Arch and Castle A110

Tourist Publicity: 25m, Decorated gourd and sun over shore, vert. 60m, Mountain road, vert. 100m, Village church.

Perf. 13½x13, 13x13½

1971, Sept. 20

371 A110 15m vio bl & multi .25 .25
372 A110 25m ocher & multi .25 .25
373 A110 60m green & multi .25 .60
374 A110 100m blue & multi .25 .65
Nos. 371-374 (4) 1.00 1.75

Virgin and Child — A111

1971, Nov. 22 *Perf. 13½x14*

375 A111 10m shown .25 .35
376 A111 50m The Three Kings .25 .35
377 A111 100m Shepherds .25 .35
a. Strip of 3, Nos. 375-377 .65 .95

Christmas.

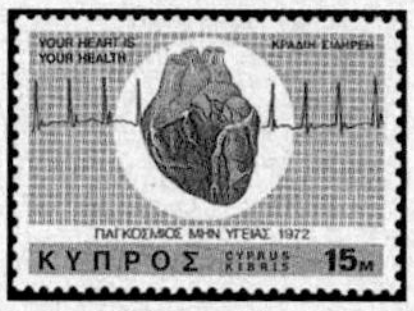

Heart and Electrocardiogram — A112

1972, Apr. 11 *Perf. 13½x12½*

378 A112 15m bister & multi .25 .25
379 A112 50m brown & multi .25 .45

"Your heart is your health," World Health Day.

Europa Issue

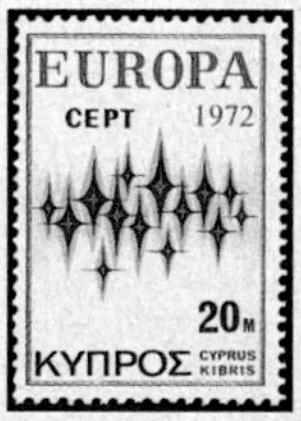

Sparkles, Symbolic of Communications CD15

1972, May 22 *Perf. 12½x13½*

380 CD15 20m brn, org & fawn *.60 .30*
381 CD15 30m pur, org & lilac *.60 .55*
382 CD15 150m dk ol, org & brt green *4.75 1.60*
Nos. 380-382 (3) 5.95 2.45

Archery, Olympic and Motion Emblems A114

1972, July 24 *Perf. 14x13½*

383 A114 10m shown .25 .25
384 A114 40m Wrestling .35 .25
385 A114 100m Soccer .65 1.75
Nos. 383-385 (3) 1.25 2.25

20th Olympic Games, Munich, 8/26-9/11.

Apollo, Silver Stater, Marion, 5th Century B.C. A115

Silver Staters of Cyprus: 30m, Eagle's head, Paphos, c. 460 B.C. 40m, Pallas Athena, Lapithos, 388-387 B.C. 100m, Sphinx (obverse) and lotus flower (reverse), Idalion, c. 460 B.C.

1972, Sept. 25 Litho. Wmk. 344
Coins in Silver

386 A115 20m lt grnsh bl & blk .25 .25
387 A115 30m pale bl & silver .25 .25
388 A115 40m ol bister & black .25 .30
389 A115 100m pale brn & blk .75 1.10
Nos. 386-389 (4) 1.50 1.90

Bathing the Christ Child — A116

Christmas: 20m, The Three Kings. 100m, Nativity. 250m, The Nativity, 1466, mural in Church of the Holy Cross, Platanistasa. The designs of the 10m, 20m, 100m, show details from mural shown entirely on 250m.

1972, Nov. 20 Litho. *Perf. 13½x14*

390 A116 10m multicolored .25 .25
391 A116 20m multicolored .25 .25
392 A116 100m multicolored .25 .40

Size: 110x90mm
Imperf

393 A116 250m multicolored 1.75 4.00
Nos. 390-393 (4) 2.50 4.90

Landscape, Troodos Mountains A117

100m, FIS Congress emblem and map of Cyprus.

Perf. 14x13½

1973, Mar. 13 Wmk. 344

394 A117 20m blue & multi .25 .25
395 A117 100m blue & multi .25 .40

29th Meeting of the Intl. Ski Fed. (FIS), Nicosia, June 1973.

Europa Issue

Post Horn of Arrows CD16

1973, May 7 Size: 37x21mm

396 CD16 20m dl bl & multi *.50 .25*
397 CD16 30m multicolored *.50 .35*
398 CD16 150m multicolored *3.25 1.50*
Nos. 396-398 (3) 4.25 2.10

Archbishop's Palace, Nicosia — A119

Traditional Architecture: 30m, Konak, Nicosia, 18th century, vert. 50m, House, Gourri, 1850, vert. 100m, House, Rizokarpaso, 1772.

1973, July 23 *Perf. 14x13, 13x14*

399 A119 20m multicolored .25 .25
400 A119 30m multicolored .25 .25
401 A119 50m multicolored .25 .25
402 A119 100m multicolored .25 .85
Nos. 399-402 (4) 1.00 1.60

No. 354 Surcharged

1973, Sept. 24 *Perf. 14x13*

403 A106 20m on 15m multi .35 .35

Cyprus Scout Emblem — A120

EEC Emblem A121

Cyprus Airways Emblem — A122

35m, FAO emblem. 100m, INTERPOL emblem.

1973, Sept. 24 *Perf. 13x14, 14x13*

404 A120 10m brn ol, ol & buff .30 .30
405 A121 25m pur, bl & plum .30 .30
406 A121 35m grn, gray grn & citron .30 .30
407 A122 50m black & blue .30 .30
408 A120 100m brown & fawn .40 .80
Nos. 404-408 (5) 1.60 2.00

60th anniv. of Cyprus Boy Scout Organ.; association of Cyprus with EEC; 10th anniv. of FAO; 25th anniv. of Cyprus Airways; 50th anniv. of Intl. Criminal Police Organization.

Archangel Gabriel — A123

Virgin and Child — A124

Christmas: 100m, Panaya tou Araka Church, horiz. Designs of 10m, 20m are from wall paintings in Arakas Church.

1973, Nov. 26 Wmk. 344

409 A123 10m multicolored .25 .25
410 A124 20m multicolored .25 .25
411 A124 100m multicolored .25 .75
Nos. 409-411 (3) .75 1.25

Grapes — A125

1974, Mar. 18 Litho. *Perf. 13x14*

412 A125 25m shown .25 .25
413 A125 50m Grapefruit .25 .50
414 A125 50m Oranges .25 .50
415 A125 50m Lemons .25 .50
a. Strip of 3, #413-415 1.00 1.75
Nos. 412-415 (4) 1.00 1.75

Europa Issue

Rape of Europa — A126

Design shows a silver stater of Marion, second half of 5th century B.C.

1974, Apr. 29

416 A126 10m org brn & multi *.60 .30*
417 A126 40m multicolored *.60 .60*
418 A126 150m dk car & multi *2.75 1.40*
Nos. 416-418 (3) 3.95 2.30

Solon, 3rd Century Mosaic A127

Designs: 10m, Front page of "History of Cyprus," by Archimandrite Kyprianos, 1788, vert. 100m, St. Neophytos, mural, vert. 250m, Maps of Cyprus and Greek Islands, by Abraham Ortelius, 1584.

Perf. 13x14, 14x13

1974, July 22 Litho. Wmk. 344

419 A127 10m multicolored .25 .25
420 A127 25m multicolored .25 .25
421 A127 100m multicolored .30 .85

Size: 110x90mm

Imperf

422 A127 250m multicolored 2.00 *4.00*
Nos. 419-422 (4) 2.80 5.35

2nd Intl. Congress of Cypriot Studies, Nicosia, Sept. 15-21. No. 422 has simulated perforations.

Nos. 353, 358-359, 362 Overprinted

Perf. 13x14, 13½x13

1974, Oct. 14 Litho.

424 A105 10m multicolored .25 .25
425 A105 40m multicolored .35 .50
426 A105 50m multicolored .35 .35
427 A107 250m multicolored .70 1.50
Nos. 424-427 (4) 1.65 2.60

UN Security Council Resolution No. 353 to end hostilities on Cyprus. Overprint is in 3 lines on No. 427.

Virgin and Child, 1466 A129

Adoration of the Kings, c. 1500 — A130

Christmas: 100m, Flight into Egypt, mural, Monastery Church of Ayios Neophytos, c. 1500. (50m is from same church). Mural on 10m is in Church of Stavros tou Agiasmati.

Perf. 14x13, 13x14

1974, Dec. 2 Wmk. 344

429 A129 10m multicolored .25 .25
430 A130 50m multicolored .25 .25
431 A129 100m multicolored .25 .45
Nos. 429-431 (3) .75 .95

Disabled Persons, Emblem — A131

Council of Europe Flag — A132

1975, Feb. 17 Unwmk. *Perf. 14½*

432 A131 30m ocher & ultra .25 .25
433 A132 100m multicolored .60 1.00

8th European Meeting of the Intl. Society for the Rehabilitation of Disabled Persons (30m; design shows society's emblem); 25th anniv. of Council of Europe (100m).

First Mail Coach in Cyprus A133

1975, Feb. 17

434 A133 20m multicolored .25 .25
435 A133 50m ultra & multi .90 .40

Centenary (in 1974) of UPU.

The Distaff, by Michael Kashalos — A134

Europa (Paintings): 30m, Still Life, by Christoforos Savva. 150m, Virgin and Child of Liopetri, by Georghios P. Georghiou.

Perf. 13½x14½

1975, Apr. 28 Photo.

436 A134 20m multicolored *.30 .25*
437 A134 30m multicolored *.35 .25*
438 A134 150m multicolored *1.00 .60*
a. Strip of 3, #436-438 *1.75 1.75*

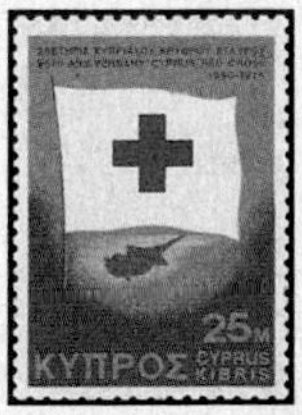

Red Cross Flag over Cyprus — A135

Nurse and Nurses Emblem A136

Steatite Female Figure, c. 3000 B.C. — A137

Perf. 12½x13½, 13½x12½

1975, Aug. 4 Litho. Wmk. 344

439 A135 25m blue green & red .25 .25
440 A136 30m dp blue & lt grn .25 .25
441 A137 75m multicolored .25 .75
Nos. 439-441 (3) .75 1.25

Cyprus Red Cross, 25th anniv.; Intl. Nurses' Day 1975; IWY.

Submarine Cable — A138

International Telephone A139

Perf. 12½x13½, 13½x12½

1975, Oct. 13 Litho.

442 A138 50m multicolored .30 .25
443 A139 100m purple & org .50 .75

Telecommunications achievements.

No. 351 Surcharged

1976, Jan. 5 *Perf. 12½x13½*

444 A104 10m on 3m multi .40 .80

Vessel in Shape of Woman, 19th Century — A140

Composite Vessel, 2100-2000 B.C. — A141

Europa: 100m, Byzantine goblet, 15th cent.

Perf. 13x14

1976, May 3 Litho. Wmk. 344

445 A140 20m violet & multi *.35 .25*
446 A141 60m gray & multi *.80 .70*
447 A140 100m brown & multi *1.60 .95*
Nos. 445-447 (3) 2.75 1.90

Self-help Housing A142

Cyprus Airways Jet — A143

Designs: 25m, Women sewing in front of tents. 30m, Aforestation.

1976, May 3 *Perf. 14x13*

448 A142 10m multicolored .25 .25
449 A142 25m multicolored .25 .25
450 A142 30m multicolored .25 .25
451 A143 60m multicolored .25 .55
Nos. 448-451 (4) 1.00 1.30

Re-activation of the economy.

Terracotta Statue, 7th-6th Centuries B.C. — A144

Bronze Plate with Inscription, Idalion, 5th Century B.C. A145

Designs: 10m, Limestone head of bearded man, 5th cent. B.C. 20m, Gold necklace, Lamboussa, 6th cent. A.D. 25m, Terracotta warrior on horseback, 7th cent. B.C. 30m, Limestone figure, priest of Aphrodite, 5th cent. B.C. 50m, Mycenaean crater, 13th cent. B.C. 60m, Limestone sarcophagus, Amathus, 550-500 B.C. 100m, Gold bracelet, Lamboussa, 6th cent. A.D. 250m, Silver dish, Lamboussa, 6th cent. A.D. 500m, Bronze stand, 12th cent. B.C. £1, Marble statue of Artemis, Larnaca, 4th cent. B.C.

Perf. 12x13½

1976, June 7 Wmk. 344

Size: 22x33mm

452 A144 5m brn & multi .25 .75
453 A144 10m gray & multi .25 .65

Size: 24x37mm, 37x24mm

Perf. 13x14, 14x13

454 A144 20m red & multi .25 .60
455 A144 25m lt brn & blk .25 .25
456 A144 30m green & multi .25 .25
457 A145 40m bis gray & blk .25 .60
458 A145 50m brn & multi .25 .25
459 A145 60m dk brn & multi .25 .25
460 A145 100m crim & multi .40 .60

Size: 28x40mm

Perf. 13x12½

461 A144 250m dk bl & multi .50 1.75
462 A144 500m yel & multi 1.00 2.00
463 A144 £1 slate & multi 2.10 3.00
Nos. 452-463 (12) 6.00 10.95

George Washington A146

1976, July 5 *Perf. 13x13½*

464 A146 100m multicolored .50 .40

American Bicentennial.

Montreal Olympic Games Emblem — A147

Various Sports A148

100m, like 60m, with different sports.

1976, July 5	Unwmk.		Perf. 14	
465	A147	20m yel, blk & dk car	.25	.25
466	A148	60m ultra & multi	.25	.30
467	A148	100m lilac & multi	.35	.40
		Nos. 465-467 (3)	.85	.95

21st Olympic Games, Montreal, Canada, July 17-Aug. 1.

Children in Library — A149

Low-cost Housing Development A150

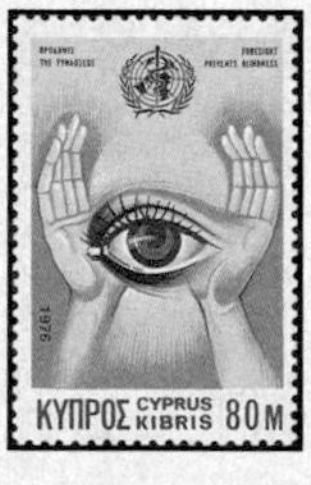

Hands Shielding Eye — A151

Perf. 13½x14, 13x13½

1976, Sept. 27	Litho.	Wmk. 344		
468	A149	40m black & multi	.25	.25
469	A150	50m multicolored	.25	.25
470	A151	80m ultra & multi	.35	.50
		Nos. 468-470 (3)	.85	1.00

Books for Children (40m); Habitat, UN Conference on Human Settlements, Vancouver, Canada, May 31-June 11 (50m); World Health Day: Foresight prevents blindness (80m).

Archangel Michael — A152

Christmas: 15m, Archangel Gabriel. 150m, Nativity. Icons in Ayios Neophytos Monastery, 16th century.

1976, Nov. 15	Unwmk.		Perf. 12½	
471	A152	10m multicolored	.25	.25
472	A152	15m multicolored	.25	.25
473	A152	150m multicolored	.30	.80
		Nos. 471-473 (3)	.80	1.30

Landscape, by A. Diamantis — A154

Europa (Paintings): 60m, Trees and Meadow, by T. Kanthos. 120m, Harbor, by V. Ioannides.

Perf. 13½x13

1977, May 2	Litho.	Unwmk.		
475	A154	20m multicolored	*.30*	*.25*
476	A154	60m multicolored	*.70*	*.40*
477	A154	120m multicolored	*1.25*	*.90*
		Nos. 475-477 (3)	*2.25*	*1.55*

Cyprus No. 196 — A155

Perf. 13x13½

1977, June 13	Litho.	Wmk. 344		
478	A155	120m multicolored	.45	.40

25th anniv. of reign of Queen Elizabeth II.

Silver Tetradrachm of Demetrios Poliorcetes — A156

Ancient Coins of Cyprus: 10m, Bronze coin of Emperor Trajan. 60m, Silver Tetradrachm of Ptolemy VIII. 100m, Gold octadrachm of Arsinoe II.

1977, June 13	Unwmk.		Perf. 14	
479	A156	10m multicolored	.25	.25
480	A156	40m multicolored	.30	.25
481	A156	60m multicolored	.35	.30
482	A156	100m multicolored	.50	.75
		Nos. 479-482 (4)	1.40	1.55

Archbishop Makarios (1913-1977), Pres. of Cyprus — A157

20m, Archbishop in full vestments. 250m, Head.

Perf. 13x14

1977, Sept. 10	Litho.	Unwmk.		
483	A157	20m multicolored	.25	.25
484	A157	60m multicolored	.25	.25
485	A157	250m multicolored	.60	1.00
		Nos. 483-485 (3)	1.10	1.50

Handicrafts A158

Sputnik over Earth — A159

Designs: 40m, Map of the Mediterranean Sea. 60m, Gold medals and sports emblems.

Perf. 13½x12

1977, Oct. 17		Wmk. 344		
486	A158	20m multicolored	.25	.25
487	A158	40m multicolored	.25	.25
488	A158	60m multicolored	.25	.25
489	A159	80m multicolored	.25	.60
		Nos. 486-489 (4)	1.00	1.35

Revitalization of handicrafts (20m); Man and the biosphere (40m); Gold medals won by secondary school students in France for long jump and 200 meter race (60m); 60th anniv. of Bolshevik Revolution (80m).

Nativity A160

Christmas (Children's Drawings): 10m, Three Kings following the star. 150m, Flight into Egypt.

Perf. 14x13½

1977, Nov. 21	Litho.	Unwmk.		
490	A160	10m multicolored	.25	.25
491	A160	40m multicolored	.25	.25
492	A160	150m multicolored	.25	.70
		Nos. 490-492 (3)	.75	1.20

Demetrios Lipertis (1866-1937) — A161

150m, Vasilis Michaelides (1849-1917).

1978, Mar. 6	Wmk. 344		Perf. 14x13	
493	A161	40m bister & olive	.25	.25
494	A161	150m gray, ver & blk	.40	.70

Cypriot poets.

Chrysorrhogiatissa Monastery — A162

Europa: 75m, Kolossi Castle. 125m, Municipal Library, Paphos.

Perf. 14½x13

1978, Apr. 24	Litho.	Unwmk.		
495	A162	25m multicolored	*.30*	*.25*
496	A162	75m multicolored	*.80*	*.40*
497	A162	125m multicolored	*1.40*	*.70*
		Nos. 495-497 (3)	*2.50*	*1.35*

Makarios as Archbishop 1950-1977 A163

"The Great Leader" — A164

Archbishop Makarios: 25m, Exiled, Seychelles, 1956-1957. 50m, President of Cyprus, 1960-1977. 75m, Soldier of Christ. 100m, Freedom fighter.

Perf. 14x14½

1978, Aug. 3	Litho.	Unwmk.		
498	A163	15m multicolored	.25	.25
499	A163	25m multicolored	.25	.25
500	A163	50m multicolored	.25	.25
501	A163	75m multicolored	.25	.35
502	A163	100m multicolored	.25	.35
a.		Strip of 5, #498-502	1.25	1.50

Size: 110x80mm

Imperf

503	A164	300m multicolored	2.00	2.50
		Nos. 498-503 (6)	3.25	3.95

Archbishop Makarios, President of Cyprus.

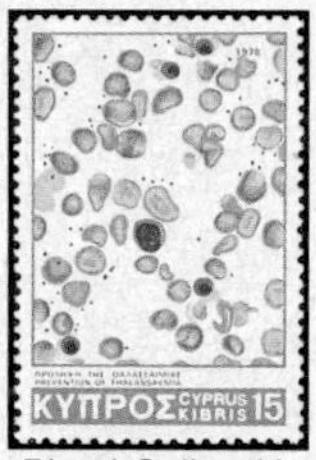

Blood Cells with Low Hemoglobin A165

Bust of Aristotle A166

Heads and Human Rights Emblem A167

Wilbur and Orville Wright, Flyer I A168

Perf. 13x14, 14x13

1978, Oct. 23	Unwmk.	Litho.		
504	A165	15m multicolored	.25	.25
505	A166	35m multicolored	.25	.25
506	A167	75m black	.25	.35
507	A168	125m multicolored	.35	.70
		Nos. 504-507 (4)	1.10	1.55

Anemia prevention (15m); 2300th death anniv. of Aristotle (35m); 30th anniv. of Universal Declaration of Human Rights (75m); 75th anniv. of first powered flight (125m).

Kiti Icon Stand — A169

Christmas: 35m, Athienou icon stand. 150m, Omodhos icon stand.

1978, Dec. 4 *Perf. 14x14½*

508	A169	15m	multicolored	.25	.25
509	A169	35m	multicolored	.25	.25
510	A169	150m	multicolored	.40	.75
			Nos. 508-510 (3)	.90	1.25

Venus Statue from Soli A170

125m, Birth of Venus, by Botticelli (detail).

1979, Mar. 12 Litho. *Perf. 14x13½*

511	A170	75m	multicolored	.30	.25
512	A170	125m	multicolored	.50	.40

Mail Coach, Envelope and Truck A171

Europa: 75m, Old telephone, dish antenna and satellite. 125m, Steamship, jet and envelopes.

1979, Apr. 30 Litho. *Perf. 14x13½*

513	A171	25m	multicolored	*.55*	*.25*
514	A171	75m	multicolored	*.95*	*.40*
515	A171	125m	multicolored	*2.75*	*1.00*
			Nos. 513-515 (3)	*4.25*	*1.65*

Peacock Wrasse A172

Designs: 50m, Black partridge, vert. 75m, Cyprus cedar, vert. 125m, Mule.

Perf. 13½x12½, 12½x13½

1979, June 25 Litho.

516	A172	25m	multicolored	.25	.25
517	A172	50m	multicolored	.40	.50
518	A172	75m	multicolored	.40	.35
519	A172	125m	multicolored	.60	.90
			Nos. 516-519 (4)	1.65	2.00

Children Holding Globe, UNESCO Emblem — A173

Dove, Magnifying Glass, Album A174

Lord Kitchener, Map of Cyprus A175

Smiling Child, IYC Emblem A176

Soccer A177

Rotary Emblem — A178

1979, Oct. 1 Litho. *Perf. 12½*

520	A173	15m	multicolored	.25	.25
521	A174	25m	multicolored	.25	.25
522	A175	50m	multicolored	.25	.25
523	A176	75m	multicolored	.25	.25
524	A177	100m	multicolored	.25	.45
525	A178	125m	multicolored	.25	.70
			Nos. 520-525 (6)	1.50	2.15

Intl. Bureau of Education, Geneva, 50th anniv.; Cyprus Philatelic Society, 20th anniv.; Horatio Herbert Kitchener's survey of Cyprus, cent.; IYC; European Soccer Assoc., 25th anniv.; Rotary Club of Cyprus, 75th anniv.

Jesus, Icon, 12th Century — A179

Christmas (Icons): 35m, Nativity, 16th cent. 150m, Virgin and Child, 12th cent.

Perf. 13½x14, 13x14

1979, Nov. 5 Litho.

Sizes: 24x37mm; 27x40mm (35m)

526	A179	15m	multicolored	.25	.25
527	A179	35m	multicolored	.25	.25
528	A179	150m	multicolored	.25	.45
			Nos. 526-528 (3)	.75	.95

Cyprus No. 1, Nicosia Cancel A180

Cyprus Stamp Centenary: 125m, #3, Kyrenia cancel. 175m, #6, Larnaca cancel. 500m, #1-6.

1980, Mar. 17 Litho. *Perf. 14x13*

529	A180	40m	multicolored	.25	.25
530	A180	125m	multicolored	.25	.40
531	A180	175m	multicolored	.75	.85

Size: 105x85mm

Imperf

532	A180	500m	multicolored	1.40	1.40
			Nos. 529-532 (4)	2.65	2.90

Holy Cross, St. Barnabas Church, Agiasmati — A181

Europa: 125m, Zeno of Citium, Ny Carsberg Glyptothek, Copenhagen.

1980, Apr. 28 *Perf. 12½*

533	A181	40m	multicolored	*.25*	.25
534	A181	125m	multicolored	*.45*	*.30*

Sailing, Moscow '80 Emblem A182

1980, June 23 Litho. *Perf. 14x13*

535	A182	40m	shown	.25	.25
536	A182	125m	Swimming	.25	.25
537	A182	200m	Gymnast	.40	.40
			Nos. 535-537 (3)	.90	.90

22nd Summer Olympic Games, Moscow, July 19-Aug. 3.

Gold Necklace — A183

Clay Amphora — A184

Archaeological finds on Cyprus, 12th cent. B.C. to 3rd cent. A.D. 15m, 40m, 150m, 500m, horiz.

Perf. 13½x14, 14x13½

1980, Sept. 15 Litho. Wmk. 344

538	A183	10m	shown	.30	.30
539	A184	15m	Bronze cow	.30	.30
540	A184	25m	shown	.30	.30
541	A184	40m	Lion, gold ring	.40	.40
542	A184	50m	Bronze cauldron	.40	.40
543	A184	75m	Stele	1.10	1.10
544	A184	100m	Clay jug	.80	.80
545	A184	125m	Warrior, terracotta bust	.80	.80
546	A184	150m	Lions attacking bull	1.25	1.25
547	A184	175m	Faience and enamel vase	.90	.90
548	A184	200m	Warrior god, bronze	.90	.90
549	A184	500m	Stone bowl	.90	.90
550	A183	£1	Ivory plaque	1.10	1.25
551	A183	£2	Leda and the swan, mosaic	1.90	2.25
			Nos. 538-551 (14)	11.35	11.85

For surcharges see Nos. 584, 600-611.

Cyprus Flag — A185

Archbishop Makarios — A187

Treaty Signing Establishing Republic, 20th Anniversary — A186

1980, Oct. 1 *Perf. 13½x14, 14x13*

552	A185	40m	multicolored	.25	.25
553	A186	125m	multicolored	.25	.25
554	A187	175m	multicolored	.35	.35
			Nos. 552-554 (3)	.85	.85

Dove and Woman A188

Perf. 14x13

1980, Nov. 29 Litho. Wmk. 344

555	A188	40m	shown	.25	.25
556	A188	125m	Dove and man	.40	.40
a.			Pair, #555-556	.65	.65

Intl. Palestinian Solidarity Day.

Pulpit, Ayios Lazaros Church, Larnaca — A189

Christmas: 25m, Pulpit, Tripiotis Church, Nicosia. 100m, Iconostatis (Holy Door), Panayia Church, Paralimni.

1980, Nov. 29 *Perf. 13½x14*

557	A189	25m	multicolored	.25	.25

Size: 24x37mm

558	A189	100m	multicolored	.25	.25

Size: 21x37mm

559	A189	125m	multicolored	.25	.25
			Nos. 557-559 (3)	.75	.75

Europa Issue

Folk Dance — A190

1981, May 4 Photo. *Perf. 14*

560	A190	40m	shown	*.35*	.25
561	A190	175m	Dance, diff.	*.75*	*.50*

Self-portrait, by Leonardo Da Vinci — A191

The Last Supper, by Da Vinci — A192

Perf. 13½x14, 12½x13½

1981, June 15 Wmk. 344 Litho.

562	A191	50m	shown	.35	.30
563	A192	125m	shown	.75	.50
564	A191	175m	Lace pattern, Milan Cathedral	.90	.70
			Nos. 562-564 (3)	2.00	1.50

Da Vinci's visit to Cyprus, 500th anniv.

Ophrys Kotschyi — A193

Designs: Orchids.

1981, July 6 *Perf. 13½x14*

565 A193 25m shown .30 .30
566 A193 50m Orchis puntulata .50 .50
567 A193 75m Ophrys argolica elegantis .80 .80
568 A193 150m Epipactis veratrifolia 1.40 1.40
a. Block of 4, #565-568 3.00 3.00
Nos. 565-568 (4) 3.00 3.00

Prince Charles and Lady Diana, St. Paul's Cathedral A194

Perf. 14x13

1981, Sept. 28 **Wmk. 344**

569 A194 200m multicolored .75 .80

Royal wedding.

Heinrich von Stephan (1831-1897), UPU Founder — A195

World Food Day (Oct. 16) A196

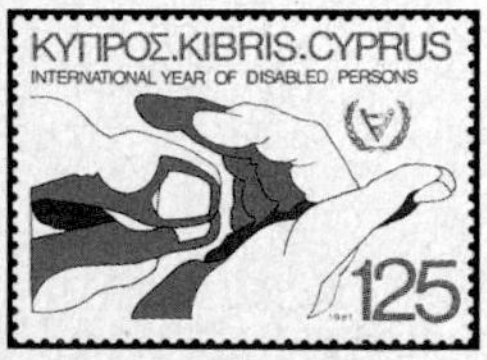

Intl. Year of the Disabled A197

European Campaign for Urban Renaissance — A198

1981, Sept. 28

570 A195 25m multicolored .25 .25
571 A196 40m multicolored .25 .25
572 A197 125m multicolored .35 .35
573 A198 150m multicolored .40 .40
Nos. 570-573 (4) 1.25 1.25

Our Lady of the Angels, Transfiguration Church, Palekhori A199

Christmas (Frescoes): 100m, Christ, Madonna of Arakas Church, Lagoudera, vert. 125m, Baptism of Christ, Our Lady of Assinou Church, Nikitari.

1981, Nov. 16 *Perf. 12½*

574 A199 25m multicolored .25 .25
575 A199 100m multicolored .60 .35
576 A199 125m multicolored .70 .45
Nos. 574-576 (3) 1.55 1.05

Bathing Aphrodite, Sculpture, Soloi, 250 B.C. — A200

Design: 175m, Aphrodite Emerging from the Water, by Titian, 16th cent.

Perf. 13½x14

1982, Apr. 12 **Litho.** **Wmk. 344**

577 A200 125m multicolored .70 .50
578 A200 175m multicolored .90 .70

Europa Issue

Liberation by Emperor Nicephorus II Phocas, 965 A.D. A201

Perf. 12½

1982, May 3 **Photo.** **Unwmk.**

579 A201 40m shown *.50* .25
580 A201 175m Conversion of Sergius Paulus, 45 A.D. *.85* *.75*

Mosaic Chrismon A202

Cultural Heritage: 125m, King of Palaepaphos (High Priest of Aphrodite), sculpture, vert. 225m, Theseus Struggling with the Minotaur, mosaic.

1982, July 5 **Litho.** **Wmk. 344**

581 A202 50m multicolored .25 .25
582 A202 125m multicolored .55 .55
583 A202 225m multicolored 1.00 1.00
Nos. 581-583 (3) 1.80 1.80

No. 543 Surcharged

1982, Sept. 6 **Litho.** *Perf. 13½x14*

584 A184 100m on 75m multi .55 .55

Scouting Year — A203

Perf. 13½x12½, 12½x13½

1982, Nov. 8 **Wmk. 344**

585 A203 100m Emblem, horiz. .40 .40
586 A203 125m Baden-Powell .50 .50
587 A203 175m Camp site, horiz. .60 .80
Nos. 585-587 (3) 1.50 1.70

A203a

Christmas — A204

Perf. 12½, 13½x14 (100m)

1982, Dec. 6

Designs: 25m, 250m, Christ Giving Holy Communion (bread, 25m: wine, 250m) to the Apostles, St. Neophytos Monastery Church, Paphos. 100m, Chalice, Church of St. Savvas, Nicosia.

588 A203a 25m multicolored .25 .25
589 A204 100m multicolored .35 .35
590 A203a 250m multicolored .80 1.25
Nos. 588-590 (3) 1.40 1.85

A204a

1983, Mar. 14 *Perf. 14x13½*

591 A204a 50m Cyprus Forest Industries, Ltd. .25 .25
592 A204a 125m Mosaic, 3rd cent. .25 .25
593 A204a 150m Dancers .25 .35
594 A204a 175m Royal Exhibition Building, Melbourne .25 .50
Nos. 591-594 (4) 1.00 1.35

Commonwealth Day.

Europa A205

50m, Cyprosyllabic script funerary stele, 6th cent. B.C. 200m, Copper ore, Enkomi ingot, 1400-1250 BC, bronze jug, 2nd cent.

1983, May 3 **Photo.** *Perf. 14½x14*

595 A205 50m multicolored *.25* .25
596 A205 200m multicolored *.75* *.50*

Local Butterflies A206

Wmk. 344

1983, June 28 **Litho.** *Perf. 12½*

597 A206 60m Pararge aegeria .35 .35
598 A206 130m Aricia medon .75 .75
599 A206 250m Glaucopsyche paphos 1.40 2.10
Nos. 597-599 (3) 2.50 3.20

Nos. 538-549 Surcharged

Perf. 13½x14, 14x13½

1983, Oct. 3 **Litho.** **Wmk. 344**

600 A183 1c on 10m multi .25 .75
601 A184 2c on 15m multi .25 1.00
602 A184 3c on 25m multi .25 .75
603 A184 4c on 40m multi .25 .75
604 A184 5c on 50m multi .30 .40
605 A184 6c on 75m multi .30 .75
606 A184 10c on 100m multi .55 .55
607 A184 13c on 125m multi .65 .60
608 A184 15c on 150m multi .65 .70
609 A184 20c on 200m multi .70 .80
610 A184 25c on 175m multi 1.10 1.30
611 A184 50c on 500m multi 1.90 2.25
Nos. 600-611 (12) 7.15 10.60

Electricity Authority of Cyprus, 30th Anniv. — A207

World Communications Year — A208

Intl. Maritime Org., 25th Anniv. — A209

Universal Declaration of Human Rights, 35th Anniv. — A210

Nicos Kazantzakis, 100th Birth Anniv. — A211

Archbishop Makarios III, 70th Birth Anniv. — A212

1983, Oct. 27 **Litho.** *Perf. 13½x14*

612 A207 3c multicolored .25 .25
613 A208 6c multicolored .25 .25
614 A209 13c multicolored .25 .25
615 A210 15c multicolored .25 .25
616 A211 20c multicolored .30 .65
617 A212 25c multicolored .30 .80
Nos. 612-617 (6) 1.60 2.45

Christmas — A213

Designs: 4c, Belfry, St. Lazaros Church, Larnaca. 13c, Belfry, St. Varvara Church, Kaimakli, Nicosia. 20c, Belfry, St. Ioannis Church, Larnaca.

1983, Dec. 12 *Perf. 12½x14*

618 A213 4c multicolored .25 .25
619 A213 13c multicolored .60 .60
620 A213 20c multicolored .85 1.10
Nos. 618-620 (3) 1.70 1.95

Waterside Cafe at the Marina, Larnaca — A214

19th Century engravings. Size of 6c: 41x27mm; 75c, 110x85mm.

Perf. 14½x14 (6c), 14, Imperf. (75c)

1984, Mar. 6

621 A214 6c shown .25 .25
622 A214 20c Bazaar, Larnaca .40 .65
623 A214 30c East Gate, Nicosia .65 1.25

624	A214	75c	St. Lazarus Church Interior, Larnaca	1.50	2.00
			Nos. 621-624 (4)	2.80	4.15

Europa (1959-1984) — A215

1984, Apr. 30 Wmk. 344 *Perf. 12½*

625	A215	6c	multicolored	.40	.25
626	A215	15c	multicolored	.90	.75

1984 Summer Olympics A216

1984, June 18 Litho. *Perf. 14*

627	A216	3c	Running	.25	.25
628	A216	4c	Olympic column	.25	.25
629	A216	13c	Swimming	.50	.70
630	A216	20c	Gymnastics	.70	1.10
			Nos. 627-630 (4)	1.70	2.30

Turkish Invasion, 10th Anniv. A217

1984, July 20 Litho. *Perf. 14x13½*

631	A217	15c	Prisoners, barbed wire	.45	.45
632	A217	20c	Map	.60	.60

Cyprus Philatelic Society, 25th Anniv. — A218

Cyprus Soccer Assoc., 50th Anniv. A219

George Papanicolaou (1883-1962), Cancer Researcher — A220

Medieval Map A221

1984, Oct. 15 Wmk. 344 *Perf. 12½*

633	A218	6c	multicolored	.25	.25
634	A219	10c	multicolored	.40	.40
635	A220	15c	multicolored	.70	.70
636	A221	25c	multicolored	1.25	1.75
			Nos. 633-636 (4)	2.60	3.10

Intl. Symposium of Cyprus Cartography and First Intl. Symposium on Medieval Paleography (25c).

Christmas — A222

1984, Nov. 26 Litho. *Perf. 12½*

637	A222	4c	St. Mark	.30	.30
638	A222	13c	Gospel page (St. Mark)	1.00	1.00
639	A222	20c	St. Luke	1.50	1.75
			Nos. 637-639 (3)	2.80	3.05

Landscapes — A223

Perf. 15x14, 14x15

1985, Mar. 18 Litho.

640	A223	1c	Autumn at Platania	.25	.65
641	A223	2c	Ayia Napa Monastery	.25	.65
642	A223	3c	Phine Village	.25	.65
643	A223	4c	Kykko Monastery	.25	.35
644	A223	5c	Beach at Makronissos	.25	.25
645	A223	6c	Village Street, Omodhos, vert.	.25	.25
646	A223	10c	Sea view	.30	.35
647	A223	13c	Water sports	.40	.30
648	A223	15c	Beach at Protaras	.45	.35
649	A223	20c	Forestry, vert.	.50	.60
650	A223	25c	Sunrise at Protaras, vert.	.80	.90
651	A223	30c	Village houses, Pera Orinis	1.10	1.10
652	A223	50c	Apollo Hylates Sanctuary	2.25	1.50
653	A223	£1	Troodos Mountain, vert.	5.00	2.75
654	A223	£5	Personification of Autumn, Dionyssos House, vert.	18.00	17.00
			Nos. 640-654 (15)	30.30	27.55

For surcharges see Nos. 684-685, 712.

Europa A224

6c, Ceramic figures playing the double flute, lyre and tambourine, 7th-6th cent. B.C. 15c, Cypriot violin, lute, flute, the Fourth Women's Dance from the Cyprus Suite.

1985, May 6 Litho. *Perf. 12½*

655	A224	6c	multicolored	.60	.40
656	A224	15c	multicolored	1.40	1.10

Republic of Cyprus, 25th Anniv. — A225

UN 40th Anniv. — A229

Natl. Liberation Movement, 30th Anniv. — A226

Intl. Youth Year A227

Solon Michaelides (1905-1979), Conductor, European Music Year — A228

Perf. 14½ (#657), 14½x14, 15 (#661)

1985, Sept. 23 Litho.

657	A225	4c	multicolored	.25	.25
658	A226	6c	multicolored	.25	.25
659	A227	13c	multicolored	.55	1.10
660	A228	15c	multicolored	.60	1.25
661	A229	20c	multicolored	.80	1.60
			Nos. 657-661 (5)	2.45	4.45

Christmas — A230

Murals of the St. Ioannis Lampadistis Monastery, Kalopanyiotis: 4c, Virgin Mary's Visit to Elizabeth. 13c, The Nativity. 20c, The Candlemas, Church of Our Lady of Assinous, Nikitari.

1985, Nov. 18 Litho. *Perf. 12½*

662	A230	4c	multicolored	.25	.25
663	A230	13c	multicolored	.50	.65
664	A230	20c	multicolored	.85	1.65
			Nos. 662-664 (3)	1.60	2.55

Hellenistic Platinum Spoon A231

Designs: 20c, Ionian helmet, foot of a sculpture. 25c, Union of Eros and Intellect personified, abstract. 30c, Statue profile.

1986, Feb. 17 *Perf. 15x14*

665	A231	15c	multicolored	.70	.70
666	A231	20c	multicolored	.95	.95
667	A231	25c	multicolored	1.20	1.20
668	A231	30c	multicolored	1.50	1.50
a.			Souv. sheet of 4, #665-668	15.00	17.00
			Nos. 665-668 (4)	4.35	4.35

Construction of the New Archaeological Museum, Nicosia. Department of Antiquities, 50th anniv. No. 668a sold for £1.

Europa Issue

Mouflon, Cedar Trees A232

1986, Apr. 28 Litho. *Perf. 14x13*

669	A232	7c	shown	.40	.35
670	A232	17c	Flamingos, Larnaca Salt Lake	1.50	1.25

Seashells A233

1986, July 1 *Perf. 14x13½*

671	A233	5c	Chlamys pesfelis	.35	.35
672	A233	7c	Charonia variegata	.40	.40
673	A233	18c	Murex brandaris	1.00	1.00
674	A233	25c	Cypraea spurca	1.30	1.30
			Nos. 671-674 (4)	3.05	3.05

Overseas Cypriots Year A234

Halley's Comet A235

Anniversaries and events.

Perf. 13½x13

1986, Oct. 13 Litho. Wmk. 344

675	A234	15c	multicolored	1.10	1.10
676	A235	18c	shown	1.60	1.60
677	A235	18c	Comet tail, Edmond Halley	1.60	1.60
a.			Pair, #676-677	3.25	3.25
			Nos. 675-677 (3)	4.30	4.30

No. 677a has continuous design.

Road Safety A236

1986, Nov. 10 *Perf. 14x13*

678	A236	5c	Pedestrian crossing	.60	.60
679	A236	7c	Helmet, motorcycle controls	1.00	1.00
680	A236	18c	Seatbelt, rearview mirror	2.40	2.40
			Nos. 678-680 (3)	4.00	4.00

Intl. Peace Year, Christmas A237

Nativity frescoes (details): 5c, Church of Panayia tou Araka. 15c, Church of Panayia tou Moutoulla. 17c, Church of St. Nicholaos tis Steyis.

1986, Nov. 24 *Perf. 13½x14*
681 A237 5c multicolored .40 .40
682 A237 15c multicolored 1.25 1.25
683 A237 17c multicolored 1.60 1.60
Nos. 681-683 (3) 3.25 3.25

Nos. 645 and 647 Surcharged
Perf. 14x15, 15x14
1986, Oct. 13 Litho. Wmk. 344
684 A223 7c on 6c multi .90 .90
685 A223 18c on 13c multi 1.75 1.75

Miniature Sheet

Troodos Churches on UNESCO World Heritage List — A238

Churches and frescoes: a, Assinou, Nikitari. b, Moutoulla, Moutoullas. c, Podithou, Galata. d, Ayios Ioannis Lampadistis, Kalopanayiotis. e, Timios Stavros, Pelentri. f, Stavros Ayiasmati, Platanistasa. g, Archangelos Pedoula, Pedoulas. h, Ayios Nicolaos tis Steyis, Kakopetria. i, Araka, Lagoudera.

Perf. 12½
1987, Apr. 22 Photo. Unwmk.
686 A238 Sheet of 9 10.00 10.00
a.-i. 15c any single 1.00 1.00

Europa Issue

Modern Architecture A239

Perf. 14x13½
1987, May 11 Litho. Wmk. 344
687 A239 7c Central Bank of Cyprus *.50 .40*
688 A239 18c Cyprus Communications Authority *1.00 .90*

Ships Named Kyrenia A240

1987, Oct. 3
689 A240 2c The Kyrenia, Kyrenia Castle .45 .30
690 A240 3c Kyrenia II, Perama Shipyard .60 .75
691 A240 5c Kyrenia II, Paphos .80 .50
692 A240 17c Kyrenia II, NY Harbor 1.75 1.50
Nos. 689-692 (4) 3.60 3.05

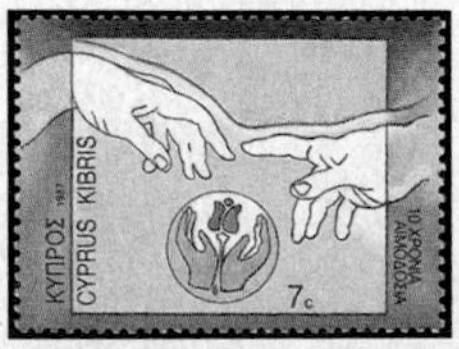

Blood Donation Coordinating Committee, 10th Anniv. — A241

European Campaign for Countryside — A242

TROODOS '87 — A243

Perf. 14x13½
1987, Nov. 2 Litho. Wmk. 344
693 A241 7c multicolored .60 .55
694 A242 15c multicolored 1.40 1.25
695 A243 20c multicolored 2.00 1.75
Nos. 693-695 (3) 4.00 3.55

Christmas A244

1987, Nov. 30 *Perf. 14*
696 A244 5c Babe in a manger .35 .35
697 A244 15c Ornament 1.25 1.25
698 A244 17c Fruit bowl 1.50 1.50
Nos. 696-698 (3) 3.10 3.10

Cyprus Customs Union in Cooperation with the EEC — A245

Perf. 13x13½
1988, Jan. 11 Wmk. 344
699 A245 15c Natl. and EEC flags 1.25 1.25
700 A245 18c Maps 1.60 1.60

A246

Europa (Communication and transportation): No. 701, Electronic mail (Intelpost). No. 702, Cellular telephone system. No. 703, Cyprus Airways, technology vs. ecology (jet, 3 flamingos). No. 704, Cyprus Airways (jet, 4 flamingos).

1988, May 9 *Perf. 14x14½*
701 A246 7c multicolored *.55 .45*
702 A246 7c multicolored *.55 .45*
a. Pair, #701-702 *1.25 1.25*
703 A246 18c multicolored *2.00 1.50*
704 A246 18c multicolored *2.00 1.50*
a. Pair, #703-704 *5.00 5.00*
Nos. 701-704 (4) 5.10 3.90

1988 Summer Olympics, Seoul — A247

Unwmk.
1988, June 27 Photo. *Perf. 12*
Granite Paper
705 A247 5c Sailing .40 .30
706 A247 7c Track .45 .45
707 A247 10c Marksmanship .50 .50
708 A247 20c Judo 1.10 1.10
Nos. 705-708 (4) 2.45 2.35

Non-Aligned Foreign Minister's Conference — A248

Designs: 10c, Natl. coat of arms. 50c, Jawaharlal Nehru, Tito, Gamal Abdel Nasser and Makarios III (1913-77).

Perf. 14x13½
1988, Sept. 5 Litho. Wmk. 344
709 A248 1c shown .25 .25
710 A248 10c multicolored .65 .65
711 A248 50c multicolored 3.00 3.00
Nos. 709-711 (3) 3.90 3.90

No. 643 Srchd.

1988, Oct. 3 Litho. *Perf. 15x14*
712 A223 15c on 4c multi 1.75 1.40

A249

Christmas.

Perf. 13½x14
1988, Nov. 28 Litho. Wmk. 344
713 A249 5c Candlemas .40 .25
714 A249 15c Madonna and child .85 .30
715 A249 17c Adoration of the Magi 1.30 1.30
Nos. 713-715 (3) 2.55 1.85

A250

1988, Dec. 10
716 A250 25c lt ultra & int blue 1.40 1.40

UN Declaration of Human Rights, 40th anniv.

3rd Games of Small European States, Nicosia A251

Perf. 13½
1989, Apr. 10 Litho. Unwmk.
717 A251 1c Discus .40 .30
718 A251 5c Javelin .40 .30
719 A251 15c Wrestling .90 .70
720 A251 18c Running 1.10 1.10

Size: 110x80mm
Imperf
721 A251 £1 Nike, laurel, bird 8.00 8.00
Nos. 717-721 (5) 10.80 10.40

Various Children's Games A252

Perf. 13x13½
1989, May 8 Litho. Unwmk.
722 A252 7c multi (5 boys) *.85 .75*
723 A252 7c multi (6 boys) *.85 .75*
a. Pair, #722-723 *1.90 1.90*
724 A252 18c multi (6 boys) *1.25 1.10*
725 A252 18c multi (5 boys) *1.25 1.10*
a. Pair, #724-725 *2.75 2.75*
Nos. 722-725 (4) 4.20 3.70

Europa.

French Revolution, Bicent. — A253

Perf. 11½
1989, July 7 Litho. Unwmk.
Granite Paper
726 A253 18c multicolored 1.40 1.40

A254

A255

1989, Sept. 4 *Perf. 13½*
727 A254 15c multicolored .65 .65
728 A255 30c multicolored 1.40 1.40

15c for Interparliamentary Union, cent. 30c for 9th Non-Aligned Summit Conf., Belgrade.

Apiculture A256

1989, Oct. 15 *Perf. 13½x14*
729 A256 3c Honeycomb .50 .30
730 A256 10c Gathering nectar .90 .60
731 A256 15c Gathering nectar, diff. 1.10 .60
732 A256 18c Queen, worker bees 1.25 1.50
Nos. 729-732 (4) 3.75 3.00

Annivs. & Events — A257

Designs: 3c, Armenian earthquake. 5c, Cyprus Philatelic Society. 7c, European Cancer Year. 17c, World Food Day.

1989, Nov. 13

733	A257	3c multicolored	.35	.75
734	A257	5c multicolored	.50	.30
735	A257	7c multicolored	.85	1.10
736	A257	17c multicolored	1.25	1.40
		Nos. 733-736 (4)	2.95	3.55

A258

A259

Mosaics, 3rd-5th Cent. A260

Details: 1c, Winter, from *The Four Seasons,* House of Dionysos. 2c, Personification of Crete, from *Theseus Slaying the Minotaur,* Villa of Theseus. 3c, Centaur and Maenad, from *The Dionysiac Procession,* House of Aion, vert. 4c, *Poseidon and Amymone,* House of Dionysos. 5c, Leda, from *Leda and the Swan,* House of Aion. 7c, Apollon, from *Apollo and Marsyas,* House of Aion. 10c, Hermes and Dionysos, from *Hermes Presenting Dionysos to Tropheus,* House of Aion, vert. 15c, Cassiopeia, from *Cassiopeia and the Nereids,* House of Aion. 18c, *Orpheus Playing the Lyre,* House of Orpheus. 20c, Nymphs preparing bath, from *Hermes Presenting Dionysos to Tropheus,* vert. 25c, Amazon holding double ax and reins, House of Orpheus, vert. 40c, Doris, one of 3 Nereids in *Cassiopeia and the Nereids.* 50c, Hercules and the lion, from *The First Labor of Hercules,* House of Orpheus. £1, *Apollon and Daphne,* House of Dionysos. £3, Cupid hunting, Villa of Theseus.

Perf. 13, 13x13½ (2c, 4c, 18c, 40c), 13½x13 (3c, 10c, 20c, 25c)

1989, Dec. 29

737	A258	1c multicolored	.50	1.25
738	A259	2c multicolored	.50	1.25
739	A259	3c multicolored	.65	1.50
740	A259	4c multicolored	.85	1.50
741	A258	5c multicolored	.85	.30
742	A258	7c multicolored	1.10	.35
743	A259	10c multicolored	1.30	.40
744	A258	15c multicolored	2.10	.65
745	A259	18c multicolored	2.10	.70
746	A259	20c multicolored	2.50	1.10
747	A259	25c multicolored	2.50	1.10
748	A259	40c multicolored	3.75	2.25

Perf. 13½x14

749	A260	50c multicolored	2.75	2.25
750	A260	£1 multicolored	6.25	4.50
751	A260	£3 multicolored	13.00	13.00
		Nos. 737-751 (15)	40.70	32.10

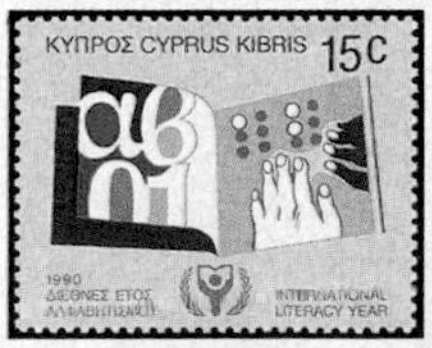

UNESCO World Literacy Year — A261

83rd Interparliamentary Conference, Nicosia — A262

Lions Europa Forum A263

Anniversaries & events.

1990, Apr. 3 ***Perf. 14x13½***

752	A261	15c multicolored	.80	.80
753	A262	17c multicolored	.95	.95
754	A263	18c multicolored	1.25	1.25
		Nos. 752-754 (3)	3.00	3.00

Europa A264

Post Offices.

1990, May 10 **Litho.** ***Perf. 13x13½***

755	A264	7c Paphos	*1.00*	*.45*
756	A264	18c Limassol City Center	*1.75*	*1.25*

European Year of Tourism — A265

Designs: 5c, Hotel and Catering Institute, 25th anniv. 7c, Holy Church of St. Lazarus, 1100th anniv. 15c, Female silhouette, butterflies. 18c, Male silhouette, birds.

1990, July 9 ***Perf. 14***

757	A265	5c multicolored	.60	.60
758	A265	7c multicolored	.75	.75
759	A265	15c multicolored	2.10	1.75
760	A265	18c multicolored	2.40	2.40
		Nos. 757-760 (4)	5.85	5.50

Republic of Cyprus, 30th Anniv. A266

1990, Sept. 29 **Photo.** ***Perf. 11½***

761	A266	15c Sun	.75	.60
762	A266	17c shown	.95	.70
763	A266	18c Fish	1.25	.80
764	A266	40c Birds, flowers	3.00	3.00

Size: 90x90mm

Imperf

765	A266	£1 Stylized bird	6.50	6.50
		Nos. 761-765 (5)	12.45	11.60

Flowers — A267

Christmas — A268

1990, Nov. 5 **Litho.** ***Perf. 13½x13***

766	A267	2c Chionodoxa lochiae	.40	*1.25*
767	A267	3c Pancrayium maritimum	.60	*1.25*
768	A267	5c Paeonia mascula	.85	.65
769	A267	7c Cyclamen cyprium	1.10	1.00
770	A267	15c Tulipa cypria	2.25	2.25
771	A267	18c Crocus cyprius	2.40	3.00
		Nos. 766-771 (6)	7.60	9.40

1990, Dec. 3 ***Perf. 13½x14***

772	A268	5c Nativity	.90	.30
773	A268	15c Virgin and Child	1.90	.45
774	A268	17c Nativity, diff.	2.25	1.90
		Nos. 772-774 (3)	5.05	2.65

Mosaics From Kanakaria Church — A269

1991, Mar. 28 **Photo.** ***Perf. 12***

Granite Paper

775	A269	5c Archangel	.80	.25
776	A269	15c Christ Child	.85	.75
777	A269	17c St. James	1.60	1.60
778	A269	18c St. Matthew	1.75	1.75
		Nos. 775-778 (4)	5.00	4.35

Europa A270

1991, May 6 **Litho.** ***Perf. 13x13½***

779	A270	7c Spacecraft Ulysses	*.75*	*.40*
780	A270	18c Spacecraft Giotto	*1.60*	*1.10*

Oenanthe Cypriaca (Cyprus Wheatear) A271

1991, July 4 **Litho.** ***Perf. 13½***

781	A271	5c Juvenile bird	1.10	.50
782	A271	7c Autumn plumage	1.25	.50
783	A271	15c Male bird	1.50	.75
784	A271	30c Female bird	2.40	3.25
		Nos. 781-784 (4)	6.25	5.00

UN High Commissioner for Refugees, 40th Anniv. — A272

1991, Oct. 7 **Litho.** ***Perf. 14x13½***

785	A272	5c shown	.35	.25
786	A272	15c Legs	1.40	.75
787	A272	18c Faces	1.75	2.10
		Nos. 785-787 (3)	3.50	3.10

Christmas A273

1991, Nov. 25 **Litho.** ***Perf. 13½***

788	A273	5c Nativity scene	.35	.25
789	A273	15c St. Basil	.85	.85
790	A273	17c Baptism of Jesus	1.10	1.50
a.		Strip of 3, #788-790	2.75	2.75

Strips of 3 are from sheets of 9.

A274

1992, Apr. 3 **Litho.** ***Perf. 12***

Granite Paper

791	A274	10c Swimming	1.10	.60
792	A274	20c Long jump	1.50	1.00
793	A274	30c Running	2.25	2.25
794	A274	35c Discus	2.50	2.50
		Nos. 791-794 (4)	7.35	6.35

1992 Summer Olympics, Barcelona.

Expo '92, Seville A275

10th Youth Under 16 European Soccer Tournament — A276

Opening of University of Cyprus A277

1992, Apr. 20 **Litho.** ***Perf. 14***

795	A275	20c multicolored	2.00	.95
796	A276	25c multicolored	2.10	1.25
797	A277	30c multicolored	2.10	2.10
		Nos. 795-797 (3)	6.20	4.30

Discovery of America, 500th Anniv. A278

1992, May 29 **Litho.** ***Perf. 13x13½***

798	A278	10c Map	*1.00*	*.90*
799	A278	10c Embarkation at Palos	*1.00*	*.90*
a.		Pair, #798-799	*2.25*	*2.25*
800	A278	30c Three ships	*1.50*	*1.25*
801	A278	30c Columbus	*1.50*	*1.25*
a.		Pair, #800-801	*3.25*	*3.25*
		Nos. 798-801 (4)	5.00	4.30

Europa.

Reptiles A279

Designs: 7c, Chamaeleo chamaeleon. 10c, Lacerta laevis troodica. 15c, Mauremys caspica. 20c, Coluber cypriensis.

1992, Sept. 14 **Litho.** ***Perf. 14x13½***

802	A279	7c multicolored	1.00	.40
803	A279	10c multicolored	1.10	.65
804	A279	15c multicolored	1.60	1.10
805	A279	20c multicolored	2.10	2.50
		Nos. 802-805 (4)	5.80	4.65

Intl. Maritime and Shipping Conference — A280

Unwmk.

1992, Nov. 9 Litho. *Perf. 14*

806	A280 50c multicolored	4.00	4.00

Christmas A281

Church wall paintings: 7c, , "Virgin Mary Greeting Elizabeth," Church of Timios Stavros, Pelendri. 15c, "The Virgin and Child," Church of Panayia tou Araka. 20c, "Holy Mother Odigitria," Church of Ayios Nicolaos tis Steyis.

1992, Nov. 9 *Perf. 13½x14*

807	A281 7c multicolored	.60	.35
808	A281 15c multicolored	1.00	.75
809	A281 20c multicolored	1.50	2.00
	Nos. 807-809 (3)	3.10	3.10

A282

1993, Feb. 15 Litho. *Perf. 14*

810	A282 10c multicolored	1.00	.80

Pancyprian Gymnasium, cent.

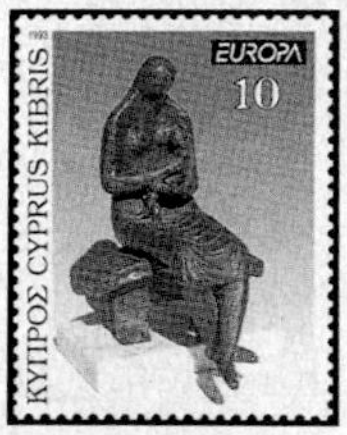

A283

Europa: 10c, Bronze sculpture, Motherhood, by N. Dymiotis (1930-1990). 30c, Applique, Motherhood, by Savva (1924-1968), horiz.

1993, Apr. 3 *Perf. 13½x14, 14x13½*

811	A283 10c multicolored	*.90*	*.65*
812	A283 30c multicolored	*1.60*	*1.25*

13th European Cup for Women Athletes A284

Scouting in Cyprus, 80th Anniv. — A285

Water Skiing Moufflon Encouragement Cup — A286

Archbishop Makarios III, 80th Anniv. of Birth — A287

Perf. 13½x14, 14x13½

1993, May 24 Litho.

813	A284 7c multicolored	.50	.40
814	A285 10c multicolored	.70	.55
815	A286 20c multicolored	1.25	1.25
a.	Inscribed "MUFFLON"	20.00	
816	A287 25c multicolored	1.75	2.25
	Nos. 813-816 (4)	4.20	4.45

Fish — A288

1993, Sept. 6 Litho. *Perf. 14x13½*

817	A288 7c Holocentrus ruber	.60	.35
818	A288 15c Scorpaena scrofa	.90	.70
819	A288 20c Serranus scriba	1.00	1.00
820	A288 30c Balistes capriscus	2.00	2.40
	Nos. 817-820 (4)	4.50	4.45

Maritime Cyprus A289

1993, Oct. 4 *Perf. 14*

821	A289 25c multicolored	2.25	2.25

12th Commonwealth Summit Conference — A290

1993, Oct. 4 *Perf. 14x13½*

822	A290 35c red brown & tan	2.10	2.10
823	A290 40c olive brown & tan	2.75	2.75

Christmas A291

7c, Carved wooden cross, Stavrovouni Monastery. 20c, Crucifixion, cross from Lefkara Church. 25c, Nativity, cross from Pedoulas Church.

1993, Nov. 22 Litho. *Perf. 13½x14*

824	A291 7c multicolored	.40	.30
825	A291 20c multicolored	.95	.95

Perf. 14x13½

826	A291 25c multi, horiz.	1.40	2.00
	Nos. 824-826 (3)	2.75	3.25

Copper Industry A292

Europa: 10c, Early smelting of copper. 30c, Map, boat, copper ingot.

1994, Mar. 1 Litho. *Perf. 13x13½*

827	A292 10c multicolored	*.70*	*1.90*
828	A292 30c multicolored	*1.25*	*1.10*

Persons with Special Needs — A293

Intl. Olympic Committee, Cent. — A294

World Gymnasiade, Nicosia — A295

Intl. Year of the Family — A296

1994, May 9 Litho. *Perf. 13*

829	A293 7c multicolored	.55	.35
830	A294 15c multicolored	1.00	.65
831	A295 20c multicolored	1.25	1.25
832	A296 25c multicolored	1.50	1.90
	Nos. 829-832 (4)	4.30	4.15

Turkish Invasion and Occupation of Cyprus, 20th Anniv. — A297

1994, June 27 Litho. *Perf. 14*

833	A297 10c Human rights	.80	.40
834	A297 50c Cultural heritage	3.25	3.25

Trees — A298

7c, Pinus nigra. 15c, Cedrus libani. 20c, Quercus alnifolia. 30c, Arbutus andrachne.

1994, Oct. 10 Litho. *Perf. 13½*

835	A298 7c multicolored	.70	.40
836	A298 15c multicolored	1.10	.80
837	A298 20c multicolored	1.25	1.40
838	A298 30c multicolored	1.90	2.25
	Nos. 835-838 (4)	4.95	4.85

ICAO, 50th Anniv. A299

1994, Nov. 21 Litho. *Perf. 14*

839	A299 30c multicolored	3.25	3.25

Christmas A300

Designs: 7c, Virgin Mary (Vlahernitissa). 20c, Nativity. 25c, Archangel Michael.

1994, Nov. 21 *Perf. 13½*

840	A300 7c multicolored	.80	.50
841	A300 20c multicolored	1.90	1.00
842	A300 25c multicolored	2.50	3.00
	Nos. 840-842 (3)	5.20	4.50

Traditional Costumes — A301

Costumes: 1c, Female, Phapos. 2c, Bridal, Karpess. 3c, Female, Phapos, diff. 5c, Female, Messaoria. 7c, Bridegroom's. 10c, Shepherd's, Messaoria. 15c, Festive female, Nicosia. 20c, Festive female, Karpass. 25c, Female, Mountain-Pitsillia. 30c, Festive female, Karpass, diff. 35c, Rural male. 40c, Plain festive male, Messaoria. 50c, Urban male. £1, Urban festive female, Sarka.

1994, Dec. 27 Litho. *Perf. 13½x13*

843	A301 1c multicolored	.40	.40
844	A301 2c multicolored	.60	.60
845	A301 3c multicolored	.65	.65
846	A301 5c multicolored	.80	.80
847	A301 7c multicolored	.85	.85
848	A301 10c multicolored	1.25	1.25
849	A301 15c multicolored	2.10	2.10
850	A301 20c multicolored	2.10	2.10
851	A301 25c multicolored	2.40	2.40
852	A301 30c multicolored	2.40	2.40
853	A301 35c multicolored	2.40	2.40
854	A301 40c multicolored	2.75	2.75
855	A301 50c multicolored	3.50	3.50
856	A301 £1 multicolored	6.00	6.00
a.	Inscribed "1998"	6.00	6.00
	Nos. 843-856 (14)	28.20	28.20

Third Intl. Congress of Cypriot Studies — A302

Excavations: 20c, Hearth room, Ashlar building, Paliotaverna. 30c, Hall, Agios Demetrios area, Kalavasos. £1, Old Nicosia Archbishorpic building, 18th cent.

1995, Feb. 27 Litho. *Perf. 14*

859	A302 20c multicolored	1.25	1.25
860	A302 30c multicolored	1.90	1.90

Size: 107x71mm

Imperf

861	A302 £1 multicolored	5.75	5.75
	Nos. 859-861 (3)	8.90	8.90

A303

A304

Liberation Monument, Nicosia: a, People walking left. b, Statue of Liberty, prisoners leaving prison. c, People walking right.

1995, Mar. 31 Litho. *Perf. 13x14*

862	Strip of 3	4.25	4.25
a.-c.	A303 20c any single	1.35	1.35

No. 862 is a continuous design.
Formation of EOKA (Natl. Organization of Cypriot Struggle), 40th anniv.

1995, May 8 Litho. *Perf. 13½*

Europa: 10c, Concentration camp prisoners, dove, rainbow, map of Europe. 30c, Prisoner, dove.

863	A304 10c multicolored	*1.00*	*.75*
864	A304 30c multicolored	*2.00*	*1.60*

Liberation of the concentration camps, 50th anniv.

Health
A305

7c, Proper nutrition, exercise. 10c, Fight against AIDS. 15c, Fight against illegal drugs. 20c, Stop smoking campaign.

1995, June 26 Litho. *Perf. 13½*

865	A305 7c multi, vert.	.35	.30
866	A305 10c multi	.75	.75
867	A305 15c multi	.80	.80
868	A305 20c multi, vert.	1.10	1.10
	Nos. 865-868 (4)	3.00	2.95

European Cultural Month
A306

1995, Sept. 18 Litho. *Perf. 13x13½*

869	A306 20c shown	.85	.85
870	A306 25c Map of Europe, building	1.10	1.10

Souvenir Sheet

Europhilex '95 — A307

Designs: a, Dove carrying letter, stars. b, Stars, exhibition emblem.

1995, Sept. 18 Litho. *Perf. 14*

871	A307 Sheet of 2	8.75	8.75
a.-b.	50c any single	4.00	4.00

A limited number were surcharged £5 on each stamp and sold at "Europhilex '95" on Oct. 27 and 28, 1995.

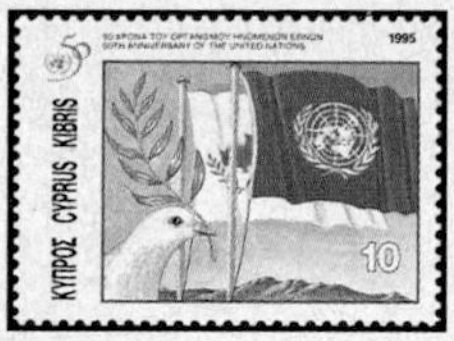

UN, 50th Anniv.
A308

Volleyball, Cent. — A309

European Conservation Year — A310

World Clay Target Shooting Championships — A311

Perf. 13x13½, 13½x13

1995, Oct. 24 Litho.

872	A308 10c multicolored	.65	.65
873	A309 15c multicolored	1.00	.75
874	A310 20c multicolored	1.40	1.10
875	A311 25c multicolored	1.60	2.10
	Nos. 872-875 (4)	4.65	4.60

Christmas
A312

Various reliquaries, Kykko Monastery.

1995, Nov. 27 Litho. *Perf. 13½x13*

876	A312 7c multicolored	.60	.45
877	A312 20c multicolored	1.40	1.10
878	A312 25c multicolored	1.75	1.75
	Nos. 876-878 (3)	3.75	3.30

A313

A314

A315

Anniversaries and Events — A316

1996, Jan. 4 Litho. *Perf. 13½x13*

879	A313 10c multicolored	.90	.65
880	A314 20c multicolored	1.50	1.10
881	A315 35c multicolored	2.25	2.25
882	A316 40c multicolored	2.25	2.25
	Nos. 879-882 (4)	6.90	6.25

Pancyprian Organization of Large Families, 25th anniv. (No. 879). Motion pictures, cent. (NO. 880). UNICEF, 50th anniv. (No. 881). 13th Conf. of Commonwealth Speakers and Presiding Officers (No. 882).

Portraits of Women
A317 A318

1996, Apr. 8 Litho. *Perf. 14*

883	A317 10c multicolored	*1.10*	*.50*
884	A318 30c multicolored	*2.40*	*1.40*

Europa.

1996 Summer Olympics, Atlanta
A319

1996, June 10 Litho. *Perf. 13*

885	A319 10c High jump	.90	.35
886	A319 20c Javelin	1.25	.70
887	A319 25c Wrestling	1.75	1.00
888	A319 30c Swimming	2.10	2.10
	Nos. 885-888 (4)	6.00	4.15

Mills of Cyprus — A320

1996, Sept. 23 Litho. *Perf. 13*

889	A320 10c Watermill	.95	.70
890	A320 15c Olivemill	1.40	1.00
891	A320 20c Windmill	1.50	1.40
892	A320 25c Handmill	2.25	2.25
	Nos. 889-892 (4)	6.10	5.35

Icons, Religious Landmarks
A321

Designs: No. 893, Icon of Our Lady of Iberia, Moscow. No. 894, Holy Monastery of Stavrovouni, Cyprus. No. 895, Icon of St. Nicholas, Cyprus. No. 896, Iveron Mother of God Resurrection Gate, Moscow.

1996, Nov. 13 Litho. *Perf. 11½*

893	A321 30c multicolored	2.10	2.10
894	A321 30c multicolored	2.10	2.10
895	A321 30c multicolored	2.10	2.10
896	A321 30c multicolored	2.10	2.10
a.	Block of 4, #893-896	9.00	9.00

See Russia No. 6356.

Christmas
A322

Paintings from Church of the Virgin of Asinou: 7c, Detail from Nativity. 20c, Virgin Mary between Archangels Gabriel and Michael. 25c, Christ bestowing blessings, vert.

1996, Dec. 2 *Perf. 13x13½, 13½x13*

897	A322 7c multicolored	1.00	.50
898	A322 20c multicolored	2.25	1.25
899	A322 25c multicolored	2.75	2.75
	Nos. 897-899 (3)	6.00	4.50

Easter
A323

1997, Mar. 24 Litho. *Perf. 13x13½*

900	A323 15c The Last Supper	1.25	.75
901	A323 25c The Crucifixion	1.75	1.75

A324

1997, Mar. 24 *Perf. 13½x13*

902	A324 30c multicolored	4.25	3.75

European Men's Clubs Basketball Cup finals.

A325

Europa (Stories and Legends): 30c, Man in red cape fighting Death, eagle above.

1997, May 5 Litho. *Perf. 13½x13*

903	A325 15c shown	*1.00*	*.50*
904	A325 30c multicolored	*2.00*	*1.10*

Insects
A326

10c, Oedipoda miniata. 15c, Acherontia atropos. 25c, Daphnis nerii. 35c, Ascalaphus macaronius.

1997, June 30 Litho. *Perf. 13x13½*
905 A326 10c multicolored 1.00 .50
906 A326 15c multicolored 1.50 .70
907 A326 25c multicolored 2.00 1.50
908 A326 35c multicolored 2.50 2.50
Nos. 905-908 (4) 7.00 5.20

Archbishop Makarios III (1913-77), 1st Pres. of Cyprus Republic
A327

1997, Aug. 1 Litho. *Perf. 13x13½*
909 A327 15c multicolored 1.50 1.50

Christmas
A328

Frescoes from Church of Ayios Ioannis Lambadestis: 10c, Nativity. 25c, Magi on way to Bethlehem. 30c, Flight into Egypt.

1997, Nov. 17 Litho. *Perf. 13½x13*
910 A328 10c multicolored .95 .65
911 A328 25c multicolored 2.40 1.40
912 A328 30c multicolored 2.75 2.75
Nos. 910-912 (3) 6.10 4.80

Minerals
A329

1998, Mar. 9 Litho. *Perf. 13x13½*
913 A329 10c Green jasper .55 .40
914 A329 15c Iron pyrite .80 .65
915 A329 25c Gypsum 1.30 1.30
916 A329 30c Chalcedony 1.60 1.60
Nos. 913-916 (4) 4.25 3.95

1998 World Cup Soccer Championships, France — A330

1998, May 4 Litho. *Perf. 14*
917 A330 35c multicolored 2.75 1.75

Europa
A331

Festivals, holidays: 15c, "Katakklysmos" Larnaca. 30c, People watching proclamation of independence, 1960.

1998, May 4
918 A331 15c multicolored *1.10 .55*
919 A331 30c multicolored *2.40 1.60*

Ovis Gmelini Ophion
A332

World Wildlife Fund: No. 920, Male, female, calf. No. 921, Group running. No. 922, Male up close. No. 923, Male with front legs up on rock, one grazing.

1998, June 22 Litho. *Perf. 13x13½*
920 A332 25c multicolored 1.40 1.40
921 A332 25c multicolored 1.40 1.40
922 A332 25c multicolored 1.40 1.40
923 A332 25c multicolored 1.40 1.40
a. Block of 4, #920-923 5.75 5.75

Issued in sheets of 16.

World Stamp Day
A333

1998, Oct. 9 Litho. *Perf. 14*
924 A333 30c multicolored 2.75 2.75
a. Booklet pane of 8 22.00
Complete booklet, #924a 25.00

A334 A335

1998, Oct. 9
925 A334 50c multicolored 2.00 2.00

Universal Declaration of Human Rights, 50th anniv.

1998, Nov. 16 Litho. *Perf. 14*

Christmas (Scenes from paintings in the Church of the Virgin of Théosképasti, Kalopanayiotis): 10c, The Annunciation. 25c, The Nativity. 30c, Baptism of Christ.

926 A335 10c multicolored .35 .35
927 A335 25c multicolored .90 .90
928 A335 30c multicolored 2.75 2.75
a. Souvenir sheet, #926-928 4.00 4.00
Nos. 926-928 (3) 4.00 4.00

Mushrooms — A336

10c, Pleurotus eryngii. 15c, Lactarius deliciosus. 25c, Sparassis crispa. 30c, Morchella elata.

1999, Mar. 4 Litho. *Perf. 13½x13*
929 A336 10c multicolored .50 .50
930 A336 15c multicolored 1.00 .60
931 A336 25c multicolored 1.50 1.50
932 A336 30c multicolored 1.60 1.60
Nos. 929-932 (4) 4.60 4.20

Natl. Parks and Nature Preserves
A337

1999, May 6 Litho. *Perf. 14*
933 A337 15c Tripylos Reserve *.90 .50*
934 A337 30c Lara Reserve *1.60 1.00*
a. Booklet pane, 4 each #933-934 *11.00*
Complete booklet, #934a *12.00*

Europa.

Council of Europe, 50th Anniv.
A338

1999, May 6
935 A338 30c multicolored 2.10 2.10

4000 Years of Hellenism — A339

a, Sanctuary of Apollo Hylates, Kourion. b, Mycenaean "Krater of the Warriors," Athens. c, Mycenaean amphoral krater, Cyprus Museum. d, Sanctuary of Apollo Epikourios, Delphi.

1999, June 28 Litho. *Perf. 13½x13*
936 A339 25c Block of 4, #a.-d. 6.25 6.25

See Greece No. 1938.

UPU, 125th Anniv.
A340

1999, Sept. 30 Litho. *Perf. 14*
937 A340 15c shown 1.00 .90
938 A340 35c "125" 2.50 2.00

Souvenir Sheet

Maritime Cyprus Shipping Conference — A341

Cyprus flag and: a, Container ship. b, Binoculars, chart, cap. c, Ship with yellow stripe on tower. d, Tanker.

1999, Sept. 30
939 A341 25c Sheet of 4, #a.-d. 5.00 5.00

Souvenir Sheet

Turkish Invasion of Cyprus, 25th Anniv. — A342

1999, Nov. 11 Litho. *Imperf.*
940 A342 30c multicolored 2.50 2.50

A343

1999, Nov. 11 *Perf. 14*
941 A343 10c Angel .70 .55
942 A343 25c Magi 1.40 1.25
943 A343 30c Madonna and child 1.60 1.60
Nos. 941-943 (3) 3.70 3.40

Christmas.

Souvenir Sheet

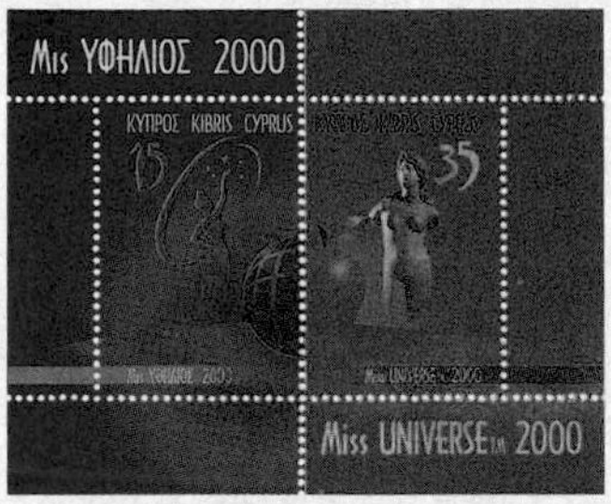

A344

Miss Universe 2000: a, 15c, Woman, stars. b, 35c, Armless nude statue of woman.

2000, Mar. 30 Litho. *Perf. 13¼x13*
944 A344 Sheet of 2, #a.-b. 3.00 3.00

Jewelry — A345

Various pieces of jewelry. Nos. 945-952 vert.

2000, Mar. 30 Litho. *Perf. 14*
945 A345 10c multi .45 .45
946 A345 15c multi .60 .60
947 A345 20c multi .80 .80
948 A345 25c multi 1.00 1.00
949 A345 30c multi 1.25 1.25
950 A345 35c multi 1.40 1.40
951 A345 40c multi 1.60 1.60
952 A345 50c multi 2.25 2.25
953 A345 75c multi 3.00 3.00
954 A345 £1 multi 4.00 4.00
955 A345 £2 multi 7.50 7.50
956 A345 £3 multi 11.00 11.00
Nos. 945-956 (12) 34.85 34.85

Cyprus Red Cross, 50th Anniv.
A346

2000, May 9 Litho. *Perf. 13x13¼*
957 A346 15c multi 2.25 2.25

Memorial to Heroes of 1955-59 Independence Struggle — A347

2000, May 9 *Perf. 13¼x13*
958 A347 15c multi 2.40 2.40

Europa, 2000
Common Design Type

2000, May 9 *Perf. 14*
959 CD17 30c multi *2.10 1.40*

World Meteorological Org., 50th Anniv. — A348

2000, May 9
960 A348 30c multi 2.25 2.25

European Convention of Human Rights, 50th Anniv. A349

2000, June 29 Litho. *Perf. 13x13¼*
961 A349 30c multi 3.00 3.00

Churches Damaged Under Turkish Occupation A350

Designs: 10c, Monastery of Antifonitis, Kalograia, vert. 15c, Church of St. Themonianos, Lysi, vert. 25c, Church of Panagia Kanakaria, Lytrhagkomi. 30c, Avgasida Monastery Church, Milia.

Perf. 13¼x13, 13x13¼
2000, June 29

962	A350 10c multi	1.10	.60
963	A350 15c multi	1.50	.80
964	A350 25c multi	2.00	1.60
965	A350 30c multi	2.40	2.40
	Nos. 962-965 (4)	7.00	5.40

2000 Summer Olympics, Sydney A351

Designs: 10c, Archery. 15c, Pommel horse. 25c, Diving. 35c, Trampoline.

2000, Sept. 14 Litho. *Perf. 13x13½*
966-969 A351 Set of 4 6.00 6.00

Christmas — A352

Gospel covers: 10c, Annunciation. 25c, Nativity. 30c, Baptism of Jesus.

2000, Nov. 2 *Perf. 13½x13*
970-972 A352 Set of 3 5.00 5.00

Pavlos Liasides (1901-85), Poet — A353

2001, Mar. 12 Litho. *Perf. 13¼x13*
973 A353 13c multi 1.25 .65

Commonwealth Day, 25th Anniv. — A354

2001, Mar. 12 *Perf. 13x13¼*
974 A354 30c multi 2.75 2.75

UN High Commissioner for Refugees, 50th Anniv. — A355

2001, Mar. 12
975 A355 30c multi 2.50 2.50

Europa A356

Designs: 20c, Bridge over Diarizos River. 30c, Akaki River.

2001, May 3

976-977	A356 Set of 2	*4.00*	*2.00*
977a	Booklet pane, 4 each #976-977	*17.00*	
	Booklet, #977a	*19.00*	

Crabs A357

Designs: 13c, Parthenope massena. 20c, Calappa granulata. 25c, Ocypode cursor. 30c, Pagurus bernhardus.

2001, June 7
978-981 A357 Set of 4 8.00 8.00

Loukis Akritas (1909-65), Writer A358

Christmas A359

2001, Oct. 25 Litho. *Perf. 13½x13*
982 A358 20c multi 2.00 .90

2001, Oct. 25

Holy Monastery of Macheras, 800th anniv.: 13c, Icon of Madonna. 25c, Monastery building. 30c, Crucifix.

983-985 A359 Set of 3 4.50 4.50

Cats — A360

No. 986, 20c: a, Red brown panel. b, Green panel.
No. 987, 25c: a, Dark brown panel. b, Orange brown panel.

2002, Mar. 21 Litho. *Perf. 13x13½*
Horiz. Pairs, #a-b
986-987 A360 Set of 2 6.75 6.75

Europa — A361

Designs: 20c, Equestrian act. 30c, Tightrope walker.

2002, May 9 *Perf. 13½x13*

988-989	A361 Set of 2	*4.00*	*2.00*
a.	Booklet pane, 4 each #988-989	*17.00*	—
	Booklet, #989a	*19.00*	

Medicinal Plants A362

Designs: 13c, Myrtus communis. 20c, Lavandula stoechas. 25c, Capparis spinosa. 30c, Ocimum basilicum.

2002, June 13 *Perf. 13x13½*
990-993 A362 Set of 4 6.50 6.50

Mother Teresa (1910-97) — A363

2002, Sept. 12 Litho. *Perf. 13½x13*
994 A363 40c multi 4.00 4.00

Intl. Teachers' Day — A364

No. 995: a, 13c, Blackboard and teachers. b, 30c, Computer and teachers.

2002, Sept. 12 *Perf. 13x13½*
995 A364 Horiz. pair, #a-b 3.75 3.75

Cyprus-Europhilex 02 Philatelic Exhibition — A365

No. 996: a, Seal, 490-470 B.C. (red brown background). b, Silver coin of Timoharis, 5th-4th cent B.C. (blue background) c, Silver coin of Stasioikos, 449 B.C. (yellow background).
No. 997: a, Clay oil lamp, 2nd cent. A.D. (olive green background). b, Clay statue of Europa on a bull, 7th-6th cent. B.C. (yellow background). c, Clay oil lamp, 1st cent. B.C. (lilac background)
No. 998: a, 15th cent. map of eastern Crete and western Cyprus, and statue of Aphrodite, 1st cent. B.C. b, Map of eastern Cyprus, and Abduction of Europe, by Francesco di Giorgio.

2002, Sept. 22

996	Horiz. strip of 3	4.50	4.50
a.-c.	A365 20c Any single	1.50	1.50
997	Horiz. strip of 3	6.75	6.75
a.-c.	A365 30c Any single	2.25	2.25

Souvenir Sheet

998	Sheet of 2, #a-b	9.00	9.00
a.-b.	A365 50c Any single	3.50	3.50

Christmas A366

Wall painting in Church of Metamorphosis Sotiros, Palechori: 13c, Nativity, detail. 25c, Angels, detail. 30c, Entire painting (37x37mm).

Perf. 13x13½, 13¾ (30c)
2002, Nov. 21
999-1001 A366 Set of 3 5.25 5.25

Antique Automobiles A367

No. 1002: a, 20c, 1946 Triumph Roadster 1800. b, 25c, 1917 Ford Model T. c, 30c, 1932 Baby Ford.

2003, Mar. 20 Litho. *Perf. 13x13½*
1002 A367 Vert. strip of 3, #a-c 6.50 6.50

Europa — A368

2003, May 8 *Perf. 13½x13*
Color of Triangles

1003	A368 20c yellow	*1.00*	*.65*
a.	Perf. 13½x13¾ on 3 sides	*1.75*	*1.10*
1004	A368 30c red	*1.60*	*1.00*
a.	Perf. 13½x13¾ on 3 sides	*3.00*	*1.60*
b.	Booklet pane, 4 each #1003a-1004a	*20.00*	—
	Complete booklet, #1004b	*24.00*	

European Ministers of Education, 7th Conference — A369

2003, June 12 Litho. ***Perf. 13½x13***
1005 A369 30c multi 2.25 2.25

Worldwide Fund for Nature (WWF) — A370

Mediterranean horseshoe bat: a, In flight. b, Close-up. c, Hanging from rock. d, With open mouth.

2003, June 12 ***Perf. 13x13½***
1006 A370 25c Block of 4, #a-b 7.00 7.00

Birds of Prey — A371

No. 1007, 20c: a, Eleonora's falcon. b, Eleonora's falcons in flight.
No. 1008, 25c: a, Head of Imperial eagle. b, Imperial eagles in flight.
No. 1009, 30c: a, Owl on branch. b, Owl in flight, eggs.

2003, Sept. 25 Litho. ***Perf. 14***
Horiz. pairs, #a-b
1007-1009 A371 Set of 3 9.50 9.50

Famous Men A372

Designs: No. 1010, 5c, Constantinos Spyridakis (1903-76), Education minister. No. 1011, 5c, Tefkros Anthias (1903-68), poet (23x31mm).

Perf. 13x13¼, 13¼x13
2003, Nov. 13
1010-1011 A372 Set of 2 1.25 1.25

Christmas A373

Details of Nativity icon from church in Kourdali: 13c, Angels. 30c, Three Magi on horses. 40c, Entire icon (37x60mm).

Perf. 13¾x13¼, 13¾x14 (40c)
2003, Nov. 13
1012-1014 A373 Set of 3 5.25 5.25

FIFA (Fédération Internationale de Football Association), Cent. — A374

Perf. 13¼x13¾
2004, Mar. 11 Litho.
1015 A374 30c multi 2.10 2.10

UEFA (European Soccer Union), 50th Anniv. — A375

2004, Mar. 11 ***Perf. 13¼x13***
1016 A375 30c multi 2.10 2.10

Yiannos Kranidiotis (1947-99), Politician A376

2004, May 1 ***Perf. 13¼x13½***
1017 A376 20c multi 1.25 1.25

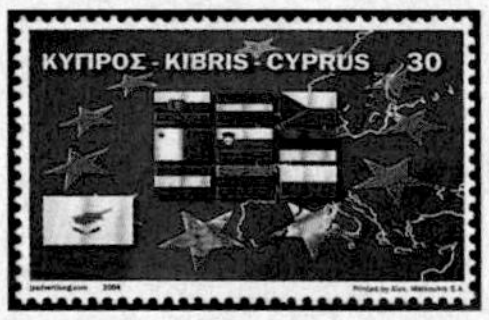

Admission to European Union — A377

2004, May 1 ***Perf. 14¼x14***
1018 A377 30c multi 2.10 2.10

Europa A378

Cliff and: 20c, Amphitheater, ship. 30c, Family at seashore, sculpture

2004, May 1 ***Perf. 13¾x13¼***
1019 A378 20c multi *1.25 .60*
a. Perf. 13¾ on 3 sides *1.50 .70*
1020 A378 30c multi *1.75 .90*
a. Perf. 13¾ on 3 sides *2.00 1.10*
b. Booklet pane, 4 each #1019a, 1020a *16.00 —*
Complete booklet, #1020b *18.00*

2004 Summer Olympics, Athens — A379

Designs: 13c, Equestrian. 20c, Runners. 30c, Swimmers. 40c, Athletes, man in robe.

2004, June 10 Litho. ***Perf. 13¼x13***
1021-1024 A379 Set of 4 5.75 5.75

Mammals — A380

No. 1025, 20c — Tursiops truncatus: a, Blue background. b, White background.
No. 1026, 30c — Vulpes vulpes indutus: a, Green background. b, White background.
No. 1027, 40c, Lepus europaeus cyprium: a, Orange brown background. b, White background.

2004, Sept. 9 Litho. ***Perf. 13¾x13½***
Horiz. Pairs, #a-b
1025-1027 A380 Set of 3 12.00 12.00

Georgios Philippou Pierides (1904-99), Writer — A381

Emilios Chourmouzios (1904-73), Writer — A382

2004, Nov. 11 ***Perf. 13¼x13***
1028 A381 5c multi .55 .55
1029 A382 5c multi .55 .55

Christmas A383

Details from icon depicting the birth of Christ, Monastery of Chrysoroyiatissa: 13c, Angels. 30c, Magi on horseback. 40c, Annunciation, vert. (37x60mm).
£1, Adoration of the Shepherds.

Perf. 13¾x13¼, 13¾x14 (40c)
2004, Nov. 11
1030-1032 A383 Set of 3 6.00 6.00

Souvenir Sheet
Perf. 13¾ on 3 Sides
1033 A383 £1 multi 6.75 6.75

No. 1033 contains one 37x38mm stamp.

Carolina Pelendritou, Swimming Gold Medalist at 2004 Paralympics A384

2005, Mar. 3 Litho. ***Perf. 13¼x13¾***
1034 A384 20c multi 1.40 1.40

Rotary International, Cent. — A385

2005, Mar. 3
1035 A385 40c multi 2.50 2.50

Natl. Organization of Cypriot Struggle (EOKA), 50th Anniv. — A386

2005, Mar. 3
1036 A386 50c multi 2.75 2.75

Europa — A387

Table with food and: 20c, Purple grapes, sailboat. 30c, Green grapes, steamship.

2005, May 5 ***Perf. 13½x13***
White Frame All Around
1037 A387 20c multi .90 .90
1038 A387 30c multi 1.40 1.40

Booklet Stamps
White Frame on 3 Sides
Perf. 13½ on 3 Sides
1039 A387 20c multi *1.25 .75*
1040 A387 30c multi *1.75 1.25*
a. Horiz. pair, #1039-1040 *3.25 2.25*
b. Booklet pane, 4 #1040a *13.50 —*
Complete booklet, #1040b *15.00*
Nos. 1037-1040 (4) 5.30 4.30

Dogs — A388

Designs: 13c, German shepherd. 20c, Hungarian vizsla. 30c, Labrador retriever. 40c, Dalmatian.

2005, June 16 Litho. ***Perf. 13¼***
1041-1044 A388 Set of 4 8.00 8.00
1044a Booklet pane, #1041-1044 8.50 —
Complete booklet, #1044a 8.50

Christmas A389

Icons: 13c, Annunciation to the Shepherds. 30c, Adoration of the Magi. 40c, Madonna and Child, vert. (38x60mm).

Perf. 13¼, 13¾x14 (40c)
2005, Nov. 10 Litho.
1045-1047 A389 Set of 3 4.25 4.25

Souvenir Sheet

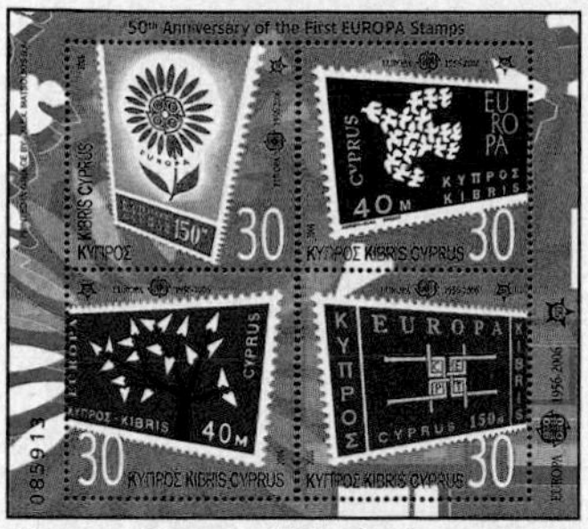

Europa Stamps, 50th Anniv. — A390

No. 1048: a, Cyprus #246. b, Cyprus #202. c, Cyprus #220. d, Cyprus #231.

2006, Feb. 23 **Litho.** ***Perf. 13¾***
1048 A390 30c Sheet of 4, #a-d 6.00 6.00

Postal Museum, 25th Anniv. A391

2006, Mar. 30 ***Perf. 13¾x13¼***
1049 A391 25c multi 1.50 1.50

Rembrandt (1606-69), Painter A392

2006, Mar. 30
1060 A392 40c multi 2.75 2.75

2006 World Cup Soccer Championships, Germany A393

2006, Mar. 30 ***Perf. 13¼x13¾***
1051 A393 50c multi 3.00 3.00

Souvenir Sheet

Folk Dances — A394

No. 1052 — Folk dancers from: a, Cyprus. b, India.

2006, Apr. 12 ***Perf. 13x13½***
1052 A394 40c Sheet of 2, #a-b 5.00 5.00

See India No. 2151.

Europa — A395

2006, May 4 ***Perf. 13½x13***
1053 A395 30c grn & multi 1.50 1.50
a. Perf. 13½x13¾ on 3 sides 1.50 1.50
1054 A395 40c red & multi 1.90 1.90
a. Perf. 13½x13¾ on 3 sides 1.90 1.90
b. Booklet pane, 4 each #1053a-1054a 14.00 —
Complete booklet, #1054b 14.00

Organ Transplantation — A396

2006, June 15 **Litho.** ***Perf. 13¼***
1055 A396 13c multi .85 .85

Fruit — A397

Designs: 20c, Elaeagnus angustifolia. 25c, Mespilus germanica, horiz. 60c, Opuntia ficus barbarica.

Perf. 13¼x13½, 13½x13¼
2006, June 15
1056-1058 A397 Set of 3 6.25 6.25

Fire Trucks A398

Designs: 13c, Bedford water carrier. 20c, Hino pump water tender. 50c, Bedford ladder truck.

2006, Sept. 14 ***Perf. 13¾x13¼***
1059-1061 A398 Set of 3 5.50 5.50

Nicos Nicolaides (1884-1956), Writer — A399

2006, Nov. 16 **Litho.** ***Perf. 13½x13***
1062 A399 5c multi .50 .50

Christmas — A400

Items from Agiou Eleftheriou Church: 13c, Carved wood iconostasis. 30c, Cross. 40c, Bas-relief of cross, spear and sponge.

2006, Nov. 16 ***Perf. 13¼x13¾***
1063-1065 A400 Set of 3 4.25 4.25

St. Xenon, the Postman — A401

Litho. & Embossed

2007, Feb. 8 ***Imperf.***
1066 A401 £1 multi 7.75 7.75

Echinoderms — A402

No. 1067: a, Antedon mediterranea. b, Centrostephanus longispinus. c, Astropecten jonstoni. d, Ophioderma longicadum.

2007, Feb. 8 **Litho.** ***Perf. 13¾x13¼***
1067 Horiz. strip of 4 6.50 6.50
a.-d. A402 25c Any single 1.60 1.60

Motorcycles A403

Designs: 13c, 1972 Triumph Daytona. 20c, 1941 Matchless. 40c, 1940 BSA. 60c, 1939 Ariel Red Hunter.

2007, Mar. 15
1068-1071 A403 Set of 4 7.00 7.00

Treaty of Rome, 50th Anniv. — A404

2007, May 3 ***Perf. 13¼x13¾***
1072 A404 30c multi 1.60 1.60

Europa — A405

Scouting emblem in gold, knot in: 30c, Light blue. 40c, Buff.

Litho. & Embossed With Foil Application

2007, May 3
1073-1074 A405 Set of 2 3.25 3.25
1074a Booklet pane, 4 each #1073-1074, perf. on 3 sides 13.00 —
Complete booklet, #1074a 13.00

Scouting, cent.

Social Insurance, 50th Anniv. — A406

No. 1075: a, Text in Greek. b, Text in English.

2007, June 14 **Litho.** ***Perf. 13x13¼***
1075 A406 40c Horiz. pair, #a-b 4.00 4.00

Miniature Sheet

Cyprus Throughout the Ages — A407

No. 1076: a, Skeleton of pygmy hippopotamus, 10,000 B.C. b, Stone vessel, 7000 B.C. c, Choirokoitia Settlement, 7000 B.C. d, Female terracotta figurine, 3000 B.C. e, Terracotta vessel, 2000 B.C. f, Greek inscriptions on bronze skewer, 1000 B.C. g, Bird-shaped vessel, 800 B.C. h, Map of ancient kingdoms of Cyprus.

2007, Oct. 2 ***Perf. 13¾***
1076 A407 25c Sheet of 8, #a-h 11.00 11.00

See Nos. 1101, 1116, 1138.

Neoclassical Buildings A408

Designs: 13c, Limassol District Administration Building. 15c, National Bank of Greece Building, Nicosia. 20c, Archaeological Research Unit Building, Nicosia. 30c, National Art Gallery, Nicosia. 40c, Paphos Municipal Library. 50c, A. G. Leventis Foundation Office Building, Nicosia. £1, Limassol Municipal Library. £3, Phaneromeni Gymnasium, Nicosia.

2007, Oct. 2 ***Perf. 13¾x13½***
1077 A408 13c multi .65 .65
1078 A408 15c multi .75 .75
1079 A408 20c multi 1.00 1.00
1080 A408 30c multi 1.50 1.50
1081 A408 40c multi 2.00 2.00
1082 A408 50c multi 2.40 2.40
1083 A408 £1 multi 5.00 5.00
1084 A408 £3 multi 14.50 14.50
Nos. 1077-1084 (8) 27.80 27.80

Christmas — A409

Murals from Chapel of St. Themonianus, Lysi: 13c, Virgin Mary. 30c, Archangel Gabriel. 40c, Christ Pantocrator (35x45mm).

Perf. 14x13¾, 13¾ (40c)

2007, Nov. 15
1085-1087 A409 Set of 3 4.50 4.50

100 Cents = 1 Euro

Souvenir Sheet

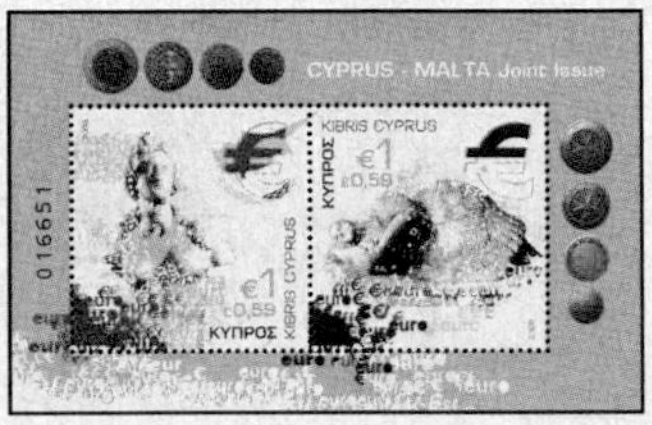

Introduction of Euro Currency — A410

No. 1088: a, Statue of Aphrodite, map of Cyprus. b, Sleeping Lady statue.

2008, Jan. 1 Litho. *Perf. 13¾*
1088 A410 €1 Sheet of 2, #a-b 5.50 5.50

See Malta No. 1329.

Anemone Flowers — A411

Variously colored Anemone coronaria flowers with background colors of: 26c, Blue. 34c, Red. 51c, Green. 68c, Yellow orange.

2008, Mar. 6 *Perf. 13¼x13¾*
1089-1092 A411 Set of 4 6.00 6.00

Europa — A412

Designs: 51c, Closed and open envelopes. 68c, Envelopes and mail boxes.

2008, May 2 Litho. *Perf. 13¼x13¾*
1093-1094 A412 Set of 2 3.75 3.75
1094a Booklet pane, 4 each #1093-1094, perf. 13¼x13¾ on 3 sides 15.00 —
Complete booklet, #1094a 15.00

Souvenir Sheet

Fourth Intl. Congress of Cypriot Studies, Nicosia — A413

2008, May 2 *Perf. 13¾ on 3 Sides*
1095 A413 85c multi 3.25 3.25

12th Francophone Summit, Quebec — A414

2008, June 5 Litho. *Perf. 13¾*
1096 A414 85c multi 3.00 3.00

2008 Summer Olympics, Beijing
A415

Designs: 22c, Sailboarding. 34c, High jump. 43c, Tennis. 51c, Shooting.

2008, June 5 *Perf. 13x13¼*
1097-1100 A415 Set of 4 4.75 4.75

Cyprus Throughout the Years Type of 2007

Miniature Sheet

No. 1101: a, Coin from Archaic period, 750 B.C.-480 B.C. b, Ship from Archaic period. c, Bust of Kimon the Athenian and ship, Classical period, 480 B.C.-310 B.C. d, Tomb of the Kings, Hellenistic period, 310 B.C.-30 B.C. e, Coin from Hellenistic period. f, Painting of St. Paul from Roman period, 30 B.C.-A.D. 324. g, Bust of Septimus Severus from Roman period. h, Granting of church privileges from Early Byzantine period, 324-841.

2008, Oct. 2 Litho. *Perf. 13¾*
1101 A407 43c Sheet of 8, #a-h 11.00 11.00

Christmas — A416

Icons from church, Pelendri: 22c, Archangel Gabriel. 51c, Archangel Michael. 68c, Madonna and Child.

2008, Nov. 13 *Perf. 13¼x13*
1102-1104 A416 Set of 3 4.75 4.75

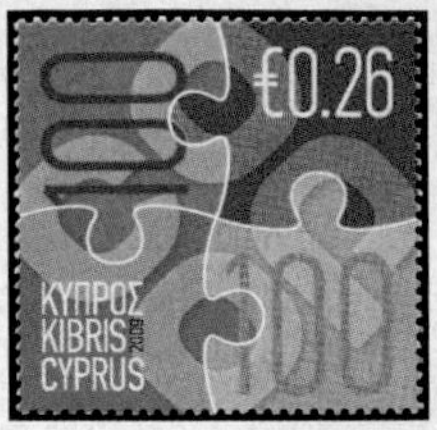

Cooperative Movement, Cent.
A417

2009, Mar. 12 Litho. *Perf. 13¾*
1105 A417 26c multi .85 .85

Louis Braille (1809-52), Educator of the Blind
A418

2009, Mar. 12 Litho. & Embossed
1106 A418 68c multi 2.25 2.25

Introduction of the Euro, 10th Anniv.
A419

Reverse of Cyprus: 51c, Cent coin. 68c, 2-euro coin.

2009, Mar. 12 Litho.
1107-1108 A419 Set of 2 4.25 4.25

Intl. Year of Planet Earth — A420

No. 1109: a, Western Hemisphere. b, Eastern Hemisphere.

2009, May 4 Litho. *Perf. 13x13¼*
1109 A420 51c Horiz. pair, #a-b 3.50 3.50

Europa — A421

Constellations: 51c, Cassiopeia. 68c, Andromeda.

2009, May 4 *Perf. 13¼x13¾*
1110-1111 A421 Set of 2 3.75 3.75
1111a Booklet pane of 8, 4 each #1110-1111, perf. 13¼x13¾ on 3 sides 15.00 —
Complete booklet, #1111a 15.00

Intl. Year of Astronomy.

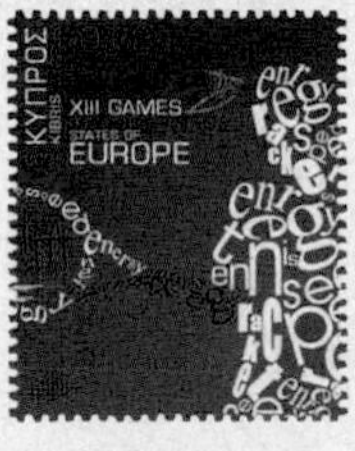

18th Games of the Small States of Europe, Cyprus — A422

Designs: 22c, Tennis. 34c, Sailing. 43c, Cycling.

2009, June 1 Litho. *Perf. 13¼x13¾*
1112-1114 A422 Set of 3 3.25 3.25

Souvenir Sheet

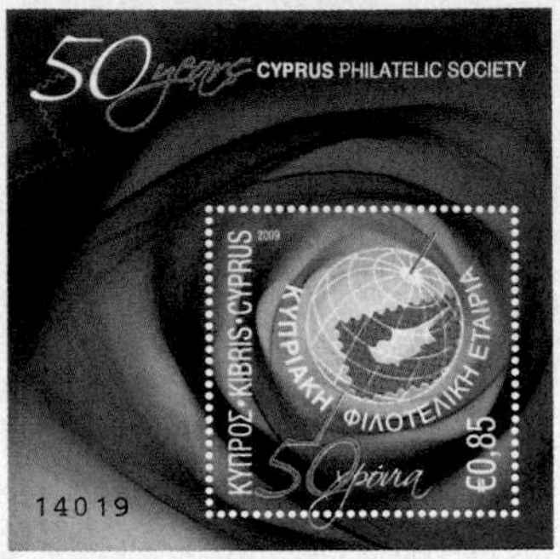

Cyprus Philatelic Society, 50th Anniv. — A423

Litho. & Embossed With Foil Application

2009, June 1 *Perf. 13¾*
1115 A423 85c multi 3.00 3.00

Cyprus Throughout the Years Type of 2007

Miniature Sheet

No. 1116: a, St. Paraskevi Church, 9th cent. b, Monastery of St. John Chrysostom, 1090-1100. c, Lusignan coat of arms, 1192-1489. d, Chronicle of Leontios Machairas, 15th cent. e, Queen Caterina Cornaro cedes Cyprus to Venice, 1489. f, Venetian Walls, Nicosia, 1567-70. g, Ottoman siege of Nicosia, 1570. h, Larnaca Aqueduct, 18th cent.

2009, Sept. 10 Litho. *Perf. 13¾*
1116 A407 43c Sheet of 8, #a-h 12.00 12.00

Domesticated Birds — A424

Designs: 22c, Pigeon. 34c, Turkey. 43c, Rooster. 51c, Duck.

2009, Sept. 10 *Perf. 13¾x13¼*
1117-1120 A424 Set of 4 5.25 5.25

European Court of Human Rights, 50th Anniv.
A425

2009, Nov. 12 Litho. *Perf. 13x13¼*
1121 A425 51c multi 1.75 1.75

A426

Christmas
A427

Perf. 13¼x13¾

2009, Nov. 12 Litho.

1122 A426 22c shown .75 .75

Litho. & Embossed With Foil Application

Perf. 13¾

1123 A427 51c shown 1.75 1.75
1124 A427 68c Solid silver star 2.50 2.50
Nos. 1122-1124 (3) 5.00 5.00

Republic of Cyprus, 50th Anniv. A428

Denomination color: 68c, Bister. 85c, Blue.

Litho. & Embossed With Foil Application

2010, Jan. 27 ***Perf. 13¾x13¼***

1125-1126 A428 Set of 2 4.25 4.25

Expo 2010, Shanghai A429

2010, Mar. 17 Litho. ***Perf. 13x13¼***

1127 A429 51c multi 1.40 1.40

2010 World Cup Soccer Championships, South Africa — A430

2010, Mar. 17 ***Perf. 13¾***

1128 A430 €1.71 multi 4.75 4.75

Barnyard Animals A431

Designs: 22c, Pig. 26c, Sheep. 34c, Goat. 43c, Cow. €1.71, Rabbit.

2010, Mar. 17 ***Perf. 13¾x13¼***

1129-1133 A431 Set of 5 8.00 8.00

Europa — A432

No. 1134 — Stack of books and: a, Sun, flowers, tree, snails, bees. b, Tree, bees.

2010, May 5 ***Perf. 13¼x13¾***

1134 A432 51c Horiz. pair, #a-b 2.75 2.75
c. Booklet pane of 8, 4 each #1134a-1134b, perf. 13¼x13¾ on 3 sides 11.00 —
Complete booklet, #1134c 11.00

Visit of Pope Benedict XVI — A433

2010, June 4 ***Perf. 13¾x14¼***

1135 A433 51c multi 1.25 1.25

Cyprus Railway — A434

No. 1136 — Locomotive with denomination in: a, Black. b, White.

85c, Train, map of stations.

2010, June 4 ***Perf. 13¾x13¼***

1136 A434 43c Pair, #a-b 2.10 2.10

Souvenir Sheet

1137 A434 85c multi 2.10 2.10

Cyprus Through the Ages Type of 2007

Miniature Sheet

No. 1138: a, Treaties of Sevres, 1920, and Lausanne, 1923. b, Burnt Government House, 1931. c, Imprisoned graves, 1955-59. d, Statue of Gregoris Afxentiou (1928-57), anti-colonialist leader. e, Presidential Palace, 1960. f, Black Summer 1974, painting by Telemachos Kanthos. g, Pres. Tassos Papadopoulos signing Treaty of Accession to the European Union, 2004. h, Flag of Cyprus.

2010, Oct. 1 Litho. ***Perf. 13¾***

1138 A407 43c Sheet of 8, #a-h 9.50 9.50

Souvenir Sheet

Viticulture — A435

No. 1139: a, Wine barrels, wine glass. b, Grapes, pitcher.

Perf. 14 on 3 Sides

2010, Nov. 10 Litho.

1139 A435 51c Sheet of 2, #a-b 2.75 2.75

See Romania Nos. 5216-5217.

Nativity — A436

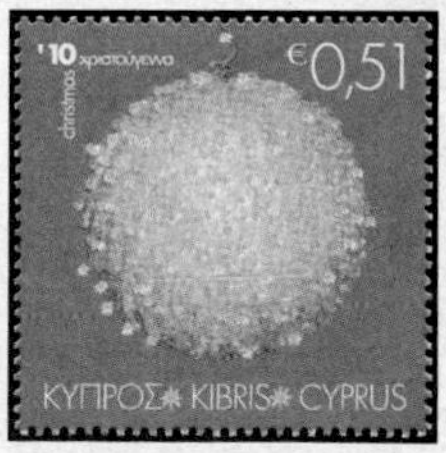

Christmas Ornament A437

Perf. 13¼x13¾

2010, Nov. 10 Litho.

1140 A436 22c shown .60 .60

Litho. & Embossed With Foil Application

Perf. 13¾

1141 A437 51c shown 1.40 1.40
1142 A437 68c Ornament, diff. 1.90 1.90
Nos. 1140-1142 (3) 3.90 3.90

Anorthosis Ammochostos Soccer Team, Cent. — A438

2011, Jan. 28 Litho. ***Perf. 13¾***

1143 A438 34c multi .95 .95

Composers — A439

No. 1144: a, Johann Sebastian Bach (1685-1750). b, Wolfgang Amadeus Mozart (1756-91). c, Ludwig van Beethoven (1770-1827).

2011, Jan. 28 ***Perf. 13¾x14¼***

1144 Horiz. strip of 3 4.25 4.25
a.-c. A439 51c Any single 1.40 1.40

Lace A440

Lace with: 26c, Floral pattern. 43c, Diamonds and squares pattern.

2011, Mar. 23 ***Perf. 13¾x14***

1145-1146 A440 Set of 2 2.00 2.00

Rosa Damascena A441

2011, Mar. 23 ***Perf. 13¾***

1147 A441 34c shown 1.00 1.00

Souvenir Sheet

1148 A441 85c Roses, diff. 2.50 2.50

Nos. 1147-1148 are impregnated with a rose scent.

Europa A442

2011, May 4 ***Perf. 14***

1149 A442 51c Blue forest 1.50 1.50
a. Perf. 13x13½ on 3 sides 1.50
1150 A442 68c Green forest 2.00 2.00
a. Perf. 13x13½ on 3 sides 2.00 2.00
b. Booklet pane of 8, 4 each #1149a-1150a 14.00 —
Complete booklet, #1150b 14.00

Intl. Year of Forests.

Lighthouses A443

Map and: 34c, Paphos Lighthouse. 43c, Cape Greco Lighthouse. €1.71 Cape Kiti Lighthouse.

2011, May 4 ***Perf. 14***

1151-1152 A443 Set of 2 2.25 2.25

Souvenir Sheet

Perf. 13½x13¼

1153 A443 €1.71 multi 5.00 5.00

Booklet Stamp Self-Adhesive

Die Cut Perf. 13¼x13

1153A A443 43c multi (RA28Ab) 1.25 1.25

No. 1153 contains one 27x35mm stamp.

Christopher A. Pissarides, 2010 Nobel Laureate in Economics — A444

2011, June 8 ***Perf. 14x14¼***

1154 A444 €1.71 multi 5.00 5.00

Tall Ships A445

Designs: 22c, Galleon. 43c, Caravel. 85c, Brig.

2011, June 8 ***Perf. 13¾***

1155-1157 A445 Set of 3 4.50 4.50

The Hare and the Tortoise — A446

No. 1158: a, Hare. b, Tortoise. c, Tortoise passing sleeping hare, horiz. d, Hare running. e, Tortoise crossing finish line.

Die Cut Perf. 11½x12, 12x11½

2011, Oct. 5 Litho.

Self-Adhesive

1158 A446 34c Booklet pane of 5, #a-e 4.75 4.75

Nativity — A447

Christmas Ornament A448

Perf. 13¼x13¾

2011, Nov. 11 **Litho.**
1159 A447 22c shown .60 .60

Litho. & Embossed With Foil Application

Perf. 13¾

1160 A448 51c shown 1.40 1.40
1161 A448 68c Ornament, diff. 1.90 1.90
Nos. 1159-1161 (3) 3.90 3.90

Horses A449

Various horses: 26c, 34c, 51c, 85c.

2012, Jan. 31 **Litho.** ***Perf. 13¾x13¼***
1162-1165 A449 Set of 4 5.25 5.25

2012 Summer Olympics, London A450

Designs: 22c, Men's gymnastics. 26c, Men's tennis. 34c, Men's high jump. 43c, Shooting.

Litho. With Foil Application

2012, Mar. 21 ***Perf. 14***
1166-1169 A450 Set of 4 3.25 3.25

Souvenir Sheet

Soccer — A451

2012, Mar. 21 **Litho.** ***Perf.***
1170 A451 €1.71 multi 4.50 4.50

Jasminum Grandiflorum — A452

2012, May 2 ***Perf. 13¾***
1171 A452 34c shown .90 .90

Souvenir Sheet

1172 A452 85c Flowers, diff. 2.25 2.25

Nos. 1171-1172 are impregnated with a jaasmine scent.

Europa A453

Various Cyprus tourist attractions and silhouette of: 51c, Family. 68c, Man and woman with bicycles.

2012, May 2 ***Perf. 13¾x13½***
1173-1174 A453 Set of 2 3.25 3.25
1174a Booklet pane of 8, 4 each #1173-1174, perf. 13¾x13½ on 3 sides 13.00 —
Complete booklet, #1174a 13.00

Cyprus Presidency of European Union Council A454

Litho. With Foil Application

2012, July 1 ***Perf. 13¾***
1175 A454 51c multi 1.25 1.25

Souvenir Sheet

1176 A454 €10 multi 25.00 25.00

The Cricket and the Ant — A455

No. 1177: a, Cricket with fiddle, sun. b, Ant with seeds. c, Ant carrying seeds. d, Cricket fiddling under tree. e, Cricket outside in winter, ant at door.

2012, Oct. 3 ***Die Cut Perf. 11¼x12***

Self-Adhesive

1177 A455 34c Booklet pane of 5, #a-e 4.50 4.50

Pavlos Kontides, Silver Medalist in Sailing at 2012 Summer Olympics A456

Litho. With Foil Application

2012, Nov. 14 ***Perf. 14***
1178 A456 34c multi .90 .90

Christmas — A457

Icons from: 22c, Madonna and Child, Christ Antiphonitis Church. 51c, Madonna and Child, Panayia Church, Lysi. 68c, Madonna and Child Enthroned Between St. George and St. Nicholas, St. George's Church, Vatyli.

Perf. 13¼x13¾

2012, Nov. 12 **Litho.**
1179 A457 22c multi .60 .60
1180 A457 51c multi 1.40 1.40

Size: 65x65mm

Imperf

1181 A457 68c multi 1.75 1.75

Admission of Cyprus Red Cross to International Red Cross, 1st Anniv. — A458

2013, Jan. 30 ***Perf. 14¼x13¾***
1182 A458 22c multi .60 .60

Cyprus Scouts Association, Cent. A459

2013, Jan. 30 ***Perf. 13¾***
1183 A459 43c multi 1.25 1.25

Archbishop Makarios (1913-77), President of Cyprus A460

2013, Jan. 30 ***Perf. 14***
1184 A460 85c multi 2.40 2.40

Easter — A461

Icons depicting: 26c, Christ's entry into Jerusalem. 34c, Crucifixion. €1.71, Resurrection (27x40mm).

2013, Apr. 3 ***Perf. 14x14¼***
1185-1187 A461 Set of 3 6.00 6.00

Origanum Dubium A462

2013, May 2 ***Perf. 13¾***
1188 A462 22c shown .60 .60

Souvenir Sheet

1189 A462 85c Flowers, diff. 2.25 2.25

Nos. 1188-1189 are impregnated with an oregano scent.

Europa A463

Mailbox and postal vehicles: 34c, Automobile, van and airplane. 51c, Automobile.

2013, May 2 ***Perf. 14***
1190-1191 A463 Set of 2 2.25 2.25
1191a Booklet pane of 8, 4 each #1190-1191, perf. 14 on 3 sides 9.00 —
Complete booklet, #1191a 9.00

Marine Life — A464

Designs: 34c, Seahorse. 43c, Sea anemone. €1.71, Sea fan coral.

2013, June 5 ***Perf. 13¾***
1192-1194 A464 Set of 3 6.75 6.75

For surcharge, see No. 1225.

Cypriot Folk Tale "Spanos and the Forty Dragons" — A465

No. 1195: a, Spanos in cloud near dragon. b, Boar chasing Spanos up a tree, vert. c, Spanos, river, woman holding flowers. d, Spanos sitting near dragon. e, Spanos pouring water on dragon.

Die Cut Perf. 13x13½, 13½x13

2013, Nov. 13 **Litho.**

Self-Adhesive

1195 A465 34c Booklet pane of 5, #a-e 4.75 4.75

Christmas A466

Winning art in children's stamp design contest: 22c, Santa Claus and Christmas tree. 34c, Snowman, Christmas trees and houses. 85c, Christmas tree and gifts, vert.

Perf. 14¼x14, 14x14¼

2013, Nov. 13 **Litho.**
1196-1198 A466 Set of 3 4.00 4.00

Olive Production A467

Designs: 34c, Olive tree and grove.
No. 1200: a, Olives. b, Olives, container of olive oil.

2014, Jan. 30 **Litho.** ***Perf. 14***
1199 A467 34c multi .95 .95
1200 A467 51c Horiz. pair, #a-b 2.75 2.75

Four Seasons A468

Designs: 22c, Child under umbrella (winter). 43c, Girl wearing butterfly costume standing in flowers (spring). 85c, Girl with balloons, fish and dolphins (summer). €1.71, Child holding fallen leaf in front of face (autumn).

2014, Mar. 12 Litho. *Perf. 13¾*
1201-1204 A468 Set of 4 9.00 9.00

For surcharges, see Nos. 1212-1214.

Europa A469

Musicians with instruments: 34c, Cyprus flute. 51c, Lute.

2014, May 2 Litho. *Perf. 14*
1205-1206 A469 Set of 2 2.40 2.40
1206a Booklet pane of 8, 4 each #1205-1206, perf. 14 on 3 sides 9.75 —
Complete booklet, #1206a 9.75

Famous Men A470

Designs: 41c, El Greco (1541-1614), painter. 50c, Michelangelo (1475-1564), painter and sculptor. 64c, Galileo Galilei (1564-1642), astronomer. 75c, Henri de Toulouse-Lautrec (1864-1901), painter.

2014, June 30 Litho. *Perf. 14*
1207-1210 A470 Set of 4 6.25 6.25

Euromed Postal Emblem and Mediterranean Sea — A471

2014, July 9 Litho. *Perf. 14*
1211 A471 60c multi 1.60 1.60

Nos. 1201, 1202 and 1204 Surcharged

Methods and Perfs. As Before
2014, Aug. 1
1212 A468 4c on 22c #1201 .25 .25
1213 A468 €1 on 43c #1202 2.75 2.75
1214 A468 €1.88 on €1.71 #1204 5.00 5.00
Nos. 1212-1214 (3) 8.00 8.00

Famous People — A472

No. 1215: a, Theodoulos Kallinikos (1904-2004), cantor and musicologist. b, Stylianos Hourmouzios (1850-1937), cantor and journalist.

No. 1216: a, Sozos Tombolis (1914-2002), cantor and music professor. b, Achilleas Lymbourides (1917-2008), composer.

No. 1217: a, Telemachos Kanthos (1910-93), painter. b, Loukia Nicolaidou (1909-94), painter.

No. 1218: a, George Pol Georgiou (1901-72), painter. b, Michael Kashalos (1885-1974), painter.

No. 1219: a, Kypros Chrysanthis (1915-98), writer. b, Antis Pernaris (1903-80), writer.

No. 1220: a, Glafkos Alithersis (1897-1965), writer. b, Costas Montis (1914-2004), writer.

2014, Oct. 10 Litho. *Perf. 14*
1215 A472 Horiz. pair .25 .25
a.-b. 4c Either single .25 .25
1216 A472 Horiz. pair 1.75 1.75
a.-b. 34c Either single .85 .85
1217 A472 Horiz. pair 2.00 2.00
a.-b. 41c Either single 1.00 1.00
1218 A472 Horiz. pair 2.50 2.50
a.-b. 50c Either single 1.25 1.25
1219 A472 Horiz. pair 3.25 3.25
a.-b. 64c Either single 1.60 1.60
1220 A472 Horiz. pair 4.25 4.25
a.-b. 85c Either single 2.10 2.10
Nos. 1215-1220 (6) 14.00 14.00

See Nos. 1226-1231.

Cypriot Folk Tale "The Prince of Venice" — A473

No. 1221: a, Prince carried by angel. b, Angel carrying sword, vert. c, Woman with veil, vert. d, Angel and woman, vert. e, Ship at sea.

Die Cut Perf. 13½
2014, Nov. 24 Litho.
Self-Adhesive
1221 A473 Booklet pane of 5 5.00
a.-e. 41c Any single 1.00 1.00

Christmas — A474

Icons depicting: 41c, Nativity. 64c, Madonna and Child. 75c, Nativity, diff.

2014, Nov. 24 Litho. *Perf. 14*
1222-1224 A474 Set of 3 4.50 4.50

No. 1193 Surcharged

Method and Perf. As Before
2015, Feb. 4
1225 A464 34c on 43c #1193 .75 .75

Famous People Type of 2014

No. 1226: a, Adamantios Diamantis (1900-94), painter. b, Theodosis Pierides (1908-68), poet.

No. 1227: a, Maria Rousia (1894-1957), writer. b, Melis Nicolaides (1892-1979), writer.

No. 1228: a, Kyriakos Hadjioannou (1909-97), folklorist. b, Polyxeni Loizia (1855-1942), educator.

No. 1229: a, Loizos Philippou (1895-1950), newspaper editor. b, Persefoni Papadopoulou (1888-1948), educator.

No. 1230: a, Georgios Frangoudes (1869-1939), politician. b, Porfyrios Dikaios (1904-71), archaeologist.

No. 1231: a, Nicos Pantelides (1906-84), actor. b, Pavlos Xioutas (1908-91), folklorist.

2015, Feb. 4 Litho. *Perf. 14*
1226 A472 Horiz. pair .25 .25
a.-b. 4c Either single .25 .25
1227 A472 Horiz. pair 2.25 2.25
a.-b. 50c Either single 1.10 1.10
1228 A472 Horiz. pair 2.80 2.80
a.-b. 60c Either single 1.40 1.40
1229 A472 Horiz. pair 3.50 3.50
a.-b. 75c Either single 1.75 1.75
1230 A472 Horiz. pair 4.50 4.50
a.-b. €1 Either single 2.25 2.25
1231 A472 Horiz. pair 7.00 7.00
a.-b. €1.50 Either single 3.50 3.50
Nos. 1226-1231 (6) 20.30 20.30

Melkonian Orphanage — A475

2015, Apr. 2 Litho. *Perf. 13¾x14¼*
1232 A475 64c multi 1.40 1.40

See Armenia No. 1034.

Preserved Fruit — A476

Designs: 34c, Bitter orange. 41c, Bitter orange, diff. €1.88, Cherry.

2015, Apr. 2 Litho. *Perf. 13¾*
1233-1235 A476 Set of 3 5.75 5.75

Souvenir Sheet

Independence Struggle of National Organization of Cypriot Fighters, 60th Anniv. — A477

Litho., Sheet Margin Litho. With Foil Application
2015, Apr. 2 *Perf. 13¾*
1236 A477 €2 multi 4.50 4.50

Europa — A478

Children and: 34c, Top. 64c, Marbles.

2015, May 5 Litho. *Perf. 14*
1237-1238 A478 Set of 2 2.25 2.25
1238a Booklet pane of 8, 4 each #1237-1238, perf. 14 on 3 sides 9.00 —
Complete booklet, #1238a 9.00

Map of Mediterranean Sea and Cypriot Boats — A479

2015, July 9 Litho. *Perf. 14*
1239 A479 75c multi 1.75 1.75

Akamas Peninsula A480

Avakas Gorge — A481

2015, July 9 Litho. *Perf. 14*
1240 A480 34c multi .75 .75
1241 A481 64c multi 1.40 1.40

International Telecommunication Union, 150th Anniv. — A482

2015, Sept. 14 Litho. *Perf. 14*
1242 A482 64c multi 1.50 1.50

Castles A483

Designs: 4c, Buffavento Castle. 34c, Kantara Castle. 41c, Agios Ilarionas (St. Hilarion) Castle. 75c, Kyrenia Castle.

Perf. 13¾x13½
2015, Sept. 14 Litho.
1243-1246 A483 Set of 4 3.50 3.50

Handicrafts — A484

No. 1247: a, Carved wooden chair. b, Decorated gourds.

No. 1248: a, Silver merrecha. b, Clay vessels.

2015, Sept. 14 Litho. *Perf. 14*
1247 A484 Pair 1.50 1.50
a.-b. 34c Either single .75 .75
1248 A484 Pair 3.00 3.00
a.-b. 64c Either single 1.50 1.50

A485

A486

Christmas — A487

Designs: 34c, Girl burning olive leaves. 41c, Madonna and Child icon. 64c, Child mailing letter to Santa Claus. €2, Nativity.

2015, Nov. 19 Litho. *Perf. 14*

1249	A485 34c multi	.75	.75
1250	A486 41c multi	.90	.90
1251	A485 64c multi	1.40	1.40
	Nos. 1249-1251 (3)	3.05	3.05

Imperf

1252	A487 €2 multi	4.25	4.25

POSTAL TAX STAMPS

Catalogue values for unused stamps in this section are for Never Hinged items.

Unless otherwise stated, Cyprus postal tax stamps are for the Refugee Fund.

No. 352 Surcharged

Perf. 12x12½

1974, Dec. 2 Wmk. 344

RA1	A104 10m on 5m multi	.60	.60

Old Woman and Child — PT1

1974, Oct. 1 *Perf. 12½x13½*

RA2	PT1 10m gray & black	.50	.50

Child and Barbed Wire — PT2

Perf. 13x12½

1977, Jan. 10 Litho. Wmk. 344

RA3	PT2 10m black	.50	.50

Inscribed 1984

1984, June 18 *Perf. 13x12½*

RA4	PT2 1c black	.50	.50

There are two types of No. RA4.

Inscribed 1988 — PT3

1988-2007 *Perf. 13x12½*

Design Size 22x28mm

RA5	PT3 1c black & pale gray	.50	.50
	Perf. 11½x12		
RA6	PT3 1c Inscribed 1989	.50	.50
RA7	PT3 1c Inscribed 1990	.50	.50
	Unwmk.		
	Perf. 13		
RA8	PT3 1c Inscribed 1991	.50	.50
RA9	PT3 1c Inscribed 1992	.50	.50
RA10	PT3 1c Inscribed 1993	.50	.50
RA11	PT3 1c Inscribed 1994	.50	.50
	Perf. 14½x13¾		
	Design Size 21x24.5mm		
RA12	PT3 1c Inscribed 1995	.50	.50
RA13	PT3 1c Inscribed 1996	.50	.50
RA14	PT3 1c Inscribed 1997	.50	.50
RA15	PT3 1c Inscribed 1998	.50	.50
RA16	PT3 1c Inscribed 1999	.50	.50
RA17	PT3 1c Inscribed 2000	.50	.50
RA18	PT3 1c Inscribed 2001	.50	.50
	Size: 22x27mm		
	Perf. 12¾		
RA19	PT3 1c Inscribed 2002	.50	.50
RA20	PT3 1c Inscribed 2003	.50	.50
	Perf. 12¾x13		
RA21	PT3 1c Inscribed 2004	.50	.50
RA22	PT3 1c Inscribed 2005	.50	.50
RA23	PT3 1c Inscribed 2006	.50	.50
	Perf. 13½x14		
RA24	PT3 1c Inscribed 2007	.40	.40
	Nos. RA5-RA24 (20)	9.90	9.90

Issued: No. RA5, 9/12/88; No. RA6, 9/4/89; No. RA7, 9/29/90; No. RA8, 10/7/91; No. RA9, 11/9/92; No. RA10, 1993; No. RA11, 11/21/94; No. RA12, 10/24/95; No. RA13, 6/10/96; No. RA14, 6/30/97; No. RA15, 1998; No. RA16, 1999; No. RA17, 2000; No. RA18, 2001. No. RA19, 2002. No. RA19, 2003. No. RA20, 2003. No. RA21, 11/11/04. No. RA22, 6/16/05. No. RA23, 5/4/06. No. RA24, 3/15/07.

Child and Barbed Wire With Denomination in Euro Currency — PT4

2008, Jan. 1 Litho. *Perf. 13½x14*

RA25	PT4 2c dk gray & gray	.40	.40

Type of 2008

2009-10 Litho. *Perf. 13½x14*

Inscribed "2009"

RA26	PT4 2c blk & lilac gray	.40	.40
	Inscribed "2010"		
RA27	PT4 2c blk & tan	.40	.40

Type of 2008

2011-13 *Perf. 13½x14*

Inscribed "2011"

RA28	PT4 2c blk & lt green	.25	.25
	Booklet Stamp		
	Self-Adhesive		
	Die Cut Perf. 13½x14¼		
RA28A	PT4 2c blk & lt grn	.25	.25
b.	Booklet pane of 12, 6 each #1153A, RA28A	9.00	
	Inscribed "2012"		
	Perf. 13½		
RA29	PT4 2c blk & lt blue	.25	.25
	Inscribed "2013"		
RA30	PT4 2c blk & dull org	.25	.25
	Inscribed "2014"		
RA31	PT4 2c blk & gray	.25	.25
	Inscribed "2015"		
RA32	PT4 2c blk & bl gray	.25	.25

Issued: Nos. RA28, RA28A, 5/4/11; No. RA29, 1/31/12; No. RA30, 1/30/13; No. RA31, 3/12/14 No. RA32, 4/2/15.

CYRENAICA

ˌsir-ə-ˈnā-ə-kə

LOCATION — In northern Africa bordering on the Mediterranean Sea
GOVT. — Italian colony
AREA — 75,340 sq. mi.
POP. — 225,000 (approx. 1934)
CAPITAL — Bengasi (Benghazi)

Cyrenaica was an Italian Colony. In 1949 Great Britain granted the Amir of Cyrenaica autonomy in internal affairs. Cyrenaica was incorporated into the kingdom of Libya in 1951.

100 Centesimi = 1 Lira
1000 Milliemes = 1 Pound (1950)

Catalogue values for unused stamps in this country are for Never Hinged items, beginning with Scott 65 in the regular postage section, Scott J1 in the postage due section.

Used values in italics are for postally used stamps. CTO's sell for about the same as unused, hinged stamps.

Watermark

Wmk. 140 — Crown

Propaganda of the Faith Issue

Italy Nos. 143-146 Overprinted

1923, Oct. 24 Wmk. 140 *Perf. 14*

1	A68 20c ol grn & brn org	11.50	*50.00*
2	A68 30c claret & brn org	11.50	*50.00*
3	A68 50c violet & brn org	7.50	*57.50*
4	A68 1 l blue & brown orange	7.50	*85.00*
	Nos. 1-4 (4)	38.00	*242.50*
	Set, never hinged	90.00	

Fascisti Issue

Italy Nos. 159-164 Overprinted in Red or Black

1923, Oct. 29 Unwmk. *Perf. 14*

5	A69 10c dk grn (R)	11.00	*19.00*
6	A69 30c dk vio (R)	11.00	*19.00*
7	A69 50c brn car	11.00	*25.00*
	Wmk. 140		
8	A70 1 l blue	11.00	*50.00*
9	A70 2 l brown	11.00	*60.00*
10	A71 5 l blk & bl (R)	11.00	*90.00*
	Nos. 5-10 (6)	66.00	*263.00*
	Set, never hinged	150.00	

Manzoni Issue

Italy Nos. 165-170 Ovptd. in Red

1924, Apr. 1 *Perf. 14*

11	A72 10c brn red & blk	12.00	*80.00*
12	A72 15c bl grn & blk	12.00	*80.00*
13	A72 30c blk & slate	12.00	*80.00*
14	A72 50c org brn & blk	12.00	*80.00*
15	A72 1 l bl & blk	72.50	*475.00*
a.	Double overprint	*1,200.*	
	Never hinged	*1,800.*	
16	A72 5 l vio & blk	475.00	*3,250.*
	Nos. 11-16 (6)	595.50	*4,045.*
	Set, never hinged	1,500.	

Vertical overprints on Nos. 11-14 are essays. On Nos. 15-16 the overprint is vertical at the left.

All examples of No. 15a are poorly centered.

Victor Emmanuel Issue

Italy Nos. 175-177 Overprinted

1925-26 Unwmk. *Perf. 11*

17	A78 60c brn car	1.60	*11.00*
18	A78 1 l dark blue	1.60	*11.00*
19	A78 1.25 l dk bl ('26)	4.75	*24.00*
a.	Perf. 13½	350.00	*1,000.*
	Never hinged	900.00	
	Nos. 17-19 (3)	7.95	*46.00*
	Set, never hinged	20.00	

Issue dates: Nov. 1925, July 1926.

Saint Francis of Assisi Issue

Italian Stamps of 1926 Ovptd.

1926, Apr. 12 Wmk. 140 *Perf. 14*

20	A79 20c gray green	2.50	*14.50*
21	A80 40c dark violet	2.50	*14.50*
22	A81 60c red brown	2.50	*26.00*

Ovptd. in Red

Unwmk.

23	A82 1.25 l dk bl, perf. 11	2.50	*35.00*
24	A83 5 l + 2.50 l ol grn	8.00	*72.50*
	Nos. 20-24 (5)	18.00	*162.50*
	Set, never hinged	40.00	

Volta Issue

Type of Italy 1927, Overprinted

1927, Oct. 10 Wmk. 140 *Perf. 14*

25	A84 20c purple	6.75	*40.00*
26	A84 50c dp org	9.50	*27.50*
27	A84 1.25 l brt bl	14.50	*62.50*
	Nos. 25-27 (3)	30.75	*130.00*
	Set, never hinged	72.50	

Monte Cassino Issue

Types of 1929 Issue of Italy, Ovptd. in Red or Blue

1929, Oct. 14

28	A96	20c dk grn (R)	6.50	*22.50*
29	A96	25c red org (Bl)	6.50	*22.50*
30	A98	50c + 10c crim (Bl)	6.50	*24.00*
31	A98	75c + 15c ol brn (R)	6.50	*24.00*
32	A96	1.25 l + 25c dk vio (R)	14.00	*42.50*
33	A98	5 l + 1 l saph (R)	14.00	*47.50*

Overprinted in Red

Unwmk.

34	A100	10 l + 2 l gray brn	14.00	*72.50*
		Nos. 28-34 (7)	68.00	*255.50*
		Set, never hinged	169.00	

Royal Wedding Issue

Type of Italian Stamps of 1930 Overprinted

1930, Mar. 17 **Wmk. 140**

35	A101	20c yel grn	3.25	*9.50*
36	A101	50c + 10c dp org	2.40	*9.50*
37	A101	1.25 l + 25c rose red	2.40	*19.00*
		Nos. 35-37 (3)	8.05	*38.00*
		Set, never hinged	20.00	

Ferrucci Issue

Types of Italian Stamps of 1930, Ovptd. in Red or Blue

1930, July 26

38	A102	20c violet (R)	6.50	*6.50*
39	A103	25c dk grn (R)	6.50	*6.50*
40	A103	50c black (R)	6.50	*12.00*
41	A103	1.25 l dp bl (R)	6.50	*22.50*
42	A104	5 l + 2 l dp car	14.50	*47.50*
		Nos. 38-42 (5)	40.50	*95.00*
		Set, never hinged	94.00	

Virgil Issue

Italian Stamps of 1930 Ovptd. in Red or Blue

1930, Dec. 4

43	A106	15c vio blk	1.25	*12.00*
44	A106	20c org brn (Bl)	1.25	*4.75*
45	A106	25c dk grn	1.25	*4.75*
46	A106	30c lt brn (Bl)	1.25	*4.75*
47	A106	50c dl vio	1.25	*4.75*
48	A106	75c rose red (Bl)	1.25	*9.50*
49	A106	1.25 l gray bl	1.25	*12.00*

Unwmk.

50	A106	5 l + 1.50 l dk vio	4.75	*47.50*
51	A106	10 l + 2.50 l ol brn (Bl)	4.75	*72.50*
		Nos. 43-51 (9)	18.25	*172.50*
		Set, never hinged	40.00	

Saint Anthony of Padua Issue

Italian Stamps of 1931 Ovptd. in Blue or Red

1931, May 7 **Wmk. 140**

52	A116	20c brown (Bl)	1.60	*22.50*
53	A116	25c green (R)	1.60	*8.00*
54	A118	30c gray brn (Bl)	1.60	*8.00*
55	A118	50c dl vio (Bl)	1.60	*8.00*
56	A120	1.25 l slate bl (R)	1.60	*22.50*

Overprinted like Nos. 23-24 in Red or Black

Unwmk.

57	A121	75c black (R)	1.60	*22.50*
58	A122	5 l + 2.50 l dk brn	11.00	*80.00*
		Nos. 52-58 (7)	20.60	*171.50*
		Set, never hinged	51.50	

Carabineer A1

1934, Oct. 16 **Photo.** **Wmk. 140**

59	A1	5c dk ol grn & brn	5.50	*22.50*
60	A1	10c brn & blk	5.50	*22.50*
61	A1	20c scar & indigo	5.50	*20.00*
62	A1	50c pur & brn	5.50	*20.00*
63	A1	60c org brn & ind	5.50	*28.00*
64	A1	1.25 l dk bl & grn	5.50	*47.50*
		Nos. 59-64 (6)	33.00	*160.50*
		Set, never hinged	81.00	

2nd Colonial Art Exhibition held at Naples. See Nos. C24-C29.

Catalogue values for unused stamps in this section, from this point to the end of the section, are for Never Hinged items.

Autonomous State

Senussi Warrior
A2 A3

Perf. 12½

1950, Jan. 16 **Unwmk.** **Engr.**

65	A2	1m dark brown	.65	*2.25*
66	A2	2m rose car	.85	*2.00*
67	A2	3m orange	.85	*2.00*
68	A2	4m dark green	4.25	*3.25*
69	A2	5m gray	1.10	*1.25*
70	A2	8m red orange	1.25	*1.50*
71	A2	10m purple	1.25	*1.50*
72	A2	12m red	1.25	*1.50*
73	A2	20m deep blue	1.25	*1.50*
74	A3	50m choc & ultra	6.75	*8.50*
75	A3	100m bl blk & car rose	21.00	*42.50*
76	A3	200m vio & pur	25.00	*67.50*
77	A3	500m dk grn & org	110.00	*135.00*
		Nos. 65-77 (13)	175.45	*270.25*

SEMI-POSTAL STAMPS

Many issues of Italy and Italian Colonies include one or more semipostal denominations. To avoid splitting sets, these issues are generally listed as regular postage unless all values carry a surtax.

Holy Year Issue

Italian Semi-Postal Stamps of 1924 Overprinted in Black or Red

1925, June 1 **Wmk. 140** ***Perf. 12***

B1	SP4	20c + 10c dk grn & brn	4.00	*24.00*
B2	SP4	30c + 15c dk brn & brn	4.00	*25.00*
B3	SP4	50c + 25c vio & brn	4.00	*24.00*
B4	SP4	60c + 30c dp rose & brn	4.00	*32.50*
B5	SP8	1 l + 50c dp bl & vio (R)	4.00	*47.50*
B6	SP8	5 l + 2.50 l org brn & vio (R)	4.00	*60.00*
		Nos. B1-B6 (6)	24.00	*213.00*
		Set, never hinged	60.00	

Colonial Institute Issue

"Peace" Substituting Spade for Sword — SP1

1926, June 1 **Typo.** ***Perf. 14***

B7	SP1	5c + 5c brown	1.20	*10.00*
B8	SP1	10c + 5c olive grn	1.20	*10.00*
B9	SP1	20c + 5c blue grn	1.20	*10.00*
B10	SP1	40c + 5c brown red	1.20	*10.00*
B11	SP1	60c + 5c orange	1.20	*10.00*
B12	SP1	1 l + 5c blue	1.20	*21.00*
		Nos. B7-B12 (6)	7.20	*71.00*
		Set, never hinged	16.00	

Surtax for Italian Colonial Institute.

Types of Italian Semi-Postal Stamps of 1926 Overprinted like Nos. 17-19

1927, Apr. 21 **Unwmk.** ***Perf. 11***

B13	SP10	40c + 20c dk brn & blk	4.00	*45.00*
B14	SP10	60c + 30c brn red & ol brn	4.00	*45.00*
B15	SP10	1.25 l + 60c dp bl & blk	4.00	*65.00*
a.		Double overprint	*1,750.*	
		Never hinged	*2,600.*	
B16	SP10	5 l + 2.50 l dk grn & blk	6.50	*100.00*
		Nos. B13-B16 (4)	18.50	*255.00*
		Set, never hinged	43.00	

The surtax on these stamps was for the charitable work of the Voluntary Militia for Italian National Defense.

Allegory of Fascism and Victory — SP2

1928, Oct. 15 **Wmk. 140** ***Perf. 14***

B17	SP2	20c + 5c bl grn	3.25	*14.50*
B18	SP2	30c + 5c red	3.25	*14.50*
B19	SP2	50c + 10c purple	3.25	*24.00*
B20	SP2	1.25 l + 20c dk bl	4.00	*32.50*
		Nos. B17-B20 (4)	13.75	*85.50*
		Set, never hinged	34.00	

46th anniv. of the Societa Africana d'Italia. The surtax aided that society.

Types of Italian Semi-Postal Stamps of 1926 Overprinted in Red or Black like Nos. 52-56

1929, Mar. 4 **Unwmk.** ***Perf. 11***

B21	SP10	30c + 10c red & blk	4.75	*27.50*
B22	SP10	50c + 20c vio & blk	4.75	*30.00*
B23	SP10	1.25 l + 50c brn & bl	7.25	*52.50*
B24	SP10	5 l + 2 l ol grn & blk (Bk)	7.25	*100.00*
		Nos. B21-B24 (4)	24.00	*210.00*
		Set, never hinged	60.00	

Surtax for the charitable work of the Voluntary Militia for Italian Natl. Defense.

Types of Italian Semi-Postal Stamps of 1926 Overprinted in Black or Red like Nos. 52-56

1930, Oct. 20 ***Perf. 14***

B25	SP10	30c + 10c dk grn & bl grn (Bk)	35.00	*65.00*
B26	SP10	50c + 10c dk grn & vio	35.00	*100.00*
B27	SP10	1.25 l + 30c ol brn & red brn	35.00	*100.00*
B28	SP10	5 l + 1.50 l ind & grn	120.00	*275.00*
		Nos. B25-B28 (4)	225.00	*540.00*
		Set, never hinged	562.50	

Surtax for the charitable work of the Voluntary Militia for Italian Natl. Defense.

Sower — SP3

1930, Nov. 27 **Photo.** **Wmk. 140**

B29	SP3	50c + 20c ol brn	4.25	*26.00*
B30	SP3	1.25 l + 20c dp bl	4.25	*26.00*
B31	SP3	1.75 l + 20c green	4.25	*27.50*
B32	SP3	2.55 l + 50c purple	9.50	*45.00*
B33	SP3	5 l + 1 l dp car	9.50	*67.50*
		Nos. B29-B33 (5)	31.75	*192.00*
		Set, never hinged	72.00	

25th anniv. of the Italian Colonial Agricultural Institute. The surtax was for the aid of that institution.

AIR POST STAMPS

Air Post Stamps of Tripolitania, 1931, Overprinted in Blue like Nos. 38-42

1932, Jan. 7 **Wmk. 140** ***Perf. 14***

C1	AP1	50c rose car	1.60	.40
C2	AP1	60c dp org	6.50	*14.00*
C3	AP1	80c dl vio	6.50	*22.50*
		Nos. C1-C3 (3)	14.60	*36.90*
		Set, never hinged	32.00	

Air Post Stamps of Tripolitania, 1931, Overprinted in Blue

1932, May 12

C4	AP1	50c rose car	1.60	2.00
C5	AP1	80c dull violet	6.50	*27.50*
		Set, never hinged	16.50	

This overprint was also applied to the 60c, Tripolitania No. C9. The overprinted stamp was never used in Cyrenaica, but was sold at Rome in 1943 by the Postmaster General for the Italian Colonies. Value $10.

Arab on Camel — AP2

Airplane in Flight
AP3

1932, Aug. 8 **Photo.**

C6	AP2 50c purple	14.50	.25
C7	AP2 75c brn rose	14.50	*16.00*
C8	AP2 80c deep blue	14.50	*30.00*
C9	AP3 1 l black	5.00	.25
C10	AP3 2 l green	5.00	*16.00*
C11	AP3 5 l deep car	10.00	*32.50*
	Nos. C6-C11 (6)	63.50	*95.00*
	Set, never hinged	140.00	

For surcharges and overprint see Nos. C20-C23.

Graf Zeppelin Issue

Zeppelin and Clouds forming Pegasus
AP4

Zeppelin and Ancient Galley
AP5

Zeppelin and Giant Bowman
AP6

1933, Apr. 15

C12	AP4 3 l dk brn	12.50	*125.00*
C13	AP5 5 l purple	12.50	*125.00*
C14	AP6 10 l dp grn	12.50	*240.00*
C15	AP5 12 l deep blue	12.50	*260.00*
C16	AP4 15 l carmine	12.50	*260.00*
C17	AP6 20 l black	12.50	*350.00*
	Nos. C12-C17 (6)	75.00	*1,360.*
	Set, never hinged	180.00	

North Atlantic Crossing Issue

Airplane Squadron and Constellations — AP7

1933, June 1

C18	AP7 19.75 l grn & dp bl	21.00	*650.00*
C19	AP7 44.75 l red & indigo	21.00	*650.00*
	Set, never hinged	105.00	

Type of 1932 Ovptd. and Srchd.

1934, Jan. 20

C20	AP3 2 l on 5 l org brn	4.75	*95.00*
C21	AP3 3 l on 5 l yel grn	4.75	*95.00*
C22	AP3 5 l ocher	4.75	*110.00*
C23	AP3 10 l on 5 l rose	6.50	*110.00*
	Nos. C20-C23 (4)	20.75	*410.00*
	Set, never hinged	52.00	

For use on mail to be carried on a special flight from Rome to Buenos Aires.

Transport Plane
AP8

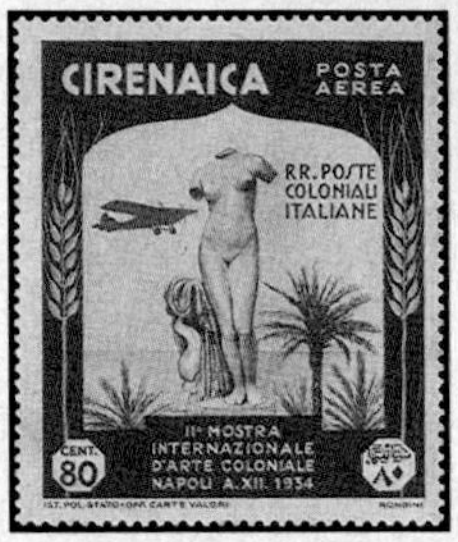

Venus of Cyrene
AP9

1934, Oct. 9

C24	AP8 25c sl bl & org red	5.50	*22.50*
C25	AP8 50c dk grn & ind	5.50	*20.00*
C26	AP8 75c dk brn & org red	5.50	*20.00*
a.	Imperf.	3,250.	
	Never hinged	4,850.	
C27	AP9 80c org brn & ol grn	5.50	*22.50*
C28	AP9 1 l scar & ol grn	5.50	*27.50*
C29	AP9 2 l dk bl & brn	5.50	*47.50*
	Nos. C24-C29 (6)	33.00	*160.00*
	Set, never hinged	81.00	

2nd Colonial Arts Exhib. held at Naples.

AIR POST SEMI-POSTAL STAMPS

King Victor Emmanuel III
SPAP1

Wmk. 104

1934, Nov. 5 **Photo.** ***Perf. 14***

CB1	SPAP1	25c + 10c gray grn	9.50	*27.50*
CB2	SPAP1	50c + 10c brn	9.50	*27.50*
CB3	SPAP1	75c + 15c rose red	9.50	*27.50*
CB4	SPAP1	80c + 15c brn blk	9.50	*27.50*
CB5	SPAP1	1 l + 20c red brn	9.50	*27.50*
CB6	SPAP1	2 l + 20c brt bl	9.50	*27.50*
CB7	SPAP1	3 l + 25c pur	27.50	*130.00*
CB8	SPAP1	5 l + 25c org	27.50	*130.00*
CB9	SPAP1	10 l + 30c dp vio	27.50	*130.00*
CB10	SPAP1	25 l + 2 l dp grn	27.50	*130.00*
		Nos. CB1-CB10 (10)	167.00	*685.00*
		Set, never hinged	415.00	

65th birthday of King Victor Emmanuel III and the non-stop flight, Rome-Mogadiscio.

AIR POST SEMI-POSTAL OFFICIAL STAMP

Type of Air Post Semi-Postal Stamps, 1934, Overprinted Crown and "SERVIZIO DI STATO" in Black

1934, Nov. 5 **Wmk. 140** ***Perf. 14***

CBO1 SPAP1 25 l + 2 l cop red *2,600.*

POSTAGE DUE STAMPS

Catalogue values for unused stamps in this section are for Never Hinged items.

D1

Perf. 12½

1950, July 1 **Unwmk.** **Engr.**

J1	D1	2m dark brown	77.50	*110.00*
J2	D1	4m deep green	77.50	*110.00*
J3	D1	8m scarlet	77.50	*110.00*
J4	D1	10m vermilion	77.50	*120.00*
J5	D1	20m orange yel	77.50	*120.00*
J6	D1	40m deep blue	77.50	*160.00*
J7	D1	100m dark gray	77.50	*250.00*
		Nos. J1-J7 (7)	542.50	*980.00*

CZECHOSLOVAKIA

ˌche-kə-slō-ˈvä-kē-ə

LOCATION — Central Europe
GOVT. — Republic
AREA — 49,355 sq. mi.
POP. — 15,395,970 (1983 est.)
CAPITAL — Prague

The Czechoslovakian Republic consists of Bohemia, Moravia and Silesia, Slovakia and Ruthenia (Carpatho-Ukraine). In March 1939, a German protectorate was established over Bohemia and Moravia, as well as over Slovakia which had meanwhile declared its independence. Ruthenia was incorporated in the territory of Hungary. These territories were returned to the Czechoslovak Republic in 1945, except for Ruthenia, which was ceded to Russia. Czechoslovakia became a federal state on Jan. 2, 1969. On Jan. 1, 1993 Czechoslovakia separated into Slovakia and the Czech Republic. See Volume 5 for the stamps of Slovakia.

100 Haleru = 1 Koruna

Catalogue values for unused stamps in this country are for Never Hinged items, beginning with Scott 142 in the regular postage section, B144 in the semi-postal section, Scott C19 in the air post section, Scott EX1 in the personal delivery section, and Scott J58 in the postage due section, Scott O1 int he officials section, and Scott P14 in the newspaper section.

Watermarks

Wmk. 107 — Linden Leaves (Vertical)

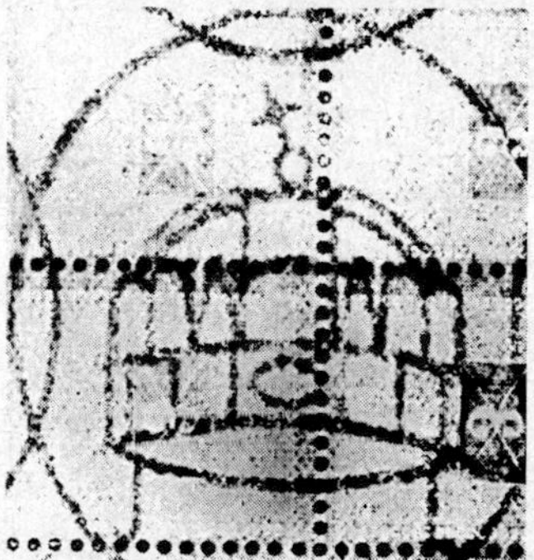

Wmk. 135 — Crown in Oval or Circle, Sideways

Wmk. 136

Wmk. 136a

Wmk. 341 — Striped Ovals

Stamps of Austria overprinted "Ceskoslovenska Republika," lion and "Cesko Slovensky Stat," "Provisorni Ceskoslovenska Vlada" and Arms, and "Ceskoslovenska Statni Posta" and Arms were made privately. A few of them were passed through the post but all have been pronounced unofficial and unauthorized by the Postmaster General.

During the occupation of part of Northern Hungary by the Czechoslovak forces, stamps of Hungary were overprinted "Cesko Slovenska Posta," "Ceskoslovenska Statni Posta" and Arms, and "Slovenska Posta" and Arms. These stamps were never officially issued though examples have passed the post.

Hradcany at Prague — A1

1918-19 Unwmk. Typo. *Imperf.*

1	A1	3h red violet	.25	.25
2	A1	5h yellow green	.25	.25
3	A1	10h rose	.25	.25
4	A1	20h bluish green	.25	.25
5	A1	25h deep blue	.25	.25
6	A1	30h bister	.45	.25
7	A1	40h red orange	.45	.25
8	A1	100h brown	1.25	.25
9	A1	200h ultra	2.25	.25
10	A1	400h purple	3.50	.25

On the 3h-40h "Posta Ceskoslovenska" is in white on a colored background; on the higher values the words are in color on a white background.

No. 5c was not valid for postage.

Nos. 1-6 exist as tete-beche gutter pairs.

See Nos. 368, 1554, 1600. For surcharges see Nos. B130, C1, C4, J15, J19-J20, J22-J23, J30.

Perf. 11½, 13½

13	A1	5h yellow green	.80	.25
a.		Perf. 11½x10¾	2.50	.55
14	A1	10h rose	.40	.25
15	A1	20h bluish green	.40	.25
a.		Perf. 11½	.40	.25
16	A1	25h deep blue	.60	.25
a.		Perf. 11½	1.50	.65
20	A1	200h ultra	4.25	.25
		Nos. 1-10,13-16,20 (15)	15.60	3.75

All values of this issue exist with various private perforations and examples have been used on letters.

The 3h, 30h, 40h, 100h and 400h formerly listed are now known to have been privately perforated.

For overprints see Eastern Silesia Nos. 2, 5, 7-8, 14, 16, 18, 30.

A2

Type II

Type III

Type IV

Type II — Sun behind cathedral. Colorless foliage in foreground.

Type III — Without sun. Shaded foliage in foreground.

Type IV — No foliage in foreground. Positions of buildings changed. Letters redrawn.

1919 *Imperf.*

23	A2	1h dark brown (II)	.25	.25
25	A2	5h blue green (IV)	.40	.25
27	A2	15h red (IV)	.85	.25
29	A2	25h dull violet (IV)	.65	.25
30	A2	50h dull violet (II)	.40	.25
31	A2	50h dark blue (IV)	.40	.25
32	A2	60h orange (III)	1.60	.25
33	A2	75h slate (IV)	1.20	.25
34	A2	80h olive grn (III)	.95	.25
36	A2	120h gray black (IV)	2.50	.35
38	A2	300h dark green (III)	8.00	.65
39	A2	500h red brown (IV)	8.50	.50
40	A2	1000h violet (III)	19.00	1.20
a.		1000h bluish violet	42.50	2.40
		Nos. 23-40 (13)	44.70	4.95

For overprints see Eastern Silesia Nos. 1, 3-4, 6, 9-13, 15, 17, 20-21.

1919-20 *Perf. 11½, 13¾, 13¾x11½*

41	A2	1h dk brown (II)	.25	.25
42	A2	5h blue grn (IV), perf. 13½	.75	.25
a.		Perf. 11½	25.00	4.00
43	A2	10h yellow grn (IV)	.40	.25
a.		Imperf.	25.00	19.00
b.		Perf. 11¾	13.00	1.25
44	A2	15h brick red (IV)	.40	.25
a.		Perf. 11½x10¾	30.00	4.50
b.		Perf. 11½x13¾	85.00	22.50
c.		Perf. 13¾x10¾	125.00	26.00
45	A2	20h rose (IV)	.40	.25
a.		Imperf.	100.00	95.00
46	A2	25h dull vio (IV), perf. 11½	.65	.25
a.		Perf. 11½x10¾	5.00	1.10
b.		Perf. 13¾x10¾	175.00	40.00
47	A2	30h red violet (IV)	.35	.25
a.		Imperf.	190.00	190.00
b.		Perf. 13¾x13½	550.00	175.00
c.		30h deep violet	.70	.25
d.		As "c," perf. 13¾x13½	625.00	190.00
e.		As "c," imperf.	190.00	140.00
50	A2	60h orange (III)	.30	.25
a.		Perf. 13¾x13½	25.00	6.25
53	A2	120h gray black (IV)	3.75	.95
		Nos. 41-53 (9)	7.25	2.95

Nos. 43a, 45a, 47a and 47e were imperforate by accident and not issued in quantities as were Nos. 23 to 40.

Rouletted stamps of the preceding issues are said to have been made by a postmaster in a branch post office at Prague, or by private firms, but without authority from the Post Office Department.

The 50, 75, 80, 300, 500 and 1000h have been privately perforated.

Unlisted color varieties of types A1 and A2 were not officially released, and some are printer's waste.

For surcharges and overprints see Nos. B131, C2-C3, C5-C6, J16-J18, J21, J24-J29, J31, J42-J43, Eastern Silesia 22-29.

Pres. Thomas Garrigue Masaryk — A4

1920 *Perf. 13½*

61	A4	125h gray blue	2.00	.25
a.		125h ultramarine	40.00	19.00
62	A4	500h slate, *grysh*	5.00	2.50
63	A4	1000h blk brn, *brnsh*	10.00	5.00
		Nos. 61-63 (3)	17.00	7.75

Nos. 61, 61a, 63 imperf. were not regularly issued. Values: unused singles, No. 61 $30; No. 61a $150; No. 62 $30; No. 63 $40.

For surcharge and overprints, see Nos. B131, Eastern Silesia 31-32.

Carrier Pigeon with Letter — A5

Czechoslovakia Breaking Chains to Freedom — A6

Hussite Priest — A7

Agriculture and Science — A8

Type I

Type II

Two types of 40h:
Type I: 9 leaves by woman's hip.
Type II: 10 leaves by woman's hip.

1920 *Perf. 14*

65	A5	5h dark blue	.25	.25
a.		Perf. 13¾	*325.00*	*150.00*
66	A5	10h blue green	.25	.25
a.		Perf. 13¾	*225.00*	110.00
67	A5	15h red brown	.25	.25
68	A6	20h rose	.25	.25
69	A6	25h lilac brown	.25	.25
70	A6	30h red violet	.25	.25
71	A6	40h red brown (I)	.60	.25
a.		As "b," tête bêche pair	6.75	2.00
b.		Perf. 13½	1.50	.25
c.		Type II	.25	.25
72	A6	50h carmine	.50	.25
73	A6	60h dark blue	.50	.25
a.		As "b," tête bêche pair	6.00	4.00
b.		Perf. 13½	2.00	.25

Photo.

74	A7	80h purple	.25	.25
75	A7	90h black brown	.30	.25

Typo.

Perf. 13¾

76	A8	100h dark green	1.00	.25
77	A8	200h violet	1.50	.25
78	A8	300h vermilion	3.50	.25
a.		Perf. 13¾x13½	7.00	.35
79	A8	400h brown	6.00	.45
80	A8	500h deep green	7.00	.45
a.		Perf. 13¾x13½	100.00	5.50
81	A8	600h deep violet	9.00	.45
a.		Perf. 13¾x13½	275.00	7.00
		Nos. 65-81 (17)	31.65	4.85

No. 69 has background of horizontal lines.

Imperfs. were not regularly issued.

Nos. 71 and 73 exist as tete-beche gutter pairs.

For surcharges and overprint see Nos. C7-C9, J44-J56.

Type I

Type II

Two types of 20h:

Type I: Base of 2 is long, interior of 0 is angular.

Type II: Base of 2 is short, interior of 0 is an oval.

Type I

Type II

Two types of 25h:

Type I: Top of 2 curves up.

Type II: Top of 2 curves down.

1920-25 *Perf. 14*

82	A5	5h violet	.25	.25
a.		As "b," tête bêche pair	2.00	1.00
b.		Perf. 13½	1.00	.35
83	A5	10h olive bister	.25	.25
a.		As "b," tête bêche pair	2.25	1.50
b.		Perf. 13½	.80	.25
84	A5	20h deep orange (II)	.25	.25
a.		As "b," tête bêche pair	30.00	14.00
b.		Perf. 13½	6.00	.60
c.		Type I	—	—
85	A5	25h blue green (I)	.25	.25
a.		Type II	.25	.25
86	A5	30h deep violet ('25)	3.00	.25
87	A6	50h yellow green	1.00	.25
a.		As "b," tête bêche pair	60.00	27.50
b.		Perf. 13½	12.00	2.00
88	A6	100h dark brown	1.00	.25
a.		Perf. 13½	15.00	.25
89	A6	150h rose	4.50	.50
a.		Perf. 13½	80.00	1.10
90	A6	185h orange	3.00	.25
91	A6	250h dark green	5.00	.25
		Nos. 82-91 (10)	18.50	2.75

Imperfs. were not regularly issued.

Nos. 82-84, 87 exist as tete-beche gutter pairs.

Type of 1920 Issue Redrawn

Type I

Type II

Type III

Type I — Rib of leaf below "O" of POSTA is straight and extends to tip. White triangle above book is entirely at left of twig. "P" has a stubby, abnormal appendage.

Type II — Rib is extremely bent; does not reach tip. Triangle extends at right of twig. "P" like Type I.

Type III — Rib of top left leaf is broken in two. Triangle like Type II. "P" has no appendage.

1923 *Perf. 13¾, 13¾x13½*

92	A8	100h red, *yellow,* III, perf. 14x13½	1.00	.25
a.		Type I, perf. 13¾	1.25	.25
b.		Type I, perf. 13¾x13½	1.25	.25
c.		Type II, perf. 13¾	1.50	.25
d.		Type II, perf. 13¾x13½	1.50	.25
e.		Type III, perf. 13¾	7.00	.25
93	A8	200h blue, *yellow,* II, perf. 14	5.00	.25
a.		Type II, perf. 13¾x13½	8.50	.25
b.		Type III, perf. 13¾	8.50	.25
c.		Type III, perf. 13¾x13½	52.50	.50
94	A8	300h violet, *yellow,* I, perf. 13¾	3.75	.25
a.		Type II, perf. 13¾	35.00	.25
b.		Type II, perf. 13¾x13½	50.00	.50
c.		Type III, perf. 13¾x13½	7.00	.25
d.		Type III, perf. 13¾	24.00	.35
		Nos. 92-94 (3)	9.75	.75

President Masaryk
A9 A10

Perf. 13¾x13½, 13¾

1925 **Photo.** **Wmk. 107**

Size: 19½x23mm

95	A9	40h brown orange	.75	.25
96	A9	50h olive green	1.50	.25
97	A9	60h red violet	1.75	.25
		Nos. 95-97 (3)	4.00	.75

Distinctive Marks of the Engravings.

I, II, III — Background of horizontal lines in top and bottom tablets. Inscriptions in Roman letters with serifs.

IV — Crossed horizontal and vertical lines in the tablets. Inscriptions in Antique letters without serifs.

I, II, IV — Shading of crossed diagonal lines on the shoulder at the right.

III — Shading of single lines only.

I — "T" of "Posta" over middle of "V" of "Ceskoslovenska." Three short horizontal lines in lower part of "A" of "Ceskoslovenska."

II — "T" over right arm of "V." One short line in "A."

III — "T" as in II. Blank space in lower part of "A."

IV — "T" over left arm of "V."

Wmk. Horizontally (107)

Engr.

I. First Engraving

Size: 19¾x22½mm

98	A10	1k carmine	.85	.25
99	A10	2k deep blue	2.00	.25
100	A10	3k brown	4.00	.65
101	A10	5k blue green	1.40	.45
		Nos. 98-101 (4)	8.25	1.60

Wmk. Vertically (107)

Size: 19¼x23mm

101A	A10	1k carmine	100.00	4.00
101B	A10	2k deep blue	100.00	12.50
101C	A10	3k brown	250.00	12.50
101D	A10	5k blue green	5.00	2.00
		Nos. 101A-101D (4)	455.00	31.00

II. Second Engraving

Wmk. Horizontally (107)

Size: 19x21½mm

102	A10	1k carmine	50.00	.50
103	A10	2k deep blue	3.50	.25
104	A10	3k brown	3.50	.50
		Nos. 102-104 (3)	57.00	1.25

III. Third Engraving

Size: 19-19½x21½-22mm

Perf. 10

105	A10	1k carmine rose	1.00	.25
a.		Perf. 14	15.00	.25

IV. Fourth Engraving

Size: 19x22mm

1926 *Perf. 10*

106	A10	1k carmine rose	1.00	.25

Perf. 14

108	A10	3k brown	4.50	.25

There is a 2nd type of No. 106: with long mustache. Same values. See No. 130, design SP3.

Karlstein Castle — A11

1926, June 1 **Engr.** *Perf. 10*

109	A11	1.20k red violet	.50	.30
110	A11	1.50k car rose	.30	.25
111	A11	2.50k dark blue	3.00	.30
		Nos. 109-111 (3)	3.80	.85

See Nos. 133, 135.

Karlstein Castle — A12

Pernstein Castle — A13

Orava Castle
A14

Masaryk
A15

Strahov Monastery — A16

Hradcany at Prague
A17

Great Tatra — A18

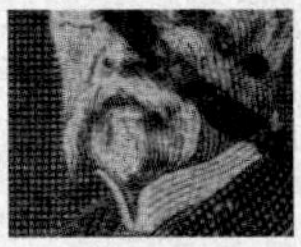
Short Mustache

Long, Wavy Mustache

1926-27 **Engr.** **Wmk. 107**

114	A13	30h gray green	1.25	.25
115	A14	40h red brown	.50	.25
116	A15	50h deep green	.50	.25
117	A15	60h red vio, *lil*	.85	.25
118	A16	1.20k red violet	4.00	1.50

Perf. 13½

119	A17	2k blue	.75	.25
a.		2k ultramarine	6.00	.75
120	A17	3k deep red	1.50	.25
121	A18	4k brn vio ('27)	4.75	.40
122	A18	5k dk grn ('27)	14.00	2.25
		Nos. 114-122 (9)	28.10	5.65

No. 116 exists in two types. The one with short, straight mustache at left sells for several times as much as that with longer wavy mustache.

See Nos. 137-140.

Coil Stamps

Perf. 10 Vertically

123	A12	20h brick red	.50	.40
a.		Vert. pair, imperf. horiz.	100.00	
124	A13	30h gray green	.35	.25
a.		Vert. pair, imperf. horiz.	100.00	
125	A15	50h deep green	.25	.25
		Nos. 123-125 (3)	1.10	.90

See No. 141.

Short Mustache

Long, Wavy Mustache

1927-31 **Unwmk.** *Perf. 10*

126	A13	30h gray green	.25	.25
127	A14	40h deep brown	.70	.25
128	A15	50h deep green	.25	.25
129	A15	60h red violet	.70	.25
130	A10	1k carmine rose	1.10	.25
131	A15	1k deep red	.75	.25
132	A16	1.20k red violet	.40	.25
133	A11	1.50k carmine ('29)	.55	.25
134	A13	2k dp grn ('29)	.50	.25
135	A11	2.50k dark blue	5.50	.30
136	A14	3k red brown ('31)	.60	.25
		Nos. 126-136 (11)	11.30	2.80

No. 130 exists in two types. The one with longer mustache at right sells for several times as much as that with the short mustache.

1927-28 *Perf. 13½*

137	A17	2k ultra	.85	.25
138	A17	3k deep red ('28)	1.90	.65
139	A18	4k brown violet ('28)	6.00	1.00
140	A18	5k dark green ('28)	6.25	.50
		Nos. 137-140 (4)	15.00	2.40

Coil Stamp

1927 *Perf. 10 Vertically*

141	A12	20h brick red	.50	.25

Catalogue values for unused stamps in this section, from this point to the end of the section, are for Never Hinged items.

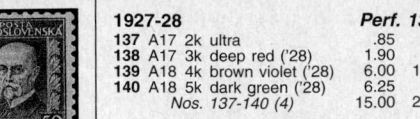

Hradec Castle
A19

Brno Cathedral
A25

Masaryk — A27

10th anniv. of Czech. independence: 40h, Town Hall, Levoca. 50h, Telephone exchange, Prague. 60h, Town of Jasina. 1k, Hluboka Castle. 1.20k, Pilgrims' House, Velehrad. 2.50k, Great Tatra. 5k, Old City Square, Prague.

1928, Oct. 22 *Perf. 13½*

142	A19	30h black	.25	.25
143	A19	40h red brown	.30	.25
144	A19	50h dark green	.35	.35
145	A19	60h orange red	.40	.40
146	A19	1k carmine	.55	.55
147	A19	1.20k brown vio	1.25	1.25
148	A25	2k ultra	1.30	1.30
149	A19	2.50k dark blue	4.00	3.25
150	A27	3k dark brown	2.25	2.25
151	A25	5k deep violet	4.25	4.25
		Nos. 142-151 (10)	14.90	14.10

From one to three sheets each of Nos. 142-148, perf 12½, appeared on the market in the early 1950's.

Coat of Arms — A29

1929-37 *Perf. 10*

152	A29	5h dark ultra ('31)	.25	.25
153	A29	10h bister brn ('31)	.25	.25
154	A29	20h red	.25	.25
155	A29	25h green	.25	.25
156	A29	30h red violet	.25	.25
157	A29	40h dk brown ('37)	1.50	.25
a.		40h red brown ('29)	4.00	.25
		Nos. 152-157 (6)	2.75	1.50

Coil Stamp

Perf. 10 Vertically

158	A29	20h red	.25	.25

For overprints, see Bohemia and Moravia Nos. 1-5, Slovakia Nos. 2-6.

St. Wenceslas
A30

Founding St. Vitus' Cathedral
A31

Design: 3k, 5k, St. Wenceslas martyred.

1929, May 14 *Perf. 13½*

159 A30 50h gray green .50 .25
160 A30 60h slate violet .80 .25
161 A31 2k dull blue 1.50 .50
162 A30 3k brown 2.00 .50
163 A30 5k brown violet 7.50 4.00
Nos. 159-163 (5) 12.30 5.50

Millenary of the death of St. Wenceslas.

Statue of St. Wenceslas and National Museum, Prague — A33

1929 *Perf. 10*

164 A33 2.50k deep blue 1.00 .25

Brno Cathedral A34

Tatra Mountain Scene A35

Design: 5k, Old City Square, Prague.

1929, Oct. 15 *Perf. 13½*

165 A34 3k red brown 3.00 .25
166 A35 4k indigo 9.50 .55
167 A35 5k gray green 11.00 .50
Nos. 165-167 (3) 23.50 1.30

See No. 183.

A37

Type I 

Type II 

Two types of 50h:
I — A white space exists across the bottom of the vignette between the coat, shirt and tie and the "HALERU" frame panel.
II — An extra frame line has been added just above the "HALERU" panel which finishes off the coat and tie shading evenly.

1930, Jan. 2 *Perf. 10*

168 A37 50h myrtle green (II) .25 .25
a. Type I 1.25 .25
169 A37 60h brown violet 1.00 .25
170 A37 1k brown red .40 .25
Nos. 168-170 (3) 1.65 .75

See No. 234.

Coil Stamp

1931 *Perf. 10 Vertically*

171 A37 1k brown red 1.25 .65

President Masaryk — A38

St. Nicholas' Church, Prague — A39

1930, Mar. 1 *Perf. 13½*

175 A38 2k gray green 2.00 .50
176 A38 3k red brown 3.25 .50
177 A38 5k slate blue 8.00 2.00
178 A38 10k gray black 22.50 5.00
Nos. 175-178 (4) 35.75 8.00

Eightieth birthday of President Masaryk.
Nos. 175-178 were each issued in sheets with ornamental tabs at the bottom. Value, set with tabs $65.50.

1931, May 15

183 A39 10k black violet 18.00 3.25

Krivoklat Castle — A40

Krumlov Castle — A42

Design: 4k, Orlik Castle.

1932, Jan. 2 *Perf. 10*

184 A40 3.50k violet 4.50 1.50
185 A40 4k deep blue 4.50 .75
186 A42 5k gray green 5.50 .75
Nos. 184-186 (3) 14.50 3.00

A43

A44

1932, Mar. 16

187 A43 50h yellow green .75 .25
188 A43 1k brown carmine 2.00 .25
189 A44 2k dark blue 12.00 .60
190 A44 3k red brown 17.50 .60
Nos. 187-190 (4) 32.25 1.70

Miroslav Tyrs — A45

1933, Feb. 1

191 A45 60h dull violet .30 .25

Miroslav Tyrs (1832-84), founder of the Sokol movement; and the 9th Sokol Congress (Nos. 187-190).

First Christian Church at Nitra
A46 A47

1933, June 20

192 A46 50h yellow green .60 .30
193 A47 1k carmine rose 9.00 .60

Prince Pribina who introduced Christianity into Slovakia and founded there the 1st Christian church in A.D. 833.
All gutter pairs are vertical. Values unused: No. 192 $350; No. 193 $10,000.

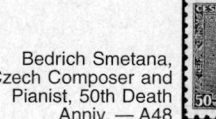

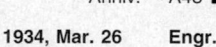

Bedrich Smetana, Czech Composer and Pianist, 50th Death Anniv. — A48

1934, Mar. 26 **Engr.** *Perf. 10*

194 A48 50h yellow green .40 .25

Consecration of Legion Colors at Kiev, Sept. 21, 1914 — A49

Ensign Heyduk with Colors A51

Legionnaires A52

1k, Legion receiving battle flag at Bayonne.

1934, Aug. 15 *Perf. 10*

195 A49 50h green .75 .25
196 A49 1k rose lake .90 .25
197 A51 2k deep blue 4.00 .60
198 A52 3k red brown 6.75 .75
Nos. 195-198 (4) 12.40 1.85

20th anniv. of the Czechoslovakian Legion which fought in WWI.

Antonin Dvorák, (1841-1904), Composer — A53

1934, Nov. 22

199 A53 50h green .40 .25

Pastoral Scene — A54

1934, Dec. 17 *Perf. 10*

200 A54 1k claret .80 .25
a. Souv. sheet of 15, perf. 13½ 200.00 *300.00*
b. As "a," single stamp 10.00 *12.50*
201 A54 2k blue 2.25 .80
a. Souv. sheet of 15, perf. 13½ 1,000. *1,000.*
b. As "a," single stamp 42.50 29.00

Centenary of the National Anthem.
Nos. 200-201 were each issued in sheets of 100 stamps and 12 blank labels. Value, set with attached labels: mint $24; used $8.
Nos. 200a & 201a have thick paper, darker shades, no gum. Forgeries exist.

President Masaryk
A55 A56

1935, Mar. 1

202 A55 50h green, *buff* .35 .25
203 A55 1k claret, *buff* .40 .25
204 A56 2k gray blue, *buff* 2.00 .60
205 A56 3k brown, *buff* 3.25 .60
Nos. 202-205 (4) 6.00 1.70

85th birthday of President Masaryk.
Nos. 204-205 were each issued in sheets of 100 stamps and 12 blank labels. Value with attached labels: mint $30; used $10.
See No. 235.

Monument to Czech Heroes at Arras, France — A57

1935, May 4

206 A57 1k rose .85 .25
207 A57 2k dull blue 3.00 .75

20th anniversary of the Battle of Arras.
Nos. 206-207 were each issued in sheets of 100 stamps and 12 blank labels. Value, set with attached labels: mint $22.50; used $22.50.

Gen. Milan Stefánik — A58

1935, May 18

208 A58 50h green .25 .25

Sts. Cyril and Methodius — A59

1935, June 22

209 A59 50h green .40 .25
210 A59 1k claret .55 .25
211 A59 2k deep blue 2.00 .50
Nos. 209-211 (3) 2.95 1.00

Millenary of the arrival in Moravia of the Apostles Cyril and Methodius.

Masaryk — A60

1935, Oct. 20 *Perf. 12½*

212 A60 1k rose lake .25 .25

No. 212 exists imperforate. See Bohemia and Moravia No. 1A. For overprints see Bohemia and Moravia Nos. 9-10, Slovakia 12.

Statue of Macha, Prague — A61

1936, Apr. 30

213 A61 50h deep green .25 .25
214 A61 1k rose lake .50 .25

Karel Hynek Macha (1810-1836), Bohemian poet.
Nos. 213-214 were each issued in sheets of 100 stamps and 12 blank labels. Value, set with attached labels: mint $2; used 80c.

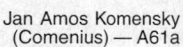

Jan Amos Komensky (Comenius) — A61a

Pres. Eduard Benes A62

Gen. Milan Stefánik A63

1936

215	A61a	40h dark blue	.25	.25
216	A62	50h dull green	.25	.25
217	A63	60h dull violet	.25	.25
		Nos. 215-217 (3)	.75	.75

See no. 252, Slovakia 23A. For overprints see Bohemia and Moravia Nos. 6, 8, Slovakia 7, 9-11.

Castle Palanok near Mukacevo A64

Town of Banska Bystrica A65

Castle at Zvikov — A66

Ruins of Castle at Strecno — A67

Castle at Cesky Raj A68

Palace at Slavkov (Austerlitz) A69

Statue of King George of Podebrad A70

Town Square at Olomouc — A71

Castle Ruins at Bratislava A72

1936, Aug. 1

218	A64	1.20k rose lilac	.25	.25
219	A65	1.50k carmine	.25	.25
220	A66	2k dark blue green	.25	.25
221	A67	2.50k dark blue	.40	.25
222	A68	3k brown	.40	.25
223	A69	3.50k dark violet	1.60	.55
224	A70	4k dark violet	.65	.25
225	A71	5k green	.65	.25
226	A72	10k blue	1.10	.55
		Nos. 218-226 (9)	5.55	2.85

Nos. 224-226 were each issued in sheets of 100 stamps and 12 blank labels. Value, with attached labels: mint $7; used $2.75.

For overprints and surcharge see Nos. 237-238, 254A, Bohemia and Moravia 11-12, 14-19, Slovakia 13-14, 16-23.

President Benes — A73

Soldiers of the Czech Legion — A74

1937, Apr. 26 Unwmk. *Perf. 12½*

227	A73	50h deep green	.25	.25

For overprints see Nos. 236, Slovakia 8.

1937, June 15

228	A74	50h deep green	.25	.25
229	A74	1k rose lake	.40	.25

20th anniv. of the Battle of Zborov.

Nos. 228-229 were each issued in sheets of 100 stamps and 12 blank labels. Value, set with attached labels: mint $4; used $2.

Cathedral at Prague — A75

Jan Evangelista Purkyne — A76

1937, July 1

230	A75	2k green	1.00	.25
231	A75	2.50k blue	1.50	.80

Founding of the "Little Entente," 16th anniv.

Nos. 230-231 were each issued in sheets with blank labels. Value, set with attached labels: mint $22.50; used $11.

1937, Sept. 2

232	A76	50h slate green	.25	.25
233	A76	1k dull rose	.30	.25

150th anniv. of the birth of Purkyne, Czech physiologist.

Nos. 232-233 were printed in sheets of 100 with 12 decorated labels. Value, set with labels, $2.50.

Masaryk Types of 1930-35

1937, Sept. *Perf. 12½*

234	A37	50h black	.25	.25

With date "14.IX. 1937" in design

235	A56	2k black	.30	.25

Death of former President Thomas G. Masaryk on Sept. 14, 1937.

No. 235 was issued in sheets of 100 stamps and 12 inscribed labels. Value, with attached label: mint $3.50; used $3.50.

International Labor Bureau Issue

Stamps of 1936-37 Overprinted in Violet or Black

1937, Oct. 6 *Perf. 12½*

236	A73	50h dp green (Bk)	.55	.50
237	A65	1.50k carmine (V)	.55	.50
238	A66	2k dp green (V)	.95	.60
		Nos. 236-238 (3)	2.05	1.60

Bratislava Philatelic Exhibition Issue

Souvenir Sheet

A77

1937, Oct. 24 *Perf. 12½*

239	A77	Sheet of 2	2.50	*3.25*
a.		50h dark blue	.80	1.20
b.		1k brown carmine	.80	1.20

The stamps show a view of Poprad Lake (50h) and the tomb of General Milan Stefanik (1k).

No. 239 overprinted with the Czechoslovak arms and "Czecho-Slovak Participation New York World's Fair 1939, Czecho-Slovak Pavilion" were privately produced to finance Czechoslovak participation in the exhibition. The overprint exists in black, green, red, blue, gold and silver.

No. 239 overprinted "Liberation de la Tchechoslovaquie, 28-X-1945" etc., was sold at a philatelic exhibition in Brussels, Belgium.

St. Barbara's Church, Kutna Hora — A79

Peregrine Falcon, Sokol Emblem — A80

1937, Dec. 4

240	A79	1.60k olive green	.25	.25

For overprints see Bohemia and Moravia Nos. 13, Slovakia 15.

1938, Jan. 21

241	A80	50h deep green	.25	.25
242	A80	1k rose lake	.25	.25

10th Intl. Sokol Games.

Nos. 241-242 were each issued in sheets of 100 stamps and 12 inscribed labels. Value, set with attached labels: mint $1.50; used $2.50.

Imperf. examples of No. 242 are essays.

Legionnaires

A81 A82

Legionnaire — A83

1938

243	A81	50h deep green	.25	.25
244	A82	50h deep green	.25	.25
245	A83	50h deep green	.25	.25
		Nos. 243-245 (3)	.75	.75

20th anniv. of the Battle of Bachmac, Vouziers and Doss Alto.

Nos. 243-245 were each issued in sheets of 100 stamps and 12 inscribed labels. Value, set with attached labels $2, mint or used.

Jindrich Fügner, Co-Founder of Sokol Movement — A84

1938, June 18 *Perf. 12½*

246	A84	50h deep green	.25	.25
247	A84	1k rose lake	.25	.25
248	A84	2k slate blue	.40	.25
		Nos. 246-248 (3)	.90	.75

10th Sokol Summer Games.

Nos. 246-248 were each issued in sheets of 100 stamps and 12 inscribed labels. Value, set with attached labels: mint $2.50; used $2.

View of Pilsen — A85

Cathedral of Kosice — A86

1938, June 24

249	A85	50h deep green	.25	.25

Provincial Economic Council meeting, Pilsen.

No. 249 was issued in sheets of 150 stamps and 10 labels depicting a flower within a cogwheel. Value, with attached label $1, mint or used.

For overprint see Bohemia & Moravia No. 7.

1938, July 15 *Perf. 12½*

250	A86	50h deep green	.25	.25

Kosice Cultural Exhibition.

No. 250 was issued in sheets of 150 stamps and 10 labels depicting grapes. Value, with attached label $1, $7.50 mint, $4.50 used.

Prague Philatelic Exhibition Issue

Souvenir Sheet

Vysehrad Castle — Hradcany — A87

1938, June 26 *Perf. 12½*

251	A87	Sheet of 2	5.00	5.00
a.		50h dark blue	1.50	1.50
b.		1k deep carmine	1.50	1.50

See No. 3036.

Stefánik Type of 1936

1938, Nov. 21

252	A63	50h deep green	.25	.25

Allegory of the Republic — A89

1938, Dec. 19 Unwmk.

253	A89	2k lt ultra	.30	.25
254	A89	3k pale brown	.50	.40

20th anniv. of Independence.

Nos. 253-254 were each issued in sheets of 100 stamps and 12 blank labels. Value, set with attached labels $2.50, mint or used.

See No. B153.

"Wir sind frei!"

Stamps of Czechoslovakia, 1918-37, overprinted with a swastika in black or red and "Wir sind frei!" were issued locally and unofficially in 1938 as Czech authorities were evacuating and German authorities arriving. They appeared in the towns of Asch, Karlsbad, Reichenberg-Maffersdorf, Rumburg, etc.

The overprint, sometimes including a surcharge or the town name (as in Karlsbad), exists on many values of postage, air post, semi-postal, postage due and newspaper stamps.

No. 226 Surcharged in Orange Red

1939, Jan. 18 Unwmk. *Perf. 12½*

254A	A72 300h on 10k blue	1.60	*2.25*

Opening of the Slovakian Parliament.

No. 254A was issued in sheets of 100 stamps with 12 blank labels. Value, set with attached labels, mint $4.

View of Jasina — A89a

Perf. 12½

1939, Mar. 15 Engr. Unwmk.

254B	A89a 3k ultra	25.00	*90.00*

Inauguration of the Carpatho-Ukraine Diet, Mar. 2, 1939.

Printed for use in the province of Carpatho-Ukraine but issued in Prague at the same time.

Used value is for red commemorative cancel.

The stamps formerly listed as Czechoslovakia Nos. 255, 256 and C18 are now listed with Bohemia and Moravia and Slovakia. No. 255 is now Slovakia 23A. No. 256 and C18 are now listed as Bohemia and Moravia 1A and C1, respectively.

Linden Leaves and Buds — A90

1945 Photo. *Perf. 14*

256A	A90	10h black	.25	.25
257	A90	30h yellow brown	.25	.25
258	A90	50h dark green	.25	.25
258A	A90	60h dark blue	.25	.25

Engr.

(Buds Open)

Perf. 12½

259	A90	60h blue	.25	.25
259A	A90	80h orange ver	.25	.25
260	A90	1.20k rose	.25	.25
261	A90	3k violet brown	.25	.25
262	A90	5k green	.25	.25
		Nos. 256A-262 (9)	2.25	2.25

Compare with Bohemia-Moravia type A1.

Thomas G. Masaryk — A91

Coat of Arms — A92

1945-46 Photo. *Perf. 12*

262A	A91	5h dull violet ('46)	.25	.25
262B	A91	10h orange yel ('46)	.25	.25
262C	A91	20h dk brown ('46)	.25	.25
263	A91	50h brt green	.25	.25
264	A91	1k orange red	.25	.25
265	A91	2k chalky blue	.25	.25
		Nos. 262A-265 (6)	1.50	1.50

1945 *Imperf.*

266	A92	50h olive gray	.25	.25
267	A92	1k brt red vio	.25	.25
268	A92	1.50k dk carmine	.25	.25
269	A92	2k deep blue	.25	.25
269A	A92	2.40k henna brn	.30	.25
270	A92	3k brown	.25	.25
270A	A92	4k dk slate grn	.25	.25
271	A92	6k violet blue	.25	.25
271A	A92	10k sepia	.40	.25
		Nos. 266-271A (9)	2.45	2.25

Nos. 266, 268, 269, 270 and 271 exist in 2 printings. Stamps of the 1st printing have a coarse impression and are on thin, hard paper in sheets of 100; all values exist in the 2nd printing, with fine impressions on thick, soft wove paper in sheets of 200. Values are the same.

Staff Capt. Ridky (British Army) — A93

Dr. Miroslav Novak (French Army) — A94

Capt. Otakar Jaros (Russian Army) — A95

Staff Capt. Stanislav Zimprich (Foreign Legion) — A96

2nd Lt. Jiri Kral (French Air Force) A97

Josef Gabcik (Parachutist) A98

Staff Capt. Alois Vasatko (Royal Air Force) A99

Private Frantisek Adamek (British Colonial Service) A100

1945, Aug. 18 Engr. *Perf. 11½x12½*

272	A93	5h intense blue	.25	.25
273	A94	10h dark brown	.25	.25
274	A95	20h brick red	.25	.25
275	A96	25h rose red	.25	.25
276	A97	30h purple	.25	.25
277	A98	40h sepia	.25	.25
278	A99	50h dark olive	.25	.25
279	A100	60h violet	.25	.25
280	A93	1k carmine	.25	.25
281	A94	1.50k lake	.25	.25
282	A95	2k ultra	.25	.25
283	A96	2.50k deep violet	.25	.25
284	A97	3k sepia	.25	.25
285	A98	4k rose lilac	.25	.25
286	A99	5k myrtle green	.25	.25
287	A100	10k brt ultra	.65	.25
		Nos. 272-287 (16)	4.40	4.00

Flags of Russia, Great Britain, US and Czechoslovakia — A101

View of Banská Bystrica A102

Patriot Welcoming Russian Soldier, Turciansky A103

Ruins of Castle at Sklabina A104

Czech Patriot, Strecno A105

1945, Aug. 29 Photo. *Perf. 10*

288	A101	1.50k brt carmine	.25	.25
289	A102	2k brt blue	.25	.25
290	A103	4k dark brown	.25	.25
291	A104	4.50k purple	.25	.25
292	A105	5k deep green	.50	.50
		Nos. 288-292 (5)	1.50	1.50

National uprising against the Germans.

A card contains one each of Nos. 288-292 on thin cardboard, ungummed. Size: 148x210mm. Sold for 50k. Value, $20 unused, $120 used. Forged cancellations exist.

Stefánik A106

Benes A107

Masaryk — A108

1945-47 Engr. *Perf. 12, 12½*

293	A106	30h rose violet	.25	.25
294	A107	60h blue	.25	.25
294A	A106	1k red org ('47)	.25	.25
295	A108	1.20k car rose	.25	.25
295A	A108	1.20(k) rose lil ('46)	.25	.25
296	A106	2.40(k) rose	.25	.25
297	A107	3k red violet	.25	.25
297A	A108	4k dark blue ('46)	.25	.25
298	A108	5k Prus green	.25	.25
299	A107	7k gray	.25	.25
300	A106	10k gray blue	.35	.25
300A	A106	20k sepia ('46)	.75	.25
		Nos. 293-300A (12)	3.60	3.00

1945 Photo. *Perf. 14*

301	A108	50h brown	.25	.25
302	A106	80h dark green	.25	.25
303	A107	1.60(k) olive green	.25	.25
304	A108	15k red violet	.55	.25
		Nos. 301-304 (4)	1.30	1.00

Statue of Kozina and Chod Castle, Domazlice A109

Red Army Soldier A110

1945, Nov. 28 Engr. *Perf. 12½*

305	A109	2.40k rose carmine	.25	.25
306	A109	4k blue	.25	.25

250th anniv. of the death of Jan Sladky Kozina, peasant leader.

Nos. 305-306 were issued in sheets of 100 stamps with 12 blank labels. Value, set with attached labels, mint $6.

1945, Mar. 26 Litho. *Imperf.*

307	A110	2k crimson rose	.40	.40
308	A110	5k slate black	1.25	1.25
309	A110	6k ultramarine	1.25	1.25
		Nos. 307-309 (3)	2.90	2.90

Souvenir Sheet

1945, July 16 Gray Burelage

310	Sheet of 3	4.00	4.00
a.	A110 2k crimson rose	.75	.75
b.	A110 5k slate black	.75	.75
c.	A110 6k ultramarine	.75	.75

Return of Pres. Benes, Apr., 1945.

Clasped Hands — A112

1945 *Rouletted 12½*

311	A112	1.50k brown red	2.25	2.25
312	A112	9k red orange	.50	.50
313	A112	13k orange brown	.65	.65
314	A112	20k blue	1.75	1.75
		Nos. 311-314 (4)	5.15	5.15

Karel Havlícek Borovsky — A113

1946, July 5 Engr. *Perf. 12½*

315	A113	1.20k gray black	.25	.25

Borovsky (1821-56), editor and writer.

Issued in sheets of 100 stamps and 12 inscribed labels. Value with attached label: $1.25.

Old Town Hall, Brno — A114

Hodonin Square — A115

Perf. 12½x12, 12x12½

1946, Aug. 3 Engr. Unwmk.

316	A114	2.40k deep rose	.25	.25
317	A115	7.40k dull violet	.30	.25

See No. B159.

President Eduard Benes — A116

1946, Oct. 28

318	A116	60h indigo	.25	.25
319	A116	1.60k dull green	.25	.25
320	A116	3k red lilac	.25	.25
321	A116	8k sepia	.25	.25
		Nos. 318-321 (4)	1.00	1.00

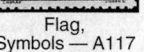

Flag, Symbols — A117

Saint Adalbert — A118

1947, Jan. 1 *Perf. 12½*

322	A117	1.20k Prus green	.25	.25
323	A117	2.40k deep rose	.25	.25
324	A117	4k deep blue	.80	.25
		Nos. 322-324 (3)	1.30	.75

Czechoslovakia's two-year reconstruction and rehabilitation program.

Nos. 322-324 each issued in sheets of 100 stamps and 12 inscribed labels. Value, set with attached labels, $3.

1947, Apr. 23

326	A118	1.60k gray	.50	.30
327	A118	2.40k rose carmine	.80	.65
328	A118	5k blue green	1.00	.40
		Nos. 326-328 (3)	2.30	1.35

950th anniv. of the death of Saint Adalbert, Bishop of Prague.

Nos. 326-328 each issued in sheets of 100 stamps and 12 monogrammed labels. Value, set with attached labels, $40.

Grief — A119

Allegorical Figure — A120

1947, June 10 **Engr.**

329	A119	1.20k black	.30	.25
330	A119	1.60k slate black	.40	.40
331	A120	2.40k brown violet	.50	.50
		Nos. 329-331 (3)	1.20	1.15

Destruction of Lidice, 5th anniversary.

Nos. 329-331 each issued in sheets of 100 stamps and 12 inscribed labels. Value, set with attached labels, $15.

World Federation of Youth Symbol — A121

Thomas G. Masaryk — A122

1947, July 20

332	A121	1.20k violet brown	.50	.40
333	A121	4k slate	.50	.40

World Youth Festival held in Prague, July 20-Aug. 17.

1947, Sept. 14

334	A122	1.20k gray blk, *buff*	.25	.25
335	A122	4k blue blk, *cream*	.40	.25

Death of Masaryk, 10th anniv.

Nos. 334-335 each issued in sheets of 100 stamps and 12 inscribed labels. Value, set with attached labels, $7.50.

Msgr. Stefan Moyses A123

1947, Oct. 19

336	A123	1.20k rose violet	.25	.25
337	A123	4k deep blue	.35	.25

150th anniversary of the birth of Stefan Moyses, first Slovakian chairman of the Slavic movement.

Each issued in sheets of 100 stamps and 12 labels with "MOYSES" and floral decoration. Value, set with attached labels, $9.50.

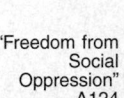

"Freedom from Social Oppression" A124

1947, Oct. 26 **Photo.** *Perf. 14*

338	A124	2.40k brt carmine	.40	.30
339	A124	4k brt ultra	.50	.25

Russian revolution of Oct., 1917, 30th anniv.

Benes A125

"Czechoslovakia" Greeting Sokol Marchers A126

1948, Feb. 15 **Photo.**

Size: 17½x21½mm

340	A125	1.50k brown	.25	.25

Size: 19x23mm

341	A125	2k deep plum	.25	.25
342	A125	5k brt ultra	.25	.25
		Nos. 340-342 (3)	.75	.75

1948, Mar. 7 **Engr.** *Perf. 12½*

343	A126	1.50k brown	.25	.25
344	A126	3k rose carmine	.25	.25
345	A126	5k blue	.60	.25
		Nos. 343-345 (3)	1.10	.75

The 11th Sokol Congress.

Nos. 343-345 each issued in sheets of 100 stamps and 12 labels depicting dates and bouquet. Values, set with attached labels: mint $5; used $3.75.

King Charles IV — A127

St. Wenceslas, King Charles IV — A128

1948, Apr. 7

346	A127	1.50k black brown	.25	.25
347	A128	2k dark brown	.25	.25
348	A128	3k brown red	.25	.25
349	A127	5k dark blue	.40	.25
		Nos. 346-349 (4)	1.15	1.00

600th anniv. of the foundation of Charles University, Prague.

Nos. 346-349 each issued in sheets of 100 stamps and 12 inscribed labels. Value, set with attached labels, $6.

Czech Peasants in Revolt A129

Jindrich Vanicek A130

Unwmk.

1948, May 14 **Photo.** *Perf. 14*

350	A129	1.50k dk olive brown	.25	.25

Centenary of abolition of serfdom.

1948, June 10 **Engr.** *Perf. 12½*

Designs: 1.50k, 2k, Josef Scheiner.

351	A130	1k dark green	.25	.25
352	A130	1.50k sepia	.25	.25
353	A130	2k gray blue	.25	.25
354	A130	3k claret	.25	.25
		Nos. 351-354 (4)	1.00	1.00

11th Sokol Congress, Prague, 1948.

Nos. 351-354 each issued in sheets of 100 stamps and 12 labels depicting a sunflower. Values, set with attached labels: $3.75 mint; $3 used.

Frantisek Palacky & F. L. Rieger — A131

Miloslav Josef Hurban — A132

1948, June 20 **Unwmk.**

355	A131	1.50k gray	.25	.25
356	A131	3k brown carmine	.25	.25

Constituent Assembly at Kromeriz, cent.

Nos. 355-356 each issued in sheets of 100 stamps and 12 labels depicting a wreath. Value, set with attached labels, $1.50.

1948, Aug. 27 *Perf. 12½*

3k, Ludovit Stur. 5k, Michael M. Hodza.

357	A132	1.50k dark brown	.25	.25
358	A132	3k carmine lake	.25	.25
359	A132	5k indigo	.25	.25
		Nos. 357-359 (3)	.75	.75

Cent. of 1848 insurrection against Hungary.

Nos. 357-359 each issued in sheets of 100 stamps and 12 labels depicting signatures. Values, set with attached labels: mint $5; used $3.50.

Eduard Benes A133

Czechoslovak Family A134

1948, Sept. 28

360	A133	8k black	.25	.25

President Eduard Benes, 1884-1948.

1948, Oct. 28 *Perf. 12½x12*

361	A134	1.50k deep blue	.25	.25
362	A134	3k rose carmine	.25	.25

Czechoslovakia's Independence, 30th anniv.

Nos. 361-362 each issued in sheets of 100 stamps and 12 labels depicting dates, leaves. Value, set with attached labels, $2.

Pres. Klement Gottwald — A135

1948-49 *Perf. 12½*

Size: 18½x23½mm

363	A135	1.50k dk brown	.25	.25
364	A135	3k car rose	.40	.25
a.		3k rose brown	1.20	.25
365	A135	5k gray blue	.25	.25

Size: 23½x29mm

366	A135	20k purple	1.10	.25
		Nos. 363-366 (4)	2.00	1.00

No. 366 was issued in sheets of 100 stamps and 12 monogrammed labels. Value, with attached label, $3.50.

See Nos. 373, 564, 600-604.

Souvenir Sheet

1948, Nov. 23 **Unwmk.** *Imperf.*

367	A135	30k rose brown	4.50	3.50

52nd birthday of Pres. Klement Gottwald (1896-1953).

Hradcany Castle Type of 1918

Souvenir Sheet

1948, Dec. 18

368	A1	10k dk blue violet	3.00	2.40

1st Czech postage stamp, 30th anniv.

Czechoslovak and Russian Workmen Shaking Hands — A138

1948, Dec. 12 *Perf. 12½*

369	A138	3k rose carmine	.25	.25

5th anniv. of the treaty of alliance between Czechoslovakia and Russia.

No. 369 issued in sheets of 100 stamps and 12 labels depicting Czech and Soviet flags. Value with attached label 60c.

Lenin — A139

1949, Jan. 21 **Engr.** *Perf. 12½*

370	A139	1.50k violet brown	.30	.25
371	A139	5k deep blue	.30	.30

25th anniversary of the death of Lenin.

Nos. 370-371 each issued in sheets of 100 stamps and 12 labels depicting torch. Value, set with attached labels: mint $1.75; used $1.50.

Gottwald Type of 1948 Inscribed: "UNOR 1948" and

Gottwald Addressing Meeting A140

1949, Feb. 25 **Photo.** *Perf. 14*

372	A140	3k red brown	.25	.25

Perf. 12½

Engr.

Size: 23½x29mm

373	A135	10k deep green	.60	.25

1st anniv. of Gottwald's speech announcing the appointment of a new government. No. 372 exists in a souvenir sheet of 1. It was not sold to the public.

No. 373 issued in sheets of 100 stamps and 12 inscribed labels. Values with attached label: mint $3; used $2.

A141

Writers: 50h, P. O. Hviezdoslav. 80h, V. Vancura. 1k, J. Sverma. 2k, Julius Fucik. 4k, Jiri Wolker. 8k, Alois Jirasek.

1949 Photo. *Perf. 14*

374 A141 50h violet brown .25 .25
375 A141 80h scarlet .25 .25
376 A141 1k dk olive green .25 .25
377 A141 2k brt blue .40 .25

Perf. 12½

Engr.

378 A141 4k violet brown .40 .25
379 A141 8k brown black .50 .25
Nos. 374-379 (6) 2.05 1.50

A142

3k, Stagecoach and Train. 5k, Postrider and post bus. 13k, Sailing ship and plane.

1949, May 20

380 A142 3k brown carmine 1.25 1.25
381 A142 5k deep blue .80 .40
382 A142 13k deep green 1.25 .80
Nos. 380-382 (3) 3.30 2.45

75th anniv. of the UPU.

Reaping A143

Communist Emblem and Workers A144

Workman, Symbol of Industry — A145

Perf. 12½x12, 12x12½

1949, May 24 Unwmk.

383 A143 1.50k deep green .50 .45
384 A144 3k brown carmine .50 .45
385 A145 5k deep blue .50 .45
Nos. 383-385 (3) 1.50 1.35

No. 384 for the 9th meeting of the Communist Party of Czechoslovakia, 5/25/49.

Nos. 383-385 each issued in sheets of 100 stamps and 12 inscribed labels. Value, set with attached labels, $15.

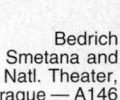

Bedrich Smetana and Natl. Theater, Prague — A146

1949, June 4 *Perf. 12½x12*

386 A146 1.50k dull green .25 .25
387 A146 5k deep blue .55 .25

Birth of Bedrich Smetana, composer, 125th anniv.

Aleksander Pushkin — A147

1949, June 6 *Perf. 12x12½*

388 A147 2k olive gray .35 .30

Birth of Aleksander S. Pushkin, 150th anniv.

Frederic Chopin and Conservatory, Warsaw A148

1949, June 24 *Perf. 12½x12*

389 A148 3k dark red .40 .25
390 A148 8k violet brown .75 .50

Cent. of the death of Frederic F. Chopin.

Globe and Ribbon — A149

1949, Aug. 20 *Perf. 12½x12*

391 A149 1.50k violet brown .45 .45
392 A149 5k ultra 1.15 1.15

50th Prague Sample Fair, Sept. 11-18, 1949.

Starting in October, 1949, some commemorative sets included one "blocked" value, which could be obtained only by purchasing the complete set. These restricted values were printed in smaller quantities than other stamps in the set and were typically sold for more than face value.

Zvolen Castle — A150

1949, Aug. 28 *Perf. 12½*

393 A150 10k rose lake .75 .25

Early Miners — A151

Miner of Today — A152

Design: 5k, Mining Machine.

1949, Sept. 11 *Perf. 12½*

394 A151 1.50k sepia .85 .65
395 A152 3k carmine rose 7.00 2.75
396 A151 5k deep blue 5.25 2.00
Nos. 394-396 (3) 13.10 5.40

700th anniv. of the Czechoslovak mining industry; 150th anniv. of the miner's laws.

Construction Workers — A153

Joseph V. Stalin — A154

1949, Dec. 11 *Perf. 12½*

397 A153 1k shown 3.50 1.60
398 A153 2k Machinist 2.50 .80

2nd Trade Union Congress, Prague, 1949.

1949, Dec. 21 Unwmk.

Design: 3k, Stalin facing left.

Cream Paper

399 A154 1.50k greenish gray 1.25 .60
400 A154 3k claret 4.75 2.00

70th birthday of Joseph V. Stalin.

Skier — A155

Efficiency Badge — A156

Engr., Photo. (3k)

1950, Feb. 15 *Perf. 12½, 13½*

401 A155 1.50k gray blue 3.50 1.75
402 A156 3k vio brn, *cr* 3.50 1.75
403 A155 5k ultramarine 2.75 1.25
Nos. 401-403 (3) 9.75 4.75

51st Ski Championship for the Tatra cup, Feb. 15-26, 1950.

Vladimir V. Mayakovsky, Poet, 20th Death Anniv. — A157

1950, Apr. 14 Engr. *Perf. 12½*

404 A157 1.50k dark brown 2.50 1.25
405 A157 3k brown red 2.50 1.25

See Nos. 414-417, 422-423, 432-433, 464-465, 477-478.

Soviet Tank Soldier and Hradcany A158

2k, Hero of Labor medal. 3k, Two workers (militiamen) and Town Hall, Prague. 5k, Text of government program and heraldic lion.

1950, May 5

406 A158 1.50k gray green .40 .25
407 A158 2k dark brown 1.25 1.25
408 A158 3k brown red .25 .25
409 A158 5k dark blue .55 .25
Nos. 406-409 (4) 2.45 2.00

5th anniv. of the Czechoslovak People's Democratic Republic.

Factory and Young Couple with Tools A159

Designs: 2k, Steam shovel. 3k, Farmer and farm scene. 5k, Three workers leaving factory.

1950, May 9 Engr.

410 A159 1.50k dark green 2.00 .95
411 A159 2k dark brown 2.00 .95
412 A159 3k rose red 1.25 .40
413 A159 5k deep blue 1.25 .40
Nos. 410-413 (4) 6.50 2.70

Canceled to Order

The government philatelic department started about 1950 to sell canceled sets of new issues. Values in the second ("used") column are for these canceled-to-order stamps. Postally used stamps are worth more.

Portrait Type of 1950

Design: S. K. Neumann.

1950, June 5 Unwmk. *Perf. 12½*

414 A157 1.50k deep blue .40 .25
415 A157 3k violet brown 1.25 .75

Stanislav Kostka Neumann (1875-1947), journalist and poet.

1950, June 21

Design: Bozena Nemcova.

416 A157 1.50k deep blue 1.25 .75
417 A157 7k dark brown .30 .25

Bozena Nemcova (1820-1862), writer.

Liberation of Colonies A160

Designs: 2k, Allegory, Fight for Peace. 3k, Group of Students. 5k, Marching Students with flags.

1950, Aug. 14

418 A160 1.50k dark green .25 .25
419 A160 2k sepia .85 .55
420 A160 3k rose carmine .25 .25
421 A160 5k ultra .40 .35
Nos. 418-421 (4) 1.75 1.40

2nd International Students World Congress, Prague, Aug. 12-24, 1950.

Portrait Type of 1950

Design: Zdenek Fibich.

1950, Oct. 15

422 A157 3k rose brown .90 .55
423 A157 8k gray green .35 .25

Zdenek Fibich, musician, birth centenary.

Miner, Soldier and Farmer A161

Czech and Soviet Soldiers A162

1950, Oct. 6

424 A161 1.50k slate 1.25 1.25
425 A162 3k carmine rose .40 .40

Issued to publicize Czech Army Day.

Prague Castle, 16th Century A163

Prague, 1493
A164

3k, Prague, 1606. 5k, Prague, 1794.

1950, Oct. 21 *Perf. 14*

426	A163	1.50k	black	5.00	3.00
427	A164	2k	chocolate	5.00	3.00
428	A164	3k	brown car	5.00	3.00
429	A164	5k	gray	5.00	3.00
a.			Block of 4, #426-429	30.00	20.00

See Nos. 434-435.

Communications Symbols — A165

1950, Oct. 25 *Perf. 12½*

430	A165	1.50k	chocolate	.40	.25
431	A165	3k	brown carmine	.85	.30

1st anniv. of the foundation of the Intl. League of P.T.T. Employees.

Portrait Type of 1950

Design: J. Gregor Tajovsky.

1950, Oct. 26

432	A157	1.50k	brown	1.00	.60
433	A157	5k	deep blue	.65	.30

10th anniversary of the death of J. Gregor Tajovsky (1874-1940), Slovakian writer.

Scenic Type of 1950

Design: Prague, 1950.

1950, Oct. 28

434	A164	1.50k	indigo	.40	.25
a.			Souvenir sheet of 4, imperf.	40.00	20.00
435	A164	3k	brown car	.80	.50

Czech and Soviet Steel Workers
A166

1950, Nov. 4 **Unwmk.**

436	A166	1.50k	chocolate	.50	.35
437	A166	5k	deep blue	.95	.60

Issued to publicize the 2nd meeting of the Union of Czechoslovak-Soviet Friendship.

Dove by Picasso
A167

1951, Jan. 20 **Photo.** *Perf. 14*

438	A167	2k	deep blue	5.25	3.00
439	A167	3k	rose brown	3.50	2.00

1st Czechoslovak Congress of Fighters for Peace, held in Prague.

Julius Fucik — A168

1951, Feb. 17 **Engr.** *Perf. 12½*

440	A168	1.50k	gray	.80	.80
441	A168	5k	gray blue	1.60	1.60

No. 441 exists in a sheet of 12. Value, $500.

Drop Hammer — A169

Installing Gear — A170

1951, Feb. 24

442	A169	1.50k	gray blk	.25	.25
443	A170	3k	violet brn	.25	.25
444	A169	4k	gray blue	.60	.50
			Nos. 442-444 (3)	1.10	1.00

Women Machinists
A171

Apprentice Miners
A172

Designs: 3k, Woman tractor operator. 5k, Women of different races.

1951, Mar. 8 **Photo.** *Perf. 14*

445	A171	1.50k	olive brown	.40	.30
446	A171	3k	brown car	1.60	1.25
447	A171	5k	blue	.80	.50
			Nos. 445-447 (3)	2.80	2.05

International Women's Day, Mar. 8.

1951, Apr. 12 **Engr.** *Perf. 12½*

448	A172	1.50k	gray	.55	.50
449	A172	3k	red brown	.25	.25

Plowing
A173

Collective Cattle Breeding
A174

1951, Apr. 28 **Photo.** *Perf. 14*

450	A173	1.50k	brown	.80	.80
451	A174	2k	dk green	1.60	1.60

Tatra Mountain Recreation Center — A175

Mountain Recreation Centers: 2k, Beskydy (Beskids). 3k, Krkonose (Carpathians).

1951, May 5 **Engr.** *Perf. 12½*

452	A175	1.50k	deep green	.25	.25
453	A175	2k	dark brown	1.10	.95
454	A175	3k	rose brown	.30	.25
			Nos. 452-454 (3)	1.65	1.45

Issued to publicize the summer opening of trade union recreation centers.

Klement Gottwald and Joseph Stalin
A176

Factory Militiaman
A177

Red Army Soldier and Partisan
A178

Marx, Engels, Lenin and Stalin
A179

1951 **Unwmk.** *Perf. 12½*

455	A176	1.50k	olive gray	.80	.25
456	A177	2k	red brown	.40	.25
457	A178	3k	rose brown	.40	.25
458	A176	5k	deep blue	2.00	1.40
459	A179	8k	gray	.80	.25
			Nos. 455-459 (5)	4.40	2.40

30th anniv. of the founding of the Czechoslovak Communist Party.

A180

Design: 1k, 2k, Antonin Dvorák. 1.50k, 3k, Bedrich Smetana.

1951, May 30

460	A180	1k	redsh brown	.40	.25
461	A180	1.50k	olive gray	1.60	.80
462	A180	2k	dk redsh brn	1.60	.80
463	A180	3k	rose brown	.40	.25
			Nos. 460-463 (4)	4.00	2.10

International Music Festival, Prague.

Nos. 461 and 462 were each issued in sheets of 10 stamps. Value, $700 for 461, $600 for 462.

Portrait Type of 1950

Portrait: Bohumir Smeral (facing right).

1951, June 21

464	A157	1.50k	dark gray	.80	.65
465	A157	3k	rose brown	.40	.25

10th anniv. of the death of Bohumir Smeral, political leader.

A181

1951, June 21

466	A181	1k	shown	.75	.35
467	A181	1.50k	Discus	.75	.35
468	A181	3k	Soccer	1.50	.35
469	A181	5k	Skier	3.50	1.50
			Nos. 466-469 (4)	6.50	2.55

Issued to honor the 9th Congress of the Czechoslovak Sokol Federation.

Scene from "Fall of Berlin"
A182

Scene from "The Great Citizen"
A183

1951, July 14

470	A182	80h	rose brown	.40	.40
471	A183	1.50k	dark gray	.40	.40
472	A182	4k	gray blue	1.60	1.25
			Nos. 470-472 (3)	2.40	2.05

Intl. Film Festival, Karlovy Vary, July 14-29.

Alois Jirásek — A184

"Fables and Fate"
A185

Design: 4k, Scene from "Reign of Tabor."

1951, Aug. 23 **Engr.** *Perf. 12½*

473	A184	1.50k	gray	.55	.25
474	A184	5k	dark blue	2.40	1.25

Photo.

Perf. 14

475	A185	3k	dark red	.55	.25
476	A185	4k	dark brown	.55	.25
			Nos. 473-476 (4)	4.05	2.00

Cent. of the birth of Alois Jirásek, author.

No. 474 was issued in a sheet of 10 stamps. Value: mint *$900.*

Portrait Type of 1950

Design: Josef Hybes (1850-1921), co-founder of Czech Communist Party.

1951, July 21 **Engr.**

477	A157	1.50k	chocolate	.25	.25
478	A157	2k	rose brown	.80	.65

"Ostrava Region" — A186

Mining Iron Ore — A187

1951, Sept. 9

479	A186	1.50k	dk brown	.25	.25
480	A187	3k	rose brown	.25	.25
481	A186	5k	deep blue	1.25	1.00
			Nos. 479-481 (3)	1.75	1.50

Miner's Day, Sept. 9, 1951.

Soldiers on Parade — A188

1k, Gunner and field gun. 1.50k, Klement Gottwald. 3k, Tankman and tank. 5k, Aviators.

Photo. (80h, 5k), Engr.
1951, Oct. 6 ***Perf. 14 (80h, 5k), 12½***
Inscribed: "Den CS Armady 1951"

482 A188 80h olive brown .35 .30
483 A188 1k dk olive grn .35 .30
484 A188 1.50k sepia .35 .30
485 A188 3k claret .80 .40
486 A188 5k blue 2.00 .80
Nos. 482-486 (5) 3.85 2.10

Issued to publicize Army Day, Oct. 6, 1951.

Stalin and Gottwald — A189

Lenin, Stalin and Soldiers — A190

1951, Nov. 3 **Engr.** ***Perf. 12½***
487 A189 1.50k sepia .25 .25
488 A190 3k red brown .25 .25
489 A189 4k deep blue 1.25 .80
Nos. 487-489 (3) 1.75 1.30

Issued to publicize the month of Czechoslovak-Soviet friendship, 1951.

Peter Jilemnicky A191

Ladislav Zapotocky A192

1951, Dec. 5 **Unwmk.**
491 A191 1.50k redsh brown .25 .25
492 A191 2k dull blue .95 .40

Peter Jilemnicky (1901-1949), writer.

1952, Jan. 12 ***Perf. 11½***
493 A192 1.50k brown red .25 .25
494 A192 4k gray 1.25 .55

Centenary of the birth of Ladislav Zapotocky, Bohemian socialist pioneer.

Jan Kollar — A193

1952, Jan. 30 **Unwmk.** ***Perf. 11½***
495 A193 3k dark carmine .25 .25
496 A193 5k violet blue 1.25 .80

Jan Kollar (1793-1852), poet.

Lenin and Lenin Hall — A194

1952, Jan. 30 ***Perf. 12½***
497 A194 1.50k rose carmine .30 .25
498 A194 5k deep blue 1.25 .80

6th All-Russian Party Conf., 40th anniv.

Emil Holub and African — A195

1952, Feb. 21 ***Perf. 11½***
499 A195 3k red brown .50 .30
500 A195 5k gray 2.00 1.10

Death of Emil Holub, explorer, 50th anniv.

Gottwald Metallurgical Plant — A196

Designs: 2k, Foundry. 3k, Chemical plant.

1952, Feb. 25 **Photo.** ***Perf. 14***
501 A196 1.50k sepia .25 .25
502 A196 2k red brown 1.50 .75
503 A196 3k scarlet .25 .25
Nos. 501-503 (3) 2.00 1.25

Student, Soldier and Miner — A197

Youths of Three Races — A198

1952, Mar. 21 **Unwmk.** ***Perf. 14***
504 A197 1.50k blue .25 .25
505 A198 2k olive black .25 .25
506 A197 3k lake 1.25 .80
Nos. 504-506 (3) 1.75 1.30

International Youth Day, Mar. 25, 1952.

Similar to Type of 1951

Portrait: Otakar Sevcik.

1952, Mar. 22 **Engr.** ***Perf. 12½***
507 A184 2k choc, *cr* .95 .50
508 A184 3k rose brn, *cr* .25 .25

Otakar Sevcik, violinist, birth cent.

Jan A. Komensky A199

Industrial and Farm Women A200

1952, Mar. 28
509 A199 1.50k dk brown, *cr* 1.60 .80
510 A199 11k dk blue, *cr* .40 .25

360th anniv. of the birth of Jan Amos Komensky (Comenius), teacher and philosopher.

1952, Mar. 8
511 A200 1.50k dp blue, *cr* 1.00 .80

International Women's Day Mar. 8, 1952.

Woman and Children A201

Antifascist A202

1952, Apr. 12
512 A201 2k chocolate, *cr* 2.00 1.25
513 A201 3k dp claret, *cr* .25 .25

Intl. Conf. for the Protection of Children, Vienna, Apr. 12-16, 1952.

1952, Apr. 11 **Photo.** ***Perf. 14***
514 A202 1.50k red brown .25 .25
515 A202 2k ultra 1.25 .75

Day of International Solidarity of Fighters against Fascism, Apr. 11, 1952.

Harvester A203

Design: 3k, Tractor and Seeders.

1952, Apr. 30
516 A203 1.50k deep blue 2.50 1.40
517 A203 2k brown .30 .30
518 A203 3k brown red .30 .30
Nos. 516-518 (3) 3.10 2.00

Youths Carrying Flags — A204

1952, May 1
519 A204 3k brown red .45 .25
520 A204 4k dk red brown 2.00 1.75

Issued to publicize Labor Day, May 1, 1952.

Crowd Cheering Soviet Soldiers — A205

1952, May 9
521 A205 1.50k dark red .65 .50
522 A205 5k deep blue 2.50 2.00

Liberation of Czechoslovakia from German occupation, 7th anniversary.

Children A206

Design: 3k, "Pioneer" teaching children.

1952, May 31 **Engr.** ***Perf. 12½***
523 A206 1.50k dk brn, *cr* .25 .25
524 A206 2k Prus grn, *cr* 1.50 1.00
525 A206 3k rose brn, *cr* .25 .25
Nos. 523-525 (3) 2.00 1.50

International Children's Day May 31, 1952.

J. V. Myslbek — A207

Design: 8k, Allegory, "Music."

1952, June 2
526 A207 1.50k red brown .30 .25
527 A207 2k dark brown 1.50 1.25
528 A207 8k gray green .25 .25
Nos. 526-528 (3) 2.05 1.75

Joseph V. Myslbek (1848-1922), sculptor.

Beethoven — A208

House of Artists — A209

1952, June 7 **Unwmk.** ***Perf. 11½***
529 A208 1.50k sepia .35 .25
530 A209 3k red brown .40 .25
531 A208 5k indigo 1.60 1.25
Nos. 529-531 (3) 2.35 1.75

International Music Festival, Prague, 1952.

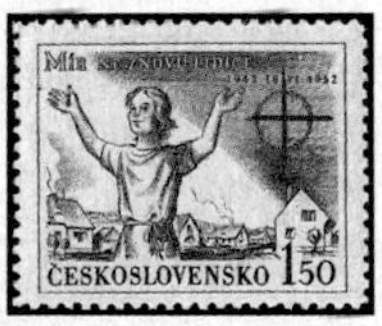

Lidice, Symbol of a New Life — A210

1952, June 10 ***Perf. 12½***
532 A210 1.50k dk violet brn .25 .25
533 A210 5k dark blue 1.25 .75

Destruction of Lidice, 10th anniversary.

Jan Hus — A211

Bethlehem Chapel — A212

1952, July 5
534 A211 1.50k brown .25 .25
535 A212 3k red brown .25 .25
536 A211 5k black 1.60 *1.00*
Nos. 534-536 (3) 2.10 1.50

550th anniv. of the installation of Jan Hus as pastor of Bethlehem Chapel, Prague.

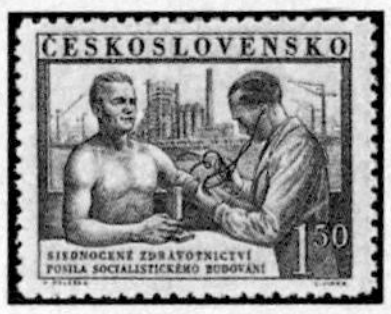

Doctor Examining Patient — A213

2k, Doctor, Nurse, Mother and child.

1952, July 31
537 A213 1.50k dark brown 1.50 1.00
538 A213 2k blue violet .35 .25
539 A213 3k rose brown .35 .25
Nos. 537-539 (3) 2.20 1.50

Czechoslovakia's Unified Health Service.

A214

United Physical Education Program — A214a

1952, Aug. 2 *Perf. 11½*

540	A214	1.50k Relay race		.95	.60
541	A214a	2k Canoeing		2.75	1.25
542	A214a	3k Cycling		.60	.55
543	A214a	4k Hockey		*4.50*	*3.25*
		Nos. 540-543 (4)		8.80	5.65

Issued to publicize Czechoslovakia's Unified Physical Education program.

F. L. Celakovski A215 — Mikulas Ales A216

1952, Aug. 5 *Perf. 12½*

544	A215	1.50k dark brown	.25	.25
545	A215	2k dark green	1.60	1.25

Centenary of the death of Frantisek L. Celakovski, poet and writer.

Perf. 11x11½

1952, Aug. 30 Engr. Unwmk.

546	A216	1.50k dk gray grn	.50	.40
547	A216	6k red brown	3.25	2.40

Birth centenary of Mikulas Ales, painter.

17th Century Mining Towers — A217

Designs: 1.50k, Coal Excavator. 2k, Peter Bezruc mine. 3k, Automatic coaling crane.

1952, Sept. 14 *Perf. 12½*

548	A217	1k sepia	1.40	.90
549	A217	1.50k dark blue	.25	.25
550	A217	2k olive gray	.25	.25
551	A217	3k violet brown	.25	.25
		Nos. 548-551 (4)	2.15	1.65

Miners' Day, Sept. 14, 1952. No. 550 also for the 85th anniv. of the birth of Peter Bezruc (Vladimir Vasek), poet.

Jan Zizka — A218

Designs: 2k, Fraternization with Russians. 3k, Marching with flag.

Inscribed: ". . . . Armady 1952,"

1952, Oct. 5 Engr. *Perf. 11½*

552	A218	1.50k rose lake	.25	.25
553	A218	2k olive bister	.25	.25
554	A218	3k dk car rose	.25	.25
555	A218	4k gray	1.90	.95
		Nos. 552-555 (4)	2.65	1.70

Issued to publicize Army Day, Oct. 5, 1952.

Souvenir Sheet

Statues to Bulgarian Partisans and to Soviet Army — A219

1952, Oct. 18 Unwmk. *Perf. 12½*

556	A219	Sheet of 2	110.00	25.00
a.		2k deep carmine	35.00	7.50
b.		3k ultramarine	35.00	7.50

National Philatelic Exhibition, Bratislava, Oct. 18-Nov. 2, 1952.

Danube River, Bratislava A220

1952, Oct. 18

557	A220	1.50k dark brown	.25	.25

National Philatelic Exhibition, Bratislava.

Conference with Lenin and Stalin — A221

1952, Nov. 7

558	A221	2k brown black	1.60	1.25
559	A221	3k carmine	.25	.25

35th anniv. of the Russian Revolution and to publicize Czechoslovak-Soviet friendship.

Worker and Nurse Holding Dove and Olive Branch — A222

1952, Nov. 15 Photo. *Perf. 14*

560	A222	2k brown	1.40	.80
561	A222	3k red	.25	.25

Issued to publicize the first State Congress of the Czechoslovak Red Cross.

Matej Louda, Hussite Leader, Painted by Mikulas Ales A223

3k, Dragon-killer Trutnov, painted by Ales.

1952, Nov. 18 Engr. *Perf. 11½*

562	A223	2k red brown	.40	.25
563	A223	3k grnsh gray	.80	.25

Mikulas Ales, painter, birth cent.

Gottwald Type of 1948-49

1952, June 2 Unwmk. *Perf. 12½*

Size: 19x24mm

564	A135	1k dark green	.60	.25

"Peace" Flags — A224 — Dove by Picasso — A225

1952, Dec. 12 Photo. *Perf. 14*

565	A224	3k red brown	.40	.25
566	A224	4k deep blue	1.50	1.00

Issued to publicize the Congress of Nations for Peace, Vienna, Dec. 12-19, 1952.

1953, Jan. 17

Design: 4k, Czech Family.

567	A225	1.50k dark brown	.25	.25
568	A225	4k slate blue	.80	.50

2nd Czechoslovak Peace Congress.

Smetana Museum — A226

Design: 4k, Jirásek Museum.

1953, Feb. 10 Engr. *Perf. 11½*

569	A226	1.50k dk violet brn	.25	.25
570	A226	4k dark gray	1.50	.90

Prof. Zdenek Nejedly, 75th birth anniv.

Martin Kukucin — A227 — Jaroslav Vrchlicky — A228

Designs: 2k, Karel Jaromir Erben. 3k, Vaclav Matej Kramerius. 5k, Josef Dobrovsky.

1953, Feb. 28

571	A227	1k gray	.25	.25
572	A228	1.50k olive	.25	.25
573	A228	2k rose lake	.25	.25
574	A228	3k lt brown	.75	.50
575	A228	5k slate blue	1.50	1.10
		Nos. 571-575 (5)	3.00	2.35

Issued to honor Czech writers and poets: 1k, 25th anniv. of death of Kukucin. 1.50k, birth cent. of Vrchlicky. 2k, cent. of completion of "Kytice" by Erben. 3k, birth bicent. of Kramerius. 5k, birth bicent. of Dobrovsky.

Militia — A229

Gottwald — A230

Design: 8k, Portraits of Stalin and Gottwald and Peoples Assembly.

Perf. 13½x14

1953, Feb. 25 Photo. Unwmk.

576	A229	1.50k deep blue	.25	.25
577	A230	3k red	.25	.25
578	A229	8k dark brown	2.40	1.00
		Nos. 576-578 (3)	2.90	1.50

5th anniv. of the defeat of the attempt to reinstate capitalism.

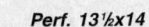

Book and Torch — A231

Design: 3k, Bedrich Vaclavek.

1953, Mar. 5 Engr. *Perf. 11½*

579	A231	1k sepia	1.60	.80
580	A231	3k orange brown	.25	.25

Bedrich Vaclavek (1897-1943), socialist writer.

Stalin Type of 1949

Inscribed "21 XII 1879-5 III 1953"

1953, Mar. 12

581	A154	1.50k black	.35	.25

Death of Joseph Stalin, Mar. 5, 1953.

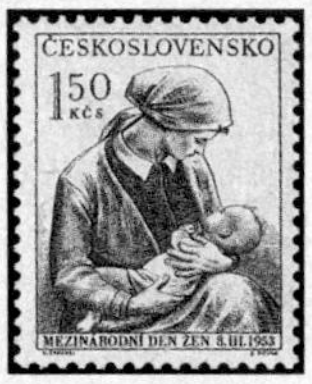
Mother and Child — A232

Girl Revolutionist A233

1953, Mar. 8

582	A232	1.50k ultra	.25	.25
583	A233	2k brown red	1.25	.75

International Women's Day.

Klement Gottwald — A234

1953, Mar. 19

584	A234	1.50k black	.25	.25
585	A234	3k black	.25	.25

Souvenir Sheet

Imperf

586	A234	5k black	6.00	4.00

Death of Pres. Klement Gottwald, 3/14/53.

Josef Pecka, Ladislav Zapotocky and Josef Hybes — A236

1953, Apr. 7 Unwmk. *Perf. 11½*

587	A236	2k lt violet brn	.25	.25

75th anniversary of the first congress of the Czech Social Democratic Party.

Cyclists — A237

1953, Apr. 29

588 A237 3k deep blue .75 .35

6th International Peace Bicycle Race, Prague-Berlin-Warsaw.

Medal of "May 1, 1890" A238

Designs: 1.50k, Lenin and Stalin. 3k, May Day Parade. 8k, Marx and Engels.

Engraved and Photogravure

1953, Apr. 30 ***Perf. 11½x11, 14***

589 A238 1k chocolate 1.50 .75
590 A238 1.50k dark gray .25 .25
591 A238 3k carmine lake .25 .25
592 A238 8k dk gray green .35 .25
Nos. 589-592 (4) 2.35 1.50

Issued to publicize Labor Day, May 1, 1953.

Sowing Grain — A239

1953, May 8 **Photo.** ***Perf. 14***

593 A239 1.50k shown .35 .25
594 A239 7k Reaper 1.60 1.40

Socialization of the village.

Dam — A240

Welder — A241

Design: 3k, Iron works.

1953, May 8 ***Perf. 11½***

595 A240 1.50k gray 1.25 .60
596 A241 2k blue gray .25 .25
597 A240 3k red brown .25 .25
Nos. 595-597 (3) 1.75 1.10

Josef Slavik — A242

Leos Janacek — A243

1953, June 19 **Photo.**

598 A242 75h dp gray blue .75 .25
599 A243 1.60k dark brown 1.00 .25

Issued on the occasion of the International Music Festival, Prague, 1953.

Gottwald Type of 1948-49

Perf. 12½ (15h, 1k), 11½ (20h, 3k)

1953

600 A135 15h yellow green .35 .25
601 A135 20h dk violet brn .50 .25
602 A135 1k purple 1.25 .25
603 A135 3k brown car .25 .25
604 A135 3k gray .80 .25
Nos. 600-604 (5) 3.15 1.25

Nos. 600-604 vary slightly in size.

Pres. Antonin Zapotocky — A244

1953, June 19 ***Perf. 14***

605 A244 30h violet blue .75 .25
606 A244 60h cerise 1.00 .25

Julius Fucik A245

Book and Carnation A246

1953, Sept. 8 **Engr.** ***Perf. 12½***

607 A245 40h dk violet brn .30 .25
608 A246 60h pink .50 .30

10th anniv. of the death of Julius Fucik, Communist leader executed by the Nazis.

Miner and Flag — A247

Design: 60h, Oil field and workers.

1953, Sept. 10 ***Perf. 11½***

609 A247 30h gray .25 .25
610 A247 60h brown vio 1.25 .50

Miner's Day, Sept. 10, 1953.

Volleyball Game — A248

Motorcyclist A249

Design: 60h, Woman throwing javelin.

1953, Sept. 15

611 A248 30h brown red 5.75 1.75
612 A249 40h dk violet brn 3.50 1.00
613 A248 60h rose violet 3.00 1.00
Nos. 611-613 (3) 12.25 3.75

Hussite Warrior A250

Pres. Antonin Zapotocky A251

Designs: 60h, Soldier presenting arms. 1k, Red army soldiers.

1953, Oct. 8

614 A250 30h brown .30 .25
615 A250 60h rose lake .65 .25
616 A250 1k brown red 1.50 1.25
Nos. 614-616 (3) 2.45 1.75

Issued to publicize Army Day, Oct. 3, 1953.

1953 **Unwmk.** ***Perf. 11½, 12½***

617 A251 30h violet blue .45 .25
618 A251 60h carmine rose .80 .25

No. 617 is perf. 11½ & measures 19x23mm, No. 618 perf. 12½ & 18½x23½mm.

See No. 780.

Charles Bridge and Prague Castle — A252

1953, Aug. 15 **Engr.** ***Perf. 11½***

619 A252 5k gray 4.00 .25

Korean and Czech Girls — A253

1953, Oct. 11 ***Perf. 11x11½***

620 A253 30h dark brown 2.40 1.60

Czechoslovakia's friendship with Korea.

Flags, Hradcany Castle and Kremlin — A254

Designs: 60h, Lomonosov University, Moscow. 1.20k, Lenin Ship Canal.

1953, Nov. 7

621 A254 30h dark gray .80 .55
622 A254 60h dark brown 1.25 1.00
623 A254 1.20k ultra 4.00 2.00
Nos. 621-623 (3) 6.05 3.55

Czechoslovak-Soviet friendship month.

Emmy Destinn, Opera Singer — A255

National Theater, Prague — A256

Portrait: 2k, Eduard Vojan, actor.

1953, Nov. 18 ***Perf. 14***

624 A255 30h blue black 1.25 .75
625 A256 60h brown .40 .40
626 A255 2k sepia 3.25 1.25
Nos. 624-626 (3) 4.90 2.40

Natl. Theater founding, 70th anniv.

Nos. 624 and 626 each were issued in sheets of 10. Values: No. 624, $100; No. 626, $75.

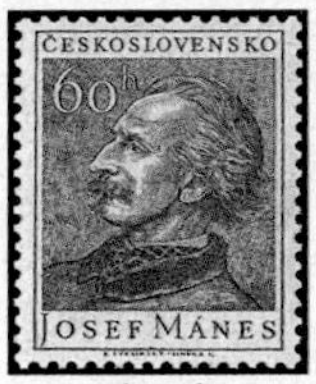
Josef Manes — A257

Vaclav Hollar — A258

1953, Nov. 28 ***Perf. 11x11½***

627 A257 60h brown carmine .35 .25
628 A257 1.20k deep blue 1.50 .90

Issued to honor Josef Manes, painter.

1953, Dec. 5

Portrait: 1.20k, Head framed, facing right.

629 A258 30h brown black .35 .25
630 A258 1.20k dark brown 1.50 .65

Vaclav Hollar, artist and etcher.

Leo N. Tolstoy — A259

1953, Dec. 29 **Unwmk.**

631 A259 60h dark green .35 .25
632 A259 1k chocolate 1.50 .65

Leo N. Tolstoi, 125th birth anniv.

Locomotive — A260

Design: 1k, Plane loading mail.

Engraved, Center Photogravure

1953, Dec. 29 ***Perf. 11½x11***

633 A260 60h brn org & gray vio 1.50 .50
634 A260 1k org brn & brt bl 4.00 1.25

Lenin — A261

Lenin Museum, Prague — A262

1954, Jan. 21 **Engr.** ***Perf. 11½***

635 A261 30h dark brown .45 .25
636 A262 1.40k chocolate 1.50 .90

30th anniversary of the death of Lenin.

Klement Gottwald — A263

Design: 2.40k, Revolutionist with flag.

1954, Feb. 18 ***Perf. 11x11½, 14x13½***

637	A263	60h dark brown	.30	.25
638	A263	2.40k rose lake	4.25	1.50

25th anniversary of the fifth congress of the Communist Party in Czechoslovakia.

No. 638 was issued in a sheet of 10 stamps. Value, $90.

Gottwald Mausoleum, Prague — A264

Gottwald and Stalin A265

1.20k, Lenin & Stalin mausoleum, Moscow.

1954, Mar. 5 ***Perf. 11½, 14x13½***

639	A264	30h olive brown	.35	.25
640	A265	60h deep ultra	.35	.25
641	A264	1.20k rose brown	2.25	1.00
		Nos. 639-641 (3)	2.95	1.50

1st anniv. of the deaths of Stalin and Gottwald.

No. 641 was issued in a sheet of 10 stamps. Value, $120.

Two Runners — A266

Group of Hikers — A267

Design: 1k, Woman swimmer.

1954, Apr. 24 ***Perf. 11½***

642	A266	30h dark brown	2.40	1.25
643	A267	80h dark green	8.00	4.00
644	A266	1k dk violet blue	2.00	.80
		Nos. 642-644 (3)	12.40	6.05

No. 643 was issued in a sheet of 10 stamps. Value, $350.

Nurse — A268

Designs: 15h, Construction worker. 40h, Postwoman. 45h, Ironworker. 50h, Soldier. 75h, Lathe operator. 80h, Textile worker. 1k, Farm woman. 1.20k, Scientist and microscope. 1.60k, Miner. 2k, Physician and baby. 2.40k, Engineer. 3k, Chemist.

1954 ***Perf. 12½x12, 11½x11***

645	A268	15h dark green	.30	.25
646	A268	20h lt violet	.35	.25
647	A268	40h dark brown	.45	.25
648	A268	45h dk gray blue	.35	.25
649	A268	50h dk gray green	.45	.25
650	A268	75h deep blue	.45	.25
651	A268	80h violet brown	.45	.25
652	A268	1k green	.75	.25
653	A268	1.20k dk violet blue	.45	.25
654	A268	1.60k brown blk	1.10	.25
655	A268	2k orange brown	1.60	.25
656	A268	2.40k violet blue	1.50	.25
657	A268	3k carmine	1.50	.25
		Nos. 645-657 (13)	9.70	3.25

Antonin Dvorák — A269

Prokop Divis — A270

40h, Leos Janacek. 60h, Bedrich Smetana.

1954, May 22 ***Perf. 11x11½***

658	A269	30h violet brown	2.50	.30
659	A269	40h brick red	3.00	.40
660	A269	60h dark blue	.80	.25
		Nos. 658-660 (3)	6.30	.95

"Year of Czech Music," 1954.

1954, June 15

661	A270	30h gray	.40	.25
662	A270	75h violet brown	1.60	.65

200th anniv. of the invention of a lightning conductor by Prokop Divis.

Slovak Insurrectionist A271

Anton P. Chekhov A272

Design: 1.20k, Partisan woman.

1954, Aug. 28 ***Perf. 11½***

663	A271	30h brown orange	.25	.25
664	A271	1.20k dark blue	.95	.75

Slovak national uprising, 10th anniv.

1954, Sept. 24

665	A272	30h dull gray grn	.30	.25
666	A272	45h dull gray brn	1.25	.65

50th anniv. of the death of Chekhov, writer.

Soviet Representative Giving Agricultural Instruction — A273

Designs: 60h, Soviet industrial instruction. 2k, Dancers (cultural collaboration).

1954, Nov. 6 ***Perf. 11½x11***

667	A273	30h yellow brown	.25	.25
668	A273	60h dark blue	.25	.25
669	A273	2k vermilion	1.40	1.25
		Nos. 667-669 (3)	1.90	1.75

Czechoslovak-Soviet friendship month.

Jan Neruda — A274

60h, Janko Jesensky. 1.60k, Jiri Wolker.

1954, Nov. 25 ***Perf. 11x11½***

670	A274	30h dark blue	.85	.25
671	A274	60h dull red	1.40	.50
672	A274	1.60k sepia	.35	.25
		Nos. 670-672 (3)	2.60	1.00

Issued to honor Czechoslovak poets.

View of Telc A275

Views: 60h, Levoca. 3k, Ceske Budejovice.

1954, Dec. 10 **Engr. & Photo.**

673	A275	30h black & bis	.65	.25
674	A275	60h brown & bis	.65	.25
675	A275	3k black & bis	2.40	1.60
		Nos. 673-675 (3)	3.70	2.10

Pres. Antonin Zapotocky A276

Attacking Soldiers A278

1954, Dec. 18 **Engr.** ***Perf. 11½***

676	A276	30h black brown	.55	.25
677	A276	60h dark blue	.55	.25

Souvenir Sheet

Imperf

678	A276	2k deep claret	20.00	8.00

70th birthday of Pres. Antonin Zapotocky. See Nos. 829-831.

1954, Oct. 3 ***Perf. 11½***

Design: 2k, Soldier holding child.

679	A278	60h dark green	.30	.25
680	A278	2k dark brown	1.60	1.25

Army Day, Oct. 6, 1954.

Woman Holding Torch — A279

Design: 45h, Ski jumper.

1955, Jan. 20 **Engr.**

681	A279	30h red	2.40	.50

Engraved and Photogravure

682	A279	45h black & blue	4.00	.50

First National Spartacist Games, 1955.

Comenius University Building A280

Design: 75h, Jan A. Komensky medal.

1955, Jan. 28 **Engr.** ***Perf. 11½***

683	A280	60h deep green	.30	.25
684	A280	75h chocolate	1.60	.80

35th anniversary of the founding of Comenius University, Bratislava.

Czechoslovak Automobile A281

60h, Textile worker. 75h, Lathe operator.

1955, Mar. 15 **Unwmk.**

685	A281	45h dull green	1.50	.45
686	A281	60h dk violet blue	.60	.25
687	A281	75h sepia	.90	.25
		Nos. 685-687 (3)	3.00	.95

Woman Decorating Soviet Soldier — A282

Stalin Memorial, Prague — A283

Designs: 35h, Tankman with flowers. 60h, Children greeting soldier.

1955, May 5 **Engr.** ***Perf. 11½***

688	A282	30h blue	.35	.25
689	A282	35h dark brown	1.50	.75
690	A282	60h cerise	.35	.25

Photo.

691	A283	60h sepia	.35	.25
		Nos. 688-691 (4)	2.55	1.50

10th anniv. of Czechoslovakia's liberation.

Music and Spring — A284

Foundry Worker — A285

Design: 1k, Woman with lyre.

1955, May 12 **Engr. & Photo.**

692	A284	30h black & pale blue	.35	.25
693	A284	1k black & pale rose	1.50	1.50

International Music Festival, Prague, 1955.

1955, May 12 **Engr.**

Design: 45h, Farm workers.

694	A285	30h violet	.25	.25
695	A285	45h green	1.40	.75

Issued to publicize the third congress of the Trade Union Revolutionary Movement.

Woman Athlete — A286

Jakub Arbes — A287

60h, Dancing couple. 1.60k, Athlete.

1955, June 21

696	A286	20h violet blue	1.00	.50
697	A286	60h green	.35	.25
698	A286	1.60k red	.75	.30
		Nos. 696-698 (3)	2.10	1.05

Issued to publicize the first National Spartacist Games, Prague, June-July, 1955.

1955

Portraits: 30h, Jan Stursa. 40h, Elena Marothy-Soltesova. 60h, Josef Vaclav Sladek.

75h, Alexander Stepanovic Popov. 1.40k, Jan Holly. 1.60k, Pavel Josef Safarik.

699	A287	20h brown	.25	.25
700	A287	30h black	.25	.25
701	A287	40h gray green	.75	.25
702	A287	60h black	.50	.25
703	A287	75h claret	1.75	.70
704	A287	1.40k black, *cr*	.50	.25
705	A287	1.60k dark blue	.50	.25
		Nos. 699-705 (7)	4.50	2.20

Various anniversaries of prominent Slavs.

Girl and Boy of Two Races — A288

Costume of Ocova, Slovakia — A289

1955, July 20

706	A288	60h violet blue	.75	.25

5th World Festival of Youth in Warsaw, July 31-Aug. 14.

1955, July 25

Regional Costumes: 75h, Detva man, Slovakia. 1.60k, Chodsko man, Bohemia. 2k, Hana woman, Moravia.

Frame and Outlines in Brown

707	A289	60h orange & rose	9.00	6.00
708	A289	75h orange & lilac	3.75	3.75
709	A289	1.60k blue & orange	11.00	6.75
710	A289	2k yellow & rose	11.00	6.75
		Nos. 707-710 (4)	34.75	23.25

Nos. 707-710 were each issued in sheets of 10 stamps. Value, $450.

Carp A290

Designs: 30h, Beetle. 35h, Gray Partridge. 1.40k, Butterfly. 1.50k, Hare.

1955, Aug. 8 **Engr. & Photo.**

711	A290	20h sepia & lt bl	2.75	.40
712	A290	30h sepia & pink	1.75	.30
713	A290	35h sepia & buff	1.75	.80
714	A290	1.40k sepia & cream	8.50	4.75
715	A290	1.50k sepia & lt grn	3.00	1.25
		Nos. 711-715 (5)	17.75	7.50

Tabor A291

45h, Prachatice. 60h, Jindrichuv Hradec.

1955, Aug. 26 **Engr.**

716	A291	30h violet brown	.35	.25
717	A291	45h rose carmine	1.50	.75
718	A291	60h sage green	.75	.25
		Nos. 716-718 (3)	2.60	1.25

Issued to publicize the architectural beauty of the towns of Southern Bohemia.

Souvenir Sheet

Various Views of Prague — A292

1955, Sept. 10 **Engr.** ***Perf. 14x13½***

719	A292	Sheet of 5	30.00	30.00
a.		30h gray black	4.75	5.25
b.		45h gray black	4.75	5.25
c.		60h rose lake	4.75	5.25
d.		75h rose lake	4.75	5.25
e.		1.60k gray black	4.75	5.25

International Philatelic Exhibition, Prague, Sept. 10-25, 1955. Size: 145x110mm. Exists imperf., value $40.

Motorcyclists A293

Workers, Soldier and Pioneer A294

1955, Aug. 28

720	A293	60h violet brown	3.00	.75

30th International Motorcycle Races at Gottwaldov, Sept. 13-18, 1955.

1955, Oct. 6 **Unwmk.** ***Perf. 11½***

Army Day: 60h, Tanks and planes.

721	A294	30h violet brown	.35	.25
722	A294	60h slate	1.75	1.25

Hans Christian Andersen — A295

Portraits: 40h, Friedrich von Schiller. 60h, Adam Mickiewicz. 75h, Walt Whitman.

1955, Oct. 27

723	A295	30h brown red	.35	.25
724	A295	40h dark blue	2.25	1.00
725	A295	60h deep claret	.35	.25
726	A295	75h greenish black	.75	.35
		Nos. 723-726 (4)	3.70	1.85

Issued in honor of these four poets and to mark the 100th anniversary of the publication of Walt Whitman's "Leaves of Grass."

Railroad Bridge A296

30h, Train crossing bridge. 60h, Train approaching tunnel. 1.60k, Miners' housing project.

Inscribed: "Stavba Socialismu"

1955, Dec. 15

727	A296	20h dull green	.40	.25
728	A296	30h violet brown	.80	.25
729	A296	60h slate	.80	.25
730	A296	1.60k carmine rose	.55	.25
		Nos. 727-730 (4)	2.55	1.00

Issued to publicize socialist public works.

Hydroelectric Plant — A297

2nd Five Year Plan: 10h, Miner with drill. 25h, Building construction. 30h, Harvester. 60h, Metallurgical plant.

Inscribed: "Druhy Petilety Plan 1956-1960."

1956, Feb. 20 ***Perf. 11½x11***

731	A297	5h violet brown	.30	.25
732	A297	10h gray black	.30	.25
733	A297	25h dk car rose	.55	.25
734	A297	30h green	.35	.25
735	A297	60h violet blue	.55	.25
		Nos. 731-735 (5)	2.05	1.25

Jewelry — A298

1956, Mar. 17 ***Perf. 11x11½***

736	A298	30h shown	.55	.25
737	A298	45h Glassware	4.00	2.00
738	A298	60h Ceramics	.80	.25
739	A298	75h Textiles	.65	.30
		Nos. 736-739 (4)	6.00	2.80

Products of Czechoslovakian industries.

Karlovy Vary (Karlsbad) A299

"We Serve our People" A300

Various Spas: 45h, Marianske Lazne (Marienbad). 75h, Piestany. 1.20k, Tatry Vysne Ruzbachy (Tatra Mountains).

1956, Mar. 17

740	A299	30h olive green	1.75	.30
741	A299	45h brown	1.25	.30
742	A299	75h claret	6.50	4.00
743	A299	1.20k ultra	.85	.30
		Nos. 740-743 (4)	10.35	4.90

Issued to publicize Czechoslovakian spas.

1956, Apr. 9 **Photo.** ***Perf. 11x11½***

Designs: 60h, Russian War Memorial, Berlin, 1k, Tank crewman with standard.

744	A300	30h olive brown	.75	.25
745	A300	60h carmine rose	.75	.25
746	A300	1k ultra	4.75	3.00
		Nos. 744-746 (3)	6.25	3.50

Exhibition: "The Construction and Defense of our Country," Prague, Apr., 1956.

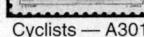

Cyclists — A301

Girl Basketball Players — A302

Athletes and Olympic Rings — A303

Engraved and Photogravure

1956, Apr. 25 **Unwmk.** ***Perf. 11½***

747	A301	30h green & lt blue	4.00	.40
748	A302	45h dk blue & car	1.60	.40
749	A303	75h brown & lemon	1.25	.80
		Nos. 747-749 (3)	6.85	1.60

9th Intl. Peace Cycling Race, Warsaw-Berlin-Prague, May 1-15, 1956 (No. 747). 5th European Womens' Basketball Championship (No. 748). Summer Olympics, Melbourne, Nov. 22-Dec. 8, 1956 (No. 749).

See No. 765.

Mozart — A304

45h, Josef Myslivecek. 60h, Jiri Benda. 1k, Bertramka House, Prague. 1.40k, Xaver Dusek (1731-99) and wife Josepha. 1.60k, Nostic Theater, Prague.

1956, May 12 **Engr.**

Design in Gray Black

750	A304	30h bister	1.50	.35
751	A304	45h gray green	13.50	9.00
752	A304	60h pale rose lilac	1.50	.35
753	A304	1k salmon	1.90	.35
754	A304	1.40k lt blue	4.50	.75
755	A304	1.60k lemon	3.00	.35
		Nos. 750-755 (6)	25.90	11.15

200th anniv. of the birth of Wolfgang Amadeus Mozart and to publicize the International Music Festival in Prague.

Home Guard — A305

1956, May 25

756	A305	60h violet blue	.75	.25

Issued to commemorate the first meeting of the Home Guard, Prague, May 25-27, 1956.

Josef Kajetan Tyl — A306

River Patrol — A307

Portraits: 20h, Ludovit Stur. 30h, Frana Sramek. 1.40k, Karel Havlicek Borovsky.

1956, June 23

757	A306	20h dull purple	.75	.25
758	A306	30h blue	.45	.25
759	A306	60h black	.45	.25
760	A306	1.40k claret	3.00	1.75
		Nos. 757-760 (4)	4.65	2.50

Issued to honor various Czechoslovakian writers. See Nos. 781-784, 873-876.

1956, July 8 ***Perf. 11x11½***

Design: 60h, Guard and dog.

761	A307	30h ultra	.85	.25
762	A307	60h green	.60	.25

Issued to honor men of Frontier Guard.

Type of 1956 and

Steeplechase — A308

1956, Sept. 8 Unwmk. *Perf. 11½*

763	A308	60h indigo & bister	3.00	.80
764	A308	80h brown vio & vio	1.75	.40
765	A303	1.20k slate & orange	3.00	1.75
		Nos. 763-765 (3)	7.75	2.95

Steeplechase, Pardubice, 1956 (No. 763). Marathon race, Kosice, 1956 (No. 764). Olympic Games, Melbourne, Nov. 22-Dec. 8 (No. 765).

Woman Gathering Grapes — A309

Fishermen — A310

35h, Women gathering hops. 95h, Logging.

1956, Sept. 20 Engr.

766	A309	30h brown lake	.35	.25
767	A309	35h gray green	.35	.25
768	A310	80h dark blue	.75	.25
769	A310	95h chocolate	2.25	1.00
		Nos. 766-769 (4)	3.70	1.75

Issued to publicize natural resources.

European Timetable Conf., Prague, Nov. 9-13 — A311

A312

Locomotives: 10h, 1846. 30h, 1855. 40h, 1945. 45h, 1952. 60h, 1955. 1k, 1954.

1956, Nov. 9 Unwmk. *Perf. 11½*

770	A311	10h brown	2.00	.30
771	A312	30h gray	3.00	.30
772	A312	40h green	5.00	.45
773	A312	45h brown car	13.50	6.75
774	A312	60h indigo	3.00	.30
775	A312	1k ultra	6.00	.45
		Nos. 770-775 (6)	32.50	8.55

Costume of Moravia — A313

Regional Costumes (women): 1.20k, Blata, Bohemia. 1.40k, Cicmany, Slovakia. 1.60k, Novohradsko, Slovakia.

1956, Dec. 15 *Perf. 13½*

776	A313	30h brn, ultra & car	1.75	1.75
777	A313	1.20k brn, car & ultra	2.75	.40
778	A313	1.40k brn, ocher & ver	9.00	3.25
779	A313	1.60k brn, car & grn	3.50	.80
		Nos. 776-779 (4)	17.00	6.20

See Nos. 832-835.

Nos. 776-779 each were issued in sheets of 10 stamps. Value, $160.

Zapotocky Type of 1953

1956, Oct. 7 Unwmk. *Perf. 12½*

780	A251	30h blue	.75	.25

Portrait Type of 1956

15h, Ivan Olbracht. 20h, Karel Toman. 30h, F. X. Salda. 1.60k, Terezia Vansova.

1957, Jan. 18 Engr. *Perf. 11½*

781	A306	15h dk red brn, *cr*	.30	.25
782	A306	20h dk green, *cr*	.30	.25
783	A306	30h dk brown, *cr*	.30	.25
784	A306	1.60k dk blue, *cr*	.60	.25
		Nos. 781-784 (4)	1.50	1.00

Issued in honor of Czechoslovakian writers.

Kolin Cathedral — A315

Views: No. 786, Banska Stiavnica. No. 787, Uherske Hradiste. No. 788, Karlstein. No. 789, Charles Bridge, Prague. 1.25k, Moravska Trebova.

1957, Feb. 23

785	A315	30h dk blue gray	.30	.25
786	A315	30h rose violet	.45	.25
787	A315	60h deep rose	.45	.25
788	A315	60h gray green	.45	.25
789	A315	60h brown	.60	.25
790	A315	1.25k gray	2.50	1.50
		Nos. 785-790 (6)	4.75	2.75

Anniversaries of various towns and landmarks.

Komensky Mausoleum, Naarden A316

Jan A. Komensky A317

Old Prints: 40h, Komensky teaching. 1k, Sun, moon, stars and earth.

Perf. 11½x11, 14 (A317)

1957, Mar. 28 Engr. Unwmk.

791	A316	30h pale brown	.45	.25
792	A316	40h dark green	.45	.25
793	A317	60h chocolate	3.00	.75
794	A316	1k carmine rose	.60	.25
		Nos. 791-794 (4)	4.50	1.50

300th anniv. of the publication of "Didactica Opera Omnia" by J. A. Komensky (Comenius). No. 793 issued in sheets of four. Value, $24.

Farm Woman — A318

1957, Mar. 22 *Perf. 11½*

795	A318	30h lt blue green	.75	.25

3rd Cong. of Agricultural Cooperatives.

Cyclists A319

Woman Archer A320

Boxers — A321

Rescue Team A322

1957, Apr. 30 *Perf. 11½x11, 11x11½*

796	A319	30h sepia & ultra	.60	.25
797	A319	60h dull grn & bis	*2.25*	*1.25*
798	A320	60h gray & emer	.45	.25
799	A321	60h sepia & org	.45	.25
800	A322	60h violet & choc	.75	.25
		Nos. 796-800 (5)	*4.50*	*2.25*

10th Intl. Peace Cycling Race, Prague-Berlin-Warsaw (Nos. 796-797). Intl. Archery Championships (No. 798). European Boxing Championships, Prague (No. 799). Mountain Climbing Rescue Service (No. 800).

Jan V. Stamic — A323

Musicians: No. 802, Ferdinand Laub. No. 803, Frantisek Ondricek. No. 804, Josef B. Foerster. No. 805, Vitezslav Novak. No. 806, Josef Suk.

1957, May 12 *Perf. 11½*

801	A323	60h purple	.35	.25
802	A323	60h black	.35	.25
803	A323	60h slate blue	.35	.25
804	A323	60h brown	.35	.25
805	A323	60h dull red brn	.90	.25
806	A323	60h blue green	.35	.25
		Nos. 801-806 (6)	2.65	1.50

Spring Music Festival, Prague.

Josef Bozek — A324

School of Engineering A325

60h, F. J. Gerstner. 1k, R. Skuhersky.

1957, May 25

807	A324	30h bluish black	.25	.25
808	A324	60h gray brown	.35	.25
809	A324	1k rose lake	.35	.25
810	A325	1.40k blue violet	.75	.25
		Nos. 807-810 (4)	1.70	1.00

School of Engineering in Prague, 250th anniv.

Pioneer and Philatelic Symbols A326

Design: 60h, Girl and carrier pigeon.

Engraved and Photogravure

1957, June 8 *Perf. 11½*

811	A326	30h olive grn & org	.50	.25

Engr. *Perf. 13½*

812	A326	60h brn & vio bl	1.50	1.00

Youth Philatelic Exhibition, Pardubice.

No. 812 was printed in miniature sheets of 4. Value $12.

"Grief" A327

Motorcyclists A328

Design: 60h, Rose, symbol of new life.

1957, June 10

813	A327	30h black	.40	.25
814	A327	60h blk & rose red	1.40	.45

Destruction of Lidice, 15th anniversary.

No. 814 was issued in a sheet of 10 stamps. Value, $28.

1957, July 5 *Perf. 11½*

815	A328	60h dk gray & blue	1.50	.30

32nd International Motorcycle Race.

Karel Klic — A329

Josef Ressel — A330

1957, July 5

816	A329	30h gray black	.60	.25
817	A330	60h violet blue	.60	.25

Klic, inventor of photogravure, and Ressel, inventor of the ship screw.

Chamois — A331

Gentian
A332

Designs: 30h, Brown bear. 60h, Edelweiss. 1.25k, Tatra Mountains.

1957, Aug. 28 Engr. *Perf. 11½*

818 A331 20h emer & brnsh gray 1.10 .35
819 A331 30h lt blue & brn 1.10 .25
820 A332 40h gldn brn & vio bl 2.00 .35
821 A332 60h yellow & grn 1.10 .25

Size: 48x28½mm

822 A332 1.25k ol grn & bis 2.00 1.00
Nos. 818-822 (5) 7.30 2.20

Tatra Mountains National Park.

"Marycka Magdonova"
A333

Man Holding Banner of Trade Union Cong.
A334

Engraved and Photogravure

1957, Sept. 15 Unwmk. *Perf. 11½*

823 A333 60h black & dull red .45 .25

90th birthday of Petr Bezruc, poet and author of "Marycka Magdonova."

1957, Sept. 28 Engr.

824 A334 75h rose red .45 .25

4th Intl. Trade Union Cong., Leipzig, 10/4-15.

Television Transmitter and Antennas — A335

Design: 60h, Family watching television.

1957, Oct. 19 Engr. *Perf. 11½*

825 A335 40h dk blue & car .30 .25
826 A335 60h redsh brown & emer .45 .25

Issued to publicize the television industry.

Worker, Globe and Lenin
A336

60h, Worker, factory, hammer and sickle.

1957, Nov. 7 *Perf. 12x11½*

827 A336 30h claret .25 .25
828 A336 60h gray blue .25 .25

Russian Revolution, 40th anniversary.

Zapotocky Type of 1954 dated: 19 XII 1884-13 XI 1957

1957, Nov. 18 Unwmk. *Perf. 11½*

829 A276 30h black .25 .25
830 A276 60h black .25 .25

Souvenir Sheet

Imperf

831 A276 2k black 4.00 2.00

Death of Pres. Antonin Zapotocky.

Costume Type of 1956

Regional Costumes: 45h, Pilsen woman, Bohemia. 75h, Slovacko man, Moravia. 1.25k, Hana woman, Moravia. 1.95k, Teshinsko woman, Silesia.

1957, Dec. 18 Engr. *Perf. 13½*

832 A313 45h brn, bl & dk red 4.25 1.50
833 A313 75h dk brn, red & grn 3.00 .80
834 A313 1.25k dk brn, scar & ocher 5.25 1.50
835 A313 1.95k sepia, bl & ver 6.00 3.75
Nos. 832-835 (4) 18.50 7.55

Nos. 832-835 each was issued in sheets of 10 stamps. Value, set $200.

A337

A338

Designs: 30h, Radio telescope and observatory. 45h, Meteorological station in High Tatra. 75h, Sputnik 2 over Earth.

1957, Dec. 20 *Perf. 11½*

836 A337 30h violet brn & yel 2.00 .65
837 A338 45h sepia & lt bl .50 .35
838 A337 75h claret & blue 2.75 1.00
Nos. 836-838 (3) 5.25 2.00

IGY, 1957-58. No. 838 also for the launching of Sputnik 2, Nov. 3, 1957.

Girl Skater — A339

Designs: 40h, Canoeing. 60h, Volleyball. 80h, Parachutist. 1.60k, Soccer.

1958, Jan. 25 Engr. *Perf. 11½x12*

839 A339 30h rose violet 3.50 .25
840 A339 40h blue .70 .25
841 A339 60h redsh brown .70 .25
842 A339 80h violet blue 2.00 .50
843 A339 1.60k brt green .65 .25
Nos. 839-843 (5) 7.55 1.50

Issued to publicize various sports championship events in 1958.

Litomysl Castle — A340

Design: 60h, Bethlehem Chapel.

1958, Feb. 10 *Perf. 11½*

844 A340 30h green .30 .25
845 A340 60h redsh brown .30 .25

80th anniversary of the birth of Zdenek Nejedly, restorer of Bethlehem Chapel.

Giant Excavator
A341

Peace Dove and: 60h, Soldiers, flame and banner, horiz. 1.60k, Harvester and rainbow, horiz.

1958, Feb. 25

846 A341 30h gray violet & yel .25 .25
847 A341 60h gray brown & car .30 .25
848 A341 1.60k green & dull yel .50 .25
Nos. 846-848 (3) 1.05 .75

10th anniv. of the "Victorious February."

Jewelry — A342

Designs: 45h, Dolls. 60h, Textiles. 75h, Kaplan turbine. 1.20k, Glass.

Engraved and Photogravure

1958 Unwmk. *Perf. 11½*

849 A342 30h rose car & blue .40 .25
850 A342 45h rose red & pale lil .40 .25
851 A342 60h violet & aqua .60 .25
852 A342 75h ultra & salmon 1.50 .75
853 A342 1.20k blue grn & pink .60 .25
Nos. 849-853 (5) 3.50 1.75

Issued for the Universal and International Exposition at Brussels.

King George of Podebrad — A343

Design: 60h, View of Prague, 1628.

1958, May 19 Engr.

854 A343 30h carmine rose .50 .25
855 A343 60h violet blue .30 .25

Issued to publicize the National Archives Exhibition, Prague, May 15-Aug. 15.

"Towards the Stars" — A344

Women of Three Races — A345

Boy, Girl and Globes
A346

1958, May 26

856 A344 30h carmine rose .95 .35
857 A345 45h rose violet .25 .25
858 A346 60h blue .25 .25
Nos. 856-858 (3) 1.45 .85

The Soc. for Dissemination of Political and Cultural Knowledge (No. 856). 4th Cong. of the Intl. Democratic Women's Fed. (No. 857). 1st World Trade Union Conf. of Working Youths, Prague, July 14-20 (No. 858).

Grain, Hammer and Sickle
A347

Atomic Reactor
A348

45h, Map of Czechoslovakia, hammer & sickle.

1958, May 26

859 A347 30h dull red .25 .25
860 A347 45h green .25 .25
861 A348 60h dark blue .25 .25
Nos. 859-861 (3) .75 .75

11th Congress of the Czech Communist Party and the 15th anniv. of the Russo-Czechoslovakian Treaty.

Karlovy Vary
A349

Various Spas: 40h, Podebrady. 60h, Marianske Lazne. 80h, Luhacovice. 1.20k, Strbske Pleso. 1.60k, Trencianske Teplice.

1958, June 25

862 A349 30h rose claret .45 .25
863 A349 40h redsh brown .45 .25
864 A349 60h gray green .30 .25
865 A349 80h sepia .45 .25
866 A349 1.20k violet blue .60 .25
867 A349 1.60k lt violet 1.20 .75
Nos. 862-867 (6) 3.45 2.00

Telephone Operator
A350

Pres. Novotny
A351

Design: 45h, Radio transmitter.

1958, June 20

868 A350 30h black & brn org .40 .25
869 A350 45h black & lt grn .50 .25

Conference of Postal Ministers of Communist Countries, Prague, June 30-July 9.

1958-59 *Perf. 12½*

870 A351 30h brt violet blue .80 .25
b. Perf. 11½ .80 .25
870A A351 30h violet ('59) 4.50 1.75
871 A351 60h carmine rose .50 .25

Perf. 11½

Redrawn

871A A351 60h rose red .50 .25
Nos. 870-871A (4) 6.30 2.50

On No. 871 the top of the "6" turns down; on No. 871A it is open.

Czechoslovak Pavilion, Brussels — A352

1958, July 15 **Engr. & Photo.**

872	A352	1.95k lt blue & bis brn	.90	.25

Czechoslovakia Week at the Universal and International Exhibition at Brussels.

Portrait Type of 1956

30h, Julius Fucik. 45h, G. K. Zechenter 60h, Karel Capek. 1.40k, Svatopluk Cech.

1958, Aug. 20 **Engr.** ***Perf. 11½***

873	A306	30h rose red	.40	.25
874	A306	45h violet	2.10	.50
875	A306	60h dk blue gray	.75	.25
876	A306	1.40k gray	.75	.25
		Nos. 873-876 (4)	4.00	1.25

Death anniversaries of four famous Czechs.

The Artist and the Muse — A353

1958, Aug. 20 ***Perf. 14***

877	A353	1.60k black	4.50	1.25

85th birthday of Max Svabinsky, artist and engraver.

No. 877 was printed in miniature sheets of 4. Value $24.

Children's Hospital, Brno — A354

Designs: 60h, New Town Hall, Brno. 1k, St. Thomas Church. 1.60k, View of Brno.

1958, Sept. 6 **Unwmk.** ***Perf. 11½***

Size: 40x23mm

878	A354	30h violet	.25	.25
879	A354	60h rose red	.25	.25
880	A354	1k brown	.45	.25

Perf. 14

Size: 50x28mm

881	A354	1.60k dk slate grn	1.90	1.75
		Nos. 878-881 (4)	2.85	2.50

Natl. Phil. Exhib., Brno, Sept. 9.

No. 881 sold for 3.10k, including entrance ticket to exhibition. Issued in sheets of four. Value, $10.

Lepiota Procera — A355

Children on Beach — A356

Mushrooms: 40h, Boletus edulis. 60h, Krombholzia rufescens. 1.40k, Amanita muscaria L. 1.60k, Armillariella mellea.

1958, Oct. 6 ***Perf. 14***

882	A355	30h dk brn, grn & buff	1.60	.80
883	A355	40h vio brn & brn org	2.40	.80
884	A355	60h black, red & buff	3.25	.80
885	A355	1.40k brown, scar & grn	4.00	2.25
886	A355	1.60k blk, red brn & ol	13.00	5.75
		Nos. 882-886 (5)	24.25	10.40

Nos. 882-886 were each issued in a miniature sheet of 10 stamps. Value, set $275.

1958, Oct. 24 **Unwmk.** ***Perf. 14***

45h, Mother, child and bird. 60h, Skier.

887	A356	30h blue, yel & red	.40	.25
888	A356	45h ultra & carmine	1.60	.85
889	A356	60h brown, blue & yel	.40	.25
		Nos. 887-889 (3)	2.40	1.35

UNESCO Headquarters in Paris opening, Nov. 3. Nos. 887-889 each were issued in sheets of 10. Value, set $75.

Bozek's Steam Car of 1815 A357

Designs: 45h, "Präsident" car of 1897. 60h, "Skoda" sports car. 80h, "Tatra" sedan. 1k, "Autocar Skoda" bus. 1.25k, Trucks.

Engraved and Photogravure

1958, Dec. 1 ***Perf. 11½x11***

890	A357	30h vio blk & buff	.75	.25
891	A357	45h ol & lt ol grn	.75	.30
892	A357	60h ol gray & sal	1.75	.25
893	A357	80h claret & bl grn	1.10	.30
894	A357	1k brn & lt yel grn	1.50	.30
895	A357	1.25k green & buff	2.25	.45
		Nos. 890-895 (6)	8.10	1.85

Issued to honor the automobile industry.

Stamp of 1918 and Allegory — A358

1958, Dec. 18 **Engr.** ***Perf. 11x11½***

896	A358	60h dark blue gray	1.25	.30

1st Czechoslovakian postage stamp, 40th anniv.

Ice Hockey A359

30h, Girl throwing javelin. 60h, Ice hockey. 1k, Hurdling. 1.60k, Rowing. 2k, High jump.

1959, Feb. 14 ***Perf. 11½x11***

897	A359	20h dk brown & gray	.65	.25
898	A359	30h red brn & org brn	.45	.25
899	A359	60h dk bl & pale grn	.80	.25
900	A359	1k maroon & citron	.65	.25
901	A359	1.60k dull vio & lt bl	.95	.25
902	A359	2k red brn & lt bl	2.00	1.00
		Nos. 897-902 (6)	5.50	2.25

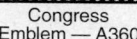

Congress Emblem — A360

"Equality of All Races" — A361

60h, Industrial & agricultural workers, emblem.

1959, Feb. 27 ***Perf. 11½***

903	A360	30h maroon & lt blue	.45	.25
904	A360	60h dk blue & yellow	.45	.25

4th Agricultural Cooperative Cong. in Prague.

1959, Mar. 23

Designs: 1k, "Peace." 2k, Mother and Child: "Freedom for Colonial People."

905	A361	60h gray green	.30	.25
906	A361	1k gray	.45	.25
907	A361	2k dk gray blue	1.50	.50
		Nos. 905-907 (3)	2.25	1.00

10th anniversary of the signing of the Universal Declaration of Human Rights.

Girl Holding Puppet — A362

Frederic Joliot Curie — A363

40h, Pioneer studying map. 60h, Pioneer with radio. 80h, Girl pioneer planting tree.

1959, Mar. 28 **Engr. & Photo.**

908	A362	30h violet bl & yel	.45	.25
909	A362	40h indigo & ultra	.45	.25
910	A362	60h black & lilac	.45	.25
911	A362	80h brown & lt green	1.00	.25
		Nos. 908-911 (4)	2.35	1.00

10th anniv. of the Pioneer organization.

1959, Apr. 17 **Engr.**

912	A363	60h sepia	1.60	.30

Frederic Joliot Curie and the 10th anniversary of the World Peace Movement.

"Reaching for the Moon" — A364

Town Hall Pilsen — A365

1959, Apr. 17

913	A364	30h violet blue	1.25	.30

2nd Cong. of the Czechoslovak Assoc. for the Propagation of Political and Cultural knowledge.

1959, May 2

Designs: 60h, Part of steam condenser turbine. 1k, St. Bartholomew's Church, Pilsen. 1.60k, Part of lathe.

914	A365	30h lt brown	.25	.25
915	A365	60h violet & lt grn	.30	.25
916	A365	1k violet blue	.40	.25
917	A365	1.60k black & yellow	1.60	1.10
		Nos. 914-917 (4)	2.55	1.85

2nd Pilsen Stamp Exhib. in connection with the centenary of the Skoda (Lenin) armament works.

Factory and Emblem A366

Inscribed: "IV Vseodborovy sjezd, 1959"

1959, May 13

918	A366	30h shown	.50	.25
919	A366	60h Dam	.30	.25

4th Trade Union Congress.

Zvolen Castle A367

1959, June 13

920	A367	60h gray olive & yel	.75	.25

Regional Stamp Exhibition, Zvolen, 1959.

Frantisek Benda — A368

Aurel Stodola — A369

30h, Vaclav Kliment Klicpera. 60h, Karel V. Rais. 80h, Antonin Slavicek. 1k, Peter Bezruc.

1959, June 22 ***Perf. 11½x11***

921	A368	15h violet blue	.25	.25
922	A368	30h orange brown	.25	.25
923	A369	40h dull green	.25	.25
924	A369	60h dull red brn	.35	.25
925	A369	80h dull violet	.65	.25
926	A368	1k dark brown	.65	.25
		Nos. 921-926 (6)	2.40	1.50

View of the Fair Grounds A370

Designs: 60h, Fair emblem and world map. 1.60k, Pavilion "Z."

Inscribed: "Mezinarodni Veletrh Brne 6.-20.IX. 1959"

Engraved and Photogravure

1959, July 20 **Unwmk.** ***Perf. 11½***

927	A370	30h lilac & yellow	.25	.25
928	A370	60h dull blue	.25	.25
929	A370	1.60k dk blue & bister	.75	.25
		Nos. 927-929 (3)	1.25	.75

International Fair at Brno, Sept. 6-20.

Revolutionist and Flag — A371

Slovakian Fighter — A372

1.60k, Linden leaves, sun and factory.

Perf. 11½

1959, Aug. 29 Unwmk. Engr.

930	A371	30h black & rose	.25	.25
931	A372	60h carmine rose	.25	.25
932	A371	1.60k dk blue & yel	.45	.25
		Nos. 930-932 (3)	.95	.75

Natl. Slovakian revolution, 15th anniv. and Slovakian Soviet Republic, 40th anniv.

Alpine Marmots A373

1959, Sept. 25 Engr. & Photo.

933	A373	30h shown	1.60	.25
934	A373	40h Bison	1.10	.40
935	A373	60h Lynx, vert.	3.25	.25
936	A373	1k Wolf	3.25	.25
937	A373	1.60k Red deer	2.75	.55
		Nos. 933-937 (5)	11.95	1.70

Tatra National Park, 10th anniv.

Lunik 2 Hitting Moon and Russian Flag A374

1959, Sept. 23 ***Perf. 11½***

938	A374	60h dk red & lt ultra	1.90	.30

Issued to commemorate the landing of the Soviet rocket on the moon, Sept. 13, 1959.

Stamp Printing Works, Peking A375

1959, Oct. 1

939	A375	30h pale green & red	.40	.25

10 years of Czechoslovakian-Chinese friendship.

Haydn — A376

Design: 3k, Charles Darwin.

1959, Oct. 16 Engr. ***Perf. 11½***

940	A376	60h violet black	.50	.25
941	A376	3k dark red brown	1.50	.70

150th death anniv. of Franz Joseph Haydn, Austrian composer, and 150th birth anniv. of Charles Darwin, English naturalist.

Great Spotted Woodpecker A377

Birds: 30h, Blue tits. 40h, Nuthatch. 60th, Golden oriole. 80h, Goldfinch. 1k, Bullfinch. 1.20k, European kingfisher.

1959, Nov. 16 ***Perf. 14***

942	A377	20h multicolored	1.50	.60
943	A377	30h multicolored	1.50	.60
944	A377	40h multicolored	6.50	1.50
945	A377	60h multicolored	1.50	.60
946	A377	80h multicolored	2.50	.90
947	A377	1k multicolored	2.75	.90
948	A377	1.20k multicolored	5.00	1.25
		Nos. 942-948 (7)	21.25	6.35

Nos. 942-948 were each issued in miniature sheets of 10. Value, set $275.

Nikola Tesla A378

Designs: 30h, Alexander S. Popov. 35h, Edouard Branly. 60h, Guglielmo Marconi. 1k, Heinrich Hertz. 2k, Edwin Howard Armstrong and research tower, Alpine, N. J.

Engraved and Photogravure

1959, Dec. 7 ***Perf. 11½***

949	A378	25h black & pink	.65	.25
950	A378	30h black & orange	.25	.25
951	A378	35h black & lt vio	.25	.25
952	A378	60h black & blue	.25	.25
953	A378	1k black & lt grn	.30	.25
954	A378	2k black & bister	1.90	.40
		Nos. 949-954 (6)	3.60	1.65

Issued to honor inventors in the fields of telegraphy and radio.

Gymnast — A379

2nd Winter Spartacist Games: 60h, Skier. 1.60k, Basketball players.

1960, Jan. 20 ***Perf. 11½***

955	A379	30h salmon pink & brn	1.10	.25
956	A379	60h lt blue & blk	1.10	.25
957	A379	1.60k bister & brn	1.00	.25
		Nos. 955-957 (3)	3.20	.75

1960, June 15 Unwmk.

Designs: 30h, Two girls in "Red Ball" drill. 60h, Gymnast with stick. 1k, Three girls with hoops.

958	A379	30h lt grn & rose claret	.65	.25
959	A379	60h pink & black	.50	.25
960	A379	1k ocher & vio bl	.85	.25
		Nos. 958-960 (3)	2.00	.75

2nd Summer Spartacist Games, Prague, June 23-July 3.

River Dredge Boat A380

Ships: 60h, River tug. 1k, Tourist steamer. 1.20k, Cargo ship "Lidice."

1960, Feb. 22 ***Perf. 11½***

961	A380	30h slate grn & sal	3.00	.30
962	A380	60h maroon & pale bl	1.60	.30
963	A380	1k dk violet & yel	2.75	.30
964	A380	1.20k lilac & pale grn	4.00	.90
		Nos. 961-964 (4)	11.35	1.80

Ice Hockey Players — A381

Design: 1.80k, Figure skaters.

1960, Feb. 27

965	A381	60h sepia & lt blue	2.40	.50
966	A381	1.80k black & lt green	7.25	2.00

8th Olympic Winter Games, Squaw Valley, Calif., Feb. 18-29, 1960.

1960, June 15 Unwmk.

Designs: 1k, Running. 1.80k, Women's gymnastics. 2k, Rowing.

967	A381	1k black & orange	1.00	.30
968	A381	1.80k black & sal pink	1.60	.40
969	A381	2k black & blue	2.50	.95
		Nos. 967-969 (3)	5.10	1.65

17th Olympic Games, Rome, 8/25-9/11.

Trencin Castle — A382

Castles: 10h, Bezdez. 20h, Kost. 30h, Pernstein. 40h, Kremnica. 50h, Krivoklát castle. 60h, Karlstein. 1k, Smolenice. 1.60k, Kokorin.

1960-63 Engr. ***Perf. 11½***

970	A382	5h gray violet	.30	.25
971	A382	10h black	.30	.25
972	A382	20h brown org	.40	.25
973	A382	30h green	.30	.25
974	A382	40h brown	.40	.25
974A	A382	50h black ('63)	4.00	.25
975	A382	60h rose red	.45	.25
976	A382	1k lilac	.45	.25
977	A382	1.60k dark blue	.90	.25
		Nos. 970-977 (9)	7.50	2.25

1961, Oct. Wmk. 341

977A	A382	30h green	3.25	.40

Lenin — A383

Soldier Holding Child — A384

1960, Apr. 22 Unwmk.

978	A383	60h gray olive	1.60	.25

90th anniversary of the birth of Lenin.

1960, May 5 Engr. & Photo.

Designs: No. 980, Child eating pie. No. 981, Soldier helping concentration camp victim. No. 982, Welder and factory, horiz. No. 983, Tractor driver and farm, horiz.

979	A384	30h maroon & lt blue	.35	.25
980	A384	30h dull red	.35	.25
981	A384	30h green & dull blue	.40	.25
982	A384	60h dk blue & buff	.35	.25
983	A384	60h redsh brn & yel grn	.40	.25
		Nos. 979-983 (5)	1.85	1.25

15th anniversary of liberation.

Steelworker — A385

Design: 60h, Farm woman and child.

1960, May 24

984	A385	30h maroon & gray	.25	.25
985	A385	60h green & pale blue	.30	.25

1960 parliamentary elections.

Red Cross Nurse Holding Dove A386

Fire Fighters A387

1960, May 26 Unwmk.

986	A386	30h brown car & bl	.40	.25
987	A387	60h dk blue & pink	.60	.25

3rd Congress of the Czechoslovakian Red Cross (No. 986), and the 2nd Fire Fighters' Congress (No. 987).

Hand of Philatelist with Tongs and Two Stamps — A388

Design: 1k, Globe and 1937 Bratislava stamp (shown in miniature on 60h).

1960, July 11 ***Perf. 11½***

988	A388	60h black & dull yel	.80	.25
989	A388	1k black & blue	1.00	.25

Issued to publicize the National Stamp Exhibition, Bratislava, Sept. 24-Oct. 9.

See Nos. C49-C50.

Stalin Mine, Ostrava-Hermanovice — A390

Designs: 20h, Power station, Hodonin. 30h, Gottwald iron works, Kuncice. 40h, Harvester. 60h, Oil refinery.

1960, July 25

992	A390	10h black & pale grn	.30	.25
993	A390	20h maroon & lt bl	.30	.25
994	A390	30h indigo & pink	.30	.25
995	A390	40h green & pale lilac	.30	.25
996	A390	60h dk blue & yel	.30	.25
		Nos. 992-996 (5)	1.50	1.25

Issued to publicize the new five-year plan.

Viktorin Cornelius, Lawyer — A391

Portraits: 20h, Karel Matej Capek-Chod, writer. 30h, Hana Kvapilova, actress. 40h, Oskar Nedbal, composer. 60h, Otakar Ostrcil, composer.

1960, Aug. 23 **Engr.**

997	A391	10h black		.40	.25
998	A391	20h red brown		.45	.25
999	A391	30h rose red		.65	.25
1000	A391	40h dull green		1.60	.80
1001	A391	60h gray violet		.45	.25
		Nos. 997-1001 (5)		3.55	1.80

See Nos. 1037-1041.

Skoda Sports Plane Flying Upside Down A392

1960, Aug. 28 **Engr. & Photo.**
1002 A392 60h violet blue & blue 1.50 .30

1st aerobatic world championships, Bratislava.

Constitution and "Czechoslovakia" — A393

1960, Sept. 18
1003 A393 30h violet bl & pink .40 .25

Proclamation of the new socialist constitution.

Workers Reading Newspaper — A394

Man Holding Newspaper — A395

1960, Sept. 18

1004	A394	30h slate & ver	.25	.25
1005	A395	60h black & rose	.25	.25

Day of the Czechoslovak Press, Sept. 21, 1960, and 40th anniv. of the Rudé Právo paper.

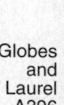

Globes and Laurel A396

1960, Sept. 18 **Engr.**
1006 A396 30h dk blue & bister .40 .25

World Federation of Trade Unions, 15th anniv.

Black-crowned Night Heron — A397

Doronicum Clusii (Thistle) — A398

Birds: 30h, Great crested grebe. 40h, Lapwing. 60h, Gray heron. 1k, Graylag goose, horiz. 1.60k, Mallard, horiz.

Engraved and Photogravure

1960, Oct. 24 **Unwmk.** ***Perf. 11½***

Designs in Black

1007	A397	25h pale vio blue	.90	.25
1008	A397	30h pale citron	.80	.25
1009	A397	40h pale blue	.90	.30
1010	A397	60h pink	.60	.25
1011	A397	1k pale yellow	1.75	.25
1012	A397	1.60k lt violet	4.50	1.25
		Nos. 1007-1012 (6)	9.45	2.55

1960, Nov. 21 **Engr.** ***Perf. 14***

Flowers: 30h, Cyclamen. 40h, Primrose. 60h, Hen-and-chickens. 1k, Gentian. 2k, Pasqueflower.

1013	A398	20h black, yel & grn	.85	.85
1014	A398	30h black, car rose & grn	.85	.85
1015	A398	40h black, yel & grn	.85	.85
1016	A398	60h black, pink & grn	.85	.85
1017	A398	1k black, bl, vio & grn	2.50	.85
1018	A398	2k black, lil, yel & grn	3.25	1.60
		Nos. 1013-1018 (6)	9.15	5.85

Nos. 1013-1018 were each issued in sheets of 10. Value, set $180.

Alfons Mucha — A399

1960, Dec. 18 **Engr.** ***Perf. 11½x12***
1019 A399 60h dk blue gray 3.25 .25

Day of the Czechoslovak Postage Stamp and birth cent. of Alfons Mucha, designer of the 1st Czechoslovakian stamp (Type A1).

Rolling-mill Control Bridge — A400

Athletes with Flags — A401

Designs: 30h, Turbo generator. 60h, Ditch-digging machine.

1961, Jan. 20 **Unwmk.** ***Perf. 11½***

1020	A400	20h blue	.30	.25
1021	A400	30h rose	.30	.25
1022	A400	60h brt green	.30	.25
		Nos. 1020-1022 (3)	.90	.75

Third Five-Year Plan.

Perf. 11x11½, 11½x11

1961, Feb. 20 **Engr. & Photo.**

Designs: No. 1024, Motorcycle race, horiz. 40h, Sculling, horiz. 60h, Ice skater. 1k, Rugby. 1.20k, Soccer. 1.60k, Long-distance runners.

1023	A401	30h rose red & bl	.30	.25
1024	A401	30h dk blue & car	.30	.25
1025	A401	40h dk gray & car	.50	.25
1026	A401	60h lilac & blue	.50	.25
1027	A401	1k ultra & yel	.50	.25
1028	A401	1.20k green & buff	.75	.25
1029	A401	1.60k sepia & salmon	2.00	1.00
		Nos. 1023-1029 (7)	4.85	2.50

Various sports events.

Exhibition Emblem A402

Rocket Launching A403

1961, Mar. 6 **Engr.** ***Perf. 11½***
1030 A402 2k dk blue & red 2.40 .25

"Praga 1962" International Stamp Exhibition, Prague, Sept. 1962.

1961, Mar. 6 **Engr. & Photo.**

30h, Sputnik III, horiz. 40h, As 20h, but inscribed "Start Kosmicke Rakety k Venusi — 12.II.1961". 60h, Sputnik I, horiz. 1.60k, Interplanetary station, horiz. 2k, Similar to type A404, without commemorative inscription.

1031	A403	20h violet & pink	.40	.25
1032	A403	30h dk green & buff	.80	.25
1033	A403	40h dk red & yel grn	.80	.30
1034	A403	60h violet & buff	.95	.25
1035	A403	1.60k dk bl & pale grn	.65	.25
1036	A403	2k mar & pale bl	2.40	1.10
		Nos. 1031-1036 (6)	6.00	2.40

Issued to publicize Soviet space research.

Portrait Type of 1960

No. 1037, Jindrich Mosna. No. 1038, Pavol Orszagh Hviezdoslav. No. 1039, Alois Mrstik. No. 1040, Joza Uprka. No. 1041, Josef Hora.

1961, Mar. 27 ***Perf. 11½***

1037	A391	60h green	.30	.25
1038	A391	60h dark blue	.65	.25
a.		"ORSZACH" instead of "ORSZAGH"	*400.00*	*100.00*
1039	A391	60h dull claret	.80	.25
1040	A391	60h gray	.65	.25
1041	A391	60h sepia	.30	.25
		Nos. 1037-1041 (5)	2.70	1.25

Man Flying into Space A404

1961, Apr. 13

1042	A404	60h car & pale bl	.80	.25
1043	A404	3k ultra & yel	2.40	.80

1st man in space, Yuri A. Gagarin, Apr. 12, 1961. See No. 1036.

Flute Player — A405

1961, Apr. 24 **Engr.**

1044	A405	30h shown	.55	.25
1045	A405	30h Dancer	.55	.25
1046	A405	60h Lyre player	.80	.25
		Nos. 1044-1046 (3)	1.90	.75

Prague Conservatory of Music, 150th anniv.

Blast Furnace and Mine, Kladno — A406

1961, Apr. 24
1047 A406 3k dull red .75 .25

City of Kladno, 400th anniv.

Marching Workers — A407

Woman with Hammer and Sickle — A408

Klement Gottwald Museum A409

Designs: No. 1050, Lenin Museum. No. 1051, Crowd with flags. No. 1053, Man saluting Red Star.

1961, May 10

1048	A407	30h dull violet	.30	.25
1049	A409	30h dark blue	.30	.25
1050	A409	30h redsh brown	.30	.25
1051	A407	60h vermilion	.30	.25
1052	A408	60h dark green	.30	.25
1053	A408	60h carmine	.30	.25
		Nos. 1048-1053 (6)	1.80	1.50

Czech Communist Party, 40th anniversary.

Puppet — A410

Designs: Various Puppets.

Engraved and Photogravure

1961, June 20 **Unwmk.** ***Perf. 11½***

1054	A410	30h ver & yel	.30	.25
1055	A410	40h sepia & bluish grn	.30	.25
1056	A410	60h vio bl & sal	.30	.25
1057	A410	1k green & lt blue	.30	.25
1058	A410	1.60k mar & pale vio	1.10	.35
		Nos. 1054-1058 (5)	2.30	1.35

Woman, Map of Africa and Flag of Czechoslovakia — A411

1961, June 26
1059 A411 60h red & blue .40 .25

Issued to publicize the friendship between the people of Africa and Czechoslovakia.

Map of Europe and Fair Emblem
A412

Fair emblem and: 60h Horizontal boring machine, vert. 1k, Scientists' meeting and nuclear physics emblem.

1961, Aug. 14 *Perf. 11½*

1060	A412	30h dk bl & pale grn		.30	.25
1061	A412	60h green & pink		.30	.25
1062	A412	1k vio brn & lt bl		.60	.25
		Nos. 1060-1062 (3)		1.20	.75

International Trade Fair, Brno, Sept. 10-24.

Sugar Beet, Cup of Coffee and Bags of Sugar
A413

Charles Bridge, St. Nicholas Church and Hradcany
A414

1961, Sept. 18 **Unwmk.** *Perf. 11½*

1063	A413	20h	shown	.25	.25
1064	A413	30h	Clover	.25	.25
1065	A413	40h	Wheat	.25	.25
1066	A413	60h	Hops	.25	.25
1067	A413	1.40k	Corn	.50	.30
1068	A413	2k	Potatoes	2.00	.80
			Nos. 1063-1068 (6)	3.50	2.10

1961, Sept. 25

1069	A414	60h violet bl & car	1.20	.25

26th session of the Governor's Council of the Red Cross Societies League, Prague.

Orlik Dam and Kaplan Turbine
A415

Designs: 30h, View of Prague, flags and stamps. 40h, Hluboká Castle, river and fish. 60h, Karlovy Vary and cup. 1k, Pilsen and beer bottle. 1.20k, North Bohemia landscape and vase. 1.60k, Tatra mountains, boots, ice pick and rope. 2k, Ironworks, Ostrava Kuncice and pulley. 3k, Brno and ball bearing. 4k, Bratislava and grapes. 5k, Prague and flags.

1961 **Unwmk.** *Perf. 11½*

Size: 41x23mm

1070	A415	20h	gray & blue	*1.60*	.55
1071	A415	30h	vio blue & red	.30	.25
1072	A415	40h	dk blue & lt grn	1.60	.85
1073	A415	60h	dk blue & yel	1.75	.85
1074	A415	1k	mar & grn	1.25	.85
1075	A415	1.20k	green & pink	1.75	.85
1076	A415	1.60k	brn & vio bl	1.75	1.25
1077	A415	2k	blk & ocher	2.00	1.25
1078	A415	3k	ultra & yel	2.00	.55
1079	A415	4k	purple & sal	2.40	1.10

Perf. 13½

Engr.

Size: 50x29mm

1080	A415	5k	multicolored	27.00	17.50
			Nos. 1070-1080 (11)	43.40	25.85

"PRAGA 1962 World Exhib. of Postage Stamps," Aug. 18-Sept. 2, 1962. No. 1080 was printed in sheet of 4. Value $150.

Globe
A416

Engraved and Photogravure

1961, Nov. 27 *Perf. 11½*

1081	A416	60h red & ultra	.50	.25

Issued to publicize the Fifth World Congress of Trade Unions, Moscow, Dec. 4-16.

Orange Tip Butterfly
A417

Bicyclists
A418

Designs (butterflies): 20h, Zerynthia hypsipyle Sch. 30h, Apollo. 40h, Swallowtail. 60h, Peacock. 80h, Mourning cloak (Camberwell beauty). 1k, Underwing (moth). 1.60k, Red admiral. 2k, Brimstone (sulphur).

1961, Nov. 27 **Engr.**

1082	A417	15h	multicolored	.90	.30
1083	A417	20h	multicolored	.90	.30
1084	A417	30h	multicolored	.90	.30
1085	A417	40h	multicolored	.90	.30
1086	A417	60h	multicolored	.90	.30
1087	A417	80h	multicolored	2.75	.90
1088	A417	1k	multicolored	3.00	.90
1089	A417	1.60k	multicolored	3.00	.90
1090	A417	2k	multicolored	7.50	3.00
			Nos. 1082-1090 (9)	20.75	7.20

Nos.1082-1090 were each issued in sheets of 10. Value, set $350.

Engraved and Photogravure

1962, Feb. 5 **Unwmk.** *Perf. 11½*

Sports: 40h, Woman gymnast. 60h, Figure skaters. 1k, Woman bowler. 1.20k, Goalkeeper, soccer. 1.60k, Discus thrower.

1091	A418	30h	black & vio bl	.25	.25
1092	A418	40h	black & yel	.25	.25
1093	A418	60h	slate & grnsh bl	.40	.25
1094	A418	1k	black & pink	.40	.25
1095	A418	1.20k	black & green	.40	.25
1096	A418	1.60k	blk & dull grn	2.00	.95
			Nos. 1091-1096 (6)	3.70	2.20

Various 1962 sports events.

No. 1095 does not have the commemorative inscription.

Karel Kovarovic — A419

Frantisek Zaviska and Karel Petr
A420

20h, Frantisek Skroup. 30h, Bozena Nemcova. 60h, View of Prague & staff of Aesculapius. 1.60k, Ladislav Celakovsky. 1.80k, Miloslav Valouch & Juraj Hronec.

1962, Feb. 26 **Engr.**

1097	A419	10h	red brown	.25	.25
1098	A419	20h	violet blue	.25	.25
1099	A419	30h	brown	.25	.25
1100	A420	40h	claret	.25	.25
1101	A419	60h	black	.25	.25
1102	A419	1.60k	slate green	.50	.25
1103	A420	1.80k	dark blue	.60	.25
			Nos. 1097-1103 (7)	2.35	1.75

Various cultural personalities and events.

Miner and Flag
A421

1962, Mar. 19 **Engr. & Photo.**

1104	A421	60h indigo & rose	.25	.25

30th anniv. of the miners' strike at Most.

"Man Conquering Space" — A422

Soviet Spaceship Vostok 2 — A423

40h, Launching of Soviet space rocket. 80h, Multi-stage automatic rocket. 1k, Automatic station on moon. 1.60k, Television satellite.

1962, Mar. 26

1105	A422	30h	dk red & lt blue	.40	.25
1106	A422	40h	dk blue & sal	.40	.25
1107	A423	60h	dk blue & pink	.40	.25
1108	A423	80h	rose vio & lt grn	.60	.25
1109	A422	1k	indigo & citron	.40	.25
1110	A423	1.60k	green & buff	2.40	.75
			Nos. 1105-1110 (6)	4.60	2.00

Issued to publicize space research.

Polar Bear — A424

Zoo Animals: 30h, Chimpanzee. 60h, Camel. 1k, African and Indian elephants, horiz. 1.40k, Leopard, horiz. 1.60k, Przewalski horse, horiz.

1962, Apr. 24 **Unwmk.** *Perf. 11½*

Design and Inscriptions in Black

1111	A424	20h	grnsh blue	.75	.25
1112	A424	30h	violet	.75	.25
1113	A424	60h	orange	.75	.25
1114	A424	1k	green	.90	.25
1115	A424	1.40k	carmine rose	.90	.25
1116	A424	1.60k	lt brown	2.00	1.25
			Nos. 1111-1116 (6)	6.05	2.50

Child and Grieving Mother — A425

Klary's Fountain, Teplice — A426

60h, Flowers growing from ruins of Lezáky.

1962, June 9 **Engr. & Photo.**

1118	A425	30h black & red	.45	.25
1119	A425	60h black & dull bl	.85	.25

20th anniversary of the destruction of Lidice and Lezáky by the Nazis.

1962, June 9

1120	A426	60h dull grn & yel	.40	.25

1,200th anniversary of the discovery of the medicinal springs of Teplice.

Malaria Eradication Emblem, Cross and Dove
A427

Soccer Goalkeeper
A428

3k, Dove and malaria eradication emblem.

1962, June 18

1121	A427	60h black & crimson	.25	.25
1122	A427	3k dk blue & yel	1.40	.60

WHO drive to eradicate malaria.

1962, June 20 **Unwmk.** *Perf. 11½*

1123	A428	1.60k green & yellow	1.50	.25

Czechoslovakia's participation in the World Cup Soccer Championship, Chile, May 30-June 17. See No. 1095.

Soldier in Swimming Relay Race
A429

"Agriculture"
A430

Designs: 40h, Soldier hurdling. 60h, Soccer player. 1k, Soldier with rifle in relay race.

1962, July 20

1124	A429	30h	green & lt ultra	.25	.25
1125	A429	40h	dk purple & yel	.25	.25
1126	A429	60h	brown & green	.25	.25
1127	A429	1k	dk blue & sal pink	.35	.25
			Nos. 1124-1127 (4)	1.10	1.00

2nd Summer Spartacist Games of Friendly Armies, Prague, Sept., 1962.

1962 **Engr.** *Perf. 13½*

Designs: 60h, Astronaut in capsule. 80h, Boy with flute, horiz. 1k, Workers of three races, horiz. 1.40k, Children dancing around tree. 1.60k, Flying bird, horiz. 5k, View of Prague, horiz.

1128	A430	30h	multicolored	1.50	.90
1129	A430	60h	multicolored	.70	.55
a.			Miniature sheet of 8	*20.00*	*20.00*
1130	A430	80h	multicolored	2.40	1.60
1131	A430	1k	multicolored	2.40	1.60
1132	A430	1.40k	multicolored	2.40	1.60
1133	A430	1.60k	multicolored	4.00	4.00
			Nos. 1128-1133 (6)	13.40	10.25

Souvenir Sheet

1134	A430	5k	multicolored	13.00	10.00
a.			Imperf.	60.00	48.00

"PRAGA 1962 World Exhib. of Postage Stamps," 8/18-9/2/62. No. 1133 also for FIP Day, Sept. 1. Printed in sheets of 10. Value: Nos. 1128-1133 $150; No. 1134 $80.

No. 1129a contains 4 each of Nos. 1128-1129 and 2 labels arranged in 2 rows of 2 se-tenant pairs of Nos. 1128-1129 with label between. Sold for 5k, only with ticket.

No. 1134 contains one 51x30mm stamp. Sold only with ticket.

Children in Day Nursery and Factory A431

Sailboat and Trade Union Rest Home, Zinkovy — A432

Engraved and Photogravure

1962, Oct. 29 Unwmk. *Perf. 11½*

1135 A431 30h black & lt blue .25 .25
1136 A432 60h brown & yellow .25 .25

Cruiser "Aurora" A433

1962, Nov. 7

1137 A433 30h black & gray bl .25 .25
1138 A433 60h black & pink .25 .25

Russian October revolution, 45th anniv.

Cosmonaut and Worker — A434

Lenin — A435

1962, Nov. 7

1139 A434 30h dark red & blue .25 .25
1140 A435 60h black & dp rose .25 .25

40th anniversary of the USSR.

Symbolic Crane — A436

40h, Agricultural products, vert. 60h, Factories.

1962, Dec. 4

1141 A436 30h dk red & yel .25 .25
1142 A436 40h gray blue & yel .25 .25
1143 A436 60h black & dp rose .30 .25
Nos. 1141-1143 (3) .80 .75

Communist Party of Czechoslovakia, 12th cong.

Ground Beetle — A437

Beetles: 30h, Cardinal beetle. 60h, Stag beetle, vert. 1k, Great water beetle. 1.60k, Alpine longicorn, vert. 2k, Ground beetle, vert.

1962, Dec. 15 Engr. *Perf. 14*

1144 A437 20h multicolored 1.00 .40
1145 A437 30h multicolored 1.00 .40
1146 A437 60h multicolored 1.00 .40
1147 A437 1k multicolored 2.00 .60
1148 A437 1.60k multicolored 4.00 .60
1149 A437 2k multicolored 6.00 2.00
Nos. 1144-1149 (6) 15.00 4.40

Nos. 1144-1149 were each printed in sheets of 10. Value, set $225.

Table Tennis — A438

Sports: 60h, Bicyclist. 80h, Skier. 1k, Motorcyclist. 1.20k, Weight lifter. 1.60k, Hurdler.

Engraved and Photogravure

1963, Jan. *Perf. 11½*

1150 A438 30h black & dp grn .25 .25
1151 A438 60h black & orange .25 .25
1152 A438 80h black & ultra .25 .25
1153 A438 1k black & violet .40 .25
1154 A438 1.20k blk & pale brn .40 .25
1155 A438 1.60k blk & car .85 .25
Nos. 1150-1155 (6) 2.40 1.50

Various 1963 sports events.

Industrial Plant, Laurel and Star — A439

Symbol of Pioneer Summer Camp — A440

Industrial Plant and Symbol of Growth — A441

1963, Feb. 25 Unwmk. *Perf. 11½*

1156 A439 30h carmine & lt bl .25 .25
1157 A440 60h black & red .25 .25
1158 A441 60h black & red .25 .25
Nos. 1156-1158 (3) .75 .75

15th anniv. of the "Victorious February" and 5th Trade Union Cong.

Artists' Guild Emblem — A442

Juraj Jánosik — A443

Eduard Urx — A444

National Theater, Prague — A445

No. 1163, Woman reading to children. No. 1164, Juraj Pálkovic. 1.60k, Max Svabinsky.

Engr. & Photo.; Engr. (A444)

1963, Mar. 25 Unwmk. *Perf. 11½*

1159 A442 20h black & Prus bl .25 .25
1160 A443 30h car & lt bl .25 .25
1161 A444 30h carmine .25 .25
1162 A445 60h dl red brn & lt bl .25 .25
1163 A444 60h green .25 .25
1164 A444 60h black .25 .25
1165 A444 1.60k brown .50 .25
Nos. 1159-1165 (7) 2.00 1.75

Various cultural personalities and events.

Boy and Girl with Flag A446

Television Transmitter A447

Engraved and Photogravure

1963, Apr. 18 *Perf. 11½*

1166 A446 30h slate & rose red .35 .25

The 4th Congress of Czechoslovak Youth.

1963, Apr. 25

40h, Television camera, mast and set, horiz.

1167 A447 40h buff & slate .40 .25
1168 A447 60h dk red & lt blue .40 .25

Czechoslovak television, 10th anniversary.

Rocket to the Sun A448

50h, Rockets & Sputniks leaving Earth. 60h, Spacecraft to & from Moon. 1k, 3k, Interplanetary station & Mars 1. 1.60k, Atomic rocket & Jupiter. 2k, Rocket returning from Saturn.

1963, Apr. 25

1169 A448 30h red brn & buff .65 .25
1170 A448 50h slate & bluish grn .65 .25
1171 A448 60h dk green & yel .65 .25
1172 A448 1k dk gray & sal .80 .25
1173 A448 1.60k gray brn & lt grn .80 .25
1174 A448 2k dk purple & yel 2.50 .75
Nos. 1169-1174 (6) 6.05 2.00

Souvenir Sheet

Imperf

1175 A448 3k Prus grn & org red 14.50 7.25

No. 1175 issued for 1st Space Research Exhib., Prague, Apr. 1963.

Studio and Radio A449

1k, Globe inscribed "Peace" & aerial mast, vert.

1963, May 18 Unwmk. *Perf. 11½*

1176 A449 30h choc & pale grn .40 .25
1177 A449 1k bluish grn & lilac .40 .25

40th anniversary of Czechoslovak radio.

Tupolev Tu-104B Turbojet A450

Design: 1.80k, Ilyushin Il-18 Moskva.

1963, May 25

1178 A450 80h violet & lt bl 1.25 .40
1179 A450 1.80k dk blue & lt grn 2.00 .40

40th anniversary of Czechoslovak airlines.

9th Cent. Ring, Map of Moravian Settlements A451

Woman Singing A452

1.60k, Falconer, 9th cent. silver disk.

1963, May 25

1180 A451 30h lt green & blk .25 .25
1181 A451 1.60k dull yel & blk .75 .25

1100th anniversary of Moravian empire.

1963, May 25 Engr.

1182 A452 30h bright red .60 .25

60th anniversary of the founding of the Moravian Teachers' Singing Club.

Kromeriz Castle and Barley — A453

Centenary Emblem, Nurse and Playing Child — A454

Engraved and Photogravure

1963, June 20 Unwmk. *Perf. 11½*

1183 A453 30h slate grn & yel .60 .25

Natl. Agricultural Exhib. and 700th anniv. of Kromeriz.

1963, June 20

1184 A454 30h dk gray & car .50 .25

Centenary of the International Red Cross.

Bee, Honeycomb and Emblem A455

1963, June 20

1185 A455 1k brown & yellow .75 .25

19th Intl. Beekeepers Cong., Apimondia, 1963.

Liberec Fair Emblem — A456

1963, July 13
1186 A456 30h black & dp rose .40 .25

Liberec Consumer Goods Fair.

Town Hall, Brno — A457

Cave, Moravian Karst — A458

Design: 60h, Town Hall tower, Brno.

1963, July 29
1187 A457 30h lt blue & maroon .35 .25
1188 A457 60h pink & dk blue .35 .25

International Trade Fair, Brno.

1963, July 29

No. 1190, Trout, Hornad Valley. 60h, Great Hawk Gorge. 80h, Macocha mountains.

1189 A458 30h brown & lt bl .80 .25
1190 A458 30h dk bl & dull grn .95 .25
1191 A458 60h green & blue .80 .25
1192 A458 80h sepia & pink .80 .25
Nos. 1189-1192 (4) 3.35 1.00

Blast Furnace A459

1963, Aug. 15 Unwmk. *Perf. 11½*
1193 A459 60h blk & bluish grn .40 .25

30th Intl. Cong. of Iron Founders, Prague.

White Mouse A460

1963, Aug. 15
1194 A460 1k black & carmine .65 .25

2nd Intl. Pharmacological Cong., Prague.

Farm Machinery for Underfed Nations — A461

1963, Aug. 15 Engr.
1195 A461 1.60k black .50 .25

FAO "Freedom from Hunger" campaign.

Wooden Toys — A462

Folk Art (Inscribed "UNESCO"): 80h, Cock and flowers. 1k, Flowers in vase. 1.20k, Janosik, Slovak hero. 1.60k, Stag. 2k, Postilion.

1963, Sept. 2 Engr. *Perf. 13½*
1196 A462 60h red & vio bl .75 .30
1197 A462 80h multi .75 .30
1198 A462 1k multi .75 .30
1199 A462 1.20k multi .75 .30
1200 A462 1.60k multi .75 .30
1201 A462 2k multi 3.25 1.75
Nos. 1196-1201 (6) 7.00 3.25

Nos. 1196-1201 were printed in sheets of 10. Value, set $175.

Canoeing A463

Sports: 40h, Volleyball. 60h, Wrestling. 80h, Basketball. 1k, Boxing. 1.60k, Gymnastics.

Engraved and Photogravure
1963, Oct. 26 *Perf. 11½*
1202 A463 30h indigo & grn .35 .25
1203 A463 40h red brn & lt bl .35 .25
1204 A463 60h brn red & yel .40 .25
1205 A463 80h dk pur & dp org .50 .25
1206 A463 1k ultra & dp rose .70 .35
1207 A463 1.60k vio bl & ultra 2.75 1.40
Nos. 1202-1207 (6) 5.05 2.75

1964 Olympic Games, Tokyo.

Tree and Star — A464

Design: 60h, Star, hammer and sickle.

1963, Dec. 11 Unwmk. *Perf. 11½*
1208 A464 30h bis brn & lt bl .30 .25
1209 A464 60h carmine & gray .30 .25

Russo-Czechoslovakian Treaty, 20th anniv.

Atom Diagrams Surrounding Head — A465

Chamois — A466

1963, Dec. 12 Engr.
1210 A465 60h dark purple .40 .25

3rd Congress of the Association for the Propagation of Scientific Knowledge.

1963, Dec. 14 *Perf. 14*

40h, Alpine ibex. 60h, Mouflon. 1.20k, Roe deer. 1.60k, Fallow deer. 2k, Red deer.

1211 A466 30h multi 1.50 .35
1212 A466 40h multi 1.50 .35
1213 A466 60h brn, yel & grn 1.50 .35
1214 A466 1.20k multi 2.50 1.00
1215 A466 1.60k multi 3.00 1.25
1216 A466 2k multi 6.00 2.50
Nos. 1211-1216 (6) 16.00 5.80

Nos. 1211-1216 were each issued in sheets of 10 stamps. Value, set $225.

Figure Skating — A467

80h, Skiing, horiz. 1k, Field ball player.

Engraved and Photogravure
1964, Jan. 20 Unwmk. *Perf. 11½*
1217 A467 30h violet bl & yel .30 .25
1218 A467 80h dk blue & org .45 .25
1219 A467 1k brown & lilac .75 .25
Nos. 1217-1219 (3) 1.50 .75

Intl. University Games (30h, 80h) and the World Field Ball Championships (1k).

Ice Hockey — A468

1964, Jan. 20
1220 A468 1k shown .85 .35
1221 A468 1.80k Toboggan 1.00 .60
1222 A468 2k Ski jump 2.50 2.25
Nos. 1220-1222 (3) 4.35 3.20

9th Winter Olympic Games, Innsbruck, Jan. 29-Feb. 9, 1964.

Magura Rest Home, High Tatra — A469

Design: 80h, Slovak National Insurrection Rest Home, Low Tatra.

1964, Feb. 19 Unwmk. *Perf. 11½*
1223 A469 60h green & yellow .30 .25
1224 A469 80h violet bl & pink .30 .25

Skiers and Ski Lift A470

60h, Automobile camp, Telc. 1k, Fishing, Spis Castle. 1.80k, Lake & boats, Cesky Krumlov.

1964, Feb. 19 Engr. & Photo.
1225 A470 30h dk vio brn & bl .40 .25
1226 A470 60h slate & car .45 .25
1227 A470 1k brown & olive .80 .25
1228 A470 1.80k slate grn & org 1.25 .35
Nos. 1225-1228 (4) 2.90 1.10

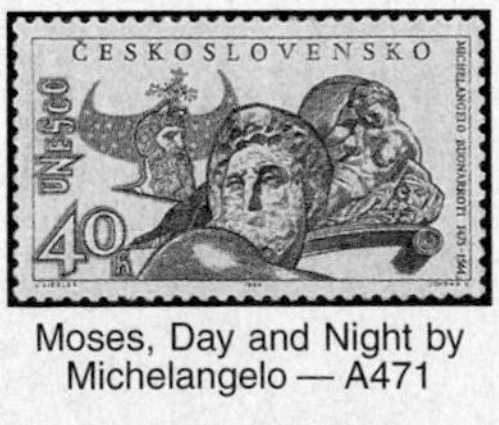

Moses, Day and Night by Michelangelo — A471

Designs: 60h, "A Midsummer Night's Dream," by Shakespeare. 1k, Man, telescope and heaven, vert. 1.60k, King George of Podebrad (1420-71).

1964, Mar. 20
1229 A471 40h black & yel grn .45 .25
1230 A471 60h slate & car .30 .25
1231 A471 1k black & lt blue 1.10 .25
1232 A471 1.60k black & yellow 1.25 .25
a. Souvenir sheet of 4, imperf. ('88) 9.50 6.50
Nos. 1229-1232 (4) 3.10 1.00

400th anniv. of the death of Michelangelo (40h); 400th anniv. of the birth of Shakespeare (60h); 400th anniv. of the birth of Galileo (1k); 500th anniv. of the pacifist efforts of King George of Podebrad (1.60k).

No. 1232a for PRAGA '88.

Yuri A. Gagarin — A472

Astronauts: 60h, Gherman Titov. 80h, John H. Glenn, Jr. 1k, Scott M. Carpenter, vert. 1.20k, Pavel R. Popovich and Andrian G. Nikolayev. 1.40k, Walter M. Schirra, vert. 1.60k, Gordon L. Cooper, vert. 2k, Valentina Tereshkova and Valeri Bykovski, vert.

1964, Apr. 27 Unwmk. *Perf. 11½*
Yellow Paper
1233 A472 30h black & vio bl .55 .25
1234 A472 60h dk grn & dk car .25 .25
1235 A472 80h dk car & vio .55 .25
1236 A472 1k ultra & rose vio .25 .25
1237 A472 1.20k ver & ol gray .55 .35
1238 A472 1.40k black & dl grn 1.40 .50
1239 A472 1.60k pale pur & Prus grn 3.25 1.50
1240 A472 2k dk blue & red 1.10 .40
Nos. 1233-1240 (8) 7.90 3.75

World's first 10 astronauts.

Creeping Bellflower A473

Film "Flower" and Karlovy Vary Colonnade A474

Flowers: 80h, Musk thistle. 1k, Chicory. 1.20k, Yellow Iris. 1.60k, Gentian. 2k, Corn poppy.

1964, June 15 Engr. *Perf. 14*
1241 A473 60h dk grn, lil & org 1.25 .25
1242 A473 80h blk, grn & red lil 1.25 .25
1243 A473 1k vio bl, grn & pink 1.25 .45
1244 A473 1.20k black, yel & grn 1.25 .30
1245 A473 1.60k violet & grn 3.00 .40
1246 A473 2k vio, red & grn 7.00 2.00
Nos. 1241-1246 (6) 15.00 3.65

Nos. 1241-1246 were each issued in sheets of 10. Value, set $250.

Engraved and Photogravure
1964, June 20 Unwmk. *Perf. 13½*
1247 A474 60h black, blue & car 2.00 .50

14th Intl. Film Festival at Karlovy Vary, July 4-19.

Issued in sheets of 10. Value, $60.

Silesian Coat of Arms — A475

1964, June 20 ***Perf. 11½***

1248	A475	30h black & yel	.30	.25

150th anniv. of the Silesian Museum, Opava.

Young Miner of 1764 — A476

1964, June 20

1249	A476	60h sepia & lt grn	.30	.25

Mining School at Banska Stiavnica, bicent.

Skoda Fire Engine A477

1964, June 20

1250	A477	60h car rose & lt bl	1.25	.25

Voluntary fire brigades in Bohemia, cent.

Gulls, Hradcany Castle, Red Cross — A478

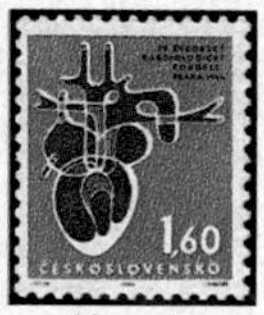

Human Heart — A479

1964, July 10

1251	A478	60h car & bluish gray	.55	.25

4th Czechoslovak Red Cross Congress at Prague.

1964, July 10

1252	A479	1.60k ultra & car	1.25	.25

4th European Cardiological Cong. at Prague.

Partisans, Girl and Factories A480

Battle Scene, 1944 — A481

Design: No. 1254, Partisans and flame.

Engraved and Photogravure

1964, Aug. 17 **Unwmk.** ***Perf. 11½***

1253	A480	30h brown & red	.25	.25
1254	A480	60h dk blue & red	.25	.25
1255	A481	60h black & red	.25	.25
		Nos. 1253-1255 (3)	.75	.75

20th anniv. of the Slovak Natl. Uprising; No. 1255, 20th anniv. of the Battles of Dukla Pass.

Hradcany at Prague — A482

Discus Thrower and Pole Vaulter — A483

Design: 5k, Charles Bridge and Hradcany.

1964, Aug. 30 ***Perf. 11½x12***

1256	A482	60h black & red	.65	.25

Souvenir Sheet

Engr. ***Imperf.***

1257	A482	5k deep claret	4.00	3.25

Millenium of the Hradcany, Prague. No. 1257 stamp size: 30x50mm.

Engraved and Photogravure

1964, Sept. 2 ***Perf. 13½***

Designs: 60h, Bicycling, horiz. 1k, Soccer. 1.20k, Rowing. 1.60k, Swimming, horiz. 2.80k, Weight lifting, horiz.

1258	A483	60h multi	1.00	.30
1259	A483	80h multi	1.00	.30
1260	A483	1k multi	1.00	.30
1261	A483	1.20k multi	1.00	.30
1262	A483	1.60k multi	1.00	.30
1263	A483	2.80k multi	*5.00*	*2.00*
		Nos. 1258-1263 (6)	*10.00*	*3.50*

Issued to commemorate the 18th Olympic Games, Tokyo, Oct. 10-25.

Nos. 1258-1263 were issued in sheets of 10. Value, set $225.

Miniature Sheet

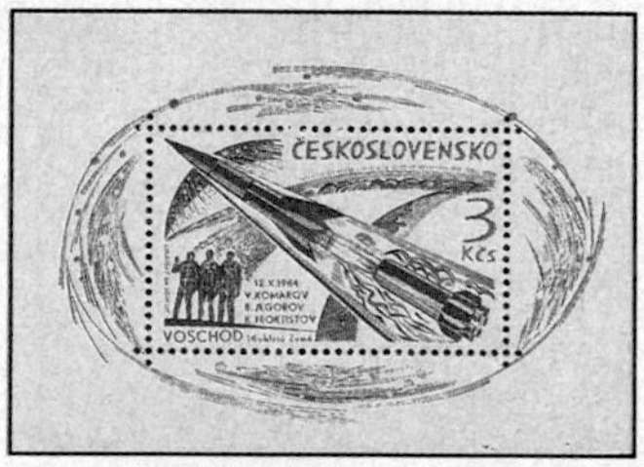

Space Ship Voskhod I, Astronauts and Globe — A484

1964, Nov. 12 **Unwmk.** ***Perf. 11½***

1264	A484	3k dk bl & dl lil, *buff*	6.00	4.00

Russian 3-man space flight of Vladimir M. Komarov, Boris B. Yegorov and Konstantin Feoktistov, Oct. 12-13.

Steam Engine and Atomic Power Plant — A485

Diesel Engine "CKD Praha" — A486

1964, Nov. 16 **Engr.**

1265	A485	30h dull red brown	.25	.25

Engraved and Photogravure

1266	A486	60h green & salmon	.75	.25

Traditions and development of engineering; No. 1265 for 150th anniv. of the First Brno Engineering Works, No. 1266 for the engineering concern CKD Praha.

European Redstart — A487

Birds: 60h, Green woodpecker. 80h, Hawfinch. 1k, Black woodpecker. 1.20k, European robin. 1.60k, European roller.

1964, Nov. 16 **Litho.** ***Perf. 10½***

1267	A487	30h multicolored	1.25	.30
1268	A487	60h black & multi	1.25	.30
1269	A487	80h multicolored	1.50	.35
1270	A487	1k multicolored	2.00	.40
1271	A487	1.20k lt vio bl & blk	2.00	.40
1272	A487	1.60k yellow & blk	4.00	1.00
		Nos. 1267-1272 (6)	12.00	2.75

Dancer A488

"In the Sun" Preschool Children A489

Designs: 60h, "Over the Obstacles," teenagers. 1k, "Movement and Beauty," woman flag twirler. 1.60k, Runners at start.

Engraved and Photogravure

1965 **Unwmk.** ***Perf. 11½***

1273	A488	30h red & lt blue	.25	.25

Perf. 11½x12

1274	A489	30h vio bl & car	.25	.25
1275	A489	60h brown & ultra	.25	.25
1276	A489	1k black & yellow	.25	.25
1277	A489	1.60k maroon & gray	.60	.25
		Nos. 1273-1277 (5)	1.60	1.25

3rd Natl. Spartacist Games. Issue dates: No. 1273, Jan. 3; Nos. 1274-1277, May 24.

Mountain Rescue Service — A490

Designs: No. 1279, Woman gymnast. No. 1280, Bicyclists. No. 1281, Women hurdlers.

1965, Jan. 15 **Unwmk.** ***Perf. 11½***

1278	A490	60h violet & blue	.30	.25
1279	A490	60h maroon & ocher	.30	.25
1280	A490	60h black & carmine	.30	.25
1281	A490	60h green & yellow	.30	.25
		Nos. 1278-1281 (4)	1.20	1.00

Mountain Rescue Service (No. 1278); 1st World Championship in Artistic Gymnastics, Prague, Dec. 1965 (No. 1279); World Championship in Indoor Bicycling, Prague, Oct. 1965 (No. 1280); "Universiada 1965," Brno (No. 1281).

Arms and View, Beroun — A491

Designs: No. 1283, Town Square, Domazlice. No. 1284, Old and new buildings, Frydek-Mystek. No. 1285, Arms and view, Lipnik. No. 1286, Fortified wall, City Hall and Arms, Policka. No. 1287, View and hops, Zatek. No. 1288, Small fortress and rose, Terezin.

1965, Feb. 15

1282	A491	30h vio bl & lt bl	.30	.25
1283	A491	30h dull pur & yel	.30	.25
1284	A491	30h slate & gray	.30	.25
1285	A491	30h green & bis	.30	.25
1286	A491	30h brown & tan	.30	.25
1287	A491	30h dk blue & cit	.30	.25
1288	A491	30h black & rose	.30	.25
		Nos. 1282-1288 (7)	2.10	1.75

Nos. 1282-1287 for 700th anniv. of the founding of various Bohemian towns; No. 1288 the 20th anniv. of the liberation of the Theresienstadt (Terezin) concentration camp.

Sun's Corona A492

Space Research: 30h, Sun. 60h, Exploration of the Moon. 1k, Twin space craft, vert. 1.40k, Space station. 1.60k, Exploration of Mars, vert. 2k, USSR and US Meteorological collaboration.

1965, Mar. 15 ***Perf. 12x11½, 11½x12***

1289	A492	20h rose & red lilac	.25	.25
1290	A492	30h rose red & yel	.25	.25
1291	A492	60h bluish blk & yel	.25	.25
1292	A492	1k pur & pale bl	.50	.25
1293	A492	1.40k black & salmon	.50	.25
1294	A492	1.60k black & pink	.50	.25
1295	A492	2k bluish blk & lt bl	*1.50*	*1.00*
		Nos. 1289-1295 (7)	*3.75*	*2.50*

Space research; Nos. 1289-1290 also for the Intl. Quiet Sun Year, 1964-65.

Frantisek Ventura, Equestrian; Amsterdam, 1928 — A493

Czechoslovakian Olympic Victories: 30h, Discus, Paris, 1900. 60h, Running, Helsinki, 1952. 1k, Weight lifting, Los Angeles, 1932. 1.40k, Gymnastics, Berlin, 1936. 1.60k, Double sculling, Rome, 1960. 2k, Women's gymnastics, Tokyo, 1964.

1965, Apr. 16 ***Perf. 11½x12***

1296	A493	20h choc & gold	.25	.25
1297	A493	30h indigo & emer	.25	.25
1298	A493	60h ultra & gold	.25	.25
1299	A493	1k red brn & gold	.35	.25
1300	A493	1.40k dk sl grn & gold	.80	.65
1301	A493	1.60k black & gold	.85	.65
1302	A493	2k maroon & gold	1.25	.50
		Nos. 1296-1302 (7)	4.00	2.80

Astronauts Virgil Grissom and John Young — A494

Designs: No. 1304, Alexei Leonov floating in space. No. 1305, Launching pad at Cape Kennedy. No. 1306, Leonov leaving space ship.

1965, Apr. 17 ***Perf. 11x11½***

1303	A494	60h slate bl & lil rose	.45	.25
1304	A494	60h vio blk & blue	.45	.25
1305	A494	3k slate bl & lil rose	1.75	1.00
a.		Pair, #1303, 1305	3.75	2.00
1306	A494	3k vio blk & blue	1.75	1.00
a.		Pair, #1304, 1306	3.75	2.00
		Nos. 1303-1306 (4)	4.40	2.50

Issued to honor American and Soviet astronauts. Printed in sheets of 25; one sheet contains 20 No. 1303 and 5 No. 1305, the other sheet contains 20 No. 1304 and 5 No. 1306.

Russian Soldier, View of Prague and Guerrilla Fighters
A495

Designs: No. 1308, Blast furnace, workers and tank. 60h, Worker and factory. 1k, Worker and new constructions. 1.60k, Woman farmer, new farm buildings and machinery.

1965, May 5 **Engr.** ***Perf. 13½***

1307 A495 30h dk red, blk & ol .40 .25
1308 A495 30h multicolored .40 .25
1309 A495 60h vio bl, red & blk .40 .25
1310 A495 1k dp org, blk & brn .65 .25
1311 A495 1.60k yel, red & blk .70 .25
Nos. 1307-1311 (5) 2.55 1.25

20th anniv. of liberation from the Nazis.
Nos. 1307-1311 were each printed in sheets of 10. Value, set $120.

Slovakian Kopov Dog
A496

Dogs: 40h, German shepherd. 60h, Czech hunting dog with pheasant. 1k, Poodle. 1.60k, Czech terrier. 2k, Afghan hound.

1965, June 10 ***Perf. 12x11½***

1312 A496 30h black & red org .50 .25
1313 A496 40h black & yellow .50 .25
1314 A496 60h black & ver .80 .25
1315 A496 1k black & dk car rose 1.10 .30
1316 A496 1.60k black & orange 1.50 .35
1317 A496 2k black & orange 3.00 1.25
Nos. 1312-1317 (6) 7.40 2.65

World Dog Show at Brno and the International Dog Breeders Congress, Prague.

UN Headquarters Building, NY — A497

Emblems: 60h, UN & inscription. 1.60k, ICY.

1965, June 24 ***Perf. 12x11½***

1318 A497 60h dk red brn & yel .30 .25
1319 A497 1k ultra & lt blue .75 .25
1320 A497 1.60k gold & dk red .70 .35
Nos. 1318-1320 (3) 1.75 .85

20th anniv. of the UN and the ICY, 1965.

Trade Union Emblem
A498

1965, June 24 **Engr.**

1321 A498 60h dk red & ultra .65 .25

Intl. Trade Union Federation, 20th anniv.

Women and Globe — A499

1965, June 24 ***Perf. 11½x12***

1322 A499 60h violet blue .40 .25

20th anniv. of the Intl. Women's Federation.

Children's House (Burgraves' Palace), Hradcany
A500

Matthias Tower — A501

1965, June 25 ***Perf. 11½***

1323 A500 30h slate green .30 .25
1324 A501 60h dark brown .30 .25

Issued to publicize the Hradcany, Prague.

Marx and Lenin — A502

1965, July 1 **Engr. & Photo.**

1325 A502 60h car rose & gold .40 .25

6th conf. of Postal Ministers of Communist Countries, Peking, June 21-July 15.

Joseph Navratil — A503

Jan Hus — A504

Gregor Johann Mendel
A505

Costume Jewelry
A506

Bohuslav Martinu
A507

Seated Woman and University of Bratislava
A508

ITU Emblem and Communication Symbols
A509

Macromolecular Symposium Emblem
A510

Design: No. 1327, Ludovit Stur (diff. frame).

1965 **Unwmk.** ***Perf. 11½***

1326 A503 30h black & fawn .25 .25
1327 A503 30h black & dull grn .25 .25
1328 A504 60h black & crimson .25 .25
1329 A505 60h vio bl & red .25 .25
1330 A506 60h purple & gold .25 .25
1331 A507 60h black & orange .25 .25
1332 A508 60h brn, *yel* .25 .25
1333 A509 1k orange & blue .35 .25
1334 A510 1k black & dp org .35 .25
Nos. 1326-1334 (9) 2.45 2.25

No. 1326, Navratil (1798-1865), painter; No. 1327, Stur (1815-56), Slovak author and historian; No. 1328, the 550th anniv. of the death of Hus, religious reformer;

No. 1329, cent. of publication of Mendel's laws of inheritance; No. 1330 publicizes the "Jablonec 1965" costume jewelry exhib.; No. 1331, Martinu (1890-1959), composer; No. 1332, 500th anniv. of the founding of the University of Bratislava as Academia Istropolitana; No. 1333, cent. of the ITU; No. 1334, Intl. Symposium on Macromolecular Chemistry, Prague, Sept. 1-8.

Issued: No. 1333, 7/10.

Miniature Sheet

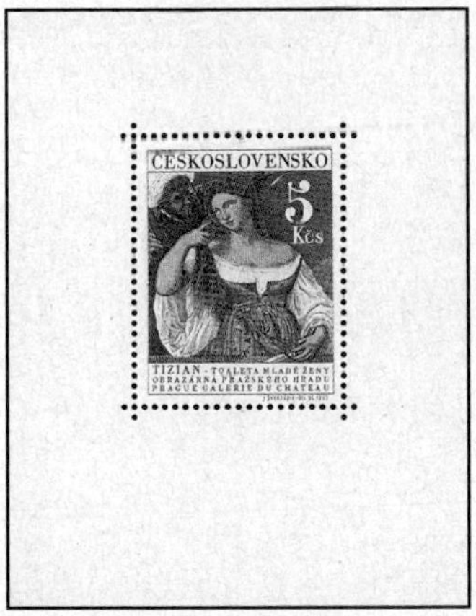

"Young Woman at her Toilette," by Titian — A512

1965, Aug. 12

1336 A512 5k multicolored 6.00 4.00

Hradcany Art Gallery. No. 1336 contains one stamp.

Help for Flood Victims — A513

Rescue of Flood Victims
A514

1965, Sept. 6 **Engr.**

1337 A513 30h violet blue .25 .25

Engraved and Photogravure

1338 A514 2k dk ol grn & ol .65 .45

Help for Danube flood victims in Slovakia.

Dotterel
A515

Mountain Birds: 60h, Wall creeper, vert. 1.20k, Lesser redpoll. 1.40k, Golden eagle, vert. 1.60k, Ring ouzel. 2k, Eurasian nutcracker, vert.

1965, Sept. 20 **Litho.** ***Perf. 11***

1339 A515 30h multi 1.50 .25
1340 A515 60h multi 1.50 .25
1341 A515 1.20k multi 1.75 .25
1342 A515 1.40k multi 2.75 .40
1343 A515 1.60k multi 1.75 .65
1344 A515 2k multi 7.00 2.75
Nos. 1339-1344 (6) 16.25 4.55

Levoca — A516

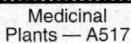

Medicinal Plants — A517

Views of Towns: 10h, Jindrichuv Hradec. 20h, Nitra. 30h, Kosice. 40h, Hradec Králové. 50h, Telc. 60h, Ostrava. 1k, Olomouc. 1.20k, Ceske Budejovice. 1.60k, Cheb. 2k, Brno. 3k, Bratislava. 5k, Prague.

Engraved and Photogravure

1965-66 ***Perf. 11½x12***

Size: 23x19mm

1345 A516 5h black & yel .25 .25
1346 A516 10h ultra & ol bis .65 .25
1347 A516 20h black & lt bl .25 .25
1348 A516 30h vio bl & lt grn .25 .25
1348A A516 40h dk brn & lt bl ('66) .25 .25
1348B A516 50h black & ocher ('66) .50 .25
1348C A516 60h red & gray ('66) 1.00 .25
1348D A516 1k pur & pale grn ('66) .65 .25

Perf. 11½x11

Size: 30x23mm

1349 A516 1.20k slate & lt bl .55 .25
1350 A516 1.60k indigo & yel .80 .25
1351 A516 2k sl grn & pale yel .75 .25
1352 A516 3k brn & yel 1.00 .25
1353 A516 5k black & pink 1.40 .25
Nos. 1345-1353 (13) 8.30 3.25

1965, Dec. 3 **Engr.** ***Perf. 14***

1354 A517 30h Coltsfoot .40 .25
1355 A517 60h Meadow saffron .40 .25
1356 A517 80h Corn poppy 1.25 .25
1357 A517 1k Foxglove 1.25 .40
1358 A517 1.20k Arnica 1.75 .75
1359 A517 1.60k Cornflower 1.75 .75
1360 A517 2k Dog rose 4.25 2.00
Nos. 1354-1360 (7) 11.05 4.65

Nos. 1354-1360 were each printed in sheets of 10. Value, set $200.

Strip of "Stamps" — A518

Engraved and Photogravure

1965, Dec. 18 ***Perf. 11½***

1361 A518 1k dark red & gold 4.00 2.25

Issued for Stamp Day, 1965.

Romain Rolland (1866-1944), French Writer A519

Symbolic Musical Instruments & Names of Composers A520

Portraits: No. 1362, Stanislav Sucharda (1866-1916), sculptor. No. 1363, Ignac Josef Pesina (1766-1808), veterinarian. No. 1365, Donatello (1386-1466), Italian sculptor.

1966, Feb. 14 Engr. *Perf. 11½*

1362	A519	30h deep green	.25	.25
1363	A519	30h violet blue	.25	.25
1364	A519	60h rose lake	.25	.25
1365	A519	60h brown	.25	.25
		Nos. 1362-1365 (4)	1.00	1.00

1966, Jan. 15 Engr. & Photo.

1366	A520	30h black & gold	.65	.25

Czech Philharmonic Orchestra, 70th anniv.

Figure Skating Pair A521

No. 1368, Man skater. No. 1369, Volleyball player, spiking, vert. 1k, Volleyball player, saving, vert. 1.60k, Woman skater. 2k, Figure skating pair.

1966, Feb. 17

1367	A521	30h dk car rose	.30	.25
1368	A521	60h green	.30	.25
1369	A521	60h carmine & buff	.30	.25
1370	A521	1k vio & lt bl	.40	.25
1371	A521	1.60k brown & yellow	.50	.25
1372	A521	2k blue & grnsh bl	2.40	.40
		Nos. 1367-1372 (6)	4.20	1.65

Nos. 1367-1368, 1371-1372 for the European Figure Skating Championships, Bratislava; Nos. 1369-1370 for the World Volleyball Championships.

Souvenir Sheet

Girl Dancing — A522

1966, Mar. 21 Engr. *Imperf.*

1373	A522	3k slate bl, red & bl	4.00	2.75

Cent. of the opera "The Bartered Bride" by Bedrich Smetana.

"Ajax" 1841 A523

Locomotives: 30h, "Karlstejn" 1865. 60h, Steam engine, 1946. 1k, Steam engine with tender, 1946. 1.60k, Electric locomotive, 1964. 2k, Diesel locomotive, 1964.

1966, Mar. 21 *Perf. 11½x11*

Buff Paper

1374	A523	20h sepia	1.40	.25
1375	A523	30h dull violet	1.75	.25
1376	A523	60h dull purple	1.25	.25
1377	A523	1k dark blue	1.40	.50
1378	A523	1.60k dk blue grn	2.40	.40
1379	A523	2k dark red	4.75	2.10
		Nos. 1374-1379 (6)	12.95	3.75

European Perch A524

30h, Brown trout, vert. 1k, Carp. 1.20k, Northern pike. 1.40k, Grayling. 1.60k, Eel.

Perf. 13x13½, 13½x13

1966, Apr. 22 Litho. Unwmk.

1380	A524	30h multi	.75	.25
1381	A524	60h multi	.75	.25
1382	A524	1k multi	1.75	.25
1383	A524	1.20k multi	.75	.25
1384	A524	1.40k multi	1.25	.25
1385	A524	1.60k multi	3.50	1.10
		Nos. 1380-1385 (6)	8.75	2.35

Intl. Fishing Championships, Svit, Sept. 3-5.

WHO Headquarters, Geneva — A525

Engraved and Photogravure

1966, Apr. 25 *Perf. 12x11½*

1386	A525	1k dk blue & lt blue	.50	.25

Opening of the WHO Headquarters, Geneva.

Symbolic Handshake and UNESCO Emblem A526

1966, Apr. 25 *Perf. 11½*

1387	A526	60h bister & olive gray	.30	.25

20th anniv. of UNESCO.

Prague Castle Issue

Belvedere Palace and St. Vitus' Cathedral A527

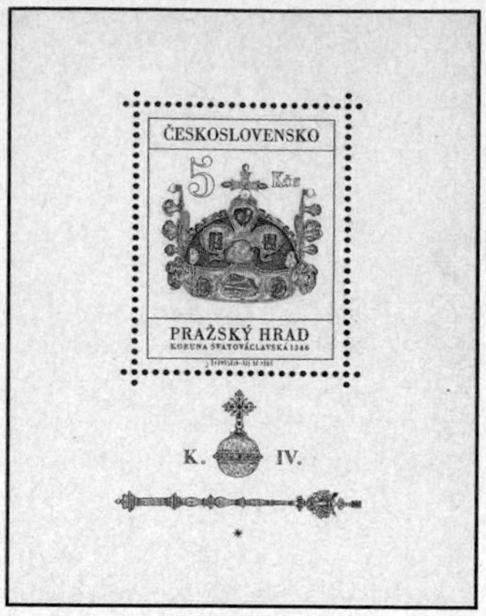

Crown of St. Wenceslas, 1346 — A528

Design: 60h, Madonna, altarpiece from St. George's Church.

1966, May 9 Engr. *Perf. 11½*

1388	A527	30h dark blue	.50	.25

Engraved and Photogravure

1389	A527	60h blk & yel bis	.75	.25

Souvenir Sheet

Engr.

1390	A528	5k multi	6.50	3.25

See Nos. 1537-1539.

Tiger Swallowtail A529

Butterflies and Moths: 60h, Clouded sulphur. 80h, European purple emperor. 1k, Apollo. 1.20k, Burnet moth. 2k, Tiger moth.

1966, May 23 Engr. *Perf. 14*

1391	A529	30h multi	.90	.25
1392	A529	60h multi	.90	.25
1393	A529	80h multi	1.25	.40
1394	A529	1k multi	1.90	.60
1395	A529	1.20k multi	1.90	.50
1396	A529	2k multi	5.50	2.00
		Nos. 1391-1396 (6)	12.35	4.00

Nos. 1391-1396 were issued in sheets of 10. Value, set $250.

Flags of Russia and Czechoslovakia — A530

Designs: 60h, Rays surrounding hammer and sickle "sun." 1.60k, Girl's head and stars.

Engraved and Photogravure

1966, May 31 *Perf. 11½*

1397	A530	30h dk bl & crim	.25	.25
1398	A530	60h dk bl & red	.25	.25
1399	A530	1.60k red & dk bl	.30	.25
		Nos. 1397-1399 (3)	.80	.75

13th Congress of the Communist Party of Czechoslovakia.

Dakota Chief — A531

Model of Molecule — A532

Designs: 20h, Indians, canoe and tepee, horiz. 30h, Tomahawk. 40h, Haida totem poles. 60h, Kachina, good spirit of the Hopis. 1k, Indian on horseback hunting buffalo, horiz. 1.20k, Calumet, Dakota peace pipe.

1966, June 20 Size: 23x40mm

1400	A531	20h vio bl & dp org	.25	.25
1401	A531	30h blk & dl org	.25	.25
1402	A531	40h blk & lt bl	.25	.25
1403	A531	60h grn & yel	.25	.25
1404	A531	1k pur & emer	.40	.25
1405	A531	1.20k vio bl & rose lil	.65	.30

Perf. 14

Engr.

Size: 23x37mm

1406	A531	1.40k multi	1.60	.90
		Nos. 1400-1406 (7)	3.65	2.45

Cent. of the Náprstek Ethnographic Museum, Prague, and "The Indians of North America" exhibition.

No. 1406 was issued in sheets of 10. Value $130.

Engraved and Photogravure

1966, July 4 Unwmk. *Perf. 11½*

1407	A532	60h blk & lt bl	.50	.25

Czechoslovak Chemical Society, cent.

"Guernica" by Pablo Picasso — A533

1966, July 5 Size: 75x30mm

1408	A533	60h blk & pale bl	3.20	1.60

30th anniversary of International Brigade in Spanish Civil War.

Sheets of 15 stamps and 5 labels inscribed "Picasso-Guernica 1937." Values: with tab attached, $6; sheet $75.

Pantheon, Bratislava — A534

Designs: No. 1410, Devin Castle and Ludovit Stur. No. 1411, View of Nachod. No. 1412, State Science Library, Olomouc.

1966, July 25 Engr.

1409	A534	30h dl pur	.30	.25
1410	A534	60h dk bl	.35	.25
1411	A534	60h green	.35	.25
1412	A534	60h sepia	.30	.25
		Nos. 1409-1412 (4)	1.30	1.00

No. 1409, Russian War Memorial, Bratislava; No. 1410, the 9th cent. Devin Castle as symbol of Slovak nationalism; No. 1411, 700th anniv. of the founding of Nachod; No. 1412, the 400th anniv. of the State Science Library, Olomouc.

Atom Symbol and Sun — A535

Engraved and Photogravure

1966, Aug. 29 *Perf. 11½*

1413	A535	60h blk & red	.40	.25

Issued to publicize Jachymov (Joachimsthal), where pitchblende was first discovered, "cradle of the atomic age."

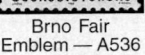

Brno Fair Emblem — A536

Olympia Coin and Olympic Rings — A537

1966, Aug. 29

1414	A536	60h blk & red	.40	.25

8th International Trade Fair, Brno.

1966, Aug. 29

Design: 1k, Olympic flame, Czechoslovak flag and Olympic rings.

1415	A537	60h blk & gold	.30	.25
1416	A537	1k dk bl & red	1.10	.30

70th anniv. of the Olympic Committee.

Missile Carrier, Tank and Jet Plane A538

1966, Aug. 31

1417	A538	60h blk & apple grn	.40	.25

Issued to commemorate the maneuvers of the armies of the Warsaw Pact countries.

Mercury A539

30h, Moravian silver thaler, 1620, reverse & obverse, vert. 1.60k, Old & new buildings of Brno State Theater. 5k, Intl. Trade Fair Administration Tower & postmark, vert.

1966, Sept. 10

1418	A539	30h dk red & blk	.45	.25
1419	A539	60h org & blk	.45	.25
1420	A539	1.60k blk & brt grn	.85	.25
		Nos. 1418-1420 (3)	1.75	.75

Souvenir Sheet

1421	A539	5k multi	3.50	3.50

Brno Philatelic Exhibition, Sept. 11-25. No. 1421 contains one 30x40mm stamp.

First Meeting in Orbit — A540

30h, Photograph of far side of Moon & Russian satellite. 60h, Photograph of Mars & Mariner 4. 80th, Soft landing on Moon. 1k, Satellite, laser beam & binary code. 1.20k, Telstar over Earth & receiving station.

1966, Sept. 26 ***Perf. 11½***

1422	A540	20h vio & lt grn	.25	.25
1423	A540	30h blk & sal pink	.25	.25
1424	A540	60h slate & lilac	.35	.25
1425	A540	80h dk pur & lt bl	.35	.25
1426	A540	1k blk & vio	.40	.25
1427	A540	1.20k red & bl	2.25	.60
		Nos. 1422-1427 (6)	3.85	1.85

Issued to publicize American and Russian achievements in space research.

Badger A541

Game Animals: 40h, Red deer, vert. 60h, Lynx. 80h, Hare. 1k, Red fox. 1.20k, Brown bear, vert. 2k, Wild boar.

1966, Nov. 28 **Litho.** ***Perf. 13½***

1428	A541	30h multi	.60	.25
1429	A541	40h multi	.60	.25
1430	A541	60h multi	.50	.25
1431	A541	80h multi *(europaens)*	1.25	.25
a.		80h multi *(europaeus)*	6.00	3.50
1432	A541	1k multi	.90	.30
1433	A541	1.20k multi	1.25	.50
1434	A541	2k multi	3.00	1.25
		Nos. 1428-1434 (7)	8.10	3.05

The sheet of 50 of the 80h contains 40 with misspelling "europaens" and 10 with "europaeus."

"Spring" by Vaclav Hollar, 1607-77 A542

Paintings: No. 1436, Portrait of Mrs. F. Wussin, by Jan Kupecky (1667-1740). No. 1437, Snow Owl by Karel Purkyne (1834-1868). No. 1438, Tulips by Vaclav Spála (1885-1964). No. 1439, Recruit by Ludovít Fulla (1902-1980).

1966, Dec. 8 **Engr.** ***Perf. 14***

1435	A542	1k black	3.75	3.50
1436	A542	1k multicolored	5.25	1.90
1437	A542	1k multicolored	2.40	1.90
1438	A542	1k multicolored	2.40	1.90
1439	A542	1k multicolored	19.00	16.00
		Nos. 1435-1439 (5)	32.80	25.20

Printed in sheets of 4 stamps and 2 labels. The labels in sheet of No. 1435 are inscribed "Vaclav Hollar 1607-1677" in fancy frame. Other labels are blank. Value, set $150.

See No. 1484.

Symbolic Bird — A543

Engraved and Photogravure

1966, Dec. 17 ***Perf. 11½***

1440	A543	1k dp blue & yel	1.25	.80

Issued for Stamp Day.

Youth — A544

1967, Jan. 16 ***Perf. 11½***

1441	A544	30h ver & lt bl	.30	.25

5th Cong. of the Czechoslovak Youth Org.

Symbolic Flower and Machinery A545

1967, Jan. 16

1442	A545	30h carmine & yel	.30	.25

6th Trade Union Congress, Prague.

Parents with Dead Child — A545a

1967, Jan. 16 ***Perf. 11½***

1442A	A545a	60h black & salmon	.30	.25

"Peace and Freedom in Viet Nam."

View of Jihlava and Tourist Year Emblem A546

Views and Tourist Year Emblem: 40h, Spielberg Castle and churches, Brno. 1.20k, Danube, castle and churches, Bratislava. 1.60k, Vlatava River bridges, Hradcany and churches, Prague.

1967, Feb. 13 **Engr.** ***Perf. 11½***

Size: 40x23mm

1443	A546	30h brown violet	.25	.25
1444	A546	40h maroon	.25	.25

Size: 75x30mm

1445	A546	1.20k violet blue	.60	.25
1446	A546	1.60k black	2.00	.80
		Nos. 1443-1446 (4)	3.10	1.55

International Tourist Year, 1967.

Black-tailed Godwit — A547

Birds: 40h, Shoveler, horiz. 60h, Purple heron. 80h, Penduline tit. 1k, Avocet. 1.40k, Black stork. 1.60k, Tufted duck, horiz.

1967, Feb. 20 **Litho.** ***Perf. 13½***

1447	A547	30h multi	.60	.30
1448	A547	40h multi	.60	.30
1449	A547	60h multi	.60	.30
1450	A547	80h multi	.60	.30
1451	A547	1k multi	.85	.30
1452	A547	1.40k multi	1.10	.60
1453	A547	1.60k multi	4.50	1.20
		Nos. 1447-1453 (7)	8.85	3.30

Solar Research and Satellite — A548

Space Research: 40h, Space craft, rocket and construction of station. 60h, Man on moon and orientation system. 1k, Exploration of solar system and rocket. 1.20k, Lunar satellites and moon photograph. 1.60k, Planned lunar architecture and moon landing.

Engraved and Photogravure

1967, Mar. 24 ***Perf. 11½***

1454	A548	30h yel & dk red	.30	.25
1455	A548	40h vio bl & blk	.45	.25
1456	A548	60h lilac & grn	.45	.25
1457	A548	1k brt pink & sl	.45	.25
1458	A548	1.20k lt violet & blk	.70	.25
1459	A548	1.60k brn lake & blk	2.40	.60
		Nos. 1454-1459 (6)	4.75	1.85

Gothic Painting, by Master Theodoric A549

Designs: 40h, "Burning of Master Hus," from Litomerice Hymnal. 60h, Modern glass sculpture. 80h, "The Shepherdess and the Chimney Sweep," Andersen fairy tale, painting by J. Trnka. 1k, Section of pressure vessel from atomic power station. 1.20k, Three ceramic figurines, by P. Rada. 3k, Montreal skyline and EXPO '67 emblem.

1967, Apr. 10 **Engr.** ***Perf. 14***

Size: 37x23mm

1460	A549	30h multi	.25	.25
1461	A549	40h multi	.25	.25
1462	A549	60h multi	.25	.25
1463	A549	80h multi	.25	.25
1464	A549	1k multi	1.00	.25
1465	A549	1.20k multi	1.25	.60
		Nos. 1460-1465 (6)	3.25	1.85

Souvenir Sheet

Perf. 11½

Size: 40x30mm

1466	A549	3k multi	3.00	2.50

EXPO '67, International Exhibition, Montreal, Apr. 28-Oct. 27, 1967.

Nos. 1460-1465 were each issued in a miniature sheet of 10 stamps. Value, set $75.

Examples of No. 1466 imperf. were not issued.

Canoe Race A550

Women Playing Basketball — A551

No. 1468, Wheels, dove & emblems of Warsaw, Berlin, Prague. 1.60k, Canoe slalom.

Perf. 12x11½, 11½x12

1967, Apr. 17 **Engr. & Photo.**

1467	A550	60h black & brt bl	.25	.25
1468	A550	60h black & salmon	.25	.25
1469	A551	60h blk & grnsh bl	.25	.25
1470	A551	1.60k black & brt vio	1.40	.55
		Nos. 1467-1470 (4)	2.15	1.30

No. 1467, 5th Intl. Wild-Water Canoeing Championships; No. 1468, 20th Warsaw-Berlin-Prague Bicycle Race: No. 1469, Women's Basketball Championships; No. 1470, 10th Intl. Water Slalom Championships.

"Golden Street" — A552

Designs: 60h, Interior of Hall of King Wenceslas. 5k, St. Matthew, from illuminated manuscript, 11th century.

1967, May 9 *Perf. 11½x11*

1471 A552 30h rose claret .25 .25
1472 A552 60h bluish black .50 .25

Souvenir Sheet

Perf. 11½

1473 A552 5k multicolored 2.75 2.50

Issued to publicize the Castle of Prague.

Stylized Lyre with Flowers — A553

1967, May 10 *Perf. 11½*

1474 A553 60h dull pur & brt grn .30 .25

Prague Music Festival.

Old-New Synagogue, Prague — A554

30h, Detail from Torah curtain, 1593. 60h, Prague Printer's emblem, 1530. 1k, Mikulov jug, 1804. 1.40k, Memorial for Concentration Camp Victims 1939-45, Pincas Synagogue (menorah & tablet). 1.60k, Tombstone of David Gans, 1613.

1967, May 22 *Perf. 11½*

1475 A554 30h dull red & lt bl .30 .25
1476 A554 60h blk & lt grn .25 .25
1477 A554 1k dk bl & rose lil .35 .25
1478 A554 1.20k dk brn & mar .65 .25
1479 A554 1.40k black & yellow .55 .25
1480 A554 1.60k green & yel 4.50 2.75
Nos. 1475-1480 (6) 6.60 4.00

Issued to show Jewish relics. The items shown on the 30h, 60h and 1k are from the State Jewish Museum, Prague.

"Lidice" — A555

1967, June 9 **Unwmk.** *Perf. 11½*

1481 A555 30h black & brt rose .30 .25

Destruction of Lidice by the Nazis, 25th anniv.

Prague Architecture — A556

1967, June 10 **Engr. & Photo.**

1482 A556 1k black & gold .45 .25

Issued to publicize the 9th Congress of the International Union of Architects, Prague.

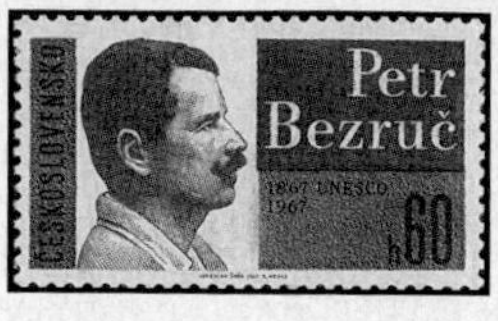

Peter Bezruc A557

1967, June 21

1483 A557 60h dull rose & blk .30 .25

Peter Bezruc, poet & writer, birth cent.

Painting Type of 1966

2k, Henri Rousseau (1844-1910), self-portrait.

Issued in sheets of 4. Value $12.50.

1967, June 22 **Engr.** *Perf. 11½*

1484 A542 2k multicolored 2.00 1.60

Praga 68, World Stamp Exhibition, Prague, June 22-July 7, 1968. Printed in sheets of 4 stamps (2x2), separated by horizontal gutter with inscription and picture of Natl. Gallery, site of Praga 68.

View of Skalitz — A558

No. 1486, Mining tower & church steeple, Pribram. No. 1487, Hands holding book & view of Presov.

1967, Aug. 21 **Engr.** *Perf. 11½*

1485 A558 30h violet blue .25 .25
1486 A558 30h slate green .25 .25
1487 A558 30h claret .25 .25
Nos. 1485-1487 (3) .75 .75

Towns of Skalitz, Pribram, Presov, annivs.

Colonnade and Spring, Karlovy Vary and Communications Emblem — A559

1967, Aug. 21 **Engr. & Photo.**

1488 A559 30h violet bl & gold .30 .25

5th Sports & Cultural Festival of the Employees of the Ministry of Communications, Karlovy Vary.

Ondrejov Observatory and Galaxy — A560

1967, Aug. 22 **Engr.**

1489 A560 60h vio bl, rose lil & sil 1.50 .25

13th Cong. of the Intl. Astronomical Union.

No. 1489 was issued in a sheet of 10 stamps. Value, set $50.

Orchid — A561

Flowers from the Botanical Gardens: 30h, Cobaea scandens. 40h, Lycaste deppei. 60h, Glottiphyllum davisii. 1k, Anthurium. 1.20k, Rhodocactus. 1.40k, Moth orchid.

1967, Aug. 30 **Litho.** *Perf. 12½*

1490 A561 20h multicolored .40 .25
1491 A561 30h pink & multi .40 .25
1492 A561 40h multicolored .55 .25
1493 A561 60h lt blue & multi .55 .25
1494 A561 1k multicolored .75 .25
1495 A561 1.20k lt yellow & multi .90 .30
1496 A561 1.40k multicolored 2.40 .70
Nos. 1490-1496 (7) 5.95 2.25

Red Squirrel A562

Animals from the Tatra National Park: 60h, Wild cat. 1k, Ermine. 1.20k, Dormouse. 1.40k, Hedgehog. 1.60k, Pine marten.

Engraved and Photogravure

1967, Sept. 25 *Perf. 11½*

1497 A562 30h black, yel & org .35 .25
1498 A562 60h black & buff .35 .25
1499 A562 1k black & lt blue .40 .25
1500 A562 1.20k brn, pale grn & yel .70 .25
1501 A562 1.40k blk, pink & yel .80 .25
1502 A562 1.60k black, org & yel 3.50 1.25
Nos. 1497-1502 (6) 6.10 2.50

Rockets and Weapons — A563

1967, Oct. 6 **Engr.** *Perf. 11½*

1503 A563 30h slate green .30 .25

Day of the Czechoslovak People's Army.

Cruiser "Aurora" Firing at Winter Palace A564

Designs: 60h, Hammer and sickle emblems and Red Star, vert. 1k, Hands reaching for hammer and sickle, vert.

1967, Nov. 7 **Engr. & Photo.**

1504 A564 30h black & dk car .25 .25
1505 A564 60h black & dk car .25 .25
1506 A564 1k black & dk car .25 .25
Nos. 1504-1506 (3) .75 .75

Russian October Revolution, 50th anniv.

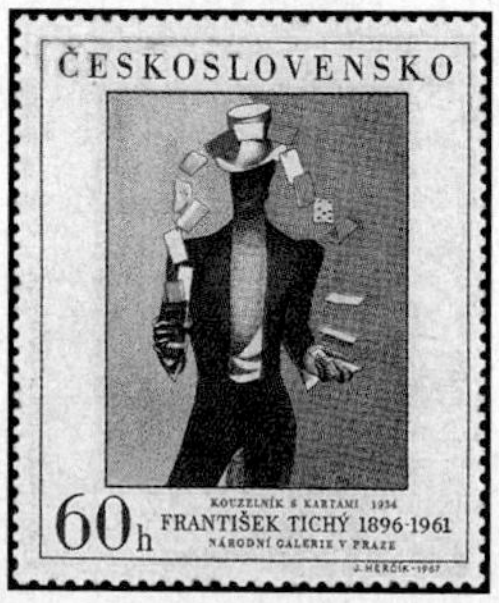

The Conjurer, by Frantisek Tichy A565

Paintings: 80h, Don Quixote, by Cyprian Majernik. 1k, Promenade in the Park, by Norbert Grund. 1.20k, Self-portrait, by Peter J. Brandl. 1.60k, Saints from Jan of Jeren Epitaph, by Czech Master of 1395.

1967, Nov. 13 **Engr.** *Perf. 11½*

1507 A565 60h multi .35 .25
1508 A565 80h multi .50 .30
1509 A565 1k multi .75 .50
1510 A565 1.20k multi .75 .50
1511 A565 1.60k multi 3.25 2.75
Nos. 1507-1511 (5) 5.60 4.30

Nos. 1507-1511 were issued in sheets of 4. Value, set $27.50.

See Nos. 1589-1593, 1658-1662, 1711-1715, 1779-1783, 1847-1851, 1908-1913, 2043-2047, 2090-2093, 2147-2151, 2265-2269, 2335-2339, 2386-2390, 2437-2441, 2534-2538, 2586-2590, 2634-2638, 2810-2813, 2843-2847, 2872-2874, 2908-2910, 2936-2938, 2973-2975, 2995, 3001-3002, 3028-3030, 3054-3055, 3075-3076, 3105-3107, 3133-3135, 3160-3162, 3188-3190, 3224-3226, 3233, 3255-3257, 3287-3289, 3323-3325, 3359-3361, 3401-3402, 3435-3436, 3478-3480, 3518-3520, 3552-3553, 3591-3593, 3616, 3618, 3656-3658.

Pres. Antonin Novotny — A566

1967, Dec. 9 **Engr.** *Perf. 11½*

1512 A566 2k blue gray 1.60 .25
1513 A566 3k brown 1.60 .25

Czechoslovakia Nos. 65, 71 and 81 of 1920 — A567

1967, Dec. 18

1514 A567 1k maroon & silver 1.60 1.10

Issued for Stamp Day.

Symbolic Flag and Dates — A568

1968, Jan. 15 **Engr.** *Perf. 11½*

1515 A568 30h red, dk bl & ultra .80 .25

50th anniversary of Czechoslovakia.

No. 1515 was issued in a sheet of 10. Value, $25.

Figure Skating and Olympic Rings — A569

Olympic Rings and: 1k, Ski course. 1.60k, Toboggan chute. 2k, Ice hockey.

1968, Jan. 29 **Engr. & Photo.**

1516 A569 60h blk, yel & ocher .30 .25
1517 A569 1k ol grn, lt bl & lem .60 .25
1518 A569 1.60k blk, lil & bl grn .80 .25
1519 A569 2k blk, ap grn & lt bl 1.25 .65
Nos. 1516-1519 (4) 2.95 1.40

10th Winter Olympic Games, Grenoble, France, Feb. 6-18.

Factories and Rising Sun — A570

Design: 60h, Workers and banner.

1968, Feb. 25 ***Perf. 11½x12***
1520 A570 30h car & dk bl .25 .25
1521 A570 60h car & dk bl .25 .25

20th anniversary of February Revolution.

Map of Battle of Sokolovo A571

Human Rights Flame — A572

1968, Mar. 8 ***Perf. 11½***
1522 A571 30h blk, brt bl & car .40 .25

Engr.

1523 A572 1k rose carmine 1.25 .50

25th anniv. of the Battle of Sokolovo, Mar. 8, 1943, against the German Army, No. 1522; Intl. Human Rights Year, No. 1523.

Janko Kral and Liptovsky Mikulas — A573

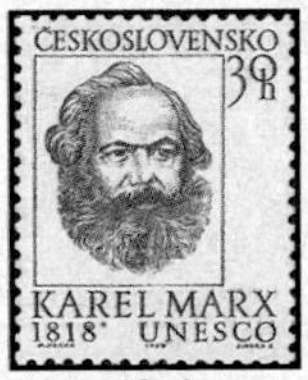

Karl Marx — A574

Girl's Head — A575

Arms and Allegory — A576

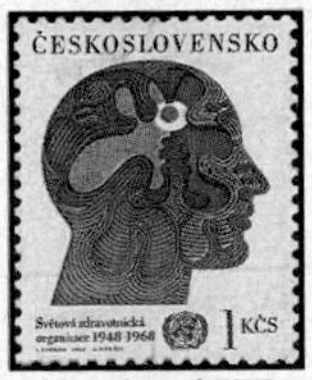

Head — A577

1968, Mar. 25 **Engr.**
1524 A573 30h green .30 .25
1525 A574 30h claret .25 .25

Engraved and Photogravure

1526 A575 30h dk red & gold .25 .25
1527 A576 30h dk blue & dp org .25 .25
1528 A577 1k multicolored .50 .25
Nos. 1524-1528 (5) 1.55 1.25

The writer Janko Kral and the Slovak town Liptovsky Mikulas (No. 1524); 150th anniv. of the birth of Karl Marx (No. 1525); cent. of the cornerstone laying of the Prague Natl. Theater (No. 1526); 150th anniv. of the Prague Natl. Museum (No. 1527); 20th anniv. of WHO (1k).

Symbolic Radio Waves A578

No. 1530, Symbolic television screens.

1968, Apr. 29 ***Perf. 11½***
1529 A578 30h blk, car & vio bl .25 .25
1530 A578 30h blk, car & vio bl .25 .25

45th anniv. of Czechoslovak broadcasting (No. 1529), 15th anniv. of television (No. 1530).

Olympic Rings, Mexican Sculpture and Diver — A579

Olympic Rings and: 40h, Runner and "The Sanctification of Quetzalcoatl." 60h, Volleyball and Mexican ornaments. 1k, Czechoslovak and Mexican Olympic emblems and carved altar. 1.60k, Soccer and ornaments. 2k, View of Hradcany, weather vane and key.

1968, Apr. 30
1531 A579 30h black, bl & car .25 .25
1532 A579 40h multi .25 .25
1533 A579 60h multi .25 .25
1534 A579 1k multi .35 .25
1535 A579 1.60k multi .35 .25
1536 A579 2k black & multi 1.75 .40
Nos. 1531-1536 (6) 3.20 1.65

19th Olympic Games, Mexico City, 10/12-27.

Prague Castle Types of 1966

Designs: 30h, Tombstone of Bretislav I. 60h, Romanesque door knocker, St. Wenceslas Chapel. 5k, Head of St. Peter, mosaic from Golden Gate of St. Vitus Cathedral.

1968, May 9 ***Perf. 11½***
1537 A527 30h multicolored .40 .25
1538 A527 60h black, red & cit .40 .25

Souvenir Sheet

Engr.

1539 A528 5k multicolored 2.50 2.50

Pres. Ludvik Svoboda — A580

1968-70 **Engr.** ***Perf. 11½***
1540 A580 30h ultramarine .25 .25
1540A A580 50h green ('70) .25 .25
1541 A580 60h maroon .25 .25
1541A A580 1k rose car ('70) .30 .25
Nos. 1540-1541A (4) 1.05 1.00

Shades exist of No. 1541A.

"Business," Sculpture by Otto Gutfreund A581

Cabaret Performer, by Frantisek Kupka — A582

Designs (The New Prague): 40h, Broadcasting Corporation Building. 60h, New Parliament. 1.40k, Tapestry by Jan Bauch "Prague 1787." 3k, Presidential standard.

Engr. & Photo.; Engr. (2k)

1968, June 5
1542 A581 30h black & multi .25 .25
1543 A581 40h black & multi .25 .25
1544 A581 60h dk brn & multi .25 .25
1545 A581 1.40k dk brn & multi .40 .25
1546 A582 2k indigo & multi .85 .70
1547 A581 3k black & multi .85 .30
Nos. 1542-1547 (6) 2.85 2.00

Designs (The Old Prague): 30h, St. George's Basilica. 60h, Renaissance fountain. 1k, Villa America-Dvorak Museum, 18th cent. building. 1.60k, Emblem from the House of Three Violins, 18th cent. 2k, Josefina, by Josef Manes. 3k, Emblem of Prague, 1475.

1968, June 21 ***Perf. 11½***
1548 A581 30h green, gray & yel .25 .25
1549 A581 60h dk vio, ap grn & gold .25 .25
1550 A581 1k black, lt bl & pink .30 .25
1551 A581 1.60k slate grn & multi .55 .25
1552 A582 2k brown & multi 1.25 .60
1553 A581 3k blk, yel, bl & pink 1.25 .60
Nos. 1548-1553 (6) 3.85 2.20

Nos. 1542-1553 publicized the Praga 68 Philatelic Exhibition. Nos. 1542-1545, 1547-1551, 1553 issued in sheets of 15 + 15 labels with Praga 68 emblem and inscription.

Nos. 1546, 1552 issued in sheets of 4 (2x2) with one horizontal label between top and bottom rows showing Praga 68 emblem. Values for sheets of 4, each $8.

Souvenir Sheet

View of Prague and Emblems — A583

Engraved and Photogravure

1968, June 22 ***Imperf.***
1554 A583 10k multicolored 3.00 2.50

Praga 68 and 50th anniv. of Czechoslovak postage stamps. Sold only together with a 5k admission ticket to the Praga 68 philatelic Exhibition. Value $20.

Madonna with the Rose Garlands, by Dürer — A584

1968, July 6 ***Perf. 11½***
1555 A584 5k multicolored 3.00 1.75

FIP Day, July 6. Issued in sheets of 4 (2x2) with one horizontal label between, showing Praga 68 emblem. Value, $25.

Stagecoach on Rails — A585

Design: 1k, Steam and electric locomotives.

1968, Aug. 6
1556 A585 60h multicolored .45 .25
1557 A585 1k multicolored 1.60 .60

No. 1556: 140th anniv. of the horse-drawn railroad Ceské Budejovice to Linz; No. 1557: cent. of the Ceské Budejovice to Plzen railroad.

6th Intl. Slavonic Cong. in Prague — A586

1968, Aug. 7 ***Perf. 11½***
1558 A586 30h vio blue & car .40 .25

Ardspach Rocks and Ammonite — A587

60h, Basalt formation & frog skeleton fossil. 80h, Rocks, basalt veins & polished agate. 1k, Pelecypoda (fossil shell) & Belanske Tatra mountains. 1.60k, Trilobite & Barrande rock formation.

1968, Aug. 8
1559 A587 30h black & citron .25 .25
1560 A587 60h black & rose cl .25 .25
1561 A587 80h black, lt vio & pink .30 .25
1562 A587 1k black & lt blue .40 .25
1563 A587 1.60k black & bister 1.40 .65
Nos. 1559-1563 (5) 2.60 1.65

Issued to publicize the 23rd International Geological Congress, Prague, Aug. 8-Sept. 3.

Raising Slovak Flag A588

60h, Slovak partisans, and mountain.

1968, Sept. 9 Engr. *Perf. 11½*
1564 A588 30h ultra .25 .25
1565 A588 60h red .25 .25

No. 1564 for the Slovak Natl. Council, No. 1565 the 120th anniv. of the Slovak national uprising.

Flowerpot, by Jiri Schlessinger (age 10) — A589

Drawings by Children in Terezin Concentration Camp: 30h, Jew and Guard, by Jiri Beutler (age 10). 60h, Butterflies, by Kitty Brunnerova (age 11).

Engraved and Photogravure
1968, Sept. 30 *Perf. 11½*
Size: 30x23mm
1566 A589 30h blk, buff & rose lil .30 .25
1567 A589 60h black & multi .30 .25

Perf. 12x11½
Size: 41x23mm
1568 A589 1k black & multi .95 .25
Nos. 1566-1568 (3) 1.55 .75

30th anniversary of Munich Pact.

Arms of Regional Capitals A590

Arms of Prague — A591

1968, Oct. 21 *Perf. 11½*
1569 A590 60h Banská Bystrica .25 .25
1570 A590 60h Bratislava .25 .25
1571 A590 60h Brno .25 .25
1572 A590 60h České Budejovice .25 .25
1573 A590 60h Hradec Králové .25 .25
1574 A590 60h Kosice .25 .25
1575 A590 60h Ostrava (horse) .25 .25
1576 A590 60h Plzen .25 .25
1577 A590 60h Ustí nad Labem .25 .25

Perf. 11½x16
1578 A591 1k shown .75 .25
Nos. 1569-1578 (10) 3.00 2.50

No. 1578 issued in sheets of 10. Value, $30.
See Nos. 1652-1657, 1742-1747, 1886-1888, 2000-2001.

Flag and Linden Leaves A592

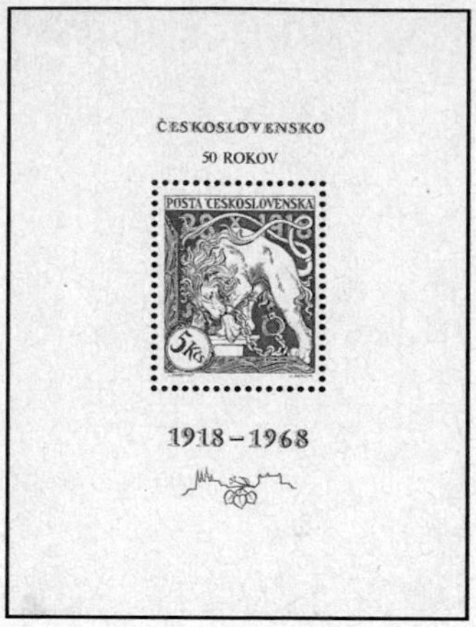

Bohemian Lion Breaking Chains (Type SP1 of 1919) — A593

Design: 60h, Map of Czechoslovakia, linden leaves, Hradcany in Prague and Castle in Bratislava.

1968, Oct. 28 *Perf. 12x11½*
1579 A592 30h dp blue & mag .30 .25
1580 A592 60h blk, gold, red & ultra .30 .25

Souvenir Sheet
Engr.
Perf. 11½x12
1581 A593 5k red 3.50 2.75

Founding of Czechoslovakia, 50th anniv.

Ernest Hemingway — A594

Caricatures: 30h, Karel Capek (1890-1938), writer. 40h, George Bernard Shaw. 60h, Maxim Gorki. 1k, Pablo Picasso. 1.20k, Taikan Yokoyama (1868-1958), painter. 1.40k, Charlie Chaplin.

Engraved and Photogravure
1968, Nov. 18 *Perf. 11½x12*
1582 A594 20h black, org & red .25 .25
1583 A594 30h black & multi .30 .25
1584 A594 40h blk, lic & car .30 .25
1585 A594 60h black, sky bl & grn .25 .25
1586 A594 1k black, brn & yel .45 .25
1587 A594 1.20k black, dp car & vio .45 .25
1588 A594 1.40k black, brn & dp org 1.75 .40
Nos. 1582-1588 (7) 3.75 1.90

Cultural personalities of the 20th cent. and UNESCO. See Nos. 1628-1633.

Painting Type of 1967

Czechoslovakian Art: 60h, Cleopatra II, by Jan Zrzavy (1890-1977). 80h, Black Lake (man and horse), by Jan Preisler (1872-1918). 1.20k, Giovanni Francisci as a Volunteer, by Peter Michal Bohun (1822-1879). 1.60k, Princess Hyacinth, by Alfons Mucha (1860-1939). 3k, Madonna and Child, woodcarving, 1518, by Master Paul of Levoca.

1968, Nov. 29 Engr. *Perf. 11½*
1589 A565 60h multi .75 .35
1590 A565 80h multi .75 .35
1591 A565 1.20k multi .75 .35
1592 A565 1.60k multi .75 .35
1593 A565 3k multi 2.50 2.50
Nos. 1589-1593 (5) 5.50 3.90

Nos. 1589-1593 were issued in sheets of 4. Value, set $30.

Cinderlad — A595

Slovak Fairy Tales: 60h, The Proud Lady. 80h, The Ruling Knight. 1k, Good Day, Little Bench. 1.20k, The Spellbound Castle. 1.80k, The Miraculous Hunter. The designs are from illustrations by Ludovit Fulla for "Slovak Stories."

1968, Dec. 18 Engr. & Photo.
1594 A595 30h multi .25 .25
1595 A595 60h multi .25 .25
1596 A595 80h multi .40 .25
1597 A595 1k multi .55 .25
1598 A595 1.20k multi .55 .25
1599 A595 1.80k multi 1.50 .65
Nos. 1594-1599 (6) 3.50 1.90

Czechoslovakia Nos. 2 and 3 — A596

1968, Dec. 18
1600 A596 1k violet bl & gold .95 .65

50th anniv. of Czechoslovakian postage stamps.

Crescent, Cross and Lion and Sun Emblems A597

ILO Emblem A598

60h, 12 crosses in circles forming large cross.

1969, Jan. 31 *Perf. 11½*
1601 A597 60h black, red & gold .25 .25
1602 A597 1k black, ultra & red .35 .25

No. 1601: 50th anniv. of the Czechoslovak Red Cross. No. 1602: 50th anniv. of the League of Red Cross Societies.

1969, Jan. 31
1603 A598 1k black & gray .30 .25

50th anniv. of the ILO.

Cheb Pistol A599

Historical Firearms: 40h, Italian pistol with Dutch decorations, c. 1600. 60h, Wheellock rifle from Matej Kubik workshop c. 1720. 1k, Flintlock pistol, Devieuxe workshop, Liege, c. 1760. 1.40k, Duelling pistols, from Lebeda workshop, Prague, c. 1835. 1.60k, Derringer pistols, US, c. 1865.

1969, Feb. 18
1604 A599 30h black & multi .25 .25
1605 A599 40h black & multi .25 .25
1606 A599 60h black & multi .25 .25
1607 A599 1k black & multi .25 .25
1608 A599 1.40k black & multi .35 .25
1609 A599 1.60k black & multi 1.00 .50
Nos. 1604-1609 (6) 2.35 1.75

Bratislava Castle, Muse and Book — A600

No. 1611, Science symbols & emblem (Brno University). No. 1612, Harp, laurel & musicians' names. No. 1613, Theatrical scene. No. 1614, Arms of Slovakia, banner & blossoms. No. 1615, School, outstretched hands & woman with linden leaves.

1969, Mar. 24 Engr. *Perf. 11½*
1610 A600 60h violet blue .25 .25

Engraved and Photogravure
1611 A600 60h blk, gold & slate .25 .25
1612 A600 60h gold, blue, blk & red .25 .25
1613 A600 60h black & rose red .25 .25
1614 A600 60h rose red, sil & bl .25 .25
1615 A600 60h black & gold .25 .25
Nos. 1610-1615 (6) 1.50 1.50

50th anniv. of: Komensky University in Bratislava (No. 1610); Brno University (No. 1611); Brno Conservatory of Music (No. 1612); Slovak Natl. Theater (No. 1613); Slovak Soviet Republic (No. 1614); cent. of the Zniev Gymnasium (academic high school) (No. 1615).

Baldachin-top Car and Four-seat Coupé of 1900-1905 — A601

Designs: 1.60k, Laurin & Klement Voiturette, 1907, and L & K touring car with American top, 1907. 1.80k, First Prague bus, 1907, and sectionalized Skoda bus, 1967.

1969, Mar. 25 Engr. & Photo.
1616 A601 30h blk, lil & lt grn .65 .25
1617 A601 1.60k blk, org brn & lt bl .80 .25
1618 A601 1.80k multi 1.40 .60
Nos. 1616-1618 (3) 2.85 1.10

Peace, by Ladislav Guderna — A602

1969, Apr. 21 *Perf. 11*
1619 A602 1.60k multi .50 .35

20th anniv. of the Peace Movement. Issued in sheets of 15 stamps and 5 tabs. Stamp with tab $2.50.

Horse and Rider, by Vaclav Hollar — A603

Old Engravings of Horses: 30h, Prancing Stallion, by Hendrik Goltzius, horiz. 80h, Groom Leading Horse, by Matthäus Merian, horiz. 1.80k, Horse and Soldier, by Albrecht Dürer. 2.40k, Groom and Horse, by Johann E. Ridinger.

1969, Apr. 24 *Perf. 11x11½, 11½x11*

Yellowish Paper

1620	A603	30h dark brown	.25	.25
1621	A603	80h violet brown	.25	.25
1622	A603	1.60k slate	.45	.25
1623	A603	1.80k sepia	.50	.25
1624	A603	2.40k multi	2.40	.60
		Nos. 1620-1624 (5)	3.85	1.60

M. R. Stefánik as Astronomy Professor and French General — A604

1969, May 4 **Engr.** *Perf. 11½*

1625	A604	60h rose claret	.40	.25

Gen. Milan R. Stefánik, 50th death anniv.

St. Wenceslas Pressing Wine, Mural by the Master of Litomerice — A605

Design: No. 1627, Coronation banner of the Estates, 1723, with St. Wenceslas and coats of arms of Bohemia and Czech Crown lands.

1969, May 9 **Engr.** *Perf. 11½*

1626	A605	3k multicolored	2.00	1.40
1627	A605	3k multicolored	2.00	1.40

Issued to publicize the art treasures of the Castle of Prague.

Issued in sheets of 4. Value, set $20.

See Nos. 1689-1690.

Caricature Type of 1968

Caricatures: 30h, Pavol Orszagh Hviezdoslav (1849-1921), Slovak writer. 40h, Gilbert K. Chesterton (1874-1936), English writer. 60h, Vladimir Mayakovski (1893-1930), Russian poet. 1k, Henri Matisse (1869-1954), French painter. 1.80k, Ales Hrdlicka (1869-1943), Czech-born American anthropologist. 2k, Franz Kafka (1883-1924), Austrian writer.

Engraved and Photogravure

1969, June 17 *Perf. 11½x12*

1628	A594	30h blk, red & bl	.25	.25
1629	A594	40h blk, bl & lt vio	.25	.25
1630	A594	60h blk, rose & yel	.25	.25
1631	A594	1k black & multi	.25	.25
1632	A594	1.80k blk, ultra & ocher	.25	.25
1633	A594	2k blk, yel & brt grn	1.50	.50
		Nos. 1628-1633 (6)	2.75	1.75

Issued to honor cultural personalities of the 20th century and UNESCO.

"Music," by Alfons Mucha — A606

Paintings by Mucha: 60h, "Painting." 1k, "Dance." 2.40k, "Ruby" and "Amethyst."

1969, July 14 *Perf. 11½x11*

Size: 30x49mm

1634	A606	30h black & multi	1.00	.25
1635	A606	60h black & multi	1.00	.25
1636	A606	1k black & multi	1.25	.25

Size: 39x51mm

1637	A606	2.40k black & multi	2.75	1.25
		Nos. 1634-1637 (4)	6.00	2.00

Alfons Mucha (1860-1930), painter and stamp designer (Type A1).

No. 1637 was issued in sheets of 4. Value $18.

Pres. Svoboda and Partisans A607

No. 1639, Slovak fighters and mourners.

1969, Aug. 29 *Perf. 11*

1638	A607	30h ol grn & red, *yel*	.25	.25
1639	A607	30h vio bl & red, *yel*	.25	.25

25th anniversary of the Slovak uprising and of the Battle of Dukla.

Tatra Mountain Stream and Gentians — A608

Designs: 60h, Various views in Tatra Mountains. No. 1644, Mountain pass and gentians. No. 1645, Houses, Krivan Mountain and autumn crocuses.

1969, Sept. 8 **Engr.** *Perf. 11*

Size: 71x33mm

1640	A608	60h gray	.25	.25
1641	A608	60h dark blue	.25	.25
1642	A608	60h dull gray vio	.25	.25

Perf. 11½

Size: 40x23mm

1643	A608	1.60k multi	.80	.25
1644	A608	1.60k multi	1.60	.50
1645	A608	1.60k multi	.80	.25
		Nos. 1640-1645 (6)	3.95	1.75

20th anniv. of the creation of the Tatra Mountains Natl. Park.

Nos. 1640-1642 are printed in sheets of 15 (3x5) with 5 labels showing mountain plants. Value, set with tabs $2.50.

Nos. 1643-1645 were issued in sheets of 10. Value, $55.

Bronze Belt Ornaments A609

Archaeological Treasures from Bohemia and Moravia: 30h, Gilt ornament with 6 masks. 1k, Jeweled earrings. 1.80k, Front and back of lead cross with Greek inscription. 2k, Gilt strap ornament with human figure.

Engraved and Photogravure

1969, Sept. 30 *Perf. 11½x11*

1646	A609	20h gold & multi	.25	.25
1647	A609	30h gold & multi	.25	.25
1648	A609	1k red & multi	.25	.25
1649	A609	1.80k dull org & multi	.65	.25
1650	A609	2k gold & multi	2.00	.40
		Nos. 1646-1650 (5)	3.40	1.40

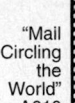

"Mail Circling the World" A610

1969, Oct. 1 **Engr.** *Perf. 12*

1651	A610	3.20k multi	.95	.60

16th UPU Cong., Tokyo, Oct. 1-Nov. 14.
Issued in sheets of 4. Value $9.

Coat of Arms Type of 1968

Engraved and Photogravure

1969, Oct. 25 *Perf. 11½*

1652	A590	50h Bardejov	.25	.25
1653	A590	50h Hranice	.25	.25
1654	A590	50h Kezmarok	.25	.25
1655	A590	50h Krnov	.25	.25
1656	A590	50h Litomerice	.25	.25
1657	A590	50h Manetin	.25	.25
		Nos. 1652-1657 (6)	1.50	1.50

Painting Type of 1967

Designs: 60h, Requiem, 1944, by Frantisek Muzika. 1k, Resurrection, 1380, by the Master of the Trebon Altar. 1.60k, Crucifixion, 1950, by Vincent Hloznik. 1.80k, Girl with Doll, 1863, by Julius Bencur. 2.20k, St. Jerome, 1357-67, by Master Theodorik.

1969, Nov. 25 *Perf. 11½*

1658	A565	60h multi	1.00	.25
1659	A565	1k multi	1.00	.25
1660	A565	1.60k multi	1.10	.40
1661	A565	1.80k multi	1.40	.50
1662	A565	2.20k multi	3.00	2.00
		Nos. 1658-1662 (5)	7.50	3.40

Nos. 1658-1662 were each issued in sheets of 4. Value, set $40.

Symbolic Sheet of Stamps — A611

1969, Dec. 18 *Perf. 11½x12*

1663	A611	1k dk brn, ultra & gold	.30	.30

Issued for Stamp Day 1969.

Ski Jump — A612

Designs: 60h, Long distance skier. 1k, Ski jump and slope. 1.60k, Woman skier.

1970, Jan. 6 *Perf. 11½*

1664	A612	50h multi	.25	.25
1665	A612	60h multi	.25	.25
1666	A612	1k multi	.25	.25
1667	A612	1.60k multi	.60	.30
		Nos. 1664-1667 (4)	1.35	1.05

Intl. Ski Championships "Tatra 1970."

Ludwig van Beethoven — A613

Portraits: No. 1669, Friedrich Engels (1820-95), German socialist. No. 1670, Maximilian Hell (1720-92), Slovakian Jesuit and astronomer. No. 1671, Lenin, Russian Communist leader. No. 1672, Josef Manes (1820-71), Czech painter. No. 1673, Comenius (1592-1670), theologian and educator.

1970, Feb. 17 **Engr.** *Perf. 11x11½*

1668	A613	40h black	.25	.25
1669	A613	40h dull red	.25	.25
1670	A613	40h yellow brn	.25	.25
1671	A613	40h dull red	.25	.25
1672	A613	40h brown	.25	.25
1673	A613	40h black	.25	.25
		Nos. 1668-1673 (6)	1.50	1.50

Anniversaries of birth of Beethoven, Engels, Hell, Lenin and Manes, 300th anniv. of the death of Comenius, and to honor UNESCO.

Bells A614

80h, Machine tools & lathe. 1k, Folklore masks. 1.60k, Angel & Three Wise Men, 17th cent. icon from Koniec. 2k, View of Orlik Castle, 1787, by F. K. Wolf. 3k, "Passing through Koshu down to Mishima" from Hokusai's 36 Views of Fuji.

Engraved and Photogravure

1970, Mar. 13 *Perf. 11½x11*

Size: 40x23mm

1674	A614	50h multi	.25	.25
1675	A614	80h multi	.25	.25
1676	A614	1k multi	.25	.25

Size: 50x40mm

Perf. 11½

1677	A614	1.60k multi	.55	.30
1678	A614	2k multi	.75	.35
1679	A614	3k multi	1.90	1.00
		Nos. 1674-1679 (6)	3.95	2.40

EXPO '70 Intl. Exhib., Osaka, Japan, Mar. 15-Sept. 13, 1970.

Nos. 1674-1676 issued in sheets of 50.

Nos. 1677-1679 in sheets of 4. Value, set of 3 sheets, $28.

Kosice Townhall, Laurel and Czechoslovak Arms — A615

1970, Apr. 5 *Perf. 11*

1680	A615	60h slate, ver & gold	.40	.25

Government's Kosice Program, 25th anniv.

"The Remarkable Horse" by Josef Lada — A616

Paintings by Josef Lada: 60h, Autumn, 1955, horiz. 1.80k, "The Water Sprite." 2.40k, Children in Winter, 1943, horiz.

1970, Apr. 21 *Perf. 11½*

1681	A616	60h black & multi	.30	.25
1682	A616	1k black & multi	.45	.25
1683	A616	1.80k black & multi	.80	.25
1684	A616	2.40k black & multi	1.60	.40
		Nos. 1681-1684 (4)	3.15	1.15

Lenin — A617

Design: 60h, Lenin without cap, facing left.

1970, Apr. 22

1685	A617	30h dk red & gold	.25	.25
1686	A617	60h black & gold	.25	.25

Lenin (1870-1924), Russian communist leader.

Fighters on the Barricades — A618

No. 1688, Lilac, Russian tank and castle.

1970, May 5 ***Perf. 11x11½***

1687	A618	30h dull pur, gold & bl	.25	.25
1688	A618	30h dull grn, gold & red	.25	.25

No. 1687: 25th anniv. of the Prague uprising. No. 1688: 25th anniv. of the liberation of Czechoslovakia from the Germans.

Prague Castle Art Type of 1969

No. 1689, Bust of St. Vitus, 1486. No. 1690, Hermes and Athena, by Bartholomy Spranger (1546-1611), mural from White Tower.

1970, May 7 Engr. ***Perf. 11½***

1689	A605	3k maroon & multi	2.40	1.50
1690	A605	3k lt blue & multi	2.40	1.50

Nos. 1689-1690 were issued in sheets of 4. Value, set of 2 sheets, $20.

Compass Rose, UN Headquarters and Famous Buildings of the World — A619

Engraved and Photogravure

1970, June 26 ***Perf. 11***

1691	A619	1k black & multi	.40	.25

25th anniv. of the UN. Issued in sheets of 15 (3x5) and 5 labels showing UN emblem. Value of single with tab attached: unused $2; used $1.50.

Cannon from 30 Years' War and Baron Munchhausen — A620

Historical Cannons: 60h, Cannon from Hussite war and St. Barbara. 1.20k, Cannon from Prussian-Austrian war, and legendary cannoneer Javurek. 1.80k, Early 20th century cannon and spaceship "La Colombiad" (Jules Verne). 2.40k, World War I cannon and "Good Soldier Schweik."

1970, Aug. 31 ***Perf. 11½***

1692	A620	30h black & multi	.25	.25
1693	A620	60h black & multi	.25	.25
1694	A620	1.20k black & multi	.25	.25
1695	A620	1.80k black & multi	.30	.25
1696	A620	2.40k black & multi	1.60	.65
		Nos. 1692-1696 (5)	2.65	1.65

"Rude Pravo" (Red Truth) A621

1970, Sept. 21 ***Perf. 11½x11***

1697	A621	60h car, gold & blk	.25	.25

50th anniv. of the Rude Pravo newspaper.

"Great Sun" House Sign and Old Town Tower Bridge, Prague — A622

60h, "Blue Lion" & Town Hall Tower, Brno. 1k, Gothic corner stone & Town Hall Tower, Bratislava. 1.40k, Coat of Arms & Gothic Tower, Bratislava, & medallion. 1.60k, Moravian Eagle & Gothic Town Hall Tower, Brno. 1.80k, "Black Sun" & "Green Frog" house signs & New Town Hall, Prague.

1970, Sept. 23 ***Perf. 11x11½***

1698	A622	40h black & multi	.25	.25
1699	A622	60h black & multi	.25	.25
1700	A622	1k black & multi	.25	.25
1701	A622	1.40k black & multi	1.40	.50
1702	A622	1.60k black & multi	.30	.25
1703	A622	1.80k black & multi	.95	.25
		Nos. 1698-1703 (6)	3.40	1.75

Germany-Uruguay Semifinal Soccer Match — A623

Designs: 20h, Sundisk Games' emblem and flags of participating nations. 60h, England-Czechoslovakia match and coats of arms. 1k, Romania-Czechoslovakia match and coats of arms. 1.20k, Brazil-Italy, final match and emblems. 1.80k, Brazil-Czechoslovakia match and emblems.

1970, Oct. 29 ***Perf. 11½***

1704	A623	20h blk & multi	.25	.25
1705	A623	40h blk & multi	.25	.25
1706	A623	60h blk & multi	.25	.25
1707	A623	1k blk & multi	.35	.25
1708	A623	1.20k blk & multi	.40	.25
1709	A623	1.80k blk & multi	1.90	.30
		Nos. 1704-1709 (6)	3.40	1.55

9th World Soccer Championships for the Jules Rimet Cup, Mexico City, 5/30-6/21.

Congress Emblem — A624

1970, Nov. 9 **Engr. & Photo.**

1710	A624	30h blk, gold, ultra & red	.25	.25

Congress of the Czechoslovak Socialist Youth Federation.

Painting Type of 1967

Paintings: 1k, Seated Mother, by Mikulas Galanda. 1.20k, Bridesmaid, by Karel Svolinsky. 1.40k, Walk by Night, 1944, by Frantisek Hudecek. 1.80k, Banska Bystrica Market, by Dominik Skutecky. 2.40k, Adoration of the Kings, from the Vysehrad Codex, 1085.

1970, Nov. 27 Engr. ***Perf. 11½***

1711	A565	1k multi	.65	.25
1712	A565	1.20k multi	.80	.45
1713	A565	1.40k multi	.65	.30
1714	A565	1.80k multi	1.00	.45
1715	A565	2.40k multi	3.25	2.10
		Nos. 1711-1715 (5)	6.35	3.55

Nos. 1711-1715 were each issued in sheets of 4. Value, set $30.

Radar A625

Designs: 40h, Interkosmos 3, geophysical satellite. 60h, Kosmos meteorological satellite. 1k, Astronaut and Vostok satellite. No. 1720, Interkosmos 4, solar research satellite. No. 1720A, Space satellite (Sputnik) over city. 1.60k, Two-stage rocket on launching pad.

1970-71 Engr. & Photo. ***Perf. 11***

1716	A625	20h black & multi	.25	.25
1717	A625	40h black & multi	.25	.25
1718	A625	60h black & multi	.25	.25
1719	A625	1k black & multi	.25	.25
1720	A625	1.20k black & multi	.25	.25
1720A	A625	1.20k black & multi ('71)	.30	.25
1721	A625	1.60k black & multi	1.40	.35
		Nos. 1716-1721 (7)	2.95	1.85

"Interkosmos," the collaboration of communist countries in various phases of space research.

Issued: No. 1720A, 11/15/71; others, 11/30/70.

Face of Christ on Veronica's Veil — A626

Slovak Ikons, 16th-18th Centuries: 60h, Adam and Eve in the Garden, vert. 2k, St. George and the Dragon. 2.80k, St. Michael, vert.

1970, Dec. 17 Engr. ***Perf. 11½***
Cream Paper

1722	A626	60h multi	.90	.40
1723	A626	1k multi	1.25	.55
1724	A626	2k multi	1.60	.70
1725	A626	2.80k multi	2.25	1.40
		Nos. 1722-1725 (4)	6.00	3.05

Nos. 1722-1725 were each issued in sheets of 4. Value, set $32.50.

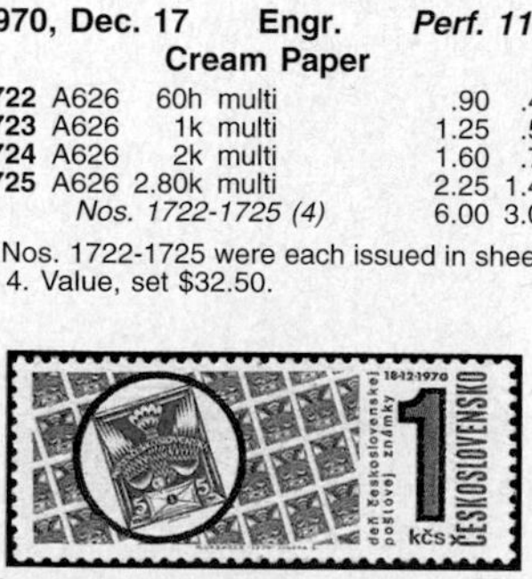

Carrier Pigeon Type of 1920 — A627

Engraved and Photogravure

1970, Dec. 18 ***Perf. 11x11½***

1726	A627	1k red, blk & yel grn	.40	.30

Stamp Day.

Song of the Barricades, 1938, by Karel Stika — A628

Czech and Slovak Graphic Art: 50h, Fruit Grower's Barge, 1941, by Cyril Bouda. 60h, Moon (woman) Searching for Lilies of the Valley, 1913, by Jan Zrzavy. 1k, At the Edge of Town (working man and woman), 1931, by Koloman Sokol. 1.60k, Summer, 1641, by Vaclav Hollar. 2k, Gamekeeper and Shepherd of Orava Castle, 1847, by Peter M. Bohun.

Engr. & Photo.; Engr. (40h, 60h, 1k)

1971, Jan. 28 ***Perf. 11½***

1727	A628	40h brown	.25	.25
1728	A628	50h black & multi	.25	.25
1729	A628	60h slate	.25	.25
1730	A628	1k black	.30	.25
1731	A628	1.60k black & buff	.30	.25
1732	A628	2k black & multi	1.40	.30
		Nos. 1727-1732 (6)	2.75	1.55

Church of St. Bartholomew, Chrudim A629

Bell Tower, Hronsek A630

Designs: 1k, Roofs and folk art, Horácko. 1.60k, Saris Church. 2.40k, House, Jicin. 3k, House and folk art, Melnik. 5k, Watch Tower, Nachod. 5.40k, Baroque house, Posumavi. 6k, Cottage, Orava. 9k, Cottage, Turnov. 10k, Old houses, Liptov. 14k, House and wayside bell stand. 20k, Houses, Cicmany.

Engraved and Photogravure

1971-72 ***Perf. 11½x11, 11x11½***

1733	A630	1k multi	.25	.25
1734	A629	1.60k multi	1.60	.25
1735	A630	2k multi	2.40	.25
1736	A629	2.40k multi	1.40	.30
1736A	A630	3k multi ('72)	2.40	.25
1737	A629	3.60k multi	1.90	.25
1737A	A630	5k multi ('72)	2.40	.25
1738	A629	5.40k multi	1.25	.25
1739	A630	6k multi	3.75	.25
1740	A630	9k multi	1.50	.25
1740A	A629	10k multi ('72)	3.50	.25
1741	A629	14k multi	3.75	.25
1741A	A629	20k multi ('72)	4.00	.30
		Nos. 1733-1741A (13)	30.10	3.35

Nos. 1736A, 1738, 1740 are horizontal. See No. 2870.

Coat of Arms Type of 1968

1971, Mar. 26 ***Perf. 11½***

1742	A590	60h Zilina	.25	.25
1743	A590	60h Levoca	.25	.25
1744	A590	60h Ceska Trebova	.25	.25
1745	A590	60h Uhersky Brod	.25	.25
1746	A590	60h Trutnov	.25	.25
1747	A590	60h Karlovy Vary	.25	.25
		Nos. 1742-1747 (6)	1.50	1.50

"Fight of the Communards and Rise of the International" — A631

Design: No. 1749, World fight against racial discrimination, and "UNESCO."

1971, Mar. 18 ***Perf. 11***

1748	A631	1k multicolored	.30	.25
1749	A631	1k multicolored	.30	.25

No. 1748 for cent. of the Paris Commune. No. 1749 for the Year against Racial Discrimination. Issued in sheets of 15 stamps and 5 labels. Value for single with attached tab, each $1.

A632

A633

Edelweiss, mountaineering map & equipment.

1971, Apr. 27 *Perf. 11½x11*

1750	A632	30h multicolored	.25	.25

50th anniversary of Slovak Alpine Club.

1971, Apr. 27 *Perf. 11½*

1751	A633	30h Singer	.25	.25

50th anniversary of Slovak Teachers' Choir.

Abbess' Crosier, 16th Century A634

No. 1753, Allegory of Music, 16th cent. mural.

1971, May 9

1752	A634	3k gold & multi	1.90	1.40
1753	A634	3k blk, dk brn & buff	2.50	1.40

Nos. 1752-1753 were each issued in sheets of 4. Value, set $22.50.

See Nos. 1817-1818, 1884-1885, 1937-1938, 2040-2041, 2081-2082, 2114-2115, 2176-2177, 2238-2239, 2329-2330, 2384-2385, 2420-2421.

Lenin A635

40h, Hammer & sickle allegory. 60h, Raised fists. 1k, Star, hammer & sickle.

1971, May 14 *Perf. 11*

1754	A635	30h blk, red & gold	.25	.25
1755	A635	40h blk, ultra, red & gold	.25	.25
1756	A635	60h blk, ultra, red & gold	.25	.25
1757	A635	1k blk, ultra, red & gold	.30	.25
		Nos. 1754-1757 (4)	1.05	1.00

Czechoslovak Communist Party, 50th anniv.

Star, Hammer-Sickle Emblems — A636

60h, Hammer-sickle emblem, fist & people, vert.

Perf. 11½x11, 11x11½

1971, May 24 **Engr. & Photo.**

1758	A636	30h blk, red, gold & yel	.25	.25
1759	A636	60h blk, red, gold & bl	.25	.25

14th Congress of Communist Party of Czechoslovakia.

Ring-necked Pheasant — A637

Designs: 60h, Rainbow trout. 80h, Mouflon. 1k, Chamois. 2k, Stag. 2.60k, Wild boar.

1971, Aug. 17 *Perf. 11½x11*

1760	A637	20h orange & multi	.25	.25
1761	A637	60h lt blue & multi	.25	.25
1762	A637	80h yellow & multi	.25	.25
1763	A637	1k lt green & multi	.35	.25
1764	A637	2k lilac & multi	.50	.25
1765	A637	2.60k bister & multi	2.25	.65
		Nos. 1760-1765 (6)	3.85	1.90

World Hunting Exhib., Budapest, Aug. 27-30.

Diesel Locomotive A638

Gymnasts and Banners A639

1971, Sept. 2 *Perf. 11x11½*

1766	A638	30h lt bl, blk & red	.40	.25

Cent. of CKD, Prague Machine Foundry.

1971, Sept. 2 *Perf. 11½x11*

1767	A639	30h red brn, gold & ultra	.25	.25

50th anniversary of Workers' Physical Exercise Federation.

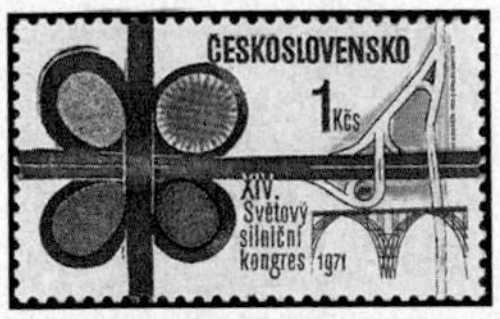

Road Intersections and Bridge — A640

1971, Sept. 2 **Engr. & Photo.**

1768	A640	1k blk, gold, red & bl	.30	.25

14th World Highways and Bridges Congress. Sheets of 25 stamps and 25 labels printed se-tenant with continuous design. Value, single with attached tab, unused $1.25; used 50c.

Chinese Fairytale, by Eva Bednarova A641

Designs: 1k, Tiger and other animals, by Mirko Hanak. 1.60k, The Miraculous Bamboo Shoot, by Yasuo Segawa, horiz.

Perf. 11½x11, 11x11½

1971, Sept. 10

1769	A641	60h multi	.25	.25
1770	A641	1k multi	.30	.25
1771	A641	1.60k multi	.45	.25
		Nos. 1769-1771 (3)	1.00	.75

Bratislava BIB 71 biennial exhibition of illustrations for children's books.

Apothecary Jars and Coltsfoot — A642

Intl. Pharmaceutical Cong.: 60h, Jars and dog rose. 1k, Scales and adonis vernalis. 1.20k, Mortars and valerian. 1.80k, Retorts and chicory. 2.40k, Mill, mortar and henbane.

1971, Sept. 20 *Perf. 11½x11*

Yellow Paper

1772	A642	30h multi	.25	.25
1773	A642	60h multi	.25	.25
1774	A642	1k multi	.25	.25
1775	A642	1.20k multi	.25	.25
1776	A642	1.80k multi	.35	.25
1777	A642	2.40k multi	1.40	.45
		Nos. 1772-1777 (6)	2.75	1.70

Painting Type of 1967

Paintings: 1k, "Waiting" (woman's head), 1967, by Imro Weiner-Král. 1.20k, Resurrection, by Master of Vyssl Brod, 14th century. 1.40k, Woman with Pitcher, by Milos Bazovsky. 1.80k, Veruna Čudova (in folk costume), by Josef Mánes. 2.40k, Detail from "Feast of the Rose Garlands," by Albrecht Dürer.

1971, Nov. 27 *Perf. 11½*

1779	A565	1k multi	.40	.30
1780	A565	1.20k multi	.95	.45
1781	A565	1.40k multi	.75	.30
1782	A565	1.80k multi	1.40	.60
1783	A565	2.40k multi	2.40	.95
		Nos. 1779-1783 (5)	5.90	2.60

Nos. 1779-1783 were each issued in sheets of 4. Value, set $28.

Workers Revolt in Krompachy, by Julius Nemcik — A643

1971, Nov. 28 *Perf. 11x11½*

1784	A643	60h multi	.30	.25

History of the Czechoslovak Communist Party.

Wooden Dolls and Birds — A644

Folk Art and UNICEF Emblem: 80h, Jug handles, carved. 1k, Horseback rider. 1.60k, Shepherd carrying lamb. 2k, Easter eggs and rattle. 3k, "Zbojnik," folk hero.

1971, Dec. 11 *Perf. 11½*

1785	A644	60h multi	.40	.25
1786	A644	80h multi	.80	.25
1787	A644	1k multi	.40	.25
1788	A644	1.60k multi	.40	.25
1789	A644	2k multi	.40	.45
1790	A644	3k multi	2.50	.60
		Nos. 1785-1790 (6)	4.90	2.05

25th anniv. of UNICEF.

Nos. 1785-1790 were each issued in sheets of 10. Value, set $50.

Runners, Parthenon, Czechoslovak Olympic Emblem — A645

Designs: 40h, Women's high jump, Olympic emblem and plan for Prague Stadium. 1.60k, Cross-country skiers, Sapporo '72 emblem and ski jump in High Tatras. 2.60k, Discus thrower, Discobolus and St. Vitus Cathedral.

1971, Dec. 16 **Engr. & Photo.**

1791	A645	30h multi	.25	.25
1792	A645	40h multi	.25	.25
1793	A645	1.60k multi	.25	.25
1794	A645	2.60k multi	1.50	.75
		Nos. 1791-1794 (4)	2.25	1.50

75th anniversary of Czechoslovak Olympic Committee (30h, 2.60k); 20th Summer Olympic Games, Munich, Aug. 26-Sept. 10, 1972 (40h); 11th Winter Olympic Games, Sapporo, Japan, Feb. 3-13, 1972 (1.60k).

Post Horns and Lion — A646

1971, Dec. 17 *Perf. 11x11½*

1795	A646	1k blk, gold, car & bl	.30	.25

Stamp Day.

Figure Skating — A647

Olympic Emblems and: 50h, Ski jump. 1k, Ice hockey. 1.60k, Sledding, women's.

1972, Jan. 13 *Perf. 11½*

1796	A647	40h pur, org & red	.25	.25
1797	A647	50h dk bl, org & red	.25	.25
1798	A647	1k mag, org & red	.35	.25
1799	A647	1.60k bl grn, org & red	1.60	.30
		Nos. 1796-1799 (4)	2.45	1.05

11th Winter Olympic Games, Sapporo, Japan, Feb. 3-13.

"Lezáky" — A648

No. 1801, Boy's head behind barbed wire, horiz. No. 1802, Hand rising from ruins. No. 1803, Soldier and banner, horiz.

1972, Feb. 16

1800	A648	30h blk, dl org & red	.25	.25
1801	A648	30h blk & brn org	.25	.25
1802	A648	60h blk, yel & red	.25	.25
1803	A648	60h sl grn & multi	.25	.25
		Nos. 1800-1803 (4)	1.00	1.00

30th anniv. of: destruction of Lezáky (No. 1800) and Lidice (No. 1802); Terezin concentration camp (No. 1801); Czechoslovak Army unit in Russia (No. 1803).

Book Year Emblem
A649

Steam and Diesel Locomotives
A650

1972, Mar. 17 ***Perf. 11½x11***

1804 A649 1k blk & org brn .30 .25

International Book Year 1972.

1972, Mar. 17 ***Perf. 11½x11***

1805 A650 30h multi .75 .25

Centenary of the Kosice-Bohumin railroad.

"Pasture," by Vojtech Sedlacek
A651

Designs: 50h, Dressage, by Frantisek Tichy. 60th, Otakar Kubin, by Vaclav Fiala. 1k, The Three Kings, by Ernest Zmetak. 1.60k, Woman Dressing, by Ludovit Fulla.

1972, Mar. 27 ***Perf. 11½x11***

1806 A651 40h multi .25 .25
1807 A651 50h multi .25 .25
1808 A651 60h multi .25 .25
1809 A651 1k multi .30 .25
1810 A651 1.60k multi 1.60 1.60
Nos. 1806-1810 (5) 2.65 2.60

Czech and Slovak graphic art.
1.60k issued in sheets of 4. Value $12.
See Nos. 1859-1862, 1921-1924.

Ice Hockey
A652

Design: 1k, Two players.

1972, Apr. 7 ***Perf. 11***

1811 A652 60h blk & multi .25 .25
1812 A652 1k blk & multi .40 .25

World and European Ice Hockey Championships, Prague.
For overprint see Nos. 1845-1846.

Bicycling, Olympic Rings and Emblem
A653

1972, Apr. 7

1813 A653 50h shown .25 .25
1814 A653 1.60k Diving .40 .25
1815 A653 1.80k Canoeing .55 .25
1816 A653 2k Gymnast 1.25 .40
Nos. 1813-1816 (4) 2.45 1.15

20th Olympic Games, Munich, 8/26-9/11.

Prague Castle Art Type of 1971

Designs: No. 1817, Adam and Eve, column capital, St. Vitus Cathedral. No. 1818, Czech coat of arms (lion), c. 1500.

1972, May 9 ***Perf. 11½***

1817 A634 3k blk & multi 3.20 1.90
1818 A634 3k blk, red, sil & gold 1.60 .95

Nos. 1817-1818 were each issued in sheets of 4. Value, set $20.

Andrej Sladkovic (1820-1872), Poet — A654

No. 1820, Janko Kral (1822-1876), poet. No. 1821, Ludmilla Podjavorinska (1872-1951), writer. No. 1822, Antonin Hudecek (1872-1941), painter. No. 1823, Frantisek Bilek (1872-1941), sculptor. No. 1824, Jan Preisler (1872-1918), painter.

1972, June 14 ***Perf. 11***

1819 A654 40h pur, ol & bl .25 .25
1820 A654 40h dk grn, bl & yel .25 .25
1821 A654 40h blk & multi .25 .25
1822 A654 40h brn, grn & bl .25 .25
1823 A654 40h choc, grn & org .25 .25
1824 A654 40h grn, sl & dp org .25 .25
Nos. 1819-1824 (6) 1.50 1.50

Men with Banners — A655

1972, June 14 ***Perf. 11x11½***

1825 A655 30h dk vio bl, red & yel .25 .25

8th Trade Union Congress, Prague.

Art Forms of Wire
A656

Ornamental Wirework: 60h, Plane and rosette. 80h, Four-headed dragon and ornament. 1k, Locomotive and loops. 2.60k, Tray and owl.

1972, Aug. 28 ***Perf. 11½x11***

1826 A656 20h sal & multi .25 .25
1827 A656 60h multi .25 .25
1828 A656 80h pink & multi .30 .25
1829 A656 1k multi .40 .25
1830 A656 2.60k rose & multi 1.40 .45
Nos. 1826-1830 (5) 2.60 1.45

"Jiskra"
A657

Engr. & Photo.
1972, Sept. 27 ***Perf. 11½x11***
Size: 40x22mm
Multicolored Design on Blue Paper

1831 A657 50h shown .25 .25
1832 A657 60h "Mir" .25 .25
1833 A657 80h "Republika" .25 .25

Size: 48x29mm
Perf. 11x11½

1834 A657 1k "Kosice" .30 .25
1835 A657 1.60k "Dukla" .45 .25
1836 A657 2k "Kladno" 1.40 .55
Nos. 1831-1836 (6) 2.90 1.80

Czechoslovak sea-going vessels.

Hussar, 18th Century Tile — A658

1972, Oct. 24 ***Perf. 11½x11***

1837 A658 30h shown .25 .25
1838 A658 60h Janissary .25 .25
1839 A658 80h St. Martin .25 .25
1840 A658 1.60k St. George .45 .25
1841 A658 1.80k Nobleman's guard .70 .25
1842 A658 2.20k Slovakian horseman 1.40 .60
Nos. 1837-1842 (6) 3.30 1.85

Horsemen from 18th-19th century tiles or enamel paintings on glass.

Worker, Flag Hoisted on Bayonet
A659

Star, Hammer and Sickle
A660

1972, Nov. 7 ***Perf. 11x11½***

1843 A659 30h gold & multi .25 .25
1844 A660 60h rose car & gold .25 .25

55th anniv. of the Russian October Revolution (30h); 50th anniv. of the Soviet Union (60h).

Nos. 1811-1812 Overprinted in Violet Blue or Black

1972 ***Perf. 11***

1845 A652 60h multi (VBl) 8.00 6.50
1846 A652 1k multi (Bk) 8.00 6.50

Czechoslovakia's victorious ice hockey team. The overprint on the 60h (shown) is in Czech and reads CSSR/MISTREM/SVETA; the overprint on the 1k is in Slovak.

Painting Type of 1967

Designs: 1k, "Nosegay" (nudes and flowers), by Max Svabinsky. 1.20k, Struggle of St. Ladislas with Kuman nomad, anonymous, 14th century. 1.40k, Lady with Fur Hat, by Vaclav Hollar. 1.80k, Midsummer Night's Dream, 1962, by Josef Liesler. 2.40k, Pablo Picasso, self-portrait.

1972, Nov. 27 **Engr. & Photo.**

1847 A565 1k multi .60 .40
1848 A565 1.20k multi .80 .55
1849 A565 1.40k blk & cream .95 .70
1850 A565 1.80k multi 1.25 1.10
1851 A565 2.40k multi 2.75 2.75
Nos. 1847-1851 (5) 6.35 5.50

Nos. 1847-1851 were each issued in sheets of 4. Value, set $30.

Goldfinch
A661

Songbirds: 60h, Warbler feeding young cuckoo. 80h, Cuckoo. 1k, Black-billed magpie. 1.60k, Bullfinch. 3k, Song thrush.

1972, Dec. 15 **Size: 30x48½mm**

1852 A661 60h yel & multi .25 .25
1853 A661 80h multi .25 .25
1854 A661 1k lt bl & multi .25 .25

Engr.
Size: 30x23mm

1855 A661 1.60k multi 1.50 .80
1856 A661 2k multi 1.50 .80
1857 A661 3k multi 1.50 .80
Nos. 1852-1857 (6) 5.25 3.15

Nos. 1855-1857 were each issued in a sheet of 10. Value, set $45.

Post Horn and Allegory — A662

1972, Dec. 18 **Engr. & Photo.**

1858 A662 1k blk, red lil & gold .30 .30

Stamp Day.

Art Type of 1972

Designs: 30h, Flowers in Window, by Jaroslav Grus. 60h, Quest for Happiness, by Josef Balaz. 1.60k, Balloon, by Kamil Lhotak. 1.80k, Woman with Viola, by Richard Wiesner.

1973, Jan. 25 ***Perf. 11½x11***

1859 A651 30h multi .25 .25
1860 A651 60h multi .25 .25
1861 A651 1.60k multi .35 .25
1862 A651 1.80k multi 1.40 .35
Nos. 1859-1862 (4) 2.25 1.10

Czech and Slovak graphic art.

Tennis Player — A663

Figure Skater — A664

Torch and Star — A665

1973, Feb. 22 ***Perf. 11***

1863 A663 30h vio & multi .25 .25
1864 A664 60h blk & multi .25 .25
1865 A665 1k multi .30 .25
Nos. 1863-1865 (3) .80 .75

80th anniversary of the tennis organization in Czechoslovakia (30h); World figure skating championships, Bratislava (60h); 3rd summer army Spartakiad of socialist countries (1k).

Star and Factories
A666

Workers' Militia, Emblem and Flag — A667

1973, Feb. 23

1866 A666 30h multi .25 .25
1867 A667 60h multi .25 .25

25th anniversary of the Communist revolution in Czechoslovakia and of the Militia.

Capt. Jan Nalepka, Major Antonin Sochor and Laurel
A668

Torch &: 40h, Evzen Rosicky, Mirko Nespor & ivy leaves. 60h, Vlado Clementis, Karol Smidke & linden leaves. 80h, Jan Osoha, Josef Molak & oak leaves. 1k, Marie Kuderikova, Jozka Jaburkova & rose. 1.60k, Vaclav Sinkule, Eduard Urx & palm leaf.

1973, Mar. 20 ***Perf. 11½x11***

Yellow Paper

1868 A668 30h blk, ver & gold .30 .25
1869 A668 40h blk, ver & grn .30 .25
1870 A668 60h blk, ver & gold .30 .25
1871 A668 80h blk, ver & gold .30 .25
1872 A668 1k blk, ver & grn .40 .25
1873 A668 1.60k blk, ver & sil .85 .25
Nos. 1868-1873 (6) 2.45 1.50

Fighters against and victims of Fascism and Nazism during German Occupation.

Virgil I. Grissom, Edward H. White, Roger B. Chaffee — A669

Designs: 20h, Soviet planetary station "Venera." 30h, "Intercosmos" station. 40h, Lunokhod on moon. 3.60k, Vladimir M. Komarov, Georgi T. Dobrovolsky, Vladislav N. Volkov, Victor I. Patsayev. 5k, Yuri A. Gagarin.
Two types of 3.60k: type I, Cosmonaut on background of cross-hatched lines; type 2, Cosmonaut on background of parallel diagonal lines.

1973, Apr. 12 ***Perf. 11½x11***

Size: 40x22mm

1874 A669 20h multi .25 .25
1875 A669 30h multi .25 .25
1876 A669 40h multi .25 .25

Engr.

Perf. 11½

Size: 49x30mm

1877 A669 3k multi .80 .50
1878 A669 3.60k multi, type 1 1.25 1.10
a. Type 2 25.00 15.00
1879 A669 5k multi 3.00 2.00
Nos. 1874-1879 (6) 5.80 4.35

In memory of American and Russian astronauts.
Nos. 1877-1879 were each issued in sheets of 4. Values: set (with No. 1878) $30; mset (with No. 1878a) $120.

Radio — A670

Telephone and Map of Czechoslovakia
A671

Television
A672

1973, May 1 ***Perf. 11½x11***

1880 A670 30h blk & multi .25 .25
1881 A671 30h lt bl, pink & blk .25 .25
1882 A672 30h dp bl & multi .25 .25
Nos. 1880-1882 (3) .75 .75

Czechoslovak anniversaries: 50 years of broadcasting (No. 1880); 20 years of telephone service to all communities (No. 1881); 20 years of television (No. 1882).

Coat of Arms and Linden Branch — A673

1973, May 9 ***Perf. 11x11½***

1883 A673 60h red & multi .25 .25

25th anniv. of the Constitution of May 9.

Prague Castle Art Type of 1971

No. 1884, Royal Legate, 14th century. No. 1885, Seal of King Charles IV, 1351.

1973, May 9 ***Perf. 11½***

1884 A634 3k blue & multi 1.50 1.10
1885 A634 3k gold, grn & dk brn 3.00 2.25

Nos. 1884-1885 were each issued in sheets of 4. Value, set $16.

Coat of Arms Type of 1968

1973, June 20

1886 A590 60h Mikulov .25 .25
1887 A590 60h Zlutice .35 .25
1888 A590 60h Smolenice .35 .25
Nos. 1886-1888 (3) .95 .75

Coats of arms of Czechoslovakian cities.

Heraldic Colors of Olomouc and Moravia — A674

1973, Aug. 23 **Engr. & Photo.**

1889 A674 30h multi .25 .25

University of Olomouc, 400th anniv.

Anthurium — A675

Sizes: 60h, 1k, 2k, 30x50mm; 1.60k, 1.80k, 3.60k, 23x39mm.

1973, Aug. 23 ***Perf. 11½***

1890 A675 60h Tulips .75 .35
1891 A675 1k Rose .75 .35
1892 A675 1.60k shown .40 .35
1893 A675 1.80k Iris .40 .35
1894 A675 2k Chrysanthemum 1.90 1.00
1895 A675 3.60k Cymbidium .75 .35
Nos. 1890-1895 (6) 4.95 2.75

Flower Show, Olomouc, Aug. 18-Sept. 2. 60h, 1k, 2k issued in sheets of 4, others in sheets of 10. Value, set $100.

Hunting Dogs
A676

1973, Sept. 5

1896 A676 20h Irish setter .45 .25
1897 A676 30h Czech terrier .45 .25
1898 A676 40h Bavarian hunting dog .65 .25
1899 A676 60h German pointer .65 .25
1900 A676 1k Cocker spaniel 1.00 .25
1901 A676 1.60k Dachshund 2.40 .50
Nos. 1896-1901 (6) 5.60 1.75

Czechoslovak United Hunting Org., 50th anniv.

St. John, the Baptist, by Svabinsky
A677

Works by Max Svabinsky: 60h, "August Noon" (woman). 80h, "Marriage of True Minds" (artist and muse). 1k, "Paradise Sonata I" (Adam dreaming of Eve). 2.60k, Last Judgment, stained glass window, St. Vitus Cathedral.

1973, Sept. 17 **Litho. & Engr.**

1902 A677 20h blk & pale grn .25 .25
1903 A677 60h black & buff .25 .25

Engr.

1904 A677 80h black .75 .25
1905 A677 1k slate green .75 .25
1906 A677 2.60k multi 1.90 1.25
Nos. 1902-1906 (5) 3.90 2.25

Centenary of the birth of Max Svabinsky (1873-1962), artist and stamp designer. 20h and 60h issued in sheets of 25; 80h and 1k se-tenant in sheets of 4 checkerwise (value $5); 2.60k in sheets of 4 (value $12).

Trade Union Emblem
A678

1973, Oct. 15 **Engr. & Photo.**

1907 A678 1k red, bl & yel .25 .25

8t (valueh Congress of the World Federation of Trade Unions, Varna, Bulgaria.

Painting Type of 1967

1k, Boy from Martinique, by Antonin Pelc. 1.20k, "Fortitude" (mountaineer), by Martin Benka. 1.80k, Rembrandt, self-portrait. 2k, Pierrot, by Bohumil Kubista. 2.40k, Ilona Kubinyiova, by Peter M. Bohun. 3.60k, Virgin and Child (Veveri Madonna), c. 1350.

1973, Nov. 27 ***Perf. 11½***

1908 A565 1k multi, vio bl inscriptions 2.50 1.25
a. 1k multi, black inscriptions 10.00 10.00
1909 A565 1.20k multi *2.50* *1.25*
1910 A565 1.80k multi .80 .80
1911 A565 2k multi .80 .80
1912 A565 2.40k multi .80 .80
1913 A565 3.60k multi .80 .80
Nos. 1908-1913 (6) 8.20 5.70

Sheets of 4. Nos. 1910-1913 printed se-tenant with gold and black inscription on gutter. Value, set $35. No. 1908a in sheet of 4, value $45.
Nos. 1908-1909 were each issued in sheets of 4. Nos. 1910-1913 were issued combined in a sheet of 4.
Central background light bluish green on No. 1908, grayish blue on No. 1908a.

Postilion — A679

1973, Dec. 18

1914 A679 1k gold & multi .30 .25

Stamp Day 1974 and 55th anniversary of Czechoslovak postage stamps. Printed with 2 labels showing telephone and telegraph. Value of single with two labels, $1.75.

"CSSR" — A680

1974, Jan. 1

1915 A680 30h red, gold & ultra .25 .25

5th anniversary of Federal Government in the Czechoslovak Socialist Republic.

Bedrich Smetana — A681

Pablo Neruda, Chilean Flag — A682

1974, Jan. 4 ***Perf. 11x11½***

1916 A681 60h shown .25 .25
1917 A681 60h Josef Suk .25 .25
1918 A682 60h shown .25 .25
Nos. 1916-1918 (3) .75 .75

Smetana (1824-84), composer; Suk (1874-1935), composer, and Pablo Neruda (Neftali Ricardo Reyes, 1904-73), Chilean poet.

Comecon Building, Moscow — A683

1974, Jan. 23

1919 A683 1k gold, red & vio bl .25 .25

25th anniversary of the Council of Mutual Economic Assistance (COMECON).

Symbols of Postal Service — A684

1974, Feb. 20 ***Perf. 11½***

1920 A684 3.60k multi .95 .45

BRNO '74 National Stamp Exhibition, Brno, June 8-23.
No. 1920 was issue both in normal sheets of 25 stamps and in sheets containing 16 stamps se-tenant with 9 labels depicting Brno. Values: single stamp with attached tab unused $3; used $2.50; full sheet of 16 stamps and 9 labels $50.

Art Type of 1972

Designs: 60h, Tulips 1973, by Josef Broz. 1k, Structures 1961 (poppy and building), by Orest Dubay. 1.60k, Bird and flowers (Golden Sun-Glowing Day), by Adolf Zabransky. 1.80k, Artificial flowers, by Frantisek Gross.

1974, Feb. 21 *Perf. 11½x11*

1921	A651	60h multi	.25	.25
1922	A651	1k multi	.30	.25
1923	A651	1.60k multi	.40	.25
1924	A651	1.80k multi	1.10	.30
		Nos. 1921-1924 (4)	2.05	1.05

Czech and Slovak graphic art.

Oskar Benes and Vaclav Prochazka — A685

40h, Milos Uher, Anton Sedlacek. 60h, Jan Hajecek, Marie Sedlackova. 80h, Jan Sverma, Albin Grznar. 1k, Jaroslav Neliba, Alois Hovorka. 1.60k, Ladislav Exnar, Ludovit Kukorelli.

1974, Mar. 21 *Perf. 11½x11*

1925	A685	30h indigo & multi	.25	.25
1926	A685	40h indigo & multi	.25	.25
1927	A685	60h indigo & multi	.25	.25
1928	A685	80h indigo & multi	.25	.25
1929	A685	1k indigo & multi	.30	.25
1930	A685	1.60k indigo & multi	.85	.25
		Nos. 1925-1930 (6)	2.15	1.50

Partisan commanders and fighters.

"Water, the Source of Energy" A686

Symbolic Designs: 1k, Importance of water for agriculture. 1.20k, Study of the oceans. 1.60k, "Hydrological Decade." 2k, Struggle for unpolluted water.

1974, Apr. 25 **Engr.** *Perf. 11½*

1931	A686	60h multi	.65	.25
1932	A686	1k multi	.65	.25
1933	A686	1.20k multi	1.25	.45
1934	A686	1.60k multi	1.25	.45
1935	A686	2k multi	2.40	1.75
		Nos. 1931-1935 (5)	6.20	3.15

Hydrological Decade (UNESCO), 1965-1974.

Nos. 1931-1935 were each issued in sheets of 4. Value $30.

Allegory Holding "Molniya," and Ground Station — A687

1974, Apr. 30 **Engr. & Photo.**

1936	A687	30h vio bl & multi	.25	.25

"Intersputnik," first satellite communications ground station in Czechoslovakia.

Prague Castle Art Type of 1971

No. 1937, Golden Cock, 17th century locket. No. 1938, Glass monstrance, 1840.

1974, May 9 **Engr.** *Perf. 11½*

1937	A634	3k gold & multi	1.60	1.25
1938	A634	3k blk & multi	2.40	1.60

Nos. 1937-1938 werre each issued in sheets of 4. Value, set $20.

Sousaphone A688

Engraved and Photogravure

1974, May 12 *Perf. 11x11½*

1939	A688	20h shown	.25	.25
1940	A688	30h Bagpipe	.25	.25
1941	A688	40h Violin, by Martin Benka	.25	.25
1942	A688	1k Pyramid piano	.25	.25
1943	A688	1.60k Tenor quinton, 1754	.80	.25
		Nos. 1939-1943 (5)	1.80	1.25

Prague and Bratislava Music Festivals. The 1.60k also commemorates 25th anniversary of Slovak Philharmonic Orchestra.

Child — A689

1974, June 1 *Perf. 11½*

1944	A689	60h multi	.25	.25

Children's Day. Design is from illustration for children's book by Adolf Zabransky.

Globe, People and Exhibition Emblems — A690

Design: 6k, Rays and emblems symbolizing "Oneness and Mutuality."

1974, June 1

1945	A690	30h multi	.25	.25
1946	A690	6k multi	1.50	.75

BRNO 74 Natl. Stamp Exhib., Brno, June 8-23.

Nos. 2171-2172 were each issued both in sheet of 50 stamps and in sheets of 16 stamps and 14 labels. Values: stamps with attached labels, $1.75; sheet of 16 stamps and 14 labels $50.

Resistance Fighter — A691

1974, Aug. 29 *Perf. 11½*

1947	A691	30h multi	.25	.25

Slovak National Uprising, 30th anniversary.

Actress Holding Tragedy and Comedy Masks — A692

1974, Aug. 29

1948	A692	30h red, sil & blk	.25	.25

Bratislava Academy of Music and Drama, 25th anniversary.

Slovak Girl with Flower — A693

1974, Aug. 29

1949	A693	30h multi	.25	.25

SLUK, Slovak folksong and dance ensemble, 25th anniversary.

Hero and Leander A694

Design: 2.40k, Hero watching Leander swim the Hellespont. No. 1952, Leander reaching shore. No. 1953, Hero mourning over Leander's body. No. 1954, Hermione, Leander's sister. No. 1955, Mourning Cupid. Designs are from 17th century English tapestries in Bratislava Council Palace.

1974-76

1950	A694	2k multi	1.25	1.10
1951	A694	2.40k multi	1.50	1.25
1952	A694	3k multi	1.00	.45
1953	A694	3k multi	1.75	1.75
1954	A694	3.60k multi	2.50	1.10
1955	A694	3.60k multi	.85	.60
		Nos. 1950-1955 (6)	8.85	6.25

Issued: Nos. 1950-1951, 9/25/74; Nos. 1952, 1954, 8/29/75; Nos. 1953, 1955, 5/9/76.

Nos. 1950-1951 were each issued in sheets of 4, with 2 blank labels; Nos. 1952-1955 were issued in sheets of 4. Value, set $50.

Soldier Standing Guard, Target, 1840 — A695

Painted Folk-art Targets: 60h, Landscape with Pierrot and flags, 1828. 1k, Diana crowning champion marksman, 1832. 1.60k, Still life with guitar, 1839. 2.40k, Salvo and stag in flight, 1834. 3k, Turk and giraffe, 1831.

1974, Sept. 26 *Perf. 11½*

Size: 30x50mm

1956	A695	30h black & multi	.25	.25
1957	A695	60h black & multi	.25	.25
1958	A695	1k black & multi	.30	.25

Engr.

Perf. 12

Size: 40x50mm

1959	A695	1.60k green & multi	.50	.45
1960	A695	2.40k sepia & multi	.90	.75
1961	A695	3k multi	*3.00*	*3.00*
		Nos. 1956-1961 (6)	*5.20*	*4.95*

Nos. 1959-1961 were each issued in sheets of 4. Value, set $28.

UPU Emblem and Postilion — A696

UPU Cent. (UPU Emblem and): 40h, Mail coach. 60h, Railroad mail coach, 1851. 80h, Early mail truck. 1k, Czechoslovak Airlines mail plane. 1.60k, Radar.

Engraved and Photogravure

1974, Oct. 9 *Perf. 11½*

1962	A696	30h multi	.25	.25
1963	A696	40h multi	.25	.25
1964	A696	60h multi	.25	.25
1965	A696	80h multi	.25	.25
1966	A696	1k multi	.40	.25
1967	A696	1.60k multi	1.25	.25
		Nos. 1962-1967 (6)	2.65	1.50

Sealed Letter — A697

Post Rider — A698

20h, Post Horn, Old Town Bridge Tower. No. 1971, Carrier pigeon.

1974, Oct. 31 *Perf. 11½x11*

1968	A698	20h multi	.25	.25
1969	A697	30h brn, bl & red	.25	.25
1970	A698	40h multi	.25	.25
1971	A697	60h bl, yel & red	.25	.25
		Nos. 1968-1971 (4)	1.00	1.00

Nos. 1968-1971 were reissued in 1979, printed on fluorescent paper. Value, set $15.

See No. 2675.

Stylized Bird — A699

No. 1977, Same design as No. 1976. No. 1979, Map of Czechoslovakia with postal code numbers.

Coil Stamps

1975 **Photo.** *Perf. 14*

1976	A699	30h brt bl	.25	.25
1977	A699	60h carmine	.25	.25

Postal Code Symbol — A699a

1976 *Perf. 11½*

1978	A699a	30h emer	.25	.25
1979	A699a	60h scar	.25	.25

Nos. 1976-1979 have black control number on back of every fifth stamp.

Ludvik Kuba, Self-portrait, 1941 — A700

Paintings: 1.20k, Violinist Frantisek Ondricek, by Vaclav Brozik. 1.60k, Vase with Flowers, by Otakar Kubin. 1.80k, Woman with Pitcher, by Janko Alexy. 2.40k, Bacchanalia, c. 1635, by Karel Skreta.

1974, Nov. 27 **Engr.** *Perf. 11½*

1980	A700	1k multi	.50	.30
1981	A700	1.20k multi	.80	.40
1982	A700	1.60k multi	.80	.60
1983	A700	1.80k multi	1.00	.40
1984	A700	2.40k multi	2.50	1.75
		Nos. 1980-1984 (5)	5.60	3.45

Czech and Slovak art.

Nos. 1980-1984 were each issued in sheets of 4. Value, set $28.

See Nos. 2209-2211, 2678-2682, 2721-2723, 2743, 2766-2768.

Post Horn — A701

Engraved and Photogravure

1974, Dec. 18 *Perf. 11x11½*

1985	A701 1k multicolored	.30	.25

Stamp Day.

Still-life with Hare, by Hollar — A702

Designs: 1k, The Lion and the Mouse, by Vaclav Hollar. 1.60k, Deer Hunt, by Philip Galle. 1.80k, Grand Hunt, by Jacques Callot.

1975, Feb. 26 *Perf. 11½x11*

1988	A702 60h blk & buff	.25	.25
1989	A702 1k blk & buff	.25	.25
1990	A702 1.60k blk & yel	.25	.25
1991	A702 1.80k blk & buff	1.25	.65
	Nos. 1988-1991 (4)	2.00	1.40

Hunting scenes from old engravings.

Guns Pointing at Family A703

Designs: 1k, Women and building on fire. 1.20k, People and roses. All designs include names of destroyed villages.

1975, Feb. 26 *Perf. 11*

1992	A703 60h multi	.25	.25
1993	A703 1k multi	.25	.25
1994	A703 1.20k multi	.30	.25
	Nos. 1992-1994 (3)	.80	.75

Destruction of 14 villages by the Nazis, 30th anniversary.

Young Woman and Globe — A704

1975, Mar. 7 *Perf. 11½x11*

1995	A704 30h red & multi	.25	.25

International Women's Year 1975.

Little Queens, Moravian Folk Custom A705

Folk Customs: 1k, Straw masks (animal heads and blackened faces), Slovak. 1.40k, The Tale of Maid Dorothea (executioner, girl, king and devil). 2k, Drowning of Morena, symbol of death and winter.

1975, Mar. 26 **Engr.** *Perf. 11½*

1996	A705 60h blk & multi	.45	.25
1997	A705 1k blk & multi	.80	.45
1998	A705 1.40k blk & multi	.90	.65
1999	A705 2k blk & multi	1.10	.85
	Nos. 1996-1999 (4)	3.25	2.20

Nos. 1996-1999 were each issued in sheets of four. Value $15.

Coat of Arms Type of 1968

Engraved and Photogravure

1975, Apr. 17 *Perf. 11½*

2000	A590 60h Nymburk	.25	.25
2001	A590 60h Znojmo	.25	.25

Coats of arms of Czechoslovakian cities.

Czech May Uprising — A706

Liberation by Soviet Army — A707

Czechoslovak-Russian Friendship — A708

Engr. & Photo.; Engr. (A707)

1975, May 9

2002	A706 1k multi	.25	.25
2003	A707 1k multi	.25	.25
2004	A708 1k multi	.25	.25
	Nos. 2002-2004 (3)	.75	.75

30th anniv. of the May uprising of the Czech people and of liberation by the Soviet Army; 5th anniv. of the Czechoslovak-Soviet Treaty of Friendship, Cooperation and Mutual Aid.

Adolescents' Exercises — A709

Designs: 60th, Children's exercises. 1k, Men's and women's exercises.

Engraved and Photogravure

1975, June 15 *Perf. 12x11½*

2005	A709 30h lil & multi	.25	.25
2006	A709 60h multi	.25	.25
2007	A709 1k vio & multi	.25	.25
	Nos. 2005-2007 (3)	.75	.75

Spartakiad 1975, Prague, June 26-29. Nos. 2005-2007 each issued in sheets of 30 stamps and 40 labels, showing different Spartakiad emblems. Value, set with tabs, $1.

Datrioides Microlepis and Sea Horse — A710

Tropical Fish (Aquarium): 1k, Beta splendens regan and Pterophyllum scalare. 1.20k, Carassius auratus. 1.60k, Amphiprion percula and Chaetodon sp. 2k, Pomacanthodes semicirculatus, Pomocanthus maculosus and Paracanthorus hepatus.

1975, June 27 *Perf. 11½*

2008	A710 60h multi	.25	.25
2009	A710 1k multi	.35	.25
2010	A710 1.20k multi	.40	.25
2011	A710 1.60k multi	.55	.25
2012	A710 2k multi	1.75	.50
	Nos. 2008-2012 (5)	3.30	1.50

Pelicans, by Nikita Charushin — A711

Book Illustrations: 30h, The Dreamer, by Lieselotte Schwarz. 40h, Hero on horseback, by Val Munteanau. 60h, Peacock, by Klaus Ensikat. 80h, Woman on horseback, by Robert Dubravec.

1975, Sept. 5

2013	A711 20h multi	.25	.25
2014	A711 30h multi	.25	.25
2015	A711 40h multi	.30	.25
2016	A711 60h multi	.30	.25
2017	A711 80h multi	.60	.25
	Nos. 2013-2017 (5)	1.70	1.25

Bratislava BIB 75 biennial exhibition of illustrations for children's books.

Nos. 2013-2017 issued in sheets of 25 stamps and 15 labels with designs and inscriptions in various languages. Value, set with attached labels, $2.50.

Strakonice, 1951 — A712

Designs: Motorcycles.

1975, Sept. 29 *Perf. 11½*

2018	A712 20h shown	.25	.25
2019	A712 40h Jawa 250, 1945	.25	.25
2020	A712 60h Jawa 175, 1935	.25	.25
2021	A712 1k ITAR, 1921	.25	.25
2022	A712 1.20k ORION, 1903	.25	.25
2023	A712 1.80k Laurin & Klement, 1898	1.40	.40
	Nos. 2018-2023 (6)	2.65	1.65

Study of Shortwave Solar Radiation — A713

Soyuz-Apollo Link-up in Space — A714

60h, Study of aurora borealis & Oréol satellite. 1k, Study of ionosphere & cosmic radiation. 2k, Copernicus, radio map of the sun & satellite.

1975, Sept. 30

2024	A713 30h multi	.25	.25
2025	A713 60h yel, rose red & vio	.25	.25
2026	A713 1k bl, yel & vio	.25	.25
2027	A713 2k red, vio & yel	.35	.25
	Engr.		
2028	A714 5k vio & multi	2.00	1.50
	Nos. 2024-2028 (5)	3.10	2.50

International cooperation in space research.

No. 2028 issued in sheets of 4. Value $15.

The design of No. 2026 appears to be inverted.

Slovnaft, Petrochemical Plant — A715

Designs: 60h, Atomic power station. 1k, Construction of Prague subway. 1.20k, Construction of Friendship pipeline. 1.40k, Combine harvesters. 1.60k, Apartment house construction.

Engraved and Photogravure

1975, Oct. 28

2029	A715 30h multi	.25	.25
2030	A715 60h multi	.25	.25
2031	A715 1k multi	.25	.25
2032	A715 1.20k multi	.25	.25
2033	A715 1.40k multi	.25	.25
2034	A715 1.60k multi	.75	.30
	Nos. 2029-2034 (6)	2.00	1.55

Socialist construction, 30th anniversary. Nos. 2029-2034 printed se-tenant with labels. Value, set with attached labels, $2.50.

Pres. Gustav Husak — A716

1975, Oct. 28 **Engr.**

2035	A716 30h ultra	.25	.25
2036	A716 60h rose red	.25	.25

Prague Castle Art Type of 1971

3k, Gold earring, 9th cent. 3.60k, Arms of Premysl Dynasty & Bohemia from lid of leather case containing Bohemian crown, 14th cent.

1975, Oct. 29

2040	A634 3k blk, grn, pur & gold	.95	.50
2041	A634 3.60k red & multi	2.00	1.60

Nos. 2040-2041 each issued in sheets of 4. Value, set $15.

Miniature Sheet

Ludvik Svoboda, Map of Journey from Buzuluk to Prague, Carnations — A717

1975, Nov. 25

2042 A717 10k multi		9.00	7.00

Pres. Ludvik Svoboda, 80th birthday. Exists imperf. Value, $40 unused, $25 used.

Painting Type of 1967

Paintings: 1k, "May 1975" (Woman and doves for 30th anniv. of peace), by Zdenek Sklenar. 1.40k, Woman in national costume, by Eugen Nevan. 1.80k, "Liberation of Prague," by Alena Cermakova, horiz. 2.40k, "Fire 1938" (woman raising fist), by Josef Capek. 3.40k, Old Prague, 1828, by Vincenc Morstadt.

1975, Nov. 27 Engr. *Perf. 11½*

2043 A565	1k blk, buff & brn	.30	.25
2044 A565	1.40k multi	.65	.30
2045 A565	1.80k multi	.65	.30
2046 A565	2.40k multi	1.60	.75
2047 A565	3.40k multi	1.60	1.25
	Nos. 2043-2047 (5)	4.80	2.85

Nos. 2043-2047 were each issued in sheets of 4. Value, set $22.50.

Carrier Pigeon — A718

Engraved and Photogravure

1975, Dec. 18 *Perf. 11½*

2048 A718 1k red & multi		.30	.25

Stamp Day 1975.

Frantisek Halas — A719

Wilhelm Pieck — A720

Frantisek Lexa — A721

Jindrich Jindrich — A722

Ivan Krasko — A723

1976, Feb. 25 *Perf. 11½*

2049 A719 60h multi		.25	.25
2050 A720 60h multi		.25	.25
2051 A721 60h multi		.25	.25
2052 A722 60h multi		.25	.25
2053 A723 60h multi		.25	.25
	Nos. 2049-2053 (5)	1.25	1.25

Halas (1901-49), poet; Pieck (1876-1960), pres. of German Democratic Republic; Lexa (1876-1960), professor of Egyptology; Jindrich (1876-1967), composer and writer; Krasko (1876-1958), Slovak poet. No. 2051 printed in sheets of 10, others in sheets of 50. Value, No. 2051 sheet, $5.00.

Ski Jump, Olympic Emblem A724

Winter Olympic Games Emblem and: 1.40k, Figure skating, women's. 1.60k, Ice hockey.

1976, Mar. 22 *Perf. 12x11½*

2054 A724	1k gold & multi	.25	.25
2055 A724	1.40k gold & multi	.25	.25
2056 A724	1.60k gold & multi	1.00	.30
	Nos. 2054-2056 (3)	1.50	.80

12th Winter Olympic Games, Innsbruck, Austria, Feb. 4-15.

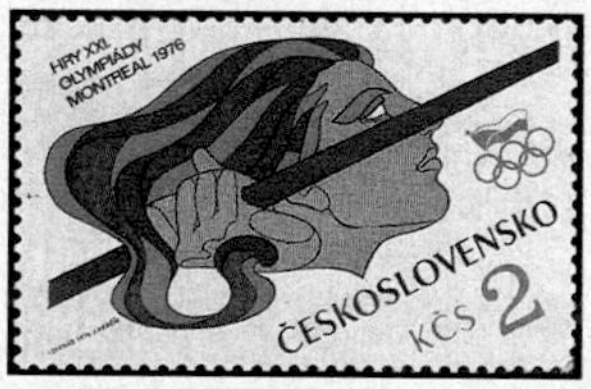

Javelin and Olympic Rings — A725

1976, Mar. 22 *Perf. 11½*

2057 A725	2k shown	.25	.25
2058 A725	3k Relay race	.40	.25
2059 A725	3.60k Shot put	1.40	.90
	Nos. 2057-2059 (3)	2.05	1.40

21st Olympic Games, Montreal, Canada, July 17-Aug. 1.

Table Tennis — A726

1976, Mar. 22 *Perf. 11x12*

2060 A726 1k multi		.30	.25

European Table Tennis Championship, Prague, Mar. 26-Apr. 4.

Symbolic of Communist Party — A727

Worker, Derrick, Emblem — A728

1976, Apr. 12 *Perf. 11x12*

2061 A727 30h gold & multi		.25	.25
2062 A728 60h gold & multi		.25	.25

15th Congress of the Communist Party of Czechoslovakia.

Radio Prague Orchestra A729

Dancer, Violin, Tragic Mask — A730

Actors — A731

Folk Dancers A732

Film Festival — A733

1976, Apr. 26 *Perf. 11½*

2063 A729	20h gold & multi	.25	.25
2064 A730	20h pink & multi	.25	.25
2065 A731	20h lt bl & multi	.25	.25
2066 A732	30h blk & multi	.25	.25
2067 A733	30h vio bl, rose & grn	.25	.25
	Nos. 2063-2067 (5)	1.25	1.25

Czechoslovak Radio Symphony Orchestra, Prague, 50th anniv. (No. 2063); Academy of Music and Dramatic Art, Prague, 50th anniv. (No. 2064); Nova Scena Theater Co., Bratislava, 30th anniv. (No. 2065); Intl. Folk Song and Dance Festival, Straznice, 30th anniv. (No. 2066); 20th Intl. Film Festival, Karlovy Vary (No. 2067).

Hammer and Sickle
A734 A735

Design: 6k, Hammer and sickle, horiz.

1976, May 14

2068 A734 30h gold, red & dk bl		.25	.25
2069 A735 60h gold, red & dp car		.25	.25

Souvenir Sheet

2070 A735 6k red & multi		1.75	1.75

Czechoslovak Communist Party, 55th anniv. No. 2070 contains a 50x30mm stamp.

Ships in Storm, by Frans Huys (1522-1562) A736

Old Engravings of Ships: 60h, by Václav Hollar (1607-77). 1k, by Regnier Nooms Zeeman (1623-68). 2k, by Francois Chereau (1680-1729).

Engraved and Photogravure

1976, July 21 *Perf. 11x11½*

2071 A736	40h buff & blk	.25	.25
2072 A736	60h gray, buff & blk	.25	.25
2073 A736	1k lt grn, buff & blk	.25	.25
2074 A736	2k lt bl, buff & blk	*1.60*	*.40*
	Nos. 2071-2074 (4)	*2.35*	*1.15*

"UNESCO" A737

1976, July 30 *Perf. 11½*

2075 A737 2k gray & multi		.40	.45

30th anniversary of UNESCO. Issued in sheets of 10. Value $8.

Souvenir Sheet

Hands Holding Infant, Globe and Dove — A738

1976, July 30

2076 A738 Sheet of 2		4.00	3.50
a. 6k multi		2.50	2.00

European Security and Cooperation Conference, Helsinki, Finland, 2nd anniv.

Merino Ram — A739

Designs: 40h, Bern-Hana milk cow. 1.60k, Kladruby stallion Generalissimus XXVII.

1976, Aug. 28 *Perf. 11½x12*

2077 A739	30h multi	.25	.25
2078 A739	40h multi	.25	.25
2079 A739	1.60k multi	.35	.25
	Nos. 2077-2079 (3)	.85	.75

Bountiful Earth Exhibition, Ceske Budejovice, Aug. 28-Sept. 12.

Couple Smoking, WHO Emblem and Skull — A740

1976, Sept. 7 *Perf. 12x11½*

2080 A740 2k multi .50 .30

Fight against smoking, WHO drive against drug addiction.

Printed in sheets of 10 (2x5) with WHO emblems and inscription in margin. Value $10.

Prague Castle Art Type of 1971

Designs: 3k, View of Prague Castle, by F. Hoogenberghe, 1572. 3.60k, Faun and Satyr, sculptured panel, 16th century.

1976, Oct. 22 **Engr.** *Perf. 11½*

2081 A634 3k multi 2.50 2.10
2082 A634 3.60k multi .90 .60

Nos. 2081-2082 were each issued in sheets of 4. Value $15.

Guernica 1937, by Imro Weiner-Kral A741

1976, Oct. 22

2083 A741 5k multi .80 .40

40th anniv. of the Intl. Brigade in Spain.

Zebras A742

20h, Elephants. 30h, Cheetah. 40h, Giraffes. 60h, Rhinoceros. 3k, Bongos.

Engraved and Photogravure

1976, Nov. 3 *Perf. 11½x11, 11x11½*

2084 A742 10h multi .25 .25
2085 A742 20h multi, vert. .25 .25
2086 A742 30h multi .30 .25
2087 A742 40h multi, vert. .45 .25
2088 A742 60h multi .45 .25
2089 A742 3k multi, vert. 2.25 .65
Nos. 2084-2089 (6) 3.95 1.90

African animals in Dvur Kralove Zoo.

Painting Type of 1967

Paintings of Flowers: 1k, by Peter Matejka. 1.40k, by Cyril Bouda. 2k, by Jan Breughel. 3.60k, J. Rudolf Bys.

1976, Nov. 27 **Engr.** *Perf. 11½*

2090 A565 1k multi .75 .50
2091 A565 1.40k multi 1.50 .90
2092 A565 2k multi 1.50 .90
2093 A565 3.60k multi .90 .50
Nos. 2090-2093 (4) 4.65 2.80

Nos. 2090-2093 were each issued in sheets of 4, with emblem and name of Praga 1978 on horizontal gutter. Value, set $25.

Postrider, 17th Century, and Satellites — A743

1976, Dec. 18 **Engr. & Photo.**

2094 A743 1k multi .25 .25

Stamp Day 1976.

Ice Hockey — A744

Arms of Vranov — A745

1977, Feb. 11 *Perf. 11½*

2095 A744 60h shown .25 .25
2096 A744 1k Biathlon .25 .25
2097 A744 1.60k Ski jump .95 .25
2098 A744 2k Downhill skiing .25 .25
Nos. 2095-2098 (4) 1.70 1.00

6th Winter Spartakiad of Socialist Countries' Armies.

1977, Feb. 20

Coats of Arms of Czechoslovak towns.

2099 A745 60h shown .25 .25
2100 A745 60h Kralupy nad Vltavou .25 .25
2101 A745 60h Jicin .25 .25
2102 A745 60h Valasske Mezirici .25 .25
Nos. 2099-2102 (4) 1.00 1.00

See Nos. 2297-2300.

Window, Michna Palace — A746

Prague Renaissance Windows: 30h, Michna Palace. 40h, Thun Palace. 60h, Archbishop's Palace, Hradcany. 5k, St. Nicholas Church.

1977, Mar. 10

2103 A746 20h multi .25 .25
2104 A746 30h multi .25 .25
2105 A746 40h multi .25 .25
2106 A746 60h multi .25 .25
2107 A746 5k multi 1.50 .60
Nos. 2103-2107 (5) 2.50 1.60

PRAGA 1978 International Philatelic Exhibition, Prague, Sept. 8-17, 1978.

Children, Auxiliary Police A747

1977, Apr. 21 *Perf. 11½*

2108 A747 60h multi .25 .25

Auxiliary Police, 25th anniversary.

Warsaw, Polish Flag, Bicyclists A748

Designs: 60h, Berlin, DDR flag, bicyclists. 1k, Prague, Czechoslovakian flag, victorious bicyclist. 1.40k, Bicyclists on highways, modern views of Berlin, Prague and Warsaw.

1977, May 7

2109 A748 30h multi .25 .25
2110 A748 60h multi .25 .25
2111 A748 1k multi .60 .25
2112 A748 1.40k multi .40 .25
Nos. 2109-2112 (4) 1.50 1.00

30th International Bicycle Peace Race Warsaw-Prague-Berlin.

Congress Emblem — A749

1977, May 25 *Perf. 11½*

2113 A749 30h car, red & gold .25 .25

9th Trade Union Congress, Prague 1977.

Prague Castle Art Type of 1971

Designs: 3k, Onyx footed bowl, 1350. 3.60k, Bronze horse, 1619.

1977, June 7 **Engr.**

2114 A634 3k multi 1.25 1.10
2115 A634 3.60k multi 1.10 1.10

Nos. 2114-2115 were each issued in sheets of 4. Value, set $13.

French Postrider, 19th Century, PRAGA '78 Emblem — A750

Postal Uniforms: 1k, Austrian, 1838. 2k, Austrian, late 18th century. 3.60k, Germany, early 18th century.

1977, June 8 **Engr. & Photo.**

2116 A750 60h multi .25 .25
2117 A750 1k multi .25 .25
2118 A750 2k multi .40 .25
2119 A750 3.60k multi 1.50 .60
Nos. 2116-2119 (4) 2.40 1.35

PRAGA 1978 International Philatelic Exhibition, Prague, Sept. 8-17, 1978.

Nos. 2116-2119 were each issued both in sheets of 50 and in sheets of 4 stamps with 4 inscribed labels and 2 blank labels. Value, set of sheets of 4, $16.

Coffeepots, Porcelain Mark — A751

Czechoslovak Porcelain and Porcelain Marks: 30h, Urn. 40h, Vase. 60h, Cup and saucer, jugs. 1k, Candlestick and plate. 3k, Cup and saucer, coffeepot.

1977, June 15

2120 A751 20h multi .25 .25
2121 A751 30h multi .25 .25
2122 A751 40h multi .25 .25
2123 A751 60h multi .25 .25
2124 A751 1k multi .25 .25
2125 A751 3k multi 1.10 .35
Nos. 2120-2125 (6) 2.35 1.60

Mlada Boleslav Costume — A752

PRAGA Emblem and Folk Costumes from: 1.60k, Vazek. 3.60k, Zavadka. 5k, Belkovice.

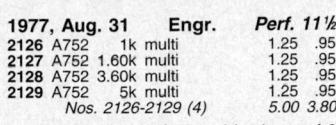

1977, Aug. 31 **Engr.** *Perf. 11½*

2126 A752 1k multi 1.25 .95
2127 A752 1.60k multi 1.25 .95
2128 A752 3.60k multi 1.25 .95
2129 A752 5k multi 1.25 .95
Nos. 2126-2129 (4) 5.00 3.80

Issued in sheets of 10 and in sheets of 8 plus 2 labels showing PRAGA '78 emblem. Value, set: sheets of 10 $50; sheets of 8 $40.

Old Woman, Devil and Spinner, by Viera Bombova A753

Book Illustrations: 60h, Bear and tiger, by Genadij Pavlisin. 1k, Coach drawn by 4 horses (Hans Christian Andersen), by Ulf Lovgren. 2k, Bear and flamingos (Lewis Carroll), by Nicole Claveloux. 3k, King with keys, and toys, by Jiri Trnka.

1977, Sept. 9 **Engr. & Photo.**

2130 A753 40h multi .25 .25
2131 A753 60h multi .25 .25
2132 A753 1k multi .25 .25
2133 A753 2k multi .25 .25
2134 A753 3k multi 1.00 .35
Nos. 2130-2134 (5) 2.00 1.35

Prize-winning designs, 6th biennial exhibition of illustrations for children's books, Bratislava.

Globe, Violin, Doves, View of Prague — A754

1977, Sept. 28 *Perf. 11½*

2135 A754 60h multi .25 .25

Congress of International Music Council of UNESCO, Prague and Bratislava.

Souvenir Sheets

"For a Europe of Peace" — A755

1.60k, "For a Europe of Cooperation." 2.40k, "For a Europe of Social Progress."

1977, Oct. 3

2136 A755 Sheet of 2 .50 .50
a. 60h multi .25 .25
2137 A755 Sheet of 2 1.00 1.00
a. 1.60k multi .25 .25
2138 A755 Sheet of 2 2.00 1.75
a. 2.40k multi .50 .50

2nd European Security and Cooperation Conference, Belgrade. Nos. 2136-2138 each contain 2 stamps and 2 blue on buff inscriptions and ornaments.

Nos. 2136-2138 were issued imperforate in sheets of 4. Value, $50.

For overprint of No. 2137, see No. 2334.

S. P. Korolev, Sputnik I Emblem — A756

30h, Yuri A. Gagarin & Vostok I. 40h, Alexei Leonov. 1k, Neil A. Armstrong & footprint on moon. 1.60k, Construction of orbital space station.

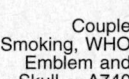

1977, Oct. 4

2139 A756 20h multi .25 .25
2140 A756 30h multi .25 .25
2141 A756 40h multi .25 .25
2142 A756 1k multi .25 .25
2143 A756 1.60k multi .60 .25
Nos. 2139-2143 (5) 1.60 1.25

Space research, 20th anniv. of 1st earth satellite.

Sailors, Cruiser Aurora — A757

1977, Nov. 7

2144 A757 30h multi .25 .25

60th anniv. of Russian October Revolution.

"Russia," Arms of USSR, Kremlin — A758

1977, Nov. 7

2145 A758 30h multi .25 .25

55th anniversary of the USSR.

"Science" — A759

1977, Nov. 17

2146 A759 3k multi .50 .25

Czechoslovak Academy of Science, 25th anniversary.

Painting Type of 1967

Paintings: 2k, "Fear" (woman), by Jan Mudroch. 2.40k, Jan Francisci, portrait by Peter M. Bohun. 2.60k, Vaclav Hollar, self-portrait, 1647. 3k, Young Woman, 1528, by Lucas Cranach. 5k, Cleopatra, by Rubens.

1977, Nov. 27 Engr. *Perf. 11½*

2147 A565 2k multi .80 .45
2148 A565 2.40k multi 1.25 1.10
2149 A565 2.60k multi 1.25 1.10
2150 A565 3k multi .80 .70
2151 A565 5k multi 1.60 1.60
Nos. 2147-2151 (5) 5.70 4.95

Nos. 2147-2151 were each issued in sheets of 4. Value, set $28.

View of Bratislava, by Georg Hoefnagel — A760

Design: 3.60k, Arms of Bratislava, 1436.

1977, Dec. 6

2152 A760 3k multi 1.90 1.60
2153 A760 3.60k multi .80 .50

Nos. 2152-21531 were each issued in sheets of 4. Value, set $12.50.

See Nos. 2174-2175, 2270-2271, 2331-2332, 2364-2365, 2422-2423, 2478-2479, 2514-2515, 2570-2571, 2618-2619.

Stamp Pattern and Post Horn — A761

1977, Dec. 18 Engr. & Photo.

2154 A761 1k multi .25 .25

Stamp Day.

Zdenek Nejedly — A762

Karl Marx — A763

1978, Feb. 10 *Perf. 11½*

2155 A762 30h multi .25 .25
2156 A763 40h multi .25 .25

Zdenek Nejedly (1878-1962), musicologist and historian; Karl Marx (1818-1883), political philosopher.

Civilians Greeting Guardsmen — A764

Intellectual, Farm Woman and Steel Worker, Flag — A765

1978, Feb. 25

2157 A764 1k gold & multi .25 .25
2158 A765 1k gold & multi .25 .25

30th anniv. of "Victorious February" (No. 2157), and Natl. Front (No. 2158). An imperforate sheet of four of No. 2157 was sold with an admission ticket to PRAGA 78 international philatelic exhibition. Value, $5. See note after 2190.

Yuri A. Gagarin, Vostok I — A766

Design: 30h, 3.60k, like No. 2140.

Engraved; Overprint Photogravure (Blue and carmine on 30h, green and lilac rose on 3.60k)

1978, Mar. 2 *Perf. 11½x12*

2159 A766 30h dk red .25 .25
2160 A766 3.60k vio bl 2.40 2.40

Capt. V. Remek, 1st Czechoslovakian cosmonaut on Russian spaceship Soyuz 28, Mar. 2-9.

10k Coin, 1964, and 25k Coin, 1965 — A767

40h, Medal for Culture, 1972. 1.40k, Charles University medal, 1948. 3k, Ferdinand I medal, 1568. 5k, Gold florin, 1335.

1978, Mar. 14 Engr. & Photo.

2161 A767 20h sil & multi .25 .25
2162 A767 40h sil & multi .25 .25
2163 A767 1.40k gold & multi 1.00 .25
2164 A767 3k gold & multi .35 .25
2165 A767 5k gold & multi .35 .25
Nos. 2161-2165 (5) 2.20 1.25

650th anniversary of Kremnica Mint.

Tire Tracks and Ball — A768

Congress Emblem — A769

1978, Mar. 15

2166 A768 60h multi .25 .25

Road safety.

1978, Apr. 16 *Perf. 11½*

2167 A769 1k multi .25 .25

9th World Trade Union Cong., Prague 1978.

Shot Put and Praha '78 Emblem A770

1k, Pole vault. 3.60k, Women runners.

1978, Apr. 26

2168 A770 40h multi .30 .30
2169 A770 1k multi .40 .30
2170 A770 3.60k multi .90 .50
Nos. 2168-2170 (3) 1.60 1.10

5th European Athletic Championships, Prague 1978.

Ice Hockey — A771

Designs: 30h, Hockey. 2k, Ice hockey play.

1978, Apr. 26

2171 A771 30h multi .30 .25
2172 A771 60h multi .25 .25
2173 A771 2k multi .40 .25
Nos. 2171-2173 (3) .95 .75

5th European Ice Hockey Championships and 70th anniversary of Bandy hockey.

Bratislava Type of 1977

Designs: 3k, Bratislava, 1955, by Orest Dubay. 3.60k, Fishpound Square, Bratislava, 1955, by Imro Weiner-Kral.

1978, May 9 Engr. *Perf. 11½*

2174 A760 3k multi .95 .80
2175 A760 3.60k multi 1.25 .80

Nos. 2174-2175 were each issued in sheets of 4. Value, set $12.

Prague Castle Art Type of 1971

3k, King Ottokar II, detail from tomb. 3.60k, Charles IV, detail from votive panel by Jan Ocka.

1978, May 9

2176 A634 3k multi 1.25 .60
2177 A634 3.60k multi 4.00 2.40

Nos. 2176-2177 were each issued in sheets of 4. Value, set $20.

Ministry of Post, Prague A772

Engraved and Photogravure

1978, May 29 *Perf. 12x11½*

2178 A772 60h multi .25 .25

14th session of permanent COMECOM Commission (Ministers of Post and Telecommunications of Socialist Countries).

Palacky Bridge A773

Prague Bridges and PRAGA '78 Emblem: 40h, Railroad bridge. 1k, Bridge of May 1. 2k, Manes Bridge. 3k, Svatopluk Cech Bridge. 5.40k, Charles Bridge.

1978, May 30

2179 A773 20h blk & multi .25 .25
2180 A773 40h blk & multi .25 .25
2181 A773 1k blk & multi .25 .25
2182 A773 2k blk & multi .25 .25
2183 A773 3k blk & multi .45 .25
2184 A773 5.40k blk & multi 1.50 .75
Nos. 2179-2184 (6) 2.95 2.00

PRAGA 1978 International Philatelic Exhibition, Prague, Sept. 8-17.

St. Peter and Apostles, Clock Tower, and Emblem A774

Town Hall Clock, Prague, by Josef Manes, and PRAGA '78 Emblem: 1k, Astronomical clock. 2k, Prague's coat of arms. 3k, Grape harvest (September). 3.60k, Libra. 10k, Arms surrounded by zodiac signs and scenes symbolic of 12 months, horiz. 2k, 3k, 3.60k show details from design of 10k.

1978, June 20 *Perf. 11½x11*

2185 A774 40h multi .25 .25
2186 A774 1k multi .25 .25
2187 A774 2k multi .25 .25
2188 A774 3k multi 1.50 .35
2189 A774 3.60k multi .75 .25
Nos. 2185-2189 (5) 3.00 1.35

Souvenir Sheet

Perf. 12x12

2190 A774 10k multi 10.00 7.50

PRAGA '78 Intl. Philatelic Exhibition, Prague, Sept. 8-17. No. 2190 contains one 50x40mm stamp. Sheet exists imperf. Value $30.

A non-valid souvenir sheet contains 4 imperf. examples of No. 2157. Sold only with PRAGA ticket.

Folk Dancers — A775

1978, July 7 *Perf. 11½x12*

2191	A775	30h multi	.25	.25

25th Folklore Festival, Vychodna.

Overpass and PRAGA Emblem — A776

1k, 2k, Modern office buildings, diff. 6k, Old & new Prague. 20k, Charles Bridge & Old Town, by Vincent Morstadt, 1828.

1978 *Perf. 12x11½*

2192	A776	60h blk & multi	.25	.25
2193	A776	1k blk & multi	.25	.25
2194	A776	2k blk & multi	.25	.25
2195	A776	6k blk & multi	1.50	.75
		Nos. 2192-2195 (4)	2.25	1.50

Souvenir Sheet

Engr.

2196	A776	20k multi	9.50	7.50

PRAGA 1978 Intl. Phil. Exhib., Prague, Sept. 8-17. No. 2196 also for 60th anniv. of Czechoslovak postage stamps. No. 2196 contains one 61x45mm stamp.

Issued: Nos. 2192-2195, 9/8; No. 2196, 9/10.

Souvenir Sheet

Titian (1488-1576), Venetian painter — A777

No. 2197a, Apollo's Companion, by Titian. No. 2197b, King Midas. Stamps show details from "Apollo Flaying Marsya" by Titian.

1978, Sept. 12 *Perf. 11½*

2197	A777	Sheet of 2	11.00	8.75
a.		10k multi	5.00	4.25
b.		10k multi	5.00	4.25

No. 2197 with dark blue marginal inscription "FIP" was sold only with entrance ticket to PRAGA Philatelic Exhibition. Value $25.

Exhibition Hall — A778

Engraved and Photogravure

1978, Sept. 13 *Perf. 11½x11*

2198	A778	30h multi	.25	.25

22nd International Engineering Fair, Brno.

Postal Newspaper Service — A779

TV Screen, Headquarters and Logo — A780

Newspaper, Microphone A781

1978, Sept. 21 *Perf. 11½*

2199	A779	30h multi	.25	.25
2200	A780	30h multi	.25	.25
2201	A781	30h multi	.25	.25
		Nos. 2199-2201 (3)	.75	.75

Postal News Service, 25th anniv.; Czechoslovakian television, 25th anniv.; Press, Broadcasting and Television Day.

Sulky Race A782

Pardubice Steeplechase: 10h, Falling horses and jockeys at fence. 30h, Race. 40h, Horses passing post. 1.60k, Hurdling. 4.40k, Winner.

1978, Oct. 6 *Perf. 12x11½*

2202	A782	10h multi	.25	.25
2203	A782	20h multi	.25	.25
2204	A782	30h multi	.25	.25
2205	A782	40h multi	.25	.25
2206	A782	1.60k multi	.25	.25
2207	A782	4.40k multi	1.50	.65
		Nos. 2202-2207 (6)	2.75	1.90

Woman Holding Arms of Czechoslovakia A783

1978, Oct. 28 *Perf. 11½*

2208	A783	60h multi	.25	.25

60th anniversary of independence.

Art Type of 1974

2.40k, Flowers, by Jakub Bohdan (1660-1724). 3k, The Dream of Salas, by Ludovit Fulla, horiz. 3.60k, Apostle with Censer, Master of the Spissko Capitals (c. 1480-90).

1978, Nov. 27 **Engr.**

2209	A700	2.40k multi	.70	.55
2210	A700	3k multi	.90	.80
2211	A700	3.60k multi	3.25	2.50
		Nos. 2209-2211 (3)	4.85	3.85

Slovak National Gallery, 30th anniversary.

Nos. 2209-2211 were each issued in sheets of 4. Value, set $25.

Musicians, by Jan Könyves — A784

Slovak Ceramics: 30h, Janosik on Horseback, by Jozef Franko. 40h, Woman in Folk Costume by Michal Polasko. 1k, Three Girls Singing, by Ignac Bizmayer. 1.60k, Janosik Dancing, by Ferdis Kostka.

Engraved and Photogravure

1978, Dec. 5 *Perf. 11½x12*

2212	A784	20h multi	.25	.25
2213	A784	30h multi	.25	.25
2214	A784	40k multi	.25	.25
2215	A784	1k multi	.25	.25
2216	A784	1.60k multi	1.00	.30
		Nos. 2212-2216 (5)	2.00	1.30

Alfons Mucha and his Design for 1918 Issue — A785

1978, Dec. 18 *Perf. 11¼*

2217	A785	1k multi	.25	.25

60th Stamp Day.

COMECON Building, Moscow — A786

1979, Jan. 1 *Perf. 11½*

2218	A786	1k multi	.25	.25

Council for Mutual Economic Aid (COMECON), 30th anniversary.

Woman's Head and Grain — A787

Woman, Workers, Child, Doves — A788

1979, Jan. 1

2219	A787	30h multi	.25	.25
2220	A788	60h multi	.25	.25

United Agricultural Production Assoc., 30th anniv. (30h); Czechoslovakian Federation, 10th anniv. (60h).

Soyuz 28, Rockets and Capsule — A789

60h, Astronauts Aleksei Gubarev and Vladimir Remek on launching pad, vert. 1.60k, Soviet astronauts J. Romanenko and G. Grecko, Salyut 6 and recovery ship. 2k, Salyut-Soyuz orbital complex, post office in space and Czechoslovakia No. 2153. 4k, Soyuz 28, crew after landing and trajectory map, vert. 10k, Gubarev and Remek, Intercosmos emblem, arms of Czechoslovakia and USSR.

1979, Mar. 2

2221	A789	30h multi	.25	.25
2222	A789	60h multi	.25	.25
2223	A789	1.60k multi	.25	.25
2224	A789	2k multi	1.60	.30
2225	A789	4k multi	.80	.25
		Nos. 2221-2225 (5)	3.15	1.30

Souvenir Sheet

2226	A789	10k multi	5.00	3.50

1st anniv. of joint Czechoslovak-Soviet space flight. Size of No. 2226: 76x93mm (stamp 39x55mm). No. 2226 has Cyrillic inscription, No. 2455a does not. No. 2226 exists imperf. Value, $22.50.

Alpine Bellflowers A790

Stylized Satellite, Dial, Tape A791

Mountain Flowers: 20h, Crocus. 30h, Pinks. 40h, Alpine hawkweed. 3k, Larkspur.

1979, Mar. 23 *Perf. 11½*

2227	A790	10h multi	.25	.25
2228	A790	20h multi	.25	.25
2229	A790	30h multi	.25	.25
2230	A790	40h multi	.25	.25

Perf. 14

2231	A790	3k multi	1.50	.75
		Nos. 2227-2231 (5)	2.50	1.75

Mountain Rescue Service, 25th anniversary.

The 3k exists perf. 11½. Value, $40 unused, $20 used.

The 3k was issued in sheets of 10. Values: perf 14 (No. 2231), $25; perf 11½, $400.

1979, Apr. 2

2232	A791	10h multi	.25	.25

Telecommunications research, 30th anniv.

Artist and Model, Dove, Bratislava Castle — A792

Cog Wheels, Transformer and Student — A793

Musical Instruments, Bratislava Castle — A794

Pioneer Scarf, IYC Emblem — A795

Red Star, Man, Child and Doves — A796

1979, Apr. 2

2233	A792	20h multi	.25	.25
2234	A793	20h multi	.25	.25
2235	A794	30h multi	.25	.25
2236	A795	30h multi	.25	.25
2237	A796	60h multi	.25	.25
		Nos. 2233-2237 (5)	1.25	1.25

Fine Arts Academy, Bratislava, 30th anniv.; Slovak Technical University, 40th anniv.; Radio Symphony Orchestra, Bratislava, 30th anniv.; Young Pioneers, 30th anniv. and IYC; Peace Movement, 30th anniversary.

Prague Castle Art Type of 1971

3k, Burial crown of King Ottokar II. 3.60k, Portrait of Mrs. Reitmayer, by Karel Purkyne.

1979, May 9 ***Perf. 11½***

2238	A634	3k multi	2.10	1.75
2239	A634	3.60k multi	1.00	.60

Nos. 2238-2239 were each issued in sheets of 4. Value, set $15.

Arms of Vlachovo Brezi, 1538 — A797

Animals in Heraldry: 60h, Jesenik, 1509 (bear and eagle). 1.20k, Vysoke Myto, 1471 (St. George slaying dragon). 1.80k,Martin, 1854 (St. Martin giving coat to beggar). 2k, Zebrak, 1674 (mythological beast).

1979, May 25 ***Perf. 11½x12***

2240	A797	30h multi	.25	.25
2241	A797	60h multi	.25	.25
2242	A797	1.20k multi	.25	.25
2243	A797	1.80k multi	*1.25*	*.40*
2244	A797	2k multi	.80	.25
		Nos. 2240-2244 (5)	*2.80*	*1.40*

Forest, Thriving and Destroyed A798

Designs: 1.80k, Water. 3.60k, City. 4k, Cattle. All designs show good and bad environment, separated by exclamation point; Man and Biosphere emblem.

1979, June 22 **Engr.** ***Perf. 11½***

2245	A798	60h multi	.25	.25
2246	A798	1.80k multi	.30	.25
2247	A798	3.60k multi	*1.75*	*.75*
2248	A798	4k multi	1.25	.40
		Nos. 2245-2248 (4)	*3.55*	*1.65*

Man and Biosphere Program of UNESCO.
Nos. 2245-2248 were each issued in sheets of 10. Value, set $40.

Refinery, Smokestacks A799

Engraved and Photogravure

1979, Aug. 29 ***Perf. 11x11½***

2249	A799	30h multi	.25	.25

Slovak National Uprising, 35th anniversary.

Frog and Goat A800

Book Illustrations (IYC Emblem and): 40h, Knight on horseback. 60h, Maidens. 1k, Boy with sled following rooster. 3k, King riding flying beast.

1979, Apr. 2 ***Perf. 11½x11***

2250	A800	20h multi	.25	.25
2251	A800	40h multi	.25	.25
2252	A800	60h multi	.25	.25
2253	A800	1k multi	.25	.25
2254	A800	3k multi	*1.50*	*.50*
		Nos. 2250-2254 (5)	*2.50*	*1.50*

Prize-winning designs, 7th biennial exhibition of illustrations for children's books, Bratislava; International Year of the Child. Printed with labels showing story characters. Value, set with attached labels, $4.75.

"Bone Shaker" Bicycles, 1870 A801

Bicycles from: 20h, 1978. 40h, 1910. 60h, 1886. 3.60k, 1820.

1979, Sept. 14 ***Perf. 12x11½***

2255	A801	20h multi	.25	.25
2256	A801	40h multi	.25	.25
2257	A801	60h multi	.25	.25
2258	A801	2k multi	.40	.25
2259	A801	3.60k multi	1.50	.50
		Nos. 2255-2259 (5)	2.65	1.50

Bracket Clock, 18th Century A802

Designs: 18th century clocks.

1979, Oct. 1 ***Perf. 11½***

2260	A802	40h multi	.25	.25
2261	A802	60h multi	.25	.25
2262	A802	80h multi	.85	.25
2263	A802	1k multi	.25	.25
2264	A802	2k multi	.50	.25
		Nos. 2260-2264 (5)	2.10	1.25

Painting Type of 1967

Paintings: 1.60k, Sunday by the River, by Alois Moravec. 2k, Self-portrait, by Gustav Mally. 3k, Self-portrait, by Ilia Yefimovic Repin. 3.60k, Horseback Rider, by Jan Bauch. 5k, Dancing Peasants, by Albrecht Dürer.

1979, Nov. 27 **Engr.** ***Perf. 12***

2265	A565	1.60k multi	.40	.35
2266	A565	2k multi	.60	.50
2267	A565	3k multi	.60	.50
2268	A565	3.60k multi	2.00	1.75
2269	A565	5k multi	1.60	1.25
		Nos. 2265-2269 (5)	5.20	4.35

Nos. 2265-2269 were each issued in sheets of 4. Value, set $25.

Bratislava Type of 1977

Designs: 3k, Bratislava Castle on the Danube, by L. Janscha, 1787. 3.60k, Bratislava Castle, stone engraving by Wolf, 1815.

1979, Dec. 5

2270	A760	3k multi	1.25	.80
2271	A760	3.60k multi	1.80	1.50

Nos. 2270-2272 were each issued in sheets of 4. Value, set $15.

Stamp Day — A803

Engraved and Photogravure

1979, Dec. 18 ***Perf. 11½x12***

2272	A803	1k multi	.25	.25

Electronic Circuits — A804

Designs: 50h, Satellite dish. 2k, Airplane. 3k, Computer punch tape.

1979-80 **Photo.** ***Perf. 11½x12***

Coil Stamps

2273	A804	50h red	.25	.25
2274	A804	1k brown	.25	.25
2275	A804	2k green ('80)	.30	.25
2276	A804	3k lake ('80)	.45	.25
		Nos. 2273-2276 (4)	1.25	1.00

The 1k comes in two shades.

Runners and Dove A805

Engraved and Photogravure

1980, Jan. 29 ***Perf. 12x11½***

2289	A805	50h multi	.25	.25

50th Intl. Peace Marathon, Kosice, Oct. 4.

Downhill Skiing — A806

1980, Jan. 29 ***Perf. 11½x12***

2290	A806	1k shown	.30	.25
2291	A806	2k Speed skating	.95	.35
2292	A806	3k Four-man bobsled	.80	.35
		Nos. 2290-2292 (3)	2.05	.95

13th Winter Olympic Games, Lake Placid, NY, Feb. 12-24.

Basketball — A807

1980, Jan. 29 ***Perf. 11½***

2293	A807	40h shown	.25	.25
2294	A807	1k Swimming	.35	.25
2295	A807	2k Hurdles	1.50	.35
2296	A807	3.60k Fencing	1.10	.30
		Nos. 2293-2296 (4)	3.20	1.15

22nd Olympic Games, Moscow, 7/19-8/3.

Arms Type of 1977

1980, Feb. 20 ***Perf. 11½***

2297	A745	50h Bystrice Nad Pernstejnem	.25	.25
2298	A745	50h Kunstat	.25	.25
2299	A745	50h Rozmital Pod Tremsinem	.25	.25
2300	A745	50h Zlata Idka	.25	.25
		Nos. 2297-2300 (4)	1.00	1.00

Theatrical Mask — A808

Slovak National Theater, Actors — A809

1980, Mar. 1

2301	A808	50h multi	.25	.25
2302	A809	1k multi	.25	.25

50th Jiraskuv Hronov Theatrical Ensemble Review; Slovak National Theater, Bratislava, 60th anniversary.

Mouse in Space, Satellite — A810

Police Corps Banner, Emblem — A811

Intercosmos: 1k, Weather map, satellite. 1.60k, Intersputnik television transmission. 4k, Camera, satellite. 5k, Czech satellite station, 1978, horiz. 10k, Intercosmos emblem, horiz.

1980, Apr. 12 ***Perf. 11½x12, 12x11½***

2303	A810	50h multi	.25	.25
2304	A810	1k multi	.35	.25
2305	A810	1.60k multi	2.10	.25
2306	A810	4k multi	.90	.50
2307	A810	5k multi	1.25	.60
		Nos. 2303-2307 (5)	4.85	1.85

Souvenir Sheet

2308	A810	10k multi	3.25	2.50

Intercosmos cooperative space program.
No. 2305 was issued in a sheet of 10. Value, $25.
No. 2308 exists imperf. Value, $40.

1980, Apr. 17 ***Perf. 11½***

2309	A811	50h multi	.25	.25

National Police Corps, 35th anniversary.

Lenin's 110th Birth Anniversary — A812

Design: No. 2311, Engels's 160th birth anniv.

1980, Apr. 22

2310	A812	1k tan & brn	.25	.25
2311	A812	1k lt grn & brn	.25	.25

Old and Modern Prague, Czech Flag, Bouquet A813

Boy Writing "Peace" A814

Pact Members' Flags, Dove — A815

Czech and Soviet Arms, Prague and Moscow Views
A816

1980, May 6 *Perf. 12x11½*

2312 A813 50h multi .25 .25
2313 A814 1k multi .25 .25
2314 A815 1k multi .25 .25
2315 A816 1k multi .25 .25
Nos. 2312-2315 (4) 1.00 1.00

Liberation by Soviet army, 35th anniv.; Soviet victory in WWII, 35th anniv.; Signing of Warsaw Pact (Bulgaria, Czechoslovakia, German Democratic Rep., Hungary, Poland, Romania, USSR), 25th anniv.; Czechoslovak-Soviet Treaty of Friendship, Cooperation and Mutual Aid, 10th anniv.

Souvenir Sheet

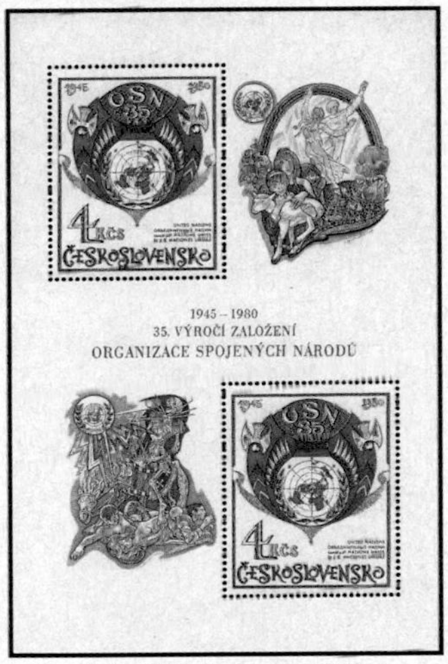

UN, 35th Anniv. — A817

1980, June 3 **Engr.** *Perf. 12*

2316 A817 Sheet of 2 3.50 2.75
a. 4k multicolored 1.50 1.25

Athletes Parading Banners in Strahov Stadium, Prague, Spartakiad Emblem — A818

Engraved and Photogravure

1980, June 3 *Perf. 12x11½*

2317 A818 50h shown .25 .25
2318 A818 1k Gymnast, vert. .25 .25

Spartakiad 1980, Prague, June 26-29.

Aechmea Fasciata — A819

A820

Flowers: 50ch, Gerbera Jamesonii. 1k, Aechmea fasciata. 2k, Strelitzia reginae. 4k, Paphiopedilum.

1980, Aug. 13 *Perf. 12*

2319 A819 50h multicolored .50 .25
2320 A819 1k multicolored 2.40 .80
2321 A819 2k multicolored .65 .25
2322 A819 4k multicolored 2.50 .40
Nos. 2319-2322 (4) 6.05 1.70

Olomouc and Bratislava Flower Shows.
Nos. 2319-2322 were each issued in sheets of 10. Value, set $70.

1980, Sept. 24 *Perf. 11½x12*

Designs: Folktale character embroideries.

2323 A820 50h Chad girl .25 .25
2324 A820 1k Punch and dog .25 .25
2325 A820 2k Dandy and Posy .75 .25
2326 A820 4k Lion and moon 1.30 .75
2327 A820 5k Wallachian dance .65 .25
Nos. 2323-2327 (5) 3.20 1.75

National Census
A821

1980, Sept. 24 *Perf. 12x11½*

2328 A821 1k multi .25 .25

Prague Castle Type of 1971

Designs: 3k, Old Palace gateway. 4k, Armorial lion, 16th century.

1980, Oct. 28 *Perf. 12*

2329 A634 3k multi 1.25 1.10
2330 A634 4k multi 1.00 .65

Nos. 2329-2330 were each issued in sheets of 4. Value, set $18.

Bratislava Type of 1977

3k, View across the Danube, by J. Eder, 1810. 4k, The Old Royal Bridge, by J.A. Lantz, 1820.

1980, Oct. 28

2331 A760 3k multi 1.60 1.40
2332 A760 4k multi 1.25 .80

Nos. 2331-2332 were each issued in sheets of 4. Value, set $16.

10th Anniversary of Socialist Youth Federation — A822

1980, Nov. 9 *Perf. 12x11½*

2333 A822 50h multi .25 .25

No. 2137 Overprinted 3. / MEZINARODNI VELETRH ZNAMEK / ESSEN '80 in Red

1980, Nov. 18

2334 A755 1.60k multi 20.00 15.00

Czechoslovak Day/ ESSEN '80, 3rd International Stamp Exhibition, No. 2334 has overprinted red marginal inscription.

Painting Type of 1967

Designs: 1k, Pavel Jozef Safarik, by Jozef B. Klemens. 2k, Peasant Revolt mosaic, Anna Podzemna. 3k, St. Lucia, 14th century statue. 4k, Waste Heaps, by Jan Zrzavy, horiz. 5k, Labor, sculpture by Jan Stursa.

1980, Nov. 27 **Engr.** *Perf. 12*

2335 A565 1k multi .95 1.10
2336 A565 2k multi 1.10 .95
2337 A565 3k multi .55 .50
2338 A565 4k multi .65 .55
2339 A565 5k multi .65 .55
Nos. 2335-2339 (5) 3.90 3.65

Nos. 2335-2339 were each issued in sheets of 4. Value, set $27.

Stamp Day — A823

Engraved and Photogravure

1980, Dec. 18 *Perf. 11½x12*

2340 A823 1k multi .25 .25

7th Five-year Plan, 1981-1985
A824

1981, Jan. 1 *Perf. 11½*

2341 A824 50h multi .25 .25

International Year of the Disabled
A825

1981, Feb. 24

2342 A825 1k multi .25 .25

Landau, 1800
A826

1981, Feb. 25 *Perf. 12x11½*

2343 A826 50h shown .25 .25
2344 A826 1k Mail coach, 1830 .25 .25
2345 A826 3.60k Mail sled, 1840 1.25 .60
2346 A826 5k 4-horse mail coach, 1860 .85 .45
2347 A826 7k Open carriage, 1840 1.25 .85
a. Sheet of 4 13.00 10.00
Nos. 2343-2347 (5) 3.85 2.40

WIPA '81 Intl. Philatelic Exhibition, Vienna, Austria, May 22-31. No. 2347a issued May 10.

Wolfgang Amadeus Mozart — A827

Famous Men: No. 2348, Josef Hlavka (1831-1908). No. 2349, Juraj Hronec (1881-1959). No. 2350, Jan Sverma (1901-44). No. 2351, Mikulas Schneider-Trnavsky (1881-1958). No. 2352, B. Bolzano (1781-1848). No. 2353, Dimitri Shostakovich, composer. No. 2354, George Bernard Shaw, playwright.

1981, Mar. 10 *Perf. 11½*

2348 A827 50h multi .25 .25
2349 A827 50h multi .25 .25
2350 A827 50h multi .25 .25
2351 A827 50h multi .25 .25
2352 A827 1k multi .75 .35
2353 A827 1k multi .25 .25
2354 A827 1k multi .25 .25
2355 A827 1k multi .25 .25
Nos. 2348-2355 (8) 2.50 2.10

Souvenir Sheet

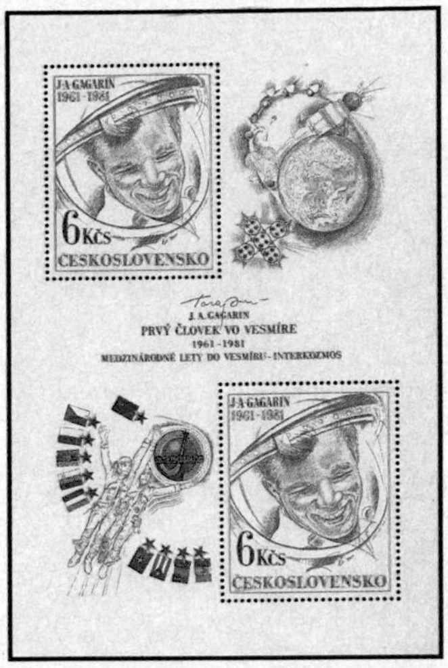

Yuri Gagarin — A828

1981, Apr. 5 *Perf. 12*

2356 A828 Sheet of 2 4.50 4.00
a. 6k multicolored 2.00 1.60

20th anniv. of 1st manned space flight.

Workers and Banner
A829

1981, Apr. 6 *Perf. 12x11½*

2357 A829 50h shown .25 .25
2358 A829 1k Hands holding banner .25 .25
2359 A829 4k Worker holding banner, vert. .35 .25
Nos. 2357-2359 (3) .85 .75

Czechoslovakian Communist Party, 60th anniv.

Congress Emblem, View of Prague — A830

1981, Apr. 6

2360 A830 50h shown .25 .25
2361 A830 1k Bratislava .25 .25

16th Communist Party Congress.

Agriculture Museum, 90th Anniv.
A831

Natl. Assembly Elections
A832

1981, May 14 *Perf. 11½x12*

2362 A831 1k multi .25 .25

1981, June 1

2363 A832 50h multi .25 .25

Bratislava Type of 1977

Designs: 3k, Bratislava Castle, by G.B. Probst, 1760. 4k, Grassalkovic Palace, by C. Bschor, 1815.

1981, June 10 *Perf. 12*

2364 A760 3k multi 1.50 1.40
2365 A760 4k multi 1.25 .90

Nos. 2364-2365 were each issued in sheets of 4. Value, set $18.

Uran and Red October (Health) Resorts A833

Successes of Socialist Achievements Exhibition: 1k, Brno-Bratislava Highway, Jihlava. 2k, Nuclear power station, Jaslovske Bohunice.

1981, June 10 *Perf. 12x11½*

2366 A833 80h multi .25 .25
2367 A833 1k multi .25 .25
2368 A833 2k multi .25 .25
Nos. 2366-2368 (3) .75 .75

Border Defense Units, 30th Anniv. A834

Civil Defense, 30th Anniv. A835

Union for Cooperation with the Army (SVAZARM), 30th Anniv. — A836

Intl.Youth Character Building Contest, Rysy Mtn., 25th Anniv. — A837

Engraved and Photogravure

1981, July 11 *Perf. 11½*

2369 A834 40h multi .25 .25
2370 A835 50h multi .25 .25
2371 A836 1k multi .25 .25
2372 A837 3.60k multi .75 .30
Nos. 2369-2372 (4) 1.50 1.05

30th Natl. Festival of Amateur Puppet Ensembles — A838

1981, July 2 *Perf. 11½*

2373 A838 2k Punch and Devil .50 .25

Souvenir Sheet

Guernica, by Pablo Picasso — A839

1981, July 2 **Engr.** *Perf. 11½x12*

2374 A839 10k multi 3.50 2.50

Picasso's birth centenary; 45th anniv. of Intl. Brigades in Spain.

Cat Holding Flower, by Etienne Delessert A840

8th Biennial Exhibition of Children's Book Illustrations (Designs by): 50h, Albin Brunovsky, vert. 1k, Adolf Born. 2k, Vive Tolli. 10k, Suekichi Akaba.

Engraved and Photogravure

1981, Sept. 5 *Perf. 11½*

2375 A840 50h multi .25 .25
2376 A840 1k multi .25 .25
2377 A840 2k multi .40 .25
2378 A840 4k multi .95 .40
2379 A840 10k multi 2.00 .75
Nos. 2375-2379 (5) 3.85 1.90

Prague Zoo, 50th Anniv. — A841

1981, Sept. 28 *Perf. 11½x12*

2380 A841 50h Gorillas .45 .25
2381 A841 1k Lions .80 .25
2382 A841 7k Przewalski's horses 2.25 .80
Nos. 2380-2382 (3) 3.50 1.30

Anti-smoking Campaign A842

1981, Oct. 27 *Perf. 12*

2383 A842 4k multi 1.00 .60

No. 2383 was issued in sheets of 10, containing 8 stamps and 2 labels. Values: single with label attached, $1.50; sheet, $14.

Prague Castle Art Type of 1971

Designs: 3k, Carved dragon, Palais Lobkovitz, 16th cent. 4k, St. Vitus Cathedral, by J. Sember and G. Dobler, 19th cent.

1981, Oct. 28

2384 A634 3k multi .75 .45
2385 A634 4k multi 1.75 1.40

Nos. 2384-2385 were each issued in sheets of 4. Value, set $13.

Painting Type of 1967

Designs: 1k, View of Prague, by Vaclav Hollar (1607-1677). 2k, Czechoslovak Academy medallion, engraved by Otakar Spaniel (1881-1955). 3k, Jihoceska Vysivka, by Zdenek Sklenar (b. 1910). 4k, Still Life, by A.M. Gerasimov (1881-1963). 5k, Standing Woman, by Pablo Picasso (1881-1973).

1981, Nov. 27 **Engr.** *Perf. 12*

2386 A565 1k multi 2.40 1.60
2387 A565 2k multi .65 .30
2388 A565 3k multi .80 .50
2389 A565 4k multi .95 .65
2390 A565 5k multi 2.40 1.25
Nos. 2386-2390 (5) 7.20 4.30

Nos. 2386-2390 were each issued in sheets of 4. Value, set $35.

Sheets of No. 2390 exist with center gutter inscribed with Philexfrance 82 and FIP emblems. Value, $22.

Stamp Day — A843

Engraved and Photogravure

1981, Dec. 18 *Perf. 11½x12*

2391 A843 1k Engraver Edward Karel .25 .25

Russian Workers' Party, Prague Congress, 70th Anniv. — A844

1982, Jan. 18 *Perf. 12*

2392 A844 2k Lenin .50 .25
a. Sheet of 4 *5.00 4.00*

No. 2392 issued in sheet of 8. Value $10.

1982 World Cup Soccer A845

Designs: Various soccer players.

1982, Jan. 29 *Perf. 12x11½*

2393 A845 1k multi .25 .25
2394 A845 3.60k multi .70 .30
2395 A845 4k multi 1.40 .50
Nos. 2393-2395 (3) 2.35 1.05

10th World Trade Union Congress, Havana — A846

Arms of Hrob — A847

1982, Feb. 10 *Perf. 11½*

2396 A846 1k multi .25 .25

1982, Feb. 10 *Perf. 12x11½*

Arms of various cities.

2397 A847 50h shown .25 .25
2398 A847 50h Nove Mesto Nad Metuji .25 .25
2399 A847 50h Trencin .25 .25
2400 A847 50h Mlada Boleslav .25 .25
Nos. 2397-2400 (4) 1.00 1.00

See Nos. 2499-2502, 2542-2544, 2595-2597, 2783-2786.

50th Anniv. of the Great Strike at Most — A848

1982, Mar. 23 *Perf. 11½*

2401 A848 1k multi .25 .25

60th Intl. Railway Union Congress — A849

1982, Mar. 23 *Perf. 12x11½*

2402 A849 6k Steam locomotive, 1922, electric, 1982 3.25 .95

10th Workers' Congress, Prague A850

George Dimitrov A851

1982, Apr. 15

2403 A850 1k multi .25 .25

1982, May 1

2404 A851 50h multi .25 .25

A852

Engravings: 40h, The Muse Euterpe Playing a Flute, by Crispin de Passe (1565-1637). 50h, The Lute Player, by Jacob de Gheyn (1565-1629). 1k, Woman Flautist, by Adriaen Collaert (1560-1618). 2k, Musicians in a Hostel, by Rembrandt (1606-1669). 3k, Hurdy-gurdy Player, by Jacques Callot (1594-1635).

1982, May 18 *Perf. 11½x12*

2405 A852 40h multi .25 .25
2406 A852 50h multi .25 .25
2407 A852 1k multi .25 .25
2408 A852 2k multi .30 .25
2409 A852 3k multi 1.10 .60
Nos. 2405-2409 (5) 2.15 1.60

10th Lidice Intl. Children's Drawing Contest — A853

1982, May 18

2410 A853 2k multi 1.60 1.25

Issued in sheets of 6. Value $10.

40th Anniv. of Destruction of Lidice and Lezaky — A854

1982, June 4 *Perf. 11½*

2411 A854 1k Girl, rose .45 .25
2412 A854 1k Hands, barbed wire .45 .25

Souvenir Sheet

UN Disarmament Conference — A855

1982, June 4 *Perf. 12*

2413 A855 Sheet of 2 12.00 8.00
a. 6k Woman holding doves 5.50 3.50

Souvenir Sheet

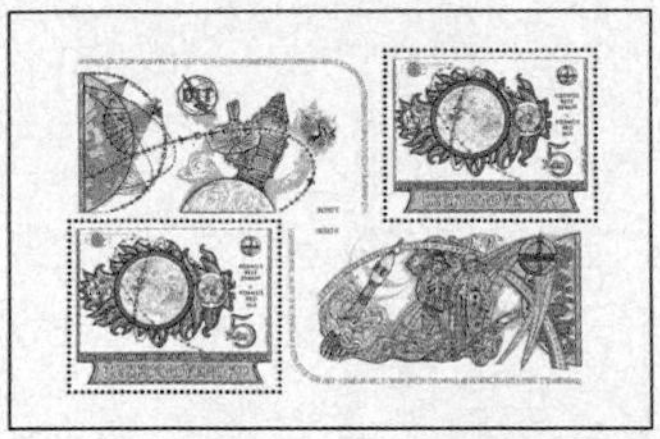

2nd UN Conference on Peaceful Uses of Outer Space, Vienna, Aug. 9-21 — A856

1982, Aug. 9 **Engr. & Photo.**

2414 A856 Sheet of 2 16.00 12.00
a. 5k multi 6.00 4.00

Krivoklat Castle A857

1982, Aug. 31 *Perf. 12x11½*

2415 A857 50h shown .25 .25
2416 A857 1k Statues (Krivoklat) .25 .25
2417 A857 2k Nitra Castle .30 .25
2418 A857 3k Pottery, lock (Nitra) .40 .35
a. Souv. sheet of 4, #2415-2418 2.00 1.60
Nos. 2415-2418 (4) 1.20 1.10

50th Anniv. of Zizkov Hill Natl. Monument — A858

1982, Sept. 16

2419 A858 1k multi .25 .25

Prague Castle Art Type of 1971

Designs: 3k, St. George and the Dragon, 1373. 4k, Tomb of King Vratislav I, 10th cent.

1982, Sept. 28 *Perf. 12*

2420 A634 3k multi 2.00 1.40
2421 A634 4k multi 1.10 1.10

Nos. 2420-2421 were each issued in sheets of 4. Value, set $13.

Bratislava Type of 1977

Designs: 3k, Paddle steamer, Parnik, 1818. 4k, View from Bridge, 19th cent.

1982, Sept. 29

2422 A760 3k multi 1.40 1.00
2423 A760 4k multi 1.10 1.00

Nos. 2422-2423 were each issued in sheets of 4. Value, set $18.

European Danube Commission — A859

1982, Sept. 29 *Perf. 11½x12*

2424 A859 3k Steamer, Bratislava Bridge .80 .35
a. Souvenir sheet of 4 5.00 4.00
2425 A859 3.60k Ferry, Budapest 1.25 .50
a. Souvenir sheet of 4 7.00 6.00

16th Communist Party Congress — A860

1982, Oct. 28 *Perf. 12x11½*

2426 A860 20h Agriculture .25 .25
2427 A860 1k Industry .25 .25
2428 A860 3k Engineering .35 .35
Nos. 2426-2428 (3) .85 .85

30th Anniv. of Academy of Sciences — A861

1982, Oct. 29 *Perf. 11½*

2429 A861 6k Emblem .90 .35

65th Anniv. of October Revolution — A862

Design: 1k, 60th anniv. of USSR.

1982, Nov. 7 *Perf. 12x11½*

2430 A862 50h multi .25 .25
2431 A862 1k multi .25 .25

Jaroslav Hasek, Writer, Sculpture by Josef Malejovsky — A863

Sculptures: 2k, Jan Zrzavy, painter and graphic artist, by Jan Simota. 4.40k, Leos Janacek, composer, by Milos Axman. 6k, Martin Kukucin, freedom fighter, by Jan Kulich. 7k, Peaceful Work, by Rudolf Pribis.

Engraved and Photogravure

1982, Nov. 26 *Perf. 11½x12*

2432 A863 1k multi .25 .25
2433 A863 2k multi .25 .25
2434 A863 4.40k multi .85 .25
2435 A863 6k multi 1.20 .30
2436 A863 7k multi 1.50 .75
Nos. 2432-2436 (5) 4.05 1.80

Nos. 2432-2436 were each issued in sheets of 4. Value, set $30.

Painting Type of 1967

1k, Revolution in Spain, by Josef Sima (1891-1971). 2k, Woman Dressing, by Rudolf Kremlicka (1886-1932). 3k, The Girl Bride, by Dezider Milly (1906-1971). 4k, Performers, by Jan Zelibsky (b. 1907). 5k, The Complaint of the Birds, by Emil Filla (1882-1953).

1982, Nov. 27 *Perf. 12*

2437 A565 1k multi .65 .45
2438 A565 2k multi 1.25 1.00
2439 A565 3k multi .85 .85
2440 A565 4k multi .85 .85
2441 A565 5k multi 2.00 1.00
Nos. 2437-2441 (5) 5.60 4.15

Nos. 2437-2441 were each issued in sheets of 4. Value, set $28.

Stamp Day — A864

1982, Dec. 8 *Perf. 11½*

2442 A864 1k Engraver Jaroslav Goldschmied (1890-1977) .25 .25

A865

A866

1983, Jan. 10 **Engr.** *Perf. 12x11½*

2443 A865 50h dark blue .25 .25

Pres. Gustav Husak, 70th birthday. See No. 2686.

1983, Feb. 24 **Engr. & Photo.**

Designs: 50h, Jaroslav Hasek (1882-1923), writer. 1k, Julius Fucik (1903-1943), antifascist martyr. 2k, Martin Luther (1483-1546). 5k, Johannes Brahms (1833-1897), composer.

2444 A866 50h multi .25 .25
2445 A866 1k multi .25 .25
2446 A866 2k multi .25 .25
a. Souvenir sheet of 4 24.00 12.50
2447 A866 5k multi .85 .25
Nos. 2444-2447 (4) 1.60 1.00

Nordposta '83 Intl. Stamp Exhibition, Hamburg.
No. 2446a issued Nov. 1.

Workers Marching A867

Family — A868

1983, Feb. 25 *Perf. 11½*

2448 A867 50h multi .25 .25
2449 A868 1k multi .25 .25

35th anniv. of "Victorious February" (50h), and Natl. Front (1k).

World Communications Year — A869

Perf. 11½, 12x11½ (2k)

1983, Mar. 16

2450 A869 40h multi .25 .25
2451 A869 1k multi .25 .25
2452 A869 2k multi .30 .25
2453 A869 3.60k multi .60 .25
Nos. 2450-2453 (4) 1.40 1.00

Various wave patterns. 2k, 40x23mm; 3.60k, 49x19mm.

7th World Ski-jumping Championships A870

1983, Mar. 16 *Perf. 11½*

2454 A870 1k multi .25 .25

Souvenir Sheet

5th Anniv. of Czechoslovak-USSR Intercosmos Cooperative Space Program — A871

1983, Apr. 12 *Perf. 12*

2455 A871 Sheet of 2 13.00 9.50
a. 10k multi 4.75 4.00

See No. 2226.

Protected Species — A872

1983, Apr. 28 *Perf. 12x11½*

2456 A872 50h Butterfly, violets .30 .25
2457 A872 1k Water lilies, frog .65 .25
2458 A872 2k Pine cones, crossbill .65 .30
2459 A872 3.60k Herons .80 .35
2460 A872 5k Gentians, lynx 1.10 .45
2461 A872 7k Stag 2.50 1.00
Nos. 2456-2461 (6) 6.00 2.60

A873

A874

Soviet Marshals.

1983, May 5 *Perf. 11½*

2462 A873 50h Ivan S. Konev .25 .25
2463 A873 1k Andrei I. Yeremenko .25 .25
2464 A873 2k Rodion J. Malinovsky .25 .25
Nos. 2462-2464 (3) .75 .75

30th anniv. of Czechoslovak-Soviet defense treaty.

1983, July 13 *Perf. 12*

2465 A874 2k multi .40 .25
a. Souvenir sheet of 4 6.50 5.50

World Peace and Life Congress, Prague.
No. 2465 issued in sheets of 8. Value $10.

Emperor Rudolf II by Adrian De Vries (1560-1626) A875

Art treasures of the Prague Castle: 5k, Kinetic relief, Timepiece, Rudolf Svoboda.

1983, Aug. 25 *Perf. 11½*

2466 A875 4k multi	.90	.60
2467 A875 5k multi	.90	.60

Nos. 2466-2467 were each issued in sheets of 6. Value, set $15.

See Nos. 2518-2519, 2610-2611, 2654-2655, 2717-2718, 2744-2745, 2792-2793.

9th Biennial of Illustrations for Children and Youth — A876

Illustrators: 50h, Oleg K. Zotov, USSR. 1k, Zbigniew Rychlicki, Poland. 4k, Lisbeth Zwerger, Austria. 7k, Antonio Dominques, Angola.

1983, Sept. 9 **Engr. & Photo.**

2468 A876 50h multi	.25	.25
2469 A876 1k multi	.25	.25
2470 A876 4k multi	.35	.25
2471 A876 7k multi	.75	.30
a. Souv. sheet of 4, #2468-2471	5.00	3.00
Nos. 2468-2471 (4)	1.60	1.05

World Communications Year — A877

Emblems and aircraft.

1983, Sept. 30 *Perf. 11½*

2472 A877 50h red & black	.25	.25
2473 A877 1k red & black, vert.	.25	.25
2474 A877 4k red & black	.75	.25
Nos. 2472-2474 (3)	1.25	.75

60th anniv. of the Czechoslovak Airlines.

16th Party Congress Achievements — A878

1983, Oct. 20 *Perf. 12x11½*

2475 A878 50h Civil engineering construction	.25	.25
2476 A878 1k Chemical industry	.25	.25
2477 A878 3k Health services	.40	.25
Nos. 2475-2477 (3)	.90	.75

Bratislava Type of 1977

Designs: 3k, Two sculptures, Viktor Tilgner (1844-96). 4k, Mirbachov Palace, 1939, by Julius Schubert (1888-1947).

1983, Oct. 28 *Perf. 12*

2478 A760 3k multi	1.50	1.25
2479 A760 4k multi	1.25	1.00

Nos. 2478-2479 were each issued in sheets of 4 stamps. Value, set $16.

Natl. Theater, Prague, Centenary — A879

1983, Nov. 8 **Engr.** *Perf. 11½*

2480 A879 50h Natl. Theater building	.25	.25
2481 A879 2k State Theater, Natl. Theater	.30	.25

Messenger of Mourning, by Mikolas Ales — A880

Designs: 2k, Genius, theater curtain by Vojtech Hynais (1854-1925). 3k, Music, Lyric drawings by Frantisek Zenisek (1849-1916). 4k, Symbolic figure of Prague, by Vaclav Brozik (1851-1901). 5k, Hradcany Castle, by Julius Marak (1832-1899).

1983, Nov. 18 **Engr.**

2482 A880 1k multi	1.20	.75
2483 A880 2k multi	1.50	1.10
2484 A880 3k multi	.90	.45
2485 A880 4k multi	1.40	.45
2486 A880 5k multi	1.10	.60
Nos. 2482-2486 (5)	6.10	3.35

Nos. 2482-2486 were each issued in sheets of 4 stamps. Value, set $35.

Warrior with Sword and Shield, Engraving, 17th Cent. — A881

Engravings of Costumes: 50h, Bodyguard of Rudolf II, by Jacob de Gheyn (1565-1629). 1k, Lady with Lace Collar, by Jacques Callot (1592-1635). 4k, Lady, by Vaclav Hollar (1607-77). 5k, Man, by Antoine Watteau (1684-1721).

Engraved and Photogravure

1983, Dec. 2 *Perf. 11½x12*

2487 A881 40h multi	.25	.25
2488 A881 50h multi	.25	.25
2489 A881 1k multi	.25	.25
2490 A881 4k multi	.75	.25
2491 A881 5k multi	1.25	.75
Nos. 2487-2491 (5)	2.75	1.75

Stamp Day — A882

1983, Dec. 18

2492 A882 1k Karl Seizinger (1889-1978), #114	.25	.25

Czechoslovak Federation, 15th Anniv. — A883

1984, Jan. 1 *Perf. 11½*

2493 A883 50h Bratislava, Prague Castles	.25	.25

35th Anniv. of COMECON A884

1984, Jan. 23

2494 A884 1k Headquarters, Moscow	.25	.25

1984 Winter Olympics A885

1984, Feb. 7 *Perf. 12x11½*

2495 A885 2k Cross-country skiing	.40	.25
2496 A885 3k Hockey	.50	.25
a. Souvenir sheet of 4	5.00	4.00
2497 A885 5k Biathlon	1.25	.35
Nos. 2495-2497 (3)	2.15	.85

Intl. Olympic Committee, 90th Anniv. — A886

1984, Feb. 7 *Perf. 11½x12*

2498 A886 7k Rings, runners, torch	1.25	.35

City Arms Type of 1982

1984, Mar. 1 *Perf. 12x11½*

2499 A847 50h Kutna Hora	.25	.25
2500 A847 50h Turnov	.25	.25
2501 A847 1k Martin	.25	.25
2502 A847 1k Milevsko	.25	.25
Nos. 2499-2502 (4)	1.00	1.00

Intercosmos Space Program — A887

Various satellites. Nos. 2503-2507 se-tenant with labels showing flags.

1984, Apr. 12 *Perf. 11½x12*

2503 A887 50h multi	.25	.25
2504 A887 1k multi	.25	.25
2505 A887 2k multi	.35	.25
2506 A887 4k multi	.75	.40
2507 A887 5k multi	1.40	.50
Nos. 2503-2507 (5)	3.00	1.65

Resistance Heroes — A888

Designs: 50h, Vendelin Opatrny (1908-44). 1k, Ladislav Novomesky (1904-76). 2k, Rudolf Jasiok (1919-44). 4k, Jan Nalepka (1912-43).

1984, May 9 *Perf. 11x11½*

2508 A888 50h multi	.25	.25
2509 A888 1k multi	.25	.25
2510 A888 2k multi	.30	.25
2511 A888 4k multi	.50	.25
Nos. 2508-2511 (4)	1.30	1.00

Music Year — A889

1984, May 11 *Perf. 11½*

2512 A889 50h Instruments	.25	.25
2513 A889 1k Organ pipes, vert.	.30	.25

Bratislava Type of 1977

Designs: 3k, Vintners' Guild arms, 19th cent. 4k, View of Bratislava (painting commemorating shooting competition, 1827).

1984, June 1 *Perf. 12*

2514 A760 3k multi	1.10	.85
2515 A760 4k multi	1.60	1.10

Nos. 2514-2515 were each issued in sheets of 4 stamps. Value, set $15.

Central Telecommunications Building, Bratislava — A890

1984, June 1 *Perf. 11½*

2516 A890 2k multi	.35	.25

A891

1984, June 12 *Perf. 12*

2517 A891 5k UPU emblem, dove, globe	3.25	2.75

1984 UPU Congress. Issued in sheet of 4 with and without Philatelic Salon text. Values, $40 with text, $12 without text.

Prague Castle Type of 1983

Designs: 3k, Crowing rooster, St. Vitus Cathedral, 19th cent. 4k, King David from the Roundnice, Book of Psalms illuminated manuscript, Bohemia, 15th cent.

1984, Aug. 9 **Engr. & Photo.**

2518 A875 3k multi	1.25	.80
2519 A875 4k multi	1.60	.50

Nos. 2518-2519 were each issued in sheets of 6 stamps. Value, set $18.

A893

Playing cards.

1984, Aug. 28 *Perf. 11½x12*

2520 A893 50h Jack of Spades, 16th cent.	.25	.25
2521 A893 1k Queen of spades, 17th cent.	.25	.25
2522 A893 2k 9 of hearts, 18th cent.	.25	.25
2523 A893 3k Jack of clubs, 18th cent.	.35	.25
2524 A893 5k King of hearts, 19th cent.	1.00	.25
Nos. 2520-2524 (5)	2.10	1.25

Slovak Natl. Uprising, 40th Anniv. A894

1984, Aug. 29 *Perf. 12x11½*

2525 A894 50h Family, factories, flowers	.25	.25

Battle of Dukla Pass (Carpathians), 40th Anniv. — A895

1984, Sept. 8 *Perf. 11½x12*
2526 A895 2k Soldiers, flag .40 .25

1984 Summer Olympics A896

1984, Sept. 9 *Perf. 12x11½*
2527 A896 1k Pole vault .25 .25
2528 A896 2k Bicycling .40 .25
2529 A896 3k Rowing .60 .35
2530 A896 5k Weight lifting 1.00 .45
a. Souv. sheet of 4, #2527-2530 4.00 3.25
Nos. 2527-2530 (4) 2.25 1.30

16th Party Congress Goals and Projects — A897

1984, Oct. 28 *Perf. 12x11½*
2531 A897 1k Communications .25 .25
2532 A897 2k Transportation .25 .25
2533 A897 3k Transgas pipeline .35 .25
a. Souvenir sheet of 3 2.00 1.60
Nos. 2531-2533 (3) .85 .75

Painting Type of 1967

1k, The Milevsky River, by Karel Stehlik (b. 1912). 2k, Under the Trees, by Viktor Barvitius (1834-1902). 3k, Landscape with Flowers, by Zolo Palugyay (1898-1935). 4k, King in Palace, Visehrad Codex miniature, 1085. 5k, View of Kokorin Castles, by Antonin Manes. Nos. 2534-2537 horiz.; issued in sheets of 4.

1984, Nov. 16 *Perf. 11½*
2534 A565 1k multi 3.00 .90
2535 A565 2k multi 3.00 .90
2536 A565 3k multi 2.00 .50
2537 A565 4k multi 3.00 .70
2538 A565 5k multi 3.00 .70
Nos. 2534-2538 (5) 14.00 3.70

Nos. 2534-2538 were each issued in sheets of 4 stamps. Value, set $60.

Students' Intl., 45th Anniv. A898

Birth Cent., Antonin Zapotocky A899

1984, Nov. 17
2539 A898 1k Head, dove .25 .25

Engr. & Photo.

1984, Dec. 18 *Perf. 11½*
2540 A899 50h multi .25 .25

Stamp Day — A900

1984, Dec. 18 *Perf. 11½x12*
2541 A900 1k Engraver Bohumil Heinz (1894-1940) .25 .25

City Arms Type of 1982

1985, Feb. 5 *Perf. 12x11½*
2542 A847 50h Kamyk nad Vltavou .25 .25
2543 A847 50h Havirov .25 .25
2544 A847 50h Trnava .25 .25
Nos. 2542-2544 (3) .75 .75

University of Applied Arts, Prague, Centenary — A901

1985, Feb. 6 *Perf. 11½x12*
2545 A901 3k Art and Pleasure, sculpture .40 .25

Trnava University, 350th Anniv. — A902

1985, Feb. 6 *Perf. 11½x12*
2546 A902 2k Town of Trnava .40 .25

Military Museum Exposition — A903

1985, Feb. 7 *Perf. 11½x12, 12x11½*
2547 A903 50h Armor, crossbow, vert. .25 .25
2548 A903 1k Medals, vert. .25 .25
2549 A903 2k Biplane, spacecraft .40 .25
Nos. 2547-2549 (3) .90 .75

Vladimir I. Lenin (1870-1924), 1st Chairman of Russia — A904

1985, Mar. 15 **Engr.** *Perf. 12*
2550 A904 2k multi .80 .40

No. 2550 printed in sheets of 6 stamps. Value $5.

UN 40th Anniv., Peace Year 1986 A905

1985, Mar. 15
2551 A905 6k UN, Peace Year emblems 2.75 2.40

Issued in sheets of 4 stamps. Value $12.

A906

A907

Engraved and Photogravure

1985, Apr. 5 *Perf. 11½*
2552 A906 4k Natl. arms, twig, crowd .60 .25

Kosice govt. plan, Apr. 5, 1945.

1985, Apr. 5
2553 A907 50h Natl. arms, flag, soldiers .25 .25

Natl. Security Forces, 40th anniv.

Halley's Comet, INTERCOSMOS Project Vega — A908

Design: Emblem, space platform, interstellar map, intercept data.

1985, Apr. 12 *Perf. 12x11½*
2554 Sheet of 2 12.00 9.50
a. A908 5k multicolored 5.00 3.25

Project Vega, a joint effort of the USSR, France, German Democratic Republic, Austria, Poland, Bulgaria and CSSR, was for the geophysical study of Halley's Comet, Dec. 1984-Mar. 1986.

European Ice Hockey Championships, Prague, Apr. 17-May 3 — A909

1985, Apr. 13
2555 A909 1k Hockey players, emblem .25 .25

No. 2555 Ovptd. "CSSR MISTREM SVETA" in Violet Blue

1985, May 31 *Perf. 12x11½*
2556 A909 1k multi 2.50 2.50

Natl. Chess Org., 80th Anniv. — A910

1985, Apr. 13 *Perf. 11½*
2557 A910 6k Emblem, game board, chessmen 1.25 .50

Anniversaries — A911

1985, May 5 *Perf. 11½x12*
2558 A911 1k May Uprising, 1945 .25 .25
2559 A911 1k Soviet Army in CSSR, 1945 .25 .25
2560 A911 1k Warsaw Treaty, 1950 .25 .25
2561 A911 1k Czech-Soviet Treaty, 1970 .25 .25
Nos. 2558-2561 (4) 1.00 1.00

Spartakiad '85, Strahov Stadium, Prague, June 27 — A912

Designs: 50h, Gymnasts warming up with rackets and balls. 1k, Rhythmic gymnastics floor exercise, Prague Castle.

1985, June 3 *Perf. 11½, 11½x12*
2562 A912 50h multi .25 .25

Size: 53x22mm

2563 A912 1k multi .25 .25

WWII Anti-Fascist Political Art — A913

Drawings and caricatures: 50h, Fire, and From the Concentration Camp, by Joseph Capek (1887-1945). 2k, The Conference on Disarmament in Geneva, 1927 and The Prophecy of Three Parrots, 1933, by Frantisek Bidlo (1895-1945). 4k, The Unknown Warrior to Order, 1936, and The Almost Peaceful Dove, 1937, by Antonin Pelc (1895-1967).

1985, June 4 *Perf. 12x11½*
2564 A913 50h multi .25 .25
2565 A913 2k multi .30 .25
2566 A913 4k multi .60 .40
Nos. 2564-2566 (3) 1.15 .90

Helsinki Conference on European Security and Cooperation, 10th Anniv. — A914

1985, July 1 **Engr. & Photo.**
2567 A914 7k multi 2.25 1.50
a. Souvenir sheet of 4 12.00 8.00

An imperf. souv. sheet similar to No. 2567a was issued June 1, 1988 for FINLANDIA '88 and PRAGA '88. Value $40.

12th World Youth Festival, Moscow A915

1985, July 2
2568 A915 1k Kremlin, youths .25 .25

A916

1985, Sept. 3 *Perf. 11½*
2569 A916 50h multi .25 .25

Federation of World Trade Unions, 40th anniv.

Bratislava Type of 1977

Designs: 3k, Castle and river, lace embroidery by Elena Holeczyova (1906-1983). 4k, Pottery cups and mugs, 1600-1500 B.C.

1985, Sept. 4 **Engr.** *Perf. 12*
2570 A760 3k multi 1.60 .45
2571 A760 4k multi 2.10 .60

Nos. 2570-2571 were each issued in sheets of 4 stamps. Value, set $18.

A918

Children's book illustrations: 1k, Rocking Horse, by Kveta Pacovska, USSR. 2k, Fairies, by Gennadij Spirin, USSR. 3k, Butterfly and Girl, by Kaarina Kaila, Finland. 4k, Boy and Animals, by Erick Ingraham, US.

Engraved and Photogravure

1985, Sept. 5 *Perf. 11½*

2572 A918 1k multi .25 .25
2573 A918 2k multi .30 .25
2574 A918 3k multi .45 .25
2575 A918 4k multi .60 .35
a. Souv. sheet of 4, #2572-2575 4.00 3.00
Nos. 2572-2575 (4) 1.60 1.10

10th biennial of illustrations.

5-Year Development Plan — A919

1985, Oct. 28 *Perf. 12x11½*

2576 A919 50h Construction machinery .25 .25
2577 A919 1k Prague subway, map .25 .25
2578 A919 2k Modern textile spinning .25 .25
Nos. 2576-2578 (3) .75 .75

16th Communist Party Congress goals.

Prague Castle — A920

A921

Engr., Engr. & Photo. (3k)

1985, Oct. 28 *Perf. 12*

2579 A920 2k Presidential Palace Gate, 1768 .40 .40
2580 A920 3k St. Vitus' Cathedral .50 .50

Nos. 2579-2580 were each issued in sheets of 6 stamps. Value, set $9.

Engraved and Photogravure

1985, Nov. 23 *Perf. 11½x12*

Glassware: 50h, Pitcher, Near East, 4th cent. 1k, Venetian pitcher, 16th cent. 2k, Bohemian goblet, c. 1720. 4k, Harrachov Bohemian vase, 18th cent. 6k, Jablonec Bohemian vase, c. 1900.

2581 A921 50h multi .25 .25
2582 A921 1k multi .25 .25
2583 A921 2k multi .30 .25
2584 A921 4k multi .50 .25
2585 A921 6k multi 1.00 .35
Nos. 2581-2585 (5) 2.30 1.35

Arts and Crafts Museum, Prague, cent.

Painting Type of 1967

Designs: 1k, Young Woman in a Blue Gown, by Jozef Ginovsky (1800-1857). 2k, Lenin on the Charles Bridge, Prague, 1952, by Martin Sladky (b. 1920). 3k, Avenue of Poplars, 1935, by Vaclav Rabas (1885-1954). 4k, The Martyrom of St. Dorothea, 1516, by Hans Baldung Grien (c. 1484-1545). 5k, Portrait of Jasper Schade van Westrum, 1645, by Frans Hals (c. 1581-1666).

1985, Nov. 27 **Engr.** *Perf. 12*

2586 A565 1k multi 1.60 .80
2587 A565 2k multi 1.10 .35
2588 A565 3k multi 1.50 .35
2589 A565 4k multi .90 .50
2590 A565 5k multi .90 .50
Nos. 2586-2590 (5) 6.00 2.50

Nos. 2586-2590 were each issued in sheets of 4 stamps. Value, set $30.

Bohdan Roule (1921-1960), Engraver — A922

Engraved and Photogravure

1985, Dec. 18 *Perf. 11½x12*

2591 A922 1k multicolored .25 .25

Stamp Day 1985.

Intl. Peace Year — A923

1986, Jan. 2

2592 A923 1k multi .25 .25

Philharmonic Orchestra, 90th Anniv. — A924

1986, Jan. 2 *Perf. 11½*

2593 A924 1k Victory Statue, Prague .25 .25

EXPO '86, Vancouver A925

Design: Z 50 LS monoplane, Cenyerth Prague-Kladno locomotive, Sahara Desert rock drawing, 5th-6th cent. B.C.

1986, Jan. 23 *Perf. 11½*

2594 A925 4k multicolored .75 .25

City Arms Type of 1982

1986, Feb. 10 *Perf. 12x11½*

Size: 42x54mm

2595 A847 50h Myjava .25 .25
2596 A847 50h Vodnany .25 .25
2597 A847 50h Zamberk .25 .25
Nos. 2595-2597 (3) .75 .75

17th Natl. Communist Party Congress, Prague, Mar. 24 — A926

1986, Mar. 20 *Perf. 11½*

2598 A926 50h shown .25 .25
2599 A926 1k Industry .25 .25

Natl. Communist Party, 65th Anniv. — A927

1986, Mar. 20 *Perf. 12x11½*

2600 A927 50h Star, man, woman .25 .25
2601 A927 1k Hammer, sickle, laborers .25 .25

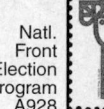

Natl. Front Election Program A928

1986, Mar. 28

2602 A928 50h multi .25 .25

Karlovy Vary Intl. Film Festival, 25th Anniv. — A929

1986, Apr. 3 *Perf. 11½*

2603 A929 1k multi .25 .25

A930

1986, Apr. 8 **Engr. & Photo.**

2604 A930 1k multi .25 .25

Spring of Prague Music Festival.

A931

1986, Apr. 25

2605 A931 50h multi .40 .25

Prague-Moscow air service, 50th anniv.

Intl. Olympic Committee, 90th Anniv. — A932

1986, May 12 *Perf. 11½x12*

2606 A932 2k multi .30 .25

1986 World Cup Soccer Championships, Mexico — A933

1986, May 15 *Perf. 12x11½*

2607 A933 4k multi .80 .40

Women's World Volleyball Championships, Prague — A934

1986, May 19

2608 A934 1k multi .25 .25

Souvenir Sheet

Intl. Philatelic Federation, FIP, 60th Anniv. — A935

1986, June 3 **Engr.** *Perf. 12*

2609 A935 20k multi 6.50 5.00

Exists imperf and with perforations between stamps omitted. Values, $12 and $25, respectively.

Prague Castle Type of 1983

Designs: 2k, Jewelled funerary pendant, 9th cent. 3k, Allegory of Blossoms, sculpture by Jaroslav Horejc (1886-1983), St. Vitus' Cathedral.

1986, June 6 **Engr.** *Perf. 12*

2610 A875 2k multi .30 .30
2611 A875 3k multi .70 .45

Nos. 2610-2611 were each issued in sheets of 6 stamps. Value, set $10.

UN Child Survival Campaign — A937

Toys.

Engraved and Photogravure

1986, Sept. 1 *Perf. 11½*

2612 A937 10h Rooster .25 .25
2613 A937 20h Horse and rider .25 .25
2614 A937 1k Doll .25 .25
2615 A937 2k Doll, diff. .50 .25
2616 A937 3k Tin omnibus, c. 1910 .65 .30
Nos. 2612-2616 (5) 1.90 1.30

UNICEF, 40th anniv.

Registration, Cent. — A938

1986, Sept. 2 *Perf. 11½x12*

2617 A938 4k Label, mail coach .45 .25

Bratislava Type of 1977

1986, Sept. 11 **Engr.** *Perf. 12*

2618 A760 3k Sigismund Gate 1.25 .80
2619 A760 4k St. Margaret, bas-relief 1.25 .65

Nos. 2618-2619 were each issued in sheets of 4 stamps. Value, set $12.

Owls — A939

Engraved and Photogravure

1986, Sept. 18 *Perf. 11½*

2620 A939 50h Bubo bubo .80 .25
2621 A939 2k Asio otus .95 .35
2622 A939 3k Strix aluco 1.60 .35
2623 A939 4k Tyto alba 1.60 .45
2624 A939 5k Asio flammeus 2.25 6.75
Nos. 2620-2624 (5) 7.20 8.15

Souvenir Sheet

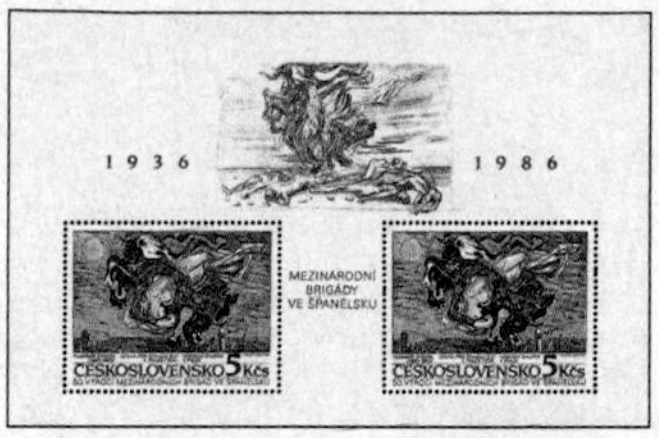

Intl. Brigades in Spain — A940

Theater curtain: Woman Savaged by Horses, 1936, by Vladimir Sychra (1903-1963), Natl Gallery, Prague.

1986, Oct. 1 Engr. *Perf. 12*
2625 A940 Sheet of 2 4.50 3.50
a. 5k multi 2.00 1.25

Locomotives and Streetcars — A941

Engraved and Photogravure

1986, Oct. 6 *Perf. 12x11½*
2626 A941 50h KT-8 .25 .25
2627 A941 1k E458.1 .25 .25
2628 A941 3k T466.2 .75 .30
2629 A941 5k M152.0 .80 .25
Nos. 2626-2629 (4) 2.05 1.05

Paintings in the Prague and Bratislava Natl. Galleries — A942

Designs: 1k, The Circus Rider, 1980, by Jan Bauch (b. 1898). 2k, The Ventriloquist, 1954, by Frantisek Tichy (1896-1961). 3k, In the Circus, 1946, by Vincent Hloznik (b. 1919). 6k, Clown, 1985, by Karel Svolinsky (1896-1986).

1986, Oct. 13 Engr. *Perf. 12*
2630 A942 1k multi 1.25 .65
2631 A942 2k multi 1.60 .85
2632 A942 3k multi 1.60 .85
2633 A942 6k multi 1.10 .95
Nos. 2630-2633 (4) 5.55 3.30

Nos. 2630-2633 were each issued in sheets of 4 stamps. Value, set $30.

Painting Type of 1967

1k, The Czech Lion, May 1918, by Vratislav H. Brunner (1886-1928). 2k, Boy with Mandolin, 1945, by Jozef Sturdik (b. 1920). 3k, Metra Building, 1984, by Frantisek Gross (1909-1985). 4k, Portrait of Maria Maximiliana at Sternberk, 1665, by Karel Skreta (1610-1674). 5k, Adam & Eve, 1538, by Lucas Cranach (1472-1553).

1986, Nov. 3 Engr. *Perf. 12*
2634 A565 1k multi 3.00 2.25
2635 A565 2k multi 3.00 2.25
2636 A565 3k multi 3.00 2.25
2637 A565 4k multi 3.00 2.25
2638 A565 5k multi 3.00 2.25
Nos. 2634-2638 (5) 15.00 11.25

Nos. 2634-2638 were each issued in sheets of 4 stamps. Value, set $100.

Stamp Day — A943

Design: V.H. Brunner (1886-1928), stamp designer, and No. 88.

Photo. & Engr.

1986, Dec. 18 *Perf. 11½x12*
2639 A943 1k multicolored .25 .25

World Cyclocross Championships, Jan. 24-25, Central Bohemia — A944

1987, Jan. 22 *Perf. 11½*
2640 A944 6k multi .80 .25

Czechoslovakian Bowling Union, 50th Anniv. — A945

1987, Jan. 22 *Perf. 11½*
2641 A945 2k multi .35 .25

State Decorations — A946

Designs: 50h, Gold Stars of Socialist Labor and Czechoslovakia. 2k, Order of Klement Gottwald. 3k, Order of the Republic. 4k, Order of Victorious February. 5k, Order of Labor.

1987, Feb. 4 *Perf. 12x11½*
2642 A946 50h multi .25 .25
2643 A946 2k multi .25 .25
2644 A946 3k multi .30 .25
2645 A946 4k multi .45 .25
2646 A946 5k multi .60 .40
Nos. 2642-2646 (5) 1.85 1.40

Butterflies — A947

1987, Mar. 4
2647 A947 1k Limenitis populi .80 .25
2648 A947 2k Smerinthus ocellatus 1.25 .30
2649 A947 3k Pericallia matronula 1.60 .45
2650 A947 4k Saturnia pyri 1.60 .45
Nos. 2647-2650 (4) 5.25 1.45

Natl. Nuclear Power Industry A948

1987, Apr. 6
2651 A948 5k multi .60 .25

11th Revolutionary Trade Union Movement Congress, Apr. 14-17, Prague — A949

1987, Apr. 7 *Perf. 11½*
2652 A949 1k multi .25 .25

Souvenir Sheet

INTERCOSMOS, 20th Anniv. — A950

Cosmonauts Alexei Gubarev of the USSR & Vladimir Remek of Czechoslovakia, rocket & emblem.

1987, Apr. 12 Engr. *Perf. 12*
2653 A950 Sheet of 2 8.00 6.50
a. 10k multi 3.25 2.00
b. Souv. sheet of 4, litho. & engr., imperf. 10.00 8.00

No. 2653b issued Nov. 15, 1987, and exists in two formats with either exhibition embelm or "Dni Nametove Filatelie" at top.

Prague Castle Type of 1983

Designs: 2k, Three Saints, stained-glass window detail, c. 1870, St. Vitus Cathedral, by Frantisek Sequens (1830-1896). 3k, Coat of Arms, New Land Rolls Hall, 1605.

1987, May 9 *Perf. 11½*
2654 A875 2k multi .40 .30
2655 A875 3k dk red, slate gray & yel org .60 .45

Nos. 2634-2638 were each issued in sheets of 6 stamps. Value, set $9.

PRAGA '88 A951

Photo. & Engr.

1987, May 12 *Perf. 12x11½*
2656 A951 3k Telephone, 1894 .80 .25
2657 A951 3k Postal van, 1924 .80 .30
2658 A951 4k Locomotive tender, 1907 .80 .30
2659 A951 4k Tram, 1900 .80 .30
2660 A951 5k Steam roller, 1936 .80 .30
Nos. 2656-2660 (5) 4.00 1.45

Printed in sheets of 8 + 2 labels picturing telephone or vehicles. Value $40.

Nos. 2657-2658 were also printed in sheets of 4 + label picturing vehicles. Value, $30 for both sheets.

Destruction of Lidice and Lezaky, 45th Anniv. — A952

Drawings: No. 2661, When the Fighting Ended, 1945, by Pavel Simon. No. 2662, The End of the game, 1945, by Ludmila Jirincova.

1987, June *Perf. 11½*
2661 A952 1k blk, cerise & vio .25 .25
2662 A952 1k blk, gold, pale lil & cerise .25 .25

Union of Czechoslovakian Mathematicians and Physicists, 125th Anniv. — A953

Designs: No. 2663, Prague Town Hall mathematical clock, Theory of Functions diagram. No. 2664, J.M. Petzval (1807-1891), C. Strouhal (1850-1922) and V. Jarnik (1897-1970). No. 2665, Geographical measurement from A.M. Malletta's book, 1672, earth fold and Brownian motion diagrams.

1987, July 6 *Perf. 11½x12*
2663 A953 50h multi .25 .25
2664 A953 50h multi .25 .25
2665 A953 50h multi .25 .25
Nos. 2663-2665 (3) .75 .75

A954

Award-winning illustrations.

1987, Sept. 3 *Perf. 11½*
2666 A954 50h Asun Balzola, Spain .25 .25
2667 A954 1k Frederic Clement, France .25 .25
2668 A954 2k Elzbieta Gaudasinska, Poland .40 .25
a. Souv. sheet of 2 + label 2.50 1.75
2669 A954 4k Marija Lucija Stupica, Yugoslavia .80 .50
Nos. 2666-2669 (4) 1.70 1.25

11th Biennial of Children's Book Illustration, Sept. 11-Oct. 30, Bratislava.

A955

1987, Sept. 23
2670 A955 50h Eternal flame, flower .25 .25

Theresienstadt Memorial for the victims from 23 European countries who died in the Small Fortress, Terezin, a Nazi concentration camp.

Socialist Communications Organization, 30th Anniv. — A956

1987, Sept. 23
2671 A956 4k Emblem, satellite, dish receiver .40 .25

Jan Evangelista Purkyne (1787-1869), Physiologist A957

1987, Sept. 30
2672 A957 7k multicolored .80 .25

Views of Bratislava — A958

Designs: 3k, Male and female figures supporting an oriel, Arkier Palace, c. 1552. 4k, View of Bratislava from Ware Conterfactur de Stadt Presburg, from an engraving by Hans Mayer, 1563.

1987, Oct. 1 Engr. *Perf. 12*
2673 A958 3k multicolored .50 .35
2674 A958 4k multicolored .70 .45

Each printed in sheets of 4 with Bratislava Castle (from Mayer's engraving) between. Value, set $6.50.

See Nos. 2719-2720, 2763-2764, 2800-2801.

Type of 1974
Photo. & Engr.

1987, Nov. 1 *Perf. 12x11½*

2675	A699	1k Post rider	.25	.25

PRAGA '88, Aug. 26-Sept. 4, 1988. No. 2675 printed se-tenant with label picturing exhibition emblem. Value for single with attached label 40c.

October Revolution, Russia, 70th Anniv. — A959

Establishment of the Union of Soviet Socialist Republics, 65th Anniv. — A960

1987, Nov. 6 *Perf. 12x11½*

2676	A959	50h multicolored	.25	.25
2677	A960	50h multicolored	.25	.25

Art Type of 1974

Paintings in national galleries: 1k, Enclosure of Dreams, by Kamil Lhotak (b. 1912). 2k, Tulips, by Ester Simerova-Martincekova (b. 1909). 3k, Triptych with Bohemian Landscape, by Josef Lada (1887-1957). 4k, Accordion Player, by Josef Capek (1887-1945). 5k, Self-portrait, by Jiri Trnka (1912-1969).

1987, Nov. 18 **Engr.** *Perf. 12*

2678	A700	1k multi	3.25	.75
2679	A700	2k multi	4.50	1.60
2680	A700	3k multi	4.00	1.10
2681	A700	4k multi	2.75	.80
2682	A700	5k multi	4.25	1.25
		Nos. 2678-2682 (5)	18.75	5.50

Czech and Slovak art.

Nos. 2678-2682 were each issued in sheets of 4. Value, set $80.

69th Stamp Day — A961

Portrait of Jacob Obrovsky (1882-1949), stamp designer, Bohemian Lion (Type SP1), sketch of a lion and PRAGA '88 emblem.

Photo. & Engr.

1987, Dec. 18 *Perf. 11½x12*

2683	A961	1k multicolored	.25	.25

No. 2683 printed in sheet of four with eight labels se-tenant with stamps, inscribed "100 Years of the National Philatelic Movement in Czechoslovakia" in Czech. The four labels between the "blocks of six" are blank. Value, sheet $3.

Czechoslovak Republic, 70th Anniv. — A962

1988, Jan. 1 *Perf. 12x11½*

2684	A962	1k Woman, natl. arms, linden branch	.25	.25

Natl. Front, 40th Anniv. — A963

1988, Feb. 25 *Perf. 11½*

2685	A963	50h multicolored	.25	.25

Husak Type of 1983
Photo. & Engr.

1988, Jan. 10 *Perf. 12x11½*

2686	A865	1k brt rose & dk carmine	.25	.25

Olympics — A965

1988, Feb. 1 *Perf. 11½x12*

2687	A965	50h Ski jumping, ice hockey	.25	.25
2688	A965	1k Basketball, soccer	.25	.25
2689	A965	6k Discus, weight lifting	.80	.40
		Nos. 2687-2689 (3)	1.30	.90

Exist in souv. sheets of 2, imperf. between and in souv. sheets of 2, imperf. Value, each set, $16.

Victorious February, 40th Anniv. — A966

Statue of Klement Gottwald by Rudolf Svoboda.

1988, Feb. 25 *Perf. 11½*

2690	A966	50h multicolored	.25	.25

No. 2690 exists in a souvenir sheet of two No. 2690 and two postally invalid imperf impressions of No. 637. Value $9. Sheet exists imperf. Value $12.

Classic Automobiles — A967

1988, Mar. 1 *Perf. 12x11½*

2691	A967	50h	1914 Laurin & Klement	.25	.25
2692	A967	1k	1902 Tatra NW Type B	.25	.25
2693	A967	2k	1905 Tatra NW Type E	.30	.25
2694	A967	3k	1929 Tatra 12 Normandie	.60	.25
2695	A967	4k	1899 Meteor	.80	.40
a.			Bklt. pane, 2 3k, 3 4k + label	6.00	6.00
			Complete booklet, #2695a	7.00	
			Nos. 2691-2695 (5)	2.20	1.40

Postal Museum, 70th Anniv. A968

Praga '88 emblem and: 50h, Postman, Malostranske Namesti Square p.o., Prague, c. 1742, and Velka Javorina television transmitter, 1979. 1k, Telecommunications Center, Mlada Boleslav, 1986, and Carmelite Street p.o., Prague, c. 1792. 2k, Prague 1 (1873) and Bratislava 56 (1984) post offices. 4k, Communications Center, Prachatice (1982), postman and Maltetske Nameski Square p.o., Prague, c. 1622.

1988, Mar. 10

2696	A968	50h multi	.25	.25
2697	A968	1k multi	.25	.25
2698	A968	2k multi	.25	.25
2699	A968	4k multi	.45	.25
a.		Souv. sheet, 2 ea #2698-2699	2.25	1.25
		Nos. 2696-2699 (4)	1.20	1.00

In No. 2699a the top pair of Nos. 2698-2699 is imperf. at top and sides.

A969

1988, Mar. 29 *Perf. 11½*

2700	A969	50h multicolored	.25	.25

Matice Slovenska Cultural Assoc., 125th anniv.

A970

PRAGA '88. (Exhibition emblem and aspects of the Museum of Natl. Literature, Prague): 1k, Gate and distant view of museum. 2k, Celestial globe, illuminated manuscript, bookshelves and ornately decorated ceiling. 5k, Illuminated "B" and decorated binder of a medieval Bible. 7k, Celestial globe, illuminated manuscript, Zodiacal signs (Aries and Leo), view of museum.

1988, May 12 **Photo. & Engr.**

2701	A970	1k multicolored	.30	.25
a.		Souvenir sheet of 4	1.50	1.25
2702	A970	2k multicolored	.65	.40
a.		Souvenir sheet of 4	3.25	2.00
2703	A970	5k multicolored	.95	.60
a.		Souvenir sheet of 4	5.75	4.75
2704	A970	7k multicolored	2.00	.95
a.		Souvenir sheet of 4	11.00	9.00
b.		Souv. sheet of 4, imperf., #2701-2704	4.00	3.50
		Nos. 2701-2704 (4)	3.90	2.20

PRAGA '88 — A971

Exhibition emblem and fountains, Prague.

1988, June 1 *Perf. 11½x12*

2705	A971	1k Waldstein Palace	.35	.25
2706	A971	2k Old town square	.45	.25
2707	A971	3k Charles University	.90	.25
2708	A971	4k Prague Castle	1.25	.30
a.		Souv. sheet of 4, #2705-2708	4.00	2.00
		Nos. 2705-2708 (4)	2.95	1.05

Souvenir Sheet

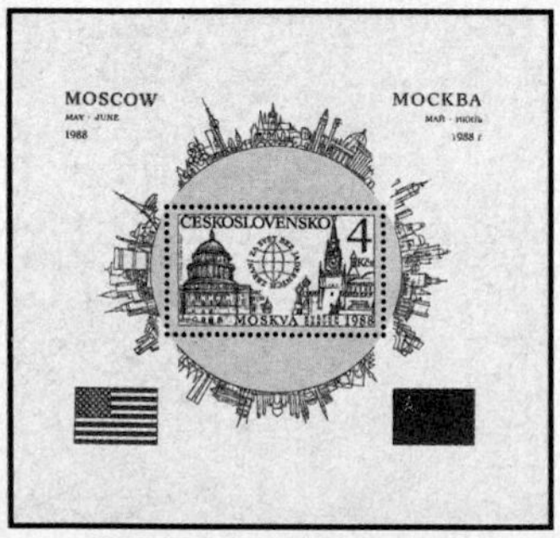

Soviet-US Summit Conference on Arms Reduction, Moscow — A972

Design: The Capitol, Washington, and the Kremlin, Moscow.

1988, June 1 *Perf. 12x11½*

2709	A972	4k blue blk, dark red & gold	2.50	1.50

Exists imperf. Value $8.

PRAGA '88 A973

Exhibition emblem and modern architecture, Prague: 50h, Trade Unions Central Recreation Center. 1k, Koospol foreign trade company. 2k, Motol Teaching Hospital. 4k, Culture Palace.

1988, July 1 *Perf. 12x11½*

2710	A973	50h multicolored	.25	.25
2711	A973	1k blk, lt blue & bister	.25	.25
2712	A973	2k multicolored	.25	.25
a.		Souv. sheet, 2 1k, 2 2k + 4 labels, imperf.	2.00	1.50
2713	A973	4k multicolored	.50	.35
a.		Souv. sheet, 2 50h, 2 4k + 4 labels, imperf.	2.00	1.50
		Nos. 2710-2713 (4)	1.25	1.10

Souvenir Sheet

PRAGA '88 — A974

Design: Exhibition emblem and Alfons Mucha (1860-1939), designer of first Czech postage stamp.

1988, Aug. 18 **Engr.** *Perf. 12*

2714	A974	Sheet of 2	5.50	3.25
a.		5k multicolored	2.40	1.25

Czech postage stamps, 70th anniv.

Souvenir Sheets

PRAGA '88 — A975

5k, *Turin, Monte Superga,* by Josef Navratil (1798-1865), Postal Museum, Prague.

Details of *Bacchus and Ariadne,* by Sebastiano Ricci (1659-1734), Natl. Gallery, Prague: No. 2716a, Ariadne. No. 2716b, Bacchus and creatures.

1988

2715	A975	Sheet of 2	6.50	4.00
a.		5k multi	2.75	1.60
2716	A975	Sheet of 2	10.50	6.00
a.-b.		10k any single	4.80	2.40

No. 2716 exists with emblem and inscription "DEN F.I.P. JOURNEE DE LA FEDERATION INTERNATIONALE DE PHILATELIE." Value $12.

Issue dates: 5k, Aug. 19; 10k, Aug. 26.

Prague Castle Type of 1983

2k, Pottery jug, 17th cent. 3k, *St. Catherine with Angel*, 1580, by Paolo Veronese.

1988, Sept. 28 Engr. *Perf. 12*

2717 A875 2k shown .50 .50
2718 A875 3k multi 1.25 .70

Nos. 2717-2718 were each issued in sheets of 6. Value, set $12.

Bratislava Views Type of 1987

3k, *Hlavne Square, circa 1840* an etching by R. Alt-Sandman, 1840. 4k, *Ferdinand House, circa 1850*, a pen-and-ink drawing by V. Reim.

1988, Oct. 19

2719 A958 3k multicolored .50 .50
2720 A958 4k multicolored 1.25 1.25

Nos. 2719-2720 were each issued in sheets of 4. Value, set $9.

Art Type of 1974

Paintings in natl. galleries: 2k, *With Bundles*, 1931, by Martin Benka (1888-1971). 6k, *Blue Bird*, 1903, by Vojtech Preissig (1873-1944). 7k, *A Jaguar Attacking a Rider*, c. 1850, by Eugene Delacroix (1798-1863).

1988, Nov. 17 Engr. *Perf. 12*

2721 A700 2k multicolored 3.00 1.40
2722 A700 6k multicolored 4.75 2.00
2723 A700 7k multicolored 4.75 2.00
Nos. 2721-2723 (3) 12.50 5.40

Czech and Slovak art.

Nos. 2721-2723 were each issued in sheets of 4. Value, set $55.

Stamp Day — A978

Design: 1k, Jaroslav Benda (1882-1970), illustrator and stamp designer.

Photo. & Engr.

1988, Dec. 18 *Perf. 11½x12*

2724 A978 1k multicolored .25 .25

Paris-Dakar Rally — A979

Trucks: 50h, Earth, Motokov Liaz. 1k, Liaz, globe. 2k, Earth, Motokov Tatra. No. 607. 4k, Map of racecourse, turban, Tatra.

1989, Jan. 2 *Perf. 12x11½*

2725 A979 50h multicolored .25 .25
2726 A979 1k multicolored .30 .25
2727 A979 2k multicolored .45 .25
2728 A979 4k multicolored .80 .30
Nos. 2725-2728 (4) 1.80 1.05

Czechoslovakian Federation, 20th Anniv. — A980

1989, Jan. 1

2729 A980 50h multicolored .25 .25

Jan Botto (1829-1881) A981

Taras Grigorievich Shevchenko (1814-1861) A982

Jean Cocteau (1889-1963) A983

Charlie Chaplin (1889-1977) A984

Jawaharlal Nehru (1889-1964) and "UNESCO" — A985

Famous men: No. 2732, Modest Petrovich Musorgsky (1839-1881).

Photo. & Engr.

1989, Mar. 9 *Perf. 12x11½*

2730 A981 50h brn blk & lt blue green .25 .25
2731 A982 50h shown .25 .25
2732 A982 50h multicolored .25 .25
2733 A983 50h red brn, grnh blk & org brn .25 .25
2734 A984 50h blk, int blue & dark red .25 .25
2735 A985 50h brn blk & lt yel green .25 .25
Nos. 2730-2735 (6) 1.50 1.50

Shipping Industry A986

1989, Mar. 27

2736 A986 50h Republika .25 .25
2737 A986 1k Pionyr, flags .25 .25
2738 A986 2k Brno, flags .35 .25
2739 A986 3k Trinec .60 .25
2740 A986 4k Flags, mast, Orlik .80 .30
2741 A986 5k Vltava, communication hardware 1.00 .30
Nos. 2736-2741 (6) 3.25 1.60

Pioneer Organization, 40th Anniv. — A987

Photo. & Engr.

1989, Apr. 20 *Perf. 11½*

2742 A987 50h multi .25 .25

Art Type of 1974

Details of *Feast of Rose Garlands*, 1506, by Albrecht Durer, Natl. Gallery, Prague: a, Virgin and Child. b, Angel playing mandolin.

1989, Apr. 21 Engr. *Perf. 12*

Miniature Sheet

2743 Sheet of 2 10.00 5.00
a.-b. A700 10k any single 4.50 2.00

Prague Castle Art Type of 1983

2k, Bas-relief picturing Kaiser Karl IV, from Kralovske tomb by Alexander Colin (c. 1527-1612). 3k, Self-portrait, by V.V. Reiner (1689-1743).

1989, May 9 Photo. & Engr.

2744 A875 2k dark red, sepia & buff .40 .30
2745 A875 3k multi .60 .40

Nos. 2744-2745 were each issued in sheets of 6. Value, set $7.

Souvenir Sheet

PHILEXFRANCE '89, French Revolution Bicent. — A988

1989, July 14 Engr. *Perf. 12*

2746 A988 5k brt blue, blk & dk red 2.00 1.50

Haliaeetus albicilla — A989

Photo. & Engr.

1989, July 17 *Perf. 12x11½*

2747 A989 1k multicolored .50 .25

World Wildlife Fund — A990

Toads and newts.

1989, July 18 *Perf. 11½x12*

2748 A990 2k Bombina bombina 1.40 .35
2749 A990 3k Bombina variegata 1.70 .45
2750 A990 4k Triturus alpestris 1.90 .65
2751 A990 5k Triturus montandoni 2.25 .85
Nos. 2748-2751 (4) 7.25 2.30

Slovak Folk Art Collective, 40th Anniv. — A991

1989, Aug. 29 *Perf. 12x11½*

2752 A991 50h multicolored .25 .25

Slovak Uprising, 45th Anniv. — A992

Photo. & Engr.

1989, Aug. 29 *Perf. 11½x12*

2753 A992 1k multicolored .25 .25

A993

A994

Award-winning illustrations.

1989, Sept. 4 *Perf. 11½*

2754 A993 50h Hannu Taina, Finland .25 .25
2755 A993 1k Aleksander Aleksov, Bulgaria .25 .25
2756 A993 2k Jurgen Spohn, West Berlin .25 .25
2757 A993 4k Robert Brun, Czechoslovakia .75 .25
a. Souvenir sheet of 2 2.00 .80
Nos. 2754-2757 (4) 1.50 1.00

12th Biennial of Children's Book Illustration, Bratislava.

1989, Sept. 5 Engr. *Perf. 11½x12*

Poisonous mushrooms: 50h, Nolanea verna. 1k, Amanita phalloides. 2k, Amanita virosa. 3k, Cortinarius orellanus. 5k, Galerina marginata.

2758 A994 50h multicolored .30 .25
2759 A994 1k multicolored .40 .40
2760 A994 2k multicolored .55 .50
2761 A994 3k multicolored .90 .70
2762 A994 5k multicolored 1.00 .70
Nos. 2758-2762 (5) 3.15 2.55

Nos. 2758-2762 were each issued in sheets of 10. Value, set $40.

Bratislava Views Type of 1987

Views of Devin, a Slavic castle above the Danube, Bratislava.

1989, Oct. 16 Engr. *Perf. 12*

2763 A958 3k Castle, flower .65 .65
2764 A958 4k Castle, urn .85 .85

Nos. 2763-2764 were each issued in sheets of 4. Value, set $7.

Jan Opletal (1915-39) — A996

Photo. & Engr.

1989, Nov. 17 *Perf. 12x11½*

2765 A996 1k multicolored .25 .25

Intl. Student's Day. Funeral of Opletal, a Nazi victim, on Nov. 15, 1939, sparked student demonstrations that resulted in the closing of all universities in occupied Bohemia and Moravia.

Art Type of 1974

Paintings in Natl. Galleries: 2k, *Nirvana*, c. 1920, by Anton Jasusch (1882-1965). 4k, *Winter Evening in Town*, c. 1907, by Jakub Schikaneder (1855-1924), horiz. 5k, *The Bakers*, 1926, by Pravoslav Kotik (1889-1970), horiz.

1989, Nov. 27 Engr. *Perf. 12*

2766 A700 2k multicolored .90 .55
2767 A700 4k multicolored 1.60 1.10
2768 A700 5k multicolored 1.50 1.10
Nos. 2766-2768 (3) 4.00 2.75

Nos. 2766-2768 were each issued in sheets of 4. Value, set $17.

Stamp Day — A997

Design: Portrait of Cyril Bouda, stamp designer, art tools and falcon.

Photo. & Engr.

1989, Dec. 18 *Perf. 11½x12*

2769 A997 1k multicolored .25 .25

A998

Photo. & Engr.

1990, Jan. 8 *Perf. 11½x12*

2770 A998 1k multicolored .60 .25

UNESCO World Literacy Year. Printed se-tenant with inscribed label picturing UN and UNESCO emblems. Value, single with label attached 75c.

A999

Famous men: No. 2771, Karel Capek, writer. No. 2772, Thomas G. Masaryk. 1k, Lenin. 2k, Emile Zola, French writer. 3k, Jaroslav Heyrovsky (1890-1987), chemical physicist. 10k, Bohuslav Martinu (1890-1959), composer.

1990, Jan. 9 *Perf. 11½*

2771 A999 50h multicolored .25 .25
2772 A999 50h multicolored .25 .25
2773 A999 1k multicolored .25 .25
2774 A999 2k multicolored .30 .25
2775 A999 3k multicolored .50 .30
2776 A999 10k multicolored 1.60 .90
Nos. 2771-2776 (6) 3.15 2.20

Nos. 2771, 2775-2776 inscribed "UNESCO."

Pres. Vaclav Havel A1000

Handball Players A1001

1990, Jan. 9 *Perf. 12x11½*

2777 A1000 50h red, brt vio & bl .30 .25

See Nos. 2879, 2948.

1990, Feb. 1 *Perf. 11½*

2778 A1001 50h multicolored .25 .25

1990 Men's World Handball Championships, Czechoslovakia.

Flora — A1002

Flowers: 50h, Antirrhinum majus. 1k, Zinnia elegans. 3k, Tigridia pavonia. 5k, Lilium candidum.

Photo. & Engr.

1990, Mar. 1 *Perf. 11½*

2779 A1002 50h multicolored .65 .25
2780 A1002 1k multicolored .90 .25
2781 A1002 3k multicolored 1.25 .30

Perf. 12x12½

2782 A1002 5k multicolored 1.60 .90
Nos. 2779-2782 (4) 4.40 1.70

No. 2782 was issued in a sheet of 10. Value, $20.

City Arms Type of 1982

Photo. & Engr.

1990, Mar. 28 *Perf. 12x11½*

2783 A847 50h Prostejov .25 .25
2784 A847 50h Bytca .25 .25
2785 A847 50h Sobeslav .25 .25
2786 A847 50h Podebrady .25 .25
Nos. 2783-2786 (4) 1.00 1.00

A1003

1990, Apr. 16 *Perf. 11½x12*

2787 A1003 1k brn vio, rose & buff .60 .25

Visit of Pope John Paul II.

World War II Liberation A1004

Photo. & Engr.

1990, May 5 *Perf. 11½*

2788 A1004 1k multicolored .25 .25

Souvenir Sheet

150th Anniv. of the Postage Stamp — A1005

1990, May 6 **Engr.** *Perf. 12*

2789 A1005 7k multicolored 4.00 1.50

Stamp World London 90.

A1006

Photo. & Engr.

1990, May 8 *Perf. 11½*

2790 A1006 1k multicolored .60 .25

World Cup Soccer Championships, Italy.

A1007

1990, June 1

2791 A1007 1k multicolored .60 .25

Free elections.

Prague Castle Type of 1983

1990, June 6, 1990 **Engr.**

2792 A875 2k Gold and jeweled hand .60 .30
2793 A875 3k King Otakar II's Seal .90 .45

Art treasures of Prague Castle.

Nos. 2792-2793 were each issued in sheets of 6. Value, set $12.

Helsinki Conference, 15th Anniv. — A1008

Photo & Engr.

1990, June 21 *Perf. 12x11½*

2794 A1008 7k multicolored 1.10 .60

Dr. Milada Horakova A1009

1990, June 25 *Perf. 12x11½*

2795 A1009 1k multicolored .30 .25

Intercanis Dog Show, Brno — A1010

Designs: 50h, Poodles, 1k, Afghan hound, Irish wolfhound, greyhound. 4k, Czech terrier, bloodhound, Hannoverian hound. 7k, Cavalier King Charles Spaniel, cocker spaniel, American cocker spaniel.

1990, July 2

2796 A1010 50h multicolored .65 .25
2797 A1010 1k multicolored 1.00 .25
2798 A1010 4k multicolored 1.60 .45
2799 A1010 7k multicolored 2.25 .75
Nos. 2796-2799 (4) 5.50 1.70

Bratislava Art Type of 1987

1990 **Engr.** *Perf. 12*

2800 A958 3k Ancient Celtic coin .80 .40
2801 A958 4k Gen. Milan Stefanik .80 .50

Issue dates: 3k, Sept. 29. 4k, July 21.

Nos. 2800-2801 were each issued in sheets of 4. Value, set $8.

Grand Pardubice Steeplechase, Cent. — A1011

Photo. & Engr.

1990, Sept. 7 *Perf. 12x11½*

2802 A1011 50h multicolored .25 .25
2803 A1011 4k multi, diff. .70 .35

Protected Animals — A1012

Litho. & Engr.

1990, Oct. 1 *Perf. 12x11*

2804 A1012 50h Marmota marmota 1.00 .25
2805 A1012 1k Felis silvestris 1.60 .25
2806 A1012 4k Castor fiber 1.75 .45
2807 A1012 5k Plecotus auritus 2.25 .75
Nos. 2804-2807 (4) 6.60 1.70

Conf. of Civic Associations, Helsinki — A1013

Litho. & Engr.

1990, Oct. 15 *Perf. 12x11½*

2808 A1013 3k blue, gold & yel .50 .30

Christmas — A1014

Photo. & Engr.

1990, Nov. 15 *Perf. 11½x12*

2809 A1014 50h multicolored .25 .25

Painting Type of 1967

Works of art: 2k, Krucemburk by Jan Zrzavy (1890-1977), horiz. 3k, St. Agnes of Bohemia from the St. Wenceslas Monument, Prague by Josef V. Myslbek (1848-1922). 4k, The Slavs in their Homeland by Alfons Mucha (1860-1939). 5k, St. John the Baptist by Auguste Rodin (1840-1917).

1990, Nov. 27 **Engr.** *Perf. 11½*

2810 A565 2k multicolored 1.50 .50
2811 A565 3k multicolored 1.75 1.75
2812 A565 4k multicolored 2.10 .60
2813 A565 5k multicolored 2.50 .60
Nos. 2810-2813 (4) 7.85 3.45

Nos. 2810-2813 were each issued in sheets of 4. Value, set $35.

Karel Svolinsky (1896-1986), Vignette from No. 1182 — A1016

1990, Dec. 18 **Photo. & Engr.**

2814 A1016 1k multicolored .25 .25

Stamp Day.

A1017

A1018

1991, Jan. 10 *Perf. 11½*

2815 A1017 1k multicolored .30 .25

European Judo Championships, Prague.

1991, Jan. 10

Design: A. B. Svojsik (1876-1938), Czech Scouting Founder.

2816 A1018 3k multicolored 1.00 .25

Scouting in Czechoslovakia, 80th Anniv.

Bethlehem Chapel, Prague, 600th Anniv. — A1019

1991, Feb. 4 *Perf. 12x11½*

2817 A1019 50h multicolored .25 .25

Wolfgang Amadeus Mozart (1756-1791), Old Theatre — A1020

1991, Feb. 4
2818 A1020 1k multicolored .25 .25

Steamship Bohemia, 150th Anniv. — A1021

1991, Feb. 4 ***Perf. 11½x12***
2819 A1021 5k multicolored 1.00 .30

Famous Men A1022

Designs: No. 2820, Antonin Dvorak (1841-1904), composer. No. 2821, Andrej Kmet (1841-1908), botanist. No. 2822, Jaroslav Seifert (1901-1986), poet, Nobel laureate for Literature. No. 2823, Jan Masaryk (1886-1948), diplomat. No. 2824, Alois Senefelder (1771-1834), lithographer.

1991, Feb. 18 ***Perf. 12x11½***
2820 A1022 1k multicolored .25 .25
2821 A1022 1k multicolored .30 .25
2822 A1022 1k multicolored .40 .25
2823 A1022 1k multicolored .50 .25
2824 A1022 1k multicolored .60 .25
Nos. 2820-2824 (5) 2.05 1.25

Nos. 2820-2824 printed with se-tenant labels.
See No. 2831.

Europa — A1023

A1024

Photo. & Engr.

1991, May 6 ***Perf. 11½x12***
2825 A1023 6k blk, bl & red 2.50 .75

Photo. & Engr.

1991, May 10 ***Perf. 11½x12***
2826 A1024 1k multicolored .25 .25

General Exhibition in Prague, cent.

Antarctic Treaty, 30th Anniv. A1025

1991, May 20 ***Perf. 12x11½***
2827 A1025 8k multicolored 1.75 .60

Castles — A1026

1991, June 3 ***Perf. 11½***
2828 A1026 50h Blatna .40 .25
2829 A1026 1k Bouzov .50 .25
2830 A1026 3k Kezmarok .60 .25
Nos. 2828-2830 (3) 1.50 .75

Famous Men Type

Design: Jan Palach (1948-1969), Student.

Photo. & Engr.

1991, Aug. 9 ***Perf. 12x11½***
2831 A1022 4k black 2.00 .30

Printed se-tenant with label.

Scenic Views — A1027

Photo. & Engr.

1991, Aug. 28 ***Perf. 11½***
2832 A1027 4k Krivan mountains 1.00 .60
2833 A1027 4k Rip mountain 1.00 .60

A1028

Illustrations by: 1k, Binette Schroeder, Germany. 2k, Stasys Eidrigevicius, Poland.

Photo. & Engr.

1991, Sept. 2 ***Perf. 11½***
2834 A1028 1k multicolored .40 .25
2835 A1028 2k multicolored .40 .25

13th Biennial Exhibition of Children's Book Illustrators, Bratislava.

A1029

Design: Father Andrej Hlinka (1864-1938), Slovak nationalist.

1991, Sept. 27 **Engr.** ***Perf. 11½***
2836 A1029 10k blue black 1.60 .30

Art of Prague and Bratislava A1030

Designs: No. 2837, Holy Infant of Prague. No. 2838, Blue Church of Bratislava.

1991, Sept. 30
2837 A1030 3k multicolored 1.25 .75
2838 A1030 3k multicolored 1.25 .75

Nos. 2837-2838 were each issued in sheets of 8. Value, set $20.

Flowers — A1031

Photo. & Engr.

1991, Nov. 3 ***Perf. 12x11½***
2839 A1031 1k Gagea bohemica .40 .25
2840 A1031 2k Aster alpinus .75 .25
2841 A1031 5k Fritillaria meleagris 2.00 .30
2842 A1031 11k Daphne cneorum 3.25 .45
Nos. 2839-2842 (4) 6.40 1.25

Painting Type of 1967

Paintings: 2k, Everyday Homelife by Max Ernst. 3k, Lovers by Auguste Renoir. 4k, Head of Christ by El Greco. 5k, Coincidence by Ladislav Guderna. 7k, Two Maidens by Utamaro.

1991, Nov. 3 **Engr.** ***Perf. 11½***
2843 A565 2k multicolored 1.25 .45
2844 A565 3k multicolored 1.60 .65
2845 A565 4k multicolored 2.40 .75
2846 A565 5k multicolored 2.40 .95
2847 A565 7k multicolored 3.25 1.60
Nos. 2843-2847 (5) 10.90 4.40

Nos. 2843-2847 were each issued in sheets of 4. Value, set $47.50.

Christmas — A1033

1991, Nov. 19
2848 A1033 50h multicolored .30 .25

Stamp Day — A1034

Martin Benka (1888-1971), stamp engraver.

Photo. & Engr.

1991, Dec. 18 ***Perf. 11½x12***
2849 A1034 2k multicolored .45 .25

1992 Winter Olympics, Albertville — A1035

1992, Jan. 6 ***Perf. 11½***
2850 A1035 1k Biathlon .25 .25

Photo. & Engr.

1992, May 21 ***Perf. 11½***
2851 A1035 2k Tennis .30 .25

1992 Summer Olympics, Barcelona.

Souvenir Sheet

Jan Amos Komensky (Comenius), Educator — A1036

1992, Mar. 5 **Engr.**
2852 A1036 10k multicolored 5.00 4.75

World Ice Hockey Championships, Prague and Bratislava — A1037

1992, Mar. 31 **Photo. & Engr.**
2853 A1037 3k multicolored .75 .25

Traffic Safety A1038

1992, Apr. 2
2854 A1038 2k multicolored .50 .25

Expo '92, Seville — A1039

1992, Apr. 2
2855 A1039 4k multicolored .75 .25

Discovery of America, 500th Anniv. — A1040

1992, May 5 **Engr.**
2856 A1040 22k multicolored 2.75 2.75

Europa. Printed in sheets of 8. Value $25.

Czechoslovak Military Actions in WWII — A1041

Designs: 1k, J. Kubis and J. Gabcik, assassins of Reinhard Heydrich, 1942. 2k, Pilots flying for France and Great Britain. 3k, Defense of Tobruk. 6k, Capture of Dunkirk, 1944-45.

1992, May 21 **Engr.** ***Perf. 12x11½***
2857 A1041 1k multicolored .50 .25
2858 A1041 2k multicolored .60 .25
2859 A1041 3k multicolored .75 .25
2860 A1041 6k multicolored 1.60 .35
Nos. 2857-2860 (4) 3.45 1.10

A1042

A1043

Photo. & Engr.

1992, June 10 ***Perf. 11½***
2861 A1042 2k multicolored .30 .25

Czechoslovakian Red Cross.

1992, June 30
2862 A1043 1k multicolored .30 .25

Junior European Table Tennis Championships, Topolcany.

Beetles A1044

1992, July 15

2863 A1044 1k Polyphylla fullo .80 .25
2864 A1044 2k Ergates faber 1.10 .40
2865 A1044 3k Meloe violaceus 2.25 .55
2866 A1044 4k Dytiscus latissimus 2.25 .75
Nos. 2863-2866 (4) 6.40 1.95

The 1k exists with denomination omitted.

Troja Castle A1045

1992, Aug. 28 Engr. *Perf. 11½*

2867 A1045 6k shown 2.75 1.00
2868 A1045 7k Statue of St. Martin, vert. 4.00 1.10
2869 A1045 8k Lednice Castle 4.00 1.25
Nos. 2867-2869 (3) 10.75 3.35

Nos. 2867-2869 were each issued in sheets of 8. Value, set $85.

Chrudim Church Type of 1971

Photo. & Engr.

1992, Aug. 28 *Perf. 11½x11*

2870 A629 50h multicolored .75 .25

Postal Bank — A1045a

Photo. & Engr.

1992, Aug. 28 *Perf. 11½x12*

2870A A1045a 20k multicolored 5.00 1.10

Antonius Bernolak, Georgius Fandly — A1046

Photo. & Engr.

1992, Oct. 6 *Perf. 12x11½*

2871 A1046 5k multicolored 1.50 .50

Slovakian Educational Society, bicent.

Cesky Krumlov — A1046a

Photo. & Engr.

1992, Oct. 19 *Perf. 11½x12*

2871A A1046a 3k brick red & brn .90 .25

See No. 2890.

Painting Type of 1967

6k Old Man on a Raft, by Koloman Sokol. 7k, Still Life of Grapes and Raisins, by Georges Braque, horiz. 8k, Abandoned Corset, by Toyen.

Perf. 11½x12, 12x11½

1992, Nov. 2 Engr.

2872 A565 6k multicolored 2.50 .95
2873 A565 7k multicolored 4.00 1.10
2874 A565 8k multicolored 4.00 1.25
Nos. 2872-2874 (3) 10.50 3.30

Nos. 2872-2874 were each issued in sheets of 4. Value, set $45.

Christmas — A1047

Photo. & Engr.

1992, Nov. 9 *Perf. 12x11½*

2875 A1047 2k multicolored .80 .25

Jindra Schmidt (1897-1984), Graphic Artist and Engraver — A1048

Photo. & Engr.

1992, Dec. 18 *Perf. 11½x12*

2876 A1048 2k multicolored .80 .25

Stamp Day.

On January 1, 1993, Czechoslovakia split into Czech Republic and Slovakia. Czech Republic listings continue here. Slovakia can be found in Volume 5.

CZECH REPUBLIC

AREA — 30,449 sq. mi.
POP. — 10,280,513 (1999 est.)

Natl. Arms A1049

Photo. & Engr.

1993, Jan. 20 *Perf. 11*

2877 A1049 3k multicolored .45 .25

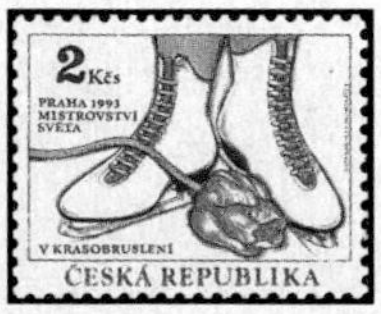

1993 World Figure Skating Championships, Prague A1050

1993, Feb. 25 *Perf. 11½x11*

2878 A1050 2k multicolored .30 .25

Havel Type of 1990 Inscribed "Ceska Republika"

Photo. & Engr.

1993, Mar. 2 *Perf. 12x11½*

2879 A1000 2k vio, vio brn & blue .30 .25

St. John Nepomuk, Patron Saint of Czechs, 600th Death Anniv. — A1051

1993, Mar. 11

2880 A1051 8k multicolored 1.00 .35

See Germany No. 1776; Slovakia No. 158.

Holy Hunger, by Mikulas Medek — A1052

1993, Mar. 11 *Perf. 11½*

2881 A1052 14k multicolored *6.00 2.00*

Europa.

Sacred Heart Church, Prague A1053

1993, Mar. 30 Engr. *Perf. 11½*

2882 A1053 5k multicolored 2.75 .35

Brevnov Monastery, 1000th Anniv. — A1054

Litho. & Engr.

1993, Apr. 12 *Perf. 12x11½*

2883 A1054 4k multicolored .55 .25

1993 Intl. Junior Weight Lifting Championships, Cheb — A1055

Photo. & Engr.

1993, May 12 *Perf. 11½*

2884 A1055 6k multicolored .85 .35

Clock Tower and Church, Brno — A1056

1993, June 16 Engr. *Perf. 12x11½*

2885 A1056 8k multicolored 3.00 3.00

Brno, 750th anniv.

Arrival of St. Cyril and St. Methodius, 1130th Anniv. — A1057

1993, June 22 Photo. & Engr.

2886 A1057 8k multicolored 1.00 .50

See Slovakia No. 167.

Souvenir Sheet

State Arms — A1058

1993, June 22 *Perf. 11½*

2887 A1058 8k Sheet of 2 2.40 2.40

Architecture Type of 1992 Inscribed "Ceska Republika" and

A1059

Cities: 1k, Ceske Budejovice. 2k, Usti Nad Labem. No. 2890, like #2871A. No. 2891, Brno. 5k, Plzen. 6k, Slany. 7k, Ostrava. 8k, Olomouc. 10k, Hradec Kralove. 20k, Prague. 50k, Opava.

Perf. 12x11½, 11½x12

1993-94 Photo. & Engr.

2888 A1059 1k dp cl & org .25 .25
2889 A1059 2k red vio & bl .75 .25
2890 A1046a 3k gray bl & red .75 .25
Complete booklet, 5 #2890 4.50
2891 A1059 3k dk bl & red .25 .25
Complete booklet, 5 #2891 3.75
2892 A1059 5k bluish green & brn .45 .25
2893 A1059 6k grn & org yel .55 .30
2894 A1059 7k blk brn & grn .65 .30
2895 A1059 8k dp vio & yel .70 .30
2896 A1059 10k olive gray & red .90 .40
2897 A1059 20k red & blue 1.90 .75
2898 A1059 50k brn & grn 4.50 1.75
Nos. 2888-2898 (11) 11.65 5.05

Issued: No. 2891, 3/30/94; 6k, 10/1/94; 7k, 11/23/94; others, 7/1/93.

World Rowing Championships, Racice A1060

Photo. & Engr.

1993, Aug. 18 *Perf. 11½*

2901 A1060 3k multicolored .50 .25

A1061

Trees — A1062

Famous men: 2k, August Sedlacek (1843-1926), historian. 3k, Eduard Cech (1893-1960), mathematician.

1993, Aug. 26 *Perf. 12x11½*

2902 A1061 2k multicolored .40 .25
2903 A1061 3k multicolored .55 .25

1993, Oct. 26 *Perf. 11½*

2904 A1062 5k Quercus robur .75 .30
2905 A1062 7k Carpinus betulus 1.00 .40
2906 A1062 9k Pinus silvestris 1.50 .50
Nos. 2904-2906 (3) 3.25 1.20

See Slovakia Nos. 160-162.

Christmas — A1063

Photo. & Engr.

1993, Nov. 8 *Perf. 11½*

2907 A1063 2k multicolored .30 .25

Painting Type of 1967 Inscribed "CESKA REPUBLIKA"

Paintings: 9k, Strahovska Madonna, by "Bohemian Master" in the year 1350. 11k, Composition, by Miro, horiz. 14k, Field of Green, by Van Gogh, horiz.

1993 **Engr.** *Perf. 11½x12*

2908 A565 9k multicolored 2.25 2.25

Perf. 12x11½

2909 A565 11k multicolored 2.25 2.25
2910 A565 14k multicolored 3.50 3.50
Nos. 2908-2910 (3) 8.00 8.00

Issued: 11k, 14k, Nov. 8; 9k, Dec. 15.

Nos. 2908-2910 were each issued in sheets of 4. Value $35.

A1064

Photo. & Engr.

1994, Jan. 19 *Perf. 11½*

2911 A1064 2k multicolored .30 .25

Intl. Year of the Family.

Jan Kubelik (1880-1940), Composer A1065

Photo. & Engr.

1994, Jan. 19 *Perf. 11½*

2912 A1065 3k multicolored .40 .25

UNESCO — A1065a

Designs: 2k, Voltaire (1694-1778), philosopher. 6k, Georgius Agricola (1494-1555), mineralogist, humanist.

1994, Feb. 2 *Perf. 12x11½*

2913 A1065a 2k multicolored .25 .25
2914 A1065a 6k multicolored .80 .35

A1066

A1067

Photo. & Engr.

1994, Feb. 2 *Perf. 11½*

2915 A1066 5k multicolored .65 .35

1994 Winter Olympics, Lillehammer.

Photo. & Engr.

1994, May 4 *Perf. 11½*

Europa (Marco Polo &): No. 2916, Stylized animals, Chinese woman. No. 2917, Stylized animals.

2916 A1067 14k multicolored 1.75 1.75
2917 A1067 14k multicolored 1.75 1.75
a. Pair, #2916-2917 3.50 3.50

A1068

1994, May 18

2918 A1068 5k Eduard Benes .60 .25

Architectural Sights — A1069

UNESCO: 8k, Houses at the square, Telč. 9k, Cubist house designed by Chochol, Prague.

1994, May 18

2919 A1069 8k multicolored 1.25 .75
2920 A1069 9k multicolored 1.50 .75

A1070

Photo. & Engr.

1994, June 1 *Perf. 11½*

2921 A1070 2k Children's Day .40 .25

Dinosaurs — A1071

Perf. 11½x11, 11x11½

1994, June 1 **Litho.**

2922 A1071 2k Stegosaurus .30 .25
2923 A1071 3k Apatosaurus .45 .25
2924 A1071 5k Tarbosaurus, vert. .55 .35
Nos. 2922-2924 (3) 1.30 .85

A1072

Photo. & Engr.

1994, June 1 *Perf. 11½x11*

2925 A1072 8k multicolored 1.10 .50

1994 World Cup Soccer Championships, US.

A1073

1994, June 15 *Perf. 11x11½*

2926 A1073 2k multicolored .35 .25

12th Pan-Sokol Rally, Prague.

Intl. Olympic Committee, Cent. — A1074

1994, June 15

2927 A1074 7k multicolored .90 .50

UPU, 120th Anniv. A1075

1994, Aug. 3 **Engr.** *Perf. 11½*

2928 A1075 11k multicolored 1.25 1.00

Songbirds — A1076

Designs: 3k, Saxicola torquata. 5k, Carpodacus erythrinus. 14k, Luscinia svecica.

Photo. & Engr.

1994, Aug. 24 *Perf. 11x11½*

2929 A1076 3k multicolored .45 .25
2930 A1076 5k multicolored .75 .30
2931 A1076 14k multicolored 1.80 .80
Nos. 2929-2931 (3) 3.00 1.35

Historic Race Cars — A1077

Photo. & Engr.

1994, Oct. 5 *Perf. 11½*

2932 A1077 2k 1900 NW .25 .25
Complete booklet, 10 #2932 3.00
2933 A1077 3k 1908 L&K .45 .25
Complete booklet, 5 #2933 2.75
2934 A1077 9k 1912 Praga 1.10 .50
Nos. 2932-2934 (3) 1.80 1.00

Christmas — A1078

Photo. & Engr.

1994, Nov. 9 *Perf. 11½*

2935 A1078 2k multicolored .45 .25

Painting Type of 1967 Inscribed "CESKA REPUBLIKA"

Engraving or paintings: 7k, Stary Posetilec A Zena, by Lucas Van Leyden. 10k, Moulin Rouge, by Henri de Toulouse-Lautrec. 14k, St. Vitus Madonna, St. Vitus Cathedral, Prague.

1994, Nov. 9 **Engr.** *Perf. 12*

2936 A565 7k multicolored .95 .95
2937 A565 10k multicolored 1.40 1.40
2938 A565 14k multicolored 2.00 2.00
Nos. 2936-2938 (3) 4.35 4.35

Nos. 2936-2938 were each printed in sheets of 4. Value, set $14.

World Tourism Organization, 20th Anniv. A1079

Czech Stamp Production A1080

Photo. & Engr.

1995, Jan. 2 *Perf. 11x12*

2939 A1079 8k green blue & red .95 .50

1995, Jan. 20

2940 A1080 3k Design N1 .60 .25

Czech Republic & European Union Association Agreement A1081

1995, Jan. 20 **Litho.** *Perf. 13½x12½*

2941 A1081 8k multicolored .95 .65

Famous Men A1082

Designs: 2k, Johannes Marcus Marci (1595-1667). 5k, Ferdinand Peroutka (1895-1978). 7k, Premysl Pitter (1895-1976).

Photo. & Engr.

1995, Feb. 1 *Perf. 12x11*

2942 A1082 2k multicolored .25 .25
2943 A1082 5k multicolored .60 .25
2944 A1082 7k multicolored .85 .35
Nos. 2942-2944 (3) 1.70 .85

Theater Personalities — A1083

Designs: No. 2945, Jiri Voskovec (1905-81). No. 2946, Jan Werich (1905-80). No. 2947, Jaroslav Jezek (1906-42). 22k, Caricatures of Voskovec, Werich, and Jezek with piano.

1995 **Photo. & Engr.** *Perf. 12x11*

2945 A1083 3k multicolored .50 .25
Complete booklet, 3 #2945 2.00
2946 A1083 3k multicolored .50 .25
Complete booklet, 3 #2946 2.00
2947 A1083 3k multicolored .50 .25
Complete booklet, 3 #2947 2.00
a. Strip of 3, #2945-2947 1.75 1.50
Complete booklet, 2 #2947a 4.00
Nos. 2945-2947 (3) 1.50 .75

Souvenir Sheet

Photo.

Perf. 12

2947B A1083 22k yellow & black 2.50 2.50

Issued: 3k, 3/15; 22k, 9/20.

Havel Type of 1990 Inscribed "Ceska Republika"

Photo. & Engr.

1995, Mar. 22 ***Perf. 12x11½***

2948 A1000 3.60k bl, vio & mag .45 .25
Complete booklet, 5 #2948 4.00

Rural Architecture A1084

1995, Mar. 22 ***Perf. 11½***

2949 A1084 40h shown .25 .25
2950 A1084 60h Homes, diff. .25 .25

European Nature Conservation Year — A1085

1995, Apr. 12

2951 A1085 3k Bombus terrestris .35 .30
Complete booklet, 5 #2951 4.00
2952 A1085 5k Mantis religiosa .60 .30
Complete booklet, 5 #2952 4.50
2953 A1085 6k Calopteryx splendens .75 .30
Complete booklet, 5 #2953 5.00
Nos. 2951-2953 (3) 1.70 .90

Peace & Freedom A1086

Photo. & Engr.

1995, May 3 ***Perf. 11½***

2954 A1086 9k Rose, profiles 1.40 .35
2955 A1086 14k Butterfly, profiles 1.75 .75

Europa.

Natural Beauties in Czech Republic A1087

Designs: 8k, "Stone Organ" scenic mountain. 9k, Largest sandstone bridge in Europe.

Photo. & Engr.

1995, May 3 ***Perf. 11½***

2956 A1087 8k multicolored .95 .95
2957 A1087 9k multicolored 1.00 1.00

Nos. 2956-2957 were each issued in sheets of 8. Value, set $17.50.

Children's Day — A1088

Photo. & Engr.

1995, June 1 ***Perf. 11½***

2958 A1088 3.60k multicolored .60 .25

First Train from Vienna to Prague, 150th Anniv. A1089

3k, Chocen Tunnel. 9.60k, Entering Prague.

1995, June 21

2959 A1089 3k multicolored .35 .25
Complete booklet, 5 #2959 2.00
2960 A1089 9.60k multicolored 1.15 .50

World Wrestling Championships, Prague A1090

Photo. & Engr.

1995, Sept. 6 ***Perf. 11½***

2961 A1090 3k multicolored .55 .25

Cartoon Characters A1091

Designs: 3k, Man playing violin, woman washing, by Vladimir Rencin. 3.60k, Angel, naked man, by Vladimir Jiranek. 5k, Circus trainer holding ring for champagne cork to pop through, by Jiri Sliva.

1995, Sept. 6

2962 A1091 3k multicolored .45 .25
Complete booklet, 5 #2962 2.00
2963 A1091 3.60k multicolored .55 .25
Complete booklet, 5 #2963 2.50
2964 A1091 5k multicolored .75 .30
Complete booklet, 5 #2964 3.50
Nos. 2962-2964 (3) 1.75 .80

A1092 A1093

1995, Sept. 20 Litho. ***Perf. 13½x13***

2965 A1092 3k multicolored .35 .25

SOS Children's Villages, 25th anniv.

Photo. & Engr.

1995-97 ***Perf. 12x11½***

Designs: 2.40k, Gothic. 3k, Secession. 3.60k, Romance. 4k, Classic portal; 4.60k, Rococo. 9.60k, Renaissance Portal. 12.60k, Cubist. 14k, Baroque.

2966 A1093 2.40k red & green .30 .25
2967 A1093 3k grn & bl .35 .25
2967A A1093 3.60k pur & grn .45 .25
2968 A1093 4k blue & red .50 .25
Complete booklet, 5 #2967A 3.00
2968A A1093 4.60k multicolored .55 .25
2969 A1093 9.60k blue & red 1.10 .45
2969A A1093 12.60k red brn & bl 1.50 .45
2970 A1093 14k grn & pur 1.60 .60
Nos. 2966-2970 (8) 6.35 2.75

Issued: 9.60k, 9/27; 2.40k, 14k, 10/11; 3k, 3.60k, 10/25; 4k, 6/12/96; 4.60k, 3/26/97; 12.60k, 6/25/97.

UN, 50th Anniv. A1094

1995, Oct. 11 Litho. ***Perf. 12x11½***

2971 A1094 14k multicolored 1.90 .80

Wilhelm Röntgen (1845-1923), Discovery of the X-Ray, Cent. — A1095

1995, Oct. 11 **Photo. & Engr.**

2972 A1095 6k blk, buff & bl vio .85 .35

Painting Type of 1967 Inscribed "CESKA REPUBLIKA"

Designs: 6k, Parisiene, by Ludek Marold. 9k, Vase of Flowers, by J.K. Hirschely. 14k, Portrait of J. Malinsky, by Antoinín Machek.

1995, Nov. 8 ***Perf. 12***

2973 A565 6k multicolored .95 .45
2974 A565 9k multicolored 1.25 .65
2975 A565 14k multicolored 2.00 1.00
Nos. 2973-2975 (3) 4.20 2.10

Nos. 2973-2975 were each printed in sheets of 4. Value, set $13.50.

Christmas — A1096

1995, Nov. 8 ***Perf. 11½***

2976 A1096 3k multicolored .60 .25
Complete booklet, 3 #2976 2.00

Czech Philharmonic Orchestra, Cent. — A1097

Photo. & Engr.

1996, Jan. 2 ***Perf. 12x11½***

2977 A1097 3.60k multicolored .55 .25

Tradition of Czech Stamp Production — A1098

Photo. & Engr.

1996, Jan. 20 ***Perf. 11½x12***

2978 A1098 3.60k Design A5 of 1920 .55 .25

Vera Mencikova (1906-44), Chess Player — A1099

Photo. & Engr.

1996, Feb. 14 ***Perf. 12x11½***

2979 A1099 6k multicolored .75 .35

Easter — A1100

1996, Mar. 13 ***Perf. 11½x12***

2980 A1100 3k multicolored .45 .25
Complete booklet, 5 #2980 2.00

Josef Sudek (1896-1976), Photographer A1101

Photo. & Engr.

1996, Mar. 13 ***Perf. 11***

2981 A1101 9.60k multicolored 1.25 .60

Rulers from House of Luxembourg — A1102

Designs: a, John of Luxembourg (1296-1346). b, Charles IV (1316-78). c, Wenceslas IV. (1361-1419). d, Sigismund (1368-1437).

1996, Mar. 27 **Engr.** ***Perf. 11½***

2982 A1102 14k Sheet of 4, #a.-d. + label 6.75 6.75

Jiri Guth-Jarkovsky, Participant in First Modern Olympic Games, Athens A1103

Photo. & Engr.

1996, Mar. 27 ***Perf. 11½***

2983 A1103 9.60k multicolored 1.25 .60

Modern Olympic Games, cent.

World Wildlife Fund — A1104

Ema Destinnova (1878-1930), Singer — A1105

Designs: a, 3.60k, Eliomys quercinus. b, 5k, Dryomys nitedula. c, 6k, Spermophilus citellus. d, 8k, Sicista betulina.

Photo. & Engr.

1996, Apr. 24 *Perf. 11½x12*
2984 A1104 Block of 4, #a.-d. 3.50 3.50

Issued in sheets of 8 stamps. Value $9.

1996, May 2 *Perf. 11½*
2985 A1105 8k multicolored .90 .40

Europa.

No. 2985 was issued in sheets of 10. Value $11.

A1106

A1107

Photo. & Engr.

1996, May 15 *Perf. 11x11½*
2986 A1106 12k multicolored 1.40 .65

Jean Gaspart Deburau (1796-1846), mime.

1996, May 29
2987 A1107 3k multicolored .35 .25

1996 Summmer Olympic Games, Atlanta.

Intl. Children's Day — A1108

Photo. & Engr.

1996, May 29 *Perf. 11½*
2988 A1108 3k multicolored .35 .25

Architectural Sites — A1109

UNESCO: 8k, St. Nepomuk Church, Zelena Hora. 9k, Loreta Tower, Prague.

1996, June 26 **Engr.** *Perf. 11½*
2989 A1109 8k multicolored 1.00 1.00
2990 A1109 9k multicolored 1.10 1.10

Nos. 2989-2990 were each issued in sheets of 8. Value, set $16.

See Nos. 3056-3057.

UNICEF, 50th Anniv. A1110

Photo. & Engr.

1996, Sept. 11 *Perf. 12x11*
2991 A1110 3k multicolored .35 .25

Horses

A1111 A1112

Photo. & Engr.

1996, Sept. 25 *Perf. 11x11½*
2992 A1111 3k multicolored .50 .25
2993 A1112 3k multicolored .50 .25
a. Pair, #2992-2993 1.00 .75
Complete booklet, 3 #2992, 2 #2993 3.00
Complete booklet, 2 #2992, 3 #2993 3.00

Souvenir Sheet

Vaclav Havel, 60th Birthday — A1113

1996, Oct. 5
2994 A1113 Sheet of 2 1.50 1.50
a. 6k red & blue .80 .50

Painting Type of 1967 Inscribed "CESKA REPUBLIKA"

The Baroque Chair, by Endre Nemes (1909-85).

1996, Oct. 5 **Engr.** *Perf. 11½*
2995 A565 20k multicolored 2.50 2.50

No. 2995 was issued in sheets of 4. Value $10.

See Slovakia No. 255; Sweden No. 2199.

Tycho Brahe (1546-1601), Astronomer — A1114

Photo. & Engr.

1996, Oct. 9 *Perf. 11½x11*
2996 A1114 5k multicolored .75 .30

Biplanes A1115

1996, Oct. 9
2997 A1115 7k Letov S1 (1920) .85 .40
2998 A1115 8k Aero A11 (1925) .95 .45
2999 A1115 10k Avia BH21 (1925) 1.20 .55
Nos. 2997-2999 (3) 3.00 1.40

Christmas A1116

Photo. & Engr.

1996, Nov. 13 *Perf. 11½*
3000 A1116 3k multicolored .45 .25
Complete booklet, 5 #3000 3.50

Painting Type of 1967 Inscribed "CESKA REPUBLIKA"

Designs: 9k, Garden of Eden, by Josef Váchal (1884-1969), horiz. 11k, Breakfast, by Georg Flegel (1566-1638).

1996, Nov. 13 **Engr.** *Perf. 11½*
3001 A565 9k multicolored 1.25 1.25
3002 A565 11k multicolored 1.60 1.60

Nos. 3001-3002 were each issued in sheets of 4. Value, set $10.

Czech Stamp Production — A1117

Photo. & Engr.

1997, Jan. 20 *Perf. 11½x12*
3003 A1117 3.60k #68, bl & red .40 .25

Easter — A1118

Flowers — A1119

Photo. & Engr.

1997, Mar. 12 *Perf. 11½*
3004 A1118 3k multicolored .65 .25
Complete booklet, 5 #3004 4.00

1997, Mar. 12 *Perf. 11x11½*

3.60k, Erythronium dens-canis. 4k, Calla palustris. 5k, Cypripedium calceolus. 8k, Iris pumila.

3005 A1119 3.60k multicolored .45 .25
Complete booklet, 5 #3005 2.50
3006 A1119 4k multicolored .45 .25
Complete booklet, 5 #3006 2.50
3007 A1119 5k multicolored .60 .30
Complete booklet, 5 #3007 3.50
3008 A1119 8k multicolored .95 .45
Complete booklet, 5 #3008 5.00
Nos. 3005-3008 (4) 2.45 1.25

A1120

A1121

Jewish Monuments in Prague: 8k, Altneuschul Synagogue. 10k, Tombstone of Rabbi Judah Loew MaHaRal.

1997, Apr. 30 *Perf. 11½*
3009 A1120 8k multicolored .90 .45
3010 A1120 10k multicolored 1.10 .55
a. Sheet, 4 each #3009-3010 8.00 4.00

See Israel Nos. 1302-1303.

1997, Mar. 26 **Litho.** *Perf. 13x13½*

Greetings stamp.

3011 A1121 4k Girl with cats .50 .25

A1122 A1123

1997, Apr. 23 **Engr.** *Perf. 11½*
3012 A1122 7k deep violet .85 .40

St. Adalbert (956-97). See Germany No. 1964, Hungary No. 3569, Poland No. 3337, Vatican City No. 1040.

Photo. & Engr.

1997, Apr. 30 *Perf. 11½x12*

Europa (Stories and Legends): No. 3013, Queen, knight with sword, lion, snakes. No. 3014, Man riding in chariot drawn by chickens, King looking through window.

3013 A1123 8k multicolored 1.25 1.25
3014 A1123 8k multicolored 1.25 1.25

Nos. 3013-3014 were each issued in sheets of 8. Value, set $16.

Souvenir Sheet

Collections of Rudolf II (1522-1612), Prague Exhibition — A1124

Designs: a, 6k, Musical instruments, flowers, face of bearded man. b, 8k, Rudolf II wearing laurel wreath, holding rose, Muses. c, 10k, Rudolf II, skull, moth's wings, tree, flowers, leaves, fruit.

1997, May 14 **Engr.** *Perf. 12*
3015 A1124 Sheet of 3, #a.-c. 2.75 2.75

Intl. Children's Day — A1125

Photo. & Engr.

1997, May 28 *Perf. 11½*
3016 A1125 4.60k multicolored .55 .25

Frantisek Krizik (1847-1941), Electrical Engineer, Inventor of Arc Lamp — A1126

Photo. & Engr.

1997, June 25 *Perf. 12x11½*
3017 A1126 6k multicolored .70 .25

European Swimming & Diving Championships, Prague — A1127

Photo. & Engr.

1997, Aug. 27 *Perf. 11½*

3018 A1127 11k multicolored 1.50 .40

"The Good Soldier Schweik," by Jaroslav Hasek, 110th Anniv. — A1128

4k, Mrs. Müller, Schweik in wheelchair. 4.60k, Lt. Lukás, Col. Kraus von Zillergut, dog. 6k, Schweik smoking pipe, winter scene.

Photo. & Engr.

1997, Sept. 10 *Perf. 12x11½*

3019 A1128 4k multicolored .50 .25
a. Booklet pane of 8 + 4 labels 4.50
Complete booklet, #3019a 4.50
3020 A1128 4.60k multicolored .55 .25
a. Booklet pane of 8 + 4 labels 5.00
Complete booklet, #3020a 5.00
3021 A1128 6k multicolored .70 .30
a. Booklet pane of 8 + 4 labels 6.00
Complete booklet, #3021a 6.00
Nos. 3019-3021 (3) 1.75 .80

Praga 1998, Intl. Stamp Exhibition — A1129

No. 3022, Lesser Town, Prague Castle. No. 3023, Old Town, bridges over Vltava River.

Photo. & Engr.

1997, Sept. 24 *Perf. 11½*

3022 A1129 15k multicolored 1.80 .70
3023 A1129 15k multicolored 1.80 .70
a. Souvenir sheet, #3022-3023 + 2 labels 3.75 3.00

Historic Service Vehicles A1130

Designs: 4k, Postal bus, Prague. 4.60k, Sentinel truck, Skoda. 8k, Fire truck, Tatra.

1997, Oct. 8 *Perf. 12x11½*

3024 A1130 4k multicolored .45 .25
Complete booklet, 5 #3024 2.50
3025 A1130 4.60k multicolored .55 .25
Complete booklet, 5 #3025 3.50
3026 A1130 8k multicolored .95 .40
Complete booklet, 5 #3026 5.00
Nos. 3024-3026 (3) 1.95 .90

A1131

A1132

Photo. & Engr.

1997, Nov. 12 *Perf. 11½*

3027 A1131 4k multicolored .50 .25
Complete booklet, 5 #3027 2.75

Christmas.

Painting Type of 1967 Inscribed "CESKA REPUBLIKA"

7k, Landscape with Chateau in Chantilly, by Antonín Chittussi (1847-91). 12k, The Prophets Came Out of the Desert, by Frantisek Bílek (1872-1941). 1 6k, Parisian Antiquarians, by T. F. Simon (1877-1942).

1997, Nov. 12 **Engr.** *Perf. 12*

3028 A565 7k multi, horiz. .85 .85
3029 A565 12k multi 1.40 1.40
3030 A565 16k multi 1.90 1.90
Nos. 3028-3030 (3) 4.15 4.15

Nos. 3028-3030 were each issued in sheets of 4. Value, set $17.

1998, Jan. 20 **Litho.** *Perf. 11½x12*

3031 A1132 7k multicolored .85 .30

1998 Winter Olympic Games, Nagano.

Tradition of Czech Stamp Production — A1133

Photo. & Engr.

1998, Jan. 20 *Perf. 12x11½*

3032 A1133 12.60k Type A8 1.50 .55
a. Booklet pane of 8 + 4 labels 12.50
Complete booklet, #3032a 12.50

Pres. Václav Havel A1134

Love A1135

1998, Jan. 22

3033 A1134 4.60k dark grn & red .55 .25

See No. 3114.

1998, Feb. 4 *Perf. 11½*

3034 A1135 4k multicolored .50 .25
Complete booklet, 5 #3034 2.50

Skibob World Championship, Spindleruv Mlyn — A1136

1998, Feb. 25

3035 A1136 8k multicolored 1.00 .35

Prague Philatelic Exhibition Type of 1938

Souvenir Sheet

1998, Feb. 25 **Engr.** *Perf. 12x11½*

3036 A87 Sheet of 2 7.00 7.00
a. 30k like #251a 4.00 2.00

Prague '98, Intl. Philatelic Exhibition.

Easter — A1137

Photo. & Engr.

1998, Mar. 25 *Perf. 11x11½*

3037 A1137 4k multicolored .55 .25
Complete booklet, 5 #3037 2.75

Ondrejov Observatory, Cent. — A1138

1998, Mar. 25 *Perf. 12x11½*

3038 A1138 4.60k multicolored .55 .25

Czech Ice Hockey Team, Gold Medalists at Nagano Winter Olympic Games — A1139

1998, Apr. 1 **Litho.** *Perf. 11½x12*

3039 A1139 23k Dominik Hasek 2.00 2.00

No. 3039 was issued in a sheet with two labels.

Charles University and New Town, Prague, 650th Anniv. — A1140

Designs: a, 15k, Hands forming arch, University seal. b, 22k, Charles IV (1316-78), Holy Roman Emperor, King of Bohemia. c, 23k, Groin vault, St. Vitus Cathedral, Prague.

1998, Apr. 1 **Engr.** *Perf. 12*

3040 A1140 Sheet of 3, #a.-c. 5.00 5.00

World Book and Copyright Day — A1141

1998, Apr. 23 **Litho.** *Perf. 12x11½*

3041 A1141 10k multicolored 1.20 .45

Nature Conservation A1142

1998, Apr. 23 *Perf. 13x13½*

3042 A1142 4.60k Perdix perdix .55 .25
3043 A1142 4.60k Lyrurus tetrix .55 .25
a. Pair, #3042-3043 1.10 .60
3044 A1142 8k Cervus elaphus .95 .35
3045 A1142 8k Alces alces .95 .35
a. Pair, #3044-3045 1.90 1.10
Nos. 3042-3045 (4) 3.00 1.20

Natl. Festivals and Holidays A1143

Europa: 11k, King's Ride. 15k, Wearing masks for Carnival.

Litho. & Engr.

1998, May 5 *Perf. 11½*

3046 A1143 11k multicolored 1.25 .55
3047 A1143 15k multicolored 1.75 .75

Intl. Children's Day — A1144

Designs: 4k, Two satyr musicians. 4.60k, Character riding on fish.

Photo. & Engr.

1998, May 27 *Perf. 11½*

3048 A1144 4k multicolored .45 .25
a. Booklet of 6 +4 labels 3.00
Complete booklet, #3048a 3.00
3049 A1144 4.60k multicolored .55 .25
a. Booklet of 6 + 4 labels 3.50
Complete booklet, #3049a 3.50

Famous Men — A1145

Designs: 4k, Frantisek Kmoch (1848-1912), bandleader, composer. 4.60k, Frantisek Palacky (1798-1876), historian, politician. 6k, Rafael Kubelík (1914-96), composer, conductor.

1998, May 27 *Perf. 11½x12*

3050 A1145 4k multicolored .45 .25
3051 A1145 4.60k multicolored .55 .25
3052 A1145 6k multicolored .70 .25
Nos. 3050-3052 (3) 1.70 .75

Revolt of 1848, 150th Anniv. A1146

1998, May 27 *Perf. 12x11½*

3053 A1146 15k multicolored 1.75 .75

Painting Type of 1967 Inscribed "CESKA REPUBLIKA"

Praga 1998 Intl. Stamp Exhibition, works of art: 22k, Amorfa Dvoubarevna Fuga, by Frantisek Kupka (1871-1957), horiz. 23k, Escape, by Paul Gauguin (1848-1903), horiz.

1998, June 17 **Engr.** *Perf. 12*

3054 A565 22k multicolored 2.50 1.75
3055 A565 23k multicolored 2.75 1.75

Nos. 3054-3055 were each issued in sheets of 4. Value, set $22.

UNESCO World Heritage Sites Type of 1996

8k, St. Barbara Cathedral, Kutná Hora, horiz. 11k, The Chateau of Valtice, horiz.

1998, Oct. 7 **Engr.** *Perf. 11½x12*

3056 A1109 8k multicolored .95 .40
3057 A1109 11k multicolored 1.25 .60

Nos. 3056-3057 were each issued in sheets of 8. Value, set $17.50.

Czechoslovak Republic, 80th Anniv. — A1147

Designs based on World War I recruitment posters by Vojtech Preissig (1873-1944): 4.60k, Soldiers holding flags, guns. 5k, Three soldiers marching. 12.60k, Flags waving from city buildings.

Perf. 11½x11¾

1998, Oct. 28 **Litho. & Engr.**

3058 A1147 4.60k multicolored .55 .40
3059 A1147 5k multicolored .60 .40
3060 A1147 12.60k multicolored 1.60 .90
Nos. 3058-3060 (3) 2.75 1.70

No. 3060 was issued in sheets of 6+2 labels. Value $30.

Christmas A1148

Designs: 4k, People following star. 6k, Angel blowing trumpet over town, vert.

Photo. & Engr.

1998, Nov. 18 ***Perf. 11½***

3061 A1148 4k multicolored .45 .25
Complete booklet, 5 #3061 2.50
3062 A1148 6k multicolored .70 .25
Complete booklet, 5 #3062 4.00

Signs of the Zodiac — A1149

1998-2000 ***Perf. 12x11½***

3063 A1149 1k Capricorn .25 .25
3064 A1149 10k Aquarius 1.20 .25
3065 A1149 9k Libra 1.00 .25
3066 A1149 8k Cancer .95 .25
3067 A1149 20k Sagittarius 2.25 .45

Photo. & Engr.

Perf. 11¾x11¼

3068 A1149 5k Taurus .55 .25
Booklet, 5 #3068 2.75
3069 A1149 5.40k Scorpio .60 .25
Booklet, 5 #3069 3.00
3070 A1149 2k Virgo .25 .25
3071 A1149 40h Pisces .25 .25
3072 A1149 12k Leo 1.40 .30
3073 A1149 17k Gemini 2.00 .65
3074 A1149 26k Aries 3.00 .95
Nos. 3063-3074 (12) 13.70 4.35

Issued: 1k, 10k, 11/18; 9k, 5/5/99; 8k, 20k, 9/8/99; 5k, 5.40k, 12/8/99; 2k, 5/9/00. 40h, 1/20/01. 12k, 2/21/01. 17k, 9/1/02. 26k, 2/12/03.

Painting Type of 1967 Inscribed "CESKA REPUBLIKA"

15k, Painting from the Greater Cycle, 1902, by Jan Preisler (1872-1918), horiz. 16k, Spinner, by Josef Navrátil (1798-1865).

1998, Dec. 9 ***Perf. 12***

3075 A565 15k multicolored 1.75 1.00
3076 A565 16k multicolored 1.80 1.00

Nos. 3075-3076 were each issued in sheets of 4. Value, set $14.50.

A1150

A1151

Photo. & Engr.

1999, Jan. 20 ***Perf. 11½x11¾***

3077 A1150 4.60k #164 .50 .25
a. Booklet pane of 8 + 4 labels 4.00
Complete booklet, #3077a 4.00

Tradition of Czech stamp production.

Photo. & Engr.

1999, Feb. 17 ***Perf. 11½***

Domestic cats.

3078 A1151 4.60k shown .55 .25
Complete booklet, 5 #3078 2.75
3079 A1151 5k Adult, kitten .55 .25
Complete booklet, 5 #3079 2.75
3080 A1151 7k Two cats .80 .30
Complete booklet, 5 #3080 4.00
Nos. 3078-3080 (3) 1.90 .80

Easter — A1152

A1153

Photo. & Engr.

1999, Mar. 10 ***Perf. 11¼x11½***

3081 A1152 3k multicolored .35 .25

Perf. 12¾x13¼

1999, Mar. 10 **Litho.**

Protected birds: No. 3082, Merops apiaster. No. 3083, Upupa epops.

Protected butterflies: No. 3084, Catocala electa. No. 3085, Euphydryas maturna.

3082 A1153 4.60k multicolored .55 .25
3083 A1153 4.60k multicolored .55 .25
a. Pair, #3082-3083 1.10 .60
Complete booklet, 3 #3082, 2 #3083 2.75
3084 A1153 5k multicolored .55 .25
3085 A1153 5k multicolored .55 .25
a. Pair, #3084-3085 1.10 .60
Complete booklet, 3 #3084, 2 #3085 2.75

Nature conservation.

Czech Republic's Entry Into NATO — A1154

Photo. & Engr.

1999, Mar. 12 ***Perf. 12x11½***

3086 A1154 4.60k multicolored .45 .25

Council of Europe, 50th Anniv. A1155

Photo. & Engr.

1999, Apr. 14 ***Perf. 11¾x11¼***

3087 A1155 7k multicolored .75 .40

Natl. Olympic Committee, Cent. — A1156

Design: Josef Rössler-Orovsky (1869-1933), founder of Czech Olympic Committee.

1999, Apr. 14 ***Perf. 11¼x11¾***

3088 A1156 9k multicolored 1.00 .35

Europa A1157

Natl. Parks: 11k, Sumava. 17k, Podyji.

1999, May 5 ***Perf. 11¾x11¼***

3089 A1157 11k multicolored 1.25 .40
3090 A1157 17k multicolored 2.00 .65

Nos. 3089-3090 were each issued in sheets of 8. Value, set $27.

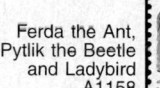

Ferda the Ant, Pytlik the Beetle and Ladybird A1158

Photo. & Engr.

1999, May 26 ***Perf. 11½x11¼***

3091 A1158 4.60k multicolored .55 .25
Complete booklet, 8 #3091 4.50

Bridges A1159

1999, May 26 **Engr.** ***Perf. 11¾***

3092 A1159 8k Stádlec, vert. .90 .40
3093 A1159 11k Cernvír 1.25 .60

Nos. 3092-3094 were each issued in sheets of 8. Value, set $17.50.

Souvenir Sheet

Paleontologist Joachim Barrande (1799-1883) and Trilobite Fossils — A1160

a, 13k, Barrande, fossils. b, 31k, Delphon forbesi, Ophioceras simplex, Carolicrinus barrandei.

1999, June 23 **Engr.** ***Perf. 11¾***

3094 A1160 Sheet of 2, #a.-b. + 2 labels 5.00 4.00

Jihlava Mining Rights, 750th Anniv. A1161

Photo. & Engr.

1999, June 23 ***Perf. 11¾x11¼***

3095 A1161 8k multicolored .90 .35
a. Bklt. pane of 8 + 4 labels 7.25
Complete booklet, #3095a 7.50

UPU, 125th Anniv. — A1162

Litho. & Engr.

1999, June 23 ***Perf. 11¾***

3096 A1162 9k multicolored 1.00 .40

Issued se-tenant with two labels.

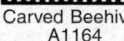

Vincenc Preissnitz (1799-1851), Hydrotherapy Advocate A1163

Photo. & Engr.

1999, Sept. 8 ***Perf. 11¼***

3097 A1163 4.60k multicolored .50 .25

UNESCO.

Carved Beehives A1164

Cartoons by Miroslav Bartak A1165

Designs: 4.60k, Woman. 5k, St. Joseph and Infant Jesus. 7k, Chimney sweep.

Photo. & Engr.

1999, Sept. 29 ***Perf. 11¼x11½***

3098 A1164 4.60k multi .55 .25
Complete booklet, 5 #3098 2.75
3099 A1164 5k multi .60 .25
Complete booklet, 5 #3099 3.00
3100 A1164 7k multi .80 .30
Complete booklet, 5 #3100 4.00
Nos. 3098-3100 (3) 1.95 .80

1999, Oct. 20

Designs: 4.60k, Doctor in clown mask, infant. 5k, Dog with pipe. 7k, Night seeping through window sill.

3101 A1165 4.60k multi .55 .25
3102 A1165 5k multi .60 .25
3103 A1165 7k multi .80 .30
Nos. 3101-3103 (3) 1.95 .80

Souvenir Sheet

Beuron Art School — A1166

Designs: a, 11k, Mater Dei, 1898. b, 13k, Pantocrator, 1911.

Litho. & Engr.

1999, Oct. 20 *Perf. 11¾*
3104 A1166 Sheet of 2, #a.-b. 2.75 2.25

Painting Type of 1967 Inscribed "CESKA REPUBLIKA"

Designs: 13k, Red Orchid, by Jindrich Styrsky (1899-1942). 17k, Landscape with Marsh, by Julius Marák (1832-99). 26k, Monument, by Frantisek Hudecek (1909-90).

1999, Nov. 10 Engr. *Perf. 11¾*
3105 A565 13k multi 1.50 1.00
3106 A565 17k multi 2.00 1.50
3107 A565 26k multi 3.00 2.00
Nos. 3105-3107 (3) 6.50 4.50

Nos. 3105-3107 were each issued in sheets of 4. Value, set $26.

A1167

A1168

Photo. & Engr.

1999, Nov. 10 *Perf. 11¼x11½*
3108 A1167 3k multi .35 .25

Christmas.

Photo. & Engr.

2000, Jan. 20 *Perf. 11¼x11¾*
3109 A1168 5.40k #B151 .60 .25
a. Bklt. pane of 8 + 4 labels 5.00
Booklet, #3109a 5.00

Tradition of Czech stamp production.

Brno 2000 Philatelic Exhibition — A1169

Designs: 5k, 1593 view of Brno. 50k, St. James's Church, vert.

2000, Jan. 20 *Perf. 11¾x11¼*
3110 A1169 5k multi .60 .25

Souvenir Sheet

Perf. 11¼x11¾

3111 A1169 50k multi 6.00 4.25

No. 3110 printed in sheets of 35 stamps and 30 labels.

Kutna Hora Royal Mining Law, 700th Anniv. — A1170

2000, Mar. 1 *Perf. 11¼x11¾*
3112 A1170 5k multi .60 .25
a. Booklet pane of 8 + 4 labels 5.00
Booklet, #3112a 5.00

Souvenir Sheet

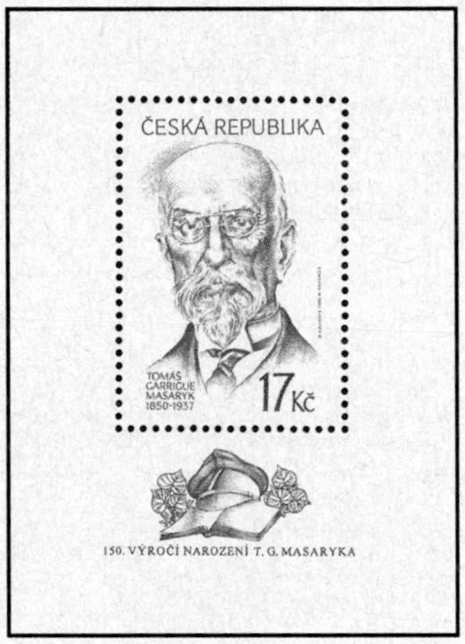

Pres. Thomas Garrigue Masaryk (1850-1937) — A1171

2000, Mar. 1 Engr. *Perf. 11¾*
3113 A1171 17k multi 2.00 1.50

Pres. Havel Type of 1998

Photo. & Engr.

2000, Mar. 1 *Perf. 11¾x11¼*
3114 A1134 5.40k Prus bl & org brn .60 .25

Easter — A1172

Photo. & Engr.

2000, Apr. 5 *Perf. 11¼x11½*
3115 A1172 5k multi .60 .25

Souvenir Sheet

Prague, 2000 European City of Culture — A1173

No. 3116: a, 9k, Statue of man. b, 11k, Statue of harpist. c, 17k, Statue of King Charles IV.

Litho. & Engr.

2000, Apr. 5 *Perf. 11¾*
3116 A1173 #a-c + 3 labels 4.00 4.00

Souvenir Sheet

Trains — A1174

No. 3117: a, 8k, Train from 1900. b, 15k, Train from 2000.

Litho. & Engr.

2000, May 5 *Perf. 11¾*
3117 A1174 Sheet of 2, #a-b, +3 labels 3.00 3.00

Czech Personalities A1175

5k, Vítezslav Nezval (1900-58), writer. 8k, Gustav Mahler (1860-1911), composer.

Photo. & Engr.

2000, May 5 *Perf. 11¼x11¾*
3118-3119 A1175 Set of 2 1.40 .50

Europa, 2000

Common Design Type

2000, May 5 Litho. *Perf. 12¾x13¼*
3120 CD17 9k multi 1.00 .40

Intl. Children's Year — A1176

Photo. & Engr.

2000, May 31 *Perf. 11½x11¼*
3121 A1176 5.40k multi .60 .25
a. Booklet pane of 8 + 2 labels 5.00
Booklet, #3121a 5.00

1995 Proof of Fermat's Last Theorem by Andrew Wiles A1177

2000, May 31 *Perf. 11¾x11¼*
3122 A1177 7k multi .80 .25

Intl. Mathematics Year.

Prague Landmarks — A1178

Designs: 9k, Charles Bridge tower. 11k, St. Nicholas's Church. 13k, Town Hall.

2000, June 28 Engr. *Perf. 11¾*
3123-3125 A1178 Set of 3 4.00 1.10

Mushrooms — A1179

No. 3126, 5k: a, Geastrum pouzarii. b, Boletus satanoides.

No. 3127, 5.40k: a, Morchella pragensis. b, Verpa bohemica.

Photo. & Engr.

2000, June 28 *Perf. 11¼x11½*

Pairs, #a-b

3126-3127 A1179 Set of 2 2.40 .70
Booklet, 3 #3126a, 2 #3126b 3.50
Booklet, 3 #3127b, 2 #3127a 3.50

Meeting of Intl. Monetary Fund and World Bank Group, Prague — A1180

2000, Aug. 30 *Perf. 11¾x11¼*
3128 A1180 7k multi .80 .25

Ancient Olympics A1181

2000, Aug. 30
3129 A1181 9k multi 1.00 .35

2000 Summer Olympics, Sydney — A1182

2000, Aug. 30
3130 A1182 13k multi 1.50 .45

Hunting — A1183

No. 3131: a, 5k, Falconry. b, 5k, Deer at feed trough.

No. 3132: a, 5.40k, Ducks and blind. b, 5.40k, Deer and blind.

Photo. & Engr.

2000, Oct. 4 *Perf. 11¼x11¾*

Horiz. Pairs, #a-b

3131-3132 A1183 Set of 2 2.40 .55
Booklet, 3 #3131a, 2 #3131b 3.50
Booklet, 3 #3132a, 2 #3132b 3.50

Painting Type of 1967 Inscribed "CESKA REPUBLIKA"

Designs: 13k, St. Luke the Evangelist, by Master Theodoricus. 17k, Simeon With Infant

Jesus, by Petr Jan Brandl. 26k, Brunette, by Alfons Mucha.

2000, Nov. 15 **Engr.** ***Perf. 11¾***
3133-3135 A565 Set of 3 6.50 4.50

Nos. 3133-3135 were each issued in sheets of 4. Value, set $27.

Christmas — A1184

Photo. & Engr.

2000, Nov. 15 ***Perf. 11¼x11½***
3136 A1184 5k multi .60 .25

End of Millennium A1185

Advent of New Millennium A1186

2000, Nov. 22
3137 A1185 9k multi 1.00 .35

2001, Jan. 2
3138 A1186 9k multi 1.00 .35

Tradition of Czech Stamp Production A1187

2001, Jan. 20 ***Perf. 11¼x11¾***
3139 A1187 5.40k #474 .50 .25
a. Booklet pane of 8 + 4 labels 4.00
Booklet, #3139a 4.00

Jan Amos Komensky (Comenius, 1592-1670), Theologian — A1188

Photo. & Engr.

2001, Mar. 14 ***Perf. 11¼x11½***
3140 A1188 9k red & black 1.00 .35

Souvenir Sheet

Architecture — A1189

No. 3141: a, 13k, Church and decorations, Jakub. b, 17k, Arcade decorations, Bucovice Castle. c, 31k, Dance Hall, Prague.

2001, Mar. 28 **Engr.** ***Perf. 11¾x11½***
3141 A1189 Sheet of 3, #a-c 7.00 4.50

Easter — A1190

Photo. & Engr.

2001, Mar. 28 ***Perf. 11¼x11½***
3142 A1190 5.40k multi .60 .25

Souvenir Sheet

Allegory of Art, by Vaclav Vavrinec Reiner — A1191

Litho. & Engr.

2001, Apr. 18 ***Perf. 11¾***
3143 A1191 50k multi 6.00 4.25

Europa A1192

Photo. & Engr.

2001, May 9 ***Perf. 11¾x11¼***
3144 A1192 9k pur & lilac 1.00 .35

European Men's Volleyball Championships, Ostrova — A1193

Photo. & Engr.

2001, May 9 ***Perf. 11¼x11½***
3145 A1193 12k multi 1.50 .50

Intl. Children's Day — A1194

Famous Men — A1195

Photo. & Engr.

2001, May 30 ***Perf. 11¼x11½***
3146 A1194 5.40k multi .60 .25
a. Booklet pane of 8 + 2 labels 5.00 —
Booklet, #3146a 5.00

2001, May 30

Designs: 5.40k, Frantisek Skroup (1801-62), composer. 16k, Frantisek Halas (1901-49), writer.

3147-3148 A1195 Set of 2 2.50 .80

Congratulations A1196

2001, June 20
3149 A1196 5.40k multi .60 .25
Booklet, 5 #3149 3.00

Dogs — A1197

No. 3150: a, West Highland terrier. b, Beagle.
No. 3151: a, German shepherd. b, Golden retriever.

Photo. & Engr.

2001, June 20 ***Perf. 11½x11¼***
3150 Pair 1.40 1.00
a.-b. A1197 5.40k Any single .65 .25
Booklet, 3 #3150a, 2 #3150b 3.25
Booklet, 3 #3150b, 2 #3150a 3.25
3151 Pair 1.40 1.00
a.-b. A1197 5.40k Any single .65 .25
Booklet, 3 #3151a, 2 #3151b 3.25

Zoo Animals A1198

No. 3152: a, Pongo pygmaeus. b, Panthera tigris altaica.
No. 3153: a, Ailurus fulgens. b, Fennecus zerda.

Photo. & Engr.

2001, Sept. 5 ***Perf. 11¾x11¼***
3152 Pair 1.40 1.00
a.-b. A1198 5.40k Any single .65 .25
Booklet, 3 #3152b, 2 #3152a 3.25
3153 Pair 1.40 1.00
a.-b. A1198 5.40k Any single .65 .25
Booklet, 3 #3153b, 2 #3153a 3.25

UNESCO World Heritage Sites A1199

Designs: 12k, Kormeríz Castle and Gardens. 14k, Holasovice Historical Village Restoration.

2001, Oct. 9 **Engr.** ***Perf. 11½x11¾***
3154-3155 A1199 Set of 2 3.00 1.25

See Nos. 3177-3178, 3267-3268.

Year of Dialogue Among Civilizations A1200

Photo. & Engr.

2001, Oct. 9 ***Perf. 11¼x11½***
3156 A1200 9k multi 1.00 .35

Mills A1201

Christmas A1202

Designs: 9k, Windmill. 14.40k, Water mill.

2001, Oct. 9
3157-3158 A1201 Set of 2 2.25 1.00

Photo. & Engr.

2001, Nov. 14 ***Perf. 11¼x11½***
3159 A1202 5.40k multi .60 .30

Painting Type of 1967 Inscribed "ČESKÁ REPUBLIKA"

Designs: 12k, The Annunciation of the Virgin Mary, by Michael J. Rentz. 17k, The Sans Souci Bar in Nimes, by Cyril Bouda. 26k, The Goose Keeper, by Vaclav Brozík.

2001, Nov. 14 **Engr.** ***Perf. 11¾***
3160-3162 A565 Set of 3 6.50 4.25

Nos. 3160-3162 were each issued in sheets of 4. Value, set $25.

Tradition of Czech Stamp Production — A1203

Photo. & Engr.

2002, Jan. 20 ***Perf. 11¼x11¾***
3163 A1203 5.40k Type A89 .60 .25
a. Booklet pane of 8 + 4 labels 5.00 —
Booklet, #3163a 5.00

2002 Winter Olympics, Salt Lake City — A1204

2002, Jan. 30 ***Perf. 11¼***
3164 A1204 12k multi 1.40 .45

For overprint, see No. 3168.

2002 Winter Paralympics, Salt Lake City — A1205

2002, Jan. 30 ***Perf. 11¼x11½***
3165 A1205 5.40k multi .60 .25

Composers Jaromír Vejvoda (1902-88), Josef Poncar (1902-86) and Karel Vacek (1902-82) — A1206

2002, Mar. 6 ***Perf. 11¾x11¼***
3166 A1206 9k multi 1.00 .35

Easter — A1207

2002, Mar. 6 ***Perf. 11¼x11½***
3167 A1207 5.40k multi .60 .25

No. 3164 Overprinted in Blue

Photo. & Engr.

2002, Mar. 8 ***Perf. 11¼***

3168 A1204 12k multi 1.40 .65

Divan, by Vlaho Bukovac (1855-1922) — A1208

Litho. & Engr.

2002, Apr. 23 ***Perf. 11¾***

3169 A1208 17k multi 2.00 1.40

Printed in sheets of 4 + 2 labels. Value $9.
See Croatia No. 487.

Europa A1209

Photo. & Engr.

2002, May 7 ***Perf. 11¾x11¼***

3170 A1209 9k multi 1.00 .35

Souvenir Sheet

Czech Culture and France — A1210

No. 3171: a, 23k, Klávesy Piana-Jezero, by Frantisek Kupka. b, 31k, Man with Broken Nose, sculpture by Auguste Rodin.

Perf. 11¾x11½

2002, May 7 **Litho. & Engr.**

3171 A1210 Sheet of 2, #a-b 6.25 4.00

Intl. Children's Day — A1211

Photo. & Engr.

2002, May 29 ***Perf. 11¼x11½***

3172 A1211 5.40k multi .60 .25

a. Booklet pane of 8 + 2 labels 5.00 —

Complete booklet, #3172a 5.00

Margaritifera Margaritifera A1212

2002, June 6

3173 A1212 9k multi 1.00 .35

Jan Hus (1372-1415), Religious Leader — A1213

2002, June 19

3174 A1213 9k multi + label 1.00 .35

Souvenir Sheet

Worldwide Fund for Nature (WWF) — A1214

Butterflies: a, 5.40k, Maculinea nausithous. b, 5.40k, Maculinea alcon. c, 9k, Maculinea teleius. d, 9k, Maculinea arion.

Litho. & Engr.

2002, June 19 ***Perf. 11¾***

3175 A1214 Sheet of 4, #a-d + 4 labels 3.50 2.75

Pansy — A1215

Photo. & Engr.

2002, Sept. 1 ***Perf. 11¾x11¼***

3176 A1215 6.40k multi .75 .25

See Nos. 3220-3221, 3262-3263, 3293-3294, 3340, 3345-3347, 3363-3366, 3467-3469, 3500.

World Heritage Sites Type of 2001

Designs: 12k, Litomysl Castle. 14k, Holy Trinity Column, Olomouc, vert.

Perf. 11½x11¾, 11¾x11½

2002, Sept. 11 **Engr.**

3177-3178 A1199 Set of 2 2.75 2.00

Nos. 3177-3178 were each issued in sheets of 8. Value, set $25.

Emil Zátopek (1922-2000), Olympic Long Distance Runner — A1216

Photo. & Engr.

2002, Sept. 11 ***Perf. 11¼x11¾***

3179 A1216 9k multi 1.00 .35

Pres. Havel Type of 1998

Photo. & Engr.

2002, Nov. 6 ***Perf. 11¾x11¼***

3180 A1134 6.40k pur & blue .75 .25

St. Nicholas' Day A1217

Christmas A1218

2002, Nov. 6 ***Perf. 11¼x11½***

3181 A1217 6.40k multi .75 .25

a. Booklet pane of 8 + 2 labels 6.00 —

Complete booklet, #3181a 6.00

2002, Nov. 13

3182 A1218 6.40k multi .75 .25

NATO Summit, Prague — A1219

2002, Nov. 14 ***Perf. 11¼x11¾***

3183 A1219 9k multi 1.00 .30

Furniture — A1220

Designs: 6.40k, Armchair, 17th cent. 9k, Sewing table with hemispheric cover, 1820. 12k, Dressing table with mirror, 1860. 17k, Art deco amchair, 1923.

2002, Dec. 11

3184-3187 A1220 Set of 4 5.00 2.25

Painting Type of 1967 Inscribed "CESKA REPUBLIKA"

Designs: 12k, The Abandoned, by Jaroslav Panuska, horiz. 20k, St. Wenceslas, by Mikolás Ales. 26k, Portrait of a Young Man with a Lute, by Jan Petr Molitor.

2002, Dec. 11 **Engr.** ***Perf. 11¾***

3188-3190 A565 Set of 3 6.50 3.75

Nos. 3188-3190 were each issued in sheets of 4. Value, set $27.

Souvenir Sheet

Czech Republic, 10th Anniv. — A1221

Litho. & Engr.

2003, Jan. 1 ***Perf. 11¾***

3191 A1221 25k multi 2.75 1.60

Tradition of Czech Stamp Production — A1222

Photo. & Engr.

2003, Jan. 20 ***Perf. 11¼x11¾***

3192 A1222 6.40k Type A75 .75 .25

a. Booklet pane of 8 + 2 labels 6.00 —

Complete booklet, #3192a 6.00

Famous Men — A1223

Designs: 6.40k, Jaroslav Vrchlicky (1853-1912), poet. 8k, Josef Thomayer (1853-1927), physician and writer.

2003, Feb. 12 ***Perf. 11½x11¼***

3193-3194 A1223 Set of 2 1.60 .50

Easter — A1224

2003, Mar. 26 ***Perf. 11¼x11½***

3195 A1224 6.40k multi .75 .25

Roses Above Prague — A1225

Perf. 12¾x13¼

2003, Mar. 26 **Litho.**

3196 A1225 6.40k multi + label .75 .35

Labels could be personalized.
Issued in sheets of 9 stamps and 12 labels. Value $9.
See No. 3517.

Lace
A1226

Designs: 6.40k, Netted lace. 9k, Bobbin lace.

Photo. & Engr.

2003, Mar. 26 *Perf. 11¼*

3197 A1226 6.40k bl, dk bl & red	.75	.25
a. Booklet pane of 6 + 4 labels	4.50	—
Complete booklet, #3197a	4.50	
3198 A1226 9k dk bl, bl & red	1.00	.35
a. Booklet pane of 6 + 4 labels	6.00	—
Complete booklet, #3197a	6.00	

Europa — A1227

Litho. & Engr.

2003, May 7 *Perf. 11¾*

3199 A1227 9k multi 1.00 .65

Geologic Attractions — A1228

Designs: 12k, Sandstone towers, Hrubá Skála Region. 14k, Punkva Caves, Moravian karst area.

2003, May 7 Engr. *Perf. 11½x11¾*

3200-3201 A1228 Set of 2 3.00 2.00

Nos. 3200-3201 were each issued in sheets of 8. Value, set $25.

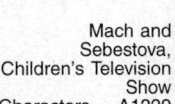

Mach and Sebestova, Children's Television Show Characters — A1229

Photo. & Engr.

2003, May 28 *Perf. 11¼x11½*

3202 A1229 6.40k multi .75 .35

First Electric Railway, Tábor — Bechyne, Cent.
A1230

2003, May 28 *Perf. 11¾x11¼*

3203 A1230 10k multi 1.25 .50

A1231

Observation towers: No. 3204, 6.40k, Klet. No. 3205, 6.40k, Slovanka.

2003, May 28 *Perf. 11¼x11½*

3204-3205 A1231 Set of 2 1.50 .50

A1232

2003, June 25 *Perf. 11¾x11¼*

3206 A1232 9k multi 1.00 .35

European Shooting Championships, Plzen and Brno.

A1233

2003, June 25 *Perf. 11¼x11½*

3207 A1233 9k multi 1.00 .35

Josef Dobrovsky (1753-1829), linguist.

Pres. Vaclav Klaus — A1234

Photo. & Engr.

2003 *Perf. 11¾x11¼*

3208 A1234 6.40k buff, red & vio bl	.75	.35
3209 A1234 6.50k Prus bl & pur	.75	.35

Issued: 6.40k, 7/30; 6.50k, 11/5.

See No. 3264.

Souvenir Sheet

Tropical Fish — A1235

No. 3210: a, 12k, Betta splendens (27x44mm). b, 14k, Pterophyllum scalare (27x44mm). c, 16k, Carassius auratus (54x44mm). d, 20k, Symphysodon aequifasciatus (54x44mm).

Litho. & Engr.

2003, Sept. 10 *Perf. 11¾*

3210 A1235 Sheet of 4, #a-d 7.25 5.00

Oriental Carpets
A1236

Designs: 9k, Turkish prayer carpet, 19th cent. 12k, Turkish carpet, 18th cent.

2003, Oct. 1 Engr. *Perf. 11¾*

3211-3212 A1236 Set of 2 2.50 1.75

Nos. 3211-3212 were each issued in sheets of 4. Value, set $10.

Tympanum, Porta Coeli Monastery, Predklásterí — A1237

Photo. & Engr.

2003, Oct. 15 *Perf. 11¾x11¼*

3213 A1237 6.50k multi	.75	.45
a. Booklet pane of 8 + 4 labels	6.00	—
Complete booklet, #3213a	6.00	

Birds of Prey — A1238

Designs: 6.50k, Milvus milvus. 8k, Falco peregrinus. 9k, Hieraaetus pennatus.

2003, Oct. 15 *Perf. 11¼x11½*

3214 A1238 6.50k multi	.75	.25
Booklet, 5 #3214	3.75	
3215 A1238 8k multi	.90	.30
Booklet, 5 #3215	4.50	
3216 A1238 9k multi	1.00	.30
Booklet, 5 #3216	5.00	
Nos. 3214-3216 (3)	2.65	.85

Czech Fire Fighters, 140th Anniv.
A1239

Fire engines: 6.50k, Wooden fire engine, 1822. 9k, Motorized fire engine, 1933. 12k, CAS 8/Avia Daewoo fire truck, 2002.

2003, Oct. 15 *Perf. 11¾x11¼*

3217-3219 A1239 Set of 3 3.25 1.50

Flower Type of 2002

Designs: 50h, Cornflower (chrpa). 6.50k, Dahlia (jirina).

2003, Oct. 22

3220 A1215 50h multi	.25	.25
3221 A1215 6.50k multi	.75	.25

Roses Over Prague Type of 2003 and

Prague Castle Lantern — A1240

2003, Oct. 22 Litho. *Perf. 12¾x13¼*

3222 A1225 6.50k multi + label	.75	.25
3223 A1240 9k multi + label	1.00	.30

Labels could be personalized.

Nos. 3222-3223 were each issued in sheets of 9 stamps and 12 labels. Value, set $17.50.

Painting Type of 1967 Inscribed "CESKA REPUBLIKA"

Designs: 17k, Poor Countryside, by Max Svabinsky, horiz. 20k, Autumn in Veltrusy, by Antonín Slavícek. 26k, Eleanora de Toledo, by Agnolo Bronzino.

2003, Nov. 5 Engr. *Perf. 11¾*

3224-3226 A565 Set of 3 7.25 4.00

Nos. 3224-3226 were each issued in sheets of 4. Value, set $30.

Christmas
A1241

Photo. & Engr.

2003, Nov. 5 *Perf. 11¼x11½*

3227 A1241 6.50k multi .75 .35

Tradition of Czech Stamp Production
A1242

Photo. & Engr.

2004, Jan. 20 *Perf. 11¼x11¾*

3228 A1242 6.50k Vignette of #1703	.75	.35
a. Booklet pane of 8 + 4 labels	6.00	—
Complete booklet, #3228a	6.00	

Church of the Assumption of the Virgin Mary, Brno — A1243

2004, Feb. 18 Engr. *Perf. 11¾*

3229 A1243 17k multi 1.90 1.00

Brno 2005 Philatelic Exhibition.

No. 3229 was issued in sheets of 4. Value $8.

Industrial Building Historical Preservation
A1244

Designs: 6.50k, Busek's Water Forging Hammer, Lniste. 17k, Iron Furnace, Stará Hut u Adamova.

Photo. & Engr.

2004, Feb. 18 *Perf. 11½x11¼*

3230-3231 A1244 Set of 2 2.75 .90

Easter
A1245

2004, Mar. 17

3232 A1245 6.50k multi .75 .25

Painting Type of 1967 Inscribed "ČESKÁ REPUBLIKA"

Design: Prometheus, by Antonín Procházka.

2004, Mar. 17 Engr. ***Perf. 11¾***
3233 A565 26k multi 3.00 1.60

Brno 2005 Philatelic Exhibition. No. 3233 was issued in sheets of 4. Value $12.

World Ice Hockey Championships, Prague and Ostrava — A1246

Photo. & Engr.

2004, Apr. 14 ***Perf. 11¼x11¾***
3234 A1246 12k multi 1.50 .50

Admission to European Union A1247

Photo. & Engr.

2004, May 1 ***Perf. 11¼***
3235 A1247 9k multi 1.00 .35

Admission to the European Union — A1248

2004, May 1 Litho. ***Perf. 11¾x11¼***
3236 A1248 9k multi 1.00 .35

No. 3236 was issued in sheets of 10. Value $8.

Europa A1249

2004, May 5 ***Perf. 11¼***
3237 A1249 9k multi 1.00 .35

Composers of Czech Operas — A1250

Designs: 6.50k, Dalibor, by Bedrich Smetana (1824-84). 8k, Jakobín, by Antonín Dvorák (1841-1904). 10k, Její Pastorkyna, by Leos Janácek (1854-1928).

Photo. & Engr.

2004, May 5 ***Perf. 11¼x11¾***
3238-3240 A1250 Set of 3 2.75 1.10

For Children A1251

Photo. & Engr.

2004, May 26 ***Perf. 11½x11¼***
3241 A1251 6.50k multi .75 .25
a. Booklet pane of 8 + 2 labels 6.00 —
Complete booklet, #3241a 6.00

Statue of Radegast, by Albín Polásek — A1252

2004, May 26 ***Perf. 11¼x11½***
3242 A1252 6.50k multi .75 .25

Brno 2005 Philatelic Exhibition.

Tourist Attractions — A1253

Designs: 12k, Holy Mountain, Príbram. 14k, Holy Shrine, Bystrice pod Hostynem.

2004, May 26 Engr. ***Perf. 11½x11¾***
3243-3244 A1253 Set of 2 3.00 1.50

Nos. 3243-3244 were each issued in sheets of 8. Value, set $24.

A1254 A1255

Photo. & Engr.

2004, June 23 ***Perf. 11¼x11¾***
3245 A1254 6.50k multi .75 .25

2004 Paralympics, Athens.

2004, June 23
3246 A1255 9k multi 1.00 .35

2004 Summer Olympics, Athens.

Petrarch (1304-74), Poet — A1256

2004, June 23 ***Perf. 11¾x11¼***
3247 A1256 14k multi 1.75 .60

Famous Trees — A1257

Designs: 6.50k, Singing lime tree, Telecí. 8k, Jan Zizka oak tree, Podhradí.

Photo. & Engr.

2004, Sept. 8 ***Perf. 11¼x11½***
3248 A1257 6.50k multi .75 .25
Complete booklet, 5 #3248 3.75
3249 A1257 8k multi .90 .30
Complete booklet, 5 #3249 4.50

Miniature Sheet

Parrots — A1258

No. 3250: a, 12k, Melopsittacus undulatus. b, 14k, Agapornis personata. c, 16k, Psittacula krameri. d, 20k, Ara chloroptera.

Litho. & Engr.

2004, Sept. 8 ***Perf. 11¾***
3250 A1258 Sheet of 4, #a-d, + 4 labels 7.00 4.50

Compulsory School Attendance, 230th Anniv. — A1259

Photo. & Engr.

2004, Sept. 29 ***Perf. 11¼x11½***
3251 A1259 6.50k multi .75 .25

Baby Carriages — A1260

Carriages made about: 12k, 1880. 14k, 1890. 16k, 1900.

2004, Oct. 20
3252-3254 A1260 Set of 3 4.75 2.00

Painting Type of 1967 Inscribed "ČESKÁ REPUBLIKA"

Designs: 20k, On the Outskirts of the Cesky Ráj Region, by Alois Bubák, horiz. 22k, The Long, the Broad and the Sharpsight, by Hanus Schwaiger. 26k, The Spring, by Vojtéch Hynais.

2004, Nov. 10 Engr. ***Perf. 11¾***
3255-3257 A565 Set of 3 7.50 4.25

Nos. 3255-3257 were each issued in sheets of 4. Value, set $32.

Christmas — A1261

Photo. & Engr.

2004, Nov. 10 ***Perf. 11¼x11½***
3258 A1261 6.50k multi .75 .25

Tradition of Czech Stamp Production A1262

2005, Jan. 18 ***Perf. 11¼x11¾***
3259 A1262 6.50k Design of #975 .75 .30
a. Booklet pane of 8 + 4 labels 6.00 —
Complete booklet, #3259a 6.00

Peacock and Bugler Portal Decoration — A1263

2005, Jan. 18 Litho. ***Perf. 12¾x13¼***
3260 A1263 7.50k multi + label .85 .30

Labels could be personalized for an additional fee.

Issued in sheets of 9 stamps and 12 labels. Value $8.

See Nos. 3372, 3516.

Souvenir Sheet

Moonscape, by Petr Ginz — A1264

Perf. 11¾x11½

2005, Jan. 18 Litho. & Engr.
3261 A1264 31k multi 3.50 2.00

Flower Type of 2002

Designs: 7.50k, Lily (lilie). 19k, Fuchsia (fuchsie).

Photo. & Engr.

2005 ***Perf. 11¾x11¼***
3262 A1215 7.50k multi .85 .30
3263 A1215 19k multi 2.25 .85

Issued: 7.50k, 1/20; 19k, 3/2.

Pres. Vaclav Klaus Type of 2003

2005, Feb. 9
3264 A1234 7.50k claret & red .85 .30

Granny, by Bozena Nemcová, 150th Anniv. of Publication A1265

2005, Feb. 9 ***Perf. 11¼x11¾***
3265 A1265 7.50k multi .85 .30

Easter — A1266

Photo. & Engr.

2005, Mar. 2 ***Perf. 11¼x11½***
3266 A1266 7.50k multi .85 .30

UNESCO World Heritage Sites Type of 2001

Designs: 14k, St. Prokop's Basilica, Trebíc, vert. 16k, Villa Tugendhat, Brno.

Perf. 11¾x11½, 11½x11¾

2005, Mar. 23 **Engr.**
3267-3268 A1199 Set of 2 3.50 1.90

Nos. 3267-32682 were each issued in sheets of 8. Value, set $28.

Famous Men — A1267

Designs: 7.50k, Bohuslav Brauner (1855-1935), chemist. 12k, Adalbert Stifter (1805-68), writer, painter. 19k, Mikulás Dacicky of Heslov (1555-1626), poet.

Photo. & Engr.

2005, Apr. 13 ***Perf. 11¼x11¾***
3269-3271 A1267 Set of 3 4.25 1.60

Europa A1268

2005, May 4 **Litho.** ***Perf. 11¼***
3272 A1268 9k multi 1.00 .35

Battle of Austerlitz, Bicent. — A1269

Napoleon Before the Battle of Austerlitz, by Louis-François Lejeune — A1270

Photo. & Engr.

2005, May 4 ***Perf. 11¾x11¼***
3273 A1269 19k multi 2.00 .90

Souvenir Sheet

Litho. & Engr.

Perf. 11¾

3274 A1270 30k multi 3.50 2.25

Brno 2005 Stamp Exhibition (No. 3274). See France No. 3115.

Kremílek and Vochomurka, by Václav Ctvrtek — A1271

Photo. & Engr.

2005, May 25 ***Perf. 11¼x11½***
3275 A1271 7.50k multi .85 .30
a. Booklet pane of 8 + 2 labels 7.00 —
Complete booklet, #3275a 7.00

A1272

A1273

2005, May 25 ***Perf. 11¼x11¾***
3276 A1272 12k multi 1.40 .75

Intl. Year of Physics.

2005, June 22
3277 A1273 9k multi 1.00 .50

2005 European Baseball Championships.

Souvenir Sheet

Protected Flora and Fauna of the Krkonose Mountains — A1274

No. 3278: a, 12k, Viola lutea sudetica, Hedysarum hedysaroides (44x28mm). b, 14k, Cinclus cinclus, Leucojum vernum (44x28mm). c, 15k, Sorex alpinus, Salamandra salamandra, Primula minima (44x54mm). d, 22k, Mt. Snezka, Luscinia svecica svecica, Aeschna coerulea, Pneumonanthe asclepiadea (44x54mm).

Litho. & Engr.

2005, June 22 ***Perf. 11¾***
3278 A1274 Sheet of 4, #a-d, + 4 labels 7.00 4.25

Church Bells — A1275

Bells from: 7.50k, Benesov, 1322, Havlíckuv Brod, 1335. 9k, Dobrs, 1561, 1596. 12k, Olomouc, 1827.

Photo. & Engr.

2005, Sept. 7 ***Perf. 11½x11¾***
3279 A1275 7.50k multi .85 .30
Complete booklet, 5 #3279 4.25
3280 A1275 9k multi 1.00 .40
Complete booklet, 5 #3280 5.00
3281 A1275 12k multi 1.40 .50
Complete booklet, 5 #3281 7.00
Nos. 3279-3281 (3) 3.25 1.20

Tractors A1276

Designs: 7.50k, 1923 John Deere 15/27. 9k, 1921 Lanz Bulldog HL-12, 1596. 18k, 1937 Skoda HT 40.

2005, Sept. 21 ***Perf. 11½x11¼***
3282 A1276 7.50k multi .85 .30
Complete booklet, 5 #3282 4.25
3283 A1276 9k multi 1.00 .35
Complete booklet, 5 #3283 5.00
3284 A1276 18k multi 2.00 .75
Complete booklet, 5 #3284 10.00
Nos. 3282-3284 (3) 3.85 1.40

World Summit on the Information Society, Tunis A1277

2005, Sept. 21 ***Perf. 11¼***
3285 A1277 9k org & violet 1.00 .35

Curling A1278

Photo. & Engr.

2005, Oct. 12 ***Perf. 11¾x11¼***
3286 A1278 17k multi 2.00 .70

Painting Type of 1967 Inscribed "CESKÁ REPUBLIKA"

Designs: 22k, Summer Landscape, by Adolf Kosárek. 25k, Deinotherium, by Zdenék Burian. 26k, Osiky Near Velké Nemcice, by Alois Kalvoda.

2005, Nov. 9 **Engr.** ***Perf. 11¾***
3287-3289 A565 Set of 3 8.00 5.25

Nos. 3287-3289 were each issued in sheets of 4. Value, set $32.50.

A1279

Christmas A1280

Photo. & Engr.

2005, Nov. 9 ***Perf. 11¼x11½***
3290 A1279 7.50k multi .85 .30

Perf. 11½x11¼

3291 A1280 9k multi 1.00 .35

Tradition of Czech Stamp Production A1281

Photo. & Engr.

2006, Jan. 20 ***Perf. 11¼x11¾***
3292 A1281 7.50k Portion of #C59 .85 .30
a. Booklet pane of 8 + 2 labels 7.00 —
Complete booklet, #3292a 7.00

Flower Type of 2002

Designs: 11k, Marshmallow (ibisek). 24k, Daffodil (narcis).

2006 ***Perf. 11¾x11¼***
3293 A1215 11k multi 1.25 .45
3294 A1215 24k multi 2.75 1.00

Issued: 11k, 2/1; 24k, 2/22.

Flowers — A1282

Flowers, Grapes, Glass of Wine — A1283

2006 **Litho.** ***Perf. 12¾x13¼***
3295 A1282 10k multi + label 1.10 .60
3296 A1283 12k multi + label 1.40 .75

Issued: 10k, 2/1; 12k, 2/22. Labels could be personalized for an additional fee.

Nos. 3295-3296 were issued in sheets of 9 stamps and 12 labels. Value, set $22.50.

See No. 3373.

Madonna of Zbraslav — A1284

2006, Feb. 8 Engr. *Perf. 11¾*

3297 A1284 25k multi 2.75 1.75

Printed in sheets of 4. Value $11.

2006 Winter Paralympics, Turin — A1285

Photo. & Engr.

2006, Feb. 8 *Perf. 11¾x11¼*

3298 A1285 7.50k multi .85 .30

2006 Winter Olympics, Turin — A1286

2006 *Perf. 11¼x11¾*

3299 A1286 9k multi 1.00 .40

With "K. NEUMANNOVA / ZLATA MEDAILE" Overprinted in Red Reading Up

3300 A1286 9k multi 1.00 .40

Issued: No. 3299, 2/8; No. 3300, 3/15.

Famous Men — A1287

Designs: 11k, Frantisek Josef Gerstner (1756-1832), mathematician and educator. 12k, Jaroslav Jezek (1906-42), composer. 19k, Sigmund Freud (1856-1939), psychoanalyst.

2006, Feb. 22 *Perf. 11½x11¼*

3301-3303 A1287 Set of 3 4.75 1.75

Easter — A1288

2006, Mar. 22 *Perf. 11¼x11½*

3304 A1288 7.50k multi .85 .30

Osek Monastery — A1289

Kokorinsko Capstones — A1290

2006, Mar. 22 Engr. *Perf. 11½x11¾*

3305 A1289 12k multi 1.40 .65

3306 A1290 15k multi 1.60 .85

Nos. 3305-3306 were each issued in sheets of 8. Value, set $25.

Love — A1291

Photo. & Engr.

2006, Apr. 26 *Perf. 11¼x11½*

3307 A1291 7.50k multi .85 .35

Complete booklet, 5 #3307 4.25

Europa A1292

Silhouette of person and: 10k, Horse. 20k, Dog.

2006, May 3 *Perf. 11¾x11¼*

3308-3309 A1292 Set of 2 3.25 1.40

Rumcajs, Manka and Cipísek, by V. Ctvrtek — A1293

Photo. & Engr.

2006, May 31 *Perf. 11¼x11½*

3310 A1293 7.50k multi .85 .35

a. Booklet pane of 8 + 2 labels 7.00 —

Complete booklet, #3310a 7.00

A1294

A1295

2006, June 14 *Perf. 11¼x11¾*

3311 A1294 19k multi 2.25 .90

Kamenice Pass, Czech Switzerland National Park.

2006, June 14

Jewelry with garnets: 15k, Silver brooch with pearl, 1904. 18k, Gold pendant, 1930.

3312-3313 A1295 Set of 2 3.75 1.75

Miniature Sheet

Bohemian Kings of Premyslid Dynasty — A1296

No. 3314: a, 12k, Otakar I Premysl (c. 1155-1230). b, 14k, Václav (Wenceslas) I (1205-53). c, 15k, Otakar II Premysl (1230-78). d, 22k, Václav (Wenceslas) II (1271-1305). e, 28k, Václav (Wenceslas) III (1289-1306).

2006, June 14 Engr. *Perf. 11¾*

3314 A1296 Sheet of 5, #a-e, + label 10.00 6.00

Souvenir Sheet

Mosaic of Prague Castle, by Giovanni Castrucci — A1297

Litho. & Engr.

2006, Sept. 13 *Perf. 11¾*

3315 A1297 35k multi 3.75 2.25

Cacti — A1298

No. 3316: a, Gymnocalycium denudatum. b, Obregonia denegrii.

No. 3317: a, Astrophytum asterias. b, Cintia knizei.

Perf. 11¼x11¾

2006, Sept. 13 Litho.

3316 A1298 7.50k Pair, #a-b 1.50 .90

Complete booklet, 2 #3316a, 3 #3316b 3.50

3317 A1298 10k Pair, #a-b 2.00 1.25

Complete booklet, 2 #3317a, 3 #3317b 5.00

Ecology A1299

2006, Sept. 27 *Perf. 11¾x11¼*

3318 A1299 7.50k multi .85 .35

Christmas — A1300

2006, Oct. 11 *Perf. 12¾x13¼*

3319 A1300 7.50k multi + label .85 .35

Printed in sheets of 9 stamps + 12 labels. Labels could be personalized.

Vrtbovská Garden, Prague — A1301

Photo. & Engr.

2006, Oct. 11 *Perf. 11½x11¾*

3320 A1301 7.50k multi .80 .35

a. Booklet pane of 8 + 4 labels 6.50 —

Complete booklet, #3320a 6.50

Praga 2008 Intl. Philatelic Exhibition, Prague.

Wooden Churches — A1302

Designs: 7.50k, Church of the Virgin Mary, Broumov. 19k, Church of St. Andrew, Hodslavice.

Photo. & Engr.

2006, Oct. 11 *Perf. 11¾x11¼*

3321-3322 A1302 Set of 2 2.75 1.60

Painting Type of 1967 Inscribed "CESKA REPUBLIKA"

Designs: 22k, Still Life with Fruit, by Jan Davidsz de Heem. 25k, Montenegrin Madonna, by Jaroslav Cermák. 28k, Pod Suchym Skalim, by Frantisek Kaván, horiz.

2006, Nov. 8 Engr. *Perf. 11¾*

3323-3325 A565 Set of 3 8.00 4.50

Christmas — A1303

Photo. & Engr.

2006, Nov. 8 *Perf. 11¾x11½*
3326 A1303 7.50k multi .75 .35

Emblem of Praga 2008 Intl. Philatelic Exhibition — A1304

2006, Dec. 1 **Litho.**
3327 A1304 7.50k multi .75 .35

See Nos. 3341, 3368.

Czech Technical University, Prague, 300th Anniv. — A1305

Photo. & Engr.

2007, Jan. 10 *Perf. 11¾x11½*
3328 A1305 9k multi 1.00 .50

Famous Men — A1306

Designs: 7.50k, Fràna Šràmek (1877-1952), writer. 19k, Karel Slavoj Amerling (1807-84), educator.

2007, Jan. 10 *Perf. 11½x11¼*
3329-3330 A1306 Set of 2 3.00 1.40

Tradition of Czech Stamp Production A1307

2007, Jan. 20 *Perf. 11½x11¾*
3331 A1307 7.50k Type A242 .70 .35
a. Booklet pane of 8 + 4 labels 5.75 —
Complete booklet, #3331a 5.75

Cancer Prevention A1308

Photo. & Engr.

2007, Feb. 21 *Perf. 11¼x11½*
3332 A1308 7.50k multi .85 .35

Snake — A1309

Perf. 11¼x11¾

2007, Feb. 21 **Litho.**
3333 A1309 12k multi 1.40 .70

Oriental Art A1310

Designs: 12k, Girl with a Puppet, by Kunisawa Utagawa. 24k, Siva, Parvati and Ganesa, 19th cent. Indian glass painting.

Litho. & Engr.

2007, Feb. 21 *Perf. 11¾*
3334-3335 A1310 Set of 2 4.00 2.10

Easter — A1311

Photo. & Engr.

2007, Mar. 14 *Perf. 11¼x11½*
3336 A1311 7.50k multi .85 .35

Model of Mala Strana Area of Prague, by Antonín Langweil — A1312

2007, Mar. 14 *Perf. 11¾x11¼*
3337 A1312 7.50k multi .85 .35

Praga 2008 Intl. Philatelic Exhibition, Prague.

Stoclet House, Brussels, Designed by Josef Hoffmann — A1313

Designs: 20k, Building interior. 35k, Building exterior.

2007, Mar. 26 *Perf. 11¼x11¾*
3338-3339 A1313 Set of 2 6.00 3.25

See Belgium Nos. 2228-2229.

Flowers Type of 2006

Perf. 12¾x13¼

2007, Mar. 26 **Litho.**
3340 A1282 11k multi + label 1.25 .60

Label could be personalized for an additional fee.

Praga 2008 Emblem Type of 2006

2007, Apr. 4 *Perf. 11¾x11½*
3341 A1304 11k blue & multi 1.25 .60

Spas A1314

Designs: 12k, Jurkovic House, Luhacovice. 15k, Gocár Pavillion, Lázne Bohdanec.

2007, Apr. 4 **Engr.** *Perf. 11½x11¾*
3342-3343 A1314 Set of 2 3.00 1.75

Europa A1315

Photo. & Engr.

2007, May 9 *Perf. 11¼*
3344 A1315 11k multi 1.25 .60

Scouting, cent.

Flowers Type of 2002

Designs: 1k, Cyclamen (brambořík). 15k, Tropaeolum (lichořeřisnice). 23k, Geranium (pelargonie).

Photo. & Engr.

2007 *Perf. 11¾x11¼*
3345 A1215 1k multi .25 .25
3346 A1215 15k multi 1.75 .90
3347 A1215 23k multi 2.50 1.25
Nos. 3345-3347 (3) 4.50 2.40

Issued: 1k, 23k, 5/9. 15k, 9/5.

Fast Arrows, Comic Strip by Jaroslav Foglar A1316

Photo. & Engr.

2007, May 30 *Perf. 11¾x11¼*
3348 A1316 7.50k multi .75 .35
a. Booklet pane of 8 + 4 labels 6.00 —
Complete booklet, #3348a 6.00

Historic Stoves — A1317

Designs: 7.50k, Gothic era stove, Olomouc, and tile. 12k, Renaissance era stove, Rícany u Prahy and tile.

Photo. & Engr.

2007, June 20 *Perf. 11½x11¾*
3349 A1317 7.50k multi .70 .35
Complete booklet, 5 #3349 3.50
3350 A1317 12k multi 1.25 .60
Complete booklet, 5 #3350 6.25

Souvenir Sheet

Vaclav Hollar (1607-77), Engraver — A1318

Litho. & Engr.

2007, June 20 *Perf. 11¾*
3351 A1318 35k multi + 2 labels 4.00 2.10

Souvenir Sheet

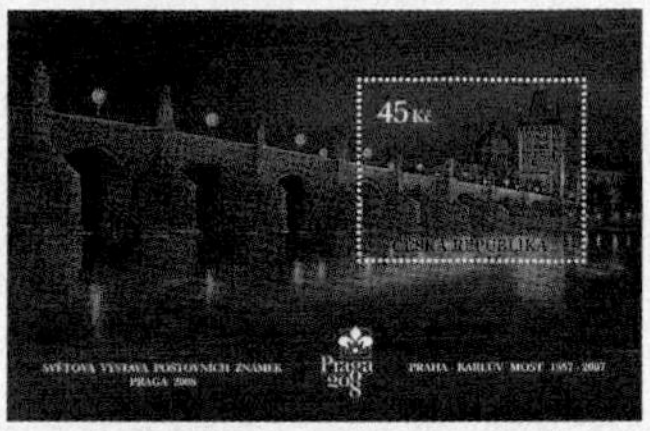

Charles Bridge, Prague, 650th Anniv. — A1319

2007, June 20
3352 A1319 45k multi 5.00 3.00

Praga 2008 World Philatelic Exhibition.

First Movie Theater in Prague, Cent. A1320

Photo. & Engr.

2007, Sept. 5 *Perf. 11¾x11¼*
3353 A1320 7.50k multi .75 .35

Didactica Opera Omnla, by Comenlus, 350th Anniv. — A1321

2007, Sept. 5
3354 A1321 12k multi 1.25 .75

Miniature Sheet

Flora and Fauna of the White Carpathians — A1322

No. 3355: a, 9k, Ophrys holosericea (27x44mm). b, 10k, Colias myrmidone, Anacamptis pyramidalis (27x44mm). c, 11k, Ophrys apifera (27x44mm). d, 12k, Coracias garrulus, Gymnadenia densiflora (54x44mm).

Litho. & Engr.

2007, Sept. 5 *Perf. 11¾*
3355 A1322 Sheet of 4, #a-d, + 4 labels 4.75 2.75

Emil Holub (1847-1902), Naturalist — A1323

Photo. & Engr.

2007, Oct. 3 *Perf. 11¾x11¼*
3356 A1323 11k multi 1.25 .65

Water Towers — A1324

Towers in: 7.50k, Karviná. 18k, Plzen.

2007, Oct. 3 *Perf. 11¼x11¾*
3357-3358 A1324 Set of 2 2.75 1.50

Painting Type of 1967 Inscribed "CESKA REPUBLIKA"

Designs: 22k, Vrbicany Castle, by Amálie Mánesova, horiz. 25k, Way to Bechnye Castle, by Otakar Lebeda. 28k, Montmartre, by Sobeslav Hippolyt Pinkas, horiz.

2007, Nov. 7 **Engr.** *Perf. 11¾*
3359-3361 A565 Set of 3 8.25 4.50

Christmas — A1325

Photo. & Engr.

2007, Nov. 7 *Perf. 11¼x11½*
3362 A1325 7.50k multi .85 .40

Flower Type of 2002

Design: 2.50k, Gaillardia (kokarda); 3k, Azalea (azalka); 10k, Rose (ruze); 21k, Gerbera daisy (gerbera).

Photo. & Engr.

2007-08 *Perf. 11¾x11¼*
3363 A1215 2.50k multi .30 .25
3364 A1215 3k multi .40 .25
3365 A1215 10k multi 1.25 .60
3366 A1215 21k multi 2.60 1.40
Nos. 3363-3366 (4) 4.55 2.50

Issued: 2.50k, 12/12/07; 3k, 3/19/08; 10k, 1/30/08; 21k, 3/5/08.

Czech Republic's Entry Into Schengen Border-Free Zone A1326

2007, Dec. 19 **Litho.** *Perf. 11¼*
3367 A1326 10k multi 1.10 .55

Praga 2008 Emblem Type of 2006

2007, Dec. 19 *Perf. 11¾x11¼*
3368 A1304 18k bl grn & blue 2.00 1.00

Tradition of Czech Stamp Production A1327

Photo. & Engr.

2008, Jan. 20 *Perf. 11¼x11¾*
3369 A1327 10k Type A311 1.25 .60
a. Booklet pane of 8 + 4 labels 10.00 —
Complete booklet, #3369a 10.00

Famous Men — A1328

Designs: 11k, Karel Klostermann (1848-1923), writer. 14k, Josef Kajetán Tyl (1808-56), playwright.

2008, Jan. 20 *Perf. 11¼x11½*
3370-3371 A1328 Set of 2 3.00 1.50

Peacock and Bugler Type of 2005 and Flowers, Grapes and Glass of Wine Type of 2006 Redrawn

2008, Jan. 30 **Litho.** *Perf. 12¾x13¼*
3372 A1263 10k multi + label 1.25 .60
3373 A1283 17k multi + label 2.00 1.00

Nos. 3372-3373 were issued in sheets of 9 stamps and 12 labels. Labels could be personalized for an additional fee.

George of Podebrady (1420-71), King of Bohemia — A1329

Photo. & Engr.

2008, Feb. 20 *Perf. 11¼x11¾*
3374 A1329 12k multi 1.50 .75

Intl. Year of Planet Earth A1330

2008, Feb. 20 **Litho.** *Perf. 11¼*
3375 A1330 18k multi 2.00 1.10

Easter A1331

Photo. & Engr.

2008, Mar. 5 *Perf. 11½x11¼*
3376 A1331 10k multi 1.25 .60

Bath Servant Zuzana Carrying King Wenceslas IV Over the Vltava River, by J. Navrátil — A1332

2008, Mar. 5 *Perf. 11¾x11¼*
3377 A1332 10k multi 1.25 .60
a. Booklet pane of 8 + 4 labels 10.00 —
Complete booklet, #3377a 10.00

Praga 2008 Intl. Philatelic Exhibition, Prague.

Publication of Orbis Pictus, Children's Picture Book, by Comenius, 350th Anniv. — A1333

2008, Mar. 19 *Perf. 11¼x11¾*
3378 A1333 10k multi 1.25 .60

Mountaintop Hotel With Broadcast Tower, Jested — A1334

Hradec Kralové Buildings and Monuments A1335

2008, Mar. 19 **Engr.** *Perf. 11½*
3379 A1334 12k multi 1.40 .75
3380 A1335 15k multi 1.75 .95

Pres. Klaus Type of 2003

Photo. & Engr.

2008, Apr. 2 *Perf. 11¾x11¼*
3381 A1234 10k multi 1.25 .60

A1336

A1337

Items in National Technical Museum: 10k, Reichenbach-Ertel astronomical theodolite, c. 1830. 14k, 1935 Jawa 750 sports car, horiz. 18k, Märky, Bromovsky-Schulz gasoline combustion engine, c. 1889.

Perf. 11¼x11¾, 11¾x11¼
2008, Apr. 16 **Photo. & Engr.**
3382-3384 A1336 Set of 3 4.50 2.60

National Technical Museum, Prague, cent.

2008, Apr. 16 *Perf. 11¼x11¾*
3385 A1337 17k multi 2.10 1.10

Czech Hockey Association, cent.

Europa A1338

2008, May 7 **Litho.** *Perf. 11¾x11¼*
3386 A1338 17k multi 2.10 1.10

The Doggy's and Pussy's Tales, Children's Book by Josef Capek A1339

Photo. & Engr.

2008, May 28 *Perf. 11½x11¼*
3387 A1339 10k multi 1.40 .70
a. Booklet pane of 8 + 2 labels 11.50 —
Complete booklet, #3387a 11.50

Souvenir Sheet

Ledeburk Gardens, Prague — A1340

Litho. & Engr.

2008, May 28 *Perf. 11¾*
3388 A1340 51k multi 6.00 3.25

Praga 2008 World Philatelic Exhibition.

Miniature Sheet

Flora and Fauna of Trebon Basin UNESCO Biosphere Reservation — A1341

No. 3389: a, 10k, Alcedo atthis (28x44mm). b, 12k, Lutra lutra and Spiraea salicifolia (54x44mm). c, 14k, Haliaeetus albicilla (54x44mm). d, 18k, Netta rufina and Nymphaea alba (54x44mm).

2008, May 28
3389 A1341 Sheet of 4, #a-d, + 3 labels 6.25 3.50

2008 Paralympics, Beijing — A1342

Perf. 11¾x11¼
2008, June 18 **Litho.**
3390 A1342 10k multi 1.25 .70

2008 Summer Olympics, Beijing — A1343

2008, June 18
3391 A1343 18k multi 2.10 1.25

Explorers — A1344

Designs: 12k, Ferdinand Stolicka (1838-74), explorer of Himalayas. 21k, Alois Musil (1868-1944), explorer of Jordanian desert.

2008, June 18 **Photo. & Engr.**

3392-3393 A1344 Set of 2 4.00 2.25

Children's Book Illustration by Josef Palacek — A1345

2008, Sept. 3 Litho. ***Perf. 12¾x13¼***

3394 A1345 10k multi + label 1.25 .60

Printed in sheets of 9 stamps + 12 labels. Labels could be personalized.

Emmaus Monastery, Prague — A1346

Photo. & Engr.

2008, Sept. 3 ***Perf. 11¼x11¾***

3395 A1346 10k multi 1.25 .60
Tete-beche pair 2.50 *2.50*

Praga 2008 World Philatelic Exhibition.

Applied Art Designers' Association, Cent. — A1347

2008, Sept. 3 ***Perf. 11¾x11¼***

3396 A1347 26k multi 3.00 1.60

Karel Plicka (1894-1987), Photographer — A1348

Litho. & Engr.

2008, Sept. 12 ***Perf. 11¾***

3397 A1348 35k multi + 2 labels 4.00 2.10

See Slovakia No. 548.

Souvenir Sheet

Mail Coach — A1349

2008, Sept. 12

3398 A1349 35k multi 4.00 2.10

Praga 2008 Intl. Stamp Exhibition, Prague, and 2008 Vienna Intl. Stamp Exhibition. See Austria No. 2172.

Stoves — A1350

Stove from: 10k, Sternberk Castle. 17k, Archbishop's Palace, Prague.

Photo. & Engr.

2008, Oct. 15 ***Perf. 11¼x11¾***

3399 A1350 10k multi 1.10 .55
Complete booklet, 5 #3399 5.50

3400 A1350 17k multi 1.90 .95
Complete booklet, 5 #3400 9.50

Painting Type of 1967 Inscribed "CESKA REPUBLIKA"

Designs: 23k, Vltava River at Klecany, by Zdenka Braunerová, horiz. 26k, Autumn Road, by Otakar Nejedly.

2008, Nov. 5 **Engr.** ***Perf. 11¾***

3401-3402 A565 Set of 2 5.75 3.00

Souvenir Sheet

Allegory of Water, by Jan Jakub Hartman — A1351

2008, Nov. 5 **Litho. & Engr.**

3403 A1351 30k multi 3.50 1.75

Basket With Apples — A1352

Winter Scene — A1353

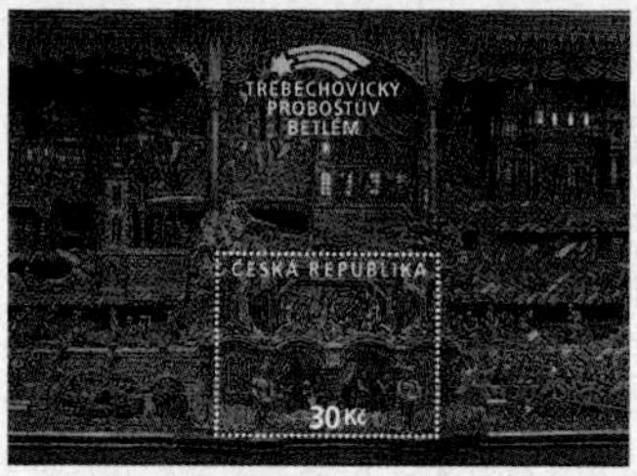

Mechanical Christmas Display — A1354

Photo. & Engr.

2008, Nov. 5 ***Perf. 11¼x11½***

3404 A1352 10k multi 1.10 .55

Litho.

Perf. 12¾x13¼

3405 A1353 10k multi + label 1.10 .55

Souvenir Sheet

Litho. & Engr.

Perf. 11¾

3406 A1354 30k multi 3.50 1.75

Christmas. No. 3405 was printed in sheets of 9 stamps + 12 labels. Labels could be personalized.

Czech Republic Presidency of European Union, January to June 2009 — A1355

Perf. 11¾x11¼

2008, Nov. 25 **Litho.**

3407 A1355 17k multi + label 2.00 .90

Louis Braille (1809-52), Educator of the Blind — A1356

Charles Darwin (1809-82), Naturalist — A1357

2009, Jan. 2 **Photo. & Engr.**

3408 A1356 10k multi 1.10 .55

3409 A1357 12k multi 1.25 .60

Tradition of Czech Stamp Production A1358

2009, Jan. 20 ***Perf. 11¼x11¾***

3410 A1358 10k Design of #980 1.00 .50
a. Booklet pane of 8 + 4 labels 8.25 —
Complete booklet, #3410a 8.25

Nordic World Skiing Championships, Liberec — A1359

Perf. 11¾x11¼

2009, Feb. 11 **Litho.**

3411 A1359 18k multi 1.75 1.75

Souvenir Sheet

Preservation of Polar Regions and Glaciers — A1360

Litho. & Engr.

2009, Feb. 11 ***Perf. 11¾***

3412 A1360 35k multi 3.50 1.90

Easter A1361

Photo. & Engr.

2009, Mar. 18 ***Perf. 11½x11¼***

3413 A1361 10k multi 1.10 .55

Lu Tung-pin, by Unknown Chinese Artist — A1362

Mythical Beings, by Unknown Balinese Artist — A1363

Litho. & Engr.

2009, Mar. 18 ***Perf. 11¾***

3414 A1362 18k multi 2.00 1.00

3415 A1363 24k multi 2.50 1.40

Souvenir Sheet

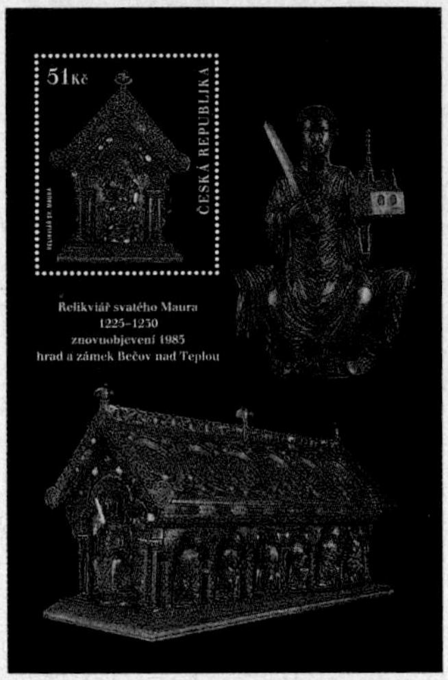

Reliquary of St. Maurus, Becov nad Teplou Castle — A1364

2009, Apr. 8
3416 A1364 51k multi 5.50 3.00

Pardubice to Liberec Rail Line, 150th Anniv. — A1365

Photo. & Engr.

2009, Apr. 22 *Perf. 11¾x11¼*
3417 A1365 10k multi 1.10 .60

Industry and Trade Ministry Building, 75th Anniv. A1366

Photo. & Engr.

2009, Apr. 22 *Perf. 11¾x11½*
3418 A1366 10k multi 1.10 .60

Europa A1367

2009, May 6 Litho. *Perf. 11¼*
3419 A1367 17k multi 2.00 1.00

Intl. Year of Astronomy.

Buildings A1368

Designs: 12k, Cistercian Monastery, Vyssí Brod. 14k, Horsovsky Castle, Tyn.

2009, May 6 Engr. *Perf. 11¾x11½*
3420-3421 A1368 Set of 2 3.00 1.50

Marionettes Spejbl and Hurvínek — A1369

Photo. & Engr.

2009, May 27 *Perf. 11¼x11½*
3422 A1369 10k multi 1.25 .60
a. Booklet pane of 8 + 2 labels 9.00 —
Complete booklet, #3422a 9.00

Rabbi Jehuda Löw (c. 1525-1609) A1370

2009, May 27 Litho. *Perf. 11¼x11¾*
3423 A1370 21k multi 2.50 1.25

Printed in sheets of 5 + 4 labels.

Granting of Religious Freedom by Rudolf II, 400th Anniv. A1371

Photo. & Engr.

2009, June 17 *Perf. 11¼*
3424 A1371 26k multi 3.00 1.50

Intl. Firefighters' Games, Ostrava — A1372

Perf. 11¾x11¼

2009, June 17 Litho.
3425 A1372 17k multi 2.00 1.00

Miniature Sheet

Krivoklát UNESCO Biosphere Reservation — A1373

No. 3426: a, 10k, Eudia pavonia (44x27mm). b, 12k, Aglia tau, Cervus elaphus (44x54mm). c, 14k, Bubo bubo, Lunaria rediviva, Ciconia nigra (44x54mm). d, 17k, Tyto alba, Krivoklát Castle (44x54mm).

Litho. & Engr.

2009, Sept. 2 *Perf. 11¾*
3426 A1373 Sheet of 4, #a-d, + 4 labels 5.75 3.25

Souvenir Sheet

Bohemian-Moravian Highlands — A1374

2009, Sept. 2
3427 A1374 43k multi 4.75 2.50

Windmill, Ruprechtov A1375

Water Mill, Hoslovice A1376

Photo. & Engr.

2009, Sept. 23 *Perf. 11¼x11½*
3428 A1375 10k multi 1.25 .60
Complete booklet, 5 #3428 6.25

Perf. 11½x11¼

3429 A1376 12k multi 1.40 .70
Complete booklet, 5 #3429 7.00

Czech National Anthem, 175th Anniv. — A1377

2009, Oct. 14 *Perf. 11¼x11¾*
3430 A1377 10k multi 1.10 .60

Barbora Markéta Eliásová (1874-1957), Travel Writer — A1378

2009, Oct. 14 *Perf. 11¾x11¼*
3431 A1378 18k multi 2.10 1.10

Stoves — A1379

Designs: 10k, Empire stove, Litomysl Castle. 14k, Biedermeier stove, Vyskov Castle.

2009, Oct. 14 *Perf. 11¼x11¾*
3432 A1379 10k multi 1.25 .60
Complete booklet, 5 #3432 6.25
3433 A1379 14k multi 1.60 .80
Complete booklet, 5 #3433 8.00

Protest Rallies of Nov. 17, 1939, and Nov. 17, 1989 — A1380

2009, Nov. 4 **Litho.**
3434 A1380 14k multi 1.60 .80

Painting Type of 1967 Inscribed "CESKÁ REPUBLIKA"

Designs: 24k, Canal Lock in Moret, by Alfred Sisley, horiz. 26k, Alley, by Alfred Justitz, horiz.

2009, Nov. 4 Engr. *Perf. 11¾*
3435-3436 A565 Set of 2 5.75 3.00

Souvenir Sheet

Oldrich and Bozena, by Frantisek Zenísek — A1381

Litho. & Engr.

2009, Nov. 4 *Perf. 11¾*
3437 A1381 34k multi 4.00 2.00

Christmas — A1382

Photo. & Engr.

2009, Nov. 4 *Perf. 11¼x11½*
3438 A1382 10k multi 1.25 .60

Tradition of Czech Stamp Production A1383

2010, Jan. 20 *Perf. 11¼x11¾*
3439 A1383 10k Vignette of #2121 1.10 .55
a. Booklet pane of 8 + 4 labels 9.00 —
Complete booklet, #3439a 9.00

Magdalena Dobromila Rettigová (1785-1845), Writer — A1384

2010, Jan. 20 ***Perf. 11¾x11¼***
3440 A1384 12k multi 1.25 .65

2010 Winter Olympics, Vancouver — A1385

2010, Feb. 10 ***Perf. 11¼x11¾***
3441 A1385 18k multi 1.90 .95

2010 Winter Paralympics, Vancouver — A1386

2010, Feb. 10
3442 A1386 18k multi 1.90 .95

Souvenir Sheet

Expo 2010, Shanghai — A1387

2010, Feb. 10 **Litho.**
3443 A1387 35k multi + 3 labels 3.75 1.90

Easter A1388

Photo. & Engr.
2010, Mar. 10 ***Perf. 11½x11¼***
3444 A1388 10k multi 1.10 .55

Martina Sáblíková, Gold Medalist at 2010 Winter Olympic Games — A1389

Perf. 11¼x11¾
2010, Mar. 24 **Litho.**
3445 A1389 10k multi 1.10 .55

Souvenir Sheet

Karel Hynek Macha (1810-36), Writer — A1390

Perf. 11½x11¾
2010, Mar. 10 **Litho. & Engr.**
3446 A1390 43k multi 4.75 2.40

Enrique Stanko Vráz (1860-1932), Travel Writer — A1391

Photo. & Engr.
2010, Apr. 14 ***Perf. 11¾x11¼***
3447 A1391 24k multi 2.50 1.25

19th Century Transcaucasian Carpets — A1392

Designs: 21k, Kasim Usak carpet. 24k, Celaberd carpet.

Litho. & Engr.
2010, Apr. 14 ***Perf. 11¾***
3448-3449 A1392 Set of 2 5.00 2.40

Ctyrlístek Comic Strip Character Fifinka — A1393

Serpentine Die Cut 15x16½
2010, Apr. 28 **Litho.**
Booklet Stamp
Self-Adhesive
3450 A1393 A multi 1.10 .55
a. Booklet pane of 10 11.00

No. 3450 sold for 10k on day of issue.

Prague Castle — A1394

2010, May 5 **Engr.** ***Perf. 11¾***
3451 A1394 17k brown 1.75 .85

Prague Castle in the Art of the Postage Stamp Exhibition, Prague. Printed in sheets of 4 + label.

Dásenka, Children's Book by Karel Capek A1395

2010, May 5 **Litho.** ***Perf. 11¼***
3452 A1395 17k multi 1.75 .85

Europa.

Children's Book Illustration by Helena Zmatlíková (1923-2005) A1396

Photo. & Engr.
2010, May 26 ***Perf. 11¼x11½***
3453 A1396 10k multi 1.10 .50
a. Booklet pane of 8 + 2 labels 9.00 —
Complete booklet, #3453a 9.00

Alphonse Mucha (1860-1939), Illustrator — A1397

Designs: E, Gismonda. Z, Zodiac.

Serpentine Die Cut 14¼x14½
2010, May 26 **Litho.**
Booklet Stamps
Self-Adhesive
3454 A1397 E multi 1.60 .80
a. Booklet pane of 6 9.75

Size: 43x54mm
Serpentine Die Cut 14½
3455 A1397 Z multi 1.75 .85
a. Booklet pane of 6 10.50

No. 3454 sold for 17k and No. 3455 sold for 18k on day of issue.

Zd'árské Hills Protected Landscape — A1398

Photo. & Engr.
2010, June 16 ***Perf. 11¾x11½***
3456 A1398 10k multi 1.10 .50

Marriage of John of Luxembourg and Elizabeth of Bohemia, 700th Anniv. — A1399

Photo. & Engr.
2010, June 16 ***Perf. 11¾x11¼***
3457 A1399 17k multi 1.75 .85

Accession to the throne of Bohemia by the House of Luxembourg. See Luxembourg No. 1292.

Astronomical Clock, Prague, 600th Anniv. — A1400

2010, June 16 **Litho.**
3458 A1400 21k multi 2.25 1.10

Towns — A1401

Designs: 12k, Klatovy. 14k, Stramberk.

2010, June 16 **Engr.**
3459-3460 A1401 Set of 2 2.75 1.25

Czech Republic, Winners of 2010 World Ice Hockey Championships A1402

Perf. 11¼x11¾
2010, June 23 **Litho.**
3461 A1402 10k multi 1.10 .50

Ctyrlístek Comic Strip Characters Fifinka, Pind'a, Bobík and Myspulín — A1403

2010, Sept. 1 **Litho.** ***Perf. 12¾x13¼***
3462 A1403 A multi + label 1.10 .55

No. 3462 was printed in sheets of 9 + 12 labels that could be personalized and had a franking value of 10k on day of issue.

Children With Magnifying Glass and Stamp Album — A1404

Boy Examining Stamp — A1405

2010, Sept. 1

3463 A1404 A multi + label 1.10 .55
3464 A1405 E multi + label 2.10 1.10

Nos. 3463-3464 each were printed in sheets of 9 + 12 labels that could be personalized. On day of issue, No. 3463 had a franking value of 10k and No. 3464 had a franking value of 20k.

2010 Women's World Basketball Championships, Czech Republic — A1406

2010, Sept. 1 ***Perf. 11¼x11¾***

3465 A1406 17k multi 1.75 .90

Miniature Sheet

Flora and Fauna of Lower Morava UNESCO Biosphere Reserve — A1407

No. 3466: a, 10k, Tichodroma muraria, Papilio machaon, Aster amellus (45x55mm). b, 12k, Saga pedo, Iris variegata (45x27mm). c, 14k, Lacerta viridis, Pulsatilla grandis (45x27mm). d, 18k, Upupa epops, Arenaria grandiflora (45x55mm).

Litho. & Engr.

2010, Sept. 1 ***Perf. 11¾***

3466 A1407 Sheet of 4, #a-d, + 3 labels 6.00 3.00

Flowers Type of 2002

Designs: 4k, Anemone (sasanka). 25k, Iris (kosatec). 30k, Tulip (tulipán).

Photo. & Engr.

2010 ***Perf. 11¾x11¼***

3467 A1215 4k multi .45 .25
3468 A1215 25k multi 3.00 1.50
3469 A1215 30k multi 3.50 1.75
Nos. 3467-3469 (3) 6.95 3.50

Issued: 4k, 9/29; 25k, 30k, 9/15.

Austrian Empire Post Office Sign, Postal Map, Dwarves with Letters, Handstamp and Posthorn A1408

2010, Sept. 29 Litho. ***Perf. 11¼***

3470 A1408 A multi 1.10 .55

Postal Musuem, Prague. No. 3470 sold for 10k on day of issue.

Famous Men — A1409

Designs: 10k, Adolf Branald (1910-2008), writer. 12k, Karel Zeman (1910-89), film director and animator.

Photo. & Engr.

2010, Sept. 29 ***Perf. 11¼x11½***

3471-3472 A1409 Set of 2 2.50 1.25

Ctyrlístek Comic Strip Character Myspulín — A1410

Serpentine Die Cut 15x16½

2010, Oct. 20 Litho.

Booklet Stamp
Self-Adhesive

3473 A1410 A multi 1.25 .60
a. Booklet pane of 10 12.50

No. 3473 sold for 10k on day of issue.

Bridges A1411

Designs: 10k, Mariánsky Bridge, Ustí nad Labem. 12k, Stone Bridge, Písek.

Photo. & Engr.

2010, Oct. 20 ***Perf. 11¾x11¼***

3474 A1411 10k multi 1.25 .60
Complete booklet, 5 #3474 6.25
3475 A1411 12k multi 1.40 .70
Complete booklet, 5 #3475 7.00

Stoves — A1412

Designs: 10k, Art Nouveau stove. 20k, Art Deco stove.

2010, Oct. 20 ***Perf. 11¼x11¾***

3476 A1412 10k multi 1.25 .60
Complete booklet, 5 #3476 6.25
3477 A1412 20k multi 2.40 1.25
Complete booklet, 5 #3477 12.00

Art Type of 1967 Inscribed "CESKA REPUBLIKA"

Designs: 24k, Paris and Helen, by Karel Skréta. 26k, Sand Bargemen, by Milos Jiránek. 30k, Spring, by Karel Spillar, horiz.

Litho. & Engr. (24k), Engr.

2010, Nov. 10 ***Perf. 11¾***

3478-3480 A565 Set of 3 9.00 4.50

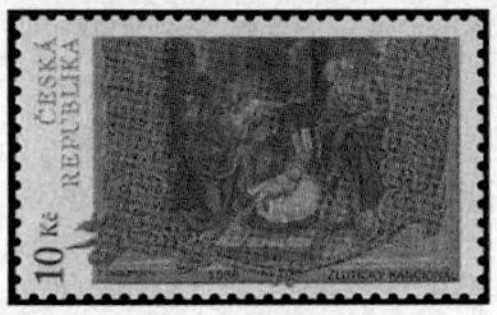

Illumination From 1558 Zlutice Hymn Book — A1413

Perf. 11¼x11¾

2010, Nov. 10 Litho.

3481 A1413 10k multi 1.10 .55

Christmas.

2011 Census — A1414

2011, Jan. 5

3482 A1414 10k black & green 1.10 .55

Souvenir Sheet

Kaspar Maria von Sternberg (1761-1838), Paleobotanist — A1415

Perf. 11¾x11½

2011, Jan. 5 Litho. & Engr.

3483 A1415 43k multi 5.00 2.40

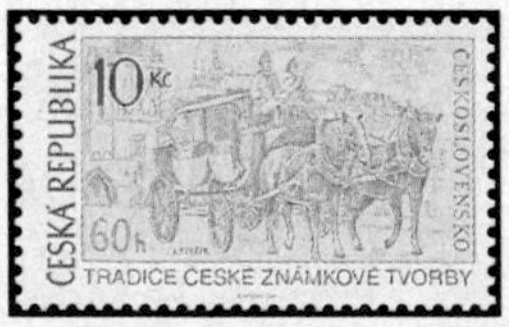

Mail Coach on Charles Bridge, 1966 Envelope Indicia by Josef Hercík — A1416

Photo. & Engr.

2011, Jan. 20 ***Perf. 11¾x11¼***

3484 A1416 10k multi 1.25 .55
a. Booklet pane of 8 + 4 labels 10.00 —
Complete booklet, #3484a 10.00

Tradition of Czech stamp production.

St. Agnes of Bohemia (1211-82) — A1417

2011, Jan. 20 ***Perf. 11¼x11¾***

3485 A1417 12k multi 1.40 .70

Ctyrlístek Comic Strip Character Pind'a — A1418

Booklet Stamp

Serpentine Die Cut 15x16½

2011, Feb. 9 Litho. Self-Adhesive

3486 A1418 A multi 1.10 .55
a. Booklet pane of 10 11.00

No. 3486 sold for 10k on day of issue.

Jirí Melantrich of Aventinum (c. 1511-80), Printer — A1419

Photo. & Engr.

2011, Feb. 9 ***Perf. 11¼x11¾***

3487 A1419 30k multi 3.50 1.75

Cheb, 950th Anniv. — A1420

Black Madonna House, Prague, Cent. — A1421

2011, Feb. 9 Engr. ***Perf. 11¾x11½***

3488 A1420 12k multi 1.40 .70

Perf. 11½x11¾

3489 A1421 14k multi 1.60 .80

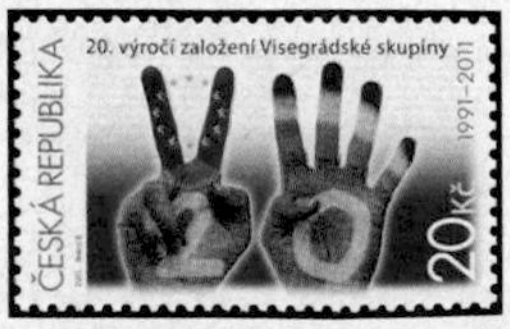

Visegrád Group, 20th Anniv. — A1422

Perf. 11¾x11¼

2011, Feb. 11 **Litho.**

3490 A1422 20k multi 2.25 1.10

See Hungary No. 4183, Poland No. 4001, and Slovakia No. 611.

Architecture A1423

Designs: A, House gables from Blatensko region, North Moravia and West Bohemia, gable shutter from North Bohemia. E, House gables from North Bohemia and South Bohemia, Wallachian cottage, Central Bohemian gate. Z, Houses from North Bohemia, West Bohemia and Wallachia, vert.

Photo. & Engr.

2011 *Perf. 11¼x11¾*

3491 A1423 A blk, lt bl & bl 1.25 .60
3492 A1423 E blk, beige & brn 2.40 1.25

Perf. 11¾x11¼

3493 A1423 Z blk, gray grn & bl grn 2.50 1.25
Nos. 3491-3493 (3) 6.15 3.10

Issued: Nos. 3491-3492, 2/23; No. 3493, 5/27. On day of issue Nos. 3491-3493 sold for 10k, 20k and 21k, respectively.

See No. 3559.

Souvenir Sheet

Petr Vok (1539-1611) and Vilém (1535-92) von Rosenberg, Aristocrats — A1424

2011, Mar. 9 **Engr.** *Perf. 11¾*

3494 A1424 49k multi 5.75 3.00

Easter — A1425

Perf. 11¼x11¾

2011, Mar. 23 **Litho.**

3495 A1425 A multi 1.25 .60

No. 3495 sold for 10k on day of issue.

Vlasta Burian (1891-1962), Actor — A1426

Photo. & Engr.

2011, Apr. 6 *Perf. 11¾x11¼*

3496 A1426 10k multi 1.25 .60

Teaching at Prague Conservatory, Bicent. — A1427

2011, Apr. 6 *Perf. 11¼x11¾*

3497 A1427 10k multi 1.25 .60

Ctyrlistek Comic Strip Character Bobík — A1428

Booklet Stamp

Serpentine Die Cut 15x16½

2011, May 4 **Litho.** **Self-Adhesive**

3498 A1428 A multi 1.25 .60
a. Booklet pane of 10 12.50

No. 3498 sold for 10k on day of issue.

Europa A1429

2011, May 4 **Litho.** *Perf. 11¼*

3499 A1429 20k multi 2.40 1.25

Intl. Year of Forests.

Flower Type of 2002

Design: 2k, Chrysanthemum (chryzantéma).

Photo. & Engr.

2011, May 27 *Perf. 11¾x11¼*

3500 A1215 2k multi .25 .25

Souvenir Sheet

Johann Gerstner (1851-1939), Violinist — A1430

Litho. & Engr.

2011, May 27 *Perf. 11¾*

3501 A1430 34k multi 4.00 2.10

See Slovenia No. 891.

The Little Witch and Abraxas, the Raven, Animated Characters by Zdenek Smetana A1431

Photo. & Engr.

2011, June 1 *Perf. 11½x11¼*

3502 A1431 10k multi 1.25 .60
a. Booklet pane of 8 + 2 labels 10.00 —
Complete booklet, #3502a 10.00

First Public Long-Distance Flight of Jan Kaspar (1883-1927), Cent. — A1432

2011, June 1 *Perf. 11¼x11¾*

3503 A1432 21k multi 2.50 1.25

Execution of 27 Protestant Leaders in Prague, 390th Anniv. — A1433

Litho. & Engr.

2011, June 1 *Perf. 11¾*

3504 A1433 26k rose pink & blk 3.00 1.60

Cricetus Cricetus A1434

Floral Arrangement A1435

Perf. 11¼x11¾

2011, June 15 **Litho.**

3505 A1434 10k multi 1.25 .60
Complete booklet, 5 #3505 6.25

2011, June 15

3506 A1435 25k multi 3.00 1.50

Europa Cup, Championships of European Federation of Professional Florist Associations, Havirov.

Men's European Volleyball Championships, Prague and Karlovy Vary — A1436

Perf. 11¼x11¾

2011, Aug. 31 **Litho.**

3507 A1436 20k multi 2.25 1.10

Wolfgang Amadeus Mozart (1756-91), Composer — A1437

Booklet Stamp

Serpentine Die Cut 11½

2011, Aug. 31 **Self-Adhesive**

3508 A1437 E multi 2.25 1.10
a. Booklet pane of 6 13.50

No. 3508 sold for 20k on day of issue.

Miniature Sheet

Flora and Fauna of Sumava UNESCO Biosphere Reserve — A1438

No. 3509: a, 10k,Turdus torquatus, Erebia euryale, Tetrao urogallus (54x44mm). b, 14k, Dactylorhiza traunsteineri, Colias palaeno (27x44mm). c, 18k, Aeshna juncea, Alces alces, Tetrao tetrix (54x44mm). d, 20k, Lynx lynx, Picoides tridactylus (54x44mm).

Litho. & Engr.

2011, Aug. 31 *Perf. 11¾*

3509 A1438 Sheet of 4, #a-d, + 4 labels 7.00 3.50

Organ, Church of the Assumption of Our Lady, Plasy — A1439

Perf. 11¼x11¾

2011, Sept. 14 **Litho.**

3510 A1439 10k multi 1.10 .55

Frantisek Alexander Elstner (1902-74), Travel Writer — A1440

Photo. & Engr.

2011, Sept. 14 *Perf. 11¾x11¼*

3511 A1440 14k multi 1.60 .80

Pat and Mat, Characters From Children's Television Show — A1441

Booklet Stamp

Serpentine Die Cut 15x16½

2011, Oct. 5 **Litho.** **Self-Adhesive**

3512 A1441 A multi 1.10 .55
a. Booklet pane of 10 11.00

No. 3512 sold for 10k on day of issue.

World Post Day
A1442

2011, Oct. 5 ***Perf. 11¼***
3513 A1442 21k multi 2.40 1.25

Film Posters
A1443

Poster for: No. 3514, 10k, Une Femme Douce, 1970. No. 3515, 10k, Markéta Lazarová, 1966.

2011, Oct. 5 **Litho.** ***Perf. 11¾x11¼***
3514-3515 A1443 Set of 2 2.25 1.10

Peacock & Bugler Type of 2005 and Roses Above Prague Type of 2003

2011, Oct. 27 ***Perf. 11¼x11¾***
3516 A1263 A multi + label 1.10 .55
3517 A1225 E multi + label 2.25 1.10

On day of issue, No. 3516 sold for 10k and No. 3517 sold for 20k. Nos. 3516-3517 each were issued in sheets of 9 stamps and 12 labels that could be personalized.

Art Type of 1967 Inscribed "CESKA REPUBLIKA"

Designs: 24k, Lovers, by Jaroslav Vozniak, horiz. 26k, Woman in Corn Field, by Joza Uprka. 30k, Winter Landscape, by August Bedrich Piepenhagen, horiz.

2011, Nov. 9 **Engr.** ***Perf. 11¾***
3518-3520 A565 Set of 3 8.75 4.50

Christmas
A1444

2011, Nov. 9 **Litho.** ***Perf. 11¾x11¼***
3521 A1444 A multi 1.10 .55

No. 3521 sold for 10k on day of issue.

House, Vidim — A1445

Photo. & Engr.
2012, Jan. 20 ***Perf. 11¼x11¾***
3522 A1445 6k multi .65 .30

Josef Liesler (1912-2005), Stamp Designer — A1446

2012, Jan. 20 ***Perf. 11¾x11¼***
3523 A1446 10k multi 1.10 .55
a. Booklet pane of 8 + 4 labels 9.00 —
Complete booklet, #3523a 9.00

Tradition of Czech stamp production.

Jirí Trnka (1912-69), Film Animator and Director — A1447

2012, Feb. 15
3524 A1447 10k multi 1.10 .55

Sokol Movement, 150th Anniv. — A1448

Perf. 11¼x11¾
2012, Feb. 15 **Litho.**
3525 A1448 14k multi 1.50 .75

Union of Czech Mathematicians and Physicists, 150th Anniv. — A1449

2012, Mar. 7 ***Perf. 11¾x11¼***
3526 A1449 10k multi 1.10 .55

Kuks
A1450

Designs: 14k, Buildings in Kuks. 18k, Statue by Matthias B. Braun, vert.

Perf. 11½x11¾, 11¾x11½
2012, Mar. 7 **Engr.**
3527-3528 A1450 Set of 2 3.50 1.75

Hiker at Signpost — A1451

Perf. 11¼x11¾
2012, Mar. 21 **Litho.**
3529 A1451 A multi + label 1.10 .55

No. 3529 was printed in sheets of 9 + 12 labels that could be personalized and had a franking value of 10k on day of issue.

Gregor Mendel (1822-84), Genetics Pioneer — A1452

Photo. & Engr.
2012, Apr. 4 ***Perf. 11¾x11¼***
3530 A1452 20k multi 2.25 1.10

First Hebrew Book Printed in Prague, 500th Anniv.
A1453

2012, Apr. 18 **Litho.** ***Perf. 11¼***
3531 A1453 25k multi 2.75 1.40

Prague Tourist Attractions
A1454

Photo. & Engr.
2012, May 2 ***Perf. 11¼x11¾***
3532 A1454 20k multi 2.10 1.10

Europa.

Scouting in Czechoslovakia, Cent. — A1455

2012, May 2 **Litho.** ***Perf. 11¼***
3533 A1455 21k multi 2.25 1.10

Boats on Bat'a Canal
A1456

2012, May 16 **Engr.** ***Perf. 11¾x11¼***
Booklet Stamp
3534 A1456 10k dark blue 1.00 .50
a. Booklet pane of 8 + 4 labels 8.00 —
Complete booklet, #3534a 8.00

The Whipping of Christ, by Tintoretto — A1457

2012, May 16 ***Perf. 11¾***
3535 A1457 30k multi 3.00 1.50

Art in Prague Castle. See Nos. 3569, 3605, 3642.

St. Wenceslas (c. 907-35)
A1458

Serpentine Die Cut 11 Syncopated
2012, June 6 **Litho.**
Self-Adhesive
3536 A1458 A multi 1.00 .50

No. 3536 sold for 10k on day of issue. See No. 3576.

Lezáky Massacre, 70th Anniv. — A1459

2012, June 6 ***Perf. 11¾x11¼***
3537 A1459 10k multi 1.00 .50

Lidice Massacre, 70th Anniv. — A1460

2012, June 6 **Photo. & Engr.**
3538 A1460 20k multi 2.00 1.00

Coronation of Statue of Our Lady of Hostyn, Cent. — A1461

Litho. & Engr.
2012, June 20 ***Perf. 11¾***
3539 A1461 21k multi 2.00 1.00

A1462

A1463

Personalized Stamps
A1464

Serpentine Die Cut 11 Syncopated

2012, June 20 Litho.

Self-Adhesive

3540 A1462 A multi .95 .50
3541 A1463 A multi .95 .50
3542 A1464 E multi 1.90 .95
Nos. 3540-3542 (3) 3.80 1.95

Nos. 3540-3542 each were printed in sheets of 25. Vignette portions of each stamp could be personalized. The generic vignettes of these stamps are shown. On day of issue, the franking value of Nos. 3540-3541 each were 10k, and of No. 3542, 20k.

2012 Summer Olympics, London — A1465

Litho. & Engr.

2012, June 20 ***Perf. 11¾***

3543 A1465 20k multi 1.90 .95

Alberto Vojtech Fric (1882-1944), Cactus Collector, Botanist and Ethnographer — A1466

2012, Sept. 5 Litho. ***Perf. 11¾x11¼***

3544 A1466 10k multi 1.10 .55

Illustrations of Antique Automobiles by Václav Zapadlík — A1467

No. 3545: a, 1933 Duesenberg SJ. b, 1931, Wikov 70. c, 1936 Mercedes-Benz 540. d, 1938 Rolls Royce Phantom III. e, 1934 Bugatti Royale 41. f, 1929 Isotta Fraschini Tipo 8A.

Serpentine Die Cut 11½

2012, Sept. 5

Self-Adhesive

3545 Booklet pane of 6 13.00
a.-f. A1467 E Any single 2.10 1.10

On day of issue, Nos. 3545a-3545f each sold for 20k. See Nos. 3580-3581, 3610-3611, 3645-3646.

Miniature Sheet

Orchids — A1468

No. 3546: a, 10k, Dendrobium peguanum (44x27mm). b, 14k, Stanhopea tigrina and Coryanthes feildingii (44x54mm). c, 18k, Cattleya aclandiae and Cattleya maxima (44x54mm). d, 20k, Paphiopedilum charlesworthii, Paphiopedilum insigne, and Paphiopedilum hirsutissimum (44x54mm).

Litho. & Engr.

2012, Sept. 5 ***Perf. 11¾***

3546 A1468 Sheet of 4, #a-d, + 4 labels 6.50 3.25

Souvenir Sheet

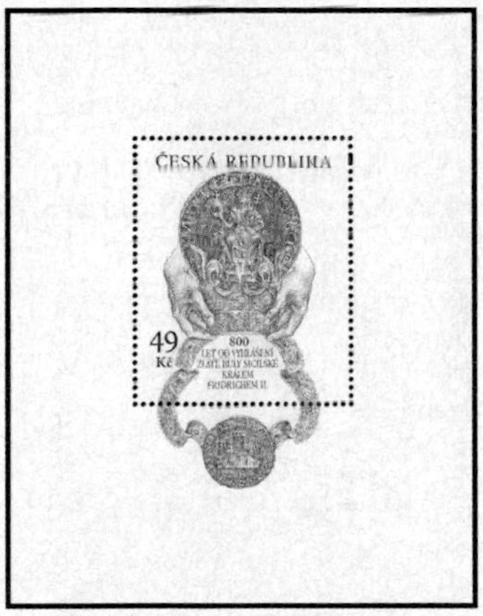

Golden Bull of Sicily, 800th Anniv. — A1469

2012, Sept. 19 Engr. ***Perf. 11¾***

3547 A1469 49k multi 5.25 2.60

Paphiopedilum Venustum — A1470

2012, Oct. 3 Litho. ***Perf. 11¼x11¾***

3548 A1470 A multi + label 1.10 .55

No. 3548 was printed in sheets of 9 + 12 labels that could be personalized. On day of issue, No. 3548 had a franking value of 10k.

Masaryk Circuit Racers — A1471

Designs: 18k, Frantisek St'astny (1927-2000), motorcycle racer. 25k, Louis Chiron (1899-1979), automobile racer.

2012, Oct. 3 Photo. & Engr.

3549-3550 A1471 Set of 2 4.50 2.25

1891 Ericsson Desk Telephone A1472

2012, Oct. 3 Litho. ***Perf. 11¼***

3551 A1472 26k multi 2.75 1.40

World Post Day.

Art Type of 1967 Inscribed "CESKA REPUBLIKA" and

Life's Pleasures, by Frantisek Kupka — A1473

Designs: 26k, A Long-haired Girl, by Kamil Lhoták. 32k, Self-portrait with Family, by Jan Kupecky. No. 3554: a, Blonde nude on horse. b, Brunette nude on pony, vert.

2012, Nov. 7 Engr. ***Perf. 11¾***

3552-3553 A565 Set of 2 6.00 3.00

Litho. & Engr.

Souvenir Sheet

3554 A1473 30k Sheet of 2, #a-b 6.00 3.00

Christmas — A1474

2012, Nov. 7 Litho. ***Perf. 11¼x11¾***

3555 A1474 A multi + label 1.00 .50

No. 3555 sold for 10k on day of issue and was printed in sheets of 9 + 12 labels that could be personalized.

Pinda, Bobik, Myspulin and Fifinka Riding Griffin A1475

Myspulin Taking Picture of Bobik, Fifinka, King Rudolf II, Aurix the Lion and Pinda — A1476

Serpentine Die Cut 16½x15

2012, Nov. 7 Self-Adhesive

Booklet Stamps

3556 A1475 A multi 1.00 .50
3557 A1476 A multi 1.00 .50
a. Booklet pane of 10, 5 each #3556-3557 10.00

On day of issue, Nos. 3556-3557 each sold for 10k.

Architecture Type of 2011 and

Building, Busanovice, 1847 — A1477

Photo. & Engr.

2012 ***Perf. 11¼x11¾***

3558 A1477 5k multi .50 .25
3559 A1423 A black & blue 1.00 .50

Issued: No. 3558, 12/19; No. 3559, 11/8. No. 3559 sold for 10k on day of issue. Compare No. 3559 with No. 3491.

Ivan Strnad (1926-2005), Stamp Designer — A1478

2013, Jan. 20 ***Perf. 11¾x11¼***

3560 A1478 10k multi 1.10 .55
a. Booklet pane of 8 + 4 labels 9.00 —
Complete booklet, #3560a 9.00

Tradition of Czech stamp production.

Bertha von Suttner (1843-1914), 1905 Nobel Peace Laureate — A1479

Perf. 11¼x11¾

2013, Feb. 13 Litho.

3561 A1479 18k multi 1.90 .95

Cottage, Novy Hrozenkov — A1480

Photo. & Engr.

2013, Mar. 6 ***Perf. 11¾x11¼***

3562 A1480 14k brn & dk brn 1.50 .75

Transportation — A1481

No. 3563: a, Aero HC2 Heli Baby helicopter. b, Pécko-18 tugboat.

2013, Mar. 6 **Litho.**
3563 A1481 25k Vert. pair, #a-b 5.25 2.60

Zlatá Koruna Monastery, 750th Anniv. — A1482

2013, Apr. 3 **Engr.** ***Perf. 11¾x11½***
3564 A1482 14k multi 1.40 .70

George Orwell (1903-50), Writer — A1483

Photo. & Engr.
2013, Apr. 3 ***Perf. 11¼x11¾***
3565 A1483 26k multi 2.60 1.40

Pres. Milos Zeman — A1484

2013, Apr. 24 ***Perf. 11¾x11¼***
3566 A1484 A red & purple 1.00 .50

No. 3566 sold for 10k on day of issue.

Europa A1485

2013, May 2 **Litho.** ***Perf. 11¼***
3567 A1485 25k multi 2.60 1.40

Fláje Dam A1486

2013, May 15 **Engr.** ***Perf. 11¾x11¼***
3568 A1486 14k green 1.50 .75
a. Booklet pane of 8 + 4 labels 12.00 —
Complete booklet, #3568a 12.00

Art in Prague Castle Type of 2012

Design: 25k, Portrait of Jacob König, Goldsmith and Bookseller, by Paolo Veronese.

2013, May 15 **Engr.** ***Perf. 11¾***
3569 A1457 25k multi 2.60 1.40

Cross of Závis of Falkenstejn A1487

2013, May 29 ***Perf. 11¾***
3570 A1487 26k multi 2.75 1.40

Krtek the Mole — A1488

Serpentine Die Cut 16½x15
2013, May 29 **Litho.**
Booklet Stamp
Self-Adhesive
3571 A1488 A multi 1.10 .55
a. Booklet pane of 10 11.00

No. 3571 sold for 10k on day of issue.

Historic Methods of Transportation — A1489

No. 3572: a, Tatra 15/30 automobile. b, Cechie 33 Böhmerland motorcycle.

Perf. 11¾x11¼
2013, June 12 **Litho.**
3572 A1489 10k Horiz. pair, #a-b 2.10 1.10

Souvenir Sheet

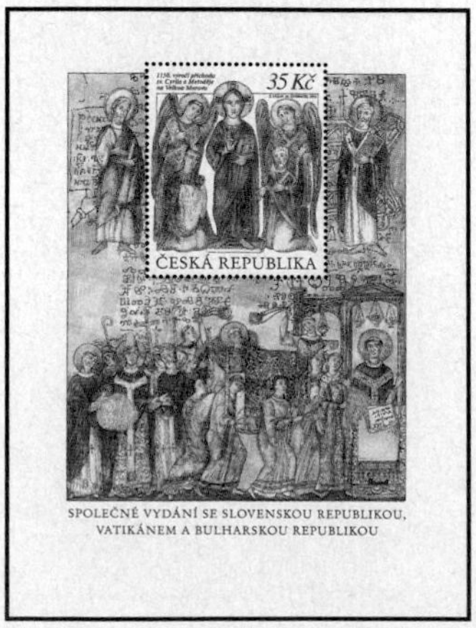

Mission of Sts. Cyril and Methodius to Slavic Lands, 1150th Anniv. — A1490

Litho. & Engr.
2013, June 12 ***Perf. 11¾***
3573 A1490 35k multi 3.75 1.90

See Bulgaria No. 4647, Slovakia No. 666 and Vatican City No. 1536.

Postal Banking Services, 130th Anniv. A1491

Perf. 11¾x11¼
2013, June 26 **Litho.**
3574 A1491 20k multi 2.00 1.00

Franz Kafka (1883-1924), Writer — A1492

Serpentine Die Cut 11½
2013, June 26 **Litho.**
Booklet Stamp
Self-Adhesive
3575 A1492 E multi 2.00 1.00
a. Booklet pane of 6 12.00

No. 3575 sold for 20k on day of issue.

St. Wenceslas Type of 2012

2013, July 31 **Litho.** ***Perf. 11¼x11¾***
3576 A1458 13k multi 1.40 .70

2013 Canoe Slalom World Championships, Prague — A1493

Photo. & Engr.
2013, Sept. 4 ***Perf. 11¾x11¼***
3577 A1493 10k multi 1.10 .55

Novy Jicín, 700th Anniv. — A1494

2013, Sept. 4 **Engr.** ***Perf. 11¾***
3578 A1494 20k multi 2.10 2.10

Miniature Sheet

Flora and Fauna of the Karlstejn Region — A1495

No. 3579: a, 10k, Dracocephalum austriacum, Chorthippus vagans (27x44mm). b, 14k, Oenanthe oenanthe, Velká Amerika Limestone Quarry (27x44mm). c, 18k, Polyommatus coridon, Pulsatilla pratensis, Colias crocea (54x44mm). d, 20k, Rosa gallica, Karlstejn Castle (54x44mm).

Litho. & Engr.
2013, Sept. 4 ***Perf. 11¾***
3579 A1495 Sheet of 4, #a-d, + 4 labels 6.50 3.25

Antique Automobiles Type of 2012

Illustrations by Václav Zapadlík: No. 3580, 1930 Skoda 860. No. 3581, 1932 Skoda 645.

Serpentine Die Cut 11¼ Syncopated
2013, Sept. 4 **Litho.**
Booklet Stamps
Self-Adhesive
3580 A1467 A multi 1.40 .70
3581 A1467 A multi 1.40 .70
a. Booklet pane of 8, 4 each #3580-3581 11.50

Nos. 3580-3581 each sold for 13k on day of issue.

A1496

Personalized Stamps — A1497

Serpentine Die Cut 11¼ Syncopated
2013, Sept. 4 **Litho.**
Booklet Stamps
Self-Adhesive
3582 A1496 A black 1.40 .70
a. Booklet pane of 8 11.50
3583 A1497 E black 2.60 1.25
a. Booklet pane of 8 21.00

On day of issue, No. 3582 sold for 13k, and No. 3583 sold for 25k. Nos. 3582 and 3583 could have the image portions of the stamp personalized for an additional fee. The horizontal generic vignettes of these stamps are shown. Nos. 3582a and 3583a contain four stamps with these horizontal generic vignettes and four stamps with similar generic vignettes but with a vertical orientation. Values for Nos. 3582 and Nos. 3583 are for stamps with images with either a horizontal or vertical orientation.

Josef Bican (1913-2001), Soccer Player — A1498

Photo. & Engr.
2013, Sept. 18 ***Perf. 11¼x11¾***
3584 A1498 13k multi 1.40 .70

Horses From Chlumetz Stud Farm — A1499

Design: 13k, Kinsky horse. 17k, Palomino horse.

Perf. 11¼x11¾

2013, Sept. 18 **Litho.**

3585-3586 A1499 Set of 2 3.25 1.60

Cottage, Salajna — A1500

2013, Oct. 2 Engr. ***Perf. 11¼x11¾***

3587 A1500 29k green 3.25 1.60

Souvenir Sheet

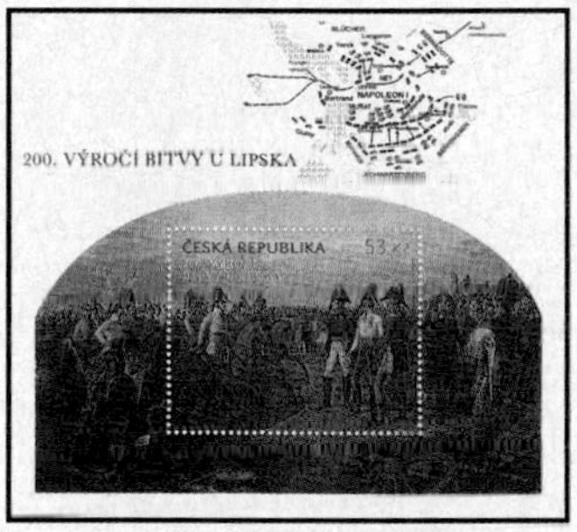

Battle of Leipzig, 200th Anniv. — A1501

Litho. & Engr.

2013, Oct. 2 ***Perf. 11¾***

3588 A1501 53k multi 5.75 3.00

Bible of Kralice, 400th Anniv. A1502

2013, Oct. 16 Litho. ***Perf. 11¼***

3589 A1502 17k multi 1.75 .85

Otto Wichterle (1912-98), Inventor of Soft Contact Lenses — A1503

Photo. & Engr.

2013, Oct. 16 ***Perf. 11¼x11¾***

3590 A1503 21k multi 2.10 1.10

Art Type of 1967 Inscribed "CESKA REPUBLIKA"

Designs: 25k, A View of Roman Churches, by Giovanni Battista Piranesi, horiz. 30k, Still Life with the Author, by Bohuslav Reynek. 35k, Round Portrait, by Max Svabinsky.

Engr., Litho & Engr. (30k)

2013, Nov. 27 ***Perf. 11¾***

3591-3593 A565 Set of 3 9.00 4.50

Ladislav Jirka (1914-86), Stamp Engraver — A1504

2014, Jan. 20 Litho. ***Perf. 11¾x11¼***

3594 A1504 13k multi 1.25 .65
a. Booklet pane of 8 + 4 labels 10.00 —
Complete booklet, #3594a 10.00

Tradition of Czech stamp production.

Dog and Four-Leaf Clover — A1505

2014, Jan. 20 Litho. ***Perf. 11¼x11¾***

3595 A1505 A multi + label 1.25 .65

No. 3595 was printed in sheets of 9 + 12 labels that could be personalized. On day of issue, No. 3595 had a franking value of 13k.

2014 Winter Olympics, Sochi, Russia — A1506

2014, Feb. 5 Litho. ***Perf. 11¾x11¼***

3596 A1506 25k multi 2.50 1.25

2014 Winter Paralympics, Sochi, Russia A1507

2014, Feb. 5 Litho. ***Perf. 11¾x11¼***

3597 A1507 13k multi 1.40 .70
a. Tête-bêche pair 2.80 1.40

Czech Firefighters, 150th Anniv. — A1508

2014, Mar. 5 Litho. ***Perf. 11¾x11¼***

3598 A1508 13k multi 1.40 .70

Transportation — A1509

No. 3599: a, Rapid, 1912 airplane of Eugen Cihák. b, Type R1 Prague Metro train.

2014, Mar. 5 Litho. ***Perf. 11¾x11¼***

3599 A1509 13k Pair, #a-b 2.60 1.40

Bohumil Hrabal (1914-97), Writer — A1510

Photo. & Engr.

2014, Mar. 26 ***Perf. 11¼x11¾***

3600 A1510 17k blk & brn 1.75 .85

Cervená Lhota Castle — A1511

2014, Mar. 26 Engr. ***Perf. 11¾***

3601 A1511 17k multi 1.75 .85

Zdenek Kopal (1914-93), Astronomer — A1512

Perf. 11¾x11¼

2014, Mar. 26 **Litho.**

3602 A1512 21k multi 2.10 1.10

Silesian Museum, Opava, 200th Anniv. — A1513

Photo. & Engr.

2014, Apr. 30 ***Perf. 11¼x11¾***

3603 A1513 13k multi 1.40 .70

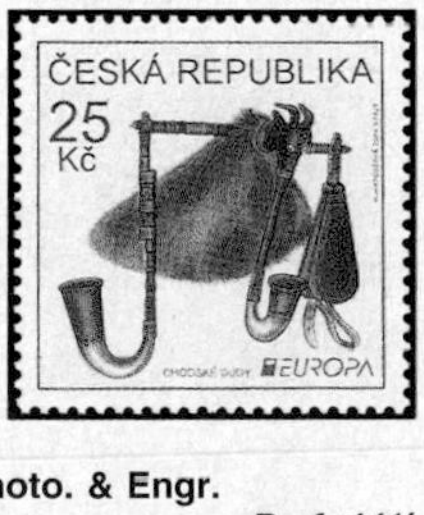

Bagpipes A1514

Photo. & Engr.

2014, Apr. 30 ***Perf. 11¼***

3604 A1514 25k multi 2.60 1.25

Europa.

Art in Prague Castle Type of 2012

Design: 37k, Assembly of Olympian Gods, by Peter Paul Rubens.

Litho. & Engr.

2014, May 28 ***Perf. 11¾***

3605 A1457 37k multi 3.75 1.90

No. 3605 was printed in sheets of 2.

Paper Mill, Velké Losiny A1515

Photo. & Engr.

2014, May 28 ***Perf. 11¾x11¼***

3606 A1515 13k multi 1.40 .70

Animated Characters Ju and Hele — A1516

Serpentine Die Cut 11 Syncopated

2014, May 28 **Litho.**

Booklet Stamp Self-Adhesive

3607 A1516 A multi 1.40 .70
a. Booklet pane of 10 14.00

No. 3607 sold for 13k on day of issue.

Historic Methods of Transportation — A1517

No. 3608: a, Paddle steamer Franz Joseph I. b, 1936 Zbrojovka Brno Z4 automobile.

Perf. 11¾x11¼

2014, June 11 **Litho.**

3608 A1517 25k Horiz. pair, #a-b 5.00 2.50

Souvenir Sheet

World War I, Cent. — A1518

No. 3609: a, Soldier carrying rifle, mother holding child. b, Soldiers, people falling into pit.

2014, June 11 Litho. ***Perf. 11¾***

3609 A1518 29k Sheet of 2, #a-b, + 3 labels 6.00 3.00

Antique Automobiles Type of 2012

Designs: No. 3610, 1938 Skoda Popular Monte Carlo. No. 3611, 1941 Skoda Superb 3000.

Serpentine Die Cut 11¼ Syncopated

2014, Sept. 3 **Litho.**

Booklet Stamps Self-Adhesive

3610 A1467 A multi 1.25 .60
3611 A1467 A multi 1.25 .60
a. Booklet pane of 8, 4 each #3610-3611 10.00

Nos. 3610-3611 each sold for 13k on day of issue.

Karel, Elder of Zierotín (1564-1636), Governor of Moravia — A1519

Photo. & Engr.

2014, Sept. 3 *Perf. 11¾x11¼*

3612 A1519 29k multi 2.75 1.40

Miniature Sheet

Flora and Fauna of the Beskid Mountains — A1520

No. 3613: a, 13k, Meles meles (44x27mm). b, 17k, Felis silvestris (44x27mm). c, 21k, Ursus arctos, Carabus variolosus (44x54mm). d, 25k, Nucifraga caryocatactes, Canis lupus (44x54mm).

Litho. & Engr.

2014, Sept. 3 *Perf. 11¾*

3613 A1520 Sheet of 4, #a-d, + 3 labels 7.00 3.50

Flower Bouquet in Wine Bottle — A1521

2014, Oct. 15 Litho. *Perf. 11¼x11¾*

3614 A1521 A multi + label 1.25 .60

No. 3614 was printed in sheets of 9 + 12 labels that could be personalized. On day of issue No. 3614 had a franking value of 13k.

Souvenir Sheet

St. Vitus Cathedral, Prague, 670th Anniv. — A1522

Litho. & Engr.

2014, Oct. 15 *Perf. 11¾*

3615 A1522 58k multi 5.25 2.60

Art Type of 1967 Inscribed "CESKA REPUBLIKA" and

Solitude and Spectacles, Photograph by Jaromír Funke — A1523

Designs: 25k, Street in Winter, by Jakub Schikaneder. 37k, Leda Atomica, by Salvador Dalí.

Engr., Litho. (29k)

2014, Nov. 5 *Perf. 11¾*

3616 A565 25k multi 2.25 1.10
3617 A1523 29k multi 2.60 1.40
3618 A565 37k multi 3.50 1.75
Nos. 3616-3618 (3) 8.35 4.25

Historical Events of November 17 — A1524

2014, Nov. 5 Litho. *Perf. 11¼x11¾*

3619 A1524 13k multi 1.25 .60

Nazi attack on Czech university students, 75th anniv.; start of Velvet Revolution, 25th anniv.

Andreas Vesalius (1514-64), Anatomist — A1525

Photo. & Engr.

2014, Nov. 5 *Perf. 11¼x11¾*

3620 A1525 25k multi 2.25 1.10

Bethlehem in Winter, by Josef Lada — A1526

2014, Nov. 5 Litho. *Perf. 11¾x11¼*

3621 A1526 A multi 1.25 .60

Christmas. No. 3621 sold for 13k on day of issue.

A1527

Personalized Stamps A1528

Serpentine Die Cut Syncopated

2014, Nov. 26 **Litho.**

Self-Adhesive

3622 A1527 A multi 1.25 .60
3623 A1528 Z multi 2.75 1.40

Nos. 3622-3623 were each printed in sheets of 25. Vignette portions of each stamp could be personalized. The generic vignettes of these stamps are shown. On day of issue, the franking value of No. 3622 was 13k; No. 3623, 30k.

Oldrich Kulhánek (1940-2013), Stamp Designer — A1529

Photo. & Engr.

2015, Jan. 20 *Perf. 11¾x11¼*

3624 A1529 13k multi 1.10 .55
a. Booklet pane of 8 + 4 labels 9.00 —
Complete booklet, #3624a 9.00

Vitezslava Kaprálová (1915-40), Composer — A1530

2015, Jan. 20 Litho. *Perf. 11¾x11¼*

3625 A1530 17k multi 1.40 .70

Military Aircraft and Vehicles — A1531

Designs: No. 3626, Supermarine Spitfire LF Mk IXE. No. 3627, T-34/76.2 tank. No. 3628, Harley-Davidson motorcycle. No. 3629, Jeep-Ford GPW.

Serpentine Die Cut 11¼ Syncopated

2015, Jan. 20 **Litho.**

Booklet Stamps

Self-Adhesive

3626 A1531 A multi 1.10 .55
3627 A1531 A multi 1.10 .55
3628 A1531 A multi 1.10 .55
3629 A1531 A multi 1.10 .55
a. Bookklet pane of 8, 2 each #3626-3629 9.00
Nos. 3626-3629 (4) 4.40 2.20

On day of issue, Nos. 3626-3629 each sold for 13k.

Cartoon Character Vecernícek, 50th Anniv. A1532

Serpentine Die Cut 11 Syncopated

2015, Feb. 18 **Litho.**

Self-Adhesive

3630 A1532 A multi 1.10 .55

No. 3630 sold for 13k on day of issue.

Plzen, 2015 European Capital of Culture A1533

Photo. & Engr.

2015, Feb. 18 *Perf. 11¼*

3631 A1533 25k multi 2.00 1.00

Historic Methods of Transportation — A1534

No. 3632: a, Walter 6B automobile. b, Monoplane of Metodej Vlach.

Perf. 11¾x11¼

2015, Feb. 18 **Litho.**

3632 A1534 13k Horiz. pair, #a-b 2.10 1.10

Easter — A1535

2015, Mar. 4 Litho. *Perf. 11¼x11¾*

3633 A1535 A multi 1.10 .55

No. 3633 sold for 13k on day of issue.

Postmen on Geese Above Charles Bridge — A1536

2015, Mar. 4 Litho. *Perf. 11¼x11¾*

3634 A1536 A multi + label 1.10 .55

No. 3633 has a franking value of 13k on day of issue and was printed in sheets of 9 + 12 labels that could be personalized.

Souvenir Sheet

The Last Supper, by Leonardo da Vinci — A1537

Perf. 11¼x11¾

2015, Mar. 18 **Litho.**

3635 A1537 25k multi 2.00 1.00

Expo 2015, Milan.

Church of St. Ignatius and Spejchar Gallery, Chomutov — A1538

Photo. & Engr.

2015, Apr. 15 *Perf. 11¼x11¾*

3636 A1538 25k multi		2.10	2.10
a.	Booklet pane of 8 + 4 labels	17.00	—
	Complete booklet, #3636a	17.00	

Sixth Czech and German Philatelic Exhibition, Chomutov.

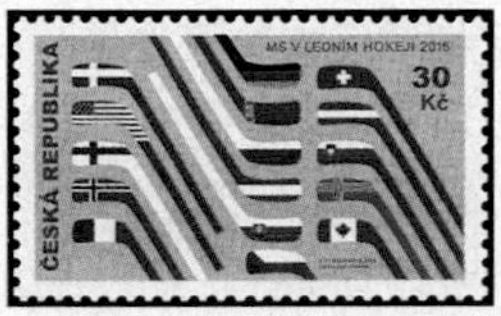

2015 Men's Ice Hockey World Championships, Czech Republic — A1539

2015, Apr. 15 Litho. *Perf. 11¾x11¼*

3637 A1539 30k multi 2.50 1.25

Animated Film Characters Bob and Bobek A1540

Bob and Bobek: No. 3638, Playing ice hockey. No. 3639, Rowing raft.

Serpentine Die Cut 11 Syncopated

2015, Apr. 29 **Litho.**

Booklet Stamps
Self-Adhesive

3638 A1540 A multi	1.10	.55
3639 A1540 A multi	1.10	.55
a. Booklet pane of 10, 5 each #3638-3639	11.00	

Nos. 3638-3639 each sold for 13k on day of issue.

Moldava Railway, 130th Anniv. A1541

2015, May 6 Engr. *Perf. 11¾x11¼*

3640 A1541 13k black	1.10	.55
a. Booklet pane of 8 + 4 labels	9.00	—
Complete booklet, #3640a	9.00	

Europa A1542

2015, May 6 Litho. *Perf. 11¼*

3641 A1542 25k multi 2.10 2.10

Art in Prague Castle Type of 2012

Design: 34k, Head of a Woman, by Hans von Aachen.

2015, May 27 Engr. *Perf. 11¾*

3642 A1457 34k multi 2.75 1.40

Rabí Castle Ruins A1543

2015, May 27 Engr. *Perf. 11¾*

3643 A1543 17k multi 1.40 .70

Jan Hus (c. 1370-1415), Church Reformer — A1544

Perf. 11¼x11¾

2015, June 17 **Litho.**

3644 A1544 13k multi 1.10 .55

Antique Automobiles Type of 2012

Illustrations by Václav Zapadlik: No. 3645, 1955 Skoda 1201. No. 3646, 1947 Skoda Rapid 1500.

Serpentine Die Cut 11¼ Syncopated

2015, Sept. 2 **Litho.**

Booklet Stamps
Self-Adhesive

3645 A1467 A multi	1.10	.55
3646 A1467 A multi	1.10	.55
a. Booklet pane of 8, 4 each #3645-3646	9.00	

Nos. 3645-3646 each sold for 13k on day of issue.

Postcrossing A1546

Serpentine Die Cut 11¼ Syncopated

2015, Sept. 2 **Litho.**

Self-Adhesive

3648 A1546 E multi 2.10 1.10

No. 3648 sold for 25k on day of issue.

Miniature Sheet

Owls — A1547

No. 3649: a, 13k, Athene noctua (27x44mm). b, 17k, Aegolius funereus (27x44mm). c, 21k, Nyctea scandiaca (27x44mm). d, 25k, Bubo bubo (44x54mm).

Litho. & Engr.

2015, Sept. 2 *Perf. 11¾*

3649 A1547 Sheet of 4, #a-d, + 4 labels 6.50 3.25

Historic Methods of Transportation — A1548

No. 3650: a, Tatra T3 tram, 1960s. b, Primátor Dittrich paddle steamer.

Perf. 11¾x11¼

2015, Sept. 23 **Litho.**

3650 A1548 25k Vert. pair, #a-b 4.25 2.10

Flag of Czech Republic A1549

Serpentine Die Cut 11¼ on 1 Side Syncopated

2015, Oct. 14 **Litho.**

Self-Adhesive

3651 A1549 A multi 1.10 .55

No. 3651 sold for 13k on day of issue.

Organ and Jakub Jan Ryba (1765-1815), Composer — A1550

Photo. & Engr.

2015, Oct. 14 *Perf. 11¼x11¾*

3652 A1550 13k multi 1.10 .55

Wedding of Oldrich and Bozena, Painting From Dalimil's Chronicle — A1551

2015, Oct. 14 Litho. *Perf. 11¾x11¼*

3653 A1551 21k multi 1.75 .85

Souvenir Sheet

World War I, Cent. — A1552

No. 3654: a, Unveiling of statue of Jan Hus burning at the stake. b, Soldier carrying dying comrade.

2015, Oct. 14 **Litho.** *Perf. 11¾*

3654 A1552 27k Sheet of 2, #a-b, + 3 labels 4.50 2.25

Jan Opletal (1915-39), Medical Student Killed in Anti-Nazi Protests — A1553

Photo. & Engr.

2015, Nov. 11 *Perf. 11¼x11¾*

3655 A1553 13k blue & red 1.10 .55

Art Type of 1967 Inscribed "CESKA REPUBLIKA"

Designs: 27k, The Bride, book illustration by Antonín Strnadel. 30k, Sitting, by Bohumír Matal. 34k, Great Dialogue, sculpture by Karel Nepras, horiz.

Engr., Litho. & Engr. (34k)

2015, Dec. 16 *Perf. 11¾*

3656-3658 A565 Set of 3 7.50 3.75

Postman With Posthorn — A1554

Perf. 11¼x11¾

2015, Dec. 16 **Litho.**

3659 A1554 Z multi + label 2.50 1.25

No. 3659 was printed in sheets of 9 + 12 labels that could be personalized. On day of issue, No. 3659 had a franking value of 30k.

SEMI-POSTAL STAMPS

Nos. B1-B123 were sold at 1 ½ times face value at the Philatelists' Window of the Prague P.O. for charity benefit. They were available for ordinary postage.

Almost all stamps between Nos. B1-B123 are known with misplaced or inverted overprints and/or in pairs with one stamp missing the overprint.

The overprints of Nos. B1-B123 have been well forged.

Austrian Stamps of 1916-18 Overprinted in Black or Blue — a

Two sizes of type A40:
Type I: 25x30mm.
Type II: 26x29mm.

1919 *Perf. 12½*

B1 A37 3h brt violet .25 *.25*
B2 A37 5h lt green .25 *.25*
B3 A37 6h dp orange (Bl) .60 *.80*
B4 A37 6h dp orange (Bk) *2,000.* *2,000.*
B5 A37 10h magenta .80 *1.00*
B6 A37 12h lt blue .80 .80
B7 A42 15h dull red .25 *.25*
B8 A42 20h dark green .25 *.25*
a. 20h green 55.00 40.00
B9 A42 25h blue .35 .25
B10 A42 30h dull violet .35 .25
B11 A39 40h olive grn .40 .40
B12 A39 50h dk green .40 .40
B13 A39 60h dp blue .40 .40
B14 A39 80h orange brn .40 .40
B15 A39 90h red violet .80 .80
B16 A39 1k car, *yel* (Bl) .60 .60
B17 A39 1k car, *yel* (Bk) 62.50 62.50
B18 A40 2k light blue (I) 3.25 3.25
a. 2k dark blue (II) 3,000. 2,000.
B19 A40 3k car rose (I) 37.50 32.50
a. 3k claret (I) 2,500. 900.00
B20 A40 4k yellow grn (I) 20.00 15.00
a. 4k deep green (I) 55.00 45.00
B21 A40 10k violet 300.00 160.00
a. 10k deep violet 375.00 275.00
b. 10k black violet 450.00 300.00

The used value of No. B18a is for a stamp that has only a Czechoslovakian cancellation. Some examples of Austria No. 160, which were officially overprinted with type "a" and sold by the post office, had previously been used and lightly canceled with Austrian cancellations. These canceled-before-overprinting stamps, which were postally valid, sell for about one-fourth as much.

Granite Paper

B22 A40 2k light blue 4.00 2.90
B23 A40 3k carmine rose 10.00 8.25

The 4k and 10k on granite paper with this overprint were not regularly issued.
Excellent counterfeits of Nos. B1-B23 exist.

Austrian Newspaper Stamps Overprinted — b

Imperf

On Stamp of 1908

B26 N8 10h carmine *3,500.* 2,000.

On Stamps of 1916

B27 N9 2h brown .25 .25
B28 N9 4h green .40 .40
B29 N9 6h deep blue .40 .40
B30 N9 10h orange 5.00 5.00
B31 N9 30h claret 1.60 1.60
Nos. B27-B31 (5) 7.65 7.65

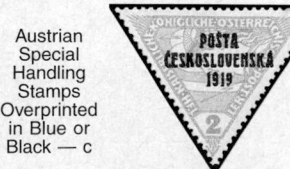

Austrian Special Handling Stamps Overprinted in Blue or Black — c

Perf. 12½

Stamps of 1916 Overprinted

B32 SH1 2h claret, *yel* (Bl) 25.00 25.00
B33 SH1 5h dp grn, *yel* (Bk) *1,900.* *825.00*

Stamps of 1917 Overprinted — d

B34 SH2 2h cl, *yel* (Bl) .25 *.35*
a. Vert. pair, imperf. btwn. *250.00*
B35 SH2 2h cl, *yel* (Bk) 60.00 35.00
B36 SH2 5h grn, *yel* (Bk) .25 .25

Austrian Air Post Stamps, #C1-C3, Overprinted Type "c" Diagonally

B37 A40 1.50k on 2k lil 175.00 175.00
B38 A40 2.50k on 3k ocher 175.00 175.00
B39 A40 4k gray 1,500. 800.00

1919

Austrian Postage Due Stamps of 1908-13 Overprinted Type "b"

B40 D3 2h carmine *6,500.* *2,750.*
B41 D3 4h carmine 25.00 15.00
B42 D3 6h carmine 12.50 8.00
B43 D3 14h carmine 90.00 35.00
B44 D3 25h carmine 45.00 20.00
B45 D3 30h carmine 600.00 300.00
B46 D3 50h carmine 1,200. 825.00

Austria Nos. J49-J56 Overprinted Type "b"

B47 D4 5h rose red .25 *.30*
B48 D4 10h rose red .25 *.30*
B49 D4 15h rose red .25 *.30*
B50 D4 20h rose red 2.00 2.00
B51 D4 25h rose red 2.00 2.00
B52 D4 30h rose red .65 .65
B53 D4 40h rose red 2.00 2.00
B54 D4 50h rose red 600.00 250.00

Austria Nos. J57-J59 Overprinted Type "a"

B55 D5 1k ultra 12.50 10.00
B56 D5 5k ultra 55.00 35.00
B57 D5 10k ultra 475.00 200.00

Austria Nos. J47-J48, J60-J63 Overprinted Type "c" Diagonally

B58 A22 1h gray 32.50 30.00
B59 A23 15h on 2h vio 150.00 110.00
B60 A38 10h on 24h blue 120.00 85.00
B61 A38 15h on 36h vio 1.00 1.00
B62 A38 20h on 54h org 90.00 85.00
B63 A38 50h on 42h choc 1.00 1.00

Hungarian Stamps Ovptd. Type "b"

1919 **Wmk. 137** ***Perf. 15***

On Stamps of 1913-16

B64 A4 1f slate 4,000. 1,600.
B65 A4 2f yellow 3.50 2.50
B66 A4 3f orange 45.00 25.00
B67 A4 6f olive green 4.50 4.50
B68 A4 50f lake, *bl* 1.25 1.00
B69 A4 60f grn, *sal* 50.00 20.00
B70 A4 70f red brn, *grn* 4,000. 1,600.

On Stamps of 1916

B71 A8 10f rose 475.00 175.00
B72 A8 15f violet 250.00 100.00

On Stamps of 1916-18

B73 A9 2f brown orange .25 .25
B74 A9 3f red lilac .25 .25
B75 A9 5f green .25 .25
B76 A9 6f grnsh blue .60 .60
B77 A9 10f rose red 1.40 *2.25*
B78 A9 15f violet .25 .25
B79 A9 20f gray brown 14.00 14.00
B80 A9 25f dull blue 1.00 .80
B81 A9 35f brown 10.00 10.00
B82 A9 40f olive green 3.25 2.50

Overprinted Type "d"

B83 A10 50f red vio & lil 1.25 *1.60*
B84 A10 75f brt bl & pale bl 1.25 *1.60*
B85 A10 80f yel grn & pale grn 1.25 *1.60*
B86 A10 1k red brn & cl 2.50 2.00
B87 A10 2k ol brn & bis 10.00 10.00
B88 A10 3k dk vio & ind 37.50 37.50
B89 A10 5k dk brn & lt brn 140.00 90.00
B90 A10 10k vio brn & vio 1,800. 800.00

Overprinted Type "b"

On Stamps of 1918

B91 A11 10f scarlet .25 .25
B92 A11 20f dark brown .30 .30
B93 A11 25f deep blue 1.40 1.25
B94 A12 40f olive grn 4.00 3.25
B95 A12 50f lilac 67.50 25.00

On Stamps of 1919

B96 A13 10f red 10.00 8.00
B97 A13 20f dk brn *10,000.* —

Same Overprint On Hungarian Newspaper Stamp of 1914

Imperf

B98 N5 (2f) orange .25 *.30*

Same Overprint On Hungarian Special Delivery Stamp

Perf. 15

B99 SD1 2f gray grn & red .25 *.35*

Same Ovpt. On Hungarian Semi-Postal Stamps

B100 SP3 10f + 2f rose red .80 .80
B101 SP4 15f + 2f violet 1.25 1.25
B102 SP5 40f + 2f brn car 7.00 3.50
Nos. B98-B102 (5) 9.55 6.20

Hungarian Postage Due Stamps of 1903-18 Overprinted Type "b"

1919 **Wmk. 135** ***Perf. 11½, 12***

B103 D1 50f green & black *525.00* *525.00*

Wmk. Crown (136, 136a)

Perf. 11½x12, 15

B104 D1 1f green & black *1,200.* *1,000.*
B105 D1 2f green & black *1,000.* *750.*
B106 D1 12f green & black *4,250.* *3,000.*
B107 D1 50f green & black 275. 150.

Wmk. Double Cross (137)

Perf. 15

On Stamps of 1914

B110 D1 1f green & black 1,250. 600.
B111 D1 2f green & black 700. 550.
B112 D1 5f green & black 1,325. 900.
B113 D1 12f green & black *5,250.* *4,000.*
B114 D1 50f green & black 275. 150.

On Stamps of 1915-18

B115 D1 1f green & red 175.00 140.00
B116 D1 2f green & red 1.00 .80
B117 D1 5f green & red 12.50 10.00
B118 D1 6f green & red 1.50 1.50
B119 D1 10f green & red .60 .60
a. Pair, one without overprint
B120 D1 12f green & red 2.00 2.00
B121 D1 15f green & red 7.50 5.00
B122 D1 20f green & red 1.00 1.00
B123 D1 30f green & red 80.00 70.00
Nos. B115-B123 (9) 281.10 230.90

Excellent counterfeits of Nos. B1-B123 exist.

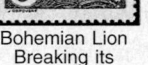

Bohemian Lion Breaking its Chains — SP1

Mother and Child — SP2

Perf. 11½, 13¾ and Compound

1919 **Typo.** **Unwmk.**

Pinkish Paper

B124 SP1 15h gray green .25 .25
a. 15h light green 32.50 25.00
B125 SP1 25h dark brown .25 .25
a. 25h light brown *5.00* 4.00
B126 SP1 50h dark blue .25 .25

Photo.

Yellowish Paper

B127 SP2 75h slate .25 .25
B128 SP2 100h brn vio .25 .25
B129 SP2 120h vio, *yel* .25 .25
Nos. B124-B129 (6) 1.50 1.50

Values are for perf 13¾. Other perfs are valued higher.
Nos. B124-B126 commemorate the 1st anniv. of Czechoslovak independence. Nos. B127-B129 were sold for the benefit of Legionnaires' orphans. Imperforates exist.
See No. 1581.

Regular Issues of Czechoslovakia Surcharged in Red

a

b

1920 *Perf. 13¾*

B130 A1(a) 40h + 20h bister 1.25 *.90*
B131 A2(a) 60h + 20h green 1.25 *.90*
B132 A4(b) 125h + 25h gray bl 5.75 *2.75*
Nos. B130-B132 (3) 8.25 *4.55*

President Masaryk — SP3

Wmk. Linden Leaves (107)

1923 **Engr.** ***Perf. 13¾x14¾***

B133 SP3 50h gray green .90 .55
B134 SP3 100h carmine 1.10 .90
B135 SP3 200h blue 3.50 3.00
B136 SP3 300h dark brown 3.50 4.25
Nos. B133-B136 (4) 9.00 8.70

5th anniv. of the Republic.
The gum was applied through a screen and shows the monogram "CSP" (Ceskoslovenska Posta). These stamps were sold at double their face values, the excess being given to the Red Cross and other charitable organizations.

International Olympic Congress Issue

Semi-Postal Stamps of 1923 Overprinted in Blue or Red

1925

B137 SP3 50h gray green 10.00 8.50
B138 SP3 100h carmine 14.50 12.00
B139 SP3 200h blue (R) 72.50 55.00
Nos. B137-B139 (3) 97.00 75.50
Set, never hinged 175.00

These stamps were sold at double their face values, the excess being divided between a fund for post office clerks and the Olympic Games Committee.

Sokol Issue

Semi-Postal Stamps of 1923 Overprinted in Blue or Red

1926

B140 SP3 50h gray green 1.60 *4.00*
B141 SP3 100h carmine 3.25 *4.00*
B142 SP3 200h blue (R) 15.00 12.50
a. Double overprint
B143 SP3 300h dk brn (R) 20.00 20.00
Nos. B140-B143 (4) 39.85 40.50
Set, never hinged 140.00

These stamps were sold at double their face values, the excess being given to the Congress of Sokols, June, 1926.

Catalogue values for unused stamps in this section, from this point to the end of the section, are for Never Hinged items.

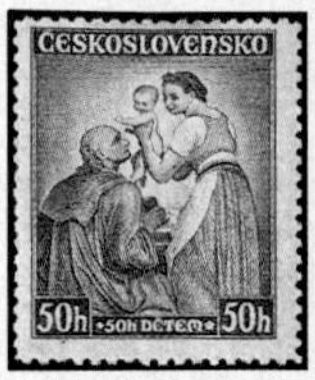

Midwife Presenting Newborn Child to its Father; after a Painting by Josef Manes

SP4 SP5

1936 Unwmk. Engr. *Perf. 12½*

B144 SP4 50h + 50h green .75 .75
B145 SP5 1k + 50h claret 1.25 1.25
B146 SP4 2k + 50h blue 2.75 2.75
Nos. B144-B146 (3) 4.75 4.75

Nos. B144-B146 were each issued in sheets of 100 with 12 labels. Value, set $40.

SP6

"Lullaby" by Stanislav Sucharda SP7

1937 *Perf. 12½*

B147 SP6 50h + 50h dull green .60 .35
B148 SP6 1k + 50h rose lake 1.10 1.10
B149 SP7 2k + 1k dull blue 2.60 1.75
Nos. B147-B149 (3) 4.30 3.20

Nos. B147-B149 were each issued in sheets of 100 with 12 labels. Value, set of singles with attached labels hinged mint $5; used $5.

President Masaryk and Little Girl in Native Costume — SP8

1938 *Perf. 12½*

B150 SP8 50h + 50h deep green .95 .95
B151 SP8 1k + 50h rose lake 1.25 1.25

Souvenir Sheet

Imperf

B152 SP8 2k + 3k black 6.25 6.25

88th anniv. of the birth of Masaryk (1850-1937).

Nos. B150-B151 were each issued in sheets of 100 stamps and 12 blank labels. Value, set of singles with attached labels: mint $6; used $4.

Allegory of the Republic Type

Souvenir Sheet

1938 *Perf. 12½*

B153 A89 2k (+ 8k) dark blue 4.00 4.00

The surtax was devoted to national relief for refugees.

"Republic" and Congress Emblem SP10

St. George Slaying the Dragon SP11

1945 Engr.

B154 SP10 1.50k + 1.50k car rose .25 .25
B155 SP10 2.50k + 2.50k blue .25 .25

Students' World Cong., Prague, 11/17/45.

1946

B156 SP11 2.40k + 2.60k car rose .25 .25
B157 SP11 4k + 6k blue .45 .25

Souvenir Sheet

Imperf

B158 SP11 4k + 6k blue 1.50 1.50

1st anniv. of Czechoslovakia's liberation. The surtax aided WW II orphans.

Nos. B156-B157 were each issued in sheets of 100 stamps and 12 inscribed labels. Value for set of singles with attached labels, mint or used $4.

Old Town Hall Type of 1946

Souvenir Sheet

1946, Aug. 3 *Imperf.*

B159 A114 2.40k rose brown 1.25 .80

Brno Natl. Stamp Exhib., Aug., 1946. The sheet was sold for 10k.

"You Went Away" — SP14

"You Remained Ours" — SP15

"You Came Back" — SP16

1946, Oct. 28 Photo. *Perf. 14*

B160 SP14 1.60k + 1.40k red brn .50 .50
B161 SP15 2.40k + 2.60k scarlet .50 .50
B162 SP16 4k + 4k deep blue 1.00 1.00
Nos. B160-B162 (3) 2.00 2.00

The surtax was for repatriated Slovaks.

Barefoot Boy — SP17

Woman and Child — SP18

2k+1k, Mother and child. 3k+1k, Little girl.

Perf. 12½

1948, Dec. 18 Unwmk. Engr.

B163 SP17 1.50k + 1k rose lilac .35 .25
B164 SP17 2k + 1k dp blue .25 .25
B165 SP17 3k + 1k rose car .35 .25
Nos. B163-B165 (3) .95 .75

The surtax was for child welfare.

Nos. B163-B165 were each issued in sheets of 100 stamps and 12 inscribed labels. Value for set of singles with attached labels: mint $5; used $3.

1949, Dec. 18 *Perf. 12½*

Design: 3k+1k, Man lifting child.

B166 SP18 1.50k + 50h gray 4.50 1.25
B167 SP18 3k + 1k claret 6.50 2.75

The surtax was for child welfare.

SP19

Dove Carrying Olive Branch — SP20

1949, Dec. 18

B168 SP19 1.50k + 50h claret 6.00 2.50
B169 SP20 3k + 1k rose red 7.25 3.00

The surtax was for the Red Cross.

AIR POST STAMPS

Nos. 9, 39-40, 20, and Types of 1919 Srchd. in Red, Blue or Green

1920 Unwmk. *Imperf.*

C1 A1 14k on 200h (R) 21.00 18.00
a. Inverted surcharge 125.00
C2 A2 24k on 500h (Bl) 50.00 30.00
a. Inverted surcharge 225.00
C3 A2 28k on 1000h (G) 32.50 30.00
a. Inverted surcharge 150.00
b. Double surcharge 200.00
Nos. C1-C3 (3) 103.50 78.00

Perf. 13¾

C4 A1 14k on 200h (R) 22.50 *30.00*
a. Perf. 13¾x13½ 95.00 95.00
C5 A2 24k on 500h (Bl) 45.00 *70.00*
a. Perf. 13¾x13½ 100.00 100.00

Perf. 13¾x13½

C6 A2 28k on 1000h (G) 20.00 27.50
a. Inverted surcharge 400.00 —
b. Perf. 13¾ 475.00 700.00
c. As "b," invtd. surcharge 350.00 —
Nos. C4-C6 (3) 87.50 127.50
Nos. C1-C6 (6) 191.00 205.50

Excellent counterfeits of the overprint are known.

Stamps of 1920 Srchd. in Black or Violet

1922, June 15 *Perf. 13¾*

C7 A8 50h on 100h dl grn 1.50 1.50
a. Inverted surcharge 150.00
b. Double surcharge 160.00
C8 A8 100h on 200h vio 4.00 3.25
a. Inverted surcharge 150.00
C9 A8 250h on 400h brn (V) 6.00 7.50
a. Inverted surcharge 275.00
Nos. C7-C9 (3) 11.50 12.25
Set, never hinged 20.00

Fokker Monoplane AP3

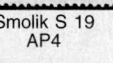

Smolik S 19 AP4

Smolik S 19 — AP5

Fokker over Prague AP6

1930, Dec. 16 Engr. *Perf. 13½*

C10 AP3 50h deep green .25 .25
C11 AP3 1k deep red .30 *.45*
C12 AP4 2k dark green .70 *1.10*
C13 AP4 3k red violet 1.50 1.30
C14 AP5 4k indigo 1.40 1.30
C15 AP5 5k red brown 2.75 *4.25*
C16 AP6 10k vio blue 5.00 4.25
a. 10k ultra 13.50 12.00
C17 AP6 20k gray violet 5.25 5.25
Nos. C10-C17 (8) 17.15 18.15

Two types exist of the 50h, 1k and 2k, and three types of the 3k, differing chiefly in the size of the printed area. A "no hill at left" variety of the 3k exists.

Imperf. examples of Nos. C10-C17 are proofs.

See Bohemia and Moravia No. C1.

Perf. 12

C10a AP3 50h deep green 3.25 *5.00*
C11a AP3 1k deep red 18.00 *22.50*
C12a AP4 2k dark green 18.00 *22.50*
C14a AP5 4k indigo 2.75 *3.75*
C17a AP6 20k gray violet 3.50 *7.50*

Perf. 12x13½, 13½x12

C11b AP3 1k deep red 4.00 *7.50*
C12b AP4 2k dark green 12.00 *20.00*

Perf. 13¾x12¼

C17b AP6 20k gray violet *1,750.*

Perf. 12½

C15a AP5 5k red brown *2,000.*

Catalogue values for unused stamps in this section, from this point to the end of the section, are for Never Hinged items.

Capt. Frantisek Novak — AP7

Plane over Bratislava Castle — AP8

Plane over Charles Bridge, Prague — AP9

1946-47 *Perf. 12½*

C19 AP7 1.50k rose red .25 .25
C20 AP7 5.50k dk gray bl .50 .25
C21 AP7 9k sepia ('47) .85 .25
C22 AP8 10k dl grn .85 .35
C23 AP7 16k violet 1.50 .60
C24 AP8 20k light blue 1.60 1.10
C25 AP9 24k dk bl, *cr* 1.00 .65
C26 AP9 24k rose lake 1.75 1.00
C27 AP9 50k dk gray bl 3.25 2.60
Nos. C19-C27 (9) 11.55 7.05

No. C25 was issued June 12, 1946, for use on the first Prague-New York flight.

Nos. C22, C24-C27 were each issued in sheets of 100 stamps and 12 labels depicting airplane over globe. Values for singles with attached labels (mint/used): C22, $2/$1.50; C24, $4/$3; C25, $7.50/$4; C26, $5.50/$4.50; C27, $9/$7.50.

Nos. C19-C24, C26-C27 Surcharged with New Value and Bars in Various Colors

1949, Sept. 1 *Perf. 12½*

C28 AP7 1k on 1.50k (Bl) .25 .25
C29 AP7 3k on 5.50k (C) .35 .25
C30 AP7 6k on 9k (Br) .55 .25
C31 AP7 7.50k on 16k (C) .75 .25
C32 AP8 8k on 10k (G) .75 .75
C33 AP8 12.50k on 20k (Bl) 1.10 .55

C34 AP9 15k on 24k rose lake (Bl) 2.75 1.00
C35 AP9 30k on 50k (Bl) 2.00 .90
Nos. C28-C35 (8) 8.50 4.20

Karlovy Vary (Karlsbad) — AP10

1951, Apr. 2 Engr. *Perf. 13½*
C36 AP10 6k shown 3.50 1.75
C37 AP10 10k Piestany 3.50 1.75
C38 AP10 15k Marienbad 6.00 1.75
C39 AP10 20k Silac 9.50 4.50
Nos. C36-C39 (4) 22.50 9.75

Nos. C36-C39 were each issued in a sheet of 10 stamps. Value, set *$950.*

View of Cesky Krumlov — AP11

Views: 1.55k, Olomouc. 2.35k, Banska Bystrica. 2.75k, Bratislava. 10k, Prague.

1955 Cream Paper *Perf. 11½*
C40 AP11 80h olive green 1.00 .25
C41 AP11 1.55k violet brn 1.40 .45
C42 AP11 2.35k violet blue 1.90 .25
C43 AP11 2.75k rose brown 2.75 .45
C44 AP11 10k indigo 5.50 2.75
Nos. C40-C44 (5) 12.55 4.15

Issue dates: 10k, Feb. 20. Others, Mar. 28.

Airline: Moscow-Prague-Paris — AP12

2.35k, Airline: Prague-Cairo-Beirut-Damascus.

Engraved and Photogravure
1957, Oct. 15 Unwmk. *Perf. 11½*
C45 AP12 75h ultra & rose .75 .25
C46 AP12 2.35k ultra & org yel .75 .25

Planes at First Czech Aviation School, Pardubice — AP13

Design: 1.80k, Jan Kaspar and flight of first Czech plane, 1909.

1959, Oct. 15
C47 AP13 1k gray & yel .25 .25
C48 AP13 1.80k blk & pale bl .75 .25

50th anniv. of Jan Kaspar's 1st flight Aug. 25, 1909, at Pardubice.

Mail Coach, Plane and Arms of Bratislava — AP14

Design: 2.80k, Helicopter over Bratislava.

1960, Sept. 24 Unwmk. *Perf. 11½*
C49 AP14 1.60k dk bl & gray 1.90 1.00
C50 AP14 2.80k grn & buff 2.40 1.35

Issued to publicize the National Stamp Exhibition, Bratislava, Sept. 24-Oct. 9.

AP15

AP16

Designs: 60h, Prague hails Gagarin. 1.80k, Gagarin, rocket and dove.

1961, June 22
C51 AP15 60h gray & car .35 .25
C52 AP15 1.80k gray & blue .55 .30

No. C51 commemorates Maj. Gagarin's visit to Prague, Apr. 28-29; No. C52 commemorates the first man in space, Yuri A. Gagarin, Apr. 12, 1961.

1962, May 14 Engr. *Perf. 14*

"PRAGA" emblem and: 80h, Dove & Nest of Eggs. 1.40k, Dove. 2.80k, Symbolic flower with five petals. 4.20k, Five leaves.

C53 AP16 80h multicolored .75 .35
C54 AP16 1.40k blk, dk red & bl 1.90 1.50
C55 AP16 2.80k multicolored 1.90 1.50
C56 AP16 4.20k multicolored 2.25 1.50
Nos. C53-C56 (4) 6.80 4.85

PRAGA 1962 World Exhibition of Postage Stamps, Aug. 18-Sept. 2, 1962.
Nos. C53-C56 were each issued in sheets of 10. Value, set $125.

Vostok 5 and Lt. Col. Valeri Bykovski AP17

2.80k, Vostok VI & Lt. Valentina Tereshkova.

1963, June 26
C57 AP17 80h slate bl & pink .50 .25
C58 AP17 2.80k dl red brn & lt bl 2.00 .30

Space flights of Valeri Bykovski, June 14-19, and Valentina Tereshkova, first woman astronaut, June 16-19, 1963.

PRAGA 1962 Emblem, View of Prague and Plane — AP18

Designs: 60h, Istanbul '63 (Hagia Sophia). 1k, Philatec Paris 1964 (Ile de la Cité). 1.40k, WIPA 1965 (Belvedere Palace, Vienna). 1.60k, SIPEX 1966 (Capitol, Washington). 2k, Amphilex '67 (harbor and old town, Amsterdam). 5k, PRAGA 1968 (View of Prague).

Engraved and Photogravure
1967, Oct. 30 *Perf. 11½*
Size: 30x50mm
C59 AP18 30h choc, yel & rose .25 .25
C60 AP18 60h dk grn, yel & lil .25 .25
C61 AP18 1k blk, brick red & lt bl .35 .25
C62 AP18 1.40k vio, yel & dp org .45 .25
C63 AP18 1.60k ind, tan & lil .45 .25
C64 AP18 2k dk grn, org & red .45 .25
Size: 40x50mm
C65 AP18 5k multi 2.50 1.60
Nos. C59-C65 (7) 4.70 3.10

PRAGA 1968 World Stamp Exhibition, Prague, June 22-July 7, 1968. No. C59-C64 issued in sheets of 15 stamps and 15 bilingual labels. Values, set of singles with attached labels: mint $6.50; used $4.50. No. C65 issued in sheets of 4 stamps and one center label. Value $15.

Glider L-13 — AP19

Airplanes: 60h, Sports plane L-40. 80h, Aero taxi L-200. 1k, Crop-spraying plane Z-37. 1.60k, Aerobatics trainer Z-526. 2k, Jet trainer L-29.

1967, Dec. 11
C66 AP19 30h multi .25 .25
C67 AP19 60h multi .25 .25
C68 AP19 80h multi .25 .25
C69 AP19 1k multi .30 .25
C70 AP19 1.60k multi .50 .25
C71 AP19 2k multi 1.60 .90
Nos. C66-C71 (6) 3.15 2.15

Charles Bridge, Prague, and Balloon — AP20

Designs: 1k, Belvedere, fountain and early plane. 2k, Hradcany, Prague, and airship.

1968, Feb. 5 Unwmk. *Perf. 11½*
C72 AP20 60h multicolored .30 .25
C73 AP20 1k multicolored .45 .30
C74 AP20 2k multicolored .75 .30
Nos. C72-C74 (3) 1.50 .85

PRAGA 1968 World Stamp Exhibition, Prague, June 22-July 7, 1968.
Nos. C72-C74 were each issued in a sheet of 10 stamps, Value, set $30.

Astronaut, Moon and Manhattan AP21

Design: 3k, Lunar landing module and J. F. Kennedy Airport, New York.

1969, July 21
C75 AP21 60h blk, vio, yel & sil .30 .25
C76 AP21 3k blk, bl, ocher & sil 1.10 .50

Man's 1st landing on the moon, July 20, 1969, US astronauts Neil A. Armstrong and Col. Edwin E. Aldrin, Jr., with Lieut. Col. Michael Collins piloting Apollo 11.
Nos. C75-C76 printed with label inscribed with names of astronauts and European date of moon landing. Values for pair of singles with attached labels: mint $2; used $1.

TU-104A over Bitov Castle AP22

Designs: 60h, IL-62 over Bezdez Castle. 1.40k, TU-13A over Orava Castle. 1.90k, IL-18 over Veveri Castle. 2.40k, IL-14 over Pernstejn Castle. 3.60k, TU-154 over Trencin Castle.

1973, Oct. 24 Engr. *Perf. 11½*
C77 AP22 30h multi .25 .25
C78 AP22 60h multi .25 .25
C79 AP22 1.40k multi .25 .25
C80 AP22 1.90k multi .40 .25
C81 AP22 2.40k multi 1.50 .75
C82 AP22 3.60k multi .70 .25
Nos. C77-C82 (6) 3.35 2.00

50 years of Czechoslovakian aviation.
Nos. C77-C82 were each printed in sheets of 10. Values, set: mint $60; used $30.

Old Water Tower and Manes Hall — AP23

Designs (Praga 1978 Emblem, Plane Silhouette and): 1.60k, Congress Hall. 2k, Powder Tower, vert. 2.40k, Charles Bridge and Old Bridge Tower. 4k, Old Town Hall on Old Town Square, vert. 6k, Prague Castle and St. Vitus' Cathedral, vert.

Engraved and Photogravure
1976, June 23 *Perf. 11½*
C83 AP23 60h ind & multi .25 .25
C84 AP23 1.60k ind & multi .25 .25
C85 AP23 2k ind & multi .35 .25
C86 AP23 2.40k ind & multi .40 .25
C87 AP23 4k ind & multi .80 .30
C88 AP23 6k ind & multi 2.00 .80
Nos. C83-C88 (6) 4.05 2.10

PRAGA 1978 International Philatelic Exhibition, Prague, Sept. 8-17, 1978.

Zeppelin, 1909 and 1928 — AP24

PRAGA '78 Emblem and: 1k, Ader, 1890, L'Eole & Dunn, 1914. 1.60k, Jeffries-Blanchard balloon, 1785. 2k, Otto Lilienthal's glider, 1896. 4.40k, Jan Kaspar's plane, Pardubice, 1911.

1977, Sept. 15 *Perf. 11½*
C89 AP24 60h multi .25 .25
C90 AP24 1k multi .30 .25
C91 AP24 1.60k multi .35 .25
C92 AP24 2k multi .45 .25
C93 AP24 4.40k multi 2.25 .50
Nos. C89-C93 (5) 3.60 1.50

History of aviation.
Nos. C89-C93 were each issued in sheets of 30 stamps, 15 labels depicting the exhibition emblem, and 5 blank labels. Values for set of singles with attached inscribed labels: mint $5; used $2.50.

SPECIAL DELIVERY STAMPS

Doves — SD1

1919-20 Unwmk. Typo. *Imperf.*

E1	SD1	2h red vio, *yel*	.25	.25
E2	SD1	5h yel grn, *yel*	.25	.25
E3	SD1	10h red brn, *yel* ('20)	.80	.80
		Nos. E1-E3 (3)	1.30	1.30

For overprints and surcharge see Nos. P11-P13, Eastern Silesia E1-E2.

1921 White Paper

E1a	SD1	2h red violet	9.50
E2a	SD1	5h yellow green	6.50
E3a	SD1	10h red brown	140.00
		Nos. E1a-E3a (3)	156.00

It is doubted that Nos. E1a-E3a were regularly issued.

PERSONAL DELIVERY STAMPS

Catalogue values for unused stamps in this section are for Never Hinged items.

PD1

Design: No. EX2, "D" in each corner.

1937 Unwmk. Photo. *Perf. 13½*

EX1	PD1	50h blue	.25	*.25*
EX2	PD1	50h carmine	.25	*.25*

PD3

1946 *Perf. 13½*

EX3	PD3	2k deep blue	.50	*.75*

POSTAGE DUE STAMPS

D1

1918-20 Unwmk. Typo. *Imperf.*

J1	D1	5h deep bister	.25	.25
J2	D1	10h deep bister	.25	.25
J3	D1	15h deep bister	.25	.25
J4	D1	20h deep bister	.30	.25
J5	D1	25h deep bister	.45	.25
J6	D1	30h deep bister	.45	.25
J7	D1	40h deep bister	.60	.25
J8	D1	50h deep bister	.75	.25
J9	D1	100h blk brn	1.50	.25
J10	D1	250h orange	11.00	1.40
J11	D1	400h scarlet	15.00	1.40
J12	D1	500h gray grn	7.50	.25
J13	D1	1000h purple	7.50	.25
J14	D1	2000h dark blue	22.50	.60
		Nos. J1-J14 (14)	68.30	6.15

For surcharges and overprints see Nos. J32-J41, J57, Eastern Silesia J1-J11.

Nos. 1, 33-34, 10 Surcharged in Blue

1922

J15	A1	20h on 3h red vio	.30	.25
J16	A2	50h on 75h slate	1.50	.25
J17	A2	60h on 80h olive grn	.80	.25
J18	A2	100h on 80h olive grn	3.00	.25
J19	A1	200h on 400h purple	4.00	.25
		Nos. J15-J19 (5)	9.60	1.25

Same Surcharge on Nos. 1, 10, 30-31, 33-34, 36, 40 in Violet

1923-26

J20	A1	10h on 3h red vio	.25	.25
J21	A1	20h on 3h red vio	.30	.25
J22	A1	30h on 3h red vio	.25	.25
J23	A1	40h on 3h red vio	.25	.25
J24	A2	50h on 75h slate	1.25	.25
J25	A2	60h on 50h dk vio ('26)	4.00	1.25
J26	A2	60h on 50h dk bl ('26)	4.00	1.50
J27	A2	60h on 75h slate	.50	.25
J28	A2	100h on 80h ol grn	27.50	.25
J29	A2	100h on 120h gray blk	1.00	.25
J30	A1	100h on 400h pur ('26)	1.00	.25
J31	A2	100h on 1000h dp vio ('26)	1.60	.25
		Nos. J20-J31 (12)	41.90	5.25

Postage Due Stamp of 1918-20 Surcharged in Violet

1924

J32	D1	50h on 400h scar	.90	.25
J33	D1	60h on 400h scar	3.25	.60
J34	D1	100h on 400h scar	2.00	.25
		Nos. J32-J34 (3)	6.15	1.10

Postage Due Stamps of 1918-20 Surcharged with New Values in Violet as in 1924

1925

J35	D1	10h on 5h bister	.25	.25
J36	D1	20h on 5h bister	.25	.25
J37	D1	30h on 15h bister	.25	.25
J38	D1	40h on 15h bister	.25	.25
J39	D1	50h on 250h org	1.10	.25
J40	D1	60h on 250h org	1.50	.60
J41	D1	100h on 250h org	2.25	.25
		Nos. J35-J41 (7)	5.85	2.10

Stamps of 1918-19 Surcharged with New Values in Violet as in 1922

1926 *Perf. 14, 11½*

J42	A2	30h on 15h red	.50	.30
J43	A2	40h on 15h red	.50	.30

Surcharged in Violet

1926 *Perf. 14*

J44	A8	30h on 100h dk grn	.25	.25
J45	A8	40h on 200h violet	.25	.25
J46	A8	40h on 300h ver	.95	.25
a.		Perf. 14x13½		60.00
J47	A8	50h on 500h dp grn	.50	.25
a.		Perf. 14x13½	2.75	
J48	A8	60h on 400h brown	1.00	.25
J49	A8	100h on 600h dp vio	2.50	.35
a.		Perf. 14x13½	30.00	1.25
		Nos. J44-J49 (6)	5.45	1.60

Surcharged in Violet

1927

J50	A6	100h dark brown	.55	.25
a.		Perf. 13½	*200.00*	10.00

Surcharged in Violet

J51	A6	40h on 185h org	.25	.25
J52	A6	50h on 20h car	.25	.25
a.		50h on 50h carmine (error)		*55,000.*
J53	A6	50h on 150h rose	.25	.25
a.		Perf. 13½	12.50	2.00
J54	A6	60h on 25h brown	.25	.25
J55	A6	60h on 185h orange	.55	.25
J56	A6	100h on 25h brown	.55	.25
		Nos. J50-J56 (7)	2.65	1.75

No. J52a is known only used.

No. J12 Surcharged in Violet

1927 *Imperf.*

J57	D1	200h on 500h gray grn	8.00	2.50

Catalogue values for unused stamps in this section, from this point to the end of the section, are for Never Hinged items.

D5

1928 *Perf. 14x13½*

J58	D5	5h dark red	.25	.25
J59	D5	10h dark red	.25	.25
J60	D5	20h dark red	.25	.25
J61	D5	30h dark red	.25	.25
J62	D5	40h dark red	.25	.25
J63	D5	50h dark red	.25	.25
J64	D5	60h dark red	.25	.25
J65	D5	1k ultra	.25	.25
J66	D5	2k ultra	.50	.25
J67	D5	5k ultra	.75	.25
J68	D5	10k ultra	1.90	.25
J69	D5	20k ultra	3.75	.30
		Nos. J58-J69 (12)	8.90	3.05

D6

1946-48 Photo. *Perf. 14*

J70	D6	10h dark blue	.25	.25
J71	D6	20h dark blue	.25	.25
J72	D6	50h dark blue	.35	.25
J73	D6	1k carmine rose	.35	.25
J74	D6	1.20k carmine rose	.35	.25
J75	D6	1.50k carmine rose ('48)	.35	.25
J76	D6	1.60k carmine rose	.35	.25
J77	D6	2k carmine rose ('48)	.35	.25
J78	D6	2.40k carmine rose	.35	.25
J79	D6	3k carmine rose	.70	.25
J80	D6	5k carmine rose	.70	.25
J81	D6	6k carmine rose ('48)	1.00	.25
		Nos. J70-J81 (12)	5.35	3.00

D7

D8

1954-55 Engr. *Perf. 12½, 11½*

J82	D7	5h gray green ('55)	.25	.25
J83	D7	10h gray green ('55)	.25	.25
J84	D7	30h gray green	.25	.25
J85	D7	50h gray green ('55)	.25	.25
J86	D7	60h gray green ('55)	.25	.25
J87	D7	95h gray green	.35	.25
J88	D8	1k violet	.35	.25
J89	D8	1.20k violet ('55)	.35	.25
J90	D8	1.50k violet	.70	.25
J91	D8	1.60k violet ('55)	.45	.25
J92	D8	2k violet	.85	.25
J93	D8	3k violet	1.10	.25
J94	D8	5k violet ('55)	1.40	.25
		Nos. J82-J94 (13)	6.80	3.25

Perf. 11½ stamps are from a 1963 printing which lacks the 95h, 1.60k, and 2k.

Stylized Flower — D9

Designs: Various stylized flowers.

Engraved and Photogravure

1971-72 *Perf. 11½*

J95	D9	10h vio bl & pink	.25	.25
J96	D9	20h vio & lt bl	.25	.25
J97	D9	30h emer & lil rose	.25	.25
J98	D9	60h pur & emer	.25	.25
J99	D9	80h org & vio bl	.25	.25
J100	D9	1k dk red & emer	.25	.25
J101	D9	1.20k grn & org	.25	.25
J102	D9	2k blue & red	.40	.25
J103	D9	3k blk & yel	.50	.25
J104	D9	4k brn & ultra	.85	.25
J105	D9	5.40k red & lilac	1.00	.25
J106	D9	6k brick red & org	1.40	.25
		Nos. J95-J106 (12)	5.90	3.00

All except 5.40k issued in 1972.

OFFICIAL STAMPS

Catalogue values for unused stamps in this section are for Never Hinged items.

Coat of Arms — O1

1945 Unwmk. Litho. *Perf. 10½x10*

O1	O1	50h dp slate grn	.25	.25
O2	O1	1k dp bl vio	.25	.25
O3	O1	1.20k plum	.25	.25
O4	O1	1.50k crimson rose	.25	.25
O5	O1	2.50k bright ultra	.25	.25
O6	O1	5k dk vio brn	.30	.25
O7	O1	8k rose pink	.30	.30
		Nos. O1-O7 (7)	1.85	1.80

Redrawn

1947 Photo. *Perf. 14*

O8	O1	60h red	.25	.25
O9	O1	80h dk olive grn	.25	.25
O10	O1	1k dk lilac gray	.25	.25
O11	O1	1.20k dp plum	.25	.25
O12	O1	2.40k dk car rose	.25	.25
O13	O1	4k brt ultra	.25	.25
O14	O1	5k dk vio brn	.25	.25
O15	O1	7.40k purple	.25	.25
		Nos. O8-O15 (8)	2.00	2.00

There are many minor changes in design, size of numerals, etc., of the redrawn stamps.

NEWSPAPER STAMPS

Windhover — N1

1918-20 Unwmk. Typo. *Imperf.*

P1	N1	2h gray green	.25	.25
P2	N1	5h green ('20)	.25	.25
a.		5h dark green	.40	.25
P3	N1	6h red	.30	.25
P4	N1	10h dull violet	.25	.25
P5	N1	20h blue	.25	.25
P6	N1	30h gray brown	.25	.25
P7	N1	50h orange ('20)	.30	.25
P8	N1	100h red brown ('20)	.40	.25
		Nos. P1-P8 (8)	2.25	2.00

Nos. P1-P8 exist privately perforated.

For surcharges and overprints see Nos. P9-P10, P14-P16, Eastern Silesia P1-P5.

Stamps of 1918-20 Surcharged in Violet

1925-26

P9	N1	5h on 2h gray green	.50	.40
P10	N1	5h on 6h red ('26)	.25	*.40*

Special Delivery Stamps of 1918-20 Overprinted in Violet

1926

P11	SD1	5h apple grn, *yel*	.25	.25
a.		5h dull green, *yellow*	.50	.40
P12	SD1	10h red brn, *yel*	.25	.25

With Additional Surcharge of New Value

P13	SD1	5h on 2h red vio, *yel*	.35	.35
		Nos. P11-P13 (3)	.85	.85

Catalogue values for unused stamps in this section, from this point to the end of the section, are for Never Hinged items.

Newspaper Stamps of 1918-20 Overprinted in Violet

1934

P14	N1	10h dull violet	.25	.25
P15	N1	20h blue	.25	.25
P16	N1	30h gray brown	.25	.25
		Nos. P14-P16 (3)	.75	.75

Overprinted for use by commercial firms only.

Carrier Pigeon — N2

1937 ***Imperf.***

P17	N2	2h bister brown	.25	.25
P18	N2	5h dull blue	.25	.25
P19	N2	7h red orange	.25	.25
P20	N2	9h emerald	.25	.25
P21	N2	10h henna brown	.25	.25
P22	N2	12h ultra	.25	.25
P23	N2	20h dark green	.25	.25
P24	N2	50h dark brown	.25	.25
P25	N2	1k olive gray	.25	.25
		Nos. P17-P25 (9)	2.25	2.25

For overprint see Slovakia Nos. P1-P9.

Bratislava Philatelic Exhibition Issue

Souvenir Sheet

1937 ***Imperf.***

P26	N2	10h henna brn, sheet of 25	4.00	4.00

Newspaper Delivery Boy — N4

1945 Unwmk. Typo. ***Imperf.***

P27	N4	5h dull blue	.25	.25
P28	N4	10h red	.25	.25
P29	N4	15h emerald	.25	.25
P30	N4	20h dark green	.25	.25
P31	N4	25h bright red vio	.25	.25
P32	N4	30h ocher	.25	.25
P33	N4	40h red orange	.25	.25
P34	N4	50h brown red	.25	.25
P35	N4	1k slate gray	.25	.25
P36	N4	5k deep vio blue	.25	.25
		Nos. P27-P36 (10)	2.50	2.50

CZECHOSLOVAK LEGION POST

The Czechoslovak Legion in Siberia issued these stamps for use on its mail and that of local residents. Forgeries exist.

For more detailed listings of Czechoslovak Legion Post issues, see the *Classic Specialized Catalogue of Stamps and Covers.*

Russia No. 79 Overprinted

1918 Typo. ***Perf. 14x14½***

A1	A15	10k dark blue	2,500.	—

No. A1 was sold for a few days in Chelyabinsk. It was withdrawn because of a spelling error ("CZESZKJA," instead of "CZESZKAJA").

This overprint was also applied to Russia Nos. 73-78, 80-81, 83-85, 119-121, 123 and 130-131. These were trial printings, never sold to the public, although favor-cancelled covers exist.

Urn and Cathedral at Irkutsk — A1

Armored Railroad Car — A2

Sentinel — A3

1919-20 Litho. ***Imperf.***

1	A1	25k carmine	10.50	—
a.		Perf 11½ ('20)	15.00	—
2	A2	50k yellow green	10.50	—
a.		Perf 11½ ('20)	15.00	—
3	A3	1r red brown	19.00	—
a.		Perf 11½ ('20)	22.50	—

Originals of Nos. 1-3 and 1a-3a have a crackled yellow gum. Ungummed remainders, which were given a white gum, exist imperforate and perforated 11½ and 13¼. Value per set, $3.

Lion of Bohemia — A4

Two types: 1 — 6 points on star-like mace head at right of goblet; large saber handle; measures 20x25¼mm. 2 — 5 points on mace head; small saber handle; measures 19½x25mm.

Perce en Arc in Blue

1920 Embossed

4	A4	(25k) blue & rose	3.00	—

No. 4 Overprinted

1920

5	A4	(25k) bl & rose	10.00	—

Both types of No. 4 received overprint.

No. 5 Surcharged with New Values in Green

6	A4	2k bl & rose	35.00
7	A4	3k bl & rose	35.00
8	A4	5k bl & rose	35.00
9	A4	10k bl & rose	35.00
10	A4	15k bl & rose	35.00
11	A4	25k bl & rose	35.00
12	A4	35k bl & rose	35.00
13	A4	50k bl & rose	35.00
14	A4	1r bl & rose	35.00
		Nos. 6-14 (9)	315.00

BOHEMIA AND MORAVIA

Catalogue values for unused stamps in this country are for never hinged items, beginning with Scott 20 in the regular postage section, Scott B1 in the semipostal section, Scott J1 in the postage due section, and Scott P1 in the newspaper section.

Masaryk Type of Czechoslovakia with hyphen in "Cesko-Slovensko" A60

1939, Apr. 23

1A	A60	1k rose lake	.25	.25

Prepared by Czechoslovakia prior to the German occupation March 15, 1939. Subsequently issued for use in Bohemia and Moravia.

See No. C1.

German Protectorate

Stamps of Czechoslovakia, 1928-39, Overprinted in Black

Perf. 10, 12½, 12x12½

1939, July 15 Unwmk.

1	A29	5h dk ultra	.25	*1.25*
2	A29	10h brown	.25	*1.25*
3	A29	20h red	.25	*1.25*
4	A29	25h green	.25	*1.25*
5	A29	30h red vio	.25	*1.25*
6	A61a	40h dk bl	2.50	*5.00*
7	A85	50h dp grn	.25	*1.25*
8	A63	60h dl vio	2.50	*5.00*
9	A60	1k rose lake (212)	.75	*1.75*
10	A60	1k rose lake (256)	.30	*1.25*
11	A64	1.20k rose lilac	3.00	*5.00*
12	A65	1.50k carmine	2.50	*5.75*
13	A79	1.60k olive grn	5.00	*5.75*
a.		"Mähnen"	32.50	*75.00*
14	A66	2k dk bl grn	1.10	*4.00*
15	A67	2.50k dk bl	3.00	*5.00*
16	A68	3k brown	3.00	*5.75*
17	A70	4k dk vio	9.50	*6.50*
18	A71	5k green	3.50	*10.00*
19	A72	10k blue	4.75	*15.00*
		Nos. 1-19 (19)	42.90	*83.25*
		Set, never hinged	60.00	

The size of the overprint varies, Nos. 1-10 measure 17½x15½mm, Nos. 11-16 19x18mm, Nos. 17 and 19 28x17½mm and No. 18 23½x23mm.

Catalogue values for unused stamps in this section, from this point to the end of the section, are for never hinged items.

Linden Leaves and Closed Buds — A1

1939-41 Photo. ***Perf. 14***

20	A1	5h dark blue	.25	*.30*
21	A1	10h blk brn	.25	*.40*
22	A1	20h crimson	.25	*.30*
23	A1	25h dk bl grn	.25	*.30*
24	A1	30h dp plum	.25	*.30*
24A	A1	30h golden brn ('41)	.25	*.30*
25	A1	40h orange ('40)	.25	.25
26	A1	50h slate grn ('40)	.25	.25
		Nos. 20-26 (8)	2.00	2.40

See Nos. 49-51.

Castle at Zvikov — A2

Karlstein Castle — A3

St. Barbara's Church, Kutna Hora — A4

Cathedral at Prague — A5

Brno Cathedral — A6

Town Square, Olomouc — A7

1939 Engr. ***Perf. 12½***

27	A2	40h dark blue	.25	*.30*
28	A3	50h dk bl grn	.25	*.30*
29	A4	60h dl vio	.25	*.30*
30	A5	1k dp rose	.25	*.30*
31	A6	1.20k rose lilac	.40	*.60*
32	A6	1.50k rose car	.25	*.30*
33	A7	2k dk bl grn	.25	*.50*
34	A7	2.50k dark blue	.25	*.30*
		Nos. 27-34 (8)	2.15	*2.90*

No. 31 measures 23½x29½mm, No. 42 measures 18½x23mm.

See #52-53, 53B. For overprints see #60-61.

Zlin — A8

Iron Works at Moravská Ostrava — A9

Prague — A10

1939-40

35	A8	3k dl rose vio	.25	*.30*
36	A9	4k slate ('40)	.25	*.40*
37	A10	5k green	.50	*.80*
38	A10	10k lt ultra	.40	*1.00*
39	A10	20k yel brn	1.25	*2.00*
		Nos. 35-39 (5)	2.65	*4.50*

Types of 1939 and

Neuhaus A11

Pernstein Castle A12

Pardubice Castle — A13

Lainsltz Bridge near Bechyne A14

Samson Fountain, Budweis — A15

Kromeriz A16

Wallenstein Palace, Prague — A17

1940 Engr. *Perf. 12½*

40	A11	50h dk bl grn	.25	.25
41	A12	80h dp bl	.25	*.40*
42	A6	1.20k vio brn	.40	.25
43	A13	2k gray grn	.25	.25
44	A14	5k dk bl grn	.25	.25
45	A15	6k brn vio	.25	*.50*
46	A16	8k slate grn	.25	*.30*
47	A17	10k blue	.45	.30
48	A10	20k sepia	1.10	*1.60*
		Nos. 40-48 (9)	3.45	*4.10*

No. 42 measures 18½x23mm; No. 31, 23½x29½mm.

Types of 1939-40

1941

49	A1	60h violet	.25	.25
50	A1	80h red org	.25	.25
51	A1	1k brown	.25	.25
52	A5	1.20k rose red	.25	.25
53	A4	1.50k lil rose	.25	*.25*
53A	A13	2k light blue	.25	.25
53B	A6	2.50k ultra	.25	.25
53C	A12	3k olive	.25	.25
		Nos. 49-53C (8)	2.00	2.00

Nos. 49-51 show buds open. Nos. 52 and 53B measure 18¾x23½mm and have no inscriptions below design.

For overprints see Nos. 60-61.

Antonin Dvorák — A18

1941, Aug. 25 Engr. *Perf. 12½*

54	A18	60h dull lilac	.50	*.60*
55	A18	1.20k sepia	.50	*.60*

Antonin Dvorák (1841-1904), composer.

Nos. 54-55 were issued in sheets of 50 stamps and 50 alternating inscribed labels. Value for set of singles with attached labels, unused or used, $1.50.

Farming Scene — A19

Factories — A20

1941, Sept. 7 Photo. *Perf. 13½*

56	A19	30h dk red brn	.25	*.30*
57	A19	60h dark green	.25	*.30*
58	A20	1.20k dk plum	.25	*.30*
59	A20	2.50k sapphire	.25	*.65*
		Nos. 56-59 (4)	1.00	*1.55*

Issued to publicize the Prague Fair.

Nos. 52 and 53B Overprinted in Blue or Red

1942, Mar. 15 *Perf. 12½*

60	A5	1.20k rose red (Bl)	.70	*.80*
61	A6	2.50k ultra (R)	.80	*1.25*

3rd anniv. of the Protectorate of Bohemia and Moravia.

Adolf Hitler A21

17th Century Messenger A22

1942 Photo. *Perf. 14*

Size: 17½x21½mm

62	A21	10(h) gray blk	.25	*.25*
63	A21	30(h) bister brn	.25	*.25*
64	A21	40(h) slate blue	.25	*.25*
65	A21	50(h) slate grn	.25	*.25*
66	A21	60(h) purple	.25	*.25*
67	A21	80(h) org ver	.25	*.25*

Perf. 12½

Engr.

Size: 18x21mm

68	A21	1k dl brn	.25	*.25*
69	A21	1.20(k) carmine	.25	*.30*
70	A21	1.50(k) claret	.25	*.30*
71	A21	1.60(k) Prus grn	.25	*.30*
72	A21	2k light blue	.25	*.30*
73	A21	2.40(k) fawn	.25	*.30*

Size: 18½x24mm

74	A21	2.50(k) ultra	.25	*.30*
75	A21	3k olive grn	.25	*.30*
76	A21	4k brt red vio	.25	*.30*
77	A21	5k myrtle grn	.25	*.30*
78	A21	6k claret brn	.25	*.40*
79	A21	8k indigo	.25	*.40*

Size: 23½x29¾mm

80	A21	10k dk gray grn	.25	*1.00*
81	A21	20k gray vio	.40	*1.00*
82	A21	30k red	.75	*2.00*
83	A21	50k deep blue	1.50	*3.00*
		Nos. 62-83 (22)	7.40	*12.25*

1943, Jan. 10 Photo. *Perf. 13½*

84	A22	60h dark rose violet	.40	.40

Stamp Day.

Scene from "Die Meistersinger" A23

Richard Wagner A24

Scene from "Siegfried" — A25

1943, May 22

85	A23	60h violet	.25	.25
86	A24	1.20k carmine rose	.25	.25
87	A25	2.50k deep ultra	.25	.25
		Nos. 85-87 (3)	.75	.75

Richard Wagner (1813-83).

St. Vitus' Cathedral, Prague — A26

Adolf Hitler — A27

1944, Nov. 21 Engr. *Perf. 12½*

88	A26	1.50k dull rose brn	.25	.25
89	A26	2.50k dull lilac blue	.25	*.35*

1944

90	A27	4.20k green	.50	.50

SEMI-POSTAL STAMPS

Catalogue values for unused stamps in this section are for never hinged items.

Nurse and Wounded Soldier — SP1

Perf. 13½

1940, June 29 Photo. Unwmk.

B1	SP1	60h + 40h indigo	.90	*1.10*
B2	SP1	1.20k + 80h deep plum	.90	*1.25*

Surtax for German Red Cross.

Nos. B1-B2 were issued in sheets of 50 stamps and 50 alternating inscribed labels. Value for set of singles with attached labels: unused $3; used $4.

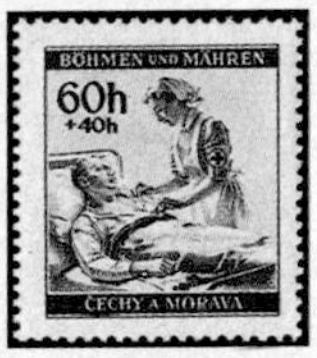

Red Cross Nurse and Patient — SP2

1941, Apr. 20

B3	SP2	60h + 40h indigo	.40	*.60*
B4	SP2	1.20k + 80h dp plum	.40	*.65*

Surtax for German Red Cross.

Nos. B3-B4 were issued in sheets of 50 stamps and 50 alternating inscribed labels. Value for set of singles with attached labels: unused $1.80; used $2.75.

Old Theater, Prague — SP3

Mozart — SP4

1941, Oct. 26

B5	SP3	30h + 30h brown	.25	.25
B6	SP3	60h + 60h Prus grn	.25	.25
B7	SP4	1.20k + 1.20k scar	.25	*.25*
B8	SP4	2.50k + 2.50k dk bl	.45	*.55*
		Nos. B5-B8 (4)	1.20	*1.30*

150th anniversary of Mozart's death.

Labels alternate with stamps in sheets of Nos. B5-B8. The labels with Nos. B5-B6 show two bars of Mozart's opera "Don Giovanni." Those with Nos. B7-B8 show Mozart's piano. Value for set of singles with attached labels: unused $2; used $3.25.

Adolf Hitler — SP5

Nurse and Soldier — SP6

1942, Apr. 20 Engr. *Perf. 12½*

B9	SP5	30h + 20h dl brn vio	.25	.25
B10	SP5	60h + 40h dl grn	.25	.25
B11	SP5	1.20k + 80h dp claret	.25	.35
B12	SP5	2.50k + 1.50k dl bl	.35	*.55*
		Nos. B9-B12 (4)	1.10	*1.40*

Hitler's 53rd birthday.

Nos. B9-B12 were issued in sheets of 100 stamps and 12 blank labels. Value for set of singles with attached labels: unused $3; used $2.25.

1942, Sept. 4 *Perf. 13½*

B13	SP6	60h + 40h deep blue	.25	.25
B14	SP6	1.20(k) + 80(h) dp plum	.25	.25

The surtax aided the German Red Cross.

Emperor Charles IV SP7

Peter Parler SP8

John the Blind, King of Bohemia — SP9

Adolf Hitler — SP10

1943, Jan. 29

B15	SP7	60h + 40h violet	.25	.25
B16	SP8	1.20k + 80h carmine	.25	.25
B17	SP9	2.50k + 1.50k vio bl	.25	.25
		Nos. B15-B17 (3)	.75	*.75*

The surtax was for the benefit of the German wartime winter relief.

1943, Apr. 20 Engr. *Perf. 12½*

B18	SP10	60h + 1.40k dl vio	.25	*.30*
B19	SP10	1.20k + 3.80k carmine	.25	*.30*

Hitler's 54th birthday.

Nos. B18-B19 were issued in sheets of 100 stamps and 12 blank labels. Value for set of singles with attached labels: unused $1.10; used 60c.

Deathmask of Reinhard Heydrich — SP11

Eagle and Red Cross — SP12

1943, May 28 Photo. *Perf. 13½*

B20	SP11	60h + 4.40k black	.75	*1.60*

No. B20 exists in a souvenir sheet containing a single stamp. It was given to high Nazi officials attending a ceremony one year after Heydrich's assassination. Value $15,000.

1943, Sept. 16 *Perf. 13*

B21	SP12	1.20k + 8.80k blk & car	.50	.50

The surtax aided the German Red Cross.

Native Costumes SP13

Nazi Emblem, Arms of Bohemia, Moravia SP14

1944, Mar. 15 *Perf. 13½*

B22	SP13	1.20(k) + 3.80(k) rose lake	.25	.25
B23	SP14	4.20(k) + 10.80(k) golden brn	.25	.25
B24	SP13	10k + 20k saph	.25	*.40*
		Nos. B22-B24 (3)	.75	*.90*

Fifth anniversary of protectorate.

Adolf Hitler — SP15

Bedrich Smetana — SP16

1944, Apr. 20

B25	SP15	60h + 1.40k olive blk	.30	.30
B26	SP15	1.20k + 3.80k slate grn	.30	.30

1944, May 12 Engr. *Perf. 12½*

B27	SP16	60h + 1.40k dk gray grn	.25	.25
B28	SP16	1.20k + 3.80k brn car	.25	.25

Bedrich Smetana (1824-84), Czech composer and pianist.

AIR POST STAMP

Catalogue values for unused stamps in this section are for never hinged items.

Type of Czechoslovakia 1930 with hyphen in "Cesko-Slovensko"

Fokker Monoplane — AP3

1939, Apr. 22 *Perf. 13½*

C1	AP3	30h rose lilac	.25	.25

Prepared by Czechoslovakia prior to the German occupation March 15, 1939. Subsequently issued for use in Bohemia and Moravia. See No. 1A.

PERSONAL DELIVERY STAMPS

PD1

1939-40 Unwmk. Photo. *Perf. 13½*

EX1	PD1	50h indigo & blue ('40)	1.25	*2.00*
EX2	PD1	50h carmine & rose	1.60	*2.50*

POSTAGE DUE STAMPS

Catalogue values for unused stamps in this section are for never hinged items.

D1

1939-40 Unwmk. Typo. *Perf. 14*

J1	D1	5h dark carmine	.25	*.30*
J2	D1	10h dark carmine	.25	*.30*
J3	D1	20h dark carmine	.25	*.30*
J4	D1	30h dark carmine	.25	*.30*
J5	D1	40h dark carmine	.25	*.30*
J6	D1	50h dark carmine	.25	*.30*
J7	D1	60h dark carmine	.25	*.30*
J8	D1	80h dark carmine	.25	*.30*
J9	D1	1k bright ultra	.25	*.40*
J10	D1	1.20k brt ultra ('40)	.30	*.40*
J11	D1	2k bright ultra	1.00	*1.25*
J12	D1	5k bright ultra	1.10	*1.60*
J13	D1	10k bright ultra	1.60	*2.00*
J14	D1	20k bright ultra	3.25	*3.25*
		Nos. J1-J14 (14)	9.50	*11.30*

OFFICIAL STAMPS

Catalogue values for unused stamps in this section are for never hinged items.

Numeral — O1

Unwmk.

1941, Jan. 1 Typo. *Perf. 14*

O1	O1	30h ocher	.25	.25
O2	O1	40h indigo	.25	.25
O3	O1	50h emerald	.25	.25
O4	O1	60h slate grn	.25	.25
O5	O1	80h org red	.80	.25
O6	O1	1k red brn	.40	.25
O7	O1	1.20k carmine	.40	.25
O8	O1	1.50k dp plum	.65	.25
O9	O1	2k brt bl	.65	.25
O10	O1	3k olive	.65	.25
O11	O1	4k red vio	.80	.50
O12	O1	5k org yel	2.00	1.00
		Nos. O1-O12 (12)	7.35	4.00

Eagle — O2

1943, Feb. 15

O13	O2	30(h) bister	.25	*.30*
O14	O2	40(h) indigo	.25	*.30*
O15	O2	50(h) yel grn	.25	*.30*
O16	O2	60(h) dp vio	.25	*.30*
O17	O2	80(h) org red	.25	*.30*
O18	O2	1k chocolate	.25	*.30*
O19	O2	1.20(k) carmine	.25	*.30*
O20	O2	1.50(k) brn red	.25	*.30*
O21	O2	2k lt bl	.25	*.30*
O22	O2	3k olive	.25	*.30*
O23	O2	4k red vio	.25	*.30*
O24	O2	5k dk grn	.25	*.50*
		Nos. O13-O24 (12)	3.00	3.80

NEWSPAPER STAMPS

Catalogue values for unused stamps in this section are for never hinged items.

Carrier Pigeon — N1

1939 Unwmk. Typo. *Imperf.*

P1	N1	2h ocher	.25	*.30*
P2	N1	5h ultra	.25	*.30*
P3	N1	7h red orange	.25	*.30*
P4	N1	9h emerald	.25	*.30*
P5	N1	10h henna brown	.25	*.30*
P6	N1	12h dark ultra	.25	*.30*
P7	N1	20h dark green	.25	*.30*
P8	N1	50h red brown	.25	*.40*
P9	N1	1k greenish gray	.25	*.80*
		Nos. P1-P9 (9)	2.25	3.30

No. P5 Overprinted in Black

1940

P10	N1	10h henna brown	.40	*.65*

Overprinted for use by commercial firms.

N2

1943, Feb. 15

P11	N2	2(h) ocher	.25	.25
P12	N2	5(h) light blue	.25	.25
P13	N2	7(h) red orange	.25	.25
P14	N2	9(h) emerald	.25	.25
P15	N2	10(h) henna brown	.25	.25
P16	N2	12(h) dark ultra	.25	.25
P17	N2	20(h) dark green	.25	.25
P18	N2	50(h) red brown	.25	.25
P19	N2	1k slate green	.25	.25
		Nos. P11-P19 (9)	2.25	2.25

DAHOMEY

də-'hō-mē

LOCATION — West coast of Africa
AREA — 43,483 sq. mi.
POP. — 3,030,000 (est. 1974)
CAPITAL — Porto-Novo

Formerly a native kingdom including Benin, Dahomey was annexed by France in 1894. It became part of the colonial administrative unit of French West Africa in 1895. Stamps of French West Africa superseded those of Dahomey in 1945. The Republic of Dahomey was proclaimed Dec. 4, 1958.

The republic changed its name to the People's Republic of Benin on Nov. 30, 1975. See Benin for stamps issued after that date.

100 Centimes = 1 Franc

Catalog values for unused stamps in this country are for Never Hinged items, beginning with Scott 137 in the regular postage section, Scott B15 in the semi-postal section, Scott C14 in the airpost section, Scott CQ1 in the airpost parcel post section, Scott J29 in the postage due section, and Scott Q1 in the parcel post section.

See French West Africa No. 71 for stamp inscribed "Dahomey" and "Afrique Occidentale Francaise."

Navigation and Commerce — A1

Perf. 14x13½

1899-1905 Typo. Unwmk.

Name of Colony in Blue or Carmine

1	A1	1c black, *lil bl* ('01)	1.60	.80
2	A1	2c brown, *buff* ('04)	1.60	.80
3	A1	4c claret, *lav* ('04)	2.40	2.40
4	A1	5c yellow grn ('04)	6.50	4.00
5	A1	10c red ('01)	8.00	4.00
6	A1	15c gray ('01)	4.00	4.00
7	A1	20c red, *grn* ('04)	20.00	16.00
8	A1	25c black, *rose* ('99)	24.00	24.00
9	A1	25c blue ('01)	20.00	16.00
10	A1	30c brown, *bis* ('04)	24.00	12.00
11	A1	40c red, *straw* ('04)	24.00	16.00
12	A1	50c brn, *az* (name in red) ('01)	40.00	24.00
12A	A1	50c brn, *az* (name in bl) ('05)	32.50	24.00
13	A1	75c dp vio, *org* ('04)	85.00	55.00
14	A1	1fr brnz grn, *straw* ('04)	40.00	32.50
15	A1	2fr violet, *rose* ('04)	110.00	72.50
16	A1	5fr red lilac, *lav* ('04)	135.00	105.00
		Nos. 1-16 (17)	578.60	413.00

Perf. 13½x14 stamps are counterfeits.
For surcharges see Nos. 32-41.

Gen. Louis Faidherbe A2

Oil Palm — A3

Dr. Noel Eugène Ballay A4

1906-07 ***Perf. 13½x14***

Name of Colony in Red or Blue

17	A2	1c slate	1.60	.80
18	A2	2c chocolate	2.40	.80
19	A2	4c choc, *gray bl*	4.00	3.25
20	A2	5c green	8.00	3.25
21	A2	10c carmine (B)	24.00	4.00
22	A3	20c black & red, *azure*	16.00	12.00
23	A3	25c blue, *pnksh*	16.00	12.00
24	A3	30c choc, *pnksh*	16.00	16.00
25	A3	35c black, *yellow*	87.50	12.00
26	A3	45c choc, *grnsh* ('07)	24.00	16.00
27	A3	50c deep violet	20.00	20.00
28	A3	75c blue, *orange*	24.00	24.00
29	A4	1fr black, *azure*	32.00	24.00
30	A4	2fr blue, *pink*	110.00	110.00
31	A4	5fr car, *straw* (B)	95.00	110.00
		Nos. 17-31 (15)	480.50	368.10

Nos. 2-3, 6-7, 9-13 Surcharged in Black or Carmine

Spacing between figures of surcharge 1.5mm (5c), 2mm (10c)

1912 ***Perf. 14x13½***

32	5c on 2c brn, *buff*	2.00	*2.40*
33	5c on 4c claret, *lav* (C)	1.60	*2.00*
a.	Double surcharge	275.00	
34	5c on 15c gray (C)	2.00	*2.40*
35	5c on 20c red, *grn*	2.00	*2.40*
36	5c on 25c blue (C)	2.00	*2.40*
a.	Inverted surcharge	240.00	
37	5c on 30c brown, *bis* (C)	2.00	*2.40*
38	10c on 40c red, *straw*	2.00	*2.40*
a.	Inverted surcharge	325.00	
39	10c on 50c brn, *az,* name in bl (C)	2.40	2.75
40	10c on 50c brn, *az,* name in red (C)	1,125.	1,300.
41	10c on 75c violet, *org*	8.00	8.00
a.	Double surcharge	*5,500.*	
	Nos. 32-39,41 (9)	24.00	27.15

Two spacings between the surcharged numerals are found on Nos. 32 to 41. For detailed listings, see the *Scott Classic Specialized Catalogue of Stamps and Covers.*

Man Climbing Oil Palm — A5

1913-39 ***Perf. 13½x14***

42	A5	1c violet & blk	.40	.30
43	A5	2c choc & rose	.40	.40
44	A5	4c black & brn	.40	.40
45	A5	5c yel grn & bl grn	1.20	.55
46	A5	5c vio brn & vio ('22)	.40	.80
47	A5	10c org red & rose	1.60	.80
a.		Half used as 5c on wrapper or printed matter		—
48	A5	10c yel grn & bl grn ('22)	.80	.80
49	A5	10c red & ol ('25)	.40	.40
50	A5	15c brn org & dk vio ('17)	.80	.80
51	A5	20c gray & red brown	.80	.75
52	A5	20c bluish grn & grn ('26)	.40	.40
53	A5	20c mag & blk ('27)	.40	.40
54	A5	25c ultra & dp blue	2.00	1.60
55	A5	25c vio brn & org ('22)	1.20	.80
56	A5	30c choc & vio	2.75	2.40
57	A5	30c red org & rose ('22)	3.25	3.25
58	A5	30c yellow & vio ('25)	.40	.40
59	A5	30c dl grn & grn ('27)	.40	.40
60	A5	35c brown & blk	.80	.80
61	A5	35c bl grn & grn ('38)	.40	.30
62	A5	40c black & red org	.80	.80
63	A5	45c gray & ultra	.80	.80
64	A5	50c chocolate & brn	6.50	6.00
a.		Half used as 25c on cover		*500.00*
65	A5	50c ultra & bl ('22)	1.60	1.60
66	A5	50c brn red & bl ('26)	1.20	1.20
67	A5	55c gray grn & choc ('38)	.80	.55
68	A5	60c vio, *pnksh* ('25)	.40	.40
69	A5	65c yel brn & ol grn ('26)	1.20	1.20
70	A5	75c blue & violet	1.20	1.20
71	A5	80c henna brn & ultra ('38)	.40	.40
72	A5	85c dk bl & ver ('26)	1.60	1.60
73	A5	90c rose & brn red ('30)	.80	.80
74	A5	90c yel bis & red org ('39)	1.20	.80
75	A5	1fr blue grn & blk	1.20	1.20
76	A5	1fr dk bl & ultra ('26)	1.60	1.60
77	A5	1fr yel brn & lt red ('28)	1.60	1.20
78	A5	1fr dk red & red org ('38)	1.05	.95
79	A5	1.10fr vio & bis ('28)	5.50	*6.00*
80	A5	1.25fr dp bl & dk brn ('33)	17.50	7.25
81	A5	1.50fr dk bl & lt bl ('30)	1.60	.80
82	A5	1.75fr dk brn & dp buff ('33)	4.00	2.00
83	A5	1.75fr ind & ultra ('38)	1.60	.95
84	A5	2fr yel org & choc	1.20	*1.60*
85	A5	3fr red violet ('30)	2.40	1.75
86	A5	5fr violet & dp bl	2.40	2.75
		Nos. 42-86 (45)	79.35	62.15

The 1c gray and yellow green and 5c dull red and black are Togo Nos. 193a, 196a.

Nos. 47a and 64a were authorized for use in Paouignan during the last part of November 1921. Other values exist as bisects but were not authorized.

For surcharges see Nos. 87-96, B1, B8-B11.

Type of 1913 Surcharged

1922-25

87	A5 60c on 75c vio, *pnksh*	1.20	1.20
a.	Double surcharge	200.00	
88	A5 65c on 15c brn org & dk vio ('25)	2.00	2.00
89	A5 85c on 15c brn org & dk vio ('25)	2.00	2.00
	Nos. 87-89 (3)	5.20	5.20

Stamps and Type of 1913-39 Surcharged with New Value and Bars

1924-27

90	A5	25c on 2fr org & choc	1.20	1.20
91	A5	90c on 75c cer & brn red ('27)	2.00	2.00
92	A5	1.25fr on 1fr dk bl & ultra (R) ('26)	1.60	1.60
93	A5	1.50fr on 1fr dk bl & grnsh bl ('27)	2.75	2.75
94	A5	3fr on 5fr olvn & dp org ('27)	10.50	10.50
95	A5	10fr on 5fr bl vio & red brn ('27)	8.00	8.00
96	A5	20fr on 5fr ver & dl grn ('27)	8.75	8.75
		Nos. 90-96 (7)	34.80	34.80

Common Design Types pictured following the introduction.

Colonial Exposition Issue

Common Design Types

1931 **Engr.** ***Perf. 12½***

Name of Country in Black

97	CD70	40c deep green	6.50	6.50
98	CD71	50c violet	6.50	6.50
99	CD72	90c red orange	6.50	6.50
100	CD73	1.50fr dull blue	6.50	6.50
		Nos. 97-100 (4)	26.00	26.00

Paris International Exposition Issue

Common Design Types

1937 **Engr.** ***Perf. 13***

101	CD74	20c deep violet	2.00	2.00
102	CD75	30c dark green	2.00	2.00
103	CD76	40c carmine rose	2.00	2.00
104	CD77	50c dark brown	1.60	1.60
105	CD78	90c red	1.60	1.60
106	CD79	1.50fr ultra	2.40	2.40
		Nos. 101-106 (6)	11.60	11.60

Souvenir Sheet

Imperf

107	CD77	3fr dp blue & blk	12.00	*16.00*
a.		Inscription inverted	1,600.	1,600.

Caillié Issue

Common Design Type

1939, Apr. 5 **Engr.** ***Perf. 12½x12***

108	CD81	90c org brn & org	.40	1.20
109	CD81	2fr brt violet	.40	1.20
110	CD81	2.25fr ultra & dk blue	.40	1.20
		Nos. 108-110 (3)	1.20	3.60

New York World's Fair Issue

Common Design Type

1939 **Engr.**

111	CD82	1.25fr carmine lake	.80	1.60
112	CD82	2.25fr ultra	.80	1.60

Man Poling a Canoe — A7

Pile House A8

Sailboat on Lake Nokoué — A9

Dahomey Warrior — A10

1941 ***Perf. 13***

113	A7	2c scarlet	.25	.25
114	A7	3c deep blue	.25	.25
115	A7	5c brown violet	.70	.70
116	A7	10c green	.30	.30
117	A7	15c black	.25	.25
118	A8	20c violet brown	.30	.30
119	A8	30c dk violet	.30	.30
120	A8	40c scarlet	.70	.70
121	A8	50c slate green	.95	.95
122	A8	60c black	.30	.30
123	A8	70c brt red violet	1.20	1.20
124	A9	80c brown black	1.20	1.20
125	A9	1fr violet	1.20	1.20
126	A9	1.30fr brown violet	1.20	1.20
127	A9	1.40fr green	1.20	1.20
128	A9	1.50fr brt rose	1.20	1.20
129	A9	2fr brown orange	1.20	1.20
130	A10	2.50fr dark blue	1.20	1.20
131	A10	3fr scarlet	1.20	1.20
132	A10	5fr slate green	1.20	1.20
133	A10	10fr violet brown	2.00	2.00
134	A10	20fr black	2.40	2.40
		Nos. 113-134 (22)	20.70	20.70

Nos. 121, 122 without "RF," see Nos. 136A-136B.

Pile House and Marshal Pétain A11

1941 ***Perf. 12½x12***

135	A11	1fr green	.80	—
136	A11	2.50fr blue	.80	—

For surcharges see Nos. B14A-B14B.

Type of 1941 without "RF"

1944 ***Perf. 13***

136A	A8	50c slate green	1.20
136B	A8	60c black	1.20

Nos. 136A-136B were issued by the Vichy government in France, but were not placed on sale in Dahomey.

Catalogue values for unused stamps in this section, from this point to the end of the section, are for Never Hinged items.

Republic

Village Ganvié — A12

Unwmk.

1960, Mar. 1 **Engr.** ***Perf. 12***

137	A12	25fr dk blue, brn & red	.65	.25

For overprint see No. 152.

Imperforates

Most Dahomey stamps from 1960 onward exist imperforate in issued and trial colors, and also in small presentation sheets in issued colors.

C.C.T.A. Issue

Common Design Type

1960, May 16

138	CD106	5fr rose lilac & ultra	.50	.25

Emblem of the Entente — A13

Prime Minister Hubert Maga — A14

Council of the Entente Issue

1960, May 29 **Photo.** ***Perf. 13x13½***

139	A13	25fr multicolored	.65	.40

1st anniv. of the Council of the Entente (Dahomey, Ivory Coast, Niger and Upper Volta).

1960, Aug. **Engr.** ***Perf. 13***

140	A14	85fr deep claret & blk	1.60	.90

Issued on the occasion of Dahomey's proclamation of independence, Aug. 1, 1960.

For surcharge see No. 149.

Weaver — A15

2fr, 10fr, Wood sculptor. 3fr, 15fr, Fisherman and net, horiz. 4fr, 20fr, Potter, horiz.

1961, Feb. 17 Engr. *Perf. 13*

141 A15 1fr rose, org & red lilac .25 .25
142 A15 2fr bister brn & choc .25 .25
143 A15 3fr green & orange .25 .25
144 A15 4fr olive bis & claret .25 .25
145 A15 6fr rose, lt vio & ver .40 .25
146 A15 10fr blue & green .55 .40
147 A15 15fr red lilac & violet .75 .40
148 A15 20fr bluish vio & Prus bl .90 .55
Nos. 141-148 (8) 3.60 2.60

For surcharges see Nos. 1374, Q1-Q7.

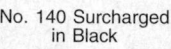

No. 140 Surcharged in Black

1961, Aug. 1

149 A14 100fr on 85fr dp cl & blk 3.25 3.25

First anniversary of Independence.

Doves, UN Building and Emblem — A16

1961, Sept. 20 Unwmk. *Perf. 13*

150 A16 5fr multicolored .35 .25
151 A16 60fr multicolored 1.20 .90

1st anniv. of Dahomey's admission to the UN. See No. C16 and souvenir sheet No. C16a.

No. 137 Overprinted in Black

1961, Dec. 24

152 A12 25fr dk blue, brn & red .65 .40

Abidjan Games, Dec 24-31.

Interior of Burned-out Fort Ouidah and Wrecked Car — A17

1962, July 31 Photo. *Perf. 12½*

153 A17 30fr multicolored .45 .45
154 A17 60fr multicolored .75 .60

Evacuation of Fort Ouidah by the Portuguese, and its occupation by Dahomey. 1st anniv.

African and Malgache Union Issue
Common Design Type

1962, Sept. 8 *Perf. 12½x12*

155 CD110 30fr red lil, bluish grn, red & gold 1.25 .90

Red Cross Nurses and Map — A18

1962, Oct. 5 Engr. *Perf. 13*

156 A18 5fr blue, choc & red .30 .25
157 A18 20fr blue, dk grn & red .60 .45
158 A18 25fr blue, brown & red .65 .45
159 A18 30fr blue, black & red .85 .70
Nos. 156-159 (4) 2.40 1.85

Ganvié Woman in Canoe — A19

Peuhl Herdsman and Cattle A20

Designs: 3fr, 65fr, Bariba chief of Nikki. 15fr, 50fr, Ouidah witch doctor, rock python. 20fr, 30fr, Nessoukoué women carrying vases on heads, Abomey. 25fr, 40fr, Dahomey girl. 60fr, Peuhl herdsman and cattle. 85fr, Ganvié woman in canoe.

1963, Feb. 18 Unwmk. *Perf. 13*

160 A19 2fr grnsh blue & vio .25 .25
161 A19 3fr blue & black .25 .25
162 A20 5fr brown, blk & grn .35 .25
163 A19 15fr brn, bl grn & red brn .35 .25
164 A19 20fr green, blk & car .30 .25
165 A20 25fr dk brn, bl & bl grn .40 .25
166 A19 30fr brn org, choc & mag .60 .40
167 A20 40fr choc, grn & brt bl 1.00 .40
168 A19 50fr blk, grn, brn & red brn 1.60 .55
169 A20 60fr choc, org red & ol 3.50 1.00
170 A19 65fr orange brn & choc 1.75 .65
171 A19 85fr brt blue & choc 2.50 1.00
Nos. 160-171 (12) 12.85 5.50

For surcharges see Nos. 211, 232, Benin 655A, 690F, 700, 722, 1375, 1417.

Boxers — A21

Designs: 1fr, 20fr, Soccer goalkeeper, horiz. 2fr, 5fr, Runners.

1963, Apr. 11 Engr.

172 A21 50c green & blue .25 .25
173 A21 1fr olive, blk & brn .25 .25
174 A21 2fr olive, blue & brn .25 .25
175 A21 5fr brown, crim & blk .25 .25
176 A21 15fr dk violet & brn .35 .25
177 A21 20fr multicolored .55 .55
Nos. 172-177 (6) 1.90 1.80

Friendship Games, Dakar, Apr. 11-21.
For surcharges & overprint see Benin Nos. 697, 704, 1372, 1382, 1384.

President's Palace, Cotonou — A22

1963, Aug. 1 Photo. *Perf. 12½x12*

178 A22 25fr multicolored .45 .25

Third anniversary of independence.

Gen. Toussaint L'Ouverture — A23

UN Emblem, Flame, "15" — A24

1963, Nov. 18 Unwmk. *Perf. 12x13*

179 A23 25fr multicolored .55 .25
180 A23 30fr multicolored .70 .25
181 A23 100fr ultra, brn & red 1.60 .80
Nos. 179-181 (3) 2.85 1.30

Pierre Dominique Toussaint L'Ouverture (1743-1803), Haitian gen., statesman and descendant of the kings of Allada (Dahomey). For overprint, see Benin No. 1367. For surcharge, see Benin No. 1466.

1963, Dec. 10 *Perf. 12*

182 A24 4fr multicolored .25 .25
183 A24 6fr multicolored .25 .25
184 A24 25fr multicolored .45 .25
Nos. 182-184 (3) .95 .75

15th anniversary of the Universal Declaration of Human Rights. For surcharge, see Benin No. 1377.

Somba Dance — A25

Regional Dances: 3fr, Nago dance, Pobe-Ketou, horiz. 10fr, Dance of the baton. 15fr, Nago dance, Ouidah, horiz. 25fr, Dance of the Sakpatassi. 30fr, Dance of the Nessouhouessi, horiz.

1964, Aug. 8 Engr. *Perf. 13*

185 A25 2fr red, emerald & blk .25 .25
186 A25 3fr dull red, blue & grn .25 .25
187 A25 10fr purple, blk & red .45 .25
188 A25 15fr magenta, blk & grn .45 .25
189 A25 25fr Prus blue, brn & org .90 .30
190 A25 30fr dk red, choc & org 1.15 .40
Nos. 185-190 (6) 3.45 1.70

Runner — A26

1964, Oct. 20 Photo. *Perf. 11*

191 A26 60fr shown 1.60 1.00
192 A26 85fr Bicyclist 2.75 1.40

18th Olympic Games, Tokyo, Oct. 10-25.

Cooperation Issue
Common Design Type

1964, Nov. 7 Engr. *Perf. 13*

193 CD119 25fr org, vio & dk brn .80 .35

UNICEF Emblem, Mother and Child — A27

IQSY Emblem and Apollo — A28

25fr, Mother holding child in her arms.

1964, Dec. 11 Unwmk. *Perf. 13*

194 A27 20fr yel grn, dk red & blk .40 .25
195 A27 25fr blue, dk red & blk .60 .45

18th anniv. of UNICEF. For overprint, see Benin No. 1368.

1964, Dec. 22 Photo. *Perf. 13x12½*

100fr, IQSY emblem, Nimbus weather satellite.

196 A28 25fr green & lt yellow .55 .25
197 A28 100fr deep plum & yellow 2.00 .95

International Quiet Sun Year, 1964-65.

Abomey Tapestry — A29

Designs (Abomey tapestries): 25fr, Warrior and fight scenes. 50fr, Birds and warriors, horiz. 85fr, Animals, ship and plants, horiz.

1965, Apr. 12 Photo. *Perf. 12½*

198 A29 20fr multicolored .80 .25
199 A29 25fr multicolored .95 .40
200 A29 50fr multicolored 1.50 .80
201 A29 85fr multicolored 3.25 1.10
a. Min. sheet of 4, #198-201 8.00 8.00
Nos. 198-201 (4) 6.50 2.55

Issued to publicize the local rug weaving industry.

Baudot Telegraph Distributor and Ader Telephone A30

1965, May 17 Engr. *Perf. 13*

202 A30 100fr lilac, org & blk 1.75 1.60

Cent. of the ITU.

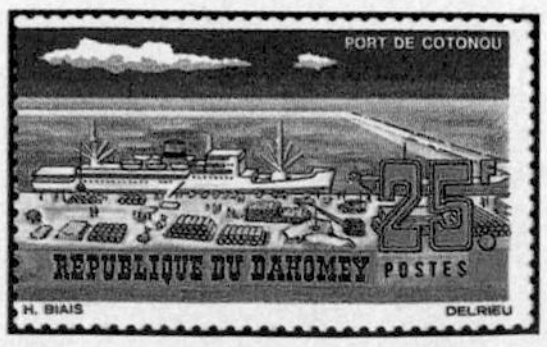

Cotonou Harbor — A31

100fr, Cotonou Harbor, denomination at left.

1965, Aug. 1 Photo. *Perf. 12½*

203 A31 25fr multicolored 1.10 .25
204 A31 100fr multicolored 2.50 1.10
a. Pair, #203-204 4.50 2.10

The opening of Cotonou Harbor. No. 204a has a continuous design.
For surcharges see Nos. 219-220.

Cybium Tritor A32

Fish: 25fr, Dentex filosus. 30fr, Atlantic sailfish. 50fr, Blackish tripletail.

1965, Sept. 20 Engr. *Perf. 13*

205 A32 10fr black & brt blue .75 .25
206 A32 25fr brt blue, org & blk 1.00 .55
207 A32 30fr violet bl & grnsh bl 1.75 .80
208 A32 50fr black, gray bl & org 2.75 1.00
Nos. 205-208 (4) 6.25 2.60

For surcharge see Benin No. 911.

Independence Monument — A33

1965, Oct. 28 Photo. *Perf. 12x12½*

209 A33 25fr gray, black & red .40 .25
210 A33 30fr lt ultra, black & red .65 .25

October 28 Revolution, 2nd anniv. For surcharge, see Benin No. 1385.

No. 165 Surcharged

1965, Nov. Engr. *Perf. 13*

211 A20 1fr on 25fr .30 .25

Porto Novo Cathedral A34

Designs: 50fr, Ouidah Pro-Cathedral, vert. 70fr, Cotonou Cathedral.

1966, Mar. 21 Engr. *Perf. 13*

212 A34 30fr Prus bl, vio brn & grn .55 .25
213 A34 50fr vio brn, Prus bl & brn .70 .50
214 A34 70fr grn, Prus bl & vio brn 1.25 .75
Nos. 212-214 (3) 2.50 1.50

Jewelry — A35

Designs: 30fr, Architecture. 50fr, Musician. 70fr, Crucifixion, sculpture.

1966, Apr. 4 Engr. *Perf. 13*

215 A35 15fr dull red brn & blk .45 .25
216 A35 30fr dk brn, ultra & brn red .70 .45
217 A35 50fr brt blue & dk brn 1.20 .55
218 A35 70fr red brown & blk 2.50 .85
Nos. 215-218 (4) 4.85 2.10

International Negro Arts Festival, Dakar, Senegal, Apr. 1-24.

Nos. 203-204 Surcharged

1966, Apr. 24 Photo. *Perf. 12½*

219 A31 15fr on 25fr multi .55 .35
220 A31 15fr on 100fr multi .55 .35
a. Pair, #219-220 1.50 1.10

Fifth anniversary of the Cooperation Agreement between France and Dahomey.

WHO Headquarters from the East — A36

1966, May 3 *Perf. 12½x13*
Size: 35x22½mm

221 A36 30fr multicolored .75 .25

Inauguration of the WHO Headquarters, Geneva. See No. C32.

Boy Scout Signaling A37

Designs: 10fr, Patrol standard with pennant, vert. 30fr, Campfire and map of Dahomey, vert. 50fr, Scouts building foot bridge.

1966, Oct. 17 Engr. *Perf. 13*

222 A37 5fr dk brn, ocher & red .30 .25
223 A37 10fr black, grn & rose cl .30 .25
224 A37 30fr org, red brn & pur .70 .35
225 A37 50fr vio bl, grn & dk brn 1.20 .45
a. Min. sheet of 4, #222-225 3.00 3.00
Nos. 222-225 (4) 2.50 1.30

Clappertonia Ficifolia — A38

Lions Emblem, Dancing Children, Bird — A39

Flowers: 3fr, Hewittia sublobata. 5fr, Butterfly pea. 10fr, Water lily. 15fr, Commelina forskalaei. 30fr, Eremomastax speciosa.

1967, Feb. 20 Photo. *Perf. 12x12½*

226 A38 1fr multicolored .25 .25
227 A38 3fr multicolored .35 .25
228 A38 5fr multicolored .55 .25
229 A38 10fr multicolored .90 .35
230 A38 15fr multicolored 1.10 .55
231 A38 30fr multicolored 2.10 .90
Nos. 226-231 (6) 5.25 2.55

For surcharges see Benin Nos. 707, 715, 1376, 1390, 1402.

Nos. 170-171 Surcharged

1967, Mar. 1 Engr. *Perf. 13*

232 A19 30fr on 65fr .85 .60
a. Double surcharge 36.00
233 A19 30fr on 85fr .85 .60
a. Double surcharge 60.00
b. Inverted surcharge 60.00

1967, Mar. 20

234 A39 100fr dl vio, dp bl & grn 1.50 1.10

50th anniversary of Lions International.

EXPO '67 "Man in the City" Pavilion A40

Design: 70fr, "The New Africa" exhibit.

1967, June 12 Engr. *Perf. 13*

235 A40 30fr green & choc .70 .25
236 A40 70fr green & brn red 1.50 .65

EXPO '67, International Exhibition, Montreal, Apr. 28-Oct. 27, 1967. See No. C57 and miniature sheet No. C57a.
For surcharges see Benin No. 897.

Europafrica Issue

Trade (Blood) Circulation, Map of Europe and Africa — A41

1967, July 20 Photo. *Perf. 12x12½*

237 A41 30fr multicolored .70 .25
238 A41 45fr multicolored 1.10 .45

For surcharge, see Benin No. 1386.

Scouts Climbing Mountain, Jamboree Emblem A42

70fr, Jamboree emblem, Scouts launching canoe.

1967, Aug. 7 Engr. *Perf. 13*

239 A42 30fr brt bl, red brn & sl .80 .25
240 A42 70fr brt bl, sl grn & dk brn 1.60 .65

12th Boy Scout World Jamboree, Farragut State Park, Idaho, Aug. 1-9. For souvenir sheet see No. C59a.
For surcharges see Benin Nos. 902, 912, 1391.

Rhone River and Olympic Emblems A43

Designs (Olympic Emblems and): 45fr, View of Grenoble, vert. 100fr, Rhone Bridge, Grenoble, and Pierre de Coubertin.

1967, Sept. 2 Engr. *Perf. 13*

241 A43 30fr bis, dp bl & grn .70 .40
242 A43 45fr ultra, grn & brn .90 .55
243 A43 100fr choc, grn & brt bl 2.25 1.00
a. Min. sheet of 3, #241-243 4.50 4.50
Nos. 241-243 (3) 3.85 1.95

10th Winter Olympic Games, Grenoble, Feb. 6-18, 1968.
For surcharges, see Benin No. 903, 1392.

Monetary Union Issue
Common Design Type

1967, Nov. 4 Engr. *Perf. 13*

244 CD125 30fr grn, dk car & dk brn .65 .65

Animals from the Pendjari Reservation A45

Designs: 15fr, Cape Buffalo. 30fr, Lion. 45fr, Buffon's kob. 70fr, African slender-snouted crocodile. 100fr, Hippopotamus.

1968, Mar. 18 Photo. *Perf. 12½x13*

245 A45 15fr multicolored .55 .25
246 A45 30fr purple & multi .65 .50
247 A45 45fr blue & multi 1.25 .60
248 A45 70fr multicolored 2.25 .75
249 A45 100fr multicolored 4.00 2.25
Nos. 245-249 (5) 8.70 4.35

See Nos. 252-256.
For surcharges see No. 310, Benin Nos. 655E, 725, 1415, 1420, 1421.

WHO Emblem A46

1968, Apr. 22 Engr. *Perf. 13*

250 A46 30fr multicolored .60 .25
251 A46 70fr multicolored 1.40 .70

20th anniv. of WHO. For surcharges, see Benin Nos. 1387, 1465.

Animals from the Pendjari Reservation A47

Animals: 5fr, Warthog. 30fr, Leopard. 60fr, Spotted hyena. 75fr, Anubius baboon. 90fr, Hartebeest.

1969, Feb. 10 Photo. *Perf. 12½x12*

252 A47 5fr dark brown & multi .25 .25
253 A47 30fr deep ultra & multi .70 .50
254 A47 60fr dark green & multi 1.25 .70
255 A47 75fr dark blue & multi 3.00 1.00
256 A47 90fr dark green & multi 4.00 2.25
Nos. 252-256 (5) 9.20 4.70

For surcharges, see Benin Nos. 708, 1438.

Heads, Symbols of Agriculture and Science, and Globe A48

1969, Mar. 10 Engr. *Perf. 13*

257 A48 30fr orange & multi .50 .25
258 A48 70fr maroon & multi 1.50 .70

50th anniv. of the ILO.
For surcharges see Benin Nos. 904, 913.

Arms of Dahomey — A49

1969, June 30 Litho. *Perf. 13½x13*
259 A49 5fr yellow & multi .35 .30
260 A49 30fr orange red & multi 1.50 .45

See No. C101.

Development Bank Issue

Cornucopia and Bank Emblem — A50

1969, Sept. 10 Photo. *Perf. 13*
261 A50 30fr black, grn & ocher .75 .55

African Development Bank, 5th anniv.
For surcharge see Benin No. 905.

Europafrica Issue

Ambary (Kenaf) Industry, Cotonou A51

Design: 45fr, Cotton industry, Parakou.

1969, Sept. 22 Litho. *Perf. 14*
262 A51 30fr multicolored 1.00 .50
263 A51 45fr multicolored 1.25 .75

See Nos. C105-C105a.

Sakpata Dance and Tourist Year Emblem — A52

Dances and Tourist Year Emblem: 30fr, Guelede dance. 45fr, Sato dance.

1969, Dec. 15 Litho. *Perf. 14*
264 A52 10fr multicolored .75 .30
265 A52 30fr multicolored 1.45 .45
266 A52 45fr multicolored 2.00 .55
Nos. 264-266 (3) 4.20 1.30

See No. C108. For surcharges see Benin Nos. 690J, 1054B, 1388, 1433.

UN Emblem, Garden and Wall — A53

1970, Apr. 6 Engr. *Perf. 13*
267 A53 30fr ultra, red org & slate .70 .25
268 A53 40fr ultra, brn & sl grn 1.25 .50

25th anniversary of the United Nations.
For surcharge see No. 294. For overprint see Benin 647B.

ASECNA Issue
Common Design Type

1970, June 1 Engr. *Perf. 13*
269 CD132 40fr red & purple .90 .55

For surcharges, see Benin Nos. 906, 1396.

Mt. Fuji, EXPO '70 Emblem, Monorail Train — A54

1970, June 15 Litho. *Perf. 13½x14*
270 A54 5fr green, red & vio bl .40 .25

EXPO '70 International Exhibition, Osaka, Japan, 3/15-9/13/70. See Nos. C124-C125.

Alkemy, King of Ardres — A55

40fr, Sailing ships "La Justice" & "La Concorde," Ardres, 1670. 50fr, Matheo Lopes, ambassador of the King of Ardres & his coat of arms. 200fr, Louis XIV & fleur-de-lis.

1970, July 6 Engr. *Perf. 13*
271 A55 40fr brt grn, ultra & brn .75 .25
272 A55 50fr dk car, choc & emer 1.05 .40
273 A55 70fr gray, lemon & choc 1.60 .65
274 A55 200fr Prus bl, dk car & choc 4.00 1.25
Nos. 271-274 (4) 7.40 2.55

300th anniv. of the mission from the King of Ardres to the King of France, and of the audience with Louis XIV on Dec. 19, 1670.
For surcharges see Benin Nos. 724, 914.

Star of the Order of Independence A56

Bariba Warrior A57

1970, Aug. 1 Photo. *Perf. 12*
275 A56 30fr multicolored .40 .25
276 A56 40fr multicolored .60 .25

10th anniversary of independence.
For surcharge see Benin Nos. 720, 1464.

1970, Aug. 24 *Perf. 12½x13*

Designs: 2fr, 50fr, Two horsemen. 10fr, 70fr, Horseman facing left.

277 A57 1fr yellow & multi .30 .25
278 A57 2fr gray grn & multi .45 .25
279 A57 10fr blue & multi .60 .25
280 A57 40fr yellow grn & multi 1.90 .35
281 A57 50fr gold & multi 2.40 .50
282 A57 70fr lilac rose & multi 3.00 .80
Nos. 277-282 (6) 8.65 2.40

For surcharges see Benin Nos. 350-351, 613, 703, 1373, 1401.

Globe and Heart A58

Design: 40fr, Hands holding heart, vert.

1971, June 7 Engr. *Perf. 13*
283 A58 40fr red, green & dk brn 2.00 .50
284 A58 100fr green, red & blue 4.00 1.25

For surcharges see Benin Nos. 617, 647A, 712, 907, 1429.

Intl. year against racial discrimination.

Ancestral Figures and Lottery Ticket — A59

1971, June 24 Litho. *Perf. 14*
285 A59 35fr multicolored .80 .25
286 A59 40fr multicolored 1.25 .35

4th anniv. of the National Lottery.
For overprint and surcharge, see Benin Nos. 710, 1430.

King Behanzin's Emblem (1889-1894) A60

Emblems of the Kings of Abomey: 25fr, Agoliagbo (1894-1900). 35fr, Ganyehoussou (1620-45), bird and cup, horiz. 100fr, Guezo (1818-58), bull, tree and birds. 135fr, Ouegbadja (1645-85), horiz. 140fr, Glèle (1858-89), lion and sword, horiz.

Photo.; Litho. (25fr, 135fr)

1971-72 *Perf. 12½*
287 A60 25fr multicolored .55 .25
288 A60 35fr green & multi .90 .25
289 A60 40fr green & multi 1.25 .55
290 A60 100fr red & multi 2.25 .90
291 A60 135fr multicolored 3.25 1.40
292 A60 140fr brown & multi 3.75 1.90
Nos. 287-292 (6) 11.95 5.25

Issued: 25fr, 135fr, 7/17/72; others, 8/3/71.
For surcharges and overprint, see Benin Nos. 614, 634B, 791, 1369, 1422, 1431, 1467, 1470.

Kabuki Actor, Long-distance Skiing — A61

1972, Feb. Engr. *Perf. 13*
293 A61 35fr dk car, brn & bl grn 2.50 .75

11th Winter Olympic Games, Sapporo, Japan, Feb. 3-13. See No. C153.

No. 268 Surcharged

1972
294 A53 35fr on 40fr multi .90 .35

Brahms and "Soir d'été" — A62

Design: 65fr, Brahms, woman at piano & music, horiz.

1972, June 29 Engr. *Perf. 13*
295 A62 30fr red brn, blk & lilac 4.00 .80
296 A62 65fr red brn, blk & lilac 6.75 1.50

75th anniversary of the death of Johannes Brahms (1833-1897), German composer.
For surcharges see Benin Nos. 654B, 718, 1389.

The Hare and The Tortoise, by La Fontaine — A63

Fables: 35fr, The Fox and The Stork, vert. 40fr, The Cat, The Weasel and Rabbit.

1972, Aug. 28 Engr. *Perf. 13*
297 A63 10fr multicolored 2.25 .75
298 A63 35fr dark red & multi 4.25 1.25
299 A63 40fr ultra & multi 5.50 1.75
Nos. 297-299 (3) 12.00 3.75

Jean de La Fontaine (1621-1695), French fabulist. For surcharges, see Benin Nos. 1380, 1393, 1397.

West African Monetary Union Issue
Common Design Type

1972, Nov. 2 Engr. *Perf. 13*
300 CD136 40fr choc, ocher & gray .65 .25

Dr. Hansen, Microscope, Bacilli — A65

Design: 85fr, Portrait of Dr. Hansen.

1973, May 14 Engr. *Perf. 13*
301 A65 35fr ultra, vio brn & brn .50 .35
302 A65 85fr yel grn, bis & ver 1.25 .75

Centenary of the discovery by Dr. Armauer G. Hansen of the Hansen bacillus, the cause of leprosy.
For surcharges see Benin Nos. 655G, 1084, 1437.

Arms of Dahomey — A66

1973, June 25 Photo. *Perf. 13*
303 A66 5fr ultra & multi .25 .25
304 A66 35fr ocher & multi .40 .25
305 A66 40fr red orange & multi .60 .25
Nos. 303-305 (3) 1.25 .75

For overprint and surcharge see Benin Nos. 690A, 1403.

INTERPOL Emblem and Spiderweb A67

Design: 50fr, INTERPOL emblem and communications symbols, vert.

1973, July **Engr.**
306 A67 35fr ver, grn & brn .60 .30
307 A67 50fr green, brn & red .85 .45

50th anniversary of International Criminal Police Organization (INTERPOL).
For overprints and surcharges, see Benin Nos. 634A, 810, 1434, 1471.

Education in Hygiene and Nutrition A68

WHO, 25th Anniv.: 100fr, Prenatal examination and care, WHO emblem.

1973, Aug. 2 **Photo.** ***Perf. 12½x13***
308 A68 35fr multicolored .50 .30
309 A68 100fr multicolored 1.50 .65

For surcharges, see Benin Nos. 655B, 1439.

No. 248 Srchd. and Ovptd. in Red

1973, Aug. 16
310 A45 100fr on 70fr multi 2.50 1.00

African solidarity in drought emergency.

African Postal Union Issue
Common Design Type

1973, Sept. 12 **Engr.** ***Perf. 13***
311 CD137 100fr red, purple & blk 1.25 .55

For surcharges, see Benin Nos. 690I, 1440.

Epinephelus Aeneus — A69

Fish: 15fr, Drepane africana. 35fr, Pragus ehrenbergi.

1973, Sept. 18
312 A69 5fr slate blue & indigo 1.00 .30
313 A69 15fr black & brt blue 1.50 .35
314 A69 35fr emerald, ocher & sep 4.00 .60
Nos. 312-314 (3) 6.50 1.25

For surcharges, see Benin No. 698, 1378, 1383, 1394.

Chameleon A70

40fr, Emblem over map of Dahomey, vert.

1973, Nov. 30 **Photo.** ***Perf. 13***
315 A70 35fr olive & multi .55 .30
316 A70 40fr multicolored 1.25 .35

1st anniv. of the Oct. 26 revolution.

The Chameleon in the Tree — A71

Designs: 5fr, The elephant, the hen and the dog, vert. 10fr, The sparrowhawk and the dog, vert. 25fr, The chameleon in the tree. 40fr, The eagle, the viper and the hen.

1974, Feb. 14 **Photo.** ***Perf. 13***
317 A71 5fr emerald & multi .75 .25
318 A71 10fr slate blue & multi .90 .25
319 A71 25fr slate blue & multi 1.75 .30
320 A71 40fr light blue & multi 2.50 .45
Nos. 317-320 (4) 5.90 1.25

Folktales of Dahomey.
For surcharges and overprint see Benin Nos. 709, 908, 1363, 1370, 1379, 1381, 1432.

German Shepherd — A72

1974, Apr. 25 **Photo.** ***Perf. 13***
321 A72 40fr shown 1.50 .35
322 A72 50fr Boxer 1.75 .35
323 A72 100fr Saluki 3.50 .80
Nos. 321-323 (3) 6.75 1.50

For surcharges, see Benin No. 1398, 1435, 1441.

Council Issue

Map and Flags of Members A73

1974, May 29 **Photo.** ***Perf. 13x12½***
324 A73 40fr blue & multi .80 .25

15th anniversary of the Council of Accord.

Locomotive 232, 1911 — A74

Designs: Locomotives.

1974, Sept. 2 **Photo.** ***Perf. 13x12½***
325 A74 35fr shown 1.00 .30
326 A74 40fr Freight, 1877 2.00 .30
327 A74 100fr Crampton, 1849 3.00 1.00
328 A74 200fr Stephenson, 1846 6.00 1.60
Nos. 325-328 (4) 12.00 3.20

For surcharges see Benin Nos. 654E, 690K, 727, 909, 1395, 1399, 1442, 1444.

Globe, Money, People in Bank A75

1974, Oct. 31 **Engr.** ***Perf. 13***
329 A75 35fr multicolored .50 .35

World Savings Day. For surcharge, see Benin No. 1468.

Dompago Dance, Hissi Tribe — A76

Folk Dances: 25fr, Fetish Dance, Vaudou-Tchinan. 40fr, Bamboo Dance, Agbehoun. 100fr, Somba Dance, Sandoua, horiz.

1975, Aug. 4 **Litho.** ***Perf. 12***
330 A76 10fr yellow & multi .65 .25
331 A76 25fr dk green & multi 1.25 .25
332 A76 40fr red & multi 1.60 .50
333 A76 100fr multicolored 3.00 .60
Nos. 330-333 (4) 6.50 1.60

For surcharges and overprints see Benin Nos. 655D, 713, 1371, 1414, 1443.

Flags of Dahomey and Nigeria over Africa — A77

Design: 100fr, Arrows connecting maps of Dahomey and Nigeria, horiz.

1975, Aug. 11 **Photo.** ***Perf. 12½x13***
334 A77 65fr multicolored .75 .25
335 A77 100fr green & multi 1.00 .45

Year of intensified cooperation between Dahomey and Nigeria.
For surcharges & overprint see Benin Nos. 690H, 701, 899, 901, 1419, 1423.

Map, Pylons, Emblem — A78

Benin Electric Community Emblem and Pylon — A79

1975, Aug. 18
336 A78 40fr multicolored .75 .35
337 A79 150fr multicolored 2.00 1.00

Benin Electric Community and Ghana-Togo-Dahomey cooperation.
For surcharges see Benin Nos. 601, 900, 910, 1400.

Map of Dahomey, Rising Sun — A80

Albert Schweitzer, Nurse, Patient — A81

1975, Aug. 25 **Photo.** ***Perf. 12½x13***
338 A80 35fr multicolored .50 .25

Cooperation Year for the creation of a new Dahoman society.
For overprint see Benin No. 690E. For surcharge, see Benin No. 1362.

1975, Sept. 22 **Engr.** ***Perf. 13***
339 A81 200fr olive, grn & red brn 6.25 1.50

Birth centenary of Albert Schweitzer (1875-1965), medical missionary and musician.
For surcharges, see Benin Nos. 655F, 1445.

Woman Speaking on Telephone, IWY Emblem — A82

150fr, IWY emblem and linked rings.

1975, Oct. 20 **Engr.** ***Perf. 12½x13***
340 A82 50fr Prus blue & lilac .75 .35
341 A82 150fr emerald, brn & org 2.00 .80

International Women's Year 1975.
For surcharges, see Benin Nos. 655C, 1436, 1469.

SEMI-POSTAL STAMPS

Regular Issue of 1913 Surcharged in Red

1915 **Unwmk.** ***Perf. 14x13½***
B1 A5 10c + 5c orange red & rose 1.60 1.60

Curie Issue
Common Design Type

1938 ***Perf. 13***
B2 CD80 1.75fr + 50c brt ultra 9.50 9.50

French Revolution Issue
Common Design Type

1939 **Photo.**
Name and Value Typo. in Black

B3 CD83 45c + 25c green 9.50 9.50
B4 CD83 70c + 30c brown 9.50 9.50
B5 CD83 90c + 35c red org 9.50 9.50
B6 CD83 1.25fr + 1fr rose pink 9.50 9.50
B7 CD83 2.25fr + 2fr blue 9.50 9.50
Nos. B3-B7 (5) 47.50 47.50

Postage Stamps of 1913-38 Surcharged in Black

1941 ***Perf. 13½x14***

B8 A5 50c + 1fr brn red & bl 3.25 3.25
B9 A5 80c + 2fr hn brn & ultra 7.25 7.25
B10 A5 1.50fr + 2fr dk bl & lt bl 7.25 7.25
B11 A5 2fr + 3fr yel org & choc 7.25 7.25
Nos. B8-B11 (4) 25.00 25.00

Common Design Type and

Radio Operator — SP1

Senegalese Artillerymen SP2

1941 **Photo.** ***Perf. 13½***

B12 SP1 1fr + 1fr red 1.20
B13 CD86 1.50fr + 3fr claret 1.20
B14 SP2 2.50fr + 1fr blue 1.20
Nos. B12-B14 (3) 3.60

Surtax for the defense of the colonies.
Nos. B12-B14 were issued by the Vichy government in France, but were not placed on sale in Dahomey.

Nos. 135-136 Srchd. in Black or Red

1944 **Engr.** ***Perf. 12½x12***

B14A 50c + 1.50fr on 2.50fr deep blue (R) .80
B14B + 2.50fr on 1fr green .80

Colonial Development Fund.
Nos. B14A-B14B were issued by the Vichy government in France, but were not placed on sale in Dahomey.

Catalogue values for unused stamps in this section, from this point to the end of the section, are for Never Hinged items.

Republic
Anti-Malaria Issue
Common Design Type

1962, Apr. 7 **Engr.** ***Perf. 12½x12***

B15 CD108 25fr + 5fr orange brn .75 .75

Freedom from Hunger Issue
Common Design Type

1963, Mar. 21 **Unwmk.** ***Perf. 13***

B16 CD112 25fr + 5fr ol, brn red & brn .80 .80

AIR POST STAMPS

Common Design Type

1940 **Unwmk.** **Engr.** ***Perf. 12½***

C1 CD85 1.90fr ultra .40 .40
C2 CD85 2.90fr dk red .40 .40
C3 CD85 4.50fr dk gray grn .80 .80
C4 CD85 4.90fr yel bister .80 .80
C5 CD85 6.90fr deep org 1.60 1.60
Nos. C1-C5 (5) 4.00 4.00

Common Design Types

1942

C6 CD88 50c car & bl .30
C7 CD88 1fr brn & blk .30
C8 CD88 2fr dk grn & red brn .50
C9 CD88 3fr dk bl & scar .95
C10 CD88 5fr vio & brn red 1.05

Frame Engr., Center Typo.

C11 CD89 10fr ultra, ind & org 1.05
C12 CD89 20fr rose car, mag & gray blk 1.10
C13 CD89 50fr yel grn, dl grn & dp bl 1.90 *3.25*
a. 50fr yellow green, dull green & pale blue 2.75 *3.75*
Nos. C6-C13 (8) 7.15

Nos. C6-C12 were issued by the Vichy government in France, but were not placed on sale in Dahomey.

Catalogue values for unused stamps in this section, from this point to the end of the section, are for Never Hinged items.

Republic

Somba House — AP4

Design: 500fr, Royal Court of Abomey.

Unwmk.

1960, Apr. 1 **Engr.** ***Perf. 13***

C14 AP4 100fr multi 3.25 .80
C15 AP4 500fr multi 13.50 4.00

For overprint see Benin No. C419. For surcharges, see Benin Nos. C541, C609.

Type of Regular Issue, 1961

1961, Sept. 20

C16 A16 200fr multi 3.50 2.25
a. Souv. sheet of 3, #150-151, C16 7.00 7.00

Air Afrique Issue
Common Design Type

1962, Feb. 17 ***Perf. 13***

C17 CD107 25fr ultra, blk & org brn .80 .40

Palace of the African and Malgache Union, Cotonou — AP5

1963, July 27 **Photo.** ***Perf. 13x12***

C18 AP5 250fr multi 5.00 2.75

Assembly of chiefs of state of the African and Malgache Union held at Cotonou in July.

African Postal Union Issue
Common Design Type

1963, Sept. 8 **Unwmk.** ***Perf. 12½***

C19 CD114 25fr brt bl, ocher & red .75 .25

See note after Cameroun No. C47.

Boeing 707 — AP6

Boeing 707: 200fr, On the ground. 300fr, Over Cotonou airport. 500fr, In the air.

1963, Oct. 25 **Engr.** ***Perf. 13***

C20 AP6 100fr multi 2.00 .60
C21 AP6 200fr multi 3.00 2.00
C22 AP6 300fr multi 5.00 2.00
C23 AP6 500fr multi 10.00 2.50
Nos. C20-C23 (4) 20.00 7.10

For surcharges see Nos. CQ1-CQ5, Benin No. C610.

Priests Carrying Funerary Boat, Isis Temple, Philae — AP7

1964, Mar. 9 **Unwmk.** ***Perf. 13***

C24 AP7 25fr vio bl & brn 2.00 .95

UNESCO world campaign to save historic monuments in Nubia.

Weather Map and Symbols — AP8

1965, Mar. 23 **Photo.** ***Perf. 12½***

C25 AP8 50fr multi .80 .55

Fifth World Meteorological Day.

ICY Emblem and Men of Various Races — AP9

1965, June 26 **Engr.** ***Perf. 13***

C26 AP9 25fr dl pur, mar & grn .65 .25
C27 AP9 85fr dp bl, mar & sl grn 1.25 .80

International Cooperation Year, 1965

Winston Churchill — AP10

1965, June 15 **Photo.** ***Perf. 12½***

C28 AP10 100fr multi 2.25 1.75

For surcharge, see Benin No. C611.

Abraham Lincoln — AP11

1965, July 15 ***Perf. 13***

C29 AP11 100fr multi 2.00 1.00

Centenary of death of Lincoln
For surcharge see No. C55.

John F. Kennedy and Arms of Dahomey — AP12

1965, Nov. 22 **Photo.** ***Perf. 12½***

C30 AP12 100fr dp grn & blk 2.75 1.10

President John F. Kennedy (1917-63).
For surcharge see No. C56.

Dr. Albert Schweitzer and Patients — AP13

1966, Jan. 17 **Photo.** ***Perf. 12½***

C31 AP13 100fr multi 3.00 1.25

Dr. Albert Schweitzer (1875-1965), medical missionary, theologian and musician.
For surcharge see Benin No. C435.

WHO Type of Regular Issue

Design: WHO Headquarters from the West.

1966, May 3 **Unwmk.** ***Perf. 13***
Size: 47x28mm

C32 A36 100fr ultra, yel & blk 1.75 1.50

Pygmy Goose — AP14

Broad-billed Rollers — AP15

Birds: 100fr, Fiery-breasted bush-shrike. 250fr, Emerald cuckoos. 500fr, Emerald starling.

1966-67 ***Perf. 12½***

C33 AP14 50fr multi 2.00 .55
C34 AP14 100fr multi 3.00 .85
C35 AP15 200fr multi 10.00 2.25
C36 AP15 250fr multi 10.00 3.00
C37 AP14 500fr multi 15.00 6.00
Nos. C33-C37 (5) 40.00 12.65

Issued: 50fr, 100fr, 500fr, 6/13/66; others, 1/20/67.
For surcharges see Nos. C107, Benin Nos. 1472, C353-C355, C357, C368, C426, C436, C550, C590.

Industrial Symbols — AP16

1966, July 21 Photo. *Perf. 12x13*

C38 AP16 100fr multi 1.75 .80

Agreement between European Economic Community & the African & Malagache Union, 3rd anniv.

Pope Paul VI and St. Peter's, Rome — AP17

Pope Paul VI and UN General Assembly AP18

70fr, Pope Paul VI and view of NYC.

1966, Aug. 22 Engr. *Perf. 13*

C39	AP17 50fr multi	.75	.45
C40	AP17 70fr multi	.95	.55
C41	AP18 100fr multi	1.75	1.00
a.	Min. sheet of 3, #C39-C41	4.50	4.50
	Nos. C39-C41 (3)	3.45	2.00

Pope Paul's appeal for peace before the UN General Assembly, Oct. 4, 1965.

Air Afrique Issue, 1966
Common Design Type

1966, Aug. 31 Photo. *Perf. 12½*

C42 CD123 30fr dk vio, blk & gray .75 .25

"Science" — AP20

Designs: 45fr, "Art" (carved female statue), vert. 100fr, "Education" (book and letters).

1966, Nov. 4 Engr. *Perf. 13*

C43	AP20 30fr mag, ultra & vio brn	.45	.25
C44	AP20 45fr mar & grn	.80	.55
C45	AP20 100fr blk, mar & brt bl	1.90	1.00
a.	Min. sheet of 3, #C43-C45	3.25	3.25
	Nos. C43-C45 (3)	3.15	1.80

20th anniversary of UNESCO.

Madonna by Alessio Baldovinetti AP21

Christmas: 50fr, Nativity after 15th century Beaune tapestry. 100fr, Adoration of the Shepherds, by José Ribera.

1966, Dec. 25 Photo. *Perf. 12½x12*

C46	AP21 50fr multi	3.25	2.25
C47	AP21 100fr multi	4.50	3.25
C48	AP21 200fr multi	9.00	5.00
	Nos. C46-C48 (3)	16.75	10.50

See Nos. C95-C96, C109-C115. For surcharge see No. C60. For overprint, see Benin No. C544

1967, Apr. 10 *Perf. 12½x12*

Paintings by Ingres: No. C49, Self-portrait, 1804. No. C50, Oedipus and the Sphinx.

C49	AP21 100fr multi	3.25	1.75
C50	AP21 100fr multi	3.25	1.75

Jean Auguste Dominique Ingres (1780-1867), French painter.

Three-master Suzanne — AP22

Windjammers: 45fr, Three-master Esmeralda, vert. 80fr, Schooner Marie Alice, vert. 100fr, Four-master Antonin.

1967, May 8 *Perf. 13*

C51	AP22 30fr multi	1.00	.50
C52	AP22 45fr multi	1.25	.75
C53	AP22 80fr multi	2.50	1.25
C54	AP22 100fr multi	3.25	1.50
	Nos. C51-C54 (4)	8.00	4.00

For overprint and surcharges see Benin Nos. C369, C420, C606, C612.

Nos. C29-C30 Surcharged

1967, May 29 Photo. *Perf. 13, 12½*

C55	AP11 125fr on 100fr	2.75	1.25
C56	AP12 125fr on 100fr	2.75	1.25

50th anniv. of the birth of Pres. John F. Kennedy.

EXPO '67 "Man In Space" Pavilion — AP23

1967, June 12 Engr. *Perf. 13*

C57	AP23 100fr dl red & Prus bl	2.00	.75
a.	Min. sheet of 3, #235-236, C57	4.00	4.00

EXPO '67, International Exhibition, Montreal, Apr. 28-Oct. 27, 1967.

Europafrica Issue

Konrad Adenauer, by Oscar Kokoschká AP24

1967, July 19 Photo. *Perf. 12½x12*

C58	AP24 70fr multi	2.00	1.25
a.	Souv. sheet of 4	8.50	8.50

Konrad Adenauer (1876-1967), chancellor of West Germany (1949-1963). For surcharges, see Benin Nos. C572, C602.

Jamboree Emblem, Ropes and World Map — AP25

1967, Aug. 7 Engr. *Perf. 13*

C59	AP25 100fr lil, sl grn & dp bl	1.60	.75
a.	Souv. sheet of 3, #239-240, C59	3.50	3.50

12th Boy Scout World Jamboree, Farragut State Park, Idaho, Aug. 1-9.

No. C48 Srchd. in Red

1967, Aug. 12 Photo. *Perf. 12½x12*

C60	AP21 150fr on 200fr	3.50	2.75
a.	"150F" omitted	300.00	300.00

Riccione, Italy Stamp Exhibition.

African Postal Union Issue, 1967
Common Design Type

1967, Sept. 9 Engr. *Perf. 13*

C61 CD124 100fr red, brt lil & emer 1.75 .95

For surcharge see Benin No. C471.

Charles de Gaulle AP26

1967, Nov. 21 Photo. *Perf. 12½x13*

C62	AP26 100fr multi	3.75	2.50
a.	Souv. sheet of 4	16.00	16.00

Pres. Charles de Gaulle of France on the occasion of Pres. Christophe Soglo's state visit to Paris, Nov. 1967.

Madonna, by Matthias Grunewald AP27

Paintings: 50fr, Holy Family by the Master of St. Sebastian, horiz. 100fr, Adoration of the Magi by Ulrich Apt the Elder. 200fr, Annunciation, by Matthias Grunewald.

1967, Dec. 11 Photo. *Perf. 12½*

C63	AP27 30fr multi	.55	.45
C64	AP27 50fr multi	1.10	.60
C65	AP27 100fr multi	2.00	1.25
C66	AP27 200fr multi	5.00	2.00
	Nos. C63-C66 (4)	8.65	4.30

Christmas 1967.

Venus de Milo and Mariner 5 — AP28

#C68, Venus de Milo and Venera 4 rocket.

1968, Feb. 17 Photo. *Perf. 13*

C67	AP28 70fr grnsh bl & multi	1.75	.75
C68	AP28 70fr dp bl & multi	1.75	.75
a.	Souv. sheet of 2, #C67-C68	4.00	4.00

Explorations of the planet Venus, Oct. 18-19, 1967.

For surcharges see Nos. C103-C104, Benin No. C587.

Gutenberg Monument, Strasbourg Cathedral AP29

Design: 100fr, Gutenberg Monument, Mainz, and Gutenberg press.

1968, May 20 Litho. *Perf. 14x13½*

C69	AP29 45fr grn & org	1.00	.40
C70	AP29 100fr dk & lt bl	2.00	1.00
a.	Souv. sheet of 2, #C69-C70	3.75	3.75

500th anniv. of the death of Johann Gutenberg, inventor of printing from movable type.

For surcharge see Benin No. C516.

Martin Luther King, Jr. — AP30

Designs: 30fr, "We must meet hate with creative love" in French, English and German. 100fr, Full-face portrait.

Perf. 12½, 13½x13

1968, June 17 **Photo.**

Size: 26x46mm

C71 AP30 30fr red brn, yel & blk .60 .35

Size: 26x37mm

C72 AP30 55fr multi 1.00 .45
C73 AP30 100fr multi 1.50 .90
a. Min. sheet of 3, #C71-C73 4.00 4.00
Nos. C71-C73 (3) 3.10 1.70

Martin Luther King, Jr. (1929-68), American civil rights leader.
For surcharges, see Benin Nos. C517, C561, C613.

Robert Schuman — AP31

45fr, Alcide de Gasperi. 70fr, Konrad Adenauer.

1968, July 20 **Photo.** ***Perf. 13***
C74 AP31 30fr dp yel, blk & grn .40 .40
C75 AP31 45fr org, dk brn & ol .85 .50
C76 AP31 70fr multi 1.40 .50
Nos. C74-C76 (3) 2.65 1.40

5th anniversary of the economic agreement between the European Economic Community and the African and Malgache Union.
For surcharges, see Benin Nos. C462, C562, C603.

Battle of Montebello, by Henri Philippoteaux — AP32

Paintings: 45fr, 2nd Zouave Regiment at Magenta, by Riballier. 70fr, Battle of Magenta, by Louis Eugène Charpentier. 100fr, Battle of Solferino, by Charpentier.

1968, Aug. 12 ***Perf. 12½x12***
C77 AP32 30fr multi 1.15 .50
C78 AP32 45fr multi 1.60 .65
C79 AP32 70fr multi 3.25 1.25
C80 AP32 100fr multi 4.00 1.00
Nos. C77-C80 (4) 10.00 3.40

Issued for the Red Cross. For surcharges, see Benin Nos. C574, C594, C614.

Mail Truck in Village — AP33

Designs: 45fr, Mail truck stopping at rural post office. 55fr, Mail truck at river bank. 70fr, Mail truck and train.

1968, Oct. 7 **Photo.** ***Perf. 13x12½***
C81 AP33 30fr multi .90 .50
C82 AP33 45fr multi 1.10 .55
C83 AP33 55fr multi 1.75 .55
C84 AP33 70fr multi 4.25 1.00
Nos. C81-C84 (4) 8.00 2.60

For surcharges see Benin Nos. C352, C357A, C584.

Aztec Stadium, Mexico City — AP34

45fr, Ball player, Mayan sculpture, vert. 70fr, Wrestler, sculpture from Uxpanapan, vert. 150fr, Olympic Stadium, Mexico City.

1968, Nov. 20 **Engr.** ***Perf. 13***
C85 AP34 30fr dp cl & sl grn .80 .30
C86 AP34 45fr ultra & dk rose brn 1.50 .60
C87 AP34 70fr sl grn & dk brn 2.10 .65
C88 AP34 150fr dk car & dk brn 3.00 1.25
a. Min. sheet of 4, #C85-C88 7.50 7.50
Nos. C85-C88 (4) 7.40 2.80

19th Olympic Games, Mexico City, Oct. 12-27. No. C88a is folded down the vertical gutter separating Nos. C85-C86 se-tenant at left and Nos. C87-C88 se-tenant at right.
For overprint and surcharges see Benin Nos. C457, C461, C513.

The Annunciation, by Foujita — AP35

Paintings by Foujita: 30fr, Nativity, horiz. 100fr, The Virgin and Child. 200fr, The Baptism of Christ.

Perf. 12x12½, 12½x12

1968, Nov. 25 **Photo.**
C89 AP35 30fr multi .80 .55
C90 AP35 70fr multi 1.60 .80
C91 AP35 100fr multi 1.75 1.25
C92 AP35 200fr multi 4.00 2.75
Nos. C89-C92 (4) 8.15 5.35

Christmas 1968. For surcharges, see Benin Nos. C563, C615, C648.

PHILEXAFRIQUE Issue

Painting: Diderot, by Louis Michel Vanloo.

1968, Dec. 16 ***Perf. 12½x12***
C93 AP35 100fr multi 3.75 3.75

PHILEXAFRIQUE, Philatelic Exhibition in Abidjan, Feb. 14-23. Printed with alternating label.
For surcharges, see Benin Nos. C522, C629.

2nd PHILEXAFRIQUE Issue

Common Design Type

50fr, Dahomey #119 and aerial view of Cotonou.

1969, Feb. 14 **Engr.** ***Perf. 13***
C94 CD128 50fr bl, brn & pur 2.25 2.25

For surcharge see Benin No. C467.

Christmas Painting Type

Paintings: No. C95, Virgin of the Rocks, by Leonardo da Vinci. No. C96, Virgin with the Scales, by Cesare da Sesto.

1969, Mar. 17 **Photo.** ***Perf. 12½x12***
C95 AP21 100fr vio & multi 2.00 1.00
C96 AP21 100fr grn & multi 2.00 1.00

Leonardo da Vinci (1452-1519).

General Bonaparte, by Jacques Louis David AP36

Paintings: 60fr, Napoleon I in 1809, by Robert J. Lefevre. 75fr, Napoleon on the Battlefield of Eylau, by Antoine Jean Gros, horiz. 200fr, Gen. Bonaparte at Arcole, by Gros.

1969, Apr. 14 **Photo.** ***Perf. 12½x12***
C97 AP36 30fr multi 1.50 1.25
C98 AP36 60fr multi 2.75 1.75
C99 AP36 75fr multi 3.25 2.50
C100 AP36 200fr multi 7.50 5.50
Nos. C97-C100 (4) 15.00 11.00

Bicentenary of the birth of Napoleon I. For surcharges, see Benin Nos. C599, C605.

Arms Type of Regular Issue, 1969

1969, June 30 **Litho.** ***Perf. 13½x13***
C101 A49 50fr multi .75 .30

For overprint and surcharge see Benin Nos. C417, C596.

Apollo 8 Trip Around the Moon — AP37

Embossed on Gold Foil

1969, July ***Die-cut Perf. 10½***
C102 AP37 1000fr gold 20.00 20.00

US Apollo 8 mission, which put the 1st men into orbit around the moon, Dec. 21-27, 1968.

Nos. C67-C68 Surcharged

1969, Aug. 1 **Photo.** ***Perf. 13***
C103 AP28 125fr on 70fr, #C67 2.50 1.75
C104 AP28 125fr on 70fr, #C68 2.50 1.75

Man's 1st landing on the moon, July 20, 1969; US astronauts Neil A. Armstrong, Col. Edwin E. Aldrin, Jr., with Lieut. Col. Michael Collins piloting Apollo 11.

Europafrica Issue

Type of Regular Issue, 1969

Design: 100fr, Oil palm industry, Cotonou.

1969, Sept. 22 **Litho.** ***Perf. 14***
C105 A51 100fr multi 2.25 .35
a. Souv. sheet of 3, #262-263, C105 4.25 4.25

For surcharge see Benin No. C523.

Dahomey Rotary Emblem — AP38

1969, Sept. 25 ***Perf. 14x13½***
C106 AP38 50fr multi 1.00 .75

For surcharge see Benin No. C468.

No. C33 Surcharged

1969, Nov. 15 **Photo.** ***Perf. 12½***
C107 AP14 10fr on 50fr multi .45 .25

Dance Type of Regular Issue

Design: Teke dance and Tourist Year emblem.

1969, Dec. 15 **Litho.** ***Perf. 14***
C108 A52 70fr multi 2.50 1.50

For surcharge see Benin No. C398.

Painting Type of 1966

Christmas: 30fr, Annunciation, by Vrancke van der Stockt. 45fr, Nativity, Swabian School, horiz. 110fr, Madonna and Child, by the Master of the Gold Brocade. 200fr, Adoration of the Kings, Antwerp School.

1969, Dec. 20 ***Perf. 12½x12, 12x12½***
C109 AP21 30fr multi .50 .40
C110 AP21 45fr red & multi .85 .65
C111 AP21 110fr multi 2.10 1.25
C112 AP21 200fr multi 3.75 2.25
Nos. C109-C112 (4) 7.20 4.55

For surcharges see Benin #C425, C463, C475, C532, C595.

1969, Dec. 27 ***Perf. 12½x12***

Paintings: No. C113, The Artist's Studio (detail), by Gustave Courbet. No. C114, Self-portrait with Gold Chain, by Rembrandt. 150fr, Hendrickje Stoffels, by Rembrandt.

C113 AP21 100fr red & multi 2.25 1.25
C114 AP21 100fr grn & multi 2.25 1.25
C115 AP21 150fr multi 3.75 1.75
Nos. C113-C115 (3) 8.25 4.25

For overprint and surcharge see Benin Nos. C458, C472.

Franklin D. Roosevelt AP39

1970, Feb. **Photo.** ***Perf. 12½***
C116 AP39 100fr ultra, yel grn & blk 1.75 .80

25th anniversary of the death of Pres. Franklin Delano Roosevelt (1882-1945). For surcharge see Benin No. C637.

Astronauts, Rocket, US Flag — AP40

Astronauts: 50fr, Riding rocket through space. 70fr, In landing module approaching moon. 110fr, Planting US flag on moon.

1970, Mar. 9 Photo. *Perf. 12½*

C117 AP40 30fr multi .65 .25

Souvenir Sheet

C118 Sheet of 4 8.00 8.00
a. AP40 50fr violet blue & multi .75 .75
b. AP40 70fr violet blue & multi 1.00 1.00
c. AP40 110fr violet blue & multi 1.25 1.25

See note after No. C104. No. C118 contains Nos. C117, C118a, C118b and C118c.
For surcharge see No. C120.

Walt Whitman and Dahoman Huts — AP41

1970, Apr. 30 Engr. *Perf. 13*

C119 AP41 100fr Prus bl, brn & emer 1.40 .80

Walt Whitman (1818-92), American poet.

No. C117 Surcharged in Silver

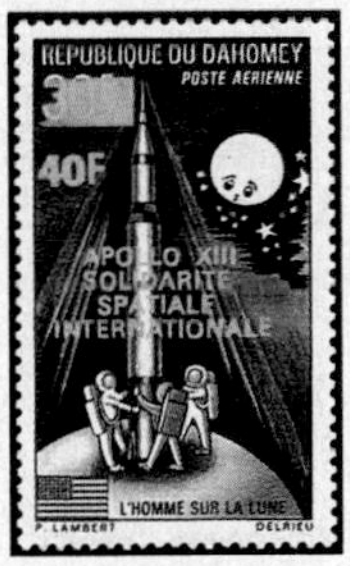

1970, May 15 Photo. *Perf. 12½*

C120 AP40 40fr on 30fr multi 1.20 .75

The flight of Apollo 13.
For surcharge see Benin No. C464.

Soccer Players and Globe — AP42

Designs: 50fr, Goalkeeper catching ball. 200fr, Players kicking ball.

1970, May 19

C121 AP42 40fr multi .75 .40
C122 AP42 50fr multi .95 .50
C123 AP42 200fr multi 3.50 1.25
Nos. C121-C123 (3) 5.20 2.15

9th World Soccer Championships for the Jules Rimet Cup, Mexico City, May 30-June 21, 1970.
For surcharge see No. C126.

EXPO '70 Type of Regular Issue

EXPO '70 Emblems and: 70fr, Dahomey pavilion. 120fr, Mt. Fuji, temple and torii.

1970, June 15 Litho. *Perf. 13½x14*

C124 A54 70fr yel, red & dk vio 1.25 .60
C125 A54 120fr yel, red & grn 2.25 1.00

For surcharges see Benin Nos. C470, C477.

No. C123 Surcharged and Overprinted

1970, July 13 Photo. *Perf. 12½*

C126 AP42 100fr on 200fr multi 2.10 1.00

Brazil's victory in the 9th World Soccer Championships, Mexico City.
For surcharge see Benin No. C515.

Mercury, Map of Africa and Europe — AP43

Europafrica Issue, 1970

1970, July 20 Photo. *Perf. 12x13*

C127 AP43 40fr multi .90 .40
C128 AP43 70fr multi 1.50 .60

For surcharges see Benin Nos. C429, C488, C566.

Ludwig van Beethoven AP44

1970, Sept. 21 Litho. *Perf. 14x13½*

C129 AP44 90fr brt bl & vio blk 1.40 .45
C130 AP44 110fr yel grn & dk brn 1.75 .65

Bicentenary of the birth of Ludwig van Beethoven (1770-1827), composer.
For surcharges, see Benin Nos. C476, C608.

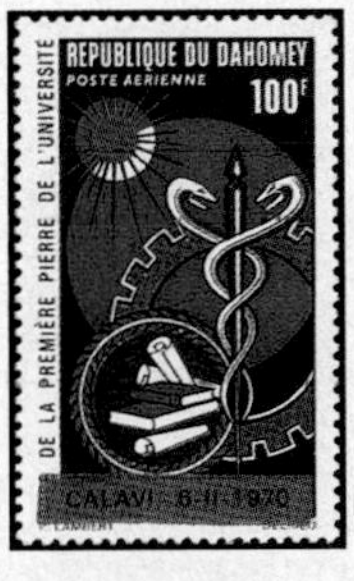

Symbols of Learning — AP45

1970, Nov. 6 Photo. *Perf. 12½*

C131 AP45 100fr multi 1.40 .75

Laying of the foundation stone for the University at Calavi.
For overprint and surcharge see Benin Nos. C356, C616.

Annunciation, Rhenish School, c.1340 — AP46

Paintings of Rhenish School, circa 1340: 70fr, Nativity. 110fr, Adoration of the Kings. 200fr, Presentation at the Temple.

1970, Nov. 9 *Perf. 12½x12*

C132 AP46 40fr gold & multi .55 .40
C133 AP46 70fr gold & multi 1.00 .55
C134 AP46 110fr gold & multi 2.40 1.25
C135 AP46 200fr gold & multi 4.00 2.00
Nos. C132-C135 (4) 7.95 4.20

Christmas 1970.
For surcharge see Benin No. C479.

Charles de Gaulle, Arc de Triomphe and Flag — AP47

Design: 500fr, de Gaulle as old man and Notre Dame Cathedral, Paris.

1971, Mar. 15 Photo. *Perf. 12½*

C136 AP47 40fr multi .80 .45
C137 AP47 500fr multi 6.50 3.25

Gen. Charles de Gaulle (1890-1970), President of France.
For surcharges see Benin Nos. C465, C567.

L'Indifférent, by Watteau — AP48

Painting: No. C139, Woman playing stringed instrument, by Watteau.

1971, May 3 Photo. *Perf. 13*

C138 AP48 100fr red brn & multi 3.25 1.75
C139 AP48 100fr red brn & multi 3.25 1.75

For overprints and surcharge see Nos. C151-C152, Benin Nos. C357D, C456, C526, C617, C638.

1971, May 29 Photo. *Perf. 13*

Dürer Paintings: 100fr, Self-portrait, 1498. 200fr, Self-portrait, 1500.

C140 AP48 100fr bl grn & multi 2.25 1.25
C141 AP48 200fr dk grn & multi 4.50 2.25

Albrecht Dürer (1471-1528), German painter and engraver. See Nos. C151-C152, C174-C175. For surcharges and overprints see Benin Nos. C357B, C381, C545, C618.

Johannes Kepler and Diagram — AP49

200fr, Kepler, trajectories, satellite and rocket.

1971, July 12 Engr. *Perf. 13*

C142 AP49 40fr brt rose lil, blk & vio bl .90 .55
C143 AP49 200fr red, blk & dk bl 3.25 1.75

Kepler (1571-1630), German astronomer.
For overprint and surcharges see Benin Nos. C342, C348, C466, C480, C568.

Europafrica Issue

Jet Plane, Maps of Europe and Africa — AP50

100fr, Ocean liner, maps of Europe and Africa.

1971, July 19 Photo. *Perf. 12½x12*

C144 AP50 50fr blk, lt bl & org 1.60 .60
C145 AP50 100fr multi 2.50 1.00

For surcharges see Benin Nos. C374, C404, C421, C585, C630.

African Postal Union Issue, 1971

Common Design Type

Design: 100fr, Dahomey coat of arms and UAMPT building, Brazzaville, Congo.

1971, Nov. 13 *Perf. 13x13½*

C146 CD135 100fr bl & multi 1.75 .80

For overprint and surcharge see Benin Nos. C357E, C619.

Flight into Egypt, by Van Dyck — AP51

Paintings: 40fr, Adoration of the Shepherds, by the Master of the Hausbuch, c. 1500, vert. 70fr, Adoration of the Kings, by Holbein the Elder, vert. 200fr, The Birth of Christ, by Dürer.

1971, Nov. 22 *Perf. 13*

C147 AP51 40fr gold & multi .85 .45
C148 AP51 70fr gold & multi 1.40 .55
C149 AP51 100fr gold & multi 2.10 .80
C150 AP51 200fr gold & multi 5.00 1.75
Nos. C147-C150 (4) 9.35 3.55

Christmas 1971
For overprint and surcharges see Benin Nos. C394, C394A, C397, C403, C405, C481, C503, C546, C581, C604, C631.

Painting Type of 1971 Inscribed: "25e ANNIVERSAIRE DE L'UNICEF"

Paintings: 40fr, Prince Balthazar, by Velasquez. 100fr, Infanta Margarita Maria, by Velázquez.

1971, Dec. 11

C151 AP48 40fr gold & multi 1.75 .55
C152 AP48 100fr gold & multi 3.00 .85

25th anniv. of UNICEF.
For surcharges see Benin Nos. C366, C418, C437, C592, C639.

Olympic Games Type

Design: 150fr, Sapporo '72 emblem, ski jump and stork flying.

1972, Feb. **Engr.** ***Perf. 13***
C153 A61 150fr brn, dp rose lil & bl 3.50 1.25

11th Winter Olympic Games, Sapporo, Japan, Feb. 3-13.
For overprint and surcharge see Benin Nos. C347, C433, C645.

Boy Scout and Scout Flag — AP52

Designs: 40fr, Scout playing marimba. 100fr, Scouts doing farm work.

1972, Mar. 19 **Photo.** ***Perf. 13***
Size: 26x35mm
C154 AP52 35fr multi .50 .25
C155 AP52 40fr multi .85 .40
Size: 26x46mm
C156 AP52 100fr yel & multi 1.75 .85
a. Souvenir sheet of 3, #C154-C156, perf. 12½ 4.25 4.25
Nos. C154-C156 (3) 3.10 1.50

World Boy Scout Seminar, Cotonou, Mar. 1972.
For overprint and surcharges see Benin Nos. C373, C414, C569.

Workers Training Institute and Friedrich Naumann — AP53

Design: 250fr, Workers Training Institute and Pres. Theodor Heuss of Germany.

1972, Mar. 29 **Photo.** ***Perf. 13x12***
C157 AP53 100fr brt rose, blk & vio 1.50 .65
C158 AP53 250fr bl, blk & vio 3.50 1.40

Laying of foundation stone for National Workers Training Institute.
For surcharges see Benin Nos. C380, C473, C640, C649, Q25A.

Mosaic Floor, St. Mark's, Venice — AP54

12th Century Mosaics from St. Mark's Basilica: 40fr, Roosters carrying fox on a pole. 65fr, Noah sending out dove.

1972, Apr. 10 ***Perf. 13***
C159 AP54 35fr gold & multi 1.35 .75
C160 AP54 40fr gold & multi 1.50 .90
C161 AP54 65fr gold & multi 3.00 1.50
Nos. C159-C161 (3) 5.85 3.15

UNESCO campaign to save Venice.
For surcharges see Benin Nos. 690G, C600.

Neapolitan and Dahoman Dancers — AP55

1972, May 3 ***Perf. 13½x13***
C162 AP55 100fr multi 1.50 .65

12th Philatelic Exhibition, Naples.
For surcharges, see Benin Nos. C395, C620.

Running, German Eagle, Olympic Rings — AP56

85fr, High jump and Glyptothek, Munich. 150fr, Shot put and Propylaeum, Munich.

1972, June 12 **Engr.** ***Perf. 13***
C163 AP56 20fr ultra, grn & brn .40 .25
C164 AP56 85fr brn, grn & ultra .95 .60
C165 AP56 150fr grn, brn & ultra 2.00 1.00
a. Min. sheet of 3, #C163-C165 4.00 4.00
Nos. C163-C165 (3) 3.35 1.85

20th Olympic Games, Munich, 8/26-9/10.
For overprints and surcharges see Nos. C170-C172, Benin C343, C346, C370, C404A, C559, C651A.

Louis Blériot and his Plane — AP57

1972, June 26
C166 AP57 100fr vio, cl & brt bl 4.00 1.75

Birth centenary of Louis Blériot (1872-1936), French aviation pioneer.
For surcharges see Benin Nos. C386, C621.

Adam, by Lucas Cranach — AP58

Design: 200fr, Eve, by Lucas Cranach.

1972, Oct. 24 **Photo.**
C167 AP58 150fr multi 2.75 1.25
C168 AP58 200fr multi 4.50 1.75

Cranach (1472-1553), German painter.
For surcharges see Benin Nos. C402, C537, C643.

Pauline Borghese, by Canova — AP59

1972, Nov. 8
C169 AP59 250fr multi 7.00 1.75

Antonio Canova (1757-1822), Italian sculptor.
For surcharge, see Benin No. 1366.

Nos. C163-C165 Overprinted

a

b

c

1972, Nov. 13 **Engr.** ***Perf. 13***
C170 AP56(a) 20fr multi .45 .25
C171 AP56(b) 85fr multi 1.25 .60
C172 AP56(c) 150fr multi 2.25 1.25
a. Miniature sheet of 3 5.25 5.25
Nos. C170-C172 (3) 3.95 2.10

Gold medal winners in 20th Olympic Games: Lasse Viren, Finland, 5,000m. and 10,000m. races (20fr); Ulrike Meyfarth, Germany, women's high jump (85fr); Wladyslaw Komar, Poland, shot put (150fr).
For surcharges, see Benin Nos. C343A, C538, C607.

Louis Pasteur — AP60

1972, Nov. 30
C173 AP60 100fr brt grn, lil & brn 2.50 1.00

Pasteur (1822-95), chemist and bacteriologist.
For surcharges see Benin Nos. C344, C622.

Painting Type of 1971

Paintings by Georges de La Tour (1593-1652), French painter: 35fr, Vielle player. 150fr, The Newborn, horiz.

1972, Dec. 11 **Photo.**
C174 AP48 35fr multi .80 .40
C175 AP48 150fr multi 2.25 1.25

For surcharges see Benin Nos. C364, C490, C578.

Annunciation, School of Agnolo Gaddi — AP61

Paintings: 125fr, Nativity, by Simone dei Crocifissi. 140fr, Adoration of the Shepherds, by Giovanni di Pietro. 250fr, Adoration of the Kings, by Giotto.

1972, Dec. 15
C176 AP61 35fr gold & multi .75 .25
C177 AP61 125fr gold & multi 2.00 .65
C178 AP61 140fr gold & multi 2.75 1.00
C179 AP61 250fr gold & multi 4.50 1.50
Nos. C176-C179 (4) 10.00 3.40

Christmas 1972. See Nos. C195-C198, C234, C251, C253-C254. For overprint and surcharges see Benin Nos. C384, C392, C401, C444, C628, C652.

Statue of St. Teresa, Basilica of Lisieux — AP62

100fr, St. Teresa, roses, and globe, vert.

1973, May 14 **Photo.** ***Perf. 13***
C180 AP62 40fr blk, gold & lt ultra .75 .45
C181 AP62 100fr gold & multi 2.50 1.00

St. Teresa of Lisieux (Therese Martin, 1873-97), Carmelite nun.
For surcharges see Benin Nos. C390, C570, C623.

Scouts, African Scout Emblem — AP63

Designs (African Scout Emblem and): 20fr, Lord Baden-Powell, vert. 40fr, Scouts building bridge.

1973, July 2 **Engr.** ***Perf. 13***
C182 AP63 15fr bl, grn & choc .45 .25
C183 AP63 20fr ol & Prus bl .75 .25
C184 AP63 40fr grn, Prus bl & brn .90 .35
a. Souvenir sheet of 3 3.00 3.00
Nos. C182-C184 (3) 2.10 .85

24th Boy Scout World Conference, Nairobi, Kenya, July 16-21. No. C184a contains 3 stamps similar to Nos. C182-C184 in changed colors (15fr in ultramarine, slate green and chocolate; 20fr in chocolate, ultramarine and indigo; 40fr in slate green, indigo and chocolate).
For surcharges see Nos. C217-C218, Benin C365, C409, C558, C560, C571.

Copernicus, Venera and Mariner Satellites — AP64

125fr, Copernicus, sun, earth & moon, vert.

1973, Aug. 20 Engr. *Perf. 13*

C185 AP64 65fr blk, dk brn & org 1.50 .55
C186 AP64 125fr bl, slate grn & pur 2.75 1.00

For surcharges see Benin Nos. C345, C375, C601, C642.

Head and City Hall, Brussels AP64a

1973, Sept. 17 Engr. *Perf. 13*

C187 AP64a 100fr blk, Prus bl & dk grn 1.10 .60

African Weeks, Brussels, Sept. 15-30, 1973.
For surcharge see Benin No. C400.

WMO Emblem, World Weather Map — AP65

1973, Sept. 25

C188 AP65 100fr ol grn & lt brn 1.40 .75

Cent. of intl. meteorological cooperation.
For surcharges and overprint see Nos. C199, Benin Nos. C382, C624.

Europafrica Issue

AP66

Design: 40fr, similar to 35fr.

1973, Oct. 1 Engr. *Perf. 13*

C189 AP66 35fr multi .55 .35
C190 AP66 40fr bl, sepia & ultra .70 .40

For overprint and surcharges, see Benin Nos. C411, C564, C593.

John F. Kennedy — AP67

1973, Oct. 18

C191 AP67 200fr bl grn, vio & sl grn 2.75 2.75
a. Souvenir sheet 5.00 5.00

Pres. John F. Kennedy (1917-63). No. C191a contains one stamp in changed colors (bright blue, magenta & brown).
For surcharge and overprint, see Benin Nos. C377, C441, C547.

Soccer — AP68

40fr, 2 soccer players. 100fr, 3 soccer players.

1973, Nov. 19 Engr. *Perf. 13*

C192 AP68 35fr multi .55 .25
C193 AP68 40fr multi .65 .25
C194 AP68 100fr multi 1.25 .65
Nos. C192-C194 (3) 2.45 1.15

World Soccer Cup, Munich 1974.
For surcharges and overprint see Nos. C219-C220, Benin Nos. C396, C591, C644.

Painting Type of 1972

Christmas: 35fr, Annunciation, by Dirk Bouts. 100fr, Nativity, by Giotto. 150fr, Adoration of the Kings, by Botticelli. 200fr, Adoration of the Shepherds, by Jacopo Bassano, horiz.

1973, Dec. 20 Photo. *Perf. 13*

C195 AP61 35fr gold & multi .80 .40
C196 AP61 100fr gold & multi 1.50 .65
C197 AP61 150fr gold & multi 3.00 1.10
C198 AP61 200fr gold & multi 3.25 1.75
Nos. C195-C198 (4) 8.55 3.90

For surcharges see Benin Nos. C378, C388, C410, C434, C442, C565, C646.

No C188 Surcharged in Violet

1974, Feb. 4 Engr. *Perf. 13*

C199 AP65 200fr on 100fr multi 2.25 1.25

Skylab US space missions, 1973-74.

Skiers, Snowflake, Olympic Rings — AP69

1974, Feb. 25 Engr. *Perf. 13*

C200 AP69 100fr vio bl, brn & brt bl 1.75 1.10

50th anniversary of first Winter Olympic Games, Chamonix, France. For surcharge, see Benin No. C625.

Marie Curie AP70

1974, June 7 Engr. *Perf. 13*

C201 AP70 50fr Lenin 1.75 .65
C202 AP70 125fr shown 2.25 .90
C203 AP70 150fr Churchill 2.50 1.40
Nos. C201-C203 (3) 6.50 2.95

50th anniv. of the death of Lenin; 40th anniv. of the death of Marie Sklodowska Curie; cent. of the birth of Winston Churchill.
For surcharges see Benin Nos. C391A, C489, C597, C632, C634.

Bishop, Persian, 18th Century — AP71

200fr, Queen, Siamese chess piece, 19th cent.

1974, June 14 Photo. *Perf. 12½x13*

C204 AP71 50fr org & multi 2.50 1.00
C205 AP71 200fr brt grn & multi 6.00 2.50

21st Chess Olympiad, Nice, 6/6-30/74.
For surcharges and overprint see Benin Nos. C469, C482, C598, Q11.

Frederic Chopin — AP72

Design: No. C207, Ludwig van Beethoven.

1974, June 24 Engr. *Perf. 13*

C206 AP72 150fr blk & copper red 4.50 1.40
C207 AP72 150fr blk & copper red 4.50 1.40

Famous musicians: Frederic Chopin and Ludwig van Beethoven.
For surcharges see Benin Nos. C376, C452, C459, C539, C579, C647.

Astronaut on Moon, and Earth AP73

1974, July 10 Engr. *Perf. 13*

C208 AP73 150fr multi 2.75 1.50

5th anniversary of the first moon walk.
For surcharges and overprint see Benin Nos. C391, C460, C635.

Litho. & Embossed 'Gold Foil' Stamps
These stamps generally are of a different design format than the rest of the issue. Since there is a commemorative inscription tying them to the issue a separate illustration is not being shown.

There is some question as to the status of 4 sets, Nos. C209-C216, C225-C232, C238-C249.

World Cup Soccer Championships, Munich — AP74

World Cup trophy and players and flags of: 35fr, West Germany, Chile, Australia, DDR. 40fr, Zaire, Scotland, Brazil, Yugoslavia. 100fr, Sweden, Bulgaria, Uruguay, Netherlands. 200fr, Italy, Haiti, Poland, Argentina. 300fr, Stadium. 500fr, Trophy and flags.

Perf. 14x13, 13x14

1974, July 16 Litho.

C209 AP74 35fr multicolored .40 .25
C210 AP74 40fr multicolored .55 .25
C211 AP74 100fr multicolored 1.10 .70
C212 AP74 200fr multicolored 2.50 1.25
C213 AP74 300fr multi, horiz. 2.50 1.50

Souvenir Sheet

C215 AP74 500fr multi, horiz. 7.25 7.25

It is uncertain if this issue was valid for postage or recognized by the Dahomey government.

Nos. C182-C183 Srchd. and Ovptd. In Black or Red

1974, July 19

C217 AP63 100fr on 15fr multi 1.25 .60
C218 AP63 140fr on 20fr multi (R) 1.75 .90

11th Pan-Arab Jamboree, Batrun, Lebanon, Aug. 1974. Overprint includes 2 bars over old denomination; 2-line overprint on No. C217, 3 lines on No. C218.

Nos. C193-C194 Overprinted and Surcharged

1974, July 26 Engr. *Perf. 13*

C219 AP68 100fr on 40fr 1.10 .65
C220 AP68 150fr on 100fr 1.60 1.00

World Cup Soccer Championship, 1974, victory of German Federal Republic.

Earth and UPU Emblem — AP75

Designs (UPU Emblem and): 65fr, Concorde in flight. 125fr, French railroad car, c. 1860. 200fr, African drummer and Renault mail truck, pre-1939.

1974, Aug. 5 Engr. *Perf. 13*

C221 AP75 35fr rose cl & vio .75 .40
C222 AP75 65fr Prus grn & cl 1.50 .95
C223 AP75 125fr multi 3.50 1.50
C224 AP75 200fr multi 3.50 2.00
Nos. C221-C224 (4) 9.25 4.85

Centenary of Universal Postal Union.
For surcharges, see Benin Nos. C422, C530, C540, C586, C653, Q17B.

UPU, Cent. — AP76

Communications and transportation: 50fr, Rocket, Indian shooting arrow. 100fr, Airplane, dog sled, vert. 125fr, Rocket launch, balloon. 150fr, Rocket re-entry into Earth's atmosphere, drum. 200fr, Locomotive, Pony Express rider. 500fr, UPU headquarters. No. C230, Train, 1829. No. C232, Astronaut canceling envelope on moon.

1974 Litho. *Perf. 13x14, 14x13*

C225 AP76 50fr multicolored .50 .30
C226 AP76 100fr multicolored .75 .60
C227 AP76 125fr multicolored 1.00 .85
C228 AP76 150fr multicolored 1.75 1.00
C229 AP76 200fr multicolored 2.50 1.25

Litho. & Embossed
Perf. 13½
Size: 48x60mm

C230 AP76 1000fr gold & multi 12.00 12.00

Souvenir Sheets
Litho.
Perf. 13x14

C231 AP76 500fr multicolored 4.50 4.50

Litho. & Embossed
Perf. 13½

C232 AP76 1000fr gold & multi 7.25 7.25

Issued: #C230, C232, Oct. 9; others, Aug. 5.
It is uncertain if this issue was valid for postage or recognized by the Dahomey government.

Painting Type of 1972 and

Lion of Belfort by Frederic A. Bartholdi — AP77

Painting: 250fr, Girl with Falcon, by Philippe de Champaigne.

1974, Aug. 20 Engr. *Perf. 13*

C233 AP77 100fr rose brn 2.50 1.00
C234 AP61 250fr multi 4.00 2.40

For surcharges see Benin Nos. C363, C387, C445, C626.

Prehistoric Animals — AP78

1974, Sept. 23 Photo.

C235 AP78 35fr Rhamphorhynchus 1.50 .80
C236 AP78 150fr Stegosaurus 5.00 2.25
C237 AP78 200fr Tyrannosaurus 7.00 2.75
Nos. C235-C237 (3) 13.50 5.80

For surcharges and overprint, see Benin Nos. C349, C350, C440, C548, C636.

Conquest of Space — AP79

Various spacecraft and: 50fr, Mercury. 100fr, Venus. 150fr, Mars. 200fr, Jupiter. 400fr, Sun.

1974, Oct. 31 Litho. *Perf. 13x14*

C238 AP79 50fr multicolored .40 .30
C239 AP79 100fr multicolored 1.00 .50
C240 AP79 150fr multicolored 1.75 .90
C241 AP79 200fr multicolored 2.25 1.25
Nos. C238-C241 (4) 5.40 2.95

Souvenir Sheet

C242 AP79 400fr multicolored 5.25 5.25

West Germany, World Cup Soccer Champions — AP80

Designs: 100fr, Team. 125fr, Paul Breitner. 150fr, Gerd Muller. 300fr, Presentation of trophy. 500fr, German team positioned on field.

1974, Nov. Litho. *Perf. 13x14*

C243 AP80 100fr multicolored .75 .50
C244 AP80 125fr multicolored 1.00 .75
C245 AP80 150fr multicolored 1.50 1.00
C246 AP80 300fr multicolored 3.25 2.00
Nos. C243-C246 (4) 6.50 4.25

Souvenir Sheet

C248 AP80 500fr multicolored 5.25 5.25

Europafrica Issue

Globe, Cogwheel, Emblem — AP81

1974, Dec. 20 Typo. *Perf. 13*

C250 AP81 250fr red & multi 3.25 2.75

Printed tête bêche in sheets of 10.
For surcharges see Benin Nos. C430, C509, C650.

Christmas Type of 1972 and

Nativity, by Martin Schongauer — AP82

Paintings: 35fr, Annunciation, by Schongauer. 100fr, Virgin in Rose Arbor, by Schongauer. 250fr, Virgin and Child, with St. John the Baptist, by Botticelli.

1974, Dec. 23 Photo. *Perf. 13*

C251 AP61 35fr gold & multi .60 .30
C252 AP82 40fr gold & multi .60 .40
C253 AP61 100fr gold & multi 1.60 .55
C254 AP61 250fr gold & multi 4.25 1.75
Nos. C251-C254 (4) 7.05 3.00

For surcharges, see Benin Nos. C413, C431, C439, C446, C641.

Apollo and Soyuz Spacecraft AP83

200fr, American and Russian flags, rocket take-off. 500fr, Apollo-Soyuz link-up.

1975, July 16 Litho. *Perf. 12½*

C255 AP83 35fr multi .50 .30
C256 AP83 200fr vio bl, red & bl 2.40 1.25
C257 AP83 500fr vio bl, ind & red 5.50 3.00
Nos. C255-C257 (3) 8.40 4.55

Apollo Soyuz space test project (Russo-American cooperation); launching July 15; link-up, July 17.
For surcharges and overprints, see Benin Nos. C406, C415-C416, C451, C542-C543, C549, C580.

Nos. C255-C256 Surcharged

No. C258

No. C259

1975, July 17 Litho. *Perf. 12½*

C258 AP83 100fr on 35fr (S) 1.25 .60
C259 AP83 300fr on 200fr 3.25 1.40

Apollo-Soyuz link-up in space, July 17, 1975.

ARPHILA Emblem, "Stamps" and Head of Ceres — AP84

1975, Aug. 22 Engr. *Perf. 13*

C260 AP84 100fr blk, bl & lilac 1.50 .75

ARPHILA 75, International Philatelic Exhibition, Paris, June 6-16.
For surcharges see Benin Nos. C383, C474.

Europafrica Issue

Holy Family, by Michelangelo AP85

1975, Sept. 29 Litho. *Perf. 12*

C261 AP85 300fr gold & multi 4.50 1.50

For surcharge and overprint, see Benin Nos. C447, C554.

Infantry and Stars — AP86

American bicentennial (Stars and): 135fr, Drummers and fifer. 300fr, Artillery with cannon. 500fr, Cavalry.

1975, Nov. 18 Engr. *Perf. 13*

C262 AP86 75fr grn car & pur 1.00 .45
C263 AP86 135fr bl, mag & sep 1.75 .90
C264 AP86 300fr vio bl, ver & choc 3.25 1.75
C265 AP86 500fr ver, dk grn & brn 5.75 2.50
Nos. C262-C265 (4) 11.75 5.60

For overprints and surcharges see Benin Nos. C247-C249, C385, C412, C453, C478, C555, C557, C576, C588.

Diving and Olympic Rings AP87

Design: 250fr, Soccer and Olympic rings.

1975, Nov. 24

C266 AP87 40fr vio, grnsh bl & ol brn .55 .25
C267 AP87 250fr red, emer & brn 2.40 1.25

Pre-Olympic Year 1975.
For surcharges see Benin Nos. C341, C393, C582.

AIR POST SEMI-POSTAL STAMPS

Maternity Hospital, Dakar — SPAP1

Dispensary, Mopti — SPAP2

Nurse Weighing Baby — SPAP3

Perf. 13½x12½, 13 (#CB3)
Photo, Engr. (#CB3)

1942, June 22

CB1	SPAP1 1.50fr + 3.50fr green	.80	*5.50*
CB2	SPAP2 2fr + 6fr brown	.80	*5.50*
CB3	SPAP3 3fr + 9fr car red	.80	*5.50*
	Nos. CB1-CB3 (3)	2.40	*16.50*

Native children's welfare fund.

Colonial Education Fund

Common Design Type
Perf. 12½x13½

1942, June 22 **Engr.**

CB4	CD86a 1.20fr + 1.80fr blue & red	.80	*5.50*

AIR POST PARCEL POST STAMPS

Catalogue values for unused stamps in this section are for Never Hinged items.

Nos. C20-C23, C14 Surcharged in Black or Red

1967-69 **Engr.** ***Perf. 13***

CQ1	AP6 200fr on 200fr	2.10	2.10
CQ2	AP6 300fr on 100fr	2.40	2.40
CQ3	AP6 500fr on 300fr	4.50	4.50
CQ4	AP6 1000fr on 500fr	9.50	9.50
CQ5	AP4 5000fr on 100fr (R) ('69)	35.00	35.00
	Nos. CQ1-CQ5 (5)	53.50	53.50

On No. CQ5, "Colis Postaux" is at top, bar at right.

POSTAGE DUE STAMPS

Dahomey Natives — D1

D2

1906 **Unwmk.** **Typo.** ***Perf. 14x13½***

J1	D1	5c grn, *grnsh*	4.00	4.00
J2	D1	10c red brn	4.00	4.00
J3	D1	15c dark blue	8.00	8.00
J4	D1	20c blk, *yellow*	8.00	8.00
J5	D1	30c red, *straw*	12.00	12.00
J6	D1	50c violet	24.00	24.00
J7	D1	60c blk, *buff*	16.00	16.00
J8	D1	1fr blk, *pinkish*	52.50	40.00
		Nos. J1-J8 (8)	128.50	116.00

1914

J9	D2	5c green	.25	.25
J10	D2	10c rose	.55	.55
J11	D2	15c gray	.55	.55
J12	D2	20c brown	1.10	1.10
J13	D2	30c blue	1.40	1.40
J14	D2	50c black	1.60	1.60
J15	D2	60c orange	2.00	2.00
J16	D2	1fr violet	2.10	2.10
		Nos. J9-J16 (8)	9.55	9.55

Type of 1914 Issue Surcharged

1927

J17	D2	2fr on 1fr lilac rose	5.50	5.50
J18	D2	3fr on 1fr org brn	5.50	5.50

Carved Mask — D3

1941 **Engr.** ***Perf. 14x13***

J19	D3	5c black	.25	.25
J20	D3	10c lilac rose	.25	.25
J21	D3	15c dark blue	.25	.25
J22	D3	20c bright yel green	.30	.30
J23	D3	30c orange	.50	.50
J24	D3	50c violet brown	.70	.70
J25	D3	60c slate green	1.10	1.10
J26	D3	1fr rose red	1.40	1.40
J27	D3	2fr yellow	1.50	1.50
J28	D3	3fr dark purple	1.90	1.90
		Nos. J19-J28 (10)	8.15	8.15

Type D3 without "RF"

1944

J28A	D3	10c lilac rose	.50
J28B	D3	15c dark blue	.55
J28C	D3	20c bright yel green	.55
		Nos. J28A-J28C (3)	1.60

Nos. J28A-J28C were issued by the Vichy government in France, but were not placed on sale in Dahomey.

Catalogue values for unused stamps in this section, from this point to the end of the section, are for Never Hinged items.

Republic

Panther and Man — D4

Perf. 14x13½

1963, July 22 **Typo.** **Unwmk.**

J29	D4	1fr green & rose	.25	.25
J30	D4	2fr brn & emerald	.30	.30
J31	D4	5fr org & vio bl	.30	.30
J32	D4	10fr magenta & blk	.65	.65
J33	D4	20fr vio bl & org	1.10	1.10
		Nos. J29-J33 (5)	2.60	2.60

Heliograph — D5

No. J35, Mail boat. No. J36, Morse receiver. No. J37, Mailman on bicycle. No. J38, Early telephone. No. J39, Autorail. No. J40, Mail truck. No. J41, Radio tower. No. J42, DC-8F jet plane. No. J43, Early Bird communications satellite.

1967, Oct. 24 **Engr.** ***Perf. 11***

J34	D5	1fr brn, dl pur & bl	.25	.25
J35	D5	1fr dl pur, brn & bl	.25	.25
a.		Pair, #J34-J35	.25	
J36	D5	3fr dk brn, dk grn & org	.25	.25
J37	D5	3fr dk grn, dk brn & org	.25	.25
a.		Pair, #J36-J37	.25	
J38	D5	5fr ol bis, lil & bl	.35	.35
J39	D5	5fr lil, ol bis & bl	.35	.35
a.		Pair, #J38-J39	.75	
J40	D5	10fr brn org, vio & grn	.50	.50
J41	D5	10fr vio, brn org & grn	.50	.50
a.		Pair, #J40-J41	1.10	
J42	D5	30fr Prus bl, mar & vio	1.00	1.00
J43	D5	30fr vio, Prus bl & mar	1.00	1.00
a.		Pair, #J42-J43	2.25	
		Nos. J34-J43 (10)	4.70	4.70

Pairs printed tete beche, se-tenant at the base.

PARCEL POST STAMPS

Catalogue values for unused stamps in this section are for Never Hinged items.

Nos. 141-146 and 148 Surcharged

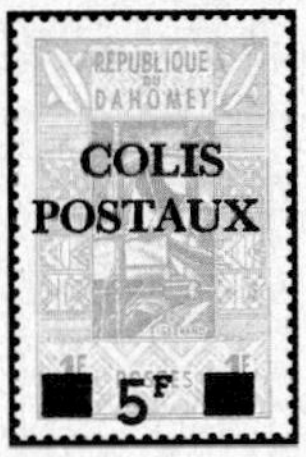

1967, Jan. **Unwmk.** **Engr.** ***Perf. 13***

Q1	A15	5fr on 1fr multi	.25	.25
Q2	A15	10fr on 2fr multi	.35	.35
Q3	A15	20fr on 6fr multi	.60	.60
Q4	A15	25fr on 3fr multi	.90	.90
Q5	A15	30fr on 4fr multi	1.00	1.00
Q6	A15	50fr on 10fr multi	1.40	1.40
a.		"20" instead of "50"	100.00	
Q7	A15	100fr on 20fr multi	2.50	2.50
		Nos. Q1-Q7 (7)	7.00	7.00

The surcharge is arranged to fit the shape of the stamp.
No. Q6a occurred once on the sheet.

DALMATIA

dal-'mā-sh,ē-,ə

LOCATION — A promontory in the northwestern part of the Balkan Peninsula, together with several small islands in the Adriatic Sea.
GOVT. — Part of the former Austro-Hungarian crownland of the same name.
AREA — 113 sq. mi.
POP. — 18,719 (1921)
CAPITAL — Zara.

Stamps were issued during Italian occupation. This territory was subsequently annexed by Italy.

100 Centesimi = 1 Corona = 1 Lira

Used values are for postally used stamps.

Issued under Italian Occupation

Italy No. 87 Surcharged

1919, May 1 **Wmk. 140** ***Perf. 14***

1	A46	1cor on 1 l brn & grn	4.00	*20.00*
a.		Pair, one without surcharge	*1,050.*	*1,050.*

Italian Stamps of 1906-08 Surcharged — a

1921-22

2	A48	5c on 5c green	4.00	*4.75*
3	A48	10c on 10c claret	4.00	*4.75*
a.		Pair, one without surcharge	875.00	
4	A49	25c on 25c blue ('22)	6.50	*8.00*
5	A49	50c on 50c vio ('22)	6.50	*8.00*
a.		Double surcharge		*250.00*
b.		Pair, one without surcharge	*1,050.*	

Italian Stamps of 1901-10 Surcharged — b

6	A46	1cor on 1 l brn & grn ('22)	8.00	*24.00*
7	A46	5cor on 5 l bl & rose ('22)	55.00	*150.00*
8	A51	10cor on 10 l gray grn & red ('22)	55.00	*150.00*
		Nos. 2-8 (7)	139.00	*349.50*

Surcharges similar to these but differing in style or arrangement of type were used in Austria under Italian occupation.

SPECIAL DELIVERY STAMPS

Italian Special Delivery Stamp No. E1 Surcharged type "a"

1921 **Wmk. 140** ***Perf. 14***

E1	SD1	25c on 25c rose red	4.75	*20.00*
a.		Double surcharge	400.00	*650.00*

Italian Special Delivery Stamp Surcharged

1922

E2	SD2	1.20 l on 1.20 l	240.00

No. E2 was not placed in use.

POSTAGE DUE STAMPS

Italian Postage Due Stamps and Type Surcharged types "a" or "b"

1922 **Wmk. 140** ***Perf. 14***

J1	D3 (a)	50c on 50c buff & mag	4.00	*9.50*
J2	D3 (b)	1cor on 1 l bl & red	9.50	*32.50*
J3	D3 (b)	2cor on 2 l bl & red	65.00	*145.00*
J4	D3 (b)	5cor on 5 l bl & red	65.00	*145.00*
		Nos. J1-J4 (4)	143.50	*332.00*

DANISH WEST INDIES

'dā-nish 'west 'in-dēs

LOCATION — Group of islands in the West Indies, lying east of Puerto Rico
GOVT. — Danish colony
AREA — 132 sq. mi.
POP. — 27,086 (1911)
CAPITAL — Charlotte Amalie

The US bought these islands in 1917 and they became the US Virgin Islands, using US stamps and currency.

100 Cents = 1 Dollar
100 Bit = 1 Franc (1905)

Wmk. 111 — Small Crown

Wmk. 112 — Crown

Wmk. 113 — Crown

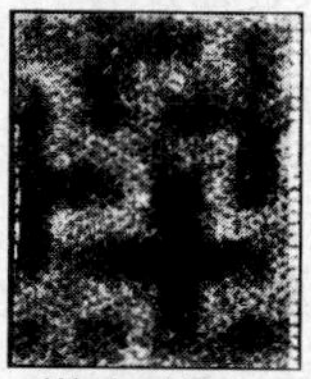
Wmk. 114 — Multiple Crosses

Coat of Arms — A1

Yellowish Paper
Yellow Wavy-line Burelage, UL to LR

1856 Typo. Wmk. 111 *Imperf.*

1	A1 3c dark carmine, brown gum	200.	*275.*
a.	3c dark carmine, yellow gum	225.	*275.*
b.	3c carmine, white gum	*4,250.*	—

The brown and yellow gums were applied locally.

Reprint: 1981, carmine, back-printed across two stamps ("Reprint by Dansk Post og Telegrafmuseum 1978"), value, pair, $10.

White Paper

1866
Yellow Wavy-line Burelage UR to LL

2	A1 3c rose	40.	*75.*

No. 2 reprints, unwatermarked: 1930, carmine, value $100. 1942, rose carmine, back-printed across each row ("Nytryk 1942 G. A. Hagemann Danmark og Dansk Vestindiens Frimaerker Bind 2"), value $50.

1872 *Perf. 12½*

3	A1 3c rose	100.	*275.*

1873 Without Burelage

4	A1 4c dull blue	250.	*475.*
a.	Imperf., pair	775.	
b.	Horiz. pair, imperf. vert.	575.	

The 1930 reprint of No. 4 is ultramarine, unwatermarked and imperf., value $100.

The 1942 4c reprint is blue, unwatermarked, imperf. and has printing on back (see note below No. 2), value $60.

A2

Normal Frame

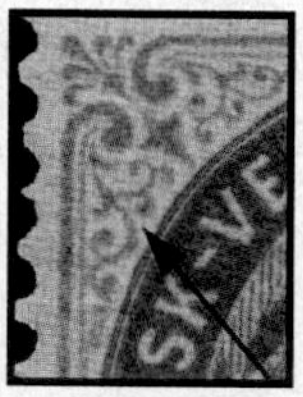
Inverted Frame

The arabesques in the corners have a main stem and a branch. When the frame is in normal position, in the upper left corner the branch leaves the main stem half way between two little leaflets. In the lower right corner the branch starts at the foot of the second leaflet. When the frame is inverted the corner designs are, of course, transposed.

White Wove Paper
Varying from Thin to Thick

1874-79 Wmk. 112 *Perf. 14x13½*

Values for inverted frames, covers and blocks are for the cheapest variety.

5	A2 1c green & brown red	22.50	*30.00*
a.	1c green & rose lilac, thin paper	80.00	*125.00*
b.	1c green & red violet, medium paper	45.00	*65.00*
c.	1c green & claret, thick paper	20.00	*30.00*
e.	As "c," inverted frame	25.00	*32.50*
f.	As "a," inverted frame	*475.00*	

No. 5 exists with a surcharge similar to the surcharge on No. 15, with 10 CENTS value and 1895 date. This stamp is an essay.

6	A2 3c blue & carmine	27.50	20.00
a.	3c light blue & rose carmine, thin paper	65.00	50.00
b.	3c deep blue & dark carmine, medium paper	40.00	17.00
c.	3c greenish blue & lake, thick paper	32.50	17.00
d.	Imperf., pair	375.00	—
e.	Inverted frame, thick paper	30.00	20.00
f.	As "a," inverted frame	*350.00*	
7	A2 4c brown & dull blue	16.00	*19.00*
b.	4c brown & ultramarine, thin paper	225.00	*225.00*
c.	Diagonal half used as 2c on cover		140.00
d.	As "b," inverted frame	*900.00*	*1,400.*
8	A2 5c grn & gray ('76)	30.00	20.00
a.	5c yellow green & dark gray, thin paper	55.00	32.50
b.	Inverted frame, thick paper	30.00	20.00
9	A2 7c lilac & orange	35.00	*95.00*
a.	7c lilac & yellow	90.00	*100.00*
b.	Inverted frame	65.00	*150.00*
10	A2 10c blue & brn ('76)	30.00	25.00
a.	10c dark blue & black brown, thin paper	70.00	40.00
b.	Period between "t" & "s" of "cents"	35.00	25.00
c.	Inverted frame	27.50	*32.50*
11	A2 12c red lil & yel grn ('77)	42.50	*175.00*
a.	12c lilac & deep green	160.00	*200.00*
12	A2 14c lilac & green	650.00	*1,250.*
a.	Inverted frame	*2,500.*	*3,500.*
13	A2 50c vio, thin paper ('79)	190.00	*300.00*
a.	50c gray violet, thick paper	250.00	*375.00*
	Nos. 5-13 (9)	1,043.	1,934.

The central element in the fan-shaped scrollwork at the outside of the lower left corner of Nos. 5a and 7b looks like an elongated diamond.

See Nos. 16-20. For surcharges see Nos. 14-15, 23-28, 40.

Nos. 9 and 13 Surcharged in Black

a

b

1887

14	A2 (a) 1c on 7c lilac & orange	100.00	*200.00*
a.	1c on 7c lilac & yellow	120.00	*225.00*
b.	Double surcharge	250.00	*500.00*
c.	Inverted frame	110.00	*350.00*

1895

15	A2 (b) 10c on 50c violet, thin paper	42.50	*67.50*

The "b" surcharge also exists on No. 5, with "10" found in two sizes. These are essays.

Type of 1874-79

1896-1901 *Perf. 13*

16	A2 1c green & red violet, inverted frame ('98)	15.00	*22.50*
a.	Normal frame	300.00	*450.00*
17	A2 3c blue & lake, inverted frame ('98)	12.00	*17.50*
a.	Normal frame	250.00	*425.00*
18	A2 4c bister & dull blue ('01)	17.50	12.50
a.	Diagonal half used as 2c on cover		100.00
b.	Inverted frame	60.00	*80.00*
c.	As "b," diagonal half used as 2c on cover		350.00
19	A2 5c green & gray, inverted frame	35.00	35.00
a.	Normal frame	800.00	*1,200.*
20	A2 10c blue & brown ('01)	80.00	*150.00*
a.	Inverted frame	1,000.	*2,000.*
b.	Period between "t" and "s" of "cents"	170.00	160.00
	Nos. 16-20 (5)	159.50	*237.50*

Arms — A5

1900

21	A5 1c light green	3.00	3.00
22	A5 5c light blue	17.50	*25.00*

See Nos. 29-30. For surcharges see Nos. 41-42.

Nos. 6, 17, 20 Surcharged

c

Surcharge "c" in Black

1902 *Perf. 14x13½*

23	A2 2c on 3c blue & carmine, inverted frame	700.00	*900.00*
a.	"2" in date with straight tail	750.00	*950.00*
b.	Normal frame		—

Perf. 13

24	A2 2c on 3c blue & lake, inverted frame	10.00	*27.50*
a.	"2" in date with straight tail	12.00	*32.50*
b.	Dated "1901"	750.00	750.00
c.	Normal frame	175.00	*300.00*
d.	Dark green surcharge	2,750.	
e.	As "d" & "a"	—	—
f.	As "d" & "c"		—

The overprint on No. 24b exists in two types: with '1901' measuring 2.5 mm or 2.2 mm high.

Only one example of No. 24f can exist.

25	A2 8c on 10c blue & brown	25.00	*42.50*
a.	"2" with straight tail	30.00	*45.00*
b.	On No. 20b	32.50	*45.00*
c.	Inverted frame	250.00	*425.00*

d

Surcharge "d" in Black

1902 *Perf. 13*

27	A2 2c on 3c blue & lake, inverted frame	12.00	*32.50*
a.	Normal frame	240.00	*425.00*
28	A2 8c on 10c blue & brown	12.00	12.50
a.	On No. 20b	18.50	*25.00*
b.	Inverted frame	225.00	*400.00*
	Nos. 23-28 (5)	759.00	1,015.

1903 Wmk. 113

29	A5 2c carmine	8.00	*22.50*
30	A5 8c brown	27.50	*35.00*

King Christian IX — A8

St. Thomas Harbor — A9

1905 Typo. *Perf. 13*

31	A8 5b green	3.75	3.25
32	A8 10b red	3.75	3.25
33	A8 20b green & blue	8.75	8.75
34	A8 25b ultramarine	8.75	*10.50*
35	A8 40b red & gray	8.25	*9.50*
36	A8 50b yellow & gray	10.00	*11.00*

Perf. 12
Wmk. Two Crowns (113)
Frame Typographed, Center Engraved

37	A9 1fr green & blue	17.50	*40.00*
38	A9 2fr orange red & brown	30.00	*55.00*
39	A9 5fr yellow & brown	77.50	*275.00*
	Nos. 31-39 (9)	168.25	*416.25*

Favor cancels exist on Nos. 37-39. Value 25% less.

Nos. 18, 22 and 30 Surcharged in Black

1905 Wmk. 112

40	A2 5b on 4c bister & dull blue	16.00	*50.00*
a.	Inverted frame	45.00	*90.00*
41	A5 5b on 5c light blue	10.00	*47.50*

Wmk. 113

42	A5 5b on 8c brown	12.50	*50.00*
	Nos. 40-42 (3)	38.50	147.50

Favor cancels exist on Nos. 40-42. Value 25% less.

Frederik VIII — A10

Frame Typographed, Center Engraved

1908

43 A10 5b green 1.90 1.90
44 A10 10b red 1.90 1.90
45 A10 15b violet & brown 3.75 *4.50*
46 A10 20b green & blue 30.00 27.50
47 A10 25b blue & dark blue 1.90 *2.50*
48 A10 30b claret & slate 50.00 *52.50*
49 A10 40b vermilion & gray 5.75 *9.50*
50 A10 50b yellow & brown 5.75 *14.00*
Nos. 43-50 (8) 100.95 114.30

Christian X — A11

1915 **Wmk. 114** ***Perf. 14x14½***

51 A11 5b yellow green 4.00 *5.50*
52 A11 10b red 4.00 *55.00*
53 A11 15b lilac & red brown 4.00 *55.00*
54 A11 20b green & blue 4.00 *55.00*
55 A11 25b blue & dark blue 4.00 *17.50*
56 A11 30b claret & black 4.00 *100.00*
57 A11 40b orange & black 4.00 *100.00*
58 A11 50b yellow & brown 3.75 *100.00*
Nos. 51-58 (8) 31.75 *488.00*

Forged and favor cancellations exist.

POSTAGE DUE STAMPS

Royal Cipher, "Christian 9 Rex" D1

1902 **Litho.** **Unwmk.** ***Perf. 11½***

J1 D1 1c dark blue 5.00 *17.50*
J2 D1 4c dark blue 12.50 *22.50*
J3 D1 6c dark blue 22.50 *60.00*
J4 D1 10c dark blue 20.00 *65.00*
Nos. J1-J4 (4) 60.00 *165.00*

There are five types of each value. On the 4c they may be distinguished by differences in the figure "4"; on the other values differences are minute.

Used values of Nos. J1-J8 are for canceled stamps. Uncanceled stamps without gum have probably been used. Value 60% of unused.

Excellent counterfeits of Nos. J1-J4 exist.

Numeral of value — D2

1905-13 ***Perf. 13***

J5 D2 5b red & gray 4.50 *6.75*
J6 D2 20b red & gray 7.50 *14.00*
J7 D2 30b red & gray 6.75 *14.00*
J8 D2 50b red & gray 6.00 *35.00*
a. Perf. 14x14½ ('13) 37.50 *140.00*
b. Perf. 11½ 325.00
Nos. J5-J8 (4) 24.75 *69.75*

All values of this issue are known imperforate, but were not regularly issued.

Used values of Nos. J5-J8 are for canceled stamps. Uncanceled examples without gum have probably been used. Value 60% of unused.

Counterfeits of Nos. J5-J8 exist.

Danish West Indies stamps were replaced by those of the U.S. in 1917, after the U.S. bought the islands.

DANZIG

ˈdanˌtˌ-sig

LOCATION — In northern Europe bordering on the Baltic Sea
AREA — 754 sq. mi.
POP. — 407,000 (approx. 1939)
CAPITAL — Danzig

Established as a "Free City and State" under the protection of the League of Nations in 1920, Danzig was seized by Germany in 1939. It became a Polish province in 1945.

100 Pfennig = 1 Gulden (1923)
100 Pfennig = 1 Mark

Watermarks

Wmk. 108 — Honeycomb

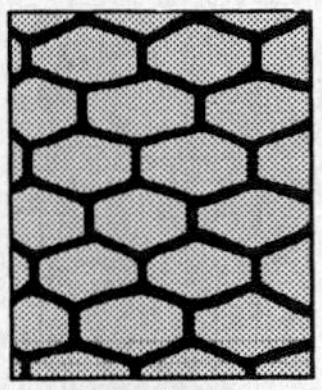

Wmk. 109 — Webbing

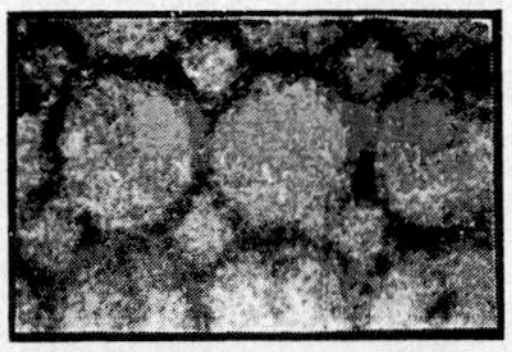

Wmk. 110 — Octagons

Wmk. 125 — Lozenges

Wmk. 237 — Swastikas

Used Values of 1920-23 are for favor-canceled stamps unless otherwise noted. Postally used examples bring much higher prices.

For additional varieties, see the *Scott Classic Catalogue.*

German Stamps of 1906-20 Overprinted in Black

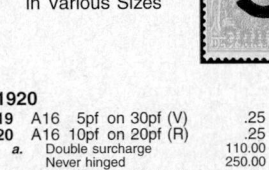

Perf. 14, 14½, 15x14½

1920 **Wmk. 125**

1 A16 5pf green .30 *.50*
a. Pair, one without overprint 100.00
b. Double overprint —
2 A16 10pf car rose .30 .30
3 A22 15pf violet brown .30 .30
4 A16 20pf blue violet .30 *1.10*
5 A16 30pf org & blk, *buff* .30 .30
a. Pair, one without overprint — —
6 A16 40pf car rose .30 .30
7 A16 50pf pur & blk, *buff* .50 .30
a. Pair, one without overprint 175.00
8 A17 1m red .50 .60
a. Pair, one without overprint 100.00
9 A17 1.25m green .50 .60
10 A17 1.50m yellow brn .90 *1.60*
11 A21 2m blue 3.25 *7.25*
a. Double overprint *375.00*
Never hinged 825.00
12 A21 2.50m lilac rose 3.00 *4.50*
c. Double overprint 1,000.
13 A19 3m black violet 7.50 *10.50*
b. Double overprint
14 A16 4m black & rose 4.75 *6.00*
15 A20 5m slate & car (25x17 holes) 2.50 *3.75*
a. Center & "Danzig" invtd. *15,000.*
Never hinged —
b. Inverted overprint *20,000.*
Nos. 1-15 (15) 25.20 37.90
Set, never hinged 122.50

The 5pf brown, 10pf orange and 40pf lake and black with this overprint were not regularly issued. Value for trio, $450.

For surcharges see Nos. 19-23, C1-C3.

Issued: 40pf, 9/13; 1.50m, 3m 7/20; 4m, 12/21; others 6/14.

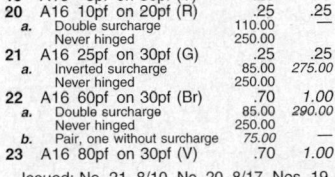

Nos. 5, 4 Surcharged in Various Sizes

1920

19 A16 5pf on 30pf (V) .25 .25
20 A16 10pf on 20pf (R) .25 .25
a. Double surcharge 110.00 —
Never hinged 250.00
21 A16 25pf on 30pf (G) .25 .25
a. Inverted surcharge 85.00 *275.00*
Never hinged 250.00
22 A16 60pf on 30pf (Br) .70 *1.00*
a. Double surcharge 85.00 *290.00*
Never hinged 250.00
b. Pair, one without surcharge *75.00* —
23 A16 80pf on 30pf (V) .70 *1.00*

Issued: No. 21, 8/10. No. 20, 8/17. Nos. 19, 22-23, 11/1.

German Stamps Surcharged in Various Styles

No. 25

No. 27

No. 30

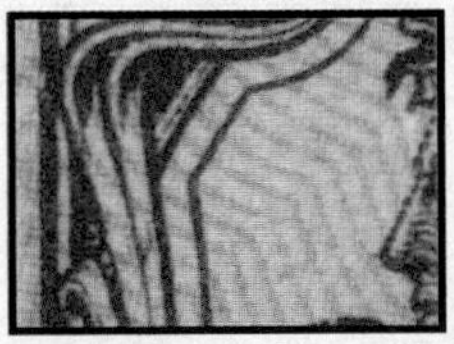

Gray Burelage With Points Up

Gray Burelage with Points Up

25 A16 1m on 30pf org & blk, *buff* (Bk) .85 *1.50*
a. Pair, one without surcharge
26 A16 1¼m on 3pf brn (R) 1.00 *1.50*
27 A22 2m on 35pf red brn (Bl) 1.50 1.50
d. Surcharge omitted 70.00 —
Never hinged 260.00
28 A22 3m on 7½pf org (G) 1.00 *1.50*
29 A22 5m on 2pf gray (R) 1.00 *2.00*
30 A22 10m on 7½pf org (Bk) 3.00 *7.00*
Nos. 19-30 (11) 10.50 *17.75*
Set, never hinged 64.00

Gray Burelage with Points Down

26a A16 1¼m on 3pf brown 36.00 *42.50*
27a A22 2m on 35pf red brn 400.00 325.00
28a A22 3m on 7½pf orange 25.00 17.00
29a A22 5m on 2pf gray 25.00 *30.00*
30a A22 10m on 7½pf orange 5.75 *11.00*
Nos. 26a-30a (5) 491.75 *425.50*
Set, never hinged 2,100.

Violet Burelage with Points Up

25b A16 1m on 30pf org & blk, *buff* 85.00 30.00
26b A16 1¼m on 3pf brown 4.50 *6.50*
27b A22 2m on 35pf red brn 11.50 *37.50*
28b A22 3m on 7½pf orange 2.50 *2.50*
29b A22 5m on 2pf gray 1.25 *2.50*
30b A22 10m on 7½pf orange 1.25 *2.50*
h. Double overprint 70.00
Nos. 25b-30b (6) 106.00 *81.50*
Set, never hinged 430.00

Violet Burelage with Points Down

25c A16 1m on 30pf org & blk, *buff* 1.25 2.50
26c A16 1¼m on 3pf brown 6.50 *11.00*
e. Double overprint 450.00
27c A22 2m on 35pf red brn 30.00 *50.00*
28c A22 3m on 7½pf orange 40.00 *85.00*
29c A22 5m on 2pf gray 6.50 *8.50*
30c A22 10m on 7½pf orange 13.50 *29.00*
Nos. 25c-30c (6) 97.75 *186.00*
Set, never hinged 380.00

Excellent counterfeits of the surcharges are known.

German Stamps of 1906-20 Overprinted in Blue

1920

31 A22 2pf gray 110.00 *200.00*
32 A22 2½pf gray 150.00 *300.00*
33 A16 3pf brown 11.00 *17.00*
a. Double overprint 75.00 —
Never hinged 180.00
34 A16 5pf green .60 *.70*
a. Double overprint 85.00
Never hinged 200.00
35 A22 7½pf orange 40.00 *57.50*
36 A16 10pf carmine 3.75 *7.00*
b. Double overprint 75.00
37 A22 15pf dk violet .60 *.70*
b. Double overprint 85.00
Never hinged 200.00
38 A16 20pf blue violet .60 *.70*

Overprinted in Carmine or Blue

39 A16 25pf org & blk, *yel* .60 *.70*
40 A16 30pf org & blk, *buff* 50.00 *92.50*
42 A16 40pf lake & blk 2.25 *2.50*
a. Inverted overprint 210.00
b. Double overprint 425.00
43 A16 50pf pur & blk, *buff* 175.00 *300.00*
44 A16 60pf mag (Bl) 1,250. *2,100.*
45 A16 75pf green & blk .60 *.70*
a. Double overprint *450.00*
46 A16 80pf lake & blk, *rose* 2.40 *4.25*
47 A17 1m carmine 1,200. *2,100.*
a. Double overprint *4,250.*

Overprinted in Carmine

48 A21 2m gray blue 1,200. *2,100.*

Counterfeit overprints of Nos. 31-48 exist.

Nos. 44, 47 and 48 were issued in small quantities and usually affixed directly to the mail by the postal clerk.

For surcharge see No. 62.

A8

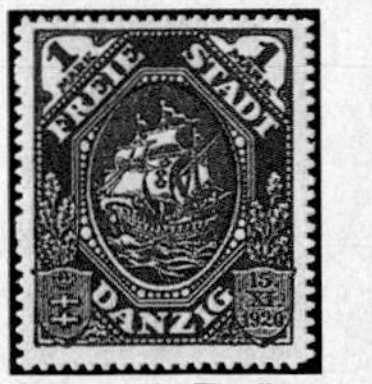

Hanseatic Trading Ship — A9

Serrate Roulette 13½

1921, Jan. 31 **Typo.** **Wmk. 108**

49 A8 5pf brown & violet .25 .25
50 A8 10pf orange & dk vio .25 .25
51 A8 25pf green & car rose .50 .65
52 A8 40pf carmine rose 3.75 3.25
53 A8 80pf ultra .50 .50
54 A9 1m car rose & blk 1.60 *2.00*

55 A9 2m dk blue & dk grn 5.00 5.00
56 A9 3m blk & grnsh bl 2.00 *2.00*
57 A9 5m indigo & rose red 2.00 *2.00*
58 A9 10m dk grn & brn org 2.50 *4.50*
Nos. 49-58 (10) 18.35 *20.40*
Set, never hinged 82.50

Issued in honor of the Constitution.
Nos. 49 and 50 with center in red instead of violet and Nos. 49-51, 54-58 with center inverted are probably proofs. All values of this issue exist imperforate but are not known to have been regularly issued in that condition.

1921, Mar. 11 *Perf. 14*
59 A8 25pf green & car rose .50 *.85*
60 A8 40pf carmine rose .50 .85
61 A8 80pf ultra 5.50 *10.00*
Nos. 59-61 (3) 6.50 *11.70*
Set, never hinged 34.00

No. 45 Surcharged in Black

1921, May 6 **Wmk. 125**
62 A16 60pf on 75pf .95 .90
Never hinged 5.50
a. Double surcharge 100.00 *110.00*
Never hinged 250.00

Surcharge on No. 62 normally appears at top of design.

Arms — A11

Coat of Arms — A12

Wmk. 108 (Upright or Sideways)
1921-22 *Perf. 14*
63 A11 5(pf) orange .25 .25
64 A11 10(pf) dark brown .25 .25
65 A11 15(pf) green .25 .25
66 A11 20(pf) slate .25 .25
67 A11 25(pf) dark green .25 .25
68 A11 30(pf) blue & car .25 .25
Never hinged .85
a. Center inverted 75.00 *150.00*
Never hinged 225.00
69 A11 40pf green & car .25 .25
Never hinged .85
a. Center inverted 75.00 *150.00*
Never hinged 225.00
70 A11 50pf dk grn & car .25 .25
71 A11 60pf carmine .45 .45
72 A11 80pf black & car .35 *.45*

Paper With Faint Gray Network
73 A11 1m org & car .50 .40
a. Center inverted 75.00 150.00
Never hinged 225.00
74 A11 1.20m blue violet 1.25 1.25
75 A11 2m gray & car 3.25 *4.25*
76 A11 3m violet & car 9.00 10.00

Serrate Roulette 13½
Wmk. 108 Upright
77 A12 5m grn, red & blk 1.25 *3.00*
78 A12 9m rose, red & org ('22) 3.00 *8.50*
79 A12 10m ultra, red & blk 1.25 *3.00*
80 A12 20m red & black 1.25 *3.00*
Nos. 63-80 (18) 23.55 *36.30*
Set, never hinged 85.00

In this and succeeding issues the mark values usually have the face of the paper covered with a gray network. This network is often very faint and occasionally is omitted.
Nos. 64-76 exist imperf. Value, each $16-$50 unused, $50-$150 never hinged.
See Nos. 81-93, 99-105. For surcharges and overprints see Nos. 96-98, O1-O33.

Type of 1921 and

A13

Coat of Arms — A13a

1922 **Wmk. 108 Upright** *Perf. 14*
81 A11 75(pf) deep vio .25 *.25*
82 A11 80(pf) green .25 *.25*
83 A11 1.25m vio & car .25 *.25*
84 A11 1.50m slate gray .25 *.40*
85 A11 2m car rose .25 *.25*
86 A11 2.40m dk brn & car 1.15 *2.00*
87 A11 3m car lake .25 *.40*
88 A11 4m dark blue 1.15 *2.00*
89 A11 5m deep grn .25 *.35*
90 A11 6m car lake .25 *.35*
a. 6m car rose, wmk. 109 sideways *1,800.*
Never hinged *3,900.*
91 A11 8m light blue .45 *1.60*
92 A11 10m orange .25 *.35*
93 A11 20m org brn .25 *.35*
94 A13 50m gold & car 2.00 *6.50*
a. 50m gold & red 57.50 *120.00*
Never hinged 220.00
95 A13a 100m metallic grn & red 3.25 *6.00*
Nos. 81-95 (15) 10.50 *21.30*
Set, never hinged 42.50

No. 95 has buff instead of gray network.
Nos. 81-83, 85-86, 88 exist imperf. Value, each $12.50.
Nos. 94-95 exist imperf. Value, each $50

Nos. 87, 88 and 91 Surcharged in Black or Carmine

1922
96 A11 6m on 3m car lake .35 *.60*
a. Double surcharge
97 A11 8m on 4m dk blue .35 *.85*
a. Double surcharge 70.00 *145.00*
Never hinged 140.00
b. Pair, one without surcharge 150.00
98 A11 20m on 8m lt bl (C) .35 *.60*
Nos. 96-98 (3) 1.05 *2.05*
Set, never hinged 4.00

Wmk. 109 Sideways
1922-23 *Perf. 14*
99 A11 4m dark blue .25 *.40*
100 A11 5m dark green .25 *.40*
102 A11 10m orange .25 *.40*
103 A11 20m orange brn .25 *.40*

Paper Without Network
Wmk. 109 Upright
104 A11 40m pale blue .25 *.60*
105 A11 80m red .25 *.60*
Nos. 99-105 (6) 1.50 *2.80*
Set, never hinged 5.40

Nos. 100, 102 and 103 also exist with watermark vertical. Values slightly higher.

Nos. 104-105 exist imperf. Value, each $12.50 unused, $32.50 never hinged.

A15

A15a

Coat of Arms A16

1922-23 Wmk. 109 Upright *Perf. 14*
Paper With Gray Network
106 A15 50m pale bl & red .25 *.40*
107 A15a 100m dk grn & red .25 *.40*
108 A15a 150m violet & red .25 *.40*
109 A16 250m violet & red .40 *.40*
110 A16 500m gray blk & red .40 *.40*
111 A16 1000m brn & red .40 *.40*
112 A16 5000m silver & red 1.50 *6.00*

Paper Without Network
113 A15 50m pale blue .40 *.60*
114 A15a 100m deep green .40 *.60*
115 A15 200m orange .40 *.60*
Nos. 106-115 (10) 4.65 *10.20*
Set, never hinged 19.00

Nos. 108-112 exist imperf. Value, each $50 unused, $125 never hinged.
Nos. 113-115 exist imperf. Value, each $35 unused, $92.50 never hinged.
See Nos. 123-125. For surcharges and overprints see Nos. 126, 137-140, 143, 156-167, O35-O38.

A17

1923 *Perf. 14*
Paper With Gray Network
117 A17 250m violet & red .25 *.55*
118 A17 300m bl grn & red .25 *.55*
119 A17 500m gray & red .25 *.55*
120 A17 1000m brown & red .25 *.55*
121 A17 3000m violet & red .25 *.55*
123 A16 10,000m orange & red .60 .60
124 A16 20,000m pale bl & red .60 *1.00*
125 A16 50,000m green & red .60 *1.00*
Nos. 117-125 (8) 3.05 *5.35*
Set, never hinged 12.50

Nos. 117, 119-121 exist imperf. Value, each $19 unused, $45 never hinged; Nos. 123-125 also exist imperf. Values each, $25 unused, $85 never hinged.
See Nos. 127-135. For surcharges & overprints see Nos. 141-142, 144-155, O39-O41.

No. 124 Surcharged in Red

1923, Aug. 14
126 A16 100,000m on #124 1.00 *6.00*
Never hinged 4.50

No. 126 exists imperf. Value $50 unused, $125 never hinged.

1923 *Perf. 14*
Paper Without Network
127 A17 1000m brown .25 *.40*
129 A17 5000m rose .25 *.40*
131 A17 20,000m pale blue .25 *.40*
132 A17 50,000m green .25 *.40*

Paper With Gray Network
133 A17 100,000m deep blue .25 *.40*
b. Double impression 80.00
134 A17 250,000m violet .25 *.40*
135 A17 500,000m slate .25 *.40*
Nos. 127-135 (7) 1.75 2.80
Set, never hinged 5.00

Abbreviations:
th=(tausend) thousand
mil=million

Nos. 115, 114, 132, and Type of 1923 Surcharged

1923 *Perf. 14*
Paper Without Network
137 A15 40th m on 200m .85 *2.00*
a. Double surcharge 85.00
Never hinged 160.00
138 A15 100th m on 200m .85 *2.00*
139 A15 250th m on 200m 6.25 *13.00*
140 A15a 400th m on 100m .60 .60
141 A17 500th m on #132 .40 *.60*

On 10,000m
142 A17 1mil m org 3.75 *6.25*

The surcharges on Nos. 140-142 differ in details from those on Nos. 137-139.

Type of 1923 Surcharged

Paper With Gray Network
On 1,000,000m
143 A16 10mil m org .40 *1.25*
Nos. 137-143 (7) 13.10 *25.70*
Set, never hinged 60.00

Nos. 142-143 exist imperf. Values: No. 142 unused $50, never hinged $125; No. 143 unused $25, never hinged $85.

Type of 1923 Surcharged

Wmk. 109 Upright
Perf. 14
10,000m rose on paper without Network
144 A17 1mil m on 10,000m .25 *.60*
145 A17 2mil m on 10,000m .25 *.60*
146 A17 3mil m on 10,000m .25 *.60*
147 A17 5mil m on 10,000m .35 *.60*
b. Double surcharge 85.00
Never hinged 160.00

10,000m gray lilac on paper without Network
148 A17 10mil m on 10,000m .40 *.75*
149 A17 20mil m on 10,000m .40 *.75*
150 A17 25mil m on 10,000m .25 *.75*
151 A17 40mil m on 10,000m .25 *.75*
a. Double surcharge 52.50
Never hinged 160.00
152 A17 50mil m on 10,000m .25 *.75*

Type of 1923 Surcharged in Red

10,000m gray lilac on paper without Network
153 A17 100mil m on 10,000m .25 *.75*
154 A17 300mil m on 10,000m .25 *.75*
155 A17 500mil m on 10,000m .25 *.75*
Nos. 144-155 (12) 3.40 *8.40*
Set, never hinged 15.00

Nos. 144-147 exist imperf. Value, each $25 unused, $85 never hinged. Nos. 148-155 exist imperf. Value, each $32.50 unused, $85 never hinged.

Types of 1923 Surcharged

1923, Oct. 31 Wmk. 110 Perf. 14

156	A15	5pf on 50m	.45	.40
157	A15	10pf on 50m	.45	.40
158	A15a	20pf on 100m	.45	.40
159	A15	25pf on 50m	3.50	*9.00*
160	A15	30pf on 50m	3.50	2.00
161	A15a	40pf on 100m	2.25	2.00
162	A15a	50pf on 100m	2.25	*3.00*
163	A15a	75pf on 100m	8.00	*16.00*

Type of 1923 Surcharged

1923, Nov. 5

164	A16	1g on 1mil m rose	4.50	*6.25*
165	A16	2g on 1mil m rose	12.00	*17.50*
166	A16	3g on 1mil m rose	22.00	*62.50*
167	A16	5g on 1mil m rose	25.00	*67.50*
		Nos. 156-167 (12)	84.35	*186.95*
		Set, never hinged	400.00	

Coat of Arms — A19

1924-37 Wmk. 109 Perf. 14

168	A19	3pf brn, *yelsh* ('35)	1.25	*1.50*
a.		3pf dp brn, *white* ('27)	2.10	1.90
		Never hinged	9.50	
170	A19	5pf org, *yelsh*	3.25	.55
a.		White paper	8.50	2.00
		Never hinged	45.00	
c.		Tête bêche pair	375.00	
		Never hinged	725.00	
d.		Syncopated perf., #170	10.50	9.25
		Never hinged	30.00	
e.		Syncopated perf., #170a	25.00	22.50
		Never hinged	120.00	
171	A19	7pf yel grn ('33)	1.60	*3.00*
172	A19	8pf yel grn ('37)	1.60	*6.00*
173	A19	10pf grn, *yelsh*	5.50	.50
a.		White paper	11.50	2.50
		Never hinged	47.50	
c.		10pf blue grn, *yellowish*	7.75	1.10
		Never hinged	27.50	
d.		Tête bêche pair	325.00	
		Never hinged	750.00	
e.		Syncopated perf., #173	18.00	11.00
		Never hinged	55.00	
f.		Syncopated perf., #173a	27.50	13.00
		Never hinged	110.00	
g.		Syncopated perf., #173c	11.00	*14.50*
		Never hinged	37.50	
175	A19	15pf gray	3.75	.65
176	A19	15pf red, *yelsh* ('35)	2.10	1.10
a.		White paper ('25)	4.50	1.10
		Never hinged	25.00	
177	A19	20pf carmine & red	15.00	.65
178	A19	20pf gray ('35)	2.25	*2.50*
179	A19	25pf slate & red	27.00	3.75
180	A19	25pf carmine ('35)	16.00	1.60
181	A19	30pf green & red	14.00	.85
182	A19	30pf dk violet ('35)	2.25	*4.25*
183	A19	35pf ultra	4.50	1.50
184	A19	40pf dk blue & blue	12.00	1.00
185	A19	40pf yel brn & red	6.50	*12.50*
186	A19	40pf dk blue ('35)	2.25	*3.75*
a.		Imperf.	60.00	
		Never hinged	170.00	
187	A19	50pf blue & red	16.00	7.50
a.		Yellowish paper	17.50	*32.50*
		Never hinged	57.50	
188	A19	55pf plum & scar	5.00	*14.50*
189	A19	60pf dk grn & red	6.25	*17.50*
190	A19	70pf yel grn & red ('35)	2.25	*7.50*
191	A19	75pf violet & red, *yellowish*	7.50	*29.00*
a.		White paper	10.00	8.50
		Never hinged	47.50	
192	A19	80pf dk org brn & red ('35)	2.25	*7.50*
		Nos. 168-192 (23)	160.05	*129.15*
		Set, never hinged	675.00	

The 5pf and 10pf with syncopated perforations (Netherlands type C) are coils.

See Nos. 225-232. For overprints and surcharges see Nos. 200-209, 211-215, 241-252, B9-B11, O42-O52.

Oliva Castle and Cathedral A20

St. Mary's Church A23

Council Chamber on the Langenmarkt A24

2g, Mottlau River & Krantor. 3g, View of Zoppot.

1924-32 Engr. Wmk. 125

193	A20	1g yel grn & blk	21.00	*45.00*
		Parcel post cancel		20.00
194	A20	1g org & gray blk ('32)	17.00	3.75
		Parcel post cancel		1.00
a.		1g red orange & blk	17.00	11.00
		Never hinged	67.50	
		Parcel post cancel		1.00
195	A20	2g red vio & blk	45.00	*110.00*
		Parcel post cancel		40.00
196	A20	2g rose & blk	3.75	*8.00*
		Parcel post cancel		1.75
197	A20	3g dk blue & blk	4.75	*5.00*
		Parcel post cancel		2.25
198	A23	5g brn red & blk	4.75	*8.50*
		Parcel post cancel		1.90
199	A24	10g dk brn & blk	21.00	*110.00*
		Parcel post cancel		18.00
		Nos. 193-199 (7)	117.25	*290.25*
		Set, never hinged	600.00	

See No. 233. For overprints and surcharges see Nos. 210, 253-254, C31-C35.

Stamps of 1924-25 Overprinted in Black, Violet or Red

1930, Nov. 15 Typo. Wmk. 109

200	A19	5pf orange	2.50	*3.50*
201	A19	10pf yellow grn (V)	3.50	4.25
202	A19	15pf red	6.00	*10.00*
203	A19	20pf carmine & red	3.00	*5.50*
204	A19	25pf slate & red	4.25	*10.00*
205	A19	30pf green & red	8.50	*22.50*
206	A19	35pf ultra (R)	32.50	*90.00*
207	A19	40pf dk bl & bl (R)	11.50	*35.00*
208	A19	50pf dp blue & red	32.50	*75.00*
209	A19	75pf violet & red	32.50	*82.50*

Engr. Wmk. (125)

210	A20	1g orange & blk (R)	32.50	*75.00*
		Nos. 200-210 (11)	169.25	*413.25*
		Set, never hinged	675.00	

10th anniv. of the Free State. Counterfeits exist.

Nos. 171 and 183 Surcharged in Red, Blue or Green

Nos. 211-214

No. 215

1934-36

211	A19	6pf on 7pf (R)	1.00	*1.50*
212	A19	8pf on 7pf (Bl)	2.00	*2.25*
213	A19	8pf on 7pf (R)	1.15	*2.40*
214	A19	8pf on 7pf (G)	.75	*2.40*
215	A19	30pf on 35pf (Bl)	11.00	*24.50*
		Nos. 211-215 (5)	15.90	*33.05*
		Set, never hinged	60.00	

Bathing Beach, Brösen A25

View of Brösen Beach A26

War Memorial at Brösen — A27

1936, June 23 Typo. Wmk. 109

216	A25	10pf deep green	.70	*.70*
217	A26	25pf rose red	1.25	*2.40*
218	A27	40pf bright blue	2.25	*4.50*
		Nos. 216-218 (3)	4.20	*7.60*
		Set, never hinged	15.00	

Village of Brösen, 125th anniversary.

Exist imperf. Value each, $40 unused, $110 never hinged.

Skyline of Danzig — A28

1937, Mar. 27

219	A28	10pf dark blue	.50	*1.40*
220	A28	15pf violet brown	1.60	*2.00*
		Set, never hinged	11.25	
		Set of 2, #219-220 on one 1st day cover		20.00

Air Defense League.

Danzig Philatelic Exhibition Issue

Souvenir Sheet

St. Mary's Church — A29

1937, June 6 Wmk. 109 Perf. 14

221	A29	50pf dark opal green	4.00	*20.00*
		Never hinged	11.00	

Danzig Philatelic Exhib., June 6-8, 1937.

Arthur Schopenhauer
A30 A31

Design: 40pf, Full-face portrait, white hair.

Unwmk.

1938, Feb. 22 Photo. Perf. 14

222	A30	15pf dull blue	1.35	*2.40*
223	A31	25pf sepia	3.25	*8.00*
224	A31	40pf orange ver	1.35	*3.25*
		Nos. 222-224 (3)	5.95	*13.65*
		Set, never hinged	20.00	
		Set of 3, #222-224 on one 1st day cover		37.50

150th anniv. of the birth of Schopenhauer.

Type of 1924-35

1938-39 Typo. Wmk. 237 Perf. 14

225	A19	3pf brown	.90	*7.25*
226	A19	5pf orange	.90	*2.00*
b.		Syncopated perf.	1.40	*7.50*
		Never hinged	5.50	
227	A19	8pf yellow grn	4.00	*32.50*
228	A19	10pf blue green	.90	*2.00*
b.		Syncopated perf.	3.00	*10.00*
		Never hinged	14.00	
229	A19	15pf scarlet	1.60	*10.00*
230	A19	25pf carmine	2.10	*7.50*
231	A19	40pf dark blue	2.10	*27.50*
232	A19	50pf brt bl & red	2.10	*130.00*

Engr.

233	A20	1g red org & blk	6.75	*110.00*
		Nos. 225-233 (9)	21.35	*328.75*
		Set, never hinged	90.00	

Sizes: No. 233, 32½x21¼mm; No. 194, 31x21mm.

Nos. 226b and 228b are coils with Netherlands type C perforation.

Knights in Tournament, 1500 — A33

French Leaving Danzig, 1814 — A35

Stamp Day: 10pf, Signing of Danzig-Sweden neutrality treaty, 1630. 25pf, Battle of Weichselmünde, 1577.

Unwmk.

1939, Jan. 7 Photo. Perf. 14

234	A33	5pf dark green	.40	*2.00*
235	A33	10pf copper brown	.85	*2.25*
236	A35	15pf slate black	1.25	*2.75*
237	A35	25pf brown violet	1.60	*3.75*
		Nos. 234-237 (4)	4.10	*10.75*
		Set, never hinged	14.00	
		Set of 4, #234-237 on one 1st day cover		30.00

Gregor Mendel — A37

15pf, Dr. Robert Koch. 25pf, Wilhelm Roentgen.

1939, Apr. 29 Photo. Perf. 13x14

238	A37	10pf copper brown	.65	*.85*
239	A37	15pf indigo	.65	*2.00*
240	A37	25pf dark olive green	1.25	*2.75*
		Nos. 238-240 (3)	2.55	*5.60*
		Set, never hinged	7.25	

Issued in honor of the achievements of Mendel, Koch and Roentgen.

Issued under German Administration

Stamps of Danzig, 1925-39, Surcharged in Black

a

b

c

1939 Wmk. 109 Perf. 14

241	A19(b)	4rpf on 35pf ultra	.75	*2.25*
242	A19(b)	12rpf on 7pf yel grn	1.50	*2.25*
243	A19(a)	20rpf gray	3.00	*8.50*

Wmk. 237

244	A19(a)	3rpf brown	.75	*2.40*
245	A19(a)	5rpf orange	.65	*3.00*
246	A19(a)	8rpf yellow grn	1.10	*4.25*
247	A19(a)	10rpf blue grn	2.25	*4.25*
248	A19(a)	15rpf scarlet	6.00	*11.00*
249	A19(a)	25rpf carmine	4.50	*10.00*
250	A19(a)	30rpf dk violet	2.00	*4.50*
251	A19(a)	40rpf dk blue	2.75	*6.00*
252	A19(a)	50rpf brt bl & red	4.00	*7.00*

Thick Paper

253 A20(c) 1rm on 1g red org & blk 14.00 *57.50*

Wmk. 125

Thin White Paper

254 A20(c) 2rm on 2g rose & blk 20.00 *62.50*
Nos. 241-254 (14) 63.25 *185.40*
Set, never hinged 190.00

Nos. 241-254 were valid throughout Germany.

SEMI-POSTAL STAMPS

St. George and Dragon — SP1

Wmk. 108

1921, Oct. 16 Typo. *Perf. 14*

Size: 19x22mm

B1 SP1 30pf + 30pf grn & org .45 .95
B2 SP1 60pf + 60pf rose & org 1.25 *1.60*

Size: 25x30mm

Serrate Roulette 13½

B3 SP1 1.20m + 1.20m dk bl & org 2.00 *2.25*
Nos. B1-B3 (3) 3.70 4.80
Set, never hinged 16.00

Nos. B1-B3 exist imperf. Value each, $45 unused, $125 never hinged.

Aged Pensioner SP2

1923, Mar. Wmk. 109 *Perf. 14*

Paper With Gray Network

B4 SP2 50m + 20m lake .25 *.60*
B5 SP2 100m + 30m red vio .25 *.60*
Set, never hinged 2.50

Nos. B4-B5 exist imperf. Value each, $50 unused, $30 used, $210 never hinged.

Philatelic Exhibition Issue

Neptune Fountain — SP3

Various Frames.

1929, July 7 Engr. Unwmk.

B6 SP3 10pf yel grn & gray 2.40 1.60
B7 SP3 15pf car & gray 2.40 1.60
B8 SP3 25pf ultra & gray 8.50 *13.00*
a. 25pf violet blue & black 25.00 *80.00*
Never hinged 92.50
Nos. B6-B8 (3) 13.30 16.20
Set, never hinged 45.00
Set of 3, #B6-B8 on one 1st day cover 200.00

These stamps were sold exclusively at the Danzig Philatelic Exhibition, June 7-14, 1929, at double their face values, the excess being for the aid of the exhibition.

Regular Issue of 1924-25 Surcharged in Black

1934, Jan. 15 Wmk. 109

B9 A19 5pf + 5pf orange 9.50 *19.00*
B10 A19 10pf + 5pf yel grn 22.50 *45.00*
B11 A19 15pf + 5pf carmine 13.50 *35.00*
Nos. B9-B11 (3) 45.50 *99.00*
Set, never hinged 220.00

Surtax for winter welfare. Counterfeits exist.

Stock Tower — SP4

George Hall — SP6

City Gate, 16th Century SP5

1935, Dec. 16 Typo. *Perf. 14*

B12 SP4 5pf + 5pf orange .65 *1.50*
B13 SP5 10pf + 5pf green 1.10 *2.25*
B14 SP6 15pf + 10pf scarlet 2.75 *3.50*
Nos. B12-B14 (3) 4.50 *7.25*
Set, never hinged 16.00
Set of 3, #B12-B14 on one 1st day cover 40.00

Surtax for winter welfare.

Milk Can Tower SP7

Frauentor SP8

Krantor — SP9

Langgarter Gate — SP10

High Gate SP11

1936, Nov. 25

B15 SP7 10pf + 5pf dk bl 1.60 *4.50*
a. Imperf. 75.00
Never hinged 180.00
B16 SP8 15pf + 5pf dull grn 1.60 *5.75*
B17 SP9 25pf + 10pf red brn 2.25 *9.00*
B18 SP10 40pf + 20pf brn & red brn 3.00 *10.00*
B19 SP11 50pf + 20pf bl & dk bl 5.25 *15.00*
Nos. B15-B19 (5) 13.70 *44.25*
Set, never hinged 80.00

Surtax for winter welfare.

SP12

SP13

1937, Oct. 30 Wmk. 109 Sideways

B20 SP12 25pf + 25pf dk car 2.75 *5.25*

Wmk. 109 Upright

B21 SP13 40pf + 40pf blue & red 2.75 *5.25*
a. Souvenir sheet of 2, #B20a-B21 60.00 *110.00*
Never hinged 110.00
Set, never hinged 27.50

Founding of Danzig community at Magdeburg. No. B21a exists imperf. Value, $1,600 unused, $3,250 never hinged.

Madonna SP14

Mercury SP15

Weather Vane, Town Hall SP16

Neptune Fountain SP17

St. George and Dragon — SP18

1937, Dec. 13

B23 SP14 5pf + 5pf brt violet 2.50 *7.50*
B24 SP15 10pf + 10pf dk brn 2.50 *5.75*
B25 SP16 15pf + 5pf bl & yel brn 2.50 *8.25*
B26 SP17 25pf + 10pf bl grn & grn 3.25 *11.00*
B27 SP18 40pf + 25pf brt car & bl 5.75 *15.00*
Nos. B23-B27 (5) 16.50 *47.50*
Set, never hinged 65.00
Set of 5, #B23-B27 on one 1st day cover 100.00

Surtax for winter welfare. Designs are from frieze of the Artushof.

"Peter von Danzig" Yacht Race — SP19

Ships: 10pf+5pf, Dredger Fu Shing. 15pf+10pf, S. S. Columbus. 25pf+10pf, S. S. City of Danzig. 40pf+15pf, Peter von Danzig, 1472.

1938, Nov. 28 Photo. Unwmk.

B28 SP19 5pf + 5pf dk bl grn 1.40 *1.50*
B29 SP19 10pf + 5pf gldn brn 1.40 *3.00*
B30 SP19 15pf + 10pf ol grn 1.60 *3.00*
B31 SP19 25pf + 10pf indigo 2.50 *4.00*
B32 SP19 40pf + 15pf vio brn 3.00 *6.75*
Nos. B28-B32 (5) 9.90 *18.25*
Set, never hinged 50.00
Set of 5, #B28-B32 on one 1st day cover 60.00

Surtax for winter welfare.

AIR POST STAMPS

No. 6 Surcharged in Blue or Carmine

1920, Sept. 29 Wmk. 125 *Perf. 14*

C1 A16 40pf on 40pf 1.25 *2.60*
a. Double surcharge 160.00 *250.00*
Never hinged 450.00
C2 A16 60pf on 40pf (C) 1.25 *2.60*
a. Double surcharge 125.00 *250.00*
Never hinged 350.00
C3 A16 1m on 40pf 1.25 *2.60*
a. Double surcharge 125.00 250.00
Never hinged 350.00
Nos. C1-C3 (3) 3.75 *7.80*
Set, never hinged 13.50

Plane faces left on No. C2.

AP3

Plane over Danzig AP4

Wmk. (108) Upright

1921-22 Typo. *Perf. 14*

C4 AP3 40(pf) blue green .25 *.45*
C5 AP3 60(pf) dk violet .25 *.45*
C6 AP3 1m carmine .25 *.45*
C7 AP3 2m org brn .25 *.45*

Serrate Roulette 13½

Size: 34½x23mm

C8 AP4 5m violet blue 1.25 *2.25*
C9 AP4 10m dp grn 2.00 *4.25*
Nos. C4-C9 (6) 4.25 *8.30*
Set, never hinged 18.00

Nos. C4-C9 exist imperf. Value, each $32.50 unused, $125 never hinged.

1923 Wmk. (109) Upright *Perf. 14*

C10 AP3 40(pf) blue green .55 *1.90*
C11 AP3 60(pf) dk violet .55 *1.90*
a. Double impression —
C12 AP3 1m carmine .55 *1.90*
C13 AP3 2m org brown .55 *1.90*
C14 AP3 25m pale blue .40 *.70*

Serrate Roulette 13½

Size: 34½x23mm

C15 AP4 5m violet blue .55 *1.00*
C16 AP4 10m deep green .55 *1.00*

Paper With Gray Network

C17 AP4 20m org brn .55 *1.00*

Size: 40x23mm

C18 AP4 50m orange .40 *.70*
C19 AP4 100m red .40 *.70*
C20 AP4 250m dark brown .60 *.70*
C21 AP4 500m car rose .60 *.70*
Nos. C10-C21 (12) 6.25 *14.10*
Set, never hinged 30.00

Nos. C11, C12, C14-C21 exist imperf. Value, Nos. C11, C12, C15-C17, each $8.50 unused, $32.50 never hinged. Value, No. C14, C18-C21, each $40 unused, $125 never hinged.

Nos. C18, C19 and C21 exist with wmk. sideways, both perf and imperf. Value each, $60 unused, $160 never hinged.

Post Horn and Airplanes — AP5

1923, Oct. 18 ***Perf. 14***

Paper Without Network

C22 AP5 250,000m scarlet .35 *1.25*
C23 AP5 500,000m scarlet .35 *1.25*
Set, never hinged 2.50

Exist imperf. Value, each: $50 unused; $125 never hinged.

Surcharged

On 100,000m

C24 AP5 2mil m scarlet .35 *1.25*

On 50,000m

C25 AP5 5mil m scarlet .35 *1.25*
b. Cliché of 10,000m in sheet of 50,000m 32.50 *160.00*
Never hinged 130.00

Exist imperf. Value, each $125 unused, $290 never hinged.

Nos. C24 and C25 were not regularly issued without surcharge, although examples have been passed through the post. Values: C24 unused $8.50, never hinged $32.50; C25 unused $12, never hinged $21.

AP6

Plane over Danzig — AP7

1924

C26 AP6 10(pf) vermilion 21.00 3.50
C27 AP6 20(pf) carmine rose 2.10 1.50
C28 AP6 40(pf) olive brown 3.00 1.75
C29 AP6 1g deep green 3.00 3.00
C30 AP7 2½g violet brown 17.50 *32.50*
Nos. C26-C30 (5) 46.60 *42.25*
Set, never hinged 175.00

Exist imperf. Value Nos. C26, C30, $85 unused, $200 never hinged; others, each $40 unused, $110 never hinged.

Nos. 193, 195, 197-199 Srchd. in Various Colors

1932 **Wmk. 125**

C31 A20 10pf on 1g (G) 9.00 *21.00*
C32 A20 15pf on 2g (V) 9.00 *21.00*
C33 A20 20pf on 3g (Bl) 9.00 *21.00*
C34 A23 25pf on 5g (R) 9.00 *21.00*
C35 A24 30pf on 10g (Br) 9.00 *21.00*
Nos. C31-C35 (5) 45.00 *105.00*
Set, never hinged 200.00

Intl. Air Post Exhib. of 1932. The surcharges were variously arranged to suit the shapes and designs of the stamps. The stamps were sold at double their surcharged values, the excess being donated to the exhibition funds.

No. C31 exists with inverted surcharge and with double surcharge. Value each, $85 unused, $210 never hinged.

Airplane
AP8 AP9

1935, Oct. 24 **Wmk. 109**

C36 AP8 10pf scarlet 1.75 .85
C37 AP8 15pf yellow 1.75 1.25
C38 AP8 25pf dark green 1.75 1.50
C39 AP8 50pf gray blue 9.00 *9.25*
C40 AP9 1g magenta 3.50 *13.00*
Nos. C36-C40 (5) 17.75 *25.85*
Set, never hinged 65.00

Nos. C36 and C40 exist imperf. Values: C36 unused $20, never hinged $62.50; C40 unused $29, never hinged $85.

See Nos. C42-C45.

Souvenir Sheet

St. Mary's Church — AP10

1937, June 6 ***Perf. 14***

C41 AP10 50pf dark grayish blue 3.75 *16.00*
Never hinged 10.50

Danzig Phil. Exhib., June 6-8, 1937.

Type of 1935

1938-39 **Wmk. 237**

C42 AP8 10pf scarlet 1.25 *3.75*
C43 AP8 15pf yellow ('39) 2.00 *12.00*
C44 AP8 25pf dark green 1.60 *6.50*
C45 AP8 50pf gray blue ('39) 4.00 *57.50*
Nos. C42-C45 (4) 8.85 *79.75*
Set, never hinged 42.50

POSTAGE DUE STAMPS

Danzig Coat of Arms — D1

1921-22 Typo. Wmk. (108) ***Perf. 14***

Paper Without Network

J1 D1 10(pf) deep violet .35 *.45*
J2 D1 20(pf) deep violet .35 *.45*
J3 D1 40(pf) deep violet .35 *.45*
J4 D1 60(pf) deep violet .35 *.45*
J5 D1 75(pf) dp violet ('22) .35 *.45*
J6 D1 80(pf) deep violet .35 *.45*
J7 D1 120(pf) deep violet .35 *.45*
J8 D1 200(pf) dp violet ('22) .95 *1.00*
J9 D1 240(pf) deep violet .35 *1.00*
J10 D1 300(pf) dp violet ('22) .95 *1.00*
J11 D1 400(pf) deep violet .95 *1.00*
J12 D1 500(pf) deep violet .95 *1.00*
J13 D1 800(pf) deep violet ('22) .95 *1.00*
J14 D1 20m dp violet ('22) .95 *1.00*
Nos. J1-J14 (14) 8.50 *10.15*
Set, never hinged 27.50

Nos. J1-J14 exist imperf. Value, each $30 unused, $75 never hinged.

1923 **Wmk. 109 Sideways**

J15 D1 100(pf) deep violet .60 *.75*
J16 D1 200(pf) deep violet 2.50 *3.75*
J17 D1 300(pf) deep violet .60 *.75*
J18 D1 400(pf) deep violet .60 *.75*
J19 D1 500(pf) deep violet .60 *.75*
J20 D1 800(pf) deep violet 1.25 *3.75*
J21 D1 10m deep violet .60 *1.00*
J22 D1 20m deep violet .60 *.75*
J23 D1 50m deep violet .60 *.75*

Paper With Gray Network

J24 D1 100m deep violet .60 *1.00*
J25 D1 500m deep violet .60 *1.00*
Nos. J15-J25 (11) 9.15 15.00
Set, never hinged 25.00

Nos. J15, J17, J22-J25 exist imperf. Value each, $12.50 unused, $40 never hinged.

Nos. J22-J23 and Type of 1923 Surcharged

1923, Oct. 1

Paper without Network

J26 D1 5000m on 50m .40 *.75*
J27 D1 10,000m on 20m .40 *.75*
J28 D1 50,000m on 500m .40 *.75*
J29 D1 100,000m on 20m .85 *1.25*
Nos. J26-J29 (4) 2.05 *3.50*
Set, never hinged 8.00

On No. J26 the numerals of the surcharge are all of the larger size.

A 1000(m) on 100m deep violet was prepared but not issued. Value, $145, never hinged $350.

Nos. J26-J28 exist imperf. Value each, $18 unused, $45 never hinged.

Danzig Coat of Arms — D2

1923-28 **Wmk. 110**

J30 D2 5(pf) blue & blk .85 .75
J31 D2 10(pf) blue & blk .40 *.75*
J32 D2 15(pf) blue & blk 1.25 1.10
J33 D2 20(pf) blue & blk 1.25 *2.00*
J34 D2 30(pf) blue & blk 9.00 2.00
J35 D2 40(pf) blue & blk 2.10 *3.00*
J36 D2 50(pf) blue & blk 2.10 *2.25*
J37 D2 60(pf) blue & blk 13.00 *18.00*
J38 D2 100(pf) blue & blk 17.50 9.75
J39 D2 3g blue & car 10.00 *40.00*
a. "Guldeu" instead of "Gulden" 325.00 *1,050.*
Never hinged 1,050.
Nos. J30-J39 (10) 57.45 *79.60*
Set, never hinged 225.00

Used values of Nos. J30-J39 are for postally used stamps.

See Nos. J43-J47.

Postage Due Stamps of 1923 Issue Surcharged in Red

1932, Dec. 20

J40 D2 5pf on 40(pf) 4.25 *7.50*
J41 D2 10pf on 60(pf) 32.50 9.00
J42 D2 20pf on 100(pf) 2.75 *7.50*
Nos. J40-J42 (3) 39.50 *24.00*
Set, never hinged 160.00

Type of 1923

1938-39 **Wmk. 237** ***Perf. 14***

J43 D2 10(pf) bl & blk ('39) 1.25 *62.50*
J44 D2 30(pf) bl & blk 2.25 *50.00*
J45 D2 40(pf) bl & blk ('39) 6.75 *100.00*
J46 D2 60(pf) bl & blk ('39) 6.75 *100.00*
J47 D2 100(pf) bl & blk 11.00 *72.50*
Nos. J43-J47 (5) 28.00 *385.00*
Set, never hinged 125.00

OFFICIAL STAMPS

Regular Issues of 1921-22 Overprinted — a

1921-22 **Wmk. 108** ***Perf. 14x14½***

O1 A11 5(pf) orange .25 .25
O2 A11 10(pf) dark brown .25 .25
a. Inverted overprint 60.00
Never hinged 170.00
O3 A11 15(pf) green .25 .25
O4 A11 20(pf) slate .25 .25
O5 A11 25(pf) dark green .25 .25
a. Pair, one without oveprint 170.00
O6 A11 30(pf) blue & car .60 .60
O7 A11 40(pf) grn & car .25 .25
O8 A11 50(pf) dk grn & car .25 .25
O9 A11 60(pf) carmine .25 .25
O10 A11 75(pf) dp vio .25 *.40*
O11 A11 80(pf) black & car .85 .85
O12 A11 80(pf) green .25 *2.40*

Paper With Faint Gray Network

O14 A11 1m org & car .25 .25
O15 A11 1.20m blue violet 1.25 1.25
O16 A11 1.25m vio & car .25 *.40*
O17 A11 1.50m slate gray .25 *.40*
O18 A11 2m gray & car 16.00 12.00
a. Inverted overprint 110.00
Never hinged 250.00
O19 A11 2m car rose .25 *.40*
O20 A11 2.40m dk brn & car 1.25 *2.40*
O21 A11 3m violet & car 8.50 *10.00*
O22 A11 3m car lake .25 *.40*
O23 A11 4m dk blue 1.25 .85
O24 A11 5m dp grn .25 *.40*
O25 A11 6m car lake .25 *.40*
O26 A11 10m orange .25 *.40*
O27 A11 20m org brn .25 *.40*
Nos. O1-O27 (26) 34.45 *36.20*
Set, never hinged 175.00

Double overprints exist on Nos. O1-O2, O5-O7, O10 and O12.

Same Overprint on No. 96

O28 A11 6m on 3m .35 *.75*
Never hinged 1.00
a. Inverted overprint 30.00
Never hinged 85.00

No. 77 Overprinted

Serrate Roulette 13½

1922 **Wmk. 108 Sideways**

O29 A12 5m grn, red & blk 3.75 *6.00*
Never hinged 18.00

Nos. 99-103, 106-107 Overprinted Type "a"

1922-23 **Wmk. 109** ***Perf. 14***

O30 A11 4m dark blue .25 *.60*
O31 A11 5m dark green .25 *.60*
O32 A11 10m orange .25 *.60*
O33 A11 20m orange brn .25 *.60*
O34 A15 50m pale blue & red .25 *.60*
O35 A15a 100m dk grn & red .25 *.60*

Nos. 113-115, 118-120 Overprinted Type "a"

O36 A15 50m pale blue .25 *.75*
a. Inverted overprint 25.00
Never hinged 62.50
O37 A15a 100m dark green .25 *.75*
O38 A15 200m orange .25 *.75*
a. Inverted overprint 25.00
Never hinged 62.50

Paper With Gray Network

O39 A17 300m bl grn & red .25 *.60*
O40 A17 500m gray & red .25 *.75*
O41 A17 1000m brn & red .25 *.75*
Nos. O30-O41 (12) 3.00 *7.95*
Set, never hinged 16.80

Regular Issue of 1924-25 Overprinted

1924-25			Perf. 14x14½	
O42	A19	5pf red orange	2.10	*3.25*
O43	A19	10pf green	2.10	*9.00*
O44	A19	15pf gray	2.10	3.25
O45	A19	15pf red	19.00	10.00
O46	A19	20pf car & red	2.10	2.10
O47	A19	25pf slate & red	19.00	27.50
O48	A19	30pf green & red	3.00	*3.75*
O49	A19	35pf ultra	60.00	50.00
O50	A19	40pf dk bl & dull bl	7.00	*8.50*
O51	A19	50pf dp blue & red	21.00	*42.50*
O52	A19	75pf violet & red	42.50	*120.00*
		Nos. O42-O52 (11)	179.90	279.85
		Set, never hinged	640.00	

Double overprints exist on Nos. O42-O44, O47, O50-O52.

DENMARK

'den-,märk

LOCATION — Northern part of a peninsula which separates the North and Baltic Seas, and includes the surrounding islands
GOVT. — Kingdom
AREA — 16,631 sq. mi.
POP. — 5,294,860 (1/1/1999)
CAPITAL — Copenhagen

96 Skilling = 1 Rigsbank Daler
100 Ore = 1 Krone (1875)

Catalogue values for unused stamps in this country are for Never Hinged items, beginning with Scott 297 in the regular postage section, Scott B15 in the semi-postal section, and Scott Q28 in the parcel post section.

Values for unused stamps are for examples with original gum as defined in the catalogue introduction. Very fine examples of Nos. 9-37 and O1-O9 will have perforations clear of the framelines but with the design noticeably off center. Well centered stamps are quite scarce and will command substantial premiums.

Watermarks

Wmk. 111 — Small Crown

Wmk. 112 — Crown

Wmk. 113 — Crown

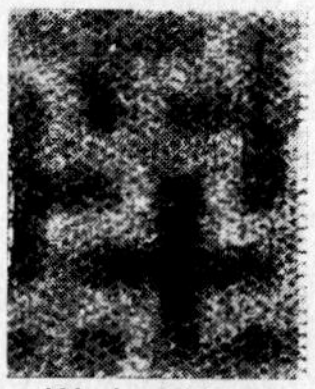

Wmk. 114 — Multiple Crosses

A1

Royal Emblems — A2

1851	Typo.	Wmk. 111	Imperf.	
		With Yellow Brown Burelage		
1	A1	2rs blue	*3,500.*	1,000.
a.		First printing	*8,250.*	*2,400.*
2	A2	4rs brown	600.00	40.00
a.		First printing	600.00	40.00
b.		4rs yellow brown	875.00	55.00

The first printing of Nos. 1 and 2 had the burelage printed from a copper plate, giving a clear impression with the lines in slight relief. The subsequent impressions had the burelage typographed, with the lines fainter and not rising above the surface of the paper.

Nos. 1-2 were reprinted in 1885 and 1901 on heavy yellowish paper, unwatermarked and imperforate, with a brown burelage. No. 1 was also reprinted without burelage, on both yellowish and white paper. Value for least costly reprint of No. 1, $50.

No. 2 was reprinted in 1951 in 10 shades with "Colour Specimen 1951" printed on the back. It was also reprinted in 1961 in 2 shades without burelage and with "Farve Nytryk 1961" printed on the back. Value for least costly reprint of No. 2, $8.50.

Dotting in Spandrels
A3

Wavy Lines in Spandrels
A4

1854-57				
3	A3	2s blue ('55)	75.00	60.00
4	A3	4s brown	325.00	15.00
a.		4s yellow brown	350.00	15.00
5	A3	8s green ('57)	300.00	67.50
a.		8s yellow green	300.00	80.00
6	A3	16s gray lilac ('57)	525.00	190.00
		Nos. 3-6 (4)	1,225.	332.50

See No. 10. For denominations in cents see Danish West Indies Nos. 1-4.

1858-62				
7	A4	4s yellow brown	65.00	8.50
a.		4s brown	67.50	8.00
b.		Wmk. 112 ('62)	62.50	9.00
8	A4	8s green	800.00	82.50

Nos. 2 to 8 inclusive are known with unofficial perforation 12 or 13, and Nos. 4, 5, 7 and 8 with unofficial roulette 9½.

Nos. 3, 6-8 were reprinted in 1885 on heavy yellowish paper, unwatermarked, imperforate and without burelage. Nos. 4-5 were reprinted in 1924 on white paper, unwatermarked, imperforate, gummed and without burelage. Value for No. 3, $15; Nos. 4-5, each $110; No. 6, $20; Nos. 7-8, each $15.

1863		Wmk. 112	Rouletted 11	
9	A4	4s brown	100.00	15.00
a.		4s deep brown	100.00	15.00
10	A3	16s violet	1,400.	650.00

Royal Emblems — A5

1864-68			Perf. 13	
11	A5	2s blue ('65)	65.00	35.00
12	A5	3s red vio ('65)	80.00	75.00
13	A5	4s red	40.00	8.00
14	A5	8s bister ('68)	275.00	95.00
15	A5	16s olive green	475.00	175.00
		Nos. 11-15 (5)	935.00	388.00

Nos. 11-15 were reprinted in 1886 on heavy yellowish paper, unwatermarked, imperforate and without gum. The reprints of all values except the 4s were printed in two vertical rows of six, inverted with respect to each other, so that horizontal pairs are always tête bêche. Value $12 each.

Nos. 13 and 15 were reprinted in 1942 with printing on the back across each horizontal row: "Nytryk 1942. G. A. Hagemann: Danmarks og Vestindiens Frimaerker, Bind 2." Value, $70 each.

Imperf, single

11a	A5	2s blue	95.00	95.00
12a	A5	3s red violet	140.00	
13a	A5	4s red	77.50	90.00
14a	A5	8s bister	375.00	
15a	A5	16s olive green	450.00	

1870			Perf. 12½	
11b	A5	2s blue	275.00	350.00
12b	A5	3s red violet	475.00	650.00
14b	A5	8s bister	475.00	475.00
15b	A5	16s olive green	725.00	*1,450.*
		Nos. 11b-15b (4)	1,950.	2,925.

A6

Normal Frame

Inverted Frame

The arabesques in the corners have a main stem and a branch. When the frame is in normal position, in the upper left corner the branch leaves the main stem half way between two little leaflets. In the lower right corner the branch starts at the foot of the second leaflet. When the frame is inverted the corner designs are, of course, transposed.

1870-71		Wmk. 112	Perf. 14x13½	
		Paper Varying from Thin to Thick		
16	A6	2s gray & ultra ('71)	70.00	27.50
a.		2s gray & blue	70.00	27.50
17	A6	3s gray & brt lil ('71)	100.00	110.00
18	A6	4s gray & car	40.00	10.00
19	A6	8s gray & brn ('71)	200.00	75.00
20	A6	16s gray & grn ('71)	275.00	175.00
		Perf. 12½		
21	A6	2s gray & bl ('71)	2,000.	*3,250.*
22	A6	4s gray & car	150.00	125.00
24	A6	48s brn & lilac	450.00	275.00

Nos. 16-20, 24 were reprinted in 1886 on thin white paper, unwatermarked, imperforate and without gum. These were printed in sheets of 10 in which 1 stamp has the normal frame (value $32.50 each) and 9 the inverted (value $11 each).

Imperf, single

16b	A6	2s	*250.*	
17a	A6	3s	*240.*	
18a	A6	4s	*200.*	
19a	A6	8s	*250.*	
20a	A6	16s	*400.*	
24a	A6	48s	*425.*	—

Inverted Frame

16c	A6	2s	1,000.	775.
17b	A6	3s	2,500.	2,000.
18b	A6	4s	775.	87.50
19b	A6	8s	1,750.	900.
20b	A6	16s	2,000.	1,750.
24b	A6	48s	2,750.	1,900.

1875-79			Perf. 14x13½	
25	A6	3o gray blue & gray	18.00	15.00
a.		1st "A" of "DANMARK" missing	60.00	150.00
b.		Imperf	*750.00*	
c.		Inverted frame	18.00	16.00
26	A6	4o slate & blue	25.00	.50
a.		4o gray & blue	25.00	1.10
b.		4o slate & ultra	90.00	17.00
c.		4o gray & ultra	75.00	16.00
d.		Imperf	75.00	—
e.		As #26, inverted frame	25.00	.50
27	A6	5o rose & blue ('79)	30.00	72.50
a.		Ball of lower curve of large "5" missing	125.00	300.00
b.		Inverted frame	1,000.	*2,250.*
28	A6	8o slate & car	22.50	.50
a.		8o gray & carmine	75.00	5.00
b.		Imperf	150.00	—
c.		Inverted frame	22.50	.50
29	A6	12o sl & dull lake	10.00	4.00
a.		12o gray & bright lilac	65.00	8.00
b.		12o gray & dull magenta	72.50	10.00
c.		Inverted frame	14.00	4.00
30	A6	16o slate & brn	77.50	6.50
a.		16o light gray & brown	77.50	17.00
b.		Inverted frame	52.50	4.50
31	A6	20o rose & gray	90.00	32.50
a.		20o carmine & gray	90.00	32.50
b.		Inverted frame	90.00	32.50
32	A6	25o gray & green	65.00	40.00
a.		Inverted frame	77.50	62.50
33	A6	50o brown & vio	70.00	37.50
a.		50o brown & blue violet	400.00	175.00
b.		Inverted frame	70.00	32.50
34	A6	100o gray & org ('77)	110.00	60.00
a.		Imperf, single	375.00	
b.		Inverted frame	150.00	60.00
		Nos. 25-34 (10)	518.00	269.00
		Set, never hinged	1,625.	

The stamps of this issue on thin semi-transparent paper are far scarcer than those on thicker paper.

See Nos. 41-42, 44, 46-47, 50-52. For surcharges see Nos. 55, 79-80, 136.

Arms — A7

Two types of numerals in corners

Small Numerals

Large Numerals

1882				
		Small Corner Numerals		
35	A7	5o green	240.00	100.00
		Never hinged	725.00	
37	A7	20o blue	190.00	70.00
		Never hinged	650.00	

1884-88				
		Larger Corner Numerals		
38	A7	5o green	15.00	3.50
a.		Imperf	—	
39	A7	10o carmine ('85)	16.00	2.50
a.		Small numerals in corners ('88)	550.00	*725.00*
b.		Imperf, single	175.00	
c.		Pair, Nos. 39, 39a	600.00	*875.00*
40	A7	20o blue	30.00	5.00
a.		Pair, Nos. 37, 40	400.00	*875.00*
b.		Imperf	—	
		Nos. 38-40 (3)	61.00	11.00
		Set, never hinged	285.00	

Stamps with large corner numerals have white line around crown and lower oval touches frame.

The plate for No. 39, was damaged and 3 clichés in the bottom row were replaced by clichés for post cards, which had small numerals in the corners.

Two clichés with small numerals were inserted in the plate of No. 40.

See Nos. 43, 45, 48-49, 53-54. For surcharge see No. 56.

1895-1901		Wmk. 112	Perf. 13	
41	A6	3o blue & gray	10.00	7.25
42	A6	4o slate & bl ('96)	4.50	.40
43	A7	5o green	12.00	.75
44	A6	8o slate & car	4.50	.45
45	A7	10o rose car	24.00	.65
46	A6	12o sl & dull lake	7.00	4.00
47	A6	16o slate & brown	19.00	4.50
48	A7	20o blue	30.00	2.40
49	A7	24o brown ('01)	7.00	6.00
50	A6	25o gray & grn ('98)	110.00	19.50
51	A6	50o brown & vio ('97)	60.00	24.00
52	A6	100o slate & org	90.00	35.00
		Nos. 41-52 (12)	378.00	104.90
		Set, never hinged	875.00	

Inverted Frame

41b	A6	3o	12.00	7.00
42a	A6	4o	4.50	.45
44a	A6	8o	4.50	.50
46a	A6	12o	14.00	4.50
47a	A6	16o	30.00	5.00
50a	A6	25o	60.00	27.50
51a	A6	50o	95.00	32.50
52a	A6	100o	90.00	57.50
		Nos. 41b-52a (8)	310.00	134.95
		Set, never hinged	635.00	

1902-04			Wmk. 113	
41c	A6	3o blue & gray	2.75	3.00
42b	A6	4o slate & blue	17.00	20.00
43a	A7	5o green	2.00	.25
44d	A6	8o slate & carmine	525.00	425.00
45a	A7	10o rose carmine	3.00	.25
48a	A7	20o blue	20.00	4.75
50b	A6	25o gray & green	10.50	4.50
51b	A6	50o brown & violet	27.50	20.00
52b	A6	100o slate & orange	30.00	15.00
		Nos. 41c-52b (9)	637.75	492.75
		Set, never hinged	1,325.	

Inverted Frame

41d	A6	3o	75.00	130.00
42c	A6	4o	140.00	130.00
50c	A6	25o	210.00	60.00
51c	A6	50o	260.00	240.00
52c	A6	100o	225.00	240.00
		Nos. 41d-52c (5)	910.00	800.00
		Set, never hinged	2,500.	

1902 **Wmk. 113**
53 A7 1o orange .75 .65
a. Imperf — —
54 A7 15o lilac 11.00 .75
a. Imperf, single 4,250.

Nos. 44d, 44, 49 Surcharged

a

b

1904-12 **Wmk. 113**
55 A6(a) 4o on 8o sl & car 3.50 4.00
a. Wmk. 112 ('12) 21.00 60.00
Never hinged 42.50
b. As "a," inverted frame — 6,000.

Wmk. 112
56 A7(b) 15o on 24o brown 5.75 17.50
a. Short "15" at right 27.50 105.00
Never hinged 60.00
Set, never hinged 16.00

A10

1905-17 **Wmk. 113** ***Perf. 13***
57 A10 1o orange ('06) 2.25 .75
58 A10 2o carmine 4.75 .40
a. Perf. 14x14½ ('17) 3.75 19.00
59 A10 3o gray 9.75 .65
60 A10 4o dull blue 7.00 .60
a. Perf. 14x14½ ('17) 11.00 37.50
61 A10 5o dp green ('12) 5.25 .35
62 A10 10o dp rose ('12) 6.75 .35
63 A10 15o lilac 25.00 2.25
64 A10 20o dk blue ('12) 35.00 .90
Nos. 57-64 (8) 95.75 6.25
Set, never hinged 310.00

The three wavy lines in design A10 are symbolical of the three waters which separate the principal Danish islands.

See Nos. 85-96, 1338-1342A, 1468-1473. For surcharges and overprints see Nos. 163, 181, J1, J38, Q1-Q2.

King Christian IX
A11

King Frederik VIII
A12

1904-05 **Engr.**
65 A11 10o scarlet 4.00 .65
66 A11 20o blue 22.50 3.00
67 A11 25o brown ('05) 27.50 8.00
68 A11 50o dull vio ('05) 110.00 120.00
69 A11 100o ocher ('05) 13.00 60.00
Nos. 65-69 (5) 177.00 191.65
Set, never hinged 565.00

1905-06 **Re-engraved**
70 A11 5o green 4.50 .35
71 A11 10o scarlet ('06) 21.00 .60
Set, never hinged 56.00

The re-engraved stamps are much clearer than the originals, and the decoration on the king's left breast has been removed.

1907-12
72 A12 5o green 1.75 .40
a. Imperf. —
73 A12 10o red 4.25 .40
a. Imperf. —
74 A12 20o indigo 19.00 .65
a. 20o bright blue ('11) 40.00 2.75
75 A12 25o olive brn 35.00 1.25
76 A12 35o dp org ('12) 6.00 10.00
77 A12 50o claret 35.00 7.00
78 A12 100o bister brn 100.00 5.00
Nos. 72-78 (7) 201.00 24.70
Set, never hinged 525.00

Nos. 47, 31 and O9 Surcharged

c

d

Dark Blue Surcharge

1912 **Wmk. 112** ***Perf. 13***
79 A6(c) 35o on 16o 17.00 50.00
a. Inverted frame 325.00 625.00

Perf. 14x13½
80 A6(c) 35o on 20o 30.00 85.00
a. Inverted frame 130.00 325.00

Black Surcharge
81 O1(d) 35o on 32o 42.50 120.00
Nos. 79-81 (3) 89.50 255.00
Set, never hinged 185.00

General Post Office, Copenhagen — A15

1912 **Engr.** **Wmk. 113** ***Perf. 13***
82 A15 5k dark red 500.00 200.00
Never hinged 1,500.

See Nos. 135, 843.

Perf. 14x14½
1913-30 **Typo.** **Wmk. 114**
85 A10 1o dp orange ('14) .40 .45
a. Bklt. pane, 2 ea #85, 91 + 2 labels 20.00
86 A10 2o car ('13) 3.75 .35
a. Imperf 150.00 300.00
b. Booklet pane, 4 + 2 labels 27.50
87 A10 3o gray ('13) 6.75 .40
88 A10 4o blue ('13) 8.00 .45
a. Half used as 2o on cover 1,250.
89 A10 5o dk brown ('21) .75 .35
a. Imperf 190.00
b. Booklet pane, 4 + 2 labels 14.00
90 A10 5o lt green ('30) 1.50 .40
a. Booklet pane, 4 + 2 labels 16.00
b. Booklet pane of 50
91 A10 7o apple grn ('26) 5.75 7.25
a. Booklet pane, 4 + 2 labels 20.00
92 A10 7o dk violet ('30) 16.00 6.50
93 A10 8o gray ('21) 7.00 3.25
94 A10 10o green ('21) .85 .35
a. Imperf 225.00
b. Booklet pane, 4 + 2 labels 37.50
95 A10 10o bister brn ('30) 2.25 .35
a. Booklet pane, 4 + 2 labels 16.00
b. Booklet pane of 50
96 A10 12o violet ('26) 25.00 9.75
Nos. 85-96 (12) 78.00 29.85
Set, never hinged 200.00

No. 88a was used with No. 97 in Faroe Islands, Jan. 3-23, 1919.

See surcharge and overprint note following No. 64.

King Christian X
A16 A17

1913-28 **Typo.** ***Perf. 14x14½***
97 A16 5o green 1.40 .35
a. Bklt. pane of 4, with P# 400.00
98 A16 7o orange ('18) 2.25 2.75
99 A16 8o dk gray ('20) 14.00 6.50
100 A16 10o red 2.40 .40
a. Imperf 300.00
b. Bklt. pane of 4, with P# 500.00
101 A16 12o gray grn ('18) 7.50 10.00
102 A16 15o violet 3.25 .40
103 A16 20o dp blue 13.00 .35
104 A16 20o brown ('21) 1.25 .40
105 A16 20o red ('26) 1.50 .40
106 A16 25o dk brown 13.50 .50
107 A16 25o brn & blk ('20) 85.00 8.75
108 A16 25o red ('22) 4.25 .95
109 A16 25o yel grn ('25) 3.00 .50
110 A16 27o ver & blk ('18) 30.00 50.00
111 A16 30o green & blk ('18) 35.00 3.25
112 A16 30o orange ('21) 3.00 2.00
113 A16 30o dk blue ('25) 1.75 1.00
114 A16 35o orange 29.00 7.50
115 A16 35o yel & blk ('19) 9.00 6.50
116 A16 40o vio & blk ('18) 18.00 4.00
117 A16 40o gray bl & blk ('20) 37.50 7.50
118 A16 40o dk blue ('22) 6.00 1.60
119 A16 40o orange ('25) 1.50 1.50
120 A16 50o claret 37.50 5.75
121 A16 50o claret & blk ('19) 75.00 2.50
122 A16 50o lt gray ('22) 9.25 .40
a. 50o olive gray ('21) 75.00 8.00
Never hinged 210.00
123 A16 60o brn & bl ('19) 60.00 3.75
a. 60o brown & ultra ('19) 225.00 12.50
Never hinged 750.00
124 A16 60o grn bl ('21) 9.00 .75
125 A16 70o brn & grn ('20) 26.00 2.25
126 A16 80o bl grn ('15) 50.00 22.50
127 A16 90o brn & red ('20) 18.00 3.25
128 A16 1k brn & bl ('22) 75.00 3.00
129 A16 2k gray & cl ('25) 67.50 15.00
130 A16 5k vio & brn ('27) 7.00 5.75
131 A16 10k ver & yel grn ('28) 325.00 65.00
Nos. 97-131 (35) 1,082. 247.00
Set, never hinged 3,085.

No. 97 surcharged "2 ORE" is Faroe Islands No. 1. Two of the 14 printings of No. 97a have no P# in the selvage. These sell for more.

Nos. 87 and 98, 89 and 94, 89 and 104, 90 and 95, 97 and 103, 100 and 102 exist se-tenant in coils for use in vending machines.

For surcharges and overprints see Nos. 161-162, 176-177, 182-184, J2-J8, M1-M2, Q3-Q10.

1913-20 **Engr.**
132 A17 1k yellow brown 95.00 1.25
133 A17 2k gray 150.00 7.00
134 A17 5k purple ('20) 15.00 10.00
Nos. 132-134 (3) 260.00 18.25
Set, never hinged 940.00

For overprint see No. Q11.

G.P.O. Type of 1912
Perf. 14x14½
1915 **Wmk. 114** **Engr.**
135 A15 5k dark red ('15) 500.00 175.00
Never hinged 1,500.

Nos. 46 and O10 Surcharged in Black type "c" and

e

1915 **Wmk. 112** **Typo.** ***Perf. 13***
136 A6 (c) 80o on 12o 40.00 100.00
a. Inverted frame 600.00 1,100.
Never hinged 825.00
137 O1 (e) 80o on 8o 47.50 140.00
a. "POSTERIM" 95.00 325.00
Never hinged 140.00
Set, never hinged 155.00

Newspaper Stamps Surcharged

On Issue of 1907

1918 **Wmk. 113** ***Perf. 13***
138 N1 27o on 1o olive 105.00 325.00
139 N1 27o on 5o blue 105.00 325.00
140 N1 27o on 7o car 105.00 325.00
141 N1 27o on 10o dp lil 105.00 325.00
142 N1 27o on 68o yel brn 7.50 37.50
143 N1 27o on 5k rose & yel grn 6.75 26.00
144 N1 27o on 10k bis & bl 7.50 35.00
Nos. 138-144 (7) 441.75 1,398.
Set, never hinged 940.00

On Issue of 1914-15
Wmk. Multiple Crosses (114)
Perf. 14x14½
145 N1 27o on 1o ol gray 5.00 15.50
146 N1 27o on 5o blue 7.50 30.00
147 N1 27o on 7o rose 5.00 12.50
148 N1 27o on 8o green 7.50 16.00
149 N1 27o on 10o dp lil 3.25 17.00
150 N1 27o on 20o green 8.00 16.50
151 N1 27o on 29o org yel 3.25 14.50
152 N1 27o on 38o orange 32.50 110.00
153 N1 27o on 41o yel brn 7.50 45.00
154 N1 27o on 1k bl grn & mar 5.00 14.50
Nos. 145-154 (10) 84.50 291.50
Set, never hinged 150.00

Kronborg Castle — A20

Sonderborg Castle — A21

Roskilde Cathedral — A22

Perf. 14½x14, 14x14½
1920, Oct. 5 **Typo.**
156 A20 10o red 7.00 .50
157 A21 20o slate 5.00 .50
158 A22 40o dark brown 17.00 4.50
Nos. 156-158 (3) 29.00 5.50
Set, never hinged 52.00

Reunion of Northern Schleswig with Denmark.

See Nos. 159-160. For surcharges see Nos. B1-B2.

1921
159 A20 10o green 9.00 .55
160 A22 40o dark blue 67.50 11.50
Set, never hinged 174.00

Stamps of 1918 Surcharged in Blue

1921-22

161 A16 8o on 7o org ('22) 2.25 *5.00*
162 A16 8o on 12o gray grn 2.25 *15.00*
Set, never hinged 15.75

No. 87 Surcharged

1921

163 A10 8o on 3o gray 3.75 *5.25*
Never hinged 8.25

Christian X
A23

Christian IV
A24

A25

A26

1924, Dec. 1 ***Perf. 14x14½***

164 A23 10o green 7.50 *7.00*
165 A24 10o green 7.50 *7.00*
166 A25 10o green 7.50 *7.00*
167 A26 10o green 7.50 *7.00*
a. Block of 4, #164-167 37.50 *50.00*
168 A23 15o violet 7.50 *7.00*
169 A24 15o violet 7.50 *7.00*
170 A25 15o violet 7.50 *7.00*
171 A26 15o violet 7.50 *7.00*
a. Block of 4, #168-171 37.50 *50.00*
172 A23 20o dark brown 7.50 *7.00*
173 A24 20o dark brown 7.50 *7.00*
174 A25 20o dark brown 7.50 *7.00*
175 A26 20o dark brown 7.50 *7.00*
a. Block of 4, #172-175 37.50 *50.00*
Nos. 164-175 (12) 90.00 84.00
Set, never hinged 180.00
#167a, 171a, 175a, never hinged 225.00

300th anniv. of the Danish postal service.

Stamps of 1921-22 Surcharged

k

l

1926

176 A16 (k) 20o on 30o org 6.75 *15.00*
177 A16 (l) 20o on 40o dk bl 9.00 *18.00*
Set, never hinged 31.00

A27

A28

1926, Mar. 11 ***Perf. 14x14½***

178 A27 10o dull green 1.50 .45
179 A28 20o dark red 2.00 .45
180 A28 30o dark blue 8.50 1.50
Nos. 178-180 (3) 12.00 2.40
Set, never hinged 24.50

75th anniv. of the introduction of postage stamps in Denmark.

Stamps of 1913-26 Surcharged in Blue or Black

No. 181

Nos. 182-184

1926-27 ***Perf. 14x14½***

181 A10 7o on 8o gray (Bl) 1.50 *4.75*
182 A16 7o on 27o ver & blk 4.50 *17.00*
183 A16 7o on 20o red ('27) .75 *2.50*
184 A16 12o on 15o violet 2.25 *6.00*

Surcharged on Official Stamps of 1914-23

185 O1 (e) 7o on 1o org 4.00 *16.00*
186 O1 (e) 7o on 3o gray 7.50 *32.50*
187 O1 (e) 7o on 4o blue 3.75 *7.75*
188 O1 (e) 7o on 5o grn 52.50 *150.00*
189 O1 (e) 7o on 10o grn 4.50 *15.50*
190 O1 (e) 7o on 15o vio 4.50 *15.50*
191 O1 (e) 7o on 20o ind 19.00 *77.50*
a. Double surcharge *750.00* *975.00*
Nos. 181-191 (11) 104.75 *345.00*
Set, never hinged 155.00

Caravel
A30

Christian X
A31

1927 **Typo.** ***Perf. 14x14½***

192 A30 15o red 6.00 .40
193 A30 20o gray 11.00 2.40
194 A30 25o light blue 1.25 .40
195 A30 30o ocher 1.25 .40
196 A30 35o red brown 25.00 1.50
197 A30 40o yel green 25.00 .40
Nos. 192-197 (6) 69.50 5.50
Set, never hinged 200.00

See Nos. 232-238J. For surcharges & overprints see Nos. 244-245, 269-272, Q12-Q14, Q19-Q25.

1930, Sept. 26

210 A31 5o apple grn 2.50 .35
a. Booklet pane, 4 + 2 labels 18.00
211 A31 7o violet 6.75 3.00
212 A31 8o dk gray 22.50 32.50
213 A31 10o yel brn 5.00 .35
a. Booklet pane, 4 + 2 labels 29.00
214 A31 15o red 10.00 .35
215 A31 20o lt gray 25.00 9.75
216 A31 25o lt blue 8.50 1.25
217 A31 30o yel buff 9.00 1.75
218 A31 35o red brown 12.00 4.50
219 A31 40o dp green 10.00 1.25
Nos. 210-219 (10) 111.25 55.05
Set, never hinged 295.00

60th birthday of King Christian X.

Wavy Lines and Numeral of Value — A32

Type A10 Redrawn

1933-40 **Unwmk.** **Engr.** ***Perf. 13***

220 A32 1o gray blk .45 .30
221 A32 2o scarlet .35 .30
222 A32 4o blue .40 .35
223 A32 5o yel grn 1.00 .35
a. 5o gray green 37.50 *60.00*
b. Tête bêche gutter pair 8.00 *15.50*
c. Booklet pane of 4 11.00
d. Bklt. pane, 1 #223a, 3 #B6 37.50 70.00
Never hinged 60.00
e. As "b," without gutter 17.50 *27.50*
224 A32 5o rose lake ('38) .30 .30
a. Booklet pane of 4 1.20
b. Booklet pane of 10 12.00
224C A32 6o orange ('40) .30 .30
225 A32 7o violet 2.00 .35
226 A32 7o yel grn ('38) 1.10 .45
226A A32 7o lt brown ('40) .35 .35
227 A32 8o gray .45 .50
227A A32 8o yellow grn ('40) .30 .35
228 A32 10o yellow org 12.50 .35
a. Tête bêche gutter pair 50.00 55.00
b. Booklet pane of 4 110.00
c. As "a," without gutter 60.00 *70.00*
Never hinged 100.00
229 A32 10o lt brown ('37) 9.50 .35
a. Booklet pane of 4 100.00
b. Booklet pane of 4, 1 #229, 3 #B7 32.50 45.00

230 A32 10o violet ('38) .75 .35
a. Booklet pane of 4 2.75
b. Bklt. pane, 2 #230, 2 #B10 2.50 7.00
Never hinged 6.00
Nos. 220-230 (14) 29.75 4.95
Set, never hinged 75.00

Design A10 was typographed. They had a solid background with groups of small hearts below the heraldic lions in the upper corners and below "DA" and "RK" of "DANMARK." The numerals of value were enclosed in single-lined ovals.

Design A32 is line-engraved and has a background of crossed lines. The hearts have been removed and the numerals of value are now in double-lined ovals. Two types exist of some values.

The 1ö, No. 220, was issued on fluorescent paper in 1969.

No. 230 with wide margins is from booklet pane No. 230b.

Surcharges of 20, 50 & 60öre on #220, 224 and 224C are listed as Faroe Islands #2-3, 5-6.

See Nos. 318, 333, 382, 416, 437-437A, 493-498, 629, 631, 688-695, 793-795, 883-886, 1111-1113, 1116. For overprints and surcharges see Nos. 257, 263, 267-268, 355-356, Q15-Q17, Q31, Q43.

Certain Tête-Bêche pairs of 1938-55 issues which reached the market in 1971, and were not regularly issued, are not listed. This group comprises 24 different major-number vertical pairs of types A32, A47, A61 and SP3 (13 with gutters, 11 without), and pairs of some minor numbers and shades. They were removed from booklet pane sheets.

Type of 1927 Issue
Type I

Type I — Two columns of squares between sail and left frame line.

1933-34 **Engr.** ***Perf. 13***

232 A30 20o gray 15.00 .35
233 A30 25o blue 85.00 30.00
234 A30 25o brown ('34) 30.00 .35
235 A30 30o orange yel 1.50 1.40
236 A30 30o blue ('34) 1.50 .40
237 A30 35o violet .60 .35
238 A30 40o yellow grn 6.25 .35
Nos. 232-238 (7) 139.85 33.20
Set, never hinged 325.00

Type II

Type II — One column of squares between sail and left frame line.

1933-40

238A A30 15o deep red 3.00 .35
k. Booklet pane of 4 26.00
l. Bklt. pane, 1 #238A, 3 #B8 45.00
Never hinged 115.00
238B A30 15o yel grn ('40) 9.00 .40
238C A30 20o gray blk ('39) 4.50 .70
238D A30 20o red ('40) .90 .35
238E A30 25o dp brown ('39) .90 .35
238F A30 30o blue ('39) 2.25 .70
238G A30 30o orange ('40) .75 .35
238H A30 35o violet ('40) 1.00 .35
238I A30 40o yel grn ('39) 15.00 .35
238J A30 40o blue ('40) 1.40 .35
Nos. 238A-238J (10) 38.70 4.25
Set, never hinged 95.00

Nos. 232-238J, engraved, have crosshatched background. Nos. 192-197, typographed, have solid background.

For No. 238A surcharged 20 ore see Denmark No. 271, Faroe Islands No. 4.

See note on surcharges and overprints following No. 197.

King Christian X — A33

1934-41 ***Perf. 13***

239 A33 50o gray 1.20 .30
240 A33 60o blue grn 2.40 .35
240A A33 75o dk blue ('41) .45 .35
241 A33 1k lt brown 3.75 .35
242 A33 2k dull red 6.00 1.00
243 A33 5k violet 9.00 3.50
Nos. 239-243 (6) 22.80 5.85
Set, never hinged 75.00

For overprints see Nos. Q26-Q27.

Nos. 233, 235 Surcharged in Black

1934, June 9

244 A30 4o on 25o blue .50 .50
245 A30 10o on 30o org yel 2.40 *3.25*
Set, never hinged 7.50

"The Ugly Duckling"
A34

Andersen
A35

"The Little Mermaid" — A36

1935, Oct. 1 ***Perf. 13***

246 A34 5o lt green 3.00 .30
a. Tête bêche gutter pair 15.00 *22.50*
b. Booklet pane of 4 40.00
c. As "a," without gutter 17.00 *21.00*
Never hinged 45.00
247 A35 7o dull vio 2.50 *2.50*
248 A36 10o orange 4.50 .30
a. Tête bêche gutter pair 18.00 *32.50*
b. Booklet pane of 4 65.00
c. As "a," without gutter 20.00 *40.00*
Never hinged 65.00
249 A35 15o red 11.00 .30
a. Tête bêche gutter pair 45.00 *52.50*
b. Booklet pane of 4 160.00
c. As "a," without gutter 42.50 *75.00*
Never hinged 110.00
250 A35 20o gray 9.50 1.25
251 A35 30o dl bl 3.00 .35
Nos. 246-251 (6) 33.50 *5.00*
Set, never hinged 87.50

Centenary of the publication of the earliest installment of Hans Christian Andersen's "Fairy Tales."

Nikolai Church
A37

Hans Tausen
A38

Ribe Cathedral — A39

1936 ***Perf. 13***

252 A37 5o green 1.40 .40
a. Booklet pane of 4 21.00
253 A37 7o violet 2.00 *4.50*
254 A38 10o lt brown 2.00 .40
a. Booklet pane of 4 25.00
255 A38 15o dull rose 3.00 .30
256 A39 30o blue 16.00 1.40
Nos. 252-256 (5) 24.40 7.00
Set, never hinged 62.50

Church Reformation in Denmark, 400th anniv.

No. 229 Overprinted in Blue

1937, Sept. 17

257 A32 10o lt brown 1.50 *1.60*
Never hinged 2.00

Jubilee Exhib. held by the Copenhagen Phil. Club on their 50th anniv. The stamps were on sale at the Exhib. only, each holder of a ticket of admission (1k) being entitled to purchase 20 stamps at face value; of a season ticket (5k), 100 stamps.

Yacht and Summer Palace, Marselisborg
A40

Christian X in Streets of Copenhagen
A41

Equestrian Statue of Frederik V and Amalienborg Palace — A42

1937, May 15 *Perf. 13*

258 A40 5o green	1.40	.30
a. Booklet pane of 4	15.00	
259 A41 10o brown	1.40	.30
a. Booklet pane of 4	15.00	
260 A42 15o scarlet	1.40	.30
a. Booklet pane of 4	17.00	
261 A41 30o blue	15.00	2.40
Nos. 258-261 (4)	19.20	3.30
Set, never hinged	42.50	

25th anniv. of the accession to the throne of King Christian X.

Emancipation Column, Copenhagen — A43

1938, June 20 *Perf. 13*

262 A43 15o scarlet	.60	.30
Never hinged	1.40	

Abolition of serfdom in Denmark, 150th anniv.

No. 223 Overprinted in Red on Alternate Stamps

1938, Sept. 2

263 A32 5o yellow grn, pair	3.25	*7.00*
Never hinged	4.50	

10th Danish Philatelic Exhibition.

Bertel Thorvaldsen
A44

Statue of Jason
A45

1938, Nov. 17 **Engr.** *Perf. 13*

264 A44 5o rose lake	.45	.30
265 A45 10o purple	.45	.30
266 A44 30o dark blue	1.50	.60
Nos. 264-266 (3)	2.40	1.20
Set, never hinged	5.25	

The return to Denmark in 1838 of Bertel Thorvaldsen, Danish sculptor.

Stamps of 1933-39 Surcharged with New Values in Black

a

b

c

1940

267 A32 (a) 6o on 7o yel grn	.30	*.35*
268 A32 (a) 6o on 8o gray	.45	*.35*
269 A30 (b) 15o on 40o #238	.90	*6.00*
270 A30 (b) 15o on 40o #238I	.75	*.95*
271 A30 (c) 20o on 15o dp red	1.10	.30
272 A30 (b) 40o on 30o #238F	1.00	.35
Nos. 267-272 (6)	4.50	*8.30*
Set, never hinged	9.25	

Bering's Ship — A46

1941, Nov. 27 **Engr.** *Perf. 13*

277 A46 10o dk violet	.35	.30
278 A46 20o red brown	.60	.30
279 A46 40o dk blue	.40	.35
Nos. 277-279 (3)	1.35	.95
Set, never hinged	3.00	

Death of Vitus Bering, explorer, 200th anniv.

King Christian X — A47

1942-46 **Unwmk.** *Perf. 13*

280 A47 10o violet	.30	.35
281 A47 15o yel grn	.35	.35
282 A47 20o red	.40	.35
283 A47 25o brown ('43)	.50	.45
284 A47 30o orange ('43)	.45	.35
285 A47 35o brt red vio ('44)	.40	.35
286 A47 40o blue ('43)	.40	.35
286A A47 45o ol brn ('46)	.35	.35
286B A47 50o gray ('45)	.60	.35
287 A47 60o bluish grn ('44)	.55	.35
287A A47 75o dk blue ('46)	.55	.35
Nos. 280-287A (11)	4.85	3.95
Set, never hinged	8.00	

For overprints see Nos. Q28-Q30.

Round Tower — A48

Condor Plane — A49

1942, Nov. 27

288 A48 10o violet	.35	.30
Never hinged	.75	

300th anniv. of the Round Tower, Copenhagen.

For surcharge see No. B14.

1943, Oct. 29

289 A49 20o red	.25	.25
Never hinged	.35	

25th anniv. of the Danish Aviation Company (Det Danske Luftfartsselskab).

Ejby Church — A50

15ö, Oesterlars Church. 20ö, Hvidbjerg Church.

1944 **Engr.** *Perf. 13*

290 A50 10o violet	.30	.25
291 A50 15o yellow grn	.30	.25
292 A50 20o red	.30	.25
Nos. 290-292 (3)	.90	.75
Set, never hinged	1.75	

Ole Roemer
A53

Christian X
A54

1944, Sept. 25

293 A53 20o henna brown	.35	.30
Never hinged	.65	

Birth of Ole Roemer, astronomer, 300th anniv.

1945, Sept. 26

294 A54 10o lilac	.25	.25
295 A54 20o red	.25	.25
296 A54 40o deep blue	.25	.25
Nos. 294-296 (3)	.75	.75
Set, never hinged	1.75	

75th birthday of King Christian X.

Catalogue values for unused stamps in this section, from this point to the end of the section, are for Never Hinged items.

Small State Seal — A55

Tycho Brahe — A56

1946-47 **Unwmk.** *Perf. 13*

297 A55 1k brown	1.00	.25
298 A55 2k red ('47)	2.40	.25
299 A55 5k dull blue	6.00	.25
Nos. 297-299 (3)	9.40	.75

Nos. 297-299 issued on ordinary and fluorescent paper. Values for ordinary paper are much higher.

See Nos. 395-400, 441A-444D, 499-506, 643-650, 716-720A, 804-815, 909, 1134-1138, 1304-1313, 1474-1478, 1508. For overprints see Nos. Q35, Q40, Q46-Q48.

1946, Dec. 14 **Engr.**

300 A56 20o dark red	.30	.25

Birth of Tycho Brahe, astronomer, 400th anniv.

First Danish Locomotive
A57

Modern Steam Locomotive
A58

Diesel Locomotive
A59

1947, June 27

301 A57 15o steel blue	.60	.35
302 A58 20o red	1.10	.35
303 A59 40o deep blue	3.50	2.25
Nos. 301-303 (3)	5.20	2.95

Inauguration of the Danish State Railways, cent.

Jacobsen
A60

Frederik IX
A61

1947, Nov. 10 *Perf. 13*

304 A60 20o dark red	.30	.25

60th anniv. of the death of Jacob Christian Jacobsen, founder of the Glyptothek Art Museum, Copenhagen.

1948-50 Unwmk. *Perf. 13*

Three types among 15ō, 20ō, 30ō:
I — Background of horizontal lines. No outline at left for cheek and ear. King's uniform textured in strong lines.
II — Background of vertical and horizontal lines. Contour of cheek and ear at left. Uniform same.
III — Background and facial contour lines as in II. Uniform lines double and thinner.

306 A61 15(o) green (II) 2.50 .30
a. Type III ('49) 1.60 .50
307 A61 20(o) dk red (I) 1.10 .25
a. Type III ('49) 1.40 .30
308 A61 25(o) lt brown 1.40 .25
309 A61 30(o) org (II) 13.00 .50
a. Type III ('50) 21.00 .50
310 A61 40(o) dl blue ('49) 4.75 1.00
311 A61 45(o) olive ('50) 2.10 .35
312 A61 50(o) gray ('49) 1.75 .30
313 A61 60(o) grnsh bl ('50) 2.50 .30
314 A61 75(o) lil rose ('50) 2.00 .30
Nos. 306-314 (9) 31.10 3.55

See Nos. 319-326, 334-341, 354. For surcharges see Nos. 357-358, 370, B20, B24-B25, Q32-Q34, Q36-Q39.

Legislative Assembly, 1849 — A62

1949, June 5
315 A62 20o red brown .35 .25

Adoption of the Danish constitution, cent.

Symbol of UPU — A63

1949, Oct. 9
316 A63 40o dull blue .65 .35

75th anniv. of the UPU.

Kalundborg Radio Station and Masts — A64

1950, Apr. 1 Engr. *Perf. 13*
317 A64 20o brown red .50 .25

Radio broadcasting in Denmark, 25th anniv.

Types of 1933-50

1950-51 Unwmk. *Perf. 13*
318 A32 10o green .30 .25
319 A61 15(o) lilac 1.00 .30
b. 15(o) gray lilac 4.00 .25
320 A61 20(o) lt brown 1.10 .30
321 A61 25(o) dark red 3.50 .25
322 A61 35(o) gray grn ('51) .95 .25
323 A61 40(o) gray .95 .25
324 A61 50(o) dark blue 3.25 .25
325 A61 55(o) brown ('51) 32.50 2.75
326 A61 70(o) deep green 3.00 .30
Nos. 318-326 (9) 46.55 4.90

Warship of 1701 — A65

Oersted — A66

1951, Feb. 26 Engr. *Perf. 13*
327 A65 25o dark red .50 .30
328 A65 50o deep blue 4.00 .80

250th anniv. of the foundation of the Naval Officers' College.

1951, Mar. 9 Unwmk.
329 A66 50o blue 1.40 .60

Cent. of the death of Hans Christian Oersted, physicist.

Post Chaise ("Ball Post") — A67

Marine Rescue — A68

1951, Apr. 1 *Perf. 13*
330 A67 15o purple .65 .25
331 A67 25o henna brown .65 .25

Cent. of Denmark's 1st postage stamp.

1952, Mar. 26
332 A68 25o red brown .45 .35

Cent. of the foundation of the Danish Life-saving Service.

Types of 1933-50

1952-53 *Perf. 13*
333 A32 12o lt yel grn .30 .25
334 A61 25(o) lt blue 1.10 .30
335 A61 30(o) brown red 1.00 .35
336 A61 50(o) aqua ('53) 1.00 .30
337 A61 60(o) dp blue ('53) 1.10 .35
338 A61 65(o) gray ('53) 1.10 .35
339 A61 80(o) orange ('53) 1.10 .35
340 A61 90(o) olive ('53) 3.00 .30
341 A61 95(o) red org ('53) 1.10 .25
Nos. 333-341 (9) 10.80 2.80

Jelling Runic Stone — A69

Designs: 15o, Vikings' camp, Trelleborg. 20o, Church of Kalundborg. 30o, Nyborg castle. 60o, Goose tower, Vordinborg.

1953-56 *Perf. 13*
342 A69 10o dp green .30 .25
343 A69 15o lt rose vio .30 .25
344 A69 20o brown .30 .25
345 A69 30o red ('54) .30 .25
346 A69 60o dp blue ('54) .35 .25

Designs: 10o, Manor house, Spottrup. 15o, Hammershus castle ruins. 20o, Copenhagen stock exchange. 30o, Statue of Frederik V, Amalienborg. 60o, Soldier statue at Fredericia.

347 A69 10o green ('54) .30 .25
348 A69 15o lilac ('55) .30 .25
349 A69 20o brown ('55) .30 .25
350 A69 30o red ('55) .30 .25
351 A69 60o deep blue ('56) .60 .25
Nos. 342-351 (10) 3.35 2.50

1000th anniv. of the Kingdom of Denmark. Each stamp represents a different century.

Telegraph Equipment of 1854 — A70

Frederik V — A71

1954, Feb. 2 *Perf. 13*
352 A70 30o red brown .40 .25

Cent. of the telegraph in Denmark.

1954, Mar. 31
353 A71 30o dark red .55 .35

200th anniv. of the founding of the Royal Academy of Fine Arts.

Type of 1948-50

1955, Apr. 27
354 A61 25o lilac 1.00 .30

Nos. 224C and 226A Surcharged with New Value in Black. Nos. 307 and 321 Surcharged with New Value and 4 Bars

1955-56
355 A32 5o on 6o org .30 .25
356 A32 5o on 7o lt brn .30 .25
357 A61 30(o) on 20(o) dk red (I) .80 .30
a. Type III 1.40 .35
b. Double surcharge 1,150. 1,150.
c. Inverted surcharge 650.00
358 A61 30(o) on 25(o) dk red ('56) .60 .25
a. Double surcharge —
Nos. 355-358 (4) 2.00 1.05

A72

A73

1955, Nov. 11 Unwmk.
359 A72 30o dark red .50 .25

100th anniv. of the death of Sören Kierkegaard, philosopher and theologian.

1956, Sept. 12 Engr.
360 A73 30o Ellehammer's plane .50 .25

50th anniv. of the 1st flight made by Jacob Christian Hansen Ellehammer in a heavier-than-air craft.

Northern Countries Issue

Whooper Swans — A74

1956, Oct. 30 *Perf. 13*
361 A74 30o rose red 1.75 .25
362 A74 60o ultramarine 1.60 .80

Issued to emphasize the close bonds among the northern countries: Denmark, Finland, Iceland, Norway and Sweden.

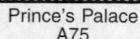

Prince's Palace — A75

Harvester — A76

Design: 60ō, Sun God's Chariot.

1957, May 15 Unwmk.
363 A75 30o dull red .90 .25
364 A75 60o dark blue .90 .75

150th anniv. of the National Museum.

1958, Sept. 4 Engr. *Perf. 13*
365 A76 30o fawn .30 .25

Centenary of the Royal Veterinary and Agricultural College.

Frederik IX — A77

Ballet Dancer — A78

1959, Mar. 11
366 A77 30o rose red .40 .25
367 A77 35o rose lilac .50 .25
368 A77 60o ultra .50 .25
Nos. 366-368 (3) 1.40 .75

King Frederik's 60th birthday.

1959, May 16
369 A78 35o rose lilac .30 .25

Danish Ballet and Music Festival, May 17-31. See Nos. 401, 422.

No. 319 Surcharged

1960, Apr. 7
370 A61 30o on 15o lilac .30 .25

World Refugee Year, 7/1/59-6/30/60.

Seeder and Farm — A79

30ō, Harvester combine. 60ō, Plow.

1960, Apr. 28 Engr. *Perf. 13*
371 A79 12o green .25 .25
372 A79 30o dull red .30 .25
373 A79 60o dk blue .65 .50
Nos. 371-373 (3) 1.20 1.00

King Frederik IX and Queen Ingrid — A80

1960, May 24 Unwmk.
374 A80 30o dull red .45 .25
375 A80 60o blue .65 .60

25th anniversary of the marriage of King Frederik IX and Queen Ingrid.

Bascule Light — A81

1960, June 8 Engr.
376 A81 30o dull red .30 .25

400th anniv. of the Lighthouse Service.

Finsen — A82

1960, Aug. 1 *Perf. 13*
377 A82 30o dark red .30 .25

Centenary of the birth of Dr. Niels R. Finsen, physician and scientist.

Nursing Mother — A83

1960, Aug. 16 **Unwmk.**
378 A83 60o ultra .55 .50

10th meeting of the regional committee for Europe of WHO, Copenhagen, Aug. 16-20.

Europa Issue, 1960
Common Design Type

1960, Sept. 19 *Perf. 13*
Size: 28x21mm
379 CD3 60o ultra .55 .50

DC-8 Airliner — A84

1961, Feb. 24
380 A84 60o ultra .75 .50

10th anniv. of the Scandinavian Airlines System, SAS.

Landscape A85

1961, Apr. 21 *Perf. 13*
381 A85 30o copper brown .30 .25

Denmark's Soc. of Nature Lovers, 50th anniv.

Fluorescent Paper
as well as ordinary paper, was used in printing many definitive and commemorative stamps, starting in 1962. These include No. 220, 224; the 15, 20, 25, 30, 35 (Nos. 386 and 387), 50 and 60ö, 1.20k, 1.50k and 25k definitives of following set, and Nos. 297-299, 318, 333, 380, 401-427, 429-435, 438-439, 493, 543, 548, B30.
Only fluorescent paper was used for Nos. 436-437, 437A and 440 onward; in semipostals from B31 onward.

Frederik IX — A86

1961-63 **Engr.** *Perf. 13*
382 A32 15o green ('63) .50 .35
383 A86 20o brown .45 .35
384 A86 25o brown ('63) .30 .35
385 A86 30o rose red .65 .35
386 A86 35o olive grn .85 .75
387 A86 35o rose red ('63) .30 .35
388 A86 40o gray 1.20 .35
389 A86 50o aqua .55 .30
390 A86 60o ultra 1.10 .35
391 A86 70o green 1.60 .35
392 A86 80o red orange 1.60 .35
393 A86 90o olive bister 4.25 .35
394 A86 95o claret ('63) 1.00 .90
Nos. 382-394 (13) 14.35 5.45

See Nos. 417-419, 438-441. For overprints see Nos. Q41-Q42, Q44-Q45.

State Seal Type of 1946-47

1962-65
395 A55 1.10k lilac ('65) 5.25 2.00
396 A55 1.20k gray 3.00 .35
397 A55 1.25k orange 3.00 .35
398 A55 1.30k green ('65) 5.50 1.75
399 A55 1.50k red lilac 2.75 .35
400 A55 25k yellow grn 8.00 .35
Nos. 395-400 (6) 27.50 5.15

Dancer Type of 1959 Inscribed "15-31 MAJ"

1962, Apr. 26
401 A78 60o ultra .30 .25

Issued to publicize the Danish Ballet and Music Festival, May 15-31.

Old Mill — A87

M.S. Selandia — A88

1962, May 10 **Unwmk.** *Perf. 13*
402 A87 10o red brown .30 .25

Cent. of the abolition of mill monopolies.

1962, June 14 **Engr.**
403 A88 60o dark blue 1.60 1.50

M.S. Selandia, the 1st Diesel ship, 50th anniv.

Violin Scroll, Leaves, Lights and Balloon A89

1962, Aug. 31
404 A89 35o rose violet .35 .25

150th anniv. of the birth of Georg Carstensen, founder of Tivoli amusement park, Copenhagen.

Cliffs on Moen Island — A90

1962, Nov. 22
405 A90 20o pale brown .30 .25

Issued to publicize preservation of natural treasures and landmarks.

Germinating Wheat — A91

1963, Mar. 21 **Engr.**
406 A91 35o fawn .35 .25

FAO "Freedom from Hunger" campaign.

Railroad Wheel, Tire Tracks, Waves and Swallow — A92

1963, May 14 **Unwmk.** *Perf. 13*
407 A92 15o green .60 .40

Inauguration of the "Bird Flight Line" railroad link between Denmark and Germany.

Sailing Vessel, Coach, Postilions and Globe — A93

1963, May 27
408 A93 60o dark blue .40 .40

Cent. of the 1st Intl. Postal Conf., Paris, 1863.

Niels Bohr and Atom Diagram — A94

Early Public School Drawn on Slate — A95

1963, Nov. 21 **Engr.**
409 A94 35o red brown .40 .35
410 A94 60o dark blue .65 .25

50th anniv. of Prof. Niels Bohr's (1885-1962) atom theory.

1964, June 19 **Unwmk.** *Perf. 13*
411 A95 35o red brown .60 .25

150th anniversary of the royal decrees for the public school system.

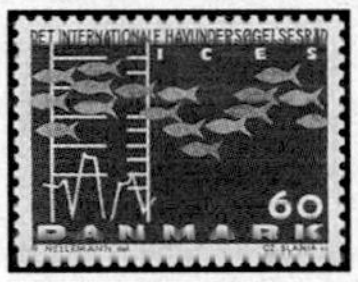

Fish and Chart — A96

1964, Sept. 7 **Engr.**
412 A96 60o violet blue .35 .40

Conference of the International Council for the Exploration of the Sea, Copenhagen.

Danish Watermarks and Perforations A97

1964, Oct. 10 *Perf. 13*
413 A97 35o pink .30 .25

25th anniv. of Stamp Day and to publicize the Odense Stamp Exhibition, Oct. 10-11.

Landscape A98

1964, Nov. 12 **Engr.**
414 A98 25o brown .30 .25

Issued to publicize preservation of natural treasures and landmarks.

Calculator, Ledger and Inkwell — A99

1965, Mar. 8 **Unwmk.**
415 A99 15o light olive green .30 .25

First Business School in Denmark, cent.

Types of 1933 and 1961

1965, May 15 **Engr.** *Perf. 13*
416 A32 25o apple green .55 .50
417 A86 40o brown .45 .35
418 A86 50o rose red .75 .35
419 A86 80o ultra .75 .65
Nos. 416-419 (4) 2.50 1.85

For overprints see Nos. Q41-Q42.

ITU Emblem, Telegraph Key, Teletype Paper A100

Carl Nielsen (1865-1931), Composer A101

1965, May 17
420 A100 80o dark blue .35 .25

Cent. of the ITU.

1965, June 9 **Engr.**
421 A101 50o brown red .40 .25

Dancer Type of 1959 Inscribed "15-31 MAJ"

1965, Sept. 23
422 A78 50o rose red .30 .25

Issued to publicize the Danish Ballet and Music Festival, May 15-31.

Bogo Windmill A102

Mylius Dalgas Surveying Wasteland A103

1965, Nov. 10 **Engr.** *Perf. 13*
423 A102 40o brown .30 .25

Issued to publicize the preservation of natural treasures and landmarks.

1966, Feb. 24
424 A103 25o olive green .50 .30

Cent. of the Danish Heath Soc. (reclamation of wastelands), founded by Enrico Mylius Dalgas.

Christen Kold (1816-70), Educator — A104

1966, Mar. 29 *Perf. 13*
425 A104 50o dull red .50 .50

Poorhouse, Copenhagen A105

Holte Allée, Bregentved A106

Dolmen (Grave) in Jutland — A107

1966 **Unwmk.**
426 A105 50o dull red .55 .50
427 A106 80o dk blue 1.00 .40
428 A107 1.50k dk slate grn 1.40 .25
Nos. 426-428 (3) 2.95 1.15

Publicizing preservation of national treasures and ancient monuments. Issued: 50o, May 12; 80o, June 16; 1.50k, Nov. 24.

George Jensen by Ejnar Nielsen A108

Music Bar and Instruments A109

1966, Aug. 31 **Engr.** ***Perf. 13***
429 A108 80o dark blue 1.00 .40

George Jensen, silversmith, birth cent.

1967, Jan. 9
430 A109 50o dark red .70 .25

Royal Danish Academy of Music, cent.

Cogwheels, and Broken Customs Duty Ribbon — A110

1967, Mar. 2
431 A110 80o dark blue .70 .25

European Free Trade Association. Industrial tariffs were abolished Dec. 31, 1966, among EFTA members: Austria, Denmark, Finland, Great Britain, Norway, Portugal, Sweden and Switzerland.

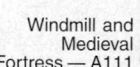

Windmill and Medieval Fortress — A111

Designs: 40ö, Ship's rigging and baroque house front. 50ö, Old Town Hall. 80ö, New building construction.

1967 **Engr.** ***Perf. 13***
432 A111 25o green .60 .25
433 A111 40o sepia .35 .25
434 A111 50o red brown .35 .40
435 A111 80o dk blue .85 .80
Nos. 432-435 (4) 2.15 1.70

The 800th anniversary of Copenhagen.
Issued: Nos. 432-433, 4/6; Nos. 434-435, 5/11.

Princess Margrethe and Prince Henri — A112

1967, June 10
436 A112 50o red .30 .25

Marriage of Crown Princess Margrethe and Prince Henri de Monpezat.

Types of 1933-1961

1967-71 **Engr.** ***Perf. 13***
437 A32 30o dk green .70 .35
437A A32 40o orange ('71) .80 .35
438 A86 50o brown 1.25 .35
Complete booklet, 4 #318, 2 each #437, 438 20.00
439 A86 60o rose red 1.25 .35
440 A86 80o green .85 .35
441 A86 90o ultra .90 .35
441A A55 1.20k Prus grn ('71) 2.00 .45
442 A55 2.20k orange 3.50 .35
443 A55 2.80k gray 3.00 .35
444 A55 2.90k rose vio 5.25 .35
444A A55 3k dk sl grn ('69) 1.00 .35
444B A55 3.10k plum ('70) 8.50 .35
444C A55 4k gray ('69) 1.40 .35
444D A55 4.10k olive ('70) 8.50 .35
Nos. 437-444D (14) 38.90 5.00

Issued: Nos. 437-441, 6/30/67; Nos. 442-443, 7/8/67; No. 444, 4/29/68; Nos. 444A, 444C, 8/28/69; Nos. 444B, 444D, 8/27/70; Nos. 437A, 441A, 6/24/71.
For overprints see Nos. Q44-Q45.

Sonne — A113

Cross-anchor and Porpoise — A114

1967, Sept. 21
445 A113 60o red .30 .25

150th anniv. of the birth of Hans Christian Sonne, pioneer of the cooperative movement in Denmark.

1967, Nov. 9 **Engr.** ***Perf. 13***
446 A114 90o dk blue .35 .25

Centenary of the Danish Seamen's Church in Foreign Ports.

Esbjerg Harbor — A115

1968, Apr. 24
447 A115 30o dk yellow grn .30 .25

Centenary of Esbjerg Harbor.

Koldinghus A116

1968, June 13
448 A116 60o copper red .65 .25

700th anniversary of Koldinghus Castle.

Shipbuilding Industry A117

Sower A118

Designs: 50o, Chemical industry. 60o, Electric power. 90o, Engineering.

1968, Oct. 24 **Engr.** ***Perf. 13***
449 A117 30o green .25 .25
450 A117 50o brown .25 .25
451 A117 60o red brown .25 .25
452 A117 90o dark blue 1.00 1.00
Nos. 449-452 (4) 1.75 1.75

Issued to publicize Danish industries.

1969, Jan. 29
453 A118 30o gray green .30 .25

Royal Agricultural Soc. of Denmark, 200th anniv.

Five Ancient Ships A119

Frederik IX A120

Nordic Cooperation Issue

1969, Feb. 28 **Engr.** ***Perf. 13***
454 A119 60o brown red .80 .25
455 A119 90o blue 1.60 1.60

50th anniv. of the Nordic Soc. and cent. of postal cooperation among the northern countries. The design is taken from a coin found at the site of Birka, an ancient Swedish town. See also Finland No. 481, Iceland Nos. 404-405, Norway Nos. 523-524 and Sweden Nos. 808-810.

1969, Mar. 11
456 A120 50o sepia .30 .25
457 A120 60o dull red .30 .25

70th birthday of King Frederik IX.

Common Design Types pictured following the introduction.

Europa Issue, 1969
Common Design Type

1969, Apr. 28
Size: 28x20mm
458 CD12 90o chalky blue .75 .75

Kronborg Castle — A121

Danish Flag — A122

1969, May 22 **Engr.** ***Perf. 13***
459 A121 50o brown .30 .25

Association of Danes living abroad, 50th anniv.

1969, June 12
460 A122 60o bluish blk, red & gray .30 .25

750th anniversary of the fall of the Dannebrog (Danish flag) from heaven.

Nexo A123

Stensen A124

1969, Aug. 28
461 A123 80o deep green .30 .25

Centenary of the birth of Martin Andersen Nexo (1869-1954), novelist.

1969, Sept. 25
462 A124 1k deep brown .35 .25

300th anniv. of the publication of Niels Stensen's geological work "On Solid Bodies."

Abstract Design — A125

Symbolic Design — A126

1969, Nov. 10 **Engr.** ***Perf. 13***
463 A125 60o rose, red & ultra .30 .25

1969, Nov. 20
464 A126 30o olive green .30 .25

Valdemar Poulsen (1869-1942), electrical engineer and inventor.

Post Office Bank — A127

School Safety Patrol — A128

1970, Jan. 15 **Engr.** ***Perf. 13***
465 A127 60o dk red & org .30 .25

50th anniv. of post office banking service.

1970, Feb. 19
466 A128 50o brown .30 .25

Issued to publicize road safety.

Candle in Window A129

Deer A130

1970, May 4 **Engr.** ***Perf. 13***
467 A129 50o slate, dull bl & yel .30 .25

25th anniv. of liberation from the Germans.

1970, May 28
468 A130 60o yel grn, red & brn .30 .25

Tercentenary of Jaegersborg Deer Park.

Elephant Figurehead, 1741 A131

"The Homecoming" by Povl Christensen A132

1970, June 15 ***Perf. 11½***
469 A131 30o multicolored .30 .25

Royal Naval Museum, tercentenary.

1970, June 15 ***Perf. 13***
470 A132 60o org, dl vio & ol grn .30 .25

Union of North Schleswig and Denmark, 50th anniv.

Electromagnet A133

1970, Aug. 13 **Engr.**
471 A133 80o gray green .30 .25

150th anniversary of Hans Christian Oersted's discovery of electromagnetism.

Bronze Age Ship A134

Ships: 50o, Viking shipbuilding, from Bayeux tapestry. 60o, Thuroe schooner with topgallant. 90o, Tanker.

1970, Sept. 24

472 A134 30o ocher & brown .25 .25
473 A134 50o brn red & rose brn .25 .25
474 A134 60o gray ol & red brn .35 .25
475 A134 90o blue grn & ultra 1.25 1.25
Nos. 472-475 (4) 2.10 2.00

UN Emblem
A135

1970, Oct. 22 **Engr.** ***Perf. 13***

476 A135 90o blue, grn & red 1.00 1.00

25th anniversary of the United Nations.

Bertel Thorvaldsen
A136

Mathide Fibiger
A137

1970, Nov. 19

477 A136 2k slate blue .60 .50

Bicentenary of the birth of Bertel Thorvaldsen (1768-1844), sculptor.

1971, Feb. 25

478 A137 80o olive green .30 .25

Danish Women's Association centenary.

Refugees
A138

Hans Egede
A139

1971, Mar. 26 **Engr.** ***Perf. 13***

479 A138 50o brown .25 .25
480 A138 60o brown red .35 .25

Joint northern campaign for the benefit of refugees.

1971, May 27

481 A139 1k brown .35 .25

250th anniversary of arrival of Hans Egede in Greenland and beginning of its colonization.

A140

1971, Oct. 14

482 A140 30o Swimming .25 .25
483 A140 50o Gymnastics .50 .25
484 A140 60o Soccer .75 .25
485 A140 90o Sailing .75 .75
Nos. 482-485 (4) 2.25 1.50

A141

1971, Nov. 11 **Engr.** ***Perf. 13***

486 A141 90o dark blue .35 .35

Centenary of first lectures given by Georg Brandes (1842-1927), writer and literary critic.

A142

1972, Jan. 27

487 A142 80o slate green .35 .25

Centenary of Danish sugar production.

A143

1972, Mar. 11 **Engr.** ***Perf. 13***

488 A143 60o red brown .30 .25

Frederik IX (1899-1972).

Abstract Design
A144

1972, Mar. 11

489 A144 1.20k brt rose lil, bl gray & brn .65 .65

Danish Meteorological Institute, cent.

Nikolai F. S. Grundtvig
A145

Locomotive, 1847, Ferry, Travelers
A146

1972, May 4 **Engr.** ***Perf. 13***

490 A145 1k sepia .50 .50

Nikolai Frederik Severin Grundtvig (1783-1872), theologian and poet.

1972, June 26

491 A146 70o rose red .30 .25

125th anniversary of Danish State Railways.

Rebild Hills
A147

"Tinker Turned Politician"
A148

1972, June 26

492 A147 1k bl, sl grn & mar .35 .25

Types of 1933-46

1972-78 **Engr.** ***Perf. 13***

493 A32 20o slate bl ('74) .35 .35
494 A32 50o sepia ('74) .30 .30
a. Bklt. pane of 12 (4 #318, 4 #493, 4 #494) ('85) 15.00
495 A32 60o apple grn ('76) 1.75 .90
496 A32 60o gray ('78) .70 .70
497 A32 70o red 1.00 .35
498 A32 70o apple grn ('77) 1.10 .35
499 A55 2.50k orange 1.75 .35
500 A55 2.80k olive ('75) 1.25 .65
501 A55 3.50k lilac 2.00 .35
502 A55 4.5k olive 5.50 .35
503 A55 6k vio blk ('76) 2.00 .35
504 A55 7k red lilac ('78) 2.10 .35
505 A55 9k brown ol ('77) 3.00 .35
506 A55 10k lemon ('76) 3.00 .35
Nos. 493-506 (14) 25.80 6.05

1972, Sept. 14

507 A148 70o dark red .30 .25

250th anniv. of the comedies of Ludvig Holberg (1684-1754) on the Danish stage.

WHO Building, Copenhagen — A149

1972, Sept. 14

508 A149 2k bl, blk & lt red brn .60 .60

Opening of WHO Building, Copenhagen.

Bridge Across Little Belt
A150

Aeroskobing House c. 1740
A151

Highway engineering (Diagrams): 60o, Hanstholm Harbor. 70o, Lim Fjord Tunnel. 90o, Knudshoved Harbor.

1972, Oct. 19 **Engr.** ***Perf. 13***

509 A150 40o dk green .25 .25
510 A150 60o dk brown .35 .25
511 A150 70o dk red .35 .25
512 A150 90o dk blue grn 1.40 .50
Nos. 509-512 (4) 2.35 1.25

1972, Nov. 23

Danish Architecture: 60o, East Bornholm farmhouse, 17th century, horiz. 70o, House, Christianshavn, c. 1710. 1.20k, Hvide Sande Farmhouse, c. 1810, horiz.

Size: 20x28mm, 27x20mm

513 A151 40o red, brn & blk .35 .25
514 A151 60o blk, vio bl & grn .35 .25

Size: 18x37mm, 36x20mm

515 A151 70o red, dk red & blk .45 .30
516 A151 1.20k dk brn, red & grn 1.40 1.00
Nos. 513-516 (4) 2.55 1.80

Jensen
A152

Guard Rails, Cogwheels
A153

1973, Feb. 22 **Engr.** ***Perf. 13***

517 A152 90o green .35 .25

Centenary of the birth of Johannes Vilhelm Jensen (1873-1950), lyric poet and novelist.

1973, Mar. 22

518 A153 50o sepia .55 .25

Centenary of first Danish Factory Act for labor protection.

Abildgaard
A154

Rhododendron
A155

1973, Mar. 22

519 A154 1k dull blue .70 .35

Bicentenary of Royal Veterinary College, Christianshaven, founded by Prof. P. C. Abildgaard.

1973, Apr. 26

Design: 70o, Dronningen of Denmark rose.

520 A155 60o brn, grn & vio .50 .25
521 A155 70o dk red, rose & grn .50 .25

Centenary of the founding of the Horticultural Society of Denmark.

Nordic Cooperation Issue

Nordic House, Reykjavik
A156

1973, June 26 **Engr.** ***Perf. 13***

522 A156 70o multicolored .50 .25
523 A156 1k multicolored 1.50 1.25

A century of postal cooperation among Denmark, Finland, Iceland, Norway and Sweden, and in connection with the Nordic Postal Conference, Reykjavik.

Sextant, Stella Nova, Cassiopeia
A157

St. Mark, from 11th Cent. Book of Dalby
A158

1973, Oct. 18 **Engr.** ***Perf. 13***

524 A157 2k dark blue 1.75 .30

400th anniversary of the publication of "De Nova Stella," by Tycho Brahe.

1973, Oct. 18 **Photo.** ***Perf. 14x14½***

525 A158 120o buff & multi 1.10 .65

300th anniversary of Royal Library.

Devil and Gossips, Fanefjord Church, 1480 — A159

Frescoes: No. 527, Queen Esther and King Ahasuerus, Tirsted Church, c.1400. No. 528, Miraculous Harvest, Jetsmark Church, c.1474. No. 529, Jesus carrying cross, and wearing crown of thorns, Biersted Church, c.1400. No. 530, Creation of Eve, Fanefjord Church, c.1480.

1973, Nov. 28 **Engr.** ***Perf. 13***

Cream Paper

526 A159 70o dk red, yel & grn 1.40 .30
527 A159 70o dk red, yel & grn 1.40 .30
528 A159 70o dk red, yel & grn 1.40 .30
529 A159 70o dk red, yel & grn 1.40 .30
530 A159 70o dk red, yel & grn 1.40 .30
a. Bklt. pane, 2 each #526-530 35.00
b. Strip of 5, #526-530 6.75

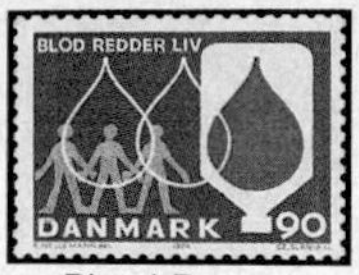

Blood Donors A160

Queen Margrethe A161

1974, Jan. 24

531	A160	90o purple & red	1.10	.25

"Blood Saves Lives."

1974-81 Engr. *Perf. 13*

532	A161	60o brown	1.00	.50
533	A161	60o orange	.60	.45
534	A161	70o red	1.00	.25
535	A161	70o dk brown	.80	.25
536	A161	80o green	.80	.25
537	A161	80o dp brn ('76)	1.10	.25
538	A161	90o red lilac	1.10	.25
539	A161	90o dull red	1.40	.30
540	A161	90o slate grn ('76)	1.10	.30
541	A161	100o dp ultra	1.10	.25
542	A161	100o gray ('75)	1.10	.25
543	A161	100o red ('76)	1.10	.35
544	A161	100o brown ('77)	1.00	.25
a.		Bklt. pane of 5 (#544, #494, 2 #493, #318)	2.50	
		Complete booklet, #544a	2.50	
545	A161	110o orange ('78)	1.20	.25
546	A161	120o slate	1.00	.50
547	A161	120o red ('77)	1.40	.25
		Complete booklet, 4 each #318, 493, 544, 547	13.50	
548	A161	130o ultra ('75)	1.60	1.40
549	A161	150o vio bl ('78)	1.40	.85
550	A161	180o slate grn ('77)	1.40	.40
551	A161	200o blue ('81)	1.40	1.00
		Nos. 532-551 (20)	22.60	8.55

See Nos. 630, 632-642. For overprint see No. Q49.

Pantomime Theater — A162

1974, May 16

552	A162	100o indigo	.40	.30

Cent. of the Pantomime Theater, Tivoli.

Hverringe A163

Views: 60o, Norre Lyndelse, Carl Nielsen's childhood home. 70o, Odense, Hans Chr. Andersen's childhood home. 90o, Hesselagergaard, vert. 120o, Hindsholm.

1974, June 20 Engr. *Perf. 13*

553	A163	50o brown & multi	.50	.50
554	A163	60o sl grn & multi	.65	.65
555	A163	70o red brn & multi	.50	.50
556	A163	90o dk green & mar	.55	.25
557	A163	120o red org & dk grn	.70	.50
		Nos. 553-557 (5)	2.90	2.40

Emblem, Runner with Map — A164

Iris — A165

1974, Aug. 22 Engr. *Perf. 13*

558	A164	70o shown	.70	.70
559	A164	80o Compass	.25	.25

World Orienteering Championships 1974.

1974, Sept. 19

560	A165	90o shown	.50	.25
561	A165	120o Purple orchid	.75	.75

Copenhagen Botanical Garden centenary.

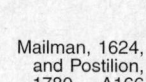

Mailman, 1624, and Postilion, 1780 — A166

Carrier Pigeon — A167

Design: 90o, Balloon and sailing ships.

1974, Oct. 9 Engr. *Perf. 13*

562	A166	70o lemon & dk brn	.40	.25
563	A166	90o dull grn & sepia	.40	.25
564	A167	120o dark blue	.65	.65
		Nos. 562-564 (3)	1.45	1.15

350th anniv. of Danish PO (70o, 90o) and cent. of UPU (120o).

Souvenir Sheet

Ferslew's Essays, 1849 and 1852 — A168

Engraved and Photogravure

1975, Feb. 27 *Perf. 13*

565	A168	Sheet of 4	7.50	*8.50*
a.		70o Coat of arms	1.75	*2.00*
b.		80o King Frederik VII	1.75	*2.00*
c.		90o King Frederik VII	1.75	*2.00*
d.		100o Mercury	1.75	*2.00*

HAFNIA 76 Intl. Stamp Exhib., Copenhagen, Aug. 20-29, 1976. Sold for 5k.

See No. 585.

Early Radio Equipment A169

Flora Danica Plate A170

1975, Mar. 20 Engr. *Perf. 13*

566	A169	90o dull red	.35	.30

Danish broadcasting, 50th anniversary.

1975, May 22

Danish China: 90o, Flora Danica tureen. 130o, Vase and tea caddy, blue fluted china.

567	A170	50o slate grn	.30	.25
568	A170	90o brown red	.65	.65
569	A170	130o violet bl	1.10	1.10
		Nos. 567-569 (3)	2.05	2.00

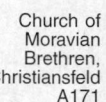

Church of Moravian Brethren, Christiansfeld A171

120o, Kongsgaard farmhouse, Lejre. 150o, Anna Queenstraede, Helsingor, vert.

1975, June 19

570	A171	70o sepia	.65	.65
571	A171	120o olive green	.80	.80
572	A171	150o violet black	.65	.25
		Nos. 570-572 (3)	2.10	1.70

European Architectural Heritage Year 1975.

Andersen A172

Watchman's Square, Abenra A173

Designs: 70o, Numbskull Jack, drawing by Vilh. Pedersen. 130o, The Marshking's Daughter, drawing by L. Frohlich.

1975, Aug. 28 Engr. *Perf. 13*

573	A172	70o brown & blk	.60	.60
574	A172	90o brn red & dk brn	.75	.30
575	A172	130o blue blk & sepia	1.75	1.75
		Nos. 573-575 (3)	3.10	2.65

Hans Christian Andersen (1805-75), writer.

1975, Sept. 25

Designs: 90o, Haderslev Cathedral, vert. 100o, Mögeltönder Polder. 120o, Mouth of Vidaaen at Höjer Floodgates.

576	A173	70o multicolored	.45	.45
577	A173	90o multicolored	.40	.25
578	A173	100o multicolored	.50	.25
579	A173	120o multicolored	.55	.50
		Nos. 576-579 (4)	1.90	1.45

European Kingfisher A174

1975, Oct. 23 Engr. *Perf. 13*

580	A174	50o shown	.45	.45
581	A174	70o Hedgehog	.45	.45
582	A174	90o Cats	.45	.45
583	A174	130o Avocets	1.25	1.25
584	A174	200o Otter	.65	.25
		Nos. 580-584 (5)	3.25	2.85

Protected animals, and for the centenary of the Danish Society for the Prevention of Cruelty to Animals (90ö).

HAFNIA Type of 1974

Souvenir Sheet

1975, Nov. 20 Engr. & Photo.

585	A168	Sheet of 4	4.50	*6.75*
a.		50o buff & brown, No. 2	1.10	*1.60*
b.		70o buff, brown & blue, No. 1	1.10	*1.60*
c.		90o buff, blue & brown, No. 11	1.10	*1.60*
d.		130o olive, brown & buff, No. 19	1.10	*1.60*

HAFNIA 76 Intl. Stamp Exhib., Copenhagen, Aug. 20-29, 1976. Sold for 5k.

Copenhagen, Center — A175

View from Round Tower — A176

Copenhagen, Views: 100o, Central Station, interior. 130o, Harbor.

1976, Mar. 25 Engr. *Perf. 12½*

586	A175	60o multicolored	.45	.45
587	A176	80o multicolored	.45	.45
588	A176	100o multicolored	.45	.25
589	A175	130o multicolored	1.50	1.50
		Nos. 586-589 (4)	2.85	2.65

Postilion, by Otto Bache A177

Emil Chr. Hansen, Physiologist, in Laboratory A178

1976, June 17 Engr. *Perf. 12½*

590	A177	130o multicolored	1.00	1.25

Souvenir Sheet

591	A177	130o multicolored	10.00	*16.00*

HAFNIA 76 Intl. Stamp Exhib., Copenhagen, Aug. 20-29. No. 591 contains one stamp similar to No. 590 with design continuous into sheet margin. Sheet shows painting "A String of Horses Outside an Inn" of which No. 590 shows a detail. Sheet sold for 15k including exhibition ticket.

1976, Sept. 23 Engr. *Perf. 13*

592	A178	100o orange red	.40	.30

Carlsberg Foundation (art and science), centenary.

Glass Blower Molding Glass — A179

Five Water Lilies — A180

Danish Glass Production: 80o, Finished glass removed from pipe. 130o, Glass cut off from foot. 150o, Glass blown up in mold.

1976, Nov. 18 Engr. *Perf. 13*

593	A179	60o slate	.50	.50
594	A179	80o dk brown	.50	.25
595	A179	130o dk blue	1.00	1.00
596	A179	150o red brown	.60	.25
		Nos. 593-596 (4)	2.60	2.00

Photogravure and Engraved

1977, Feb. 2 *Perf. 12½*

597	A180	100o brt green & multi	.50	.35
598	A180	130o ultra & multi	2.00	2.00

Nordic countries cooperation for protection of the environment and 25th Session of Nordic Council, Helsinki, Feb. 19.

Road Accident — A181

1977, Mar. 24 Engr. *Perf. 12½*

599	A181	100o brown red	.40	.30

Road Safety Traffic Act, May 1, 1977.

Europa — A182

1977, May 2 Engr. *Perf. 12½*

600	A182	1k Allinge	*.60*	*.30*
601	A182	1.30k View, Ringsted	*3.00*	*3.00*

Kongeaen
A183

Landscapes, Southern Jutland: 90o, Skallingen. 150o, Torskind. 200o, Jelling.

1977, June 30 Engr. *Perf. 12½*

602 A183	60o multicolored	1.25	1.25
603 A183	90o multicolored	.65	.65
604 A183	150o multicolored	.60	.50
605 A183	200o multicolored	.75	.50
Nos. 602-605 (4)		3.25	2.90

See Nos. 616-619, 655-658, 666-669.

Hammers and Horseshoes
A184

Designs: 1k, Chisel, square and plane. 1.30k, Trowel, ceiling brush and folding ruler.

1977, Sept. 22 Engr. *Perf. 12½*

606 A184 80o dk brown	.30	.25
607 A184 1k red	.40	.25
608 A184 1.30k violet bl	.75	.60
Nos. 606-608 (3)	1.45	1.10

Danish crafts.

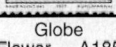

Globe Flower — A185

Handball — A186

Endangered Flora: 1.50k, Cnidium dubium.

1977, Nov. 17 Engr. *Perf. 12½*

609 A185 1k multicolored	.40	.25
610 A185 1.50k multicolored	1.25	1.25

1978, Jan. 19 *Perf. 12½*

611 A186 1.20k red	.40	.30

Men's World Handball Championships.

Christian IV, Frederiksborg Castle
A187

Frederiksborg Museum
A188

1978, Mar. 16

612 A187 1.20k brown red	.50	.50
613 A188 1.80k black	.60	.30

Frederiksborg Museum, centenary.

Europa Issue

Jens Bang's House, Aalborg
A189

Frederiksborg Castle, Ground Plan and Elevation
A190

1978, May 11 Engr. *Perf. 12½*

614 A189 1.20k red	*.30*	.25
615 A190 1.50k dk bl & vio bl	*1.25*	*1.25*

Landscape Type of 1977

Landscapes, Central Jutland: 70o, Kongenshus Memorial Park. 120o, Post Office, Old Town in Aarhus. 150o, Lignite fields, Soby. 180o, Church wall, Stadil Church.

1978, June 15 Engr. *Perf. 12½*

616 A183 70o multicolored	.50	.50
617 A183 120o multicolored	.55	.25
Complete booklet, 10 #617	9.00	
618 A183 150o multicolored	.80	.80
619 A183 180o multicolored	.60	.60
Nos. 616-619 (4)	2.45	2.15

Boats in Harbor — A191

Edible Morel — A192

Danish fishing industry: 1k, Eel traps. 1.80k, Boats in berth. 2.50k, Drying nets.

1978, Sept. 7 Engr. *Perf. 12½*

620 A191 70o olive gray	.50	.50
621 A191 1k redsh brown	.50	.25
622 A191 1.80k slate	.60	.50
623 A191 2.50k sepia	.85	.60
Nos. 620-623 (4)	2.45	1.85

1978, Nov. 16 Engr. *Perf. 12½*

Design: 1.20k, Satan's mushroom.

624 A192 1k sepia	.65	.55
625 A192 1.20k dull red	.65	.55

Telephones — A193

1979, Jan. 25 Engr. *Perf. 12½*

626 A193 1.20k dull red	.40	.30

Centenary of Danish telephone.

University Seal
A194

Pentagram: University Faculties
A195

1979, Apr. 5 Engr. *Perf. 12½*

627 A194 1.30k vermilion	.40	.25
628 A195 1.60k dk vio blue	.55	.55

University of Copenhagen, 500th anniv.

Types of 1933-1974

1979-82 Engr. *Perf. 13*

629 A32 80o green	.35	.40
630 A161 90o slate	3.00	3.25
631 A32 100o dp green ('81)	.50	.40
632 A161 110o brown	.65	.40
a. Bklt. pane, #493-494, 632, 2 #318 ('79)	1.50	
complete booklet, #632a	1.50	
633 A161 130o red	.65	.40
a. Bklt. pane, 2 ea #494, 629, 632, 4 #633 ('79)	7.50	
Complete booklet, #633a	8.00	
634 A161 130o brown ('81)	.65	.60
635 A161 140o red org ('80)	2.00	2.50
636 A161 150o red org ('81)	.65	.80
637 A161 160o ultra	1.25	1.25
638 A161 160o red ('81)	.65	.40
a. Bklt. pane, 2 ea #318, 634, 638, 8 #494)	12.00	
Complete booklet, #638a	12.00	
639 A161 180o ultra ('80)	1.40	1.40
640 A161 210o gray ('80)	2.00	2.50
641 A161 230o ol grn ('81)	1.00	.65
642 A161 250o blue grn ('81)	1.40	1.00
643 A55 2.80k dull grn	1.40	1.10
644 A55 3.30k brn red ('81)	1.40	.80
645 A55 3.50k grnsh bl ('82)	2.50	3.00
646 A55 4.30k brn red ('80)	4.00	5.25
647 A55 4.70k rose lil ('81)	3.50	5.25
648 A55 8k orange	2.75	.40
649 A55 12k red brn ('81)	5.00	.65
650 A55 14k dk red brn ('82)	5.75	.80
Nos. 629-650 (22)	42.45	33.20

A196

A197

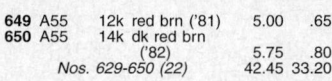

Europa: 1.30k, Mail cart, 1785. 1.60k, Morse key and amplifier.

1979, May 10 *Perf. 12½*

651 A196 1.30k red	*1.00*	.25
652 A196 1.60k dark blue	*3.00*	1.10

1979, June 14 Engr. *Perf. 13*

Viking Art: 1.10k, Gripping beast pendant. 2k, Key with gripping beast design.

653 A197 1.10k sepia	.40	.40
654 A197 2k grnsh gray	.50	.40

Landscape Type of 1977

Landscapes, Northern Jutland: 80o, Mols Bjerge. 90o, Orslev Kloster. 200o, Trans. 280o, Bovbjerg.

1979, Sept. 6 Engr. *Perf. 12½*

655 A183 80o multicolored	.50	.50
656 A183 90o multicolored	1.60	1.60
657 A183 200o multicolored	.90	.35
658 A183 280o multicolored	1.10	1.10
Nos. 655-658 (4)	4.10	3.55

Adam Oehlenschläger (1799-1850), Poet and Dramatist
A198

1979, Oct, 4 Engr. *Perf. 13*

659 A198 1.30k dk carmine	.40	.30

Score, Violin, Dancing Couple — A199

Ballerina — A200

1979, Nov. 8 Engr. *Perf. 13x12½*

660 A199 1.10k brown	.40	.30
661 A200 1.60k ultra	.60	.65

Jacob Gade (1879-63), composer; August Bournonville (1805-79), ballet master.

Royal Mail Guards' Office, Copenhagen, 1779 — A201

1980, Feb. 14 Engr. *Perf. 13*

662 A201 1.30k brown red	.50	.35

National Postal Service, 200th anniversary.

Symbols of Occupation, Health and Education
A202

1980, May 5 Engr. *Perf. 13*

663 A202 1.60k dark blue	.65	.50

World Conference of the UN Decade for Women, Copenhagen, July 14-30.

Karen Blixen (1885-1962), Writer (Pen Name Isak Dinesen) — A203

Europa: 1.60k, August Krogh (1874-1949), physiologist.

1980, May 5

664 A203 1.30k red	*.65*	.25
665 A203 1.60k blue	*1.40*	*1.40*

Landscape Type of 1977

Northern Jutland: 80o, Viking ship burial grounds, Lindholm Hoje. 110o, Lighthouse, Skagen, vert. 200o, Boreglum Monastery. 280o, Fishing boats, Vorupor Beach.

1980, June 19 Engr. *Perf. 13*

666 A183 80o multicolored	.50	.50
667 A183 110o multicolored	.50	.50
668 A183 200o multicolored	.70	.30
669 A183 280o multicolored	2.00	2.00
Nos. 666-669 (4)	3.70	3.30

Nordic Cooperation Issue

Silver Tankard, by Borchardt Rollufse, 1641 — A204

1.80K, Bishop's bowl, Copenhagen faience, 18th cent.

1980, Sept. 9 Engr. *Perf. 13*

670 A204 1.30k shown	.50	.35
671 A204 1.80k multicolored	1.40	1.40

Frisian Sceat Facsimile, Obverse and Reverse, 9th Century
A205

Coins: 1.40k Silver coin of Valdemar the Great and Absalom, 1157-1182, 1.80k, Gold 12-mark coin of Christian VII, 1781.

1980, Oct. 9 Engr. *Perf. 13*

672 A205 1.30k red & redsh brn	.50	.45
673 A205 1.40k ol gray & sl grn	1.60	1.40
674 A205 1.80k dk bl & sl bl	1.25	1.25
Nos. 672-674 (3)	3.35	3.10

Tonder Lace Pattern, North Schleswig — A206

Designs: Tonder lace patterns.

1980, Nov. 13 Engr. *Perf. 13*

675 A206 1.10k brown	.65	.65
676 A206 1.30k brown red	.50	.30
677 A206 2k olive gray	.70	.30
Nos. 675-677 (3)	1.85	1.25

Nyboder Development, Copenhagen, 350th Anniversary
A207

Design: 1.30k, View of Nyboder, diff.

1981, Mar. 19

678 A207 1.30k dp org & ocher	.90	.90
679 A207 1.60k dp org & ocher	.55	.30

Tilting at a Barrel on Shrovetide A208

Design: 2k, Midsummer's Eve bonfire.

1981, May 4 Engr. *Perf. 13*

680 A208 1.60k brown red *.40* .25
Complete booklet, 10 #680 *4.00*
681 A208 2k dk blue *1.25* *.75*

Soro Lake and Academy, Zealand — A209

Designs: Views of Zealand.

1981, June 18 Engr. *Perf. 13*

682 A209 100o shown .50 .50
683 A209 150o Poet N.F.S. Grundtvig's home, Udby .65 .65
684 A209 160o Kaj Munk's home, Opager .65 .30
685 A209 200o Gronsund .80 .80
686 A209 230o Bornholm Isld. 1.10 .85
Nos. 682-686 (5) 3.70 3.10

European Urban Renaissance Year — A210

1981, Sept. 10 Engr. *Perf. 12½x13*

687 A210 1.60k dull red .65 .35

Type of 1933

1981-85 Engr. *Perf. 13*

688 A32 30o orange .60 .40
a. Bklt. pane 10 (2 #318, 2 #688, 6 #494)('84) 30.00
Complete booklet, #688a, 6 #708 30.00
689 A32 40o purple .50 .40
a. Bklt. pane of 10 (4 #318, 2 #689, 4 #494) ('89) 4.50
690 A32 80o ol bis ('85) 1.00 .80
691 A32 100o blue ('83) .85 .40
b. Bklt. pane of 8 (2 #494, 4 #691, 2 #706) ('83) 21.00
Complete booklet, #691b 21.00
692 A32 150o dk green ('82) .85 .40
693 A32 200o green ('83) 1.00 .90
694 A32 230o brt yel grn ('84) 1.50 .60
695 A32 250o brt yel grn ('85) 1.50 .60
Nos. 688-695 (8) 7.80 4.50

Ellehammer's 18-horsepower Biplane, 1906 — A211

1981, Oct. 8 Engr. *Perf. 13*

696 A211 1k shown .65 .65
697 A211 1.30k R-1 Fokker CV reconnaissance plane, 1926 1.10 1.10
698 A211 1.60k Bellanca J-300, 1931 .65 .30
699 A211 2.30k DC-7C, 1957 .90 .70
Nos. 696-699 (4) 3.30 2.75

Arms Type of 1946 and

Queen Margrethe II, 10th Anniv. of Accession — A212

1982-85 Engr. *Perf. 13*

700 A212 1.60k dull red .65 .40
701 A212 1.60k dk ol grn 2.50 3.00
702 A212 1.80k sepia .85 .70
703 A212 2k dull red .90 .30
b. Bklt. pane, 4 #494, 2 ea #493, 702, 703 20.00
704 A212 2.20k ol grn ('83) 1.50 2.75
705 A212 2.30k violet 1.00 1.20
706 A212 2.50k org red ('83) .85 .30
707 A212 2.70k dk blue 1.20 .80
708 A212 2.70k cop red ('84) 1.25 .40
c. Booklet pane, 3 #688, 2 #494, 3 #708 ('84) 13.00
709 A212 2.80k cop red ('85) 1.00 .50
Complete booklet, #494a, 6 #709 13.50
b. Booklet pane, 3 #493, 2 #494, 3 #709 ('85) 6.75
Complete booklet, #709b 7.00
710 A212 3k violet ('83) 1.20 .50
711 A212 3.30k bluish blk ('84) 1.75 1.00
712 A212 3.50k blue ('83) 1.50 .65
713 A212 3.50k dk vio ('85) 1.50 .80
714 A212 3.70k dp blue ('84) 1.75 .80
715 A212 3.80k dk blue ('85) 1.40 .60
716 A55 4.30k dk ol grn ('84) 4.50 4.75
717 A55 5.50k dk bl grn ('84) 2.75 1.25
718 A55 16k cop red ('83) 6.00 .90
719 A55 17k cop red ('84) 7.75 1.25
720 A55 18k brn vio ('85) 8.50 1.25
720A A55 50k dk red ('85) 17.00 3.25
Nos. 700-720A (22) 67.30 27.35

See Nos. 796-803, 887, 889, 896, 899.

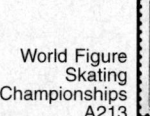

World Figure Skating Championships A213

1982, Feb. 25

721 A213 2k dark blue .80 .50

A214

1982, Feb. 25 Engr. *Perf. 12½*

722 A214 1.60k Revenue schooner Argus .65 .35

Customs Service centenary

A215

1982, May 3 Engr. *Perf. 12½*

723 A215 2k Abolition of adscription, 1788 *.75* .25
Complete booklet, 10 #723 7.50
724 A215 2.70k Women's voting right, 1915 *1.75* *1.00*

Europa.

Butter Churn, Barn, Hjedding — A216

1982, June 10 Engr. *Perf. 13*

725 A216 1.80k brown .80 .65

Cooperative dairy farming centenary.

Records Office, 400th Anniv. — A217

1982, June 10

726 A217 2.70k green 1.20 .50

Steen Steensen Blicher (1782-1848), Poet, by J.V. Gertner — A218

1982, Aug. 26 Engr. *Perf. 13*

727 A218 2k brown red .35 .30

Robert Storm Petersen (1882-1949), Cartoonist A219

Printing in Denmark, 500th Anniv. A220

Characters: 1.50k, Three little men and the number man. 2k, Peter and Ping the penguin, horiz.

1982, Sept. 23 Engr. *Perf. 12½*

728 A219 1.50k dk bl & red .70 .50
729 A219 2k red & ol grn 1.10 .40

1982, Sept. 23

730 A220 1.80k Press, text, ink balls .80 .85

A221 A222

1982, Nov. 4

731 A221 2.70k Library seal 1.20 .50

500th anniv. of University Library.

1983, Jan. 27 Engr. *Perf. 13*

732 A222 2k multicolored .80 .35

World Communications Year.

Amusement Park, 400th Anniv. A223

Badminton Championship A224

1983, Feb. 24

733 A223 2k multicolored .80 .35

1983, Feb. 24

734 A224 2.70k multicolored 1.20 .50

Nordic Cooperation Issue — A225

1983, Mar. 24

735 A225 2.50k Egeskov Castle .90 .40
736 A225 3.50k Troll Church, North Jutland 1.40 .75

50th Anniv. of Steel Plate Printed Stamps — A226

1983, Mar. 24 Engr. *Perf. 13*

737 A226 2.50k car rose 1.00 .35

Europa 1983 — A227

Weights and Measures Ordinance, 300th Anniv. — A228

2.50k, Kildekovshallen Recreation Center, Copenhagen. 3.50k, Salling Sound Bridge.

1983, May 5 Engr. *Perf. 13*

738 A227 2.50k multicolored *1.10* .25
739 A227 3.50k multicolored *2.00* *1.00*

1983, June 16

740 A228 2.50k red 1.00 .35

A229 A230

1983, Sept. 8 Engr.

741 A229 5k Codex titlepage 2.00 1.00

Christian V Danish law, 300th anniv.

1983, Oct. 6 Engr. *Perf. 13*

742 A230 1k Car crash, police .50 .50
743 A230 2.50k Fire, ambulance service 1.00 .35
744 A230 3.50k Sea rescue 1.25 .85
Nos. 742-744 (3) 2.75 1.70

Life saving and salvage services.

Elderly in Society — A231

1983, Oct. 6

745 A231 2k Stages of life .80 .80
746 A231 2.50k Train passengers 1.00 .30

N.F.S. Grundtvig (1783-1872), Poet — A232

Street Scene, by C.W. Eckersberg (1783-1853) — A233

1983, Nov. 3 Engr.

747 A232 2.50k brown red 1.20 .50
748 A233 2.50k brown red 1.00 .35

A234 A235

1984, Jan. 26 Litho. & Engr.

749 A234 2.70k Shovel, sapling 1.20 .35

Plant a tree campaign.

1984, Jan. 26 Engr.

750 A235 3.70k Game 1.75 .50

1984 Billiards World Championships, Copenhagen, May 10-13.

Hydrographic Dept. Bicentenary
A236

Pilotage Service, 300th Anniv. — A237

1984, Mar. 22 **Engr.** ***Perf. 13***

751 A236 2.30k Compass	1.25	.90
752 A237 2.70k Boat	1.25	.50

2nd European Parliament Elections
A238

Scouts Around Campfire, Emblems
A239

Litho. & Engr.

1984, Apr. 12 ***Perf. 13***

753 A238 2.70k org & dk bl	1.75	.35
754 A239 2.70k multi	1.20	.35

Europa (1959-84)
A240

1984, May 3 **Engr.** ***Perf. 12½***

755 A240 2.70k red	*1.75*	.25
756 A240 3.70k blue	*2.25*	*1.60*

Prince Henrik, 50th Birthday
A241

D Day, 40th Anniv.
A242

1984, June 6 **Engr.**

757 A241 2.70k brown red	1.20	.35
758 A242 2.70k War Memorial, Copenhagen	1.20	.35

See Greenland No. 160.

17th Cent. Inn — A243

1984, June 6

759 A243 3k multicolored	1.50	1.40

Fishing and Shipping
A244

1984, Sept. 6 **Engr.**

760 A244 2.30k Research (Herring)	1.60	1.75
761 A244 2.70k Sea transport	1.10	.60
762 A244 3.30k Deep-sea fishing	1.60	1.75
763 A244 3.70k Deep-sea, diff.	1.60	1.75
Nos. 760-763 (4)	5.90	5.85

A245 A246

1984, Oct. 5 **Litho. & Engr.**

764 A245 1k Post bird	.35	.35

1984, Oct. 5

Holberg Meets with an Officer, by Wilhelm Marstrand (1810-73).

765 A246 2.70k multicolored	1.20	.35

Ludvig Holberg (1684-1754), writer.

Jewish Community in Copenhagen, 300th Anniv. — A247

1984, Oct. 5

766 A247 3.70k Woman blessing Sabbath candles	1.75	1.40

Carnival in Rome, by Christoffer W. Eckersberg (1783-1853) — A248

Paintings: 10k, Ymer and Odhumble (Nordic mythology figures), by Nicolai A. Abildgaard (1743-1809), vert.

Perf. 12½x13, 13x12½

1984, Nov. 22 **Litho. & Engr.**

767 A248 5k multicolored	3.25	3.25
768 A248 10k multicolored	5.75	5.75

German and French Reform Church, 300th Anniv. — A249

1985, Jan. 24 **Engr.** ***Perf. 13***

769 A249 2.80k magenta	1.75	.35

Bonn-Copenhagen Declaration, 30th Anniv. — A250

1985, Feb. 21 **Litho.** ***Perf. 14***

770 A250 2.80k Map, flags	1.90	.65

A251 A252

1985, Mar. 14 ***Perf. 13***

771 A251 3.80k multicolored	1.75	.90

Intl. Youth Year.

Early postal ordinances.

Souvenir Sheet

1985, Mar. 14 **Litho. & Engr.**

772 Sheet of 4	5.50	*6.50*
a. A252 1k Christian IV's Ordinance on Postmen, 1624	1.25	*1.60*
b. A252 2.50k Plague Mandate, 1711	1.25	*1.60*
c. A252 2.80k Ordinance on Prohibition of Mail by Means other than the Post, 1775	1.25	*1.60*
d. A252 3.80k Act on Postal Articles, 1831	1.25	*1.60*

HAFNIA '87 phil. exhib. Sold for 15k.

Europa 1985 — A253

1985, May 2

773 A253 2.80k Musical staff	*1.50*	*.50*
774 A253 3.80k Musical staff, diff.	*1.90*	*1.25*

Arrival of Queen Ingrid in Denmark, 50th Anniv. — A254

1985, May 21

775 A254 2.80k Queen Mother, chrysanthemums	1.20	.35

See Greenland No. 163.

Opening of the Faro Bridges — A255

1985, May 21 **Litho.** ***Perf. 13***

776 A255 2.80k Faro-Falster Bridge	1.20	.35

St. Cnut's Land Grant to Lund Cathedral, 900th Anniv. — A256

Seal of King Cnut and: 2.80k, Lund Cathedral. 3k, City of Helsingdorg, Sweden.

1985, May 21 **Engr.**

777 A256 2.80k multi	1.10	.45
778 A256 3k multi	2.00	2.00

See Sweden Nos. 1538-1539.

UN Decade for Women
A257

Sports
A258

1985, June 27 **Litho. & Engr.**

779 A257 3.80k Cyclist	1.75	1.00

1985, June 27

780 A258 2.80k Women's floor exercise	1.25	.30
781 A258 3.80k Canoe & kayak	1.75	.95
782 A258 6k Cycling	2.90	1.75
Nos. 780-782 (3)	5.90	3.00

Kronborg Castle, Elsinore, 400th Anniv. — A259

UN 40th Anniv. — A260

1985, Sept. 5

783 A259 2.80k multi	1.75	.35

1985, Sept. 5

784 A260 3.80k Dove, emblem	1.75	1.20

Niels Bohr (1885-1962), Physicist — A261

1985, Oct. 3 ***Perf. 13x12½***

785 A261 2.80k With wife Margrethe	1.75	1.40

Winner of 1922 Nobel Prize in Physics for theory of atomic structure.

Hand Signing "D" — A262

Boat, by Helge Refn — A263

1985, Nov. 7 **Engr.** ***Perf. 13***

786 A262 2.80k multicolored	1.40	.35

Danish Assoc. for the Deaf, 50th anniv.

1985, Nov. 7 **Litho.**

787 A263 2.80k multicolored	1.40	.35

Abstract Iron Sculpture by Robert Jacobsen
A264

Lithographed and Engraved

1985, Nov. 7 ***Perf. 13x12½***

788 A264 3.80k multicolored	3.50	3.75

Painting by Bjorn Wiinblad A265

1986, Jan. 23 Litho. *Perf. 13x12½*
789 A265 2.80k multicolored 1.75 1.40

Amnesty Intl., 25th Anniv. A266

Lithographed and Engraved
1986, Jan. 23 *Perf. 13*
790 A266 2.80k multicolored 1.20 .35

Miniature Sheet

HAFNIA '87 — A267

1986, Feb. 20
791 A267 Sheet of 4 7.50 11.00
a. 100o Holstein carriage, c. 1840 1.75 2.50
b. 250o Iceboat, c. 1880 1.75 2.50
c. 280o 1st mail van, 1908 1.75 2.50
d. 380o Airmail service 1919 1.75 2.50

Sold for 15k.

Changing of the Guard — A268

1986, Mar. 20 *Perf. 13*
792 A268 2.80k multicolored 1.20 .35

Royal Danish Life Guards barracks and Rosenborg Drilling Ground, bicent.

Types of 1933-85

1986-90 Engr. *Perf. 13*
793 A32 5o brn org ('89) .35 .40
794 A32 270o brt yel grn 1.90 1.75
b. Bklt. pane, 6 #318, 2 #691, 2 #794 18.00
795 A32 300o brt yel grn 1.75 .40
Complete booklet, #794b, 4 #795 22.50
796 A212 3k cop red 1.20 .60
Complete booklet, #691, #794, 3 #318, 2 #796 6.00
797 A212 3.20k deep vio 1.00 .80
798 A212 3.20k carmine 1.25 .40
c. Bklt. pane, 2 #693, 4 #798 9.00
Complete booklet, #689a, #798c 15.00
Complete booklet, #693, 2 #798, 2 #318, #689, 2 #494 15.50
799 A212 3.40k dk grn 2.25 3.00
800 A212 3.80k dark vio 1.20 2.90
801 A212 4.10k dark blue 1.40 .60
802 A212 4.20k dk pur 3.50 3.00
803 A212 4.40k dp bl 2.50 .60
804 A55 4.60k gray 5.00 5.50
805 A55 6.50k dp grn 2.50 1.00
806 A55 6.60k green 5.00 5.50
807 A55 7.10k brn vio 3.50 3.50
808 A55 7.30k green 4.75 5.50
809 A55 7.70k dk brn vio 4.50 2.10
810 A55 11k brown 5.50 5.25
811 A55 20k dp ultra 6.75 .80
812 A55 22k henna brn 7.25 2.25
813 A55 23k dark olive grn 10.50 2.25
814 A55 24k dark olive grn 10.50 2.00
815 A55 26k dark olive grn 12.50 2.25
Nos. 793-815 (23) 96.55 52.35

Issued: 6.50k, 20k, 1/9/86; 22k, 1/3/87; 270o, 3k, No. 797, 3.80k, 4.10k, 4.60k, 6.60k, 7.10k, 24k, 1/7/88; No. 794b, 1/28/88; 300o, No. 798, 3.40k, 4.20k, 4.40k, 7.30k, 7.70k, 11k, 26k, 1/26/89; 5o, 1989; 23k, 1/11/90.

No. 793 issued for use in lieu of currency of the same face value.

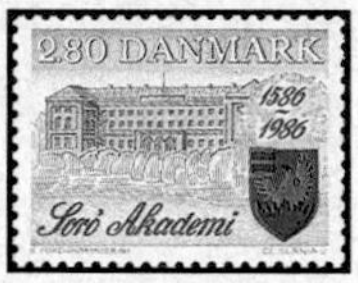

Soro Academy, 400th Anniv. — A269

1986, Apr. 28 Litho. & Engr.
816 A269 2.80k multi 1.40 .50

A270

A271

1986, Apr. 28
817 A270 3.80k multi 1.60 1.10

Intl. Peace Year.

1986, May 26 Litho.
818 A271 2.80k multi 1.75 .50

Crown Prince Frederik, 18th birthday.

Nordic Cooperation Issue 1986 — A272

Sister towns.

1986, May 27 Engr.
819 A272 2.80k Aalborg Harbor 1.40 .35
820 A272 3.80k Thisted Church and Town Hall 1.60 1.25

Hoje Tastrup Train Station Opening, May 31 — A273

1986, May 27 Litho.
821 A273 2.80k multi 1.20 .35

Mailbox, Telegraph Lines, Telephone — A274

1986, June 19 Litho. *Perf. 13*
822 A274 2.80k multi 1.00 .35

19th European Intl. PTT Congress, Copenhagen, Aug. 12-16.

Natl. Bird Candidates — A275

Finalists: a, Corvus corax. b, Sturnus vulgaris. c, Cygnus olor (winner). d, Vanellus vanellus. e, Alauda arvensis.

1986, June 19 Litho. & Engr.
823 Strip of 5 10.50 24.00
a.-e. A275 2.80k any single 2.00 1.00
Complete booklet, 2 #823 21.00

A276

1986, June 19
824 A276 2.80k multi 1.20 .35

Danish Rifle, Gymnastics and Sports Club, 125th anniv.

Souvenir Sheet

HAFNIA '87 — A277

1986, Sept. 4
825 Sheet of 4 10.00 12.50
a. A277 100o Mailcoach, c. 1841 2.25 3.00
b. A277 250o Postmaster, c. 1840 2.25 3.00
c. A277 280o Postman, c. 1851 2.25 3.00
d. A277 380o Rural postman, c. 1893 2.25 3.00

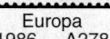

Sold for 15k.

Europa 1986 — A278

Cupid — A279

1986, Sept. 4 Engr.
826 A278 2.80k Street sweeper *2.50 .25*
827 A278 3.80k Garbage truck *3.50 1.50*

1986, Oct. 9 Litho.
828 A279 3.80k multi 1.50 1.00

Premiere of The Whims of Cupid and the Ballet Master, by Vincenzo Galeotti, bicent.

Refugee — A280

A281

1986, Oct. 9 Litho. & Engr.
829 A280 2.80k multi 1.20 .35

Danish Refugee Council Relief Campaign.

1986, Oct. 9 Litho. *Perf. 13*

Protestant Reformation in Denmark, 450th Anniv.: Sermon, altarpiece detail, 1561, Thorslunde Church, Copenhagen.

830 A281 6.50k multi 2.50 1.75

A282

Abstract by Lin Utzon — A283

1986, Nov. 6 Litho. & Engr.
831 A282 3.80k multi 3.00 3.00

Organization for Economic Cooperation and Development, 25th anniv.

1987, Jan. 22 Litho. *Perf. 13*
832 A283 2.80k multi 1.00 .35
Complete booklet, 10 #832 11.00

Art appreciation.

A284

A285

1987, Feb. 26 Engr. *Perf. 13*
833 A284 2.80k lake & black 1.00 .35

Danish Consumer Council, 40th anniv.

1987, Apr. 9 Litho. *Perf. 13*

Religious art (details) from Ribe Cathedral.

834 A285 3k Fresco 1.40 .60
835 A285 3.80k Stained-glass window 2.10 2.10
Complete booklet, 10 #835 21.00
836 A285 6.50k Mosaic 3.50 3.50
Nos. 834-836 (3) 7.00 6.20

Ribe Cathedral redecoration, 1982-1987, by Carl-Henning Pedersen.

A286

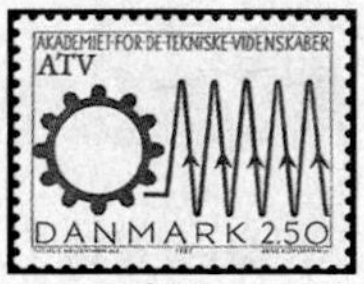

A287

Europa (Modern architecture): 2.80k, Central Library, Gentofte, 1985. 3.80k, Hoje Tastrup High School, 1985, horiz.

1987, May 4 Engr. *Perf. 13*
837 A286 2.80k rose claret *2.50 .35*
838 A286 3.80k bright ultra *3.50 2.25*

1987, May 4
839 A287 2.50k dk red & bl blk 2.00 2.00

Danish Academy of Technical Sciences (ATV), 50th anniv.

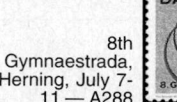

8th Gymnaestrada, Herning, July 7-11 — A288

1987, June 18 Litho. & Engr.
840 A288 2.80k multi 1.00 .35
Complete booklet, 10 #840 10.00

A289 A290

1987, June 18
841 A289 3.80k multi 1.60 1.40

Danish Cooperative Bacon Factories, cent.

1987, Aug. 27 **Litho.**
842 A290 3.80k Single-sculler 1.60 1.20

World Rowing Championships, Aug. 23-30.

HAFNIA '87, Bella Center, Copenhagen, Oct. 16-25 — A291

Litho. & Engr.

1987, Aug. 27 ***Perf. 13x12½***
843 A291 280o Type A15, mail train c. 1912 1.90 1.50

Souvenir Sheet

843A A291 280o like No. 843 20.00 26.00

Purchase of No. 843A included admission to the exhibition. Sold for 45k.

Due to a color shift, some examples of No. 843A have a green lawn and locomotive.

Abstact by Ejler Bille — A292

1987, Sept. 24 **Litho.** ***Perf. 13***
844 A292 2.80k multi 1.00 .35
Complete booklet, 10 #844 10.00

Rasmus Rask (1787-1832), Linguist — A293

1987, Oct. 15 **Engr.** ***Perf. 13x12½***
845 A293 2.80k dark henna brown 1.00 .45

A294

Emblem: Miraculous Catch (Luke 5:4-7), New Testament.

1987, Oct. 15 ***Perf. 13***
846 A294 3k carmine lake 1.25 .50

Clerical Assoc. for the Home Mission in Denmark, 125th anniv.

A295

Designs: 3k, Two lions from the gate of Rosenburg Castle around the monogram of Christian IV. 4.10k, Portrait of the monarch painted by P. Isaacsz, vert.

Photo. & Engr., Litho. (4.10k)

1988, Feb. 18 ***Perf. 13***
847 A295 3k blue gray & gold 1.25 .30
Complete booklet, 10 #847 12.50
848 A295 4.10k multi 1.60 .75

Accession of Christian IV (1577-1648), King of Denmark and Norway (1588-1648), 400th anniv.

Ole Worm (1588-1654), Archaeologist, and Runic Artifacts — A296

1988, Feb. 18 **Engr.**
849 A296 7.10k chocolate 2.75 2.75

Odense, 1000th Anniv. — A297 A298

Design: St. Cnut's Church and statue of Hans Christian Andersen, Odense.

1988, Mar. 10 **Engr.**
850 A297 3k multi 1.00 .35
Complete booklet, 10 #850 10.00

1988, Apr. 7 **Litho.**
851 A298 2.70k multi 1.25 1.25

Danish Civil Defense and Emergency Planning Agency, 50th Anniv.

WHO, 40th Anniv. — A299

Abolition of *Stavnsbaand,* 200th Anniv. — A300

1988, Apr. 7 **Litho. & Engr.**
852 A299 4.10k multi 1.75 1.00

1988, May 5 **Litho.**

Painting: King Christian VII riding past the Liberty Memorial, Copenhagen, by C.W. Eckersberg (1783-1853).

853 A300 3.20k multi 1.40 1.00

Stavnsbaand (adscription) provided that all Danish farmers' sons from age 4 to 40 would be bound as villeins to the estates on which they were born, thus providing landowners with free labor.

A301 A302

Europa: Transport and communication.

1988, May 5
854 A301 3k Postwoman on bicycle *1.75* .25
855 A301 4.10k Mobile telephone *2.50* *1.00*

1988, June 16 **Litho.**
856 A302 4.10k multi 1.60 .75

1988 Individual Speedway World Motorcycle Championships, Denmark, Sept. 3.

Federation of Danish Industries, 150th Anniv. — A303

Painting (detail): *The Industrialists,* by P.S. Kroyer.

1988, June 16 ***Perf. 13½x13***
857 A303 3k multi 1.00 .50

Danish Metalworkers' Union, Cent. — A304

1988, Aug. 18 **Litho.** ***Perf. 13***
858 A304 3k Glass mosaic by Niels Winkel 1.00 .50

Tonder Teachers' Training College, 200th Anniv. — A305

1988, Aug. 18 **Engr.** ***Perf. 13x12½***
859 A305 3k lake 1.00 .50

Homage to Leon Degand, Sculpture by Robert Jacobsen A306

1988, Sept. 22 ***Perf. 11½x13***
860 A306 4.10k blk, lake & gray 3.75 *5.00*

Danish-French cultural exchange program, 10th anniv. See France No. 2130.

Preservation of Historic Sites — A307

1988, Oct. 13 **Engr.** ***Perf. 13x12½***
861 A307 3k Lumby Windmill, 1818 1.60 .50
Complete booklet, 10 #861 16.00
862 A307 7.10k Vejstrup Water Mill, 1837 4.00 2.75

Paintings in the State Museum of Art, Copenhagen — A308

4.10k, *Bathing Boys,* 1902, by Peter Hansen (1868-1928). 10k, *The Hill at Overkaerby,* 1917, by Fritz Syberg (1862-1939).

Litho. & Engr.

1988, Nov. 3 ***Perf. 13***
863 A308 4.10k multi 3.25 *4.50*
864 A308 10k multi 6.50 *8.00*

See Nos. 881-882, 951-952, 972-973, 1018-1019.

The Little Mermaid, Sculpture by Edvard Eriksen — A309

1989, Feb. 16 **Engr.**
865 A309 3.20k dark green 1.75 .50
Complete booklet, 10 #865 17.50

Tourism industry, cent.

Danish Soccer Assoc., Cent. — A310

NATO Membership, 40th Anniv. — A311

1989, Mar. 16 **Litho.**
866 A310 3.20k multi 1.60 .50
Complete booklet, 10 #866 16.00

1989, Mar. 16
867 A311 4.40k dk blue, gold & lt blue 2.00 1.25

Nordic Cooperation Issue — A312

Folk costumes.

1989, Apr. 20 **Litho. & Engr.**
868 A312 3.20k Woman from Valby 1.40 .40
869 A312 4.40k Pork butcher 2.10 1.60

European Parliament 3rd Elections A313

1989, May 11 **Litho.**
870 A313 3k blue & yellow 1.60 1.50

Europa 1989 — A314

Children's toys.

1989, May 11 Litho. & Engr.

871 A314 3.20k Lego blocks *1.90* .25
872 A314 4.40k Wooden soldiers, by Kay Bojesen *3.00* *.90*

Agricultural Museum, Cent. A315

1989, June 15 Engr. *Perf. 13*

873 A315 3.20k Tractor, 1889 1.25 .50

Interparliamentary Union, Cent. — A316

1989, June 15 Litho. & Engr.

874 A316 3.40k Folketing Chamber layout 3.50 4.00

Danish Fishery and Marine Research Institute, Cent. A317

1989, Aug. 24 Litho. & Engr.

875 A317 3.20k multi 1.25 .50

Bernhard Severin Ingemann (1789-1862), Poet and Novelist — A318

1989, Aug. 24 Engr.

876 A318 7.70k dark green 3.00 1.90

A319

A320

Danish Film Office, 50th Anniv.: 3k, Scene from the short feature film *They Reached the Ferry*, 1948. 3.20k, Bodil Ipsen (d. 1964), actress. 4.40k, Carl Th. Dreyer (1889-1968), screenwriter and director.

1989, Sept. 28 Litho.

877 A319 3k multi 1.40 1.40
878 A319 3.20k multi 1.25 .50
879 A319 4.40k multi 1.75 1.00
Nos. 877-879 (3) 4.40 2.90

1989, Nov. 10 Litho. & Engr.

880 A320 3.20k multi 1.25 .50

Stamp Day, 50th anniv.

Art Type of 1988

Paintings: 4.40k, *Part of the Northern Gate of the Citadel Bridge*, c. 1837, by Christen Kobke (1810-1848). 10k, *A Little Girl, Elise Kobke, With a Cup in Front of Her*, c. 1850, by Constantin Hansen (1804-1880).

1989, Nov. 10 *Perf. 12½x13*

881 A308 4.40k multi 3.00 4.00
882 A308 10k multi 6.25 8.50

Types of 1933-82 and

A321

A321a

Queen Margrethe II

1990-98 Engr. *Perf. 12¾*

883 A32 25o bluish black .55 .40
a. Bklt. pane, 4 #691, 2 #883 4.75
884 A32 125o carmine lake .95 .40
885 A32 325o lt yel grn 2.10 1.75
886 A32 350o yellow green 2.00 .95
887 A212 3.50k dark red 1.25 .40
a. Bklt. pane, 2 each #691, 885, 887 8.00
Complete booklet, #883, #885, #887, 3 #691 16.00
Complete booklet, #883a, #887a 13.50
888 A321 3.50k henna brown 1.40 .40
b. Bklt. pane, 4 each #883, #884, #888 ('91) 20.00
Complete booklet, #888b 20.00
Complete booklet, 2 each #883, #884, #888 16.00
889 A212 3.75k dark green 2.25 2.40
890 A321 3.75k green 4.00 3.75
891 A321 3.75k red 3.00 .40
a. Bklt. pane, 4 each #884, #891 17.50
Complete booklet, #891a 17.50
b. Booklet pane, 2 each #691, 883, 891 8.75
Complete booklet, #891b 8.75
892 A321a 3.75k red 2.25 .50
a. Booklet pane, 2 each #691, 883, 892 14.50
Complete booklet, #892a 14.50
b. Booklet pane, 2 #883, 4 #494, 2 #892 12.00
Complete booklet, #892b 12.00
893 A321 4k brown 2.50 1.20
894 A321a 4k deep bl grn 2.25 .80
895 A321a 4.25k olive brown 2.90 1.90
896 A212 4.50k brown violet 2.75 3.25
897 A321 4.50k violet 2.50 2.40
898 A321a 4.50k deep bl blk 2.60 2.40
899 A212 4.75k dark blue 1.90 .40
900 A321 4.75k blue 2.50 .40
901 A321 4.75k violet 3.50 2.00
902 A321a 4.75k brown *3.50* 2.10
903 A321a 5k violet 2.50 1.75
904 A321 5k blue 3.50 .40
905 A321 5.25k black 3.50 1.75
906 A321a 5.25k deep blue 3.25 .80
907 A321 5.50k green 3.25 3.75
908 A321a 5.50k henna brown 3.50 2.75
909 A55 7.50k dark bl grn 3.00 2.75
Nos. 883-909 (27) 69.15 42.15

Queen Margrethe II's 50th birthday (No. 888).

Issued: No. 888, 4/5; Nos. 890, 897, 900, 1990; No. 888a, 2/14/91; Nos. 886, 891, 891a, 901, 904, 6/10/92; 5.50k, 1/13/94; 4k, 5.25k, 6/27/96; Nos. 892, 892a, 1/14/97; Nos. 894, 902, 903, 906, 8/28/97; Nos. 895, 898, 908, 909, 3/26/98; others, 1/11/90.

See Nos. 1114, 1125, 1130.

A322

A323

Design: Silver coffee pot designed by Axel Johannes Kroyer, Copenhagen, 1726.

1990, Feb. 15 Engr. *Perf. 13*

911 A322 3.50k dark blue & blk 1.20 .80
Complete booklet, 10 #911 12.00

Museum of Decorative Art, cent.

1990, Feb. 15

Steam engine, 200th anniv.: Steam engine built by Andrew Mitchell, 1790.

912 A323 8.25k dull red brown 2.75 1.75

Nyholm, 300th Anniv. A324

1990, Apr. 5 Engr.

913 A324 4.75k black 1.75 .90

Europa 1990 — A325

1990, Apr. 5 Litho.

914 A325 3.50k Royal Monogram, Haderslev P.O. *1.10* .25
915 A325 4.75k Odense P.O. *1.75* *.60*

A326

A327

Pieces from the Flora Danica Banquet Service produced for King Christian VII.

1990, May 3 Litho.

916 A326 3.50k Bell-shaped lid, dish 1.25 1.90
917 A326 3.50k Gravy boat, dish 1.25 1.90
918 A326 3.50k Ice pot, casserole, lid 1.25 1.90
919 A326 3.50k Serving dish 1.25 1.90
a. Strip of 4, #916-919 5.00 8.50

Flora Danica porcelain, 200th anniv.

1990, June 14

Endangered plant species.

920 A327 3.25k Marshmallow 1.25 1.25
921 A327 3.50k Red helleborine 2.25 *35.00*
Complete booklet, 10 #921 30.00
922 A327 3.75k Purple orchis 1.50 1.50
923 A327 4.75k Lady's slipper 1.90 .65
Nos. 920-923 (4) 6.90 38.40

Village Churches, Jutland — A328

Perf. 13x12½, 12½x13

1990, Aug. 30 Engr.

924 A328 3.50k Gjellerup 1.20 .35
Complete booklet, 10 #924 12.00
925 A328 4.75k Veng 1.60 .75
926 A328 8.25k Bredsten, vert. 3.00 2.00
Nos. 924-926 (3) 5.80 3.10

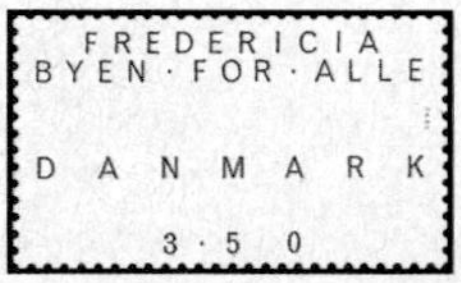

Fredericia, "The Town for Everybody" A329

Engr. & Embossed

1990, Oct. 5 *Perf. 13*

927 A329 3.50k black & red 1.20 .90

Tordenskiold (Peter Wessel, 1690-1720), Admiral — A330

1990, Oct. 5 Litho. *Perf. 13½x13*

928 A330 3.50k multicolored 1.20 .60
Complete booklet, 10 #928 12.00

Prevent Bicycle Thefts — A331

Design: 3.50k, Stop drunk driving.

1990, Nov. 8 Litho. *Perf. 13x12½*

930 A331 3.25k shown 1.10 1.10
931 A331 3.50k Automobile, wine glass 1.10 .30

Locomotives — A332

1991, Mar. 14 Engr. *Perf. 13*

932 A332 3.25k IC3 1990 1.40 1.50
933 A332 3.50k Class A 1882 1.10 .35
Complete booklet, 10 #933 11.00
934 A332 3.75k Class MY 1954 1.25 1.75
935 A332 4.75k Class P 1907 1.50 1.50
Nos. 932-935 (4) 5.25 5.10

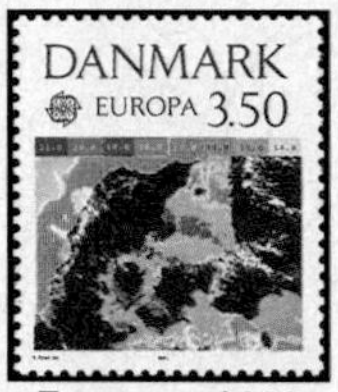

Europa — A333

Jutland Law, 750th Anniv. — A334

Satellite photographs showing temperatures of Danish: 3.50k, Waters. 4.75k, Land.

1991, May 2 Litho. *Perf. 13*

936 A333 3.50k multicolored *1.75* *.25*
937 A333 4.75k multicolored *2.10* *1.00*

1991, May 2

938 A334 8.25k multicolored 3.00 2.75

Danish Islands — A335

1991, June 6

939 A335 3.50k Fano 1.40 .30
Complete booklet, 10 #939 18.00
940 A335 4.75k Christianso 1.60 .90

Decorative Art — A336

Keep Denmark Clean — A337

Designs: 3.25k, Earthenware bowl and jars by Christian Poulsen. 3.50k, Chair by Hans Wegner, vert. 4.75k, Silver cutlery by Kay Bojesen, vert. 8k, Lamp by Poul Henningsen.

1991, Aug. 22 Litho. *Perf. 13*

941 A336 3.25k multicolored 1.10 1.50
942 A336 3.50k multicolored 1.00 .35
Complete booklet, 10 #942 10.00
943 A336 4.75k multicolored 1.25 1.75
944 A336 8.25k multicolored 3.00 4.50
Nos. 941-944 (4) 6.35 8.10

1991, Sept. 19 Engr. *Perf. 13*

Designs: 3.50k, Cleaning up after dog. 4.75k, Picking up litter.

945 A337 3.50k red 2.00 .30
Complete booklet, 10 #945 20.00
946 A337 4.75k blue 2.00 1.00

Posters from Danish Museum of Decorative Arts — A338

Posters for: 3.50k, Nordic Advertising Congress, by Arne Ungermann (1902-1981). 4.50k, Poster Exhibition at Copenhagen Zoo (baboon), by Valdemar Andersen (1875-1928). 4.75k, Danish Air Lines, by Ib Andersen (1907-1969). 12k, The Sinner, by Sven Brasch (1886-1970).

1991, Sept. 19 **Litho.**

947 A338 3.50k multicolored 1.00 .30
948 A338 4.50k multicolored 1.75 2.50
949 A338 4.75k multicolored 1.25 1.50
950 A338 12k multicolored 4.00 3.50
Nos. 947-950 (4) 8.00 7.80

Art Type of 1988

Designs: 4.75k, Lady at her Toilet by Harald Giersing (1881-1927), vert. 14k, Road through a Wood by Edvard Weie (1879-1943), vert.

Litho. & Engr.

1991, Nov. 7 ***Perf. 13x12½***

951 A308 4.75k multicolored 1.75 1.75
952 A308 14k multicolored 4.50 4.00

A339 A340

Treasures of Natl. Museum: 3.50k, Earthenware bowl, Skarpsalling. 4.50k, Bronze dancer, Grevensvaenge. 4.75k, Bottom plate of silver cauldron, Gundestrup. 8.25k, Flint knife, Hindsgavl.

1992, Feb. 13 **Engr.** ***Perf. 13***

953 A339 3.50k dk vio & brown 1.10 .30
Complete booklet, 10 #953 11.00
954 A339 4.50k dk bl & dk ol green 2.40 2.40
955 A339 4.75k brown & black 1.25 1.10
956 A339 8.25k dk ol grn & vio brown 2.75 2.75
Nos. 953-956 (4) 7.50 6.55

1992, Mar. 12 ***Perf. 13½x13***

957 A340 3.50k rose carmine 1.25 .65

Danish Society of Chemical, Civil, Electrical, and Mechanical Engineers, cent.

Souvenir Sheet

Queen Margaret I (1353-1412) — A341

Litho. & Engr.

1992, Mar. 12 ***Perf. 12½***

958 A341 Sheet of 2 6.25 7.25
a. 3.50k Fresco 3.00 3.50
b. 4.75k Alabaster bust 3.00 3.50

Nordia '94, Scandinavian Philatelic Exhibition. No. 958 sold for 12k to benefit the exhibition.

Discovery of America, 500th Anniv. — A342

1992, May 7 **Engr.** ***Perf. 12½***

959 A342 3.50k Potato plant *2.25* *.40*
Complete booklet, 10 #959 *22.50*
960 A342 4.75k Ear of corn *4.25* *1.75*

Europa.

Protect the Environment — A343

Litho. & Engr.

1992, June 10 ***Perf. 13***

961 A343 3.75k Hare beside road 1.25 .30
Complete booklet, 10 #961 12.50
962 A343 5k Fish, water pollution 1.75 .70
963 A343 8.75k Cut trees, vert. 3.50 2.00
Nos. 961-963 (3) 6.50 3.00

Queen Margrethe II and Prince Henrik, 25th Wedding Anniv. — A344

1992, June 10 **Litho.** ***Perf. 12½x13***

964 A344 3.75k multicolored .90 1.60

See Greenland No. 253.

A345 A346

1992, July 16 ***Perf. 13***

965 A345 3.75k multicolored 1.75 .75

Denmark, European soccer champions.

1992, Aug. 27 **Engr.** ***Perf. 13***

966 A346 3.75k blue 1.50 .75

Danish Pavilion, Expo '92, Seville.

A347 A348

1992, Oct. 8 **Litho. & Engr.** ***Perf. 13***

967 A347 3.75k blue & org 1.50 .75

Single European market.

Litho. & Engr.

1992, Oct. 8 ***Perf. 12½***

Cartoon characters: 3.50k, A Hug, by Ivar Gjorup. 3.75k, Love Letter, by Phillip Stein Jonsson. 4.75k, Domestic Triangle, by Nikoline Werdelin. 5k, Poet and His Little Wife, by Jorgen Mogensen.

968 A348 3.50k multicolored 1.75 1.00

Engr.

969 A348 3.75k red & purple 1.40 .30
970 A348 4.75k blk & red brn 2.50 2.50
971 A348 5k blue & red brn 1.75 .70
Nos. 968-971 (4) 7.40 4.50

Art Type of 1988

5k, Landscape from Vejby, 1843, by John Thomas Lundbye. 10k, Motif from Halleby Brook, 1847, by Peter Christian Skovgaard.

Litho. & Engr.

1992, Nov. 12 ***Perf. 12½x13***

972 A308 5k multicolored 2.10 2.00
973 A308 10k multicolored 4.00 3.25

A349 A350

1992, Nov. 12 ***Perf. 13***

974 A349 3.75k Jacob's fight with angel 1.75 1.20

Publication of new Danish bible.

Litho. & Engr.

1993, Feb. 4 ***Perf. 13***

Archaeological Treasures. Anthropomorphic gold foil figures found in: 3.75k, Lundeborg, horiz. 5k, Bornholm.

975 A350 3.75k multicolored 1.40 .30
976 A350 5k multicolored 1.90 .70

A351 A352

Butterflies.

1993, Mar. 11 **Litho.**

977 A351 3.75k Small tortoise-shell 1.75 .40
Complete booklet, 10 #977 17.50
978 A351 5k Large blue 2.50 .80
979 A351 8.75k Marsh fritillary 5.25 3.50
980 A351 12k Red admiral 5.25 3.50
Nos. 977-980 (4) 14.75 8.20

1993, May 6 **Litho.** ***Perf. 12½***

Posters: 3.75k, Pierrot, by Thor Bogelund, 1947, horiz. 5k, Balloons, by Wilhelm Freddie, 1987.

981 A352 3.75k multicolored 1.75 1.00
Complete booklet, 10 #981 17.50
982 A352 5k multicolored 1.75 .90

Tivoli Gardens, 150th anniv.

A353

Europa (Contemporary paintings by): 3.75k, Troels Worsel, horiz. 5k, Stig Brogger.

1993, May 6 ***Perf. 13***

983 A353 3.75k multicolored *1.40* *1.10*
984 A353 5k multicolored *1.90* *.90*

A354

1993, June 17 **Engr.** ***Perf. 13***

985 A354 5k dark blue green 4.00 1.00

Danish-Russian relations, 500th anniv. See Russia No. 6154.

Training Ships
A355 A356

Perf. 13, 13½x13 (#987)

1993, June 17 **Litho. & Engr.**

986 A355 3.75k Danmark 2.00 .30
987 A356 4.75k Jens Krogh 4.00 4.50
988 A355 5k Georg Stage, horiz. 3.00 1.75

Size: 39x28mm

Perf. 13x13½

989 A356 9.50k Marilyn Anne, horiz. 5.50 5.25
Nos. 986-989 (4) 14.50 11.80

Child's Drawing of Viking Ships — A357

Letter Writing Campaign — A358

1993, Aug. 19 **Litho.** ***Perf. 13***

990 A357 3.75k multicolored 2.25 .65
991 A358 5k lt & dk bl & blk 2.50 1.40

Ethnic Jewelry — A359

1993, Sept. 16 **Litho.** ***Perf. 13***

992 A359 3.50k Falster 1.75 1.25
993 A359 3.75k Amager 1.75 .30
Complete booklet, 10 #993 17.50
994 A359 5k Laeso 2.00 .90
995 A359 8.75k Romo 4.50 3.00
Nos. 992-995 (4) 10.00 5.45

Cubist Paintings
A360

5k, Assemblage, by Vilhelm Lundstrom, 1929. 15k, Composition, by Franciska Clausen, 1929.

Litho. & Engr.

1993, Nov. 11 *Perf. 12½*
996 A360 5k multicolored 2.75 2.25
997 A360 15k multicolored 6.75 5.00

See Nos. 1033-1034, 1080-1081.

Conservation — A361

1994, Jan. 27 **Litho.** *Perf. 13*
998 A361 3.75k Save water *3.50 .30*
999 A361 5k CO2 *4.50 1.10*

Castles
A362

Castles: 3.50k, Marselisborg, Aarhus. 3.75k, Amalienborg, Copenhagen. 5k, Fredensborg, North Zealand. 8.75k, Graasten, South Jutland.

Litho. & Engr.

1994, Mar. 17 *Perf. 13x12½*
1000 A362 3.50k multicolored 1.50 .70
1001 A362 3.75k multicolored 1.75 .30
Complete booklet, 10 #1001 17.50
1002 A362 5k multicolored 2.25 .30
1003 A362 8.75k multicolored 3.75 3.50
a. Bklt. pane, #1000-1003 30.00 30.00

No. 1003a printed with 2 different labels. One shows a marching band, the other shows a ship.

Danmark Expedition, 1906-08 — A363

Europa: 3.75k, Expedition ship, Danmark, Alfred Wegener's weather balloon. 5k, Theodolite, Johan Peter Koch, cartographer.

1994, May 5 **Engr.** *Perf. 13*
1004 A363 3.75k deep brn vio *1.90 .25*
1005 A363 5k dp slate grn *2.60 1.25*
Complete booklet, 10 #1005 *35.00*

Trams — A364

Designs: 3.75k, Copenhagen tram (Engelhardt). 4.75k, Aarhus car. 5k, Odense tram, vert. 12k, Horse-drawn tram.

Litho. & Engr.

1994, June 9 *Perf. 13*
1006 A364 3.75k multicolored 1.25 .30
1007 A364 4.75k multicolored 2.25 2.75
1008 A364 5k multicolored 1.75 1.40

Size: 38x21mm

1009 A364 12k multicolored 5.25 5.25
Nos. 1006-1009 (4) 10.50 9.70

Children's Stamp Competition
A365

ILO, 75th Anniv.
A366

1994, Aug. 25 **Litho.** *Perf. 12½*
1010 A365 3.75k multicolored 1.50 .70

1994, Aug. 25 *Perf. 13*
1011 A366 5k multicolored 2.00 1.00

A367

Wild animals.

Litho. & Engr.

1994, Oct. 20 *Perf. 12½*
1012 A367 3.75k House sparrows 2.00 .35
1013 A367 4.75k Badger 3.00 2.25
1014 A367 5k Squirrel, vert. 2.60 1.00
1015 A367 9.50k Black grouse 5.00 4.50

Size: 36x26mm

Perf. 13

1016 A367 12k Grass snake 6.00 5.25
Nos. 1012-1016 (5) 18.60 13.35

A368

1994, Nov. 10 **Litho.** *Perf. 13*
1017 A368 3.75k multicolored 1.75 .70

Folk High Schools, 150th anniv.

Painting Type of 1988

Designs: 5k, Study of Italian Woman and Sleeping Child, by Wilhelm Marstrand. 15k, Interior from Amaliegade with the Artist's Brothers, by Wilhelm Bendz.

Litho. & Engr.

1994, Nov. 10 *Perf. 12½x13*
1018 A308 5k multicolored 2.00 1.40
1019 A308 15k multicolored 6.00 3.25

Aarhus Cathedral School, 800th Anniv. — A369

Litho. & Engr.

1995, Jan. 26 *Perf. 13*
1020 A369 3.75k multicolored 1.75 .70

UN, 50th Anniv. — A370

Litho. & Engr.

1995, Jan. 26 *Perf. 13*
1021 A370 5k multicolored 2.50 1.20
Complete booklet, 10 #1021 35.00

Danish Islands
A371

1995, Mar. 16 **Engr.** *Perf. 13*
1022 A371 3.75k Avernako 2.25 .30
Complete booklet, 10 #1022 22.50
1023 A371 4.75k Fejo 2.75 2.50
1024 A371 5k Fur 3.50 .90
1025 A371 9.50k Endelave 4.50 4.50
a. Booklet pane, #1022-1025 + 2 labels 15.00
Complete booklet, 2 #1025a 32.50
Nos. 1022-1025 (4) 13.00 8.20

No. 1025a printed with four different large labels. Labels with one pane are MF Faaborg II and MF Endelave. The other pane has MF Bukken-bruse and MF Fursund.

Liberation of Denmark, 50th Anniv.
A372

Designs: 3.75k, Gen. Montgomery, Town Hall Square, vert. 5k, White busses returning from concentration camps. 8.75k, Airplane dropping supplies to resistance. 12k, Jews escape across the Sound to Sweden.

1995, May 4 **Litho.** *Perf. 13*
1026 A372 3.75k multicolored 2.10 .30
Complete booklet, 10 #1026 21.00
1027 A372 5k multicolored 2.75 1.00
1028 A372 8.75k multicolored 4.25 4.00
1029 A372 12k multicolored 6.00 6.00
Nos. 1026-1029 (4) 15.10 11.30

Europa (Nos. 1026-1027).

A373 A374

1995, June 8 **Litho.** *Perf. 13*
1030 A373 3.50k multicolored 1.50 .70

Danish Rhymed Chronicle, 500th anniv.

1995, June 8

3.75k, Roskilde Festival. 5k, Tonder Festival.

1031 A374 3.75k multi, horiz. 1.60 .30
Complete booklet, 10 #1031 16.00
1032 A374 5k multi 2.25 1.00

No. 1031 is 28x21mm.

Paintings
A375

Designs: 10k, "Sct. Hans Aften, 1955," by Jens Sondergaard. 15k, "Landskab-Gudhjem, 1939," by Niels Lergaard.

Litho. & Engr.

1995, Aug. 24 *Perf. 13x12½*
1033 A375 10k multicolored 5.00 5.75
1034 A375 15k multicolored 7.50 7.50

Tycho Brahe (1546-1601), Astronomer
A376

3.75k, Uranienborg Observatory. 5.50k, Sextant.

Litho. & Engr.

1995, Oct. 27 *Perf. 13*
1035 A376 3.75k multicolored 2.00 .65
1036 A376 5.50k multicolored 2.75 2.75

See Sweden Nos. 2149-2150.

Toys
A377

Designs: 3.75k, Tekno cars. 5k, Dolls, teddy bear. 8.75k, Model trains. 12k, Glud & Marstrand tin horse-drawn carriage & fire pumper.

1995, Nov. 9 *Perf. 13x12½*
1037 A377 3.75k multicolored 1.60 .30
Complete booklet, 10 #1037 16.00
1038 A377 5k multicolored 2.10 1.00
1039 A377 8.75k multicolored 3.25 3.25
1040 A377 12k multicolored 4.25 4.25
Nos. 1037-1040 (4) 11.20 8.80

A378 A379

Cartoonlike views of Copenhagen: 3.75k, Round Tower as music box. 5k, Christiansborg Castle. 8.75k, Marble Church as top of balloon. 12k, The Little Mermaid statue on stage.

1996, Jan. 25 **Litho.** *Perf. 13*
1041 A378 3.75k multicolored 1.25 .30
Complete booklet, 10 #1041 13.00
1042 A378 5k multicolored 1.75 .70
1043 A378 8.75k multicolored 3.00 3.00
1044 A378 12k multicolored 4.00 4.50
Nos. 1041-1044 (4) 10.00 8.50

Copenhagen, 1996 cultural capital of Europe.

1996, Mar. 21 **Litho.** *Perf. 13*
1045 A379 3.75k Sports for disabled 1.25 .30
Complete booklet, 10 #1045 13.00
1046 A379 4.75k Swimming 1.60 1.60
1047 A379 5k Sailing 1.75 .50
1048 A379 9.50k Cycling 3.25 3.25
a. Bklt. pane of 4, #1045-1048 + 2 labels 14.00
Complete booklet, 2 #1048a 28.00

No. 1048a printed with two different large labels. One shows hands and soccer ball, second shows tennis racket and tennis balls.

Danish Federation for Sports for the Disabled (No. 1045). Modern Olympic Games, cent., Sports Confederation of Denmark, cent., 1996 Summer Olympics, Atlanta (Nos. 1046-1048).

A380 A381

1996, May 9 **Litho.** *Perf. 13*
1049 A380 3.75k multicolored 1.50 1.00

Danish Employers' Confederation, cent.

1996, May 9

Famous Danish Women (Europa): 3.75k, Karen Blixen (1885-1962), writer. 5k, Asta Nielsen (1881-1972), silent screen actress.

1050 A381 3.75k lt brn & dk brn *1.50 .50*
1051 A381 5k gray & dk blue *2.00 .75*
Complete booklet, 10 #1051 *20.00*

A382

A383

Wooden Dinghies: 3.50k, Roskilde Fjord sail boat. 3.75k, Limfjorden skiff. 12.25k, Two-masted smack, South Funen Archipelago.

Perf. 13, 12½ (#1053)

1996, June 13 Engr.

1052 A382 3.50k multicolored 1.25 1.00
1053 A382 3.75k multicolored 1.50 .50
Complete booklet, 10 #1053 16.00
1054 A382 12.25k multicolored 4.50 5.25
Nos. 1052-1054 (3) 7.25 6.75

No. 1053 is 20x39mm.

Litho. & Engr.

1996, Sept. 12 ***Perf. 13x12½***

Lighthouses.

1055 A383 3.75k Fornaes 1.50 .30
Complete booklet, 10 #1055 16.00
1056 A383 5k Blavandshuk 1.75 .50
a. Bklt. pane, 8 #1055, 2 #1056 22.00
Complete booklet, #1056a 22.00
1057 A383 5.25k Bovbjerg 2.00 2.00
1058 A383 8.75k Mon 3.00 3.00
Nos. 1055-1058 (4) 8.25 5.80

Art Works of Thorvald Bindesboll (1846-1908) — A384

Litho. & Engr.

1996, Oct. 10 ***Perf. 13***

1059 A384 3.75k Pitcher 1.50 .30
Complete booklet, 10 #1059 16.00

Litho.

1060 A384 4k Portfolio cover 1.60 1.10

Paintings A385

Designs: 10k, "At Lunch," by P.S. Kroyer, 1893. 15k, "The Girl with Sunflowers," by Michael Ancher, 1889.

Litho. & Engr.

1996, Nov. 7 ***Perf. 13x12½***

1061 A385 10k multicolored 4.00 4.00
1062 A385 15k multicolored 5.25 5.25

A386

A387

Queen Margrethe II: 3.50k, With Prince Henrik. 3.75k, With Crown Prince Frederik. 4k, Delivering New Year speech. 5.25k, Waving to crowd.

1997, Jan. 14 Litho. ***Perf. 13***

1063 A386 3.50k multicolored 1.25 1.25
1064 A386 3.75k multicolored 1.50 .30
Complete booklet, 10 #1064 16.00
1065 A386 4k multicolored 1.40 .70
1066 A386 5.25k multicolored 2.00 1.50
a. Sheet of 4, #1063-1066 + 2 labels 6.50 6.50
Nos. 1063-1066 (4) 6.15 3.75

Queen Margrethe II, 25th anniv. of coronation.

1997, Mar. 13 Engr. ***Perf. 13***

Open Air Museum, Copenhagen, Cent.: 3.50k, Kalstrup post mill. 3.75k, Ellested water mill. 5k, Fjellerup manor barn. 8.75k, Romo farm.

1067 A387 3.50k multicolored 1.25 1.00
1068 A387 3.75k multicolored 1.25 .30
Complete booklet, 10 #1068 12.50
1069 A387 5k multicolored 1.75 .75
Complete booklet, 10 #1069 17.50
1070 A387 8.75k multicolored 3.00 2.50
a. Booklet pane, #1067-1070 + label 14.00
Complete booklet, 2 #1070a 28.00
Nos. 1067-1070 (4) 7.25 4.55

No. 1070a printed with two different large labels. One shows a view of Ellested water mill, the other shows a farm in Ejersted.

Great Belt Railway Link — A388

1997, May 15 Litho. ***Perf. 13***

1071 A388 3.75k East Tunnel 1.50 .50
Complete booklet, 10 #1071 15.00
1072 A388 4.75k West Bridge 1.75 1.75

A389

Kalmar Union, 600th Anniv.: No. 1073, Margrete I and Eric of Pomerania. No. 1074, The Three Graces symbolizing Denmark, Norway and Sweden.

1997, June 12 Litho. ***Perf. 13***

1073 A389 4k multicolored 2.60 2.75
1074 A389 4k multicolored 2.60 2.75
a. Pair, #1073-1074 5.25 6.50

No. 1074a is a continuous design.

Copenhagen-Roskilde Railway, 150th Anniv. — A390

Designs: 3.75k, Two modern trains under Carlsberg Bridge. 8.75k, Early steam train going under Carlsberg Bridge.

Litho. & Engr.

1997, June 12 ***Perf. 13***

1075 A390 3.75k multicolored 2.75 .30
Complete booklet, 10 #1075 27.50
1076 A390 8.75k multicolored 5.00 2.50

End of Railway Mail Service A391

1997, June 12 Litho.

1077 A391 5k multicolored 1.75 .70

Stories and Legends A392

Europa: 3.75k, Large cat on top of treasure chest, from "The Tinder Box." 5.25k, Butterfly, pond, frog, from "Thumbelina."

1997, Aug. 28 Engr. ***Perf. 13***

1078 A392 3.75k multicolored *1.40 .40*
1079 A392 5.25k multicolored *1.75 1.50*

Painting Type of 1993

Designs: 9.75k, "Dust Dancing in the Sun," by Vilhelm Hammershoi (1864-1916). 13k, "Woman Mountaineer," by J.F. Willumsen (1863-1958).

Litho. & Engr.

1997, Sept. 18 ***Perf. 13x12½***

1080 A360 9.75k multicolored 4.75 5.50
1081 A360 13k multicolored 6.25 7.00

A393

Danish Design: 3.75k, Faaborg chair, vert. 4k, Margrethe bowl, vert. 5k, The Ant (chair). 12.25k, Georg Jensen silver bowl, vert.

1997, Nov. 6 Litho. ***Perf. 13***

1082 A393 3.75k multicolored 1.25 .30
Complete booklet, 10 #1082 12.50
1083 A393 4k multicolored 1.25 .75
1084 A393 5k multicolored 2.00 .45
1085 A393 12.25k multicolored 4.50 5.25
Nos. 1082-1085 (4) 9.00 6.75

A394

A395

Danish Confederation of Trade Unions, Cent.: 3.50k, General Workers Union in Denmark (SiD). 3.75k, Danish Confederation of Trade Unions (LO). 4.75k, Danish Nurse's Organization. 5k, Union of Commercial and Clerical Employees in Denmark (HK).

1998, Jan. 22 Litho. ***Perf. 13***

1086 A394 3.50k multicolored 1.10 .90
1087 A394 3.75k multicolored 1.25 .30
Complete booklet, 10 #1087 12.50
1088 A394 4.75k multicolored 1.90 2.50
1089 A394 5k multicolored 2.00 .65
Complete booklet, 10 #1089 20.00
Nos. 1086-1089 (4) 6.25 4.35

Litho. & Engr.

1998, Mar. 26 ***Perf. 13***

1090 A395 3.75k multicolored 1.50 .90
Complete booklet, 10 #1090 15.00

City of Roskilde, 1000th anniv.

A396

A397

1998, Mar. 26 Litho. ***Perf. 13***

1091 A396 5k Ladybug 1.75 .50

Reduce poison.

1998, May 28 Litho. ***Perf. 13***

New Post & Tele Museum, Copenhagen: 3.75k, Postman, 1922. 4.50k, Morse code operator, c. 1910. 5.50k, Telephone operator, 1910. 8.75k, Modern postman.

1092 A397 3.75k multicolored 1.25 .30
Complete booklet, 10 #1092 12.50
a. Booklet pane, 2 each #1087, 1089, 3 ea. 1090, 1092 30.00
Complete booklet, #1092a 30.00
1093 A397 4.50k multicolored 1.50 1.50
1094 A397 5.50k multicolored 2.00 2.00
1095 A397 8.75k multicolored 2.75 2.75
a. Booklet pane, #1092-1095 14.00
Complete booklet, 2 #1095a 28.00
Nos. 1092-1095 (4) 7.50 6.55

No. 1095a is printed with two backgrounds. One shows part of King Christian IV's "Order Concerning Postmen," 1624. The other shows part of Copenhagen c. 1923. Complete booklets contain panes with each background.

Bridges over Great Belt A398

1998, May 28 Engr. ***Perf. 13***

1096 A398 5k West Bridge (shown) 2.75 .75
1097 A398 5k East Bridge (suspension) 2.75 .75
a. Pair, #1096-1097 + label 6.00 1.50

Nordic Stamps — A399

Shipping: No. 1098, Signal flags, harbor master with binoculars. No. 1099, Radar image of entrance to Copenhagen harbor, sextant.

1998, May 28 Litho. ***Perf. 13***

1098 A399 6.50k multicolored 3.50 3.50
1099 A399 6.50k multicolored 3.50 3.50
a. Pair, #1098-1099 7.25 7.25
b. Souvenir sheet, #1099a 8.00 10.00

National Festivals — A400

Europa: 3.75k, Horse at Danish agricultural show. 4.50k, Theater, tents at Arhus Festival Week, Arhus.

Litho. & Engr.

1998, Sept. 3 ***Perf. 13***

1100 A400 3.75k multicolored *1.50 .60*
Complete booklet, 10 #1100 *15.00*
1101 A400 4.50k multicolored *1.75 1.00*

Contemporary Art — A401

Paintings: 3.75k, Danish Autumn, by Per Kirkeby. 5k, Alpha, by Mogens Andersen, vert. 8.75k, Imagery, by Ejler Bille, vert. 19k, Celestial Horse, by Carl-Henning Pedersen.

Perf. 12½x13, 13x12½

1998, Oct. 15 **Litho. & Engr.**

1102 A401 3.75k multicolored 1.25 1.25

Litho.

1103 A401 5k multicolored 2.00 1.50
1104 A401 8.75k multicolored 3.25 3.25
1105 A401 19k multicolored 6.50 7.75
Nos. 1102-1105 (4) 13.00 13.75

See Nos. 1160-1161, 1190-1191, 1204-1205, 1235-1236, 1255-1256, 1282-1283, 1333-1336.

A402

Fossil, name of Danish geologist: 3.75k, Ammonite, Ole Worm (1588-1654). 4.50k, Shark's teeth, Niels Stensen (1638-86). 5.50k, Sea Urchin, Soren Abildgaard (1718-91). 15k, Slit-shell snail, Erich Pontoppidan (1698-1764).

1998, Nov. 5 **Engr.** ***Perf. 13***

1106 A402 3.75k multicolored 1.25 .30
Complete booklet, 10 #1106 12.50
1107 A402 4.50k multicolored 1.75 1.75
1108 A402 5.50k multicolored 1.75 1.75
1109 A402 15k multicolored 5.00 4.50
a. Souvenir sheet, #1106-1109 12.00 12.50

Wavy Lines and Queen Types of 1933, 1997 and

Queen Margrethe II — A402a

1999-2004 **Engr.** ***Perf. 12¾***

1111 A32 150o purple *.60* .25
1112 A32 375o green 2.60 .70
1113 A32 400o green 1.75 .65
1114 A321a 4k red 2.60 .50
a. Booklet pane, 4 #883, 2 #494, 2 #1114 6.75
Complete booklet, #1114a 7.00
1115 A402a 4k red 1.75 .50
b. Booklet pane, 4 #883, 2 #494, 2 #1115 5.00
Booklet, #1115b 5.00
c. Sheet of 8 + label 16.00
1116 A32 425o green 2.75 .65
1117 A402a 4.25k blue 2.60 1.00
1118 A402a 4.25k red 1.75 .70
b. Booklet pane, 6 #883, 2 #1118 5.00
c. Sheet of 8 + central label 36.00 —
1119 A402a 4.50k orange 2.00 1.50
a. Vert. strip of 10 + 10 etiquettes 24.00
1120 A402a 4.50k red 2.90 1.10
a. Booklet pane, 2 #494, 2 #1120 6.00 —
Complete booklet, #1120a 6.00
b. Sheet of 8 + central label 26.00 —
1121 A402a 4.75k sepia 3.25 1.75
1122 A402a 5k dk green 2.00 1.00
a. Sheet of 8 + 8 etiquettes *65.00* —
1123 A402a 5.25k ultra 2.10 1.00
1124 A402a 5.50k violet 2.50 .90
a. Sheet of 8 + label 24.00
b. Sheet of 8 + 8 etiquettes 30.00
1125 A321a 5.75k blue 2.25 1.25
1126 A402a 5.75k emerald 2.50 1.25
1127 A402a 6k bister 2.50 .75
a. Sheet of 10 + 10 etiquettes 45.00 —
1128 A402a 6.25k green 4.00 2.00
1129 A402a 6.50k slate grn *2.50* .90
a. Sheet of 8 + 8 etiquettes 32.00
b. Sheet of 8 + central label 42.00 —
1130 A321a 6.75k slate green 4.25 2.75
1131 A402a 6.75k henna brn 3.25 2.50
1132 A402a 7k rose lilac 3.00 2.50
1133 A402a 8.50k bright blue *3.00* 3.00
1134 A55 10.50k dk bl gray *4.00* 2.50
1135 A55 11.50k dk bl gray 5.75 4.00
1136 A55 12.50k gray 6.00 4.50
1137 A55 13k orange 5.50 4.50
1138 A55 15k blue 6.50 5.25
Nos. 1111-1138 (28) 86.15 49.85

Issued: 375o, Nos. 1114, 1118, 1130, 1/13/99; No. 1125, 1/3/00; Nos. 1115, 1119, 1119a, 4.25k, 4.50k, 5k, 5.25k, 5.50k, Nos. 1126, 1131, 4/12/00; No. 1119b, 6k, 7k, 5/9/01; Nos. 1119c, 1121a, 1124a, 4/17/01; 150o, 4.75k, 6.50k, 10.50k, 1/2/02. 400o, No. 1120, 6.25k, 8.50k, 11.50k, 1/2/03. No. 1120b, 3/12. Nos. 1124b, 1129a, 3/12/03. Nos. 1128b, 1/2/03; No. 1122a, 4/2/02; 425o, No. 1120, 12.50k, 13k, 15k, 1/2/04. Nos. 1120b, 1127a, 1/2/04.
See Nos. 1295, 1296-1303.

A403

1999, Jan. 13 **Litho.** ***Perf. 13***

1143 A403 4k Oersted Satellite 1.40 .90

Deciduous Trees A404

4k, Fagus sylvatica. 5k, Fraxinus excelsior, vert. 5.25k, Tilia cordata, vert. 9.25k, Quercus robur.

1999, Jan. 13 **Litho. & Engr.**

1144 A404 4k multicolored 1.25 .30
Complete booklet, 10 #1144 12.50
1145 A404 5k multicolored 1.75 1.00
1146 A404 5.25k multicolored 1.75 .65
1147 A404 9.25k multicolored 3.00 3.00
Nos. 1144-1147 (4) 7.75 4.95

50th Anniversaries — A405

Litho. & Engr.

1999, Feb. 24 ***Perf. 13***

1148 A405 3.75k Home Guard 1.40 .90
1149 A405 4.25k NATO 2.00 1.00

A406

A407

Harbingers of spring.

1999, Feb. 24 **Litho.**

1150 A406 4k Lapwing in flight 1.60 .30
Complete booklet, 10 #1150 16.00
1151 A406 5.25k Geese 1.75 .90
a. Souvenir sheet, #1150-1151 6.50 5.00

Litho. & Engr.

1999, Apr. 28 ***Perf. 13***

Nature Reserves.

1152 A407 4.50k Vejlerne *1.75* *1.00*
1153 A407 5.50k Langli *2.00* *1.25*

Europa.

Council of Europe, 50th Anniv. A408

1999, Apr. 28 **Engr.**

1154 A408 9.75k blue 3.00 3.00

Danish Constitution, 150th Anniv. — A409

1999, June 2 **Litho.** ***Perf. 13***

1155 A409 4k red & black 1.40 .70

Danish Revue, 150th Anniv. A410

Performers: 4k, Kjeld Petersen and Dirch Passer, comedians. 4.50k, Osvald Helmuth, singer. 5.25k, Preben Kaas and Jorgen Ryg, comedians, singers. 6.75k, Liva Weel, singer.

1999, June 2 **Engr.** ***Perf. 13***

1156 A410 4k deep red 1.60 .50
Complete booklet, 10 #1156 16.00
1157 A410 4.50k slate 1.75 1.40
1158 A410 5.25k deep blue 1.75 .85
Complete booklet, 10 #1158 17.50
1159 A410 6.75k deep claret 2.25 1.60
a. Bklt. pane, #1156-1159 + 2 labels 14.00 15.00
Complete booklet, 2 #1159a 28.00
Nos. 1156-1159 (4) 7.35 4.35

No. 1159a printed with two different pairs of labels. One version has showgirl label at left, the second version has showgirl label at right. Complete booklets contain one of each pane.

Contemporary Paintings Type

9.25k, Fire Farver, by Thomas Kluge. 16k, Dreng, by Lise Malinovsky.

1999, Aug. 25 **Litho.** ***Perf. 12¾***

1160 A401 9.25k multi, vert. 3.25 4.00
1161 A401 16k multi, vert. 5.25 5.25

Opening of New Extension of the Royal Library, "The Black Diamond" A411

1999, Aug. 25 **Engr.** ***Perf. 13¾***

1162 A411 8.75k black 4.00 3.00

Migratory Birds — A412

Litho. & Engr.

1999, Sept. 29 ***Perf. 12¾***

1163 A412 4k Swallows 1.60 .30
Complete booklet, 10 #1163 16.00
1164 A412 5.25k Gray-lag geese 1.75 1.00
a. Souvenir sheet, #1163-1164 5.25 6.50
1165 A412 5.50k Common eider 1.75 .90
1166 A412 12.25k Arctic tern 4.50 5.25
a. Souvenir sheet, #1165-1166 9.00 10.00
Nos. 1163-1166 (4) 9.60 7.45

Stamps from Nos. 1164a and 1166a lack white border found on Nos. 1163-1166.

New Year 2000 — A413

1999, Nov. 10 **Litho.** ***Perf. 13¼***

1167 A413 4k Hearts 1.40 .50
1168 A413 4k Wavy lines 1.40 .50
a. Bklt. pane, 5 ea #1167-1168 35.00
Complete booklet, #1168a 35.00

The 20th Century — A414

4k, Prof. J.H. Deuntzer on front page of newspaper, 1901. 4.50k, Newspaper illustration, 1903. 5.25k, Asta Nielsen and Poul Reumert in the film "The Abyss," 1910. 5.75k, Advertising sticker showing woman on telephone, 1914.
See sheet of 16, #1184a.

2000, Jan. 12 **Litho. & Engr.**

1169 A414 4k buff & blk 1.40 .50
Complete booklet, 10 #1169 14.00
1170 A414 4.50k multicolored 1.75 1.00
1171 A414 5.25k multicolored 1.75 1.00
Complete booklet, 10 #1171 17.50
1172 A414 5.75k multicolored 1.75 1.25
Nos. 1169-1172 (4) 6.65 3.75

2000, May 9

4k, Allegory of women suffrage on front page of newspaper, 1915. 5k, Newspaper caricature of the Kanslergade Agreement, 1933. 5.50k, Film "Long and Short," 1927. 6.75k, Front page of Radio Weekly Review, 1925.

1173 A414 4k multi 1.40 .55
Booklet, 10 #1173 14.00
1174 A414 5k multi 1.75 1.00
1175 A414 5.50k multi 2.00 1.60
1176 A414 6.75k multi 2.25 2.50
Nos. 1173-1176 (4) 7.40 5.65

2000, Aug. 23

4k, Liberation of Denmark on front page of newspaper, 1945. 5.75k, Newspaper caricature of new constitution, 1953. 6.75k, Poster for film "Café Paradise," 1950. 12.25k, Advertisement for Arena television, 1957.

1177 A414 4k multi 1.40 .90
Booklet, 10 #1177 14.00
1178 A414 5.75k multi 2.00 1.60
1179 A414 6.75k multi 2.25 2.50
1180 A414 12.25k multi 4.00 4.25
Nos. 1177-1180 (4) 9.65 9.25

2000, Nov. 8

4k, Entry of Denmark into European Community on front page of newspaper, 1972. 4.50k, Newspaper caricature of youth revolt, 1969. 5.25k, Poster for film "The Olsen Gang," 1968. 5.50k, Denmark Post website on Internet, 1999.

1181 A414 4k multi 1.40 .90
Booklet, 10 #1181 14.00
1182 A414 4.50k multi 1.60 1.60
1183 A414 5.25k multi 1.75 1.00
Booklet, 10 #1183 17.50
a. Booklet pane, #1171, 1175, 1179, 1183 + label 8.00
Booklet, 2 #1183a 16.00
1184 A414 5.50k multi 2.00 1.25
a. Sheet of 16, #1169-1184 47.50 42.50
Nos. 1181-1184 (4) 6.75 4.75

No. 1183a comes with two different labels. Booklet contains one of each.

60th Birthday of Queen Margrethe II — A415

2000, Apr. 12 Litho. *Perf. 12¾*
1185 A415 4k blk & car 1.60 .60
Complete booklet, 10 #1185 16.00
1186 A415 5.25k blk & blue 1.75 .90
a. Souvenir sheet, #1185-1186 4.00 4.25

Oresund Bridge, Sweden-Denmark — A416

Litho. & Engr.
2000, May 9 *Perf. 12¾*
1187 A416 4.50k shown 2.00 1.90
Litho.
1188 A416 4.50k Map 2.00 1.90
a. Pair, #1187-1188 4.25 3.75

See Sweden Nos. 2391-2393.

Europa, 2000
Common Design Type
2000, May 9 Litho. *Perf. 13*
1189 CD17 9.75k multi *3.50 2.25*

Contemporary Art Type of 1998
Designs: 4k, Pegasus, by Kurt Trampedach. 5.25k, Landscape, by Nina Sten-Knudsen.

2000, Sept. 27 *Perf. 12¾*
1190 A401 4k multi 1.50 1.50
1191 A401 5.25k multi 1.50 1.50

Royal Danish Air Force, 50th Anniv. A417

2000, Sept. 27 Engr.
1192 A417 9.75k black & red 3.00 2.50
a. Souvenir sheet of 1 3.00 3.50

Botanical Gardens, Copenhagen — A418

Litho. & Engr.
2001, Jan. 24 *Perf. 12¾*
1193 A418 4k Palm House 1.40 .60
Booklet, 10 #1193 14.00
Size: 28x21mm
1194 A418 6k Lake 2.00 .85
1195 A418 12.25k Water lilies 4.00 4.50
Nos. 1193-1195 (3) 7.40 5.95

"Use the Language" A419

2001, Mar. 28 Litho. *Perf. 13*
1196 A419 4k "A," text 1.40 .55
Booklet, 10 #1196 14.00
1197 A419 7k "Z," text 2.75 .90

Danish Postage Stamps, 150th Anniv. — A420

Portion of #2 and: 4k, Engraver Martinus Willam Ferslew. 5.50k, Printer Andreas Thiele. 6k, Head Copenhagen postmaster Frantz Christopher von Jessen. 10.25k, Postmaster General Magrius Otto Spohus Count Danneskjold-Samsoe.

Litho. & Engr.
2001, Apr. 1 *Perf. 13¼x13*
1198 A420 4k multi 1.50 1.00
1199 A420 5.50k multi 1.90 1.25
Booklet, 10 #1199 19.00
1200 A420 6k multi 2.00 1.25
1201 A420 10.25k multi 4.00 2.50
a. Booklet pane, #1198-1201 + label 20.00 21.00
Booklet, 2 #1201a 40.00
Nos. 1198-1201 (4) 9.40 6.00

No. 1201a printed with two different labels. One version has proof of stamp design, sketch of proposed design and Ferslew's letter to Danneskjold-Samsoe, and other shows two essays and letter from M. T. C. Bartholdy.

Europa — A421

Designs: 4.50k, Hands in water. 9.75k, Woman's head, water.

2001, May 9 Litho. *Perf. 13¼x13*
1202 A421 4.50k multi 1.25 .90
a. Booklet pane of 5 + 5 etiquettes 7.50
Booklet, 2 #1202a 15.00
1203 A421 9.75k multi 3.00 3.50

Contemporary Paintings Type of 1998
Designs: 18k, Missus, by Jorn Larsen, horiz. 22k, Postbillede, by Henning Damgaard-Sorensen.

Perf. 13x12½, 12½x13
2001, Aug. 22 Litho.
1204 A401 18k multi 6.00 6.50
1205 A401 22k multi 7.25 7.75

Youth Culture A422

Designs: 4k, Skateboarding. 5.50k, Kissing. 6k, Creating music. 10.25k, Tongue piercing.

2001, Aug. 22 *Perf. 13*
1206 A422 4k multi 1.60 .60
Booklet, 10 #1206 16.00
1207 A422 5.50k multi 1.75 1.10
Booklet, 10 #1207 17.50
1208 A422 6k multi 1.90 1.90
1209 A422 10.25k multi 4.00 4.00
a. Souvenir sheet, #1206-1209 9.00 9.75
Nos. 1206-1209 (4) 9.25 7.60

Hafnia 01 Philatelic Exhibition, Copenhagen A423

Monarch and stamps: 4k, Queen Margrethe II, #757, 1000. 4.50k, King Frederik IX, #775, 1003. 5.50k, King Christian X, #1001, B10. 7k, King Christian IX, #1002, 66.

Litho. & Engr.
2001, Oct. 16 *Perf. 13x13¼*
1210 A423 4k multi 1.60 .75
1211 A423 4.50k multi 1.75 1.75
1212 A423 5.50k multi 1.75 1.75
1213 A423 7k multi 2.50 2.75
a. Souvenir sheet, #1210-1213 6.50 7.50
b. Strip, #1210-1213 + central label 10.00 11.50
Nos. 1210-1213 (4) 7.60 7.00

Island Ferries A424

Designs: 3.75k, Bukken-Bruse. 4k, Ouro. 4.25k, Hjarno. 6k, Barsofaergen.

2001, Nov. 7 *Perf. 12¾*
1214 A424 3.75k multi 1.25 1.60
1215 A424 4k multi 1.60 .60
Booklet, 10 #1215 16.00
1216 A424 4.25k multi 1.60 1.60
1217 A424 6k multi 2.00 2.25
Nos. 1214-1217 (4) 6.45 6.05

Comics and Cartoons — A425

Designs: 4k, Rasmus Klump, by Vilhelm Hansen. 5.50k, Valhalla, by Peter Madsen. 6.50k, Jungledyret Hugo, by Flemming Quist Moller. 10.50k, Cirkeline, by Hanne Hastrup.

2002, Jan. 16 Litho. *Perf. 13¼x13*
1218 A425 4k multi 1.50 .55
Booklet, 10 #1218 15.00
a. Sheet of 8 + label 50.00
1219 A425 5.50k multi 1.75 1.00
Booklet, 10 #1219 17.50
a. Sheet of 8 + label 27.50
1220 A425 6.50k multi 2.10 1.75
1221 A425 10.50k multi 4.00 4.50
a. Souvenir sheet, #1218-1221 8.00 9.00
Nos. 1218-1221 (4) 9.35 7.80

The Girls in the Airport, Sculpture by Hanne Varming — A426

Designs: 4k, Rear view. 5k, Front view.

Photo. & Engr.
2002, Mar. 13 *Perf. 12¾*
1222 A426 4k multi, *cream* 1.60 .55
Booklet, 10 #1222 16.00
1223 A426 5k multi, *cream* 1.75 1.60

Europa — A427

Winning drawings in children's stamp design contest: 4k, Clown, by Luna Ostergard. 5k, Clown, by Camille Wagner Larsen.

2002, May 15 Litho. *Perf. 13*
1224 A427 4k multi *1.50 .90*
Booklet, 10 #1224 *15.00*
1225 A427 5k multi *1.75 1.75*
a. Booklet pane of 5 + 5 etiquettes *8.75* —
Booklet, 2 #1225a *17.50*

Landscapes A428

2002, May 15 Engr.
1226 A428 4k Bornholm 1.60 .90
1227 A428 6k West Jutland 1.90 1.90
1228 A428 6.50k Langeland 1.75 2.25
1229 A428 12.50k Thy 4.50 4.50
Nos. 1226-1229 (4) 9.75 9.55

Historic Postal Vehicles A429

Designs: 4k, 1953 Nimbus motorcycle. 5.50k, 1962 Bedford van. 10k, 1984 Renault 4 van. 19k, 1998 Volvo FH12 tractor trailer.

Litho. & Engr.
2002, Aug. 21 *Perf. 13x13¼*
1230 A429 4k multi 1.60 .65
Booklet, 10 #1230 16.00
a. Sheet of 8 + central label 36.00 —
1231 A429 5.50k multi 1.90 1.50
Booklet, 10 #1231 19.00
1232 A429 10k multi 4.00 4.00
1233 A429 19k multi 7.00 7.00
a. Booklet pane of 4, #1230-1233 20.00
Booklet, 2 #1233a 40.00
Nos. 1230-1233 (4) 14.50 13.15

No. 1233a is printed with two different labels. One shows a 1908 Berliet van and the other a 2002 Peugeot Partner. Both are included in the booklet.

Opening of Copenhagen Metro — A430

2002, Sept. 25 Engr. *Perf. 12¾*
1234 A430 5.50k multi, *tan* 1.50 1.40

Contemporary Paintngs Type of 1998
Designs: 5k, Children's Corner, by Jens Birkemose, vert. 6.50k, Maleren og Modellen, by Frans Kannik, vert.

2002, Sept. 25 *Perf. 13x12½*
1235 A401 5k red & blue 1.75 1.75
1236 A401 6.50k multi 2.25 2.25

Intl. Council for the Exploration of the Sea, Cent. — A431

Atlantic cod and: 4k, Exploration ship Dana. 10.50k, Hirtshals lighthouse.

Litho. & Engr.
2002, Sept. 25 *Perf. 13¼x13*
1237 A431 4k multi 1.60 .65
1238 A431 10.50k multi 4.00 4.00
a. Souvenir sheet, #1237-1238 4.50 5.00

See Faroe Islands No. 426, Greenland Nos. 401-402.

Danish House Architecture A432

Designs: 4k, Dianas Have, Horsholm, by Vandkusten Design Studio, 1992. 4.25k, Blangstedgard, Odense, by Poul Ingemann, 1988. 5.50k, Dansk Folkeferie, Karrebaeksminde, by Stephan Kappel, 1979. 6.50k, Fredensborg Terraces, Fredensborg, by Jorn Utzon, 1963. 9k, Soholm, Klampenborg, by Arne Jacobsen, 1950.

Litho. & Engr.

2002, Nov. 8 *Perf. 12¾*

1239 A432 4k multi 1.60 1.00
Booklet, 10 #1239 16.00
1240 A432 4.25k multi 1.60 .70
1241 A432 5.50k multi 1.90 1.50
1242 A432 6.50k multi 2.25 1.75
1243 A432 9k multi 3.00 3.00
Nos. 1239-1243 (5) 10.35 7.95

See Nos. 1257-1261, 1267-1271, 1317-1321.

Youth Sports — A433

2003, Jan. 15 **Litho.** *Perf. 12¾*

1244 A433 4.25k Soccer 1.50 .70
Booklet, 10 #1244 16.00
a. Sheet of 8 + central label *13.00 13.00*
1245 A433 5.50k Swimming 1.75 1.50
Booklet, 10 #1245 17.50
1246 A433 8.50k Gymnastics 3.25 3.25
1247 A433 11.50k Handball 4.00 4.25
Nos. 1244-1247 (4) 10.50 9.70

Danish Literary Greenland Expedition, Cent. — A434

Designs: 4.25k, Expedition members Harald Moltke, Knud Rasmussen, Jorgen Bronlund, Ludvig Mylius-Erichsen and Gabriel Olsen. 7k, Campsite.

2003, Mar. 12 **Engr.** *Perf. 12¾*

1248 A434 4.25k blue gray 1.25 .70

Size: 61x22mm

1249 A434 7k multi 2.25 2.25
a. Souvenir sheet, #1248-1249 + label *5.00 5.00*

See Greenland Nos. 407-408.

Europa — A435

Poster art: 4.25k, Poster for Copenhagen International Theater Festival, by Ole Fick, 1985. 5.50k, Poster for Bertel Thorvaldsen Museum, by Ole Woldbye, 1970.

2003, May 14 **Litho.** *Perf. 12¾*

1250 A435 4.25k multi *1.50* .60
Booklet, 10 #1250 *15.00*

Engr.

1251 A435 5.50k black *1.75 1.40*
Booklet, 10 #1251 *17.50*
a. Sheet of 8 + central label *40.00*

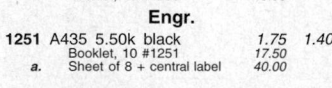

Insects — A436

Designs: 4.25k, Ephemera danica. 6.50k, Dytiscus latissimus. 12k, Cordulegaster boltoni, vert.

2003, May 14 **Litho. & Engr.**

1252 A436 4.25k multi 1.50 .50
a. Sheet of 8 + central label 25.00 —
1253 A436 6.50k multi 2.00 2.00
a. Sheet of 8 + central label 50.00 —

Size: 21x39mm

1254 A436 12k multi 3.75 3.75
a. Souvenir sheet, #1252-1254 7.00 7.50
Nos. 1252-1254 (3) 7.25 6.25

Contemporary Art Type of 1998

Designs: 5.50k, Baering, by Sys Hindsbo. 19k, Det Forjaettede Land, by Poul Anker Bech.

Litho. & Engr.

2003, Aug. 27 *Perf. 12½x13*

1255 A401 5.50k multi 1.75 1.75

Litho.

1256 A401 19k multi 6.50 6.50

Danish House Architecture Type of 2002

Designs: 4k, Bellahoj Apartment Complex, Copenhagen, by Tage Nielsen and Mogens Irming, 1944-58. 4.25k, Anchersvej, Klampenborg, by Mogens Lassen, 1935. 5.25k, Gerthasminde, Odense, by Anton Rosen, 1912-35. 9k, Solvang, Vallekilde College, by Andreas Bentsen and Martin Nyrop, 1889. 15k, Stenbrogard, Brorup, by Peter Holdensen, 1868.

Litho. & Engr.

2003, Aug. 27 *Perf. 12¾*

1257 A432 4k multi 1.60 1.60
1258 A432 4.25k multi 1.60 .90
Complete booklet, 10 #1258 16.00
1259 A432 5.25k multi 1.75 1.75
1260 A432 9k multi 3.25 3.25
1261 A432 15k multi 4.50 4.50
Nos. 1257-1261 (5) 12.70 12.00

A437

A438

2003, Nov. 7 **Engr.** *Perf. 12¾*

1262 A437 6.50k gray blue 2.00 1.75

Awarding of first Nobel Prize to a Dane (Niels Finsen for Physiology and Medicine), cent.

2003, Nov. 7 **Litho. & Engr.**

Artifacts from Royal Jelling World Heritage Site: 4.25k, Queen Thyra's stone. 5.50k, King Gorm's cup. 8.50k, King Harald's stone. 11.50k, Wall paintings, Jelling Church.

1263 A438 4.25k multi 1.50 1.25
Booklet, 10 #1263 17.50
1264 A438 5.50k multi 1.75 1.50
Booklet, 10 #1264 22.50
1265 A438 8.50k multi 2.75 2.75
1266 A438 11.50k multi 3.75 3.75
Nos. 1263-1266 (4) 9.75 9.25

A spiral-bound booklet, enclosed in a slipcase, with four booklet panes containing single stamps of Nos. 1263-1266, and a booklet pane containing a strip of Nos. 1263-1266, sold for 99k. Value, $35.

Danish House Architecture Type of 2002

Designs: 4.50k, Spurveskjul, Virum, by Nicolai Abildgaard, 1805. 6k, Liselund, Mon, by Andreas Kirkerup, 1792. 7k, Kampmann's Yard, Varde, by Hans Wolff Ollgaard, Hack Kampmann and Mikkel Stobberup, 1781. 12.50k, Harsdorff's House, Copenhagen, by Caspar Frederik Harsdorff, 1780. 15k, Nyso Manor, Praesto, by Jens Lauridsen.

Litho. & Engr.

2004, Jan.14 *Perf. 12¾*

1267 A432 4.50k multi 1.60 1.00
Booklet, 10 #1267 16.00
1268 A432 6k multi 2.40 1.60
1269 A432 7k multi 2.50 2.50
1270 A432 12.50k multi 4.00 4.00
1271 A432 15k multi 5.25 5.25
Nos. 1267-1271 (5) 15.75 14.35

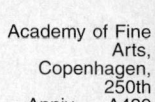

Academy of Fine Arts, Copenhagen, 250th Anniv. — A439

Litho. & Engr.

2004, Mar. 26 *Perf. 13¼x13*

1272 A439 5.50k multi 2.10 1.25
Booklet, 10 #1272 21.00

Norse Gods — A440

Designs: 4.50k, Heimdal guarding Bifrost bridge. 6k, Gefion plowing Sjaelland out of Sweden.

2004, Mar. 26

1273 A440 4.50k multi 1.75 .85
a. Sheet of 8 + central label 35.00 35.00
1274 A440 6k multi 2.40 1.10
a. Souvenir sheet, #1273-1274 8.00 8.00
b. Sheet of 8 + central label 55.00 55.00

Wedding of Crown Prince Frederik and Mary Donaldson — A441

No. 1275: a, Couple facing right. b, Couple facing left.

Litho. & Photo.

2004, May 14 *Perf. 13x13¼*

1275 A441 Horiz. pair 3.50 3.50
Booklet, 5 #1275 20.00
a.-b. 4.50k Either single, denomination 8½ mm wide 1.75 1.25
c.-d. 4.50k Either single, denomination 7½ mm wide 1.75 1.25
e. Souvenir sheet, #1275c-1275d + central label *4.00 4.00*

Frederiksberg Palace, 300th Anniv. — A442

Designs: 4.25k, Doorway overlooking Sondermarken Park. 4.50k, Gatehouse archway, castle yard. 6.50k, Aerial view.

Litho. & Engr.

2004, May 14 *Perf. 13*

1276 A442 4.25k multi 1.60 1.60
1277 A442 4.50k multi 1.75 1.00

Size: 55x32mm

1278 A442 6.50k multi 2.50 2.00
a. Souvenir sheet, #1276-1278 6.00 7.00
Nos. 1276-1278 (3) 5.85 4.60

Prince Henrik, 70th Birthday — A443

2004, June 9 **Litho.** *Perf. 12¾*

1279 A443 4.50k multi 1.60 1.00

Europa A444

2004, June 9 *Perf. 13*

1280 A444 6k Cyclists 2.50 1.60
1281 A444 9k Sailboats 3.50 3.00

Contemporary Paintings Type of 1998

Designs: 13k, Senses the Body Landscape, by Lars Ravn, vert. 21k, The Dog Bites, by Lars Norgard, vert.

Litho. & Engr.

2004, Aug. 25 *Perf. 13x12½*

1282 A401 13k multi 5.00 5.00

Litho.

1283 A401 21k multi 7.50 7.50

Viking Ship Museum, Roskilde A445

Designs: 4.50k, Skuldelev 1 on Roskilde Fjord. 5.50k, Reconstruction of Skuldelev 2. 6.50k, Cross-section of ship. 12.50k, Excavation of archaeological site where ships were found.

Litho. & Engr.

2004, Aug. 25 *Perf. 13x13¼*

1284 A445 4.50k multi 1.60 1.00
Complete booklet, 10 #1284 16.00
1285 A445 5.50k multi 2.00 1.60
Complete booklet, 10 #1285 20.00
1286 A445 6.50k multi 2.40 2.00
1287 A445 12.50k multi 4.50 4.50
Nos. 1284-1287 (4) 10.50 9.10

A spiral-bound booklet, enclosed in a slipcase, with four booklet panes containing single stamps of Nos. 1284-1287 and a booklet pane containing a strip of Nos. 1284-1287, sold for 99k. Value, $40.

Birds of Prey A446

Designs: 4.50k, Falco tinnunculus. 5.50k, Accipiter nisus. 6k, Buteo buteo. 7k, Circus aeruginosus.

Litho. & Engr.

2004, Nov. 5 *Perf. 13*

1288 A446 4.50k multi 1.75 .90
Complete booklet, 10 #1288 17.50
a. Sheet of 8 + central label 17.50 17.50
1289 A446 5.50k multi 2.10 1.00
a. Sheet of 8 + central label 22.50 22.50
1290 A446 6k multi 2.40 2.00
1291 A446 7k multi 2.75 2.25
Nos. 1288-1291 (4) 9.00 6.15

Queen and Small State Seal Types of 1946-2000

2005-09 **Engr.** *Perf. 12¾*

1295 A402a 4.75k red 1.90 1.00
a. Sheet of 8 + central label 17.00 —
1296 A402a 5.50k red 2.25 .50
b. Sheet of 8 #1296 + central label 20.00 —
1296A A402a 6.50k blue 2.75 .50
1297 A402a 7.25k black violet 3.00 2.50
1298 A402a 7.50k blue 3.25 2.50
1299 A402a 7.75k vio blk 3.50 .90
1300 A402a 8k indigo 4.00 2.50
1301 A402a 8.25k Prussian blue *2.50* 2.50
1302 A402a 8.75k Prus blue 3.75 1.00
1303 A402a 9k blue 3.25 3.25
1304 A55 10k lemon 3.50 1.25
1304A A55 10.50k car rose 4.00 3.25
1305 A55 13.50k green 5.00 4.25
1308 A55 16k Prus grn 7.25 1.25
1309 A55 16.50k red brown 6.00 5.25

1310	A55	17k slate green	6.25	5.25
1311	A55	17.50k purple	6.25	5.25
1312	A55	20k blue	8.25	1.75
1312A	A55	20.50k purple	9.25	1.75
1313	A55	22k brown violet	8.25	6.00
		Nos. 1295-1313 (20)	94.15	52.40

Issued: 7.50k, 16.50k, 22k, 1/3. 4.75k, 8k, 11/11. 4.75k, 10k, 17k, 1/2/06. 7.25k, 8.25k, 11/10/06. 13.50k, 17.50k, 1/2/07. 20k, 11/8/07. 5.50k, 6.50k, 7.75k, 8.75k, 1/2/08. Nos. 1296b, 1308, 1312, 3/27/08. Nos. 1303, 1304A, 1/2/09. This is an expanding set. Numbers may change.

Danish House Architecture Type of 2002

Designs: 4.25k, Hjarup Manse, Vamdrup, c. 1665. 4.50k, Ejdersted Farm, Southwest Schleswig, 1653. 7.50k, Provstegade, Randers, c. 1650. 9.50k, Smith's Yard, Koge, c. 1550. 16.50k, Carmelite Monastery, Elsinore, c. 1500.

Litho. & Engr.

2005, Jan. 12 *Perf. 12¾*

1317	A432	4.25k multi	1.75	1.75
1318	A432	4.50k multi	1.75	.65
		Complete booklet, 10 #1318	17.50	
a.		Booklet pane, 4 #691, 8 #1318	17.00	—
		Complete booklet, #1318a	17.00	
1319	A432	7.50k multi	2.90	2.90
1320	A432	9.50k multi	3.50	3.50
1321	A432	16.50k multi	7.25	7.25
		Nos. 1317-1321 (5)	17.15	16.05

Bonn-Copenhagen Declaration, 50th Anniv. — A447

2005, Mar. 2 **Litho.**

1322	A447	6.50k multi	2.50	2.00

See Germany No. 2330.

Hans Christian Andersen (1805-75), Author — A448

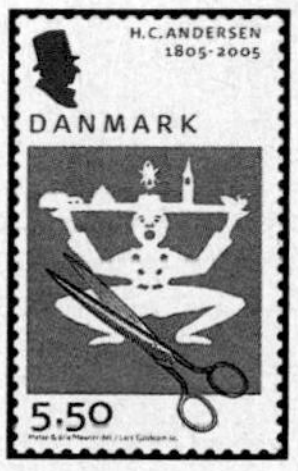

Paper Cutting by Andersen, Scissors — A449

Designs: 6.50k, Pen, inkwell, illustration of duckling, manuscript handwritten by Andersen. 7.50k, Andersen's drawing of Casino dell'Orlogio, Rome, and boots.

2005, Mar. 2 **Engr.**

1323	A448	4.50k black	1.60	1.60
a.		Sheet of 8 + central label	20.00	20.00

Litho. & Engr.

1324	A449	5.50k multi	2.00	2.00
		Complete booklet, 10 #1324	20.00	
a.		Sheet of 8 + central label	25.00	25.00
1325	A449	6.50k multi	2.25	2.00
1326	A449	7.50k multi	3.00	2.50
		Nos. 1323-1326 (4)	8.85	8.10

A spiral-bound booklet, enclosed in a slipcase, with four booklet panes containing single stamps of Nos. 1323-1326, and a booklet pane containing a strip of Nos. 1323-1326, sold for 99k. Value, $40.

See Malta Nos. 1196-1199.

August Bournonville (1805-79), Choreographer A450

Bournonville and: 4.50k, Dancer. 5.50k, Dancers.

Litho. & Engr.

2005, May 4 *Perf. 13¼x13*

1327	A450	4.50k multi	1.75	1.75
		Complete booklet, 10 #1327	17.50	
a.		Sheet of 8 + central label	19.00	—
1328	A450	5.50k multi	2.00	2.00
a.		Sheet of 8 + central label	17.50	—
b.		Souvenir sheet, #1327-1328	4.00	4.00

Sailors in World War II — A451

Designs: 4.50k, Ship convoy. 7.50k, Unloading of ship's cargo.

2005, May 4 **Litho.** *Perf. 13*

1329	A451	4.50k multi	1.60	1.60
1330	A451	7.50k multi	2.75	2.75

Europa — A452

2005, May 4 *Perf. 12¾*

1331	A452	6.50k Hot dog	*3.00*	*1.90*
1332	A452	9.50k Fish	*4.50*	*3.75*

Contemporary Art Type of 1998

Designs: 5.50k, Telepathy, by Anna Fro Vodder, vert. 6.50k, Home Again, by Kaspar Bonnén, vert. 7.50k, Unrest, by John Korner, vert. 12.50k, Palace in the Morning, by Tal Rosenzweig.

Perf. 13x12½, 12½x13

2005, Aug. 24 **Litho.**

1333	A401	5.50k multi	2.40	2.40
1334	A401	6.50k multi	2.75	2.75
1335	A401	7.50k multi	3.00	3.00
1336	A401	12.50k multi	6.00	6.00
		Nos. 1333-1336 (4)	14.15	14.15

INDEX:2005 Intl. Design Exhibition, Copenhagen A453

2005, Aug. 24 **Engr.** *Perf. 13¼*

1337	A453	4.50k black	1.75	1.25
		Complete booklet, 10 #1337	17.50	

Wavy Lines Type of 1905-17

2005-08 **Engr.** *Perf. 12¾*

1338	A10	25o indigo	.25	.25
a.		Booklet pane, 2 each #1295, 1338 ('06)	4.00	—
		Complete booklet, #1338a	4.00	
1339	A10	50o brown	.25	.25
1340	A10	100o bright blue	.35	.25
1341	A10	200o dark green	.70	.25
1342	A10	450o green	1.60	.65
1342A	A10	500o brt yel grn	2.25	.65
		Nos. 1338-1342A (6)	5.40	2.30

Wavy Line stamps, cent.

Issued: Nos. 1338-1342, 10/28/05. No. 1338a, 1/2/06. No. 1342A, 3/27/08.

Seals A454

Designs: 4.50k, Phoca vitulina. 5.50k, Halichoerus grypus.

2005, Nov. 11 **Engr.** *Perf. 13x13¼*

1343	A454	4.50k multi	1.75	1.25
		Complete booklet, 10 #1343	17.50	
1344	A454	5.50k indigo	2.00	1.50
a.		Souvenir sheet, #1343-1344	4.00	4.00

Flowers — A455

Designs: 4.75k, Calanthus nivalis. 5.50k, Eranthis hyemalis. 7k, Crocus vernus hybrid. 8k, Anemone nemorosa.

2006, Jan. 11 **Engr.** *Perf. 12¾*

1345	A455	4.75k multi	1.60	.90
		Complete booklet, 10 #1345	16.00	
a.		Sheet of 8 + central label	15.00	—
1346	A455	5.50k multi	1.75	1.75
		Complete booklet, 10 #1346	17.50	
a.		Sheet of 8 + central label	17.00	—
1347	A455	7k multi	2.25	2.25
1348	A455	8k multi	2.50	2.50
		Nos. 1345-1348 (4)	8.10	7.40

Creatures in Norse Mythology — A456

Designs: 4.75k, Elf king and elf girls. 7k, Incubi, werewolves, hel-horse, gnome and troll.

Litho. & Engr.

2006, Mar. 29 *Perf. 13¼x13*

1349	A456	4.75k multi	1.60	1.60
1350	A456	7k multi	2.40	2.40
a.		Souvenir sheet, #1349-1350	4.50	7.00

Rosenborg Castle, 400th Anniv. — A457

Designs: 4.75k, Castle exterior. 5.50k, Silver lion, thrones of king and queen. 13k, Royal coat of arms ceiling decoration.

2006, Mar. 29

1351	A457	4.75k multi	1.60	1.60
		Complete booklet, 10 #1351	16.00	
1352	A457	5.50k multi	2.00	2.00
1353	A457	13k multi	4.50	4.50
		Nos. 1351-1353 (3)	8.10	8.10

A spiral-bound booklet, enclosed in a slipcase, with four booklet panes containing single stamps of Nos. 1351-1353 and a booklet pane containing a strip of Nos. 1351-1353, sold for 99k. Value, $35.

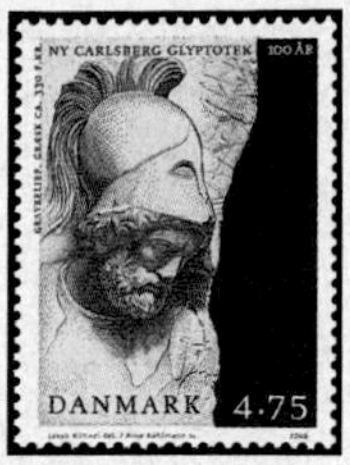

New Carlsberg Glyptotek, Cent. — A458

Designs: 4.75k, Marble relief from Athenian graveyard. 5.50k, Conservatory dome. 8k, Dancer Looking at the Sole of Her Right Foot, sculpture by Edgar Degas.

2006, June 7

1354	A458	4.75k multi	1.60	1.60
		Complete booklet, 10 #1354	16.00	
1355	A458	5.50k multi	2.00	2.00
1356	A458	8k multi	2.75	2.75
a.		Souvenir sheet, #1354-1356	6.50	6.50
		Nos. 1354-1356 (3)	6.35	6.35

Race Cars A459

Designs: 4.75k, 1958 Alfa Dana Midget, Swebe Jap. 5.50k, 1965 Austin Mini Cooper S, 1965 Ford Cortina GT, 1965 Alfa Romeo 1600 GTA. 10k, 1963 Jaguar E Type, 1967 Volvo P 1800. 17k, 1965 Lotus Elan, Renault Alpine A 110.

2006, June 7 *Perf. 13x13¼*

1357	A459	4.75k multi	1.75	1.75
		Complete booklet, 10 #1357	17.50	
1358	A459	5.50k multi	2.00	2.00
		Complete booklet, 10 #1358	20.00	
1359	A459	10k multi	3.75	3.75
1360	A459	17k multi	6.00	6.00
		Nos. 1357-1360 (4)	13.50	13.50

Europa — A460

Winning designs in children's stamp design contest: 4.75k, Smiling children, by Rikke Veber Rasmussen. 7k, Two smiling children, by Anette Bertram Nielsen.

2006, Aug. 23 **Litho.** *Perf. 13¼x13*

1361	A460	4.75k multi	1.90	.90
		Booklet, 10 #1361	19.00	
1362	A460	7k blk & dull grn	2.75	1.25

Airplanes A461

Designs: 4.50k, J. C. H. Ellehammer's 1906 biplane. 4.75k, KZ II, 1946. 5.50k, KZ IV, 1944. 13k, KZ VII, 1947.

Litho. & Engr.

2006, Aug. 23 *Perf. 12¾*

1363	A461	4.50k multi	1.75	1.75
1364	A461	4.75k multi	1.75	1.75
a.		Miniature sheet of 8 + central label	14.00	14.00
1365	A461	5.50k multi	2.00	2.00
a.		Miniature sheet of 8 + central label	16.00	16.00
1366	A461	13k multi	4.50	4.50
		Nos. 1363-1366 (4)	10.00	10.00

Paintings by COBRA Group Artists A462

Designs: 4.75k, Untitled, by Asger Jorn. 5.50k, Landscape of the Night, by Else Alfelt, vert. 7k, New Skin, by Pierre Alechinsky. 8k, The Olive Eater, by Egill Jacobsen, vert.

Perf. 13x13¼, 13¼x13

2006, Nov. 10 **Litho.**

1367	A462	4.75k multi	1.75	1.75
		Booklet, 10 #1367	17.50	
1368	A462	5.50k multi	2.00	2.00
1369	A462	7k multi	2.75	2.75
1370	A462	8k multi	3.00	3.00
		Nos. 1367-1370 (4)	9.50	9.50

See Belgium Nos. 2168-2169.

Danish Soldiers in United Nations Peace-keeping Forces, 50th Anniv. — A463

Litho. & Engr.

2007, Jan. 10 ***Perf. 13***

1371	A463	4.75k multi	1.75	1.75

Intl. Polar Year A464

Designs: 7.25k, Wooden and walrus tusk carvings of Norse, Late Dorset and Thule cultures of Greenland. 13.50k, Research airplane used for measuring thickness of polar ice.

2007, Jan. 10 ***Perf. 13¼***

1372	A464	7.25k multi	2.50	2.50
1373	A464	13.50k multi	4.75	4.75
a.		Souvenir sheet, #1372-1373	5.00	5.00

Windmills — A465

Designs: 4.50k, Askov Mill, 1891. 4.75k, Gedser Mil, 1957. 6k, Bogo Mill, 1989. 8.25k, Middelgrunden, 2000.

2007, Jan. 10 **Engr.**

1374	A465	4.50k brown	1.75	1.75
1375	A465	4.75k red	1.75	1.75
		Complete booklet, 10 #1375	17.50	
a.		Sheet of 8 + central label	15.00	15.00
1376	A465	6k green	2.00	2.00
		Complete booklet, 10 #1376	20.00	
a.		Sheet of 8 + central label	19.00	19.00
1377	A465	8.25k blue	3.00	3.00
		Nos. 1374-1377 (4)	8.50	8.50

Galathea 3 Scientific Expedition — A466

Satellite, ship and: 4.75k, Marine life. 7.25k, Globe showing route of expedition.

Litho. & Engr.

2007, Mar. 28 ***Perf. 12¾***

1378	A466	4.75k multi	1.75	1.75
1379	A466	7.25k multi	2.50	2.50
a.		Souvenir sheet, #1378-1379	4.50	4.50

National Museum, Bicent. — A467

Designs: 4.75k, Ceremonial axes. 6k, Funen aquaemanale. 8.25k, Armillary sphere. 10.25k, Wooden mask, Borneo.

2007, Mar. 28 ***Perf. 13¼***

1380	A467	4.75k Prus bl & blk	1.75	1.75
		Complete booklet, 10 #1380	17.50	
1381	A467	6k brn lake & blk	2.00	2.00
1382	A467	8.25k orange & blk	3.00	3.00
1383	A467	10.25k bl gray, blk & org	3.75	3.75
		Nos. 1380-1383 (4)	10.50	10.50

A spiral-bound booklet, enclosed in a slipcase, with four booklet panes containing single stamps of Nos. 1380-1383 and a booklet pane containing a strip of Nos. 1380-1383, sold for 109k. Value, $40.

Europa A468

Scouts: 4.75k, On hike. 7.25k, Around campfire.

2007, June 6 ***Perf. 13x13¼***

1384	A468	4.75k multi	1.75	1.75
		Complete booklet, 10 #1384	17.50	
1385	A468	7.25k multi	2.75	2.75

Scouting, cent.

Modern Art A469

Designs: 4.75k, The Traveler, by Arne Haugen Sorensen. 8.25k, Trionfale, by Seppo Mattinen.

2007, June 6 **Litho.** ***Perf. 13x12½***

1386	A469	4.75k multi	1.75	1.60
a.		Miniature sheet of 8 + central label	15.00	15.00
1387	A469	8.25k multi	3.00	2.50

Mandatory Use of Metric System in Denmark, Cent. A470

Litho. & Engr.

2007, Aug. 22 ***Perf. 12¾***

1388	A470	4.75k black & red	1.90	.85

Nature of Denmark A471

Flora and fauna of Rabjerg Dune: 4.75k, Niobe fritillary butterfly (klitperlemorsommerfugl). 6k, Northern dune tiger beetle (sandspringer). 7.25k, Sand lizard (markfirben). 13.50k, Seaside pansy (klitstedmoderblomst).

2007, Aug. 22

1389	A471	4.75k multi	1.75	.70
		Complete booklet, 10 #1389	17.50	
1390	A471	6k multi	2.25	.90
		Complete booklet, 10 #1390	22.50	
1391	A471	7.25k multi	2.75	1.00
1392	A471	13.50k multi	5.00	1.75
a.		Souvenir sheet, #1389-1392	12.50	12.50
		Nos. 1389-1392 (4)	11.75	4.35

Famous Men — A472

Designs: 4.75k, Poul Henningsen (1894-1967), designer, and Artichoke lamp. 6k, Victor Borge (1909-2000), comedian, and piano keys. 7.25k, Arne Jacobsen (1902-71), architect, and Egg chair. 8.25k, Piet Hein (1905-96), inventor, and superellipse.

2007, Nov. 8 **Engr.** ***Perf. 12¾***

1393	A472	4.75k multi	1.75	.85
		Complete booklet, 10 #1393	17.50	
1394	A472	6k blk & blue	2.00	1.00
1395	A472	7.25k multi	2.75	1.25
1396	A472	8.25k blk & purple	3.00	1.60
		Nos. 1393-1396 (4)	9.50	4.70

See Nos. 1412-1415, 1502-1505.

Danish National Theater A473

Designs: 5.50k, Old Stage. 6.50k, Playhouse. 7.75k, Copenhagen Opera House.

Litho. & Engr.

2008, Jan. 9 ***Perf. 13x13¼***

1397	A473	5.50k multi	2.25	1.10
		Complete booklet, 10 #1397	22.50	
a.		Sheet of 8 + central label	19.00	—
1398	A473	6.50k multi	2.60	1.25
		Complete booklet, 10 #1398	26.00	
1399	A473	7.75k multi	3.25	1.60
		Nos. 1397-1399 (3)	8.10	3.95

Royal Life Guards, 350th Anniv. — A474

Guards in: 5.50k, Red dress uniforms. 10k, Camouflage uniforms.

Litho. & Engr.

2008, Mar. 27 ***Perf. 13¼x13***

1400	A474	5.50k multi	2.50	1.25
		Complete booklet, 10 #1400	25.00	
1401	A474	10k multi	4.50	2.10
a.		Souvenir sheet, #1400-1401	7.00	7.00

Nordic Mythology A475

Places associated with mythology: 5.50k, Lindholm Hoje burial grounds. 7.75k, Feggeklit.

2008, Mar. 27 **Litho.**

1402	A475	5.50k black	2.40	1.25
1403	A475	7.75k black	3.25	1.60
a.		Souvenir sheet, #1402-1403	6.00	6.00

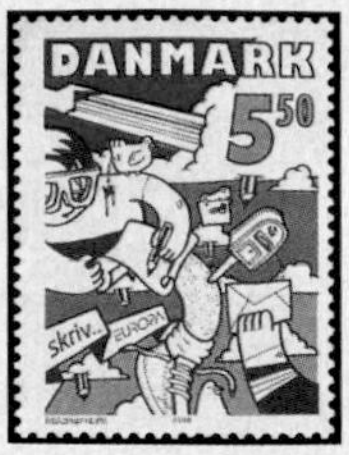

Europa — A476

Designs: 5.50k, Boy writing letter. 7.75k, Girl reading letter.

2008, June 4 **Litho.** ***Perf. 13***

1404	A476	5.50k multi	2.40	1.25
		Complete booklet, 10 #1404	24.00	
1405	A476	7.75k multi	3.25	1.60

Allotment Gardens A477

Designs: 5.50k, Man tending Hjelm Allotment Association garden. 6.50k, Men sitting in Vennelyst Allotment Association garden.

Litho. & Engr.

2008, June 4 ***Perf. 13x13¼***

1406	A477	5.50k multi	2.40	1.25
		Complete booklet, 10 #1406	24.00	
a.		Miniature sheet of 8 + central label	20.00	
1407	A477	6.50k multi	2.75	1.40
a.		Miniature sheet of 8 + central label	23.00	

Louisiana Museum of Art, Humlebaek, 50th Anniv. — A478

Designs: 5.50k, Original Museum building, Figures in Landscape, by Roy Lichtenstein, I Am in You, by Doug Aitken. 7.75k, I Am in You, glass corridor, A Closer Grand Canyon, by David Hockney. 8.75k, Reclining Figure No. 5, by Henry Moore, Walking Man, by Albert Giacometti, Big Head, by Giacometti, Slender Ribs, by Alexander Calder. 16k, Slender Ribs, people in concert hall, Untitled, by Sam Francis, seat designed by Poul Kjaerholm.

2008, June 4

1408	A478	5.50k multi	2.40	1.25
1409	A478	7.75k multi	3.25	1.60
a.		Booklet pane, #1408-1409	8.00	—
1410	A478	8.75k multi	3.75	1.90
1411	A478	16k multi	6.75	3.50
a.		Booklet pane, #1410-1411	14.50	—
b.		Booklet pane, #1408-1411	22.00	—
c.		Horiz. strip of 4, #1408-1411	19.00	19.00
		Complete booklet, #1409a, 1411a, 1411b	50.00	
		Nos. 1408-1411 (4)	16.15	8.25

Complete booklet sold for 102.40k.

Famous Men Type of 2007

Designs: 5k, Halfdan Rasmussen (1915-2002), poet, and line from poem. 5.50k, Erik Balling (1924-2005), film and television director, and actors in movie. 6.50k, Bodil Kjer (1917-2003), actress. 10k, Niels-Henning Orsted Pedersen (1946-2005), jazz musician, and bass.

2008, Aug. 27 **Engr.** ***Perf. 12¾***

1412	A472	5k blk & claret	2.40	.90
1413	A472	5.50k multi	2.75	1.10
		Complete booklet, 10 #1413	27.50	
1414	A472	6.50k multi	3.25	1.10
		Complete booklet, 10 #1414	32.50	
1415	A472	10k multi	4.50	1.75
		Nos. 1412-1415 (4)	12.90	4.85

Art Photography — A479

Designs: 5.50k, Trappe, by Viggo Rivad. 7.75k, Berlin, by Krass Clement, horiz.

2008, Aug. 27 Litho. *Perf. 13x12¾*

1416 A479 5.50k black 2.50 2.00

Perf. 12¾x13

1417 A479 7.75k black 3.25 2.50

Winter Berries and Flowers — A480

Designs: 5.50k, Ilex aquifolium berries. 6.50k, Helleborus niger flower. 7.75k, Taxus baccata berries. 8.75k, Symphoricarpos rivularis berries.

Litho. & Engr.

2008, Nov. 7 *Perf. 13*

1418 A480 5.50k multi 1.90 .95
Complete booklet, 10 #1418 19.00
a. Booklet pane of 4 7.75 —
1419 A480 6.50k multi 2.25 1.10
1420 A480 7.75k multi 2.75 1.40
1421 A480 8.75k multi 3.00 1.50
a. Souvenir sheet, #1418-1421 10.00 5.00
b. Booklet pane of 4, #1418-1421 10.00 —
Complete booklet, #1418a, 1421b 18.00
Nos. 1418-1421 (4) 9.90 4.95

No. 1421b is No. 1421a sewn into the booklet.

COP15 Climate Change Conference, Copenhagen — A481

Designs: 5.50k, Bioenergy. 9k, Low-energy building.

2009, Jan. 7 Engr. *Perf. 13x13¼*

1422 A481 5.50k blue 2.00 1.00
1423 A481 9k blue 3.25 1.75

Old Town Open-Air Museum, Aarhus, Cent. A482

Designs: 5.50k, Mintmaster's Mansion, drummer. 6.50k, Mayor's House, woman in period costume. 8k, Museum of Clocks and Watches and Danish Poster Museum, painter. 10.50k, Steps to Kerteminde School, farm hand.

Litho. & Engr.

2009, Jan. 7 *Perf. 13x13¼*

1424 A482 5.50k multi 2.00 1.00
Complete booklet, 10 #1424 20.00
1425 A482 6.50k multi 2.40 1.25
Complete booklet, 10 #1425 24.00
1426 A482 8k multi 3.00 1.50
1427 A482 10.50k multi 3.75 1.90
a. Souvenir sheet, #1424-1427 11.00 11.00
Nos. 1424-1427 (4) 11.15 5.65

Europa — A483

Designs: 5.50k, Round Tower, Copenhagen. 8k, Tycho Brahe Planetarium.

2009, Mar. 25 Litho. *Perf. 13¼*

1428 A483 5.50k multi 2.00 .95
Complete booklet, 10 #1428 20.00
1429 A483 8k multi 3.25 1.40

Flora and Fauna — A484

Designs: 5k, Anacamptus pyramidalis. 5.50k, Falco peregrinus. 8k, Zygaena purpuralis. 17k, Tooth of Mosasaurus lemonnieri.

2009, Mar. 25 Litho. *Perf. 12¾*

1430 A484 5k multi 1.90 .85
1431 A484 5.50k multi 2.40 .95
Complete booklet, 10 #1431 24.00
a. Miniature sheet of 8 + central label 17.00 17.00
1432 A484 8k multi 3.00 1.40
1433 A484 17k multi 6.75 3.00
a. Souvenir sheet, #1430-1433 13.50 13.50
Nos. 1430-1433 (4) 14.05 6.20

Copenhagen Zoo, 150th Anniv. — A485

Designs: 5.50k, Zoo Tower, rhinoceros. 6.50k, Elephants. 8k, Red-eyed tree frog, flamingos. 9k, Tiger python, golden lion tamarin.

2009, June 10 Litho. *Perf. 13¼x13*

1434 A485 5.50k multi 2.10 1.10
Complete booklet, 10 #1434 21.00
a. Miniature sheet of 8 + central label 17.00 17.00
1435 A485 6.50k multi 2.50 1.25
a. Miniature sheet of 8 + central label 20.00 20.00
b. Booklet pane of 2, #1434-1435 8.00 —
1436 A485 8k multi 3.00 1.50
1437 A485 9k multi 3.50 1.75
a. Booklet pane of 2, #1436-1437 12.00 —
b. Booklet pane of 4, #1434-1437 20.00 —
Complete booklet, #1435b, 1437a, 1437b 40.00
Nos. 1434-1437 (4) 11.10 5.60

Complete booklet containing Nos. 1435b, 1437a, 1437b sold for 109k.

Historic Maps A486

Maps of Denmark by: 5.50k, Royal Danish Academy of Sciences and Letters, 1841. 6.50k, Johannes Mejer, 1650. 12k, Marcus Jordan, 1585. 18k, Abraham Ortelius, 1570.

2009, July 15 Litho. *Perf. 12½*

1438 A486 5.50k multi 2.10 1.10

Size: 41x24mm

Perf. 12¾

1439 A486 6.50k multi 2.50 1.25
1440 A486 12k multi 4.75 2.40
1441 A486 18k multi 7.00 3.50
Nos. 1438-1441 (4) 16.35 8.25

Intl. Conference on the History of Cartography, Copenhagen.

Metropolitanskole, 800th Anniv. — A487

Designs: 5.50k, Author Hans Scherfig as boy and Metropolitanskole building, Copenhagen. 6.50k, Two students and current school building, Norrebro.

2009, Sept. 9 Engr. *Perf. 13x13¼*

1442 A487 5.50k red & black 2.25 1.10
1443 A487 6.50k black & grn 2.60 1.40

COP15, United Nations Climate Conference, Copenhagen — A488

Designs: 5.50k, Fuel cell technology. 8k, Wind turbine.

2009, Sept. 9

1444 A488 5.50k blue 2.25 1.10
Complete booklet, 10 #1444 22.50
1445 A488 8k gray 3.25 1.60

Modern Art — A489

Designs: 5.50k, Houses in Motion, by Jes Fomsgaard. 12k, Garlic, by Karin Birgitte Lund, vert.

2009 Litho. *Perf. 12¾x13*

1446 A489 5.50k multi 2.25 1.10
a. Sheet of 8 + central label 18.00 18.00

Perf. 12½x12¾

1447 A489 12k multi 5.00 2.40

Issued: 5.50k, 9/9; 12k, 10/27.

Children Playing in Snow — A490

Designs: 5.50k, Child rolling snow into large ball, snowman. 6.50k, Child in snow, child sledding. 8k, Child throwing snowball at two children. 9k, Two children making snow angels.

2009, Oct. 27 Litho. *Perf. 12½x12¾*

1448 A490 Sheet of 4 12.50 12.50
a. 5.50k multi 2.25 1.10
b. 6.50k multi 2.60 1.40
c. 8k multi 3.25 1.60
d. 9k multi 3.75 1.90

Self-Adhesive

Die Cut Perf. 13x13½

1449 A490 5.50k multi 2.40 1.10
a. Booklet pane of 12 29.00
1450 A490 6.50k multi 2.75 1.40
a. Booklet pane of 12 33.00
1451 A490 8k multi 3.25 1.60
1452 A490 9k multi 3.75 1.90
a. Sheet of 8, 2 each #1449-1452 25.00
Nos. 1449-1452 (4) 12.15 6.00

Nos. 1449a and 1450a each exist with six different booklet covers.

Flora and Fauna — A491

Designs: 8.50k, Bufo calamita. 9.50k, Lycaena phlaeas. 12.50k, Alauda arvensis. 18.50k, Astragalus danicus.

2010, Jan. 2 Litho. *Perf. 12¼*

1453 Souvenir sheet of 4 19.00 19.00
a. A491 8.50k multi 3.25 1.60
b. A491 9.50k multi 3.50 1.75
c. A491 12.50k multi 4.75 2.40
d. A491 18.50k multi 7.00 3.50

Self-Adhesive

Die Cut Perf. 13x13½

1454 A491 8.50k multi 3.25 1.60
1455 A491 9.50k multi 3.50 1.75
1456 A491 12.50k multi 5.00 2.40
1457 A491 18.50k multi 7.00 3.50
Nos. 1454-1457 (4) 18.75 9.25

Queen Margrethe II — A492

Die Cut Perf. 13

2010, Feb. 10 Litho. & Engr.

Self-Adhesive

Panel Color

1458 A492 5.50k red 2.25 1.00
1459 A492 6.50k Prus blue 2.60 1.25
a. Booklet pane of 10 26.00
1460 A492 8.50k yel green 3.25 1.60
1461 A492 9.50k dark blue 3.75 1.75
a. Miniature sheet of 8, 2 each #1458-1461 25.00
Nos. 1458-1461 (4) 11.85 5.60

No. 1458 was issued in coils as well as sheets. Every fifth coil stamp has a control number printed on the backing paper.

No. 1461a sold for 99k. See Nos. 1516-1519, 1574-1575, 1619-1620, 1635, 1665-1666, 1697-1700.

Issued: No. 1459a, 1/2/14.

Queen Margrethe II and Family A493

Die Cut Perf. 13¼

2010, Mar. 24 Litho. & Engr.

Self-Adhesive

1462 A493 5.50k multi 2.25 2.00
a. Booklet pane of 12 27.00

Queen Margrethe II, 70th birthday.

Ribe, 1300th Anniv. — A494

Designs: 5.50k, Ribe Cathedral. 6.50k, Statue of Queen Dagmar.

2010, Mar. 24 **Engr.**

Self-Adhesive

1463 A494 5.50k black 2.25 1.00
1464 A494 6.50k black 2.40 1.25
a. Booklet pane of 12 29.00
b. Miniature sheet of 6, 3 each #1463-1464 16.00

Nordic Coastlines A495

Designs: 5.50k, Ship at Lindo Shipyard. 8.50k, Crane, Port of Aarhus.

Perf. 12¼x12½

2010, Mar. 24 **Litho.**

1465 Sheet of 2 5.50 6.00
a. A495 5.50k multi 2.00 1.00
b. A495 8.50k multi 3.25 1.60

Self-Adhesive

Die Cut Perf. 13¼

1466 A495 5.50k multi 2.00 1.00
1467 A495 8.50k multi 3.25 1.60

Wavy Lines Type of 1905 and Small State Seal Type of 1946

2010 **Engr.** ***Die Cut Perf. 13***

Self-Adhesive

1468 A10 50o brown .25 .25
1469 A10 100o blue .40 .25
1470 A10 200o dark green .75 .25
1471 A10 300o orange 1.20 .25
1472 A10 400o purple 1.60 .35
1473 A10 500o green 1.90 .45
1474 A55 10k lemon 3.75 .80
1475 A55 15k blue 5.50 1.25
1476 A55 20k dark blue 7.50 1.60
1477 A55 30k red brown 11.50 2.75
1478 A55 50k red 18.00 4.00
Nos. 1468-1478 (11) 52.35 12.20

Issued: 50o, 100o, 200o, 500o, 4/28; 300o, 400o, 30k, 3/24; 10k, 15k, 20k, 50k, 6/1.

Album Cover for Gasolin' 3, by Gasolin' A496

Die Cut Perf. 13½x13¼

2010, Apr. 28 **Litho.**

Self-Adhesive

1479 A496 5.50k multi 2.25 1.50
a. Booklet pane of 12 27.00
b. Sheet of 4 19.00 15.00

Klampenborg Racetrack, Cent. — A497

Designs: 5.50k, Horses at finish line. 24k, Spectators watching race.

2010, June 1

Self-Adhesive

1480 A497 5.50k multi 2.25 1.10
1481 A497 24k multi 9.25 4.50

Europa — A498

Children's book characters: 5.50k, Sporge-Jorgen. 8.50k, Orla Fro-Snapper, horiz.

Die Cut Perf. 13¼x13½

2010, June 1

Self-Adhesive

1482 A498 5.50k multi 2.10 1.00
a. Sheet of 8 18.00

Die Cut Perf. 13½x13¼

1483 A498 8.50k multi 3.25 2.00

Booklet Stamp

Serpentine Die Cut 13½

1484 A498 5.50k multi 8.00 3.50
a. Booklet pane of 12 96.00
b. Serpentine Die Cut 10 8.00 3.50
c. Booklet pane of 12 #1484b 96.00

Royal Danish Navy, 500th Anniv. A499

Designs: 5.50k, Frigate Iver Huitfeldt. 6.50k, Artillery ship Niels Iuel. 8.50k, Ironclad warship Todenskjold. 9.50k, Screw frigate Jylland. 16k, Caravel Maria.

Die Cut Perf. 13¼x13

2010, June 1 **Litho. & Engr.**

Self-Adhesive (#1485-1489, 1491-1495)

1485 A499 5.50k red & black 2.00 .90
1486 A499 6.50k red & black 2.50 1.10
a. Booklet pane of 12 25.00
1487 A499 8.50k red & black 3.25 1.40
1488 A499 9.50k red & black 4.00 1.60
1489 A499 16k red & black 6.25 2.60
Nos. 1485-1489 (5) 18.00 7.60

Booklet Stamps

Perf. 12¼x12½

1490 Booklet pane of 5 30.00 —
a. A499 5.50k red & black 3.00 2.60
b. A499 6.50k red & black 3.75 3.00
c. A499 8.50k red & black 5.25 4.25
d. A499 9.50k red & black 5.75 4.75
e. A499 16k red & black 9.50 7.75

Booklet Panes of 1

Serpentine Die Cut 13¼x13½

1491 A499 5.50k red & black 3.25 2.75
1492 A499 6.50k red & black 4.00 3.50
1493 A499 8.50k red & black 5.50 4.50
1494 A499 9.50k red & black 6.25 5.00
1495 A499 16k red & black 10.00 8.00
Complete booklet, #1490-1495 60.00
Nos. 1491-1495 (5) 29.00 23.75

Complete booklet sold for 139k.

Greetings — A500

Die Cut Perf. 13x13¼

2010, June 1 **Litho.**

Self-Adhesive

1496 A500 5.50k Heart 2.25 .90
1497 A500 5.50k Danish Flag 2.25 .90
1498 A500 5.50k "Tillykke" 2.25 .90
1499 A500 5.50k Gift 2.25 .90
1500 A500 5.50k Flower 2.25 .90
a. Sheet of 10, 2 each #1496-1500 22.50
Nos. 1496-1500 (5) 11.25 4.50

The right third of Nos. 1496-1500 has straight-edged die cutting. See Nos. 1552-1556.

A501

A502

A503

A504

A505

A506

A507

A508

A509

Post Danmark Rundt Bicycle Race — A510

2010, Aug. 4 ***Die Cut Perf. 13x13¼***

1501 Sheet of 10 *65.00*
a. A501 5.50k multi *6.50 3.25*
b. A502 5.50k multi *6.50 3.25*
c. A503 5.50k multi *6.50 3.25*
d. A504 5.50k multi *6.50 3.25*
e. A505 5.50k multi *6.50 3.25*
f. A506 5.50k multi *6.50 3.25*
g. A507 5.50k multi *6.50 3.25*
h. A508 5.50k multi *6.50 3.25*
i. A509 5.50k multi *6.50 3.25*
j. A510 5.50k multi *6.50 3.25*

The right third of Nos. 1501a-1501j has straight-edged die cutting.

Famous Men Type of 2007

Designs: 5.50k, Dan Turèll (1946-93), writer, and lines from poem. 6.50k, Tove Ditlevsen (1917-76), poet, and her childhood home. 9.50k, Henry Heerup (1907-93), and "Love in the Coffee Pot." 12.50k, Dea Trier Morch (1941-2001), writer and artist, and illustration from her novel, *Winter's Child.*

Die Cut Perf. 13½x12¾

2010, Aug. 25 **Litho. & Engr.**

Self-Adhesive

1502 A472 5.50k multi 2.25 .80
a. Souvenir sheet of 8 17.50
b. Booklet pane of 12 27.50

1503 A472 6.50k multi 2.50 1.10
1504 A472 9.50k multi 3.50 1.60
1505 A472 12.50k multi 5.00 3.25
Nos. 1502-1505 (4) 13.25 6.75

Art — A511

Designs: 5.50k, Two Roses, by Inge Ellegaard. 18.50k, Night Flower, by Kirstine Roepstorff, vert.

Die Cut Perf. 13¼x13½

2010, Aug. 25 **Litho.**

Self-Adhesive

1506 A511 5.50k multi 2.25 1.50

Die Cut Perf. 13½x13¼

1507 A511 18.50k multi 7.25 5.00

Small State Seal Type of 1946

Die Cut Perf. 13

2010, Oct. 26 **Engr.**

1508 A55 25k green 9.50 4.75

"Winter Tales" — A512

Designs: 5.50k, Woman on park bench, ducks. 6.50k, Woman on park bench hugging snowman. 8.50k, Woman kissing snowman. 12.50k, Snowman coming to life, dog.

2010, Oct. 26 **Litho.** ***Perf. 12¼x13***

1509 Sheet of 4 13.00 6.50
a. A512 5.50k multi 2.10 1.10
b. A512 6.50k multi 2.50 1.25
c. A512 8.50k multi 3.25 1.60
d. A512 12.50k multi 4.75 2.40

Self-Adhesive

Die Cut Perf. 13¼

1510 A512 5.50k multi 2.10 1.10
1511 A512 6.50k multi 2.50 1.25
1512 A512 8.50k multi 3.25 1.60
1513 A512 12.50k multi 4.75 2.40
a, Sheet of 8, #1511-1513, 5 #1510 21.00
Nos. 1510-1513 (4) 12.60 6.35

Booklet Stamps

Serpentine Die Cut 13½

1514 A512 5.50k multi 5.00 5.00
a. Booklet pane of 12 60.00
1515 A512 6.50k multi 5.00 5.00
a. Booklet pane of 12 60.00

Queen Margrethe II Type of 2010

Die Cut Perf. 13

2011, Mar. 9 **Litho. & Engr.**

Self-Adhesive

Panel Color

1516 A492 6k Prus blue 2.50 1.10
1517 A492 8k red 3.25 1.50
1518 A492 9k yel green 3.75 1.75
1519 A492 11k dark blue 4.50 2.10
Nos. 1516-1519 (4) 14.00 6.45

Nos. 1516 and 1517 were issued in coils as well as sheets. Every fifth coil stamp has a control number printed on the backing paper.

Art A513

Designs: 8k, Untitled (for Karl Pichert), by Claus Carstensen. 13k, Det Her Sted (This Place), by Lise Harlev.

Die Cut Perf. 13½x13¼

2011, Mar. 23 Litho. & Engr.

Self-Adhesive

1520 A513 8k sil & black 3.25 1.60

Litho.

1521 A513 13k multi 5.00 2.50

Supreme Court, 350th Anniv. — A514

Designs: 6k, Supreme Court decree of King Frederik III, 1661. 8k, Court and judges.

Litho. & Engr.

2011, Mar. 23 ***Perf. 13x12½***

1522 Sheet of 2 5.75 6.25
a. A514 6k multi 2.40 2.40
b. A514 8k multi 3.25 1.60

Self-Adhesive

Die Cut Perf. 13x13½

1523 A514 6k multi 2.40 1.25
1524 A514 8k multi 3.25 1.60

Camping — A515

Designs: 6k, Man wearing t-shirt and shorts in front of trailer. 8k, Garden gnome in front of trailer.

Die Cut Perf. 13x13¼

2011, Mar. 23 Litho.

Self-Adhesive

1525 A515 6k multi 2.50 1.25
1526 A515 8k multi 3.25 1.60

Serpentine Die Cut 13½

1527 A515 6k multi 2.50 1.25
a. Booklet pane of 12 30.00
1528 A515 8k multi 3.25 1.60
a. Booklet pane of 12 39.00
b. Pair, #1527-1528 5.75
Nos. 1525-1528 (4) 11.50 5.70

Nos. 1527-1528 were printed in sheets of 8 containing four of each stamp. Sheet sold for 56k.

Europa — A516

Designs: 8k, Caterpillar on branch in spring. 11k, Squirrel, tree in autumn.

2011, May 4 ***Die Cut Perf. 13x13¼***

Self-Adhesive

1529 A516 8k multi 3.25 1.60
1530 A516 11k multi 4.25 2.10

Booklet Stamp

Serpentine Die Cut 13½

1531 A516 8k multi 3.25 3.00
a. Booklet pane of 12 39.00

Intl. Year of Forests.

Manor Houses A517

Designs: No. 1532, Norre Vosborg, near Holstebro. No. 1533, Voergaard Castle, Vendsyssel. No. 1534, Englesholm Castle, near Vejle. No. 1535, Gammel Estrup, near Randers.

Die Cut Perf. 13¼x13

2011, May 4 Litho. & Engr.

Self-Adhesive

1532 A517 6k multi 2.40 1.25
1533 A517 6k multi 2.40 1.25
1534 A517 8k multi 3.25 1.60
1535 A517 8k multi 3.25 1.60
Nos. 1532-1535 (4) 11.30 5.70

Arabian Expedition of Carsten Niebuhr, 250th Anniv. — A518

Compass rose and: 8k, Niebuhr (1733-1815), explorer. 13k, Horse-drawn grain mill from Egypt.

2011, May 4 ***Die Cut Perf. 13x13¼***

Self-Adhesive

1536 A518 8k multi 3.50 1.60
1537 A518 13k multi 5.25 2.50
a. Souvenir sheet of 2, #1536-1537, + label 8.75

Booklet Stamp

Serpentine Die Cut 13½

1538 A518 8k multi 3.25 1.60
a. Booklet pane of 12 39.00

Paddle Steamer SS Hjejlen, 150th Anniv. A519

2011, June 8 ***Die Cut Perf. 13***

Self-Adhesive

1539 A519 8k multi 3.50 1.60
a. Miniature sheet of 6 21.00

Children's Television Characters A520

Designs: 6k, Bruno the Bear and French fries. 8k, Bamse the Bear and balloons.

Die Cut Perf. 13¼x13

2011, June 8 Litho.

Self-Adhesive

1540 A520 6k multi 2.50 1.25
a. Miniature sheet of 6 15.00
1541 A520 8k multi 3.50 1.60
a. Miniature sheet of 6 21.00

Booklet Stamps

Serpentine Die Cut 13½

1542 A520 6k multi 2.50 2.00
a. Booklet pane of 10 + 10 etiquettes 25.00
1543 A520 8k multi 3.50 3.00
a. Booklet pane of 12 35.00

Summer Flowers — A521

Designs: 2k, Papaver rhoeas. 6k, Geranium. 8k, Astrantia major. 10k, Papaver nudicaule.

2011, June 8 ***Perf. 12x12¾***

1544 Miniature sheet of 4 11.00 11.00
a. A521 2k multi .80 .40
b. A521 6k multi 2.40 1.25
c. A521 8k multi 3.25 1.60
d. A521 10k multi 4.00 2.00

Self-Adhesive

Die Cut Perf. 13x13¼

1545 A521 2k multi .80 .40
1546 A521 6k multi 2.40 1.25
1547 A521 8k multi 3.25 1.60
1548 A521 10k multi 4.00 2.00
Nos. 1545-1548 (4) 10.45 5.25

Booklet Stamp

Serpentine Die Cut 13½

1549 A521 6k multi 2.50 2.25
a. Booklet pane of 10 + 10 etiquettes 25.00

Sketch of Woman's Clothing Designed by Malene Birger — A522

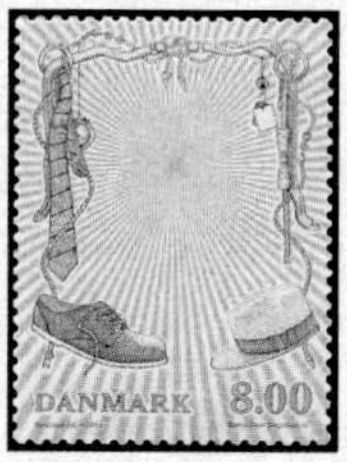

Fashion Accessories Designed by Silas Adler — A523

Die Cut Perf. 13x13¼

2011, Aug. 4 Litho. & Engr.

Self-Adhesive

1550 A522 6k black 2.40 1.25
1551 A523 8k multi 3.25 1.60
a. Souvenir sheet of 2, #1550-1551 5.75

Greetings Type of 2010

Die Cut Perf. 13x13¼

2011, Aug. 4 Litho.

Self-Adhesive

1552 A500 8k Heart 3.25 1.60
1553 A500 8k Danish Flag 3.25 1.60
1554 A500 8k "Tillykke" 3.25 1.60
1555 A500 8k Open envelope 3.25 1.60
1556 A500 8k Flower 3.25 1.60
a. Sheet of 10, 2 each #1552-1556 32.50
Nos. 1552-1556 (5) 16.25 8.00

The right third of Nos. 1552-1556 has straight-edged die cutting.

International Cycling Union Road World Championships, Denmark — A524

2011, Aug. 4 ***Die Cut Perf. 13x13¼***

Self-Adhesive

1557 A524 8k multi 3.25 1.60
a. Souvenir sheet of 6 19.50

Copenhagen Central Railway Station, Cent. — A525

People and: 6k, Station's front. 8k, Clock. 9k, Arches. 16k, Train at platform.

Litho. & Engr.

2011, Sept. 10 ***Perf. 13x12¼***

Booklet Stamps (#1558-1561, 1566)

1558 A525 6k multi 6.00 6.00
1559 A525 8k multi 6.00 6.00
a. Booklet pane of 2, #1558-1559 12.00 —
1560 A525 9k multi 9.00 9.00
1561 A525 16k multi 9.00 9.00
a. Booklet pane of 4, #1558-1561 30.00 —
b. Booklet pane of 2, #1560-1561 18.00 —
Complete booklet, #1559a, 1561a, 1561b 60.00
Nos. 1558-1561 (4) 30.00 30.00

Self-Adhesive

Die Cut Perf. 13¼x13

1562 A525 6k multi 2.25 1.25
1563 A525 8k multi 3.00 1.75
1564 A525 9k multi 3.50 2.00
1565 A525 16k multi 6.00 3.00
Nos. 1562-1565 (4) 14.75 8.00

Serpentine Die Cut 13½

1566 A525 8k multi 3.25 3.00
a. Booklet pane of 12 39.00

The complete booklet sold for 139k.

People in Winter — A526

Designs: 6k, Bathing Viking. 8k, Woman feeding duck. 11k, Man walking dog. 13k, Ice fisherman.

2011, Oct. 25 Litho. ***Perf. 12¼***

1567 Sheet of 4 15.00 7.50
a. A526 6k multi 2.40 1.25
b. A526 8k multi 3.00 1.75
c. A526 11k multi 4.25 2.90
d. A526 13k multi 5.00 3.25

Self-Adhesive

Die Cut Perf. 13x13¼

1568 A526 6k multi 2.40 1.25
1569 A526 8k multi 3.00 1.75
1570 A526 11k multi 4.25 2.90
1571 A526 13k multi 5.00 3.25
Nos. 1568-1571 (4) 14.65 9.15

Booklet Stamps

Serpentine Die Cut 13½

1572 A526 6k multi 2.50 2.25
a. Booklet pane of 10 + 10 etiquettes 25.00
1573 A526 8k multi 3.50 3.25
a. Booklet pane of 12 42.50

Queen Margrethe II Type of 2010

Die Cut Perf. 13

2012, Jan. 2 Litho. & Engr.

Self-Adhesive

Panel Color

1574 A492 12k purple 4.50 3.75
1575 A492 14k black 5.25 2.90

Armillary Spheres A527

Designs: No. 1576, Equatorial armillary sphere built by Tycho Brahe, 1595. No. 1577, Simplified armillary sphere built by Guo Shoujing, 1276.

Die Cut Perf. 13¾

2012, Jan. 4 Litho. & Engr.

Self-Adhesive

1576 A527 6k multi 2.50 1.50
1577 A527 6k multi 2.50 1.50

See People's Republic of China Nos. 3980-3981.

Reign of Queen Margrethe II, 40th Anniv. — A528

2012, Jan. 4 ***Perf. 13½***

Souvenir Sheet

1578 A528 8k multi 3.00 3.00

Self-Adhesive

Die Cut Perf. 13¼x13½

1579 A528 8k multi 3.00 3.00

Bridges A529

Designs: 6k, Queen Alexandrine Bridge. 8k, Faro Bridge.

2012, Jan. 4 Litho. ***Perf. 13¼***

Souvenir Sheet

1580 Sheet of 2 8.25 8.25
a. A529 6k multi 3.00 2.00
b. A529 8k multi 5.00 3.00

Self-Adhesive

Die Cut Perf. 13¼

1581 A529 6k multi 2.10 1.40
1582 A529 8k multi 3.25 2.00

Booklet Stamps

Serpentine Die Cut 13½

1583 A529 6k multi 2.10 1.40
a. Booklet pane of 10 + 10 etiquettes 21.00
1584 A529 8k multi 3.25 2.00
a. Booklet pane of 10 + 10 etiquettes 32.50

Nordia 2012 Stamp Exhibition, Roskilde.

Europa — A530

2012, Mar. 21 ***Perf. 14***

Souvenir Sheet

1585 A530 12k multi 4.50 4.50

Self-Adhesive

Die Cut Perf. 14

1586 A530 12k multi 4.50 2.75

No. 1586 was printed in sheets of 30.

Sea Rescue — A531

Designs: 6k, Helicopter and rescue boat. 11k, Helicopter over Copenhagen University Hospital helipad.

2012, Mar. 21 ***Perf. 13½x13¼***

Souvenir Sheet

1587 A531 Sheet of 2 6.50 6.50
a. 6k multi 2.40 1.60
b. 11k multi 4.00 2.40

Self-Adhesive

Die Cut Perf. 13½x13¼

1588 A531 6k multi 2.40 1.60
1589 A531 11k multi 4.00 2.40

Scenes From Tales by Hans Christian Andersen A532

Designs: 2k, The Shepherdess and the Chimney Sweep. 3k, The Nightingale. 6k, The Wild Swans. 8k, What the Old Man Does Is Always Right.

Die Cut Perf. 13½x13¼

2012, June 1 Litho. & Engr.

Self-Adhesive

1590 A532 2k multi 1.10 .70
1591 A532 3k multi 1.00 1.00
1592 A532 6k multi 2.10 1.40
1593 A532 8k multi 2.75 1.75
Nos. 1590-1593 (4) 6.95 4.85

Booklet Stamps

Serpentine Die Cut 13½x13¼

1594 A532 6k multi 2.25 1.50
a. Booklet pane of 10 + 10 etiquettes 22.50
1595 A532 8k multi 3.00 1.75
a. Booklet pane of 10 + sticker 30.00

Sandwiches
A533 A534

Designs: Nos. 1596, 1600, 1604, Egg and shrimp sandwich. Nos. 1597, 1601, 1605, Rolled sausage sandwich. 8k, Potato sandwich. 16k, Roast beef sandwich.

2012, June 1 Litho. ***Perf. 13x13¼***

Booklet Stamps

1596 A533 6k multi 4.00 4.00
a. Booklet pane of 1 4.00 —
1597 A534 6k multi 4.00 4.00
a. Booklet pane of 1 4.00 —
1598 A534 8k multi 5.25 5.25
a. Booklet pane of 1 5.25 —
1599 A534 16k multi 10.50 10.50
a. Booklet pane of 1 10.50 —
b. Booklet pane of 4, #1596-1599 24.00 —
Complete booklet, #1596a, 1597a, 1598a, 1599a, 1599b 48.00
Nos. 1596-1599 (4) 23.75 23.75

Self-Adhesive

Die Cut Perf. 13x13¼

1600 A533 6k multi 2.00 1.00
1601 A534 6k multi 2.00 1.00
1602 A534 8k multi 2.75 1.40
1603 A534 16k multi 5.50 2.75
Nos. 1600-1603 (4) 12.25 6.15

Serpentine Die Cut 13½

1604 A533 6k multi 2.10 1.10
1605 A534 6k multi 2.10 1.10
a. Booklet pane of 10, 5 each #1604-1605 + 10 etiquettes 20.00
1606 A534 8k multi 2.90 1.75
a. Booklet pane of 10 27.50
Nos. 1604-1606 (3) 7.10 3.95

Complete booklet sold for 139k. Nos. 1604-1606 weree printed in a sheet of 8 containing 3 each nos. 1604-1605 and 2 No. 1606.

Portrait of Johanne Luise Heiberg, by Emilius Baerentzen — A535

Die Cut Perf. 14x13¾

2012, Sept. 5 Litho. & Engr.

Self-Adhesive

1607 A535 8k multi 3.00 1.75

Heiberg (1812-90), theater actress and director.

Flowers — A536

Designs: 8k, Saponaria officinalis. 12k, Centaurea scabiosa. 14k, Leontodon autumnalis.

Die Cut Perf. 13x13½

2012, Sept. 5 Litho.

Self-Adhesive

1608 A536 8k multi 3.00 1.75
1609 A536 12k multi 4.50 2.40
1610 A536 14k multi 5.25 3.75
Nos. 1608-1610 (3) 12.75 7.90

Booklet Stamp

Serpentine Die Cut 13½

1611 A536 8k multi 3.00 2.50
a. Booklet pane of 10 30.00

Copenhagen Central Post Office, Cent. — A537

2012, Sept. 12 Engr. ***Perf. 13x13¼***

1612 A537 8k dark red 3.00 3.00

Post Scriptum, by Christian Vind — A538

Die Cut Perf. 14x13¾

2012, Nov. 2 Litho. & Engr.

Self-Adhesive

1613 A538 16k blk & yel org 5.75 4.00

Tree in Winter — A539

Tree and: 6k, Bird and musical notes. 8k, Birdhouse, bird. 12k, Moon, bird on branch of bush.

Die Cut Perf. 13x13¼

2012, Nov. 2 Litho. Self-Adhesive

1614 A539 6k blue 2.10 1.10
1615 A539 8k dull blue 2.90 1.75
1616 A539 12k blue 4.25 3.50
Nos. 1614-1616 (3) 9.25 6.35

Booklet Stamps

Serpentine Die Cut 13½

1617 A539 6k blue 2.10 1.10
a. Booklet pane of 10 + 10 etiquettes 21.00
1618 A539 8k dull blue 2.90 1.75
a. Booklet pane of 10 29.00

Queen Margrethe II Type of 2010

Self-Adhesive

Die Cut Perf. 13

Litho. & Engr.

2013, Jan. 2 Panel Color

1619 A492 12.50k purple 4.75 2.75
1620 A492 14.50k dark gray 5.25 2.75

Kaj and Andrea A540

Mr. Beard — A541

Die Cut Perf. 13½x13¼

2013, Jan. 7 Self-Adhesive Litho.

1621 A540 8k multi 3.00 2.50
a. Sheet of 6 18.00 15.00

Die Cut Perf. 13¼x13½

1622 A541 8k multi 3.00 2.50

Booklet Stamps

Serpentine Die Cut 13½

1623 A540 8k multi 3.00 2.50
1624 A541 8k multi 3.00 2.50
a. Booklet pane of 10, 5 each #1623-1624 30.00

Characters on children's television programs.

Fish — A542

Designs: 6k, Clupea harengus. 8k, Gadus morhua. 12.50k, Platichthys flesus. 14.50k, Anguilla anguilla.

Booklet Stamps (#1625-1628, 1633-1634)

2013, Jan. 7 Litho. ***Perf. 13***

1625 A542 6k multi	3.50	3.50
a. Booklet pane of 1	3.50	—
1626 A542 8k multi	5.00	5.00
a. Booklet pane of 1	5.00	—
1627 A542 12.50k multi	7.50	7.50
a. Booklet pane of 1	7.50	—
1628 A542 14.50k multi	9.00	9.00
a. Booklet pane of 1	9.00	—
b. Booklet pane of 4, #1625-1628	25.00	—
Complete booklet, #1625a, 1626a, 1627a, 1628a, 1628b	50.00	
Nos. 1625-1628 (4)	25.00	25.00

Self-Adhesive

Die Cut Perf. 13

1629 A542 6k multi	2.25	1.20
1630 A542 8k multi	3.00	1.75
1631 A542 12.50k multi	4.50	3.75
1632 A542 14.50k multi	5.25	3.75
Nos. 1629-1632 (4)	15.00	10.45

Serpentine Die Cut 13½

1633 A542 6k multi	2.25	1.20
a. Booklet pane of 10 + 10 etiquettes	22.50	
1634 A542 8k multi	3.00	1.75
a. Booklet pane of 10	30.00	

Complete booklet sold for 139k.

Queen Margrethe II Type of 2010

Die Cut Perf. 13

2013, Mar. 4 Litho. & Engr.

Self-Adhesive
Panel Color

1635 A492 16k orange	6.00	5.00

Soren Kierkegaard (1813-55), Philosopher A543

2013, Mar. 4 ***Die Cut Perf. 13¼x13***

1636 A543 8k multi	3.00	2.50

Electric Postal Bicycle A544

2013, Mar. 4 ***Perf. 13½x13***

Souvenir Sheet

1637 A544 12.50k multi	4.75	3.00

Self-Adhesive

Die Cut Perf. 13¼x13

1638 A544 12.50k multi	4.75	2.25

Manor Houses A545

Designs: Nos. 1639, 1641, Egeskov Castle. Nos. 1640, 1642, Valdemar's Castle.

2013, Mar. 4 ***Die Cut Perf. 13¼x13***

Self-Adhesive

1639 A545 8k multi	3.00	2.50
1640 A545 8k multi	3.00	2.50

Booklet Stamps

Serpentine Die Cut 13½

1641 A545 8k multi	3.00	2.50
1642 A545 8k multi	3.00	2.50
a. Booklet pane of 10, 5 each #1641-1642	30.00	

The Little Mermaid Statue, Copenhagen, Cent. — A546

Litho. & Engr.

2013, May 27 ***Perf. 13½x13***

Souvenir Sheet

1643 A546 14.50k multi	*5.25*	5.25

Self-Adhesive

Die Cut Perf. 13¼x13

1644 A546 14.50k multi	5.25	4.50

Danish Rock Music A547

Designs: Nos. 1645, 1647, Crowd at rock concert. Nos. 1646, 1648, Electric guitar of Kasper Eistrup.

Die Cut Perf. 13¼x13

2013, May 27 Litho.

Self-Adhesive

1645 A547 8k multi	3.00	1.75
1646 A547 8k multi	3.00	1.75

Serpentine Die Cut 13½

1647 A547 8k multi	3.00	1.75
1648 A547 8k multi	3.00	1.75
a. Booklet pane of 10, 5 each #1647-1648	30.00	
Nos. 1645-1648 (4)	12.00	7.00

Nos. 1647-1648 were printed in sheets containing 3 of each stamp.

Culture Yard, Elsinore — A548

Designs: 8k, Wing of building and reflecting pond. 12.50k, Building entrance and reflecting pond.

2013, Aug. 29 Litho. ***Perf. 13x13¼***

Souvenir Sheet

1649 A548 Sheet of 2	7.50	4.50
a. 8k multi	3.00	1.75
b. 12.50k multi	4.50	2.75

Self-Adhesive

Die Cut Perf. 13x13¼

1650 A548 8k multi	3.00	1.75
1651 A548 12.50k multi	4.50	2.75

Fifth INDEX: Intl. Design award ceremonies, Elsinore.

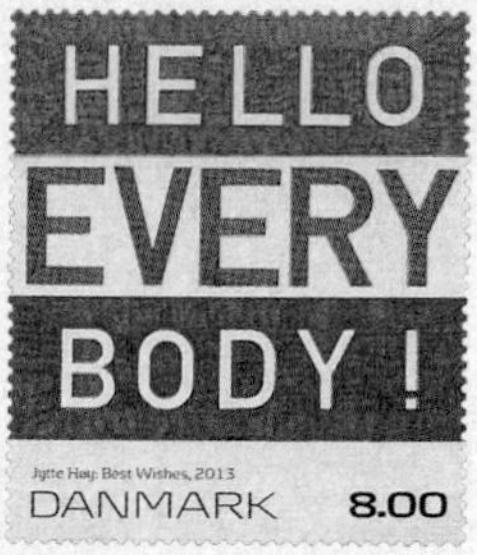

Best Wishes, by Jytte Hoy A549

Die Cut Perf. 13¼x13½

2013, Sept. 2 Litho. & Engr.

Self-Adhesive

1652 A549 8k multi	3.00	1.75

Scenes from Stories by Hans Christian Andersen A550

Scenes from: 6k, The Tinderbox. 8k, The Flying Trunk. 12.50k, The Sweethearts (The Top and the Ball). 14.50k, The Little Match Girl.

Die Cut Perf. 13¼x13

2013, Sept. 2 Litho. & Engr.

Self-Adhesive

1653 A550 6k multi	2.25	1.50
a. Booklet pane of 10 + 10 etiquettes	22.50	
1654 A550 8k multi	3.00	1.75
a. Booklet pane of 10	30.00	
1655 A550 12.50k multi	4.50	3.00
1656 A550 14.50k multi	5.25	3.75
Nos. 1653-1656 (4)	15.00	10.00

Christmas — A551

Designs: 6k, Christmas rose. 8k, Skating girl. 12.50k, Robins.

2013, Oct. 29 Litho. ***Perf. 13x12¾***

Souvenir Sheet

1657 Sheet of 3	9.75	9.75
a. A551 6k multi	2.25	1.20
b. A551 8k multi	3.00	1.75
c. A551 12.50k multi	4.50	3.75

Self-Adhesive

Die Cut Perf. 13x13¼

1658 A551 6k multi	2.25	1.20
1659 A551 8k multi	3.00	1.75
1660 A551 12.50k multi	4.50	3.00
Nos. 1658-1660 (3)	9.75	5.95

Booklet Stamps

Serpentine Die Cut 13½

1661 A551 6k multi	2.25	1.20
a. Booklet pane of 10 + 10 etiquettes	22.50	
1662 A551 8k multi	3.00	1.75
a. Booklet pane of 10	30.00	

Trade Treaty Between Denmark and France, 350th Anniv. A552

Map and compass rose with ship at: 8k, Right. 12.50k, Left.

Die Cut Perf. 13½x13¼

2013, Nov. 7 Litho. & Engr.

Self-Adhesive

1663 A552 8k rose & blue	3.00	1.75
1664 A552 12.50k blue & rose	4.50	2.75

See France Nos. 4526-4527.

Queen Margrethe II Type of 2010

Die Cut Perf. 13

2014, Jan. 2 Litho. & Engr.

Self-Adhesive
Panel Color

1665 A492 9k red	3.75	2.50
a. Booklet pane of 10	37.50	
1666 A492 18k blue	7.50	4.50
a. Booklet pane of 10	75.00	

Nordic Cuisine — A553

Aebleflaesk: 6.50k, Raw ingredients (Pig and apples). 14k, Finished dish.

Die Cut Perf. 13½x13

2014, Jan. 2 Litho.

Self-Adhesive

1667 A553 6.50k multi	2.50	1.50
a. Booklet pane of 10	25.00	
1668 A553 14k multi	5.25	2.60

Flowers — A554

Designs: No. 1669, Fritillaria meleagris. No. 1670, Muscari botryoides.

Die Cut Perf. 13¾

2014, Jan. 2 Litho.

Self-Adhesive

1669 A554 9k multi	3.50	1.75
1670 A554 9k multi	3.50	1.75
a. Horiz. pair, #1669-1670 on backing paper without printing	7.00	
b. Booklet pane of 10, 5 each #1669-1670	35.00	

Nos. 1669 and 1670 were printed in sheets of 6 containing 3 of each stamp.

PH Grand Piano — A555

Die Cut Perf. 13½x13

2014, Mar. 15 Litho. & Engr.

Self-Adhesive

1671 A555 14k multi	5.25	3.75

Europa.

General Peter du Plat (1809-64) — A556

Prussian Soldiers at Battle of Dybbol — A557

Litho. & Engr.
2014, Mar. 15 *Perf. 13x12¾*
Souvenir Sheet

1672 Sheet of 2 + label 10.50 10.50
a. A556 9k multi 3.50 1.75
b. A557 18k multi 6.75 3.50

Self-Adhesive
Die Cut Perf. 13½

1673 A556 9k multi 3.50 1.75
a. Booklet pane of 10 35.00

Die Cut Perf. 13x13½

1674 A557 18k multi 6.75 3.50

Battle of Dybbol, 150th anniv,

Danish School System, 200th Anniv. — A561

Die Cut Perf. 13½
2014, June 11 **Litho.**
Self-Adhesive

1681 A561 6.50k multi 2.40 1.50
a. Booklet pane of 10 24.00

Chairs — A558

Prince Henrik, 80th Birthday A562

Designs: 6.50k, Three-legged shell chair, designed by Hans J. Wegner (1914-2007). 16k, Spanish chair, designed by Borge Mogensen (1914-72).

Die Cut Perf. 13½x13
2014, Mar. 15 **Litho. & Engr.**
Self-Adhesive

1675 A558 6.50k org & gray 2.40 1.50
a. Booklet pane of 10 24.00
1676 A558 16k brn & lt brn 6.00 3.00
a. Booklet pane of 5 30.00

A booklet containing perf. 13½x13 stamps with water-activated gum having designs identical to Nos. 1675 and 1676 sold for 139k. The booklet contained a pane containing one example of the 6.50k, another containing one example of the 16k, and another containing one example each of the 6.50k and 16k.

Die Cut Perf. 13½
2014, June 11 **Litho.**
Self-Adhesive

1682 A562 9k multi 3.50 1.75
a. Booklet pane of 4 14.00

Den Frie Center of Contemporary Art, Cent. — A563

Die Cut Perf. 13½
2014, June 11 **Litho. & Engr.**
Self-Adhesive

1683 A563 9k multi 3.50 1.75
a. Booklet pane of 2 7.00

Sailboats A559

Designs: 6.50k, Laser Radial dinghy. 14k, Hanse 430e yacht.

Perf. 12½x12¾
2014, Mar. 17 **Litho.**
Souvenir Sheet

1677 Sheet of 2 7.75 7.75
a. A559 6.50k multi 2.40 1.50
b. A559 14k multi 5.25 2.75

Self-Adhesive
Die Cut Perf. 13x13½

1678 A559 6.50k multi 2.40 1.50
a. Booklet pane of 10 24.00
1679 A559 14k multi 5.25 2.60

Manor Houses A564

Designs: 6.50k, Knuthenborg. 9k, Ledreborg Palace.

Die Cut Perf. 13x13½
2014, June 11 **Litho. & Engr.**
Self-Adhesive

1684 A564 6.50k multi 2.40 1.25
a. Booklet pane of 10 24.00
1685 A564 9k multi 3.50 1.75
a. Booklet pane of 10 35.00

Princess Benedikte and Scouts A560

Die Cut Perf. 13x13½
2014, Apr. 29 **Litho.**
Self-Adhesive

1680 A560 9k multi + label 3.50 3.50
a. Booklet pane of 5 + 5 labels 17.50

Princess Benedikte, 70th birthday.

Guard Hussar Regiment, 400th Anniv. — A565

Die Cut Perf. 13½
2014, Aug. 30 **Litho. & Engr.**
Self-Adhesive

1686 A565 6.50k multi 2.40 1.25
a. Booklet pane of 10 24.00

Blank Space for Greetings, by Olafur Eliasson — A566

Serpentine Die Cut 10¼
2014, Aug. 30 **Litho. & Engr.**
Self-Adhesive

1687 A566 9k blk & olive 3.25 1.60
a. Booklet pane of 4 13.00

The central portion of the stamp is die cut.

Characters from Stories by Hans Christian Andersen — A567

Designs: 6.50k, Klods-Hans (Clumsy Hans) and dead crow. 9k, Tommelise (Thumbelina) and toad.

Perf. 12¾x13¼
2014, Aug. 30 **Litho. & Engr.**
Souvenir Sheet

1688 Sheet of 2 5.75 3.00
a. A567 6.50k multi 2.40 1.25
b. A567 9k multi 3.25 1.60

Self-Adhesive
Die Cut Perf. 13½x13

1689 A567 6.50k multi 2.40 1.25
a. Booklet pane of 10 24.00
1690 A567 9k multi 3.25 1.60
a. Booklet pane of 10 32.50

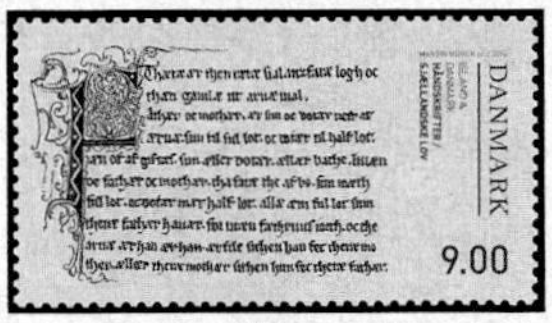

Manuscripts — A568

Designs: 9k, Valdemar's Law of Zealand, 13th cent. 14k, Njáls Saga, c. 1350.

Litho. & Engr.
2014, Aug. 30 *Perf. 13x12¾*
Souvenir Sheet

1691 Sheet of 2 8.25 4.25
a. A568 9k multi 3.25 1.60
b. A568 14k multi 5.00 2.50

Self-Adhesive
Die Cut Perf. 13½

1692 A568 9k multi 3.25 1.60
a. Booklet pane of 10 32.50
1693 A568 14k multi 5.00 2.50
a. Booklet pane of 5 25.00

See Iceland Nos. 1350-1352.

Berries — A569

Designs: 6.50k, Snowberries. 9k, Lingonberries. 14k, Firethorn.

Die Cut Perf. 13½x13¼
2014, Oct. 18 **Litho.**
Self-Adhesive

1694 A569 6.50k multi 2.25 1.10
a. Booklet pane of 10 22.50
1695 A569 9k multi 3.00 1.50
a. Booklet pane of 10 30.00
1696 A569 14k multi 4.75 2.40
a. Booklet pane of 5 24.00
Nos. 1694-1696 (3) 10.00 5.00

Queen Margrethe II Type of 2010
Die Cut Perf. 13
2014, Nov. 17 **Litho. & Engr.**
Self-Adhesive
Panel Color

1697 A492 7k Prus blue 2.40 1.25
a. Booklet pane of 10 24.00
1698 A492 10k red 3.50 1.75
a. Booklet pane of 10 35.00
1699 A492 16.50k orange 5.50 2.75
a. Booklet pane of 10 55.00
1700 A492 19k blue 6.50 3.25
a. Booklet pane of 10 65.00
Nos. 1697-1700 (4) 17.90 9.00

Children's Poems by Halfdan Rasmussen (1915-2002) — A570

Poems from *Halfdans ABC*: No. 1701, Bennys Bukser Braendte (Benn's Trouser's Burned). No. 1702, Kanonkongen Knold (Cannon King Knold).

Die Cut Perf. 13¾x13½
2015, Jan. 2 **Litho. & Engr.**
Self-Adhesive

1701 A570 7k blue & multi 2.25 1.10
1702 A570 7k dl grn & multi 2.25 1.10
a. Booklet pane of 10, 6 #1701, 4 #1702 22.50

Lego Blocks — A571

Blocks of various colors and: 10k, Boy. 14.50k, Girl.

Die Cut Perf. 13½x13
2015, Jan. 2 **Litho.**
Self-Adhesive

1703 A571 10k multi 3.25 1.60
a. Booklet pane of 10 32.50
b. Sheet of 6 + 20 stickers 22.50
1704 A571 14.50k multi 4.75 2.40
a. Booklet pane of 10 4.75 2.40

No. 1703b sold for 70k.

Animals in Wadden Sea National Park — A572

Designs: Nos. 1705a, 1706, Texel sheep. Nos. 1705b, 1707, Black-tailed godwit, vert. Nos. 1705c, 1708, Harbor seals.

Litho. & Engr.
2015, Jan. 2 *Perf. 13*

1705 Souvenir sheet of 3 9.75 5.00
a.-c. A572 10k Any single 3.25 1.60

Self-Adhesive
Die Cut Perf. 13¼x13½, 13½x13¼

1706 A572 10k multi 3.25 1.60
1707 A572 10k multi 3.25 1.60
1708 A572 10k multi 3.25 1.60
a. Booklet pane of 10, 4 #1706, 6 #1708 32.50
Nos. 1706-1708 (3) 9.75 4.80

Herlufsholm, 450th Anniv. — A573

Die Cut Perf. 13½x13

2015, Mar. 14 **Litho.**

Self-Adhesive

1709 A573 10k multi 3.00 1.50
a. Booklet pane of 10 30.00 —

Inventions — A574

Inventions: Nos. 1710a, 1711, Dry cell battery, by Wilhelm Hellesen, 1887. Nos. 1710b, 1712, Ready-mix concrete truck, by Kristian Hindhede, 1929, horiz. Nos. 1710c, 1713, Long John delivery bicycle, by Morten Rasmussen Mortensen, 1929, horiz. Nos. 1710d, 1714, Writing ball, by Rasmus Mallin-Hansen, 1867.

2015, Mar. 14 **Litho.** ***Perf. 13***

Souvenir Sheet

1710 Sheet of 4 12.00 6.00
a.-d. A574 10k Any single 3.00 1.50

Booklet Stamps

Self-Adhesive

Litho. & Engr.

Die Cut Perf. 13½x13, 13x13½

1711 A574 10k multi 3.00 1.50
1712 A574 10k multi 3.00 1.50
1713 A574 10k multi 3.00 1.50
a. Booklet pane of 10, 6 #1713, 4 #1712 30.00
1714 A574 10k multi 3.00 1.50
a. Booklet pane of 10, 6 #1711, 4 #1714 30.00
Nos. 1711-1714 (4) 12.00 6.00

Medal of Merit — A575

Order of the Elephant — A576

Order of Dannebrog — A577

Die Cut Perf. 13½x13

2015, Mar. 14 **Litho. & Engr.**

Self-Adhesive

1715 A575 7k multi 2.10 1.10

Booklet Stamps

1716 A576 7k multi 2.10 1.10
1717 A577 7k multi 2.10 1.10
a. Booklet pane of 10, 6 #1716, 4 #1717 21.00
Nos. 1715-1717 (3) 6.30 3.30

A booklet containing perforated examples of Nos. 1715-1717 (three booklet panes containing one of each stamp and one booklet pane containing all three stamps) sold for 199k.

Woman Suffrage, Cent. A578

Die Cut Perf. 13¼

2015, June 13 **Litho.**

Self-Adhesive

1718 A578 10k multi 3.00 1.50

Samosvej 8, 2300 Kobenhaven S, Danmark, by Jesper Christiansen — A579

Die Cut Perf. 13¼

2015, June 13 **Litho. & Engr.**

Self-Adhesive

1719 A579 10k multi 3.00 1.50

Copenhagen Carpenters' Guild, 500th Anniv. — A580

Die Cut Perf. 13½x13

2015, June 13 **Litho. & Engr.**

Self-Adhesive

1720 A580 10k multi 3.00 1.50
a. Booklet pane of 10 30.00

Ships — A581

Designs: Nos. 1721a, 1723, Georg Stage. Nos. 1721b, 1722, Danmark. Nos. 1721c, 1724, Kobenhavn. Nos. 1721d, 1725, Fulton.

2015, June 13 **Litho.** ***Perf. 13x12¾***

1721 A581 Sheet of 4 8.50 8.50
a.-d. 7k Any single 2.10 1.10

Self-Adhesive

Die Cut Perf. 13x13½

1722 A581 7k multi 2.10 1.10
1723 A581 7k multi 2.10 1.10
a. Vert. pair, #1722-1723, on backing paper without printing 4.25
1724 A581 7k multi 2.10 1.10
1725 A581 7k multi 2.10 1.10
a. Vert. pair, #1724-1725, on backing paper without printing 4.25
b. Booklet pane of 10, 2 each #1723-1725, 4 #1722 21.00
Nos. 1722-1725 (4) 8.40 4.40

Miniature Sheet

25th Post Danmark Rundt Bicycle Race — A582

No. 1726: a, Moreno Argentin. b, Jakob Fuglsang. c, Cyclists in Randers. d, Matti Breschel. e, Cyclists on Kiddesvej climb, Velje. f, Fabian Cancellara. g, Cyclists on Storebaelts Bridge. h, Cyclist on Frederiksberg Allé, Copenhagen. i, Mark Cavendish. j, Michael Valgren.

Die Cut Perf. 13x13¼ on 3 Sides

2015, June 27 **Litho.**

Self-Adhesive

1726 A582 Sheet of 10 25.50
a.-e. 7k Any single 2.10 1.10
f.-j. 10k Any single 3.00 1.50

Christmas — A583

Honey cakes shaped as: Nos. 1727a, 1728, Man. Nos. 1727b, 1729, Woman. Nos. 1727c, 1730, Heart.

2015, Oct. 17 **Litho.** ***Perf. 12¾x13¼***

Souvenir Sheet

1727 Sheet of 3 7.25 3.75
a.-b. A583 7k Either single 2.10 1.10
c. A583 10k multi 3.00 1.50

Self-Adhesive

Die Cut Perf. 13½x13

1728 A583 7k multi 2.10 1.10
1729 A583 7k multi 2.10 1.10
a. Booklet pane of 10, 6 #1728, 4 #1729 21.00

Size:22x32mm

Die Cut Perf. 12¼x13 Syncopated

1730 A583 10k multi 3.00 1.50
Nos. 1728-1730 (3) 7.20 3.70

Maribo Cathedral, 600th Anniv. — A584

Litho. & Engr.

2016, Jan. 4 ***Perf. 13½x13***

Self-Adhesive

1731 A584 19k multi 5.50 2.75
a. Booklet pane of 10 55.00

Nordic Food Culture
A585 A586

2016, Jan. 4 **Litho.** ***Perf. 13***

Souvenir Sheet

1732 Sheet of 2 4.80 2.50
a. A585 8k multi 2.40 1.25
b. A586 8k multi 2.40 1.25

Self-Adhesive

Die Cut Perf. 13

1733 A585 8k multi 2.40 1.25
a. Booklet pane of 5 12.00
1734 A586 8k multi 2.40 1.25
a. Booklet pane of 5 12.00

SEMI-POSTAL STAMPS

Nos. 159, 157 Surcharged in Red

Wmk. Multiple Crosses (114)

1921, June 17 ***Perf. 14½x14***

B1 A20 10o + 5o green 27.50 *60.00*
B2 A21 20o + 10o slate 30.00 *77.50*
Set, never hinged 167.50

Crown and Staff of Aesculapius SP1

Dybbol Mill SP2

1929, Aug. 1 **Engr.**

B3 SP1 10o yellow green 4.50 *7.00*
a. Booklet pane of 2 27.50
B4 SP1 15o brick red 9.00 *12.00*
a. Booklet pane of 2 32.50
B5 SP1 25o deep blue 25.00 *40.00*
a. Booklet pane of 2 135.00
Nos. B3-B5 (3) 38.50 *59.00*
Set, never hinged 100.00

These stamps were sold at a premium of 5 öre each for benefit of the Danish Cancer Committee.

1937, Jan. 20 **Unwmk.** ***Perf. 13***

B6 SP2 5o + 5o green .60 *1.40*
B7 SP2 10o + 5o lt brown 2.25 *9.00*
B8 SP2 15o + 5o carmine 3.25 *9.00*
Nos. B6-B8 (3) 6.10 *19.40*
Set, never hinged 13.00

The surtax was for a fund in memory of H. P. Hanssen, statesman.

Nos. 223a and B6, Nos. 229 and B7, Nos. 238A and B8 are found se-tenant in booklets. For booklet panes, see Nos. 223d, 229b and 238Al.

Queen Alexandrine — SP3

1939-40 ***Perf. 13***

B9 SP3 5o + 3o rose lake & red ('40) .25 .35
a. Booklet pane of 4 2.00 2.00
B10 SP3 10o + 5o dk violet & red .35 .25
B11 SP3 15o + 5o scarlet & red .30 *.50*
Nos. B9-B11 (3) .90 1.10
Set, never hinged 1.35

The surtax was for the Danish Red Cross.

Nos. 230 and B10 have been issued se-tenant in booklets. See No. 230b. In this pane No. 230 measures 23½x31mm from perf. to perf.

Crown Princess Ingrid and Princess Margrethe — SP4

1941-43

B12 SP4 10o + 5o dk violet .25 .25
a. Booklet pane of 10 32.50
B13 SP4 20o + 5o red ('43) .25 .25
Set, never hinged .60

Surtax for the Children's Charity Fund.

No. 288 Surcharged in Red

1944, May 11

B14 A48 10o + 5o violet .25 .25
Never hinged .30
a. Booklet pane of 10 27.50

The surtax was for the Danish Red Cross.

Catalogue values for unused stamps in this section, from this point to the end of the section, are for Never Hinged items.

Symbols of Freedom SP5

Explosions at Rail Junction SP6

Danish Flag SP7

Princess Anne-Marie SP8

1947, May 4 Engr. *Perf. 13*

B15 SP5 15o + 5o green .35 .35
B16 SP6 20o + 5o dark red .35 .35
B17 SP7 40o + 5o deep blue .85 .85
Nos. B15-B17 (3) 1.55 1.55

Issued in memory of the Danish struggle for liberty and the liberation of Denmark. The surtax was for the Liberty Fund.

For surcharges see Nos. B22-B23.

1950, Oct. 19 Unwmk.

B18 SP8 25o + 5o rose brown .55 .50

The surtax was for the National Children's Welfare Association.

S. S. Jutlandia — SP9

1951, Sept. 13 *Perf. 13*

B19 SP9 25o + 5o red .65 .60

The surtax was for the Red Cross.

No. 335 Surcharged in Black

1953, Feb. 13

B20 A61 30o + 10o brown red 1.50 1.50

The surtax was for flood relief in the Netherlands.

Stone Memorial — SP10

1953, Mar. 26 *Perf. 13*

B21 SP10 30o + 5o dark red 1.40 1.25

The surtax was for cultural work of the Danish Border Union.

Nos. B15 and B16 Surcharged in Black

1955, Feb. 17

B22 SP5 20o + 5o on No. B15 1.00 .85
B23 SP6 30o + 5o on No. B16 1.00 .85

The surtax was for the Liberty Fund.

No. 341 Surcharged

1957, Mar. 25

B24 A61 30o + 5o on 95o red org .65 .65

The surtax went to the Danish Red Cross for aid to Hungary.

No. 335 Surcharged in Black

1959, Feb. 23

B25 A61 30o + 10o brown red .80 .90

The surtax was for the Greenland Fund.

Globe Encircled by Red Cross Flags — SP11

1959, June 24 Engr. *Perf. 13*

B26 SP11 30o + 5o rose red .50 .50
B27 SP11 60o + 5o lt ultra & car .75 .75

Centenary of the Intl. Red Cross idea. The surtax was for the Red Cross. Crosses photogravure on No. B27.

Queen Ingrid — SP12

1960, Oct. 25 Unwmk.

B28 SP12 30o + 10o dark red 1.00 1.00

Queen Ingrid's 25th anniv. as a Girl Scout. The surtax was for the Scouts' fund for needy and sick children.

African Mother, Child — SP13

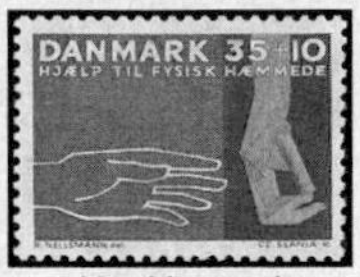

Healthy and Crippled Hands — SP14

1962, May 24

B29 SP13 30o + 10o dark red .75 1.00

Issued to aid underdeveloped countries.

1963, June 24 *Perf. 13*

B30 SP14 35o + 10o dark red 1.10 1.10

The surtax was for the benefit of the Cripples' Foundation.

Old Bridge at Danish-German Border — SP15

1964, May 28 Engr.

B31 SP15 35o + 10o henna brn .85 .90

Surtax for the Danish Border Union.

Princesses Margrethe, Benedikte, Anne-Marie — SP16

Happy Child — SP17

1964, Aug. 24

B32 SP16 35o + 10o dull red .85 .75
B33 SP16 60o + 10o dk bl & red 1.10 .95

The surtax was for the Red Cross.

1965, Oct. 21 Engr. *Perf. 13*

B34 SP17 50o + 10o brick red .65 .65

The surtax was for the National Children's Welfare Association.

"Red Cross" in 32 Languages and Red Cross, Red Lion and Sun, and Red Crescent Emblems SP18

1966, Jan. 20 Engr. *Perf. 13*

B35 SP18 50o + 10o red .65 .65

Engraved and Photogravure

B36 SP18 80o + 10o dk bl & red .80 .80

The surtax was for the Red Cross.

"Refugees 66" — SP19

Symbolic Rose — SP20

1966, Oct. 24 Engr. *Perf. 13*

B37 SP19 40o + 10o sepia .80 .80
B38 SP19 50o + 10o rose red .80 .80
B39 SP19 80o + 10o blue 1.60 1.60
Nos. B37-B39 (3) 3.20 3.20

The surtax was for aid to refugees.

1967, Oct. 12

B40 SP20 60o + 10o brown red .50 .55

The surcharge was for the Salvation Army.

Two Greenland Boys in Round Tower — SP21

1968, Sept. 12 Engr. *Perf. 13*

B41 SP21 60o + 10o dark red .65 .65

The surtax was for child welfare work in Greenland.

Princess Margrethe and Prince Henrik with Prince Frederik — SP22

1969, Dec. 11

B42 SP22 50o + 10o brn & red .65 .65
B43 SP22 60o + 10o brn red & red .65 .65

The surtax was for the Danish Red Cross.

Child Seeking Help — SP23

1970, Mar. 13

B44 SP23 60o + 10o brown red .65 .65

Surtax for "Save the Children Fund."

Child — SP24

1971, Apr. 29 Engr. *Perf. 13*

B45 SP24 60o + 10o copper red .65 .65

Surtax was for the National Children's Welfare Association.

Marsh Marigold — SP25

1972, Aug. 17

B46 SP25 70o + 10o green & yel .50 .55

Soc. and Home for the Disabled, cent.

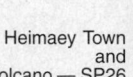

Heimaey Town and Volcano — SP26

1973, Oct. 17 Engr. *Perf. 13*

B47 SP26 70o + 20o vio blue & red 1.00 1.00

The surtax was for the victims of the eruption of Heimaey Volcano, Jan. 23, 1973.

Queen Margrethe, IWY Emblem — SP27

1975, Mar. 20 **Engr.** ***Perf. 13***
B48 SP27 90o + 20o red & buff .95 .80

International Women's Year 1975. Surtax was for a foundation to benefit women primarily in Greenland and Faroe Islands.

Skuldelev I SP28

Ships: 90o+20o, Thingvalla, emigrant steamer. 100o+20o, Liner Frederick VIII, c. 1930. 130o+20o, Three-master Danmark.

1976, Jan. 22 **Engr.** ***Perf. 13***
B49 SP28 70 + 20o olive brown .75 .85
B50 SP28 90 + 20o brick red .75 .85
B51 SP28 100 + 20o olive green .85 1.10
B52 SP28 130 + 20o violet blue .90 1.60
Nos. B49-B52 (4) 3.25 4.40

American Declaration of Independence, 200th anniv.

People and Red Cross SP29

Invalid in Wheelchair SP30

1976, Feb. 26 **Engr.** ***Perf. 13***
B53 SP29 100o + 20o red & black .65 .65
B54 SP29 130o + 20o bl, red & blk .80 .80

Centenary of Danish Red Cross.

1976, May 6 **Engr.** ***Perf. 13***
B55 SP30 100o + 20o ver & blk .65 .65

The surtax was for the Foundation to Aid the Disabled.

Mother and Child — SP31

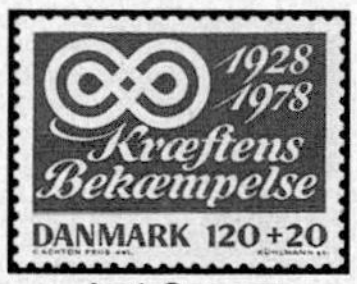

Anti-Cancer Campaign — SP32

1977, Mar. 24 **Engr.** ***Perf. 12½***
B56 SP31 1k + 20o multicolored .80 .80

Danish Society for the Mentally Handicapped, 25th anniv. Surtax was for the Society.

1978, Oct. 12 **Engr.** ***Perf. 13***
B57 SP32 120o + 20o red .65 .65

Danish Anti-Cancer Campaign, 50th anniversary. Surtax was for campaign.

Child and IYC Emblem — SP33

1979, Jan. 25 **Engr.** ***Perf. 12½***
B58 SP33 1.20k + 20o red & brown .65 .65

International Year of the Child.

Foundation for the Disabled, 25th Anniversary SP34

1980, Apr. 10 **Engr.** ***Perf. 13***
B59 SP34 130o + 20o brown red .65 .70

Children Playing Ball SP35

Intl. Year of the Disabled SP36

1981, Feb. 5 **Engr.** ***Perf. 12½x13***
B60 SP35 1.60k + 20o brown red .70 .90

Surtax was for child welfare.

1981, Sept. 10 **Engr.** ***Perf. 12½x13***
B61 SP36 2k + 20o dark blue 1.00 1.10

Stem and Broken Line — SP37

1982, May 3 **Engr.** ***Perf. 13***
B62 SP37 2k + 40o dull red 1.10 1.20

Surtax was for Danish Multiple Sclerosis Society.

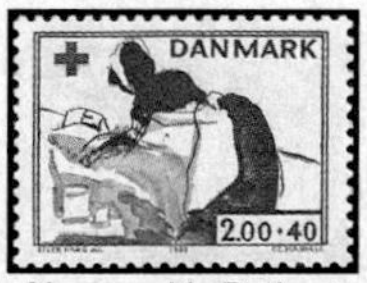

Nurse with Patient SP38

1984 Olympic Games SP39

1983, Jan. 27 **Engr.**
B63 SP38 2k + 40o multicolored 1.40 1.40

1984, Feb. 23 **Litho. & Engr.**
B64 SP39 2.70k + 40o multi 1.75 1.40

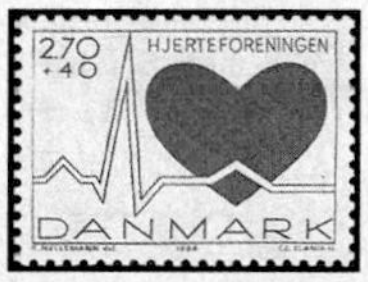

Electrocardiogram Reading, Heart — SP40

1984, Sept. 6 **Engr.** ***Perf. 12½***
B65 SP40 2.70k + 40o red 1.75 2.00

Surtax was for Heart Foundation.

SP41

SP42

1985, May 2 **Litho.** ***Perf. 13***
B66 SP41 2.80k + 50o multi 1.40 2.25

Liberation from German Occupation, 40th Anniv. Surtax for benefit of World War II veterans.

1985, Oct. 3 **Litho. & Engr.**

Design: Tapestry detail, by Caroline Ebbeson (1852-1936), former patient, St. Hans Hospital, Roskilade.

B67 SP42 2.80k + 40o multi 1.40 1.90

Natl. Soc. for the Welfare of the Mentally Ill, 25th Anniv. Surtax benefited the mentally ill.

Danish Arthritis Assoc., 50th Anniv. — SP43

1986, Mar. 20 **Litho.** ***Perf. 13***
B68 SP43 2.80k + 50o multi 2.25 2.25

Surtax for the Arthritis Assoc.

Poul Reichhart (1913-1985), as Papageno in The Magic Flute — SP44

1986, Feb. 6 **Litho.** ***Perf. 13***
B69 SP44 2.80k + 50o multicolored 2.25 2.25

Surtax for the physically handicapped.

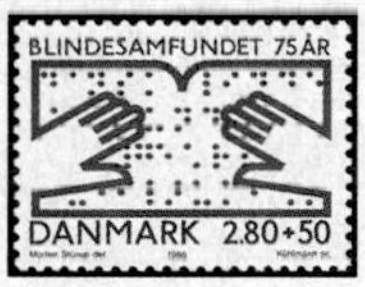

Danish Society for the Blind, 75th Anniv. — SP45

Litho. & Engr.

1986, Feb. 20 ***Perf. 13***
B70 SP45 2.80k +50o blk, vio brn & dk red 2.25 2.75

Danish Assoc. of Epileptics, 25th Anniv. SP46

1987, Sept. 24 **Engr.** ***Perf. 13***
B71 SP46 2.80k +50o dk red, brt ultra & dk grn 2.40 3.00

Folkekirkens Nodhjaelp Relief Organization — SP47

1988, Mar. 10 **Engr.**
B72 SP47 3k +50o multicolored 2.25 2.75

Surtax for the relief organization.

Natl. Council for Unwed Mothers, 5th Anniv. — SP48

1988, Sept. 22 **Photo.**
B73 SP48 3k +50o dk rose brn 2.50 3.25

SP49

SP50

1989, Feb. 16 **Litho.**
B74 SP49 3.20k +50o multi 2.50 3.00

Salvation Army.

1990, Aug. 30 **Litho.** ***Perf. 13***
B75 SP50 3.50k +50o Insulin crystal 3.25 4.50

Danish Diabetes Assoc., 50th anniv.

Children's Telephone SP51

1991, June 6 **Engr.** ***Perf. 13***
B76 SP51 3.50k +50o dark blue 2.40 2.75

Surtax benefits Borns Vilkar, children's welfare organization.

Danish Dyslexia Assoc., 50th Anniv. SP52

Litho. & Engr.

1992, Aug. 27 ***Perf. 13***
B77 SP52 3.75k +50o multi 3.75 5.00

SP53

SP54

1993, Aug. 19 **Litho.** ***Perf. 13***
B78 SP53 3.75k +50o multi 2.75 3.25

YMCA Social Work, 75th anniv.

Litho. & Engr.

1994, June 9 ***Perf. 13***
B79 SP54 3.75k +50o multi 2.10 3.00

Prince Henrik, 60th birthday. Surtax for Danish Red Cross.

Natl. Society of Polio and Accident Victims, 50th Anniv. SP55

1995, June 8 **Litho.** ***Perf. 13***
B80 SP55 3.75k +50o red 1.90 2.75

SP56

SP57

1996, Oct. 10 Litho. *Perf. 13*

B81 SP56 3.75k +50o red & black 3.50 2.25

The AIDS Foundation.

1997, May 15 Litho. *Perf. 13*

B82 SP57 3.75k +50o multi 2.50 2.75

Asthma-Allergy Assoc.

Danish Cancer Society SP58

1998, Sept. 3 Litho. *Perf. 13*

B83 SP58 3.75k +50o multi 2.25 2.50

SP59

1999, Aug. 25 Litho. *Perf. 13*

B84 SP59 4k +50o blue & red 2.00 2.25

For the Alzheimer's Association.

SP60

2000, Sept. 27 Engr. *Perf. 13*

B85 SP60 4k +50o red & blue 1.60 2.00

For the Cerebral Palsy Association.

Amnesty International — SP61

2001, Jan. 24 Engr. *Perf. 12¾*

B86 SP61 4k +50o blk & red 2.25 2.25

LEV National Association SP62

2002, Mar. 13 Engr. *Perf. 12¾*

B87 SP62 4k + 50o multi, *greenish* 2.25 2.25

Doctors Without Borders SP63

2003, Mar. 12 Litho. *Perf. 12¾*

B88 SP63 4.25k +50o multi 1.60 1.25
Booklet, 10 #B88 16.00

Children's Aid Day — SP64

2004, Jan. 14 Litho. *Perf. 12¾*

B89 SP64 4.50k +50o multi 1.75 2.10
Booklet, 10 #B89 17.50

SOS Children's Villages SP65

2005, Jan. 12 Litho. *Perf. 12¾*

B90 SP65 4.50k +50o multi 2.40 2.75
Complete booklet, 10 #B90 24.00

Surtax was originally intended for an SOS Children's Village in Burundi, but surtax went to the relief fund for Dec. 26, 2004 tsunami victims. A sticker noting this change was to be applied to the front covers of the booklets.

Danish Refugee Council, 50th Anniv. SP66

2006, Jan. 11 Engr. *Perf. 12¾*

B91 SP66 4.75k +50o blk & red, *tan* 2.75 2.75
Complete booklet, 10 #B91 27.50

Crown Prince Frederik, Crown Princess Mary, and Prince Christian SP67

2007, Jan. 10 Engr. *Perf. 13x13¼*

B92 SP67 4.75k +50o multi 2.75 2.40
Complete booklet, 10 #B92 27.50

Surtax for Crown Prince Frederik and Crown Princess Mary's Fund for Charitable and Humanitarian Purposes.

Danish Cancer Society, 80th Anniv. — SP68

2008, Jan. 9 Engr. *Perf. 12¾*

B93 SP68 5.50k +50o blk & red 2.50 2.40
Complete booklet, 10 #B93 25.00

Prince Henrik, Farm Field, Viet Nam, Emblem of Worldwide Fund for Nature (WWF) SP69

2009, Jan. 7 Litho. *Perf. 13x13¼*

B94 SP69 5.50k + 50o multi 2.75 3.25
Complete booklet, 10 #B94 27.50

Surtax for Worldwide Fund for Nature.

Danish Children's Cancer Foundation SP70

Die Cut Perf. 13¼x13½

2010, Jan. 6 Litho.

Self-Adhesive

B95 SP70 5.50k +50o multi 2.40 2.50
a. Souvenir sheet of 4 9.75

Booklet Stamp

Serpentine Die Cut 10

B96 SP70 5.50k +50o multi 2.40 2.50
a. Booklet pane of 12 29.00

Issued: No. B95a, 8/4.

Eight People SP71

2011 Litho. *Die Cut Perf. 13½x13*

Self-Adhesive

B97 SP71 5.50k+50o blk & red 2.50 2.50

B98 SP71 8k+50o blk & red 3.50 3.50

Booklet Stamps

Serpentine Die Cut 13½

B99 SP71 5.50k+50o blk & red 2.50 2.50
a. Booklet pane of 10 25.00

B100 SP71 8k+50o blk & red 3.50 3.50
a. Booklet pane of 10 35.00
b. Sheet of 6 + 7 labels 21.00 21.00

Surtax for Danish Rheumatism Association. Issued: Nos. B97, B99, 1/6; Nos. B98, B100, 3/9. No. B100b, 8/4.

Crown Princess Mary — SP72

2012, June 10 *Die Cut Perf. 13x13½*

Self-Adhesive

B101 SP72 8k+50o multi 3.00 3.00

Booklet Stamp

Serpentine Die Cut 13½

B102 SP72 8k+50o multi 3.00 3.00
a. Booklet pane of 10 + sticker 30.00

Surtax for Danish Heart Foundation.

Crown Princess Mary Type of 2012

Serpentine Die Cut 13½

2012, June 10

Self-Adhesive

Stochastic Litho. Printing

B103 SP72 8k+50o multi 3.50 3.50

The black dots that make up the design on No. B102 are arranged in lines, but are randomly placed on No. B103. No. B103 was printed in sheets of 6.

Girl's Head — SP73

Die Cut Perf. 13x13¼

2013-14 Litho.

B104 SP73 8k+1k multi 3.25 3.25

Booklet Stamp

Serpentine Die Cut 13½

B105 SP73 8k+1k multi 3.25 3.25
a. Booklet pane of 10 32.50

Self-Adhesive

Die Cut Perf. 13½x13

B106 SP73 9k+1k multi 3.75 3.75
a. Booklet pane of 10 37.50

Surtax for Save the Children charity.

Issued: Nos. B104-B105, 5/27; No. B106, 1/2/14.

No. B106 was printed in sheets of 6. Surtax was for Save the Children charity.

Red Cross, 150th Anniv. — SP74

2014-15 Litho. *Die Cut Perf. 13½*

Self-Adhesive

B107 SP74 9k+1k gray & red 3.75 3.75
a. Booklet pane of 10 37.50

B108 SP74 10k+1k gray & red 3.50 3.50
a. Booklet pane of 10 35.00

Surtax for Red Cross. Issued: No. B107, 6/3; No. B108, 1/2/15.

Worldwide Fund for Nature (WWF) — SP75

Sun, bird and: No. B109, Deer. No. B110, Farmhouse and wind generator.

Die Cut Perf. 13¼ Syncopated

2015, May 7 Litho.

Self-Adhesive

B109 SP75 10k+1k multi 3.25 3.25

B110 SP75 10k+1k multi 3.25 3.25
a. Booklet pane of 10, 6 #B109, 4 #B110 32.50

Surtax for Worldwide Fund for Nature. See Sweden No. B63.

WWF Type of 2015

Designs: No. B111, Like #B109. No. B112, Like #B110.

Die Cut Perf. 13½ Syncopated

2016, Jan. 4 Litho.

Self-Adhesive

B111 SP75 8k+1k multi 2.60 2.60

B112 SP75 8k+1k multi 2.60 2.60
a. Booklet pane of 5, 3 #B111, 2 #B112 13.00

AIR POST STAMPS

Airplane and Plowman — AP1

Wmk. Multiple Crosses (114)

1925-29 Typo. *Perf. 12x12½*

C1	AP1	10o yellow green	27.50	*50.00*
C2	AP1	15o violet ('26)	70.00	*110.00*
C3	AP1	25o scarlet	45.00	*72.50*
C4	AP1	50o lt gray ('29)	130.00	*315.00*
C5	AP1	1k choc ('29)	105.00	*300.00*
		Nos. C1-C5 (5)	377.50	*847.50*
		Set, never hinged	975.00	

Towers of Copenhagen — AP2

Unwmk.

1934, June 9 Engr. Perf. 13
C6 AP2 10o orange .75 1.10
C7 AP2 15o red 2.60 5.50
C8 AP2 20o Prus blue 2.60 5.50
C9 AP2 50o olive black 2.60 5.50
C10 AP2 1k brown 10.50 19.00
Nos. C6-C10 (5) 19.05 36.60
Set, never hinged 40.00

LATE FEE STAMPS

LF1

Coat of Arms — LF2

Perf. 14x14½

1923 Typo. Wmk. 114
I1 LF1 10o green 17.00 5.25
Never hinged 50.00
a. Double overprint 3,000.

No. I1 was, at first, not a postage stamp but represented a tax for the services of the post office clerks in filling out postal forms and writing addresses. In 1923 it was put into use as a Late Fee stamp.

1926-31
I2 LF2 10o green 13.50 1.00
I3 LF2 10o brown ('31) 9.00 .70
Set, never hinged 60.00

1934 Unwmk. Engr. Perf. 13
I4 LF2 5o green .35 .30
I5 LF2 10o orange .35 .30
Set, never hinged 1.30

POSTAGE DUE STAMPS

Regular Issues of 1913-20 Overprinted

Perf. 14x14½

1921, May 1 Wmk. 114
J1 A10 1o deep orange 2.50 7.00
J2 A16 5o green 7.00 7.00
J3 A16 7o orange 4.50 8.50
J4 A16 10o red 30.00 17.00
J5 A16 20o deep blue 22.50 14.00
J6 A16 25o brown & blk 30.00 10.00
J7 A16 50o claret & blk 13.50 8.50
Nos. J1-J7 (7) 110.00 72.00
Set, never hinged 300.00

Same Overprint in Dark Blue On Military Stamp of 1917

1921, Nov. 23
J8 A16 10o red 15.00 20.00
Never hinged 37.50
a. "S" inverted 175.00 240.00
Never hinged 350.00

Numeral of Value — D1

Typographed (Solid Panel)

1921-30 Perf. 14x14½
J9 D1 1o orange ('22) 2.00 2.50
J10 D1 4o blue ('25) 3.75 3.25
J11 D1 5o brown ('22) 3.25 2.50
J12 D1 5o lt green ('30) 3.75 2.50
J13 D1 7o apple grn ('27) 18.00 24.00
J14 D1 7o dk violet ('30) 50.00 40.00
J15 D1 10o yellow grn ('22) 4.50 2.25
J16 D1 10o lt brown ('30) 4.50 2.25
J17 D1 20o grnsh blue ('21) 3.50 3.25
a. Double impression 2,700.
J18 D1 20o gray ('30) 4.75 5.00
J19 D1 25o scarlet ('23) 4.50 6.00
J20 D1 25o violet ('26) 3.75 7.75
J21 D1 25o lt blue ('30) 7.25 10.75
J22 D1 1k dk blue ('21) 90.00 20.00
J23 D1 1k brn & dk bl ('25) 10.00 18.00
J24 D1 5k purple ('25) 22.50 18.00
Nos. J9-J24 (16) 236.00 168.00
Set, never hinged 615.00

Engraved (Lined Panel)

1934-55 Unwmk. Perf. 13
J25 D1 1o slate .30 .30
J26 D1 2o carmine .35 .30
J27 D1 5o yellow green .45 .30
J28 D1 6o dk olive ('41) .45 .30
J29 D1 8o magenta ('50) 2.00 4.00
J30 D1 10o orange .35 .30
J31 D1 12o dp ultra ('55) .55 1.50
J32 D1 15o lt violet ('54) .85 .30
J33 D1 20o gray .65 .30
J34 D1 25o blue .75 .30
J35 D1 30o green ('53) .50 .30
J36 D1 40o claret ('49) .60 .25
J37 D1 1k brown .80 .30
Nos. J25-J37 (13) 8.60 8.75
Set, never hinged 14.50

No. 96 Surcharged in Black

1934 Wmk. 114 Perf. 14x14½
J38 A10 15o on 12o violet 6.00 4.50
Never hinged 18.00

MILITARY STAMPS

Nos. 97 and 100 Overprinted in Blue

1917 Wmk. 114 Perf. 14x14½
M1 A16 5o green 19.00 40.00
a. "S" inverted 300.00 375.00
M2 A16 10o red 16.00 27.00
a. "S" inverted 225.00 375.00
Set, never hinged 70.00
#M1a, M2a, never hinged 975.00

The letters "S F" are the initials of "Soldater Frimaerke" (Soldier's Stamp).
For overprint see No. J8.

OFFICIAL STAMPS

Small State Seal — O1

Wmk. Crown (112)

1871 Typo. Perf. 14x13½
O1 O1 2s blue 275.00 200.00
a. 2s ultra 275.00 200.00
b. Imperf 450.00
O2 O1 4s carmine 77.50 40.00
a. Imperf 450.00
O3 O1 16s green 450.00 350.00
a. Imperf 450.00

Perf. 12½
O4 O1 4s carmine 6,500. 650.00
O5 O1 16s green 450.00 600.00
#O1-O3, O5, never hinged 3,575.

Nos. O4-O5 values are for stamps with defective perfs.

Nos. O1-O3 were reprinted in 1886 upon white wove paper, unwatermarked and imperforate. Value $10 each.

1875 Perf. 14x13½
O6 O1 3o violet 15.00 55.00
O7 O1 4o grnsh blue 18.00 6.25
O8 O1 8o carmine 15.00 2.00
a. Imperf —
O9 O1 32o green 32.50 30.00
Nos. O6-O9 (4) 80.50 93.25
Set, never hinged 245.00

For surcharge see No. 81.

1899-02 Perf. 13
O9A O1 3o red lilac ('02) 4.50 15.00
c. Imperf 400.00
As "c," pair 1,100.
O9B O1 4o blue 3.75 4.50
O10 O1 8o carmine 20.00 26.00
Nos. O9A-O10 (3) 28.25 45.50
Set, never hinged 85.00

For surcharge see No. 137.

1902-06 Wmk. 113
O11 O1 1o orange 2.25 3.25
O12 O1 3o red lilac ('06) 1.50 1.90
O13 O1 4o blue ('03) 3.00 4.50
O14 O1 5o green 3.00 .85
O15 O1 10o carmine 4.50 3.50
Nos. O11-O15 (5) 14.25 14.00
Set, never hinged 36.00

1914-23 Wmk. 114 Perf. 14x14½
O16 O1 1o orange 1.25 2.75
O17 O1 3o gray ('18) 4.50 17.00
O18 O1 4o blue ('16) 30.00 60.00
O19 O1 5o green ('15) 3.00 2.25
O20 O1 5o choc ('23) 7.50 30.00
O21 O1 10o red ('17) 15.00 8.00
O22 O1 10o green ('21) 5.25 6.00
O23 O1 15o violet ('19) 20.00 37.50
O24 O1 20o indigo ('20) 22.50 20.00
Nos. O16-O24 (9) 109.00 183.50
Set, never hinged 250.00

For surcharges see Nos. 185-191.
No. O20 is valued CTO.
Official stamps were discontinued Apr. 1, 1924.

NEWSPAPER STAMPS

Numeral of Value — N1

1907 Typo. Wmk. 113 Perf. 13
P1 N1 1o olive 20.00 3.00
P2 N1 5o blue 30.00 15.00
P3 N1 7o carmine 18.00 1.25
P4 N1 10o deep lilac 57.50 5.00
P5 N1 20o green 45.00 1.50
P6 N1 38o orange 62.50 2.50
P7 N1 68o yellow brown 150.00 27.50
P8 N1 1k bl grn & claret 37.50 6.00
P9 N1 5k rose & yel grn 225.00 45.00
P10 N1 10k bister & blue 225.00 45.00
Nos. P1-P10 (10) 870.50 151.75
Set, never hinged 3,050.

For surcharges see Nos. 138-144.

1914-15 Wmk. 114 Perf. 14x14½
P11 N1 1o olive gray 18.00 2.00
P12 N1 5o blue 45.00 12.50
P13 N1 7o rose 45.00 3.00
P14 N1 8o green ('15) 45.00 7.00
P15 N1 10o deep lilac 75.00 3.00
P16 N1 20o green 300.00 3.25
a. Imperf., pair 1,200.
P17 N1 29o orange yel ('15) 75.00 8.00
P18 N1 38o orange 2,000. 190.00
P19 N1 41o yellow brn ('15) 95.00 5.75
P20 N1 1k blue grn & mar 125.00 3.25
Nos. P11-P17,P19-P20 (9) 823.00 47.75
Set, never hinged 3,200.

For surcharges see Nos. 145-154.

PARCEL POST STAMPS

These stamps were for use on postal packets sent by the Esbjerg-Fano Ferry Service.

Regular Issues of 1913-30 Overprinted

1919-41 Wmk. 114 Perf. 14x14½
Q1 A10 10o green ('22) 20.00 20.00
Q2 A10 10o bister brn ('30) 15.00 8.50
Q3 A16 10o red 45.00 90.00
a. "POSFFAERGE" 200.00 500.00
Q4 A16 15o violet 20.00 35.00
a. "POSFFAERGE" 250.00 525.00
Q5 A16 30o orange ('22) 22.50 47.50
Q6 A16 30o dk blue ('26) 4.50 8.00
Q7 A16 50o cl & blk ('20) 300.00 350.00
Q8 A16 50o lt gray ('22) 30.00 30.00
a. 50o olive gray ('22) 225.00 450.00
Q9 A16 1k brn & bl ('24) 60.00 30.00
Q9A A16 5k vio & brn ('41) 3.75 3.25
Q10 A16 10k ver & grn ('30) 80.00 150.00

Engr.
Q11 A17 1k yellow brn 120.00 225.00
a. "POSFFAERGE" 1,500. 2,600.
Nos. Q1-Q11 (12) 720.75 997.25
Set, never hinged 1,750.

1927-30
Q12 A30 15o red ('27) 27.00 15.00
Q13 A30 30o ocher ('27) 18.00 20.00
Q14 A30 40o yel grn ('30) 27.00 17.00
Nos. Q12-Q14 (3) 72.00 52.00
Set, never hinged 180.00

Overprinted on Regular Issues of 1933-40

1936-42 Unwmk. Perf. 13
Q15 A32 5o rose lake ('42) .35 .35
Q16 A32 10o yellow org 35.00 35.00
Q17 A32 10o lt brown ('38) 1.50 2.75
Q18 A32 10o purple ('39) .35 .35
Q19 A30 15o deep red 1.50 2.00
Q20 A30 30o blue, I 4.50 7.50
Q21 A30 30o blue, II ('40) 15.00 32.50
Q22 A30 30o org, II ('42) .60 1.25
Q23 A30 40o yel grn, I 4.50 7.00
Q24 A30 40o yel grn, II ('40) 15.00 32.50
Q25 A30 40o blue, II ('42) .60 1.10
Q26 A33 50o gray 1.20 2.40
Q27 A33 1k lt brown 1.40 1.40
Nos. Q15-Q27 (13) 81.50 126.10
Set, never hinged 160.00

Catalogue values for unused stamps in this section, from this point to the end of the section, are for Never Hinged items.

Overprinted on Nos. 284, 286, 286B

1945
Q28 A47 30o orange 4.00 2.40
Q29 A47 40o blue 1.90 1.90
Q30 A47 50o gray 2.00 2.00
Nos. Q28-Q30 (3) 7.90 6.30

Ovptd. on #318, 309, 310, 312, 297

1949-53
Q31 A32 10o green ('53) .65 .50
Q32 A61 30o orange 5.50 2.25
Q33 A61 40o dull blue 4.50 2.25
Q34 A61 50o gray ('50) 24.00 1.25
Q35 A55 1k brown ('50) 2.40 1.50
Nos. Q31-Q35 (5) 37.05 7.75

Ovptd. on #335, 323, 336, 326, 397

1955-65
Q36 A61 30o brown red 2.25 2.25
Q37 A61 40o gray 2.25 2.25
Q38 A61 50o aqua 2.25 2.25
Q39 A61 70o deep green 2.25 2.25
Q40 A55 1.25k orange ('65) 10.00 12.00
Nos. Q36-Q40 (5) 19.00 21.00

Overprinted on Nos. 417 and 419

1967 **Engr.** *Perf. 13*

Q41	A86	40o brown	.65	1.25
Q42	A86	80o ultra	.65	1.25

Nos. 224, 438, 441, 297-299 Overprinted

1967-74 **Engr.** *Perf. 13*

Q43	A32	5o rose lake	.60	.50
Q44	A86	50o brown ('74)	.65	.90
Q45	A86	90o ultra ('70)	1.10	1.60
Q46	A55	1k brown	2.50	2.75
Q47	A55	2k red ('72)	2.90	4.25
Q48	A55	5k dull bl ('72)	3.50	4.50
		Nos. Q43-Q48 (6)	11.25	14.50

Nos. Q44-Q45, Q47-Q48 are on fluorescent paper.

Overprinted on No. 541

1975, Feb. 27

Q49	A161	100o deep ultra	1.60	2.40

DIEGO-SUAREZ

dē-ˌā-gō ˈswär-əs

LOCATION — A town at the northern end of Madagascar
GOVT. — French colony
POP. — 12,237

From 1885 to 1896 Diego-Suarez, (Antsirane), a French naval base, was a separate colony and issued its own stamps. These were succeeded by stamps of Madagascar.

100 Centimes = 1 Franc

Values for unused stamps are for examples with original gum as defined in the catalogue introduction except for Nos. 6-10 and J1-J2 which are valued without gum.

Stamps of French Colonies Handstamp Surcharged in Violet

1890 **Unwmk.** *Perf. 14x13½*

1	A9	15c on 1c blk, *bl*	300.00	100.00
2	A9	15c on 5c grn, *grnsh*	650.00	100.00
3	A9	15c on 10c blk, *lav*	300.00	92.50
4	A9	15c on 20c red, *grn*	650.00	80.00
5	A9	15c on 25c blk, *rose*	130.00	52.50

This surcharge is found inverted, double, etc. See the *Scott Classic Catalogue*. Counterfeits exist.

Ship Flying French Flag — A2

France — A5

Symbolical of Union of France and Madagascar
A3 A4

1890 **Litho.** *Imperf.*

6	A2	1c black	1,150.	240.00
7	A3	5c black	1,100.	200.00
8	A4	15c black	210.00	95.00
9	A5	25c black	225.00	110.00

Counterfeits exist of Nos. 6-9.

A6

1891

10	A6	5c black	350.00	100.00

Excellent counterfeits exist of No. 10.

Stamps of French Colonies Surcharged in Red or Black

No. 11

No. 12

1892 *Perf. 14x13½*

11	A9	5c on 10c blk, *lav* (R)	210.00	105.00
a.		Inverted surcharge	475.00	400.00
12	A9	5c on 20c red, *grn*	190.00	72.50
a.		Inverted surcharge	450.00	400.00

Stamps of French Colonies Overprinted in Black or Red

1892

13	A9	1c blk, *lilac blue* (R)	32.50	20.00
14	A9	2c brown, *buff*	32.50	20.00
15	A9	4c claret, *lav*	55.00	45.00
16	A9	5c green, *grnsh*	120.00	80.00
17	A9	10c black, *lavender*	40.00	32.50
b.		Double overprint	240.00	180.00
18	A9	15c blue, *pale blue*	32.50	20.00
19	A9	20c red, *grn*	40.00	32.50
20	A9	25c black, *rose*	36.00	20.00
21	A9	30c brown, *bis* (R)	1,300.	925.00
22	A9	35c black, *yellow*	1,300.	925.00
23	A9	75c carmine, *rose*	72.50	52.50
a.		Double overprint		400.00
24	A9	1fr brnz grn, *straw* (R)	80.00	52.50
a.		Double overprint	240.00	210.00

Inverted Overprint

13a	A9	1c	225.00	190.00
14a	A9	2c	225.00	190.00
15a	A9	4c		325.00
16a	A9	5c	240.00	200.00
17a	A9	10c	240.00	200.00
20a	A9	25c	240.00	200.00
21a	A9	30c		1,700.
22a	A9	35c		1,700.

Navigation and Commerce
A10 A11

1892 **Typo.** *Perf. 14x13½*
Name of Colony in Blue or Carmine

25	A10	1c black, *blue*	2.00	2.00
26	A10	2c brown, *buff*	2.75	2.75
27	A10	4c claret, *lav*	3.25	3.25
28	A10	5c green, *grnsh*	6.50	6.50
29	A10	10c black, *lavender*	8.75	7.25
30	A10	15c bl, quadrille paper	16.50	11.00
31	A10	20c red, *green*	22.50	16.00
32	A10	25c black, *rose*	17.50	14.50
33	A10	30c brown, *bister*	22.50	16.00
34	A10	40c red, *straw*	27.50	21.00
35	A10	50c carmine, *rose*	45.00	35.00
36	A10	75c violet, *org*	52.50	45.00
37	A10	1fr brnz grn, *straw*	75.00	60.00
		Nos. 25-37 (13)	302.25	240.25

Perf. 13½x14 stamps are counterfeits.

1894 *Perf. 14x13½*

38	A11	1c black, *blue*	2.00	2.00
39	A11	2c brown, *buff*	2.75	2.40
40	A11	4c claret, *lav*	3.25	2.75
41	A11	5c green, *grnsh*	5.50	4.75
42	A11	10c black, *lavender*	7.25	7.25
43	A11	15c blue, quadrille paper	12.00	6.50
44	A11	20c red, *grn*	20.00	13.50
45	A11	25c black, *rose*	12.00	9.50
46	A11	30c brown, *bister*	13.50	6.50
47	A11	40c red, *straw*	13.50	6.50
48	A11	50c carmine, *rose*	20.00	13.50
49	A11	75c violet, *org*	12.00	8.75
50	A11	1fr brnz grn, *straw*	27.50	24.00
		Nos. 38-50 (13)	151.25	107.90

Bisected stamps of type A11 are mentioned in note after Madagascar No. 62.

For surcharges see Madagascar Nos. 56-57, 61-62.

Perf. 13½x14 stamps are counterfeits.

POSTAGE DUE STAMPS

D1

D2

1891 **Unwmk.** **Litho.** *Imperf.*

J1	D1	5c violet	240.00	120.00
J2	D2	50c black	260.00	140.00

Excellent counterfeits exist of Nos. J1-J2.

Postage Due Stamps of French Colonies Ovptd. Like Nos. 13-24

1892

J3	D1	1c black	130.00	72.50
J4	D1	2c black	130.00	65.00
a.		Inverted overprint	450.00	300.00
J5	D1	3c black	130.00	65.00
J6	D1	4c black	130.00	60.00
J7	D1	5c black	130.00	72.50
J8	D1	10c black	40.00	32.50
a.		Inverted overprint	460.00	450.00
J9	D1	15c black	36.00	32.50
a.		Double overprint	575.00	500.00
J10	D1	20c black	200.00	135.00
a.		Double overprint	600.00	500.00
J11	D1	30c black	120.00	60.00
a.		Inverted overprint	450.00	300.00
J12	D1	60c black	1,200.	775.00
J13	D1	1fr brown	2,800.	1,500.

DJIBOUTI

jə-ˈbü-tē

LOCATION — East Africa
GOVT. — Republic
AREA — 8,958 sq. mi.
POP. — 447,439 (1999 est.)
CAPITAL — Djibouti

The French territory of Afars and Issas became the Republic of Djibouti June 27, 1977. For 1894-1902 issues with "Djibouti" or "DJ," see Somali Coast.

Catalogue values for all unused stamps in this country are for Never Hinged items.

Afars and Issas Issues of 1972-1977 Ovptd. and Srchd. in Black, Dark Green, Blue or Brown — No. 452

Printing and Perforations as Before

1977

439	A63	1fr on 4fr (#358;B)	3.00	.25
440	A81	2fr on 5fr (#433;B)	3.00	.25
441	A75	5fr on 20fr (#421;B)	.40	.25
442	A70	8fr (#380;B)	.40	.25
443	A71	20fr (#387;DG)	3.75	1.00
444	A81	30fr (#434;B)	5.00	.80
445	A71	40fr (#388;DG)	4.50	1.25
446	A71	45fr (#389;Bl)	5.00	1.50
447	A78	45fr (#428;B)	8.00	1.50
448	A72	50fr (#394;B)	9.00	1.75
449	A71	60fr (#391;Br)	7.50	1.75
450	A79	70fr (#430;B)	8.00	2.50
451	A81	70fr (#435;B)	6.50	2.25
452	A74	100fr (#418;B)	12.00	3.50
453	A72	150fr (#399;B)	12.00	3.50
454	A76	200fr (#422;B)	7.00	4.50
455	A80	200fr (#432;B)	8.00	5.00
456	A74	300fr (#419;B)	10.00	6.50
		Nos. 439-456,C106-C108 (21)	141.80	57.55

Map and Flag of Djibouti — A83

Design: 65fr, Map and flag of Djibouti, map of Africa, horiz.

1977, June 27 **Litho.** *Perf. 12½*

457	A83	45fr multicolored	1.50	.70
458	A83	65fr multicolored	2.25	.80

Independence, June 27.

A84

1977, July 4

459	A84	10fr Headrest, horiz.	.35	.25
460	A84	20fr Water Pipe	.70	.25
461	A84	25fr Pitcher	1.00	.45
		Nos. 459-461 (3)	2.05	.95

Ostrich — A85

1977, Aug. 11 **Litho.** *Perf. 12½*

462	A85	90fr shown	3.75	.80
463	A85	100fr Weaver	4.75	1.25

Snail
A86

Designs: 15fr, Fiddler crab. 50fr, Klipspringers. 70fr, Green turtle. 80fr, Priacanthus hamrur (fish). 150fr, Dolphinfish.

1977 Litho. *Perf. 12½*

464 A86 15fr multicolored .85 .25
465 A86 45fr multicolored 1.60 .40
466 A86 50fr multicolored 2.00 .50
467 A86 70fr multicolored 2.25 .60
468 A86 80fr multicolored 2.75 .75
469 A86 150fr multicolored 4.50 2.00
Nos. 464-469 (6) 13.95 4.50

Issued: 45fr, 70fr, 80fr, 9/14; others, 12/5.

Pres. Hassan Gouled Aptidon and Djibouti Flag — A87

1978, Feb. 12 Litho. *Perf. 13*

470 A87 65fr multicolored 2.00 .50

Charaxes Hansali — A88

Necklace — A89

Butterflies: 20fr, Colias electo. 25fr, Acraea chilo. 150fr, Junonia hierta.

1978, Mar. 13 Litho. *Perf. 12½x13*

471 A88 5fr multicolored .50 .25
472 A88 20fr multicolored 1.25 .25
473 A88 25fr multicolored 1.75 .50
474 A88 150fr multicolored 7.00 1.75
Nos. 471-474 (4) 10.50 2.75

1978, May 29 Litho. *Perf. 12½x13*

Design: 55fr, Necklace, diff.

475 A89 45fr pink & multi 1.25 .35
476 A89 55fr blue & multi 1.60 .45

Bougainvillea
A90

Flowers: 35fr, Hibiscus schizopetalus. 250fr, Caesalpinia pulcherrima.

1978, July 10 Photo. *Perf. 12½x13*

477 A90 15fr multicolored .55 .25
478 A90 35fr multicolored 1.10 .25
479 A90 250fr multicolored 6.50 .90
Nos. 477-479 (3) 8.15 1.40

Charonia Nodifera — A91

Sea Shell: 80fr, Charonia variegata.

1978, Oct. 9 Litho. *Perf. 13*

480 A91 10fr multicolored 1.25 .35
481 A91 80fr multicolored 4.00 .95

Chaetodon
A92

30fr, Yellow surgeonfish. 40fr, Harlequinfish.

1978, Nov. 20 Litho. *Perf. 13x12½*

482 A92 8fr multicolored .75 .25
483 A92 30fr multicolored 1.40 .35
484 A92 40fr multicolored 2.75 .65
Nos. 482-484 (3) 4.90 1.25

Alsthom BB 1201 at Dock — A93

55fr, Steam locomotive 231. 60fr, Steam locomotive 130 and map of route. 75fr, Diesel.

1979, Jan. 29 Litho. *Perf. 13*

485 A93 40fr multicolored 1.25 .25
486 A93 55fr multicolored 1.40 .30
487 A93 60fr multicolored 1.75 .30
488 A93 75fr multicolored 2.25 .40
Nos. 485-488 (4) 6.65 1.25

Djibouti-Addis Ababa railroad.

Children and IYC Emblem — A94

Design: 200fr, Mother, child, IYC emblem.

1979, Feb. 26 Litho. *Perf. 13*

489 A94 20fr multicolored .50 .25
490 A94 200fr multicolored 4.00 1.10

International Year of the Child.

Plane over Ardoukoba Volcano — A95

30fr, Helicopter over Ardoukoba Volcano.

1979, Mar. 19

491 A95 30fr multi, vert. 1.00 .35
492 A95 90fr multi 3.00 .65

Rowland Hill, Postal Clerks, No. C109 — A96

100fr, Somali Coast #22, Djibouti #457, letters, Rowland Hill. 150fr, Letters hoisted onto ship, smoke signals, Rowland Hill.

1979, Apr. 17 Litho. *Perf. 13x12½*

493 A96 25fr multicolored .40 .25
494 A96 100fr multicolored 2.00 .45
495 A96 150fr multicolored 3.00 .70
Nos. 493-495 (3) 5.40 1.40

Sir Rowland Hill (1795-1879), originator of penny postage.

View of Djibouti, Bird and Local Woman — A97

Design: 80fr, Map and flag of Djibouti, UPU emblem, Concorde, train and mail runner.

1979, June 8 Litho. *Perf. 13x12½*

496 A97 55fr multicolored 4.00 .85
497 A97 80fr multicolored 4.75 1.10

Philexafrique II, Libreville, Gabon, June 8-17. Nos. 496, 497 each printed in sheets of 10 with 5 labels showing exhibition emblem.

Solanacea
A98

Flowers: 2fr, Opuntia, vert. 15fr, Trichodesma. 45fr, Acacia etbaica. 50fr, Thunbergia alata, vert.

Perf. 13x13½, 13½x13

1979, June 18

498 A98 2fr multicolored .25 .25
499 A98 8fr multicolored .25 .25
500 A98 15fr multicolored .50 .25
501 A98 45fr multicolored 1.00 .25
502 A98 50fr multicolored 1.25 .25
Nos. 498-502 (5) 3.25 1.25

Running — A99

Olympic Emblem and: 70fr, Basketball, vert. 200fr, Soccer.

Perf. 12½x13, 13x12½

1979, Oct. 22 Litho.

503 A99 70fr multicolored 1.50 .25
504 A99 120fr multicolored 2.25 .50
505 A99 200fr multicolored 3.75 .75
Nos. 503-505 (3) 7.50 1.50

Pre-Olympic Year.

Cypraecassis Rufa — A100

Shells: 40fr, Lambis chiragra arthritica. 300fr, Harpa connaidalis.

1979, Dec. 22 Litho. *Perf. 13*

506 A100 10fr multicolored .25 .25
507 A100 40fr multicolored 1.00 .25
508 A100 300fr multicolored 6.50 1.50
Nos. 506-508 (3) 7.75 2.00

Rotary International, 75th Anniversary — A101

1980, Feb. 19 Litho. *Perf. 13x12½*

509 A101 90fr multicolored 2.25 .75
a. Souvenir sheet of 1 #509 15.00 15.00

Lions Club of Djibouti — A102

1980, Feb. 19

510 A102 100fr multicolored 2.25 .75

Colotis Danae — A103

1980, Mar. 17 *Perf. 13x13½*

511 A103 5fr shown .75 .50
512 A103 55fr Danaus chrysippus 3.50 1.50

Chess Players, Knight — A104

Chess Federation Creation: 75fr, Chess Game, Florence, 1493.

1980, June 9 Litho. *Perf. 13*

513 A104 20fr multicolored 1.25 .25
514 A104 75fr multicolored 3.25 .35

Cribraria
A105

1980, Aug. 12 Litho. *Perf. 13*
515 A105 15fr shown .75 .25
516 A105 85fr Nautilius pompilius 2.75 .50

Alexander Fleming, Discoverer of Penicillin — A106

Design: 130fr, Jules Verne, French science fiction writer; earth, moon and spacecraft.

1980, Sept. 1
517 A106 20fr multicolored 1.10 .35
518 A106 130fr multicolored 3.25 .60

Capt. Cook and Endeavor — A107

Capt. James Cook Death Bicentenary: 90fr, Ships and Maps of voyages.

1980, Nov. 20 Litho. *Perf. 13*
519 A107 55fr multicolored 1.40 .65
520 A107 90fr multicolored 2.25 .90

Souvenir sheets of 1 exist, perf. 12½x12. Value, each $10.

Angel Fish A108

1981, Apr. 13 Litho. *Perf. 12½*
521 A108 25fr shown 1.75 .25
522 A108 55fr Moorish idol 3.25 .50
523 A108 70fr Scad 3.75 1.50
Nos. 521-523 (3) 8.75 2.25

13th World Telecommunications Day — A109

1981, May 17 Litho. *Perf. 13*
524 A109 140fr multicolored 2.75 .70

Type 231 Steam Locomotive, Germany, 1958 and Amtrak, US, 1980 — A110

Locomotives: 55fr, Stephenson and his Rocket, Djibouti Railways 230 engine. 65fr, Type TGV, France, Type 962, Japan.

1981, June 9 Litho. *Perf. 13*
525 A110 40fr multicolored 1.50 .30
526 A110 55fr multicolored 2.00 .35
527 A110 65fr multicolored 2.50 .40
Nos. 525-527 (3) 6.00 1.05

Radio Amateurs Club — A111

1981, June 25
528 A111 250fr multicolored 5.00 1.00

Prince Charles and Lady Diana — A112

1981, June 29
529 A112 180fr shown 2.50 .75
530 A112 200fr Couple, diff. 3.00 1.00

Royal Wedding.

Lord Nelson and Victory — A113

1981, July 6 Litho. *Perf. 13x12½*
531 A113 100fr multicolored 1.90 .45
532 A113 175fr multicolored 3.25 .90

Lord Horatio Nelson (1758-1805).

Scout Tending Campfire — A114

1981, July 16 Litho. *Perf. 13*
533 A114 60fr shown 3.00 .70
534 A114 105fr Scout giving sign 3.75 .80

28th World Scouting Conference, Dakar, Aug. (60fr); 4th Pan-African Scouting Conference, Abidjan, Aug. (105fr).

Pawn and Queen, Swedish Bone Chess Pieces, 13th Cent. — A115

1981, Oct. 15 Litho. *Perf. 13*
535 A115 50fr shown 1.50 .35
536 A115 130fr Pawn, knight, Chinese, 19th cent., vert. 3.00 .85

For overprints see Nos. 542-543.

Sheraton Hotel Opening — A116

1981, Nov. 15 Litho. *Perf. 13x12½*
537 A116 75fr multicolored 1.50 .45

For surcharge see No. 623.

Acacia Mellifera A117

1981, Dec. 21 *Perf. 13*
538 A117 10fr Clitoria ternatea, vert. .40 .25
539 A117 30fr shown .80 .25
540 A117 35fr Punica granatum 1.15 .25
541 A117 45fr Malvaceous plant, vert. 1.40 .30
Nos. 538-541 (4) 3.75 1.05

See Nos. 558-560.

Nos. 535-536 Overprinted

1981, Dec. Litho. *Perf. 13*
542 A115 50fr multicolored 2.00 .50
543 A115 130fr multicolored 4.00 1.00

World Chess Championship.

TB Bacillus Centenary A117a

1982, Mar. 24 Litho. *Perf. 13*
544 A117a 305fr Koch, slide, microscope 7.00 1.50

A117b

1982, Apr. 8 Litho. *Perf. 13*
545 A117b 125fr Ivory bishop 3.50 .75
546 A117b 175fr Queen, pawn, 19th cent. 4.25 1.25

1982 World Chess Championship.

A118

1982, May 17
547 A118 150fr multicolored 3.00 .85

14th World Telecommunications Day.
For surcharge see No. 647.

Bus and Jeep — A119

1982, July 27 Litho. *Perf. 13*
548 A119 20fr shown .55 .25
549 A119 25fr Dhow, ferry .70 .25
550 A119 55fr Train, jet 1.50 .45
Nos. 548-550 (3) 2.75 .95

Shells from the Red Sea A120

1982, Nov. 20 Litho. *Perf. 12½*
551 A120 10fr Cypraea erythraeensis .45 .25
552 A120 15fr Conus sumatrensis .75 .30
553 A120 25fr Cypraea pulchra .90 .35
554 A120 30fr Conus inscriptus 1.10 .40
555 A120 70fr Casmaria ponderosa 2.25 .50
556 A120 150fr Cypraea exusta 4.50 1.50
a. Strip of 6, #551-556 9.95 3.30
Nos. 551-556 (6) 9.95 3.30

See Nos. 563-567.

Intl. Palestinian Solidarity Day — A121

1982, Nov. 29 Litho. *Perf. 13*
557 A121 40fr multicolored 1.00 .25

Local Flowers type of 1981

Various flowers. 5fr, 55fr, vert.

1983, Apr. 14 Litho. *Perf. 13*
558 A117 5fr multicolored .25 .25
559 A117 50fr multicolored 1.25 .40
560 A117 55fr multicolored 1.40 .40
Nos. 558-560 (3) 2.90 1.05

World Communications Year — A123

1983, June 20 Litho. *Perf. 13*
561 A123 500fr multicolored 9.00 2.25

Conference of Donors, Nov. 21-23 — A124

1983, Nov. 21 Litho. *Perf. 13x12½*
562 A124 75fr multicolored 1.50 .40

Shell Type of 1982

1983, Dec. 20 Litho. *Perf. 12½*
563 A120 15fr Marginella obtusa .50 .25
564 A120 30fr Conus jickelli 1.00 .25
565 A120 55fr Cypraea macandrewi 1.60 .40
566 A120 80fr Conus cuvieri 2.25 .50
567 A120 100fr Turbo petholatus 2.50 .65
Nos. 563-567 (5) 7.85 2.05

Local Butterflies A125

1984, Jan. 24 Litho. *Perf. 13½x13*
568 A125 5fr Colotis chrysonome .50 .25
569 A125 20fr Colias erate 1.00 .25
570 A125 30fr Junonia orithyia 1.50 .35
571 A125 75fr Acraea doubledayi 4.25 1.00
572 A125 110fr Byblia ilithya 5.50 1.50
Nos. 568-572 (5) 12.75 3.35

Landscapes and Animals — A126

1984, Apr. 29 Litho. *Perf. 13*
573 A126 2fr Randa Klipspringer .25 .25
574 A126 8fr Ali Sabieh, gazelles .25 .25
575 A126 10fr Lake Assal, oryx .25 .25
576 A126 15fr Tadjoura, gazelle .25 .25
577 A126 40fr Alaila Dada, jackal, vert. .75 .25
578 A126 45fr Lake Abbe, warthog .75 .30
579 A126 55fr Obock, seagull 1.90 .75
580 A126 125fr Presidential Palace, bird 3.75 1.25
Nos. 573-580 (8) 8.15 3.55

For surcharges see Nos. 646, 657-658, 660.

Fire Prevention — A127

1984, Sept. 9 Litho. *Perf. 13*
581 A127 25fr Fire truck 1.00 .25
582 A127 95fr Hook & ladder 3.25 .50
583 A127 100fr Fire plane 3.25 1.00
Nos. 581-583 (3) 7.50 1.75

International Olympic Committee Membership A128

1984, July 22 Litho. *Perf. 13*
584 A128 45fr Runners .90 .35

Motor Carriage, 1886 A128a

1984, Nov. 11 Litho. *Perf. 12½*
585 A128a 35fr shown .80 .30
586 A128a 65fr Cabriolet, 1896 1.60 .65
587 A128a 90fr Phoenix, 1900 2.25 .95
Nos. 585-587 (3) 4.65 1.90

Gottlieb Daimler (1834-1900), pioneer automobile manufacturer.

Marie and Pierre Curie — A129

1984, Dec. 3 Litho. *Perf. 12½*
588 A129 150fr Pierre Curie 3.25 1.10
589 A129 150fr Marie Curie 3.25 1.10

A130

Audubon Bicentenary — A130a

1985, Jan. 27 Litho. *Perf. 13*
590 A130 5fr Merops albicollis .75 .35
591 A130 15fr Pterocles exustus 3.25 .85
592 A130 20fr Trachyphonus margaritatus somalicus 3.75 1.00
593 A130 25fr Coracias garrulus 4.50 1.10
Nos. 590-593 (4) 12.25 3.30

Souvenir Sheet
Self-Adhesive
Perf. 12½

593A A130a 200fr Pandion haliaetus, vert. 26.00 26.00

No. 593A is airmail and printed on wood.

Intl. Youth Year — A131

1985, Mar. 26 Litho. *Perf. 13*
594 A131 10fr multicolored .30 .25
595 A131 30fr multicolored .65 .30
596 A131 40fr multicolored .90 .40
Nos. 594-596 (3) 1.85 .95

German Railways, 150th Anniv. — A132

Designs: 55fr, Engine No. 29, Addis Ababa-Djibouti Railways. 75fr, Adler, museum facsimile of the first German locomotive.

1985, Apr. 22 Litho. *Perf. 13*
597 A132 55fr multicolored 2.00 .65
598 A132 75fr multicolored 3.00 .90

A133

1985, May 23
599 A133 35fr Planting saplings 1.00 .45
600 A133 65fr Hygiene, family health care 1.75 .75

Scouting.

A134

80fr, Victor Hugo (1802-1885), Novelist. 100fr, Arthur Rimbaud (1854-1891), poet.

1985, June 24 Litho.
601 A134 80fr brt blue & slate 1.60 .80
602 A134 100fr multicolored 2.00 1.00

Sea Shells A135

1985, July 15 Litho. *Perf. 12½*
603 A135 10fr Cypraea nebrites .40 .25
604 A135 15fr Cypraea turdus .60 .25
605 A135 30fr Conus acuminatus 1.50 .30
606 A135 40fr Cypraea camelopardalis 1.75 .55
607 A135 55fr Conus terebra 2.75 .70
Nos. 603-607 (5) 7.00 2.05

1st World Cup Marathon '85, Hiroshima A136

1985, Sept. 2 *Perf. 12½x13*
608 A136 75fr Winners 1.25 .75
609 A136 100fr Approaching finish 2.00 1.00

Halley's Comet — A137

Designs: 85fr, Bayeux Tapestry, Comet and Halley. 90fr, Vega I, Giotto space probes, map of planets, comet trajectory.

1986, Jan. 27 Litho. *Perf. 13*
610 A137 85fr multicolored 1.50 .50
611 A137 90fr multicolored 1.75 .85

ISERST Solar Energy Installation — A138

Designs: 50fr, Runners on beach. 150fr, Windmill, headquarters, power control station.

1986, Mar. 20
612 A138 50fr multicolored .95 .40
613 A138 150fr multicolored 2.75 1.25

Ships from Columbus's Fleet, 1492 — A139

1986, Apr. 14

614	A139	60fr	Santa Maria	1.75	.55
615	A139	90fr	Nina, Pinta	3.00	.95

Fish, Red Sea — A140

1986, June 16 Litho. *Perf. 13½x13*

616	A140	20fr	Elagatis bipinnulatus	.65	.30
617	A140	25fr	Valamugil seheli	.75	.45
618	A140	55fr	Lutjanus rivulatus	2.00	.75
			Nos. 616-618 (3)	3.40	1.50

Public Buildings — A141

105fr, People's Palace. 115fr, Ministry of the Interior, Posts & Telecommunications.

1986, July 21 Litho. *Perf. 13*

619	A141	105fr	multicolored	1.75	.90
620	A141	115fr	multicolored	2.10	1.00

Sea-Me-We Building, Keyboard — A142

1986, Sept. 8 Litho. *Perf. 13*

621	A142	100fr	multicolored	2.00	.70

Souvenir Sheet

Perf. 12½

622	A142	250fr	multicolored	13.50	13.50

Southeast Asia, Middle East, Western Europe Submarine Cable System inauguration.

No. 537 Surcharged

1986, Nov. 15 *Perf. 13x12½*

623	A116	55fr	on 75fr multi	1.40	.50

Pasteur Institute, Cent. — A143

1987, Feb. 19 Litho. *Perf. 13*

624	A143	220fr	multicolored	5.00	1.60

Natl. Vaccination Campaign.

Edible Mushrooms A144

1987, Apr. 16 Litho. *Perf. 13x12½*

625	A144	35fr	Macrolepiota imbricata	1.50	.65
626	A144	50fr	Lentinus squarrosulus	2.25	.85
627	A144	95fr	Terfezia boudieri	3.00	1.50
			Nos. 625-627 (3)	6.75	3.00

Wildlife A145

1987, May 14 *Perf. 12½x13*

628	A145	5fr	Hare	.50	.25
629	A145	30fr	Dromedary	1.25	.30
630	A145	140fr	Cheetah	5.00	1.00
			Nos. 628-630 (3)	6.75	1.55

1988 Olympics, Seoul and Calgary — A146

85fr, Pierre de Coubertin (1863-1937), founder of the modern Olympics, & lighting of the flame. 135fr, Ski jumping. 140fr, Running.

1987, July 16 *Perf. 13*

631	A146	85fr	multicolored	1.50	.55
632	A146	135fr	multicolored	2.50	.95
633	A146	140fr	multicolored	2.75	1.00
			Nos. 631-633 (3)	6.75	2.50

Traditional Art — A147

1988, Jan. 20 Litho. *Perf. 13*

634	A147	30fr	Nomad's comb	.60	.30
635	A147	70fr	Wash jug	1.25	.60

UN Universal Immunization by 1990 Campaign A148

1988, Apr. 10 *Perf. 12½*

636	A148	125fr	multicolored	2.50	1.00

16th Africa Cup Soccer Championships, Morocco — A149

1988, Mar. 13 *Perf. 13*

637	A149	55fr	Athletes, view of Rabat	1.20	.50

1988 Winter Olympics, Calgary — A150

1988, May 7 Litho. *Perf. 13*

638	A150	45fr	Ski jump	1.00	.40

Campaign Against Thirst A151

1988, Sept. 10 Litho. *Perf. 12½x13*

639	A151	50fr	multicolored	1.25	.45

Intl. Fund for Agricultural Development, 10th Anniv. — A152

1988, Nov. 14 *Perf. 13*

640	A152	135fr	multicolored	2.50	1.00

Michel Lafoux Air Club, 40th Anniv. — A153

1988, Dec. 6

641	A153	145fr	1948 Tiger Moth, 1988 Tobago-10	2.75	1.00

Marine Life A154

1989, Jan. 20 Litho. *Perf. 12½*

642	A154	90fr	Lobophyllia costata	2.25	.30
643	A154	160fr	Lambis truncata	4.25	1.40

Colotis protomedia A155

1989, Feb. 15

644	A155	70fr	multicolored	5.00	2.10

Nos. 573 and 547 Surcharged

1989 *Perf. 13*

646	A126	70fr	on 2fr No. 573	2.25	.50
647	A118	70fr	on 150fr No. 547	2.25	.50

Issued: 646, 12/20; 647, 12/29.

Folk Dances — A157

1989, Mar. 20

648	A157	30fr	shown	.50	.25
649	A157	70fr	multicolored, diff.	1.40	.50

Francolin of Djibouti — A159

1989, Apr. 10 Litho. *Perf. 12½*

651	A159	35fr	multicolored	2.50	.75

Rare Flora A160

1989, June 12

652	A160	25fr	Calotropis procera	.90	.25

A161

1989, Aug. 10 Litho. *Perf. 13*
653 A161 70fr multicolored 1.60 .75

Interparliamentary Union, cent.

A162

1989, Oct. 1
654 A162 145fr multicolored 2.75 1.10

Intl. Literacy Year.

Petroglyph — A163

1989, Nov. 18 Litho. *Perf. 13*
655 A163 5fr multicolored 1.00 .40

Girl — A164

1989, Dec. 6
656 A164 55fr multicolored 1.60 .65

Nos. 574, 576-577 Surcharged

1989-1990 Litho. *Perf. 13*

657	A126	30fr on 8fr multi	.50	.30
658	A126	50fr on 40fr multi	2.00	.55
660	A126	120fr on 15fr multi	2.25	1.00
		Nos. 657-660 (3)	4.75	1.85

Issue dates: 30fr, 12/20/89; 50fr, 7/3/90; 120fr, 3/17/90.

Water Conservation — A165

1990, May 5 Litho. *Perf. 11½*
665 A165 120fr multicolored 2.25 .90

Traditional Jewelry A166

1990, Mar. 10
666 A166 70fr multicolored 1.75 .45

Commiphora — A167

1990, Feb. 20 *Perf. 12*
667 A167 30fr multicolored .60 .35

Baskets — A168

1990, July 3
668 A168 30fr multicolored .70 .40

A169

1990, June 12 *Perf. 11½*
669 A169 100fr multicolored 2.00 .80

World Cup Soccer Championships, Italy.

A170

1990, Apr. 16 *Perf. 11½*
670 A170 55fr shown 1.50 .45

20 kilometer race of Djibouti.

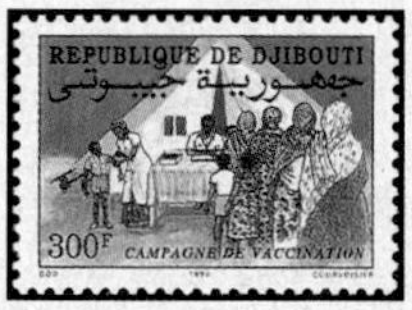
Vaccination Campaign A171

1990, Aug. 22 Litho. *Perf. 11½*
Granite Paper
671 A171 300fr multicolored 4.75 2.00

Charles de Gaulle — A172

African Tourism Year — A173

1990, Sept. 16 Granite Paper
672 A172 200fr multicolored 4.00 1.25

1991, Jan. 23 Litho. *Perf. 13*
673 A173 115fr multicolored 2.25 .80

Corals — A174

1991, Jan. 28 *Perf. 12½*

674	A174	40fr Acropora	.90	.50
675	A174	45fr Seriatopora hytrise	1.25	.50

Aquatic Birds — A175

1991, Feb. 12

676	A175	10fr Pelecanus rufescens	.60	.25
677	A175	15fr Egretta gularis	1.25	.25
678	A175	20fr Ardea goliath, horiz.	1.45	.30
679	A175	25fr Platalea leucorodia, horiz.	1.60	.35
		Nos. 676-679 (4)	4.90	1.15

UNO Development Conference A176

Fossils A177

1990, Oct. 9 Litho. *Perf. 11½x12*
Granite Paper
680 A176 45fr multicolored 1.10 .45

1990, Nov. 1 Granite Paper
681 A177 90fr pur, org & blk 5.25 1.75

Papio Hamadryas — A178

1990, Dec. 6 Granite Paper
682 A178 50fr multicolored 1.75 .55

Pandion Haliaetus A179

1991, Mar. 20 Litho. *Perf. 12x11½*
683 A179 200fr multicolored 5.00 1.60

Traditional Game A180

1991, Apr. 4
684 A180 250fr multicolored 5.25 3.25

See No. 696.

Djibouti-Ethiopia Railroad — A181

1991, May 25 Litho. *Perf. 11½*
685 A181 85fr multicolored 4.00 2.25

World Environment Day — A182

1991, June 10
686 A182 110fr multicolored 2.75 .65

Philexafrique — A183

1991, Jul. 16 Litho. *Perf. 11½*
687 A183 120fr Islands 3.25 1.75

A184

1991, Sept. 25
688 A184 175fr Handball 4.50 3.00

Pre-Olympic year.

A185

1991, Oct. 16 Litho. *Perf. 11½x12*
689 A185 105fr multicolored 2.50 1.10

World Food Day.

Underwater Cable Network — A186

1991, Nov. 28 *Perf. 12x11½*
690 A186 130fr multicolored 3.00 1.00

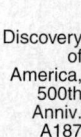

Discovery of America, 500th Anniv. A187

1991, Dec. 19 Litho. *Perf. 11½*
691 A187 145fr multicolored 3.25 1.60

Arthur Rimbaud (1854-1891) Poet and Merchant — A188

1991-92 *Perf. 11½*
692 A188 90fr Young man, ship 2.75 .90
693 A188 150fr Old man, camels 3.00 .90

Issued: 90fr, 2/5/92; 150fr, 12/23/91.

Djibouti-Ethiopia Railroad — A189

Design: 250fr, Locomotive, map.

1992 Litho. *Perf. 12x11½*
694 A189 70fr multicolored 2.75 1.10

Souvenir Sheet
Perf. 13x12½
695 A189 250fr multicolored 5.25 5.25

Issue dates: 70fr, Feb. 2; 250fr, Jan. 30.

Traditional Game Type of 1991

1992, Feb. 10 *Perf. 11½*
696 A180 100fr Boys playing Go 2.10 .85

A190

1992, June 9 Litho. *Perf. 14*
697 A190 80fr multicolored 2.10 1.25

1992 Summer Olympics, Barcelona.

A191

Traditional food preparation.

1992 Litho. *Perf. 14x13½*
698 A191 30fr Pounding grain 1.25 .50
698A A191 45fr Preparing mofo 90.00 —
699 A191 70fr Winnowing grain 1.25 .65
699A A191 75fr Cooking mofo 90.00 —

Issued: Nos. 698, 699, 4/20; No. 698A, 12/6.

Discovery of America, 500th Anniv. A192

1992, May 16 Litho. *Perf. 11½*
700 A192 125fr multicolored 3.25 .95

African Soccer Championships A193

1992, July 22 *Perf. 14*
701 A193 15fr multicolored .75 .25

Intl. Space Year — A194

Perf. 14x13½, 13½x14
1992, Sept. 28
702 A194 120fr Rocket, satellite 2.75 .85
703 A194 135fr Astronaut, satellite, horiz. 2.75 .95

Wildlife—A195

1992, Nov. 11 *Perf. 14*
704 A195 5fr Dik-dik 1.25 .25
705 A195 200fr Caretta caretta 5.00 1.60

Taeniura Lymma — A195a

Perf. 11½x11¾
1990, Mar. 24 Litho.

Panel Color
705A A195a 30fr pink — —
705B A195a 70fr yellow — —
705C A195a 100fr green — —
705D A195a 120fr lilac — —

Nomad Girls in Traditional Costumes A196

1993, Jan. 26 Litho. *Perf. 13*
706 A196 70fr Girl beside hut 1.75 .45
707 A196 120fr shown 2.75 .75

White-eyed Seagull A197

1993, Feb. 28 Litho. *Perf. 12½*
708 A197 300fr multicolored 5.25 1.75

Amin Salman Mosque — A198

1993, Feb. 17 Litho. *Perf. 13¾x14*
709 A198 500fr multicolored *52.50 5.50*

Handcrafts — A199

1993, Apr. 23 Litho. *Perf. 13¾x14*
710 A199 100fr Neck rest 100.00 15.00
711 A199 125fr Sword 100.00 15.00

Cercopithecus Aethiops — A200

1993, May 29 Litho. *Perf. 14¼x13½*
712 A200 150fr multi 80.00 5.00

Organization of African Unity, 30th Anniv. — A201

Perf. 14¼x13½
1993, June 20 Litho.
713 A201 200fr multi 100.00 2.25

Water Carriers — A202

1993, July 6 Litho. *Perf. 14x13¾*
714 A202 30fr Woman 100.00 —
715 A202 50fr Man 100.00 —

Conquest of Space — A203

1993, Sept. 30 Litho. *Perf. 14x13¾*
716 A203 90fr multicolored — —

A204

Traditional utensils.

1993, Sept. 30 Litho. *Perf. 13½*
717 A204 15fr Weyso .45 .25
718 A204 20fr Hangol .90 .25
719 A204 25fr Saqaf 1.00 .25
720 A204 30fr Subrar 1.40 .45
Nos. 717-720 (4) 3.75 1.20

A205

Traditional musical instruments.

1993, Nov. 10 Litho. *Perf. 14*
721 A205 5fr Flute 1.00 1.00
722 A205 10fr Drum 1.00 1.00

Souvenir Sheet

Wedding of Japan's Crown Prince Naruhito and Masako Owada — A206

1994, Jan. 10 Litho. *Perf. 13x12½*
Self-Adhesive
723 A206 500fr multicolored 22.50 22.50

No. 723 printed on wood.

20 Kilometer Race of Djibouti A207

Promotion of Breastfeeding A208

1994 Litho. *Perf. 11½*
724 A207 50fr multicolored 2.50 1.00

1994
725 A208 40fr shown 1.90 .40
726 A208 45fr Mother, infant 2.10 .40

Hassan Gouled Aptidon Stadium A209

1994
727 A209 70fr multicolored 2.50 1.10

Stenella Longirostris A210

1994, May 1 Litho. *Perf. 11¾x11½*
728 A210 120fr multicolored — —

World Housing Day — A211

1994, May 9 Litho. *Perf. 11½x11¾*
729 A211 30fr multi *100.00* —

Eupodotis Senegalensis — A212

Perf. 11¾x11½
1994, June 16 Litho.
730 A212 10fr multicolored 180.00 —

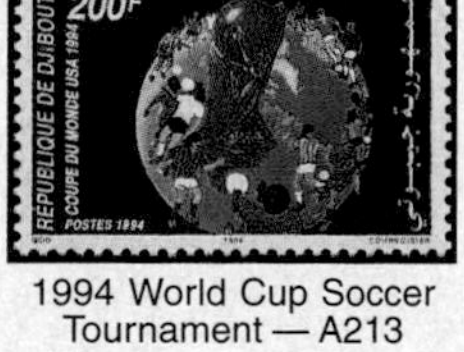

1994 World Cup Soccer Tournament — A213

1994, Sept. 7
731 A213 200fr multicolored *150.00* —

Dress of a Village Leader — A214

Design: 100fr, Traditional nomad costume.

Perf. 11½x11¾
1994, Sept. 18 Litho.
732 A214 100fr multicolored *100.00* —
Perf. 11¾
733 A214 150fr multicolored *10.00* —

Canis Aureus A215

Perf. 11¾x11½
1994, Sept. 28 Litho.
734 A215 400fr multi *135.00* —

World Walking Day A216

1994, Oct. 19 Litho. *Perf. 11¾x11½*
735 A216 75fr multicolored *150.00* —

A217

1994, Nov. 26 Litho. *Perf. 11¾*
736 A217 55fr Book stand 150.00 —

A218

1994, Dec. 6 Litho. *Perf. 11½x11¾*
737 A218 35fr Traditional dance 60.00 12.00

Souvenir Sheet

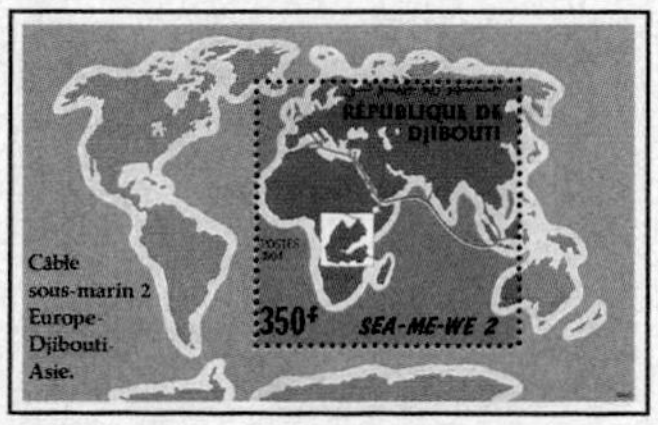

Sea-Me-We 2 Submarine Cable — A218a

1994 *Perf. 12½*
737A A218a 350fr multi *175.00* —

A219

A220

1995, Feb. 25 Litho. *Perf. 11¾*
738 A219 70fr multicolored — —

Volleyball, cent.

1995, Feb. 25
739 A220 120fr multicolored — —

United Nations, 50th anniv.

Fight Against Thirst A221

Perf. 11¾x11½
1995, Mar. 29 Litho.
740 A221 100fr multicolored — —

Threskiornis Aethiopica — A222

1995, Apr. 5 Litho. *Perf. 11¾*
742 A222 50fr multicolored — —

A number has been reserved for a 30fr stamp in this set. The editors would like to examine it.

World Telecommunications Day — A223

Perf. 11¾x11½
1995, June 10 Litho.
743 A223 125fr multicolored *70.00* 1.25

Crocuta Crocuta A224

1995, June 12 Litho. *Perf. 11¾*
744 A224 200fr multi *105.00* —

People Meeting Under Tree A225

1995, July 3 Litho. *Perf. 11¾x11½*
745 A225 150fr multi *65.00* —

A226

A227

1995, Aug. 9 ***Perf. 11¾***
746 A226 45fr Nomads around fire *60.00* 12.00

1995, Sept. 27 ***Perf. 11½x11¾***
747 A227 250fr multi *70.00* 12.00

FAO, 50th anniv.

Traditional Costume — A228

1995, Dec. 6 ***Perf. 11¾***
748 A228 90fr multicolored — 12.00

African Development Bank, 30th Anniv. — A229

1995. Dec. 18 ***Perf. 11¾x11½***
749 A229 300fr multi *60.00* 12.00

African Soccer Cup — A230

1996, Feb. 28
750 A230 70fr multicolored *180.00* —

Ostrich — A231

1996, Apr. 23
751 A231 120fr multi *100.00* —

Leopard A232

1996, May 6
752 A232 70fr multi 105.00 —

Amber Necklace — A233

1996, June 13 **Litho.**
753 A233 30fr multi 100.00 —

1996 Summer Olympic Games, Atlanta — A234

Perf. 11½x11¾
1996, Sept. 21 **Litho.**
754 A234 105fr multicolored *125.00* 12.00

Commicarpus Grandiflorus A236

1996, Oct. 6 **Litho.** ***Perf. 11½x11¾***
756 A236 350fr multi *60.00* 12.00

Djibouti Folklore — A237

1996, Nov. 28 **Litho.** ***Perf. 11¾***
757 A237 95fr multi *60.00* —

Legend of the Lion and Three Bulls A238

1996, Nov. 28 **Litho.** ***Perf. 11¾***
758 A238 95fr multi *70.00* 12.00

Children's Day A239

1996, Dec. 17 ***Perf. 11¾x11½***
759 A239 130fr multi *60.00* 12.00

A240

A241

Legend of the Tortoise and the Fox: No. 760, Tortoise and fox at starting line. No. 761, Fox leaves tortoise behind. No. 762, Tortoise passes sleeping fox.

1997, Jan. 17 ***Perf. 11¾***
760 A240 60fr multi — —
761 A240 60fr multi — —
762 A240 60fr multi — —
a. Horiz. strip, #760-762 *135.00*

1997, Feb. 9 **Litho.** ***Perf. 11¾***
763 A241 80fr Mother, child *50.00* 10.00
764 A241 90fr Hands around globe *100.00* 12.00

UNICEF, 50th anniv.

Dancers — A242

1997, May 14 **Litho.** ***Perf. 11¾***
765 A242 70fr multi *70.00* 12.00

Fortune Teller A243

Designs: 200fr, Fortune teller and woman. 300fr, Fortune teller, camel.

1997, May 29 **Litho.** ***Perf. 11¾***
766 A243 200fr multi 70.00 12.00
767 A243 300fr multi 70.00 12.00

Woman's Day — A244

1997, May 30 **Litho.** ***Perf. 11¾***
768 A244 250fr multi *175.00 12.00*

Traditional Objects A245

Design: 30fr, Writing board, horiz. 400fr, Bowl and spoon.

1997, June 5 **Litho.** ***Perf. 11¾***
769 A245 30fr multi 57.50 10.00
770 A245 400fr multi 57.50 10.00

Telecommunications A246

Designs: 30fr, Arta post office. 100fr, Map, building with antenna and satellite dishes. 120fr, Ships, map showing submarine cable route, horiz.

1997, June 27 **Litho.** ***Perf. 11¾***
771 A246 30fr multi — 12.00
772 A246 100fr multi — 12.00
773 A246 120fr multi — 12.00

Goats in Tree A247

1997, July 26 **Litho.** ***Perf. 11¾***
774 A247 120fr multi 50.00 15.00

A248

Portrait of Diana: a, 125fr. b, 130fr. c, 150fr.

1998, Mar. 25 **Litho.** ***Perf. 13½***
775 A248 Strip of 3, #a.-c. 7.00 7.00

Diana, Princess of Wales (1961-97).
No. 775 was isssued in sheets of 6 stamps.

A249

1998 **Litho.** ***Perf. 13½***
776 A249 130fr multicolored 2.75 1.40

Mother Teresa (1910-97). No. 776 was issued in sheets of 4.

Intl. Year of the Ocean A250

a, Tangara chilensis. b, Agalychnis callidryas. c, Delphinus delphis, megaptera novaeangliae. d, Cercopithecus aethiops (h). e, Laticaudia colubrina (i), sphyrna mokarran. f, Lactoria cornuta, delphinus delphis (g). g, Delphinus delphis (k). h, Aspidontus taeniatus, lo vulpinus. i, Sepioteuthis lessoniana. j, Prionace glauca (i), chaetodon ornatissimus. k, Eupagurus bernherdus. l, Octopus vulgaris (k).

1998, Apr. 20 **Litho.** ***Perf. 13½***
777 A250 75fr Sheet of 12, #a.-l. 16.00 16.00

Mahatma Gandhi (1869-1948) A251

1998, Apr. 20 Litho. *Perf. 11¾*
778 A251 250fr multi *80.00* *12.00*

Traditional Art — A252

1998, Apr. 25 Litho. *Perf. 11½x11¾*
779 A252 30fr multicolored *120.00* 12.00

Women's Rights and International Peace — A253

1998, May 3 *Perf. 11¾x11½*
780 A253 70fr multicolored *60.00* 12.00

World Water Day A254

1998, May 10 Litho. *Perf. 11¾*
781 A254 45fr multi *60.00* 12.00

1998 World Cup Soccer Championships, France — A255

1998, June 10 Litho. *Perf. 11¾*
782 A255 200fr multi 160.00 —

Marine Life — A256

Cats and Bush — A257

Perf. 11½x11¾, 11¾x11½
1998, July 2 Litho.
783 A256 20fr Octopus *135.00* —
784 A256 25fr Shark, horiz. *135.00* —

1998, Aug. 30 *Perf. 11½x11¾*
785 A257 120fr multi *135.00* —

World Telecommunications Day — A258

1996, Sept. 27 Litho. *Perf. 11¾*
786 A258 150fr multi 100.00 —

National Bank — A259

1998, Sept. 30 Litho. *Perf. 11¾*
787 A259 100fr multi 135.00 12.00

Flags and IGAD Emblem — A260

Perf. 11½x11¾
1998, Sept. 30 Litho.
788 A260 85fr multi *60.00* —

Traditional Game Goos A261

1998, Oct. 1 *Perf. 11¾x11½*
789 A261 110fr multi *60.00* —

Fishing Port A262

1998
790 A262 100fr multi *115.00* —

Maskali Island A263

1998
791 A263 500fr multi *140.00* —

Fish A264

1999 Litho. *Perf. 13¼x13½*
792 A264 70fr multi *115.00* —

Antelope — A264a

Perf. 13¼x13½
1999, Mar. 16 Litho.
792A A264a 120fr multi 105.00 —

Djibouti Franc, 50th Anniv. A265

1999
793 A265 100fr multi *60.00* —

World Telecommunications Day — A266

1999
794 A266 125fr multi *55.00* —

Worldwide Fund for Nature (WWF) — A267

Phacochoerus africanus aeliani: a, Adult and young. b, Adult standing. c, Head. d, Adult walking.

2000, Apr. 13 Litho. *Perf. 14*
795 A267 100fr Block of 4, #a-d 9.00 9.00

Wild Animals — A268

No. 796: a, Flamingo. b, Ostrich. c, Sifaka. d, Yellow-billed stork. e, Scarlet macaw. f, Dwarf puff adder. g, Toucan. h, Whooping crane.

2000, Apr. 13
796 A268 100fr Sheet of 8, #a-h 20.00 20.00

Butterflies — A269

No. 797: a, Doxocopa cherubina. b, Heliconius charitonius. c, Cantonephele numili. d, Danaus gilippus. e, Morpho peleides. f, Heliconius doris.

No. 798, 250fr, Agraulis vanillae. No. 799, 250fr, Strymon melinus.

2000, Apr. 13
797 A269 100fr Sheet of 6, #a-f 12.00 12.00

Souvenir Sheets

798-799 A269 Set of 2 11.00 11.00

No. 797 contains six 28x42mm stamps.

Water Resources — A270

2000, Apr. 13
800 A270 500fr multi 8.00 8.00

Trains and Landmarks — A271

No. 801: a, 5fr, Class OJ 2-10-2, China. b, 25fr, Eurostar, France-England. c, 15fr, Glacier Express, Switzerland. d, 40fr, Unidentified train. e, 35fr, Class WP 4-6-2, India.

No. 802, 110fr: a, Nord Chapelon Pacific, France. b, Class 23 2-6-2, Germany. c, Class GS-4 4-8-4, US. d, Class A4 4-6-2, Great Britain. e, Pacific 4-6-2, South Africa. f, Class HP, India.

No. 803, 120fr: a, VT601, Germany. b, ICIII Bo-Bo EMU, Netherlands. c, TGV, France. d, ETR 450, Italy. e, AVE, Spain. f, Bullet Train, Japan.

No. 804, 250fr, GM War Bonnet, US. No. 805, 250fr, Class 8 Pacific, Great Britain.

2000, Apr. 28
801 A271 Horiz. strip of 5, #a-e 2.40 2.40

Sheets of 6, #a-f

802-803 A271 Set of 2 20.00 20.00

Souvenir Sheets

804-805 A271 Set of 2 9.50 9.50

Dancers
A272

2000, Apr. 28

806 A272 75fr multi *5.50 1.50*

Blacksmith — A273

2000, May 14

807 A273 100fr multi 6.00 2.50

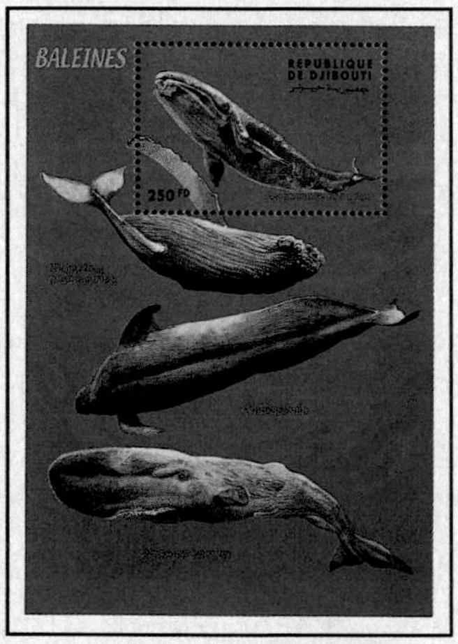

Marine Life — A274

No. 808, vert.: a, Dendrochirus biocellatus. b, Hippocampus. c, Amphiprion ocellaris, Amphiprion percula. d, Periclimenes imperator. e, Pomacnetridae. f, Octopus vulgaris.

No. 809, 50fr: a, Cephalopholis miniata. b, Ptereleotris hanae. c, Sphyraena genie. d, Tripterygion segmentatum. e, Odontaspididae. f, Cirrhitidae. g, Amphiprion. h, Capros aper. i, Balistidae. j, Trygonorhina fasciata. k, Cephalopholis. l, Corythoichthys ocellatus.

No. 810, 60fr: a, Lutjanus kasmira. b, Chaetodon fasciatus. c, Epinephelinae. d, Hypoplectrus gutavarius. e, Loligo opalescens. f, Diodontinae. g, Coelenterata. h, Sargocentron xantherythrum. i, Thalassoma lunare. j, Hemichromis bimaculatus. k, Dasyatis. l, Fromia monilis.

No. 811, 250fr, Eschrichtis robustus. No. 812, 250fr, Cheloniidae.

2000, May 14

808 A274 55fr Sheet of 6, #a-f 10.00 10.00

Sheets of 12, #a-l

809-810 A274 Set of 2 24.00 24.00

Souvenir Sheets

811-812 A274 Set of 2 8.00 8.00

Camels
and
Tender
A275

2000, June 26

813 A275 35fr multi *5.25 .90*

Ships
A276

Designs: 10fr, Thomas W. Lawson, 1902. 15fr, BT Global Challenge, 2000. 20fr, Reliance and Shamrock III, 1903. 25fr, Archibald Russell, 1905. 50fr, Greek merchantman, 8th cent. B.C.

No. 819, 130fr: a, Norman warship, 1066. b, Hanseatic cog, c. 1300. c, Santa Maria, 1492. d, Mary Rose, 1510. e, Golden Hind, 1577. f, Sovereign of the Seas, 1637.

No. 820:, 135fr: a, HMS Endeavour, 1768. b, USS Constitution, 1797. c, Chasse-Maree, 1800. d, Baltimore clipper, 1812. e, Lightning, 1853. f, Bluenose, 1921.

No. 821, 250fr, HM Yacht Britannia, 1893. No. 822, 250fr, Herzogin Cecilie, 1902.

2000, June 26

814-818 A276 Set of 5 2.00 2.00

Sheets of 6, #a-f

819-820 A276 Set of 2 25.00 25.00

Souvenir Sheets

821-822 A276 Set of 2 8.00 8.00

Millennium
A277

2000, July 18

823 A277 125fr multi 2.75 2.75

Birds
A278

2000, Aug. 23

824 Horiz. strip of 5 2.75 2.75
- *a.* A278 5fr Lanius excubitor .35 .35
- *b.* A278 10fr Phoenicopterus minor .35 .35
- *c.* A278 15fr Eupodatis senegalensis .35 .35
- *d.* A278 40fr Noephron perchopterus .60 .60
- *e.* A278 50fr Pterocles lichtensteinii .75 .75

Space Exploration — A279

No. 825, 100fr, vert.: a, John Glenn and Mercury capsule, 1962. b, Soyuz capsule, Apollo-Soyuz mission, 1975. c, Hubble Telescope, 1990. d, Apollo capsule, Apollo-Soyuz mission. e, Glenn at speaker's stand, 1974. f, Space Shuttle Columbia, 1981.

No. 826, 100fr, vert.: a, Apollo 11 service module, 1969. b, Telstar, 1962. c, Ariane 4, 1988. d, Apollo 11 lunar module. e, Neil Armstrong, 1969. f, Splashdown of Apollo 11, 1969.

No. 827, 200fr, Astronaut on moon saluting. No. 828, 250fr, Astronauts conducting experiments on moon. No. 829, 250fr, Space Shuttle Challenger.

2000, Aug. 23 **Sheets of 6, #a-f**

825-826 A279 Set of 2 20.00 20.00

Souvenir Sheets

827-829 A279 Set of 3 12.00 12.00

2000
Summer
Olympics,
Sydney
A280

Olympic flame, flag and: 80fr, Runner. 90fr, Tennis player.

2000 ***Perf. 14***

830-831 A280 Set of 2 4.00 4.00

Unknown Soldier
Monument

2004, Apr. 18 **Litho.** ***Perf. 13x12¾***

832 A280a 175fr multi 40.00 20.00

Independence, 27th Anniv. — A281

2004, June 27 **Litho.** ***Perf. 13***

833 A281 45fr multi — —

Dragon
Tree
A282

Pregnant Woman
at
Hospital — A283

Camel
Caravan
A284

Natl. Union of
Djibouti
Women — A285

National
Arms
A286

Perf. 12¾x13, 13x12¾

2004, Dec. 18 **Litho.**

834 A282 15fr multi 30.00 20.00
835 A283 25fr multi 30.00 20.00
836 A284 45fr multi 30.00 20.00
837 A285 70fr multi 30.00 20.00
838 A286 100fr multi 20.00 20.00
Nos. 834-838 (5) 140.00 100.00

Friendship
Between
Djibouti
and
People's
Republic of
China,
25th Anniv.

Designs: 5fr, Djibouti Electricity Building. 10fr, Hassan Gouled Stadium. 15fr, Djibouti Central Bank. 30fr, People's Palace. 45fr, Ministry of Foreign Affairs Building.

2004, Dec. 27 ***Perf. 12***

839-843 A286a Set of 5 100.00 100.00

Items commemorating the death of Pope John Paul II were declared as "fraudulent" by Djibouti Post.

2006 World Cup Soccer
Championships, Germany — A287

2005, June 8 **Litho.** ***Perf. 13***

844 A287 100fr multi *80.00* —

Tanker in Port of Doraleh — A288

2006, Nov. 6 **Litho.** ***Perf. 13***

845 A288 120fr multi *25.00* —

Printed in sheets of 4.

Common Market for Eastern and
Southern Africa Summit,
Djibouti — A289

2006, Nov. 6 **Litho.** ***Perf. 13¼x13***

846 A289 150fr multi 25.00 —

Djibouti Chamber
of Commerce,
Cent. — A290

2007 **Litho.** ***Perf. 12¾***

847 A290 50fr multi — —
- *a.* Souvenir sheet of 2 — —

Independence, 30th Anniv. — A291

2007, June 27 Litho. *Perf. 13*
848 A291 75fr multi 25.00 —
a. Souvenir sheet of 2 50.00 —

Mahamoud Harbi (1921-60), Politician — A292

2007, Aug. 17 Litho. *Perf. 13x12¾*
849 A292 165fr multi 30.00 5.00

Indo-Suez Red Sea Bank — A293

2008, Oct. 19 Litho. *Perf. 13x13½*
850 A293 220fr multi —

2010 World Cup Soccer Championships, South Africa — A295

2010, May Litho. *Perf. 13*
852 A295 105fr multi 25.00 —

Djibouti postal authorities have declared "illegal" the following items:
Sheets of 8 stamps of various values: Mushrooms
Sheets of 6 stamps of various values: Fire trucks and Scouts (3 different)
Sheets of 6 700f stamps: Butterflies and Orchids, Butterflies and Scouts, Trains
Sheets of 6 300f stamps: Birds
Sheets of 4 800f stamps: Bonsai
Sheets of 4 700f stamps: Dogs (4 different), Cats (4 different), Babe Ruth and Tiger Woods, Dinosaurs
Sheets of 2 stamps of various values: Fire trucks (2 different).

2014 Africa Internet Summit, Djibouti — A296

2014 Litho. *Perf. 13*
853 A296 170fr multi — —

AIR POST STAMPS

Afars and Issas Nos. C104-C105, C103 Overprinted in Brown or Black

1977 Engr. *Perf. 13*
C106 AP37 55fr multi (Br) 2.75 1.75
C107 AP37 75fr multi 11.00 4.00

Litho. *Perf. 12*
C108 AP36 500fr multi 15.00 13.50
Nos. C106-C108 (3) 22.25 18.25

Map of Djibouti, Dove, UN Emblem — AP38

1977, Oct. 19 Photo. *Perf. 13*
C109 AP38 300fr multi 6.50 4.25

Djibouti's admission to the United Nations.

Marcel Brochet MB 101, 1955 — AP39

Djibouti Aero Club: 85fr, Tiger Moth, 1960. 200fr, Rallye-Commodore, 1973.

1978, Feb. 27 Litho. *Perf. 13*
C110 AP39 60fr multi 1.25 .40
C111 AP39 85fr multi 1.75 .65
C112 AP39 200fr multi 4.00 1.10
Nos. C110-C112 (3) 7.00 2.15

Old Man, by Rubens AP40

500fr, Hippopotamus Hunt, by Rubens.

1978, Apr. 24 Photo. *Perf. 13*
C113 AP40 50fr multi 1.50 .35
C114 AP40 500fr multi, horiz. 11.00 3.25

Peter Paul Rubens (1577-1640).

Player Holding Soccer Cup — AP41

Design: 300fr, Soccer player, map of South America with Argentina, Cup and emblem.

1978, June 20 Litho. *Perf. 13*
C115 AP41 100fr multi 2.00 .50
C116 AP41 300fr multi 6.00 1.75

11th World Cup Soccer Championship, Argentina, June 1-25.
For overprints see Nos. C117-C118.

Nos. C115-C116 Overprinted

a

b

1978, Aug. 20 Litho. *Perf. 13*
C117 AP41 (a) 100fr multi 3.00 .40
C118 AP41 (b) 300fr multi 7.25 1.25

Argentina's victory in 1978 Soccer Championship.

Tahitian Women, by Gauguin — AP42

Young Hare, by Dürer AP43

Perf. 13x12½, 12½x13
1978, Sept. 25 Litho.
C119 AP42 100fr multi 3.00 .40
C120 AP43 250fr multi 6.50 1.50

Paul Gauguin (1848-1903) and Albrecht Dürer (1471-1528), painters.

Common Design Types pictured following the introduction.

Philexafrique II-Essen Issue
Common Design Types

Designs: No. C121, Lynx and Djibouti No. 456. No. C122, Jay and Brunswick No. 3.

1978, Dec. 13 Litho. *Perf. 13x12½*
C121 CD138 90fr multi 4.00 1.75
C122 CD139 90fr multi 4.00 1.75
a. Pair, Nos. C121-C122 + label 8.50 8.50

UPU Emblem, Map of Djibouti, Dove — AP44

1978, Dec. 18 Engr. *Perf. 13*
C123 AP44 200fr multi 3.75 1.10

Centenary of Congress of Paris.

Junkers JU-52 and Dewoitine D-338 — AP45

Powered Flight, 75th Anniversary: 250fr, Potez P63-11, 1941 and Supermarine Spitfire HF-VII, 1942. 500fr, Conoorde, 1969 and Sikorsky S-40 "American Clipper," 1931.

1979, May 21 Litho. *Perf. 13x12½*
C124 AP45 140fr multi 3.00 .60
C125 AP45 250fr multi 4.50 1.00
C126 AP45 500fr multi 9.00 1.75
Nos. C124-C126 (3) 16.50 3.35

The Laundress, by Honore Daumier AP46

1979, July 10 Litho. *Perf. 12½x13*
C127 AP46 500fr multi 12.00 3.00

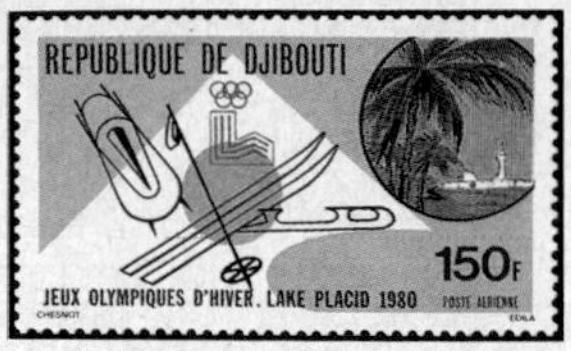

Olympic Emblem, Skis, Sleds — AP47

1980, Jan. 21 **Litho.** ***Perf. 13***

C128 AP47 150fr multi 3.00 .60

13th Winter Olympic Games, Lake Placid, N.Y., Feb. 12-24.

For surcharges see Nos. C133-C134.

Cathedral of the Archangel, Basketball, Moscow '80 Emblem — AP48

120fr, Lomonossov Univ., Moscow, soccer. 250fr, Cathedral of the Annunciation, running.

1980, Apr. 10 **Litho.** ***Perf. 13***

C129 AP48 60fr multi 1.05 .25
C130 AP48 120fr multi 2.10 .40
C131 AP48 250fr multi 4.25 1.00
Nos. C129-C131 (3) 7.40 1.65

22nd Summer Olympic Games, Moscow, July 18-Aug. 3.

Air Djibouti, 1st Anniversary — AP49

1980, Mar. 29 **Litho.** ***Perf. 13x12½***

C132 AP49 400fr multi 9.00 2.50

No. C128 Surcharged in Black and Blue or Purple

1980, Apr. 5 **Litho.** ***Perf. 13***

C133 AP47 80fr on 150fr 1.75 .50
C134 AP47 200fr on 150fr (P) 4.00 1.50

Apollo 11 Moon Landing, 10th Anniversary — AP50

Space Conquests: 300fr, Apollo-Soyuz space project, 5th anniversary.

1980, May 8

C135 AP50 200fr multi 4.00 .75
C136 AP50 300fr multi 6.50 1.25

Satellite Earth Station Inauguration — AP51

1980, July 3 **Litho.** ***Perf. 13***

C137 AP51 500fr multi 9.50 1.75

Graf Zeppelin — AP52

1980, Oct. 2 **Litho.** ***Perf. 13***

C138 AP52 100fr shown 2.25 .40
C139 AP52 150fr Ferdinand von Zeppelin, blimp 3.25 .60

Zeppelin flight, 80th anniversary.

Voyager Passing Saturn — AP53

1980, Dec. 21 **Litho.** ***Perf. 13***

C140 AP53 250fr multi 5.50 1.00

AP54

World Cup Soccer Preliminary Games: 200fr, Players, diff.

1981, Jan. 14

C141 AP54 80fr multi 1.75 .30
C142 AP54 200fr multi 4.25 .65

AP55

1981, Feb. 10 **Litho.** ***Perf. 13***

C143 AP55 100fr multi 3.00 .50

European-African Economic Convention.

5th Anniversary of Viking I Take-off to Mars — AP56

20th Anniversary of Various Space Flights: 75fr, Vostok I, Yuri Gagarin, vert. 150fr, Freedom 7, Alan B. Shepard, vert.

1981, Mar. 9 **Litho.** ***Perf. 13***

C144 AP56 75fr multi 1.75 .35
C145 AP56 120fr multi 2.25 .45
C146 AP56 150fr multi 3.00 .65
Nos. C144-C146 (3) 7.00 1.45

Football Players, by Picasso (1881-1973) — AP57

Design: 400fr Man Wearing a Turban, by Rembrandt (1606-1669), vert.

Perf. 13x12½, 12½x13

1981, Aug. 3 **Litho.**

C147 AP57 300fr multi 7.00 1.40
C148 AP57 400fr multi 7.50 1.75

Columbia Space Shuttle — AP58

1981, Sept. 24 **Litho.** ***Perf. 13***

C149 AP58 90fr Shuttle, diff., vert. 1.75 .40
C150 AP58 120fr shown 2.50 .60

Nos. C149-C150 Overprinted in Brown

1981, Nov. 12 **Litho.** ***Perf. 13***

C151 AP58 90fr multi 1.75 .50
C152 AP58 120fr multi 2.50 .75

1982 World Cup Soccer — AP59

Designs: Various soccer players.

1982, Jan. 20

C153 AP59 110fr multi 2.10 .60
C154 AP59 220fr multi 4.75 1.25

For overprints see Nos. C166-C167.

Space Anniversaries — AP60

Designs: 40fr, Luna 9 moon landing, 15th, vert. 60fr, John Glenn's flight, 20th, vert. 180fr, Viking I Mars landing, 5th.

1982, Feb. 15

C155 AP60 40fr multi .70 .25
C156 AP60 60fr multi 1.10 .30
C157 AP60 180fr multi 3.00 1.00
Nos. C155-C157 (3) 4.80 1.55

21st Birthday of Princess Diana of Wales AP61

1982, Apr. 29 **Litho.** ***Perf. 12½x13***

C158 AP61 120fr Portrait 2.25 .75
C159 AP61 180fr Portrait, diff. 3.50 1.00

For overprints see Nos. C168-C169.

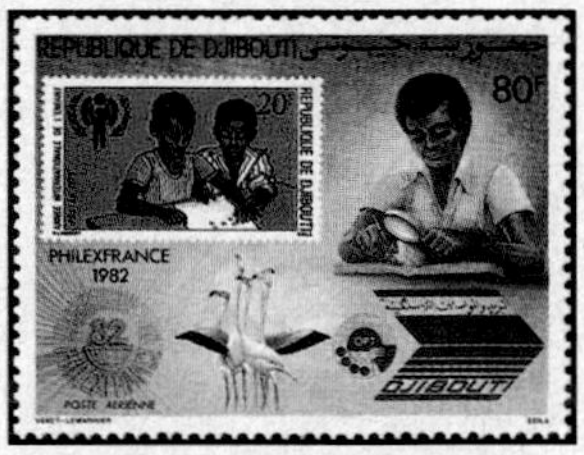

No. 489, Boy Examining Collection — AP62

1982, May 10 ***Perf. 13x12½***

C160 AP62 80fr shown 2.50 .75
C161 AP62 140fr No. 495 3.75 1.00
a. Pair, Nos. C160-C161 + label 6.50 6.50

PHILEXFRANCE '82 Stamp Exhibition, Paris, June 11-21.

1350th Anniv. of Mohammed's Death at Medina — AP63

1982, June 8 **Litho.** ***Perf. 13***

C162 AP63 500fr Medina Mosque 9.00 2.00

Scouting Year — AP64

1982, June 28

C163 AP64 95fr Baden-Powell 1.75 .50
C164 AP64 200fr Camp, scouts 4.00 1.25

2nd UN Conference on Peaceful Uses of Outer Space, Vienna, Aug. 9-21 — AP65

1982, Aug. 19
C165 AP65 350fr multi 6.75 3.00

Nos. C153-C154 Overprinted

1982, July 21 Litho. *Perf. 13*
C166 AP59 110fr multi 2.00 .60
C167 AP59 220fr multi 4.00 1.10

Italy's victory in 1982 World Cup.

Nos. C158-C159 Overprinted in Blue or Red

No. C168

No. C169

1982, Aug. 9 *Perf. 12½x13*
C168 AP61 120fr multi 2.50 .75
C169 AP61 180fr multi (R) 3.50 1.00

Birth of Prince William of Wales, June 21.

Franklin D. Roosevelt (1882-1945) AP66

1982, Oct. 7 Litho. *Perf. 13*
C170 AP66 115fr shown 2.00 .50
C171 AP66 250fr George Washington 5.25 1.00

Manned Flight Bicentenary AP67

1983, Jan. 20 Litho.
C172 AP67 35fr Montgolfiere, 1783 .80 .25
C173 AP67 45fr Giffard, Paris Exposition, 1878 1.35 .30
C174 AP67 120fr Double Eagle II, 1978 3.50 .80
Nos. C172-C174 (3) 5.65 1.35

Pre-olympic Year — AP68

1983, Feb. 15
C175 AP68 75fr Volleyball 1.50 .55
C176 AP68 125fr Wind surfing 2.75 .85

50th Anniv. of Air France — AP69

1983, Mar. 20 Litho. *Perf. 13*
C177 AP69 25fr Bloch 220 .50 .25
C178 AP69 100fr DC-4 1.75 .70
C179 AP69 175fr Boeing 747 3.50 1.10
Nos. C177-C179 (3) 5.75 2.05

AP70

180fr, Martin Luther King, Jr. (1929-68), civil rights leader. 250fr, Alfred Nobel (1833-96)

1983, May 18 Litho. *Perf. 13*
C180 AP70 180fr multi 3.50 1.25
C181 AP70 250fr multi 4.50 2.00

AP71

Service Clubs: 90fr, Rotary Club Intl., Sailing Show, Toronto, June 5-9. 150fr, Lions Club Intl., Honolulu Meeting, June 22-24, Djibouti lighthouse.

1983, July 18 Litho. *Perf. 13*
C182 AP71 90fr multi 3.00 1.50
C183 AP71 150fr multi 3.00 1.00
a. Pair, Nos. C182-C183 + label 5.50 5.50

Vintage Motor Cars — AP72

1983, Sep. 20 Litho. *Perf. 13x12½*
C184 AP72 60fr Renault, 1904 1.90 .50
C185 AP72 80fr Mercedes, 1910, vert. 2.50 .65
C186 AP72 110fr Lorraine-Dietrich, 1912 3.00 .85
Nos. C184-C186 (3) 7.40 2.00

Souvenir Sheet

Air France, 50th Anniv. — AP73

1983, Oct. 7 Litho. *Perf. 12½*
Self-Adhesive
C187 AP73 250fr multicolored 25.00 25.00

Printed on wood.

Vostok VI AP74

1983, Oct. 20 Litho. *Perf. 12*
C188 AP74 120fr shown 2.25 .80
C189 AP74 200fr Explorer I 3.75 1.10

1984 Winter Olympics — AP75

1984, Feb. 14 Litho. *Perf. 13*
C190 AP75 70fr Speed skating 1.50 .55
C191 AP75 130fr Figure skating 2.50 1.10

For overprints see Nos. C196-C197.

Souvenir Sheet

Ship — AP76

1984, Feb. 14 Litho. *Perf. 12½*
C192 AP76 250fr multi 11.00 11.00

Sea-Me-We (South-east Asia-Middle East-Western Europe) submarine cable construction agreement.

Motorized Hang Gliders — AP77

Various hang gliders.

1984, Mar. 12 *Perf. 13x12½*
C193 AP77 65fr multi 1.25 .50
C194 AP77 85fr multi 1.60 .60
C195 AP77 100fr multi 2.10 .75
Nos. C193-C195 (3) 4.95 1.85

Nos. C190-C191 Overprinted with Winners' Names and Country

1984, Mar. 28 *Perf. 13*
C196 AP75 70fr multi 1.50 .50
C197 AP75 130fr multi 2.75 1.00

Portrait of Marguerite Matisse, 1910, by Henri Matisse AP78

Design: 200fr, Portrait of Mario Varvogli, by Amedeo Modigliani.

1984, Apr. 15 Litho. *Perf. 12½x13*
C198 AP78 150fr multi 3.75 1.00
C199 AP78 200fr multi 4.75 1.40

1984 Summer Olympics — AP79

1984, May 24 *Perf. 13*
C200 AP79 50fr Running 1.00 .40
C201 AP79 60fr High jump 1.25 .40
C202 AP79 80fr Swimming 1.50 .60
Nos. C200-C202 (3) 3.75 1.40

Battle Scene — AP80

1984, June 16 Litho. ***Perf. 13x12½***

C203 AP80 300fr multi 6.00 2.75

125th anniv. of Battle of Solferino and 120th anniv. of Red Cross.

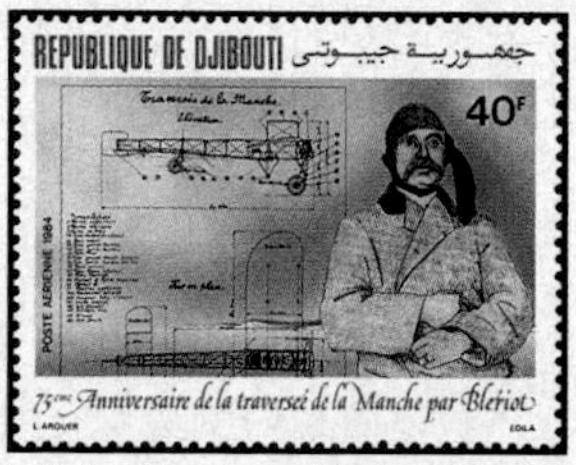

Bleriot's Flight over English Channel, 75th Anniv. — AP81

1984, July 8

C204 AP81 40fr 14-Bis plans .90 .40
C205 AP81 75fr Britten-Norman Islander 1.40 .75
C206 AP81 90fr Air Djibouti jet 1.50 1.00
Nos. C204-C206 (3) 3.80 2.15

375th Anniv., Galileo's Telescope AP82

1984, Oct. 7 Litho. ***Perf. 13***

C207 AP82 120fr Telescopes, spacecraft 2.50 .80
C208 AP82 180fr Galileo, telescopes 3.50 1.10

1984 Soccer Events — AP83

1984, Oct. 20 Litho. ***Perf. 13***

C209 AP83 80fr Euro Cup 2.50 .60
C210 AP83 80fr Los Angeles Olympics 2.50 .60
a. Pair, Nos. C209-C210 + label 4.50 4.00

Service Clubs — AP84

1985, Feb. 23 Litho. ***Perf. 13***

C211 AP84 50fr Lions, World Leprosy Day 1.40 .50
C212 AP84 60fr Rotary, chess board, pieces 1.60 .55

#C211-C212 exist in souvenir sheets of 1.

Telecommunications Technology — AP85

No. C213, Technician, researchist, operator. No. C214, Offshore oil rig, transmission tower, government building.

1985, July 2 ***Perf. 13x12½***

C213 AP85 80fr multi 2.50 .55
C214 AP85 80fr multi 2.50 .55
a. Pair, Nos. C213-C214 + label 6.25 1.25

PHILEXAFRICA '85, Lome.

Telecommunications Development — AP86

1985, Oct. 2 ***Perf. 13***

C215 AP86 50fr Intl. transmission center .90 .35
C216 AP86 90fr Ariane rocket, vert. 1.60 .65
C217 AP86 120fr ARABSAT satellite 2.00 .90
Nos. C215-C217 (3) 4.50 1.90

Youths Windsurfing, Playing Tennis — AP87

No. C219, Tadjoura Highway construction.

1985, Nov. 13 ***Perf. 13x12½***

C218 AP87 100fr multi 2.50 1.00
C219 AP87 100fr multi 2.50 1.00
a. Pair, Nos. C218-C219 + label 6.00 5.00

PHILEXAFRICA '85, Lome, Togo, 11/16-24.

1986 World Cup Soccer Championships, Mexico — AP88

1986, Feb. 24 Litho. ***Perf. 13***

C220 AP88 75fr shown 1.50 .50
C221 AP88 100fr Players, stadium 2.00 .70

For overprints see Nos. C223-C224.

Statue of Liberty, Cent. — AP89

1986, May 21

C222 AP89 250fr multi 4.50 1.75

Nos. C220-C221 Ovptd. with Winners

1986, Sept. 15 Litho. ***Perf. 13***

C223 75fr "FRANCE - BELGIQUE / 4-2" 1.25 .65
C224 100fr "3-2 ARGENTINE-RFA" 1.75 .80

1986 World Chess Championships, May 1-19 — AP89a

Malayan animal chess pieces.

1986, Oct. 13 Litho. ***Perf. 13***

C225 AP89a 80fr Knight, bishops 2.00 .60
C226 AP89a 120fr Rook, king, pawn 3.25 .90

Yuri Gagarin, Sputnik Spacecraft — AP90

1986, Nov. 27 Litho. ***Perf. 13***

C227 AP90 150fr shown 3.00 1.10
C228 AP90 200fr Space rendezvous, 1966 4.25 1.25

First man in space, 25th anniv.; Gemini 8-Agena link-up, 20th anniv.

Historic Flights — AP91

1987, Jan. 22 Litho. ***Perf. 13***

C229 AP91 55fr Amiot 370 1.25 .40
C230 AP91 80fr Spirit of St. Louis 1.75 .55
C231 AP91 120fr Voyager 2.50 .90
Nos. C229-C231 (3) 5.50 1.85

First flight from Istria to Djibouti, 1942; Lindbergh's Transatlantic flight, 1927; nonstop world circumnavigation without refueling.

For surcharge see No. C240.

Souvenir Sheet

Fight Against Leprosy — AP91a

Design: Raoul Follereau (b. 1903), care giver to lepers, Gerhard Hansen (1841-1912), discoverer of bacillus of leprosy.

1987, Mar. 23 Litho. ***Perf. 13x12½***

Self-Adhesive

C231A AP91a 500fr multi 20.00 15.00

No. C231A printed on wood.

Pres. Aptidon, Natl. Crest and Flag AP92

1987, June 27 Litho. ***Perf. 12½x13***

C232 AP92 250fr multi 4.50 1.50

Natl. independence, 10th anniv.

Telstar, 25th Anniv. — AP93

1987, Oct. 1 ***Perf. 13***

C233 AP93 190fr shown 3.50 1.25
a. Souvenir sheet, 1 #C233 14.00 —
C234 AP93 250fr Samuel Morse, telegraph key 4.50 1.50
a. Souvenir sheet, 1 #C234 14.00 —

Invention of the telegraph, 150th anniv. (250fr).

Nos. C233a and C234a also exist imperf. Value, set of 2, $40.

City of Djibouti, Cent. — AP94

100fr, Djibouti Creek & quay, 1887. 150fr, Aerial view of city, 1987. 250fr, Somali Coast #6, 20, postmarks of 1898 & 1903.

1987, Nov. 15 Litho. ***Perf. 13x12½***

C235 AP94 100fr blk & buff 2.00 1.10
C236 AP94 150fr multi 3.00 1.60
a. Pair, Nos. C235-C236 + label 6.00 2.75

Souvenir Sheet

237 AP94 250fr multi 5.50 5.50

No. C237 has decorative margin like design of 100fr.

Intl. Red Cross and Red Crescent Organizations, 125th Anniv. — AP95

1988, Feb. 17 **Litho.** ***Perf. 13***
C238 AP95 300fr multi 6.00 3.25

1988 Summer Olympics, Seoul — AP96

1988, June 15 **Litho.** ***Perf. 13***
C239 AP96 105fr multi 3.00 1.00

For overprint see No. C242.

No. C229 Surcharged in Black

1988, June 28
C240 AP91 70fr on 55fr multi 3.00 1.50

Air race in memory of the Paris-Djibouti-St. Denis flight of French aviator Roland Garros (1888-1913).

World Post Day — AP97

1988, Oct. 9 **Litho.** ***Perf. 13***
C241 AP97 1000fr multi 18.00 10.00

No. C239 Overprinted

1988, Dec. 15 **Litho.** ***Perf. 13***
C242 AP96 105fr multi 2.25 1.50

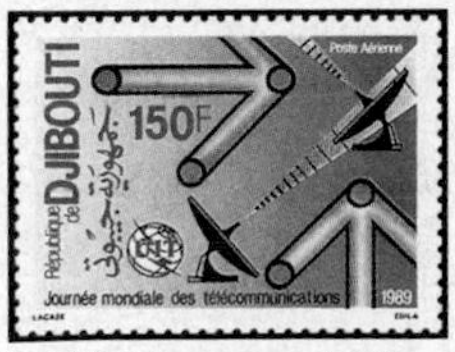

World Telecommunications Day — AP98

1989, May 17 **Litho.** ***Perf. 12½***
C243 AP98 150fr multi 2.75 1.50

PHILEXFRANCE '89, Declaration of Human Rights and Citizenship Bicent. — AP99

1989, July 14 **Litho.** ***Perf. 12½x13***
C244 AP99 120fr multi 2.75 1.25

Salt, Lake Assal — AP100

1989, Sept. 15 **Litho.** ***Perf. 13***
C245 AP100 300fr multicolored 6.75 3.50

POSTAGE DUE STAMP

Urn for Milking Camel — D1

1988, Jan. 20 **Litho.** ***Perf. 13***
J1 D1 60fr multi 1.20 .65

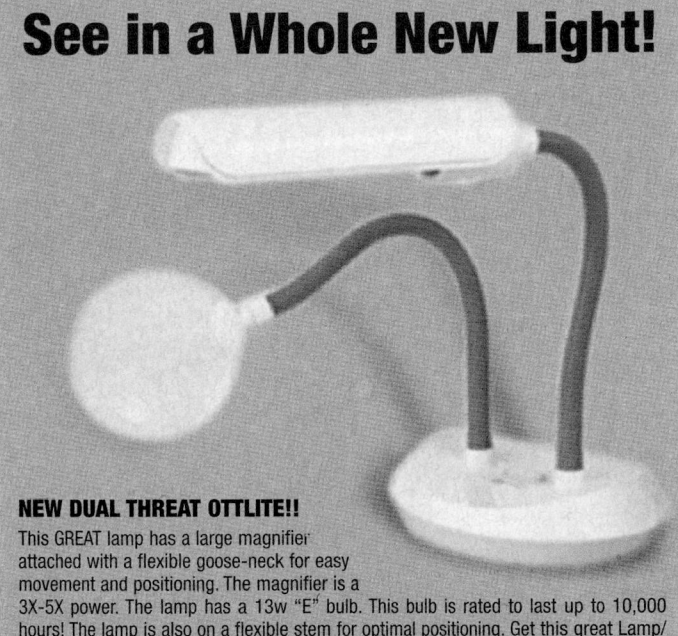

DOMINICA

ˌdä-mə-ˈnē-kə

LOCATION — The largest island of the Windward group in the West Indies. Southeast of Puerto Rico.
GOVT. — Republic in British Commonwealth
AREA — 290 sq. mi.
POP. — 64,881 (1999 est.)
CAPITAL — Roseau

Formerly a Presidency of the Leeward Islands, Dominica became a separate colony under the governor of the Windward Islands on January 1, 1940. Dominica joined the West Indies federation April 22, 1958. In 1968, Dominica became an associate state of Britain; in 1978, an independent nation.

12 Pence = 1 Shilling
20 Shillings = 1 Pound
100 Cents = 1 Dollar (1949)

Catalogue values for unused stamps in this country are for Never Hinged items, beginning with Scott 112.

Watermark

Wmk. 334 — Rectangles

Queen Victoria — A1

Perf. 12½

1874, May 4 Typo. Wmk. 1

1	A1	1p violet	170.00	55.00
a.		Vertical half used as ½p on cover		9,000.
2	A1	6p green	625.00	115.00
3	A1	1sh deep lilac rose	375.00	80.00
		Nos. 1-3 (3)	1,170.	250.00

During 1875-87 some issues were manuscript dated with village names. These are considered postally used. Stamps with entire village names sell for much more, starting at $100.

1877-79 *Perf. 14*

4	A1	½p bister ('79)	17.00	62.50
5	A1	1p violet	16.00	3.75
a.		Diagonal or vertical half used as ½p on cover		2,600.
6	A1	2½p red brown ('79)	275.00	40.00
7	A1	4p blue ('79)	130.00	4.00
8	A1	6p green	170.00	22.50
9	A1	1sh dp lilac rose	140.00	57.50
		Nos. 4-9 (6)	748.00	190.25

For surcharges see Nos. 10-15.

No. 5 Bisected and Surcharged in Black or Red

a b c

1882

10	A1(a)	½p on half of 1p	240.00	57.50
a.		Inverted surcharge	1,150.	900.00
b.		Surcharge tete beche pair	2,600.	2,000.
11	A1(b)	½p on half of 1p	72.50	36.00
a.		Surch. reading downward	72.50	36.00
b.		Double surcharge	900.00	
12	A1(c)	½p on half of 1p (R)	35.00	20.00
a.		Inverted surcharge	1,150.	550.00
b.		Double surcharge	1,850.	750.00
		Nos. 10-12 (3)	347.50	113.50

The existence of genuine examples of No. 10b has been questioned.

Nos. 8 and 9 Surcharged in Black

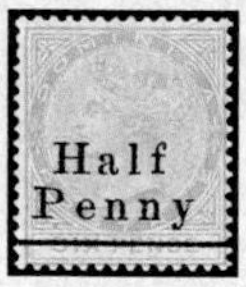

1886

13	A1	½p on 6p green	10.00	11.00
14	A1	1p on 6p green	45,000.	12,500.
15	A1	1p on 1sh	22.00	22.00
a.		Double surcharge	11,500.	4,250.

All examples of No. 14 may have small pin marks which may have been part of the surcharging process.

1883-89 Wmk. 2

16	A1	½p bister ('83)	6.00	11.50
17	A1	½p green ('86)	5.75	6.25
18	A1	1p violet ('86)	60.00	16.00
a.		Half used as ½p on cover		2,350.
19	A1	1p dp carmine ('89)	4.25	14.00
a.		1p rose ('87)	19.00	26.00
b.		Vert. half used as ½p on cover		2,100.
20	A1	2½p red brn ('84)	160.00	4.00
21	A1	2½p ultra ('88)	4.25	6.00
22	A1	4p gray ('86)	5.50	7.75
23	A1	6p orange ('88)	21.00	92.50
24	A1	1sh dp lil rose ('88)	200.00	500.00
		Nos. 16-24 (9)	466.75	658.00

Roseau, Capital of Dominica — A6

King Edward VII — A7

1903 Wmk. 1 *Perf. 14*
Ordinary Paper

25	A6	½p gray green	5.25	4.25
26	A6	1p car & black	13.00	.80
27	A6	2p brn & gray grn	4.50	6.50
28	A6	2½p ultra & blk	9.50	5.25
29	A6	3p black & vio	10.50	4.50
30	A6	6p org brn & blk	12.00	22.50
31	A6	1sh gray grn & red vio	35.00	52.50
32	A6	2sh red vio & blk	32.50	35.00
33	A6	2sh6p ocher & gray grn	23.00	92.50
34	A7	5sh brown & blk	125.00	175.00
		Nos. 25-34 (10)	270.25	398.80

Nos. 25 to 29 and 31 are on both ordinary and chalky paper. For detailed listings, see the *Scott Classic Specialized Catalogue of Stamps & Covers.*

1907-20 Chalky Paper Wmk. 3

35	A6	½p gray green	12.00	8.00
36	A6	1p car & black	2.50	.55
37	A6	2p brn & gray grn	13.00	20.00
38	A6	2½p ultra & black	5.50	27.50
39	A6	3p black & vio	5.00	17.00
40	A6	3p vio, *yel*, chalky paper ('09)	3.75	5.25
41	A6	6p org brn & blk ('08)	65.00	100.00
42	A6	6p vio & dl vio, chalky paper ('09)	12.50	19.00
43	A6	1sh gray grn & red vio	4.75	67.50
44	A6	1sh blk, *green*, chalky paper ('10)	3.75	5.00
45	A6	2sh red vio & blk ('08)	30.00	40.00
46	A6	2sh ultra & vio, *bl* ('19)	32.50	110.00
47	A6	2sh6p ocher & gray grn ('08)	27.50	75.00
48	A6	2sh6p red & blk, *bl* ('20)	32.50	125.00
49	A7	5sh brn & blk ('08)	75.00	75.00
		Nos. 35-49 (15)	325.25	694.80

Nos. 40, 42 and 44 are on both ordinary and chalky paper. For detailed listings, see the *Scott Classic Specialized Catalogue of Stamps & Covers.*
For type surcharged see No. 55.

1908-09 Ordinary Paper

50	A6	½p green	9.50	6.25
51	A6	1p scarlet	2.00	.75
a.		1p carmine	4.50	.45
52	A6	2p gray ('09)	4.50	17.50
53	A6	2½p ultramarine	9.50	9.75
a.		2½p bright blue ('18)	5.75	10.50
		Nos. 50-53 (4)	25.50	34.25

King George V — A8

1914 Chalky Paper *Perf. 14*

54	A8	5sh grn & scar, *yel*	70.00	100.00

Type of 1903 Surcharged

1920

55	A6	1½p on 2½p orange	7.50	4.75

1921 Ordinary Paper Wmk. 4

56	A6	½p green	3.50	22.00
57	A6	1p rose red	3.00	4.00
58	A6	1½p orange	4.75	18.00
59	A6	2p gray	4.25	4.00
60	A6	2½p ultra	2.75	15.00
61	A6	6p vio & dl vio	4.00	45.00
62	A6	2sh ultra & vio, *bl*	50.00	130.00
63	A6	2sh6p red & blk, *bl*	45.00	150.00
		Nos. 56-63 (8)	117.25	388.00

No. 61 is on chalky paper.

Seal of Colony and George V — A9

1923-33 Chalky Paper Wmk. 4

65	A9	½p green & blk	2.50	.85
66	A9	1p violet & blk	6.50	2.25
67	A9	1p scar & black	17.00	1.40
68	A9	1½p car & black	6.50	.90
69	A9	1½p dp brn & blk	15.50	.95
70	A9	2p gray & black	4.25	.65
71	A9	2½p org & black	3.75	10.00
72	A9	2½p ultra & black	7.75	2.25
73	A9	3p ultra & black	4.00	17.50
74	A9	3p red & blk, *yel*	4.00	1.40
75	A9	4p brown & blk	4.50	7.25
76	A9	6p red vio & blk	4.75	9.00
77	A9	1sh blk, *emerald*	3.50	3.75
78	A9	2sh ultra & blk, *bl*	22.50	32.50
79	A9	2sh6p red & blk, *bl*	25.00	32.50
80	A9	3sh vio & blk, *yel*	4.50	15.00
81	A9	4sh red & blk, *emer*	22.00	35.00
82	A9	5sh grn & blk, *yel*	40.00	62.50
		Nos. 65-82 (18)	198.50	235.65

Issue years: Nos. 80, 82, 1927; Nos. 72, 74, 1928; Nos. 67, 69, 1933; others, 1923.
Many values of this set are known with a forged G.P.O. cancellation dated "MY 19 27".

1923 Wmk. 3

83	A9	3sh vio & blk, *yel*	5.75	72.50
84	A9	5sh grn & blk, *yel*	10.00	65.00
85	A9	£1 vio & blk, *red*	260.00	375.00
		Nos. 83-85 (3)	275.75	512.50

Common Design Types pictured following the introduction.

Silver Jubilee Issue
Common Design Type
Perf. 13½x14

1935, May 6 Wmk. 4 Engr.

90	CD301	1p car & blue	1.60	.35
91	CD301	1½p gray blk & ultra	5.75	3.25
92	CD301	2½p blue & brn	5.75	4.75
93	CD301	1sh brt vio & ind	5.75	11.50
		Nos. 90-93 (4)	18.85	19.85
		Set, never hinged	27.50	

Coronation Issue
Common Design Type

1937, May 12 *Perf. 11x11½*

94	CD302	1p dark carmine	.25	.25
95	CD302	1½p brown	.25	.25
96	CD302	2½p deep ultra	.35	1.90
		Nos. 94-96 (3)	.85	2.40
		Set, never hinged	1.50	

Fresh-Water Lake — A10

Layou River — A11

Picking Limes — A12

Boiling Lake — A13

1938-47 Wmk. 4 *Perf. 12½*

97	A10	½p grn & red brn	.25	.25
98	A11	1p car & gray	.25	.25
99	A12	1½p rose vio & grn	.25	.75
100	A13	2p brn blk & dp rose	.35	2.25
101	A12	2½p ultra & rose vio	.25	2.25
a.		2½p bl & rose vio	2.75	1.90
102	A11	3p red brn & ol	.25	.60
103	A12	3½p red vio & brt ultra	1.00	2.10
104	A10	6p vio & yel grn	.50	1.60
105	A10	7p org brn & grn	1.00	1.60
106	A13	1sh olive & vio	2.50	1.60
107	A11	2sh red vio & blk	4.50	12.50
108	A10	2sh6p scar ver & blk	10.00	5.75
109	A11	5sh dk brn & bl	8.00	12.00
110	A13	10sh dl org & blk	10.00	22.50
		Nos. 97-110 (14)	39.10	66.00
		Set, never hinged	80.00	

Issued: No. 101, 8/42; 3½p, 7p, 2sh, 10sh, 10/15/47; others, 8/15/38.

King George VI — A14

1940, Apr. 15 Photo. *Perf. 14½x14*
111 A14 ¼p brown violet 1.00 *.25*
a. Ordinary paper ('42) .25 *1.50*

No. 111 is on chalky paper.

Catalogue values for unused stamps in this section, from this point to the end of the section, are for Never Hinged items.

Peace Issue
Common Design Type

1946, Oct. 14 Engr. *Perf. 13½x14*
112 CD303 1p carmine .25 .25
113 CD303 3½p deep blue .25 .25

Silver Wedding Issue
Common Design Types

1948, Dec. 1 Photo. *Perf. 14x14½*
114 CD304 1p scarlet .25 .25

Engraved; Name Typographed
Perf. 11½x11
115 CD305 10sh orange brn 25.00 *32.50*

UPU Issue
Common Design Types

Engr.: Name Typo. on 6c and 12c
1949, Oct. 10 *Perf. 13½, 11x11½*
116 CD306 5c blue .25 .25
117 CD307 6c chocolate 1.25 *3.00*
118 CD308 12c rose violet .50 *2.10*
119 CD309 24c olive .30 .30
Nos. 116-119 (4) 2.30 5.65

University Issue
Common Design Types

1951, Feb. 16 Engr. *Perf. 14x14½*
120 CD310 3c purple & green .60 *1.25*
121 CD311 12c dp car & dk bl grn .80 .50

George VI A15

Drying Cocoa A16

Picking Oranges — A17

Designs: 2c and 60c, Carib Baskets. 3c and 48c, Lime Plantation. 4c, Picking Oranges. 5c, Bananas. 6c, Botanical Gardens. 8c, Drying Vanilla Beans. 12c and $1.20, Fresh Water Lake. 14c, Layou River. 24c, Boiling Lake.

Perf. 14½x14
1951, July 1 Photo. Wmk. 4
122 A15 ½c brown .25 .25

Perf. 13x13½
Engr.
123 A16 1c red org & blk .25 .30
124 A16 2c dp grn & red brn .25 .25
125 A16 3c red vio & bl grn .25 *3.50*
126 A16 4c dk brn & brn org .75 *3.75*
127 A16 5c rose red & blk .85 .30
128 A16 6c org brn & ol grn 1.00 .30
129 A16 8c dp bl & dp grn 3.00 1.75
130 A16 12c emer & gray .75 *1.25*
131 A16 14c pur & blue 1.25 *3.50*
132 A16 24c rose car & red vio 1.00 .40
133 A16 48c red org & bl grn 5.00 *13.50*
134 A16 60c gray & car 4.00 *9.25*
135 A16 $1.20 gray & emer 8.25 *7.25*

Perf. 13½x13
136 A17 $2.40 gray & org 30.00 *52.50*
Nos. 122-136 (15) 56.85 *98.05*

Nos. 125, 127, 129 and 131 Overprinted in Black or Carmine

1951, Oct. 15 *Perf. 13x13½*
137 A16 3c red vio & bl green .25 *.60*
138 A16 5c rose red & black .25 *1.75*
139 A16 8c dp blue & dp grn (C) .30 .25
140 A16 14c purple & blue (C) 1.75 .30
Nos. 137-140 (4) 2.55 2.90

Adoption of a new constitution for the Windward Islands, 1951.

Coronation Issue
Common Design Type

1953, June 2 Engr. *Perf. 13½x13*
141 CD312 2c dk green & black .40 .40

Types of 1951 with Portrait of Queen Elizabeth II

1954, Oct. 1 Photo. *Perf. 14½x14*
142 A15 ½c brown .25 1.25

Perf. 13x13½
Engr.
143 A16 1c red org & blk .25 .30
144 A16 2c dp grn & red brn 1.10 *2.00*
145 A16 3c red vio & bl grn 1.50 .40
146 A16 4c dk brn & brn org .25 .30
147 A16 5c rose red & blk 2.75 1.00
148 A16 6c org brn & ol grn .55 .30
149 A16 8c dp bl & dp grn 1.50 .30
150 A16 12c emer & gray .60 .25
151 A16 14c pur & bl .45 .25
152 A16 24c rose car & red vio .55 .30
153 A16 48c red org & bl grn 2.75 *11.00*
154 A16 60c gray & car 3.50 1.50
155 A16 $1.20 gray & emer 22.50 7.00

Perf. 13½x13
156 A17 $2.40 gray & org 22.50 14.00
Nos. 142-156 (15) 61.00 40.15

Mat Making — A18

5c, Canoe making. 10c, Bananas.

1957, Oct. 15 Wmk. 4 *Perf. 13x13½*
157 A18 3c car rose & black 4.00 2.50
158 A18 5c brown & blue 12.00 1.10
159 A18 10c redsh brn & brt grn 6.00 3.25
160 A18 48c violet & brown 3.25 2.75
Nos. 157-160 (4) 25.25 9.60

West Indies Federation
Common Design Type

Perf. 11½x11
1958, Apr. 22 Wmk. 314
161 CD313 3c green .50 .35
162 CD313 6c blue .60 *1.10*
163 CD313 12c car rose .85 .40
Nos. 161-163 (3) 1.95 1.85

Sailing Canoe — A19

Traditional Costume — A20

Designs: 1c, Seashore, Rosalie. 2c, 5c, Queen Elizabeth II by Annigoni. 4c, Sulphur Springs. 6c, Road making. 8c, Dugout canoe. 10c, Frog (mountain chicken). 12c, Boats and Scotts Head. 15c, Bananas. 24c, Imperial parrot. 48c, View of Goodwill. 60c, Cacao tree. $1.20, Coat of Arms. $2.40, Trafalgar Falls. $4.80, Coconut palm.

Two types of 14c:
I — Mountain light violet. Girl's eyes look straight out.
II — Mountain blue. Eyes look sideways.

Perf. 14½x14, 14x14½
1963, May 16 Photo. Wmk. 314
164 A19 1c bl, brn & grn .25 *.90*
165 A20 2c ultramarine .30 .25
166 A19 3c lt ultra & blk 1.50 1.10
167 A19 4c sl, grn & brn .25 .25
168 A20 5c magenta .30 .25
169 A19 6c lt grn, vio & buff .25 .50
170 A19 8c tan, blk & lt grn .30 .25
171 A19 10c pink & brn .25 .25
172 A19 12c bl, blk, grn & brn .90 .25
173 A20 14c multi (II) 2.50 2.50
a. Type I .90 .30
174 A19 15c grn, yel & brn 1.25 .25
175 A20 24c multicolored 8.50 .25
176 A19 48c bl, blk & grn .90 .90
177 A19 60c blk, grn, org & brn 1.00 .75
178 A19 $1.20 multicolored 6.25 1.60
179 A20 $2.40 grn, bl, brn & blk 4.75 4.00
180 A20 $4.80 bl, brn & grn 20.00 *30.00*
Nos. 164-180 (17) 49.45 44.25

For overprints see Nos. 211-232.

1966-67 Wmk. 314 Sideways
167a A19 4c ('67) 1.25 .90
169a A19 6c .25 .80
170a A19 8c .45 .90
171a A19 10c ('67) .70 .95
174a A19 15c ('67) .85 1.50
Nos. 167a-174a (5) 3.50 5.05

Freedom from Hunger Issue
Common Design Type

1963, June 4 *Perf. 14x14½*
181 CD314 15c lilac .30 .30

Red Cross Centenary Issue
Common Design Type

Wmk. 314
1963, Sept. 2 Litho. *Perf. 13*
182 CD315 5c black & red .25 .25
183 CD315 15c ultra & red .45 *.80*

Shakespeare Issue
Common Design Type

1964, Apr. 23 Photo. *Perf. 14x14½*
184 CD316 15c lilac rose .35 .35

ITU Issue
Common Design Type

1965, May 17 Litho. *Perf. 11x11½*
185 CD317 2c emerald & blue .25 .25
186 CD317 48c grnsh blue & slate .30 .30

Intl. Cooperation Year Issue
Common Design Type

1965, Oct. 25 *Perf. 14½*
187 CD318 1c blue grn & claret .25 .25
188 CD318 15c lt violet & grn .30 .30

Churchill Memorial Issue
Common Design Type

1966, Jan. 24 Photo. *Perf. 14*
Design in Black, Gold and Carmine Rose
189 CD319 1c bright blue .25 .25
a. Gold omitted *2,000.*
190 CD319 5c green .25 .25
191 CD319 15c brown .30 .30
192 CD319 24c violet .35 .35
Nos. 189-192 (4) 1.15 1.15

Royal Visit Issue
Common Design Type

1966, Feb. 4 Litho. *Perf. 11x12*
193 CD320 5c violet blue .75 .25
194 CD320 15c dk car rose 2.25 .35

World Cup Soccer Issue
Common Design Type

1966, July 1 Litho. *Perf. 14*
195 CD321 5c multicolored .35 .25
196 CD321 24c multicolored .85 .50

WHO Headquarters Issue
Common Design Type

1966, Sept. 20 Litho. *Perf. 14*
197 CD322 5c multicolored .25 .25
198 CD322 24c multicolored .50 .50

UNESCO Anniversary Issue
Common Design Type

1966, Dec. 1 Litho. *Perf. 14*
199 CD323 5c "Education" .35 .25
200 CD323 15c "Science" .45 .25
201 CD323 24c "Culture" .80 .25
Nos. 199-201 (3) 1.60 .75

Carib, Negro and Caucasian Children — A21

10c, Columbus' ship Santa Maria & banderol. 15c, Hands with banderol. 24c, Belaire dancers.

Perf. 14½x14
1967, Nov. 3 Photo. Wmk. 314
202 A21 5c multicolored .25 .25
203 A21 10c multicolored .25 .25
204 A21 15c multicolored .25 .25
205 A21 24c multicolored .25 .25
Nos. 202-205 (4) 1.00 1.00

Issued for National Day, Nov. 3.

John F. Kennedy and Human Rights Flame — A22

Human Rights Flame and: 10c, Cecil E. A. Rawle (1891-1938), Dominican crusader for human rights. 12c, Pope John XXIII. 48c, Florence Nightingale. 60c, Dr. Albert Schweitzer.

Wmk. 314 Sideways
1968, Apr. 20 Litho. *Perf. 14*
206 A22 1c multicolored .25 .25
207 A22 10c multicolored .25 .25
208 A22 12c multicolored .25 .25
209 A22 48c multicolored .25 .25
210 A22 60c multicolored .25 .25
Nos. 206-210 (5) 1.25 1.25

International Human Rights Year.

Stamps and Types of 1963-67 Overprinted in Silver or Black: "ASSOCIATED / STATEHOOD"

Perf. 14½x14, 14x14½
1968, July 8 Photo. Wmk. 314
211 A19 1c multi .25 .25
212 A20 2c ultra .25 .25
213 A19 3c lt ultra & blk .25 .25
214 A19 4c multi .25 .25
215 A20 5c magenta .25 .25
216 A19 6c multi (B) .25 .25
217 A19 8c multi (B) .25 .25
218 A19 10c pink & brn .55 .25
219 A19 12c multi .25 *.50*
a. Watermark upright .25 .25
220 A20 14c multi (II) .25 .25
221 A19 15c multi .25 .25
222 A20 24c multi 4.00 .25
223 A19 48c multi .55 *2.25*
a. Watermark upright .50 *1.00*
224 A19 60c multi (B) .90 .75
225 A19 $1.20 multi (B) 1.00 *3.00*
226 A20 $2.40 multi 1.00 *2.25*
227 A20 $4.80 multi 1.25 8.00
Nos. 211-227 (17) 11.75 19.50

In this set, overprint was applied to 2c, 3c, 12c, 14c, 24c, 48c, 60c, $1.20, $2.40 and $4.80 with watermark upright. A reprinting of the 1c, 4c, 6c, 8c, 10c, 12c, No. 219, 15c and 48c, No. 223 on paper with watermark sideways was made. Same value.

Nos. 164-166, 173 and 178 Overprinted: "NATIONAL DAY / 3 NOVEMBER 1968"

Perf. 14½x14, 14x14½
1968, Nov. 3 Photo. Wmk. 314
228 A19 1c blue, brn & grn .25 .25
229 A20 2c ultra .25 .25
230 A19 3c lt ultra & blk .25 .25
231 A20 14c multi (I) .25 .25
232 A19 $1.20 multicolored .55 .55
Nos. 228-232 (5) 1.55 1.55

A23

No. 233: a, 3 soccer players; b, Soccer player, goalie. No. 234: a, Swimmers at start; b, Divers. No. 235: a, Javelin thrower, hurdlers; b, Hurdlers. No. 236: a, Basketball; b, 3 basketball players.

Perf. 11½

1968, Nov. 23 Unwmk. Litho.

233 A23 1c Pair, #a-b .25 .25
234 A23 5c Pair, #a-b .25 .25
235 A23 48c Pair, #a-b .50 .50
236 A23 60c Pair, #a-b 1.40 1.40
Nos. 233-236 (4) 2.40 2.40

19th Olympic Games, Mexico City, 10/12-27.

The Small Cowper Madonna, by Raphael A24

Perf. 12½x12

1968, Dec. 23 Photo. Unwmk.

241 A24 5c multicolored .30 .30

Christmas. No. 241 printed in sheets of 20. Sheets of 6 (3x2) exist containing two each of 12c, 24c, and $1.20 stamps, each picturing a different madonna painting. Value $6.

Venus and Adonis, by Rubens — A25

Paintings: 15c, The Death of Socrates, by Louis Jacques David. 24c, Christ at Emmaus, by Velazquez. 50c, Pilate Washing his Hands, by Rembrandt.

Perf. 14½x15

1969, Jan. 30 Litho. Wmk. 314

242 A25 5c lilac & multi .25 .25
243 A25 15c emerald & multi .25 .25
244 A25 24c lt blue & multi .25 .25
245 A25 50c crimson & multi .45 .45
Nos. 242-245 (4) 1.20 1.20

20th anniv. (in 1968) of the WHO.

Citrus Fruit Picker — A26

No. 247, Woman and child. No. 248, Hotel. No. 249, Red-necked parrots. No. 250, Calypso band. No. 251, Women dancers. No. 252, Tropical fish and coelenterates. No. 253, Diver and turtle.

1969, Mar. 10 *Perf. 14½*

246 A26 10c multicolored .25 .25
247 A26 10c multicolored .25 .25
a. Pair, #246-247 .25 .25
248 A26 12c multicolored .25 .25
249 A26 12c multicolored .25 .25
a. Pair, #248-249 .25 .25
250 A26 24c multicolored .25 .25
251 A26 24c multicolored .25 .25
a. Pair, #250-251 .50 .50
252 A26 48c multicolored .65 .65
253 A26 48c multicolored .65 .65
a. Pair, #252-253 1.30 1.30
Nos. 246-253 (8) 2.80 2.80

Tourist publicity.

Spinning, by Millet, Flags and ILO Emblem — A27

50th anniv. of the ILO (Etchings by Jean F. Millet, Flags and ILO Emblem): 30c, Threshing. 30c, Flax pulling.

1969, July Unwmk. ***Perf. 13½***

254 A27 15c multicolored .25 .25
255 A27 30c multicolored .30 .30
256 A27 38c multicolored .30 .30
Nos. 254-256 (3) .85 .85

"Strength in Unity," Bananas and Cacao A28

"Strength in Unity" Emblem and: 8c, Map of Dominica and Hawker Siddeley 748. 12c, Map of Caribbean. 24c, Ships in harbor.

1969, July Litho.

257 A28 5c orange & multi .30 .30
258 A28 8c gray & multi .30 .30
259 A28 12c lilac & multi .30 .30
260 A28 24c lt blue & multi .30 .30
Nos. 257-260 (4) 1.20 1.20

Caribbean Free Trade Area (CARIFTA).

Gandhi at Spinning Wheel and Big Ben, London A29

38c, Gandhi, Nehru and Fatehpur Sikri Mausoleum. $1.20, Gandhi & Taj Mahal.

1969, Oct. Litho. ***Perf. 14½***

261 A29 6c multicolored .55 .25
262 A29 38c multicolored .75 .25
263 A29 $1.20 multicolored .85 .85
Nos. 261-263 (3) 2.15 1.35

Mohandas K. Gandhi (1869-1948), leader in India's fight for independence. "Gandhi" is misspelled "Ghandi" on Nos. 261-263.

St. Joseph — A30

Stained Glass Windows, from 17th Century French Churches: 8c, St. John. 12c, St. Peter. 60c, St. Paul.

1969, Nov. 10 Litho. ***Perf. 14***

264 A30 6c black & multi .25 .25
265 A30 8c black & multi .25 .25
266 A30 12c black & multi .25 .25
267 A30 60c black & multi .40 .40
Nos. 264-267 (4) 1.15 1.15

National Day, Nov. 3. Issued in sheets of 16 (4x4) with control numbers and 4 tabs with a patriotic poem by W. O. M. Pond.

Queen Elizabeth II — A31

Purplethroated Carib (Hummingbird) — A32

2c, Poinsettia. 3c, Red-necked pigeon. 4c, Imperial parrot. 5c, Swallowtail butterfly. 6c, Brown Julia butterfly. 8c, Banana shipment. 10c, Portsmouth Harbor. 12c, Copra processing plant. 15c, Women with straw work. 25c, Timber plant. 30c, Mining pumice. 38c, Cricket, Grammar School. 50c, Roman Catholic Cathedral. 60c, Government headquarters. $1.20, Melville Hall Airport. $2.40, Coat of Arms. $4.80, Queen Elizabeth II.

Perf. 13½

1969, Nov. 26 Unwmk. Photo.

Chalky Paper

268 A31 ½c silver & multi .25 *1.50*
269 A32 1c yellow & multi .75 *2.00*
270 A32 2c yellow & multi .25 .25
271 A32 3c yellow & multi 2.50 2.50
272 A32 4c yellow & multi 2.50 2.50
273 A32 5c yellow & multi 2.50 2.50
274 A32 6c brown & multi 2.00 *3.50*
275 A32 8c brown & multi .25 .25
276 A32 10c yellow & multi .25 .25
277 A32 12c citron & multi .25 .25
278 A32 15c blue & multi .25 .25
279 A32 25c pink & multi .40 .25
280 A32 30c olive & multi 1.50 .25
281 A32 38c multicolored 8.50 1.75
282 A32 50c brown & multi .65 .65

Wmk. Rectangles (334)

Perf. 14

Size: 38x26mm, 26x38mm

283 A32 60c yel & multi 1.00 *1.50*
284 A32 $1.20 yel & multi 2.00 2.00
285 A32 $2.40 gold & multi 1.50 *4.00*
286 A31 $4.80 gold & multi 3.00 *7.50*
Nos. 268-286 (19) 30.30 *33.65*

1972 On glazed Paper

268a A31 ½c silver & multi .30 *2.00*
269a A32 1c yellow & multi 1.40 *1.50*
270a A32 2c yellow & multi .50 .50
271a A32 3c yellow & multi 3.00 1.50
272a A32 4c yellow & multi 3.00 1.50
273a A32 5c yellow & multi 2.75 1.25
274a A32 6c brown & multi 2.75 2.75
275a A32 8c brown & multi .45 *.60*
276a A32 10c yellow & multi .35 .25
277a A32 12c citron & multi .35 .25
278a A32 15c blue & multi .35 .30
279a A32 25c pink & multi .30 .25
280a A32 30c olive & multi 1.50 .65
281a A32 38c multicolored 8.00 *14.00*
282a A32 50c brown & multi .85 *1.25*
Nos. 268a-282a (15) 25.85 *28.55*

Madonna and Child, by Filippino Lippi — A33

Paintings: 10c, Holy Family with Lamb, by Raphael. 15c, Virgin and Child, by Perugino. $1.20, Madonna of the Rose Hedge, by Botticelli.

Perf. 14½

1969, Dec. Unwmk. Litho.

287 A33 6c lt blue & multi .25 .25
288 A33 10c multicolored .25 .25
289 A33 15c lilac & multi .25 .25
290 A33 $1.20 lt grn & multi .25 .25
a. Souvenir sheet of 2 1.25 1.25
Nos. 287-290 (4) 1.00 1.00

Christmas. No. 290a contains 2 imperf. stamps with simulated perforations similar to Nos. 289-290.

Neil A. Armstrong, First Man on the Moon — A34

Designs: 5c, American flag and astronauts on moon. 8c, Astronauts collecting moon rocks. 30c, Landing module, moon and earth. 50c, Memorial tablet left on moon. 60c, Astronauts Armstrong, Aldrin and Collins.

1970, Feb. 2 Litho. ***Perf. 12½***

291 A34 ½c lilac & multi .25 .25
292 A34 5c lt blue & multi .25 .25
293 A34 8c orange & multi .25 .25
294 A34 30c blue & multi .25 .25
295 A34 50c red brn & multi .40 .30
296 A34 60c rose & multi .50 .45
a. Souvenir sheet of 4 2.60 2.60
Nos. 291-296 (6) 1.90 1.75

See note after US No. C76. No. 296a contains 4 stamps similar to Nos. 293-296, but imperf. with simulated perforations.

Giant Green Turtle — A35

Designs: 24c, Flying fish. 38c, Anthurium lily. 60c, Imperial and red-necked parrots.

1970, Sept. 6 Litho. ***Perf. 13½x13***

297 A35 6c lt green & multi .50 .50
298 A35 24c multicolored .65 .65
299 A35 38c green & multi .75 .75
300 A35 60c yellow & multi 3.50 3.50
a. Souvenir sheet of 4, #297-300 8.50 8.50
Nos. 297-300 (4) 5.40 5.40

Women in 18th Century Dress A36

Natl. Day: 8c, Carib mace & wife leader, 18th cent. $1, Map & flag of Dominica.

1970, Nov. 3 Litho. ***Perf. 14***

301 A36 5c yellow & multi .25 .25
302 A36 8c green & multi .25 .25
303 A36 $1 lt blue & multi .40 .40
a. Souv. sheet of 3, #301-303 + 3 labels 1.25 *1.50*
Nos. 301-303 (3) .90 .90

Marley's Ghost — A37

Designs (from A Christmas Carol, by Dickens): 15c, Fezziwig's Ball. 24c, Scrooge and his Nephew's Christmas Party. $1.20, The Ghost of Christmas Present.

1970, Nov. 23 Litho. ***Perf. 14x14½***

304 A37 2c blue & multi .25 .25
305 A37 15c multicolored .25 .25
306 A37 24c red & multi .25 .25
307 A37 $1.20 multicolored .75 .75
a. Souvenir sheet of 4, #304-307 2.75 2.75
Nos. 304-307 (4) 1.50 1.50

Christmas; Charles Dickens (1812-1870).

Hands and Red Cross A38

Designs: 8c, The Doctor, by Sir Luke Fildes. 15c, Dominica flag and Red Cross. 50c, The Sick Child, by Edvard Munch.

1970, Dec. 28 ***Perf. 14½x14***

308	A38	8c multicolored	.25	.25
309	A38	10c multicolored	.25	.25
310	A38	15c multicolored	.25	.25
311	A38	50c multicolored	.50	.50
a.		Souvenir sheet of 4, #308-311	2.00	2.00
		Nos. 308-311 (4)	1.25	1.25

Centenary of the British Red Cross Society.

Marigot Primary School — A39

Education Year Emblem and: 8c, Goodwill Junior High School. 14c, University of the West Indies. $1, Trinity College, Cambridge, England.

1971, Mar. 1 **Litho.** ***Perf. 13½***

312	A39	5c multicolored	.25	.25
313	A39	8c multicolored	.25	.25
314	A39	14c multicolored	.25	.25
315	A39	$1 multicolored	.45	.45
a.		Souvenir sheet of 2, #314-315	1.50	1.50
		Nos. 312-315 (4)	1.20	1.20

International Education Year.

Waterfall and Bird-of-Paradise Flower — A40

Tourist Publicity: 10c, Boat building. 30c, Sailboat along North Coast. 50c, Speed boat and steamer.

1971, Mar. 22 ***Perf. 13½x14***

316	A40	5c multicolored	.25	.25
317	A40	10c multicolored	.25	.25
318	A40	30c multicolored	.25	.25
319	A40	50c multicolored	.35	.35
a.		Souvenir sheet of 4, #316-319	1.10	1.10
		Nos. 316-319 (4)	1.10	1.10

UNICEF Emblem, Letter "D" A41

1971, June 14 **Litho.** ***Perf. 14***

320	A41	5c multicolored	.25	.25
321	A41	10c multicolored	.25	.25
322	A41	38c multicolored	.25	.25
323	A41	$1.20 multicolored	.25	.25
a.		Souvenir sheet of 2, #321, 323	.85	.85
		Nos. 320-323 (4)	1.00	1.00

25th anniv. of UNICEF.

Boy Scout, Jamboree Emblem, Torii, Camp and Mt. Fuji — A42

24c, British Scout, flag. 30c, Japanese Scout, flag. $1, Dominican Scout, flag.

1971, Oct. 18 **Unwmk.** ***Perf. 11***

324	A42	20c bister & multi	.25	.25
325	A42	24c green & multi	.30	.30
326	A42	30c red lilac & multi	.40	.40
327	A42	$1 blue & multi	.80	.80
a.		Souvenir sheet of 2, #326-327	1.75	1.75
		Nos. 324-327 (4)	1.75	1.75

13th Boy Scout World Jamboree, Asagiri Plain, Japan, Aug. 2-10.

Boats at Portsmouth — A43

15c, Carnival street scene. 20c, $1.20, Anthea Mondesire, Carifta Queen. 50c, Rock of Atkinson.

Perf. 13½x14, 14x13½

1971, Nov. 15 **Litho.**

328	A43	8c multi	.25	.25
329	A43	15c multi	.25	.25
330	A43	20c multi, vert.	.25	.25
331	A43	50c multi, vert.	.25	.25
		Nos. 328-331 (4)	1.00	1.00

Souvenir Sheet

Perf. 15

332	A43	$1.20 multi, vert.	.85	.85

National Day.

First Dominica Coin, 8 Reals, 1761 — A44

Early Dominica Coins: 30c, Eleven and 3-bit pieces, 1798. 35c, Two-real coin, 1770, vert. 50c, Three "mocos" and piece of 8, 1798.

1972, Feb. 7 **Litho.** ***Perf. 14***

333	A44	10c violet, silver & blk	.25	.25
334	A44	30c green, silver & blk	.25	.25
335	A44	35c ultra, silver & blk	.25	.25
336	A44	50c red, silver & blk	.25	.25
a.		Souvenir sheet of 2, #335-336	1.00	1.00
		Nos. 333-336 (4)	1.00	1.00

Margin of No. 336a inscribed "Christmas 1971."

Common Opossum, Environment Emblem — A45

Environment Emblem and: 35c, Agouti. 60c, Oncidium papillo (orchid). $1.20, Hibiscus.

1972, June 5

337	A45	½c yel grn & multi	.25	.25
338	A45	35c org brn & multi	.30	.30
339	A45	60c lt blue & multi	2.25	2.25
340	A45	$1.20 yellow & multi	1.75	1.75
a.		Souvenir sheet of 4, #337-340	6.75	6.75
		Nos. 337-340 (4)	4.55	4.55

UN Conf. on Human Environment, Stockholm, June 5-16.

100-meter Sprint, Olympic Rings — A46

Olympic Rings and: 35m, 400-meter hurdles. 58c, Hammer throw, vert. 72c, Broad jump, vert.

1972, Oct. 9 **Litho.** ***Perf. 14***

341	A46	30c dp org & multi	.25	.25
342	A46	35c blue & multi	.25	.25
343	A46	58c lilac rose & multi	.30	.30
344	A46	72c yel green & multi	.40	.40
a.		Souv. sheet, #343-344, perf. 15	1.25	1.25
		Nos. 341-344 (4)	1.20	1.20

20th Olympic Games, Munich, Aug. 26-Sept. 11.

General Post Office — A47

1972, Nov. 1 ***Perf. 13½***

345	A47	10c shown	.25	.25
346	A47	20c Morne Diablotin Mountain	.25	.25
347	A47	30c Rodney's Rock	.25	.25
a.		Souv. sheet, #346-347, perf. 15	.60	.60
		Nos. 345-347 (3)	.75	.75

National Day.

Adoration of the Shepherds, by Caravaggio A48

Paintings: 14c, Madonna and Child, by Rubens. 30c, Madonna and Child, with St. Anne by Orazio Gentileschi. $1, Adoration of the Kings, by Jan Mostaert. (On 8c, painting is mistakenly attributed to Boccaccino, according to Fine Arts Philatelist.)

1972, Dec. 4.

348	A48	8c gold & multi	.25	.25
349	A48	14c gold & multi	.25	.25
350	A48	30c gold & multi	.25	.25
351	A48	$1 gold & multi	.35	.35
a.		Souvenir sheet of 2	1.10	1.10
		Nos. 348-351 (4)	1.10	1.10

Christmas. No. 351a contains one each of Nos. 350-351 with simulated perforations.

Silver Wedding Issue, 1972

Common Design Type

Design: Queen Elizabeth II, Prince Philip, bananas, sisseron parrot.

Perf. 14x14½

1972, Nov. 13 **Photo.** **Wmk. 314**

352	CD324	5c olive & multi	.25	.25
353	CD324	$1 multicolored	.40	.40

See note after Antigua No. 296.

Launching of Tiros Weather Satellite — A49

1c, Nimbus satellite. 2c, Radiosonde balloon & equipment. 30c, Radarscope. 35c, General circulation of atmosphere. 50c, Picture of hurricane transmitted by satellite. $1, Computer weather map. 30c, 35c, 50c, $1, horiz.

Perf. 14½

1973, July 16 **Unwmk.** **Litho.**

354	A49	½c black & multi	.25	.25
355	A49	1c black & multi	.25	.25
356	A49	2c black & multi	.25	.25
357	A49	30c black & multi	.25	.25
358	A49	35c black & multi	.25	.25
359	A49	50c black & multi	.30	.30
360	A49	$1 black & multi	.55	.55
a.		Souvenir sheet of 2, #359-360	1.40	1.40
		Nos. 354-360 (7)	2.10	2.10

Intl. meteorological cooperation, cent.

Going to the Hospital A50

WHO Emblem and: 1c, Maternity and infant care. 2c, Inoculation against smallpox. 30c, Emergency service. 35c, Waiting patients. 50c, Examination. $1, Traveling physician.

1973, Aug. 20 **Unwmk.** ***Perf. 14½***

361	A50	½c lt blue & multi	.25	.25
362	A50	1c gray grn & multi	.25	.25
363	A50	2c yellow & multi	.25	.25
364	A50	30c lt vio & multi	.25	.25
365	A50	35c yel grn & multi	.30	.30
366	A50	50c multicolored	.30	.30
367	A50	$1 bister & multi	.45	.45
a.		Souvenir sheet of 2, #366-367, perf. 14x14½	1.25	1.25
		Nos. 361-367 (7)	2.05	2.05

WHO, 25th anniv. No. 367a exists perf. 14½.

Cyrique Crab — A51

1973, Oct.

368	A51	½c shown	.25	.25
369	A51	22c Blue land crab	.35	.35
370	A51	25c Breadfruit	.45	.45
371	A51	$1.20 Sunflower	1.00	1.00
a.		Souvenir sheet of 4, #368-371	2.75	2.75
		Nos. 368-371 (4)	2.05	2.05

Princess Anne and Mark Phillips — A52

1973, Nov. 14 ***Perf. 13½***

372	A52	25c salmon & multi	.25	.25
373	A52	$2 blue & multi	.60	.60
a.		Souv. sheet of 2 (75c, $1.20)	.60	.60

Wedding of Princess Anne and Capt. Mark Phillips.

Nos. 372-373 were issued in sheets of 5 + label. No. 373a contains 2 stamps of type A52: 75c in colors of the 25c, and $1.20 in colors of the $2.

Nativity, by Brueghel A53

Paintings of the Nativity by: 1c, Botticelli. 2c, Dürer. 12c, Botticelli. 22c, Rubens. 35c, Dürer. $1, Giorgione (inscribed "Giorgeone").

1973 Unwmk. *Perf. 14½x15*

374	A53	½c gray & multi	.25	.25
375	A53	1c gray & multi	.25	.25
376	A53	2c gray & multi	.25	.25
377	A53	12c gray & multi	.25	.25
378	A53	22c gray & multi	.25	.25
379	A53	35c gray & multi	.25	.25
380	A53	$1 gray & multi	.60	.60
a.		Souvenir sheet of 2	1.30	1.30
		Nos. 374-380 (7)	2.10	2.10

Christmas. No. 380a contains one each of Nos. 379-380 in changed colors.

Carib Basket Weaving — A54

Designs: 10c, Staircase of the Snake. 50c, Miss Caribbean Queen, Kathleen Telemacque, vert. 60c, Miss Carifta Queen, Esther Fadelle, vert. $1, La Jeune Etoille Dancers.

1973, Dec. 17 *Perf. 13½x14, 14x13½*

381	A54	5c buff & multi	.25	.25
382	A54	10c multicolored	.25	.25
383	A54	50c multicolored	.25	.25
384	A54	60c multicolored	.25	.25
385	A54	$1 multicolored	.25	.25
a.		Souv. sheet of 3, #381-382, 385	.75	.75
		Nos. 381-385 (5)	1.25	1.25

National Day.

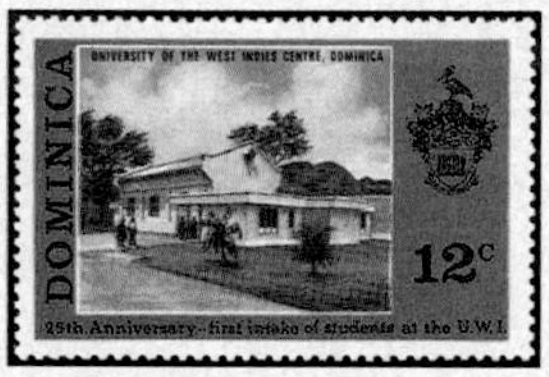

U.W.I. Center, Dominica — A55

30c, Graduation. $1, University coat of arms.

1974, Jan. 21 Litho. *Perf. 13½x14*

386	A55	12c dp orange & multi	.25	.25
387	A55	30c violet & multi	.25	.25
388	A55	$1 multicolored	.35	.35
a.		Souvenir sheet of 3, #386-388	.50	*.50*
		Nos. 386-388 (3)	.85	.85

University of the West Indies, 25th anniv.

Dominica No. 1 and Map of Island A56

Designs: 1c, 50c, No. 8 and post horn. 2c, $1.20, No. 9 and coat of arms. 10c, Like ½c.

1974, May 4 Litho. *Perf. 14½*

389	A56	½c brt pur & multi	.25	.25
390	A56	1c salmon & multi	.25	.25
391	A56	2c ultra & multi	.25	.25
392	A56	10c violet & multi	.25	.25
393	A56	50c yel grn & multi	.40	.40
394	A56	$1.20 rose & multi	.65	.65
a.		Souv. sheet, #392-394, perf. 15	1.60	1.60
		Nos. 389-394 (6)	2.05	2.05

Centenary of Dominican postage stamps.

Soccer Player and Cup, Brazilian Flag — A57

Soccer cup, various players and flags.

1974, July Litho. *Perf. 14½*

395	A57	½c shown	.25	.25
396	A57	1c Germany, Fed. Rep.	.25	.25
397	A57	2c Italy	.25	.25
398	A57	30c Scotland	.25	.25
399	A57	40c Sweden	.30	.30
400	A57	50c Netherlands	.75	.75
401	A57	$1 Yugoslavia	1.10	1.10
a.		Souvenir sheet of 2, #400-401, perf. 13½	1.25	1.25
		Nos. 395-401 (7)	3.15	3.15

World Cup Soccer Championship, Munich, June 13-July 7.

Indian Hole A58

40c, Teachers' Training College. $1, Petite Savane Co-operative Bay Oil Distillery.

1974, Nov. 1 Litho. *Perf. 13½x14*

402	A58	10c multicolored	.25	.25
403	A58	40c multicolored	.25	.25
404	A58	$1 multicolored	.50	.50
a.		Souvenir sheet of 3, #402-404	.80	.80
		Nos. 402-404 (3)	1.00	1.00

Churchill at Race Track A59

Sir Winston Churchill (1874-1965): 1c, with Gen. Eisenhower. 2c, with Franklin D. Roosevelt. 20c, as First Lord of the Admiralty. 45c, painting outdoors. $2, giving "V" sign.

1974, Nov. 25 Litho. *Perf. 14½*

405	A59	½c multicolored	.25	.25
406	A59	1c multicolored	.25	.25
407	A59	2c multicolored	.25	.25
408	A59	20c multicolored	.25	.25
409	A59	45c multicolored	.25	.25
410	A59	$2 multicolored	.50	.50
a.		Souvenir sheet of 2, #409-410, perf. 13½	1.25	1.25
		Nos. 405-410 (6)	1.75	1.75

Virgin and Child, by Oronzo Tiso — A60

Paintings (Virgin and Child): 1c, by Lorenzo Costa. 2c, by unknown Master. 10c, by G. F. Romanelli. 25c, Holy Family, by G. S. da Sermoneta. 45c, Adoration of the Shepherds, by Guido Reni. $1, Adoration of the Kings, by Cristoforo Caselli.

1974, Dec. 16 Litho. *Perf. 14*

411	A60	½c multicolored	.25	.25
412	A60	1c multicolored	.25	.25
413	A60	2c multicolored	.25	.25
414	A60	10c multicolored	.25	.25
415	A60	25c multicolored	.25	.25
416	A60	45c multicolored	.35	.25
417	A60	$1 multicolored	.65	.50
a.		Souvenir sheet of 2, #416-417	1.10	1.10
		Nos. 411-417 (7)	2.25	2.00

Christmas.

Seamail, "Orinoco," 1851, and "Geesthaven," 1966 — A61

Cent. of UPU: $2, $2.40, Airmail, De Havilland 4, 1918, and Boeing 747, 1974.

1974, Dec. 4 Litho. *Perf. 13½*

418	A61	10c multicolored	.25	.25
419	A61	$2 multicolored	1.25	1.25

Souvenir Sheet

419A		Sheet of 2	1.50	1.50
b.		A61 $1.20 multicolored	.45	.45
c.		A61 $2.40 multicolored	.90	.90

Nos. 418-419 were each printed in sheets of 50 and 5 + label.

Oldwife A62

1975, June 2 Litho. *Perf. 14½*

421	A62	½c shown	.25	.25
422	A62	1c Ocyurus chrysurus	.25	.25
423	A62	2c Blue marlin	.25	.25
424	A62	3c Swordfish	.25	.25
425	A62	20c Great barracuda	.90	.90
426	A62	$2 Grouper	2.75	2.75
a.		Souvenir sheet, perf. 13½	4.00	4.00
		Nos. 421-426 (6)	4.65	4.65

Myscelia Antholia A63

Designs: Butterflies.

1975, July 28 Litho. *Perf. 14½*

427	A63	½c shown	.25	.25
428	A63	1c Lycorea ceres	.25	.25
429	A63	2c Siderone nemesis	.25	.25
430	A63	6c Battus polydamas	.75	.75
431	A63	30c Anartia lytrea	1.50	1.00
432	A63	40c Morpho peleides	1.50	1.00
433	A63	$2 Dryas julia	2.25	*6.75*
a.		Souvenir sheet, perf. 13½	4.00	4.00
		Nos. 427-433 (7)	6.75	10.25

Royal Mail Ship Yare A64

Ships Tied in with Dominican History: 1c, Royal mail ship Thames. 2c, Canadian National S.S. Lady Nelson. 20c, C.N. S.S. Lady Rodney. 45c, Harrison Line M.V. Statesman. 50c, Geest Line M.V. Geestcape. $2, Geest Line M.V. Geeststar.

1975, Sept. 1 *Perf. 14*

434	A64	½c black & multi	.40	.35
435	A64	1c black & multi	.40	.35
436	A64	2c black & multi	.45	.40
437	A64	20c black & multi	1.25	.60
438	A64	45c black & multi	1.50	.80
439	A64	50c black & multi	1.50	1.00
440	A64	$2 black & multi	2.50	*4.50*
a.		Souvenir sheet of 2, #439-440	4.00	4.00
		Nos. 434-440 (7)	8.00	8.00

IWY Emblem, Farm Women A65

$2, IWY emblem, dressmaker & saleswoman.

1975, Oct. 30 Litho. *Perf. 14*

441	A65	10c pink & multi	.25	.25
442	A65	$2 yellow & multi	.65	.65

International Women's Year.

Public Library — A66

5c, Miss Caribbean Queen 1975. 30c, Citrus factory. $1, National Day Cup.

1975, Nov. 6

443	A66	5c multi, vert.	.25	.25
444	A66	10c multi	.25	.25
445	A66	30c multi	.25	.25
446	A66	$1 multi, vert.	.40	.40
a.		Souvenir sheet of 3	.90	.90
		Nos. 443-446 (4)	1.15	1.15

National Day. No. 446a contains 3 stamps similar to Nos. 444-446 with simulated perforations.

Virgin and Child, by Mantegna — A67

Christmas: Paintings of the Virgin and Child.

1975, Nov. 24

447	A67	½c shown	.25	.25
448	A67	1c Fra Filippo Lippi	.25	.25
449	A67	2c Bellini	.25	.25
450	A67	10c Botticelli	.25	.25
451	A67	25c Bellini	.25	.25
452	A67	45c Correggio	.25	.25
453	A67	$1 Durer	.50	.50
a.		Souvenir sheet of 2, #452-453	1.25	1.25
		Nos. 447-453 (7)	2.00	2.00

Hibiscus A68

Queen Elizabeth II — A69

Designs: 1c, African tulip. 2c, Castor oil tree. 3c, White cedar flower. 4c, Eggplant. 5c, Garfish. 6c, Okra. 8c, Zenaida doves. 10c, Screw pine. 20c, Mangoes. 25c, Crayfish. 30c, Manicou. 40c, Bay leaf groves. 50c, Tomatoes. $1, Lime factory. $2, Rum distillery. $5, Bay oil distillery.

1975, Dec. 8 Litho. *Perf. 14½*

454	A68	½c ultra & multi	.25	*.80*
455	A68	1c lilac & multi	.25	*.80*
456	A68	2c orange & multi	.25	*.80*
457	A68	3c multicolored	.25	*.80*
458	A68	4c pink & multi	.25	*.80*
459	A68	5c multicolored	.25	*.80*
460	A68	6c gray & multi	.25	*1.00*
461	A68	8c multicolored	3.25	1.10
462	A68	10c violet & multi	.25	.25
a.		Perf. 13½	30.00	—
463	A68	20c yellow & multi	.35	.25
464	A68	25c lemon & multi	.40	.25
465	A68	30c salmon & multi	.85	.80
466	A68	40c multicolored	.85	.80
467	A68	50c red & multi	.50	.50
468	A68	$1 citron & multi	.75	.65
469	A68	$2 multicolored	1.30	*3.25*
470	A68	$5 multicolored	1.60	*5.00*

Perf. 14

471	A69	$10 blue & multi	2.25	*14.50*
		Nos. 454-471 (18)	14.10	*33.15*

For overprints see Nos. 584-601, 640-643.
All except 3c and 25c exist imperf.

American Infantry — A70

Designs: 1c, English three-decker, 1782. 2c, George Washington. 45c, English sailors. 75c, English ensign with regimental flag. $2, Admiral Hood. All designs have old maps in background.

1976, Apr. 12 Litho. *Perf. 14½*

472	A70	½c green & multi	.25	.25
473	A70	1c purple & multi	.25	.25
474	A70	2c orange & multi	.25	.25
475	A70	45c brown & multi	.45	.25
476	A70	75c ultra & multi	.75	.75
477	A70	$2 red & multi	.90	*1.50*
a.		Souvenir sheet of 2	2.75	2.75
		Nos. 472-477 (6)	2.85	3.25

American Bicentennial. No. 477a contains 2 stamps similar to Nos. 476-477, perf. 13.

Rowing — A71

1c, Shot put. 2c, Swimming. 40c, Relay race. 45c, Gymnastics. 60c, Sailing. $2, Archery.

1976, May 24 Litho. *Perf. 14½*

478	A71	½c ocher & multi	.25	.25
479	A71	1c ocher & multi	.25	.25
480	A71	2c ocher & multi	.25	.25
481	A71	40c ocher & multi	.25	.25
482	A71	45c ocher & multi	.25	.25
483	A71	60c ocher & multi	.25	.25
484	A71	$2 ocher & multi	.65	.65
a.		Souv. sheet, #483-484, perf 13	1.75	1.75
		Nos. 478-484 (7)	2.15	2.15

21st Olympic Games, Montreal, Canada, July 17-Aug. 1.

Ringed Kingfisher A72

Birds: 1c, Mourning dove. 2c, Green heron. 15c, Broad-winged hawk. 30c, Blue-headed hummingbird. 45c, Banana-quit. $2, Imperial parrot. 15c, 30c, 45c, $2, vert.

1976, June 28

485	A72	½c multicolored	.25	.25
486	A72	1c multicolored	.25	.25
487	A72	2c multicolored	.25	.25
488	A72	15c multicolored	.90	.90
489	A72	30c multicolored	1.25	1.25
490	A72	45c multicolored	1.50	1.50
491	A72	$2 multicolored	3.00	3.00
a.		Souv. sheet of 3, #489-491, perf. 13	7.00	7.00
		Nos. 485-491 (7)	7.40	7.40

Map of West Indies, Bats, Wicket and Ball A72a

Prudential Cup — A72b

1976, July 26 Litho. *Perf. 14*

492	A72a	15c lt blue & multi	.45	.45
493	A72b	25c lilac rose & black	.85	.85

World Cricket Cup, won by West Indies Team, 1975.

Viking Spacecraft — A73

Virgin and Child, by Giorgione — A74

1c, Titan launch center, horiz. 2c, Titan 3-D & Centaur D-IT. 3c, Orbiter & landing capsule. 45c, Capsule with closed parachute. 75c, Capsule with open parachute. $1, Landing capsule descending on Mars, horiz. $2, Viking on Mars, horiz.

1976, Sept. 20 Litho. *Perf. 15*

494	A73	½c multicolored	.25	.25
495	A73	1c multicolored	.25	.25
496	A73	2c multicolored	.25	.25
497	A73	3c multicolored	.25	.25
498	A73	45c multicolored	.25	.25
499	A73	75c multicolored	.30	.30
500	A73	$1 multicolored	.35	.35
501	A73	$2 multicolored	.60	.60
a.		Souvenir sheet of 2, #500, 501, perf. 13½	1.75	1.75
		Nos. 494-501 (8)	2.50	2.50

Viking mission to Mars.

1976, Nov. 1 Litho. *Perf. 14*

Virgin and Child by: 1c, Bellini. 2c, Mantegna. 6c, Mantegna. 25c, Memling. 45c, 50c, Correggio. $1, $3, Raphael.

502	A74	½c multicolored	.25	.25
503	A74	1c multicolored	.25	.25
504	A74	2c multicolored	.25	.25
505	A74	6c multicolored	.25	.25
506	A74	25c multicolored	.25	.25
507	A74	45c multicolored	.25	.25
508	A74	$3 multicolored	.60	.60
		Nos. 502-508 (7)	2.10	2.10

Souvenir Sheet

509		Sheet of 2	1.10	1.10
a.	A74	50c multicolored	.35	.35
b.	A74	$1 multicolored	.75	.75

Christmas.

Island Craft Co-operative — A75

National Day: 50c, Banana harvest, Castle Bruce Co-operative. $1, Banana shipping plant, Bourne Farmers' Co-operative.

1976, Nov. 22 Litho. *Perf. 13½x14*

510	A75	10c multicolored	.25	.25
511	A75	50c multicolored	.25	.25
512	A75	$1 multicolored	.30	.30
a.		Souvenir sheet of 3, #510-512	.75	.75
		Nos. 510-512 (3)	.80	.80

Common Sundial — A76

Sea Shells: 1c, Flame helmet. 2c, Mouse cone. 20c, Caribbean vase. 40c, West Indian fighting conch. 50c, Short coral shell. $2, Long-spined star shell. $3, Apple murex.

1976, Dec. 20 Litho. *Perf. 14*

513	A76	½c black & multi	.25	.25
514	A76	1c black & multi	.25	.25
515	A76	2c black & multi	.25	.25
516	A76	20c black & multi	.30	.25
517	A76	40c black & multi	.55	.45
518	A76	50c black & multi	.60	.50
519	A76	$3 black & multi	2.25	2.25
		Nos. 513-519 (7)	4.45	4.20

Souvenir Sheet

520	A76	$2 black & multi	2.00	2.00

Queen Enthroned — A77

Designs: 1c, Imperial crown. 45c, Elizabeth II and Princess Anne. $2, Coronation ring. $2.50, Ampulla and spoon. $5, Royal visit to Dominica.

1977, Feb. 7 *Perf. 14*

521	A77	½c multicolored	.25	.25
522	A77	1c multicolored	.25	.25
523	A77	45c multicolored	.25	.25
524	A77	$2 multicolored	.35	.35
525	A77	$2.50 multicolored	.50	.50
		Nos. 521-525 (5)	1.60	1.60

Souvenir Sheet

526	A77	$5 multicolored	1.40	1.40

25th anniv. of the reign of Elizabeth II.
Nos. 521-525 were printed in sheets of 40 (4x10), perf. 14, and sheets of 5 plus label, perf. 12, in changed colors.
For overprints see Nos. 549-554.

Joseph Haydn — A78

Designs: 1c, Fidelio, act I, scene IV. 2c, Dancer Maria Casentini. 15c, Beethoven working on Pastoral Symphony. 30c, "Wellington's Victory." 40c, Soprano Henriette Sontag. $2, Young Beethoven.

1977, Apr. 25 Litho. *Perf. 14*

527	A78	½c multicolored	.25	.25
528	A78	1c multicolored	.25	.25
529	A78	2c multicolored	.25	.25
530	A78	15c multicolored	.50	.50
531	A78	30c multicolored	.50	.50
532	A78	40c multicolored	.50	.50
533	A78	$2 multicolored	1.60	1.60
a.		Souvenir sheet of 3, #531-533	2.60	2.60
		Nos. 527-533 (7)	3.85	3.85

Ludwig van Beethoven (1770-1827), composer.

Boy Scouts on Hike A79

Saluting Boy Scout and: 1c, First aid. 2c, Scouts setting up camp. 45c, Rock climbing. 50c, Kayaking. 75c, Map reading. $2, Campfire. $3, Sailing.

1977, Aug. 8 Litho. *Perf. 14*

534	A79	½c multicolored	.25	.25
535	A79	1c multicolored	.25	.25
536	A79	2c multicolored	.25	.25
537	A79	45c multicolored	.35	.35
538	A79	50c multicolored	.50	.50
539	A79	$3 multicolored	2.00	2.00
		Nos. 534-539 (6)	3.60	3.60

Souvenir Sheet

540		Sheet of 2	1.90	1.90
a.		A79 75c multicolored	.55	.55
b.		A79 $2 multicolored	1.35	1.35

6th Caribbean Jamboree, Kingston, Jamaica, Aug. 5-14.

Nativity A80

Christmas: 1c, Annunciation to the Shepherds. 2c, 45c, Presentation at the Temple (different). 6c, $2, $3, Flight into Egypt (different). 15c, Adoration of the Kings. 50c, Virgin and Child with Angels. ½c to 45c are illustrations from De Lisle Psalter, 14th century. 50c, $2, $3 are from other Psalters.

1977, Nov. 14 Litho. *Perf. 14*

541	A80	½c multicolored	.25	.25
542	A80	1c multicolored	.25	.25
543	A80	2c multicolored	.25	.25
544	A80	6c multicolored	.25	.25
545	A80	15c multicolored	.25	.25
546	A80	45c multicolored	.35	.35
547	A80	$3 multicolored	.85	.85
		Nos. 541-547 (7)	2.45	2.45

Souvenir Sheet

548		Sheet of 2	1.35	1.35
a.		A80 50c multicolored	.25	.25
b.		A80 $2 multicolored	1.10	1.10

Nos. 521-526 Overprinted

1977, Nov. 24 Litho. *Perf. 12, 14*

549	A77	½c multicolored	.25	.25
550	A77	1c multicolored	.25	.25
551	A77	45c multicolored	.25	.25
552	A77	$2 multicolored	.40	.40
553	A77	$2.50 multicolored	.45	.45
		Nos. 549-553 (5)	1.60	1.60

Souvenir Sheet

Perf. 14

554	A77	$5 multicolored	1.10	1.10

Caribbean visit of Queen Elizabeth II. Nos. 549-550 are perf. 12, others perf. 12 and 14.

Two types of No. 554: I. Overprinted only on stamp. II. Overprinted "W.I. 1977" on stamp and "Royal Visit W.I. 1977" on margin.

Masqueraders — A81

Designs: 1c, Sensay costume. 2c, Street musicians. 45c, Douiette band. 50c, Pappy Show wedding. $2, $2.50, Masquerade band.

1978, Jan. 9 *Perf. 14*

555	A81	½c multicolored	.25	.25
556	A81	1c multicolored	.25	.25
557	A81	2c multicolored	.25	.25
558	A81	45c multicolored	.25	.25
559	A81	50c multicolored	.30	.30
560	A81	$2 multicolored	.50	.50
		Nos. 555-560 (6)	1.80	1.80

Souvenir Sheet

561	A81	$2.50 multicolored	1.50	1.50

History of Carnival.

Lindbergh and Spirit of St. Louis A82

Designs: 10c, Spirit of St. Louis take-off, Long Island, May 20, 1927. 15c, Lindbergh and map of route New York to Paris. 20c, Lindbergh and plane in Paris. 40c, 1st Zeppelin, trial over Lake Constance. 50c, Spirit of St. Louis. 60c, Count Zeppelin and Zeppelin LZ-2, 1906. $2, Graf Zeppelin, 1928. $3, LZ-127, 1928.

1978, Mar. 13 **Litho.** *Perf. 14½*

562	A82	6c multicolored	.25	.25
563	A82	10c multicolored	.25	.25
564	A82	15c multicolored	.30	.30
565	A82	20c multicolored	.40	.40
566	A82	40c multicolored	.60	.60
567	A82	60c multicolored	.85	.85
568	A82	$3 multicolored	2.25	2.25
		Nos. 562-568 (7)	4.90	4.90

Souvenir Sheet

569		Sheet of 2	2.00	2.00
a.		A82 50c multicolored	.40	.40
b.		A82 $2 multicolored	1.60	1.60

Charles A. Lindbergh's solo transatlantic flight from New York to Paris, 50th anniv., and flights of Graf Zeppelin.

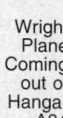

Royal Family on Balcony — A83

Designs: 45c, Coronation. $2.50, Elizabeth II and Prince Philip. $5, Elizabeth II.

1978, June 2 **Litho.** *Perf. 14*

570	A83	45c multicolored	.25	.25
571	A83	$2 multicolored	.45	.45
572	A83	$2.50 multicolored	.55	.55
		Nos. 570-572 (3)	1.25	1.25

Souvenir Sheet

573	A83	$5 multicolored	1.00	1.00

Coronation of Queen Elizabeth II, 25th anniv. Nos. 570-572 were issued in sheets of 50, and in sheets of 3 stamps and label, in changed colors, perf. 12.

Wright Plane Coming out of Hangar A84

Designs: 40c, 1908 plane. 60c, Flyer I gliding. $2, Flyer I taking off. $3, Wilbur and Orville Wright and Flyer I.

1978, July 10 **Litho.** *Perf. 14½*

574	A84	30c multicolored	.25	.25
575	A84	40c multicolored	.25	.25
576	A84	60c multicolored	.30	.30
577	A84	$2 multicolored	1.25	1.25
		Nos. 574-577 (4)	2.05	2.05

Souvenir Sheet

578	A84	$3 multicolored	1.75	1.75

75th anniv. of first powered flight.

A set of 30 stamps embossed on gold foil exists. Value, $400.

Two Apostles, by Rubens — A85

Rubens Paintings: 45c, Descent from the Cross. 50c, St. Ildefonso Receiving Chasuble. $2, Holy Family. $3, Assumption of the Virgin.

1978, Oct. 16 **Litho.** *Perf. 14*

579	A85	20c multicolored	.25	.25
580	A85	45c multicolored	.25	.25
581	A85	50c multicolored	.25	.25
582	A85	$2 multicolored	.90	.90
		Nos. 579-582 (4)	1.65	1.65

Souvenir Sheet

583	A85	$2 multicolored	1.00	1.00

Christmas.

Nos. 454-471 Overprinted

1978 Nov. 1 **Litho.** *Perf. 14½*

584	A68	½c ultra & multi	.25	.25
585	A68	1c lilac & multi	.25	.25
586	A68	2c orange & multi	.30	.25
587	A68	3c multicolored	.30	.25
588	A68	4c pink & multi	.30	.25
589	A68	5c multicolored	.30	.25
590	A68	6c gray & multi	.35	.25
591	A68	8c multicolored	3.00	.25
592	A68	10c violet & multi	1.00	.25
a.		Perf. 13½ ('79)	.50	.25
593	A68	20c yellow & multi	.60	.25
594	A68	25c lemon & multi	.65	.25
595	A68	30c salmon & multi	.70	.30
596	A68	40c multicolored	.70	.55
597	A68	50c red & multi	.75	.75
598	A68	$1 citron & multi	.80	1.40
599	A68	$2 multicolored	1.50	2.75
600	A68	$5 multicolored	2.00	5.50

Perf. 14

601	A69	$10 blue & multi	3.00	12.50
		Nos. 584-601 (18)	16.75	26.50

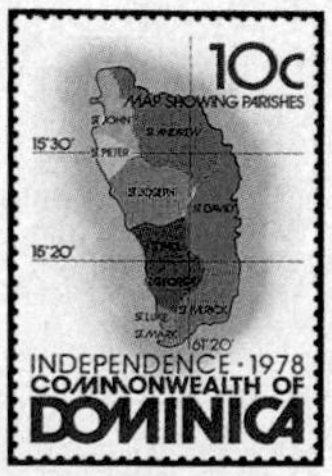

Map of Dominica with Parishes — A86

25c, Sabinea carinalis, natl. flower, & map. 45c, New flag & map. 50c, Coat of arms & map. $2, Prime Minister Patrick John.

1978, Nov. 1 *Perf. 14*

602	A86	10c multicolored	.75	.40
603	A86	25c multicolored	.55	.25
604	A86	45c multicolored	1.50	.35
605	A86	50c multicolored	.65	.35
606	A86	$2 multicolored	1.50	*2.75*
		Nos. 602-606 (5)	4.95	4.10

Souvenir Sheet

607	A86	$2.50 multicolored	2.60	2.60

Dominican independence.

Rowland Hill — A87

45c, Great Britain #2. 50c, Dominica #1. $2, Maltese Cross handstamps. $5, Penny Black.

1979, Mar. 19

608	A87	25c multicolored	.25	.25
609	A87	45c multicolored	.25	.25
610	A87	50c multicolored	.25	.25
611	A87	$2 multicolored	.35	.35
		Nos. 608-611 (4)	1.10	1.10

Souvenir Sheet

612	A87	$5 multicolored	1.40	1.40

Sir Rowland Hill (1795-1879), originator of penny postage.

Nos. 608-611 printed in sheets of 5 plus label, perf. 12x12½, in changed colors.

For overprints see Nos. 663A-663D.

Boys and Dugout Canoe A88

IYC Emblem and: 40c, Children carrying bananas. 50c, Boys playing cricket. $3, Child feeding rabbits. $5, Boy showing catch of fish.

1979, Apr. 23 **Litho.** *Perf. 14*

613	A88	30c multicolored	.30	.30
614	A88	40c multicolored	.45	.45
615	A88	50c multicolored	.50	.50
616	A88	$3 multicolored	2.00	2.00
		Nos. 613-616 (4)	3.25	3.25

Souvenir Sheet

617	A88	$5 multicolored	2.00	2.00

Grouper A89

30c, Striped dolphin. 50c, White-tailed tropic birds. 60c, Brown pelicans. $1, Pilot whale. $2, Brown booby. $3, Elkhorn coral.

1979, May 21 **Litho.** *Perf. 14*

618	A89	10c multicolored	.50	.25
619	A89	30c multicolored	1.00	.50
620	A89	50c multicolored	1.75	.75
621	A89	60c multicolored	2.00	2.00
622	A89	$1 multicolored	2.50	2.50
623	A89	$2 multicolored	4.25	4.25
		Nos. 618-623 (6)	12.00	10.25

Souvenir Sheet

624	A89	$3 multicolored	2.75	2.75

Wildlife protection.

Capt. Cook, Bark Endeavour — A90

Capt. Cook and: 50c, Resolution, map of 2nd voyage. 60c, Discovery, map of 3rd voyage. $2, Cook's map of New Zealand, 1770. $5, Portrait.

1979, July 16 **Litho.** *Perf. 14*

625	A90	10c multicolored	.60	.40
626	A90	50c multicolored	1.00	1.00
627	A90	60c multicolored	1.25	1.25
628	A90	$2 multicolored	1.50	*2.50*
		Nos. 625-628 (4)	4.35	5.15

Souvenir Sheet

629	A90	$5 multicolored	2.00	2.00

200th death anniv. of Capt. James Cook (1728-1779).

Girl Guides Cooking A91

Girl Guides: 20c, Setting up emergency rain tent. 50c, Raising flag of independent Dominica. $2.50, Playing accordion and singing. $3, Leader and Guides of different ages.

1979, July 30

630	A91	10c multicolored	.25	.25
631	A91	20c multicolored	.25	.25
632	A91	50c multicolored	.30	.30
633	A91	$2.50 multicolored	1.25	1.25
		Nos. 630-633 (4)	2.05	2.05

Souvenir Sheet

634	A91	$3 multicolored	1.50	1.50

50th anniv. of Dominican Girl Guides.

Colvillea — A92

Flowering Trees: 40c, Lignum vitae. 60c, Dwarf poinciana. $2, Fern tree. $3, Perfume tree.

1979, Sept. 3 **Litho.** *Perf. 14*

635	A92	20c multicolored	.25	.25
636	A92	40c multicolored	.25	.25
637	A92	60c multicolored	.35	.35
638	A92	$2 multicolored	.90	.90
		Nos. 635-638 (4)	1.75	1.75

Souvenir Sheet

639	A92	$3 multicolored	1.75	1.75

Nos. 459, 466, 470-471 Overprinted

Perf. 14½, 13½, 13½x14, 14

1979, Oct. 29 **Litho.**

640	A68	5c multicolored	.25	.25
641	A68	40c multicolored	.30	.30
642	A68	$5 multicolored	2.00	2.00
643	A68	$10 multicolored	3.50	3.50
		Nos. 640-643 (4)	6.05	6.05

Hurricane devastation, Aug. 29. Vertical overprint on No. 643, others horizontal.

Music Scenes A92a

1979, Nov. 2 Litho. *Perf. 11*

644	A92a	½c	Mickey Mouse	.25	.25
645	A92a	1c	Goofy playing guitar	.25	.25
646	A92a	2c	Mickey Mouse and Goofy	.25	.25
647	A92a	3c	Donald Duck	.25	.25
648	A92a	4c	Minnie Mouse	.25	.25
649	A92a	5c	Goofy playing accordion	.25	.25
650	A92a	10c	Horace Horsecollar and Dale	.25	.25
651	A92a	$2	Huey, Dewey, Louie	1.50	1.50
652	A92a	$2.50	Donald and Huey	1.50	1.50
			Nos. 644-652 (9)	4.75	4.75

Souvenir Sheet

Perf. 13

653	A92a	$3	Mickey Mouse playing piano	3.25	3.25

Cathedral of the Assumption — A93

Cathedrals: 40c, St. Patrick's, New York. 45c, St. Paul's, London, vert. 60c, St. Peter's, Rome. $2, Cologne Cathedral. $3, Notre Dame, Paris, vert.

1979, Nov. 26 Litho. *Perf. 14*

654	A93	6c	multicolored	.25	.25
655	A93	45c	multicolored	.25	.25
656	A93	60c	multicolored	.25	.25
657	A93	$3	multicolored	.90	.90
			Nos. 654-657 (4)	1.65	1.65

Souvenir Sheet

658		Sheet of 2	.80	.80
a.	A93 40c multicolored		.25	.25
b.	A93 $2 multicolored		.55	.55

Christmas.

Nurse and Patients, Rotary Emblem A94

1980, Mar. 31 Litho. *Perf. 14*

659	A94	10c	shown	.25	.25
660	A94	20c	Electrocardiogram machine	.25	.25
661	A94	40c	Mental hospital	.25	.25
662	A94	$2.50	Paul Harris, founder	.75	.75
			Nos. 659-662 (4)	1.50	1.50

Souvenir Sheet

663	A94	$3	Map of Africa and Europe	1.25	1.25

Rotary International, 75th anniv. Nos. 659-662 each contain quadrant of Rotary emblem.

Nos. 608-611 Overprinted in Black

1980, May 6 Litho. *Perf. 12*

663A	A87	25c	multicolored	.35	.35
663B	A87	45c	multicolored	.55	.55
663C	A87	50c	multicolored	.60	.60
663D	A87	$2	multicolored	1.50	1.50
			Nos. 663A-663D (4)	3.00	3.00

London 80 Intl. Stamp Exhib., May 6-14.

Shot Put, Moscow '80 Emblem A95

1980, May 27 Litho. *Perf. 14*

664	A95	30c	shown	.25	.25
665	A95	40c	Basketball	.60	.30
666	A95	60c	Swimming	.40	.40
667	A95	$2	Gymnast	.70	.70
			Nos. 664-667 (4)	1.95	1.65

Souvenir Sheet

668	A95	$3	Running	1.25	1.25

22nd Summer Olympic Games, Moscow, July 19-Aug. 3.

Embarkation for Cythera, by Watteau — A96

Paintings: 20c, Supper at Emmaus, by Caravaggio. 25c, Charles I Hunting, by Van Dyck, vert. 30c, The Maids of Honor, by Velazquez, vert. 45c, Rape of the Sabine Women, by Poussin. $1, Embarkation for Cythera, by Watteau. $3, Holy Family, by Rembrandt. $5, Girl before a Mirror, by Picasso, vert.

Perf. 14x13½, 13½x14

1980, July 22 Litho.

669	A96	20c	multicolored	.25	.25
670	A96	25c	multicolored	.25	.25
671	A96	30c	multicolored	.25	.25
672	A96	45c	multicolored	.25	.25
673	A96	$1	multicolored	.40	.40
674	A96	$5	multicolored	1.50	1.50
			Nos. 669-674 (6)	2.90	2.90

Souvenir Sheet

675	A96	$3	multicolored	1.10	1.10

Queen Mother Elizabeth, 80th Birthday A97

1980, Aug. 4 *Perf. 12, 14*

676	A97	40c	multicolored	.25	.25
677	A97	$2.50	multicolored	.50	.50

Souvenir Sheet

678	A97	$3	multicolored	.75	.75

Tinkerbell — A98

Designs: Scenes from Disney's Peter Pan.

1980, Oct. 1 Litho. *Perf. 11*

679	A98	½c	multicolored	.25	.25
680	A98	1c	multicolored	.25	.25
681	A98	2c	multicolored	.25	.25
682	A98	3c	multicolored	.25	.25
683	A98	4c	multicolored	.25	.25
684	A98	5c	multicolored	.25	.25
685	A98	10c	multicolored	.25	.25
686	A98	$2	multicolored	2.25	1.60
687	A98	$2.50	multicolored	2.25	1.75
			Nos. 679-687 (9)	6.25	5.10

Souvenir Sheet

688	A98	$4	multicolored	5.00	5.00

Christmas.

Douglas Bay A99

1981, Feb. 12 Litho. *Perf. 14*

689	A99	20c	shown	.25	.25
690	A99	30c	Valley of Desolation	.25	.25
691	A99	40c	Emerald Pool, vert.	.25	.25
692	A99	$3	Indian River, vert.	.70	.70
			Nos. 689-692 (4)	1.45	1.45

Souvenir Sheet

693	A99	$4	Trafalgar Falls	1.40	1.40

Pluto and Fifi — A100

$4, Pluto in Blue Note (1947 cartoon).

1981, Apr. 30 Litho. *Perf. 13½x14*

694	A100	$2	multicolored	1.75	1.75

Souvenir Sheet

695	A100	$4	multicolored	2.75	2.75

50th anniversary of Walt Disney's Pluto.

Forest Thrush A101

1981, Apr. 30 *Perf. 14*

696	A101	20c	shown	.60	.25
697	A101	30c	Stolid flycatcher	.70	.35
698	A101	40c	Blue-hooded euphonia	.80	.45
699	A101	$5	Lesser antillean peewee	4.75	4.75
			Nos. 696-699 (4)	6.85	5.80

Souvenir Sheet

700	A101	$3	Sisserou parrot	3.75	3.75

Royal Wedding Issue

Common Design Type

1981, June 16 Litho. *Perf. 14*

701	CD331a	45c	Couple	.25	.25
702	CD331a	60c	Windsor Castle	.25	.25
703	CD331a	$4	Charles	.60	.60
			Nos. 701-703 (3)	1.10	1.10

Souvenir Sheet

704	CD331	$5	Helicopter	1.25	1.25

Booklet

705	CD331		6.00	
a.	Pane of 6 (3x25c, Lady Diana, 3x$2, Charles)		2.25	*4.50*
b.	Pane of 1, $5, Couple		3.00	*3.50*

No. 705 contains imperf., self-adhesive stamps.

Nos. 701-703 also printed in sheets of 5 plus label, perf. 12, in changed colors. Value, set of three sheets $10.

Elves Repairing Santa's Sleigh — A102

Christmas: Scenes from Walt Disney's Santa's Workshop.

1981, Nov. 2 Litho. *Perf. 14*

706	A102	½c	multicolored	.25	.25
707	A102	1c	multicolored	.25	.25
708	A102	2c	multicolored	.25	.25
709	A102	3c	multicolored	.25	.25
710	A102	4c	multicolored	.25	.25
711	A102	5c	multicolored	.25	.25
712	A102	10c	multicolored	.25	.25
713	A102	45c	multicolored	2.00	.40
714	A102	$5	multicolored	4.00	*5.50*
			Nos. 706-714 (9)	7.75	7.65

Souvenir Sheet

715	A102	$4	multicolored	5.75	5.75

Ixora A103

1981, Dec. 1 Litho. *Perf. 14*

716	A103	1c	shown	.25	.90
717	A103	2c	Flamboyant	.25	.90
718	A103	4c	Poinsettia	.25	.90
719	A103	5c	Sabinea carinalis	.25	.60
720	A103	8c	Annatto roucou	.25	.90
721	A103	10c	Passion fruit	.30	.25
722	A103	15c	Breadfruit	.50	.50
723	A103	20c	Allamanda buttercup	.35	.25
724	A103	25c	Cashew	.40	.25
725	A103	35c	Soursop	.45	.40
726	A103	40c	Bougainvillea	.45	.65
727	A103	45c	Anthurium	.50	.70
728	A103	60c	Cacao	1.00	.95
729	A103	90c	Pawpaw tree	.75	1.40
730	A103	$1	Coconut palm	2.00	1.50
731	A103	$2	Coffee tree	1.50	3.00
732	A103	$5	Lobster claw	2.00	*7.00*
c.			Perf. 12½x12 ('85)	3.25	*5.00*
733	A103	$10	Banana fig	3.50	*13.00*
			Nos. 716-733 (18)	14.95	34.05

For overprints see Nos. 852-853.

1984 Inscribed "1984" *Perf. 12*

721a	A103	10c		1.75	.40
730a	A103	$1		2.50	*3.00*
732a	A103	$5		3.25	*5.00*
733a	A103	$10		5.25	*10.00*
			Nos. 721a-733a (4)	12.75	*18.40*

1985 Inscribed "1985" *Perf. 14*

721b	A103	10c		1.00	.65
722b	A103	15c	Breadfruit	4.00	2.00
728b	A103	60c	Cacao	5.00	3.50
732b	A103	$5	Lobster claw	3.25	*5.00*
			Nos. 721b-732b (4)	13.25	11.15

Intl. Year of the Disabled — A104

Bathers, by Picasso — A105

1981, Dec. 22 Litho. *Perf. 14*

734	A104	45c	Ramp curb	.45	.30
735	A104	60c	Bus steps	.55	.40
736	A104	75c	Hand-operated car	.65	.50
737	A104	$4	Bus lift	2.00	*2.40*
			Nos. 734-737 (4)	3.65	3.60

Souvenir Sheet

738	A104	$5	Elevator buttons	5.00	5.00

1981, Dec. 30 *Perf. 14½*

739	A105	45c	Olga in Armchair	.30	.30
740	A105	60c	shown	.40	.40
741	A105	75c	Woman in Spanish Costume	.50	.50
742	A105	$4	Dog and Cock	2.25	2.25
			Nos. 739-742 (4)	3.45	3.45

Souvenir Sheet

743	A105	$5	Sleeping Peasants	4.00	4.00

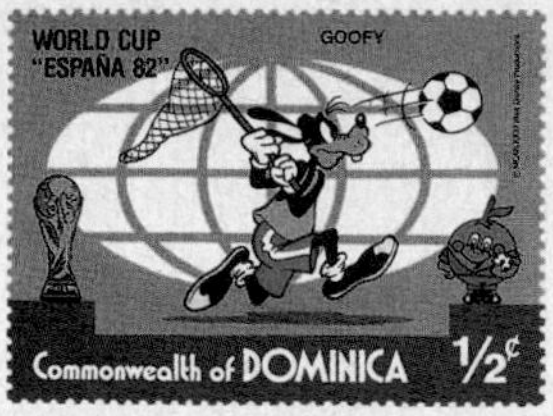

1982 World Cup Soccer — A106

Various Disney characters playing soccer.

1982, Jan. 29 *Perf. 14*

744 A106 ½c multicolored .25 .25
745 A106 1c multicolored .25 .25
746 A106 2c multicolored .25 .25
747 A106 3c multicolored .25 .25
748 A106 4c multicolored .25 .25
749 A106 5c multicolored .25 .25
750 A106 10c multicolored .25 .25
751 A106 60c multicolored 1.25 1.25
752 A106 $5 multicolored 6.25 6.25
Nos. 744-752 (9) 9.25 9.25

Souvenir Sheet

753 A106 $4 multicolored 5.75 5.75

Golden Days, by Norman Rockwell A107

1982, Mar. 10 Litho. *Perf. 14x13½*

754 A107 10c shown .25 .25
755 A107 25c The Morning News .25 .25
756 A107 45c The Marbles Champ .30 .30
757 A107 $1 Speeding Along .55 .55
Nos. 754-757 (4) 1.35 1.35

Intl. Decade for Women (1975-85) A108

Famous Women: 10c, Elma Napier (1890-1973), first woman elected to Legislative Council in British West Indies, 1940. 45c, Margaret Mead (1901-1978), anthropologist. $1, Mabel Caudiron (1909-1968), musician and folk historian. $3, Florence Nightingale, founder of modern nursing. $4, Eleanor Roosevelt.

1982, Apr. 15 Litho. *Perf. 14*

758 A108 10c multicolored .25 .25
759 A108 45c multicolored .35 .35
760 A108 $1 multicolored .60 .60
761 A108 $4 multicolored 2.50 2.50
Nos. 758-761 (4) 3.70 3.70

Souvenir Sheet

762 A108 $3 multicolored 3.00 3.00

George Washington and Independence Hall, Philadelphia — A109

Washington or Roosevelt and: 60c, Capitol Building. 90c, The Surrender of Cornwallis, by John Trumbull. $2, Dam construction during New Deal (mural by William Gropper). $5, Washington, Roosevelt.

1982, May 1 *Perf. 14½*

763 A109 45c multicolored .35 .35
764 A109 60c multicolored .40 .40
765 A109 90c multicolored .55 .55
766 A109 $2 multicolored 1.00 1.00
Nos. 763-766 (4) 2.30 2.30

Souvenir Sheet

767 A109 $5 multicolored 3.00 3.00

George Washington's 250th birth anniv. and Franklin D. Roosevelt's birth cent.

Godman's Leaf Butterfly — A110

1982, June 1 Litho. *Perf. 14*

768 A110 15c shown 1.75 1.75
769 A110 45c Zebra 2.75 2.75
770 A110 60c Mimic 3.00 3.00
771 A110 $3 Red rim 6.25 6.25
Nos. 768-771 (4) 13.75 13.75

Souvenir Sheet

772 A110 $5 Southern dagger tail 7.00 7.00

Princess Diana Issue

Common Design Type

1982, July 1 Litho. *Perf. 14½x14*

773 CD332 45c Buckingham Palace .30 .30
774 CD332 $2 Engagement portrait 1.00 1.00
775 CD332 $4 Wedding 2.25 2.25
Nos. 773-775 (3) 3.55 3.55

Souvenir Sheet

776 CD332 $5 Diana, diff. 3.50 3.50

Also issued in sheet of 5 plus label.
For overprints see Nos. 782-785.

Scouting Year A111

1982, July 1 Litho. *Perf. 14*

777 A111 45c Cooking 1.25 1.25
778 A111 60c Meteorological study 1.75 1.75
779 A111 75c Sisserou parrot, cub scouts 2.25 2.25
780 A111 $3 Canoeing, Indian River 5.25 5.25
Nos. 777-780 (4) 10.50 10.50

Souvenir Sheet

781 A111 $5 Flagbearer 3.50 3.50

Nos. 773-776 Overprinted

1982, Sept. 1 Litho. *Perf. 14½x14*

782 CD332 45c multicolored .30 .30
783 CD332 $2 multicolored 1.00 1.00
784 CD332 $4 multicolored 2.25 2.25
Nos. 782-784 (3) 3.55 3.55

Souvenir Sheet

785 CD332 $5 multicolored 3.50 3.50

Birth of Prince William of Wales, June 21.
Also issued in sheet of 5 plus label.

Christmas — A112

Holy Family Paintings by Raphael.

1982, Oct. 18 Litho. *Perf. 14*

786 A112 25c multicolored .25 .25
787 A112 30c multicolored .25 .25
788 A112 90c multicolored .40 .40
789 A112 $4 multicolored 1.75 1.75
Nos. 786-789 (4) 2.65 2.65

Souvenir Sheet

790 A112 $5 multicolored 3.50 3.50

Goosebeak Whale Eating Squid — A113

1983, Feb. 15 Litho. *Perf. 14*

791 A113 45c shown 1.75 1.75
792 A113 60c Humpback whale 2.00 2.00
793 A113 75c Great right whale 2.25 2.25
794 A113 $3 Melonhead whale 7.50 7.50
Nos. 791-794 (4) 13.50 13.50

Souvenir Sheet

795 A113 $5 Pygmy sperm whale 6.25 6.25

A113a

1983, Mar. 14

796 A113a 25c Banana industry .25 .25
797 A113a 30c Road construction .25 .25
798 A113a 90c Community nursing .40 .40
799 A113a $3 Basket weavers 1.25 1.25
Nos. 796-799 (4) 2.15 2.15

Commonwealth Day.

World Communications Year — A114

1983, Apr. 18 Litho. *Perf. 14*

800 A114 45c Hurricane pattern, map .30 .30
801 A114 60c Air-to-ship communication .35 .35
802 A114 90c Columbia shuttle, dish antenna .50 .50
803 A114 $2 Walkie-talkie 1.00 1.00
Nos. 800-803 (4) 2.15 2.15

Souvenir Sheet

804 A114 $5 Satellite 2.50 2.50

Manned Flight Bicentenary — A115

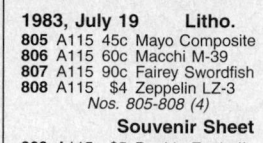

1983, July 19 Litho. *Perf. 15*

805 A115 45c Mayo Composite .50 .50
806 A115 60c Macchi M-39 .60 .60
807 A115 90c Fairey Swordfish .85 .85
808 A115 $4 Zeppelin LZ-3 3.00 3.00
Nos. 805-808 (4) 4.95 4.95

Souvenir Sheet

809 A115 $5 Double Eagle II, vert. 3.00 3.00

Duesenberg SJ, 1935 — A116

1983, Sept. 1 Litho. *Perf. 14*

810 A116 10c shown .35 .35
811 A116 45c Studebaker Avanti, 1962 .45 .45
812 A116 60c Cord 812, 1936 .50 .50
813 A116 75c MG-TC, 1945 .55 .55
814 A116 90c Camaro 350-SS, 1967 .60 .60
815 A116 $3 Porsche 356, 1948 1.75 1.75
Nos. 810-815 (6) 4.20 4.20

Souvenir Sheet

816 A116 $5 Ferrari 312-T, 1975 3.00 3.00

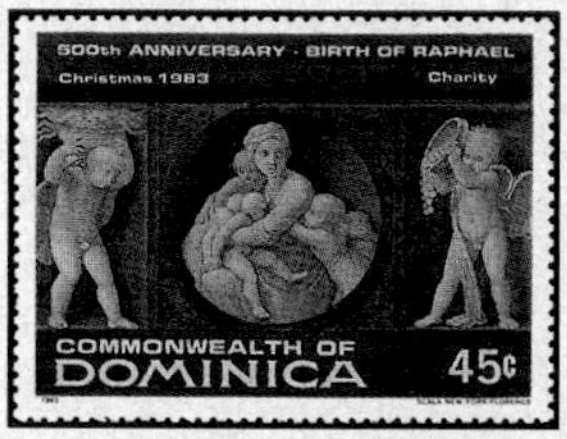

Christmas — A117

Raphael Paintings.

1983, Oct. 4 Litho. *Perf. 13½*

817 A117 45c multicolored .30 .30
818 A117 60c multicolored .35 .35
819 A117 90c multicolored .50 .50
820 A117 $4 multicolored 2.00 2.00
Nos. 817-820 (4) 3.15 3.15

Souvenir Sheet

821 A117 $5 multicolored 3.00 3.00

23rd Olympic Games, Los Angeles, July 28-Aug. 12 — A118

1984, Mar. Litho. *Perf. 14*

822 A118 30c Gymnastics .25 .25
823 A118 45c Javelin .35 .35
824 A118 60c Diving .45 .45
825 A118 $4 Fencing 2.50 2.50
Nos. 822-825 (4) 3.55 3.55

Souvenir Sheet

826 A118 $5 Equestrian 3.75 3.75

Local Birds A119

1984, May Litho.

827 A119 5c Plumbeous warbler 3.00 3.00
828 A119 45c Imperial parrot 7.00 7.00
829 A119 60c Blue-headed hummingbird 8.50 8.50
830 A119 90c Red-necked parrot 11.00 11.00
Nos. 827-830 (4) 29.50 29.50

Souvenir Sheet

831 A119 $5 Roseate flamingoes 9.00 9.00

Easter
A120

Various Disney characters and Easter bunnies.

1984, Apr. 15 **Litho.** ***Perf. 11***

832 A120 ½c multicolored .25 .25
833 A120 1c multicolored .25 .25
834 A120 2c multicolored .25 .25
835 A120 3c multicolored .25 .25
836 A120 4c multicolored .25 .25
837 A120 5c multicolored .25 .25
838 A120 10c multicolored .25 .25
839 A120 $2 multicolored 3.00 3.00
840 A120 $4 multicolored 6.25 6.25
Nos. 832-840 (9) 11.00 11.00

Souvenir Sheet
Perf. 14

841 A120 $5 multicolored 5.75 5.75

Ships
A121

1984, June 14 **Litho.** ***Perf. 14***

842 A121 45c Atlantic Star 1.75 1.75
843 A121 60c Atlantic 2.00 2.00
844 A121 90c Carib fishing pirogue 2.50 2.50
845 A121 $4 Norway 6.75 6.75
Nos. 842-845 (4) 13.00 13.00

Souvenir Sheet

846 A121 $5 Santa Maria 5.00 5.00

Local
Plants — A122

1984, Aug. 13

847 A122 45c Guzmania lingulata .40 .40
848 A122 60c Pitcairnia angustifolia .50 .50
849 A122 75c Tillandsia fasciculata .60 .60
850 A122 $3 Aechmea smithiorum 2.40 2.40
Nos. 847-850 (4) 3.90 3.90

Souvenir Sheet

851 A122 $5 Tillandsia utriculata 3.75 3.75

Ausipex Intl. Stamp Exhibition.

Nos. 721, 732 Overprinted

1984 **Litho.** ***Perf. 14***

852 A103 10c multicolored .25 .25
853 A103 $5 multicolored 4.00 4.00

Correggio &
Degas — A122a

Correggio: 25c, Virgin and Child with Young St. John. 60c, Christ Bids Farewell to the Virgin Mary. 90c, Do Not Touch Me. $4, The Mystical Marriage of St. Catherine. No. 862, Adoration of the Magi,

Degas, horiz.: 30c, Before the Start. 45c, On the Racecourse. $1, Jockeys at the Flagpole. $3, Racehorses at Longchamp. No. 863, Self-portrait.

1984, Nov. **Litho.** ***Perf. 15***

854 A122a 25c multicolored .35 .35
855 A122a 30c multicolored .40 .40
856 A122a 45c multicolored .45 .45
857 A122a 60c multicolored .50 .50
858 A122a 90c multicolored .65 .65
859 A122a $1 multicolored .75 .75
860 A122a $3 multicolored 1.75 1.75
861 A122a $4 multicolored 1.90 1.90
Nos. 854-861 (8) 6.75 6.75

Souvenir Sheets

862 A122a $5 multicolored 3.00 3.00
863 A122a $5 multicolored 3.00 3.00

A123

1984, Dec. ***Perf. 14***

864 A123 30c Avro 748 1.25 1.25
865 A123 60c Twin Otter 2.25 2.25
866 A123 $1 Islander 2.50 2.50
867 A123 $3 Casa 4.75 4.75
Nos. 864-867 (4) 10.75 10.75

Souvenir Sheet

868 A123 $5 Boeing 747 5.50 5.50

Intl. Civil Aviation Org., 40th anniv.

A124

Scenes from various Donald Duck movies.

1984, Nov. **Litho.**

869 A124 45c multicolored 1.25 1.25
870 A124 60c multicolored 1.50 1.50
871 A124 90c multicolored 2.00 2.00
872 A124 $2 multicolored, perf. 12x12½ 3.50 3.50
873 A124 $4 multicolored 5.75 5.75
Nos. 869-873 (5) 14.00 14.00

Souvenir Sheet
Perf. 13½x14

874 A124 $5 multicolored 5.50 5.50

Christmas and 50th anniv. of Donald Duck.

Cats
A125

1984, Nov. 12 **Litho.** ***Perf. 15***

875 A125 10c Tabby .25 .25
876 A125 15c Calico shorthair .25 .25
877 A125 20c Siamese .25 .25
878 A125 25c Manx .25 .25
879 A125 45c Abyssinian .40 .40
880 A125 60c Tortoise shell longhair .50 .50
881 A125 $1 Rex .75 .75
882 A125 $2 Persian 1.00 1.00
883 A125 $3 Himalayan 2.00 2.00
884 A125 $5 Burmese 3.50 3.50
Nos. 875-884 (10) 9.15 9.15

Souvenir Sheet

885 A125 $5 Gray Burmese, Persian, American shorthair 5.50 5.50

Girl
Guides,
75th
Anniv.
A126

1985, Feb. 18 ***Perf. 14***

886 A126 35c Lady Baden-Powell .60 .60
887 A126 45c Inspecting Dominican troop .70 .70
888 A126 60c With Dominican troop leaders .90 .90
889 A126 $3 Lord and Lady Baden-Powell, vert. 3.50 3.50
Nos. 886-889 (4) 5.70 5.70

Souvenir Sheet

890 A126 $5 Flag ceremony 5.50 5.50

John
James
Audubon
A127

1985, Apr. 4

891 A127 45c King rails 1.25 1.25
892 A127 $1 Black & white warbler, vert. 2.00 2.00
893 A127 $2 Broad-winged hawks, vert. 3.25 3.25
894 A127 $3 Ring-necked ducks 4.25 4.25
Nos. 891-894 (4) 10.75 10.75

Souvenir Sheet

895 A127 $5 Reddish egrets, vert. 5.50 5.50

Nos. 891-894 exist vertically se-tenant with labels showing additional bird species.

See Nos. 965-969.

Duke of Edinburgh
Awards,
1984 — A128

1985, Apr. 30

896 A128 45c Woman at computer terminal .50 .50
897 A128 60c Medical staff, patient 1.60 1.60
898 A128 90c Runners 2.00 2.00
899 A128 $4 Family jogging 3.25 3.25
Nos. 896-899 (4) 7.35 7.35

Souvenir Sheet

900 A128 $5 Duke of Edinburgh 4.00 4.00

Intl. Youth
Year
A129

1985, July 8 **Litho.** ***Perf. 14***

901 A129 45c Cricket match 3.00 2.00
902 A129 60c Environmental study, parrot 3.75 2.50
903 A129 $1 Stamp collecting 4.00 3.50
904 A129 $3 Boating, leisure 5.25 *7.50*
Nos. 901-904 (4) 16.00 15.50

Souvenir Sheet

905 A129 $5 Youths join hands 4.00 4.00

Queen Mother,
85th
Birthday — A130

60c, Visiting Sadlers Wells. $1, Fishing. $3, At Clarence House, 1984.

$5, Attending Windsor Castle Garter Ceremony.

1985, July 15

906 A130 60c multicolored 1.00 .75
907 A130 $1 multicolored 1.50 .75
908 A130 $3 multicolored 2.00 2.00
Nos. 906-908 (3) 4.50 3.50

Souvenir Sheet

909 A130 $5 multicolored 3.75 3.75

Johann Sebastian
Bach — A131

Portrait, signature, music from Explication and: 45c, Cornett 60c, Coiled trumpet. $1, Piccolo. $3, Violoncello piccolo.

1985, Sept. 2

910 A131 45c multicolored 1.00 1.00
911 A131 60c multicolored 1.50 1.50
912 A131 $1 multicolored 2.00 2.00
913 A131 $3 multicolored 4.25 4.25
Nos. 910-913 (4) 8.75 8.75

Souvenir Sheet

914 A131 $5 Portrait 4.00 4.00

State Visit of Elizabeth II,
Oct. 25 — A132

1985, Oct. 25 ***Perf. 14½***

915 A132 60c Flags of UK, Dominica .75 .75
916 A132 $1 Elizabeth II, vert. .75 .75
917 A132 $4 HMS Britannia 3.50 3.50
Nos. 915-917 (3) 5.00 5.00

Souvenir Sheet

918 A132 $5 Map 3.75 3.75

Mark Twain — A133

Disney characters in Tom Sawyer.

1985, Nov. 11 Litho. *Perf. 14*

919 A133 20c multicolored .75 .35
920 A133 60c multicolored 1.50 .35
921 A133 $1 multicolored 2.00 2.00
922 A133 $1.50 multicolored 2.50 2.50
923 A133 $2 multicolored 3.00 3.00
Nos. 919-923 (5) 9.75 8.20

Souvenir Sheet

924 A133 $5 multicolored 6.50 6.50

Christmas.

The Brothers Grimm — A134

Disney characters in Little Red Cap (Little Red Riding Hood).

1985, Nov. 11

925 A134 10c multicolored .40 .40
926 A134 45c multicolored 1.00 .50
927 A134 90c multicolored 2.00 2.00
928 A134 $1 multicolored 2.25 2.25
929 A134 $3 multicolored 4.25 4.25
Nos. 925-929 (5) 9.90 9.40

Souvenir Sheet

930 A134 $5 multicolored 7.75 7.75

Christmas.

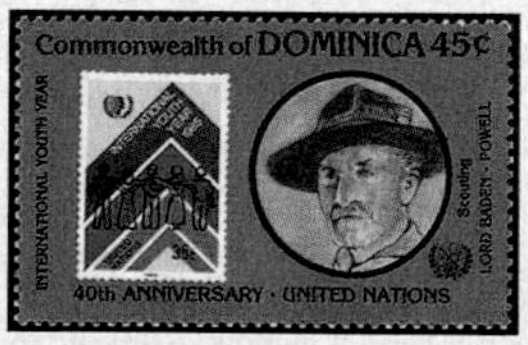

UN, 40th Anniv. A135

Stamps of UN, famous men and events: 45c, No. 442 and Lord Baden-Powell. $2, No. 157 and Maimonides (1135-1204) Judaic scholar. $3, No. 278 and Sir Rowland Hill. $5, Apollo-Soyuz Mission, 10th anniv.

1985, Nov. 22 *Perf. 14½*

931 A135 45c multicolored .90 .90
932 A135 $2 multicolored 2.00 2.00
933 A135 $3 multicolored 2.00 2.00
Nos. 931-933 (3) 4.90 4.90

Souvenir Sheet

934 A135 $5 multicolored 3.75 3.75

1986 World Cup Soccer Championships, Mexico — A136

Various soccer plays.

1986, Mar. 26 *Perf. 14*

935 A136 45c multicolored 1.25 1.25
936 A136 60c multicolored 1.75 1.75
937 A136 $1 multicolored 2.25 2.25
938 A136 $3 multicolored 5.50 5.50
Nos. 935-938 (4) 10.75 10.75

Souvenir Sheet

939 A136 $5 multicolored 8.50 8.50

For overprints see Nos. 974-978.

Statue of Liberty, Cent. A137

Statue and: 15c, New York police pursuing river pirates, c. 1890. 25c, Police patrol boat. 45c, Hoboken Ferry Terminal, c. 1890. $4, Holland Tunnel.

1986, Mar. 26

940 A137 15c multicolored 1.50 .75
941 A137 25c multicolored 1.50 1.00
942 A137 45c multicolored 2.50 1.00
943 A137 $4 multicolored 5.00 5.00
Nos. 940-943 (4) 10.50 7.75

Souvenir Sheet

944 A137 $5 Statue, vert. 5.50 5.50

Halley's Comet A138

5c, Jantal Mantar Observatory, Delhi, India, Nasir al Din al Tusi (1201-1274), astronomer. 10c, US Bell X-1 rocket plane breaking sound barrier. 45c, Astronomicum Caesareum, 1540, manuscript diagram of comet's trajectory, 1531. $4, Mark Twain, comet appeared at birth and death. $5, Comet.

1986, Apr. 17

945 A138 5c multicolored .60 .60
946 A138 10c multicolored .60 .60
947 A138 45c multicolored 1.25 1.25
948 A138 $4 multicolored 3.25 3.25
Nos. 945-948 (4) 5.70 5.70

Souvenir Sheet

949 A138 $5 multicolored 3.75 3.75

For overprints see Nos. 984-988.

Queen Elizabeth II, 60th Birthday

Common Design Type

1986, Apr. 21 Litho. *Perf. 14*

950 CD339 2c Wedding, 1947 .25 .25
951 CD339 $1 With Pope John Paul II, 1982 .75 .75
952 CD339 $4 Royal visit, 1971 2.50 2.50
Nos. 950-952 (3) 3.50 3.50

Souvenir Sheet

953 CD339 $5 Age 10 3.75 3.75

AMERIPEX '86 — A139

Walt Disney characters involved in stamp collecting.

1986, May 22 *Perf. 11*

954 A139 25c Mickey Mouse and Pluto .75 .75
955 A139 45c Donald Duck .95 .95
956 A139 60c Chip-n-Dale 1.25 1.25
957 A139 $4 Donald, nephews 4.00 4.00
Nos. 954-957 (4) 6.95 6.95

Souvenir Sheet

Perf. 14

958 A139 $5 Uncle Scrooge 6.00 6.00

British Monarchs — A140

1986, June 9 *Perf. 14*

959 A140 10c William I .40 .40
960 A140 40c Richard II .75 .75
961 A140 50c Henry VIII .90 .90
962 A140 $1 Charles II 1.00 1.00
963 A140 $2 Queen Anne 1.50 1.50
964 A140 $4 Queen Victoria 3.00 3.00
Nos. 959-964 (6) 7.55 7.55

Audubon Type of 1985

Perf. 12½x12, 12x12½

1986, June 18

965 A127 25c Black-throated diver 1.25 .50
966 A127 60c Great blue heron 1.75 1.75
967 A127 90c Yellow-crowned night heron 2.25 2.25
968 A127 $4 Shoveler duck 4.50 4.50
Nos. 965-968 (4) 9.75 9.00

Souvenir Sheet

Perf. 14

969 A127 $5 Goose 10.00 10.00

Nos. 966-967 vert.

Royal Wedding Issue, 1986

Common Design Type

1986, July 23 *Perf. 14*

970 CD340 45c Couple .40 .40
971 CD340 60c Prince Andrew .60 .60
972 CD340 $4 Prince, aircraft 2.50 2.50
Nos. 970-972 (3) 3.50 3.50

Souvenir Sheet

973 CD340 $5 Couple, diff. 3.75 3.75
Nos. 970-973 (4) 7.25 7.25

Nos. 935-939 Overprinted in Gold

1986, Sept. 15 Litho. *Perf. 14*

974 A136 45c multicolored 1.25 .50
975 A136 60c multicolored 1.50 1.50
976 A136 $1 multicolored 2.00 2.00
977 A136 $3 multicolored 4.75 4.75
Nos. 974-977 (4) 9.50 8.75

Souvenir Sheet

978 A136 $5 multicolored 8.75 8.75

Paintings by Albrecht Durer — A141

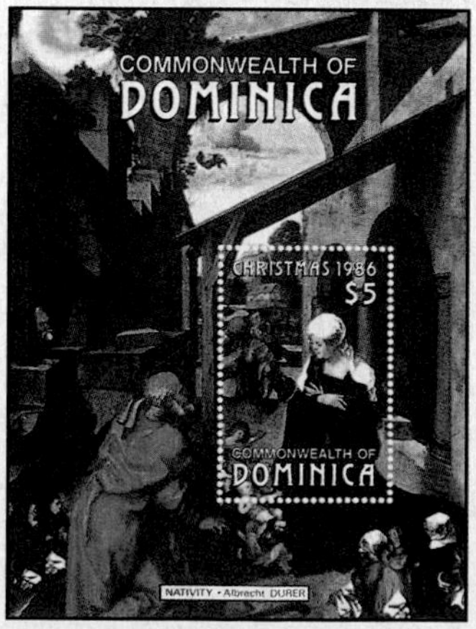

A142

1986, Dec. 2 Litho. *Perf. 14*

979 A141 45c Virgin in Prayer .85 .35
980 A141 60c Madonna and Child 1.40 1.40
981 A141 $1 Madonna and Child, diff. 2.00 2.00
982 A141 $3 Madonna and Child with St. Anne 5.50 5.50
Nos. 979-982 (4) 9.75 9.25

Souvenir Sheet

983 A142 $5 Nativity 8.75 8.75

Nos. 945-949 Printed with Halley's Comet Logo in Black or Silver

1986, Dec. 16

984 A138 5c multicolored .25 .25
985 A138 10c multicolored .25 .25
986 A138 45c multicolored .50 .50
987 A138 $4 multicolored 3.75 3.75
Nos. 984-987 (4) 4.75 4.75

Souvenir Sheet

988 A138 $5 multi (S) 4.50 4.50

Birds — A143

1987, Jan. 20 Litho. *Perf. 15*

989 A143 1c Broad-winged hawk .25 *.75*
990 A143 2c Ruddy quail dove .25 *.75*
991 A143 5c Red-necked pigeon .30 *.75*
992 A143 10c Green heron .30 .25
993 A143 15c Common gallinule .40 .30
994 A143 20c Ringed kingfisher .40 .30
995 A143 25c Brown pelican .40 .25
996 A143 35c White-tailed tropicbird .40 .30
997 A143 45c Red-legged thrush .50 .40
998 A143 60c Purple throated carib .60 .55
999 A143 90c Magnificent frigatebird .70 .70
1000 A143 $1 Trembler .80 .80
1001 A143 $2 Black-capped petrel 1.50 1.50
1002 A143 $5 Barn owl 3.75 3.75
1003 A143 $10 Imperial parrot 6.25 6.25
Nos. 989-1003 (15) 16.80 17.60

Inscribed "1989" and "Questa"

1989, Aug. 31 Litho. *Perf. 14*

990a A143 2c .35 *.90*
991a A143 5c .35 *.80*
992a A143 10c .40 .25
993a A143 15c .55 .30
994a A143 20c .65 .35
995a A143 25c .65 .35
996a A143 35c .85 .30
997a A143 45c 1.00 .30
998a A143 60c 1.50 .50
1000a A143 $1 1.75 1.00
1001a A143 $2 3.00 3.00
1002a A143 $5 6.00 6.00
1003a A143 $10 8.00 8.00
Nos. 990a-1003a (13) 25.05 22.05

Inscribed "1990" and "Questa"

1990 Litho. *Perf. 12*

990b A143 2c .40 *.95*
991b A143 5c .40 *.85*
992b A143 10c .45 .35
993b A143 15c .45 .35
994b A143 20c .70 .40
995b A143 25c .70 .40
996b A143 35c .85 .35
997b A143 45c 1.00 .35
998b A143 60c 1.50 1.60
1000b A143 $1 1.75 1.00
1001b A143 $2 3.00 3.00
1002b A143 $5 6.25 6.25
1003b A143 $10 8.25 8.25
Nos. 990b-1003b (13) 25.70 24.10

Inscribed "1991" and "Questa"

1991 Litho. *Perf. 13x11½*

990c A143 2c .50 *1.10*
991c A143 5c .50 *.95*
992c A143 10c .55 .40
993c A143 15c .55 .35
994c A143 20c .75 .35
995c A143 25c .75 .40
996c A143 35c .85 .40
997c A143 45c 1.40 1.25
998c A143 60c 2.00 1.40
1000c A143 $1 2.00 1.50
1001c A143 $2 3.50 3.50
1002c A143 $5 7.00 7.00
1003c A143 $10 10.00 10.00
Nos. 990c-1003c (13) 30.35 28.60

Paintings by Marc Chagall (1887-1985) A144

Designs: 25c, Artist and His Model. 35c, Midsummer Night's Dream. 45c, Joseph the Shepherd. 60c, the Cellist. 90c, Woman with Pigs. $1, the Blue Circus. $3, For Vava. $4, the Rider. No. 1012, Purim. No. 1013, Firebird design for the curtain of the Stravinsky Ballet production.

1987, Mar. 2 *Perf. 14*

1004	A144	25c	multicolored	.50	.25
1005	A144	35c	multicolored	.65	.30
1006	A144	45c	multicolored	.85	.35
1007	A144	60c	multicolored	1.00	.50
1008	A144	90c	multicolored	1.10	.70
1009	A144	$1	multicolored	1.25	1.25
1010	A144	$3	multicolored	2.50	2.50
1011	A144	$4	multicolored	3.50	3.50

Size: 110x95mm

Imperf

1012	A144	$5	multicolored	4.00	4.00
1013	A144	$5	multicolored	4.00	4.00
			Nos. 1004-1013 (10)	19.35	17.35

A145

Conch Shells — A147

America's Cup — A146

1987, Feb. 5 *Perf. 15*

1014	A145	45c	Reliance, 1903	.60	.45
1015	A145	60c	Freedom, 1980	.70	.50
1016	A145	$1	Mischief, 1881	.90	1.00
1017	A145	$3	Australia, 1977	2.75	2.00
			Nos. 1014-1017 (4)	4.95	3.95

Souvenir Sheet

1018	A146	$5	Courageous, Australia, 1977	3.75	3.75

1987, Apr. 13 **Litho.**

Designs: 35c, Morch Poulsen's triton. 45c, Swainson globe purple sea snail. 60c, Banded tulip. No. 1022, Lamarck deltoid rock shell. No. 1023, Junoia volute.

1019	A147	35c	multicolored	.35	.35
1020	A147	45c	multicolored	.45	.45
1021	A147	60c	multicolored	.55	.55
1022	A147	$5	multicolored	3.50	3.50
			Nos. 1019-1022 (4)	4.85	4.85

Souvenir Sheet

1023	A147	$5	multicolored	4.50	4.50

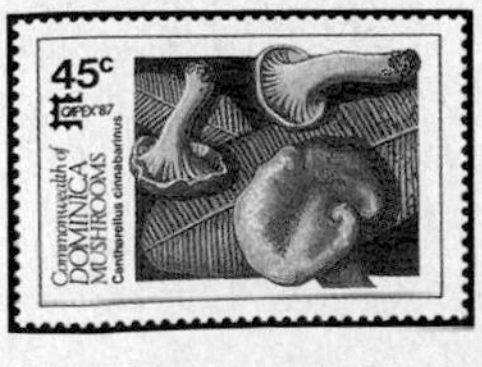

CAPEX '87 A148

Mushrooms.

1987, June 15 **Litho.** *Perf. 14*

1024	A148	45c	Cantharellus cinnabarinus	1.50	.75
1025	A148	60c	Boletellus cubenis	2.00	2.00
1026	A148	$2	Eccilia cystiophorus	3.75	3.75
1027	A148	$3	Xerocomus guadelupae	4.50	4.50
			Nos. 1024-1027 (4)	11.75	11.00

Souvenir Sheet

1028	A148	$5	Gymnopilus chrysopellus	10.00	10.00

A149

Discovery of America, 500th Anniv. (in 1992) — A150

Explorations of Christopher Columbus: 10c, Discovery of Dominica. 15c, Ships greeted by Carib Indians. 45c, Claiming New World for Spain. 60c, Wrecking of the Santa Maria. 90c, Fleet setting sail. $1, Sighting land. $3, Trading with the Indians. No. 1036, First settlement. No. 1037, Arrival of Second Fleet at Dominica, Nov. 3, 1493. No. 1038, Map of exploration of the Leeward Islands.

1987, July 27 *Perf. 15*

1029	A149	10c	multicolored	.40	.40
1030	A149	15c	multicolored	.50	.50
1031	A149	45c	multicolored	.75	.75
1032	A149	60c	multicolored	.95	.95
1033	A149	90c	multicolored	1.20	1.20
1034	A149	$1	multicolored	1.25	1.25
1035	A149	$3	multicolored	2.50	2.50
1036	A149	$5	multicolored	3.25	3.25
			Nos. 1029-1036 (8)	10.80	10.80

Souvenir Sheets

1037	A150	$5	multicolored	4.75	4.75
1038	A150	$5	multicolored	4.75	4.75

For overprints see Nos. 1083-1084.

Transportation — A151

10c, Warrior, 1st iron-clad warship. 15c, Maglev-MLU 001, fastest passenger train. 25c, Clipper Flying Cloud, fastest NYC-San Francisco voyage, 1852. 35c, 1st elevated railway, NYC. 45c, Tom Thumb, 1st US passenger train locomotive. 60c, Joshua Slocum, 1st solo circumnavigation of the world in a sloop. 90c, Se-Land Commerce, fastest Pacific crossing. $1, 1st cable car, San Francisco. $3, Orient Express. $4, The North River Steamboat of Clermont, invented by Robert Fulton, 1st successful commercial steamboat.

1987 **Litho.** *Perf. 14*

1039	A151	10c	multicolored	.50	.50
1040	A151	15c	multicolored	.75	.75
1041	A151	25c	multi, vert.	.80	.80
1042	A151	35c	multi, vert.	1.00	1.00
1043	A151	45c	multicolored	1.10	1.10
1044	A151	60c	multi, vert.	1.25	1.25
1045	A151	90c	multi, vert.	1.40	1.40
1046	A151	$1	multicolored	1.50	1.50
1047	A151	$3	multicolored	3.75	3.75
1048	A151	$4	multicolored	4.00	4.00
			Nos. 1039-1048 (10)	16.05	16.05

Issued: 10c, 15c, 45c, 60c, $4, 9/28; others 8/1.

For overprints see Nos. 1081-1082.

Christmas — A152

Paintings (details): 20c, Virgin and Child with St. Anne, by Durer. 25c, The Virgin and Child, by Murillo. $2, Madonna and Child, by Vincenzo Foppa (c. 1427-1516). $4, Madonna and Child, by Paolo Veronese (1528-1588). $5, Angel of the Annunciation, anonymous.

1987, Nov. 16

1049	A152	20c	multicolored	.30	.30
1050	A152	25c	multicolored	.30	.30
1051	A152	$2	multicolored	2.00	2.00
1052	A152	$4	multicolored	4.25	4.25
			Nos. 1049-1052 (4)	6.85	6.85

Souvenir Sheet

1053	A152	$5	multicolored	3.75	3.75

Mickey Mouse, 60th Anniv. A153

Disney theme parks and trains: 20c, People Mover, Disney World. 25c, Horse-drawn Trolley, Disneyland. 45c, Roger E. Broggie, Disney World. 60c, Big Thunder Mountain, Disneyland. 90c, Walter E. Disney, Disneyland. $1, Monorail, Disney World. $3, Casey Jr. from Dumbo. $4, Lilly Belle, Disney World. No. 1062, Rainbow Caverns Mine Train, Disneyland, horiz. No. 1063, Toy train from movie Out of Scale, horiz.

1987, Dec. 7 **Litho.** *Perf. 14*

1054	A153	20c	multicolored	.55	.55
1055	A153	25c	multicolored	.55	.55
1056	A153	45c	multicolored	.90	.90
1057	A153	60c	multicolored	1.00	1.00
1058	A153	90c	multicolored	1.60	1.60
1059	A153	$1	multicolored	1.75	1.75
1060	A153	$3	multicolored	4.00	4.00
1061	A153	$4	multicolored	5.25	5.25
			Nos. 1054-1061 (8)	15.60	15.60

Souvenir Sheets

1062	A153	$5	multicolored	4.00	4.00
1063	A153	$5	multicolored	4.00	4.00

40th Wedding Anniv. of Queen Elizabeth II and Prince Philip — A154

1988 Summer Olympics, Seoul — A155

1988, Feb. 15 **Litho.** *Perf. 14*

1064	A154	45c	Couple, wedding party, 1947	.75	.75
1065	A154	60c	Elizabeth, Charles, c. 1952	.80	.80
1066	A154	$1	Royal Family, c. 1952	1.00	1.00
1067	A154	$3	Queen with tiara, c. 1960	2.40	2.40
			Nos. 1064-1067 (4)	4.95	4.95

Souvenir Sheet

1068	A154	$5	Elizabeth, 1947	3.50	3.50

1988, Mar. 15

1069	A155	45c	Kayaking	.85	.85
1070	A155	60c	Tae kwon-do	1.25	1.25
1071	A155	$1	Diving	1.40	1.40
1072	A155	$3	Parallel bars	2.50	2.50
			Nos. 1069-1072 (4)	6.00	6.00

Souvenir Sheet

1073	A155	$5	Soccer	3.25	3.25

For overprints see Nos. 1151-1155.

Reunion '88 Tourism Campaign A156

1988, Apr. 13 **Litho.** *Perf. 15*

1074	A156	10c	Carib Indian, vert.	.25	.25
1075	A156	25c	Mountainous interior	.25	.25
1076	A156	35c	Indian River, vert.	.25	.25
1077	A156	60c	Belaire dancer, vert.	.25	.25
1078	A156	90c	The Boiling Lake, vert.	.30	.30
1079	A156	$3	Coral reef	.90	.90
			Nos. 1074-1079 (6)	2.20	2.20

Souvenir Sheet

1080	A156	$5	Belaire dancer, diff., vert.	3.00	3.00

Independence, 10th anniv.

Nos. 1046-1047, 1037-1038 Ovptd. for Philatelic Exhibitions in Black

a

b

c

d

1988, June 1 **Litho.** *Perf. 14*

1081	A151(a)	$1	multi	1.00	1.00
1082	A151(b)	$3	multi	3.75	3.75

Souvenir Sheets

Perf. 15

1083	A150(c)	$5	multi	4.00	4.00
1084	A150(d)	$5	multi	4.00	4.00

Miniature Sheet

Rain Forest Flora and Fauna — A157

Designs: a, White-tailed tropicbirds. b, Blue-throated euphonia. c, Smooth-billed ani. d, Scaly-breasted thrasher. e, Purple-throated carib. f, Southern daggertail and Clench's hairstreak. g, Trembler. h, Imperial parrot. i, Mangrove cuckoo. j, Hercules beetle. k, Orion. l, Red-necked parrot. m, Tillandsia. n, Polystacha luteola and bananaquit. o, False chameleon. p, Iguana. q, Hypolimnas. r, Green-throated carib. s, Heliconia. t, Agouti.

1988, July 25 *Perf. 14½*

1085 A157 Sheet of 20 14.00 14.00
a.-t. 45c any single .60 .60

Intl. Fund for Agricultural Development (IFAD), 10th Anniv. — A158

1988, Sept. 5 **Litho.** *Perf. 14*

1086 A158 45c Hen house .65 .65
1087 A158 60c Pig farm .90 .90
1088 A158 90c Cattle 1.25 1.25
1089 A158 $3 Black-belly sheep 3.50 3.50
Nos. 1086-1089 (4) 6.30 6.30

Souvenir Sheet

1090 A158 $5 Mixed crops, vert. 3.75 3.75

Entertainers A159

1988, Sept. 8

1091 A159 10c Gary Cooper .40 .25
1092 A159 35c Josephine Baker .50 .25
1093 A159 45c Maurice Chevalier .55 .30
1094 A159 60c James Cagney .75 .30
1095 A159 $1 Clark Gable 1.00 .30
1096 A159 $2 Louis Armstrong 1.75 1.75
1097 A159 $3 Liberace 2.00 2.00
1098 A159 $4 Spencer Tracy 2.50 2.50
Nos. 1091-1098 (8) 9.45 7.65

Souvenir Sheets

1099 A159 $5 Elvis Presley 4.25 4.25
1100 A159 $5 Humphrey Bogart 4.25 4.25

Flowering Trees and Shrubs A160

1988, Sept. 29 **Litho.** *Perf. 14*

1101 A160 15c Sapodilla .25 .25
1102 A160 20c Tangerine .25 .25
1103 A160 25c Avocado pear .25 .25
1104 A160 45c Amherstia .30 .30
1105 A160 90c Lipstick tree .55 .55
1106 A160 $1 Cannonball tree .60 .60
1107 A160 $3 Saman 1.50 1.50
1108 A160 $4 Pineapple 2.00 2.00
Nos. 1101-1108 (8) 5.70 5.70

Souvenir Sheets

1109 A160 $5 Lignum vitae 3.75 3.75
1110 A160 $5 Sea grape 3.75 3.75

Paintings by Titian A161

Designs: 25c, Jacopo Strada, c. 1567. 35c, Titian's Daughter Lavinia, c. 1565. 45c, Andrea Navagero, c. 1515. 60c, Judith with Head of Holoferenes, c. 1570. $1, Emilia di Spilimbergo, c. 1560. $2, Martyrdom of St. Lawrence, c. 1548. $3, Salome With the Head of St. John the Baptist, 1560. $4, St. John the Baptist, c. 1540. No. 1119, Self-portrait, c. 1555. No. 1120, Sisyphus, 1549.

1988, Oct. 10 **Litho.** *Perf. 13½x14*

1111 A161 25c multicolored .25 .25
1112 A161 35c multicolored .25 .25
1113 A161 45c multicolored .35 .35
1114 A161 60c multicolored .45 .45
1115 A161 $1 multicolored .90 .90
1116 A161 $2 multicolored 1.25 1.25
1117 A161 $3 multicolored 2.00 2.00
1118 A161 $4 multicolored 2.50 2.50
Nos. 1111-1118 (8) 7.95 7.95

Souvenir Sheets

1119 A161 $5 multicolored 3.50 3.50
1120 A161 $5 multicolored 3.50 3.50

A162

A163

1988, Oct. 31 **Litho.** *Perf. 14*

1121 A162 20c Imperial parrot 1.75 .50
1122 A162 45c No. 1, landscape 1.00 .40
1123 A162 $2 No. 602, waterfall 1.75 1.75
1124 A162 $3 Carib wood 2.00 3.00
Nos. 1121-1124 (4) 6.50 5.65

Souvenir Sheet

1125 A162 $5 Natl. band performing 3.75 3.75

Independence, 10th Anniv. Nos. 1122-1123 horiz.

1988, Nov. 22

1126 A163 20c With Jackie .25 .25
1127 A163 25c Sailing Vicuna .25 .25
1128 A163 $2 Walking in Hyannis Port .95 .95
1129 A163 $4 Berlin Wall speech 2.25 2.25
Nos. 1126-1129 (4) 3.70 3.70

Souvenir Sheet

1130 A163 $5 Portrait 3.50 3.50

John F. Kennedy. Nos. 1126-1128 horiz.

Miniature Sheet

Christmas, Mickey Mouse 60th Anniv. — A164

No. 1131: a, Huey, Dewey, Louie. b, Daisy Duck. c, Winnie-the-Pooh. d, Goofy. e, Donald Duck. f, Mickey Mouse. g, Minnie Mouse. h, Chip-n-Dale.

No. 1132, Mickey, Morty and Ferdy. No. 1133, Characters visiting shopping mall Santa.

1988, Dec. 1 *Perf. 13½x14*

1131 A164 Sheet of 8 6.75 6.75
a.-h. 60c any single .80 .80

Souvenir Sheets

1132 A164 $6 multi 5.00 5.00
1133 A164 $6 multi, horiz. 5.00 5.00

UN Declaration of Human Rights, 40th Anniv. — A165

Designs: $3, Flag of Sweden and Raoul Wallenberg, who helped save 100,000 Jews in Budapest from deportation to Nazi concentration camps. $5, Human Rights Flame.

1988, Dec. 12 *Perf. 14*

1134 A165 $3 multicolored 3.00 3.00

Souvenir Sheet

1135 A165 $5 multi, vert. 4.00 4.00

Coastal Game Fish A166

1988, Dec. 22 **Litho.** *Perf. 14*

1136 A166 10c Greater amberjack .25 .25
1137 A166 15c Blue marlin .25 .25
1138 A166 35c Cobia .40 .40
1139 A166 45c Dolphin .50 .50
1140 A166 60c Cero .75 .75
1141 A166 90c Mahogany snapper 1.00 1.00
1142 A166 $3 Yellowfin tuna 2.50 2.50
1143 A166 $4 Rainbow parrotfish 3.50 3.50
Nos. 1136-1143 (8) 9.15 9.15

Souvenir Sheets

1144 A166 $5 Manta ray 5.00 5.00
1145 A166 $5 Tarpon 5.00 5.00

Caribbean Insects and Reptiles A167

1988, Dec. 29

1146 A167 10c Leatherback turtle .60 .60
1147 A167 25c Monarch butterfly 1.75 1.75
1148 A167 60c Green anole 2.00 2.00
1149 A167 $3 Praying mantis 5.50 5.50
Nos. 1146-1149 (4) 9.85 9.85

Souvenir Sheet

1150 A167 $5 Hercules beetle 5.00 5.00

Nos. 1069-1073 Overprinted

a

b

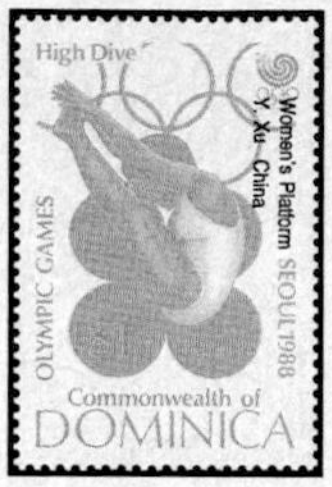

c

d

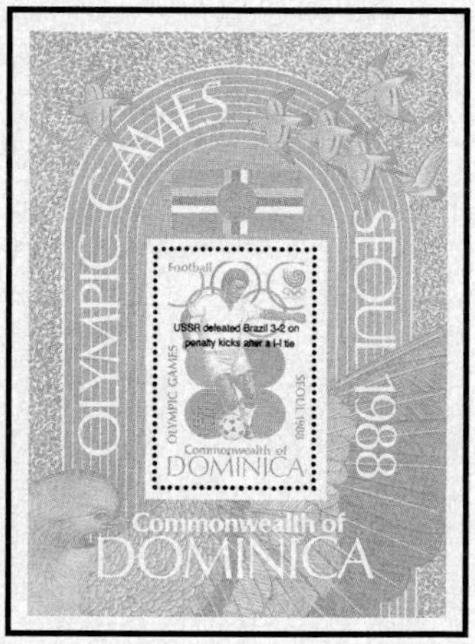

e

1989, Mar. 20 **Litho.** *Perf. 14*

1151 A155(a) 45c multi .30 .30
1152 A155(b) 60c multi .40 .40
1153 A155(c) $1 multi .75 .75
1154 A155(d) $3 multi 1.90 1.90
Nos. 1151-1154 (4) 3.35 3.35

Souvenir Sheet

1155 A155(e) $5 multi 3.75 3.75

Pre-Columbian Societies and Their Customs — A168

UPAE and discovery of America anniv. emblems and: 20c, Carib Indians canoeing. 35c, Bow hunting. $1, Canoe making. $3, Shield wrestling. $6, Dancing.

1989, May 8 **Litho.** *Perf. 14*

1156 A168 20c multicolored .25 .25
1157 A168 35c multicolored .35 .35
1158 A168 $1 multicolored 1.00 1.00
1159 A168 $3 multicolored 2.75 2.75
Nos. 1156-1159 (4) 4.35 4.35

Souvenir Sheet

1160 A168 $6 multicolored 4.25 4.25

Discovery of America 500th anniv. (in 1992).

Paintings by Yokoyama Taikan (1868-1958) A169

Designs: 10c, Lao-tzu. 20c, Red Maple Leaves (panels 1-2). 45c, King Wen Learns a Lesson from His Cook. 60c, Red Maple Leaves (panels 3-4). $1, Wild Flowers. $2, Red Maple Leaves (panels 5-6). $3, Red Maple Leaves (panels 7-8). $4, The Indian Ceremony of Floating Lamps on the River. No. 1169, Innocence. No. 1170, Red Maple Leaves (4 panels).

1989, Aug. 8 Litho. *Perf. 13½x14*

1161	A169	10c multicolored	.25	.25
1162	A169	20c multicolored	.25	.25
1163	A169	45c multicolored	.30	.30
1164	A169	60c multicolored	.40	.40
1165	A169	$1 multicolored	.65	.65
1166	A169	$2 multicolored	1.25	1.25
1167	A169	$3 multicolored	1.75	1.75
1168	A169	$4 multicolored	2.25	2.25
		Nos. 1161-1168 (8)	7.10	7.10

Souvenir Sheets

1169	A169	$5 multicolored	3.75	3.75
1170	A169	$5 multicolored	3.75	3.75

Hirohito (1901-89) and enthronement of Akihito as emperor of Japan.

PHILEXFRANCE '89, July 7-17, Paris — A170

Designs: 10c, Map of Dominica with French place names, 1766. 35c, French coin, 1688. $1, French ship, 1720. $4, Introduction of coffee to Dominica by the French, 1772. $5, Text.

1989, July 17 Litho. *Perf. 14*

1171	A170	10c multi, vert.	1.00	1.00
1172	A170	35c shown	1.00	1.00
1173	A170	$1 multicolored	1.50	1.50
1174	A170	$4 multicolored	3.00	3.00
		Nos. 1171-1174 (4)	6.50	6.50

Souvenir Sheet

1175	A170	$5 multicolored	5.25	5.25

Butterflies A171

Designs: 10c, Homerus swallowtail. 15c, *Morpho peleides.* 25c, Julia. 35c, Gundlach's swallowtail. 60c, Monarch. $1, Gulf fritillary. $3, Red-splashed sulphur. $5, *Papilio andraemon.* No. 1184, *Heliconius doris, Adelpha cytherea, Calliona argenissa, Eurema proterpia.* No. 1185, *Adelpha iphicla, Dismorphia spio, Lucinia sida.*

1989, Sept. 11 Litho. *Perf. 14*

1176	A171	10c multicolored	.40	.40
1177	A171	15c multicolored	.40	.40
1178	A171	25c multicolored	.70	.70
1179	A171	35c multicolored	.80	.80
1180	A171	60c multicolored	1.10	1.10
1181	A171	$1 multicolored	1.50	1.50
1182	A171	$3 multicolored	3.50	3.50
1183	A171	$5 multicolored	6.00	6.00
		Nos. 1176-1183 (8)	14.40	14.40

Souvenir Sheets

1184	A171	$6 multicolored	6.50	6.50
1185	A171	$6 multicolored	6.50	6.50

Misspellings: No. 1181, "Frittillary"; No. 1182, "Sulper."

Orchids — A172

1989, Sept. 28

1186	A172	10c Oncidium pusillum	.40	.40
1187	A172	35c Epidendrum cochleata	.75	.75
1188	A172	45c Epidendrum ciliare	.85	.85
1189	A172	60c Cyrtopodium andersonii	1.10	1.10
1190	A172	$1 Habenaria pauciflora	1.50	1.50
1191	A172	$2 Maxillaria alba	2.50	2.50
1192	A172	$3 Selenipedium palmifolium	3.00	3.00
1193	A172	$4 Brassavola cucullata	4.75	4.75
		Nos. 1186-1193 (8)	14.85	14.85

Souvenir Sheets

1194	A172	$5 Oncidium lanceanum	6.50	6.50
1195	A172	$5 Comparettia falcata	6.50	6.50

1st Moon Landing, 20th Anniv. A173

1989, Oct. 31 Litho. *Perf. 14*

1196	A173	10c Columbia in lunar orbit	.35	.35
1197	A173	60c Aldrin descending ladder	.80	.80
1198	A173	$2 Aldrin, Sea of Tranquillity	2.25	2.25
1199	A173	$3 Flag raising	3.25	3.25
		Nos. 1196-1199 (4)	6.65	6.65

Souvenir Sheet

1200	A173	$6 Liftoff	7.00	7.00

Souvenir Sheets

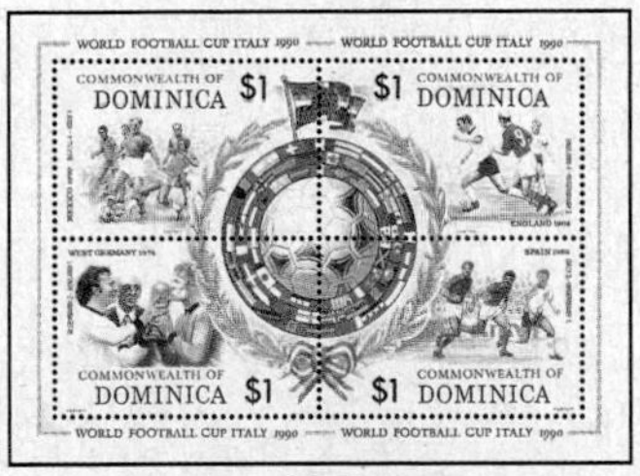

A174

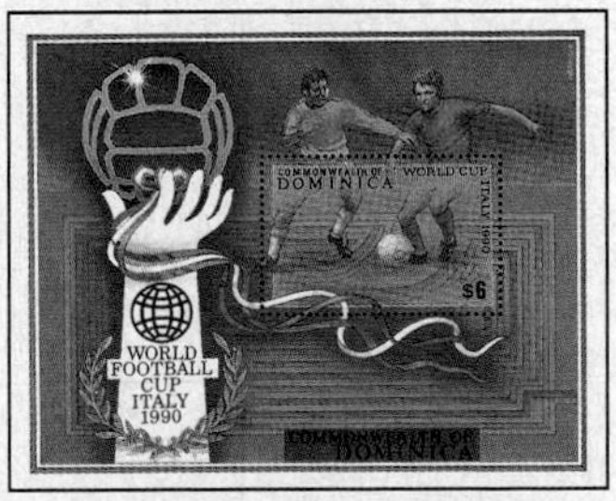

1990 World Cup Soccer Championships, Italy — A175

Past championship match scenes, flags and soccer ball: a, Brazil vs. Italy, Mexico, 1970. b, England vs. West Germany, England, 1966. c, West Germany vs. Netherlands, West Germany, 1974. d, Italy vs. West Germany, Spain, 1982.

1989, Nov. 7 *Perf. 14*

1201	A174	Sheet of 4	8.75	8.75
a.-d.		$1 any single	2.00	2.00

Perf. 14

1202	A175	$6 shown	6.00	6.00

Souvenir Sheet

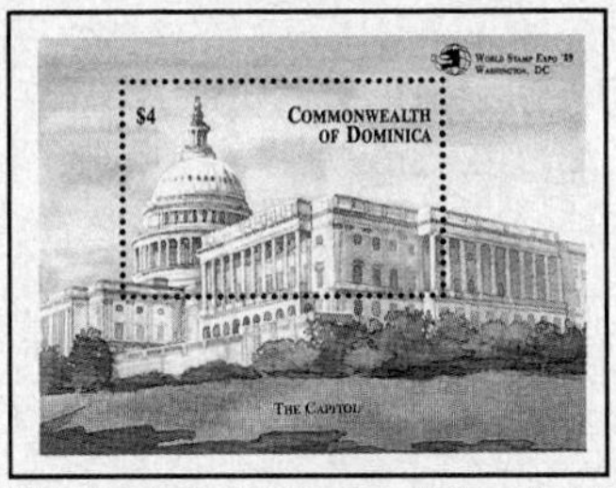

The Capitol, Washington, DC — A176

1989, Nov. 17 Litho. *Perf. 14*

1203	A176	$4 multicolored	3.75	3.75

World Stamp Expo '89.

Miniature Sheets

American Presidency, 200th Anniv. — A177

US presidents, historic events and monuments.

No. 1204: a, Washington, 1st inauguration. b, John Adams, presidential mansion, 1800. c, Jefferson, Graff House in Philadelphia, excerpt from the 1st draft of the Declaration of Independence. d, Madison, USS *Constitution* at the defeat of HMS *Guerriere,* 1812. e, Monroe, freed slaves settle Liberia, 1822. f, John Quincy Adams, opening of the Erie Canal, 1825.

No. 1205: a, Fillmore, Commodore Perry laying groundwork for US trade agreement with Japan. b, Pierce, Jefferson Davis and San Xavier del Bac mission, Tucson, AZ, Gadsden Purchase, 1853. c, Buchanan, Pony Express stamp, Buffalo Bill Cody as express rider. d, Lincoln, UPU emblem, Intl. Postal Congress, Paris, 1863. e, Andrew Johnson, polar bear, purchase of Alaska from Russia, 1867. f, Grant, 1st transcontinental railway link, Promontory Point, Utah, 1869.

No. 1206: a, Theodore Roosevelt, construction of the Panama Canal, 1904. b, Taft, Adm. Peary becomes 1st man to reach the North Pole, 1909. c, Wilson, US #C3, cancel commemorating 1st scheduled airmail service, 1918. d, Harding, airship USS *Shenandoah* at Lakehurst, NJ. e, Coolidge, Lindbergh's solo transatlantic flight, 1927. f, Mt. Rushmore, by Gutzon Borglum, 1927.

No. 1207: a, Lyndon B. Johnson, space exploration. b, Nixon visiting PRChina, 1971. c, Ford, tall ship in NY Harbor for Operation Sail, 1976, US bicentennial celebrations. d, Carter, Sadat of Egypt and Begin of Israel during the Camp David Accords, 1979. e, Reagan, European Space Agency emblem, flags and *Columbia* space shuttle. f, Bush, Grumman Avenger bomber he piloted during WWII.

1989, Nov. 17 *Perf. 14*

1204	A177	Sheet of 6	6.50	6.50
a.-f.		60c any single	1.00	1.00
1205	A177	Sheet of 6	6.50	6.50
a.-f.		60c any single	1.00	1.00
1206	A177	Sheet of 6	6.50	6.50
a.-f.		60c any single	1.00	1.00
1207	A177	Sheet of 6	6.50	6.50
a.-f.		60c any single	1.00	1.00

Mickey Mouse as a Hollywood Star — A178

Walt Disney characters: 20c, Reading script. 35c, Television interview. 45c, Named a star in tabloid headline. 60c, Signing autographs. $1, In dressing room, holding fans at bay. $2, Riding in limousine. $3, With Minnie in the limelight. $4, Accepting award. No. 1216, Giving interview during celebrity tennis tournament. No. 1217, Footprint impression in cement outside theater.

1989, Nov. 30 Litho. *Perf. 14x13½*

1208	A178	20c multicolored	.50	.50
1209	A178	35c multicolored	.70	.70
1210	A178	45c multicolored	.80	.80
1211	A178	60c multicolored	.90	.90
1212	A178	$1 multicolored	1.25	1.25
1213	A178	$2 multicolored	2.25	2.25
1214	A178	$3 multicolored	3.00	3.00
1215	A178	$4 multicolored	4.00	4.00
		Nos. 1208-1215 (8)	13.40	13.40

Souvenir Sheets

1216	A178	$5 multicolored	5.50	5.50
1217	A178	$5 multicolored	5.50	5.50

Christmas — A179

Religious paintings by Botticelli: 20c, *Madonna in Glory with Seraphim.* 25c, *The Annunciation.* 35c, *Madonna of the Pomegranate.* 45c, *Madonna of the Rose Garden.* 60c, *Madonna of the Book.* $1, *Madonna and Child Under a Baldachin with Three Angels.* $4, *Madonna and Child with Angels.* No. 1225, *Bardi Madonna.* No. 1226, *The Mystic Nativity.* No. 1227, *The Adoration of the Magi.*

1989, Dec. 4 *Perf. 14*

1218	A179	20c multicolored	.45	.45
1219	A179	25c multicolored	.45	.45
1220	A179	35c multicolored	.60	.60
1221	A179	45c multicolored	.75	.75
1222	A179	60c multicolored	.90	.90
1223	A179	$1 multicolored	1.10	1.10
1224	A179	$4 multicolored	3.00	3.00
1225	A179	$5 multicolored	4.75	4.75
		Nos. 1218-1225 (8)	12.00	12.00

Souvenir Sheets

1226	A179	$5 multicolored	5.00	5.00
1227	A179	$5 multicolored	5.00	5.00

Nehru — A180

Girl Guides — A181

1989, Dec. 27 Litho. *Perf. 14*

1228	A180	60c shown	2.00	2.00

Souvenir Sheet

1229	A180	$5 Parliament House, New Delhi, horiz.	6.00	6.00

Jawaharlal Nehru (1889-1964), 1st prime minister of independent India.

1989, Dec. 29

Guide movement in Dominica, 60th anniv.: 60c, Lady Baden-Powell and Agatha Robinson, former Guide leader on Dominica. $5, Dorris Stockmann, chairman of the world committee of the World Assoc. of Girl Guides and Girl Scouts, and Judith Pestaina, chief commissioner of the Dominica Girl Guides Assoc., horiz.

1230	A181	60c multicolored	1.25	1.25

Souvenir Sheet

1231	A181	$5 multi, horiz.	5.25	5.25

Miniature Sheet

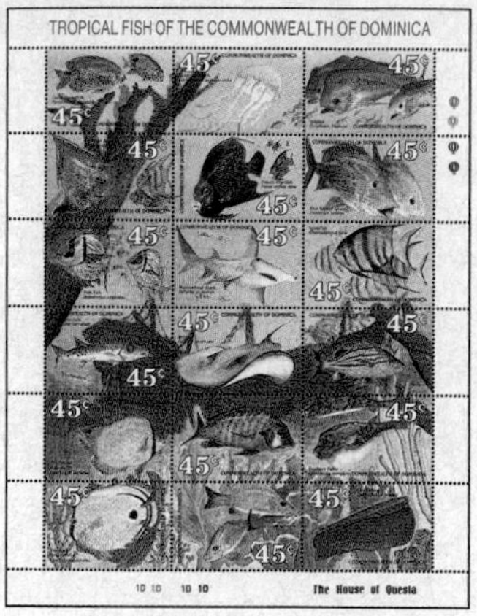

Marine Life — A182

Designs: a, Cocoa damselfish. b, Stinging jellyfish. c, Dolphin. d, Queen angelfish. e, French angelfish. f, Blue striped grunt. g, Pork fish. h, Hammerhead shark. i, Spadefish. j, Great barracuda. k, Stingray. l, Black grunt. m, Two-spotted butterflyfish. n, Dog snapper. o, Southern puffer. p, Four-eyed butterflyfish. q, Lane snapper. r, Green moray.

1990 **Litho.** ***Perf. 14***

1232 A182 Sheet of 18 11.00 11.00
a.-r. 45c any single .55 .55

Penny Black, 150th Anniv. A183

Stamp World London '90: 50c, Post Office accelerator, 1830. 60c, $4, No. 1239, London skyline, St. Paul's Cathedral. 90c, Railway post car, 1838. $3, Center cycle, 1883. No. 1240, Mail truck, 1899.

1990, May 3 **Litho.** ***Perf. 13½***

1233 A183 45c green & black .60 .60
1234 A183 50c blk & slate blue .80 .80
1235 A183 60c dk blue & blk .85 .85
1236 A183 90c black & green 1.50 1.50
1237 A183 $3 blk & dk bl vio 2.75 2.75
1238 A183 $4 dk bl vio & blk 3.75 3.75
Nos. 1233-1238 (6) 10.25 10.25

Souvenir Sheet

1239 A183 $5 beige & black 4.50 4.50
1240 A183 $5 gray & red brn 4.50 4.50

A184

A185

Birds: 10c, Blue-headed hummingbird. 20c, Black-capped petrel. 45c, Red-necked parrot. 60c, Black swift. $1, Troupial. $2, Brown noddy. $4, Lesser Antillean pewee. $5. Little blue heron. No. 1249, House wren. No. 1250, Imperial parrot.

1990, July 16 **Litho.** ***Perf. 14***

1241 A184 10c multicolored .40 .40
1242 A184 20c multicolored .55 .55
1243 A184 45c multicolored .75 .75
1244 A184 60c multicolored .95 .95
1245 A184 $1 multicolored 1.60 1.60
1246 A184 $2 multicolored 2.25 2.25
1247 A184 $4 multicolored 3.75 3.75
1248 A184 $5 multicolored 4.25 4.25
Nos. 1241-1248 (8) 14.50 14.50

Souvenir Sheets

1249 A184 $6 multicolored 5.00 5.00
1250 A184 $6 multicolored 5.00 5.00

1990, July 19

Shells: 10c, Reticulated cowrie-helmet. 20c, West Indian chank. 35c, West Indian fighting conch. 60c, True tulip. $1, Sunrise tellin. $2, Crown cone. $3, Common dove shell. $4, Atlantic fig shell. No. 1259, Giant tun. No. 1260, King helmet.

1251 A185 10c multicolored .40 .40
1252 A185 20c multicolored .55 .55
1253 A185 35c multicolored .70 .70
1254 A185 60c multicolored 1.00 1.00
1255 A185 $1 multicolored 1.40 1.40
1256 A185 $2 multicolored 2.25 2.25
1257 A185 $3 multicolored 3.00 3.00
1258 A185 $4 multicolored 3.75 3.75
Nos. 1251-1258 (8) 13.05 13.05

Souvenir Sheets

1259 A185 $5 multicolored 5.00 5.00
1260 A185 $5 multicolored 5.00 5.00

A186

A187

Queen Mother, 90th Birthday: various photos.

1990, Sept. 10

1261 A186 20c multicolored .25 .25
1262 A186 45c multicolored .40 .40
1263 A186 60c multicolored .60 .60
1264 A186 $3 multicolored 2.50 2.50
Nos. 1261-1264 (4) 3.75 3.75

Souvenir Sheet

1265 A186 $5 multicolored 3.50 3.50

1990, Nov. 5 **Litho.** ***Perf. 14***

1266 A187 45c Men's singles, tennis 1.25 1.25
1267 A187 60c Men's foil fencing 1.40 1.40
1268 A187 $2 100m freestyle swimming 2.25 2.25
1269 A187 $3 Star class yachting 3.25 3.25
Nos. 1266-1269 (4) 8.15 8.15

Souvenir Sheet

1270 A187 $5 Coxless pairs, rowing 6.75 6.75

1992 Summer Olympics, Barcelona.

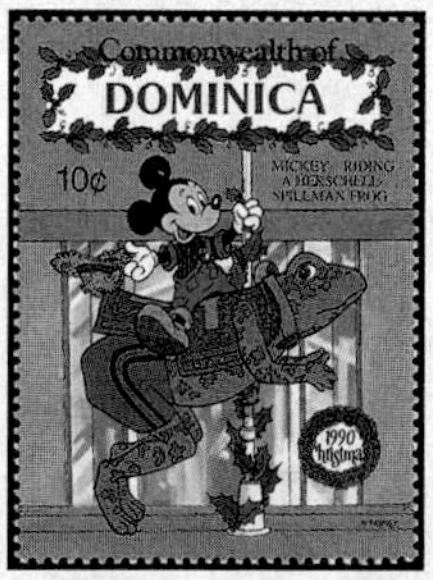

Christmas A188

Walt Disney characters on carousel animals: 10c, Mickey, frog. 15c, Huey, Dewey & Louie, white elephant. 25c, Donald, polar bear. 45c, Goofy, goat. $1, Donald, giraffe. $2, Daisy, stork. $4, Goofy, lion. $5, Daisy, horse. No. 1279, Mickey, swan chariot, horiz. No. 1280, Mickey, Minnie & Goofy, griffin chariot.

1990, Dec. 13 ***Perf. 13½x14***

1271 A188 10c multicolored .40 .40
1272 A188 15c multicolored .50 .50
1273 A188 25c multicolored .60 .60
1274 A188 45c multicolored .90 .90
1275 A188 $1 multicolored 1.25 1.25
1276 A188 $2 multicolored 2.00 2.00
1277 A188 $4 multicolored 4.00 4.00
1278 A188 $5 multicolored 5.00 5.00
Nos. 1271-1278 (8) 14.65 14.65

Souvenir Sheets

Perf. 14x13½

1279 A188 $6 multicolored 7.00 7.00
1280 A188 $6 multicolored 7.00 7.00

World Cup Soccer Championships, Italy — A189

Players and coaches from participating countries.

1990, Dec. 28 **Litho.** ***Perf. 14***

1281 A189 15c England .45 .45
1282 A189 45c Brazil .75 .75
1283 A189 60c West Germany 1.00 1.00
1284 A189 $4 Austria 4.25 4.25
Nos. 1281-1284 (4) 6.45 6.45

Souvenir Sheets

1285 A189 $6 Ireland, vert. 5.00 5.00
1286 A189 $6 USSR, vert. 5.00 5.00

Cog Trains of Switzerland — A190

Designs: 10c, Glion-Roches de Naye, 1890. 35c, Electric cog rail car ascending Mt. Pilatus. 45c, Cog railway to Schynige Platte, view of Eiger, Monch and Jungfrau Mountains. 60c, Furka-Oberalp train on Bugnli Viaduct, vert. $1, 1910 Jungfraubahn Cog Railway, Jungfrau Mountain, 1910. $2, Testing Swiss rail cars built for Pike's Peak on Arth-Rigibahn, 1963. $4, Brienz-Rothorn Bahn, 1991. $5, Private 1870 Rigi-Scheideck Hotel post stamp, 1890 Arth-Rigi Railway Engine. No. 1295, Sherlock Holmes watching Brunigline train descending from Brunig Pass. No. 1296, Switzerland #738 and first passenger train to ascend Mt. Rigi, 1871.

1991, Mar. 26 **Litho.** ***Perf. 14***

1287 A190 10c multicolored .60 .60
1288 A190 35c multicolored 1.00 1.00
1289 A190 45c multicolored 1.10 1.10
1290 A190 60c multicolored 1.25 1.25
1291 A190 $1 multicolored 1.40 1.40
1292 A190 $2 multicolored 2.00 2.00
1293 A190 $4 multicolored 3.00 3.00
1294 A190 $5 multicolored 3.50 3.50
Nos. 1287-1294 (8) 13.85 13.85

Souvenir Sheets

Perf. 13½

1295 A190 $6 multicolored 6.00 6.00
1296 A190 $6 multicolored 6.00 6.00

Nos. 1295-1296 each contain one 50x37mm stamp.

Voyages of Discovery A191

Explorer's ships: 10c, Gil Eannes, 1433-1434. 25c, Alfonso Gonclaves Baldaya, 1436. 45c, Bartolomeu Dias, 1487. 60c, Vasco da Gama, 1497-1499. $1, Vallarte the Dane. $2, Aloisio Cadamosto, 1456-1458. $4, Diogo Gomes, 1457. $5, Diogo Cao, 1482-1485.

1991, Apr. 8 **Litho.** ***Perf. 14***

1297 A191 10c multicolored .45 .45
1298 A191 25c multicolored .55 .55
1299 A191 45c multicolored .65 .65
1300 A191 60c multicolored .75 .75
1301 A191 $1 multicolored 1.10 1.10
1302 A191 $2 multicolored 1.60 1.60
1303 A191 $4 multicolored 2.75 2.75
1304 A191 $5 multicolored 3.25 3.25
Nos. 1297-1304 (8) 11.10 11.10

Souvenir Sheets

1305 A191 $6 Blue and yellow macaw 4.75 4.75
1306 A191 $6 Red and yellow macaw 4.75 4.75

Discovery of America, 500th anniv. (in 1992).

Japanese Costumes — A192

Walt Disney characters wearing Japanese costumes: 10c, Donald as soldier. 15c, Mickey as Kabuki actor. 25c, Mickey, Minnie in traditional wedding clothes. 45c, Daisy as Geisha girl, vert. $1, Mickey in sokutai dress of high government official, vert. $2, Goofy as mino farmer, vert. $4, Pete as shogun, vert. $5, Donald as warlord. No. 1315, Mickey, as Noh player, vert. No. 1316, Goofy as Kabubei-Jishi street performer, vert.

1991, May 22 **Litho.** ***Perf. 14***

1307 A192 10c multicolored .65 .65
1308 A192 15c multicolored .75 .75
1309 A192 25c multicolored .90 .90
1310 A192 45c multicolored 1.10 1.10
1311 A192 $1 multicolored 2.00 2.00
1312 A192 $2 multicolored 2.75 2.75
1313 A192 $4 multicolored 3.50 3.50
1314 A192 $5 multicolored 4.25 4.25
Nos. 1307-1314 (8) 15.90 15.90

Souvenir Sheets

1315 A192 $6 multicolored 7.50 7.50
1316 A192 $6 multicolored 7.50 7.50

Phila Nippon '91.

Mushrooms A193

1991, June 3 **Litho.** ***Perf. 14***

1318 A193 10c Horn of plenty .25 .25
1319 A193 15c Shaggy mane .45 .45
1320 A193 45c Yellow morel .55 .55
1321 A193 60c Chanterelle .65 .65
1322 A193 $1 Blewit 1.00 1.00
1323 A193 $2 Slippery jack 1.75 1.75
1324 A193 $4 Emetic russula 3.00 3.00
1325 A193 $5 Honey mushroom 4.00 4.00
Nos. 1318-1325 (8) 11.65 11.65

Souvenir Sheets

1326 A193 $6 Beefsteak polypore 5.00 5.00
1327 A193 $6 Voluminous-latex milky 5.00 5.00

Royal Family Birthday, Anniversary

Common Design Type

1991, June 17 **Litho.** ***Perf. 14***

1328 CD347 10c multicolored .45 .45
1329 CD347 15c multicolored .90 .90
1330 CD347 40c multicolored 1.00 1.00
1331 CD347 60c multicolored 1.10 1.10
1332 CD347 $1 multicolored 2.00 2.00
1333 CD347 $2 multicolored 2.75 2.75
1334 CD347 $4 multicolored 4.00 4.00
1335 CD347 $5 multicolored 4.50 4.50
Nos. 1328-1335 (8) 16.70 16.70

Souvenir Sheets

1336 CD347 $5 Elizabeth, Philip 5.00 5.00
1337 CD347 $5 Charles, Diana, sons 8.50 8.50

10c, 60c, $2, $4, No. 1336, Queen Elizabeth II, 65th birthday. Others, Charles and Diana, 10th wedding anniversary.

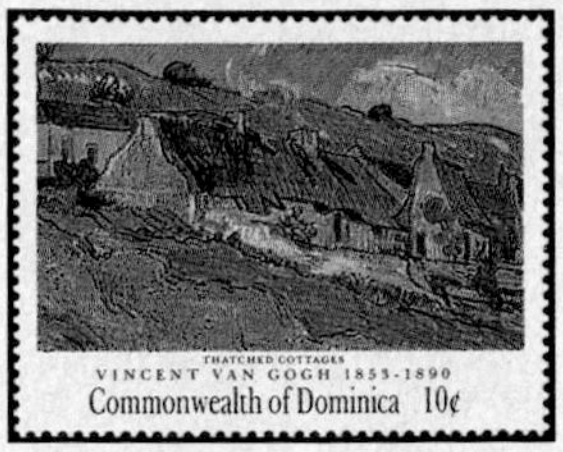

Vincent Van Gogh (1853-1890), Painter — A194

Paintings: 10c, Thatched Cottages. 25c, The House of Pere Eloi. 45c, The Midday Siesta. 60c, Portrait of a Young Peasant, vert. $1, Still Life: Vase with Irises Against a Yellow Background, vert. $2, Still Life Vase with Irises. $4, Blossoming Almond Tree. $5, Irises. No. 1346, A Meadow in the Mountains: Le Mas De Saint-Paul. No. 1347, Doctor Gachet's Garden in Auvers, vert.

1991, July 8 Litho. *Perf. 13½*

1338 A194 10c multicolored .65 .65
1339 A194 25c multicolored .90 .90
1340 A194 45c multicolored 1.10 1.10
1341 A194 60c multicolored 1.40 1.40
1342 A194 $1 multicolored 2.00 2.00
1343 A194 $2 multicolored 2.50 2.50
1344 A194 $4 multicolored 3.75 3.75
1345 A194 $5 multicolored 4.00 4.00
Nos. 1338-1345 (8) 16.30 16.30

Size: 101x75mm

Imperf

1346 A194 $6 multicolored 6.50 6.50
1347 A194 $6 multicolored 6.50 6.50

Intl. Literacy Year — A195

Scenes from Walt Disney's "The Little Mermaid": 10c, Ariel with Flounder and Sebastian. 25c, King Triton. 45c, Sebastian drums in "Kiss De Girl" concert. 60c, Flotsam and Jetsam taunt Ariel. $1, Scuttle, Flounder and Ariel. $2, Ariel and Flounder discover a book. $4, Prince Eric, dog Max, manservant Grimsby, and crew. $5, Ursula the sea witch. No. 1356, Ariel transformed into human being. No. 1357, Ariel and Prince Eric dancing in town, vert.

1991, Aug. 6 *Perf. 14*

1348 A195 10c multicolored .35 .35
1349 A195 25c multicolored .45 .45
1350 A195 45c multicolored .65 .65
1351 A195 60c multicolored .90 .90
1352 A195 $1 multicolored 1.50 1.50
1353 A195 $2 multicolored 2.75 2.75
1354 A195 $4 multicolored 4.50 4.50
1355 A195 $5 multicolored 5.50 5.50
Nos. 1348-1355 (8) 16.60 16.60

Souvenir Sheets

1356 A195 $6 multicolored 6.50 6.50
1357 A195 $6 multicolored 6.50 6.50

World Landmarks — A196

Designs: 10c, Empire State Building, US, vert. 25c, Kremlin, USSR. 45c, Buckingham Palace, United Kingdom. 60c, Eiffel Tower, France, vert. $1, Taj Mahal, India. $2, Sydney Opera House, Australia. $4, Colosseum, Italy. $5, Pyramids, Egypt. No. 1366, Galileo demonstrating laws of physics from Tower of Pisa, Italy. No. 1367, Great Wall of China and Emperor Shi Huang Ti.

1991, Aug. 12 Litho. *Perf. 14*

1358 A196 10c multicolored .45 .45
1359 A196 25c multicolored .55 .55
1360 A196 45c multicolored .90 .90
1361 A196 60c multicolored 1.10 1.10
1362 A196 $1 multicolored 2.00 2.00
1363 A196 $2 multicolored 3.00 3.00
1364 A196 $4 multicolored 4.75 4.75
1365 A196 $5 multicolored 5.50 5.50
Nos. 1358-1365 (8) 18.25 18.25

Souvenir Sheets

1366 A196 $6 multicolored 8.00 8.00
1367 A196 $6 multicolored 8.00 8.00

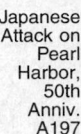

Japanese Attack on Pearl Harbor, 50th Anniv. A197

Designs: 10c, 6:00am, First wave of Japanese planes leave carrier Akagi. 15c, 6:40am, Destroyer Ward and PBY attack midget submarine. 45c, 7:00am, Second wave of Japanese planes leave carriers. 60c, 7:48am, Japanese Zeros attack on Kaneohe Air Station. $1, 8:30am, Destroyers Breeze, Medusa and Curtiss sink midget submarine. $2, 8:45am, Damaged battleship Nevada sorties. $4, 8:10am, Battleship Arizona explodes, killing 1,177 men. $5, 9:45am, Japanese attack ends. No. 1376, 8:00am, Japanese fighters and bombers attack Hickam Air Base. No. 1377, 7:55am, Pearl Harbor attack begins.

1991, Sept. 2

1368 A197 10c multicolored .60 .60
1369 A197 15c multicolored .70 .70
1370 A197 45c multicolored 1.10 1.10
1371 A197 60c multicolored 1.25 1.25
1372 A197 $1 multicolored 1.50 1.50
1373 A197 $2 multicolored 2.00 2.00
1374 A197 $4 multicolored 2.75 2.75
1375 A197 $5 multicolored 3.00 3.00
Nos. 1368-1375 (8) 12.90 12.90

Souvenir Sheets

1376 A197 $6 multicolored 5.25 5.25
1377 A197 $6 multicolored 5.25 5.25

Butterflies — A198

A199

Perf. 13½x13, 13½x14 (2c, 10c, 15c, 25c, 45c, 90c, $1, $20)

1991-93

1378 A198 1c Little yellow .35 *.90*
1379 A198 2c Gulf fritillary .35 *.90*
1380 A198 5c Monarch .65 *.90*
1381 A198 10c Red rim .65 .25
1382 A198 15c Flambeau .75 .25
1383 A198 20c Large orange sulphur .75 .25
1384 A198 25c Caribbean buckeye .75 .25
1385 A198 35c Polydamas swallowtail .85 .35
1386 A198 45c Cassius blue .85 .35
1386A A198 55c Great southern white 1.25 .60
1387 A198 60c Godman's leaf 1.00 .40
1387A A198 65c Hanno blue 1.25 .60
1388 A198 90c Mimic 1.40 .60
1389 A198 $1 Long-tailed skipper 1.40 .75
1389A A198 $1.20 Orion 1.50 1.50
1390 A198 $2 Cloudless sulphur 2.25 2.25
1391 A198 $5 Painted lady 3.75 *5.50*
1391A A198 $10 Southern daggertail 9.00 *11.00*
1391B A198 $20 White peacock 14.00 *16.00*
Nos. 1378-1391B (19) 42.75 43.60

Issued: 55c, 65c, $1.20, 1/11/93; others, 10/14/91.

1991, Nov. 1

1392 A199 45c shown 2.25 2.25

Souvenir Sheet

1393 A199 $5 blk & bl, horiz. 6.00 6.00

Charles de Gaulle, birth cent.

Creole Week — A200

Credit Union, 40th Anniv. — A201

45c, Man in 18th cent. costume. 60c, Accordion player. $1, Dancers. $5, Stick fight c. 1785.

1991, Nov. 1 *Perf. 14*

1394 A200 45c multicolored .60 .60
1395 A200 60c multicolored .90 .90
1396 A200 $1 multicolored 1.50 1.50
Nos. 1394-1396 (3) 3.00 3.00

Souvenir Sheet

1397 A200 $5 multicolored 6.50 6.50

1991, Nov. 1

1398 A201 10c black .55 .55
1399 A201 60c Emblem, founder, horiz. 1.50 1.50

Year of the Environment and Shelter — A202

15c, Keep the beaches clean. 60c, No. 1402, Amazona imperialis. No. 1403, Lagoon outlet.

1991, Nov. 18

1400 A202 15c multicolored .50 .50
1401 A202 60c multicolored 2.75 2.75

Souvenir Sheets

1402 A202 $5 multicolored 7.75 7.75
1403 A202 $5 multicolored 7.75 7.75

Christmas A203

Paintings by Jan van Eyck: 10c, The Virgin Enthroned with Child (detail). 20c, The Madonna at the Fountain. 35c, The Virgin in a Church. 45c, The Madonna with Canon van der Paele. 60c, The Madonna with Canon van der Paele (detail). $1, The Madonna in an Interior. $3, The Annunciation. $5, The Annunciation, diff. No. 1412, The Madonna with Chancellor Rolin. No. 1413, Virgin and Child with Saints and Donor.

1991, Dec. 2 *Perf. 12*

1404 A203 10c multicolored .55 .55
1405 A203 20c multicolored .75 .75
1406 A203 35c multicolored .90 .90
1407 A203 45c multicolored 1.00 1.00
1408 A203 60c multicolored 1.50 1.50
1409 A203 $1 multicolored 1.75 1.75
1410 A203 $3 multicolored 2.75 2.75
1411 A203 $5 multicolored 4.00 4.00
Nos. 1404-1411 (8) 13.20 13.20

Souvenir Sheets

Perf. 14x14½

1412 A203 $6 multicolored 6.50 6.50
1413 A203 $6 multicolored 6.50 6.50

Queen Elizabeth II's Accession to the Throne, 40th Anniv.

Common Design Type

1992, Feb. 6 Litho. *Perf. 14*

1414 CD348 10c multicolored .25 .25
1415 CD348 15c multicolored .25 .25
1416 CD348 $1 multicolored .75 .75
1417 CD348 $5 multicolored 3.75 3.75
Nos. 1414-1417 (4) 5.00 5.00

Souvenir Sheets

1418 CD348 $6 River scene 3.75 3.75
1419 CD348 $6 Seaside village 3.75 3.75

Botanical Gardens, Cent. — A204

Designs: 10c, Cricket match. 15c, Scenic entrance. 45c, Traveller's tree. 60c, Bamboo house. $1, Old pavilion. $2, Ficus benjamina. $4, Cricket ground. $5, Thirty-five steps. No. 1428, Fountain. No. 1429, Cricket masters.

1992, Mar. 30 Litho. *Perf. 14*

1420 A204 10c multicolored .40 .40
1421 A204 15c multicolored .40 .40
1422 A204 45c multicolored .40 .40
1423 A204 60c multicolored .60 .60
1424 A204 $1 multicolored 1.00 1.00
1425 A204 $2 multicolored 1.75 1.75
1426 A204 $4 multicolored 4.25 4.25
1427 A204 $5 multicolored 4.50 4.50
Nos. 1420-1427 (8) 13.30 13.30

Souvenir Sheets

1428 A204 $6 multicolored 5.00 5.00
1429 A204 $6 multicolored 5.00 5.00

Spanish Art — A205

Paintings or details from paintings by Velazquez: 10c, Pope Innocent X. 15c, 45c The Forge of Vulcan (different details). 60c, Queen Mariana of Austria. $1, Pablo de Valladolid. $2, Sebastian de Morra. $3, Felipe IV (detail). $4, Felipe IV. No. 1438, Surrender of Breda. No. 1439, The Drunkards.

1992, May 4 *Perf. 13*

1430 A205 10c multicolored .25 .25
1431 A205 15c multicolored .25 .25
1432 A205 45c multicolored .45 .45
1433 A205 60c multicolored .55 .55
1434 A205 $1 multicolored .80 .80
1435 A205 $2 multicolored 1.50 1.50
1436 A205 $3 multicolored 2.25 2.25
1437 A205 $4 multicolored 2.75 2.75

Size: 120x95mm

Imperf

1438 A205 $6 multicolored 4.75 4.75
1439 A205 $6 multicolored 4.75 4.75
Nos. 1430-1439 (10) 18.30 18.30

Granada '92.

Easter — A206

Paintings: 10c, The Supper at Emmaus, studio of Gerrit Van Honthorst. 15c, Christ before Caiaphas, by Van Honthorst, vert. 45c, The

Taking of Christ, by Valentin de Boulogne. 60c, Pilate Washing his Hands, by Mattia Preti, vert. $1, The Last Supper (detail), by Master of the Reredos of The Chapel of the Church of S. Francisco D'Evora. $2, The Three Marys at the Tomb (detail), by Adolphe William Bouguereau, vert. $3, Denial of St. Peter, by Hendrik Terbrugghen. $5, Doubting Thomas, by Bernardo Strozzi, vert. No. 1448, The Crucifixion (detail), by Mathias Grunewald, vert. No. 1449, The Resurrection (detail), by Caravaggio, vert.

1992 *Perf. 14*

1440	A206	10c multicolored	.25	.25
1441	A206	15c multicolored	.25	.25
1442	A206	45c multicolored	.50	.50
1443	A206	60c multicolored	.75	.75
1444	A206	$1 multicolored	.90	.90
1445	A206	$2 multicolored	1.50	1.50
1446	A206	$3 multicolored	2.25	2.25
1447	A206	$5 multicolored	3.75	3.75
		Nos. 1440-1447 (8)	10.15	10.15

Souvenir Sheets

1448	A206	$6 multicolored	5.00	5.00
1449	A206	$6 multicolored	5.00	5.00

Columbus and New World Flora and Fauna — A207

1992, May 18

1450	A207	10c Hercules beetle	.50	.50
1451	A207	25c Crapaud frog	1.00	1.00
1452	A207	75c Parrot	1.75	1.75
1453	A207	$2 Anole	2.00	2.00
1454	A207	$4 Royal gramma	2.75	2.75
1455	A207	$5 Hibiscus	3.50	3.50
		Nos. 1450-1455 (6)	11.50	11.50

Souvenir Sheets

1456	A207	$6 Giant katydid	5.00	5.00
1457	A207	$6 Columbus' fleet	5.00	5.00

Nos. 1456-1457 are horiz.

Hummingbirds — A208

10c, Purple throated carib. 15c, Rufous breasted hermit. 45c, Puerto Rican emerald. 60c, Antillean mango. $1, Green throated carib. $2, Blue headed. $4, Eastern streamertail. $5, Antillean crested. No. 1466, Green mango. No. 1467, Vervain hummingbird.

1992, May 28

1458	A208	10c multicolored	.50	.50
1459	A208	15c multicolored	.50	.50
1460	A208	45c multicolored	.75	.75
1461	A208	60c multicolored	.90	.90
1462	A208	$1 multicolored	1.25	1.25
1463	A208	$2 multicolored	2.25	2.25
1464	A208	$4 multicolored	3.75	3.75
1465	A208	$5 multicolored	4.50	4.50
		Nos. 1458-1465 (8)	14.40	14.40

Souvenir Sheets

1466	A208	$6 multicolored	6.75	6.75
1467	A208	$6 multicolored	6.75	6.75

Genoa '92.

Dinosaurs A209

1992, June 23 Litho. *Perf. 14*

1468	A209	10c Camptosaurus	.50	.50
1469	A209	15c Edmontosaurus	.60	.60
1470	A209	25c Corythosaurus	.75	.75
1471	A209	60c Stegosaurus	.85	.85
1472	A209	$1 Torosaurus	1.00	1.00
1473	A209	$3 Euoplocephalus	1.90	1.90
1474	A209	$4 Tyrannosaurus	3.00	3.00
1475	A209	$5 Parasaurolophus	3.50	3.50
		Nos. 1468-1475 (8)	12.10	12.10

Souvenir Sheets

1476	A209	$6 like #1472	4.75	4.75
1477	A209	$6 like #1470	4.75	4.75

Marine Life A210

No. 1478: a, Copper sweeper (b). b, Sea wasp (c). c, Nassau grouper. d, Glasseye snapper, margate. e, Green moray (f). f, Reef squid. g, Octopus. h, Porkfish (g, i). i, Reef squirrelfish (h). j, Coral crab, flower coral. k, Red coral shrimp, sea star, pillar coral (l, n). l, Cubbyu, brain coral (o). m, Basket starfish, thick finger coral. n, Belted cardinal fish, boulder coral (k, m). o, Fire worm, crenelated fire coral.

No. 1479: a, Trumpetfish, blue chromis. b, Queen triggerfish. c, Hawksbill turtle. d, Sergeant major, rock beauty. e, Sharksucker. f, Lemon shark. g, Spotted trunkfish, bluehead. h, Blue tang, yellowtail damselfish. i, Queen angelfish, banded butterflyfish. j, Spotted seahorse, flower coral. k, Stoplight parrotfish, pillar coral. l, Smallmouth grunt, brain coral. m, Flamingo tongue, thick finger coral. n, Arrow crab, boulder coral. o, Sharknose goby, crenelated fire coral.

No. 1480, Harlequin bass. No. 1481, Flamefish.

1992, July 20 Litho. *Perf. 14*

1478	A210	65c Sheet of 15, #a.-o.	7.75	7.75
1479	A210	65c Sheet of 15, #a.-o.	7.75	7.75

Souvenir Sheets

1480	A210	$6 multicolored	6.50	6.50
1481	A210	$6 multicolored	6.50	6.50

A211

1992, Aug. 10 Litho. *Perf. 14*

1482	A211	10c Archery	.30	.30
1483	A211	15c Two-man canoeing	.35	.35
1484	A211	25c 110-meter hurdles	.40	.40
1485	A211	60c Men's high jump	.65	.65
1486	A211	$1 Greco-Roman wrestling	.90	.90
1487	A211	$2 Men's rings	1.50	1.50
1488	A211	$4 Men's parallel bars	2.75	2.75
1489	A211	$5 Equestrian	3.25	3.25
		Nos. 1482-1489 (8)	10.10	10.10

Souvenir Sheets

1490	A211	$6 Field hockey	5.50	5.50
1491	A211	$6 Women's platform diving	5.50	5.50

1992 Summer Olympics, Barcelona.

A212

1992 Litho. *Perf. 14½*

1492	A212	$1 Coming ashore	1.00	1.00
1493	A212	$2 Natives, ships	1.75	2.00

Discovery of America, 500th anniv. Organization of East Caribbean States.

Walt Disney's Goofy, 60th Anniv. — A213

Scenes from Disney cartoon films: 10c, Two Weeks Vacation, 1952. 15c, Aquamania, 1961. 25c, Goofy Gymnastics, 1949. 45c, How to Ride a Horse, 1941. $1, Foul Hunting, 1947. $2, For Whom the Bulls Toil, 1953. $4, Tennis Racquet, 1949. $5, Double Dribble, 1946. No. 1502, Aquamania, 1961, vert. No. 1503, The Goofy Sports Story, 1956, vert.

1992, Nov. 11 Litho. *Perf. 14x13½*

1494	A213	10c multicolored	.45	.45
1495	A213	15c multicolored	.55	.55
1496	A213	25c multicolored	.80	.80
1497	A213	45c multicolored	.90	.90
1498	A213	$1 multicolored	1.50	1.50
1499	A213	$2 multicolored	2.75	2.75
1500	A213	$4 multicolored	4.75	4.75
1501	A213	$5 multicolored	5.25	5.25
		Nos. 1494-1501 (8)	16.95	16.95

Souvenir Sheets

Perf. 13½x14

1502	A213	$6 multicolored	7.75	7.75
1503	A213	$6 multicolored	7.75	7.75

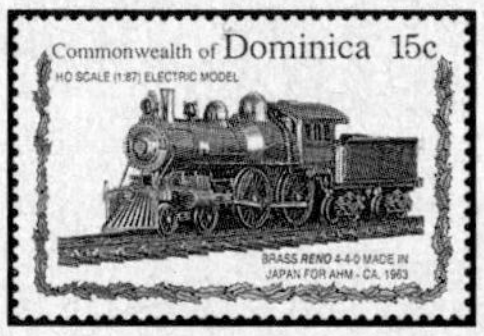

Model Trains A214

15c, Brass Reno 4-4-0, HO scale, c. 1963. 25c, Union Pacific Golden Classic, G gauge, 1992. 55c, LMS 3rd class brake coach, OO scale, 1970s. 65c, Brass Wabash 2-6-0, HO scale, c. 1958. 75c, Pennsylvania RR T-1 duplex, O gauge, 1991. $1, Streamline engine 2-6-0, O gauge, post World War II. $3, Japanese Natl. Railways class C62, HO scale, c. 1960. $5, Tinplate friction-drive floor trains, 1960s. No. 1512, 1st "toy" train in Japan, 1854. No. 1513, Stephenson's Rocket, 1:26 scale, c. 1972, vert.

1992, Nov. 11 *Perf. 14*

1504	A214	15c multicolored	.45	.45
1505	A214	25c multicolored	.50	.55
1506	A214	55c multicolored	.75	.75
1507	A214	65c multicolored	.90	.90
1508	A214	75c multicolored	1.00	1.00
1509	A214	$1 multicolored	1.25	1.25
1510	A214	$3 multicolored	2.75	2.75
1511	A214	$5 multicolored	4.50	4.50
		Nos. 1504-1511 (8)	12.10	12.15

Souvenir Sheets

Perf. 13

1512	A214	$6 multicolored	5.50	5.50
1513	A214	$6 multicolored	5.50	5.50

No. 1512 contains one 52x40mm stamp, No. 1513 one 39x51mm stamp.

Hummel Figurines — A215

Angel: 20c, Playing violin. 25c, Playing horn. 55c, Playing mandolin. 65c, Seated, playing trumpet. 90c, On cloud with lantern. $1, Holding candle. $1.20, Flying. $6, On cloud with candle.

1992, Nov. 2 *Perf. 14*

1514	A215	20c multicolored	.35	.35
1515	A215	25c multicolored	.35	.35
1516	A215	55c multicolored	.55	.55
1517	A215	65c multicolored	.70	.70
a.		Sheet of 4, #1514-1517	2.25	2.25
1518	A215	90c multicolored	1.00	1.00
1519	A215	$1 multicolored	1.25	1.25
1520	A215	$1.20 multicolored	1.50	1.50
1521	A215	$6 multicolored	3.25	3.25
a.		Sheet of 4, #1518-1521	8.00	8.00
		Nos. 1514-1521 (8)	8.95	8.95

Anniversaries and Events
A216 A217

Designs: 25c, Graf Zeppelin, 1929. No. 1523, Elderly man, plant. No. 1524, Elderly man on bicycle. No. 1525, Elderly man helping boy bait hook. No. 1526, Konrad Adenauer. No. 1527, Space shuttle. No. 1528, Wolfgang Amadeus Mozart. No. 1529, Snowy egret. No. 1530, Sir Thomas Lipton, Shamrock V, 1930. $2, Men pulling fishing net toward beach. $3, Helen Keller. No. 1533, Earth Resources Satellite. No. 1534, Map of Germany, 1949. No. 1535, Eland. $5, Count Ferdinand von Zeppelin. No. 1537, Cologne Cathedral, Germany. No. 1538, Scene from the Magic Flute. No. 1539, Mir Space Station. No. 1540, Engine of Graf Zeppelin. No. 1541, Rhinoceros hornbill.

1992 Litho. *Perf. 14*

1522	A216	25c multicolored	.60	.60
1523	A216	45c multicolored	.80	.80
1524	A216	45c multicolored	.80	.80
1525	A216	45c multicolored	.80	.80
1526	A216	90c multicolored	.90	.90
1527	A216	90c multicolored	.90	.90
1528	A217	$1.20 multicolored	2.00	2.00
1529	A216	$1.20 multicolored	1.50	1.50
1530	A216	$1.20 multicolored	1.75	1.75
1531	A216	$2 multicolored	1.75	1.75
1532	A216	$3 multicolored	3.00	3.00
1533	A216	$3 multicolored	3.00	3.00
1534	A216	$4 multicolored	4.25	4.25
1535	A216	$4 multicolored	4.25	4.25
1536	A216	$5 multicolored	5.00	5.00
		Nos. 1522-1536 (15)	31.30	31.30

Souvenir Sheets

1537	A216	$6 multicolored	6.25	6.25
1538	A217	$6 multicolored	6.75	6.75
1539	A216	$6 multicolored	6.25	6.25
1540	A216	$6 multicolored	6.25	6.25
1541	A216	$6 multicolored	5.75	5.75

Konrad Adenauer, 25th anniv. of death (Nos. 1526, 1534, 1537). Intl. Space Year (Nos. 1527, 1533, 1539). Mozart, 200th anniv. of death (in 1991) (Nos. 1528, 1538). Count Zeppelin, 75th anniv. of death (Nos. 1522, 1536, 1540). Intl. Day of the Elderly (Nos. 1523-1525). UN Earth Summit, Rio (Nos. 1529, 1535, 1541). America's Cup yacht race (No. 1530). WHO Intl. Conference on Nutrition, Rome (No. 1531). Lions Intl., 75th anniv. (No. 1532).

Issued: Nos. 1528, 1539, Oct.; Nos. 1523-1527, 1533-1534, 1537-1538, Nov.; Nos. 1522, 1529, 1535-1536, 1540-1541, Dec.

Miniature Sheet

Louvre Museum, Bicent. — A218

Details or entire paintings by Titian: a-b, Madonna and Child with St. Catherine and a Rabbit (diff. details). c, A Woman at Her Toilet. d-e, The Supper at Emmaus (diff. details). f, The Pastoral Concert. g-h, An Allegory, Perhaps of Marriage (diff. details).

Painting by Hieronymus Bosch: $6, The Ship of Fools.

1993, Mar. 24 Litho. *Perf. 12*

1542 A218 $1 Sheet of 8, #a.-h. + label 9.50 9.50

Souvenir Sheet

Perf. 14½

1543 A218 $6 multicolored 5.75 5.75

No. 1543 contains one 55x88mm stamp.

Elvis Presley, 15th Anniv. of Death (in 1992) A219

a, Portrait. b, With guitar. c, Holding microphone.

1993, Feb. *Perf. 14*

1544 A219 $1 Strip of 3, #a.-c. 3.75 3.75

Miniature Sheet

Birds of Dominica — A220

a, Plumbeous warbler. b, Black swift. c, Blue-hooded euphonia. d, Rufous-throated solitaire. e, Ringed kingfisher. f, Blue-headed hummingbird. g, Bananaquit. h, Trembler. i, Forest thrush. j, Purple-throated carib. k, Ruddy quail dove. l, Least bittern.

No. 1546, Imperial parrot. No. 1547, Red-necked parrot (Amazona arausiaca).

1993, Apr. 30

1545 A220 90c Sheet of 12, #a.-l. 18.00 18.00

Souvenir Sheets

1546 A220 $6 multicolored 6.50 6.50
1547 A220 $6 multicolored 6.50 6.50

Turtles A221

25c, Leatherback laying eggs. 55c, Hawksbill. 65c, Atlantic Ridley. 90c, Green turtle laying eggs. $1, Green turtle at sea. $2, Hawksbill, diff. $4, Loggerhead. $5, Leatherback at sea. No. 1556, Green turtle hatchling. No. 1557, Head of hawksbill.

1993, May 26 Litho. *Perf. 14*

1548 A221 25c multicolored .45 .45
1549 A221 55c multicolored .55 .55
1550 A221 65c multicolored .75 .75
1551 A221 90c multicolored .95 .95
1552 A221 $1 multicolored 1.10 1.10
1553 A221 $2 multicolored 1.75 1.75
1554 A221 $4 multicolored 3.25 3.25
1555 A221 $5 multicolored 4.25 4.25
Nos. 1548-1555 (8) 13.05 13.05

Souvenir Sheets

1556 A221 $6 multicolored 5.75 5.75
1557 A221 $6 multicolored 5.75 5.75

For overprints see Nos. 2103-2107.

Automobiles — A222

Designs: 90c, 1928 Model A Ford. $1.20, Mercedes-Benz winning Swiss Grand Prix, 1936. $4, Mercedes-Benz winning German Grand Prix, 1935. $5, 1915 Model T Ford.

No. 1562: a, 1993 Mercedes-Benz coupe/roadster. b, 1893 Benz Viktoria.

No. 1563, Ford GT-40.

1993, May Litho. *Perf. 14*

1558 A222 90c multicolored .80 .80
1559 A222 $1.20 multicolored 1.10 1.10
1560 A222 $4 multicolored 2.75 2.75
1561 A222 $5 multicolored 3.75 3.75
Nos. 1558-1561 (4) 8.40 8.40

Souvenir Sheets

1562 A222 $3 Sheet of 2, #a.-b. 5.00 5.00
1563 A222 $6 multicolored 5.00 5.00

No. 1563 contains one 57x42mm stamp.

First Ford gasoline engine, cent. (Nos. 1558, 1561, 1563). Benz's first four-wheeled vehicle, cent. (Nos. 1559-1560, 1562).

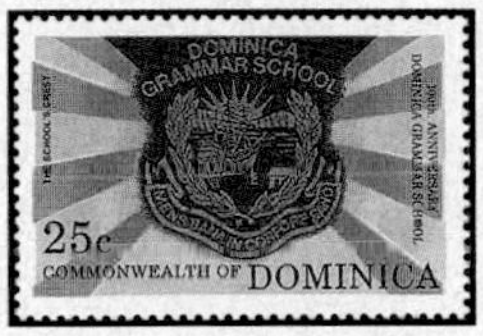

Dominica Grammar School, Cent. A223

Designs: 25c, School crest. 30c, V. A. A. Archer, first West Indian headmaster. 65c, Hubert A. Charles, first Dominican headmaster. 90c, Present school building.

1993, May

1564 A223 25c multicolored .25 .25
1565 A223 30c multicolored .30 .30
1566 A223 65c multicolored .60 .60
1567 A223 90c multicolored .85 .85
Nos. 1564-1567 (4) 2.00 2.00

Aviation Anniversaries — A224

Designs: 25c, New York ticker tape parade, 1928. 55c, BAC Lightning F2. 65c, Graf Zeppelin over Sphinx, pyramids, 1929. $1, Boeing 314 flying boat. $2, Astronaut stepping onto moon. $4, Viktoria Louise over Kiel harbor, 1912. $5, Supermarine Spitfire, vert. No. 1575, Royal Air Force Crest, vert. No. 1576, Hugo Eckener in airship cockpit, vert. No. 1577, Jean-Pierre Blanchard's hot air balloon, 1793, vert.

1993, May 28 Litho. *Perf. 14*

1568 A224 25c multicolored .90 .90
1569 A224 55c multicolored 1.10 1.10
1570 A224 65c multicolored 1.50 1.50
1571 A224 $1 multicolored 1.75 1.75
1572 A224 $2 multicolored 3.00 3.00
1573 A224 $4 multicolored 4.00 4.00
1574 A224 $5 multicolored 4.25 4.25
Nos. 1568-1574 (7) 16.50 16.50

Souvenir Sheets

1575 A224 $6 multicolored 6.25 6.25
1576 A224 $6 multicolored 6.25 6.25
1577 A224 $6 multicolored 5.75 5.75

Zeppelin Capt. Hugo Eckener, 125th anniv. of birth (Nos. 1568, 1570, 1573, 1576). Royal Air Force, 75th anniv. (Nos. 1569, 1574-1575).

Nos. 1575-1576 each contain one 42x57mm stamp.

Miniature Sheet

Coronation of Queen Elizabeth II, 40th Anniv. — A225

Designs: No. 1578a, 20c, Official coronation photograph. b, 25c, Ceremony. c, 65c, Gold State Coach. d, $5, Queen Elizabeth II, Queen Mother.

$6, Portrait, by Norman Hutchinson, 1969.

1993, June 2 Litho. *Perf. 13½x14*

1578 A225 Sheet, 2 each #a.-d. 13.00 13.00

Souvenir Sheet

Perf. 14

1579 A225 $6 multicolored 6.75 6.75

No. 1579 contains one 28x42mm stamp.

For overprints see Nos. 1688-1689.

Wedding of Japan's Crown Prince Naruhito and Masako Owada A226

Cameo photos of couple and: 90c, Crown Prince holding flowers. $5, Princess wearing full-length coat.

$6, Princess riding in limousine.

1993, June 14 Litho. *Perf. 14*

1580 A226 90c multicolored .75 .75
1581 A226 $5 multicolored 5.00 5.00

Souvenir Sheet

1582 A226 $6 multicolored 6.00 6.00

Inauguration of Pres. William J. Clinton — A227

$5, Bill, Hillary Clinton. $6, Bill Clinton, vert.

1993, July 30 Litho. *Perf. 14*

1583 A227 $5 multicolored 4.25 4.25

Souvenir Sheet

1584 A227 $6 multicolored 6.00 6.00

Willy Brandt (1913-92), German Chancellor — A228

Brandt and: 65c, Pres. Eisenhower, 1959. $5, N.K. Winston, 1964. $6, Portrait.

1993, July 30

1585 A228 65c black & brown .90 .90
1586 A228 $5 black & brown 4.75 4.75

Souvenir Sheet

1587 A228 $6 black & brown 6.00 6.00

Picasso (1881-1973) A229

Polska '93 A230

Paintings: 25c, Bather with Beach Ball, 1929. 90c, Portrait of Leo Stein, 1906. $5, Portrait of Wilhelm Unde, 1910. $6, Man with a Pipe, 1915.

1993, July 30

1588 A229 25c multicolored .40 .40
1589 A229 90c multicolored .85 .85
1590 A229 $5 multicolored 4.75 4.75
Nos. 1588-1590 (3) 6.00 6.00

Souvenir Sheet

1591 A229 $6 multicolored 6.00 6.00

1993, July 30

Paintings: 90c, Self-portrait, by Marian Szczyrbula, 1921. $3, Portrait of Bruno Jasienski, by Tytus Czyzewski, 1921. $6, Miser, by Tadeusz Makowski, 1973.

1592 A230 90c multicolored 1.50 1.50
1593 A230 $3 multicolored 3.50 3.50

Souvenir Sheet

1594 A230 $6 multicolored 6.00 6.00

A231

A232

90c, Monika Holzner, speedskating, 1984. $4, US hockey players, Ray Leblanc, Tim Sweeney, 1992. $6, Men's ski jump.

1993, July 30

1595 A231 90c multicolored 1.50 1.50
1596 A231 $4 multicolored 4.00 4.00

Souvenir Sheet

1597 A231 $6 multicolored 5.75 5.75

1994 Winter Olympics, Lillehammer, Norway.

1993, July 30

Designs: $1.20, Astronomer using quadrant. $3, Observatory. $5, Copernicus.

1598 A232 $1.20 multicolored 1.50 1.50
1599 A232 $3 multicolored 3.75 3.75

Souvenir Sheet

1600 A232 $5 multicolored 6.00 6.00

Copernicus (1473-1543).

Opening of New General Post Office A233

New General Post Office and: 25c, Prince Philip. 90c, Queen Elizabeth II.

1993, July 30

1601 A233 25c multicolored .25 .25
1602 A233 90c multicolored 1.00 1.00

1994 World Cup Soccer Championships, US — A234

1993, Sept. 8 Litho. *Perf. 14*

1603 A234 25c Maradona, Buchwald .65 .65
1604 A234 55c Gullit .75 .75
1605 A234 65c Chavarria, Bliss .85 .85
1606 A234 90c Maradona 1.00 1.00
1607 A234 90c Alvares 1.00 1.00
1608 A234 $1 Altobelli, Yong-hwang 1.25 1.25
1609 A234 $2 Referee, Stopyra 2.00 2.00
1610 A234 $5 Renquin, Yaremtchuk 3.00 3.00
Nos. 1603-1610 (8) 10.50 10.50

Souvenir Sheets

1611 A234 $6 Brehme 4.50 4.50
1612 A234 $6 Fabbri 4.50 4.50

Taipei '93 — A235

Chinese kites: No. 1617a, Chang E Rising up to the Moon. b, Red Phoenix and Rising Sun. c, Heavenly Judge. d, Monkey King. e, Goddess of the Luo River. f, Heavenly Maiden Scatters Flowers.

1993, Oct. 4 Litho. *Perf. 13½x14*

1613 A235 25c Tiger Balm Gardens .30 .30
1614 A235 65c Building, Kenting Park .55 .55
1615 A235 90c Tzu-en Tower 1.00 1.00
1616 A235 $5 Villa, Lan Tao Island 4.25 4.25
Nos. 1613-1616 (4) 6.10 6.10

Miniature Sheet

1617 A235 $1.65 Sheet of 6, #a.-f. 10.00 10.00

Souvenir Sheet

1618 A235 $6 Jade Girl, Liao Dynasty 5.25 5.25

With Bangkok '93 Emblem

Puppets: No. 1623a, Thai, Rama and Sita. b, Burmese, Tha Khi Lek. c, Burmese, diff. d, Thai, Demons, Wat Phra Kaew. e, Thai, Hun Lek performing Khun Chang, Khun Phaen. f, Thai, Hun Lek performing Ramakien.

1993

1619 A235 25c Tugu Monument, Java .30 .30
1620 A235 55c Candi Cangkuang, West Java .55 .55
1621 A235 90c Pura Taman Ayun, Mengwi 1.00 1.00
1622 A235 $5 Stone mosaics, Ceto 4.00 4.00
Nos. 1619-1622 (4) 5.85 5.85

Miniature Sheet

1623 A235 $1.65 Sheet of 6, #a.-f. 10.00 10.00

Souvenir Sheet

1624 A235 $6 Stone carving, Thailand 5.25 5.25

With Indopex '93 Emblem

Designs: 25c, Ornate Chedi, Wat Phra Boromathat Chaiya. 55c, Preserved temple ruins, Sukhothai Historical Park. 90c, Prasat Hin Phimai, Thailand. $5, Main sanctuary, Prasat Phanom Rung, Thailand.

Indonesian puppets — No. 1629: a, Arjuna & Prabu Gilling Wesi. b, Loro Blonyo. c, Yogyanese puppets, Menak cycle. d, Wayang gedog, Ng Setro. e, Wayang golek, Kencana Wungu. f, Wayang gedog, Raden Damar Wulan.

$6, Sculpture of Majapahit noble, Pura Sada, Kapel.

1993, Oct. 4 Litho. *Perf. 13½x14*

1625 A235 25c multicolored .40 .40
1626 A235 55c multicolored .60 .60
1627 A235 90c multicolored 1.25 1.25
1628 A235 $5 multicolored 4.00 4.00
Nos. 1625-1628 (4) 6.25 6.25

Miniature Sheet

1629 A235 $1.65 Sheet of 6, #a.-f. 10.00 10.00

Souvenir Sheet

1630 A235 $6 multicolored 5.25 5.25

Miniature Sheet

Willie the Operatic Whale — A236

Nos. 1631-1633, Characters and scenes from Disney's animated film Willie the Operatic Whale.

1993, Nov. 1 Litho. *Perf. 14x13½*

1631 A236 $1 Sheet of 9, #a.-i. 14.00 14.00

Souvenir Sheets

1632 A236 $6 multicolored 5.00 5.00

Perf. 13½x14

1633 A236 $6 multi, vert. 5.00 5.00

Christmas A237

25c, 55c, 65c, 90c (No. 1637), Details or entire woodcut, The Adoration of the Magi, by Durer.

90c (No. 1638), $1, $3, $5, Details or entire painting, The Foligni Madonna, by Raphael.

Souvenir Sheets: No. 1642, $6, The Adoration of the Magi, by Durer. No. 1643, $6, The Foligni Madonna, by Raphael.

1993, Nov. 8 Litho. *Perf. 13*

1634-1643 A237 Set of 10 20.00 20.00

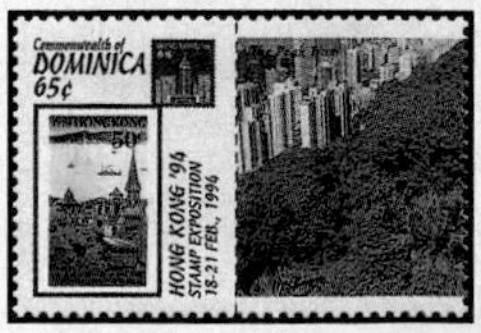

A238

Hong Kong '94 — A239

Stamps, scene from Peak Tram: No. 1644, Hong Kong #527, city buildings, trees. No. 1645, Trees, tram, #1292.

Chinese jade: No. 1646a, Horse. b, Cup with handle. c, Vase with birthday peaches. d, Vase. e, Fu dog and puppy. f, Drinking vessel.

1994, Feb. 18 Litho. *Perf. 14*

1644 A238 65c multicolored .50 .50
1645 A238 65c multicolored .50 .50
a. Pair, #1644-1645 1.10 1.10

Miniature Sheet

1646 A239 65c Sheet of 6, #a.-f. 5.75 5.75

Nos. 1644-1645 issued in sheets of 5 pairs. No. 1645a is a continuous design.

New Year 1994 (Year of the Dog) (No. 1646e).

Insects, Butterflies, & Birds — A240

Various Hercules beetles: 20c, 25c, 65c, Male. 90c, Female.

$1, Imperial parrot. $2, Southern dagger tail. $3, The mimic. $5, Purple-throated carib.

Each $6: No. 1655, Snout butterfly. No. 1656, Blue-headed hummingbird.

1994, Mar. 15 Litho. *Perf. 14*

1647-1654 A240 Set of 8 11.00 11.00
1650a Min. sheet, 3 each #1647-1650 10.00 10.00

Souvenir Sheets

1655-1656 A240 Set of 2 12.00 12.00

World Wildlife Fund (Nos. 1647-1650).

Mushrooms A241

Designs: 20c, Russula matoubenis. 25c, Leptonia caeruleocapita. 65c, Inocybe littoralis. 90c, Russula hygrophytica. $1, Pyrrhoglossum lilaceipes. $2, Hygrocybe konradii. $3, Inopilus magnificus. $5, Boletellus cubensis.

No. 1665, Gerronema citrinum. No. 1666, Lentinus strigosus.

1994, Apr. 18

1657 A241 20c multicolored .45 .45
1658 A241 25c multicolored .50 .50
1659 A241 65c multicolored .65 .65
1660 A241 90c multicolored .80 .80
1661 A241 $1 multicolored .95 .95
1662 A241 $2 multicolored 1.50 1.50
1663 A241 $3 multicolored 2.00 2.00
1664 A241 $5 multicolored 3.00 3.00
Nos. 1657-1664 (8) 9.85 9.85

Souvenir Sheets

1665 A241 $6 multicolored 4.75 4.75
1666 A241 $6 multicolored 4.75 4.75

Orchids — A242

Designs: 20c, Laeliocattleya. 25c, Sophrolaeliocattleya. 65c, Odontocidium. 90c, Laeliocattleya, diff. $1, Cattleya. $2, Odontocidium, diff. $3, Epiphronitis. $4, Oncidium.

Each $6: No. 1675, Schombocattleya. No. 1676, Cattleya, diff.

1994, May 3

1667-1674 A242 Set of 8 10.00 10.00

Souvenir Sheets

1675-1676 A242 Set of 2 10.00 10.00

New Year 1994 (Year of the Dog) — A243

Designs: 20c, Dachshund. 25c, Beagle. 55c, Greyhound. 90c, Jack Russell terrier. $1, Pekingese. $2, White fox terrier. $4, English toy spaniel. $5, Irish setter.

No. 1686, Welsh corgi. No. 1687, Labrador retriever.

1994, May 17

1678 A243 20c multicolored .30 .30
1679 A243 25c multicolored .35 .35
1680 A243 55c multicolored .50 .50
1681 A243 90c multicolored .80 .80
1682 A243 $1 multicolored 1.00 1.00
1683 A243 $2 multicolored 1.50 1.50
1684 A243 $4 multicolored 2.50 2.50
1685 A243 $5 multicolored 3.00 3.00
Nos. 1678-1685 (8) 9.95 9.95

Souvenir Sheets

1686 A243 $6 multicolored 5.00 5.00
1687 A243 $6 multicolored 5.00 5.00

Nos. 1578-1579 Ovptd. in Black or Silver

1994, June 27 Litho. *Perf. 13½x14*

1688 A225 Sheet, 2 ea #a-d 15.00 15.00

Souvenir Sheet

1689 A225 $6 multicolored (S) 7.25 7.25

Overprint on No. 1689 appears in sheet margin.

Miniature Sheet

1994 World Cup Soccer Championships, US — A244

No. 1690: a, Dos Armstrong, US. b, Dennis Bergkamp, Netherlands. c, Roberto Baggio, Italy. d, Rai, Brazil. e, Cafu, Brazil. f, Marco Van Baston, Netherlands.

Each $6: No. 1691, Roberto Mancini, Italy. No. 1692, Stanford Stadium, Palo Alto.

1994, July 5 *Perf. 14*

1690 A244 $1 Sheet of 6, #a.-f. 6.00 6.00

Souvenir Sheets

1691-1692 A244 Set of 2 10.00 10.00

Butterflies A245

1994, May 3 Litho. *Perf. 14*

1693 A245 20c Florida white .40 .40
1694 A245 25c Red rim .40 .40
1695 A245 55c Barred sulphur .75 .75
1696 A245 65c Mimic .80 .80
1697 A245 $1 Large orange sulphur 1.00 1.00
1698 A245 $2 Southern dagger tail 1.50 1.50
1698A A245 $3 Dominican snout butter-fly 2.00 2.00
1699 A245 $5 Caribbean buckeye 3.50 3.50
Nos. 1693-1699 (8) 10.35 10.35

Souvenir Sheets

1700 A245 $6 Clench's hair-streak 5.50 5.50
1701 A245 $6 Painted lady 5.50 5.50

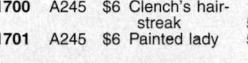

10th Caribbean Scout Jamboree A246

Designs: 20c, Backpacking. 25c, Cooking over campfire. 55c, Making camp. 65c, Camping. $1, Scout drum unit. $2, Planting trees. $4, Sailing. $5, Scout salute.
Each $6: No. 1710, Early Scout troop. No. 1711, Pres. C.A. Sorhaindo, vert.

1994, July 18 Litho. *Perf. 14*

1702-1709 A246 Set of 8 11.50 11.50

Souvenir Sheets

1710-1711 A246 Set of 2 11.50 11.50

For overprints see Nos. 1762-1766.

D-Day, 50th Anniv. A247

Designs: 65c, US Waco glider brings reinforcements. $2, British Horsa gliders land more troops. $3, Glider troops take Pegasus Bridge.
$6, Hadrian glider.

1994, July 26

1712-1714 A247 Set of 3 5.00 5.00

Souvenir Sheet

1715 A247 $6 multicolored 4.75 4.75

A248

Intl. Olympic Committee, Cent. — A249

Designs: 55c, Ulrike Meyfarth, Germany, high jump, 1984. $1.45, Dieter Baumann, Germany, 5000-meter run, 1992.
$6, Ji Hoon Chae, South Korea, 500-meter short track speed skating, 1994.

1994, July 26

1716 A248 55c multicolored .90 .90
1717 A248 $1.45 multicolored 2.00 2.00

Souvenir Sheet

1718 A249 $6 multicolored 5.75 5.75

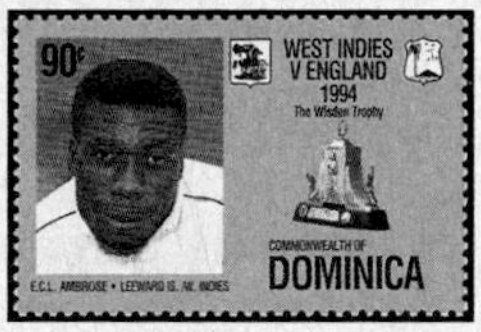

English Touring Cricket, Cent. A250

Designs: 55c, D.I. Goweer Leics, England, vert. 90c, E.C.L. Ambrose, Leeward Islands. $1, G.A. Gooch, England, vert.
$3, First English team, 1895.

1994, July 26

1719-1721 A250 Set of 3 4.00 4.00

Souvenir Sheet

1722 A250 $3 multicolored 5.75 5.75

Miniature Sheet of 6

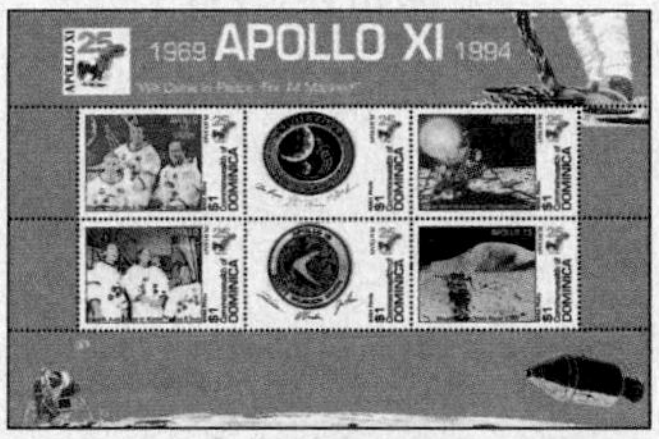

First Manned Moon Landing, 25th Anniv. — A251

No. 1723: a, Apollo 14 crew. b, Apollo 14 patch. c, Apollo 14 lunar module Antares at Fra Mauro Crater. d, Apollo 15 crew. e, Apollo 15 patch. f, Apollo 15 mission, Mount Hadley from rover.
$6, 25th anniv. emblem, lunar surface.

1994, July 26

1723 A251 $1 #a.-f. 7.75 7.75

Souvenir Sheet

1724 A251 $6 multicolored 6.50 6.50

A252

PHILAKOREA '94 — A253

Designs: 65c, P'alsang-jon Hall, Korea. 90c, Popchu-sa Temple. $2, Uhwajong Pavillion, Korea.
Screen, Late Choson Dynasty showing flowers and: No. 1728a, c, e, Birds. b, g, Butterfly. d, Roosters. f, Duck. h, Pheasant. i, Cranes. j, Deer.
$4, Stylized "spirit post" guardian.

1994, July 26 *Perf. 14, 13 (#1728)*

1725-1727 A252 Set of 3 3.50 3.50

Miniature Sheet of 10

1728 A253 55c #a.-j. 6.00 6.00

Souvenir Sheet

1729 A252 $4 multicolored 3.00 3.00

Mickey Mouse, 65th Birthday A254

Disney characters: 20c, Dippy dawg. 25c, Clarabelle Cow. 55c, Horace Horsecollar. 65c, Mortimer Mouse. $1, Joe Piper. $3, Mr. Casey. $4, Chief O'Hara. $5, Mickey and the Blot.
Each $6: No. 1738, Minnie, Tanglefoot. No. 1739, Pluto, Minnie, horiz.

Perf. 13½x14, 14x13½ (#1739)

1994, Oct. 3

1730-1737 A254 Set of 8 14.00 14.00

Souvenir Sheets

1738-1739 A254 Set of 2 13.00 13.00

A255

Local Entertainers: 20c, Sonia Llyod, folk singer. 25c, Ophelia Marie, singer. 55c, Edney Francis, accordionist. 65c, Norman Letang, saxophonist. 90c, Edie Andre, steel drummer.

1994, Dec. 1 Litho. *Perf. 14*

1740-1744 A255 Set of 5 3.25 3.25

Miniature Sheet

A256

Marilyn Monroe (1926-62), Actress: Nos. 1745a-1745i, Various portraits. No. 1746, $6, Hands above head. No. 1747, $6, Holding hat.

1994, Dec. 1

1745 A256 90c #a.-i. 11.50 11.50

Souvenir Sheets

1746-1747 A256 Set of 2 10.00 10.00

Christmas A257

Details or entire Spanish paintings: 20c, Madonna and child, by Luis de Morales. 25c, Madonna and Child with Yarn Winder, by Morales. 55c, Our Lady of the Rosary, by Zurbaran. 65c, Dream of the Patrician, by Bartolome Murillo. 90c, Madonna of Charity, by El Greco. $1, The Annunciation, by Zurbaran. $2, Mystical Marriage of St. Catherine, by Jusepe de Ribera. $3, The Holy Family with St. Bruno and Other Saints, by Ribera.
Each $6: No. 1756, Vision of the Virgin to St. Bernard, by Murillo. No. 1757, Adoration of the Shepherds, by Murillo.

1994, Dec. 2 *Perf. 13½x14*

1748-1755 A257 Set of 8 7.00 7.00

Souvenir Sheets

1756-1757 A257 Set of 2 10.00 10.00

Order of the Caribbean Community — A258

First award recipients: 25c, Sir Shridath Ramphal, statesman, Guyana. 65c, William Gilbert Demas, economist, Trinidad & Tobago. 90c, Derek Walcott, writer, St. Lucia.

1994, Dec. 16 *Perf. 14*

1758-1760 A258 Set of 3 2.00 2.00

Jeffrey Edmund, 1994 World Cup Soccer Player A259

1994, Dec. 28

1761 A259 25c multicolored .35 .35

Nos. 1705, 1708-1711 Ovptd.

1995, Mar. 21 Litho. *Perf. 14*

1762-1764 A246 Set of 3 7.00 7.00

Souvenir Sheets

1765-1766 A246 Set of 2 10.00 10.00

Location of overprint varies.

New Year 1995 (Year of the Boar) — A260

Stylized boars: a, 25c, Facing right. b, 65c, Facing forward. c, $1, Facing left.
$2, Two facing each other, horiz.

1995, Apr. 15 Litho. *Perf. 14½*

1767 A260 Strip of 3, #a.-c. 1.60 1.60
d. Souv. sheet of 3, #1767a-1767c 1.60 1.60

Souvenir Sheet

1768 A260 $2 multicolored 1.50 1.50

No. 1767 was issued in sheets of 4 strips.

Birds A261

Designs: 25c, Wood duck. 55c, Mallard. 65c, Blue-winged teal. $5, Blood eared parakeet.

No. 1773, vert.: a, Cattle egret. b, Snow goose (a, c). c, Peregrine falcon. d, Barn owl. e, Black-crowned night heron. f, Common grackle. g, Brown pelican. h, Great egret. i, Ruby-throated hummingbird. j, Laughing gull. k, Greater flamingo. l, Common moorhen.

No. 1774, Trumpeter swan, vert. No. 1775, White-eyed vireo.

1995, Apr. 15 Litho. *Perf. 14*

1769-1772 A261 Set of 4 5.00 5.00

Miniature Sheet of 12

1773 A261 65c #a.-l. 16.00 16.00

Souvenir Sheets

1774 A261 $5 multicolored 5.00 5.00
1775 A261 $6 multicolored 6.00 6.00

Miniature Sheets

End of World War II, 50th Anniv. — A262

No. 1776: a, Mitsubishi A6M2 Zero. b, Aichi D3A1 Type 99 "Val." c, Nakajima 97-B5N "Kate." d, Zuikaku. e, Akagi. f, Ryuho.

No. 1777: a, German Panther tank, Ardennes. b, Allied fighter bomber. c, Patton's army crosses the Rhine. d, Rocket-powered ME 163. e, V-2 rocket on launcher. f, German U-boat surrenders in North Atlantic. g, Round the clock bombardment of Berlin. h, Soviet soldiers reach center of Berlin.

Each $6: No. 1778, Statue atop Dresden's town hall after Allied bombing. No. 1779, Japanese attack plane.

1995 Litho. *Perf. 14*

1776 A262 $2 #a.-f. + label 9.00 9.00
1777 A262 $2 #a.-h. + label 13.00 13.00

Souvenir Sheets

1778-1779 A262 Set of 2 14.00 14.00

Issued: Nos. 1777-1778, 5/18; others, 7/21.

1996 Summer Olympics, Atlanta A263

Designs: 15c, Mark Breland, boxing. 20c, Lou Banach, Joseph Atiyeh, freestyle wrestling. 25c, Judo. 55c, Fencing. 65c, Matt Biondi, swimming. $1, Gushiken on rings, vert. $2, Cycling, vert. $5, Volleyball.

Each $6: No. 1788, Joe Fargis on Touch of Class, equestrian. No. 1789, Soccer, vert.

1995, July 21

1780-1787 A263 Set of 8 9.50 9.50

Souvenir Sheets

1788-1789 A263 Set of 2 10.50 10.50

UN, 50th Anniv. — A264

No. 1790: a, 65c, Signatures on UN charter, attendee. b, $1, Attendee. $2, Attendees. $6, Winston Churchill.

1995, Aug. 16 Litho. *Perf. 14*

1790 A264 Strip of 3, #a.-c. 2.75 2.75

Souvenir Sheet

1791 A264 $6 multicolored 5.00 5.00

No. 1790 is a continuous design.

Souvenir Sheets

FAO, 50th Anniv. — A265

Street market scene: a, 90c, Woman in red dress. b, $1, Woman seated. c, $2, Vendors, women.

$6, Woman in field, woman holding water cans, vert.

1995, Aug. 16

1792 A265 Sheet of 3, #a.-c. 2.50 2.50
1793 A265 $6 multicolored 4.50 4.50

No. 1792 is a continuous design.

Queen Mother, 95th Birthday A266

No. 1794: a, Drawing. b, Wearing crown, green dress. c, Formal portrait. d, Blue dress. $6, Portrait as younger woman.

1995, Aug. 16 *Perf. 13½x14*

1794 A266 $1.65 Strip or block of 4, #a.-d. 5.50 5.50

Souvenir Sheet

1795 A266 $6 multicolored 5.50 5.50

No. 1794 was issued in sheets of 8 stamps. Sheet margins of Nos. 1794-1795 exist with black frame and text "In Memoriam — 1900-2002" overprinted in sheet margins.

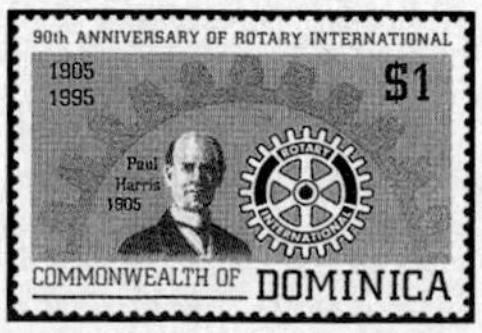

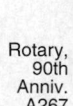

Rotary, 90th Anniv. A267

1995 *Perf. 14*

1796 A267 $1 Paul Harris, emblem 1.00 1.00

Souvenir Sheet

1797 A267 $6 Rotary emblems 4.75 4.75

Dinosaurs A268

20c, Monoclonius. 25c, Euoplocephalus. 55c, Coelophysis. 65c, Compsognathus.

No. 1802: a, Dimorphodon. b, Ramphorynchus. c, Giant alligator. d, Pentaceratops.

No. 1803, vert: a, Ceratosaurus. b, Comptosaurus (a). c, Stegosaur. d, Camarasaurs. e, Baronyx. f, Dilophosaurus. g, Dromaeosaurids (f). h, Deinonychus. i, Dinicthys. j, Carcharodon (k). k, Nautiloid. l, Trilobite.

$5, Sauropelta. $6, Triceratops, vert.

1995, Sept. 8

1798-1801 A268 Set of 4 1.75 1.75
1802 A268 90c Strip of 4, #a.-d. 3.00 3.00

Miniature Sheet of 12

1803 A268 $1 #a.-l. 10.00 10.00

Souvenir Sheets

1804 A268 $5 multicolored 5.00 5.00
1805 A268 $6 multicolored 5.00 5.00

Singapore '95 (Nos. 1798-1801, 1803-1805).

Miniature Sheets of 6

Nobel Prize Fund Established, Cent. — A269

Recipients, each $2: No. 1806a, Oscar A. Sanchez, peace, 1987. b, Ernst B. Chain, medicine, 1945. c, Aage Bohr, physics, 1975. d, Jaroslav Seifert, literature, 1984. e, Joseph E. Murray, medicine, 1990. f, Jaroslav Heyrovsky, chemistry, 1959.

No. 1807, each $2: a, Adolf von Baeyer, chemistry, 1905. b, Edward Buchner, chemistry, 1907. c, Carl Bosch, chemistry, 1931. d, Otto Hahn, chemistry, 1944. e, Otto Paul Herman Diels, chemistry, 1950. f, Kurt Alder, chemistry, 1950.

No. 1808, Emil A. von Behring, medicine, 1901.

1995, Oct. 24 Litho. *Perf. 14*

1806-1807 A269 Set of 2 19.00 19.00

Souvenir Sheet

1808 A269 $2 multicolored 1.75 1.75

Christmas A270

Details or entire paintings: 20c, Madonna and Child, by Pontormo. 25c, The Immaculate Conception, by Murillo. 55c, The Adoration of the Magi, by Filippino Lippi. 65c, Rest on the Flight into Egypt, by Van Dyck. 90c, Sacred Family, by Van Dyck. $5, The Annunciation, by Van Eyck.

No. 1815, The Virgin and the Infant, by Van Eyck. No. 1816, The Holy Family, by Ribera.

1995, Nov. 30 Litho. *Perf. 13½x14*

1809-1814 A270 Set of 6 6.00 6.00

Souvenir Sheets

1815 A270 $5 multicolored 3.75 3.75
1816 A270 $6 multicolored 4.75 4.75

Miniature Sheets

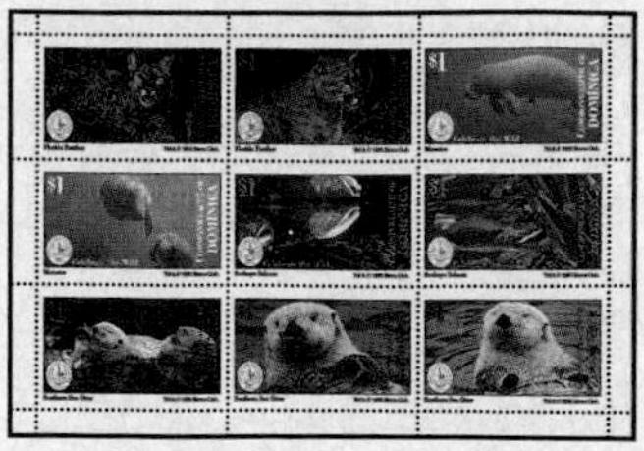

Sierra Club, Cent. — A271

Designs: No. 1817, each $1: a, Florida panther with mouth open. b, Florida panther looking right. c, Manatee. d, Two manatees. e, Three sockeye salmon. f, Group of sockeye salmon. g, Two southern sea otters. h, Southern sea otter. i, Southern sea otter showing both front paws.

No. 1818, vert, each $1: a, Florida panther. b, Manatee. c, Sockeye salmon. d, Key deer facing left. e, Key deer. f, Key deer with antlers, up close. g, Wallaby with young in pouch. h, Wallaby. i, Wallaby with young.

1995, Dec. 10 *Perf. 14*

1817-1818 A271 Set of 2 13.00 13.00

Chinese Paintings, A City of Cathay A272

No. 1819, brown lettering, each 90c: a, Boats docked, people on shore. b, River, bridge. c, Two boats on river. d, River, pavilion along shore. e, Open sea, people in courtyard.

No. 1820, black lettering, each 90c: a, City scene. b, City scene, wall. c, Outside wall, river. d, Large boat on river. e, People crossing over bridge.

No. 1821, $2: a, Boat on river, city above. b, People walking across bridge.

No. 1822, $2: a, Lifting ramp to another boat, vert. b, Holding lines in water, tree, vert.

1995, Dec. 27 Litho. *Perf. 14½*

Strips of 5

1819-1820 A272 Set of 2 7.50 7.50

Souvenir Sheets of 2

1821-1822 A272 Set of 2 6.00 6.00

Nos. 1819-1822 are each continuous designs.

Classic Western Art — A273

Paintings by Raphael: No. 1823, Agony in the Garden. No. 1824, Pope Leo X with Two Cardinals. No. 1825, Bindo Altoviti.

$6, Triumphant entry of Constantine into Rome, by Rubens.

1995, Dec. 27 *Perf. 14*

1823-1825 A273 $2 Set of 3 5.25 5.25

Souvenir Sheet

1826 A273 $6 multicolored 5.25 5.25

New Year 1996 (Year of the Rat) — A274

Stylized rats, Chinese inscriptions: No. 1827a, 25c, purple & brown. b, 65c, orange & green. c, $1, red lilac & blue.

$2, Two rats, horiz.

1996, Jan. 16 ***Perf. 14½***
1827 A274 Strip of 3, #a.-c. 1.90 1.90

Miniature Sheet

1828 A274 Sheet of 1 #1827 1.60 1.60

Souvenir Sheet

1829 A274 $2 multicolored 1.75 1.75

No. 1827 was issued in sheets of 12 stamps.

Miniature Sheet

Disney Lunar New Year — A275

Disney characters representing year of the: No. 1830a, Rat. b, Ox. c, Tiger. d, Hare. e, Dragon. f, Snake. g, Horse. h, Sheep. i, Monkey. j, Rooster. k, Dog. l, Pig.
$3, Rat character. $6, Pig, rat, ox characters on lunar calendar wheel.

1996, Jan. 16 ***Perf. 14x13½***
1830 A275 55c Sheet of 12, #a.-l. 11.00 11.00

Souvenir Sheets

1831 A275 $3 multicolored 4.00 4.00
1832 A275 $6 multicolored 8.00 8.00

Methods of Transportation — A276

Designs: 65c, Donkey cart, 1965. 90c, 1910 Car. $2, 1950 Taxi. $3, 1955 Bus.

1996, Jan. 29 **Litho.** ***Perf. 14***
1833-1836 A276 Set of 4 8.00 8.00

Miniature Sheets

Locomotives — A277

No. 1837, each $2: a, "Dragon," Hawaii. b, "Regina," Italy. c, Calazo to Padua, Italy. d, "Mogul," Philippines. e, Nuremberg, Germany. f, "Stanislas," French Natl. Railway. g, "Black Five," Scotland. h, SNCF diesel electric, France. i, "Sir Nigel Gresley," England.
No. 1838, each $2: a, Hohi Line 9600 class, Japan. b, Peloponnese Express, Greece. c, Porter 2-4-0S, Hawaii. d, Norway-Swedish Jodemans Railway. e, 220 Diesel, Federal German Railway. f, 2-8-4T Indian Railways. g, East African Railways. h, Electrical trains, USSR. i, 0-8-0, Austria.
$5, "Duchess of Hamilton," England. $6, Diesel engine, China.

1996, Jan. 29
1837-1838 A277 Set of 2 28.00 28.00

Souvenir Sheets

1839 A277 $5 multicolored 4.75 4.75
1840 A277 $6 multicolored 5.25 5.25

No. 1837h has a face value of $1.

Giant Panda A278

Designs: a, With right leg up on rock. b, Front legs up on rock. c, Seated. d, Holding head down.

1996, May 15 **Litho.** ***Perf. 13½x14***
1841 A278 55c Block of 4, #a.-d. 4.50 4.50

Souvenir Sheet

Perf. 14x13½

1842 A278 $3 Panda, horiz. 3.75 3.75

CHINA '96, 9th Asian Intl. Philatelic Exhibition. No. 1841 was issued in sheets of 8 stamps.
See No. 1911.

Queen Elizabeth II, 70th Birthday A279

No. 1843: a, Portrait. b, Wearing regalia of Order of the Garter. c, Wearing bright blue dress, pearls.
$6, In uniform.

1996, May 16 **Litho.** ***Perf. 13½x14***
1843 A279 $2 Strip of 3, #a.-c. 4.25 4.25

Souvenir Sheet

1844 A279 $6 multicolored 4.25 4.25

No. 1843 was issued in sheets of 9 stamps.

Legendary Film Detectives A280

Designs: a, Humphrey Bogart as Sam Spade. b, Sean Connery as James Bond. c, Warren Beatty as Dick Tracy. d, Basil Rathbone as Sherlock Holmes. e, William Powell as the Thin Man. f, Sidney Toler as Charlie Chan, g, Peter Sellers as Inspector Clouseau. h, Robert Mitchum as Philip Marlowe. i, Peter Ustinov as Inspector Poirot.
$6, Margaret Rutherford as Miss Marple.

1996, July
1845 A280 $1 Sheet of 9, #a.-i. 13.00 13.00

Souvenir Sheet

1846 A280 $6 multicolored 6.00 6.00

1996 Summer Olympics, Atlanta A281

Designs: 20c, Olympic Stadium, Moscow, 1980. 25c, Hermine Joseph, vert. 55c, Women's field hockey, Zimbabwe, 1980. 90c, Jerome Romain, vert. $1, Polo, discontinued sport, vert. $2, Greg Louganis, diving.

1996 ***Perf. 14***
1847-1852 A281 Set of 6 4.25 4.25

See Nos. 1897-1900.

Local Entertainers A282

Designs: 25c, Irene Peltier, national dress of Dominica. 55c, Rupert Bartley, street band player. 65c, Rosemary Cools-Lartigue, pianist. 90c, Celestine "Orion" Theophile, belle queen, Grand Bay. $1, Cecil Bellot, former government band master.

1996, July 31 **Litho.** ***Perf. 14***
1853-1857 A282 Set of 5 2.75 2.75

Jerusalem, 3000th Anniv. — A283

Designs: a, 90c, Shrine of the Book, Israel Museum. b, $1, Church of All Nations. c, $2, The Great Synagogue.
$5, Hebrew University, Mount Scopus.

1996, July 31
1858 A283 Sheet of 3, #a.-c. 3.00 3.00

Souvenir Sheet

1859 A283 $5 multicolored 4.50 4.50

Radio, Cent. A284

Entertainers: 90c, Artie Shaw. $1, Benny Goodman. $2, Duke Ellington. $4, Harry James.
$6, Tommy Dorsey, Jimmy Dorsey, horiz.

1996, July 31
1860-1863 A284 Set of 4 6.25 6.25

Souvenir Sheet

1864 A284 $6 multicolored 5.00 5.00

UNICEF, 50th Anniv. A285

20c, Girl looking at globe. 55c, Boy with stethoscope, syringe. $5, Doctor examining child.
No. 1868, Girl, vert.

1996, July 31
1865-1867 A285 Set of 3 4.25 4.25

Souvenir Sheet

1868 A285 $5 multicolored 4.50 4.50

World Post Day — A286

Scenes of 18th cent. life in Dominica: 10c, Captain of ship taking letters by hand. 25c, Anthony Trollope visits Dominica to organize postal service. 55c, Steam vessel "Yare" carries mail around island. 65c, Post offices and agencies. 90c, Country postman carrying mail around mountain tracks. $1, West Indies Federation stamp, first airmail sent on German "goose" seaplane. $2, #602, General Post Office, old and new.
$5, Captain of ship.

1996, Oct. 1 **Litho.** ***Perf. 14***
1869-1875 A286 Set of 7 6.25 6.25

Souvenir Sheet

1876 A286 $5 multicolored 5.50 5.50

Fish — A287

Designs: 1c, Scrawled filefish. 2c, Lion fish. 5c, Porcupine fish. 10c, Powder blue surgeonfish. 15c, Red hind. 20c, Golden butterfly fish. 25c, Long-nosed butterfly fish. 35c, Pennant butterfly fish. 45c, Spotted drum. 55c, Blue-girdled angelfish. 60c, Scorpion fish. 65c, Harlequin sweetlips. 90c, Flame angelfish. $1, Queen trigger. $1.20, Stoplight parrot. $1.45, Black durgon. $2, Glasseye snapper. $5, Balloon fish. $10, Creole wrasse. $20, Seabass.

1996, Oct. 1 **Litho.** ***Perf. 14***

1877	A287	1c	multicolored	.30	.50
1878	A287	2c	multicolored	.30	.50
1879	A287	5c	multicolored	.35	.50
1880	A287	10c	multicolored	.45	.45
1881	A287	15c	multicolored	.50	.50
1882	A287	20c	multicolored	.55	.55
1883	A287	25c	multicolored	.55	.55
1884	A287	35c	multicolored	.70	.70
1885	A287	45c	multicolored	.90	.90
1886	A287	55c	multicolored	1.00	1.00
1887	A287	60c	multicolored	1.00	1.00
1888	A287	65c	multicolored	1.00	1.00
1889	A287	90c	multicolored	1.25	1.00
1890	A287	$1	multicolored	1.50	1.00
1891	A287	$1.20	multicolored	1.60	1.00
1892	A287	$1.45	multicolored	1.75	1.25
1893	A287	$2	multicolored	2.00	2.00
1894	A287	$5	multicolored	5.00	5.00
1895	A287	$10	multicolored	10.00	10.00
1896	A287	$20	multicolored	19.00	19.00
			Nos. 1877-1896 (20)	49.70	48.40

See Nos. 2024-2039B for size 20x18mm stamps.

1996 Summer Olympic Games Type

Past Olympic medalists, vert, each 90c: No. 1897a, Ulrike Meyfarth, high jump. b, Pat McCormick, diving. c, Takeichi Nishi, equestrian. d, Peter Farkas, Greco-Roman wrestling. e, Carl Lewis, track & field. f, Agnes Keleti, gymnastics. g, Yasuhiro Yamashita, judo. h, John Kelly, single sculls. i, Naim Suleymanoglu, weight lifting.
No. 1898, vert, each 90c: a, Sammy Lee, diving. b, Bruce Jenner, decathlon. c, Olga

Korbut, gymnastics. d, Steffi Graf, tennis. e, Florence Griffith-Joyner, track and field. f, Mark Spitz, swimming. g, Li Ning, gymnastics. h, Erika Salumae, cycling. i, Abebe Bikila, marathon.

#1899, $5, Joan Benoit, 1st women's marathon, vert.

#1900, $5, Milt Campbell, discus.

1996, June 7 Litho. *Perf. 14*

Sheets of 9

1897-1898 A281 Set of 2 15.00 15.00

Souvenir Sheets

1899-1900 A281 Set of 2 8.25 8.25

A288

A289

Christmas (Details or entire paintings): 25c, Enthroned Madonna and Child, by Stefano Veneziano. 55c, Noli Me Tangere, by Beato Angelico. 65c, Madonna and Child, by Angelico. 90c, Madonna of Corneta Tarquinia, by Filippo Lippi. $2, Annunciation, by Angelico. $5, Madonna with Child, by Angelico, diff.

Each $6: No. 1907, Coronation of the Virgin, by Beato Angelico. No. 1908, Holy Family with St. Barbara, by Veronese, horiz.

1996, Nov. 25

1901-1906 A288 Set of 6 8.50 8.50

Souvenir Sheets

1907-1908 A288 Set of 2 10.00 10.00

1997 Litho. *Perf. 14*

Paintings of "Herdboy and Buffalo," by Li Keran (1907-89): No. 1909: a, f, Herdboy Plays the Flute. b, g, Playing Cricket in the Autumn. c, h, Listen to the Summer Cicada. d, i, Grazing in the Spring.

$2, Return in Wind and Rain.

1909 A289 90c Strip of 4, #a.-d. 3.25 3.25

Souvenir Sheets

1909E A289 55c Sheet of 4, #f.-i. 2.00 2.00

Perf. 15x14½

1910 A289 $2 multicolored 2.00 2.00

New Year 1997 (Year of the Ox).

No. 1909 was printed in sheets of 8 stamps.

No. 1910 contains one 34x52mm stamp.

Souvenir Sheet

Huangshan Mountain, China — A290

1996, May 15 Litho. *Perf. 12*

1911 A290 $2 multicolored 2.25 2.25

China '96. No. 1911 was not available until March 1997.

A291

Lee Lai-Shan, 1996 Olympic Gold Medalist in Wind Surfing — A291a

1997 Litho. *Perf. 15x14*

1912 A291 $2 multicolored 1.75 1.75

Souvenir Sheet

Perf. 14

1913 A291 $5 multicolored 4.25 4.25

No. 1912 was issued in sheets of 3.

No. 1913 contains one 38x51mm stamp.

Litho. & Embossed

Perf. 9

Without Gum

1913A A291a $35 gold & multi, like #1913

Butterflies A292

No. 1914: a, Meticalla metis. b, Coeliades forestan. c, Papilio dardanus. d, Mylothris chloris. e, Poecilmitis thyshe. f, Myrina silenus. g, Bematistes aganice. h, Euphaedra neophron. i, Precis hierta.

No. 1915, vert: a, Striped policeman. b, Mountain sandman. c, Brown-veined white. d, Bowker's widow. e, Foxy charaxes. f, Pirate. g, African clouded yellow. h, Garden inspector.

Each $6: No. 1916, Acraea natalica. No. 1917, Eurytela dryope.

1997, Apr. 1 Litho. *Perf. 14*

1914 A292 55c Sheet of 9, #a.-i. 4.75 4.75

1915 A292 90c Sheet of 8, #a.-h. 6.75 6.75

Souvenir Sheets

1916-1917 A292 Set of 2 12.00 12.00

UNESCO, 50th Anniv. A293

55c, View from temple, China. 65c, Palace of Diocletian, Croatia. 90c, St. Mary's Cathedral, Hildesheim, Germany. $1, Monastery of Rossanou, Mount Athos, Greece. $2, Scandola Nature Reserve, France. $4, Church of San Antao, Portugal.

No. 1924: a, Ruins of Copan, Honduras. b, Cuzco Cathedral, Peru. c, Olinda, Brazil, d, Canaima Natl. Park, Venezuela. e, Galapagos Islands Natl. Park, Ecuador. f, Ruins of Church, Jesuit missions of Santisima, Paraguay. g, Fortress, San Lorenzo, Panama. h, Natl. Park, Fortress, Haiti.

Each $6: No. 1925, Chengde Lakes, China. No. 1926, Kyoto, Japan.

1997, Apr. 7 *Perf. 13½x14*

1918-1923 A293 Set of 6 8.75 8.75

1924 A293 $1 Sheet of 8, #a.-h. + label 7.75 7.75

Souvenir Sheets

1925-1926 A293 Set of 2 10.50 10.50

Disney Scenes "Sealed with a Kiss" A294

Cartoon film, year released: 25c, Mickey's Horse, Tanglefoot, 1933. 35c, Shanghaied, 1935. 55c, Pluto's Judgment Day, 1935. 65c, Race for Riches, 1935. 90c, Elmer Elephant, 1936. $1, Brave Little Tailor, 1938. $2, Donald's Crime, 1945. $4, In Dutch, 1946.

Each $6: No. 1935, Nifty Nineties, 1941. No. 1936, Mickey's Surprise Party, 1939.

1997, Apr. 15 *Perf. 13½x14*

1927-1934 A294 Set of 8 11.00 11.00

Souvenir Sheets

1935-1936 A294 Set of 2 10.00 10.00

Cats — A295

Dogs — A296

25c, Cream Burmese. $1, Snowshoe. $2, Sorrell Abyssinian. $5, Torbie Persian.

No. 1941: a, British bicolor shorthair (d, e). b, Maine coon kitten, Somali kitten (c). c, Maine coon kitten, diff. d, Lynx point Siamese (e). e, Blue Burmese kitten, white Persian (odd-eyed) (f). f, Persian kitten.

No. 1942, Silver tabby.

1997, Apr. 24 *Perf. 14*

1937-1940 A295 Set of 4 7.00 7.00

1941 A295 $2 Sheet of 6, #a.-f. 10.50 10.50

Souvenir Sheet

1942 A295 $6 multicolored 5.50 5.50

1997, Apr. 24

Designs: 20c, Afghan hound. 55c, Cocker spaniel. 65c, Smooth fox terrier. 90c, West Highland white terrier.

No. 1947a, St. Bernard. b, Boy with grand basset. c, Rough collie. d, Golden retriever. e, Golden retriever, Tibetan spaniel, smooth fox terrier. f, Smooth fox terrier, diff.

$6, Shetland sheepdog.

1943-1946 A296 Set of 4 2.00 2.00

1947 A296 90c Sheet of 6, #a.-f. 5.25 5.25

Souvenir Sheet

1948 A296 $6 multicolored 5.50 5.50

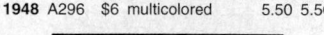

Queen Elizabeth II and Prince Philip, 50th Wedding Anniv. A297

No. 1949: a, Queen Elizabeth II. b, Royal Arms. c, Prince, Queen walking among crowd. d, Queen, Prince in military attire. e, Buckingham Palace. f, Prince Philip.

$6, Portrait of Queen and Prince on balcony.

1997, May 29 Litho. *Perf. 14*

1949 A297 $1 Sheet of 6, #a.-f. 5.50 5.50

Souvenir Sheet

1950 A297 $6 multicolored 5.00 5.00

Paintings by Hiroshige (1797-1858) A298

No. 1951: a, Ichigaya Hachiman Shrine. b, Blossoms on the Tama River Embankment. c, Kumano Junisha Shrine, Tsunohazu ("Juniso"). d, Benkei Moat from Soto-Sakurada to Kojimachi. e, Kinokuni Hill & View of Akasak Tameike. f, Naito Shinjuku, Yotsuya.

Each $6: No. 1952, Kasumigaseki. No. 1952A, Sanno Festival Procession at Kojimachi I-chome.

1997, May 29

1951 A298 $1.55 Sheet of 6, #a.-f. 10.50 10.50

Souvenir Sheets

1952-1952A A298 Set of 2 12.50 12.50

Orchids A299

Designs, vert: 20c, Oncidium altissimum. 25c, Oncidium papilio. 55c, Epidendrum fragrans. 65c, Oncidium lanceanum. 90c, Campylocentrum micranthum. $4, Pogonia rosea.

No. 1959: a, Brassavola cucculata. b, Epidendrum ibaguense. c, Ionopsis utriculari-odes. d, Rodriguezia lanceolata. e, Oncidium cebolleta. f, Epidendrum ciliare.

Each $5: No. 1960, Stanhopea grandiflora. No. 1961, Oncidium ampliatum.

1997, May 10 Litho. *Perf. 14*

1953-1958 A299 Set of 6 8.00 8.00

1959 A299 $1 Sheet of 6, #a.-f. 7.00 7.00

Souvenir Sheets

1960-1961 A299 Set of 2 11.00 11.00

Paul P. Harris (1868-1947), Founder of Rotary, Intl. — A300

Portrait of Harris and: $2, Rotary Village Corps, irrigation project, Honduras. $6, Emblems, world community service.

1997, May 29

1962 A300 $2 multicolored 1.60 1.60

Souvenir Sheet

1963 A300 $6 multicolored 6.00 6.00

Heinrich von Stephan (1831-97) A301

Portraits of Von Stephan and: No. 1964 a, Kaiser Wilhelm II. b, UPU emblem. c, Postal messenger, ancient Japan.

$6, Von Stephan, Russian dog team carrying post, 1859.

1997, May 29

1964 A301 $2 Sheet of 3, #a.-c. 4.25 4.25

Souvenir Sheet

1965 A301 $6 multicolored 4.50 4.50

PACIFIC 97.

Chernobyl Disaster, 10th Anniv. A302

Designs: No. 1966, Chabad's Children of Chernobyl. No. 1967, UNESCO.

1997, May 29 *Perf. 13½x14*
1966 A302 $2 multicolored 2.25 2.25
1967 A302 $2 multicolored 2.25 2.25

Grimm's Fairy Tales A303

Mother Goose Rhymes — A304

The Goose Girl: No. 1968: a, Girl with horse. b, Geese, pond, castle. c, Girl. No. 1969, Girl, horiz.

No. 1970: Mary, Mary, Quite Contrary.

1997, May 29 *Perf. 13½x14*
1968 A303 $2 Sheet of 3, #a.-c. 6.00 6.00

Souvenir Sheets

Perf. 14x13½

1969 A303 $6 multicolored 6.00 6.00

Perf. 14

1970 A304 $6 multicolored 5.00 5.00

Return of Hong Kong to China — A305

Designs: $1, View of Hong Kong at night. $1.45, View of Hong Kong in daytime. $2, View of Hong Kong at night, diff.

Hong Kong skyline at dusk: No. 1974: a, 65c. b, 90c. c, $1. d, $3.

1997, July 1 *Perf. 14*
1971-1973 A305 Set of 3 3.75 3.75
1974 A305 Sheet of 4, #a.-d. 5.00 5.00

Nos. 1971-1973 were issued in sheets of 4.

1998 Winter Olympics, Nagano — A306

Medal winners: 20c, Yukio Kasaya, 1972 ski jump. 25c, Jens Weissflog, 1994 ski jump. No. 1977, 55c, Anton Maier, 1968 men's speed skating. No. 1978, 55c, Ljubov Egorova, 1994 women's cross-country skiing. 65c, 1994 Ice hockey, Sweden. 90c, Bernhard Glass, 1980 men's luge. $4, Frank-Peter Roetsch, 1988 men's biathlon.

No. 1982: a, like #1975. b, like #1976. c, like #1977. d, Christa Rothenburger, 1988 women's speed skating.

Each $5: No. 1983, Jacob Tullin Thams, 1924 ski jumping. No. 1984, Charles Jewtraw, 1924 men's speed skating.

1997, July 15
1975-1981 A306 Set of 7 8.75 8.75
1982 A306 $1 Strip or block of 4, #a.-d. 5.00 5.00

Souvenir Sheets

1983-1984 A306 Set of 2 9.00 9.00

No. 1982 issued in sheets of 8 stamps.

1998 World Cup Soccer Championships, France — A307

Players, vert: 20c, Klinsmann, Germany. 55c, Bergkamp, Holland. 65c, Ravanelli, Italy. 90c, Kinkladze, Georgia. $2, Shearer, England. $4, Dani, Portugal.

Stadiums: No. 1991, each 65c: a, Wembley, England. b, Bernabeu, Spain. c, Maracana, Brazil. d, Torino, Italy. e, Centenary, Uruguay. f, Olympic, Germany. g, Rose Bowl, US. h, Azteca, Mexico.

Team Captains: No. 1992, each 65c: a, Meazza, Italy, 1934. b, Matthaus, Germany, 1990. c, Walter, W. Germany, 1954. d, Maradona, Argentina, 1986. e, Beckenbauer, Germany, 1974. f, Moore, England, 1966. g, Dunga, Brazil, 1994. h, Zoff, Italy, 1982.

$5, Mario Kempes, Argentina, vert. $6, Ally McCoist, Scotland, vert.

1997, July 21 **Litho.** *Perf. 14*
1985-1990 A307 Set of 6 8.00 8.00

Sheets of 8 + Label

1991-1992 A307 Set of 2 9.00 9.00

Souvenir Sheets

1993 A307 $5 multicolored 4.50 4.50
1994 A307 $6 multicolored 5.50 5.50

Dominica Credit Union — A308

25c, Joffre Robinson, former Credit Union president. 55c, Sister Alicia, founder credit union movement in Dominica. 65c, Lorrel Bruce, 1st Cooperative Credit Union president. 90c, Roseau Credit Union Building.

$5, Bruce, Robinson, Sister Alicia.

1997, Aug. 15 **Litho.** *Perf. 14x13½*
1995-1998 A308 Set of 4 2.25 2.25

Souvenir Sheet

Perf. 14

1999 A308 $5 multicolored 4.50 4.50

No. 1999 contains one 28x60mm stamp.

A309

Medical Pioneers: 20c, Louis Pasteur, father of bacteriology. 25c, Christiaan Barnard, performed first heart transplant. 55c, Sir Alexander Fleming, developer of penicillin. 65c, Camillo Golgi, neurologist. 90c, Jonas Salk, developer of polio vaccine. $1, Har Ghobind Khorana, geneticist. $2, Elizabeth Blackwell, first woman physician. $3, Sir Frank Macfarlane Burnet, immunologist.

$5, Fleming, diff. $6, Pasteur, diff.

1997, Sept. 1 **Litho.** *Perf. 14*
2000-2007 A309 Set of 8 10.00 10.00

Souvenir Sheets

2008 A309 $5 multicolored 5.25 5.25
2009 A309 $6 multicolored 6.25 6.25

A310

Diana, Princess of Wales (1961-97): Various portraits.

1997, Oct. 20 **Litho.** *Perf. 14*
2010 A310 $2 Sheet of 4, #a.-d. 6.50 6.50

Souvenir Sheet

2011 A310 $5 multicolored 4.75 4.75

Christmas — A311

Entire paintings or details: 20c, Echo and Narcissus, by Poussin. 55c, Angel Departing from the Family of Tobias, by Rembrandt. 65c, Seated Nymphs with Flute, by Francois Boucher. 90c, Angel, by Rembrandt. $2, Dispute of the Holy Sacrament, by Raphael. $4, Garden of Love, by Rubens.

Each $6: No. 2018, Annunciation, by Botticelli. No. 2019, Christ on the Mount of Olives, by El Greco.

1997, Nov. 10 **Litho.** *Perf. 14*
2012-2017 A311 Set of 6 7.00 7.00

Souvenir Sheets

2018-2019 A311 Set of 2 11.00 11.00

The $4 is incorrectly inscribed Holy Trinity, by Raphael. No. 2018 is incorrectly inscribed Study of a Muse, by Raphael.

A312

Paintings of tigers, by Ling-Nan School: No. 2020: a, 55c, Gao Qifeng. b, 65c, Zhao Shao'ang. c, 90c, Gao Jianfu. d, $1.20, Gao Jianfu, diff.

$3, Tiger running down mountain, by Gao Jianfu.

1998, Jan. 5 **Litho.** *Perf. 14½*
2020 A312 Sheet of 4, #a.-d. 3.00 3.00

Souvenir Sheet

Perf. 14x14½

2021 A312 $3 multicolored 2.25 2.25

New Year 1998 (Year of the Tiger). No. 2021 contains one 44x36mm stamp.

Fish Type of 1996

1998 *Perf. 13x13½*

Size: 20x18mm

2024	A287	5c	Porcupine fish	.30	.50
2025	A287	10c	Powder-blue surge-onfish	.30	.50
2026	A287	15c	Red hind	.40	.50
2027	A287	20c	Golden but-terflyfish	.40	.40
2028	A287	25c	Long-nosed butterf-lyfish	.45	.45
2029	A287	35c	Pennant butterf-lyfish	.50	.50
2030	A287	45c	Spotted drum	.70	.70
2031	A287	55c	Blue-girdled angelfish	.80	.80
2032	A287	60c	Scorpion fish	.90	.90
2033	A287	65c	Harlequin sweetlips	.90	.90
2034	A287	90c	Flame an-gelfish	1.00	.90
2035	A287	$1	Queen trig-ger	1.25	1.25
2036	A287	$1.20	Stoplight parrot	1.50	1.40
2037	A287	$1.45	Black durgon	1.75	1.75
2038	A287	$2	Glasseye snapper	2.25	2.25
2039	A287	$5	Balloon fish	5.00	5.00
2039A	A287	$10	Creole wrasse	9.50	9.50
2039B	A287	$20	Seabass	20.00	20.00
			Nos. 2024-2039B (18)	47.90	48.20

A313

Famous 20th cent. athletes — No. 2040: a, Jesse Owens. b, Owens jumping in 1936 Summer Olympic Games, Berlin. c, Isaac Berger lifting weights. d, Berger. e, Boris Becker. f, Becker playing tennis. g, Arthur Ashe playing tennis, holding Wimbledon trophy. h, Ashe.

No. 2041, Franz Beckenbauer, soccer player, horiz.

1998, Feb. 9 Litho. *Perf. 14*

Sheet of 8

2040 A313 $1 #a.-h. 7.50 7.50

Souvenir Sheet

2041 A313 $6 multi 6.25 6.25

Nos. 2040b-2040c, 2040f-2040g are each 53x38mm.

A314

Japanese Cinema Stars — No. 2042: a, Akira Kurosawa. b, Kurosawa's 1950 film, "Rashomon." c, Toshiro Mifune in 1954 film, "Seven Samurai." d, Mifune. e, Yasujiro Ozu. f, Ozu's 1949 film, "Late Spring." g, Sessue Hayakawa in 1957 film, "Bridge on the River Kwai." h, Hayakawa.

No. 2043, Akira Kurosawa, director.

1998, Feb. 9 Litho. *Perf. 14*

Sheet of 8

2042 A314 $1 #a.-h. 7.50 7.50

Souvenir Sheet

2043 A314 $6 multi 6.25 6.25

Nos. 2042b-2042c, 2042f-2042g are each 53x38mm.

A315

Mushrooms: 10c, Omphalotus illudens. 15c, Inocybe fastigiata. 20c, Marasmius plicatulus. 50c, Mycena lilacifolia. 55c, Armillaria straminea. 90c, Tricholomopsis rutilans.

No. 2050, each $1: a, Lepiota naucina. b, Cortinarius violaceus. c, Boletus aereus. d, Tricholoma aurantium. e, Lepiota procera. f, Clitocybe geotropa. g, Lepiota acutesquamosa. h, Tricholoma saponaceum. i, Lycoperdon gemmatum.

No. 2051, each $1: a, Boletus ornatipes. b, Russula xerampelina. c, Cortinarius collinitus. d, Agaricus meleagris. e, Coprinus comatus. f, Amanita caesarea. g, Amanita brunnescens. h, Amanita muscaria. i, Morchella esculenta.

$6, Cortinarius violaceus.

1998, Mar. 2 Litho. *Perf. 14*

2044-2049 A315 Set of 6 3.00 3.00

Sheets of 9

2050-2051 A315 Set of 2 17.50 17.50

Souvenir Sheet

2052 A315 $6 multicolored 5.25 5.25

Sailing Ships A316

Designs: 65c, Greek bireme. 90c, Egyptian felucca. $1, Viking longboat. $2, Chinese junk.

No. 2057: a, Two-masted topsail schooner. b, The Golden Hinde. c, Roman merchant ship. d, Gazela Primeiro. e, Moshulu. f, Bluenose.

Each $5: No. 2058, Pinta. No. 2059, Chesapeake Bay skipjack.

1998, Mar. 16 Litho. *Perf. 14*

2053-2056 A316 Set of 4 4.50 4.50

2057 A316 55c Block of 6, #a.-f. 3.25 3.25

Souvenir Sheets

2058-2059 A316 Set of 2 10.00 10.00

No. 2053 incorrectly inscribed "Egyptian felucca."

No. 2057 was issued in sheets of 12 stamps.

Mickey & Minnie Mouse's 70th Anniv. — A317

25c, Steamboat Willie, 1928. 55c, The Brave Little Tailor, 1938. 65c, Nifty Nineties, 1941. 90c, Mickey Mouse Club, 1955. $1, Mickey, Minnie at the opening of Walt Disney World, 1971. $1.45, Mousercise Mickey & Minnie, 1980.

Each $5: No. 2061, Walt Disney, Mickey, Minnie. No. 2062, Surprise Party for Mickey & Minnie.

1998, June 16 Litho. *Perf. 14x13½*

2060A A317 25c black .30 .30
2060B A317 55c multi .60 .60
2060C A317 65c multi .75 .75
2060D A317 90c multi 1.00 1.00
2060E A317 $1 multi 1.10 1.10
2060F A317 $1.45 multi 1.60 1.60
Nos. 2060A-2060F (6) 5.35 5.35

Souvenir Sheet of 7

2060G #2060A-2060F, 2060h 11.50 11.50
h. $5 Runaway brain, perf 13½ at left 3.50 3.50

Size: 130x104mm

Imperf

2061-2062 A317 Set of 2 10.00 10.00

Souvenir Sheet

Disney's The Lion King — A318

1998, June 16 Litho. *Perf. 13½x14*

2063 A318 $5 multicolored 7.00 7.00

Sea Birds A319

25c, Erect crested penguin. 65c, Humboldt penguin. 90c, Red knot. $1, Audubon's shearwater.

No. 2068: a, Crested tern. b, Franklin's gull. c, Australian pelican. d, Fairy prion. e, Andean gull. f, Imperial shag. g, Red phalarope. h, Hooded grebe. i, Least auklet. j, Little grebe. k, Cape petrel. l, Horned grebe.

Each $5: No. 2069, Sula nebouxii. No. 2070, Fulmarus glacialis.

1998, Aug. 4 *Perf. 14*

2064-2067 A319 Set of 4 2.50 2.50
2068 A319 90c Sheet of 12, #a.-l. 10.00 10.00

Souvenir Sheets

2069-2070 A319 Set of 2 10.50 10.50

Airplanes A320

20c, Jetstar II. 25c, AN 225. 55c, Dash-8. 65c, Beech-99. 90c, American Eagle. $2, HFB 320 Itansa Jet.

No. 2077, each $1: a, SR 71 "Blackbird." b, Stealth bomber. c, Northrop YF23. d, F-14 A "Tomcat." e, F-15 "Eagle S." f, MiG 29 "Fulcrum." g, Europa X5. h, Camion.

No. 2078, each $1: a, E400. b, CL-215 C-GKDN Amphibian. c, Piper jet. d, Beech Hawker. e, Lockheed YF22. f, Piper Seneca V. g, CL-215 Amphibian. h, Vantase.

Each $6: No. 2079, F-1 Fighter. No. 2080, Sea Hopper.

1998, Aug. 17

2071-2076 A320 Set of 6 4.50 4.50

Sheets of 8

2077-2078 A320 Set of 2 17.00 17.00

Souvenir Sheets

2079-2080 A320 Set of 2 11.00 11.00

Intl. Year of the Ocean A321

Marine life: 25c, Fridman fish. 55c, Hydrocoral. 65c, Feather star. 90c, Royal angelfish.

No. 2085, each $1: a, Monk seal. b, Galapagos penguin. c, Manta ray. d, Hawksbill turtle. e, Moorish idol. f, Nautilus. g, Giant clam. h, Tubeworms. i, Nudibranch.

No. 2086, each $1: a, Spotted dolphin. b, Atlantic sailfish. c, Sailfin flying fish. d, Fairy basslet. e, Atlantic spadefish. f, Leatherback turtle. g, Blue tang. h, Coral banded shrimp. i, Rock beauty.

No. 2087, Humpback whale. No. 2088, Leafy sea dragon.

1998, Sept. 7 Litho. *Perf. 14*

2081-2084 A321 Set of 4 2.50 2.50

Sheets of 9

2085-2086 A321 Set of 2 19.00 19.00

Souvenir Sheets

2087 A321 $5 multicolored 4.75 4.75
2088 A321 $6 multicolored 5.50 5.50

Organization of American States, 50th Anniv. A322

1998, Sept. 1 Litho. *Perf. 14*

2089 A322 $1 multicolored 1.25 1.25

Ferrari Sports Cars A323

55c, 365 GT 2+2. 90c, Boano/Ellena 250 GT. $1, 375 MM coupe. $5, 212.

1998, Sept. 1

2090-2092 A323 Set of 3 3.75 3.75

Souvenir Sheet

2093 A323 $5 multicolored 5.50 5.50

No. 2093 contains one 91x35mm stamp.

Gandhi — A324

1998, Sept. 1

2094 A324 90c shown 1.50 1.50

Souvenir Sheet

2095 A324 $6 Seated 5.25 5.25

No. 2094 was issued in sheets of 4.

Pablo Picasso A325

Paintings: 90c, The Painter and His Model, 1926. $1, The Crucifixion, 1930. $2, Nude with Raised Arms, 1908, vert.

$6, Cafe at Royan, 1940.

1998, Sept. 1 *Perf. 14½*

2096-2098 A325 Set of 3 4.50 4.50

Souvenir Sheet

2099 A325 $6 multicolored 5.75 5.75

Royal Air Force, 80th Anniv. A326

No. 2100: a, Nimrod MR2P. b, C-130 Hercules Mk3. c, Panavia Tornado GR1. d, C-130 Hercules landing.

$5, Biplane, hawk. $6, Hawker Hart, jet.

1998, Sept. 1 *Perf. 14*

2100 A326 $2 Sheet of 4, #a.-d. 7.00 7.00

Souvenir Sheets

2101 A326 $5 multicolored 4.75 4.75
2102 A326 $6 multicolored 5.25 5.25

No. 2100d incorrectly inscribed Panavia Tornado GR1.

Nos. 1548-1549, 1551-1552, 1554 Ovptd.

1998, Sept. 14

2103-2107 A221 Set of 5 6.00 6.00

A327

1998 World Scouting Jamboree, Chile: 65c, Scout sign. $1, Scout handshake. $2, World Scout flag.

$5, Lord Baden-Powell.

1998

2108-2110 A327 Set of 3 3.25 3.25

Souvenir Sheet

2111 A327 $5 multicolored 5.25 5.25

A328

Birds: 25c, Northern cardinal. 55c, Eastern bluebird. 65c, Carolina wren. 90c, Blue jay. $1, Evening grosbeak. $2, Bohemian waxwing.
$5, Northern parula. $6, Painted bunting.

1998, Dec. 1 Litho. *Perf. 14*

2112-2117 A328 Set of 6 5.50 5.50

Souvenir Sheets

2118 A328 $5 multicolored 5.25 5.25
2119 A328 $6 multicolored 6.25 6.25

Christmas.

New Year 1999 (Year of the Rabbit) A329

1999, Jan. 4 Litho. *Perf. 14*

2120 A329 $1.50 multicolored 2.00 2.00

No. 2120 was issued in sheets of 4.

Orchids — A330

55c, Broughtonia sanguinea. 65c, Cattleyonia Keith Roth "Roma." 90c, Comparettia falcata. $2, Cochleanthes discolor.

No. 2125, each $1: a, Dracula erythiochaete. b, Lycasle aromatica. c, Masdevallla marguerile. d, Encyclia marfae. e, Laelia gouldiana. f, Huntleya meleagris. g, Galeandria baueri. h, Lycale deppei.

No. 2126, each $1: a, Anguloa clowesii. b, Lemboglossum cervantesii. c, Oncidium cebolleta. d, Millonia. e, Pescatorea lehmannll. f, Sophronitis coccinea. g, Pescatorea cerina. h, Encyclia vitellina.

Each $5: No. 2127, Lepanthes ovalis. No. 2128, Encyclia cochleata.

1999, Apr. 26 Litho. *Perf. 14*

2121-2124 A330 Set of 4 4.50 4.50

Sheets of 8

2125-2126 A330 Set of 2 17.50 17.50

Souvenir Sheets

2127-2128 A330 Set of 2 10.00 10.00

Trains A331

No. 2129, each $1: a, Class 103.1 Co-Co, Germany. b, Class .24, "Trans Pennine," UK. c, GG1 2-Co-Co-2, US. d, LRC Bo-Bo, Canada. e, Class EW, New Zealand. f, Class SS1 "Shao-Shani," China. g, Gulf, Mobile Ohio, US. h, Class 9100 2-Do-2, France.

No. 2130, each $1: a, County Donegal Petrol Rail Car No. 10, Ireland. b, RDC Single Rail Car, US. c, WDM Class Co-Co, India. d, Bi-Polar No. E-2, US. e, Class X Co-Co, Australia. f, Beijing Bo-Bo, China. g, Class E428 2-Bo-Bo-2, Italy. h, Class 581 Twelve-Car Train, Japan.

$5, X-2000 Tilting Express Train, Sweden, vert. $6, Class 87 Bo-Bo, Great Britain, vert.

1999, May 10 Litho. *Perf. 14*

Sheets of 8

2129-2130 A331 Set of 2 13.00 13.00

Souvenir Sheets

2131 A331 $5 multicolored 4.00 4.00
2132 A331 $6 multicolored 5.00 5.00

Australia '99, World Stamp Expo.

Prehistoric Animals — A332

25c, Tyrannosaurus, vert. 65c, Hypacrosaurus. 90c, Sauropelta. $2, Zalambdalestes.

No. 2137, each $1: a, Barosaurus. b, Rhamphorhynchus. c, Apatosaurus. d, Archaeopteryx. e, Diplodocus. f, Ceratosaurus. g, Stegosaurus. h, Elaphrosaurus. i, Vulcanodon.

No. 2138, each $1: a, Psittacosaurus. b, Pteranodon. c, Ichthyornis. d, Spinosaurus. e, Parasaurolophus. f, Ornithomimus. g, Anatosaurus. h, Triceratops. i, Baronyx.

$5, Yangchuanosaurus. $6, Brachiosaurus.

1999, June 1 Litho. *Perf. 14*

2133-2136 A332 Set of 4 3.50 3.50

Sheets of 9

2137-2138 A332 Set of 2 18.00 18.00

Souvenir Sheets

2139 A332 $5 multicolored 4.50 4.50
2140 A332 $6 multicolored 5.50 5.50

Wedding of Prince Edward and Sophie Rhys-Jones A333

No. 2141: a, Sophie. b, Sophie, Edward. c, Edward.

$6, like No. 2141b.

1999, June 19 Litho. *Perf. 13½*

2141 A333 $3 Sheet of 3, #a.-c. 7.25 7.25

Souvenir Sheet

2142 A333 $6 multicolored 5.00 5.00

IBRA '99, World Philatelic Exhibition, Nuremberg — A334

Exhibition emblem, sailing ship Eendraght and: 65c, Cameroun #58, #56. 90c, Cameroun #11, #9.

Emblem, early German train and: $1, Cameroun #19. $2, Cameroun #6.

$6, Cover with Cameroun #19.

1999, June 22 *Perf. 14*

2143-2146 A334 Set of 4 4.00 4.00

Souvenir Sheet

2147 A334 $6 multicolored 6.25 6.25

Souvenir Sheets

PhilexFrance '99 — A335

Trains: $5, L'Aigle, 1855. $6, Mainline diesel locomotive, 1963.

1999, June 22 *Perf. 13¾*

2148 A335 $5 multicolored 4.50 4.50
2149 A335 $6 multicolored 5.50 5.50

Apollo 11 Moon Landing, 30th Anniv. A336

No. 2150: a, Command Module separation b, Service Module separation. c, 3rd Stage Booster separation. d, Landing, Command Modules go to the moon. e, Apollo Ground Tracker. f, Goldstone Radio Telescope.

$6, Apollo 11 after splashdown.

1999, June 22 *Perf. 14*

2150 A336 $1.45 Sheet of 6, #a.-f. 9.00 9.00

Souvenir Sheet

2151 A336 $6 multicolored 6.00 6.00

Paintings by Hokusai (1760-1849) A337

Details or entire paintings — No. 2152:, each $2 a, Pilgrims at Kirifuri Waterfall. b, Kakura-Sato (rats looking at book, pulling on rope). c, Travelers on the Bridge by Ono Waterfall. d, Fast Cargo Boat Battling the Waves. e, Kakura-Sato (rats working with bales). f, Buufinfinh and Weeping cherry.

No. 2153, each $2: a, Cuckoo and Azalea. b, Soldiers (spear in left hand). c, Lover in the snow. d, Ghost of Koheiji. e, Soldiers (spear in right hand). f, Chinese Poet in Snow.

$5, Empress Jitó. $6, One Hundred Poems by One Hundred Poets.

Perf. 13½x13¾

1999, June 22 Litho.

Sheets of 6

2152-2153 A337 Set of 2 19.00 19.00

Souvenir Sheets

2154 A337 $5 multicolored 4.50 4.50
2155 A337 $6 multicolored 5.50 5.50

Johann Wolfgang von Goethe (1749-1832), Poet — A338

No. 2156: a, Faust perceives an astrological sign. b, Portrait of Goethe and Friedrich von Schiller (1759-1805). c, Faust tempted by Mephistopheles.

$6, Profile portrait of Goethe.

1999, June 22 *Perf. 14*

2156 A338 $2 Sheet of 3, #a.-c. 5.00 5.00

Souvenir Sheet

2157 A338 $6 multicolored 5.00 5.00

Rights of the Child — A339

No. 2158: a, Woman, child. b, Child in blue sweater. c, Two children.

$6, Dove, horiz.

1999, June 22 Litho. *Perf. 14*

2158 A339 $3 Sheet of 3, #a.-c. 7.50 7.50

Souvenir Sheet

2159 A339 $6 multicolored 5.00 5.00

Queen Mother (b. 1900) — A340

A340a

Gold Frames

No. 2160: a, In 1939. b, In Australia, 1958. c, At Badminton, 1982. d, Hatless, in 1982.

$6, In 1953.

1999, Aug. 4 *Perf. 14*

2160 A340 $2 Sheet of 4, #a.-d. + label 7.50 7.50

Souvenir Sheet

Perf. 13¾

2161 A340 $6 multicolored 5.00 5.00

No. 2161 contains one 38x51mm stamp.

Compare with Nos. 2345-2346. Backdrop of photo is more pink on No. 2161 than on No. 2346. No. 2161 has embossed arms in margin, while No. 2346 does not.

Litho. & Embossed

Die Cut Perf. 8¾

Without Gum

2161A A340a $20 gold & multi 20.00 20.00

See Nos. 2345-2346.

Flora & Fauna A341

Designs: 25c, Heliconia lobster claw. 65c, Broad winged hawk. $1, Anthurium. $1.55, Blue-headed hummingbird. $2, Bananaquit. $4 Agouti.

No. 2168: a, White-throated sparrow. b, Blue-winged teal. c, Raccoon. d, Alfalf butterfly. e, Bridge. f, Whitetail deer. g, Gray squirrel. h, Banded purple butterfly. i, Snowdrop. j, Bullfrog. k, Mushrooms. l, Large-blotched ensatina.

$5, Eastern chipmunk. $6, Black-footed ferret.

1999

2162-2167 A341 Set of 6 9.00 9.00

Sheet of 12

2168 A341 90c #a.-l. 10.00 10.00

Souvenir Sheets

2169 A341 $5 multicolored 5.00 5.00
2170 A341 $6 multicolored 6.00 6.00

A342

Dominica Festival Commission: 25c, Domfesta. 55c, $5, Dominica's 21st anniv. as a republic. 65c, Carnival development committee. 90c, World Creole Music Festival.

1999 ***Perf. 12½***

2171-2174 A342 Set of 4 2.00 2.00

Souvenir Sheet

Perf. 13¼

2175 A342 $5 multicolored 4.50 4.50

No. 2175 contains one 38x51mm stamp.

A343

Intl. Year of the Elderly: 25c, Family. 65c, Four people. 90c, Four people, one in chair.

1999, Aug. 4 ***Perf. 14***

2176 A343 Sheet of 3, #a.-c. 1.50 1.50

A345

Christmas: 25c, Yellow-crowned parrot. 55c, Red bishop. 65c, Troupial. 90c, Puerto Rican woodpecker. $2, Mangrove cuckoo. $3, American robin.

$6, Mary with Child Beside the Wall, by Albrecht Dürer.

1999, Dec. 7 **Litho.** ***Perf. 14***

2178-2183 A345 Set of 6 6.75 6.75

Souvenir Sheet

2184 A345 $6 multi 5.25 5.25

Inscription on No. 2181 is misspelled.

A346

Millennium (Highlights of the early 13th Cent.) — No. 2185: a, Leonardo Fibonacci publishes "Liber Abaci," 1202. b, St. Francis of Assisi. c, Mongols conquer China. d, Children's Crusade begins, 1212. e, Magna Carta signed, 1215. f, Founding of Salamanca University, 1218. g, Snorri Sturluson writes "Prose Edda". h, Chinese painter Ma Yuan dies, 1225. i, Genghis Khan dies, 1227. j, Zen Buddhism in Japan. k, Sixth Crusade. l, Lubeck-Hamburg League. m, Inquisitions begin, 1231. n, Cordoba conquered by Castilians, 1236. o, Democracy in San Marino. p, Maimonides (60x40mm). q, Notre Dame Cathedral, Paris.

Highlights of the 1940s — No. 2186: a, Japan bombs Pearl Harbor. b, Churchill becomes Prime Minister of Great Britain. c, Regular television broadcasting begins in the US. d, Anne Frank hid in Amsterdam. e, D-Day Invasion. f, Yalta Conference. g, Establishment of the UN. h, Germany surrenders, concentration camps exposed. i, Russians hoist flag over gutted Reichstag building. j, Eniac computer. k, Independence for India. l, Bell Laboratories produce 1st transistor. m, Gandhi assassinated. n, Israel achieves statehood. o, Blockade of West Berlin, Berlin Airlift. p, Atomic bomb tested in New Mexico (60x40mm). q, Establishment of People's Republic of China.

Perf. 12¾x12½

1999, Dec. 31 **Sheets of 17** **Litho.**

2185 A346 55c #a.-q. + label 8.50 8.50
2186 A346 55c #a.-q. + label 8.50 8.50

See Nos. 2249-2252.

New Year 2000 (Year of the Dragon) A347

2000, Feb. 5 ***Perf. 13¾***

2187 A347 $1.50 shown 1.25 1.25

Souvenir Sheet

2188 A347 $4 Dragon, horiz. 3.75 3.75

No. 2187 printed in sheets of 4.

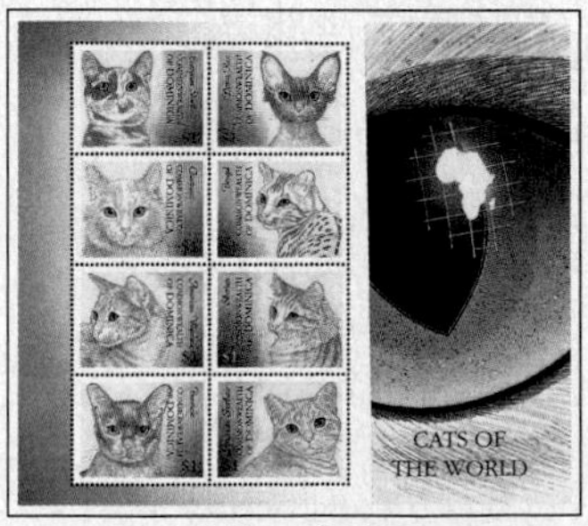

Cats — A348

No. 2189, each $1: a, European Shorthair. b, Devon Rex. c, Chartreux. d, Bengal. e, American Wirehair. f, Siberian. g, Burmese. h, American Shorthair.

No. 2190, each $1: a, Asian Longhair. b, Burmilla. c, Snowshoe. d, Pekeface Persian. e, Himalayan Persian. f, Japanese Bobtail. g, Seychelles Longhair. h, Exotic Shorthair.

Each $6: No. 2191, Awake cat. No. 2192, Sleeping cat.

2000, Feb. 21 ***Perf. 14¼***

Sheets of 8, #a.-h.

2189-2190 A348 Set of 2 16.00 16.00

Souvenir Sheets

2191-2192 A348 Set of 2 12.00 12.00

Puppies — A349

No. 2193: a, Jack Russell Terrier. b, Shar Peis. c, Basset Hound. d, Boxers. e, Wire-haired Terrier. f, Golden Retrievers.

No. 2194, Beagle.

2000, Feb. 21 ***Perf. 14½x14¼***

2193 A349 $1 Sheet of 6, #a.-f. 6.00 6.00

Souvenir Sheet

2194 A349 $6 multi 6.00 6.00

Flowers A350

Various flowers making up a photomosaic of Princess Diana.

2000, Apr. 3 ***Perf. 13¾***

2195 A350 $1 Sheet of 8, #a.-h. 7.50 7.50

See No. 2225.

Butterflies A351

No. 2196, each $1.50: a, Giant swallowtail. b, Tiger pierid. c, Orange theope. d, White peacock. e, Blue tharops. f, Mosaic.

No. 2197, each $1.50: a, Banded king shoemaker. b, Figure-of-eight. c, Grecian shoemaker. d, Blue night. e, Monarch. f, Common morpho.

No. 2198, each $1.50: a, Orange-barred sulphur. b, Clorinde. c, Small flambeau. d, Small lace-wing. e, Polydamas swallowtail. f, Atala.

Each $6: No. 2199, Polydamas swallowtail, vert. No. 2200, Sloane's urania, vert. No. 2201, Blue-green reflector, vert.

2000, Apr. 10 ***Perf. 14***

Sheets of 6, #a.-f.

2196-2198 A351 Set of 3 24.00 24.00

Souvenir Sheets

2199-2201 A351 Set of 3 17.50 17.50

Flowers — A352

Designs: 65c, Passion flower. 90c, Spray orchid. $1, Peach angel's trumpet. $4, Allamanda.

No. 2206, each $1.65: a, Bird of paradise. b, Lobster claw heliconia. c, Candle bush. d, Flor de San Miguel. e, Hibiscus. f, Oleander.

No. 2207, each $1.65: a, Anthurium. b, Fire ginger. c, Shrimp plant. d, Sky vine thunbergia. e, Ceriman. f, Morning glory.

Each $6: No. 2208, Bird of paradise, diff. No. 2109, Hibiscus, diff.

2000, Apr. 25 **Litho.** ***Perf. 14***

2202-2205 A352 Set of 4 6.00 6.00

Sheets of 6, #a-f

Perf. 13¾

2206-2207 A352 Set of 2 17.00 17.00

Souvenir Sheets

Perf. 13½x 13¾

2208-2209 A352 Set of 2 12.00 12.00

Size of stamps: Nos. 2106-2107, 32x48mm; Nos. 2108-2109, 38x51mm.

Paintings of Anthony Van Dyck — A353

No. 2210, each $1.65: a, Lady Jane Goodwin. b, Philip Herbert, 4th Earl of Pembroke. c, Philip, Lord Wharton. d, Sir Thomas Hammer. e, Olivia Porter, Wife of Enymion Porter. f, Sir Thomas Chaloner.

No. 2211, horiz, each $1.65: a, Ladies in Waiting. b, Thomas Wentworth, Earl of Strafford, with Sir Philip Mainwaring. c, Dorothy Rivers Savage, Viscountess Andover and Her Sister Lady Elizabeth Thimbleby. d, Mountjoy Blount, Earl of Newport, and Lord George Goring with a Page. e, Thomas Killigrew and an Unidentified Man. f, Elizabeth Villiers, Lady Dalkeith, and Cecilia Killigrew.

No. 2212, horiz, each $1.65: a, The Ages of Man. b, Portrait of a Girl as Erminia Accompanied by Cupid. c, Cupid and Psyche. d, Vertumnus and Pomona. e, The Continence of Scipio. f, Diana and Endymion Surprised by a Satyr.

No. 2213, $5, Achilles and the Daughters of Lycomedes. No. 2214, $5, Amaryllis and Mirtillo. No. 2215, $6, Thomas Howard, 2nd Earl of Arundel, with Alathea, Countess of Arundel.

2000, May 29 ***Perf. 13¾***

Sheets of 6, #a-f

2210-2212 A353 Set of 3 27.00 27.00

Souvenir Sheets

2213-2214 A353 Set of 2 9.00 9.00
2215 A353 $6 multi 5.50 5.50

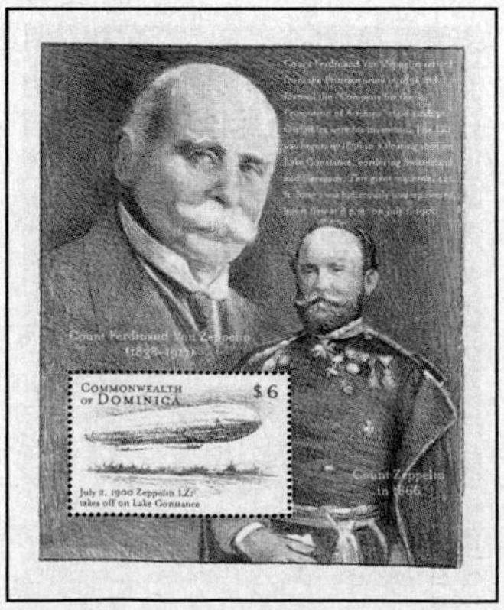

First Zeppelin Flight, Cent. — A354

No. 2216: a, Count Ferdinand von Zeppelin (1838-1917). b, First takeoff of LZ-1. c, LZ-10 over field. d, LZ-6 and Deutschland in hangar. e, Arrival of Z-4 at Luneville. f, Victoria Luise.

No. 2217, LZ-1, diff.

2000, June 21 **Litho.** ***Perf. 14***

2216 A354 $1.65 Sheet of 6, #a-f 9.00 9.00

Souvenir Sheet

2217 A354 $6 multi 5.50 5.50

Berlin Film Festival, 50th Anniv. — A355

No. 2218: a, Director Satyajit Ray. b, Mahangar. c, Fanfan La Tulipe. d, Le Salaire de la Peur. e, Les Cousins. f, Hon Dansade en Sommar.
No. 2219, Buffalo Bill and the Indians.

2000, June 21
2218 A355 $1.65 Sheet of 6, #a-f 9.00 9.00

Souvenir Sheet

2219 A355 $6 multi 5.50 5.50

100th Test Match at Lord's Ground — A356

2000, June 21
2220 A356 $4 Norbert Phillip 3.50 3.50

Souvenir Sheet

2221 A356 $6 Lord's Ground 5.50 5.50

Souvenir Sheets

2000 Summer Olympics, Sydney — A357

a, Jesse Owens. b, Pole vault. c, Lenin Stadium Moscow, Soviet Union flag. d, Ancient Greek discus thrower.

2000, June 21
2222 A357 $2 Sheet of 4, #a-d 8.00 8.00

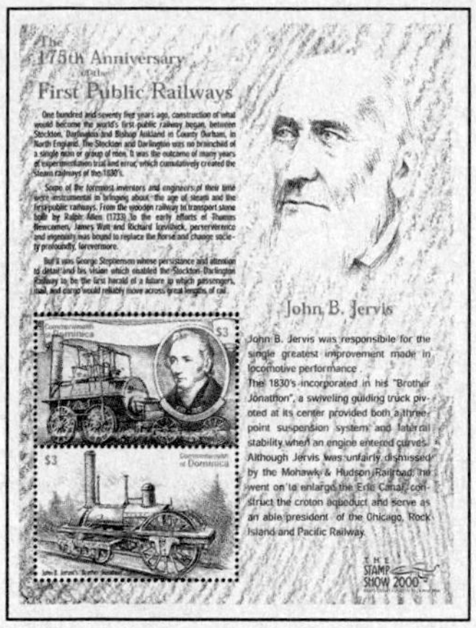

Public Railways, 175th Anniv. — A358

No. 2223: a, Locomotion No. 1, George Stephenson. b, Brother Jonathon.

2000, June 21
2223 A358 $3 Sheet of 2, #a-b 6.25 6.25

The Stamp Show 2000, London.

Johann Sebastian Bach — A359

2000, June 21
2224 A359 $6 multi 5.50 5.50

Flower Type of 2000

Various pictures of religious sites making up a photomosaic of Pope John Paul II.

2000, June 21 Litho. *Perf. 13¾*
2225 A350 $1 Sheet of 8, #a-h 8.00 8.00

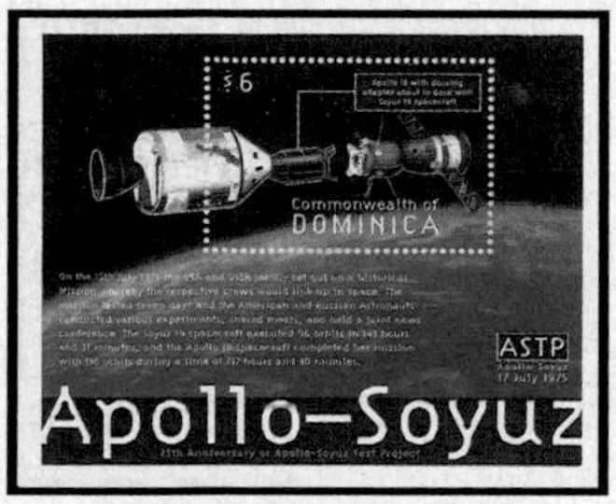

Apollo-Soyuz Mission, 25th Anniv. — A360

No. 2226, vert.: a, Saturn IB launch vehicle. b, Apollo 18. c, Donald K. Slayton.
$6, Apollo and Soyuz docking.

2000, June 21 *Perf. 14*
2226 A360 $3 Sheet of 3, #a-c 9.50 9.50

Souvenir Sheet

2227 A360 $6 multi 6.00 6.00

Souvenir Sheet

Albert Einstein (1879-1955) — A361

2000, June 21 *Perf. 14¼*
2228 A361 $6 multi 5.50 5.50

Prince William, 18th Birthday — A362

No. 2229: a, In ski gear. b, In jacket and red sweater. c, In suit and tie. d, In plaid shirt.
$6, With Prince Harry.

2000, June 22 *Perf. 14*
2229 A362 $1.65 Sheet of 4, #a-d 6.25 6.25

Souvenir Sheet

Perf. 13¾

2230 A362 $6 multi 5.50 5.50

No. 2229 contains four 28x42mm stamps.

Bob Hope — A363

No. 2231: a, Microphone at right. b, Entertaining troops. c, Wearing bowler. d, Standing in cake. e, Microphone at left. f, With moon.

2000, Aug. 7 *Perf. 14*
2231 A363 $1.65 Sheet of 6, #a-f 10.00 10.00

Monty Python and the Holy Grail, 25th Anniv. — A364

No. 2232: a, Close-up of Eric Idle. b, Terry Jones, Graham Chapman and John Cleese as three-headed giant, horiz. c, Knights facing castle wall. d, Chapman as King Arthur, with helmeted knight. e, Beheaded knight. f, Armless and legless Black Knight and King Arthur.

2000, Aug. 7 *Perf. 13¾*
2232 A364 90c Sheet of 6, #a-f 5.25 5.25

Popes — A365

No. 2233: a, Clement X, 1670-76. b, Innocent X, 1644-55. c, Nicholas V, 1447-55. d, Martin V, 1417-31. e, Julius III, 1550-55. f, Innocent XII, 1691-1700.
$6, Clement XIV, 1769-74.

2000, Sept. 5
2233 A365 $1.65 Sheet of 6, #a-f 10.00 10.00

Souvenir Sheet

2234 A365 $6 multi 5.50 5.50

Monarchs — A366

No. 2235: a, Edward IV of England, 1461-83. b, Peter the Great of Russia, 1682-1725. c, Henry VI of England, 1422-61. d, Henry III of England, 1216-72. e, Richard III of England, 1483-85. f, Edward I of England, 1272-1307.
$6, Henry VIII of England, 1509-47.

2000, Sept. 5
2235 A366 $1.65 Sheet of 6, #a-f 10.00 10.00

Souvenir Sheet

2236 A366 $6 multi 5.50 5.50

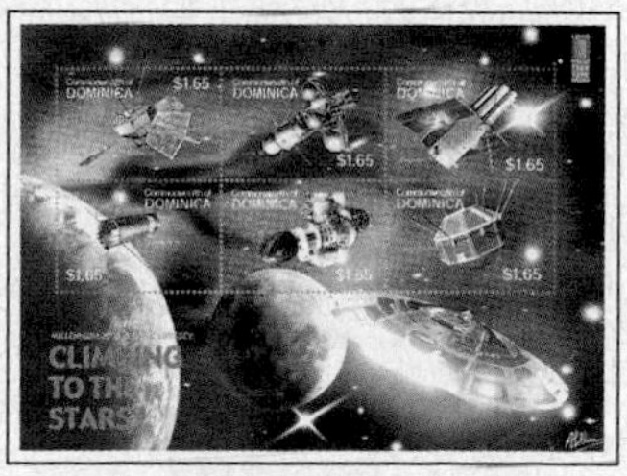

World Stamp Expo 2000, Anaheim — A367

Spacecraft — No. 2237, $1.65: a, Explorer 14. b, Luna 16. c, Copernicus. d, Explorer 16. e, Luna 10. f, Arybhattan.
No. 2238, $1.65: a, ESSA 8. b, Echo 1. c, Topex Poseidon. d, Diademe. e, Early Bird. f, Molniya.
No. 2239, $6, Hipparcos. No. 2240, $6, Eole.

2000, June 21 Litho. *Perf. 14¼x14*

Sheets of 6, #a-f

2237-2238 A367 Set of 2 20.00 20.00

Souvenir Sheets

2239-2240 A367 Set of 2 11.00 11.00

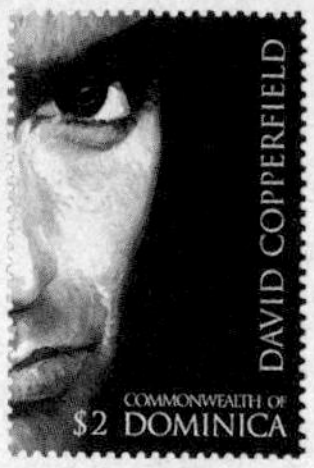

David Copperfield, Magician — A368

2000, Aug. 8 ***Perf. 14***

2241 A368 $2 multi 1.75 1.75

Printed in sheets of 4.

Souvenir Sheet

Female Recording Groups of the 1960s — A369

No. 2242 — The Crystals, yellow spotlight covering: a, UR, LL and LR corners. b, UL and LL corners. c, UR and LR corners. d, UL, LL and LR corners.

2000, Aug. 8

2242 A369 90c Sheet of 4, #a-d 3.50 3.50

Christmas — A370

Angel: 25c, No. 2247a, Looking right, purple and yellow green background. 65c, No. 2247b, At left, looking left, purple background. 90c, No. 2247c, At right, purple and orange background. $5, No. 2247d, At center, blue and purple background.

2000, Dec. 4

2243-2246 A370 Set of 4 6.25 6.25

Sheet of 4

2247 A370 $1.90 #a-d 7.00 7.00

Souvenir Sheet

2248 A370 $6 Angel 5.50 5.50

Millennium Type of 1999

Chinese Art — No. 2249, 55c: a, Eight Prize Steeds, by Giuseppe Castiglione. b, Oleanders, by Wu Hsi Tsai. c, Mynah and Autumn Flowers, by Chang Hsiung. d, Hen and Chicks Beneath Chrysanthemums, by Chu Ch'ao. e, Long Living Pine and Crane, by Xugu. f, Flowers and Fruits, by Chu Lien. g, Lotus and Willow, by Pu Hua. h, Kuan-Yin, by Ch'ien Hui-An. i, Human Figures, by Jen hsun. j, Han-Shan and Shih-Te, by Ren Yi. k, Landscape and Human Figure, by Jen Yu. l, Poetic Thoughts While Walking With a Staff, by Wangchen. m, Peony, by Chen Heng-Ko. n, Plum and Orchids, by Wu Chang-Shih. o, Monkey, by Kao Chi-Feng. p, Grapes and Locust, by Ch'i Pai-Shih and Galloping Horse, by Xu Beihong (60x40mm). q, The Beauty, by Lin Fengmian.

History of Change — No. 2250, 55c: a, Star charts. b, Precision tools. c, Science of the stars. d, Investigation into healing a human being. e, Sharing of medical information. f, Church. g, Water alarm clock. h, Weighted clock. i, Spring-loaded miniature clock. j, New technology of glass blowing. k, First screws. l, Wood lathe. m, New systems for assembly blocks for ships. n, Interchangeable parts for rifles. o, Study of movement. p, Efficiency and the Industrial Revolution (60x40mm). q, Concept of efficiency.

Highlights of the 1960s — No. 2251, 55c: a, First birth control pill developed. b, Yuri Gagarin becomes first man in space. c, The first hit for the Beatles in Britain. d, Assassination of John F. Kennedy. e, Dr. Martin Luther King's "I Have a Dream" speech. f, Betty Friedan writes "The Feminine Mystique." g, Kenya gains independence. h, U.S. Surgeon General warns about smoking-related health hazards. i, U.S. Congress passes Civil Rights Act. j, U.S. increases military presence in South Viet Nam. k, Ernesto "Che" Guevara. l, First heart transplant. m, Israel wins Six-day War. n, Ho Chi Minh dies. o, First man on the Moon. p, Communists build wall to divide East and West Berlin (60x40mm). q, Woodstock rock concert.

Highlights of the late 14th Century — No. 2252: a, Minnesingers. b, Acampitzin, King of the Aztecs. c, Black Death eases. d, Giotto's campanile built. e, First French franc. f, Ming Dynasty in China. g, Tamerlane begins conquest of Asia. h, Triumph of Death painted by Francesco Traini. i, Robin Hood. j, Geoffrey Chaucer writes "The Canterbury Tales." k, Succession dispute in Japan. l, Jewish exodus from France. m, Temple of the Golden Pavilion built . n, Strasbourg Cathedral built. o, Alhambra Palace (60x40mm). p, Ife bronzes in Nigeria.

2000, Dec. 31 ***Perf. 12¾x12½***

Sheets of 17, #a-q

2249-2251 A346 Set of 3 26.00 26.00
2252 A347 65c Sheet of 17, #a-h, j-p, 2 #i 10.00 10.00

Hummingbirds — A371

No. 2253, $1.25: a, Green-throated carib. b, Bee, on branch. c, Bee, in flight. d, Bahama woodstar. e, Antillean mango. f, Blue-headed.

No. 2254, $1.65: a, Eastern streamertail. b, Purple-throated carib. c, Vervain. d, Bahama woodstar. e, Puerto Rican emerald. f, Antillean crested.

No. 2255, $5, Feeders. No. 2256, $6, Hispaniolan.

2000, Dec. 18 Litho. ***Perf. 14***

Sheets of 6, #a-f

2253-2254 A371 Set of 2 16.00 16.00

Souvenir Sheets

2255-2256 A371 Set of 2 10.00 10.00

Misspellings abound on Nos. 2253-2254.

New Year 2001 (Year of the Snake) A372

2001, Jan. 2 ***Perf. 12x12¼***

2257 A372 $1.20 multi 1.00 1.00

Printed in sheets of 4.

Fauna A373

Designs: 15c, Puerto Rican crested toad. 20c, Axolotl. $1.90, Panamanian golden frog. $2.20, Manatee.

No. 2262, $1.45: a, St. Vincent parrot. b, Indigo macaw. c, Cock of the rock. d, Cuban solenodon. e, Cuban hutia. f, Chinchilla.

No. 2263, $1.45: a, South American flamingo. b, Golden conure. c, Ocelot. d, Giant armadillo. e, Margay. f, Maned wolf.

No. 2264, $6, Anteater. No. 2265, $6, Hawksbill turtle.

2000, Dec. 18 Litho. ***Perf. 14***

2258-2261 A373 Set of 4 4.75 4.75

Sheets of 6, #a-f

2262-2263 A373 Set of 2 17.00 17.00

Souvenir Sheets

2264-2265 A373 Set of 2 12.00 12.00

Pokémon — A374

No. 2266, horiz.: a, Butterfree. b, Bulbasaur. c, Caterpie. d, Charmander. e, Squirtle. f, Pidgeotto.

2001, Feb. ***Perf. 13¾***

2266 A374 $1.65 Sheet of 6, #a-f 7.00 7.00

Souvenir Sheet

2267 A374 $6 Nidoking 4.25 4.25

A375

Marine Life A376

Designs: No. 2268, 15c, Banded sea snake. 25c, Soldier fish. 55c, Banner fish. No. 2271, 90c, Crown of thorns starfish.

No. 2272, 15c, Fish. 65c, Ray. No. 2274, 90c, Octopus. $3, Fish, diff.

No. 2276, $1.65: a, White-tip reef shark, lionfish, sergeant major. b, Blue-striped snappers. c, Great hammerhead shark, stovepipe sponge, pink vase sponge. d, Hawaiian monk seal, blue tube coral. e, Seahorse, common clownfish, red feather star coral. f, Bat starfish, brown octopus.

No. 2277, $1.65: a, Red sponge, shoal of Anthias. b, Orange-striped triggerfish. c, Coral grouper, soft tree coral. d, Peacock fan worms, gorgonian sea fan. e, Sweetlips, sea fan. f, Giant clam, golden cup coral.

No. 2278: a, Shark. b, Starfish. c, Seahorse. d, Fish. e, Crab. f, Eel.

No. 2279, $5, Royal angelfish. No. 2280, $5, Pink anemone fish. No. 2281, Turtle.

2001, Feb. 27 ***Perf. 14***

2268-2271 A375 Set of 4 2.00 2.00
2272-2275 A376 Set of 4 5.00 5.00

Sheets of 6, #a-f

2276-2277 A375 Set of 2 19.00 19.00
2278 A376 $2 Sheet of 6, #a-f 11.00 11.00

Souvenir Sheets

2279-2280 A375 Set of 2 10.00 10.00
2281 A376 $5 multi 5.00 5.00

Phila Nippon '01, Japan — A377

Art: 25c, Gathering of Chinese Women, by Tsuji Kako. 55c, Village by Bamboo Grove, by Takeuchi Seiho. 65c, Mountain Village in Spring, by Suzuki Hyakunen. 90c, Gentleman Amusing Himself, by Domoto Insho. $1, Calmness of Spring Light, by Seiho. $2, Su's Embankment on a Spring Morning, by Tomioka Tessai.

No. 2288, $1.65: a, Thatched Cottages in the Willows, by Kako. b, Joy in the Garden, by Kako. c, Azalea and butterfly, by Kikuchi Hobun. d, Pine Grove, by Kako. e, Woodcutters Talking in Autumn Valley, by Kubota Beisen.

No. 2289, $1.65: a, Waterfowl in Snow, by Kako. b, Heron and Willow, by Kako. c, Crow and Cherry Blossoms, by Hobun. d, Chrysanthemum Immortal, by Yamamoto Shunkyo. e, Cranes of Immortality, by Kako.

No. 2290, $6, Kamo Riverbank in the Misty Rain, by Kako. No. 2291, $6, Diamond Gate, by Kako. No. 2292, $6, Woman, by Suzuki Harunobu.

2001, May 15 Litho. ***Perf. 14***

2282-2287 A377 Set of 6 5.25 5.25

Sheets of 5, #a-e

2288-2289 A377 Set of 2 15.00 15.00

Souvenir Sheets

Perf. 13¾

2290-2292 A377 Set of 3 12.00 12.00

Nos. 2290-2292 each contain one 38x51mm stamp.

Queen Victoria (1819-1901) — A378

No. 2293: a, Prince Albert in uniform. b, Victoria with silver crown. c, Victoria with gold crown. d, Albert in suit.

$6, Victoria as old woman.

2001, May 15 ***Perf. 14***

2293 A378 $2 Sheet of 4, #a-d 7.25 7.25

Souvenir Sheet

Perf. 13¾

2294 A378 $6 multi 5.50 5.50

No. 2294 contains one 38x51mm stamp.

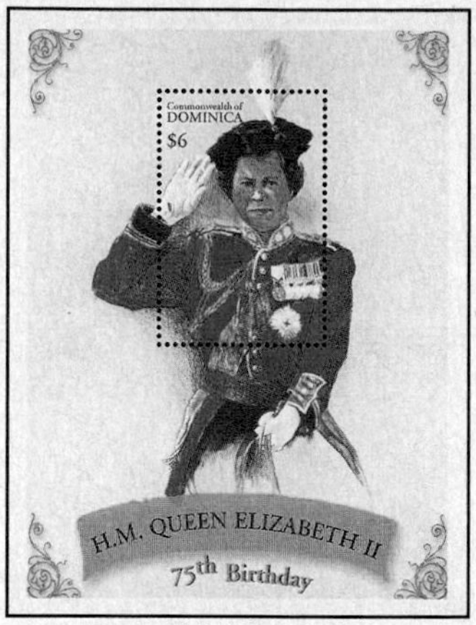

Queen Elizabeth II, 75th Birthday — A379

No. 2295: a, With crown. b, With white dress. c, Formal portrait by Pietro Annigoni. d, With orange coat. e, With child. f, With green dress.

$6, In uniform.

2001, May 15 *Perf. 14*

2295 A379 $1.20 Sheet of 6, #a-f 6.25 6.25

Souvenir Sheet

2296 A379 $6 multi 5.50 5.50

Toulouse-Lautrec Paintings — A380

No. 2297: a, Two Women Waltzing. b, The Medical Inspection. c, The Two Girlfriends. d, Woman Pulling Up Her Stocking.

2001, May 15 **Litho.** *Perf. 13¾*

2297 A380 $2 Sheet of 4, #a-d 7.25 7.25

Souvenir Sheet

2298 A380 $6 Self-portrait 5.50 5.50

Giuseppe Verdi (1813-1901), Opera Composer — A381

No. 2299: a, Verdi. b, Lady Macbeth. c, Orchestra. d, Score.

2001, May 15 *Perf. 14*

2299 A381 $2 Sheet of 4, #a-d 7.25 7.25

Souvenir Sheet

2300 A381 $6 Verdi, score 5.50 5.50

Mushrooms A382

Designs: 15c, Cantharellus cibarius. 25c, Hygrocybe pratensis. 55c, Leccinum aurantiacum. $3, Mycena haematopus.

No. 2305, 90c, horiz.: a, Caesar's amanita. b, Agaricus augustus. c, Clitocybe nuda. d, Hygrocybe plavescens. e, Stropharia kaufmanii. f, Hygrophorus speciosus.

No. 2306, $2: a, Marasmiellus candidus. b, Calostoma cinnabarina. c, Cantharellus infundibuliformis. d, Hygrocybe punicea. e, Basket stinkhorn. f, Agrocybe praecox.

No. 2307, $5, Fly agaric, horiz. No. 2308, $5, Gymnopilus spectabilis, horiz.

2001, June 18

2301-2304 A382 Set of 4 4.50 4.50

Sheets of 6, #a-f

2305-2306 A382 Set of 2 18.00 18.00

Souvenir Sheets

2307-2308 A382 Set of 2 10.00 10.00

Mao Zedong (1893-1976) — A383

No. 2309 — Picture from: a, 1945. b, 1926. c, 1949.

$3, 1930.

2001, May 15 **Litho.** *Perf. 14*

2309 A383 $2 Sheet of 3, #a-c 5.25 5.25

Souvenir Sheet

2310 A383 $3 multi 2.75 2.75

Monet Paintings — A384

No. 2311, horiz.: a, The Basin of Argenteuil. b, The Bridge at Argenteuil. c, The Railway Bridge, Argenteuil. d, The Seine Bridge at Argenteuil.

$6, Woman with a Parasol — Madame Monet and Her Son.

2001, May 15 *Perf. 13¾*

2311 A384 $2 Sheet of 4, #a-d 7.25 7.25

Souvenir Sheet

2312 A384 $6 multi 5.25 5.25

Fauna — A385

No. 2313: a, St. Vincent parrot. b, Painted bunting. c, Jamaican giant anole. d, White-fronted capuchin. e, Strand racerunner. f, Agouti.

No. 2314: a, Cook's tree boa. b, Tamandua. c, Common iguana. d, Solenodon.

No. 2315, $5, Purple gallinule. No. 2316, $5, Rufous-tailed jacamar. No. 2317, $5, Ruby-throated hummingbird, horiz. No. 2318, $5, Bottlenose dolphins, horiz.

2001, Sept. 3 *Perf. 14*

2313 A385 $1.45 Sheet of 6, #a-f 8.75 8.75

2314 A385 $2 Sheet of 4, #a-d 8.25 8.25

Souvenir Sheets

2315-2318 A385 Set of 4 19.00 19.00

Birds — A386

Designs: 5c, Yellow warbler. 10c, Palmchat. 15c, Snowy cotinga. 20c, Blue-gray gnatcatcher. 25c, Belted kingfisher. 55c, Red-legged thrush. 65c, Bananaquit. 90c, Yellow-bellied sapsucker. $1, White-tailed tropicbird. $1.45, Ruby-throated hummingbird. $1.90, Painted bunting. $2, Great frigatebird. $5, Brown trembler. $10, Red-footed booby. $20, Sooty tern.

2001, Sept. 3 **Litho.** *Perf. 14¾x14*

2319	A386	5c	multi	.30	.80
2320	A386	10c	multi	.30	.80
2321	A386	15c	multi	.35	.35
2322	A386	20c	multi	.35	.35
2323	A386	25c	multi	.35	.35
2324	A386	55c	multi	.65	.65
2325	A386	65c	multi	.75	.75
2326	A386	90c	multi	1.00	.80
2327	A386	$1	multi	1.25	1.25
2328	A386	$1.45	multi	1.60	1.60
2329	A386	$1.90	multi	2.00	2.00
2330	A386	$2	multi	2.50	2.50
2331	A386	$5	multi	5.00	5.00
2332	A386	$10	multi	8.50	8.50
2333	A386	$20	multi	17.50	17.50
	Nos. 2319-2333 (15)			42.40	43.20

No. 2323 exists dated "2005."

See No. 2513.

Photomosaic of Queen Elizabeth II — A387

2001, Nov. 15 *Perf. 14*

2334 A387 $1 multi 1.00 1.00

Issued in sheets of 8.

Christmas — A388

Paintings by Giovanni Bellini: 25c, Madonna and Child. 65c, Madonna and Child, diff. 90c, Baptism of Christ. $1.20, Madonna and Child, diff. $4, Madonna and Child, diff.

$6, Madonna and Child with Sts. Catherine and Mary Magdalene.

2001, Dec. 3

2335-2339 A388 Set of 5 6.75 6.75

Souvenir Sheet

2340 A388 $6 multi 5.50 5.50

2002 World Cup Soccer Championships, Japan and Korea — A389

No. 2341, $2: a, US team, 1950. b, Poster, 1954. c, Poster, 1958. d, Zozimo, 1962. e, Gordon Banks, 1966. f, Pelé, 1970.

No. 2342, $2: a, Daniel Passarella, 1978. b, Paolo Rossi, 1982. c, Diego Maradona, 1986. d, Poster, 1990. e, Seo Jungulon, 1994. f, Jürgen Klinsmann, 1998.

No. 2343, $5, Face on World Cup, 1930. No. 2344, $5, Face and globe on Jules Rimet Trophy, 2002.

2001, Dec. 13 *Perf. 13¾x14¼*

Sheets of 6, #a-f

2341-2342 A389 Set of 2 21.00 21.00

Souvenir Sheets

Perf. 14¼

2343-2344 A389 Set of 2 10.00 10.00

Queen Mother Type of 1999 Redrawn

No. 2345: a, In 1939. b, In Australia, 1958. c, At Badminton, 1982. d, Hatless, in 1982.

$6, In 1953.

2001, Dec. *Perf. 14*

Yellow Orange Frames

2345 A340 $2 Sheet of 4, #a-d, + label 7.00 7.00

Souvenir Sheet

Perf. 13¾

2346 A340 $6 multi 5.25 5.25

Queen Mother's 101st birthday. No. 2346 contains one 38x51mm stamp with a bluer backdrop than that found on No. 2161. Sheet margins of Nos. 2345-2346 lack embossing and gold arms and frames found on Nos. 2160-2161.

Souvenir Sheets

Betty Boop — A390

Betty Boop: No. 2347, $5, In chair, pink rose background. No. 2348, $5, Wearing blue blouse, in jungle. No. 2349, $5, With heart and stars, cat with film reel. No. 2350, $5, Wearing nurse's cap.

2001, Oct. 1 **Litho.** ***Perf. 13¾***
2347-2350 A390 Set of 4 18.00 18.00

The Three Stooges — A391

No. 2351: a, Man, Larry, Moe with sledgehammer, Joe Besser. b, Larry, woman, Joe Besser, Moe. c, Joe Besser, Larry and Moe on hands and knees. d, Larry grabbing throat of woman holding Joe Besser and Moe. e, Joe Besser drinking from baby bottle, pony, Moe and Larry. f, Military policeman, Joe Besser, Larry, woman. g, Larry. h, Joe Besser. i, Moe.
No. 2352, $5, Moe and Larry, "On the air" sign. No. 2353, $5, Larry and pony.

2001, Oct. 1 **Litho.** ***Perf. 13¾***
2351 A391 $1 Sheet of 9, #a-i 8.00 8.00

Souvenir Sheets

2352-2353 A391 Set of 2 9.00 9.00

Souvenir Sheet

New Year 2002 (Year of the Horse) — A392

No. 2354: a, Man with pole, horse. b, Horses grazing. c, Man currying horse. d, Horses with heads up.

2001, Dec. 17 ***Perf. 14***
2354 A392 $1.65 Sheet of 4, #a-d 6.00 6.00

Reign of Queen Elizabeth II, 50th Anniv. — A393

No. 2355: a, Wearing blue coat. b, With Prince Philip. c, Wearing tiara. d, Wearing flowered hat.
$6, With Prince Philip, diff.

2002, Feb. 6 ***Perf. 14¼***
2355 A393 $2 Sheet of 4, #a-d 7.00 7.00

Souvenir Sheet

2356 A393 $6 multi 5.00 5.00

United We Stand — A394

2002, Feb. ***Perf. 13½x13¼***
2357 A394 $2 multi 1.50 1.50

Printed in sheets of 4.

Shirley Temple in "Just Around the Corner" — A395

No. 2358, horiz.: a, Temple, woman with dogs. b, Temple, man and woman. c, Temple and man. d, Boy eating turkey leg, Temple carving turkey. e, Temple with old man. f, Temple with group of boys.
No. 2359: a, Boy, Temple with purse. b, Man and Temple using fingers as guns. c, Temple and man. d, Temple cutting boy's hair.
$6, Temple with black man on toadstool.

2002, Apr. 8 ***Perf. 12¼***
2358 A395 $1.90 Sheet of 6, #a-f 10.00 10.00
2359 A395 $2 Sheet of 4, #a-d 7.25 7.25

Souvenir Sheet

2360 A395 $6 multi 5.25 5.25

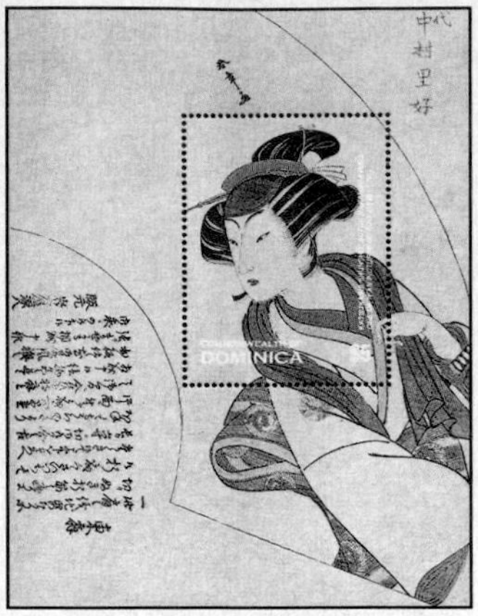

Japanese Art — A396

No. 2361, $1.20: a, The Courtesan Tsukioka of the Teahouse Hyogo-Ya, by Eisui Ichirakutei. b, Woman and Servant in the Snow, by Choki Eishosai. c, The Courtesan Shiratsuyu of the Teahouse Wakana-Ya, by Eisho Chokosai. d, Ohisa of the Takashima-Ya, by Toyokuni Utagawa. e, Woman and a Cat, by Kunimasa Utagawa. f, One of "Genre Scenes of Beauties," by Eizen Keisai.
No. 2362, $1.65: a, Women Inside and Outside a Mosquito Net, by Harushige Suzuki. b, Komachi at Shimizu, by Harushige Suzuki. c, Women Viewing Plum Blossoms, by Harunobu Suzuki. d, Women Cooling Themselves at Shijogawara in Kyoto, by Toyohiro Utagawa. e, Woman Reading a Letter, by Utamaro Kitagawa. f, Women Dressed for the Kashima Dance at the Niwaka Festival, by Utamaro Kitagawa.
No. 2363, $1.90: a, Actor Kiyotaro Iwai, by Kunimasa Utagawa. b, Actors Hiriji Otani III and Ryuzo Arashi, by Sharaku Toshusai. c, Actor Komazo Ichikawa II, by Shunko Katsukawa. d, Actors Yaozo Ichikawa and Hangoro Sakata III, by Sharaku Toshusai. e, Actor Torazo Tanimura, by Sharaku Toshusai. f, Actor Kiyotaro Iwai as Oishi, by Toyokuni Utagawa.
No. 2464, $5, Actor Riko Nakamura, by Shunsho Katsukawa. No. 2365, $5, Actors Hanshiro Iwai IV and Sojuro Sawamura III, by Kiyonaga Torii, horiz. No. 2366, $6, Ofuji, Daughter of the Motoyanagi-Ya, by Harunobu Suzuki.

2002, June 17 ***Perf. 14¼***

Sheets of 6, #a-f

2361-2363 A396 Set of 3 24.00 24.00

Souvenir Sheets

2364-2366 A396 Set of 3 12.00 12.00

Souvenir Sheet

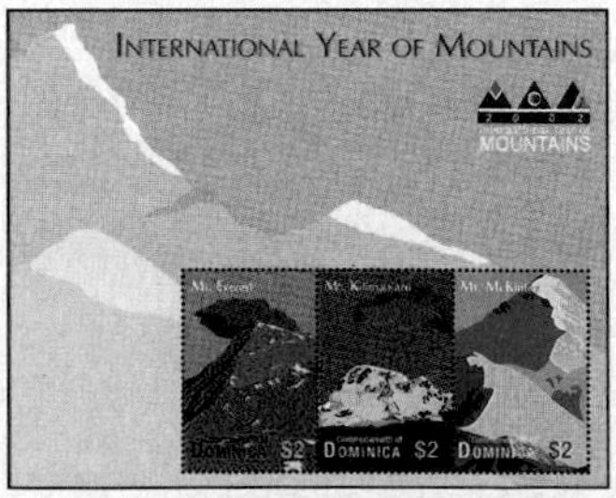

Intl. Year of Mountains — A397

No. 2367: a, Mt. Everest. b, Mt. Kilimanjaro. c, Mt. McKinley.

2002, July 15 ***Perf. 14***
2367 A397 $2 Sheet of 3, #a-c 5.00 5.00

2002 Winter Olympics, Salt Lake City
A398

Designs: No. 2368, $2, Skiing. No. 2369, $2, Bobsled.

2002, July 15 ***Perf. 13½***
2368-2369 A398 Set of 2 3.50 3.50
a. Souvenir sheet, #2368-2369 3.50 3.50

First Solo Trans-Atlantic Flight, 75th Anniv. — A399

No. 2370: a, Charles Lindbergh and Spirit of St. Louis. b, Charles and Anne Morrow Lindbergh.
$6, Charles Lindbergh and Spirit of St. Louis, diff.

2002, July 15 ***Perf. 14***
2370 A399 $3 Sheet of 2, #a-b 5.00 5.00

Souvenir Sheet

2371 A399 $6 multi 5.00 5.00

Popeye in New York — A400

No. 2372, $1: a, Olive Oyl. b, Brutus. c, Sweet Pea. d, Wimpy. e, Jeep. f, Popeye.
No. 2373, $1.90: a, Popeye and Olive Oyl, giraffe at Bronx Zoo. b, Popeye and Olive Oyl, Statue of Liberty. c, Popeye, Olive Oyl, Empire State Building. d, Popeye skating at Rockefeller Center. e, Popeye at Yankee Stadium. f, Popeye helping firefighters.
No. 2374, $6, Popeye, Atlas Statue, Rockefeller Center. No. 2375, $6, Popeye, Olive Oyl and Radio City Music Hall Rockettes, horiz.

2002, July 22

Sheets of 6, #a-f

2372-2373 A400 Set of 2 15.00 15.00

Souvenir Sheets

2374-2375 A400 Set of 2 10.50 10.50

20th World Scout Jamboree, Thailand — A401

No. 2376: a, Lord Robert Baden-Powell (facing forward). b, Lady Olave Baden-Powell. c, Maceo Johnson.
$6, Lord Baden-Powell (profile).

2002, July 15 Litho. *Perf. 14¼x14*

2376 A401 $3 Sheet of 3, #a-c 8.00 8.00

Souvenir Sheet

2377 A401 $6 multi 5.25 5.25

Birds, Insects, Moths and Whales — A402

No. 2378, $1.50, vert. — Birds: a, Brown trembler. b, Snowy ctinga. c, Bananaquit. d, Painted bunting. e, Belted kingfisher. f, Ruby-throated hummingbird.

No. 2379, $1.50, vert. — Insects: a, Field cricket. b, Migratory grasshopper. c, Honey bee. d, Hercules beetle. e, Black ant. f, Cicada.

No. 2380, $1.50, vert. — Moths: a, Carolina sphinx. b, White-lined sphinx. c, Orizaba silkmoth. d, Hieroglyphic moth. e, Hickory tussock moth. f, Diva moth.

No. 2381, $1.50, vert. — Whales: a, Sei. b, Killer. c, Blue. d, White. e, Pygmy. f, Sperm.

No. 2382, $6, Yellow-bellied sapsucker. No. 2383, $6, Bumble bee. No. 2384, $6, Ornate moth. No. 2385, $6, Gray whale.

2002, July 29 *Perf. 14*

Sheets of 6, #a-f

2378-2381 A402 Set of 4 28.00 28.00

Souvenir Sheets

2382-2385 A402 Set of 4 22.00 22.00

A403

A404

Amphilex 2002 Intl. Stamp Exhibition, Amsterdam — A405

No. 2386 — Dutch Nobel Prize winners: a, Willem Einthoven, Medicine, 1924. b, Nobel Economics medal. c, Peter J. W. Debye, Chemistry, 1936. d, Frits Zernike, Physics, 1953. e, Jan Tinbergen, Economics, 1969. f, Simon van der Meer, Physics, 1984.

No. 2387 — Dutch lighthouses: a, Marken. b, Harlingen. c, Den Oever. d, De Ven. e, Urk. f, Oosterleek.

No. 2388 — Traditional women's costumes: a, South Holland woman with small white head covering (facing forward). b, Zeeland woman with large white head covering (facing backwards). c, Limburg woman with black scarf.

2002, Aug. 30 *Perf. 13½x13¼*

2386 A403 $1.50 Sheet of 6, #a-f 8.00 8.00

2387 A404 $1.50 Sheet of 6, #a-f 8.00 8.00

Perf. 13½

2388 A405 $3 Sheet of 3, #a-c 8.00 8.00

Intl. Year of Ecotourism A406

Island scenes and cartoon characters: 45c, Detective H2O. 50c, Factman. 55c, B.B. 60c, Stanley the Starfish. 90c, Toxi. $1.20, Adopt. $6, Litterbit.

2002, Oct. 16 *Perf. 14¼*

2389-2394 A406 Set of 6 3.25 3.25

Souvenir Sheet

2395 A406 $6 multi 5.00 5.00

Elvis Presley (1935-77) A407

2002, Oct. 28 *Perf. 13¾*

2396 A407 $1.50 multi 1.10 1.10

Printed in sheets of 6 stamps with slightly differing frames.

Amerigo Vespucci (1454-1512), Explorer — A408

No. 2397: a, Compass rose. b, Vespucci with map. c, Map scroll.

$5, Two men.

2002, Nov. 28 *Perf. 13¾*

2397 A408 $3 Sheet of 3, #a-c 8.00 8.00

Souvenir Sheet

Perf. 14

2398 A408 $5 multi 4.50 4.50

No. 2397 contains three 50x38mm stamps.

Pres. John F. Kennedy (1917-63) — A409

No. 2399, $1.90: a, Wearing military uniform. b, With red denomination at UL. c, With blue denomination at UR. d, Wearing tan suit.

No. 2400, $1.90 (denominations at UL in blue): a, Wearing red tie. b, Wearing blue tie (profile). c, Wearing black tie. d, With hand on chin.

2002, Dec. 16 *Perf. 14*

Sheets of 4, #a-d

2399-2400 A409 Set of 2 13.50 13.50

Pres. Ronald Reagan — A410

No. 2401, $1.90: a, Wearing cowboy hat. b, Wearing blue green sweater. c, Wearing red sweater. d, Wearing blue sweater.

No. 2402, $1.90, horiz.: a, Wearing blue shirt, and with wife, Nancy. b, Nancy and US flag. c, Ronald. d, Wearing pink shirt, and with wife.

2002, Dec. 16 Litho. *Perf. 14*

Sheets of 4, #a-d

2401-2402 A410 Set of 2 13.50 13.50

Princess Diana (1961-97) — A411

No. 2403 — Various depictions of Princess Diana with background colors of: a, Tan. b, Pink. c, Light blue. d, Light green.

2002, Dec. 16

2403 A411 $1.90 Sheet of 4, #a-d 7.00 7.00

Souvenir Sheet

2404 A411 $5 multi 4.50 4.50

Elizabeth "Ma Pampo" Israel, 128th Birthday — A412

2003, Jan. 27 *Perf. 13½x13¼*

2405 A412 90c multi .70 .70

New Year 2003 (Year of the Ram) — A413

2003, Feb. 10 *Perf. 13¾*

2406 A413 $1.65 multi 1.25 1.25

Printed in sheets of 4.

Souvenir Sheets

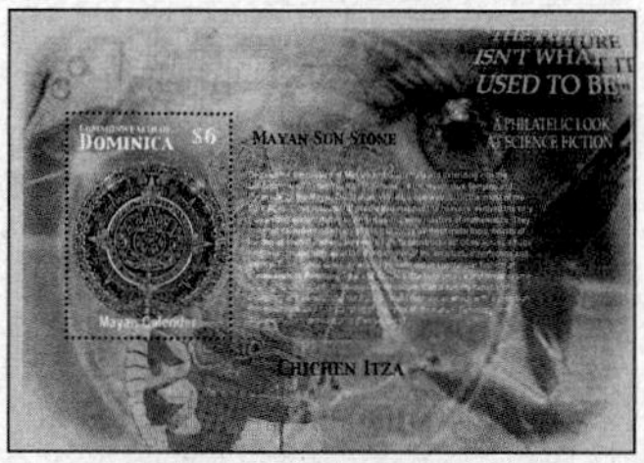

Science Fiction — A414

Designs: No. 2407, $6, Mayan calendar. No. 2408, $6, Atlas. No. 2409, $6, Confucius. No. 2410, $6, Nazca Lines. No. 2411, $6, Pres. Franklin D. Roosevelt and Pres. John F. Kennedy. No. 2412, $6, Zoroaster.

2003, Feb. 10 *Perf. 13¼*

2407-2412 A414 Set of 6 27.50 27.50

A415

Coronation of Queen Elizabeth II, 50th Anniv. — A416

No. 2413: a, Wearing white dress, no crown. b, Wearing black robe. c, Wearing crown.

$6, Wearing crown, diff. $20, Wearing red robe.

2003 Litho. *Perf. 14*

2413 A415 $3 Sheet of 3, #a-c 6.25 6.25

Souvenir Sheet

2414 A415 $6 multi 4.25 4.25

Miniature Sheet

Litho. & Embossed

Perf. 13¼x13

2415 A416 $20 gold & multi 14.00 14.00

Issued: Nos. 2413-2414, 5/13; No. 2415, 2/24.

Prince William, 21st Birthday — A417

No. 2416: a, Wearing dark blue shirt. b, Wearing blue suit, holding flowers. c, In polo uniform.
$6, Wearing black suit.

2003, June 21 **Litho.** ***Perf. 14***

2416 A417 $3 Sheet of 3, #a-c 6.50 6.50

Souvenir Sheet

2417 A417 $6 multi 4.50 4.50

Intl. Year of Fresh Water — A418

No. 2418: a, Trafalgar Falls. b, YS Falls. c, Dunn's River.
$6, Annandale Falls.

2003, June 21 ***Perf. 13½***

2418 A418 $3 Sheet of 3, #a-c 6.75 6.75

Souvenir Sheet

2419 A418 $6 multi 4.50 4.50

Teddy Bears, Cent. — A419

No. 2420 — Bear with: a, Purple shirt. b, Pink shirt and party favor. c, Green shirt and party favor. d, Black hat. e, Purple hat. f, Pink shirt and birthday cake.
No. 2421 — Bear with: a, Reindeer sweater, text at top. b, Santa Claus costume, text at top. c, Santa Claus costume, text at bottom. d, Reindeer sweater, text at bottom.

2003, June 21 ***Perf. 13½***

2420 A419 $1.65 Sheet of 6, #a-f 7.50 7.50

2421 A419 $2 Sheet of 4, #a-d 6.00 6.00

No. 2421 contains four 37x51mm stamps.

General Motors Automobiles — A420

No. 2422, $2 — Cadillacs: a, 1903 Model A Runabout. b, 1912 Model 30. c, 1918 Type 57 Victoria Coupe. d, 1927 Lasalle Convertible Coupe.
No. 2423, $2 — Corvettes: a, 1953. b, 1956. c, 1957. d, 1962.
No. 2424, $5, 1933 Cadillac 355-C V8 sedan. No. 2425, $5, 1959 Corvette.

2003, June 21 ***Perf. 13¼***

Sheets of 4, #a-d

2422-2423 A420 Set of 2 12.00 12.00

Souvenir Sheets

2424-2425 A420 Set of 2 7.50 7.50

Tour de France Bicycle Race, Cent. — A421

No. 2426 — Champions: a, Firmin Lambot, 1919. b, Phillippe Thys, 1920. c, Léon Scieur, 1921. d, Lambot, 1922.
$5, François Faber.

2003, June 21

2426 A421 $2 Sheet of 4, #a-d 6.00 6.00

Souvenir Sheet

2427 A421 $5 multi 3.75 3.75

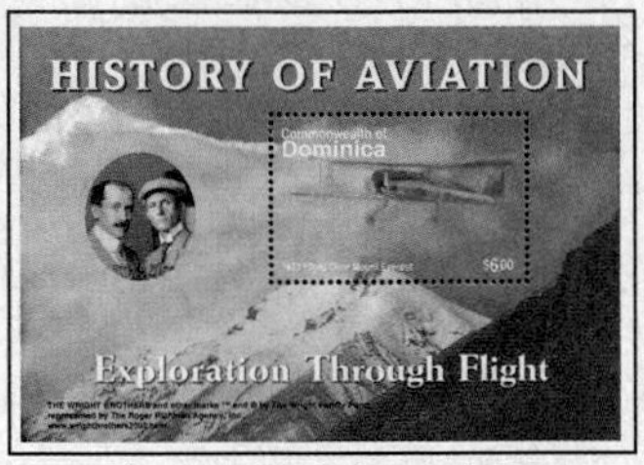

History of Aviation — A422

No. 2428: a, Sputnik, first orbiting satellite, 1957. b, Yuri Gagarin, first man in space, 1961. c, Neil Armstrong, first man on the Moon, 1969. d, Skylab 1, 1973.
$6, Flight over Mt. Everest, 1933.

2003, June 21 ***Perf. 14***

2428 A422 $2 Sheet of 4, #a-d 6.50 6.50

Souvenir Sheet

2429 A422 $6 multi 5.00 5.00

Lewis & Clark Expedition A423

Designs: 20c, Dealing with the Chinook Indians. 50c, Compass used in expedition. 55c, Rocky Mountains. 65c, Medals presented to the Indians, vert. 90c, First encounter with grizzly bear. $1, Befriending Shoshone Indians. $2, Lewis after the expedition, vert. $4, Lewis & Clark, vert.
No. 2438, $5, Meriwether Lewis, vert. No. 2439, $5, William Clark, vert.

2003, June 21

2430-2437 A423 Set of 8 7.50 7.50

Souvenir Sheets

2438-2439 A423 Set of 2 7.00 7.00

2002 World Cup Soccer Championships, Japan and Korea — A424

No. 2440, $1.45: a, Danny Mills. b, Paul Scholes. c, Darius Vassell. d, Michael Owen. e, Emile Heskey. f, Rio Ferdinand.
No. 2441, $1.45: a, Bobby Moore. b, Roger Hunt. c, Gordon Banks. d, Bobby Charlton. e, Alan Ball. f, Geoff Hurst.
No. 2442, $3: a, Ashley Cole. b, David Seaman.
No. 2443, $3: a, Sven-Goran Eriksson. b, Nikki Butt.
No. 2444, $3: a, Robbie Fowler. b, Sol Campbell.
No. 2445, $3: a, Charlton, Ball and Hunt. b, Nobby Stiles.
No. 2446, $3: a, Franz Beckenbauer. b, Oliver Kahn.

2003, June 21 ***Perf. 13¼***

Sheets of 6, #a-f

2440-2441 A424 Set of 2 11.00 11.00

Souvenir Sheets of 2, #a-b

2442-2446 A424 Set of 5 20.00 20.00

CARICOM, 30th Anniv. — A425

2003, July 25 ***Perf. 13½***

2447 A425 $1 multi .75 .75

Christmas A426

Painting details: 50c, Madonna and Child with the Young St. John, by Correggio. 90c, Madonna in Glory with the Christ Child and Sts. Frances and Alvise with the Donor, by Titian. $1.45, Madonna and Child with Angels Playing Musical Instruments, by Correggio. $3, Madonna of the Cherries, by Titian.
$6, Holy Family with John the Baptist, by Andrea del Sarto.

2003, Nov. 17 **Litho.** ***Perf. 14¼***

2448-2451 A426 Set of 4 4.50 4.50

Souvenir Sheet

2452 A426 $6 multi 4.50 4.50

New Year 2004 (Year of the Monkey) — A427

No. 2453: a, Orange monkey, hindquarters of brown monkey. b, Monkey with brown face. c, Brown monkey drinking water. d, Monkey with blue face.

2004, Jan. 5 **Litho.** ***Perf. 14***

2453 A427 $1.50 Sheet of 4, #a.-d. 4.50 4.50

Paintings of Pablo Picasso — A428

No. 2454, vert.: a, Portrait of Manuel Pallarés. b, Woman with Vase of Flowers. c, Woman with a Fan (Fernande). d, Portrait of Clovis Sagot.
$5, Brick Factory at Torosa (The Factory).

2004, Mar. 8 ***Perf. 14¼***

2454 A428 $1 Sheet of 4, #a.-d. 3.00 3.00

Imperf

2455 A428 $5 multi 3.75 3.75

No. 2454 contains four 38x50mm stamps.

Paintings of Paul Gauguin — A429

No. 2456: a, Village Tahitien avec la Femme en Marche. b, La Barriere. c, Bonjour, Monsieur Gauguin. d, Vegetation Tropicale.
$5, Petites Bretonnes Devant la Mer.

2004, Mar. 8 ***Perf. 14¼***
2456 A429 $2 Sheet of 4, #a.-d. 6.00 6.00

Imperf

2457 A429 $5 multi 3.75 3.75

No. 2456 contains four 38x50mm stamps.

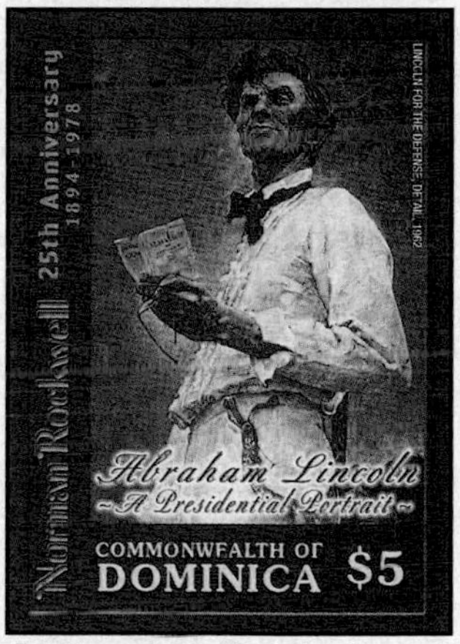

Paintings of Presidents by Norman Rockwell — A430

No. 2458: a, Dwight D. Eisenhower. b, John F. Kennedy. c, Lyndon B. Johnson. d, Richard M. Nixon.
$5, Abraham Lincoln.

2004, Mar. 8 ***Perf. 14¼***
2458 A430 $2 Sheet of 4, #a.-d. 6.00 6.00

Imperf

2459 A430 $5 multi 3.75 3.75

No. 2458 contains four 38x50mm stamps.

Paintings of James McNeill Whistler — A431

Designs: 50c, Symphony in White No. 3. $1, The Artist's Studio, vert. $1.65, The Thames in Ice, vert. No. 2463, $2, Arrangement in Black: Portrait of F. R. Leyland, vert.
No. 2464, $2, vert.: a, Arrangement in Brown & Black: Portrait of Miss Rosa Corder. b, Harmony in Red: Lamplight. c, Symphony in Flesh Color & Pink: Portrait of Mrs. Frances Leyland. d, Arrangement in Yellow & Gray: Effie Deans.
$5, Harmony in Gray and Green: Miss Cicely Alexander, vert.

2004, Mar. 8 ***Perf. 14¼***
2460-2463 A431 Set of 4 4.00 4.00

Perf. 13½

2464 A431 $2 Sheet of 4, #a-d 6.00 6.00

Imperf

Size: 71x103mm

2465 A431 $5 multi 3.75 3.75

No. 2464 contains four 35x70mm stamps.

Fish A432

Designs: 20c, Banded butterflyfish. 25c, Queen angelfish. 55c, Porkfish. No. 2469, $5, Redband parrotfish.
No. 2470: a, Beaugregory. b, Porkfish, diff. c, Bicolor cherubfish. d, Rock beauty. e, Blackfin snapper. f, Blue tang.
No. 2471, $5, Indigo hamlet.

2004, Mar. 8 ***Perf. 14¼x14¾***
2466-2469 A432 Set of 4 4.50 4.50

Perf. 14

2470 A432 $2 Sheet of 6, #a-f 9.00 9.00

Souvenir Sheet

2471 A432 $5 multi 3.75 3.75

Nos. 2470-2471 each contain 42x28mm stamps.

Shells A433

Designs: 20c, Siratus perelegans. 90c, Polystira albida. $1.45, Cypraea cervus. $2, Strombus gallus.
No. 2476: a, Strombus pugilis. b, Cittarium pica. c, Distorsio clathrata. d, Melongena morio. e, Prunum labiata. f, Chione paphla.
$5, Strombus alatus, vert.

2004, Mar. 8 ***Perf. 14¼x14¾***
2472-2475 A433 Set of 4 3.50 3.50

Perf. 14

2476 A433 $1.90 Sheet of 6, #a-f 8.50 8.50

Souvenir Sheet

2477 A433 $5 multi 3.75 3.75

No. 2476 contain six 42x28mm stamps; No. 2477 contains one 28x42mm stamp.

Orchids — A434

Designs: 25c, Epidendrum pseudepidendrum. 55c, Aspasia epidendroides. $1.50, Cochleanthes discolor. $4, Brassavola nodosa.
No. 2482: a, Laelia anceps. b, Caularthron bicornutum. c, Cattleya velutina. d, Cattleya warneri. e, Oncidium splendidum. f, Psychlis atropurpurea.
$5, Maxillaria cuculata, vert.

2004, Mar. 8 ***Perf. 14¼x14¾***
2478-2481 A434 Set of 4 4.75 4.75

Perf. 14

2482 A434 $1.90 Sheet of 6, #a-f 8.50 8.50

Souvenir Sheet

2483 A434 $5 multi 3.75 3.75

No. 2482 contains six 42x28mm stamps; No. 2483 contains one 28x42mm stamp.

Butterflies — A435

Designs: 50c, Small flambeau. 90c, Tiger pierid. $1, White peacock. No. 2469, $2, Cramer's mesene.
No. 2488, $2: a, Figure-of-eight. b, Orange theope. c, Clorinde. d, Grecian shoemaker. e, Orange-barred sulphur. f, Common morpho.
$5, Giant swallowtail, vert.

2004, Mar. 8 ***Perf. 14¼x14¾***
2484-2487 A435 Set of 4 3.00 3.00

Perf. 14

2488 A435 $2 Sheet of 6, #a-f 8.00 8.00

Souvenir Sheets

2489 A435 $5 multi 3.75 3.75

No. 2488 contains six 42x28mm stamps; No. 2489 contains one 28x42mm stamp.

Olympic Gold Medalists A436

Designs: 20c, Elizabeth Robinson, Amsterdam, 1928. 25c, Károly Takács, London, 1948. 55c, Bob Beamon, Mexico City, 1968. 65c, Mildred Didrikson, Los Angeles, 1932. $1, Ville Ritola, Paris, 1924. $1.65, Alfred Hajós (Guttman), Athens, 1896. $2, Paavo Nurmi, Antwerp, 1920. $4, Nedo Nadi, Antwerp, 1920.

2004, Apr. 12 ***Perf. 13¼***
2490-2497 A436 Set of 8 7.75 7.75

Election of Pope John Paul II, 25th Anniv. (in 2003) — A437

No. 2498: a, Praying for peace in Falkland Islands, 1982. b, In Croatia, 1998. c, Seated, 1998. d, With Franciscan monks, 1999. e, Remembering the Holocaust, 2001.

2004, June 21 **Litho.** ***Perf. 14***
2498 A437 $2 Sheet of 5, #a-e 7.50 7.50

European Soccer Championships, Portugal — A438

No. 2499, vert.: a, Jose Luis Villalonga. b, Lev Yashin. c, Marcelino Martinez. d, Santiago Bernabeu Stadium.
$6, 1964 Spain team.

2004, June 21 ***Perf. 14***
2499 A438 $2 Sheet of 4, #a-d 6.00 6.00

Souvenir Sheet

Perf. 14¼

2500 A438 $6 multi 4.50 4.50

No. 2499 contains four 28x42mm stamps.

Trains — A439

No. 2501, $1: a, Engine #22, V7 T4-4-0, V7T4-6-0. b, Don J12. c, Baldwin 2-D-D. d, Southern Engine #20. e, 143-890 2DB class electric locomotive. f, Engine #1.
No. 2502, $1: a, Canadian Pacific freight train. b, Queensland Rail IM U railroad. c, Green and white Shinkansen locomotive. d, Amtrak locomotive. e, Shinkansen locomotive in station. f, YPDMU rail cars.
No. 2503, $1: a, Santa Fe Railroad locomotive. b, Via Rail train, Canada. c, Two Conrail road switchers. d, Strasburg Railroad #90. e, Deltic diesel-electric engine. f, Brighton Belle.
No. 2504, $6, Golsdorf two cylinder compound locomotive 4-4-0. No. 2505, $6, Southern Pacific 4449 4-8-4. No. 2506, $6, White, yellow and blue Shinkansen.

2004, July 12 ***Perf. 13¼x13½***

Sheets of 6, #a-f

2501-2503 A439 Set of 3 13.50 13.50

Souvenir Sheets

2504-2506 A439 Set of 3 13.50 13.50

D-Day, 60th Anniv. A440

Designs: $1, Eddie Hannath. $4, Pres. Franklin D. Roosevelt.
No. 2509: a, Rangers make their way towards the cliffs of Pointe du Hoo. b, Rangers begin scaling the cliffs of Pointe du Hoc. c, British troops advance on Sword Beach. d, An AVRE Petard heads inland off Sword Beach.
$6, British troops landing on Sword Beach.

2004, July 22 ***Perf. 14***

Stamp + Label (#2507-2508)

2507-2508 A440 Set of 2 3.75 3.75
2509 A440 $2 Sheet of 4, #a-d 6.00 6.00

Souvenir Sheet

2510 A440 $6 multi 4.50 4.50

George Herman "Babe" Ruth (1895-1948), Baseball Player — A441

No. 2511: a, Swinging bat. b, Swinging bat, looking up. c, Holding three bats. d, Hand on knee.

2004, Aug. 18 ***Perf. 13½x13¼***
2511 A441 $2 Sheet of 4, #a-d 6.00 6.00

Marilyn Monroe (1926-62), Actress — A442

No. 2512: a, Wearing earrings and necklace. b, Wearing earrings. c, Wearing no earrings or necklace. d, Wearing necklace.

2004, Aug. 18
2512 A442 $2 Sheet of 4, #a-d 6.00 6.00

Bird Type of 2001

2004, Sept. 3 ***Perf. 14¾x14***
2513 A386 50c Baltimore oriole .45 .45

Exists dated "2005."

Queen Juliana of the Netherlands (1909-2004) A443

2004, Sept. 21 ***Perf. 13¼***
2514 A443 $2 multi 1.50 1.50

Printed in sheets of 6.

Intl. Year of Peace — A444

No. 2515: a, Mother Teresa, UN emblem. b, Mother Teresa feeding poor. c, Dove.

2004, Sept. 21 ***Perf. 14***
2515 A444 $2 Sheet of 3, #a-c 4.50 4.50

Souvenir Sheet

Deng Xiaoping (1904-97) and Mao Zedong (1893-1976), Chinese Leaders — A445

2004, Sept. 21 ***Perf. 14***
2516 A445 $6 multi 4.50 4.50

National Soccer Team — A446

2004, Nov. 8 **Litho.** ***Perf. 12***
2517 A446 90c multi .70 .70

FIFA (Fédération Internationale de Football Association), Cent. — A447

No. 2518: a, Ferenc Puskas. b, Rivaldo. c, Carsten Jancker. d, Johan Cruyff.
$6, George Best.

2004, Nov. 8 ***Perf. 12¾x12½***
2518 A447 $2 Sheet of 4, #a-d 6.00 6.00

Souvenir Sheet

2519 A447 $6 multi 4.50 4.50

Worldwide Fund for Nature (WWF) — A448

No. 2520: a, Green-throated Carib (denomination in blue). b, Purple-throated Carib (denomination in white). c, Green-throated Carib (denomination in white). d, Purple-throated Carib (denomination in red).

2005, Jan. 10 ***Perf. 14***
2520 A448 $2 Block of 4, #a-d 5.50 5.50
e. Miniature sheet, 2 each #2520a-2520d 11.00 11.00

Prehistoric Animals — A449

No. 2521, $2: a, Tyrannosaurus rex. b, Velociraptor. c, Stegosaurus. d, Psittacosaurus.

No. 2522, $2: a, Mammuthus columbi. b, Spinosaurus. c, Ankylosaurus. d, Mammuthus primigenius.

No. 2523, $2: a, Pterodactylus. b, Pteranodon. c, Sordes. d, Caudipteryx zoui.

$3, Compsognathus. $5, Archaeopteryx. $6, Mammuthus primigenius, diff.

2005, Jan. 10 ***Perf. 12¾***

Sheets of 4, #a-d

2521-2523 A449 Set of 3 18.00 18.00

Souvenir Sheets

2524-2526 A449 Set of 3 10.50 10.50

Birds A450

Designs: 25c, Brown booby. 90c, Brown pelican. $1, Red-billed tropicbird. $4, Northern gannet.

No. 2531: a, Great egret. b, Black-necked grebe. c, Turkey vulture. d, Snail kite.

$6, Red knot.

2005, Jan. 10 ***Perf. 14***
2527-2530 A450 Set of 4 4.50 4.50
2531 A450 $2 Sheet of 4, #a-d 5.75 5.75

Souvenir Sheet

2532 A450 $6 multi 4.00 4.00

Mushrooms — A451

No. 2533: a, Cortinarius mucosus. b, Cortinarius splendens. c, Cortinarius rufoolivaceus. d, Inocybe erubescens.

$6, Split fibercap.

2005, Jan. 10
2533 A451 $2 Sheet of 4, #a-d 6.00 6.00

Souvenir Sheet

2534 A451 $6 multi 4.50 4.50

Miniature Sheet

Flowers — A452

No. 2535: a, Sweetshrub. b, Pink turtleheads. c, Flowering quince. d, Water lily.

$6, Glory of the snow, vert.

2005, Jan. 10 **Litho.** ***Perf. 14***
2535 A452 $2 Sheet of 4, #a-d 6.00 6.00

Souvenir Sheet

2535E A452 $6 multi 4.50 4.50

New Year 2005 (Year of the Rooster) — A453

2005, Jan. 24 ***Perf. 12¾x12½***
2536 A453 $1 shown .75 .75

Souvenir Sheet

Perf. 12

2537 A453 $4 Roosters 3.00 3.00

No. 2537 contains one 56x36mm stamp.

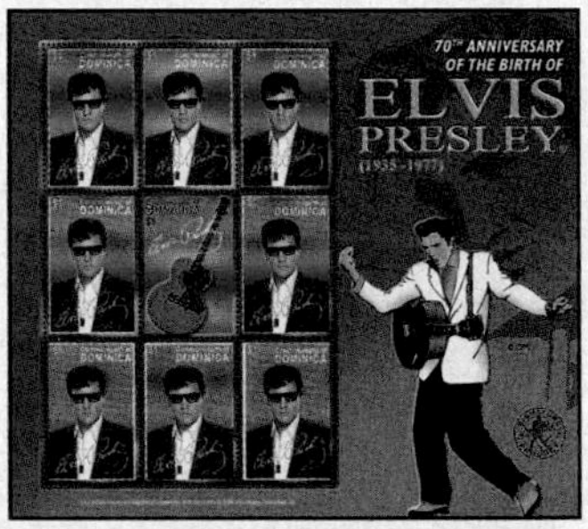

A454

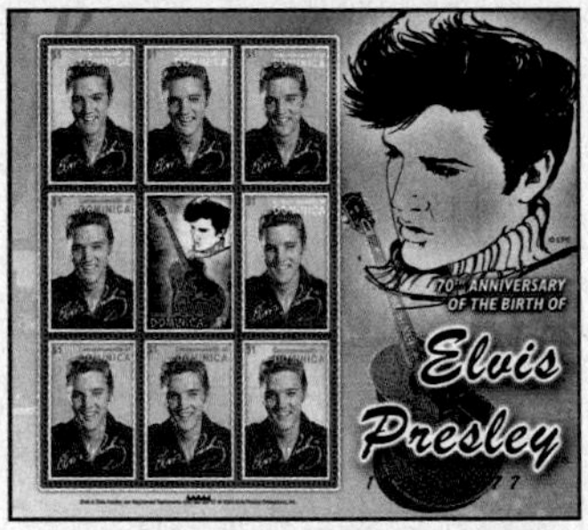

Elvis Presley (1935-77) — A455

Elvis Presley (1935-77) — A455a

No. 2538: a, Green background under country name and near shirt collar. b, Guitar. c, Large red violet areas at side of head. d, Dark green background under country name, blue background near shirt collar. e, Purple background near shirt collar. f, Small red violet areas at side of head.

No. 2539: a, Country name in white, blue background at UR. b, Country name in white, pink background at UR. c, Country name in white, orange background at UR. d, Country name in blue, green background at UR. e, Presley and guitar. f, Country name in blue, yellow background at UR. g, Country name in blue, blue background at UR.

No. 2539H illustration reduced.

2005, Apr. 5 ***Perf. 13½***
2538 A454 $1 Sheet of 9, #a-c, 2 each #d-f 6.75 6.75
2539 A455 $1 Sheet of 9, #a, c, e-g, 2 each #b, d 6.75 6.75

Litho. & Embossed
Variable Serpentine Die Cut
Without Gum

2539H A455a $20 gold & multi 14.00 14.00

No. 2539H was not available in the marketplace until 2006.

Miniature Sheet

Rotary International, Cent. — A456

No. 2540: a, Globe and Rotary emblem. b, Rotary emblem. c, Women and children.

2005, Sept. 7 ***Perf. 12½x12¾***
2540 A456 $3 Sheet of 3, #a-c 6.75 6.75

Battle of Trafalgar, Bicent. — A457

Designs: 55c, Admiral Horatio Nelson explaining plan of attack before battle. 65c, Orient explodes during the Battle of the Nile, vert. $1, Nelson and his men board San Nicolas during the Battle of Cape St. Vincent, vert. $2, Ships Agamemnon and Ca Ira in battle.
$6, HMS Victory.

2005, Sept. 7 ***Perf. 13¼***
2541-2544 A457 Set of 4 3.25 3.25

Souvenir Sheet
Perf. 12

2545 A457 $6 multi 4.50 4.50

Hans Christian Andersen (1805-75), Author — A458

No. 2546: a, The Swineherd. b, The Nightingale. c, The Fir Tree.
$6, The Ugly Duckling.

2005, Sept. 7 ***Perf. 12¾***
2546 A458 $2 Sheet of 3, #a-c 4.50 4.50

Souvenir Sheet
Perf. 12

2547 A458 $6 multi 4.50 4.50

No. 2546 contains three 42x28mm stamps.

Friedrich von Schiller (1759-1805), Writer — A459

No. 2548, vert. — Schiller and German Democratic Republic stamps: a, #241. b, #242. c, #243.
$6, Statue of Schiller.

2005, Sept. 7 ***Perf. 12¾***
2548 A459 $3 Sheet of 3, #a-c 6.75 6.75

Souvenir Sheet

2549 A459 $6 multi 4.50 4.50

Jules Verne (1828-1905), Writer — A460

No. 2550: a, Men, dog and rooster in space. b, Astronauts. c, Men looking at undersea creature. d, Submarine.
$6, Portrait of Verne.

2005, Sept. 7
2550 A460 $2 Sheet of 4, #a-d 6.00 6.00

Souvenir Sheet

2551 A460 $6 multi 4.50 4.50

World Cup Soccer Championships, 75th Anniv. — A461

No. 2552: a, 1934 Italy team. b, Scene from 1934 Italy victory over Czechoslovakia. c, Flaminio Stadium. d, Angelos Schiavo.
$6, Italian team celebrating.

2005, Sept. 7 ***Perf. 12***
2552 A461 $2 Sheet of 4, #a-d 6.00 6.00

Souvenir Sheet

2553 A461 $6 multi 4.50 4.50

Christmas — A462

Painting details: 25c, Madonna and Child with Two Angels, by Sandro Botticelli. 50c, Madonna and Child with Angels, by Botticelli. 65c, Madonna and Child, by Pietro Lorenzetti. 90c, Madonna del Roseto, by Botticelli. $1.20, Adoration of the Magi, by Lorenzetti. $3, Madonna in Glory with the Seraphim, by Botticelli.
$5, Madonna of Frari, by Titian, horiz.

2005, Nov. 15 ***Perf. 12¾***
2554-2559 A462 Set of 6 5.00 5.00

Souvenir Sheet

2560 A462 $5 multi 3.75 3.75

Pope John Paul II (1920-2005) and Princess Diana (1961-97) — A463

2005 ***Perf. 13½x13¼***
2561 A463 $3 multi 2.25 2.25

Pope Benedict XVI — A464

2005 **Litho.** ***Perf. 13½x13¼***
2562 A464 $2 multi 1.50 1.50

Printed in sheets of 4.

Souvenir Sheet

New Year 2006 (Year of the Dog) — A465

No. 2563 — Dog figurines with background colors of: a, Pale green and green. b, Orange and pink. c, Rose pink and yellow.

2006, Jan. 3 ***Perf. 13¼x13½***
2563 A465 $1 Sheet of 3, #a-c 2.25 2.25

Miniature Sheets

National Basketball Association Players and Team Emblems — A466

No. 2564, 90c: a, Orlando Magic emblem. b, Hedo Turkoglu.
No. 2565, 90c: a, Denver Nuggets emblem. b, Kenyon Martin.
No. 2566, 90c: a, Miami Heat emblem. b, Antoine Walker.
No. 2567, 90c: a, Golden State Warriors emblem. b, Jason Richardson.
No. 2568, 90c: a, Phoenix Suns emblem. b, Amaré Stoudemire.
No. 2569, 90c: a, Los Angeles Clippers emblem. b, Elton Brand.

2006, Feb. 14 ***Perf. 14***
Sheets of 12, 2 each #a, 10 each #b
2564-2569 A466 Set of 6 47.50 47.50

Léopold Sédar Senghor (1906-2001), First President of Senegal — A467

2006, Mar. 20 ***Perf. 13¼***
2570 A467 $2 multi 1.50 1.50

2006 Winter Olympics, Turin — A468

Designs: 75c, Yugoslavia #1670. 90c, 1984 Sarajevo Winter Olympics poster, vert. $2, Japan #2607g, vert. $3, 1998 Nagano Winter Olympics poster, vert.

2006, Mar. 29
2571-2574 A468 Set of 4 5.00 5.00

Each stamp printed in sheets of 4.

Queen Elizabeth II, 80th Birthday — A469

No. 2575: a, As infant, with mother. b, As young child. c, As baby, wearing bonnet. d, As young girl, wearing jacket.
$5, Wearing tiara and sash.

2006, Mar. 29

2575 A469 $2 Sheet of 4, #a-d 6.00 6.00

Souvenir Sheet

2576 A469 $5 multi 3.75 3.75

Marilyn Monroe (1926-62), Actress — A470

2006, Apr. 7

2577 A470 $3 multi 2.25 2.25

Printed in sheets of 4.

Space Achievements — A471

No. 2578 — Viking I: a, Trenches dug by Viking I. b, Sunset at Viking I landing site. c, Chryse Planitia looking northwest over Viking I. d, First panoramic image of Chryse Planitia, country name and denomination in white. e, As "d," country name in black, denomination in white. f, As "d", country name and denomination in black.

No. 2579, $3, vert. — Luna 9: a, Flight apparatus. b, Modified SS-6 Sapwood rocket. c, Luna 9 Soft Lander. d, Tyuratam.

No. 2580, $3, vert. — Giotto Comet Probe: a, Launch of Giotto. b, Giotto during solar simulation test. c, Halley's Comet develops seven tails. d, Giotto and Comet Grigg-Skjellerup approach trajectories.

No. 2581, $6, Intl. Space Station. No. 2582, $6, Mars Reconnaissance Orbiter. No. 2583, $6, Venus Express Orbiter.

2006, June 6 Litho. *Perf. 14*

2578 A471 $2 Sheet of 6, #a-f 9.00 9.00

Sheets of 4, #a-d

2579-2580 A471 Set of 2 18.00 18.00

Souvenir Sheets

2581-2583 A471 Set of 3 13.50 13.50

Miniature Sheet

Wolfgang Amadeus Mozart (1756-91), Composer — A472

No. 2584: a, Oval portrait. b, Playing harpsichord. c, Wearing red coat. d, Head of Mozart.

2006, Sept. 1 *Perf. 13¼*

2584 A472 $3 Sheet of 4, #a-d 9.00 9.00

Miniature Sheet

Purchase of Graceland by Elvis Presley, 50th Anniv. — A473

No. 2585: a, View of path leading to front door. b, Graceland, columns at right. c, Graceland, columns at left. d, Room with Presley's costumes.

2006, Sept. 1 *Perf. 13¼*

2585 A473 $3 Sheet of 4, #a-d 9.00 9.00

Miniature Sheets

Pres. John F. Kennedy (1917-63) — A474

No. 2586, $3: a, Supporters holding campaign sign. b, Kennedy campaigning. c, Kennedy waiting for concession. d, Kennedy addressing the nation.

No. 2587, $3: a, Kennedy on crutches from war injuries. b, Kennedy on stretcher. c, Dust jacket of *Profiles in Courage.* d, Kennedy as senator.

2006, Oct. 1 *Perf. 13¼*

Sheets of 4, #a-d

2586-2587 A474 Set of 2 18.00 18.00

Shells — A475

Designs: 5c, Turbinella angulata. 10c, Vasum muricatum. 15c, Fusinus closter. 20c, Crasispira gibbosa. 25c, Terebra strigata. 50c, Prunum carneum. 65c, Purpura patula. 90c, C. chrysostoma. $1, M. nodulosa. $2, Conus regius. $3.50, Conus hieroglyphus. $5, Anodontia alba, vert. $10, C. cassidiformis. $20, Strigilla carnaria, vert.

2006, Oct. 1 *Perf. 14x15, 15x14*

2588	A475	5c multi	.30	*.50*
2589	A475	10c multi	.30	*.50*
2590	A475	15c multi	.40	*.80*
2591	A475	20c multi	.40	.30
2592	A475	25c multi	.40	.30
2593	A475	50c multi	.55	.35
2594	A475	65c multi	.75	.50
2595	A475	90c multi	1.00	.75
2596	A475	$1 multi	1.25	1.25
2597	A475	$2 multi	2.00	2.00
2598	A475	$3.50 multi	3.25	3.25
2599	A475	$5 multi	4.00	4.00
2600	A475	$10 multi	7.00	7.00
2601	A475	$20 multi	14.00	14.00
	Nos. 2588-2601 (14)		35.60	35.50

Souvenir Sheet

Ludwig Durr (1878-1956), Engineer — A476

2006, Nov. 15 Litho. *Perf. 12¾*

2602 A476 $5 multi 3.75 3.75

Betty Boop — A477

No. 2603, vert.: a, Betty Boop with black background and leg raised. b, Lips. c, Betty Boop with black background. d, Dog on leash, star. e, Betty Boop, white background. f, Dog, two stars.

No. 2604 — Betty Boop with: a, Light blue panel at top. b, Light yellow panel at top.

2006, Nov. 15

2603 A477 $2 Sheet of 6, #a-f 9.00 9.00

Souvenir Sheet

2604 A477 $3.50 Sheet of 2, #a-b 5.25 5.25

Christmas A478

Christmas stocking showing: No. 2605, 25c, No. 2609a, $2, Christmas tree. No. 2606, 50c, No. 2609b, $2, Bell. No. 2607, 90c, No. 2609c, $2, Candy canes. No. 2608, $1, No. 2609d, $2, Stars.

2006, Dec. 1 *Perf. 14¼*

2605-2608 A478 Set of 4 2.00 2.00

Souvenir Sheet

2609 A478 $2 Sheet of 4, #a-d 5.00 3.00

Souvenir Sheet

Christopher Columbus (1451-1506), Explorer — A479

2007, Jan. 10 *Perf. 12*

2610 A479 $5 brn & black 3.75 3.75

Scouting, Cent. — A480

2007, Jan. 10

2611 A480 $3.50 blue & multi 2.60 2.60

Souvenir Sheet

2612 A480 $5 org & multi 3.75 3.75

No. 2611 was printed in sheets of 3.

Concorde Prototype 001 F-WTSS — A481

No. 2613: a, $1, Airplane in hangar. b, $2, Airplane out of hangar.

2007, Jan. 23 *Perf. 13¼*

2613 A481 Pair, #a-b 2.25 2.25

Printed in sheets containing 3 of each stamp.

Rembrandt (1606-69), Painter — A482

No. 2614, vert. — Details from Christ Driving the Money Changers from the Temple: a, Christ. b, Man with moustache looking up. c, Man with striped headdress. d, Man protecting face with hands.

$5, Jesus and His Disciples.

2007, Jan. 23 *Perf. 13¼*

2614 A482 $2 Sheet of 4, #a-d 6.00 6.00

Imperf

2615 A482 $5 shown 3.75 3.75

No. 2614 contains four 38x50mm stamps.

Cricket World Cup — A483

Designs: 90c, Cricket bats, ball and wicket, map and flag of Dominica. $1, Umpire Billy Doctrove.

$5, Cricket bats, ball and wicket.

2007, Apr. 11 ***Perf. 14***

2616-2617 A483 Set of 2 2.50 2.50

Souvenir Sheet

2618 A483 $5 multi 4.00 4.00

Birds A484

Designs: 10c, Great frigatebird. 25c, Peruvian booby. 90c, Black stork, vert. No. 2622, $5, Lipkin, vert.

No. 2623: a, Antillean crested hummingbird. b, Rufous-breasted hermit. c, Cuban hummingbird. d, Blue-headed hummingbird.

No. 2624, $5, Red-capped manakin, vert.

2007, Apr. 11 ***Perf. 12¾***

2619-2622 A484 Set of 4 5.25 5.25

2623 A484 $2 Sheet of 4, #a-d 7.50 7.50

Souvenir Sheet

2624 A484 $5 multi 5.25 5.25

Flowers — A485

Designs: 10c, Red jasmine. 25c, Bougainvillea. 90c, Portia tree. No. 2628, $5, Rose bay.

No. 2629 — Orchids: a, $1, Tolumnia urophylla. b, $1, Brassavola cucullata. c, $2, Isochilus linearis. d, Spathoglottis plicata.

No. 2630, horiz.: a, Red ginger. b, Baobab. c, Purple wreath. d, Thunbergia.

No. 2631, $5, Flamboyant. No. 2632, $5, Oncidium altissimum.

2007, Apr. 11 **Litho.** ***Perf. 12¾***

2625-2628 A485 Set of 4 4.75 4.75

2629 A485 Sheet of 4, #a-d 4.50 4.50

2630 A485 $2 Sheet of 4, #a-d 6.00 6.00

Souvenir Sheets

2631-2632 A485 Set of 2 7.50 7.50

Princess Diana (1961-97) — A486

No. 2633: a, Holding flowers, wearing purple hat. b, Without hat. c, Not holding flowers, wearing purple hat. d, Close-up of #2633a, lines on face. e, Close-up of #2633b, lines on face. f, Close-up of #2633c, lines on face.

$5, Wearing purple sweater.

2007, June 11 ***Perf. 13½***

2633 A486 $1 Sheet of 6, #a-f 4.50 4.50

Souvenir Sheet

2634 A486 $5 multi 3.75 3.75

No. 2633 contains six 28x42mm stamps.

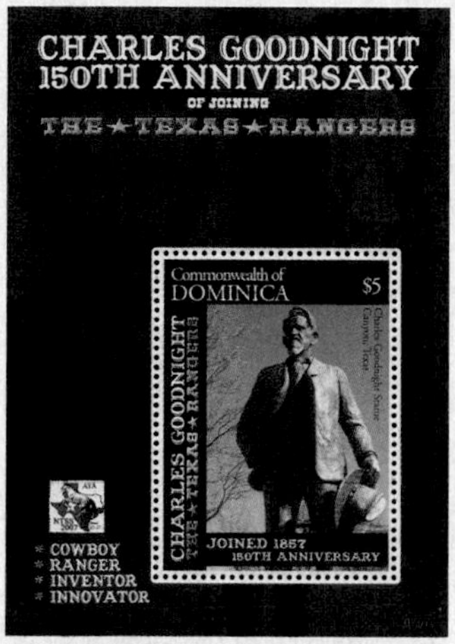

Texas Rangers — A487

No. 2635, horiz.: a, Two Rangers on horses. b, Seven Rangers in front of building with pillars. c, Ten rangers showing rifles. d, Rangers on horses. e, Rangers around still. f, Three Rangers at Justice of the Peace office. g, Rangers and tents. h, Rangers and locomotive. i, Five Rangers on horses near house.

$5, Statue of Charles Goodnight.

2007, June 15 ***Perf. 13½***

2635 A487 $1 Sheet of 9, #a-i 6.75 6.75

Souvenir Sheet

2636 A487 $5 multi 3.75 3.75

American Topical Association National Topical Stamp Show, Irving, TX.

Miniature Sheet

New Year 2007 (Year of the Pig) — A488

No. 2637 — Text in: a, Red. b, Green. c, Blue green. d, Purple.

2007, July 2

2637 A488 $2 Sheet of 4, #a-d 6.00 6.00

A489

A490

A491

Christmas A492

2007, Nov. 19 **Litho.** ***Perf. 14¾x14***

2638 A489 25c multi .25 .25

2639 A490 50c multi .40 .40

2640 A491 90c multi .70 .70

2641 A492 $1 multi .75 .75

Nos. 2638-2641 (4) 2.10 2.10

New Year 2008 (Year of the Rat) — A493

2008, Feb. 28 ***Perf. 12***

2642 A493 $1 multi .75 .75

Printed in sheets of 4.

University of the West Indies, 60th Anniv. A494

University crest, Dr. Bernard A. Sorhaindo and denomination in: 50c, Red brown. 65c, Green. 90c, Brown.

No. 2646, $5, Crest, Sorhaindo, denomination in black. No. 2647, $5, Crest, Sorhaindo, denomination in blue. No. 2648, $5, Crest, diploma, 60th anniversary emblem.

2008, Apr. 8 ***Perf. 13¼***

2643-2645 A494 Set of 3 1.60 1.60

Souvenir Sheets

2646-2648 A494 Set of 3 11.50 11.50

Miniature Sheet

2008 Summer Olympics, Beijing — A495

No. 2649: a, Archery. b, Men's gymnastics. c, Badminton. d, Boxing.

2008, Apr. 8 ***Perf. 13¼x13***

2649 A495 $1.40 Sheet of 4, #a-d 4.25 4.25

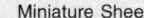

Miniature Sheet

Visit of Pope Benedict XVI to New York — A496

No. 2650 — Pope and part of St. Patrick's Cathedral in background: a, Small circular window under spire. b, Large central circular window. c, Archway below spire. d, Archway above main door.

2008, June 16 **Litho.** ***Perf. 13½***

2650 A496 $1.40 Sheet of 4, #a-d 4.25 4.25

Miniature Sheet

Wedding of Queen Elizabeth II and Prince Philip, 60th Anniv. — A497

No. 2651: a, Couple, denomination in white. b, Queen, denomination in red violet. c, Couple, denomination in black. d, Queen, denomination in white. e, Couple, denomination in red violet. f, Queen, denomination in black.

2008, June 16

2651 A497 $1 Sheet of 6, #a-f 4.50 4.50

Miniature Sheet

Elvis Presley (1935-77) — A498

No. 2652 — Presley and: a, Black and red background, Prussian blue denomination. b, Gray and black background, purple denomination. c, Blue and black background, Prussian blue denomination. d, Purple and black background, purple denomination. e, Gray and black background, Prussian blue denomination. f, Brown and black background, purple denomination.

2008, June 16

2652 A498 $1.50 Sheet of 6 #a-f 6.75 6.75

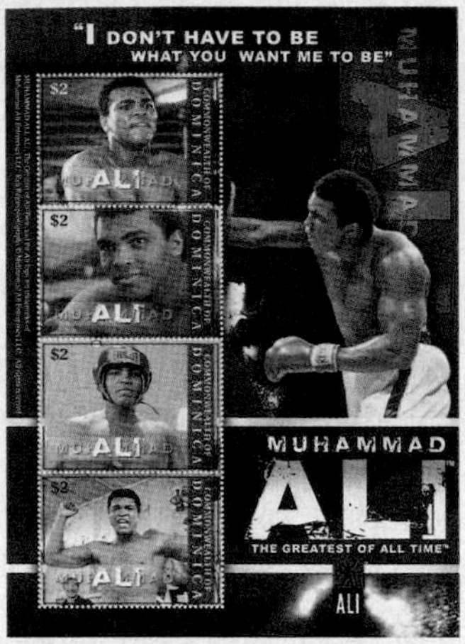

A499

Muhammad Ali, Boxer — A500

No. 2653 — Ali: a, Sweating, denomination in white. b, Smiling, denomination in black. c, Wearing headgear. d, With arms raised.

No. 2654 — Ali: a, Seated in corner of boxing ring. b, Speaking to the press. c, Punching bag. d, Wearing headgear and mouth guard.

2008, July 7

2653 A499 $2 Sheet of 4, #a-d 6.25 6.25
2654 A500 $2 Sheet of 4, #a-d 6.25 6.25

Convent High School, 150th Anniv. A501

Panel color: 50c, Red violet. 65c, Yellow orange. 90c, Blue. $1, Red.

$5, Denomination in LR corner.

2008, Oct. 1 ***Perf. 12½***

2655-2658 A501 Set of 4 2.40 2.40

Souvenir Sheet

2659 A501 $5 multi 4.00 4.00

Dogs — A502

Designs: 25c, Dandie Dinmont terrier. 50c, Alaskan malamute. 90c, Welsh Springer spaniel. $1, Pug. $2, Norfolk terrier. $5, Vizsla.

No. 2666: a, Akita. b, Australian cattle dog. c, Border collie. d, Staffordshire bull terrier cross.

Perf. 14¼x14¾

2008, Dec. 11 **Litho.**

2660-2665 A502 Set of 6 8.50 8.50
2666 A502 $2.50 Sheet of 4, #a-d 9.00 9.00

Miniature Sheet

Marilyn Monroe (1926-62), Actress — A503

No. 2667 — Monroe wearing: a, Purple sweater, hand on arm. b, Orange sweater, looking in mirror. c, Purple sweater, holding post. d, Orange sweater, holding wine glass.

2008, Dec. 11 ***Perf. 14***

2667 A503 $2 Sheet of 4, #a-d 6.00 6.00

Christmas A504

Designs: 25c, Santa Claus. 50c, Palm tree with Christmas ornaments. 90c, Christmas stocking. $1, Poinsettias.

2008, Dec. 15 ***Perf. 12***

2668-2671 A504 Set of 4 2.00 2.00

New Year 2009 (Year of the Ox) A505

2009, Jan. 5 ***Perf. 14¾x14¼***

2672 A505 $2 multi 1.50 1.50

Printed in sheets of 4.

Inauguration of Barack Obama as US President A506

Pres. Obama: 65c, With raised hand. 90c, Hand not showing.

No. 2675: a, $2.25, Like 65c. b, $2.25, Looking over shoulder. c, $2.25, Like 90c. d, $2.50, Like 90c. e, $2.50, Looking over shoulder. f, $2.50, Like 65c.

2009, Jan. 20 ***Perf. 11½***

2673-2674 A506 Set of 2 1.25 1.25
2675 A506 Sheet of 6, #a-f 11.00 11.00

Diplomatic Relations Between Dominica and People's Republic of China, 5th Anniv. A507

Denominations: 50c, 65c, 90c, $1.

2009, Mar. 23 ***Perf. 14¾x14¼***

2676-2679 A507 Set of 4 2.40 2.40

Souvenir Sheet

2680 A507 $5 multi 3.75 3.75

Peony A508

2009, Apr. 10 ***Perf. 13¼***

2681 A508 75c shown .55 .55

Souvenir Sheet

2682 A508 $5 Peonies 3.75 3.75

No. 2682 contains one 44x44mm stamp.

Miniature Sheet

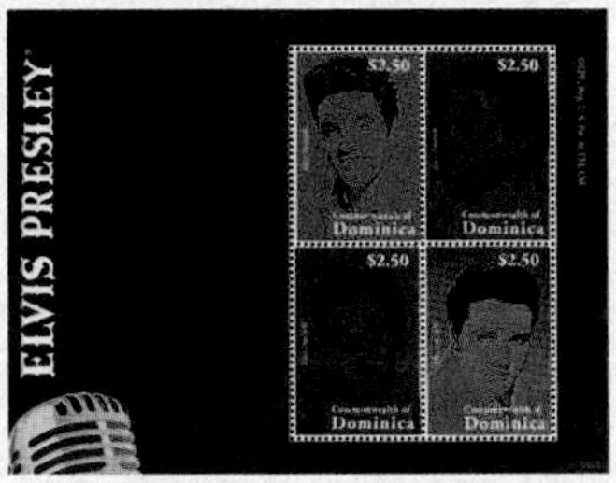

Elvis Presley (1935-77) — A509

No. 2683 — Various photos of Presley with background colors of: a, Yellow orange. b, Gray and blue. c, Blue. d, Gray.

2009, May 23 ***Perf. 13¼***

2683 A509 $2.50 Sheet of 4, #a-d 7.75 7.75

Miniature Sheet

Joseph Haydn (1732-1809), Composer — A510

No. 2684: a, Haydn. b, Haydn's birthplace, Rohrau, Austria. c, Wolfgang Amadeus Mozart. d, St. Stephen's Cathedral, Vienna. e, Nikolaus Esterházy, sponsor of Haydn. f, Esterházy Palace, Fertod, Hungary.

2009, June 10 ***Perf. 11½***

2684 A510 $2.25 Sheet of 6, #a-f 10.00 10.00

Mushrooms A511

Designs: 50c, Leucopaxillus gracillimus. 65c, Calvatia cyathiformis. 90c, Hygrocybe viridiphylla. $1, Boletellus coccineus.

No. 2689, $2: a, Hygrocybe acutoconica. b, Lepiota sulphureocyanescens. c, Lactarius rubrilacteus. d, Lactarius ferrugineus. e, Asterophora lycoperdoides. f, Amanita polypyramis.

2009, Sept. 8 **Litho.** ***Perf. 14x14¾***

2685-2688 A511 Set of 4 2.25 2.25
2689 A511 $2 Sheet of 6, #a-f 9.00 9.00

A512

Corals and Marine Life — A513

Designs: 50c, Lobed star coral and shark. 65c, Orange cup coral and fish. 90c, Grooved brain coral and turtle. $1, Elkhorn coral and fish.

No. 2694, $2: a, Rough star coral and fish. b, Branched finger coral and fish. c, Wire coral and ray. d, Great star coral and fish. e, Pillar coral and fish. f, Rose lace coral and fish.

2009, Sept. 8 ***Perf. 14¾x14***

2690-2693 A512 Set of 4 2.25 2.25
2694 A513 $2 Sheet of 6, #a-f 9.00 9.00

Butterflies A514

Designs: 90c, Banded orange heliconian. $1, Gulf fritillary. $2, Julia longwing. $5, Zebra longwing.

No. 2699: a, Cuban cattleheart. b, White peacock. c, Bahamian swallowtail. d, Tropical buckeye.

No. 2700, $6, Purple emperor. No. 2701, $6, Atala black.

2009, Sept. 8 ***Perf. 14¾x14***

2695-2698 A514 Set of 4 6.75 6.75
2699 A514 $2.50 Sheet of 4, #a-d 7.50 7.50

Souvenir Sheets

Perf. 14¼

2700-2701 A514 Set of 2 9.00 9.00

Nos. 2700-2701 each contain one 50x38mm stamp.

Dolphins and Whales A515

Designs: 50c, Irawaddy dolphin. 65c, Pantropical spotted dolphin. 90c, Atlantic humpback dolphin. $1, Indian humpback dolphin.

No. 2706: a, Melon-headed whale. b, Striped dolphin. c, Atlantic spotted dolphin. d, Clymene dolphin. e, Pantropical spotted dolphin (Stenella attenuata graffmani). f, Pantropical spotted dolphin (Stenella attenuata).

2009, Sept. 8 **Litho.** ***Perf. 14¾x14***

2702-2705 A515 Set of 4 2.25 2.25
2706 A515 $2 Sheet of 6, #a-f 9.00 9.00

See No. 2732.

Shells A516

Designs: 50c, Oliva reticularis. 65c, Vasum muricatum. 90c, Olivella nivea. $1, Olivella mutica.

No. 2711: a, Hyalina avena. b, Persicula fluctuata. c, Agatrix agassizi. d, Trigonostoma rugosum. e, Olivella floralia. f, Marginella eburneola.

2009, Sept. 8

2707-2710 A516	Set of 4	2.25	2.25
2711 A516 $2 Sheet of 6, #a-f		9.00	9.00

Miniature Sheet

Expo 2010, Shanghai — A517

No. 2712: a, Bund. b, Shanghai Museum. c, Yangpu Bridge. d, Shanghai Theater.

2009, Oct. 16 ***Perf. 13x12¾***

2712 A517 $1.50 Sheet of 4, #a-d	4.50	4.50

Discovery of Manhattan Island by Henry Hudson, 400th Anniv. — A518

No. 2713, horiz.: a, Panoramic view of New York City, 1913. b, Hudson, the Dreamer, by Jean L.G. Ferris. c, Henry Hudson. d, Hudson's ship, Half Moon. e, Map of Hudson River, c. 1600. f, Henry Hudson Memorial Column, Bronx, NY.

$6, Hudson, aerial view of New York City.

2009, Oct. 16 ***Perf. 13x12¾***

2713 A518 $2.25 Sheet of 6, #a-f	10.00	10.00

Souvenir Sheet

Perf. 12¾x13

2714 A518	$6 multi	4.50	4.50

Miniature Sheet

Pres. John F. Kennedy (1917-63) — A519

No. 2715 — Pres. Kennedy: a, On telephone. b, With family. c, With Vice-president Lyndon B. Johnson. d, Pointing.

2009, Oct. 30 ***Perf. 11½x12***

2715 A519 $2.50 Sheet of 4, #a-d	7.50	7.50

Miniature Sheet

First Man on the Moon, 40th Anniv. — A520

No. 2716: a, Apollo 11 crew. b, Moon landing on television. c, Apollo 11 capsule with parachutes. d, Earth, Apollo 11 modules and patch. e, Command Module in Moon orbit. f, Project Orion.

2009, Nov. 2 ***Perf. 11½***

2716 A520 $2 Sheet of 6, #a-f	9.00	9.00

Chinese Aviation, Cent. — A521

No. 2717: a, H-5. b, H-6. c, H-6H. d, H-6L. $6, H-6U.

2009, Nov. 12 ***Perf. 14***

2717 A521 $2 Sheet of 4, #a-d	6.50	6.50

Souvenir Sheet

Perf. 14¼

2718 A521	$6 multi	4.75	4.75

Aeropex 2009 Intl. Philatelic Exhibition, Beijing. No. 2717 contains four 42x28mm stamps.

Christmas A522

Designs: 50c, Bell-shaped Christmas tree ornament. 65c, Candles and poinsettia. 90c, Gingerbread man. $1.10, Decorated palm tree. $2.25, Christmas tree ornaments. $2.75, Women dancers.

2009, Nov. 16 ***Perf. 11½***

2719-2724 A522	Set of 6	6.25	6.25

Personalized Stamp — A523

2009, Dec. 18 ***Perf. 14x14¾***

2725 A523 $3 gray	2.25	2.25

The vignette on the stamp shown is a generic image. Stamps without a vignette were also made available. Printed in sheets of 12.

Pope John Paul II (1920-2005) A524

2010, Jan. 4 ***Perf. 12x11½***

2726 A524 $2.75 multi	2.10	2.10

Printed in sheets of 4.

Miniature Sheet

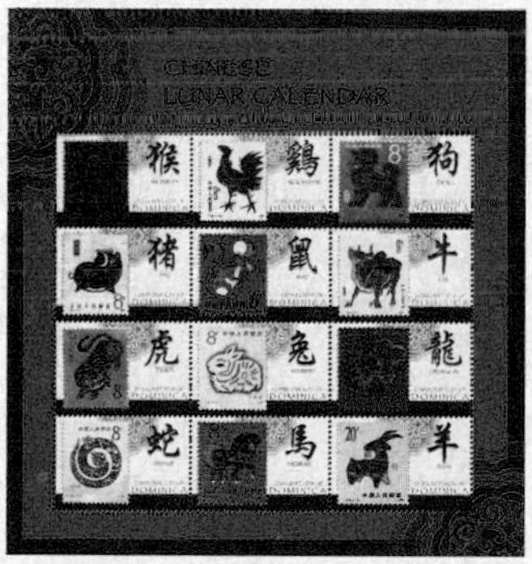

Chinese Zodiac Animals — A524a

No. 2726A — Various stamps of People's Republic of China depicting Zodiac animals: b, Monkey. c, Rooster. d, Dog. e, Pig. f, Rat. g, Ox. h, Tiger. i, Rabbit. j, Dragon. k, Snake. l, Horse. m, Ram.

2010, Jan. 4 **Litho.** ***Perf. 12¾***

2726A A524a 60c Sheet of 12, #b-m	6.00	6.00

Souvenir Sheet

New Year 2010 (Year of the Tiger) — A525

2010, Jan. 4 ***Perf. 12¾***

2727 A525 $5 multi	4.00	4.00

Miniature Sheet

Elvis Presley (1935-77) — A526

Various drawings of Presley.

2010, Jan. 8 ***Perf. 11½***

2728 A526 $2.50 Sheet of 4, #a-d	7.75	7.75

Miniature Sheet

NASCAR Drivers and Their Cars — A527

No. 2729: a, Denny Hamlin. b, Kyle Busch. c, Joey Logano. d, Hamlin's car (#11). e, Busch's car (#18). f, Logano's car (#20).

2010, Jan. 19 **Litho.**

2729 A527 $3.25 Sheet of 6, #a-f	15.00	15.00

Miniature Sheets

Dogs — A528

No. 2730, $2.50 — Dalmatian and: a, Books. b, Stone wall. c, Swimming pool. d, Stack of logs.

No. 2731, $2.50 — Boxer and: a, Brick wall. b, Bush. c, Window. d, Fence.

2010, Jan. 19 ***Perf. 11½x11¾***

Sheets of 4, #a-d

2730-2731 A528	Set of 2	15.50	15.50

No. 2706 With "Haiti Earthquake Relief Fund" and Map of Haiti Added to Stamps and Sheet Margin

Miniature Sheet

Designs as before.

2010, Feb. 4 ***Perf. 14¾x14***

2732 A515 $2 Sheet of 6, #a-f	9.25	9.25

Position of added text varies on each stamp.

Ferraris and Their Parts
A529

No. 2733, $1.25: a, Engine of 1982 208 GTB Turbo. b, 1982 208 GTB Turbo.
No. 2734, $1.25: a, Engine of 1983 126 C3. b, 1983 126 C3.
No. 2735, $1.25: a, Side panel and rear wheel of 1984 Testarossa. b, 1984 Testarossa.
No. 2736, $1.25: a, Suspension of 1987 408 4RM. b, 1987 408 4RM.

2010, Feb. 17 ***Perf. 12***
Vert. Pairs, #a-b

2733-2736 A529 Set of 4 8.00 8.00

Nos. 2733-2736 each were printed in sheets containing four pairs.

Miniature Sheet

Mother Teresa (1910-97), Humanitarian — A530

No. 2737 — Mother Teresa: a, Denomination in black. b, Holding rosary. c, Wearing white habit. d, Kissing hand of Pope John Paul II.

2010, Feb. 24 ***Perf. 11¼x11½***

2737 A530 $2.50 Sheet of 4, #a-d 8.00 8.00

Boy Scouts of America, Cent. — A531

No. 2738, $2.50: a, Outdoor skills. b, Campfire inspirations.
No. 2739, $2.50: a, Emergency one-man carry. b, Swimming fun with safety.

2010, Feb. 24 ***Perf. 13¼***
Pairs, #a-b

2738-2739 A531 Set of 2 8.00 8.00

Nos. 2738-2739 each were printed in sheets containing two pairs.

Miniature Sheet

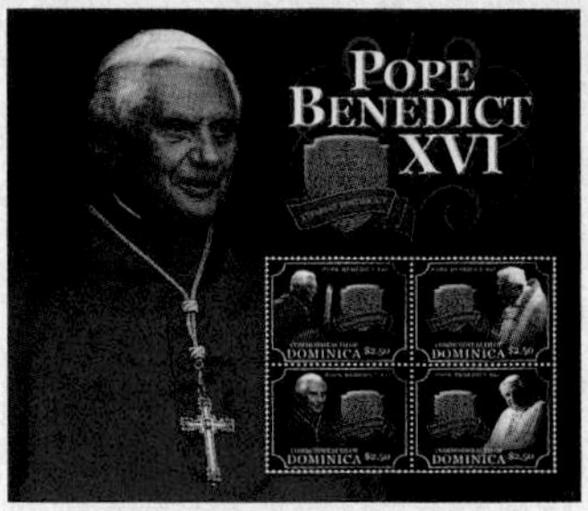

Pope Benedict XVI — A532

No. 2740 — Pope Benedict XVI: a, Wearing red, holding candle. b, Wearing white, hands clasped. c, Wearing red, not holding candle. d, Wearing white, hands not clasped.

2010, Mar. 23 ***Perf. 11½x12***

2740 A532 $2.50 Sheet of 4, #a-d 7.50 7.50

Caravaggio Paintings — A533

No. 2741, vert.: a, Mary Magdalene. b, Sick Bacchus. c, Bacchus. d, The Inspiration of Saint Matthew.
$6, Saint Gerolamo.

2010, Mar. 23 ***Perf. 12x11½***

2741 A533 $2.50 Sheet of 4, #a-d 7.50 7.50

Souvenir Sheet
Perf. 11½

2742 A533 $6 multi 4.50 4.50

Miniature Sheet

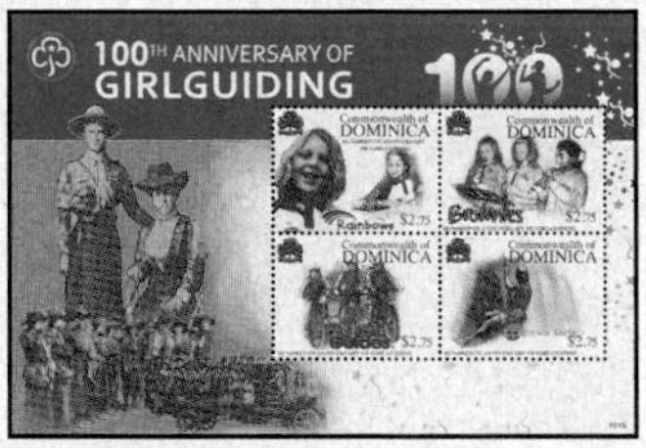

Girl Guides, Cent. — A534

No. 2743: a, Rainbows. b, Brownies. c, Guides. d, Senior Section. $6, Girl Guide, vert.

2010, Apr. 19 ***Perf. 11½x12***

2743 A534 $2.75 Sheet of 4, #a-d 8.25 8.25

Souvenir Sheet
Perf. 11¼x11½

2743E A534 $6 multi 4.50 4.50

Souvenir Sheets

A535

A536

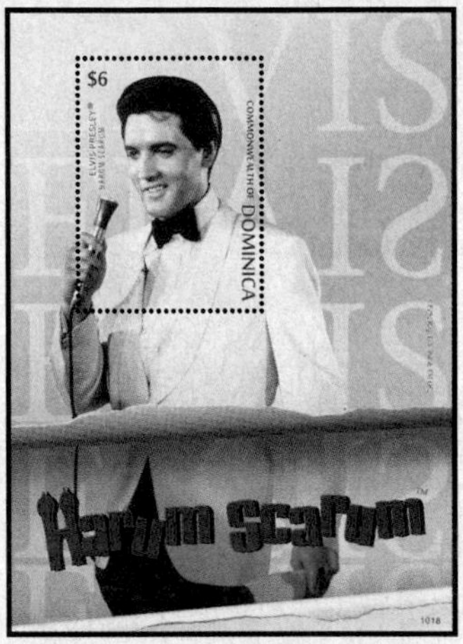

A537

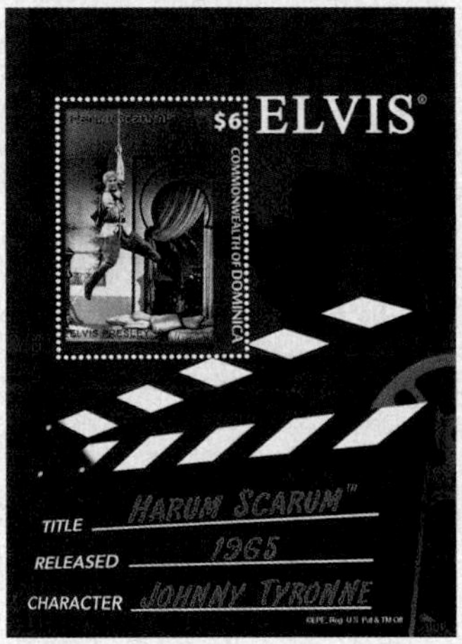

Elvis Presley (1935-77) — A538

2010, May 12 ***Perf. 13½***

2744	A535	$6 multi	4.50	4.50
2745	A536	$6 multi	4.50	4.50
2746	A537	$6 multi	4.50	4.50
2747	A538	$6 multi	4.50	4.50
	Nos. 2744-2747 (4)		18.00	18.00

Miniature Sheets

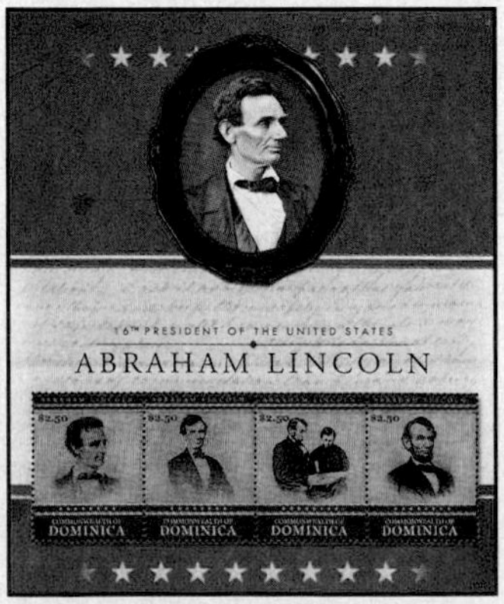

Pres. Abraham Lincoln (1809-65) — A539

No. 2748, $2.50 — Photographs of Lincoln: a, Without beard. b, Without beard, arms crossed. c, Reading to son, Tad. d, With beard.

No. 2749, $2.50: a, Statue of Lincoln, Bascom Hill, University of Wisconsin. b, Aerial view of Lincoln Memorial. c, Statue of Lincoln in Lincoln Memorial. d, Sculpture of Lincoln, Mount Rushmore.

2010, June 22 **Litho.** ***Perf. 11½***
Sheets of 4, #a-d

2748-2749 A539 Set of 2 15.00 15.00

Whales — A540

No. 2750: a, Sowerby's beaked whale. b, Blainville's beaked whale. c, Short-finned pilot whale. d, True's beaked whale. e, False killer whale. f, Dwarf sperm whale.
$6, Sperm whale.

2010, June 22 **Litho.** ***Perf. 13x13½***

2750 A540 $2 Sheet of 6, #a-f 9.00 9.00

Souvenir Sheet

2751 A540 $6 multi 4.50 4.50

Miniature Sheets

A541

Princess Diana (1961-97) — A542

No. 2752 — Princess Diana wearing: a, Plaid jacket. b, Wedding gown. c, Black jacket. d, Red and white dress.
No. 2753 — Princess Diana with: a, Prince Charles. b, Princes Charles, William and Harry. c, Crowd, holding flowers. d, Small child.

2010, May 12 **Litho.** ***Perf. 13x13¼***

2752 A541 $2.75 Sheet of 4, #a-d 8.25 8.25
2753 A542 $2.75 Sheet of 4, #a-d 8.25 8.25

Christmas — A543

Painting details: 90c, Geburt Christi (Birth of Christ), by Hans Baldung. $1.45, Thomas Altar, by Meister Francke. $2, Nativity, by Baldung.

2010, Dec. 1 ***Perf. 13x13½***

2754-2756 A543 Set of 3 3.25 3.25

Nos. 2754-2756 each were printed in sheets of 6.

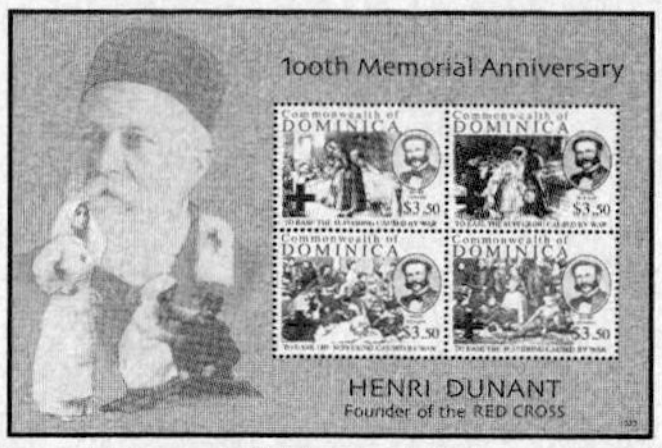

Henri Dunant (1828-1910), Founder of Red Cross — A544

No. 2757 — Red Cross, nurses aiding wounded and portrait of Dunant in: a, Green. b, Brown. c, Purple. d, Blue.
$5, Red Cross, nurses, Dunant in purplish gray.

2010, Dec. 15 *Perf. 12½x12*

2757 A544 $3.50 Sheet of 4, #a-d 10.50 10.50

Souvenir Sheet

2758 A544 $5 multi 3.75 3.75

Tenth Cricket World Cup, India, Sri Lanka and Bangladesh A545

Designs: 90c, Chris Gayle. $2, Windsor Park Sports Stadium, Roseau, horiz.
$5, Cricket World Cup.

2011, June 1 **Litho.** *Perf. 12½*

2759-2760 A545 Set of 2 2.25 2.25

Souvenir Sheet

Perf. 12

2761 A545 $5 multi 3.75 3.75

No. 2761 contains one 30x40mm stamp.

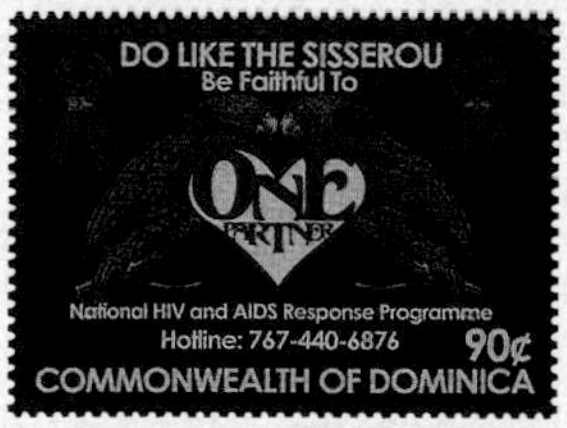

National HIV and AIDS Response Program — A545a

2011, June 1 **Litho.** *Perf. 13½*

2761A A545a 90c multi — —

Lizards — A546

Designs: 5c, Golden skink. 10c, Dominican ground lizard. 15c, Crested anole. 20c, Dominican tree lizard. 25c, Pygmy skink. 50c, House gecko. 65c, Fantastic gecko. 90c, Iguana. $1, Vincent's least gecko. $2, Turnip-tailed gecko. $5, House gecko, diff. $10, Fantastic gecko, diff. $20, Vincent's least gecko, diff.

2011, Oct. 1 *Perf. 14*

2762	A546	5c multi	.25	.25
2763	A546	10c multi	.25	.25
2764	A546	15c multi	.25	.25
2765	A546	20c multi	.25	.25
2766	A546	25c multi	.25	.25
2767	A546	50c multi	.40	.40
2768	A546	65c multi	.50	.50
2769	A546	90c multi	.70	.70
2770	A546	$1 multi	.75	.75
2771	A546	$2 multi	1.50	1.50
2772	A546	$5 multi	3.75	3.75
2773	A546	$10 multi	7.50	7.50
2774	A546	$20 multi	15.00	15.00
		Nos. 2762-2774 (13)	31.35	31.35

Christmas A547

Paintings: 90c, The Annunciation, by Andrea del Sarto. $1.45, Madonna with Child, by Jacopo Bellini. $2, The Virgin, by Carlo Dolci.

2011, Nov. 1

2775-2777 A547 Set of 3 3.25 3.25

Christmas A548

Paintings: 50c, Virgin in Adoration Before the Christ Child, by Peter Paul Rubens. 90c, Altarpiece of the Rose Garlands, by Albrecht Dürer. $3.50, Crowning of St. Catherine, by Rubens. $5, Adoration of the Magi, by Dürer.

2012, Nov. 19 *Perf. 13¾*

2778-2781 A548 Set of 4 7.50 7.50

New Year 2011 (Year of the Rabbit) A549

2013, Aug. 29 **Litho.** *Perf. 12*

2782 A549 $4 multi 3.00 3.00

No. 2782 was printed in sheets of 2.

Cats — A550

No. 2783: a, Cat with brown-tipped tail, eyes not visible. b, Cat with black tail and four white paws. c, Head of cat and two front paws. d, Cat with black tail, paw touching "A" in "Cats." e, Cat with white tail, with one black paw visible. f, Cat with one black and three white paws.
$5, Cat, diff.

2013, Sept. 2 **Litho.** *Perf. 14*

2783 A550 $1 Sheet of 6, #a-f 4.50 4.50

Souvenir Sheet

Perf. 12

2784 A550 $5 multi 3.75 3.75

Dogs — A551

No. 2785, $1.45: a, Airedale terrier. b, Bernese mountain dog. c, Pekingese. d, Samoyed.
No. 2786, $1.45, horiz.: a, Labrador retriever. b, Border collie. c, Cocker spaniel. d, Dalmatian.
No. 2787, $5, Rottweiler. No. 2788, $5, Great Dane.

2013, Sept. 2 **Litho.** *Perf. 12*

Sheets of 4, #a-d

2785-2786 A551 Set of 2 8.75 8.75

Souvenir Sheets

2787-2788 A551 Set of 2 7.50 7.50

Bees and Wasps — A552

No. 2789: a, Carpenter bee. b, Golden digger wasp. c, Bumblebee. d, Yellowjacket.
$5, Golden paper wasp.

2013, Sept. 2 **Litho.** *Perf. 13¾*

2789 A552 $2 Sheet of 4, #a-d 6.00 6.00

Souvenir Sheet

2790 A552 $5 multi 3.75 3.75

Corals — A553

No. 2791 — Various unnamed corals with colors of; a, Pink (with anemone-like tips). b, Purple and pink (small bead-like appearance). c, Dark red. d, Blue (tubes). e, Purple and pink (with lines). f, Pink (with branches). g, Yellow green. h, Blue (with black curved lines).
$5, Nephthyigorgia sp.

2013, Sept. 2 **Litho.** *Perf. 14*

2791 A553 90c Sheet of 8, #a-h 5.50 5.50

Souvenir Sheet

Perf. 12¾x12½

2792 A553 $5 multi 3.75 3.75

No. 2792 contains one 38x51mm stamp.

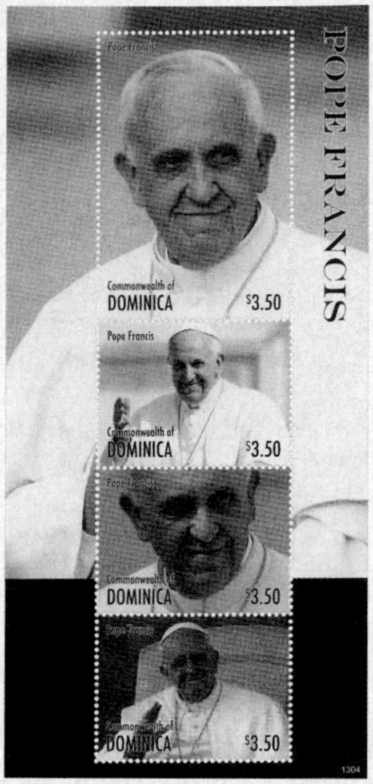

Election of Pope Francis — A554

No. 2793 — Pope Francis: a, With top of head visible (40x60mm). b, Waving, without eyeglasses, horiz. (40x30mm). c, With top of head not visible, horiz. (40x30mm). d, Waving, wearing eyeglasses, horiz. (40x30mm).
$5, Pope Francis, horiz.

2013, Sept. 2 **Litho.** *Perf. 14*

2793 A554 $3.50 Sheet of 4, #a-d 10.50 10.50

Souvenir Sheet

Perf. 12¾x12½

2794 A554 $5 multi 3.75 3.75

No. 2794 contains one 51x38mm stamp.

Painting of Marine Life — A555

Painting of Parrot — A556

No. 2795: a, Coral, denomination on coral (30x40mm). b, Coral, denomination on blue background (30x40mm). c, Ray (60x40mm). d, Fish and coral (60x40mm). e, Sea grass (30x40mm). f, Jellyfish (30x40mm). g, Sea grass and starfish (60x40mm).

2013, Sept. 2 **Litho.** *Perf. 14*

2795 A555 65c Sheet of 7, #a-g 3.50 3.50

Souvenir Sheet

Perf. 12

2796 A556 $5 multi 3.75 3.75

Butterflies A577

No. 2797, $2: a, Malachite. b, Silver-banded hairstreak.

No. 2798, $2: a, Gold rim swallowtail. b, Mangrove buckeye.

2013, Sept. 2 Litho. *Perf. 13¾*

Pairs, #a-b

2797-2798 A577 Set of 2 6.00 6.00

Nos. 2797 and 2798 each were printed in sheets containing two pairs.

Birth of Prince George of Cambridge — A558

No. 2799: a, Duke and Duchess of Cambridge, Prince George. b, Duke of Cambridge holding Prince George. c, Duchess of Cambridge holding Prince George. d, Close-up of Prince George.

$6, Duke and Duchess of Cambridge, Prince George, diff.

2013 Litho. *Perf. 14*

2799 A558 $2 Sheet of 4, #a-d 6.00 6.00

Souvenir Sheet

2800 A558 $6 multi 4.50 4.50

A559

Nelson Mandela (1918-2013), President of South Africa — A560

No. 2801 — Mandela: a, Holding loudspeaker. b, Wearing green and black shirt and jacket. c, With arms raised, color photograph. d, With arms raised, black-and-white photograph. e, Wearing black and gray shirt. f, Wearing black shirt.

$5, Mandela wearing gray shirt. $20, Mandela wearing shirt with leaf design.

2014, Jan. 6 Litho. *Perf. 13¾*

2801 A559 $2.50 Sheet of 6, #a-f 11.00 11.00

Souvenir Sheets

2802 A559 $5 multi 3.75 3.75

Litho., Margin Embossed With Foil Application

Imperf

2803 A560 $20 multi 15.00 15.00

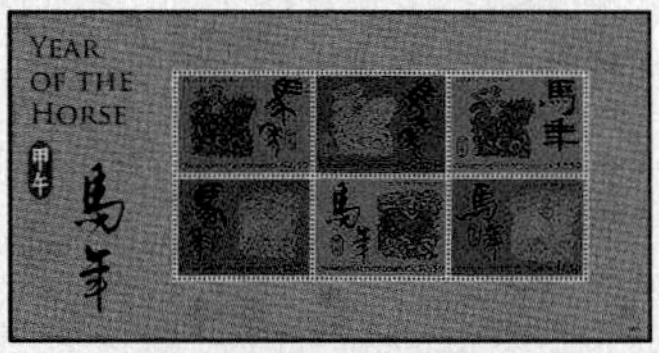

New Year 2014 (Year of the Horse) — A561

No. 2804 — Various Chinese characters for "horse" and: a, Horse in red at left, red chop at right, orange background. b, Horse in yellow at left, yellow chop at left, red orange background. c, Horse in red at left, red chop at left, yellow orange background. d, Horse in yellow at right, red chop at left, brown background. e, Horse in red at right, red chop at left, yellow orange background. f, Horse in yellow at right, red chop at left, dull orange background.

No. 2805 — Chinese characters for "horse" and: a, Horse in red at right. b, Horse in yellow brown at right.

2014, Jan. 8 Litho. *Perf. 14*

2804 A561 $2.50 Sheet of 6, #a-f 11.00 11.00

Souvenir Sheet

2805 A561 $5 Sheet of 2, #a-b 7.50 7.50

Sea Turtles — A562

No. 2806: a, Leatherback turtle. b, Green sea turtle. c, Hawksbill turtle.

$5, Green sea turtle, diff.

2014, May 1 Litho. *Perf. 11½x12*

2806 A562 $3.50 Sheet of 3, #a-c 7.75 7.75

Souvenir Sheet

2807 A562 $5 multi 3.75 3.75

WAR TAX STAMPS

No. 50 Surcharged in Red

1916 Wmk. 3 *Perf. 14*

MR1 A6 ½p on ½p green 3.50 .85

No. 50 Overprinted in Black

1918

MR2 A6 ½p green 7.50 *6.25*

Nos. 50, 40 in Black or Red

1918

MR3 A6 ½p green .25 *.30*

MR4 A6 3p violet, *yel* (R) 5.50 *4.50*

Type of 1908-09 Surcharged in Red

1919

MR5 A6 1½p on 2½p orange .25 *.60*

DOMINICAN REPUBLIC

də-ˈmi-ni-kən ri-ˈpə-blik

LOCATION — Comprises about two-thirds of the island of Hispaniola in the West Indies

GOVT. — Republic

AREA — 18,700 sq. mi.

POP. — 8,129,734 (1999 est.)

CAPITAL — Santo Domingo

8 Reales = 1 Peso

100 Centavos = 1 Peso (1880)

100 Centimos = 1 Franco (1883)

100 Centavos = 1 Peso (1885)

Catalogue values for unused stamps in this country are for Never Hinged items, beginning with Scott 437 in the regular postage section, Scott B1 in the semi-postal section, Scott C75 in the airpost section, Scott CB1 in the airpost semi-postal section, Scott E7 in the special delivery section, Scott G13 in the insured letter section, Scott J14 in the postage due section, Scott O26 in the officials section, and Scott RA20 in the postal tax section.

Watermarks

Wmk. 115 Diamonds

Wmk. 116 Crosses and Circles

Coat of Arms

A1 A2

1865 Unwmk. Typo. *Imperf.*

Wove Paper

1 A1 ½r black, *rose* 700. 650.

2 A1 1r black, *dp green* 1,100. 1,000.

Twelve varieties of each.

Laid Paper

3 A2 ½r black, *pale green* 550. 475.

4 A2 1r black, *straw* 1,800. 1,200.

Twelve varieties of the ½r, ten of the 1r.

A3

A4

1866 Laid Paper Unwmk.

5 A3 ½r black, *straw* 200.00 160.00

6 A3 1r black, *pale green* 2,500. 2,000.

7 A4 1r black, *pale green* 175.00 125.00

Nos. 5-8 have 21 varieties (sheets of 21).

Wmk. 115

8 A3 1r black, *pale green* 13,000. 13,000.

a. "CORREOS" and "Un Real" doubled 21,000.

The unique example of No. 8a is centered in the grade of fine, has a shallow thin spot and pinhole.

1866-67 Wove Paper Unwmk.

9 A3 ½r black, *rose* ('67) 60.00 60.00

10 A3 1r blk, *pale green* 85.00 75.00

a. Inscription dbl., top & bottom *400.00* *400.00*

11 A3 1r black, *blue* ('67) 60.00 37.50

a. 1r black, *light blue* ('67) 50.00 30.00

b. No space btwn. "Un" and "real" *600.00* 500.00

c. Without inscription at top & bottom *1,500.* 1,000.

d. Inscription invtd., top & bottom —

Nos. 9-11 (3) 205.00 172.50

1867-71 Pelure Paper

13 A3 ½r black, *rose* 150.00 75.00

15 A3 ½r black, *lav* ('68) 250.00 210.00

a. Without inscription at top and bottom 525.00

b. Dbl. inscriptions, one invtd. *425.00*

16 A3 ½r black, *grnsh gray* ('68) 260.00 225.00

17 A3 ½r black, *yellow* ('68) 12,000.

18 A3 ½r black, *ol* ('69) 3,000. 5,500.

22 A3 1r black, *blue* 4,000.

23 A3 1r black, *lavender* 225.00 200.00

24 A4 1r black, *rose* ('68) 225.00 225.00

25 A4 1r black, *mag* ('69) 2,250. 1,300.

26 A4 1r black, *sal* ('71) 300.00 225.00

Value for No. 17 is for an example with very fine centering and small faults. Value for No. 22 is for a faulty example with very fine centering and appearance.

1870-73 Ordinary Paper

27	A3	½r black, *magenta*	2,500.	4,750.
28	A3	½r blue, *rose* (blk inscription) ('71)	50.00	42.50
a.		Blue inscription	500.00	500.00
b.		Without inscription at top and bottom		
29	A3	½r black, *yel* ('73)	30.00	21.00
a.		Without inscription at top and bottom	700.00	700.00
30	A4	1r black, *vio* ('73)	30.00	21.00
a.		Without inscription at top and bottom	700.00	700.00
31	A4	1r black, *dk grn*	60.00	50.00

Nos. 9-31 have 21 varieties (sheets of 21). Nos. 29 and 30 are known pin-perforated, unofficially.

Bisects are known of several of the early 1r stamps.

A5

A6

1879 *Perf. 12½x13*

32	A5	½r violet	3.00	2.10
a.		Imperf., pair	9.00	9.00
b.		Horiz. pair, imperf. vert.	17.00	
33	A5	½r violet, *bluish*	2.50	1.80
a.		Imperf., pair	9.00	7.50
34	A5	1r carmine	4.50	2.10
a.		Imperf., pair	11.50	9.00
b.		Perf. 13	11.50	7.50
c.		Perf. 13x12½	11.50	7.50
35	A5	1r carmine, *sal*	2.50	1.50
a.		Imperf., pair	8.25	8.25
		Nos. 32-35 (4)	12.50	7.50

In 1891 15 stamps of 1879-83 were surcharged "U P U," new values and crossed diagonal lines.

1880 Typo. *Rouletted in Color*

36	A6	1c green	1.40	.90
b.		Laid paper	50.00	50.00
37	A6	2c red	1.00	.75
a.		Pelure paper	40.00	40.00
b.		Laid paper	40.00	40.00
38	A6	5c blue	1.50	.70
39	A6	10c rose	3.25	.90
40	A6	20c brown	2.00	.85
41	A6	25c violet	2.25	1.25
42	A6	50c orange	3.00	1.75
43	A6	75c ultra	5.75	3.00
a.		Laid paper	40.00	40.00
44	A6	1p gold	7.50	4.50
a.		Laid paper	50.00	50.00
b.		Double impression	42.50	42.50
		Nos. 36-44 (9)	27.65	14.60

1881 Network Covering Stamp

45	A6	1c green	.90	.50
46	A6	2c red	.90	.50
47	A6	5c blue	1.25	.50
48	A6	10c rose	1.50	.65
49	A6	20c brown	1.50	.90
50	A6	25c violet	1.75	1.00
51	A6	50c orange	2.00	1.40
52	A6	75c ultra	6.00	4.50
53	A6	1p gold	8.00	7.00
		Nos. 45-53 (9)	23.80	16.95

Preceding Issues (Type A6) Srch. with Value in New Currency

a

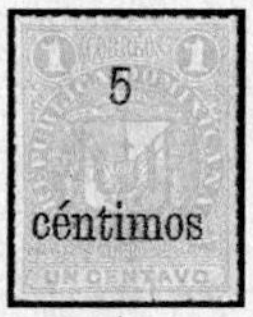

b

c

d

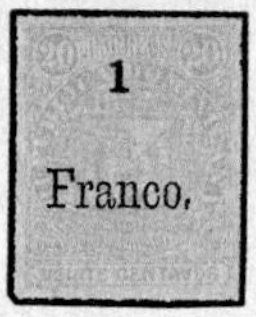

e

f

g

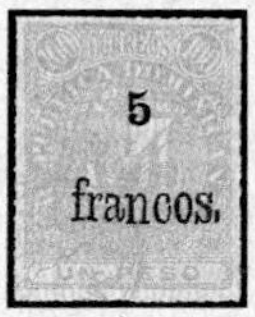

h

i

1883 Without Network

54	(a)	5c on 1c green	1.50	1.60
b.		Inverted surcharge	21.00	21.00
c.		Surcharged "25 céntimos"	50.00	50.00
d.		Surcharged "10 céntimos"	27.50	27.50
55	(b)	5c on 1c green	25.00	9.00
b.		Double surcharge	100.00	
c.		Inverted surcharge	65.00	65.00
56	(c)	5c on 1c green	17.00	9.50
b.		Surcharged "10 céntimos"	35.00	35.00
c.		Surcharged "25 céntimos"	37.50	37.50
57	(a)	10c on 2c red	5.00	3.00
a.		Inverted surcharge	27.50	27.50
d.		Surcharged "5 céntimos"	52.50	52.50
e.		Surcharged "25 céntimos"	75.00	75.00
58	(e)	10c on 2c red	4.50	3.50
a.		"Céntimso"		
b.		Inverted surcharge	37.50	37.50
c.		Surcharged "25 céntimos"	60.00	60.00
d.		"10" omitted	60.00	
59	(a)	25c on 5c blue	7.00	4.50
a.		Surcharged "5 céntimos"	52.50	
b.		Surcharged "10 céntimos"	52.50	52.50
c.		Surcharged "50 céntimos"	75.00	75.00
d.		Inverted surcharge	50.00	50.00
60	(c)	25c on 5c blue	7.50	3.50
a.		Inverted surcharge	45.00	37.50
b.		Surcharged "10 céntimos"	45.00	37.50
e.		"25" omitted	75.00	
f.		Surcharged on back		75.00
61	(a)	50c on 10c rose	27.50	12.50
a.		Inverted surcharge	50.00	45.00
62	(c)	50c on 10c rose	35.00	17.50
a.		Inverted surcharge	52.50	52.50
63	(d)	1fr on 20c brown	15.00	9.75
64	(e)	1fr on 20c brown	17.50	9.75
a.		Comma after "Franco,"	27.50	27.50
65	(f)	1fr on 20c brown	25.00	17.50
a.		Inverted surcharge		75.00
66	(g)	1fr25c on 25c violet	21.00	15.00
a.		Inverted surcharge	65.00	65.00
67	(g)	2fr50c on 50c orange	16.00	12.00
a.		Inverted surcharge	35.00	27.50
68	(g)	3fr75c on 75c ultra	27.50	25.00
b.		Inverted surcharge	60.00	60.00
c.		Laid paper	75.00	75.00
70	(i)	5fr on 1p gold	550.00	500.00
a.		"s" of "francos" inverted	700.00	700.00

With Network

71	(a)	5c on 1c green	3.00	2.50
b.		Inverted surcharge	22.50	22.50
c.		Double surcharge	22.50	22.50
d.		Surcharged "25 céntimos"	42.50	42.50
e.		"5" omitted	75.00	75.00
72	(b)	5c on 1c green	21.00	9.00
b.		Inverted surcharge	60.00	60.00
73	(c)	5c on 1c green	27.50	11.50
b.		Surcharged "10 céntimos"	50.00	42.50
c.		Surcharged "25 céntimos"	60.00	
74	(a)	10c on 2c red	3.75	2.25
a.		Surcharged "5 céntimos"	52.50	45.00
b.		Surcharged "25 céntimos"	67.50	67.50
c.		"10" omitted	57.50	
75	(c)	10c on 2c red	3.00	2.00
a.		Inverted surcharge	30.00	17.00
76	(a)	25c on 5c blue	7.50	3.50
a.		Surcharged "10 céntimos"	75.00	
b.		Surcharged "5 céntimos"	60.00	
c.		Surcharged "50 céntimos"	67.50	
77	(c)	25c on 5c blue	60.00	30.00
a.		Inverted surcharge		
b.		Surcharged on back		
78	(a)	50c on 10c rose	25.00	7.50
a.		Inverted surcharge	50.00	30.00
b.		Surcharged "25 céntimos"	60.00	
79	(c)	50c on 10c rose	30.00	9.50
a.		Inverted surcharge	60.00	
80	(d)	1fr on 20c brown	12.00	9.75
81	(e)	1fr on 20c brown	14.50	12.50
a.		Comma after "Franco"	35.00	35.00
b.		Inverted surcharge	75.00	
82	(f)	1fr on 20c brown	25.00	20.00
83	(g)	1fr25c on 25c violet	45.00	30.00
a.		Inverted surcharge	75.00	
84	(g)	2fr50c on 50c orange	19.00	12.50
a.		Inverted surcharge	35.00	27.50
85	(g)	3fr75c on 75c ultra	45.00	42.50
86	(h)	5fr on 1p gold	140.00	140.00
a.		Inverted surcharge		
87	(i)	5fr on 1p gold	190.00	190.00

Many minor varieties exist in Nos. 54-87: accent on "i" of "centimos"; "5" with straight top; "1" with straight serif.

A7

A7a

1885-91 Engr. *Perf. 12*

88	A7	1c green	1.00	.50
89	A7	2c vermilion	1.00	.50
90	A7	5c blue	1.40	.50
91	A7a	10c orange	2.25	.65
92	A7a	20c dark brown	2.25	.80
93	A7a	50c violet ('91)	7.50	6.50
94	A7	1p carmine ('91)	20.00	13.50
95	A7	2p red brown ('91)	25.00	16.00
		Nos. 88-95 (8)	60.40	38.95

Nos. 93, 94, 95 were issued without gum.
Imperf. varieties are proofs.
For surcharges see Nos. 166-168.

Coat of Arms — A8

1895 *Perf. 12½x14*

96	A8	1c green	1.25	.50
97	A8	2c orange red	1.25	.50
98	A8	5c blue	1.40	.50
99	A8	10c orange	3.25	1.60
		Nos. 96-99 (4)	7.15	3.10

Exist imperforate but were not issued.

1897 *Perf. 14*

96a	A8	1c green	1.40	.50
97a	A8	2c orange red	8.00	.75
98a	A8	5c blue	1.40	.75
99a	A8	10c orange	2.75	1.50
		Nos. 96a-99a (4)	13.55	3.50

Voyage of Diego Méndez from Jamaica — A9

Enriquillo's Revolt — A10

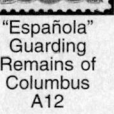

Sarcophagus of Columbus A11

"Española" Guarding Remains of Columbus A12

Toscanelli Replying to Columbus A13

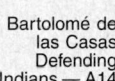

Bartolomé de las Casas Defending Indians — A14

Columbus at Salamanca A15

Columbus' Mausoleum A16

1899, Feb. 27 Litho. *Perf. 11½*

100	A9	1c brown violet	7.25	5.25
102	A10	2c rose red	1.75	.70
103	A11	5c blue	2.00	.70
104	A12	10c orange	5.00	1.60
a.		Tête bêche pair	42.50	42.50
105	A13	20c brown	10.00	8.25
106	A14	50c yellow green	11.50	9.75
a.		Tête bêche pair	60.00	60.00
107	A15	1p black, *gray bl*	27.00	22.00
108	A16	2p bister brown	45.00	47.50

1900, Jan.

109	A11	¼c black	.75	*1.60*
110	A15	½c black	.75	*1.60*
110A	A9	1c gray green	.75	.65
		Nos. 100-110A (11)	111.75	99.60

Nos. 100-110A were issued to raise funds for a Columbus mausoleum.

Imperf., Pairs

100a	A9	1c brown violet	16.50	16.50
102a	A10	2c rose red	5.00	
103a	A11	5c blue	5.75	
104b	A12	10c orange	8.75	
105a	A13	20c brown	15.00	
106b	A14	50c yellow green	17.50	
c.		As "b," tête bêche pair	125.00	
107a	A15	1p black, *gray blue*	42.50	
108a	A16	2p bister brown	70.00	
109a	A11	¼c black	3.75	*4.25*
110b	A15	½c black	3.75	*4.25*
110c	A9	1c gray green	3.50	

Map of Hispaniola A17

1900, Oct. 21 Unwmk. *Perf. 14*

111	A17	¼c dark blue	.75	.40
112	A17	½c rose	.75	.40
113	A17	1c olive green	.75	.40
114	A17	2c deep green	.75	.40
115	A17	5c red brown	.75	.40
a.		Vertical pair, imperf. between	17.50	

Perf. 12

116	A17	10c orange	.75	.40
117	A17	20c lilac	3.00	2.50
a.		20c rose (error)	6.00	6.00
118	A17	50c black	2.75	2.50
119	A17	1p brown	3.00	2.50
		Nos. 111-119 (9)	13.25	9.90

Several varieties in design are known in this issue. They were deliberately made. Counterfeits of Nos. 111-119 abound.

A18

1901-06 Typo. *Perf. 14*

120	A18	½c carmine & vio	.70	.40
121	A18	½c blk & org ('05)	1.80	.95
122	A18	½c grn & blk ('06)	.85	.30
123	A18	1c ol grn & vio	.70	.25
124	A18	1c blk & ultra ('05)	1.80	.85
125	A18	1c car & blk ('06)	1.00	.45
126	A18	2c dp grn & vio	.80	.25
127	A18	2c blk & vio ('05)	2.25	.70
128	A18	2c org brn & blk ('06)	1.40	.25
129	A18	5c org brn & vio	.80	.25
130	A18	5c black & cl ('05)	2.50	1.25
131	A18	5c blue & blk ('06)	1.25	.30
132	A18	10c orange & vio	1.40	.45
133	A18	10c blk & grn ('05)	4.25	2.25

134 A18 10c red vio & blk ('06) 1.40 .40
135 A18 20c brn vio & vio 2.50 .95
136 A18 20c blk & ol ('05) 13.50 8.75
137 A18 20c ol grn & blk ('06) 7.25 3.25
138 A18 50c gray blk & vio 8.00 5.50
139 A18 50c blk & red brn ('05) 47.50 34.00
140 A18 50c brn & blk ('06) 8.75 7.75
141 A18 1p brn & vio 18.00 10.00
142 A18 1p blk & gray ('05) 200.00 *225.00*
143 A18 1p violet & blk ('06) 21.00 13.50
Nos. 120-143 (24) 349.40 318.00

Issued: 11/15/01; 5/11/05; 8/17/06.

See Nos. 172-176. For surcharges see Nos.151-156.

Francisco Sánchez — A19

Juan Pablo Duarte — A20

Ramón Mella — A21

Ft. Santo Domingo — A22

1902, Feb. 25 Engr. *Perf. 12*

144 A19 1c dk green & blk .35 .35
145 A20 2c scarlet & blk .35 .35
146 A20 5c blue & blk .35 .35
147 A19 10c orange & blk .35 .35
148 A21 12c purple & blk .35 .35
149 A21 20c rose & blk .60 .60
150 A22 50c brown & blk .90 .90
Nos. 144-150 (7) 3.25 3.25

Center Inverted

144a A19 1c 17.50 *17.50*
145a A20 2c 17.50 *17.50*
146a A20 5c 17.50 *17.50*
148a A21 12c 17.50 *17.50*
149a A21 20c 17.50 *17.50*
150a A22 50c 17.50 *17.50*
Nos. 144a-150a (6) 105.00 *105.00*

400th anniversary of Santo Domingo.

Imperforate varieties of Nos. 144 to 150 were never sold to the public.

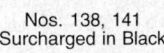

Nos. 138, 141 Surcharged in Black

1904, Aug.

151 A18 2c on 50c 9.25 7.25
152 A18 2c on 1p 13.50 9.25
b. "2" omitted 50.00 50.00
153 A18 5c on 50c 4.25 2.25
154 A18 5c on 1p 5.25 4.00
155 A18 10c on 50c 8.25 6.75
156 A18 10c on 1p 8.75 6.75
Nos. 151-156 (6) 49.25 36.25

Inverted Surcharge

151a A18 2c on 50c 15.00 15.00
152a A18 2c on 1p 15.00 15.00
c. As "a," "2" omitted 85.00 85.00
153a A18 5c on 50c 5.50 5.50
154a A18 5c on 1p 7.00 6.50
155a A18 10c on 50c 14.00 14.00
156a A18 10c on 1p 10.00 10.00
Nos. 151a-156a (6) 66.50 66.00

Official Stamps of 1902 Overprinted

1904, Aug. 16 Red Overprint

157 O1 5c dk blue & blk 5.75 3.00
a. Inverted overprint 7.25 5.75

Black Overprint

158 O1 2c scarlet & blk 17.00 5.25
a. Inverted overprint 20.00 6.50
159 O1 5c dk blue & blk 3,500. 3,500.
160 O1 10c yellow grn & blk 10.50 10.50
a. Inverted overprint 14.00 14.00

Official Stamps of 1902 Surcharged

161 O1 1c on 20c yellow & blk 4.75 3.00
a. Inverted surcharge 7.25 5.50

Nos. J1-J2 Surcharged or Overprinted in Black

1904-05 Surcharged "CENTAVOS"

162 D1 1c on 2c olive gray 250.00 200.00
a. "entavos" —
b. "Dominican" 350.00 300.00
c. "Centavo" 350.00 300.00

Carmine Surcharge or Overprint

163 D1 1c on 2c olive gray 3.50 1.10
a. Inverted surcharge 4.75 2.50
b. "Domihicana" 15.00 15.00
c. As "b," inverted 40.00 40.00
d. "Dominican" 10.50 10.50
e. "Centavos" omitted 30.00 30.00
g. "entavos" 30.00
163F D1 1c on 4c olive gray 35.00 7.00
164 D1 2c olive gray .95 .60
a. "Domihicana" 11.00 11.00
b. Inverted overprint 1.90 1.90
c. As "a," inverted 25.00 25.00
d. "Dominican" 5.75 5.75
e. "Centavo" omitted 12.50 10.00
f. "entavos" 12.50 12.50
g. As "f," inverted 40.00 40.00
h. As "d," inverted 40.00 40.00

Surcharged "CENTAVO"

165 D1 1c on 4c olive gray .95 .70
a. "Domihicana" 10.00 10.00
c. Inverted surcharge 1.75 1.75
d. "1" omitted 3.50 3.50
e. As "a," inverted 32.50 32.50
f. As "d," inverted 40.00 40.00
g. Double surcharge 30.00 30.00

No. 92 Surcharged in Red

1905, Apr. 4

166 A7a 2c on 20c dk brown 8.75 7.25
a. Inverted surcharge 15.00 15.00
167 A7a 5c on 20c dk brown 4.75 2.50
a. Inverted surcharge 16.00 16.00
b. Double surcharge 25.00 25.00
168 A7a 10c on 20c dk brown 8.75 7.25
Nos. 166-168 (3) 22.25 17.00

Nos. 166-168 exist with inverted "A" for "V" in "CENTAVOS" in surcharge.

No. J2 Surcharged in Red

1906, Jan. 16 *Perf. 14*

169 D1 1c on 4c olive gray .95 .50
a. Inverted surcharge 10.50 10.50
b. Double surcharge 25.00

Nos. J4, J3 Surcharged in Black

1906, May 1

170 D1 1c on 10c olive gray 1.10 .40
a. Inverted surcharge 10.50 10.50
b. Double surcharge 14.00 14.00
c. "OMINICANA" 20.00 20.00
d. As "c," inverted 150.00
171 D1 2c on 5c olive gray 1.10 .40
a. Inverted surcharge 10.50 10.50
b. Double surcharge 35.00

The varieties small "C" or small "A" in "REPUBLICA" are found on Nos.169, 170, 171.

Arms Type of 1901-06

1907-10 Wmk. 116

172 A18 ½c grn & blk ('08) .85 .25
173 A18 1c carmine & blk .85 .25
174 A18 2c orange brn & blk .85 .25
175 A18 5c blue & blk .85 .25
176 A18 10c red vio & blk ('10) 8.00 1.00
Nos. 172-176 (5) 11.40 2.00

No. O6 Overprinted in Red

1911, July 11 *Perf. 13½x14, 13½x13*

177 O2 2c scarlet & black 1.60 .60
a. "HABILITAOO" 8.75 6.00
b. Inverted overprint 21.00
c. Double overprint 21.00

A23

Juan Pablo Duarte — A24

1911-13 Center in Black *Perf. 14*

178 A23 ½c orange ('13) .25 .25
179 A23 1c green .25 .25
180 A23 2c carmine .25 .25
181 A23 5c gray blue ('13) .80 .25
182 A23 10c red violet 1.60 .45
183 A23 20c olive green 11.50 11.50
184 A23 50c yellow brn ('12) 3.75 3.75
185 A23 1p violet ('12) 5.75 4.25
Nos. 178-185 (8) 24.15 20.95

See Nos. 230-232.

1914, Apr. 13 *Perf. 13x14*

Background Red, White and Blue

186 A24 ½c orange & blk .60 .30
187 A24 1c green & blk .60 .30
188 A24 2c rose & blk .60 .30
189 A24 5c slate & blk .60 .40
190 A24 10c magenta & blk 1.40 .70
191 A24 20c olive grn & blk 2.50 1.90
192 A24 50c brown & blk 3.50 2.75
193 A24 1p dull lilac & blk 5.50 4.00
Nos. 186-193 (8) 15.30 10.65

Cent. of the birth of Juan Pablo Duarte (1813-1876), patriot and revolutionary.

Official Stamps of 1909-12 Surcharged in Violet or Overprinted in Red

a

b

1915, Feb. *Perf. 13½x13, 13½x14*

194 O2 (a) ½c on 20c orange & blk .50 .35
a. Inverted surcharge 6.00 6.00
b. Double surcharge 8.75 8.75
c. "Habilitado" omitted 5.25 5.25
195 O2 (b) 1c blue grn & blk .80 .25
a. Inverted overprint 6.00 6.00
b. Double overprint 7.00
c. Overprinted "1915" only 12.50
196 O2 (b) 2c scarlet & blk 1.25 .25
a. Inverted overprint 5.25 5.25
b. Double overprint 7.75 7.75
c. Overprinted "1915" only 8.75
d. "1915" double
197 O2 (b) 5c dk blue & blk 1.00 .25
a. Inverted overprint 7.00 7.00
b. Double overprint 8.75 8.75
c. Double ovpt., one invtd. 27.50
d. Overprinted "1915" only 8.50
198 O2 (b) 10c yel grn & blk 2.75 2.50
a. Inverted overprint 15.00
199 O2 (b) 20c orange & blk 9.25 7.25
a. "Habilitado" omitted
Nos. 194-199 (6) 15.55 10.85

Nos. 194, 196-198 are known with both perforations. Nos. 195, 199 are only perf. 13½x13.

The variety capital "I" for "1" in "Habilitado" occurs once in each sheet in all denominations.

A25

Type of 1911-13 Redrawn Overprinted "1915" in Red

TWO CENTAVOS:

Type I — "DOS" in small letters.

Type II — "DOS" in larger letters with white dot at each end of the word.

1915 Unwmk. Litho. *Perf. 11½*

200 A25 ½c violet & blk .85 .25
a. Imperf., pair 5.75
201 A25 1c yel brn & blk .85 .25
a. Imperf., pair 6.50
b. Vert. pair, imperf. horiz. 10.50
c. Horiz. pair, imperf. vert. 10.50
202 A25 2c ol grn & blk (I) 3.75 .25
a. Imperf., pair 10.00
203 A25 2c ol grn & blk (II) 6.00 .25
a. Center omitted 87.50
b. Frame omitted 87.50
c. Imperf., pair 15.00
d. Horiz. pair, imperf. vert. 15.00
204 A25 5c magenta & blk 3.75 .25
a. Pair, one without overprint 65.00
b. Imperf., pair 6.50
205 A25 10c gray blue & blk 3.75 .50
a. Imperf., pair 7.75
b. Horiz. pair, imperf. vert. 35.00
206 A25 20c rose red & blk 8.25 1.40
a. Imperf., pair 12.50
207 A25 50c green & blk 10.50 4.00
a. Imperf., pair 25.00
208 A25 1p orange & blk 21.00 7.00
a. Imperf., pair 52.50
Nos. 200-208 (9) 58.70 14.15

Type of 1915 Overprinted "1916" in Red

1916

209 A25 ½c violet & blk 2.25 .25
a. Imperf., pair 21.00
210 A25 1c green & blk 3.25 .25
a. Imperf., pair 21.00

Type of 1915 Overprinted "1917" in Red

1917-19

213 A25 ½c red lilac & blk 3.50 .30
a. Horiz. pair, imperf. btwn. 47.50 47.50
214 A25 1c yellow grn & blk 1.60 .25
a. Vert. pair, imperf. btwn. 50.00
215 A25 2c olive grn & blk 2.25 .25
a. Imperf., pair 35.00
216 A25 5c magenta & blk 23.00 .85
Nos. 213-216 (4) 30.35 1.65

Type of 1915 Overprinted "1919" in Red

1919

219 A25 2c olive grn & blk 17.00 .25

Type of 1915 Overprinted "1920" in Red

1920-27

220 A25 ½c lilac rose & blk .60 .25
a. Horiz. pair, imperf. btwn. 25.00 25.00
b. Inverted overprint
c. Double overprint
d. Double overprint, one invtd.
221 A25 1c yellow grn & blk .75 .25
a. Overprint omitted 70.00
b. Horiz. pair, imperf. btwn. 40.00
222 A25 2c olive grn & blk .75 .25
a. Vertical pair, imperf. between 27.50
223 A25 5c dp rose & blk 9.00 .50
224 A25 10c blue & black 5.75 .25

225 A25 20c rose red & blk ('27) 7.75 .50
226 A25 50c green & blk ('27) 65.00 21.00
Nos. 220-226 (7) 89.60 23.00

Type of 1915 Overprinted "1921" in Red

1921
227 A25 1c yellow grn & blk 5.25 .30
a. Horiz. pair, imperf. btwn. 45.00 45.00
b. Imperf., pair 45.00 45.00
228 A25 2c olive grn & blk 5.75 .40
a. Vert. pair, imperf. btwn. 45.00

Redrawn Design of 1915 without Overprint

1922
230 A25 1c green 3.75 .25
231 A25 2c carmine (II) 3.75 .25
232 A25 5c blue 5.75 .25
Nos. 230-232 (3) 13.25 .75

Nos. 230-232 exist imperf.

A26 A27
Second Redrawing

TEN CENTAVOS:
Type I — Numerals 2mm high. "DIEZ" in thick letters with large white dot at each end.
Type II — Numerals 3mm high. "DIEZ" in thin letters with white dot with colored center at each end.

1924-27
233 A26 1c green 1.60 .25
a. Vert. pair, imperf. btwn. 35.00 35.00
234 A26 2c red .85 .25
235 A26 5c blue 2.25 .25
236 A26 10c pale bl & blk (I) ('26) 12.00 3.00
236A A26 10c pale bl & blk (II) 22.50 1.10
236B A26 50c gray grn & blk ('26) 60.00 33.00
237 A26 1p orange & blk ('27) 19.00 12.50
Nos. 233-237 (7) 118.20 50.35

In the second redrawing the shield has a flat top and the design differs in many details from the stamps of 1911-13 and 1915-22.

1927
238 A27 ½c lilac rose & blk .30 .25

Exhibition Pavilion — A28

1927 **Unwmk.** ***Perf. 12***
239 A28 2c carmine 1.10 .50
240 A28 5c ultra 2.10 .50

Natl. and West Indian Exhib. at Santiago de los Caballeros.

Ruins of Columbus' Fortress A29

1928
241 A29 ½c lilac rose .95 .35
242 A29 1c deep green .70 .25
a. Horiz. pair, imperf. btwn. 25.00
243 A29 2c red .95 .25
244 A29 5c dark blue 2.75 .35
245 A29 10c light blue 2.75 .30
246 A29 20c rose 4.75 .40
247 A29 50c yellow green 13.50 8.25
248 A29 1p orange yellow 35.00 27.00
Nos. 241-248 (8) 61.35 37.15

Reprints exist of 1c, 2c and 10c.
Issued: 1c, 2c, 10c, Oct. 1; others, Dec.

Horacio Vasquez — A30

Convent of San Ignacio de Loyola — A31

1929, May-June
249 A30 ½c dull rose .60 .30
250 A30 1c gray green .60 .25
251 A30 2c red .70 .25
252 A30 5c dark ultra 1.40 .35
253 A30 10c pale blue 2.10 .50
Nos. 249-253 (5) 5.40 1.65

Signing of the "Frontier" treaty with Haiti.
Issue dates: 2c, May; others, June.

Imperf., Pairs

249a A30 ½c 12.50
250a A30 1c 12.50
251a A30 2c 12.50
252a A30 5c 14.00

1930, May 1 ***Perf. 11½***
254 A31 ½c red brown .70 .45
a. Imperf., pair 55.00 55.00
255 A31 1c deep green .65 .25
256 A31 2c vermilion .65 .25
a. Imperf., pair 60.00
257 A31 5c deep blue 2.10 .35
258 A31 10c light blue 4.25 1.25
Nos. 254-258 (5) 8.35 2.55

Cathedral of Santo Domingo, First Church in America A32

1931 ***Perf. 12***
260 A32 1c deep green .85 .25
a. Imperf., pair 50.00
261 A32 2c scarlet .60 .25
a. Imperf., pair 50.00
262 A32 3c violet .85 .25
263 A32 7c dark blue 2.50 .25
264 A32 8c bister 3.00 .85
265 A32 10c light blue 5.75 1.25
a. Imperf., pair 35.00
Nos. 260-265 (6) 13.55 3.10

Issued: 3c-7c, Aug. 1; others, July 11.
For overprint see No. RAC8.

A33

Overprinted or Surcharged in Black

1932, Dec. 20 ***Perf. 12***

Cross in Red

265B A33 1c yellow green .55 .50
265C A33 3c on 2c violet .80 .60
265D A33 5c blue 4.50 4.75
265E A33 7c on 10c turq bl 6.00 6.25
Nos. 265B-265E (4) 11.85 12.10

Proceeds of sale given to Red Cross. Valid Dec. 20 to Jan. 5, 1933.
Inverted and pairs, one without surcharge or overprint, exist on Nos. 265B-265D, as well as missing letters.

Fernando Arturo de Merino (1833-1906) as President — A35

Cathedral of Santo Domingo A36

Designs: ½c, 5c, 8c, Tomb of Merino. 1c, 3c, 10c, as Archbishop.

1933, Feb. 27 **Engr.** ***Perf. 14***
266 A35 ½c lt violet .45 .35
267 A35 1c yellow green .60 .25
268 A35 2c lt red 1.00 .75
269 A35 3c deep violet .70 .30
270 A35 5c dark blue .80 .35
271 A35 7c ultra 1.40 .50
272 A35 8c dark green 1.75 1.00
273 A35 10c orange yel 1.50 .60
274 A35 20c carmine rose 3.00 1.75
275 A36 50c lemon 11.25 7.75
276 A36 1p dark brown 26.00 19.00
Nos. 266-276 (11) 48.45 32.60

For surcharges see Nos. G1-G7.

Tower of Homage, Ozama Fortress — A37

1932 **Litho.** ***Perf. 12***
278 A37 1c green 1.75 .25
279 A37 3c violet 1.10 .25

Issue dates: 1c, July 2; 3c, June 22.

"CORREOS" added at left

1933, May 28
283 A37 1c dark green .50 .25

President Rafael L. Trujillo
A38 A39

1933, Aug. 16 **Engr.** ***Perf. 14***
286 A38 1c yellow grn & blk .75 .35
287 A39 3c dp violet & blk .90 .35
288 A38 7c ultra & blk 2.00 .75
Nos. 286-288 (3) 3.65 1.45

42nd birthday of President Rafael Leonidas Trujillo Molina.

San Rafael Bridge — A40

1934 **Litho.** ***Perf. 12***
289 A40 ½c dull violet .70 .40
290 A40 1c dark green 1.00 .25
291 A40 3c violet 1.75 .25
Nos. 289-291 (3) 3.45 .90

Opening of San Rafael Bridge.
Issue dates: ½c, 3c, Mar. 3; 1c, Feb. 17.

Trujillo Bridge A41

1934
292 A41 ½c red brown .70 .25
293 A41 1c green 1.00 .25
294 A41 3c purple 1.40 .25
Nos. 292-294 (3) 3.10 .75

Opening of the General Trujillo Bridge near Ciudad Trujillo.
Issue dates: 1c, Aug. 24. Others, Sept. 7.

Ramfis Bridge A42

1935, Apr. 6
295 A42 1c green .70 .25
296 A42 3c yellow brown .70 .25
297 A42 5c brown violet 2.10 1.00
298 A42 10c rose 4.25 1.40
Nos. 295-298 (4) 7.75 2.90

Opening of the Ramfis Bridge over the Higuamo River.

President Trujillo — A43

A44

A45

1935 ***Perf. 11***
299 A43 3c yellow & brown .30 .25
300 A44 5c org red, bl, red & bis .40 .25
301 A45 7c ultra, bl, red & brn .60 .25
302 A44 10c red vio, bl, red & bis 1.00 .25
Nos. 299-302 (4) 2.30 1.00

Ratification of a treaty setting the frontier between Dominican Republic and Haiti.
Issued: 3c, 10/29; 5c, 10c, 11/25; 7c, 11/8.

National Palace A46

1935, Apr. 1 ***Perf. 11½***
303 A46 25c yellow orange 3.75 .30

Obligatory for all mail addressed to the president and cabinet ministers.

Post Office, Santiago A47

1936
304 A47 ½c bright violet .30 .35
305 A47 1c green .30 .25

Issue dates: ½c, Jan. 14; 1c, Jan. 4.

George Washington Ave., Ciudad Trujillo — A48

1936, Feb. 22
306 A48 ½c brn & vio brn .40 .45
a. Imperf., pair 52.50
307 A48 2c carmine & brn .40 .30
308 A48 3c yellow org & red brn .70 .25

309 A48 7c ultra, blue & brn 1.60 1.25
a. Imperf., pair 52.50
Nos. 306-309 (4) 3.10 2.25

Dedication of George Washington Avenue, Ciudad Trujillo.

José Nuñez de Cáceres — A49

Felix M. del Monte — A55

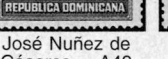

Proposed National Library — A56

1c, Gen. Gregorio Luperon. 2c, Emiliano Tejera. 3c, Pres. Trujillo. 5c, Jose Reyes. 7c, Gen. Antonio Duverge. 25c, Francisco J. Peynado. 30c, Salome Urena. 50c, Gen. Jose M. Cabral. 1p, Manuel de Jesus Galvan. 2p, Gaston F. Deligne.

1936 Unwmk. Engr. ***Perf. 13½, 14***

310 A49 ½c dull violet .40 .25
311 A49 1c dark green .30 .25
312 A49 2c carmine .30 .25
313 A49 3c violet .40 .25
314 A49 5c deep ultra .70 .30
315 A49 7c slate blue 1.25 .60
316 A55 10c orange 1.25 .30
317 A56 20c olive green 5.75 3.00
318 A55 25c gray violet 6.75 8.75
319 A55 30c scarlet 8.25 11.50
320 A55 50c black brown 9.75 6.25
321 A55 1p black 27.50 35.00
322 A55 2p yellow brown 80.00 90.00
Nos. 310-322 (13) 142.60 156.70

The funds derived from the sale of these stamps were returned to the National Treasury Fund for the erection of a building for the National Library and Archives.

Issued: 3c, 7c, Mar. 18; others, May 22.

President Trujillo and Obelisk — A62

1937, Jan. 11 Litho. ***Perf. 11½***

323 A62 1c green .30 .25
324 A62 3c violet .40 .25
325 A62 7c blue & turq blue 1.10 1.10
Nos. 323-325 (3) 1.80 1.60

1st anniv. of naming Ciudad Trujillo.

Discus Thrower and Flag — A63

Flag in Red and Blue

1937, Aug. 14

326 A63 1c dark green 11.50 1.00
327 A63 3c violet 14.50 1.00
328 A63 7c dark blue 26.00 5.25
Nos. 326-328 (3) 52.00 7.25

1st Natl. Olympic Games, Aug. 16, 1937.

Symbolical of Peace, Labor and Progress — A64

1937, Sept. 18 ***Perf. 12***

329 A64 3c purple .50 .25

"8th Year of the Benefactor."

Monument to Father Francisco Xavier Billini (1837-90) — A65

1937, Dec. 29

330 A65 ½c deep orange .25 .25
331 A65 5c purple .60 .25

Globe and Torch of Liberty — A66

1938, Feb. 22 ***Perf. 11½***

332 A66 1c green .50 .25
333 A66 3c purple .70 .25
334 A66 10c orange 1.40 .25
Nos. 332-334 (3) 2.60 .75

150th anniv. of the Constitution of the US.

Pledge of Trinitarians, City Gate and National Flag — A67

1938, July 16 ***Perf. 12***

335 A67 1c green, red & dk bl .50 .25
336 A67 3c purple, red & bl .60 .25
337 A67 10c orange, red & bl 1.25 .40
Nos. 335-337 (3) 2.35 .90

Trinitarians and patriots, Francisco Del Rosario Sanchez, Matías Ramón Mella and Juan Pablo Duarte, who helped free their country from foreign domination.

Seal of the University of Santo Domingo — A68

1938, Oct. 28

338 A68 ½c orange .40 .25
339 A68 1c dp green & lt green .40 .25
340 A68 3c purple & pale vio .50 .25
341 A68 7c dp blue & lt blue 1.00 .50
Nos. 338-341 (4) 2.30 1.25

Founding of the University of Santo Domingo, on Oct. 28, 1538.

Trylon and Perisphere, Flag and Proposed Columbus Lighthouse — A69

Flag in Blue and Red

1939, Apr. 30 Litho. ***Perf. 12***

342 A69 ½c red org & org .35 .25
343 A69 1c green & lt green .40 .25
344 A69 3c purple & pale vio .40 .25
345 A69 10c orange & yellow 1.40 .65
Nos. 342-345,C33 (5) 4.55 2.25

New York World's Fair.

A70

A71

1939, Sept. **Typo.**

346 A70 ½c black & pale gray .40 .25
347 A70 1c black & yel grn .50 .25
348 A70 3c black & yel brn .50 .25
349 A70 7c black & dp ultra 1.10 .90
350 A70 10c black & brt red vio 2.10 .40
Nos. 346-350 (5) 4.60 2.05

José Trujillo Valdez (1863-1935), father of President Trujillo Molina.

Flags in National Colors

Map of the Americas and flags of 21 American republics.

1940, Apr. 14 Litho. ***Perf. 11½***

351 A71 1c deep green .35 .25
352 A71 2c carmine .45 .25
353 A71 3c red violet .60 .25
354 A71 10c orange 1.25 .25
355 A71 1p chestnut 18.00 13.50
Nos. 351-355 (5) 20.65 14.50

Pan American Union, 50th anniv.

Sir Rowland Hill — A72

1940, May 6 ***Perf. 12***

356 A72 3c brt red vio & rose lil 3.25 .40
357 A72 7c dk blue & lt blue 6.75 1.75

Centenary of first postage stamp.

Julia Molina Trujillo A73

1940, May 26

358 A73 1c grn, lt grn & dk grn .40 .25
359 A73 2c brt red, buff & dp rose .40 .25
360 A73 3c org, dl org & brn org .55 .25
361 A73 7c bl, pale bl & dk bl 1.10 .35
Nos. 358-361 (4) 2.45 1.10

Issued in commemoration of Mother's Day.

Map of Caribbean A74

1940, June 6 ***Perf. 11½***

362 A74 3c brt car & pale rose .50 .25
363 A74 7c dk blue & lt blue 1.00 .25
364 A74 1p yel grn & pale grn 10.00 9.00
Nos. 362-364 (3) 11.50 9.50

2nd Inter-American Caribbean Conf. held at Ciudad Trujillo, May 31 to June 6.

Marion Military Hospital — A75

1940, Dec. 24

365 A75 ½c chestnut & fawn .25 .25

Fortress, Ciudad Trujillo A76

Statue of Columbus, Ciudad Trujillo — A77

1941

366 A76 1c dk green & lt green .25 .25
367 A77 2c brt red & rose .25 .25
368 A77 10c orange brn & buff .70 .25
Nos. 366-368 (3) 1.20 .75

Issue dates: 1c, Mar. 27; others, Apr. 7.

Sánchez, Duarte, Mella and Trujillo — A78

1941, May 16

369 A78 3c brt red lil & red vio .30 .25
370 A78 4c brt red, crim & pale rose .40 .25
371 A78 13c dk blue & lt blue .85 .35
372 A78 15c orange brn & buff 2.75 2.10
373 A78 17c lt bl, bl & pale bl 2.75 2.10
374 A78 1p org, yel brn & pale org 11.50 10.50
375 A78 2p lt gray & pale gray 25.00 10.50
Nos. 369-375 (7) 43.55 26.05

Trujillo-Hull Treaty signed Sept. 24, 1940 and effective Apr. 1, 1941.

Bastion of February 27 — A79

1941, Oct. 20

376 A79 5c brt blue & lt blue .50 .25

School, Torch of Knowledge, Pres. Trujillo — A80

1941

377 A80 ½c chestnut & fawn .25 .25
378 A80 1c dk green & lt green .25 .25

Education campaign.
Issue dates: ½c, Dec. 12, 1c, Dec. 2.

Reserve Bank of Dominican Republic A81

1942 **Unwmk.**

379 A81 5c lt brown & buff .50 .25
380 A81 17c dp blue & lt blue 1.00 .45

Founding of the Reserve Bank, 10/24/41.

Representation of Transportation A82

Virgin of Altagracia A83

1942, Aug. 15

381 A82 3c dk brn, grn yel & lt bl 4.25 .50
382 A82 15c pur, grn, yel & lt bl 11.00 5.50

Day of Posts and Telegraph, 8th anniv.

1942, Aug. 15

383 A83 ½c gray & pale gray 1.00 .25
384 A83 1c dp grn & lt grn 2.10 .25
385 A83 3c brt red lil & lil 13.50 .25
386 A83 5c dk vio brn & vio brn 2.75 .25
387 A83 10c rose pink & pink 4.75 .25
388 A83 15c dp blue & lt blue 10.50 .30
Nos. 383-388 (6) 34.60 1.55

20th anniv. of the coronation of Our Lady of Altagracia.

Bananas — A84

Cows — A85

1942-43

389 A84 3c dk brn & grn ('43) .60 .25
390 A84 4c vermilion & blk ('43) .60 .40
391 A85 5c dp blue & cop brn .60 .25
392 A85 15c dk pur & blue grn 1.00 .50
Nos. 389-392 (4) 2.80 1.40

Issue date: 5c, 15c, Aug. 18.

Emblems of Dominican and Trujillista Parties A86

1943, Jan. 15

393 A86 3c orange .50 .25
394 A86 4c dark red .60 .25
395 A86 13c brt red lilac 1.40 .25
396 A86 1p lt blue 6.75 1.60
Nos. 393-396 (4) 9.25 2.35

Re-election of President Rafael Trujillo Molina, May 16, 1942.

Model Market, Ciudad Trujillo A87

1944

397 A87 2c dk brown & buff .25 .25

Bastion of Feb. 27 and National Flag — A88

1944, Feb. 27 **Unwmk.**

Flag in Dark Blue and Carmine

398 A88 ½c ocher .25 .25
399 A88 1c yellow green .25 .25
400 A88 2c scarlet .25 .25
401 A88 3c brt red vio .25 .25
402 A88 5c yellow orange .25 .25
403 A88 7c brt blue .25 .25
404 A88 10c orange brown .40 .30
405 A88 20c olive green .65 .60
406 A88 50c lt blue 1.90 1.75
Nos. 398-406,C46-C48 (12) 7.25 6.15

Souvenir Sheet

Imperf

407 A88 Sheet of 12 110.00 110.00
a.-l. Single stamp 3.00 3.00

Centenary of Independence.
No. 407 contains 1 each of Nos. 398-406 and C46-C48 with simulated perforations. Size: 141x205mm.

Battlefield and Nurse with Child A90

1944, Aug. 1

408 A90 1c dk bl grn, buff & car .25 .25
a. Vertical pair, imperf. btwn. 15.00
b. Horiz. pair, imperf. vert. 15.00
409 A90 2c dk brn, buff & car .40 .25
410 A90 3c brt bl, buff & car .40 .25
411 A90 10c rose car, buff & car .80 .25
Nos. 408-411 (4) 1.85 1.00

80th anniv. of the Intl. Red Cross.

Municipal Building, San Cristobal A91

Emblem of Communications A92

Unwmk.

1945, Jan. 10 **Litho.** ***Perf. 12***

412 A91 ½c blue & lt blue .25 .25
413 A91 1c dk green & green .25 .25
414 A91 2c red org & org .25 .25
415 A91 3c dk brown & brown .25 .25
416 A91 10c ultra & gray blue 1.25 .25
Nos. 412-416 (5) 2.25 1.25

Centenary of the constitution.

1945, Sept. 1

Center in Dark Blue and Carmine

417 A92 3c orange .25 .25
418 A92 20c yellow green .85 .25
419 A92 50c light blue 1.75 .70
Nos. 417-419,C53-C56 (7) 5.00 2.20

Palace of Justice, Ciudad Trujillo A93

1946 ***Perf. 11½***

420 A93 3c dk red brown & buff .25 .25

Map of Hispaniola — A94

1946, Aug. 4 ***Perf. 12***

421 A94 10c multicolored .75 .25
Nos. 421,C62-C63 (3) 3.20 .75

450th anniv. of the founding of Santo Domingo.

Waterfall of Jimenoa — A95

1946-47 **Center Multicolored**

422 A95 1c yellow grn ('47) .25 .25
423 A95 2c carmine ('47) .25 .25
424 A95 3c deep blue .25 .25
425 A95 13c red violet ('47) .45 .35
426 A95 20c chocolate ('47) .80 .35
427 A95 50c orange ('47) 1.75 1.25
Nos. 422-427,C64-C67 (10) 11.45 5.50

Nos. 422-423, 425-427 issued Mar. 18.
For surcharge see No. 540.

Executive Palace A96

1948, Feb. 27

428 A96 1c yellow green .25 .25
429 A96 3c deep blue .25 .25
Nos. 428-429,C68-C69 (4) 8.35 3.60

Church of San Francisco Ruins — A97

1949, Apr. 13 ***Perf. 11½***

430 A97 1c dk grn & pale grn .25 .25
431 A97 3c dp bl & pale bl .25 .25
Nos. 430-431,C70-C73 (6) 4.30 1.90

Gen. Pedro Santana — A98

1949, Aug. 10

432 A98 3c deep blue & blue .25 .25

Battle of Las Carreras, cent. See No. C74.

Pigeon and Globe — A99

Center and Inscriptions in Brown

1950, Mar. 23

433 A99 1c green & pale green .25 .25
434 A99 2c yel grn & yel .25 .25
435 A99 5c blue & pale blue .25 .25
436 A99 7c dk vio bl & pale bl .40 .25
Nos. 433-436 (4) 1.15 1.00

75th anniv. of the UPU.

Catalogue values for unused stamps in this section, from this point to the end of the section, are for Never Hinged items.

Hotel Jimani A100

Hotels: 1c, 2c, Hamaca. 5c, Montana. 15c, San Cristobal. 20c, Maguana.

1950-52

437 A100 ½c org brn & buff .25 .25
438 A100 1c dp grn & grn ('51) .25 .25
439 A100 2c red org & sal ('52) .25 .25
440 A100 5c blue & lt blue .40 .25
441 A100 15c dp orange & yel .60 .25
442 A100 20c lilac & rose lilac 1.10 .25
443 A100 1p chocolate & yel 4.50 1.90
Nos. 437-443,C75-C76 (9) 11.70 6.15

Issue dates: 1c, Dec. 1, 1951; 2c, Jan. 11, 1952; others, Sept. 8, 1950.
The ½c, 15c and 20c exist imperf.

Ruins of Church and Hospital of San Nicolas de Bari A101

School of Medicine — A102

1950, Oct. 2

444 A101 2c dk green & rose brn .25 .25
445 A102 5c vio blue & org brn .50 .25
Nos. 444-445,C77 (3) 1.60 .75

13th Pan-American Health Conference.
Nos. 444-445 and C77 exist imperf.

Queen Isabella I — A103

1951, Oct. 12

446 A103 5c dk blue & red brn .70 .25

500th anniversary of the birth of Queen Isabella I of Spain. Exists imperf.

Dr. Salvador B. Gautier Hospital A104

1952, Aug.

447 A104 1c dark green .25 .25
448 A104 2c red .25 .25
449 A104 5c violet blue .50 .25
Nos. 447-449,C78-C79 (5) 4.10 3.10

Columbus Lighthouse and Flags of 21 Republics A105

1953, Jan. 6 Engr. *Perf. 13*

450 A105 2c dark green .25 .25
451 A105 5c deep blue .40 .25
452 A105 10c deep carmine .70 .25
Nos. 450-452,C80-C86 (10) 6.65 4.80

Treasury Building, Ciudad Trujillo A106

Sugar Industry, "Central Rio Haina" A107

1953 Litho. *Perf. 11½*

453 A106 ½c brown .25 .25
454 A106 2c dark blue .25 .25
455 A107 5c blue & vio brn .25 .25
456 A106 15c orange 1.00 .25
Nos. 453-456 (4) 1.75 1.00

For surcharge see No. 539.

José Marti — A108

1954 *Perf. 12½*

457 A108 10c dp blue & dk brown .60 .25

Centenary of the birth of Jose Marti (1853-1895), Cuban patriot.

Monument to the Peace of Trujillo — A109

1954, May 25

458 A109 2c green .25 .25
459 A109 7c blue .30 .25
460 A109 20c orange 1.10 .25
Nos. 458-460 (3) 1.65 .75

See No. 493.

Rotary Emblem A110

1955, Feb. 23 *Perf. 12*

461 A110 7c deep blue .70 .25

50th anniv., Rotary Intl. See No. C90.

Gen. Rafael L. Trujillo — A111

4c, Trujillo in civilian clothes. 7c, Trujillo statue. 10c, Symbols of culture & prosperity.

1955, May 16 Engr. *Perf. 13½x13*

462 A111 2c red .40 .25
463 A111 4c lt olive green .40 .25
464 A111 7c indigo .50 .25
465 A111 10c brown 1.10 .25
Nos. 462-465,C91-C93 (7) 6.10 2.05

25th anniversary of the Trujillo era.

General Rafael L. Trujillo — A112

1955, Dec. 20 Unwmk. *Perf. 13*

466 A112 7c deep claret .40 .25
467 A112 10c dark blue .60 .25
Nos. 466-467,C94 (3) 1.40 .75

Angelita Trujillo — A113

1955, Dec. 20 Litho. *Perf. 12½*

468 A113 10c blue & ultra .50 .25

Nos. 466-468 were issued to publicize the International Fair of Peace and Brotherhood in Ciudad Trujillo, Dec. 1955.

Airport A114

1956, Apr. 6 *Perf. 12½*

469 A114 1c brown .25 .25
470 A114 2c red orange .25 .25
Nos. 469-470,C95 (3) 1.00 .75

3rd Caribbean conf. of the ICAO.

Cedar — A115

1956, Dec. 8 *Perf. 11½x12*

471 A115 5c car rose & grn *1.60* .25
472 A115 6c red vio & grn *1.90* .25
Nos. 471-472,C96 (3) 5.75 .75

Reforestation program.

Fair Emblem — A116

1957, Jan. 10 *Perf. 12½*

473 A116 7c blue, lt brn & ver .35 .25

2nd International Livestock Show, Ciudad Trujillo, Jan. 10-20, 1957. Exists imperf.

Fanny Blankers-Koen, Netherlands A117

Olympic Winners and Flags: 2c, Jesse Owens, US. 3c, Kee Chung Sohn, Japan. 5c, Lord Burghley, England. 7c, Bob Mathias, US.

Flags in National Colors

Engraved & Lithographed

1957, Jan. 24 *Perf. 11½, Imperf.*

474 A117 1c brn, lt bl, vio & mar .25 .25
475 A117 2c dk brn, lt bl & vio .25 .25
476 A117 3c red lilac & red .30 .25
477 A117 5c red org & vio .40 .25
478 A117 7c green & violet .50 .25
Nos. 474-478,C97-C99 (8) 2.65 2.00

16th Olympic Games, Melbourne, Nov. 22-Dec. 8, 1956.

Miniature sheets of 5 exist, perf. and imperf., containing Nos. 474-478. Value, 2 sheets, perf. and imperf., $15.

For surcharges see Nos. B1-B5, B26-B30, CB1-CB3, CB16-CB18.

Lars Hall, Sweden, Pentathlon — A118

Olympic Winners and Flags: 2c, Betty Cuthbert, Australia, 100 & 200 meter dash. 3c, Egil Danielsen, Norway, javelin. 5c, Alain Mimoun, France, marathon. 7c, Norman Read, New Zealand, 50 km. walk.

Perf. 13½, Imperf.

1957, July 18 Photo. Unwmk.

Flags in National Colors

479 A118 1c brn & brt bl .30 .25
480 A118 2c org ver & dk bl .30 .25
481 A118 3c dark blue .30 .25
482 A118 5c ol & dk bl .30 .25
483 A118 7c rose brn & dk bl .30 .30
Nos. 479-483,C100-C102 (8) 2.40 2.05

1956 Olympic winners.

Miniature sheets of 8 exist, perf. and imperf., containing Nos. 479-483 and C100-C102. The center label in these sheets is printed in two forms: Olympic gold medal or Olympic flag. Sheets measure 140x140mm. Value, 4 sheets, perf. and imperf., medal and flag, $18.

A third set of similar miniature sheets (perf. and imperf.) with center label showing an incorrect version of the Dominican Republic flag (colors transposed) was printed. These sheets are said to have been briefly sold on the first day, then withdrawn as the misprint was discovered. Value, 2 sheets, perf. & imperf., $150.

For surcharges see Nos. B6-B10, CB4-CB6.

Gerald Ouellette, Canada, Small Bore Rifle, Prone — A119

Ron Delaney, Ireland, 1,500 Meter Run — A120

Olympic Winners and Flags: 3c, Tenley Albright, US, figure skating. 5c, Joaquin Capilla, Mexico, platform diving. 7c, Ercole Baldini, Italy, individual road race (cycling).

Engraved and Lithographed

1957, Nov. 12 *Perf. 13½, Imperf.*

Flags in National Colors

484 A119 1c red brown .25 .25
485 A120 2c gray brown .25 .25
486 A119 3c violet .25 .25
487 A120 5c red orange .25 .25
488 A119 7c Prus green .25 .25
Nos. 484-488,C103-C105 (8) 2.30 2.00

1956 Olympic winners.

Miniature sheets of 5 exist, perf. and imperf., containing Nos. 484-488. Value, 2 sheets, perf. and imperf., $5.50.

For surcharges see Nos. B11-B20, CB7-CB12.

Mahogany Flower — A121

1957-58 Litho. *Perf. 12½*

489	A121	2c green & maroon	.25	.25

Perf. 12

490	A121	4c lilac & rose ('58)	.25	.25
491	A121	7c ultra & gray grn	.40	.25
492	A121	25c brown & org ('58)	1.00	.35
		Nos. 489-492 (4)	1.90	1.10

Sizes: No. 489, 25x29¼mm; Nos. 490-492, 24x28¾mm. In 1959, the 2c was reissued in size 24¼x28½mm with slightly different tones of green and maroon.

Issued: 2c, 10/24; 7c, 11/6; 4c, 25c, 4/7/58.

For surcharges see Nos. 537-538.

Type of 1954, Redrawn

Perf. 12x11½

1957, June 12 Unwmk.

493	A109	7c bright blue	.55	.25

On No. 493 the cent symbol is smaller, the shading of the sky and steps stronger and the letters in "Correos" shorter and bolder.

Cervantes, Globe, Book — A122

1958, Apr. 23 Litho. *Perf. 12½*

494	A122	4c yellow green	.25	.25
495	A122	7c red lilac	.25	.25
496	A122	10c lt olive brown	.35	.25
		Nos. 494-496 (3)	.85	.75

4th Book Fair, Apr. 23-28. Exist imperf.

Gen. Rafael L. Trujillo — A123

1958, Aug. 16 *Perf. 12*

497	A123	2c red lilac & yel	.25	.25
498	A123	4c green & yel	.25	.25
499	A123	7c brown & yel	.25	.25
a.		Souv. sheet of 3, #497-499, imperf.	1.00	.80
		Nos. 497-499 (3)	.75	.75

25th anniv. of Gen. Trujillo's designation as "Benefactor of his country."

S. S. Rhadames A124

1958, Oct. 27 *Perf. 12½*

500	A124	7c bright blue	1.25	.30

Day of the Dominican Merchant Marine. Exists imperf.

Shozo Sasahara, Japan, Featherweight Wrestling — A125

Olympic Winners and Flags: 1c, Gillian Sheen, England, fencing, vert. 2c, Milton Campbell, US, decathlon, vert. 5c, Madeleine Berthod, Switzerland, downhill skiing. 7c, Murray Rose, Australia, 400 & 1,500 meter freestyle.

Perf. 13½, Imperf.

1958, Oct. 30 Photo.

Flags in National Colors

501	A125	1c rose, ind & ultra	.30	.25
502	A125	2c brown & blue	.30	.25
503	A125	3c gray, vio, blk & buff	.30	.25
504	A125	5c rose, dk bl, brn & red	.30	.25
505	A125	7c lt brn, dk bl & red	.30	.25
		Nos. 501-505,C106-C108 (8)	2.60	2.00

1956 Olympic winners.

Miniature sheets of 5 exist, perf. and imperf. containing Nos. 501-505. Value, 2 sheets, perf. and imperf., $5.

For surcharges see Nos. B21-B25, CB13-CB15.

Globe and Symbolic Fire — A126

1958, Nov. 3 Litho. *Perf. 11½*

506	A126	7c blue & dp carmine	.40	.25

UNESCO Headquarters in Paris opening, Nov. 3.

Dominican Republic Pavilion, Brussels Fair — A127

1958, Dec. 9 Unwmk. *Perf. 12½*

507	A127	7c blue green	.30	.25
		Nos. 507,C109-C110 (3)	1.45	.90

Universal & Intl. Exposition at Brussels.

Gen. Trujillo Placing Wreath on Altar of the Nation — A128

1959, July 10 *Perf. 12*

508	A128	9c brn, grn, red & gold	.30	.25
a.		Souv. sheet of 1, imperf.	1.10	.75

29th anniversary of the Trujillo regime.

Lt. Leonidas Rhadames Trujillo, Team Captain — A129

Jamaican Polo Team A130

Design: 10c, Lt. Trujillo on polo pony.

1959, May 15

509	A129	2c violet	.25	.25
510	A130	7c yellow brown	.50	.25
511	A130	10c green	.60	.25
		Nos. 509-511,C111 (4)	1.75	1.05

Jamaica-Dominican Republic polo match at Ciudad Trujillo.

Symbolical of Census A131

1959, Aug. 15 Litho. *Perf. 12½*

Flag in Ultramarine and Red

512	A131	1c blue & black	.25	.25
513	A131	9c green & black	.40	.25
514	A131	13c orange & black	.60	.30
		Nos. 512-514 (3)	1.25	.80

Issued to publicize the 1960 census.

Trujillo Stadium — A132

1959, Aug. 27

515	A132	9c green & gray	.50	.25

Issued to publicize the 3rd Pan American Games, Chicago, Aug. 27-Sept. 7.

Charles V A133

1959, Oct. 12 Unwmk. *Perf. 12*

516	A133	5c bright pink	.30	.25
517	A133	9c violet blue	.45	.25

400th anniv. of the death of Charles V (1500-1558), Holy Roman Emperor.

Rhadames Bridge — A134

1c and No. 520, Different view of bridge.

1959-60 Litho. *Perf. 12*

518	A134	1c green & gray ('60)	.30	.25
519	A134	2c ultra & gray	.30	.25
520	A134	2c red & gray ('60)	.30	.25
521	A134	5c brn & dull red brn	.30	.25
		Nos. 518-521 (4)	1.20	1.00

Issued: No. 519, 10/22; 5c, 11/30; 1c, No. 520, 2/6.

For surcharge see No. 536.

Sosua Refugee Settlement and WRY Emblem — A135

1960, Apr. 7 *Perf. 12½*

Center in Gray

522	A135	5c red brn & yel grn	.25	.25
523	A135	9c carmine & lt blue	.25	.25
524	A135	13c orange & green	.50	.25
		Nos. 522-524,C113-C114 (5)	2.55	1.35

World Refugee Year, 7/1/59-6/30/60.

For surcharges see Nos. B31-B33.

Sholam Takhti, Iran, Lightweight Wrestling — A136

Olympic Winners: 2c, Masaru Furukawa, Japan, 200 meter breast stroke. 3c, Mildred McDaniel, US, high jump. 5c, Terence Spinks, England, featherweight boxing. 7c, Carlo Pavesi, Italy, fencing.

Perf. 13½, Imperf.

1960, Sept. 14 Photo.

Flags in National Colors

525	A136	1c red, yel grn & blk	.30	.25
526	A136	2c org, grnsh bl & brn	.30	.25
527	A136	3c henna brn & bl	.30	.25
528	A136	5c brown & ultra	.30	.25
529	A136	7c grn, bl & rose brn	.30	.25
		Nos. 525-529,C115-C117 (8)	2.45	2.20

17th Olympic Games, Rome, 8/25-9/11.

Miniature sheets of 5 exist, perf. and imperf., containing Nos. 525-529. Value, 2 sheets, perf. & imperf., $5.

For surcharges see Nos. B34-B38, CB21-CB23.

Post Office, Ciudad Trujillo A137

1960, Aug. 26 Litho. *Perf. 11½x12*

530	A137	2c ultra & gray	.30	.25

Exists imperf.

Cattle A138

1960, Aug. 30

531	A138	9c carmine & gray	.30	.25

Issued to publicize the Agricultural and Industrial Fair, San Juan de la Maguana.

Nos. 518, 490-491, 453, 427 Surcharged in Red, Black or Blue

1960-61 *Perf. 12*

536	A134	2c on 1c grn & gray (R)	.25	.25
537	A121	9c on 4c lilac & rose	.60	.25
a.		Inverted surcharge	21.00	
538	A121	9c on 7c ultra & gray grn (R)	.60	.25

539 A106 36c on ½c brown 1.90 1.75
a. Inverted surcharge 18.00
540 A95 1p on 50c multi (Bl) 4.25 3.25
Nos. 536-540 (5) 7.60 5.75

Issue dates: No. 536, Dec. 30, 1960; No. 537, Dec. 20, 1960; others, Feb. 4, 1961.

Trujillo Memorial A139

Coffee, Cacao A140

1961 Unwmk. *Perf. 11½*
548 A139 1c brown .25 .25
549 A139 2c green .25 .25
550 A139 4c rose lilac .50 .30
551 A139 5c light blue .50 .25
552 A139 9c red orange .50 .25
Nos. 548-552 (5) 2.00 1.30

Gen. Rafael L. Trujillo (1891-1961). Issued: 2c, 8/7; 4c, 10/24; others 8/30.

1961, Dec. 30 Litho. *Perf. 12½*
553 A140 1c blue green .30 .25
554 A140 2c orange brown .30 .25
555 A140 4c violet .30 .25
556 A140 5c blue .30 .25
557 A140 9c gray .40 .25
Nos. 553-557,C118-C119 (7) 2.60 2.25

Nos. 553-557 exist imperf.

Dagger Pointing at Mosquito — A141

1962, Apr. 29 Photo. *Perf. 12*
558 A141 10c brt pink & red lilac .30 .25
559 A141 20c pale brn & brn .60 .30
560 A141 25c pale grn & yel grn .85 .40
Nos. 558-560,B39-B40,C120-C121,CB24-CB25 (#) * *

WHO drive to eradicate malaria.

Broken Fetters and Laurel A142

"Justice," Map of Dominican Republic — A143

Design: 20c, Flag, torch and inscription.

1962, May 30 Litho. *Perf. 12½*
561 A142 1c grn, yel, ultra & red .25 .25
562 A143 9c bister ultra & red .40 .25
563 A142 20c lt blue, ultra & red .85 .25
a. Souvenir sheet of 3, #561-563 1.90 1.90
564 A143 1p lilac, ultra & red 4.50 2.50
Nos. 561-564,C122-C123 (6) 7.80 4.55

1st anniv. of end of Trujillo era. Nos. 561-564 exist imperf.

Farm, Factory and Flag — A144

1962, May 22
565 A144 1c ultra, red & green .25 .25
566 A144 2c ultra & red .25 .25
567 A144 3c ultra, red & brown .25 .25
568 A144 5c ultra, red & blue .25 .25
569 A144 15c ultra, red & orange .40 .30
Nos. 565-569 (5) 1.40 1.30

Map and Laurel A145

1962, June 14 Litho.
570 A145 1c black .40 .25

Honoring the martyrs of June 1959 revolution.

Western Hemisphere and Carrier Pigeon — A146

Archbishop Adolfo Alejandro Nouel — A147

1962, Oct. 23 Unwmk. *Perf. 12½*
571 A146 2c rose red .25 .25
572 A146 9c orange .25 .25
573 A146 14c blue green .50 .25
Nos. 571-573,C124-C125 (5) 1.90 1.50

50th anniv. of the founding of the Postal Union of the Americas and Spain, UPAE.

1962, Dec. 18
574 A147 2c bl grn & dull bl .25 .25
575 A147 9c orange & red brn .30 .25
576 A147 13c maroon & vio brn .40 .25
Nos. 574-576,C126-C127 (5) 2.05 1.50

Cent. of the birth of Archbishop Adolfo Alejandro Nouel, President of Dominican Republic in 1911.

Globe, Banner and Emblems A148

1963, Apr. 15 Unwmk. *Perf. 11½*
Banner in Dark Blue & Red
577 A148 2c green .25 .25
578 A148 5c brt rose lilac .25 .25
579 A148 9c orange .50 .25
Nos. 577-579,B41-B43 (6) 1.90 1.50

FAO "Freedom from Hunger" campaign.

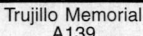

Juan Pablo Duarte — A149

1963, July 7 Litho. *Perf. 12x11½*
580 A149 2c shown .25 .25
581 A149 7c Francisco Sanchez .30 .25
582 A149 9c Ramon Mella .40 .25
Nos. 580-582 (3) .95 .75

120th anniv. of separation from Haiti. See No. C128.

Ulises F. Espaillat, Benigno F. de Rojas and Pedro F. Bono — A150

Designs: 4c, Generals Santiago Rodriguez, Jose Cabrera and Benito Moncion. 5c, Capotillo monument. 9c, Generals Gaspar Polanco, Gregorio Luperon and Jose A. Salcedo.

1963, Aug. 16 Unwmk. *Perf. 11½*
583 A150 2c green .25 .25
584 A150 4c red orange .25 .25
585 A150 5c brown .70 .25
586 A150 9c bright blue .30 .25
a. Souvenir sheet of 4 1.10 1.00
Nos. 583-586 (4) 1.50 1.00

Cent. of the Restoration. No. 586a contains 4 imperf. stamps similar to Nos. 583-586.

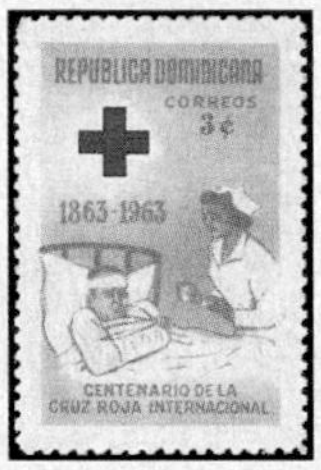

Patient and Nurse — A151

1963, Oct. 25 Unwmk. *Perf. 12½*
587 A151 3c gray & carmine .30 .25
588 A151 6c emerald & red .30 .25
Nos. 587-588,C129 (3) 1.00 .75

Centenary of International Red Cross. Nos. 587-588 exist imperf. See No. C129.

Scales, Globe, UNESCO Emblem A152

1963, Dec. 10 Litho.
589 A152 6c pink & deep pink .25 .25
590 A152 50c lt green & green .85 .85
Nos. 589-590,C130-C131 (4) 1.70 1.60

Universal Declaration of Human Rights, 15th anniv. Nos. 589-590 exist imperf.

Ramses II Battling the Hittites (from Abu Simbel) — A153

Design: 6c, Two heads of Ramses II.

1964, Mar. 8 Unwmk. *Perf. 12½*
591 A153 3c pale pink & ver .25 .25
592 A153 6c pale blue & ultra .25 .25
593 A153 9c pale rose & red brn .25 .25
Nos. 591-593,C132-C133 (5) 1.35 1.25

UNESCO world campaign to save historic monuments in Nubia.
For surcharges see Nos. B44-B46.

Maximo Gomez — A154

Palm Chat — A155

1964, Apr. 30 Litho.
594 A154 2c lt blue & blue .25 .25
595 A154 6c dull pink & dull claret .25 .25

Bicent. of the founding of the town of Bani.

1964, June 8 Unwmk. *Perf. 12½*

Design: 6c, Hispaniolan parrot.

Size: 27x37½mm
596 A155 3c ultra, brn & yel 2.50 .25
597 A155 6c gray & multi 3.25 .25
Nos. 596-597,C134 (3) 11.50 .75

See Nos. 602-604.

Rocket Leaving Earth A156

Designs: 1c, Launching of rocket, vert. 3c, Space capsule orbiting earth. 6c, As 2c.

1964, July 28 Litho.
598 A156 1c sky blue .25 .25
599 A156 2c emerald .25 .25
600 A156 3c blue .25 .25
601 A156 6c sky blue .35 .25
Nos. 598-601,C135-C136 (6) 1.80 1.55

Conquest of space.

Bird Type of 1964

Designs: 1c, Narrow-billed tody. 2c, Hispaniolan emerald hummingbird. 6c, Hispaniolan trogon.

1964, Nov. 7 *Perf. 11½*
Size: 26x37mm
Birds in Natural Colors
602 A155 1c bright pink 2.50 .25
603 A155 2c dark brown 2.50 .25
604 A155 6c blue 4.25 .25
Nos. 602-604 (3) 9.25 .75

Universal Postal Union and United Nations Emblems A157

1964, Dec. 5 Litho. *Perf. 12½*
605 A157 1c red .30 .25
606 A157 4c green .30 .25
607 A157 5c orange .30 .25
Nos. 605-607,C138 (4) 1.20 1.00

15th UPU Cong., Vienna, May-June 1964.

International Cooperation Year Emblem A158

1965, Feb. 16 Unwmk. *Perf. 12½*
608 A158 2c lt blue & ultra .30 .25
609 A158 3c emerald & dk grn .30 .25
610 A158 6c salmon pink & red .30 .25
Nos. 608-610,C139 (4) 1.25 1.05

UN Intl. Cooperation Year.

Virgin of Altagracia A159

Design: 2c, Hands holding lily.

1965, Mar. 18 Unwmk. *Perf. 12½*

611 A159 2c grn, emer & dp rose .30 .25
612 A159 6c multicolored .35 .25
Nos. 611-612,C140 (3) 1.05 .75

4th Mariological Cong. and 11th Intl. Marian Cong. No. 612 exists imperf.

Flags of 21 American Nations — A160

1965, Apr. 14 Litho. *Perf. 11½*

613 A160 2c brown, yel & multi .25 .25
614 A160 6c red lilac & multi .35 .25

Organization of American States.

Stamp of 1865 (No. 1) — A161

1965, Dec. 28 Litho. *Perf. 12½*

615 A161 1c pink, buff & blk .30 .25
616 A161 2c blue, buff & blk .30 .25
617 A161 6c emerald, buff & blk .30 .25
a. Souvenir sheet of 2 1.10 1.10
Nos. 615-617,C142-C143 (5) 1.50 1.30

Cent. of 1st Dominican postage stamps. No. 617a shows replicas of Nos. 1-2. Sold for 50c.

WHO Headquarters, Geneva — A162

1966, May 21 Litho. *Perf. 12½*

618 A162 6c blue .25 .25
619 A162 10c red lilac .35 .25

New WHO Headquarters, Geneva.

Man Holding Map of Republic — A163

1966, May 23

620 A163 2c black & brt green .25 .25
621 A163 6c black & dp orange .35 .25

General elections, June 1, 1966.

Ascia Monuste — A164

Natl. Altar — A165

1966 Litho. *Perf. 12½*
Various Butterflies in Natural Colors
Size: 31x21mm

622 A164 1c blue & vio bl 1.50 .25
623 A164 2c lt grn & brt grn 1.40 .25
624 A164 3c lt gray & gray 1.40 .25
625 A164 6c pink & magenta 2.25 1.00
626 A164 8c buff & brown 3.50 1.40
Nos. 622-626,C146-C148 (8) 37.05 7.90

Issued: 1c, 9/7; 3c, 9/11; others, 11/8.
For surcharges see Nos. B47-B51, CB28-CB30.

1967, Jan. 18 Litho. *Perf. 11½*

627 A165 1c bright blue .25 .25
628 A165 2c carmine rose .25 .25
629 A165 3c emerald .25 .25
630 A165 4c gray .25 .25
631 A165 5c orange yellow .25 .25
632 A165 6c orange .25 .25
Nos. 627-632,C149-C151 (9) 2.40 2.30

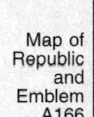

Map of Republic and Emblem A166

1967, Mar. 30 Litho. *Perf. 12½*

633 A166 2c yellow, blue & blk .25 .25
634 A166 6c orange, blue & blk .25 .25
635 A166 10c emerald, blue & blk .70 .45
Nos. 633-635 (3) 1.20 .95

Development Year, 1967.

Rook and Knight A167

1967, June 23 Litho. *Perf. 12½*

636 A167 25c multicolored 3.00 .50

5th Central American Chess Championships, Santo Domingo. See Nos. C152-C152a.

Alliance for Progress A168

Institute Emblem A169

1967, Sept. 16 Litho. *Perf. 12½*

637 A168 1c bright green .30 .25
Nos. 637,C153-C154 (3) 1.20 .85

6th anniv. of the Alliance for Progress.

1967, Oct. 7

638 A169 3c bright green .30 .25
639 A169 6c salmon pink .30 .25
Nos. 638-639,C155 (3) 1.20 .80

25th anniversary of the Inter-American Agriculture Institute.

Globe and Satellite A170

1968, June 15 Typo. *Perf. 12*

640 A170 6c black & multi .30 .25
Nos. 640,C156-C157 (3) 1.00 .80

World Meteorological Day, Mar. 23.

Boxers A171

1968, June 29

641 A171 6c rose red & dp claret .30 .25
Nos. 641,C158-C159 (3) 1.40 .75

Fight between Carlos Ortiz, Puerto Rico, and Teo Cruz, Dominican Republic, for the World Lightweight Boxing Championship.

Lions Emblem — A172

1968, Aug. 9 Litho. *Perf. 11½*

642 A172 6c brown & multi .25 .25

Lions Intl., 50th anniv. (in 1967). See No. C160.

Wrestling and Olympic Emblem A173

1968, Nov. 12 Litho. *Perf. 11½*

643 A173 1c shown .25 .25
644 A173 6c Running .30 .25
645 A173 25c Boxing 1.00 .40
Nos. 643-645,C161-C162 (5) 2.85 1.90

19th Olympic Games, Mexico City, 10/12-27.

Map of Americas and House — A174

1969, Jan. 25 Litho. *Perf. 12½*

646 A174 6c brt bl, lt bl & grn .30 .25

7th Inter-American Conference for Savings and Loans, Santo Domingo, Jan. 25-31. See No. C163.

Stool in Human Form A175

Taino Art: 2c, Wood carved mother figure, vert. 3c, Face carved on 3-cornered stone. 4c, Stone hatchet, vert. 5c, Clay pot.

1969, Jan. 31 Litho. *Perf. 12½*

647 A175 1c yellow, org & blk .30 .25
648 A175 2c lt grn, grn & blk .30 .25
649 A175 3c citron, ol & brt grn .30 .25
650 A175 4c lt lil, lil & brt grn .30 .25
651 A175 5c yellow, org & brn .30 .25
Nos. 647-651,C164-C166 (8) 2.85 2.05

Taino art flourished in the West Indies at the time of Columbus.

Community Day Emblem — A176

1969, Mar. 25 Litho. *Perf. 12½*

652 A176 6c dull green & gold .25 .25

Community Development Day, Mar. 22.

COTAL Emblem — A177

Headquarters Building and COTAL Emblem — A178

Design: 2c, Boy and COTAL emblem.

1969, May 25 Litho. *Perf. 12½*

653 A177 1c lt & dk blue & red .30 .25
654 A177 2c emerald & dk grn .30 .25
655 A178 6c vermilion & pink .30 .25
Nos. 653-655,C167 (4) 1.20 1.00

12th Congress of the Confederation of Latin American Tourist Organizations (COTAL), Santo Domingo, May 25-29.

ILO Emblem — A179

1969, June 27 Litho. *Perf. 12½*

656 A179 6c lt grnsh bl, grnsh bl & blk .30 .25

50th anniv. of the ILO. See No. C168.

Sliding into Base — A180

Designs: 1c, Catching a fly ball. 2c, View of Cibao Stadium, horiz.

Size: 21x31mm (1c, 3c); 43x30mm (2c)

1969, Aug. 15 Litho. *Perf. 12½*

657 A180 1c green & gray	.30	.25
658 A180 2c green & lt green	.30	.25
659 A180 3c purple & red brown	.30	.25
Nos. 657-659,C169-C171 (6)	7.05	4.85

17th World Amateur Baseball Championships, Santo Domingo.

Las Damas Dam A181

Tavera Dam — A182

Designs: 2c, Las Damas hydroelectric station, vert. 6c, Arroyo Hondo substation.

1969 Litho. *Perf. 12*

660 A181 2c green & multi	.30	.25
661 A181 3c dk blue & multi	.30	.25
662 A181 6c brt rose lilac	.30	.25
663 A182 6c multicolored	.50	.25
Nos. 660-663,C172-C173 (6)	2.25	1.50

National electrification plan.

Issued: Nos. 660-662, Sept. 15; No. 663, Oct. 15.

Juan Pablo Duarte — A183

1970, Jan. 26 Litho. *Perf. 12*

664 A183 1c emerald & dk grn	.30	.25
665 A183 2c sal pink & dp car	.30	.25
666 A183 3c brt pink & plum	.30	.25
667 A183 6c blue & violet blue	.30	.25
Nos. 664-667,C174 (5)	1.85	1.25

Issued for Duarte Day in memory of Juan Pablo Duarte (1813-1876), liberator.

Map of Republic, People, Census Emblem A184

Design: 6c, Census emblem and inscription.

1970, Feb. 6 *Perf. 11*

668 A184 5c emerald & blk	.30	.25
669 A184 6c ultra & blue	.30	.25
Nos. 668-669,C175 (3)	1.25	.75

Census of 1970.

Abelardo Rodriguez Urdaneta — A185

"One of Many" A186

1970, Feb. 20 Litho. *Perf. 12½*

670 A185 3c ultramarine	.30	.25
671 A186 6c green & yel grn	.30	.25
Nos. 670-671,C176 (3)	1.05	.75

Issued to honor Abelardo Rodriguez Urdaneta, sculptor.

Masonic Symbols — A187

1970, Mar. 2

672 A187 6c green	.30	.25

8th Inter-American Masonic Conference, Santo Domingo, Mar. 1-7. See No. C177.

Communications Satellite — A188

1970, May 25 Litho. *Perf. 12½*

673 A188 20c olive & gray	.65	.30

World Telecommunications Day. See No. C178.

UPU Headquarters, Bern — A189

1970, June 5 *Perf. 11*

674 A189 6c gray & brown	.30	.25

Inauguration of the new UPU headquarters in Bern. See No. C179.

Education Year Emblem — A190

Pedro Alejandrino Pina — A191

1970, June 26 Litho. *Perf. 12½*

675 A190 4c rose lilac	.30	.25

Issued for International Education Year, 1970. See No. C180.

1970, Aug. 24 Litho. *Perf. 12½*

676 A191 6c lt red brn & blk	.30	.25

Pedro Alejandrino Pina (1820-70), author.

Children Reading A192

1970, Oct. 12 Litho. *Perf. 12½*

677 A192 5c dull green	.30	.25
Nos. 677,C181-C182 (3)	1.05	.75

1st World Exhibition of Books and Culture Festival, Santo Domingo, Oct. 11-Dec. 11.

Virgin of Altagracia A193

1971, Jan. 20 Litho. *Perf. 12½*

678 A193 3c multicolored	.30	.25

Inauguration of the Basilica of Our Lady of Altagracia. See No. C184.

Rodriguez Objio — A194

1971, June 18 Litho. *Perf. 11*

679 A194 6c light blue	.30	.25

Manuel Rodriguez Objio (1838-1871), poet.

Boxing and Canoeing — A195

1971, Sept. 10

680 A195 2c shown	.25	.25
681 A195 5c Basketball	.25	.25
Nos. 680-681,C186 (3)	.80	.75

2nd National Games.

Goat and Fruit A196

Designs: 2c, Cow and goose. 3c, Cacao and horse. 6c, Bananas, coffee and pig.

1971, Sept. 29 *Perf. 12½*

682 A196 1c brown & multi	.25	.25
683 A196 2c plum & multi	.25	.25
684 A196 3c green & multi	.25	.25
685 A196 6c blue & multi	.25	.25
Nos. 682-685,C187 (5)	1.65	1.35

6th Natl. agriculture and livestock census.

José Nuñez de Cáceres — A197

1971, Dec. 1 *Perf. 11*

686 A197 6c lt bl, lil & dk bl	.30	.25

Sesquicentennial of first national independence. See No. C188.

Shepherds and Star — A198

1971, Dec. 10 *Perf. 12½*

687 A198 6c blue, brown & yel	.30	.25

Christmas 1971. See No. C189.

UNICEF Emblem, Child on Beach — A199

1971, Dec. 14 Litho. *Perf. 11*

688 A199 6c gray blue & multi	.25	.25

UNICEF, 25th anniv. See No. C190.

Book Year Emblem A200

1972, Jan. 25 *Perf. 12½*

689 A200 1c green, ultra & red	.25	.25
690 A200 2c brown, ultra & red	.25	.25
Nos. 689-690,C191 (3)	.95	.80

Intl. Book Year 1972.

Taino Mask — A201

4c, Ladle and amulet. 6c, Human figure.

1972, May 10 Litho. *Perf. 11*

691 A201 2c pink & multi	.40	.25
692 A201 4c black, bl & ocher	.40	.25
693 A201 6c gray & multi	.40	.25
Nos. 691-693,C194-C196 (6)	3.70	1.70

Taino art. See note after No. 651.

Globe A202

1972, May 17 ***Perf. 12½***

694 A202 6c blue & multi .30 .25

4th World Telecommunications Day. See No. C197.

"1972," Stamps and Map of Dominican Republic A203

1972, June 3

695 A203 2c green & multi .30 .25

First National Philatelic Exhibition, Santo Domingo, June 3-17. See No. C198.

Basketball — A204

1972, Aug. 25 Litho. ***Perf. 12½***

696 A204 2c blue & multi .30 .25

20th Olympic Games, Munich, Aug. 26-Sept. 11. See No. C199.

Club Emblem A205

1972, Sept. 29 Litho. ***Perf. 10½***

697 A205 1c lt green & multi .30 .25

50th anniversary of the Club Activo 20-30 International. See No. C200.

Emilio A. Morel A206

1972, Oct. 20 ***Perf. 12½***

698 A206 6c brt pink & multi .30 .25

Emilio A. Morel (1884-1958), poet and journalist. See No. C201.

Central Bank Building A207

1972, Oct. 23

699 A207 1c shown .25 .25

700 A207 5c 1-peso note .25 .25

Nos. 699-700,C202 (3) 1.35 1.05

25th anniv. of Central Bank.

Holy Family — A208

Poinsettia A209

1972, Nov. 21

701 A208 2c rose lil, pur & gold .25 .25

702 A209 6c red & multi .25 .25

Nos. 701-702,C203 (3) 1.15 .75

Christmas 1972.

Mail Box and Student A210

1972, Dec. 15

703 A210 2c rose red .25 .25

704 A210 6c blue .25 .25

705 A210 10c emerald .35 .25

Nos. 703-705 (3) .85 .75

Publicity for correspondence schools.

Tavera Dam A211

1973, Feb. 26 Litho. ***Perf. 12½***

706 A211 10c multicolored .30 .25

Inauguration of the Tavera Dam.

Various Sports — A212

Designs: a, UL. b, UR. c, LL. d, LR.

1973, Mar. 30 ***Perf. 13½x13***

707 A212 Block of 4 .50 .50

a.-d. 2c, any single .25 .25

708 A212 Block of 4 5.25 4.50

a.-d. 25c, any single 1.00 .35

Nos. 707-708,C204-C205 (4) 9.75 9.00

12th Central American and Caribbean Games, Santo Domingo, Summer 1974.

Christ Carrying the Cross A213

6c, Belfry of Church of Our Lady of Carmen.

1973, Apr. 18 Litho. ***Perf. 10½***

709 A213 2c multicolored .30 .25

710 A213 6c multicolored, vert. .30 .25

Nos. 709-710,C206 (3) 1.15 .75

Holy Week, 1973.

WMO Emblem, Weather Satellite, "Weather" A214

1973, Aug. 10 Litho. ***Perf. 13½x13***

711 A214 6c magenta & multi .30 .25

Centenary of international meteorological cooperation. See No. C208.

Mask, Cibao — A215

1973, Oct. 12 Litho. ***Perf. 10½***

712 A215 1c Maguey drum, horiz .30 .25

713 A215 2c Carved amber, horiz .30 .25

714 A215 4c shown .30 .25

715 A215 6c Pottery .30 .25

Nos. 712-715,C210-C211 (6) 1.90 1.50

Opening of Museum of Mankind in Santo Domingo.

Nativity A216

Christmas: 6c, Stained glass window, vert.

Perf. 13½x13, 13x13½

1973, Nov. 26

716 A216 2c black, bl & yel .30 .25

717 A216 6c rose & multi .30 .25

Nos. 716-717,C212 (3) .90 .75

No. 717 exists imperf.

Dominican Scout Emblem A217

Design: 5c, Scouts and flag.

1973, Dec. 7 Litho. ***Perf. 12***

Size: 35x35mm

718 A217 1c ultra & multi .30 .25

Size: 26x36mm

719 A217 5c black & multi .30 .25

Nos. 718-719,C213 (3) 1.45 1.25

Dominican Republic Boy Scouts, 50th anniv.

Sports Palace, Basketball Players A218

Design: 6c, Bicyclist and race track.

1974, Feb. 25 Litho. ***Perf. 13½***

720 A218 2c red brown & multi .25 .25

721 A218 6c yellow & multi .25 .25

Nos. 720-721,C214-C215 (4) 1.35 1.00

12th Central American and Caribbean Games, Santo Domingo, 1974.

Bell Tower, Cathedral of Santo Domingo — A219

Mater Dolorosa — A220

1974, June 27 Litho. ***Perf. 13½***

722 A219 2c multicolored .25 .25

723 A220 6c multicolored .30 .25

Nos. 722-723,C216 (3) 1.00 .75

Holy Week 1974.

Francisco del Rosario Sanchez Bridge — A221

1974, July 12 ***Perf. 12***

724 A221 6c multicolored .35 .25

See No. C217.

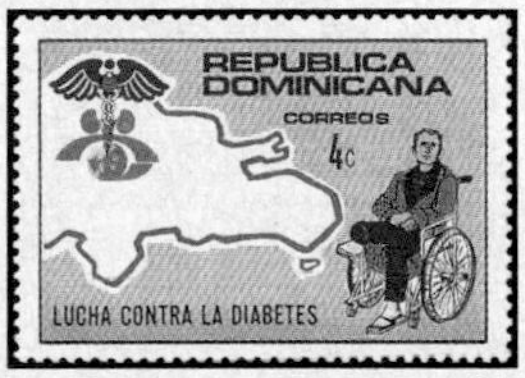

Map, Emblem and Patient — A222

Design: 5c, Map of Dominican Republic, diabetics' emblem and pancreas.

1974, Aug. 22 Litho. ***Perf. 13***

725 A222 4c blue & multi .25 .25

726 A222 5c yellow grn & multi .25 .25

Nos. 725-726,C218-C219 (4) 2.55 1.50

Fight against diabetes.

Train and UPU Emblem A223

Design: 6c, Mail coach and UPU emblem.

1974, Oct. 9 Litho. *Perf. 13½*

727 A223 2c blue & multi .60 .60
728 A223 6c brown & multi .45 .25
Nos. 727-728,C220-C221 (4) 5.05 1.95

Cent. of UPU.

Golfers — A224

Design: 2c, Championship emblem and badge of Dominican Golf Association, horiz.

1974, Oct. 24 *Perf. 13x13½, 13½x13*

729 A224 2c yellow & blk 1.00 .25
730 A224 6c blue & multi 1.25 .25
Nos. 729-730,C222-C223 (4) 3.55 1.15

World Amateur Golf Championships.

Christmas Decorations A225

Virgin and Child — A226

1974, Dec. 3 Litho. *Perf. 12*

731 A225 2c multicolored .30 .25
732 A226 6c multicolored .30 .25
Nos. 731-732,C224 (3) 1.00 .75

Christmas 1974.

Tomatoes, FAO Emblem — A227

1974, Dec. 5

733 A227 2c shown .95 .25
734 A227 3c Avocados .95 .25
735 A227 5c Coconuts .95 .25
Nos. 733-735,C225 (4) 4.35 1.00

World Food Program, 10th anniv.

Fernando A. Defillo A228

Tower, Our Lady of the Rosary Convent A229

1975, Feb. 14 Litho. *Perf. 13½x13*

736 A228 1c dull brown .25 .25
737 A228 6c dull green .25 .25

Dr. Defillo (1874-1949), physician.

1975, Mar. 26 Litho. *Perf. 13½*

Design: 2c, Jesus saying "I am the Resurrection and the Life."

738 A229 2c brown & multi .25 .25
739 A229 6c multicolored .25 .25
Nos. 738-739,C226 (3) .95 .75

Holy Week 1975.

Hands (Steel Beams) with Symbols of Agriculture, Industry A230

1975, May 19 Litho. *Perf. 10½x10*

740 A230 6c dull blue & multi .30 .25

16th Assembly of the Governors of the International Development Bank, Santo Domingo, May 1975. See No. C228.

Satellite Tracking Station — A231

1975, June 21 Litho. *Perf. 13½*

741 A231 5c multicolored .25 .25

Opening of first earth satellite tracking station in Dominican Republic. See No. C229.

Apollo A232

1975, July 24 Size: 35x25mm

742 A232 1c shown .30 .25
743 A232 4c Soyuz .30 .25
Nos. 742-743,C230 (3) 6.60 4.50

Apollo Soyuz space test project (Russo-American cooperation), launching July 15; link-up, July 17.

Father Rafael C. Castellanos A233

1975, Aug. 6 Litho. *Perf. 12*

744 A233 6c brown & buff .30 .25

Castellanos (1875-1934), 1st Apostolic Administrator in Dominican Republic.

Women and Men Around IWY Emblem — A234

1975, Aug. 6 *Perf. 13*

745 A234 3c orange & multi .25 .25

International Women's Year 1975.

Guacanagarix A235

Indian Chiefs: 2c, Guarionex. 3c, Caonabo. 4c, Bohechio. 5c, Cayacoa. 6c, Anacona (woman). 9c, Hatuey.

1975, Sept. 27 Litho. *Perf. 12*

746 A235 1c yellow & multi .25 .25
747 A235 2c salmon & multi .25 .25
748 A235 3c violet bl & multi .25 .25
749 A235 4c green & multi .30 .25
750 A235 5c blue & multi .30 .25
751 A235 6c violet & multi .30 .25
752 A235 9c rose & multi .45 .25
Nos. 746-752,C231-C233 (10) 3.40 2.60

Basketball A236

Design: 6c, Baseball and Games' emblem.

1975, Oct. 24 Litho. *Perf. 12*

753 A236 2c pink & multi .30 .25
754 A236 6c orange & multi .30 .25
Nos. 753-754,C234-C235 (4) 1.45 1.05

7th Pan-American Games, Mexico City, Oct. 13-26.

Carolers — A237

6c, Dominican nativity with farmers & shepherds.

1975, Dec. 12 Litho. *Perf. 13x13½*

755 A237 2c yellow & multi .30 .25
756 A237 6c blue & multi .30 .25
Nos. 755-756,C236 (3) .90 .75

Christmas 1975.

Abudefdul Marginatus — A238

1976, Jan. 23 Litho. *Perf. 13*

757 A238 10c shown .65 .25
758 A238 10c Doncella .65 .25
759 A238 10c Carajuelo .65 .25
760 A238 10c Reina de los Angeles .65 .25
761 A238 10c Pargo Colorado .65 .25
a. Strip of 5, #757-761 5.75 5.75

Ascension, by J. Priego — A239

2c, Mary Magdalene, by Enrique Godoy.

1976, Apr. 14 Litho. *Perf. 13½*

762 A239 2c blue & multi .30 .25
763 A239 6c yellow & multi .30 .25
Nos. 762-763,C238 (3) 1.05 .80

Holy Week 1976.

"Separacion Dominicana" and Adm. Cambiaso A240

1976, Apr. 15 *Perf. 13½x13*

764 A240 20c multicolored 1.25 .45

Naval Battle off Tortuga, Apr. 15, 1844.

Maps of US and Dominican Republic — A241

Design: 9c, Maps within cogwheels.

1976, May 29 Litho. *Perf. 13½*

765 A241 6c violet bl & multi .30 .25
766 A241 9c violet bl & multi .30 .25
Nos. 765-766,C239-C240 (4) 2.65 2.00

American Bicentennial.

Flags of Dominican Republic and Spain A242

1976, May 31

767 A242 6c multicolored .55 .25

Visit of King Juan Carlos I and Queen Sofia of Spain. See No. C241.

Various Telephones A243

1976, July 15 *Perf. 12x12½*

768 A243 6c multicolored .30 .25

Cent. of 1st telephone call by Alexander Graham Bell, Mar. 10, 1876. See No. C242.

Vision of Duarte, by Luis Desangles — A244

Juan Pablo Duarte, by Rhadames Mejia — A245

1976, July 20 Litho. *Perf. 13x13½*

769 A244 2c multicolored .25 .25

Perf. 13½

770 A245 6c multicolored .25 .25

Nos. 769-770,C243-C244 (4) 2.45 1.85

Juan Pablo Duarte, liberation hero, death centenary.

Fire Hydrant — A246

Design: 6c, Firemen's emblem.

1976, Sept. 13 Litho. *Perf. 12*

771 A246 4c multicolored .25 .25

772 A246 6c multicolored .25 .25

Nos. 771-772,C245 (3) .95 .80

Honoring firemen. Nos. 771-772 inscribed "Corrreos."

Radio and Atom Symbols A247

1976, Oct. 8 Litho. *Perf. 13½*

773 A247 6c red & black .25 .25

Dominican Radio Club, 50th anniv. See No. C246.

Spain, Central and South America, Galleon A248

1976, Oct. 22 Litho. *Perf. 13½*

774 A248 6c multicolored .30 .25

Spanish heritage. See No. C247.

Boxing and Montreal Emblem A249

Design: 3c, Weight lifting.

1976, Oct. 22 *Perf. 12*

775 A249 2c blue & multi .25 .25

776 A249 3c multicolored .25 .25

Nos. 775-776,C248-C249 (4) 2.20 1.50

21st Olympic Games, Montreal, Canada, July 17-Aug. 1.

Virgin and Child — A250

Three Kings — A251

1976, Dec. 8 Litho. *Perf. 13½*

777 A250 2c multicolored .30 .25

778 A251 6c multicolored .30 .25

Nos. 777-778,C250 (3) 1.05 .80

Christmas 1976.

Cable Car and Beach Scenes A252

1977, Jan. 7

779 A252 6c multicolored .25 .25

Nos. 779,C251-C253 (4) 1.60 1.20

Tourist publicity.

Championship Emblem — A253

1977, Mar. 4 Litho. *Perf. 13½*

780 A253 3c rose & multi .25 .25

781 A253 5c yellow & multi .25 .25

Nos. 780-781,C254-C255 (4) 2.20 1.50

10th Central American and Caribbean Children's and Young People's Swimming Championships, Santo Domingo.

Christ Carrying Cross — A254

Design: 6c, Head with crown of thorns.

1977, Apr. 18 Litho. *Perf. 13½x13*

782 A254 2c multicolored .30 .25

783 A254 6c black & rose .30 .25

Nos. 782-783,C256 (3) 1.05 .75

Holy Week 1977.

Doves, Lions Emblem A255

1977, May 6 *Perf. 13½x13*

784 A255 2c lt blue & multi .25 .25

785 A255 6c salmon & multi .25 .25

Nos. 784-785,C257 (3) .80 .75

12th annual Dominican Republic Lions Convention.

Battle Scene A256

1977, June 15 Litho. *Perf. 13x13½*

786 A256 20c multicolored 1.20 .35

Dominican Navy.

Water Lily — A257

National Botanical Garden: 4c, "Flor de Mayo" (orchid). 6c, Sebesten.

1977, Aug. 19 Litho. *Perf. 12*

787 A257 2c multicolored .40 .25

788 A257 4c multicolored .40 .25

789 A257 6c multicolored .45 .25

Nos. 787-789,C259-C260 (5) 3.30 2.10

Chart and Computers — A258

1977, Nov. 30 Litho. *Perf. 13*

790 A258 6c multicolored .30 .25

7th Interamerican Statistics Conf. See No. C261.

Solenodon Paradoxus — A259

Design: 20c, Iguana and Congress emblem.

1977, Dec. 29 Litho. *Perf. 13*

791 A259 6c multicolored 2.10 .25

792 A259 20c multicolored 3.75 .30

Nos. 791-792,C262-C263 (4) 12.85 1.35

8th Pan-American Veterinary and Zoo-technical Congress.

Main Gate, Casa del Cordon, 1503 — A260

Crown of Thorns, Tools at the Cross — A261

1978, Jan. 19 *Perf. 13x13½*

Size: 26x36mm

793 A260 6c multicolored .30 .25

Spanish heritage. See No. C264.

1978, Mar. 21 Litho. *Perf. 12*

6c, Head of Jesus with crown of thorns.

Size: 22x33mm

794 A261 2c multicolored .30 .25

795 A261 6c slate .35 .25

Nos. 794-795,C265-C266 (4) 1.50 1.05

Holy Week 1978.

Cardinal Octavio A. Beras Rojas — A262

1978, May 5 Litho. *Perf. 13*

796 A262 6c multicolored .25 .25

First Cardinal from Dominican Republic, consecrated May 24, 1976. See No. C268.

Pres. Manuel de Troncoso — A263

1978, June 12 Litho. *Perf. 13½*

797 A263 2c black, rose & brn .30 .25

798 A263 6c black, gray & brn .40 .25

Manuel de Jesus Troncoso de la Concha (1878-1955), pres. of Dominican Republic, 1940-42.

Father Juan N. Zegri y Moreno — A264

1978, July 11 Litho. ***Perf. 13x13½***
799 A264 6c multicolored .25 .25

Congregation of the Merciful Sisters of Charity, centenary. See No. C273.

Boxing and Games' Emblem A265

1978, July 21 ***Perf. 12***
800 A265 2c shown .30 .25
801 A265 6c Weight lifting .35 .25
Nos. 800-801,C274-C275 (4) 1.50 1.00

13th Central American & Caribbean Games, Medellin, Colombia.

Sun over Landscape A266

Design: 6c, Sun over beach and boat.

1978, Sept. 12 Litho. ***Perf. 12***
802 A266 2c multicolored .35 .25
803 A266 6c multicolored .35 .25
Nos. 802-803,C280-C281 (4) 1.70 1.00

Tourist publicity.

Ships of Columbus, Map of Dominican Republic — A267

1978, Oct. 12 Litho. ***Perf. 13½***
804 A267 2c multicolored .25 .25

Spanish heritage. See No. C282.

Dove, Lamp, Poinsettia A268

Design: 6c, Dominican family and star, vert.

1978, Dec. 5 Litho. ***Perf. 12***
805 A268 2c multicolored .35 .25
806 A268 6c multicolored .45 .25
Nos. 805-806,C284 (3) 1.20 .80

Christmas 1978.

Starving Child, IYC Emblem — A269

1979, Feb. 26 Litho. ***Perf. 12***
807 A269 2c orange & black .25 .25
Nos. 807,C287-C289 (4) 2.55 1.85

Intl. Year of the Child.

Crucifixion A270

Design: 3c, Jesus carrying cross, horiz.

1979, Apr. 9 Litho. ***Perf. 13½***
808 A270 2c multicolored .30 .25
809 A270 3c multicolored .45 .25
Nos. 808-809,C290 (3) 2.50 1.75

Holy Week.

Stigmaphyllon Periplocifolium — A271

1979, May 17 Litho. ***Perf. 12***
810 A271 50c multicolored 1.40 .50
Nos. 810,C293-C295 (4) 3.15 1.80

Dr. Rafael M. Moscoso National Botanical Garden.

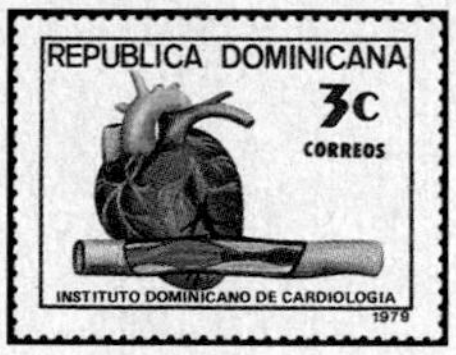

Heart, Diseased Blood Vessel A272

Design: 1p, Cardiology Institute and heart.

1979, June 2 Litho. ***Perf. 13½***
811 A272 3c multicolored .25 .25
812 A272 1p multicolored 2.40 .75
Nos. 811-812,C296 (3) 3.25 1.40

Dominican Cardiology Institute.

Baseball, Games' Emblem A273

3c, Bicycling and Games' emblem, vert.

1979, June 20
813 A273 2c multicolored .25 .25
814 A273 3c multicolored .25 .25
Nos. 813-814,C297 (3) .95 .80

8th Pan American Games, Puerto Rico, June 30-July 15.

Soccer — A274

Design: 25c, Swimming, horiz.

1979, Aug. 9 Litho. ***Perf. 12***
815 A274 2c multicolored .25 .25
816 A274 25c multicolored .35 .25
Nos. 815-816,C298 (3) 1.05 .80

Third National Games.

Thomas A. Edison — A275

1979, Aug. 27 ***Perf. 13½***
817 A275 25c multicolored .85 .45

Cent. of invention of electric light. See No. C300.

Hand Holding Electric Plug A276

Design: 6c, Filling automobile gas tank.

1979, Aug. 30
818 A276 2c multicolored .25 .25
819 A276 6c multicolored .30 .25

Energy conservation.

Parrot A277

Birds: 6c, Temnotrogon roseigaster.

1979, Sept. 12 Litho. ***Perf. 12***
820 A277 2c multicolored 2.10 .25
821 A277 6c multicolored 2.10 .25
Nos. 820-821,C301-C303 (5) 20.20 2.10

A278

Lions Emblem, Map of Dominican Republic.

1979, Nov. 13 Litho. ***Perf. 12***
822 A278 20c multicolored .65 .40

Lions International Club of Dominican Republic, 15th anniversary. See No. C304.

A279

1979, Dec. 18 Litho. ***Perf. 12***
823 A279 2c Holy Family .25 .25

Christmas 1979. See No. C305.

A280

Design: Jesus Carrying Cross.

1980, Mar. 27 Litho. ***Perf. 12***
824 A280 3c multicolored .25 .25
Nos. 824,C306-C307 (3) .95 .80

Holy Week.

A281

1980, May 15 Litho. ***Perf. 13½***
825 A281 1c shown .45 .25
826 A281 2c Coffee .45 .25
827 A281 3c Plantain .45 .25
828 A281 4c Sugar cane .45 .25
829 A281 5c Corn .45 .25
Nos. 825-829 (5) 2.25 1.25

Cacao Harvest (Agriculture Year)

Cotuf Gold Mine, Pueblo Viejo, Flag of Dominican Republic A282

1980, July 8 Litho. ***Perf. 13½***
830 A282 6c multicolored .30 .25
Nos. 830,C310-C311 (3) 2.20 1.15

Nationalization of gold mining.

Blind Man's Buff A283

1980, July 21 ***Perf. 12***
831 A283 3c shown .25 .25
832 A283 4c Marbles .25 .25
833 A283 5c Drawing in sand .30 .25
834 A283 6c Hopscotch .30 .25
Nos. 831-834 (4) 1.10 1.00

Iguana
A284

1980, Aug. 30 Litho. *Perf. 12*
835 A284 20c multicolored 2.75 .45
Nos. 835,C314-C317 (5) 16.15 2.80

Dance, by Jaime Colson
A285

Perf. 13x13½, 13½x13
1980, Sept. 23 Litho.
836 A285 3c *shown* .25 .25
837 A285 50c *Woman, by Gilberto Hernandez Ortega*, vert. 1.30 .90
Nos. 836-837,C318-C319 (4) 2.75 2.00

Three Kings — A286

1980, Dec. 5 Litho. *Perf. 13½*
838 A286 3c shown .25 .25
839 A286 6c Carolers .25 .25
Nos. 838-839,C327 (3) .95 .80

Christmas 1980.

Salcedo Province Cent. — A287

1981, Jan. 14 Litho. *Perf. 13½*
840 A287 6c multicolored .25 .25

See No. C328.

Juan Pablo Duarte, Liberation Hero, 105th Anniv. of Death — A288

1981, Feb. 6 Litho. *Perf. 12*
841 A288 2c sepia & deep bister .30 .25

Gymnast — A289

1981, Mar. 31 Litho. *Perf. 13½*
842 A289 1c shown .30 .25
843 A289 2c Running .30 .25
844 A289 3c Pole vault .30 .25
845 A289 6c Boxing .45 .25
Nos. 842-845,C331 (5) 1.90 1.35

5th National Games.

Mother Mazzarello
A290

1981, Apr. 14 *Perf. 12*
846 A290 6c multicolored .30 .25

Mother Maria Mazzarello (1837-1881), founder of Daughters of Mary.

A291

1981, May 18 Litho. *Perf. 13½*
847 A291 6c gray vlo & lt gray .30 .25

Pedro Henriquez Urena, Historian (1884-1946)

A292

1981, June 30 Litho. *Perf. 12*
848 A292 2c shown .30 .25
849 A292 6c River, forest .30 .25

Forest conservation.

Family in House, Census Emblem
A293

1981, Aug. 14 Litho. *Perf. 12*
850 A293 3c shown .25 .25
851 A293 6c Farmer .30 .25

1981 natl. population and housing census.

A294

1981, Dec. 23 Litho. *Perf. 13½*
852 A294 2c Bells .25 .25
853 A294 3c Poinsettia .25 .25
Nos. 852-853,C353 (3) 1.25 .95

Christmas.

A295

1982, Jan. 29 Litho. *Perf. 13½*
854 A295 2c Juan Pablo Duarte .70 .25

National Elections
A296

Designs: Voters casting votes. 3c, 6c vert.

1982, Mar. 30 Litho. *Perf. 13½*
855 A296 2c multicolored .25 .25
856 A296 3c multicolored .25 .25
857 A296 6c multicolored .30 .25
Nos. 855-857 (3) .80 .75

A297

Energy Conservation: Various forms of energy.

1982, May 10 Litho. *Perf. 12*
858 A297 1c multicolored .25 .25
859 A297 2c multicolored .25 .25
860 A297 3c multicolored .25 .25
861 A297 4c multicolored .35 .25
862 A297 5c multicolored .35 .25
863 A297 6c multicolored .35 .25
Nos. 858-863 (6) 1.80 1.50

A298

1982, Aug. 2 *Perf. 12x12½*
864 A298 6c multicolored .25 .25

Emilio Prud'Homme (1856-1932), composer.

Pres. Antonio Guzman Fernandez (1911-1982)
A299

1982, Aug. 4 *Perf. 13x13½*
865 A299 6c multicolored .25 .25

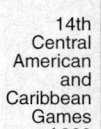

14th Central American and Caribbean Games
A300

1982, Aug. 13 *Perf. 12, Imperf.*
866 A300 3c Baseball .50 .25

See Nos. C368-C370.

San Pedro de Macoris Province Centenary — A301

1982, Aug. 26 *Perf. 13*
867 A301 1c Wagon .30 .25
868 A301 2c Stained-glass window .30 .25
869 A301 5c Views .40 .25
Nos. 867-869,C375 (4) 1.45 1.05

Size of 2c, 25x35mm.

St. Teresa of Jesus of Avila (1515-1582)
A302

1982, Nov. 17 Litho. *Perf. 13½*
870 A302 6c multicolored .45 .25

Christmas 1982 — A303

Various Christmas balls.

1982, Dec. 8
871 A303 6c multicolored .30 .25

See No. C380.

Environmental Protection
A304

1982, Dec. 15 *Perf. 12*
872 A304 2c Bird .25 .25
873 A304 3c Water .25 .25
874 A304 6c Forest .25 .25
875 A304 20c Fish .75 .35
Nos. 872-875 (4) 1.50 1.10

Natl. Literacy Campaign A305

1983, Mar. 9 Litho. *Perf. 13½*

876 A305 2c Vowels on blackboard	.25	.25
877 A305 3c Writing, reading	.25	.25
878 A305 6c Children, pencil	.35	.25
Nos. 876-878 (3)	.85	.75

A306

5c, similar arms, incorporating stylized centenary monument.

1983, Apr. 4 *Perf. 12*

879 A306 1c multicolored	.25	.25
880 A306 5c multicolored	.30	.25

Mao City centenary.

A307

Dominican Historians: 2c, Antonio del Monte y Tejada (1780-1861). 3c, Manuel Ubaldo Gomez (1857-1941). 5c, Emiliano Tejera (1841-1923). 6c, Bernardo Pichardo (1877-1924). 7c, Americo Lugo (1870-1952). 10c, José Gabriel Garcia (1834-1910). 7c, 10c airmail.

1983, Apr. 25 Litho. *Perf. 12*

881 A307 2c multicolored	.25	.25
882 A307 3c multicolored	.25	.25
883 A307 5c multicolored	.25	.25
884 A307 6c multicolored	.25	.25
885 A307 7c multicolored	.30	.25
886 A307 10c multicolored	.45	.30
Nos. 881-886 (6)	1.75	1.55

National Anthem, 100th Anniv. A308

Emilio Prud'Homme, & Jose Reyes, composer.

1983, Sept. 13 Litho. *Perf. 13½*

887 A308 6c copper red & blk	.30	.25

Free Masons, 125th Anniv. — A309

1983, Oct. 24 Litho. *Perf. 12*

888 A309 4c Emblem	.25	.25

Church of Our Lady of Regla, 300th Anniv. — A310

1983, Nov. 5 *Perf. 13½*

889 A310 3c Church	.30	.25
890 A310 6c Statue	.30	.25

450th Anniv. of Monte Cristi Province — A311

1983, Nov. 25 *Perf. 12*

891 A311 1c Tower	.30	.25
892 A311 2c Arms	.30	.25
893 A311 5c Cuban independence site, horiz.	.30	.25
894 A311 7c Workers, horiz.	.30	.25
Nos. 891-894 (4)	1.20	1.00

6th Natl. Games — A312

1983, Dec. 9

895 A312 6c Bicycling, boxing, baseball	.25	.25
896 A312 10c Runner, weight lifting, swimming	.30	.25

10c airmail.

Restoration of the Republic, 120th Anniv. — A313

1983, Dec. 30 Litho. *Perf. 13½*

897 A313 1c Capotillo Heroes Monument	.30	.25

140th Anniv. of Independence — A314

Designs: 6c, Matia Ramon Mella (Patriot), flag. 25c, Mella's Blunderbuss rifle, Gate of Deliverance (independence deolaration site).

1984, Feb. 24 Litho. *Perf. 13½*

898 A314 6c multicolored	.30	.25
899 A314 25c multicolored	.90	.35

Heriberto Pieter (1884-1972), Physician, First Negro Graduate — A315

1984, Mar. 16

900 A315 3c multicolored	.35	.25

Battle of Barranquita, 67th Anniv. — A316

1983, Dec. 30 *Perf. 12*

901 A316 5c multicolored	.30	.25

Battle of Santiago, 140th Anniv. A317

1984, Mar. 29 *Perf. 13½*

902 A317 7c multicolored	.35	.25

Coast Guard Ship DC-1, 1934 A318

1984, Apr. 13 Litho.

903 A318 10c multicolored	.45	.25

Navy Day and 140th anniv. of Battle of Tortuguero.

Birth Centenary of Pedro Henriquez Urena — A319

1984, June 29 Litho. *Perf. 12*

904 A319 7c Salome Urena	.30	.25
905 A319 10c Text	.35	.25
906 A319 22c Urena	.40	.25
Nos. 904-906 (3)	1.05	.75

Monument to Heroes of June 1959 A320

1984, June 20 *Perf. 13½*

907 A320 6c silver & blue	.40	.25

Costal towns of Constanza, Maimon and Estero Hondo - sites of attempted overthrow of Rafael Trujillo, 25th anniv.

1984 Summer Olympics A321

1984, Aug. 1

908 A321 1p Hurdles	2.10	1.90
909 A321 1p Weightlifting	2.10	1.90
910 A321 1p Boxing	2.10	1.90
911 A321 1p Baseball	2.10	1.90
a. Block of 4, #908-911	15.00	15.00
Nos. 908-911 (4)	8.40	7.60

Protection of Fauna — A322

1984, Oct. 3 Litho. *Perf. 12*

912 A322 10c Owl	3.00	.25
913 A322 15c Flamingo	3.75	.35
914 A322 25c Wild Pig	5.00	.50
915 A322 35c Solenodon	6.75	.70
Nos. 912-915 (4)	18.50	1.80

500th Anniv. of Discovery of America A323

1984, Oct. 10 Litho. *Perf. 13½x13*

916 A323 10c Landing on Hispaniola	.25	.25
917 A323 35c Destruction of Ft. Navidad	.65	.35
918 A323 65c First Mass in America	1.00	.80
919 A323 1p Battle of Santo Cerro	1.60	1.10
Nos. 916-919 (4)	3.50	2.50

Visit of Pope John Paul II — A324

1984, Oct. 11 Litho. *Perf. 13x13½*

920 Block of 4	9.00	9.00
a. A324 75c shown	1.90	1.90
b. A324 75c Pope, map of Caribbean	1.90	1.90
c. A324 75c Pope, globe	1.90	1.90
d. A324 75c Bishop's crozier	1.90	1.90

150th Anniv. of Birth of Maximo Gomez (1986) A325

1984, Dec. 6 **Litho.** ***Perf. 13½***
921 A325 10c Gomez on horseback .25 .25
922 A325 20c Maximo Gomez .35 .25

Christmas 1984 A326

Perf. 13½x13, 13x13½
1984, Dec. 14 **Litho.**
923 A326 5c multicolored .25 .25
924 A326 10c multicolored, vert. .30 .25

Sacrifice of the Goat, by Eligio Pichardo A327

Paintings and sculpture: 10c, The Pumpkin Sellers, by Gaspar Mario Cruz; 25c, The Market, by Celeste Woss y Gil; 50c, Horses in the Rain, by Dario Suro.

1984, Dec. 19 **Litho.** ***Perf. 13½***
925 A327 5c multi .50 .25
926 A327 10c multi, vert. .50 .25
927 A327 25c multi .75 .45
928 A327 50c multi 1.40 .65
Nos. 925-928 (4) 3.15 1.60

Day of Our Lady of Altagracia A328

1985, Jan. 21
929 A328 5c Old church at Higuey, 1572 .30 .25
930 A328 10c Our Lady of Altagracia 1514, vert. .35 .25
931 A328 25c Basilica of the Protector, Higuey 1971, vert. .55 .35
Nos. 929-931 (3) 1.20 .85

Independence, 141st Anniv. — A329

Painting: The Fathers of Our Country (Duarte, Sanchez and Mella).

1985, Mar. 8 ***Perf. 12½***
932 A329 5c multicolored .25 .25
933 A329 10c multicolored .30 .25
934 A329 25c multicolored .55 .25
Nos. 932-934 (3) 1.10 .75

Battle of Azua, 141st Anniv. A330

1985, Apr. 8 **Litho.** ***Perf. 13½***
935 A330 10c Gen. Antonio Duverge, Statue .45 .25

A331

1985, Apr. 15 **Litho.**
936 A331 25c Santo Domingo Lighthouse, 1853 .50 .25

Battle of Tortuguero, 141st anniv.

A332

1985, Apr. 15 **Litho.** ***Perf. 12***
937 A332 35c multicolored 1.10 .45

American Airforces Cooperation System, 25th anniv.

A333

1985, May 24 **Litho.** ***Perf. 13½***
938 A333 10c Don Carlos M. Rojas, 1st gov. .45 .30

Espaillat Province cent.

A334

1985, July 5 **Litho.** ***Perf. 12***
939 A334 5c Table tennis .25 .25
940 A334 10c Walking race .35 .30

MOCA '85, 7th Natl. Games.

Intl. Youth Year A335

1985, July 29 ***Perf. 13½***
941 A335 5c Youth .35 .25
942 A335 25c The Haitises 1.10 .45
943 A335 35c Mt. Duarte summit 1.25 .50
944 A335 2p Mt. Duarte 7.25 2.75
Nos. 941-944 (4) 9.95 3.95

Interamerican Development Bank, 25th Anniv. — A336

10c, Haina Harbor. 25c, Map of development sites. 1p, Tavera-Bao-Lopez Hydroelectric Complex.

1985, Aug. 23
945 A336 10c multicolored .25 .25
946 A336 25c multicolored .75 .40
947 A336 1p multicolored 2.75 1.75
Nos. 945-947 (3) 3.75 2.40

Intl. Decade for Women — A337

Design: Evangelina Rodriguez (1879-1947), first Dominican woman doctor.

1985, Sept. 26
948 A337 10c multicolored .45 .25

15th Central American and Caribbean Games, Santiago — A338

1985, Oct. 9 ***Perf. 12***
949 A338 5c multicolored .45 .25
950 A338 25c multicolored 1.20 .45

4th Adm. Christopher Columbus Regatta, Casa de Espana A339

Designs: 50c, Founding of Santo Domingo, 1496. 65c, Chapel of Our Lady of the Rosary, 1496, Santo Domingo. 1p, Columbus, American Indian and old Spanish coat of arms.

1985, Oct. 10 ***Perf. 13½***
951 A339 35c multicolored 1.40 .85
952 A339 50c multicolored 1.80 1.20
953 A339 65c multicolored 2.50 1.50
954 A339 1p multicolored 4.50 2.40
Nos. 951-954 (4) 10.20 5.95

Discovery of America, 500th anniv. (in 1992).

Cacique Enriquillo — A340

Designs: 5c, Enriquillo in the Bahuroco Mountains, mural detail.

1985, Oct. 31
955 A340 5c multicolored .25 .25
956 A340 10c multicolored .45 .25

Enriquillo (d. 1536), leader of revolution against Spain. Size of No. 955: 47x33mm.

Archbishop Fernando Arturo de Merino — A341

1985, Dec. 3 ***Perf. 12***
957 A341 25c multicolored .55 .40

Cent. of holy orders granted to Merino (1833-1906), pres. of the republic 1880-82.

Mirabal Sisters, Political Martyrs 1960 A342

1985, Dec. 18 ***Perf. 13½***
958 A342 10c multicolored .35 .25

Christmas A343

1985, Dec. 18
959 A343 10c multicolored .30 .25
960 A343 25c multicolored .75 .35

Day of Independence, Feb. 27 — A344

Design: Mausoleum of founding fathers Duarte, Sanchez and Mella.

1986, Feb. 26 **Litho.** ***Perf. 13½***
961 A344 5c multicolored .25 .25
962 A344 10c multicolored .30 .25

Holy Week A345

Colonial churches.

1986, Apr. 10
963 A345 5c San Miguel .45 .25
964 A345 5c San Andres .45 .25
965 A345 10c Santa Barbara .50 .25
966 A345 10c San Lazaro .50 .25
967 A345 10c San Carlos .50 .25
Nos. 963-967 (5) 2.40 1.25

Navy Day A346

Design: Juan Bautista Cambiaso, Juan Bautista Maggiolo and Juan Alejandro Acosta, 1844 independence battle heroes.

1986, Apr. 15

968 A346 10c multicolored .35 .25

Natl. Elections — A347

1986, Apr. 29

969 A347 5c Voters, map .25 .25
970 A347 10c Ballot box .30 .25

Natl. Postal Institute Inauguration A348

1986, June 10

971 A348 10c gold, blue & red .35 .25
972 A348 25c silver, blue & red .90 .30
973 A348 50c black, blue & red 1.75 .65
Nos. 971-973 (3) 3.00 1.20

Central America and Caribbean Games, Santiago — A349

1986, July 17 Litho. *Perf. 13½*

974 A349 10c Weight lifting .35 .25
975 A349 25c Gymnastics .75 .30
976 A349 35c Diving 1.10 .45
977 A349 50c Equestrian 1.40 .70
Nos. 974-977 (4) 3.60 1.70

Historians A350

Designs: 5c, Ercilia Pepin (b. 1886), vert. 10c, Ramon Emilio Jimenez (b. 1886) and Victor Garrido (1886-1972).

1986, Aug. 1 Litho. *Perf. 13½*

978 A350 5c silver & dull brn .25 .25
979 A350 10c silver & dull brn .30 .25

A351

A352

Discovery of America, 500th Anniv. (in 1992) — A353

Designs: 25c, Yachts racing, 5th Adm. Christopher Columbus Regatta, Casa de Espana. 50c, Columbus founding La Isabela City. 65c, Exploration of the hidalgos. 1p, Columbus returning to the Court of Ferdinand and Isabella. 1.50p, Emblems.

1986, Oct. 10 Litho. *Perf. 13½*

980 A351 25c multicolored .65 .35
981 A352 50c multicolored 1.40 .55
982 A352 65c multicolored 1.90 .95
983 A352 1p multicolored 3.00 1.30

Textured Paper

Size: 86x58mm

Imperf

984 A353 1.50p multicolored 6.25 6.00
Nos. 980-984 (5) 13.20 9.15

1986 World Cup Soccer Championships, Mexico — A354

Various soccer plays.

1986, Oct. 21 *Perf. 13½*

985 A354 50c multicolored 1.40 .65
986 A354 75c multicolored 3.00 1.10

Medicinal Plants — A355

1986, Dec. 5

987 A355 5c Zea mays .25 .25
988 A355 10c Bixa orellana .25 .25
989 A355 25c Momordica charantia .65 .25
990 A355 50c Annona muricata 1.40 .55
Nos. 987-990 (4) 2.55 1.30

Second Caribbean Pharmacopeia Seminar.

Christmas A356

1986, Dec. 19

991 A356 5c Urban scene .50 .25
992 A356 25c Rural scene 1.30 .35

A357

1986, Dec. 31 Litho. *Perf. 13½*

993 A357 10c shown .40 .25
994 A357 25c Portrait, c. 1900 .85 .40

Maximo Gomez (1836-1905), revolutionary, statesman.

A358

1987, Mar. 30 Litho. *Perf. 13½*

995 A358 50c brt blue, blk & red 1.40 .65

16th Pan American Ophthalmological Conf., Apr. 5-10.

A359

Stained-glass window, San Juan Bosco church, Santo Domingo: Ascension of Christ to Heaven.

1987, May 28

996 A359 35c multicolored 1.40 .50

A360

Edible plants.

1987, Aug. 21

997 A360 5c Sorghum bicolor .25 .25
998 A360 25c Martanta arundinacea .60 .30
999 A360 65c Calathaea allouia 1.90 .95
1000 A360 1p Voandzeia subterranea 3.00 1.40
Nos. 997-1000 (4) 5.75 2.90

Activo 20-30 Intl., 25th Anniv. A361

1987, Aug. 26

1001 A361 35c multicolored 1.75 .50

Adm. Christopher Columbus Regatta A362

A363

Columbus Memorial, Santo Domingo — A364

1987, Oct. 14

1002 A362 50c shown 1.50 .70
1003 A363 75c shown 2.25 1.00
1004 A363 1p Building Ft. Santiago 3.00 1.30
1005 A363 1.50p Columbus imprisoned by Bombadilla 4.50 2.00

Size: 82x70mm

Imperf

1006 A364 2.50p shown 9.00 6.50
Nos. 1002-1006 (5) 20.25 11.50

Discovery of America, 500th anniv. in 1992.

A365

1987, Sept. 28

1007 A365 40c multicolored 1.10 .50

Junior Olympics, La Vega, 50th anniv.

A366

Historians and authors: 10c, Jose Antonio Hungria. 25c, Joaquin Sergio Inchaustegui.

1987, Nov. 10 Litho. *Perf. 13½*

1008 A366 10c buff & brown .25 .25
1009 A366 25c pale grn & grn .75 .25

SAN CRISTOBAL '87, 8th Natl. Games — A367

1987, Nov. 19

1010 A367 5c Baseball .65 .25
1011 A367 10c Boxing .30 .25
1012 A367 50c Judo 1.40 .70
Nos. 1010-1012 (3) 2.35 1.20

Christmas 1987
A368

1987, Dec. 9 Litho. *Perf. 13½*

1013 A368 10c Roasting pig .55 .25
1014 A368 50c Arriving at airport 1.50 .60

Fr. Xavier Billini (b. 1837) — A369

1987, Dec. 18 Litho. *Perf. 13½*

1015 A369 10c Statue .25 .25
1016 A369 25c Portrait .60 .35
1017 A369 75c Ana Hernandez de Billini, his mother 2.10 1.10
Nos. 1015-1017 (3) 2.95 1.70

Frank Feliz, Sr., and Aircraft
A370

1987, Dec. 22

1018 A370 25c shown .60 .25

Size: 86x106mm

Imperf

1019 A370 2p No. C30, map 11.00 6.50

Pan-American goodwill flight to South American countries by the planes Colon, Pinta, Nina and Santa Maria, 50th anniv.

Flora
A371

1988, Feb. 3 Litho. *Perf. 13½*

1020 A371 50c Bromelia pinguin 1.80 .70
1021 A371 50c Tillandsia fasciculata 1.80 .70
1022 A371 50c Tillandsia hotteana, vert. 1.80 .70
1023 A371 50c Tillandsia compacta, vert. 1.80 .70
Nos. 1020-1023 (4) 7.20 2.80

St. John Bosco (1815-1888)
A372

1988, Feb. 23 Litho. *Perf. 13½*

1024 A372 10c shown .35 .25
1025 A372 70c Stained-glass window 2.50 .95

Dominican Rehabilitation Assoc., 25th Anniv. — A373

1988, Mar. 1

1026 A373 20c multicolored .55 .30

A374

1988, Apr. 6 Litho. *Perf. 13½*

1027 A374 20c dk red brn & lt fawn .55 .30

Dr. Manuel Emilio Perdomo (b.1886).

A375

1988, Apr. 29 Litho. *Perf. 13½*

1028 A375 20c multicolored .55 .30

Dominican College of Engineers, Architects and Surveyors (CODIA), 25th Anniv.

Independence Day, Mexico — A376

Flags and: No. 1029, Fr. Miguel Hidalgo y Costilla (1753-1811), Mexican revolutionary. No. 1030, Juan Pablo Duarte (1813-1876), father of Dominican independence.

1988, Sept. 12 Litho. *Perf. 13½*

1029 A376 50c multicolored 1.30 .65
1030 A376 50c multicolored 1.30 .65

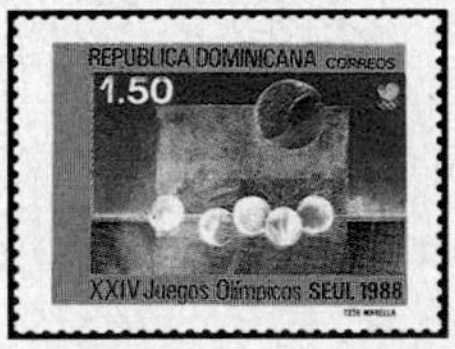

1988 Summer Olympics, Seoul
A377

1988, Sept. 21 Litho. *Perf. 13½*

1031 A377 50c Running, vert. 1.10 .50
1032 A377 70c Table tennis, vert. 1.60 .75
1033 A377 1p Judo, vert. 2.50 .95
1034 A377 1.50p Mural by Tete Marella 3.75 1.50
Nos. 1031-1034 (4) 8.95 3.70

A378

Discovery of America, 500th Anniv. (in 1992) — A379

Designs: 50c, 7th Adm. Christopher Columbus Regatta, Casa de Espana, 1988. 70c, La Concepcion Fortress, La Vega Real, 1494. 1.50p, Ft. Bonao. 2p, Nicolas de Ovando (c. 1451-1511), governor of Spanish possessions in America from 1502 to 1509. 3p, Mausoleum of Christopher Columbus, Santo Domingo Cathedral.

1988, Oct. 14 *Perf. 13½*

1035 A378 50c multicolored 1.10 .65
1036 A378 70c multicolored 1.75 .95
1037 A378 1.50p multicolored 3.50 1.90
1038 A378 2p multicolored 5.00 2.40

Size: 78x109mm

Imperf

1039 A379 3p multicolored 6.25 5.50
Nos. 1035-1039 (5) 17.60 11.40

Discovery of America, 500th anniv. (in 1992). No. 1038 inscribed "1501-1509."

Duverge Parish, Cent. — A380

1988, July 13 Litho. *Perf. 13½*

1040 A380 50c multicolored 1.25 .40

A381

Trinitarians, 150th Anniv. — A382

1988, Nov. 11

1041 A381 10c shown .45 .25
1042 A382 1p Trinitarian Plaza 2.00 .45
1043 A382 5p Independence Plaza 13.00 4.75
Nos. 1041-1043 (3) 15.45 5.45

See footnote after No. 337.

Pharmacology and Biochemistry
A383

1988, Nov. 28 Litho. *Perf. 13½*

1044 A383 1p multicolored 1.60 1.40

13th Pan American and 16th Central American Congresses.

The Holy Family, 1504, by Miguel Angel — A384

1988, Dec. 12

1045 A384 10c shown .30 .25
1046 A384 20c Stained-glass window .55 .30

Christmas.

Municipal Technical Advisory Organization (LIGA), 50th Anniv. — A385

1988, Dec. 23

1047 A385 20c multicolored .55 .35

Ana Teresa Paradas (1890-1960), 1st Female Lawyer of the Republic, 1913 — A386

1988, Dec. 26

1048 A386 20c deep claret .55 .35

French Revolution Bicent.
A387

1989, Mar. 10 Litho. *Perf. 13½*

1049 A387 3p red & violet blue 3.00 2.75

Battle of Tortuga, Apr. 15, 1844
A388

1989, Apr. 14 Litho. *Perf. 13½*

1050 A388 40c multicolored .90 .50

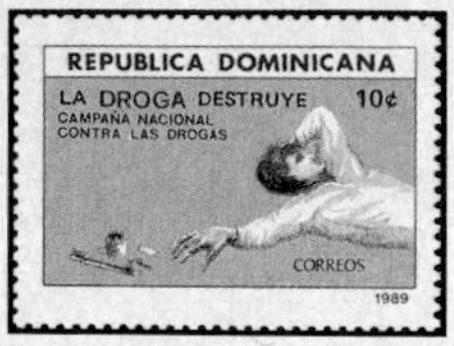

Natl. Anti-drug Campaign A389

1989, May 15

1051	A389	10c	multicolored	.30	.25
1052	A389	20c	multicolored	.35	.25
1053	A389	50c	multicolored	.60	.25
1054	A389	70c	multicolored	.85	.30
1055	A389	1p	multicolored	1.25	.45
1056	A389	1.50p	multicolored	1.75	.50
1057	A389	2p	multicolored	2.40	.70
1058	A389	5p	multicolored	6.00	1.50
1059	A389	10p	multicolored	11.50	3.75
			Nos. 1051-1059 (9)	25.00	7.95

Mother's Day A390

1989, May 30 Litho. *Perf. 13½*

1060 A390 20c multicolored .30 .25

Eugenio Maria de Hostos (b. 1839) — A391

1989, Aug. 22 Litho. *Perf. 13½*

1061 A391 20c multicolored .50 .25

Gen. Gregorio Luperon (b. 1839) — A392

1989, Aug. 28

1062 A392 20c multicolored .50 .25

Little League Baseball, 50th Anniv. A393

1989, Sept. 29

1063 A393 1p multicolored 1.75 1.00

Diabetes '89, 7th Latin American Congress A394

1989, Oct. 9 Litho. *Perf. 13½*

1064 A394 1p multicolored 1.50 .60

America Issue A395

UPAE emblem, pre-Columbian artifacts and customs: 20c, Cohoba silver statue and ritual dance. 1p, Taina mortar, pestle and family preparing cazabe.

1989, Oct. 12

1065 A395 20c multicolored .75 .25
1066 A395 1p multicolored 3.75 2.10

8th Adm. Christopher Columbus Regatta, Casa de Espana — A396

European Colonization of the Americas — A397

Designs: 70c, Fr. Pedro de Cordoba converting the Indians to Catholicism. 1p, Christopher Columbus trading with the Indians. 3p, Sermon of Pedro de Cordoba.

1989, Oct. 13

1067	A396	50c	shown	.60	.30
1068	A397	70c	shown	.75	.55
1069	A397	1p	multicolored	1.60	.75
1070	A397	3p	multicolored	3.25	2.10
			Nos. 1067-1070 (4)	6.20	3.70

Discovery of America, 500th anniv. (in 1992).

Natl. Afforestation A398

1989, Oct. 30 Litho. *Perf. 13½*

1071	A398	10c	shown	.25	.25
1072	A398	20c	Tree	.30	.25
1073	A398	50c	Forest	.90	.55
1074	A398	1p	Sapling, mature trees	1.90	1.20
			Nos. 1071-1074 (4)	3.35	2.25

9th Natl. Games, La Vega — A399

1990, Mar. 20 Litho. *Perf. 13½*

1075	A399	10c	Cycling	.25	.25
1076	A399	20c	Running	.35	.30
1077	A399	50c	Basketball	1.10	.75
			Nos. 1075-1077 (3)	1.70	1.30

Holy Week (Easter) — A400

1990, Apr. 5

1078 A400 20c shown .40 .30
1079 A400 50c Jesus carrying cross 1.10 .75

Labor Day, Cent. A401

1990, Apr. 30 Litho. *Perf. 13½*

1080 A401 1p multicolored 1.50 .65

Urban Renewal A402

1990, May 10

1081	A402	10c	shown	.25	.25
1082	A402	20c	Highway underpass	.35	.25
1083	A402	50c	Library	.70	.25
1084	A402	1p	City street	1.75	.80
			Nos. 1081-1084 (4)	3.05	1.55

No. 1084 inscribed $100 instead of $1.00.

Penny Black, 150th Anniv. — A403

1990, May 29

1085 A403 1p multicolored 2.25 1.60

Size: 62x80mm

Imperf

1086 A403 3p Sir Rowland Hill, Penny Black 6.25 6.25

Organization of American States, Cent. — A404

1990, Oct. 5 Litho. *Perf. 13½*

1087 A404 2p Flags 4.00 2.40

Children's Drawings A405

1990, Aug. 7

1088 A405 50c House of Tostado 1.10 .75
1089 A405 50c Ruins of St. Nicolas of Bari 1.10 .75

Discovery of America, 500th Anniv. (in 1992) A406

Designs: 1p, Fight at the Gulf of Arrows. 2p, Columbus talking with Guacanagari Indians. 5p, Columbus and Caonabo Indian prisoner.

1990, Oct. 12

1090	A406	1p	multicolored	2.25	1.40
1091	A406	2p	multicolored	4.50	3.00
1092	A406	5p	multicolored	11.00	7.50
			Nos. 1090-1092 (3)	17.75	11.90

9th Adm. Christopher Columbus Regatta — A407

1990, Oct. 12

1093 A407 50c multicolored 1.50 .70

America Issue A408

UPAE emblem and: 50c, Men in canoe. 3p, Man on hammock.

1990, Nov. 7 Litho. *Perf. 13½*

1094 A408 50c multicolored 1.90 .70
1095 A408 3p multicolored 8.00 4.75

A409

Discovery of Hispaniola: 50c, 1st official mass in Americas. 1p, Arms of 1st religious order in Americas. 3p, Map of island, horiz. 4p, Christopher Columbus, 1st viceroy and governor in Americas.

1991, July 17 Litho. *Perf. 13½*

1096	A409	50c	multicolored	.90	.55
1097	A409	1p	multicolored	1.75	1.20
1098	A409	3p	multicolored	4.75	2.75
1099	A409	4p	multicolored	8.25	5.00
			Nos. 1096-1099 (4)	15.65	9.50

A410

1991

1100	A410	30c	Boxing	.40	.25
1101	A410	50c	Cycling	1.25	.50
1102	A410	1p	Bowling	2.50	1.00
			Nos. 1100-1102 (3)	4.15	1.75

11th Pan American Games, Havana.

Dr. Tomas Eudoro Perez Rancier, Birth Cent. — A411

1991, July 3
1103 A411 2p yellow & black 7.50 1.90

10th Columbus Regatta, Casa de Espana — A412

Discovery of America, 500th Anniv. (in 1992) A413

Designs: 50c, Encounter of three cultures. 3p, Columbus and Dr. Alvarez Chanca caring for sick. 4p, Rebellion of Enriquillo.

1991, Oct. 15 Litho. ***Perf. 13½***
1104 A412 30c multicolored .65 .25
1105 A413 50c multicolored .90 .50
1106 A413 3p multicolored 5.50 3.00
1107 A413 4p multicolored 7.50 4.00
Nos. 1104-1107 (4) 14.55 7.75

See No. 1116.

A414

1991, Nov. 18
1108 A414 3p black & red 4.75 2.10

Cornea Bank.

A415

1991 Litho. ***Perf. 13½***
1109 A415 1p Santa Maria 3.00 .85
1110 A415 3p Christopher Columbus 7.00 3.50

America issue.

33rd Meeting of Inter-American Development Bank Governors, Santo Domingo — A416

1992 Litho. ***Perf. 13½***
1111 A416 1p multicolored 1.75 .85

A417

1992 Litho. ***Perf. 13½***
1112 A417 3p multicolored 5.25 2.75

Espanola '92 Philatelic Exposition.

A418

Valentin Salinero, Order of the Apostles founder.

1992 Litho. ***Perf. 13½***
1113 A418 1p blue & brown 1.75 .90

Order of the Apostles, cent.

Ruins of Monastery of San Francisco A419

Designs: 3p, Ruins of San Nicolas hospital, first in the Americas.

1992, July 28
1114 A419 50c multicolored .75 .50
1115 A419 3p multicolored 5.50 3.25

Type of 1991 and

A420

Designs: 50c, Racing yacht. 1p, Native women, Columbus. 2p, Natives offering Columbus tobacco. 3p, Native woman, Columbus, corn.

1992, Oct. 6 Litho. ***Perf. 13½***
1116 A412 50c multicolored .70 .35
1117 A420 1p multicolored 1.60 .75
1118 A420 2p multicolored 4.50 2.75
1119 A420 3p multicolored 6.50 3.25
Nos. 1116-1119 (4) 13.30 7.10

11th Columbus Regatta (No. 1116), Discovery of America, 500th anniv. (Nos. 1117-1119).

23rd Convention of the Alliance of Panamerican Round Tables, Santo Domingo — A421

1992, Oct. 14
1120 A421 1p multicolored 1.75 .85

Visit by Pope John Paul II A422

Cathedrals: 50c, Vega. 3p, Santo Domingo.

1992, Oct. 1 **Photo.**
1121 A422 50c multicolored 1.40 .60
1122 A422 3p multicolored 4.75 2.25

Columbus Lighthouse A423

1992, Oct. 12 **Litho.**
1123 A423 30c multicolored .90 .45
1124 A423 1p multicolored 1.90 .70

Size: 70x133mm

Imperf

1125 A423 3p Lighthouse at night 10.00 10.00

America Issue A424

Designs: 50c, First royal residence in America, Santo Domingo. 3p, First viceregal residence in America, Royal Palace, Colon.

1992, Nov. 13 Litho. ***Perf. 13½***
1126 A424 50c multicolored .75 .40
1127 A424 3p multicolored 4.00 2.50

A425

1992, Dec. 2 Litho. ***Perf. 13½***
1128 A425 30c Torch bearer .45 .25
1129 A425 1p Emblems 1.50 .80
1130 A425 4p Judo 7.00 3.50
Nos. 1128-1130 (3) 8.95 4.55

1992 Natl. Sports Games, San Juan. Secretary of Sports, Education, Exercise and Recreation (No. 1129).

Natl. Census — A426

1992-93 Litho. ***Perf. 13½***
1131 A426 50c black, buff & blue .70 .25
1132 A426 1p blk, brn & blue 1.40 .75
1133 A426 3p blk, gray & bl 4.75 2.50
1134 A426 4p blk, yel grn & bl 6.00 3.00
Nos. 1131-1134 (4) 12.85 6.50

Issued: 50c, 1p, 5/12/92; 3p, 4p, 9/9/93.

A427

1993, May 30
1135 A427 30c multicolored .45 .25
1136 A427 50c multicolored .75 .30
1137 A427 1p multicolored 1.60 .80
Nos. 1135-1137 (3) 2.80 1.35

Ema Balaguer, humanitarian.

A428

1993, Oct. 7 Litho. ***Perf. 13½***
1138 A428 30c shown .90 .45
1139 A428 1p Emblem, flags 2.75 1.00

Rotary Club of Santo Domingo, 50th anniv.

17th Central American & Caribbean Games, Ponce A429

1993, Dec. 21 Litho. ***Perf. 13½***
1140 A429 50c Tennis .65 .25
1141 A429 4p Swimming 7.00 2.00

Natl. Education Plan — A430

1993, Dec. 8
1142 A430 1.50p multicolored 2.40 .90

Spanish America — A431

1993, Dec. 28

1143 A431 50c First university lecturn .75 .25
1144 A431 3p First city coat of arms 5.25 1.50

America Issue A432

1993, Dec. 30

1145 A432 1p Aratinga chloroptera 1.25 .50
1146 A432 3p Cyclura cornuta 5.25 2.75

Opening of New Natl. Post Office A433

1993, Nov. 12

Color of Inscription

1147 A433 1p olive 1.00 .55
1148 A433 3p red 3.00 1.60
1149 A433 4p blue 3.75 1.90
1150 A433 5p green 4.75 2.25
1151 A433 10p black 9.50 4.50

Size: 105x96mm

Imperf

1152 A433 5p black 12.50 12.50
Nos. 1147-1152 (6) 34.50 23.30

First Mass in America, 500th Anniv. — A434

1994, Feb. 3 Litho. *Perf. 13½*

1153 A434 2p multicolored 3.00 1.25

5th Natl. Philatelic Exhibition A435

1994, Feb. 25

1154 A435 3p multicolored 4.50 1.60

Natl. Independence, 150th Anniv. — A436

No. 1155: a, Men with document, left side of table. b, Document on right side of table, men. c, Flag. d, Couple at window. e, Child holding material, mother making flag.

No. 1156: a, Men looking upward, shooting muskets. b, Men with guns, swords looking backwards. c, Natl. coat of arms. d, Men with guns, swords, one pointing upward. e, Men with weapons, one with flag.

10p, Three men, angel carrying musket, flag.

1994, Feb. 26

Strips of 5

1155 A436 2p #a.-e. 8.25 4.00
1156 A436 3p #a.-e. 12.50 6.00

Size: 161x104mm

Imperf

1157 A436 10p multicolored 11.50 11.50
Nos. 1155-1157 (3) 32.25 21.50

Nos. 1155a-1155b, 1155d-1155e, 1156a-1156b, 1156d-1156e have a continuous design.

Solenodon Paradoxus A437

Designs: a, Crawling on rock. b, Walking in leaves. c, Looking up. d, With food in mouth.

1994, Mar. 15 Litho. *Perf. 13½*

1158 A437 1p Block of 4, #a.-d. 9.00 5.25

World Wildlife Fund.

Battle of March 19, 150th Anniv. A438

No. 1160, Soldiers advancing uphill toward fort.

1994

1159 A438 2p multicolored 3.00 1.50
1160 A438 2p multicolored 3.00 1.50

Issued: No. 1159, Mar. 18; No. 1160, Mar. 29.

Virgin of Amparo — A439

1994, Apr. 15 Litho. *Perf. 13½*

1161 A439 3p multicolored 4.50 1.75

Battle of Puerto Tortuguero, 150th anniv.

Natl. Elections, May 16 — A440

1994, Apr. 4

1162 A440 2p multicolored 3.00 1.50

1994 World Cup Soccer Championships, US — A441

1994, June 24 Litho. *Perf. 13½*

1163 A441 4p multicolored 5.00 2.25
1164 A441 6p multicolored 7.00 3.25

Ema Balaguer City of Children A442

1994, July 20 Litho. *Perf. 13½*

1165 A442 1p magenta & brown 2.75 .60

Stamp Day A443

1994, Oct. 18 Litho. *Perf. 13½*

1166 A443 5p Type A3 7.75 3.00

America Issue — A444

1994, Oct. 28

1167 A444 2p Pony Express 3.00 1.50
1168 A444 6p Sailing ship 10.00 4.00

Province of LaVega, 500th Anniv. A445

3p, Ruins of San Francisco Monastery.

1994, Nov. 24 Litho. *Perf. 13½*

1169 A445 3p multicolored 7.25 1.60

First Church the New World, 500th Anniv. — A446

a, "La Isabela," cradle of evangelization. b, "Temple of the Americas," first mission.

1994, Dec. 5 *Perf. 11½*

1170 A446 3p Pair, #a.-b. 10.00 3.00

A447

1994, Nov. 6 *Perf. 13½*

1171 A447 3p multicolored 5.00 1.60

Constitution, 150th anniv.

A448

Christmas: 2p, Holy family's flight into Egypt. 3p, Modern family of three standing at river's edge.

1994, Nov. 18

1172 A448 2p multicolored 3.50 1.25
1173 A448 3p multicolored 4.75 1.60

Intl. Year of the Family.

Firsts in America — A449

1994, Dec. 21 Litho. *Perf. 13½*

1174 A449 2p Circulating coins 3.50 .75
1175 A449 5p Sermon for Justice 7.75 2.00

Snakes A450

No. 1176, Hypsirhynchus ferox. No. 1177, Antillophis parvifrons. No. 1178, Uromacer catesbyi. No. 1179, Epicrates striatus.

1994, Dec. 26

1176 A450 2p multicolored 3.00 1.00
1177 A450 2p multicolored 3.00 1.00
a. Pair, #1176-1177 6.00 5.50
1178 A450 2p multicolored 3.00 1.00
1179 A450 2p multicolored 3.00 1.00
a. Pair, #1178-1179 6.00 5.50

Nos. 1177a, 1179a are continuous designs.

Pan American Games, Mar Del Plata, Argentina A451

1995, Apr. 20 *Perf. 13½*

1180 A451 4p Tae kwon do 4.75 1.75
1181 A451 13p Tennis 14.50 5.00

FAO, 50th Anniv. — A452

1995, Apr. 21 Litho. *Perf. 11½*

1182 A452 4p multicolored 4.50 2.25

A453

Designs: 2p, Jose Marti, Maximo Gomez. 3p, Marti. 4p, Marti seated at desk, Gomez.

1995, May 19 Litho. *Perf. 13½*

1183 A453 2p multicolored 1.90 .75
1184 A453 3p multicolored 2.50 1.40
1185 A453 4p multicolored 3.75 2.00
Nos. 1183-1185 (3) 8.15 4.15

Jose Marti (1853-95), Monteoristi Manifesto, cent.

A454

1995, May 22

1186 A454 3p multicolored 3.00 .45

Basketball, cent.

Medicinal Plants — A455

1995, May 26

1187 A455 2p Pimenta ozua 2.00 1.00
1188 A455 2p Melocactus communis 2.00 1.00
1189 A455 3p Smilax 3.00 1.50
1190 A455 3p Zamia 3.00 1.50
Nos. 1187-1190 (4) 10.00 5.00

Tourism A456

4p, San Souci Port. 5p, Barahona Airport. 6p, G. Luperon Airport. 13p, Airport of the Americas.

1995, June 21

1191 A456 4p multicolored 3.00 .50
1192 A456 5p multicolored 3.75 .75
1193 A456 6p multicolored 4.75 .85
1194 A456 13p multicolored 10.00 1.75
Nos. 1191-1194 (4) 21.50 3.85

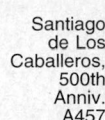

Santiago de Los Caballeros, 500th Anniv. A457

1995, July 29 Litho. *Perf. 13½*

1195 A457 3p Jacagua ruins 4.75 .90

Whales A458

Designs: No. 1196, Physeter macrocephalus. No. 1197, Balaenoptera borealis. No. 1198, Ziphius cavirostris. No. 1199, Megaptera novaeangliae.

1995, Aug. 14

1196 A458 3p multicolored 3.00 .50
1197 A458 3p multicolored 3.00 .50
1198 A458 3p multicolored 3.00 .50
1199 A458 3p multicolored 3.00 .50
Nos. 1196-1199 (4) 12.00 2.00

Stamp Day A459

1995, Oct. 18 Litho. *Perf. 13½*

1200 A459 4p No. 37 3.25 .50

Popular Singers — A460

1995, Oct. 8

1201 A460 2p Rafael Colon 1.75 .75
1202 A460 3p Casandra Damiron 2.25 1.10

Cathedral of Santiago, Cent. A461

1995, Dec. 28 Litho. *Perf. 13½*

1203 A461 3p multicolored 2.50 1.10

4th World Conference of Women, Beijing — A462

1995, Nov. 23

1204 A462 2p multicolored 5.25 1.10

Volleyball, Cent. — A463

Norceca '95 — A464

1995, Oct. 19 *Imperf.*

1205 A463 5p multicolored 4.75 1.90

Perf. 13½

1206 A464 6p multicolored 5.00 4.25

Singers — A465

1995, Dec. 27 *Perf. 13½*

1207 A465 2p Antonio Mesa 1.75 .80
1208 A465 2p Julieta Otero 1.75 .80
1209 A465 2p Susano Polanco 1.75 .80
Nos. 1207-1209 (3) 5.25 2.40

Columbus Lighthouse A466

1995, Dec. 5

1210 A466 10p dk bl, bl & gray 11.00 3.50

See Nos. 1241, 1265, 1299, 1337, 1371, 1375, 1382.

A467

UN, 50th Anniv. A468

1995, Oct. 24

1211 A467 2p multicolored 1.75 .75

Perf. 11½

1212 A468 6p multicolored 5.00 1.00

Environmental Protection — A469

America issue: 2p, Flamingos, sea gull. 6p, Manglar.

1995, Dec. 19 Litho. *Perf. 13½*

1213 A469 2p multicolored 1.75 .65
1214 A469 6p multicolored 5.00 1.00

Dominican Republic Air Force, 50th Anniv. A470

Aircraft: a, O2U-35D Corsair. b, PT-17 Stearman. c, AT-6 Texan. d, PBY-5A Catalina. e, TF-10 Beaufighter. f, FB-6 Mosquito. g, P-38 Lightning. h, P-51D Mustang. i, B-17G Flying Fortress. j, P-47D Thunderbolt. k, FB-5 Vampire. l, C-46 Commander. m, B-26 Invader. n, C-47 Skytrain. o, T-28D Trojan. p, T-33A Silverstar. q, Cessna T-41D. r, T-34 Mentor. s, Cessna O-2A. t, A-37B Dragonfly.

1995, Dec. 30

1215 A470 2p Sheet of 20, #a-t 30.00 17.00

See No. 1228.

UNICEF, 50th Anniv. — A471

1996, Feb. 23

1216 A471 2p shown 1.40 .45
1217 A471 4p Mirror image of #1216 2.75 1.40

Intl. Sailing Competition A472

1996, Mar. 8

1218 A472 5p multicolored 3.25 1.60

Eduardo Brito, Singer, 50th Death Anniv. — A473

1996, Jan. 15

1219 A473 1p shown .60 .30
1220 A473 2p With maracas 1.25 .75
1221 A473 3p Portrait 1.90 1.10
Nos. 1219-1221 (3) 3.75 2.15

No. 1220 is 54x35mm.

Natl. Journalist Day — A474

Design: Arturo J. Pellerano Alfau, Dr. Freddy Gaton Arce, Rafael Herrera Cabral.

1996, Apr. 17 Litho. ***Perf. 13½***

1222 A474 5p multicolored 3.75 1.75

ESPAMER '96, Seville — A475

1996, June 7 Litho. ***Perf. 13½***

1223 A475 15p multicolored 9.50 4.75

1996 Summer Olympic Games, Atlanta — A476

1996, July 5

1224 A476 5p Judo 3.75 1.40
1225 A476 15p Torch 9.75 4.25

Modern Olympic Games, Cent. — A477

1996, July 5

1226 A477 6p Greece No. 118 3.75 1.90
1227 A477 15p No. 328 9.00 4.25

Dominican Republic Air Force, 50th Anniv. Type of 1995

Helicoptors: a, Sikorsky S-55. b, Alouette II. c, Alouette III. d, OH-6A Cayuse. e, Bell 205 A-1. f, Dauphin II SA.365C.

1996, July 31 Litho. ***Perf. 13½***

1228 A470 3p Sheet of 6, #a.-f. 8.00 8.00

World Day Against Illegal Drugs — A478

1996, Sept. 23 Litho. ***Perf. 13½***

1229 A478 15p multicolored 9.75 4.25

Mail Delivery A479

No. 1230, World delivery, putting mail in letter box, mailman receiving mail on motorcycle. No. 1231, Woman giving mail to man on horseback, vert. No. 1232, Child holding letter beside mailbox.

1996, July 17 Litho. ***Perf. 13½***

1230 A479 3p multicolored 2.50 1.25
1231 A479 3p multicolored 2.50 1.25
1232 A479 3p multicolored 2.50 1.25
Nos. 1230-1232 (3) 7.50 3.75

America Issue — A480

1996, Oct. 15 Litho. ***Perf. 13½***

1233 A480 2p Men's costume 1.40 .65
1234 A480 6p Women's costume 3.75 1.75

Stamp Day A481

1996, Oct. 18

1235 A481 5p No. 142 3.25 1.40

26th Intl. Sunfish Championships — A482

6p, Sun, natl. flag, sailboat, vert. 10p, Man sailing boat.

1996, Oct. 16

1236 A482 6p multicolored 3.75 1.75
1237 A482 10p multicolored 6.25 3.25

A483

1996, Nov. 25 Litho. ***Perf. 13½***

1238 A483 5p green & multi 3.25 1.60
1239 A483 10p pink & multi 6.25 3.25

Intl. Day to End Violence Against Women.

A484

Birds: a, Buteo ridgwayi. b, Aratinga chloroptera. c, Amazona ventralis. d, Hyetornis rufigularis. e, Saurothera longirostris. f, Siphonorhis brewsteri. g, Chlorostilbon swainsonii. h, Todus angustirostris. i, Todus subulatus. j, Temnotrogon roseigaster. k, Nesoctites micromegas. l, Melanerpes striatus. m, Turdus swalesi. n, Carduelis dominicensis. o, Dulus dominicus. p, Microligea palustris. q, Vireo nanus. r, Xenoligea montanta. s, Turdus swalesi dodae. t, Calyptophilus frugivorus tertius. u, Corvus leucognaphalus. v, Calyptophilus frugivorus neibae.

1996, Nov. 11

1240 A484 2p Sheet of 22, #a.-v 45.00 30.00

Lighthouse Type of 1995

1996, Dec. 27 Litho. ***Perf. 13½***

1241 A466 10p grn, sil & gray 7.00 3.50

Turtles A485

a, Dermochelys coriacea. b, Caretta caretta. c, Chelonia mydas. d, Eretmochelys imbricata.

1996, Dec. 30

1242 A485 5p Block of 4, #a.-d. 12.00 10.00

Natl. Youth Day — A486

1997, Jan. 31

1243 A486 3p multicolored 1.90 1.00

National Anthem — A487

Designs: 2p, Lyrics, by Emilio Prudhome. 3p, Music, by Jose Reyes.

1997, Feb. 26

1244 A487 2p multicolored 1.40 .65
1245 A487 3p multicolored 1.90 .95

Salomé Urena (1850-97), Poet — A488

1997, Mar. 6 ***Perf. 13½***

1246 A488 3p multicolored 1.90 .95

Comet Hale-Bopp A489

1997, Apr. 1

1247 A489 5p multicolored 4.25 1.60

Size: 72x47mm

Imperf

1248 A489 10p multicolored 11.00 11.00

A490

11th Natl. Sports Games, Mao '97 — A491

2p, Mascot running with torch. 3p, Mascot in batting stance, vert. 5p, Runner breaking finish line.

1997, Apr. 3

1249 A490 2p multicolored 1.75 .65
1250 A491 3p multicolored 2.75 1.00
1251 A491 5p multicolored 4.25 1.60
Nos. 1249-1251 (3) 8.75 3.25

A492

Design: 10p, 5p, Heinrich von Stephan (1831-97), founder of UPU.

1997, Apr. 8 Litho. ***Perf. 13½***

1252 A492 10p multicolored 6.25 3.25

Souvenir Sheet

Imperf

1253 A492 5p like #1252 3.25 2.75

No. 1253 has simulated perforations.

A493

1997, Apr. 29 *Perf. 13½*
1254 A493 10p multicolored 9.50 3.25

25th Intl. Congress of CLAHT (Caracas and Latin American Group of Hemostasis and Thrombosis).

Gregorio Luperón (1839-1897), Politician — A494

1997, May 21
1255 A494 3p multicolored 1.90 1.00

House of Spain, 80th Anniv. — A495

1997, July 4
1256 A495 5p multicolored 3.25 1.60

First Peso Coin, Cent. A496

1997, Aug. 6 **Litho.** *Perf. 13½*
1257 A496 2p multicolored 1.50 .65

A497

Coronation of the Image of Our Lady of Alta Gracia, 75th Anniv. — A498

1997, Aug. 12
1258 A497 3p multicolored 1.90 .85
1259 A498 5p multicolored 3.25 1.60

America Issue A499

Life of a postman: 2p, Dog grabbing pants leg of postman on motorcycle. 6p, Dog tearing pants leg of postman with letter.

1997, Oct. 9 **Litho.** *Perf. 13½*
1260 A499 2p multicolored 1.25 .65

Size: 35½x35½mm

1261 A499 6p multicolored 3.25 1.60

Mother Teresa (1910-97) A500

1997, Oct. 17
1262 A500 5p multicolored 3.00 1.60

Stamp Day — A501

1997, Oct. 18
1263 A501 5p Nos. 108, 322 2.75 1.60

Central Bank of the Dominican Republic, 50th Anniv. — A502

1997, Oct. 30 *Perf. 11½*
1264 A502 10p multicolored 5.50 3.25

Lighthouse Type of 1995

1997, Dec. 15 **Litho.** *Perf. 13½*
1265 A466 10p bright rose & gray 7.50 3.25

Bats A503

a, Erophylius bombifrons. b, Brachyphylla nana. c, Molossus molossus. d, Lasiurus borealis.

1997, Nov. 11
1266 A503 5p Block of 4, #a.-d. 11.00 11.00

Dominican Air Force, 50th Anniv. A504

Insignias: a, Air Force, red, white, and blue target. b, Northern Air Command, "shark plane." c, Air Command, eagle's wings over target. d, Rescue Force, eagle. e, Maintenance Command. f, Combat Force, dragon, target.

1997, Dec. 19
1267 A504 3p Sheet of 6, #a.-f. 11.00 11.00

Construction of the National Palace, 50th Anniv. — A505

1997, Dec. 30 **Litho.** *Perf. 13½*
1268 A505 10p multicolored 6.25 3.50

First Regional Symposium on Pre-Columbian Culture and Caribbean Contemporary Art — A506

1998, Jan. 28
1269 A506 6p multicolored 3.75 1.60

A507

1998, Apr. 2 **Litho.** *Perf. 13½*
1270 A507 10p multicolored 6.25 3.25

American Chamber of Commerce of the Dominican Republic, 75th anniv.

A508

Book Fair: 3p, Natl. Book Fair, 25th anniv. 5p, Intl. Book Fair, Santo Domingo '98.

1998, Apr. 26
1271 A508 3p black, blue & red 1.90 .85

Size: 35x33mm

1272 A508 5p black, blue & red 3.25 1.60

Organization of American States, 50th Anniv. — A509

1998, Apr. 30
1273 A509 5p blue & multi 3.25 1.60
1274 A509 5p pink & multi 3.25 1.60

Establishment of the State of Israel, 50th Anniv. — A510

1998, Apr. 30
1275 A510 10p multicolored 9.00 4.50

Dominican Air Force, 50th Anniv. — A511

a, Gen. Frank Felix Miranda, portrait at left. b, Early aircraft. c, Col. Ernesto Tejeda, portrait at right. d, As "c," portrait at left. e, As "a," portrait at right.

1998, June 26 **Sheet of 6**
1276 A511 3p #a, c-e, 2 b 10.00 10.00

City of Santo Domingo, 500th Anniv. A512

2p, Sun clock. 3p, St. Lazaro Church & Hospital. 4p, First Cathedral in America. 5p, Royal Palace. 6p, Tower of Honor. 10p, St. Nicolas of Bari Church & Hospital.

1998, Aug. 6 **Litho.** *Perf. 13½*
1277 A512 2p multi, vert. 1.25 .65
1278 A512 3p multi 1.90 .90
1279 A512 4p multi 2.50 1.25
1280 A512 5p multi 3.25 1.60
1281 A512 6p multi 3.75 1.90
1282 A512 10p multi, vert. 6.25 3.25
Nos. 1277-1282 (6) 18.90 9.55

National Theater, 25th Anniv. — A513

1998, Aug. 14 *Perf. 13x13½*
1283 A513 10p multicolored 6.25 3.00

Latin Union, 44th Anniv. A514

1998, Aug. 26 ***Perf. 13½***
1284 A514 10p multicolored 6.25 3.00

ICCO (Intl. Cocoa Organization of America & Europe), 25th Anniv. — A515

1998, Sept. 3
1285 A515 10p multicolored 7.75 3.50

Nino Ferrua (1909-79), Stamp Designer A516

1998, Oct. 18 Litho. ***Perf. 13½x13***
1286 A516 5p multicolored 3.25 1.50

Stamp Day.

Pontificate of John Paul II, 20th Anniv. A517

1998, Oct. 22 ***Perf. 13½***
1287 A517 5p shown 3.25 1.50
1288 A517 10p Portrait, diff. 6.75 2.10

Medicinal Plants — A518

a, Pimenta racemosa. b, Pimenta haitiensis. c, Cymbopogon citratus. d, Citrus aurantium.

1998, Nov. 2
1289 A518 3p Block of 4, #a.-d. 6.50 3.25

Famous Women A519

America Issue: 2p, Juana Saltitopa standing with cannon. 6p, Anacaona, Indian maiden, group of Indians.

1998, Nov. 5
1290 A519 2p multicolored 1.90 .65
1291 A519 6p multicolored 4.50 2.00

A520

1998, Nov. 20
1292 A520 5p multicolored 4.00 1.50

Intl. Year of the Ocean.

A521

1998, Nov. 23
1293 A521 5p multicolored 2.75 1.50

Expofila '98, Santo Domingo. Santo Domingo, 500th anniv.

National Military Heroes — A522

Designs: a, Fernando Valerio. b, Benito Moncion. c, Jose Maria Cabral. d, Antonio Duverge. e, Gregorio Luperon. f, Jose A. Salcedo. g, Fco. A. Salcedo. h, Gaspar Polanco. i, Santiago Rodriguez. j, Juan Bta. Cambiaso. k, Jose J. Puello. l, Jose Ma. Imbert. m, Juan A. Acosta. n, Marcos Adon. o, Matias R. Mella. p, Francisco R. Sanchez. q, Juan Pablo Duarte. r, Olegario Tenares. s, Pedro Santana. t, Juan Sanchez Ramirez.

1998, Nov. 29
1294 A522 3p Sheet of 20, #a.-t. 27.50 24.50

1st Natl. Paper Money, 150th Anniv. — A523

1998, Nov. 30 ***Perf. 11½***
1295 A523 10p multicolored 4.75 2.10

Christmas A524

1998, Dec. 7 ***Perf. 13½***
1296 A524 2p Roasting hog .90 .45
1297 A524 5p Magi 2.25 1.10

Universal Declaration of Human Rights, 50th Anniv. A525

1998, Dec. 10
1298 A525 10p multicolored 4.50 2.10

Columbus Lighthouse Type of 1995

1998, Dec. 11
1299 A466 10p orange & black 6.00 3.00

Shells A526

Designs: a, Lyria vegai. b, Strombus gigas. c, Cittarium pica. d, Nerita peloronta.

1998, Dec. 16
1300 A526 5p Block of 4, #a.-d. 11.00 5.25

Gaspar Hernández (1798-1858), Priest — A527

1998, Dec. 18
1301 A527 3p multicolored 1.40 .70

Dominican Society of Endocrinology and Nutrition, 25th Anniv. — A528

1999, Feb. 24 Litho. ***Perf. 13¼***
1302 A528 10p multicolored 4.00 2.00

Office of Comptroller General — A529

1999, May 4 Litho. ***Perf. 13¼***
1303 A529 2p multicolored .90 .45

Export Industries A530

Perf. 13½x13¼, 13¼x13½
1999, Apr. 30 Litho.
1304 A530 6p Tobacco 2.25 1.10
1305 A530 10p Textiles, vert. 3.75 1.60

Pan American Games, Winnipeg A530a

1999, July 29 Litho. ***Perf. 13¼x13½***
1306 A530a 5p Baseball 2.50 1.25
1307 A530a 6p Weight lifting 3.00 1.50

Native Plants — A531

Designs: a, Pseudophoenix ekmanii. b, Murtigia calabura. c, Pouteria dominguensis. d, Rubus dominguensis focke.

1999, July 13
1308 A531 5p Block of 4, #a.-d. 9.50 9.50

Presidents of the Dominican Republic A532

Designs: a, Tomas Bobadilla y Briones. b, Pedro Santana. c, Manuel Jimenez. d, Buenaventura Baez. e, Manuel de Regla Mota. f, José Desiderio Valverde. g, José A. Salcedo. h, Gaspar Polanco.

1999, Aug. 31 ***Perf. 13½x13¼***
1309 A532 3p Sheet of 8, #a.-h. + label 10.00 10.00

A533

Sovereign Military Order of Malta A534

Perf. 13¼x13½
1999, Sept. 20 Litho.
1310 A533 2p multicolored .85 .45
Perf. 13½
1311 A534 10p multicolored 4.50 2.75

Paintings by José Vela Zanetti (1913-99) — A535

Various paintings.

Perf. 13½x13¼, 13¼x 13½

1999, Sept. 8

1312	A535	2p multi, vert.	.70	.45
1313	A535	3p multi, vert.	1.25	.80
1314	A535	5p multi	1.90	1.10
1315	A535	6p multi, vert.	2.40	1.40
1316	A535	10p multi, vert.	3.75	2.10
		Nos. 1312-1316 (5)	10.00	5.85

Insects A536

Designs: a, Strataegus quadrifoveatus. b, Anetia jaegeri. c, Polyancistroydes tettigonidae. d, Aploppus phasmidae.

1999, Sept. 10 *Perf. 13½x13¼*

1317	A536	5p Block of 4, #a.-d.	8.00	8.00

SOS Children's Villages, 50th Anniv. — A537

1999, Sept. 29 *Perf. 13¼x13½*

1318	A537	10p multicolored	4.00	2.10

Intl. Year of the Elderly — A538

1999, Oct. 1

1319	A538	2p Man	.75	.25
1320	A538	5p Woman	2.00	1.00

A539

1999, Oct. 5

1321	A539	5p multicolored	2.00	.90

World Education Day.

A540

Designs: 2p, Skull and crossbones, land mines, shattered gun. 6p, Mushroom cloud.

1999, Oct. 18

1322	A540	2p multicolored	.75	.50
1323	A540	6p multicolored	2.50	1.25

America Issue, a new millennium without arms.

Stamp Day — A541

1999, Oct. 22

1324	A541	5p Luis F. Thomen	2.00	.90

Account of Gen. Juan Pablo Duarte A542

1999, July 16 *Perf. 13½*

1325	A542	3p multicolored	1.25	.25

A543

Contemporary Writers — A544

Perf. 13¼x13½, 13½x13¼

1999, June 23

1326	A543	2p multicolored	.65	.25
1327	A544	10p multicolored	4.75	2.25

Dermatological Society, 50th Anniv. — A545

1999, Sept. 15 **Litho.** *Perf. 13¼*

1328	A545	3p multi	1.25	.80

Millennium — A546

3p, Earth, trees. 5p, Scientific achievements.

Perf. 13¼x13½

1999, Nov. 10 **Litho.**

1329	A546	3p multi	1.25	.75
1330	A546	5p multi	2.25	1.10

2nd Summit of African, Caribbean and Pacific Heads of State — A547

Emblem and: 5p, Map of Caribbean area, whale. 6p, Map of Pacific area, Easter Island statues. 10p, Map of Africa, lion.

1999, Nov. 23

1331	A547	5p multi	2.00	1.00
1332	A547	6p multi	2.50	1.10
1333	A547	10p multi	4.00	2.00
		Nos. 1331-1333 (3)	8.50	4.10

UPU, 125th Anniv. A548

6p, Globe, envelope, computer, electronic circuits. 10p, Envelope, electronic circuits.

1999, Nov. 29

1334	A548	6p multi	2.25	1.00

Size: 50x75mm

Imperf

1335	A548	10p multi	4.50	2.10

Union of Latin American Universities, 50th Anniv. — A549

1999, Dec. 3 *Perf. 13½x13¼*

1336	A549	6p multi	2.25	1.00

Lighthouse Type of 1995

1999, Dec. 14 *Perf. 13¼x13½*

1337	A466	10p brown & silver	4.50	2.10

Classical Musicians A550

No. 1338, José de Jésus Ravelo (1876-1951), clarinet. No. 1339, Juan Francisco Garcia (1892-1974), cornet. No. 1340, Manuel Simo (1916-88), saxophone.

1999, Dec. 17

1338	A550	5p multi	2.00	1.00
1339	A550	5p multi	2.00	1.00
1340	A550	5p multi	2.00	1.00
		Nos. 1338-1340 (3)	6.00	3.00

Municipal Notes, Cent. — A551

Notes and background colors — No. 1341: a, Santo Domingo, San Pedro de Macorís, deep purple. b, Puerto Plata, Moca, purple.

No. 1342, vert.: a, Santiago, Cotui, blue green. b, San Francisco de Macorís, La Vega, golden brown. c, San Cristobal, Samana, peacock blue.

No. 1343: a, As No. 1342a, green background. b, As No. 1342b, brown background. c, As No. 1342c, Prussian blue background.

1999, Dec. 30 *Perf. 13¼*

1341	A551	2p Pair, #a.-b.	2.00	1.00
1342	A551	2p Strip of 3, #a.-c.	2.50	1.10

Souvenir Sheet

Imperf

1343	A551	2p Sheet of 5, Nos. 1341a-1341b, 1343a-1343c	4.50	2.25

Chamber of Spanish Commerce and Industry, 75th Anniv. — A552

1999, Dec. 30 *Perf. 13¼x13½*

1344	A552	10p multi	4.50	2.40

Fight Against Drugs A553

2000, Feb. 17 **Litho.** *Perf. 13½*

1345	A553	5p multi	2.25	1.10

Hogar Crea Dominicana Inc., 25th anniv.

Duarte Institute — A554

2000, Feb. 25 *Perf. 13¼*

1346	A554	2p multi	1.00	.50

Prevention of Child Abuse — A555

2000, Mar. 31

1347 A555 2p multi .90 .45

National Police A556

2000, Apr. 6 ***Perf. 13½***

1348 A556 2p shown .90 .45

Size: 37x28mm

Perf. 13½x13¼

1349 A556 5p Crest 2.25 1.10

Dominican Institute of Industrial Technology, 25th Anniv. A557

2000, Apr. 11 ***Perf. 13½***

1350 A557 2p multi .90 .45

Independencia Province, 50th Anniv. — A558

2000, Apr. 15

1351 A558 3p multi 1.25 .65

A559

12th Natl. Games, La Romana A560

2000, Apr. 27 ***Perf. 13½x13¼***

1352 A559 2p Baseball .75 .45
1353 A559 3p Boxing 1.50 .80

Perf. 13½

1354 A560 5p Emblem 2.25 1.00
Nos. 1352-1354 (3) 4.50 2.25

Paintings A561

Designs: 5p, The Violinist, by Darío Suro. 10p, Self-portrait, by Théodore Chassériau.

2000, May 5 ***Perf. 13¼***

1355 A561 5p multi 2.50 1.10
1356 A561 10p multi 4.25 2.50

Presidential Elections A562

2000, May 12

1357 A562 2p multi .90 .45

Classical Musicians A563

No. 1358, Julio Alberto Hernandez Camejo (1900-99), pianist. No. 1359, Ramon Diaz (1901-76), bassoonist. No. 1360, Enrique de Marchena Dujarric (1908-88), pianist.

2000, May 31 ***Perf. 13½***

1358 A563 5p multi 2.25 1.10
1359 A563 5p multi 2.25 1.10
1360 A563 5p multi 2.25 1.10
Nos. 1358-1360 (3) 6.75 3.30

Expo 2000, Hanover A564

2000, June 1

1361 A564 5p shown 2.25 1.10
1362 A564 10p Emblem, diff. 4.50 2.10

Art by Jaime Colson — A565

Designs: 2p, Woman on horseback. 3p, Abstract. 5p, Musicians and dancers, horiz. 6p, Nudes. 10p, Colson.

2000 **Litho.** ***Perf. 13¼***

1363-1367 A565 Set of 5 13.50 6.75

Holy Year 2000 A566

Churches: 2p, Santo Cristo de los Milagros de Bayaguana Sanctuary. 5p, Santa Maria la Menor Cathedral, first in the Americas, vert. 10p, Nuestra Señora de la Altagracia Basilica, vert.

2000 ***Perf. 13½x13¼, 13¼x13½***

1368-1370 A566 Set of 3 8.00 4.00

Lighthouse Type of 1995

2000 ***Perf. 13¼x13½***

1371 A466 10p buff, brn & sil 5.25 3.50

Dominican Republic — Republic of China Diplomatic Relations A566a

Flags of Dominican Republic and Republic of China and: 5p, Illustration of dragon. 10p, Carved dragon.

Serpentine Die Cut 11¼

2000, Dec. 15 **Litho.**

Self-Adhesive

1371A-1371B A566a Set of 2 7.25 3.50

America Issue — Campaign Against AIDS — A566b

Designs: 2p, Child. 6p, AIDS patient (38x38mm).

2000, Dec. 21 **Self-Adhesive**

1371C-1371D A566b Set of 2 4.00 2.00

UN High Commissioner for Refugees, 50th Anniv. — A566c

2000, Dec. 29 **Self-Adhesive**

1371E A566c 10p multi 4.50 2.25

Environmental Protection — A567

Designs: 2p, Lizard on leaf, vert. $3, House. $5, River rapids, vert.

Serpentine Die Cut 11¼

2000 **Litho.**

Self-Adhesive

1372-1374 A567 Set of 3 5.00 2.50

Lighthouse Type of 1995

2001 **Litho.** ***Perf. 13¼x13½***

1375 A466 15p lt bl, dk bl & sil 7.25 3.50

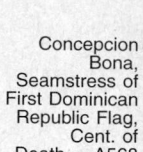

Concepcion Bona, Seamstress of First Dominican Republic Flag, Cent. of Death — A568

2001 ***Perf. 13½x13¼***

1376 A568 10p multi 4.50 2.75

Stamp Day — A569

2001

1377 A569 5p multi 2.25 1.10

Year of Dialogue Among Civilizations A570

2001 ***Perf. 13¼x13½***

1378 A570 12p multi 5.50 2.50

America Issue — UNESCO World Heritage A571

Designs: 4p, San Felipe Fort. 15p, Ruins of San Nicolas de Bari Hospital (27x37mm).

2001 ***Perf. 13½, 13¼x13½ (15p)***

1379-1380 A571 Set of 2 8.50 4.25

Lighthouse Type of 1995

2002, Oct. 17 **Litho.** ***Perf. 13½x13¾***

1382 A466 15p yel & multi 4.00 2.00

Mushrooms — A572

No. 1383: a, Pycnoporus sanguineus. b, Morchella elata. c, Mycena epipterygia. d, Coriolopsis polyzona.

Perf. 13¼x13½

2001, Sept. 13 **Litho.**
1383 A572 6p Block of 4, #a-d 13.00 6.50

National Botanical Gardens, 25th Anniv. — A573

No. 1384: a, Isidorea pungens. b, Pereskia quisqueyana. c, Goetzea ekmanii. d, Cubanola domingensis.

Perf. 13¼x13½

2001, Sept. 20 **Litho.**
1384 A573 4p Block of 4, #a-d *8.00 8.00*

Presidents of the Dominican Republic — A574

No. 1385: a, Gen. José María Cabral. b, Gen. Gregório Luperón. c, Gen. Ignacio María González. d, Ulises Espaillat. e, Pedro A. Pimentel. f, Federico de Jesús García. g, Frenando Arturo de Mariño. h, Gen. Ulises Heureaux.

2001, Sept. 27 **Litho.** ***Perf. 13¼***
1385 A574 6p Sheet of 8, #a-h, + label 22.50 11.00

Blessed Josemaría Escrivá de Balaguer (1902-75), Founder of Opus Dei — A575

2002, Aug. 29 ***Perf. 13½x13¼***
1386 A575 10p multi 4.00 1.90

Loyola Polytechnic Institute, 50th Anniv. — A576

2002, Oct. 24 ***Perf. 13¼x13½***
1387 A576 6p multi 2.00 1.40

12th Iberoamerican Heads of State Summit — A577

Designs: 12p, Flags below map. 15p, Flags above map.

Perf. 13¾x13½

2002, Nov. 14 **Litho.**
1388-1389 A577 Set of 2 9.00 4.75

America Issue — Youth Education and LIteracy — A578

Designs: 4p, Teacher helping child write. 15p, Child writing on blackboard.

2002, Dec. 20 ***Perf. 13¼x13½***
1390-1391 A578 Set of 2 6.00 3.00

Coccothrinax Spissa — A579

Perf. 13¼x13½

2002, Dec. 20 **Litho.**
1392 A579 10p multi 3.00 1.50

2003 Pan American Games, Santo Domingo — A580

Color of "2003" in design: 4p, Light green blue. 6p, Blue. 12p, Red.

2003, Feb. 25
1393-1395 A580 Set of 3 6.25 3.00

Medicinal Plants — A581

No. 1396: a, Hymenaea courbaril. b, Spondias mombin. c, Genipa americana. d, Guazuma ulmifonia.

2003, June 17
1396 A581 5p Block of 4, #a-d 5.50 2.75

Dr. José Francisco Peña Gomez (1937-98), Politician A582

Litho. & Engr.

2003, Dec. 17 ***Perf. 11½***
1397 A582 10p multi 3.25 1.40

José Marti (1853-95), Cuban Patriot — A583

2003, Nov. 5 **Litho.** ***Perf. 13x13¼***
1398 A583 15p multi 4.50 2.25

Pan American Health Organization, Cent. (in 2002) — A583a

Perf. 13½x13¼

2003, Sept. 12 **Litho.**
1398A A583a 20p multi 4.00 2.00

America Issue — Flora and Fauna — A584

Designs: 5p, Aristelliger lar. 15p, Corpernicia berteroana, vert.

Perf. 13½x13¼, 13¼x13½

2004, Jan. 19
1399-1400 A584 Set of 2 6.00 3.00

Nos. 1399-1400 are dated "2003."

Election of Pope John Paul II, 25th Anniv. — A585

Pope John Paul II: 10p, With hand touching face. 15p, Blessing crowd, horiz.
25p, Vignettes of 10p and 15p stamps.

Perf. 13¼x13½, 13½x13¼

2005, Nov. 26
1401-1402 A585 Set of 2 6.75 3.25

Size: 57x85mm

Imperf

1403 A585 25p multi 7.25 3.50

National Council for Children A586

2004, Mar. 10 ***Perf. 13½x13¼***
1404 A586 7p multi 2.25 1.10

Exfilna National Philatelic Exhibition A587

2004, Dec. 8 **Litho.** ***Perf. 13½x13¼***
1405 A587 7p multi 2.50 1.10

America Issue — Fight Against Poverty A588

Design: 10p, Shack. 20p, Poor woman.

2004, Dec. 23
1406-1407 A588 Set of 2 9.50 5.75

Dominican Republic - Canada Diplomatic Relations, 50th Anniv. A589

2004, Dec. 31
1408 A589 20p multi 6.50 3.75

Interexpo '05 Intl. Philatelic Exhibition A590

Designs: 7p, Dove and stamp. 20p, Map highlighting Dominican Republic, vert.

Perf. 13½x13¼, 13¼x13½

2005 **Litho.**

1409-1410 A590 Set of 2 8.75 4.75

Souvenir Sheet

Design: 10p, Similar to 7p.

1410A A590 10p multi 2.50 2.00

Dominican Republic Philatelic Society, 50th anniv.

Issued: 20p, 10/16; 7p, 10/17; 10p, 2005.

America Issue — Environmental Protection A591

Prevention of: 10p, Water pollution. 20p, Air pollution.

2005 *Perf. 13¼x13½*

1411-1412 A591 Set of 2 8.75 4.75

Monte Plata Maternity Clinic A592

Perf. 13½x13¼

2005, Nov. 14 **Litho.**

1413 A592 15p multi 5.00 2.50

Proclamation of Sister City Status of Santo Domingo and La Guardia, Spain — A593

2005, Nov. 11

1414 A593 10p multi 3.00 1.50

Stamp Day A594

2005 **Litho.** *Perf. 13½x13¼*

1415 A594 10p multi 3.00 1.50

Palace of Fine Arts, 50th Anniv. A595

2006, Oct. 10 **Litho.** *Perf. 13¾x13¼*

1416 A595 7p multi 2.25 1.10

Dominican History Academy, 75th Anniv. — A596

2006, Oct. 30 *Perf. 13¼*

1417 A596 10p multi 3.00 1.50

16th Intl. Boxing Congress, Santo Domingo — A597

2006, Nov. 2 *Perf. 13¼x13½*

1418 A597 20p multi 5.00 2.50

Pope John Paul II (1920-2005) A598

Pope and: 10p, Crucifix. 20p, Dove, horiz.

2006, Nov. 4 *Perf. 13½*

1419-1420 A598 Set of 2 9.00 4.50

Blessing of Natl. Sacred Heart of Jesus Sanctuary, 50th Anniv. — A599

2006, Nov. 24 *Perf. 13½x13¼*

1421 A599 10p multi 3.00 1.50

Ninth Latin American Botanical Congress A600

2006 *Perf. 13¼x13½*

1422 A600 20p multi 6.00 3.00

America Issue, Energy Conservation — A601

Designs: 10p, Light bulb in hands. 20p, Transmission lines and tower.

2006 *Perf. 13x13¼*

1423-1424 A601 Set of 2 9.00 4.50

Pres. Joaquin Balaguer (1906-2002) A602

Balaguer: 7p, Wearing bow tie. 10p, Holding book.

2006, Sept. 1 *Perf. 13¼x13½*

1425-1426 A602 Set of 2 5.50 2.75

Office of the First Lady A603

Emblem and: 10p, Tree. 25p, Computer and keyboard.

2007, Mar. 1 *Perf. 13½x13¼*

1427-1428 A603 Set of 2 9.00 4.75

Selection of Nicolás de Jesus Cardinal López Rodríguez as Archbishop of Santo Domingo, 25th Anniv. — A604

López Rodríguez: 10p, Standing next to chair. 15p, With Pope John Paul II. 25p, Holding crucifix.

2007, May 25 *Perf. 13¼x13½*

1429-1431 A604 Set of 3 12.00 6.00

2007 Pan American Games, Rio de Janeiro — A605

Designs: 15p, High jump. 20p, Weight lifting.

2007, July 6 **Litho.**

1432-1433 A605 Set of 2 9.00 4.50

Podilymbus Podiceps A606

2007 **Litho.** *Perf. 13½x13¼*

1434 A606 20p multi 6.00 3.00

Dated 2006.

Stamp Day — A607

2007, Oct. *Perf. 13¼x13½*

1435 A607 15p multi 4.00 2.00

America Issue, Education For All — A608

Top panel in: 10p, Red. 20p, Blue.

2007, Oct.

1436-1437 A608 Set of 2 9.00 4.50

Treaty of Friendship With the Netherlands, 150th Anniv. — A609

2007, Nov. *Perf. 13½x13¼*

1438 A609 25p multi 6.00 3.00

Palace of Columbus A610

2007

1439 A610 10p multi 3.00 1.50

Barahona Province, Cent. — A611

2007 *Perf. 13¼x13*

1440 A611 10p multi 2.00 1.00

Salvaléon de Higuey, 500th Anniv. A612

2007 *Perf. 13½*

1441 A612 15p multi 3.00 1.50

Friendship and Cooperation Between Dominican Republic and Republic of China — A613

Designs: 10p, Prunus mume, Swietenia mahagonni. 15p, Urocissa caeruela, Dulus dominicus. 35p, Buildings from China and Dominican Republic.

2007
1442-1444 A613 Set of 3 11.00 5.50

Children's Book Illustrations by Dr. Sophie Jakowska A614

Initials of Dr. Jakowska and: No. 1445, 7p, Trichechus manatus manatus. No. 1446, 7p, Eretmochelys imbricata, horiz. No. 1447, 10p, Photograph of Jakowska. No. 1448, 10p, Amazona ventralis. 15p, Crocodylus acutus, horiz.

2007 ***Perf. 13¼x13, 13x13¼***
1445-1449 A614 Set of 5 10.00 5.00

Scouting, Cent. — A615

Designs: 10p, Dominican Republic Scouting emblem. 15p, Scouts, knotted rope.

2007 **Litho.** ***Perf. 13½***
1450-1451 A615 Set of 2 5.00 2.50

Dominican Diaspora — A616

2008 ***Perf. 13¼x13***
1452 A616 15p multi 3.00 1.50

Freemasonry in Dominican Republic, 150th Anniv. — A617

2008 ***Perf. 13¼x13½***
1453 A617 25p multi 5.00 2.50

Stamp Day A618

2008 ***Perf. 13¼***
1454 A618 20p brown 4.00 2.00

2008 Summer Olympics, Beijing — A619

No. 1455: a, Taekwondo. b, Boxing. c, Table tennis. d, Judo.

2008 ***Perf. 13x13¼***
1455 A619 10p Block of 4, #a-d 8.00 4.00

Women Involved in Fight for Independence A620

No. 1456: a, Juana de la Merced Trinidad (d. 1860). b, Joaquina Filomena Gomez de la Cova (1800-93). c, Maria Baltasara de los Reyes (1789-1867). d, Rosa Protomartir Duarte y Diaz (1820-88). e, Manuela Diaz y Jimenez (1786-1858). f, Petronila Abreu y Delgado (1815-1904). g, Micaela de Rivera de Santana (1785-1854). h, Froilana Febles de Santana (1814-88). i, Rosa Montas de Duvergé (1813-95). j, Josefa Antonia Perez de la Paz (1788-1855). k, Ana Valverde (1798-1864). l, Maria de la Concepción Bona y Hernandez (1824-1901). m, Maria de Jesus Pina y Benitez (1825-58). n, Maria Trinidad Sanchez y Ramona (1794-1845).

2008 ***Perf. 13¼x13½***
1456 Sheet of 14 + 31 labels 25.00 12.50
a.-n. A620 10p Any single 1.75 .90

Arms of Santiago, 500th Anniv. A621

2008 **Litho.** ***Perf. 13x13¼***
1457 A621 10p multi 1.10 .50

Discovery of Quisqueya (Hispaniola) by Christopher Columbus, 1492 — A622

2008
1458 A622 10p multi 1.10 .50

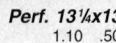

General Timoteo Ogando Encarnación (1818-1908) A623

2008 ***Perf. 13¼x13***
1459 A623 10p multi 1.10 .50

Campaign Against Commercial Sexual Exploitation A624

2008
1460 A624 10p multi 1.10 .50

Intl. Swimming Federation, Cent. — A625

2008 ***Perf. 13½***
1461 A625 15p multi 1.10 .50

America Issue, National Festivals — A626

No. 1462: a, 15p, Shot of Independence. b, 25p, Sword of the Restoration.

2008 ***Perf. 13¼x13***
1462 A626 Horiz. pair, #a-b 5.00 2.50

Duarte y Díez Family Tree — A627

No. 1463: a, Juan J. Duarte (1768-1843) and wife, Manuela Díez (1786-1858). b, Juan J. Duarte's sons, Juan Pablo (1813-76), Dominican independence leader, and Vicente (1802-65). c, Juan J. Duarte's son, Manuel (1826-90), and daughter, Rosa (1820-88). d, Juan J. Duarte's daughters, Francisca (1831-99), and Filomena (1818-65).

2009, Feb. 26 ***Perf. 13½x13¼***
1463 A627 10p Block of 4, #a-d 5.00 2.50

Chinatown, Santo Domingo A628

Designs: 15p, Confucius Plaza. 20p, Gateway.

2009, Apr. 17
1464-1465 A628 Set of 2 6.00 3.00

De La Salle Schools in Dominican Republic, 75th Anniv. A629

St. Jean Baptiste de la Salle (1651-1719) A630

2009, May 14 ***Perf. 13½x13¼***
1466 A629 7p multi 1.25 .60
Perf. 13¼x13½
1467 A630 10p multi 2.25 1.10

Invasion of Constanza, Maimón and Estero Hondo by Dominican Exiles, 50th Anniv. A631

2009, June 17 ***Perf. 13½***
1468 A631 10p multi 2.25 1.10

Pres. Juan Bosch (1909-2001) A632

2009 ***Perf. 13¼x13***
1469 A632 20p multi 3.75 1.90

Crabs — A633

No. 1470: a, Epilobocera haytensis. b, Gecarcinus ruricola. c, Coenobita clypeatus. d, Callinectes sapidus.

2009 Litho. *Perf. 13½x13¼*
1470 A633 10p Block of 4, #a-d 3.50 2.25

Winning Designs in Children's Christmas Stamp Design Contest — A634

No. 1471: a, Dancers and musicians in front of house. b, Parade. c, Family and livestock. d, Villagers, manger and Christmas tree.

2009, Oct. 5 Litho. *Perf. 13x13¼*
1471 A634 10p Block of 4, #a-d 4.00 2.25

Plazas A635

Designs: 15p, Galicia Plaza, Santo Domingo. 25p, Santo Domingo Plaza, La Guardia, Spain.

2009, Oct. 15 *Perf. 13¼*
1472-1473 A635 Set of 2 4.00 2.25

15th American Genealogical Reunion — A636

2009, Nov. 3 *Perf. 13x13¼*
1474 A636 75p multi 8.50 4.25

Natl. School of Judicature A637

2009, Nov. 4 *Perf. 13½*
1475 A637 7p multi .60 .40

America Issue, Toys and Games — A638

Designs: 10p, Fu-fu. 15p, Hopscotch, horiz. 20p, Pañuelo, horiz.

2009 *Perf. 13x13, 13x13¼*
1476-1477 A638 Set of 2 1.75 1.40

Imperf

Size: 76x50mm

1478 A638 20p multi 1.40 1.10

Miniature Sheet

Dominican Republic Presidents — A639

No. 1479: a, Benigno Filomeno De Rojas. b, Jacinto B. De Castro. c, Maetos Cabral. d, Gen. Cesáreo Guillermo. e, Francisco G. Billini. f, Alejandro Woss y Gil. g, Carlos Felipe Morales Languasco. h, Ramón Cáceres.

2009 *Perf. 13¼*
1479 A639 7p Sheet of 8, #a-h, + central label 6.00 3.25

See No. 1531.

National Coat of Arms — A640

2010, Feb. 10 *Perf. 13¼x13½*
1480 A640 50p multi 4.00 2.75

14th Ibero-American Notaries Meeting — A641

2010, June 3 Litho. *Perf. 13¼x13*
1481 A641 26p multi 2.75 1.40

Preservation of Polar Regions — A642

2010, July 7 *Perf. 13½x13¼*
1482 A642 20p multi 1.90 1.10

Solenodon Paradoxus A643

2010, July 28
1483 A643 25p multi 2.50 1.40

Biodiversity protection.

National Philatelic and Numismatic Museum, 25th Anniv. — A644

2010, Aug. 10 *Perf. 13¼x13*
1484 A644 33p ocher & black 4.00 1.90

Juan Pablo Duarte (1813-76), Independence Leader, and Birthplace, Santo Domingo — A645

2010, Aug. 30 *Perf. 11½x13¼*
1485 A645 25p multi 3.00 1.40

Delivery of the Flag A646

National Pantheon A647

2010, Oct. 12 Litho. *Perf. 13½*
1486 A646 26p multi 3.00 1.40

Perf. 13¼x13

1487 A647 33p multi 4.00 1.75

America Issue.

Stamp Day A648

2010, Oct. 18 *Perf. 13x13¼*
1488 A648 15p multi 1.50 .80

Miniature Sheet

Tourism — A649

No. 1489 — Tourist attractions: a, Los Tres Ojos. b, Juan Dolio Beach. c, Altos de Chavón. d, Bayahibe Beach. e, Bávaro Beach. f, Cayo Levantado. g, Las Terrenas Beach. h, Cabarete Beach. i, River rafters, Jarabacoa. j, Lake Enriquillo.

2010, Nov. 4
1489 A649 10p Sheet of 10, #a-j, + 2 labels 5.50 5.50

Veritas Odd Fellows Lodge, Santo Domingo A650

2010, Nov. 26 *Perf. 13½x13¼*
1490 A650 60p multi 3.25 3.25

World AIDS Day — A651

Designs: 15p, Hands with AIDS ribbons on thumbs. 46p, Flower with AIDS ribbon petals.

2010, Dec. 1 *Perf. 13¼x13*
1491-1492 A651 Set of 2 3.25 3.25

Dominican Order in the Americas, 500th Anniv. A652

Designs: 15p, Monastery. 26p, Dominican monk and native boy, vert.

2010, Dec. 7 *Perf. 13x13¼, 13¼x13*
1493-1494 A652 Set of 2 2.25 2.25

National Archives, 75th Anniv. A653

2010, Dec. 14 *Perf. 13½x13¼*
1495 A653 20p multi 1.10 1.10

Santo Domingo, 2010 American Capital of Culture — A654

2010, Dec. 16 *Imperf.*
1496 A654 26p multi 1.40 1.40

Santo Domingo Gates — A655

No. 1497: a, Puerta de la Misericordia, "Republica" at bottom. b, Puerta del Conde, "Republica" at left. c, Puerta del Conde, "Republica" at top. d, Puerta de la Misericordia, "Republica" at left.

20p, Puerta de la Misericordia, Puerta del Conde, arms of Domincan Republic.

2011, Feb. 21 *Perf. 13x13¼*
1497 A655 10p Block of 4, #a-d 2.25 2.25

Size: 90x70mm

Imperf

1498 A655 20p multi 1.10 1.10

Sur Futuro Foundation A656

Designs: 15p, Tree and rainbow. 20p, Lake.

2011, Mar. 3 *Perf. 13¼x13½*
1499-1500 A656 Set of 2 1.90 1.90

Caves — A657

No. 1501: a, Pomier Caves, San Cristobal. b, Fun Fun Cave, Hato Mayor del Rey. c, Guácara de Hernando Alonzo, La Mata, Sánchez Ramírez. d, Golondrinas Cave, Río San Juan.

2011, Mar. 15 *Perf. 13½x13¼*
1501 A657 10p Block of 4, #a-d 2.25 2.25

Dated 2010.

Postal Union of the Americas, Spain and Portugal (UPAEP), Cent. A658

Designs: 20p, "100" with map of Americas and Iberian peninsula in zeroes. 26p, Map of Americas and Iberian peninsula, doves with letters.

2011, Mar. 18 **Litho.**
1502-1503 A658 Set of 2 2.50 2.50

Flowers — A659

No. 1504: a, Pereskia quisqueyana. b, Cereus hexagonus. c, Catalpa longissima. d, Tolumnia variegata.

2011, Mar. 31 *Perf. 13¼x13*
1504 A659 10p Block of 4, #a-d 2.25 2.25

Dated 2010.

Colonel Rafael T. Fernandez Dominguez (1934-65) A660

2011, May 19 **Litho.** *Perf. 13¼x13*
1505 A660 15p multi .80 .80

Liberty Day, 50th Anniv. — A661

2011, June 2 *Imperf.*
1506 A661 33p multi 1.75 1.75

Assassination of Pres. Rafael Trujillo, 50th anniv.

Aviation A662

No. 1507: a, 20p, Airplane of Zoilo H. Garcia. b, 25p, Garcia (1849-1922), first Dominican pilot.

2011, June 16 *Perf. 13x13¼*
1507 A662 Vert. pair, #a-b 2.40 2.40

Places Associated With Independence Leader Juan Pablo Duarte — A663

Designs: 15p, Santa Barbara Church, Santo Domingo. 20p, Baptismal font.

2011, Aug. 30
1508-1509 A663 Set of 2 1.90 1.90

Worldwide Fund for Nature (WWF) — A664

No. 1510 — Hypsiboas heilprini: a, Blue denomination at LR. b, Red denomination at LL. c, Red denomination at LR. d, Blue denomination at LL.

2011, Sept. 7
1510 A664 10p Block of 4, #a-d 2.10 2.10

Father of the Fatherland, by Martin de San Juan — A665

2011, Nov. 9 **Litho.** *Imperf.*
1511 A665 20p multi 1.10 1.10

Execution of Francisco del Rosario Sánchez, 150th anniv.

Pastoral and Social Work in Dominican Rpeublic of Bishop Francisco José Arnáiz, 50th Anniv. — A666

2011, Dec. 21
1512 A666 33p multi 1.75 1.75

Juan Pablo Duarte and Camara de Cuentas (Governmental Accounting Office) Document — A667

2011
1513 A667 20p multi 1.10 1.10

Sermon Denouncing Mistreatment of Indians of Friar Antonio de Montesinos, 500th Anniv. (in 2011) — A668

2012, Jan. 5 *Perf. 11½*
1514 A668 60p multi 3.25 3.25

Dated 2011.

National Police, 75th Anniv. (in 2011) A669

2012, Jan. 12 *Perf. 13x13¼*
1515 A669 20p multi 1.10 1.10

Dated 2011.

Order of the Pilgrims of the Way of St. James — A670

2012, Feb. 8 *Perf. 13¼x13½*
1516 A670 33p multi 1.75 1.75

Miniature Sheets

A671

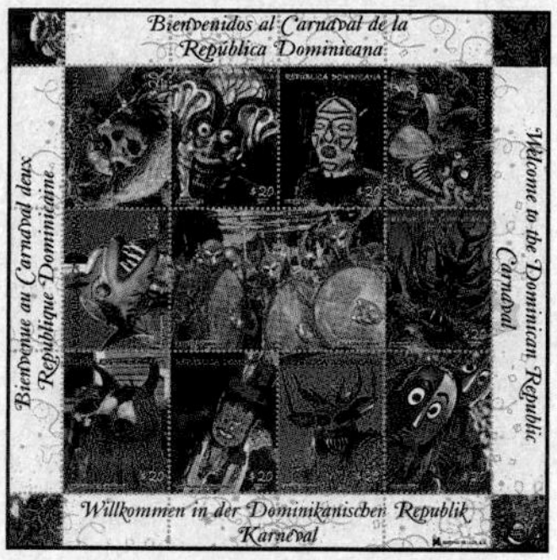

A672

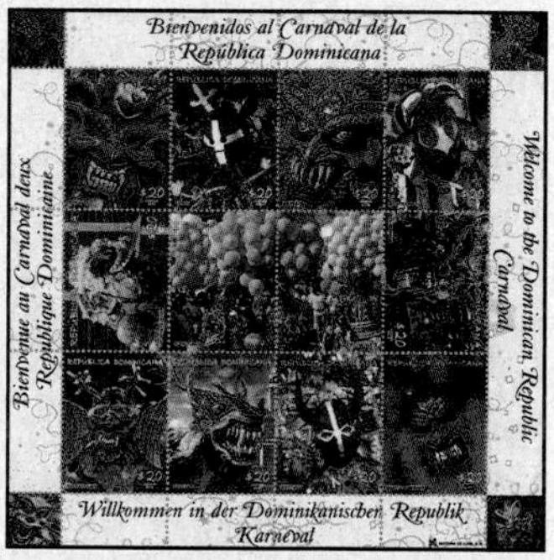

A673

A674

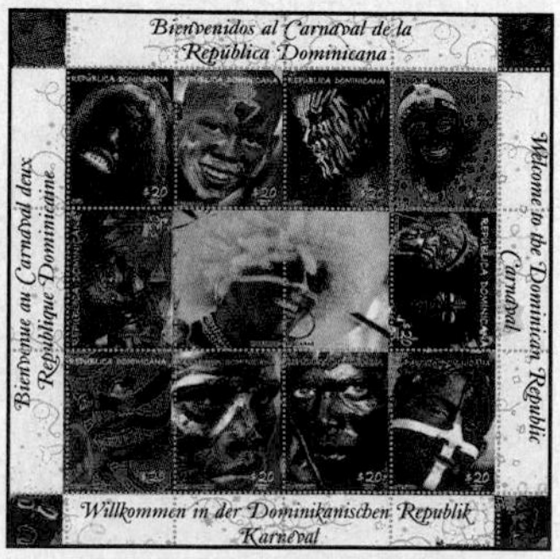

Carnival Masks and Painted Faces — A675

No. 1517: a, Azua (white face with headband). b, Bani. c, Barahona (red and black face). d, Barahona (green, yellow and red face). e, Cotuí (black and red face). f, La Romana (red, white and blue face with hat). g, La Romana (red and blue face with flower). h, Montecristi (yellow face with black and yellow hat). i, San Luis. j, Santo Domingo (red and yellow face with blue spots).

No. 1518: a, Cotuí (pink and red woman's face mask with blue eye lashes), horiz. b, Navarrette. c, Puerto Plata (white and brown mask). d, La Vega (mask with large pointed teeth), horiz. e, Rio San Juan (fish-head mask with large teeth), horiz. f, Samaná. g, San Juan de la Maguana. h, San Pedro de Macoris. i, Santo Domingo (green mask with horns). j, Villa Rivas.

No. 1519: a, Bonao (blue, green and red dragon's head mask). b, Cotuí (hat in flag colors with slits for eyes and mouth). c, La Vega (green and red dragon's head mask). d, Montecristi (red, gold, white, black and green mask). e, La Joya, Guerra, horiz. f, La Romana (yellow and blue bull's head mask with open mouth), horiz. g, Rio San Juan (blue, yellow, green and red demon-head mask with projections). h, Salcedo. i, Santiago (red, white and blue mask with spiked horns). j, Santo Domingo (mask with yellow beard).

No. 1520: a, Barahona (red, white and blue bull's head mask with horns), horiz. b, Bonao (mask with beard, moustache and gold hat). c, Constanza. d, Cabral, horiz. e, Elias Piña. f, La Vega (black, green and red cat's head mask). g, Valverde-Mao, horiz. h, Santiago (white, red and orange mask with spiked horns). i, Santo Domingo (red and yellow mask with horns). j, Puerto Plata (green, white and black pottery head mask), horiz.

No. 1521: a, Azua (red face with green hair). b, Barahona (blue, red, white and black face). c, Cotuí (black and white striped face with green hat). d, Cotuí (black face with flag hat). e, Cotuí (yellow, green, red and black face), horiz. f, Puerto Plata (brown and red mask, black, red and white face). g, Santo Domingo (yellow and black striped face). h, Santo Domingo (red, blue, white, green and black face). i, Rio San Juan (black face). j, Santiago (red, white and blue face).

Perf. 13¼x13 (vert. stamps), 13x13¼ (horiz. stamps)

2012, Feb. 27

1517 A671 20p	Sheet of 10, #a-j, + 2 central labels		10.50	10.50
1518 A672 20p	Sheet of 10, #a-j, + 2 central labels		10.50	10.50
1519 A673 20p	Sheet of 10, #a-j, + 2 central labels		10.50	10.50
1520 A674 20p	Sheet of 10, #a-j, + 2 central labels		10.50	10.50
1521 A675 20p	Sheet of 10, #a-j, + 2 central labels		10.50	10.50
	Nos. 1517-1521 (5)		52.50	52.50

Diplomatic Relations Between Dominican Republic and Ecuador, 125th Anniv.
A676

2012, Mar. 1 ***Perf. 13½x13¼***
1522 A676 20p multi 1.10 1.10

Dated 2011.

Pontifical Catholic University, Santo Domingo, 50th Anniv. — A677

2012, Apr. 17 ***Perf. 13¼x13***
1523 A677 25p multi 1.40 1.40

Mailboxes
A678

Designs: 20p, Mailbox with legs. 25p, Mailbox without legs.

2012, May 8 ***Perf. 13¼x13½***
1524-1525 A678 Set of 2 2.40 2.40

America Issue. Dated 2011.

Maria Montez (1912-51), Actress — A679

2012, June 2 ***Perf. 13¼x13***
1526 A679 100p multi 5.25 5.25

Juan Pablo Duarte (1813-76), Patriot — A680

No. 1527: a, 15p, Photograph of Duarte in Hamburg. b, 25p, Oath of the Trinitaria.

2012, July 24 ***Perf. 13½x13¼***
1527 A680 Pair, #a-b 2.10 2.10

Expo Cibao, 25th Anniv. — A681

2012, Sept. 5 ***Perf. 13¼x13***
1528 A681 20p multi 1.10 1.10
a. Tete-beche pair 2.20 2.20

Miniature Sheet

Birds — A682

No. 1529: a, Caprimulgus eckmani. b, Contopus hispaniolensis. c, Phaenicophilus palmarum. d, Icterus dominicensis. e, Loxia megaplaga. f, Calyptophilus frugivorus. g, Geotrygon leucometopia. h, Spindalis dominicensis. i, Corvus palmarum. j, Tyto glaucops.

2012, Sept. 19
1529 A682 20p Sheet of 10, #a-j, + 2 central labels 10.50 10.50

Orchids — A683

No. 1530: a, Sudamerylcaste peguerol. b, Tolumnia calochila. c, Quisqueya ekmanii. d, Tolumnia henekenii.

2012, Oct. 18
1530 A683 15p Block of 4, #a-d 3.00 3.00

Presidents Type of 2009
Miniature Sheet

No. 1531: a, Pedro Guillermo. b, Wenceslao Figuereo. c, Horacio Vásquez. d, Juan Isidro Jiménez. e, Eladio Victoria. f, Adolfo Alejandro Nouel. g, José Bordas Valdéz. h, Ramón Báez Machado.

2012 ***Perf. 13¼***
1531 A639 15p Sheet of 8, #a-h, + central label 6.00 6.00

America Issue — A684

No. 1532 — Legend of: a, El Caracaracol. b, La Ciguapa.

2012, Dec. 18 ***Perf. 13¼x13***
1532 A684 20p Horiz. pair, #a-b 2.00 2.00

Miniature Sheet

Tourism — A685

No. 1533: a, Beach, Saona Island. b, Beach, Bahia de las Aguilas. c, San Rafael Beach. d, Gri-Gri Lagoon. e, Dominican Republic flag. f, Playa Dorada. g, El Morro Beach. h, Puerto Plata. i, Monument to the Heroes of the Restoration, Santiago. j, Historic center of Santiago. k, Jordobadas Whale Sanctuary. l, Beach, Punta Cana.

2013, May 23 ***Perf. 13½x13¼***
1533 A685 10p Sheet of 12, #a-l 6.00 6.00

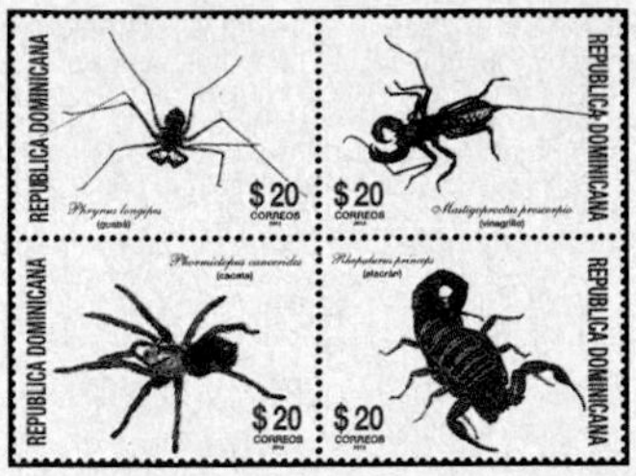

Arachnids — A686

No. 1534: a, Phrynus longipes. b, Mastigoproctus proscorpio. c, Phormictopus cancerides. d, Rhopalurus princeps.

2013, May 28
1534 A686 20p Block of 4, #a-d 4.00 4.00

Pedro Mir (1913-2000), Poet — A687

2013, June 24 ***Perf. 13¼x13***
1535 A687 50p multi 2.40 2.40

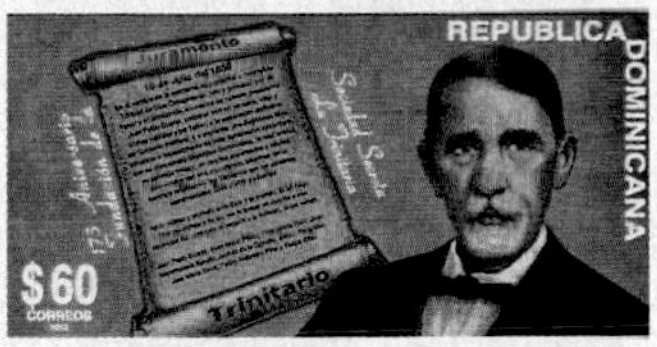

La Trinitaria Secret Society, 175th Anniv. — A688

2013, July 15 ***Imperf.***
1536 A688 60p multi 3.00 3.00

María Ugarte (1914-2011), Investigative Reporter — A689

2013, July 31 Litho. ***Perf. 13¼x13***
1537 A689 33p multi 1.60 1.60

A690

General Gregoio Luperón (1839-97) — A691

Perf. 13½x13¼
2013, Aug. 12 Litho.
1538 A690 15p multi .70 .70

Imperf

1539 A691 33p multi 1.60 1.60

Dominican War of the Restoration, 150th anniv.

Dominican Rehabilitation Association, Inc., 50th Anniv. — A692

2013, Oct. 23 Litho. ***Perf. 13½x13***
1540 A692 15p red & blue .70 .70

Dominican Postal Institute (Inposdom), 50th Anniv. — A693

Designs: 15p, Emblem for InposPak service. 20p, Inposdom emblem, vert. 25p, Exhibit frames at stamp exhibition. 80p, Inposdom Headquarters.

2013, Nov. 28 Litho. ***Perf. 13¼***
1541 A693 15p multi .70 .70

Size: 30x40mm
Perf. 13¼x13½

1542 A693 20p multi .95 .95

Size: 40x30mm
Perf. 13½x13¼

1543 A693 25p multi 1.25 1.25
Nos. 1541-1543 (3) 2.90 2.90

Size: 80x50mm
Imperf

1544 A693 80p multi 3.75 3.75

Campaign Against Discrimination — A696

Designs: 15p, Five children. 20p, Map of Dominican Republic, hands.

2014, Jan. 30 Litho. ***Perf. 13x13¼***
1547-1548 A696 Set of 2 1.75 1.75

America issue. Dated 2013.

Founding of St. Thomas Aquinas University, Santo Domingo, 475th Anniv. (in 2013) A697

Designs: 20p, Building. 25p, Buildings and university crest.

2014, Feb. 14 Litho. ***Perf. 13x13¼***
1549 A697 20p multi .95 .95

Size: 89x60mm
Imperf

1550 A697 25p multi 1.25 1.25

Reopening of university as Autonomous University of Santo Domingo, cent. Dated 2013.

Julia de Burgos (1914-53), Poet — A698

2014, Mar. 28 Litho. ***Perf. 13¼x13***
1551 A698 100p multi 4.75 4.75

Souvenir Sheets

Centro León Museum — A699

National Botanical Gardens — A700

Bellapart Museum — A701

Numismatic and Philatelic Museum — A702

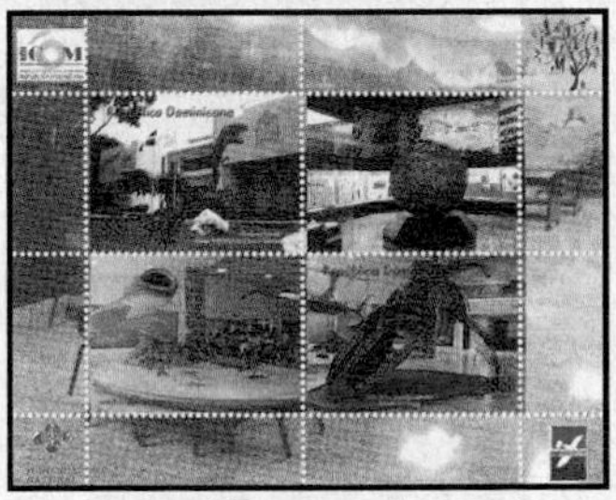

National Museum of Natural History — A703

Museum of Modern Art — A704

No. 1552: a, Entrance to Jimenes Cultural Center. b, Caribeño Patio of Eduardo León Jimenes Cultural Center.
No. 1553: a, Bridge in Japanese Garden. b, Path in Japanese Garden.
No. 1554: a, Permanent Gallery. b, Merengue, painting by Jaime Colson.
No. 1555: a, Exhibit of money with metal ingot. b, Display case in Numismatics Gallery.
No. 1556: a, Museum entrance. b, Skeleton of humpback whale.
No. 1557: a, Sculptures. b, Sculptures and paintings in Permanent Gallery.

2014, May 21 Litho. ***Perf. 13½***
1552 A699 50p Sheet of 2, #a-b, + 2 labels 4.75 4.75
1553 A700 50p Sheet of 2, #a-b, + 2 labels 4.75 4.75
1554 A701 50p Sheet of 2, #a-b, + 2 labels 4.75 4.75
1555 A702 50p Sheet of 2, #a-b, + 2 labels 4.75 4.75
1556 A703 50p Sheet of 2, #a-b, + 2 labels 4.75 4.75
1557 A704 50p Sheet of 2, #a-b, + 2 labels 4.75 4.75
Nos. 1552-1557 (6) 28.50 28.50

World Museum Day.

Duarte Institute, 50th Anniv. A705

2014, June 24 Litho. ***Perf. 13½***
1558 A705 50p multi 2.40 2.40

Flowers — A706

No. 1559: a, Salcedoa mirabaliarum. b, Ekmanianthe longiflora, vert. c, Coccothrinax jienezii, vert. d, Rhytidophyllum daisyanum.

2014, Aug. 27 Litho. ***Perf. 13x13¼***
1559 A706 20p Block of 4, #a-d 3.75 3.75

Dated 2013.

National Literacy Plan A707

2014, Sept. 8 Litho. ***Perf. 13½***
1560 A707 15p multi .70 .70

Dated 2013.

Miniature Sheets

Heroes and Flags of Nations of North and South America — A708

No. 1561, 50p: a, José de San Martín, flag of Argentina. b, Joaquim José Da Silva Xavier (Tiradentes), flag of Brazil. c, Francisco de Paula Santander, flag of Colombia. d, Pedro Alvarado y Bonilla, flag of Costa Rica. e, José Martí, flag of Cuba. f, Juan Pablo Duarte (standing), flag of Dominican Republic. g, Quote by Duarte, flag of Dominican Republic. h, Bernardo O'Higgins Riquelme, flag of Chile. i, José Matías Delgado de León, flag of El Salvador. j, George Washington, flag of United States. k, Jean Jacques Dessalines, flag of Haiti. l, Francisco Morazán Quezada, flag of Honduras.

No. 1562, 50p: a, Simón Bolívar, flag of Bolivia. b, Georges-Etienne Cartier, flag of Canada. c, Máximo Gómez y Báez, flag of Cuba. d, Manuela Sáenz y Aizpuru, flag of Ecuador. e, Pedro Molina Mazariegos, flag of Guatemala. f, Miguel Hidalgo y Costilla, flag of Mexico. g, Head of Duarte, flag of Dominican Republic. h, Augusto César Sandino, flag of Nicaragua. i, Gaspar Rodríguez de Francia, flag of Paraguay. j, José Gabriel Condorcanqui (Túpac Amaru II), flag of Peru. k, José Gervado Artigas Arnal, flag of Uruguay. l, Bolívar, flag of Venezuela.

2014, Sept. 30 Litho. *Perf. 13¼x13*
Sheets of 12, #a-l

1561-1562 A708 Set of 2 55.00 55.00

America issue.

World Food Day — A709

No. 1563: a, Boy holding apple. b, Boy eating broccoli, vert. c, Fruit picker on ladder. d, Girl eating cob of corn, vert.

2014, Oct. 15 Litho. *Perf. 13½*

1563 A709 25p Block of 4, #a-d 4.50 4.50

Miniature Sheet

Wildlife — A710

No. 1564, 25p — Fish: a, Pomacanthus paru. b, Holacanthus ciliaris. c, Serranus tigrinus. d, Nandopsis haitensis. e, Haemulon flavolineatum. f, Anisotremus virginicus. g, Cantherhines macrocerus. h, Agonostomus monticola. i, Epinephelus striatus. j, Gymnothorax funebris. k, Aulostomus maculatus. l, Dasyatis americana.

No. 1565, 25p — Butterflies: a, Anaea troglodyta. b, Anartia lytrea. c, Burca stillmani. d, Burca hispaniolae. e, Myscelia aracynthia. f, Archimestra teleboas. g, Atlante cryptadia. h, Greta diaphanus quisqueya. i, Heraclides machaonides. j, Choranthus haitensis. k, Memphis verticordia. l, Pyrisitia pyro.

Perf. 13½x13¼
2014, Nov. 20 Litho.
Sheets of 12, #a-l

1564-1565 A710 Set of 2 28.00 28.00

Miniature Sheet

Merengue Musicians and Instruments — A711

No. 1566: a, Nico Lora playing accordion. b, Accordion, horiz. c, Tatico Henriquez playing accordion, horiz. d, Güira. e, Tambora. f, Trio Reynosa performing, horiz. g, Marimba. g, Guandulito playing accordion, horiz.

Perf. 13¼x13½, 13½x13¼
2014, Nov. 26 Litho.

1566 A711 15p Sheet of 8, #a-h, + central label 5.50 5.50

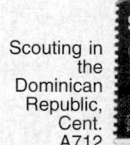

Scouting in the Dominican Republic, Cent. A712

2014, Dec. 3 Litho. *Perf. 13½x13¼*

1567 A712 20p multi .90 .90

ISA University, 50th Anniv. (in 2014) A713

2015, May 5 Litho. *Perf. 13½*

1568 A713 200p multi 9.00 9.00

Bani, 250th Anniv. (in 2014) A714

2015, Mar. 6 Litho. *Perf. 13¼*

1569 A714 100p multi 4.50 4.50

Dated 2014.

Gustavo A. Moré González (1925-2002), President of Dominican Philatelic Society — A715

2015, Apr. 9 Litho. *Perf. 13½*

1570 A715 75p multi 3.50 3.50

Stamp Day. Dated 2014.

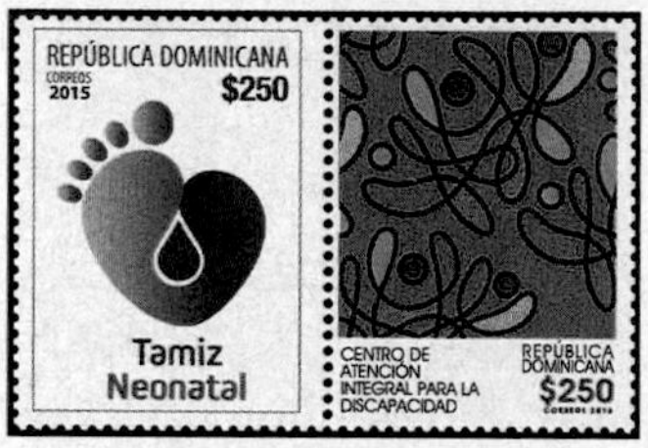

Programs Run Through Office of the First Lady — A716

No. 1571: a, Newborn Screening Program. b, Comprehensive Care Center for Disability.

2015, Apr. 28 Litho. *Perf. 13¼x13*

1571 A716 250p Horiz. pair, #a-b 22.50 22.50

Miniature Sheets

National Parks — A717

No. 1572, 20p: a, Pyramids, Valle Nuevo National Park. b, Rio Grande Waterfall, Francisco Alberto Caamaño Deñó National Park. c, Coral reef and fish, Monte Cristi Underwater National Park. d, Hatillo Dam Reservoir with small islands at left, Aniana Vargas National Park. e, Hoyo de Pelempito, Sierra de Bahoruco National Park. f, Aerial view of El Morro Beach, El Morro National Park. g, Coastal hills, Los Haitises National Park. h, Sierra de Neiba, Sierra de Neiba National Park. i, Salado de Neiba, La Gran Sabana National Park. j, Haemulon spp., La Caleta Underwater National Park. k, Quita Coraza, Anacona National Park. l, La Isabela ruins, La Hispaniola National Park.

No. 1573, 20p: a, Baiguate Waterfall, Baiguate National Park. b, Punta Aguila Cliffs, Jaragua National Park. c, Waterfall, Saltos de la Jalda National Park, vert. d, Cliffs, Sierra Martin García National Park. e, Cyclura ricordii, Lago Enriquillo e Isla Cabritos National Park. f, Offshore rocks, Los Haitises National Park. g, Rock art, Aniana Vargas National Park, vert. h, Whales, Cabo Cabrón National Park. i, Plagiodontia aedium, Sierra de Bahoruco National Park. j, Mountains, Nalga de Maco National Park. k, Sea level view of cliffs and El Morro Beach, El Morro National Park. l, Palm trees, Sierra Martin García National Park.

No. 1574, 20p: a, Tetero Valley, José del Carmen Ramírez National Park. b, Isla Saona, Este National Park. c, Fregata magnificens, Este National Park. d, Mountains, Armando Bermúdez National Park. e, Sun over water, Lago Enriquillo e Isla Cabritos National Park. f, Cabo Cabrón, Cabo Cabrón National Park. g, Epilobocera wetherbeei, Valle Nuevo National Park. h, Punta Espada, Punta Espada National Park. i, Río Amina, Manolo Tavárez Justo National Park. j, La Humeadora, La Humeadora National Park. k, Rivers, Humedales del Ozama National Park. l, Río Mana, Máximo Gómez National Park, vert.

No. 1575, 20p: a, Balsa Estuary, Mangiares de Estero Balsa National Park. b, Río Mao, Piky Lora National Park. c, Lakes, Humedales del Ozama National Park. d, Shoreline, Mangiares del Bajo Yuna National Park. e, Foggy landscape, Valle Nuevo National Park. f, Bahia de las Aguilas, Jaragua National Park. g, Siproeta stelenes, Máximo Gómez National Park, vert. h, Hatillo Dam Reservoir with rocks at LR, Aniana Vargas National Park. i, Phaenicophilus palmarum, Luis Quin National Park. j, Loma La Tachuela, Luis Quin National Park. k, Shoreline, Este National Park. l, Mountains, Manolo Tavárez Justo National Park.

2015, May 22 Litho. *Perf. 13½*
Sheets of 12, #a-l

1572-1575 A717 Set of 4 42.50 42.50

Dominican Chapter of Lions International, 50th Anniv. — A718

2015, May 24 Litho. *Perf. 13¼*

1576 A718 50p multi 2.25 2.25

Matías Ramón Mella Castillo (1816-64), Vice-President — A719

2015, June 10 Litho. *Imperf.*

1577 A719 300p multi 13.50 13.50

Dated 2014.

Cooperation Between Brazilian and Dominican Republic Universities, 50th Anniv. — A720

2015, June 22 Litho. *Perf. 13½*

1578 A720 50p multi 2.25 2.25

Santiago Chamber of Commerce, Cent. — A721

2015, July 9 Litho. *Perf. 13¼*

1579 A721 50p multi 2.25 2.25

Oscar de la Renta (1932-2014), Fashion Designer — A722

2015, Oct. 13 Litho. *Perf. 13¼x13*

1580 A722 250p multi 11.00 11.00

St. Teresa of Avila (1515-82) — A723

2015, Oct. 16 Litho. *Perf. 13¼x13½*
1581 A723 45p multi 2.00 2.00

Rights for Disabled People — A724

2015, Nov. 16 Litho. *Perf. 13¼*
1582 A724 100p multi 4.50 4.50

Campaign to End Violence Against Women — A725

Perf. 13¼x13½
2015, Nov. 25 Litho.
1583 A725 35p multi 1.60 1.60

See Ecuador No. , Guatemala No. , El Salvador No. , and Venezuela No.

Religious Objects — A726

No. 1584: a, Pax, 17th cent. (portapaz). b, Processional cross, 18th cent. (cruz procesional). c, Monstrance, 19th cent. (custodia). d, Eucharistic ark, 16th cent. (arca eucarística). e, Chalice, 16th cent. (cáliz).

2015, Dec. 1 Litho. *Perf. 13¼x13½*
1584 Strip of 5 10.00 10.00
a.-e. A726 45p Any single 2.00 2.00

SEMI-POSTAL STAMPS

Catalogue values for unused stamps in this section are for Never Hinged items.

Nos. 474-478 Surcharged in Red

Engraved and Lithographed
1957, Feb. 8 Unwmk. *Perf. 11½*
Flags in National Colors

B1 A117 1c + 2c brn, lt bl, vio & mar .30 .25
B2 A117 2c + 2c dk brn, lt bl & vio .30 .25
B3 A117 3c + 2c red lilac & red .30 .25
B4 A117 5c + 2c red orange & vio .30 .25
B5 A117 7c + 2c green & violet .35 .30
Nos. B1-B5,CB1-CB3 (8) 2.85 2.60

The surtax was to aid Hungarian refugees. A similar 25c surcharge was applied to the miniature sheets described in the footnote following No. 478. Value, 2 sheets, perf. and imperf., $32.50

Nos. 479-483 Surcharged in Red Orange

1957, Sept. 9 Photo. *Perf. 13½*
Flags in National Colors

B6 A118 1c + 2c brown & brt bl .25 .25
B7 A118 2c + 2c org ver & dk bl .30 .30
B8 A118 3c + 2c dark blue .35 .35
B9 A118 5c + 2c olive & dk bl .45 .45
B10 A118 7c + 2c rose brn & dk bl .50 .50
Nos. B6-B10,CB4-CB6 (8) 4.00 3.55

Cent. of the birth of Lord Baden Powell and the 50th anniv. of the Scout Movement. The surtax was for the Dominican Republic Boy Scouts.

A similar 5c surcharge was applied to the miniature sheets described in the footnote following No. 483. Value 4 sheets, perf. and imperf., medal and flag, $62.50

Types of Olympic Regular Issue, 1957, Surcharged in Carmine

a

b

1958, May 26 Engr. & Litho.
Flags in National Colors
Pink Paper

B11 A119(a) 1c + 2c red brown .25 .25
B12 A119(b) 1c + 2c red brown .25 .25
B13 A120(a) 2c + 2c gray brown .30 .30
B14 A120(b) 2c + 2c gray brown .30 .30
B15 A119(a) 3c + 2c violet .30 .30
B16 A119(b) 3c + 2c violet .30 .30
B17 A120(a) 5c + 2c red orange .40 .40
B18 A120(b) 5c + 2c red orange .40 .40
B19 A119(a) 7c + 2c Prus green .50 .50
B20 A119(b) 7c + 2c Prus green .50 .50
Nos. B11-B20,CB7-CB12 (16) 5.90 5.90

Surtax for the UN Relief and Works Agency for Palestine Refugees.

A similar 5c surcharge, plus marginal United Nations emblem and "UNRWA," was applied to the miniature sheets described in the footnote following No. 488. Value, 4 sheets, perf. and imperf., $20.

Nos. 501-505 Surcharged

Perf. 13½
1959, Apr. 13 Photo. Unwmk.
Flags in National Colors

B21 A125 1c + 2c rose, indigo & ultra .40 .40
B22 A125 1c + 2c brown & blue .40 .40
B23 A125 3c + 2c gray, vio, blk & buff .50 .50
B24 A125 5c + 2c rose, dk bl, brn & red .60 .60
B25 A125 7c + 2c lt brn, dk bl & red .70 .70
Nos. B21-B25,CB13-CB15 (8) 5.65 5.65

International Geophysical Year, 1957-58.

A similar 5c surcharge was applied to the miniature sheets described in the footnote following No. 505. Value, 2 sheets, perf. and imperf., $40.

Type of 1957 Surcharged in Red

Engraved and Lithographed
1959, Sept. 10 Unwmk. *Imperf.*
Flags in National Colors

B26 A117 1c + 2c brn, lt bl, vio & mar .30 .30
B27 A117 2c + 2c dk brn, lt bl & vio .30 .30
B28 A117 3c + 2c red lilac & red .35 .35
B29 A117 5c + 2c red org & vio .35 .35
B30 A117 7c + 2c green & violet .45 .45
Nos. B26-B30,CB16-CB18 (8) 3.75 3.75

3rd Pan American Games, Chicago, Aug. 27-Sept. 7, 1959.

Nos. 522-524 Surcharged in Red

1960, Apr. 7 Litho. *Perf. 12½*
Center in Gray

B31 A135 5c + 5c red brn & yel grn .30 .30
B32 A135 9c + 5c car & lt bl .30 .30
B33 A135 13c + 5c org & grn .65 .65
Nos. B31-B33,CB19-CB20 (5) 2.00 2.00

World Refugee Year, July 1, 1959-June 30, 1960. The surtax was for aid to refugees.

Souvenir sheets exist perf. and imperf., containing one each of Nos. B31-B33 and CB19-CB20. Value, 2 sheets, perf. and imperf., $12.50

Nos. 525-529 Surcharged

1962, Jan. 8 Photo. *Perf. 13½*
Flags in National Colors

B34 A136 1c + 2c red, yel grn & blk .30 .25
B35 A136 2c + 2c org, grnsh bl & brn .30 .25
B36 A136 3c + 2c henna brn & bl .30 .25
B37 A136 5c + 2c brown & ultra .30 .25
B38 A136 7c + 2c grn, bl & rose brn .30 .25
Nos. B34-B38,CB21-CB23 (8) 2.60 2.35

15th anniv. (in 1961) of UNESCO.

A similar 5c surcharge was applied to the miniature sheets described in the footnote following No. 529. Value, 2 sheets, perf. and imperf., $16.

Anti-Malaria Type of 1962

1962, Apr. 29 Litho. *Perf. 12*
B39 A141 10c + 2c brt pink & red lil .40 .30
B40 A141 20c + 2c pale brn & brn .60 .45

Freedom from Hunger Type of 1963

1963, Apr. 15 Unwmk. *Perf. 11½*
Banner in Dark Blue & Red

B41 A148 2c + 1c green .30 .25
B42 A148 5c + 2c brt rose lil .30 .25
B43 A148 9c + 2c orange .30 .25
Nos. B41-B43 (3) .70 .70

A souvenir sheet contains three imperf. stamps similar to Nos. B41-B43. Value, $1.50.

Nos. 591-593 Surcharged

1964, Mar. 8 *Perf. 12½*
B44 A153 3c + 2c pale pink & ver .25 .25
B45 A153 6c + 2c pale bl & ultra .25 .25
B46 A153 9c + 2c pale rose & red brn .25 .25
Nos. B44-B46,CB26-CB27 (5) 1.30 1.25

UNESCO world campaign to save historic monuments in Nubia.

Nos. 622-626 Surcharged

1966, Dec. 9 Litho. *Perf. 12½*
Size: 31x21mm

B47 A164 1c + 2c multi *8.50* *1.25*
B48 A164 2c + 2c multi *8.50* *1.25*
B49 A164 3c + 2c multi *8.50* *1.25*
B50 A164 6c + 4c multi *8.50* *1.25*
B51 A164 8c + 4c multi *8.50* *1.25*
Nos. B47-B51,CB28-CB30 (8) 56.00 14.00

Surtax for victims of Hurricane Inez.

AIR POST STAMPS

Map of Hispaniola — AP1

Perf. 11½

1928, May 31 Litho. Unwmk.

C1 AP1 10c deep ultra 5.25 2.50

1930

C2 AP1 10c ocher 3.50 3.00
a. Vert. pair, imperf. btwn. *600.00*
C3 AP1 15c scarlet 6.75 4.00
C4 AP1 20c dull green 3.25 .85
C5 AP1 30c violet 6.75 4.50
Nos. C2-C5 (4) 20.25 12.35

Nos. C2-C5 have only "CENTAVOS" in lower panel. Issued: 10c, 20c, 1/24; 15c, 30c, 2/14.

1930

C6 AP1 10c light blue 1.75 .60
C7 AP1 15c blue green 3.25 1.00
C8 AP1 20c yellow brown 3.50 .85
a. Horiz. pair, imperf. vert. 450.00 450.00
C9 AP1 30c chocolate 6.25 1.75
Nos. C6-C9 (4) 14.75 4.20

Issue dates: 10c, 15c, 20c, Sept.; 30c, Oct.

Batwing Sundial Erected in 1753 — AP2

1931-33 *Perf. 12*

C10 AP2 10c carmine 3.50 .50
C11 AP2 10c light blue 1.75 .50
C12 AP2 10c dark green 6.25 2.75
C13 AP2 15c rose lilac 2.75 .50
C14 AP2 20c dark blue 6.25 2.25
a. Numerals reading up at left and down at right 5.75 2.75
b. Imperf., pair 250.00
C15 AP2 30c green 2.50 .25
C16 AP2 50c red brown 6.25 .50
C17 AP2 1p deep orange 10.00 2.75
Nos. C10-C17 (8) 39.25 10.00

Issued: No. C11, 7/2/32; No. C12, 5/28/33; others 8/16.

Airplane and Ozama Fortress AP3

1933, Nov. 20

C18 AP3 10c dark blue 3.50 .60

Airplane and Trujillo Bridge AP4

1934, Sept. 20

C19 AP4 10c dark blue 3.00 .50

Symbolic of Flight AP5

1935, Apr. 29

C20 AP5 10c lt blue & dk blue 1.60 .50

AP6

1936, Feb. 11 *Perf. 11½*

C21 AP6 10c dk bl & turq bl 2.50 .50

Allegory of Flight AP7

1936, Oct. 17

C22 AP7 10c dk bl, bl & turq bl 2.25 .40

Macoris Airport AP8

1937, Oct. 22

C23 AP8 10c green 1.00 .25

Fleet of Columbus AP9

Air Fleet AP10

Proposed Columbus Lighthouse — AP11

1937, Nov. 9 *Perf. 12*

C24 AP9 10c rose red 1.75 1.40
C25 AP10 15c purple 1.40 .95
C26 AP11 20c dk bl & lt bl 1.40 1.25
C27 AP10 25c red violet 2.00 1.25
C28 AP11 30c yellow green 1.75 1.25
C29 AP10 50c brown 3.50 1.75
C30 AP11 75c dk olive grn 10.50 10.50
C31 AP9 1p orange 6.25 2.50
Nos. C24-C31 (8) 28.55 20.85

Goodwill flight to all American countries by the planes "Colon," "Pinta," "Nina" and "Santa Maria."

No. C30 was reproduced imperf. on No. 1019.

Pan American Clipper AP12

1938, July 30

C32 AP12 10c green 1.25 .25

Trylon and Perisphere, Plane and Proposed Columbus Lighthouse — AP13

1939, Apr. 30

C33 AP13 10c green & lt green 2.00 .85

New York World's Fair.

Airplane AP14

1939, Oct. 18

C34 AP14 10c green & dp green 1.60 .25
a. Pair, imperf. btwn. *450.00*

Proposed Columbus Lighthouse, Plane and Caravels — AP15

Christopher Columbus and Proposed Lighthouse — AP16

Proposed Lighthouse — AP17

Christopher Columbus — AP18

Caravel — AP19

1940, Oct. 12

C35 AP15 10c sapphire & lt bl 1.10 .60
C36 AP16 15c org brn & brn 1.60 1.00
C37 AP17 20c rose red & red 1.60 1.00
C38 AP18 25c brt red lil & red vio 1.60 .50
C39 AP19 50c green & lt green 3.00 1.75
Nos. C35-C39 (5) 8.90 4.85

Discovery of America by Columbus and proposed Columbus memorial lighthouse in Dominican Republic.

Posts and Telegraph Building, San Cristobal AP20

1941, Feb. 21

C40 AP20 10c brt red lil & pale lil rose .50 .25

Globe, Wing and Letter AP21

1942, Feb. 13

C41 AP21 10c dark violet brn .60 .30
C42 AP21 75c deep orange 3.25 2.00

Plane AP22

1943, Sept. 1

C43 AP22 10c brt red lilac .40 .25
C44 AP22 20c dp blue & lt blue .40 .25
C45 AP22 25c yellow olive 5.75 3.25
Nos. C43-C45 (3) 6.55 3.75

Plane, Flag, Coat of Arms and Torch of Liberty — AP23

1944, Feb. 27 *Perf. 11½*

Flag in Gray, Dark Blue, Carmine

C46 AP23 10c multicolored .35 .25
C47 AP23 20c multicolored .45 .25
C48 AP23 1p multicolored 2.00 1.50
Nos. C46-C48 (3) 2.80 1.90

Centenary of Independence. See No. 407 for souvenir sheet listing.

Communications Building, Ciudad Trujillo — AP24

1944, Nov. 12 Litho. *Perf. 12*

C49 AP24 9c yel grn & blue .25 .25
C50 AP24 13c dull brn & rose car .25 .25
C51 AP24 25c org & dull red .35 .25
b. Vert. pair, imperf. btwn. 45.00
C52 AP24 30c black & ultra .75 .65
Nos. C49-C52 (4) 1.60 1.40

Twenty booklets of 100 (25 panes of 4) of the 25c were issued. All booklets are still intact.

Communications Type

1945, Sept. 1

Center in Dark Blue and Carmine

C53 A92 7c deep yellow green .35 .25
C54 A92 12c red orange .40 .25
C55 A92 13c deep blue .50 .25
C56 A92 25c orange brown .90 .25
Nos. C53-C56 (4) 1.90 .85

AP26

Flags and National Anthem AP27

Unwmk.

1946, Feb. 27 Litho. *Perf. 12*

Center in Dark Blue, Deep Carmine and Black

C57 AP26 10c carmine .95 .40
C58 AP26 15c blue 2.10 .85
C59 AP26 20c chocolate 2.50 .85
C60 AP26 35c orange 3.00 .95
C61 AP27 1p grn, yel grn & cit 25.00 10.00
Nos. C57-C61 (5) 33.55 13.05

Nos. C57-C61 exist imperf.

Map Type of Regular Issue

1946, Aug. 4

C62 A94 10c multicolored .85 .25
C63 A94 13c multicolored 1.60 .25

Waterfall Type of Regular Issue

1947, Mar. 18 Litho.

Center Multicolored

C64 A95 18c light blue 1.00 .50
C65 A95 23c carmine 1.60 .60
C66 A95 50c red violet 2.10 .60
C67 A95 75c chocolate 3.00 1.10
Nos. C64-C67 (4) 5.45 2.40

Palace Type of Regular Issue

1948, Feb. 27

C68 A96 37c orange brown 2.10 1.00
C69 A96 1p orange yellow 5.75 2.10

Ruins Type of Regular Issue

1949 Unwmk. *Perf. 11½*

C70 A97 7c ol grn & pale ol grn .40 .25
C71 A97 10c orange brn & buff .40 .25
C72 A97 15c brt rose & pale pink 1.25 .30
C73 A97 20c green & pale green 1.75 .60
Nos. C70-C73 (4) 2.75 1.10

Issue dates: 10c, Apr. 4; others, Apr. 13.

Las Carreras Monument — AP32

1949, Aug. 10

C74 AP32 10c red & pink .60 .25

Cent. of the Battle of Las Carreras.

Catalogue values for unused stamps in this section, from this point to the end of the section, are for Never Hinged items.

Hotel Type of Regular Issue

Hotels: 12c, Montana. 37c, San Cristobal.

1950, Sept. 8

C75 A100 12c dk blue & blue .60 .25
C76 A100 37c carmine & pink 3.75 2.50

Map, Plane and Caduceus AP34

1950, Oct. 2

C77 AP34 12c orange brn & yel .85 .25

13th Pan-American Health Conf. Exists imperf.

Hospital Type of Regular Issue

1952, Aug.

C78 A104 23c deep blue .85 .85
C79 A104 29c carmine 2.25 1.50

Columbus Lighthouse and Plane — AP36

1953, Jan. 6 Engr. *Perf. 13*

C80 AP36 12c ocher .30 .25
C81 AP36 14c dark blue .25 .25
C82 AP36 20c black brown .70 .60
C83 AP36 23c deep plum .40 .40
C84 AP36 25c dark blue .95 .70
C85 AP36 29c deep green .70 .60
C86 AP36 1p red brown 2.00 1.25
a. Miniature sheet of 10 21.00 21.00
Nos. C80-C86 (7) 4.15 3.00

No. C86a is lithographed and contains Nos. 450-452 and C80-C86, in slightly different shades. Sheet measures 190x130mm and is imperf. with simulated perforations.

A miniature sheet similar to No. C86a, but measuring 200x163mm and in folder, exists. Value $100.

Ano Mariano Initials in Monogram — AP37

1954, Aug. 5 Litho. *Perf. 11½*

C87 AP37 8c claret .25 .25
C88 AP37 11c blue .30 .25
C89 AP37 33c brown orange 1.00 .60
Nos. C87-C89 (3) 1.55 1.10

Marian Year. Nos. C87-C89 exist imperf.

Rotary Type of Regular Issue

1955, Feb. 23 *Perf. 12*

C90 A110 11c rose red .50 .25

Flags — AP39

Portraits of General Hector B. Trujillo: 25c, In civilian clothes. 33c, In uniform.

1955, May 16 Engr. *Perf. 13½x13*

C91 AP39 11c blue, yel & car .70 .25
C92 AP39 25c rose violet 1.25 .30
C93 AP39 33c orange brown 1.75 .60
Nos. C91-C93 (3) 2.70 1.00

The center of No. C91 is litho. 25th anniv. of the inauguration of the Trujillo era.

Fair Type of Regular Issue

1955, Dec. 20 Unwmk. *Perf. 13*

C94 A112 11c vermilion .40 .25

ICAO Type of Regular Issue

1956, Apr. 6 Litho. *Perf. 12½*

C95 A114 11c ultra .50 .25

Tree Type of Regular Issue

Design: 13c, Mahogany tree.

1956, Dec. 8 Litho. *Perf. 11½x12*

C96 A115 13c orange & green 2.25 .25

Type of Regular Issue, 1957

Olympic Winners and Flags: 11c, Paavo Nurmi, Finland. 16c, Ugo Frigerio, Italy. 17c, Mildred Didrikson ("Didrickson" on stamp), US.

Engraved and Lithographed

Perf. 11½, Imperf.

1957, Jan. 24 Unwmk.

Flags in National Colors

C97 A117 11c ultra & red org .25 .25
C98 A117 16c carmine & lt grn .30 .25
C99 A117 17c black, vio & red .40 .25
Nos. C97-C99 (3) .75 .75

16th Olympic Games, Melbourne, Nov. 22-Dec. 8, 1956.

Souvenir sheets of 3 exist, perf. and imperf., containing Nos. C97-C99. Value, 2 sheets, perf. & imperf., $15.

For surcharges see Nos. CB1-CB3, CB16-CB18.

Type of Regular Issue

Olympic Winners and Flags: 11c, Robert Morrow, US, 100 & 200 meter dash. 16c, Chris Brasher, England, steeplechase. 17c, A. Ferreira Da Silva, Brazil, hop, step and jump.

Perf. 13½, Imperf.

1957, July 18 Photo.

Flags in National Colors

C100 A118 11c yellow grn & dk bl .25 .25
C101 A118 16c lilac & dk blue .30 .25
C102 A118 17c brown & blue grn .35 .25
Nos. C100-C102 (3) .75 .75

1956 Olympic winners.

See note on miniature sheets following No. 483.

For surcharges see Nos. CB4-CB6.

Types of Regular Issue

Olympic Winners and Flags: 11c, Hans Winkler, Germany, individual jumping. 16c, Alfred Oerter, US, discus throw. 17c, Shirley Strickland, Australia, 800 meter hurdles.

Engraved and Lithographed

Perf. 13½, Imperf.

1957, Nov. 12 Unwmk.

Flags in National Colors

C103 A119 11c ultra .25 .25
C104 A120 16c rose carmine .40 .25
C105 A119 17c claret .40 .25
Nos. C103-C105 (3) .75 .75

1956 Olympic winners.

Miniature sheets of 3 exist, perf. and imperf., containing Nos. C103-C105. Value, 2 sheets, perf. and imperf., $5.50.

For surcharges see Nos. CB7-CB12.

Type of Regular Issue

Olympic Winners and Flags: 11c, Charles Jenkins, 400 & 800 meter run, and Thomas Courtney, 1,600 meter relay, US. 16c, Field hockey team, India. 17c, Yachting team, Sweden.

Perf. 13½, Imperf.

1958, Oct. 30 Unwmk. Photo.

Flags in National Colors

C106 A125 11c blue, olive & brn .30 .25
C107 A125 16c lt grn, org & dk bl .40 .25
C108 A125 17c ver, blue & yel .40 .25
Nos. C106-C108 (3) .75 .75

1956 Olympic winners.

Miniature sheets of 3 exist, perf. and imperf., containing Nos. C106-C108. Value, 2 sheets, perf. and imperf., $3.

For surcharges see Nos. CB13-CB15.

Fair Type of Regular Issue

1958, Dec. 9 Litho. *Perf. 12½*

C109 A127 9c gray .30 .25
C110 A127 25c lt violet .85 .40
a. Souv. sheet of 3, #C109-C110, 507, imperf. 2.25 2.25

Polo Type of Regular Issue

1959, May 15 *Perf. 12*

C111 A130 11c Dominican polo team .40 .30

"San Cristobal" Plane — AP42

Perf. 11½

1960, Feb. 25 Unwmk. Litho.

C112 AP42 13c org, bl, grn & gray .35 .25

Dominican Civil Aviation.

Children and WRY Emblem AP43

1960, Apr. 7 *Perf. 12½*

C113 AP43 10c plum, gray & grn .65 .30
C114 AP43 13c gray & green .90 .30

World Refugee Year, 7/1/59-6/30/60.

For surcharges see Nos. CB19-CB20.

Olympic Type of Regular Issue

Olympic Winners: 11c, Pat McCormick, US, diving. 16c, Mithat Bayrack, Turkey, welter-weight wrestling. 17c, Ursula Happe, Germany, 200 meter breast stroke.

Perf. 13½, Imperf.

1960, Sept. 14 Photo.

Flags in National Colors

C115 A136 11c blue, gray & brn .25 .25
C116 A136 16c red, brown & ol .30 .30
C117 A136 17c black, blue & ocher .40 .40
Nos. C115-C117 (3) .70 .70

17th Olympic Games, Rome, 8/25-9/11.

Miniature sheets of 3 exist, perf. and imperf., containing Nos. C115-C117. Value, 2 sheets, perf. and imperf., $3.75.

For surcharges see Nos. CB21-CB23.

Coffee-Cacao Type of Regular Issue

1961, Dec. 30 Litho. *Perf. 12½*

C118 A140 13c orange ver .30 .30
C119 A140 33c brt yellow .70 .70

Nos. C118-C119 exist imperf.

Anti-Malaria Type of Regular Issue

1962, Apr. 29 Unwmk. *Perf. 12*

C120 A141 13c pink & red .50 .25
C121 A141 33c org & dp org .95 .50

See Nos. CB24-CB25.

Type of Regular Issue

Designs: 13c, Broken fetters and laurel. 50c, Flag, torch and inscription.

1962, May 30 *Perf. 12½*

C122 A142 13c brn, yel, ol, ultra & red .40 .30
C123 A142 50c rose lilac, ultra & red 1.40 1.00

No. C122 exists imperf.

UPAE Type of Regular Issue

1962, Oct. 23 *Perf. 12½*

C124 A146 13c bright blue .40 .25
C125 A146 22c dull red brown .50 .50

Nos. C124-C125 exist imperf.

Nouel Type of Regular Issue

Design: Frame altered with rosary and cross surrounding portrait.

1962, Dec. 18

C126 A147 13c blue & pale blue .40 .25
C127 A147 25c vio & pale vio .70 .50
a. Souv. sheet, #C126-C127, imperf 1.25 1.25

Nos. C126-C127 exist imperf.

Sanchez, Duarte, Mella AP44

1963, July 7 Litho. *Perf. 11½x12*

C128 AP44 15c orange .40 .25

120th anniv. of separation from Haiti.

World Map
AP45

1963, Oct. 25 Unwmk. *Perf. 12½*
C129 AP45 10c gray & carmine .40 .25

Cent. of Intl. Red Cross. Exists imperf.

Human Rights Type

1963, Dec. 10 Litho.
C130 A152 7c fawn & red brn .30 .25
C131 A152 10c lt blue & blue .30 .25

Nos. C130-C131 exist imperf.

Ramses II Battling the Hittites (from Abu Simbel) — AP46

1964, Mar. 8 *Perf. 12½*
C132 AP46 10c brt violet .30 .25
C133 AP46 13c yellow .30 .25

UNESCO world campaign to save historic monuments in Nubia.
Nos. C132-C133 exist imperf.
For surcharges see Nos. CB26-CB27.

Striated Woodpecker — AP47

1964, June 8 Litho.
C134 AP47 10c multicolored 5.75 .25

Type of Space Issue

Designs: 7c, Rocket leaving earth. 10c, Space capsule orbiting earth.

1964, July 28 Unwmk. *Perf. 12½*
C135 A156 7c brt green .30 .25
C136 A156 10c violet blue .40 .30
a. Souvenir sheet 4.25 3.50

No. C136a contains 7c and 10c stamps similar to Nos. C135-C136 with simulated perforations.

Pres. John F. Kennedy — AP48

1964, Nov. 22 *Perf. 11½*
C137 AP48 10c buff & dk brown .50 .25

President John F. Kennedy (1917-63). Sheets of 10 (5x2) and sheets of 50.

UPU Type of Regular Issue

1964, Dec. 5 Litho. *Perf. 12½*
C138 A157 7c blue .30 .25

ICY Type of Regular Issue

1965, Feb. 16 Unwmk. *Perf. 12½*
C139 A158 10c lilac & violet .35 .30

Basilica of Our Lady of Altagracia — AP49

1965, Mar. 18 Unwmk. *Perf. 12½*
C140 AP49 10c multicolored .40 .25

Fourth Mariological Congress and the Eleventh International Marian Congress.

Abraham Lincoln — AP50

1965, Apr. 15 Litho. *Perf. 12½*
C141 AP50 17c bright blue .55 .40

Cent. of the death of Abraham Lincoln.

Stamp Centenary Type of 1965

Design: Stamp of 1865, (No. 2).

1965, Dec. 28 Litho. *Perf. 12½*
C142 A161 7c violet, lt grn & blk .30 .25
C143 A161 10c yellow, lt grn & blk .30 .30

ITU Emblem, Old and New Communication Equipment — AP51

1966, Apr. 6 Litho. *Perf. 12½*
C144 AP51 28c pink & carmine .85 .85
C145 AP51 45c brt grn & grn 1.25 1.25

Cent. (in 1965) of the ITU.

Butterfly Type of Regular Issue

1966, Nov. 8 Litho. *Perf. 12½*
Various Butterflies in Natural Colors
Size: 35x24mm

C146 A164 10c lt violet & violet 7.75 .75
C147 A164 50c org & dp org 8.25 1.50
C148 A164 75c pink & rose red 11.00 2.50
Nos. C146-C148 (3) 25.00 4.75

For surcharges see Nos. CB28-CB30.

Altar Type of Regular Issue

1967, Jan. 18 Litho. *Perf. 11½*
C149 A165 7c lt olive green .25 .25
C150 A165 10c lilac .25 .25
C151 A165 20c yellow brown .40 .30
Nos. C149-C151 (3) .70 .65

Chess Type of Regular Issue

Design: 10c, Pawn and Bishop.

1967, June 23 Litho. *Perf. 12½*
C152 A167 10c ol, lt ol & blk 1.25 .30
a. Souvenir sheet 10.00 1.90

No. C152a contains 2 imperf. stamps similar to Nos. 636 and C152.

Alliance for Progress Type

1967, Sept. 16 Litho. *Perf. 12½*
C153 A168 8c gray .40 .30
C154 A168 10c blue .50 .30

Cornucopia and Emblem — AP52

1967, Oct. 7
C155 AP52 12c multicolored .60 .30

25th anniversary of the Inter-American Agriculture Institute.

Satellite Type of Regular Issue

1968, June 15 Typo. *Perf. 12*
C156 A170 10c dp blue & multi .30 .25
C157 A170 15c purple & multi .40 .30

Boxing Type of Regular Issue

Designs: Two views of boxing match.

1968, June 29
C158 A171 7c orange yel & grn .50 .25
C159 A171 10c gray & blue .60 .25

See note after No. 641.

Lions Type of Regular Issue

1968, Aug. 9 Litho. *Perf. 11½*
C160 A172 10c ultra & multi .30 .25

Olympic Type of Regular Issue

Designs (Olympic Emblem and): 10c, Weight lifting. 33c, Pistol shooting.

1968, Nov. 12 Litho. *Perf. 11½*
C161 A173 10c buff & multi .30 .25
C162 A173 33c pink & multi 1.00 .75

Latin American Flags — AP53

1969, Jan. 25 Litho. *Perf. 12½*
C163 AP53 10c pink & multi .30 .25

7th Inter-American Savings and Loan Conference, Santo Domingo, Jan. 25-31.

Taino Art Type of Regular Issue

7c, Various vomiting spoons with human heads, vert. 10c, Female torso forming drinking vessel. 20c, Vase with human head, vert.

1969, Jan. 31 Litho. *Perf. 12½*
C164 A175 7c lt bl, bl & lem .25 .25
C165 A175 10c pink, ver & brn .50 .25
C166 A175 20c yellow, org & brn .60 .30
Nos. C164-C166 (3) .75 .70

COTAL Type of Regular Issue

10c, Airport of the Americas and COTAL emblem.

1969, May 25 Litho. *Perf. 12½*
C167 A178 10c brown & pale fawn .30 .25

ILO Type of Regular Issue

1969, June 27 Litho. *Perf. 12½*
C168 A179 10c rose, red & black .30 .25

Baseball Type of Regular Issue

Designs: 7c, Bleachers, Tetelo Vargas Stadium, horiz. 10c, Batter, catcher and umpire. 1p, Quisqueya Stadium, horiz.

1969, Aug. 15 Litho. *Perf. 12½*
Size: 43x30mm (7c, 1p); 21x31mm (10c)

C169 A180 7c magenta & org .50 .30
C170 A180 10c mar & rose red .65 .30
C171 A180 1p violet blue & brn 5.00 3.50
Nos. C169-C171 (3) 5.30 3.60

Electrification Types of Regular Issue

Design: No. C172, Rio Haina steam plant. No. C173, Valdesa Dam.

1969 Litho. *Perf. 12*
C172 A181 10c orange ver .40 .25
C173 A182 10c multicolored .45 .25

Issued: No. C172, Sept. 15; No. C173, Oct. 15.

Duarte Type of Regular Issue

1970, Jan. 26 Litho. *Perf. 12*
C174 A183 10c brown & dk brown .65 .25

Census Type of Regular Issue

Design: 10c, Buildings and census emblem.

1970, Feb. 6 *Perf. 11*
C175 A184 10c lt blue & multi .65 .25

Sculpture Type of Regular Issue

Design: 10c, The Prisoner, by Abelardo Rodriguez Urdaneta, vert.

1970, Feb. 20 Litho. *Perf. 12½*
C176 A186 10c bluish gray .45 .25

Masonic Type of Regular Issue

1970, Mar. 2
C177 A187 10c brown .30 .25

Satellite Type of Regular Issue

1970, May 25 Litho. *Perf. 12½*
C178 A188 7c blue & gray .30 .25

UPU Type of Regular Issue

1970, June 5 *Perf. 11*
C179 A189 10c yellow & brown .30 .25

Education Year Type of Regular Issue

1970, June 26 Litho. *Perf. 12½*
C180 A190 15c bright pink .50 .25

Dancers
AP54

Design: 10c, UN emblem and wheel.

1970, Oct. 12 Litho. *Perf. 12½*
C181 AP54 7c blue & multi .30 .25
C182 AP54 10c pink & multi .45 .25

1st World Exhib. of Books and Culture Festival, Santo Domingo, Oct. 11-Dec. 11.

Album, Globe and Emblem — AP55

1970, Oct. 26 Litho. *Perf. 11*
C183 AP55 10c multicolored .40 .25

EXFILCA 70, 2nd Interamerican Philatelic Exhibition, Caracas, Venezuela, 11/27-12/6.

Basilica of Our Lady of Altagracia — AP56

1971, Jan. 20 Litho. *Perf. 12½*
C184 AP56 17c multicolored .90 .45

Inauguration of the Basilica of Our Lady of Altagracia.

Map of Dominican Republic, CARE Package AP57

1971, May 28 Litho. *Perf. 12½*
C185 AP57 10c blue & green .30 .25

25th anniversary of CARE, a US-Canadian Cooperative for American Relief Everywhere.

Sports Type of Regular Issue

1971, Sept. 10 *Perf. 11*
C186 A195 7c Volleyball .30 .25

Animal Type of Regular Issue

Design: 25c, Cock and grain.

1971, Sept. 29 *Perf. 12½*
C187 A196 25c black & multi .65 .35

Independence Type

10c, Dominican-Colombian flag of 1821.

1971, Dec. 1 *Perf. 11*
C188 A197 10c vio bl, yel & red .65 .30

Christmas Type of Regular Issue

1971, Dec. 10 *Perf. 12½*
C189 A198 10c Bell, 1493 .30 .25

UNICEF Type of Regular Issue

Design: UNICEF emblem & child on beach.

1971, Dec. 14 *Perf. 11*
C190 A199 15c multicolored .65 .45

Book Year Type of Regular Issue

1972, Jan. 25 Litho. *Perf. 12½*
C191 A200 12c lilac, dk bl & red .45 .30

Magnifying Glass over Peru on Map of Americas — AP58

1972, Mar. 7 Litho. *Perf. 12*
C192 AP58 10c blue & multi .45 .30

EXFILIMA '71, 3rd Inter-American Philatelic Exposition, Lima, Peru, Nov. 6-14, 1971.

"Your Heart is your Health" — AP59

1972, Apr. 27 Litho. *Perf. 11*
C193 AP59 7c red & multi .30 .25

World Health Day.

Taino Art Type of 1972

Taino Art: 8c, Ritual vessel showing human figures. 10c, Trumpet (shell). 25c, Carved vomiting spoons. All horiz.

1972, May 10 Litho. *Perf. 11*
C194 A201 8c multicolored .40 .25
C195 A201 10c lt blue & multi .60 .25
C196 A201 25c multicolored 1.50 .45
Nos. C194-C196 (3) 2.50 .85

Telecommunications Type of Regular Issue

1972, May 17 *Perf. 12½*
C197 A202 21c yellow & multi .85 .45

Exhibition Type of Regular Issue

1972, June 3
C198 A203 33c orange & multi .85 .55

Olympic Type of Regular Issue

1972, Aug. 25 Litho. *Perf. 12½*
C199 A204 33c Running 1.00 .75

Club Type of Regular Issue

1972, Sept. 29 Litho. *Perf. 10½*
C200 A205 20c blue & multi .55 .25

Morel Type of Regular Issue

1972, Oct. 20 Litho. *Perf. 12½*
C201 A206 10c multicolored .30 .25

Bank Type of Regular Issue

25c, 1947 silver coin, entrance to the Mint.

1972, Oct. 23
C202 A207 25c ocher & multi .85 .55

"La Navidad" Fortress, 1492 AP60

1972, Nov. 21 Litho. *Perf. 12½*
C203 AP60 10c multicolored .65 .25

Christmas 1972.

Sports Type of Regular Issue

Various sports; a, UL. b, UR. c, LL. d, LR.

1973, Mar. 30 Litho. *Perf. 13½x13*
C204 A212 Block of 4 1.50 1.50
a.-d. 8c, any single .25 .25
C205 A212 Block of 4 2.50 2.50
a.-d. 10c, any single .50 .30

Easter Type 1973

10c, Belfry of Church of Our Lady of Help.

1973, Apr. 18 Litho. *Perf. 10½*
C206 A213 10c multicolored, vert. .55 .25

North and South America on Globe — AP61

1973, May 29 Litho. *Perf. 12*
C207 AP61 7c multicolored .30 .25

Pan-American Health Organization, 70th anniversary (in 1972).

WMO Type of Regular Issue

1973, Aug. 10 Litho. *Perf. 13½x13*
C208 A214 7c green & multi .30 .25

INTERPOL Emblem Police Scientist AP62

1973, Sept. 28 Litho. *Perf. 10½*
C209 AP62 10c vio bl, bl & emer .45 .25

50th anniversary of International Criminal Police Organization.

Handicraft Type of Regular Issue

1973, Oct. 12
C210 A215 7c Sailing ship, mosaic .25 .25
C211 A215 10c Maracas rattles, horiz. .45 .25

Christmas Type of Regular Issue

Design: 10c, Angels adoring Christ Child.

1973, Nov. 26 Litho. *Perf. 13½x13*
C212 A216 10c multicolored .30 .25

Scout Type of Regular Issue

21c, Scouts cooking, Lord Baden-Powell.

1973, Dec. 7 Litho. *Perf. 12*
C213 A217 21c red & multi .85 .75

Sport Type of Regular Issue

10c, Olympic swimming pool and diver. 25c, Olympic Stadium, soccer and discus.

1974, Feb. 25 Litho. *Perf. 13½*
C214 A218 10c blue & multi .30 .25
C215 A218 25c multicolored .55 .25

The Last Supper AP63

1974, June 27 Litho. *Perf. 13½*
C216 AP63 10c multicolored .45 .25

Holy Week 1974.

Bridge Type

Design: 10c, Higuamo Bridge.

1974, July 12 *Perf. 12*
C217 A221 10c multicolored .45 .25

Diabetes Type

Map of Dominican Republic, Diabetics' Emblem and: 7c, Kidney. 33c, Eye & heart.

1974, Aug. 22 Litho. *Perf. 13*
C218 A222 7c yellow & multi .30 .25
C219 A222 33c lt blue & multi 1.75 .75

UPU Type

1974, Oct. 9 Litho. *Perf. 13½*
C220 A223 7c Ships 1.50 .35
C221 A223 33c Jet 2.50 .75
a. Souvenir sheet of 4 7.50 7.50

No. C221a contains Nos. 727-728, C220-C221 forming continuous design.

Golfers and Championship Emblem — AP64

20c, Golfer and Golf Association emblem.

1974, Oct. 24 Litho. *Perf. 13x13½*
C222 AP64 10c green & multi .50 .25
C223 AP64 20c green & multi .80 .40

World Amateur Golf Championships.

Hand Holding Dove AP65

1974, Dec. 3 Litho. *Perf. 12*
C224 AP65 10c multicolored .40 .25

Christmas 1974.

FAO Type

10c, Bee, beehive and barrel of honey.

1974, Dec. 5
C225 A227 10c multicolored 1.50 .25

Chrismon, Lamb, Candle and Palm — AP66

Spain No. 1, España 75 Emblem — AP67

1975, Mar. 26 Litho. *Perf. 13½*
C226 AP66 10c gold & multi .45 .25

Holy Week 1975.

1975, Apr. 10
C227 AP67 12c red, yel & blk .55 .30

Espana 75, International Philatelic Exhibition, Madrid, Apr. 4-13.

Development Bank Type

1975, May 19 Litho. *Perf. 10½x10*
C228 A230 10c rose car & multi .45 .25

Three Satellites and Globe AP68

1975, June 21 Litho. *Perf. 13½*
C229 AP68 15c multicolored .60 .35

Opening of first earth satellite tracking station in Dominican Republic.

Apollo Type

Design: 2p, Apollo-Soyuz link-up over earth.

1975, July 24 *Perf. 13*
Size: 42x28mm
C230 A232 2p multicolored 6.00 4.00

Indian Chief Type

7c, Mayobanex. 8c, Cotubanama & Juan de Esquivel. 10c, Enriquillo & Mencia.

1975, Sept. 27 Litho. *Perf. 12*
C231 A235 7c lt green & multi .30 .25
C232 A235 8c orange & multi .45 .30
C233 A235 10c gray & multi .55 .30
Nos. C231-C233 (3) .85 .75

Volleyball AP69

10c, Weight lifting and Games' emblem.

1975, Oct. 24 Litho. *Perf. 12*
C234 AP69 7c blue & multi .30 .25
C235 AP69 10c multicolored .55 .30

7th Pan-American Games, Mexico City, Oct. 13-26.

Christmas Type

Design: 10c, Dove and peace message.

1975, Dec. 12 Litho. *Perf. 13x13½*
C236 A237 10c yellow & multi .30 .25

Valdesia Dam — AP70

1976, Jan. 26 Litho. *Perf. 13*
C237 AP70 10c multicolored .40 .25

Holy Week Type 1976

Design: 10c, Crucifixion, by Eliezer Castillo.

1976, Apr. 14 Litho. *Perf. 13½*
C238 A239 10c multicolored .45 .30

Bicentennial Type and

George Washington, Independence Hall — AP71

Design: 10c, Hands holding maps of US and Dominican Republic.

1976, May 29 Litho. *Perf. 13½*
C239 A241 10c vio bl, grn & blk .45 .25
C240 AP71 75c black & orange 1.60 1.25

American Bicentennial; No. C240 also for Interphil 76 International Philatelic Exhibition, Philadelphia, Pa., May 29-June 6.

King Juan Carlos I and Queen Sofia — AP72

1976, May 31
C241 AP72 21c multicolored 1.10 .85

Visit of King Juan Carlos I and Queen Sofia of Spain.

Telephone Type

Design: 10c, Alexander Graham Bell and telephones, 1876 and 1976.

1976, July 15
C242 A243 10c multicolored .45 .25

Duarte Types

10c, Scroll with Duarte letter and Dominican flag. 33c, Duarte return from Exile, by E. Godoy.

1976, July 20 Litho. *Perf. 13½*
C243 A245 10c blue & multi .45 .25

Perf. 13x13½
C244 A244 33c brown & multi 1.50 1.10

Fire Engine AP73

1976, Sept. 13 Litho. *Perf. 12*
C245 AP73 10c multicolored .45 .30

Honoring firemen.

Radio Club Type

1976, Oct. 8 Litho. *Perf. 13½*
C246 A247 10c blue & black .45 .25

Various People — AP74

1976, Oct. 22 Litho. *Perf. 13½*
C247 AP74 21c multicolored .70 .55

Spanish heritage.

Olympic Games Type

1976, Oct. 22 *Perf. 12*
C248 A249 10c Running .45 .25
C249 A249 25c Basketball 1.25 .75

Christmas Type

Design: 10c, Angel with bells.

1976, Dec. 8 Litho. *Perf. 13½*
C250 A251 10c multicolored .45 .30

Tourist Activities AP75

Tourist publicity: 12c, Angling and hotel. 25c, Horseback riding and waterfall, vert.

1977, Jan. 7 Size: 36x36mm
C251 AP75 10c multicolored .30 .25

Size: 34x25½mm, 25½x34mm
C252 AP75 12c multicolored .30 .25
C253 AP75 25c multicolored .75 .45
Nos. C251-C253 (3) 1.00 .70

Championship Type

1977, Mar. 4 Litho. *Perf. 13½*
C254 A253 10c yel grn & multi .45 .25
C255 A253 25c lt brown & multi 1.25 .75

Holy Week Type 1977

Design: 10c, Belfry and open book.

1977, Apr. 18 Litho. *Perf. 13½x13*
C256 A254 10c multicolored .45 .25

Lions Type

1977, May 6 *Perf. 13½x13*
C257 A255 7c lt green & multi .30 .25

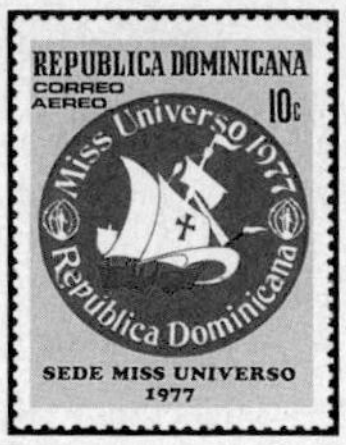

Caravel under Sail — AP76

1977, July 16 Litho. *Perf. 13*
C258 AP76 10c multicolored .45 .30

Miss Universe Contest, held in Dominican Republic.

Melon Cactus — AP77

Design: 33c, Coccothrinax (tree).

1977, Aug. 19 Litho. *Perf. 12*
C259 AP77 7c multicolored .45 .25
C260 AP77 33c multicolored 1.60 1.10

National Botanical Garden.

Chart and Factories — AP78

1977, Nov. 30 Litho. *Perf. 13x13½*
C261 AP78 28c multicolored .85 .65

7th Interamerican Statistics Conference.

Animal Type

Congress Emblem and: 10c, "Dorado," red Roman stud bull. 25c, Flamingo, vert.

1977, Dec. 29 Litho. *Perf. 13*
C262 A259 10c multicolored 2.50 .30
C263 A259 25c multicolored 4.50 .50

Spanish Heritage Type

21c, Window, Casa del Tostado, 16th cent.

1978, Jan. 19 *Perf. 13x13½*
Size: 28x41mm
C264 A260 21c multicolored .65 .55

Holy Week Type, 1978

7c, Facade, Santo Domingo Cathedral. 10c, Facade of Dominican Convent.

1978, Mar. 21 Litho. *Perf. 12*
Size: 27x36mm
C265 A261 7c multicolored .30 .25
C266 A261 10c multicolored .55 .30

Schooner Duarte AP79

1978, Apr. 15 Litho. *Perf. 13½*
C267 AP79 7c multicolored .55 .25

Dominican naval forces training ship.

Cardinal Type

1978, May 5 Litho. *Perf. 13*
C268 A262 10c multicolored .45 .25

Antenna AP80

1978, May 17 Litho. *Perf. 13½*
C269 AP80 25c silver & multi .75 .55

10th World Telecommunications Day.

No. C1 and Map AP81

1978, June 6
C270 AP81 10c multicolored .45 .25

1st Dominican Rep. airmail stamp, 50th anniv.

Globe, Soccer Ball, Emblem — AP82

33c, Soccer field, Argentina '78 emblem, globe.

1978, June 29
C271 AP82 12c multicolored .55 .35
C272 AP82 33c multicolored 1.25 1.00

11th World Cup Soccer Championship, Argentina, June 1-25.

Crown, Cross and Rosary Emblem — AP83

1978, July 11 *Perf. 13x13½*
C273 AP83 21c multicolored .75 .65

Congregation of the Merciful Sisters of Charity, centenary.

Sports Type

1978, July 21 Litho. *Perf. 13½*
C274 A265 7c Baseball, vert. .40 .25
C275 A265 10c Basketball, vert. .45 .25

Wright Brothers and Glider, 1902 AP84

Designs: 7c, Diagrams of Flyer I and jet, vert. 13c, Diagram of air flow over wing. 45c, Flyer I over world map.

1978, Aug. 8 *Perf. 12*
C276 AP84 7c multicolored .25 .25
C277 AP84 10c multicolored .55 .25
C278 AP84 13c multicolored .75 .30
C279 AP84 45c multicolored 2.10 1.40
Nos. C276-C279 (4) 3.65 2.20

75th anniversary of first powered flight.

Tourist Type

Designs: 7c, Sun and musical instruments. 10c, Sun and plane over Santo Domingo.

1978, Sept. 12 Litho. *Perf. 12*

C280 A266 7c multicolored .45 .25
C281 A266 10c multicolored .55 .25

People and Globe AP85

1978, Oct. 12 Litho. *Perf. 13½*

C282 AP85 21c multicolored .80 .70

Spanish heritage.

Dominican Republic and UN Flags AP86

1978, Oct. 23 *Perf. 12*

C283 AP86 33c multicolored 1.10 .75

33rd anniversary of the United Nations.

Statue of the Virgin — AP87

Pope John Paul II — AP88

1978, Dec. 5 Litho. *Perf. 12*

C284 AP87 10c multicolored .40 .30

Christmas 1978.

1979, Jan. 25 Litho. *Perf. 13½*

C285 AP88 10c multicolored 3.75 3.25

Visit of Pope John Paul II to the Dominican Republic, Jan. 25-26.

Map of Beata Island AP89

1979, Jan. 25 *Perf. 12*

C286 AP89 10c multicolored .50 .30

1st expedition of radio amateurs to Beata Is.

Year of the Child Type, 1979

Designs (ICY Emblem and): 7c, Children reading book. 10c, Symbolic head and protective hands. 33c, Hands and jars.

1979, Feb. 26

C287 A269 7c multicolored .25 .25
C288 A269 10c multicolored .45 .25
C289 A269 33c multicolored 1.60 1.10
Nos. C287-C289 (3) 1.60 1.15

Pope John Paul II Giving Benediction AP90

1979, Apr. 9 Litho. *Perf. 13½*

C290 AP90 10c multicolored 1.75 1.25

Holy Week.

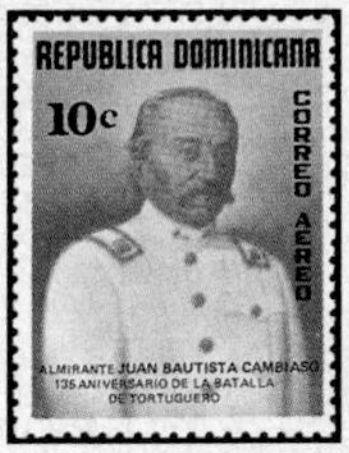

Adm. Juan Bautista Cambiaso AP91

1979, Apr. 14 *Perf. 12*

C291 AP91 10c multicolored .45 .25

135th anniv. of the Battle of Tortuguero.

Map of Dominican Rep., Album, Magnifier AP92

1979, Apr. 18

C292 AP92 33c multicolored 1.10 .75

EXFILNA, 3rd National Philatelic Exhibition, Apr. 18-22.

Flower Type

Designs: 7c, Passionflower. 10c, Isidorea pungens. 13c, Calotropis procera.

1979, May 17 Litho. *Perf. 12*

C293 A271 7c multicolored .45 .30
C294 A271 10c multicolored .55 .35
C295 A271 13c multicolored .75 .65
Nos. C293-C295 (3) 1.25 1.00

Cardiology Type, 1979

10c, Figure of man showing blood circulation.

1979, June 2 Litho. *Perf. 13½*

C296 A272 10c multicolored, vert. .60 .40

Sports Type

7c, Runner and Games' emblem, vert.

1979, June 20

C297 A273 7c multicolored .45 .30

Soccer Type

1979, Aug. 9 Litho. *Perf. 12*

C298 A273 10c Tennis, vert. .45 .30

Rowland Hill, Dominican Republic No. 1 — AP93

1979, Aug. 21 *Perf. 13½*

C299 AP93 2p multicolored 4.75 3.25

Sir Rowland Hill (1795-1879), originator of penny postage.

Electric Light Type

Design: 10c, "100" and light bulb, horiz.

1979, Aug. 27 *Perf. 13½*

C300 A275 10c multicolored .40 .30

Bird Type

Birds: 7c, Phaenicophilus palmarum. 10c, Calyptophilus frugivorus tertius. 45c, Icterus dominicensis.

1979, Sept. 12 Litho. *Perf. 12*

C301 A277 7c multicolored 2.75 .30
C302 A277 10c multicolored 3.75 .30
C303 A277 45c multicolored 9.50 1.00
Nos. C301-C303 (3) 12.60 1.60

Lions Type

10c, Melvin Jones, organization founder.

1979, Nov. 13 Litho. *Perf. 12*

C304 A278 10c multicolored .50 .30

Christmas Type

Christmas: 10c, Three Kings riding camels.

1979, Dec. 18 Litho. *Perf. 12*

C305 A279 10c multicolored .30 .25

Holy Week Type

1980, Mar. 27 Litho. *Perf. 12*

C306 A280 7c Crucifixion .25 .25
C307 A280 10c Resurrection .45 .30

Navy Day — AP94

1980, Apr. 15 Litho. *Perf. 13½*

C308 AP94 21c multicolored .65 .55

Dominican Philatelic Society, 25th Anniversary AP95

1980, Apr. 18

C309 AP95 10c multicolored .45 .30

Gold Type

1980, July 8 Litho. *Perf. 13½*

C310 A282 10c Drag line mining .65 .35
C311 A282 33c Mine 1.25 .55

Tourism Secretariat Emblem — AP96

1980, Aug. 26 Litho. *Perf. 13½*

C312 AP96 10c shown .45 .30
C313 AP96 33c Conf. emblem 1.60 1.10

World Tourism Conf., Manila, Sept. 27.

Iguana Type

1980, Aug. 30 *Perf. 12*

C314 A284 7c American crocodile 2.00 .35
C315 A284 10c Cuban rat 2.40 .40
C316 A284 25c Manatee 3.75 .65
C317 A284 45c Turtle 5.25 .95
Nos. C314-C317 (4) 10.90 2.35

Painting Type

1980, Sept. 23 Litho. *Perf. 13½x13*

C318 A285 10c Abstract, by Paul Guidicelli, vert. .45 .30
C319 A285 17c Farmer, by Yoryi Morel, vert. .75 .55

Visit of Radio Amateurs to Catalina Island AP97

1980, Oct. 3

C320 AP97 7c multicolored .50 .50

Rotary International, 75th Anniversary — AP98

1980, Oct. 23 Litho. *Perf. 12*

C321 AP98 10c Globe, emblem, vert. .55 .45
C322 AP98 33c shown 1.10 .85

Carrier Pigeons, UPU Emblem AP99

1980, Oct. 31 *Perf. 13½*

C323 AP99 33c shown .75 .50
C324 AP99 45c Pigeons, diff. .95 .65
C325 AP99 50c Pigeon, stamp 1.25 .75
Nos. C323-C325 (3) 2.95 1.90

Souvenir Sheet

Imperf

C326 AP99 1.10p UPU emblem 2.00 2.00

UPU cent. No. C326 contains one 48½x31mm stamp.

Christmas Type

1980, Dec. 5 Litho. *Perf. 13½*

C327 A286 10c Holy Family .45 .30

Christmas 1980.

Salcedo Type

Design: Map and arms of Salcedo.

1981, Jan. 14 Litho. *Perf. 13½*

C328 A287 10c multicolored .30 .25

AP100

Industrial Symbols, Seminar Emblem.

1981, Feb. 18 Litho. *Perf. 13½*

C329 AP100 10c shown .45 .30
C330 AP100 33c Seminar emblem .75 .55

CODIA Chemical Engineering Seminar.

National Games Type

1981, Mar. 31 Litho. *Perf. 13½*

C331 A289 10c Baseball .55 .35

AP101

Design: Admiral Juan Alejandro Acosta.

1981, Apr. 15

C332 AP101 10c multicolored .30 .25

Battle of Tortuguero anniversary.

13th World Telecommunications Day — AP102

1981, May 16 **Litho.** ***Perf. 12***

C333 AP102 10c multicolored .30 .25

Heinrich von Stephan AP103

1981, July 15 **Litho.** ***Perf. 13½***

C334 AP103 33c tan & lt red brn 1.10 .75

Birth sesquicentennial of UPU founder.

Worker in Wheelchair AP104

1981, July 24

C335 AP104 7c Stylized people .45 .30
C336 AP104 33c shown 1.10 .75

Intl. Year of the Disabled.

EXPURIDOM '81 Intl. Stamp Show, Santo Domingo, July 31-Aug. 2 — AP105

1981, July 31

C337 AP105 7c multicolored .50 .35

Bullet Holes in Target, Competition Emblem AP106

1981, Aug. 12

C338 AP106 10c shown .30 .25
C339 AP106 15c Riflemen .45 .30
C340 AP106 25c Pistol shooting .75 .65
Nos. C338-C340 (3) 1.50 1.20

2nd World Sharpshooting Championship.

Exports — AP107

1981, Oct. 16 **Litho.** ***Perf. 12***

C341 AP107 7c Jewelry .45 .25
C342 AP107 10c Handicrafts .55 .30
C343 AP107 11c Fruit .65 .30
C344 AP107 17c Vegetables .85 .35
Nos. C341-C344 (4) 2.50 1.20

World Food Day — AP108

1981, Oct. 16 **Litho.** ***Perf. 13½***

C345 AP108 10c Fruits .65 .30
C346 AP108 50c Vegetables 1.50 1.40

5th Natl. Games AP109

1981, Dec. 5 **Litho.** ***Perf. 13½***

C347 AP109 10c Javelin, vert. .45 .35
C348 AP109 50c Cycling 2.10 1.75

Orchids AP110

1981, Dec. 14

C349 AP110 7c Encyclia cochleata .65 .25
C350 AP110 10c Broughtonia domingensis .85 .30
C351 AP110 25c Encyclia truncata 1.25 .75
C352 AP110 75c Elleanthus capitatus 3.25 2.25
Nos. C349-C352 (4) 6.00 3.55

Christmas Type

1981, Dec. 23

C353 A294 10c Dove, sun .75 .45

Battle of Tortuguero Anniv. AP111

1982, Apr. 15 **Litho.** ***Perf. 13½***

C354 AP111 10c Naval Academy, cadets .45 .30

1982 World Cup Soccer — AP112

Designs: Various soccer players.

1982, Apr. 19

C355 AP112 10c multicolored .45 .35
C356 AP112 21c multicolored .55 .45
C357 AP112 33c multicolored 1.10 .90
Nos. C355-C357 (3) 2.10 1.70

American Air Forces Cooperation System — AP113

1982, Apr. 12 ***Perf. 12***

C358 AP113 10c multicolored .45 .30

Scouting Year AP114

1982, Apr. 30 **Litho.** ***Perf. 13½***

C359 AP114 10c Baden-Powell, vert. .30 .25
C360 AP114 15c Globe .45 .30
C361 AP114 25c Baden-Powell, scout, vert. .65 .45
Nos. C359-C361 (3) 1.40 1.00

Dancers — AP115

1982, June 1 **Litho.** ***Perf. 13½***

C362 AP115 7c Emblem .25 .25
C363 AP115 10c Cathedral, Casa del Tostado, Santo Domingo .30 .25
C364 AP115 33c shown 1.25 .85
Nos. C362-C364 (3) 1.80 1.35

Tourist Org. of the Americas, 25th Congress (COTAL '82), Santo Domingo.

Espamer '82 Emblem — AP116

Espamer '82 Intl. Stamp Exhibition, San Juan, Oct. 12-17: Symbolic stamps.

1982, July 5

C365 AP116 7c multi .25 .25
C366 AP116 13c multi, horiz. .45 .30
C367 AP116 50c multi 1.90 1.60
Nos. C365-C367 (3) 2.60 2.15

Sports Type

1982, Aug. 13 ***Perf. 12, Imperf.***

C368 A300 10c Basketball .30 .25
C369 A300 13c Boxing .65 .30
C370 A300 25c Gymnast .75 .45
Nos. C368-C370 (3) 1.70 1.00

Harbor, by Alejandro Bonilla — AP117

Paintings: 10c, Portrait of a Woman, by Leopoldo Navarro. 45c, Amelia Francasci, by Luis Desangles. 2p, Portrait, by Abelardo Rodriguez Urdaneta. 10c, 45c, 2p vert.

1982, Aug. 20 ***Perf. 13, Imperf.***

C371 AP117 7c multicolored .30 .25
C372 AP117 10c multicolored .45 .30
C373 AP117 45c multicolored 2.10 1.40
C374 AP117 2p multicolored 9.00 6.00
Nos. C371-C374 (4) 11.85 7.95

San Pedro de Macoris Type

1982, Aug. 26

Size: 42x29mm

C375 A301 7c Lake .45 .30

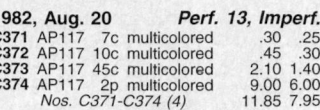

35th Anniv. of Central Bank AP118

1982, Oct. 22 **Litho.** ***Perf. 13½x13***

C376 AP118 10c multicolored .50 .35

490th Anniv. of Discovery of America AP119

1982, Oct. 7 **Litho.** ***Perf. 13½***

C377 AP119 7c Map 1.25 .95
C378 AP119 10c Santa Maria, vert. 1.60 1.10
C379 AP119 21c Columbus, vert. 2.10 1.10
Nos. C377-C379 (3) 4.95 3.15

Christmas Type

1982, Dec. 8

C380 A303 10c multicolored .55 .35

French Alliance Centenary AP120

1983, Mar. 31 **Litho.** ***Perf. 13½***

C381 AP120 33c multicolored .75 .55

Battle of Tortuguero Anniv. AP121

1983, Apr. 15 **Litho.** ***Perf. 13½***

C382 AP121 15c Frigate Mella-451 .85 .35

World Communications Year — AP122

1983, May 6 **Litho.** ***Perf. 13½***

C383 AP122 10c dk blue & blue .45 .30

AP123

1983, July 5 Litho. *Perf. 13½*
C384 AP123 9c multicolored .50 .35

Simon Bolivar (1783-1830).

AP124

1983, Aug. 22 Litho. *Perf. 12*
C385 AP124 7c Gymnast, basketball .55 .25
C386 AP124 10c Highjump, boxing .65 .25
C387 AP124 15c Baseball, weight lifting, bicycling .75 .30
Nos. C385-C387 (3) 1.95 .80

9th Pan American Games, Caracas, Aug. 13-28.

491st Anniv. of Discovery of America AP125

1983, Oct. 11 Litho. *Perf. 13½*
C388 AP125 10c Columbus' ships, map 1.25 .45
C389 AP125 21c Santa Maria (trophy) 1.90 .75
C390 AP125 33c Yacht Sotavento, vert. 2.10 .85
Nos. C388-C390 (3) 5.25 2.05

Size: 103x103mm

Imperf

C391 AP125 50c Ship models 15.00 15.00

10th Anniv. of Latin American Civil Aviation Commission AP126

1983, Dec. 7
C392 AP126 10c dark blue .50 .35

Funeral Procession, by Juan Bautista Gomez — AP127

Designs: 15c, Meeting of Maximo Gomez and Jose Marti in Guayubin, by Enrique Garcia Godoy. 21c, St. Francis, by Angel Perdomo, vert. 33c, Portrait of a Girl, by Adriana Billini, vert.

1983, Dec. 26 *Perf. 13½*
C393 AP127 10c multicolored .35 .25
C394 AP127 15c multicolored .35 .25
C395 AP127 21c multicolored .45 .25
C396 AP127 33c multicolored .70 .25
Nos. C393-C396 (4) 1.85 1.00

Christmas 1983 — AP128

1983, Dec. 13 Litho. *Perf. 13½*
C397 AP128 10c Bells, ornaments .30 .25

AIR POST SEMI-POSTAL STAMPS

Catalogue values for unused stamps in this section are for Never Hinged items.

Nos. C97-C99 Surcharged in Red like Nos. B1-B5

Engraved and Lithographed

1957, Feb. 8 Unwmk. *Perf. 11½*

Flags in National Colors

CB1 A117 11c + 2c ultra & red org .30 .30
CB2 A117 16c + 2c car & lt grn .50 .50
CB3 A117 17c + 2c blk, vio & red .50 .50
Nos. CB1-CB3 (3) 1.10 1.10

The surtax was to aid Hungarian refugees.
A similar 25c surcharge was applied to the souvenir sheets described in the footnote following No. C99. Value, 2 sheets, perf. and imperf., $17.50.

Nos. C100-C102 Surcharged in Red Orange like Nos. B6-B10

1957, Sept. 9 Photo. *Perf. 13½*

Flags in National Colors

CB4 A118 11c + 2c yel grn & dk bl .60 .45
CB5 A118 16c + 2c lilac & dk bl .70 .60
CB6 A118 17c + 2c brn & bl grn .85 .65
Nos. CB4-CB6 (3) 1.75 1.70

See note after No. B10.
A similar 5c surcharge was applied to the miniature sheets described in the footnote following No. 483. Value, 4 sheets, perf. & imperf., medal and flag, $40.

Types of Olympic Air Post Stamps, 1957, Surcharged in Carmine like Nos. B11-B20

1958, May 26 Engr. & Litho.

Flags in National Colors

Pink Paper

CB7 A119(a) 11c + 2c ultra .30 .30
CB8 A119(b) 11c + 2c ultra .30 .30
CB9 A120(a) 16c + 2c rose car .40 .40
CB10 A120(b) 16c + 2c rose car .40 .40
CB11 A119(a) 17c + 2c claret .50 .50
CB12 A119(b) 17c + 2c claret .50 .50
Nos. CB7-CB12 (6) 2.10 2.10

A similar 5c surcharge, plus marginal UN emblem and "UNRWA," was applied to the miniature sheets described in the footnote following No. C105. Value, 4 sheets, perf. and imperf., $20.

Nos. C106-C108 Surcharged like Nos. B21-B25

1959, Apr. 13 Photo. *Perf. 13½*

Flags in National Colors

CB13 A125 11c + 2c blue, ol & brn .70 .70
CB14 A125 16c + 2c lt grn, org & dk bl .95 .95
CB15 A125 17c + 2c ver bl & yel 1.40 1.40
Nos. CB13-CB15 (3) 2.20 2.20

A similar 5c surcharge was applied to the miniature sheets described in the footnote following No. C108. Value, 2 sheets, perf. and imperf., $25.

Type of Regular Issue 1957 Surcharged in Red like Nos. B26-B30

Engraved and Lithographed

1959, Sept. 10 *Imperf.*

Flags in National Colors

CB16 A117 11c + 2c ultra & red org .60 .60
CB17 A117 16c + 2c carmine & lt grn .70 .70
CB18 A117 17c + 2c black, vio & red .70 .70
Nos. CB16-CB18 (3) 1.50 1.50

Nos. C113-C114 Surcharged in Red like Nos. B31-B33

1960, Apr. 7 Litho. *Perf. 12½*
CB19 AP43 10c + 5c plum, gray & grn .30 .30
CB20 AP43 13c + 5c gray & green .45 .45

World Refugee Year.
For souvenir sheets see note after No. B33.

Nos. C115-C117 Surcharged

Perf. 13½

1962, Jan. 8 Unwmk. Photo.

Flags in National Colors

CB21 A136 11c + 2c blue, gray & brn .30 .30
CB22 A136 16c + 2c red, brn & ol .40 .40
CB23 A136 17c + 2c blk, bl & ocher .40 .40
Nos. CB21-CB23 (3) .85 .85

See note after No. B38.
A similar 5c surcharge was applied to the miniature sheets described in the footnote following No. C117. Value, 2 sheets, perf. and imperf., $7.50.

Anti-Malaria Type of 1962

1962, Apr. 29 Litho. *Perf. 12*
CB24 A141 13c + 2c pink & red .40 .30
CB25 A141 33c + 2c org & dp org .95 .60

Souvenir sheets exist, perf. and imperf. containing one each of Nos. B39-B40, CB24-CB25 and a 25c+2c pale grn and yel grn. Value, 2 sheets, perf. and imperf., $7.50.

Nos. C132-C133 Surcharged like Nos. B44-B46

1964, Mar. 8
CB26 AP46 10c + 2c brt violet .25 .25
CB27 AP46 13c + 2c yellow .30 .25

Nos. C146-C148 Surcharged like Nos. B47-B51

1966, Dec. 9 Litho. *Perf. 12½*

Size: 35x24mm

CB28 A164 10c + 5c multi *3.00* *1.00*
CB29 A164 50c + 10c multi *4.50* *3.00*
CB30 A164 75c + 10c multi *6.00* *3.75*
Nos. CB28-CB30 (3) *13.50* *7.75*

AIR POST OFFICIAL STAMPS

Nos. O13-O14 Overprinted in Blue

Unwmk.

1930, Dec. 3 Typo. *Perf. 12*
CO1 O3 10c light blue 15.00 *17.50*
a. Pair, one without ovpt. *900.00*
CO2 O3 20c orange 15.00 *17.50*

SPECIAL DELIVERY STAMPS

Biplane SD1

Perf. 11½

1920, Apr. Unwmk. Litho.
E1 SD1 10c deep ultra 6.75 1.40
a. Imperf., pair

Special Delivery Messenger — SD2

1925
E2 SD2 10c dark blue 21.00 5.75

SD3

1927
E3 SD3 10c red brown 6.75 1.40
a. "E EXPRESO" at top 55.00 55.00

Type of 1927

1941 Redrawn
E4 SD3 10c yellow green 3.00 3.25
E5 SD3 10c dark blue green 2.75 .60

The redrawn design differs slightly from SD3.
Issue dates: No. E4, Mar. 27; No. E5, Aug. 7.

Emblem of Communications — SD4

1945, Sept. 1 *Perf. 12*
E6 SD4 10c rose car, car & dk bl 1.25 .25

Catalogue values for unused stamps in this section, from this point to the end of the section, are for Never Hinged items.

SD5

1950 Litho. Unwmk.
E7 SD5 10c multicolored .60 .25

Exists imperf.

Modern Communications System — SD6

1956, Aug. 18 *Perf. 11½*
E8 SD6 25c green 1.25 .30

Carrier Pigeon SD7

1967 **Litho.** ***Perf. 11½***
E9 SD7 25c light blue .70 .30

Carrier Pigeon, Globe — SD8

Messenger, Plane — SD9

1978, Aug. 2 **Litho.** ***Perf. 13½***
E10 SD8 25c multicolored 1.10 .45

1979, Nov. 30 ***Perf. 13½***
E11 SD9 25c multicolored .65 .45

Motorcycling — SD10

1989, May **Litho.** ***Perf. 13½***
E12 SD10 1p multicolored 2.50 1.10

Postman SD11

1999 **Litho.** ***Perf. 13½x13¼***
E13 SD11 8p multicolored 3.25 2.75

INSURED LETTER STAMPS

Merino Issue of 1933 Surcharged in Red or Black

1935, Feb. 1 **Unwmk.** ***Perf. 14***
G1 A35 8c on 7c ultra .60 .25
a. Inverted surcharge 18.00
G2 A35 15c on 10c org yel .65 .25
a. Inverted surcharge 18.00
G3 A35 30c on 8c dk green 2.25 .90
G4 A35 45c on 20c car rose (Bk) 3.25 1.10
G5 A36 70c on 50c lemon 7.75 1.75
Nos. G1-G5 (5) 14.50 4.25

Merino Issue of 1933 Surcharged in Red

1940
G6 A35 8c on ½c lt vio 2.75 2.75
G7 A35 8c on 7c ultra 3.25 3.25

Coat of Arms — IL1

1940-45 **Litho.** ***Perf. 11½***
Arms in Black
G8 IL1 8c brown red .85 .25
a. 8c dk red, no shading on inner frame 1.10 .25
G9 IL1 15c dp orange ('45) 1.75 .25
G10 IL1 30c dk green ('41) 2.00 .25
a. 30c yellow green 2.00 .25
G11 IL1 45c ultra ('44) 2.25 .30
G12 IL1 70c olive brn ('44) 2.10 .30
Nos. G8-G12 (5) 8.95 1.35

See Nos. G13-G16, G24-G27.

Catalogue values for unused stamps in this section, from this point to the end of the section, are for Never Hinged items.

Redrawn Type of 1940-45
1952-53 **Arms in Black**
G13 IL1 8c car lake ('53) 3.25 .50
G14 IL1 15c red orange ('53) 1.75 .75
G15 IL1 70c dp brown car 7.25 1.75
Nos. G13-G15 (3) 12.25 3.00

Larger and bolder numerals on 8c and 15c. Smaller and bolder "70." There are many other minor differences in the design.

Type of 1940-45
1954 **Arms in Black, 15x16mm**
G16 IL1 10c carmine .75 .25

Coat of Arms — IL2

1955-69 **Unwmk.** **Litho.** ***Perf. 11½***
Arms in Black, 13½x11½mm
G17 IL2 10c carmine rose .40 .25
G18 IL2 15c red orange ('56) 5.25 2.25
G19 IL2 20c red orange ('58) 1.25 .30
a. 20c orange ('69) 1.25 .30
b. 20c orange, retouched ('69) 3.50 1.25
G20 IL2 30c dark green ('55) 2.00 .40
G21 IL2 40c dark green ('58) 2.10 .90
a. 40c lt yellow grn ('62) 2.10 .45
G22 IL2 45c ultra ('56) 4.00 3.75
G23 IL2 70c dp brn car ('56) 6.75 2.25
Nos. G17-G23 (7) 21.75 10.10

On No. G19b the horizontal shading lines of shield are omitted.
See Nos. G28-G37.

Type of 1940-45
Second Redrawing
1963 ***Perf. 12½***
Arms in Black, 17x16mm
G24 IL1 10c red orange 1.25 .30
G25 IL1 20c orange 1.90 1.25

Third Redrawing
1966 **Litho.** ***Perf. 12½***
Arms in Black, 14x14mm
G26 IL1 10c violet .40 .25
G27 IL1 40c orange 1.50 1.00

Type of 1955-62
1968 **Litho.** ***Perf. 11½***
Arms in Black, 13½x11½mm
G28 IL2 20c red 2.50 1.00
G29 IL2 60c yellow 2.10 2.10

1973-76 **Litho.** ***Perf. 12½***
Arms in Black, 11x11mm
G30 IL2 10c car rose ('76) .50 .35
G31 IL2 20c yellow 1.40 .90
G32 IL2 20c orange ('76) 1.75 .50
G33 IL2 40c yel grn 1.60 1.00
a. 40c green ('76) 3.00 3.00
G34 IL2 70c blue 1.90 1.90
Nos. G30-G34 (5) 7.15 4.65

1973 ***Perf. 11½***
Arms in Black, 13½x11½mm
G35 IL2 10c dark violet .90 .30

1978, Aug. 9 ***Perf. 10½***
Arms in Black, 11x11mm
G36 IL2 10c rose magenta .35 .25
G37 IL2 40c bright green 1.50 1.50

IL3

1982-83 **Litho.** ***Perf. 10½***
Arms in Black
G38 IL3 10c deep magenta .25 .25
G39 IL3 20c deep orange .35 .30
G40 IL3 40c bluish green .75 .50
Nos. G38-G40 (3) 1.35 1.05

IL4

1986 **Litho.** ***Perf. 10½***
Arms in Black
G41 IL4 20c brt rose lilac .35 .25
G42 IL4 60c orange 1.20 .85
G43 IL4 1p light blue 2.10 1.40
G44 IL4 1.25p pink 2.75 1.75
G45 IL4 1.50p vermilion 3.25 2.50
G46 IL4 3p light green 6.25 4.25
G47 IL4 3.50p olive bister 7.00 4.50
G48 IL4 4p yellow 8.75 5.50
G49 IL4 4.50p lt blue grn 9.75 6.25
G50 IL4 5p brown olive 10.50 7.00
G51 IL4 6p gray 12.50 8.50
G52 IL4 6.50p lt ultra 14.50 9.50
Nos. G41-G52 (12) 78.90 52.25

Issue dates: Nos. G42-G43, G45, July 16. Nos. G46-G52, Sept. 2. Nos. G41, G44, Nov. 6.

Coat of Arms — IL5

1989-90 **Litho.** ***Perf. 13½***
Arms in Black
G53 IL5 20c brt lilac rose .35 .25
G54 IL5 60c orange ('90) 1.00 .45
G55 IL5 1p sky blue 1.60 .75
G56 IL5 1.25p lt salmon pink 1.90 .90
G57 IL5 1.50p dark red 2.40 1.40
Nos. G53-G57 (5) 7.25 3.75

"RD$" in lower left square on Nos. G55-G57.

IL6

1994, Oct. **Litho.** ***Perf. 13½***
Arms in Black
G58 IL6 50c lilac rose .25 .25
G59 IL6 1p sky blue .35 .25
G60 IL6 1.50p red .45 .30
G61 IL6 2p pink .65 .50
G62 IL6 3p violet blue .90 .60
G63 IL6 5p yellow 1.25 .90
G64 IL6 6p apple green 1.75 1.25
G65 IL6 8p green 2.00 1.50
G66 IL6 10p silver gray 2.75 2.00
Nos. G58-G66 (9) 10.35 7.55

POSTAGE DUE STAMPS

D1

1901 **Unwmk.** **Typo.** ***Perf. 14***
J1 D1 2c olive gray .90 .25
J2 D1 4c olive gray 1.10 .25
J3 D1 5c olive gray 1.90 .30
J4 D1 10c olive gray 3.25 .95
Nos. J1-J4 (4) 7.15 1.75

For surcharges and overprint see Nos. 162-165, 169-171.

1909 **Wmk. 116**
J5 D1 2c olive gray 1.50 .50
J6 D1 4c olive gray 1.50 .50
J7 D1 6c olive gray 2.00 .75
J8 D1 10c olive gray 4.00 2.50
Nos. J5-J8 (4) 9.00 4.25

1913
J9 D1 2c olive green .60 .30
J10 D1 4c olive green .70 .40
J11 D1 6c olive green 1.10 .50
J12 D1 10c olive green 1.25 .60
Nos. J9-J12 (4) 3.65 1.80

1922 **Unwmk.** **Litho.** ***Perf. 11½***
J13 D1 1c olive green .70 .70

Catalogue values for unused stamps in this section, from this point to the end of the section, are for Never Hinged items.

D2

D3

1942
J14 D2 1c dk red & pale pink .30 .25
J15 D2 2c dk bl & pale bl .30 .25
J16 D2 4c dk grn & pale grn .30 .25
J17 D2 6c green & buff .40 .25
J18 D2 8c yel org & pale yel .40 .30
J19 D2 10c mag & pale pink .50 .50
Nos. J14-J19 (6) 2.20 1.80

1955 **Size: 20½x25mm**
J20 D2 2c dark blue 1.40 1.00

1959 **Litho.** ***Perf. 11½***
Size: 21x25½mm
J21 D3 1c dark car rose 1.25 1.25
J22 D3 2c dark blue 1.25 1.25
J23 D3 4c green 3.00 3.00
Nos. J21-J23 (3) 5.50 5.50

OFFICIAL STAMPS

Bastion of February 27 O1

Unwmk.
1902, Feb. 25 **Litho.** ***Perf. 12***
O1 O1 2c scarlet & blk .65 .30
O2 O1 5c dk blue & blk .85 .25
O3 O1 10c yel grn & blk 1.00 .55
O4 O1 20c yellow & blk 1.25 .55
a. Imperf., pair 11.00
Nos. O1-O4 (4) 3.75 1.65

For overprints and surcharge see Nos. 157-161.

Bastion of Feb. 27
O2

Columbus Lighthouse
O3

Perf. 13½x13, 13½x14

1909-12 Wmk. 116 Typo.

O5	O2	1c blue grn & blk	.40	.25
O6	O2	2c scarlet & blk	.50	.30
O7	O2	5c dk blue & blk	1.00	.40
O8	O2	10c yel grn & blk ('12)	1.60	.95
O9	O2	20c orange & blk ('12)	2.75	2.25
		Nos. O5-O9 (5)	6.25	4.15

The 2c, 5c are found in both perforations; 1c, 20c perf. 13½x13; 10c perf. 13½x14.

For overprints and surcharge see Nos. 177, 194-199.

1928 Unwmk. *Perf. 12*

O10	O3	1c green	.25	.25
O11	O3	2c red	.25	.25
O12	O3	5c ultramarine	.30	.30
O13	O3	10c light blue	.40	.40
O14	O3	20c orange	.60	.60
		Nos. O10-O14 (5)	1.80	1.80

For overprints see Nos. CO1-CO2.

Proposed Columbus Lighthouse
O4

1937 Litho. *Perf. 11½*

O15	O4	3c dark purple	1.10	.30
O16	O4	7c indigo & blue	1.20	.40
O17	O4	10c orange yellow	1.30	.60
		Nos. O15-O17 (3)	3.60	1.30

Proposed Columbus Lighthouse
O5

1939-41

O18	O5	1c dp grn & lt grn	.50	.25
O19	O5	2c crim & pale pink	.50	.25
O20	O5	3c purple & lt vio	.50	.25
O21	O5	5c dk bl & lt bl ('40)	.85	.40
O21A	O5	5c lt blue ('41)	1.50	1.00
O22	O5	7c brt bl & lt bl ('41)	1.40	.25
O23	O5	10c yel org & pale org ('41)	1.40	.35
O24	O5	20c brn org & buff ('41)	4.25	.70
O25	O5	50c brt red lil & pale lil ('41)	5.00	2.10
		Nos. O18-O25 (9)	15.90	5.55

Catalogue values for unused stamps in this section, from this point to the end of the section, are for Never Hinged items.

Type of 1939

1950 Redrawn

O26	O5	50c dp car & rose	8.75	1.75

The numerals "50" measure 3mm, and are close to left and right frames; numerals measure 4mm on No. O25. There are other minor differences.

Denominations in "Centavos Oro"

1950

O27	O5	5c light blue	.85	.25
O28	O5	10c yel & pale yel	.90	.40
O29	O5	20c dl org brn & buff	1.90	1.90
		Nos. O27-O29 (3)	3.65	2.55

Letters of top inscription are 1½mm high.

Second Redrawing

Type of 1939-41 Denominations in "Centavos Oro"

1956 Unwmk. *Perf. 11½*

O30	O5	7c blue & lt blue	.85	.85
O31	O5	20c yellow brn & buff	1.90	1.90
O32	O5	50c red lil & brt pink	4.75	4.75
		Nos. O30-O32 (3)	7.50	7.50

The letters of top inscription are 2mm high, the trees at base of monument have been redrawn, etc. On No. O32 the numerals are similar to No. O26.

POSTAL TAX STAMPS

Santo Domingo after Hurricane
PT1

Hurricane's Effect on Capital
PT2

1930, Dec. Unwmk. Litho. *Perf. 12*

RA1	PT1	1c green & rose	.25	.25
RA2	PT1	2c red rose	.25	.25
RA3	PT2	5c ultra & rose	.30	.25
RA4	PT2	10c yellow & rose	.40	.30

Imperf

RA5	PT1	1c green & rose	.40	.30
RA6	PT1	2c red & rose	.50	.30
RA7	PT2	5c ultra & rose	.60	.50
RA8	PT2	10c yellow & rose	.90	.75
		Nos. RA1-RA8 (8)	3.60	2.90

For surcharges see Nos. RAC1-RAC7.

Tête bêche Pairs

RA1a	PT1	1c green & rose	1.75	1.75
RA2a	PT1	2c red rose	1.75	1.50
RA3a	PT1	5c ultra & rose	1.75	2.10
RA4a	PT1	10c yellow & rose	2.10	2.10
RA5a	PT1	1c green & rose	1.75	1.75
RA6a	PT1	2c red & rose	1.75	1.75
RA7a	PT1	5c ultra & rose	2.10	2.10
RA8a	PT1	10c yellow & rose	2.10	2.10
		Nos. RA1a-RA8a (8)	15.05	15.15

Dr. Martos Sanatorium — PT3

Nurse and Child — PT4

1944, Apr. 1 Litho. *Perf. 11½*

RA9	PT3	1c dp bl, sl bl & red	.40	.30

1947, Apr. 1 Unwmk.

RA10	PT4	1c dp bl, pale bl & car	.50	.30

Sanatorium of the Holy Help — PT5

1949, Apr. 1

RA11	PT5	1c dp bl, pale bl & car	.35	.25

Youth Holding Banner
PT6

"Suffer Little Children to Come Unto Me"
PT7

1950, Apr. 1 *Perf. 11½*

RA12	PT6	1c dp bl, pale bl & car	.30	.25

1950, Dec. 1 *Perf. 12*

Size: 22½x32mm

RA13	PT7	1c lt bl & pale bl	1.25	.30
b.		Perf. 12½ ('52)	4.50	.25

Vertical line centering side borders merges into dots toward the bottom. See Nos. RA13A, RA17, RA19, RA26, RA32, RA35.

The tax was for child welfare.

1951, Dec. 1 Redrawn

RA13A	PT7	1c lt blue & pale blue	6.25	.30

In the redrawn stamp, the standing child, a blonde in No. RA13, is changed to a brunette; more foliage has been added above child's head and to branches showing in upper right corner. Vertical dashes in side borders.

Tuberculosis Sanatorium, Santiago — PT8

1952, Apr. 1 Litho. *Perf. 11½*

RA14	PT8	1c lt blue & car	.30	.25

Sword, Serpent and Crab — PT9

1953, Feb. 1 Unwmk. *Perf. 12.*

RA15	PT9	1c carmine	.50	.30

The tax was for the Dominican League Against Cancer. See Nos. RA18, RA21, RA43, RA46, RA51, RA56, RA61, RA67, RA72, RA76, RA82, RA88, RA93, RA96.

Tuberculosis Dispensary for Children — PT10

1953, Apr. 1 Litho. *Perf. 12½*

RA16	PT10	1c dp bl, pale bl & red	.40	.30

See No. RA22.

Jesus Type of 1950

Second Redrawing

1953, Dec. 1 *Perf. 11½*

Size: 22x31mm

RA17	PT7	1c blue	.35	.25

Solid shading in sky reduced to a few scattered dots. Girl's left arm indicated. Rough white dots in side borders.

Cancer Type of 1952

1954, Oct. 1 Redrawn *Perf. 12½*

RA18	PT9	1c rose carmine	.30	.25
a.		1c red orange ('58)	.40	.25
b.		1c carmine ('70)	1.25	.25

Upper right serif of numeral "1" eliminated; diagonal line added through "C" and period removed; sword extended, placing top on a line with top of "1." Dots of background screen arranged diagonally. Many other differences.

The tax was for the Dominican League Against Cancer. No. RA18a exists imperf.

On No. RA18b background screen eliminates white outline of crab.

Jesus Type of 1950

1954, Dec. 1 Third Redrawing

Size: 23x32¾mm

RA19	PT7	1c bright blue	.40	.30
a.		1c pale blue ('59)	.40	.30

Center completely screened. Tiny white horizontal rectangles in side borders.

Catalogue values for unused stamps in this section, from this point to the end of the section, are for Never Hinged items.

Lorraine Cross as Bell Clapper — PT11

1955, Apr. 1 Litho. *Perf. 11½x12*

RA20	PT11	1c black, yel & red	.40	.30

Cancer Type of 1952

Second Redrawing

1956, Oct. 1 *Perf. 12½*

RA21	PT9	1c carmine	.60	.30
a.		1c red orange ('64)	1.00	.50

Similar to No. RA18, but dots of background screen arranged in vertical and horizontal rows. Outlines of central device, lettering and frame clearly delineated. "C" of cent-sign smaller. Upper claw in solid color.

TB Dispensary Type of 1953

Redrawn

1954, Apr. 1

RA22	PT10	1c blue & red	.70	.25
a.		Red (cross) omitted	55.00	

No. RA22 has third color omitted; clouds added; bolder letters and numerals.

Angelita Trujillo — PT12

1955, Dec. 1 Unwmk. *Perf. 12½*

RA23	PT12	1c violet	.85	.30

The tax was for child welfare.

Lorraine Cross — PT13

1956, Apr. 1 Litho. *Perf. 11½*
RA24 PT13 1c blk, grn, lem & red .40 .30

The tax was for the Anti-Tuberculosis League. Inscribed: B.C.G. (Bacillus Calmette-Guerin).

PT14

1957, Apr. 1
RA25 PT14 1c red, blk, yel, grn & bl .40 .30

Jesus Type of 1950
Fourth Redrawing

1956, Dec. 1 Unwmk. *Perf. 12*
Size: 21¾x31¼mm
RA26 PT7 1c blue .30 .25

Thin white lines around numeral boxes. Girl's bouquet touches Jesus' sleeve. Tiny white squares or rectangles in side borders. Foliage at either side of "Era de Trujillo" panel.

PT15

1958, Apr. 1 Litho. *Perf. 12½*
RA27 PT15 1c brown car & red .25 .25

1959, Apr. 1 Inscribed "1959"
RA28 PT15 1c brown car & red .30 .25

PT16

1960, Apr. 1 Litho. *Perf. 12*
RA29 PT16 1c bl, pale yel & red .40 .30

PT17

1961, Apr. 1 Unwmk. *Perf. 11½*
RA30 PT17 1c blue & red .30 .25

Nos. RA29-RA30: tax was for the Anti-Tuberculosis League.
See No. RA33.

Maria de los Angeles M. de Trujillo and Housing Project PT18

1961, Aug. 1 Litho. *Perf. 12*
RA31 PT18 1c carmine rose .30 .25

The tax was for aid to the needy.
Nos. RA31-RA33 exist imperf.

Jesus Type of 1950
Fifth Redrawing

1961, Dec. 1 Unwmk. *Perf. 12½*
RA32 PT7 1c blue .30 .25

No. RA32 is similar to No. RA19, but "Era de Trujillo" has been replaced by a solid color panel.

Type of 1961 Dated "1962"

1962, Apr. 2 *Perf. 12½*
RA33 PT17 1c blue & red .85 .30

Tax for the Anti-Tuberculosis League.

Man's Chest — PT19

1963, Apr. 1 *Perf. 12x11½*
RA34 PT19 1c ultra & red .40 .30

Jesus Type of 1950
Sixth Redrawing

1963, Dec. 1 *Perf. 11½*
Size: 21¾x32mm
RA35 PT7 1c blue .30 .25
a. 1c deep blue ('64) .30 .25

No. RA35 is similar to No. RA26, but "Era de Trujillo" panel has been omitted.

Hibiscus — PT20

1966, Apr. 1 Litho. *Perf. 11½*
RA36 PT20 1c emerald & car .30 .25

Tax for the Anti-Tuberculosis League.

Domingoa Nodosa — PT21

1967, Apr. 1 Litho. *Perf. 12½*
RA37 PT21 1c lilac & red 1.00 .30

Tax for the Anti-Tuberculosis League.

Civil Defense Emblem — PT22

1967, July 1 Litho. *Rouletted 13*
RA38 PT22 1c multicolored .30 .25

Tax for the Civil Defense Organization.

Boy, School and Yule Bells — PT23

1967, Dec. 1 Litho. *Perf. 12½*
RA39 PT23 1c rose red & pink .40 .30

1968 *Perf. 11*
RA40 PT23 1c vermilion .35 .25

No. RA40 has screened background; No. RA39, smooth background.
The tax was for child welfare.
See Nos. RA49A, RA52, RA57, RA62, RA68, RA73, RA77, RA81.

Hand Holding Invalid — PT24

1968, Mar. 19 Litho. *Perf. 12½*
RA41 PT24 1c green & yellow .30 .25
a. 1c olive green & deep yellow, perf. 11½x12 ('69) .30 .25

The tax was for the rehabilitation of the handicapped. See Nos. RA47, RA50, RA54.

Dogbane — PT25

1968, Apr. 25 Litho. *Perf. 12½*
RA42 PT25 1c emerald, yel & red .30 .25

The tax was for the Anti-Tuberculosis League. See Nos. RA45, RA49.

Redrawn Cancer Type of 1955

1968, Oct. 1 Litho. *Perf. 12*
RA43 PT9 1c emerald .25 .25

The tax was for the Dominican League against Cancer.

Schoolyard, Torch — PT26

1969, Feb. 1 Litho. *Perf. 12½*
RA44 PT26 1c light blue .30 .25

Issued for Education Year 1969.

Flower Type of 1968
Design: No. RA45, Violets.

1969, Apr. 25 Litho. *Perf. 12½*
RA45 PT25 1c emerald, lil & red .60 .30

Tax for the Anti-Tuberculosis League.

Redrawn Cancer Type of 1955

1969, Oct. 1 Litho. *Perf. 11*
RA46 PT9 1c brt rose lilac .25 .25

Tax for Dominican League against Cancer.

Invalid Type of 1968

1970, Mar. 2 *Perf. 12½*
RA47 PT24 1c blue .30 .25

The tax was for the rehabilitation of the handicapped.

Book, Sun and Education Year Emblem — PT27

1970, Feb. 6 *Perf. 11*
RA48 PT27 1c bright pink .30 .25

International Education Year.

Flower Type of 1968
Design: 1c, Elleanthus capitatus; cross in upper left corner, denomination in lower right.

1970, Apr. 30 *Perf. 11*
RA49 PT25 1c emerald, red & yel 1.00 .30

Tax for Anti-Tuberculosis League.

Boy Type of 1967

1970, Dec. 1 *Perf. 12½*
RA49A PT23 1c orange .35 .30

Communications Emblem — PT28

1971, Jan. 2 Litho. *Perf. 11*
Size: 17½x20½mm
RA49B PT28 1c vio bl & red (white frame) .45 .30

Tax was for Postal and Telegraph Communications School.
See Nos. RA53, RA58, RA63, RA69, RA78, RA91.

Invalid Type of 1968

1971, Mar. 1 Litho. *Perf. 11*
RA50 PT24 1c brt rose lilac .30 .25

Tax for rehabilitation of the handicapped.

Cancer Type of 1952
Third Redrawing

1971, Oct. 1 *Perf. 11½*
RA51 PT9 1c dp yellow green .30 .25

Background of No. RA51 appears white and design stands out. No. RA43 has greenish background and design appears faint. Numeral "1" on No. RA51 is 3½mm high, on No. RA43 it is 3mm.

Boy Type of 1967

1971, Dec. 1 Litho. *Perf. 11*
RA52 PT23 1c green .30 .25

Communications Type of 1971

1972, Jan. 3 Litho. *Perf. 12½*
Size: 19x22mm
RA53 PT28 1c dk bl & red (bl frame) .25 .25

Tax was for the Postal and Telegraph Communications School.

Invalid Type of 1968

1972, Mar. 1 Litho. *Perf. 11½*
RA54 PT24 1c brown .60 .25

Orchid — PT29

1972, Apr. 2 *Perf. 11*
RA55 PT29 1c lt grn, red & yel 1.60 .45

Tax was for the Anti-Tuberculosis League.

Redrawn Cancer Type of 1954-58

1972, Oct. 2 ***Perf. 12½***
RA56 PT9 1c orange .25 .25

Tax for Dominican League against Cancer.

Boy Type of 1967

1972, Dec. 1 ***Perf. 12***
RA57 PT23 1c violet .30 .25

Tax was for child welfare.

Communications Type of 1971

1973, Jan. 2 ***Perf. 10½***
Size: 19x22mm
RA58 PT28 1c dk bl & red (red frame) .30 .25

Tax was for Postal and Telegraph Communications School.

Invalid PT30

Hibiscus PT31

1973, Mar. 1 Litho. ***Perf. 12½***
Size: 21x25mm
RA59 PT30 1c olive .30 .25

Tax was for the Dominican Rehabilitation Association. See Nos. RA66, RA70, RA74, RA79, RA86.

1973, Apr. 17 Litho. ***Perf. 10½***
RA60 PT31 1c multicolored 1.10 .30

Tax was for Anti-Tuberculosis League. Exists imperf.

Cancer Type of 1952 Redrawn and "1973" Added

1973, Oct. 1 ***Perf. 13½***
RA61 PT9 1c olive green .45 .30

Tax was for Dominican League Against Cancer.

Boy Type of 1967

1973, Dec. 1 Litho. ***Perf. 13x13½***
RA62 PT23 1c blue .60 .25

Communications Type of 1971

1973, Nov. 3 ***Perf. 10½***
Size: 19x22mm
RA63 PT28 1c bl & red (lt grn frame) .30 .25

Tax was for Postal and Telegraph Communications School. Exists imperf.

Invalid Type of 1973

1974, Mar. 1 Litho. ***Perf. 10½***
Size: 22x27½mm
RA66 PT30 1c light ultra .45 .30

See note after No. RA59.

Cancer Type of 1952 Redrawn and "1974" Added

1974, Oct. 1 ***Perf. 12***
RA67 PT9 1c orange .45 .30

Tax for Dominican League Against Cancer.

Boy Type of 1967

1974, Dec. 2 Litho. ***Perf. 11½***
RA68 PT23 1c dk brown & buff .30 .25

Communications Type of 1971

1974, Nov. 13 ***Perf. 10½***
RA69 PT28 1c blue & red (yel frame) .30 .25

Invalid Type of 1973 Dated "1975"

1975, Mar. 1 ***Perf. 13½x13***
Size: 21x32mm
RA70 PT30 1c olive brown .45 .30

See note after No. RA59.

Catteeyopsis Rosea — PT32

1975, Apr. 1 ***Perf. 12***
RA71 PT32 1c blue & multi 1.40 .95

Tax was for Anti-Tuberculosis League.

Cancer Type of 1952 Redrawn and "1975" Added

1975, Oct. 1 Litho. ***Perf. 12***
RA72 PT9 1c violet blue .45 .30

Tax was for Dominican League Against Cancer. Exists imperf.

Boy Type of 1967

1975, Dec. 1 Litho. ***Perf. 12***
RA73 PT23 1c red orange .30 .25

Tax was for child welfare.

Invalid Type of 1973 Dated "1976"

1976, Mar. 1 Litho. ***Perf. 12***
Size: 21x31mm
RA74 PT30 1c ultra .45 .30

See note after No. RA59.

Oncidium Colochilum — PT33

1976, Apr. 6 ***Perf. 13x13½***
RA75 PT33 1c green & multi .85 .30

Tax was for Anti-Tuberculosis League. See Nos. RA80, RA84.

Cancer Type of 1952 Redrawn and "1976" Added

1976, Oct. 1 Litho. ***Perf. 13½***
RA76 PT9 1c green .45 .30

Tax was for Dominican League Against Cancer.

Boy Type of 1967

1976, Dec. 1 Litho. ***Perf. 13½***
RA77 PT23 1c purple .45 .30

Tax was for child welfare.

Communications Type of 1971

1977, Jan. 7 Litho. ***Perf. 10½***
Size: 19x22mm
RA78 PT28 1c blue & red (lil frame) .30 .25

Tax was for Postal and Telegraph Communications School.

Invalid Type of 1973 Dated "1977"

1977, Mar. 11 ***Perf. 12***
Size: 21x31mm
RA79 PT30 1c ultra .45 .30

See note after No. RA59.

Orchid Type of 1976 Dated "1977"

Orchid: Oncidium variegatum.

1977, Apr. 22 Litho. ***Perf. 13½***
RA80 PT33 1c multicolored 1.10 .30

Tax was for Anti-Tuberculosis League.

Boy Type of 1967

1977, Dec. 27 Litho. ***Perf. 12***
RA81 PT23 1c emerald .30 .25

Tax was for child welfare.

Cancer Type of 1952 Redrawn and "1977" Added

1978, Oct. 2 Litho. ***Perf. 13½***
RA82 PT9 1c lilac rose .45 .30

Tax for Dominican League Against Cancer.

Mother, Child, Holly — PT34

1978, Dec. 1 Litho. ***Perf. 13½***
RA83 PT34 1c green .30 .25

Tax was for child welfare. See Nos. RA89, RA92, RA97.

Orchid Type of 1973 Dated "1978"

Flower: Yellow alder.

1979, Apr. Litho. ***Perf. 13½***
RA84 PT33 1c lt blue & multi 1.10 .30

Tax was for Anti-Tuberculosis League.

University Seal — PT35

1979, Feb. 10 Litho. ***Perf. 13½***
RA85 PT35 2c ultra & gray .30 .25

450th anniv. of University of Santo Domingo.

Invalid Type of 1973 Dated "1978"

1979, Mar. 1 Litho. ***Perf. 12***
RA86 PT30 1c emerald .85 .30

See note after No. RA59.

Invalid — PT36

1980, Mar. 28 Litho. ***Perf. 13½***
RA87 PT36 1c olive & citron .85 .30

Cancer Type of 1952 Redrawn and "1980" Added

1980, Oct. 1
RA88 PT9 1c violet & dk pur .30 .25

Mother and Child Type of 1978

1980, Dec. 1 Litho. ***Perf. 13½***
RA89 PT34 1c bright blue .30 .25

Turnera Ulmifolia (Marilope) — PT37

1981, Apr. 27 Litho. ***Perf. 12***
RA90 PT37 1c multicolored .30 .25

Tax was for Anti-Tuberculosis League. See Nos. RA98-RA99.

Communications Type of 1971

1981, Feb. Litho. ***Perf. 10½***
RA91 PT28 1c blue & red (lt bl frame) .60 .25

Mother and Child Type of 1978

1982, Dec. 1 Litho. ***Perf. 12x12½***
RA92 PT34 1c lt bluish green .30 .25

Inscribed 1981.

Cancer Type of 1952 Redrawn and "1981" Added

1982 Litho. ***Perf. 13½***
RA93 PT9 1c blue & dp blue .85 .30

PT38

1983, Apr. 29 Litho. ***Perf. 12***
RA94 PT38 1c multicolored .30 .25

Tax was for Red Cross.

Disabled — PT39

1984 Litho. ***Perf. 13½***
RA95 PT39 1c sky blue .30 .25

Cancer Type of 1952 Redrawn and "1983" Added

1983, Oct. 1 Litho. ***Perf. 13½***
RA96 PT9 1c lt bluish grn & dk grn .30 .25

Mother and Child Type of 1978

1983, Dec. 1 Litho. ***Perf. 12***
RA97 PT34 1c light green .30 .25

Inscribed 1983.

Flower Type of 1981 Dated "1983" or "1984"

1983-85 Litho. ***Perf. 12x12½***
RA98 PT37 1c 1983 .30 .25
RA99 PT37 1c 1984 .30 .25

Issued: #RA98, 4/19/83; #RA99, 4/1/85.

POSTAL TAX AIR POST STAMPS

Postal Tax Stamps Surcharged in Red or Gold

1930, Dec. 3 Unwmk. ***Perf. 12***
RAC1 PT2 5c + 5c blk & rose (R) 27.00 31.00
a. Tête bêche pair 125.00
b. "Habilitado Para" missing 52.50
RAC2 PT2 10c + 10c blk & rose (R) 27.00 31.00
a. Tête bêche pair 125.00
b. "Habilitado Para" missing 52.50
c. Gold surcharge 95.00 95.00
d. As "c," tête bêche pair 450.00
e. As "c" and "b" 250.00

Nos. RAC1-RAC2 were on sale one day.

RAC4 PT2 5c + 5c ultra & rose (R) 6.75 6.75
a. Tête bêche pair 45.00
b. Inverted surcharge 42.50
c. Tête bêche pair, inverted surcharge 600.00
d. Pair, one without surcharge 190.00
e. "Habilitado Para" missing 15.00
RAC5 PT2 10c + 10c yel & rose (G) 5.25 5.25
a. Tête bêche pair 42.50

b.		"Habilitado Para" missing	18.00	

Imperf

RAC6	PT2	5c + 5c ultra & rose (R)	6.75	6.75
a.		Tête bêche pair	52.50	
b.		"Habilitado Para" missing	18.00	
RAC7	PT2	10c + 10c yel & rose (G)	6.75	6.75
a.		Tête bêche pair	52.50	
b.		"Habilitado Para" missing	18.00	
		Nos. RAC1-RAC7 (6)	79.50	87.50

It was obligatory to use Nos. RA1-RA8 and RAC1-RAC7 on all postal matter, in amounts equal to the ordinary postage.
This surtax was for the aid of sufferers from the hurricane of Sept. 3, 1930.

No. 261 Overprinted in Green

1933, Oct. 11

RAC8	A32	2c scarlet	.50	.40
a.		Double overprint	9.00	
b.		Pair, one without overprint	375.00	

By official decree this stamp, in addition to the regular postage, had to be used on every letter, etc., sent by the internal air post service.

DUBAI

dü-'bī

LOCATION — Oman Peninsula, Arabia, on Persian Gulf
GOVT. — Sheikdom under British protection
AREA — 1,500 sq. mi.
POP. — 60,000
CAPITAL — Dubai

Dubai is one of six Persian Gulf sheikdoms to join the United Arab Emirates which proclaimed its independence Dec. 2, 1971. See United Arab Emirates.

100 Naye Paise = 1 Rupee
100 Dirhams = 1 Riyal (1966)

Imperforate
Many issues were accompanied by smaller quantities of imperforate stamps.

Catalogue values for all unused stamps in this country are for Never Hinged items.

Hermit Crab — A1

Sheik Rashid bin Said al Maktum — A2

2np, 20np, Cuttlefish. 3np, 25np, Snail. 4np, 30np, Crab. 5np, 35np, Sea urchin. 10np, 50np, Sea shell. 1r, Fortress wall. 2r, View of Dubai. 3r, Fortress wall. 5r, View of Dubai.

Perf. 12x11½

1963, June 15 Litho. Unwmk.

1	A1	1np dl bl & car rose	.30	.25
2	A1	2np lt bl & bis brn	.35	.25
3	A1	3np green & sepia	.35	.25
4	A1	4np pink & orange	.35	.25
5	A1	5np violet & blk	.35	.25
6	A1	10np brn org & blk	.35	.25
7	A1	15np gray ol & dp car	.70	.25
8	A1	20np rose red & org brn	.75	.40
9	A1	25np ap grn & red brn	.90	.40
10	A1	30np gray & red	1.50	.40
11	A1	35np dl lil & dl vio	1.50	.40
12	A1	50np org & sepia	2.25	.75
13	A1	1r brt bl & red org	6.00	1.50
14	A1	2r dull yel & brn	9.50	3.50
15	A1	3r rose car & blk	16.00	5.50
16	A1	5r grn & dl red brn	27.50	9.50

Perf. 12

17	A2	10r rose lake, grnsh bl & blk	60.00	19.00
		Nos. 1-17 (17)	128.65	43.10

Nos. 13-17 exist perf 10½. Values are much higher.

Dhows A3

Designs: 2np, First-aid tent. 3np, Camel caravan. 4np, Butterfly.

1963, Sept. 1 Unwmk. *Perf. 12*

18	A3	1np ultra, yel & red	.70	.35
19	A3	2np brn, yel & red	.70	.35
20	A3	3np red brn, org & red	.70	.35
21	A3	4np brn, brt grn & red	.70	.35
		Nos. 18-21,C9-C12 (8)	9.90	4.10

Intl. Red Cross, cent. Exist perf. 10½. Values, each $1.75.
Four imperf. souvenir sheets exist in the denominations and designs of Nos. C9-C12, with "Air-Mail" omitted and colors changed. Size: 119x99mm. Value $50.
For overprints see Nos. C52-C54.

A4

Anopheles Mosquito: 2np, Mosquito and entwined snakes. 3np, Mosquitoes over swamp.

1963, Dec. 20 Unwmk. *Perf. 12*

22	A4	1np emer & red brn	.30	.25
23	A4	1np red & dark brn	.30	.25
24	A4	1np blue & carmine	.30	.25
25	A4	2np brn & orange	.30	.25
26	A4	2np carmine & blue	.30	.25
27	A4	3np org brn & blue	.30	.25
		Nos. 22-27,C13-C15 (9)	3.95	2.35

WHO drive to eradicate malaria.

A5

Designs: 1np, Scouts forming pyramid. 2np, Bugler. 3np, Cub Scouts. 4np, Scouts and bugler. 5np, Scouts presenting flag.

1964 Unwmk.

28	A5	1np dk brn & ocher	.25	.25
29	A5	2np car rose & sep	.25	.25
30	A5	3np blue & red org	.25	.25
31	A5	4np carmine & blue	.25	.25
32	A5	5np ind & bluish grn	.35	.25
		Nos. 28-32,C20-C24 (10)	6.75	3.20

11th Boy Scout Jamboree, Marathon, Greece, Aug., 1963.
For overprints see Nos. C47-C51.

Unisphere, New York Skyline and Dubai Harbor — A6

2np, 4np, 10np, Views of NYC and Dubai.

1964, Apr. 22 Litho. *Perf. 12*

33	A6	1np dk bl & rose red	.25	.25
34	A6	2np dl red, lil rose & bl	.25	.25
35	A6	3np brown & green	.25	.25
36	A6	4np emer, brt grn & red	.25	.25
37	A6	5np ol, sl grn & lil	.25	.25
38	A6	10np brn org, red org & blk	.80	.50
		Nos. 33-38,C36-C38 (9)	6.80	4.05

New York World's Fair, 1964-65.

Gymnast — A8

Designs: 2np, 5np, 20np, 40np, Various exercises on bar. 3np, 30np, Various exercises on vaulting horse. 4np, 10np, 1r, Various exercises on rings.

1964 Photo. *Perf. 14*

43	A8	1np org brn & yel grn	.25	.25
44	A8	2np dk brn & grnsh bl	.25	.25
45	A8	3np ultra & org brn	.25	.25
46	A8	4np dk pur & yel	.25	.25
47	A8	5np ocher & dk bl	.30	.25
48	A8	10np brt bl & ocher	.35	.25
49	A8	20np ol & lil rose	.55	.25
50	A8	30np dk bl & yel	1.25	.25
51	A8	40np Prus grn & dl org	2.00	.50
52	A8	1r rose vio & grnsh bl	5.25	1.25
		Nos. 43-52 (10)	10.70	3.75

18th Olympic Games, Tokyo, Oct. 10-25, 1964. An imperf. miniature sheet contains a 67x67mm stamp similar to No. 52. Value $11.

Palace — A9

Sheik Rashid bin Said — A10

Designs: 20np, 25np, View of new Dubai. 35np, 40np, Bridge and dhow. 60np, 1r, Bridge. 1.25r, Minaret. 1.50r, 3r, Old Dubai.

1966, May 30 Photo. *Perf. 14x14½*

Size: 23x18mm

53	A9	5np brown & indigo	.25	.25
54	A9	10np black & orange	.30	.25
55	A9	15np ultra & brown	.40	.25

Perf. 13

Size: 27½x20½mm

56	A9	20np blue & red brn	.50	.30
57	A9	25np org ver & ultra	.55	.40
58	A9	35np violet & emer	.75	.50
59	A9	40np grnsh bl & bl	1.25	.50

Perf. 14½

Size: 31½x24mm

60	A9	60np yel grn & org ver	2.00	1.00
61	A9	1r ultra & blue	3.00	1.50
62	A9	1.25r brn org & blk	3.25	2.00
63	A9	1.50r rose lil & yel grn	6.00	2.10
64	A9	3r dk ol bis & vio	11.00	4.00

Engr.

Perf. 14

65	A10	5r rose carmine	20.00	7.50
66	A10	10r dark blue	40.00	16.00
		Nos. 53-66 (14)	89.25	36.55

Nos. 53-62, 64-66 Overprinted with New Currency Names and Bars

1967

67	A9	5d on 5np	.30	.25
68	A9	10d on 10np	.35	.25
69	A9	15d on 15np	.50	.25
70	A9	20d on 20np	1.00	.25
71	A9	25d on 25np	1.25	.25
72	A9	35d on 35np	1.50	.25
73	A9	40d on 40np	1.75	.30
74	A9	60d on 60np	3.00	.40
75	A9	1r on 1r	4.00	.95
76	A9	1.25r on 1.25r	7.25	1.30
77	A9	3r on 3r	15.00	3.75
78	A10	5r on 5r	27.50	7.50
79	A10	10r on 10r	40.00	14.00
		Nos. 67-79 (13)	103.40	29.70

Sheik and Falcon — A11

Dhow — A12

Litho. & Engr.

1967, Aug. 21 *Perf. 13½*

80	A11	5d dp car & org	1.25	.30
81	A11	10d sepia & green	1.40	.25
82	A11	20d dp cl & bl gray	1.50	.30
83	A11	35d slate & car	2.00	.30
84	A11	60d vio bl & emer	3.50	.50
85	A11	1r green & lilac	5.00	.50
86	A12	1.25r lt bl & claret	6.00	.65
87	A12	3r dull vio & claret	12.00	1.75
88	A12	5r brt grn & vio	25.00	3.75
89	A12	10r lil rose & grn	32.50	6.75
		Nos. 80-89 (10)	90.15	15.05

S. S. Bamora, 1914 — A13

35d, De Havilland 66 plane, 1930. 60d, S. S. Sirdhana, 1947. 1r, Armstrong Whitworth 15 "Atlanta," 1938. 1.25r, S. S. Chandpara, 1949. 3r, BOAC Sunderland amphibian plane, 1943. No. 96, Freighter Bombala, 1961, and BOAC Super VC10, 1967.

1969, Feb. 12 Litho. *Perf. 14x13½*

90	A13	25d lt grn, bl & blk	.25	*.25*
91	A13	35d multicolored	.25	*.25*
92	A13	60d multicolored	.80	*.25*
93	A13	1r lil, blk & dl yel	1.25	*.25*
94	A13	1.25r gray, blk & dp org	1.75	*.25*
95	A13	3r pink, blk & bl grn	2.75	*.35*
		Nos. 90-95 (6)	7.05	*1.60*

Miniature Sheet

Imperf

96	A13	1.25r pink, blk & bl grn	18.00	18.00

60 years of postal service.

Mother and Children, by Rubens
A14

Arab Mother's Day: 60d, Madonna and Child, by Murillo. 1r, Mother and Child, by Francesco Mazzuoli. 3r, Madonna and Child, by Correggio.

1969, Mar. 21 Litho. *Perf. 13½*

97	A14	60d silver & multi	.75	*.25*
98	A14	1r silver & multi	1.50	*.25*
99	A14	1.25r silver & multi	1.75	*.25*
100	A14	3r silver & multi	3.50	*.45*
		Nos. 97-100 (4)	7.50	*1.20*

Porkfish — A15

1969, May 26 Litho. *Perf. 11*

101	A15	60d shown	2.25	*.35*
102	A15	60d Spotted grouper	2.25	*.35*
103	A15	60d Moonfish	2.25	*.35*
104	A15	60d Sweetlips	2.25	*.35*
105	A15	60d Blue angel	2.25	*.35*
106	A15	60d Texas skate	2.25	*.35*
107	A15	60d Striped butterflyfish	2.25	*.35*
108	A15	60d Imperial angelfish	2.25	*.35*
a.		Block of 8, #101-108	35.00	
		Nos. 101-108 (8)	18.00	*2.80*

Nos. 101-108 printed in se-tenant blocks of 8, each sheet containing two such blocks.

Explorers and Map of Arabia — A16

1969, July 21 Litho. *Perf. 13½x13*

109	A16	35d brown & green	1.50	*.35*
110	A16	60d vio & sepia	2.00	*.45*
111	A16	1r green & dl bl	5.50	*.55*
112	A16	1.25r gray & rose car	7.00	*.65*
		Nos. 109-112 (4)	16.00	*2.00*

European explorers of Arabia: Sir Richard Francis Burton (1821-1890), Charles Montagu Doughty (1843-1926), Johann Ludwig Burckhardt (1784-1817) and Wilfred Patrick Thesiger (1910-).

Construction of World's First Underwater Oil Storage Tank — A17

Designs: 20d, Launching of oil storage tank. 35d, Oil storage tank in place on ocean ground. 60d, Sheik Rashid bin Said, offshore drilling platform and monument commemorating first oil export. 1r, Offshore production platform and helicopter port.

1969, Oct. 13 Litho. *Perf. 11*

113	A17	5d blue & multi	.25	*.25*
114	A17	20d blue & multi	.85	*.25*
115	A17	35d blue & multi	1.60	*.25*
116	A17	60d blue & multi	2.50	*.25*
117	A17	1r blue & multi	3.50	*.25*
		Nos. 113-117 (5)	8.70	*1.25*

Astronauts Collecting Moon Rocks — A18

Designs: 1r, Astronaut at foot of ladder. 1.25r, Astronauts planting American flag.

1969, Dec. 15 Litho. *Perf. 14½*

118		Strip of 3	4.50	*.30*
a.	A18	60d multicolored	.45	*.25*
b.	A18	1r multicolored	.90	*.25*
c.	A18	1.25r multicolored (airmail)	1.90	*.25*

The 1.25r is inscribed "AIRMAIL."

Sizes: 60d and 1r, 28½x41mm; 1.25r, 60½x41mm.

See note after US No. C76.

Ocean Weather Ship Launching Radio Sonde, and Hastings Plane — A19

WMO Emblem and: 1r, Kew-type radio sonde, weather balloon and radar antenna. 1.25r, Tiros satellite and weather sounding rocket. 3r, Ariel satellite and rocket launching.

1970, Mar. 23 Litho. *Perf. 11*

121	A19	60d dl grn, brn & blk	.50	*.25*
122	A19	1r brown & multi	.90	*.25*
123	A19	1.25r dk blue & multi	1.10	*.25*
124	A19	3r multicolored	2.50	*.30*
		Nos. 121-124 (4)	5.00	*1.05*

10th World Meteorological Day.

UPU Headquarters and Monument, Bern — A20

60d, UPU monument, Bern, telecommunications satellite and London PO tower.

1970, May 20 Litho. *Perf. 13½x14*

125	A20	5d lt green & multi	.65	*.25*
126	A20	60d dp blue & multi	1.60	*.25*

UPU Headquarters opening, May 20.

Charles Dickens, London Skyline — A21

60d, Dickens' portrait, vert. 1.25r, Dickens & "Old Curiosity Shop." 3r, Bound volumes.

1970, July 23 Litho. *Perf. 13½*

127	A21	60d olive & multi	.70	*.25*
128	A21	1r multicolored	.85	*.25*
129	A21	1.25r buff & multi	1.00	*.25*
130	A21	3r multicolored	3.25	*.50*
		Nos. 127-130 (4)	5.80	*1.25*

Dickens (1812-70), English novelist.

The Graham Children, by William Hogarth — A22

Paintings: 60d, Caroline Murat and her Children, by François Pascal Gerard, vert. 1r, Napoleon with the Children on the Terrace in St. Cloud, by Louis Ducis.

1970, Oct. 1 Litho. *Perf. 13½*

131	A22	35d multicolored	.75	.25
132	A22	60d multicolored	1.25	.25
133	A22	1r multicolored	2.00	.25
		Nos. 131-133 (3)	4.00	.75

Issued for Children's Day.

National Bank of Dubai
A24

Sheik Rashid bin Said — A23

Television Station — A25

Designs: 10d, Boat building. 20d, Al Maktum Bascule Bridge. 35d, Great Mosque, Dubai, vert. 1r, Dubai International Airport, horiz. 1.25r, Port Rashid harbor project, horiz. 3r, Rashid Hospital, horiz. 5r, Dubai Trade School, horiz.

Perf. 14x14½, 14½x14

1970-71 Litho.

134	A23	5d multi ('71)	.30	.25
135	A24	10d multi ('71)	.30	.25
136	A24	20d multi ('71)	.50	.25
137	A24	35d multi ('71)	.65	.25
138	A24	60d multicolored	1.00	.25

Perf. 14

139	A25	1r multicolored	1.50	.25
140	A25	1.25r multicolored	1.50	.25
141	A25	3r multicolored	4.50	.25
142	A25	5r multicolored	7.25	.40
143	A25	10r multi ('71)	17.50	.85
		Nos. 134-143 (10)	35.00	3.25

Dubai Airport
A26

Designs: 1.25r, Airport entrance.

1971, May 15 Litho. *Perf. 13½x14*

144	A26	1r multicolored	3.25	.25
145	A26	1.25r multicolored	4.00	.25

Opening of Dubai International Airport.

Map With Tracking Stations, Satellites
A27

1971, June 21 Litho. *Perf. 14½*

146	A27	60d multicolored	.60	.30

Outer Space Telecommunications Cong., Paris, Mar. 29-Apr. 2. See Nos. C55-C56.

Fan, Scout Emblem, Map of Japan — A28

Designs: 1r, Boy Scouts in kayaks. 1.25r, Mountaineering. 3r, Campfire, horiz.

Perf. 14x13½, 13½x14

1971, Aug. 30 Litho.

147	A28	60d multicolored	.50	*.25*
148	A28	1r multicolored	1.00	*.25*
149	A28	1.25r multicolored	1.25	*.25*
150	A28	3r multicolored	2.75	*.30*
		Nos. 147-150 (4)	5.50	*1.05*

13th Boy Scout World Jamboree, Asagiri Plain, Japan, Aug. 2-10.

Albrecht Dürer, Self-portrait
A29

1971, Oct. 18 *Perf. 14x13½*

151	A29	60d gold & multi	.80	*.25*

See Nos. C57-C59.

Boy in Meadow
A30

5r, Boys playing and UNICEF emblem.

1971, Dec. 11 *Perf. 13½*

152	A30	60d multi	.45	*.25*
153	A30	5r multi, horiz.	3.50	*.50*

25th anniv. of UNICEF. See No. C60.

Ludwig van Beethoven A31

Portrait: 10d, Leonardo da Vinci.

1972, Feb. 7

154	A31	10d lt tan & multi	.30	*.25*
155	A31	35d lt tan & multi	.45	*.25*

See Nos. C61-C62.

Olympic Emblems, Gymnast on Rings — A32

1972, July 31 Litho. *Perf. 13½*

156	A32	35d shown	.55	*.25*
157	A32	40d Fencing	.65	*.25*
158	A32	65d Hockey	.80	*.25*
		Nos. 156-158,C65-C67 (6)	7.50	1.50

20th Olympic Games, Munich, 8/26-9/11.

Stamps of Dubai were replaced in 1972 by those of United Arab Emirates.

AIR POST STAMPS

Type of Regular Issue and

Peregrine Falcon — AP1

Design: A1, Falcon over bridge.

Perf. 12x11½, 11½x12

1963, June 15 Litho. Unwmk.

C1	A1	20np dk red brn & lt blue	2.50	.35
C2	AP1	25np ol & blk brn	2.75	.45
C3	A1	30np red org & blk	3.25	.55
C4	AP1	40np grayish brn & dk violet	3.50	.65
C5	A1	50np emer & rose cl	4.25	.75
C6	AP1	60np brn org & blk	5.25	.85
C7	A1	75np vio & dp grn	6.50	1.00
C8	AP1	1r org & red brn	9.00	1.25
		Nos. C1-C8 (8)	37.00	5.85

Red Cross Type

Designs: 20np, Dhows. 30np, First-aid tent. 40np, Camel caravan. 50np, Butterfly.

1963, Sept. 1 Unwmk. *Perf. 12*

C9	A3	20np brown, yel & red	1.25	.50
C10	A3	30np dk bl, buff & red	1.25	.50
C11	A3	40np black, yel & red	1.60	.60
C12	A3	50np vio, lt bl & red	3.00	1.10
		Nos. C9-C12 (4)	7.10	2.70

Malaria Type

Designs: 30np, Anopheles mosquito. 40np, Mosquito and coiled arrows. 70np, Mosquitoes over swamp.

1963, Dec. 20 Unwmk. *Perf. 12*

C13	A4	30np purple & emer	.55	.25
C14	A4	40np red & dull grn	.65	.25
C15	A4	70np slate & citron	.95	.35
		Nos. C13-C15 (3)	2.00	.80

Three imperf. souv. sheets exist containing 4 stamps each in changed colors similar to Nos. C13-C15. Value $30.

Wheat — AP2

40np, Wheat and palm tree. 70np, Hands holding wheat. 1r, Woman carrying basket.

1963, Dec. 30 Litho.

C16	AP2	30np vio bl & ocher	.55	.30
C17	AP2	40np red & olive	.80	.45
C18	AP2	70np green & orange	1.25	.65
C19	AP2	1r org brn & Prus bl	1.90	1.00
		Nos. C16-C19 (4)	4.50	2.40

Boy Scout Type

Designs: 20np, Human pyramid. 30np, Bugler. 40np, Cub Scouts. 70np, Scouts and bugler. 1r, Scouts presenting flag.

1964, Jan. 20

C20	A5	20np green & dk brn	.30	.25
C21	A5	30np lilac & ocher	.65	.25
C22	A5	40np vio bl & yel grn	.85	.30
C23	A5	70np dk grn & gray	1.50	.45
C24	A5	1r vio bl & red org	2.10	.70
		Nos. C20-C24 (5)	5.15	1.90

Five imperf. souv. sheets exist containing 4 stamps each in changed colors similar to Nos. C20-C24. Value $60.

For overprints see Nos. C47-C51.

John F. Kennedy and US Seal AP3

1964, Jan. 15 Litho.

C25	AP3	75np grn & blk, *lt grn*	.90	.55
C26	AP3	1r ocher & blk, *tan*	1.25	.60
C27	AP3	1.25r mag & blk, *gray*	1.60	.85
		Nos. C25-C27 (3)	3.75	2.00

Pres. John F. Kennedy (1917-1963). A souvenir sheet contains one imperf. 1.25r in buff and black with simulated perforations. Value $6.

For overprints see Nos. C52-C54.

Spacecraft — AP4

Designs: 1np, 5np, Ascending rocket, vert. 2np, 1r, Mercury capsule, vert. 4np, 2r, Twin spacecraft.

1964, Jan. 25 Unwmk. *Perf. 12*

C28	AP4	1np emerald & org	.25	.25
C29	AP4	2np multicolored	.30	.25
C30	AP4	3np multicolored	.35	.25
C31	AP4	4np multicolored	.40	.25
C32	AP4	5np blue & orange	.45	.25
C33	AP4	1r vio bl, dp car & buff	1.25	.70
C34	AP4	1.50r vio bl, dp car & buff	2.00	1.25
C35	AP4	2r blue, yel & red	2.75	1.50
		Nos. C28-C35 (8)	7.75	4.70

Issued to honor the astronauts. An imperf. souvenir sheet contains one stamp similar to No. C35. Value $7.

New York World's Fair Type

Statue of Liberty and ships in Dubai harbor.

1964, Apr. 22 Litho.

C36	A6	75np gray bl, ultra & blk	.90	.40
C37	A6	2r gray grn, dk brn & bis	1.60	.80
C38	A6	3r dl grn, gray ol & dp org	2.25	1.10
		Nos. C36-C38 (3)	4.75	2.30

An imperf. souvenir sheet contains 2 stamps in Statue of Liberty design: 2r dark brown and rose carmine, and 3r ultramarine and gold. Value $10.

Scales and Flame AP5

1964, Apr. 30 Litho. *Perf. 12*

C39	AP5	35np bl, brn & scar	.60	.30
C40	AP5	50np lt bl, dk grn & scar	.75	.35
C41	AP5	1r grnsh bl, blk & scar	1.40	.60
C42	AP5	3r lt ultra, ultra, & scar	4.00	2.00
		Nos. C39-C42 (4)	6.75	3.25

15th anniv. of the Universal Declaration of Human Rights. An imperf. souvenir sheet contains one 3r light green, ultramarine and scarlet stamp. Value $7.50.

Nos. C20-C24 Overprinted in Red and Black (Shield in Red)

1964, June 20

C47	A5	20np green & dk brn	1.25	.40
C48	A5	30np lilac & ocher	1.50	.50
C49	A5	40np vio bl & yel grn	2.25	.75
C50	A5	70np dk grn & gray	3.50	1.50
C51	A5	1r vio bl & red org	5.00	2.00
		Nos. C47-C51 (5)	13.50	5.15

9th Winter Olympic Games, Innsbruck, Austria, Jan. 29-Feb. 9, 1964.

A similar but unauthorized overprint, with shield in black, exists on Nos. 28-32, C20-C24, and the five souvenir sheets mentioned below No. C24. The Dubai G.P.O. calls this black-shield overprint "bogus."

Nos. C25-C27 Overprinted in Brown or Green

1964, Sept. 15

C52	AP3	75np (Br)	2.00	2.00
C53	AP3	1r (G)	2.40	2.40
C54	AP3	1.25r (G)	3.00	3.00
		Nos. C52-C54 (3)	7.40	7.40

Pres. John F. Kennedy 48th birth anniv. The same overprint in black was applied to the souv. sheet noted after No. C27.

Communications Type

Designs: 1r, Intelsat 4, tracking station on globe and rocket. 5r, Eiffel Tower, Syncom 3 and Goonhilly radar station.

1971, June 21 Litho. *Perf. 14½*

C55	A27	1r lt brown & multi	.60	*.25*
C56	A27	5r multicolored	3.00	*.45*

Portrait Type

1r, Newton. 1.25r, Avicenna. 3r, Voltaire.

1971, Oct. 18 Litho. *Perf. 14x13½*

C57	A29	1r gold & multi	1.10	*.25*
C58	A29	1.25r gold & multi	1.40	*.25*
C59	A29	3r gold & multi	4.00	*.50*
		Nos. C57-C59 (3)	6.50	*1.00*

UNICEF Type

1r, Mother, children, UNICEF emblem.

1971, Dec. 11 *Perf. 13½*

C60	A30	1r gold & multi	1.00	*.25*

Portrait Type

75d, Khalil Gibran. 5r, Charles de Gaulle.

1972, Feb. 7 Litho. *Perf. 13½*

C61	A31	75d lt tan & multi	.75	*.25*
C62	A31	5r lt tan & multi	5.25	*.35*

Infant Health Care AP6

Design: 75d, Nurse supervising children at meal, and WHO emblem, vert.

1972, Apr. 7 Litho. *Perf. 14x13½*

C63	AP6	75d multicolored	1.60	*.25*
C64	AP6	1.25r multicolored	2.40	*.25*

World Health Day.

Olympic Type

1972, July 31 Litho. *Perf. 13½*

C65	A32	75d Water polo	1.50	*.25*
C66	A32	1r Steeplechase	1.75	*.25*
C67	A32	1.25r Running	2.25	*.25*
		Nos. C65-C67 (3)	5.50	*.60*

POSTAGE DUE STAMPS

Type of Regular Issue

Designs: 1np, 4np, 15np, Clam. 2np, 5np, 25np, Mussel. 3np, 10np, 35np, Oyster.

Perf. 12x11½

1963, June 15 Litho. Unwmk.

J1	A1	1np gray grn & ver	1.00	.35
J2	A1	2np lemon & brt bl	1.50	.45
J3	A1	3np dl rose & green	1.75	.75
J4	A1	4np light grn & mag	2.50	1.00
J5	A1	5np vermilion & blk	3.00	1.25
J6	A1	10np citron & violet	3.50	1.50
J7	A1	15np brt ultra & ver	4.50	1.90
J8	A1	25np buff & olive grn	6.00	2.00
J9	A1	35np turq bl & dp org	6.50	2.75
		Nos. J1-J9 (9)	30.25	11.95

Sheik Rashid bin Said — D1

1972, May 22 Litho. *Perf. 14x14½*

J10	D1	5d blk & gray grn	2.00	.75
J11	D1	10d vio bl, blk & bis	2.50	.85
J12	D1	20d sl grn, blk & brick red	4.25	1.50
J13	D1	30d grnsh gray, blk & lil	7.00	2.25
J14	D1	50d lilac, brn & bis	11.00	4.50
		Nos. J10-J14 (5)	26.75	9.85

EAST AFRICA & UGANDA PROTECTORATES

ˈest ˈa-fri-kə and ü-ˈgan-də
prə-ˈtek-tˌə-ˌrəts

LOCATION — Central East Africa, bordering on the Indian Ocean
GOVT. — British Protectorate
AREA — 350,000 sq. mi. (approx.)
POP. — 6,503,507 (approx.)
CAPITAL — Mombasa

This territory, formerly administered by the British East Africa Colony, was divided between Kenya Colony and the Uganda Protectorate. See Kenya, Uganda and Tanzania.

16 Annas = 1 Rupee
100 Cents = 1 Rupee (1907)

Altered high value stamps of East Africa and Uganda are plentiful.
Expertization by competent authorities is recommended.

A1 A2

King Edward VII

1903 Typo. Wmk. 2 *Perf. 14*

1	A1	½a gray green	5.50	*21.00*
2	A1	1a car & black	2.25	1.50
3	A1	2a vio & dull vio	10.50	3.00
4	A1	2½a ultramarine	14.50	*60.00*
5	A1	3a gray grn & brn	27.50	*70.00*
6	A1	4a blk & gray grn	13.50	*27.50*
7	A1	5a org brn & blk	22.50	*60.00*
8	A1	8a pale blue & blk	26.00	*50.00*

Wmk. 1

9	A2	1r gray green	25.00	*65.00*
10	A2	2r vio & dull vio	87.50	*100.00*
11	A2	3r blk & gray grn	160.00	*275.00*
12	A2	4r lt green & blk	160.00	*300.00*
13	A2	5r car & black	160.00	*300.00*
14	A2	10r ultra & black	425.00	*550.00*
15	A2	20r ol gray & blk	750.00	*1,800.*
16	A2	50r org brn & blk	2,250.	*4,250.*
		Nos. 1-14 (14)	1,139.	*1,883.*

Nos. 9 and 14 are on both ordinary and chalky paper. Values are for examples on ordinary paper. Values are for the least expensive varieties. See *Scott Classic Specialized Catalogue of Stamps & Covers* for detailed listings.

1904-07 Wmk. 3 Chalky Paper

17	A1	½a gray green	14.00	3.75
18a	A1	1a car & black	4.50	1.00
19	A1	2a vio & dull vio	3.50	3.25
20	A1	2½a blue	10.00	37.50
a.		2½a blue & ultramarine	9.50	*21.00*
21	A1	3a gray grn & brn	4.75	*45.00*
22	A1	4a blk & gray grn	9.25	*22.50*
23	A1	5a org brn & blk	8.00	*18.50*
24a	A1	8a pale blue & blk	8.75	10.50
25	A2	1r gray green	35.00	*75.00*
26	A2	2r vio & dl vio	47.50	*67.50*
27	A2	3r blk & gray grn	90.00	*140.00*
28	A2	4r lt green & blk	100.00	*180.00*
29	A2	5r car & black	160.00	*180.00*
29A	A2	10r ultra & black	350.00	*400.00*
30	A2	20r ol gray & blk	800.00	*1,400.*
30A	A2	50r org brn & blk	2,750.	*4,250.*
		Nos. 17-29 (10)	472.00	*735.50*

Nos. 17-19, 21-24 are on both ordinary and chalky paper. No. 20 is on ordinary paper. Values are for the least expensive varieties. See *Scott Classic Specialized Catalogue of Stamps & Covers* for detailed listings.

1907-08

31	A1	1c brown ('08)	3.00	.25
32	A1	3c gray green	20.00	.80
33	A1	6c carmine	3.25	.25
34	A1	10c citron & violet	11.00	10.00
35	A1	12c red vio & dl vio	12.00	3.50
36	A1	15c ultramarine	30.00	11.00
37	A1	25c blk & blue green	21.00	*8.50*
38	A1	50c org brn & green	16.00	14.50
39	A1	75c pale bl & gray blk ('08)	5.50	*40.00*
		Nos. 31-39 (9)	121.75	*88.80*

Nos. 31-33, 36 are on ordinary paper.
There are two dies of the 6c differing very slightly in many details.

King George V
A3 A4

1912-18 Ordinary Paper Wmk. 3

40	A3	1c black	.40	*2.10*
41	A3	3c green	2.50	.75
a.		Booklet pane of 6		
42	A3	6c carmine	1.50	.70
a.		Booklet pane of 6		
43	A3	10c yel orange	2.50	.65
44	A3	12c gray	3.25	.65
45	A3	15c ultramarine	3.25	1.00

Chalky Paper

46	A3	25c scar & blk, *yel*	.65	*1.60*
47	A3	50c violet & black	1.90	1.60
48	A3	75c black, *green*	1.90	*21.00*
a.		75c black, *emerald*	13.50	*65.00*
b.		75c blk, *bl grn*, olive back	7.25	9.25
c.		75c blk, *emer*, olive back	50.00	*175.00*
49	A4	1r black, *green*	2.25	*5.25*
a.		1r black, *emerald*	6.00	*60.00*
50	A4	2r blk & red, *bl*	24.50	*45.00*
51	A4	3r gray grn & vio	27.50	*130.00*
52	A4	4r grn & red, *yel*	55.00	*125.00*
53	A4	5r dl vio & ultra	65.00	*160.00*
54	A4	10r grn & red, *grn*	180.00	*275.00*
55	A4	20r vio & blk, *red*	425.00	425.00
56	A4	20r bl & violet, *blue* ('18)	500.00	*550.00*
57	A4	50r gray grn & rose red	900.00	*975.00*
58	A4	100r blk & vio, *red*	*9,750.*	*3,000.*
59	A4	500r red & grn, *grn*	*37,500.*	
		Nos. 40-54 (15)	372.10	*770.30*

1914 Surface-colored Paper

60	A3	25c scarlet & blk, *yel*	.65	*5.50*
61	A3	75c black, *green*	1.25	*19.50*

Stamps of types A3 and A4 with watermark 4 are listed under Kenya, Uganda and Tanzania.
The 1r through 50r with revenue cancellations sell for minimal prices. The 100r and 500r were available for postage but were nearly always used fiscally.
For surcharge see No. 62.

No. 42 Surcharged

1919

62	A3	4c on 6c carmine	1.50	.25
a.		Double surcharge	150.00	*240.00*
b.		Without squares over old value	50.00	*85.00*
c.		Pair, one without surcharge	2,000.	*2,250.*
d.		Inverted surcharge	325.00	*475.00*

For later issues see Kenya, Uganda and Tanzania.
For stamps of East Africa and Uganda overprinted "G. E. A." see German East Africa.

EASTERN RUMELIA

ˈē-stərn rü-ˈmēl-yə

(South Bulgaria)

LOCATION — In southern Bulgaria
GOVT. — An autonomous unit of the Turkish Empire.
CAPITAL — Philippopolis (Plovdiv)

In 1885 the province of Eastern Rumelia revolted against Turkish rule and united with Bulgaria, adopting the new name of South Bulgaria. This union was assured by the Treaty of Bucharest in 1886, following the war between Serbia and Bulgaria.

40 Paras = 1 Piaster

Counterfeits of all overprints are plentiful.

Stamps of Turkey, 1876-84, Overprinted in Blue

No. 1

A2 A3

1880 Unwmk. *Perf. 13½*

1	A5	½pi on 20pa yel grn	67.50	57.50
a.		Horiz. pair, one without overprint		*400.00*
3	A2	10pa blk & rose	*55.00*	
4	A2	20pa vio & grn	87.50	67.50
6	A2	2pi blk & buff	115.00	100.00
7	A2	5pi red & bl	450.00	*500.00*
8	A3	10pa blk & red lil	57.50	

Nos. 3 & 8 were not placed in use.
Inverted and double overprints of all values exist.

Same, with Extra Overprint "R. O."

9	A3	10pa blk & red lil	97.50	95.00

Crescent and Turkish Inscriptions of Value — A4

1881 Typo. *Perf. 13½*

10	A4	5pa blk & olive	17.00	1.35
11	A4	10pa blk & green	65.00	1.35
12	A4	20pa blk & rose	1.75	1.25
13	A4	1pi blk & blue	5.75	4.50
14	A4	5pi rose & blue	57.50	*82.50*

Tête bêche pairs, imperforates and all perf. 11½ examples of Nos. 10-14 were not placed in use, and were found only in the remainder stock. This is true also of a 10pa cliché in the 20pa plate, and of a cliché of Turkey No. 63 in the 1pi plate. See the *Scott Classic Catalogue.*

1884 *Perf. 11½*

15	A4	5pa lil & pale lil	.55	.45
16	A4	10pa grn & pale grn	.25	.45
17	A4	20pa car & pale rose	.55	
18	A4	1pi bl & pale bl	1.15	
19	A4	5pi brn & pale brn	*400.00*	

Nos. 17-19 were not placed in use, and were found only in the remainder stock.
Nos. 15-19 imperf. are from remainders.
See the *Scott Classic Catalogue for perf 13½ listings.*
For overprints see Turkey Nos. 542-545.

South Bulgaria

Counterfeits of all overprints are plentiful.

Nos. 10-14 Overprinted in Two Types

a b

Type a — Four toes on each foot.
Type b — Three toes on each foot.

Blue Overprint

1885 Unwmk. *Perf. 13½*

20	A4 (a)	5pa blk & olive	*325.00*	*375.00*
21	A4 (a)	10pa blk & grn	*875.00*	*825.00*
22	A4 (a)	20pa blk & rose	325.00	—
23	A4 (a)	1pi blk & blue	37.50	*72.50*
24	A4 (b)	5pi rose & blue	*1,100.*	—

See the *Scott Classic Catalogue* for Nos. 22-23, type b, No. 24, type a, and No. 22, perf 11½, types a and b.

Black Overprint

24B	A4 (a)	20pa blk & rose	275.00	—
25	A4 (a)	1pi blk & bl	55.00	*115.00*
26	A4 (b)	5pi rose & bl	*675.00*	—

See the *Scott Classic Catalogue* for No. 25 type b.

Same Overprint on Nos. 15-17

Blue Overprint

Perf. 11½

27	A4 (b)	5pa lil & pale lil, type "b"	22.50	*57.50*
28	A4 (b)	10pa grn & pale grn	40.00	*75.00*
29	A4 (b)	20pa car & pale rose	275.00	*375.00*

Black Overprint

Perf. 13½

30	A4 (b)	5pa lil & pale lil	40.00	*67.50*

Perf. 11½

31	A4 (a)	10pa grn & pale grn	42.50	*85.00*
32	A4 (b)	20pa car & pale rose	55.00	*65.00*

See the *Scott Classic Catalogue* for detailed listings of Nos. 27-32.

Nos. 10-17 Handstamped in Black in Two Types

a b

Type a — First letter at top circular.
Type b — First letter at top oval.

1885 *Perf. 13½*

33	A4 (b)	5pa blk & olive	*300.00*	250.00
34	A4 (b)	10pa blk & grn	*225.00*	250.00
35	A4 (b)	20pa blk & rose	72.50	*85.00*
36	A4 (a)	1pi blk & bl	87.50	*115.00*
37	A4 (a)	5pi rose & blue, type "a"	*2,500.*	—

Perf. 13½

38	A4 (a)	5pa lil & pale lil	26.00	*44.00*

Perf. 11½

39	A4 (a)	10pa grn & pale grn	29.00	*35.00*
40	A4 (a)	20pa car & pale rose	29.00	*50.00*

See the *Scott Classic Catalogue* for Nos. 38-40, type b, and No. 38, perf 11½, types a and b.
Nos. 20-40 exist with inverted and double handstamps. Overprints in unlisted colors are proofs.
The stamps of South Bulgaria were superseded in 1886 by those of Bulgaria.

EASTERN SILESIA

ˈē-stərn sī-ˈlē-zhˌē-ˌə

LOCATION — In central Europe
GOVT. — Austrian crownland
AREA — 1,987 sq. mi.
POP. — 680,422 (estimated 1920)
CAPITAL — Troppau

After World War I, this territory was occupied by Czechoslovakia and eventually was divided between Poland and Czechoslovakia, the dividing line running through Teschen.

100 Heller = 1 Krone
100 Fennigi = 1 Marka

Plebiscite Issues

Stamps of Czechoslovakia 1918-20, Overprinted in Black, Blue, Violet or Red

1920		Unwmk.		*Imperf.*
1	A2	1h dark brown	.25	.30
2	A1	3h red violet	.25	.25
3	A2	5h blue green	23.50	22.50
4	A2	15h red	11.50	11.00
5	A1	20h blue green	.25	.25
6	A2	25h dull violet	.75	.75
7	A1	30h bister (R)	.25	.25
8	A1	40h red orange	.30	.30
9	A2	50h dull violet	.60	.45
10	A2	50h dark blue	2.60	1.50
11	A2	60h orange (Bl)	.75	.75
12	A2	75h slate (R)	.50	.75
13	A2	80h olive grn (R)	.50	.75
14	A1	100h brown	1.10	1.10
15	A2	120h gray blk (R)	1.60	*2.25*
16	A1	200h ultra (R)	1.60	*2.00*
17	A2	300h green (R)	6.25	*7.50*
18	A1	400h purple (R)	2.60	*3.00*
20	A2	500h red brn (Bl)	5.25	*6.00*
a.		Black overprint	6.25	*9.00*
21	A2	1000h violet (Bl)	13.00	*13.50*
a.		Black overprint	62.50	*75.00*
		Nos. 1-21 (20)	73.40	75.15

Perf. 11½, 13¾				
22	A2	1h dark brown	.25	.25
23	A2	5h blue green	.30	.25
24	A2	10h yellow green	.30	.25
a.		Imperf.	*260.00*	*210.00*
25	A2	15h red	.50	.25
26	A2	20h rose	.50	.35
a.		Imperf.	*300.00*	*250.00*
27	A2	25h dull violet	.50	.35
28	A2	30h red violet (Bl)	.35	.35
29	A2	60h orange (Bl)	.50	.50
30	A1	200h ultra (R)	3.00	3.00
		Nos. 22-30 (9)	6.20	5.55

The letters "S. O." are the initials of "Silésie Orientale."

Forged cancellations are found on Nos. 1-30.

Overprinted in Carmine or Violet

31	A4	500h sl, *grysh* (C)	40.00
32	A4	1000h blk brn, *brnsh*	40.00

Excellent counterfeits of this overprint exist.

Stamps of Poland, 1919, Overprinted

1920				*Perf. 11½*
41	A10	5f green	.25	.25
42	A10	10f red brown	.25	.25
43	A10	15f light red	.25	.25
44	A11	25f olive green	.25	.25
45	A11	50f blue green	.25	.25

Overprinted

46	A12	1k deep green	.25	.25
47	A12	1.50k brown	.25	.25
48	A12	2k dark blue	.25	.25
49	A13	2.50k dull violet	.30	.25
50	A14	5k slate blue	.50	.25
		Nos. 41-50 (10)	2.80	2.50

SPECIAL DELIVERY STAMPS

Czechoslovakia Special Delivery Stamps Ovptd. in Blue

1920		Unwmk.		*Imperf.*
E1	SD1	2h red violet, *yel*	.25	.25
a.		Black overprint	4.75	.80
E2	SD1	5h yellow green, *yel*	.25	.25
a.		Black overprint	8.00	5.00

Nos. E1-E2a exist on white paper.

POSTAGE DUE STAMPS

Czechoslovakia Postage Due Stamps Overprinted In Blue or Red

1920		Unwmk.		*Imperf.*
J1	D1	5h deep bis (Bl)	.25	.25
a.		Black overprint	72.50	62.50
J2	D1	10h deep bister	.25	.25
J3	D1	15h deep bister	.25	.25
J4	D1	20h deep bister	.25	.25
J5	D1	25h deep bister	.25	.25
J6	D1	30h deep bister	.25	.25
J7	D1	40h deep bister	.50	.25
J8	D1	50h deep bister	2.60	3.00
J9	D1	100h blk brn (R)	2.60	3.00
J10	D1	500h gray grn (R)	5.75	4.50
J11	D1	1000h purple (R)	8.50	11.50
		Nos. J1-J11 (11)	21.45	23.75

Forged cancellations exist.

NEWSPAPER STAMPS

Czechoslovakia Newspaper Stamps Overprinted in Black like Nos. 1-30

1920		Unwmk.		*Imperf.*
P1	N1	2h gray green	.30	.30
P2	N1	6h red	.25	.25
P3	N1	10h dull violet	.40	.25
P4	N1	20h blue	.65	.25
P5	N1	30h gray brown	.65	.25
		Nos. P1-P5 (5)	2.25	1.30

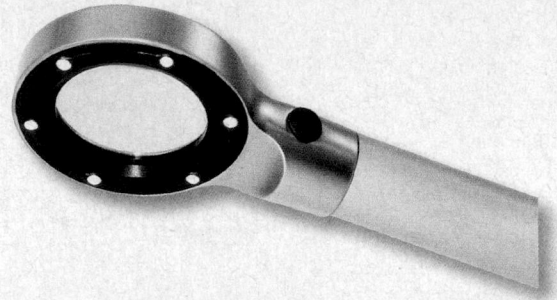

ECUADOR

ˈe-kwə-ˌdor

LOCATION — Northwest coast of South America, bordering on the Pacific Ocean
GOVT. — Republic
AREA — 116,270 (?) sq. mi.
POP. — 12,562,496 (1999 est.)
CAPITAL — Quito

The Republic of Ecuador was so constituted on May 11, 1830, after the Civil War that separated the original members of the Republic of Colombia, founded by Simon Bolivar by uniting the Presidency of Quito with the Viceroyalty of New Grenada and the Captaincy of Venezuela. The Presidency of Quito became the Republic of Ecuador.

8 Reales = 1 Peso
100 Centavos = 1 Sucre (1881)
100 Cents = 1 Dollar (2000)

Catalogue values for unused stamps in this country are for Never Hinged items, beginning with Scott 453 in the regular postage section, Scott C147 in the airpost section, Scott CO19 in the airpost officials section, Scott O201 in the officials section, Scott RA60 in the postal tax section, and all entries in the Galapagos section.

Watermarks

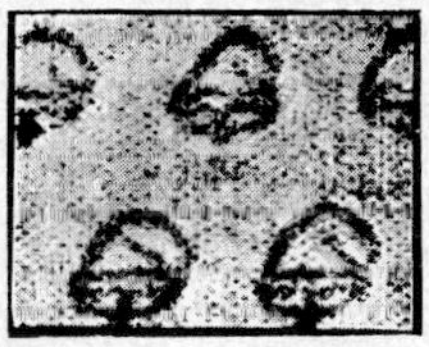
Wmk. 117 — Liberty Cap

Wmk. 127 Quatrefoils

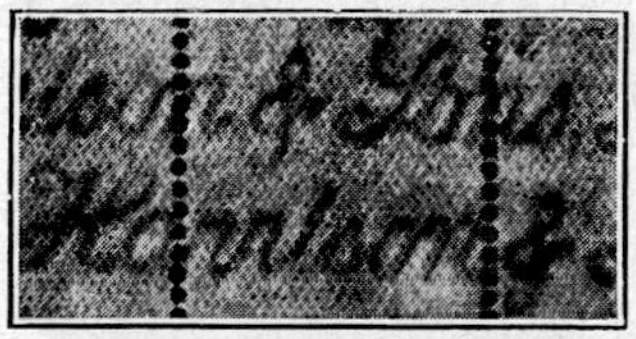
Wmk. 233 — "Harrison & Sons, London" in Script Letters

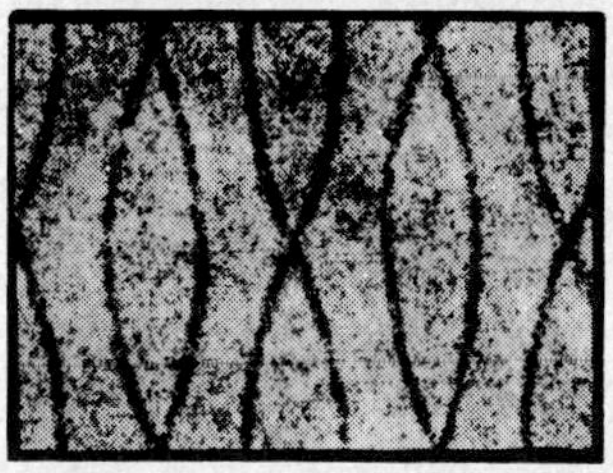
Wmk. 340 — Alternating Interlaced Wavy Lines

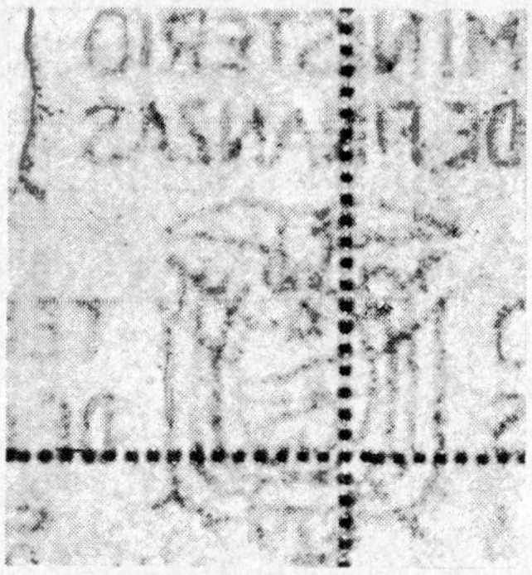
Wmk. 367 — Liberty Cap, Emblem, Inscription

Wmk. 377 — Interlocking Circles

Wmk. 395 — Emblem, Inscription

Coat of Arms
A1 A2

1865-72 Unwmk. Typo. *Imperf.*

Quadrille Paper

1	A1	1r yellow ('72)	60.00	55.00

Wove Paper

2	A1	½r ultra	40.00	20.00
a.		½r gray blue ('67)	40.00	15.00
b.		Batonne paper ('70)	50.00	25.00
c.		Blue paper ('72)	250.00	100.00
3	A1	1r buff	25.00	18.00
a.		1r orange buff	30.00	20.00
4	A1	1r yellow	25.00	15.00
a.		1r olive yellow ('66)	32.50	22.50
b.		Laid paper	175.00	110.00
c.		Half used as ½r on cover		900.00
d.		Batonne paper	40.00	30.00
5	A1	1r green	300.00	55.00
a.		Half used as ½r on cover		*900.00*
6	A2	4r red ('66)	500.00	200.00
a.		4r red brown ('66)	700.00	200.00
b.		Arms in circle	500.00	250.00
c.		Printed on both sides	550.00	—
d.		Half used as 2r on cover		1,600.
		Nos. 1-6 (6)	950.00	363.00

Letter paper embossed with arms of Ecuador was used in printing a number of sheets of Nos. 2, 4-6.

On the 4r the oval holding the coat of arms is usually 13½-14mm wide, but on about one-fifth of the stamps in the sheet it is 15-15½mm wide, almost a circle.

The 2r, 8r and 12r, type A1, are bogus.

Proofs of the ½r, type A1, are known in black and green.

An essay of type A2 shows the condor's head facing right.

1871-72 Blue-surface Paper

7	A1	½r ultra	50.00	25.00
8	A1	1r yellow	300.00	100.00

Unofficial reprints of types A1-A2 differ in color, have a different sheet makeup and lack gum. Type A1 reprints usually have a double frameline at left. All stamps on blue paper with horiz. blue lines are reprints.

A3 A4

1872 White Paper Litho. *Perf. 11*

9	A3	½r blue	30.00	5.00
10	A4	1r orange	40.00	7.00
11	A3	1p rose	5.00	*25.00*
		Nos. 9-11 (3)	75.00	*37.00*

The 1r surcharged 4c is fraudulent.

A5 A6

A7 A8

A9 A10

1881, Nov. 1 Engr. *Perf. 12*

12	A5	1c yellow brn	.40	.25
13	A6	2c lake	.40	.25
14	A7	5c blue	10.00	.50
15	A8	10c orange	.40	.25
16	A9	20c gray violet	.40	.25
17	A10	50c blue green	2.00	*3.00*
		Nos. 12-17 (6)	13.60	*4.50*

The 1c surcharged 3c, and 20c surcharged 5c are fraudulent.

For overprints see Nos. O1-O6.

No. 17 Surcharged in Black

1883, Apr.

18	A10	10c on 50c blue grn	50.00	30.00
a.		Double surcharge		

Dangerous forgeries exist.

A12 A13

A14 A15

1887

19	A12	1c blue green	.50	.40
20	A13	2c vermilion	1.00	.40
21	A14	5c blue	3.00	.50
22	A15	80c olive green	6.00	*15.00*
		Nos. 19-22 (4)	10.50	*16.30*

For overprints see Nos. O7-O10.

President Juan Flores — A16

1892

23	A16	1c orange	.30	1.00
24	A16	2c dk brown	.30	1.00
25	A16	5c vermilion	.30	1.00
26	A16	10c green	.30	1.00
27	A16	20c red brown	.30	1.00
28	A16	50c maroon	.30	*2.00*
29	A16	1s blue	.30	*4.00*
30	A16	5s purple	1.00	*8.00*
		Nos. 23-30 (8)	3.10	*19.00*

The issues of 1892, 1894, 1895 and 1896 were printed by the Hamilton Bank Note Co., New York, to the order of N. F. Seebeck, who held a contract for stamps with the government of Ecuador.

No. 30 in green is said to be an essay or color trial.

For surcharges and overprints see Nos. 31-37, O11-O17.

Nos. 29 and 30 Surcharged in Black

1893

Surcharge Measures 25½x2½mm

31	A16	5c on 1s blue	6.00	6.00
32	A16	5c on 5s purple	10.00	9.00
a.		Double surcharge		

Surcharge Measures 24x2¼mm

33	A16	5c on 1s blue	3.00	3.00
a.		Double surcharge, one inverted		
34	A16	5c on 5s purple	12.00	10.00
a.		Double surcharge, one invtd.		

Nos. 28-30 Surcharged in Black

35	A16	5c on 50c maroon	2.00	2.00
a.		Inverted surcharge	5.00	
36	A16	5c on 1s blue	2.50	2.00
37	A16	5c on 5s purple	10.00	10.00
		Nos. 31-37 (7)	45.50	42.00

Pres. Juan Flores — A19

38	A19	5c on 5s lake	4.00	4.00

It is stated that No. 38 was used exclusively as a postage stamp and not for telegrams.

Pres. Vicente Rocafuerte — A20

Dated "1894"

1894 Various Frames *Perf. 12*

39	A20	1c blue	.40	.40
40	A20	2c yellow brn	.40	.40
41	A20	5c green	.40	.40
b.		Perf. 14	6.00	2.00
42	A20	10c vermilion	.70	.60
43	A20	20c black	1.10	.70
44	A20	50c orange	6.00	2.00
45	A20	1s carmine	9.50	4.00
46	A20	5s dark blue	12.00	6.00
		Nos. 39-46 (8)	30.50	14.50

1895 Same, Dated "1895"

47	A20	1c	blue	.90	.70
48	A20	2c	yellow brn	.90	.70
49	A20	5c	green	.70	.50
50	A20	10c	vermilion	.70	.40
51	A20	20c	black	1.00	1.00
52	A20	50c	orange	3.50	2.25
53	A20	1s	carmine	21.00	8.00
54	A20	5s	dark blue	8.50	4.00
			Nos. 47-54 (8)	37.20	17.55

Reprints of the 2c, 10c, 50c, 1s and 5s of the 1894-95 issues are generally on thick paper. Original issues are on thin to medium thick paper. To distinguish reprints from originals, a comparison of paper thickness, paper color, gum, printing clarity and direction of paper weave is necessary. Value 20 cents each.

For overprints see Nos. 77-112, O20-O33, O50-O91.

A21

A22

A23

A24

A25

A26

A27

A28

1896 Wmk. 117

55	A21	1c	dk green	.70	.60
56	A22	2c	red	.70	.40
57	A23	5c	blue	.70	.40
58	A24	10c	bister brn	.60	*.90*
59	A25	20c	orange	1.40	*2.00*
60	A26	50c	dark blue	5.00	3.00
61	A27	1s	yellow brn	4.00	*4.00*
62	A28	5s	violet	14.00	5.50
			Nos. 55-62 (8)	27.10	*16.80*

Unwmk.

62A	A21	1c	dk green	1.00	.40
62B	A22	2c	red	1.10	.40
62C	A23	5c	blue	1.10	.70
62D	A24	10c	bister brn	.70	*1.40*
62E	A25	20c	orange	6.00	5.50
62F	A26	50c	dark blue	2.00	*2.75*
62G	A27	1s	yellow brn	6.00	*8.00*
62H	A28	5s	violet	15.00	6.00
			Nos. 62A-62H (8)	*32.90*	*25.15*

Reprints of Nos. 55-62H are on very thick paper, with paper weave direction vertical. Value 20 cents each.

For surcharges and overprints see Nos. 74, 76, 113-114, O34-O49.

Vicente Roca, Diego Noboa and José Olmedo — A28a

General Juan Francisco Elizalde — A28b

Perf. 11½

1896, Oct. 9 Unwmk. Litho.

63	A28a	1c	rose	.55	.55
64	A28b	2c	blue	.55	.55
65	A28a	5c	green	.75	.75
66	A28b	10c	ocher	.75	.75
67	A28a	20c	red	1.10	*3.25*
68	A28b	50c	violet	1.75	*4.75*
69	A28a	1s	orange	3.25	*8.00*
			Nos. 63-69 (7)	8.70	*18.60*

Success of the Liberal Party in 1845 & 1895.
For overprints see Nos. 115-125.

A29

Black Surcharge

1896, Nov. *Perf. 12*

70	A29	1c on 1c ver, "1893-1894"	1.00	.60
	a.	Inverted surcharge	2.50	2.00
	b.	Double surcharge	8.00	7.00
71	A29	2c on 2c bl, "1893-1894"	2.00	1.75
	a.	Inverted surcharge	4.00	3.50
72	A29	5c on 10c org, "1887-1888"	2.00	.60
	a.	Inverted surcharge	4.00	1.75
	b.	Double surcharge	7.00	4.00
	c.	Surcharged "2cts"	1.00	.80
	d.	"1893-1894"	6.00	5.00
73	A29	10c on 4c brn, "1887-1888"	2.00	1.10
	a.	Inverted surcharge	4.00	1.75
	b.	Double surcharge	6.00	3.50
	c.	Double surcharge, one inverted		
	d.	Surcharged "1 cto"	2.00	*2.75*
	e.	"1891-1892"	17.00	13.50
		Nos. 70-73 (4)	7.00	4.05

Similar surcharges of type A29 include: Dated "1887-1888" — 1c on 1c blue green, 1c on 2c red, 1c on 4c brown, 1c on 10c yellow; 2c on 2c red, 2c on 10c yellow; 10c on 1c green.

Dated "1891-1892" — 1c on 1c blue green, 1c on 4c brown.

Dated "1893-1894" — 2c on 10c yellow; 10c on 1c vermilion, 10c on 10s black.

For overprints see Nos. O18-O19.

Nos. 59-60 Surcharged in Black or Red

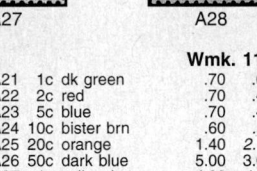

1896, Oct. Wmk. 117

74	A25	5c	on 20c orange	40.00	40.00
76	A26	10c	on 50c dk bl (R)	50.00	50.00
	a.		Double surcharge		

The surcharge is diag., horiz. or vert.

Nos. 39-54 Overprinted

On Issue of 1894

1897 Unwmk.

77	A20	1c	blue	2.25	2.25
78	A20	2c	yellow brn	1.90	1.30
79	A20	5c	green	.90	.90
80	A20	10c	vermilion	2.75	2.25
81	A20	20c	black	3.00	2.75
82	A20	50c	orange	6.50	3.25
83	A20	1s	carmine	19.00	6.50
84	A20	5s	dark blue	110.00	90.00
			Nos. 77-84 (8)	146.30	109.20

On Issue of 1895

85	A20	1c	blue	6.00	5.50
86	A20	2c	yellow brn	2.25	2.25
87	A20	5c	green	1.90	1.60
88	A20	10c	vermilion	7.00	6.00
89	A20	20c	black	1.90	1.75
90	A20	50c	orange	32.50	13.00
91	A20	1s	carmine	14.50	7.50
92	A20	5s	dark blue	14.50	14.50
			Nos. 85-92 (8)	80.55	52.10

Nos. 39-54 Overprinted

On Issue of 1894

93	A20	1c	blue	1.40	.90
94	A20	2c	yellow brn	1.20	.75
95	A20	5c	green	.60	.50
96	A20	10c	vermilion	3.50	1.75
97	A20	20c	black	3.75	2.50
98	A20	50c	orange	7.00	2.75
99	A20	1s	carmine	13.00	8.50
100	A20	5s	dark blue	115.00	85.00
			Nos. 93-100 (8)	145.45	102.65

On Issue of 1895

101	A20	1c	blue	3.25	1.60
102	A20	2c	yellow brn	1.60	1.60
103	A20	5c	green	1.75	1.00
104	A20	10c	vermilion	5.50	4.50
105	A20	20c	black	5.00	1.20
106	A20	50c	orange	1.75	1.75
107	A20	1s	carmine	8.00	7.00
108	A20	5s	dark blue	9.50	9.50
			Nos. 101-108 (8)	36.35	28.15

Overprints on Nos. 77-108 are to be found reading upward from left to right and downward from left to right, as well as inverted.

Overprinted

1897 On Issue of 1894

109	A20	10c	vermilion	—	—

On Issue of 1895

110	A20	2c	yellow brn	—	—
111	A20	1s	carmine	—	—
112	A20	5s	dark blue	—	—

Nos. 56, 59 Overprinted like Nos. 93-108

1897, June Wmk. 117

113	A22	2c	red	—	—
114	A25	20c	orange	—	—

Many forged overprints on Nos. 77-114 exist, made on original stamps and reprints.

Stamps or Types of 1896 Overprinted in Black

1897 Unwmk. *Perf. 11½*

115	A28a	1c	rose	3.75	3.75
116	A28b	2c	blue	3.00	3.00
117	A28b	10c	ocher	3.00	3.00
118	A28a	1s	yellow	15.00	15.00
			Nos. 115-118 (4)	24.75	24.75

No. 63 Overprinted in Black

1897

119	A28a	1c	rose	.60	.50

Nos. 63-66 Overprinted in Black

1897

122	A28a	1c	rose	4.50	4.00
123	A28b	2c	blue	4.50	4.00
124	A28a	5c	green	4.50	4.00
125	A28b	10c	ocher	4.50	4.00
	a.		Double overprint	10.50	9.50
			Nos. 122-125 (4)	18.00	16.00

The 20c, 50c and 1s with this overprint in black and all values of the issue overprinted in blue are reprints.

Overprint Inverted

122a	A28a	1c	6.00	5.50
123a	A28b	2c	6.00	5.50
124a	A28a	5c	6.00	5.50
125b	A28b	10c	6.00	5.50

Coat of Arms — A33

1897, June 23 Engr. *Perf. 14-16*

127	A33	1c	dk yellow grn	.35	.25
128	A33	2c	orange red	.35	.25
129	A33	5c	lake	.35	.25
130	A33	10c	dk brown	.35	.25
131	A33	20c	yellow	.45	.40
132	A33	50c	dull blue	.45	*.65*
133	A33	1s	gray	.90	*1.25*
134	A33	5s	dark lilac	4.00	*5.00*
			Nos. 127-134 (8)	7.20	*8.30*

No. 135

No. 136

1899, May

135	A33	1c on 2c orange red	3.00	1.50
136	A33	5c on 10c brown	2.50	1.00
	a.	Double surcharge		

Luis Vargas Torres A36

Abdón Calderón A37

Juan Montalvo A38

José Mejia A39

Santa Cruz y Espejo — A40

Pedro Carbo — A41

José Joaquin Olmedo
A42

Pedro Moncayo
A43

1899 *Perf. 12½-16*

137	A36	1c gray blue & blk	.40	.25
a.		Horiz. pair, imperf. vert.		
138	A37	2c brown lil & blk	.40	.25
139	A38	5c lake & blk	.70	.25
140	A39	10c violet & blk	.70	.25
141	A40	20c green & blk	.70	.25
142	A41	50c lil rose & blk	1.75	.55
143	A42	1s ocher & blk	8.00	2.75
144	A43	5s lilac & blk	14.50	7.50
		Nos. 137-144 (8)	27.15	12.05

1901

145	A36	1c scarlet & blk	.45	.25
146	A37	2c green & blk	.45	.25
147	A38	5c gray lil & blk	.45	.25
148	A39	10c dp blue & blk	.50	.25
149	A40	20c gray & blk	.50	.25
150	A41	50c lt blue & blk	1.75	.95
151	A42	1s brown & blk	6.00	2.75
152	A43	5s gray blk & blk	9.00	5.75
		Nos. 145-152 (8)	19.10	10.70

In July, 1902, following the theft of a quantity of stamps during a fire at Guayaquil, the Government authorized the governors of the provinces to handstamp their stocks. Many varieties of these handstamps exist.

Other control marks were used in 1907.

For overprints see Nos. O103-O106, O167.

A44

Surcharged on Revenue Stamp Dated 1901-1902

1903-06 *Perf. 14, 15*

153	A44	1c on 5c gray lil ('06)	.75	.40
154	A44	1c on 20c gray ('06)	10.00	4.50
155	A44	1c on 25c yellow	1.50	.40
a.		Double surcharge		
156	A44	1c on 1s bl ('06)	77.50	50.00
157	A44	3c on 5c gray lil ('06)	10.00	4.00
158	A44	3c on 20c gray ('06)	25.00	15.00
159	A44	3c on 25c yel ('06)	24.00	15.00
159A	A44	3c on 1s blue ('06)	3.75	2.25
		Nos. 153-159A (8)	152.50	91.55

Counterfeits are plentiful.

See Nos. 191-197.

Capt. Abdón Calderón
A45 A46

1904, July 31 *Perf. 12*

160	A45	1c red & blk	.45	.30
161	A45	2c blue & blk	.50	.35
162	A46	5c yellow & blk	1.90	1.00
163	A45	10c red & blk	6.00	2.00
164	A45	20c blue & blk	10.00	8.00
165	A46	50c yellow & blk	85.00	*120.00*
		Nos. 160-165 (6)	103.85	131.65

Centenary of the birth of Calderón.

Presidents

Vicente Roca — A47

Diego Noboa — A48

Francisco Robles — A49

José M. Urvina — A50

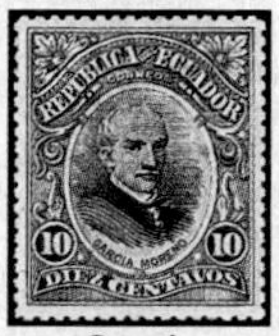

García Moreno — A51

Jerónimo Carrión — A52

Javier Espinoza
A53

Antonio Borrero
A54

1907, July *Perf. 14, 15*

166	A47	1c red & blk	1.00	.25
167	A48	2c pale blue & blk	2.00	.25
168	A49	3c orange & blk	3.00	.25
169	A50	5c lilac rose & blk	3.75	.25
170	A51	10c dp blue & blk	7.50	.25
171	A52	20c yellow grn & blk	10.00	.35
172	A53	50c violet & blk	22.50	.70
173	A54	1s green & blk	30.00	2.00
		Nos. 166-173 (8)	79.75	4.30

The stamps of the 1907 issue frequently have control marks similar to those found on the 1899 and 1901 issues. These marks were applied to distinguish the stamps issued in the various provinces and to serve as a check on local officials.

Locomotive — A55

García Moreno — A56

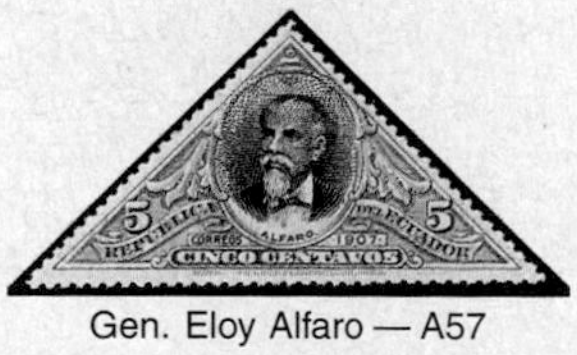

Gen. Eloy Alfaro — A57

Abelardo Moncayo — A58

Archer Harman — A59

James Sivewright — A60

Mt. Chimborazo
A61

1908, June 25

174	A55	1c red brown	1.10	*2.10*
175	A56	2c blue & blk	1.30	*2.25*
176	A57	5c claret & blk	2.75	*5.25*
177	A58	10c ocher & blk	1.75	*2.75*
178	A59	20c green & blk	1.75	*3.75*
179	A60	50c gray & blk	1.75	*3.75*
180	A61	1s black	3.50	*8.00*
		Nos. 174-180 (7)	13.90	*27.85*

Opening of the Guayaquil-Quito Railway.

José Mejía Vallejo — A62

Principal Exposition Building — A70

Designs: 2c, Francisco J. E. Santa Cruz y Espejo. 3c, Francisco Ascásubi. 5c, Juan Salinas. 10c, Juan Pio de Montúfar, el Marques de Selva Alegre. 20c, Carlos de Montúfar. 50c, Juan de Dios Morales. 1s, Manuel R. de Quiroga.

1909, Aug. 10 *Perf. 12*

181	A62	1c green	.35	*.65*
182	A62	2c blue	.35	*.65*
183	A62	3c orange	.35	*.75*
184	A62	5c claret	.35	*.75*
185	A62	10c yellow brn	.45	*.75*
186	A62	20c gray	.45	*1.10*
187	A62	50c vermilion	.45	*1.10*
188	A62	1s olive grn	.45	*1.40*
189	A70	5s violet	1.25	*2.75*
		Nos. 181-189 (9)	4.45	*9.90*

National Exposition of 1909.

No. 187 Surcharged

1909

190	A62	5c on 50c vermilion	.90	.75

Revenue Stamps Surcharged as in 1903

1910 *Perf. 14, 15*

Stamps Dated 1905-1906

191	A44	1c on 5c green	2.25	1.75
192	A44	5c on 20c blue	9.50	2.00
193	A44	5c on 25c violet	18.00	3.50

Stamps Dated 1907-1908

194	A44	1c on 5c green	.40	.40
195	A44	5c on 20c blue	14.00	9.50
196	A44	5c on 25c violet	1.20	.40

Stamp Dated 1909-1910

197	A44	5c on 20c blue	*80.00*	*60.00*
		Nos. 191-197 (7)	*125.35*	*77.55*

Presidents

Roca — A71

Noboa — A72

Robles — A73

Urvina — A74

Moreno — A75

Borrero — A76

1911-28 *Perf. 12*

198	A71	1c scarlet & blk	.80	.25
199	A71	1c orange ('16)	.80	.25
200	A71	1c lt blue ('25)	.40	.25
201	A72	2c blue & blk	1.10	.25
202	A72	2c green ('16)	1.10	.25
203	A72	2c dk violet ('25)	1.10	.25
204	A73	3c orange & blk ('13)	2.25	.30
205	A73	3c black ('15)	1.50	.25
206	A74	5c scarlet & blk	1.90	.25
207	A74	5c violet ('15)	1.90	.25
208	A74	5c rose ('25)	.70	.25
209	A74	5c dk brown ('28)	.70	.25
210	A75	10c dp blue & blk	2.25	.25
211	A75	10c dp blue ('15)	2.25	.25
212	A75	10c yellow grn ('25)	.70	.25
213	A75	10c black ('28)	1.60	.25
214	A76	1s green & blk	12.00	1.50
215	A76	1s orange & blk ('27)	8.00	.25
		Nos. 198-215 (18)	41.05	5.80

For overprints see Nos. 260-262, 264-265, O107-O122, O124-O134, O156-O157, O160-O162, O164-O166, O168-O173, O175-O178, O183-O184, O189, RA1.

A77

1912 *Perf. 14, 15*

216	A77	1c on 1s green	1.00	1.00
217	A77	2c on 2s carmine	2.50	1.50
218	A77	2c on 5s dull blue	1.50	1.50
219	A77	2c on 10s yellow	5.00	5.00
a.		Inverted surcharge	16.00	12.00
		Nos. 216-219 (4)	10.00	9.00

No. 216 exists with narrow "V" and small "U" in "UN" and Nos. 217, 218 and 219 with "D" with serifs or small "O" in "DOS."

Enrique Váldez — A78

Jerónimo Carrión — A79

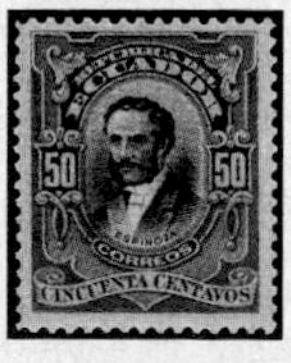

Javier Espinoza — A80

1915-17 *Perf. 12*

220 A78 4c red & blk .40 .25
221 A79 20c green & blk ('17) 3.50 .25
222 A80 50c dp violet & blk 6.00 .45
Nos. 220-222 (3) 9.90 .95

For overprints see Nos. O123, O135, O163, O174.

Olmedo — A86

Monument to "Fathers of the Country" — A95

Laurel Wreath and Star — A104

Designs: 2c, Rafael Ximena. 3c, Roca. 4c, Luis F. Vivero. 5c, Luis Febres Cordero. 6c, Francisco Lavayen. 7c, Jorge Antonio de Elizalde. 8c, Baltazar Garcia. 9c, Jose de Antepara. 15c, Luis Urdaneta. 20c, Jose M. Villamil. 30c, Miguel Letamendi. 40c, Gregorio Escobedo. 50c, Gen. Antonio Jose de Sucre. 60c, Juan Illingworth. 70c, Roca. 80c, Rocafuerte. 1s, Simon Bolivar.

1920

223 A86 1c yellow grn .35 .25
224 A86 2c carmine .35 .25
225 A86 3c yellow brn .35 .25
226 A86 4c myrtle green .55 .25
227 A86 5c pale blue .55 .25
228 A86 6c red orange .90 .30
229 A86 7c brown 2.25 .75
230 A86 8c apple green 1.25 .35
231 A86 9c lake 4.25 1.50
232 A95 10c lt blue 1.50 .25
233 A86 15c dk gray 2.25 .35
234 A86 20c dk violet 2.25 .25
235 A86 30c brt violet 4.25 1.40
236 A86 40c dk brown 7.50 2.10
237 A86 50c dk green 5.25 .55
238 A86 60c dk blue 9.50 2.10
239 A86 70c gray 16.00 4.75
240 A86 80c orange yel 16.50 4.75
241 A104 90c green 17.00 4.75
242 A86 1s pale blue 24.00 8.50
Nos. 223-242 (20) 116.80 33.90

Cent. of the independence of Guayaquil.
For overprints and surcharges see Nos. 263, 274-292, O136-O155, O179-O182, O185-O188.

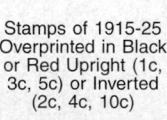

Postal Tax Stamp of 1924 Overprinted

1925

259 PT6 20c bister brown 4.00 1.50

Stamps of 1915-25 Overprinted in Black or Red Upright (1c, 3c, 5c) or Inverted (2c, 4c, 10c)

1926

260 A71 1c lt blue 12.50 10.50
261 A72 2c dk violet 12.50 10.50
262 A73 3c black (R) 12.50 10.50
263 A86 4c myrtle green 12.50 10.50
264 A74 5c rose 17.50 10.50
265 A75 10c yellow grn 17.50 10.50
Nos. 260-265 (6) 85.00 63.00

Quito-Esmeraldas railway opening.
Upright overprints on 2c, 4c, 10c and inverted overprints on 1c, 3c, 5c sell for more.

Postal Tax Stamps of 1920-24 Overprinted

1927

266 PT6 1c olive green .50 .25
a. "POSTAl" 1.40 .85
b. Double overprint 2.00 .85
c. Inverted overprint 2.00 .85
267 PT6 2c deep green .50 .25
a. "POSTAl" 1.40 .85
b. Double overprint 2.00 .85
268 PT6 20c bister brown 1.00 .25
a. "POSTAl" 8.50 5.00
Nos. 266-268 (3) 2.00 .75

Quito Post Office — A109

1927, June

269 A109 5c orange .50 .25
270 A109 10c dark green .70 .25
271 A109 20c violet .80 .25
Nos. 269-271 (3) 2.00 .75

Opening of new Quito P.O.
For overprint see No. O190.

Postal Tax Stamp of 1924 Overprinted in Dark Blue

1928

273 PT6 20c bister brown .50 .25
a. Double overprint, one inverted 2.00 .70

See No. 339 for 10c with same overprint.

Nos. 235, 239-240 Ovptd. in Red Brown and Srchd. in Dark Blue

1928, July 8

274 A86 10c on 30c violet 16.00 16.00
275 A86 50c on 70c gray 20.00 20.00
276 A86 1s on 80c org yel 22.50 22.50
Nos. 274-276 (3) 58.50 58.50

Quito-Cayambe railway opening.

Stamps of 1920 Surcharged

1928, Oct. 9

277 A86 1c on 1c yel grn 15.00 15.00
278 A86 1c on 2c car .30 .30
279 A86 2c on 3c yel brn 2.25 2.25
a. Dbl. surch., one reading up 30.00 30.00
280 A86 2c on 4c myr grn 1.50 1.50
281 A86 2c on 5c lt blue .60 .45
a. Dbl. surch., one reading up 30.00 30.00
282 A86 2c on 7c brown 75.00 75.00
283 A86 5c on 6c red org .40 .30
a. "5 ctvos." omitted 37.50 37.50
284 A86 10c on 7c brown 1.25 1.25
285 A86 20c on 8c apple grn .35 .30
a. Double surcharge
286 A95 40c on 10c blue 4.25 4.25
287 A86 40c on 15c dk gray 1.25 1.25
288 A86 50c on 20c dk vio 13.25 13.25
289 A86 1s on 40c dk brown 4.50 4.50
290 A86 5s on 50c dk green 5.25 5.25
291 A86 10s on 60c dk blue 19.50 19.50

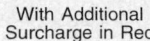

With Additional Surcharge in Red

292 A86 10c on 2c on 7c brn .55 .55
a. Red surcharge double 30.00 30.00
Nos. 277-292 (16) 145.20 144.90

National Assembly of 1928.
Counterfeit overprints exist of Nos. 277-291.

A111

Surcharged in Various Colors

1928, Oct. 31 *Perf. 14*

293 A111 5c on 20c gray lil (Bk) 3.00 1.75
294 A111 10c on 20c gray lil (R) 3.00 1.75
295 A111 20c on 1s grn (O) 3.00 1.75
296 A111 50c on 1s grn (Bl) 3.75 1.40
297 A111 1s on 1s grn (V) 4.75 1.75
298 A111 5s on 2s red (G) 15.00 9.00
299 A111 10s on 2s red (Br) 18.00 12.00
a. Black surcharge 15.00 10.00
Nos. 293-299 (7) 50.50 29.40

Quito-Otavalo railway opening.
See Nos. 586-587.

Postal Tax Stamp of 1924 Overprinted in Red

1929 *Perf. 12*

302 PT6 2c deep green .50 .25

There are two types of overprint on No. 302 differing slightly.

A112

1929 **Red Overprint**

303 A112 1c dark blue .50 .25
a. Overprint reading down .75 .50

See Nos. 586-587.

Plowing — A113

Cultivating Cacao — A114

Cacao Pod — A115

Growing Tobacco — A116

Exportation of Fruits — A117

Landscape — A118

Loading Sugar Cane — A119

Scene in Quito A120

Scene in Quito A121

Olmedo — A122

Monument to Simón Bolívar — A125

Designs: 2s, Sucre. 5s, Bolivar.

1930, Aug. 1 *Perf. 12½*

304	A113	1c yellow & car	.30	.25
305	A114	2c yellow & grn	.30	.25
306	A115	5c dp grn & vio brn	.35	.25
307	A116	6c yellow & red	.45	.25
308	A117	10c orange & ol grn	.45	.25
309	A118	16c red & yel grn	.55	.25
310	A119	20c ultra & yel	.90	.25
311	A120	40c orange & sepia	1.10	.35
312	A121	50c orange & sepia	1.10	.40
313	A122	1s dp green & blk	4.25	.45
314	A122	2s dk blue & blk	6.50	2.00
315	A122	5s dk violet & blk	11.50	3.00
316	A125	10s car rose & blk	40.00	6.50
		Nos. 304-316 (13)	67.75	14.45

Centenary of founding of republic.
For surcharges and overprints see Nos. 319-320, 331-338, RA25, RA33, RA43.

A126

A127

1933 **Red Overprint** *Perf. 15*

317	A126	10c olive brown	1.15	.25

Blue Overprint

318	A127	10c olive brown	.70	.25
a.		Inverted overprint	5.00	5.00

For overprint see No. 339.

Nos. 307, 309 Surcharged in Black

1933 *Perf. 12½*

319	A116	5c on 6c yellow & red	1.00	.25
320	A118	10c on 16c red & yel grn	2.00	.25
a.		Inverted overprint	4.00	4.00

Landscape A128

Mt. Chimborazo A129

1934-45 *Perf. 12*

321	A128	5c violet	1.40	.55
322	A128	5c blue	1.40	.55
323	A128	5c dark brown	1.40	.55
323A	A128	5c slate blk ('45)	1.40	.55
324	A128	10c rose	1.40	.55
325	A128	10c dark green	1.40	.55
326	A128	10c brown	1.40	.55
327	A128	10c orange	1.40	.55
328	A128	10c olive green	1.40	.55
329	A128	10c gray blk ('35)	1.40	.55
329A	A128	10c red lilac ('44)	1.40	.55

Perf. 14

330	A129	1s carmine rose	1.60	.55
		Nos. 321-330 (12)	17.00	6.60

Stamps of 1930 Srchd. or Ovptd. in various colors

1935 *Perf. 12½*

331	A116	5c on 6c (Bl)	.90	.35
332	A116	10c on 6c (G)	1.25	.35
333	A119	20c (R)	1.75	.35
334	A120	40c (G)	2.50	.35
335	A121	50c (G)	3.00	.45
336	A122	1s on 5s (Gold)	7.00	1.25
337	A122	2s on 5s (Gold)	9.50	1.75
338	A125	5s on 10s (Bl)	12.00	5.00
		Nos. 331-338,C35-C38 (12)	87.90	29.85

Unveiling of a monument to Bolivar at Quito, July 24, 1935.

A129a

1935, Oct. 13 **Photo.** *Perf. 11½x11*

338A	A129a	5c ultra & black	.25	.25
338B	A129a	10c orange & blue	.25	.25
338C	A129a	40c dk carmine & red	.25	*.30*
338D	A129a	1S blue green & red	.30	*.70*
338E	A129a	2S violet & red	.55	*1.20*
		Nos. 338A-338E,C38A-C38E (10)	4.35	*7.60*

Columbus Day. Nos. 338A-338E and C38A-C38E were prepared by the Sociedad Colombista Panamericana and were sold by the Ecuadorian post office through Oct. 30.

Telegraph Stamp Overprinted Diagonally in Red like No. 273

1935 *Perf. 14½*

339	A126	10c olive brown	.75	.25

Map of Galápagos Islands A130

Galapagos Land Iguana A131

Galápagos Tortoise — A132

Charles R. Darwin — A133

Columbus A134

Island Scene A135

1936 *Perf. 14*

340	A130	2c black	1.00	.25
341	A131	5c olive grn	1.25	.25
342	A132	10c brown	2.40	.30
343	A133	20c dk violet	2.75	.45
344	A134	1s dk carmine	5.00	.85
345	A135	2s dark blue	7.75	1.40
		Nos. 340-345 (6)	20.15	3.50

Cent. of the visit of Charles Darwin to the Galápagos Islands, Sept. 17, 1835.
For overprints see Nos. O191-O195.

Tobacco Stamp Overprinted in Black

1936 ***Rouletted 7***

346	PT7	1c rose red	.50	.25
a.		Horiz. pair, imperf. vert.		
b.		Double surcharge		

No. 346 is similar to type PT7 but does not include "CASA CORREOS."

Louis Godin, Charles M. de la Condamine and Pierre Bouguer A136

Portraits: 5c, 20c, Antonio Ulloa, La Condamine and Jorge Juan.

1936 **Engr.** *Perf. 12½*

347	A136	2c deep blue	.50	.30
348	A136	5c dark green	.50	.30
349	A136	10c deep orange	.50	.30
350	A136	20c violet	.80	.30
351	A136	50c dark red	1.25	.30
		Nos. 347-351,C39-C42 (9)	6.60	2.60

Bicentenary of Geodesical Mission to Quito.

Independence Monument — A137

1936 *Perf. 13½x14*

352	A137	2c green	2.25	1.25
353	A137	5c dark violet	2.25	1.25
354	A137	10c carmine rose	2.25	1.25
355	A137	20c black	2.25	1.25
356	A137	50c blue	3.25	2.10
357	A137	1s dark red	3.75	3.25
		Nos. 352-357,C43-C50 (14)	50.50	41.35

1st Intl. Philatelic Exhibition at Quito.

Coat of Arms — A138

Overprint in Black or Red

1937 *Perf. 12½*

359	A138	5c olive green	2.00	.30
360	A138	10c dark blue (R)	2.00	.25

For overprint see No. 562.

Andean Landscape A139

Atahualpa, the Last Inca A140

Hat Weavers — A141

Coast Landscape A142

Gold Washing A143

1937, Aug. 19 *Perf. 11½*

361	A139	2c green	.50	.25
362	A140	5c deep rose	.50	.25
363	A141	10c blue	.50	.25
364	A142	20c deep rose	1.50	.30
365	A143	1s olive green	2.00	.35
		Nos. 361-365 (5)	5.00	1.40

For overprints see Nos. O196-O200.

"Liberty" Carrying Flag of Ecuador — A144

Engraved and Lithographed

1938, Feb. 22 *Perf. 12*

Center Multicolored

366	A144	2c blue	.25	.25
367	A144	5c violet	.35	.25
368	A144	10c black	.55	.25
369	A144	20c brown	.65	.25
370	A144	50c black	1.10	.25
371	A144	1s olive blk	1.75	.30
372	A144	2s dk brn	3.25	.55
		Nos. 366-372,C57-C63 (14)	22.40	4.50

US Constitution, 150th anniversary.
For overprints and surcharges see Nos. 413-415, 444-446, RA46, RA52.

A145

A146

A147

A148

Designs: 10c, Winged figure holding globe. 50c, Cactus, winged wheel. 1s, "Communications," 2s, "Construction."

Perf. 13, 13x13½

1938, Oct. 30 **Engr.**

373	A145	10c bright ultra	.40	.25
374	A146	50c deep red violet	.40	.25
375	A147	1s copper red	.70	.25
376	A148	2s dark green	1.10	.25
		Nos. 373-376 (4)	2.60	1.00

Progress of Ecuador Exhibition.
For overprints see Nos. C105-C113.

Parade of Athletes — A149

Runner — A150

Basketball — A151

Wrestlers A152

Diver A153

1939, Mar. *Perf. 12*

377 A149 5c carmine rose 3.00 .55
378 A150 10c deep blue 3.50 .65
379 A151 50c gray olive 5.75 .85
380 A152 1s dull violet 7.75 .85
381 A153 2s dull olive green 12.50 .95
Nos. 377-381,C65-C69 (10) 78.35 6.15

First Bolivarian Games (1938), Bogota.

Dolores Mission A154

Trylon and Perisphere A155

1939, June 16 *Perf. 12½x13*

382 A154 2c blue green .50 .25
383 A154 5c rose red .50 .25
384 A154 10c ultra .50 .25
385 A154 50c yellow brown 1.20 .25
386 A154 1s black 1.90 .25
387 A154 2s purple 1.25 .40
Nos. 382-387,C73-C79 (13) 11.25 3.40

Golden Gate International Exposition.
For surcharges see Nos. 429, 436.

1939, June 30

388 A155 2c lt olive green .80 .35
389 A155 5c red orange .80 .35
390 A155 10c ultra .80 .35
391 A155 50c slate gray 1.10 .35
392 A155 1s rose carmine 1.90 .35
393 A155 2s black brown 2.25 .40
Nos. 388-393,C80-C86 (13) 16.55 4.20

New York World's Fair.
For surcharge see No. 437.

Flags of the 21 American Republics — A156

1940 *Perf. 12*

394 A156 5c dp rose & blk 1.00 .25
395 A156 10c dk blue & blk .40 .25
396 A156 50c Prus green & blk .60 .25
397 A156 1s dp violet & blk 1.00 .30
Nos. 394-397,C87-C90 (8) 8.30 2.75

Pan American Union, 50th anniversary.

Francisco J. E. Santa Cruz y Espejo — A157

1941, Dec. 15

398 A157 30c blue 1.25 .25
399 A157 1s red orange 2.50 .35
Nos. 398-399,C91-C92 (4) 21.50 1.30

Exposition of Journalism held under the auspices of the Natl. Newspaper Men's Union.

Francisco de Orellana A158

Gonzalo Pizarro A159

View of Guayaquil A160

View of Quito — A161

1942, Jan. 30

400 A158 10c sepia .90 .35
401 A159 40c deep rose 2.50 .35
402 A160 1s violet 3.50 .35
403 A161 2s dark blue 4.50 .45
Nos. 400-403,C93-C96 (8) 23.45 3.35

400th anniv. of the discovery and exploration of the Amazon River by Orellana.

Remigio Crespo Toral A162

Alfredo Baquerizo Moreno A163

1942 *Perf. 13½*

404 A162 10c green .60 .25
405 A162 50c brown 1.00 .25
Nos. 404-405,C97 (3) 2.85 1.00

1942

406 A163 10c green .25 .25

Mt. Chimborazo A164

1942-47 *Perf. 12*

407 A164 30c red brown .60 .30
407A A164 30c lt blue ('43) .60 .30
407B A164 30c red orange ('44) .60 .30
407C A164 30c green ('47) .60 .30
Nos. 407-407C (4) 2.40 1.20

View of Guayaquil A165

1942-44

408 A165 20c red .55 .25
408A A165 20c deep blue ('44) .55 .25

Gen. Eloy Alfaro — A166

Devil's Nose — A167

President Alfaro (1842-1912): 30c, Military College. 1s, Montecristi, Alfaro's birthplace.

1942

409 A166 10c dk rose & blk .60 .25
410 A167 20c ol blk & red brn .60 .25
411 A167 30c ol gray & grn .75 .25
412 A167 1s slate & salmon 1.80 .25
Nos. 409-412,C98-C101 (8) 20.15 4.40

Nos. 370-372 Overprinted in Red Brown

1943, Apr. 15 *Perf. 11½*

413 A144 50c multicolored .65 .65
414 A144 1s multicolored 1.25 1.25
415 A144 2s multicolored 2.75 2.75
Nos. 413-415,C102-C104 (6) 14.65 10.25

Visit of US Vice-Pres. Henry A. Wallace.

"30 Centavos" — A170

1943 Black Surcharge *Perf. 12½*

416 A170 30c on 50c red brn 1.00 .25
a. Without bars 1.00 .25

Map Showing US and Ecuador — A171

1943, Oct. 9 *Perf. 12*

417 A171 10c dull violet .75 .50
418 A171 20c red brown .75 .50
419 A171 30c orange .75 .50
420 A171 50c olive green .90 .60
421 A171 1s deep violet 1.00 .65
422 A171 10s olive bister 8.25 5.25
Nos. 417-422,C114-C118 (11) 32.70 15.10

Good will tour of Pres. Arroyo del Rio in 1942.

1944, Feb. 7

423 A171 10c yellow green .65 .45
424 A171 20c rose pink .65 .45
425 A171 30c dark gray brown .65 .45
426 A171 50c deep red lilac .65 .45
427 A171 1s olive gray 1.00 .65
428 A171 10s red orange 10.50 6.00
Nos. 423-428,C119-C123 (11) 24.90 13.40

For surcharges see Nos. B1-B6.

No. 385 Surcharged in Black

1944 Unwmk. *Perf. 12½x13*

429 A154 30c on 50c yel brn 2.00 .25

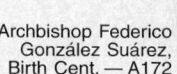

Archbishop Federico González Suárez, Birth Cent. — A172

1944 *Perf. 12*

430 A172 10c deep blue .40 .25
431 A172 20c green .40 .25
432 A172 30c dk violet brn .50 .25
433 A172 1s dull violet .90 .25
Nos. 430-433,C124-C127 (8) 15.50 4.30

Air Post Stamps Nos. C76 and C83 Surcharged in Black

1944 *Perf. 12½x13*

434 AP15 30c on 50c rose vio .40 .25
435 AP16 30c on 50c sl grn .40 .25

Nos. 382 and 388 Surcharged in Black

1944-45

436 A154 5c on 2c bl grn .50 .25
a. Double surcharge 4.00
437 A155 5c on 2c lt ol grn ('45) .50 .25

Government Palace, Quito — A173

1944 Engr. *Perf. 11*

438 A173 10c dark green .50 .25
439 A173 30c blue .50 .25

See Nos. C128-C130, C221. For surcharges see Nos. 452, RAC1-RAC2.

Symbol of the Red Cross A174

1945, Apr. 25 *Perf. 12*

Cross in Rose

440 A174 30c bister brown 1.90 .35
441 A174 1s red brown 2.75 .45
442 A174 5s turq green 4.75 1.10
443 A174 10s scarlet 13.00 3.00
Nos. 440-443,C131-C134 (8) 58.40 14.75

International Red Cross, 80th anniversary.

Nos. 370 to 372 Overprinted in Dark Blue and Gold

1945, Oct. 2 *Perf. 11½*

Center Multicolored

444 A144 50c black .80 .70
a. Double overprint 22.50

445 A144 1s olive black 1.40 1.40
446 A144 2s dark brown 2.75 2.50
a. Double overprint *22.50*
Nos. 444-446,C139-C141 (6) 10.45 8.25

Visit of Pres. Juan Antonio Rios of Chile.

General Antonio José de Sucre, 150th Birth Anniv. — A175

1945, Nov. 14 Engr. *Perf. 12*
447 A175 10c olive .55 .25
448 A175 20c red brown .55 .25
449 A175 40c olive gray .55 .25
450 A175 1s dark green 1.10 .25
451 A175 2s sepia 2.25 .75
Nos. 447-451,C142-C146 (10) 13.20 6.10

No. 438 Surcharged in Blue

1945 *Perf. 11*
452 A173 20c on 10c dark green .50 .25
a. Fancy bar omitted

Catalogue values for unused stamps in this section, from this point to the end of the section, are for Never Hinged items.

Map of Pan-American Highway and Arms of Loja — A176

1946, Apr. 22 Engr. *Perf. 12*
453 A176 20c red brown .60 .40
454 A176 30c bright green .60 .45
455 A176 1s bright ultra .60 .45
456 A176 5s deep red lilac 1.90 1.50
457 A176 10s scarlet 3.50 2.00
Nos. 453-457,C147-C151 (10) 14.55 7.95

Torch of Democracy — A177

Popular Suffrage A178

Flag of Ecuador — A179

Pres. José M. Velasco Ibarra — A180

1946, Aug. 9 Unwmk. *Perf. 12½*
458 A177 5c dark blue .25 .25
459 A178 10c Prus green .25 .25
460 A179 20c carmine .30 .25
461 A180 30c chocolate .45 .25
Nos. 458-461,C152-C155 (8) 3.45 2.20

Revolution of May 28, 1944, 2nd anniv.

"30 Ctvs." — A181

1946 Black Surcharge
462 A181 30c on 50c red brown .50 .25

For overprint see No. 484.

Nos. CO13-CO14 With Additional Ovpt. in Black

1946 *Perf. 11½*
463 AP7 10c chestnut .50 .25
464 AP7 20c olive black .50 .25

Instructor and Student — A182

1946, Sept. 16 *Perf. 12½*
465 A182 10c deep blue .40 .30
466 A182 20c chocolate .40 .30
467 A182 30c dark green .40 .30
468 A182 50c bluish blk .55 .45
469 A182 1s dark red 1.10 .75
470 A182 10s dark violet 6.50 1.40
Nos. 465-470,C156-C160 (11) 21.00 6.85

Campaign for adult education.

Mariana de Jesus Paredes y Flores — A183

Urn — A184

1946, Nov. 28
471 A183 10c black brown .35 .25
472 A183 20c green .35 .25
473 A183 30c purple .35 .25
474 A184 1s rose brown .45 .30
Nos. 471-474,C161-C164 (8) 5.00 3.10

300th anniv. of the death of the Blessed Mariana de Jesus Paredes y Flores.

Pres. Vicente Rocafuerte A185

Jesuits' Church Quito A186

45c, 50c, 80c, F.J.E. de Santa Cruz y Espejo.

1947, Nov. 27 *Perf. 12*
475 A185 5c redsh brown .25 .25
476 A185 10c sepia .25 .25
477 A185 15c gray black .25 .25
478 A186 20c redsh brown .30 .25
479 A186 30c red violet .50 .25
480 A186 40c brt ultra .65 .25
481 A185 45c dk slate grn .80 .30
482 A185 50c olive black .85 .30
483 A185 80c orange red 1.20 .35
Nos. 475-483,C165-C171 (16) 8.60 4.20

For overprints and surcharges see Nos. 489, 496, 525-527.

Type of 1946, Overprinted "POSTAL" in Black but Without Additional Surcharge

1948 Engr.
484 A181 10c orange .50 .25

Andrés Bello — A188

1948, Apr. 21 *Perf. 13*
485 A188 20c lt blue .30 .25
486 A188 30c rose carmine .30 .25
487 A188 40c blue green .30 .25
488 A188 1s black brown .60 .25
Nos. 485-488,C172-C174 (7) 3.20 1.75

83rd anniversary of the death of Andrés Bello (1781-1865), educator.

No. 480 Overprinted in Black

1948, May 24 *Perf. 12*
489 A186 40c bright ultra .60 .35

See No. C175.

Flagship of Columbus — A189

1948 *Perf. 14*
490 A189 10c dark blue green .50 .25
491 A189 20c brown .50 .25
492 A189 30c dark purple 1.20 .25
493 A189 50c deep claret 1.60 .25
494 A189 1s ultra 2.40 .40
495 A189 5s carmine 6.50 .80
Nos. 490-495,C176-C180 (11) 25.65 7.55

Issued to publicize the proposed Columbus Memorial Lighthouse near Ciudad Trujillo, Dominican Republic.

No. 483 Overprinted in Blue, "MANANA" Reading Down

1948 *Perf. 12*
496 A185 80c orange red .25 .25

Issued to publicize the National Fair of Today and Tomorrow, 1948. See No. C181.

Telegrafo I in Flight — A190

Book and Pen — A191

1948 Engr. *Perf. 12½*
497 A190 30c red orange .65 .25
498 A190 40c rose lilac .65 .25
499 A190 60c violet blue .65 .25
500 A190 1s brown red .65 .25
501 A190 3s brown 2.00 .35
502 A190 5s gray black 2.40 .35
Nos. 497-502,C182-C187 (12) 13.80 3.50

25th anniversary (in 1945) of the first postal flight in Ecuador.

1948, Oct. 12 Unwmk. *Perf. 14*
503 A191 10c deep claret .60 .25
504 A191 20c brown .60 .25
505 A191 30c dark green 1.25 .25
506 A191 50c red 2.00 .25
507 A191 1s purple 3.00 .30
508 A191 10s dull blue 8.00 1.00
Nos. 503-508,C188-C192 (11) 32.45 7.80

Campaign for adult education.

A192

Franklin D. Roosevelt and Two of "Four Freedoms" — A193

1948, Oct. 24 *Perf. 12½*
509 A192 10c rose brn & gray .40 .30
510 A192 20c brn ol & bl .50 .40
511 A193 30c ol bis & car rose .50 .40
512 A193 40c red vio & sep .65 .40
513 A193 1s org brn & car .70 .50
Nos. 509-513,C193-C197 (10) 7.05 3.70

Maldonado and Map — A194

Riobamba Aqueduct A195

Maldonado on Bank of Riobamba A196

Pedro V. Maldonado A197

1948, Nov. 17 Engr. Unwmk.
514 A194 5c gray blk & ver .40 .25
515 A195 10c car & gray blk .50 .25
516 A196 30c bis brn & ultra .60 .25

517 A195 40c sage grn & vio .75 .25
518 A194 50c grn & car 1.00 .30
519 A197 1s brn & slate bl 1.25 .35
Nos. 514-519,C198-C201 (10) 8.10 2.65

Bicentenary of the death of Pedro Vicente Maldonado, geographer.

For overprints and surcharges see Nos. 537-540.

A198

Miguel de Cervantes Saavedra
A199

1949, May 2 *Perf. 12½x12*

520 A198 30c dk car rose & dp ultra .75 .25
521 A199 60c bis & brn vio 1.25 .30
522 A198 1s grn & rose car 1.75 .25
523 A199 2s gray blk & red brn 3.25 .30
524 A198 5s choc & aqua 6.50 1.25
Nos. 520-524,C202-C206 (10) 25.75 5.95

400th anniv. of the birth of Miguel de Cervantes Saavedra, novelist, playwright and poet.

No. 480 Surcharged in Carmine

1949, June 15 *Perf. 12*

525 A186 10c on 40c brt ultra .40 .25
526 A186 20c on 40c brt ultra .55 .25
a. Double surcharge
527 A186 30c on 40c brt ultra .55 .25
Nos. 525-527,C207-C209 (6) 3.05 1.50

2nd Natl. Eucharistic Cong., Quito, 6/49.
No. 526 exists se-tenant with No. 527.

Monument on Equator — A200

1949, June **Engr.** *Perf. 12½x12*

528 A200 10c deep plum .40 .25

For overprint see No. 536.

No. 542 Surcharged in Black and Carmine

1949 *Perf. 12x12½*

529 A203 10c on 50c green .55 .25
530 A203 20c on 50c green .55 .25
531 A203 30c on 50c green .65 .25
Nos. 529-531,C210-C213 (7) 6.05 2.25

Universal Postal Union, 75th anniversary.

Consular Service Stamps Surcharged in Black

Arms of Ecuador — R1

1949 *Perf. 12*

532 R1 20c on 25c red brown .75 .25
533 R1 30c on 50c gray .75 .25

For other overprints and surcharges on type R1 see Nos. 544-549, 566-570, C245, C249-C252, RA60-RA62, RA72.

Nos. RA49A and RA55 Overprinted in Black — a

1950 **Unwmk.** *Perf. 12*

534 PT18 5c green .30 .25
535 PT21 5c blue .30 .25

Overprint 15mm on No. 534.

Nos. 528 and 517 to 519 Ovptd. or Srchd. in Black or Carmine

1950, Feb. 10 *Perf. 12½x12*

536 A200 10c dp plum .50 .50

Perf. 12½

537 A195 20c on 40c sage grn & vio 1.00 1.00
538 A195 30c on 40c sage grn & vio 1.25 1.25
539 A194 50c grn & car 2.00 2.00
540 A197 1s brn & slate bl (C) 2.50 2.50

No. C220 Overprinted Type "a" in Carmine

Perf. 11

Overprint 15mm long

541 A173 10s violet 6.00 3.00
Nos. 536-541,C216-C220 (11) 33.00 22.25

Nos. 536-541 publicize adult education.

San Pablo Lake — A203

Perf. 12x12½

1950, May **Engr.** **Unwmk.**

542 A203 50c green .50 .25

For surcharges see Nos. 529-531.

Consular Service Stamp Surcharged Vertically in Black

1950 *Perf. 12*

544 R1 30c on 50c gray .50 .25

Consular Service Stamps Overprinted or Surcharged in Black

b

c

d

e

f

g

1951 **Unwmk.** *Perf. 12*

545 R1 (b) 5c on 10c car rose .50 .25
546 R1 (c) 10c car rose .50 .25
547 R1 (d) 10c car rose .50 .25
548 R1 (e) 20c on 25c red brn .50 .25
549 R1 (e) 30c on 50c gray .50 .25
550 R2 (f) 40c on 25c blue .50 .25
551 R2 (g) 50c on 25c blue .50 .25
Nos. 545-551 (7) 3.50 1.75

See Nos. 552-554, C233-C234, C246-C248, RA67.

Consular Service Stamps Surcharged in Black

1951

552 R2 20c on 25c blue .50 .25
553 R2 30c on 25c blue .50 .25

Adult education. See Nos. C225-C226.

Consular Service Stamp Surcharged in Black

1951

554 R2 $0.30 on 50c car rose .50 .25

Reliquary of St. Mariana and Vatican — A204

Perf. 12½x12

1952, Feb. **Engr.** **Unwmk.**

555 A204 10c emer & red brn .90 .70
556 A204 20c dp bl & pur .90 .70
557 A204 30c car & bl grn .90 .70
Nos. 555-557,C227-C230 (7) 6.00 3.30

Issued to publicize the canonization of Mariana de Jesus Paredes y Flores.

Presidents Galo Plaza and Harry Truman — A205

2s, Pres. Plaza addressing US Congress.

1952, Mar. 26 *Perf. 12*

558 A205 1s rose car & gray blk .70 .60
559 A205 2s dl bl & sepia 1.75 .90
Nos. 558-559,C231-C232 (4) 5.15 3.70

1951 visit of Pres. Galo Plaza y Lasso to the US.

Fiscal Stamps Srchd. or Ovptd. Horiz. in Carmine or Black

R3

No. 562 Ovptd. Diagonally

1952 **Unwmk.** **Engr.** *Perf. 12*

560 R3 20c on 30c dp bl (C) .75 .25
561 R3 30c deep blue .75 .25
562 A138 50c purple .75 .25
Nos. 560-562 (3) 2.25 .75

For overprints and surcharge see Nos. RA68-RA69, RA71.

Pres. José M. Urvina, Slave and "Liberty" A206

Hyphen-hole Perf. 7x6½

1952 **Litho.**

563 A206 20c red & green .65 .45
564 A206 30c red & vio bl .80 .45
565 A206 50c blue & car 1.40 .45
Nos. 563-565,C236-C239 (7) 16.85 3.15

Centenary of abolition of slavery in Ecuador. Counterfeits exist.

Consular Service Stamps Surcharged in Black — h

1952-53 **Unwmk.** *Perf. 12*

566 R1 10c on 20s blue ('53) .75 .25
567 R1 20c on 10s gray ('53) .75 .25
568 R1 20c on 20s blue .75 .25
569 R1 30c on 10s gray ('53) .75 .25
570 R1 30c on 20s blue .75 .25
Nos. 566-570 (5) 3.75 1.25

Similar surcharges of 60c and 90c on the 20s blue are said to be bogus.

Teacher and Students — A207

New Citizens Voting — A208

Designs: 10c, Instructor with student. 30c, Teaching the alphabet.

1953, Apr. 13 **Engr.**

571	A207	5c	lt bl	.30	.25
572	A207	10c	dk car rose	.45	.25
573	A208	20c	brt brn org	.50	.25
574	A208	30c	dp red lil	.75	.25
			Nos. 571-574,C240-C241 (6)	4.70	1.50

1952 adult education campaign.

A209

1953 **Black Surcharge**

575	A209	40c on 50c	purple	1.00	.25

Cuicocha Lagoon — A210

Designs: 10c, Equatorial Line monument. 20c, Quininde countryside. 30c, Tomebamba river. 40c, La Chilintosa rock. 50c, Iliniza Mountains.

Frames in Black

1953 **Engr.** ***Perf. 13x12½***

576	A210	5c	brt bl	.50	.50
577	A210	10c	brt grn	.50	.50
578	A210	20c	purple	.50	.50
579	A210	30c	brown	.50	.50
580	A210	40c	orange	.50	.50
581	A210	50c	dp car	.90	.50
			Nos. 576-581 (6)	3.40	3.00

A211

A212

Carlos Maria Cardinal de la Torre and arches.

1954, Jan. **Photo.** ***Perf. 8½***

582	A211	30c	blk & ver	.65	.65
583	A211	50c	blk & rose lil	.65	.65
			Nos. 582-583,C253-C255 (5)	3.80	2.35

1st anniv. of the elevation of Archbishop de la Torre to Cardinal.

1954, Apr. 22

584	A212	30c	blk & gray	1.40	1.40
585	A212	50c	blk brn & yel	1.40	1.40
			Nos. 584-585,C256-C260 (7)	6.75	4.80

Queen Isabella I (1451-1504) of Spain, 500th birth anniv.

Type of 1929 Overprint Larger, No Letterspacing

1954-55 **Unwmk.** ***Perf. 12***

586	A112	5c	ol grn ('55)	.75	.25
587	A112	10c	orange	.75	.25

The normal overprint on Nos. 586-587 reads up. It also exists reading down.

Indian Messenger A213

Products of Ecuador A214

1954, Aug. 2 **Litho.** ***Perf. 11***

588	A213	30c	dk brn	1.00	.25

Day of the Postal Employee. See No. C263.

1954, Sept. 24 **Photo.**

589	A214	10c	orange	.40	.25
590	A214	20c	vermilion	.40	.25
591	A214	30c	rose pink	.40	.25
592	A214	40c	dk gray grn	.60	.25
593	A214	60c	yel brn	.80	.25
			Nos. 589-593 (5)	2.60	1.25

José Abel Castillo — A215

Babahoyo River Los Rios — A216

Perf. 11½x11

1955, Oct. 19 **Engr.** **Unwmk.**

594	A215	30c	olive bister	.60	.25
595	A215	50c	dk gray	.60	.25
			Nos. 594-595,C282-C286 (7)	10.20	2.10

30th anniv. of the 1st flight of the "Telegrafo I" and to honor Castillo, aviation pioneer.

1955-56 **Photo.** ***Perf. 13***

Designs: 5c, Palms, Esmeraldas. 10c, Fishermen, Manabi. 30c, Guayaquil, Guayas. 50c, Pital River, El Oro. 70c, Cactus, Galapagos Isls. 80c, Orchids, Napo-Pastaza. 1s, Aguacate Mission, Zamora-Chinchipe. 2s, Jibaro Indian, Morona-Santiago.

596	A216	5c	yel grn ('56)	1.50	.30
597	A216	10c	blue ('56)	1.50	.30
598	A216	20c	brown	1.50	.30
599	A216	30c	dk gray	1.50	.30
600	A216	50c	bl grn	1.50	.30
601	A216	70c	ol ('56)	1.50	.30
602	A216	80c	dp vio ('56)	3.75	.30
603	A216	1s	org ('56)	2.00	.30
604	A216	2s	rose red ('56)	3.75	.30
			Nos. 596-604 (9)	18.50	2.70

See Nos. 620-630, 670, C288-C297, C310-C311.

Brother Juan Adam Schwarz, S. J. — A217

1956, Aug. 27 **Engr.** ***Perf. 13½***

605	A217	5c	yel grn	.45	.25
606	A217	10c	org red	.45	.25
607	A217	20c	lt vio	.45	.25
608	A217	30c	dk grn	.45	.25
609	A217	40c	blue	.45	.25
610	A217	50c	dp ultra	.45	.25
611	A217	70c	orange	.45	.25
			Nos. 605-611,C302-C305 (11)	5.55	2.75

Bicentennial of printing in Ecuador and honoring Brother Juan Adam Schwarz, S.J.

Andres Hurtado de Mendoza — A218

Gil Ramirez Davalos A219

Designs: 20c, Brother Vincent Solano.

1957, Apr. 7 **Unwmk.** ***Perf. 12***

612	A218	5c	dk bl, *pink*	.65	.25
613	A219	10c	grn, *grnsh*	.65	.25
614	A218	20c	choc, *buff*	.65	.25
a.			Souvenir sheet of 4, imperf.	3.50	3.50
			Nos. 612-614,C312-C314 (6)	2.85	1.50

4th cent. of the founding of Cuenca.

No. 614a contains 2 5c gray & 2 20c brown red stamps in designs similar to #612, 614. It was printed on white ungummed paper.

Francisco Marcos, Gen. Pedro Alcantara Herran and Santos Mlchelena A220

1957, Sept. 5 **Engr.** ***Perf. 14½x14***

615	A220	40c	yellow	.40	.25
616	A220	50c	ultra	.40	.25
617	A220	2s	dk red	1.00	.25
			Nos. 615-617 (3)	1.80	.75

7th Postal Congress of the Americas and Spain (in 1955).

Souvenir Sheets

Various Railroad Scenes — A221

1957 **Litho.** ***Perf. 10½x11***

618	A221	20c	Sheet of 5	9.25	4.25
619	A221	30c	Sheet of 5	9.25	4.25

Issued to commemorate the opening of the Quito-Ibarra-San Lorenzo railroad.

Nos. 618-619 contain 2 orange yellow, 1 ultramarine and 2 carmine stamps, each in a different design.

Scenic Type of 1955-56.

Designs as before, except: 40c, as 70c. 90c, as 80c. No. 629, San Pablo, Imbabura.

1957-58 **Photo.** ***Perf. 13***

620	A216	5c	light blue	1.75	.25
621	A216	10c	brown	1.75	.25
622	A216	20c	crimson rose	1.75	.25
623	A216	20c	yel green	1.75	.25
624	A216	30c	rose red	2.50	.25
625	A216	40c	chalky blue	1.75	.25
626	A216	50c	lt vio	2.50	.25
627	A216	90c	brt ultra	1.75	.25
628	A216	1s	dark brown	1.75	.25
629	A216	1s	gray blk ('58)	1.75	.25
630	A216	2s	brown	2.75	.25
			Nos. 620-630 (11)	21.75	2.75

Blue and Yellow Macaw — A222

Birds: 20c, Red-breasted toucan. 30c, Condor. 40c, Black-tailed and sword-tailed hummingbirds.

Perf. 13½x13

1958, Jan. 7 **Litho.** **Unwmk.**

Birds in Natural Colors

634	A222	10c	red brn	1.40	.25
635	A222	20c	dk gray	1.40	.25
636	A222	30c	brt yel grn	3.50	.25
637	A222	40c	red org	3.50	.25
			Nos. 634-637 (4)	9.80	1.00

Carlos Sanz de Santamaria A223

Richard M. Nixon and Flags — A224

No. 640, Dr. Ramon Villeda Morales, flags. 2.20s, José Carlos de Macedo Soares, horizontal flags.

1958 ***Perf. 12***

Flags in Red, Blue, Yellow & Green

638	A223	1.80s	dl vio	.65	.25
639	A224	2s	dk grn	.65	.25
640	A224	2s	dk brn	.65	.25
641	A223	2.20s	blk brn	.65	.25
			Nos. 638-641 (4)	2.60	1.00

Visits: Colombia's Foreign Minister Dr. Carlos Sanz de Santamaria; US Vice Pres. Nixon, May 9-10; Pres. Ramon Villeda Morales of Honduras; Brazil's Foreign Minister José Carlos de Macedo Soares. See Nos. C419-C421. For overprints and surcharges see Nos. 775-775C, C419-C421, C460.

Locomotive of 1908 A225

Garcia Moreno, Jose Caamano, L. Plaza and Eloy Alfaro — A226

Design: 50c, Diesel locomotive.

Perf. 13½x14, 14

1958, Aug. 9 Photo. Unwmk.

642 A225 30c brn blk .25 .25
643 A225 50c dk car .35 .25
644 A226 5s dk brn 1.75 .70
Nos. 642-644 (3) 2.35 1.20

Guayaquil-Quito railroad, 50th anniv.

Cardinal — A227

Birds: 30c, Andean cock-of-the-rock. 50c, Glossy cowbird. 60c, Red-fronted Amazon.

1958 Litho. *Perf. 13½x13*

Birds in Natural Colors

645 A227 20c bluish grn, blk & red 1.40 .25
646 A227 30c buff, blk & brt bl 1.65 .25
647 A227 50c org, blk & grn 1.90 .55
648 A227 60c pale rose, blk & bluish grn 3.75 .55
Nos. 645-648 (4) 8.70 1.60

UNESCO Building and Eiffel Tower, Paris — A228

1958, Nov. 3 Engr. *Perf. 12½*

649 A228 80c brown .50 .25

UNESCO Headquarters in Paris opening, Nov. 3.

Globe and Satellites — A229

1958, Dec. 20 Photo. *Perf. 14x13½*

650 A229 1.80s dark blue 1.00 .45

International Geophysical Year, 1957-58. For overprints see Nos. 718, C422.

Virgin of Quito — A230

1959, Sept. 8 Unwmk. *Perf. 13*

651 A230 5c ol grn .25 .25
652 A230 10c yel brn .25 .25
653 A230 20c purple .25 .25
654 A230 30c ultra .25 .25
655 A230 80c dk car rose .25 .25
Nos. 651-655 (5) 1.25 1.25

See No. C290. For surcharges and overprint see Nos. 695-699.

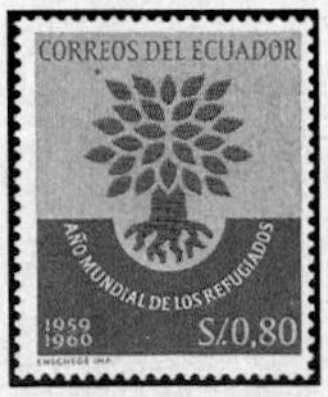

Uprooted Oak Emblem — A231

1960, Apr. 7 Litho. *Perf. 14x13*

656 A231 80c rose car & grn .25 .25

World Refugee Year, 7/1/59-6/30/60. For overprints see Nos. 709, 719, O205.

Great Anteater and Arms — A232

Animals: 40c, Tapir and map. 80c, Spectacled bear and arms. 1s, Puma and map.

1960, May 14 Photo. *Perf. 13*

657 A232 20c org, grn & blk .60 .25
658 A232 40c yel grn, bl grn & brn .90 .25
659 A232 80c bl, blk & red brn 1.50 .25
660 A232 1s Prus bl, plum & ocher 2.75 .60
Nos. 657-660 (4) 5.75 1.35

Founding of the city of Baeza, 4th cent. See Nos. 676-679.

Hotel Quito A233

No. 662, Dormitory, Catholic University. No. 663, Dormitory, Central University. No. 664, Airport, Quito. No. 665, Overpass on Highway to Quito. No. 666, Security Bank. No. 667, Ministry of Foreign Affairs. No. 668, Government Palace. No. 669, Legislative Palace.

Perf. 11x11½

1960, Aug. 8 Engr. Unwmk.

661 A233 1s dk pur & redsh brn .45 .25
662 A233 1s dk bl & brn .45 .25
663 A233 1s blk & red .45 .25
664 A233 1s dk bl & ultra .45 .25
665 A233 1s dk pur & dk car rose .45 .25
666 A233 1s blk & ol bis .45 .25
667 A233 1s dk pur & turq .45 .25
668 A233 1s dk bl & grn .45 .25
669 A233 1s blk & vio .45 .25
Nos. 661-669 (9) 4.05 2.25

11th Inter-American Conference, Quito. For surcharges see Nos. 700-708.

Type of Regular Issue, 1955-56

Souvenir Sheet

Design: Orchids, Napo-Pastaza.

1960 Photo. *Perf. 13*

Yellow Paper

670 Sheet of 2 5.00 5.00
a. A216 80c deep violet .85 .45
b. A216 90c deep green .85 .45

25th anniv. of Asociacion Filatelica Ecuatoriana. Marginal inscription in silver. Exists with silver inscription omitted.

"Freedom of Expression" — A234

Manabi Bridge A235

10c, "Freedom to vote." 20c, "Freedom to work." 30c, Coins, "Monetary stability."

1960, Aug. 29 Litho. *Perf. 13*

671 A234 5c dk bl .75 .25
672 A234 10c lt vio .75 .25
673 A234 20c orange .75 .25
674 A234 30c bluish grn .75 .25
675 A235 40c brn & bluish grn .75 .25
Nos. 671-675 (5) 3.75 1.25

Achievements of President Camilo Ponce Enriquez. See Nos. C370-C374.

Animal Type of 1960

Animals: 10c, Collared peccary. 20c, Kinkajou. 80c, Jaguar. 1s, Mountain coati.

Unwmk.

1961, July 13 Photo. *Perf. 13*

676 A232 10c grn, rose red & blk .55 .25
677 A232 20c vio, grnsh bl & brn 1.00 .25
678 A232 80c red org, dl yel & blk 1.60 .55
679 A232 1s brn, brt grn & org 2.10 .65
Nos. 676-679 (4) 5.25 1.70

Founding of the city of Tena, 400th anniv.

Graphium Pausianus A236

Butterflies: 30c, Papilio torquatus leptalea. 50c, Graphium molops molops. 80c, Battus lycidas.

1961, July 13 Litho. *Perf. 13½*

680 A236 20c pink & multi .65 .25
681 A236 30c lt ultra & multi 1.10 .25
682 A236 50c org & multi 1.25 .25
683 A236 80c bl grn & multi 2.25 .25
Nos. 680-683 (4) 5.25 1.00

See Nos. 711-713.

Galapagos Islands Nos. L1-L3 Overprinted in Black or Red

1961, Oct. 31 Photo. *Perf. 12*

684 A1 20c dk brn 1.00 .25
685 A2 50c violet 1.00 .25
686 A1 1s dk ol grn (R) 2.40 1.50
Nos. 684-686,C389-C391 (6) 12.05 3.25

Establishment of maritime biological stations on Galapagos Islands by UNESCO. Overprint arranged differently on 20c, 1s. See Nos. C389-C391.

Daniel Enrique Proano School A237

Designs: 60c, Loja-Zamora highway, vert. 80c, Aguirre Abad College, Guayaquil. 1s, Army quarters, Quito.

Perf. 11x11½, 11½x11

1962, Jan. 10 Engr. Unwmk.

687 A237 50c dl bl & blk .45 .25
688 A237 60c ol grn & blk .45 .25
689 A237 80c org red & blk .45 .25
690 A237 1s rose lake & blk .45 .25
Nos. 687-690 (4) 1.80 1.00

Pres. Arosemena, Flags of Ecuador, US — A238

Designs (Arosemena and): 10c, Flags of Ecuador. 20c, Flags of Ecuador and Panama.

1963, July 1 Litho. *Perf. 14*

691 A238 10c buff & multi .25 .25
692 A238 20c multi .25 .25
693 A238 60c multi .25 .25
Nos. 691-693,C409-C411 (6) 2.60 1.60

Issued to commemorate Pres. Carlos J. Arosemena's friendship trip, July 1962. Imperfs exist. Value $9.

Protection for The Family — A239

1963, July 9 Unwmk. *Perf. 14*

694 A239 10c ultra, red, gray & blk .25 .25

Social Insurance, 25th anniv. See No. C413.

No. 655 Ovptd. or Srchd. in Black or Blue

1963 Photo. *Perf. 13*

695 A230 10c on 80c dk car rose .25 .25
696 A230 20c on 80c dk car rose .25 .25
697 A230 50c on 80c dk car rose .25 .25
698 A230 60c on 80c dk car rose (Bl) .25 .25
699 A230 80c dk car rose .30 .25
Nos. 695-699 (5) 1.30 1.25

Nos. 661-669 Surcharged

1964, Apr. 20 Engr. *Perf. 11x11½*

700 A233 10c on 1s dk pur & redsh brn .40 .25
701 A233 10c on 1s dk pur & turq .40 .25
702 A233 20c on 1s dk bl & brn .40 .25
703 A233 20c on 1s dk bl & grn .40 .25
704 A233 30c on 1s dk pur & dk car rose .40 .25
705 A233 40c on 1s blk & ol bis .40 .25
706 A233 60c on 1s blk & red .40 .25
707 A233 80c on 1s dk bl & ultra .40 .25
708 A233 80c on 1s blk & vio .40 .25
Nos. 700-708 (9) 3.60 2.25

No. 656 Overprinted in Black or Light Ultramarine

1964 Litho. *Perf. 14x13*

709 A231 80c rose car & grn 4.50 1.25

Butterfly Type of 1961

Butterflies: Same as on Nos. 680, 682-683.

1964, June Litho. *Perf. 13½*

711 A236 20c brt grn & multi .75 .25
712 A236 50c sal pink & multi 1.50 .25
713 A236 80c lt red brn & multi 3.00 .25
Nos. 711-713 (3) 5.25 .75

Alliance for Progress Emblem, Agriculture and Industry A240

Designs: 50c, Emblem, gear wheels, mountain and seashore. 80c, Emblem, banana worker, fish, factory and ship.

1964, Aug. 26 Unwmk. *Perf. 12*

715 A240 40c bis brn & vio .25 .25
716 A240 50c red org & blk .25 .25
717 A240 80c bl & dk brn .40 .25
Nos. 715-717 (3) .90 .75

Issued to publicize the Alliance for Progress which aims to stimulate economic growth and raise living standards in Latin America.

No. 650 Overprinted in Red

1964 **Photo.** ***Perf. 14x13½***
718 A229 1.80s dark blue 2.75 2.25

No. 656 Overprinted

1964, July **Litho.** ***Perf. 14x13***
719 A231 80c block of 4 4.00 4.00

Organization of American States.

World Map and Banana Tree — A241

1964, Oct. 26 ***Perf. 12½x12***
720 A241 50c dk brn, gray & gray ol .30 .25
721 A241 80c blk, org & gray ol .30 .25

Issued to publicize the Banana Conference, Oct.-Nov. 1964. See Nos. C427-C428a.

King Philip II of Spain and Map of Upper Amazon River A242

Designs (Map and): 20c, Juan de Salinas de Loyola. 30c, Hernando de Santillan.

1964, Dec. 6 **Litho.** ***Perf. 13½***
722 A242 10c rose, blk & buff .30 .25
723 A242 20c bl grn, blk & buff .30 .25
724 A242 30c bl, blk & buff .30 .25
Nos. 722-724 (3) .90 .75

4th centenary of the establishment of the Royal High Court in Quito.

Pole Vaulting A243

1964, Dec. 16 ***Perf. 14x13½***
725 A243 80c vio bl, yel grn & brn .35 .25

18th Olympic Games, Tokyo, Oct. 10-25. See Nos. C432-C434.

Peter Fleming and Two-toed Sloth — A244

Designs: 20c, James Elliot and armadillo. 30c, T. Edward McCully, Jr., and squirrel. 40c, Roger Youderian and deer. 60c, Nathaniel (Nate) Saint and plane over Napo River.

1965 **Unwmk.** ***Perf. 13½***
726 A244 20c emerald & multi 1.00 .25
727 A244 30c yellow & multi 1.00 .25
728 A244 40c lilac & multi 1.00 .25
729 A244 60c multi 1.00 .25
730 A244 80c multi 1.00 .25
Nos. 726-730 (5) 5.00 1.25

Issued in memory of five American Protestant missionaries, killed by the Auca Indians, 1/8/56.
Issue dates: 80c, May 11; others, July 8.

Juan B. Vázquez and Benigno Malo College — A245

1965, June 6 **Litho.** ***Perf. 14***
731 A245 20c blk, yel & vio bl .25 .25
732 A245 60c blk, red, yel & vio bl .25 .25
733 A245 80c blk, emer, yel & vio bl .25 .25
Nos. 731-733 (3) .75 .75

Centenary (in 1964) of the founding of Benigno Malo National College.

National Anthem, Juan Leon Mera and Antonio Neumane A246

1965, Aug. 10 **Litho.** ***Perf. 13½***
734 A246 50c pink & blk .25 .25
735 A246 80c lt grn & blk .35 .25
736 A246 5s bis & blk .80 .35
737 A246 10s lt ultra & blk 1.40 .90
Nos. 734-737 (4) 2.80 1.75

Cent. of the national anthem. The name of the poet Juan Leon Mera is misspelled on the stamps.
For surcharges see Nos. 766C, 766H.

Torch and Athletes (Shot Put, Discus, Javelin and Hammer Throw) — A247

50c, 1s, Runners. 60c, 1.50s, Soccer.

1965, Nov. 20 ***Perf. 12x12½***
738 A247 40c org, gold, & blk .25 .25
739 A247 50c org ver, gold & blk .25 .25
740 A247 60c bl, gold & blk .25 .25
741 A247 80c brt yel grn, gold & blk .45 .25
742 A247 1s lt vio, gold & blk .45 .25
743 A247 1.50s brt pink, gold & blk .75 .50
Nos. 738-743,C435-C440 (12) 6.25 3.75

Issued to publicize the 5th Bolivarian Games, held at Guayaquil and Quito.
For surcharges see Nos. 766B, 766D, C449.

Stamps of 1865 A248

1965, Dec. 30 **Litho.** ***Perf. 13½***
Stamps of 1865 in Yellow, Ultramarine & Green
744 A248 80c rose red .35 .25
745 A248 1.30s rose lilac .40 .25
746 A248 2s chocolate .55 .25
747 A248 4s black .80 .25
a. Souv. sheet, #744-747, imperf. 4.00 4.00
Nos. 744-747 (4) 2.10 1.00

Cent. of Ecuadorian postage stamps.

The postal validity of some of the following sets has been questioned.

ITU Centenary — A248a

1966, Jan. 27 **Litho.** ***Perf. 12x12½***
748 A248a 10c Telstar .25 .25
748A A248a 10c Syncom .25 .25
748B A248a 80c Relay .25 .25
748C A248a 1.50s Luna 3 .40 .35
748D A248a 3s Echo II 2.00 1.25
f. Souv. sheet of 3, #748, 748B, 748D, perf. 14x12½ 15.00
748E A248a 4s E. Branly, Marconi, Bell, E. Belin 2.00 1.50
g. Souv. sheet of 3, #748A, 748C, 748E, perf. 14x12½ 15.00
Nos. 748-748E (6) 5.15 3.85

1.50s, 3s, 4s are airmail.
Nos. 748Df, 748Eg are printed on surface colored paper. Exist imperf. Value, each $18.

Space Exploration — A248b

10c, Edward White's space walk, June 8, 1965. 1s, Gemini 5, Aug. 21, 1965. 1.30s, Solar system. 2s, Charles Conrad, L. Gordon Cooper, Gemini 5, Aug. 21-29, 1965. 2.50s, Gemini 6. 3.50s, Alexei L. Leonov's space walk, Mar. 18, 1965.

1966, Jan. 27 ***Perf. 12x12½***
749 A248b 10c multi .25 .25
749A A248b 1s multi .35 .25
749B A248b 1.30s multi .35 .25
749C A248b 2s multi 1.20 .65
749D A248b 2.50s multi 1.20 .65
749E A248b 3.50s multi 2.75 2.50
f. Souv. sheet of 3, #749, 749B, 749E, perf. 14x12½ 15.00 10.00
Nos. 749-749E (6) 6.10 4.55

1.30s, 2s, 2.50s, 3.50s are airmail.
No. 749Ef is printed on surface colored paper. Exists imperf. Value $15.

Dante's Dream by Rossetti — A248c

Designs: 80c, Dante and Beatrix by Holliday. 2s, Galileo Galilei, 400th birth cent., vert. 3s, Dante, 700th birth cent., vert.

1966, June ***Perf. 13½x14, 14x13½***
750 A248c 10c multicolored .25 .25
750A A248c 80c multicolored .25 .25
750B A248c 2s multicolored 2.40 1.50
750C A248c 3s multicolored 2.50 1.60
d. Souv. sheet of 3, #750, 750A, 750C, perf. 12x12½ 18.00 18.00
Nos. 750-750C (4) 5.40 3.60

Nos. 750A-750B are airmail. No. 750Cd exists imperf. Value $18.

Pavonine Quetzal — A249

Birds: 50c, Blue-crowned motmot. 60c, Paradise tanager. 80c, Wire-tailed manakin.

1966, June 17 **Litho.** ***Perf. 13½***
Birds in Natural Colors
751 A249 40c dl rose & blk 1.60 .25
751A A249 50c sal & blk 1.60 .25
751B A249 60c lt ocher & blk 1.60 .25
751C A249 80c lt bl & blk 1.60 .25
Nos. 751-751C,C441-C448 (12) 31.70 6.25

For surcharges see Nos. 766E-766F, C450, C455-C457.

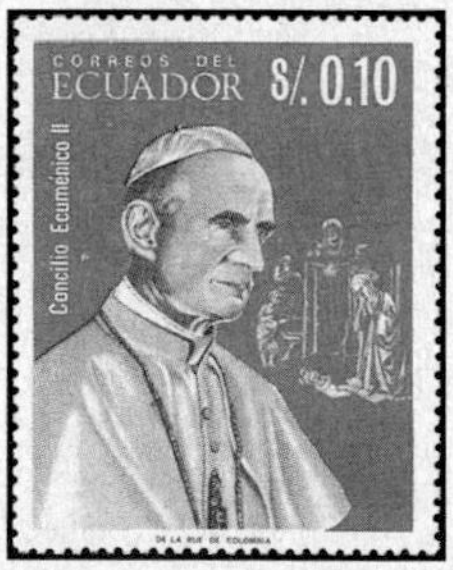

Pope Paul VI — A249a

Pope Paul VI and: 1.30s, Nativity. 3.50s, Virgin of Merced.

1966, June 24 ***Perf. 12½x12***
752 A249a 10c multicolored .25 .25
752A A249a 1.30s multicolored .75 .35
752B A249a 3.50s multicolored 2.25 .75
c. Souv. sheet of 3, #752, perf. 14x13½, 752A-752B, perf. 12½x12 15.00 15.00
Nos. 752-752B (3) 3.25 1.35

Nos. 752A-752B are airmail.
No. 752Bc is printed on surface colored paper. Exists imperf. Value $18.

Sir Winston Churchill, (1874-1965) — A249b

Famous Men: 10c, Dag Hammarskjold, vert. 1.50s, Albert Schweitzer, vert. 2.50s, John F. Kennedy, vert. 4s, Churchill, Kennedy.

Perf. 14x13½, 13½x14

1966, June 24

753 A249b 10c vio bl, brn & blk .25 .25
753A A249b 1s ver, bl & blk .35 .25
753B A249b 1.50s brn, lil rose & blk .80 .30
753C A249b 2.50s ver, bl & blk 2.00 1.00
753D A249b 4s bl, blk & brn 2.25 1.50
e. Souv. sheet of 3, #753, 753B, 753D 27.50 27.50
Nos. 753-753D (5) 5.65 3.30

Nos. 753C-753D are airmail.

No. 753De is printed on surface colored paper. 10c stamp is perf. 14x13½, 1.50s is perf. 14x13½x14x12, 4s is perf. 12x12½x13x12½. Exists imperf. Value $27.50.

History of Summer Olympics — A249c

1966, June 27 *Perf. 12x12½*

754 A249c 10c Long jump .25 .25
754A A249c 10c Wrestling .25 .25
754B A249c 80c Discus, javelin .50 .25
754C A249c 1.30s Chariot racing 1.25 .45
754D A249c 3s High jump 2.00 .90
f. Souv. sheet of 3, #754, 754B, 754D 12.00 5.00
754E A249c 3.50s Discus 3.25 1.10
g. Souv. sheet of 3, #754A, 754C, 754E 12.50 5.00
Nos. 754-754E (6) 7.50 3.20

Nos. 754C-754D are airmail.

Nos. 754Df, 754Eg are printed on surface colored paper.

Nos. 754Df and 754Eg exist imperf. Value $13.50.

1968 Winter Olympics, Grenoble — A249d

1966, June 27 *Perf. 14*

755 A249d 10c Speedskating .25 .25
755A A249d 1s Ice hockey .40 .25
755B A249d 1.50s Ski jumping .60 .30
755C A249d 2s Cross country skiing 1.20 .45
755D A249d 2.50s Downhill skiing 1.60 1.25
755E A249d 4s Figure skating 2.00 1.50
f. Souv. sheet of 3, #755, 755B, 755E, perf. 14x13½ 8.00 6.00
Nos. 755-755E (6) 6.05 4.00

Nos. 755B-755E are airmail.

No. 755Ef is printed on surface colored paper. Exists imperf. Value same as perf.

French-American Cooperation in Space — A249e

Designs: 1.50s, French satellite D-1, Mt. Gros observatory, vert. 4s, John F. Kennedy, satellites.

1966 *Perf. 13½x14, 14x13½*

756 A249e 10c multicolored .25 .25
756A A249e 1.50s multicolored 1.60 1.10
756B A249e 4s multicolored 3.75 2.25
c. Sheet of 3, #756-756B 15.00 12.00
Nos. 756-756B (3) 5.60 3.60

Nos. 756A-756B are airmail.

No. 756Bc exists imperf. Value same as perf.

Italian Space Program — A249n

Designs: 10c, San Marco satellite. 1.30s, San Marco satellite, diff. 3.50s, Leonardo da Vinci, Moon, and Johannes Kepler.

1966 **Litho.** **Unwmk.** *Perf. 14*

757 A249n 10c multi .25 .25
757A A249n 1.30s multi .75 .45
757B A249n 3.50s multi 2.00 1.10
c. Souvenir sheet of 3, #757, 757A, 757B 12.00 8.00
Nos. 757- (3) 3.00 1.80

Nos. 757A and 757B are airmail. No. 757Bc is printed on paper with a gray pattern, and exists imperforate on paper printed with a green pattern.

Moon Exploration A249f

1966 *Perf. 14*

758 A249f 10c Surveyor .25 .25
758A A249f 80c Luna 10 .25 .25
758B A249f 1s Luna 9 .25 .25
758C A249f 2s Astronaut flight trainer .80 .45
758D A249f 2.50s Ranger 7 1.00 .75
758E A249f 3s Lunar Orbiter 1 1.20 .90
f. Sheet of 3, #758, 758A, 758E 12.00 6.00
Nos. 758-758E (6) 3.75 2.85

Nos. 758C-758E are airmail. Stamps in No. 758Ef have colored pattern in border.

No. 758Ef exists imperf. Value same as perf.

1968 Summer Olympics, Mexico City — A249g

Paintings by Mexican artists: 10c, Wanderer by Diego Rivera. 1s, Workers by Jose Orozco. 1.30s, Pres. Juarez by Orozco. 2s, Mother and Child by David Siqueiros. 2.50s, Two Women by Rivera. 3.50s, New Democracy by Siqueiros.

1967, Mar. 13 *Perf. 14*

759 A249g 10c multicolored .25 .25
759A A249g 1s multicolored .55 .25
759B A249g 1.30s multicolored .80 .30
759C A249g 2s multicolored 1.00 .50
759D A249g 2.50s multicolored 1.20 .90
759E A249g 3.50s multicolored 2.25 1.75
f. Sheet of 3, #759, 759B, 759E 15.00
Nos. 759-759E (6) 6.05 3.95

Nos. 759B-759E are airmail.

No. 759f is printed on surface colored paper that differs slightly from Nos. 759-759E. Exists imperf. Value same as perf.

1968 Summer Olympics, Mexico City — A249h

1967, Mar. 13

760 A249h 10c Soccer .25 .25
760A A249h 10c Hurdles .25 .25
760B A249h 80c Track .25 .25
760C A249h 1.50s Fencing .75 .30
760D A249h 3s High jump 1.50 1.00
f. Souv. sheet of 3, #760A, 760B, 760D 15.00 7.50
760E A249h 4s Swimming 3.25 1.50
g. Souv. sheet of 3, #760, 760C, 760E 12.00 7.00
Nos. 760-760E (6) 6.25 3.55

Nos. 760C-760E are airmail.

Nos. 760f-760g are printed on surface colored paper. Exist imperf. Value same as perf.

4th Natl. Eucharistic Congress A249i

Paintings: 10c, Madonna and Child by unknown artist. 60c, Holy Family by Rodriguez. 80c, Madonna and Child by Samaniego. 1s, Good Shepherd by Samaniego. 1.50s, Assumption of the Virgin by Vargas. 2s, Man in Prayer by Santiago.

10s, Chalice, eucharist, church, wheat.

1967, May 10

761 A249i 10c multicolored .25 .25
761A A249i 60c multicolored .55 .30
761B A249i 80c multicolored .80 .30
761C A249i 1s multicolored .80 .50
761D A249i 1.50s multicolored 1.50 .75
761E A249i 2s multicolored 2.50 .75
Nos. 761-761E (6) 6.40 2.85

Souvenir Sheet

761F A249i 10s multi 6.50 6.50

Nos. 761D-761E are airmail. Frames and inscriptions vary greatly.

No. 761F exists imperf. with an orange margin color. Value, same.

Madonna and Child Enthroned by Guido Reni A249j

Paintings of the Madonna and Child by: 40c, van Hemesen. 50c, Memling. 1.30s, Durer. 2.50s, Raphael. 3s, Murillo.

1967, May 25 *Perf. 14x13½*

762 A249j 10c multicolored .25 .25
762A A249j 40c multicolored .25 .25
762B A249j 50c multicolored .25 .25
762C A249j 1.30s multicolored .70 .30
762D A249j 2.50s multicolored 1.75 .95
762E A249j 3s multicolored 2.75 1.20
Nos. 762-762E (6) 5.95 3.20

Nos. 762C-762E are airmail.

Portrait of a Young Woman by Rogier van der Weyden A249k

Designs: 1s, Helene Fourment by Rubens. 1.50s, Venetian Woman by Durer. 2s, Lady Sheffield by Gainsborough. 2.50s, Suzon by Manet. 4s, Lady with a Unicorn by Raphael.

1967, Sept. 9 *Perf. 14x13½*

763 A249k 10c multicolored .25 .25
763A A249k 1s multicolored .55 .30
763B A249k 1.50s multicolored 1.20 .50
763C A249k 2s multicolored 1.60 .65
763D A249k 2.50s multicolored 2.40 .80
763E A249k 4s multicolored 2.75 1.25
f. Sheet of 3, #763, 763B, 763E, perf. 14 12.00 8.00
Nos. 763-763E (6) 8.75 3.75

Nos. 763B-763E are airmail.

Stamps in No. 763f have colored pattern in border. Exists imperf. Value same as perf.

John F. Kennedy, 50th Birth Anniv. A249l

JFK and: No. 764A, Dag Hammarskjold. 80c, Pope Paul VI. 1.30s, Konrad Adenauer. 3s, Charles de Gaulle. 3.50s, Winston Churchill.

Perf. 14x13½, 13½x14

1967, Sept. 11

764 A249l 10c lil, brn & bl .25 .25
764A A249l 10c yel, brn & sky bl .25 .25
764B A249l 80c yel, brn & sal .25 .25
764C A249l 1.30s yel, brn & pink 2.00 .75
764D A249l 3s yel, brn & yel grn 2.90 1.25
764E A249l 3.50s yel, brn & bl 4.00 1.75
Nos. 764-764E (6) 9.65 4.50

Souvenir Sheets

764F Sheet of 3 16.00 8.00
h. like #764, 35x27mm
i. like #764B, 35x27mm
j. like #764D, 35x27mm
764G Sheet of 3 16.00 8.00
k. like #764A, 35x27mm
l. like #764C, 35x27mm
m. like #764E, 35x27mm

Nos. 764C-764E are airmail. Nos. 764A-764E horiz. Stamps in Nos. 764F-764G have colored pattern in border.

Nos. 764F and 764G exist imperf. Values same as perf.

Christmas — A249m

Designs: No. 765A, Children's procession. 40c, Candlelight procession. 50c, Children singing. 60c, Processional. 2.50s, Christmas celebration.

1967, Dec. 29 *Perf. 13x14*

765 A249m 10c multi .40 .25
765A A249m 10c multi .40 .25
765B A249m 40c multi .40 .25
765C A249m 50c multi .40 .25

765D	A249m	60c multi	.40	.25
765E	A249m	2.50s multi	11.00	9.75
		Nos. 765-765E (6)	13.00	11.00

No. 765E is airmail. See Nos. 768-768F.

Various Surcharges on Issues of 1956-66

1967-68

766	AP72	30c on 1.10s (C337)	.35	.25
766A	AP66	40c on 1.70s (C292)	.35	.25
766B	A247	40c on 3.50s (C438)	.35	.25
766C	A246	50c on 5s (736) ('68)	.35	.25
766D	A247	80c on 1.50s (743)	.40	.25
766E	A249	80c on 2.50s (C445)	.40	.25
766F	A249	1s on 4s (C447)	.50	.25
766G	AP66	1.30s on 1.90s (C293)	.65	.55
766H	A246	2s on 10s (737) ('68)	.80	.25
		Nos. 766-766H,C449-C450 (11)	4.95	3.15

The surcharge on Nos. 766B-766C, 766E and 766G-766H includes "Resello." The obliteration of old denomination and arrangement of surcharges differ on each stamp.

Bust of Peñaherrera, Central University, Quito — A250

50c, Law books. 80c, Open book, laurel, horiz.

Perf. 12x12½, 12½x12

1967, Dec. 29 **Litho.**

767	A250	50c brt grn & blk	.25	.25
767A	A250	60c rose & blk	.25	.25
767B	A250	80c rose lil & blk	.25	.25
		Nos. 767-767B,C451-C452 (5)	1.35	1.25

Cent. (in 1964) of the birth of Dr. Victor Manuel Peñaherrera (1864-1932), author of the civil and criminal codes of Ecuador.

Christmas Type of 1967

Native Christian Art: 10c, Mourning of the Death of Christ, by Manuel Chili. 80c, Ascension of the Holy Virgin, vert. 1s, The Holy Virgin. 1.30s, Coronation of the Holy Virgin, by Bernardo Rodriguez, vert. 1.50s, Madonna and Child with the Heavenly Host, vert. 2s, Madonna and Child, by Manuel Samaniego, vert. 3s, Immaculate Conception, by Bernardo de Legranda, vert. 3.50s, Passion of Christ, by Chili, vert. 4s, The Holy Virgin of Quito, by de Legranda, vert.

1968 Jan. 19 ***Perf. 13½x14, 14x13½***

768	A249m	10c multi	.25	.25
768A	A249m	80c multi	.25	.25
768B	A249m	1s multi	.25	.25
768C	A249m	1.30s multi	.25	.25
768D	A249m	1.50s multi	.50	.30
768E	A249m	2s multi	.80	.75
		Nos. 768-768E (6)	2.30	2.05

Souvenir Sheet

Perf. 14

768F	Sheet of 3	16.00	8.00
g.	A249m 3s multicolored		
h.	A249m 3.50s multicolored		
i.	A249m 4s multicolored		

Nos. 768C-768F are airmail. No. 768F exists imperf. Value same.

Tourism Year — A250a

20c, Woman from Otavalo. 30c, Colorado Indian. 40c, Petroglyph of a cat. 50c, Petroglyph of a mythological predator. 60c, Woman in a bazaar. 80c, 1s, 1.30s, Petroglyphs, diff. 1.50s, Colonial street, Quito. 2s, Amulet.

1968, Apr. 1 ***Perf. 13½x14***

769	A250a	20c multicolored	.25	.25
769A	A250a	30c multicolored	.25	.25
769B	A250a	40c multicolored	.25	.25
769C	A250a	50c multicolored	.25	.25
769D	A250a	60c multicolored	.25	.25
769E	A250a	80c multicolored	.25	.25
769F	A250a	1s multicolored	.30	.25
769G	A250a	1.30s multicolored	.25	.25
769H	A250a	1.50s multicolored	.30	.25
769I	A250a	2s multicolored	.35	.25
		Nos. 769-769I (10)	2.70	2.50

Eleventh Congress of the Confederation of Latin American Tourist Organizations (COTAL). Nos. 769G-769I are airmail.

Otto Arosemena Gomez — A251

Design: 1s, Page from the Constitution.

1968, May 9 **Litho.** ***Perf. 13½x14***

770	A251	80c lil & multi	.25	.25
770A	A251	1s multi	.25	.25
		Nos. 770-770A,C453-C454 (4)	1.05	1.00

First anniversary of the administration of Pres. Otto Arosemena Gomez.

Lions Emblem — A252

1968, May 24 **Litho.** ***Perf. 13½x14***

771	A252	80c multi	.25	.25
771A	A252	1.30s multi	.25	.25
771B	A252	2s pink & multi	.30	.25
c.		Souvenir sheet of 1	4.75	4.75
		Nos. 771-771B (3)	.80	.75

50th anniv. (in 1967) of Lions Intl.

No. 771c contains one 5s 39x49mm stamp. Exists imperf. Value same as perf.

Pope Paul VI, Visit to Latin America — A252a

39th Intl. Eucharistic Congress, Bogota, Colombia A252b

60c, Pope Paul VI, vert. 1s, Madonna by Botticelli. 1.30s, Pope Paul VI with flags of South American nations. 2s, Madonna and Child by Durer.

1969 ***Perf. 13½x14, 14x13½***

772	A252a	40c multicolored	.25	.25
772A	A252a	60c multicolored	.35	.25
772B	A252b	1s multicolored	1.10	.30
772C	A252a	1.30s multicolored	.80	.40
e.		Souv. sheet of 3, #772, 772A, 772C, imperf.	4.00	2.50
772D	A252b	2s multicolored	1.75	.75
f.		Souv. sheet of 2, #772B, 772D, imperf.	4.75	2.50
		Nos. 772-772D (5)	4.25	1.95

Nos. 772C-772D are airmail. Nos. 772-772f overprinted in silver with the national coat of arms.

Madonna with the Angel by Rogier van der Weyden A252c

Paintings by various artists showing the life of the Virgin Mary.

1969 ***Perf. 14x13½, 13½x14***

773	A252c	40c shown	.25	.25
773A	A252c	60c Van der Weyden, diff.	.25	.25
773B	A252c	1s Raphael	.35	.25
773C	A252c	1.30s Veronese	1.25	.65
e.		Souv. sheet of 2, #773B-773C, imperf.	5.75	2.50
773D	A252c	2s Van der Weyden, horiz.	2.00	.80
f.		Souv. sheet of 3, #773-773A, 773D, imperf.	5.75	2.50
		Nos. 773-773D (5)	4.10	2.20

Nos. 773-773Df overprinted in silver with the national coat of arms. Nos. 773C-773D are airmail.

Nos. C331 and C326 Surcharged in Violet and Dark Blue

a

b

1969, Jan. 10 ***Perf. 11½, 14x13½***

774	AP79 (a)	40c on 1.30s (V)	.55	.25
774A	AP76 (b)	50c on 1.30s (DBl)	.55	.25

Types of 1958

No. 775 & 775B Srchd. and Ovptd. in Plum and Black

No. 775A Srchd. and Ovptd. in Plum and Black

No. 775C Overprinted in Red & Black

Design: Ignacio Luis Arcaya, Foreign Minister of Venezuela.

1969, Mar. **Litho.** ***Perf. 12***

Flags in Red, Blue and Yellow

775	A223	50c on 2s sepia	.30	.25
775A	A223	80c on 2s sepia	.30	.25
775B	A223	1s on 2s sepia	.30	.25
775C	A223	2s sepia	.30	.25
		Nos. 775-775C,C455-C457 (7)	2.70	1.75

Nos. 775-775C were not issued without overprint. The obliteration of old denomination on No. 775A is a small square around a star. Overprint is plum, except for the black small coat of arms on right flag.

Map of Ecuador and Oriental Region — A253

Surcharge typographed in Dark Blue, Red Brown, Black or Lilac

1969 **Litho.** ***Perf. 14***

776	A253	20c on 30c (DBl)	.35	.25
776A	A253	40c on 30c (RBr)	.35	.25
777	A253	50c on 30c (DBl)	.35	.25
778	A253	60c on 30c (DBl)	.35	.25
778A	A253	60c on 30c (Bk)	.40	.40
778B	A253	80c on 30c (DBl)	—	20.00
779	A253	80c on 30c (Bk)	.35	.25
780	A253	1s on 30c (L)	.35	.25
780A	A253	1s on 30c (DBl)	1.20	.80
781	A253	1.30s on 30c (Bk)	.50	.25
782	A253	1.50s on 30c (Bk)	.50	.25
783	A253	2s on 30c (DBl)	.65	.25
784	A253	3s on 30c (DBl)	.75	.25
784A	A253	4s on 30c (DBl)	2.00	2.00
785	A253	4s on 30c (Bk)	.80	.25
786	A253	5s on 30c (Bk)	1.00	.35
		Nos. 776-786 (16)	9.90	26.30

Not issued without surcharge.

M. L. King, John and Robert Kennedy — A254

1969-70 **Typo.** ***Perf. 12½***

787	A254	4s blk, bl, grn & buff	.50	.25

Perf. 13½

788	A254	4s blk, lt bl & grn ('70)	.50	.25

In memory of John F. Kennedy, Robert F. Kennedy and Martin Luther King, Jr.

Thecla Coronata — A255

Butterflies: 20c, Papilio zabreus. 30c, Heliconius chestertoni. 40c, Papilio pausanias. 50c, Pereute leucodrosime. 60c, Metamorpha dido. 80c, Morpho cypris. 1s, Catagramma astarte.

1970 **Litho.** ***Perf. 12½***

789	A255	10c buff & multi	3.25	.45
790	A255	20c lt grn & multi	3.25	.45
791	A255	30c pink & multi	3.25	.45
792	A255	40c lt bl & multi	3.25	.25
793	A255	50c gold & multi	3.25	.25
794	A255	60c salmon & multi	3.25	.25
795	A255	80c silver & multi	3.25	.25
796	A255	1s lt grn & multi	3.25	.25

Same, White Background

Perf. 13½

797	A255	10c multi	3.25	.45
798	A255	20c multi	3.25	.45
799	A255	30c multi	3.25	.45
800	A255	40c multi	3.25	.25
801	A255	50c multi	3.25	.25
802	A255	60c multi	3.25	.25
803	A255	80c multi	3.25	.25
804	A255	1s multi	3.25	.25
		Nos. 789-804,C461-C464 (20)	66.00	6.20

Surcharged Revenue Stamps
A256 A257

1970, June 16 Litho. *Perf. 14*

Red Surcharge

805 A256 1s on 1s light blue .25 .25
806 A256 1.30s on 1s light blue .25 .25
807 A256 1.50s on 1s light blue .30 .30
808 A256 2s on 1s light blue .35 .25
809 A256 5s on 1s light blue .75 .30
810 A256 10s on 1s light blue 1.50 .55
Nos. 805-810 (6) 3.40 1.90

1970 Typo. *Perf. 12*

Black Surcharge

811 A257 60c on 1s violet .30 .25
812 A257 80c on 1s violet .30 .25
813 A257 1s on 1s violet .30 .25
814 A257 1.10s on 1s violet .30 .25
815 A257 1.30s on 1s violet .30 .25
816 A257 1.50s on 1s violet .35 .25
817 A257 2s on 1s violet .35 .25
818 A257 2.20s on 1s violet .40 .25
819 A257 3s on 1s violet .50 .25
Nos. 811-819 (9) 3.10 2.25

1970

820 A257 1.10s on 2s green .30 .25
821 A257 1.30s on 2s green .30 .25
822 A257 1.50s on 2s green .35 .25
823 A257 2s on 2s green .35 .25
824 A257 3.40s on 2s green .50 .25
825 A257 5s on 2s green .75 .25
826 A257 10s on 2s green 1.25 .25
827 A257 20s on 2s green 2.10 .70
828 A257 50s on 2s green 5.00 2.25
Nos. 820-828 (9) 10.90 4.70

1970

829 A257 3s on 5s blue .50 .25
830 A257 5s on 5s blue .65 .35
831 A257 10s on 40s orange 1.25 .65
Nos. 829-831 (3) 2.40 1.25

In the surcharge applied to Nos. 811-831, the word "POSTAL" is not locked into horizontal and vertical position relative to the "1970". On some stamps the "P" is directly below the numeral "1", on others the "O" is below the "1". The top of "POSTAL" can vary from 1mm-8mm from the bottom of the date.

Arms of Zamora Chinchipe — A258 Flags of Ecuador and Chile — A259

Design: 1s, Arms and flag of Esmeraldas.

1971 Litho. *Perf. 10½*

832 A258 50c pale yel & multi .25 .25
833 A258 1s sal & multi .25 .25
Nos. 832-833,C465-C469 (7) 3.50 2.00

1971, Sept. *Perf. 12½*

840 A259 1.30s blk & multi .25 .25
Nos. 840,C481-C482 (3) .75 .75

Visit of Pres. Salvador Allende of Chile, Aug. 24.

Ismael Pérez Pazmiño — A260

1971, Sept. 16 *Perf. 12x11½*

841 A260 1s grn & multi .25 .25
Nos. 841,C485-C486 (3) .85 .75

"El Universo," newspaper founded by Ismael Pérez Pazmiño, 50th anniv.

CARE Package — A261 Flags of Ecuador and Argentina — A262

1971-72 *Perf. 12½*

842 A261 30c lilac ('72) .25 .25
843 A261 40c emerald ('72) .25 .25
844 A261 50c blue .25 .25
845 A261 60c carmine .25 .25
846 A261 80c lt brn ('72) .25 .25
Nos. 842-846 (5) 1.25 1.25

25th anniversary of CARE, a US-Canadian Cooperative for American Relief Everywhere.

1972 *Perf. 11½*

847 A262 1s blk & multi .25 .25
Nos. 847,C491-C492 (3) 1.00 .80

Visit of Lt. Gen. Alejandro Agustin Lanusse, president of Argentina, Jan. 25.

Jesus Giving Keys to St. Peter, by Miguel de Santiago A263

Ecuadorian Paintings: 1.10s, Virgin of Mercy, Quito School. 2s, Virgin Mary, by Manuel Samaniego.

1972, Apr. 24 Litho. *Perf. 14x13½*

848 A263 50c black & multi .25 .25
849 A263 1.10s black & multi .35 .30
850 A263 2s black & multi .55 .50
a. Souvenir sheet of 3 2.50 2.50
Nos. 848-850,C494-C495 (5) 2.60 1.95

No. 850a contains 3 imperf. stamps similar to Nos. 848-850.

1972, May 4

Ecuadorian Statues: 50c, Our Lady of Sorrow, by Caspicara. 1.10s, Nativity, Quito School, horiz. 2s, Virgin of Quito, anonymous.

851 A263 50c blk & multi .25 .25
852 A263 1.10s blk & multi .35 .35
853 A263 2s blk & multi .50 .50
a. Souv. sheet of 3 2.90 2.40
Nos. 851-853,C496-C497 (5) 2.45 2.00

Letters of "Ecuador" 3mm high on Nos. 851-853, 7mm high on Nos. 848-850. No. 853a contains 3 imperf. stamps similar to Nos. 851-853.

A264

Designs: 30c, Gen. Juan Ignacio Pareja. 40c, Juan José Flores. 50c, Leon de Febres Cordero. 60c, Ignacio Torres. 70c, Francisco de Paula Santander. 1s, José M. Cordova.

1972, May 24 *Perf. 12½*

854 A264 30c blue & multi .25 .25
855 A264 40c blue & multi .25 .25
856 A264 50c blue & multi .25 .25
857 A264 60c blue & multi .25 .25
858 A264 70c blue & multi .25 .25
859 A264 1s blue & multi .25 .25
Nos. 854-859,C498-C503 (12) 5.90 4.10

Sesquicentennial of the Battle of Pichincha and the liberation of Quito.

A265

Designs: 2s, Woman Wearing Poncho. 3s, Striped poncho. 5s, Embroidered poncho. 10s, Metal vase.

1972, July Photo. *Perf. 13*

860 A265 2s multicolored .25 .25
861 A265 3s multicolored .50 .25
862 A265 5s multicolored .65 .40
863 A265 10s dp blue & multi 1.40 .90
a. Souvenir sheet of 4 4.00 4.00
Nos. 860-863,C504-C507 (8) 5.75 3.60

Handicraft of Ecuador. No. 863a contains 4 imperf. stamps similar to Nos. 860-863.

Sucre Statue, Santo Domingo — A266 Radar Station — A267

1.80s, San Agustin Convent. 2.30s, Plaza de la Independencia. 2.50s, Bolivar statue, La Alameda. 4.75s, Chapel door.

1972, Dec. 6 Litho. *Perf. 11½*

864 A266 1.20s yel & multi .25 .25
865 A266 1.80s yel & multi .25 .25
866 A266 2.30s yel & multi .30 .25
867 A266 2.50s yel & multi .45 .25
868 A266 4.75s yel & multi .60 .30
Nos. 864-868,C518-C524 (12) 6.00 3.95

Sesquicentennial of the Battle of Pichincha.

1973, Apr. 5 Wmk. 367

869 A267 1s multicolored .35 .25

Inauguration of earth telecommunications station, Oct. 19, 1972.

Blue-footed Boobies A268

Wmk. 367, Unwmkd. (#872)

1973 Litho. *Perf. 11½x12*

870 A268 30c shown .55 .25
871 A268 40c Blue-faced booby .55 .25
872 A268 50c Oyster-catcher .55 .25
873 A268 60c California sea lions 1.10 .25
874 A268 70c Galapagos giant tortoise 1.25 .25
875 A268 1s California sea lion 1.75 .25
Nos. 870-875,C527-C528 (8) 9.95 2.00

Elevation of Galapagos Islands to a province of Ecuador.

Issue dates: 50c, Oct. 3; others Aug. 16.

Black-chinned Mountain Tanager — A269

Birds of Ecuador: 2s, Moriche oriole. 3s, Toucan barbet, vert. 5s, Masked crimson tanager, vert. 10s, Blue-necked tanager, vert.

Perf. 11x11½, 11½x11

1973, Dec. 6 Litho. Unwmk.

876 A269 1s brick red & multi .65 .25
877 A269 2s lt blue & multi 1.10 .25
878 A269 3s lt green & multi 1.10 .25
879 A269 5s pale lilac & multi 2.40 .65
880 A269 10s pale yel grn & multi 4.75 1.40
Nos. 876-880 (5) 10.00 2.80

Two souvenir sheets exist: one contains 2 imperf. stamps similar to Nos. 876-877 with yellow margin and black inscription; the other 3 stamps similar to Nos. 878-880; gray margin and black inscription including "Aereo." Both sheets dated "1972." Size: 143x84mm. Value, each $9.

Marco T. Varea, Botanist — A270

Portraits: 60c, Pio Jaramillo Alvarado, writer. 70c, Prof. Luciano Andrade M. No. 883, Marco T. Varea, botanist. No. 884, Dr. Juan Modesto Carbo Noboa, medical researcher. No. 885, Alfredo J. Valenzuela. No. 886, Capt. Edmundo Chiriboga G. 1.20s, Francisco Campos R., scientist. 1.80s, Luis Vernaza Lazarte, philanthropist.

1974 Unwmk. *Perf. 12x11½*

881 A270 60c crimson rose .35 .25
882 A270 70c lilac .35 .25
883 A270 1s ultra .25 .25
884 A270 1s orange .25 .25
885 A270 1s emerald .25 .25
886 A270 1s brown .25 .25
887 A270 1.20s apple green .35 .25
889 A270 1.80s lt blue .40 .25
Nos. 881-889 (8) 2.45 2.00

Arcade A271

Designs: 30c, Monastery, entrance. 40c, Church. 50c, View of Church through gate, vert. 60c, Chapel, vert. 70c, Church and cemetery, vert.

Perf. 11½x12, 12x11½

1975, Feb. 4 Litho.

896 A271 20c yellow & multi .30 .25
897 A271 30c yellow & multi .30 .25
898 A271 40c yellow & multi .30 .25
899 A271 50c yellow & multi .30 .25
900 A271 60c yellow & multi .30 .25
901 A271 70c yellow & multi .30 .25
Nos. 896-901 (6) 1.80 1.50

Colonial Monastery, Tilipulo, Cotopaxi Province.

Angel Polibio Chaves, Founder of Bolivar Province — A272

Portrait: No. 903, Emilio Estrada Ycaza (1916-1961), archeologist.

1975 Litho. *Perf. 12x11½*

902 A272 80c violet bl & lt bl .25 .25
903 A272 80c vermilion & pink .25 .25

Issue dates: No. 902, 2/21; No. 903, 3/25.

R. Rodriguez Palacios and A. Duran Quintero — A273

"Woman of Action" — A274

1975, Apr. 1 Litho. *Perf. 12x11½*

910	A273 1s multicolored	.25	.25
	Nos. 910,C547-C548 (3)	.85	.75

Meeting of the Ministers for Public Works of Ecuador and Colombia, July 27, 1973.

1975, June

Design: No. 912, "Woman of Peace."

911	A274 1s yellow & multi	.35	.25
912	A274 1s blue & multi	.45	.25

International Women's Year 1975.

Planes, Soldier and Ship — A275

1975, July 9 *Perf. 11½x12*

913	A275 2s multicolored	.40	.25

3 years of Natl. Revolutionary Government.

Hurdling — A276

Designs: Modern sports drawn Inca style.

1975, Sept. 11 Litho. *Perf. 11½*

914	A276 20c shown	.50	.35
915	A276 20c Chess	.50	.35
916	A276 30c Basketball	.50	.35
917	A276 30c Boxing	.50	.35
918	A276 40c Bicycling	.50	.35
919	A276 40c Steeplechase	.50	.35
920	A276 50c Soccer	.50	.35
921	A276 50c Fencing	.50	.35
922	A276 60c Golf	.50	.35
923	A276 60c Vaulting	.50	.35
924	A276 70c Judo (standing)	.50	.35
925	A276 70c Wrestling	.50	.35
926	A276 80c Swimming	.50	.35
927	A276 80c Weight lifting	.50	.35
928	A276 1s Table Tennis	.50	.35
929	A276 1s Paddle ball	.50	.35
	Nos. 914-929,C554-C558 (21)	11.35	6.85

3rd Ecuadorian Games.

Genciana A277

Designs: Ecuadorian plants.

Perf. 12x11½, 11½x12

1975, Nov. 18 Litho.

930	A277 20c Orchid, vert	.25	.25
931	A277 30c shown	.25	.25
932	A277 40c Bromeliaceae cactacceae, vert	.35	.25
933	A277 50c Orchid	.35	.25
934	A277 60c Orchid	.45	.25
935	A277 80c Flowering cactus	.45	.25
936	A277 1s Orchid	.75	.25
	Nos. 930-936,C559-C563 (12)	7.20	3.95

Venus, Chorrera Culture — A278

Female Mask, Tolita Culture — A279

Designs: 30c, Venus, Valdivia Culture. 40c, Seated man, Chorrera Culture. 50c, Man with poncho, Panzaleo Culture (late). 60c, Mythical head, Cashaloma Culture. 80c, Musician, Tolita Culture. No. 943, Chief Priest, Mantefia Culture. No. 945, Ornament, Tolita Culture. No. 946, Angry mask, Tolita Culture.

1976, Feb. 12 Litho. *Perf. 11½*

937	A278 20c multicolored	.40	.25
938	A278 30c multicolored	.40	.25
939	A278 40c multicolored	.40	.25
940	A278 50c multicolored	.40	.25
941	A278 60c multicolored	.40	.25
942	A278 80c multicolored	.40	.25
943	A278 1s multicolored	.40	.25
944	A279 1s multicolored	.40	.25
945	A279 1s multicolored	.40	.25
946	A279 1s multicolored	.40	.25
	Nos. 937-946,C568-C572 (15)	7.65	4.35

Archaeological artifacts.

Strawberries A280

Carlos Amable Ortiz (1859-1937) A281

1976, Mar. 30

947	A280 1s blue & multi	.35	.25
	Nos. 947,C573-C574 (3)	1.55	.90

25th Flower and Fruit Festival, Ambato.

1976, Mar. 15 Litho. *Perf. 11½*

No. 949, Sixto Maria Duran (1875-1947). No. 950, Segundo Cueva Celi (1901-1969). No. 951, Cristobal Ojeda Davila (1910-1952). No. 952, Luis Alberto Valencia (1918-1970).

948	A281 1s ver & multi	.35	.25
949	A281 1s orange & multi	.35	.25
950	A281 1s lt green & multi	.35	.25
951	A281 1s blue & multi	.35	.25
952	A281 1s lt brn & multi	.35	.25
	Nos. 948-952 (5)	1.75	1.25

Ecuadorian composers and musicians.

Institute Emblem A282

1977, Aug. 15 Litho. *Perf. 11½x12*

953	A282 2s multicolored	.35	.25

11th General Assembly of Pan-American Institute of Geography and History, Quito, Aug. 15-30. See Nos. C597-C597a.

Hands Holding Rotary Emblem A283

1977, Aug. 31 Litho. *Perf. 12*

954	A283 1s multicolored	.25	.25
955	A283 2s multicolored	.45	.25

Souvenir Sheets

Imperf

956	A283 5s multicolored	1.25	1.25
957	A283 10s multicolored	1.50	1.50

Rotary Club of Guayaquil, 50th anniv.

José Peralta — A284

Design: 2.40s, Peralta statue.

1977 Litho. *Perf. 11½*

958	A284 1.80s multi	.25	.25
959	A284 2.40s multi	.25	.25
	Nos. 958-959,C609 (3)	.90	.75

José Peralta (1855-1937), writer.

Blue-faced Booby A285

Galapagos Birds: 1.80s, Red-footed booby. 2.40s, Blue-footed boobies. 3.40s, Gull. 4.40s, Galapagos hawk. 5.40s, Map of Galapagos Islands and boobies, vert.

Perf. 11½x12, 12x11½

1977, Nov. 29 Litho.

960	A285 1.20s multi	.45	.25
961	A285 1.80s multi	.60	.25
962	A285 2.40s multi	1.00	.25
963	A285 3.40s multi	1.40	.25
964	A285 4.40s multi	2.10	.30
965	A285 5.40s multi	2.75	.30
	Nos. 960-965 (6)	8.30	1.60

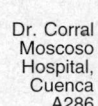

Dr. Corral Moscoso Hospital, Cuenca A286

1978, Apr. 12 Litho. *Perf. 11½x12*

966	A286 3s multicolored	.30	.25
	Nos. 966,C613-C614 (3)	1.95	1.00

Inauguration (in 1977) of Dr. Vicente Corral Moscoso Regional Hospital, Cuenca.

Surveyor Plane over Ecuador — A287

Latin-American Lions Emblem — A288

1978, Apr. 12 Litho. *Perf. 11½*

967	A287 6s multicolored	.75	.35
	Nos. 967,C619-C620 (3)	3.60	2.65

Military Geographical Institute, 50th anniv.

1978, May 24

968	A288 3s multi	.60	.25
969	A288 4.20s multi	.90	.25
	Nos. 968-969,C621-C623 (5)	5.65	2.40

7th meeting of Latin American Lions, Jan. 25-29.

70th Anniversary Emblem — A289

1978, Sept. Litho. *Perf. 11½*

970	A289 4.20s gray & multi	.55	.30

70th anniversary of Filanbanco (Philanthropic Bank). See No. C626.

Goalmouth and Net — A290

Designs: 1.80s, "Gauchito" and Games emblem, vert. 4.40s, "Gauchito," vert.

1978, Nov. 1 Litho. *Perf. 12*

971	A290 1.20s multi	.25	.25
972	A290 1.80s multi	.25	.25
973	A290 4.40s multi	.65	.25
	Nos. 971-973,C627-C629 (6)	3.35	2.05

11th World Cup Soccer Championship, Argentina, June 1-25.

Symbols for Male and Female — A291

1979, Feb. 15 Litho. *Perf. 12x11½*

974	A291 3.40s multi	.55	.30

Inter-American Women's Commission, 50th anniversary.

Emblem A292

1979, June 21 Litho. *Perf. 11½x12*

975 A292 4.40s multi .45 .30
976 A292 5.40s multi .55 .30

Ecuadorian Mortgage Bank, 16th anniv.

Street Scene, Quito — A293

Perf. 12x11½

1979, Aug. 3 Litho. Unwmk.

977 A293 3.40s multi .35 .25
Nos. 977,C651-C653 (4) 8.00 3.70

Natl. heritage: Quito & Galapagos Islands.

Jose Joaquin de Olmedo (1780-1847), Physician — A294

Chief Enriquillo, Dominican Republic — A295

1980, Apr. 29 Litho. *Perf. 12x11½*

978 A294 3s multi .35 .25
979 A294 5s multi .55 .40
Nos. 978-979,C662 (3) 2.15 1.30

First Pres. of Free State of Guayaquil, 1820.

Wmk. 367, Unwmkd. (#981-983)

1980, May 12

Indo-American Tribal Chiefs: 3.40s, Guaycaypuro, Venezuela. No. 982, Abayuba, Uruguay. No. 983, Atlacatl, Salvador.

980 A295 3s multi .60 .25
981 A295 3.40s multi .75 .30
982 A295 5s multi 1.50 .45
983 A295 5s multi 1.50 .45
Nos. 980-983,C663-C678 (20) 39.85 9.70

King Juan Carlos and Queen Sofia, Visit to Ecuador A296

Perf. 11½x12

1980, May 18 Unwmk.

984 A296 3.40s multi .55 .30

See No. C679.

Cofan Indian, Napo Province — A297

1980, June 10 Litho. *Perf. 12x11½*

985 A297 3s shown .45 .25
986 A297 3.40s Zuleta man, Imbabura .45 .25
987 A297 5s Chota woman, Imbabura .70 .30
Nos. 985-987,C681-C684 (7) 7.10 4.55

Basilica, Our Lady of Mercy Church, Quito A298

1980, July 7 Litho. *Perf. 11½*

988 A298 3.40s shown .45 .25
989 A298 3.40s Balcony .45 .25
989A A298 3.40s Dome and cupolas .45 .25

Sizes: 91x116mm, 116x91mm

Imperf

990 A298 5s multi 1.75 1.60
990A A298 5s multi, horiz. 1.75 1.60
990B A298 5s multi 1.75 1.60
Nos. 988-990B,C685-C691 (13) 15.60 10.05

Virgin of Mercy, patron saint of Ecuadorian armed forces. No. 990 contains designs of Nos. C686, C685, 989. No. 990A contains designs of Nos. C688, C691, C690. No. 990B contains designs of Nos. C689, C687, 989A, 988.

Olympic Torch and Rings — A299

Coronation of Virgin of Cisne, 50th Anniv. — A300

Perf. 12x11½

1980, July 19 Wmk. 395

991 A299 5s multi .70 .25
992 A299 7.60s multi .80 .30
Nos. 991-992,C695-C696 (4) 3.65 2.05

Souvenir Sheet

Imperf

993 A299 30s multi 6.75 6.75

22nd Summer Olympic Games, Moscow, July 19-Aug. 3.

No. 993 contains vignettes in designs of Nos. 991 and C695.

1980 Litho. *Perf. 11½*

994 A300 1.20s shown .25 .25
995 A300 3.40s Different statue .50 .30

J.J. Olmedo, Father de Velasco, Flags of Ecuador and Riobamba, Constitution A301

1980, Sept. 20 Litho. *Perf. 11½*

996 A301 3.40s multi .25 .25
997 A301 5s multi .70 .40
Nos. 996-997,C700-C701 (4) 2.60 1.35

Souvenir Sheet

Imperf

998 A301 30s multi 3.00 3.00

Constitutional Assembly of Riobamba sesquicentennial. No. 998 contains vignettes in designs of #996-997.

Young Indian Girl — A302

Perf. 12x11½

1980, Oct. 9 Litho. Wmk. 395

999 A302 1.20s multi .25 .25
1000 A302 3.40s multi .50 .25
Nos. 999-1000,C703-C704 (4) 2.85 1.45

Democratic government, 1st anniversary.

OPEC Emblem A303

1980, Nov. 8 *Perf. 11½x12*

1001 A303 3.40s multi .50 .25

20th anniversary of OPEC. See No. C706.

Decorative Hedges, Capitol Gardens, Carchi A304

1980, Nov. 21 *Perf. 13*

1002 A304 3s multi .45 .25
Nos. 1002,C707-C708 (3) 3.60 1.55

Carchi province centennial.

Cattleya Maxima A305

Orchids: 3s, Comparattia speciosa. 3.40s, Cattleya iricolor.

1980, Nov. 22 *Perf. 11½x12*

1003 A305 1.20s shown .75 .25
1004 A305 3s multicolored 1.00 .30
1005 A305 3.40s multicolored 1.10 .35
Nos. 1003-1005,C709-C712 (7) 21.60 5.20

Souvenir Sheet

Imperf

1006 A305 20s multi 14.00 10.00

No. 1006 contains vignettes in designs of Nos. 1003-1005.

Pope John Paul II and Children — A306

1980, Dec. 27 *Perf. 12*

1007 A306 3.40s multi .60 .30
Nos. 1007,C715-C716 (3) 2.85 1.40

Christmas and visit of Pope John Paul II.

Carlos and Jorge Mantilla Ortega, Editors of El Comercio — A307

El Comercio Newspaper, 75th Anniv.: 3.40s, Editors Cesar & Carlos Mantilla Jacome.

1981, Jan. 6

1008 A307 2s multi .30 .25
1009 A307 3.40s multi .50 .25

Soldier on Map of Ecuador A308

1981, Mar. 10 Litho. *Perf. 13*

1010 A308 3.40s shown .30 .25
1011 A308 3.40s Pres. Roldos .30 .25
a. Pair, #1010-1011 1.40 .90

National defense.

Theodore E. Gildred and Ecuador I A309

1981, Mar. 31 Litho. *Perf. 13*

1012 A309 2s lt bl & blk .35 .25

Ecuador-US flight, 50th anniv.

A310 A311

1981, Apr. 10

1013 A310 2s multi .45 .25

Octavio Cordero Palacios (1870-1930), humanist.

1981 Litho. *Perf. 13*

1014 A311 2s multi .30 .30
Nos. 1014,C721-C722 (3) 3.30 1.85

Radio station HCJB, 50th anniv.

Virgin of Dolorosa A312

1981, Apr. 30 Litho. *Perf. 12*

1015 A312 2s shown .30 .25
1016 A312 2s San Gabriel College Church .30 .25

Miracle of the painting of the Virgin of Dolorosa at San Gabriel College, 75th anniv.

Dr. Rafael Mendoza Aviles Bridge Inauguration A313

1981, July 25 *Perf. 13*

1017 A313 2s multi .45 .25

Pablo Picasso (1881-1973), Painter — A313a

1981, Oct. 26 **Litho.** ***Imperf.***

1017A A313a 20s multi 2.75 2.75
Nos. 1017A,C728-C731 (5) 9.30 7.50

No. 1017A contains design of No. C728, additional portrait.

World Food Day — A314

1981, Dec. 31 **Litho.** ***Perf. 13½x13***

1018 A314 5s multi .60 .25

See No. C732

Transnave Shipping Co. 10th Anniv. — A315

Intl. Year of the Disabled — A316

1982, Jan. 21 **Litho.** ***Perf. 13***

1019 A315 3.50s Freighter Isla Salango .60 .25

1982, Feb. 25

1020 A316 3.40s Man in wheelchair .35 .25
Nos. 1020,C733-C734 (3) 1.95 1.10

Arch — A317

1982, May **Litho.** ***Perf. 13***

1021 A317 2s shown .30 .25
1022 A317 3s Houses .45 .25

Miniature Sheet

Perf. 12½ on 2 Sides

1023 Sheet of 4, 18th cent. map of Quito 4.50 3.50
a.-d. A317 6s multi .90 .50

QUITEX '82, 4th Natl. Stamp Exhib., Quito, Apr. 16-22. No. 1023 contains 4 48x31mm stamps.

Juan Montalvo Birth Sesqui. — A318

1982 ***Perf. 13***

1024 A318 2s Portrait .35 .25
1025 A318 3s Mausoleum .35 .25
Nos. 1024-1025,C735 (3) 1.95 1.15

American Air Forces Cooperation System — A319

1982

1026 A319 5s Emblem .55 .35

4th World Swimming Champ., Guayaquil A320

1982, July 30

1027 A320 1.80s Stadium .30 .25
1028 A320 3.40s Water polo .35 .25
Nos. 1027-1028,C736-C737 (4) 2.85 1.55

A321

A322

1982, Dec. **Litho.** ***Perf. 13***

1029 A321 5.40s shown .35 .25
1030 A321 6s Statue .45 .25

Juan L. Mera (1832-?), Writer, by Victor Mideros.

1983, Mar. 28 **Litho.** ***Perf. 13***

1031 A322 2s multi .45 .25

St. Teresa of Jesus of Avila (1515-82).

Sea Lions A323

Flamingoes A324

1983, June 17 **Litho.** ***Perf. 13***

1032 A323 3s multi 1.40 .25
1033 A324 5s multi 2.25 .25

Ecuadorian rule over Galapagos Islds., sesqui. (3s); Charles Darwin (1809-1882).

Pres. Rocafuerte A325

Simon Bolivar A326

Perf. 13x13½

1983, Aug. 26 **Litho.** **Wmk. 395**

1034 A325 5s Statue .25 .25
1035 A325 20s Portrait .85 .35
1036 A326 20s Portrait .85 .35
Nos. 1034-1036 (3) 1.95 .95

Vicente Rocafuerte Bejarano, president, 1833-39 (Nos. 1034-1035).

A327

A328

1983, Sept. 3

1037 A327 5s River .70 .25
1038 A327 10s Dam 1.10 .85

Size: 110x89mm

Imperf

1039 A327 20s Dam, river 3.50 2.50
Nos. 1037-1039 (3) 5.30 3.60

Paute hydroelectric plant opening. No. 1039 is airmail.

Wmk. 395

1983, Oct. 11 **Litho.** ***Perf. 13***

1040 A328 2s multi .45 .30

World Communication Year.

A329

A330

1983, Sept. **Litho.** ***Perf. 13***

1041 A329 3s multi .45 .30

Cent. of Bolivar and El Oro Provinces (1984).

1984, Mar. **Litho.** ***Perf. 13***

1042 A330 15s Engraving .55 .45

Atahualpa (1497-1529), last Incan ruler.

A331

Christmas 1983 — A331a

Creche figures.

Perf. 13½x13, 13x13½

1984, July 7 **Litho.**

1043 A331 5s Jesus & the teachers .30 .25
1044 A331 5s Three kings .30 .25
1045 A331 5s Holy Family .30 .25
1046 A331a 6s Priest .30 .25
Nos. 1043-1046 (4) 1.20 1.00

Foreign Policy of Pres. Hurtado A332

State visits.

1984, July 10 ***Perf. 13½x13***

1047 A332 8s Brazil .35 .25
1048 A332 9s PRC .40 .25
1049 A332 24s UN 1.10 .75
1050 A332 28s US 1.40 .80
1051 A332 29s Venezuela 1.40 .80
1052 A332 37s Latin American Economic Conf., Quito 1.75 1.25
Nos. 1047-1052 (6) 6.40 4.10

Miguel Diaz Cueva (1884-1942), Lawyer A333

1984, Aug. 8 **Litho.** ***Perf. 13½x13***

1053 A333 10s multicolored .75 .30

1984 Winter Olympics A334

Manned Flight Bicentenary A335

Perf. 13x13½, 12x11½ (6s)

1984, Aug. 15

1054 A334 2s Emblem .35 .25
1055 A334 4s Ice skating .35 .25
1056 A334 6s Skating, diff. .35 .25
1057 A334 10s Skiing .65 .25
Nos. 1054-1057 (4) 1.70 1.00

Size: 90x100mm

1057A A334 20s Figure skating 40.00 17.50

1984, Aug. 15 ***Perf. 13x13½***

1058 A335 3s Montgolfier .25 .25
1059 A335 6s Charlier's balloon, Paris, 1789 .50 .25

Souvenir Sheet

1060 A335 20s Graf Zeppelin, Montgolfier 2.50 1.50

No. 1060 is airmail and contains one imperf. stamp (50x37mm).

SAN MATEO '83, Esmeraldas A336

1984 **Litho.** ***Perf. 13***

1061 A336 8s La Marimba folk dance 1.75 .25

Size: 89x110mm

Imperf

1061A A336 15s La Marimba, diff. 2.50 1.50

No. 1061A is airmail.

Jose Maria de Jesus Yerovi (b. 1824), 4th Archbishop of Quito — A337

1984

1062 A337 5s multi .45 .30

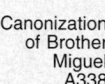

Canonization of Brother Miguel A338

1984 Litho. *Perf. 13*

1063 A338 9s Academy of Languages .35 .25
1064 A338 24s Vatican City, vert. 1.00 .60

Imperf

Size: 110x90mm

1065 A338 28s Home of Brother Miguel 3.50 1.50
Nos. 1063-1065 (3) 4.85 2.35

No. 1065, airmail, has black control number.

State Visit of Pope John Paul II — A339

Beatification of Mercedes de Jesus Molina — A340

1985, Jan. 23 Litho. *Perf. 13x13½*

1066 A339 1.60s Papal arms .85 .25
1067 A339 5s Blessing crowd .85 .25
1068 A339 9s World map, itinerary .85 .25
1069 A339 28s Pope waving 2.25 .40
1070 A339 29s Portrait 2.50 .40

Size: 90x109mm

Imperf

1071 A339 30s Pope holding crosier 8.00 6.00
Nos. 1066-1071 (6) 15.30 7.55

1985, Jan. 23

Paintings, sculpture.

1072 A340 1.60s Portrait .30 .25
1073 A340 5s Czestochowa Madonna .30 .25
1074 A340 9s Alborada Madonna .50 .25

Size: 90x110mm

Imperf

1075 A340 20s Mercedes de Jesus, children 3.00 3.00
Nos. 1072-1075 (4) 4.10 3.75

Visit of Pope John Paul II, birth bimillennium of the Virgin Mary.

Samuel Valarezo Delgado, Naturalist, Politician — A341

1985, Feb.

1076 A341 2s Bird .25 .25
1077 A341 3s Swordfish, tuna .25 .25
1078 A341 6s Portrait .40 .25
Nos. 1076-1078 (3) .90 .75

ESPANA '84, Madrid A342

1985, Apr. 25 *Perf. 13½x13*

1079 A342 6s Emblem .30 .25
1080 A342 10s Spanish royal family .50 .25

Size: 110x90mm

Imperf

1081 A342 15s Retiro Park, exhibition site 1.50 1.50

Dr. Pio Jaramillo Alvarado (1884-1968), Historian A343

1985, May 17

1082 A343 6s multi .35 .25

Ingenio Valdez Sugar Refinery — A344

Designs: 50s, Sugar cane, emblem. 100s, Rafael Valdez Cervantes, founder.

1985, June Litho. *Perf. 13*

1082A A344 50s multi 1.10 .50
1082B A344 100s multi 2.40 1.00

Size: 110x90mm

Imperf

1083 A344 30s multi 1.50 1.50
Nos. 1082A-1083 (3) 5.00 3.00

Chamber of Commerce, 10th Anniv. A345

50s, Natl. and American Statues of Liberty.

1985, Aug. 15 *Perf. 13½x13*

1084 A345 24s multicolored .80 .30
1085 A345 28s multicolored .90 .45

Size: 110x90mm

Imperf

1086 A345 50s multicolored 2.25 2.25
Nos. 1084-1086 (3) 3.95 3.00

Natl. Philatelic Assoc., AFE, 50th Anniv. — A346

1985, Aug. 25 *Perf. 12*

1087 A346 25s AFE emblem .75 .45
1088 A346 30s No. 357, horiz. 1.10 .50

Guayaquil Fire Dept., 150th Anniv. A347

1985, Oct. 10 *Perf. 13½x13*

1089 A347 6s Steam fire pump, 1882 .45 .25
1090 A347 10s Fire Wagon, 1899 .75 .25
1091 A347 20s Anniv. emblem, natl. flag 1.50 .75
Nos. 1089-1091 (3) 2.70 1.25

Natl. Infant Survival Campaign — A348

1985, Oct. *Perf. 13x13½*

1092 A348 10s Boy, girl, tree .55 .30

1st Natl. Phil. Cong., Quito, Nov. 25-28 — A349

20th cent. illustrations, natl. cultural collection: 5s, Supreme Court, Quito, by J. M. Roura. 10s, Riobamba Cathedral, by O. Munaz. 15s, House of 100 Windows, by J. M. Roura, horiz. 20s, Rural cottage near Cuenca, by J. M. Roura.

No. 1097: a, Stampless cover, 1779, Riobamba. b, Hand press, 1864, Quito. c, Postrider, 1880, Cuenca. d, Monoplane, 1st airmail flight, 1919, Guayaquil.

1985, Nov. *Perf. 13x13½, 13½x13*

1093 A349 5s multi .25 .25
1094 A349 10s multi .55 .25
1095 A349 15s multi .65 .40
1096 A349 20s multi .95 .50
Nos. 1093-1096 (4) 2.40 1.40

Souvenir Sheet

1097 Sheet of 4 1.25 1.25
a.-d. A349 5s, any single .25 .25

AFE, 50th anniv. No. 1097 contains 53x42mm stamps, perf. 13x12½ on 2 sides.

10th Bolivarian Games, Cuenca A350

1985, Nov. *Perf. 13½x13*

1098 A350 10s Boxing .45 .25
1099 A350 25s Women's gymnastics .75 .30
1100 A350 30s Discus .90 .45
Nos. 1098-1100 (3) 2.10 1.00

BAE Calderon, Navy Cent. — A351

Military anniv.: No. 1102, Fighter plane, Air Force 65th anniv. No. 1103, Army & paratroops emblems, Special Forces 30th anniv.

1985, Dec. *Perf. 13x13½*

1101 A351 10s multi .50 .30
1102 A351 10s multi .50 .30
1103 A351 10s multi .50 .30
Nos. 1101-1103 (3) 1.50 .90

UN, 40th Anniv. A352

1985, Oct. Litho. *Perf. 13*

1104 A352 10s UN flag .50 .30
1105 A352 20s Natl. flag .50 .30

Size: 110x90mm

Imperf

1106 A352 50s UN Building 1.50 1.50
Nos. 1104-1106 (3) 2.50 2.10

Christmas A353

Indigenous Flowers A354

1985, Nov.

1107 A353 5s Child riding donkey .25 .25
1108 A353 10s Baked goods .50 .30
1109 A353 15s Riding donkey, diff. .70 .50

Size: 90x110mm

Imperf

1110 A353 30s like 5s 1.75 1.50
Nos. 1107-1110 (4) 3.20 2.55

1986, Feb.

1111 A354 24s Embotrium grandiforum 1.00 .30
1112 A354 28s Topobea sp. 1.50 .30
1113 A354 29s Befaria resinosa mutis 2.00 .40

Size: 110x90mm

Imperf

1114 A354 15s multi 6.50 3.50
Nos. 1111-1114 (4) 11.00 4.50

No. 1114 contains designs of Nos. 1111, 1113, 1112; black control number.

Discovery of the Galapagos Islds., 450th Anniv. A355

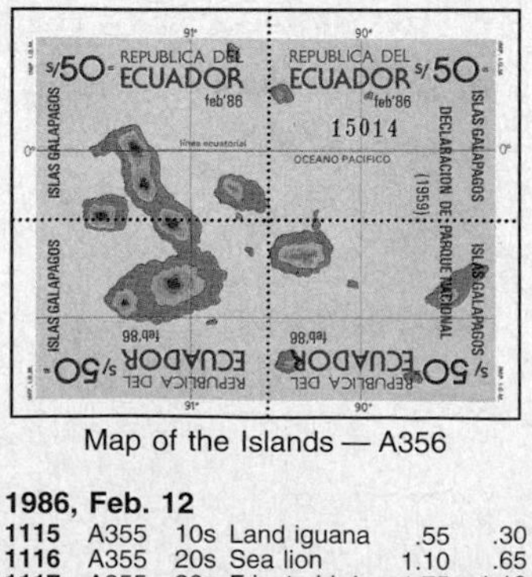

Map of the Islands — A356

1986, Feb. 12

1115 A355 10s Land iguana .55 .30
1116 A355 20s Sea lion 1.10 .65
1117 A355 30s Frigate birds 1.75 1.10
1118 A355 40s Penguins 2.25 1.50
1119 A355 50s Giant tortoise 2.75 1.75
1120 A355 100s Charles Darwin 5.50 3.75
1121 A355 200s Bishop Tomas de Berlenga, discoverer 11.00 7.00

Perf. 12½ on 2 Sides

1122 A356 Sheet of 4 13.00 13.00
a.-d. 50s, any single 1.75 1.75
Nos. 1115-1122 (8) 37.90 29.05

No. 1122 contains 53x42mm stamps.

Inter-American Development Bank, 25th Anniv. — A357

5s, Antonio Ortiz Mena, pres. 1971-88. 10s, Felipe Herrera, pres. 1960-71. 50s, Emblem.

1986, Mar. 6

1123 A357 5s multi .45 .25
1124 A357 10s multi .65 .25
1125 A357 50s multi 1.25 .80
Nos. 1123-1125 (3) 2.35 1.30

Guayaquil Tennis Club, 75th Anniv. A358

1986, Mar. 7

1126 A358 10s Emblem .55 .30
1127 A358 10s Francisco Segura Cano, vert. .55 .30
1128 A358 10s Andres Gomez Santos, vert. .55 .30
Nos. 1126-1128 (3) 1.65 .90

1986 World Cup Soccer Championships, Mexico — A359

1986, May 5

1129 A359 5s Shot .35 .25
1130 A359 10s Block .80 .25

An imperf. stamp exists picturing flags, player and emblem. Value $8.50.

Meeting of Presidents Cordero and Betancourt of Colombia, Feb. 1985 A360

1986 **Litho.** *Perf. 13½x13*

1131 A360 20s Presidents .55 .30
1132 A360 20s Embracing .55 .30

Exports A361

35s, No. 1137c, Shrimp. 40s, No. 1137b, Tuna. 45s, No. 1137a, Sardines. No. 1137d, MICIP emblem.

1986, Apr. 12

1133 A361 35s ultra & ver 1.10 .40
1134 A361 40s red & yel grn 1.10 .40
1135 A361 45s car & dk yel 1.25 .60

Perf. 12½ on 2 Sides

1137 Sheet of 4 2.50 2.50
a.-d. A361 10s, any single .40 .40
Nos. 1133-1137 (4) 5.95 3.90

No. 1137 contains 4 53x42mm stamps.

A362

La Condamine's First Geodesic Mission, 250th Anniv. — A363

No. 1141a, Triangulation map for determining equatorial meridian, 1736. No. 1141b, Partial map of the Maranon & Amazon Rivers, by Samuel Fritz, 1743-1744. No. 1141c, Base of measurement, Yaruqui plains. No. 1141d, Caraburo & Dyambaru Pyramids near Quito. No. 1141 has a continuous design.

1986, July 10 **Litho.** *Perf. 13½x13*

1138 A362 10s La Condamine .45 .25
1139 A362 15s Maldonado .55 .30
1140 A362 20s Middle of the World, Quito .65 .30
Nos. 1138-1140 (3) 1.65 .85

Souvenir Sheet

Perf. 12½ on 2 Sides

1141 A363 Sheet of 4 3.25 3.25
a.-d. 10s any single .46 .45

Chambers of Commerce A364

1986 **Litho.** *Perf. 13½x13*

1142 A364 10s Pichincha .35 .25
1143 A364 10s Cuenca .35 .25
1144 A364 10s Guayaquil .35 .25
Nos. 1142-1144 (3) 1.05 .75

Civil Service and Communications Ministry, 57th Anniv. — A365

Organization emblems.

1986, Dec. **Litho.** *Perf. 13x13½*

1145 A365 5s State railway .25 .25
1146 A365 10s Post office .35 .25
1147 A365 15s Communications .65 .25
1148 A365 20s Ministry of Public Works .75 .55
Nos. 1145-1148 (4) 2.00 1.30

A366

A367

1987, Feb. 16 **Litho.** *Perf. 13x13½*

1149 A366 5s multi .45 .25

Chamber of Agriculture of the 1st Zone, 50th anniv.

Litho. & Typo.

1988, Jan. 6 *Perf. 13*

Col. Luis Vargas Torres (d. 1887): 50s, Portrait. No. 1151, Combat unit, c. 1885. No. 1152a, Torres & his mother, Delfina. No. 1152b, Letter to Delfina written by Torres during Imprisonment, 1882. No. 1152c, Arms of Ecuador & combat unit.

1150 A367 50s yel grn, blk & gold 1.25 .80
1151 A367 100s ver, gold & ultra 2.75 1.40

Size: 95x140mm

Perf. 12 on One or Two Sides

1152 Block of 3 8.25 8.25
a.-c. A367 100s any single 1.50 1.50
Nos. 1150-1152 (3) 12.25 10.45

Sizes: Nos. 1152a, 1152c, 95x28mm, No. 1152b, 95x83mm.

Founding of Guayaquil, 450th Anniv. A368

15s, Street in Las Penas. 30s, Rafael Mendoza Aviles Bridge. 40s, Francisco de Orellana (c. 1490-1546), Spanish explorer, founder, & reenactment of landing, 1538.

1988, Feb. 19 **Litho.** *Perf. 13*

1153 A368 15s multi, vert. .30 .25
1154 A368 30s multi .55 .25
1155 A368 40s multi .65 .25
Nos. 1153-1155 (3) 1.50 .75

Social Security Foundation (IESS), 60th Anniv. A369

1988, Mar. 11

1156 A369 50s shown .90 .55
1157 A369 100s multi, diff. 1.90 1.10

Dr. Pedro Moncayo y Esparza (1807-1888), Author, Politician A370

1988, Apr. 28 **Litho.** *Perf. 14x13½*

1158 A370 10s Yaguarcocha Lake .25 .25
1159 A370 15s shown .35 .25
1160 A370 20s Residence .35 .25

Size: 89x110mm

Imperf

1161 A370 100s Full-length portrait 1.50 1.50
Nos. 1158-1161 (4) 2.45 2.25

A371

Avianca Airlines, 60th Anniv. — A372

1988, May 12 **Litho.** *Perf. 14x13½*

1162 A371 10s Junkers F-13 .35 .25
1163 A371 20s Dornier Wal seaplane .35 .25
1164 A371 30s Ford 5AT trimotor .45 .25
1165 A371 40s Boeing 247-D .55 .25
1166 A371 50s Boeing 720-059B .65 .45
1167 A371 100s Douglas DC-3 1.50 .60
1168 A371 200s Boeing 727-200 2.75 1.50
1169 A371 300s Sikorsky S-38 4.75 2.00

Perf. 13½x14

1170 A372 500s shown 7.25 3.75
Nos. 1162-1170 (9) 18.60 9.30

San Gabriel College, 125th Anniv. A373

1988, July 25 **Litho.** *Perf. 14x13½*

1171 A373 15s Contemporary facility .25 .25
1172 A373 35s College entrance, 19th cent. .75 .30

A374

Military Geographical Institute, 60th Anniv. A375

1988, July 25 *Perf. 12½ on 2 Sides*

Size of No. 1173: 110x90mm

1173 A374 Block of 4 2.25 2.25
a.-d. 5s any single .30 .30

Perf. 13½

1174 A375 25s Planetarium .55 .30
1175 A375 50s Zeiss projector 1.00 .30
1176 A375 60s Anniv. emblem 1.25 .40
1177 A375 500s Creation, mural by E. Kingman 7.75 3.75
Nos. 1173-1177 (5) 12.80 7.00

In 1996 Nos. 1174, 1183, 1265 were surcharged 800s, 2600s 400s respectively. Only a few sets were sold to the public. The balance were sold by postal employees at greatly inflated prices.

Salesian Brothers in Ecuador, Cent. A376

Designs: 10s, St. John Bosco (1815-88), vert. 50s, 1st Salesian Cong. in Ecuador. 100s, Bosco, Salesian Brothers monument and Andes Mountains.

1988, July 29 **Litho.** *Perf. 13½*

1178 A376 10s multi .25 .25
1179 A376 50s multi 1.00 .40

Size: 89x110mm

Imperf

1180 A376 100s multi 2.75 1.60
Nos. 1178-1180 (3) 4.00 2.25

Francisco Coello, Founder — A377

Social Services Council, Guayaquil, Cent. — A378

Flag: a, Emblem (upper left portion). b, Emblem (upper right portion). c, Emblem (lower left portion) and "100 ANOS." d, Emblem (lower right portion) and "DE TRADICION DE FE, AMPARO Y ESPERANZA."

1988, Nov. 24 Litho. *Perf. 13½x14*

1181 A377 15s shown .25 .25
1182 A377 20s Eduardo Arosemena, 1st Director .30 .25
1183 A377 45s Emblem .65 .25

Size: 110x90mm

Perf. 12½ on 2 Sides

1184 A378 Block of 4 1.75 1.75
a.-d. 10s any single .25 .25
Nos. 1181-1184 (4) 2.95 2.50

For surcharge see note following No. 1177.

A379

Azuay Bank, 75th Anniv. — A380

Perf. 14x13½, 13½x14

1989, Mar. 1 Litho.

1185 A379 20s shown .30 .25
1186 A379 40s multi, vert. .40 .25

Size: 90x110mm

Imperf

1187 A380 500s shown 11.00 2.75
Nos. 1185-1187 (3) 11.70 3.25

1988 Summer Olympics, Seoul — A381

Character trademark demonstrating sports.

1989, Mar. 20 *Perf. 13½x14*

1188 A381 10s Running .30 .25
1189 A381 20s Boxing .30 .25
1190 A381 30s Cycling .50 .25
1191 A381 40s Shooting .50 .25
1192 A381 100s Diving 1.25 .65
1193 A381 200s Weight lifting 2.25 1.40
1194 A381 300s Tae kwon do 3.50 2.10

Size: 90x110mm

Imperf

1195 A381 200s Emblems 3.50 3.25
Nos. 1188-1195 (8) 12.10 8.40

RUMINAHUI '88 — A382

Designs: 50s, *Bird,* by Joaquin Tinta, vert. 70s, Matriz Church, Sangolqui. 300s, Monument to Ruminahui in Sangolqui, Pichincha.

Perf. 14x13½, 13½x14

1989, May 2 Litho. Wmk. 395

1196 A382 50s multi .90 .30
1197 A382 70s multi 1.25 .45

Size: 90x111mm

Imperf

1198 A382 300s multi 7.25 2.10
Nos. 1196-1198 (3) 9.40 2.85

Cantonization, 50th anniv.

Benjamin Carrion Mora, Educator A383

Perf. 13½x14, 14x13½

1989, May 10 Litho.

1199 A383 50s Portrait, vert. .45 .25
1200 A383 70s Loja landscape .65 .25
1201 A383 1000s University 10.50 5.25

Size: 110x90mm

Imperf

1202 A383 200s Portrait, diff. 2.00 2.00
Nos. 1199-1202 (4) 13.60 7.75

2nd Intl. Art Biennial A384

Prize-winning art: 40s, *The Gilded Frame,* by Myrna Baez. 70s, *Paraguay III,* by Carlos Colorabino, vert. 100s, Ordinance establishing the art exhibition. 180s, *Modulation 892,* by Julio Le Parc, vert.

Perf. 14x13½, 13½x14, Imperf. (100s)

1989, June 2 Litho.

Size of No. 1205: 110x90mm

1203 A384 40s multi .55 .25
1204 A384 70s multi 1.10 .25
1205 A384 100s multi 2.25 .75
1206 A384 180s multi 1.75 .95
Nos. 1203-1206 (4) 5.65 2.20

Guayaquil Chamber of Commerce, Cent. A385

Perf. 13½x14, 14x13½, Imperf. (No. 1208)

1989, June 20 Litho.

Size of No. 1208: 110x91mm

1207 A385 50s Founder Ignacio Molestina, vert. .85 .35
1208 A385 200s Flags 3.50 2.00
1209 A385 300s Headquarters 2.50 2.25
1210 A385 500s Flags, diff. 1.75 1.50
Nos. 1207-1210 (4) 8.60 6.10

French Revolution, Bicent. A386

20s, French natl. colors, anniv. emblem. 50s, Cathedral fresco. 100s, Rooster. 200s, Symbols of the revolution. 600s, Story board showing events of the revolution.

1989, July 11 *Perf. 13½x14, 14x13½*

1211 A386 20s multi, vert. .25 .25
1212 A386 50s multi .55 .25
1213 A386 100s multi, vert. .90 .45

Size: 90x110mm

Imperf

1214 A386 200s multi, vert. 1.75 1.75
1215 A386 600s multi, vert. 6.75 6.75
Nos. 1211-1215 (5) 10.20 9.45

A387

Ministry of Public Works and Communications A388

No. 1216a, MOP emblem, 2-lane roadway. No. 1216b, State railway emblem, train. No. 1216c, Postal service emblem, airmail cover. No. 1216d, Telecommunications (IETEL) emblem, wall telephone. No. 1217, MOP, IETEL, postal service & state railway emblems. 100s, IETEL emblem. 200s, MOP emblem.

1989, July 7 *Perf. 12½ on 2 Sides*

1216 A387 Block of 4 2.00 2.00
a.-d. 50s any single .40 .40

Perf. 13½x14

1217 A388 50s shown .45 .25
1218 A388 100s multi .90 .55
1219 A388 200s multi 1.90 1.10
Nos. 1216-1219 (4) 5.25 3.90

MOP, 60th anniv.; national communications, 105th anniv. (No. 1216d, 100s).

Natl. Red Cross, Intl. Red Cross and Red Crescent Societies, 125th Annivs. A389

1989, Sept. 14 Litho. *Perf. 13½*

1220 A389 10s Medical volunteer, vert. .25 .25
1221 A389 30s shown .25 .25
1222 A389 200s Two volunteers 2.00 .85
Nos. 1220-1222 (3) 2.50 1.35

Juan Montalvo (1832-1889), Writer A390

1989, Nov. 11 Litho. *Perf. 14x13½*

1223 A390 50s Mausoleum, Ambato .45 .25
1224 A390 100s Portrait (detail) 1.25 .65
1225 A390 200s Monument, Ambato 2.10 1.40

Size: 90x110mm

Imperf

1226 A390 200s Portrait 1.75 1.75
Nos. 1223-1226 (4) 5.55 4.05

America Issue A391

UPAE emblem and pre-Columbian pottery.

1990, Mar. 6 Litho. *Perf. 13½*

1227 A391 200s La Tolita incensory, vert. 2.10 1.25
1228 A391 300s Warrior (plate) 3.25 2.00

Dated 1989.

Dr. Luis Carlos Jaramillo Leon, Founder A392

No. 1233a, Dr. Leon. Nos. 1230, 1233b, Federico Malo Andrade, honorary president. 130s, No. 1233c, Roberto Crespo Toral, 1st president. 200s, Alfonso Jaramillo Leon, founder.

1990, Jan. 17 Litho. *Perf. 13½*

1229 A392 100s shown .90 .60
1230 A392 100s multicolored .90 .60
1231 A392 130s multicolored 1.25 .75
1232 A392 200s multicolored 1.75 1.25

Size: 91x38mm

Perf. 12½ Horiz. on 1 or 2 sides

1233 Block of 3 3.00 3.00
a.-c. A392 100s any single .50 .50
Nos. 1229-1233 (5) 7.80 6.20

Chamber of Commerce, 70th anniversary.

World Cup Soccer, Italy — A393

1990, July 12 Litho. *Perf. 13½*

1234 A393 100s shown .60 .25
1235 A393 200s Soccer player 1.25 .60
1236 A393 300s Map of Italy, trophy 1.90 .90

Imperf

Size: 110x90mm

1237 A393 200s Player, flags 1.75 1.75

Size: 60x90mm

1238 A393 300s World Cup Trophy 2.50 2.50
Nos. 1234-1238 (5) 8.00 6.00

Nos. 1235-1236, 1238 vert.

A394

1990, June 12 *Perf. 13½*

1239	A394	100s multi	.70	.25
1240	A394	200s Church tower, book	1.25	.60

College of St. Mariana, cent.

A395

Tourism: No. 100s, No. 1244c, Iguana. 200s, No. 1244b, La Compania Church, Quito. 300s, No. 1244a, Old man from Vilcabamba. No. 1244d, Locomotive.

1990, Sept. 7 **Litho.** *Perf. 13½*

1241	A395	100s multi	.85	.25
1242	A395	200s multi, vert.	1.75	.55
1243	A395	300s multi	2.50	.75

Size: 111x90mm

Perf. 12½ on 2 sides

1244	Block of 4	7.50	3.25
a.-d.	A395 100s any single	.35	.25
	Nos. 1241-1244 (4)	12.60	4.80

A396

National Census: 100s, No. 1248a, People and house. 200s, No. 1248b, Map. 300s, No. 1248c, Census breakdown, pencil.

1990, Sept. 1 *Perf. 13½*

1245	A396	100s multicolored	.60	.25
1246	A396	200s multicolored, horiz.	1.25	.55
1247	A396	300s multicolored	1.75	.75

Size: 109x88mm

Perf. 12½ on 2 sides

1248	Block of 3	1.90	1.90
a.-c.	A396 100s any single	.30	.30
	Nos. 1245-1248 (4)	5.50	3.45

A397

A398

1990, Nov. 2 **Litho.** *Perf. 14*

1249	A397	200s Flags	1.25	.55
1250	A397	300s shown	1.90	.75

Organization of Petroleum Exporting Countries (OPEC), 30th anniv.

1990, Oct. 31 *Perf. 13½x14*

1251	A398	200s Emblem	1.25	.55
1252	A398	300s Wooden parrots	1.90	.75

Size: 92x110mm

Imperf

1253	A398	200s Wooden parrots, diff.	2.10	2.10
		Nos. 1251-1253 (3)	5.25	3.40

Artisans' Organization, 25th anniv.

Flowers — A399

Wmk. 395

1990, Nov. 12 **Litho.** *Perf. 13½*

1254	A399	100s Sobralia	1.25	.25
1255	A399	100s Blakea, vert.	1.25	.25
1256	A399	100s Cattleya, vert.	1.25	.25
1257	A399	100s Loasa, vert.	1.25	.25
		Nos. 1254-1257 (4)	5.00	1.00

Discovery of America, 500th Anniv. (in 1992) A400

1990, Dec. 31 **Litho.** *Perf. 13½*

1258	A400	100s Ancient dwelling	.70	.25
1259	A400	200s Mangrove swamp	1.60	.35

Natl. Union of Journalists, 50th Anniv. A401

1991, Feb. 28

1260	A401	200s shown	1.10	.70
1261	A401	300s Eugenio Espejo, writer	1.75	.80
1262	A401	400s Union emblem	1.90	1.10
		Nos. 1260-1262 (3)	4.75	2.60

Radio Quito, 50th Anniv. A402

Designs: 200s, Man with microphone, vert. 500s, Family listening to radio.

1991, Apr. 10

1263	A402	200s multicolored	.85	.35
1264	A402	500s multicolored	1.75	.95

Dr. Pablo A. Suarez, Birth Cent. — A403

1991, Sept. 16 **Wmk. 395**

1265	A403	70s multicolored	.45	.25

Dated 1990.

For surcharge see note following No. 1177. Value $20.

America Issue A404

UPAEP emblem and: 200s, Columbus' ships. 500s, Columbus, landing in America.

1991, Oct. 18 **Litho.** *Perf. 13½x13*

1266	A404	200s multicolored	1.25	.65
1267	A404	500s multicolored	2.25	1.25

A405

A406

Designs: Cultural artifacts.

Wmk. 395

1991, Nov. 14 **Litho.** *Perf. 13½*

1268	A405	100s Cat censer	.50	.25
1269	A405	200s Statue of old man's head	1.00	.35
1270	A405	300s Zoomorphic statue	1.75	.60
		Nos. 1268-1270 (3)	3.25	1.20

Dated 1990. See No. 1291.

1991 *Perf. 13*

Design: 500s, Woman in profile.

1271	A406	300s shown	1.00	.55
1272	A406	500s multicolored	1.90	1.00

Day of Non-violence Toward Women.

Jacinto Jijon y Caamano, Archaeologist, Birth Cent. — A407

1991, Dec. 11 *Perf. 13½*

1273	A407	200s Portrait, vert.	.70	.35
1274	A407	300s shown	1.10	.55

Pres. Rodrigo Borja, Ecuador and Pres. Jaime Paz Zamora, Bolivia — A408

1991, Dec. 10 *Perf. 14x13½*

1275	A408	500s multicolored	2.00	1.00

Pres. Rodrigo Borja's Visit to the UN — A409

Wmk. 395

1992, Jan. 24 **Litho.** *Perf. 14*

1276	A409	100s multicolored	.40	.25
1277	A409	1000s Flags, world map	3.00	1.60

Battle of Jambeli, 50th Anniv. — A410

No. 1278, Gunboat Calderon and Capt. Raphael Moran Valverde. No. 1279, Dispatch boat Atahualpa and Ens. Victor Naranjo Fiallo. No. 1280, Valverde, Fiallo and ships.

1992, Apr. 7

1278	A410	300s multicolored	.55	.40
1279	A410	500s multicolored	1.25	.90

Size: 110x90mm

Imperf

1280	A410	500s multicolored	2.75	2.40
		Nos. 1278-1280 (3)	4.55	3.70

Galapagos Islands Wildlife — A411

Designs: No. 1281, Giant tortoise. No. 1282, Galapagos penguin, vert. No. 1283, Zalophus californianus, vert. No. 1284, Swallow-tailed gull. No. 1285, Fregata minor. No. 1286, Land iguana.

1992, Apr. 10 **Litho.** *Perf. 13½*

1281	A411	100s multicolored	1.75	.80
1282	A411	100s multicolored	1.75	.80
1283	A411	100s multicolored	1.75	.80
1284	A411	100s multicolored	1.75	.80
1285	A411	100s multicolored	1.75	.80
1286	A411	100s multicolored	1.75	.80
		Nos. 1281-1286 (6)	10.50	4.80

Vicente Rocafuerte National College, 150th Anniv. (in 1991) A412

Perf. 14x13½

1992, Apr. 29 **Litho.** **Wmk. 395**

1287	A412	200s shown	.85	.35
1288	A412	400s Vicente Rocafuerte	1.40	.65

Eloy Alfaro (1842-1912), President — A413

Designs: 300s, Portrait, vert.

Perf. 13½x14, 14x13½

1992, Aug. 26 **Litho.** **Wmk. 395**

1289	A413	300s multicolored	.90	.70
1290	A413	700s multicolored	1.60	1.00

Cultural Artifacts Type of 1991

1992, Sept. 6 **Litho.** *Perf. 13½*

1291	A405	400s Ceremonial mask	1.40	.75

Dated 1990.

Discovery of America, 500th Anniv. A414

Wmk. 395

1992, Oct. 15 **Litho.** *Perf. 13½*

1292	A414	200s Sailing ship	.75	.50
1293	A414	400s Columbus, map, vert.	1.40	.85

Andres F. Cordova (b. 1892)
A415

1992, Nov. 17 Litho. *Perf. 13½*
1294 A415 300s multicolored 1.10 .60

Beatification of Narcisa of Jesus — A416

1992, Nov. 30 *Perf. 13½*
1295 A416 100s multicolored .45 .30

A417 A418

Christmas: 300s, Infant Jesus of Saqueo, 18th cent. 600s, Stable scene, Infant Jesus asleep on hay.

1992, Dec. 14 *Perf. 13½*
1296 A417 300s multicolored 1.10 .60
1297 A417 600s multicolored 1.90 1.25

1992, Dec. 29
1298 A418 200s multicolored .80 .45

Father Juan de Velasco, Death Bicent.

Frogs — A419

A420

Perf. 13½x14
1993, Jan. 28 Litho. Wmk. 395
1299 A419 300s Agalychnis spurelli .85 .35
1300 A419 300s Atelopus bomolochos .85 .35
1301 A419 600s Gastrotheca plumbea 2.00 .90
1302 A419 600s Hyla picturata 2.00 .90
1303 A419 900s Dendrobates sp. 2.75 1.40
1304 A419 900s Sphae-norhyncus lacteus 2.75 1.40
Nos. 1299-1304 (6) 11.20 5.30

1993, Feb. 16 Litho. *Perf. 13x13½*
1305 A420 300s blue .80 .25

J. Roberto Paez, (1893-1983), co-founder of social security.

A421 A422

1993, Mar. 16 *Perf. 13½x14*
1306 A421 500s No. 168 1.50 .55

Francisco Robles (1811-93).

Perf. 13½x14
1993, Mar. 25 Litho. Wmk. 395
1307 A422 300s Natl. police 1.00 .60

Pres. Jose Maria Velasco Ibarra (1893-1979)
A423

Perf. 14x13½
1993, Mar. 31 Litho. Wmk. 395
1308 A423 500s multicolored 1.50 .55

Insects — A424

Wmk. 395
1993, May 27 Litho. *Perf. 13½*
1309 A424 150s Fulgora laternaria .75 .25
1310 A424 200s Semiotus ligneus 1.00 .25
1311 A424 300s Taeniotes pulverulenta 1.50 .45
1312 A424 400s Danaus plexippus 2.00 .60
1313 A424 600s Erotylus onaga 3.00 .95
1314 A424 700s Xylocopa darwini 3.25 1.10
Nos. 1309-1314 (6) 11.50 3.60

A425

Wmk. 395
1993, May 31 Litho. *Perf. 13½*
1315 A425 1000s multicolored 3.00 1.50

Pedro Fermin Cevallos Villacreces (1812-93), historian and founder of Academy of Language.

First Latin-American Children's Peace Assembly, Quito — A426

1993, June 7
1316 A426 300s multicolored .80 .45

Juan Benigno Vela Hervas (1843-97), Jurist
A427

Perf. 13x13½
1993, July 8 Litho. Wmk. 395
1317 A427 2000s multicolored 5.00 3.00

Guillermo Bustamante, Birth Cent.
A428

1993, Sept. 23 *Perf. 13½*
1318 A428 1500s multicolored 4.00 1.75

University of Ecuador School of Medicine, 300th Anniv.
A429

Perf. 14x13½
1993, Sept. 7 Litho. Wmk. 395
1319 A429 300s multicolored .80 .45

Maldonado-La Condamine Amazon Expedition, 250th Anniv. — A430

Designs: 150s, Cinchona cordifolia. 200s, Pedro V. Maldonado, 1500s, Charles La Condamine (1701-74), explorer.

1993, Aug. 20
1320 A430 150s multicolored .35 .25
1321 A430 200s multicolored .50 .25
1322 A430 1500s multicolored 4.25 2.10
Nos. 1320-1322 (3) 5.10 2.60

A431 A432

Wmk. 395
1993, Nov. 27 Litho. *Perf. 13*
1323 A431 500s multicolored 1.10 .55

Dr. Carlos A. Arroyo del Rio, birth cent.

1993, Oct. 15 *Perf. 13½x13, 13x13½*

Endangered species: 400s, Dinomys branickii, horiz. 800s, Ara severa.

1324 A432 400s multicolored 2.00 .60
1325 A432 800s multicolored 3.00 1.25

America issue.

Christmas
A433

600s, Holy Family, 18th cent. Tagua miniatures. 900s, Mother and child, vert.

Wmk. 395
1993, Dec. 1 Litho. *Perf. 13*
1326 A433 600s multicolored 1.40 .90
1327 A433 900s multicolored 2.25 1.40

A434 A435

Wmk. 395
1994, Jan. 18 Litho. *Perf. 13*
1328 A434 300s grn, blk & org .40 .35

Intl. Year of the Family.

1994, Jan. 25
1329 A435 500s multicolored 1.75 .90

Dr. Julio Tobar Donoso, birth cent.

Orchids — A436

Wmk. 395
1994, Feb. 7 Litho. *Perf. 13½*
1330 A436 150s Dracula hirtzii .35 .25
1331 A436 150s Sobralia dichotoma .35 .25
1332 A436 300s Encyclia pulcherrima .85 .40
1333 A436 300s Lepanthes delhierroi .85 .40
1334 A436 600s Masdevallia rosea 1.75 .90
1335 A436 600s Telipogon andicola 1.75 .90
Nos. 1330-1335 (6) 5.90 3.10

First Convention on the Conservation of Andean Orchids.

A437 A438

1994, Apr. 12 *Perf. 13*
1336 A437 200s multicolored .55 .25

Federico Gonzalez Suarez (1844-1917).

1994, Jan. 11
1337 A438 400s multicolored 1.25 .60

Scouting in Ecuador.

Dr. Miguel Egas Cabezas (1823-94)
A439

Wmk. 395
1994, Mar. 10 Litho. *Perf. 13*
1338 A439 100s multicolored .50 .25

A440

A441

1994, July 12

1339 A440 200s multicolored .70 .45

Fr. Aurelio Espinosa, birth cent.

Wmk. 395

1994, June 10 Litho. *Perf. 13*

Nos. 1341, 1343d, Mascot. 900s, Player.
No. 1343: a, Emblem. b, "COPA MUNDIAL FUTBOL '94," emblem. c, "COPA MUNDIAL, USA 94."

1340 A441 300s shown 1.25 .60
1341 A441 600s Mascot 2.40 1.25
1342 A441 900s Soccer player 3.75 1.75

Perf. 12 on 2 Sides

1343 A441 600s Block of 4, #a.-d. 9.75 7.50
Nos. 1340-1343 (4) 17.15 11.10

1994 World Cup Soccer Championships, US.
No. 1343 contains two 50x25mm stamps, two 50x51mm stamps.

Ecuador In Antarctica
A442

1994, July 19 *Perf. 13*

1344 A442 600s Outpost 2.25 1.10
1345 A442 900s Ship, B/1 Orion 3.50 1.75

ILO, 75th Anniv.
A443

1994 Litho. Wmk. 395 *Perf. 13*

1346 A443 100s multicolored .50 .25

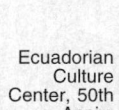

Ecuadorian Culture Center, 50th Anniv.
A444

1994

1347 A444 700s Benjamin Carrion, vert. 2.40 1.40
1348 A444 900s Cultural center 3.50 1.60

Natl. Lottery, Cent.
A445

1994

1349 A445 1000s multicolored 3.75 1.75

Junior World Cycling Championships, Quito — A446

Wmk. 395

1994, June 22 Litho. *Perf. 13*

1350 A446 300s shown .75 .35
1351 A446 400s Stylized cyclist, vert. 1.00 .50

Postal Transportation
A447

Christmas
A448

America Issue: No. 1352, Van, airplane, ship, horiz. No. 1353, Airplane, mail bag.

1994

1352 A447 600s multicolored .80 .40
1353 A447 600s multicolored 1.00 .50

1994

No. 1354, Simulated stamp showing globe circled by envelope, horiz. No. 1355, Nativity.

1354 A448 600s multicolored 1.10 .75
1355 A448 900s multicolored 1.60 .85

Juan Leon Mera, Death Cent.
A449 A450

Wmk. 395

1994, Dec. 21 Litho. *Perf. 13*

1356 A449 600s Mera's home 1.00 .65
1357 A450 900s multicolored 2.25 1.40

Gen. Antonio Jose de Sucre (1795-1830) — A451

Perf. 14x13½

1995, Mar. 14 Litho. Wmk. 395

1358 A451 1500s shown 3.75 1.75
1359 A451 2000s Portrait at right 5.00 2.50

Size: 80x105

Imperf

1360 A451 3000s In military uniform 5.50 5.50
Nos. 1358-1360 (3) 14.25 9.75

Beatification of Josemaria Escriva, 3rd Anniv. — A452

1995, May 17 *Perf. 13x13½*

1361 A452 900s multicolored 1.50 .90

Gen. Eloy Alfaro (1842-1912), Alfarista Revolution, Cent.
A453

1995, June 5 *Perf. 13½x13*

1362 A453 800s multicolored 1.40 .80

A454

Conflict Between Ecuador & Peru — A455

Designs: 200s, Soldier writing to children. 400s, Hand holding flag of Ecuador. 800s, Soldier in wilderness.

1995, July *Perf. 13½, 13 (#1364)*

1363 A454 200s multicolored .50 .25
1364 A455 400s multicolored 1.00 .45
1365 A454 800s multicolored 1.75 .90
Nos. 1363-1365 (3) 3.25 1.60

CARE, 50th Anniv. — A456

1995, July 14 *Perf. 13½*

1366 A456 400s Girl, vert. .60 .30
1367 A456 800s shown 1.75 1.00

CAF (Andes Development Corporation), 25th Anniv. — A457

1995, Aug. 22 *Perf. 13*

1368 A457 1000s multicolored 3.00 1.25

A458

A459

1995, Sept. 2 Litho. *Perf. 13*

1369 A458 500s Virgin of Cisne .75 .50

1995, Sept. 28

1370 A459 400s multicolored .85 .45

Natl. Institute of Children and Families (INNFA), 35th anniv.

UN, 50th Anniv.
A460

Wmk. 395

1995, Oct. 6 Litho. *Perf. 13*

1371 A460 1000s bl, blk & bis 2.00 1.00

Intl. Decade for Natural Disaster Reduction
A461

Civil defense emblem and: No. 1372, House surrounded by flood waters. No. 1373, Family leaving site of erupting volcano. No. 1374, People under table during earthquake. No. 1375, Couple planting seedlings on hillside. No. 1376, Man reading instruction booklet for natural disaster preparation.

1995, Oct. 11

1372 A461 1000s multicolored 2.00 1.00
1373 A461 1000s multicolored 2.00 1.00
1374 A461 1000s multicolored 2.00 1.00
1375 A461 1000s multicolored 2.00 1.00
1376 A461 1000s multicolored 2.00 1.00
Nos. 1372-1376 (5) 10.00 5.00

FAO, 50th Anniv.
A462

1995, Oct. 16

1377 A462 1300s multicolored 2.75 1.50

Women's Culture Club, 50th Anniv.
A463

1995, Oct. 20

1378 A463 1500s multicolored 2.75 1.50

29th Assembly of Inter-America Philatelic Federation, Quito — A464

1995, Nov. 11

1379 A464 1000s blue & red 1.75 1.00

A465

A466

Christmas: 2000s, Santa, sleigh, reindeer on top of world. 2600s, Man on decorated horse, children.

Wmk. 395

1995, Dec. Litho. *Perf. 13*

1380 A465 2000s multicolored 5.00 2.40
1381 A465 2600s multicolored 6.00 2.40

1995, Dec.

Indigenous Birds: No. 1382, Aglaiocercus kingi.

No. 1383: a, Coeligena torquata. b, Phaethornis superciliosus. c, Ocreatus underwoodii. d, Oreotrochilus chimborazo. e, Aglaiocercus coelestis.

1382 A466 1000s multicolored 2.25 .85
1383 A466 1000s Strip of 5, #a.-e. 11.25 6.25

Ecuadoran Air Force, 75th Anniv. A467

1995, Dec.
1384 A467 1000s multicolored 2.00 .95

Year of Folk Music — A468

2000s, Julio Jaramillo (1935-78), musician, composer. 3000s, Jaramillo, wall.

1996, Jan. 16 Litho. ***Perf. 13***
1385 A468 2000s multicolored 3.75 2.00

Imperf

1386 A468 3000s multicolored 5.00 4.25

Advancement of Ecuador, 4 Year Program A469

Designs show symbols for: 1500s, Mail delivery. 2000s, Customs crossing. 2600s, Telecommunications. 3000p, Ports.

Wmk. 395

1996, July 23 Litho. ***Perf. 13***
1387 A469 1000s multicolored 1.75 .80
1388 A469 1500s multicolored 2.75 1.25
1389 A469 2000s multicolored 3.25 1.75
1390 A469 2600s multicolored 4.50 1.90
a. Pair, #1388, #1390 8.00 8.00
b. Pair, #1389, #1390 8.50 8.50
1391 A469 3000s multicolored 5.50 3.00
a. Pair, #1387, #1391 8.00 8.00
b. Pair, #1389, #1391 9.50 9.50
Nos. 1387-1391 (5) 17.75 8.70
Nos. 1390a-1391b (4) 34.00 34.00

Nos. 1387-1391 were issued in strips of 2 each.

Esmeraldas '96, 8th National Games A470

Mascot depicting two sports on each stamp: No. 1392, Tennis, boxing. No. 1393, Basketball, socccer. 600s, Racketball, swimming. 800s, Weight lifting, karate. 1000s, Volleyball, gymnastics. 1200s, Athletics, judo. No. 1398, Chess, wrestling.

No. 1399, Mascot holding flag, emblem, surrounded by flags.

1996, July 30
1392 A470 400s multicolored .55 .25
1393 A470 400s multicolored .55 .25
1394 A470 600s multicolored .90 .45
a. Pair, #1392, #1394 1.50 1.50
1395 A470 800s multicolored 1.25 .60
a. Pair, #1394-1395 2.25 2.25
1396 A470 1000s multicolored 1.60 .75
a. Pair, #1393, #1396 2.40 2.40
b. Pair, #1395-1396 3.00 3.00
1397 A470 1200s multicolored 1.75 .95
1398 A470 2000s multicolored 3.25 1.40
Nos. 1392-1398 (7) 9.85 4.65
Nos. 1394a-1396b (4) 9.15 9.15

Size: 120x100mm

1399 A470 2000s multicolored 4.00 3.50

Nos. 1392-1396 were printed in strips of 2 each.

Civil Aviation, 50th Anniv. A471

1996, Aug. 8
1400 A471 2000s multicolored 3.00 1.25

1996 Summer Olympic Games, Atlanta A472

Atlanta Games emblem and: 1000s, Mascot carrying torch. No. 1402, Emblem of Olympic Committee of Ecuador. 3000s, Jefferson Perez, vert.

No. 1404, Perez, gold medalist, 20-kilometer walk, walking.

1996
1401 A472 1000s multicolored 2.00 .75
1402 A472 2000s multicolored 4.00 2.25
a. Pair, #1401-1402 6.00 6.00
1403 A472 3000s multicolored 5.00 2.50
Nos. 1401-1403 (3) 11.00 5.50

Size: 100x120mm

Imperf

1404 A472 2000s multicolored 4.50 3.50

Fight Against Drug Abuse — A473

Dr. Eduardo Salazar Gomez, Birth Cent. — A474

1996 Litho. Wmk. 395 ***Perf. 13***
1408 A473 2000s multicolored 4.00 2.00

1996
1409 A474 1000s multicolored 2.50 1.25

Catholic University, Quito, 50th Anniv. A475

Junior Chamber International A476

Designs: 400s, Outside view of building, horiz. 800s, Entrance.

1996
1410 A475 400s multicolored .90 .45
1411 A475 800s multicolored 1.75 .85

1996
1412 A476 2000s Children's faces, horiz. 4.50 2.75
1413 A476 2600s shown 5.50 3.50

Catholic University, Quito, 50th Anniv. A477

1996, Nov.
1414 A477 2000s multicolored 4.00 2.00

The Universe Daily Newspaper, 75th Anniv. — A478

1996, Dec.
1415 A478 2000s multicolored 4.00 2.00

Private Technical University, Loja — A479

1996, Dec. 9
1416 A479 4700s multicolored 11.00 5.50

UNICEF, 50th Anniv. A480

1996, Dec. 11
1417 A480 2000s multicolored 4.50 2.25

Christmas A481

Children's paintings: 600s, Merry Chrismas All Over the World. 800s, World of Peace and Love. 2000s, Christmas.

1996, Dec. 19
1418 A481 600s multicolored 1.50 1.00
1419 A481 800s multicolored 2.00 1.25

Size: 51x31mm

Perf. 13½

1420 A481 2000s multicolored 5.00 2.50
Nos. 1418-1420 (3) 8.50 4.75

Preserving the Ecological System A482

America '95: 1000s, Voltur grypus. 1500s, Harpia harpyja, vert.

1996, Dec. 30 ***Perf. 13***
1421 A482 1000s multicolored 2.50 1.50
1422 A482 1500s multicolored 3.75 2.00

Typical Children's Costumes — A483

America '96: No. 1423, "Bordando" girl, Zuleta. No. 1424, Girl from Otavalo.

1996, Dec. 30
1423 A483 2600s multicolored 5.00 1.75
1424 A483 2600s multicolored 5.00 4.25
a. Pair, #1423-1424 12.50 12.50

Mejia Natl. Institute, Cent. A484

Design: Jose Mejia Lequerica, building.

1997, Jan. 10
1425 A484 1000s multicolored 2.25 1.25

Army Polytechnical School, 75th Anniv. A485

Wmk. 395

1997, June 16 Typo. ***Perf. 13***
1426 A485 400s multicolored 1.10 .75

Natl. Experimental College, Ambato, 50th Anniv. A486

1997, June 20
1427 A486 600s multicolored 1.50 1.00

Vicente Rocafuerte (1783-1847), First Constitutional President of Ecuador — A487

1997, July 1
1428 A487 400s multicolored 1.25 .75

49th Intl. Congress of the Americanists A488

1997, July 3
1429 A488 2000s multicolored 5.00 3.25

Butterflies A489

Designs: 400s, Actinote equatoria. 600s, Dismorphia amphione. 800s, Marpesia corinna. 2000s, Marpesia berania. 2600s, Morpho helenor.

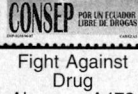

1997, July 21

1430 A489 400s multicolored 1.25 .80
1431 A489 600s multicolored 1.50 1.00
1432 A489 800s multicolored 2.00 1.25
1433 A489 2000s multicolored 5.00 3.25
1434 A489 2600s multicolored 7.00 4.75
Nos. 1430-1434 (5) 16.75 11.05

Air Club of Ecuador, 66th Anniv. A490

1997, July 23

1435 A490 2600s multicolored 6.00 3.00

Orchids — A491

400s, Epidendrum secundum. 600s, Epidendrum. 800s, Oncidium cultratrum. 2000s, Oncidium sp mariposa. 2600s, Pleurothalis corrulensis.

1997, Aug. 14 Litho. *Perf. 13*

1436 A491 400s multicolored 1.25 .80
1437 A491 600s multicolored 1.50 1.00
1438 A491 800s multicolored 2.00 1.25
1439 A491 2000s multicolored 5.00 3.25
1440 A491 2600s multicolored 7.00 4.75
Nos. 1436-1440 (5) 16.75 11.05

Rocks and Minerals — A492

1997, Oct. 6 Litho. *Perf. 13*

1441 A492 400s Quartz 1.25 .80
1442 A492 600s Chalcopyrite 1.50 1.00
1443 A492 800s Gold 2.00 1.25
1444 A492 2000s Petrified wood 5.00 3.25
1445 A492 2600s Pyrite 7.00 4.75
Nos. 1441-1445 (5) 16.75 11.05

A493

A494

Christmas (Children's designs): 400s, Santa as postman delivering letters over world. 2600s, Star on Christmas tree reaching for letters, airplane under tree. 3000s, Child dreaming of angels carrying letters.

1997, Dec. 22 Litho. *Perf. 13*

1446 A493 400s multicolored 1.25 .80
1447 A493 2600s multicolored 7.00 4.75
1448 A493 3000s multicolored 8.25 5.50
Nos. 1446-1448 (3) 16.50 11.05

1997, Dec. 29

1449 A494 800s Life of a Postman 2.00 1.00
1450 A494 2000s On bicycle 5.00 2.50

America issue.

A495

A496

Matilde Hidalgo de Procel (1889-1974), physician, social reformer.

1998, Mar. 6 Litho. *Perf. 13*

1451 A495 2000s multicolored 4.75 3.25

Intl. Women's Day.

Wmk. 395

1998, Apr. 22 Litho. *Perf. 13*

1452 A496 2000s multicolored 8.25 5.50

Dr. Misael Acosta Solis, botanist.

Organization of American States (OAS), 50th Anniv. A497

1998, Apr. 30

1453 A497 2600s multicolored 5.00 3.25

1998 World Cup Soccer Championships, France — A498

Designs: 2600s, Trophy, mascot, vert. 3000s, Two players, trophy.

1998, May

1454 A498 2000s multicolored 4.00 2.25
1455 A498 2600s multicolored 5.00 2.75
1456 A498 3000s multicolored 6.00 3.25
Nos. 1454-1456 (3) 15.00 8.25

Flowers — A499

Galapagos Flora — A500

600s, Gypsophila paniculata. 800s, Banana flowers. 2000s, Roses. 2600s, Asters.

1998, June

1457 A499 600s multicolored 1.40 .60
1458 A499 800s multicolored 1.75 .90
1459 A499 2000s multicolored 4.00 2.25
1460 A499 2600s multicolored 5.00 2.75
Nos. 1457-1460 (4) 12.15 6.50

1998, July

Designs: 600s, Jasminocereus thouarsii. 1000s, Cordia lutea lamarck. 2600s, Momordica charantia.

1461 A500 600s multicolored 1.10 .60
1462 A500 1000s multicolored 1.90 1.00
1463 A500 2600s multicolored 5.00 2.75
Nos. 1461-1463 (3) 8.00 4.35

Tourism A501

Designs: 600s, St. Augustine Church, Quito. 800s, Monument to the Heroes of the Independence, Guayaquil. 2000s, Equator Monument, Quito. 2600s, Mojanda Lake.

1998, July

1464 A501 600s multi, vert. 1.25 .60
1465 A501 800s multi, vert. 1.50 .90
1466 A501 2000s multi 3.50 2.25
1467 A501 2600s multi 4.50 2.75
Nos. 1464-1467 (4) 10.75 6.50

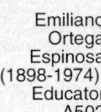

Emiliano Ortega Espinosa (1898-1974), Educator A502

Perf. 13¼x13, 13x13¼

1998 Litho. Wmk. 395

1468 A502 400s shown .90 .50
1469 A502 4700s Portrait, vert. 11.00 8.25

A503

A504

Carlos Cueva Tamariz (1898-1991), educator.

Perf. 13x13¼

1998, Nov. Litho. Wmk. 395

1470 A503 2600s multicolored 5.00 3.50

Wmk. 395

1998, Nov. 20 Litho. *Perf. 13*

1471 A504 600s multicolored 1.25 .90

Radio Club of Guayaquil, 75th anniv.

6th South American Games — A505

Designs: 400s, Mascot. 1000s, Games poster, tennis rackets, hurdles, sailing, hammer throw, bowling, boxing. 2600s, Mascot, parallel bars, wrestling, judo, fencing, running, swimming, shooting, cycling.

1998

1472 A505 400s multicolored 1.10 .50
1473 A505 1000s multicolored 1.90 1.00
1474 A505 2600s multicolored 5.00 2.75
Nos. 1472-1474 (3) 8.00 4.25

Paintings by Eduardo Kingman (1913-85) A506

Designs: 600s, Ecuadoran Woman, vert. 800s, World Without Answers.

1998, Dec. 10

1475 A506 600s multicolored 1.25 .65
1476 A506 800s multicolored 1.90 1.00

Manuela Sáenz (1797-1856), Mistress of Simon Bolívar — A507

1999, Jan. 19

1477 A507 1000s multicolored 2.00 .95

America issue. Exists imperf.

Christmas A508

Children's drawings: 1000s, Santa posting letters on tree. 2600s, People holding up giant letter, vert. 3000s, Santas parachuting with letters, nativity scene, tree, vert.

1998, Dec. 22

1478 A508 1000s multicolored 1.75 .95
1479 A508 2600s multicolored 4.50 2.50
1480 A508 3000s multicolored 5.00 2.75
Nos. 1478-1480 (3) 11.25 6.20

Los Tayos Caves A509

1999, Feb. 25 Litho. *Perf. 13*

1481 A509 1000s Man in cave, vert. 1.75 .90
1482 A509 2600s shown 4.75 2.50

Napal, the Age of Wrath, by Oswaldo Guayasamin (1919-99) — A510

Wmk. 395

1999, May 12 Litho. *Perf. 13*

1483 A510 2000s multicolored 4.25 2.10

Iberoamerica art exhibition.

Universal Day of Human Rights A511

1999, May 28

1484 A511 4000s multicolored 7.50 4.50

Eloy Alfaro Superior Military College, Cent. A512

5200s, Cannon, monument, flags, buildings. 9400s, Honor Guard, modern building.

1999, June 4

1485 A512 5200s multicolored 10.50 7.00
1486 A512 9400s multicolored 17.50 11.50

Puyo, 100th Anniv. — A513

Designs: a, Bromeliad. b, Ara chloroptera.

1999, June 2

1487 A513 4000s Pair, #a.-b. 14.50 10.00

Dr. Rafael Barahona Andrade (1827-98) A514

Perf. 13¼x13

1999, June 17 Litho. Wmk. 395
1488 A514 5200s multi 9.00 4.50

Generals — A515

Designs: 2000s, Manuel Antonio de Luzarraga y Echezurria (1776-1859). 4000s, Tomas Carlos Wright (1799-1868).

1999, Aug. 11 *Perf. 13x13¼*
1489-1490 A515 Set of 2 11.00 6.00

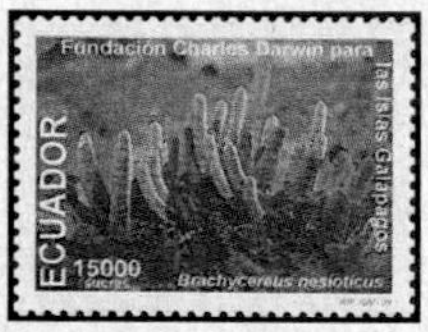

Galapagos Islands Flora and Fauna A516

No. 1491, vert.: a, Phoenicopterus ruber. b, Buteo galapagoensis. c, Amblyrhynchus cristatus. d, Conolophus subcristatus. e, Opuntia galapageia. f, Pyrocephalus rubinus. g, Sula nebouxii. h, Sula dactylatra. i, Scalesia villosa. j, G. elephantopus abingdoni.

No. 1492: a, Brachycereus nesioticus. b, Dendroica petechia. c, Nannopterum harrisi. d, Tursiops truncatus. e, Pentaceraster cumingi. f, G. elephantopus porteri. g, Microlophus albemarlensis. h, Arctocephalus galapagoensis. i, Spheniscus mendiculus. j, Geospiza scandens.

Perf. 13x13¼, 13¼x13

1999, Sept. 3 Litho. Wmk. 395
1491 Strip of 10 90.00 75.00
a.-j. A516 7000s Any single 5.50 1.75
1492 Strip of 10 175.00 125.00
a.-j. A516 15,000s Any single 12.00 5.00

Intl. Year of Older Persons A517

Designs: No. 1493, 1000s, Hands of child and old person. No. 1494, 1000s, Emblem.

Perf. 13¼x13

1999, Sept. 22 Litho. Wmk. 395
1493-1494 A517 Set of 2 3.00 1.75

SOS Children's Villages, 50th Anniv. — A518

a, 2000s, Two children. b, 2000s, One child.

1999, Sept. 30
1495 A518 Pair, #a-b 5.00 2.50

America Issue, A World Without Arms — A519

No. 1496: a, World map. b, Tree, bird, Earth.

Perf. 13¼x13

1999, Dec. 11 Litho. Wmk. 395
1496 A519 4000s Pair, #a-b *14.50 10.00*

UPU, 125th Anniv. A520

Designs: 1000s, Ecuadorian Postal Service mascot, vert. 4000s, Dove with letter, vert. 8000s, UPU emblem.

Perf. 13¼x12¾

1999, Dec. 11 Litho. Wmk. 395
1497 A520 1000s multi .90 .45
1498 A520 4000s multi 3.50 1.75
1499 A520 8000s multi 7.00 4.00
Nos. 1497-1499 (3) 11.40 6.20

Ecuador as Secretary General of Permanent South Pacific Commission A521

Perf. 13x13¼

1999, Dec. 21 Litho. Wmk. 395
1500 A521 7000s multi *7.50 5.50*

Machala Tourism A522

Designs: No. 1501, Banana flower and city. No. 1502, vert.: a, Monument to banana plantation workers. b, City Hall.

1999, Dec. 28 *Perf. 13¼x13, 13x13¼*
1501 A522 3000s multi *3.25 1.60*
1502 A522 3000s Pair, #a-b *6.50 3.25*

EMELEC Soccer Team — A523

No. 1503: a, Jorge Bolanos. b, Carlos Raffo. No. 1504, EMELEC team photo, 1957. No. 1505, Player, vert.

Perf. 13x13¼, 13¼x13

2000, Jan. 7 Litho.
1503 A523 1000s Pair, #a-b *3.00 2.25*
1504 A523 2000s multi *3.00 1.50*
1505 A523 2000s multi *3.00 1.50*

Guayas Philanthropic Society, 150th Anniv. A524

Designs: 1000s, Building. 2000s, Founder Juan Maria Martinez Coello. 4000s, Emblem.

Perf. 13¼x13

2000, Jan. 19 Litho. Wmk. 395
1506-1508 A524 Set of 3 *3.00 1.50*

Dual Nationality Day — A525

2000, Jan. 24 *Perf. 13x13¼*
1509 A525 7000s multi *3.00 1.50*

Cuenca, World Heritage Site — A526

No. 1510: a, Buildings. b, Puente Roto and Tomebamba River. c, Church bell gable, Concepcion Monastery. d, Cathedral and city skyline. e, San José Church.

2000, Mar. 24 *Perf. 13¼x13*
1510 Strip of 5 *7.00 6.00*
a.-e. A526 4000s Any single *.75 .50*

Nicolas Lapentti, Tennis Player — A527

2000, Mar. 26 *Perf. 13x13¼*
1511 A527 8000s multi *3.00 1.50*

Birds — A528

No. 1512: a, Diglossa cyanea. b, Oreotrochilus chimborazo. c, Trogon personatus. d, Colibri coruscans. e, Atlapetes rufinucha.

2000, Apr. 7
1512 Horiz. strip of 5 *13.00 11.50*
a.-e. A528 8000s Any single *2.25 1.50*

Relocation of Riobamba, Bicent. A529

Designs: No. 1513, Mt. Chimborazo. No. 1514: a, Riobamba Cathedral. b, Statue of Pedro Vicente Maldonado.

2000, Apr. 13 *Perf. 13¼x13, 13x13¼*
1513 A529 8000s multi *2.75 1.00*
1514 A529 8000s Pair, #a-b 5.25 3.50

Gen. Eloy Alfaro, Founder of Natl. Music Conservatory A530

2000, Apr. 19 *Perf. 13x13¼*
1515 A530 10,000s multi *4.00 1.60*

Natl. Music Conservatory, cent.

Climbing of Mt. Everest by Ivan Vallejo Ricaurte A531

2000, May 23 *Perf. 13¼x13*
1516 A531 8000s multi *3.50 2.00*

100 Cents=1 Dollar

Dolores Sucre Fiscal College, 50th Anniv. — A532

Perf. 13x13¼

2000 Litho. Wmk. 395
1517 A532 32c multi 2.50 1.25

Training Ship Guayas — A533

2000, July 5 *Perf. 13x13¼*
1518 A533 68c multi 1.60 .80

Imperf

Size: 90x110mm

1519 A533 $1 multi 7.00 3.25

Battle of Jambeli, 59th Anniv., Navy Day — A534

2000 *Perf. 13¼x13*
1520 A534 16c multi 1.50 .25

Guayaquil Civic Renovation A535

2000, July *Perf. 13x13¼*
1521 A535 84c multi 7.50 3.75

Megaptera Novaeangliae — A536

2000, Aug. 3 *Perf. 13¼x13*
1522 A536 84c multi 8.50 4.25

Imperf

Size: 90x110mm

1523 A536 $1 Two whales 11.50 5.75

American and Caribbean Dog Show, Quito
A537

2000, Aug. ***Perf. 13¼x13***
1524 A537 68c multi 4.50 2.25

Guayaquil Tennis Club, 90th Anniv.
A538

2000, Aug. **Wmk. 395**
1525 A538 84c multi 5.50 2.50

Alberto Spencer, Soccer Player — A539

2000 ***Perf. 13x13¼***
1526 A539 68c multi 5.00 2.50

Imperf

Size: 69x99mm

1527 A539 $1 Spencer, crowd 9.00 4.50

2000 Summer Olympics, Sydney — A540

Ecuadoran team emblem, Games emblem and: 32c Mascots. 68c, Runner Jefferson Perez Marchista. 84c, Weight lifter Boris Burov, Olympic flag, horiz.

2000, Sept. ***Perf. 13x13¼, 13¼x13***
1528-1530 A540 Set of 3 12.00 6.00

Salinas Yacht Club, 60th Anniv.
A541

Designs: No. 1531a, Lighthouse, vert. Nos. 1531b, 1533, Sailboat, vert. 68c, Sailboats, fisherman, waterskier, scuba diver.

2000, Oct. ***Perf. 13x13¼***
1531 A541 32c Horiz. pair, #a-b 5.50 2.75

Perf. 13¼x13

1532 A541 68c multi 5.75 2.75

Imperf

Size: 69x100mm

1533 A541 $1 multi 9.00 4.50

Inter-American Development Bank, 40th Anniv. — A542

Designs: No. 1534a, 68c, No. 1536a, 25c, Salsipuedes Bridge, Felipe Herrera. No. 1534b, 68c, No. 1536b, 25c, Daule-Peripa Dam, Antonio Ortiz Mena. No. 1535a, 84c, No. 1536c, 25c, Enrique Iglesias, Ucubamba Water Treatment Plant. No. 1535b, 84c, No. 1536d, 25c, Bank emblem, History Museum, Quito.

2000, Oct. 27 ***Perf. 13¼x13***

Horiz. Pairs, #a-b

1534-1535 A542 Set of 2 20.00 10.00

Rouletted 14 on 2 sides

1536 A542 25c Sheet of 4, #a-d 7.50 3.75

Size of Nos. 1536a-1536b, 75x48mm; Nos. 1536c-1536d, 75x42mm.

National Union of Journalists
A543

2000, Nov. 1 ***Perf. 13¼x13***
1537 A543 16c multi 1.25 .25

Civil Registry, Cent. — A544

No. 1538: a, People, flag, computer. b, Fingerprint, family.

2000, Oct. 27 ***Perf. 13x13¼***
1538 A544 68c Horiz. pair, #a-b 9.00 4.50

Mama Negra Festival, Latacunga — A545

No. 1539: a, Mama Negra with doll. b, Man in Moor King costume.

2000, Nov. ***Perf. 13x13¼***
1539 A545 32c Horiz. pair, #a-b 5.50 2.75

Imperf

Size: 100x68mm

1540 A545 $1 Mama Negra, doll, diff. 6.50 3.00

Ministry of Labor, 75th Anniv. — A546

2000, Nov. 15 ***Perf. 13x13¼***
1541 A546 68c multi 4.75 2.25

Intl. Fruits and Flowers Festival, Ambato, 50th Anniv.
A547

No. 1542, horiz.: a, Tungurahua Volcano. b, Aerial view of Ambato.
No. 1544, horiz.: a, Flower. b. Fruit.

2000, Nov. ***Perf. 13¾***
1542 A547 32c Vert. pair, #a-b 4.25 2.10
1543 A547 84c shown 5.75 2.75
1544 A547 84c Vert. pair, #a-b 12.00 6.00
Nos. 1542-1544 (3) 22.00 10.85

Imperf

Size: 68x100mm

1545 A547 $1 Ambato 6.25 3.00

Christmas — A548

Children's art by — No. 1546, 68c: a, Giannina Rhor Isaias. b, Josue Remache Romero.
No. 1547, 84c: a, Maria Cedeño Bazurtto. b, Juan Alban Salazar.
$1, Walther Carvache.

2000, Dec. 15 ***Perf. 13¼x13***

Horiz. Pairs, #a-b

1546-1547 A548 Set of 2 21.50 11.00

Imperf

Size: 100x69mm

1548 A548 $1 multi 6.25 3.00

Expoflores Flower Producer and Exporter Association
A549

2000 ***Perf. 13x13¼***
1549 A549 68c multi 5.00 2.50

Man's Chapel, Guayasamin
A550

2000 ***Perf. 13¼x13***
1550 A550 16c multi 1.25 .25

Spanish Chamber of Commerce in Ecuador, 80th Anniv. — A551

2000, Dec. ***Perf. 13x13¼***
1551 A551 16c multi 1.25 .25

Intl. Volunteers Year — A552

2000 **Wmk. 395**
1552 A552 16c multi 1.25 .25

Restoration of Bolivar Theater, Quito — A553

Designs: 16c, Piano, banquet room. 32c, Stage, orchestra, horiz.

2000, Dec. ***Perf. 13x13¼, 13¼x13***
1553-1554 A553 Set of 2 3.75 1.75

Spondylus Princeps
A554

2000, Dec. 16 ***Perf. 13¾***
1555 A554 84c multi 6.00 3.00

Imperf

Size: 69x99mm

1556 A554 $1 multi 7.00 3.50

America Issue, Fight Against AIDS — A555

No. 1557: a, Strands. b, Earth.

2000 ***Perf. 13x13¼***
1557 A555 84c Horiz. pair, #a-b 15.00 7.50

Guayas Province Red Cross, 90th Anniv.
A556

2000 ***Perf. 13¼x13***
1558 A556 16c multi 1.25 .60

Guayas Sports Federation, 78th Anniv. — A557

2000, Dec. ***Perf. 13x13¼***
1559 A557 16c multi 1.25 .60

Landscapes A557a

Designs: No. 1559A, 16c, Andean region. No. 1559B, 16c, Pacific coast. 32c, Tourism emblem. 68c, Amazonia. 84c, Galápagos Islands.

Perf. 13¼x12¾

2001, Jan. 24 Litho. Wmk. 395

1559A	A557a	16c multi	1.25	.60
1559B	A557a	16c multi	1.25	.60
1559C	A557a	32c multi	2.50	1.10
1559D	A557a	68c multi	4.75	2.40
1559E	A557a	84c multi	4.75	2.40
		Nos. 1559A-1559E (5)	14.50	7.10

Guayas Soccer Team, 50th Anniv. A558

2001, Mar. 8 ***Perf. 13¼x13***
1560 A558 68c multi 5.00 2.50

Census — A558a Census — A558b

Perf. 12¾x13¼

2001, Mar. 12 Litho. Wmk. 395

1560A	A558a	68c multi	4.50	4.50
1560B	A558b	68c multi	4.50	4.50
c.		Horiz. pair, #1560A-1560B	10.00	10.00

Dr. Raúl Clemente Huerta A559

2001, Apr. 4 ***Perf. 13¼x13***
1561 A559 68c multi 5.50 2.75

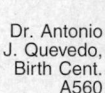

Dr. Antonio J. Quevedo, Birth Cent. A560

2001, Apr. 5 **Litho.**
1562 A560 84c multi 6.50 3.25

Military Geographic Institute A560a

No. 1562A: b, Soldier, building. c, Computer, printing press.

Perf. 13¼x12¾

2001, Apr. 11 Litho. Wmk. 395
1562A A560a 68c Vert. pair, #b-c 12.00 6.00

Automobile Club of Ecuador, 50th Anniv. A561

2001, May 15 **Wmk. 395**
1563 A561 84c multi 6.50 3.25

San Francisco de Peleusí Church, Azogues — A561a

Perf. 12¾x13¼

2001, May Litho. Wmk. 395
1563A A561a 84c multi 6.50 3.25

Women's Training Institute — A562

2001, Apr. 10 ***Perf. 13x13¼***
1564 A562 84c multi 6.50 3.25

Intl. Women's Day A563

No. 1565: a, Woman, child, corn. b, Woman, emblem.

2001, Apr. 2 ***Perf. 13¼x13***
1565 A563 84c Vert. pair, #a-b 12.50 6.25

Secular Education at Manuela Cañizares University, Cent. A564

2001, Mar. 29 **Wmk. 395**
1566 A564 84c multi 6.50 3.25

Ecuador Merchant Marines, Cent. — A565

2001, Jan. 2001 ***Perf. 13x13¼***
1567 A565 16c multi 1.25 .60

Ambato Technical University, 32nd Anniv. A566

No. 1568: a, Building. b, Painting.

2001 ***Perf. 13¼x13***
1568 A566 32c Vert. pair, #a-b 5.50 2.75

Galapagos Islands Scenes — A567

No. 1569: a, Española Island (shown). b, San Cristobal Island. c, Bartolome Island. d, Española Island, diff. e, Bartolome and Santiago Islands.
$1, Bird on rock, Española Island.

2001, Feb. 17 ***Perf. 13¾***

1569		Horiz. strip of 5	6.00	3.00
a.-e.	A567	16c Any single	.50	.25

Imperf

Size: 100x70mm

1570 A567 $1 multi 8.00 4.00

Alexander von Humboldt (1769-1859), Naturalist — A568

Perf. 13x13¼

2001, June 14 Litho. Wmk. 395
1571 A568 84c multi 6.00 3.00

Ecuadorian Atomic Energy Commission A568a

2001, Aug. 3 Litho. ***Perf. 12¾x13¼***
1571A A568a 70c multi 5.50 2.75

Lebanese Union, 80th Anniv. — A569

No. 1572: a, Building and emblem. b, Emblem.

2001, Aug. 30 ***Perf. 13¼x13***
1572 A569 16c Horiz. pair, #a-b 3.00 1.50

Manta Port Authority — A570

No. 1573: a, Emblem. b, Ships in port.

2001, Sept. 28
1573 A570 68c Horiz. pair, #a-b 10.00 5.00

Esmereldas Province Tourism — A571

No. 1574: a, Beach. b, Musicians and dancers on beach.

2001
1574 A571 86c Horiz. pair, #a-b 12.50 6.25

Latin American Writers — A572

No. 1575: a, Claudia Lars (1899-1974), Salvadoran poet. b, Federico Proaño (1848-94), Ecuadoran journalist.

2001, Aug. 28 ***Perf. 13x13¼***
1575 A572 86c Horiz. pair, #a-b 13.50 6.75

Andean Condor Preservation — A573

No. 1576: a, Condor and chick. b, Condor heads, FRAPZOO emblem.
$1, Condor in flight, FRAPZOO emblem.

2001, July 23 ***Perf. 13x13¼***
1576 A573 86c Horiz. pair, #a-b 12.50 6.25

Imperf

Size: 68x99mm

1577 A573 $1 multi 7.50 3.75

Ecuador — Peru Peace Accords A574

No. 1578: a, Map of Ecuador and Peru. b, Soldier. c, Flags of military obeservers. d, Amazon River. e, Men in field.

2001, May 22 ***Perf. 13¼x13***

1578 Horiz. strip of 5 22.50 11.00
a.-e. A574 68c Any single 4.00 2.00

Archidona Canton — A575

No. 1579: a, Phragmipedium orchid. b, Saimiri sciureus. c, B. macrophylla. d, Church. e, Kichwa Indian family.

2001, Apr. 28 ***Perf. 13x13¼***

1579 Vert. strip of 5 30.00 15.00
a.-e. A575 84c Any single 5.00 2.40

Ecotourism in Baños A576

No. 1580: a, Orchid. b, Basilica, Baños. c, Tungurahua Volcano. d, Pailon del Diablo Waterfall. e, Statue of Virgin of Rosario de Agua Santa.
$1, Pailon del Diablo Waterfall, orchid.

2001 ***Perf. 13¼x13***

1580 Horiz. strip of 5 27.50 13.50
a.-e. A576 86c Any single 5.00 2.40

Imperf

Size: 68x99mm

1581 A576 $1 multi 7.50 3.75

Guayas Educational Journalists Association, 30th Anniv. A577

Perf. 13¼x13

2001, Oct. 15 Litho. Wmk. 395

1582 A577 16c multi 1.25 .60

Foundation for Development of Cattle Ranching, 15th Anniv. — A578

2001, Aug. 15 ***Perf. 13x13¼***

1583 A578 16c multi 1.25 .60

City Gates, Loja — A579

2001 ***Perf. 13¼x13***

1584 A579 32c multi 2.50 1.25

Quito Municipal District Directorate of Security A580

2001, Nov. 26

1585 A580 68c multi 5.00 2.50

Salvador Bustamante Celi (1876-1935), Musician A581

2001

1586 A581 68c multi 5.50 2.75

Marcel Laniado de Wind (1927-98), First Pres. of Natl. Modernization Council — A582

2001, Aug. 6 ***Perf. 13x13¼***

1587 A582 70c multi 5.50 2.75

Bernardino Cardinal Echeverrla (1912-2000) A583

2001, Nov. 14

1588 A583 84c multi 6.50 3.25

José Joaquin Olmedo (1780-1847), Statesman and Poet — A584

2001, Nov. 8

1589 A584 84c multi 6.50 3.25

El Angel Ecological Reserve — A585

No. 1590: a, Paja de Paramo. b, Frailejón.

2001 ***Perf. 13¼x13***

1590 A585 16c Horiz. pair, #a-b 2.75 1.40

Yahuarcocha Race Track — A586

No. 1591: a, Race track and lake. b, Lake.

2001, Nov. 30

1591 A586 68c Horiz. pair, #a-b 10.00 5.00

World Food Day — A587

No. 1592: a, Wheat ears. b, Food baskets.

2001, Nov. 5

1592 A587 84c Horiz. pair, #a-b 12.50 6.25

Art of Voroshilov Bazante A588

No. 1593: a, Spatial composition. b, Abstract, artists name at LR. c, Urban landscape. d, Abstract, diff., "Abstracto" at UL, denomination at LL. e, Abstract, denomination at LR.

2001, Nov.

1593 Horiz. strip of 5 27.50 12.50
a.-e. A588 84c Any single 5.00 2.50

Wilson Popenoe Private Foundation A589

2001, Nov. 19 Litho. ***Perf. 13¼x13***

1594 A589 16c multi 1.25 .60

FAO Food Program A590

2001, Aug. 15

1595 A590 84c multi 6.50 3.25

Rotary District 4400, 75th Anniv. — A591

2001, Nov. 30 ***Perf. 13x13¼***

1596 A591 84c multi 6.50 3.25

Pres. Camilo Ponce Enriquez (1912-76) — A592

2001

1597 A592 84c multi 6.50 3.25

Pedro Vicente Maldonado (1702-48), Geographer A593

2001, Dec. 12

1598 A593 84c multi 6.50 3.25

Otonga Foundation — A595

No. 1599: a, Frog on branch. b, Mustela frenata.

2001, Oct. 31

1599 A595 16c Horiz. pair, #a-b 2.75 1.40

Tourism in Zaruma — A596

No. 1600: a, Virgen del Carmen. b, Orchid.

2001, Dec. 12 ***Perf. 13¼x13***

1600 A596 68c Horiz. pair, #a-b 10.00 5.00

Radio HCJB, 70th Anniv. — A597

No. 1601: a, Microphone. b, Announcer.

2001, Dec. 21

1601 A597 68c Horiz. pair, #a-b 10.00 5.00

Tennis A598

No. 1602: a, Davis Cup. b, K. Lapentti, G. Lapentti, L.A. Morejón, A. Intriago and R. Viver. c, Francisco Guzman and Miguel Olvera. d, Pancho Segura. e, Andres Gomez.

2001, Nov. 1

1602 Horiz. strip of 5 24.00 12.00
a.-e. A598 68c Any single 4.50 2.25

Church Paintings of Wilfrido Martínez — A599

No. 1603: a, San Francisco (artist's name is vert.). b, Guapulo. c, San Francisco (artist's name is horiz.). d, La Compania. e, El Rosario.

2002, Apr. 9 ***Perf. 13¾***

1603 Horiz. strip of 5 27.00 13.50
a.-e. A599 90c Any single 5.00 2.50

First Judicial Summit of the Americas, Quito
A600

Perf. 13¼x13

2002, Jan. 8 Litho. Wmk. 395
1604 A600 68c multi 5.00 2.50

Union Club, Guayaquil — A601

2002, Apr. 25 ***Perf. 13x13¼***
1605 A601 90c multi 5.75 2.75

South American Soccer Confederation
A602

Designs: 25c, Confederation Pres. Nicolás Leoz. 40c, Confederation emblem, soccer players. 70c, Emblem of Emelec team.

2002, Jan. 29
1606-1608 A602 Set of 3 10.00 5.00

World Conservation Union — A603

Designs: 70c, Fish, man's head. 85c, Leopard, man, horiz.
$1, Bird, animals, women and children, horiz.

2002, Feb. 21 ***Perf. 13x13¼, 13¼x13***
1609-1610 A603 Set of 2 11.50 5.75

Imperf

Size: 100x70mm

1611 A603 $1 multi 7.50 3.75

UN High Commissioner for Refugees — A604

Designs: 70c, Emblem. 85c, Child.
$1, Refugees carrying belongings, horiz.

2002, Feb. 28 ***Perf. 13x13¼***
1612-1613 A604 Set of 2 11.50 5.75

Imperf

Size: 100x70mm

1614 A604 $1 multi 7.50 3.75

Ecuadorian Educational Credit and Scholarship Institute — A605

No. 1615: a, Student using microscope. b, Emblem.

2002, Apr. 30 ***Perf. 13x13¼***
1615 A605 25c Horiz. pair, #a-b 3.00 1.50

Cuenca Soccer Team — A606

No. 1616: a, Team photo. b, Emblem, player dribbling.

2002, Apr. 19 ***Perf. 13¼x13***
1616 A606 25c Horiz. pair, #a-b 3.00 1.50

Imbabura Province History — A607

No. 1617: a, Building. b, Statue.

2002, Mar. 27 ***Perf. 13x13¼***
1617 A607 40c Horiz. pair, #a-b 6.00 3.00

Crucita — A608

No. 1618: a, Parachutist with sun on horizon. b, Prachutist above beach.

2002, Mar. 28 ***Perf. 13¼x13***
1618 A608 40c Horiz. pair, #a-b 6.00 3.00

Mountains
A609

No. 1619: a, Mt. Altar (trees in foreground). b, Mt. Chimborazo. c, Mt. Carihuayrazo. d, Mt. Altar (lake in foreground). e, Mt. Cubillin.

2002, Apr. 19
1619 Horiz. strip of 5 29.00 15.00
a.-e. A609 90c Any single 5.00 2.25

Endangered Frogs
A610

No. 1620: a, Atelopus bomolochos. b, Atelopus longirostris. c, Atelopus pachydermus. d, Atelopus arthuri. e, Atelopus sp.
$1, Atelopus ignescens.

2002, Mar. 25 ***Perf. 13¼x13***
1620 Horiz. strip of 5 29.00 15.00
a.-e. A610 $1.05 Any single 5.00 2.25

Imperf

Size: 100x70mm

1621 A610 $1 multi 10.00 8.00

National Anti-narcotics Police — A611

No. 1622: a, Policeman and dog. b, Emblem.

Perf. 13x13¼

2002, Apr. 23 Litho. Wmk. 395
1622 A611 40c Horiz. pair, #a-b 6.00 3.00

2002 World Cup Soccer Championships, Japan and Korea — A612

Designs: 90c, Ecuadorian Soccer Federation emblem, vert. $1.05, $2, Emblem, team photo, players in action.

2002, Apr. 28 ***Perf. 13x13¼, 13¼x13***
1623-1624 A612 Set of 2 9.00 4.50

Imperf

Size: 100x70mm

1625 A612 $2 multi 9.00 4.50

Dr. Servio Aguirre Villamagua, Forest Conservationist — A613

No. 1626: a, Aguirre. b, Plant.

2002, May 22 ***Perf. 13¼x13***
1626 A613 40c Horiz. pair, #a-b 4.00 2.00

Food and Agriculture Organization in Ecuador, 50th Anniv.
A614

2002, May 30
1627 A614 $1.05 multi 5.00 2.50

Galapagos Islands Fauna
A615

No. 1628: a, Grapsus grapsus. b, Conolophus subcristatus.
No. 1629, vert.: a, Sula sula websteri. b, Phoenicopterus ruber.
No. 1630, Amblyrhynchus cristatus.
No. 1631, vert.: a, Pair of Zalophus californianus wollebacki. b, One Zalophus californianus wollebacki.
No. 1632, Sula nebouxxi excisa, vert.
No. 1633, vert.: a, Sula dactylatra granti. b, Emblem of Iberoamerican Summit on Tourism and Environment.
$2, Bird, tourists, tourist ship.

2002, May 31 ***Perf. 13¼x13, 13x13¼***
1628 A615 25c Horiz. pair, #a-b 3.00 1.50
1629 A615 40c Horiz. pair, #a-b 4.00 2.00
1630 A615 90c multi 6.00 3.00
1631 A615 90c Horiz. pair, #a-b 9.00 4.50
1632 A615 $1.05 multi 5.00 2.50
1633 A615 $1.05 Horiz. pair, #a-b 10.00 5.00
Nos. 1628-1633 (6) 37.00 18.50

Imperf

Size: 100x68mm

1634 A615 $2 multi 11.50 7.00

Ministry of Foreign Relations — A616

2002, June 5 ***Perf. 13x13¼***
1635 A616 90c multi 4.50 2.25

Army Polytechnic School, 80th Anniv.
A617

2002, June 13 ***Perf. 13¼x13***
1636 A617 25c multi 1.75 .90

Military Engineers, Cent.
A618

Designs: No. 1637, 40c, Castle of Engineering. No. 1638, 40c, Castle of Engineering, Military engineers in action, vert.
$2, Castle of Engineering, engineers in action, emblems of military groups.

Perf. 13¼x13, 13x13¼

2002, June 19
1637-1638 A618 Set of 2 4.00 2.00

Imperf

Size: 100x68mm

1639 A618 $2 multi 9.00 4.50

Dr. Alfredo Pérez Guerrero (1901-66), Academic — A619

2002, July 4 ***Perf. 13x13¼***
1640 A619 25c multi 1.75 .90

20th Anniv. of Ecuador's Second Place Finish In World Taekwondo Championships — A620

2002, July 18 ***Perf. 13¼x13***
1641 A620 40c multi 2.00 1.00

Orellana Province — A621

No. 1642: a, Three native men. b, Man in tree.

2002, July 30 **Wmk. 395**

1642 A621 25c Horiz. pair, #a-b 3.00 1.50

CARE in Ecuador, 40th Anniv. — A622

No. 1643: a, Two children. b, Boy.

2002, July 30 ***Perf. 13x13¼***

1643 A622 90c Horiz. pair, #a-b 9.00 4.50

Macará Region A623

2002, Aug. 10 ***Perf. 13¼x13***

1644 A623 40c multi 2.00 1.00

Intl. Organization for Migration, 50th Anniv. — A624

Quito Philharmonic Society, 50th Anniv. — A625

2002, Aug. 18 ***Perf. 13x13¼***

1645 A624 $1.05 multi 5.00 2.50

2002, Aug. 29

1646 A625 25c multi 1.75 .90

Comptroller General, 75th Anniv. — A625a

Perf. 13x13¼

2002, Sept. 26 **Litho.** **Wmk. 395**

1646A A625a 40c multi 2.00 1.00

Second World Meeting of Mountain People — A626

No. 1647 — Emblem of World Meeting and: a, Mountain. b, Group of people. c, Houses in valley. d, Town. e, Other emblems.

2002, Sept. 18

1647 Horiz. strip of 5 22.50 11.00
a.-e. A626 90c Any single 4.00 2.00

Pujili Dancer — A627

Perf. 13x13¼

2002, Oct. 14 **Litho.** **Wmk. 395**

1648 A627 $1.05 multi 5.00 2.50

Paintings of Milton Estrella Gavidia — A628

No. 1649 — Various paintings with background colors of: a, Blue violet. b, Brown violet. c, Olive green. d, Blue. e, Gray lilac.

Wmk. 395

2002, May 17 **Litho.** ***Perf. 13¾***

1649 Horiz. strip of 5 22.50 11.00
a.-e. A628 90c Any single 4.00 2.00

Paintings of Leonardo Hidalgo A629

No. 1650: a, La Dolorosa. b, El Hombre Cargando su Fruto. c, Frida Kahlo. d, El Hombre Fuerte del Mar. e, Jesus.

Wmk. 395

2002, Oct. 3 **Litho.** ***Perf. 13¾***

1650 Horiz. strip of 5 22.50 11.00
a.-e. A629 90c Any single 4.00 2.00

Pan-American Health Organization, Cent. — A630

2002, Dec. 2 ***Perf. 13¼x12¾***

1651 A630 $1.05 multi 5.00 2.50

Lo Nuestro Art Exhibition — A631

No. 1652: a, Wall with six works of art. b, Walls with 16 works of art.

2002, Dec. 15

1652 A631 25c Horiz. pair, #a-b 2.50 1.25

Catholic University, 40th Anniv. A632

2002, Dec. 18

1653 A632 40c multi 2.00 1.00

America Issue — UNESCO World Heritage Sites — A633

No. 1654: a, Cupola of San Blas Church, Cuenca. b, Society of Jesus Church, Quito.

2002, Dec. 18 ***Perf. 12¾x13¼***

1654 A633 25c Horiz. pair, #a-b 3.00 1.50

Dated 2001.

America Issue — Youth, Education and Literacy — A634

No. 1655: a, Students and blackboard. b, Toddler and books.

2002, Dec. 18 ***Perf. 13¼x12¾***

1655 A634 25c Horiz. pair, #a-b 3.00 1.50

Second Meeting of South American Presidents, Guayaquil — A635

No. 1656: a, Meeting emblem. b, Emblem, presidents and flags.

2003, Jan. 13

1656 A635 $1.05 Horiz. pair, #a-b 8.00 4.00

Papal Benediction for Ecuadorian Emigrants — A636

2003, Jan. 24 ***Perf. 12¾x13¼***

1657 A636 $1.05 multi 4.50 2.25

Size: 68x100mm

Imperf

1658 A636 $2 multi 9.00 4.50

World Vision — A637

2003, Feb. 6 ***Perf. 12¾x13¼***

1659 A637 40c multi 1.90 .95

Intl. Women's Day — A638

2003, Mar. 8 **Wmk. 395**

1660 A638 $1.05 multi 5.00 2.50

Agustin Cueva Vallejo (1820-73), Physician — A639

2003, Mar. 13 **Litho.**

1661 A639 40c multi 1.90 .95

Blasco Moscoso Cuesta, Founder of Pichincha Sports Writers Association — A640

2003, Mar. 14

1662 A640 25c multi 1.50 .75

Cuenca Artisan Products A641

No. 1663: a, Azuay University domes. b, Tinware. c, Jewelry. d, Fireworks. e, Saddles.

No. 1664: a, Engraving. b, Metallurgy. c, Baskets. d, Embroidery. e, Ceramics.

$2, Assorted products.

2003, Mar. 27 ***Perf. 13¼x12¾***

1663 Horiz. strip of 5 6.00 3.00
a.-e. A641 25c Any single 1.00 .50
1664 Horiz. strip of 5 22.50 11.00
a.-e. A641 $1.05 Any single 4.00 2.00

Size: 100x68mm

Imperf

1665 A641 $2 multi 9.00 4.50

Flora and Fauna A642

No. 1666: a, Curculionidae. b, Lycidae. c, Acridoidea. d, Aracnidae. e, Liliacea.

2003, Apr. 4 ***Perf. 13¼x12¾***

1666 Horiz. strip of 5 22.50 11.00
a.-e. A642 $1.05 Any single 4.00 2.00

Military Geographic Institute, 75th Anniv. A643

Designs: No. 1667, 40c, No. 1669, $2, Painting by Eduardo Kingman. No. 1668, 40c, Institute emblem, vert.

Perf. 13¼x12¾, 12¾x13¼

2003, Apr. 11

1667-1668 A643 Set of 2 3.50 1.75

Size: 100x68mm

Imperf

1669 A643 $2 multi 9.00 4.50

Galápagos Marine Reserve — A644

Designs: 40c, Stylized butterfly.

No. 1671, $1.05, horiz.: a, Sphyrna lewini. b, Chelonia mydas agassisi.

No. 1672, $1.05, horiz.: a, Xanthichthys mento. b, Zanclus cornutus.

$2, Tubastrea coccinea, horiz.

Perf. 12¾x13¼, 13¼x12¾

2003, May 9

1670 A644 40c multi 1.75 .90

Horiz. Pairs, #a-b

1671-1672 A644 Set of 2 17.50 8.75

Size: 100x68mm

Imperf

1673 A644 $2 multi 9.00 4.50

Intl. Tourism Trade Fair of Ecuador A645

No. 1674: a, Monkey in tree. b, Birds. c, Embroidery. d, Mountain. e, Hat seller on beach.

2003, May 14 ***Perf. 13¼x12¾***

1674 Vert. strip of 5 6.00 3.00

a.-e. A645 25c Any single 1.00 .50

Artifacts of Pre-Columbian Cultures — A646

No. 1675, 25c: a, Gold bell with monkey. b, Amphora.

No. 1676, 25c: a, Sculpture of a man. b, Three-footed pot.

Perf. 13x13¼

2003, May 16 Litho. Wmk. 395

Horiz. pairs, #a-b

1675-1676 A646 Set of 2 4.50 2.25

Central Bank of Ecuador A647

No. 1677, vert.: a, Tolita Culture mask. b, Guayaquil Historic Park.

$1.05, Pumapungo Museum.

Perf. 13x13¼, 13¼x13

2003, June 5 Litho.

1677 A647 25c Horiz. pair, #a-b 1.50 .75

1678 A647 $1.05 multi 2.75 1.40

Philately and Guayaquil A648

No. 1679, horiz.: a, British consular cover to Veracruz with British stamp and cancel. b, Stampless cover.

No. 1680, horiz.: a, SCADTA first flight cover. b, French consular cover to Lima with French stamps and cancels.

$1.05, Philatelic magazines.

$2, Guayaquil Philatelic Club emblem, Ecuadoran stamps, horiz.

2003, July 22 ***Perf. 13¾***

1679 A648 40c Vert. pair, #a-b 3.25 1.60

1680 A648 40c Vert. pair, #a-b 3.25 1.60

1681 A648 $1.05 multi 4.00 2.00

Nos. 1679-1681 (3) 10.50 5.20

Size: 100x69mm

Imperf

1682 A648 $2 multi 9.00 4.50

Guayaquil Urban Renewal A649

No. 1683: a, Punta Cerro Santa Ana. b, Plaza Colón. c, Malecón Gardens. d, Crystal Palace. e, Plaza de San Francisco.

2003, July 26 ***Perf. 13¼x13***

1683 Horiz. strip of 5 19.00 9.50

a.-e. A649 90c Any single 3.50 1.75

World Bird Festival A650

Designs: No. 1684, $1.05, Geranoaetus melanoleucus. No. 1685, $1.05, Harpia harpyja, vert.

2003, Sept. 2 ***Perf. 13¼x13, 13x13¼***

1684-1685 A650 Set of 2 9.00 4.50

Zamora-Chinchipe Province, 50th Anniv. — A651

No. 1686: a, Shown. b, Eira barbara. c, Boa constrictor. d, Tapirus terrestris. e, Psophia crepitans.

2003, Nov. 7 ***Perf. 13¼x13***

1686 Vert. strip of 5 6.00 3.00

a.-e. A651 25c Any single 1.00 .50

America Issue — Flora and Fauna — A652

No. 1687: a, Semnornis ramphastinus. b, Bomarea glaucescens.

Perf. 13x13¼

2003, Nov. 1 Litho. Wmk. 395

1687 A652 $1.05 Horiz. pair, #a-b 7.50 3.75

Selection of Quito as World Heritage Site, 25th Anniv. A653

Churches: 40c, El Sagrario. No. 1689a, La Compañia de Jesus. No. 1689b, Santa Barbara. $1.05, San Francisco, vert.

2003, Nov. 1 ***Perf. 13¼x13, 13x13¼***

1688 A653 40c multi 1.25 .60

1689 A653 90c Horiz. pair, #a-b 6.00 3.00

1690 A653 $1.05 multi 3.75 1.90

Nos. 1688-1690 (3) 11.00 5.50

Christmas A654

Children's art by: No. 1691a, Stephanie Pacheco. No. 1691b, Sebastián Tejada. 40c, María Claudia Iturralde, vert. 90c, Luis Antonio Ortega. $1.05, Angel Andrés Castro, vert.

2003, Nov. 1

1691 A654 25c Horiz. pair, #a-b 1.90 .95

1692 A654 40c multi 1.50 .75

1693 A654 90c multi 3.50 1.75

1694 A654 $1.05 multi 3.75 1.90

Nos. 1691-1694 (4) 10.65 5.35

Treasures of Guayaquil Municipal Museum A655

No. 1695: a, Santiago de Guayaquil Act of Independence. b, Punaes ceremonial stone. c, Proclamation of Mariano Donoso. d, Tzantzas. e, Manteño-Huancavilca totem.

2003, Dec. 1 ***Perf. 13¼x13***

1695 Horiz. strip of 5 7.00 3.50

a.-e. A655 40c Any single 1.25 .65

Selection of Galapagos Islands as World Heritage Site, 25th Anniv. — A656

No. 1696: a, Zalophus californianus wollebacki. b, Fregata minor palmerstoni. c, Sula nebouxxi excisa. d, Isla Bartolomé. e, Two Sula nebouxxi excisa shaped as "25."

2003, Nov. 26 ***Perf. 13x13¼***

1696 Horiz. strip of 5 7.00 3.50

a.-e. A656 40c Any single 1.25 .65

Army Aviation Instruction, 50th Anniv. — A657

No. 1697, 40c: a, Mountain, airplanes, emblem. b, Airplane in flight, men on ground.

No. 1698, 40c, horiz.: a, Helicopter and soldiers. b, Airplanes, mountain, people.

2004, Jan. 21 ***Perf. 13x13¼, 13¼x13***

Horiz. pairs, #a-b

1697-1698 A657 Set of 2 6.00 3.00

Military Geographical Institute's Role in National Development — A658

2004, Apr. 14 ***Perf. 13¼x13***

1699 A658 $1.05 multi 3.25 1.90

Commander Rafael Morán Valverde, Military Hero — A659

2004, Apr. 5 ***Perf. 13x13¼***

1700 A659 $1.05 multi 3.75 1.90

Intl. Philately Day — A660

No. 1701: a, Ecuador #2, Greece #1. b, Cover with six stamps.

$2, Various stamps, tongs, magnifying glass, stamp catalogues.

2004, May 6 ***Perf. 13¼x13***

1701 A660 75c Horiz. pair, #a-b 6.00 3.00

Imperf

Size: 100x68mm

1702 A660 $2 multi 7.50 3.75

Ecuadorian Volleyball Federation A661

Perf. 13x13¼

2004, May 27 Litho. Wmk. 395

1703 A661 75c multi 3.00 1.50

2004 Miss Universe Pageant A662

2004, May 29 ***Perf. 13¾***

1704 A662 75c multi 3.00 1.50

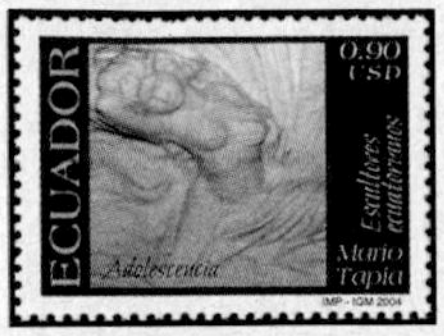

Sculpture by Mario Tapia
A663

No. 1705: a, Adolescencia. b, Beato Chaminade. c, Delfin de Galapagos. d, Pelicano. e, Homenaje a Carlo Vidano.
$2, Similar to No. 1705b.

2004, June 1 ***Perf. 13¼x13***

1705	Horiz. strip of 5		16.00	8.00
a.-e.	A663 90c Any single		2.25	1.10

Imperf

Size: 100x69mm

1706	A663	$2 multi	9.00	4.50

Pedro Vicente Maldonado (1704-48), Cartographer
A664

2004, June 25 ***Perf. 13x13¼***

1707	A664	90c multi	3.00	1.50

Dr. Agustín Cueva Tamariz (1903-79) — A665

2004, June 30 **Litho.**

1708	A665	90c multi	3.00	1.50

34th General Assembly of the Organization of American States — A666

2004, July 4 **Wmk. 395**

1709	A666	75c multi	3.00	1.50

Dr. Angel Felicísmo Rojas (b. 1909), Writer — A667

2004, July 11

1710	A667	50c multi	2.00	1.00

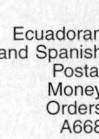

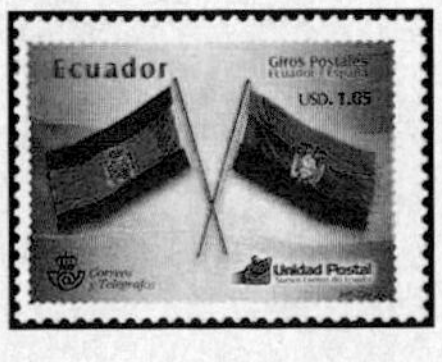

Ecuadoran and Spanish Postal Money Orders
A668

2004, Aug. 3 ***Perf. 13¼x13***

1711	A668	$1.05 multi	3.25	1.90

2004 Summer Olympics, Athens — A669

No. 1712 — 2004 Summer Olympics emblem, Ecuadoran Olympic Committee emblem and: a, 2004 Olympics mascots. b, Alexandra Escobar Guerrero.

2004, Aug. 3 ***Perf. 13x13¼***

1712	A669	$1.05 Horiz. pair, #a-b	7.50	3.75

Ecuador Orchid Association, 30th Anniv. — A670

Designs: 25c, Cattleya maxima. $1.05, Epidendrum bracteolatum.

2004, Sept. 30

1713-1714	A670	Set of 2	5.00	2.50

Guayaquil Symphony Orchestra — A671

Perf. 13x13¼

2004, Nov. 19 **Litho.** **Wmk. 395**

1715	A671	90c multi	3.00	1.50

Christmas — A672

Children's art: 40c, Christmas stocking with envelopes. $1.05, Santa Claus giving letter to Christmas tree, horiz.

2004, Dec. 12 ***Perf. 13x13¼, 13¼x13***

1716-1717	A672	Set of 2	5.00	2.50

America Issue - Environmental Protection — A673

Designs: 40d, Buddha and trees. $1.05, Mother Earth.

2004, Dec. 23 ***Perf. 13x13¼***

1718-1719	A673	Set of 2	5.00	2.50

Galapagos Islands Fauna
A674

Designs: 40c, Chelonoidis abingdonii. 90c, Amblyfhynchus cristatus, vert. $2.15, Sula granti. $3, Fregata magnifiscens.
$2, Creagrus furcatus, vert.

2005, Feb. 18 ***Perf. 13¼x13, 13x13¼***

1720-1723	A674	Set of 4	24.00	12.00

Imperf

Size: 68x98mm

1724	A674	$2 multi	7.50	3.75

El Mercurio Newspaper, 80th Anniv.
A675

Designs: $1.25, Masthead. $2, Dr. Nicanor Merchan Bermeo, newspaper co-founder. $2.25, Miguel Merchan Ochoa.

2005, Mar. 4 ***Perf. 13¼x13, 13x13¼***

1725-1727	A675	Set of 3	22.50	11.00

Tourism
A676

2005, Mar. 22 ***Perf. 13¼x13***

1728	A676	$3.75 multi	14.00	7.00

Ecuadorian Chess Federation, 25th Anniv. — A677

2005, Apr. 1 ***Perf. 13x13¼***

1729	A677	$1.25 multi	5.00	2.50

Ecuadorian Olympic Academy, 25th Anniv. — A678

Perf. 13x13¼

2005, June 20 **Litho.** **Wmk. 395**

1730	A678	$1.25 shown	5.00	2.50

Imperf

Size: 69x100mm

1731	A678	$2 Emblems	9.00	4.50

Rotary International, Cent.
A679

Rotary emblem and: 40c, Man on Mt. Chimborazo. 90c, People on Mt. Cotopaxi. $2, Man on Mt. Shisha Pangma, Nepal.

2005, June 29 ***Perf. 13¼x13***

1732-1734	A679	Set of 3	12.50	6.25

Guayaquil Conference, 183rd Anniv. — A680

No. 1735 — Guayaquil Philatelic Club emblem and: a, José de San Martín, Argentina #1. b, Simón Bolívar, Venezuela #1.
$2, Bolívar, San Martín, monument.

2005, July 22 ***Perf. 13¼x13***

1735	A680	90c Horiz. pair, #a-b	7.50	3.75

Imperf

Size:98x68mm

1736	A680	$2 multi	9.00	4.50

Intl. Year of Books and Reading — A681

Perf. 13x13¼

2005, July 22 **Litho.** **Wmk. 395**

1737	A681	25c multi	1.25	.60

Dr. Juan Isaac Lovato Vargas (1904-2001), Judge — A682

Perf. 13¼x13

2005, July 28 **Litho.** **Wmk. 395**

1738	A682	$1.25 multi	6.00	3.00

Mountain and Eastern Cattleman's Association — A683

No. 1739 — Emblem and: a, Mountains. b, Head of cow.

2005, Aug. 4 ***Perf. 13x13¼***

1739	A683	40c Horiz. pair, #a-b	3.00	3.00

University Sports League of Quito, 75th Anniv.
A684

No. 1740: a, University Sports League Stadium. b, 1969 University Sports League soccer team. c, Emblem. d, Children playing at school. e, Statue of emblem, League Country Club.
$2, Soccer shirt, vert.

2005, Aug. 4 ***Perf. 13¼x13***

1740	Horiz. strip of 5		8.00	4.00
a.-e.	A684 40c Any single		1.40	.70

Imperf

Size: 68x98mm

1741	A684	$2 multi	9.00	4.50

15th Bolivarian Games, Armenia and Pereira A685

2005, Aug. 8 ***Perf. 13¼x13***
1742 A685 25c multi 1.25 .60

1938 South American Swimming Champions, Trophy and Swimming Federation Emblem A686

2005, Aug. 8 **Litho.**
1743 A686 25c multi 1.25 .60

First Ecuadoran victory in international sports competition.

Virgin of Cisne — A687

2005, Sept. 6 ***Perf. 13¾***
1744 A687 $1.25 multi 6.00 3.00

History of the Ecuadoran Army A688

No. 1745: a, Troops in Esmeraldas, 1916. b, Military school cadets, 1928. c, Cayambe Battalion. d, Arms and Grandsons of Gen. Eloy Alfaro. e, Imbabura Battalion.

$2, Battle for emancipation of Guayaquil.

2005, Sept. 15 ***Perf. 13¼x13***
1745 Horiz. strip of 5 8.00 4.00
a.-e. A688 40c Any single 1.00 .50

Imperf

Size: 98x67mm

1746 A688 $2 multi 9.00 4.50

Carchi Province Arms — A689

No. 1747: a, Tulcán Canton. b, Bolívar Canton.

No. 1748: a, Carchi Province. b, Huaca Canton. c, Mira Canton. d, Espejo Canton. e, Montúfar Canton.

2005, Sept. 26 ***Perf. 13x13¼***
1747 Horiz. pair 3.00 1.50
a.-b. A689 40c Either single 1.40 .70
1748 Horiz. strip of 5 7.50 3.75
a.-e. A689 40c Any single 1.40 .70

Tourism — A690

No. 1749: a, Cerro Santa Ana, Guayaquil. b, Esmereldas. c, Misahualli. d, Tsunki Shuar, Pastaza.

No. 1750: a, Cisne Church, Loja. b, Ingapirca Ruins. c, Seal, Galapagos Islands. d, Sea turtle, Galapagos Islands.

Perf. 13¼x13

2005, Sept. 26 **Litho.** **Wmk. 395**
1749 A690 30c Block of 4, #a-d 5.00 2.50
1750 A690 40c Block of 4, #a-d 6.50 3.25

St. Mariana de Jesús Paredes y Flores A691

2005, Oct. 19
1751 A691 25c multi 1.25 .60

Popes Reigning in 2005 — A692

No. 1752: a, $1.25, Pope John Paul II (1920-2005). b, $2, Pope Benedict XVI.

2005, Oct. 19
1752 A692 Horiz. pair, #a-b 12.50 6.25

Cenepa War With Peru, 10th Anniv. — A693

No. 1753: a, Mirage F1-JA airplanes. b, Cessna A-37B airplanes. c, Kfir-C2 airplanes. d, Lt. Col. Carlos Uscategui and airplane.

2005, Oct. 26
1753 A693 $1.25 Block of 4, #a-d 22.50 11.00

First Guayaquil to Cuenca Airmail Flight, 85th Anniv. — A694

No. 1754: a, 25c, Tail of Telegrafo I airplane, flight manager José Abel Castillo. b, $1, Front of Telegrafo I airplane, pilot Elia Liut.

2005, Nov. 12
1754 A694 Horiz. pair, #a-b 5.50 2.75

Ecuadorian Armed Forces in United Nations Peacekeeping Forces — A695

No. 1755: a, Female soldier. b, Two soldiers wearing helmets. c, Soldiers with flags. d, United Nations and Ecuadorian flags, beret of Peacekeeping forces.

2005, Nov. 25 ***Perf. 13x13¼***
1755 A695 75c Block of 4, #a-d 12.00 6.00

Christmas — A696

No. 1756 — Children's drawings by: a, Pamela Alejandra Castillo Rocha. b, Kira Cedeño. c, Silvia Moran Burgos. d, Carol Garcia.

2005, Nov. 25
1756 A696 $1.25 Block of 4, #a-d 22.50 11.00

19th Cent. Watercolors of Ecuadorians A697

No. 1757: a, Water bearer. b, Indian governor's wife. c, Dancer. d, Cuenca Indian. e, Municipal council piper. f, Indian carrying skyrockets. g, Woman (Mina gigante). h, Majordomo. i, Society woman (Chola pinganilla). j, Street sweeper.

2005, Nov. 30 ***Perf. 13¾***
1757 Block of 10 12.50 6.25
a.-j. A697 25c Any single 1.00 .50

Publication of Don Quixote, 400th Anniv. — A698

No. 1758 — Drawings of Don Quixote and: a, Windmills. b, Tree.

2005, Dec. 7 ***Perf. 13x13¼***
1758 A698 $2 Horiz. pair, #a-b 17.00 8.50

Colonial Religious Art — A699

Colonial Religious Art — A700

No. 1759: a, St. Joseph and Baby Jesus. b, Resurrected Christ. c, Virgin of Quito. d, St. Augustine.

No. 1760: $2, The Divine Shepherd.

2005, Dec. 9
1759 A699 40c Block of 4, #a-d 6.00 3.00

Souvenir Sheet

Imperf

1760 A700 $2 multi 9.00 4.50

El Comercio Newspaper, Cent. (in 2006) A701

"100" and: No. 1761, Statue at LL, newspaper masthead. No. 1762a, Statue at LR. No. 1762b, Statue in "0." No. 1763, Statue in seal. No. 1764, Statue at LL, newspaper masthead, simulated perforations.

Perf. 13¼x13

2006, Jan. 2 **Litho.** **Wmk. 395**
1761 A701 40c multi 1.75 .85
1762 A701 40c Horiz. pair, #a-b 3.25 1.60

Size: 55x35mm

Perf. 13¾

1763 A701 50c multi 2.00 1.00
Nos. 1761-1763 (3) 7.00 3.45

Size: 100x69mm

Imperf

1764 A701 $2 multi 8.00 4.00

Dated 2006.

Quito Tourism A702

2006, Jan. 11 ***Perf. 13¼x13***
1765 A702 25c multi 1.25 .60

Dated 2005.

35th Latin American and Caribbean Lions' Club Forum, Quito — A703

Color of oceans: 90c, White. $2, Orange.

2006, Jan. 19 *Perf. 13x13¼*
1766 A703 90c multi 4.00 2.00

Size: 68x99mm

Imperf

1767 A703 $2 multi 8.00 4.00

Biodiversity of Puyo A704

Designs: $1, Cromacris sp. $1.20, Desmodus rotundus.

2006, Mar. 22 *Perf. 13¼x13*
1768-1769 A704 Set of 2 10.00 5.00

America Issue, Fight Against Poverty A705

Various Pre-Columbian Guayasamin figurines: 40c, 80c, $1, $1.20.

2006, Feb. 12
1770-1773 A705 Set of 4 14.50 7.25

Benito Juarez (1806-72), President of Mexico — A706

2006, Mar. 21 *Perf. 13x13¼*
1774 A706 $1.20 multi 5.00 2.50

Manteña Raft A707

2006, Mar. 23 *Perf. 13¼x13*
1775 A707 $1 multi 4.50 2.25

Straw Hat Makers A708

Designs: No. 1776, 40c, Hat maker. No. 1777, 40c, Hat maker wearing hat, vert.

2006, Apr. 8 *Perf. 13¼x13, 13x13¼*
1776-1777 A708 Set of 2 3.75 1.90

Federation of University Students — A709

2006, Apr. 21 *Perf. 13x13¼*
1778 A709 30c multi 1.25 .60

Miracle of Colegio San Gabriel, Cent. — A710

2006, Apr. 21 **Wmk. 395**
1779 A710 80c multi 3.75 1.90

Ibarra, 400th Anniv. A711

2006, Apr. 28 *Perf. 13¼x13*
1780 A711 20c shown .80 .25

Size: 68x100mm

Imperf

1781 A711 $2.50 Painting, diff. 11.00 5.50

Baltazara Calderon — A712

2005, May 16 *Perf. 13x13¼*
1782 A712 $1 multi 4.50 2.25

18th Cent. Military Uniforms A713

No. 1783: a, Compañia Fija de Quito. b, Dragones de Quito. c, Infanteria de Quito. d, Dragones de Guayaquil (gray horse). e, Dragones de Guayaquil (brown horse).

2006, May 18 *Perf. 13¾*
1783 Horiz. strip of 5 4.25 2.10
a.-e. A713 20c Any single .70 .25

Mushrooms and Fauna of Podocarpus Park — A714

Designs: 20c, Basidiomicetes. 25c, Tremarctus ornatus. 90c, Harpya harpyja, vert.

Perf. 13¼x13, 13x13¼

2006, May 22 **Litho.** **Wmk. 395**
1784-1786 A714 Set of 3 6.00 3.00

Wolfgang Amadeus Mozart (1756-91), Composer A715

2006, May 31 *Perf. 13¼x13*
1787 A715 20c multi .80 .25

UNICEF, 60th Anniv. A716

Designs: 75c, Child, butterfly, and sun. $1, Children and books.

Perf. 13¼x13

2006, June 1 **Litho.** **Wmk. 395**
1788-1789 A716 Set of 2 8.00 4.00

Eloy Alfaro Military School A717

2006, June 5
1790 A717 80c multi 3.75 1.90

Banco Pichincha, Cent. A718

Designs: No. 1791, 1906 1-sucre banknote. No. 1792 — First bank building: a, Denomination at left. b, Denomination at right.

2006, June 8
1791 A718 40c shown 1.80 .90
1792 A718 40c Horiz. pair, #a-b 3.75 1.90

2006 World Cup Soccer Championships, Germany — A719

FIFA emblem and: 40c, World Cup. 80c, 2006 World Cup emblem. $1, Mascot. $1.20, World Cup and flags of competing countries.

Perf. 13¼x13

2006, June 9 **Litho.** **Wmk. 395**
1793-1796 A719 Set of 4 14.50 7.25

Designs: No. 1797C, Like #1796. No. 1797D, Similar to #1796, but with scores of Ecuador team's first round victories.

2006 **Litho.** **Wmk. 395** ***Imperf.***

Size: 60x40mm

1797C A719 $2 multi 8.00 4.00
1797D A719 $2 multi 8.00 4.00

A720

Plaza de Mayo Mothers of Argentina — A721

Perf. 13¼x13

2006, June 19 **Litho.** **Wmk. 395**
1798 A720 80c multi 3.75 1.90

Imperf

1799 A721 $2.50 multi 11.00 5.50

Machala Canton, 182nd Anniv. A722

2006, June 20 *Perf. 13¼x13*
1800 A722 30c multi 1.25 .60

Machala Canton, 182nd Anniv. — A723

Flags of 2006 World Cup Soccer Championship participants, FIFA emblem and: No. 1801, Flag of Ecuador. No. 1802, Soccer shoes and ball.

2006 **Litho.** **Wmk. 395** ***Imperf.***
1801 A723 $2 multi 8.00 4.00
1802 A723 $2 multi 8.00 4.00

2006 World Cup Soccer Championships, Germany.

Garibaldi Italian Assistance Society — A724

2006, July 7 *Perf. 13x13¼*
1803 A724 90c multi 4.00 2.00

Souvenir Sheet

Municipal Railroads — A726

Wmk. 395

2006, July 20 Litho. ***Imperf.***

1806 A726 $2 multi 8.00 4.00

Simón Bolívar Experimental College — A727

Bolívar A728

2006, July 25 Litho. ***Perf. 13x13¼***

1807 A727 20c multi .80 .25

Imperf

1808 A728 $10 multi 40.00 20.00

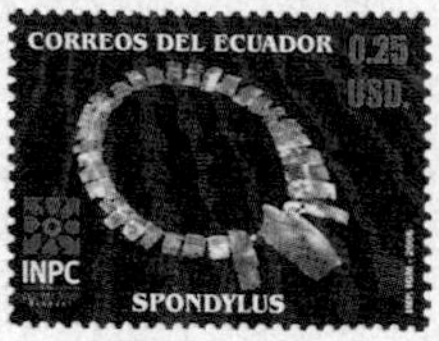

Spondylus Shell Carvings in National Institute of Cultural Heritage A729

Designs: 25c, Necklace.

No. 1810, vert.: a, Figurine of trader. b, Figurine of fishermen in boat.

2006, July 26 ***Perf. 13¼x13, 13x13¼***

1809 A729 25c multi 1.50 .75

1810 A729 $1 Horiz. pair, #a-b 8.00 8.00

Indian Postal Runner and Ecuador Post Emblem — A730

Background colors: 25c, White. 30c, Dark blue. 40c, Black. 60c, Beige. 80c, Olive green

2006, Aug. 5 ***Perf. 13x13¼***

1811-1815 A730 Set of 5 10.00 5.00

Ecuadorian Olympic Committee A731

2006, Aug. 15 Litho.

1816 A731 30c multi 1.25 .60

Writers — A732

Designs: $1, Jorge Icaza (1906-78). $1.20, Pablo Palacio (1906-47).

2006, Sept. 18 Wmk. 395

1817-1818 A732 Set of 2 10.00 5.00

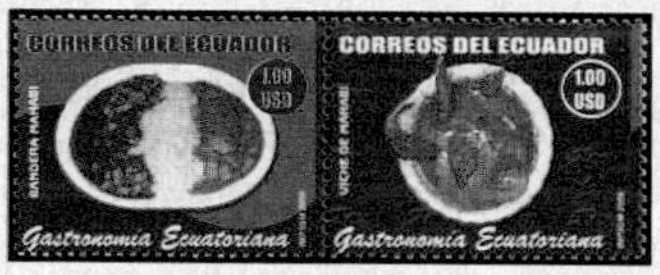

Ecuadorian Food — A733

No. 1819: a, Bandera Manabi. b, Viche de Manabi.

2006, Sept. 23 ***Perf. 13¼x13***

1819 A733 $1 Horiz. pair, #a-b 8.50 4.25

Orchids — A734

No. 1820: a, Caucaea olivaceum. b, Cyrtochilum macranthum. c, Miltoniopsis vexillaria. d, Odontoglossum harryanum. e, Cyrtochilum pastasae. f, Cyrtochilum loxense. g, Cyrtochilum eduardii. h, Odontoglossum epidendroides. i, Cyrtochilum retusum. j, Cyrtochilum geniculatum.

$2, Cyrtochilum macranthum, diff.

2006, Sept. 29 ***Perf. 13x13¼***

1820 Block of 10 13.00 6.50

a.-j. A734 30c Any single 1.25 .60

Imperf

Size: 66x95mm

1821 A734 $2 multi 8.50 4.25

America Issue, Energy Conservation — A735

Background color: $1, Brown. $1.20, Blue.

2006, Oct. 4 ***Perf. 13¼x13***

1822-1823 A735 Set of 2 10.00 5.00

Natural Fiber Art, by Giti Neuman — A736

Designs: No. 1824, En la Ventana.

No. 1825: a, Forma en Movimiento. b, Caminantes.

No. 1826, horiz.: a, Caminando. b, Cabezas Huecas.

2006, Oct. 4 ***Perf. 13x13¼, 13¼x13***

1824 A736 30c multi 1.25 .60

1825 A736 30c Vert. pair, #a-b 2.75 1.40

1826 A736 30c Horiz. pair, #a-b 2.75 1.40

Nos. 1824-1826 (3) 6.75 3.40

Tourism in Otovalo A737

Designs: 25c, El Lechero tree. 30c, El Jordan Church. 75c, Young girl, vert. $1, Costume for El Coraza Festival, vert.

2006, Oct. 18 ***Perf. 13¼x13, 13x13¼***

1827-1830 A737 Set of 4 10.50 5.25

Eruption of Tungurahua Volcano — A738

No. 1831: a, Ash cloud above volcano. b, Lava flowing down volcano.

2006, Oct. 20 ***Perf. 13x13¼***

1831 A738 $1 Horiz. pair, #a-b 8.50 4.25

Urban Renewal of Guayaquil A739

No. 1832: a, Municipal Palace, denomination at left. b, Municipal Palace, denomination at right. c, Vulcan forge. d, José Joaquín de Olmedo Airport. e, Bus station.

2006, Oct. 24 ***Perf. 13¼x13***

1832 Horiz. strip of 5 21.50 11.00

a.-e. A739 $1 Any single 3.75 1.90

Radio Station HCJB, 75th Anniv. A740

2006, Oct. 26 Wmk. 395

1833 A740 $1 multi 4.50 2.25

Millennium Development Objectives of the United Nations — A741

2006, Oct. 27 ***Perf. 13¾***

1834 A741 $2 multi 8.50 4.25

Pres. Galo Plaza Lasso (1906-87) — A742

Designs: 40c, Photograph. 80c, Tree.

2006, Oct. 27 ***Perf. 13x13¼***

1835-1836 A742 Set of 2 5.00 2.50

German Shepherd Breeding Association A743

2006, Oct. 28 Litho. ***Perf. 13¼x13***

1837 A743 $1 multi 4.50 2.25

Military Parachuting, 50th Anniv. A744

Designs: 20c, Soldiers. 40c, Soldiers and airplane. 60c, Soldier and troop emblem. 80c, Paratrooper in air.

Perf. 13¼x13, 13x13¼

2006, Oct. 31 Litho. Wmk. 395

1838-1841 A744 Set of 4 8.50 4.25

Galapagos Islands Fauna — A745

No. 1842, horiz.: a, Sea turtle. b, Sea gull. c, Marine iguana. d, Blue-footed boobies. e, Sea lion.

80c, Flamingo. $1, Crab. $1.20, Fish.

2006, Nov. 1

1842 A745 30c Horiz. strip of 5, #a-e 6.50 3.25

1843 A745 80c multi 3.25 1.60

1844 A745 $1 multi 4.00 2.00

1845 A745 $1.20 multi 5.00 2.50

Nos. 1842-1845 (4) 18.75 9.35

Christmas — A746

2006, Nov. 28 ***Perf. 13x13¼***
1846 A746 80c multi 3.25 1.60

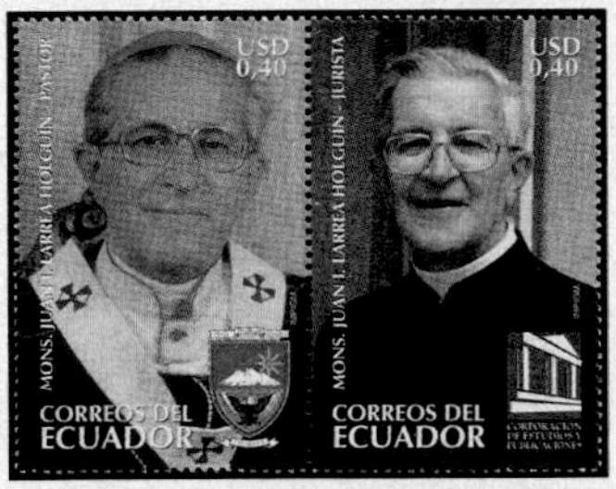

Monsignor Juan I. Larrea Holguín (1927-2006) — A747

No. 1847: a, In bishop's robes. b, In judicial robes.

2006, Dec. 8 ***Perf. 13¾***
1847 A747 40c Horiz. pair, #a-b 3.75 1.90

Freemasonry A748

Designs: 25c, Masonic altar, beehive. 40c, Compass and square.

2006, Dec. 11 ***Perf. 13x13¼***
1848-1849 A748 Set of 2 3.00 1.50

Quito Zoo Animals — A749

No. 1850: a, Parrot. b, Frog.
No. 1851: a, Harpy eagle. b, Jaguar.
$2, Parrot on branch.

2006, Dec. 11 ***Perf. 13x13¼***
1850 A749 60c Horiz. pair, #a-b 4.75 2.40
1851 A749 80c Horiz. pair, #a-b 6.50 3.25

Imperf

Size: 40x65mm

1852 A749 $2 multi 8.50 4.25

Erotic and Fertility Figurines — A750

Designs: 10c, Nursing mother. 20c, Copulating couple. $1.20, Pregnant woman. $2, Man with erect penis.

2006, Dec. 12 ***Perf. 13x13¼***
1853-1856 A750 Set of 4 15.00 7.50

Admiral Juan Illingworth Naval Museum — A751

Emblem of Ecuador Navy and Illingworth: 20c, On rope ladder, 1880. 25c, As Marine Guard, 1854.

2006, Dec. 15 **Litho.**
1857-1858 A751 Set of 2 2.00 1.00

Colors of Ecuador Flag — A752

2006, Dec. 15 **Wmk. 395**
1859 A752 $10 multi 37.50 19.00

Postmen and Bicycles A753

Color of photograph: 20c, Gray brown. 40c, Gray blue. 80c, Red.

2006, Dec. 17 ***Perf. 13¼x13***
1860-1862 A753 Set of 3 6.00 3.00

Pets A754

Designs: 25c, Puppy. 40c, Dog, vert. 50c, Cat with brown and blue eyes, vert. 80c, Dog running. $1, Cat with blue eyes, vert.

2006, Dec. 17 ***Perf. 13¼x13, 13x13¼***
1863-1867 A754 Set of 5 12.00 6.00

Cuenca Biennale A755

Art by: 5c, Alexander Apóstol. 15c, Ricardo González Elias, vert.

2006, Dec. 20
1868-1869 A755 Set of 2 .55 .25

Independence Monument, 50th Anniv. — A756

No. 1870: a, Head of statue. b, Entire statue.

2006, Dec. 21 ***Perf. 13¾***
1870 A756 20c Horiz. pair, #a-b 1.80 .90

Quito Fair — A757

Designs: No. 1871, Matador Manolo Caena.
No. 1872 — Matadors: a, Sebastián Castella. b, El Juli.
No. 1873, horiz. — Quito Bull Ring: a, At right. b, At left.
$3, Sculpture of Jesus, horiz.

Perf. 13x13¼, 13¼x13

2006, Dec. 27 **Litho.**
1871 A757 50c multi 2.50 1.25
1872 A757 50c Horiz. pair, #a-b 4.25 2.10
1873 A757 50c Horiz. pair, #a-b 4.25 2.10
Nos. 1871-1873 (3) 11.00 5.45

Litho. With Foil Application

Imperf

Size: 65x40mm

1874 A757 $3 multi 13.00 6.50

Pirates A758

No. 1875, vert.: a, Jolly Roger flag, ship, sea lions. b, Sea lions, ships. c, Ships, Jolly roger flag. d, Armed pirate on ship. e, Ship, Jolly Roger flag.
No. 1876: a, Map of Galapagos Islands, Jolly Roger flag, Sir Francis Drake. b, Ship, map, skull.
$1, Ship, map, skull, William Dampier.

Perf. 13x13¼, 13¼x13

2006, Dec. 27 **Litho.**
1875 A758 30c Horiz. strip of 5, #a-e 7.25 3.50
1876 A758 40c Horiz. pair, #a-b 3.75 1.90
1877 A758 $1 multi 5.00 2.50
Nos. 1875-1877 (3) 16.00 7.90

SEK International University, Quito A759

Perf. 13¼x13

2006, Dec. 29 **Wmk. 395**
1878 A759 10c multi .50 .40

Scouting, Cent. — A760

Scout emblem and: 25c, Circles. $2, Scout and circles.

Perf. 13x13¼

2007, Mar. 29 **Litho.** **Wmk. 395**
1879-1880 A760 Set of 2 8.00 4.00

Hispanic-American Poetry Festival — A761

2007, Apr. 19
1881 A761 10c multi .40 .30

Cuenca, 450th Anniv. — A762

Designs: 40c, Casa de los Arcos (Arch House). 75c, Vergel Plaza. 80c, Tomebamba River Gorge, horiz. $3, Cathedral of the Immaculate Conception.

2007, Apr. 27 ***Perf. 13x13¼, 13¼x13***
1882-1885 A762 Set of 4 17.50 8.75

Prehistoric Animals — A763

Designs: No. 1886, 80c, Megatherium. No. 1887, 80c, Smilodon, horiz.

2007, May 10
1886-1887 A763 Set of 2 5.75 3.75

Beetles A764

Designs: No. 1888, Golopha eaucus.
No. 1889: a, Chrysophora chrysochlora. b, Dynastes hercules.

2007, May 10 ***Perf. 13¼x13***
1888 A764 40c multi 1.50 .75
1889 A764 40c Horiz. pair, #a-b 3.00 1.50

Guayaquil Rotary Club, 80th Anniv. A765

2007, June 1 **Wmk. 395**
1890 A765 25c multi .90 .45

America Issue, Education For All — A766

Designs: 40c, Children on school bus. 80c, Girl doing geometry work. $1, Children flying kites, vert. $1.20, Student in wheelchair, vert. $2, Girl and handprints, vert.

2007, June 6 ***Perf. 13¼x13, 13x13¼***
1891-1894 A766 Set of 4 12.00 6.00

Imperf

Size: 40x65mm

1895 A766 $2 multi 7.50 3.75

Naval Institute of Oceanography, 75th Anniv. — A767

Antarctic research: 10c, Penguin, ship. $3, Scientists and scientific equipment, horiz.

2007, July 18 ***Perf. 13x13¼***
1896 A767 10c multi .40 .30

Perf. 12

Size: 52x32mm

1897 A767 $3 multi 11.00 5.50

Central Bank of Ecuador, 80th Anniv. — A768

2007, Aug. 28 ***Perf. 12***
1898 A768 $2 multi 7.50 3.75

Guayaquil Firefighters A769

Various firefighters at fires: 5c, 10c, 15c, 25c, $1. 25c and $1 are horiz.

2007, Oct. 10 ***Perf. 13x13¼, 13¼x13***
1899-1903 A769 Set of 5 5.50 2.75

Breast Cancer Prevention A770

2007, Oct. 15 ***Perf. 13¼x13***
1904 A770 $3 multi 11.00 5.50

Guayaquil Tourism — A771

Designs: 5c, Las Peñas. 10c, Lighthouse, Santa Ana Hill. 15c, El Velero Bridge. 25c, Mercado Sur, horiz. $1, June 5 Bridge, horiz.

2007, Oct. 23 ***Perf. 13x13¼, 13¼x13***
1905-1909 A771 Set of 5 5.50 2.25

Cuenca Chamber of Industries, 70th Anniv. A772

2007, Oct. 25 ***Perf. 13¼x13***
1910 A772 $1.20 multi 4.25 2.10

Operation Smile A773

2007, Nov. 16 **Litho.**
1911 A773 $1 multi 3.75 1.90

Vistazo Magazine, 50th Anniv. A774

2007, Nov. 29 ***Perf. 12***
1912 A774 20c multi .75 .25

Galapagos Islands Fauna A775

Designs: 40c, Sea turtle. 80c, Penguin. $1, Dolphin. $1.20, Tropicbird.

2007, Nov. 30 ***Perf. 13¼x13***
1913-1916 A775 Set of 4 12.00 6.00

Compare with type A780.

Comptroller General, 80th Anniv. A776

2007, Dec. 3 ***Perf. 12***
1917 A776 20c multi .75 .25

2007 Pan American Games, Rio de Janeiro — A777

No. 1918 — Athletes and text noting gold medalists: a, Alexandra Escobar. b, Seledina Nieve. c, Jefferson Perez. d, Xavier Moreno. e, Under-18 soccer team.

2007, Dec. 18 ***Perf. 13x13¼***
1918 Horiz. strip of 5 7.25 3.00
a.-e. A777 40c Any single 1.25 .60

Christmas — A778

No. 1919: a, The Annunciation. b, The Three Magi. c, Nativity. d, Flight into Egypt.

2007, Dec. 20 ***Perf. 13¼x13***
1919 A778 20c Block of 4, #a-d 2.75 1.40

Guayas Province Transit Commission, 60th Anniv. — A779

Perf. 13x13¼

2008, Jan. 29 **Litho.** **Wmk. 395**
1920 A779 $1 multi 3.75 1.90

Galapagos Islands A780

Map of islands and: 40c, Pelecanus occidentalis. 80c, Aetobatus narinari. $1, Carcharhinus galapagensis. $1.20, San Cristóbal Windmill Project.

2008, Mar. 18 ***Perf. 13¼x13***
1921-1924 A780 Set of 4 12.00 6.00

Compare with Type A775.

Free Maternity and Infant Care — A781

2008, Mar. 28 ***Perf. 12***
1925 A781 $1 multi 3.75 1.90

Guayaquil Port Authority, 50th Anniv. A782

2008, Apr. 8
1926 A782 20c multi .75 .25

Tungurahua Chamber of Industry, 80th Anniv. — A783

Wmk. 395

2008, Apr. 24 **Litho.** ***Perf. 12***
1927 A783 $3 multi 11.00 5.50

Father Carlos Crespi (1891-1982) — A784

2008, Apr. 30
1928 A784 $2 multi 7.25 3.00

Santiago de Guayaquil Medallion A785

2008, June 3
1929 A785 30c multi 1.10 .55

Intl. Philately Day.

Jorge Pérez Concha, Historian and Diplomat, Birth Cent. — A786

2008, June 4
1930 A786 $3 multi 11.00 5.50

Los Pinos College, Quito, 40th Anniv. A787

2008, June 6
1931 A787 20c multi .75 .25

Guayaquil-Quito Railway, Cent. — A788

Ecuador No. 174 and: 56c, Steam locomotive. $5, Steam locomotives, Gabriel García Moreno and Gen. Eloy Alfaro.

2008, June 23 ***Perf. 12***
1932 A788 56c multi 2.00 1.00

Imperf

Size: 100x70mm

1933 A788 $5 multi 18.00 9.00

Polytechnic School of the Coast, 50th Anniv. — A789

Wmk. 395

2008, July 28 **Litho.** ***Perf. 12***
1934 A789 32c multi 1.10 .55

Latin American Youth Year — A790

2008, Aug. 20
1935 A790 30c multi 1.10 .55

Ecuadorian Cacao — A791

No. 1936: a, Cacao pod, UL corner of #306. b, Cacao flower, UR corner of #306. c, Cacao processing, LL corner of #306. d, Cacao pods and beans, chocolate candy, LR corner of #306.

2008, Oct. 1 ***Perf. 13¼x13***
1936 A791 56c Block of 4, #a-d 8.00 4.00

Meridiano Newspaper, 25th Anniv. — A792

2008, Oct. 22 ***Perf. 13x13¼***
1937 A792 60c multi 2.00 1.00

Intl. Swimming Federation, Cent. A793

No. 1938: a, World Map. b, Ecuadorian swimmer.
30c, Swimmer from underwater.

2008, Oct. 31 ***Perf. 13¼x13***
1938 A793 24c Horiz. pair, #a-b 1.25 .60
1939 A793 30c multi .70 .30

Office of the Procurator General, 80th Anniv. — A794

2008, Nov. 11 ***Perf. 13x13¼***
1940 A794 25c multi .60 .25

Guayaquil Chamber of Construction, 40th Anniv. A795

2008, Nov. 27 ***Perf. 13¼x13***
1941 A795 $1 multi 2.25 1.10

New Constitution — A796

Flag and: 32c, Sun behind clouds. $5, People, vert.

2008, Nov. 29 ***Perf. 12***
1942 A796 32c multi .75 .30

Size: 66x95mm

Imperf

1943 A796 $5 multi 12.00 6.00

Santiago de Guayaquil Municipal Museum, Cent. A797

No. 1944: a, Old musuem building. b, New museum building with murals.
$2, Entrance to old musuem building.

2008, Dec. 16 ***Perf. 13¼x13***
1944 A797 60c Horiz. pair, #a-b 3.00 1.50
1945 A797 $2 multi 5.00 2.50

Friendship Between Ecuador and Japan, 90th Anniv. — A798

No. 1945: a, Cotopaxi Volcano, Ecuador. b, Mt. Fuji, Japan.

2008, Dec. 17
1946 A798 30c Horiz. pair, #a-b 1.50 .75

America Issue, National Festivals — A799

No. 1947 — Festival of Sts. Peter and Paul: a, Dancers. b, Guitarist.
No. 1948, vert. — Diablada Pillareña: a, Figure with red mask. b, Figure with black mask.

2008, Dec. 23 ***Perf. 13¼x13***
1947 A799 20c Horiz. pair, #a-b 1.00 .50

Perf. 13x13¼

1948 A799 $1 Horiz. pair, #a-b 5.00 2.50

Christmas A800

Various creche figurines of Holy Family and animals with background color of: 30c, Blue.
No. 1949: a, Green. b, Yellow brown.

2008, Dec. 23 ***Perf. 13¼x13***
1949 A800 30c multi .75 .30
1950 A800 80c Horiz. pair, #a-b 4.00 2.00

A801

A802

A803

A804

Jacchigua National Folk Ballet A805

Perf. 13¼x13

2009, Feb. 18 **Litho.** **Wmk. 395**
1951 Horiz. strip of 5 12.00 6.00
a. A801 $1 multi 2.00 1.00
b. A802 $1 multi 2.00 1.00
c. A803 $1 multi 2.00 1.00
d. A804 $1 multi 2.00 1.00
e. A805 $1 multi 2.00 1.00

Preservation of Polar Regions and Glaciers A806

Designs: 20c, Feet of polar bear. 80c, Earth in water.

2009, Mar. 31
1952-1953 A806 Set of 2 2.50 1.25

A807

Tourism — A808

Designs: No. 1954, Babahoyo River, Los Ríos Province. No. 1955, Ingapirca Ruins, Cañar Province. No. 1956, Rafters on Quijos River, Napo Province. No. 1957, Marimba group, Esmeraldas Province. $1.25, Tulcán cemetery, Carchi Province. $2, Train and Mt. Chimborazo, Chimborazo Province. $3, Alcea rosea flowers, Morona-Santiago Province. $5, Acrocinus longimanus, Sucumbíos Province.
No. 1962: a, Like #1954. b, Like #1957. c, Like #1958. d, Like #1955. e, Like #1959. f, Like #1956. g, Like #1960. h, Like #1961.
No. 1963: a, Equator Monument, Pichincha Province. b, Colorado Indians, Santo Domingo de los Tsáchilas Province. c, Los Frailes Beach, Manabí Province. d, Banana plantation, El Oro Province. e, Arctocephalus galapagoensis, Galápagos Province. f, Cuicocha Lake, Imbabura Province. g, Harpia harpyja, Pastaza Province. h, Shuar community, Orellana Province.
No. 1964: a, Bolívar and San Martín Monument, Guayas Province. b, The Lovers of Sumpa, Santa Elena Province. c, Pillaro devil, Tungurahua Province. d, Mt. Cotopaxi, Cotopaxi Province. e, Guaranga Indian Monument, Bolívar Province. f, Virgin of Cisne, Loja Province. g, Tomebamba River, Azuay Province. h, Leopardus pardalis, Zamora Province.

Perf. 13¼x13

2009 **Litho.** **Wmk. 395**
1954 A807 25c multi .60 .25
1955 A807 50c multi 1.25 .60
1956 A807 75c multi 1.75 .90
1957 A807 $1 multi 2.50 1.25
1958 A807 $1.25 multi 3.00 1.50
1959 A807 $2 multi 4.75 2.40
1960 A807 $3 multi 7.25 3.50
1961 A807 $5 multi 12.00 6.00
Nos. 1954-1961 (8) 33.10 16.40

Booklet Stamps

Self-Adhesive

Die Cut

Unwmk.

1962 Booklet pane of 8 + 2 labels 12.50
a.-b. A808 25c Either single .60 .25
c.-d. A808 50c Either single 1.25 .50
e.-f. A808 75c Either single 1.75 .75
g.-h. A808 $1 Either single 2.50 1.00
1963 Booklet pane of 8 + 2 labels 12.50
a.-b. A808 25c Either single .60 .25
c.-d. A808 50c Either single 1.25 .50
e.-f. A808 75c Either single 1.75 .75
g.-h. A808 $1 Either single 2.50 1.00
1964 Booklet pane of 8 + 2 labels 12.50
a.-b. A808 25c Either single .60 .25
c.-d. A808 50c Either single 1.25 .50
e.-f. A808 75c Either single 1.75 .75
g.-h. A808 $1 Either single 2.50 1.00
Nos. 1962-1964 (3) 37.50

Issued: Nos. 1954-1961, 4/29; Nos. 1962-1964, July.
See Nos. 1985-2000, 2021-2022.

Intl. Philately Day — A809

Perf. 13¼x13

2009, May 6 **Wmk. 395**
1965 A809 75c multi 1.75 .90

Icons of Santa Clara Monastery A810

No. 1966: a, Angel. b, Jesus Christ. c, Pensive child. d, Protective Virgin. e, Virgin of Quito.

2009, June 9 *Perf. 13x13¼*
1966 Horiz. strip of 5 12.00 6.00
a.-e. A810 $1 Any single 2.00 1.00

National Finance Corporation, 45th Anniv. A811

2009, June 22 *Perf. 13¼x13*
1967 A811 $1.25 multi 3.00 1.50

Ambato Electric Company, 50th Anniv. A812

2009, June
1968 A812 $1 multi 2.50 1.25

Paute-Molino Dam, 25th Anniv. A813

2009, July 22
1969 A813 $2 multi 5.00 2.50

El Telégrafo Newspaper, 125th Anniv. A814

2009, July 30 *Perf. 12*
1970 A814 $1.75 multi 4.25 2.10

Call for Independence, Bicent. — A815

Nos. 1971 and 1972 — Doves, butterflies, bell and: a, Open mouth. b, Monument.

2009, Aug. 14 *Perf. 13¼x13*
1971 A815 $3 Horiz. pair, #a-b 14.50 7.25

Souvenir Sheet

With Horizontal Blue Stripe Added to Middle of Stamps

1972 A815 $3 Sheet of 2, #a-b 14.50 7.25

Call for Independence, Bicent. — A816

Serpentine Die Cut 12½x12¼
2009, Aug. 14 Litho. Unwmk.
Self-Adhesive
Printed on Cork
1973 A816 $3.50 multi 8.50 4.25

Chinese Benevolent Society, Cent. — A817

No. 1974: a, Galápagos tortoise. b, Giant panda.

Perf. 13¼x13
2009, Aug. 18 **Wmk. 395**
1974 A817 25c Horiz. pair, #a-b 1.25 .60

Famous People A818

No. 1975: a, Carlos Silva Pareja (1909-68), musician. b, Tránsito Amaguaña (1909-2009), Indian rights advocate. c, Demetrio Aguilera Malta (1909-81), writer, diplomat. d, Carlos Zevallos Menéndez (1909-81), archaeologist. e, Humberto Salvador Guerra (1909-82), writer.

2009, Aug. 28 **Litho.**
1975 Horiz. strip of 5 3.00 1.50
a.-e. A818 25c Any single .50 .25

Ecuadorian Olympic Committee, 50th Anniv. A819

Designs: No. 1976, 25c, Shooting, cycling, equestrian, wrestling, archery, and basketball. No. 1977, 25c, Diving, running, weight lifting, tennis, boxing and soccer, vert.

2009, Oct. 17 *Perf. 13¼x13, 13x13¼*
1976-1977 A819 Set of 2 1.25 .60

Exportation of Cooperative Open Banking Information System A820

Perf. 13¼x13
2009, Nov. 5 Litho. Wmk. 395
1978 A820 50c multi 1.25 1.00

Loja National University, 150th Anniv. — A821

Wmk. 395
2009, Nov. 27 Litho. *Perf. 12*
1979 A821 $2 multi 5.00 2.50

Independence, Bicent. — A822

No. 1980: a, Juan Pío Montúfar (1758-1818), Chairman of Supreme Council of Government. b, José Mejía Lequerica (1777-1813), representative to Cortes of Cadiz. c, Eugenio Espejo (1747-95), journalist, medical pioneer. d, Manuela Cañizares (1769-1814), patriot. e, Bicentenary emblem.

2009, Nov. 28
1980 Horiz. strip of 5 9.00 4.50
a.-e. A822 75c Any single 1.50 .75

A823

Charles Darwin (1809-82), Naturalist — A824

No. 1982 — Darwin and: a, Phoenicopterus ruber. b, Ardea herodias. c, Calandria galapagosa. d, Conolopus marthae. e, Sula granti. f, Rhincodon typus. g, Zalophus wollebaeki. h, Phalacrocorax harrisi. i, Geochelone nigra abingdoni. Nos. 1982a-1982h are 35x35mm, No. 1982i is 38mm diameter.

Perf. 13¾x14
2009, Nov. 30 **Unwmk.**
Granite Paper
1981 A823 $5 multi 12.00 6.00
Perf. 13¼ ($1), 13¾ ($2)
1982 A824 Sheet of 9 24.00 12.00
a.-h. $1 Any single 2.00 1.00
i. $2 multi 4.00 2.00

Christmas A825

Perf. 13¼x13
2009, Dec. 10 **Wmk. 395**
1983 A825 $1 multi 2.50 1.25

America Issue, Toys and Games — A826

No. 1984: a, Paddle and ball. b, Go-cart.

2009, Dec. 18
1984 A826 $1 Horiz. pair, #a-b 5.00 2.50

Tourism Type of 2009

Designs: No. 1985, The Lovers of Sumpa, Santa Elena Province. No. 1986, Colorado Indians, Santo Domingo de los Tsáchilas Province. No. 1987, Shuar community, Orellana Province. No. 1988, Guaranga Indian Monument, Bolívar Province. No. 1989, Banana plantation, El Oro Province. No. 1990, Virgin of Cisne, Loja Province. No. 1991, Pillaro devil, Tungurahua Province. No. 1992, Equator Monument, Pichincha Province. No. 1993, Cuicocha Lake, Imbabura Province. $1.75, Bolívar and San Martín Monument, Guayas Province. No. 1995, Tomebamba River, Azuay Province. No. 1996, Leopardus pardalis, Zamora Province. No. 1997, Los Frailes Beach, Manabí Province. No. 1998, Harpia harpyja, Pastaza Province. No. 1999, Arctocephalus galapagoensis, Galápagos Province. $5, Mt. Cotopaxi, Cotopaxi Province.

Wmk. 395, 377 (#1986-1987, 1989, 1992, 1993, 1997-1999)

2010-11 Litho. *Perf. 13¼x13*

1985	A807	25c	multi	.50	.25
1986	A807	25c	multi	.50	.25
1987	A807	25c	multi	.50	.25
1988	A807	50c	multi	1.00	.50
1989	A807	50c	multi	1.00	.50
1990	A807	$1	multi	2.00	1.00
1991	A807	$1.25	multi	2.50	1.25
1992	A807	$1.25	multi	2.50	1.25
1993	A807	$1.25	multi	2.50	1.25
1994	A807	$1.75	multi	3.50	1.75
1995	A807	$2	multi	4.00	2.00
1996	A807	$2	multi	4.00	2.00
1997	A807	$2	multi	4.00	2.00
1998	A807	$3	multi	6.00	3.00
1999	A807	$3	multi	6.00	3.00
2000	A807	$5	multi	10.00	5.00
	Nos. 1985-2000 (16)			50.50	25.25

Issued: Nos. 1985, 1988, 1991, 1995, 1/20; Nos. 1990, 1994, 1996, 2000, 4/12; Nos. 1986, 1992, 1997, 1998, 9/30; Nos. 1987, 1989, 1993, 1999, 1/24/11.

Miniature Sheet

First Unmanned Ecuadorian Airship — A827

No. 2001: a, $1, Pilot with remote-control device (40x18mm). b, $1, Airship over coastline (40x18mm). c, $1, Airship and mountain (40x18mm). d, $3, Airship (115x42mm).

Wmk. 395
2010, Feb. 7 Litho. *Perf. 14*
2001 A827 Sheet of 4, #a-d 12.00 6.00

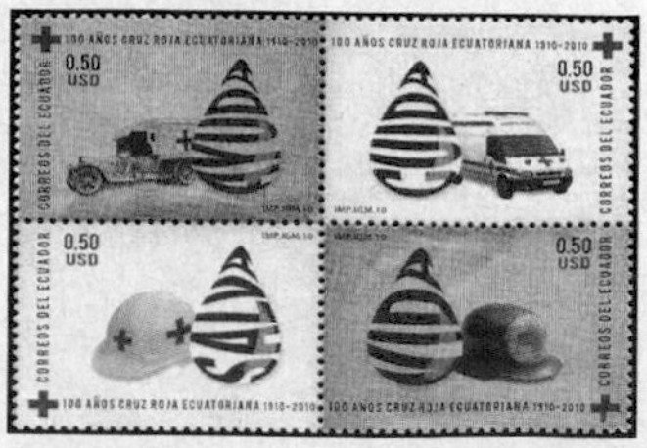

Ecuadorian Red Cross, Cent. — A828

No. 2002: a, Old ambulance, blood drop inscribed "Ayuda." b, New ambulance, blood drop inscribed "Cuida." c, Modern Red Cross hard hat, blood drop inscribed "Salva." d, Old Red Cross hard hat, blood drop inscribed "Vida."

Perf. 13¼x13

2010, Mar. 18 — Wmk. 395

2002 A828 50c Block of 4, #a-d 4.00 2.00

Birds — A829

No. 2003: a, Tachycineta albiventer. b, Momotus momota. c, Semnornis ramphastinus. d, Aulacorhynchus haematopygus.

No. 2004, horiz.: a, Ramphocelus carbo. b, Tangara vitriolina.

2010, Apr. 16 — Wmk. 395 — *Perf. 14*

2003 A829 25c Block of 4, #a-d 2.00 1.00

Souvenir Sheet

Perf. 13¼x13

2004 A829 $1.50 Sheet of 2, #a-b 6.00 3.00

No. 2004 contains two 38x27mm stamps. Birdpex 2010, Antwerp, Belgium (No. 2004).

Tall Ships in Velas Sudamérica 2010 — A830

No. 2005, vert. (27x38mm) — Various knots, ships and flags: a, Cisne Branco, Brazil. b, Libertad, Argentina. c, Sagres, Portugal. d, Capitán Miranda, Uruguay. e, Europa, Netherlands. f, Esmerelda, Chile. g, Gloria, Colombia. h, Simón Bolívar, Venezuela. i, Cuauhtémoc, Mexico. j, Juan Sebastián Elcano, Spain.

$1, Training Ship Guayas, Ecuador.

Perf. 13x13¼

2010, May 7 — Wmk. 377

2005 Block of 10 15.00 7.50

a.-j. A830 75c Any single 1.50 .75

Perf. 12

2006 A830 $1 shown 2.00 1.00

Miniature Sheet

Manuela Sáenz (c. 1797-1856), Mistress of Simón Bolívar — A831

Litho. with Foil Application

2010, May 24 — *Imperf.*

2007 A831 $3 multi 6.00 3.00

See Venezuela No. 1707.

2010 World Cup Soccer Championships, South Africa — A832

No. 2008 — Emblem of 2010 World Cup, soccer player, ball and: a, Lion. b, Elephant. c, Zebra.

$5, Mascot of 2010 World Cup, giraffe.

2010, June 9 — Litho. — *Perf. 13¼x13*

2008 Horiz. strip of 3 6.00 3.00

a.-c. A832 $1 Any single 2.00 1.00

Souvenir Sheet

Imperf

2009 A832 $5 multi 10.00 5.00

No. 2009 contains one 45x36mm stamp with simulated perforations. Animals on No. 2009 have blurred appearance, but have a three-dimensional appearance when seen through 3-D glasses.

Creation of Tungurahua Province, 150th Anniv. — A833

No. 2010: a, Atelopus ignescens. b, Mt. Tungurahua, flag at Parque de la Familia. c, Casa del Portal Museum.

Perf. 13¼x13

2010, July 1 — Wmk. 377

2010 Horiz. strip of 3 1.50 .75

a.-c. A833 25c Any single .50 .25

Las Floristas, by Camilo Egas — A834

2010, July 21 — *Perf. 12*

2011 A834 $1.25 multi 2.50 1.25

Campaign against illegal trafficking in historical objects.

Souvenir Sheet

Massacre of Patriots, Bicent. — A835

No. 2012: a, Soldier with sword threatening woman, man and child. b, Soldier threatening to shoot man.

2010, Aug. 2 — *Perf. 13x13¼*

2012 A835 $2 Sheet of 2, #a-b, + central label 8.00 4.00

Souvenir Sheet

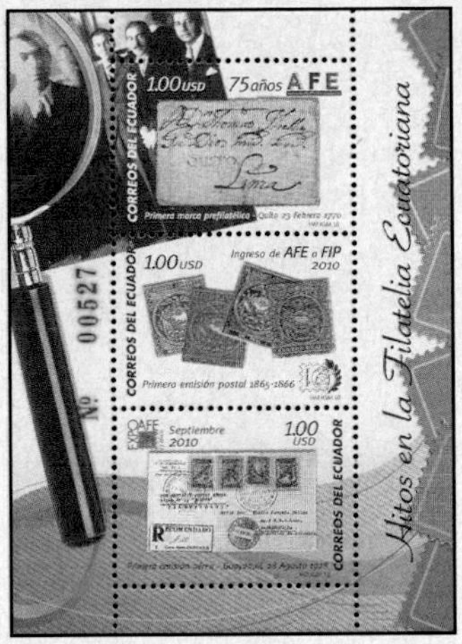

Philatelic Firsts of Ecuador — A836

No. 2013: a, First postmark of Ecuador, 1770, emblem of Philatelic Association of Ecuador. b, First Ecuadorian stamps (#2, 3, 5, 6), emblem of Intl. Federation of Philately. c, Cover from first SCADTA flight, 1928, emblem of 2010 Philatelic Association of Ecuador Expo.

2010, Aug. 25 — *Perf. 13¼x13*

2013 A836 $1 Sheet of 3, #a-c 6.00 3.00

Philatelic Association of Ecuador, 75th anniv., and its admission to Intl. Federation of Philately.

Organization of Petroleum Exporting Countries, 50th Anniv. — A837

2010, Sept. 14 — Wmk. 377 — *Perf. 12*

2014 A837 50c multi 1.00 .50

Citigroup in Ecuador, 50th Anniv. — A838

2010, Oct. 7 — *Perf. 13¼x13*

2015 A838 $1 multi 2.00 1.00

General Directorate of Civil Registration, Identification and Certification — A839

2010, Oct. 29 — Litho. — *Perf. 12*

2016 A839 50c multi 1.00 .50

America Issue, National Symbols — A840

No. 2017 — National: a, Flag. b, Coat of arms. c, Anthem.

2010, Nov. 24 — *Perf. 13¼x13*

2017 Horiz. strip of 3 6.00 3.00

a.-c. A840 $1 Any single 2.00 1.00

Christmas — A841

2010, Dec. 3 — *Perf. 13x13¼*

2018 A841 $2 multi 4.00 2.00

San José-La Salle College, Guayaquil, Cent. — A842

2010, Dec. 16 — Litho. — Wmk. 377

2019 A842 25c multi .50 .25

Children's Christmas Parade, Cuenca — A843

2010, Dec. 21 — *Perf. 13¼x13*

2020 A843 50c multi 1.00 .50

Tourism Type of 2009

No. 2021 — Galapagos Islands fauna: a, Fregata magnificens. b, Sula dactylatra. c, Spheniscíforme. d, Sula nebouxi. e, Conolophus subcristatus. f, Geochelone nigra. g, Chelonia mydas agassisi. h, Oxycirrhites typus.

No. 2022 — Galapagos Islands sites and fauna: a, Bartolomé Island, denomination at L. b, Bartolomé Island, denomination at R. c, Zoluphus wallebaeki, denomination at L. d, Zoluphus wallebaeki, denomination at R. e, Darwin's Arch, denomination at L. f, Darwin's Arch, denomination at R. g, Amblyrhynchus cristatus, denomination at L. h, Amblyrhynchus cristatus, denomination at R.

2011, Mar. 18 — Unwmk. — *Die Cut*

Self-Adhesive

2021 Booklet pane of 8 + 2 labels 10.00

a.-b. A808 25c Either single .50 .25

c.-d. A808 50c Either single 1.00 .50

e.-f. A808 75c Either single 1.50 .75

g.-h. A808 $1 Either single 2.00 1.00

i. Booklet pane of 8, #a-h, with lilac pane margins 10.00

2022 Booklet pane of 8 + 2 labels 10.00

a.-b. A808 25c Either single .50 .25

c.-d. A808 50c Either single 1.00 .50

e.-f. A808 75c Either single 1.50 .75

g.-h. A808 $1 Either single 2.00 1.00

i. Booklet pane of 8, #a-h, with lilac pane margins 10.00

Issued: Nos. 2021i, 2022i, 1/13/12. Nos. 2021 and 2022 have gray pane margins.

Souvenir Sheet

Postal Union of the Americas, Spain and Portugal (UPAEP), Cent. — A844

2011, Mar. 18 Wmk. 377 *Perf. 12*
2023 A844 $3 multi 6.00 3.00

Souvenir Sheet

Yuri Gagarin, First Man in Space, 50th Anniv. — A845

2011, May 6 *Perf. 13x13¼*
2024 A845 $5 multi 10.00 5.00

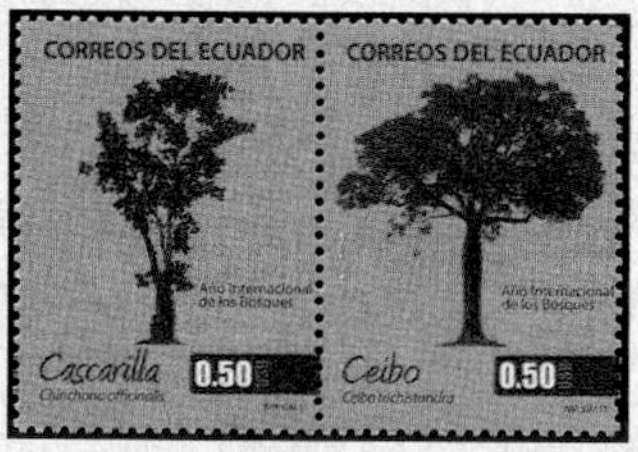

Intl. Year of Forests — A846

No. 2025, 50c: a, Chinchona officinalis. b, Ceiba tichistandra.
No. 2026, 75c, horiz.: a, Jacaranda sp. b, Prosopis sp.

2011, May 19 *Perf. 13x13¼, 13¼x13*
Horiz. pairs, #a-b
2025-2026 A846 Set of 2 5.00 2.50

Pichincha Chamber of Industries and Production, 75th Anniv. — A847

Wmk. 377
2011, June 16 Litho. *Perf. 12*
2027 A847 $2 multi 4.00 4.00

Christopher Columbus College, Guayaquil, Cent. — A848

2011, July 7 *Perf. 13¼x13*
2028 A848 $1 multi 2.00 2.00

National Telecommunications Day — A849

No. 2029: a, First Bell telephone, 1876. b, Western Electric magneto wall telephone, 1894. c, Ericsson wall pay telephone, 1970. d, Apple iPhone, 2011.

2011, July 8
2029 A849 50c Block of 4, #a-d 4.00 4.00

Miniature Sheet

Seven Wonders of Quito — A850

No. 2030: a, Basilica of the National Vow. b, Virgin of the Panecillo. c, Chimbacalle Railway Station. d, San Francisco Convent. e, Independence Plaza. f, Church of the Society of Jesus. g, Sanctuary of the Virgin of El Quinche.

2011, Sept. 8
2030 A850 75c Sheet of 7, #a-g, + label 10.50 10.50

Quito, 2011 American Capital of Culture.

Yasuni- ITT Initiative — A851

No. 2031 — Reptiles: a, Chelonoidis denticulata. b, Anolis trachyderma. c, Thecadactylus solimoensis. d, Epicrates cenchria. e, Dendropsophus bifurcus. f, Osteocephalus taurinus. g, Ranitomeya ventrimaculata. h, Melanosuchus niger.

No. 2032: a, Clavija procera. b, Duguetia hadrantha. c, Hymenaea oblongifolia. d, Connarus ruber. e, Fungi. f, Theobroma speciosum. g, Brownea gradiceps. h, Apeiba membranacea.

Unwmk.
2011, Sept. 20 Litho. *Die Cut*
Self-Adhesive

2031	Booklet pane of 8 + 2 labels	10.00	
a.-b.	A851 25c Either single	.50	.25
c.-d.	A851 50c Either single	1.00	.50
e.-f.	A851 75c Either single	1.50	.75
g.-h.	A851 $1 Either single	2.00	1.00
2032	Booklet pane of 8 + 2 labels	10.00	
a.-b.	A851 25c Either single	.50	.25
c.-d.	A851 50c Either single	1.00	.50
e.-f.	A851 75c Either single	1.50	.75
g.-h.	A851 $1 Either single	2.00	1.00

See Nos. 2061-2062.

Intl. Year For People of African Descent — A852

No. 2033 — Musical instruments: a, Marimba. b, Guasá. c, Maracas. d, Cununos.

Perf. 13¼x13
2011, Sept. 26 Litho. Wmk. 395
2033 A852 $1 Block of 4, #a-d 8.00 4.00

Flowers — A853

Designs: 25c, Passiflora manicata. $2, Passiflora pinnatistipula. $3, Herrania balaensis. $5, Passiflora arborea.

Perf. 13x13¼
2011, Sept. 26 Litho. Wmk. 377
2034-2037 A853 Set of 4 20.50 20.50

Trains — A854

Railroad Stations — A855

No. 2038 — Locomotives: a, 1992 GEC Alsthon. b, 1900 Baldwin. c, 1900 Baldwin, diff. d, 1935 Baldwin. e, 1992 GEC Alsthon on hillside. f, Front of 1992 GEC Alsthon. g, 1953 Baldwin. h, Baldwin XXXX.
No. 2039 — Stations at: a, Machachi. b, Latacunga. c, Sibambe. d, Durán. e, El Tambo. f, Riobamba. g, Chimbacalle. h, Boliche.

2011, Oct. 3 Unwmk. *Die Cut*
Self-Adhesive

2038	Booklet pane of 8 + 2 labels	10.00	
a.-b.	A854 25c Either single	.50	.25
c.-d.	A854 50c Either single	1.00	.50
e.-f.	A854 75c Either single	1.50	.75
g.-h.	A854 $1 Either single	2.00	1.00
2039	Booklet pane of 8 + 2 labels	10.00	
a.-b.	A855 25c Either single	.50	.25
c.-d.	A855 50c Either single	1.00	.50
e.-f.	A855 75c Either single	1.50	.75
g.-h.	A855 $1 Either single	2.00	1.00

Exports — A856

No. 2040: a, Wicker basket. b, Chocolate. c, Wooden automobile. d, Hats. e, Textiles. f, Leather goods. g, Filigree. h, Tagua carvings.

Perf. 13¼x13
2011, Oct. 11 Wmk. 395
2040 A856 50c Block of 8, #a-h, + central label 8.00 8.00

Intl. Day for Disaster Reduction — A857

No. 2041: a, Volcano eruption. b, Landslide. c, Flood, d, Earthquake.

2011, Oct. 12 *Perf. 13¼*
2041 A857 $1.25 Block of 4, #a-d 10.00 10.00

Mail Boxes and Postal Transportation — A858

Designs: No. 2042, $1.75, 1928 mailbox, bicycle. No. 2043, $1.75, 2011 mailbox, motorcycle.
$5, Mailbox, Post Office Bay, Galápagos Islands, vert.

Perf. 13½x13¾
2011, Nov. 28 Wmk. 377
2042-2043 A858 Set of 2 7.00 7.00

Souvenir Sheet
Perf. 13x13¼
2044 A858 $5 multi 10.00 10.00

America issue. No. 2044 contains one 28x38mm stamp.

Christmas — A859

No. 2045: a, Holy Family. b, Angel.

2011, Nov. 29 *Perf. 13½x13¾*
2045 A859 $1 Horiz. pair, #a-b 4.00 4.00

2011 Pan-American Games, Guadalajara, Mexico — A860

Emblem, sports equipment and athletes: a, Karate. b, Weight lifting. c, Kayaking. d, Boxing. e, Rollerblading.

2011, Nov. 30
2046 Horiz. strip of 5 2.50 2.50
a.-e. A860 25c Any single .50 .50

Guayaquil Chamber of Industries, 75th Anniv. — A861

2011, Dec. 14 Wmk. 377
2047 A861 $2 multi 4.00 4.00

Ecuador Cancer Society, 60th Anniv. — A862

2011, Dec. 19 *Perf. 13¼x13*
2048 A862 75c multi 1.50 .75

Pres. Luis Cordero (1833-1912) A864

2012, Mar. 1 *Perf. 13¾x13½*
2051 A864 $1 multi 2.00 2.00

Flowers — A865

Designs: $1, Barnadesia spinosa. $2, Bixa orellana. $3, Espeletia pyonophylla. $5, Brugmansia sanguinea.

Perf. 13½x13¾
2012, Mar. 28 **Unwmk.**
2052-2055 A865 Set of 4 22.00 22.00

Souvenir Sheets

Sinking of the Titanic, Cent. — A866

Designs: No. 2056, $4, Titanic, sepia-toned image. No. 2056, $4, Titanic and Olympic at dock.

Perf. 13¾x13½
2012, Apr. 20 **Wmk. 377**
2056-2057 A866 Set of 2 16.00 16.00

Bananas — A867

Perf. 13½x13¾
2012, May 17 **Litho.** **Wmk. 377**
2058 A867 $2 multi 4.00 4.00

Banco de Machala, 50th anniv.

Catholic University of Santiago, Guayaquil, 50th Anniv. A868

2012, May 31 *Perf. 13¾*
2059 A868 $1 multi 2.00 2.00

Miniature Sheet

Guayaquil Tourist Attractions — A869

No. 2060: a, Hemiciclo la Rotonda (monument honoring meeting of Simón Bolívar and José de San Martín). b, Malecón del ío Guayas (Guayas River Walk). c, Metropolitan Cathedral. d, Torre del Reloj (Clock Tower). e, Malecón del Salado (Salado Walk). f, Edificio del Municipio (City Hall). g, Las Peñas Cerro Santa Ana (Santa Ana Hill).

2012, June 8 **Wmk. 377**
2060 A869 75c Sheet of 7, #a-g, + label 10.50 10.50

Yasuni-ITT Type of 2011

No. 2061 — Flora and fauna: a, Dasypodidae. b, Saimiri sciureus. c, Tettigoniidae. d, Automeris postalbida. e, Brownea sp. f, Aristolochia sp. g, Hypsiboas sp. h, Hypsiboas geographicus.

No. 2062 — Birds: a, Morphnus guianensis. b, Sarcorhamphus papa. c, Ara ararauna. d, Harpia harpyja. e, Trochilidae sp. f, Ramphastos tucanus. g, Pteroglossus pluricinctus. h, Pionus menstruus.

2012, June 11 **Unwmk.** ***Die Cut***
Self-Adhesive

2061	Booklet pane of 8 + 2 labels	10.00	
a.-b.	A851 25c Either single	.50	.50
c.-d.	A851 50c Either single	1.00	1.00
e.-f.	A851 75c Either single	1.50	1.50
g.-h.	A851 $1 Either single	2.00	2.00
2062	Booklet pane of 8 + 2 labels	10.00	
a.-b.	A851 25c Either single	.50	.50
c.-d.	A851 50c Either single	1.00	1.00
e.-f.	A851 75c Either single	1.50	1.50
g.-h.	A851 $1 Either single	2.00	2.00

Galapagos Islands Landscapes and Fauna — A870

No. 2063: a, Rocks in surf. b, Head of Amblyrhynchus cristatus. c, Numenius phaeopus. d, South Plaza Island. e. Pinnacle Rock, Bartolomé Island. f, Sula nebouxi. g, Chelonoidis sp. h, Kicker Rock (Leon Dormido), San Cristóbal Island.

No. 2064: a, Zalophus wollebaeki. b, Geospiza magnirostris. c, Sula granti. d, Fregata magnificens. e, Microlophus bivittatus. f, Spheniscus mendiculus. g, Anas bahamensis. h, Sphyrna lewini.

2012, July 11 **Unwmk.** ***Die Cut***
Self-Adhesive
Water Droplets on Blue Depicted in Frames Around Stamps

2063	Booklet pane of 8	10.00	
a.-b.	A870 25c Either single	.50	.25
c.-d.	A870 50c Either single	1.00	.50
e.-f.	A870 75c Either single	1.50	.75
g.-h.	A870 $1 Either single	2.00	1.00
i.	Booklet pane of 8, #a-h, with pane margins depiciting rocks	10.00	
2064	Booklet pane of 8	10.00	
a.-b.	A870 25c Either single	.50	.25
c.-d.	A870 50c Either single	1.00	.50
e.-f.	A870 75c Either single	1.50	.75
g.-h.	A870 $1 Either single	2.00	1.00
i.	Booklet pane of 8, #a-h, with pane margins depiciting rocks	10.00	

Issued: Nos. 2063i, 2064i, 10/8. See Nos. 2094-2095.

Guayas Sports Federation, 90th Anniv. A871

No. 2065: a, Shooting (tiro). b, Wrestling (lucha). c, Kayaking (canotaje). d, Boxing (boxeo). e, Weight lifting (pesas).

Perf. 13¾x13½
2012, July 25 **Wmk. 377**
2065 Horiz. strip of 5 5.00 2.50
a.-e. A871 50c Any single 1.00 .50

A872

Legacy of the Revolution of 1895 — A873

No. 2066: a, Ecuador #129, Matilde Huerta, first Ecuadoran female postal official, 1895. b, Bolívar College, Tulcán, first lay college, 1896. c, Civil Registration Law, 1900. d, School of Fine Arts, Quito, 1904. e, Opening of Guayaquil-Quito Railroad, 1908. f, Founding of Guayaquil Worker's Society, 1903. g, Creation of Independence Plaza, Quito, 1909. h, Map of South America, José Marti, Eloy Alfaro, and Augusto César Sandino, 1911.

$3, Alfaro, locomotive.

2012, July 31 *Perf. 13¾x13½*
2066 A872 25c Sheet of 8, #a-h 4.00 2.00

Souvenir Sheet
Imperf
2067 A873 $3 multi 6.00 3.00

Enrique Gil Gilbert (1912-73), Writer A874

2012, Aug. 8 *Perf. 13¾x13½*
2068 A874 $1 multi 2.00 1.00

Souvenir Sheet

Steamship Ecuador — A875

No. 2069 — Emblem of 2012 Ecuador Philatelic Society Stamp Exposition and: a, Ship's stern and flag. b, Ship's bow.

Litho. (Foil Application in Margin)
2012, Aug. 16 *Perf. 13½x13¾*

2069	A875 $3 Sheet of 2, #a-b, gold inscription in sheet margin	12.00	6.00
c.	As #2069, silver inscription in sheet margin	12.00	6.00
d.	As #2069, red metallic inscription in sheet margin	12.00	6.00

Miniature Sheet

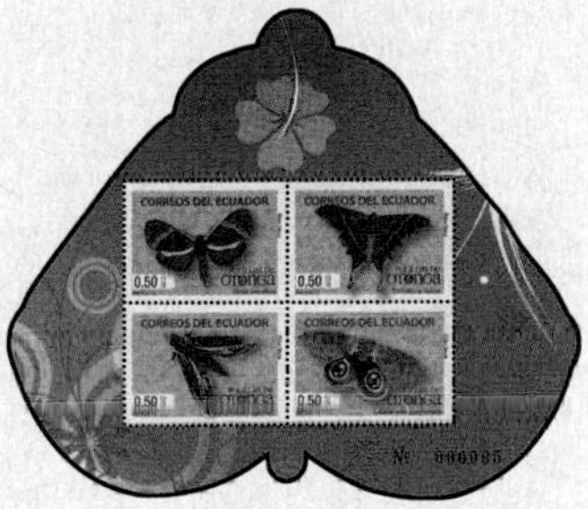

Moths — A876

No. 2070: a, Getta baetifica. b, Sematura diana. c, Xylophanes pyrrhus. d, Leucanella contempta.

Perf. 13¾x13½
2012, Aug. 28 **Litho.**
2070 A876 50c Sheet of 4, #a-d 4.00 2.00

Quito Chamber of Construction, 50th Anniv. — A877

Construction materials: No. 2071, $1, Timber (madera). No. 2072, $1, Bamboo (guadua). No. 2073, $1, Wattle (bahareque). No. 2074, $1, Compacted mud (tapial).

2012, Sept. 4 *Perf. 13½x13¾*
2071-2074 A877 Set of 4 8.00 4.00

America Issue A878

Myths and legends: No. 2075, $2, Legend of Ayer. No. 2076, $2, Legend of the Rooster of the Cathedral, vert.

Perf. 13¾x13½, 13½x13¾
2012, Sept. 17
2075-2076 A878 Set of 2 8.00 4.00

Nelson Estupiñán Bass (1912-2002), Writer — A879

2012, Sept. 20 ***Perf. 13¾x13½***
2077 A879 $2 multi 4.00 2.00

Alexander von Humboldt (1769-1859), Naturalist A880

Denominations: 50c, $2.

2012, Sept. 26 **Wmk. 377**
2078-2079 A880 Set of 2 5.00 2.50

Friendship between Ecuador and Germany, 125th anniv.

A881

Trains — A882

No. 2080: a, Baldwin No. 3 Ingenio Valdez. b, Baldwin No. 2 Inés María. c, Baldwin No. 12 C.F.F.E. d, Baldwin No. 37 G&Q. e. Baldwin No. 7 G&Q. f, Baldwin No. 3 Quito-Esmeraldas train. g, Baldwin No. 2 Yaguachi train. h, Baldwin No. 1 Curaray train.

No. 2081: a, Baldwin No. 53. b, Gec Alsthom No. 2408. c, Gec Alsthom No. 2405. d, Baldwin No. 17. e, Baldwin No. 58. f, Gec Alsthom No. 2407 and station. g, Gec Alsthom No. 2404. h, Gec Alsthom No. 2407.

No. 2082: a, Baldwin No. 58, diff. b, Gec Alsthom No. 2404, diff. c, Gec Alsthom No. 2406. d, Baldwin No. 53, diff. e, Gec Alsthom No. 2402. f, Baldwin No. 58 on bridge. g, Baldwin No. 17, diff. h, Gec Alsthom No. 2405, diff.

2012, Oct. 8 **Unwmk.** ***Die Cut***
Self-Adhesive

2080 Booklet pane of 8 10.00
a.-b. A881 25c Either single .50 .25
c.-d. A881 50c Either single 1.00 .50
e.-f. A881 75c Either single 1.50 .75
g.-h. A881 $1 Either single 2.00 1.00
2081 Booklet pane of 8 10.00
a.-b. A882 25c Either single .50 .25
c.-d. A882 50c Either single 1.00 .50
e.-f. A882 75c Either single 1.50 .75
g.-h. A882 $1 Either single 2.00 1.00
2082 Booklet pane of 8 10.00
a.-b. A882 25c Either single .50 .25
c.-d. A882 50c Either single 1.00 .50
e.-f. A882 75c Either single 1.50 .75
g.-h. A882 $1 Either single 2.00 1.00

Jesuit Institutions A883

Schools: No. 2083, $1, Unidad Educativa Borja, 75th anniv. No. 2084, $1, Unidad Educativa San Felipe Neri, 175th anniv. No. 2085, $1.25, Colegio San Gabriel, 150th anniv. $5, Jesuit church and emblem.

Perf. 13¾x13½

2012, Oct. 29 **Wmk. 377**
2083-2085 A883 Set of 3 6.50 3.25

Size: 100x70mm

Imperf

2086 A883 $5 multi 10.00 10.00

Permanent return of Jesuits to Ecuador, 150th anniv.

Renovation of Guayas Government Palace — A884

2012, Nov. 6 ***Perf. 13½x13¾***
2087 A884 $5 multi 10.00 10.00

Ecuadorian Army's Communications Group, 50th Anniv. — A885

No. 2088: a, Indian messenger. b, Men and wagon transporting radiotelegraphic station, 1924. c, Bicycle messengers, 1932. d, Communication transmission school building, 1942.

2012, Nov. 14
2088 Horiz. strip of 4 2.00 2.00
a.-d. A885 25c Any single .50 .50

Guayaquil Beneficence Council, 125th Anniv. — A886

2012, Nov. 27 ***Perf. 13¾x13½***
2089 A886 $3 multi 6.00 6.00

Miniature Sheet

Guayas Tourism — A887

No. 2090: a, Crucifix. b, Rock climbers. c, Fishermen in boats. d, Rice farmer. e, Cacao farmer. f, Sugar processing.

2012, Nov. 29
2090 A887 75c Sheet of 6, #a-f, + 2 labels 9.00 9.00

Christmas A888

Icons: No. 2091, $1, Bethlehem Portal, Concepción Monastery, Quito. No. 2092, $1, Mystery, Carmen Alto Monastery, Quito.

2012, Dec. 3 **Wmk. 377**
2091-2092 A888 Set of 2 4.00 4.00

Military Leaders A889

No. 2093: a, Gen. Eloy Alfaro (1842-1912). b, Col. Carlos Concha Torres (1864-1919). c, Col. Luis Vargas Torres (1855-87).

2012, Dec. 14 ***Rouletted 13½***
2093 Horiz. strip of 3 7.50 7.50
a.-c. A889 $1.25 Any single 2.50 2.50

Galapagos Islands Type of 2012

No. 2094: a, Rock with carving of face, Isla Floreana. b, Phoebastria irrorata. c, Carcharinus galapagensis. d, Chelonia mydas. e, Pterophyllum scalare. f, Sleeping Lion Rock, San Cristóbal. g, Flower. h, Isla Plaza Sur.

No. 2095: a, Fregata magnificens. b, Post barrel, Post Office Bay, Isla Floreana. c, Camarhynchus pallidus. d, Pyrocephalus rubinus. e, Buteo galapagoensis. f, Isla Bartolomé. g, Red reef fish. h, Vicente Roca Point.

2013, Jan. 16 **Unwmk.** ***Die Cut***
Self-Adhesive

2094 Booklet pane of 8 10.00
a.-b. A870 25c Either single .50 .50
c.-d. A870 50c Either single 1.00 1.00
e.-f. A870 75c Either single 1.50 1.50
g.-h. A870 $1 Either single 2.00 2.00
2095 Booklet pane of 8 10.00
a.-b. A870 25c Either single .50 .50
c.-d. A870 50c Either single 1.00 1.00
e.-f. A870 75c Either single 1.50 1.50
g.-h. A870 $1 Either single 2.00 2.00

Miniature Sheet

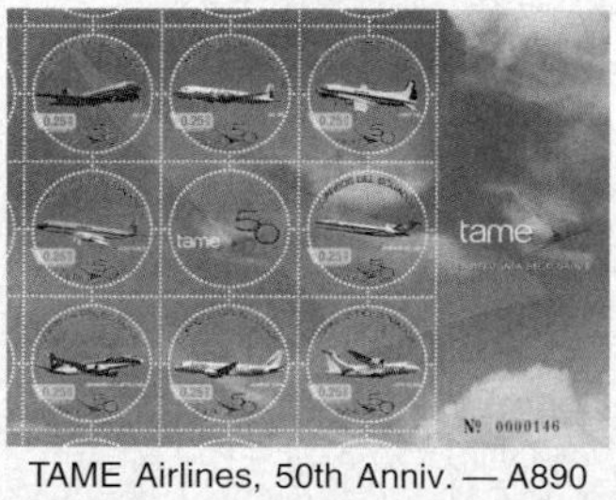

TAME Airlines, 50th Anniv. — A890

No. 2096: a, DC-3. b, DC-6B. c, Avro 748. d, Electra II. e, Boeing 727-200. f, Embraer E-190. g, Airbus A320. h, ATR 42-500.

2013, Feb. 8 **Wmk. 377** ***Perf. 13½***
2096 A890 25c Sheet of 8, #a-h, + central label 4.00 4.00

Hat Making — A891

No. 2097: a, Unfinished hats (orange panel). b, Hat maker (blue panel). c, Hat maker, diff. (red panel).

2013, Mar. 18 ***Perf. 13¼***
2097 Horiz. strip of 3 3.00 3.00
a.-c. A891 50c Any single 1.00 1.00

Scout Group No. 14, Guayaquil, 50th Anniv. — A892

Litho. With Foil Application
Perf. 13½x13¾

2013, June 21 **Wmk. 377**
2098 A892 $1 multi 2.00 2.00

Launch of Pegasus NEE-01 (First Ecuadorian Satellite) A893

Perf. 13¾x13½

2013, June 28 **Litho.**
2099 A893 $2 multi 4.00 4.00

Diplomatic Relations Between Dominican Republic and Ecuador, 75th Anniv. — A894

2013, July 2 ***Perf. 13½x13¾***
2100 A894 $1 multi 2.00 2.00

Popes Francis and Benedict XVI — A895

Litho. With Foil Application

2013, July 3 **Wmk. 377**
2101 A895 $5 multi 10.00 10.00

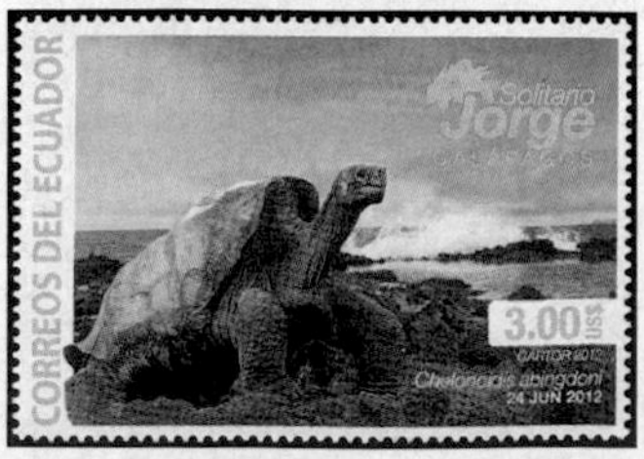

June 24, 2012 Death of Pinta Island Tortoise, Lonesome George — A896

Lonesome George and: $3, Surf spray. $25, Trees.

Litho. With Grit Affixed

Perf. 13½x13¼

2013, July 4 Unwmk.

2102 A896 $3 multi 6.00 6.00

Litho.

Wmk. 377

Size: 91x71mm

Imperf

2103 A896 $25 multi 50.00 50.00

Dr. Ricardo Descalzi (1912-90), Writer and Physician — A897

Perf. 13½x13¾

2013, Aug. 1 Litho. Wmk. 377

2104 A897 $3 multi 6.00 6.00

Volcanos A898

No. 2105: a, Mt. Chimborazo. b, Mt. Cotopaxi. c, Mt.Tungurahua.

Perf. 13¾x13½

2013, Aug. 21 Litho. Wmk. 377

2105 Horiz. strip of 3 1.50 1.50
a.-c. A898 25c Any single .50 .50

Flower With Black and White Faces, Dr. Martin Luther King, Jr. — A899

Perf. 13¾x13½

2013, Oct. 22 Litho. Wmk. 377

2106 A899 $1 multi 2.00 2.00

America issue (campaign against discrimination).

Royal Audience of Quito, 450th Anniv. — A900

Designs: 25c, Hernando de Santillán y Figueroa (1519-75), First President of the Royal Audience of Quito. $5, Map of the Royal Audience of Quito.

Perf. 13¾x13½

2013, Nov. 13 Litho. Wmk. 377

2107 A900 25c multi .50 .50

Size: 74x94mm

Imperf

2108 A900 $5 multi 10.00 10.00

Ecuadorian Presence in the Antarctic, 25th Anniv. — A901

No. 2109: a, Pygoscelis papua. b, Leptonychotes weddellii. c, Catharacta lonnbergi.

Wmk. 377

2013, Nov. 21 Litho. *Perf. 13½*

2109 Horiz. strip of 3 3.00 3.00
a.-c. A901 50c Any single 1.00 1.00

Miniature Sheet

Christmas — A902

No. 2110: a, Annunciation (Primer día). b, Visitation of St. Elizabeth (Segundo día). c, St. Joseph's dream (Tercer día). d, Journey to Bethlehem (Cuarto día). e, Arrival at the inn (Quinto día). f, Star of Bethlehem (Sexto día). g, Shepherds (Séptimo día). h, Angels (Octavo día). i, Holy Family (Noveno día).

Perf. 13½x13¼

2013, Nov. 29 Litho. Wmk. 377

2110 A902 25c Sheet of 9, #a-i 4.50 4.50

Intl. Year of Quinoa A903

No. 2111: a, Chenopodium quinoa. b, Amaranthus caudatus. c, Lupinus mutabilis.

Perf. 13¾x13½

2013, Dec. 16 Litho. Wmk. 377

2111 Horiz. strip of 3 12.00 12.00
a.-c. A903 $2 Any single 4.00 4.00

Imbabura Textile Mill — A904

No. 2112: a, Workers near weaving machines. b, Workers near machines with thread spools.

Rouletted 12¼

2014, Jan. 27 Litho. Wmk. 377

2112 A904 $1 Horiz. pair, #a-b 4.00 4.00

Resolution of Ecuador-Peru Border Dispute, 15th Anniv. — A905

Rouletted 12¼

2014, Jan. 30 Litho. Wmk. 377

2113 A905 $5 multi 10.00 10.00

Presidents of Ecuador — A906

No. 2114: a, Juan José Flores A. (1800-64). b, Vicente Rocafuerte B. (1783-1847). c, Vicente Roca R. (1792-1858). d, Diego Noboa A, (1789-1870). e, José M. Urbina V. (1808-91). f, Francisco Robles G. (1811-93). g, Gabriel García M. (1821-75). h, Jerónimo Carrión P. (1804-73). i, Javier Espinosa E. (1815-70). j, Antonio Borrero C. (1827-1911). k, Ignacio de Vientemilla V. (1828-1908). l, José M. Camaño (1837-1900). m, Antonio Flores J. (1833-1915). n, Luis Cordero C. (1833-1912). o, Eloy Alfaro D. (1842-1912). p, Leonidas Plaza G. (1865-1932). q, Lizardo García S. (1844-1937). r, Emilio Estrada C. (1855-1911). s, Alfredo Baquerizo M. (1859-1951). t, José L. Tamayo T. (1858-1947). u, Gonzalo S. córdova R. (1863-1928). v, Isidro Ayora C. (1879-1978). w, Juan D. Martínez M. (1875-1955). x, José M. Velasco I. (1893-1979). y, Aurelio Mosquera N. (1880-1939). z, Carlos A. Arroyo (1893-1969). aa, Mariano Suárez V. (1897-1980). ab, Carlos J. Arosemena T. (1888-1952). ac, Galo Plaza L. (1906-87). ad, Camilo Ponce E. (1912-76). ae, Carlos J. Arosemena M. (1919-2004). af, Otto Arosemena G. (1925-84). ag, Jaime Roldós A. (1940-81). ah, León Febres Cordero R. (1931-2008).

Perf. 13¾x13½

2014, Apr. 1 Litho. Wmk. 377

2114 Sheet of 34 + label 17.00 17.00
a.-ah. A906 25c Any single .50 .50

Hugo R. Chávez (1954-2013), President of Venezuela A907

Perf. 13¾x13½

2014, Apr. 14 Litho. Wmk. 377

2115 A907 50c multi 1.00 1.00

Parade of Tall Ships, Manabí — A908

No. 2116 — Ship and national flag: a, Cisne Branco, Brazil. b, Cuauhtémoc, Mexico. c, Gloria, Colombia. d, Libertad, Argentina. e, Esmerelda, Chile. f, Guayas, Ecuador. g, Simón Bolívar, Venezuela.

Perf. 13½x13¾

2014, May 3 Litho. Wmk. 377

2116 Sheet of 7 + label 10.50 10.50
a.-g. A908 75c Any single 1.50 1.50

Intl. Philately Day — A909

Magnifying glass over: $2, Ecuadorian stamps. $3, Text from *El Nacional.*

2014, May 22 Litho. *Perf. 13½x13¾*

2117 A909 $2 multi 4.00 4.00

Size: 90x70mm

Wmk. 395

Imperf

2118 A909 $3 multi 6.00 6.00

Regional Platform for Disaster Risk Reduction in the Americas, Guayaquil — A910

Perf. 13½x13¾

2014, May 27 Litho. Wmk. 377

2119 A910 $1 multi 2.00 2.00

2014 World Cup Soccer Championships, Brazil — A911

Designs: 50c, Stadium and stylized Ecuador soccer player. $3, Stylized Ecuador soccer player in stadium, Christ the Redeemer Statue, Rio de Janeiro, horiz.
$5, Soccer player and field, horiz.

Perf. 13½x13¾, 13¾x13½

2014, June 18 Litho. Wmk. 377

2120-2121 A911 Set of 2 7.00 7.00

Size: 55x35mm

Imperf

2122 A911 $5 multi 10.00 10.00

Pancho Segura, Ecuadorian-born Tennis Player — A912

Designs: 25c, Segura on tennis court as young man. $5, Segura, tennis ball and racquet, Ecuadoran flag.

Perf. 13½x13¾

2014, July 25 Litho. Wmk. 377

2123-2124 A912 Set of 2 10.50 10.50

Intl. Year of Family Farming A913

Designs: 75c, Woman near tree. $1, Woman spinning yarn from wool. $2, Man pulling down cacao pod from tree.

Perf. 13¾x13½

2014, Aug. 11 Litho. Wmk. 377

2125-2127 A913 Set of 3 7.50 7.50

2014 Latin American Integration Association Expo, Montevideo, Uruguay — A914

Perf. 13½x13¾

2014, Aug. 28 Litho. Wmk. 377

2128 A914 $3 multi 6.00 6.00

Mural by Oswaldo Guayasamín — A915

No. 2129: a, Denomination at left. b, Denomination at right.

Perf. 13¾x13½

2014, Aug. 29 Litho. Wmk. 377

2129 A915 25c Horiz. pair, #a-b 1.00 1.00

Latin American Parliament, 50th anniv.

Luis Vernaza Hospital, 450th Anniv. — A916

No. 2130: a, Hospital building. b, Doctor examining patient.

Perf. 13½x13¾

2014, Sept. 10 Litho. Wmk. 377

2130 A916 50c Horiz. pair, #a-b 2.00 2.00

Miniature Sheet

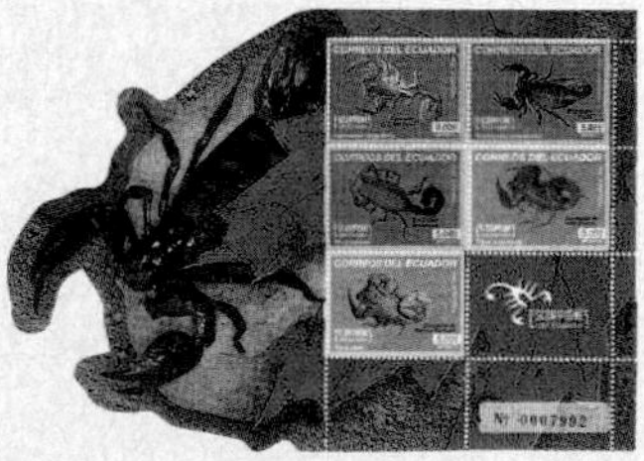

Scorpions — A917

No. 2131: a, Centruroides margaritatus. b, Teuthraustes atramentarius. c, Tityus asthenes. d, Tityus crassicauda. e, Tityus ythieri.

Perf. 13¾x13½

2014, Sept. 30 Litho. Wmk. 377

2131 A917 $5 Sheet of 5, #a-e, + label 50.00 50.00

Yachay University Buildings — A918

No. 2132: a, Capitular Building, b, Library.

Perf. 13¾x13½

2014, Oct. 21 Litho. Wmk. 377

2132 A918 $2 Horiz. pair, #a-b 8.00 8.00

Oryx Leucoryx, Vultur Gryphus, Flags of Ecuador and Qatar — A919

Litho. With Foil Application

Perf. 13½x13¾

2014, Oct. 22 Wmk. 377

2133 A919 $10 multi 20.00 20.00

See Qatar No.

Manuela Espejo (c. 1757-c. 1829), Writer — A920

Litho. With Foil Application

Perf. 13½x13¾

2014, Oct. 28 Wmk. 377

2134 A920 $5 metallic blue & blue 10.00 10.00

America issue.

Electricity Generation Projects — A921

Designs: 75c, Baba Dam. $1.25, Wind generators, Villonaco. $2, Mazar Dam.

Perf. 13½x13¾

2014, Oct. 31 Litho. Wmk. 377

2135-2137 A921 Set of 3 8.00 8.00

Fall of the Berlin Wall, 25th Anniv. — A922

Perf. 13¾x13½

2014, Nov. 10 Litho. Wmk. 377

2138 A922 75c multi 1.50 1.50

Christmas A923

Designs: 50c, Ivory creche figurines, 18th cent. $1, Wood carving of Infant Jesus, by Caspicara, vert.

Perf. 13¾x13½, 13½x13¾

2014, Nov. 25 Litho. Wmk. 377

2139-2140 A923 Set of 2 3.00 3.00

Miniature Sheet

Cuenca Tourist Attractions — A924

No. 2141: a, Rio Tomebamba. b, Mayor's office (Alcaldía). c, Benigno Malo College. d, Interamerican Artisans Center. e, New Cathedral. f, Azuay Provincial Court. g, Plaza de las Flores.

Perf. 13¾x13½

2014, Dec. 2 Litho. Wmk. 377

2141 A924 75c Sheet of 7, #a-g, + label 10.50 10.50

Miniature Sheet

First Ecuadorian Postage Stamps, 150th Anniv. — A925

No. 2142: a, Emilia Rivadeneira (1839-1916), engraver. b, Printing press, Ecuador #3. c, Printing press, Ecuador #2. d, Printing press, Ecuador #5. e, Manuel Rivadeneira (1814-94), printer.

Litho. With Foil Application

Perf. 13¾x13½

2015, Mar. 19 Wmk. 377

2142 A925 $5 Sheet of 5, #a-e, + 4 labels 50.00 50.00

Insects — A926

No. 2143: a, Antianthe expansa. b, Heteronotus abbreviatus. c, Cyphonia clavata. d, Guayaquila gracilicornis. e, Stegaspis fronditia. f, Thuris depressus. g, Tritropidia galeata. h, Membracis mexicana.

Unwmk.

2015, Apr. 21 Litho. *Die Cut*

Self-Adhesive

2143	Booklet pane of 8	10.00	
a.-b.	A926 25c Either single	.50	.50
c.-d.	A926 50c Either single	1.00	1.00
e.-f.	A926 75c Either single	1.50	1.50
g.-h.	A926 $1 Either single	2.00	2.00

Pres. Sixto Durán Ballén and Dove — A927

Perf. 13½x13¾

2015, May 15 Litho. Wmk. 377

2144 A927 $1.25 multi 2.50 2.50

Insects — A928

No. 2145: a, Alchisme grossa. b, Membracis foliata. c, Cladonota apicalis. d, Cyphonia trifida. e, Adippe histrio.

Perf. 13½x13¾

2015, May 28 Litho. Wmk. 377

2145	Horiz. strip of 5	30.00	30.00
a.-e.	A928 $3 Any single	6.00	6.00

Cattle — A929

Breeds: 75c, Aberdeen Angus. $1.25, Brahman. $3, Holstein Friesian.

Perf. 13½x13¾

2015, June 2 Litho. Wmk. 377

2146-2148 A929 Set of 3 10.00 10.00

Eradication of hoof-and-mouth disease in Ecuador.

Renovation of San Francisco Monastery, Quito — A930

Designs: 25c, Friar Jodoco Ricke baptizing indigenous people. 50c, Icon of Jesus, San Francisco Church. $1, San Francisco Church and Plaza. $1.75, Franciscan monk making beer. $2, Religious procession.

Perf. 13½x13¾

2015, June 11 Litho. Wmk. 377

2149-2153 A930 Set of 5 11.00 11.00

Birds — A931

Designs: 25c, Grallaria ridgelyi. 50c, Amazona lilacina. $1, Atlapetes pallidiceps. $2, Pyrrhura albipectus. $3, Chaetocercus berlepschi.

Perf. 13½x13¾

2015, June 16 Litho. Wmk. 377

2154-2158 A931 Set of 5 13.50 13.50

Visit of Pope Francis to Ecuador A932

Perf. 13¾x13½

2015, June 30 Litho. Wmk. 377

2159 A932 $3 multi 6.00 6.00

Litho. With Foil Application
Size: 100x70mm
Imperf

2160 A932 $5 Pope Francis, diff. 10.00 10.00

Official Registrar, 120th Anniv. A933

Perf. 13¾x13½

2015, Sept. 1 Litho. Wmk. 377
2161 A933 $1.50 multi 3.00 3.00

Famous People A934

No. 2162: a, Antonio Bastidas y Carranza (1615-81), poet. b, Raúl Clemente Huerta (1915-91), politician. c, Morayma Ofyr Carvajal (1915-51), writer. d, José Modesto Espinosa (1833-1915), writer. e, José Cuero y Caicedo (1735-1815), bishop of Quito.

Perf. 13¾x13½

2015, Sept. 22 Litho. Wmk. 377
2162 Horiz. strip of 5 12.50 12.50
a.-e. A934 $1.25 Any single 2.50 2.50

Miniature Sheet

ExpoAFE,150th Anniv. — A935

No. 2163: a, Argentina #594, flag of Argentina. b, Unissued Bolivia stamp of 1863, flag of Bolivia. c, Brazil #3252c, flag of Brazil. d, Canada #322, flag of Canada. e, Chile #348A, flag of Chile. f, Colombia #C56, flag of Colombia. g, Costa Rica #1, flag of Costa Rica. h, Cuba #432, flag of Cuba. i, Ecuador #306, flag of Ecuador. j, El Salvador #509, flag of El Salvador. k, Cover of *El Coleccionista Ecuatoriano*, emblem of Ecuadorian Philatelic Association. l, Block of six of Ecuador #2, ExpoAFE 80th anniv. emblem. m, Cover to Lima, emblem of ExpopAFE thematic stamp exhibition. n, Cover depicting airplane, emblem of FIAF thematic stamp exhibition. o, Postal card, FIAF emblem. p, Spain #345, flag of Spain. q, United States #C3a, flag of United States. r, Guatemala #21, flag of Guatemala. s, Mexico #246, flag of Mexico. t, Panama #214, flag of Panama. u, Paraguay #407, flag of Paraguay. v, Peru #C338, flag of Peru. w, St. Pierre & Miquelon #136, flag of St. Pierre & Miquelon. x, Uruguay #1167, flag of Uruguay. y, Venezuela #C9, flag of Venezuela.

Perf. 13½x13¾

2015, Sept. 29 Litho. Wmk. 377
2163 A935 Sheet of 25 37.50 37.50
a.-y. 75c Any single 1.50 1.50

Birds — A936

No. 2164: a, Tangara florida. b, Acropternis orthonyx. c, Pipreola jucunda. d, Pionopsitta pyrilia. e, Semnornis ramphastinus. f, Trogon chionurus. g, Pipra filicauda. h, Dacnis egregia.

No. 2165: a, Thryothorus nigricapillus. b, Neomorphus radiolosus. c, Phoenicircus nigricollis. d, Tangara gyrola. e, Aegolius harrisii. f, Grallaricula lineifrons. g, Melanopareia elegans. h, Piculus rivolii.

Unwmk.

2015, Oct. 20 Litho. *Die Cut*
Self-Adhesive

2164 Booklet pane of 8 10.00
a.-b. A936 25c Either single .50 .50
c.-d. A936 50c Either single 1.00 1.00
e.-f. A936 75c Either single 1.50 1.50
g.-h. A936 $1 Either single 2.00 2.00
2165 Booklet pane of 8 10.00
a.-b. A936 25c Either single .50 .50
c.-d. A936 50c Either single 1.00 1.00
e.-f. A936 75c Either single 1.50 1.50
g.-h. A936 $1 Either single 2.00 2.00

Don Quixote in Art — A937

No. 2166, $1 — Depictions of Don Quixote by: a, Carlos Monsalve. b, Ernesto Saá Sevilla.

No. 2167, $1.50 — Depictions of Don Quixote by: a, Oswaldo Viteri. b, Vilma Vargas.

No. 2168, $1.75, horiz. — Depictions of Don Quixote by: a, Joaquín Pinto. b, Karlomán Villota.

Perf. 13½x13¾, 13¾x13½

2015, Oct. 30 Litho. Wmk. 377
Horiz. Pairs, #a-b

2166-2168 A937 Set of 3 17.00 17.00

SEMI-POSTAL STAMPS

Nos. 423-428 Surcharged in Carmine or Blue

1944, May 9 Unwmk. *Perf. 12*
B1 A171 10c + 10c yel grn (C) .60 .30
B2 A171 20c + 20c rose pink .60 .30
B3 A171 30c + 20c dk gray brn .60 .30
B4 A171 50c + 20c dp red lil 1.20 .60
B5 A171 1s + 50c ol gray (C) 2.00 1.00
B6 A171 10s + 2s red orange 7.00 3.50
Nos. B1-B6 (6) 12.00 6.00

The surtax aided Mendez Hospital.

AIR POST STAMPS

In 1928-30, the internal airmail service of Ecuador was handled by the Sociedad Colombo-Alemana de Transportes Aereos ("SCADTA") under government sanction. During this period SCADTA issued stamps which were the only legal franking for airmail service except that handled under contract with Pan American-Grace Airways. SCADTA issues are Nos. C1-C6, C16-C25, CF1-CF2.

Colombia Air Post Stamps of 1923 Surcharged in Carmine

"Provisional" at 45 degree Angle

Perf. 14x14½

1928, Aug. 28 Wmk. 116
C1 AP6 50c on 10c green 110.00 70.00
C2 AP6 75c on 15c car 210.00 160.00
C3 AP6 1s on 20c gray 70.00 42.50
C4 AP6 1½s on 30c blue 45.00 35.00
C5 AP6 3s on 60c brown 85.00 52.50
Nos. C1-C5 (5) 520.00 360.00

"Provisional" at 41 degree Angle

1929, Mar. 20
C1a AP6 50c on 10c green 125.00 110.00
C2a AP6 75c on 15c carmine 225.00 175.00
C3a AP6 1s on 20c gray 225.00 175.00
Nos. C1a-C3a (3) 575.00 460.00

C6 AP6 50c on 10c green *700.00 1,700.*

A 75c on 15c carmine with "Cts." between the surcharged numerals exists. There is no evidence that it was regularly issued or used.

For overprints see Nos. CF1-CF1a.

Plane over River Guayas — AP1

Unwmk.

1929, May 5 Engr. *Perf. 12*
C8 AP1 2c black .40 .25
C9 AP1 5c carmine rose .40 .25
C10 AP1 10c deep brown .40 .25
C11 AP1 20c dark violet .90 .25
C12 AP1 50c deep green 1.60 .45
C13 AP1 1s dark blue 6.00 2.75
C14 AP1 5s orange yellow 25.00 11.00
C15 AP1 10s orange red 135.00 57.50
Nos. C8-C15 (8) 169.70 72.70

Establishment of commercial air service in Ecuador. The stamps were available for all forms of postal service and were largely used for franking ordinary letters.

Nos. C13-C15 show numerals in color on white background. Counterfeits of No. C15 exist.

See Nos. C26-C31. For overprints and surcharge see Nos. C32-C38, C287, CO1-CO12.

Jesuit Church La Compania AP2

Mount Chimborazo AP3

Wmk. 127

1929, Apr. 1 Litho. *Perf. 14*
C16 AP2 50c red brown 4.50 2.25
C17 AP2 75c green 4.50 2.25
C18 AP2 1s rose 7.00 2.25
C19 AP2 1½s gray blue 7.00 2.25
C20 AP2 2s violet 11.50 4.50
C21 AP2 3s brown 11.50 4.50
C22 AP3 5s lt blue 40.00 14.00
C23 AP3 10s lt red 85.00 30.00
C24 AP3 15s violet 140.00 60.00
C25 AP3 25s olive green 190.00 70.00
Nos. C16-C25 (10) 501.00 192.00

For overprint see No. CF2.

Plane Type of 1929

1930-44 Unwmk. Engr. *Perf. 12*
C26 AP1 1s carmine lake 6.50 .55
C27 AP1 1s green ('44) 1.00 .25
C28 AP1 5s olive green 10.00 3.75
C29 AP1 5s purple ('44) 2.00 .25
C30 AP1 10s black 30.00 5.50
C31 AP1 10s brt ultra ('44) 4.50 .30
Nos. C26-C31 (6) 54.00 10.60

Nos. C26-C31 show numerals in color on white background.

For surcharge see No. C287.

Type of 1929 Overprinted in Various Colors

AP4

1930, June 4
C32 AP4 1s car lake (Bk) 22.50 22.50
a. Double ovpt. (R Br + Bk) 75.00
C33 AP4 5s olive grn (Bl) 22.50 22.50
C34 AP4 10s black (R Br) 22.50 22.50
Nos. C32-C34 (3) 67.50 67.50

Flight of Capt. Benjamin Mendez from Bogota to Quito, bearing a crown of flowers for the tomb of Grand Marshal Sucre.

Air Post Official Stamps of 1929-30 Ovptd. in Various Colors or Srchd. Similarly in Upper & Lower Case

1935, July 24
C35 AP1 50c deep green (Bl) 12.50 5.00
C36 AP1 50c olive brn (R) 12.50 5.00
C37 AP1 1s on 5s ol grn (Bk) 12.50 5.00
a. Double surcharge 95.00
C38 AP1 2s on 10s black (R) 12.50 5.00
Nos. C35-C38 (4) 50.00 20.00

Unveiling of a monument to Bolívar at Quito, July 24th, 1935.

AP5

1935, Oct. 13 Photo. *Perf. 11½x11*
C38A AP5 5c ultra & red .25 *.30*
C38B AP5 10c brown & black .25 *.50*
C38C AP5 50c green & red .25 *.50*
C38D AP5 1S carmine & blue .80 *1.20*
C38E AP5 5S gray grn & red 1.20 *2.40*
Nos. C38A-C38E (5) 2.75 *4.90*

Columbus Day. Nos. 338A-338E and C38A-C38E were prepared by the Sociedad Colombista Panamericana and were sold by the Ecuadorian post office through Oct. 30. Nos. C38B-C38E exist imperf.

Geodesical Mission Issue

Nos. 349-351 Overprinted in Blue or Black and Type of Regular issue

1936, July 3 *Perf. 12½*
C39 A136 10c deep orange (Bl) .60 .25
C40 A136 20c violet (Bk) .60 .25
C41 A136 50c dark red (Bl) .60 .25
C42 A136 70c black 1.25 .35
Nos. C39-C42 (4) 3.05 1.10

For surcharge see No. RA42.

Philatelic Exhibition Issue

Type of Regular Issue Overprinted "AEREA"

1936, Oct. 20 *Perf. 13½x14*

C43 A137 2c rose 5.00 5.00
C44 A137 5c brown orange 5.00 5.00
C45 A137 10c brown 5.00 5.00
C46 A137 20c ultra 5.00 5.00
C47 A137 50c red violet 5.00 5.00
C48 A137 1s green 5.00 5.00
Nos. C43-C48 (6) 30.00 30.00

Condor and Plane — AP6

Perf. 13½

C49 AP6 70c orange brown 2.25 .50
C50 AP6 1s dull violet 2.25 .50

Nos. C43-C50 were issued for the 1st Intl. Phil. Exhib. at Quito.

Condor over "El Altar" — AP7

1937-46 *Perf. 11½, 12*

C51 AP7 10c chestnut 5.00 .25
C52 AP7 20c olive black 6.50 .25
C53 AP7 40c rose car ('46) 6.50 .25
C54 AP7 70c black brown 9.00 .25
C55 AP7 1s gray black 14.00 .25
C56 AP7 2s dark violet 24.00 .65
Nos. C51-C56 (6) 65.00 1.90

Issue dates: 40c, Oct. 7; others, Aug. 19.
For overprints see Nos. 463-464, CO13-CO17.

Portrait of Washington, American Eagle and Flags — AP8

Engraved and Lithographed

1938, Feb. 9 *Perf. 12*

Center Multicolored

C57 AP8 2c brown .40 .25
C58 AP8 5c black .40 .25
C59 AP8 10c brown .40 .25
C60 AP8 20c dark blue .80 .25
C61 AP8 50c violet 1.75 .25
C62 AP8 1s black 3.25 .25
C63 AP8 2s violet 7.50 .90
Nos. C57-C63 (7) 14.50 2.40

150th anniv. of the US Constitution.
In 1947, Nos. C61-C63 were overprinted in dark blue: "Primero la Patria!" and plane. These revolutionary propaganda stamps were later renounced by decree. Value $20.
For overprints see Nos. C102-C104, C139-C141.

No. RA35 Surcharged in Red

1938, Nov. 16 *Perf. 13½*

C64 PT12 65c on 3c ultra .40 .25

A national airmail concession was given to the Sociedad Ecuatoriano de Transportes Aereos (SEDTA) in July, 1938. No. RA35 was surcharged for SEDTA postal requirements. SEDTA operated through 1940.

Army Horseman — AP9

Woman Runner — AP10

Tennis — AP11

Boxing — AP12

Olympic Fire — AP13

1939, Mar. **Engr.** *Perf. 12*

C65 AP9 5c lt green 1.60 .25
C66 AP10 10c salmon 2.25 .25
C67 AP11 50c redsh brown 11.50 .25
C68 AP12 1s black brown 13.50 .45
C69 AP13 2s rose carmine 17.00 1.10
Nos. C65-C69 (5) 45.85 2.30

First Bolivarian Games (1938).

Plane over Chimborazo AP14

1939, May 1 *Perf. 13x12½*

C70 AP14 1s yellow brown .40 .25
C71 AP14 2s rose violet .70 .25
C72 AP14 5s black 1.90 .25
Nos. C70-C72 (3) 3.00 .75

Golden Gate Bridge and Mountain Peak — AP15

Empire State Building and Mountain Peak — AP16

1939 *Perf. 12½x13*

C73 AP15 2c black .40 .25
C74 AP15 5c rose red .40 .25
C75 AP15 10c indigo .40 .25
C76 AP15 50c rose violet .40 .25
C77 AP15 1s chocolate .80 .25
C78 AP15 2s yellow brown 1.00 .25
C79 AP15 5s emerald 2.00 .25
Nos. C73-C79 (7) 5.40 1.75

Golden Gate International Exposition.
For surcharge & overprint see Nos. 434, CO18.

1939

C80 AP16 2c brown orange .65 .30
C81 AP16 5c dark carmine .65 .25
C82 AP16 10c indigo .65 .30
C83 AP16 50c slate green .65 .30
C84 AP16 1s deep orange 1.30 .30
C85 AP16 2s dk red violet 1.50 .30
C86 AP16 5s dark gray 3.50 .30
Nos. C80-C86 (7) 8.90 2.00

New York World's Fair.
For surcharge see No. 435.

Map of the Americas and Airplane — AP17

1940, July 9

C87 AP17 10c red org & blue .45 .25
C88 AP17 70c sepia & blue .45 .25
C89 AP17 1s copper brn & blue .90 .25
C90 AP17 10s black & blue 3.50 .95
Nos. C87-C90 (4) 5.30 1.70

Pan American Union, 50th anniversary.

Journalism Type

1941, Dec. 15

C91 A157 3s rose carmine 5.75 .25
C92 A157 10s yellow orange 12.00 .45

See note after No. 399.

Old Map of South America Showing Amazon River — AP19

Panoramic View of Amazon River — AP20

Designs: 70c, Gonzalo de Pineda. 5s, Painting of the expedition.

1942, Jan. 30

C93 AP19 40c black & buff 1.90 .25
C94 AP19 70c olive 2.90 .25
C95 AP20 2s dark green 3.25 .25
C96 AP19 5s rose 4.00 1.10
Nos. C93-C96 (4) 12.05 1.85

See note after No. 403.

Remigio Crespo Toral Type

1942, Sept. 1 *Perf. 13½*

C97 A162 10c dull violet 1.25 .50

Alfaro Types

70c, Gen. Eloy Alfaro. 1s, Devils's Nose. 3s, Military College. 5s, Montecristi, Alfaro's birthplace.

1943, Feb. 16 *Perf. 12*

C98 A166 70c dk rose & blk 1.90 .25
C99 A167 1s ol blk & red brn 3.25 .75
C100 A167 3s ol gray & grn 4.50 1.10
C101 A167 5s slate & salmon 6.75 1.30
Nos. C98-C101 (4) 16.40 3.40

Nos. C61-C63 Overprinted in Red Brown

1943, Apr. 15 *Perf. 11½*

Center Multicolored

C102 AP8 50c violet 2.75 1.50
C103 AP8 1s black 3.25 1.60
C104 AP8 2s violet 4.00 2.50
Nos. C102-C104 (3) 10.00 5.60

Visit of US Vice-Pres. Henry A. Wallace.

Nos. 374-376 Overprinted "AEREO LOOR A BOLIVIA JUNIO 11-1943" (like Nos. C111-C113)

1943, June 11 *Perf. 13*

C105 A146 50c dp red violet .40 .25
C106 A147 1s copper red .60 .25
C107 A148 2s dark green .70 .25
Nos. C105-C107 (3) 1.70 .75

Visit of Pres. Eurique Penaranda of Bolivia.
Vertical overprints on Nos. C105-C106.

Nos. 374-376 Overprinted "AEREO LOOR A PARAGUAY JULIO 5-1943" (like Nos. C111-C113)

1943, July 5

C108 A146 50c dp red violet .45 .25
a. Double overprint 75.00
C109 A147 1s copper red 1.10 .50
C110 A148 2s dark green 1.50 .70
Nos. C108-C110 (3) 3.05 1.45

Visit of Pres. Higinio Morinigo of Paraguay.
Vertical overprints on Nos. C108-C109.

Nos. 374-376 Overprinted in Black

1943, July 23

C111 A146 50c dp red violet .45 .25
C112 A147 1s copper red .65 .25
C113 A148 2s dark green .75 .25
Nos. C111-C113 (3) 1.85 .75

Issued to commemorate the visit of President Isaias Medina Angarita of Venezuela.
Vertical overprint on Nos. C111-C112.
See Nos. C105-C110.

President Arroyo del Rio Addressing US Congress — AP26

1943, Oct. 9 *Perf. 12*

C114 AP26 50c dark brown 1.00 .50
C115 AP26 70c brt rose 1.30 .50
C116 AP26 3s dark blue 1.50 .65
C117 AP26 5s dark green 3.50 1.20
C118 AP26 10s olive black 13.00 4.25
Nos. C114-C118 (5) 20.30 7.10

Good will tour of Pres. Arroyo del Rio in 1942.
For surcharges see Nos. CB1-CB5.

1944, Feb. 7

C119 AP26 50c dp red lilac .90 .65
C120 AP26 70c red brown 1.75 .65
C121 AP26 3s turq green 1.75 .65
C122 AP26 5s brt ultra 2.90 1.40
C123 AP26 10s scarlet 3.50 1.60
Nos. C119-C123 (5) 10.80 4.95
Nos. C114-C123 (10) 31.10 12.05

Church of San Francisco, Quito — AP27

1944, Feb. 13

C124 AP27 70c turq green 1.90 .45
C125 AP27 1s olive 1.90 .45
C126 AP27 3s red orange 4.25 1.10
C127 AP27 5s carmine rose 5.25 1.30
Nos. C124-C127 (4) 13.30 3.30

See note after No. 433.

Palace Type

1944 **Engr.** *Perf. 11*

C128 A173 3s orange 1.00 .25
C129 A173 5s dark brown 1.75 .25
C130 A173 10s dark red 4.00 .25
Nos. C128-C130 (3) 6.75 .75

See No. C221. For overprints and surcharges see Nos. 541, C136-C138, C210-C213, C218-C220, C223-C224, C277-C279.

Red Cross Type

1945, Apr. 25 **Unwmk.** *Perf. 12*

Cross in Rose

C131 A174 2s deep blue 4.00 1.10
C132 A174 3s green 4.50 1.25
C133 A174 5s dark violet 6.50 1.75
C134 A174 10s carmine rose 21.00 5.75
Nos. C131-C134 (4) 36.00 9.85

No. RA55 Surcharged in Black

1945, June 8

C135 PT21 40c on 5c blue 1.00 .25
a. Double surcharge 10.00

Counterfeits exist.

Nos. C128-C130 Overprinted in Green

1945, Sept. 6 ***Perf. 11***

C136 A173 3s orange 1.00 .50
a. Inverted overprint 50.00
b. Double overprint 50.00
C137 A173 5s dark brown 1.25 .65
C138 A173 10s dark red 3.25 1.25
Nos. C136-C138 (3) 5.50 2.40

Nos. C61-C63 Overprinted in Dark Blue and Gold like Nos. 444-446

1945, Oct. 2 ***Perf. 12***

Center Multicolored

C139 AP8 50c violet 1.40 .25
C140 AP8 1s black 1.60 1.50
C141 AP8 2s violet 2.50 1.90
Nos. C139-C141 (3) 5.50 3.65

Visit of Pres. Juan Antonio Rios of Chile.

Monument to Liberty — AP30

1945, Nov. 14 **Engr.**

C142 AP30 30c blue .45 .25
C143 AP30 40c rose carmine .45 .25
C144 AP30 1s dull violet 1.30 .55
C145 AP30 3s gray black 2.50 1.40
C146 AP30 5s purple brown 3.50 1.90
Nos. C142-C146 (5) 8.20 4.35

Gen. Antonio Jose de Sucre, 150th birth anniv.

Catalogue values for unused stamps in this section, from this point to the end of the section, are for Never Hinged items.

Highway Type

1946, Apr. 22 **Unwmk.**

C147 A176 1s carmine rose .65 .40
C148 A176 2s violet .80 .55
C149 A176 3s turq green 1.40 .60
C150 A176 5s red orange 1.75 .80
C151 A176 10s dark blue 2.75 .80
Nos. C147-C151 (5) 7.35 3.15

Revolution Types

1946, Aug. 9 ***Perf. 12½***

C152 A177 40c deep claret .25 .25
C153 A178 1s sepia .25 .25
C154 A179 2s indigo .60 .25
C155 A180 3s olive green 1.10 .45
Nos. C152-C155 (4) 2.20 1.20

National Union of Journalists, Initials and Quill Pen — AP36

1946, Sept. 16

C156 AP36 50c dull purple .75 .30
C157 AP36 70c dark green .90 .45
C158 AP36 3s red 1.50 .60
C159 AP36 5s indigo 2.00 .75
C160 AP36 10s chocolate 6.50 1.25
Nos. C156-C160 (5) 11.65 3.35

Campaign for adult education.

The Blessed Mariana Teaching Children — AP37

"Lily of Quito" — AP38

1946, Nov. 28 **Unwmk.**

C161 AP37 40c chocolate .30 .25
C162 AP37 60c deep blue .40 .35
C163 AP38 3s orange yellow .80 .60
C164 AP38 5s green 2.00 .85
Nos. C161-C164 (4) 3.50 2.05

300th anniv. of the death of the Blessed Mariana de Jesus Paredes y Flores.

Rocafuerte Type

60c-1.10s, Jual de Velasco. 1.30s-2s, Riobamba Irrigation Canal.

1947, Nov. 27 ***Perf. 12***

C165 A185 60c dark green .25 .25
C166 A185 70c purple .25 .25
C167 A185 1s black brown .25 .25
C168 A185 1.10s car rose .25 .25
C169 A185 1.30s deep blue .35 .25
C170 A185 1.90s olive bister 1.00 .25
C171 A185 2s olive green 1.20 .25
Nos. C165-C171 (7) 3.55 1.75

For overprints & surcharges see Nos. C175, C181, C207-C209, C215, C216-C217, C222, C235.

Bello Type

1948, Apr. 21 ***Perf. 13***

C172 A188 60c magenta .40 .25
C173 A188 1.30s dk blue grn .70 .25
C174 A188 1.90s dk rose car .60 .25
Nos. C172-C174 (3) 1.70 .75

No. C166 Overprinted in Black

1948, May 24 ***Perf. 12***

C175 A185 70c purple .65 .35

Columbus — AP42

1948, May 26 ***Perf. 14***

C176 AP42 50c olive green .25 .25
C177 AP42 70c rose carmine .50 .40
C178 AP42 3s ultra 1.60 1.10
C179 AP42 5s brown 2.60 1.60
C180 AP42 10s deep violet 8.00 2.00
Nos. C176-C180 (5) 12.95 5.35

See note after No. 495.

No. C169 Overprinted in Carmine like No. 496 (MANANA reads up)

1948, Aug. 26 **Unwmk.** ***Perf. 12***

C181 A185 1.30s deep blue .40 .25

National Fair of Today and Tomorrow, 1948.

Elia Liut and Telegrafo I AP43

Teacher and Pupils AP44

1948, Sept. 10 ***Perf. 12½***

C182 AP43 60c rose red .80 .25
C183 AP43 1s green .80 .25
C184 AP43 1.30s deep claret .80 .25
C185 AP43 1.90s deep violet .80 .25
C186 AP43 2s dark brown 1.20 .30
C187 AP43 5s blue 2.40 .50
Nos. C182-C187 (6) 6.80 1.80

25th anniv. (in 1945) of the 1st postal flight in Ecuador.

1948, Oct. 12 ***Perf. 14***

C188 AP44 50c violet 1.50 .50
C189 AP44 70c deep blue 1.50 .50
C190 AP44 3s dark green 2.50 1.00
C191 AP44 5s red 4.00 1.50
C192 AP44 10s brown 7.50 2.00
Nos. C188-C192 (5) 17.00 5.50

Campaign for adult education.

AP45

Franklin D. Roosevelt and Two of "Four Freedoms" — AP46

1948, Oct. 24 ***Perf. 12½***

C193 AP45 60c emer & org brn .40 .25
C194 AP45 1s car rose & slate .60 .30
C195 AP46 1.50s grn & red brn .75 .55
C196 AP46 2s red & black .80 .30
C197 AP46 5s ultra & blk 1.75 .30
Nos. C193-C197 (5) 4.30 1.70

Maldonado Types

1948, Nov. 17

C198 A196 60c dp org & rose car .80 .25
C199 A197 90c red & gray blk .80 .25
C200 A196 1.30s pur & dp org 1.00 .25
C201 A197 2s dp bl & dull grn 1.00 .25
Nos. C198-C201 (4) 3.60 1.00

See note after No. 519.

Juan Montalvo and Cervantes AP47

Don Quixote — AP48

1949, May 2 **Engr.** ***Perf. 12½x12***

C202 AP47 1.30s ol brn & ultra 3.00 2.50
C203 AP48 1.90s grn & rose car 1.00 .30
C204 AP47 3s vio & org brn 1.50 .30
C205 AP48 5s red & gray blk 2.75 .25
C206 AP47 10s red lil & aqua 4.00 .25
Nos. C202-C206 (5) 12.25 3.60

400th anniv. of the birth of Miguel de Cervantes Saavedra, novelist, playwright and poet, and the 60th anniv. of the death of Juan Montalvo (1832-89), Ecuadorean writer.

For surcharges see Nos. C225-C226.

No. C168 Surcharged in Blue

1949, June 15 ***Perf. 12***

C207 A185 50c on 1.10s car rose .45 .25
C208 A185 60c on 1.10s car rose .45 .25
C209 A185 90c on 1.10s car rose .65 .25
Nos. C207-C209 (3) 1.55 .75

2nd Eucharistic Cong., Quito, June 1949.

No. C128 Surcharged in Black

1949, Oct. 11 ***Perf. 11***

C210 A173 60c on 3s orange .75 .40
a. Double surcharge 30.00
C211 A173 90c on 3s orange .80 .30
C212 A173 1s on 3s orange 1.00 .40
C213 A173 2s on 3s orange 1.75 .40
Nos. C210-C213 (4) 4.30 1.50

"SUCRE(S)" in capitals on Nos. C212-C213.
75th anniv. of the UPU.

AP49

Black Surcharge

1950 **Unwmk.** ***Perf. 12***

C214 AP49 60c on 50c gray .75 .25
a. Double surcharge 15.00

No. C170 Surcharged with New Value in Black

C215 A185 90c on 1.90s ol bis .75 .25

Nos. C168, C128-C129 and Type of 1944 Srchd. or Ovptd. in Black or Carmine

1950, Feb. 10 ***Perf. 12***

C216 A185 50c on 1.10s 1.75 1.75
C217 A185 70c on 1.10s 2.25 1.75

Perf. 11

C218 A173 3s orange 3.25 3.00
C219 A173 5s dark brown (C) 5.00 2.50
C220 A173 10s violet (C) 7.50 3.00
Nos. C216-C220 (5) 19.75 12.00

Issued to publicize adult education.
For overprint see No. 541.

Govt. Palace Type of 1944

1950, May 15 **Engr.** ***Perf. 11***

C221 A173 10s violet 2.00 .25

For surcharges see Nos. C277-C279.

No. C169 Surcharged with New Value in Black

1950 ***Perf. 12***

C222 A185 90c on 1.30s dp blue .30 .25

See No. C235.

Nos. C128-C129 Overprinted in Black

1951, July 28 Unwmk. *Perf. 11*

C223 A173 3s orange 1.25 .90
C224 A173 5s dark brown 2.50 1.25

20,000th crossing of the equator by Pan American-Grace Airways planes.

Nos. C202-C203 Surcharged in Black

1951 Unwmk. *Perf. 12½x12*

C225 AP47 60c on 1.30s .30 .25
C226 AP48 1s on 1.90s .30 .25
a. Inverted surcharge 20.00

Issued to publicize adult education.

St. Mariana de Jesus — AP50

1952, Feb. 15 Engr.

C227 AP50 60c plum & aqua .60 .30
C228 AP50 90c dk grn & lt ultra .80 .30
C229 AP50 1s car & dk grn .90 .30
C230 AP50 2s indigo & rose lil 1.00 .30
Nos. C227-C230 (4) 3.30 1.20

Canonization of Mariana de Jesus Paredes y Flores.

Plaza Visit to US Issue

3s, as No. 558. 5s, as No. 559.

1952, Mar. 26 *Perf. 12*

C231 A205 3s lilac & bl grn .70 .45
C232 A205 5s red brn & ol gray 2.00 1.75
a. Souv. sheet of 2, #C231-C232 4.50 *9.00*

Consular Service Stamps Surcharged in Black

1952 Unwmk. *Perf. 12*

C233 R2 60c on 1s green .30 .25
C234 R2 1s on 1s green .30 .25

Type R2 illustrated above No. 545.

No. C169 Surcharged with New Value in Carmine

C235 A185 90c on 1.30s dp bl .30 .25
Nos. C233-C235 (3) .90 .75

See No. C222.

Pres. José M. Urvina and Allegory of Freedom — AP52

Hyphen-hole Perf. 7x6½

1952, Nov. 18 Litho.

C236 AP52 60c rose red & blue 3.50 .45
C237 AP52 90c lilac & red 3.50 .60
C238 AP52 1s orange & green 3.50 .30
C239 AP52 2s red brn & blue 3.50 .45
Nos. C236-C239 (4) 14.00 1.80

Centenary of abolition of slavery in Ecuador. Counterfeits exist.

Torch of Knowledge AP53

Design: 2s, Aged couple studying alphabet.

Unwmk.

1953, Apr. 13 Engr. *Perf. 12*

C240 AP53 1s dark blue 1.20 .25
C241 AP53 2s red orange 1.50 .25

1952 adult education campaign.

Globe Showing Part of Western Hemisphere AP54

1953, June 5 *Perf. 12½x12*

C242 AP54 60c orange yellow .30 .25
C243 AP54 90c dark blue .40 .30
C244 AP54 3s carmine .70 .45
Nos. C242-C244 (3) 1.40 1.00

Issued to publicize the crossing of the equator by the Pan-American highway.

Consular Service Stamps Surcharged in Black

a

b

1953-54 *Perf. 12*

C245 R1 (a) 60c on 2s brown .35 .25
C246 R2 (a) 60c on 5s sep ('54) .35 .25
C247 R2 (a) 70c on 5s sep ('54) .35 .25
C248 R2 (a) 90c on 50c car rose ('54) .35 .25
C249 R1 (b) 1s on 2s brown .35 .25
C250 R1 (a) 1s on 2s brn ('54) .35 .25
C251 R1 (a) 2s on 2s brn ('54) .65 .25
C252 R1 (a) 3s on 5s vio ('54) .90 .25
Nos. C245-C252 (8) 3.65 2.00

Surcharge is horizontal on Nos. C245-C248.

Carlos Maria Cardinal de la Torre — AP55

Queen Isabella I — AP56

1954, Jan. 13 Photo. *Perf. 8½*

Center in Black

C253 AP55 60c rose lilac .50 .30
C254 AP55 90c green .80 .30
C255 AP55 3s orange 1.20 .45
Nos. C253-C255 (3) 2.50 1.05

1st anniv. of the elevation of Archbishop de la Torre to Cardinal.

1954, Apr. 22

C256 AP56 60c dk grn & grn .50 .40
C257 AP56 90c lil rose .50 .40
C258 AP56 1s blk & pale lil .50 .40
C259 AP56 2s blk brn & pale bl .70 .40
C260 AP56 5s blk brn & buff 1.75 .40
Nos. C256-C260 (5) 3.95 2.00

See note with No. 585.

Post Office, Guayaquil AP57

1954, May 19 Engr. *Perf. 12½x12*

Black Surcharge

C261 AP57 80c on 20c red .30 .25
C262 AP57 1s on 20c red .30 .25

25th anniversary of Pan American-Grace Airways' operation in Ecuador.

Plane, Gateway and Wheel — AP58

Unwmk.

1954, Aug. 2 Litho. *Perf. 11*

C263 AP58 80c blue .35 .25

Day of the Postal Employee.

San Pablo Lagoon AP59

1954, Sept. 24 Photo.

C264 AP59 60c orange .30 .25
C265 AP59 70c rose pink .30 .25
C266 AP59 90c dp grn .30 .25
C267 AP59 1s dk gray grn .30 .25
C268 AP59 2s blue .40 .25
C269 AP59 3s yel brn .75 .25
Nos. C264-C269 (6) 2.35 1.50

Glorification of Abdon Calderon Garaicoa AP60

Capt. Calderon — AP61

1954, Oct. 1

C270 AP60 80c rose pink .45 .25
C271 AP61 90c blue .45 .25

150th anniversary of the birth of Capt. Abdon Calderon Garaicoa.

El Cebollar College AP62

Brother Miguel Instructing Boys — AP63

Designs: 90c, Francisco Febres Cordero (Brother Miguel). 2.50s, Tomb of Brother Miguel. 3s, Monument to Brother Miguel.

1954, Dec. 3 Unwmk. *Perf. 11*

C272 AP62 70c dk grn .25 .25
C273 AP63 80c dk brn .25 .25
C274 AP63 90c dk gray bl .25 .25
C275 AP63 2.50s indigo .45 .25
C276 AP62 3s lil rose .55 .35
Nos. C272-C276 (5) 1.75 1.35

Centenary of the birth of Francisco Febres Cordero (Brother Miguel).

No. C221 Surcharged in Various Colors

1955, May 25

C277 A173 1s on 10s vio (Bk) .30 .25
C278 A173 1.70s on 10s vio (C) .40 .25
C279 A173 4.20s on 10s vio (Br) .65 .35
Nos. C277-C279 (3) 1.35 .85

Denomination in larger type on No. C279. National Exhibition of Daily Periodicals.

"La Rotonda," Guayaquil, and Rotary Emblem AP64

Design: 90c, Eugenio Espejo hospital, Quito, and Rotary emblem.

1955, July 9 Engr. *Perf. 12½*

C280 AP64 80c dark brown .30 .25
C281 AP64 90c dark green .50 .35

50th anniv. of the founding of Rotary Intl.

José Abel Castillo AP65

2s, 5s, José Abel Castillo, Map of Ecuador.

1955, Oct. 19 *Perf. 11x11½*

C282 AP65 60c chocolate 1.10 .25
C283 AP65 90c light olive green 1.25 .25
C284 AP65 1s lilac 1.40 .25
C285 AP65 2s vermilion 1.75 .30
C286 AP65 5s ultra 3.50 .55
Nos. C282-C286 (5) 9.00 1.60

See note after No. 595.

No. C29 Surcharged in Black

1955, Oct. 24 *Perf. 12*

C287 AP1 1s on 5s purple .65 .25

A similar surcharge on No. C29, set in two lines with letters 5mm high and no X's or black-out line of squares, was privately applied.

San Pablo, Imbabura — AP66

50s, Rumichaca Caves. 1.30s, Virgin of Quito. 1.50s, Cotopaxi Volcano. 1.70s, Tungurahua Volcano, Tungurahua. 1.90s, Guanacos. 2.40s, Mat market. 2.50s, Ruins at Ingapirca. 4.20s, El Carmen, Cuenca, Azuay. 4.80s, Santo Domingo Church.

1956, Jan. 2 Photo. *Perf. 13*
C288 AP66 50c slate blue 2.75 .25
C289 AP66 1s ultra 2.75 .25
C290 AP66 1.30s crimson 4.25 .25
C291 AP66 1.50s dp grn 2.75 .25
C292 AP66 1.70s yel brn 1.75 .25
C293 AP66 1.90s olive 3.50 .25
C294 AP66 2.40s red org 3.75 .25
C295 AP66 2.50s violet 3.75 .25
C296 AP66 4.20s black 4.75 .25
C297 AP66 4.80s yel org 7.50 .30
Nos. C288-C297 (10) 37.50 2.55

See Nos. C310-C311. For surcharges see Nos. 766A, 766G.

Honorato Vazquez — AP67

Title Page of First Book — AP68

1956, May 28 Engr.
Various Portraits
C298 AP67 1s yellow green .50 .25
C299 AP67 1.50s red .50 .25
C300 AP67 1.70s bright blue .50 .25
C301 AP67 1.90s slate blue .50 .25
Nos. C298-C301 (4) 2.00 1.00

Birth centenary (in 1955) of Honorato Vazquez, statesman.

1956, Aug. 27 Unwmk. *Perf. 13½*
C302 AP68 1s black .60 .25
C303 AP68 1.70s slate bl .60 .25
C304 AP68 2s blk brn .60 .25
C305 AP68 3s redsh brn .60 .25
Nos. C302-C305 (4) 2.40 1.00

Bicentenary of printing in Ecuador.

Hands Reaching for UN Emblem AP69

1956, Oct. 24 *Perf. 14*
C307 AP69 1.70s red org 1.10 .25

10th anniv. of the UN (in 1955).
See No. C319. For overprint see No. C426.

Coat of Arms and Basketball Player — AP70

Designs: 1.70s, Map of South America with flags and girl basketball players.

1956, Dec. 28 Photo. *Perf. 14½x14*
C308 AP70 1s red lilac .65 .25
C309 AP70 1.70s deep green 1.00 .25

6th South American Women's Basketball Championship, Aug. 1956.

Scenic Type of 1956

1957, Jan. 2 *Perf. 13*
C310 AP66 50c bl grn 1.75 .25
C311 AP66 1s orange 1.75 .25

Type of Regular Issue, 1957

Designs: 50c, Map of Cuenca, 16th century. 80c, Cathedral of Cuenca. 1s, Modern City Hall.

Unwmk.
1957, Apr. 7 Photo. *Perf. 12*
C312 A219 50c brn, *cr* .30 .25
a. Souvenir sheet of 4 1.00 1.00
C313 A219 80c red, *bluish* .30 .25
C314 A219 1s pur, *yel* .30 .25
a. Souvenir sheet of 3 2.00 2.00
Nos. C312-C314 (3) .90 .75

No. C312a contains 4 imperf. 50c stamps similar to No. 613, but inscribed "AEREO" and printed in green. The sheet is printed on white ungummed paper.

No. C314a contains 3 imperf. stamps in designs similar to Nos. C312-C314, but with colors changed to orange (50c), brown (80c), violet (1s). The sheet is printed on white ungummed paper.

Gabriela Mistral — AP71

Arms of Espejo, Carchi — AP72

Unwmk.
1957, Sept. 18 Litho. *Perf. 14*
C315 AP71 2s lt bl, blk & red .55 .25

Issued to honor Gabriela Mistral (1889-1957), Chilean poet and educator.
See Nos. C406-C407.

1957, Nov. 16 *Perf. 14½x13½*

Arms of Cantons: 2s, Montufar. 4.20s, Tulcan.

Coat of Arms Multicolored
C316 AP72 1s carmine .55 .25
C317 AP72 2s black .55 .25
C318 AP72 4.20s ultra 1.00 .25
Nos. C316-C318 (3) 2.10 .75

Province of Carchi.
See Nos. C334-C337, C355-C364, C392-C395. For surcharge see No. 766.

Redrawn UN Type of 1956

1957, Dec. 10 Engr. *Perf. 14*
C319 AP69 2s greenish blue .55 .25

Honoring the UN. Dates, as on No. C307, are omitted; inscribed: "Homenaje a las Naciones Unidas."

Mater Dolorosa, San Gabriel College — AP73

Rafael Maria Arizaga — AP74

No. C321, 1s, Door of San Gabriel College, Quito.

1958, Apr. 27 Engr. *Perf. 14*
C320 AP73 30c rose cl, *dp rose* .30 .25
C321 AP73 30c rose cl, *dp rose* .30 .25
a. Pair, #C320-C321 .75 .60
C322 AP73 1s dk bl, *lt bl* .30 .25
C323 AP73 1.70s dk bl, *lt bl* .30 .25
a. Pair, #C322-C323 .75 .60

Miracle of San Gabriel College, Quito, 50th anniv.

1958, July 21 Litho.
C324 AP74 1s multi .45 .30

Rafael Maria Arizaga (1858-1933), writer.
See Nos. C343, C350, C412.

Daule River Bridge AP75

1958, July 25 Engr. *Perf. 13½x14*
C325 AP75 1.30s green .50 .25

Issued to commemorate the opening of the River Daule bridge in Guayas province.
See Nos. C367-C369.

Basketball Player — AP76

1958, Sept. 1 Photo. *Perf. 14x13½*
C326 AP76 1.30s dk grn & lt brn .55 .45

South American basketball championships.
For surcharge see No. 774A.

Symbolical of the Eucharist — AP77

Design: 60c, Cathedral of Guayaquil.

1958, Sept. 25 Litho. Unwmk.
C327 AP77 10c vio & buff .40 .30
C328 AP77 60c org & vio brn .40 .30
C329 AP77 1s brn & lt bl .40 .30
Nos. C327-C329 (3) 1.20 .90

Souvenir Sheet

Symbolical of the Eucharist — AP78

Perf. 13½x14
C330 AP78 Sheet of 4 2.75 2.25
a.-d. 40c dark blue, any single .25 .25

3rd National Eucharistic Congress.

Stamps of 1865 and 1920 — AP79

Designs: 2s, Stamps of 1920 and 1948. 4.20s, Municipal museum and library.

1958, Oct. 8 Photo. *Perf. 11½*
Granite Paper
C331 AP79 1.30s grn & brn red .35 .25
C332 AP79 2s bl & vio .70 .30
C333 AP79 4.20s dk brn .90 .40
Nos. C331-C333 (3) 1.95 .95

National Philatelic Exposition (EXFIGUA), Guayaquil, Oct. 4-14.
For surcharge see No. 774.

Coat of Arms Type of 1957
Province of Imbabura

Arms of Cantons: 50c, Cotacachi. 60c, Antonio Ante. 80c, Otavalo. 1.10s, Ibarra.

1958, Nov. 9 Litho. *Perf. 14½x13½*
Coats of Arms Multicolored
C334 AP72 50c blk & red .50 .25
C335 AP72 60c blk, bl & red .50 .25
C336 AP72 80c blk & yel .50 .25
C337 AP72 1.10s blk & red .50 .25
Nos. C334-C337 (4) 2.00 1.00

Charles V — AP80

Paul Rivet — AP81

Engr. & Photo.
1958, Dec. 12 *Perf. 14x13½*
C338 AP80 2s brn red & dk brn .45 .30
C339 AP80 4.20s dk gray & red brn .55 .45

400th anniv. of the death of Charles V, Holy Roman Emperor.

1958, Dec. 29 Photo. *Perf. 11½*
Granite Paper
C340 AP81 1s brown .45 .30

Issued in honor of Paul Rivet (1876-1958), French anthropologist.

1959, May 6

Portrait: 2s, Alexander von Humboldt.

C341 AP81 2s slate .35 .25

Cent. of the death of Alexander von Humboldt, German naturalist and geographer.

Front Page of "El Telegrafo" — AP82

1959, Feb. Litho. *Perf. 13½*
C342 AP82 1.30s bl grn & blk .35 .25

75th anniv. of Ecuador's oldest newspaper.

Portrait Type of 1958

José Luis Tamayo (1858-1947), lawyer.

1959, June 26 Unwmk. *Perf. 14*
Portrait Multicolored
C343 AP74 1.30s lt grn, bl & sal .45 .30

El Sagrario & House of Manuela Canizares AP83

Condor — AP84

Designs: 80c, Hall at San Agustin. 1s, First words of the constitutional act. 2s, Entrance to Cuartel Real. 4.20s, Allegory of Liberty.

Unwmk.

1959, Aug. 28 Photo. *Perf. 14*

C344	AP83	20c	ultra & lt brn	.25	.25
C345	AP83	80c	brt bl & dp org	.25	.25
C346	AP83	1s	dk red & dk ol	.25	.25
C347	AP84	1.30s	brt bl & org	.25	.25
C348	AP84	2s	ultra & org brn	.25	.25
C349	AP84	4.20s	scar & brt bl	.65	.45
			Nos. C344-C349 (6)	1.90	1.70

Sesquicentennial of the revolution.

Portrait Type of 1958

1s, Alfredo Baquerizo Moreno (1859-1951), statesman.

1959, Sept. 26 Litho. *Perf. 14*

C350	AP74	1s	gray, red & salmon	.45	.30

Pope Pius XII — AP85

1959, Oct. 9 Unwmk. *Perf. 14½*

C351	AP85	1.30s	multi	.45	.30

Issued in memory of Pope Plus XII.

Flags of Argentina, Bolivia, Brazil, Guatemala, Haiti, Mexico and Peru — AP86

Flags of: 80c, Chile, Costa Rica, Cuba, Dominican Republic, Panama, Paraguay, United States. 1.30s, Colombia, Ecuador, Honduras, Nicaragua, Salvador, Uruguay, Venezuela.

1959, Oct. 12 *Perf. 13½.*

C352	AP86	50c	multi	.25	.25
C353	AP86	80c	yel, red & bl	.30	.25
C354	AP86	1.30s	multi	.40	.25
			Nos. C352-C354 (3)	.95	.75

Organization of American States.

For overprints see Nos. C423-C425, CO19-CO21.

Arms of the Cantons Type of 1957

Province of Pichincha

10c, Rumiñahui. 40c, Pedro Moncayo. 1s, Mejia. 1.30s, Cayambe. 4.20s, Quito.

Perf. 14½x13½

1959-60 Unwmk. Litho.

Coat of Arms Multicolored

C355	AP72	10c	blk & dk red ('60)	.50	.30
C356	AP72	40c	blk & yel	.50	.30
C357	AP72	1s	blk & brn ('60)	.50	.30
C358	AP72	1.30s	blk & grn ('60)	.50	.30
C359	AP72	4.20s	blk & org	.50	.30
			Nos. C355-C359 (5)	2.50	1.50

Province of Cotopaxi

40c, Pangua. 60c, Pujili. 70c, Saquisili. 1s, Salcedo. 1.30s, Latacunga.

1960 Coat of Arms Multicolored

C360	AP72	40c	blk & car	.30	.25
C361	AP72	60c	blk & bl	.30	.25
C362	AP72	70c	blk & turq	.30	.25
C363	AP72	1s	blk & red org	.30	.25
C364	AP72	1.30s	blk & org	.35	.25
			Nos. C360-C364 (5)	1.55	1.25

Flags of American Nations — AP87

1960, Feb. 23 *Perf. 13x12½*

C365	AP87	1.30s	multi	.30	.25
C366	AP87	2s	multi	.30	.25

11th Inter-American Conference, Feb. 1960.

Bridge Type of 1958.

Bridges: No. C367, Juntas. No. C368, Saracay. 2s, Railroad bridge, Ambato.

1960 Litho. *Perf. 13½*

C367	AP75	1.30s	chocolate	.30	.25

Photo. *Perf. 12½*

C368	AP75	1.30s	emerald	.30	.25
C369	AP75	2s	brown	.50	.25
			Nos. C367-C369 (3)	1.10	.75

Building of three new bridges.

Bahia-Chone Road — AP88

Pres. Camilo Ponce Enriquez AP89

Designs: 4.20s, Public Works Building, Cuenca. 5s, El Coca airport. 10s, New Harbor, Guayaquil.

1960, Aug. Litho. *Perf. 14*

C370	AP88	1.30s	blk & dl yel	.30	.25
C371	AP88	4.20s	rose car & lt grn	.45	.45
C372	AP88	5s	dk brn & yel	.65	.55
C373	AP88	10s	dk bl & bl	1.50	.55

Perf. 11x11½

C374	AP89	2s	org brn & blk	2.25	.30
			Nos. C370-C374 (5)	5.15	2.10

Nos. C370-C374 publicize the achievements of Pres. Camilo Ponce Enriquez (1956-1960).

Issued: Nos. C370-C373, 8/24; No. C374, 8/31.

Red Cross Building, Quito and Henri Dunant AP90

1960, Oct. 5 Unwmk. *Perf. 13x14*

C375	AP90	2s	rose vio & car	.60	.25

Centenary (in 1959) of Red Cross idea.

For overprint see No. C408.

El Belen Church, Quito — AP91

1961, Jan. 14 *Perf. 12½*

C376	AP91	3s	multi	.50	.25

Ecuador's participation in the 1960 Barcelona Philatelic Congress.

Map of Ecuador and Amazon River System AP92

1961, Feb. 27 Litho. *Perf. 10½*

C377	AP92	80c	salmpn, claret & grn	.35	.25
C378	AP92	1.30s	gray, slate & grn	.55	.25
C379	AP92	2s	beige, red & grn	.75	.25
			Nos. C377-C379 (3)	1.65	.75

Amazon Week, and the 132nd anniversary of the Battle of Tarqui against Peru.

Juan Montalvo, Juan Leon Mera, Juan Benigno Vela — AP93

1961, Apr. 13 Unwmk. *Perf. 13*

C380	AP93	1.30s	salmon & blk	.50	.25

Centenary of Tungurahua province.

Hugo Ortiz G. — AP94

Design: No. C382, Ortiz monument.

1961, May 25 *Perf. 14x14½*

C381	AP94	1.30s	grnsh bl, blk & yel	.35	.25
C382	AP94	1.30s	grnsh bl, pur, ol & brn	.35	.25

Lt. Hugo Ortiz G., killed in battle 8/2/41.

Condor and Airplane Stamp of 1936 AP95

1.30s, Map of South America and stamp of 1865. 2s, Bolivar monument stamp of 1930.

Perf. 10½

1961, May 25 Litho. Unwmk.

Size: 41x28mm

C383	AP95	80c	org & vio	.50	.25

Size: 41x34mm

C384	AP95	1.30s	bl, yel, ol & car	.80	.35

Size: 40½x37mm

C385	AP95	2s	car rose & blk	1.25	.35
			Nos. C383-C385 (3)	2.55	.95

Third National Philatelic Exhibition, Quito, May 25-June 3, 1961.

Arms of Los Rios and Egret — AP96

1961, May 27 *Perf. 14½x13½*

Coat of Arms Multicolored

C386	AP96	2s	bl & blk	.50	.30

Centenary (in 1960) of Los Rios province.

Gabriel Garcia Moreno — AP97

Remigio Crespo Toral — AP98

1961, Sept. 24 Unwmk. *Perf. 12*

C387	AP97	1s	bl, brn & buff	.45	.25

Centenary of the restoration of national integrity.

1961, Nov. 3 Unwmk. *Perf. 14*

C388	AP98	50c	multi	.35	.25

Centenary of the birth of Remigio Crespo Toral, poet laureate of Ecuador.

Galapagos Islands Nos. LC1-LC3 Overprinted in Black or Red (Similar to #684-686)

"ESTACION DE BIOLOGIA MARITIMA DE GALAPAGOS" and " UNESCO 1961"

1961, Oct. 31 Photo. *Perf. 12*

C389	A1	1s	dp bl	1.75	.25
a.			"de Galapagos" on top line	6.00	6.00
C390	A1	1.80s	rose vio	2.40	.40
a.			UNESCO emblem omitted	6.00	6.00
C391	A1	4.20s	blk (R)	3.50	.60
			Nos. C389-C391 (3)	7.65	1.25

Establishment of maritime biological stations on Galapagos Islands by UNESCO.

Arms of the Cantons Type of 1957

Province of Tungurahua

50c, Pillaro. 1s, Pelileo. 1.30s, Baños. 2s, Ambato.

Perf. 14½x13½

1962, Mar. 30 Litho. Unwmk.

Coats of Arms Multicolored

C392	AP72	50c	black	.25	.25
C393	AP72	1s	black	.35	.25
C394	AP72	1.30s	black	.45	.25
C395	AP72	2s	black	.75	.25
			Nos. C392-C395 (4)	1.80	1.00

Pres. Arosemena and Prince Philip, Arms of Ecuador and Great Britain and Equator Monument AP99

Perf. 14x13½

1962, Feb. 17 Wmk. 340

C396	AP99	1.30s	bl, sepia, red & yel	.30	.25
C397	AP99	2s	multi	.50	.25

Visit of Prince Philip, Duke of Edinburgh, to Ecuador, Feb. 17-20, 1962.

Mountain Farming — AP100

Perf. 12½

1963, Mar. 21 Unwmk. Litho.

C398 AP100 30c emer, yel & blk .30 .25
C399 AP100 3s dl red, grn & org .70 .25
C400 AP100 4.20s bl, blk & yel 1.10 .55
Nos. C398-C400 (3) 2.10 1.05

FAO "Freedom from Hunger" campaign. Exist imperf. Value $32.50.

Mosquito and Malaria Eradication Emblem AP101

1963, Apr. 17 Unwmk. *Perf. 12½*

C401 AP101 50c multi .25 .25
C402 AP101 80c multi .25 .25
C403 AP101 2s multi .40 .25
Nos. C401-C403 (3) .90 .75

WHO drive to eradicate malaria.

Stagecoach and Jet Plane AP102

1963, May 7 Litho.

C404 AP102 2s org & car rose .40 .30
C405 AP102 4.20s claret & ultra .70 .50

1st Intl. Postal Conference, Paris, 1863.

Type of 1957 Inscribed "Islas Galapagos," Surcharged with New Value and Overprinted "Ecuador" in Black or Red

1963, June 19 Unwmk. *Perf. 14*

C406 AP71 5s on 2s gray, dk bl & red 1.10 .80
C407 AP71 10s on 2s gray, dk bl & red (R) 2.00 1.60

The basic 2s exists without surcharge and overprint. No. C407 exists with "ECUADOR" omitted, and with both "ECUADOR" and "10 SUCRES" double.

No. C375 Overprinted: "1863-1963/Centenario/de la Fundación/ de la Cruz Roja/Internacional"

1963, June 21 Photo. *Perf. 13x14*

C408 AP90 2s rose vio & car .40 .25

Intl. Red Cross, centenary.

Type of Regular Issue, 1963

Arosemena and: 70c, Flags of Ecuador. 2s, Flags of Ecuador, Panama. 4s, Flags of Ecuador, US.

1963, July 1 Litho. *Perf. 14*

C409 A238 70c pale bl & multi .25 .25
C410 A238 2s pink & multi .50 .25
C411 A238 4s lt bl & multi 1.10 .35
Nos. C409-C411 (3) 1.85 .85

Imperfs exist. Value $15.

Portrait Type of 1958

Portrait: 2s, Dr. Mariano Cueva (1812-82).

Unwmk.

1963, July 4 Litho. *Perf. 14*

C412 AP74 2s lt grn & multi .45 .25

Social Insurance Symbol — AP103

Mother and Child — AP104

1963, July 9 Litho.

C413 AP103 10s brn, bl, gray & ocher 1.10 .90

25th anniversary of Social Insurance. Exists imperf. Value $9.

1963, July 28 *Perf. 12½*

C414 AP104 1.30s org, dk bl & blk .30 .25
C415 AP104 5s gray, red & brn .60 .60

7th Pan-American and South American Pediatrics Congresses, Quito.

Simon Bolivar Airport, Guayaquil AP105

1963, July 25 *Perf. 14*

C416 AP105 60c gray .25 .25
C417 AP105 70c dl grn .30 .25
C418 AP105 5s brn vio .50 .35
Nos. C416-C418 (3) 1.05 .85

Opening of Simon Bolivar Airport, Guayaquil, July 15, 1962. Exist imperf. Value $4.50.

Nos. 638, 640-641 Overprinted "AEREO"

1964 *Perf. 12*

Flags in National Colors

C419 A223 1.80s dl vio .60 .35
C420 A224 2s dk brn .60 .35
C421 A223 2.20s blk brn .60 .35
Nos. C419-C421 (3) 1.80 1.05

On 1.80s and 2.20s, "AEREO" is vertical, reading down.

No. 650 Overprinted in Gold: "FARO DE COLON / AEREO"

1964 Photo. *Perf. 14x13½*

C422 A229 1.80s dk bl 3.00 2.00

Nos. C352-C354 Overprinted

1964 Litho. *Perf. 13½*

C423 AP86 50c bl & multi .80 .45
C424 AP86 80c yel & multi .80 .45
C425 AP86 1.30s pale grn & multi .80 .45
Nos. C423-C425 (3) 2.40 1.35

No. C307 Overprinted: "DECLARACION / DERECHOS HUMANOS / 1964 / XV-ANIV"

Unwmk.

1964, Sept. 29 Engr. *Perf. 14*

C426 AP69 1.70s red org .40 .25

15th anniversary (in 1963) of the Universal Declaration of Human Rights.

Banana Type

1964, Oct. 26 Litho. *Perf. 12½x12*

C427 A241 4.20s blk, bis & gray ol .40 .30
C428 A241 10s blk, scar & gray ol .70 .50
a. Souv. sheet of 4 3.25 3.00

No. C428a contains imperf. stamps similar to Nos. 720-721 and C427-C428.

John F. Kennedy, Flag-draped Coffin and John Jr. — AP106

1964, Nov. 22 Litho. *Perf. 14*

C429 AP106 4.20s multi 1.25 .95
C430 AP106 5s multi 1.60 1.25
C431 AP106 10s multi 3.00 1.60
a. Souv. sheet of 3 10.00 10.00
Nos. C429-C431 (3) 5.85 3.80

President John F. Kennedy (1917-63).
No. C431a contains stamps similar to Nos. C429-C431, imperf.

Olympic Type

1.30s, Gymnast, vert. 1.80s, Hurdler. 2s, Basketball.

Perf. 13½x14, 14x13½

1964, Dec. 16 Unwmk.

C432 A243 1.30s vio bl, ver & brn .45 .25
C433 A243 1.80s vio bl & multi .45 .25
C434 A243 2s red & multi .45 .25
a. Souv. sheet of 4 3.25 3.25
Nos. C432-C434 (3) 1.35 .75

No. C434a contains stamps similar to Nos. 725 and C432-C434, imperf.

Sports Type

Torch and Athletes: 2s, 3s, Diver, gymnast, wrestlers and weight lifter. 2.50s, 4s, Bicyclists. 3.50s, 5s, Jumpers.

1965, Nov. 20 Litho. *Perf. 12x12½*

C435 A247 2s bl, gold & blk .60 .25
C436 A247 2.50s org, gold & blk .60 .25
C437 A247 3s brt pink, gold & blk .60 .25
C438 A247 3.50s lt vio, gold & bl .65 .65
C439 A247 4s brt yel grn, gold & blk .65 .25
C440 A247 5s red org, gold & blk .75 .35
a. Souv. sheet of 12 12.00 12.00
Nos. C435-C440 (6) 3.85 2.00

No. C440a contains 12 imperf. stamps similar to Nos. 738-743 and C435-C440.
For surcharges see Nos. 766B, C449.

Bird Type

Birds: 1s, Yellow grosbeak. 1.30s, Black-headed parrot. 1.50s, Scarlet tanager. 2s, Sapphire quail-dove. 2.50s, Violet-tailed sylph. 3s, Lemon-throated barbet. 4s, Yellow-tailed oriole. 10s, Collared puffbird.

1966, June 17 Litho. *Perf. 13½*

Birds in Natural Colors

C441 A249 1s lt red brn & blk 1.10 .25
C442 A249 1.30s pink & blk 1.10 .25
C443 A249 1.50s pale grn & blk 1.10 .25
C444 A249 2s sal & blk 2.75 .45
C445 A249 2.50s lt yel grn & blk 2.75 .45
C446 A249 3s sal & blk 3.75 .65
C447 A249 4s gray & blk 5.00 .85
C448 A249 10s beige & blk 7.75 2.10
Nos. C441-C448 (8) 25.30 5.25

For surcharges see Nos. 766E-766F, C450, C455-C457.

Nos. C436 and C443 Surcharged

1967

C449 A247 80c on 2.50s multi .40 .35
C450 A249 80c on 1.50s multi .40 .25

Old denomination on No. C449 is obliterated with heavy bar; the surcharge on No. C450 includes "Resello" and an ornament over old denomination.

Peñaherrera Monument, Quito — AP107

Design: 2s, Peñaherrera statue.

1967, Dec. 29 Litho. *Perf. 12x12½*

C451 AP107 1.30s blk & org .30 .25
C452 AP107 2s blk & lt ultra .30 .25

See note after No. 767B.

Arosemena Type

1.30s, Inauguration. 2s, Pres. Arosemena speaking in Punta del Este.

1968, May 9 Litho. *Perf. 13½x14*

C453 A251 1.30s multi .25 .25
C454 A251 2s multi .30 .25

No. C448 Srchd. in Plum, Dark Blue or Green

1969, Jan. 9 Litho. *Perf. 13½*

Bird in Natural Colors

C455 A249 80c on 10s beige (P) .50 .25
C456 A249 1s on 10s beige (DBl) .50 .25
C457 A249 2s on 10s beige (G) .50 .25
Nos. C455-C457 (3) 1.50 .75

"Operation Friendship" AP108

1969-70 Typo. *Perf. 13½*

C458 AP108 2s yel, blk, red & lt bl .30 .25
a. Perf. 12½ .30 .25
C459 AP108 2s bl, blk, car & yel ('70) .30 .25

Friendship campaign. Medallion background on Nos. C458 and C458a is blue; on No. C459, yellow.
No. C459 exists imperf. Value $5.

No. 639 Surcharged in Gold "S/. 5 AEREO" and Bar

1969, Nov. 25 Litho. *Perf. 12*

C460 A224 5s on 2s multi 2.00 .75

Butterfly Type

Butterflies: 1.30s, Morpho peleides. 1.50s, Anartia amathea.

1970 Litho. *Perf. 12½*

C461 A255 1.30s multi 3.50 .25
C462 A255 1.50s pink & multi 3.50 .25

Same, White Background

1970 *Perf. 13½*

C463 A255 1.30s multi 3.50 .25
C464 A255 1.50s multi 3.50 .25

Arms Type

Provincial Arms and Flags: 1.30s, El Oro. 2s, Loja. 3s, Manabi. 5s, Pichincha. 10s, Guayas.

1971 Litho. *Perf. 10½*

C465 A258 1.30s pink & multi .25 .25
C466 A258 2s multi .35 .25
C467 A258 3s multi .50 .30
C468 A258 5s multi .65 .30
C469 A258 10s multi 1.25 .40
Nos. C465-C469 (5) 3.00 1.50

Presentation of the Virgin — AP109

Art of Quito: 1.50s, Blessed Anne at Prayer. 2s, St. Theresa de Jesus. 2.50s, Altar of Carmen, horiz. 3s, Descent from the Cross. 4s, Christ of St. Mariana de Jesus. 5s, Shrine of St. Anthony. 10s, Cross of San Diego.

1971 *Perf. 11½*

Inscriptions in Black

C473	AP109	1.30s multi		.25	.25
C474	AP109	1.50s multi		.25	.25
C475	AP109	2s multi		.25	.25
C476	AP109	2.50s multi		.40	.25
C477	AP109	3s multi		.50	.25
C478	AP109	4s multi		.65	.25
C479	AP109	5s multi		.65	.35
C480	AP109	10s multi		1.25	.65
	Nos. C473-C480 (8)			4.20	2.50

Pres. Allende and Chilean Flag AP110

2.10s, Pres. José M. Velasco Ibarra of Ecuador, Pres. Salvador Allende of Chile, national flags.

1971, Aug. 24 *Perf. 12½*

C481	AP110	2s multi	.25	.25
C482	AP110	2.10s multi	.25	.25

Visit of Pres. Salvador Allende of Chile, Aug. 24.

Globe and Emblem AP111

1971

C483	AP111	5s black	1.10	.45
C484	AP111	5.50s dl pur & blk	1.10	.45

Opening of Postal Museum, Aug. 24, 1971. Exist imperf. Value $7.50.

Pazmiño Type

1971, Sept. 16 *Perf. 12x11½*

C485	A260	1.50s grn & multi	.25	.25
C486	A260	2.50s grn & multi	.35	.25

AP112

Designs: 5s, Map of Americas. 10s, Converging roads and map. 20s, Map of Americas and Equator. 50s, Mountain road and monument on Equator.

1971 *Perf. 11½*

C487	AP112	5s org & multi	.80	.30
C488	AP112	10s org & blk	1.25	.55
C489	AP112	20s blk, bl & brt rose	2.00	1.00
C490	AP112	50s bl, blk & gray	3.25	1.50
	Nos. C487-C490 (4)		7.30	3.35

11th Pan-American Road Congress.
Issued: 5s, 10s, 50s, 11/15; 20s, 11/22.
No. C488 exists imperf. Value $8.

AP113

Design: 3s, Arms of Ecuador and Argentina. 5s, Presidents José M. Velasco Ibarra and Alejandro Agustin Lanusse.

1972

C491	AP113	3s blk & multi	.25	.25
C492	AP113	5s blk & multi	.50	.30

Visit of Lt. Gen. Alejandro Agustin Lanusse, president of Argentina, Jan. 25.

Flame, Scales, Map of Americas AP114

1972, Apr. 24 **Litho.** *Perf. 12½*

C493	AP114	1.30s bl & red	.50	.25

17th Conference of the Interamerican Federation of Lawyers, Quito, Apr. 24.

Religious Paintings Type of Regular Issue

Ecuadorian Paintings: 3s, Virgin of the Flowers, by Miguel de Santiago. 10s, Virgin of the Rosary, by Quito School.

1972, Apr. 24 *Perf. 14x13½*

C494	A263	3s blk & multi	.35	.35
C495	A263	10s blk & multi	1.10	.55
a.		Souv. sheet of 2, #C494-C495	1.90	1.90

1972, May 4

Ecuadorian Statues: 3s, St. Dominic, Quito School. 10s, St. Rosa of Lima, by Bernardo de Legarda.

C496	A263	3s blk & multi	.35	.35
C497	A263	10s blk & multi	1.00	.55
a.		Souv. sheet of 2, #C496-C497	2.50	2.10

Letters of "Ecuador" 3mm high on Nos. C496-C497, 7mm high on Nos. C494-C495.

Portrait Type

Designs (Generals, from Paintings): 1.30s, José Maria Saenz. 3s, Tomás Wright. 4s, Antonio Farfan. 5s, Antonio José de Sucre. 10s, Simon Bolivar. 20s, Arms of Ecuador.

1972, May 24

C498	A264	1.30s bl & multi	.25	.25
C499	A264	3s bl & multi	.25	.25
C500	A264	4s bl & multi	.35	.25
C501	A264	5s bl & multi	.55	.30
C502	A264	10s bl & multi	1.00	.55
C503	A264	20s bl & multi	2.00	1.00
	Nos. C498-C503 (6)		4.40	2.60

Artisan Type

Handicraft of Ecuador: 2s, Woman wearing flowered poncho. 3s, Striped poncho. 5s, Poncho with roses. 10s, Gold sunburst sculpture.

1972, July **Photo.** *Perf. 13*

C504	A265	2s multi	.25	.25
C505	A265	3s multi	.50	.25
C506	A265	5s multi	.80	.40
C507	A265	10s org red & multi	1.40	.90
a.		Souv. sheet of 4, #C504-C507	4.00	4.00
	Nos. C504-C507 (4)		2.95	1.80

Epidendrum Orchid — AP115

1972 **Photo.** *Perf. 12½*

C508	AP115	4s shown	.90	.90
C509	AP115	6s Canna	1.40	1.40
C510	AP115	10s Jimson weed	2.00	2.00
a.		Souv. sheet of 3, #C508-C510	6.00	6.00
	Nos. C508-C510 (3)		4.30	4.30

Exists imperf.

Oil Drilling Towers — AP116

1972, Oct. 17 **Litho.** *Perf. 11½*

C511	AP116	1.30s bl & multi	.50	.25

Ecuadorian oil industry.

Coat of Arms — AP117

Arms Multicolored

1972, Nov. 18 **Litho.** *Perf. 11½*

C512	AP117	2s black	.25	.25
C513	AP117	3s black	.25	.25
C514	AP117	4s black	.30	.25
C515	AP117	4.50s black	.30	.25
C516	AP117	6.30s black	.75	.30
C517	AP117	6.90s black	.75	.30
	Nos. C512-C517 (6)		2.60	1.60

Pichincha Type

Designs: 2.40s, Corridor, San Agustin. 4.50s, La Merced Convent. 5.50s, Column base. 6.30s, Chapter Hall, San Agustin. 6.90s, Interior, San Agustin. 7.40s, Crucifixion, Cantuña Chapel. 7.90s, Decorated ceiling, San Agustin.

1972, Dec. 6 **Wmk. 367**

C518	A266	2.40s yel & multi	.25	.25
C519	A266	4.50s yel & multi	.45	.30
C520	A266	5.50s yel & multi	.45	.30
C521	A266	6.30s yel & multi	.60	.35
C522	A266	6.90s yel & multi	.60	.35
C523	A266	7.40s yel & multi	.90	.55
C524	A266	7.90s yel & multi	.90	.55
	Nos. C518-C524 (7)		4.15	2.65

UN Emblem — AP118

OAS Emblem — AP119

1973, Mar. 23 **Unwmk.**

C525	AP118	1.30s lt bl & blk	.30	.25

25th anniversary of the Economic Committee for Latin America (CEPAL).

1973, Apr. 14 **Wmk. 367**

C526	AP119	1.50s multi	.30	.25
a.		Unwatermarked	.30	.25

Day of the Americas and "Philately for Peace."

Bird Type

1973 **Unwmk.** *Perf. 11½x11*

C527	A268	1.30s Blue-footed booby	2.10	.25
C528	A268	3s Brown pelican	2.10	.25

Presidents Lara and Caldera AP120

1973, June 15 **Wmk. 367**

C529	AP120	3s multi	.45	.30

Visit of Venezuela Pres. Rafael Caldera, Feb. 5-7.

Silver Coin, 1934 — AP121

Globe, OPEC Emblem, Oil Derrick — AP122

Ecuadorian Coins: 10s, Silver coin, obverse. 50s, Gold coin, 1928.

Unwmk.

1973, Dec. 14 **Photo.** *Perf. 14*

C530	AP121	5s multi	.60	.40
C531	AP121	10s multi	1.00	.60
C532	AP121	50s multi	4.50	2.50
a.		Souvenir sheet of 3	7.25	7.25
	Nos. C530-C532 (3)		6.10	3.50

No. C532a contains one each of Nos. C530-C532; Dated "1972." Exists imperf. Value, same.

A gold marginal overprint was applied in 1974 to No. C532a (perf. and imperf.): "X Campeonato Mundial de Football / Munich - 1974." Value, each $75.

A carmine overprint was applied in 1974 to No. C532a (perf. and imperf.): "Seminario de Telecommunicaciones Rurales, / Septiembre-1974 / Quito-Ecuador" and ITU emblem. Value, each $10.

1974, June 15 **Litho.** *Perf. 11½*

C533	AP122	2s multi	.45	.30

Meeting of Organization of Oil Exporting Countries, Quito, June 15-24.

Ecuadorian Flag, UPU Emblem — AP123

1974, July 15 **Litho.** *Perf. 11½*

C534	AP123	1.30s multi	.30	.25

Centenary of Universal Postal Union.

Two 25s souvenir sheets exist. These were sold on a restricted basis. Value, each $75.

Teodoro Wolf AP124

Capt. Edmundo Chiriboga AP125

1974 **Litho.** *Perf. 12x11½*

C535	AP124	1.30s blk & ultra	.25	.25
C536	AP125	1.50s gray	.30	.25

Teodoro Wolf, geographer; Edmundo Chiriboga, national hero.

Issued: No. C535, 11/29; No. C536, 12/4.

Congress Emblem AP126

1974, Dec. 8 **Litho.** *Perf. 11½x12*

C537	AP126	5s bl & multi	.45	.30

8th Inter-American Postmasters' Cong., Quito.

Map of Americas and Coat of Arms AP127

Prominent Ecuadorians AP128

1975, Feb. 1 *Perf. 12x11½*

C538 AP127 3s bl & multi .45 .30

EXFIGUA Stamp Exhibition and 5th General Assembly of Federation Inter-Americana de Filatelia, Guayaquil, Nov. 1973.

1975 *Perf. 12x11½*

No. C539, Manuel J. Calle, Journalist. No. C540, Leopoldo Benites V., president of UN General Assembly, 1973-74; No. C541, Adolfo H. Simmonds G. (1892-1969), journalist; No. C542, Juan de Dios Martinez Mera, President of Ecuador, birth centenary.

C539 AP128 5s lilac rose .60 .30
C540 AP128 5s gray .60 .30
C541 AP128 5s violet .60 .30
C542 AP128 5s blk & rose red .60 .30
Nos. C539-C542 (4) 2.40 1.20

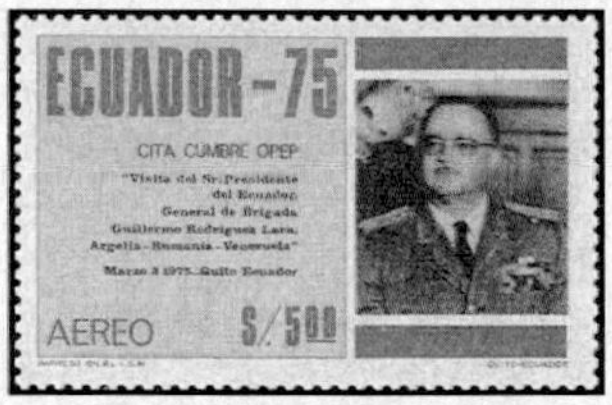

Pres. Guillermo Rodriguez Lara — AP129

1975 **Unwmk.** *Perf. 12*

C546 AP129 5s vermilion & blk .60 .30

State visit of Pres. Guillermo Rodriguez Lara to Algeria, Romania and Venezuela.

Meeting Type of 1975

1.50s, Rafael Rodriguez Palacios & Argelino Duran Quintero meeting at border in Rumichaca. 2s, Signing border agreement.

1975, Apr. 1 **Litho.** *Perf. 12x11½*

C547 A273 1.50s multi .30 .25
C548 A273 2s multi .30 .25

Sacred Heart (Painting) AP130

Quito Cathedral AP131

Design: 2s, Monstrance.

1975, Apr. 28 **Litho.** *Perf. 12x11½*

C549 AP130 1.30s yel & multi .25 .25
C550 AP130 2s bl & multi .30 .25
C551 AP131 3s multi .40 .25
Nos. C549-C551 (3) .95 .75

3rd Bolivarian Eucharistic Congress, Quito, June 9-16, 1974.

J. Delgado Panchana with Trophy — AP132

J. Delgado Panchana Swimming AP133

Perf. 12x11½, 11½x12

1975, June 12 **Unwmk.**

C552 AP132 1.30s bl & multi .25 .25
C553 AP133 3s blk & multi .30 .25

Jorge Delgado Panchana, South American swimming champion, 1971 and 1974.

Sports Type of 1975

1975, Sept. 11 **Litho.** *Perf. 11½*

C554 A276 1.30s Tennis .40 .25
C555 A276 2s Target shooting .55 .25
C556 A276 2.80s Volleyball .65 .25
C557 A276 3s Raft with sails .65 .25
C558 A276 5s Mask 1.10 .25
Nos. C554-C558 (5) 3.35 1.25

Flower Type of 1975

1975, Nov. 18 **Litho.** *Perf. 11½x12*

C559 A277 1.30s Pitcairnia pungens .35 .25
C560 A277 2s Scarlet sage .55 .25
C561 A277 3s Amaryllis .75 .40
C562 A277 4s Opuntia quitense 1.10 .55
C563 A277 5s Amaryllis 1.60 .75
Nos. C559-C563 (5) 4.35 2.20

Tail Assemblies and Emblem — AP134

Planes over Map of Ecuador — AP135

1975, Dec. 17 **Litho.** *Perf. 11½*

C564 AP134 1.30s bl & multi .45 .30
C565 AP135 3s multi .55 .30

TAME, Military Transport Airline, 13th anniv.

Benalcázar Statue — AP136

1976, Feb. 6 **Litho.** *Perf. 11½*

C566 AP136 2s multi .35 .25
C567 AP136 3s multi .35 .25

Sebastián de Benalcázar (1495-1550), Spanish conquistador, founder of Quito.

Archaeology Type of 1975

1.30s, Seated man, Carchi Culture. 2s, Funerary urn, Tuncahuan Culture. 3s, Priest, Bahia de Caraquez Culture. 4s, Snail's shell, Cuasmal Culture. 5s, Bowl supported by figurines, Guangala Culture.

1976, Feb. 12 **Litho.** *Perf. 11½*

C568 A278 1.30s multi .35 .25
C569 A278 2s multi .45 .25
C570 A278 3s multi .65 .45
C571 A278 4s multi .95 .45
C572 A278 5s multi 1.25 .45
Nos. C568-C572 (5) 3.65 1.85

Fruit Type of 1976

1976, Mar. 30

C573 A280 2s Apples .40 .25
C574 A280 5s Rose .80 .40

Lufthansa Jet — AP137

1976, June 25 **Litho.** *Perf. 12*

C575 AP137 10s bl & multi 1.50 .50

Lufthansa, 50th anniversary.

An imperf. 20s miniature sheet exists, similar to No. C575 enlarged, with overprinted black bar covering line below "Lufthansa." Size: 90x115mm.

Projected PO, Quito — AP138

Fruit Peddler — AP139

1976, Aug. 10 **Litho.** *Perf. 12*

C576 AP138 5s blk & multi .40 .25

Design for new General Post Office, Quito.

1976, July 25

No. C578, Longshoreman. No. C579, Cerros del Carmen & Santa Ana, hills of Guayaquil, horiz. No. C580, Sebastián de Belalcázar. No. C581, Francisco de Orellana. No. C582, Chief Guayas & his wife Quila.

C577 AP139 1.30s red & multi .25 .25
C578 AP139 1.30s red & multi .25 .25
C579 AP139 1.30s red & multi .25 .25
C580 AP139 2s red & multi .25 .25
C581 AP139 2s red & multi .25 .25
C582 AP139 2s red & multi .25 .25
Nos. C577-C582 (6) 1.50 1.50

Founding of Guayaquil, 441st anniversary.

Emblem and Laurel AP140

1976, Aug. 9

C583 AP140 1.30s yel & multi .35 .25

Bolivarian Soc. of Ecuador, 50th anniv.

Western Hemisphere and Equator Monument AP141

Congress Emblem AP142

1976, Sept. 6

C584 AP141 2s multi .35 .25

Souvenir Sheet

Imperf

C585 AP141 5s multi 4.00 4.00

3rd Conf. of Pan-American Transport Ministers, Quito, Sept. 6-11. No. C585 contains design similar to No. C584 with black denomination and red control number in margin.

1976, Sept. 27 **Litho.** *Perf. 11½*

C586 AP142 1.30s bl & multi .40 .25
C587 AP142 3s bl & multi .50 .30

Souvenir Sheet

Imperf

C588 AP142 10s bl & multi 1.75 1.00

10th Inter-American Congress of the Construction Industry, Quito, Sept. 27-30.

George Washington AP143

American Bicentennial: 5s, Naval battle, Sept. 23, 1779, in which the Bonhomme Richard, commanded by John Paul Jones, defeated and captured the Serapis, British man-of-war, off Yorkshire coast, horiz.

1976, Oct. 18 **Litho.** *Perf. 12*

C589 AP143 3s blk & multi .65 .30
C590 AP143 5s red brn & yel 1.25 .60

Dr. Hideyo Noguchi — AP144

Luis Cordero — AP145

1976 **Litho.** *Perf. 11½*

C591 AP144 3s yel & multi .40 .25

Dr. Hideyo Noguchi (1876-1928), bacteriologist (at Rockefeller Institute). A 10s imperf. miniature sheet in same design exists without "Aereo." Size: 95x114mm. Value $6.

1976, Dec. **Litho.** *Perf. 11½*

C592 AP145 2s multi .35 .25

Luis Cordero (1833-1912), president of Ecuador.

Mariuxi Febres Cordero — AP146

1976, Dec. *Perf. 11½*

C593 AP146 3s multi .35 .25

Mariuxi Febres Cordero, South American swimming champion.

Flags and Monument AP147

1976, Nov. 9 *Perf. 12*

C594 AP147 3s multi .35 .25

Miniature Sheet

Imperf

C595 AP147 5s multi 2.50 1.50

2nd Meeting of the Agriculture Ministers of the Andean Countries, Quito, Nov. 8-10.

Sister Catalina — AP148

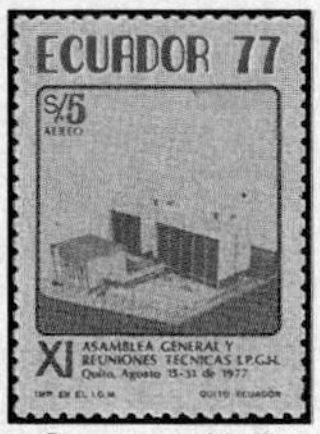

Congress Hall, Quito — AP149

1977, June 17 Litho. ***Perf. 12x11½***

C596 AP148 1.30s blk & pale salmon .45 .30

Sister Catalina de Jesus Herrera (1717-1795), writer.

1977, Aug. 15 Litho. ***Perf. 12x11½***

C597 AP149 5s multi .60 .30
a. 10s souvenir sheet 2.00 2.00

11th General Assembly of Pan-American Institute of Geography and History, Quito, Aug. 15-30. No. C597a contains the designs of types A282 and AP149 without denominations and with simulated perforations.

Pres. Alfonso López Michelsen, Flag of Colombia — AP150

Designs: 5s, Pres. López Michelsen of Colombia, Pres. Alfredo Poveda Burbano of Ecuador and aide. 7s, as 5s, vert. 9s, 10s, Presidents with aides.

1977, Sept. 13 ***Perf. 12***

C598 AP150 2.60s multi .50 .25
C599 AP150 5s multi .75 .30
C600 AP150 7s multi .90 .40
C601 AP150 9s multi 1.25 .60

Imperf

C602 AP150 10s multi 1.25 1.00
Nos. C598-C602 (5) 4.65 2.55

Meeting of the Presidents of Ecuador and Colombia and Declaration of Putumayo, Feb. 25, 1977. Nos. C598-C602 are overprinted in multiple fluorescent, colorless rows: INSTITUTO GEOGRAFICO MILITAR GOBIERNO DEL ECUADOR.

Ceramic Figure, Tolita Culture AP151

9s, Divine Shepherdess, sculpture by Bernardo de Legarda. 11s, The Fruit Seller, sculpture by Legarda. 20s, Sun God, pre-Columbian gold mask.

1977, Aug. 24 ***Perf. 12***

C603 AP151 7s gold & multi 1.20 .30
C604 AP151 9s gold & multi 1.50 .35
C605 AP151 11s gold & multi 2.00 .70
Nos. C603-C605 (3) 4.70 1.35

Souvenir Sheet
Gold Embossed

Imperf

C606 AP151 20s vio, bl, blk & gold 8.50 3.50

Central Bank of Ecuador, 50th anniversary. Nos. C603-C605 overprinted like Nos. C598-C602.

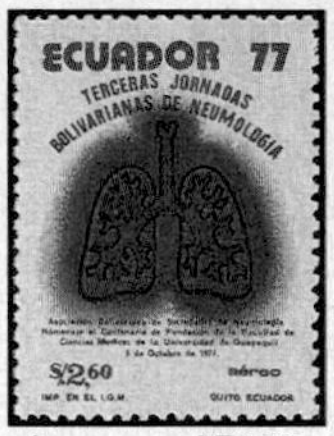

Lungs — AP152

Brother Miguel, St. Peter's, Rome — AP153

1977, Oct. 5 Litho. ***Perf. 12x11½***

C607 AP152 2.60s multi .35 .25

3rd Cong. of the Bolivarian Pneumonic Soc. and cent. of the founding of the medical faculty of the University of Guayaquil.

1977

C608 AP153 2.60s multi .35 .25

Beatification of Brother Miguel.

Peralta Type

2.60s, Titles of works by Peralta & his bookmark.

1977 ***Perf. 11½***

C609 A284 2.60s multi .40 .25

Broadcast Tower — AP154

Remigio Romero y Cordero — AP155

1977, Dec. 2 Litho. ***Perf. 12x11½***

C610 AP154 5s multi .45 .45

9th World Telecommunications Day.

1978, Mar. 2 Litho. ***Perf. 12½x11½***

C611 AP155 3s multi .40 .25
C612 AP155 10.60s multi .55 .30

Imperf

C612A AP155 10s multi 1.40 1.40
Nos. C611-C612A (3) 2.35 1.95

Remigio Romero y Cordero (1895-1967), poet.

No. C612A contains a vignette similar to Nos. C611-C612.

Dr. Vicente Corral Moscoso AP156

Faces AP157

5s, Hospital emblem with Caduceus.

1978, Apr. 12 Litho. ***Imperf.***

C613 AP156 5s multi .55 .25

Perf. 12x11½

C614 AP156 7.60s multi 1.10 .50

Inauguration (in 1977) of Dr. Vicente Corral Moscoso Regional Hospital, Cuenca.

1978, Mar. 17

Designs: 9s, Emblems and flags of Ecuador. 10s, 11s, Hands reaching for light.

C615 AP157 7s multicolored .70 .25
C616 AP157 9s multicolored 1.00 .25
C617 AP157 11s multicolored 1.25 .25

Imperf

C618 AP157 10s multicolored 1.25 1.25
Nos. C615-C618 (4) 4.20 2.00

Ecuadorian Social Security Institute, 50th anniv.

Geographical Institute Type

7.60s, Plane over map of Ecuador with mountains.

1978, Apr. 12 Litho. ***Perf. 11½***

C619 A287 7.60s multi 1.10 .55

Imperf

C620 A287 10s multi 1.75 1.75

No. C620 contains 2 vignettes with simulated perforations in designs of Nos. 967 and C619.

Lions Type

1978 ***Perf. 11½***

C621 A288 5s multi .75 .25
C622 A288 6.20s multi .90 .40

Imperf

C623 A288 10s multi 2.50 1.25
Nos. C621-C623 (3) 4.15 1.90

No. C623 contains a vignette similar to Nos. C621-C622.

San Martin — AP158

1978, Apr. 13 Litho. ***Perf. 12***

C624 AP158 10.60s multi 1.60 .50

Imperf

C625 AP158 10s multi 1.75 1.75

Gen. José de San Martin (1778-1850), soldier and statesman. No. C625 contains a vignette similar to No. C624.

Bank Type

Design: 5s, Bank emblem.

1978, Sept. Litho. ***Perf. 11½***

C626 A289 5s gray & multi .45 .30

Soccer Type

Designs: 2.60s, "Gauchito" and Games' emblem. 5s, "Gauchito." 7s, Soccer ball. 9s, Games' emblem, vert. 10s, Games' emblem.

1978, Nov. 1 ***Perf. 12***

C627 A290 2.60s multi .30 .25
C628 A290 7s multi .80 .40
C629 A290 9s multi 1.10 .65

Imperf

C630 A290 5s blk & bl 6.00 6.00
C631 A290 10s blk & bl 6.00 6.00
Nos. C627-C631 (5) 14.20 13.30

Bernardo O'Higgins AP159

Old Men of Vilcabamba AP160

1978, Nov. 11 Litho. ***Perf. 12x11½***

C632 AP159 10.60s multi .80 .30

Imperf

C633 AP159 10s multi 1.50 .90

Gen. Bernardo O'Higgins (1778-1842), Chilean soldier and statesman. No. C633 contains a vignette similar to No. C632.

1978, Nov. 11 ***Perf. 12x11½***

C634 AP160 5s multi .50 .30

Vilcabamba, valley of longevity.

Humphrey AP161

Virgin and Child AP162

1978, Nov. 27 Litho. ***Perf. 12x11½***

C635 AP1615s multi .50 .30

Hubert H. Humphrey (1911-1978), Vice President of the US.

1978

Children's Drawings: 4.60s, Holy Family. 6.20s, Candle and children.

C636 AP162 2.20s multi .30 .25
C637 AP162 4.60s multi .50 .25
C638 AP162 6.20s multi .85 .40
Nos. C636-C638 (3) 1.65 .90

Christmas 1978.

Village, by Anibal Villacis AP163

Ecuadorian Painters: No. C640, Mountain Village, by Gilberto Almeida. No. C641, Bay, by Roura Oxandaberro. No. C642, Abstract, by Luis Molinari. No. C643, Statue, by Oswaldo Viteri. No. C644, Tools, by Enrique Tabara.

1978, Dec. 9 ***Perf. 12***

C639 AP163 5s multi .60 .25
C640 AP163 5s multi .60 .25
C641 AP163 5s multi .60 .25
C642 AP163 5s multi .60 .25
C643 AP163 5s multi .60 .25
C644 AP163 5s multi .60 .25
Nos. C639-C644 (6) 3.60 1.50

House and Monument AP164

Design: 3.40s, Monument, vert.

1979, Feb. 27 Litho. ***Perf. 12***

C645 AP164 2.40s multi .30 .25
C646 AP164 3.40s multi .30 .25

Imperf

C647 AP164 10s multi .90 .90
Nos. C645-C647 (3) 1.50 1.40

Sesquicentennial of Battle of Portete and Tarqui. No. C647 contains vignettes similar to #C645-C646.

Fish and Ship — AP165

7s, Map of Ecuador & Galapagos showing territorial waters. 9s, Map of South America with west-coast territorial waters.

Perf. 12x11½, 11½x12

1979, July 23 Litho. Wmk. 367

C648 AP165 5s multi .75 .25
C649 AP165 7s multi, horiz. 1.00 .35
C650 AP165 9s multi 1.40 .50
Nos. C648-C650 (3) 3.15 1.10

Declaration of 200-mile territorial limit, 25th anniversary.

National Heritage Type

Designs: 10.60s, Bells in Quito clock tower, horiz. 13.60s, Aerial view of Galapagos coast.

1979, Aug. 3 ***Perf. 12x11½***

C651 A293 10.60s multi 1.25 .60
C652 A293 13.60s multi 1.40 .75

Size: 115x91mm

Imperf

Unwmk.

C653 A293 10s multi 5.00 2.10
Nos. C651-C653 (3) 7.65 3.45

National heritage: Quito and Galapagos Islands. No. C653 contains vignettes similar to Nos. 977, C651-C652.

Flags of Ecuador and U.S. — AP166

1979, Aug. Wmk. 367 ***Perf. 11½x12***

C654 AP166 7.60s multi .50 .50
C655 AP166 10.60s multi .75 .75

Size: 115x91mm

Imperf

Unwmk.

C656 AP166 10s multi .90 .75
Nos. C654-C656 (3) 2.15 2.00

5th anniv. of Ecuador-US Chamber of Commerce. No. C656 contains vignettes similar to Nos. C654-C655.

Smiling Girl, IYC Emblem — AP167

Perf. 12x11½

1979, Sept. 7 Litho. Wmk. 367

C657 AP167 10s multi .85 .40

International Year of the Child.

Citizens and Flag of Ecuador AP168

Design: 10.60s, Pres. Jaime Roldos Aguilera, flag of Ecuador, vert.

Perf. 11½

1979, Sept. 27 Litho. Unwmk.

C658 AP168 7.60s multi 1.00 .45

Wmk. 367

C659 AP168 10.60s multi 1.25 .40

Restoration of democracy to Ecuador.

Ecuador Coat of Arms, Olympic Rings and Eagle — AP169

Perf. 12x11½

1979, Nov. 23 Unwmk.

C660 AP169 28s multi 2.00 1.25

5th National Games, Cuenca.

CIESPAL Building, Quito AP170

Perf. 11½x12½

1979, Dec. 26 Wmk. 367

C661 AP170 10.60s multi .80 .40

Opening of Ecuadorian Institute of Engineers building.

Olmedo Type

Perf. 12x11½

1980, Apr. 29 Litho. Unwmk.

C662 A294 10s multi 1.25 .65

Tribal Chief Type

Indo-American Tribal Chiefs: No. C663, Cuauhtemoc, Mexico. No. C664, Lempira, Honduras. No. C665, Nicaragua. No. C666, Lambaré, Paraguay. No. C667, Urraca, Panama. No. C668, Anacaona, Haiti. #C669, Caupolican, Chile. No. C670, Tacun-Uman, Guatemala. No. C671, Calarca, Colombia. No. C672, Garabito, Costa Rica. No. C673, Hatuey, Cuba. No. C674, Cmarao, Brazil. No. C675, Tehuelche, Argentina. No. C676, Tupaj Katri, Bolivia. 17.80s, Sequoyah, US. 22.80s, Ruminahui, Ecuador.

Wmk. 367 (#C663, C667), Unwmkd.

1980, May 12

C663 A295 7.60s multi 1.50 .35
C664 A295 7.60s multi 1.50 .35
C665 A295 7.60s multi 1.50 .35
C666 A295 10s multi 1.90 .40
C667 A295 10s multi 1.90 .40
C668 A295 10.60s multi 1.90 .40
C669 A295 10.60s multi 1.90 .40
C670 A295 10.60s multi 1.90 .40
C671 A295 12.80s multi 2.50 .55
C672 A295 12.80s multi 2.50 .55
C673 A295 12.80s multi 2.50 .55
C674 A295 13.60s multi 2.50 .55
C675 A295 13.60s multi 2.50 .55
C676 A295 13.60s multi 2.50 .55
C677 A295 17.80s multi 3.00 .65
C678 A295 22.80s multi 3.50 1.25
Nos. C663-C678 (16) 35.50 8.25

Royal Visit Type

Perf. 11½x12

1980, May 18 Unwmk.

C679 A296 10.60s multi .75 .40

Pichincha Provincial Development Council Building — AP171

1980, June 1 ***Perf. 12x11½***

C680 AP171 10.60s multi 1.25 .60

Progress in Pichincha Province.

Indian Type

1980, June 10 Litho. ***Perf. 12x11½***

C681 A297 7.60s Salasaca boy, Tungurahua 1.00 .75
C682 A297 10s Amula woman, Chimborazo 1.25 .85
C683 A297 10.60s Canar woman, Canar 1.50 .90
C684 A297 13.60s Colorado Indian, Pichincha 1.75 1.25
Nos. C681-C684 (4) 5.50 3.75

Virgin of Mercy Type

1980, July 7 Litho. ***Perf. 11½***

C685 A298 7.60s Cupola, cloisters 1.00 .50
C686 A298 7.60s Gold screen 1.00 .50
C687 A298 7.60s Quito from basilica tower 1.00 .50
C688 A298 10.60s Retable 1.25 .60
C689 A298 10.60s Pulpit 1.25 .60
C690 A298 13.60s Cupola 1.75 .90
C691 A298 13.60s Statue of Virgin 1.75 .90
Nos. C685-C691 (7) 9.00 4.50

Nos. C685-C691 are vert.

UPU Monument AP172

Design: 17.80s, Mail box, 1880.

1980, July 7 ***Perf. 12***

C692 AP172 10.60s multi 1.50 .75
C693 AP172 17.80s multi 2.50 1.25

Souvenir Sheet

C694 AP172 25s multi 3.50 3.00

UPU membership cent. No. C694 contains designs of C692 and C693, horiz., perf. 11½.

Olympic Type.

Design: 10.60s, 13.60s, Moscow '80 emblem, Olympic rings.

Perf. 12x11½

1980, July 19 Wmk. 395

C695 A299 10.60s multi .90 .65
C696 A299 13.60s multi 1.25 .85

Souvenir Sheet

C697 A299 30s multi 7.00 7.00

No. C697 contains vignettes in designs of Nos. 991 and C695.

Marshal Sucre, by Marco Sales — AP173

1980

C698 AP173 10.60s multi .90 .60

Marshal Antonio Jose de Sucre, death sesquicentennial.

Rotary International, 75th Anniversary AP174

1980, Aug. 4 ***Perf. 11½***

C699 AP174 10s multi 1.40 .50

Riobamba Type

Design: 7.60s, 10.60s, Monstrance, Riobamba Cathedral, vert.

1980, Sept. 20 Litho. ***Perf. 11½***

C700 A301 7.60s multi .70 .30
C701 A301 10.60s multi .95 .40

Souvenir Sheet

Imperf

C702 A301 30s multi 2.25 2.25

No. C702 contains vignettes in designs of Nos. 996 and C701.

Democracy Type

7.60s, 10.60s, Pres. Aguilera and voter.

Perf. 12x11½

1980, Oct. 9 Litho. Wmk. 395

C703 A302 7.60s multi .90 .45
C704 A302 10.60s multi 1.20 .50

Souvenir Sheet

Imperf

C705 A302 15s multi 1.50 1.50

No. C705 contains vignettes in designs of Nos. 999 and C703.

OPEC Type

20th Anniversary of OPEC: 7.60s, Men holding OPEC emblem, vert.

1980, Nov. 8 ***Perf. 11½x12***

C706 A303 7.60s multi .60 .45

Carchi Province Type

10.60s, Governor's Palace, vert. 17.80s, Victory Museum, Central Square, vert.

1980, Nov. 21 ***Perf. 13***

C707 A304 10.60s multi 1.25 .50
C708 A304 17.80s multi 1.90 .80

Orchid Type

Perf. 12x11½, 11½x12

1980, Nov. 22

C709 A305 7.60s Anguloa uniflora 2.25 .60
C710 A305 10.60s Scuticaria salesiana 3.25 .35
C711 A305 50s Helcia sanguinolenta, vert. 5.75 1.10
C712 A305 100s Anguloa virginalis 7.50 2.25
Nos. C709-C712 (4) 18.75 4.30

Souvenir Sheets

Imperf

C713 A305 20s multi 7.50 5.25
C714 A305 20s multi 7.50 5.25

Nos. C713-C714 contain vignettes in designs of Nos. C709, C711 and C710, C712 respectively.

Christmas Type

7.60s, Pope blessing crowd. 10.60s, Portrait.

1980, Dec. 27 ***Perf. 12***

C715 A306 7.60s multi, vert. 1.00 .50
C716 A306 10.60s multi, vert. 1.25 .60

Isidro Cueva — AP175

Simon Bolivar, by Marco Salas — AP176

1980, Nov. 20 ***Perf. 13***

C717 AP175 18.20s multi 2.50 1.25

Dr. Isidro Ayora Cueva, former president, birth centenary.

1980, Dec. 17 ***Perf. 11½***

C718 AP176 13.60s multi 2.00 1.00

Simon Bolivar death sesquicentennial.

Turtle, Galapagos Islands AP177

100s, Oldest Ecuadorian mail box, 1793.

1981, Feb. 12 **Litho.** ***Perf. 13***
C719 AP177 50s multi 6.50 4.00
C720 AP177 100s multi, vert. 8.00 5.00

HCJB Type

1981 **Litho.** ***Perf. 13***
C721 A311 7.60s Emblem, horiz. 1.25 .65
C722 A311 10.60s Emblem, diff. 1.75 .90

Soccer Players — AP178

1981, July 8
C723 AP178 7.60s Emblem .90 .45
C724 AP178 10.60s shown 1.20 .45
C725 AP178 13.60s World Cup 1.40 .75
Nos. C723-C725 (3) 3.50 1.65

Souvenir Sheets
C726 AP178 20s multi 3.50 3.50
C727 AP178 20s multi 3.50 3.50

1982 World Cup Soccer Championship. Nos. C726-C727 contain vignettes in designs of Nos. C723 and C725 respectively.

Picasso Type

1981, Oct. 26 **Litho.** ***Perf. 13***
C728 A313a 7.60s Still-life .90 .45
C729 A313a 10.60s First Communion, vert. 1.25 .60
C730 A313a 13.60s Las Meninas, vert. 1.40 .70

Size: 110x90mm
Imperf
C731 A313a 20s multi 3.00 3.00
Nos. C728-C731 (4) 5.30 4.10

No. C731 contains designs of Nos. C730, C729.

World Food Day Type

1981, Dec. 31 **Litho.** ***Perf. 13x13½***
C732 A314 10.60s Farming, vert. 1.40 .70

IYD Type

1982, Feb. 25 **Litho.** ***Perf. 13***
C733 A316 7.60s Emblem .70 .30
C734 A316 10.60s Man with crutch .90 .55

Montalvo Type

1982 **Litho.** ***Perf. 13***
C735 A318 5s Home, horiz. 1.25 .65

Swimming Type

1982, July 30
C736 A320 10.20s Emblem, vert. .95 .45
C737 A320 14.20s Diving, vert. 1.25 .60

Pres. Jaime Roldos, (1940-81), Mrs. Martha Roldos, Independence Monument, Quito — AP179

1983, May 25 **Litho.** ***Perf. 12***
C738 AP179 13.60s multi .65 .50

Souvenir Sheet
Imperf
C739 AP179 20s multi 2.00 2.00

AIR POST SEMI-POSTAL STAMPS

Nos. C119-C123 Surcharged in Blue or Red

1944, May 9 **Unwmk.** ***Perf. 12***
CB1 AP26 50c + 50c 7.00 3.50
CB2 AP26 70c + 30c 7.00 3.50
CB3 AP26 3s + 50c (R) 7.00 3.50
CB4 AP26 5s + 1s (R) 7.00 3.50
CB5 AP26 10s + 2s 7.00 3.50
Nos. CB1-CB5 (5) 35.00 17.50

The surtax aided Mendez Hospital.

AIR POST REGISTRATION STAMPS

Issued by Sociedad Colombo-Alemana de Transportes Aereos (SCADTA)

Nos. C3 and C3a Overprinted in Carmine

1928-29 **Wmk. 116** ***Perf. 14x14½***
CF1 AP6 1s on 20c (#C3) 110.00 100.00
a. 1s on 20c (#C3a) ('29) 140.00 110.00

No. C18 Overprinted in Black

1929, Apr. 1 **Wmk. 127** ***Perf. 14***
CF2 AP2 1s rose 85.00 55.00

AIR POST OFFICIAL STAMPS

Nos. C8-C15 Overprinted in Red or Black

1929, May **Unwmk.** ***Perf. 12***
CO1 AP1 2c black (R) 1.00 .50
CO2 AP1 5c carmine rose 1.00 .50
CO3 AP1 10c deep brown 1.00 .50
CO4 AP1 20c dark violet 1.00 .50
CO5 AP1 50c deep green 4.00 2.00
CO6 AP1 1s dark blue 4.00 2.00
a. Inverted overprint 240.00
CO7 AP1 5s orange yellow 18.00 7.75
CO8 AP1 10s orange red 210.00 75.00
Nos. CO1-CO8 (8) 240.00 88.75

Establishment of commercial air service in Ecuador.

Counterfeits of No. CO8 exist.

See Nos. CO9-CO12. For overprints and surcharges see Nos. C35-C38.

1930, Jan. 9
CO9 AP1 50c olive brown 3.50 1.75
CO10 AP1 1s carmine lake 4.50 2.25
CO11 AP1 5s olive green 11.00 5.50
CO12 AP1 10s black 21.00 10.50
Nos. CO9-CO12 (4) 40.00 20.00

For surcharges and overprint see Nos. C36-C38.

Air Post Stamps of 1937 Overprinted in Black

1937, Aug. 19
CO13 AP7 10c chestnut .50 .25
CO14 AP7 20c olive black .50 .25
CO15 AP7 70c black brown .60 .25
CO16 AP7 1s gray black .70 .25
CO17 AP7 2s dark violet .70 .30
Nos. CO13-CO17 (5) 3.00 1.30

For overprints see Nos. 463-464.

No. C79 Overprinted in Black

1940, Aug. 1 ***Perf. 12½x13***
CO18 AP15 5s emerald 2.00 .60

Catalogue values for unused stamps in this section, from this point to the end of the section, are for Never Hinged items.

Nos. C352-C354 Overprinted

1964 ***Perf. 13½***
CO19 AP86 50c multi 2.00 .85
CO20 AP86 80c multi 2.00 .85
CO21 AP86 1.30s multi 2.00 .85
Nos. CO19-CO21 (3) 6.00 2.55

SPECIAL DELIVERY STAMPS

SD1

1928 **Unwmk.** ***Perf. 12***
E1 SD1 2c on 2c blue 8.00 *9.00*
E2 SD1 5c on 2c blue 7.00 *9.00*
E3 SD1 10c on 2c blue 7.00 6.00
a. "10 CTVOS" inverted 21.00 *25.00*
E4 SD1 20c on 2c blue 10.00 9.00
E5 SD1 50c on 2c blue 12.00 9.00
Nos. E1-E5 (5) 44.00 *42.00*

No. RA49A Surcharged in Red

1945
E6 PT18 20c on 5c green 3.00 2.00

LATE FEE STAMP

No. RA49A Surcharged in Black

1945 **Unwmk.** ***Perf. 12***
I1 PT18 10c on 5c green 1.00 1.00

POSTAGE DUE STAMPS

Numeral — D1

1896 **Engr.** **Wmk. 117** ***Perf. 12***
J1 D1 1c blue green 6.00 *6.50*
J2 D1 2c blue green 6.00 *6.50*
J3 D1 5c blue green 6.00 *6.50*
J4 D1 10c blue green 6.00 *6.50*
J5 D1 20c blue green 6.00 *8.50*
J6 D1 50c blue green 6.00 *13.00*
J7 D1 100c blue green 6.00 *17.00*
Nos. J1-J7 (7) 42.00 *64.50*

Reprints are on very thick paper with distinct watermark and vertical paper-weave direction. Value 15c each.

Unwmk.
J8 D1 1c blue green *5.00* *6.00*
J9 D1 2c blue green *5.00* *6.00*
J10 D1 5c blue green *5.00* *6.00*
J11 D1 10c blue green *5.00* *6.00*
J12 D1 20c blue green *5.00* *7.50*
J13 D1 50c blue green *5.00* *10.50*
J14 D1 100c blue green *5.00* *15.00*
Nos. J8-J14 (7) 35.00 *57.00*

Coat of Arms — D2

1929
J15 D2 5c deep blue .40 .40
J16 D2 10c orange yellow .40 .40
J17 D2 20c red .60 .60
Nos. J15-J17 (3) 1.40 1.40

Numeral — D3

Perf. 13½
1958, Nov. **Unwmk.** **Litho.**
J18 D3 10c bright lilac .50 .40
J19 D3 50c emerald .50 .40
J20 D3 1s maroon .60 .40
J21 D3 2s red .70 .40
Nos. J18-J21 (4) 2.30 1.60

OFFICIAL STAMPS

Regular Issues of 1881 and 1887 Handstamped in Black

1886 **Unwmk.** ***Perf. 12***
O1 A5 1c yellow brown 2.50 2.50
O2 A6 2c lake 3.00 3.00
O3 A7 5c blue 6.75 *8.75*
O4 A8 10c orange 5.25 3.25

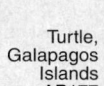

O5 A9 20c gray violet 5.25 5.25
O6 A10 50c blue green 15.00 11.50
Nos. O1-O6 (6) 37.75 34.25

1887

O7 A12 1c green 3.25 2.50
O8 A13 2c vermilion 3.25 3.25
O9 A14 5c blue 5.25 2.50
O10 A15 80c olive green 17.50 10.00
Nos. O7-O10 (4) 29.25 18.25

Nos. O1-O10 are known with red handstamp but these are believed to be speculative.

The overprint on the 1886-87 issues is handstamped and is found in various positions.

Flores — O1

Arms — O1a

1892 **Carmine Overprint**

O11 O1 1c ultramarine .25 *.40*
O12 O1 2c ultramarine .25 *.40*
O13 O1 5c ultramarine .25 *.40*
O14 O1 10c ultramarine .25 *.60*
O15 O1 20c ultramarine .25 *.90*
O16 O1 50c ultramarine .25 *.90*
O17 O1 1s ultramarine .35 *1.00*
Nos. O11-O17 (7) 1.85 4.60

1894

O18 O1a 1c slate green (R) 15.00
O19 O1a 2c lake (Bk) 20.00

Nos. O18 and O19 were not placed in use.

Rocafuerte — O2

Dated "1894"

1894 **Carmine Overprint**

O20 O2 1c gray black .60 *1.00*
O21 O2 2c gray black .60 .60
O22 O2 5c gray black .60 .60
O23 O2 10c gray black .75 *1.00*
O24 O2 20c gray black 1.00 1.00
O25 O2 50c gray black 3.75 3.75
O26 O2 1s gray black 6.00 6.00
Nos. O20-O26 (7) 13.30 13.95

Dated "1895"

1895 **Carmine Overprint**

O27 O2 1c gray black 5.25 5.25
O28 O2 2c gray black 7.50 7.50
O29 O2 5c gray black 1.50 1.50
O30 O2 10c gray black 7.50 7.50
O31 O2 20c gray black 11.00 10.50
O32 O2 50c gray black *75.00 75.00*
O33 O2 1s gray black 3.75 3.75
Nos. O27-O33 (7) *111.50 111.00*

Reprints of 1894-95 issues are on very thick paper with paper weave found both horizontal and vertical for all denominations. Values: Nos. O20-O26, 35c each; O27-O33, 20c each.Generally they are blacker than originals.

For overprints see Nos. O50-O91.

Types of 1896 Overprinted in Carmine

1896 **Wmk. 117**

O34 A21 1c olive bister 1.00 1.00
O35 A22 2c olive bister 1.00 1.00
O36 A23 5c olive bister 1.00 1.00
O37 A24 10c olive bister 1.00 1.00
O38 A25 20c olive bister 1.00 1.00
O39 A26 50c olive bister 1.00 1.00
O40 A27 1s olive bister 3.00 3.00
O41 A28 5s olive bister 6.00 6.00
Nos. O34-O41 (8) 15.00 15.00

Reprints of Nos. O34-O41 are on thick paper with vertical paper weave direction.

Unwmk.

O42 A21 1c olive bister 3.00 3.00
O43 A22 2c olive bister 3.00 3.00
O44 A23 5c olive bister 3.00 3.00
O45 A24 10c olive bister 3.00 3.00
O46 A25 20c olive bister 3.00 3.00
O47 A26 50c olive bister 3.00 *3.00*
O48 A27 1s olive bister 7.50 7.50
O49 A28 5s olive bister 10.50 10.50
Nos. O42-O49 (8) 36.00 36.00

Reprints of Nos. O42-O49 all have overprint in black. Value 20 cents each.

Nos. O20-O26 Overprinted

1897-98

O50 O2 1c gray black *20.00 20.00*
O51 O2 2c gray black *35.00 35.00*
O52 O2 5c gray black *200.00 200.00*
O53 O2 10c gray black *30.00 30.00*
O54 O2 20c gray black *20.00 20.00*
O55 O2 50c gray black *35.00 35.00*
O56 O2 1s gray black *55.00 55.00*
Nos. O50-O56 (7) *395.00 395.00*

Nos. O20-O26 Overprinted

O57 O2 1c gray black *4.00 4.00*
O58 O2 2c gray black *9.00 9.00*
O59 O2 5c gray black *90.00 90.00*
O60 O2 10c gray black *100.00 100.00*
O61 O2 20c gray black *25.00 25.00*
O62 O2 50c gray black *15.00 15.00*
O63 O2 1s gray black *165.00 165.00*
Nos. O57-O63 (7) *408.00 408.00*

Nos. O20-O26 Overprinted

O64 O2 1c gray black *40.00 40.00*
O65 O2 2c gray black *40.00 40.00*
O66 O2 5c gray black *40.00 40.00*
O67 O2 10c gray black *40.00 40.00*
O68 O2 20c gray black *40.00 40.00*
O69 O2 50c gray black *40.00 40.00*
O70 O2 1s gray black *40.00 40.00*
Nos. O64-O70 (7) *280.00 280.00*

Nos. O27-O33 Overprinted in Black like Nos. O50-O56

O71 O2 1c gray black *20.00 20.00*
O72 O2 2c gray black *20.00 20.00*
O73 O2 5c gray black *20.00 20.00*
O74 O2 10c gray black *20.00 20.00*
O75 O2 20c gray black *30.00 30.00*
O76 O2 50c gray black *275.00 275.00*
O77 O2 1s gray black *100.00 100.00*
Nos. O71-O77 (7) *485.00* 485.00

Nos. O27-O33 Overprinted

O78 O2 1c gray black *35.00 35.00*
O79 O2 2c gray black *30.00 30.00*
O80 O2 5c gray black *30.00 30.00*
O81 O2 10c gray black *32.50 32.50*
O82 O2 20c gray black *42.50 42.50*
O83 O2 50c gray black *30.00 30.00*
O84 O2 1s gray black *30.00 30.00*
Nos. O78-O84 (7) *230.00 230.00*

Nos. O27-O33 Overprinted like #O64-O70

O85 O2 1c gray black *90.00 90.00*
O86 O2 2c gray black *20.00 20.00*
O87 O2 5c gray black *80.00 80.00*
O88 O2 10c gray black *80.00 80.00*
O89 O2 20c gray black *140.00 140.00*
O90 O2 50c gray black *85.00 85.00*
O91 O2 1s gray black *165.00 165.00*
Nos. O85-O91 (7) *660.00 660.00*

Many forged overprints of Nos. O50-O91 exist, made on the original stamps and reprints.

O3

1898-99 ***Perf. 15, 16***

Black Surcharge

O92 O3 5c on 50c lilac 10.00 10.00
a. Inverted surcharge 25.00 25.00
O93 O3 10c on 20s org 15.00 15.00
a. Double surcharge 40.00 30.00
O94 O3 10c on 50c lilac *140.00 140.00*
O95 O3 20c on 50c lilac 30.00 30.00
O96 O3 20c on 50s green 30.00 30.00
Nos. O92-O96 (5) *225.00 225.00*

Green Surcharge

O97 O3 5c on 50c lilac 10.00 10.00
a. Double surcharge 5.00
b. Double surcharge, blk and grn 12.00
c. Same as "b," blk surch. invtd. 5.00

1899 **Red Surcharge**

O98 O3 5c on 50c lilac 10.00 10.00
a. Double surcharge 20.00
b. Dbl. surch., blk and red 25.00
O99 O3 20c on 50s green 15.00 15.00
a. Inverted surcharge 40.00
b. Dbl. surch., red and blk 60.00

Similar Surcharge in Black Value in Words in Two Lines

O100 O3 1c on 5c blue *650.00*

Red Surcharge

O101 O3 2c on 5c blue *1,150.*
O102 O3 4c on 20c blue *800.00*

Types of Regular Issue of 1899 Ovptd. in Black

1899 ***Perf. 14, 15***

O103 A37 2c orange & blk .70 *1.60*
O104 A39 10c orange & blk .70 *1.60*
O105 A40 20c orange & blk .50 *2.50*
O106 A41 50c orange & blk .50 *3.25*
Nos. O103-O106 (4) 2.40 *8.95*

For overprint see No. O167.

The above overprint was applied to remainders of the postage stamps of 1904 with the idea of increasing their salability. They were never regularly in use as official stamps.

Regular Issue of 1911-13 Overprinted in Black

1913 ***Perf. 12***

O107 A71 1c scarlet & blk 3.50 3.50
O108 A72 2c blue & blk 3.50 3.50
O109 A73 3c orange & blk 2.25 2.25
O110 A74 5c scarlet & blk 4.50 4.50
O111 A75 10c blue & blk 4.50 4.50
Nos. O107-O111 (5) 18.25 18.25

Regular Issue of 1911-13 Overprinted

1916-17 **Overprint 22x3 ½mm**

O112 A72 2c blue & blk 25.00 18.00
O113 A74 5c scarlet & blk 25.00 18.00
O114 A75 10c blue & blk 15.00 12.00
Nos. O112-O114 (3) 65.00 48.00

Overprint 25x4mm

O115 A71 1c scarlet & blk 1.10 1.10
O116 A72 2c blue & blk 1.60 1.60
a. Inverted overprint 5.00 5.00
O117 A73 3c orange & blk 1.00 1.00
O118 A74 5c scarlet & blk 1.60 1.60
O119 A75 10c blue & blk 1.60 1.60
Nos. O115-O119 (5) 6.90 6.90

Same Overprint On Regular Issue of 1915-17

O120 A71 1c orange 1.40 1.40
O121 A72 2c green 1.40 1.40
O122 A73 3c black 2.25 2.25
O123 A78 4c red & blk 2.25 2.25
a. Inverted overprint 15.00
O124 A74 5c violet 1.40 1.40
O125 A75 10c blue 2.75 2.75
O126 A79 20c green & blk 15.00 15.00
Nos. O120-O126 (7) 26.45 26.45

Regular Issues of 1911-17 Overprinted in Black or Red

O127 A71 1c orange .90 .90
O128 A72 2c green .70 .70
O129 A73 3c black (Bk) .90 .90
O130 A73 3c black (R) .90 .70
a. Inverted overprint
O131 A78 4c red & blk .90 .90
O132 A74 5c violet 1.75 .90
O133 A75 10c blue & blk 4.50 1.75
O134 A75 10c blue .90 .90
O135 A79 20c green & blk 4.50 1.75
Nos. O127-O135 (9) 15.95 9.40

Regular Issue of 1920 Overprinted

1920

O136 A86 1c green 1.25 1.25
a. Inverted overprint 17.00 —
O137 A86 2c carmine 1.00 1.00
O138 A86 3c yellow brn 1.25 1.25
O139 A86 4c dark green 2.00 2.00
a. Inverted overprint 17.00 —
O140 A86 5c blue 2.00 2.00
O141 A86 6c orange 1.25 1.25
O142 A86 7c brown 2.00 2.00
O143 A86 8c yellow green 2.50 2.50
O144 A86 9c red 3.25 3.25
O145 A95 10c blue 2.00 2.00
O146 A86 15c gray 11.00 11.00
O147 A86 20c deep violet 14.50 14.50
O148 A86 30c violet 17.00 17.00
O149 A86 40c dark brown 21.00 21.00
O150 A86 50c dark green 14.50 14.50
O151 A86 60c dark blue 17.00 17.00
O152 A86 70c gray 17.00 17.00
O153 A86 80c yellow 21.00 21.00
O154 A104 90c green 21.00 21.00
O155 A86 1s blue 45.00 45.00
Nos. O136-O155 (20) 217.50 217.50

Cent. of the independence of Guayaquil.

Stamps of 1911 Overprinted

1922

O156 A71 1c scarlet & blk 9.00 9.00
O157 A72 2c blue & blk 4.50 4.50

Revenue Stamps of 1919-1920 Overprinted like Nos. O156 and O157

1924

O158 PT3 1c dark blue 2.00 2.00
O159 PT3 2c green 12.50 12.50

Regular Issues of 1911-17 Overprinted

1924

O160 A71 1c orange 7.00 7.00
a. Inverted overprint 15.00

Overprinted in Black or Red

O161 A72 2c green .60 .60
O162 A73 3c black (R) .80 .80
O163 A78 4c red & blk 1.25 1.25
O164 A74 5c violet 1.25 1.25
O165 A75 10c deep blue 1.25 1.25
O166 A76 1s green & blk 7.00 7.00
Nos. O160-O166 (7) 19.15 19.15

No. O106 with Additional Overprint

1924 *Perf. 14, 15*

O167 A41 50c orange & blk 2.25 2.25

Nos. O160-O167 exist with inverted overprint.

No. 199 Overprinted

1924 *Perf. 12*

O168 A71 1c orange 5.50 5.50

Regular Issues of 1911-25 Overprinted

1925

O169 A71 1c scarlet & blk 10.00 4.25
a. Inverted overprint 15.00
O170 A71 1c orange .60 .60
a. Inverted overprint 4.00
O171 A72 2c green .60 .60
a. Inverted overprint 4.00
O172 A73 3c black (Bk) .60 .60
O173 A73 3c black (R) 1.10 1.10
O174 A78 4c red & blk .60 .60
O175 A74 5c violet .80 .80
O176 A74 5c rose .80 .80
O177 A75 10c deep blue .60 .60
Nos. O169-O177 (9) 15.70 9.95

Regular Issues of 1916-25 Ovptd. Vertically Up or Down

1927, Oct.

O178 A71 1c orange 2.00 2.00
O179 A86 2c carmine 2.00 2.00
O180 A86 3c yellow brown 2.00 2.00
O181 A86 4c myrtle green 2.00 2.00
O182 A86 5c pale blue 2.00 2.00
O183 A75 10c yellow green 2.00 2.00
Nos. O178-O183 (6) 12.00 12.00

Regular Issues of 1920-27 Overprinted

1928

O184 A71 1c lt blue 1.25 1.25
O185 A86 2c carmine 1.25 1.25
O186 A86 3c yellow brown 1.25 1.25
a. Inverted overprint 5.00
O187 A86 4c myrtle green 1.25 1.25
O188 A86 5c lt blue 1.25 1.25
O189 A75 10c yellow green 1.25 1.25
O190 A109 20c violet 11.00 2.50
a. Overprint reading up 3.50 2.25
Nos. O184-O190 (7) 18.50 10.00

The overprint is placed vertically reading down on No. O190.

Regular Issue of 1936 Overprinted in Black

1936 *Perf. 14*

O191 A131 5c olive green 1.50 1.50
O192 A132 10c brown 1.50 1.50
O193 A133 20c dark violet 1.90 .70
O194 A134 1s dark carmine 2.25 1.10
O195 A135 2s dark blue 2.50 1.75
Nos. O191-O195 (5) 9.65 6.55

Regular Postage Stamps of 1937 Overprinted in Black

1937 *Perf. 11½*

O196 A139 2c green .40 .40
O197 A140 5c deep rose .40 .40
O198 A141 10c blue .40 .40
O199 A142 20c deep rose .40 .40
O200 A143 1s olive green .40 .40
Nos. O196-O200 (5) 2.00 2.00

Catalogue values for unused stamps in this section, from this point to the end of the section, are for Never Hinged items.

Tobacco Stamp, Overprinted in Black

1946 **Unwmk.** *Rouletted*

O201 PT7 1c rose red 1.75 1.75

Communications Building, Quito — O4

1947 **Unwmk.** **Litho.** *Perf. 11*

O202 O4 30c brown .60 .40
O203 O4 30c greenish blue .60 .40
a. Imperf., pair
O204 O4 30c purple .60 .40
Nos. O202-O204 (3) 1.80 1.20

Nos. O202 to O204 overprinted "Primero la Patria!" and plane in dark blue were issued in August, 1947, by a revolutionary group. They were later repudiated by decree.

No. 719 with Additional Diagonal Overprint

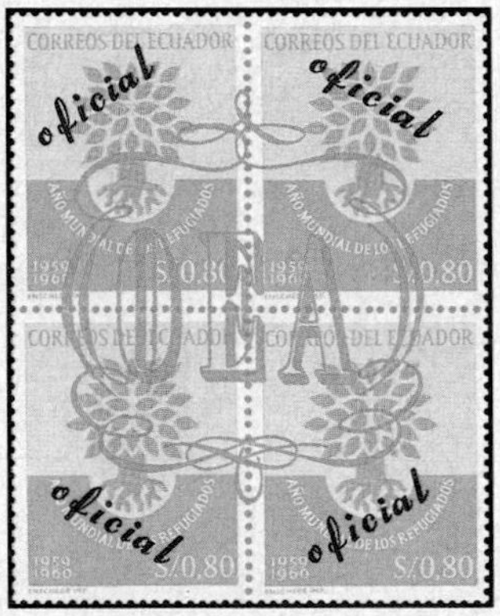

1964 *Perf. 14x13*

O205 A231 80c block of 4 6.00 6.00

The "OEA" overprint covers four stamps, the "oficial" overprint is applied to every stamp.

A set of 20 imperforate items in the above Roosevelt design, some overprinted with the initials of various government ministries, was released in 1949. Later that year a set of 8 miniature sheets, bearing the same design plus a marginal inscription, "Presidencia (or Vicepresidencia) de la Republica," and a frame-line were released. In the editors' opinion, information justifying the listing of these issues has not been received.

POSTAL TAX STAMPS

Roca — PT1

1920 **Unwmk.** *Perf. 12*

RA1 PT1 1c orange .75 .30

PT2

PT3

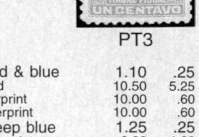

RA2 PT2 1c red & blue 1.10 .25
a. "de" inverted 10.50 5.25
b. Double overprint 10.00 .60
c. Inverted overprint 10.00 .60
RA3 PT3 1c deep blue 1.25 .25
a. Inverted overprint 6.00 1.00
b. Double overprint 6.00 1.00

For overprints see Nos. O158-O159.

PT4

PT5

Red or Black Surcharge or Overprint

Stamp Dated 1911-1912

RA4 PT4 20c deep blue — 30.00

Stamp Dated 1913-1914

RA5 PT4 20c deep blue (R) 2.25 .35

Stamp Dated 1917-1918

RA6 PT4 20c olive green (R) 6.50 .55
a. Dated 1919-20 *25.00*
RA7 PT5 1c on 2c green .90 .25

Stamp Dated 1911-1912

RA8 PT5 1c on 5c green .90 .25
a. Double surcharge

Stamp Dated 1913-1914

RA9 PT5 1c on 5c green 8.00 .55
a. Double surcharge 12.00 4.00

On Nos. RA7, RA8 and RA9 the surcharge is found reading upward or downward.
For surcharges see Nos. RA15-RA16.

Post Office — PT6

1920-24 **Engr.**

RA10 PT6 1c olive green .40 .25
RA11 PT6 2c deep green .40 .25
RA12 PT6 20c bister brn ('24) 1.75 .25
RA13 PT6 2s violet 11.50 3.25
RA14 PT6 5s blue 20.00 5.75
Nos. RA10-RA14 (5) 34.05 9.75

For overprints and surcharge see Nos. 259, 266-268, 273, 302, RA17, RA28.

Revenue Stamps of 1917-18 Srchd. Vertically in Red reading up or down

1921-22

RA15 PT5 20c on 1c dk blue 55.00 6.50
RA16 PT5 20c on 2c green 55.00 6.50

No. RA12 Surcharged in Green

1924

RA17 PT6 2c on 20c bis brn .60 .25
a. Inverted surcharge 14.00 5.00
b. Double surcharge 4.00 2.00

PT7

1924 ***Rouletted 7***

RA18 PT7 1c rose red .90 .25
a. Inverted overprint 3.50

Similar Design, Eagle at left

Perf. 12

RA19 PT7 2c blue .90 .25
a. Inverted overprint 3.50 1.75

For overprints and surcharges see Nos. 346, O201, RA32, RA34, RA37, RA44-RA45, RA47.

PT8

Inscribed "Timbre Fiscal"

1924

RA20 PT8 1c yellow 4.50 .85
RA21 PT8 2c dark blue 1.40 .35

Inscribed "Region Oriental"

RA22 PT8 1c yellow .70 .30
RA23 PT8 2c dark blue 1.40 .35
Nos. RA20-RA23 (4) 8.00 1.85

Overprint on No. RA22 reads down or up.

Revenue Stamp Overprinted in Blue

1934

RA24 2c green .50 .25
a. Blue overprint inverted 3.50 1.75
b. Blue ovpt. dbl., one invtd. 4.00 1.25

Postage Stamp of 1930 Overprinted in Red

Perf. 12½

RA25 A119 20c ultra & yel .50 .25

Telegraph Stamp Overprinted in Red, like No. RA24, and Surcharged diagonally in Black

1934 ***Perf. 14***

RA26 2c on 10c olive brn .70 .25
a. Double surcharge 5.50

Overprint Blue, Surcharge Red

RA27 2c on 10c olive brn .70 .25

PT9

1934-36 ***Perf. 12***

RA28 PT9 2c green .60 .25
a. Both overprints in red ('36) .60 .25

Postal Tax stamp of 1920-24, overprinted in red "POSTAL" has been again overprinted "CASA de Correos y Teleg. de Guayaquil" in black.

PT10

Perf. 14½x14

1934 **Photo.** **Wmk. 233**

RA29 PT10 2c yellow green .50 .25

For the rebuilding of the GPO at Guayaquil.
For surcharge see No. RA31.

Symbols of Post and Telegraph Service PT11

1935

RA30 PT11 20c claret .50 .25

For the rebuilding of the GPO at Guayaquil.

No. RA29 Surcharged in Red and Overprinted in Black

1935

RA31 PT10 3c on 2c yel grn .40 .25
a. Double surcharge

Social and Rural Workers' Insurance Fund.

Tobacco Stamp Surcharged in Black

1936 **Unwmk.** ***Rouletted 7***

RA32 PT7 3c on 1c rose red .60 .25
a. Lines of words reversed 2.00 .25
b. Horiz. pair, imperf. vert.

Issued for the Social and Rural Workers' Insurance Fund.

No. 310 Overprinted in Black

1936 ***Perf. 12½***

RA33 A119 20c ultra & yel .60 .25
a. Double overprint

Tobacco Stamp Surcharged in Black

1936 ***Rouletted 7***

RA34 PT7 3c on 1c rose red .60 .25

Social and Rural Workers' Insurance Fund.

Worker — PT12

1936 **Engr.** ***Perf. 13½***

RA35 PT12 3c ultra .40 .25

Social and Rural Workers' Insurance Fund.
For surcharges see Nos. C64, RA36, RA53-RA54.

Surcharged in Black

1936

RA36 PT13 5c on 3c ultra .60 .25

This combines the 2c for the rebuilding of the post office with the 3c for the Social and Rural Workers' Insurance Fund.

National Defense Issue
Tobacco Stamp Surcharged in Black

1936 ***Rouletted 7***

RA37 PT7 10c on 1c rose .90 .25
a. Double surcharge

Symbolical of Defense — PT14

1937-42 ***Perf. 12½***

RA38 PT14 10c deep blue .90 .25

A 1s violet and 2s green exist in type PT14.
For surcharge see No. RA40.

Overprinted or Surcharged in Black

PT15

1937 **Engr. & Typo.** ***Perf. 13½***

RA39 PT15 5c lt brn & red 2.00 .25
d. Inverted overprint 20.00

1942 ***Perf. 12, 11½***

RA39A PT15 20c on 5c rose pink & red 75.00 20.00
RA39B PT15 20c on 1s yel brn & red 75.00 20.00
e. Surcharge omitted —
RA39C PT15 20c on 2s grn & red 75.00 20.00
Nos. RA39A-RA39C (3) 225.00 60.00

A 50c dark blue and red exists.

No. RA38 Surcharged in Red

1937 **Engr.** ***Perf. 12½***

RA40 PT14 5c on 10c dp blue 1.10 .25

Map of Ecuador — PT16

1938 ***Perf. 14x13½***

RA41 PT16 5c carmine rose .70 .25

Social and Rural Workers' Insurance Fund.

No. C42 Surcharged in Red

1938 ***Perf. 12½***

RA42 A136 20c on 70c black 1.10 .25

No. 307 Surcharged in Red

1938

RA43 A116 5c on 6c yel & red .40 .25

This stamp was obligatory on all mail from Nov. 23rd to 30th, 1938. The tax was for the Intl. Union for the Control of Cancer.

Tobacco Stamp Surcharged in Black

1939 ***Rouletted***

RA44 PT7 5c on 1c rose .70 .25
a. Double surcharge
b. Triple surcharge

Tobacco Stamp Surcharged in Blue

1940

RA45 PT7 5c on 1c rose red 1.00 .25
a. Double surcharge 3.50 3.50

No. 370 Surcharged in Carmine

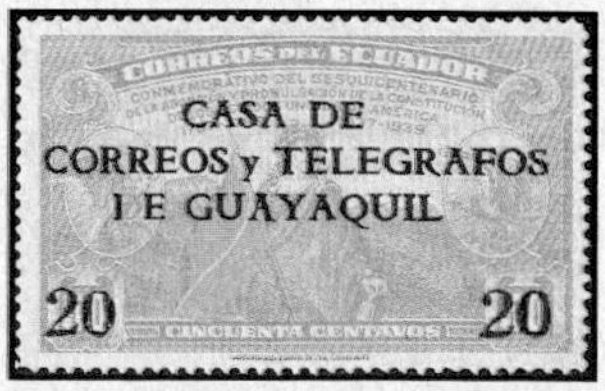

1940 ***Perf. 11½***

RA46 A144 20c on 50c blk & multi .50 .25
a. Double surcharge, one inverted

Tobacco Stamp Surcharged in Black

1940 ***Rouletted***
RA47 PT7 20c on 1c rose red 6.00 .50

Farmer Plowing — PT17

1940 ***Perf. 13x13½***
RA48 PT17 5c carmine rose .70 .25

Communication Symbols — PT18

1940-43 ***Perf. 12***
RA49 PT18 5c copper brown .70 .25
RA49A PT18 5c green ('43) .70 .25

For overprint and surcharges see #534, E6, I1.

Pursuit Planes — PT19

1941 ***Perf. 11½x13***
RA50 PT19 20c ultra 1.10 .25

The tax was used for national defense.

Warrior Shielding Women — PT20

1942-46 **Engr.** ***Perf. 12***
RA51 PT20 20c dark blue 1.10 .25
RA51A PT20 40c black brown ('46) 1.10 .25

The tax was used for national defense.
A 20c carmine, 20c brown and 30c gray exist lithographed in type PT20.

No. 370 Surcharged in Carmine

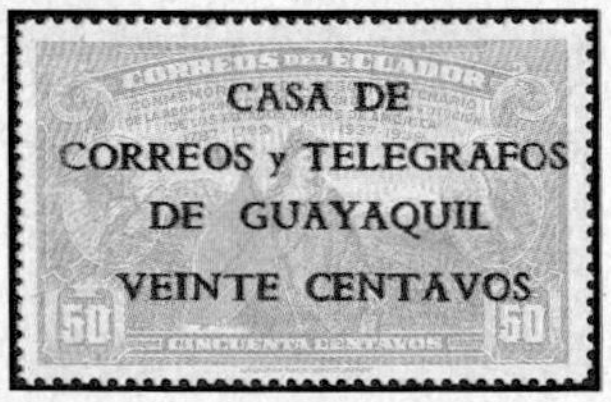

1942 ***Perf. 11½***
RA52 A144 20c on 50c multi 1.10 .25
a. Double surcharge 10.00

No. RA35 Surcharged in Red

1943 ***Perf. 13½***
RA53 PT12 5c on 3c ultra .60 .25

No. RA53 with Additional Surcharge in Black

1943
RA54 PT12 5c on 5c on 3c ultra 1.10 .25

Peons — PT21

1943 ***Perf. 12***
RA55 PT21 5c blue .90 .25

The tax was for farm workers.
For overprint & surcharge see #535, C135.

Revenue Stamp (as No. RA64) Overprinted or Surcharged in Black

No. RA56

No. RA57

1943 ***Perf. 12½***
RA56 20c red orange *75.00* 1.50

1943 ***Perf. 12***
RA57 20c on 10c orange 2.25 .25
a. Double surcharge

Coat of Arms — PT22

1943 ***Perf. 12½***
RA58 PT22 20c orange red .70 .25

The tax was for national defense.

No. RA58 Surcharged in Black

1944
RA59 PT22 30c on 20c org red .70 .25
a. Double surcharge

Catalogue values for unused stamps in this section, from this point to the end of the section, are for Never Hinged items.

Consular Service Stamps Surcharged in Black

1951 **Unwmk.** ***Perf. 12***
RA60 R1 20c on 1s red .60 .25
RA61 R1 20c on 2s brown .60 .25
RA62 R1 20c on 5s violet .60 .25
Nos. RA60-RA62 (3) 1.80 .75

Teacher and Pupils in Schoolyard — PT23

1952 **Engr.** ***Perf. 13***
RA63 PT23 20c blue green .60 .25

Revenue Stamp Overprinted — PT24

1952 ***Perf. 12***
RA64 PT24 40(c) olive green 1.10 .25

For overprints & surcharges see #RA56-RA57

Woman Holding Flag — PT25

1953 ***Perf. 12½***
RA65 PT25 40c ultra 1.25 .25

Telegraph Stamp Surcharged in Black — PT26

1954 **Unwmk.** ***Perf. 13***
RA66 PT26 20c on 30c red brn 1.00 .25

Revenue Stamps Surcharged or Overprinted Horizontally in Black

PT26a

PT26b

PT26c

1954 **Unwmk.** ***Perf. 12***
RA67 PT26a 10c on 25c blue 1.25 .25
RA68 PT26b 10c on 50c org red 1.25 .25
RA69 PT26c 10c carmine 1.25 .25
Nos. RA67-RA69 (3) 3.75 .75

Telegraph Stamp Surcharged — PT27

1954 ***Perf. 13***
RA70 PT27 10c on 30c red brn 2.25 .25

Revenue Stamp Overprinted in Black

1954 ***Perf. 12***
RA71 R3 20c olive black 1.75 .25

Consular Service Stamp Surcharged in Black

1954
RA72 R1 20c on 10s gray 1.75 .25

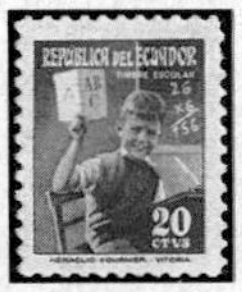
Young Student at Desk — PT28

Imprint: "Heraclio Fournier.-Vitoria"

1954 **Photo.** ***Perf. 11***
RA73 PT28 20c rose pink 1.25 .25

See No. RA76.

Globe, Ship, Plane — PT29

1954 **Engr.** ***Perf. 12***
RA74 PT29 10c dp magenta 2.25 .25

Soldier Kissing Flag — PT30

1955 **Photo.** ***Perf. 11***
RA75 PT30 40c blue 2.25 .25

See No. RA77.

Types of 1954-55 Redrawn.
Imprint: "Thomas de la Rue & Co. Ltd."

1957 **Unwmk.** ***Perf. 13***
RA76 PT28 20c rose pink 1.10 .25

Perf. 14x14½
RA77 PT30 40c blue 2.25 .25

No. RA77 is inscribed "Republica del Ecuador."

The above stamp is believed to have been used only for fiscal purposes.

AIR POST POSTAL TAX STAMPS

No. 438 Surcharged in Black or Carmine

1945	Unwmk.	*Perf. 11*	
RAC1 A173 20c on 10c dk grn		.75	.25
a. Pair, one without surcharge		90.00	
RAC2 A173 20c on 10c dk grn (C)		.75	.25

Obligatory on letters and parcel post carried on planes in the domestic service.

Liberty, Mercury and Planes PTAP1

1946	Engr.	*Perf. 12*	
RAC3 PTAP1 20c orange brown		.75	.25

GALAPAGOS ISLANDS

Issued for use in the Galapagos Islands (Columbus Archipelago), a province of Ecuador, but were commonly used throughout the country.

Catalogue values for unused stamps in this section are for Never Hinged items.

Sea Lions — A1

Map — A2

Design: 1s, Marine iguana.

Unwmk.

1957, July 15	Photo.	*Perf. 12*	
L1 A1 20c dark brown		1.50	.30
L2 A2 50c violet		1.00	.30
L3 A1 1s dull olive green		4.75	.80
Nos. L1-L3 (3)		7.25	1.40
Nos. L1-L3,LC1-LC3 (6)		18.50	3.65

125th anniv. of Ecuador's possession of the Galapagos Islands, and publicizing the islands.

See Nos. LC1-LC3. For overprints see Nos. 684-686, C389-C391.

GALAPAGOS AIR POST STAMPS

Type of Regular Issue

1s, Santa Cruz Island. 1.80s, Map of Galapagos archipelago. 4.20s, Galapagos giant tortoise.

Unwmk.

1957, July 19	Photo.	*Perf. 12*	
LC1 A1 1s deep blue		1.25	.30
LC2 A1 1.80s rose violet		2.50	.70
LC3 A1 4.20s black		7.50	1.25
Nos. LC1-LC3 (3)		11.25	2.25

For overprints see Nos. C389-C391.

Redrawn Type of Ecuador, 1956

1959, Jan. 3	Engr.	*Perf. 14*	
LC4 AP69 2s lt olive green		1.25	.70

Issued to honor the United Nations. See note after No. C407.

EGYPT

'ē-jəpt

LOCATION — Northern Africa, bordering on the Mediterranean and the Red Sea
GOVT. — Republic
AREA — 386,900 sq. mi.
POP. — 61,404,000 (1997 est.)
CAPITAL — Cairo

Modern Egypt was a part of Turkey until 1914 when a British protectorate was declared over the country and the Khedive was deposed in favor of Hussein Kamil under the title of sultan. In 1922 the protectorate ended and the reigning sultan was declared king of the new monarchy. Egypt became a republic on June 18, 1953. Egypt merged with Syria in 1958 to form the United Arab Republic. Syria left this union in 1961. In 1971 Egypt took the name of Arab Republic of Egypt.

40 Paras = 1 Piaster
1000 Milliemes = 100 Piasters = 1 Pound (1888)
1000 Milliemes = 1 Pound (1953)
1000 Milliemes = 100 Piasters = 1 Pound (1982)

Catalogue values for unused stamps in this country are for Never Hinged items, beginning with Scott 241 in the regular postage section, Scott B1 in the semi-postal section, Scott C38 in the airpost section, Scott CB1 in the airpost semi-postal section, Scott E5 in the special delivery section, Scott J40 in the postage due section, Scott M16 in the military stamps section, Scott O60 in the officials section, Scott N1 in the occupation section, Scott NC1 in the occupation airpost section, Scott NE1 in the occupation special delivery section, and Scott NJ1 in the occupation postage due section.

Watermarks

Wmk. 118 — Pyramid and Star

Wmk. 119 — Crescent and Star

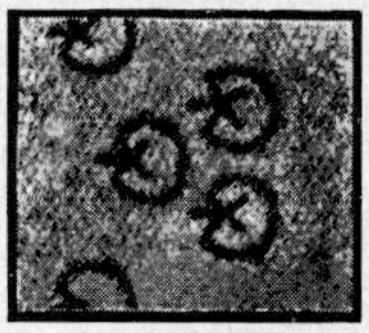

Wmk. 120 — Triple Crescent and Star

Wmk. 195 — Multiple Crown and Arabic F

"F" in watermark stands for Fuad.

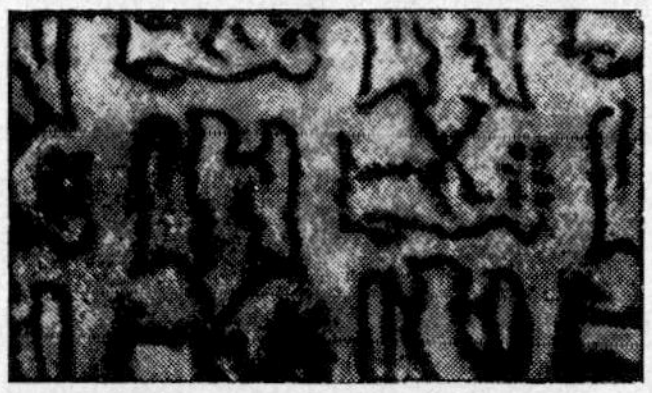

Wmk. 315 — Multiple Eagle

Wmk. 318 — Multiple Eagle and "Misr"

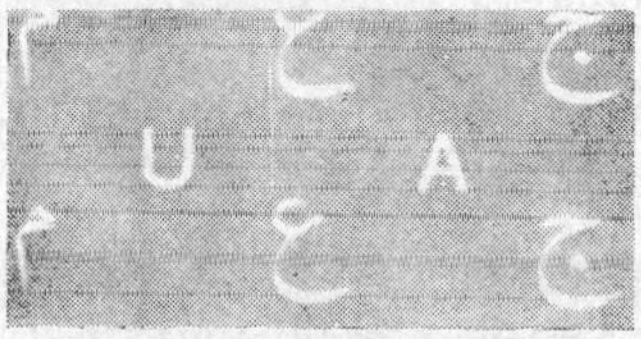

Wmk. 328 — U A R

Wmk. 342 — Coat of Arms, Multiple

Values for unused stamps are for examples with original gum as defined in the catalogue introduction. Very fine examples of Nos. 1-15 will have perforations that are clear of the framelines but with the design noticeably off center. Well centered stamps are extremely scarce and will command substantial premiums.

Turkish Numerals

١ ٢ ٣ ٤ ٥
1 2 3 4 5
٦ ٧ ٨ ٩ ٠
6 7 8 9 0

Turkish Suzerainty

A1

A2

A3

A4

A5

A6

A7

Surcharged in Black

Wmk. 118

1866, Jan. 1	Litho.	*Perf. 12½*	
1 A1 5pa greenish gray		57.50	37.50
a. Imperf., pair		250.00	
b. Pair, imperf. between		400.00	
c. Perf. 12½x13		77.50	57.50
d. Perf. 13		325.00	365.00
2 A2 10pa brown		75.00	37.50
a. Imperf., pair		210.00	
b. Pair, imperf. between		450.00	
c. Perf. 13		240.00	*260.00*
d. Perf. 12½x15		325.00	*350.00*
e. Perf. 12½x13		100.00	57.50
3 A3 20pa blue		105.00	40.00
a. Imperf., pair		300.00	
b. Pair, imperf. between		500.00	
c. Perf. 12½x13		125.00	95.00
d. Perf. 13		500.00	325.00
4 A4 2pi yellow		125.00	52.50
a. Imperf.		*150.00*	*125.00*
b. Imperf. vert. or horiz., pair		500.00	425.00
c. Perf. 12½x15		190.00	
d. Diagonal half used as 1pi on cover			*3,000.*
e. Perf. 12½x13, 13x12½		165.00	67.50
5 A5 5pi rose		325.00	250.00
a. Imperf.		425.00	375.00
b. Imperf. vert. or horiz., pair		*1,250.*	
d. Inscription of 10pi, imperf.		950.00	850.00
e. Perf. 12½x13, 13x12½		350.00	275.00
f. As "d," perf. 12½x15		1,050.	1,000.
g. Perf. 13		650.00	
6 A6 10pi slate bl		375.00	325.00
a. Imperf.		*550.00*	450.00
b. Pair, imperf. between		*2,500.*	
c. Perf. 12½x13, 13x12½		550.00	550.00
d. Perf. 13		*2,000.*	

Unwmk.

Typo.

7 A7 1pi rose lilac		80.00	5.50
a. Imperf.		125.00	
b. Horiz. pair, imperf. vert.		500.00	
c. Perf. 12½x13, 13x12½		110.00	25.00
d. Perf. 13		400.00	250.00
e. Perf. 12½x15		*350.00*	
Nos. 1-7 (7)		1,142.	748.00

Single imperforates of types A1-A10 are sometimes simulated by trimming wide-margined examples of perforated stamps.

No. 4d must be dated between July 16 and July 31, 1867.

Proofs of Nos. 1-7 are on smooth white paper, unwatermarked and imperforate. Proofs of No. 7 are on thinner paper than No. 7a.

Sphinx and Pyramid — A8

Perf. 15x12½

1867 Litho. Wmk. 119

8	A8 5pa orange	42.50	*11.00*
a.	Imperf.	250.00	—
b.	Horiz. pair, imperf between	190.00	
c.	Vert. pair, imperf between	—	
9	A8 10pa lilac ('69)	70.00	11.00
a.	10pa violet	95.00	14.00
b.	Half used as 5pa on news-paper piece		850.00
11	A8 20pa yellow green ('69)	135.00	14.00
a.	20pa blue green	135.00	17.00
13	A8 1pi rose red	27.50	1.10
a.	Imperf, pair	150.00	
b.	Pair, imperf. between	300.00	
d.	Rouletted	70.00	
e.	1pi lake red	175.00	32.50
14	A8 2pi blue	150.00	18.00
a.	Imperf.	325.00	
b.	Horiz. pair, imperf. vert.	500.00	
d.	Perf. 12½	275.00	
15	A8 5pi brown	375.00	200.00
	Nos. 8-15 (6)	800.00	255.10

There are 4 types of each value, so placed that any block of 4 contains all types.

A9

A10

Clear Impressions

Thick Opaque Paper

Typographed by the Government at Boulac

Perf. 12½x13½ Clean-cut

1872 Wmk. 119

19	A9 5pa brown	10.00	5.50
20	A9 10pa lilac	9.00	3.75
21	A9 20pa blue	67.50	4.75
22	A9 1pi rose red	72.50	2.25
h.	Half used as 20pa on cover		750.00
23	A9 2pi dull yellow	100.00	15.00
j.	Half used as 1p on cover		1,200.
24	A9 2½pi dull violet	95.00	25.00
25	A9 5pi green	325.00	42.50
i.	Tête bêche pair	*8,000.*	
	Nos. 19-25 (7)	679.00	98.75

Perf. 13½ Clean-cut

19a	A9 5pa brown	27.50	10.00
20a	A9 10pa dull lilac	7.00	3.50
21a	A9 20pa blue	95.00	22.00
22a	A9 1pi rose red	95.00	4.00
23a	A9 2pi dull yellow	20.00	4.50
24a	A9 2½pi dull violet	800.00	225.00
25a	A9 5pi green	325.00	62.50

Litho.

21m	A9 20pa blue, perf. 12½x13½	160.00	80.00
21n	A9 20pa blue, perf. 13½	250.00	65.00
21p	A9 20pa blue, imperf.	—	
21q	A9 20pa blue, pair, imperf. between	—	2,000.
22m	A9 1pi rose red, perf. 12½x13½	550.00	20.00
22n	A9 1pi rose red, perf. 13½	875.00	50.00

Typographed

Blurred Impressions

Thinner Paper

Perf. 12½ Rough

1874-75 Wmk. 119

26	A10 5pa brown ('75)	22.50	3.75
e.	Imperf.	200.00	200.00
f.	Vert. pair, imperf. horiz.	1,000.	—
g.	Tête bêche pair	45.00	45.00
20b	A9 10pa gray lilac	16.00	3.75
g.	Tête bêche pair	225.00	225.00
21b	A9 20pa gray blue	105.00	4.00
k.	Half used as 10pa on cover		—
22b	A9 1pi vermilion	12.00	1.75
f.	Imperf.	—	150.00
g.	Tête bêche pair	150.00	125.00
23b	A9 2pi yellow	90.00	5.75
i.	Tête bêche pair	600.00	600.00
24b	A9 2½pi deep violet	9.25	6.25
e.	Imperf.	—	
f.	Tête bêche pair	600.00	600.00
25b	A9 5pi yellow green	65.00	22.50
e.	Imperf.	400.00	—

No. 26f normally occurs tête-bêche.

Perf. 13½x12½ Rough

26c	A10 5pa brown	24.00	4.50
i.	Tête bêche pair	62.50	62.50
20c	A9 10pa gray lilac	37.50	3.50
i.	Tête bêche pair	225.00	*225.00*
21c	A9 20pa gray blue	11.00	3.75
h.	Pair, imperf. between	350.00	
22c	A9 1pi vermilion	90.00	3.25
i.	Tête bêche pair	500.00	500.00
23c	A9 2pi yellow	10.00	6.25
g.	Tête bêche pair	500.00	500.00

k.	Half used as 1pi on cover		*4,000.*

Perf. 12½x13½ Rough

23d	A9 2pi yellow ('75)	80.00	17.00
h.	Tête bêche pair	*1,250.*	
24d	A9 2½pi dp violet ('75)	80.00	20.00
l.	Tête bêche pair	*1,150.*	*800.00*
25d	A9 5pi yel green ('75)	375.00	300.00

Nos. 24b, 24d Surcharged in Black

1879, Jan. 1 ***Perf. 12½ Rough***

27	A9 5pa on 2½pi dull vio	10.00	*12.00*
a.	Imperf.	450.00	450.00
b.	Tête bêche pair	*7,500.*	
c.	Inverted surcharge	125.00	75.00
d.	Perf. 12½x13½ rough	12.00	*12.00*
e.	As "d," tête bêche pair	7,500.	
f.	As "d," inverted surcharge	150.00	150.00
28	A9 10pa on 2½pi dull vio	12.50	12.50
a.	Imperf.	400.00	400.00
b.	Tête bêche pair	*2,500.*	
c.	Inverted surcharge	125.00	82.50
d.	Perf. 12½x13½ rough	17.00	17.00
e.	As "d," tête bêche pair	3,000.	
f.	As "d," inverted surcharge	150.00	125.00

A11

A12

A13

A14

A15

A16

1879-1902 Typo. ***Perf. 14x13½***

Ordinary Paper

29	A11 5pa brown	4.25	1.25
30	A12 10pa violet	57.50	5.00
31	A12 10pa lilac rose ('81)	70.00	10.00
32	A12 10pa gray ('82)	8.00	1.75
33	A12 10pa green ('84)	2.50	2.00
34	A13 20pa ultra	67.50	2.25
35	A13 20pa rose ('84)	22.00	1.25
36	A14 1pi rose	42.50	.30
37	A14 1pi ultra ('84)	5.75	.30
38	A15 2pi orange yel	42.50	1.50
39	A15 2pi orange brn	27.50	.50
40	A16 5pi green	77.50	11.50
41	A16 5pi gray ('84)	25.00	.50
	Nos. 29-41 (13)	452.50	38.10

Nos. 29-31, 35-41 imperf are proofs.

Nos. 37, 39, 41, exist on both ordinary and chalky paper. See *Scott Classic Specialized Catalogue of Stamps & Covers* for detailed listings.

For overprints see Nos. 42, O6-O7.

A17

1884, Feb. 1

42	A17 20pa on 5pi green	14.00	2.25
a.	Inverted surcharge	70.00	62.50
b.	Double surcharge		—

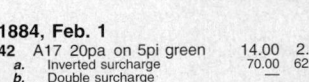

A18

A19

A20

A21

A22

A23

1888-1906 Ordinary Paper

43	A18 1m pale brown ('02)	3.50	.25
44	A19 2m green ('02)	3.00	.25
45	A20 3m maroon ('92)	8.00	2.25
46	A20 3m yel org ('02)	5.75	.25
48	A22 5m carmine rose	6.50	.25
49	A23 10p purple ('89)	35.00	1.00
	Nos. 43-49 (6)	61.75	4.25

Chalky Paper

43a	A18 1m pale brown ('02)	4.00	.25
44a	A19 2m green ('02)	1.25	.25
46a	A20 3m yel org ('02)	3.00	.25
47	A21 4m brown red ('06)	4.75	.25
a.	Half used as 2m on cover		—
48b	A22 5m rose ('02)	3.00	.25
49b	A23 10p mauve ('02)	22.50	.55

Nos. 43-44, 47-48 imperf are proofs.

For overprints see Nos. O2-O5, O8-O10, O14-O15.

Boats on Nile A24

Cleopatra A25

Ras-el-Tin Palace A26

Giza Pyramids A27

Sphinx A28

Colossi of Thebes A29

Pylon of Karnak and Temple of Khonsu — A30

Citadel at Cairo — A31

Rock Temple of Abu Simbel — A32

Aswan Dam — A33

Perf. 13½x14

1914, Jan. 8 Wmk. 119

Chalk-surfaced Paper

50	A24 1m olive brown	1.25	*.80*
51	A25 2m dp green	3.75	.25
52	A26 3m orange	3.50	.50
53	A27 4m red	4.50	.75
54	A28 5m lake	4.25	.25
a.	Booklet pane of 6	250.00	
55	A29 10m dk blue	7.50	.40

Perf. 14

56	A30 20m olive grn	8.00	.70
57	A31 50m red violet	24.00	1.10
58	A32 100m black	25.00	1.40
59	A33 200m plum	42.50	4.00
	Nos. 50-59 (10)	124.25	10.15

All values of this issue exist imperforate on both watermarked and unwatermarked paper but are not known to have been issued in that condition.

See Nos. 61-69, 72-74. For overprints and surcharge see Nos. 60, 78-91, O11-O13, O16-O27, O30.

British Protectorate

No. 52 Surcharged

1915, Oct. 15

60	A26 2m on 3m orange	1.25	2.25
a.	Inverted surcharge	250.00	250.00

Scenic Types of 1914 and

Statue of Ramses II

A34 A35

1921-22 Wmk. 120 ***Perf. 13½x14***

Chalk-surfaced Paper

61	A24 1m olive brown	1.50	*3.00*
62	A25 2m dp green	9.00	4.75
63	A25 2m red ('22)	6.00	2.50
64	A26 3m orange	9.00	6.00
65	A27 4m green ('22)	8.00	*6.50*
66	A28 5m lake	7.00	1.75
67	A28 5m pink	14.00	.25
68	A29 10m dp blue	12.00	.70
69	A29 10m lake ('22)	3.50	.70
70	A34 15m indigo ('22)	10.00	.30
71	A35 15m indigo ('22)	40.00	5.00

Perf. 14

72	A30 20m olive green	12.50	.40
73	A31 50m maroon	10.00	1.25
74	A32 100m black	95.00	7.50
	Nos. 61-74 (14)	237.50	40.60

For overprints see Nos. O28-O29.

Independent Kingdom

Stamps of 1921-22 Overprinted

1922, Oct. 10

78	A24 1m olive brown	1.50	1.10
a.	Inverted overprint	475.00	450.00
b.	Double overprint	225.00	—
79	A25 2m red	1.10	.65
a.	Double overprint	225.00	—
80	A26 3m orange	2.25	1.10
81	A27 4m green	1.50	1.00
b.	Inverted overprint	225.00	—
82	A28 5m pink	2.75	.25
83	A29 10m lake	2.75	.25
84	A34 15m indigo	5.75	1.10
85	A35 15m indigo	4.50	1.10

Perf. 14

86	A30 20m olive green	6.00	1.10
a.	Inverted overprint	200.00	—
b.	Double overprint	300.00	—
87	A31 50m maroon	9.00	1.10
a.	Inverted overprint	400.00	500.00
88	A32 100m black	22.50	1.25
a.	Inverted overprint	500.00	160.00
b.	Double overprint	400.00	150.00
	Nos. 78-88 (11)	59.60	10.00

Same Overprint on Nos. 58-59

Wmk. Crescent and Star (119)

90	A32 100m black	90.00	50.00
91	A33 200m plum	30.00	1.60

Proclamation of the Egyptian monarchy.

The overprint signifies "The Egyptian Kingdom, March 15, 1922." It exists in four types, one lithographed and three typographed on Nos. 78-87, but lithographed only on Nos. 88-91.

A36

King Fuad — A37

Wmk. 120

1923-24 Photo. *Perf. 13½*

Size 18x22½mm

92 A36 1m orange .35 .25
93 A36 2m black 1.10 .25
94 A36 3m brown 1.00 .65
a. Imperf., pair 225.00
95 A36 4m yellow grn .90 .50
96 A36 5m orange brn .45 .25
a. Imperf., pair 50.00
97 A36 10m rose 2.00 .25
98 A36 15m ultra 3.25 .25

Perf. 14

Size: 22x28mm

99 A36 20m dk green 6.25 .25
100 A36 50m myrtle grn 10.00 .25
101 A36 100m red violet 25.00 .55
102 A36 200m violet ('24) 45.00 2.00
a. Imperf., pair 325.00
103 A37 £1 ultra & dk vio ('24) 175.00 27.50
a. Imperf., pair 1,750.
Nos. 92-103 (12) 270.30 32.95

For overprints & surcharge see Nos. 167, O31-O38.

Thoth Carving Name of King Fuad — A38

1925, Apr. Litho. *Perf. 11*

105 A38 5m brown 11.00 6.00
106 A38 10m rose 22.50 12.50
107 A38 15m ultra 22.50 14.00
Nos. 105-107 (3) 56.00 32.50

International Geographical Congress, Cairo.
Nos. 106-107 exist with both white and yellowish gum.

Oxen Plowing A39

1926 Wmk. 195 *Perf. 13x13½*

108 A39 5m lt brown 3.00 2.00
109 A39 10m brt rose 2.75 2.00
110 A39 15m dp blue 3.00 2.00
111 A39 50m Prus green 14.00 5.00
112 A39 100m brown vio 22.50 8.00
113 A39 200m brt violet 32.50 17.50
Nos. 108-113 (6) 77.75 36.50

12th Agricultural and Industrial Exhibition at Gezira.
For surcharges see Nos. 115-117.

King Fuad — A40

Perf. 14x14½

1926, Apr. 2 Photo. Wmk. 120

114 A40 50p brn vio & red vio 140.00 22.50

58th birthday of King Fuad.
For overprint and surcharge see Nos. 124, 166.

Nos. 111-113 Surcharged

Perf. 13x13½

1926, Aug. 24 Wmk. 195

115 A39 5m on 50m Prus green 2.50 2.50
116 A39 10m on 100m brown vio 2.50 2.50
117 A39 15m on 200m brt violet 2.50 2.50
a. Double surcharge 300.00
Nos. 115-117 (3) 7.50 7.50

Ship of Hatshepsut — A41

1926, Dec. 9 Litho. *Perf. 13x13½*

118 A41 5m brown & blk 3.00 1.40
119 A41 10m dp red & blk 3.50 1.50
120 A41 15m dp blue & blk 4.00 1.50
Nos. 118-120 (3) 10.50 4.40

International Navigation Congress, Cairo.
For overprints see Nos. 121-123.

Nos. 118-120, 114 Overprinted — a

No. 114 Overprinted — b

1926, Dec. 21

121 A41 (a) 5m 300.00 250.00
122 A41 (a) 10m 300.00 250.00
123 A41 (a) 15m 300.00 250.00

Perf. 14x14½

Wmk. 120

124 A40 (b) 50p 1,600. *875.00*

Inauguration of Port Fuad opposite Port Said.
Nos. 121-123 have a block over "Le Caire" at lower left.
Forgeries of Nos. 121-124 exist.

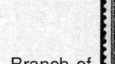

Branch of Cotton A42

Perf. 13x13½

1927, Jan. 25 Wmk. 195

125 A42 5m dk brown & sl grn 1.75 .80
126 A42 10m dp red & slate grn 2.75 1.50
127 A42 15m dp blue & slate grn 3.50 1.50
Nos. 125-127 (3) 8.00 3.80

International Cotton Congress, Cairo.

King Fuad
A43 A44

A45

A46

Type I

Type II

Early printings of the seven values indicated were printed from plates with screens of vertical dots in the vignettes (type I). All values were printed later from plates with screens of diagonal dots (type II).

Perf. 13x13½

1927-37 Wmk. 195 Photo.

Type II

128 A43 1m orange .35 .25
a. Type I 3.25 .60
129 A43 2m black .35 .25
a. Type I 11.00 6.00
130 A43 3m olive brn .35 .55
a. Type I 2.50 1.00
131 A43 3m dp green ('30) .65 .25
132 A43 4m yellow grn 1.25 1.10
a. Type I 65.00 12.50
133 A43 4m brown ('30) 1.10 .55
134 A43 4m dp green ('34) .85 .40
135 A43 5m dk red brn ('29) .95 .40
a. Type I 3.50 1.00
136 A43 10m dk red ('29) 1.40 .25
a. 10m orange red, type I 2.50 .45
137 A43 10m purple ('34) 3.75 .25
138 A43 13m car rose ('32) 1.50 .40
139 A43 15m ultra 2.50 .25
a. Type I 12.00 .65
140 A43 15m dk violet ('34) 5.25 .25
141 A43 20m ultra ('34) 9.25 .30

Perf. 13½x14

142 A44 20m olive grn 3.25 .40
143 A44 20m ultra ('32) 7.50 .25
144 A44 40m olive brn ('32) 4.25 .25
145 A44 50m Prus green 3.50 .25
a. 50m greenish blue 6.00 .35
146 A44 100m brown vio 10.00 .35
a. 100m claret 14.00 .50
147 A44 200m deep violet 9.00 1.25

Printings of Nos. 142, 145 and 146, made in 1929 and later, were from new plates with stronger impressions and darker colors.

Perf. 13x13½

148 A45 500m choc & Prus bl, entirely photo ('32) 100.00 25.00
a. Frame litho, vignette photo 125.00 11.50
149 A46 £1 dk grn & org brn, entirely photo ('37) 125.00 8.25
a. Frame litho, vignette photo 140.00 7.00
Nos. 128-149 (22) 292.00 41.45

Statue of Amenhotep, Son of Hapu — A47

1927, Dec. 29 Photo. *Perf. 13½x13*

150 A47 5m orange brown 1.50 1.00
151 A47 10m copper red 2.00 1.00
152 A47 15m deep blue 3.25 1.00
Nos. 150-152 (3) 6.75 3.00

Statistical Congress, Cairo.

Imhotep — A48

Mohammed Ali Pasha — A49

1928, Dec. 15

153 A48 5m orange brown 1.10 .65
154 A49 10m copper red 1.25 .65

Intl. Congress of Medicine at Cairo and the cent. of the Faculty of Medicine at Cairo.

Prince Farouk — A50

1929, Feb. 11 Litho.

155 A50 5m choc & gray 2.00 1.40
156 A50 10m dull red & gray 3.00 1.50
157 A50 15m ultra & gray 3.00 1.50
158 A50 20m Prus blue & gray 3.50 1.50
Nos. 155-158 (4) 11.50 5.90

Ninth birthday of Prince Farouk.
Nos. 155-158 with black or brown centers are trial color proofs. They were sent to the UPU, but were never placed on sale to the public, although some are known used.

Tomb Fresco at El-Bersheh — A51

1931, Feb. 15 *Perf. 13x13½*

163 A51 5m brown 1.50 1.00
164 A51 10m copper red 2.50 1.75
165 A51 15m dark blue 3.50 2.00
Nos. 163-165 (3) 7.50 4.75

14th Agricultural & Industrial Exhib., Cairo.

Nos. 114 and 103 Surcharged in Black

1932 Wmk. 120 *Perf. 14x14½*

166	A40	50m on 50p	20.00	2.75

Perf. 14

167	A37	100m on £1	250.00	190.00

Locomotive of 1852 — A52

Perf. 13x13½

1933, Jan. 19 Litho. Wmk. 195

168	A52 5m shown		14.00	7.00
169	A52 13m 1859		21.00	12.00
170	A52 15m 1862		21.00	12.00
171	A52 20m 1932		21.00	12.00
	Nos. 168-171 (4)		77.00	43.00

International Railroad Congress, Heliopolis.

Commercial Passenger Airplane — A56

Dornier Do-X A57

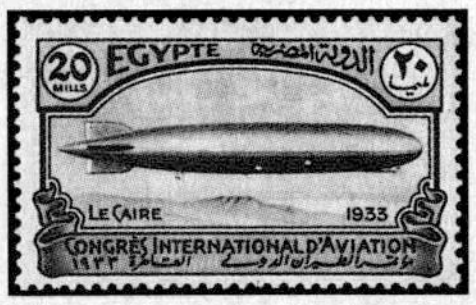

Graf Zeppelin A58

1933, Dec. 20 Photo.

172	A56	5m brown	6.50	3.00
173	A56	10m brt violet	15.00	12.00
174	A57	13m brown car	18.00	15.00
175	A57	15m violet	18.00	13.00
176	A58	20m blue	24.00	20.00
		Nos. 172-176 (5)	81.50	63.00

International Aviation Congress, Cairo.

A59

Khedive Ismail Pasha — A60

1934, Feb. 1 *Perf. 13½*

177	A59	1m dp orange	.60	*1.10*
178	A59	2m black	.60	*1.10*
179	A59	3m brown	.75	*1.25*
180	A59	4m blue green	1.25	.40
181	A59	5m red brown	1.40	.25
182	A59	10m violet	2.50	.35
183	A59	13m copper red	4.00	2.25
184	A59	15m dull violet	4.50	1.75
185	A59	20m ultra	3.00	.40
186	A59	50m Prus blue	9.50	.65
187	A59	100m olive grn	9.50	1.25
188	A59	200m dp violet	75.00	7.25

Perf. 13½x13

189	A60	50p brown	225.00	90.00
190	A60	£1 Prus blue	400.00	150.00
		Nos. 177-190 (14)	737.60	258.00

10th Congress of UPU, Cairo.

King Fuad — A61

1936-37 *Perf. 13½*

191	A61	1m dull orange	.55	*.90*
192	A61	2m black	1.75	.25
193	A61	4m dk green	2.00	.25
194	A61	5m chestnut	1.40	.55
195	A61	10m purple ('37)	2.50	.35
196	A61	15m brown violet	2.75	.50
197	A61	20m sapphire	3.25	.35
		Nos. 191-197 (7)	14.20	3.15

Entrance to Agricultural Building — A62

Agricultural Building — A63

Design: 15m, 20m, Industrial Building.

1936, Feb. 15 *Perf. 13½x13*

198	A62	5m brown	1.75	1.00

Perf. 13x13½

199	A63	10m violet	2.00	1.10
200	A63	13m copper red	3.25	2.25
201	A63	15m dark violet	1.75	1.25
202	A63	20m blue	3.75	2.25
		Nos. 198-202 (5)	12.50	7.85

15th Agricultural & Industrial Exhib., Cairo.

Signing of Treaty — A65

1936, Dec. 22 *Perf. 11*

203	A65	5m brown	.80	.80
204	A65	15m dk violet	1.00	1.00
205	A65	20m sapphire	1.75	1.75
		Nos. 203-205 (3)	3.55	3.55

Signing of Anglo-Egyptian Treaty, Aug. 26, 1936.

King Farouk — A66

Medal for Montreux Conf. — A67

1937-44 Wmk. 195 *Perf. 13x13½*

206	A66	1m brown org	.30	.25
207	A66	2m vermilion	.30	.25
208	A66	3m brown	.30	.25
209	A66	4m green	.30	.25
210	A66	5m red brown	.50	.25
211	A66	6m lt yel grn ('40)	.60	.25
212	A66	10m purple	.30	.25
213	A66	13m rose car	.60	.35
214	A66	15m dk vio brn	.50	.25
215	A66	20m blue	.75	.35
216	A66	20m lil gray ('44)	.75	.25
		Nos. 206-216 (11)	5.20	2.95

For overprints see Nos. 301, 303, 345, 348, 360E, N3, N6, N8, N22, N25, N27.

1937, Oct. 15 *Perf. 13½x13*

217	A67	5m red brown	.75	.55
218	A67	15m dk violet	1.25	1.10
219	A67	20m sapphire	1.50	1.25
		Nos. 217-219 (3)	3.50	2.90

Intl. Treaty signed at Montreux, Switzerland, under which foreign privileges in Egypt were to end in 1949.

Eye of Ré — A68

1937, Dec. 8 *Perf. 13x13½*

220	A68	5m brown	.90	.80
221	A68	15m dk violet	1.00	.90
222	A68	20m sapphire	1.25	1.00
		Nos. 220-222 (3)	3.15	2.70

15th Ophthalmological Congress, Cairo, December, 1937.

King Farouk, Queen Farida — A69

1938, Jan. 20 *Perf. 11*

223	A69	5m red brown	6.50	5.00

Royal wedding of King Farouk and Farida Zulficar.

Inscribed: "11 Fevrier 1938"

1938, Feb. 11

224	A69	£1 green & sepia	200.00	*150.00*

King Farouk's 18th birthday.

Cotton Picker — A70

1938, Jan. 26 *Perf. 13½x13*

225	A70	5m red brown	.75	.75
226	A70	15m dk violet	2.25	1.50
227	A70	20m sapphire	2.00	1.75
		Nos. 225-227 (3)	5.00	4.00

18th International Cotton Congress at Cairo.

Pyramids of Giza and Colossus of Thebes A71

1938, Feb. 1 *Perf. 13x13½*

228	A71	5m red brown	1.40	1.00
229	A71	15m dk violet	2.00	1.25
230	A71	20m sapphire	2.25	1.25
		Nos. 228-230 (3)	5.65	3.50

Intl. Telecommunication Conf., Cairo.

Branch of Hydnocarpus — A72

1938, Mar. 21 *Perf. 13x13½*

231	A72	5m red brown	1.25	1.25
232	A72	15m dk violet	1.75	1.25
233	A72	20m sapphire	1.75	1.25
		Nos. 231-233 (3)	4.75	3.75

International Leprosy Congress, Cairo.

King Farouk and Pyramids — A73

King Farouk

A74 A75

Backgrounds: 40m, Hussan Mosque. 50m, Cairo Citadel. 100m, Aswan Dam. 200m, Cairo University.

1939-46 Photo. *Perf. 14x13½*

234	A73	30m gray	.75	.25
a.		30m slate gray	.75	.25
234B	A73	30m ol grn ('46)	.80	.25
235	A73	40m dk brown	.85	.25
236	A73	50m Prus green	1.00	.25
237	A73	100m brown vio	1.40	.25
238	A73	200m dk violet	5.00	.25

Perf. 13½x13

239	A74	50p green & sep	11.00	3.25
240	A75	£1 dp bl & dk brn	26.00	6.00
		Nos. 234-240 (8)	46.80	10.75

For £1 with A77 portrait, see No. 269D. See Nos. 267-269D. For overprints see Nos. 310-314, 316, 355-358, 360, 363-364, N13-N19, N32-N38.

Catalogue values for unused stamps in this section, from this point to the end of the section, are for Never Hinged items.

King Fuad — A76

1944, Apr. 28 *Perf. 13½x13*

241	A76	10m dk violet	.50	.25

8th anniv. of the death of King Fuad.

King Farouk — A77

1944-50 Wmk. 195 *Perf. 13x13½*

242	A77	1m yellow brn ('45)	.45	.25
243	A77	2m red org ('45)	.45	.25
244	A77	3m sepia ('46)	1.00	1.00
245	A77	4m dp green ('45)	.45	.25
246	A77	5m red brown ('46)	.45	.25
247	A77	10m dp violet	.45	.25
247A	A77	13m rose red ('50)	12.00	4.25
248	A77	15m dk violet ('45)	1.25	.25
249	A77	17m olive grn	1.25	.25
250	A77	20m dk gray ('45)	1.40	.25
251	A77	22m dp blue ('45)	1.40	.25
		Nos. 242-251 (11)	20.55	7.50

For overprints see Nos. 299-300, 302, 304-309, 343-344, 346-347, 349-354, 360B, 361-362, N1-N2, N4-N5, N7, N9-N12, N20-N21, N23-N24, N26, N28-N31.

King Farouk — A78

Khedive Ismail Pasha — A79

1945, Feb. 10 *Perf. 13½x13*

252	A78	10m deep violet	.40	.25

25th birthday of King Farouk.

1945, Mar. 2 Photo.

253	A79	10m dark olive	.35	.25

50th anniv. of death of Khedive Ismail Pasha.

Flags of Arab Nations — A80

1945, July 29

254	A80	10m violet	.35	.25
255	A80	22m dp yellow grn	.45	.25

League of Arab Nations Conference, Cairo, Mar. 22, 1945.

Flags of Egypt and Saudi Arabia A81

Perf. 13x13½

1946, Jan. 10 Wmk. 195

256	A81	10m dp yellow grn	.35	.25

Visit of King Ibn Saud, Jan. 1946.

Citadel, Cairo A82

1946, Aug. 9

257	A82	10m yel brn & dp yel grn	.40	.25

Withdrawal of British troops from Cairo Citadel, Aug. 9, 1946.

King Farouk and Inchas Palace, Cairo A83

2m, Prince Abdullah, Yemen. 3m, Pres. Bechara el-Khoury, Lebanon. 4m, King Abdul Aziz ibn Saud, Saudi Arabia. 5m, King Faisal II, Iraq. 10m, Amir Abdullah ibn Hussein, Jordan. 15m, Pres. Shukri el Kouatly, Syria.

1946, Nov. 9

258	A83	1m dp yellow grn	.60	.25
259	A83	2m sepia	.60	.25
260	A83	3m deep blue	.60	.25
261	A83	4m brown orange	.60	.25
262	A83	5m brown red	.60	.25
263	A83	10m dark gray	.75	.25
264	A83	15m deep violet	.75	.25
		Nos. 258-264 (7)	4.50	1.75

Arab League Cong. at Cairo, May 28, 1946.

Parliament Building, Cairo — A84

1947, Apr. 7 Photo.

265	A84	10m green	.35	.25

36th conf. of the Interparliamentary Union, Apr. 1947.

Raising Egyptian Flag over Kasr-el-Nil Barracks — A85

1947, May 6 *Perf. 13½x13*

266	A85	10m dp plum & yel grn	.40	.25

Withdrawal of British troops from the Nile Delta.

Farouk Types 1939 Redrawn and

King Farouk — A85a

1947-51 Wmk. 195 *Perf. 14x13½*

267	A73	30m olive green	.75	.25
268	A73	40m dk brown	.60	.25
269	A73	50m Prus grn ('48)	.90	.25
269A	A73	100m dk brn vio ('49)	6.00	.90
269B	A73	200m dk violet ('49)	14.00	1.40

Perf. 13½x13

269C	A85a	50p green & sep ('51)	27.50	9.50
269D	A75	£1 dp bl & dk brn ('50)	37.50	3.75
		Nos. 267-269D (7)	87.25	16.30

The king faces slightly to the left and clouds have been added in the sky on Nos. 267-269B. Backgrounds as in 1939-46 issue. Portrait on £1 as on type A77.

For overprints see Nos. 315, 359.

Field and Branch of Cotton — A86

Perf. 13½x13

1948, Apr. 1 Wmk. 195

270	A86	10m olive green	.65	.25

Intl. Cotton Cong. held at Cairo in Apr. 1948.

Map and Infantry Column — A87

1948, June 15 *Perf. 11½x11*

271	A87	10m green	1.40	.25

Arrival of Egyptian troops at Gaza, 5/15/48.

Ibrahim Pasha (1789-1848) — A88

1948, Nov. 10 *Perf. 13x13½*

272	A88	10m brn red & dp grn	.40	.25

Statue, "The Nile" A89

Protection of Industry and Agriculture — A90

Perf. 13x13½

1949, Mar. 1 Photo. Wmk. 195

273	A89	1m dk green	.40	.25
274	A89	10m purple	1.00	.25
275	A89	17m crimson	1.00	.25
276	A89	22m deep blue	1.00	.45

Perf. 11½x11

277	A90	30m dk brown	1.50	.60
		Nos. 273-277 (5)	4.90	1.80

Souvenir Sheets

Photo. & Litho.

Imperf

278	Sheet of 4	3.75	3.75
a.	A89 1m red brown	.75	.75
b.	A89 10m dark brown	.75	.75
c.	A89 17m brown orange	.75	.75
d.	A89 22m dark Prussian green	.75	.75
279	Sheet of 2	3.75	3.75
a.	A90 10m violet gray	1.60	1.60
b.	A90 30m red orange	1.60	1.60

16th Agricultural & Industrial Expo., Cairo.

Mohammed Ali and Map — A93

Perf. 11½x11

1949, Aug. 2 Photo. Wmk. 195

280	A93	10m orange brn & grn	.60	.25

Centenary of death of Mohammed Ali.

Globe — A94

1949, Oct. 9 *Perf. 13½x13*

281	A94	10m rose brown	1.00	.60
282	A94	22m violet	2.00	.90
283	A94	30m dull blue	2.75	1.20
		Nos. 281-283 (3)	5.75	2.70

75th anniv. of the UPU.

Scales of Justice A95

1949, Oct. 14 *Perf. 13x13½*

284	A95	10m deep olive green	.40	.25

End of the Mixed Judiciary System, 10/14/49.

Desert Scene A96

1950, Dec. 27

285	A96	10m violet & red brn	.90	.75

Opening of the Fuad I Institute of the Desert.

Fuad I University A97

1950, Dec. 27

286	A97	22m dp green & claret	.90	.75

Founding of Fuad I University, 25th anniv.

Globe and Khedive Ismail Pasha A98

1950, Dec. 27

287 A98 30m claret & dp grn .90 .75

75th anniv. of Royal Geographic Society of Egypt.

Picking Cotton — A99

1951, Feb. 24

290 A99 10m olive green .40 .35

International Cotton Congress, 1951.

King Farouk and Queen Narriman — A100

1951, May 6 Photo. *Perf. 11x11½*

291 A100 10m green & red brn 3.00 2.25
a. Souvenir sheet 17.50 *19.00*

Marriage of King Farouk and Narriman Sadek, May 6, 1951.

Stadium Entrance A101

Arms of Alexandria and Olympic Emblem — A102

King Farouk A103

1951, Oct. 5 *Perf. 13x13½, 13½x13*

292 A101 10m brown 1.10 1.10
293 A102 22m dp green 1.40 1.40
294 A103 30m blue & dp grn 1.40 1.40
a. Souvenir sheet of 3, #292-294 14.00 *16.00*
Nos. 292-294 (3) 3.90 3.90

Issued to publicize the first Mediterranean Games, Alexandria, Oct. 5-20, 1951.

Winged Figure and Map — A105

Designs: 22m, King Farouk and Map. 30m, King Farouk and Flag.

Dated "16 Oct. 1951"

1952, Feb. 11 *Perf. 13½x13*

296 A105 10m dp green .75 .40
297 A105 22m plum & dp grn 1.00 .75
298 A105 30m green & brown 1.25 .95
a. Souvenir sheet of 3, #296-298 14.00 14.00
Nos. 296-298 (3) 3.00 2.10

Abrogation of the Anglo-Egyptian treaty.

Stamps of 1937-51 Overprinted in Various Colors

Perf. 13x13½

1952, Jan. 17 Wmk. 195

299 A77 1m yellow brown .85 .25
300 A77 2m red org (Bl) .35 .25
301 A66 3m brown (Bl) .35 .50
302 A77 4m dp green (RV) .35 .25
303 A66 6m lt yel grn (RV) 1.25 1.25
304 A77 10m dp vio (C) .45 .25
305 A77 13m rose red (Bl) 1.75 1.60
306 A77 15m dk violet (C) 2.75 1.75
307 A77 17m olive grn (C) 2.00 .35
308 A77 20m dk gray (RV) 1.60 .35
309 A77 22m dp blue (C) 3.00 3.00

No. 244, the 3m sepia, exists with this overprint but was not regularly issued or used.

Same Overprint, 24½mm Wide, on Nos. 267 to 269B

310 A73 30m olive grn (DkBl) 3.75 .25
a. Black overprint 2.25 1.00
311 A73 40m dk brown (G) .90 .25
312 A73 50m Prus grn (C) 1.75 .25
313 A73 100m dk brn vio (C) 3.00 .50
314 A73 200m dk violet (C) 15.00 2.25

Same Overprint, 19mm Wide, on Nos. 269C-269D

315 A85a 50p grn & sep (C) 25.00 8.00
316 A75 £1 dp bl & dk brn (Bl) 45.00 9.00
Nos. 299-316 (18) 109.10 30.30

The overprint translates: King of Egypt and the Sudan, Oct. 16, 1951.

Overprints in colors other than as listed are color trials.

Egyptian Flag — A106

Perf. 13½x13

1952, May 6 Photo. Wmk. 195

317 A106 10m org yel, dp bl & dp grn 1.00 .25
a. Souvenir sheet of 1 7.50 5.25

Issued to commemorate the birth of Crown Prince Ahmed Fuad, Jan. 16, 1952.

"Dawn of New Era" A107

Symbolical of Egypt Freed — A108

Designs: 10m, "Egypt" with raised sword. 22m, Citizens marching with flag.

Perf. 13x13½, 13½x13

1952, Nov. 23

Dated: "23 Juillet 1952"

318 A107 4m dp green & org .35 .25
319 A107 10m dp grn & cop brn .35 .75
320 A108 17m brn org & dp grn .75 .90
321 A108 22m choc & dp grn 1.25 .60
Nos. 318-321 (4) 2.70 2.50

Change of government, July 23, 1952.

Republic

Farmer A109

Soldier A110

Mosque of Sultan Hassan — A111

Queen Nefertiti — A112

1953-56 *Perf. 13x13½*

322 A109 1m red brown .50 .25
323 A109 2m dk lilac .35 .25
324 A109 3m brt blue .50 .45
325 A109 4m dk green .35 .25
326 A110 10m dk brown *("Defence")* .40 .40
327 A110 10m dk brown *("Defense")* .80 .25
328 A110 15m gray .55 .25
329 A110 17m dk grnsh blue .75 .25
330 A110 20m purple .35 .25

Perf. 13½

331 A111 30m dull green .35 .25
332 A111 32m brt blue .90 .25
333 A111 35m violet ('55) 1.10 .25
334 A111 37m gldn brn ('56) 1.75 .60
335 A111 40m red brown .90 .25
336 A111 50m violet brn 1.75 .25
337 A112 100m henna brn 2.75 .30
338 A112 200m dk grnsh blue 4.50 .75
339 A112 500m purple 12.00 1.75
340 A112 £1 dk grn, blk & red 22.50 3.25
Nos. 322-340 (19) 53.05 10.50

Nos. 327-330 are inscribed "Defense."

See No. 490. For overprints and surcharges see Nos. 460, 500, N44-N56, N72.

Stamps of 1939-51 Overprinted in Black

1953 *Perf. 13x13½, 13½x13*

343 A77 1m yellow brn .35 .25
344 A77 2m red orange .35 .25
345 A66 3m brown .75 .75
346 A77 3m sepia .35 .25
347 A77 4m dp green .35 .25
348 A66 6m lt yellow grn .35 .25
349 A77 10m dp violet .35 .25
350 A77 13m rose red 1.00 1.00
351 A77 15m dk violet .75 .25
352 A77 17m olive grn .75 .25
353 A77 20m dk gray .90 .25
354 A77 22m deep blue 1.25 .25
355 A73 30m ol grn (#267) .75 .35
356 A73 50m Prus grn (#269) 1.20 .35
357 A73 100m dk brn vio (#269A) 2.00 .75
358 A73 200m dk violet (#269B) 7.50 1.60
359 A85a 50p grn & sepia 19.00 7.00
360 A75 £1 dp bl & dk brn (#269D) 24.00 4.75
Nos. 343-360 (18) 61.95 19.05

No. 206 with this overprint is a forgery.

Same Overprint on Nos. 300, 303-305, 311 and 314

360B A77 2m red orange .40 .25
360E A66 6m lt yel grn *35.00*
361 A77 10m dp violet 4.00 4.00
362 A77 13m rose red 1.25 .75
363 A73 40m dk brown 6.00 .75
364 A73 200m dk violet 4.00 .90
Nos. 360B,361-364 (5) 15.65 6.65

Practically all values of Nos. 343-364 exist with double overprint. Other values of the 1952 overprinted issue are known only with counterfeit bars.

Symbols of Electronic Progress A113

1953, Nov. 23 Photo. *Perf. 13x13½*

365 A113 10m brt blue .75 .50

Electronics Exposition, Cairo, Nov. 23.

Crowd Acclaiming the Republic — A114

Design: 30m, Crowd, flag and eagle.

Perf. 13½x13

1954, June 18 Wmk. 195

366 A114 10m brown .55 .25
367 A114 30m deep blue .90 .60

Proclamation of the republic, 1st anniv.

Farmer — A115

1954-55 *Perf. 13x13½*

368 A115 1m red brown .35 .25
369 A115 2m dark lilac .35 .25
370 A115 3m brt blue .35 .25
371 A115 4m dk green ('55) 1.25 .95
372 A115 5m dp car ('55) .35 .25
Nos. 368-372 (5) 2.65 1.95

For overprints see Nos. N39-N43.

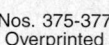

Egyptian Flag, Map — A116

Design: 35m, Bugler, soldier and map.

1954, Nov. 4 *Perf. 13½x13*

373 A116 10m rose vio & grn .50 .30
374 A116 35m ver, blk & bl grn .80 .70

Agreement of Oct. 19, 1954, with Great Britain for the evacuation of the Suez Canal zone by British troops.

Arab Postal Union Issue

Globe — A117

1955, Jan. 1

375 A117 5m yellow brn .60 .30
376 A117 10m green .60 .50
377 A117 37m violet 1.25 .95
Nos. 375-377 (3) 2.45 1.75

Founding of the Arab Postal Union, 7/1/54.
For overprints see Nos. 381-383.

Paul P. Harris and Rotary Emblem — A118

35m, Globe, wings and Rotary emblem.

Perf. 13½x13

1955, Feb. 23 **Wmk. 195**

378 A118 10m claret 1.10 .35
379 A118 35m blue 1.50 .75

50th anniv. of the founding of Rotary Intl.

Nos. 375-377 Overprinted

1955, Nov. 1

381 A117 5m yellow brown 1.00 .80
382 A117 10m green 1.25 1.00
383 A117 37m violet 1.75 1.25
Nos. 381-383 (3) 4.00 3.05

Arab Postal Union Congress held at Cairo, Mar. 15, 1955.

Map of Africa and Asia, Olive Branch and Rings A119

Globe, Torch, Dove and Olive Branch — A120

1956, July 29 *Perf. 13x13½, 13½x13*

384 A119 10m chestnut & green .40 .25
385 A120 35m org yel & dull pur 1.00 .70

Afro-Asian Festival, Cairo, July, 1956.

Map of Suez Canal and Ship — A121

Perf. 11½x11

1956, Sept. 26 **Wmk. 195**

386 A121 10m blue & buff .60 .60

Nationalization of the Suez Canal, July 26, 1956. See No. 393.

Queen Nefertiti — A122

1956, Oct. 15 *Perf. 13½x13*

387 A122 10m dark green 1.40 1.25

Intl. Museum Week (UNESCO), Oct. 8-14.

Egyptians Defending Port Said — A123

1956, Dec. 20 Litho. *Perf. 11x11½*

388 A123 10m brown violet 1.00 .75

Honoring the defenders of Port Said.

No. 388 Overprinted in Carmine Rose

1957, Jan. 14

389 A123 10m brown violet 1.00 .60

Evacuation of Port Said by British and French troops, Dec. 22, 1956.

Old and New Trains A124

1957, Jan. 30 Photo. *Perf. 13x13½*

390 A124 10m red violet & gray 1.10 1.00

100th anniv. of the Egyptian Railway System (in 1956).

Mother and Children A125

1957, Mar. 21

391 A125 10m crimson .90 .35

Mother's Day, 1957.

Battle Scene A126

Perf. 13x13½

1957, Mar. 28 **Wmk. 195**

392 A126 10m bright blue .40 .35

Victory over the British at Rosetta, 150th anniv.

Type of 1956; New Inscriptions in English

1957, Apr. 15 *Perf. 11½x11*

393 A121 100m blue & yel grn 1.60 1.25

Reopening of the Suez Canal.
No. 393 is inscribed: "Nationalisation of Suez Canal Co. Guarantees Freedom of Navigation" and "Reopening 1957."

Map of Gaza Strip — A127

Perf. 13½x13

1957, May 4 Photo. **Wmk. 195**

394 A127 10m Prus blue 1.50 .70

"Gaza Part of Arab Nation."
For overprint see No. N57.

Al Azhar University A128

1957, Apr. 27 *Perf. 13x13½*

New Arabic Date in Red

395 A128 10m brt violet .50 .40
396 A128 15m violet brown .80 .60
397 A128 20m dark gray 1.30 .90
Nos. 395-397 (3) 2.60 1.90

Millenary of Al Azhar University, Cairo.

Shepheard's Hotel, Cairo — A129

Perf. 13½x13

1957, July 20 **Wmk. 195**

398 A129 10m brt violet .70 .45

Reopening of Shepheard's Hotel, Cairo.

Gate, Palace and Eagle — A130

Perf. 11½x11

1957, July 22 **Wmk. 315**

399 A130 10m yellow & brown .70 .40

First meeting of New National Assembly.

Amasis I in Battle of Avaris, 1580 B.C. A131

Designs: No. 401, Sultan Saladin, Hitteen, 1187 A. D. No. 402, Louis IX of France in chains, Mansourah, 1250, vert. No. 403, Map of Middle East, Ein Galout, 1260. No. 404, Port Said, 1956.

Inscribed: "Egypt Tomb of Aggressors 1957"

1957, July 26 *Perf. 13x13½, 13½x13*

400 A131 10m carmine rose 1.50 1.50
401 A131 10m dk olive grn 1.50 1.50
402 A131 10m brown violet 1.50 1.50
403 A131 10m grnsh blue 1.50 1.50
404 A131 10m yellow brown 1.50 1.50
Nos. 400-404 (5) 7.50 7.50

No. 400 exists with Wmk. 195.

Ahmed Arabi Speaking to the Khedive A132

Perf. 13x13½

1957, Sept. 16 **Wmk. 315**

405 A132 10m deep violet .80 .25

75th anniversary of Arabi Revolution.

Hafez Ibrahim — A133

Portrait: No. 407, Ahmed Shawky.

1957, Oct. 14 *Perf. 13½x13*

406 A133 10m dull red brn	.30	.25
407 A133 10m olive green	.30	.25
a. Pair, #406-407	1.00	*1.00*

25th anniv. of the deaths of Hafez Ibrahim and Ahmed Shawky, poets.

MiG and Ilyushin Planes A134

Design: No. 409, Viscount plane.

1957, Dec. 19 *Perf. 13x13½*

408 A134 10m ultra	.70	.50
409 A134 10m green	.70	.50
a. Pair, #408-409	1.60	1.60

25th anniv. of the Egyptian Air Force and of Misrair, the Egyptian airline.

Pyramids, Dove and Globe A135

1957, Dec. 26 **Photo.** **Wmk. 315**

410 A135 5m brown orange	.60	.40
411 A135 10m green	.60	.30
412 A135 15m brt violet	.50	.40
Nos. 410-412 (3)	1.70	1.10

Afro-Asian Peoples Conf., Cairo, 12/26-1/2.

Farmer's Wife A136

Ramses II A137

1957-58 **Wmk. 315** *Perf. 13½*

413 A136 1m blue green ('58)	.30	.25
414 A137 10m violet	.30	.25

"Industry" — A138

1958 **Wmk. 318**

415 A136 1m lt blue green	.30	.25
416 A138 5m brown	.35	.25
417 A137 10m violet	.60	.25
Nos. 413-417 (5)	1.85	1.25

See Nos. 438-444, 474-488, 535. For overprints see Nos. N58-N63, N66-N68, N75, N77-N78.

Cyclists — A139

Perf. 13½x13

1958, Jan. 12 **Wmk. 315**

418 A139 10m lt red brown	.65	.45

5th Intl. Bicycle Race, Egypt, Jan. 12-26.

Mustafa Kamel — A140

1958, Feb. 10 **Photo.** **Wmk. 318**

419 A140 10m blue gray	.80	.25

50th anniversary of the death of Mustafa Kamel, orator and politician.

United Arab Republic

Linked Maps of Egypt and Syria — A141

Perf. 11½x11

1958, Mar. 22 **Wmk. 318**

436 A141 10m yellow & green	.75	.25

Birth of United Arab Republic. See No. C90. See also Syria-UAR Nos. 1 and C1.

Cotton — A142

1958, Apr. 5 *Perf. 13½x13*

437 A142 10m Prussian blue	.35	.25

Intl. Fair for Egyptian Cotton, Apr., 1958.

Types of 1957-58 Inscribed "U.A.R. EGYPT" and

Princess Nofret — A143

Designs: 1m, Farmer's wife. 2m, Ibn-Tulun's Mosque. 4m, 14th century glass lamp (design lacks "1963" of A217). 5m, "Industry" (factories and cogwheel). 10m, Ramses II. 35m, "Commerce" (eagle, ship and cargo).

1958 *Perf. 13½x14*

438 A136 1m crimson	.30	.30
439 A138 2m blue	.25	.25
440 A143 3m dk red brown	.25	.25
441 A217 4m green	.30	.25
442 A138 5m brown	.30	.25
443 A137 10m violet	.85	.30
444 A138 35m lt ultra	3.75	.45
Nos. 438-444 (7)	6.00	2.05

See Nos. 474-488, 532-533, N62-N68, N75-N78.

Qasim Amin — A144

1958, Apr. 23 *Perf. 13½x13*

445 A144 10m deep blue	.60	.25

50th anniversary of the death of Qasim Amin, author of "Emancipation of Women."

Doves, Broken Chain and Globe — A145

1958, June 18

446 A145 10m violet	.60	.25

5th anniv. of the republic and to publicize the struggle of peoples and individuals for freedom.

For overprint see No. N69.

Cement Industry — A146

UAR Flag — A147

Industries: No. 448, Textile. No. 449, Iron & steel. No. 450, Petroleum (Oil). No. 451, Electricity and fertilizers.

Perf. 13½x13

1958, July 23 **Photo.** **Wmk. 318**

447 A146 10m red brown	.40	.25
448 A146 10m blue green	.40	.25
449 A146 10m bright red	.40	.25
450 A146 10m olive green	.40	.25
451 A146 10m dark blue	.40	.25
a. Strip of 5, #447-451	2.75	2.75

Souvenir Sheet

Imperf

452 A147 50m grn, dp car & blk	16.00	14.00

Revolution of July 23, 1952, 6th anniv.

Sayed Darwich A148

Hand Holding Torch, Broken Chain and Flag A149

1958, Sept. 15 *Perf. 13½x13*

453 A148 10m violet brown	.50	.25

35th anniv. of the death of Sayed Darwich, Arab composer.

1958, Oct. 14 **Photo.** **Wmk. 318**

454 A149 10m carmine rose	.40	.25

Establishment of the Republic of Iraq. See Syria-UAR No. 13.

Maps and Cogwheels — A150

1958, Dec. 8 *Perf. 13x13½*

455 A150 10m blue	.50	.25

Issued to publicize the Economic Conference of Afro-Asian Countries, Cairo, Dec. 8.

Ovptd. in Red in English and Arabic in 3 Lines "Industrial and Agricultural Production Fair"

1958, Dec. 9

456 A150 10m lt red brown	.50	.25

Issued to publicize the Industrial and Agricultural Production Fair, Cairo, Dec. 9.

Dr. Mahmoud Azmy and UN Emblem A151

1958, Dec. 10

457 A151 10m dull violet	.45	.25
458 A151 35m green	1.00	.75

10th anniv. of the signing of the Universal Declaration of Human Rights.

For overprints see Nos. N70-N71.

University Building, Sphinx, "Education" and God Thoth — A152

1958, Dec. 21 **Photo.** **Wmk. 318**

459 A152 10m grnsh black	.40	.25

50th anniversary of Cairo University.

No. 337 Surcharged

1959, Jan. 20 **Wmk. 195** *Perf. 13½*

460 A112 55m on 100m henna brn	3.00	.75

For overprint see No. N72.

Emblem A153

1959, Feb. 2 ***Perf. 13x13½***

461 A153 10m lt olive green .35 .25

Afro-Asian Youth Conf., Cairo, Feb. 2.

See Syria UAR issues for stamps of designs A141, A149, A154, A156, A157, A162, A170, A172, A173, A179 with denominations in piasters (p).

Arms of UAR — A154

Perf. 13½x13

1959, Feb. 22 Photo. Wmk. 318

462 A154 10m green, blk & red .35 .25

First anniversary, United Arab Republic.
See Syria UAR No. 17.

Nile Hilton Hotel A155

1959, Feb. 22 ***Perf. 13x13½***

463 A155 10m dark gray .35 .25

Opening of the Nile Hilton Hotel, Cairo.

Globe, Radio and Telegraph A156

1959, Mar. 1

464 A156 10m violet .40 .25

Arab Union of Telecommunications.
See Syria-UAR Nos. C20-C21.

United Arab States Issue

Flags of UAR and Yemen A157

1959, Mar. 8

465 A157 10m sl grn, car & blk .35 .25

First anniversary of United Arab States.
See Syria-UAR No. 16.

Oil Derrick and Pipe Line — A158

Perf. 13½x13

1959, Apr. 16 Litho. Wmk. 318

466 A158 10m lt bl & dk bl .65 .25

First Arab Petroleum Congress, Cairo.

Railroad A159

Designs: No. 468, Bus on highway. No. 469, River barge. No. 470, Ocean liner. No. 471, Telecommunications on map. No. 472, Stamp printing building, Heliopolis. No. 472A, Ship, train, plane and motorcycle mail carrier.

1959, July 23 Photo. ***Perf. 13x13½***

Frame in Gray

467	A159	10m maroon	1.10	.50
468	A159	10m green	1.10	.50
469	A159	10m violet	1.10	.50
470	A159	10m dark blue	1.10	.50
471	A159	10m dull purple	1.10	.50
472	A159	10m scarlet	1.10	.50
		Nos. 467-472 (6)	6.60	3.00

Souvenir Sheet

Imperf

472A A159 50m green & red *12.00 12.00*

No. 472A for the 7th anniv. of the Egyptian revolution of 1952 and was sold only with 5 sets of Nos. 467-472.

Globe, Swallows and Map — A160

1959, Aug. 8 ***Perf. 13½x13***

473 A160 10m maroon .40 .25

Convention of the Assoc. of Arab Emigrants in the US.

Types of 1953-58 without "Egypt" and

St. Simon's Gate, Bosra, Syria — A161

Designs: 1m, Farmer's wife. 2m, Ibn-Tulun's Mosque. 3m, Princess Nofret. 4m, 14th century glass lamp (design lacks "1963" of A217). 5m, "Industry" (factories and cogwheel). 10m, Ramses II. 15m, Omayyad Mosque, Damascus. 20m, Lotus vase, Tutankhamun treasure. 35m, Eagle, ship and cargo. 40m, Scribe statue. 45m, Saladin's citadel, Aleppo. 55m, Eagle, cotton and wheat. 60m, Dam and factory. 100m, Eagle, hand, cotton and grain. 200m, Palmyra ruins, Syria. 500m, Queen Nefertiti, inscribed "UAR" (no ovpt.).

Perf. 13½x14, 14x13½

1959-60 Wmk. 328 Photo.

474	A136	1m	vermilion	.25	.25
475	A138	2m	dp blue ('60)	.25	.25
476	A143	3m	maroon	.25	.25
477	A217	4m	green ('60)	.25	.25
478	A138	5m	black ('60)	.25	.25
479	A137	10m	dk ol grn	.30	.25
480	A138	15m	deep claret	.30	.25
481	A138	20m	crimson ('60)	.90	.25
482	A161	30m	brown vio	.65	.25
483	A138	35m	lt vio bl ('60)	.75	.25
484	A143	40m	sepia	1.10	.25
485	A161	45m	lil gray ('60)	2.25	.35
486	A138	55m	brt blue grn	2.00	.25
487	A138	60m	dp purple ('60)	2.75	.25
488	A138	100m	org & sl grn ('60)	2.25	.30
489	A161	200m	lt blue & mar	4.50	.50
490	A112	500m	dk gray & red ('60)	14.00	1.60
			Nos. 474-490 (17)	33.00	6.00

See Nos. 532-535.

Shield and Cogwheel — A162

Perf. 13½x13

1959, Oct. 20 Photo. Wmk. 328

491 A162 10m brt car rose .35 .25

Issued for Army Day, 1959.
See Syria-UAR No. 32.

Cairo Museum A163

1959, Nov. 18 ***Perf. 13x13½***

492 A163 10m olive gray .40 .25

Centenary of Cairo museum.

Abu Simbel Temple of Ramses II — A164

1959, Dec. 22 ***Perf. 11x11½***

493 A164 10m lt red brn, *pnksh* .70 .30

Issued as propaganda to save historic monuments in Nubia threatened by the construction of Aswan High Dam.

Postrider, 12th Century A165

1960, Jan. 2 ***Perf. 13x13½***

494 A165 10m dark blue .35 .25

Issued for Post Day, Jan. 2.

Hydroelectric Power Station, Aswan Dam — A166

1960, Jan. 9

495 A166 10m violet blk .35 .25

Inauguration of the Aswan Dam hydroelectric power station, Jan. 9.

A167

10m, Arabic and English Description of Aswan High Dam. 35m, Architect's Drawing of Aswan High Dam.

1960, Jan. 9 ***Perf. 11x11½***

496		10m claret	.75	.60
497		35m claret	1.10	.75
a.		A167 Pair, #496-497	2.00	2.00

Start of work on the Aswan High Dam.

Symbols of Agriculture and Industry — A169

Arms and Flag — A170

1960, Jan. 16 ***Perf. 13½x13***

498 A169 10m gray grn & sl grn .35 .25

Industrial and Agricultural Fair, Cairo.

1960, Feb. 22 Photo. Wmk. 328

499 A170 10m green, blk & red .35 .25

2nd anniversary of the proclamation of the United Arab Republic.
See Syria-UAR No. 38.

No. 340 Overprinted in Red

1960 Wmk. 195 ***Perf. 13½***

500 A112 £1 dk grn, blk & red 19.00 4.25

"Art" — A171

Perf. 13½x13

1960, Mar. 1 Wmk. 328

501 A171 10m brown .35 .25

Issued to publicize the 3rd Biennial Exhibition of Fine Arts in Alexandria.

Arab League Center, Cairo A172

1960, Mar. 22 Photo. ***Perf. 13x13½***

502 A172 10m dull grn & blk .35 .25

Opening of Arab League Center and Arab Postal Museum, Cairo.
See Syria-UAR No. 40.

Refugees Pointing to Map of Palestine A173

1960, Apr. 7

503 A173 10m orange ver .55 .30
504 A173 35m Prus blue .80 .65

World Refugee Year, 7/1/59-6/30/60.

See Nos. N73-N74. See also Syria-UAR Nos. 43-44.

Weight Lifter — A174

Stadium, Cairo — A175

Sports: No. 506, Basketball. No. 507, Soccer. No. 508, Fencing. No. 509, Rowing. 30m, Steeplechase, horiz. 35m, Swimming, horiz.

Perf. 13½x13

1960, July 23 Photo. Wmk. 328

505 A174	5m gray	.60	.30
506 A174	5m brown	.60	.30
507 A174	5m dp claret	.60	.30
508 A174	10m brt carmine	.60	.30
509 A174	10m gray green	.60	.30
a.	Vert. or horiz. strip, #505-509	3.75	
510 A174	30m purple	.85	.50
511 A174	35m dark blue	1.10	.60
	Nos. 505-511 (7)	4.95	2.60

Souvenir Sheet

Imperf

512 A175	100m car & brown	3.25	3.25

Nos. 505-511 for the 17th Olympic Games, Rome, Aug. 25-Sept. 11.

Dove and UN Emblem — A176

35m, Lights surrounding UN emblem, horiz.

Perf. 13½x13

1960, Oct. 24 Wmk. 328

513 A176	10m purple	.25	.25
514 A176	35m brt rose	.50	.30

15th anniversary of United Nations.

Abu Simbel Temple of Queen Nefertari — A177

Perf. 11x11½

1960, Nov. 14 Photo. Wmk. 328

515 A177	10m ocher, *buff*	.80	.50

Issued as propaganda to save historic monuments in Nubia and in connection with the UNESCO meeting, Paris, Nov. 14.

Model Post Office A178

1961, Jan. 2 ***Perf. 13x13½***

516 A178	10m brt car rose	.40	.25

Issued for Post Day, Jan. 2.

Eagle, Fasces and Victory Wreath — A179

Wheat and Globe Surrounded by Flags — A180

1961, Feb. 22 ***Perf. 13½x13***

517 A179	10m dull violet	.35	.25

3rd anniversary of United Arab Republic. See Syria-UAR No. 50.

1961, Mar. 21 Wmk. 328

518 A180	10m vermilion	.35	.25

Intl. Agricultural Exhib., Cairo, 3/21-4/20.

Patrice Lumumba and Map A181

Reading Braille and WHO Emblem A182

1961, Mar. 30 ***Perf. 13½x13***

519 A181	10m black	.35	.25

Africa Day, Apr. 15 and 3rd Conf. of Independent African States, Cairo, Mar. 25-31.

1961, Apr. 6 Photo.

520 A182	10m red brown	.35	.25

WHO Day. See Nos. B21, N80.

Tower of Cairo — A183

Arab Woman and Son, Palestine Map — A184

1961, Apr. 11 ***Perf. 13½x13***

521 A183	10m grnsh blue	.35	.25

Opening of the 600-foot Tower of Cairo, on island of Gizireh. See No. C95.

1961, May 15 Wmk. 328

522 A184	10m brt green	.45	.30

Issued for Palestine Day.

See No. N79.

Symbols of Industry and Electricity A185

Chart and Workers — A186

No. 524, New buildings and family. No. 525, Ship, train, bus and radio. No. 526, Dam, cotton and field. No. 527, Hand holding candle and family.

1961, July 23 Photo. ***Perf. 13x13½***

523 A185	10m dp carmine	.65	.30
524 A185	10m brt blue	.65	.30
525 A185	10m dk vio brown	.65	.30
526 A185	35m dk green	.85	.40
527 A185	35m brt purple	.85	.40
	Nos. 523-527 (5)	3.65	1.70

Souvenir Sheet

Imperf

528 A186	100m red brown	4.00	3.75

9th anniv. of the revolution.

Map of Suez Canal and Ships — A187

Perf. 11½x11

1961, July 26 Unwmk.

529 A187	10m olive	.50	.30

Suez Canal Co. nationalization, 5th anniv.

Various Enterprises of Misr Bank — A188

Perf. 13x13½

1961, Aug. 22 Wmk. 328

530 A188	10m red brn, *pnksh*	.35	.25

The 41st anniversary of Misr Bank.

Flag, Ship's Wheel and Battleship — A189

1961, Aug. 29 Photo. ***Perf. 13½x13***

531 A189	10m deep blue	.45	.25

Issued for Navy Day.

Type A136 Redrawn, Type A138, Type A217 and

Eagle of Saladin over Cairo — A190

Designs: 1m, Farmer's wife. 4m, 14th cent. glass lamp. 35m, "Commerce."

1961, Aug. 31 Unwmk. ***Perf. 11½***

532 A136	1m blue	.25	.25
533 A217	4m olive	.25	.25
534 A190	10m purple	.40	.25
535 A138	35m slate blue	.70	.25
	Nos. 532-535 (4)	1.60	1.00

Smaller of two Arabic inscriptions in new positions: 1m, at right above Egyptian numeral; 4m, upward to spot beside waist of lamp; 35m, upper left corner below "UAR." On 4m, "UAR" is 2mm deep instead of 1mm. "Egypt" omitted as in 1959-60.

UN Emblem, Book, Cogwheel, Corn — A191

Design: 35m, Globe and cogwheel, horiz.

Perf. 13½x13

1961, Oct. 24 Photo. Wmk. 328

536 A191	10m black & ocher	.30	.25
537 A191	35m blue grn & brn	.65	.35

UN Technical Assistance Program and 16th anniv. of the UN.

See Nos. N81-N82.

Trajan's Kiosk, Philae — A192

1961, Nov. 4 Unwmk. ***Perf. 11½***

Size: 60x27mm

538 A192	10m dp vio blue	.85	.40

15th anniv. of UNESCO, and to publicize UNESCO's help in safeguarding the monuments of Nubia.

Palette, Brushes, Map of Mediterranean
A193

Atom and Educational Symbols
A194

1961, Dec. 14 Wmk. 328 *Perf. 13½*
539 A193 10m dk red brown .35 .25

Issued to publicize the 4th Biennial Exhibition of Fine Arts in Alexandria.

1961, Dec. 18
540 A194 10m dull purple .35 .25

Issued to publicize Education Day.
See No. N83.

Arms of UAR
A195

1961, Dec. 23 Unwmk. *Perf. 11½*
541 A195 10m brt pink, brt grn & blk .35 .25

Victory Day. See No. N84.

Sphinx at Giza — A196

1961, Dec. 27 *Perf. 11x11½*
542 A196 10m black .55 .35

Issued to publicize the "Sound and Light" Project, the installation of floodlights and sound equipment at the site of the Pyramids and Sphinx.

Post Office Printing Plant, Nasser City
A197

1962, Jan. 2 Photo. *Perf. 11½x11*
543 A197 10m dk brown .40 .25

Issued for Post Day, Jan. 2.

Map of Africa, King Mohammed V of Morocco and Flags — A198

1962, Jan. 4 *Perf. 11x11½*
544 A198 10m indigo .35 .25

African Charter, Casablanca, 1st anniv.

Girl Scout Saluting and Emblem
A199

Perf. 13x13½
1962, Feb. 22 Wmk. 328
545 A199 10m bright blue .95 .30

Egyptian Girl Scouts' 25th anniversary.

Arab Refugees, Flag and Map — A200

Mother and Child — A201

1962, Mar. 7 *Perf. 13½x13*
546 A200 10m dark slate green .40 .25

5th anniv. of the liberation of the Gaza Strip.
See No. N85.

1962, Mar. 21 Photo.
547 A201 10m dk violet brn .40 .25

Issued for Arab Mother's Day, Mar. 21.

Map of Africa and Post Horn — A202

1962, Apr. 23 Wmk. 328
548 A202 10m crimson & ocher .40 .30
549 A202 50m dp blue & ocher .80 .55

Establishment of African Postal Union.

Cadets on Parade and Academy Emblem
A203

1962, June 18 *Perf. 13x13½*
550 A203 10m green .35 .25

Egyptian Military Academy, 150th anniv.

Malaria Eradication Emblem — A204

Theodor Bilharz — A205

1962, June 20 *Perf. 13½x13*
551 A204 10m dk brown & red .25 .25
552 A204 35m dk green & blue .70 .50

WHO drive to eradicate malaria.

See Nos. N87-N88.

1962, June 24 *Perf. 11x11½*
553 A205 10m brown orange .55 .25

Dr. Theodor Bilharz (1825-1862), German physician who first described bilharziasis, an endemic disease in Egypt.

Patrice Lumumba and Map of Africa — A206

Hand on Charter — A207

1962, July 1 Photo. Wmk. 342
554 A206 10m rose & red .35 .25

Issued in memory of Patrice Lumumba (1925-61), Premier of Congo.

1962, July 10 *Perf. 11x11½*
555 A207 10m brt blue & dk brn .35 .25

Proclamation of the National Charter.

"Birth of the Revolution"
A208

Symbolic Designs: No. 557, Proclamation (Scroll and book). No. 558, Agricultural Reform (Farm and crescent). No. 559, Bandung Conference (Dove, globe and olive branch). No. 560, Birth of UAR (Eagle and flag). No. 561, Industrialization (cogwheel, factory, ship and bus). No. 562, Aswan High Dam. No. 563, Social Revolution (Modern buildings and emblem). 100m, Arms of UAR, emblems of Afro-Asian and African countries and UN.

1962, July 23 *Perf. 11½*

556	A208	10m	brn, dk red brn & pink	.40	.30
557	A208	10m	dk blue & sepia	.40	.30
558	A208	10m	sepia & brt bl	.40	.30
559	A208	10m	olive & dk ultra	.40	.30
560	A208	10m	grn, blk & red	.40	.30
561	A208	10m	brn org & indigo	.40	.30
562	A208	10m	brn org & vio blk	.40	.30
563	A208	10m	orange & blk	.40	.30
			Nos. 556-563 (8)	3.20	2.40

Souvenir Sheets

Perf. 11½

564 A208 100m grn, pink, red & blk 2.75 2.50

10th anniv. of the revolution.
No. 564 exists imperf. Same value.

Mahmoud Moukhtar, Museum and Sculpture
A209

1962, July 24 *Perf. 11½x11*
565 A209 10m lt vio bl & olive .40 .25

Opening of the Moukhtar Museum, Island of Gezireh. The sculpture is "La Vestale de Secrets" by Moukhtar.

Flag of Algeria and Map of Africa Showing Algeria — A210

1962, Aug. 15 *Perf. 11x11½*
566 A210 10m multicolored .35 .25

Algeria's independence, July 1, 1962.

Rocket, Arms of UAR and Atom Symbol — A211

1962, Sept. 1 Photo. Wmk. 342
567 A211 10m brt grn, red & blk .45 .25

Launching of UAR rockets.

Rifle and Target — A212

Map of Africa, Table Tennis Paddle, Net and Ball — A213

1962, Sept. 18 *Perf. 11½*

568	A212	5m	green, blk & red	.55	.45
569	A213	5m	green, blk & red	.55	.45
a.			Pair, #568-569	1.25	1.25
570	A212	10m	bister, bl & dk grn	.65	.55
571	A213	10m	bister, bl & dk grn	.65	.55
a.			Pair, #570-571	1.50	1.50
572	A212	35m	dp ultra, red & blk	1.50	1.50
573	A213	35m	dp ultra, red & blk	1.50	1.50
a.			Pair, #572-573	3.25	3.25
			Nos. 568-573 (6)	5.40	5.00

38th World Shooting Championships and the 1st African Table Tennis Tournament. Types A212 and A213 are printed se-tenant at the base.

Dag Hammarskjold and UN Emblem — A214

Perf. 11½x11
1962, Oct. 24 Photo. Wmk. 342
Portrait in Slate Blue

574	A214	5m	deep lilac	.65	.25
575	A214	10m	olive	.75	.25
576	A214	35m	deep ultra	1.10	.50
			Nos. 574-576 (3)	2.50	1.00

Dag Hammarskjold, Secretary General of the UN, 1953-61, and 17th anniv. of the UN.
See Nos. N89-N91.

Queen Nefertari Crowned by Isis and Hathor — A215

1962, Oct. 31 *Perf. 11½*

577 A215 10m blue & ocher 1.25 .40

Issued to publicize the UNESCO campaign to safeguard the monuments of Nubia.

Jet Trainer, Hawker Hart Biplane and College Emblem
A216

1962, Nov. 2 *Perf. 11½x11*

578 A216 10m bl, dk bl & crim .40 .25

25th anniversary of Air Force College.

14th Century Glass Lamp and "1963" — A217

Yemen Flag and Hand with Torch — A218

1963, Feb. 20 *Perf. 11x11½*

579 A217 4m dk brn, grn & car .35 .25

Issued for use on greeting cards.
See Nos. 441, 477, 533, N76, N92. For overprint see No. N65.

1963, Mar. 14 Photo. Wmk. 342

580 A218 10m olive & brt car .45 .25

Establishment of Yemen Arab Republic.

Tennis Player, Pyramids and Globe A219

Perf. 11½x11

1963, Mar. 20 Unwmk.

581 A219 10m gray, blk & brn .75 .30

Intl. Lawn Tennis Championships, Cairo.

Cow, UN and FAO Emblems A220

Designs: 10m, Corn, wheat and emblems, vert. 35m, Wheat, corn and emblems.

Perf. 11½x11, 11x11½

1963, Mar. 21 Wmk. 342

582 A220 5m violet & dp org .45 .30
583 A220 10m ultra & yel .55 .30
584 A220 35m blue, yel & blk .75 .75
Nos. 582-584 (3) 1.75 1.35

FAO "Freedom from Hunger" campaign.
See Nos. N93-N95.

Centenary Emblem — A221

Design: 35m, Globe and emblem.

1963, May 8 Unwmk. *Perf. 11x11½*

585 A221 10m lt blue, red & mar .30 .25
586 A221 35m lt blue & red .85 .85

Centenary of the Red Cross.
See Nos. N96-N97.

Arab Socialist Union Emblem A222

50m, Tools, torch & symbol of National Charter.

Wmk. 342

1963, July 23 Photo. *Perf. 11½*

587 A222 10m slate & rose pink .35 .25

Souvenir Sheets

Perf. 11½

588 A222 50m vio bl & org yel 2.25 2.25

11th anniv. of the revolution and to publicize the Arab Socialist Union.
No. 588 exists imperf. Same value.

Television Station, Cairo, and Screen A223

1963, Aug. 1 *Perf. 11½x11*

589 A223 10m dk blue & yel .35 .25

2nd Intl. Television Festival, Alexandria, 9/1-10.

Queen Nefertari A224

Swimmer and Map of Suez Canal A225

Designs: 10m, Great Hypostyle Hall, Abu Simbel. 35m, Ramses in moonlight.

Wmk. 342

1963, Oct. 1 Photo. *Perf. 11*

Size: 25x42mm (5m, 35m); 28x61mm (10m)

590 A224 5m brt vio blue & yel .65 .40
591 A224 10m gray, blk & red org .75 .45
592 A224 35m org yel & blk 1.60 .85
Nos. 590-592 (3) 3.00 1.70

UNESCO world campaign to save historic monuments in Nubia.
See Nos. N98-N100.

1963, Oct. 15

593 A225 10m blue & sal rose .35 .25

Intl. Suez Canal Swimming Championship.

Ministry of Agriculture — A226

Perf. 11½x11

1963, Nov. 20 Wmk. 342

594 A226 10m multicolored .35 .25

50th anniv. of the Ministry of Agriculture.

Modern Building and Map of Africa and Asia A227

1963, Dec. 7

595 A227 10m multicolored .35 .25

Afro-Asian Housing Congress, Dec. 7-12.

Scales, Globe, UN Emblem A228

1963, Dec. 10

596 A228 5m dk green & yel .30 .25
597 A228 10m blue, gray & blk .35 .25
598 A228 35m rose red, pink & red .85 .45
Nos. 596-598 (3) 1.50 .95

15th anniv. of the Universal Declaration of Human Rights.
See Nos. N101-N103.

Sculpture, Arms of Alexandria and Palette with Flags — A229

1963, Dec. 12 *Perf. 11x11½*

599 A229 10m pale bl, dk bl & brn .35 .25

Issued to publicize the 5th Biennial Exhibition of Fine Arts in Alexandria.

Lion and Nile Hilton Hotel — A230

Vase, 13th Century — A231

Pharaoh Userkaf (5th Dynasty) A232

Designs: 1m, Vase, 14th century. 2m, Ivory headrest. 3m, Pharaonic calcite boat. 4m, Minaret and gate. 5m, Nile and Aswan High Dam. 10m, Eagle of Saladin over pyramids. 15m, Window, Ibn Tulun's mosque. No. 608, Mitwalli Gate, Cairo. 35m, Nefertari. 40m, Tower Hotel. 55m, Sultan Hassan's Mosque. 60m, Courtyard, Al Azhar University. 200m, Head of Ramses II. 500m, Funerary mask of Tutankhamun.

1964-67 Unwmk. Photo. *Perf. 11*

Size: Nos. 608, 612, 19x24mm; others, 24x29mm

600 A231 1m citron & ultra .25 .25
601 A230 2m magenta & bis .25 .25
602 A230 3m sal, org & bl .25 .25
603 A235 4m och, blk & ultra .35 .25
604 A230 5m brn & brt blue .25 .25
a. 5m brown & dark blue .50 .25
605 A231 10m green, dk brn & lt brn .30 .25
606 A230 15m ultra & yel .30 .25
607 A230 20m brn org & blk .90 .25
608 A231 20m lt olive grn ('67) 1.60 .25
609 A231 30m yellow & brown .75 .25
610 A231 35m sal, och & ultra .90 .25
611 A231 40m ultra & yellow 1.75 .40
612 A231 55m brt red lil ('67) 2.00 .25
613 A231 60m grnsh bl & yel brn 1.25 .55

Wmk. 342

614 A232 100m dk vio brn & sl 3.50 .85
615 A232 200m bluish blk & yel brn 8.00 1.00
616 A232 500m ultra & dp org 17.50 3.25
Nos. 600-616 (17) 40.10 9.05

Nos. 603 & N107 lack the vertically arranged dates which appear at lower right on No. 619.
See Nos. N104-N116.

HSN Commission Emblem — A233

Perf. 11x11½

1964, Jan. 10 Wmk. 342

617 A233 10m dull bl, dk bl & yel .35 .25

1st conf. of the Commission of Health, Sanitation and Nutrition.

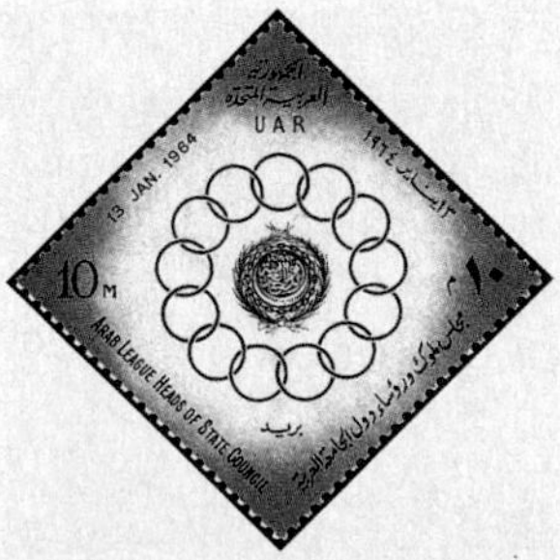

Arab League Emblem — A234

1964, Jan. 13 *Perf. 11*

618 A234 10m brt green & blk .35 .25

1st meeting of the Heads of State of the Arab League, Cairo, January.
See No. N117.

Minaret at Night — A235

1964 Unwmk. *Perf. 11*
619 A235 4m emerald, blk & red .35 .25

Issued for use on greeting cards.
See Nos. 603, N107, N118.

Old and New Dwellings and Map of Nubia A236

Perf. 11½x11
1964, Feb. 27 Photo. Wmk. 342
620 A236 10m dull vio & yel .35 .25

Resettlement of Nubian population.

Map of Africa and Asia and Train A237

1964, Mar. 21
621 A237 10m dull bl, dk bl & yel .90 .50

Asian Railway Conference, Cairo, Mar. 21.

Ikhnaton and Nefertiti with Children — A238

1964, Mar. 21 *Perf. 11x11½*
622 A238 10m dk brown & ultra .90 .30

Issued for Arab Mother's Day, Mar. 21.

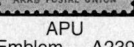

APU Emblem — A239

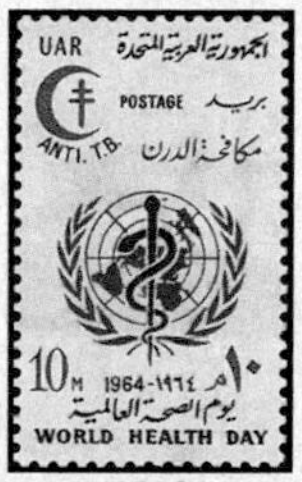

WHO Emblem — A240

1964, Apr. 1 Photo. Wmk. 342
623 A239 10m org brn & bl, *sal* .35 .25

Permanent Office of the APU, 10th anniv.
See No. N119.

1964, Apr. 7
624 A240 10m dk blue & red .35 .25

World Health Day (Anti-Tuberculosis).
See No. N120.

Statue of Liberty, World's Fair Pavilion and Pyramids A241

1964, Apr. 22 *Perf. 11½x11*
625 A241 10m brt green & ol, *grysh* .35 .25

New York World's Fair, 1964-65.

Nile and Aswan High Dam A242

1964, May 15 Unwmk. *Perf. 11½*
626 A242 10m black & blue .35 .25

The diversion of the Nile.

"Land Reclamation" — A243

Design: No. 628, "Electricity," Aswan High Dam hydroelectric station.

1964, July 23 *Perf. 11½*
627 A243 10m yellow & emer .35 .25
628 A243 10m green & blk .35 .25

Land reclamation and hydroelectric power due to the Aswan High Dam.
An imperf. souvenir sheet, issued July 23, contains two 50m black and blue stamps showing Aswan High Dam before and after diversion of the Nile. Value $2.

Map of Africa and 34 Flags — A244

1964, July 17 Photo.
629 A244 10m brn, brt bl & blk .40 .25

Assembly of Heads of State and Government of the Organization for African Unity at Cairo in July.

Jamboree Emblem — A245

Design: No. 631, Emblem of Air Scouts.

1964, Aug. 28 Unwmk. *Perf. 11½*
630 A245 10m red, grn & blk .60 .40
631 A245 10m green & red .60 .40
a. Pair, #630-631 2.50 2.50

The 6th Pan Arab Jamboree, Alexandria.

Flag of Algeria A246

1964, Sept. 5 *Perf. 11½x11*
Flags in Original Colors

632	A246	10m	Algeria	.75	.40
633	A246	10m	Iraq	.75	.40
634	A246	10m	Jordan	.75	.40
635	A246	10m	Kuwait	.75	.40
636	A246	10m	Lebanon	.75	.40
637	A246	10m	Libya	.75	.40
638	A246	10m	Morocco	.75	.40
639	A246	10m	Saudi Arabia	.75	.40
640	A246	10m	Sudan	.75	.40
641	A246	10m	Syria	.75	.40
642	A246	10m	Tunisia	.75	.40
643	A246	10m	UAR	.75	.40
644	A246	10m	Yemen	.75	.40
			Nos. 632-644 (13)	9.75	5.20

2nd meeting of the Heads of State of the Arab League, Alexandria, Sept. 1964.

World Map, Dove, Olive Branches and Pyramids — A247

1964, Oct. 5 *Perf. 11½*
645 A247 10m slate blue & yel .35 .25

Conference of Heads of State of Non-Aligned Countries, Cairo, Oct. 1964.

Pharaonic Athletes A248

Designs from ancient decorations: 10m, Four athletes, vert. 35m, Wrestlers, vert. 50m, Pharaoh in chariot hunting.

Perf. 11½x11, 11x11½
1964, Oct. 10 Photo. Unwmk.
Sizes: 39x22mm, 22x39mm
646 A248 5m lt green & org .40 .25
647 A248 10m slate bl & lt brn .45 .25
648 A248 35m dull vio & lt brn 1.10 .75
Size: 58x24mm
649 A248 50m ultra & brn org 1.75 1.00
Nos. 646-649 (4) 3.70 2.25

18th Olympic Games Tokyo, Oct. 10-25.

Emblem, Map of Africa and Asia A249

Map of Africa, Communication Symbols A250

1964, Oct. 10 *Perf. 11x11½*
650 A249 10m violet & yellow .35 .25

First Afro-Asian Medical Congress.

1964, Oct. 24
651 A250 10m green & blk .35 .25

Pan-African and Malagasy Posts and Telecommunications Cong., Cairo, Oct. 24-Nov. 6.

Horus and Facade of Nefertari Temple, Abu Simbel A251

Ramses II — A252

Designs: 35m, A god holding rope of life, Abu Simbel. 50m, Isis of Kalabsha, horiz.

1964, Oct. 24 *Perf. 11½, 11x11½*
652 A251 5m grnsh bl & yel brn .70 .35
653 A252 10m sepia & brt yel 1.10 .40
654 A251 35m brown org & indigo 2.50 1.25
Nos. 652-654 (3) 4.30 2.00

Souvenir Sheet
Imperf
655 A252 50m olive & vio blk 15.00 15.00

"Save the Monuments of Nubia" campaign. No. 655 contains one horiz. stamp.

Emblems of Cooperation, Rural Handicraft and Women's Work — A253

Perf. 11½x11
1964, Dec. 8 Photo. Unwmk.
656 A253 10m yellow & dk blue .35 .25

25th anniv. of the Ministry of Social Affairs.

UN, UNESCO Emblems, Pyramids — A254

1964, Dec. 24 *Perf. 11x11½*
657 A254 10m ultra & yellow .35 .25

Issued for UNESCO Day.

Minaret, Mardani Mosque — A255

1965, Jan. 20 Photo. *Perf. 11*
658 A255 4m blue & dk brown .35 .25

Issued for use on greeting cards.
See No. N121.

Police Emblem over City
A256

Oil Derrick and Emblem
A257

Perf. 11x11½

1965, Jan. 25 **Wmk. 342**
659 A256 10m black & yellow .85 .40

Issued for Police Day.

1965, Mar. 16 **Photo.**
660 A257 10m dk brown & yellow .45 .25

5th Arab Petroleum Congress and the 2nd Arab Petroleum Exhibition.

Flags and Emblem of the Arab League — A258

Red Crescent and WHO Emblem — A259

Design: 20m, Arab League emblem, horiz.

1965, Mar. 22 **Wmk. 342**
661 A258 10m green, red & blk .80 .40
662 A258 20m ultra & brown 1.00 .55

20th anniversary of the Arab League. See Nos. N122-N123.

1965, Apr. 7 **Photo.**
663 A259 10m blue & crimson .55 .35

World Health Day (Smallpox: Constant Alert). See No. N124.

Dagger in Map of Palestine — A260

1965, Apr. 9 *Perf. 11x11½*
664 A260 10m black & red 1.50 .35

Deir Yassin massacre, Apr. 9, 1948. See No. N125.

ITU Emblem, Old and New Communication Equipment — A261

1965, May 17 *Perf. 11½x11*
665 A261 5m violet blk & yel .40 .30
666 A261 10m red & yellow .65 .30
667 A261 35m dk blue, ultra & yel 1.75 .80
Nos. 665-667 (3) 2.80 1.40

Cent. of the ITU. See Nos. N126-N128.

Library Aflame and Lamp
A262

1965, June 7 **Photo.** **Wmk. 342**
668 A262 10m black, grn & red .60 .25

Burning of the Library of Algiers, 6/7/62.

Sheik Mohammed Abdo (1850-1905), Mufti of Egypt — A263

1965, July 11 *Perf. 11x11½*
669 A263 10m Prus blue & bis brn .35 .25

Pouring Ladle (Heavy Industry)
A264

President Gamal Abdel Nasser and Emblems of Arab League, African Unity Organization, Afro-Asian Countries and UN — A265

No. 670, Search for off-shore oil. No. 672, Housing, construction in Nasser City (diamond shaped).

1965, July 23 *Perf. 11½*
670 A264 10m indigo & lt blue .85 .50
671 A264 10m brown & yellow .85 .50
672 A264 10m yel brn & blk .85 .50
673 A265 100m lt green & blk 5.75 3.25
Nos. 670-673 (4) 8.30 4.75

13th anniversary of the revolution.
The 100m was printed in sheets of six, consisting of two singles and two vertical pairs. Margins and gutters contain multiple UAR coat of arms in light green. Size: 240x330mm.

4th Pan Arab Games Emblem
A266

Map and Emblems of Previous Games — A267

No. 675, Swimmers Zeitun & Abd el Gelil, arms of Alexandria. 35m, Race horse "Saadoon."

Perf. 11½x11; 11½ (#676)

1965, Sept. 2 **Photo.** **Wmk. 342**
674 A266 5m blue & red .40 .40
675 A266 10m dp blue & dk brn .65 .30
676 A267 10m org brn & dp bl .80 .45
677 A266 35m green & brown 1.40 1.00
Nos. 674-677 (4) 3.25 2.15

4th Pan Arab Games, Cairo, Sept. 2-11. No. 675 for the long-distance swimming competition at Alexandria, a part of the Games.

Map of Arab Countries, Emblem of Arab League and Broken Chain
A268

1965, Sept. 13 **Photo.** *Perf. 11½*
678 A268 10m brown & yellow .40 .25

3rd Arab Summit Conf., Casablanca, 9/13.

Land Forces Emblem and Sun — A269

Perf. 11x11½

1965, Oct. 20 **Wmk. 342**
679 A269 10m bister brn & blk .65 .30

Issued for Land Forces Day.

Map of Africa, Torch and Olive Branches — A270

1965, Oct. 21 *Perf. 11½*
680 A270 10m dull pur & car rose .40 .25

Assembly of Heads of State of the Organization for African Unity.

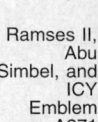

Ramses II, Abu Simbel, and ICY Emblem
A271

Pillars, Philae, and UN Emblem — A272

Designs: 35m, Two Ramses II statues, Abu Simbel and UNESCO emblem. 50m, Cartouche of Ramses II and ICY emblem, horiz.

Wmk. 342

1965, Oct. 24 **Photo.** *Perf. 11½*
681 A271 5m yellow & slate grn 1.00 .50
682 A272 10m blue & black 2.00 .50
683 A271 35m dk violet & yel 3.75 2.00
Nos. 681-683 (3) 6.75 3.00

Souvenir Sheet

Imperf

684 A272 50m brt ultra & dk brn 5.00 4.00

Intl. cooperation in saving the Nubian monuments. No. 684 also for the 20th anniv. of the UN. No. 684 contains one 42x25mm stamp.

Al-Maqrizi, Buildings and Books
A273

Perf. 11½x11

1965, Nov. 20 **Photo.** **Wmk. 342**
685 A273 10m olive & dk slate grn .40 .25

Ahmed Al-Maqrizi (1365-1442), historian.

Flag of UAR, Arms of Alexandria and Art Symbols — A274

1965, Dec. 16 *Perf. 11x11½*
686 A274 10m multicolored .40 .25

6th Biennial Exhibition of Fine Arts in Alexandria, Dec. 16, 1965-Mar. 31, 1966.

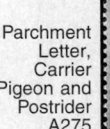

Parchment Letter, Carrier Pigeon and Postrider
A275

1966, Jan. 2 **Wmk. 342** *Perf. 11½*
687 A275 10m multicolored .80 .25
Nos. 687,CB1-CB2 (3) 8.30 6.50

Post Day, Jan. 2.

Lamp and Arch — A276

Exhibition Poster — A277

1966, Jan. 10 Unwmk. *Perf. 11*
688 A276 4m violet & dp org .40 .25

Issued for use on greeting cards.

Perf. 11x11½
1966, Jan. 27 Wmk. 342
689 A277 10m lt blue & blk .40 .25

Industrial Exhibition, Jan. 29-Feb.

Arab League Emblem — A278

Printed Page and Torch — A279

1966, Mar. 22 Photo. Wmk. 342
690 A278 10m brt yellow & pur .40 .25

Arab Publicity Week, Mar. 22-28.

1966, Mar. 25 *Perf. 11x11½*
691 A279 10m dp orange & sl blue .40 .25

Centenary of the national press.

Traffic Signal at Night — A280

Hands Holding Torch, Flags of UAR & Iraq — A281

1966, May 4 Photo. Wmk. 342
692 A280 10m green & red .85 .25

Issued for Traffic Day.

1966, May 26 *Perf. 11x11½*
693 A281 10m dp claret, rose red & brt grn .40 .25

Friendship between UAR and Iraq.

Workers and UN Emblem A282

Perf. 11½x11
1966, June 1 Photo. Wmk. 342
694 A282 5m blue grn & blk .35 .25
695 A282 10m brt rose lil & grn .40 .25
696 A282 35m orange & black 1.25 .85
Nos. 694-696 (3) 2.00 1.35

50th session of the ILO.

Mobilization Dept. Emblem, People and City — A283

1966, June 30 *Perf. 11x11½*
697 A283 10m dull pur & brn .35 .25

Population sample, May 31-June 16.

"Salah el Din," Crane and Cogwheel A284

Present-day Basket Dance and Pharaonic Dance — A285

No. 699, Transfer of first stones of Abu Simbel. No. 700, Development of Sinai (map of Red Sea area and Sinai Peninsula). No. 701, El Maadi Hospital and nurse with patient.

Wmk. 342
1966, July 23 Photo. *Perf. 11½*
698 A284 10m orange & multi .65 .30
699 A284 10m brt green & multi .65 .30
700 A284 10m yellow & multi .65 .30
701 A284 10m lt blue & multi .65 .30
Nos. 698-701 (4) 2.60 1.20

Souvenir Sheet
Imperf
702 A285 100m multicolored 5.00 3.75

14th anniv. of the revolution.

Suez Canal Headquarters, Ships and Map of Canal — A286

1966, July 26 *Perf. 11½*
703 A286 10m blue & crimson 1.10 .50

Suez Canal nationalization, 10th anniv.

Cotton, Farmers with Plow and Tractor A287

Perf. 11½x11
1966, Sept. 9 Photo. Wmk. 342
704 A287 5m shown .35 .25
705 A287 10m Rice .35 .25
706 A287 35m Onions 1.10 .90
Nos. 704-706 (3) 1.80 1.40

Issued for Farmer's Day.

WHO Headquarters, Geneva — A288

Designs: 10m, UN refugee emblem. 35m, UNICEF emblem.

Perf. 11½x11
1966, Oct. 24 Wmk. 342
707 A288 5m olive & brt pur .40 .25
708 A288 10m orange & brt pur .40 .25
709 A288 35m lt blue & brt pur .90 .80
Nos. 707-709 (3) 1.70 1.30

21st anniversary of the United Nations. See Nos. N129-N131.

World Map and Festival Emblem A289

1966, Nov. 8 Photo.
710 A289 10m brt purple & yellow .55 .25

5th Intl. Television Festival, Nov. 1-10.

Arms of UAR, Rocket and Pylon A290

1966, Dec. 23 Wmk. 342 *Perf. 11½*
711 A290 10m brt grn & car rose .55 .25

Issued for Victory Day. See No. N132.

Jackal A291

35m, Alabaster head from Tutankhamun treasure.

1967, Jan. 2 Photo.
712 A291 10m slate, yel & brn 1.50 .35
713 A291 35m bl, dk vio & ocher 2.75 .70

Issued for Post Day, Jan. 2.

Carnations A292

Workers Planting Tree A293

1967, Jan. 10 Unwmk. *Perf. 11*
714 A292 4m citron & purple .50 .25

Issued for use on greeting cards.

Perf. 11x11½
1967, Mar. 15 Wmk. 342
715 A293 10m brt green & blk vio .40 .25

Issued to publicize the Tree Festival.

Gamal el-Dine el-Afaghani and Arab League Emblem — A294

1967, Mar. 22 Photo. Wmk. 342
716 A294 10m dp green & dk brn .40 .25

Arab Publicity Week, Mar. 22-28. See No. N133.

Census Emblem, Man, Woman and Factory A295

1967, Apr. 23 *Perf. 11½x11*
717 A295 10m black & dp org .40 .25

First industrial census.

Brickmaking Fresco, Tomb of Rekhmire, Thebes, 1504-1450 B.C. — A296

1967, May 1 Photo. Wmk. 342
718 A296 10m olive & orange .55 .30

Issued for Labor Day, 1967. See No. N134.

Ramses II and Queen Nefertari — A297

Design: 35m, Shooting geese, frieze from tomb of Atet at Meidum, c. 2724 B. C.

Perf. 11½x11
1967, June 7 Photo. Wmk. 342
719 A297 10m multicolored 1.00 .50
720 A297 35m dk green & org 4.25 1.40
Nos. 719-720,C113-C115 (5) 13.60 6.15

Issued for International Tourist Year, 1967.

President Nasser, Crowd and Map of Palestine A298

1967, June 22 *Perf. 11½*
721 A298 10m dp org, yel & ol 2.75 1.50

Issued to publicize Arab solidarity for "the defense of Palestine."

Souvenir Sheet

National Products — A299

1967, July 23 Wmk. 342 *Imperf.*

722 A299 100m multicolored 4.00 3.50

15th anniv. of the revolution.

Salama Higazi — A300

Perf. 11x11½

1967, Oct. 14 Photo. Wmk. 342

723 A300 20m brown & dk blue .80 .40

50th anniversary of the death of Salama Higazi, pioneer of Egyptian lyric stage.

Stag on Ceramic Disk A301

Design: 55m, Apse showing Christ in Glory, Madonna and Saints, Coptic Museum, and UNESCO Emblem.

1967, Oct. 24 *Perf. 11½*

724 A301 20m dull rose & dk bl .95 .40
725 A301 55m dk slate grn & yel 1.75 .85
Nos. 724-725,C117 (3) 4.20 2.15

22nd anniv. of the UN.

Savings Bank and Postal Authority Emblems A302

1967, Oct. 31 *Perf. 11½x11*

726 A302 20m sal pink & dk blue .60 .30

International Savings Day.

Rose — A303

Unwmk.

1967, Dec. 15 Photo. *Perf. 11*

727 A303 5m green & rose lilac .50 .25

Issued for use on greeting cards.

Pharaonic Dress — A304

Aswan High Dam and Power Lines — A305

Designs: Various pharaonic dresses from temple decorations.

Perf. 11x11½

1968, Jan. 2 Wmk. 342

728 A304 20m brown, grn & buff 1.40 .35
729 A304 55m lt grn, yel & sepia 2.25 .85
730 A304 80m dk brn, bl & brt rose 3.75 1.25
Nos. 728-730 (3) 7.40 2.45

Issued for Post Day, Jan. 2.
See Nos. 752-755.

1968, Jan. 9

731 A305 20m yel, bl & dk brn .35 .25

1st electricity generated by the Aswan Hydroelectric Station.

Alabaster Vessel, Tutankhamun Treasure — A306

Capital of Coptic Limestone Pillar A307

Perf. 11x11½, 11½

1968, Jan. 20 Photo. Wmk. 342

732 A306 20m dk ultra, yel & brn .75 .30
733 A307 80m lt grn, dk pur & ol grn 1.60 1.00

2nd International Festival of Museums.

Girl, Moon and Paint Brushes — A308

1968, Feb. 15 *Perf. 11x11½*

734 A308 20m brt blue & black .40 .30

7th Biennial Exhibition of Fine Arts, Alexandria, Feb. 15.

Cattle and Veterinarian — A309

Perf. 11½x11

1968, May 4 Photo. Wmk. 342

735 A309 20m brown, yel & grn .75 .25

8th Arab Veterinary Congress, Cairo.

Human Rights Flame — A310

Perf. 11x11½

1968, July 1 Photo. Wmk. 342

736 A310 20m citron, crim & grn .50 .25
737 A310 60m sky blue, crim & grn 1.00 .90

International Human Rights Year, 1968.

Open Book with Symbols of Science, Victory Election Result A311

Workers, Cogwheel with Coat of Arms and Open Book — A312

1968, July 23 *Perf. 11½*

738 A311 20m rose red & sl grn .50 .25

Souvenir Sheet

Imperf

739 A312 100m lt grn, org & pur 3.25 3.00

16th anniversary of the revolution.

Imhotep and WHO Emblem A313

No. 741, Avicenna and WHO emblem.

Perf. 11½x11

1968, Sept. 1 Photo. Wmk. 342

740 A313 20m blue, yel & brn 1.10 .55
741 A313 20m yellow, bl & brn 1.10 .55
a. Pair, #740-741 3.00 3.00

20th anniv. of the WHO. Nos. 740-741 printed in checkerboard sheets of 50 (5x10).

Table Tennis — A314

Perf. 11x11½

1968, Sept. 20 Photo. Wmk. 342

742 A314 20m lt green & dk brn .90 .35

First Mediterranean Table Tennis Tournament, Alexandria, Sept. 20-27.

Factories and Fair Emblem A315

1968, Oct. 20 Wmk. 342 *Perf. 11½*

743 A315 20m bl gray, red & sl bl .45 .25

Cairo International Industrial Fair.

Temples of Philae — A316

Refugees, Map of Palestine, Refugee Year Emblem A317

55m, Temple at Philae & UNESCO emblem.

1968, Oct. 24 Photo.

744 A316 20m multicolored 1.25 .30
745 A317 30m multicolored 1.75 .85
746 A317 55m lt blue, yel & blk 3.00 1.10
Nos. 744-746 (3) 6.00 2.25

Issued for United Nations Day, Oct. 24.

Egyptian Boy Scout Emblem — A318

1968, Nov. 1

747 A318 10m dull org & vio bl .80 .30

50th anniversary of Egyptian Boy Scouts.

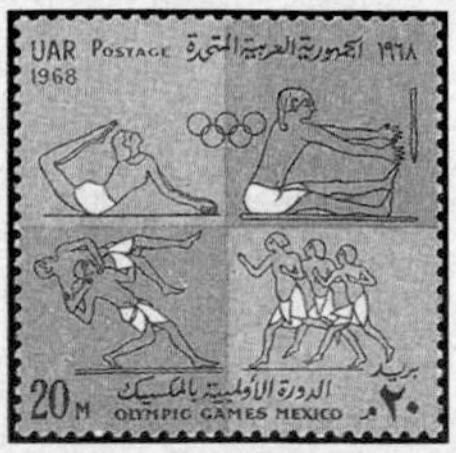

Pharaonic Sports A319

Design: 30m, Pharaonic sports, diff.

1968, Nov. 1

748 A319 20m pale ol, pale sal & blk .80 .25
749 A319 30m pale blue, buff & pur 1.25 .75

19th Olympic Games, Mexico City, 10/12-27.

Aly Moubarak — A320

1968, Nov. 9 ***Perf. 11½***

750 A320 20m green, brn & bister .55 .25

Aly Moubarak (1823-93), founder of the modern educational system in Egypt.

Lotus — A321

1968, Dec. 11 Photo. Wmk. 342

751 A321 5m brt blue, grn & yel .55 .25

Issued for use on greeting cards.

Ramses IV — A322

Pharaonic Dress: No. 753, Ramses III. No. 754, Girl carrying basket on her head. 55m, Queen of the New Empire in transparent dress.

1969, Jan. 2 Photo. ***Perf. 11½***

752 A322 5m blue & multi .75 .30
753 A322 20m blue & multi 1.25 .50
754 A322 20m blue & multi 1.50 .60
755 A322 55m blue & multi 3.75 1.75
Nos. 752-755 (4) 7.25 3.15

Issued for Post Day, Jan. 2.

Hefni Nassef — A323

Portrait: No. 757, Mohammed Farid.

Perf. 11x11½

1969, Mar. 2 Photo. Wmk. 342

756 A323 20m purple & brown .55 .30
757 A323 20m emerald & brown .55 .30
a. Pair, #756-757 1.25 1.25

50th anniv. of the death of Hefni Nassef (1860-1919) writer and government worker, and Mohammed Farid (1867-1919), lawyer and Speaker of the Nationalist Party.

Teacher and Children — A324

1969, Mar. 2 ***Perf. 11x11½***

758 A324 20m multicolored .55 .25

Arab Teacher's Day.

ILO Emblem and Factory Chimneys — A325

1969, Apr. 11 Photo. Wmk. 342

759 A325 20m brown, ultra & car .55 .25

50th anniv. of the ILO.

Flag of Algeria, Africa Day and Tourist Year Emblems A326

Perf. 11½x11

1969, May 25 Litho. Wmk. 342

760 A326 10m Algeria .95 .55
761 A326 10m Botswana .95 .55
762 A326 10m Burundi .95 .55
763 A326 10m Cameroun .95 .55
764 A326 10m Cent. Afr. Rep. .95 .55
765 A326 10m Chad .95 .55
766 A326 10m Congo (Brazzaville) .95 .55
767 A326 10m Congo (Kinshassa) .95 .55
768 A326 10m Dahomey .95 .55
769 A326 10m Equatorial Guinea .95 .55
770 A326 10m Ethiopia .95 .55
771 A326 10m Gabon .95 .55
772 A326 10m Gambia .95 .55
773 A326 10m Ghana .95 .55
774 A326 10m Guinea .95 .55
775 A326 10m Ivory Coast .95 .55
776 A326 10m Kenya .95 .55
777 A326 10m Lesotho .95 .55
778 A326 10m Liberia .95 .55
779 A326 10m Libya .95 .55
780 A326 10m Malagasy .95 .55
781 A326 10m Malawi .95 .55
782 A326 10m Mali .95 .55
783 A326 10m Mauritania .95 .55
784 A326 10m Mauritius .95 .55
785 A326 10m Morocco .95 .55
786 A326 10m Niger .95 .55
787 A326 10m Nigeria .95 .55
788 A326 10m Rwanda .95 .55
789 A326 10m Senegal .95 .55
790 A326 10m Sierra Leone .95 .55
791 A326 10m Somalia .95 .55
792 A326 10m Sudan .95 .55
793 A326 10m Swaziland .95 .55
794 A326 10m Tanzania .95 .55
795 A326 10m Togo .95 .55
796 A326 10m Tunisia .95 .55
797 A326 10m Uganda .95 .55
798 A326 10m UAR .95 .55
799 A326 10m Upper Volta .95 .55
800 A326 10m Zambia .95 .55
Nos. 760-800 (41) 38.95 22.55

El Fetouh Gate, Cairo A327

Sculptures from the Egyptian Museum, Cairo — A328

Millenary of Cairo — A329

No. 802, Al Azhar University. No. 803, The Citadel. No. 805, Sculptures, Coptic Museum. No. 806, Glass plate and vase, Fatimid dynasty, Islamic Museum.
No. 807: a, Islamic coin. b, Fatimist era jewelry. c, Copper vase. d, Coins and plaque.

Perf. 11½x11

1969, July 23 Photo. Wmk. 342

801 A327 10m dk brown & multi .55 .25
802 A327 10m green & multi .55 .25
803 A327 10m blue & multi .55 .25

Perf. 11½

804 A328 20m yellow grn & multi .95 .40
805 A328 20m dp ultra & multi .95 .40
806 A328 20m brown & multi .95 .40
Nos. 801-806 (6) 4.50 1.95

Souvenir Sheet

807 A329 Sheet of 4 15.00 14.00
a. 20m dark blue & multi 2.50 2.00
b. 20m lilac & multi 2.50 2.00
c. 20m yellow & multi 2.50 2.00
d. 20m dark green & multi 2.50 2.00

Millenium of the founding of Cairo.

African Development Bank Emblem — A330

Perf. 11x11½

1969, Sept. 10 Photo. Wmk. 342

808 A330 20m emerald, yel & vio .40 .25

African Development Bank, 5th anniv.

Pharaonic Boat and UN Emblem A331

Temple of Philae Inundated and UNESCO Emblem A332

Design: 5m, King and Queen from Abu Simbel Temple and UNESCO Emblem (size: 21x38mm).

Perf. 11x11½, 11½x11

1969, Oct. 24 Photo. Wmk. 342

809 A332 5m brown & multi .45 .30
810 A331 20m yellow & ultra 1.40 .55

Perf. 11½

811 A332 55m yellow & multi 1.60 .75
Nos. 809-811 (3) 3.45 1.60

Issued for United Nations Day.

Ships of 1869 and 1967 and Maps of Africa and Suez Canal — A333

1969, Nov. 15 ***Perf. 11½x11***

812 A333 20m lt blue & multi 1.50 .55

Centenary of the Suez Canal.

Cairo Opera House and Performance of Aida — A334

1969, Nov. 15

813 A334 20m multicolored 1.00 .45

Centenary of the Cairo Opera House.

Crowd with Egyptian and Revolutionary Flags — A335

1969, Nov. 15 ***Perf. 11½x11***

814 A335 20m brt grn, dull lil & red 1.00 .45

Revolution of 1919.

Ancient Arithmetic and Computer Cards A336

Perf. 11½x11

1969, Dec. 17 Photo. Wmk. 342

815 A336 20m multicolored .55 .30

Intl. Congress for Scientific Accounting, Cairo, Dec. 17-19.

Poinsettia A337

Sakkara Step Pyramid A338

El Fetouh Gate, Cairo — A339

Fountain, Sultan Hassan Mosque, Cairo — A340

King Khafre (Ruled c. 2850 B.C.) A341

1969, Dec. 24 Unwmk. *Perf. 11*

816 A337 5m yellow, grn & car .30 .25

Issued for use on greeting cards.

Wmk. 342 (20m, £1), Unwmkd.
Photo.; Engr. (20m, 55m)

1969-70 *Perf. 11*

Designs: 5m, Al Azhar Mosque. 10m, Luxor Temple. 50m, Qaitbay Fort, Alexandria.

817 A338 1m multi ('70) .30 *.40*
818 A338 5m multi ('70) .50 .25
819 A338 10m multi ('70) .50 .25
820 A339 20m dark brown 2.25 .35
821 A338 50m multi ('70) 2.25 .50
822 A340 55m slate green 3.50 .30

Perf. 11½

Photo. & Engr.

823 A341 £1 org & sl grn ('70) 40.00 9.50
Nos. 817-823 (7) 49.30 11.55

See Nos. 889-891, 893-897, 899, 901-902, 904.

Veiled Women, by Mahmoud Said — A342

Perf. 11x11½

1970, Jan. 2 Photo. Wmk. 342

824 A342 100m blue & multi 3.50 3.00

Post Day. Sheet of 8 with 2 panes of 4.

Parliament, Scales, Globe and Laurel — A343

1970, Feb. 2 *Perf. 11½x11*

825 A343 20m blue, vio bl & ocher .75 .25

Intl. Conf. of Parliamentarians on the Middle East Crisis, Cairo, Feb. 2-5.

Map of Arab League Countries, Flag and Emblem A344

Perf. 11½x11

1970, Mar. 22 Photo. Wmk. 342

826 A344 30m brn org, grn & dk pur .65 .40

Arab League, 25th anniv. See No. B42.

Mena House and Sheraton Hotel — A345

1970, Mar. 23

827 A345 20m olive, org & bl .55 .25

Centenary of Mena House and the inauguration of the Cairo Sheraton Hotel.

Manufacture of Medicine — A346

1970, Apr. 20

828 A346 20m brown, yel & bl 1.25 .35

Production of medicines in Egypt, 30th anniv.

Mermaid — A347

1970, Apr. 20 *Perf. 11x11½*

829 A347 20m orange, blk & ultra .65 .25

8th Biennial Exhibition of Fine Arts, Alexandria, March 12.

Misr Bank and Talaat Harb A348

ITU Emblem A349

1970, May 7 Photo. Wmk. 342

830 A348 20m multicolored .65 .25

50th anniversary of Misr Bank.

1970, May 17 *Perf. 11x11½*

831 A349 20m dk brn, yel & dull bl .65 .25

World Telecommunications Day.

UPU Headquarters, Bern — A350

1970, May 20 *Perf. 11½x11*

832 A350 20m multicolored .80 .35

Inauguration of the UPU Headquarters in Bern. See No. C128.

Basketball Player and Map of Africa — A351

UPU, UN and U.P.A.F. Emblems A352

No. 834, Soccer player, map of Africa & cup, horiz.

Perf. 11x11½, 11½x11

1970, May 25 Photo. Wmk. 342

833 A351 20m lt blue, yel & brn 1.25 .40
834 A351 20m yellow & multi .80 .35
835 A352 20m ocher, grn & blk .70 .25
Nos. 833-835 (3) 2.75 1.00

Africa Day. No. 833 also for the 5th African basketball championship for men; No. 834 the annual African Soccer championship; No. 835 publicizes the African Postal Union seminar.

Fist and Freed Bird — A353

1970, July 23 Photo. *Perf. 11*

836 A353 20m lt green, org & blk .95 .25

Souvenir Sheet

Imperf

837 A353 100m lt blue, dp org & blk 3.25 2.40

18th anniv. of the revolution.

Al Aqsa Mosque on Fire — A354

1970, Aug. 21 Wmk. 342 *Perf. 11*

838 A354 20m multicolored 1.25 .40
839 A354 60m brt blue & multi 2.75 1.60

1st anniv. of the burning of Al Aqsa Mosque, Jerusalem.

Standardization Emblems — A355

1970, Oct. 14 Wmk. 342 *Perf. 11*

840 A355 20m yellow, ultra & grn .75 .25

World Standards Day and 25th anniv. of the Intl. Standardization Organization, ISO.

UN Emblem, Scales and Dove — A356

Temple at Philae A357

Child, Education Year and UN Emblems A358

Designs: 10m, UN emblem. No. 845, 2nd Temple at Philae (denomination at left).

Perf. 11 (5m), 11½ (others)

1970, Oct. 24 Photo. Wmk. 342

841 A356 5m lt bl, rose lil & sl .25 .25
842 A357 10m yel, brn & lt bl .25 .25
843 A358 20m slate & multi .65 .30
844 A357 55m brn, bl & ocher 1.10 .75
845 A357 55m brn, bl & ocher 1.10 .75
a. Strip of 3, #842, 844-845 4.00 4.00
Nos. 841-845,B43 (6) 4.25 3.10

25th anniv. of the UN. No. 843 also for Intl. Education Year; Nos. 842, 844-845, the work of UNESCO in saving the Temples of Philae. No. 845a printed in sheets of 35 (15 No. 842, 10 each Nos. 844-845). Nos. 844-845 show continuous picture of the Temples at Philae.

Gamal Abdel Nasser — A359

1970, Nov. 6 Wmk. 342 *Perf. 11*

846 A359 5m sky blue & blk .25 .25
847 A359 20m gray green & blk .55 .25
Nos. 846-847,C129-C130 (4) 4.55 2.15

Gamal Abdel Nasser (1918-70), Pres. of Egypt.

Medical Association Building — A360

No. 849, Old & new National Library. No. 850, Egyptian Credo (Nasser quotation). No. 851, Engineering Society, old & new buildings. No. 852, Government Printing Offices, old & new buildings.

1970, Dec. 20 Photo. *Perf. 11*

848 A360 20m yel, grn & brn .80 .40
849 A360 20m green & multi .80 .40
850 A360 20m lt blue & brn .80 .40
851 A360 20m blue, yel & brn .80 .40
852 A360 20m blue, yel & brn .80 .40
a. Strip of 5, #848-852 4.50 4.25

50th anniv. of Egyptian Medical Assoc. (No. 848); cent. of Natl. Library (No. 849); Egyptian Engineering Assoc. (No. 851); sesqui. of Government Printing Offices (No. 852).

Map and Flags of UAR, Libya, Sudan
A361

1970, Dec. 27 *Perf. 11½*
853 A361 20m lt grn, car & blk .75 .25

Signing of the Charter of Tripoli affirming the unity of UAR, Libya & the Sudan, 12/27/70.

Qalawun Minaret — A362

Designs (Minarets): 10m, As Saleh. 20m, Isna. 55m, Al Hakim.

1971, Jan. 2 **Wmk. 342** *Perf. 11*
854 A362 5m green & multi .60 .25
855 A362 10m green & multi 1.25 .40
856 A362 20m green & multi 2.50 .80
857 A362 55m green & multi 4.00 2.25
a. Strip of 4, #854-857 + label 10.00 9.00

Post Day, 1971.
See Nos. 905-908, 932-935.

Gamal Abdel Nasser
A363

Photogravure and Engraved

1971 **Wmk. 342** *Perf. 11½*
858 A363 200m brn vio & dk bl 5.00 1.25
859 A363 500m blue & black 12.00 3.25

Souvenir Sheet

Design: Portrait facing right.

Imperf

860 Sheet of 2 13.00 13.00
a. A363 100m light green & black 4.00 2.75
b. A363 200m blue & black 6.00 4.50

No. 860 commemorates inauguration of the Aswan High Dam, which is shown in margin.
Issued: No. 860, 1/15; Nos. 858-859, 2/1.
See No. 903.

Cotton and Globe
A364

1971, Mar. 6 **Photo.** *Perf. 11½x11*
861 A364 20m lt green, blue & brn .65 .25

Egyptian cotton.

Arab Countries, and Arab Postal Union Emblem
A365

1971, Mar. 6 **Wmk. 342**
862 A365 20m lt bl, org & sl grn .65 .25

9th Arab Postal Cong., Cairo, 3/6-25. See No. C131.

Cairo Fair Emblem — A366

1971, Mar. 6 *Perf. 11x11½*
863 A366 20m plum, blk & org .65 .25

Cairo International Fair, March 2-23.

Nesy Ra, Apers Papyrus and WHO Emblem
A367

Perf. 11½x11

1971, Apr. 30 **Photo.** **Wmk. 342**
864 A367 20m yellow bis & pur 1.25 .30

World Health Organization Day.

Gamal Abdel Nasser — A368

1971, May 1 *Perf. 11*
865 A368 20m purple & bl gray .90 .30
866 A368 55m blue & purple 2.75 .95

Map of Africa, Telecommunications Symbols — A369

1971, May 17 *Perf. 11½x11*
867 A369 20m blue & multi .65 .25

Pan-African telecommunications system.

Wheelwright
A370

Hand Holding Wheat and Laurel
A371

Candle Lighting Africa — A372

Perf. 11x11½

1971, July 23 **Photo.** **Wmk. 342**
868 A370 20m yellow & multi .60 .25
869 A371 20m tan, grn & ocher .60 .25

Souvenir Sheet

Imperf

870 A372 100m blue & multi 6.00 4.75

19th anniv. of the July Revolution. No. 870 contains one stamp with simulated perforations in gold.

Arab Postal Union Emblem
A373

1971, Aug. 3 *Perf. 11½*
871 A373 20m black, yel & grn .65 .25

25th anniv. of the Conf. of Sofar, Lebanon, establishing the APU. See No. C135.

Arab Republic of Egypt

Three Links
A374

Perf. 11½x11

1971, Sept. 28 **Photo.** **Wmk. 342**
872 A374 20m gray, org brn & blk .65 .30

Confederation of Arab Republics (Egypt, Syria and Libya). See No. C136.

Gamal Abdel Nasser
A375

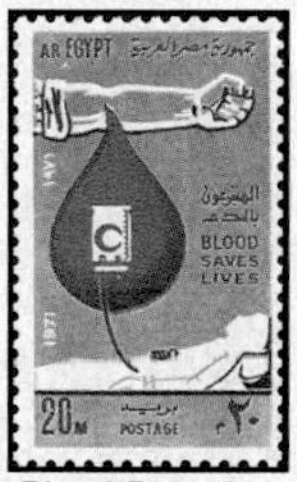

Blood Donation
A376

1971, Sept. 28 *Perf. 11x11½*
873 A375 5m slate grn & vio brn .45 .25
874 A375 20m violet brn & ultra .65 .25
875 A375 30m ultra & brown 1.25 .75
876 A375 55m brown & emerald 2.10 1.10
Nos. 873-876 (4) 4.45 2.35

Death of Pres. Gamal Abdel Nasser, 1st anniv.

1971, Oct. 24
877 A376 20m green & carmine 1.10 .25

"Blood Saves Lives."

Princess Nursing Child, UNICEF Emblem
A377

Submerged Pillar, Philae, UNESCO Emblem
A379

Equality Year Emblem
A378

Perf. 11x11½, 11½x11

1971, Oct. 24 **Photo.** **Wmk. 342**
878 A377 5m buff, blk & org brn .55 .30
879 A378 20m red brn, grn, yel & blk .90 .30
880 A379 55m black, lt bl, yel & brn 2.25 .30
Nos. 878-880,C137 (4) 5.45 1.35

UN Day. No. 878 honors UN Intl. Children's Fund; No. 879 for Intl. Year Against Racial Discrimination; No. 880 honors UNESCO.

Postal Traffic Center, Alexandria
A380

1971, Oct. 31 *Perf. 11½x11*
881 A380 20m blue & bister 1.00 .30

Opening of Postal Traffic Center in Alexandria.

Sunflower
A381

Abdalla El Nadim
A382

1971, Nov. 13 *Perf. 11*
882 A381 5m lt blue & multi .45 .25

For use on greeting cards.

1971, Nov. 14 *Perf. 11x11½*
883 A382 20m green & brown .65 .25

Abdalla El Nadim (1845-1896), journalist, publisher, connected with Orabi Revolution.

Section of Earth's Crust, Map of Africa on Globe
A383

1971, Nov. 27 *Perf. 11½x11*
884 A383 20m ultra, yel & brn 1.25 .25

75th anniv. of Egyptian Geological Survey and Intl. Conference, Nov. 27-Dec. 1.

Postal Union Emblem, Letter and Dove
A384

55m, African Postal Union emblem and letter.

1971, Dec. 2

885 A384 5m multicolored .45 .25
886 A384 20m olive, blk & org .90 .25
887 A384 55m red, blk & blue 2.00 1.10
Nos. 885-887,C138 (4) 4.75 2.00

10th anniversary of African Postal Union.

Money and Safe Deposit Box
A385

1971, Dec. 23 ***Perf. 11½***

888 A385 20m rose, brn & grn .85 .30

70th anniversary of Postal Savings Bank.

Types of 1969-70, 1971 Inscribed "A. R. Egypt" and

Ramses II — A385a

Designs as before and: No. 894, King Citi I. No. 897, View of Alexandria. No. 898, Queen Nefertari. No. 900, Sphinx and Middle Pyramid. 100m, Cairo Mosque. 200m, Head of Pharaoh Userkaf.

Wmk. 342 (892A, 901-904)

1972-76 Photo. Unwmk. ***Perf. 11***

889 A338 1m multi .25 .25
890 A338 1m dk brn ('73) .30 .25
891 A338 5m multi .40 .25
892 A385a 5m olive ('73) .45 .25
892A A385a 5m bister ('76) .45 .25
893 A338 10m multi .70 .25
894 A338 10m lt brn ('73) .70 .25
895 A339 20m olive 1.10 .25
896 A339 20m purple ('73) 1.10 .25
897 A338 50m multi 2.25 .30
898 A385a 50m dull bl ('73) 2.25 .30
899 A340 55m red lilac 4.00 .90
900 A340 55m green ('74) 2.00 .50
901 A339 100m lt blue, dp org & blk 3.00 .70

Perf. 11½

Photo. & Engr.

902 A341 200m yel grn & brn 6.75 1.50
903 A363 500m bl & choc 17.50 4.00
904 A341 £1 orange & sl grn 32.50 9.00
Nos. 889-904 (17) 75.70 19.45

Minaret Type of 1971

5m, West Minaret, Nasser Mosque. 20m, East Minaret, Nasser Mosque. 30m, Minaret, Al Gawli Mosque. 55m, Minaret, Ibn Tulun Mosque.

Wmk. 342

1972, Jan. 2 Photo. ***Perf. 11***

905 A362 5m dk green & multi .45 .25
906 A362 20m dk green & multi 1.25 .25
907 A362 30m dk green & multi 2.75 .50
908 A362 55m dk green & multi 3.75 1.50
a. Strip of 4, #905-908 + label 11.00 3.50

Post Day, 1972.

Police Emblem and Activities — A386

1972, Jan. 25 ***Perf. 11½***

909 A386 20m dull blue, brn & yel 2.25 .35

Police Day 1972.

UNESCO, UN and Book Year Emblems — A387

1972, Jan. 25 ***Perf. 11x11½***

910 A387 20m lt yel grn, vio bl & yel 1.10 .25

International Book Year 1972.

Alexandria Biennale
A388

1972, Feb. 15 Wmk. 342 ***Perf. 11½***

911 A388 20m black, brt rose & yel .85 .30

9th Biennial Exhibition of Fine Arts, Alexandria, Mar., 1972.

Fair Emblem
A389

Abdel Moniem Riad
A390

1972, Mar. 5 ***Perf. 11x11½***

912 A389 20m blue, org & yel grn 1.10 .30

International Cairo Fair.

1972, Mar. 21 Photo. Wmk. 342

913 A390 20m blue & brown 1.25 .30

In memory of Brig. Gen. Abdel Moniem Riad (1919-1969), military hero.

Bird Feeding Young
A391

1972, Mar. 21 ***Perf. 11½***

914 A391 20m yellow & multi 1.00 .25

Mother's Day.

Tutankhamun — A392

Design: 55m, Back of chair with king's name and symbols of eternity.

1972, May 22 **Unwmk.**

915 A392 20m gray, blk & ocher 2.25 .65
916 A392 55m purple & yellow 6.25 1.75
Nos. 915-916,C142-C143 (4) 28.50 13.40

Discovery of the tomb of Tutankhamun by Howard Carter & Lord Carnarvon, 50th anniv. See No. C144.

Queen Nefertiti
A393

Wmk. 342

1972, May 22 Photo. ***Perf. 11½***

917 A393 20m red, blk & gold 1.25 .30

Soc. of the Friends of Art, 50th anniv.

Map of Africa — A394

1972, May 25 ***Perf. 11x11½***

918 A394 20m purple, bl & brn .75 .30

Africa Day.

Atom Symbol, "Faith and Science"
A395

Design: No. 920, Egyptian coat of arms.

1972, July 23 ***Perf. 11½***

919 A395 20m blue, claret & blk 1.10 .30
920 A395 20m ol grn, gold & blk 1.10 .30

20th anniversary of the revolution.

Boxing, Olympic and Motion Emblems — A396

Designs (Olympic and Motion Emblems and): 10m, Wrestling. 20m, Basketball.

1972, Aug. 17 ***Perf. 11½x11***

921 A396 5m blue & multi .35 .25
922 A396 10m yellow & multi .50 .25
923 A396 20m ver & multi .60 .30
Nos. 921-923,C149-C152 (7) 6.65 3.70

20th Olympic Games, Munich, 8/26-9/11.

Flag of Confederation of Arab Republics — A397

1972, Sept. 1 Wmk. 342 ***Perf. 11½***

924 A397 20m carmine, bis & blk .85 .30

Confederation of Arab Republics, 1st anniv.

Red Crescent, TB and UN Emblems — A398

Heart and WHO Emblem
A399

Refugees, UNRWA Emblem, Map of Palestine — A400

Design: 55m, Inundated Temple of Philae, UNESCO emblem.

Perf. 11x11½ (#925), 11½ (#926, 928), 11 (#927)

1972, Oct. 24 **Photo.**

925 A398 10m brn org, red & bl .55 .30
926 A399 20m green, yel & blk 1.00 .40
927 A400 30m lt bl, pur & lt brn 3.00 .75
928 A399 55m brn, gold & bluish gray 3.25 1.00
Nos. 925-928 (4) 7.80 2.45

UN Day. No. 925 is for the 14th Regional Tuberculosis Conf., Cairo, 1972; No. 926 World Health Month; No. 927 publicizes aid to refugees and No. 928 the UN campaign to save the Temples at Philae.

Morning Glory — A401

1972, Oct. 24 ***Perf. 11***

929 A401 10m yel, lilac & grn .65 .25

For use on greeting cards.

"Seeing Eye" A402

1972, Nov. 30 ***Perf. 11½***

930 A402 20m multicolored 1.00 .25

Social Work Day.

Sculling Race, View of Luxor — A403

1972, Dec. 17 **Wmk. 342** ***Perf. 11***

931 A403 20m blue & brown 1.40 .40

3rd Nile Intl. Rowing Festival, Dec. 1972.

Minaret Type of 1971

10m, Al Maridani, 1338. 20m, Bashtak, 1337. 30m, Qusun, 1330. 55m, Al Gashankir, 1306.

1973, Jan. 2

Frame in Bright Yellow Green

932 A362 10m multicolored	.80	.25
933 A362 20m multicolored	1.25	.30
934 A362 30m multicolored	2.75	.75
935 A362 55m multicolored	3.75	2.00
a. Strip of 4, #932-935 + Label	11.00	10.00

Post Day, 1973.

Cairo Fair Emblem A404

Perf. 11½x11

1973, Mar. 21 **Photo.** **Wmk. 342**

936 A404 20m gray & multi .55 .25

International Cairo Fair.

Family — A405

1973, Mar. 21 ***Perf. 11x11½***

937 A405 20m multicolored .65 .25

Family planning.

Sania Girls' School and Hoda Sharawi A406

Perf. 11½x11

1973, July 15 **Photo.** **Wmk. 342**

938 A406 20m ultra & green .65 .25

Centenary of education for girls and 50th anniversary of the Egyptian Women's Union, founded by Hoda Sharawi.

Rifaa el Tahtawi — A407

1973, July 15 ***Perf. 11x11½***

939 A407 20m brt green, ol & brn .70 .30

Centenary of the death of Rifaa el Tahtawi, champion of democracy and principal of language school.

Omar Makram A408

Abdel Rahman al Gabarti, Historian A409

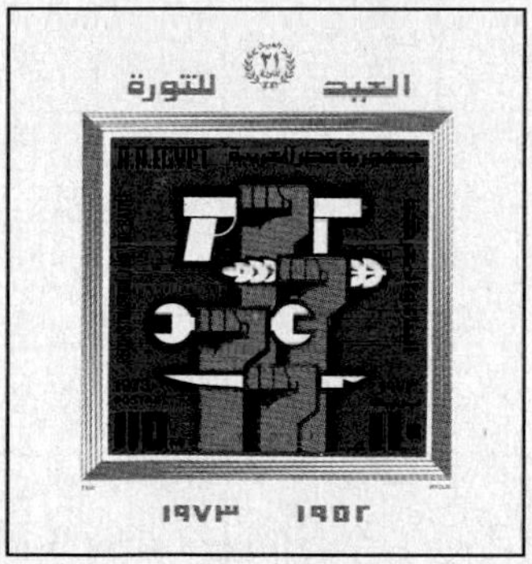

"Reconstruction and Battle" — A410

No. 941, Mohamed Korayem, martyr.

1973, July 23

940 A408 20m yel grn, bl & brn	.65	.30
941 A408 20m lt grn, bl & brn	.65	.30
942 A409 20m ocher & brown	.65	.30
Nos. 940-942 (3)	1.95	.90

Souvenir Sheet

Imperf

943 A410 110m gold, bl & blk 3.25 3.00

Revolution establishing the republic, 21st anniv.

Grain, Cow, FAO Emblem A411

Perf. 11½x11

1973, Oct. 24 **Wmk. 342**

944 A411 10m brn, dk bl & yel grn .65 .25

10th anniv. of the World Food Org.

Inundated Temples at Philae A412

1973, Oct. 24 ***Perf. 11½***

945 A412 55m blue, pur & org 4.00 1.40

UNESCO campaign to save the temples at Philae.

Bank Building A413

1973, Oct. 24

946 A413 20m brn org, grn & blk .75 .30

75th anniv. of the National Bank of Egypt.

Rose — A414

1973, Oct. 24 ***Perf. 11***

947 A414 10m blue & multi .55 .25

For use on greeting cards.

Human Rights Flame — A415

Perf. 11x11½

1973, Dec. 8 **Photo.** **Wmk. 342**

948 A415 20m yel grn, dk bl & car .75 .25

25th anniversary of the Universal Declaration of Human Rights.

Taha Hussein — A416

1973, Dec. 10

949 A416 20m dk blue, brn & emer .75 .25

Dr. Taha Hussein (1893-1973), "Father of Education" in Egypt, writer, philosopher.

Pres. Sadat, Flag and Battle of Oct. 6 — A417

1973, Dec. 23 ***Perf. 11x11½***

950 A417 20m yellow, blk & red 1.25 .60

October War against Israel (crossing of Suez Canal by Egyptian forces, Oct. 6, 1973). See No. 959.

WPY Emblem and Chart — A418

Cairo Fair Emblem — A419

1974, Mar. 21 **Wmk. 342** ***Perf. 11***

951 A418 55m org, grn & dk bl 1.10 .50

World Population Year.

1974, Mar. 21 **Photo.**

952 A419 20m blue & multi .65 .25

Cairo International Fair.

Nurse and Medal of Angels of Ramadan 10 — A420

1974, May 15 ***Perf. 11½***

953 A420 55m multicolored 2.00 .65

Nurses' and World Hospital Day.

Workers, Relief Carving from Queen Tee's Tomb, Sakhara — A421

1974, May 15 ***Perf. 11***

954 A421 20m yellow, blue & brn .85 .30

Workers' Day.

Pres. Sadat, Troops Crossing Suez Canal — A422

"Reconstruction," Map of Suez Canal and New Building — A423

Sheet of Aluminum A424

Design: 110m, Pres. Sadat's "October Working Paper," symbols of science and development.

1974, July 23 Photo. *Perf. 11x11½*

955 A422 20m multicolored .75 .40
956 A423 20m blue, gold & blk .75 .40

Perf. 11½

957 A424 20m plum & silver .75 .40
Nos. 955-957 (3) 2.25 1.20

Souvenir Sheet

Imperf

958 A424 110m green & multi 3.75 3.75

22nd anniv. of the revolution establishing the republic and for the end of the October War. No. 958 contains one 52x59mm stamp.

Pres. Sadat and Flag — A425

Perf. 11x11½

1974, Oct. 6 Wmk. 342

959 A425 20m yellow, blk & red 1.50 .75

1st anniv. of Battle. See No. 950.

Palette and Brushes A426

1974, Oct. 6 *Perf. 11½*

960 A426 30m purple, yel & blk 1.00 .40

6th Exhibition of Plastic Art.

Teachers and Pupils — A427

1974, Oct. 6 *Perf. 11x11½*

961 A427 20m multicolored .75 .25

Teachers' Day.

Souvenir Sheet

UPU Monument, Bern — A428

1974, Oct. 6 *Imperf.*

962 A428 110m gold & multi 5.50 5.00

Cent. of the UPU.

Emblems, Cogwheel and Calipers — A429

Refugee Camp under Attack and UN Refugee Organization Emblem — A430

Child and UNICEF Emblem A431

Temple of Philae — A432

1974, Oct. 24 *Perf. 11½, 11x11½*

963 A429 10m black, bl & yel .55 .25
964 A430 20m dp org, bl & blk .85 .25
965 A431 30m green, bl & brn 1.25 .40
966 A432 55m black, bl & yel 3.00 .85
Nos. 963-966 (4) 5.65 1.75

UN Day. World Standards Day (10m); Palestinian refugee repatriation (20m); Family Planning (30m); Campaign to save Temple of Philae (55m).

Calla Lily — A433

1974, Nov. 7 *Perf. 11*

967 A433 10m ultra & multi .55 .25

For use on greeting cards.

10m-coins, Smokestacks and Grain — A434

1974, Nov. 7 *Perf. 11½x11*

968 A434 20m yel grn, dk bl & sil .60 .25

International Savings Day.

Organization Emblem and Medical Services — A435

1974, Nov. 7 *Perf. 11½*

969 A435 30m vio, red & gold .90 .30

Health Insurance Organization, 10th anniv.

Mustafa Lutfy El Manfalouty A436

Abbas Mahmoud El Akkad A437

Perf. 11x11½

1974, Dec. 8 Photo. Wmk. 342

970 A436 20m blue blk & brn .55 .30
971 A437 20m brown & bl blk .55 .30
a. Pair, #970-971 1.30 1.30

Arab writers; El Manfalouty (1876-1924) and El Akkad (1889-1964).

Goddess Maat Facing God Thoth — A438

Fish-shaped Vase — A439

Pharaonic Golden Vase — A440

Sign of Life, Mirror — A441

Wmk. 342

1975, Jan. 2 Photo. *Perf. 11½*

972 A438 20m silver & multi 1.00 .30
973 A439 30m multicolored 1.25 .30
974 A440 55m multicolored 1.75 1.00
975 A441 110m blue & multi 3.00 1.75
Nos. 972-975 (4) 7.00 3.35

Post Day 1975. Egyptian art works from 12th-5th centuries B.C.

Om Kolthoum — A442

Perf. 11½

1975, Mar. 3 Photo. Unwmk.

976 A442 20m brown .85 .25

In memory of Om Kolthoum, singer.

Crescent, Globe, Al Aqsa and Kaaba — A443

Cairo Fair Emblem — A444

1975, Mar. 25

977 A443 20m multicolored .85 .25

Mohammed's Birthday.

Perf. 11x11½

1975, Mar. 25 Wmk. 342

978 A444 20m multicolored .65 .25

International Cairo Fair.

Kasr El Ainy Hospital WHO Emblem A445

Perf. 11½x11

1975, May 7 Photo. Wmk. 342

979 A445 20m dk brown & blue .85 .25

World Health Organization Day.

Children Reading Book — A446

Children and Line Graph — A447

1975, May 7 ***Perf. 11x11½***

980 A446 20m multicolored 1.00 .40
981 A447 20m multicolored 1.00 .40

Science Day.

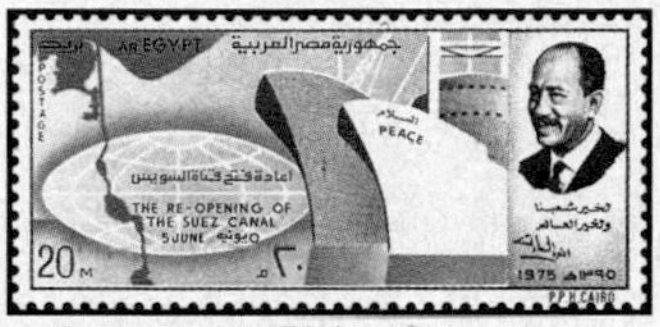

Suez Canal, Globe, Ships, Pres. Sadat — A448

1975, June 5 ***Perf. 11½***

982 A448 20m blue, brn & blk .85 .30
Nos. 982,C166-C167 (3) 5.35 2.90

Reopening of the Suez Canal, June 5.

Belmabgoknis Flowers — A449

1975, July 30 Photo. Wmk. 342

983 A449 10m green & blue .65 .25

For use on greeting cards.

Sphinx and Pyramids Illuminated — A450

Rural Electrification — A451

Map of Egypt with Tourist Sites — A452

1975, July 23

984 A450 20m black, org & grn .75 .25
985 A451 20m dk blue & brown .75 .25

Perf. 11

986 A452 110m multicolored 5.75 5.00
Nos. 984-986 (3) 7.25 5.50

23rd anniversary of the revolution establishing the republic. No. 986 printed in sheets of 6 (2x3). Size: 71x80mm.

Volleyball — A453

1975, Aug. 2 Photo. ***Perf. 11x11½***

987 A453 20m shown .90 .45
988 A453 20m Running .90 .45
989 A453 20m Torch and flag bearers .90 .45
990 A453 20m Basketball .90 .45
991 A453 20m Soccer .90 .45
a. Strip of 5, #987-991 5.75 5.75

6th Arab School Tournament.

Egyptian Flag and Tanks A454

1975 Photo. Unwmk. ***Perf. 11½***

992 A454 20m multicolored 1.40 .40

Two-line Arabic Inscription in Bottom Panel, "M" over "20"

992A A454 20m multicolored 1.40 .40

No. 992 for 2nd anniv. of October War against Israel, "The Spark;" No. 992A, the Intl. Symposium on October War against Israel 1973, Cairo University, Oct. 27-31.

Issue dates: No. 992, Oct. 6; No. 992A, Oct. 24.

Arrows Pointing to Fluke, and Emblems A455

Submerged Wall and Sculpture, UNESCO Emblem A456

Perf. 11x11½

1975, Oct. 24 Wmk. 342

993 A455 20m multicolored .95 .40
994 A456 55m multicolored 2.50 1.25

UN Day. 20m for Intl. Conf. on Schistosomiasis (Bilharziasis); 55m for UNESCO help in saving temples at Philae. See Nos. C169-C170.

Pharaonic Gate, University Emblem — A457

1975, Nov. 15 Photo. Wmk. 342

995 A457 20m multicolored .55 .25

Ain Shams University, 25th anniversary.

Al Biruni — A458

Arab Philosophers: No. 997, Al Farabi and lute. No. 998, Al Kanady, book and compass.

1975, Dec. 23 Photo. ***Perf. 11x11½***

996 A458 20m blue, brn & grn 1.50 .50
997 A458 20m blue, brn & grn 1.50 .50
998 A458 20m blue, brn & grn 1.50 .50
Nos. 996-998 (3) 4.50 1.50

Ibex (Prow) — A459

Post Day (from Tutankhamun's Tomb): 30m, Lioness. 55m, Cow's head (Goddess Hawthor). 110m, Hippopotamus' head (God Horus).

1976, Jan. 2 Unwmk. ***Perf. 11½***

999 A459 20m multicolored 4.75 2.00

Wmk. 342

1000 A459 30m brown, gold & ultra 7.50 2.50
1001 A459 55m multicolored 12.50 6.50
1002 A459 110m multicolored 18.00 13.50
Nos. 999-1002 (4) 42.75 24.50

Lake, Aswan Dam, Industry and Agriculture — A460

Perf. 11½x11

1976, Jan. 27 Photo. Wmk. 342

1003 A460 20m multicolored .90 .25

Filling of lake formed by Aswan High Dam.

Fair Emblem — A461

1976, Mar. 15 ***Perf. 11x11½***

1004 A461 20m orange & purple .50 .25

9th International Cairo Fair, Mar. 8-27.

Commemorative Medal — A462

1976, Mar. 15 Wmk. 342

1005 A462 20m olive, yel & blk .60 .25

11th Biennial Exhibition of Fine Arts, Alexandria.

Hands Shielding Invalid A463

1976, Apr. 7 Photo. ***Perf. 11½***

1006 A463 20m dk grn, lt grn & yel .65 .30

Founding of Faithfulness and Hope Society.

Eye and WHO Emblem A464

1976, Apr. 7

1007 A464 20m dk brn, yel & grn .85 .25

World Health Day: "Foresight prevents blindness."

Pres. Sadat, Legal Department Emblem — A465

Perf. 11½x11

1976, May 15 Photo. Wmk. 342

1008 A465 20m olive & multi .65 .30

Centenary of State Legal Department.

Scales of Justice — A466

1976, May 15 *Perf. 11x11½*
1009 A466 20m carmine, blk & grn .60 .30

5th anniversary of Rectification Movement.

Al-Ahram Front Page, First Issue A467

Perf. 11½x11

1976, June 25 Photo. Wmk. 342
1010 A467 20m bister & multi .65 .30

Centenary of Al-Ahram newspaper.

World Map, Pres. Sadat and Emblems — A468

1976, July 23 *Perf. 11x11½*
1011 A468 20m bl, blk & yel .85 .35

Size: 240x216mm

Imperf

1012 A468 110m bl, brn & yel 7.00 6.75

24th anniv. of the revolution. No. 1012 design is similar to No. 1011.

Scarborough Lily — A469

1976, Sept. 10 Photo. *Perf. 11*
1013 A469 10m multicolored .55 .25

For use on greeting cards.

Reconstruction of Sinai by Irrigation — A470

Abu Redice Oil Wells and Refinery — A471

Unknown Soldier, Memorial Pyramid for October War — A472

1976, Oct. 6 *Perf. 11x11½*
1014 A470 20m multicolored .85 .40
1015 A471 20m multicolored .85 .40

Size: 65x77mm

1016 A472 110m grn, bl & blk 7.50 7.00

October War against Israel, 3rd anniv.

Papyrus with Children's Animal Story — A473

Al Aqsa Mosque, Palestinian Refugees — A474

55m, Isis, from Philae Temple, UNESCO emblem, vert. 110m, UNESCO emblem & "30."

Perf. 11½, 11½x11

1976, Oct. 24 Photo. Wmk. 342
1017 A473 20m dk bl, bis & brn .65 .30
1018 A474 30m brn, grn & blk .80 .35
1019 A473 55m dk blue & bister 1.50 .50
1020 A474 110m lt grn, vio bl & red 2.50 1.40
Nos. 1017-1020 (4) 5.45 2.55

30th anniversary of UNESCO.

Census Chart A475

1976, Nov. 22 Photo. *Perf. 11½x11*
1021 A475 20m multicolored .65 .25

10th General Population and Housing Census.

A476

A477

Design: Nile and commemorative medal.

1976, Nov. 22 *Perf. 11x11½*
1022 A476 20m green & brown .65 .25

Geographical Soc. of Egypt, cent. (in 1975).

1977, Jan. 2 Photo. *Perf. 11x11½*

Post Day: 20m, Akhnaton. 30m, Akhnaton's daughter. 55m, Nefertiti, Akhnaton's wife. 110m, Akhnaton, front view.

1023 A477 20m multicolored .65 .30
1024 A477 30m multicolored .65 .35
1025 A477 55m multicolored 1.10 .55
1026 A477 110m multicolored 3.50 1.50
Nos. 1023-1026 (4) 5.90 2.70

Policeman, Emblem and Emergency Car — A478

Perf. 11½x11

1977, Feb. 25 Photo. Wmk. 342
1027 A478 20m multicolored 1.10 .30

Police Day.

Map of Africa, Arab League Emblem — A479

1977, Mar 7 *Perf. 11x11½*
1028 A479 55m multicolored .90 .50

First Afro-Arab Summit Conference, Cairo.

Fair Emblem, Pharaonic Ship A480

1977, Mar. 7 *Perf. 11½x11*
1029 A480 20m green, blk & red .65 .30

10th International Cairo Fair.

King Faisal — A481

Healthy and Crippled Children — A482

1977, Mar. 22 Photo. *Perf. 11x11½*
1030 A481 20m indigo & brown .65 .25

King Faisal Ben Abdel-Aziz Al Saud of Saudi Arabia (1906-1975).

1977, Apr. 12 Wmk. 342
1031 A482 20m multicolored .95 .30

National campaign to fight poliomyelitis.

APU Emblem, Members' Flags A483

1977, Apr. 12 *Perf. 11½*
1032 A483 20m blue & multi .45 .25
1033 A483 30m gray & multi .65 .25

25th anniv. of Arab Postal Union (APU).

Children's Village A484

Perf. 11½x11

1977, May 7 Photo. Wmk. 342
1034 A484 20m multicolored .55 .35
1035 A484 55m multicolored 1.25 .70

Inauguration of Children's Village, Cairo.

Loom, Spindle and Factory A485

1977, May 7
1036 A485 20m multicolored .55 .25

Egyptian Spinning and Weaving Company, El Mehalla el Kobra, 50th anniv.

Satellite, Globe, ITU Emblem — A486

1977, May 17 *Perf. 11x11½*
1037 A486 110m dk blue & multi 2.00 .50

World Telecommunications Day.

Flag and "25" A487

Egyptian Flag and Eagle — A488

Perf. 11½x11

1977, July 23 Photo. Wmk. 342
1038 A487 20m silver, car & blk .65 .25

Perf. 11x11½

1039 A488 110m multicolored 3.00 3.00

25th anniversary of July 23rd Revolution. No. 1039 printed in sheets of six. Size: 75x83mm.

Saad Zaghloul
A489

Archbishop Capucci, Map of Palestine
A490

Perf. 11x11½

1977, Aug. 23 Photo. Wmk. 342

1040 A489 20m dk green & dk brn .40 .25

Saad Zaghloul, leader of 1919 Revolution, 50th death anniversary.

1977, Sept. 1

1041 A490 45m emerald & blue 1.10 .50

Palestinian Archbishop Hilarion Capucci, jailed by Israel in 1974.

Bird-of-Paradise Flower — A491

1977, Sept. 3

1042 A491 10m multicolored .45 .25

For use on greeting cards.

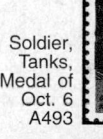

Proclamation Greening the Land — A492

Perf. 11x11½

1977, Sept. 25 Photo. Wmk. 342

1043 A492 20m multicolored .50 .25

Agrarian Reform Law, 25th anniversary.

Soldier, Tanks, Medal of Oct. 6
A493

Anwar Sadat — A494

1977, Oct. 6 *Perf. 11½x11*

1044 A493 20m multicolored .55 .25

Unwmk.

Perf. 11

1045 A494 140m dk brn, gold & red 8.50 8.50

October War against Israel, 4th anniv. No. 1045 printed in sheets of 16.

Refugees Looking at Al Aqsa Mosque
A495

Goddess Taueret and Spirit of Flight (Horus)
A496

Mural Relief, Temple of Philae — A497

Wmk. 342

1977, Oct. 24 Photo. *Perf. 11*

1046 A495 45m green, red & blk .80 .35

1047 A496 55m dp blue & yellow 1.50 .45

1048 A497 140m ol bis & dk brn 2.50 1.25

Nos. 1046-1048 (3) 4.80 2.05

United Nations Day.

Electric Trains, First Egyptian Locomotive — A498

1977, Oct. 22

1049 A498 20m multicolored 1.75 .40

125th anniversary of Egyptian railroads.

Film and Eye
A499

1977, Nov. 16 *Perf. 11½x11*

1050 A499 20m gray, blk & gold .75 .25

50th anniversary of Egyptian cinema.

Natural Gas Well and Refinery — A500

1977, Nov. 17 Photo.

1051 A500 20m multicolored 1.25 .30

National Oil Festival, celebrating the acquisition of Sinai oil wells.

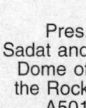

Pres. Sadat and Dome of the Rock
A501

Perf. 11½x11

1977, Dec. 31 Photo. Wmk. 342

1052 A501 20m green, brn & blk .60 .25

1053 A501 140m green, blk & brn 2.00 .80

Pres. Sadat's peace mission to Israel.

Ramses II — A502

Post Day: 45m, Queen Nefertari, bas-relief.

1978, Jan. 2 *Perf. 11½*

1054 A502 20m green, blk & gold .85 .40

1055 A502 45m orange, blk & ol 1.75 .90

Post Day 1978.

Water Wheels, Fayum — A503

Flying Duck, from Floor in Ikhnaton's Palace
A504

5m, Birdhouse, 10m, Statue of Horus. 20m, 30m, Al Rifa'i Mosque, Cairo. 50m, Monastery, Wadi al-Natrun. 55m, Ruins of Edfu Temple. 70m, 80m, Bridge of Oct. 6. 85m, Medum pyramid. 100m, Facade, El Morsi Mosque, Alexandria. 200m, Column, Alexandria, Sphinx. 500m, Arabian stallion.

Wmk. 342, Unwmkd. (30m, 70m, 80m)

1978-85 *Perf. 11½*

1056	A503	1m slate blue	.25	.25
a.		Unwmkd. ('79)	.25	.25
b.		1m gray ('83)	.25	.25
c.		1m gray, unwmkd. ('83)	.25	.25
1057	A503	5m bister brn	.25	.25
a.		5m dull brn, unwmkd. (79)	.25	.25
1058	A503	10m brt green	.25	.25
a.		Unwmkd. ('79)	.25	.25
1059	A503	20m dk brown	.25	.25
b.		Unwmkd. ('79)	.25	.25
1059A	A503	30m sepia	.60	.50
c.		Wmk. 342 ('82)	—	—
1060	A503	50m Prus blue	.25	.25
a.		Unwmkd. ('79)	.25	.25
b.		Unwmkd., brt blue ('87)	.25	.25
1061	A503	55m olive	.25	.25
1062	A503	70m olive ('79)	.40	.25
1062A	A503	80m olive ('82)	.50	.30
1063	A503	85m dp purple	.70	.30
a.		Unwmkd. ('85)	.70	.35
1064	A503	100m brown	.95	.30
a.		Unwmkd. ('85)	1.25	.40
1065	A503	200m bl & indigo	2.25	.80
a.		Unwmkd. ('85)	2.25	.85
1066	A504	500m multicolored	7.00	2.00
a.		Unwmkd. ('85)	7.00	2.00
1067	A504	£1 multicolored	11.00	4.00
a.		Unwmkd. ('85)	11.00	4.00
		Nos. 1056-1067 (14)	24.90	9.95

Issued: 500m, £1, 2/27/78; 70m, 8/22/79; others, 7/23/78.

Fair Emblem and Wheat
A505

1978, Mar. 15 *Perf. 11½*

1072 A505 20m multicolored .45 .25

11th Cairo International Fair, Mar. 11-25.

Emblem, Kasr El Ainy School
A506

1978, Mar. 18 *Perf. 11½x11*

1073 A506 20m lt blue, blk & gold .55 .25

Kasr El Ainy School of Medicine, 150th anniv.

A507

No. 1074, Soldiers and Emblem. No. 1075, Youssef El Sebai.

1978, Mar. 30 *Perf. 11x11½*

1074 20m multicolored .50 .30

1075 20m bister brown .50 .30

a. A507 Pair, #1074-1075 1.25 1.25

Youssef El Sebai, newspaper editor, assassinated on Cyprus and in memory of the commandos killed in raid on Cyprus.

Biennale Medal, Statue for Entrance to Port Said
A509

1978, Apr. 1 *Perf. 11½*

1076 A509 20m blue, grn & blk .55 .25

12th Biennial Exhibition of Fine Arts, Alexandria.

Child with Smallpox, UN Emblem
A510

1978, Apr. 7 Photo. *Perf. 11½*

1077 A510 20m multicolored .55 .35

Eradication of smallpox.

Heart & Arrow, UN Emblem — A511

Anwar Sadat — A512

1978, Apr. 7 **Wmk. 342**
1078 A511 20m multicolored .55 .35

Fight against hypertension.

1978, May 15 **Photo.** ***Perf. 11½x11***
1079 A512 20m green, brn & gold .65 .30

7th anniversary of Rectification Movement.

Social Security Emblem — A513

1978, May 16 ***Perf. 11***
1080 A513 20m lt green & dk brn .35 .25

General Organization of Insurance and Pensions (Social Security), 25th anniversary.

New Cities on Map of Egypt — A514

Map of Egypt and Sudan, Wheat — A515

Wmk. 342
1978, July 23 **Photo.** ***Perf. 11½***
1081 A514 20m multicolored .85 .30
1082 A515 45m multicolored 1.75 .50

26th anniversary of July 23rd revolution.

Symbols of Egyptian Ministries — A516

1978, Aug. 28 **Photo.** ***Perf. 11½x11***
1083 A516 20m multicolored .65 .30

Centenary of Egyptian Ministerial System.

Pres. Sadat and "Spirit of Egypt" Showing Way — A517

1978, Oct. 6 **Photo.** ***Perf. 11x11½***
1084 A517 20m multicolored .85 .30

October War against Israel, 5th anniv.

Fight Against Racial Discrimination Emblem — A518

Kobet al Sakra Mosque, Refugee Camp — A519

Dove and Human Rights Emblem — A520

UN Day: 55m, Sanctuary of Isis at Philae and UNESCO emblem, horiz.

Perf. 11, 11½ (45m)
1978, Oct. 24 **Photo.** **Wmk. 342**
1085 A518 20m multicolored .45 .25
1086 A519 45m multicolored .90 .50
1087 A518 55m multicolored 1.00 .60
1088 A520 140m multicolored 2.25 1.00
Nos. 1085-1088 (4) 4.60 2.35

Pilgrims, Mt. Arafat and Holy Kaaba — A521

1978, Nov. 7 **Photo.** ***Perf. 11***
1089 A521 45m multicolored 1.00 .40

Pilgrimage to Mecca.

Tahtib Horse Dance — A522

1978, Nov. 7
1090 A522 10m multicolored .50 .25
1091 A522 20m multicolored .50 .25

For use on greeting cards.

UN Emblem, Globe and Grain — A523

1978, Nov. 11 **Photo.** ***Perf. 11½***
1092 A523 20m green, dk bl & yel .45 .25

Technical Cooperation Among Developing Countries Conf., Buenos Aires, Sept. 1978.

Pipes, Map and Emblem of Sumed Pipeline — A524

1978, Nov. 11
1093 A524 20m brown, bl & yel .65 .25

Inauguration of Sumed pipeline from Suez to Alexandria, 1st anniversary.

Mastheads — A525

Abu el Walid — A526

1978, Dec. 24 ***Perf. 11x11½***
1094 A525 20m brown & black .65 .25

El Wakea el Masriya newspaper, 150th anniv.

1978, Dec. 24
1095 A526 45m brt green & indigo .85 .30

800th death anniv. of Abu el Walid ibn Rashid.

Helwan Observatory and Sky — A527

1978, Dec. 30 **Wmk. 342**
1096 A527 20m multicolored .95 .35

Helwan Observatory, 75th anniversary.

Second Daughter of Ramses II — A528

Ramses Statues, Abu Simbel, and Cartouches — A529

1979, Jan. 2 **Photo.** ***Perf. 11***
1097 A528 20m brown & yellow .65 .30

Perf. 11½x11
1098 A529 140m multicolored 2.25 .80

Post Day 1979.

Book, Reader and Globe — A530

Perf. 11½x11
1979, Feb. 1 **Photo.** **Wmk. 342**
1099 A530 20m yellow grn & brown .45 .25

Cairo 11th International Book Fair.

Wheat, Globe, Fair Emblem — A531

Perf. 11x11½
1979, Mar. 17 **Photo.** **Unwmk.**
1100 A531 20m blue, org & blk .50 .25

12th Cairo International Fair, Mar.-Apr.

Skull, Poppy, Agency Emblem — A532

1979, Mar. 20 ***Perf. 11***
1101 A532 70m multicolored 1.90 .65

Anti-Narcotics General Administration, 50th anniv.

Isis Holding Horus — A533

1979, Mar. 21
1102 A533 140m multicolored 3.25 1.00

Mother's Day.

World Map and Book — A534

Perf. 11x11½
1979, Mar. 22 **Wmk. 342**
1103 A534 45m yellow, bl & brn .55 .25

Cultural achievements of the Arabs.

Pres. Sadat's Signature, Peace Doves A535

Wmk. 342
1979, Mar. 31 **Photo.** ***Perf. 11½***
1104 A535 70m brt green & red 1.25 .45
1105 A535 140m yellow grn & red 2.25 1.00

Signing of Peace Treaty between Egypt and Israel, Mar. 26.

1979, May 26 **Photo.** ***Perf. 11½***
1106 A535 20m yellow & dk brn .55 .30

Return of Al Arish to Egypt.

Honeycomb with Food Symbols A536

1979, May 15
1107 A536 20m multicolored .35 .25

8th anniversary of movement to establish food security.

Coins, 1959, 1979 A537

Perf. 11½x11
1979, June 1 **Wmk. 342** **Photo.**
1108 A537 20m yellow & gray .45 .25

25th anniversary of the Egyptian Mint.

Egypt No. 1104 under Magnifying Glass — A538

1979, June 1 ***Perf. 11***
1109 A538 20m green, blk & brn .55 .25

Philatelic Society of Egypt, 50th anniversary.

Book, Atom Symbol, Rising Sun — A539

"23 July," "Revolution" and "Peace" — A540

Perf. 11½x11
1979, July 23 **Wmk. 342**
1110 A539 20m multicolored .50 .25

Miniature Sheet

Imperf

1111 A540 140m multicolored 3.75 3.75

27th anniversary of July 23rd revolution.

Musicians — A541

1979, Aug. 22 ***Perf. 11½***
1112 A541 10m multicolored .25 .25

For use on greeting cards.

Dove over Map of Suez Canal A542

Wmk. 342
1979, Oct. 6 **Photo.** ***Perf. 11½***
1113 A542 20m blue & brown .65 .30

October War against Israel, 6th anniv.

Prehistoric Mammal Skeleton, Map of Africa — A543

Perf. 11½x11
1979, Oct. 9 **Photo.** **Wmk. 342**
1114 A543 20m multicolored 2.00 .35

Egyptian Geological Museum, 75th anniv.

T Square on Drawing Board — A544

1979, Oct. 11 ***Perf. 11***
1115 A544 20m multicolored .65 .25

Engineers Day.

Human Rights Emblem Over Globe — A545

Boy Balancing IYC Emblem — A546

Perf. 11½
1979, Oct. 24 **Photo.** **Unwmk.**
1116 A545 45m multicolored .65 .30
1117 A546 140m multicolored 1.50 1.25

UN Day and Intl. Year of the Child.

International Savings Day — A547

1979, Oct. 31
1118 A547 70m multicolored 1.00 .45

A548

Design: Shooting championship emblem.

1979, Nov. 16
1119 A548 20m multicolored .65 .25

20th International Military Shooting Championship, Cairo.

A549

1979, Nov. 29 ***Perf. 11x11½***
1120 A549 45m multicolored .85 .30

International Palestinian Solidarity Day.

Dove Holding Olive Branch, Rotary Emblem, Globe A550

1979, Dec. 3 **Photo.** ***Perf. 11½***
1121 A550 140m multicolored 1.60 1.00

Rotary Intl., 75th anniv,; Cairo Rotary Club, 50th anniv.

Arms Factories, 25th Anniversary — A551

Perf. 11½x11
1979, Dec. 23 **Photo.** **Wmk. 342**
1122 A551 20m lt olive grn & brn .55 .25

Aly El Garem (1881-1949) A552

Pharaonic Capital A553

Poets: No. 1124, Mahmoud Samy El Baroudy (1839-1904).

1979, Dec. 25 ***Perf. 11x11½***

1123 A552 20m dk brn & yel brn .50 .30
1124 A552 20m brown & dk brown .50 .30
a. Pair, #1123-1124 1.25 1.25

1980, Jan. 2 Unwmk. ***Perf. 11½***

Post Day: Various Pharaonic capitals.

1125 A553 20m multicolored .45 .30
1126 A553 45m multicolored .65 .65
1127 A553 70m multicolored 1.00 .75
1128 A553 140m multicolored 2.75 1.50
a. Strip of 4, #1125-1128 6.50 .650

Golden Goddess of Writing, Fair Emblem — A554

1980, Feb. 2 Photo. ***Perf. 11½***

1129 A554 20m multicolored 1.10 .25

12th Cairo Intl. Book Fair, Jan. 24-Feb. 4.

Exhibition Catalogue and Medal — A555

1980, Feb. 2

1130 A555 20m multicolored .60 .30

13th Biennial Exhibition of Fine Arts, Alexandria.

13th Cairo International Fair — A556

1980, Mar. 8 Photo. ***Perf. 11x11½***

1131 A556 20m multicolored .60 .25

Kiosk of Trajan — A557

a, Kiosk of Tratan. b, Temple of Korasy, entry at right. c, Temple of Ksalabsha, carvings on frame. d, Temple of Philae, 5 columns..

1980, Mar. 10 ***Perf. 11½***

1132 Strip of 4 + label 5.50 5.50
a.-d. A557 70m, any single 1.10 .85

UNESCO campaign to save Nubian monuments, 20th anniversary. Shown on stamps are Temples of Philae, Kalabsha, Korasy.

Physicians' Day — A558

1980, Mar. 18 ***Perf. 11x11½***

1133 A558 20m multicolored .60 .25

Rectification Movement, 9th Anniversary — A559

Perf. 11½x11

1980, May 15 Photo. Wmk. 342

1134 A559 20m multicolored .60 .25

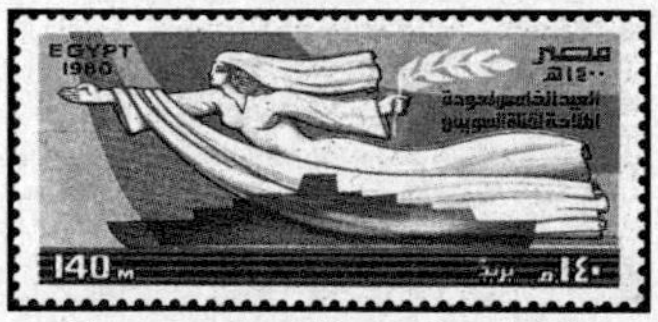

Re-opening of Suez Canal, 5th Anniversary — A560

1980, June 5 ***Perf. 11½***

1135 A560 140m multicolored 1.50 1.00

Prevention of Cruelty to Animals Week A561

1980, June 5

1136 A561 20m lt yel grn & gray .85 .25

Industry Day A562

Perf. 11½x11

1980, July 12 Photo. Wmk. 342

1137 A562 20m multicolored .55 .25

Leaf with Text A563

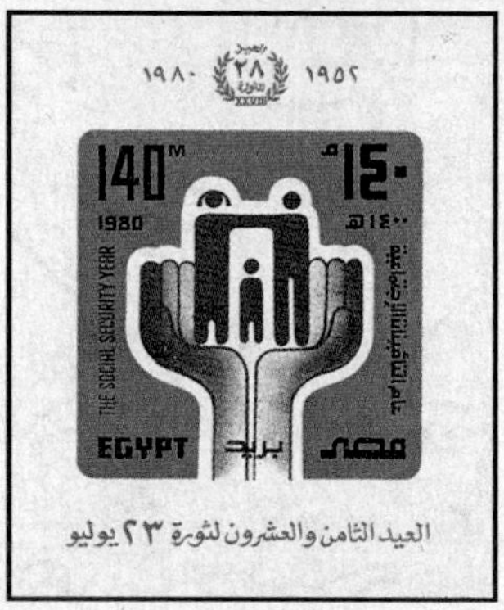

Family Protection Emblem — A564

1980, July 23 ***Perf. 11½***

1138 A563 20m multicolored .60 .25

Souvenir Sheet

Imperf

1139 A564 140m multicolored 3.75 3.75

July 23rd Revolution, 28th anniv.; Social Security Year.

Erksous Seller and Nakrazan Player — A565

Perf. 11½

1980, Aug. 8 Unwmk. Photo.

1140 A565 10m multicolored .50 .25

For use on greeting cards.

October War Against Israel, 7th Anniv. — A566

1980, Oct. 6 Litho.

1141 A566 20m multicolored .75 .25

Islamic and Coptic Columns A567

International Telecommunications Union Emblem — A568

Wmk. 342

1980, Oct. 24 Photo. ***Perf. 11½***

1142 A567 70m multicolored .80 .60
1143 A568 140m multicolored 1.60 1.25

UN Day. Campaign to save Egyptian monuments (70m), Intl. Telecommunications Day (140m).

Hegira (Pilgrimage Year) A569

1980, Nov. 9 Litho. ***Perf. 11x11½***

1144 A569 45m multicolored .70 .30

Opening of Suez Canal Third Branch A570

Perf. 11½x11

1980, Dec. 16 Photo. Wmk. 342

1145 A570 70m multicolored 1.10 .60

Mustafa Sadek El-Rafai (1880-1927), Writer — A571

No. 1147, Ali Mustafa Mousharafa (1898-1950), mathematician (with glasses). No. 1148, Ali Ibrahim (1880-1947), surgeon.

1980, Dec. 23 ***Perf. 11x11½***

1146 A571 20m green & brown .50 .30
1147 A571 20m green & brown .50 .30
1148 A571 20m green & brown .50 .30
a. Strip of 3, #1146-1148 2.00 2.00

See Nos. 1178-1179.

Ladybug Scarab Emblem — A572

von Stephan, UPU — A573

Perf. 11½

1981, Jan. 2 Photo. Unwmk.

1149 A572 70m shown 1.25 .50
1150 A572 70m Scarab, reverse 1.25 .50

Post Day.

Perf. 11x11½

1981, Jan. 7 **Wmk. 342**
1151 A573 140m grnsh bl & dk brn 1.75 .70

Heinrich von Stephan (1831-97), founder of UPU.

13th Cairo International Book Fair — A574

1981, Feb. 1 ***Perf. 11½x11***
1152 A574 20m multicolored .60 .25

14th Cairo International Fair, Mar. 14-28 — A575

Perf. 11x11½

1981, Mar. 14 **Photo.** **Wmk. 342**
1153 A575 20m multicolored .60 .25

Rural Electrification Authority, 10th Anniversary — A576

1981, Mar. 18
1154 A576 20m multicolored .60 .25

Veterans' Day — A577

Intl. Dentistry Conf., Cairo — A578

1981, Mar. 26
1155 A577 20m multicolored .60 .25

Perf. 11x11½

1981, Apr. 14 **Photo.** **Wmk. 342**
1156 A578 20m red & olive .60 .25

Trade Union Emblem — A579

Nurses' Day — A580

Perf. 11x11½

1981, May 1 **Photo.** **Wmk. 342**
1157 A579 20m brt blue & dk brn .60 .25

International Confederation of Arab Trade Unions, 25th anniv.

1981, May 12
1158 A580 20m multicolored .60 .25

Irrigation Equipment (Electrification Movement) — A581

1981, May 15 ***Perf. 11½***
1159 A581 20m multicolored .60 .25

Air Force Day — A582

Perf. 11x11½

1981, June 30 **Photo.** **Wmk. 342**
1160 A582 20m multicolored .60 .25

Flag Surrounding Map of Suez Canal — A583

Wmk. 342

1981, July 23 **Photo.** ***Perf. 11½***
1161 A583 20m multicolored .60 .25
1162 A583 20m Emblems .60 .25

July 23rd Revolution, 29th anniv.; Social Defense Year.

Lotus — A584

Wmk. 342

1981, July 29 **Photo.** ***Perf. 11***
1163 A584 10m multicolored .60 .25

For use on greeting cards.

A585

1981, Aug. 10 ***Perf. 11x11½***
1164 A585 140m Kemal Ataturk 2.25 1.25

A586

Perf. 11x11½

1981, Sept. 9 **Photo.** **Wmk. 342**
1165 A586 20m Orabi Pasha, Leader of Egyptian Force .60 .25

Orabi Revolution centenary.

A587

A588

1981, Sept. 14
1166 A587 45m Athlete, Pyramids, Sphinx .85 .25

World Muscular Athletics Championships, Cairo.

Perf. 11x11½

1981, Sept. 26 **Photo.** **Wmk. 342**
1167 A588 45m multicolored .60 .25

Ministry of Industry and Mineral Resources, 25th anniv.

20th Intl. Occupational Health Congress, Cairo — A589

1981, Sept. 28 ***Perf. 11½x11***
1168 A589 20m multicolored .60 .25

October War Against Israel, 8th Anniv. A590

1981, Oct. 6
1169 A590 20m multicolored .65 .25

World Food Day A591

13th World Telecommunications Day — A592

Intl. Year of the Disabled — A593

Fight Against Apartheid A594

Perf. 11½x11, 11x11½

1981, Oct. 24 **Photo.** **Wmk. 342**
1170 A591 10m multicolored .45 .25
1171 A592 20m multicolored .60 .25
1172 A593 45m multicolored .80 .55
1173 A594 230m multicolored 3.75 1.10
Nos. 1170-1173 (4) 5.60 2.15

United Nations Day.

Pres. Anwar Sadat (1917-81) — A595

Perf. 11x11½

1981, Nov. 14 **Unwmk.**
1174 A595 30m multicolored 1.25 .75
1175 A595 230m multicolored 5.50 3.00

Establishment of Shura Council — A596

Perf. 11½x11

1981, Dec. 12 **Photo.** **Wmk. 342**
1176 A596 45m purple & yellow .60 .30

Agricultural Credit and Development Bank, 50th Anniv. — A597

1981, Dec. 15 ***Perf. 11x11½***
1177 A597 20m multicolored .50 .25

Famous Men Type of 1980

30m, Ali el-Ghayati (1885-1956), journalist. 60m, Omar Ebn sl-Fared (1181-1234), Sufi poet.

Perf. 11x11½

1981, Dec. 21 **Photo.** **Wmk. 342**
1178 A571 30m green & brown .40 .30
1179 A571 60m green & brown .65 .45
a. Pair, #1178-1179 1.50 1.50

20th Anniv. of African Postal Union A598

1981, Dec. 21 *Perf. 11½x11*

1180 A598 60m multicolored .95 .35

14th Cairo Intl. Book Fair — A599

Arab Trade Union of Egypt, 25th Anniv. — A600

1982, Jan. 28

1181 A599 3p brown & yellow .65 .25

1982, Jan. 30

1182 A600 3p multicolored .45 .25

Khartoum Branch of Cairo University, 25th Anniv. A601

Perf. 11½x11

1982, Mar. 4 **Wmk. 342**

1183 A601 6p blue & green .75 .35

15th Cairo Intl. Fair — A602

1982, Mar. 13 *Perf. 11x11½*

1184 A602 3p multicolored .60 .25

50th Anniv. of Al-Ghardaka Marine Biological Station — A603

Fish of the Red Sea.

1982, Apr. 24 Litho. *Perf. 11½x11*

1185 10m Lined butterfly fish .90 .60
1186 30m Blue-banded sea perch 1.10 .70
1187 60m Batfish 1.50 .90
1188 230m Blue-spotted boxfish 3.50 2.00
a. A603 Block of 4, #1185-1188 7.50 7.50

Liberation of the Sinai — A604

1982, Apr. 25 Photo. *Perf. 11x11½*

1189 A604 3p multicolored .65 .25

50th Anniv. of Egypt Air A605

1982, May 7 Photo. *Perf. 11½x11*

1190 A605 23p multicolored 3.25 2.25

Minaret — A606

Al Azhar Mosque — A607

a, shown. b, Two terraces. c, Three terraces. d, Two turrets at top.

Perf. 11x11½

1982, June 28 Photo. Wmk. 342

1191 Strip of 4 + label 5.00 5.00
a.-d. A606 6p any single, multi .75 .55

Souvenir Sheet

Unwmk. *Imperf.*

1192 A607 23p multicolored 6.25 6.25

Al Azhar Mosque millennium.
No. 1192 airmail.

Dove — A608

Flower in Natl. Colors — A609

Perf. 11x11½

1982, July 23 Photo. Wmk. 342

1193 A608 3p multicolored .50 .25

Souvenir Sheet

Imperf

1194 A609 23p multicolored 4.00 4.00

30th anniv. of July 23rd Revolution.

World Tourism Day A610

Design: Sphinx, pyramid of Cheops, St. Catherine's Tower.

Perf. 11½x11

1982, Sept. 27 Photo. Wmk. 342

1195 A610 23p multicolored 3.50 2.25

October War Against Israel, 9th Anniv. A611

1982, Oct. 6

1196 A611 3p Memorial, map .65 .25

Biennale of Alexandria Art Exhibition — A612

1982, Oct. 17 *Perf. 11x11½*

1197 A612 3p multicolored .60 .25

10th Anniv. of UN Conference on Human Environment — A613

2nd UN Conference on Peaceful Uses of Outer Space, Vienna, Aug. 9-21 — A614

Scouting Year A615

TB Bacillus Centenary A616

Perf. 11½x11, 11½ (A615)

1982, Oct. 24

1198 A613 3p multicolored .50 .35
1199 A614 6p multicolored .80 .55
1200 A615 6p multicolored 1.10 .55
1201 A616 8p multicolored 1.25 .75
Nos. 1198-1201 (4) 3.65 2.20

United Nations Day.

50th Anniv. of Air Force A617

1982, Nov. 2 *Perf. 11½x11*

1202 A617 3p Jet, plane .70 .25

Ahmed Chawki (1868-1932) and Hafez Ibrahim (1871-1932), Poets — A618

Perf. 11½x11

1982, Nov. 25 Photo. Wmk. 342

1203 A618 6p multicolored .65 .50

Natl. Research Center, 25th Anniv. — A619

1982, Dec. 12 Photo. *Perf. 11x11½*

1204 A619 3p red & blue .70 .30

50th Anniv. of Arab Language Society A620

1982, Dec. 25 *Perf. 11½x11*

1205 A620 6p multicolored .80 .50

Year of the Aged — A621

1982, Dec. 25 *Perf. 11x11½*
1206 A621 23p multicolored 3.25 2.00

Post Day A622

1983, Jan. 2 *Perf. 11½*
1207 A622 3p multicolored .60 .25

15th Cairo Intl. Book Fair — A623

Perf. 11x11½
1983, Jan. 26 Photo. Wmk. 342
1208 A623 3p blue & red .65 .25

Police Day A624

1983, Jan. 25 *Perf. 11½x11*
1209 A624 3p multicolored .65 .25

16th Cairo Intl. Fair — A625

5th UN African Map Conf., Cairo — A626

Perf. 11x11½
1983, Mar. 2 Photo. Wmk. 342
1210 A625 3p multicolored .65 .30

1983, Mar. 2
1211 A626 3p lt green & blue .70 .30

African Ministers of Transport, Communications and Planning, 3rd Conference — A627

1983, Mar. 8 *Perf. 11½x11*
1212 A627 23p green & blue 1.75 1.00

A628

A629

1983, Mar. 20 *Perf. 11x11½*
1213 A628 3p Heading .55 .30
1214 A628 3p Kick .55 .30
a. Pair, #1213-1214 1.25 1.25

Victory in African Soccer Cup.

Perf. 11x11½
1983, Apr. 2 Photo. Wmk. 342
1215 A629 3p olive & red .70 .25

World Health Day and Natl. Blood Donation Campaign.

Org. of African Trade Union Unity A630

Perf. 11½x11
1983, Apr. 21 Photo. Wmk. 342
1216 A630 3p multicolored .65 .30

1st Anniv. of Sinai Liberation A631

75th Anniv. of Entomology Society A632

1983, Apr. 25 *Perf. 11x11½*
1217 A631 3p multicolored .70 .30

1983, May 23
1218 A632 3p Emblem (Holy Scarab) .70 .30

Chrysanthemums A633

1983, June 11 Photo. *Perf. 11½x11*
1219 A633 20m green & org red .40 .25

For use on greeting cards.

5th African Handball Championship, Cairo — A634

Perf. 11½x11
1983, July 22 Photo. Wmk. 342
1220 A634 6p brown & dk grn .65 .30

31st Anniv. of Revolution A635

Simon Bolivar (1783-1830) A636

1983, July 23 *Perf. 11½*
1221 A635 3p multicolored .45 .25

1983, Aug. *Perf. 11x11½*
1222 A636 23p brown & dull grn 1.75 1.00

Centenary of Arrival of Natl. Hero Orabi in Ceylon A637

Perf. 11½x11
1983, Aug. 25 Photo. Wmk. 342
1223 A637 3p Map, Orabi, El-Zahra School .55 .25

Islamic Vase, Museum Building A638

1983, Sept. 14 Photo. *Perf. 11½x11*
1224 A638 3p yel brn & dk brn .85 .30

Reopening of Islamic Museum.

October War Against Israel, 10th Anniv. — A639

2nd Pharaonic Race — A640

1983, Oct. 6 *Perf. 11½*
1225 A639 3p multicolored .70 .25

1983, Oct. 17 *Perf. 11½*
1226 A640 23p multicolored 2.25 1.25

United Nations Day — A641

1983, Oct. 24 Photo. *Perf. 11*
1227 A641 3p IMO, ships, horiz. .60 .25
1228 A641 6p ITU, UPU .75 .50
1229 A641 6p FAO, UN, grain .75 .50
1230 A641 23p UN, ocean 2.50 1.75
Nos. 1227-1230 (4) 4.60 3.00

4th World Karate Championship, Cairo — A642

1983, Nov. Photo. *Perf. 13*
1231 A642 3p multicolored .70 .30

Intl. Palestinian Cooperation Day — A643

1983, Nov. 29 Photo. *Perf. 13x13½*
1232 A643 6p Dome of the Rock 1.00 .30

75th Anniv. of Faculty of Fine Arts, Cairo A644

1983, Nov. 30 *Perf. 13*
1233 A644 3p multicolored .55 .25

75th Anniv. of Cairo University — A645

1983, Nov. 30 *Perf. 11x11½*
1234 A645 3p multicolored .55 .25
a. Perf. 13¼x12¾

Intl. Egyptian Society of Mother and Child Care A646

1983, Nov. 30 *Perf. 11½x11*
1235 A646 3p multicolored .55 .25

Org. of African Unity, 20th Anniv. — A647

World Heritage Convention, 10th Anniv. — A648

Perf. 11x11½
1983, Dec. 20 Photo. Wmk. 342
1236 A647 3p multicolored .55 .25

1983, Dec. 24

1237 Strip of 3 2.25 2.25
a. A648 3p Wood carving, Islamic .70 .45
b. A648 3p Coptic tapestry .70 .45
c. A648 3p Ramses II Thebes .70 .45

Post Day
A649

Restored Forts: 6p, Quatbay. 23p, Mosque, Salah El-Din.

1984, Jan. 2 ***Perf. 13***

1238 A649 6p multicolored .80 .45
1239 A649 23p multicolored 2.50 1.25

Misr Insurance Co., 50 Anniv.
A650

1984, Jan. 14 ***Perf. 11½x11***

1240 A650 3p multicolored .55 .30

16th Cairo Intl. Book Fair — A651

Perf. 13½x13

1984, Jan. 26 Photo. Wmk. 342

1241 A651 3p multicolored .55 .25

17th Cairo Intl. Fair
A652

Perf. 11½x11

1984, Mar. 10 Photo. Wmk. 342

1242 A652 3p multicolored .55 .30

25th Anniv. of Asyut University
A653

75th Anniv. of Cooperative Unions
A654

1984, Mar. 10 ***Perf. 11x11½***

1243 A653 3p multicolored .55 .25

1984, Mar. 17

1244 A654 3p multicolored .55 .25

World Theater Day — A655

Mahmoud Mokhtar (1891-1934), Sculptor — A656

Perf. 11x11½, 11½x11

1984, Mar. 27 Photo. Unwmk.

1245 A655 3p Masks .55 .25
1246 A656 3p Pride of the Nile .55 .25

World Health Day and Fight Against Polio — A657

Perf. 11½x11

1984, Apr. 7 Photo. Wmk. 342

1247 A657 3p Polio vaccine 1.00 .30

2nd Anniv. of Sinai Liberation — A658

1984, Apr. 25

1248 A658 3p Doves, map .55 .25

Africa Day
A659

Perf. 12½x13½

1984, May 25 Photo. Wmk. 342

1249 A659 3p Map, UN emblem .55 .25

Satellite, Waves
A660

Carnations
A661

1984, May 31 ***Perf. 11x11½***

1250 A660 3p multicolored .55 .25

Radio broadcasting in Egypt, 50th anniv.

1984, June 1

1251 A661 2p red & green .45 .25

For use on greeting cards.

Intl. Cairo Arab Arts Biennale — A662

1984, June 1 ***Perf. 13½x12½***

1252 A662 3p multicolored .55 .25

July Revolution, 32nd Anniv. — A663

Wmk. 342

1984, July 23 Photo. ***Perf. 11***

1253 A663 3p Atomic energy, agriculture .55 .25

A664

A665

1984 Summer Olympics: a, Boxing. b, Basketball. c, Volleyball. d, Soccer.

1984, July 28

1254 Strip of 4 + label 5.75 5.75
a.-d. A664 3p any single .45 .25

Size: 130x80mm

Imperf

1255 A664 30p like No. 1254 4.25 4.25

Wmk. 342

1984, Aug. 13 Photo. ***Perf. 11***

1256 A665 3p bl & multi .55 .25
1257 A665 23p grn & multi 2.50 1.40

2nd Genl. Conference of Egyptians Abroad, Aug. 11-15, Cairo.

Youth Hostels, 30th Anniv. — A666

Egypt Tour Co., 50th Anniv. — A667

Perf. 11x11½

1984, Sept. 22 Photo. Wmk. 342

1258 A666 3p Youths, emblem .55 .25

1984, Sept. 27

1259 A667 3p Emblem, sphinx .60 .25

October War Against Israel, 11th Anniv. — A668

Egypt-Sudan Unity — A669

1984, Oct. 6

1260 A668 3p Map, eagle .55 .25

1984, Oct. 12

1261 A669 3p Map of Nile, arms .55 .25

UN Day — A670

Tanks, Emblem — A671

Perf. 13½x12½

1984, Oct. 24 Photo. Wmk. 342

1262 A670 3p UNICEF Emblem, child .55 .25

UN campaign for infant survival.

1984, Nov. 10

1263 A671 3p multicolored .60 .25

Military Equipment Exhibition, Cairo, Nov. 10-14.

Tolon Mosque, Egypt
A672

1984, Dec. 23 Photo. ***Perf. 11½x11***

1264 A672 3p multicolored .65 .25

Ahmed Ebn Tolon (A.D. 835-884), Gov. of Egypt, founder of Kataea City.

A673

A674

1984, Dec. 23 ***Perf. 11x11½***

1265 A673 3p multicolored .55 .25

Kamel el-Kilany (1897-1959), author.

Perf. 11x11½

1984, Dec. 26 Photo. Wmk. 342

Globe and congress emblem.

1266 A674 3p lt blue, ver & blk .65 .25

29th Intl. Congress on the History of Medicine, Dec. 27, 1984-Jan. 1, 1985, Cairo.

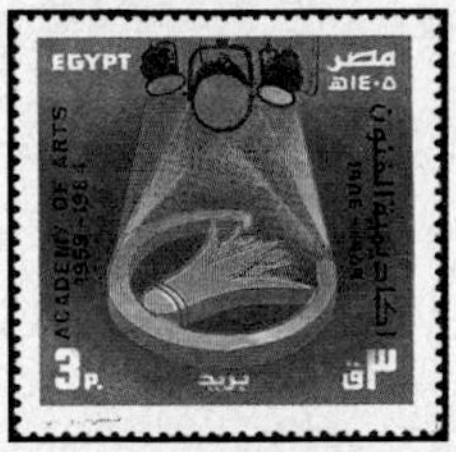

Academy of the Arts, 25th Anniv. A675

1984, Dec. 31 *Perf. 13*

1267 A675 3p Emblem in spotlights .60 .25

Pharaoh Receiving Message, Natl. Postal Museum, Cairo A676

1985, Jan. 2 *Perf. 11½x11*

1268 A676 3p brown, lt bl & ver .65 .25

Postal Museum, 50th anniv.

Intl. Union of Architects, 15th Conference, Jan. 14-Feb. 15 — A677

1985, Jan. 20

1269 A677 3p multicolored .60 .25

Seated Pharaonic Scribe — A678

Wheat, Cogwheels, Fair Emblem — A679

1985, Jan. 22 *Perf. 11x11½*

1270 A678 3p brt org & dk blue grn .70 .30

17th Intl. Book Fair, Jan. 22-Feb. 3, Cairo.

1985, Mar. 9 *Perf. 13½x13*

1271 A679 3p multicolored .60 .25

18th Intl. Fair, Mar. 9-22, Cairo.

Return of Sinai to Egypt, 3rd Anniv. — A680

1985, Apr. 25 Wmk. 342 Litho.

1272 A680 5p multicolored 1.00 .30

Ancient Artifacts — A681

A681a

Designs: 1p, God Mout, limestone sculpture, 360-340 B.C. 2p, No. 1281, Five wading birds, bas-relief. 3p, No. 1276, Seated statue, Ramses II, Temple of Luxor. No. 1276A, Vase. 8p, 15p, Slave bearing votive fruit offering, mural. 10p, Double-handled flask. 11p, Sculpted head of woman. No. 1282, Pitcher. 30p, 50p, Decanter. 35p, Temple of Karnak carved capitals. £1, Mosque.

1985-90 Photo. Unwmk. *Perf. 11½*

1273	A681	1p	brown olive	.40	.25
1274	A681	2p	brt grnsh bl	.40	.25
1275	A681	3p	yellow brown	.40	.25
1276	A681	5p	dk violet	.50	.25
1276A	A681	5p	lemon	.40	.25
1277	A681	8p	pale ol grn, sep & brn	.75	.25
1278	A681	10p	dk vio & bl	.60	.25
1279	A681	11p	dk violet	.90	.30
1280	A681	15p	pale yel, sep & brn	1.40	.30
1281	A681	20p	yellow green	.60	.30
1282	A681	20p	dk grn & yel	.60	.30
1283	A681	30p	ol bis & buff	.70	.30
1284	A681	35p	sep & pale yel	1.00	.60
1285	A681	50p	purple & buff	1.25	.50
1285A	A681a	£1	brown & buff	3.00	1.25
1286	A681a	£2	sepia & yel	6.00	2.00
			Nos. 1273-1286 (16)	18.90	7.60

Issued: 1p, 2p, 3p, No. 1276, 8p, 11p, 15p, 5/1/85; 35p, 7/7/85; No. 1281, 4/1/86; 10p, 10/1/89; £2, 12/1/89; No. 1282, 2/1/90; 30p, 50p, 2/5/90; £1, 2/8/90; No. 1276A, 12/15/90.

No. 1276A is 18x23mm.

No. 1278 exists dated "1990."

See Nos. 1467, 1470, 1472.

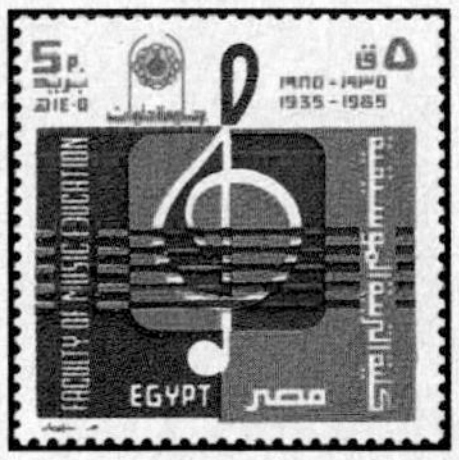

Helwan University School of Music, 50th Anniv. A682

1985, May 15

1287 A682 5p multicolored .75 .30

El-Moulid Bride, Folk Doll — A683

1985

1288 A683 2p orange & multi .50 .25

1289 A683 5p red & multi .60 .30

Festivals 1985. Issued: 2p, 6/11; 5p, 8/10. For use on greeting cards.

A684

A685

Winning teams: a, b, Cairo Sports Stadium. c, El-Zamalek Club, white uniform, 1983. d, Natl. Club, red uniform, 1984. e, El-Mokawiloon Club (Arab Contractor Club), orange uniform, 1984.

1985, June 17 *Perf. 13½x13*

1290 Strip of 5 5.50 5.50

a.-e. A684 5p any single .80 .50

1985 Africa Cup Soccer Championships. Cairo Sports Stadium, 25th anniv. Nos. 1290a-1290b have continuous design.

1985, July 23 *Perf. 11½x11*

1291 A685 5p blue, brn & yel .80 .30

Egyptian Television, 25th anniv. Egyptian Revolution, 33rd anniv.

Suez Canal Reopening, 10th Anniv. — A686

Perf. 13x13½

1985, July 23 Litho. Wmk. 342

1292 A686 5p multicolored .80 .30

Egyptian Revolution, 33rd anniv.

Ahmed Hamdi Memorial Underwater Tunnel — A687

1985, July 23 *Perf. 13½x13*

1293 A687 5p blue, vio & org .60 .25

Egyptian Revolution, 33rd anniv.

Souvenir Sheet

Aswan High Dam, 25th Anniv. — A688

Wmk. 342

1985, July 23 Photo. *Imperf.*

1294 A688 30p multicolored 4.00 4.00

Heart, Map, Olive Laurel, Conference Emblem — A689

1985, Aug. 10 Litho. *Perf. 13½x13*

1295 A689 15p multicolored 1.25 .85

Egyptian Emigrants, 3rd general conference, Aug. 10-14, Cairo.

Natl. Tourism Ministry, 50th Anniv. — A690

1985, Sept. 10 *Perf. 13x13½*

1296 A690 5p multicolored .55 .30

October War Against Israel, 12th Anniv. — A691

1985, Oct. 6

1297 A691 5p multicolored .60 .30

Air Scouts Assoc., 30th Anniv. — A692

1985, Oct. 15 Photo. *Perf. 11½*

1298 A692 5p Emblem .80 .30

A693

1985, Oct. 24

1299 A693 5p UN emblem, weather map .55 .25

UN Day, Meteorology Day.

UN, 40th Anniv. — A694

1985, Oct. 24

1300 A694 15p multicolored 1.25 .85

Intl. Youth Year — A695

1985, Oct. 24
1301 A695 5p multicolored .55 .25

A696

1985, Oct. 24
1302 A696 15p blue & int blue 1.25 .85

Intl. Communications Development Program.

A697

A698

Emblem, hieroglyphics of Hassi Raa, 1st known dentist.

1985, Oct. 29 ***Perf. 11x11½***
1303 A697 5p beige & pale bl vio .75 .30

2nd Intl. Dentistry Conference.

1985, Nov. 18 Photo. ***Perf. 11½***
1304 A698 5p Emblem, squash player .65 .25

1985 World Squash Championships, Nov. 18-Dec. 4.

A699

A700

1985, Nov. 2 Litho. ***Perf. 13½x13***
1305 A699 5p multicolored .55 .30

4th Intl. Conference on the Biography and Sunna of Mohammed.

1985, Dec. 1 Photo. ***Perf. 11x11½***
1306 A700 5p multicolored .55 .25

1st Conference on the Development of Vocational Training.

Natl. Olympic Committee, 75th Anniv. — A701

18th Intl. Book Fair, Cairo — A702

1985, Dec. 28 Photo. ***Perf. 13x13½***
1307 A701 5p multicolored .60 .30

1986, Jan. 21 ***Perf. 11x11½***
1308 A702 5p Pharaonic scribe .55 .25

CODATU III — A703

1986, Jan. 26 ***Perf. 11½***
1309 A703 5p lt ol grn, ver & grnsh bl .55 .25

3rd Intl. Conference on Urban Transportation in Developing Countries, Cairo.

Central Bank, 25th Anniv. — A704

1986, Jan. 30 ***Perf. 13x13½***
1310 A704 5p multicolored .55 .25

Cairo Postal Traffic Center Inauguration — A705

1986, Jan. 30 ***Perf. 11½x11***
1311 A705 5p blue & dk brown .55 .25

Pharaonic Mural, Btah Hotteb's Tomb at Saqqara A706

1986, Feb. 27 Photo. ***Perf. 11½x11***
1312 A706 5p yel, gldn brn & brn .70 .35

Faculty of Commerce, Cairo Univ., 75th anniv.

Cairo Intl. Fair, Mar. 8-21 — A707

1986, Mar. 8 Litho. ***Perf. 13½x13***
1313 A707 5p multicolored .55 .25

Queen Nefertiti, Sinai — A708

Perf. 13x13½
1986, Apr. 25 Litho. Wmk. 342
1314 A708 5p multicolored .70 .30

Return of the Sinai to Egypt, 4th anniv.

Ministry of Health, 50th Anniv. — A709

1986, Apr. 10 ***Perf. 13½x13***
1315 A709 5p multicolored .55 .30

1986 Census — A710

1986, May 26 Photo. ***Perf. 11½***
1316 A710 15p brn, grnsh bl & yel bis 1.00 .50

Egypt, Winner of African Soccer Cup — A711

Festivals, Roses — A712

1986, May 31 ***Perf. 13½x13***
1317 A711 5p English inscription below cup .65 .45
1318 A711 5p Arabic .65 .45
a. Pair, #1317-1318 1.50 1.50

1986, June 2 ***Perf. 11½***
1319 A712 5p multicolored .55 .25

For use on greeting cards.

World Environment Day — A713

1986, June 5 ***Perf. 13½x13***
1320 A713 15p Emblem, smoke-stacks 1.25 .50

July 23rd Revolution, 34th Anniv. A714

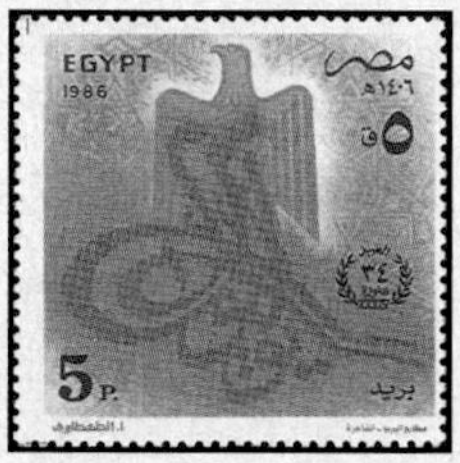

1986, July 23 Litho. ***Perf. 13***
1321 A714 5p gray grn, scar & yel bis .60 .25

6th African Roads Conference, Cairo, Sept. 22-26 — A715

Perf. 13½x13
1986, Sept. 21 Litho. Wmk. 342
1322 A715 15p multicolored 1.25 .55

October War Against Israel, 13th Anniv. A716

1986, Oct. 6 Litho. ***Perf. 13***
1323 A716 5p multicolored 1.00 .30

Engineers' Syndicate, 40th Anniv. A717

1986, Oct. 11 Photo. ***Perf. 11½***
1324 A717 5p lt blue, brn & pale grn .55 .25

Workers' Cultural Education Assoc., 25th Anniv. — A718

Intl. Peace Year — A719

1986, Oct. 11 ***Perf. 11x11½***
1325 A718 5p orange & rose vio .55 .25

1986, Oct. 24
1326 A719 5p blue, grn & pale sal .55 .25

First Oil Well in Egypt, Cent. — A720

1986, Nov. 7 **Photo.** ***Perf. 11½***
1327 A720 5p dull grn, blk & pale yel .65 .25

UN Child Survival Campaign A721

1986, Nov. 20 **Litho.** ***Perf. 13***
1328 A721 5p multicolored .60 .25

Ahmed Amin, Philosopher A722

1986, Dec. 20 ***Perf. 11½***
1329 A722 5p pale grn, pale yel & brn .55 .25

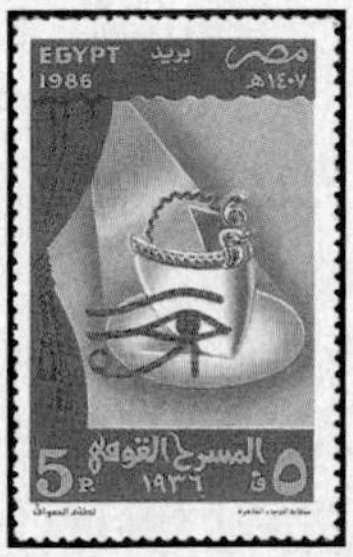

National Theater, 50th Anniv. — A723

1986, Dec. 20 ***Perf. 13½x13***
1330 A723 5p multicolored .55 .25

Post Day A724

Step Pyramid, Saqqara, King Zoser.

Perf. 13x13½
1987, Jan. 2 **Litho.** **Wmk. 342**
1331 A724 5p multicolored .65 .30

19th Intl. Book Fair, Cairo A725

1987, Jan. 25 **Litho.** ***Perf. 13***
1332 A725 5p multicolored .60 .30

5th World Conference on Islamic Education A726

Wmk. 342
1987, Mar. 8 **Litho.** ***Perf. 13***
1333 A726 5p multicolored .55 .25

20th Intl. Fair, Cairo — A727

1987, Mar. 21 **Photo.** ***Perf. 11½***
1334 A727 5p Good workers medal .55 .25

Veteran's Day A728

1987, Mar. 26
1335 A728 5p multicolored .55 .30

Intl. Gardens Inauguration, Nasser City — A729

1987, Mar. 30 **Litho.** ***Perf. 13***
1336 A729 15p multicolored 1.10 .60

World Health Day A730

1987, Apr. 7 **Photo.** ***Perf. 11½***
1337 A730 5p Mother feeding child .55 .30

Litho.
Perf. 13
1338 A730 5p Oral rehydration therapy .55 .30

A731

Natl. Team Victory at 1986 Intl. Soccer Championships — A732

Trophies: No. 1339a, Al Ahly Cup. No. 1339b, National Cup. No. 1339c, Al Zamalek Cup. No. 1340, Natl. flag, Cairo Stadium and trophies pictured on No. 1339.

1987, Apr. 19 **Litho.** ***Perf. 13½x13***
1339 Strip of 3 1.75 1.75
a.-c. A731 5p any single .55 .30

Size: 115x85mm
Imperf
1340 A732 30p multicolored 4.00 4.00

A733

Salah El Din Citadel, Pharoah's Is., Sinai.

1987, Apr. 25
1341 A733 5p sky blue & lt brown .65 .30

Return of the Sinai to Egypt, 5th anniv.

A734

Festivals.

1987, May 21 **Photo.** ***Perf. 11½***
1342 A734 5p Dahlia .55 .25

Cultural Heritage Exhibition — A735

1987, June 17 **Litho.** ***Perf. 13x13½***
1343 A735 15p multicolored 1.00 1.00

Tourism Year — A736

a, Column and Sphinx, Alexandria. b, St. Catherine's Monastery, Mt. Sinai. c, Colossi of Thebes. d, Temple of Theban Triad, Luxor.

1987, June 18
1344 Block of 4 5.25 5.25
a.-d. A736 15p any single 1.10 .90

See No. C187.

Loyalty Day A737

1987, June 26 ***Perf. 13***
1345 A737 5p multicolored .55 .25

General Intelligence Service, 32nd anniv.

Industry-Agriculture Exhibition — A738

1987, July 23 **Photo.** ***Perf. 11½***
1346 A738 5p grn, dull org & blk .55 .25

Intl. Year of Shelter for the Homeless A739

1987, Sept. 2 **Litho.** ***Perf. 13***
1347 A739 5p multicolored .55 .25

World Architects' Day.

Aida, Performed at Al Ahram Pyramid, Giza A740

Radamis and troops returning from Ethiopia.

1987, Sept. 21
1348 A740 15p multicolored 1.50 .65

Size: 70x70mm

Imperf

1349 A740 30p multicolored 10.00 10.00

Greater Cairo Subway Inauguration — A741

1987, Sept. 27 ***Perf. 13x13½***
1350 A741 5p multicolored 1.20 .30

Industry Day A742

1987, Oct. 1 ***Perf. 13***
1351 A742 5p multicolored .55 .25

Battle of Hettin, 800th Anniv. — A743

1987, Oct. 6 **Photo.** ***Perf. 11x11½***
1352 A743 5p multicolored .70 .30

UPU Emblem A744

Perf. 11½

1987, Oct. 24 **Unwmk.** **Photo.**
1353 A744 5p multicolored .55 .25

UN Executive Council, 40th anniv.; UPU Consultative Council, 30th anniv.

16th Art Biennial of Alexandria A745

1987, Nov. 7 **Litho.** ***Perf. 13½x13***
1354 A745 5p multicolored .55 .25

Second Intl. Defense Equipment Exhibition, Cairo, Nov. 9-13 — A746

Perf. 13x13½

1987, Nov. 9 **Litho.** **Unwmk.**
1355 A746 5p multicolored .60 .25

2nd Pan-Arab Congress on Anaesthesia and Intensive Care — A747

Unwmk.

1987, Dec. 1 **Litho.** ***Perf. 13***
1356 A747 5p multicolored .65 .30

Intl. Orthopedic and Traumatology Conference A748

1987, Dec. 1 ***Perf. 13½x13***
1357 A748 5p gray, red brn & bl .55 .25

Selim Hassan (1887-1961), Egyptologist, and Hieroglyphs A749

Abdel Hamid Badawi (1887-1965), Jurist, and Scales of Justice — A750

Perf. 13½x13

1987, Dec. 30 **Litho.** **Unwmk.**
1358 A749 5p multicolored .55 .25
1359 A750 5p multicolored .55 .25

Stamp Day 1988 — A751

Pyramids of the Pharaohs and: a, Cheops. b, Chefren. c, Mycerinus. No. 1360 has a continuous design.

1988, Jan. 2
1360 A751 Strip of 3 5.50 5.50
a.-c. 15p, any single 1.40 .90

Afro-Asian Peoples Solidarity Organization, 30th Anniv. — A752

1988, Jan. 10 ***Perf. 13x13½***
1361 A752 15p multicolored 1.00 .55

20th Intl. Book Fair, Cairo — A753

1988, Jan. 26 ***Perf. 13½x13***
1362 A753 5p multicolored .55 .25

Martrans (Natl. Shipping Line), 25th Anniv. A754

Unwmk.

1988, Mar. 3 **Litho.** ***Perf. 13***
1363 A754 5p multicolored .85 .25

Cairo Intl. Fair A755

1988, Mar. 12 **Photo.** ***Perf. 11½x11***
1364 A755 5p multicolored .55 .25

World Health Day 1988: Diabetes — A756

Perf. 11x11½

1988, Apr. 7 **Photo.** **Unwmk.**
1365 A756 5p multicolored .55 .25

Prince, Fig Tree — A757

1988, Apr. 17 ***Perf. 11½***
1366 A757 5p grn, brn org & brn .55 .25

1988 Festival. For use on greeting cards.

African Postal Union, 25th Anniv. — A758

1988, Apr. 23 **Litho.** ***Perf. 13x13½***
1367 A758 15p brt blue 1.00 1.00

Oppose Racial Discrimination — A759

1988, May 25 **Photo.** ***Perf. 11½***
1368 A759 5p multicolored .50 .25

Taw Fek-Hakem (1902-1987), Playwright, Novelist — A760

1988, Aug. 5 **Photo.** ***Perf. 11½***
1369 A760 5p brt grn bl & org brn .60 .25

See Nos. 1383-1384, 1479-1480, 1486, 1500-1502, 1543-1546.

Faculty of Art Education, 50th Anniv. A761

Perf. 11½

1988, Sept. 10 Photo. Unwmk.

1370 A761 5p multicolored .50 .25

A762

1988 Summer Olympics, Seoul — A763

1988, Sept. 17 Litho. *Perf. 13*

1371 A762 15p multicolored 1.25 1.25

Size: 96x91mm

Imperf.

1372 A763 30p multicolored 6.25 6.25

No. 1371 is airmail.

October War Against Israel, 15th Anniv. — A764

Perf. 13x13½

1988, Oct. 6 Litho. Unwmk.

1373 A764 5p multicolored .55 .35

A765

Opening of the Opera House — A766

1988, Oct. 10 *Perf. 11½*

1374 A765 5p multicolored .55 .30

Size: 112x75mm

Imperf

1375 A766 50p multicolored 3.50 3.50

Intl. Red Cross and Red Crescent Organizations, 125th Annivs. — A767

Perf. 11½

1988, Oct. 24 Photo. Unwmk.

1376 A767 5p green, blk & red .50 .25

WHO, 40th Anniv. — A768

1988, Oct. 24 *Perf. 11x11⅛*

1377 A768 20p multicolored 1.25 1.10

Naguib Mahfouz, 1988 Nobel Prize Winner for Literature — A769

1988, Nov. 7 Litho. *Perf. 13x13½*

1378 A769 5p multicolored .50 .25

See No. C190.

Arab Scouting Organization, 75th Anniv. — A770

1988, Nov. 10

1379 A770 25p multicolored 1.25 1.25

Return of Taba to Egypt — A771

1988, Nov. 15

1380 A771 5p multicolored .50 .25

Intl. Conference on Orthopedic Surgery, Cairo, Nov. 15-18 — A772

1988, Nov. 15 Photo. *Perf. 11½x11*

1381 A772 5p buff, brt yel grn & brn .60 .25

A773

1988, Dec. 3 *Perf. 11½*

1382 A773 5p multicolored .50 .25

Ministry of Agriculture, 75th anniv.

A774

Famous Men: No. 1383, Mohamed Hussein Hekal (1888-1956), author, politician. No. 1384, Ahmed Lotfi El Sayed (1872-1963), educator, politician.

Perf. 13½x13

1988, Dec. 29 Litho. Unwmk.

1383 A774 5p green & red brn .45 .25

1384 A774 5p green & red brn .45 .25

a. Pair, #1383-1384 1.00 1.00

A775

Statues: 5p, Statue of K. Abr, a priest, 5th cent. No. 1386, Queen Nefert, 4th Dynasty. No. 1387, King Ra Hoteb, 4th Dynasty.

1989, Jan. 2

1385 A775 5p multicolored .50 .30

1386 A775 25p multicolored 1.60 1.00

1387 A775 25p multicolored 1.60 1.00

a. Pair, #1386-1387 3.50 3.50

Nos. 1385-1387 (3) 3.70 2.30

Stamp Day.

A776

1989, Jan. 10

1388 A776 5p dull green .55 .25

Jawaharlal Nehru (1889-1964), 1st Prime Minister of independent India.

Nile Hilton Hotel, 30th Anniv. — A777

1989, Feb. 22 Litho. *Perf. 13x13½*

1389 A777 5p multicolored .45 .25

Return of Taba to Egypt A778

Unwmk.

1989, Mar. 15 Litho. *Perf. 13*

1390 A778 5p multicolored .45 .25

2nd Stage of Cairo Subway A779

1989, Apr. 12 Litho. *Perf. 13*

1391 A779 5p multicolored 1.00 .30

Lantern — A780

1989, May 4 Photo. *Perf. 11½*

1392 A780 5p multicolored .45 .25

1989 Festival. For use on greeting cards.

1st Arab Olympic Day A781

1989, May 24

1393 A781 5p tan, blk & dull grn .50 .25

Interparliamentary Union, Cent. — A782

Pyramids and the Parliament Building, Cairo.

1989, June 29 Litho. *Perf. 13x13½*

1394 A782 25p shown 1.60 1.25

Size: 87x76mm

Imperf

1395 A782 25p multi, diff. 2.75 2.75

French Revolution, Bicent. — A783

1989, July 14 Photo. *Perf. 11½*

1396 A783 25p multicolored 1.50 1.25

No. 1396 is an airmail issue.

African Development Bank, 25th Anniv. — A784

Perf. 11½

1989, Oct. 1 Photo. Unwmk.

1397 A784 10p multicolored .45 .25

A785

October War Against Israel, 16th Anniv. — A786

1989, Oct. 6 *Perf. 13*

1398 Strip of 3 1.50 1.50

a. A785 10p shown .50 .25

b. A786 10p shown .50 .25

c. A785 10p Battle scene .50 .25

See No. 1424.

Aga Khan Award for Architecture A788

Perf. 11½

1989, Oct. 15 Photo. Unwmk.

1400 A788 35p multicolored 1.25 .60

Natl. Health Insurance Plan, 25th Anniv. A789

1989, Oct. 24

1401 A789 10p blk, gray & ver .50 .25

World Post Day — A790

1989, Oct. 24 *Perf. 11x11½*

1402 A790 35p blue, blk & brt yel 1.00 .50

Statues of Memnon, Thebes — A791

Perf. 11½

1989, Nov. 12 Photo. Unwmk.

1403 A791 10p lt vio, blk & brt yel grn .50 .25

Intl. Cong. & Convention Assoc. (ICCA) annual convention, Nov. 11-18, Cairo.

Cairo University School of Agriculture, Cent. — A792

1989, Nov. 15

1404 A792 10p pale grn, blk & brt yel .45 .25

Cairo Intl. Conference Center — A793

1989, Nov. 20 *Perf. 11½x11*

1405 A793 5p multicolored .45 .25

Road Safety Soc., 20th Anniv. — A794

1989, Nov. 20 *Perf. 11½*

1406 A794 10p multicolored .45 .25

Alexandria University, 50th Anniv. — A795

1989, Nov. 30 *Perf. 11x11½*

1407 A795 10p pale blue & tan .45 .25

Portrait of Pasha, Monument in Opera Square, Cairo A796

Perf. 11½x11

1989, Dec. 31 Photo. Unwmk.

1408 A796 10p multicolored .45 .25

Ibrahim Pasha (d. 1838), army commander from 1825 to 1828.

Famous Men

A797 A798

1989, Dec. 31 *Perf. 11x11½*

1409 A797 10p grn & dk ol grn .45 .25

1410 A798 10p golden brown .45 .25

Abd El-Rahman El-Rafei (b. 1889), historian (No. 1409); Abdel Kader El Mazni (b. 1889), man of letters (No. 1410).

See Nos. 1431-1432.

Statue of Priest Ranofr — A799

Relief Sculpture of Betah Hoteb — A800

1990, Jan. 2 *Perf. 13½x13*

1411 A799 30p multicolored 1.00 .40

1412 A800 30p multicolored 1.00 .40

a. Pair, #1411-1412 2.75 2.75

Stamp Day.

Arab Cooperation Council, 1st Anniv. — A801

Perf. 13x13½

1990, Feb. 16 Photo. Unwmk.

1413 A801 10p multicolored .45 .25

1414 A801 35p multicolored 1.25 .60

Emblem, Conference Center A802

Road Safety Emblems A803

Perf. 13½x13

1990, Mar. 10 Litho. Unwmk.

1415 A802 10p brt yel grn, red & blk .50 .25

Size: 80x59mm

Imperf

1416 A802 30p multicolored 1.50 1.50

African Parliamentary Union 13th general conference, Mar. 10-15.

1990, Mar. 19 Photo. *Perf. 11x11½*

1417 A803 10p multicolored .60 .25

Intl. Conference on Road Safety & Accidents in Developing Countries, Mar. 19-22.

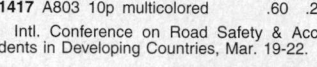

Egyptian Wild Daisies — A804

1990, Apr. 24 *Perf. 11½*

1418 A804 10p multicolored .45 .25

1990 Festival. For use on greeting cards.

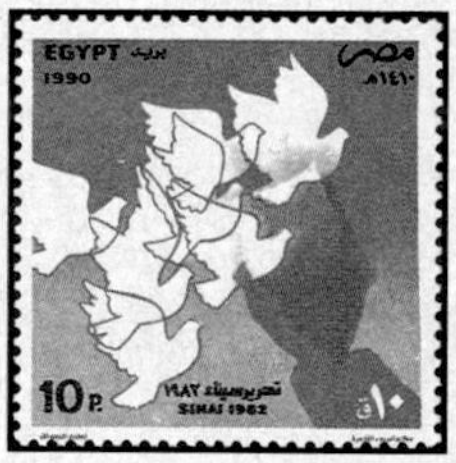

Sinai Liberation, 8th Anniv. A805

1990, Apr. 25

1419 A805 10p blue, blk & yel grn .50 .25

World Cup Soccer Championships, Italy — A806

1990, May 26 Litho. *Perf. 13½x13*

1420 A806 10p multicolored .40 .25

Souvenir Sheet

Imperf

1421 A806 50p Flags, trophy 2.25 2.25

World Basketball Championships, Argentina — A807

1990, Aug. 8 *Perf. 13x13½*
1422 A807 10p multicolored .50 .25

Natl. Population Council, 5th Anniv. — A808

1990, Sept. 15 *Perf. 13½x13*
1423 A808 10p brown & yel grn .50 .25

October War Against Israel Type

1990, Oct. 6 Litho. *Perf. 13x13½*
1424 Strip of 3 1.75 1.75
a. A785 10p Bunker, tank .40 .25
b. A786 10p like #1398b .40 .25
c. A785 10p Troops with flag, flame thrower .40 .25

Egyptian Postal Service, 125th Anniv. — A809

1990, Oct. 9
1425 A809 10p lt blue, blk & red .50 .25

Dar El Eloum Faculty, Cent. A810

1990, Oct. 13 Litho. *Perf. 13*
1426 A810 10p multicolored .45 .25

UN Development Program, 40th Anniv. — A811

ITU, 125th Anniv. — A812

1990, Oct. 24 *Perf. 11½*
1427 A811 30p yel, bl grn & yel grn .90 .30

Perf. 13

1428 A812 30p multicolored .90 .30

UN Day.

Ras Mohammed Natl. Park — A813

Designs: a, Crown butterfly fish. b, Lionfish. c, Twobar anemone fish. d, Grouper.

1990, Dec. 22 Litho. *Perf. 13*
1429 A813 Block of 4 3.50 3.50
a.-b. 10p any single .50 .30
c.-d. 20p any single .80 .40

Day of the Disabled — A814

1990. Dec. 15 Photo. *Perf. 11*
1430 A814 10p multicolored .50 .25

Mohamed Fahmy Abdel Meguid Bey, Medical Reformer A815

Nabaweya Moussa (1890-1951), Educator A816

Perf. 11x11½

1990, Dec. 30 **Unwmk.**
1431 A815 10p Prus bl, brn & org .40 .25
1432 A816 10p grn, org brn & blk .40 .25

Stamp Day — A817

1991, Jan. 1 Litho. *Perf. 13½x13*
1433 A817 5p No. 1 .30 .25
1434 A817 10p No. 2 .45 .25
1435 A817 20p No. 3 .60 .40
a. Strip of 3, #1433-1435 1.75 1.75

See Nos. 1443-1446, 1459-1460.

Veterinary Surgeon Syndicate, 50th Anniv. — A818

1991, Feb. 28 Photo. *Perf. 11½*
1436 A818 10p multicolored .45 .25

Syndicate of Journalists, 50th Anniv. — A819

1991, Apr. Photo. *Perf. 11½*
1437 A819 10p multicolored .40 .25

Narcissus — A820

1991, Apr. 13
1438 A820 10p multicolored .40 .25

1991 Festival. For use on greeting cards.

Giza Zoo, Cent. — A821

1991, June 15 Litho. *Imperf.*
Size: 80x63mm
1439 A821 50p multicolored 4.00 4.00

Mahmoud Mokhtar (1891-1934), Sculptor — A822

Mohamed Nagi (1888-1956), Painter — A823

Perf. 13x13½, 13½x13

1991, June 11 **Litho.**
1440 A822 10p multicolored .40 .25
1441 A823 10p multicolored .40 .25

Faculty of Engineering — A824

1991, June 30 *Perf. 13x13½*
1442 A824 10p multicolored .40 .25

Stamp Day Type

Designs: No. 1443, No. 5. No. 1444, No. 4. No. 1445, No. 7. No. 1446, Sphinx, pyramid, No. 6.

1991, July 23 *Perf. 13*
1443 A817 10p orange & blk .40 .25
1444 A817 10p yellow & blk .40 .25
1445 A817 10p lilac & blk .40 .25
a. Strip of 3, #1443-1445 1.40 1.40

Size: 80x60mm

Imperf

1446 A817 50p multicolored 2.25 1.75
Nos. 1443-1446 (4) 3.45 2.50

Mohamed Abdel el Wahab, Musician A825

1991, Aug. 28 *Perf. 13*
1447 A825 10p multicolored .55 .25

5th Africa Games, Cairo — A826

No. 1448, Karate, judo. No. 1449, Table tennis, field hockey, tennis. No. 1450, Running, gymnastics, swimming. No. 1451, Soccer, basketball, shooting. No. 1452, Boxing, wrestling, weightlifting. No. 1453, Handball, cycling, volleyball. No. 1454, Games mascot, vert. No. 1455, Mascot, emblem, torch.

Perf. 13x13½

1991, Sept. Litho. Unwmk.
1448 A826 10p multicolored .40 .25
1449 A826 10p multicolored .40 .25
a. Pair, #1448-1449 .90 .90
1450 A826 10p multicolored .40 .25
1451 A826 10p multicolored .40 .25
a. Pair, #1450-1451 .90 .90
1452 A826 10p multicolored .40 .25
1453 A826 10p multicolored .40 .25
a. Pair, #1452-1453 .90 .90

Perf. 13½x13

1454 A826 10p multicolored .45 .25

Size: 80x60mm

Imperf

1455 A826 50p multicolored 1.75 1.75
Nos. 1448-1455 (8) 4.60 3.50

Intl. Statistics Institute, 48th Session A827

1991, Sept. 9
1456 A827 10p multicolored .40 .25

Opening of Dar Al Eftaa Religious Center — A828

1991, Oct. 1 **Litho.** ***Perf. 13***
1457 A828 10p multicolored .40 .25

October War Against Israel, 18th Anniv. — A829

1991, Oct. 6 ***Perf. 13x13½***
1458 A829 10p multicolored .55 .25

Stamp Day Type

Designs: 10p, No. 6. £1, Stamp exhibition emblem, hieroglyphics, pyramids, sphinx.

1991, Oct. 7 ***Perf. 13***
1459 A817 10p blue & black .50 .25

Size: 90x60mm

Imperf

1460 A817 £1 multicolored *5.50 5.50*

Natl. Philatelic Exhibition, Cairo, 10/7-12 (No. 1460). No. 1460 sold only with £1 admission ticket at exhibition.

Ancient Artifacts Type of 1985

Perf. 11½x11

1990-92 **Unwmk.** **Photo.**

Size: 18x23mm

1467 A681 10p like #1278 .60 .25
1470 A681 30p like #1283 1.00 1.00
1472 A681 50p like #1285 1.75 1.75
Nos. 1467-1472 (3) 3.35 3.00

Issued: 10p, 1/20/90; 30p, 9/1/91; 50p, 7/11/92.

United Nations Day — A830

No. 1477, Brick hands housing people. No. 1478, Woman learning to write, fingerprint, vert.

Perf. 13x13½, 13½x13

1991, Oct. 24 **Litho.**
1476 A830 10p shown .40 .25
1477 A830 10p multicolored .40 .25
1478 A830 10p multicolored .40 .25
Nos. 1476-1478 (3) 1.20 .75

Famous Men Type of 1988
Inscribed "1991"

Designs: No. 1479, Dr. Zaki Mubarak (1891-1952), writer and poet. No. 1480, Abd El Kader Hamza (1879-1941), journalist.

1991, Dec. 23 **Photo.** ***Perf. 13½x13***
1479 A760 10p olive brown .40 .25
1480 A760 10p gray .40 .25

A831

Post Day — A832

1992, Jan. 2 **Litho.** ***Perf. 13***
1481 A831 10p shown .40 .25
1482 A831 45p Bird mosaic 1.00 1.00

Perf. 14

1483 A832 70p shown 1.75 1.75
Nos. 1481-1483 (3) 3.15 3.00

Nos. 1482-1483 are airmail.

Police Day — A833

1992, Jan. 25 ***Perf. 14***
1484 A833 10p multicolored .40 .25

25th Cairo Intl. Fair A834

1992, Feb. 15 **Litho.** ***Perf. 14***
1485 A834 10p multicolored .40 .25

Famous Men Type of 1988
Inscribed "1992"

10p, Sayed Darwish (1882-1923), musician.

1992, Mar. 17 **Photo.** ***Perf. 14x13½***
1486 A760 10p dull org & olive .40 .25

Festivals — A835

1992, Mar. 18 ***Perf. 11½***
1487 A835 10p Egyptian hoopoe .40 .25

For use on greeting cards.

World Health Day A836

1992, Apr. 20 **Litho.** ***Perf. 13***
1488 A836 10p multicolored .50 .25

Aswan Dam, 90th Anniv. A837

1992, July **Litho.** ***Perf. 13***
1489 A837 10p No. 487 .50 .25

20th Arab Scout Jamboree — A838

1992, July 10 ***Perf. 13x13½***
1490 A838 10p multicolored .50 .25

A839

1992, July 20 ***Perf. 13½x13***
1491 A839 10p multicolored .45 .25

Size: 80x60mm

Imperf

1492 A839 70p Summer Games' emblem 5.00 2.50

1992 Summer Olympics, Barcelona.

El Helal Magazine, Cent. — A840

1992, Sept. 14 **Litho.** ***Perf. 13½x13***
1493 A840 10p multicolored .45 .25

Alexandria World Festival — A841

1992, Sept. 27 ***Perf. 13x13½***
1494 A841 70p multicolored 1.60 1.60

Congress of Federation of World and American Travel Companies, Cairo — A842

1992, Sept. 20
1495 A842 70p multicolored 1.50 1.50

World Post Day A843

1992, Oct. 9 **Litho.** ***Perf. 13***
1496 A843 10p dk bl, lt bl & blk .45 .25

Children's Day — A844

1992, Oct. 24 **Litho.** ***Perf. 13½x13***
1497 A844 10p multicolored .55 .25

Intl. Conference on Food, Agriculture and World Health A845

1992, Oct. 24 ***Perf. 13***
1498 A845 70p multicolored 1.50 1.50

A846

1992, Nov. 21 ***Perf. 13½x13***
1499 A846 10p multicolored .50 .25

20th Arab Scout Conference, Cairo.

Famous Men Type of 1988
Inscribed "1992"

No. 1500, Talaat Harb, economist. No. 1501, Mohamed Taymour, writer. No. 1502, Dr. Ahmed Zaki Abu Shadi (with glasses), physician & poet.

1992, Dec. 23 Photo. ***Perf. 13½x13***

1500 A760 10p blue & brown .40 .25
1501 A760 10p citron & blue gray .40 .25
1502 A760 10p citron & blue gray .40 .25
a. Pair, #1501-1502 .90 .90
Nos. 1500-1502 (3) 1.20 .75

A847

Pharaohs: 10p, Sesostris I. 45p, Amenemhet III. 70p, Hur I.

1993, Jan. 2 Litho. ***Perf. 13½x13***

1503 A847 10p brown & yellow .45 .25
1504 A847 45p brown & yellow .75 .65
1505 A847 70p brown & yellow 1.20 1.00
a. Strip of 3, #1503-1505 3.00 3.00

Post Day.

25th Intl. Book Fair, Cairo — A848

1993, Jan. 26 Litho. ***Perf. 13½x13***

1506 A848 15p multicolored .40 .25

A849

A849a

A849b

A849c

A849d

A849e

A849f

A849g

A849h

Artifacts: A849, Bust. A849a, Sphinx. A849b, Bust of princess. A849c, Ramses II. A849d, Queen Ti. A849e, Horemheb. A849f, As A849b. A849g, Amenhotep III. £1, Head of a woman. £2, Woman wearing headdress. £5, Pharaonic capital.

Photo., Litho. (#1511)

1993-99 Unwmk. ***Perf. 11½x11,***

1507 A849 5p multi .55 .25
1508 A849a 15p brn & bis .55 .25
1509 A849a 15p brn & bis .30 .25
1510 A849b 25p brn & org brn .35 .25
1511 A849c 55p blk & bl .90 .50

Size: 21x25mm

Perf. 11¼

1512 A849 5p dp cl & brick red .50 .25
1513 A849d 5p brown .30 .25
a. Wmk. 342 .30 .25
1514 A849a 15p brn & bis .50 .25
1515 A849e 20p blk & gray .30 .25
a. Wmk. 342 .30 .25
1516 A849f 25p brn & org brn .70 .30
1517 A849f 25p black brown .30 .25
1518 A849c 55p blk & lt bl .60 .60
1519 A849g 75p blk & brn .90 .80

Perf. 11½

1520 A849h £1 slate & blk 2.25 2.25
1521 A849h £2 brn & grn 5.00 5.00
1521A A849h £5 brn & gold 10.00 10.00
Nos. 1507-1521A (16) 24.00 21.70

Warning: Avoid using watermark fluid on Nos. 1513-1513a and 1515-1515a. Images will be adversely affected.

Body of Sphinx on Nos. 1509, 1514 stops above value, and extends through value on No. 1508.

Issued: Nos. 1507-1508, 2/1; No. 1509, 3/10; £1, £2, 4/1; No. 1511, 7/1/93; £5, 8/1/93; Nos. 1512, 1514, 1518, 10/30/94; No. 1516, 6/25/94; 20p, 2/1/97; 75p, 3/25/97; No. 1517, 1998; Nos. 1513a, 1515a, 1999.

See Nos. C204-C206.

Architects' Association, 75th Anniv. — A850

1993, Feb. 28 Litho. ***Perf. 13x13½***

1522 A850 15p multicolored .45 .25

New Building for Ministry of Foreign Affairs A851

1993, Mar. 15 ***Perf. 13***

1523 A851 15p multicolored .45 .25
1524 A851 80p multicolored 1.50 1.50

Diplomacy Day (No. 1523). No. 1524 is airmail.

Feasts — A852

1993, Mar. 20 Litho. ***Perf. 13x13½***

1525 A852 15p Opuntia .45 .25

For use on greeting cards.

Newspaper, Le Progres Egyptien, Cent. — A853

1993, Apr. 15 Litho. ***Perf. 13x13½***

1526 A853 15p multicolored .40 .25

A854

A855

1993, May 15 Litho. ***Perf. 13½x13***

1527 A854 15p multicolored .50 .25

World Telecommunications Day.

1993, June 15 Litho. ***Perf. 13½x13***

1528 A855 15p multicolored .45 .25

UN Conference on Human Rights, Vienna.

Organization of African Unity — A856

1993, June 26 ***Perf. 13***

1529 A856 15p yel grn & multi .45 .25
1530 A856 80p red violet & multi 1.10 1.10

No. 1530 is airmail.

World PTT Conference, Cairo — A857

1993, Sept. 4 Litho. ***Perf. 13***

1531 A857 15p multicolored .45 .25

Salah El-Din El Ayubi (1137-1193), Dome of the Rock — A858

1993, Sept. 4

1532 A858 55p multicolored 1.10 1.10

A859

1993, Oct. 6

1533 A859 15p multicolored .50 .25

October War Against Israel, 20th Anniv.

A860

1993, Oct. 12 ***Perf. 13½x13***

1534 A860 15p cream & multi .45 .25
1535 A860 55p silver & multi 1.10 .55
1536 A860 80p gold & multi 1.50 .85

Imperf

Size: 90x70mm

1537 A860 80p multicolored 2.00 2.00
Nos. 1534-1537 (4) 5.05 3.65

Pres. Mohamed Hosni Mubarak, Third Term.

Reduction of Natural Disasters A861

1993, Oct. 24 Litho. ***Perf. 13***

1538 A861 80p multicolored 1.10 1.10

Electricity in Egypt, Cent. — A862

1993, Oct. 24 ***Perf. 13½x13***

1539 A862 15p multicolored .45 .25

Intl. Conference on Big Dams, Cairo — A863

1993, Nov. 19 **Litho.** ***Perf. 13***
1540 A863 15p multicolored .45 .25

35th Military Intl. Soccer Championship — A864

1993, Dec. 1 **Litho.** ***Perf. 13x13½***
1541 A864 15p orange & multi .40 .25
1542 A864 15p Trophy, emblem .40 .25

9th Men's Junior World Handball Championship (No. 1542).

Famous Men Type of 1988
Inscribed "1993"

No. 1543, Abdel Azis Al-Bishry. No. 1544, Mohammad Farid Abu Hadid. No. 1545, Mahmud Beyram el-Tunsi. No. 1546, Ali Moubarak.

1993, Dec. 25 ***Perf. 13½x13***
1543 A760 15p blue .40 .25
1544 A760 15p blue black .40 .25
1545 A760 15p light violet .40 .25
1546 A760 15p green .40 .25
Nos. 1543-1546 (4) 1.60 1.00

Post Day — A865

1994, Jan. 2
1547 A865 15p Amenhotep III .45 .25
1548 A865 55p Queen Hatshepsut 1.10 .30
1549 A865 80p Thutmose III 1.75 .40
Nos. 1547-1549 (3) 3.30 .95

Congress of Egyptian Sedimentary Geology Society — A866

1994, Jan. 4 **Litho.** ***Perf. 13x13½***
1550 A866 15p multicolored .45 .25

Birds A867

1994, Mar. 3 **Litho.** ***Perf. 13***
1551 A867 Block of 4, #a.-d. 2.75 2.75
a. 15p Egyptian swallow .45 .30
b. 15p Fire crest .45 .30
c. 15p Rose-ringed parrot .45 .30
d. 15p Goldfinch .45 .30

Festivals 1994.

A868

1994, Mar. 25 ***Perf. 13½x13***
1552 A868 15p multicolored .45 .25

Arab Scouting, 40th anniv.

A869

1994, Apr. 9 **Litho.** ***Perf. 13½x13***
1553 A869 15p multicolored .45 .25

27th Cairo Intl. Fair.

A870

1994, Apr. 15 **Litho.** ***Perf. 13***
1554 A870 15p green & brown .45 .25

1994 African Telecommunications Exhibition, Cairo.

A871

1994, Apr. 30 **Litho.** ***Perf. 13***
1555 A871 15p grn, blk & blue .45 .25

Natl. Afforestation Campaign.

5th Arab Energy Conference, Cairo. — A872

1994, July 5 **Litho.** ***Perf. 13***
1556 A872 15p multicolored .45 .25

Signing of Washington Accord for Palestinian Self-Rule in Gaza and Jericho — A873

1994, May 4 **Litho.** ***Perf. 13***
1557 A873 15p multicolored .60 .25

18th Biennial Art Exhibition, Alexandria — A874

1994, May 21
1558 A874 15p yel, blk & gray .45 .25

Organization of African Unity — A875

1994, May 25
1559 A875 15p multicolored .45 .25

Natl. Reading Festival — A876

1994, June 15
1560 A876 15p multicolored .45 .25

ILO, 75th Anniv. — A877

1994, June 28 **Litho.** ***Perf. 13½x13***
1561 A877 15p multicolored .45 .25

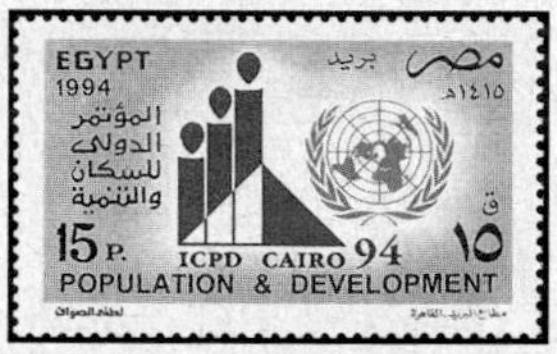

Intl. Conference on Population and Development, Cairo — A878

15p, Conference, UN emblems. 80p, Drawings, hieroglyphics, conference emblem.

1994, Sept. 5 **Litho.** ***Perf. 13***
1562 A878 15p multi .45 .25
1563 A878 80p multi, vert. 1.10 .75

No. 1563 is airmail.

World Junior Squash Championships — A879

1994, Sept. 14 **Litho.** ***Perf. 13***
1564 A879 15p multicolored .45 .25

World Post Day A880

1994, Oct. 9 **Litho.** ***Perf. 13***
1565 A880 15p multicolored .50 .25

Intl. Red Cross & Red Crescent Societies, 75th Anniv. — A881

1994, Oct. 24
1566 A881 80p multicolored 1.50 .90

Akhbar El-Yom Newspaper, 50th Anniv. — A882

1994, Nov. 11
1567 A882 15p multicolored .45 .25

African Field Hockey Club Championships — A883

1994, Nov. 14 Litho. ***Perf. 13***
1568 A883 15p multicolored .45 .25

A884

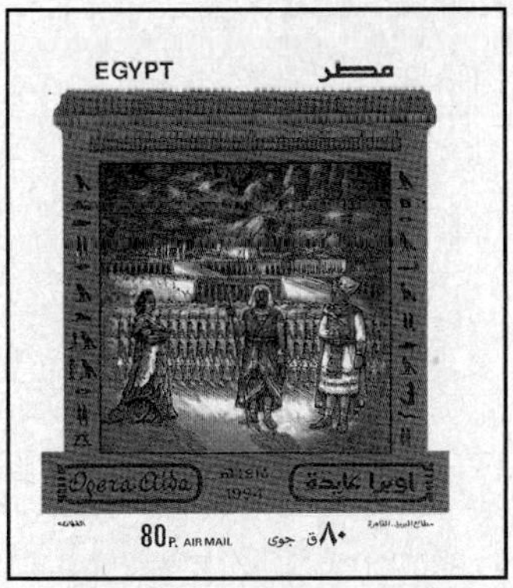

Opera Aida, by Verdi — A885

1994, Nov. 26
1569 A884 15p multicolored .45 .25

Imperf

Size: 58x69mm

1570 A885 80p multicolored 2.25 2.25

No. 1570 is airmail.

Intl. Olympic Committee, Cent. — A886

1994, Dec. 10 ***Perf. 13***
1571 A886 15p multicolored .45 .25

Egyptian Youth Hostels Assoc., 40th Anniv. — A887

1994, Dec. 24
1572 A887 15p multicolored .45 .25

Intl. Speed Ball Federation, 10th Anniv. — A888

1994, Dec. 25
1573 A888 15p multicolored .45 .25

African Development Bank, 30th Anniv. — A889

1994, Dec. 26
1574 A889 15p multicolored .45 .25

Opening of Suez Canal, 125th Anniv. — A890

Design: 80p, Map, inaugural ceremony.

1994, Dec. 27
1575 A890 15p multicolored .65 .25
1576 A890 80p multicolored 1.25 .75

No. 1576 is airmail.

Famous Men — A891

1994, Dec. 29
1577 A891 15p Hassan Fathy, engineer .40 .25
1578 A891 15p Mahmoud Taimour, writer .40 .25

Post Day — A892

15p, Statue of Akhenaton. 55p, Golden mask of King Tutankhamun. 80p, Statue of Nefertiti.

1995, Jan. 2 Litho. ***Perf. 13½x13***
1579 A892 15p multicolored .50 .25
1580 A892 55p multicolored 1.10 .40
1581 A892 80p multicolored 1.50 .50
Nos. 1579-1581 (3) 3.10 1.15

World Tourism Organization, 20th Anniv. — A893

1995, Jan. 2 ***Perf. 13x13½***
1582 A893 15p multicolored .45 .25

Festivals — A894

1995, Feb. 25 Litho. ***Perf. 13x13½***
1583 A894 15p multicolored .45 .25

For use on greeting cards.

Egyptian Women's Day — A895

1995, Mar. 16 Litho. ***Perf. 13x13½***
1584 A895 15p multicolored .45 .25

Arab League, 50th Anniv. — A896

1995, Mar. 22 ***Perf. 13½x13***
1585 A896 15p blue & multi .45 .25
1586 A896 55p green & multi .75 .75

Sheraton Hotel, Cairo, 25th Anniv. — A897

1995, Mar. 28 ***Perf. 13x13½***
1587 A897 15p multicolored .45 .25

Misr Bank, 75th Anniv. — A898

1995, May 7 Litho. ***Perf. 13½x13***
1588 A898 15p multicolored .50 .25

World Telecommunications Day — A899

1995, May 31 ***Perf. 13x13½***
1589 A899 80p multicolored 1.00 .50

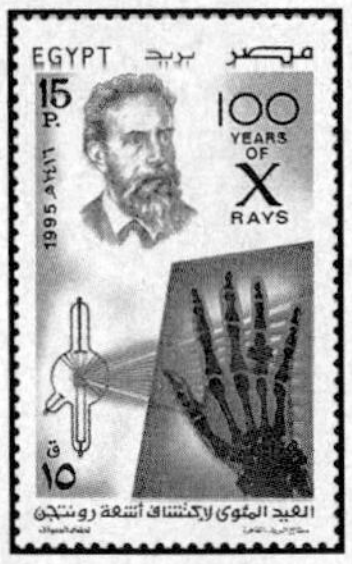

Wilhelm Roentgen (1845-1923), Discovery of the X-Ray, Cent. — A900

1995, May Litho. ***Perf. 13½x13***
1590 A900 15p multicolored .50 .25

Membership in World Heritage Committee, 20th Anniv. (in 1994) — A901

Artifacts from the Shaft of Luxor: No. 1591, Goddess Hathor. No. 1592, God Atoum. 80p, God Amon and Horemheb.

1995, July 23 Litho. ***Perf. 13½x13***
1591 15p multicolored .45 .25
1592 15p multicolored .45 .25
a. A901 Pair, #1591-1592 1.10 1.10
1593 A901 80p multicolored 1.10 1.10
Nos. 1591-1593 (3) 2.00 1.60

No. 1592a is a continuous design. No. 1593 is airmail.

21st Intl. Conference on Pediatrics, Cairo
A902

1995, Sept. 10 Litho. *Perf. 13*
1594 A902 15p multicolored .50 .25

Intl. Ozone Day — A903

1995, Sept. 16 Litho. *Perf. 13x12½*
1595 A903 15p green & multi .45 .25
1596 A903 55p brown & multi .90 .45
1597 A903 80p blue & multi 1.40 .55
Nos. 1595-1597 (3) 2.75 1.25

See Nos. 1622-1623.

World Tourism Day
A904

1995, Sept. 25 *Perf. 12½x13*
1598 A904 15p multicolored 1.00 .25

Government Printing House, 175th Anniv. — A905

1995, Sept. 27
1599 A905 15p multicolored .45 .25

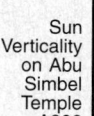

Sun Verticality on Abu Simbel Temple
A906

1995, Oct. 22 Litho. *Perf. 12½x13*
1600 A906 15p multicolored .95 .30

Opening of New Esna Dam — A907

1995, Nov. 25 *Perf. 12½*
1601 A907 15p multicolored .75 .30

Egyptian Engineers Assoc., 75th Anniv.
A908

1995, Dec. 20 *Perf. 13*
1602 A908 15p multicolored .45 .25

A909

A910

Famous entertainers.

1995, Dec. 9 Litho. *Perf. 13x12½*
1603 A909 15p Abdel Halim Hafez .40 .25
1604 A909 15p Youssef Wahbi .40 .25
1605 A909 15p Naquib el-Rihani .40 .25
Nos. 1603-1605 (3) 1.20 .75

1995, Dec. 23 Litho. *Perf. 13x12½*
1606 A910 15p multicolored .45 .25

Motion Pictures, cent.

Post Day
A911

Ancient paintings: 55p, Man facing right. 80p, Man facing left. 100p, Playing flute, dancers.

1996, Jan. 2 Litho. *Perf. 13½x13*
1607 55p multicolored 1.10 .60
1608 80p multicolored 1.50 .90
a. A911 Pair, Nos. 1607-1608 2.75 2.75

Imperf

Size: 88x72mm

1609 A911 100p multicolored 3.00 3.00

Nos. 1607-1608 are airmail.

Feasts — A912

1996, Feb. 15 *Perf. 12½*
1610 A912 15p Blue convolvulus .45 .25
1611 A912 15p Red poppies .45 .25
a. Pair, No. 1610-1611 .95 .95

For use on greeting cards.

A913

A914

1996, Mar. 13 Litho. *Perf. 13x12½*
1612 A913 15p pink & multi .40 .25
1613 A913 80p brown & multi .90 .60

Summit of Peace Makers, Sharm al-Sheikh. No. 1613 is airmail.

1996, Mar. 16
1614 A914 15p multicolored .45 .25

29th Intl. Fair, Cairo.

Egyptian Geological Survey, Cent.
A915

1996, Mar. 18 *Perf. 12½x13*
1615 A915 15p multicolored .45 .25

A916

A917

1996, Apr. 11 Litho. *Perf. 13x12½*
1616 A916 15p blue & multi .45 .25
1617 A916 80p pink & multi .95 .50

Signing of African Nuclear Weapon-Free Zone Treaty.

1996, Apr. 20 Litho. *Perf. 13x12½*
1618 A917 15p multicolored .45 .25

Egyptian Society of Accountants and Auditors, 50th anniv.

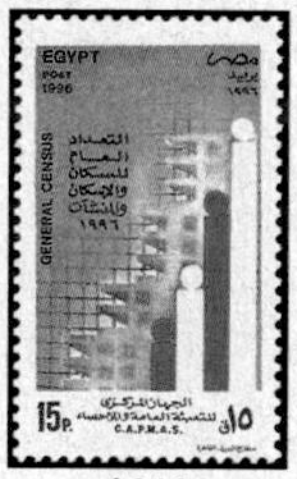

A918

A919

1996, May 4
1619 A918 15p multicolored .45 .25

General census.

1996, July 15 Litho. *Perf. 13x12½*

1996 Summer Olympics, Atlanta: 15p, Atlanta 1996 emblem. £1, Emblem surrounded by sports pictograms.

1620 A919 15p lilac & multi .50 .25

Size: 63x103mm

Imperf

1621 A919 £1 black & multi 2.75 2.75

No. 1621 is airmail.

Intl. Ozone Day Type of 1995

1996, Sept. 16 Litho. *Perf. 13x12½*
1622 A903 15p pink & multi .40 .25
1623 A903 80p gray & multi 1.10 .55

No. 1623 is airmail.

A920

A921

1996, Sept. 19
1624 A920 80p multicolored .75 .45

2nd Alexandria World Festival.

1996, Sept. 21
1625 A921 15p grn, blk & bl .45 .25

Scientific Research and Technology Academy, 25th anniv.

Opening of 2nd Line of Greater Cairo Subway System
A922

1996, Oct. 7 *Perf. 12½x13*
1626 A922 15p multicolored .50 .25

Rowing Festival
A923

1996, Sept. 27
1627 A923 15p multicolored .75 .25

Intl. Tourism Day. See Nos. C215-C216.

Courts of the State Council, 50th Anniv.
A924

1996, Nov. 2 Litho. *Perf. 12½x13*
1628 A924 15p blue & claret .45 .25

A925

A926

1996, Nov. 4 *Perf. 13x12½*
1629 A925 15p yel, blk & blue .40 .25

25th World Conference of Intl. Federation of Training and Development Organizations.

1996, Nov. 12 Litho. *Perf. 13x12½*

Cairo Economic Summit (MENA): £1, Graph, earth, gear, olive branch, wheat.

1630 A926 15p shown .45 .25

Size: 65x45mm

Imperf

1631 A926 £1 multicolored 1.75 1.75

No. 1631 is airmail.

A927

A928

1996, Nov. 13 ***Perf. 13x12½***
1632 A927 15p multicolored .45 .25

1996 World Food Summit, Rome.

1996, Nov. 16

National Day of El-Gharbia Governorate: Al Sayd Ahmed El-Badawy mosque, Tanta.

1633 A928 15p multicolored .45 .25

A929

A930

Famous artists.

1996, Dec. 28 Llitho. ***Perf. 13x12½***
1634 A929 20p Ali El-Kassar .45 .25
1635 A929 20p George Abyad .45 .25
1636 A929 20p Mohamed Kareem .45 .25
1637 A929 20p Fatma Roshdi .45 .25
Nos. 1634-1637 (4) 1.80 1.00

See Nos. 1666-1669.

1997, Jan. 2
1638 A930 20p multicolored .45 .25

Size: 61x80mm

Imperf

1639 A930 £1 multicolored 2.00 2.00

Post Day; Discovery of Tutankhamun's tomb, 75th anniv.
No. 1639 is airmail.

Police Day
A931

1997, Jan. 25 Litho. ***Perf. 13x13½***
1640 A931 20p multicolored .45 .25

Feasts — A932

1997, Feb. 1 ***Perf. 13***
1641 A932 20p Pink asters .40 .25
1642 A932 20p White asters .40 .25
a. Pair, #1641-1642 .95 .95

For use on greeting cards.

World Civil Defense Day
A933

1997, Mar. 10 Litho. ***Perf. 13x13½***
1643 A933 20p multicolored .45 .25

30th Cairo Intl. Fair — A934

1997, Mar. 19 ***Perf. 13½x13***
1644 A934 20p multicolored .45 .25

Mahmoud Said, Photographer, Artist, Birth Cent. — A935

The City, By Mahmoud Said — A936

1997, Apr. 12 Litho. ***Perf. 12½***
1645 A935 20p multicolored .45 .25

Size: 80x60mm

Imperf

1646 A936 £1 multicolored 1.25 1.25

No. 1646 is airmail.

Institute of African Research and Studies, 50th Anniv. — A937

1997, May 27 Litho. ***Perf. 13***
1647 A937 75p multicolored .65 .65

New Headquarters of State Information Service — A938

1997, Aug. 16 Litho. ***Perf. 12½***
1648 A938 20p multicolored .45 .25

A939

A940

£1, Mascot, soccer ball, playing field, emblems.

1997, Sept. 4 ***Perf. 13x12½***
1649 A939 20p multicolored .45 .25
1650 AP81 75p multicolored .70 .65

Size: 75x55mm

Imperf

1651 A939 £1 multicolored 1.75 1.75

Nos. 1650-1651 are airmail. Under 17 FIFA World Soccer Championships, Egypt.

1997, Sept. 16 ***Perf. 13***
1652 A940 20p lt bl grn & multi .60 .30
1653 A940 £1 pink & multi 1.60 1.25

Montreal Protocol on Substances that Deplete the Ozone Layer, 10th anniv. No. 1653 is airmail.

Completion of Second Stage of Metro Line No. 2 — A941

1997, Sept. 27 ***Perf. 12½x13***
1654 A941 20p multicolored .45 .25

Premiere in Egypt of Opera Aida, by Verdi, 125th Anniv. A942

1997, Oct. 12 ***Perf. 13***
1655 A942 20p multicolored .60 .25

Size: 80x75mm

Imperf

1656 A942 £1 like #1655 4.00 4.00

No. 1656 is airmail.

Queen Nefertari — A943

1997, Oct. 25 Litho. ***Perf. 13***
1657 A943 £1 multicolored 1.25 1.25
a. Perf. 14¼x14 — —

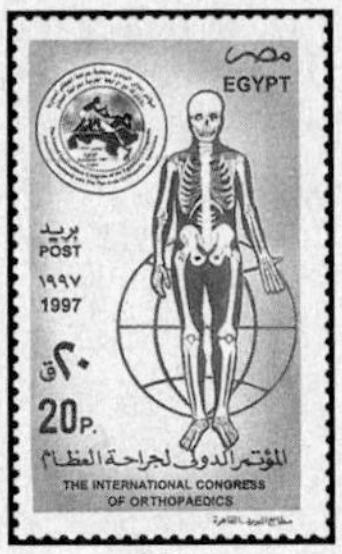

A944

A945

1997, Nov. 17 Litho. ***Perf. 13***
1658 A944 20p multicolored .50 .25

Intl. Congress of Orthopedics, Cairo.

1997, Nov. 22 ***Perf. 13x12½***

Designs: 20p, Goddess Selket. £1, Scarab, baboon pendant.

1659 A945 20p black & gold .50 .25

Size: 73x62mm

Imperf

1660 A945 £1 multicolored 1.50 1.50

No. 1660 is airmail. Discovery of King Tutanhkamen's tomb, 75th anniv.

Inauguration of Nubia Monument Museum — A946

1997, Nov. 23 ***Perf. 13***
1661 A946 20p multicolored .95 .25

Arab Land Bank, 50th Anniv. — A947

1997, Dec. 10 ***Perf. 12½***
1662 A947 20p multicolored .60 .25

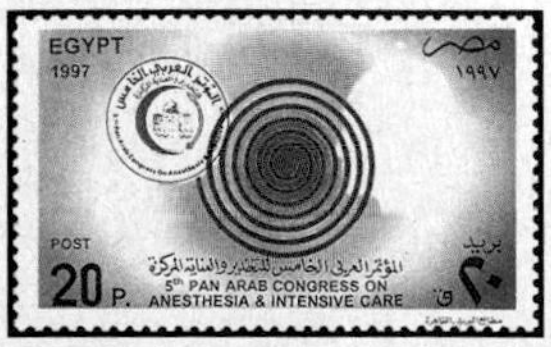

5th Pan Arab Congress on Anesthesia and Intensive Care — A948

1997, Dec. 9 Litho. ***Perf. 13***
1663 A948 20p multicolored .45 .25

El Salaam Canal — A949

1997, Dec. 28
1664 A949 20p multicolored .60 .25

Liberation of Sinai, 15th anniv.

Famous Artists Type of 1996 and

A950

1997, Dec. 23 Litho. *Perf. 13x12½*

1665	A950	20p	blue	.40	.25
1666	A929	20p	Zaky Tolaimat	.40	.25
1667	A929	20p	Ismael Yassen	.40	.25
1668	A929	20p	Zaky Roustom	.40	.25
1669	A929	20p	Soliman Naguib	.40	.25
a.			Strip of 5, #1665-1669	2.00	2.00

A951

Post Day: 20p, King Tutankhamun's guard. 75p, King Ramses III. £1, Cover of King Tutankhamun's coffin.

1998, Jan. 2 *Perf. 13*

1670	A951	20p	multicolored	.45	.25
1671	A951	75p	multicolored	1.10	.65

Size: 26x43mm

1672	A951	£1	multicolored	1.75	.85

Nos. 1671-1672 are airmail.

Feasts — A952

1998, Jan. 20

1673	20p multicolored		.40	.25
1674	20p multicolored		.40	.25
a.	A952	Pair, #1673-1674	.80	.80

For use on greeting cards.

Intl. Cairo Fair — A954

1998, Mar. 11 Litho. *Perf. 13*

1675	A954	20p	multicolored	.50	.25

Natl. Bank of Egypt, Cent. — A955

1998, Mar. 12

1676	A955	20p	multicolored	.50	.25

Tutankhamun A956

Thutmose IV A957

1998 Litho. *Perf. 13½x12½*

1677	A956	£2	pink & multi	1.75	1.75
1677A	A956	£2	Like #1677, with white background	—	—
b.			Perf. 14x14¼	—	—
1678	A957	£5	purple & black	5.00	3.75
			Nos. 1677-1678 (3)	6.75	5.50

Issued: £2, 4/23; £5, 3/23.

A958

1998, Apr. 14 *Perf. 13*

1679	A958	20p	green & multi	.45	.25
1680	A958	75p	blue & multi	1.10	.75

Size: 70x52mm

Imperf

1681	A958	£1	Natl. flags, map, trophy	1.50	1.00

Egypt, winners of 21st African Cup of Nations soccer competition.

Nos. 1680-1681 are airmail.

A959

1998, May 30 Litho. *Perf. 13*

1682	A959	20p	Egyptian Satellite "Nile Sat"	.50	.25

World Environment Day — A960

1998, June 5

1683	A960	20p	shown	.60	.25

Size: 43x62mm

Imperf

1684	A960	£1	Fauna, emblems	3.75	3.75

No. 1684 is airmail.

A961

1998, June 14

1685	A961	20p	blue & black	.40	.25
1686	A961	£1	yellow, green & black	1.10	.80

Dr. Ahmed Zewail, winner of Franklin Institute award.

No. 1686 is airmail.

A962

Imam Sheikh Mohamed Metwalli Al-Shaarawi.

1998, July 15

1687	A962	20p	buff & multi	.40	.25
1688	A962	£1	green & multi	1.10	.80

No. 1688 is airmail.

A963

1998, Sept. 12 Litho. *Perf. 13*

1689	A963	20p	multicolored	.50	.25

Day of the Nile Flood.

A964

1998, Sept. 30 Litho. *Perf. 13*

1690	A964	20p	multicolored	.50	.25

Chemistry Administration, cent.

October War Against Israel, 25th Anniv. — A965

1998, Oct. 6 Litho. *Perf. 13*

1691	A965	20p	multicolored	.60	.25

Size: 50x70mm

Imperf

1692	A965	£2	like No. 1691	3.25	3.25

No. 1692 is airmail.

Egyptian Survey Authority, Cent. — A966

1998, Oct. 15 *Perf. 13*

1693	A966	20p	multicolored	.50	.25

Cairo University, 90th Anniv. — A967

1998, Dec. 7 Litho. *Perf. 13*

1694	A967	20p	multicolored	.50	.25

A968

1998, Dec. 17 Litho. *Perf. 13*

1695	A968	20p	multicolored	.45	.25

Egyptian trade unions, cent.

A970

Post Day (19th Dynasty): 20p, Queen Nefertari, Goddess Isis. 125p, God Osiris, Goddess Isis.

1999, Jan. 2 Litho. *Perf. 13*

1696 A970 20p multicolored .50 .25

Size: 41x61mm

Imperf

1697 A970 125p multicolored 2.00 2.00

No. 1697 is airmail.

Feasts — A971

1999, Jan. 5 *Perf. 13*

1698 20p multicolored 1.00 .30

1699 20p multicolored .40 .25

a. A971 Pair, #1698-1699 1.75 *1.75*

For use on greeting cards.

Intl. Women's Day — A973

1999, Mar. 7 Litho. *Perf. 13*

1700 A973 20p multicolored .50 .25

Cairo Intl. Fair — A974

1999, Mar. 9

1701 A974 20p multicolored .50 .25

Opening of Metro Line Beneath Nile River — A975

1999, Apr. Litho. *Perf. 13*

1702 A975 20p multicolored .60 .25

A976

UPU, 125th Anniv. — A977

1999, Apr. 21

1703 A976 20p shown .45 .25

1704 A976 £1 multi 1.25 .85

1705 A977 125p shown 1.50 1.20

Size: 50x70mm

Imperf

1706 A977 125p multi 2.10 2.10

Nos. 1703-1706 (4) 5.30 4.40

Nos. 1704-1706 are airmail.

A978

1999, May 8 *Perf. 13*

1707 A978 20p green & multi .45 .25

1708 A978 125p buff, red & multi 1.25 1.00

Geneva Conventions, 50th anniv. No. 1708 is airmail.

A980

1999, May 20 Litho. *Perf. 13x12¾*

1710 A980 20p green & multi .45 .25

1711 A980 £1 buff & multi .95 .85

African Development Bank, 35th Meeting, Cairo. No. 1711 is airmail.

16th Men's Handball World Championship — A981

20p, Stylized player with ball, pyramids. 1£, Mascot with ball, Sphinx, pyramids, globe. 125p, Mascot with ball, goalie, pyramids.

1999, June 1 *Perf. 13*

1712 A981 20p multicolored .45 .25

1713 A981 £1 multicolored .90 .85

1714 A981 125p multicolored 1.10 1.00

Nos. 1712-1714 (3) 2.45 2.10

Nos. 1713-1714 are airmail.

Goddess Selket — A982

1999, June 23 Litho. *Perf. 13*

1715 A982 25p multicolored .40 .25

See Nos. 1750, 1754.

SOS Children's Village, 50th Anniv. — A983

1999, June 23 *Perf. 12¾x13¼*

1716 A983 20p grn, blk & blue .45 .25

1717 A983 125p buff, blk & bl 1.25 1.10

No. 1717 is airmail.

A984

No. 1718, Sameera Moussa (1917-52), Physicist. No. 1719, Aisha Abdul Rahman (1913-98), writer. No. 1720, Ahmed Eldemerdash Touny (1907-97), member of Intl. Olympic Committee.

1999 Litho. *Perf. 13x12¾*

1718 A984 20p multicolored .45 .25

1719 A984 20p multicolored .45 .25

1720 A984 20p multicolored .45 .25

Nos. 1718-1720 (3) 1.35 .75

Issued: Nos. 1718-1719, 7/23; No. 1720, 8/13.

See Nos. 1730-1733.

A985

1999, Oct. 5 Litho. *Perf. 13x12¾*

1721 A985 20p org & multi .45 .25

1722 A985 £1 silver & multi .90 .85

1723 A985 125p gold & multi 1.10 1.00

Imperf

1724 A985 125p multicolored 2.00 2.00

Nos. 1721-1724 (4) 4.45 4.10

Pres. Hosni Mubarak, 4th term.

Nos. 1722-1724 are airmail.

A986

1999, Nov. 15 Litho. *Perf. 13¼x13*

Background Color

1725 A986 20p green .45 .25

1726 A986 £1 red vio .90 .85

1727 A986 125p purple 1.10 1.00

Nos. 1725-1727 (3) 2.45 2.10

Intl. Year of the Elderly. Nos. 1726-1727 are airmail.

A987

1999, Nov. 20

1728 A987 20p multi .50 .25

Children's Day.

Famous People Type of 1999

No. 1730, Farid El Attrash (1913-76), singer, movie star. No. 1731, Laila Mourad (1918-95), singer, movie star. No. 1732, Anwar Wagdi (1911-55), actor, director. No. 1733, Asia Dagher (1901-86), actor, producer.

1999, Dec. 30 Litho. *Perf. 13x12¾*

1730 A984 20p lt bl & blk .40 .25

1731 A984 20p lt bl & blk .40 .25

1732 A984 20p lt bl & blk .40 .25

1733 A984 20p lt bl & blk .40 .25

Nos. 1730-1733 (4) 1.60 1.00

Millennium A989

20p, "1999" & "2000." 125p, Countdown of years. £2, Holy Family, Virgin Tree.

2000, Jan. 1 *Perf. 13x12¾*

1734 A989 20p multi .45 .25

1735 A989 125p multi 1.25 1.10

Size: 70x50mm

Imperf

1736 A989 £2 multi, horiz. 4.00 4.00

Nos. 1734-1736 (3) 5.70 5.35

Nos. 1735-1736 are airmail.

A990

Post Day — A991

2000, Jan. 2 *Perf. 13¼x12¾*

1737 A990 20p multi .50 .25
1738 A991 20p multi .50 .25
a. Pair, #1737-1738 1.25 1.25

Size: 70x50mm

Imperf

1739 A991 125p Chariot, horiz. 2.00 2.00
Nos. 1737-1739 (3) 3.00 2.50

Ain Shams University, 50th Anniv. — A992

2000, Jan. 3 *Perf. 13¼x13*

1740 A992 20p multi .50 .25

Feasts

A993 A994

2000, Jan. 5 *Perf. 13x13¼*

1741 A993 20p multi .40 .25
1742 A994 20p multi .40 .25
a. Pair, #1741-1742 .90 .90

For use on greeting cards.

A995

2000, Jan. 20 *Perf. 13¼x13*

1743 A995 20p multi .50 .25

Islamic Development Bank, 25th anniv.

A996

2000, Feb. 28 *Perf. 13¼x12¾*

1744 A996 125p multi 1.25 1.25

Common Market for Eastern and Southern Africa Economic Conference.

Death of Om Kolthoum, 25th Anniv. — A997

2000, Mar. 11 *Perf. 13¼x13*

1745 A997 20p multi .50 .25

8th Intl. Congress of Egyptologists — A998

2000, Mar. 28 *Perf. 13x13¼*

1746 A998 20p multi .50 .25

Europe-Africa Summit, Cairo — A999

2000, Apr. 3 *Perf. 13¼x13*

1747 A999 125p multi 1.25 1.25

Group of 15 Developing Nations, 10th Summit, Cairo — A1000

Perf. 12¾x13¼

2000, June 19 **Litho.**

1748 A1000 125p multi 1.25 1.25

Goddess Selket Type of 1999 and

Scene from 20th Dynasty A1003

Nofret, Wife of Rahotep A1004

King Seostris A1005

Princess Merit Aton A1006

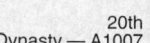

20th Dynasty — A1007

Pyramid at Snefru A1008

Wife of Sheikh-el-Balad A1009

King Psusennes I A1010

King Tutankhamun A1011

Obelisk of Ramses II A1011a

Temple of Karnak A1012

Perf. 12¾x13¼, 11¼ (#1750A, 1752-1755, 1757), 11x11½ (#1758-1760), 13¼x12¾ (#1756, 1761, 1763)

Photo., Litho. (#1750, 1750A, 1751, 1754, 1754A, 1761, 1763)

2000-2002

1750	A982	10p multi, type I	.40	.25
1750A	A982	10p multi, Type II	*3.00*	*3.00*
1751	A1003	10p multi	.40	.25
1752	A1004	20p multi	.40	.25
a.		With dot pattern in headdress and on chest and face ('07)	—	—
1753	A1005	25p multi	.40	.25
1754	A982	30p multi, Type I	.60	.45
1754A	A982	30p multi, Type II	—	—
1755	A1006	30p multi	.50	.35
1756	A1007	50p multi	.65	.45
1757	A1008	£1 multi	.60	.25
1758	A1009	110p multi	1.25	.95
1759	A1010	125p multi	1.40	1.00
1760	A1011	150p multi	1.75	1.25
1761	A1011a	225p multi	2.75	2.00
1763	A1012	£5 multi	5.75	5.50
a.		Perf. 14x14¼	—	—
		Nos. 1750-1763 (15)	19.85	16.20

Issued: 20p, 6/25; No. 1750, 3/25/01; No. 1750A, 2001 (?); 30p, 6/11/01. Nos. 1751, 1755, 225p, 5/25/02; 110p, 6/4/02; 125p, 6/20/02; 150p, 6/15/02; £5, 6/1/02. 30p, 50p, £1, 6/30/02.

Type I (Nos. 1750, 1754), has "Goddess" in smaller type than "Silakht." Type II (No. 1750A, 1754A), has "Goddess" and "Silakht" in type the same height.

Intl. Day Against Drug Abuse — A1013

Perf. 12¾x13¼

2000, June 26 **Litho.**

1764 A1013 20p multi .50 .25

See No. 1796.

Natl. Insurance Company, Cent. — A1014

Perf. 13¼x12¾

2000, Aug. 20 **Litho.**

1765 A1014 20p shown .50 .25

Imperf

Size: 96x75mm

1766 A1014 125p Emblem, building, horiz. 2.25 2.25

2000 Summer Olympics, Sydney A1015

Background colors: 20p, Light blue. 125p, Pink.

2000, Sept. 9 *Perf. 13¼x12¾*

1767-1768 A1015 Set of 2 1.75 1.50

No. 1768 is airmail.

Productive Cooperative Union, 25th Anniv. — A1016

2000, Sept. 15 *Perf. 12¾x13¼*

1769 A1016 20p multi .50 .25

Opening of Fourth Stage of Second Cairo Subway Line — A1017

2000, Oct. 7

1770 A1017 20p multi .60 .25

World Post Day — A1018

2000, Oct. 9
1771 A1018 125p multi 1.40 1.40

Solidarity with Palestinians — A1019

Palestinian Authority flag and: 20p, Dome of the Rock, Jerusalem, vert. No. 1773, 125p, shown. No. 1774, 125p, Dome of the Rock, father and boy, vert.

Perf. 13¼x12¾, 12¾x13¼
2000, Nov. 29
1772-1774 A1019 Set of 3 3.25 3.25
No. 1774 is airmail.

Opening of El-Ferdan Railway Bridge — A1020

2000, Dec. 2 ***Perf. 12¾x13¼***
1775 A1020 20p multi .70 .25

Disabled Person's Day — A1021

2000, Dec. 9 ***Perf. 13¼x12¾***
1776 A1021 20p multi .50 .25

Opening of Al-Azhar Professorial Building — A1022

2000, Dec. 10 ***Perf. 12¾x13¼***
1777 A1022 20p multi .50 .25

Famous Egyptians A1023

No. 1778: a, Karem Mahmoud, artist (yellow background). b, Mahmoud El-Miligi, artist (green background). c, Mohamed Fawzi, musician (pink background). d, Hussein Riyad, artist (lilac background). e, Abdel Wares Asser, artist (light blue background).

2000, Dec. 24 ***Perf. 13¼x12¾***
1778 Horiz. strip of 5 2.00 2.00
a.-e. A1023 20p Any single .40 .25

Feasts — A1024

a, Red and yellow flowers. b, Purple flowers.

Perf. 12¾x13¼
2000, Dec. 23 **Litho.**
1779 A1024 20p Pair, #a-b .90 .90
For use on greeting cards.

Jerusalem, City of Peace — A1025

2001, Jan. 1 ***Imperf.***
1780 A1025 £2 multi 2.00 2.00

Post Day — A1026

Ancient Egyptian art: 20p, 8 standing figures. No. 1782, 125p, 3 large standing figures.

2001, Jan. 2 ***Perf. 12¾x13¼***
1781-1782 A1026 Set of 2 1.75 1.75
Imperf
Size: 80x60mm
1783 A1026 125p Chariot 2.00 2.00
No. 1782 is airmail.

Arab Labor Organization, 36th Anniv. — A1027

Perf. 13¼x12¾
2001, Feb. 10 **Litho.**
1784 A1027 20p multi .50 .25

Postal Savings Bank, Cent. — A1028

2001, Mar. 1
1785 A1028 20p multi .50 .25

Natl. Council for Women, 1st Anniv. — A1029

Background colors: 30p, Pink. 125p, Blue.

2001, Mar. 16 ***Perf. 12¾x13¼***
1786-1787 A1029 Set of 2 2.00 1.40
No. 1787 is airmail.

Cairo Intl. Fair — A1030

2001, Mar. 21 ***Perf. 13¼x12¾***
1788 A1030 30p multi .50 .25

Helwan University, 25th Anniv. — A1031

2001, May 4 ***Perf. 12¾x13¼***
1789 A1031 30p multi .50 .25

Inauguration of Alexandria Library — A1032

2001, May 20
1790 A1032 125p multi 1.40 1.25

African Conference on the Future of Children A1033

Background color: 30p, Blue. 125p, Red.

2001, May 28 ***Perf. 13¼x12¾***
1791-1792 A1033 Set of 2 1.75 1.40
No. 1792 is airmail.

World Environment Day — A1034

2001, June 5 **Litho.** ***Perf. 13¼x12¾***
1793 A1034 125p multi 1.40 1.25

World Military Soccer Championships A1035

Designs: 30p, Emblem. 125p, Emblem and map.

Perf. 13¼x12¾
2001, June 21 **Litho.**
1794-1795 A1035 Set of 2 1.75 1.50

Intl. Day Against Drug Abuse Type of 2000

2001, June 26 ***Perf. 12¾x13¼***
1796 A1013 30p multi .50 .25

Egypt's Victory in World Military Soccer Championships — A1036

2001, July 6 **Litho.** ***Imperf.***
1797 A1036 125p multi 1.75 1.75

Egyptian Railways, 150th Anniv. — A1037

2001, July 12 ***Perf. 12¾x13¼***
1798 A1037 30p multi .75 .25

Poets — A1038

No. 1799: a, Aziz Abaza Pasha (1898-73), blue background. b, Ahmed Rami (1892-1981), pink background.

2001, July 28 ***Perf. 13¼x12¾***
1799 A1038 30p Horiz. pair, #a-b .80 .80

Intl. Volunteers Year — A1039

2001, Aug. 18
1800 A1039 125p multi 1.40 1.10

Ismailia Folklore Festival — A1040

2001, Aug. 20
1801 A1040 30p multi .60 .25

Satellite Telecommunications Ground Stations, 25th Anniv. — A1041

2001, Sept. 8 ***Perf. 12¾x13¼***
1802 A1041 30p multi .60 .25

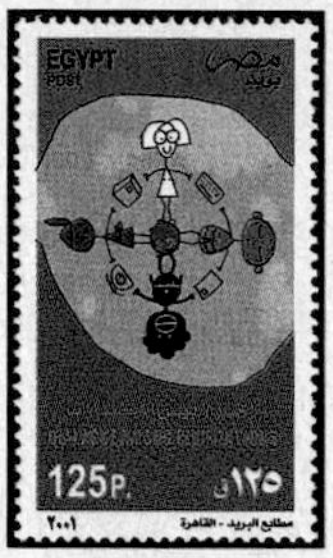

Year of Dialogue Among Civilizations A1042

Designs: No. 1803, 125p, Emblem. No. 1804, 125p, UN emblem, globe, symbols of various civilizations, horiz.

Perf. 13¼x12¾, 12¾x13¼
2001, Oct. 9
1803-1804 A1042 Set of 2 3.00 2.50

Opening of Suez Canal Bridge — A1043

No. 1805: a, 30p, Bridge, ship. b, 125p, Bridge, road.

No. 1806, Bridge, ship and flags of Egypt and Japan.

2001, Oct. 10 ***Perf. 12¾x13¼***
1805 A1043 Horiz. pair, #a-b 1.75 1.75

Imperf

Size: 81x60mm

1806 A1043 125p multi 2.00 2.00

Ancient Gold Masks — A1044

Designs: No. 1807, 30p, Mask of San Xing Dui, China, green background. No. 1808, 30p, Funerary mask of King Tutankhamun, brown background.

2001, Oct. 12 ***Perf. 12¾x13¼***
1807-1808 A1044 Set of 2 .80 .60

See People's Republic of China 3141-3142.

Opening of Azhar Tunnels, Cairo — A1045

2001, Oct. 28 ***Perf. 13¼x12¾***
1809 A1045 30p multi .60 .25

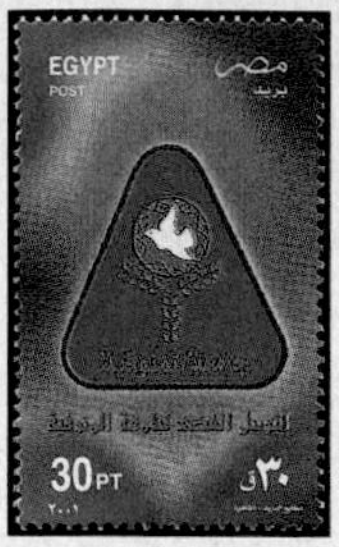

El-Menoufia University, 25th Anniv. — A1046

2001, Nov. 25
1810 A1046 30p multi .60 .25

Feasts — A1047

No.1811: a, Black and white bird on branch. b, Sea gulls. c, Parrot. d, Blue bird on branch.

2001, Dec. 5
1811 A1047 30p Block of 4, #a-d 2.50 2.00

For use on greeting cards.

Musicians — A1048

No. 1812: a, Zakaria Ahmed (1896-1961) with scarf around neck (4). b, Riyadh El-Sonbati (1908-81) with glasses with rectangular lenses (3). c, Mahmoud El-Sherif (1912-90) (2). d, Mohamed El-Kasabgi (1898-1966) with glasses with round lenses (1). Stamp numbers, shown in parentheses, are found at the bottom center in Arabian script.

2001, Dec.
1812 A1048 30p Horiz. strip of 4 2.00 1.40

Painting From Tomb of Anhur Khawi — A1049

Painting from Tomb of Irinefer — A1050

2002, Jan. 2 **Litho.** ***Perf. 12¾x13¼***
1813 A1049 30p multi .45 .25

Imperf

Size: 79x60mm

1814 A1050 125p multi 2.25 2.25

Post Day.

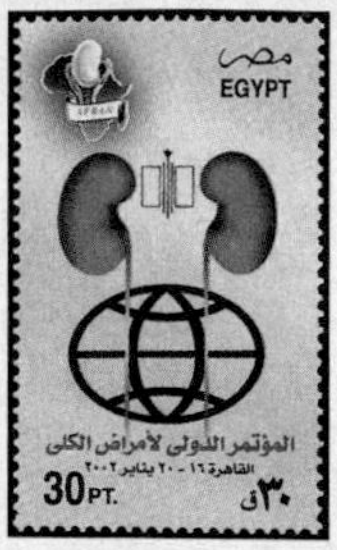

Intl. Nephrology Congress A1051

2002, Jan. 16 **Litho.** ***Perf. 13¼x12¾***
1815 A1051 30p multi .45 .25

Police Day, 50th Anniv. A1052

2002, Jan. 25 ***Perf. 12¾x13¼***
1816 A1052 30p multi .45 .25

Imperf

Size: 79x50mm

1817 A1052 30p multi 1.60 1.50

Return of Sinai to Egypt, 20th Anniv. — A1053

2002, Apr. 25 ***Perf. 13¼x12¾***
1818 A1053 30p multi .60 .25

Cairo Bank, 50th Anniv. — A1054

2002, May 15
1819 A1054 30p multi .50 .25

Weight Lifters — A1055

No. 1820: a, Ibrahim Shams, 1948 (weights over head). b, Khidre el Touney, 1936 (weights at knees).

2002, June 1
1820 A1055 30p Horiz. pair, #a-b .80 .80

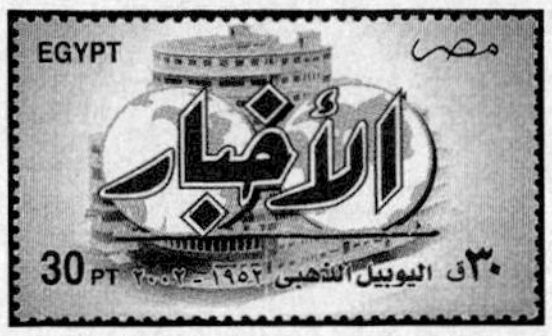

Al Akhbar Newspaper, 50th Anniv. — A1056

2002, June 15 ***Perf. 12¾x13¼***

1821 A1056 30p multi .45 .25

Nos. 318-321 and Egyptian Arms — A1057

2002, July 23 **Litho.** ***Imperf.***

1822 A1057 125p multi 1.40 1.40

July 23rd Revolution, 50th anniv.

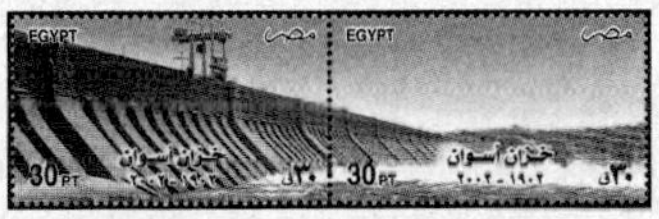

Aswan Dam, Cent. — A1058

No. 1823: a, Dam. b, Dam and buildings.

2002, Aug. 15 ***Perf. 12¾x13¼***

1823 A1058 30p Horiz. pair, #a-b .90 .90

Intl. Day for Preservation of the Ozone Layer — A1059

2002, Sept. 16 ***Perf. 13¼x12¾***

1824 A1059 125p multi 1.40 1.25

18th Intl. Conference on Road Safety, Cairo — A1060

2002, Sept. 22

1825 A1060 30p multi .50 .25

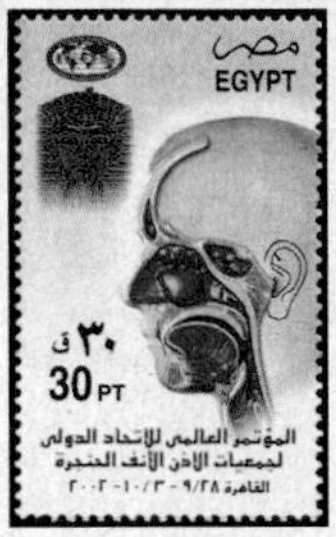

17th Congress of Intl. Federation of Otorhinolaryngological Societies, Cairo — A1061

2002, Sept. 28

1826 A1061 30p multi .50 .25

World Post Day — A1062

2002, Oct. 9

1827 A1062 125p multi 1.10 1.10

Opening of Alexandria Library — A1063

Ancient Alexandria Library — A1064

Designs: 30p, Library exterior. 125p, Pillar, sun on horizon, vert.

Perf. 12¾x13¼, 13¼x12¾

2002, Oct. 16

1828-1829 A1063 Set of 2 1.75 1.50

Size: 60x80mm

Imperf

1830 A1064 125p multi 1.60 1.60

Hassan Faek, Actor — A1065

Aziza Amir, Actress — A1066

Farid Shawki, Actor — A1067

Mary Mounib, Actress — A1068

2002, Nov. 23 ***Perf. 13¼x12¾***

1831 Horiz. strip of 4 1.75 1.60
- *a.* A1065 30p tan & black .40 .25
- *b.* A1066 30p tan & black .40 .25
- *c.* A1067 30p tan & black .40 .25
- *d.* A1068 30p tan & black .40 .25

A1069

A1070

A1071

Birds — A1072

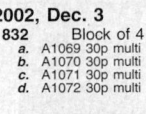

2002, Dec. 3 ***Perf. 13¼x12¾***

1832 Block of 4 1.75 1.60
- *a.* A1069 30p multi .40 .25
- *b.* A1070 30p multi .40 .25
- *c.* A1071 30p multi .40 .25
- *d.* A1072 30p multi .40 .25

Egyptian Museum, Cent. — A1073

2002, Dec. 11 ***Perf. 12¾x13¼***

1833 A1073 30p shown .50 .25

Size: 80x60mm

Imperf

1834 A1073 125p Entrance, statue of Cheops 1.40 1.40

Opening of Aswan Suspension Bridge — A1074

No. 1835: a, Bridge and support cables. b, Bridge towers.

2002, Dec. 17 ***Perf. 12¾x13¼***

1835 A1074 30p Horiz. pair, #a-b .90 .90

Suez Canal University, 25th Anniv. — A1075

2002, Dec. 29 ***Perf. 13¼x12¾***

1836 A1075 30p multi .45 .25

Toshka Land Reclamation Project — A1076

2002, Dec. 31 ***Perf. 12¾x13¼***

1837 A1076 30p multi .45 .25

A1077

A1078

Post Day — A1079

2003, Jan. 2
1838 A1077 30p multi .45 .25
1839 A1078 30p multi .45 .25
1840 A1079 125p multi 1.10 1.00
Nos. 1838-1840 (3) 2.00 1.50

Cairo Intl. Communications and Information Technology Fair — A1080

2003, Jan. 12 Litho. *Perf. 13¼x12¾*
1841 A1080 30p multi .50 .25

Intl. Nile Children's Song Festival — A1081

Background color: 30p, Brown. 125p, Green.

2003, Jan. 28 *Perf. 12¾x13¼*
1842-1843 A1081 Set of 2 1.50 1.25

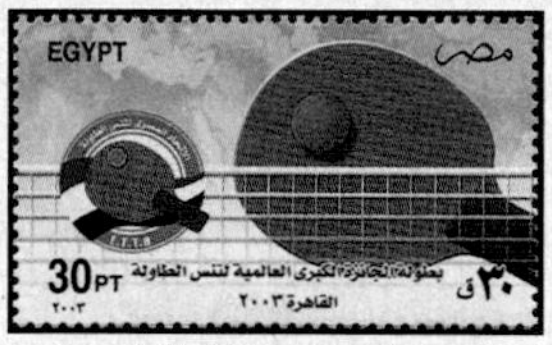

Intl. Table Tennis Championships — A1082

Background color: 30p, Blue. 125p, Orange.

2003, Feb. 3
1844-1845 A1082 Set of 2 1.50 1.25

Tenth Intl. Building and Construction Conference A1083

Background color: 30p, Orange. 125p, Blue.

2003, Apr. 1 *Perf. 13¼x12¾*
1846-1847 A1083 Set of 2 1.50 1.10

Arab Lawyer's Union, 60th Anniv. — A1084

Background color: 30p, Blue. 125p, Lilac.

2003, Apr. 25 *Perf. 12¾x13¼*
1848-1849 A1084 Set of 2 1.40 1.10

Inauguration of First Phase of Smart Village Project — A1085

Denomination color: 30p, White. 125p, Yellow. £1, White.

2003, July 1 *Perf. 12¾x13¼*
1850-1851 A1085 Set of 2 1.50 1.50

Size: 79x59mm

Imperf

1852 A1085 £1 multi 1.50 1.50

Writers — A1086

No. 1853: a, Ihsan Abdul Qudous (1919-90) (wearing checked tie). b, Youssef Idris (1927-91) (wearing solid tie).

2003, July 28 *Perf. 13¼x12¾*
1853 A1086 30p Horiz. pair, #a-b .90 .90

African Men's Basketball Championships A1087

Background color: 30p, Black. 125p, Blue.

2003, Aug. 12
1854-1855 A1087 Set of 2 1.50 1.10

Natl. Institute of Astronomical and Geophysical Research, Cent. — A1088

2003, Sept. 7 *Perf. 12¾x13¼*
1856 A1088 30p multi .60 .30

World Tourism Day — A1089

Denomination color: 30p, White. 125p, Red.

Perf. 12¾x13¼
2003, Sept. 27 Litho.
1857-1858 A1089 Set of 2 1.50 1.10

Egypt's Bid for Hosting 2010 World Cup Soccer Championships — A1090

Designs: 30p, Emblem, vert. 125p, Emblem, funerary mask of King Tutankhamun.

Perf. 13¼x12¾, 12¾x13¼
2003, Sept. 27
1859-1860 A1090 Set of 2 1.50 1.10

October War Against Israel, 30th Anniv. — A1091

2003, Oct. 6 *Perf. 13¼x12¾*
1861 A1091 30p multi 1.00 .30

World Post Day — A1092

2003, Oct. 9
1862 A1092 125p multi 1.00 .80

National Bar Association, 91st Anniv. — A1093

2003, Oct. 30
1863 A1093 30p multi .60 .25

Festivals — A1094

No. 1864: a, Pink orchids. b, White rose. c, Red rose. d, Sunflower.

2003, Nov. 23 *Perf. 14*
1864 A1094 30p Block of 4, #a-d 1.50 1.50

For use on greeting cars.

Film Directors — A1095

No. 1865: a, Salah Abou Seif (balding man with open collar). b, Kamal Selim (round eyeglasses) c, Henri Barakat (square eyeglasses). d, Hassan El Emam.

2003, Dec. 1 *Perf. 13¼x12¾*
1865 A1095 30p Horiz. strip of 4, #a-d 1.50 1.50

El Gomhoreya Newspaper, 50th Anniv. — A1096

2003, Dec. 7
1866 A1096 30p multi .50 .25

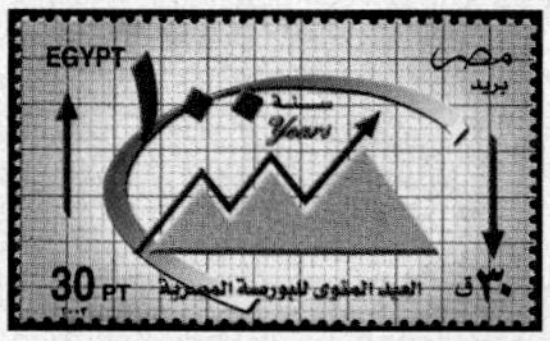

Cairo Bourse, Cent. — A1097

2003, Dec. 7 *Perf. 12¾x13¼*
1867 A1097 30p multi .45 .25

Mrs. Suzanne Mubarak, Emblems of Fifth E-9 Ministerial Review Meeting and UNESCO — A1098

Background color: 30p, Blue. 125p, Orange. £2, Blue.

Perf. 12¾x13¼
2003, Dec. 18 Litho.
1868-1869 A1098 Set of 2 1.50 1.10

Imperf

Size: 79x60mm

1870 A1098 £2 multi 2.00 2.00

Delta International Bank, 25th Anniv. — A1099

Background color: 30p, Green. 125p, Blue. £2, Green and blue, horiz.

2004, Jan. 1 *Perf. 12¾x13¼*
1871-1872 A1099 Set of 2 1.40 1.00

Imperf

Size: 80x60mm

1873 A1099 £2 multi 2.00 2.00

Post Day
A1100

Denominations: 30p, 125p.

2004, Jan. 2 ***Perf. 12¾x13¼***

1874-1875 A1100 Set of 2 1.50 1.25

Eighth Intl. Telecommunications Conference — A1101

2004, Jan. 17

1876 A1101 30p multi .80 .30

Treasures of Egypt
A1102

No. 1877: a, Sinai. b, Pyramids at dusk. c, Egyptian Bedouin. d, Red Sea corals. e, Suez Canal, Ferdinand-Marie de Lesseps, Khedive Ismail. f, Ramadan lanterns. g, Nile felucca. h, White Western Desert. i, Maydum Pyramid.

No. 1878: a, St. Catherine Monastery, Sinai. b, Icon of Sts. Paul and Anthony. c, Mosque of Muhammad Ali. d, Lamp, Old Cairo. e, Emblem of Sultan Qaytbay. f, Minaret, Cairo. g, Mosque of al-Azhar. h, Coptic priest and icon, Cairo. i, Ben Ezra Synagogue.

No. 1879: a, Ankh. b, Rosetta Stone. c, Sarcophagus of Ahmes Meritamun. d, Stela of Amenmhat. e, Sphinx. f, Udjat. g, Canopic jars of Tutankhamun. h, Cartouche of Tutankhamun. i, Egyptian scribe.

No. 1880: a, Sphinx, diff. b, Queen Nefertiti. c, Tutankhamun.

2004, Jan. 22 Litho. ***Perf. 13x13¼***

1877	Booklet pane of 9	*2.25*	—
a.-i.	A1102 30p Any single	.40	.25
1878	Booklet pane of 9	*8.25*	—
a.-i.	A1102 125p Any single	.90	.80

Litho. & Embossed, Litho. & Embossed With Foil Application (£10)

1879	Booklet pane of 9	*13.50*	—
a.-i.	A1102 £2 Any single	1.50	1.25

Perf. 13¼

1880	Booklet pane of 3	*15.00*	—
a.-b.	A1102 £5 Either single, 38x51mm	3.75	3.75
c.	A1102 £10 gold & multi, 38x51mm	7.00	7.00
	Complete booklet, #1877-1880	*39.00*	

Complete booklet sold for £80.

Morkos Hanna — A1103

Ahmed Lotfi — A1104

Mahmoud Abu el Nasr — A1105

Abd el Aziz Fahmy — A1106

Ibrahim el Helbawi — A1107

Makram Ebeid — A1108

Mohammad Naguib el Gharabli — A1109

Mohammad Bassiouni
A1110

Mohammad Hafez Ramadan
A1111

Mohammad Abu Shadi — A1112

Mahmoud Fahmi Goundia — A1113

Kamel Youssof Saleh — A1114

Abd el Hamid Abd el Hakk — A1115

Mohammad Ali Allouba — A1116

Kamel Sedki Beck — A1117

Bar Association Emblem — A1118

Abd el Rahman el Rafei — A1119

Abd el Fattah el Shalkany
A1120

Mohammad Sabri Abu Alam — A1121

Omar Omar — A1122

Sameh Ashour — A1123

Ahmed el Khawaga A1124

Abd el Aziz el Shorgabi A1125

Mostafa el Baradei — A1126

2004, Feb. **Litho.** ***Perf. 13¼x12¾***

1881	Block of 25	8.75	8.75
a.	A1103 30p bright blue & black	.35	.25
b.	A1104 30p bright blue & black	.35	.25
c.	A1105 30p bright blue & black	.35	.25
d.	A1106 30p bright blue & black	.35	.25
e.	A1107 30p bright blue & black	.35	.25
f.	A1108 30p pink & black	.35	.25
g.	A1109 30p pink & black	.35	.25
h.	A1110 30p pink & black	.35	.25
i.	A1111 30p pink & black	.35	.25
j.	A1112 30p pink & black	.35	.25
k.	A1113 30p orange & black	.35	.25
l.	A1114 30p orange & black	.35	.25
m.	A1115 30p orange & black	.35	.25
n.	A1116 30p orange & black	.35	.25
o.	A1117 30p orange & black	.35	.25
p.	A1118 30p green & multi	.35	.25
q.	A1119 30p green & black	.35	.25
r.	A1120 30p green & black	.35	.25
s.	A1121 30p green & black	.35	.25
t.	A1122 30p green & black	.35	.25
u.	A1118 30p dark blue & multi	.35	.25
v.	A1123 30p dark blue & black	.35	.25
w.	A1124 30p dark blue & black	.35	.25
x.	A1125 30p dark blue & black	.35	.25
y.	A1126 30p dark blue & black	.35	.25

National Bar Association, 92nd anniv.

IBM Corporation in Egypt, 50th Anniv. — A1127

2004, Feb. 24
1882 A1127 30p multi .60 .25

Cairo Rotary Club, 75th Anniv. — A1128

2004, Mar. 11
1883 A1128 30p multi .60 .25

Egyptian Victory in Regional Computer Programming and Information Technology Competition A1129

2004, Mar. 15
1884 A1129 30p multi .60 .25

National Women's Day — A1130

Background colors: 30p, Blue. 125p, Red orange.

2004, Mar. 16 **Litho.**
1885-1886 A1130 Set of 2 1.50 1.00

Anti-Narcotics General Administration, 75th Anniv. — A1131

2004, Mar. 20 ***Perf. 12¾x13¼***
1887 A1131 30p multi .75 .30

Imperf

Size: 80x60mm

1888 A1131 125p multi 1.50 1.50

Orphan's Day — A1132

2004, Apr. 2 ***Perf. 13¼x12¾***
1889 A1132 30p multi .60 .25

Compare with Types A1169 and A1199.

Telecom Africa Fair and Conference, Cairo — A1133

2004, May 4 ***Perf. 12¾x13¼***
1890 A1133 30p multi .60 .25

Egyptian Philatelic Society, 75th Anniv. — A1134

Designs: 30p, Emblem. 125p, Emblem, stamp, magnifying glass, tongs.

2004, May 20 ***Perf. 13¼x12¾***
1891 A1134 30p multi .60 .25

Imperf

Size: 80x60mm

1892 A1134 125p multi 1.50 1.50

State Information Service, 50th Anniv. — A1135

2004, May 30 ***Perf. 12¾x13¼***
1893 A1135 30p multi .75 .25

Tenth Radio and Television Festival, Cairo — A1136

Designs: 30p, Festival emblem, green background. £1, Fesitval emblem, brown background. 125p, Sphinx, festival emblem, film, horiz.
£2, Like 125p, horiz.

Perf. 13¼x12¾, 12¾x13¼

2004, June 1
1894-1896 A1136 Set of 3 2.00 2.00

Imperf

Size: 80x60mm

1897 A1136 £2 multi 2.00 2.00

Pres. Hosni Mubarak, "Education for All" Arab Regional Conference Emblem — A1137

Stylized Children, Emblems A1138

Perf. 12¾x13¼, 13¼x12¾

2004, June 1

1898	A1137	30p yel & multi	.35	.25
1899	A1137	125p red org & multi	.60	.60
1900	A1138	125p multi	.60	.60
		Nos. 1898-1900 (3)	1.55	1.45

Imperf

Size: 80x60mm

1901 A1137 £2 blue & multi 1.75 1.75

Construction and Housing Bank, 25th Anniv. — A1139

2004, June 24 ***Perf. 13¼x12¾***
1902 A1139 30p multi .60 .25

2004 Summer Olympics, Athens — A1140

Background color: 30p, Gray. 150p, Orange yellow.

Perf. 13¼x12¾

2004, Aug. 13 **Litho.**
1903-1904 A1140 Set of 2 1.50 1.40

Scouting in Egypt, 90th Anniv. — A1141

2004, Aug. 15 *Perf. 12¾x13¼*
1905 A1141 30p multi .80 .30

14th Intl. Folklore Festival, Ismailia — A1142

2004, Aug. 24 *Perf. 13¼x12¾*
1906 A1142 30p multi .70 .25

Administrative Attorneys, 50th Anniv. — A1143

2004, Sept. 16 *Perf. 13¼x12¾*
1907 A1143 30p multi .60 .25

Imperf

Size: 60x80mm

1908 A1143 £1 multi 1.50 1.50

Egyptian National Archives, 50th Anniv. — A1144

2004, Sept. 20 *Perf. 12¾x13¼*
1909 A1144 30p multi .75 .25

Light and Hope Society, 50th Anniv. — A1145

2004, Sept. 26
1910 A1145 30p multi .70 .25

General Arab Journalists Union, 10th Conference A1146

2004, Oct. 2 *Perf. 13¼x12¾*
1911 A1146 125p multi 1.00 .80

Telecom Egypt, 150th Anniv. A1146a

2004, Oct. 3 Litho. *Perf. 12¾x13¼*
1911A A1146a 30p multi *18.50 18.50*

No. 1911A was withdrawn from sale after a few days as anniversary emblem was incorrect.

Military Production Day, 50th Anniv. — A1147

2004, Oct. 6 *Perf. 12¾x13¼*
1912 A1147 30p multi .90 .30

World Post Day — A1148

2004, Oct. 9
1913 A1148 150p multi 1.10 1.00

Egyptian Youth Hostels Association, 50th Anniv. — A1149

2004, Oct. 20 *Perf. 13¼x12¾*
1914 A1149 30p multi .80 .25

Rose — A1150

Songbird A1151

Perf. 12¾x13¼

2004, Nov. 10 Litho.
1915 A1150 30p multi .50 .25

Perf. 13¼x12¾

1916 A1151 30p multi .50 .25

24th Arab Scouting Congress — A1152

2004, Nov. 27 *Perf. 12¾x13¼*
1917 A1152 30p multi .65 .25

Arab Scouting Organization, 50th Anniv. — A1153

2004, Dec. 4
1918 A1153 30p multi .65 .25

Islamic Art Museum Foundation, Cent. — A1154

2004, Dec. 15 *Perf. 13¼x12¾*
1919 A1154 30p multi .65 .25

FIFA (Fédération Internationale de Football Association), Cent. — A1155

2004, Dec. 15 *Perf. 12¾x13¼*
1920 A1155 150p multi 1.25 1.00

Fekri Abaza (1896-1979), Journalist A1156

Abd El Rahman El Sharqawi (1920-87), Journalist A1157

2004, Dec. 28 *Perf. 13¼x12¾*
1921 A1156 30p multi .40 .25
1922 A1157 30p multi .40 .25

Telecom Egypt, 150th Anniv. — A1158

Color of central panel: 30p, White. 125p, Gray.

2004, Dec. 30 *Perf. 12¾x13¼*
1923-1924 A1158 Set of 2 1.50 1.10

First Sale of Natural Gas to Jordan — A1159

2005, Jan. 1
1925 A1159 30p multi .90 .30

Post Day — A1160

2005, Jan. 2 *Perf. 13¼x12¾*
1926 A1160 30p multi .80 .30

Opening of Om El Massrean — El Moneib Subway Line, Cairo — A1161

2005, Jan. 16 *Perf. 12¾x13¼*
1927 A1161 30p multi .65 .30

Imperf

Size: 80x59mm

1928 A1161 150p multi 1.40 1.40

Police Day — A1162

Pres. Hosni Mubarak and flag stripes aligned: 30p, Vertically. £1, Horizontally.

2005, Jan. 25 ***Perf. 13¼x12¾***
1929 A1162 30p multi .60 .25

Imperf

Size: 80x59mm

1930 A1162 £1 multi 1.25 1.25

El Mohandes Insurance Company, 25th Anniv. — A1163

2005, Jan. 26 ***Perf. 13¼x12¾***
1931 A1163 30p multi .65 .30

9th Intl. Telecommunications and Information Conference, Cairo — A1164

2005, Feb. 1
1932 A1164 30p multi .65 .25

7th University Youth Week — A1165

2005, Feb. 5
1933 A1165 30p multi .65 .25

Rotary International, Cent. — A1166

2005, Feb. 23 **Litho.**
1934 A1166 30p multi .75 .30

38th Intl. Fair, Cairo — A1167

2005, Mar. 15
1935 A1167 30p multi .50 .25

Arab League, 60th Anniv. — A1168

2005, Mar. 22
1936 A1168 30p multi .55 .25

Orphan's Day — A1169

2005, Apr. 2
1937 A1169 30p multi .70 .30

Compare with Types A1132 and A1199. See also Nos. 2035, 2053.

Heliopolis Foundation, Cent. — A1170

2005, May 5 ***Perf. 12¾x13¼***
1938 A1170 30p multi .65 .25

National Center of Social and Criminological Research, 50th Anniv. — A1171

2005, May 22 **Litho.** ***Perf. 13¼x12¾***
1939 A1171 30p multi .70 .30

Egyptian-European Association Agreement, 1st Anniv. — A1172

2005, June 1
1940 A1172 150p multi .90 .50

World Environment Day — A1173

2005, June 5 ***Perf. 12¾x13¼***
1941 A1173 30p multi .80 .30

World Summit on the Information Society, Tunis — A1174

2005, July 31 **Litho.** ***Perf. 13¼x12¾***
1942 A1174 150p multi 1.40 1.40

Ministry of Youth, 50th Anniv. — A1175

Background colors: 30p, Green. 125p, Olive green.

2005, Aug. 13
1943-1944 A1175 Set of 2 1.25 1.10

Presidential Elections A1176

2005, Sept. 7
1945 A1176 30p multi .65 .30

13th World Psychiatry Congress, Cairo — A1177

Designs: 30p, Emblem. 150p, Emblem and funerary mask of King Tutankhamun, horiz.

2005, Sept. 10 ***Perf. 13¼x12¾***
1946 A1177 30p multi .65 .30

Imperf

Size: 80x60mm

1947 A1177 150p multi 1.90 1.90

World Literacy Day — A1178

2005, Sept. 24 ***Perf. 12¾x13¼***
1948 A1178 30p multi .70 .30

Re-election of Pres. Hosni Mubarak A1179

2005, Sept. 27 ***Perf. 13¼x12¾***
1949 A1179 30p multi .60 .25

Mohamed El-Baradei, Director General of Intl. Atomic Energy Agency — A1180

Background colors: 30p, Blue green. 150p, Rose lilac.

2005, Oct. 8
1950-1951 A1180 Set of 2 1.75 1.50

Awarding of 2005 Nobel Peace Prize to El-Baradei and IAEA.

World Post Day — A1181

Denominations: 30p, 150p.

2005, Oct. 9

1952-1953 A1181 Set of 2 1.40 1.25

Intl. Year of Sports and Physical Education A1182

2005, Oct. 24

1954 A1182 150p multi 1.25 1.00

United Nations, 60th Anniv. — A1183

2005, Oct. 24 ***Perf. 12¾x13¼***

1955 A1183 150p multi 1.25 1.00

Festivals A1184

2005, Nov. 1 ***Perf. 13¼x12¾***

1966 A1184 30p multi .70 .30

Alexandria Biennale, 50th Anniv. — A1185

2005, Dec. 1

1957 A1185 30p multi .65 .30

K-8 Training Airplane — A1186

Denominations: 30p, 150p.

Perf. 12¾x13¼

2005, Dec. 26 **Litho.**

1958-1959 A1186 Set of 2 2.00 1.50

Saved Mekawi, Musician A1187

Mohamed El Mogi (1923-95), Musician A1188

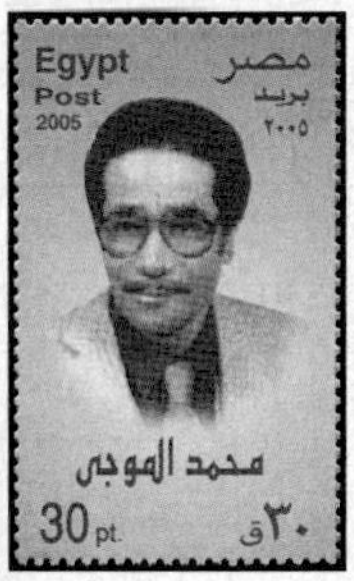

Kamal El Taweel, Composer A1189

Ali Ismael (1921-75), Composer A1190

Mohamed Roshdi, Folk Singer — A1191

2005, Dec. 31 ***Perf. 13¼x12¾***

1960 Horiz. strip of 5 1.75 1.75
- *a.* A1187 30p green & multi .30 .25
- *b.* A1188 30p blue & multi .30 .25
- *c.* A1189 30p lilac & black .30 .25
- *d.* A1190 30p org & black .30 .25
- *e.* A1191 30p brt org & black .30 .25

Post Day — A1192

2006, Jan. 2

1961 A1192 30p multi .75 .30

25th Africa Cup of Nations Soccer Tournament A1193

2006, Jan. 20

1962 A1193 30p multi .60 .25

Arab University Youth Week — A1194

2006, Feb. 4 ***Perf. 12¾x13¼***

1963 A1194 30p multi .55 .25

Intl. Telecommunications, Information and Networking Exhibition, Cairo — A1195

2006, Feb. 5 ***Perf. 13¼x12¾***

1964 A1195 30p multi .55 .25

Pres. Hosni Mubarak Holding African Cup of Nations — A1196

2006, Feb. 10 ***Perf. 12¾x13¼***

1965 A1196 30p multi .75 .35

Size: 80x60mm

Imperf

1966 A1196 150p multi 1.75 1.60

Information and Decision Support Center, 20th Anniv. — A1197

2006, Mar. 27 ***Perf. 13¼x12¾***

1967 A1197 30p multi .55 .25

Total Solar Eclipse of March 29, 2006 — A1198

2006, Mar. 29 ***Perf. 12¾x13¼***

1968 A1198 30p multi .55 .35

Size: 82x60mm

Imperf

1969 A1198 150p multi 2.25 1.90

Orphan's Day — A1199

2006, Apr. 2 ***Perf. 13¼x12¾***

1970 A1199 30p multi .70 .30

Compare with types A1132 and A1169. See also Nos. 2035, 2053.

Gamal Hemdan (1928-93), Geographical Historian A1200

2006, Apr. 16

1971 A1200 30p lilac & black .55 .30

Abd El-Rahman ibn Khaldun (1332-1406), Historian A1201

2006, May 27

1972 A1201 30p multi .70 .30

World Environment Day — A1202

Designs: 30p, Stone pillar in White Desert. 150p, Trees in desert.

2006, June 5 ***Perf. 12¾x13¼***
1973-1974 A1202 Set of 2 1.50 1.25

Diplomatic Relations Between Egypt and People's Republic of China, 50th Anniv. — A1203

No. 1975: a, Abu Simbel Temple, Egypt. b, South Gate Pavilion, China.

2006, July 13 Litho. ***Perf. 12***
1975 A1203 £1.50 Horiz. pair, #a-b, + central label 1.75 1.75
c. Souvenir sheet, #1975 *25.00 25.00*

Military Academy Headquarters, Heliopolis, 50th Anniv. — A1204

2006, July 19 ***Perf. 12¾x13¼***
1976 A1204 30p multi .70 .30

Nationalization of the Suez Canal, 50th Anniv. — A1205

2006, July 26 ***Perf. 13¼x12¾***
1977 A1205 30p multi .55 .25

World Post Day — A1206

Denominations: 30p, 150p.

2006, Oct. 9
1978-1979 A1206 Set of 2 1.50 1.25

China - Africa Summit — A1206a

No. 1979A: b, Chinese mask. c, African mask.

2006, Nov. 5 Litho. ***Perf. 12***
1979A Horiz. pair with central label 2.25 2.25
b.-c. A1206a £1.50 Either single .80 .60

National Housing Census — A1207

2006, Nov. 21 Litho. ***Perf. 13¼x13***
1980 A1207 30p multi .55 .25

Al-Ahram Newspaper — A1208

No. 1981: a, Newspaper headquarters. b, Newspaper emblem.
150p, Headquarters and emblem.

2006, Nov. 26 ***Perf. 13x13¼***
1981 A1208 30p Horiz. pair, #a-b, + central label 1.00 1.00

Imperf

Size: 80x60mm

1982 A1208 150p multi 1.00 1.00

Egyptian Initiative to Support Lebanon — A1209

2006, Dec. 27 ***Perf. 13x13¼***
1983 A1209 150p multi 1.00 1.00

Feasts — A1210

2006, Dec. 30
1984 A1210 30p multi .45 .25

Post Day — A1211

2007, Jan. 2
1985 A1211 30p multi .45 .25

Ali El Kassar (1888-1957), Artist — A1212

2007, Jan. 15 ***Perf. 13¼x13***
1986 A1212 30p multi .45 .25

Automobile and Touring Club of Egypt — A1213

2007, Jan. 14 Litho. ***Perf. 12¾x13¼***
1987 A1213 30p multi .55 .30

Imperf

Size: 80x60mm

1988 A1213 150p multi 1.50 1.50

Police Day — A1214

2007, Jan. 25 ***Perf. 12¾x13¼***
1989 A1214 30p multi .55 .30

Imperf

Size: 80x60mm

1990 A1214 150p multi 1.00 1.00

Rededication of National Library — A1215

2007, Feb. 25 ***Perf. 12¾x13¼***
1991 A1215 30p multi .55 .30

Arabic Language Academy, 75th Anniv. — A1216

2007, Mar. 17 ***Perf. 13¼x12¾***
1992 A1216 30p multi .55 .30

World Health Day — A1217

2007, Apr. 7 Litho. ***Perf. 12¾x13¼***
1993 A1217 30p multi .55 .30

Egyptian Trade Union Federation, 50th Anniv. — A1218

2007, May 1 ***Perf. 13¼x12¾***
1994 A1218 30p multi .45 .25

Egypt Air, 75th Anniv. — A1219

Anniversary emblem and: 30p, Biplane. 150p, Biplane and jet.

2007, May 7 ***Perf. 12¾x13¼***
1995-1996 A1219 Set of 2 1.00 .75

Return of Sinai to Egypt, 25th Anniv. — A1220

No. 1997: a, Monastery of St. Catherine. b, Salah el Din Castle. c, Sharm el-Sheikh. d, Oasis of Nabq.

2007, Apr. 25 Litho. ***Perf. 12¾x13¼***
1997 A1220 30p Block of 4, #a-d 1.90 1.25

Mevlana Jalal ad-Din Rumi (1207-73), Islamic Philosopher
A1221

2007, May 8 ***Perf. 13¼x12¾***

1998 A1221 150p multi .55 .30

World Environment Day — A1222

Designs: 30p, Sinai baton blue butterfly. 150p, Melting ice, horiz.

Perf. 13¼x12¾, 12¾x13¼

2007, June 5

1999-2000 A1222 Set of 2 1.50 .75

Scouting, Cent. — A1223

2007, June 6 ***Perf. 12¾x13¼***

2001 A1223 150p multi 1.25 .80

EuroMed Postal Conference, Marseille, France — A1224

2007, July 9

2002 A1224 150p multi 1.10 .75

Diplomatic Relations Between Egypt and Nepal, 50th Anniv. — A1225

2007, July 16

2003 A1225 150p multi 1.10 .75

Egyptian Air Force, 75th Anniv. — A1226

2007, Oct. 14 Litho. ***Perf. 13x13¼***

2004 A1226 30p multi .55 .25

A1227

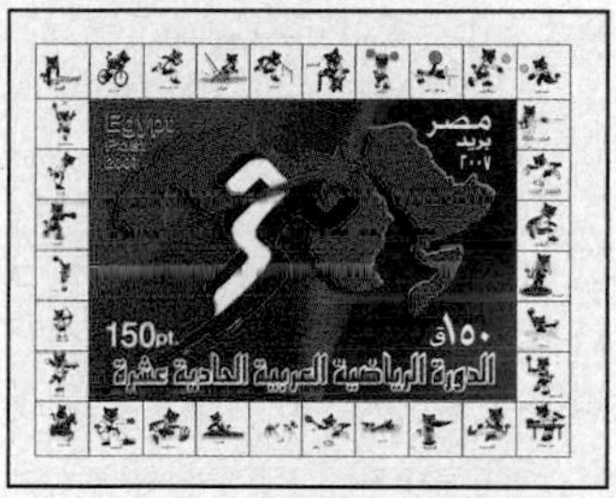

11th Arab Games — A1228

2007, Oct. 26 Litho. ***Perf. 13¼x12¾***

2005 A1227 150p multi 1.25 .90

Imperf

Size: 95x75mm

2006 A1228 150p multi 1.25 1.00

Assiut University, 50th Anniv. — A1229

2007, Nov. 27 ***Perf. 13¼x12¾***

2007 A1229 30p brn & blk .45 .25

Hafez Ibrahim (1872-1932), Poet — A1230

Ahmed Shawky (1868-1932), Poet — A1231

2007, Dec. 16

2008 A1230 30p multi .45 .25

2009 A1231 30p multi .45 .25

A 150p stamp issued in December 2007 depicting riders on horses on a beach with a se-tenant label was created exclusively for the Utopia Resort in Marsa Alam. The resort sold the stamps to its guests.

Egyptian Handball Federation, 50th Anniv. — A1232

2007, Dec. 30

2010 A1232 30p multi .50 .25

Musicians — A1233

2008, Jan. 1 ***Perf. 12¾x13¼***

2011 A1233 30p multi .45 .25

Post Day — A1234

2008, Feb. 7 Litho. ***Imperf.***

2012 A1234 150p multi 1.00 1.00

Africa Cup of Nations Soccer Championships, Ghana — A1235

2008, Feb. 10 ***Perf. 13¼x13***

2013 A1235 30p multi .45 .25

Wadi El-Hitan UNESCO World Heritage Site — A1236

No. 2014: a, Whale bones on ground. b, Reconstructed whale skeleton.

2008, Feb. 10 ***Perf. 13x13¼***

2014 Horiz. pair with central label 1.00 1.00

a.-b. A1236 30p Either single .45 .25

Cairo University, Cent. — A1237

2008, Apr. 14 ***Perf. 13¼x13***

2015 A1237 30p multi .45 .25

Land Mine Clearance in Northwest Egypt — A1238

No. 2016 — Map and: a, Amputee surrounded by land mines. b, Hand, "no land mines" symbol, vert.

Perf. 13x13¼, 13¼x13 (#2016b)

2008, Apr. 22

2016 A1238 150p Pair, #a-b 1.10 1.10

Telecom Africa Conference
A1239

2008, May 12 ***Perf. 13¼x13***

2017 A1239 30p multi .45 .25

World Environment Day — A1240

Background colors: 30p, Blue. 150p, Lilac.

2008, June 5
2018-2019 A1240 Set of 2 1.00 .70

Faculty of Fine Arts, Cent. — A1241

No. 2020 — Background color: a, 30p, Blue. b, 150p, Green.

2008, June 21 Litho. ***Perf. 13¼x13***
2020 A1241 Horiz. pair, #a-b 1.25 1.25

Pan African Postal Union Plenipotentiary Conference, Cairo — A1242

2008, June 28 ***Perf. 13x13¼***
2021 A1242 150p multi 1.25 .60

Egypt Air Joining Star Alliance — A1243

2008, July 11
2022 A1243 150p multi 1.25 .85

Alexandria, 2008 Islamic Cultural Capital — A1244

2008, July 26
2023 A1244 150p multi .85 .60

Arab Post Day — A1245

No. 2024 — Emblem and: a, World map, pigeon. b, Camel caravan.

2008, Aug. 3
2024 Horiz. pair 2.00 2.00
a.-b. A1245 150p Either single .75 .60

24th Universal Postal Union Congress, Geneva, Switzerland — A1246

2008, Aug. 4 Litho. ***Perf. 12¾x13¼***
2025 A1246 150p multi 1.00 .75

Men's Sports Education Faculty, 50th Anniv. — A1247

2008, Oct. 15 Litho. ***Perf. 13¼x13***
2026 A1247 30p multi .50 .30

Postech 2008 Intl. Postal Technology Conference, Sharm El-Sheikh — A1248

Map and: 30p, Queen Nefertari holding Postech 2008 emblem. 150p, Statue of King Tutankhamun, hand holding Postech emblem.

Perf. 12¾x13¼

2008, Nov. 17 **Litho.**
2027-2028 A1248 Set of 2 1.40 .90

Egyptian Cooperative Movement, Cent. — A1249

2008, Dec. 22 ***Perf. 13¼x12¾***
2029 A1249 30p multi .45 .25

Natl. Telecommunications Institute, 25th Anniv. — A1250

2008, Dec. 31 ***Perf. 12¾x13¼***
2030 A1250 30p multi .55 .30

Natl. Sports Council — A1251

2009, Mar. 3 ***Perf. 13¼x12¾***
2031 A1251 150p multi .95 .75

Constitutional Judiciary, 40th Anniv. — A1252

Designs: 30p, Emblem, text below. 150p, Emblem, text at right, horiz.

2009, Mar. 7 ***Perf. 13¼x12¾***
2032 A1252 30p multi .65 .40

Size:80x60mm

Imperf

2033 A1252 150p multi 1.00 1.00

Intl. Francophone Day — A1253

2009, Mar. 20 ***Perf. 12¾x13¼***
2034 A1253 150p multi .95 .55

Orphan's Day — A1254

2009, Apr. 3 ***Perf. 13¼x12¾***
2035 A1254 150p multi 1.00 .60

Compare with Types A1132, A1169 and A1199. See also No. 2053.

Intl. Labor Organization, 90th Anniv. — A1255

2009, Apr. 21 ***Perf. 12¾x13¼***
2036 A1255 150p multi .90 .60

Suzanne Mubarak Women's International Peace Movement A1256

2009, May 14 ***Perf. 13¼x12¾***
2037 A1256 150p multi .75 .55

Yehia Hakki (1905-92), Writer — A1257

2009, May 11 Litho. ***Perf. 12¾x13¼***
2038 A1257 150p multi .95 .55

Nobel Laureates From Africa — A1258

No. 2039: a, Ahmed Zewail, Chemistry, 1999. b, Bishop Desmond Tutu, Peace, 1984. c, Wangari Maathai, Peace 2004. d, Anwar al-Sadat, Peace, 1978. e, Naguib Mahfouz, Literature, 1988. f, Allan M. Cormack, Physiology or Medicine, 1979. g, Nelson Mandela, Peace, 1993. h, Wole Soyinka, Literature, 1986. i, Sydney Brenner, Physiology or Medicine, 2002. j, F.W. de Klerk, Peace, 1993. k, Nadine Gordimer, Literature, 1991. l, Max Theiler, Physiology or Medicine, 1951. m, Mohamed El Baradei, Peace, 2005. n, Albert Luthuli, Peace, 1960. o, Kofi Annan, Peace, 2001. p, J.M. Coetzee, Literature, 2003.

2009, June 9
2039 Sheet of 16, #a-p, + 9 labels 22.50 22.50
a.-p. A1258 150p Any single .95 .75

Fourth Extraordinary Session of the Pan-African Postal Union Plenipotentiary Conference, Cairo.

Fifteenth Non-Aligned Movement Summit, Sharm el-Sheikh A1259

2009, July 15 ***Perf. 13¼x12¾***
2040 A1259 150p multi .55 .55

Opening of Mubarak Public Library, Damanhour — A1260

2009, May 7 Litho. ***Perf. 13x13¼***
2041 A1260 150p multi .95 .70

Jerusalem, Capital of Arab Culture — A1261

2009, Aug. 3 ***Perf. 13¼x13***

2042 A1261 150p multi .95 .75

FIFA Under-20 World Cup Soccer Championships, Egypt — A1262

No. 2042 — Tournament emblem, trophy and flag of participating team: a, Paraguay. b, Brazil. c, Uruguay. d, Germany. e, Nigeria. f, South Korea. g, Venezuela. h, Ghana. i, United Arab Emirates. j, South Africa. k, Egypt. l, Spain. m, Italy. n, Hungary. o, Czech Republic. p, Costa Rica.

2009, Oct. 5 ***Perf. 13x13¼***

2043 Sheet of 16, #a-p, + 9 labels 19.50 19.50

a.-p. A1262 150p Any single .95 .75

Fourth Ministerial Conference of Forum on China-African Cooperation, Sharm El Sheikh — A1263

2009, Nov. 8

2044 A1263 150p multi .95 .75

Fourth Meeting of Internet Governance Forum, Sharm El Sheikh — A1264

2009, Nov. 15

2045 A1264 150p multi .95 .75

Luxor Governate — A1264a

2009, Dec. 9 Litho. ***Perf. 12¾x13¼***

2045A A1264a 250p multi 1.25 1.25

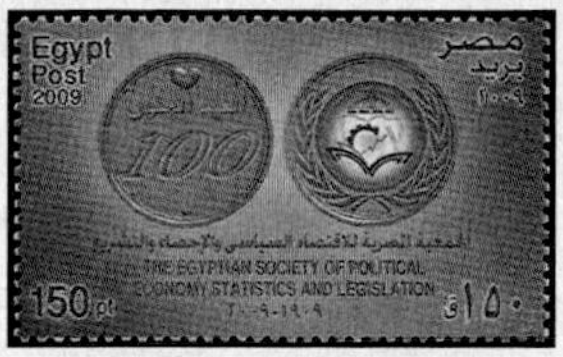

Egyptian Society of Political Economy, Statistics and Legislation, Cent. — A1265

2009, Dec. 19

2046 A1265 150p multi .95 .95

Pharmaceutical Industry Drug Holding Company, 75th Anniv. — A1266

Background colors: 30p, Pink, yellow and pale green. 150p, Green.

2009, Dec. 19 ***Perf. 13¼x13***

2047-2048 A1266 Set of 2 .95 .95

Egyptian Stock Exchange, 125th Anniv. — A1267

Stock Exchange Building with anniversary emblem at left in: 30p, Gold and white. 150p, Gold (75x30mm).

2009, Dec. 21 ***Perf. 13x13¼***

2049-2050 A1267 Set of 2 .95 .95

Pan-African Postal Union, 30th Anniv. — A1268

2010, Jan. 18

2051 A1268 150p multi .85 .85

National Council for Women, 10th Anniv. — A1269

2010, Mar. 16

2052 A1269 30p multi .65 .65

Orphan's Day — A1270

2010, Jan. 4 Litho. ***Perf. 13¼x12¾***

2053 A1270 30p multi .55 .55

Compare with Types A1132, A1169 and A1199. See also No. 2035.

Edfu Temple — A1271

2010, Jan. 5 ***Perf. 12¾x13¼***

2054 A1271 250p multi 1.50 1.50

Aswan High Dam, 50th Anniv. — A1272

No. 2055 — Part of dam: a, 30p. b, £1.

2010, Jan. 15

2055 A1272 Horiz. pair, #a-b 1.50 1.50

Arab League Center, 50th Anniv. — A1273

2010, Mar. 22

2056 A1273 200p multi 1.25 1.25

Egyptian Soccer Team, 2010 Winner of African Cup of Nations — A1274

No. 2057 — Pyramid, African Cup of Nations, tournament emblems and: a, 30p, Crocodile mascot. b, 200p, Eagle mascot. c, 250p, Antelope mascot.

No. 2058, 250p, Soccer players, African Cup of Nations, years of Egyptian championships, horiz.

2010, Jan. 31 Litho. ***Perf. 13¼x12¾***

2057 A1274 Horiz. strip of 3, #a-c 4.50 4.50

Size: 80x60mm

Imperf

2058 A1274 250p multi 1.50 1.50

Egyptian Gazette, 130th Anniv. — A1275

2010, Apr. 20 ***Perf. 13¼x12¾***

2059 A1275 30p multi .55 .55

Egypt Pavilion, Expo 2010, Shanghai — A1276

2010, May 1 Litho. ***Perf. 12¾x13¼***

2060 A1276 £2.50 multi 1.75 1.75

Opening of Road to Red Sea — A1277

2010, May 27 ***Perf. 13¼x12¾***

2061 A1277 £1 multi .95 .95

World Environment Day — A1278

2010, June 5 ***Perf. 12¾x13¼***

2062 A1278 £2.50 multi 1.50 1.50

Tawfiq al-Hakim (1898-1987), Writer — A1279

2010, June 6 Litho. ***Perf. 13¼x12¾***

2063 A1279 150p multi .95 .95

Second Egyptian Post Innovation Meeting.

Reading for All, 20th Anniv. — A1280

2010, June 21

2064 A1280 £1 multi .95 .95

Egyptian Television, 50th Anniv. — A1281

2010, July 21

2065 A1281 £1.50 multi 1.25 1.25

Alexandria, 2010 Captial of Arab Tourism — A1282

2010, July 22 ***Perf. 12¾x13¼***

2066 A1282 150p multi 1.25 1.25

2010 Asia-Pacific Broadcasting Union Robotics Competition, Cairo — A1283

2010, Sept. 19

2067 A1283 £2.50 multi 1.50 1.50

2010 Euromed Postal Conference, Alexandria — A1284

2010, Sept. 28

2068 A1284 £2.50 multi 1.75 1.75

Alabaster Canopic Jar — A1285

2010, Oct. 8 ***Perf. 13¼x12¾***

2069 A1285 £2.50 multi 1.75 1.75

See Slovakia No. 601.

Second Arab University Games, Cairo — A1286

2010, Oct. 17 ***Perf. 13¼x12¾***

2070 A1286 30p multi .55 .55

World Statistics Day — A1287

2010, Oct. 20

2071 A1287 30p multi .55 .55

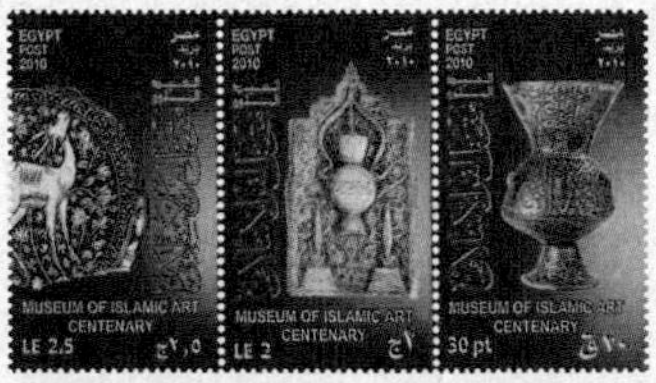

Reopening of Museum of Islamic Art, Cairo — A1288

No. 2072: a, 30p, Goblet. £2, Bas-relief. £2.50, Plate with antelope design.

2010, Oct. 25

2072 A1288 Horiz. strip of 3, #a-c 2.50 2.50

Egyptian Olympic Committee, Cent. — A1289

2010, Dec. 11

2073 A1289 30p multi .60 .60

Information and Decision Support Center, 25th Anniv. — A1290

2010, Dec. 20 ***Perf. 12¾x13¼***

2074 A1290 30p multi .55 .55

Cairo Stadium, 50th Anniv. — A1291

2010, Dec. 30 ***Imperf.***

2075 A1291 £2.50 multi 1.50 1.50

Post Day A1292

No. 2076 — Egyptian stamps: a, #3. b, #57. c, #107. d, #183. e, #271. f, #321. g, #386. h, #389. i, #873. j, #C1.

2011, Jan. 2 ***Perf. 13***

2076 Block of 10 5.50 5.50

a.-h. A1292 30p Any single .40 .30

i. A1292 £2 multi 1.00 .75

j. A1292 £2.50 multi 1.25 1.00

Cairo Tower, 50th Anniv. — A1293

No. 2077 — Tower: a, 30p, In daylight. b, £2.50, At night.

2011, Apr. 11 ***Perf. 13¼x12¾***

2077 A1293 Horiz. pair, #a-b 2.25 2.25

World Environment Day — A1294

2011, June 5

2078 A1294 £2.50 multi 1.50 1.50

War Academy, 200th Anniv. — A1295

2011, July 20 ***Perf. 12¾x13¼***

2079 A1295 30p multi .80 .80

Rivers — A1296

No. 2080: a, 30p, Pyramids, Nile River. b, 30p, Downtown Singapore, Singapore River. c, £2, Ancient Egyptian boat, Nile River. d, £2, Modern boat, Singapore River. e, £2.50, Cairo skyline, yellow flowers, Nile River. f, £2.50, Singapore buildings, pink flowers, Singapore River.

2011, Oct. 17

2080 A1296 Block of 6, #a-f 3.25 3.25

See Singapore Nos. 1513-1515.

Post Day — A1297

No. 2081: a, Dove, flowers, Egypt Post emblem. b, Post office, air mail envelopes. c, Eye of Horus, flowers, Egypt Post emblem.

2012, Jan. 2 ***Perf. 13¼x12¾***

2081 A1297 £2.50 Horiz. strip of 3, #a-c 2.50 2.50

Temple — A1297a

2011 **Litho.** ***Perf. 11¼***

2081D A1297a £2.50 multi — —

January 25 Revolution, 1st Anniv. — A1298

2012, Jan. 25 ***Imperf.***

2082 A1298 £2.50 multi .85 .85

Pope Shenouda III of Alexandria (1923-2012) — A1299

2012, Mar. 17 ***Imperf.***
2083 A1299 £5 multi 1.75 1.75

Diplomatic Relations Between Egypt and Azerbaijan, 20th Anniv. — A1300

No. 2084: a, Arches and Maiden Tower, Baku, Azerbaijan. b, Sphinx and Pyramids, Egypt.

2012, May 28 ***Perf. 12¾x13¼***
2084 A1300 £2.50 Horiz. pair, #a-b 1.75 1.75

Environment Day — A1301

2012, June 5 ***Perf. 13¼x12¾***
2085 A1301 £2 multi .70 .70

A1302

Overthrow of King Farouk by Gamal Abdel Nasser, 60th Anniv. — A1303

2012, July 23 ***Perf. 12¾x13¼***
2086 A1302 £2 multi .65 .65

Imperf

2087 A1303 £4 multi 1.40 1.40

2012 Summer Olympics, London — A1304

No. 2088 — Mascot and: a, Cycling. b, Running. c, Emblem of 2012 Summer Olympics. d, Basketball. e, Soccer.

2012, July 27 ***Perf. 13¼x12¾***
2088 Horiz. strip of 5 4.25 4.25
a.-e. A1304 £2.50 Any single .85 .85

Arab Postal Day — A1305

2012, Aug. 3 ***Perf. 12¾x13¼***
2089 A1305 £3 multi 1.00 1.00

Festivals — A1306

No. 2090: a, Rider on blue gray horse, heads of white and black horses. b, Two riders, black horse, head of brown horse. c, Rider on brown horse.

2012, Aug. 18 ***Perf. 13¼x12¾***
2090 A1306 £1 Horiz. strip of 3, #a-c 1.00 1.00

Lawyers Trade Union, Cent. — A1307

2012, Sept. 12 ***Perf. 12¾x13¼***
2091 A1307 £1 multi .35 .35

Tourism and Sustainable Energy — A1308

2012, Sept. 27 ***Perf. 13¼x12¾***
2092 A1308 £1 multi .35 .35

Helwan University Art Education Faculty, 75th Anniv. — A1309

2012, Nov. 12 **Litho.**
2093 A1309 £2 multi .65 .65

Post Day — A1310

No. 2094: a, Ancient Egyptian art with Isis seated at right, envelopes. b, Lotus flowers. funerary mask of King Tutankhamun. c, Anceint Egyptian art with Isis seated at left.

2013, Jan. 2 ***Perf. 13¼x13***
2094 A1310 £3 Horiz. strip of 3, #a-c 3.00 3.00

January 25th Revolution, 2nd Anniv. — A1311

2013, Jan. 25 ***Perf. 13x13¼***
2095 A1311 £1 multi .30 .30

Victory of Egyptian Team at African Cup of Nations Youth Soccer Championships A1312

2013, Apr. 24 ***Perf. 13¼x13***
2096 A1312 £3 multi .90 .90

Return of Sinai to Egypt, 31st Anniv. — A1313

No. 2097 — Various tourist attractions and Sinai Peninsula map showing: a, Northwestern section. b, Northeastern section. c, Southwestern section. d, Southeastern section.

2013, Apr. 25 ***Perf. 13x13¼***
2097 A1313 £2 Block of 4, #a-d 2.40 2.40

World Environment Day — A1314

2013, June 5 ***Perf. 13¼x13***
2098 A1314 £3 multi .85 .85

July 23rd Revolution, 61st Anniv. — A1315

2013, July 23 **Litho.** ***Perf. 12¾x13¼***
2099 A1315 £3 multi .85 .85

Day of the Nile Inundation — A1316

2013, Aug. 25 **Litho.** ***Imperf.***
2100 A1316 £4 multi 1.25 1.25

Intl. Islamic Council for Da'wa and Relief — A1317

Perf. 13¼x12¾

2013, Sept. 21 **Litho.**
2101 A1317 £2 multi .60 .60

World Tourism Day — A1318

Perf. 13¼x12¾

2013, Sept. 27 **Litho.**
2102 A1318 £3 multi .90 .90

A1319

October War Against Israel, 40th Anniv. — A1320

2013, Oct. 6 Litho. *Perf. 12¾x13¼*

2103	A1319	£1 multi	.30	.30
2104	A1320	£4 multi	1.25	1.25

Sculptures of Egyptian Pharaohs
A1321 A1322

Designs: Nos. 2105, 2106, Thutmosis III. £1, Senusret I. £3, Ramesses II. £4, Akhenaten.

2013, Oct. 7 Litho. *Perf. 11¼*

2105	A1321	50p org & multi	.25	.25
2106	A1321	50p grn & multi	.25	.25

Perf. 11x11½

2107	A1322	£1 multi	.30	.30
2108	A1322	£3 lil & multi	.90	.90
2108A	A1322	£3 blue & multi	—	—
2109	A1322	£4 brn & multi	1.25	1.25
2109A	A1322	£4 rose brn & multi	—	—
		Nos. 2105-2109A (7)	2.95	2.95

World Post Day — A1323

2013, Oct. 9 Litho. *Perf. 12¾x13¼*

2110	A1323	£4 multi	1.25	1.25

Tourists on Horseback, Utopia Resort, Marsa Alam — A1324

Old Town, Hurghada — A1325

Madinat Makadi Resort, Hurghada — A1326

Perf. 12¾x13¼

2013, Dec. 17 Litho.

2111	A1324	£4 multi	1.25	1.25
2112	A1325	£4 multi	1.25	1.25
2113	A1326	£4 multi	1.25	1.25
		Nos. 2111-2113 (3)	3.75	3.75

Nile Meter, by M. Sabry — A1327

2014, Jan. 2 Litho. *Imperf.*

2114	A1327	£4 multi	1.25	1.25

Post Day.

January 25th Revolution, 3rd Anniv. — A1328

2014, Jan. 25 Litho. *Perf. 12¾x13¼*

2115	A1328	£2 multi	.60	.60

Intl. Women's Day — A1329

2014, Mar. 8 Litho. *Perf. 12¾x13¼*

2116	A1329	£2 multi	.60	.60

World Heritage Day — A1330

No. 2117: a, Two women. b, Men and camel. c, Men playing board game. d, Man, pottery in windows.

2014, Apr. 18 Litho. *Perf. 12¾x13¼*

2117	A1330	£1 Block of 4 #a-d	1.25	1.25

Diversion of the Nile River, 50th Anniv. — A1331

2014, May 15 Litho. *Imperf.*

2118	A1331	£4 multi	1.10	1.10

African Regional Postal Training Center — A1332

2014, June 1 Litho. *Perf. 12¾x13¼*

2119	A1332	£2 multi	.55	.55

Day of the African Child — A1333

Perf. 12¾x13¼

2014, June 17 Litho.

2120	A1333	£3 multi	.85	.85

Euromed Postal Emblem and Mediterranean Sea — A1334

2014, July 9 Litho. *Perf. 13x13¼*

2121	A1334	£4 multi	1.10	1.10

July 23rd Revolution, 62nd Anniv. — A1335

2014, July 23 Litho. *Perf. 13¼x13*

2122	A1335	£2 multi	.55	.55

Start of Construction on Second Suez Canal — A1336

No. 2123: a, Suez Canal emblem, ship, map of northern portion of canal. b, Map of central portion of canal, ships near locks of Panama Canal. c, Map of southern portion of canal, Administration building, ship.

2014, Aug. 5 Litho. *Perf. 13¼x13*

2123	A1336	£2 Horiz. strip of 3, #a-c	*55.00*	*37.50*

No. 2123 was withdrawn shortly after the error in stamp design (the Suez Canal has no locks) was made known to Egypt Post.

General Arab Insurance Federation, 50th Anniv. — A1337

50th anniversary emblem: No. 2124, Above map of Arab countries. No. 2125, To left of map of Arab countries.

2014, Sept. 1 Litho. *Perf. 13¼x13*

2124	A1337	£4 multi	1.10	1.10

Imperf

Size: 90x70mm

2125	A1337	£4 multi	1.10	1.10

Start of Construction on New Suez Canal — A1338

No. 2126: a, Map of canal, Adminisration Building, ship in canal. b, Map of canal, ship approaching canal. c, Suez Canal emblem, ship in canal.

2014, Sept. 16 Litho. *Perf. 13¼x13*

2126	A1338	£2 Horiz. strip of 3, #a-c	1.75	1.75

No. 2126 replaces the hastily withdrawn No. 2123. First day covers of No. 2126 show the Aug. 5 first day cancel of No. 2123, though the stamps were printed after the discovery of the design error on No. 2123.

Shali Siwa Oasis — A1339

Perf. 12¾x13¼

2014, Sept. 27 Litho.

2127	A1339	£4 multi	1.10	1.10

October War Against Israel, 41st Anniv. — A1340

2014, Oct. 6 Litho. *Perf. 12¾x13¼*

2128	A1340	£2 multi	.55	.55

World Post Day — A1341

2014, Oct. 9 Litho. *Perf. 13¼x12¾*

2129	A1341	£4 multi	1.10	1.10

Scouting in Egypt, Cent. — A1342

2014, Oct. 15 Litho. ***Perf. 12¾x13¼***
2130 A1342 £1.25 multi .35 .35

Arabic Calligraphy — A1343

2014, Dec. 6 Litho. ***Imperf.***
2131 A1343 £5 multi 1.40 1.40

Central Agency for Public Mobilization and Statistics, Cent. — A1344

2014, Dec. 8 Litho. ***Perf. 13¼x12¾***
2132 A1344 £3 multi .85 .85

Birds — A1345

No. 2133: a, Palm dove. b, Hoopoe. c, Roller. d, Bee-eater. e, Sooty falcon. f, Golden oriole.

Perf. 13¼x12¾
2014, Dec. 10 Litho.
2133 A1345 £1.25 Block of 6, #a-f, + 3 central labels 2.10 2.10

Re-opening of National Theater — A1346

Perf. 12¾x13¼
2014, Dec. 20 Litho.
2134 A1346 £1.50 multi .45 .45

Amenhotep, Son of Hapu — A1347

2015 Litho. ***Perf. 11¼***
2135 A1347 £3 multi .85 .85

A1348

Egyptian Post, 150th Anniv. — A1349

2015, Jan. 2 Litho. ***Perf. 12¾x13¼***
2136 A1348 £1.50 multi .45 .45
Imperf
2137 A1349 £4 multi 1.10 1.10

January 25 Revolution, 4th Anniv. — A1350

2015, Jan. 25 Litho. ***Perf. 12¾x13¼***
2138 A1350 £2 multi .55 .55

Faten Hamama (1931-2015), Actress — A1351

2015, Mar. 8 Litho. ***Perf. 13¼x12¾***
2139 A1351 £3 black .80 .80

Egypt Economic Development Conference — A1352

Perf. 12¾x13¼
2015, Mar. 13 Litho.
2140 A1352 £2 multi .55 .55

26th Arab Summit, Sharm el-Sheikh A1353

Perf. 13¼x12¾
2015, Mar. 23 Litho.
2141 A1353 £3 multi .80 .80

International Telecommunication Union, 150th Anniv. — A1354

2015, May 17 Litho. ***Perf. 12¾x13¼***
2142 A1354 £4 multi 1.10 1.10

Dar al-Ifta al-Misriyyah Educational Institute, 120th Anniv. — A1355

2015, June 1 Litho. ***Perf. 12¾x13¼***
2143 A1355 £2 multi .55 .55

July 23rd Revolution, 63rd Anniv. — A1356

2015, July 23 Litho. ***Perf. 12¾x13¼***
2144 A1356 £2 multi .55 .55

Campaign to Save the Nile River — A1357

2015, July 25 Litho. ***Perf. 12¾x13¼***
2145 A1357 £2 multi .55 .55

A1358

New Suez Canal — A1359

2015, Aug. 6 Litho. ***Perf. 12¾x13¼***
2146 Horiz. strip of 3 2.40 2.40
a. A1358 £3 lilac & multi .80 .80
b. A1358 £3 beige & multi .80 .80
c. A1358 £3 lt blue green & multi .80 .80
Imperf
2147 A1359 £4 multi 1.10 1.10

Poets — A1360

No. 2148: a, Fouad Hadad (1927-85). b, Salah Jaheen (1930-86). c, Abd el Rahman El Abnody (1938-2015).

Perf. 13¼x12¾
2015, Aug. 10 Litho.
2148 A1360 £2 Horiz. strip of 3, #a-c 1.60 .80

Food and Agricultural Organization, 70th Anniv. — A1361

2015, Oct. 1 Litho. ***Perf. 12¾x13¼***
2149 A1361 £3 multi .80 .40

October War With Israel, 42nd Anniv. — A1362

2015, Oct. 6 Litho. ***Perf. 12¾x13¼***
2150 A1362 £2 multi .50 .25

A1363

Federation of Afro-Asian Insurers and Reinsurers, 50th Anniv. — A1364

2015, Oct. 12 Litho. ***Perf. 13¼x12¾***

2151 A1363 £4 multi 1.00 .50

Imperf

2152 A1364 £4 multi 1.00 .50

World Statistics Day — A1365

2015, Oct. 20 Litho. ***Perf. 12¾x13¼***

2153 A1365 £3 multi .75 .35

SEMI-POSTAL STAMPS

Catalogue values for unused stamps in this section are for Never Hinged items.

Princess Ferial — SP1

Perf. 13½x14

1940, May 17 Photo. Wmk. 195

B1 SP1 5m + 5m copper brown 4.50 1.25

No. B1 Overprinted in Green

1943, Nov. 17

B2 SP1 5m + 5m 14.00 9.00
a. Arabic date "1493" 300.00 300.00

The surtax on Nos. B1 and B2 was for the children's fund.

First Postage Stamp of Egypt SP2

King Fuad SP3

No. B4, Khedive Ismail Pasha. No. B6, King Farouk.

Perf. 13x13½

1946, Feb. 28 Wmk. 195

B3 SP2 1m + 1m gray .40 .25
B4 SP3 10m + 10m violet .50 .25
B5 SP3 17m + 17m brown .50 .40
B6 SP3 22m + 22m yel grn .75 .60
a. Souv. sheet, #B3-B6, perf. 8½ 85.00 85.00
b. As "a," imperf. 85.00 85.00
Nos. B3-B6 (4) 2.15 1.50

80th anniv. of Egypt's 1st postage stamp. Nos. B6a, B6b measure 129x171mm.

Goddess Hathor, King Men-kau-Re (Mycerinus) and Jackalheaded Goddess — SP7

Ramesseum, Thebes — SP8

Queen Nefertiti SP9

Funerary Mask of King Tutankhamun SP10

Perf. 13½x13

1947, Mar. 9 Wmk. 195

B9 SP7 5m + 5m slate 1.75 .80
B10 SP8 15m + 15m dp blue 2.00 1.00
B11 SP9 30m + 30m henna brn 2.50 1.75
B12 SP10 50m + 50m brown 3.50 2.25
Nos. B9-B12 (4) 9.75 5.80

Intl. Exposition of Contemporary Art, Cairo.

Boy Scout Emblem — SP11

Scout Emblems: 20m+10m, Sea Scouts. 35m+15m, Air Explorers.

1956, July 25 Photo. ***Perf. 13½x13***

B13 SP11 10m + 10m green 1.00 .55
B14 SP11 20m + 10m ultra 1.50 .85
B15 SP11 35m + 15m blue 2.00 1.25
Nos. B13-B15 (3) 4.50 2.65

2nd Arab Scout Jamboree, Alexandria-Aboukir, 1956.

Souvenir sheets, perf. and imperf., contain one each of Nos. B13-B15. Size: 118x158mm. Values: $1,750 unused each, $1,100 used each.

Ambulance — SP12

1957, May 13 ***Perf. 13x13½***

B16 SP12 10m + 5m rose red .80 .55

50th anniv. of the Public Aid Society.

United Arab Republic

Eye and Map of Africa, Europe and Asia SP13

Postal Emblem SP14

Perf. 13½x13

1958, Mar. 1 Photo. Wmk. 318

B17 SP13 10m + 5m orange 1.25 1.00

1st Afro-Asian Cong. of Ophthalmology, Cairo.

The surtax was for centers to aid the blind.

1959, Jan. 2

B18 SP14 10m + 5m bl grn, red & blk .40 .30

Post Day. The surtax went to the social fund for postal employees.

See Syria UAR issues No. B1 for similar stamp with denominations in piasters (p).

Children and UN Emblem — SP15

1959, Oct. 24 Wmk. 328

B19 SP15 10m + 5m brown lake .60 .30
B20 SP15 35m + 10m dk blue .90 .40

Issued for International Children's Day and to honor UNICEF.

Braille Type of Regular Issue, 1961

1961, Apr. 6 ***Perf. 13½x13***

B21 A182 35m + 15m yel & brn .80 .50

Arab League Building, Cairo, and Emblem — SP16

1962, Mar. 22 Photo. Wmk. 328

B22 SP16 10m + 5m gray .60 .40

Arab Publicity Week, Mar. 22-28.

See No. N86.

Postal Emblem — SP17

Stamp of 1866 — SP18

1963, Jan. 2 Wmk. 342 ***Perf. 11½***

B23 SP17 20m +10m brt grn, red & blk 1.25 1.25
B24 SP18 40m +20m blk & brn org 1.75 1.75
B25 SP18 40m +20m brn org & blk 1.75 1.75
a. Pair, #B24-B25 4.00 4.00
Nos. B23-B25 (3) 4.75 4.75

Post Day, Jan. 2 and 1966 exhibition of the FIP.

Arms of UAR and Pyramids SP19

1964, Jan. 2 Wmk. 342 ***Perf. 11***

B26 SP19 10m + 5m org yel & grn 1.75 1.00
B27 SP19 80m + 40m grnsh bl & blk 3.00 1.75
B28 SP19 115m + 55m org brn & blk 4.00 2.25
Nos. B26-B28 (3) 8.75 5.00

Issued for Post Day. Jan. 2.

Type of 1963 and

SP20

Postal Emblem — SP20a

No. B30, Emblem of Postal Secondary School. 80m+40m, Postal emblem, gear-wheel, laurel wreath.

Perf. 11½

1965, Jan. 2 Unwmk. Photo.

B29 SP20 10m + 5m lt grn & car 1.00 .50
B30 SP20 10m + 5m ultra, car & blk 1.00 .50
a. Pair, #B29-B30 2.50 2.00
B31 SP20a 80m + 40m rose, brt grn & blk 2.75 2.00
Nos. B29-B31 (3) 4.75 3.00

Issued for Post Day, Jan. 2. No. B31 also publicizes the Stamp Centenary Exhibition.

Souvenir Sheet

Stamps of Egypt, 1866 — SP21

1966, Jan. 2 Wmk. 342 *Imperf.*
B32 SP21 140m + 60m blk, sl bl & rose 4.50 4.50

Post Day, 1966, and cent. of the 1st Egyptian postage stamps.

Pharaonic "Mediator" — SP22

Design: 115m+40m, Pharaonic guard.

1967, Jan. 2 Wmk. 342 *Perf. 11½*
B33 SP22 80m + 20m multi 3.75 2.75
B34 SP22 115m + 40m multi 6.00 3.50

Issued for Post Day, Jan. 2.

Grand Canal, Doges' Palace, Venice, and Santa Maria del Fiore, Florence — SP23

115m+30m, Piazetta and Campanile, Venice, and Palazzo Vecchio, Florence.

Perf. 11½x11
1967, Dec. 9 Photo. Wmk. 342
B35 SP23 80m + 20m grn, yel & brn 1.75 1.25
B36 SP23 115m + 30m ol, yel & sl bl 2.75 2.00

The surtax was to help save the cultural monuments of Venice and Florence, damaged in the 1966 floods.

Boy and Girl — SP24

Design: No. B38, Five children and arch.

Wmk. 342
1968, Dec. 11 Photo. *Perf. 11*
B37 SP24 20m + 10m car, bl & lt brn .80 .60
B38 SP24 20m + 10m vio bl, sep & lt grn .80 .60

Children's Day & 22nd anniv. of UNICEF.

Emblem and Flags of Arab League — SP25

1969, Mar. 22 *Perf. 11x11½*
B39 SP25 20m + 10m multi .80 .60

Arab Publicity Week, Mar. 22-28.

Refugee Family SP26

1969, Oct. 24 Photo. *Perf. 11½*
B40 SP26 30m + 10m multi .80 .60

Issued for United Nations Day.

Men of Three Races, Human Rights Emblem SP27

1970, Mar. 21 *Perf. 11½x11*
B41 SP27 20m + 10m multi 1.00 .75

Issued to publicize the International Day for the Elimination of Racial Discrimination.

Arab League Type

1970, Mar. 22 Wmk. 342
B42 A344 20m + 10m bl, grn & brn .90 .60

Map of Palestine and Refugees SP28

Perf. 11½x11
1970, Oct. 24 Photo. Wmk. 342
B43 SP28 20m + 10m multi .90 .80

25th anniv. of the UN and to draw attention to the plight of the Palestinian refugees.

Arab Republic of Egypt

Blind Girl, WHO and Society Emblems — SP29

1973, Oct. 24 Photo. *Perf. 11x11½*
B44 SP29 20m + 10m blue & gold .85 .75

25th anniv. of WHO and for the Light and Hope Soc., which educates and helps blind girls.

Map of Africa, OAU Emblem SP30

Social Work Day Emblem SP31

Perf. 11x11½
1973, Dec. 8 Photo. Wmk. 342
B45 SP30 55m + 20m multi 2.25 1.50

Organization for African Unity, 10th anniv.

1973, Dec. 8
B46 SP31 20m + 10m multi .75 .65

Social Work Day.

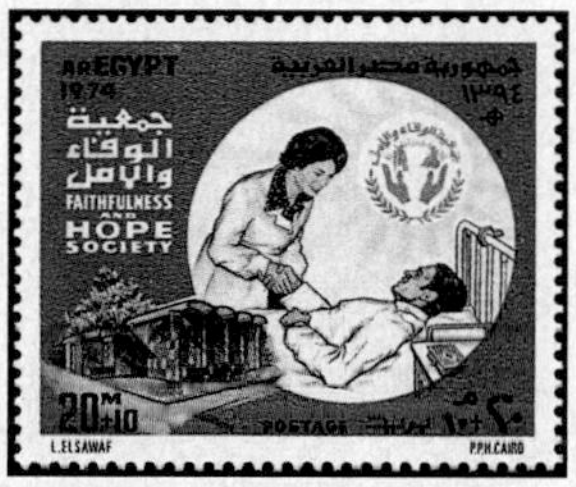

Jihan al Sadat Consoling Wounded Man — SP32

1974, Mar. 21 Wmk. 342 *Perf. 11*
B47 SP32 20m + 10m multi 1.25 .90

Faithfulness and Hope Society.

Afghan Solidarity SP33

Wmk. 342
1981, July 15 Photo. *Perf. 11½*
B48 SP33 20m + 10m multi 1.00 .75

Size: 30x25mm
1981 Photo. *Perf. 11½*
B49 SP33 20m + 10m multi 4.25 3.75

Map of Sudan, Dunes, Dead Tree — SP34

1986, Mar. 25 Photo. *Perf. 13x13½*
B50 SP34 15p + 5p multi 1.75 1.25

Fight against drought and desertification of the Sudan. Surtax for drought relief.

Organization of African Unity, 25th Anniv. — SP35

1988, May 25 Litho. *Perf. 13*
B51 SP35 15p +10p multi 1.25 1.00

AIR POST STAMPS

Mail Plane in Flight AP1

Perf. 13x13½
1926, Mar. 10 Wmk. 195 Photo.
C1 AP1 27m deep violet 30.00 30.00

1929, July 17
C2 AP1 27m orange brown 9.00 2.25

Zeppelin Issue
No. C2 Surcharged in Blue or Violet

1931, Apr. 6
C3 AP1 50m on 27m (Bl) 85.00 75.00
a. "1951" instead of "1931" 110.00 100.00
C4 AP1 100m on 27m (V) 85.00 *80.00*

Airplane over Giza Pyramids AP2

1933-38 Litho. *Perf. 13x13½*

C5	AP2	1m orange & blk	.30	.50
C6	AP2	2m gray & blk	.80	1.50
C7	AP2	2m org red & blk ('38)	2.75	2.00
C8	AP2	3m ol brn & blk	.60	.35
C9	AP2	4m green & blk	.90	.90
C10	AP2	5m dp brown & blk	.75	.25
C11	AP2	6m dk green & blk	1.50	1.25
C12	AP2	7m dk blue & blk	1.25	1.00
C13	AP2	8m violet & blk	.80	.25
C14	AP2	9m dp red & blk	2.00	1.50
C15	AP2	10m violet & brn	.75	.70
C16	AP2	20m dk green & brn	.60	.25
C17	AP2	30m dull blue & brn	.75	.25
C18	AP2	40m dp red & brn	15.00	.60
C19	AP2	50m orange & brn	13.00	.25
C20	AP2	60m gray & brn	6.00	1.10
C21	AP2	70m dk blue & bl grn	3.50	1.00
C22	AP2	80m ol brn & bl grn	3.50	1.00
C23	AP2	90m org & bl grn	4.00	1.00
C24	AP2	100m vio & bl grn	9.00	.80
C25	AP2	200m dp red & bl grn	12.00	1.75
		Nos. C5-C25 (21)	79.75	18.20

See #C34-C37. For overprint see #C38.

Type of 1933

1941-43 Photo.

C34	AP2	5m copper brn ('43)	.30	.30
C35	AP2	10m violet	.55	.30
C36	AP2	25m dk vio brn ('43)	.55	.30
C37	AP2	30m green	.70	.30
		Nos. C34-C37 (4)	2.10	1.20

Catalogue values for unused stamps in this section, from this point to the end of the section, are for Never Hinged items.

No. C37 Overprinted in Black

1946, Oct. 1

C38	AP2 30m green	.70	.35
a.	Double overprint	400.00	—
b.	Inverted overprint	400.00	—

Middle East Intl. Air Navigation Congress, Cairo, Oct. 1946.

King Farouk, Delta Dam and DC-3 Plane AP3

Perf. 13x13½

1947, Feb. 19 Photo. Wmk. 195

C39	AP3	2m red orange	.30	*.85*
C40	AP3	3m dk brown	.30	*1.00*
C41	AP3	5m red brown	.30	.30
C42	AP3	7m dp yellow org	.60	.30
C43	AP3	8m green	.60	*.90*
C44	AP3	10m violet	.60	.30
C45	AP3	20m brt blue	.90	.30
C46	AP3	30m brown violet	1.20	.30
C47	AP3	40m carmine rose	2.00	.75
C48	AP3	50m Prus green	2.50	.85
C49	AP3	100m olive green	4.25	1.00
C50	AP3	200m dark gray	10.00	3.75
		Nos. C39-C50 (12)	23.55	10.60

For overprints see Nos. C51-C64, C67-C89, NC1-NC30.

Nos. C49 and C50 Surcharged in Black

1948, Aug. 23

C51	AP3 13m on 100m	.60	.55
C52	AP3 22m on 200m	.85	*.85*
a.	Date omitted		

Inaugural flights of "Services Aeriens Internationaux d'Egypte" from Cairo to Athens and Rome, Aug. 23, 1948.

Nos. C39 to C50 Overprinted in Various Colors

Overprint 27mm Wide

1952, Jan. Wmk. 195 *Perf. 13x13½*

C53	AP3	2m red orange (Bl)	.45	.30
C54	AP3	3m dark brown (RV)	1.60	1.25
C55	AP3	5m red brown	.55	.55
C56	AP3	7m dp yel org (Bl)	.85	.50
C57	AP3	8m green (RV)	2.50	1.60
C58	AP3	10m violet (G)	1.75	1.60
C59	AP3	20m brt blue (RV)	4.25	2.50
C60	AP3	30m brown vio (G)	1.90	1.60
C61	AP3	40m carmine rose	4.00	2.50
C62	AP3	50m Prus green (RV)	4.25	2.75
C63	AP3	100m olive green	6.75	3.75
C64	AP3	200m dark gray (RV)	13.50	7.50
		Nos. C53-C64 (12)	42.35	26.40

See notes after No. 316.

Delta Dam and Douglas DC-3 AP4

1953 Photo.

C65	AP4 5m red brown	.60	.60
C66	AP4 15m olive green	1.50	1.25

For overprints see Nos. NC31-NC32.

Nos. C39-C49 Overprinted in Black

1953

C67	AP3	2m red orange	3.00	3.00
C68	AP3	3m dk brown	1.25	1.25
C69	AP3	5m red brown	1.60	1.60
C70	AP3	7m dp yellow org	.60	.60
C71	AP3	8m green	2.00	2.00
C72	AP3	10m violet	*32.50*	*37.50*
C73	AP3	20m brt blue	2.10	.60
C74	AP3	30m brown violet	3.00	1.60
C75	AP3	40m carmine rose	3.00	1.90
C76	AP3	50m Prus green	5.00	2.00
C77	AP3	100m olive green	9.25	4.75
C77A	AP3	200m gray	*55.00*	

No. C77A is in question. It is not known postally used.

Nos. C53-C64 Overprinted in Black with Three Bars to Obliterate Portrait

1953

C78	AP3	2m red orange	.90	.50
C79	AP3	3m dark brown	1.90	1.60
C80	AP3	5m red brown	.50	.35
C82	AP3	8m green	1.10	*2.50*
C83	AP3	10m violet	.90	*2.00*
C85	AP3	30m brown violet	2.00	2.00
C87	AP3	50m Prus green	4.25	1.60
C88	AP3	100m olive green	6.25	3.75
C89	AP3	200m dark gray	12.50	12.50
		Nos. C78-C89 (9)	30.30	26.80

Practically all values of Nos. C67-C89 exist with double overprint. The 7m, 20m and 40m with this overprint have been considered forgeries. Values: 7m, $8 mint and used; 20m, $5 mint and used; 40m, $20 mint, $25 used.

United Arab Republic Type of Regular Issue

Perf. 11½x11

1958, Mar. 22 Photo. Wmk. 318

C90	A141 15m ultra & red brn	.65	.30

Pyramids at Giza AP5

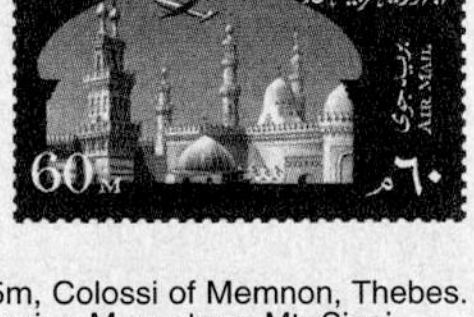

Al Azhar University AP6

Designs: 15m, Colossi of Memnon, Thebes. 90m, St. Catherine Monastery, Mt. Sinai.

1959-60 Wmk. 328 *Perf. 13x13½*

C91	AP5 5m bright red	.35	.25
C92	AP5 15m dk dull violet	.40	.35
C93	AP6 60m dk green	.95	.60
C94	AP5 90m brown car ('60)	2.00	1.25
	Nos. C91-C94 (4)	3.70	2.45

Nos. C91-C93 exist imperf. See Nos. C101, C105, NC33.

Tower of Cairo Type, Redrawn

1961, May 1 *Perf. 13½x13*

C95	A183 50m bright blue	1.10	.55

Top inscription has been replaced by two airplanes.

Weather Vane, Anemometer and UN World Meteorological Organization Emblem — AP7

Perf. 11½x11

1962, Mar. 23 Photo. Unwmk.

C96	AP7 60m yellow & dp blue	2.00	1.00

2nd World Meteorological Day, Mar. 23.

Patrice Lumumba and Map of Africa — AP8

Perf. 13½x13

1962, July 1 Wmk. 328

C97	AP8 35m multicolored	.65	.40

Patrice Lumumba (1925-61), Premier of Congo.

Maritime Station, Alexandria — AP9

Designs: 30m, International Airport, Cairo. 40m, Railroad Station, Luxor.

1963, Mar. 18 *Perf. 13x13½*

C98	AP9 20m dark brown	.70	.30
C99	AP9 30m carmine rose	.95	.40
C100	AP9 40m black	1.50	1.00
	Nos. C98-C100 (3)	3.15	1.70

Type of 1959-60 and

Temple of Queen Nefertari, Abu Simbel AP10

Arch and Tower of Cairo — AP11

Designs: 80m, Al Azhar University seen through arch. 140m, Ramses II, Abu Simbel.

Perf. 11½x11, 11x11½

1963-65 Photo. Wmk. 342

C101	AP6 80m vio blk & brt bl	3.75	1.60
C102	AP10 115m brown & yel	4.00	1.50
C103	AP10 140m pale vio, blk & org red	4.00	2.00

Unwmk.

C104	AP11 50m yel brn & brt bl	2.25	1.00
C105	AP6 80m vio bl & lt bl	3.75	1.60
	Nos. C101-C105 (5)	17.75	7.70

Issued: 50m, 11/2/64; No. C105, 2/13/65; others, 10/24/63.

See Nos. NC34-NC36.

Weather Vane, Anemometer and WMO Emblem — AP12

Perf. 11½x11

1965, Mar. 23 Wmk. 342

C106	AP12 80m dk blue & rose lil	2.75	1.50

Fifth World Meteorological Day.

See No. NC37.

Game Board from Tomb of tutankhamun — AP13

1965, July 1 Photo. Unwmk.

C107	AP13 10m yellow & dk blue	2.00	.45

See No. NC38.

Temples at Abu Simbel — AP14

1966, Apr. 28 Wmk. 342 *Perf. 11½*

C108	AP14 20m multicolored	1.10	.55
C109	AP14 80m multicolored	2.50	1.75

Issued to commemorate the transfer of the temples of Abu Simbel to a hilltop, 1963-66.

Scout Camp and Jamboree Emblem AP15

1966, Aug. 10 *Perf. 11½x11*

C110	AP15 20m olive & rose	1.60	.50

7th Pan-Arab Boy Scout Jamboree, Good Daim, Libya, Aug. 12.

St. Catherine Monastery, Mt. Sinai — AP16

1966, Nov. 30 Photo. Wmk. 342

C111	AP16 80m multicolored	2.25	1.75

St. Catherine Monastery, Sinai, 1400th anniv.

Cairo Airport AP17

1967, Apr. 26 *Perf. 11½x11*

C112	AP17 20m sky bl, sl grn & lt brn	1.00	.40

Hotel El Alamein and Map of Nile Delta AP18

Intl. Tourist Year: 80m, The Virgin's Tree, Virgin Mary and Child. 115m, Fishing in the Red Sea.

1967, June 7 Wmk. 342 *Perf. 11½*

C113	AP18	20m dull pur, sl grn & dl org	1.10	.50
C114	AP18	80m blue & multi	2.50	1.50
C115	AP18	115m brown, org & bl	4.75	2.25
		Nos. C113-C115 (3)	8.35	4.25

Oil Derricks, Map of Egypt AP19

1967, July 23 Photo.

C116	AP19	50m org & bluish blk	1.25	.85

15th anniversary of the revolution.

Type of Regular Issue, 1967

Design: 80m, Back of tutankhamun's throne and UNESCO emblem.

1967, Oct. 24 Wmk. 342 *Perf. 11½*

C117	A301	80m blue & yellow	1.50	.90

Koran — AP20

1968, Mar. 25 Wmk. 342 *Perf. 11½*

C118	AP20	30m lilac, bl & yel	1.25	1.00
C119	AP20	80m lilac, bl & yel	2.25	1.25
a.		Pair, #C118-C119 + label	4.50	3.50

1400th anniv. of the Koran. Nos. C118-C119 are printed in miniature sheets of 4 containing 2 each of Nos. C118-C119.

St. Mark and St. Mark's Cathedral — AP21

1968, June 25 Wmk. 342 *Perf. 11½*

C120	AP21	80m brt grn, dk brn & dp car	1.75	1.00

Martyrdom of St. Mark, 1900th anniv. and the consecration of St. Mark's Cathedral, Cairo.

Map of United Arab Airlines and Boeing 707 AP22

Design: No. C122, Ilyushin 18 and routes of United Arab Airlines.

1968-69 Photo. *Perf. 11½x11*

C121	AP22	55m blue, ocher & car	1.75	.90
C122	AP22	55m bl, yel & vio blk ('69)	1.25	.90

1st flights of a Boeing 707 and an Ilyushin 18 for United Arab Airlines.

Mahatma Gandhi, Arms of India and UAR AP23

Imam El Boukhary AP24

1969, Sept. 10 *Perf. 11x11½*

C123	AP23	80m lt blue, ocher & brn	4.00	1.75

Mohandas K. Gandhi (1869-1948), leader in India's fight for independence.

1969, Dec. 27 Photo. Wmk. 342

C124	AP24	30m lt olive & dk brown	.70	.25

1100th anniv. of the death of the Imam El Boukhary (824-870), philosopher and writer.

Azzahir Beybars Mosque AP25

1969, Dec. 27 Engr. *Perf. 11½x11*

C125	AP25	30m red lilac	.70	.25

700th anniv. of the founding of the Azzahir Beybars Mosque, Cairo.

Lenin (1870-1924) — AP26

Perf. 11x11½

1970, Apr. 22 Photo. Wmk. 342

C126	AP26	80m lt green & brown	2.00	1.25

Phantom Fighters and Destroyed Factory AP27

1970, May 1 *Perf. 11½x11*

C127	AP27	80m yel, grn & dk vio brn	2.00	1.00

Issued to commemorate the destruction of the Abu-Zaabal factory by Israeli planes.

UPU Type of Regular Issue

1970, May 20 Photo. Wmk. 342

C128	A350	80m multicolored	1.40	.85

Nasser and Burial Mosque — AP28

1970, Nov. 6 Wmk. 342 *Perf. 11*

C129	AP28	30m olive & blk	1.00	.40
C130	AP28	80m brown & blk	2.75	1.25

Gamal Abdel Nasser (1918-70), Pres. of Egypt.

Postal Congress Type

Perf. 11½x11

1971, Mar. 6 Photo. Wmk. 342

C131	A365	30m lt ol, org & sl grn	.90	.45

Nasser, El Rifaei and Sultan Hussein Mosques AP29

Designs: 85m, Nasser and Ramses Square, Cairo. 110m, Nasser, Sphinx and pyramids.

Perf. 11½x11

1971, July 1 Photo. Wmk. 342

C132	AP29	30m multicolored	2.50	.80
C133	AP29	85m multicolored	4.50	1.25
C134	AP29	110m multicolored	5.75	2.50
		Nos. C132-C134 (3)	12.75	4.55

APU Type of Regular Issue

1971, Aug. 3 Wmk. 342 *Perf. 11½*

C135	A373	30m brown, yel & bl	1.40	.50

Arab Republic of Egypt Confederation Type

Perf. 11½x11

1971, Sept. 28 Photo. Wmk. 342

C136	A374	30m gray, sl grn & dk pur	1.25	.50

Al Aqsa Mosque and Woman AP30

Wmk. 342

1971, Oct. 24 Photo. *Perf. 11½*

C137	AP30	30m bl, yel, brn & grn	1.75	.45

25th anniv. of the UN (in 1970) and return of Palestinian refugees.

Postal Union Type

30m, African Postal Union emblem & letter.

1971, Dec. 2 *Perf. 11½x11*

C138	A384	30m green, blk & bl	1.40	.40

Aida, Triumphal March AP31

1971, Dec. 23 Wmk. 342 *Perf. 11½*

C139	AP31	110m dk brn, yel & sl grn	5.75	3.00

Centenary of the first performance of the opera Aida, by Giuseppe Verdi.

Globe, Glider, Rocket Club Emblem — AP32

1972, Feb. 11 *Perf. 11x11½*

C140	AP32	30m blue, ocher & yel	1.50	.50

International Aerospace Education Conference, Cairo, Jan. 11-13.

St. Catherine's Monastery on Fire — AP33

Perf. 11½x11

1972, Feb. 15 Unwmk.

C141	AP33	110m dp car, org & blk	4.75	4.00

The burning of St. Catherine's Monastery in Sinai Desert, Nov. 30, 1971.

Tutankhamun in Garden — AP34

Tutankhamun, from 2nd Sarcophagus — AP35

Design: No. C143, Ankhesenamun.

1972, May 22 Photo. *Perf. 11½*

C142	AP34	110m brn org, bl & grn	10.00	5.50
C143	AP34	110m brn org, bl & grn	10.00	5.50
a.		Pair, #C142-C143	26.00	22.50

Souvenir Sheet

Imperf

C144	AP35	200m gold & multi	32.50	32.50

50th anniv. of the discovery of the tomb of Tutankhamun. No. C143a has continuous design.

Souvenir Sheet

Flag of Confederation of Arab Republics — AP36

1972, July 23 Photo. *Imperf.*

C145 AP36 110m gold, dp car & blk 4.50 4.25

20th anniversary of the revolution.

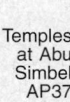

Temples at Abu Simbel AP37

Designs: 30m, Al Azhar Mosque and St. George's Church. 110m, Pyramids at Giza.

1972 Wmk. 342 *Perf. 11½x11*

C146 AP37 30m blue, brn & buff 2.50 .40
C147 AP37 85m bl, brn & ocher 3.50 1.75
C148 AP37 110m multicolored 5.25 1.75
Nos. C146-C148 (3) 11.25 3.90

Issued: Nos. C146, C148, 11/22; No. C147, 8/1.

Olympic Type of Regular Issue

Olympic and Motion Emblems and: No. C149, Handball. No. C150, Weight lifting. 50m, Swimming. 55m, Gymnastics. All vertical.

1972, Aug. 17 *Perf. 11x11½*

C149 A396 30m multicolored .80 .40
C150 A396 30m yellow & multi .80 .40
C151 A396 50m blue & multi 1.60 1.00
C152 A396 55m multicolored 2.00 1.10
Nos. C149-C152 (4) 5.20 2.90

Champollion, Rosetta Stone, Hieroglyphics — AP38

1972, Oct. 16

C153 AP38 110m gold, grn & blk 7.50 2.50

Sesquicentennial of the deciphering of Egyptian hieroglyphics by Jean-François Champollion.

World Map, Telephone, Radar, ITU Emblem — AP39

1973, Mar. 21 Photo. *Perf. 11*

C154 AP39 30m lt bl, dk bl & blk .90 .25

5th World Telecommunications Day.

Karnak Temple, Luxor — AP40

Hand Dripping Blood and Falling Plane — AP41

1973, Mar. 21

C155 AP40 110m dp ultra, blk & rose 4.75 2.50

Sound and light at Karnak.

1973, May 1 *Perf. 11x11½*

C156 AP41 110m multicolored 6.25 3.00

Israeli attack on Libyan civilian plane, Feb. 1973.

WMO Emblem, Weather Vane — AP42

1973, Oct. 24 *Perf. 11x11½*

C157 AP42 110m blue, gold & pur 3.00 1.75

Cent. of intl. meteorological cooperation.

Refugees, Map of Palestine AP43

1973, Oct. 24 *Perf. 11½*

C158 AP43 30m dk brn, yel & bl 1.60 .50

Plight of Palestinian refugees.

INTERPOL Emblem AP44

Postal and UPU Emblems AP45

Perf. 11x11½

1973, Dec. 8 Photo. Wmk. 342

C159 AP44 110m black & multi 3.75 2.00

Intl. Criminal Police Organization, 50th anniv.

1974, Jan. 2 Unwmk. *Perf. 11*

Post Day (UPU Emblems and): 30m, APU emblem. 55m, African Postal Union emblem. 110m, UPU emblem.

Size: 26x46½mm

C160 AP45 20m gray, red & blk .45 .25
C161 AP45 30m sal, blk & pur .65 .25
C162 AP45 55m emerald, blk & brt mag 1.25 .85

Size: 37x37½mm

Perf. 11½

C163 AP45 110m lt bl, blk & gold 1.75 1.50
Nos. C160-C163 (4) 4.10 2.85

Solar Bark of Khufu (Cheops) — AP46

Wmk. 342

1974, Mar. 21 Photo. *Perf. 11½*

C164 AP46 110m blue, gold & brn 3.75 2.25

Solar Bark Museum.

Hotel Meridien AP47

1974, Oct. 6 *Perf. 11½x11*

C165 AP47 110m multicolored 2.25 1.25

Opening of Hotel Meridien, Cairo.

Suez Canal Type of 1975

1975, June 5 *Perf. 11½*

C166 A448 30m bl, yel grn & ind 1.75 .60
C167 A448 110m indigo & blue 2.75 2.00

Irrigation Commission Emblem — AP48

1975, July 20

C168 AP48 110m orange & dk grn 2.25 1.25

9th Intl. Congress on Irrigation and Drainage, Moscow, and 25th anniv. of the Intl. Commission on Irrigation and Drainage.

Refugees and UNWRA Emblem — AP49

Woman and IWY Emblem — AP50

Perf. 11x11½

1975, Oct. 24 Photo. Wmk. 342

C169 AP49 30m multicolored 1.40 .50

Unwmk.

C170 AP50 110m olive, org & blk 3.50 2.00

UN Day. 30m publicizes UN help for refugees; 110m is for Intl. Women's Year 1975.

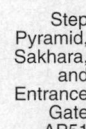

Step Pyramid, Sakhara, and Entrance Gate AP51

Designs: 45m, 60m, Plane over Giza Pyramids. 140m, Plane over boats on Nile.

Perf. 11½x11

1978-82 Photo. Wmk. 342

C171 AP51 45m yel & brown .60 .25
b. Unwatermarked — —
C171A AP51 60m olive 2.00 1.00
c. Unwatermarked — —
C172 AP51 115m blue & brown 1.10 .55
C173 AP51 140m blue & purple 2.00 1.00
C173A AP51 185m bl, sep & gray brn 5.00 2.25
Nos. C171-C173A (5) 10.70 5.05

Issued: 60m, 1/15/82; 185m, 1982; others, 1/1/78.

Flyer and UN ICAO Emblem — AP52

Perf. 11x11½

1978, Dec. 30 Photo. Wmk. 342

C174 AP52 140m blue, blk & brn 2.50 1.25

75th anniversary of 1st powered flight.

Seeing Eye Medallion AP53

Perf. 11½x11

1981, Oct. 1 Photo. Wmk. 342

C175 AP53 230m multicolored 2.50 1.25

Hilton Ramses Hotel Opening — AP54

Perf. 11x11½

1982, Mar. 15 Photo. Wmk. 342

C176 AP54 18½p multi 2.00 1.00

Temple of Horus, Edfu AP55

Designs: 15p, like 6p. 18½p, 25p, Statue of Akhnaton, Thebes, hieroglyphics, vert. 23p, 30p, Giza pyramids.

Perf. 11½x11, 11x11½

1985 Photo. Wmk. 342

C177 AP55 6p lt blue & dk bl grn 1.00 .40
C178 AP55 15p grnsh bl & brn 1.75 .50
a. Unwatermarked — —
C179 AP55 18½p grn, sep & dp yel 2.00 1.25
C180 AP55 23p grnsh bl, sep & yel bis 2.50 1.50
C181 AP55 25p lt bl, sep & yel bis 2.10 .95
a. Unwmkd. ('87) 2.75 1.10
C182 AP55 30p grnsh bl, sep & org yel 2.10 .85
a. Unwmkd. ('87) 2.75 1.10
Nos. C177-C182 (6) 11.45 5.45

Issued: 6p, 18½p, 23p, 3/1; 15p, 25p, 30p, 5/1.

See No. C236.

Post Day — AP56

Narmer Board, oldest known hieroglyphic inscriptions: No. C183a, Tablet obverse. No. C183b, Reverse.

1986, Jan. 2 Photo. *Perf. 13½x13*

C183 AP56 Pair 2.50 2.50
a.-b. 15p any single 1.10 1.00

Map, Jet, AFRAA Emblem AP57

1986, Apr. 7 Photo. *Perf. 11½*

C184 AP57 15p blue, yel & blk 1.25 .50

African Airlines Assoc., 18th General Assembly, Cairo, Apr. 7-10.

World Food Day AP58

UNESCO, 40th Anniv. — AP59

Perf. 13½x13, 13x13½

1986, Oct. 24 Litho.

C185 AP58 15p multicolored 1.00 1.00
C186 AP59 15p multicolored 1.00 1.00

UN Day.

Tourism Year — AP60

Design: Column and Sphinx in Alexandria, St. Catherine's Monastery in Mt. Sinai, Colossi of Thebes and Temple of Theban Triad in Luxor.

Unwmk.

1987, Sept. 30 Litho. *Imperf.*

Size: 140x90mm

C187 AP60 30p multicolored 4.25 4.25

Palestinian Uprising — AP61

1988, Sept. 28 Litho. *Perf. 12x13½*

C188 AP61 25p multicolored 1.60 1.40

UN Day AP62

1988, Oct. 20 Litho. *Perf. 13x13½*

C189 AP62 25p multicolored 1.60 1.40

Nobel Prize Type of 1988

1988, Nov. 7

C190 A769 25p multicolored 1.60 1.40

Arab Cooperation Council — AP63

Architecture and Art — AP64

1989, May 10 Litho. *Perf. 13½x13*

C191 AP63 25p Flags 1.25 .55

Size: 89x80mm

Imperf

C192 AP63 50p Flags, seal 3.50 3.50

1989-91 Photo. *Perf. 11x11½*

C193 AP64 20p Balcony .75 .45
C194 AP64 25p Brazier 1.10 .60
C195 AP64 35p shown 1.25 .75
C196 AP64 45p Tapestry 1.60 .75
C197 AP64 45p like #C195 1.40 .40
C198 AP64 50p Stag (dish) 2.00 1.00
C199 AP64 55p 4 animals (plate) 1.90 .90
C200 AP64 60p like #C198 2.25 1.25
C201 AP64 65p like #C198 2.50 1.50
C202 AP64 70p like #C193 2.50 1.50
C203 AP64 85p like #C199 3.00 1.75
Nos. C193-C203 (11) 20.25 10.85

Issued: 35p, 60p, 10/1/89; 55p, 1/1/90; No. C197, C202, 1/25/91; 65p, 85p, 7/20/91; others, 4/1/89.

AP65

Funerary Mask of King Tutankhamun — AP66

King Tutankhamun AP66a

1993-2000 Litho. *Perf. 11½*

C204 AP65 55p multicolored 2.00 .95
C205 AP66 80p multi, 21mm between "EGYPT" and Arabic text at top 3.25 1.25
C205A AP66 80p multi, 17mm between "Egypt" and Arabic text at top ('00) — —

Photo.

Perf. 11x11¼

C206 AP66a £1 black & brown 1.50 1.25
b. Wmk. 342 2.00 1.25
Nos. C204-C206 (4) 6.75 3.45

Issued: 55p, 80p, 3/1/93; £1, 1997; No. C206b, 1999.

See No. C231.

ICAO, 50th Anniv. — AP67

1994, Sept. 16 Litho. *Perf. 13*

C207 AP67 80p multicolored 1.00 .45

Intl. Year of the Family — AP68

1994, Oct. 24 Litho. *Perf. 13*

C208 AP68 80p multicolored 1.50 1.00

Arab League for Education, Culture, & Science Organization — AP69

1995, July 25 Litho. *Perf. 13x13½*

C209 AP69 55p multicolored .80 .50

UN Organizations, 50th Anniv. — AP70

Perf. 12½x13, 13x12½

1995, Oct. 24 Litho.

C210 AP70 80p UN 2.00 1.00
C211 AP70 80p FAO 2.00 1.00
C212 AP70 80p UNESCO, vert. 2.00 1.00
Nos. C210-C212 (3) 6.00 3.00

Arab Summit, Cairo — AP71

1996, June 21 Litho. *Perf. 13x12½*

C213 AP71 55p multicolored .70 .30

16th Intl. Conference on Irrigation and Drainage, Cairo — AP72

1996, Sept. 15 Litho. *Perf. 12½x13*

C214 AP72 80p multicolored 1.10 1.10

Intl. Tourism Day — AP73

1996, Sept. 27 *Perf. 13*

C215 AP73 80p multicolored 1.50 .60

Arabian Horse Day — AP74

World Post Day — AP75

1996, Sept. 27 *Perf. 13x12½*

C216 AP74 55p grn, blk & gray 1.00 .35

1996, Oct. 9 Litho. *Perf. 13x12½*

C217 AP75 80p multicolored 1.25 .60

AP76

AP77

1996, Oct. 24

C218 AP76 55p multicolored .70 .40

Cairo, Arab cultural capital of 1996.

1996, Oct. 24

C219 AP77 80p multicolored 1.10 .55

UNICEF, 50th anniv.

World Meteorological Day — AP78

Thutmose III — AP79

1997, Mar. 23 Litho. *Perf. 13x12½*
C220 AP78 £1 multicolored 1.75 1.00

1997, Mar. 25 Photo. *Perf. 11x11½*
C221 AP79 75p blk, bl & gray 1.10 1.10

Heinrich von Stephan (1831-97) — AP80

1997, Apr. 15 Litho. *Perf. 13*
C222 AP80 £1 multicolored 1.60 1.25

AP81

1997, Sept. 11
C223 AP81 £1 multicolored 1.00 .90

98th Intl. Parliamentary Conference, Cairo.

AP82

AP83

1997, Sept. 10 Litho. *Perf. 13*
C224 AP82 75p multicolored 1.00 .90

1997 Egyptian Team, top medal winners of 8th Pan Arab Games, Beirut, Lebanon.

1997, Sept. 27 *Perf. 13x12½*
C225 AP83 £1 multicolored 1.90 1.00

Sarabas (180-211), mumified Egyptian.

World Book and Copyright Day AP84

1997, Oct. 24 Litho. *Perf. 12½x13*
C226 AP84 £1 multicolored 1.75 1.00

African Ministries of Transport and Communications, 11th Conference — AP85

1997, Nov. 22 Litho. *Perf. 13x12½*
C227 AP85 75p multicolored .80 .70

Arab Scout Movement, 85th Anniv. — AP86

1997, Nov. 24 *Perf. 12½x13*
C228 AP86 75p multicolored 1.00 .90

8th G-15 Summit Meeting — AP87

1998, May 11 Litho. *Perf. 13*
C229 AP87 £1 multicolored 1.10 .90

Lighthouse of Alexandria AP88

1998, May 20 Litho. *Perf. 13*
C230 AP88 £1 multicolored 1.75 1.00

King Tut Type of 1997

1998, July 25 Litho. *Perf. 11x11¼*
C231 AP66a 125p Tutankhamun 1.75 1.25
a. Wmk. 342 ('99) 5.50 4.00

AP90

1998, Aug. 3 *Perf. 13*
C232 AP90 £1 multicolored 1.10 .90

Arab Post Day.

AP91

1998, Oct. 9 Litho. *Perf. 13*
C233 AP91 125p multicolored 1.40 1.25

World Post Day.

AP92

1998, Oct. 22
C234 AP92 125p multicolored 1.40 1.25

67th Interpol Meeting, Cairo.

AP93

1998, Oct. 24
C235 AP93 125p multicolored 1.40 1.25

Universal Declaration of Human Rights, 50th anniv.

Statue of Akhnaton Type of 1985

1998 Litho. *Perf. 13*
C236 AP55 25p lt bl, brn & tan 1.75 1.00

AP94

1999, Oct. 12 Litho. *Perf. 13x12¾*
C237 AP94 125p multicolored 2.25 1.75

Performance of opera "Aida" at the Pyramids.

AP95

1999, Oct. 16
C238 AP95 125p multicolored 2.50 1.75

Discovery of the Rosetta Stone, bicent.

World Tourism Day — AP96

Perf. 13¼x12¾

2000, Sept. 27 Litho.
C239 AP96 125p multi 1.50 1.25

Awarding of Nobel Prize for Chemistry to Dr. Ahmed Zewail — AP97

1999, Dec. 10 *Imperf.*
C240 AP97 125p multi 2.00 2.00

UN High Commissioner for Refugees, 50th Anniv. — AP98

2000, Dec. 13
C241 AP98 125p multi 1.50 1.25

AIR POST SEMI-POSTAL STAMPS

Catalogue values for unused stamps in this section are for Never Hinged items.

United Arab Republic

Pharaonic Mail Carriers and Papyrus Plants SPAP1

Design: 115m+55m, Jet plane, world map and stamp of Egypt, 1926 (No. C1).

Wmk. 342

1966, Jan. 2 Photo. *Perf. 11½*

CB1 SPAP1 80m + 40m multi 3.25 2.75
CB2 SPAP1 115m + 55m multi 4.25 3.50
a. Pair, #CB1-CB2 10.00 8.00

Post Day, Jan. 2.

SPECIAL DELIVERY STAMPS

Motorcycle Postman — SD1

Perf. 13x13½

1926, Nov. 28 Photo. Wmk. 195

E1 SD1 20m dark green 35.00 9.50

1929, Sept.

E2 SD1 20m brown red & black 6.75 1.75

Inscribed "Postes Expres"

1943-44 Litho.

E3 SD1 26m brn red & gray blk 6.75 *6.75*
E4 SD1 40m dl brn & pale gray ('44) 6.00 4.00

For overprints see Nos. E5, NE1.

Catalogue values for unused stamps in this section, from this point to the end of the section, are for Never Hinged items.

No. E4 Overprinted in Black

1952, Jan. Overprint 27mm Wide

E5 SD1 40m dl brn & pale gray 3.50 2.00

See notes after No. 316.

POSTAGE DUE STAMPS

D1

D2

Wmk. Crescent and Star (119)

1884, Jan. 1 Litho. *Perf. 10½*

J1 D1 10pa red 57.50 9.50
a. Horiz. pair, imperf. vert. 150.00
J2 D1 20pa red 175.00 50.00
J3 D1 1pi red 145.00 52.50
J4 D1 2pi red 240.00 12.50
J5 D1 5pi red 20.00 *60.00*
Nos. J1-J5 (5) 637.50 184.50

1886, Aug. 1 Unwmk.

J6 D1 10pa red 75.00 17.50
a. Horiz. pair, imperf. vert. 135.00
J7 D1 20pa red 260.00 50.00
J8 D1 1pi red 37.50 10.00
a. Pair, imperf. between 200.00 135.00
J9 D1 2pi red 37.50 5.00
a. Pair, imperf. between 175.00
Nos. J6-J9 (4) 410.00 82.50

1888, Jan. 1 *Perf. 11½*

J10 D2 2m green 22.50 *27.50*
a. Horiz. pair, imperf. between 225.00 200.00
J11 D2 5m rose red 45.00 27.50
J12 D2 1pi blue 145.00 40.00
a. Pair, imperf. between 300.00
J13 D2 2pi yellow 155.00 20.00
J14 D2 5pi gray 240.00 210.00
a. Period after "PIASTRES" 325.00 250.00
Nos. J10-J14 (5) 607.50 325.00

Excellent counterfeits of #J1-J14 are plentiful.

There are 4 types of each of Nos. J1-J14, so placed that any block of 4 contains all types.

D3

Perf. 14x13½

1889 Wmk. 119 Typo.

J15 D3 2m green 10.00 .70
a. Half used as 1m on cover 350.00
J16 D3 4m maroon 3.75 .70
J17 D3 1pi ultra 7.75 .70
J18 D3 2pi orange 7.50 1.00
a. Half used as 1p on cover —
Nos. J15-J18 (4) 29.00 3.10

Nos. J15-J18 exist on both ordinary and chalky paper. Imperf. examples of Nos. J15-J17 are proofs.

Black Surcharge

Type I — D4

1898

J19 D4 3m on 2pi orange 2.10 *6.25*
a. Inverted surcharge 65.00 *82.50*
b. Pair, one without surcharge —
f. Double surcharge 225.00 —

There are two types of this surcharge. In type I, the spacing between the last two Arabic characters at the right is 2mm. In type II, this spacing is 3mm, and there is an added sign on top of the second character from the right. See *Scott Classic Specialized Catalogue of Stamps & Covers* for detailed listing.

D5

D6

1921 Wmk. 120 *Perf. 14x13½*

J20 D5 2m green 3.75 *6.75*
J21 D5 4m vermilion 7.50 *19.00*
J22 D6 10m deep blue 12.50 *25.00*
Nos. J20-J22 (3) 23.75 50.75

1921-22

J23 D5 2m vermilion 1.00 *2.25*
J24 D5 4m green 6.00 2.00
J25 D6 10m lake ('22) 6.50 1.50
Nos. J23-J25 (3) 13.50 5.75

Nos. J18, J23-J25 Overprinted

1922, Oct. 10 Wmk. 119

J26 D3 2pi orange 7.50 *10.50*
a. Overprint right side up 30.00 *30.00*

Wmk. 120

J27 D5 2m vermilion 1.00 *3.00*
J28 D5 4m green 1.60 *3.00*
J29 D6 10m lake 2.50 1.90
Nos. J26-J29 (4) 12.60 18.40

Overprint on Nos. J26-J29 is inverted.

Arabic Numeral — D7

Perf. 13x13½

1927-56 Litho. Wmk. 195

Size: 18x22½mm

J30 D7 2m slate .85 .50
J31 D7 2m orange ('38) 1.00 1.10
J32 D7 4m green .85 .55
J33 D7 4m ol brn ('32) 8.00 5.25
J34 D7 5m brown 4.25 1.10
J35 D7 6m gray grn ('41) 2.75 2.10
J36 D7 8m brn vio 1.60 .65
J37 D7 10m brick red ('29) 1.25 .35
a. 10m deep red 1.90 1.00
J38 D7 12m rose lake ('41) 1.90 *3.75*
J38A D7 20m dk red ('56) 2.50 2.50

Perf. 13½x14

Size: 22x28mm

J39 D7 30m purple 5.25 3.75
Nos. J30-J39 (11) 30.20 21.60

See Nos. J47-J59. For overprints see Nos. J40-J46, NJ1-NJ7.

Catalogue values for unused stamps in this section, from this point to the end of the section, are for Never Hinged items.

Postage Due Stamps and Type of 1927 Overprinted in Various Colors

1952, Jan. 16 *Perf. 13x13½*

J40 D7 2m orange (Bl) 1.60 1.60
J41 D7 4m green 1.60 1.60
J42 D7 6m gray grn (RV) 1.90 1.90
J43 D7 8m brn vio (Bl) 2.50 2.50
J44 D7 10m dl rose (Bl) 4.25 3.50
a. 10m brown red (Bk) 4.00 3.75
J45 D7 12m rose lake (Bl) 2.10 2.10

Perf. 14

J46 D7 30m purple (C) 3.50 3.50
Nos. J40-J46 (7) 17.45 16.70

See notes after No. 316.

United Arab Republic

1960 Wmk. 318 *Perf. 13x13½*

Size: 18x22½mm

J47 D7 2m orange 1.00 1.00
J48 D7 4m light green 1.50 1.50
J49 D7 6m green 2.50 2.50
J50 D7 8m brown vio 5.00 5.00
J51 D7 12m rose brown 12.00 10.00
J52 D7 20m dull rose brn 2.00 .50

Perf. 14

Size: 22x28mm

J53 D7 30m violet 12.00 6.00
Nos. J47-J53 (7) 36.00 26.50

1962 Wmk. 328 *Perf. 13x13½*

Size: 18x22½mm

J54 D7 2m salmon 1.00 1.00
J55 D7 4m light green 1.50 1.50
J56 D7 10m red brown 2.50 2.50
J57 D7 12m rose brown 5.00 5.00
J58 D7 20m dull rose brn 11.00 11.00

Perf. 14

Size: 22x28mm

J59 D7 30m light violet 16.00 16.00
Nos. J54-J59 (6) 37.00 37.00

D8

1965 Unwmk. Photo. *Perf. 11*

J60 D8 2m org & vio blk 1.25 1.00
J61 D8 8m lt bl & dk bl 1.50 1.50
J62 D8 10m yel & emer 2.25 1.50
J63 D8 20m lt bl & vio blk 2.75 2.25
J64 D8 40m org & emer 4.75 2.00
Nos. J60-J64 (5) 12.50 8.25

MILITARY STAMPS

The "British Forces" and "Army post" stamps were special issues provided at a reduced rate for the purchase and use by the British military forces in Egypt and their families for ordinary letters sent to Great Britain and Ireland by a concessionary arrangement made with the Egyptian government. From Nov. 1, 1932 to Feb. 29, 1936, in order to take advantage of the concessionary rate, it was mandatory to use #M1-M11 by affixing them to the backs of envelopes. An "Egypt Postage Prepaid" handstamp was applied to the face of the envelopes. Envelopes bearing these stamps were to be posted only at British military post boxes. Envelopes bearing the 1936-39 "Army Post" stamps (#M12-M15, issued by the Egyptian Postal Administration) also were sold at the concessionary rate and also were to be posted only at British military post boxes. The "Army Post" stamps were withdrawn in 1941, but the concession continued without the use of special stamps. The concession was finally canceled in 1951.

Imperf examples of Nos. M1-M4, M6, M9 (without overprint) and M10 are proofs.

M1

Unwmk.

1932, Nov. 1 Typo. *Perf. 11*

M1 M1 1pi red & deep blue 70.00 4.50

For similar design see No. M3.

M2

1932, Nov. 26 Typo. *Perf. 11½*

M2 M2 3m blk, *sage grn* 57.50 *80.00*

See Nos. M4, M6, M10.

M3

1933, Aug. Typo. *Perf. 11*

M3 M3 1pi red & deep blue 47.50 1.10

Camel Type of 1932

1933, Nov. 13 Typo. *Perf. 11½*

M4 M2 3m brown lake 40.00 *57.50*

M4

1934, June 1 Photo. *Perf. 14½x14*

M5 M4 1pi bright carmine 40.00 1.25

See Nos. M7-M8. For overprint and surcharge see Nos. M9, M11.

Camel Type of 1932

1934, Nov. 17 Typo. *Perf. 11½*

M6 M2 3m deep blue 8.25 *30.00*

Type of 1934

1934, Dec. 5 Photo. *Perf. 14½x14*

M7 M4 1pi green 6.00 6.00

Type of 1934

1935, Apr. 24 *Perf. 13½x14*

M8 M4 1pi bright carmine 2.90 *3.75*

Type of 1934 Overprinted in Red

1935, May 6			***Perf. 14***
M9 M4 1pi ultramarine		350.00	275.00

Camel Type of 1932

1935, Nov. 23	**Typo.**		***Perf. 11½***
M10 M2 3m vermilion		30.00	*45.00*

No. M8 Surcharged

1935, Dec. 16	**Photo.**		***Perf. 13½x14***
M11 M4 3m on 1pi brt car		25.00	*100.00*

Fuad Type of 1927
Inscribed "Army Post"

M5

1936, Mar. 1			**Wmk. 195**
M12 M5 3m green		2.50	2.50
M13 M5 10m carmine		7.00	.25

King Farouk — M6

1939, Dec. 16			***Perf. 13x13½***
M14 M6 3m green		6.00	*12.00*
M15 M6 10m carmine rose		8.00	.25

Catalogue values for unused stamps in this section, from this point to the end of the section, are for Never Hinged items.

United Arab Republic

Arms of UAR and Military Emblems — M7

Perf. 11x11½

1971, Apr. 15	**Photo.**		**Wmk. 342**
M16 M7 10m purple		.75	.50

OFFICIAL STAMPS

O1

Wmk. Crescent and Star (119)

1893, Jan. 1	**Typo.**		***Perf. 14x13½***
O1 O1 orange brown		3.75	.25

No. O1 exists on ordinary and chalky paper. Imperf. examples of No. O1 are proofs.

Regular Issues of 1884-93 Overprinted

1907

O2 A18 1m brown	2.40	.35
O3 A19 2m green	4.25	.25
O4 A20 3m orange	4.75	1.25
O5 A22 5m car rose	7.75	.25
O6 A14 1pi ultra	4.75	.25
O7 A16 5pi gray	17.00	6.00
Nos. O2-O7 (6)	40.90	8.35

Nos. O2-O3, O5-O7 imperf. are proofs.

No. 48 Overprinted

1913

O8 A22 5m carmine rose	9.50	.70
a. Inverted overprint		90.00
b. No period after "S"	65.00	19.00

Regular Issues Overprinted

1914-15 **On Issues of 1888-1906**		
O9 A19 2m green	5.00	*10.00*
a. Inverted overprint	42.50	42.50
b. Double overprint	450.00	
c. No period after "S"	16.00	16.00
O10 A21 4m brown red	7.50	5.50
a. Inverted overprint	225.00	160.00
On Issue of 1914		
O11 A24 1m olive brown	2.50	*5.00*
a. No period after "S"	14.00	*30.00*
O12 A26 3m orange	3.75	*6.00*
a. No period after "S"	16.00	*30.00*
O13 A28 5m lake	4.75	2.75
a. No period after "S"	17.50	*26.00*
b. Two periods after "S"	17.50	*26.00*
Nos. O9-O13 (5)	23.50	29.25

Regular Issues Overprinted

1915, Oct. **On Issues of 1888-1906**		
O14 A19 2m green	5.50	*5.00*
a. Inverted overprint	24.00	24.00
b. Double overprint	30.00	
O15 A21 4m brown red	11.00	*11.00*
On Issue of 1914		
O16 A28 5m lake	15.00	1.75
a. Pair, one without overprint	325.00	
Nos. O14-O16 (3)	31.50	17.75

Nos. 50, 63, 52, 67 Overprinted

1922		**Wmk. 120**
O17 A24 1m olive brown	4.25	*16.00*
O18 A25 2m red	10.00	*24.00*
O19 A26 3m orange	77.50	*150.00*
O20 A28 5m pink	21.00	6.00
Nos. O17-O20 (4)	112.75	196.00

Regular Issues of 1921-22 Overprinted

1922

O21 A24 1m olive brn	1.50	*3.25*
O22 A25 2m red	2.00	*4.50*
O23 A26 3m orange	3.25	*5.00*
O24 A27 4m green	7.00	*9.00*
a. Two periods after "H" none after "S"	175.00	175.00
O25 A28 5m pink	4.00	1.00
a. Two periods after "H" none after "S"	75.00	75.00
O26 A29 10m deep blue	7.00	*8.00*
O27 A29 10m lake ('23)	10.00	4.00
a. Two periods after "H" none after "S"	100.00	100.00
O28 A34 15m indigo	8.00	7.00
O29 A35 15m indigo	160.00	160.00
a. Two periods after "H" none after "S"	250.00	250.00
O30 A31 50m maroon	20.00	18.00

Regular Issue of 1923 Overprinted in Black or Red

1924		***Perf. 13½x14***
O31 A36 1m orange	2.10	*2.25*
O32 A36 2m gray (R)	2.75	*3.50*
O33 A36 3m brown	6.75	*6.75*
O34 A36 4m yellow green	8.50	8.50
O35 A36 5m orange brown	2.00	1.05
O36 A36 10m rose	5.50	4.00
O37 A36 15m ultra	9.25	6.75
Perf. 14		
O38 A36 50m myrtle green	25.00	13.50
Nos. O31-O38 (8)	61.85	46.30

O2

Perf. 13x13½

1926-35 **Litho.**		**Wmk. 195**
Size: 18½x22mm		
O39 O2 1m lt orange	1.05	.55
O40 O2 2m black	.70	.40
O41 O2 3m olive brn	2.00	1.35
O42 O2 4m lt green	1.75	1.60
O43 O2 5m brown	2.10	.55
O44 O2 10m dull red	5.25	.55
O45 O2 10m brt vio ('34)	3.00	.60
O46 O2 15m dp blue	5.25	1.25
O47 O2 15m brown vio ('34)	5.25	1.10
O48 O2 20m dp blue ('35)	5.50	1.60
Perf. 13½		
Size: 22½x27½mm		
O49 O2 20m olive green	7.50	2.75
O50 O2 50m myrtle green	10.00	2.00
Nos. O39-O50 (12)	49.35	14.30

O3

1938, Dec.		**Size: 22½x19mm**
O51 O3 1m orange	.35	.35
O52 O3 2m red	.35	.35
O53 O3 3m olive brown	1.60	1.60
O54 O3 4m yel green	1.00	1.00
O55 O3 5m brown	.50	.50
O56 O3 10m brt violet	.60	.60
O57 O3 15m rose violet	1.60	1.60
O58 O3 20m blue	1.60	1.60
Perf. 14x13½		
Size: 26½x22mm		
O59 O3 50m myrtle green	3.75	3.00
Nos. O51-O59 (9)	11.35	10.60

Catalogue values for unused stamps in this section, from this point to the end of the section, are for Never Hinged items.

Nos. O51 to O59 Overprinted in Various Colors

Overprint 19mm Wide

1952, Jan.		***Perf. 13x13½***
O60 O3 1m orange (Br)	2.10	2.10
O61 O3 2m red (Br)	2.10	2.10
O62 O3 3m olive brn (Bl)	2.50	2.50
O63 O3 4m yel green (Bl)	2.50	2.50
O64 O3 5m brown (Bl)	2.50	2.50
O65 O3 10m brt violet (Bl)	2.50	2.50
O66 O3 15m rose violet (Bl)	3.00	3.00
O67 O3 20m blue	3.75	3.75

Overprint 24½mm Wide

Perf. 14x13½

O68 O3 50m myrtle grn (RV)	8.00	8.00
Nos. O60-O68 (9)	28.95	28.95

See notes after No. 316.

United Arab Republic

O4

Arms of UAR — O5

Perf. 13x13½

1959	**Litho.**		**Wmk. 318**
O69 O4 10m brown violet		.65	.25
O70 O4 35m chalky blue		1.75	.30

1962-63		**Wmk. 328**
O71 O4 1m orange ('63)	.30	.30
O72 O4 4m yel grn ('63)	.60	.60
O73 O4 5m brown	.60	.25
O74 O4 10m dk brown	.75	.30
O75 O4 35m dark blue	2.25	.50
O76 O4 50m green	3.50	.60
O77 O4 100m violet ('63)	7.00	1.75
O78 O4 200m rose red ('63)	15.00	8.00
O79 O4 500m gray ('63)	22.50	15.00
Nos. O71-O79 (9)	52.50	27.30

Perf. 11½x11

1966-68 **Unwmk.**		**Photo.**
O80 O5 1m ultra	.25	.25
O81 O5 4m brown	.25	.25
O82 O5 5m olive	.30	.25
O83 O5 10m brown blk	1.00	.35
O84 O5 20m magenta	.60	.30
O85 O5 35m dk purple	1.00	.35
O86 O5 50m orange	1.10	.45
O87 O5 55m dk purple	1.10	.45
Wmk. 342		
O88 O5 100m brt grn & brick red	2.25	1.00
O89 O5 200m blue & brick red	4.50	2.00
O90 O5 500m olive & brick red	10.00	6.25
Nos. O80-O90 (11)	22.35	11.90

1969		**Wmk. 342**
O91 O5 10m magenta	1.10	.65

Arab Republic of Egypt

Arms of Egypt
O6 O7

Wmk. 342

1972, June 30 **Photo.**		***Perf. 11***
O92 O6 1m black & vio blue	.30	.25
a. 1m black & light blue ('75)	.25	.25
O93 O6 10m black & car	.65	.30
a. 10m black & rose red ('76)	.25	.25
O94 O6 20m black & olive	.90	.40
O95 O6 50m black & orange	.60	.55
O96 O6 55m black & purple	3.00	1.00
1973		
O97 O6 20m lilac & sepia	.90	.40
a. 20m purple & light brown ('76)	2.50	.75
O98 O6 70m black & grn ('79)	.85	.45
1982 **Photo.** **Unwmk.**		***Perf. 11***
O99 O6 30m purple & brown	.60	.30
O100 O6 60m black & orange	.70	.30
O101 O6 80m black & green	.95	.35
Nos. O92-O101 (10)	9.45	4.30

Issued: 30m, 2/12; 60m, 2/24; 80m, 2/18.

1985-89 **Photo.**		***Perf. 11½***
Size: 21x25mm		
O102 O7 1p vermilion	.25	.25
O103 O7 2p brown	.25	.25
O104 O7 3p sepia	.25	.25
O105 O7 5p orange yel	.35	.30
O106 O7 8p green	.70	.35

O107 O7 10p brown olive .25 .25
O108 O7 15p dull violet 1.50 .70
O109 O7 20p blue .85 .80
O110 O7 25p red 1.50 1.00
O111 O7 30p dull violet .90 .70
O112 O7 50p green 2.25 2.25
O113 O7 60p myrtle green 2.00 1.40
Nos. O102-O113 (12) 11.05 8.50

Issued: 1p, 3p, 5p, 8p, 15p, 5/1/85; 20p, 50p, 4/88; 10p, 30p, 60p, 12/1/89; 2p, 25p, 1989.

1991-99 Wmk. 342 *Perf. 11½x11*
Size: 18x22mm

O114 O7 5p orange yellow .25 .25
O115 O7 10p brown violet .25 .25
O116 O7 15p brown .25 .25
O117 O7 20p blue .35 .25
O118 O7 20p violet .25 .25
O119 O7 25p purple .45 .25
O120 O7 30p dk violet .50 .25
O121 O7 50p green .80 .60
O122 O7 55p red .70 .55
O123 O7 75p brown .75 .55
O124 O7 £1 green blue 1.25 .75
O125 O7 £2 green 2.50 1.50
Nos. O114-O125 (12) 8.30 5.70

Issued: 10p, 30p, 7/1/91; 50p, 12/1/91; 55p, 4/1/93; £1, £2, 3/22/94; No. O123, 75p, 2/1/97; No. O118, 4/11/99.

Arms Type of 1985-89

Perf. 11½x11
2001, Mar. 25 Photo. Unwmk.
Size: 18x22mm

O127 O7 10p brown 2.75 .50

Issued: 10p, 3/25.

Arms Type of 1985-89

Perf. 11½x11
2002 ? Photo. Unwmk.

O131 O7 30p violet 3.75 .60

OCCUPATION STAMPS

Catalogue values for unused stamps in this section are for Never Hinged Items.

For Use in Palestine

Stamps of 1939-46 Overprinted in Red, Green or Black — a

Perf. 13x13½, 13½x13
1948, May 15 Wmk. 195

N1 A77 1m yellow brn (G) .35 .35
N2 A77 2m red org (G) .35 .35
N3 A66 3m brown (G) .35 .35
N4 A77 4m dp green .35 .35
N5 A77 5m red brown (Bk) .35 .35
N6 A66 6m lt yel grn (Bk) .35 .35
N7 A77 10m dp violet .35 .35
N8 A66 13m rose car (G) .45 .45
N9 A77 15m dk violet .45 .45
N10 A77 17m olive green .45 .45
N11 A77 20m dk gray .45 .45
N12 A77 22m deep blue .50 .50
N13 A74 50pi green & sep 30.00 30.00
N14 A75 £1 dp bl & dk brn 50.00 50.00

The two lines of the overprint are more widely separated on Nos. N13 and N14.

Nos. 267-269, 237 and 238 Ovptd. in Red — b

Perf. 14x13½

N15 A73 30m olive green 1.25 1.25
N16 A73 40m dark brown 1.60 1.60
N17 A73 50m Prus green 3.00 3.00
N18 A73 100m brown violet 5.00 5.00
N19 A73 200m dark violet 15.00 15.00
Nos. N1-N19 (19) 110.60 110.60

Overprint arranged to fit size of stamps.

Nos. N1-N19 Overprinted in Black with Three Bars to Obliterate Portrait

Perf. 13x13½, 13½x13, 14x13½
1953 Wmk. 195

N20 A77 1m yellow brown .70 .70
N21 A77 2m red orange .70 .70
N22 A66 3m brown .70 .70
N23 A77 4m deep green .70 .70
N24 A77 5m red brown .70 .70
N25 A66 6m lt yel grn .80 .80
N26 A77 10m deep violet .85 .85
N27 A66 13m rose carmine .90 .90
N28 A77 15m dark violet .95 .95
N29 A77 17m olive green .95 .95
N30 A77 20m dark gray 1.10 1.10
N31 A77 22m deep blue 1.45 1.45
N32 A73 30m olive green 1.45 1.45
N33 A73 40m dark brown 2.60 2.60
N34 A73 50m Prus green 8.00 8.00
N35 A73 100m brown violet 17.00 17.00
N36 A73 200m dark violet 40.00 40.00
N37 A74 50pi green & sepia 80.00 75.00
N38 A75 £1 dp bl & dk brn 170.00 170.00
Nos. N20-N38 (19) 329.55 324.55

Regular Issue of 1953-55 Overprinted Type "a" in Blue or Red

1954-56 *Perf. 13x13½*

N39 A115 1m red brown .45 .45
N40 A115 2m dark lilac .45 .45
N41 A115 3m brt blue (R) .45 .45
N42 A115 4m dark green (R) .45 .45
N43 A115 5m deep carmine .45 .45
N44 A110 10m dark brown .45 .45
N45 A110 15m gray (R) .45 .45
N46 A110 17m dk grnsh bl (R) .45 .45
N47 A110 20m purple (R) ('54) .60 .60

Nos. 331-333 and 335-340 Overprinted in Blue or Red — c

Perf. 13½

N48 A111 30m dull green (R) .85 .85
N49 A111 32m brt blue (R) .95 .95
N50 A111 35m violet (R) 1.25 1.25
N51 A111 40m red brown 1.90 1.90
N52 A111 50m violet brown 2.25 2.25
N53 A112 100m henna brown 5.50 5.50
N54 A112 200m dk grnsh bl (R) 20.00 20.00
N55 A112 500m purple (R) 70.00 70.00
N56 A112 £1 dk grn, blk & red (R) ('56) 115.00 115.00
Nos. N39-N56 (18) 221.90 221.90

Type of 1957 Overprinted in Red — d

1957 Wmk. 195 *Perf. 13½x13*

N57 A127 10m blue green 5.00 5.00

Nos. 414-417 Overprinted Type "d" in Red

1957-58 Wmk. 315 *Perf. 13½*

N58 A137 10m violet 3.00 3.00

Wmk. 318

N59 A136 1m lt bl grn ('58) .60 .60
N60 A138 5m brown ('58) .60 .60
N61 A137 10m violet ('58) .90 .90
Nos. N58-N61 (4) 5.10 5.10

United Arab Republic Nos. 438-444 Overprinted Type "d" in Red or Green

Perf. 13½x14
1958 Wmk. 318 Photo.

N62 A136 1m crimson .35 .35
N63 A138 2m blue .35 .35
N64 A143 3m dk red brn (G) .35 .35
N65 A217 4m green .35 .35
N66 A138 5m brown .35 .35
N67 A137 10m violet .45 .35
N68 A138 35m lt ultra 3.50 3.25
Nos. N62-N68 (7) 5.70 5.35

Same Overprint in Red on Freedom Struggle Type of 1958

1958 *Perf. 13½x13*

N69 A145 10m dark brown 2.00 2.00

Same Overprint in Green on Declaration of Human Rights Type

1958 *Perf. 13x13½*

N70 A151 10m rose violet 3.00 3.00
N71 A151 35m red brown 8.00 8.00

No. 460 Overprinted Type "d" in Green

1959 Wmk. 195 *Perf. 13½*

N72 A112 55m on 100m henna brn 4.00 4.00

World Refugee Year Type "PALESTINE" Added in English and Arabic to Stamps of Egypt

OS1

1960 Wmk. 328 *Perf. 13x13½*

N73 OS1 10m orange brown .75 .75
N74 OS1 35m dk blue gray 1.75 1.50

Type of Regular Issue 1959-60

1960 *Perf. 13½x14*

N75 A136 1m brown orange .35 .35
N76 A217 4m olive gray .35 .35
N77 A138 5m dk dull pur .35 .35
N78 A137 10m dk olive grn .35 .35
Nos. N75-N78 (4) 1.40 1.40

Palestine Day Type

1961, May 15 *Perf. 13½x13*

N79 A184 10m purple 1.00 1.00

WHO Day Type

1961 Wmk. 328 *Perf. 13½x13*

N80 A182 10m blue 1.25 .75

U.N.T.A.P. Type

1961, Oct. 24

N81 A191 10m dk blue & org .50 .50
N82 A191 35m vermilion & blk .75 .75

Education Day Type

1961, Dec. 18 Photo. *Perf. 13½*

N83 A194 10m red brown .50 .50

Victory Day Type

1961, Dec. 23 Unwmk. *Perf. 11½*

N84 A195 10m brn org & brn .40 .40

Gaza Strip Type

Perf. 13½x13
1962, Mar. 7 Wmk. 328

N85 A200 10m red brown .40 .40

Arab Publicity Week Type

1962, Mar. 22 *Perf. 13½x13*

N86 SP16 10m dark purple .30 .30

Anti-Malaria Type

1962, June 20 Photo.

N87 A204 10m brn & dk car rose .45 .45
N88 A204 35m black & yellow .55 .55

Hammarskjold Type

Perf. 11½x11
1962, Oct. 24 Wmk. 342
Portrait in Slate Blue

N89 A214 5m bright rose .35 .35
N90 A214 10m brown .45 .45
N91 A214 35m blue .75 .75
Nos. N89-N91 (3) 1.55 1.55

Lamp Type of Regular Issue

Perf. 11x11½
1963, Feb. 20 Unwmk.

N92 A217 4m dk brn, org & ultra .35 .35

"Freedom from Hunger" Type

Perf. 11½x11, 11x11½
1963, Mar. 21 Wmk. 342

N93 A220 5m lt grn & dp org .35 .35
N94 A220 10m olive & yellow .45 .45
N95 A220 35m dull pur, yel & blk .65 .65
Nos. N93-N95 (3) 1.45 1.45

Red Cross Centenary Type

Designs: 10m, Centenary emblem, bottom panel added. 35m, Globe and emblem, top and bottom panels added.

1963, May 8 Unwmk. *Perf. 11x11½*

N96 A221 10m dk blue & crim .35 .35
N97 A221 35m crim & dk blue .60 .60

"Save Abu Simbel" Type, 1963

1963, Oct. 15 Wmk. 342 *Perf. 11*

N98 A224 5m black & yellow .40 .40
N99 A224 10m gray, blk & yellow .50 .50
N100 A224 35m org yel & violet 1.25 .95
Nos. N98-N100 (3) 2.15 1.85

Human Rights Type

1963, Dec. 10 Photo. *Perf. 11½x11*

N101 A228 5m dk brown & yellow .35 .35
N102 A228 10m dp claret, gray & blk .40 .40
N103 A228 35m lt grn, pale grn & blk .95 .95
Nos. N101-N103 (3) 1.70 1.70

Types of Regular Issue

1964 Unwmk. *Perf. 11*

N104 A231 1m citron & lt vio .40 .40
N105 A230 2m orange & slate .40 .40
N106 A230 3m blue & ocher .40 .40
N107 A235 4m ol gray, ol, brn & rose .40 .40
N108 A230 5m rose & brt blue .40 .40
a. 5m rose & dark blue 1.25 1.25
N109 A231 10m ol, rose & brn .40 .40
N110 A230 15m lilac & yellow .50 .50
N111 A230 20m brown blk & ol .80 .80
N112 A231 30m dp org & ind 1.60 1.60
N113 A231 35m buff, ocher & emer 1.40 1.40
N114 A231 40m ultra & emer 1.75 1.75
N115 A231 60m grnsh bl & brn org 2.50 2.50

Wmk. 342

N116 A232 100m bluish blk & yel brn 3.50 3.50
Nos. N104-N116 (13) 14.45 14.45

Arab League Council Type

1964, Jan. 13 Photo.

N117 A234 10m olive & black .35 .35

Minaret Type

1964 Unwmk. *Perf. 11*

N118 A235 4m ol, red brn & red .35 .35

Arab Postal Union Type

1964, Apr. 1 Wmk. 342 *Perf. 11*

N119 A239 10m emer & ultra, *lt grn* .35 .35

WHO Type

1964, Apr. 7

N120 A240 10m violet blk & red .35 .35

Minaret Type

1965, Jan. 20 Unwmk. *Perf. 11*

N121 A255 4m green & dk brn .35 .35

Arab League Type

1965, Mar. 22 Wmk. 342 *Perf. 11*

N122 A258 10m green, red & blk .35 .35
N123 A258 20m green & brown .35 .35

World Health Day Type

1965, Apr. 7 Wmk. 342 *Perf. 11*

N124 A259 10m brt green & crim .35 .35

Massacre Type

1965, Apr. 9 Photo.

N125 A260 10m slate blue & red .60 .60

ITU Type

1965, May 17 Wmk. 342 *Perf. 11*

N126 A261 5m sl grn, sl bl & yel .40 .40
N127 A261 10m car, rose red & gray .50 .50
N128 A261 35m vio bl, ultra & yel 1.40 .95
Nos. N126-N128 (3) 2.30 1.85

United Nations Type

5m, WHO Headquarters Building, Geneva. 10m, UN Refugee emblem. 35m, UNICEF emblem.

1966, Oct. 24 Wmk. 342 *Perf. 11*

N129 A288 5m rose & brt pur .35 .35
N130 A288 10m yel brn & brt pur .40 .40
N131 A288 35m brt green & brt pur .80 .80
Nos. N129-N131 (3) 1.55 1.55

Victory Day Type

Wmk. 342

1966, Dec. 23 Photo. *Perf. 11½*

N132 A290 10m olive & car rose .40 .40

Arab Publicity Week Type

Perf. 11x11½

1967, Mar. 22 Photo. Wmk. 342

N133 A294 10m vio blue & brn .35 .35

Labor Day Type

Perf. 11½x11

1967, May 1 Photo. Wmk. 342

N134 A296 10m olive & sepia .35 .35

OCCUPATION AIR POST STAMPS

Catalogue values for unused stamps in this section are for Never Hinged items.

Nos. C39-C50 Overprinted Type "b" in Black, Carmine or Red

Perf. 13x13½

1948, May 15 Wmk. 195

NC1 AP3 2m red org (Bk) .75 .75
NC2 AP3 3m dk brn (C) .75 .75
NC3 AP3 5m red brn (Bk) .75 .75
NC4 AP3 7m dp yel org (Bk) 1.05 1.05
NC5 AP3 8m green (C) 1.05 1.05
NC6 AP3 10m violet 1.20 1.20
NC7 AP3 20m brt bl 1.90 1.90
NC8 AP3 30m brn vio (Bk) 4.50 4.50
NC9 AP3 40m car rose (Bk) 3.00 3.00
NC10 AP3 50m Prus grn 4.00 4.00
NC11 AP3 100m olive grn 6.75 6.75
NC12 AP3 200m dark gray 34.00 34.00
Nos. NC1-NC12 (12) 59.70 59.70

Nos. NC1-NC12 Overprinted in Black with Three Bars to Obliterate Portrait

1953

NC13 AP3 2m red org 1.90 1.90
NC14 AP3 3m dk brn 1.20 1.20
NC15 AP3 5m red brn 20.00 20.00
NC16 AP3 7m dp yel org 1.25 1.25
NC17 AP3 8m green 3.75 3.75
NC18 AP3 10m violet 3.75 3.75
NC19 AP3 20m brt bl 3.75 3.75
NC20 AP3 30m brn vio 3.75 3.75
NC21 AP3 40m car rose 6.75 6.75
NC22 AP3 50m Prus grn 28.00 28.00
NC23 AP3 100m olive grn 115.00 115.00
NC24 AP3 200m dk gray 15.00 15.00
Nos. NC13-NC24 (12) 204.10 204.10

Nos. NC1-NC3, NC6, NC10, NC11 with Additional Overprint in Various Colors

1953

NC25 AP3 2m red org (Bk + Bl) 1.00 1.00
NC26 AP3 3m dk brn (Bk + RV) 19.00 19.00
NC27 AP3 5m red brn (Bk) 2.75 2.75
NC28 AP3 10m vio (R + G) 28.00 28.00
NC29 AP3 50m Prus grn (R + RV) 8.75 8.75
NC30 AP3 100m ol grn (R + Bk) 62.50 62.50
Nos. NC25-NC30 (6) 122.00 122.00

Nos. C65-C66 Overprinted Type "b" in Black or Red

1955 Wmk. 195 *Perf. 13x13½*

NC31 AP4 5m red brn 7.00 5.75
NC32 AP4 15m ol grn (R) 10.00 8.25

United Arab Republic

OAP1

Designs: 80m, Al Azhar University. 115m, Temple of Queen Nefertari, Abu Simbel. 140m, Ramses II, Abu Simbel.

Perf. 11½x11

1963, Oct. 24 Photo. Wmk. 342

NC33 OAP1 80m blk & brt bl 2.50 2.50
NC34 OAP1 115m blk & yel 3.50 3.50
NC35 OAP1 140m bl, ultra & org red 4.00 4.00
Nos. NC33-NC35 (3) 10.00 10.00

Cairo Tower Type, 1964

1964, Nov. 2 Unwmk. *Perf. 11x11½*

NC36 AP11 50m dl vio & lt bl 1.25 1.25

World Meteorological Day Type

1965, Mar. 23 Wmk. 342 *Perf. 11*

NC37 AP12 80m dk bl & org 3.00 3.00

Tutankhamun Type of 1965

1965, July 1 Photo. *Perf. 11*

NC38 AP13 10m brn org & brt grn 1.75 1.75

OCCUPATION SPECIAL DELIVERY STAMP

Catalogue values for unused stamps in this section are for Never Hinged items.

No. E4 Overprinted Type "b" in Carmine

1948 Wmk. 195 *Perf. 13x13½*

NE1 SD1 40m dl brn & pale gray 12.50 12.50

OCCUPATION POSTAGE DUE STAMPS

Catalogue values for unused stamps in this section are for Never Hinged items.

Postage Due Stamps of Egypt, 1927-41, Overprinted Type "a" in Black or Rose

1948 Wmk. 195 *Perf. 13x13½*

NJ1 D7 2m orange 2.25 *2.40*
NJ2 D7 4m green (R) 1.60 *2.00*
NJ3 D7 6m gray green 1.60 *2.00*
NJ4 D7 8m brown violet 1.60 *2.00*
NJ5 D7 10m brick red 1.60 *2.00*
NJ6 D7 12m rose lake 1.60 *2.00*

Overprinted Type "b" in Red

Perf. 14

Size: 22x28mm

NJ7 D7 30m purple 5.00 *9.00*
Nos. NJ1-NJ7 (7) 15.25 *21.40*

ELOBEY, ANNOBON & CORISCO

ˌel-ə-ˈbā, ˌan-ə-ˈbän and kə-ˈris-ˌkō

LOCATION — A group of islands near the Guinea Coast of western Africa.
GOVT. — Spanish colonial possessions administered as part of the Continental Guinea District. A second district under the same governor-general included Fernando Po.
AREA — 13¾ sq. mi.
POP. — 2,950 (estimated 1910)
CAPITAL — Santa Isabel

100 Centimos = 1 Peseta

King Alfonso XIII — A1

1903 Unwmk. Typo. *Perf. 14*

Control Numbers on Back

1 A1 ¼c carmine .80 .55
2 A1 ½c dk violet .80 .55
3 A1 1c black .80 .55
4 A1 2c red .80 .55
5 A1 3c dk green .80 .55
6 A1 4c dk blue grn .80 .55
7 A1 5c violet .80 .55
8 A1 10c rose lake 1.60 1.60
9 A1 15c orange buff 4.75 1.75
10 A1 25c dark blue 8.25 6.00
11 A1 50c red brown 10.00 10.50
12 A1 75c black brn 10.00 *14.50*
13 A1 1p orange red 16.00 *20.00*
14 A1 2p chocolate 44.00 *60.00*
15 A1 3p dp olive grn 65.00 *75.00*
16 A1 4p claret 150.00 100.00
17 A1 5p blue green 175.00 110.00
18 A1 10p dull blue 325.00 165.00
Nos. 1-18 (18) 815.20 568.20
Set, never hinged 1,500.

Dated "1905"

1905 Control Numbers on Back

19 A1 1c carmine 1.40 .70
20 A1 2c dp violet 5.25 .70
21 A1 3c black 1.40 .70
22 A1 4c dull red 1.40 .70
23 A1 5c dp green 1.40 .70
24 A1 10c blue grn 4.75 .90
25 A1 15c violet 5.25 4.75
26 A1 25c rose lake 5.25 4.75
27 A1 50c orange buff 9.50 7.25
28 A1 75c dark blue 9.50 7.25
29 A1 1p red brown 19.50 16.00
30 A1 2p black brn 21.00 22.50
31 A1 3p orange red 21.00 23.00
32 A1 4p dk brown 160.00 72.50
33 A1 5p bronze grn 170.00 80.00
34 A1 10p claret 375.00 225.00
Nos. 19-34 (16) 811.60 467.40
Set, never hinged 1,500.

Nos. 19-22 Surcharged in Black or Red

1906

35 A1 10c on 1c rose (Bk) 11.50 6.50
a. Inverted surcharge 11.50 6.50
b. Value omitted 30.00 16.00
c. Frame omitted 16.00 7.50
d. Double surcharge 11.50 6.50
e. Surcharged "15 cents" 30.00 16.00
f. Surcharged "25 cents" 52.50 22.50
g. Surcharged "50 cents" 37.50 22.50
h. "1906" omitted 17.50 7.50
36 A1 15c on 2c dp vio (R) 11.50 6.50
a. Frame omitted 12.50 6.50
b. Surcharged "25 cents" 16.00 9.00
c. Inverted surcharge 11.50 6.50
d. Double surcharge 11.50 6.50
37 A1 25c on 3c blk (R) 11.50 6.50
a. Inverted surcharge 11.50 6.50
b. Double surcharge 11.50 6.50
c. Surcharged "15 cents" 16.00 6.50
d. Surcharged "50 cents" 25.00 11.00
38 A1 50c on 4c red (Bk) 11.50 6.50
a. Inverted surcharge 11.50 6.50
b. Value omitted 35.00 17.50
c. Frame omitted 17.50 8.00
e. Double surcharge 11.50 6.50
f. "1906" omitted 17.50 8.00
g. Surcharged "10 cents" 32.50 16.00
h. Surcharged "25 cents" 32.50 16.00
Nos. 35-38 (4) 46.00 26.00

Eight other surcharges were prepared but not issued: 10c on 50c, 75c, 1p, 2p and 3p; 15c on 50c and 5p; 50c on 5c.

Exist with surcharges in different colors; #35 in blue, red or violet, #36 in black or violet, #37 in black or violet, #38 in blue, violet or red. Value, set of 10, $135.

King Alfonso XIII — A2

1907 Control Numbers on Back

39 A2 1c dk violet .60 .45
40 A2 2c black .60 .45
41 A2 3c red orange .60 .45
42 A2 4c dk green .60 .45
43 A2 5c blue green .60 .45
44 A2 10c violet 6.25 5.50
45 A2 15c carmine 2.00 1.75
46 A2 25c orange 2.00 1.75
47 A2 50c blue 2.00 1.75
48 A2 75c brown 6.75 2.75
49 A2 1p black brn 11.00 4.75
50 A2 2p orange red 14.50 8.00
51 A2 3p dk brown 14.00 9.00
52 A2 4p bronze grn 22.50 8.50
53 A2 5p claret 27.50 10.00
54 A2 10p rose 60.00 27.50
Nos. 39-54 (16) 171.50 83.50
Set, never hinged 350.00

Stamps of 1907 Surcharged

1908-09 Black Surcharge

55 A2 5c on 3c red org ('09) 2.25 1.25
56 A2 5c on 4c dk grn ('09) 2.25 1.25
57 A2 5c on 10c violet 4.50 5.00
58 A2 25c on 10c violet 22.50 15.00
Nos. 55-58 (4) 31.50 22.50

1910 Red Surcharge

59 A2 5c on 1c dark violet 1.75 .90
60 A2 5c on 2c black 1.75 .90

Nos. 55-60 exist with surcharge inverted (value set, $125 unused or used); with double surcharge, one black, one red (value set, $300 unused or used); with "PARA" omitted (value set, $150.00 unused or used)

The same 5c surcharge was also applied to Nos. 45-54, but these were not issued (value set, $250).

In 1909, stamps of Spanish Guinea replaced those of Elobey, Annobon and Corisco.

Revenue stamps surcharged as above were unauthorized although some were postally used.

For postally valid examples similar to the item shown above see Rio de Oro Nos. 44-45 and Spanish Guinea Nos. 98-101C.

For revenue stamps with the arms at the left surcharged for postal use see Spanish Guinea Nos. 8A-8J.

EPIRUS

i-ˈpī-rəs

LOCATION — A region of southeastern Europe, now divided between Greece and Albania.

During the First Balkan War (1912-13), this territory was occupied by the Greek army, and the local Greek majority wished to be united with Greece. Italy and Austria-Hungary favored its inclusion in the newly created Albania, however, which both powers expected to dominate. Greek forces were withdrawn subsequently in early 1914. The local population resisted inclusion in Albania and established the Autonomous Republic of Northern Epirus on Feb. 28, 1914. Resistance to Albanian control continued until October, when Greece reoccupied the country. Northern Epirus was administered as an integral part of Greece, and it was expected that Greece's annexation of the territory would become official following World War I. Instead, in 1916, Italian pressure and its own military reverses in Anatolia caused Greece to withdraw from Epirus and to formally cede the territory to Albania.

100 Lepta = 1 Drachma

Chimarra Issue

Double-headed Eagle, Skull and Crossbones — A1

Handstamped

1914, Feb. 10 Unwmk. *Imperf.*

Control Mark in Blue

Without Gum

1	A1	1 l black & blue		*475.00*	250.00
a.		Tête-bêche pair			3,000.
2	A1	5 l blue & red		*475.00*	250.00
3	A1	10 l red & blk		*475.00*	250.00
4	A1	25 l blue & red		*475.00*	250.00
		Nos. 1-4 (4)		*1,900.*	1,000.

All values exist without control mark. This mark is a solid blue oval, about 12x8mm, containing the colorless Greek letters "SP," the first two letters of Spiromilios, the Chimarra commander.

All four exist with denomination inverted and the 1 l, 5 l and 10 l with denomination double.

The values above are for the first printing on somewhat transparent shiny, white, thin, wove paper, which is sometimes known as "rice paper."

A second printing was made from original handstamps, on similar thin wove paper, but not transluscent, known as "Spetsiotis Reprints." Value, unused or canceled to order, each $55. Later printings were made from original handstamps on other papers, generally thicker and whiter, sometimes surfaced. Value, unused or canceled to order, each $45.

Values above are for genuine stamps expertized by knowledgeable authorities. Most of the stamps offered as Nos. 1-4 in the marketplace are forgeries. Most resemble the stamps from the second reprinting, but the designs differ in details of the lettering, monogram and skull. Such forgeries have only nominal commercial value.

Some experts question the official character of this issue.

Argyrokastro Issues

Stamps of Turkey surcharged "AUTONOMOUS EPIRUS" and new denominations in several formats in Greek currency.

On Turkish stamps of 1908

No. 4A

No. 4B

1914, Mar. 2

4A	A19	1d on 2½pi (#137)	9.50	10.00
4B	A19	2d on 2½pi (#137)	9.50	10.00

No. 4C

No. 4D

4C	A19	5d on 25pi (#140)	75.00	80.00
4D	A19	5d on 50pi (#141)	115.00	120.00

On Turkish stamps of 1909-10

4E	A21	5 l on 5pa (#151)	75.00	—

No. 4F

No. 4G

4F	A21	5 l on 10pa (#152)	3.00	3.00
4G	A21	10 l (oval "O") on 20pa (#153)	2.00	2.00
a.		Double surcharge	75.00	

No. 4H

No. 4I

4H	A21	10 l (round "O") on 20pa (#153)	2.00	2.00
a.		Double surcharge	75.00	
4I	A21	20 l on 1pi (#154)	2.00	2.00
a.		Double surcharge	75.00	

No. 4J

No. 4K

4J	A21	25 l on 1pi (#154)	2.00	2.00
a.		Double surcharge	75.00	
4K	A21	40 l on 2pi (#155)	3.00	3.00

No. 4L

No. 4M

4L	A21	80 l on 2pi (#155)	3.00	3.00
4M	A21	1d on 5pi (#157)	12.00	12.00

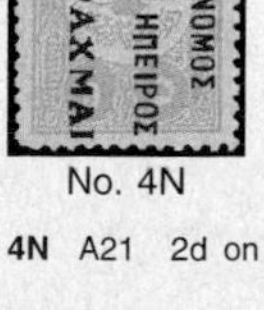

No. 4N

No. 4O

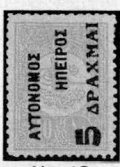

4N	A21	2d on 5pi (#157)	12.00	12.00
4O	A21	5d on 10pi (#158)	75.00	*80.00*
a.		Double surcharge		
4P	A21	5d on 10pa (#152)	125.00	*150.00*
4Q	A21	5d on 20pa (#153)	125.00	*150.00*
4R	A21	5d on 1pi (#154)	125.00	*150.00*
4S	A21	5d on 50pi (#160)	125.00	*150.00*

On Turkish stamps of 1909-11 (with "Béhié")

4T	A21	5 l on 10pa (#161)	75.00
4U	A21	10 l (oval "O") on 20pa (#162)	75.00
4V	A21	10 l (round "O") on 20pa (#162)	75.00
4W	A21	20 l on 1pi (#163)	75.00
4X	A21	25 l on 1pi (#163)	75.00
4Y	A21	40 l on 2pi (#164)	75.00
4Z	A21	80 l on 2pi (#164)	75.00
4AA	A21	5d on 10pa (#161)	125.00
4BB	A21	5d on 20pa (#162)	125.00
4CC	A21	5d on 1pi (#163)	125.00

On Turkish Printed Matter stamps of 1910-11

No. 4DD

No. 4EE

4DD	A21	30 l on 2pa on 5pa (#P67)	80.00
4EE	A21	50 l on 2pa on 5pa (#P67)	80.00

No. 4FF

4FF	A21	30 l on 2pa (#P68)	2.00	2.00
4GG	A21	50 l on 2pa (#P68)	2.00	2.00

Provisional Government Issues

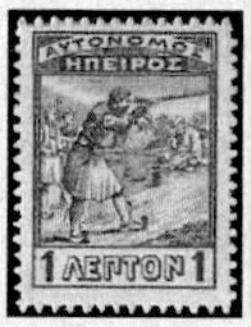

Infantryman with Rifle
A2 A3

Serrate Roulette 13½

1914, Mar. Litho.

5	A2	1 l orange	.50	.95
6	A2	5 l green	.50	.95
7	A3	10 l carmine	.50	.95
8	A3	25 l deep blue	.50	.95
9	A2	50 l brown	1.35	1.25
10	A2	1d violet	2.00	2.25
11	A2	2d blue	13.50	13.50
12	A2	5d gray green	17.50	17.50
		Nos. 5-12 (8)	36.35	38.30

Issue dates: 10 l, 25 l, Mar. 5; balance of set, Mar. 26.

Flag of Epirus — A5

1914, Aug. 28

15	A5	1 l brown & blue	.40	*.40*
16	A5	5 l green & blue	.40	*.40*
17	A5	10 l rose red & blue	.45	*.65*
18	A5	25 l dk blue & blue	1.00	1.00
19	A5	50 l violet & blue	1.00	1.00
20	A5	1d carmine & blue	5.75	*6.00*
21	A5	2d orange & blue	1.50	*2.00*
22	A5	5d dk green & blue	9.50	10.00
		Nos. 15-22 (8)	20.00	*21.45*

Koritsa Issue

A7

1914, Sept. 25

26	A7	25 l dk blue & blue	6.00	5.00
27	A7	50 l violet & blue	12.00	*13.00*

Nos. 26 and 27 were issued at Koritsa (Korce) to commemorate that city's occupation by Epirot forces.

Chimarra Issues

King Constantine I — A8

1914, Oct.

28	A8	1 l yellow green	130.00	75.00
29	A8	2 l red	115.00	42.50
30	A8	5 l dark blue	115.00	75.00
31	A8	10 l orange brown	77.50	27.50
32	A8	20 l carmine	85.00	60.00
33	A8	25 l gray blue	110.00	75.00
33A	A8	50 l yellow green	165.00	85.00
33B	A8	1d carmine	165.00	85.00
33C	A8	2d pale yellow green	250.00	120.00
33D	A8	5d orange brown	425.00	280.00
		Nos. 28-33D (10)	1,637.	925.00

Nos. 28-33D were printed by Papachrysanthou, Athens. The papermaker's watermark "PARCHIMINE JOHANNOT" appears on some stamps in the set.

1911-23 Issues of Greece Overprinted

1914, Aug. 24 *Perf. Perf. 11 ½*

34	A24	1 l green	62.50	62.50
35	A25	2 l carmine	52.50	52.50
36	A24	3 l vermilion	52.50	52.50
37	A26	5 l green	52.50	52.50
38	A24	10 l carmine	65.00	65.00
39	A25	20 l slate	87.50	87.50
40	A25	25 l blue	185.00	185.00
41	A26	50 l violet brn	225.00	225.00
		Nos. 34-41 (8)	782.50	782.50

The 2 l and 3 l are engraved stamps of the 1911-21 issue; the others are lithographed stamps of the 1912-23 issue.

Overprint reads: "Greek Chimarra 1914."

Stamps of this issue are with or without a black monogram (S.S., for S. Spiromilios) in manuscript. Counterfeits are plentiful.

Moschopolis Issue

A9
Arms

A10
Ancient Epirot Coins/Medals

1914, Sept. Engr. *Perf. 14 ½*

42	A9	1 l yellow brown	.80	*3.00*
43	A9	2 l black	.80	*3.00*
44	A9	3 l yellow	.80	*3.00*
45	A9	5 l green	.80	*3.00*
46	A9	10 l red	.80	*3.00*
47	A9	25 l deep blue	.80	*3.00*
48	A9	30 l violet	.80	*3.00*
49	A9	40 l olive gray	.80	*3.00*
50	A9	50 l violet black	.80	*3.00*
51	A10	1d yellow brown & olive	4.75	*10.00*
52	A10	2d carmine & gray	4.50	*10.00*
53	A10	3d gray green & red brown	5.00	*10.00*
54	A10	5d olive & yellow brown	4.00	*10.00*

55	A10	10d orange & blue	5.00	*13.00*
56	A10	25d violet & black	5.00	*18.00*
		Nos. 42-56 (15)	35.45	*98.00*

Nos. 42-56 were privately printed in early 1914. In June 1914, the Epirots occupied Moschopolis (Voskopoj), and these stamps were authorized for use by the local military commander in Sept. After the occupation of Moschopolis by Greek forces in Nov., remaining stocks of this issue were sent to Athens, where they were destroyed in 1931.

All values exist imperf., and all but the 5 l and 10 l stamps exist in different colors. For details, see the *Scott Classic Specialized Catalogue of Stamps and Covers.*

The 1d exists with center omitted. Value $100. The 1d, 2d, 10d and 25d exist with center inverted. Values, each $65.

Stamps of the following designs were locals, privately produced. Issued primarily for propaganda and for philatelic purposes, their postal use is in dispute. The 1920 design is a fantasy item, created long after Epirus was annexed by Albania.

From 1914: 1st design, 3 varieties. 2nd design, 6 varieties. 3rd design, 7 varieties.

From 1920: 4th design, 4 varieties.

OCCUPATION STAMPS

Issued under Greek Occupation

Greek Occupation Stamps of 1913 Overprinted Horizontally

Serrate Roulette 13½

1914-15 Black Overprint Unwmk.

N1	O1	1 l brown	.80	.80
b.		Inverted overprint	25.00	25.00
c.		Double overprint	25.00	25.00
d.		Double overprint, one inverted	25.00	25.00
N2	O2	2 l red	.80	.80
b.		2 l rose	1.25	1.25
c.		As #N2, inverted overprint	25.00	25.00
d.		As "b", inverted overprint	30.00	30.00
e.		As #N2, double overprint	25.00	*30.00*
f.		As "b", double overprint	30.00	30.00
g.		As #N2, double overprint, one inverted	25.00	25.00
N4	O2	3 l orange	.80	.80
b.		Inverted overprint	19.00	16.50
c.		Double overprint	19.00	16.50
d.		Double overprint, one inverted	25.00	25.00
N5	O1	5 l green	2.00	2.00
b.		Inverted overprint	35.00	35.00
N6	O1	10 l rose red	2.75	2.75
a.		Inverted overprint	50.00	50.00
b.		Double overprint	50.00	50.00
N7	O1	20 l violet	6.50	6.50
a.		Inverted overprint	50.00	50.00
b.		Double overprint	85.00	65.00
N8	O2	25 l pale blue	2.75	3.00
N9	O1	30 l gray green	14.00	14.50
N10	O2	40 l indigo	19.00	20.00
N11	O1	50 l dark blue	21.00	23.00
N12	O2	1d violet brown	135.00	145.00
a.		Inverted overprint	300.00	*225.00*
b.		Double overprint	375.00	*300.00*
		Nos. N1-N12 (11)	205.40	219.15

Red Overprint

N1a	O1	1 l brown	5.75
N2a	O2	2 l red	5.75
N4a	O2	3 l orange	5.75
N5a	O1	5 l green	5.75

Nos. N1a-N5a were not issued. Exist canceled.

Regular Issues of Greece, 1911-23, Ovptd. Reading Up

On Issue of 1911-21

1916 Engr.

N17	A24	3 l vermilion	11.50	11.50
a.		Overprint reading down	14.50	
N18	A26	30 l carmine rose	40.00	40.00
a.		Overprint reading down	225.00	
N19	A27	1d ultra	85.00	85.00
N20	A27	2d vermilion	95.00	95.00
N21	A27	3d carmine rose	130.00	130.00
N22	A27	5d ultra	—	—
a.		Double overprint	1,950.	1,950.
b.		Overprint reading down	725.00	
		Nos. N17-N22 (6)	361.50	361.50

On Issue of 1912-23

1916 Litho.

N23	A24	1 l green	2.75	2.75
a.		Overprint reading down	9.50	
N24	A25	2 l carmine	2.75	2.75
a.		Overprint reading down	9.50	
N25	A24	3 l vermilion	2.75	2.75
a.		Overprint reading down	14.00	
N26	A26	5 l green	2.75	2.75
a.		Overprint reading down	14.00	
N27	A24	10 l carmine	2.75	2.75
a.		Overprint reading down	27.50	
N28	A25	20 l slate	2.75	2.75
N29	A25	25 l blue	3.75	3.75
N30	A26	30 l rose	21.00	21.00
a.		Overprint reading down	250.00	
N31	A25	40 l indigo	16.00	16.00
a.		Overprint reading down	475.00	
N32	A26	50 l violet brown	25.00	25.00
		Nos. N23-N32 (10)	82.25	82.25

In each sheet, there are two varieties in the overprint. For listings, see the *Scott Classic Catalogue.*

Counterfeits exist of Nos. N1-N32.

Postage stamps issued in 1940-41, during Greek occupation, are listed under Greece.

EQUATORIAL GUINEA

ˌē-kwə-ˈtō-ē-əl ˈgi-nē

LOCATION — Gulf of Guinea, West Africa
GOVT. — Republic
AREA — 10,832 sq. mi.
POP. — 465,746 (1999 est.)
CAPITAL — Malabo

The Spanish provinces Fernando Po and Rio Muni united and became independent as the Republic of Equatorial Guinea, Oct. 12, 1968.

100 Centimos = 1 Peseta
100 centimos = 1 ekuele, bipkwele is plural (1973)
100 centimes = 1 CFA franc (1985)

Catalogue values for all unused stamps in this country are for Never Hinged items.

Clasped Hands and Laurel — A1

Unwmk.

1968, Oct. 12 Photo. *Perf. 13*

1	A1	1p	dp bl, gold & sep	.30	.30
2	A1	1.50p	dk grn, gold & brn	.30	.30
3	A1	6p	cop red, gold & brn	.30	.30
			Nos. 1-3 (3)	.90	.90

Attainment of independence, Oct. 12, 1968.

Torch, Bow and Arrows — A4

1972 Photo. *Perf. 11½*

15	A4	50p	ocher & multi	1.50	.50

"3rd Triumphal Year."

Pres. Francisco Macias Nguema — A2

1970, Jan. 27 *Perf. 13x12½*

4	A2	50c	dl org, brn & crim	.25	.25
5	A2	1p	pink, grn & lil	.25	.25
6	A2	1.50p	pale ol, brn & bl grn	.25	.25
7	A2	2p	buff, grn & ol	.25	.25
8	A2	2.50p	pale grn, dk grn & dk bl	.30	.25
9	A2	10p	bis, Prus bl & vio brn	1.00	.25
10	A2	25p	gray, blk & brn	2.10	.25
			Nos. 4-10 (7)	4.40	1.75

Pres. Macias Nguema and Cock — A3

1971, Apr. Photo. *Perf. 13*

11	A3	3p	lt bl & multi	.25	.25
12	A3	5p	buff & multi	.30	.25
13	A3	10p	pale lilac & multi	.75	.25
14	A3	25p	pale grn & multi	1.50	.35
			Nos. 11-14 (4)	2.80	1.10

2nd anniv. of independence, Oct. 12, 1970.

Upon achieving independence from Spain in 1968, Francisco Macias Nguema was elected the first president of Equatorial Guinea. By May 1971, Nguema controlled a government that essentially performed no functions except internal security. From 1972 to 1979, the country's main post office was padlocked and completely inoperative. Nonetheless, European agents continued to produce postage stamps for Equatorial Guinea that were promoted by so-called press releases from Madrid, Spain.

With the exception of Nos. 16-25, the editors question whether any of the stamps described below could have reached Equatorial Guinea or been placed on sale in that country. As such, they do not meet the criteria for listing in the Scott catalogue. See the Catalogue Listing Policy section in the catalogue introduction for additional details.

Apollo 15, set of seven, 1p, 3p, 5p, 8p, 10p, airmail 15p, 25p, plus two airmail semi-postal gold foil perf. 200p+25p, imperf. 250p+50p, and two souv. sheets, perf. 25p+200p, imperf. 50p+250p, issued Jan. 28. Nos. 7201-7211.

1972 Winter Olympics, Sapporo, set of seven, 1p, 2p, 3p, 5p, 8p, airmail 15p, 50p, plus two airmail semi-postal gold foil perf., imperf., 200p+25p, 250p+50p, and two souv. sheets, perf. 200p+25p, imperf. 250p+50p, issued Feb. 3, 1972. Nos. 7212-7222.

Christmas, paintings, set of seven, 1p, 3p, 5p, 8p, 10p, airmail 15p, 25p, plus two airmail semi-postal gold foil perf. 200p+25p, imperf. 250p+50p, and two souv. sheets, perf. 25p+200p, imperf. 50p+250p (Virgin and Child by da Vinci, Murillo, Raphael, Mabuse, van der Weyden, Durer), issued Feb. 20. Nos. 7223-7233.

Easter, set of seven, 1p, 3p, 5p, 8p, 10p, airmail 15p, 25p, plus two airmail semi-postal gold foil perf., imperf., 200p+25p, 250p+50p (designs by Velazquez and El Greco), two souv. sheets, perf. (25p, 200p), and imperf. 250p+50p, issued Apr. 28. Nos. 7234-7244.

1972 Summer Olympics, Munich, set of seven, 1p, 2p, 3p, 5p, 8p, airmail 15p, 50p, plus two airmail semi-postal souv. sheets, perf. 200p+25p, imperf. 250p+50p, and presentation folder with two gold foil, perf. 200p+25p, imperf. 250p+50p, issued May 5, 1972. Nos. 7245-7255.

Gold Medal Winners, Sapporo, set of seven, 1p, 2p, 3p, 5p, 8p, airmail 15p, 50p, plus 12 airmail semi-postal gold foil perf. 200p+25p (6), imperf. 250p+50p (6), imperf. souv. sheet 250p+50p, and perf. souv. sheet of two (25p, 200p), issued May 25. Nos. 7256-7276.

Black Gold Medal Winners, Munich, set of seven, 1p, 2p, 3p, 5p, 8p, airmail 15p, 50p, plus 18 gold foil airmail semi-postal perf. 200p+25p (9), imperf. 250p+50p (9), and two souv. sheets, perf. 200p+25p, imperf. 250p+50p, issued June 26. Nos. 7277-72103.

Olympic Games, Regatta in Kiel and Oberschleissheim, set of seven, 1p, 2p, 3p, 5p, 8p, airmail 15p, 50p, plus four airmail semi-postal gold foil, perf. 200p+25p (2), imperf. 250p+50p (2), and two souv. sheets, perf. 200p+25p, imperf. 250p+50p, issued July 25. Nos. 72104-72116.

1972 Summer Olympics, Munich, set of seven, 1p, 2p, 3p, 5p, 8p, airmail 15p, 50p, plus two airmail semi-postal souv. sheets, perf. 200p+25p, imperf. 250p+50p, issued Aug. 10, 1972; and 20 gold foil, perf. 200p+25p (10), imperf. 250+50p (10), issued Aug. 17. Nos. 72117-72145.

Olympic Equestrian Events, set of seven, 1p, 2p, 3p, 5p, 8p, airmail 15p, 50p, plus two airmail semi-postal souv. sheets, perf. 200p+25p, imperf. 250p+50p, two gold foil, perf. 200p+25p, imperf. 250p+50p, four gold foil souv. sheets of two, 200p+25p (2 perf., 2 imperf.), and 16 souv. sheets, perf. 200p+25p (8), imperf. 250p+50p (8), issued Aug. 24. Nos. 72146-72176.

Japanese Railroad Cent. (locomotives), set of seven, 1p, 3p, 5p, 8p, 10p, airmail 15p, 25p, plus 2 airmail semi-postal souv. sheets, perf. 200p+25p, imperf. 250p+50p, 11 gold foil souv. sheets of 1, perf. 200p+25p (9), imperf. 200p+25p (2), and 2 souv. sheets of 2, perf., imperf., 200p+25p, issued Sept. 21. Nos. 72177-72198.

Gold Medal Winners, Munich, set of seven, 1p, 2p, 3p, 5p, 8p, airmail 15p, 50p, plus two airmail semi-postal souv. sheets, perf. 200p+25p, imperf. 250p+50p, and four gold foil souv. sheets, perf. 200p+25p (2), imperf. 250p+50p (2), issued Oct. 30. Nos. 72199-72211.

Christmas and 500th Birth Anniv. of Lucas Cranach, Madonnas and Christmas seals, set of seven, 1p, 3p, 5p, 8p, 10p, airmail 15p, 25p (Giotto, Schongauer, Fouquet, de Morales, Fini, David, Sassetta), plus two airmail semi-postal souv. sheets, perf. 200p+25p, imperf. 250p+50p, 12 gold foil souv. sheets, perf. 200p+25p (6), imperf. 250p+50p (6), two souv. sheets of two, perf., imperf., 200p+25p, and ovptd. 200p+25p stamp, issued Nov. 22. Nos. 72212-72234.

American and Russian Astronaut Memorial, set of seven, 1p, 3p, 5p, 8p, 10p, airmail 15p, 25p, plus two airmail semi-postal souv. sheets, perf. 200p+25p, imperf. 250p+50p, and four gold foil ovptd. "Apollo 16 and 17" perf. 200p+25p (2), imperf. 250p+50p (2), issued Dec. 14. Nos. 72235-72247.

United Natl. Workers' Party Emblem — A5

1973	Litho.		*Perf. 13½x13*	
16 A5	1p	multi	.25	.25
17 A5	1.50p	multi	.25	.25
18 A5	2p	multi	.25	.25
19 A5	4p	multi	.30	.25
20 A5	5p	multi	.40	.25
	Nos. 16-20 (5)		1.45	1.25

Natl. Independence, 4th Anniv. — A6

Pres. Macias Nguema and: 1.50p, Agriculture. 2p, 4p, Education. 3p, 5p, Natl. defense.

1973			*Perf. 13½*	
21 A6	1.50p	multi	.25	.25
22 A6	2p	multi	.25	.25
23 A6	3p	multi	.35	.25
24 A6	4p	multi	.40	.25
25 A6	5p	multi	.60	.35
	Nos. 21-25 (5)		1.85	1.35

1973

Transatlantic Yacht Race, set of seven, 1p, 2p, 3p, 5p, 8p, airmail 15p, 50p, and two airmail semi-postal souv. sheets, perf. 200p+25p, imperf. 250p+50p, issued Jan. 22. Nos. 7301-7309.

Renoir paintings, set of seven, 1p, 2p, 3p, 5p, 8p, airmail 15p, 50p, plus two airmail semi-postal gold foil, perf. 200p+25p, imperf. 250p+50p, and two souv. sheets, perf. 200p+25p, imperf. 250p+50p, issued Feb. 22. Nos. 7310-7320.

Conquest of Venus (spacecraft), set of seven, 1p, 3p, 5p, 8p, 10p, airmail 5p, 25p, and two airmail semi-postal souv. sheets, perf. 200p+25p, imperf. 250p+50p, issued Mar. 22. Nos. 7321-7329.

Apollo 11-17 Flights, gold foil airmail semi-postal souv. sheets, perf. 200p+25p (7), 250p+50p (7), and four souv. sheets of two, perf. 200p+25p (2), imperf. 250p+50p (2), issued Mar. 22. Nos. 7330-7347.

Easter, paintings, set of seven, 1p, 3p, 5p, 8p, 10p, airmail 15p, 25p (Verrocchio, Perugino, Tintoretto, Witz, Pontormo), plus two airmail semi-postal souv. sheets, perf. 200p+25p, imperf. 250p+50p, and four gold foil issue of 1972 souv. sheets ovptd., perf. 200p+25p (2), imperf. 250p+50p (2), issued Apr. 25. Nos. 7348-7360.

Copernicus, 500th birth anniv. (US and USSR space explorations), four gold foil airmail semi-postal souv. sheets, perf. 200p+25p (2), imperf. 250p+50p (2), issued May 15. Nos. 7361-7364.

Tour de France bicycle race, set of seven, 1p, 2p, 3p, 5p, 8p, airmail 15p, 50p, and two airmail semi-postal souv. sheets, perf. 200p+25p, imperf. 250p+50p, issued May 22. Nos. 7365-7373.

Paintings, set of seven, 1p, 2p, 3p, 5p, 8p, airmail 15p, 50p, and two airmail semi-postal souv. sheets, 200p+25p, imperf. 250p+50p, issued June 29. Nos. 7374-7382.

1974 World Cup Soccer Championships, Munich, set of nine, 5c, 10c, 15c, 20c, 25c, 55c, 60c, airmail 5p, 70p, and two airmail souv. sheets, perf. 130p, imperf. 200p, issued Aug. 30. Nos. 7383-7393.

Rubens paintings, set of seven, 1p, 2p, 3p, 5p, 8p, airmail 15p, 50p, and two airmail semi-postal souv. sheets, perf. (25p, 200p), imperf. (50p, 250p), issued Sept. 23. Nos. 7394-73102.

1974 World Cup Soccer Championships, Munich, four gold foil airmail souv. sheets, perf. 130e (2), imperf. 200e (2), and two souv. sheets of two, perf. 130e, imperf. 200e, issued Oct. 24. Nos. 73103-73108.

Christmas, paintings, set of seven, 1p, 3p, 5p, 8p, 10p, airmail 15p, 25p, and two airmail semi-postal souv. sheets, perf. 200p+25p, imperf. 250p+50p (Nativity, by van der Weyden, Bosco, de Carvajal, Mabuse, Lucas Jordan, P. Goecke, Maino, Fabriano, Lochner), issued Oct. 30. Nos. 73109-73117.

Apollo Program and J.F. Kennedy, two gold foil airmail semi-postals, perf. 200p+25p, imperf. 250p+50p, and two souv. sheets, perf. 200p+25p, imperf. 250p+50p, issued Nov. 10. Nos. 73118-73121.

World Cup Soccer (famous players), set of nine, 30c, 35c, 40c, 45c, 50c, 65c, 70c, airmail 8p, 60p, and two airmail souv. sheets, perf. 130p, imperf. 200p, issued Nov. 20. Nos. 73122-73132.

Princess Anne's Wedding, six gold foil airmail souv. sheets, perf., imperf., two sheets of one, each 250e, one sheet of two 250e, issued Dec. 17. Nos. 73133-73141.

Pablo Picasso Memorial (Blue Period paintings), set of seven, 30c, 35c, 40c, 45c, 50c, airmail 8e, 60e, and two airmail souv. sheets, perf. 130e, imperf. 200e, issued Dec. 20. Nos. 73142-73150.

1974

Copernicus, 500th birth anniv., set of seven, 5c, 10c, 15c, 20c, 4e, airmail 10e, 70e, two airmail souv. sheets, perf. 130e, imperf. 200e, issued Feb. 8, 1974; eight gold foil airmail souv. sheets, perf. 130e (3), 250e, imperf. 200e (3), 300e, and four souv. sheets of two, perf. 250e (2), imperf. 250e (2), issued Apr. 10. Nos. 7401-7421.

World Cup Soccer Championships (final games), set of nine, 75c, 80c, 85c, 90c, 95c, 1e, 1.25e, airmail 10e, 50e, and two airmail souv. sheets, perf. 130e, imperf. 200e, issued Feb. 28. Nos. 7422-7432.

Easter, paintings, set of seven, 1p, 3p, 5p, 8p, 10p, airmail 15p, 25p (Fra Angelico, Castagno, Allori, Multscher, della Francesca, Pleydenwurff, Correggio), and two airmail semi-postal souv. sheets, perf. 200p+25p, imperf. 250p+50p, issued Mar. 27. Nos. 7433-7441.

Holy Year 1975 (famous churches), set of seven, 5c, 10c, 15c, 20c, 3.50e, airmail 10e, 70e, and two airmail souv. sheets, perf. 130e, imperf. 200e, issued Apr. 11. Nos. 7442-7450.

World Cup Soccer (contemporary players), set of nine, 1.50, 1.75, 2, 2.25, 2.50, 3, 3.50e, airmail 10, 60e, and 2 airmail souv. sheets of 2, perf. (2x65e), imperf. (2x100e), issued Apr. 30. Nos. 7451-7461.

UPU Cent. (transportation from messenger to rocket), set of seven, 60c, 70c, 80c, 1e, 1.50e, airmail 30e, 50e, and two airmail souv. sheets, perf. 225e, imperf. (150e, 150e), issued May 30; three airmail deluxe souv. sheets, 130e, and 2x130e, issued June 8. Nos. 7462-7472A.

Picasso Memorial (Pink Period paintings), set of seven, 55c, 60c, 65c, 70c, 75c, airmail 10e, 50e, and two airmail souv. sheets, perf. 130e, imperf. 200e, issued June 28. Nos. 7473-7481.

World Cup Soccer Championships, gold foil airmail souv. sheets, four sheets of one, 130e (2), 250e (2), two sheets of two (2x130e; 2x250e), issued July 8. Nos. 7482-7487.

Aleksander Solzhenitsyn, two gold foil airmail souv. sheets, perf. 250e, imperf. 300e, issued July 25. Nos. 7488-7489.

Opening of American West, set of seven, 30c, 35c, 40c, 45c, 50c, airmail 8p, 60p, and two souv. sheets, perf. 130p, imperf. 200p, issued July 30. Nos. 7490-7498.

Flowers, set of 14, 5c, 10c, 15c, 20c, 25c, 1p, 3p, 5p, 8p, 10p, airmail 5p, 15p, 25p, 70p, and 4 airmail souv. sheets, perf. 130p, 25p+200p, imperf. 200p, 50p+250p, issued Aug. 20. Nos. 7499-74116.

Christmas, set of seven, 60c, 70c, 80c, 1e, 1.50e, airmail 30e, 50e, and two souv. sheets, perf. 225e, imperf. 300e, issued Sept. 16. Nos. 74117-74125.

Barcelona Soccer Team, 75th anniv., set of seven, 1e, 3e, 5e, 8e, 10e, airmail 15e, 60e, miniature sheet of seven plus label, two airmail souv. sheets, perf. 200e, imperf. 300e, and two gold foil airmail souv. sheets, perf., imperf., 200e each, issued Sept. 25. Nos. 74126-74137.

UPU Cent. and ESPANA 75, set of seven, 1.25e, 1.50e, 1.75e, 2e, 2.25e, airmail 35e, 60e, and 2 airmail souv. sheets, perf. 225e, imperf. 300e, issued Oct. 9; 6 gold foil sheets, perf. 250e, 250e, 2x250e, imperf. 300e, 300e, 2x300e, issued Oct. 14. Nos. 74138-74152.

Nature Protection

Australian Animals, set of seven, 80c, 85c, 90c, 95c, 1e, airmail 15e, 40e, and two airmail souv. sheets, perf. 130e, imperf. 200e, issued Oct. 25. Nos. 74153-74161.

African Animals, set of seven, 55c, 60c, 65c, 70c, 75c, airmail 10e, 70e, and two airmail souv. sheets, perf. 130e, imperf. 200e, issued Nov. 6. Nos. 74162-74170.

Australian and South American Birds, set of 14, 1.25p, 1.50p, 1.75p, 2p, 2.25p, 2.50p, 2.75p, 3p, 3.50p, 4p, airmail 20p, 25p, 30p, 35p, and four souv. sheets, perf. 130p (2), imperf. 200p (2), issued Nov. 26. Nos. 74171-74188.

Endangered Species, set of 15, 10c, 15c, 20c, 25c, 30c, 35c, 40c, 45c, 50c, 55c, 60c, 1e, 2e, airmail 10e, 70e, se-tenant in sheet of 15, issued Dec. 17. Nos. 74189-74203.

Monkeys, various species, set of 16, 5c, 10c, 15c, 20c, 25c, 30c, 35c, 40c, 45c, 50c, 55c, 60c, 1e, 2e, airmail 10e, 70e, se-tenant in sheet of 16, issued Dec. 27. Nos. 74204-74219.

Cats, various species, set of 16, 5c, 10c, 15c, 20c, 25c, 30c, 35c, 40c, 45c, 50c, 55c, 60c, 1e, 2e, airmail 10e, 70e, se-tenant in sheet of 16, issued Dec. 27. Nos. 74220-74235.

Fish, various species, set of 16, 5c, 10c, 15c, 20c, 25c, 30c, 35c, 40c, 45c, 50c, 55c, 60c, 1e, 2e, airmail 10e, 70e, se-tenant in sheet of 16, issued Dec. 27. Nos. 74236-74251.

Butterflies, various species, set of 16, 5c, 10c, 15c, 20c, 25c, 30c, 35c, 40c, 45c, 50c, 55c, 60c, 1e, 2e, airmail 10e, 70e, se-tenant in sheet of 16, issued Dec. 27. Nos. 74252-74267.

1975

Picasso Memorial (paintings from last period), set of seven, 5c, 10c, 15c, 20c, 25c, airmail 5e, 70e, and two souv. sheets, perf. 130e, imperf. 200e, issued Jan. 27. Nos. 7501-7509.

ARPHILA 75 Phil. Exhib., Paris, 8 gold foil airmail souv. sheets: perf. 3 sheets of 1 250e, 1 sheet of 2 250e, imperf. 3 sheets of 1 300e, 1 sheet of 2 300e, issued Jan. 27. Nos. 7510-7517.

Easter and Holy Year 1975, set of seven, 60c, 70c, 80c, 1e, 1.50e, airmail 30e, 50e, and two airmail souv. sheets, perf. 225e, imperf. 300e, issued Feb. 15. Nos. 7518-7526.

1976 Winter Olympics, Innsbruck, set of 11, 5c, 10c, 15c, 20c, 25c, 30c, 35c, 40c, 45c, 25e, 70e, two airmail souv. sheets, perf. 130e, imperf. 200e, and two gold foil airmail souv. sheets, 1 sheet of 1 250e, 1 sheet of 2 250e, issued Mar. 10. Nos. 7527-7541.

Don Quixote, set of seven, 30c, 35c, 40c, 45c, 50c, airmail 25e, 60e, and two airmail souv. sheets, perf. 130e, imperf. 200e, issued Apr. 4. Nos. 7542-7550.

American Bicent. (1st issue), set of nine, 5c, 20c, 40c, 75c, 2e, 5e, 8e, airmail 25e, 30e, and two airmail souv. sheets, perf. 130e, imperf. 200e, issued Apr. 30. Nos. 7551-7561.

American Bicent. (2nd issue), set of nine, 10c, 30c, 50c, 1e, 3e, 6e, 10e, airmail 12e, 40e, and two airmail souv. sheets, perf. 130e, imperf. 200e, issued Apr. 30. Nos. 7562-7572.

American Bicent. (Presidents), set of 18, 5c, 10c, 20c, 30c, 40c, 50c, 75c, 1e, 2e, 3e, 5e, 6e, 8e, 10e, airmail 12e,

25e, 30e, 40e, four airmail souv. sheets, perf. 225e (2), imperf. 300e (2), and six embossed gold foil airmail souv. sheets, perf. 200e, 200e, 2x200e, imperf. 300e, 300e, 2x300e, issued July 4. Nos. 7573-75100.

Bull Fight, set of seven, 80c, 85c, 90c, 95c, 8e, airmail 35e, 40e, and two airmail souv. sheets, perf. 130e, imperf. 200e, issued May 26. Nos. 75101-75109.

Apollo-Soyuz Space Project, set of 11, 1e, 2e, 3e, 5e, 5.50e, 7e, 7.50e, 9e, 15e, airmail 20e, 30e, and two airmail souv. sheets, perf. 225e, imperf. 300e, issued June 20, 1975; airmail souv. sheet, perf. 250e, issued July 17. Nos. 75110-75123.

Famous Painters, Nudes, set of 16, 5c, 10c, 15c, 20c, 25c, 30c, 35c, 40c, 45c, 50c, 55c, 60c, 1e, 2e, airmail 10e, 70e (Egyptian Greek, Roman, Indian art, Goes, Durer, Liss, Beniort, Renoir, Gauguin, Stenlen, Picasso, Modigliani, Matisse, Padua), se-tenant in sheet of 16, and 20 airmail embossed gold foil souv. sheetlets, perf. 200p+25p (10), imperf. 250p+50p (10), issued Aug. 10. Nos. 75124-75159.

Conquerors of the Sea, set of 14, 30c, 35c, 40c, 45c, 50c, 55c, 60c, 65c, 70c, 75c, airmail 8p, 10p, 50p, 60p, and four airmail souv. sheets, perf. 130p (2), imperf. 200p (2), issued Sept. 5. Nos. 75160-75177.

Christmas and Holy Year, 1975, set of seven, 60c, 70c, 80c, 1e, 1.50e, airmail 30e, 50e (Jordan, Barocci, Vereycke, Rubens, Mengs, Del Castillo, Cavedone), two airmail souv. sheets, perf. 225e, imperf. 300e, plus four embossed gold foil souv. sheets, perf. 200e (2), imperf. 300e (2), and two gold foil miniature sheets of two, perf. 200e+200e, imperf. 300e+300e, issued Oct. Nos. 75178-75192.

President Macias, IWY, set of eight, 1.50e, 3e, 3.50e, 5e, 7e, 10e, airmail 100e, 300e, and two imperf. airmail souv. sheets (world events), 100e (US 2c Yorktown), 300e, issued Dec. 25. Nos. 75193-75202.

1976

Cavalry Uniforms, set of seven, 5c, 10c, 15c, 20c, 25c, airmail 5p, 70p, and two airmail souv. sheets, perf. 130p, imperf. 200p, issued Feb. 2. Nos. 7601-7609.

1976 Winter Olympics, Innsbruck, set of 11, 50c, 55c, 60c, 65c, 70c, 75c, 80c, 85c, 90c, airmail 35e, 60e, and two airmail souv. sheets, perf. 130e, imperf. 200e, issued Feb. Nos. 7610-7622.

1976 Summer Olympics, Montreal, Ancient to Modern Games, set of seven, 50c, 60c, 70c, 80c, 90c, airmail 35e, 60e, and two airmail souv. sheets, perf. 225e, imperf. 300e, issued Feb. Nos. 7623-7631.

1976 Summer Olympics, Montreal, set of seven, 50c, 60c, 70c, 80c, 90c, airmail 30e, 60e, plus two airmail souv. sheets, perf. 225e, imperf. 300e, four embossed gold foil airmail souv. sheets, per. 250e (2), imperf. 300e (2), and two imperf. miniature sheets of two, perf. 2x250e, imperf. 2x300e, issued Mar. 5. Nos. 7632-7646.

El Greco, paintings, set of seven, 1e, 3e, 5e, 8e, 10e, airmail 15e, 25e, and two airmail semi-postal souv. sheets, perf. 200e+25e, imperf. 250e+50e, issued Apr. 5. Nos. 7647-7655.

1976 Summer Olympics, modern games, set of 11, 50c, 55c, 60c, 65c, 70c, 75c, 80c, 85c, 90c, airmail 35e, 60e, plus two airmail souv. sheets, perf. 225e, imperf. 300e, four embossed gold foil airmail souv. sheets, perf. 250e (2), imperf. 300e (2), and two miniature sheets of two, perf. 2x250e, imperf. 2x300e, issued May 7. Nos. 7656-7674.

UN 30th Anniv., airmail souv. sheet, 250e, issued June. No. 7675.

Contemporary Automobiles, set of seven, 1p, 3p, 5p, 8p, 10p, airmail 15p, 25p, and two airmail semi-postal souv. sheets, perf. 200p+25p, imperf. 250p+50p, issued June 10. Nos. 7675-7684.

Nature Protection

European Animals, set of seven, 5c, 10c, 15c, 20c, 25c, airmail 5p, 70p, and two airmail souv. sheets, perf. 130p, imperf. 200p, issued July 1. Nos. 7685-7693.

Asian Animals, set of seven, 30c, 35c, 40c, 45c, 8p, airmail 50c, 60p, and two airmail souv. sheets, perf. 130p, imperf. 200p, issued Sept. 20. Nos. 7694-74102.

Asian Birds, set of seven, 55c, 60c, 65c, 70c, 75c, airmail 10p, 50p, and two airmail souv. sheets, perf. 130p, imperf. 200p, issued Sept. 20. Nos. 76103-76111.

European Birds, set of seven, 5c, 10c, 15c, 20c, 25c, airmail 5p, 70p, and two airmail souv. sheets, perf. 130p, imperf. 200p, issued Sept. 20. Nos. 76112-76120.

North American Birds, set of seven, 80c, 85c, 90c, 95c, 1p, airmail 15p, 40p, and two airmail souv. sheets, perf. 130p, imperf. 200p, issued Sept. 20. Nos. 76121-76129.

Motorcycle Aces, set of 16, two each 1e, 2e, 3e, 4e, 5e, 10e, 30e, 40e, in se-tenant blocks of eight diff. values, issued July 22. Nos. 76130-76145.

1976 Summer Olympics, Montreal, set of five, 10e, 25e se-tenant strip of 3, airmail 200e, and imperf. airmail souv. sheet, 300e, issued Aug. 7. Nos. 76146-76151.

South American Flowers, set of seven, 30c, 35c, 40c, 45c, 50c, airmail 8p, 60p, and two airmail souv. sheets, perf. 130p, imperf. 200p, issued Aug. 16. Nos. 76152-76160.

Oceania, set of seven, 80c, 85c, 90c, 95c, 1p, airmail 15p, 40p, and two airmail souv. sheets, perf. 130p, imperf. 200p, issued 1976. Nos. 76161-76169.

1977

Butterflies, set of seven, 80c, 85c, 90c, 95c, 8e, airmail 35e, 40e, and two airmail souv. sheets, perf. 130e, imperf. 200e, issued Jan. Nos. 7701-7709.

Madrid Real, 75th Anniv., set of nine, 2e, 4e, 5e, 8e, 10e, 15e, airmail 20e, 35e, 150e, issued Jan. Nos. 7710-7718.

Ancient Carriages, set of 16, 5c, 10c, 15c, 20c, 25c, 30c, 35c, 40c, 45c, 50c, 55c, 60c, 1e, 2e, airmail 10e, 70e, issued Feb. Nos. 7719-7734.

Chinese Art, set of seven, 60c, 70c, 80c, 1e, 1.50e, airmail 30e, 50e, and two airmail souv. sheets, perf. 130e, imperf. 200e, issued Feb. Nos. 7735-7743.

African Masks, set of seven, 5c, 10c, 15c, 20c, 25c, airmail 5e, 70e, and two airmail souv. sheets, perf. 130e, imperf. 200e, issued Mar. Nos. 7744-7752.

North American Animals, set of seven, 1.25e, 1.50e, 1.75e, 2e, 2.25e, airmail 20e, 50e, and two airmail souv. sheets, perf. 130e, imperf. 200e, issued 1977. Nos. 7753-7761.

World Cup Soccer Championships, Argentina '78 (famous players), set of eight, 2e, 4e, 5e, 8e, 10e, 15e, airmail 20e, 35e, and two airmail souv. sheets, perf. 150e, imperf. 250e, issued July 25. Nos. 7762-7771.

World Cup Soccer (famous teams), se-tenant set of eight, 2e, 4e, 5e, 8e, 10e, 15e, airmail 20e, 35e, and two gold foil embossed souv. sheets, 500e (AMPHILEX '77, Cutty Sark, Concorde), airmail 500e (World Cup), issued Aug. 25.Nos. 7772-7781.

Napoleon, Life and Battle Scenes, se-tenant sheet of 16, 5c, 10c, 15c, 20c, 25c, 30c, 35c, 40c, 45c, 50c, 55c, 60c, 1e, 2e, airmail 10e, 70e, issued Aug. 20. Nos. 7782-7797.

Napoleon, Military Uniforms, se-tenant sheet of 16, 5c, 10c, 15c, 20c, 25c, 30c, 35c, 40c, 45c, 50c, 55c, 60c, 1e, 2e, airmail 10e, 70e, issued Aug. 20. Nos. 7798-77113.

South American Animals, set of seven, 2.50e, 2.75e, 3e, 3.50e, 4e, airmail 25e, 35e, and two airmail souv. sheets, perf. 130e, imperf. 200e, issued Aug. Nos. 77114-77122.

USSR Space Program, 20th Anniv., set of eight, 2e, 4e, 5e, 8e, 10e, 15e, airmail 20e, 35e, and two airmail souv. sheets, imperf. 150e, perf. 250e, issued Dec. 15. Nos. 77123-77132.

1978

Ancient Sailing Ships, set of 12, 5c, 10c, 15c, 20c, 25c, airmail 5e, 70e, also 5e, 10e, 20e, 25e, 70e, plus four airmail souv. sheets, perf. 150e, 225e, imperf. 250e, 300e, and two embossed gold foil airmail souv. sheets, perf., imperf., 500e, issued Jan. 6. Nos. 7801-7818.

1980 Winter Olympics, Lake Placid, set of five, 5e, 10e, 20e, 25e, airmail 70e, two airmail souv. sheets, perf. 150e, imperf. 250e, and two embossed gold foil airmail souv. sheets, perf., imperf., 500e, issued Jan. 17. Nos. 7819-7827.

1980 Summer Olympics, Moscow, set of eight, 2e, 3e, 5e, 8e, 10e, 15e, airmail 30e, 50e, two airmail souv. sheets, perf. 150e, imperf. 250e, and two embossed gold foil airmail souv. sheets, perf., imperf., 500e, issued Jan. 17. Nos. 7828-7839.

1980 Summer Olympic Water Games, Tallinn, set of five, 5e, 10e, 20e, 25e, airmail 70e, two airmail souv. sheets, perf. 150e, imperf. 250e, and two embossed gold foil airmail souv. sheets, perf., imperf., 500e, issued Jan. 17. Nos. 7840-7848.

Eliz. II Coronation, 25th Anniv., set of eight, 2e, 5e, 8e, 10e, 12e, 15e, airmail 30e, 50e, and two airmail souv. sheets, perf. 150e, imperf. 250e, issued Apr. 25. Nos. 7849-7858.

English Knights of 1200-1350 A.D., set of seven, 5e, 10e, 15e, 20e, 25e, airmail 15e, 70e, and two airmail souv. sheets, perf. 130e, imperf. 200e, issued Apr. 25. Nos. 7859-7867.

Old Locomotives, set of seven, 1e, 2e, 3e, 5e, 10e, airmail 25e, 70e, and two airmail souv. sheets, perf. 150e, imperf. 250e, issued Aug. Nos. 7868-7876.

Prehistoric Animals, set of seven, 30e, 35e, 40e, 45e, 50e, airmail 25e, 60e, and airmail souv. sheets, 130e, 200e, issued Aug. Nos. 7877-7884, 7884A.

Francisco Goya, "Maja Vestida," airmail souv. sheet, 150e, issued Aug. No. 7885.

Peter Paul Rubens — UNICEF, airmail souv. sheet, 250e, issued Aug. No. 7886.

Europa — CEPT — Europhila '78, airmail souv. sheet, 250e, issued Aug. No. 7887.

30th Intl. Stamp Fair, Riccione, airmail souv. sheet, 150e, issued Aug. No. 7888.

Eliz. II Coronation, 25th anniv., airmail souv. sheet of three, 150e, issued

CEPT, airmail souv. sheet, 250e, issued Aug. Nos. 7890.

World Cup Soccer Championships, Argentina '78 and Spain '82, airmail souv. sheet, 150e, issued Aug. Nos. 7891.

Christmas, Titian painting, "The Virgin," airmail souv. sheet, 150e, issued Aug. Nos. 7892.

Natl. Independence, 5th Anniv. (in 1973) — A7

1979 *Perf. 13x13½*

26 A7 1e Ekuele coin 1.10 .25

Natl. Independence, 5th Anniv. (in 1973) — A8

1979

27	A8	1e	Port Bata	.25	.25
28	A8	1.50e	State Palace	.25	.25
29	A8	2b	Central Bank, Bata	.30	.30
30	A8	2.50b	Nguema Biyogo Bridge	.35	.35
31	A8	3b	Port, palace, bank, bridge	.60	.60
			Nos. 27-31 (5)	1.75	1.75

Pres. Nguema — A9

1979 *Perf. 13½x13*

32 A9 1.50e multi .50 .35

United Natl. Workers's Party (PUNT), 3rd Congress.

Independence Martyrs — A10

1979

33	A10	1e	Enrique Nvo	.25	.25
34	A10	1.50e	Salvador Ndongo Ekang	.30	.30
35	A10	2b	Acacio Mane	.40	.40
			Nos. 33-35 (3)	.95	.95

Agricultural Experiment Year — A11

1979 *Perf. 13x13½*

36	A11	1e	multi	.65	.25
37	A11	1.50e	multi, diff.	.95	.35

Independence Martyrs — A12

Natl. Coat of Arms — A13

1981, Mar. Photo. *Perf. 13½x12½*

38 A12 5b Obiang Esono Nguema .55 .25
39 A12 15b Fermando Nvara Engonga .55 .25
40 A12 25b Ela Edjodjomo Mangue .55 .25
41 A12 35b Obiang Nguema Mbasogo, president .75 .25
42 A12 50b Hipolito Micha Eworo 1.10 .25
43 A13 100b multi 2.25 .35
Nos. 38-43 (6) 5.75 1.60

Dated 1980.

Christmas 1980 A14

1981, Mar. 30 *Perf. 13½*

44 A14 8b Cathedral, infant .25 .25
45 A14 25b Bells, youth .30 .25

Dated 1980.

Souvenir Sheet

Pres. Obiang Nguema Mbasogo — A15

1981, Aug. 30 Litho. *Imperf.*

46 A15 400b multi 5.50 2.25

State Visit of King Juan Carlos of Spain — A16

Perf. 13x13½, 13½x13

1981, Nov. 30

47 A16 50b Government reception 1.00 .25
48 A16 100b Arrival at airport 2.00 .50
49 A16 150b King, Pres. Mbasogo, vert. 3.00 .75
Nos. 47-49 (3) 6.00 1.50

State Visit of Pope John Paul II — A17

1982, Feb. 18

50 A17 100b Papal and natl. arms 1.50 .70
51 A17 200b Pres. Mbasogo greeting Pope 3.25 1.40
52 A17 300b Pope, vert. 4.75 2.10
Nos. 50-52 (3) 9.50 4.20

Christmas 1981 A18

1982, Feb. 25 Photo.

53 A18 100b Carolers, vert. 1.25 .35
54 A18 150b Magi, African youth 1.90 .60

Dated 1981.

1982 World Cup Soccer Championships, Spain — A19

1982, June 13 *Perf. 13½*

55 A19 40b Emblem .55 .25
56 A19 60b Naranjito character trademark .90 .35
57 A19 100b World Cup trophy 1.50 .70
58 A19 200b Players, palm tree, emblem 3.00 1.25
Nos. 55-58 (4) 5.95 2.55

Fauna A20

1983, Feb. 4 Litho.

59 A20 40b Gorilla .75 .25
60 A20 60b Hippopotamus 1.25 .40
61 A20 80b Atherurus africanus 1.75 .55
62 A20 120b Felis pardus 2.75 .85
Nos. 59-62 (4) 6.50 2.05

Dated 1982.

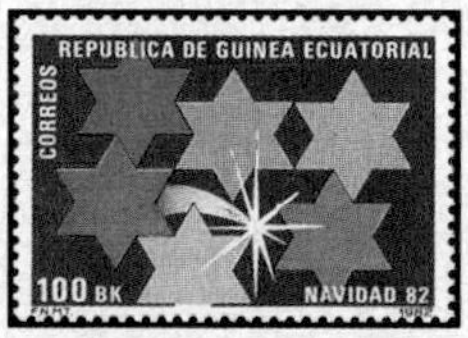

Christmas 1982 A21

1983, Feb. 25 Photo.

63 A21 100b Stars .95 .35
64 A21 200b King offering frankincense 2.25 .75

Dated 1982.

World Communications Year — A22

1983, July 18 Litho.

65 A22 150b Postal runner 1.00 .45
66 A22 200b Microwave station, drummer 2.40 1.00

Banana Trees A23

1983, Oct. 8

67 A23 300b shown 3.25 1.00
68 A23 400b Forest, vert. 4.50 1.40

Christmas 1983 A24

1984

69 A24 80b Folk dancer, musical instruments 1.00 .35
70 A24 100b Holy Family 1.25 .50

Dated 1983.

Constitution of State Powers — A25

Scales of justice, fundamental lawbook and various maps.

1984, Feb. 15

71 A25 50b Annobon and Bioko .75 .40
72 A25 100b Mainland regions 1.75 .75

Inscription at the UR on No. 71 reads "Region Insular". No. 71 also exists with inscription reading "Regiones Insulares".

Turtle Hunting, Rio Muni — A26

1984, May 1

73 A26 125b Hunting Whales, horiz. 1.75 .75
74 A26 150b shown 2.00 .85

World Food Day — A27

1984, Sept.

75 A27 60b Papaya 1.25 .50
76 A27 80b Malanga 1.50 .65

Abstract Wood-Carved Figurines and Art — A28

Designs: 25b, *Black Gazelle* and *Anxiety.* 30b, *Black Gazelle,* diff., and *Woman.* 60b, *Man and woman,* vert. 75b, *Poster,* vert. 100b, *Mother and Child,* vert. 150b, *Man and Woman,* diff., and *Bust of a Woman.*

1984, Nov. 15

77 A28 25b multi .25 .25
78 A28 30b multi .35 .25
79 A28 60b multi .75 .35
80 A28 75b multi 1.00 .40
81 A28 100b multi 1.50 .50
82 A28 150b multi 2.00 .90
Nos. 77-82 (6) 5.85 2.65

Christmas A29

1984, Dec. 24

83 A29 60b Mother and child, vert. .75 .25
84 A29 100b Musical instruments 1.25 .55

Immaculate Conception Missions, Cent. — A30

50fr, Emblem, vert. 60fr, Map, nun and youths, vert. 80fr, First Guinean nuns. 125fr, Missionaries landing at Bata Beach, 1885.

1985, Apr. *Perf. 14*

85 A30 50fr multi .45 .25
86 A30 60fr multi .60 .25
87 A30 80fr multi .90 .30
88 A30 125fr multi 1.40 .60
Nos. 85-88 (4) 3.35 1.40

Jose Mavule Ndjong, First Postmaster A31

1985, July *Perf. 13½*

89 A31 50fr Postal emblem, vert. .95 .25
90 A31 80fr shown 1.60 .45

Equatorial Guinea Postal Service.

Christmas A32

1985, Dec.

91 A32 40fr Nativity .65 .25
92 A32 70fr Folk band, dancers, mother and child 1.10 .35

Nature Conservation — A33

1985

93 A33 15fr Crab, snail .85 .25
94 A33 35fr Butterflies, bees, birds 2.25 .75
95 A33 45fr Flowering plants 2.25 .75
96 A33 65fr Spraying and harvesting cacao 3.25 .80
Nos. 93-96 (4) 8.60 2.55

Folklore — A34

1986, Apr. 15

97 A34 10fr Ndowe dance, Mekuyo, horiz. .25 .25
98 A34 50fr Fang dance, Mokom .60 .25
99 A34 65fr Cacha Bubi, Bisila .90 .30
100 A34 80fr Fang dance, Ndong-Mba 1.00 .50
Nos. 97-100 (4) 2.75 1.30

A35

1986 World Cup Soccer Championships, Mexico: Various soccer plays.

1986, June 25

101 A35 50fr multi, horiz. .25 .25
102 A35 100fr multi, horiz. .75 .25
103 A35 150fr multi 1.10 .40
104 A35 200fr multi 1.40 .55
Nos. 101-104 (4) 3.50 1.45

Christmas — A36

1986, Dec. 12

105 A36 100fr Musical instruments, horiz. 1.10 .35
106 A36 150fr Holy Family, lamb 1.60 .60

Conf. of the Union of Central African States — A37

1986, Dec. 29

107 A37 80fr Flags, map .90 .35
108 A37 100fr Emblem, map, horiz. 1.25 .40

Campaign Against Hunger A38

1987, June 5

109 A38 60fr Chicken .65 .25
110 A38 80fr Fish .95 .35
111 A38 100fr Wheat 1.25 .45
Nos. 109-111 (3) 2.85 1.05

Intl. Peace Year A39

1987, July 15 Litho. *Perf. 13½*

112 A39 100fr shown .75 .40
113 A39 200fr Hands holding dove 1.60 .80

Stamp Day 1987 A40

1987, Oct. 5 Litho. *Perf. 13½*

114 A40 150fr shown 1.25 .50
115 A40 300fr Posting envelope 2.25 .85

Christmas 1987 — A41

Mother and child (wood carvings).

1987, Dec. 22 Litho. *Perf. 13½*

116 A41 80fr multi 1.00 .35
117 A41 100fr multi, diff. 1.40 .55

Climbing Palm Tree — A42

1988, May 4 Litho. *Perf. 13½*

118 A42 50fr shown .50 .25
119 A42 75fr Woman carrying fish .70 .35
120 A42 150fr Chopping down trees 1.50 .75
Nos. 118-120 (3) 2.70 1.35

Democratic Party — A43

1988, Nov. 16

121 A43 40fr Crest .35 .25
122 A43 75fr Torch, motto, horiz. .60 .30
123 A43 100fr Torch, flag, weaving, horiz. .85 .40
Nos. 121-123 (3) 1.80 .95

Cultural Revolution Day — A44

Geometric shapes.

1988, June 4

124 A44 35fr shown .25 .25
125 A44 50fr Squares, sphere .35 .25
126 A44 100fr Bird .75 .50
Nos. 124-126 (3) 1.35 1.00

Christmas — A45

1988, Dec. 22

127 A45 50fr shown .45 .25
128 A45 100fr Mother and child .95 .40

Natl. Independence, 20th Anniv. — A46

Designs: 10fr, Lumber on truck. 35fr, Folk dancers. 45fr, Officials on dais.

1989, Apr. 14 Litho. *Perf. 14*

129 A46 10fr multicolored .35 .25
130 A46 35fr multicolored .40 .35
131 A46 45fr multicolored .55 .40
Nos. 129-131 (3) 1.30 1.00

Youths Bathing, Ilachi Falls — A47

25fr, Waterfall in the jungle. 60fr, Boy drinking from fruit, boys swimming at Luba Beach.

1989, July 7 *Perf. 13½*

132 A47 15fr shown .45 .25
133 A47 25fr multicolored .50 .25
134 A47 60fr multicolored .75 .50
Nos. 132-134 (3) 1.70 1.00

1st Congress of the Democratic Party of Equatorial Guinea A48

1989, Oct. 23 Litho. *Perf. 13½*

135 A48 25fr shown .30 .25
136 A48 35fr Torch, vert. .50 .25
137 A48 40fr Pres. Nguema, vert. .60 .25
Nos. 135-137 (3) 1.40 .75

Christmas — A49

1989, Dec. 18 Litho. *Perf. 13½*

138 A49 150fr shown 1.60 .75
139 A49 300fr Nativity, horiz. 2.00 1.00

Boy Scouts A50

1990, Mar. 23 Litho. *Perf. 13*

140 A50 100fr Lord Baden-Powell 1.50 .50
141 A50 250fr Salute 3.50 1.10
142 A50 350fr Bugler 4.75 1.50
Nos. 140-142 (3) 9.75 3.10

World Cup Soccer Championships, Italy — A51

1990, June 8 Litho. *Perf. 13*

143 A51 100fr Soccer player, map .60 .35
144 A51 250fr Goalkeeper 1.50 .65
145 A51 350fr Trophy 2.00 1.00
Nos. 143-145 (3) 4.10 2.00

Musical Instruments of the Ndowe People — A52

Instruments of the: 250fr, Fang. 350fr, Bubi.

1990, June 19

146 A52 100fr multicolored .90 .30
147 A52 250fr multicolored 1.75 .75
148 A52 350fr multicolored 2.75 1.00
Nos. 146-148 (3) 5.40 2.05

Discovery of America, 500th Anniv. (in 1992) A53

1990, Oct. 10

149 A53 170fr Arrival in New World 1.75 .60
150 A53 300fr Columbus' fleet 2.25 1.00

Christmas — A54

1990, Dec. 23 Litho. *Perf. 13½*

151 A54 170fr shown 1.00 .45
152 A54 300fr Bubi tribesman 2.00 .90

1992 Summer Olympics, Barcelona A55

1991, Apr. 22 Litho. *Perf. 13½x14*

153 A55 150fr Tennis 2.50 .90
154 A55 250fr Cycling 4.25 1.50

Souvenir Sheet

155 A55 500fr Equestrian 13.50 6.00

La Maja Desnuda by Goya
A56

Designs: 250fr, Eve by Durer, vert. 350fr, The Three Graces by Rubens, vert.

1991, May 6 **Litho.** ***Perf. 14***

156	A56	100fr shown	1.50	.50
157	A56	250fr multicolored	2.75	1.00
158	A56	350fr multicolored	3.75	1.25
		Nos. 156-158 (3)	8.00	2.75

Madrillus Sphinx — A57

1991, July 1 **Litho.** ***Perf. 13½x14***

159	A57	25fr shown	2.50	1.25
160	A57	25fr Face	2.50	1.25
161	A57	25fr Seated	2.50	1.25
162	A57	25fr Walking, horiz.	2.50	1.25
		Nos. 159-162 (4)	10.00	5.00

World Wildlife Fund.

Discovery of America, 500th Anniv.
A58

Captains, ships: 150fr, Vicente Yanez Pinzon, Nina. 260fr, Martin Alonso Pinzon, Pinta. 350fr, Christopher Columbus, Santa Maria.

1991 **Litho.** ***Perf. 13½x14***

163	A58	150fr multicolored	1.50	.60
164	A58	250fr multicolored	2.75	1.00
165	A58	350fr multicolored	3.75	1.50
		Nos. 163-165 (3)	8.00	3.10

Locomotives — A59

150fr, Electric, Japan, 1932. 250fr, Steam, US, 1873. 500fr, Steam, Germany, 1841.

1991, Sept. 10

166	A59	150fr multicolored	1.50	.65
167	A59	250fr multicolored	3.00	.75

Souvenir Sheet

168	A59	500fr multicolored	19.00	6.00

1992 Summer Olympics, Barcelona
A60

1992, Feb. 12 **Litho.** ***Perf. 13½x14***

169	A60	200fr Basketball	1.75	.75
170	A60	300fr Swimming	2.50	1.10

Souvenir Sheet

171	A60	400fr Baseball	19.00	12.50

Souvenir Sheet

Discovery of America, 500th Anniv. — A61

Columbus: a, 300fr, Departing from Palos, Spain. b, 500fr, Landing in New World.

1992, Apr. 8

172	A61	Sheet of 2, #a.-b.	22.50	12.50

Motion Pictures, Cent.
A61a

Scenes from movies: 100fr, Humphrey Bogart, Ingrid Bergman, Dooley Wilson in "Casablanca," 1942. 250fr, "Viridiana," 1961. 350fr, Laurel and Hardy in "Sons of the Desert," 1933.

1992, Sept. **Litho.** ***Perf. 14***

172C	A61a	100fr multicolored	2.00	.75
172D	A61a	250fr multicolored	3.00	1.25
172E	A61a	350fr multicolored	5.00	1.75
		Nos. 172C-172E (3)	10.00	3.75

A62

Mushrooms: 75fr, Termitomyces globulus. 125fr, Termitomyces le testui. 150fr, Termitomyces robustus.

1992, Nov. **Litho.** ***Perf. 14x13½***

173	A62	75fr multicolored	1.00	.25
174	A62	125fr multicolored	1.50	.50
175	A62	150fr multicolored	2.00	.65
		Nos. 173-175 (3)	4.50	1.40

A62a

Wildlife Protection: 150fr, Halcyon malimbicus. 250fr, Corythaeola cristata. 500fr, Mariposa nymphalidae, horiz.

1992 **Litho.** ***Perf. 14x13½***

175A	A62a	150fr multicolored	2.75	1.00
175B	A62a	250fr multicolored	4.75	1.50

Souvenir Sheet

Perf. 13½x14

175C	A62a	500fr multicolored	17.50	8.00

Virgin and Child with Virtuous Saints, by Claudio Coello (c. 1635-1693) — A63

Paintings, by Jacob Jordaens (1593-1678): 300fr, Apollo Conquering Marsias. 400fr, Meleager and Atalanta.

1993, Mar. **Litho.** ***Perf. 13½x14***

176	A63	200fr multicolored	2.25	.75
177	A63	300fr multicolored	3.25	1.25

Souvenir Sheet

178	A63	400fr multicolored	15.00	8.00

1992 Olympic Gold Medalists
A64

Designs: 100fr, Quincy Watts, 400-meter dash, US. 250fr, Martin Lopez Zubero, swimming, Spain. 350fr, Petra Kronberger, women's slalom, Austria. 400fr, Flying Dutchman class yachting, Spain.

1993 **Litho.** ***Perf. 13½x14***

179	A64	100fr multicolored	.90	.35
180	A64	250fr multicolored	2.25	.75
181	A64	350fr multicolored	3.25	1.00
182	A64	400fr multicolored	4.00	1.25
		Nos. 179-182 (4)	10.40	3.35

Scene from Romeo and Juliet, by Tchaikovsky — A65

Design: 200fr, Scene from Faust, by Charles-Francois Gounod (1818-93).

1993, June **Litho.** ***Perf. 13½x14***

183	A65	100fr multicolored	1.10	.50
184	A65	200fr multicolored	2.00	.80

First Ford Gasoline Engine, Cent.
A66

1993 ***Perf. 13½x14, 14x13½***

185	A66	200fr First Ford vehicle	3.00	1.00
186	A66	300fr Ford Model T	4.00	1.25
187	A66	400fr Henry Ford, vert.	6.00	1.50
		Nos. 185-187 (3)	13.00	3.75

25th Anniv. of Independence — A67

Designs: 150fr, Pres. Obiang Nguema Mbasogo, vert. 250fr, Cargo ship, map, communications . 300fr, Hydroelectric plant, Riaba. 350fr, Bridge.

Perf. 14x13½, 13½x14

1993, Oct. 12 **Litho.**

188	A67	150fr multicolored	1.00	.50
189	A67	250fr multicolored	1.75	.75
190	A67	300fr multicolored	2.25	.85
191	A67	350fr multicolored	2.75	.95
		Nos. 188-191 (4)	7.75	3.05

1994 World Cup Soccer Championships, US — A68

Designs: 200fr, German team, 1990 champions. 300fr, Rose Bowl Stadium, Pasadena, Calif. 500fr, Player kicking ball, vert.

1994 **Litho.** ***Perf. 13½x14, 14x13½***

192	A68	200fr multicolored	1.25	.45
193	A68	300fr multicolored	1.75	.65
194	A68	500fr multicolored	3.25	1.10
		Nos. 192-194 (3)	6.25	2.20

First Manned Moon Landing, 25th Anniv.
A69

Designs: 500fr, Lunar module, Eagle. 700fr, "Buzz" Aldrin, Michael Collins, Neil Armstrong. 900fr, Footprint on moon, astronaut.

1994 ***Perf. 13½x14***

195	A69	500fr multicolored	2.75	.70
196	A69	700fr multicolored	4.25	1.00
197	A69	900fr multicolored	6.50	1.75
		Nos. 195-197 (3)	13.50	3.45

Dinosaurs
A70

Designs: 300fr, Chasmosaurus. 500fr, Tyrannosaurus rex. 700fr, Triceratops. 800fr, Styracosaurus, deinonychus.

1994

198	A70	300fr multicolored	2.00	.65
199	A70	500fr multicolored	3.25	1.10
200	A70	700fr multicolored	6.00	1.60
		Nos. 198-200 (3)	11.25	3.35

Souvenir Sheet

201	A70	800fr multicolored	19.00	17.50

Famous Men
A71

Designs: 300fr, Jean Renoir (1894-1979), French film director. 500fr, Ferdinand de Lesseps (1805-94), French diplomat, promoter of Suez Canal. 600fr, Antoine de Saint Exupery (1900-44), French aviator, writer. 700fr, Walter Gropius (1883-1969), architect.

1994 **Litho.** ***Perf. 13½x14***

202	A71	300fr multicolored	2.25	.75
203	A71	500fr multicolored	3.75	1.40
204	A71	600fr multicolored	4.50	1.50
205	A71	700fr multicolored	5.50	2.00
		Nos. 202-205 (4)	16.00	5.65

Establishment of The Bauhaus, 75th anniv. (#205).

Minerals
A72

1994 **Litho.** ***Perf. 13½x14***

206	A72	300fr Aurichalcite	2.50	1.00
207	A72	400fr Pyromorphite	3.50	1.40
208	A72	600fr Fluorite	5.00	1.90
209	A72	700fr Halite	6.00	2.25
		Nos. 206-209 (4)	17.00	6.55

Domestic Animals
A73

Designs: a, Cat. b, Dog. c, Pig.

1995	**Litho.**	***Perf. 13½x14***	
210	Strip of 3, #a.-c.	9.50	9.50
a.-c.	A73 500fr Any single	1.75	1.50

Butterflies & Orchids
A74

a, Hypolimnas salmacis. b, Myrina silenus. c, Palla ussheri. d, Pseudacraea boisduvali.

1995			
211	Strip of 4, #a.-d.	14.00	14.00
a.-d.	A74 400fr Any single	2.75	1.50

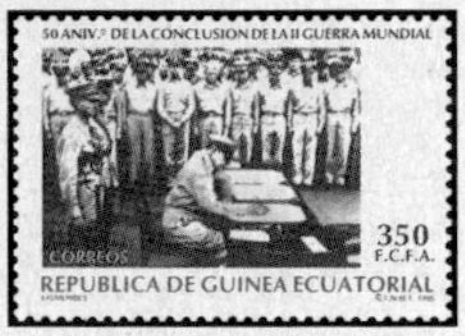

Anniversaries — A75

Designs: a, 350fr, End of World War II, 50th Anniv. b, 450fr, UN, 50th anniv. c, 600fr, Sir Rowland Hill, birth bicent.

1995	**Litho.**	***Perf. 13½x14***	
212	Strip of 3, #a.-c.	11.00	11.00
a.	A75 350fr multi	2.50	1.25
b.	A75 450fr multi	3.25	1.50
c.	A75 600fr multi	4.00	2.25

Trains
A76

Designs: No. 213a, English steam engine. b, German diesel engine. c, Japanese Shinkansen train.
800fr, Swiss electric locomotive.

1995			
213	Strip of 3, #a.-c.	12.00	12.00
a.-c.	A76 500fr Any single	2.50	2.00

Souvenir Sheet

214	A76 800fr multicolored	10.00	9.00

Formula 1 Driving Champions
A77

Designs: a, Juan Manuel Fangio. b, Ayrton Senna. c, Jim Clark. d, Jochen Rindt.

1995	**Litho.**	***Perf. 14***	
215	Strip of 4, #a.-d.	12.00	12.00
a.-d.	A77 400fr Any single	2.25	1.50

Motion Pictures, Cent.
A78

Designs: a, Marilyn Monroe. b, Elvis Presley. c, James Dean. d, Vittorio de Sica.

1996	**Litho.**	***Perf. 14***	
216	Strip of 4, #a.-d.	9.00	9.00
a.-d.	A78 350fr Any single	1.50	1.50

Famous People
A79

Designs: a, Alfred Nobel (1833-96), inventor, philanthropist. b, Anton Bruckner (1824-96), composer. c, Abraham and Three Angels, by Giovanni B. Tiepolo (1696-1770).
800fr, Family of Charles IV, by Francisco de Goya, (1746-1828).

1996			
217	Strip of 3, #a.-c.	13.50	13.50
a.-c.	A79 500fr Any single	2.75	2.00

Souvenir Sheet

218	A79 800fr multicolored	8.00	7.75

Chess
A80

Designs: a, World Chess Festival for youth and children, Minorca, Spain. b, Women's World Chess Championship, Jaén, Spain. c, Men's World Chess Championship, Karpov versus Kamsky, Elista, Kalmyk. d, Chess Olympiad, Yerevan, Armenia.

1996	**Litho.**	***Perf. 14***	
219	Strip of 4, #a.-d.	14.00	14.00
a.-d.	A80 400fr Any single	3.00	1.50

1996 Summer Olympic Games, Atlanta
A81

Designs: a, Olympic Stadium, Athens, 1896. b, Cycling. c, Tennis. d, Equestrian show jumping.

1996	**Litho.**	***Perf. 14***	
220	Strip of 4, #a.-d.	10.00	10.00
a.-d.	A81 400fr Any single	1.75	1.50

Ships
A82

Designs: a, Paddle steamer with sails, 19th cent. b, Bark "Galatea," 1896. c, Modern ferry.

1996			
221	Strip of 3, #a.-c.	12.00	12.00
a.-c.	A82 500fr Any single	2.75	2.00

Franz Schubert (1797-1828), Composer — A83

Miguel de Cervantes (1547-1616), Novelist — A84

Designs: a, shown. b, Chinese Lunar New Year, 1997, (Year of the Ox). c, Johannes Brahms (1833-97), composer.

1997, Apr. 23	**Litho.**	***Perf. 14***	
222	Strip of 3, #a.-c.	10.00	10.00
a.-c.	A83 500fr Any single	2.50	2.00

Souvenir Sheet

223	A84 800fr multicolored	5.50	5.50

Mushrooms — A85

a, Sparassis laminosa. b, Amanita pantherina. c, Morchella esculenta. d, Aleuria aurantia.

1997			
224	Strip of 4, #a.-d.	13.50	13.50
a.-d.	A85 400fr Any single	2.25	1.75

1998 World Cup Soccer Championships, France — A86

Designs: a, Players with ball on field. b, Stadium. c, Kicking ball.

1997	**Litho.**	***Perf. 14***	
225	Strip of 3, #a.-c.	7.00	7.00
a.-c.	A86 300fr Any single	1.50	1.10

Fauna
A88

a, Snake. b, Snail. c, Turtle. d, Monitor lizard.

1998	**Litho.**	***Perf. 14***	
230	Strip of 4, #a.-d.	14.00	14.00
a.-d.	A88 400fr Any single	2.25	1.50

A89

Military Uniforms: a, Alsace Regiment, French Infantry, 18th cent. b, English Marine, 18th cent. c, Georgian Hussars Regiment, Russian Calvary, 18th cent. d, Prussian Artillery, 19th cent.

1998			
231	Strip of 4, #a.-d.	11.00	11.00
a.-d.	A89 400fr Any single	1.75	1.50

A90

Easter (Museum paintings): a, Crucifixion of Christ, by Velázquez. b, Adoration of the Magi, by Rubens. c, Holy Family, by Michelangelo.

1999	**Litho.**	***Perf. 14***	
232	Strip of 3, #a.-c.	10.00	10.00
a.-c.	A90 500fr Any single	2.25	2.00

Orchids — A91

Designs: a, Angraecum eburneum. b, Paphiopedilum insigne. c, Ansellia africana. d, Cattleya leopoldii.

1999			
233	Strip of 4, #a.-d.	16.00	16.00
a.-d.	A91 400fr Any single	3.00	1.50

Birth and Death Anniversaries
A92

No. 234: a, 750fr, Portrait of Frederic Chopin (1810-49), by Eugene Delacroix. b, 100fr, Christ Crowned With Thorns, by Anthony Van Dyck (1599-1641). c, 250fr, Portrait of Johann Wolfgang von Goethe (1749-1832), by Joseph Carl Stieler. d, 500fr, Jacques-Etienne Montgolfiere (1745-1799) and balloon.

1999	**Litho.**	***Perf. 14x13¾***	
234	Horiz. strip of 4, #a-d	11.00	11.00
a.	A92 750fr multi	4.00	3.00
b.	A92 100fr multi	.45	.35
c.	A92 250fr multi	1.25	1.10
d.	A92 500fr multi	2.75	2.00

Parrots — A93

No. 235: a, Aratinga guarouba. b, Ara ambigua. c, Anodorhynchus hyacinthinus.
800fr, Alisterus amboinensis.

1999			
235	Vert. strip of 3, #a-c	11.50	11.50
a.-c.	A93 500fr any single	2.75	2.00

Souvenir Sheet

236	A93 800fr multi	8.50	7.50

Economic and Monetary Community of Central Africa Week — A93a

Designs: 100fr, Map of Africa, flags of member nations.

1999 Litho. *Perf. 14½*

236A	A93a 100fr multi		—

An additional stamp was issued in this set. The editors would like to examine any example.

Locomotives — A94

No. 237: a, Swiss. b, German. c, Japanese.

2000 Litho. *Perf. 13¾x14*

237	Horiz. strip of 3	11.00	11.00
a.-c.	A94 500fr Any single	2.75	2.25

Souvenir Sheet

238	A94 800fr AVE Train	5.00	5.00

Butterflies A95

a, Fabriciana niobe. b, Palaeochrysophanus hippothoe. c, Inachis io. d, Apatura iris.

2000

239	Horiz. strip of 4	16.00	16.00
a.-d.	A95 400fr Any single	3.00	1.75

UPU, 125th Anniv. (in 1999) A96

2000 Litho. *Perf. 13¾*

240	A96 400fr multi	2.00	1.75

Mushrooms A97

No. 241: a, Gyroporus cyanescens. b, Terfezia arenaria. c, Battarrea stevenii. d, Amanita muscaria.

2001 Litho. *Perf. 13¾*

241	Horiz. strip of 4	11.00	11.00
a.-d.	A97 400fr Any single	2.00	1.60

Fire Trucks A98

No. 242: a, Truck, 1915. b, Tanker, 1943. c, Ladder truck, 1966. d, Merryweather pumper, 1888.

2001

242	Horiz. strip of 4	12.00	12.00
a.-d.	A98 400fr Any single	2.25	1.75

Soldiers — A99

No. 243: a, Infantry officer, 1700. b, Harquebusier, 1534. c, Musketeer, 17th cent. d, Fusilier, 1815.

2001 Litho. *Perf. 14x13¾*

243	Horiz. strip of 4	11.00	11.00
a.-d.	A99 400fr Any single	2.25	1.60

Prehistoric Animals A100

No. 244: a, Carnotaurus sastrei. b, Iberomesornis romerali. c, Troodon.
800fr, Diplodocus carneglei.

2001 *Perf. 13¾x14*

244	Horiz. strip of 3	8.25	8.25
a.-c.	A100 500fr Any single	2.25	2.00

Souvenir Sheet

245	A100 800fr multi	5.75	4.00

Millennium A101

Designs: No. 246, 200fr, Intl. Conference Center. No. 247, 200fr, Offshore petroleum exploration. No. 248, 200fr, Women's Plaza, Malabo.
400fr, Statue at Intl. Conference Center, vert.

2001 Litho. *Perf. 13¾x14*

246-248	A101 Set of 3	3.50	3.50

Souvenir Sheet

Perf. 14x13¾

249	A101 400fr multi	1.75	1.75

Flora — A102

No. 250: a, Alstonia congensis. b, Harongana madagascariensis. c, Caloncoba glauca. d, Cassia occidentalis.

2002 *Perf. 14x13¾*

250	Horiz. strip of 4	8.50	8.50
a.-d.	A102 400fr Any single	2.00	1.60

Automobiles — A103

No. 251: a, 1924 Rochet Schneider 20,000. b, 1930 Bugatti T49. c, 1931 Ford Model A. d, 1925 Alfa Romeo RLSS.

2002 *Perf. 13¾x14*

251	Vert. strip of 4	9.00	9.00
a.-d.	A103 400fr Any single	2.00	1.60

Butterflies A104

No. 252: a, Papilio menestheus canui. b, Papilio policenes. c, Papilio tynderaeus. d, Papilio zalmoxis.

2002

252	Strip of 4	9.00	9.00
a.-d.	A104 400fr Any single	2.00	1.60

Famous Men A105

No. 253: a, Victor Hugo (1802-85), writer. b, Santiago Ramón y Cajal (1852-1934), histologist. c, Emile Zola (1840-1902), writer.

2002

253	Horiz. strip of 3	6.50	6.50
a.-c.	A105 400fr Any single	1.75	1.60

2002 World Cup Soccer Championships, Japan and Korea — A106

No. 254: a, Player with yellow shirt with knee on ground. b, Stadium. c, Player with yellow shirt on ground.

2002

254	Horiz. strip of 3	8.00	8.00
a.-c.	A106 500fr Any single	2.25	2.10

Souvenir Sheet

2002 Chess Olympiad, Bled, Slovenia — A107

2002

255	A107 800fr multi	5.75	5.75

Anniversaries and Events — A108

No. 256: a, Painting by Henri de Toulouse-Lautrec (1864-1901). b, Year of Dialogue Among Civilizations. c, Giuseppe Verdi (1813-1901), composer.

2004 ? Litho. *Perf. 14x13¾*

256	Vert. strip of 3	6.50	6.50
a.-c.	A108 400fr Any single	2.00	1.75

Dated 2001. Stamps did not appear in philatelic market until 2004.

Anniversaries and Events — A109

No. 257: a, Tour de France bicycle race, cent. b, Painting by Vincent van Gogh (1853-90). c, Wright Brothers and Wright Flyer.

2004 ? *Perf. 13¾x14*

257	Horiz. strip of 3	8.50	8.50
a.	A109 400fr multi	2.25	2.25
b.	A109 500fr multi	2.75	2.75
c.	A109 600fr multi	3.50	3.50

Dated 2003. Stamps did not appear in philatelic market until 2004.

Minerals A110

2004 ?

258	Vert. strip of 4	9.50	9.50
a.	A110 400fr Realgar	1.75	1.75
b.	A110 450fr Gypsum	2.25	2.00
c.	A110 550fr Red quartz	2.50	2.25
d.	A110 600fr Chrysoberyl	2.75	2.60

Dated 2003. Stamps did not appear in philatelic market until 2004.

Lighthouses A111

Designs: a, Marina Lighthouse, Luba, Equatorial Guinea. b, La Plata Lighthouse, Spain. c, Prodecao Lighthouse, Luba. d, Torre de Hércules, Spain.

2004 ? *Perf. 14x13¾*

259	Horiz. strip of 4	12.50	12.50
a.	A111 400fr multi	2.50	2.25
b.	A111 450fr multi	2.75	2.50
c.	A111 550fr multi	3.00	2.75
d.	A111 600fr multi	3.75	3.50

Dated 2003. Stamps did not appear in philatelic market until 2004.

Space Shuttle Columbia Accident — A112

No. 260: a, Rocket lift-off. b, Rocket on launch pad. c, Flight crew patch.
1000fr, View of earth from outer space.

2004 ?

260	Vert. strip of 3	9.00	9.00
a.	A112 500fr multi	2.50	2.25
b.	A112 600fr multi	2.75	2.50
c.	A112 700fr multi	3.25	3.00

Souvenir Sheet

261	A112 1000fr multi	5.00	5.00

Dated 2003. Stamps did not appear in philatelic market until 2004.

Motorcycles — A113

No. 262: a, 1944-47 Soriano Tigre. b, 1970 Derbi 50 Grand Prix. c, 1938 DKW 250 with sidecar.
1000fr, Harley-Davidson VRSCA V-Rod.

2004 ? ***Perf. 13¾x14***
262 Horiz. strip of 3 8.50 8.50
a. A113 450fr multi 2.00 1.90
b. A113 500fr multi 2.50 2.25
c. A113 550fr multi 3.00 2.75

Souvenir Sheet

263 A113 1000fr multi 6.50 6.50

Dated 2003. Stamps did not appear in philatelic market until 2004.

Souvenir Sheet

Wedding of Spanish Prince Felipe and Letizia Ortiz Rocasolano — A114

2004 **Litho.** ***Perf. 13¾x14***
264 A114 1400fr multi 6.00 6.00

2004 Summer Olympics, Athens A115

2004
265 Horiz. strip of 4 8.25 8.25
a. A115 400fr Basketball 1.60 1.60
b. A115 450fr Track 1.90 1.90
c. A115 550fr Tennis 2.25 2.25
d. A115 600fr Cycling 2.50 2.50

2004 Anniversaries A116

No. 266: a, FIFA (Fédération Internationale de Football Association), cent. b, Pablo Neruda (1904-73), poet. c, Anton Dvorak (1841-1904), composer.

2005 ? **Litho.** ***Perf. 14x13¾***
266 Vert. strip of 3 6.75 6.75
a. A116 450fr multi 1.90 1.90
b. A116 500fr multi 2.10 2.10
c. A116 550fr multi 2.40 2.40

Dated 2004. Stamps did not appear in philatelic marketplace until 2005.

Airplanes A117

No. 267: a, Concorde. b, Airbus A340-600. c, Boeing 747-400. d, Eurofighter C-16 Typhoon.

2005 ? ***Perf. 13¾x14***
267 Vert. strip of 4 8.50 8.50
a. A117 400fr multi 1.60 1.60
b. A117 450fr multi 1.90 1.90
c. A117 500fr multi 2.10 2.10
d. A117 600fr multi 2.50 2.50

Dated 2004. Stamps did not appear in philatelic marketplace until 2005.

Churches — A118

No. 268: a, Cathedral, Pisa, Italy. b, Notre-Dame-la-Grande Church, Poitiers, France. c, Speyer Cathedral, Germany. d, Cathedral, Santiago de Compostela, Spain.

2005 ***Perf. 14x13¾***
268 Horiz. strip of 4 9.00 9.00
a. A118 400fr multi 1.60 1.60
b. A118 450fr multi 1.90 1.90
c. A118 550fr multi 2.40 2.40
d. A118 600fr multi 2.50 2.50

Paintings by Salvador Dali (1904-89) — A119

Various unnamed paintings.

2005 ***Perf. 14x13¾***
269 Vert. strip of 3 8.00 8.00
a. A119 500fr multi 2.00 2.00
b. A119 600fr multi 2.50 2.50
c. A119 700fr multi 2.75 2.75

Souvenir Sheet

270 A119 1000fr multi 4.50 4.50

Art and Architecture — A120

No. 271: a, Statue of African Woman, Malabo. b, Building, Bioko Sur. c, Eyi Muan Ndong, troubador.

2005 **Litho.** ***Perf. 13¾x14***
271 Horiz. strip of 3 7.25 7.25
a. A120 450fr multi 2.00 2.00
b. A120 550fr multi 2.40 2.40
c. A120 600fr multi 2.75 2.75

Trains A121

No. 272: a, Tren Basculante. b, Tren Talgo Pendular. c, Tren Electrotrén. d, Tren T. A. F.

2005
272 Strip of 4 9.00 9.00
a. A121 400fr multi 1.75 1.75
b. A121 450fr multi 1.90 1.90
c. A121 550fr multi 2.40 2.40
d. A121 600fr multi 2.50 2.50

Publication of Don Quixote, 400th Anniv. — A122

No. 273: a, Emblem. b, Don Quixote and Sancho Panza riding. c, Quixote catching falling Panza. d, Quixote on horse, windmill.

2005 ***Perf. 14x13¾***
273 Horiz. strip of 4 9.00 9.00
a. A122 400fr multi 1.75 1.75
b. A122 450fr multi 1.90 1.90
c. A122 550fr multi 2.40 2.40
d. A122 600fr multi 2.50 2.50

Famous People A123

No. 274: a, Christopher Columbus (1451-1506), explorer. b, Federico García Lorca (1898-1936), poet. c, Wolfgang Amadeus Mozart (1756-91), composer.

2006 ***Perf. 13¾x14***
274 Horiz. strip of 3 7.25 7.25
a. A123 450fr multi 2.00 2.00
b. A123 550fr multi 2.25 2.25
c. A123 600fr multi 2.50 2.50

Pope Benedict XVI A124

No. 275: a, Coat of Arms. b, St. Peter's Basilica.
1000fr, Pope Benedict XVI.

2006
275 Vert. pair 4.50 4.50
a. A124 450fr multi 2.00 2.00
b. A124 550fr multi 2.40 2.40

Souvenir Sheet

276 A124 1000fr multi 6.50 6.50

Tourism A125

No. 277: a, Road from Boloko to Luba. b, Malabo Intl. Airport Terminal. c, Sculpture, Avenida de Juan Pablo II. d, National Parliament.

2006 **Litho.** ***Perf. 13¾x14***
277 Strip of 4 8.00 8.00
a. A125 400fr multi 1.60 1.60
b. A125 450fr multi 1.75 1.75
c. A125 550fr multi 2.25 2.25
d. A125 600fr multi 2.40 2.40

Spain, 2006 World Basketball Champions A126

No. 278: a, Emblem of Spanish Basketball Federation. b, Basketball and hoop. c, Players.

2006 ***Perf. 14x13¾***
278 Vert. strip of 3 7.00 7.00
a. A126 450fr multi 1.75 1.75
b. A126 550fr multi 2.25 2.25
c. A126 600fr multi 2.40 2.40

Christmas A127

No. 279 — Baby and: a, People and drummer. b, People. c, People and airplane.

2006 ***Perf. 13¾x14***
279 Horiz. strip of 3 6.75 6.75
a. A127 450fr multi 1.75 1.75
b. A127 550fr multi 2.25 2.25
c. A127 600fr multi 2.40 2.40

European Economic Community, 50th Anniv. — A128

No. 280: a, Orchard, Spain. b, Mountain, France. c, Farm fields, Italy. d, Village, Germany.

2007 **Litho.** ***Perf. 13¾x14***
280 Horiz. strip of 4 11.50 11.50
a. A128 400fr multi 2.00 1.75
b. A128 500fr multi 2.50 2.25
c. A128 550fr multi 2.75 2.50
d. A128 600fr multi 3.00 2.75

Locomotives in Madrid Train Museum — A129

No. 281: a, Steam locomotive 242F-2009. b, Diesel locomotive 1615. c, Electric locomotive 6101. d, Talgo II train.
1000fr, Steam locomotive, diff.

2007
281 Strip of 4 11.50 11.50
a. A129 450fr multi 2.00 2.00
b. A129 550fr multi 2.50 2.50
c. A129 600fr multi 3.00 2.75
d. A129 650fr multi 3.25 3.00

Souvenir Sheet

282 A129 1000fr multi 5.75 5.75

Native Toys A130

2007 **Litho.** ***Perf. 13¾x14***
283 Horiz. strip of 4 8.50 8.50
a. A130 400fr Airplane 1.75 1.75
b. A130 450fr Car 2.00 2.00
c. A130 500fr Scooter 2.25 2.25
d. A130 550fr Songo game 2.50 2.50

Flora A131

No. 284: a, Artocarpus communis. b, Hibiscus sabdariffa. c, Spathodea campanulata. d, Theobroma cacao.

2007 Litho. *Perf. 13¾x14*

284	Horiz. strip of 4	9.00	9.00
a.	A131 400fr multi	1.75	1.75
b.	A131 450fr multi	2.00	2.00
c.	A131 550fr multi	2.50	2.50
d.	A131 600fr multi	2.75	2.75

African Children A132

No. 285: a, Child and basket. b, Five children and toy cars. c, Six children and net.

2008 Litho. *Perf. 13¾*

285	Horiz. strip of 3	6.50	6.50
a.	A132 400fr multi	1.90	1.90
b.	A132 450fr multi	2.10	2.10
c.	A132 500fr multi	2.40	2.40

2008 African Cup of Nations Soccer Championships, Ghana — A133

No. 286 — Emblem and: a, Soccer ball and player's foot. b, Soccer ball being caught. c, Goalie. d, Goalie, diff.

2008

286	Horiz. strip of 4	9.25	9.25
a.	A133 400fr multi	1.90	1.90
b.	A133 450fr multi	2.10	2.10
c.	A133 500fr multi	2.40	2.40
d.	A133 600fr multi	2.75	2.75

Flora and Fauna A134

No. 287: a, Sitatunga. b, Passiflora quadrangularis. c, Pachylobus edulis.

2008

287	Horiz. strip of 3	6.25	6.25
a.	A134 450fr multi	1.75	1.75
b.	A134 500fr multi	2.00	2.00
c.	A134 600fr multi	2.40	2.40

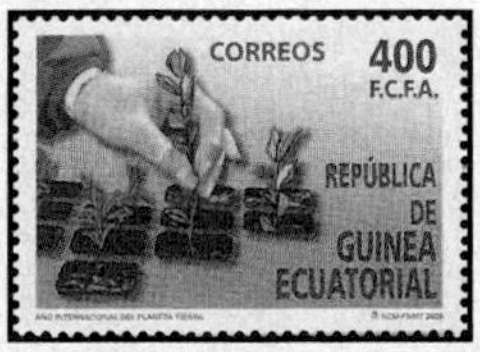

Intl. Year of Planet Earth A135

No. 288: a, Seedlings. b, Parched earth. c, Waterfall.

2008

288	Horiz. strip of 3	5.50	5.50
a.	A135 400fr multi	1.60	1.60
b.	A135 450fr multi	1.75	1.75
c.	A135 550fr multi	2.10	2.10

Declaration of the Rights of Children, 50th Anniv. — A136

No. 289: a, Child drinking glass of milk. b, Children playing with ball. c, Children reading. d, Child coloring.

2009, Mar. 27 Litho. *Perf. 14x13¾*

289	Horiz. strip of 4	8.50	8.50
a.	A136 400fr multi	1.60	1.60
b.	A136 500fr multi	2.10	2.10
c.	A136 550fr multi	2.25	2.25
d.	A136 600fr multi	2.50	2.50

Women's Soccer A137

No. 290: a, Cheering crowd. b, Soccer ball hitting net. c, Players battling for ball. d, Corner of field.

2009, May 14 Litho. *Perf. 13¾*

290	Vert. strip of 4	9.75	9.75
a.	A137 450fr multi	1.90	1.90
b.	A137 550fr multi	2.40	2.40
c.	A137 600fr multi	2.60	2.60
d.	A137 650fr multi	2.75	2.75

Medicinal Plants — A138

No. 291: a, Asystasia gangetica. b, Bryophyllum pinnatum. c, Solanum torvum. 1000fr, Cassia alata.

2009, Aug. 14

291	Vert. strip of 3	6.25	6.25
a.	A138 400fr multi	1.75	1.75
b.	A138 450fr multi	2.00	2.00
c.	A138 550fr multi	2.40	2.40

Souvenir Sheet

292	A138 1000fr multi	4.50	4.50

Christmas — A139

No. 293 — Paintings: a, Birth of Christ, by Federico Barocci. b, Adoration of the Kings, by J. B. Maíno. c, Adoration of the Shepherds, by Maíno. d, Nativity, by Master of Sopetrán.

2009, Sept. 25

293	Horiz. strip of 4	8.50	8.50
a.	A139 400fr multi	1.75	1.75
b.	A139 450fr multi	2.00	2.00
c.	A139 500fr multi	2.25	2.25
d.	A139 550fr multi	2.50	2.50

Paintings by Joaquin Sorolla y Bastida A140

No. 294: a, Paseo a Orillas del Mar. b, El Balandrito. c, La Hora del Baño. d, Self-portrait.

Perf. 13¾x13¼

2010, Mar. 15 Litho.

294	Horiz. strip of 4	9.75	9.75
a.	A140 475fr multi	2.00	2.00
b.	A140 575fr multi	2.40	2.40
c.	A140 625fr multi	2.60	2.60
d.	A140 675fr multi	2.75	2.75

Architecture — A141

No. 295: a, La Paz Medical Center, Bata. b, Gepetrol Building, Malabo. c, Gecotel Building, Bata. d, Central African Economic and Monetary Community Parliament Building, Malabo.

2010, June 15

295	Horiz. strip of 4	9.25	9.25
a.	A141 475fr multi	1.90	1.90
b.	A141 575fr multi	2.25	2.25
c.	A141 625fr multi	2.40	2.40
d.	A141 675fr multi	2.60	2.60

2010 World Cup Soccer Championships, South Africa — A142

No. 296: a, Emblem of 2010 tournament. b, Mascot. c, World Cup. d, Colors of Spain, World Cup champions.

2010 Litho. *Perf. 13¼x13¾*

296	Horiz. strip of 4	9.75	9.75
a.	A142 475fr multi	2.00	2.00
b.	A142 575fr multi	2.40	2.40
c.	A142 625fr multi	2.60	2.60
d.	A142 675fr multi	2.75	2.75

Miniature Sheet

Christmas — A143

No. 297: a, 375fr, Adoration of the Shepherds, by Anton Rafael Mengs. b, 425fr, Adoration of the Magi, by Diego Velázquez. c, 475fr, Nativity, by Hans Memling. d, 525fr, Adoration of the Shepherds, by El Greco.

2010

297	A143 Sheet of 4, #a-d	7.50	7.50

Intl. Women's Day, Cent. A144

No. 298 — Stylized woman as: a, Doctor. b, Police officer. c, Chemist. d, Chef.

2011 *Perf. 13¾x14*

298	Horiz. strip of 4	11.50	11.50
a.	A144 525fr black	2.40	2.40
b.	A144 625fr green	2.75	2.75
c.	A144 675fr red violet	3.00	3.00
d.	A144 725fr blue	3.25	3.25

Intl. Year of Chemistry — A145

No. 299 — Emblem and: a, Chemical glassware. b, Molecular model and textbook. c, Children in school. d, Water.

2011 *Perf. 14x13¾*

299	Horiz. strip of 4	11.50	11.50
a.	A145 525fr multi	2.40	2.40
b.	A145 625fr multi	2.75	2.75
c.	A145 675fr multi	3.00	3.00
d.	A145 725fr multi	3.25	3.25

Gustavo Adolfo Bécquer (1836-70), Poet — A146

No. 300: a, Drawing of Woman. b, Windows of Veruela Monastery. c, Portrait of Bécquer by his brother, Valeriano.

2011

300	Horiz. strip of 3	7.75	7.75
a.	A146 525fr multi	2.25	2.25
b.	A146 625fr multi	2.60	2.60
c.	A146 675fr multi	2.75	2.75

Christmas A147

No. 301 — Christmas-themed paintings by: a, Nicolás Francés. b, Fra Angelico. c, Luca di Tommè. d, Jaume Serra.

2011 *Perf. 13¾x14*

301	Horiz. strip of 4	11.00	11.00
a.	A147 525fr multi	2.25	2.25
b.	A147 625fr multi	2.60	2.60
c.	A147 675fr multi	2.75	2.75
d.	A147 725fr multi	3.00	3.00

Paintings by Juan Gris (1887-1927) A148

Various paintings.

2012 *Perf. 14x13¾*

302	Horiz. strip of 4	9.75	9.75
a.	A148 525fr multi	2.00	2.00
b.	A148 625fr multi	2.40	2.40
c.	A148 675fr multi	2.60	2.60
d.	A148 725fr multi	2.75	2.75

Spices — A149

No. 303: a, Xylopia aethiopica. b, Piper guineense. c, Capsicum frutescens. d, Zingiber officinale.

2012

303	Horiz. strip of 4	10.50	10.50
a.	A149 525fr multi	2.10	2.10
b.	A149 625fr multi	2.50	2.50
c.	A149 675fr multi	2.75	2.75
d.	A149 725fr multi	3.00	3.00

Sports A150

No. 304: a, Gymnastics. b, Table tennis. c, Running. d, Kayaking.

2012 ***Perf. 14x13¾***

304	Horiz. strip of 4	10.50	10.50
a.	A150 525fr multi	2.10	2.10
b.	A150 625fr multi	2.50	2.50
c.	A150 675fr multi	2.75	2.75
d.	A150 725fr multi	3.00	3.00

Christmas A151

No. 305 — Religious painting by: a, Pietro de Lignis. b, Francisco and Rodrigo de Osona. c, Pietro da Cortona. d, Hans Memling.

2012 ***Perf. 14x13¾***

305	Horiz. strip of 4	10.50	10.50
a.	A151 525fr multi	2.10	2.10
b.	A151 625fr multi	2.50	2.50
c.	A151 675fr multi	2.75	2.75
d.	A151 725fr multi	3.00	3.00

Tourist Areas A152

No. 306: a, Sipopo. b, Luba. c, Mbini. d, Bata.

2013 ***Perf. 13¾x13¼***

306	Horiz. strip of 4	10.00	10.00
a.	A152 550fr multi	2.25	2.25
b.	A152 600fr multi	2.40	2.40
c.	A152 650fr multi	2.60	2.60
d.	A152 700fr multi	2.75	2.75

Intl. Red Cross, 150th Anniv. A153

No. 307: a, Students in classroom. b, Man carrying large pot on head. c, Red Cross worker. d, Flags on building.

2013 ***Perf. 13¾x14***

307	Horiz. strip of 4	10.00	10.00
a.	A153 550fr multi	2.25	2.25
b.	A153 600fr multi	2.40	2.40
c.	A153 650fr multi	2.60	2.60
d.	A153 700fr multi	2.75	2.75

Pope John XXIII (1881-1963) A154

No. 307: a, Pope John XXIII. b, Pope John XXIII, diff. c, Pope John XXIII, diff. d, Arms of Pope John XXIII.

2013 ***Perf. 13¼x13¾***

308	Horiz. strip of 4	10.50	10.50
a.	A154 550fr multi	2.25	2.25
b.	A154 600fr multi	2.50	2.50
c.	A154 650fr multi	2.75	2.75
d.	A154 700fr multi	3.00	3.00

Christmas — A155

No. 308: a, Nativity. b, Adoration of the Magi. c, Nativity, diff. d, Nativity, diff.

2013 ***Perf. 13¼x13¾***

309	Horiz. strip of 4	10.50	10.50
a.	A155 550fr multi	2.25	2.25
b.	A155 600fr multi	2.50	2.50
c.	A155 650fr multi	2.75	2.75
d.	A155 700fr multi	3.00	3.00

Bolondo-Mbini Bridge — A156

Various views of bridge.

2014 **Litho.** ***Perf. 13¼x13¾***

310	Horiz. strip of 4	11.50	11.50
a.	A156 600fr multi	2.50	2.50
b.	A156 650fr multi	2.75	2.75
c.	A156 700fr multi	3.00	3.00
d.	A156 750fr multi	3.25	3.25

Intl. Year of Family Farms A157

No. 311: a, Hands leveling earth. b, Woman tending cows. c, Woman tending goats. d, Farmer inspecting crops.

2014 **Litho.** ***Perf. 13¾x13¼***

311	Horiz. strip of 4	11.50	11.50
a.	A157 600fr multi	2.50	2.50
b.	A157 650fr multi	2.75	2.75
c.	A157 700fr multi	3.00	3.00
d.	A157 750fr multi	3.25	3.25

Religious Paintings by El Greco (1541-1614) A158

No. 312: a, St. Andrew and St. Francis. b, Christ Carrying the Cross. c, St. Peter. d, The Disrobing of Christ.

2014 **Litho.** ***Perf. 13¼x13¾***

312	Horiz. strip of 4	10.50	10.50
a.	A158 600fr multi	2.25	2.25
b.	A158 650fr multi	2.50	2.50
c.	A158 700fr multi	2.75	2.75
d.	A158 750fr multi	3.00	3.00

Christmas A159

No. 313: a, Adoration of the Shepherds, by Bartolomé Esteban Murillo. b, Adoration of the Magi, by Peter Paul Rubens. c, Adoration of the Magi, by Luis de Morales. d, Adoration of the Shepherds, by de Morales.

2014 **Litho.** ***Perf. 13¼x13¾***

313	Horiz. strip of 4	10.50	10.50
a.	A159 600fr multi	2.25	2.25
b.	A159 650fr multi	2.50	2.50
c.	A159 700fr multi	2.75	2.75
d.	A159 750fr multi	3.00	3.00

Sipopo Congresws Center, Malabo — A160

No. 314: a, Seats and video screen in meeting hall (29x41mm). b, Seats in auditorium (29x41mm). c, Building exterior (29x41mm). d, Building entrance (58x41mm).

2015 **Litho.** ***Perf. 13¼x13¾***

314	Horiz. strip of 4	14.50	14.50
a.	A160 650fr multi	2.25	2.25
b.	A160 700fr multi	2.40	2.40
c.	A160 750fr multi	2.60	2.60
d.	A160 2100fr multi	7.25	7.25

Paintings of Women by Federico de Madrazo y Kuntz (1815-94) — A161

No. 315 — Various women wearing: a, Blue dress. b, White dress. c, Lilac dress. d, Black dress.

2015 **Litho.** ***Perf. 13¾***

315	Horiz. strip of 4	9.25	9.25
a.	A161 600fr multi	2.00	2.00
b.	A161 650fr multi	2.25	2.25
c.	A161 700fr multi	2.40	2.40
d.	A161 750fr multi	2.60	2.60

International Year of Light — A162

No. 316: a, Fiber optic cord connector. b, Ends of optical fibers. c, Ends of optical fibers, diff. d, Close-up of ends of bound optical fibers.

2015 **Litho.** ***Perf. 13¾x13¼***

316	Horiz. strip of 4	8.75	8.75
a.	A162 600fr multi	2.00	2.00
b.	A162 650fr multi	2.10	2.10
c.	A162 700fr multi	2.25	2.25
d.	A162 750fr multi	2.40	2.40

Christmas — A163

No. 317 — Various Nativity paintings by unknown artists from: a, Prado, Madrid. b, Museum of Fine Arts, Bilbao. c, Prado, diff. d, Museum of Fine Arts, diff.

2015 **Litho.** ***Perf. 13¼x13¾***

317	Horiz. strip of 4	8.75	8.75
a.	A163 600fr multi	2.00	2.00
b.	A163 650fr multi	2.10	2.10
c.	A163 700fr multi	2.25	2.25
d.	A163 750fr multi	2.40	2.40

SPECIAL DELIVERY STAMPS

Archer with Crossbow — SD1

1971, Oct. 12 **Photo.** ***Perf. 12½x13***

E1	SD1 4p blue & multi	1.00	.25
E2	SD1 8p rose & multi	1.50	.35

3rd anniversary of independence.

ERITREA

ˌer-ə-ˈtrē-ə

LOCATION — In northeast Africa, bordering on the Red Sea, Sudan, Ethiopia and Djibouti.
GOVT. — Independent state
AREA — 45,300 (?) sq. mi.
POP. — 3,984,723 (1999 est.)
CAPITAL — Asmara

Formerly an Italian colony, Eritrea was incorporated as a State of Italian East Africa in 1936.

Under British occupation (1941-52) until it became part of Ethiopia as its northernmost region. Eritrea became independent May 24, 1993.

100 Centesimi = 1 Lira
100 cents = 1 birr (1991)
100 cents = 1 nakfa (1997)

Catalogue values for unused stamps in this country are for Never Hinged items, beginning with Scott 200 in the regular postage section.

All used values to about 1916 are for postally used stamps. From 1916-1934, used values in italics are for postally used stamps. CTO's, for stamps valued postally used, sell for about the same as unused, hinged stamps.

Watermark

Wmk. 140 — Crown

Stamps of Italy Overprinted

a

b

1892 Wmk. 140 *Perf. 14*

Overprinted Type "a" in Black

1 A6 1c bronze grn 10.00 10.00
a. Inverted overprint 675.00 675.00
b. Double overprint 1,900.
Never hinged 2,400.
c. Vert. pair, one without overprint 4,500.
Never hinged 5,750.
2 A7 2c org brn 5.00 5.00
a. Inverted overprint 600.00 600.00
b. Double overprint 1,900.
Never hinged 2,400.
3 A33 5c green 160.00 17.50
a. Inverted overprint 8,000. 4,500.
Never hinged 10,000.

Overprinted Type "b" in Black

4 A17 10c claret 210.00 17.50
5 A17 20c orange 375.00 12.00
6 A17 25c blue 1,450. 55.00
7 A25 40c brown 13.50 *32.50*
8 A26 45c slate grn 13.50 *32.50*
9 A27 60c violet 13.50 72.50
10 A28 1 l brn & yel 65.00 *80.00*
11 A38 5 l bl & rose 650.00 550.00
Nos. 1-11 (11) 2,965. *884.50*
Set, never hinged 7,300.

1895-99

Overprinted type "a" in Black

12 A39 1c brown ('99) 22.50 12.00
13 A40 2c org brn ('99) 4.75 2.40
14 A41 5c green 4.75 2.40
a. Inverted overprint 525.00 *4,250.*

Overprinted type "b" in Black

15 A34 10c claret ('98) 4.75 2.40
16 A35 20c orange 4.75 3.25
17 A36 25c blue 4.75 4.75
18 A37 45c olive grn 37.50 *27.50*
Nos. 12-18 (7) 83.75 *54.70*
Set, never hinged 215.00

1903-28

Overprinted type "a" in Black

19 A42 1c brown 1.60 *1.25*
a. Inverted overprint 125.00 125.00
20 A43 2c orange brn 1.60 .60
21 A44 5c blue green 120.00 .60
22 A45 10c claret 140.00 .60
23 A45 20c orange 6.50 1.25
24 A45 25c blue 1,200. 18.00
a. Double overprint 1,100. —
25 A45 40c brown 1,300. 30.00
26 A45 45c olive grn 8.00 *10.00*
27 A45 50c violet 475.00 32.50
28 A46 75c dk red & rose ('28) 80.00 20.00
29 A46 1 l brown & grn 8.00 .85
30 A46 1.25 l bl & ultra ('28) 40.00 20.00
31 A46 2 l dk grn & org ('25) 87.50 *100.00*
32 A46 2.50 l dk grn & org ('28) 175.00 72.50
33 A46 5 l blue & rose 55.00 *45.00*
Nos. 19-33 (15) 3,698. 353.15
Set, never hinged 9,250.

Surcharged in Black

1905

34 A45 15c on 20c orange 80.00 20.00
Never hinged 200.00

1908-28

Overprinted type "a" in Black

35 A48 5c green 1.20 1.00
36 A48 10c claret ('09) 1.20 1.00
37 A48 15c slate ('20) 22.50 14.50
38 A49 20c green ('25) 16.00 11.00
39 A49 20c lilac brn ('28) 8.00 3.25
40 A49 25c blue ('09) 6.50 2.25
41 A49 30c gray ('25) 16.00 14.50
42 A49 40c brown ('16) 55.00 40.00
43 A49 50c violet ('16) 16.00 2.10
44 A49 60c brown car ('18) 27.50 *28.00*
a. Printed on both sides *1,750.*
45 A49 60c brown org ('28) 110.00 *225.00*
46 A51 10 l gray grn & red ('16) 425.00 *775.00*
Nos. 35-46 (12) 704.90 *1,117.*
Set, never hinged 1,750.

See No. 53.

A1

Government Building at Massaua — A2

1910-29 Unwmk. Engr. *Perf. 13½*

47 A1 15c slate 390.00 30.00
a. Perf. 11 ('29) 40.00 *55.00*
Never hinged 100.00
48 A2 25c dark blue 7.25 *17.50*
a. Perf. 12 875.00 875.00

For surcharges see Nos. 51-52.

A3

Farmer Plowing — A4

1914-28

49 A3 5c green 1.20 *2.50*
a. Perf. 11 ('28) 210.00 75.00
Never hinged 525.00
50 A4 10c carmine 4.75 *4.25*
a. Perf. 11 ('28) 12.00 *47.50*
Never hinged 30.00
b. Perf. 13½x14 62.50 62.50

No. 47 Surcharged in Red or Black

1916

51 A1 5c on 15c slate (R) 8.75 *15.00*
52 A1 20c on 15c slate 4.00 4.25
a. "CEN" for "CENT" 47.50 47.50
b. "CENT" omitted 190.00 190.00
c. "ENT" 47.50 *47.50*
Set, never hinged 32.00

Italy No. 113 Overprinted in Black — f

1921 Wmk. 140 *Perf. 14*

53 A50 20c brown orange 4.75 *15.00*
Never hinged 12.00

Victory Issue

Italian Victory Stamps of 1921 Overprinted type "f" 13mm long

1922

54 A64 5c olive green 2.00 *7.25*
55 A64 10c red 2.00 *7.25*
56 A64 15c slate green 2.00 *11.00*
57 A64 25c ultra 2.00 *11.00*
Nos. 54-57 (4) 8.00 *36.50*
Set, never hinged 20.00

Somalia Nos. 10-16 Overprinted In Black g

1922 Wmk. 140

58 A1 2c on 1b brn 4.75 *17.50*
a. Pair, one missing "ERITREA" 2,250.
59 A1 5c on 2b bl grn 4.75 *13.00*
60 A2 10c on 1a claret 4.75 2.40
61 A2 15c on 2a brn org 4.75 2.40
62 A2 25c on 2½a blue 4.75 2.40
63 A2 50c on 5a yellow 22.50 13.50
a. "ERITREA" double *1,600.*
64 A2 1 l on 10a lilac 22.50 22.50
a. "ERITREA" double 1,600. 1,600.
b. Pair, one missing "ERITREA" *3,000.*
Nos. 58-64 (7) 68.75 *73.70*
Set, never hinged 170.00

See Nos. 81-87.

Propagation of the Faith Issue

Italy Nos. 143-146 Overprinted

1923

65 A68 20c ol grn & brn org 12.00 *52.50*
66 A68 30c claret & brn org 12.00 *52.50*
67 A68 50c vio & brn org 8.00 *60.00*
68 A68 1 l bl & brn org 8.00 *92.50*
Nos. 65-68 (4) 40.00 *257.50*
Set, never hinged 100.00

Fascisti Issue

Italy Nos. 159-164 Overprinted in Red or Black — j

1923 Unwmk. *Perf. 14*

69 A69 10c dk green (R) 11.00 *20.00*
70 A69 30c dk violet (R) 11.00 *20.00*
71 A69 50c brown carmine 11.00 *27.50*

Wmk. 140

72 A70 1 l blue 11.00 *52.50*
73 A70 2 l brown 11.00 *65.00*
74 A71 5 l black & blue (R) 11.00 *95.00*
Nos. 69-74 (6) 66.00 *280.00*
Set, never hinged 165.00

Manzoni Issue

Italy Nos. 165-170 Overprinted in Red

1924 *Perf. 14*

75 A72 10c brown red & blk 12.00 *80.00*
76 A72 15c blue grn & blk 12.00 *80.00*
77 A72 30c black & slate 12.00 *80.00*
78 A72 50c org brn & blk 12.00 *80.00*
79 A72 1 l blue & blk 72.50 *475.00*
80 A72 5 l violet & blk 475.00 *3,250.*
Nos. 75-80 (6) 595.50 *4,045.*
Set, never hinged 1,500.

On Nos. 79 and 80 the overprint is placed vertically at the left side.

Somalia Nos. 10-16 Overprinted type "g" in Blue or Red

1924

Bars over Original Values

81 A1 2c on 1b brn 17.50 *27.50*
a. Pair, one without "ERITREA" 2,400.
82 A1 5c on 2b bl grn (R) 17.50 *17.50*
83 A2 10c on 1a rose red 9.50 *16.00*
84 A2 15c on 2a brn org 9.50 *16.00*
a. Pair, one without "ERITREA" 2,400.
b. "ERITREA" inverted 1,750. 1,750.
85 A2 25c on 2½a bl (R) 9.50 *11.00*
a. Double surcharge 1,200.
86 A2 50c on 5a yellow 9.50 *20.00*
87 A2 1 l on 10a lil (R) 9.50 *27.50*
Nos. 81-87 (7) 82.50 *135.50*
Set, never hinged 200.00

Stamps of Italy, 1901-08 Overprinted type "j" in Black

1924

88 A42 1c brown 9.50 *9.50*
a. Inverted overprint 325.00
b. Vertical pair, one without ovpt. 1,750.

89 A43 2c orange brown 6.50 *8.00*
b. Vertical pair, one without ovpt. 1,750.
90 A48 5c green 9.50 *8.75*
Nos. 88-90 (3) 25.50 *26.25*
Set, never hinged 60.00

Victor Emmanuel Issue

Italy Nos. 175-177 Overprinted — k

1925-26 **Unwmk.** ***Perf. 11***

91 A78 60c brown car 2.40 *9.50*
a. Perf. 13½ 13.00 40.00
92 A78 1 l dark blue 2.40 *14.50*
a. Perf. 13½ 24,000. 9,500.
Never hinged 36,000.

Perf. 13½

93 A78 1.25 l dk blue ('26) 4.00 *32.50*
a. Perf. 11 8.00 40.00
Nos. 91-93 (3) 8.80 *56.50*
Set, never hinged 22.00

Saint Francis of Assisi Issue

Italian Stamps of 1926 Overprinted

1926 **Wmk. 140** ***Perf. 14***

94 A79 20c gray green 2.40 *14.00*
95 A80 40c dark violet 2.40 *14.00*
96 A81 60c red violet 2.40 *26.00*

Overprinted in Red

Unwmk. ***Perf. 11***

97 A82 1.25 l dark blue 2.40 *36.00*

Perf. 14

98 A83 5 l + 2.50 l ol grn 8.00 *72.50*
Nos. 94-98 (5) 17.60 *162.50*
Set, never hinged 44.00

Italian Stamps of 1926 Overprinted type "f" in Black

1926 **Wmk. 140** ***Perf. 14***

99 A46 75c dk red & rose 80.00 20.00
a. Double overprint 450.00
100 A46 1.25 l blue & ultra 40.00 20.00
101 A46 2.50 l dk green & org 175.00 72.50
Nos. 99-101 (3) 295.00 112.50
Set, never hinged 725.00

Volta Issue

Type of Italy, 1927, Overprinted — o

1927

102 A84 20c purple 6.50 *40.00*
103 A84 50c deep orange 9.50 *27.50*
a. Double overprint 200.00
104 A84 1.25 l brt blue 14.00 *65.00*
Nos. 102-104 (3) 30.00 *132.50*
Set, never hinged 75.00

Italian Stamps of 1925-28 Overprinted type "a" in Black

1928-29

105 A86 7½c lt brown ('29) 24.00 *72.50*
106 A86 50c brt violet 87.50 65.00
Set, never hinged 270.00

Italian Stamps of 1927-28 Overprinted type "f"

1928-29

107 A86 50c brt violet 72.50 *60.00*
Never hinged 175.00

Unwmk. ***Perf. 11***

107A A85 1.75 l deep brown 95.00 52.50
Never hinged 240.00

Italy No. 192 Overprinted type "o"

1928 **Wmk. 140** ***Perf. 14***

108 A85 50c brown & slate 24.00 12.00
Never hinged 60.00

Monte Cassino Issue

Types of 1929 Issue of Italy Overprinted in Red or Blue

1929 ***Perf. 14***

109 A96 20c dk green (R) 6.50 *22.50*
110 A96 25c red orange (Bl) 6.50 *22.50*
111 A98 50c + 10c crim (Bl) 6.50 *24.00*
112 A98 75c + 15c ol brn (R) 6.50 *24.00*
113 A96 1.25 l + 25c dl vio (R) 14.50 *45.00*
114 A98 5 l + 1 l saph (R) 14.50 *47.50*

Overprinted in Red

Unwmk.

115 A100 10 l + 2 l gray brn 14.50 *72.50*
Nos. 109-115 (7) 69.50 *258.00*
Set, never hinged 170.00

Royal Wedding Issue

Type of Italian Stamps of 1930 Overprinted

1930 **Wmk. 140**

116 A101 20c yellow green 3.25 *9.50*
117 A101 50c + 10c dp orange 2.40 *9.50*
118 A101 1.25 l + 25c rose red 2.40 *19.00*
Nos. 116-118 (3) 8.05 *38.00*
Set, never hinged 20.00

Lancer — A5

Scene in Massaua A6

2c, 35c, Lancer. 5c, 10c, Postman. 15c, Lineman. 25c, Askari (infantryman). 2 l, Railroad viaduct. 5 l, Asmara Deghe Selam. 10 l, Camels.

1930 **Wmk. 140** **Litho.** ***Perf. 14***

119 A5 2c brt bl & blk 4.75 *20.00*
120 A5 5c dk vio & blk 8.00 2.40
121 A5 10c yel brn & blk 8.00 1.25
122 A5 15c dk grn & blk 8.00 1.60
123 A5 25c gray grn & blk 8.00 1.25
124 A5 35c red brn & blk 12.50 *35.00*
125 A6 1 l dk bl & blk 8.00 1.25
126 A6 2 l choc & blk 12.50 *40.00*
127 A6 5 l ol grn & blk 24.00 *52.50*
128 A6 10 l dl bl & blk 32.50 *100.00*
Nos. 119-128 (10) 126.25 *255.25*
Set, never hinged 310.00

Ferrucci Issue

Types of Italian Stamps of 1930 Overprinted type "f" in Red or Blue

1930

129 A102 20c violet (R) 6.50 *6.50*
130 A103 25c dk green (R) 6.50 *6.50*
131 A103 50c black (R) 6.50 *12.00*
132 A103 1.25 l dp blue (R) 6.50 *22.50*
133 A104 5 l + 2 l dp car (Bl) 14.50 *47.50*
Nos. 129-133 (5) 40.50 *95.00*
Set, never hinged 99.00

Virgil Issue

Types of Italian Stamps of 1930 Overprinted in Red or Blue

1930 **Photo.**

134 A106 15c violet black 1.25 *12.00*
135 A106 20c orange brown 1.25 *4.75*
136 A106 25c dark green 1.25 *4.75*
137 A106 30c lt brown 1.25 *4.75*
138 A106 50c dull violet 1.25 *4.75*
139 A106 75c rose red 1.25 *9.50*
140 A106 1.25 l gray blue 1.25 *12.00*

Unwmk. **Engr.**

141 A106 5 l + 1.50 l dk vio 4.75 *47.50*
142 A106 10 l + 2.50 l ol brn 4.75 *72.50*
Nos. 134-142 (9) 18.25 *172.50*
Set, never hinged 44.00

Saint Anthony of Padua Issue

Types of Italian Stamps of 1931 Overprinted type "f" in Blue, Red or Black

1931 **Photo.** **Wmk. 140**

143 A116 20c brown (Bl) 1.60 *22.50*
144 A116 25c green (R) 1.60 *8.00*
145 A118 30c gray brn (Bl) 1.60 *8.00*
146 A118 50c dl violet (Bl) 1.60 *8.00*
147 A120 1.25 l slate bl (R) 1.60 *40.00*

Unwmk. **Engr.**

148 A121 75c black (R) 1.60 *22.50*
149 A122 5 l + 2.50 l dk brn (Bk) 11.00 *80.00*
Nos. 143-149 (7) 20.60 *189.00*
Set, never hinged 55.00

Victor Emmanuel III — A13

1931 **Photo.** **Wmk. 140**

150 A13 7½c olive brown 1.60 *6.50*
151 A13 20c slate bl & car 1.60 .25
152 A13 30c ol grn & brn vio 1.60 .25
153 A13 40c bl & yel grn 2.40 .25
154 A13 50c bis brn & ol 1.60 .25
155 A13 75c carmine rose 4.75 .25
156 A13 1.25 l violet & indigo 6.50 6.50
157 A13 2.50 l dull green 6.50 14.50
Nos. 150-157 (8) 26.55 28.75
Set, never hinged 65.00

Camel A14

Temple Ruins — A18

Designs: 2c, 10c, Camel. 5c, 15c, Shark fishery. 25c, Baobab tree. 35c, Pastoral scene. 2 l, African elephant. 5 l, Eritrean man. 10 l, Eritrean woman.

1934 **Photo.** **Wmk. 140**

158 A14 2c deep blue 2.40 *4.75*
159 A14 5c black 4.00 .40
160 A14 10c brown 4.00 .35
161 A14 15c orange brn 4.75 *1.60*
162 A14 25c gray green 4.00 .35
163 A14 35c purple 12.50 *9.50*
164 A18 1 l dk blue gray .80 .35
165 A14 2 l olive black 35.00 3.25
166 A18 5 l carmine rose 19.00 6.50
167 A18 10 l red orange 27.50 *22.50*
Nos. 158-167 (10) 113.95 *49.55*
Set, never hinged 275.00

Abruzzi Issue

Types of 1934 Issue Overprinted in Black or Red

1934

168 A14 10c dull blue (R) 22.50 *32.50*
169 A14 15c blue 16.00 *32.50*
170 A14 35c green (R) 9.50 *32.50*
171 A18 1 l copper red 9.50 *32.50*
172 A14 2 l rose red 27.50 *32.50*
173 A18 5 l purple (R) 19.00 *55.00*
174 A18 10 l olive grn (R) 19.00 *72.50*
Nos. 168-174 (7) 123.00 *290.00*
Set, never hinged 300.00

Grant's Gazelle A22

1934 **Photo.**

175 A22 5c ol grn & brn 5.50 *22.50*
176 A22 10c yel brn & blk 5.50 *22.50*
177 A22 20c scar & indigo 5.50 *20.00*
178 A22 50c dk vio & brn 5.50 *20.00*
179 A22 60c org brn & ind 5.50 *27.50*
180 A22 1.25 l dk bl & grn 5.50 *47.50*
Nos. 175-180 (6) 33.00 *160.00*
Set, never hinged 80.00

Second Colonial Arts Exhibition, Naples. See Nos. C1-C6.

Between 1981 and 1986 unofficial labels appeared showing such non-Eritrean subjects as the British royal weddings, Queen Mother, Queen's birthday, and the Duke & Duchess of York. These labels are not listed.

In 1978, two sets of stamps were issued for use within liberated areas of Eritrea and to publicize the liberation effort. A May 26 set of 5c, 10c, 80c and 1b commemorated the 8th anniv. of the Eritrean People's Liberation Front (EPLF). An August 1 set of 80c, 1b, 1.50b featured the Future of Eritrea theme. A September 1, 1991 set of 5c, 15c and 20c was issued with a Freedom Fighter design in orange and black almost identical to design A24. Although the 80c from the 1st 1978 issue was available at the Asmara post office in late 1992 and early 1993, there is no evidence that any of these stamps were available at the time of independence. Thus these stamps are more properly considered locals and provisionals.

A23

Freedom Fighter with EPLF Flags

1991, Jan. 16 Typo. *Perf. 11 rough*

192 A23 5c lt bl, blk & org *30.00 40.00*
193 A23 15c pale green, blk & org *30.00 40.00*
194 A23 20c pale yel, blk & org *30.00 40.00*
195 A23 3b silver, blk & org *25.00 25.00*
196 A23 5b gold, blk & org *25.00 25.00*

See footnotes following No. 199.

A24

1993, Feb. 1 Litho. *Perf. 10*

197 A24 5c lt bl, blk & org *25.00 25.00*
198 A24 15c pale grn, blk & org *25.00 25.00*
199 A24 20c pale yel, blk & org *25.00 25.00*

Nos. 192-199 commemorate 30 years of the war for national liberation.

Nos. 192-199 were issued for local use, and became valid for International mail on Sept. 13, 1993.

Catalogue values for unused stamps in this section, from this point to the end of the section, are for Never Hinged items.

Referendum for Independence A25

Designs: 15c, Placing ballot in box. 60c, Group of arrows pointing right, one pointing left. 75c, Signs indicating "yes" & "no." 1b, Candle burning. 2b, Peace dove, horn over country map.

Perf. 14x15

1993, Apr. 22 Litho. Wmk. 373

200 A25 15c multicolored *1.50 1.50*
201 A25 60c multicolored *2.75 2.75*
202 A25 75c multicolored *4.00 4.00*
203 A25 1b multicolored *7.50 7.50*
204 A25 2b multicolored *10.00 10.00*
Nos. 200-204 (5) 25.75 25.75

Natl. Flag — A26

1993 Litho. *Perf. 11 rough*

Blue Border

205 A26 5c multicolored *2.50 .50*
206 A26 20c multicolored — —
207 A26 35c multicolored *4.25 2.00*
208 A26 50c multicolored *11.00 2.50*
209 A26 70c multicolored *3.50 3.50*
210 A26 80c multicolored *3.50 4.00*

The border of the 40c, No. 215, is similar to that of this issue but it was issued with next set. And the type face of the "0.40" matches that set.

1994 Litho. *Perf. 11 rough*

Color of Border

211 A26 5c brown *2.00 1.50*
212 A26 15c red *2.00 1.50*
213 A26 20c gold *15.00 —*
214 A26 25c lt blue *2.00 1.50*
215 A26 40c blue *15.00 15.00*
216 A26 60c yellow *3.00 2.00*
217 A26 70c purple *3.00 2.25*
218 A26 3b light green *7.50 6.00*
219 A26 5b silver *9.00 6.00*

Flag & Map — A27

1994, Sept. 2 Litho. *Perf. 13½x14*

Color of Border

220 A27 5c deep yellow *.45 .40*
221 A27 10c yellow green *.50 .45*
222 A27 20c salmon *.70 .65*
223 A27 25c red *1.25 1.25*
224 A27 40c lilac rose *1.40 1.25*
225 A27 60c blue green *1.50 1.25*
226 A27 70c dark green *1.60 1.50*
227 A27 1b yellow *1.60 1.50*
228 A27 2b orange *1.75 1.50*
229 A27 3b blue violet *1.90 1.75*
230 A27 5b red lilac *2.25 2.00*
231 A27 10b pale violet *3.75 3.50*
Nos. 220-231 (12) 18.65 17.00

See Nos. 277A-277D.

World Tourism Organization, 20th Anniv. — A29

Perf. 14x13½, 13½x14

1995, Jan. 2 Litho.

232 A29 10c Fishing from boat *1.50 1.50*
233 A29 35c Monument, vert. *1.50 1.50*
234 A29 85c Winding road *3.00 3.00*
235 A29 2b Stone dwelling, vert. *5.00 5.00*
Nos. 232-235 (4) 11.00 11.00

Fish — A30

Designs: 30c, Horned butterflyfish, 55c, Gonochaetodon larvatus. 70c, Shrimp lobster. 1b, Bluestripe snapper.

1995, Apr. 1 *Perf. 14x13½*

236 A30 30c multicolored *.60 .60*
237 A30 55c multicolored *.85 .85*
238 A30 70c multicolored *1.25 1.25*
239 A30 1b multicolored *1.50 1.50*
Nos. 236-239 (4) 4.20 4.20

Independence Day — A31

Designs: 25c, Breaking chains, mountain, buildings, animals. 40c, Raising natl. flag, vert. 70c, Three men, holding natl. flag, sword, vert. 3b, Natl. flag, fireworks, vert.

Perf. 14x13½, 13½x14

1995, May 23 Litho.

240 A31 25c multicolored *.40 .40*
241 A31 40c multicolored *.45 .45*
242 A31 70c multicolored *.70 .70*
243 A31 3b multicolored *1.40 1.40*
Nos. 240-243 (4) 2.95 2.95

Future Development Plan — A32

1995, Aug. 28 Litho. *Perf. 13*

244 A32 60c Building bridge *.60 .60*
245 A32 80c Trees *.75 .75*
246 A32 90c Rural village *.90 .90*
247 A32 1b Camels *1.00 1.00*
Nos. 244-247 (4) 3.25 3.25

A33

1995, Oct. 23 *Perf. 13½x14*

248 A33 40c shown *.30 .30*
249 A33 60c Tree, emblem *.40 .40*
250 A33 70c Dove, "50," emblem *.50 .50*
251 A33 2b like No. 248 *2.25 2.25*
Nos. 248-251 (4) 3.45 3.45

UN, 50th anniv.

A34

COMESA, Committee for Economic Growth and Development in Southern Africa: 40c, Map of African member countries. 50c, Tree with country names on branches. 60c, Emblem, 3b, Emblem surrounded by country flags, horiz.

1995, Oct. 2 *Perf. 13½x14, 14x13½*

252 A34 40c multicolored *.30 .30*
253 A34 50c multicolored *.50 .50*
254 A34 60c multicolored *.60 .60*
255 A34 3b multicolored *2.25 2.25*
Nos. 252-255 (4) 3.65 3.65

FAO, 50th Anniv. — A35

5c, Food bowl with world map on it, spoon. 25c, Men with tractor. 80c, Mother bird feeding chicks. 3b, Vegetables in horn of plenty.

1995, Dec. 18 Litho. *Perf. 13x14*

256 A35 5c multicolored *.40 .40*
257 A35 25c multicolored *.40 .40*
258 A35 80c multicolored *.80 .80*
259 A35 3b multicolored *2.50 2.50*
Nos. 256-259 (4) 4.10 4.10

Endangered Fauna — A36

No. 260: a, Green monkey. b, Aardwolf. c, Dugong. d, Maned rat.

Beisa oryx: No. 261: a, With young. b, One facing left. c, Two with heads together. d, One facing right.

White-eyed gull: No. 262: a, Preening. b, In flight. c, Two standing. d, One facing right.

1996, July 15 Litho. *Perf. 14*

260-262 A36 3b Set of 3 strips 26.00 26.00

Nos. 260-262 were each issued in sheets of 12 stamps, containing three strips of four stamps, Nos. a.-d. No. 261 for World Wildlife Fund.

Martyrs Day — A37

1996, June 17 Litho. *Perf. 13½x14*

263 A37 40c People, flag .40 .40
264 A37 60c At grave .40 .40
265 A37 70c Mother, child .80 .80
266 A37 80c Planting crops 1.00 1.00
Nos. 263-266 (4) 2.60 2.60

1996 Summer Olympic Games, Atlanta A38

No. 267, Cycling. No. 268, Basketball, vert. No. 269, Volleyball, vert. No. 270, Soccer.

No. 271, vert: a, Volleyball. b, Laurel wreath. c, Basketball. d, Torch. e, Cycling, yellow shirt. f, Torch, diff. g, Cycling, green shirt. h, Gold medal. i, Soccer.

Each 10b: No. 272, Soccer, vert. No. 273, Cycling, vert.

1996, Nov. 20 Litho. *Perf. 14*

267-270 A38 3b Set of 4 7.50 7.50
271 A38 2b Sheet of 9, #a.-i. 11.00 11.00

Souvenir Sheets

272-273 A38 Set of 2 11.00 11.00

UNICEF, 50th Anniv. A39

UNICEF emblem and: 40c, Mother with child. 55c, Nurse helping child. 60c, Weighing baby. 95c, Boy with one leg walking with crutch.

1996, Dec. 9 Litho. *Perf. 14x13½*

274 A39 40c multicolored .45 .45
275 A39 55c multicolored .45 .45
276 A39 60c multicolored 1.00 1.00
277 A39 95c multicolored 1.00 1.00
Nos. 274-277 (4) 2.90 2.90

Flag and Map Type of 1994 Redrawn With Islands Added on Map at Lower Right

1996, Dec. 25 Litho. *Perf. 13½x14*

Color of Border

277A A27 20c salmon — —
277B A27 40c lilac rose — —
277C A27 60c blue green — —
277D A27 3b blue violet — —

Revival of Eritrea Railway A40

Designs: 40c, Repairing track. 55c, Steam train arriving at station. 60c, Train shuttle transporting people. 95c, Train tunnel.

1997, Jan. 10

278 A40 40c multicolored .50 .50
279 A40 55c multicolored .50 .50
280 A40 60c multicolored .50 .50
281 A40 95c multicolored 1.50 1.50
Nos. 278-281 (4) 3.00 3.00

National Service A41

40c, Service members, speaker's platform, flags, vert. 55c, People looking over mountainside, vert. 60c, People digging ditches: 95c, Man standing on mountain top, overlooking valley, lake.

1996, Dec. 28 *Perf. 13½x14, 14x13½*

282 A41 40c multicolored .75 .75
283 A41 55c multicolored .75 .75
284 A41 60c multicolored 1.25 1.25
285 A41 95c multicolored 2.00 2.00
Nos. 282-285 (4) 4.75 4.75

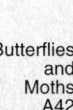

Butterflies and Moths A42

1b, Pieris napi. 2b, Heliconius melpomerie. 4b, Ornithoptera goliath. 8b, Heliconius astraea.

No. 290, vert, each 3b: a, Psaphis eusehemoides. b, Papilio brookiana. c, Parnassius charitonius. d, Morpho cypris. e, Dariaus plexippus. f, Precis octavia. g, Teinopalpus imperialis. h, Samia gloreri. i, Automeris nyctimene.

No. 291, each 3b: a, Papilio polymnestar. b, Ornithoptera paradiseo. c, Graphium marcellus. d, Panaxia quadripunctaria. e, Cardui japonica. f, Papilio childrence. g, Philosamea cynthis. h, Actias luna. i, Heticopis acit.

Each 10b: No. 292, Papilio glaucus. No. 293, Parnassius phoebus.

1997, June 16 Litho. *Perf. 14*

286-289 A42 Set of 4 12.00 12.00

Sheets of 9

290-291 A42 3b Set of 2 Sheets, #a.-i. 30.00 30.00

Souvenir Sheets

292-293 A42 10b Set of 2 Sheets 15.00 15.00

Environmental Protection — A43

1997, Aug. 15 Litho. *Perf. 14x13½*

294 A43 60c Irrigation .90 .90
295 A43 90c Reforestation .90 .90
296 A43 95c Preventing erosion 2.00 2.00
Nos. 294-296 (3) 3.80 3.80

Marine Life A44

No. 297, each 3n: a, Sergeant major, white tipped reef shark. b, Hawksbill turtle, devil ray (e). c, Surgeonfish. d, Red sea houndfish, humpback whale (a, g). e, Devil ray (b, f, h). f, Devil ray (e, c), two-banded clownfish. g, Long-nosed butterflyfish. h, Red sea houndfish (g), yellow sweetlips (i). i, White moray eel.

No. 298, each 3n: a, Masked butterflyfish. b, Suckerfish (a), whale shark (a). c, Sunrise dottyback, bluefin trevally. d, Moon wrasse (a), purple moon angel (a), two-banded anemonefish. e, Lionfish (b, f). f, White tipped shark, sand diver fish. g, Golden jacks (d), lunar tailed grouper. h, Batfish (e, i). i, Black triggerfish.

Each 10n: No. 299, Powder-blue surgeonfish. No. 300, Twin-spot wrasse.

1997, Dec. 29 Litho. *Perf. 14*

Sheets of 9, #a.-i.

297-298 A44 Set of 2 20.00 20.00

Souvenir Sheets

299-300 A44 Set of 2 Sheets 12.50 12.50

A45

Natl. Constitution: 10c, Speaker, crowd seated beneath tree. 40c, Dove, scales of justice. 85c, Hands holding constitution.

1997, Oct. 24 Litho. *Perf. 13½x14*

301-303 A45 Set of 3 3.50 3.50

A46

Birds — No. 304, each 3n: a, African darter (b, d, e). b, White-headed vulture (e). c, Egyptian vulture (f). d, Yellow-billed hornbill (g). e, Helmeted guineafowl (d, f). f, Secretary bird (d, e, i). g, Martial eagle (h). h, Bateleur eagle (i). i, Red-billed queleas.

No. 305, each 3n: a, Black-headed weaver. b, Abyssinian roller (c, f). c, Abyssinian ground hornbill (b, e, f). d, Lichtenstein's sandgrouse. e, Erckel's francolin (d, g, h). f, Arabian bustard (e, i). g, Chestnut-backed finch-lark. h, Desert lark. i, Bifasciated lark.

Each 10n: #306, Peregrine falcon. #307, Hoopoe.

1998, Mar. 16 Litho. *Perf. 14*

Sheets of 9, #a.-i.

304-305 A46 Set of 2 25.00 25.00

Souvenir Sheets

306-307 A46 Set of 2 Sheets 12.00 12.00

Dwellings — A47

1998, July 1 Litho. *Perf. 13½x14*

308 A47 50c Highlanders 1.50 1.50
309 A47 60c Lowlanders 1.50 1.50
310 A47 85c Danakils (Afars) 1.50 1.50
Nos. 308-310 (3) 4.50 4.50

Traditional Hair Styles — A48

1998, Nov. 23 Litho. *Perf. 13½x14*

311 A48 10c Cunama .30 .30
312 A48 50c Tignnys .60 .60
313 A48 85c Bllen 1.00 1.00
314 A48 95c Tigre 1.25 1.25
Nos. 311-314 (4) 3.15 3.15

Dated 1997.

A49

Traditional Musical Instruments: 15c, Chirawata. 60c, Imbilta, malaket, shambeko. 75c, Kobero. 85c, K'rar.

1998, Dec. 28 Litho. *Perf. 13½x14*

315 A49 15c multicolored .35 .35
316 A49 60c multicolored .60 .60
317 A49 75c multicolored .80 .80
318 A49 85c multicolored 1.00 1.00
Nos. 315-318 (4) 2.75 2.75

A50

1999, May 25 Litho. *Perf. 13¼x14*

319 A50 60c green & multi .60 .60
320 A50 1n red & multi 1.00 1.00
321 A50 3n blue & multi 4.00 4.00
Nos. 319-321 (3) 5.60 5.60

Independence, 8th Anniv.

1997 Introduction of Nakfa Currency — A51

Bank notes: 10c, 1 Nakfa. 60c, 5 Nakfa. 80c, 10 Nakfa. 1n, 20 Nakfa. 2n, 50 Nakfa. 3n, 100 Nakfa.

1999, Nov. 8 Litho. *Perf. 13¼*

322 A51 10c multicolored .45 .45
323 A51 60c multicolored .60 .60
324 A51 80c multicolored .75 .75
325 A51 1n multicolored 1.00 1.00
326 A51 2n multicolored 2.00 2.00
327 A51 3n multicolored 3.50 3.50
Nos. 322-327 (6) 8.30 8.30

Natl. Union of Eritrean Women, 20th Anniv. A52

Designs: 5c, Woman and child, vert. 10c, Three women. 25c, Women and flag. 1n, Woman with binoculars.

Perf. 13¼x14, 14x13¼

1999, Nov. 26

328 A52 5c multicolored .35 .35
329 A52 10c multicolored .35 .35
330 A52 25c multicolored .50 .50
331 A52 1n multicolored .75 .75
Nos. 328-331 (4) 1.95 1.95

A53

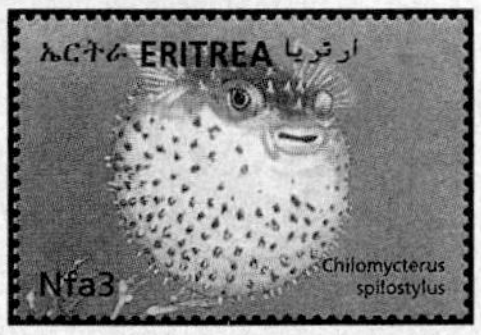

Marine Life A54

No. 332, each 3n: a, Coachwhip ray. b, Sulfur damselfish. c, "Gray moray." d, Sabre squirrelfish. e, Rusty parrotfish. f, "Striped eel catfish."

No. 333, each 3n: a, Spangled emperor. b, Devil scorpionfish. c, Crown squirrelfish. d, Vanikoro sweeper. e, Sergeant major. f, Giant manta.

No. 334, each 3n: a, Chilomycterus spilostylus. b, Dascyllus marginatus. c, Balistapus undulatus. d, Pomacanthus semicirculatus. e, Rhinecanthus assasi. f, Millepora.

No. 335, each 3n: a, Epinephalus fasciata. b, Pygoplites diacanthus. c, Cephalopholis miniata. d, Centropyge eibli. e, Ostracion cubicus. f, Heniochus acuminatus.

Each 10n: No. 336, Centropyge flavissimus. No. 337, Larabicus quadrilineatus. No. 338, Anthias squamipinnis. 15n, Pomacanthus maculosus.

2000, Apr. 17 Litho. *Perf. 14*

Sheets of 6, #a.-f.

332-333 A53 Set of 2 13.50 13.50
334-335 A54 Set of 2 13.50 13.50

Souvenir Sheets

336-338 A54 Set of 3 15.00 15.00
339 A54 15n multi 6.00 6.00

Illustrations on Nos. 332c and 332f were switched.

A55

Flag and: 5c, Man with sword. 10c, Ship Denden Assab. 25c, Independence Day festivities. 60c, Soldiers and barracks. 1n, Finger, heart and map. 2n, People under tree. 3n, Ballot box. 5n, Eritrean seal, military plane, tank, ship. 7n, Seal. 10n, Ten-nakfa note.

Perf. 13¾x13¼

2000, Mar. 17 Litho.

Denominations in Sans-Serif Type

340-349 A55 Set of 10 16.00 16.00

See Nos. 363A-363F.

Worldwide Fund for Nature (WWF) — A56

Proteles cristatus: a, Laying down. b. Pair in den. c, Walking. d, Close-up.

2001, Oct. 1 Litho. *Perf. 14*

350 A56 3n Block or strip of 4, #a-d 4.50 4.50

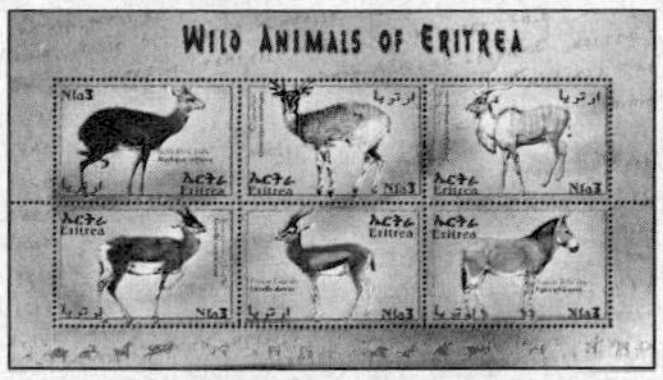

Wild Animals — A57

No. 351, 3n: a, Salt's dik-dik. b, Klipspringer. c, Greater kudu. d, Soemmering's gazelle. e, Dorcas gazelle. f, Somali wild ass.

No. 352, 3n: a, Aardvark. b, Black-backed jackal. c, Striped hyena. d, Spotted hyena. e, East African leopard. f, African elephant.

2001, Oct. 29

Sheets of 6, #a-f

351-352 A57 Set of 2 10.00 10.00

Struggle for Independence, 10th Anniv. — A58

Designs: 20c, Women, flag, jewelry. 60c, Doves, stylized flag, vert. 1n, Bees, honeycomb, flag, vert. 3n, Men with sticks, vert.

Perf. 13x13¼, 13¼x13

2001, May 23 Litho.

353-356 A58 Set of 4 3.00 3.00

Liberation of Nakfa, 25th Anniv. A59

Designs: 50c, Denden. 1n, Town of Nakfa, 1977 (77x27mm). 3n, First Organizational Congress of the Eritrean People's Liberation Front (77x27mm).

2002, Mar. 23 Litho. *Perf. 14x13¼*

357-359 A59 Set of 3 2.00 2.00

Martyr's Day — A60

Designs: 1n, People and map. 2n, Hand, map of Badma area, and flag. 3n, Map and ship. 5n, Dove, map and dead man (49x29mm, triangular).

Perf. 14x13¼, 13½ (5n)

2002, June 20

360-363 A60 Set of 4 4.50 4.50

Type of 2000 Redrawn

Flag and: 30c, People under tree. 45c, Man with sword. 50c, Independence Day festivities. 60c, Soldiers and barracks. 75c, Ship Denden Assab. 3n, Ballot box.

2002, Oct. 21 Litho. *Perf. 13¼x14¼*

Denominations in Serifed Type

363A	A55	30c multi	—	—
363B	A55	45c multi	—	—
363C	A55	50c multi	—	—
363D	A55	60c multi	—	—
363E	A55	75c multi	—	—
363F	A55	3n multi	—	—

Denominations on Nos. 340-349 are in sans-serif type.

Dr. Fred C. Hollows (1929-93), Ophthalmologist A61

Designs: 50c, Portrait. 1n, Hollows wearing ophthalmological equipment. 2n, Hollows with man.

2003, Feb. 10 *Perf. 13¼x14*

364-366 A61 Set of 3 2.00 2.00

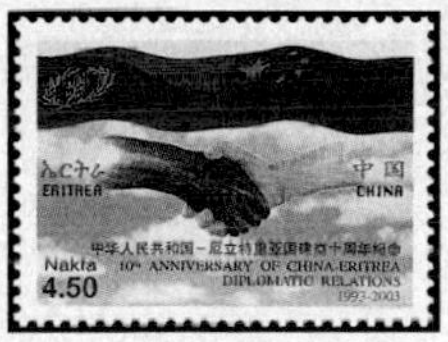

Eritrea — People's Republic of China Diplomatic Relations, 10th Anniv. A62

2003, May 24 *Perf. 12*

367 A62 4.50n multi 2.50 2.50

Eritrean postal authorities have declared "illegal" the following items:

Sheetlet of nine 5n stamps depicting Trains;

Sheetlets of nine 3n stamps depicting Marilyn Monroe (two different), Dogs, The Beatles "Yellow Submarine," September 11 firefighters, Brigitte Bardot, Grace Kelly, Sophia Loren, Golf etiquette, Sexy actresses, Sexy models, Boris Vallejo nudes, Dorian Cleavenger, Michael Möbius, Olivia, Ricky Carralero, Concorde;

Sheetlets of six stamps with various denominations depicting Lighthouses (with Rotary emblem) (two different), Hopper paintings (two different), Vettriano paintings (two different), Marilyn Monroe (two different), Elvgren pin-ups (two different), Teddy bears (two different);

Sheetlets of six 3n stamps depicting Van Gogh paintings, Paintings of nudes;

Sheetlets of five 3n stamps depicting Corot paintings, Pisarro paintings, Renoir paintings, Elvis Presley, Marilyn Monroe;

Sheetlets of four stamps with various denominations depicting Pandas (with Scouting emblem), Crocodiles (with Scouting emblem), Buffalos (with Rotary emblem), Elephants (with Rotary emblem), Monkeys (with Scouting emblem), Lizards (with Scouting emblem), Snakes (with Scouting Emblem), Turtles (with Rotary emblem), Wild cats (with Scouting emblem), Birds of prey (with Rotary emblem), Fowl (with Rotary emblem), Parrots (with Scouting emblem), Penguins (with Rotary emblem), Fish (with Rotary emblem), Marine life (with Scouting emblem), Mushrooms (with Rotary emblem), Butterflies (with Scouting emblem), Bees (with Scouting emblem), Spiders (with Scouting emblem);

Sheetlets of four 3n stamps depicting Dinosaurs (with Scouting emblem), Dinosaurs (with Rotary emblem) Elephants (with Scouting emblem), Elephants (with Rotary emblem), Horses (with Scouting emblem), Horses (with Rotary emblem), Birds (with Scouting emblem), Birds (with Rotary emblem), Penguins (with Scouting emblem), Penguins (with Rotary emblem), Orchids (with Scouting emblem), Orchids (with Rotary emblem), Butterflies (with Scouting emblem), Butterflies (with Rotary emblem), Cars (with Scouting emblem), Cars (with Rotary emblem), Motorcycles (with Scouting emblem), Motorcycles (with Rotary emblem), Trains (with Scouting emblem), Trains (with Rotary emblem);

Sheetlets of three 5n stamps depicting Dinosaurs (with Rotary emblem) (two different), Pandas;

Strips of three 5n stamps depicting Steam trains (four different);

Souvenir sheet with one 8n stamp depicting Steam Trains (with Rotary emblem) (two different), Dinosaurs (with Rotary emblem), Pandas (with Scouting emblem), Elephants (with Scouting emblem), Tigers (with Scouting emblem), Birds of prey (with Scouting emblem);

Souvenir sheets with one 5n stamp depicting Marilyn Monroe (six different), Lighthouses (with Rotary emblem) (four different), Teddy bears (four different), Hopper paintings (two different), Vettriano paintings (two different).

Eritrean Railway A63

Independence Celebrations A63a

Massawa A63b

2003 Litho. *Perf. 14x13¼*

Denomination Color

368	A63	5c	Prussian blue	.25	.25
369	A63	10c	greenish blk	.25	.25
370	A63	15c	lilac	.25	.25
371	A63	35c	violet	.25	.25
372	A63	50c	orange	.25	.25
373	A63	90c	olive green	.25	.25
374	A63	1n	red	.25	.25
375	A63	2n	blue violet	.55	.55
376	A63	10n	red	2.75	2.75
376A	A63a	50n	white	12.00	12.00
376B	A63b	75n	white	18.00	18.00
376C	A63	100n	white	24.00	24.00
	Nos. 368-376C (12)			59.05	59.05

Issued: 50n, 75n, 100n, 8/29.

Liberation of Massawa, 14th Anniv. A64

Designs: 40c, Tanks as fountains. 50c, Boat with soldiers.

No. 379: a, 3n, Crashed airplane, people, soldiers in shallow water. b, 3n, Tank, soldier, flag, boat. c, 4n, People, buildings at shore.

2004

377-378 A64 Set of 2 1.00 1.00

Miniature Sheet

379 A64 Sheet of 3, #a-c 4.00 4.00

Man and Camels — A65

Man and Cattle A66

Highland Woman, Child and Camel — A67

2004, July 12 Litho. *Perf. 12*

Frame Color

380	A65	20c violet blue	.25	.25
381	A65	25c red violet	.25	.25
382	A65	40c brown	.25	.25
383	A66	50c red	.25	.25
384	A66	55c green	.25	.25
385	A66	60c light blue	.25	.25
386	A67	80c olive green	.50	.50
387	A67	1n orange	.50	.50
388	A67	4.50n blue	1.25	1.25
		Nos. 380-388 (9)	3.75	3.75

A68

A69

Monuments and Statues — A70

Perf. 13¼x14, 14x13¼

2006, Jan. 5 Litho.

389	A68	1.50n multi	.25	.25
390	A69	6n multi	.80	.80
391	A70	25n multi	3.50	3.50
		Nos. 389-391 (3)	4.55	4.55

China - Africa Cooperation Forum, Beijing — A71

2006, Nov. 3 Litho. *Perf. 12*

392	A71	7n multi	.95	.95

African Soccer Confederation, 50th Anniv. — A72

Anniversary emblem and: 3n, Eritrean soccer players and flags. 5n, Soccer field. 10n, Soccer players in action.

2007, May 29 Litho. *Perf. 13x13¼*

393-395	A72	Set of 3	2.40	2.40

Soldiers Carrying Flag — A73

2008, Dec. 31 Litho. *Perf. 14x13¼*

Denomination Color

396	A73	15c dark blue	.25	.25
397	A73	35c green	.25	.25
398	A73	50c orange	.25	.25
399	A73	70c red	.25	.25
400	A73	75c blue	.25	.25
401	A73	90c brown	.25	.25
402	A73	1.50n red violet	.25	.25
403	A73	2n indigo	.25	.25
404	A73	3n org yellow	.40	.40
405	A73	5n gray	.65	.65
406	A73	10n yel green	1.25	1.25
		Nos. 396-406 (11)	4.30	4.30

Eritrean National Festival A74

Ethnic groups in costume: 5c, Afars. 10c, Bilens. 30c, Hedarebs. 95c, Kunamas. 1n, Naras. 1.50n, Rashaidas. 4n, Sahos. 7n, Tigres. 8n, Tigrinyas.

2010, Nov. 15

407-415	A74	Set of 9	4.25	4.25

Independence, 20th Anniv. — A75

Designs: 70c, Eritrean flag, stylized people defining border. 95c, Map of Eritrea, hand holding torch, vert. 8n, Map of Africa, flag of Eritrea, vert.

2011, Mar. 24 *Perf. 14x13¼, 13¼x14*

416-418	A75	Set of 3	2.00	2.00

Eritrean Martyr's Day, 20th Anniv. — A76

Designs: 80c, Eritreans and woman holding shining square. 9n, Woamn and child lighting candles

2011, June 17 *Perf. 13¾x13¼*

419-420	A76	Set of 2	2.10	2.10

Eritrean Armed Struggle, 50th Anniv. — A77

Designs: 1.50n, Arm holding rifle, "50," flame, stylized people. 7n, Flame, arms holding rifles.

2011, Sept. 3 *Perf. 13¼x14*

421-422	A77	Set of 2	1.75	1.75

SEMI-POSTAL STAMPS

Many issues of Italy and Italian Colonies include one or more semipostal denominations. To avoid splitting sets, these issues are generally listed as regular postage, airmail, etc., unless all values carry a surtax.

Italy Nos. B1-B3 Overprinted type "f"

1915-16 Wmk. 140 *Perf. 14*

B1	SP1	10c + 5c rose	4.00	*16.00*
a.		"EPITREA"	32.50	*45.00*
b.		Inverted overprint	800.00	800.00
B2	SP2	15c + 5c slate	32.50	*27.50*
B3	SP2	20c + 5c orange	4.75	*35.00*
a.		"EPITREA"	80.00	*110.00*
b.		Inverted overprint	800.00	800.00
c.		Pair, one without ovpt.	—	*4,500.*
		Nos. B1-B3 (3)	41.25	*78.50*
		Set, never hinged	102.00	

No. B2 Surcharged

1916

B4	SP2	20c on 15c+5c slate	32.50	*35.00*
		Never hinged	80.00	
a.		"EPITREA"	80.00	*110.00*
b.		Pair, one without overprint	2,000.	
		Never hinged	2,500.	

Counterfeits exist of the minor varieties of Nos. B1, B3-B4.

Holy Year Issue

Italy Nos. B20-B25 Overprinted in Black or Red

1925 *Perf. 12*

B5	SP4	20c + 10c dk grn & brn	4.00	*24.00*
B6	SP4	30c + 15c dk brn & brn	4.00	*27.50*
a.		Double overprint		
B7	SP4	50c + 25c vio & brn	4.00	*24.00*
B8	SP4	60c + 30c dp rose & brn	4.00	*32.50*
a.		Inverted overprint		
B9	SP8	1 l + 50c dp bl & vio (R)	4.00	*40.00*
B10	SP8	5 l + 2.50 l org brn & vio (R)	4.00	*60.00*
		Nos. B5-B10 (6)	24.00	*208.00*
		Set, never hinged	60.00	

Colonial Institute Issue

"Peace" Substituting Spade for Sword — SP1

1926 Typo. *Perf. 14*

B11	SP1	5c + 5c brown	1.20	*9.50*
B12	SP1	10c + 5c olive grn	1.20	*9.50*
B13	SP1	20c + 5c blue grn	1.20	*9.50*
B14	SP1	40c + 5c brown red	1.20	*9.50*
B15	SP1	60c + 5c orange	1.20	*9.50*
B16	SP1	1 l + 5c blue	1.20	*20.00*
		Nos. B11-B16 (6)	7.20	*67.50*
		Set, never hinged	18.00	

The surtax of 5c on each stamp was for the Italian Colonial Institute.

Italian Semi-Postal Stamps of 1926 Overprinted

1927 Unwmk. *Perf. 11½*

B17	SP10	40c + 20c dk brn & blk	4.00	*45.00*
B18	SP10	60c + 30c brn red & ol brn	4.00	*45.00*
B19	SP10	1.25 l + 60c dp bl & blk	4.00	*65.00*
B20	SP10	5 l + 2.50 l dk grn & blk	6.50	*100.00*
		Nos. B17-B20 (4)	18.50	*255.00*
		Set, never hinged	46.00	

The surtax on these stamps was for the charitable work of the Voluntary Militia for Italian National Defense.

Fascism and Victory — SP2

1928 Wmk. 140 Typo. *Perf. 14*

B21	SP2	20c + 5c blue grn	3.25	*14.00*
B22	SP2	30c + 5c red	3.25	*14.00*
B23	SP2	50c + 10c purple	3.25	*24.00*
B24	SP2	1.25 l + 20c dk blue	4.00	*32.50*
		Nos. B21-B24 (4)	13.75	*84.50*
		Set, never hinged	34.00	

The surtax was for the Society Africana d'Italia, whose 46th anniv. was commemorated by the issue.

Types of Italian Semi-Postal Stamps of 1928 Overprinted type "f"

1929 Unwmk. *Perf. 11*

B25	SP10	30c + 10c red & blk	4.75	*27.50*
B26	SP10	50c + 20c vio & blk	4.75	*30.00*
B27	SP10	1.25 l + 50c brn & bl	7.25	*52.50*
B28	SP10	5 l + 2 l olive grn & blk	7.25	*100.00*
		Nos. B25-B28 (4)	24.00	*210.00*
		Set, never hinged	60.00	

Surtax for the charitable work of the Voluntary Militia for Italian Natl. Defense.

Types of Italian Semi-Postal Stamps of 1930 Overprinted type "f" in Black or Red

1930 *Perf. 14*

B29	SP10	30c + 10c dk grn & bl grn (Bk)	35.00	*65.00*
B30	SP10	50c + 10c dk grn & vio	35.00	*100.00*
B31	SP10	1.25 l + 30c ol brn & red brn	35.00	*100.00*
B32	SP10	5 l + 1.50 l ind & grn	120.00	*275.00*
		Nos. B29-B32 (4)	225.00	*540.00*
		Set, never hinged	560.00	

Surtax for the charitable work of the Voluntary Militia for Italian Natl. Defense.

Agriculture — SP3

1930 Photo. Wmk. 140

B33	SP3	50c + 20c ol brn	4.00	*25.00*
B34	SP3	1.25 l + 20c dp bl	4.00	*25.00*
B35	SP3	1.75 l + 20c green	4.00	*27.50*
B36	SP3	2.55 l + 50c purple	9.50	*45.00*
B37	SP3	5 l + 1 l dp car	9.50	*67.50*
		Nos. B33-B37 (5)	31.00	*190.00*
		Set, never hinged	76.00	

Italian Colonial Agricultural Institute, 25th anniv. The surtax aided that institution.

AIR POST STAMPS

Desert Scene
AP1

Design: 80c, 1 l, 2 l, Plane and globe.

Wmk. Crowns (140)

1934, Oct. 17 Photo. *Perf. 14*

C1 AP1 25c sl bl & org red 5.50 *22.50*
C2 AP1 50c grn & indigo 5.50 *20.00*
C3 AP1 75c brn & org red 5.50 *20.00*
C4 AP1 80c org brn & ol grn 5.50 *22.50*
C5 AP1 1 l scar & ol grn 5.50 *27.50*
C6 AP1 2 l dk bl & brn 5.50 *47.50*
Nos. C1-C6 (6) 33.00 *160.00*
Set, never hinged 81.00

Second Colonial Arts Exhibition, Naples.

Plowing
AP3

Plane and Cacti
AP6

Designs: 25c, 1.50 l, Plowing. 50c, 2 l, Plane over mountain pass. 60c, 5 l, Plane and trees. 75c, 10 l, Plane and cacti. 1 l, 3 l, Bridge.

1936 Photo.

C7 AP3 25c deep green 4.75 *4.75*
C8 AP3 50c dark brown 3.25 .35
C9 AP3 60c brown orange 6.50 *16.00*
C10 AP6 75c orange brown 4.75 1.60
C11 AP3 1 l deep blue 1.60 .35
C12 AP3 1.50 l purple 6.50 .85
C13 AP3 2 l gray blue 6.50 *3.25*
C14 AP3 3 l copper red 25.00 27.50
C15 AP3 5 l green 19.00 8.00
C16 AP6 10 l rose red 45.00 27.50
Nos. C7-C16 (10) 122.85 90.15
Set, never hinged 300.00

AIR POST SEMI-POSTAL STAMPS

King Victor Emmanuel III — SPAP1

1934 Wmk. 140 Photo. *Perf. 14*

CB1 SPAP1 25c + 10c 9.50 *27.50*
CB2 SPAP1 50c + 10c 9.50 *27.50*
CB3 SPAP1 75c + 15c 9.50 *27.50*
CB4 SPAP1 80c + 15c 9.50 *27.50*
CB5 SPAP1 1 l + 20c 9.50 *27.50*
CB6 SPAP1 2 l + 20c 9.50 *27.50*
CB7 SPAP1 3 l + 25c 27.50 *125.00*
CB8 SPAP1 5 l + 25c 27.50 *125.00*
CB9 SPAP1 10 l + 30c 27.50 *125.00*
CB10 SPAP1 25 l + 2 l 27.50 *125.00*
Nos. CB1-CB10 (10) 167.00 *665.00*
Set, never hinged 410.00

65th birthday of King Victor Emmanuel III and the nonstop flight from Rome to Mogadiscio. Used values are for stamps canceled to order.

AIR POST SEMI-POSTAL OFFICIAL STAMP

Type of Air Post Semi-Postal Stamps, 1934, Overprinted in Black

1934 Wmk. 140 *Perf. 14*

CBO1 SPAP1 25 l + 2 l cop red *2,800.*
Never hinged *5,500.*

SPECIAL DELIVERY STAMPS

Special Delivery Stamps of Italy, Overprinted type "a"

1907 Wmk. 140 *Perf. 14*

E1 SD1 25c rose red 24.00 20.00
Never hinged 60.00
a. Double overprint — —

1909

E2 SD2 30c blue & rose 145.00 *240.00*
Never hinged 375.00

1920

E3 SD1 50c dull red 4.00 *24.00*
Never hinged 10.00

"Italia" SD1

1924 Engr. Unwmk.

E4 SD1 60c dk red & brn 6.50 *24.00*
a. Perf. 13½ 14.00 *40.00*
E5 SD1 2 l dk blue & red 17.50 *27.50*
Set, never hinged 59.00

For surcharges see Nos. E6-E8.

Nos. E4 and E5 Surcharged In Dark Blue or Red

v

w

1926

E6 SD1 70c on 60c (Bl) 6.50 *16.00*
E7 SD1 2.50 l on 2 l (R) 17.50 *27.50*
Set, never hinged 60.00

Type of 1924 Surcharged in Blue or Black

1927-35 *Perf. 11*

E8 SD1 1.25 l on 60c dk red & brn (Bl) 16.00 4.00
Never hinged 40.00
a. Perf. 14 (Bl) ('35) 110.00 24.00
Never hinged 275.00
b. Perf. 11 (Bk) ('35) *9,500.* 1,250.
Never hinged *14,500.*
c. Perf. 14 (Bk) ('35) 400.00 65.00
Never hinged 1,000.

AUTHORIZED DELIVERY STAMP

Authorized Delivery Stamp of Italy, No. EY2, Overprinted Type "f" in Black

1939-41 Wmk. 140 *Perf. 14*

EY1 AD2 10c dk brown ('41) .80
Never hinged 2.00
a. 10c reddish brown 27.50 *47.50*
Never hinged 72.50

On No. EY1a, which was used in Italian East Africa, the overprint hits the figures "10." On No. EY1, which was sold in Rome, the overprint falls above the 10's.

POSTAGE DUE STAMPS

Postage Due Stamps of Italy Overprinted type "a" at Top

1903 Wmk. 140 *Perf. 14*

J1 D3 5c buff & mag 24.00 *47.50*
a. Double overprint 550.00
J2 D3 10c buff & mag 16.00 *47.50*
J3 D3 20c buff & mag 16.00 *32.50*
J4 D3 30c buff & mag 24.00 *35.00*
J5 D3 40c buff & mag 80.00 *72.50*
J6 D3 50c buff & mag 87.50 72.50
J7 D3 60c buff & mag 24.00 *72.50*
J8 D3 1 l blue & mag 16.00 *40.00*
J9 D3 2 l blue & mag 200.00 *180.00*
J10 D3 5 l blue & mag 325.00 340.00
J11 D3 10 l blue & mag 3,600. 875.00
Never hinged 7,200.
Set, #J1-J10, never hinged 1,600.

Same with Overprint at Bottom

1920-22

J1b D3 5c buff & magenta 4.75 *16.00*
c. Numeral and ovpt. inverted 550.00 550.00
J2a D3 10c buff & magenta 8.00 *16.00*
J3a D3 20c buff & magenta 950.00 475.00
J4a D3 30c buff & magenta 65.00 65.00
J5a D3 40c buff & magenta 47.50 52.50
J6a D3 50c buff & magenta 24.00 *47.50*
J7a D3 60c buff & magenta 24.00 *47.50*
J8a D3 1 l blue & magenta 40.00 47.50
J9a D3 2 l blue & magenta 1,900. 1,450.
J10a D3 5 l blue & magenta 475.00 350.00
J11a D3 10 l blue & magenta 47.50 *100.00*
Set, never hinged 7,125.

1903 Wmk. 140

J12 D4 50 l yellow 875.00 300.00
J13 D4 100 l blue 475.00 180.00
Set, never hinged 2,700.

1927

J14 D3 60c buff & brown 160.00 *240.00*
Never hinged 325.00

Postage Due Stamps of Italy, 1934, Overprinted type "j" in Black

1934

J15 D6 5c brown .80 *16.00*
J16 D6 10c blue .80 *3.25*
J17 D6 20c rose red 4.00 *4.75*
a. Inverted overprint —
J18 D6 25c green 4.00 *6.50*
J19 D6 30c red orange 4.00 *16.00*
J20 D6 40c black brown 4.00 *16.00*
J21 D6 50c violet 4.00 2.40
J22 D6 60c black 8.00 *24.00*
J23 D7 1 l red orange 4.00 3.25
a. Inverted overprint 550.00 —
J24 D7 2 l green 16.00 *47.50*
J25 D7 5 l violet 28.00 *55.00*
J26 D7 10 l blue 32.50 *65.00*
J27 D7 20 l carmine rose 40.00 *72.50*
a. Inverted overprint 550.00
Nos. J15-J27 (13) 150.10 *332.15*
Set, never hinged 375.00

PARCEL POST STAMPS

These stamps were used by affixing them to the way bill so that one half remained on it following the parcel, the other half staying on the receipt given the sender. Most used halves are right halves. Complete stamps were obtainable canceled, probably to order. Both unused and used values are for complete stamps.

Parcel Post Stamps of Italy, 1914-17, Overprinted type "j" in Black on Each Half

1916 Wmk. 140 *Perf. 13½*

Q1 PP2 5c brown 145.00 *225.00*
Q2 PP2 10c deep blue *2,600.* *4,250.*
Never hinged 5,250.
Q3 PP2 25c red 290.00 *350.00*
Q4 PP2 50c orange 72.50 *225.00*
Q5 PP2 1 l violet 145.00 *225.00*
Q6 PP2 2 l green 110.00 *225.00*
Q7 PP2 3 l bister 875.00 *625.00*
Q8 PP2 4 l slate 875.00 *625.00*
Set #Q1, Q3-Q8, never hinged 5,200.

Halves Used, Each

Q1 4.25
Q2 85.00
Q3 5.50
Q4 3.00
Q5 3.00
Q6 8.50
Q7 19.00
Q8 19.00

Overprinted type "f" on Each Half

1917-24

Q9 PP2 5c brown 3.25 *8.00*
Q10 PP2 10c deep blue 3.25 *8.00*
Q11 PP2 20c black 3.25 *8.00*
Q12 PP2 25c red 3.25 *8.00*
Q13 PP2 50c orange 6.50 *12.00*
Q14 PP2 1 l violet 6.50 *12.00*
Q15 PP2 2 l green 6.50 *12.00*
Q16 PP2 3 l bister 6.50 *12.00*
Q17 PP2 4 l slate 6.50 *20.00*
Q18 PP2 10 l rose lil ('24) 87.50 *190.00*
Q19 PP2 12 l red brn ('24) 240.00 *375.00*
Q20 PP2 15 l olive grn ('24) 240.00 *375.00*
Q21 PP2 20 l brn vio ('24) 325.00 *525.00*
Nos. Q9-Q21 (13) 938.00 *1,565.*
Set, never hinged 1,860.

Halves Used, Each

Q9 1.20
Q10 1.20
Q11 1.20
Q12 1.20
Q13 1.20
Q14 1.20
Q15 1.60
Q16 4.25
Q17 4.25
Q18 8.50
Q19 12.50
Q20 12.50
Q21 17.00

Parcel Post Stamps of Italy, 1927-39, Overprinted type "f" on Each Half

1927-37

Q21A PP3 10c dp blue ('37) *8,750.* 1,250.
Never hinged *13,500.*
Q22 PP3 25c red ('37) 550.00 72.50
Q23 PP3 30c ultra ('29) 4.00 *24.00*
Q24 PP3 50c orange ('36) 725.00 47.50
Q25 PP3 60c red ('29) 4.00 *24.00*
Q26 PP3 1 l brown vio ('36) 325.00 47.50
a. 1 l lilac 400.00 47.50
Q27 PP3 2 l green ('36) 325.00 47.50
Q28 PP3 3 l bister 9.50 *40.00*
Q29 PP3 4 l gray 9.50 *40.00*
Q30 PP3 10 l rose lilac ('36) 525.00 800.00
Q31 PP3 20 l lilac brn ('36) 525.00 800.00
Nos. Q22-Q31 (10) 3,002.
Set, never hinged 6,000.
Nos. Q21A-Q31 (11) 3,193.

Halves Used, Each

Q21A 27.50
Q22 1.20
Q23 .65
Q24 1.70
Q25 .85
Q26 1.25
Q26a 1.25
Q27 1.25
Q28 1.25
Q29 1.25
Q30 37.50
Q31 37.50

ESTONIA

e-'stō-nē-ə

LOCATION — Northern Europe, bordering on the Baltic Sea and the Gulf of Finland
GOVT. — Independent republic
AREA — 17,462 sq. mi.
POP. — 1,408,523 (1999 est.)
CAPITAL — Tallinn

Formerly a part of the Russia empire, Estonia declared its independence in 1918. In 1940 it was incorporated in the Union of Soviet Socialist Republics.

Estonia declared the restoration of its independence from the USSR on Aug. 20, 1991. Estonian independence was recognized by the Soviet Union on Sept. 6, 1991.

100 Kopecks = 1 Ruble (1918, 1991)
100 Penni = 1 Mark (1919)
100 Sents = 1 Kroon (1928, 1992)

Catalogue values for unused stamps in this country are for Never Hinged items, beginning with Scott 200 in the regular postage section, Scott B60 in the semi-postal section, and Scott F1 in the registration section.

Watermark

Wmk. 207 — Arms of Finland in the Sheet

Watermark covers a large part of sheet.

A1

A2

1918-19 Unwmk. Litho. *Imperf.*

1	A1	5k pale red	1.00	.85
2	A1	15k bright blue	1.00	.85
3	A2	35p brown ('19)	1.00	.90
a.		Printed on both sides	*200.00*	
b.		35p olive	80.00	80.00
4	A2	70p olive grn ('19)	1.60	*2.10*
		Nos. 1-4 (4)	4.60	4.70

Nos. 1-4 exist privately perforated.

Russian Stamps of 1909-17 Handstamped in Violet or Black

1919, May 7 *Perf. 14, 14½x15, 13½*

8	A14	1k orange	*5,500.*	*5,500.*
9	A14	2k green	45.00	*45.00*
10	A14	3k red	52.50	*52.50*
11	A14	5k claret	45.00	*45.00*
12	A15	10k dk bl (Bk)	85.00	*85.00*
13	A15	10k dk bl	500.00	*500.00*
14	A14	10k on 7k lt bl	*1,500.*	*1,500.*
15	A11	15k red brn & bl	67.50	*67.50*
16	A11	25k grn & vio	77.50	*77.50*
17	A11	35k red brn & grn	5,500.	*5,500.*
18	A8	50k vio & grn	190.00	190.00
19	A9	1r pale brn, brn & org	325.00	325.00
20	A13	10r scar, yel & gray	*9,500.*	*9,500.*

Imperf

21	A14	1k orange	62.50	*62.50*
22	A14	2k green	*950.00*	*950.00*
23	A14	3k red	85.00	85.00
24	A9	1r pale brn, brn & red org	*425.00*	*425.00*
25	A12	3½r maroon & grn	*1,200.*	*1,200.*
26	A13	5r dk bl, grn & pale bl	*1,500.*	*1,500.*

Provisionally issued at Tallinn. This overprint has been extensively counterfeited. Values are for genuine examples competently expertized. No. 20 is always creased.

Gulls — A3

1919, May 13 *Imperf.*

27	A3	5p yellow	2.50	*5.50*

A4

A5

A6

A7

Viking Ship — A8

1919-20 *Perf. 11½*

28	A4	10p green	.45	.80

Imperf

29	A4	5p orange	.25	.25
30	A4	10p green	.25	.25
31	A5	15p rose	.25	.30
32	A6	35p blue	.25	.30
33	A7	70p dl vio ('20)	.25	.30
34	A8	1m bl & blk brn	4.25	1.60
a.		Gray granite paper ('20)	1.60	.80
35	A8	5m yel & blk	6.25	4.75
a.		Gray granite paper ('20)	3.25	1.25
36	A8	15m yel grn & vio ('20)	3.50	2.40
37	A8	25m ultra & blk brn ('20)	6.50	5.50
		Nos. 28-37 (10)	22.20	16.45
		Set, never hinged	32.50	

The 5m exists with inverted center. Not a postal item.

See Nos. 76-77. For surcharges see Nos. 55, 57.

Skyline of Tallinn — A9

1920-24 Pelure Paper *Imperf.*

39	A9	25p green	.35	.40
40	A9	25p yellow ('24)	.35	.30
41	A9	35p rose	.40	.40
42	A9	50p green ('21)	.40	.25
43	A9	1m vermilion	1.25	.80
44	A9	2m blue	.80	.40
45	A9	2m ultramarine	1.00	1.25
46	A9	2.50m blue	1.25	.80
		Nos. 39-46 (8)	5.80	4.60
		Set, never hinged	16.50	

Nos. 39-46 with sewing machine perforation are unofficial.

For surcharge see No. 56.

Stamps of 1919-20 Surcharged

1920 *Imperf.*

55	A5	1m on 15p rose	.50	.50
56	A9	1m on 35p rose	.70	.50
57	A7	2m on 70p dl vio	.85	.60
		Nos. 55-57 (3)	2.05	1.60
		Set, never hinged	4.25	

Weaver A10

Blacksmith A11

1922-23 Typo. *Imperf.*

58	A10	½m orange ('23)	2.75	*8.00*
59	A10	1m brown ('23)	4.75	*11.00*
60	A10	2m yellow green	4.75	*8.00*
61	A10	2½m claret	5.50	*8.00*
62	A11	5m rose	8.00	8.00
63	A11	9m red ('23)	12.00	*24.00*
64	A11	10m deep blue	6.00	*16.00*
		Nos. 58-64 (7)	43.75	83.00
		Set, never hinged	105.00	

1922-25 *Perf. 14*

65	A10	½m orange ('23)	1.25	.80
66	A10	1m brown ('23)	2.40	.80
67	A10	2m yellow green	2.40	.40
68	A10	2½m claret	4.75	.80
69	A10	3m blue green ('24)	2.00	.40
70	A11	5m rose	2.75	.40
71	A11	9m red ('23)	4.75	1.60
72	A11	10m deep blue	6.00	.40
73	A11	12m red ('25)	6.00	1.75
74	A11	15m plum ('25)	8.00	1.40
75	A11	20m ultra ('25)	20.00	.80
		Nos. 65-75 (11)	60.30	9.55
		Set, never hinged	130.00	

See No. 89. For surcharges see Nos. 84-88.

Viking Ship Type of 1920

1922, June 8 *Perf. 14x13½*

76	A8	15m yel grn & vio	8.00	.80
77	A8	25m ultra & blk brn	10.00	3.25
		Set, never hinged	35.00	

Map of Estonia — A13

1923-24 Paper with Lilac Network

78	A13	100m ol grn & bl	20.00	3.50

Paper with Buff Network

79	A13	300m brn & bl ('24)	72.50	17.50
		Set, never hinged	210.00	

For surcharges see Nos. 106-107.

National Theater, Tallinn — A14

Paper with Blue Network

1924, Dec. 9 *Perf. 14x13½*

81	A14	30m violet & blk	10.00	4.00

Paper with Rose Network

82	A14	70m car rose & blk	15.00	8.00
		Set, never hinged	50.00	

For surcharge see No. 105.

Vanemuine Theater, Tartu — A15

Paper with Lilac Network

1927, Oct. 25

83	A15	40m dp bl & ol brn	10.00	3.50
		Never hinged	20.00	

Stamps of 1922-25 Surcharged in New Currency in Red or Black

1928 *Perf. 14*

84	A10	2s yellow green	1.50	1.25
85	A11	5s rose red (B)	1.50	1.25
86	A11	10s deep blue	2.40	1.25
a.		Imperf., pair	*1,300.*	—
87	A11	15s plum (B)	6.50	1.25
88	A11	20s ultra	4.50	1.25
		Nos. 84-88 (5)	16.40	6.25
		Set, never hinged	35.00	

10th anniversary of independence.

3rd Philatelic Exhibition Issue
Blacksmith Type of 1922-23

1928, July 6

89	A11	10m gray	4.50	*7.50*
		Never hinged	9.00	

Sold only at Tallinn Philatelic Exhibition. Exists imperf. Value $1,000.

Arms — A16

Paper with Network in Parenthesis

1928-40 *Perf. 14, 14½x14*

90	A16	1s dk gray (bl)	.50	.25
a.		Thick gray-toned laid paper ('40)	10.00	*27.50*
91	A16	2s yel grn (org)	.60	.25
92	A16	4s grn (brn) ('29)	1.25	.25
93	A16	5s red (grn)	.35	.25
a.		5 feet on lowest lion	45.00	32.50
94	A16	8s vio (buff) ('29)	3.00	.25
95	A16	10s lt bl (lilac)	3.00	.25
96	A16	12s crimson (grn)	2.25	.25
97	A16	15s yel (blue)	3.00	.25
98	A16	15s car (gray) ('35)	14.50	1.75
99	A16	20s slate bl (red)	4.25	.25
100	A16	25s red vio (grn) ('29)	10.50	.25
101	A16	25s bl (brn) ('35)	12.00	1.75
102	A16	40s red org (bl) ('29)	11.00	.60
103	A16	60s gray (brn) ('29)	15.00	.60
104	A16	80s brn (bl) ('29)	15.00	.60
		Nos. 90-104 (15)	96.20	7.80
		Set, never hinged	175.00	

Types of 1924 Issues Surcharged

1930, Sept. 1 *Perf. 14x13½*

Paper with Green Network

105	A14	1k on 70m car & blk	12.00	5.50

Paper with Rose Network

106	A13	2k on 300m brn & bl	30.00	16.00

Paper with Blue Network

107 A13 3k on 300m brn & bl 60.00 27.50
Nos. 105-107 (3) 102.00 49.00
Set, never hinged 210.00

University Observatory A17

University of Tartu A18

Paper with Network as in Parenthesis

1932, June 1 *Perf. 14*
108 A17 5s red (yellow) 5.25 .80
109 A18 10s light bl (lilac) 2.40 .80
110 A17 12s car (blue) 8.25 4.00
111 A18 20s dk bl (green) 6.00 1.60
Nos. 108-111 (4) 21.90 7.20
Set, never hinged 55.00

University of Tartu tercentenary.

Narva Falls — A19

1933, Apr. 1 Photo. *Perf. 14x13½*
112 A19 1k gray black 7.00 3.00
Never hinged 15.00

See No. 149.

Ancient Bard Playing Harp — A20

Paper with Network as in Parenthesis

1933, May 29 Typo. *Perf. 14*
113 A20 2s green (orange) 1.60 .30
114 A20 5s red (green) 2.75 .30
115 A20 10s blue (lilac) 3.50 .30
Nos. 113-115 (3) 7.85 .90
Set, never hinged 17.00

Tenth National Song Festival.
Nos. 113-115 exist imperf. Value $125.

Woman Harvester — A21

1935, Mar. 1 Engr. *Perf. 13½*
116 A21 3k black brown .80 *6.50*
Never hinged 1.60

Pres. Konstantin Päts — A22

1936-40 Typo. *Perf. 14*
117 A22 1s chocolate .80 .25
118 A22 2s yellow green .80 .25
119 A22 3s dp org ('40) 8.00 6.00
120 A22 4s rose vio 1.25 .80
121 A22 5s lt blue grn 1.50 .30
122 A22 6s rose lake 1.25 .25
123 A22 6s dp green ('40) 27.50 42.00
124 A22 10s greenish blue 1.50 .25
125 A22 15s crim rose ('37) 1.90 .40
126 A22 15s dp bl ('40) 3.25 2.50
127 A22 18s dp car ('39) 20.00 7.00
128 A22 20s brt vio 3.00 .35
129 A22 25s dk bl ('38) 8.00 1.25
130 A22 30s bister ('38) 14.00 1.25
131 A22 30s ultra ('39) 16.00 5.00
132 A22 50s org brn 7.00 1.00
133 A22 60s brt pink 16.00 4.50
Nos. 117-133 (17) 131.75 73.35
Set, never hinged 255.00

St. Brigitta Convent Entrance A23

Ruins of Convent, Pirita River A24

Front View of Convent — A25

Seal of Convent — A26

Paper with Network as in Parenthesis

1936, June 10 *Perf. 13½*
134 A23 5s green (buff) .40 .40
135 A24 10s blue (lil) .40 .40
136 A25 15s red (org) 1.25 *4.00*
137 A26 25s ultra (brn) 1.60 *5.50*
Nos. 134-137 (4) 3.65 *10.30*
Set, never hinged 8.00

St. Brigitta Convent, 500th anniversary.

Harbor at Tallinn — A27

1938, Apr. 11 Engr. *Perf. 14*
138 A27 2k blue 1.00 *8.00*
Never hinged 1.75

Friedrich R. Faehlmann A28

Friedrich R. Kreutzwald A29

1938, June 15 Typo. *Perf. 13½*
139 A28 5s dark green .70 .50
140 A29 10s deep brown .70 .50
141 A29 15s dark carmine 1.00 .90
142 A28 25s ultra 1.60 1.40
a. Sheet of 4, #139-142 10.00 *80.00*
Nos. 139-142 (4) 4.00 3.30
Set, never hinged 10.00

Society of Estonian Scholars centenary.

Hospital at Pärnu — A30

Beach Hotel — A31

1939, June 20 Typo. *Perf. 14x13½*
144 A30 5s dark green 1.60 1.60
145 A31 10s deep red violet .80 1.60
146 A30 18s dark carmine 1.50 *5.50*
147 A31 30s deep blue 1.75 *7.25*
a. Sheet of 4, #144-147 15.00 *87.50*
Nos. 144-147 (4) 5.65 15.95
Set, never hinged 11.00

Cent. of health resort and baths at Pärnu.

Narva Falls Type of 1933

1940, Apr. 15 Engr.
149 A19 1k slate green 1.40 *12.00*
Never hinged 2.50

The sky consists of heavy horizontal lines and the background consists of horizontal and vertical lines.

Carrier Pigeon and Plane — A32

1940, July 30 Typo.
150 A32 3s red orange .25 .25
151 A32 10s purple .25 .25
152 A32 15s rose brown .25 .25
153 A32 30s dark blue 1.60 1.25
Nos. 150-153 (4) 2.35 2.00
Set, never hinged 5.00

Centenary of the first postage stamp.
The 15s exists imperf. Value $6.25.

Catalogue values for unused stamps in this section, from this point to the end of the section, are for Never Hinged items.

Natl. Arms — A40

A41

1991, Oct. 1 Litho. *Perf. 13x12½*
200 A40 5k salmon & red .30 .30
201 A40 10k lt grn & dk bl grn .30 .30
202 A40 15k lt bl & dk bl .30 .30
203 A40 30k vio & gray .35 .35
204 A40 50k org & brn .45 .45
205 A40 70k pink & purple .55 .55
206 A40 90k pur & rose lilac .65 .65

Size: 20½x27mm
Engr.
Perf. 12½ Horiz.

207 A40 1r dark brown .80 .80
208 A40 2r lt bl & dk bl 1.75 1.75
Nos. 200-208 (9) 5.45 5.45

See Nos. 211-213, 215, 216, 230, 299-301, 314-314A, 317, 333-334, 339-340. For surcharge, see No. 217.

Perf. 13½x14, 14x13½
1991, Nov. 1 Litho.
209 A41 1.50r Flag, vert. 1.25 1.25
210 A41 2.50r shown 2.10 2.10

National Arms — A42

1992, Mar. 16 Litho. *Perf. 13x12½*
211 A42 E (1r) lemon .25 .25
212 A42 I (20r) blue green 1.00 1.00
213 A42 A (40r) blue 2.25 2.25
Nos. 211-213 (3) 3.50 3.50

No. 211 was valid for postage within Estonia. No. 212 was valid for postage within Europe. No. 213 was valid for overseas mail. See Nos. 214, 219, 220, 224-229.

No. 202 Surcharged

Arms Types of 1991-1992 and

Natl. Arms — A42a

Perf. 14, 13x12½ (#214, 217, 219-220)

1992-96
214 A42 E (10s) orange .25 .25
215 A40 10s blue & gray .25 .25
216 A40 50s gray & brt bl .25 .25
a. Perf. 13x13¼ —
217 A40 60s on 15k #202 .25 .25
218 A40 60s lilac & olive .25 .25
219 A42 I (1k) emerald .75 .75
220 A42 A (2k) violet blue 1.50 1.50
221 A42a 5k bis & red vio 1.25 1.25
a. 5k yel orange & red violet 2.75 2.75
222 A42a 10k blue & olive 2.50 2.50
223 A42a 20k pale lilac & slate grn 4.25 4.25
Nos. 214-223 (10) 11.50 11.50

Coil Stamps
Engr.
Size: 20½x27mm
Perf. 12½ Horiz.

224 A42 X (10s) brown .30 .30
225 A42 X (10s) olive .30 .30
226 A42 X (10s) black .30 .30
227 A42 Z (30s) red lilac .30 .30
228 A42 Z (30s) red .30 .30
229 A42 Z (30s) dark blue .30 .30

Litho.

230 A40 60s lilac brown .30 .30
Nos. 224-230 (7) 2.10 2.10

Issued: Nos. 214, 219-220, 6/22; No. 224, 8/29; No. 225, 9/25; No. 226, 10/31; No. 227, 11/16; No. 228, 12/1; No. 229, 12/22; No. 230, 1/8/93; No. 217, 3/5/93; 10s, 50s, 3/23 1993; 10k, 5/25/93; 5k, 7/7/93; No. 218, 8/5/93; 20k, 9/8/93; No. 221a, 9/19/96; No. 216a, 3/5/96.

See note after No. 213. Nos. 224-229 were valid for postage within Estonia.
See No. F1.

A44

Birds of the Baltic shores.

1992, Oct. 3 Litho. & Engr. *Perf. 13*
Booklet Stamps
231 A44 1k Pandion haliaetus .75 .75
232 A44 1k Limosa limosa .75 .75
233 A44 1k Mergus merganser .75 .75
234 A44 1k Tadorna todorna .75 .75
a. Booklet pane of 4, #231-234 3.00

See Latvia Nos. 332-335a, Lithuania Nos. 427-430a and Sweden Nos. 1975-1978a.

A45

1992, Dec, 15 Litho. *Perf. 14*
235 A45 30s gray & multi .30 .30
236 A45 2k light brown & multi .70 .70

Christmas.
Exist on ordinary and fluorescent paper. Values are for former. Value for set on fluorescent paper, $27.50.

Friendship A46

1993, Feb. 8 Litho. *Perf. 14*

237 A46 1k multicolored .30 .30
a. Booklet pane of 6 1.60

See Finland No. 906.

A47

A48

1993, Feb. 16 *Perf. 13x13½*

238 A47 60s black & multi .25 .25
239 A47 1k violet & multi .25 .25
240 A47 2k blue & multi .50 .50
Nos. 238-240 (3) 1.00 1.00

First Republic, 75th anniv.

1993, June 9 Litho. *Perf. 13½x14*

241 A48 60s Wrestling .25 .25
242 A48 1k +25s Viking ship, map .30 .30
243 A48 2k Shot put with rock .45 .45
Nos. 241-243 (3) 1.00 1.00

First Baltic sea games.

Tallinn Castle — A49

Designs: 1k, Toolse Castle. No. 245, Paide Castle, vert. No. 246, Purtse Castle. No. 247, Haapsalu Castle and Cathedral. 2.70k, Narva Fortress. 2.90k, Haapsalu Cathedral. 3k, Monks' Tower, Kiiu. 3.20k, Rakvere Castle. 4k, Kuressaare Castle. 4.80k, Viljandi Castle.

1993-97 Litho. *Perf. 14*

244 A49 1k gray & black .40 .40
245 A49 2k tan & brown .40 .40
246 A49 2.50k lt vio & dk vio .55 .55
247 A49 2.50k gray .55 .55
248 A49 2.70k lt blue & dk blue .55 .55
249 A49 2.90k lt grn & dk grn .60 .60
250 A49 3k rose & brown .60 .60
251 A49 3.20k lt grn & dk grn .85 .85
252 A49 4k lt gray vio & gray vio .90 .90
253 A49 4.80k dull org & brn .95 .95
Nos. 244-253 (10) 6.35 6.35

Issued: 1k, 2/22/94; 2k, 10/12/93; 2.70k, 12/10/93; 2.90k, 12/23/93; 3k, 3/31/94; 3.20, 12/28/94; 4k, 9/20/94; No. 246, 1/25/96; 247, 7/25/96; 4.80k, 1/21/97.

First Estonian Postage Stamp, 75th Anniv. — A50

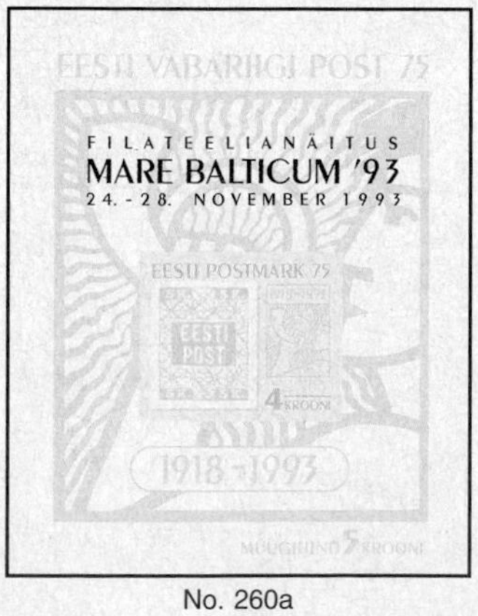

No. 260a

1993, Nov. 13 Litho. *Perf. 14*

259 A50 1k multicolored .40 .40

Souvenir Sheet

Imperf

260 A50 4k multicolored 3.25 3.25
a. Ovptd. in sheet margin 11.50 11.50

No. 260 sold for 5k.

Christmas A51

80s, Haapsalu Cathedral. 2k, Tallinn Church.

1993, Nov. Litho. *Perf. 14*

261 A51 80s red .25 .25
262 A51 2k blue, vert. .40 .40

See Nos. 279-280.

Lydia Koidula — A52

1993, Dec. 14 Litho. *Perf. 14*

263 A52 1k multicolored .25 .25

A53

A54

1994, Jan. 26

264 A53 1k +25s Ski jumping .30 .30
265 A53 2k Speed skating .40 .40

1994 Winter Olympics, Lillehammer.

1994, May 31 Litho. *Perf. 13½x14*

Festival badges: 1k+25s, Tartu, 1869. 2k, Tallinn, 1923. 3k, Tallinn, 1969.
15k, Anniversary badge.

266 A54 1k +25s olive & multi .25 .25
267 A54 2k blue & brown .45 .45
268 A54 3k brown, buff & bister .60 .60
Nos. 266-268 (3) 1.30 1.30

Souvenir Sheet

269 A54 15k multicolored 3.25 3.25

All Estonian Song Festival, 125th anniv.

Flying Squirrel — A55

1994, June 27 Litho. *Perf. 13½x14*

270 A55 1k shown .40 .40
271 A55 2k On leafy branch .50 .50
272 A55 3k In fir tree .85 .85
273 A55 4k With young 1.10 1.10
Nos. 270-273 (4) 2.85 2.85

World Wildlife Fund.

A56

Europa (Estonian Inventions): 1k, Rotating horizontal millstones, by Aleksander Mikiver. 2.70k, First mini-camera, by Walter Zapp.

1994, July 19

274 A56 1k multicolored *.25 .25*
275 A56 2.70k multicolored *.50 .50*

A57

A58

Folk Costumes.

1994, Aug. 23 Litho. *Perf. 14*

276 A57 1k Jamaja .25 .25
277 A57 1k Mustjala .25 .25

See Nos. 286-287, 303-304, 325-326, 347-348, 369-370, 476-477, 497-498, 524-525.

1994, Sept. 27 Litho. *Perf. 13½*

278 A58 1.70k multicolored .35 .35

Estonian Art Museum, 75th anniv.

Christmas Type of 1993

Designs: 1.20k, Ruhnu Church, vert. 2.50k, Urvaste Church.

1994, Nov. 15 Litho. *Perf. 14*

279 A51 1.20k brown .30 .30
280 A51 2.50k green .55 .55

For surcharge see No. B63.

A59

A60

1994, Oct. 18

281 A59 1.70k multicolored .40 .40

Intl. Year of the Family.

1994, Dec. 9

Gustavus II Adolphus (1594-1632), King of Sweden.

282 A60 2.50k lilac .80 .80

A61

A62

1995, Jan. 26 Litho. *Perf. 14*

283 A61 1.70k Branta leucopsis .35 .35
284 A61 3.20k Anser anser .60 .60

Matsalu Nature Reserve.

1995, Feb. 28 Litho. *Perf. 14*

Farm Laborer's Family at Table, by Efraim Allsalu.

285 A62 2.70k multicolored .60 .60

FAO, 50th anniv.

Folk Costumes Type of 1994

1995, Mar. 30 Litho. *Perf. 14*

286 A57 1.70k Muhu couple .40 .40
287 A57 1.70k Three Muhu girls .40 .40

A63

Via Baltica Highway Project: Nos. 288, 289a, Beach Hotel, Parnu. No. 289b, Castle, Bauska, Latvia. No. 289c, Kaunas, Lithuania.

1995, Apr. 20 Litho. *Perf. 14*

288 A63 1.70k multicolored .45 .45

Souvenir Sheet

289 A63 3.20k Sheet of 3, #a.-c. 2.00 2.00

See Latvia Nos. 394-395, Lithuania Nos. 508-509.

A64

1995, Apr. 20 Litho. *Perf. 14*

290 A64 2.70k multicolored *.75 .75*

Europa. Liberation of Nazi Concentration Camps, 50th anniv.

UN, 50th Anniv. — A65

1995, June 1 Litho. *Perf. 14*

291 A65 4k multicolored .75 .75

Pakri Lighthouse A66

1995, July 5 Litho. *Perf. 14*

292 A66 1.70k multicolored .45 .45

See Nos. 309, 318, 338, 356, 388-389, 408, 434, 452, 501-502.

Vanemuine Theater, 125th Anniv. — A67

1995, Aug. 14 Litho. *Perf. 14*

293 A67 1.70k multicolored .45 .45

Louis Pasteur (1822-95) A68

1995, Sept. 20 Litho. *Perf. 14*

294 A68 2.70k multicolored .60 .60

Miniature Sheet

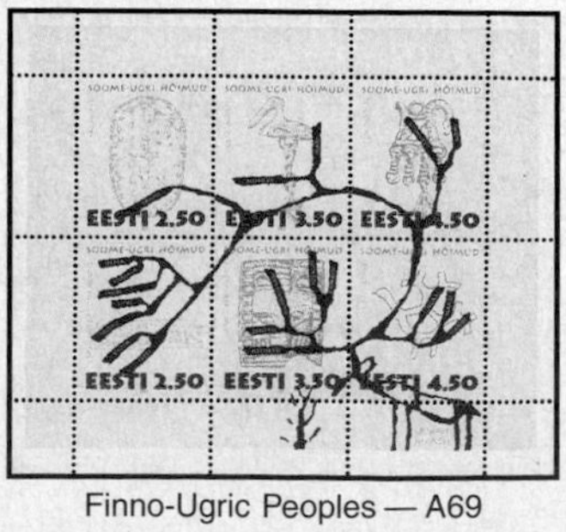

Finno-Ugric Peoples — A69

Ethnographic object, languages: a, 2.50k, Drawing on shaman's drum, Saami. b, 3.50k,

Duck-shaped brooch, Mordva, Mari. c, 4.50k, Duck-feet necklace pendant, Udmurdi, Komi. d, 2.50k, Khanty band ornament, Ungari, Mansi, Handi. e, 3.50k, Bronze amulet, Neenetsi, Eenetsi, Nganassaani, Solkupi, Kamassi. f, 4.50k, Karelian writing on birchbark, Eesti, Vadia, Soome, Liivi, Isuri, Karjala, Vespa.

1995, Oct. 17 Litho. *Perf. 14*
295 A69 Sheet of 6, #a.-f. 4.00 4.00

Aleksander Kunileid (1845-75), Composer — A70

1995, Nov. 1 Engr. *Perf. 12½ Horiz.*
296 A70 2k dark blue black .50 .50

Christmas — A71

Churches: 2k, St. Martin's, Türi. 3.50k, Charles' Church of the Toompea Congregation, Tallinn.

1995, Nov. 15 Litho. *Perf. 14*
297 A71 2k yellow orange .60 .60
298 A71 3.50k dull carmine 1.00 1.00

See Nos. 315-316, 331.

Natl. Arms Type of 1991

1995, Oct. 26 Litho. *Perf. 14*
299 A40 20s blue green & black .25 .25
300 A40 30s gray & magenta .25 .25
301 A40 80s lilac & blue black .25 .25
a. Perf. 13 .25 .25
Nos. 299-301 (3) .75 .75

No. 301a issued in 1996.

Submarine *Lembit* — A72

1996, Feb. 29 Litho. *Perf. 14*
302 A72 2.50k multicolored .50 .50

See No. 308, 328.

Folk Costume Type of 1994

1996, Mar. 26 Litho. *Perf. 14*
303 A57 2.50k Emmaste .70 .70
304 A57 2.50k Reigi .70 .70

A73

Designs: a, 2.50k, First gold medal, 1896. b, 3.50k, Alfred Neuland, weight lifter, first to win gold medal for Estonia, 1920. c, 4k, Cyclist.

1996, Apr. 25 Litho. *Perf. 14*
305 A73 Sheet of 3, #a.-c. 2.00 2.00

Modern Olympic Games, Cent. & 1996 Summer Olympics, Atlanta.

A74

Europa: Marie Under (1883-1980), poet.

1996, May 10
306 A74 2.50k multicolored *1.00 1.00*

Radio, Cent. — A75

1996, June 27 Litho. *Perf. 14*
307 A75 3.50k Guglielmo Marconi .95 .95

Ship Type of 1996

Design: Icebreaker, Suur Toll.

1996, Aug. 30 Litho. *Perf. 14*
308 A72 2.50k multicolored .60 .60

Lighthouse Type of 1995

1996, Sept. 25 Litho. *Perf. 14*
309 A66 2.50k Vaindloo .50 .50

Estonian Narrow Gauge Railway, Cent. — A76

Designs: 3.20k, Class Gk steam locomotive. 3.50k, DeM 1 diesel motor wagon. 4.50k, Class Sk steam locomotive.

1996, Oct. 17 Litho. *Perf. 14*
310 A76 3.20k multicolored .60 .60
311 A76 3.50k multicolored .65 .65
312 A76 4.50k multicolored .75 .75
Nos. 310-312 (3) 2.00 2.00

See No. 397.

Christmas A77

1996, Nov. 27 Litho. *Perf. 14*
313 A77 2.50k multicolored .50 .50

Natl. Arms Type of 1991

1996-97 *Perf. 14*
314 A40 3.30k lilac and claret .80 .80

Perf. 13x13¼
314A A40 3.30k blue & lt claret .80 .80

Issued: No. 314, 12/2; No. 314A, 12/10/97.

Church Type of 1995

Christmas: 3.30k, Harju-Madise Church. 4.50k, Holy Spirit Church, Tallinn.

1996, Dec. 12
315 A71 3.30k blue .65 .65
316 A71 4.50k pink .80 .80

Natl. Arms Type of 1991

1996, Oct. 24 Litho. *Perf. 13½*
317 A40 2.50k grn & dark grn .50 .50

Lighthouse Type of 1995

1997, Feb. 11 Litho. *Perf. 14*
318 A66 3.30k Ruhnu .75 .75

Tallinn Zoo — A78

a, Haliaeetus pelagicus. b, Mustela lutreola. c, Aegypius monachus. d, Panthera pardus orientalis. e, Diceros bicornis. f, Capra cylindricornis.

1997, Mar. 26 Litho. *Perf. 14*
319 A78 3.30k Sheet of 6, #a.-f. 3.50 3.50

Heinrich von Stephan (1831-97), Founder of UPU — A79

1997, Apr. 8 Litho. *Perf. 14*
320 A79 7k black & bister 1.25 1.25

A80

1997, May 5 Litho. *Perf. 14*
321 A80 4.80k Goldspinners Fairy Tale *1.00 1.00*

Europa.

A81

No. 323: a, like #322. b, Linijkugis, 17th cent. c, Kurenas, 16th cent.

1997, May 10
322 A81 3.30k multicolored .80 .80

Perf. 14x14½
323 A81 4.50k Sheet of 3, #a.-c. 5.00 5.00

Maasilinn ship, 16th cent.

See Latvia Nos. 443-444, Lithuania Nos. 571-572.

Folk Costume Type of 1994

1997, June 10 Litho. *Perf. 14*
325 A57 3.30k Ruhnu .60 .60
326 A57 3.30k Vormsi .60 .60

One Kroon Coin — A82

1997, June 12 Litho. *Perf. 14*
327 A82 50k bl grn, blk & gray 9.00 9.00

See Nos. 345, 363, 391.

Ship Type of 1996

Design: Four-masted barkentine, Tormilind.

1997, July 2
328 A72 5.50k multicolored 1.10 1.10

Stone Bridge, Tartu — A83

1997, Sept. 16 Litho. *Perf. 14*
329 A83 3.30k multicolored .65 .65

Wastne Testament, Estonian Bible Translation, 1686 — A84

1997, Oct. 14 Litho. *Perf. 14*
330 A84 3.50k multicolored .65 .65

Church Type of 1995

Christmas: St. Anne's, Halliste.

1997, Nov. 27 Litho. *Perf. 14*
331 A71 3.30k brown .65 .65

Christmas A85

1997, Dec. 3
332 A85 2.90k Elves .60 .60

Natl. Arms Type of 1991

1998, Jan. 19 Litho. *Perf. 13x13½*
333 A40 3.10k lt violet & rose .65 .65
334 A40 3.60k lt blue & ultra .75 .75
a. 3.60k gray & vio bl .75 .75

Issued: No. 334a, 8/4/98.

1998 Winter Olympic Games, Nagano — A86

1998, Jan. 28 Litho. *Perf. 14*
335 A86 3.60k multicolored .75 .75

Republic of Estonia, 80th Anniv. — A87

1998, Feb. 6 Litho. *Imperf.*
336 A87 7k Proclamation, arms 1.50 1.50

Eduard Wiiralt (1898-1954), Print Artist — A88

Various sections of print, "Hell," showing faces: a, 3.60k, shown. b, 3.60k, Explosion coming from center figure. c, 5.50k, Cat on top of one figure's head. d, 5.50k, Faces within faces.

1998, Feb. 18 *Perf. 14*
337 A88 Sheet of 4, #a.-d. 4.00 4.00

Lighthouse Type of 1995

1998, Mar. 12 Litho. *Perf. 14*
338 A66 3.60k Kunda .70 .70

Natl. Arms Type of 1991

1998, Mar. 16 *Perf. 13*
339 A40 10s grn bl & brn blk .25 .25
340 A40 4.50k pale orange & brick red .80 .80

Issued: 10s, 3/25/97; 4.50k, 3/16/98.

A88a

1998, Apr. 16 Litho. *Perf. 14*
341 A88a 7k multicolored 1.30 1.30

1998 World Cup Soccer Championship, France.

A89

1998, May 5 Litho. *Perf. 14*
342 A89 5.20k St. John's Day *1.25 1.25*

Europa.

Use of Lübeck Charter in Tallinn, 750th Anniv. — A90

1998, June 1
343 A90 4.80k multicolored 1.10 1.10

Beautiful Homes Year — A91

1998, June 16 Litho. *Perf. 14*
344 A91 3.60k multicolored 1.00 1.00

One Kroon Coin Type of 1997

1998, June 18
345 A82 25k green, gray & black 5.25 5.25

A92

1998, Aug. 4 Litho. *Perf. 14*
346 A92 5.50k multicolored 1.25 1.25

470 Class World Yachting Championships.

Folk Costume Type of 1994

1998, Aug. 21 Litho. *Perf. 14*
347 A57 3.60k Kihnu couple .70 .70
348 A57 3.60k Kihnu family .70 .70

A93

1998, Sept. 3
349 A93 3.60k yel, blue & blk .80 .80

Juhan Jaik (1899-1948), author.

Tallinn Zoo — A94

Design: Panthera tigris altaica.

1998, Sept. 17
350 A94 3.60k multicolored .80 .80

See No. 357.

Estonian Post, 80th Anniv. — A95

1998, Oct. 22 Litho. *Perf. 14*
351 A95 3.60k multicolored .80 .80

Military Aid from Finland, 90th Anniv. — A96

1998, Nov. 5 Litho. *Perf. 14*
352 A96 4.50k Freedom Cross 1.00 1.00

Christmas A97

1998, Nov. 26 Litho. *Perf. 14*
353 A97 3.10k Santa, child, vert. .60 .60
354 A97 5k shown .90 .90

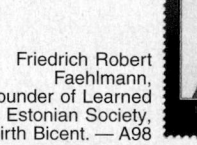

Friedrich Robert Faehlmann, Founder of Learned Estonian Society, Birth Bicent. — A98

1998, Dec. 2
355 A98 3.60k multicolored .85 .85

Lighthouse Type of 1995

1999, Jan. 20 Litho. *Perf. 14*
356 A66 3.60k Vilsandi .85 .85

Tallinn Zoo Type of 1998

1999, Feb. 18 Litho. *Perf. 14*
357 A94 3.60k Uncia uncia .70 .70

Council of Europe, 50th Anniv. — A99

1999, Mar. 24 Litho. *Perf. 14*
358 A99 5.50k multicolored 1.10 1.10

Estonian Pres. Lennart Meri, 70th Birthday A100

1999, Mar. 29
359 A100 3.60k multicolored .85 .85

Tolkuse Bog — A101

1999, Apr. 27 Litho. *Perf. 14*
360 A101 5.50k multicolored *1.25 1.25*

Europa.

Bank of Estonia, 80th Anniv. — A102

1999, May 3 Litho. *Perf. 14*
361 A102 5k multicolored 1.00 1.00

Olustvere Manor — A103

1999, June 1
362 A103 3.60k multicolored .80 .80

See Nos. 395, 414, 433, 456, 490, 520, 551, 562, 603, 627, 648.

One Kroon Coin Type of 1997

1999, June 18 Litho. *Perf. 14*
363 A82 100k bl, bister & blk 17.00 17.00

Estonian Natl. Anthem — A104

1999, June 30 Litho. *Perf. 14*
364 A104 3.60k multicolored .70 .70

No. 364 is printed se-tenant with label.

Tower on Suur Munamägi, Highest Point in Baltic Countries A105

1999, July 17
365 A105 5.20k multicolored 1.00 1.00

A106

Families holding hands and: 3.60k, Estonian flag.

No. 367: a, like #366. b, Latvian flag. c, Lithuanian flag.

1999, Aug. 23 Litho. *Perf. 14*
366 A106 3.60k multicolored .75 .75

Souvenir Sheet

367 A106 5.50k Sheet of 3, #a.-c. 3.25 3.25

Baltic Chain, 10th Anniv.

See Latvia Nos.493-494, Lithuania Nos. 639-640.

A107

1999, Sept. 23 Litho. *Perf. 14x13¾*
368 A107 7k multicolored 1.40 1.40

UPU, 125th Anniv.

Folk Costumes Type of 1994

1999, Oct. 12 Litho. *Perf. 13¾x14*
369 A57 3.60k Setu couple .65 .65
370 A57 5k Setu man, boy .90 .90

Three Lions — A108

Perf. 13x13¼, 13¾x14 (#371, 373, 374, 378-382)

1999-2002 Litho.
371 A108 10s brn & dk brn .25 .25
372 A108 30s lt bl & dk bl .25 .25
a. Perf. 13¾x14 .25 .25
373 A108 30s blue & slate blue, dated 2003 .25 .25
374 A108 50s olive & dk grn .25 .25
375 A108 1k brown & fawn .25 .25
376 A108 2k gray .40 .40
377 A108 3.60k sky bl & dk bl .65 .65
a. Bright blue green ('00) .65 .65
378 A108 4.40k grn & bl grn .85 .70
a. Inscribed "2001" .85 .70
b. Inscribed "2002" .85 .70
379 A108 4.40k bl grn & brt bl grn, wide 2001 date .85 .25
380 A108 4.40k Prus bl & lt bl, narrow 2001 date .85 .25
381 A108 4.40k green & lt grn, dated 2002 .85 .25
382 A108 4.40k grn & apple grn, dated 2002 .85 .25
382A A108 4.40k ol grn & apple grn, dated 2003 .85 .30
382B A108 5k grn & lt grn, dated "2001" 1.10 1.10
a. Inscribed "2002" 1.00 1.00
b. Inscribed "2004" .65 .65

382C A108 6k bis & yel 1.25 1.25
382D A108 6.50k bis & org 1.25 1.25
382E A108 8k lake & pink 1.50 1.50
Nos. 371-382E (17) 12.50 9.40

Issued: 30s, 2k, 11/4; No. 377, 10/22; No. 377a, 3/31/00; No. 378, 8/21/00; 6k, 10/12/00; 6.50k, 10/5/00; 8k, 10/19/00; No. 372a: 4/17/01; 1k, 5k, 8/28/01; 10s, 2/2/02. 50s, 1/7/03; No. 373, 3/11/03; No. 379, 4/17/01; No. 380, 9/24/01; No. 381, 2/2/02; No. 382, 11/14/02; No. 382A, 3/11/03.

The background color of No. 379 is bolder than that on No. 380.

See Nos. 467, 472-474.

Christmas A109

1999, Nov. 25 Litho. ***Perf. 14x13¾***
383 A109 3.10k multicolored .70 .70

A110

1999, Nov. 25 ***Perf. 13¾x14***
384 A110 7k multicolored 1.50 1.50

1st public Christmas tree in Tallinn, 1441.

Christmas Lottery A110a

1999, Dec. 1 Litho. ***Perf. 14x13¾***
384A A110a 3.10k + 1.90k multi 1.10 1.10

A111

1999, Dec. 14 Litho. ***Perf. 13¾x14***
385 A111 5.50k Millennium 1.10 1.10

2000 Census — A112

2000, Jan. 5
386 A112 3.60k multicolored .80 .80

Tartu Peace Treaty, 80th Anniv. — A113

2000, Feb. 2 Litho. ***Perf. 14x13¾***
387 A113 3.60k multi .80 .80

Lighthouse Type of 1995

2000, Feb. 25
388 A66 3.60k Ristna .75 .75
389 A66 3.60k Kopu .75 .75
a. Pair, #388-389 1.25 1.25

Congress, 10th Anniv. — A114

2000, Mar. 9 ***Perf. 13¾x14***
390 A114 3.60k multi .75 .75

One Kroon Coin Type of 1997

2000, Mar. 14 ***Perf. 14x13¾***
391 A82 10k red, sil & blk 2.00 2.00

Cornflower (Natl. Flower) — A115

2000, Apr. 7
392 A115 4.80k multi 1.00 1.00

Natl. Book Year — A116

2000, Apr. 22 ***Perf. 13¾x14***
393 A116 3.60k multi .65 .65

First book printed in Estonian language, 475th anniv.

Europa, 2000
Common Design Type

2000, May 9
394 CD17 4.80k multi *1.25 1.25*

Manor Type of 1999

2000, May 23 Litho. ***Perf. 14x13¾***
395 A103 3.60k Palmse Hall .75 .75

Tallinn Zoo — A117

2000, June 13 Litho. ***Perf. 14x13¾***
396 A117 3.60k Naemorhedus caudatus .75 .75

Railway Type of 1996

4.50k, Viljandi-Tallinn Railway, cent.

2000, June 30
397 A76 4.50k multi .80 .80

9th Intl. Finno-Ugric Congress A118

2000, Aug. 1
398 A118 5k multi 1.00 1.00

2000 Summer Olympics, Sydney — A119

2000, Sept. 5 Litho. ***Perf. 13¾x14***
399 A119 8k multi 1.50 1.50

Folk Costume Type of 1994

Designs: 4.40k, Hargla. 8k, Polva.

2000, Sept. 12
400-401 A57 Set of 2 2.25 2.25

August Mälk (1900-87), Writer — A120

2000, Sept. 20 ***Perf. 14x13¾***
402 A120 4.40k multi .90 .90

Lake Peipus Fish — A121

No. 403: a, Osmerus eperlanus spirinchus. b, Stizostedion lucioperka.

2000, Oct. 25
403 Horiz. pair + central label 2.50 2.50
a.-b. A121 6.50k Any single 1.10 1.10

See Russia No. 6607.

Souvenir Sheet

Estonian Bookplates, Cent. — A122

Various bookplates. Denominiations in: a, LR. b, UR.

2000, Nov. 11 ***Perf. 13¾x14***
404 A122 6k Sheet of 2, #a-b 2.25 2.25

Christmas A123

3.60k, Horn and bow. 6k, Ornament.

2000, Nov. 29 ***Perf. 14x13¾***
405-406 A123 Set of 2 1.70 1.70

Erki Nool, Olympic Decathlon Champion A124

2001, Jan. 10 Litho. ***Perf. 14x13¾***
407 A124 4.40k multi .80 .80

Lighthouse Type of 1995

2001, Jan. 24
408 A66 4.40k Mohni .85 .85

Valentine's Day — A125

2001, Feb. 6 Litho. ***Perf. 13¾x14***
409 A125 4.40k multi .85 .85

Stenbock House, Seat of Government A126

2001, Feb. 20 ***Perf. 14x13¾***
410 A126 6.50k multi 1.20 1.20

Souvenir Sheet

Paintings of Johann Köler (1826-99) — A127

No. 411: a, Girl on the Spring, 1858-62. b, Eve of the Pomegranate, 1879-80.

2001, Feb. 27
411 A127 4.40k Sheet of 2, #a-b 1.50 1.50

European Year of Languages A128

2001, Mar. 6
412 A128 4.40k multi .85 .85

Vanellus Vanellus A129

2001, Apr. 4 ***Perf. 12¾x13***
413 A129 4.40k multi .90 .90

See No. 435.

Manor Type of 1999

2001, Apr. 17 ***Perf. 14x13¾***
414 A103 4.40k Laupa Hall .90 .90

Europa — A130

2001, May 9 *Perf. 13¾x14*
415 A130 6.50k multi *1.30 1.30*

Kalev Sports Association, Cent. — A131

2001, May 24
416 A131 6.50k multi 1.25 1.25

Pärnu, 750th Anniv. — A132

2001, June 5 Litho. *Perf. 14x13¾*
417 A132 4.40k multi .90 .90

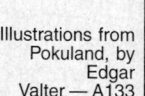

Illustrations from Pokuland, by Edgar Valter — A133

Characters and — No. 418: a, Lake. b, Owl. c, Crane. d, Bird in nest.
No. 419: a, Fence. b, Flowers. c, Dog. d, Moon.

2001, June 19

418	Booklet pane of 4	2.75	
a.-d.	A133 3.60k Any single	.75	.75
419	Booklet pane of 4	3.75	
a.-d.	A133 4.40k Any single	.90	.90
	Booklet, #418-419	7.25	

Entire booklet sold for 35k, 3k of which went to the Pokuland Project of the Estonian Nature Fund.

Restoration of Independence, 10th Anniv. — A134

2001, Aug. 7 *Perf. 13¾x14*
420 A134 4.40k multi .90 .90

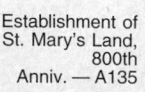

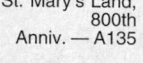

Establishment of St. Mary's Land, 800th Anniv. — A135

2001, Aug. 15 *Perf. 14x13¾*
421 A135 6.50k multi 1.25 1.25

Resumption of Issuing Stamps, 10th Anniv. — A136

2001, Sept. 4 *Perf. 13¾x14*
422 A136 4.40k #200 .90 .90

Baltic Coast Landscapes A137

Designs: 4.40k, No. 424a, Lahemaa. No. 424b, Vidzeme. No. 424c, Palanga.

2001, Sept. 15 *Perf. 14x13¾*
423 A137 4.40k multi .90 .90

Souvenir Sheet

Perf. 13¼x13½

424	Sheet of 3	3.50	3.50
a.-c.	A137 6k Any single	1.10	1.10

No. 424 contains three 35x29mm stamps. See Lithuania Nos.
See Latvia Nos. 534-535, Lithuania Nos. 698-699.

Tallinn Zoo — A138

2001, Oct. 4 *Perf. 14x13¾*
425 A138 4.40k Alligator sinensis .90 .90

Estonia 26/9 Racing Car — A139

2001, Oct. 23
426 A139 6k multi 1.25 1.25

Folk Costume Type of 1994

Designs: 4.40k, Paistu woman. 7.50k, Tarvastu man.

2001, Nov. 7 Litho. *Perf. 13¾x14*
427-428 A57 Set of 2 2.25 2.25

A140

Christmas A141

Perf. 13¾x14, 14x13¾

2001, Nov. 22

429	A140 3.60k multi	.70	.70
430	A141 6.50k multi	1.40	1.40

Radio Broadcasting in Estonia, 75th Anniv. — A142

2001, Dec. 4 *Perf. 14x13¾*
431 A142 4.40k multi .90 .90

2002 Winter Olympics, Salt Lake City — A143

2002, Jan. 10 Litho. *Perf. 14x13¾*
432 A143 8k multi 1.40 1.40

Manor Type of 1999

2002, Jan. 22
433 A103 4.40k Sangaste Hall .80 .80

Lighthouse Type of 1995

2002, Feb. 20
434 A66 4.40k Laidunina .80 .80

Bird Type of 2001

Design: Passer domesticus and Passer montanus.

2002, Mar. 7 *Perf. 12¾x13*
435 A129 4.40k multi .80 .80

Spring Flowers — A144

2002, Mar. 20 *Perf. 14x13¾*
436 A144 4.40k multi .80 .80

Estonian Puppet Theater, 50th Anniv. — A145

2002, Mar. 27 *Perf. 13¾x14*
437 A145 4.40k multi + label .80 .80

PTO-4 Training Airplane — A146

2002, Apr. 10 *Perf. 14x13¾*
438 A146 6k multi 1.10 1.10

Andrus Veerpalu, Gold Medalist at 2002 Winter Olympics A147

2002, Apr. 12
439 A147 4.40k multi .80 .80

Tartu University Anniversaries — A148

No. 440: a, Main building, 1806-09, founding act of 1632. b, University Library, 1982, text from Biblia Latina.

2002, Apr. 24
440 A148 4.40k Horiz. pair, #a-b, + central label 2.25 2.25

Europa A149

2002, May 9 *Perf. 12¾x13*
441 A149 6.50k multi *1.60 1.60*

Re-adoption of Constitution, 10th Anniv. — A150

2002, May 23 *Perf. 13¾x14*
442 A150 4.40k multi .80 .80

Adoption of Lübeck Charter by Town of Rakvere, 700th Anniv. — A151

2002, June 5
443 A151 4.40k multi .80 .80

Souvenir Sheet

Re-introduction of the Kroon, 10th Anniv. — A152

No. 444 — Portraits from bank notes: a, Lydia Koidula, poet. b, Carl Rober Jakobson, journalist.

2002, June 10 *Perf. 14x13¾*
444 A152 4.40k Sheet of 2, #a-b 2.40 2.40

Souvenir Sheet

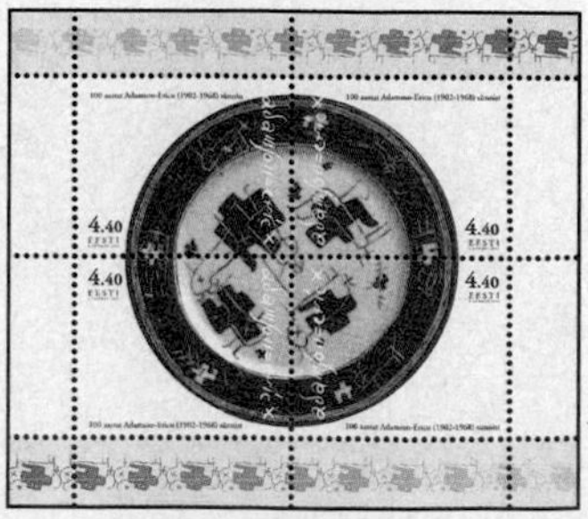

Adamson-Eric (1902-68), Painter — A153

Denomination at: a, LL. b, LR. c, UL. d, UR.

2002, Aug. 8 Litho. ***Perf. 14x13¾***
445 A153 4.40k Sheet of 4, #a-d 3.25 3.25

Sus Scrofa
A154

2002, Aug. 21 ***Perf. 12¾x13***
446 A154 4.40k multi .80 .80

Limestone, Estonia's National Stone
A155

2002, Sept. 18
447 A155 4.40k multi .80 .80

Folk Costume Type of 1994

Designs: 4.40k, Kolga-Jaani women. 5.50k, Suure-Jaani boy and girl.

2002, Oct. 1 ***Perf. 13¾x14***
448-449 A57 Set of 2 1.75 1.75

A156

Christmas — A157

Perf. 14x13¾, 13¾x14
2002, Nov. 20 Litho.
450 A156 3.60k Reindeer .60 .60
451 A157 6.50k Christmas tree 1.15 1.15

Lighthouse Type of 1995

2003, Jan. 15 ***Perf. 14x13¾***
452 A66 4.40k Keri .80 .80

Anton Hansen Tammsaare (1878-1940), Novelist — A158

2003, Jan. 30 Litho. ***Perf. 14x13¾***
453 A158 4.40k multi .80 .80

Pica Pica
A159

2003, Feb. 13 ***Perf. 12¾x13***
454 A159 4.40k multi .80 .80

See Nos. 485, 509, 540, 566, 595, 625.

Spring Flowers — A160

No. 455: a, Tulips. b, Helleborus purpurascens. c, Narcissus poeticus. d, Crocus vernus.

2003, Mar. 20 ***Perf. 13¾x14***
455 A160 4.40k Sheet of 4, #a-d 7.50 7.50
e. Booklet pane, like #455, without date in margin 3.25 —
Complete booklet, #455e 3.25

See No. 484.

Manor Type of 1999

2003, Apr. 9 ***Perf. 14x13¾***
456 A103 4.40k Alatskivi Hall .80 .80

Pres. Arnold Rüütel, 75th Birthday — A161

2003, Apr. 24
457 A161 4.40k multi + label .80 .80

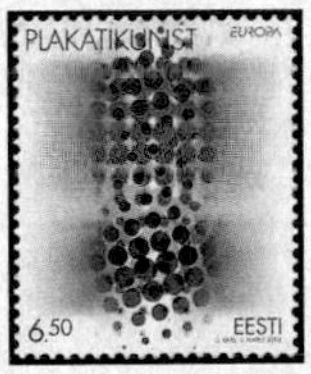

Europa — A162

2003, May 8 ***Perf. 13¾x14***
458 A162 6.50k multi *1.60 1.60*

Tartu University Botanical Gardens, Bicent. — A163

2003, June 11 Litho. ***Perf. 14x13¾***
459 A163 4.40k multi .80 .80

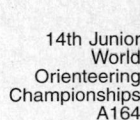

14th Junior World Orienteering Championships
A164

2003, June 27
460 A164 7.50k multi 1.35 1.35

Circumnavigation of Adam Johann von Krusenstern (1770-1846) — A165

2003, Aug. 6 ***Perf. 12½***
461 A165 8k multi 1.40 1.40

Phoca Hispida
A166

2003, Aug. 27 ***Perf. 12¾x13***
462 A166 4.40k multi .80 .80

Adm. Fabian Gottlieb von Bellingshausen (1778-1852) — A167

2003, Sept. 10
463 A167 8k multi 1.50 1.50

Ancient Trade Routes — A168

Map and: No. 464, 6.50k, Silver coin of Prince Volodymyr Sviatoslavovych, Slavic warship with sail. No. 465, 6.50k, Arrival of Scandinavian Seamen, coin of Danish King Svend Estridsen.

2003, Sept. 10 ***Perf. 11½***
464-465 A168 Set of 2 2.25 2.25

See Ukraine No. 524.

Three Lions Type of 1999-2002

2003-04 Litho. ***Perf. 13¾x14***
467 A108 20s blk & gray .25 .25
472 A108 4.40k ol grn & apple grn .75 .75
473 A108 5k dk grn & apple grn, dated 2004 1.00 1.00
474 A108 5.50k dk grn & yel grn 1.10 1.10

Issued: 20s, 4.40k, 8/22; 5k, 1/20/04; 5.50k, 3/25/04.

Folk Costume Type of 1994

Designs: 4.40k, Aksi woman and girl. 6.50k, Otepää man, woman and girl.

2003, Oct. 9 Litho. ***Perf. 13¾x14***
476-477 A57 Set of 2 1.90 1.90

A169

Christmas
A170

2003, Nov. 26 ***Perf. 14x13¾***
478 A169 3.60k multi .75 .75
479 A170 6k multi 1.00 1.00

Souvenir Sheet

Friedrich Reinhold Kreutzwald (1803-82), Writer — A171

No. 480: a, 4.40k, Illustration by Kristjan Raud of "Voyage to the End of the World," from "Kalevipoeg," by Kreutzwald. b, 6.50k, Portrait of Kreutzwald.

2003, Dec. 4 ***Perf. 13x12¾***
480 A171 Sheet of 2, #a-b 2.10 2.10

Lighthouse Type of 1995

2004, Jan. 7 Litho. ***Perf. 14x13¾***
481 A66 4.40k Sorgu .80 .80

Canis Lupus
A172

2004, Feb. 3 ***Perf. 12¾x13***
482 A172 4.40k multi .80 .80

Voyage Around Cape Horn of the Hioma, 150th Anniv. — A173

2004, Feb. 18 ***Perf. 13¾x14***
483 A173 8k multi 1.50 1.50

Spring Flowers Type of 2003

No. 484: a, Viola riviniana. b, Anemone nemorosa. c, Hepatica nobilis. d, Trollius europaeus.

2004, Mar. 17
484 A160 4.40k Sheet of 4, #a-d 3.25 3.25
e. Booklet pane, like #484 without date in margin 3.25
Complete booklet, #484e 3.25

Bird Type of 2003

2004, Apr. 6 ***Perf. 12¾x13***
485 A159 4.40k Ciconia ciconia .80 .80

Admission to European Union
A174

2004, May 1 ***Perf. 13¼x13***
486 A174 6.50k multi 1.25 1.25

Europa — A175

2004, May 4 ***Perf. 13***
487 A175 6.50k multi *1.25 1.25*

Tallinn Town Hall, 600th Anniv. A176

2004, May 13 Litho. ***Perf. 12¾x13***
488 A176 4.40k multi .80 .80

Consecration of Estonian Flag, 120th Anniv. — A177

2004, June 4 ***Perf. 13¾x14***
489 A177 4.40k multi .80 .80

Manor Type of 1999

2004, June 15 ***Perf. 14x13¾***
490 A103 4.40k Vasalemma Hall .80 .80

Admission to NATO — A178

2004, June 28 ***Perf. 13¾x14***
491 A178 6k multi 1.10 1.10

2004 Summer Olympics, Athens — A179

2004, July 15 Litho. ***Perf. 13¾x14***
492 A179 8k multi 1.40 1.40

Dragon Class Yachting European Championships — A180

2004, Aug. 17 ***Perf. 14x13¾***
493 A180 6k multi 1.10 1.10

Taraxacum Officinale — A181

Serpentine Die Cut 12½
2004, Sept. 14 Self-Adhesive
494 A181 30s multi .25 .25

See Nos. 547, 560, 572.

County Arms — A182

2004, Sept. 28 Self-Adhesive
495 A182 4.40k Harjumaa .80 .80
496 A182 4.40k Hiiumaa .80 .80

See Nos. 506-507, 518-519, 532-533, 536, 552, 561, 573, 588, 594, 608.

Folk Costumes Type of 1994

Designs: 4.40k, Viru-Jaagupi boy and girl. 7.50k, Jõhvi woman and girl.

2004, Oct. 5 Litho. ***Perf. 13¾x14***
497-498 A57 Set of 2 2.10 2.10

A183

Christmas A184

2004, Nov. 23 ***Perf. 13¾x14***
499 A183 4.40k multi .90 .90

Perf. 14x13¾
500 A184 6.50k multi 1.00 1.00

Lighthouse Type of 1995

Norrby Lighthouse with: 4.40k, White top, vert. 6.50k, Red top, vert.

2005, Jan. 11 Litho. ***Perf. 14***
501-502 A66 Set of 2 1.90 1.90

Castor Fiber A185

2005, Jan. 25 ***Perf. 12¾x13***
503 A185 4.40k multi .80 .80

Rotary International, Cent. — A186

2005, Feb. 11 ***Perf. 13¾x14***
504 A186 8k multi 1.50 1.50

Flag Over Pikk Hermann Tower, Tallinn — A187

Serpentine Die Cut 12½
2005, Feb. 22 Self-Adhesive
505 A187 5k multi 1.00 1.00

See Nos. 530, 559, 574.

County Arms Type of 2004

2005 Self-Adhesive Litho.
506 A182 4.40k Ida-Virumaa .80 .80
507 A182 4.40k Järvamaa .80 .80

Issued: No. 506, 3/8; No. 507, 3/15.

Souvenir Sheet

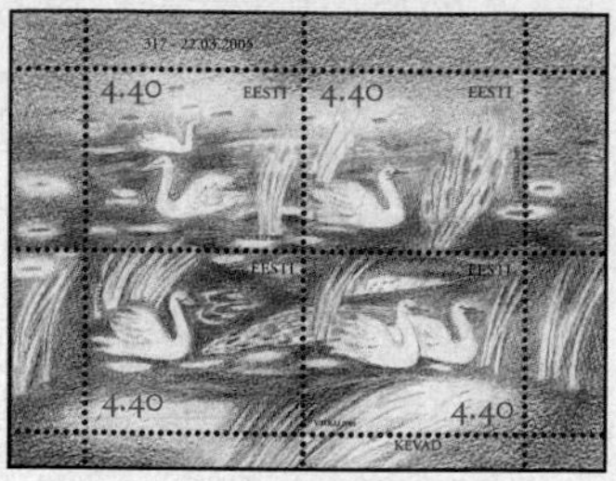

Spring — A188

No. 508: a, Two swans, denomination at UL. b, One swan, denomination at UL. c, One swan, denomination at LL. d, Two swans, denomination at LR.

2005, Mar. 22 Litho. ***Perf. 14x13¾***
508 A188 4.40k Sheet of 4, #a-d 3.10 3.10

Bird Type of 2003

2005, Apr. 5 ***Perf. 12¾x13***
509 A159 4.40k Accipiter gentilis .80 .80

Mother's Day — A189

2005, Apr. 20 ***Perf. 14x13¾***
510 A189 4.40k multi .80 .80

Europa — A190

Designs: 6k, Vegetable wrap. 6.50k, Tomato, carrots, egg yolk, parsley, fish, onion, beet.

2005, May 3
511-512 A190 Set of 2 *2.25 2.25*

Eduard Tubin (1905-82), Composer A191

2005, May 18
513 A191 6k multi 1.10 1.10

Intl. Children's Day — A192

No. 514: a, Birds. b, Butterflies.

2005, June 1 ***Perf. 13¼x13¾***
514 A192 4.40k Horiz. pair, #a-b, + central label 1.50 1.50

Orchids — A193

Designs: 4.40k, Epipactis palustris. 8k, Epipogium aphyllum.

2005, June 16 Litho. ***Perf. 13¾x14***
515-516 A193 Set of 2 2.10 2.10

Restoration of St. John's Cathedral, Tartu — A194

2005, June 29
517 A194 4.40k multi .80 .80

Tartu, 975th anniv.

County Arms Type of 2004

Serpentine Die Cut 12½
2005 Self-Adhesive Litho.
518 A182 4.40k Jõgevamaa .80 .80
519 A182 4.40k Läänemaa .80 .80

Issued: No. 518, 7/5; No. 519, 7/8.

Manor Type of 1999

2005, July 12 ***Perf. 14x13¾***
520 A103 4.40k Kiltsi Hall .80 .80

St. Catherine's Church, Karja — A195

2005, Sept. 20
521 A195 4.40k multi .80 .80

Souvenir Sheet

Sculptures by Amandus Adamson (1855-1929) — A196

No. 522: a, Igavesti Voidutsev Armastus, 1889. b, Lüüriline Muusika, 1891. c, Memento Mori, 1907. d, Koit ja Hämarik, 1895.

2005, Oct. 12 ***Perf. 13½***
522 A196 650s Sheet of 4, #a-d 4.75 4.75

Dogs — A197

No. 523: a, Kazakh hound (Kasaahi hurt). b, Estonian hound (Eesti hagijas).

2005, Oct. 19 ***Perf. 14x13¾***
523 A197 6.50k Horiz. pair, #a-b 2.40 2.40

See Kazakhstan No. 495.

Folk Costumes Type of 1994

Designs: 4.40k, Ambla man, woman and girl. 8k, Türi women.

2005, Oct. 28 ***Perf. 13¾x14***
524-525 A57 Set of 2 2.10 2.10

New Year's Goat — A198

Adoration of the Magi — A199

2005, Nov. 22
526 A198 4.40k multi .75 .75
527 A199 8k sil & red lil 1.35 1.35

Christmas and New Year's Day.

Due to the postponed conversion to the euro, originally scheduled for Jan. 1, 2007, Estonian stamps issued between 2006 and 2010 show denominations in kroons and the at-that-time-uncirculating euros.

Europa Stamps, 50th Anniv. — A200

CEPT emblem and: 6k, Superimposed letters. 6.50k, Map of Europe.

2006, Jan. 4 Litho. *Perf. 14x13¾*
528 A200 6k multi *1.00 1.00*

Souvenir Sheet
529 A200 6.50k multi *1.10 1.10*

Flag Over Pikk Hermann Tower Type of 2005 With Euro Denominations Added

2006, Jan. 11 *Die Cut Perf. 12½*
Self-Adhesive
530 A187 11k multi 1.90 1.90

2006 Winter Olympics, Turin, Italy — A201

2006, Jan. 18 *Perf. 14x13¾*
531 A201 8k multi 1.35 1.35

County Arms Type of 2004 With Euro Denominations Added

2006 *Die Cut Perf. 12½*
Self-Adhesive
532 A182 4.40k Lääne-Virumaa .85 .85
533 A182 4.40k Polvamaa .85 .85

Issued: No. 532, 1/25; No. 533, 2/8.

Alces Alces A202

2006, Feb. 1 *Perf. 12¾x13*
534 A202 4.40k multi .85 .85

Opening of KUMU Art Museum — A203

2006, Feb. 17 Litho. *Perf. 13¾x14*
535 A203 4.40k multi .85 .85

County Arms Type of 2004 With Euro Denominations Added

2006, Mar. 8 *Die Cut Perf. 12½*
Self-Adhesive
536 A182 4.40k Pärnumaa .85 .85

Souvenir Sheet

National Opera, Cent. — A204

No. 537: a, Characters from Vikerlased, first opera staged in 1928. b, Ballerina.

2006, Mar. 27 *Perf. 13¾x14*
537 A204 6.50k Sheet of 2, #a-b, + central label 2.25 2.25

A205

Gold Medalists at 2006 Winter Olympics — A206

No. 539: a, Andrus Veerpalu. b, Kristina Smigun.

2006, Mar. 30 *Perf. 14x13¾*
538 A205 4.40k multi .85 .85

Souvenir Sheet
539 A206 8k Sheet of 2, #a-b 2.75 2.75

Bird Type of 2003 With Euro Denominations Added

2006, Apr. 5 *Perf. 12¾x13*
540 A159 4.40k multi .85 .85

Lighthouses A207

Designs: 4.40k, Tallinn Bay lower lighthouse. 6.50k, Tallinn Bay upper lighthouse.

2006, Apr. 12 *Perf. 13¾x14*
541-542 A207 Set of 2 1.90 1.90

See Nos. 564, 587, 624.

Estonian Shooting Sport Federation, 75th Anniv. — A208

2006, Apr. 26
543 A208 4.40k car & sil .85 .85

Europa — A209

2006, May 3
544 A209 6.50k multi 1.10 1.10

Confectionery Industry in Estonia, Bicent. A210

2006, May 18 *Perf. 14x13¾*
545 A210 4.40k multi .85 .85

Posthorns — A211

2006, May 22 *Die Cut Perf. 10*
Self-Adhesive
546 A211 4.40k gray brn + label .85 .85

Labels could be personalized.
See No. 563.

Flower Type of 2004 with Euro Denominations Added

2006, May 24 *Die Cut Perf. 12½*
Self-Adhesive
547 A181 30s Hepatica nobilis .25 .25

Souvenir Sheet

Tori Stud Farm, 150th Anniv. — A212

No. 548: a, Three horses, denomination at UL. b, Pony and three horses, denomination at UR.

2006, June 7 *Perf. 14x13¾*
548 A212 4.40k Sheet of 2, #a-b 1.60 1.60

Victory Day — A213

2006, June 23
549 A213 4.40k multi .85 .85

20th Intl. Organ Music Festival, Tallinn — A214

2006, July 28 Litho. *Perf. 14x13¾*
550 A214 4.40k multi .85 .85

Manor Type of 1999 With Added Euro Denomination

2006, Aug. 16
551 A103 4.40k Taagepera Hall .85 .85

County Arms Type of 2004 With Added Euro Denomination

2006, Sept. 6 *Die Cut Perf. 12½*
Self-Adhesive
552 A182 4.40k Raplamaa .85 .85

St. Lawrence's Church, Noo — A215

2006, Sept. 20 *Perf. 13¾x14*
553 A215 4.40k multi .85 .85

Betti Alver (1906-89), Writer — A216

2006, Oct. 11 *Perf. 13*
554 A216 4.40k multi .85 .85

Antarctic Wildlife — A217

No. 555 — Estonian and Chilean flags and: a, Aptenodytes forsteri. b, Balaenoptera acutorostrata.

2006, Oct. 25 *Perf. 13½*
555 A217 8k Pair, #a-b 2.75 2.75

See Chile No. 1468.

A218

Christmas — A219

2006, Nov. 22 Litho. *Perf. 13¾x14*
556 A218 4.40k multi .75 .75
557 A219 6k multi 1.00 1.00

Lotte From Gadgetville A220

2007, Jan. 4 *Perf. 14x13¾*
558 A220 4.40k multi .85 .85

Flag Over Pikk Hermann Tower Type of 2005 With Euro Denomination Added

2007, Jan. 11 *Die Cut Perf. 12½*
Self-Adhesive
559 A187 5k tan & multi .85 .85

Flower Type of 2004 With Euro Denomination Added

2007, Jan. 17 ***Die Cut Perf. 12½***

Self-Adhesive

560 A181 30s Leucanthemum vulgare .25 .25

County Arms Type of 2004 With Euro Denomination Added

2007, Jan. 25 ***Die Cut Perf. 12½***

Self-Adhesive

561 A182 4.40k Saaremaa .85 .85

Manor Type of 1999 With Euro Denomination Added

2007, Feb. 14 ***Perf. 14x13¾***

562 A103 5.50k Sagadi Hall .90 .90

Posthorns Type of 2006

2007, Feb. 22 ***Die Cut Perf. 10***

Self-Adhesive

563 A211 5.50k bl grn + label .90 .90

Labels could be personalized.

Lighthouse Type of 2006

2007, Mar. 8 ***Perf. 14x13¾***

564 A207 6k Juminda, horiz. .90 .90

Meles Meles A221

2007, Mar. 22 ***Perf. 12¾x13***

565 A221 4.40k multi .90 .90

Bird Type of 2003 With Euro Denomination Added

2007, Apr. 5 ***Perf. 12¾x13***

566 A159 4.40k Cygnus bewickii .90 .90

Miniature Sheet

Summer Flowers — A222

No. 567: a, Paeonia officinalis. b, Lilium lancifolium. c, Rosa ecae Golden Chersonese. d, Iris latifolia.

2007, Apr. 19 ***Perf. 13¾x14***

567 A222 4.40k Sheet of 4, #a-d 3.00 3.00

Europa — A223

2007, May 3 ***Perf. 12½***

568 A223 20.50k multi 3.50 3.50

Scouting, cent.

Intl. Children's Day — A224

2007, June 1 **Litho.** ***Perf. 13½***

569 A224 10k multi 1.60 1.60

Souvenir Sheet

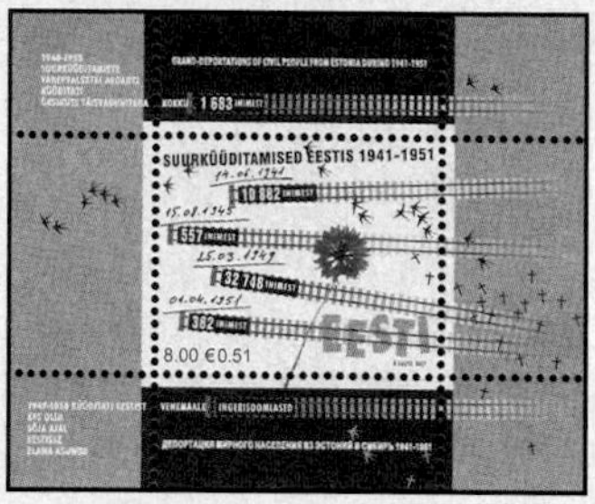

1941-51 Deportation of Estonians — A225

2007, June 14 ***Perf. 13***

570 A225 8k multi 1.40 1.40

Pirita Convent, 600th Anniv. — A226

2007, June 15 **Litho.** ***Perf. 12½***

571 A226 5.50k multi 1.00 1.00

Flower Type of 2004 With Euro Denominations Added

2007, July 2 ***Die Cut Perf. 12½***

Self-Adhesive

572 A181 1.10k Centaurea phrygia .25 .25

County Arms Type of 2004 With Euro Denominations Added

2007, July 2 **Self-Adhesive**

573 A182 5.50k Tartumaa 1.00 1.00

Flag Over Pikk Hermann Tower Type of 2005 With Euro Denominations Added

2007, Aug. 1 **Self-Adhesive**

574 A187 10k multi 1.75 1.75

Hellenurme Mill — A227

2007, Aug. 9 ***Perf. 14x13¾***

575 A227 5.50k multi .95 .95

Hirvepark Demonstration, 20th Anniv. — A228

2007, Aug. 23 ***Perf. 14x14¼***

576 A228 5.50k multi .95 .95

Souvenir Sheet

Matthias Johann Eisen (1857-1934), Folklorist — A229

2007, Sept. 14 ***Imperf.***

577 A229 10k multi 1.75 1.75

No. 577 has simulated perforations.

Ragnar Nurkse (1907-59), Economist — A230

2007, Oct. 5 ***Perf. 13***

578 A230 10k multi 1.75 1.75

St. John's Church, Kanepi — A231

2007, Oct. 11 ***Perf. 13¾x14***

579 A231 5.50k multi .95 .95

Arms of Viljandi — A232

2007, Oct. 25 **Litho.** ***Perf. 13¾x14***

580 A232 5.50k multi .95 .95

A233

Christmas A234

Die Cut Perf. 11¼ Syncopated

2007, Nov. 22 **Self-Adhesive**

581 A233 5.50k multi .90 .90
582 A234 8k multi 1.40 1.40

Post Horn — A235

2008 **Litho.** ***Die Cut Perf. 12½***

Self-Adhesive

583 A235 5.50k brt orange .95 .95
584 A235 6.50k brt yel green 1.10 1.10
585 A235 9k blue 1.50 1.50
Nos. 583-585 (3) 3.55 3.55

Issued: 5.50k, 1/10; 6.50k, 3/6; 9k, 4/1.

See Nos. 600, 638, 649, 658-662, 675-677, 682-684, 696-697, 708, 719-721.

Gustav Ernesaks (1908-93), Composer A236

2008, Jan. 17 **Litho.** ***Perf. 13***

586 A236 5.50k multi .95 .95

Lighthouse Type of 2006

2008, Jan. 24 ***Perf. 14x13¾***

587 A207 5.50k Mehikoorma, horiz. .95 .95

County Arms Type of 2004 With Euro Denominations Added

2008, Feb. 7 ***Die Cut Perf. 12½***

Self-Adhesive

588 A182 5.50k Valgamaa .95 .95

Plecotus Auritus A237

2008, Feb. 14 ***Perf. 12¾x13***

589 A237 5.50k multi .95 .95

Oak Tree — A238

2008, Feb. 23 ***Perf. 13***

590 A238 5.50k multi .95 .95

Republic of Estonia, 90th anniv.

Kristjan Palusalu (1908-87), Olympic Wrestling Gold Medalist — A239

2008, Mar. 10 ***Perf. 12½***

591 A239 10k multi 1.75 1.75

State Awards of the Baltic Countries — A240

Designs: Nos. 592, 593a, Order of the National Coat of Arms, Estonia. No. 593b, Order of Three Stars, Latvia. No. 593c, Order of Vytautas the Great, Lithuania.

2008, Mar. 15 Litho. *Perf. 13¾*
592 A240 5.50k multi .95 .95

Souvenir Sheet

593 A240 10k Sheet of 3, #a-c, + label 5.00 5.00

See Latvia Nos. 701-702, Lithuania Nos. 862-863.

County Arms Type of 2004 With Euro Denominations Added

2008, Mar. 27 *Die Cut Perf. 12½*
Self-Adhesive
594 A182 5.50k Viljandimaa .95 .95

Bird Type of 2003 With Euro Denomination Added

2008, Apr. 3 *Perf. 12¾x13*
595 A159 5.50k Tetrao tetrix .95 .95

Europa A241

2008, Apr. 30 *Perf. 14x14¼*
596 A241 9k multi 1.60 1.60

Otto Strandman (1875-1941), Statesman — A242

2008, May 9 Litho. *Perf. 13¾x14*
597 A242 5.50k brown .95 .95

Wavy Lines — A243

2008, May 22 *Serpentine Die Cut 10*
Self-Adhesive
598 A243 9k multi + label 1.60 1.60

The label shown is generic. Labels could be personalized for a fee.

Peasant War at Mahtra, 150th Anniv. — A244

2008, May 31 *Perf. 14x13¾*
599 A244 5.50k multi .95 .95

Posthorn Type of 2008

Die Cut Perf. 12½

2008, May 31 Litho.
Self-Adhesive
600 A235 50s gray .30 .30

2008 Summer Olympics, Beijing — A245

2008, Aug. 8 Litho. *Perf. 13¾x14*
601 A245 9k multi 1.60 1.60

Polma Windmill A246

2008, Aug. 28 *Perf. 14x13¾*
602 A246 5.50k multi .95 .95

Manor Type of 1999 With Euro Denomination Added

2008, Sept. 18 Litho. *Perf. 14x13¾*
603 A103 5.50k Kalvi Hall .95 .95

Gerd Kanter, Olympic Discus Champion A247

2008. Sept. 25 *Perf. 13½*
604 A247 5.50k multi .95 .95

Church of the Holy Cross, Audru — A248

2008, Oct. 16 Litho. *Perf. 13¾x14*
605 A248 5.50k multi .95 .95

County Arms Type of 2004 With Euro Denominations Added

2008, Oct. 30 *Die Cut Perf. 12½*
Self-Adhesive
606 A182 5.50k Vorumaa .95 .95

Estonia Post, 90th Anniv. — A249

2008, Nov. 13 *Perf. 13¾x14*
607 A249 5.50k multi .95 .95

Christmas A250

Designs: 5.50k, Gift on skis. 9k, Snowman on gift.

Die Cut Perf. 11¼ Syncopated

2008, Nov. 20 Litho.
Booklet Stamps Self-Adhesive
608 A250 5.50k multi .90 .90
a. Booklet pane of 10 8.25
609 A250 9k multi 1.60 1.60
a. Booklet pane of 10 13.50

Souvenir Sheet

International Polar Year — A251

No. 610 — Antarctic glacier with snowflake emblem in: a, White. b, Blue.

2009, Jan. 15 Litho. *Perf. 13x12¾*
610 A251 15k Sheet of 2, #a-b 5.25 5.25

Battle of Paju, 90th Anniv. A252

2009, Jan. 29 *Perf. 12¾x13*
611 A252 5.50k multi 1.00 1.00

Gen. Johan Laidoner (1884-1953) — A253

2009, Feb. 12 Litho. *Perf. 13*
612 A253 5.50k multi 1.00 1.00

Ants Piip (1884-1942), Prime Minister — A254

2009, Feb. 26 *Perf. 14*
613 A254 5.50k maroon 1.00 1.00

Pres. Lennart Meri (1929-2006) A255

2009, Mar. 26 Litho. *Perf. 14*
614 A255 5.50k blue 1.00 1.00

Estonian National Museum, Cent. — A256

2009, Apr. 14 *Perf. 13*
615 A256 5.50k multi 1.00 1.00

Estonian Parliament, 90th Anniv. — A257

2009, Apr. 23 *Perf. 14*
616 A257 5.50k multi 1.00 1.00

Europa — A258

No. 617: a, Galaxies and hexagonal cells. b, Galaxy and hexagonal cells at left.

2009, May 5 Litho. *Perf. 13¾x14*
617 A258 9k Horiz. pair, #a-b 3.25 3.25

Intl. Year of Astronomy.

Räpina Paper Mill, 275th Anniv. — A259

2009, May 14
618 A259 5.50k multi 1.00 1.00

Estonian Flag, 125th Anniv. — A260

Die Cut Perf. 11¼ Syncopated

2009, June 5
Booklet Stamp Self-Adhesive
619 A260 9k multi 1.50 1.50
a. Booklet pane of 10 15.00

25th Song Festival — A261

2009, June 18 *Perf. 14x13¾*
620 A261 5.50k multi 1.00 1.00

Alexander Church, Narva, 125th Anniv. — A262

2009, July 10 Litho. *Perf. 13¾x14*
621 A262 5.50k multi 1.25 1.25

Ursus Arctos A263

2009, Sept. 10 *Perf. 12¾x13*
622 A263 5.50k multi 1.00 1.00

First Track and Field Competition in Estonia, Cent. — A264

2009, Sept. 22 *Perf. 14x13¾*
623 A264 5.50k multi 1.10 1.10

Lighthouse Type of 2006

2009, Sept. 24 *Perf. 14x13¾*
624 A207 5.50k Hara Tuletorn, horiz. 1.10 1.10

Bird Type of 2003 With Euro Denomination Added

2009, Oct. 8 Litho. *Perf. 12¾x13*
625 A159 5.50k Strix aluco 1.10 1.10

Windmill, Angla — A265

2009, Oct. 22 *Perf. 13¾x14*
626 A265 5.50k multi 1.10 1.10

Manor Type of 1999 With Euro Denomination Added

2009, Nov. 5 *Perf. 14x13¾*
627 A103 5.50k Saku Hall 1.10 1.10

A266

Christmas A267

Die Cut Perf. 11¼ Syncopated
2009, Nov. 19
Booklet Stamps Self-Adhesive
628 A266 5.50k multi .90 .90
a. Booklet pane of 10 9.00
629 A267 9k multi 1.50 1.50
a. Booklet pane of 10 15.00 15.00

Fabric Design — A268

Die Cut Perf. 11¼ Syncopated
2010, Jan. 7 Litho.
Booklet Stamp Self-Adhesive
630 A268 50k orange & multi 8.50 8.50
a. Booklet pane of 10 85.00

See Nos. 646, 650.

Jüri Jaakson (1870-1942), Politician — A269

2010, Jan. 15 *Perf. 14*
631 A269 5.50k multi .95 .95

2010 European Figure Skating Championships, Tallinn — A270

2010, Jan. 19 *Perf. 12¾x13*
632 A270 9k multi 1.50 1.50
a. Tete-beche pair 3.00 3.00

Tartu Peace Treaty, 90th Anniv. A271

2010, Feb. 2 *Perf. 13*
633 A271 5.50k multi 1.00 1.00

Post Horn Type of 2008

2010, Feb. 4 *Die Cut Perf. 12½*
Self-Adhesive
634 A235 9k deep blue 1.50 1.50

Dated 2010. Compare with No. 585.

2010 Winter Olympics, Vancouver — A272

2010, Feb. 4 *Perf. 14*
635 A272 9k multi 1.60 1.60

Platanthera Bifolia — A273

2010, Feb. 19
636 A273 5.50k multi 1.00 1.00

Estonia Pavilion, Expo 2010, Shanghai A274

2010, Mar. 11
637 A274 9k multi 1.50 1.50

Posthorn Type of 2008
Die Cut Perf. 12½
2010, Mar. 23 Litho.
Self-Adhesive
638 A235 5.50k bright pink 1.00 1.00

St. Catherine's Church, Pärnu — A275

2010, Mar. 23 *Perf. 13¾x14*
639 A275 6.50k multi 1.10 1.10

Juhan Kukk (1885-1942), State Elder — A276

2010, Apr. 13
640 A276 5.50k olive brown 1.00 1.00

Lighthouses Type of 2006

Designs: 6.50k, Suurupi front lighthouse. 8k, Suurupi rear lighthouse.

2010, Apr. 22
641-642 A207 Set of 2 2.50 2.50

Europa — A277

Children's book illustrations: No. 643, 9k, Family of mice, by Jüri Mildeberg. No. 644, 9k, Skaters in snow, by Viive Noor.

2010, May 6 *Perf. 14x13¾*
643-644 A277 Set of 2 2.50 2.50

Bird Type of 2003 With Euro Denominations Added

2010, May 13 *Perf. 12¾x13*
645 A159 5.50k Lanius collurio 1.00 1.00

Fabric Design Type of 2010
Die Cut Perf. 11¼ Syncopated
2010, June 1
Booklet Stamp Self-Adhesive
646 A268 26k brt yel grn & multi 4.50 4.50
a. Booklet pane of 10 45.00

Intl. Children's Day — A278

2010, June 1 Litho.
Booklet Stamp
Self-Adhesive
647 A278 5.50k multi 1.00 1.00
a. Booklet pane of 10 10.00

Manor Type of 1999 With Euro Denominations Added

2010, Aug. 5 Litho. *Perf. 14x13¾*
648 A103 5.50k Suuremõisa Hall .95 .95

Posthorn Type of 2008

2010, Aug. 18 *Die Cut Perf. 12*
Self-Adhesive
649 A235 9k bright yellow 1.50 1.50

Fabric Design Type of 2010
Die Cut Perf. 11¼ Syncopated
2010, Aug. 18
Booklet Stamp
Self-Adhesive
650 A268 26k lilac & multi 4.50 4.50
a. Booklet pane of 10 45.00

Tallinn, 2011 European Capital of Culture — A279

2010, Sept. 9 Litho.
Self-Adhesive
651 A279 5.50k multi 1.00 1.00

Eliomys Quercinus A280

2010, Sept. 23 *Perf. 12¾x13*
652 A280 5.50k multi .75 .75

A281

A282

A283

Worldwide Fund for Nature (WWF) — A284

Various views of Triturus cristatus.

2010, Oct. 14 *Perf. 14x13¾*
653 Horiz. strip of 4 6.50 6.50
a. A281 9k multi 1.60 1.60
b. A282 9k multi 1.60 1.60
c. A283 9k multi 1.60 1.60
d. A284 9k multi 1.60 1.60
e. Sheet of 8 stamps with two tete-beche strips 13.00 13.00

Lennuk, by Nikolai Triik — A285

2010, Nov. 17 Litho. *Perf. 14*
654 A285 9k multi 1.60 1.60

A286

Christmas — A287

Die Cut Perf. 11¼ Syncopated
2010, Nov. 25
Booklet Stamps
Self-Adhesive

655 A286 5.50k multi .95 .95
a. Booklet pane of 10 9.50
656 A287 9k multi 1.60 1.60
a. Booklet pane of 10 16.00

Stamps in No. 655a are tete-beche in relation to adjacent stamps. Vertical pairs of stamps in No. 656a are tete-beche.

100 Cents = 1 Euro

Introduction of Euro Currency A288

Die Cut Perf. 11¼ Syncopated
2011, Jan. 1
Booklet Stamp
Self-Adhesive

657 A288 €1 multi 2.75 2.75
a. Booklet pane of 10 27.50

Post Horn Type of 2008 with Euro Denominations Only

2011, Jan. 3 *Die Cut Perf. 12½*
Self-Adhesive

658 A235 1c orange .25 .25
659 A235 5c salmon pink .25 .25
660 A235 10c lilac .25 .25
661 A235 50c blue 1.40 1.40
662 A235 65c green 1.75 1.75
Nos. 658-662 (5) 3.90 3.90

New Year 2011 (Year of the Rabbit) A289

2011, Feb. 3 Litho. *Perf. 12¾x13*
663 A289 58c multi 1.60 1.60

Friedebert Tuglas (1886-1971), Writer — A290

2011, Mar. 2 *Perf. 13¾x14*
664 A290 58c multi 1.60 1.60

Villem Reiman (1861-1917), Historian — A291

2011, Mar. 9
665 A291 35c multi 1.00 1.00

Peony A292

2011, Mar. 24 *Perf. 13x12¾*
666 A292 58c multi 1.60 1.60

Printed in sheets of 4 having each stamp rotated 90 degrees in relation to each other.

Folk Costumes — A293

Designs: 35c, Man and woman from Rapla. 58c, Two women from Joelähtme.

2011, Apr. 14 *Perf. 13¾x14*
667-668 A293 Set of 2 2.50 2.50

Hirundo Rustica A294

2011, Apr. 21 *Perf. 12¾x13*
669 A294 35c multi 1.00 1.00

Europa A295

Designs: No. 670, 58c, Elk in forest. No. 671, 58c, Cut logs.

2011, Apr. 28 *Perf. 13*
670-671 A295 Set of 2 3.00 3.00
Intl. Year of Forests.

Souvenir Sheet

Struve Geodetic Arc — A296

No. 672 — Map of arc and: a, Friedrch Georg Wilhelm Struve (1793-1864), astronomer. b, Tartu Observatory.

2011, May 6 *Perf. 14x13¾*
672 A296 58c Sheet of 2, #a-b 3.00 3.00

Lepus Europaeus — A297

2011, May 19 *Perf. 12¾x13*
673 A297 35c multi 1.00 1.00

Vergi Lighthouse A298

2011, June 2 *Perf. 14x13¾*
674 A298 35c multi 1.00 1.00

Posthorn Type of 2008 With Euro Denominations Only

2011 *Die Cut Perf. 12½*
Self-Adhesive

675 A235 35c brt yel grn 1.00 1.00
676 A235 58c lt purple 1.75 1.75
677 A235 58c green 1.60 1.60

Issued: 35c, No. 676, 6/2. No. 677, 8/25.

21st European Junior Track and Field Championships, Tallinn — A299

2011, July 20 Litho. *Perf. 14x13¾*
678 A299 35c multi 1.00 1.00

Restoration of Independence, 20th Anniv. — A300

2011, Aug. 20 *Perf. 13¾x14¼*
679 A300 35c multi 1.00 1.00

St. Margaret's Church, Karuse — A301

2011, Aug. 25 *Perf. 14x13¾*
680 A301 35c multi 1.00 1.00

Friedrich Karl Akel (1871-1941), State Elder — A302

2011, Sept. 5 *Perf. 13¾x14*
681 A302 35c brown 1.00 1.00

Posthorn Type of 2008 With Euro Denominations Only

2011 *Die Cut Perf. 12½*
Self-Adhesive

682 A235 10c sage green .30 .30
683 A235 35c cerise .95 .95
684 A235 45c rose 1.25 1.25
Nos. 682-684 (3) 2.50 2.50

Issued: 10c, 45c, 11/1; 35c, 9/15.

Heinrich Mark (1911-2004), Prime Minister — A303

2011, Sept. 30 *Perf. 13¾x14*
685 A303 35c blue .95 .95

Michael Andreas Barclay de Tolly (1761-1818), Military Leader — A304

2011, Oct. 20 *Perf. 14x13¾*
686 A304 €1 multi 2.75 2.75

10-Cent and 2-Euro Coins — A305

Die Cut Perf. 11¼ Syncopated
2011, Nov. 1
Booklet Stamp
Self-Adhesive

687 A305 €2.10 multi 5.50 5.50
a. Booklet pane of 10 55.00

Market, Painting by Henn-Olavi Roode (1924-74) A306

2011, Nov. 17 *Perf. 14*
688 A306 €1 multi 2.75 2.75

Christmas — A307

Die Cut Perf. 11¼ Syncopated
2011, Nov. 24
Booklet Stamps
Self-Adhesive

689 A307 45c Angel 1.25 1.25
a. Booklet pane of 10 12.50
690 A307 €1 Ornament 2.75 2.75
a. Booklet pane of 10 27.50

Vertical pairs of stamps in Nos. 689a and 690a are tete-beche.

Oskar Luts (1887-1953), Writer — A308

2012, Jan. 7 **Litho.** *Perf. 13*
691 A308 45c multi 1.25 1.25

Population and Housing Census — A309

Die Cut Perf. 11¼x11½ Syncopated
2012, Jan. 12 **Self-Adhesive**
692 A309 45c multi 1.25 1.25

New Year 2012 (Year of the Dragon) A310

2012, Jan. 23 *Perf. 12¾x13*
693 A310 €1.10 multi 3.00 3.00

Capreolus Capreolus A311

2012, Feb. 16 *Perf. 12¾x13*
694 A311 45c multi 1.25 1.25

Heino Eller (1887-1970), Composer A312

2012, Mar. 7 *Perf. 14x13¾*
695 A312 45c multi 1.25 1.25

Posthorn Type of 2008 With Euro Denominations Only

2012, Mar. 29 ***Die Cut Perf. 12½***
Self-Adhesive
Dated "2012"

696 A235 10c dull blue green .25 .25
697 A235 50c pale yel grn 1.40 1.40

Compare Nos. 696 and 750.

Personalized Stamp — A313

Die Cut Perf. 8¾ Syncopated
2012, Mar. 29 **Self-Adhesive**
698 A313 45c multi 1.25 1.25

The generic vignette shown, depicting a map of Saaremaa, could be personalized for an additional fee.
See No. 773.

Folk Costumes — A314

Designs: 45c, Woman and girl from Hageri. €1, Woman from Nissi.

2012, Apr. 14 **Litho.** *Perf. 13¾x14*
699-700 A314 Set of 2 4.00 4.00

Charadrius Dubius — A315

2012, Apr. 19 *Perf. 12¾x13*
701 A315 45c multi 1.25 1.25

Johannes Pääsuke (1892-1918), Creator of First Estonian Film in 1912 — A316

2012, Apr. 30
702 A316 45c multi 1.25 1.25

Europa A317

Inscriptions: No. 703, €1, "wild est." No. 704, €1, "smart est."

2012, May 3 *Perf. 14x13¾*
703-704 A317 Set of 2 5.25 5.25

Church of St. Simeon and the Prophet Anne, Tallinn — A318

2012, May 17 *Perf. 13¾x14*
705 A318 45c multi 1.25 1.25

2012 Summer Olympics, London A319

2012, June 1 *Perf. 14x13¾*
706 A319 €1.10 multi 2.75 2.75

Martin Klein (1884-1947), First Estonian Olympic Medalist — A320

2012, July 13 *Perf. 14x14¼*
707 A320 €1 multi 2.50 2.50

Posthorn Type of 2008 With Euro Denominations Only

2012, Aug. 10 ***Die Cut Perf. 12½***
Self-Adhesive

708 A235 45c citron 1.25 1.25

One-Euro Coin — A321

Die Cut Perf. 11¼ Syncopated
2012, Aug. 10 **Self-Adhesive**
709 A321 €1 multi 2.60 2.60

Amanita Virosa — A322

2012, Aug. 30 *Perf. 13¾x14*
710 A322 45c red & black 1.25 1.25

Käsmu Lighthouse A323

2012, Sept. 13 *Perf. 14x13¾*
711 A323 45c multi 1.25 1.25

Jaan Teemant (1872-1941), State Elder — A324

2012, Sept. 24 *Perf. 13¾x14*
712 A324 45c brown 1.25 1.25

Railway Bridges A325

Train and: Nos. 713, 714a, Narva Bridge, Estonia. No. 714b, Carnikava Bridge, Latvia. No. 714c, Lyduvenai Bridge, Lithuania.

2012, Oct. 25 *Perf. 13¼*
713 A325 45c multi 1.25 1.25

Souvenir Sheet

714 A325 €1 Sheet of 3, #a-c 7.75 7.75

See Latvia Nos. 815-816, Lithuania Nos. 985-986.

Scouting in Estonia, Cent. — A326

2012, Nov. 7 *Perf. 14x13¾*
715 A326 45c multi 1.25 1.25

Still Life with Mandolin, by Lepo Mikko — A327

2012, Nov. 16 *Perf. 14*
716 A327 €1.10 multi 3.00 3.00

Santa Claus on Skis — A328

Poinsettia A329

Die Cut Perf. 11¼ Syncopated

2012, Nov. 22 Self-Adhesive

717	A328	45c multi	1.25	1.25
718	A329	€1 multi	2.60	2.60

Christmas.

Posthorn Type of 2008 With Euro Denominations Only

Self-Adhesive

2013, Jan. 10 ***Die Cut Perf. 12½***

719	A235	5c light blue	.25	.25
720	A235	50c green	1.40	1.40
721	A235	65c red violet	1.75	1.75
		Nos. 719-721 (3)	3.40	3.40

Kiipsaare Lighthouse A330

2013, Jan. 31 ***Perf. 14x13¾***

722	A330	45c multi	1.25	1.25

New Year 2013 (Year of the Snake) A331

2013, Feb. 8 ***Perf. 12¾x13***

723	A331	€1.10 multi	3.00	3.00

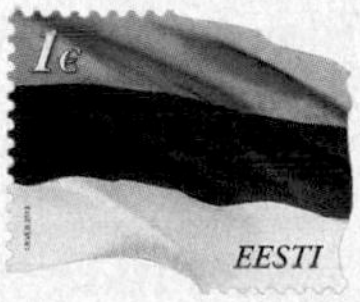

Estonian Flag — A332

Die Cut Perf. 11¼ Syncopated

2013, Feb. 22

Self-Adhesive

724	A332	€1 multi	2.60	2.60
a.		Dated "2014"	2.75	2.75

See No. 754.

Issued No. 724a, 5/22/14.

Perdix Perdix A333

2013, Mar. 7 ***Perf. 12¾x13***

725	A333	45c multi	1.25	1.25

Folk Costumes — A334

Man and woman from: 45c, Kihelkonna. €1, Karja.

2013, Apr. 12 ***Perf. 13¾x14***

726-727	A334	Set of 2	3.75	3.75

Icebreaker "Tarmo" — A335

2013, Apr. 25 ***Perf. 14x13¾***

728	A335	€1 multi	2.60	2.60

Europa — A336

No. 729 — Postal vehicles: a, Horse-drawn stagecoach, 1840s. b, Modern van.

2013, May 2 **Litho.**

729	A336	€1 Horiz. pair, #a-b	5.25	5.25

Souvenir Sheet

Estcube-1 Satellite — A337

2013, May 2

730	A337	€1.10 multi	3.00	3.00

Kuressaare, 450th Anniv. A338

2013, May 8 ***Perf. 14x14¼***

731	A338	45c multi	1.25	1.25

Kaarel Eenpalu (1888-1942), State Elder and Prime Minister — A339

2013, May 28 ***Perf. 13¾x14***

732	A339	45c dk brn violet	1.25	1.25

Mustela Nivalis A340

2013, June 6 ***Perf. 12¾x13***

733	A340	45c multi	1.25	1.25

St. Catherine's Church, Voru — A341

2013, July 24 ***Perf. 13¾x14***

734	A341	45c multi	1.25	1.25

Souvenir Sheet

Cultural Heritage Year — A342

2013, Aug. 3 ***Perf.***

735	A342	€1.10 multi	3.00	3.00

Finn Class Sailing World Championships, Tallinn — A343

2013, Aug. 23 ***Perf. 14¼x13¾***

736	A343	€1.10 multi	3.00	3.00

Estonia Theater and Concert House, Tallinn, Cent. — A344

2013, Sept. 6 ***Perf. 13***

737	A344	€1.10 multi	3.00	3.00

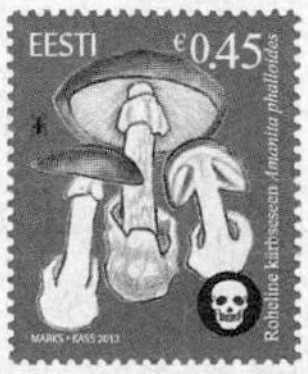

Amanita Phalloides — A345

2013, Sept. 12 ***Perf. 13¾x14***

738	A345	45c multi	1.25	1.25

Raimond Valgre (1913-49), Composer — A346

2013, Oct. 7 **Litho.** ***Perf. 13***

739	A346	45c multi	1.25	1.25

Arms of Moisaküla — A347

Die Cut Perf. 12½

2013, Oct. 31 **Litho.**

Self-Adhesive

740	A347	45c sil & black	1.25	1.25

Regular Postal Services in Estonia, 375th Anniv. A348

Perf. 14¼x13¾

2013, Nov. 13 **Litho.**

741	A348	45c multi	1.25	1.25

Aadu (Ado) Birk (1883-1942), Prime Minister — A349

2013, Nov. 14 **Litho.** ***Perf. 13¾x14***

742	A349	45c dull brown	1.25	1.25

After Dinner, by Elmar Kits (1913-72) A350

2013, Nov. 15 **Litho.** ***Perf. 14***

743	A350	€1.10 multi	3.00	3.00

A351

Christmas A352

Serpentine Die Cut 11¼ Syncopated

2013, Nov. 22 **Litho.**

Self-Adhesive

744	A351	45c multi	1.25	1.25
745	A352	€1 multi	2.75	2.75

Estonian Olympic Committee, 90th Anniv. — A353

2013, Dec. 9 **Litho.** ***Perf. 13¾x14***

746	A353	45c multi	1.25	1.25

Jaan Tonisson (1888-c. 1941), Prime Minister — A354

2013, Dec. 20 Litho. ***Perf. 13¾x14***
747 A354 45c brown 1.25 1.25

2014 Winter Olympics, Sochi, Russia — A355

2014, Jan. 16 Litho. ***Perf. 14x13¾***
748 A355 €1.10 multi 3.00 3.00

New Year 2014 (Year of the Horse) A356

2014, Jan. 31 Litho. ***Perf. 12¾x13***
749 A356 €1.10 multi 3.00 3.00

Post Horn Type of 2008 With Euro Denomination Only
Die Cut Perf. 12½
2014, Feb. 19 Litho.
Self-Adhesive
Dated "2014"
750 A235 10c brt bl grn .30 .30
a. Dated "2015" .25 .25

Issued: No. 750a, 10/16/15. Compare with No. 696.

Estonian History Museum, 150th Anniv. A357

2014, Feb. 19 Litho. ***Perf. 12¾x13***
751 A357 45c multi 1.25 1.25

Pres. Konstantin Päts (1874-1956) A358

2014, Feb. 21 Litho. ***Perf. 13¾x14***
752 A358 45c blue 1.25 1.25

Arms of Voru — A359

Die Cut Perf. 12½
2014, Mar. 5 Litho.
Self-Adhesive
753 A359 45c multi 1.25 1.25

Estonian Flag Type of 2013
Die Cut Perf. 11¼ Syncopated
2014, Mar. 5 Litho.
Self-Adhesive
754 A332 €2 multi 5.50 5.50

Alcedo Atthis A360

2014, Mar. 20 Litho. ***Perf. 12¾x13***
755 A360 45c multi 1.25 1.25

Folk Costumes — A361

Designs: 45c, Man and woman from Mihkli. €1, Women from Vigala.

2014, Apr. 12 Litho. ***Perf. 13¾x14***
756-757 A361 Set of 2 4.00 4.00

Juhan Liiv (1864-1913), Poet — A362

2014, Apr. 30 Litho. ***Perf. 13***
758 A362 45c multi 1.25 1.25

Inachis Io — A363

Serpentine Die Cut 12½
2014, May 2 Litho.
Booklet Stamp
Self-Adhesive
759 A363 45c multi 1.25 1.25
a. Booklet pane of 4 5.00

Europa A364

Musical instruments: No. 760, €1, Väikekannel (zither). No. 761, €1, Lootspill (accordion).

2014, May 8 Litho. ***Perf. 14x13¾***
760-761 A364 Set of 2 5.50 5.50

Erinaceus Europaeus A365

2014, May 30 Litho. ***Perf. 12¾x13***
762 A365 45c multi 1.25 1.25

Estonian Herdbook, Cent. A366

2014, July 19 Litho. ***Perf. 14x13½***
Textured and Flocked Granite Paper
763 A366 €1 multi 2.75 2.75

Baltic Chain Demonstration, 25th Anniv. — A367

Designs: 55c, Man and child.
No. 765: a, Five adults and one child. b, Three women. c, Like #764

2014, Aug. 23 Litho. ***Perf. 13¼***
764 A367 55c multi 1.50 1.50

Souvenir Sheet
765 A367 €1 Sheet of 3, #a-c 8.00 8.00

See Latvia Nos. 883-884; Lithuania No. 1031.

Souvenir Sheet

Tallinn Zoo, 75th Anniv. — A368

No. 766: a, Gypaetus barbatus. b, Panthera pardus orientalis.

Perf. 14¼x13¾
2014, Aug. 25 Litho.
766 A368 55c Sheet of 2, #a-b 3.00 3.00

Estonian Academy of Arts, Cent. — A369

2014, Sept. 1 Litho. ***Perf. 14x13¾***
767 A369 55c multi 1.50 1.50

Inocybe Erubescens A370

2014, Sept. 11 Litho. ***Perf. 13¾x14***
768 A370 55c red & black 1.40 1.40

Arms of Saue — A371

Die Cut Perf. 12½
2014, Sept. 11 Litho.
Self-Adhesive
769 A371 55c multi 1.40 1.40

1-Euro and 20-Cent Coins — A372

Die Cut Perf. 11¼ Syncopated
2014, Oct. 2 Litho.
Self-Adhesive
770 A372 €1.20 multi 3.00 3.00

Lighthouses A373

Designs: 55c, Northern Soru Lighthouse. €1.30, Southern Soru Lighthouse.

2014, Oct. 17 Litho. ***Perf. 13¾x14***
771-772 A373 Set of 2 4.75 4.75

Personalized Stamp Type of 2012
Die Cut Perf. 8¾ Syncopated
2014, Nov. 17 Litho.
Self-Adhesive
773 A313 55c multi 1.40 1.40

The generic vignette, depicting a map of Hüumaa, could be personalized for an additional fee.

Courtyard, by Herbert Lukk (1892-1919) A374

2014, Nov. 17 Litho. ***Perf. 14***
774 A374 €1.30 multi 3.25 3.25

Christmas A375

Christmas tree, ornaments and: 55c, Ribbon. €1.20, Pine cone.

Die Cut Perf. 11¼ Syncopated
2014, Nov. 20 Litho.
Self-Adhesive
775-776 A375 Set of 2 4.50 4.50

Jüri Uluots (1890-1945), Prime Minister — A376

2015, Jan. 13 Litho. ***Perf. 13¾x14***
777 A376 55c blue 1.25 1.25

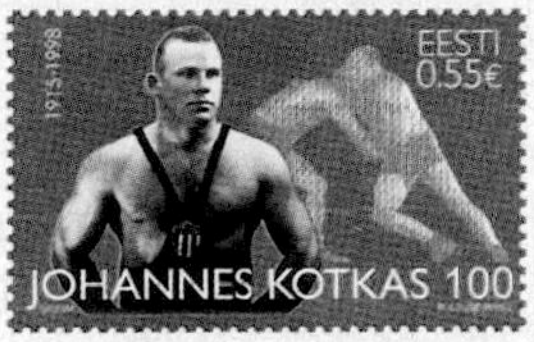

Johannes Kotkas (1915-88), Wrestler — A377

2015, Feb. 3 Litho. ***Perf. 12½***
778 A377 55c multi 1.25 1.25

New Year 2015 (Year of the Ram) A378

2015, Feb. 19 Litho. ***Perf. 12¾x13***
779 A378 €1.30 multi 3.00 3.00

Eduard Vilde (1865-1933), Writer — A379

2015, Mar. 4 Litho. ***Perf. 13***
780 A379 55c multi 1.25 1.25

Arms of Elva — A380

Die Cut Perf. 12½
2015, Mar. 12 Litho.
Self-Adhesive
781 A380 55c multi 1.25 1.25

Souvenir Sheet

Seal and Map of Baltic Sea — A381

2015, Mar. 12 Litho. ***Perf.***
782 A381 €2.55 multi 5.75 5.75

Folk Costumes — A382

Designs: 55c, Man, woman and girl from Lihula. €1.20, Women from Kirbla.

2015, Apr. 14 Litho. ***Perf. 13¾x14***
783-784 A382 Set of 2 4.00 4.00

Europa A383

Designs: No. 785, €1.20, Toy horses. No. 786, €1.20, Stuffed animals.

2015, May 6 Litho. ***Perf. 14***
785-786 A383 Set of 2 5.50 5.50

Pernis Apivorus A384

2015, May 21 Litho. ***Perf. 12¾x13***
787 A384 55c multi 1.25 1.25

Characters From Animated Film *Lotte From Gadgetville* — A385

No. 788: a, Bruno the Kitten. b, Albert the Bunny. c, Bruno, Albert and Lotte. d, Lotte the Puppy.

Serpentine Die Cut 5x6
2015, May 30 Litho.
Self-Adhesive
788 A385 Booklet pane of 4 + 6 stickers 5.00
a.-d. 55c Any single 1.25 1.25

Giraffe With Head Above Cloud — A386

Serpentine Die Cut 5x6
2015, June 4 Litho.
Booklet Stamp
Self-Adhesive
789 A386 €1.20 multi 2.75 2.75
a. Booklet pane of 4 11.00

Aleksander Warma (1890-1970), Prime Minister — A387

2015, June 22 Litho. ***Perf. 13¾x14***
790 A387 55c Prus grn 1.25 1.25

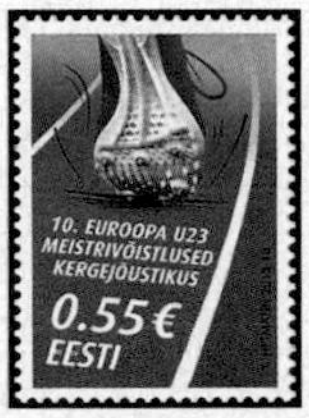

European Under-23 Track and Field Championships, Tallinn — A388

2015, July 1 Litho. ***Perf. 14x13¾***
791 A388 55c multi 1.25 1.25

Estonian Business Innovations — A389

No. 792: a, Fortumo. b, GrabCAD. c, Skype. d, TransferWise.

Die Cut Perf. 12½
2015, July 6 Litho.
Self-Adhesive
792 A389 Booklet pane of 4 12.00
a.-d. €1.30 Any single 3.00 3.00

Lutra Lutra A390

2015, Aug. 25 Litho. ***Perf. 12¾x13***
793 A390 55c multi 1.25 1.25

Arms of Paide — A391

Die Cut Perf. 12½
2015, Sept. 10 Litho.
Self-Adhesive
794 A391 55c multi 1.25 1.25

Cortinarius Rubellus — A392

2015, Sept. 10 Litho. ***Perf. 13¾x14***
795 A392 55c multi 1.25 1.25

Tahkuna Lighthouse A393

2015, Oct. 16 Litho. ***Perf. 14x13¾***
796 A393 55c multi 1.25 1.25

Penny Black, 175th Anniv. — A394

2015, Nov. 13 Litho. ***Perf. 13½***
797 A394 55c multi 1.25 1.25

A Girl and the Moon, by Karl Pärsimägi (1902-42) — A395

2015, Nov. 17 Litho. ***Perf. 14***
798 A395 55c multl 1.25 1.25

SEMI-POSTAL STAMPS

Assisting Wounded Soldier — SP1

Offering Aid to Wounded Hero — SP2

1920, June Unwmk. Litho. ***Imperf.***
B1 SP1 35p + 10p red & ol grn .75 *2.00*
B2 SP2 70p + 15p dp bl & brn .75 *2.00*

Surcharged

1920
B3 SP1 1m on No. B1 .50 .30
B4 SP2 2m on No. B2 .50 .30

Nurse and Wounded Soldier — SP3

1921, Aug. 1 *Imperf.*
B5 SP3 2½ (3½)m org, brn & car 2.00 *7.25*
B6 SP3 5 (7)m ultra, brn & car 2.00 *7.25*

1922, Apr. 26 *Perf. 13½x14*
B7 SP3 2½ (3½)m org, brn & car 2.00 *7.25*
a. Vert. pair, imperf. horiz. 30.00 *80.00*
B8 SP3 5 (7)m ultra, brn & car 2.00 *7.25*
a. Vert. pair, imperf. horiz. 30.00 *80.00*

Nos. B5-B8 Overprinted

1923, Oct. 8 *Imperf.*
B9 SP3 2½ (3½)m 60.00 *160.00*
B10 SP3 5 (7)m 60.00 *160.00*

Perf. 13½x14
B11 SP3 2½ (3½)m 60.00 *160.00*
a. Vert. pair, imperf. horiz. 200.00 *800.00*
B12 SP3 5 (7)m 60.00 *160.00*
a. Vert. pair, imperf. horiz. 200.00 *800.00*
Nos. B9-B12 (4) 240.00 640.00

Excellent forgeries are plentiful.

Nos. B7 and B8 Surcharged

1926, June 15
B13 SP3 5 (6)m on #B7 3.75 *8.00*
a. Vert. pair, imperf. horiz. 24.00 *120.00*
B14 SP3 10 (12)m on #B8 4.50 *8.00*
a. Vert. pair, imperf. horiz. 24.00 *120.00*

Nos. B5-B14 had the franking value of the lower figure. They were sold for the higher figure, the excess going to the Red Cross Society.

Kuressaare Castle SP4

Tartu Cathedral SP5

Tallinn Castle SP6

Narva Fortress SP7

View of Tallinn — SP8

Laid Paper

Perf. 14½x14
1927, Nov. 19 **Typo.** **Wmk. 207**
B15 SP4 5m + 5m bl grn & ol, *grysh* .90 *8.00*
B16 SP5 10m + 10m dp bl & brn, *cream* .90 *8.00*
B17 SP6 12m + 12m rose red & ol grn, *bluish* .90 *8.00*

Perf. 14x13½
B18 SP7 20m + 20m bl & choc, *gray* 1.75 *8.00*
B19 SP8 40m + 40m org brn & slate, *buff* 1.75 *8.00*
Nos. B15-B19 (5) 6.20 *40.00*

The money derived from the surtax was donated to the Committee for the commemoration of War for Liberation.

Red Cross Issue

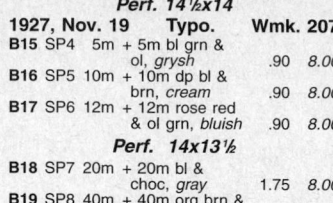

Symbolical of Succor to Injured — SP9

Symbolical of "Light of Hope" — SP10

1931, Aug. 1 **Unwmk.** *Perf. 13½*
B20 SP9 2s + 3s grn & car 8.00 8.00
B21 SP10 5s + 3s red & car 8.00 8.00
B22 SP10 10s + 3s lt bl & car 8.00 8.00
B23 SP9 20s + 3s dk bl & car 12.00 *20.00*
Nos. B20-B23 (4) 36.00 44.00
Set, never hinged 75.00

Nurse and Child SP11

Taagepera Sanatorium SP12

Lorraine Cross and Flower — SP13

Paper with Network as in Parenthesis

1933, Oct. 1 *Perf. 14, 14½*
B24 SP11 5s + 3s ver (grn) *6.00* *8.00*
B25 SP12 10s + 3s lt bl & red (vio) 6.00 *8.00*
B26 SP13 12s + 3s rose & red (grn) 8.00 *12.00*
B27 SP12 20s + 3s dk bl & red (org) 10.00 *16.00*
Nos. B24-B27 (4) 30.00 44.00
Set, never hinged 72.50

The surtax was for a fund to combat tuberculosis.

Coats of Arms

Narva — SP14

Pärnu — SP15

Tartu — SP16

Tallinn — SP17

Paper with Network as in Parenthesis

1936, Feb. 1 *Perf. 13½*
B28 SP14 10s + 10s grn & ultra (gray) 3.50 *8.00*
B29 SP15 15s + 15s car & bl (gray) 3.50 *12.00*
B30 SP16 25s + 25s gray bl & red (brn) 4.50 *16.00*
B31 SP17 50s + 50s blk & dl org (ol) 17.00 *52.50*
Nos. B28-B31 (4) 28.50 *88.50*
Set, never hinged 52.50

Paide SP18

Rakvere SP19

Valga SP20

Viljandi SP21

Paper with Network as in Parenthesis

1937, Jan. 2 *Perf. 13½x14*
B32 SP18 10s + 10s grn (gray) 3.00 *6.50*
B33 SP19 15s + 15s red brn (gray) 3.00 *6.50*
B34 SP20 25s + 25s dk bl (lil) 5.00 *9.50*
B35 SP21 50s + 50s dk vio (gray) 9.00 *24.00*
Nos. B32-B35 (4) 20.00 *46.50*
Set, never hinged 40.00

Baltiski — SP22

Võru — SP23

Haapsalu SP24

Kuressaare SP25

Designs are the armorial bearings of various cities

1938, Jan. 21
Paper with Gray Network
B36 SP22 10s + 10s dk brn 3.00 *8.00*
B37 SP23 15s + 15s car & grn 3.50 12.00
B38 SP24 25s + 25s dk bl & car 5.00 20.00
B39 SP25 50s + 50s blk & org yel 8.00 *40.00*
a. Sheet of 4, #B36-B39 35.00 *80.00*
Nos. B36-B39 (4) 19.50 *80.00*
Set, never hinged 40.00

Annual charity ball, Tallinn, Jan. 2, 1938.

Viljandimaa SP27

Pärnumaa SP28

Tartumaa SP29

Harjumaa SP30

Designs are the armorial bearings of various cities

1939, Jan. 10 *Perf. 13½*
Paper with Gray Network
B41 SP27 10s + 10s dk bl grn 3.50 *8.00*
B42 SP28 15s + 15s carmine 4.00 *8.00*
B43 SP29 25s + 25s dk blue 5.50 *20.00*
B44 SP30 50s + 50s brn lake 14.00 *47.50*
a. Sheet of 4, #B41-B44 45.00 *175.00*
Nos. B41-B44 (4) 27.00 *83.50*
Set, never hinged 47.50

Võrumaa SP32

Järvamaa SP33

Läänemaa SP34

Saaremaa SP35

Designs are the armorial bearings of various cities

1940, Jan. 2 **Typo.** *Perf. 13½*
Paper with Gray Network
B46 SP32 10s + 10s dp grn & ultra 2.50 *12.00*
B47 SP33 15s + 15s dk car & ultra 2.50 *16.00*
B48 SP34 25s + 25s dk bl & scar 3.00 *24.00*
B49 SP35 50s + 50s ocher & ultra 8.00 *32.50*
Nos. B46-B49 (4) 16.00 *84.50*
Set, never hinged 30.00

Catalogue values for unused stamps in this section, from this point to the end of the section, are for Never Hinged items.

1992 Summer Olympics, Barcelona — SP40

1992, June 22 **Litho.** *Perf. 14*
B60 SP40 1r +50k red .40 .40
B61 SP40 3r +1.50r green 1.75 1.75
B62 SP40 5r +2.50r blue & blk .80 .80
Nos. B60-B62 (3) 2.95 2.95

While face values are shown in kopecks and rubles, the stamps were sold in the new currency at the rate of 1 ruble = 10 sents.

No. 280 Surcharged

1994, Nov. 18 Litho. *Perf. 14*

B63 A51 2.50k +20k green		4.50	4.50

Surtax for benefit of survivors of sinking of ferry "Estonia."

Haliaeetus Albicilla — SP41

1995, Aug. 29 Litho. *Perf. 14*

B64 SP41 2k +25k black & blue	.45	.45

Surtax for Keep the Estonian Sea Clean Assoc.

UNICEF, 60th Anniv. SP42

2006, June 1 Litho. *Perf. 13½*

B65 SP42 4.40k +1k multi	.90	.90

AIR POST STAMPS

Airplane AP1

Unwmk.

1920, Mar. 13 Typo. *Imperf.*

C1 AP1 5m yel, blk & lt grn	3.00	*5.50*
Never hinged	7.00	

No. C1 Overprinted "1923" in Red

1923, Oct. 1

C2 AP1 5m multicolored	8.00	*32.50*
Never hinged	15.00	

No. C1 Surcharged in Red

1923, Oct. 1

C3 AP1 15m on 5m multi	16.00	*47.50*
Never hinged	30.00	

Pairs of No. C1 Surcharged in Black or Red

1923, Oct.

C4 AP1 10m on 5m+5m (B)	10.00	*35.00*
C5 AP1 20m on 5m+5m	20.00	*55.00*
C6 AP1 45m on 5m+5m	80.00	*200.00*

Rough Perf. 11½

C7 AP1 10m on 5m+5m (B)	*550.00*	*1,200.*
C8 AP1 20m on 5m+5m	*200.00*	*525.00*
Nos. C4-C8 (5)	*860.00*	*2,015.*
Set, never hinged	*1,700.*	

The pairs comprising Nos. C7 and C8 are imperforate between. Forged surcharges and perforations abound. Authentication is required.

Monoplane In Flight — AP2

Designs: Various views of planes in flight.

1924, Feb. 12 *Imperf.*

C9 AP2 5m yellow & blk	2.00	*8.00*
C10 AP2 10m blue & blk	2.00	*8.00*
C11 AP2 15m red & blk	2.00	*8.00*
C12 AP2 20m green & blk	2.00	*8.00*
C13 AP2 45m violet & blk	2.00	*16.00*
Nos. C9-C13 (5)	10.00	*48.00*
Set, never hinged	15.00	

The paper is covered with a faint network in pale shades of the frame colors. There are four varieties of the frames and five of the pictures.

1925, July 15 *Perf. 13½*

C14 AP2 5m yellow & blk	1.50	*8.00*
C15 AP2 10m blue & blk	1.50	*8.00*
C16 AP2 15m red & blk	1.50	*8.00*
C17 AP2 20m green & blk	1.50	*8.00*
C18 AP2 45m violet & blk	1.50	*16.00*
Nos. C14-C18 (5)	7.50	*48.00*
Set, never hinged	11.00	

Counterfeits of Nos. C1-C18 are plentiful.

REGISTRATION STAMP

Catalogue values for unused stamps in this section are for Never Hinged items.

Arms Type of 1992

1992, Mar. 16 Litho. *Perf. 13x12½*

F1 A42 R (10r) pink & red	.70	.70

OCCUPATION STAMPS

Issued under German Occupation

For Use in Tartu (Dorpat)

Russian Stamps of 1909-12 Surcharged

1918 Unwmk. *Perf. 14x14½*

N1 A15 20pf on 10k dk bl	35.00	*80.00*
N2 A8 40pf on 20k bl & car	35.00	*80.00*
Set, Never Hinged	130.00	

Forged overprints exist.

Estonian Arms and Swastika — OS1

Perf. 11½

1941, Aug. Typo. Unwmk.

N3 OS1 15k brown	10.00	10.00
N4 OS1 20k green	10.00	10.00
N5 OS1 30k dark blue	10.00	10.00
Nos. N3-N5 (3)	30.00	30.00
Set, never hinged	50.00	

Exist imperf. Value, set, $200.

Nos. N3-N5 were issued on both ordinary paper with colorless gum and thick chalky paper with yellow gum. Same values.

OCCUPATION SEMI-POSTAL STAMPS

Castle Tower, Tallinn — OSP1

Designs: 20k+20k, Stone Bridge, Tartu, horiz. 30k+30k, Narva Castle, horiz. 50k+50k, Tallinn view, horiz. 60k+60k, Tartu University. 100k+100k, Narva Castle, close view.

Paper with Gray Network

Perf. 11½

1941, Sept. 29 Photo. Unwmk.

NB1 OSP1 15k + 15k dk brn	.60	*4.75*
NB2 OSP1 20k + 20k red lil	.60	*4.75*
NB3 OSP1 30k + 30k dk bl	.60	*4.75*
NB4 OSP1 50k + 50k bluish grn	.70	*9.50*
NB5 OSP1 60k + 60k car	1.00	*8.00*
NB6 OSP1 100k + 100k gray	1.50	*9.50*
Nos. NB1-NB6 (6)	5.00	*41.25*
Set, never hinged	12.00	

Nos. NB1-NB6 exist imperf. Value, set unused $70, used $200.

A miniature sheet containing one each of Nos. NB1-NB6, imperf., exists in various colors. Value, mint $40, used $60. It was not postally valid. Reproductions are common.

ETHIOPIA

ˌē-thē-ˈō-pē-ə

(Abyssinia)

LOCATION — Northeastern Africa
GOVT. — Republic (1988)
AREA — 426,260 sq. mi.
POP. — 59,680,383 (1999 est.)
CAPITAL — Addis Ababa

During the Italian occupation (1936-1941) Nos. N1-N7 were used, also stamps of Italian East Africa, Eritrea and Somalia.

During the British administration (1941-42) stamps of Great Britain and Kenya were used when available.

16 Guerche = 1 Menelik Dollar or 1 Maria Theresa Dollar
100 Centimes = 1 Franc (1905)
40 Paras = 1 Piaster (1908)
16 Mehalek = 1 Thaler or Talari (1928)
100 Centimes = 1 Thaler (1936)
100 Cents = 1 Ethiopian Dollar (1946)
100 Cents = 1 Birr (1978)

Catalogue values for unused stamps in this country are for Never Hinged items, beginning with Scott 247 in the regular postage section, Scott B6 in the semi-postal section, Scott C18 in the airpost section, Scott E1 in the special delivery section, and Scott J57 in the postage due section.

Watermarks

Wmk. 140 — Crown

Wmk. 282 — Ethiopian Star and Amharic Characters, Multiple

Excellent forgeries of Nos. 1-86 exist.

Very Fine examples of Nos. 1-86 and J1-J42 will have perforations touching the design on one or more sides due to the narrow spacing of the stamps on the plates and imperfect perforating methods. Stamps with margins clear on all sides are scarce and command high premiums.

On March 9, 1894 Menelik II awarded Alfred Ilg a concession to develop a railway, including postal service. Ilg's stamps, Nos. 1-79, were valid locally and to Djibouti. Mail to other countries had to bear stamps of Obock, Somali Coast, etc.

Ethiopia joined the UPU Nov. 1, 1908.

Menelik II A1

Lion of Judah A2

Anharic numeral "8"

Perf. 14x13½

1895, Jan. Unwmk. Typo.

1	A1	¼g green	4.00	2.00
2	A1	½g red	4.00	2.00
3	A1	1g blue	4.00	2.00
4	A1	2g dark brown	4.00	2.00
5	A2	4g lilac brown	4.00	2.00
6	A2	8g violet	4.00	2.00
7	A2	16g black	4.00	2.00
		Nos. 1-7 (7)	28.00	14.00

For 4g, 8g and 16g stamps of type A1, see Nos. J3a, J4a and J7a.

Earliest reported use is Jan. 29, 1895.

Forged cancellations are plentiful.

For overprints see Nos. 8-86, J8-J28, J36-J42. For surcharges see Nos. 94-100, J29-J35.

Nos. 1-7 Handstamped in Violet or Blue

Overprint 9¼x2½mm, Serifs on "E"

1901, July 18

8	A1	¼g green	27.50	27.50
9	A1	½g red	27.50	27.50
10	A1	1g blue	27.50	27.50
11	A1	2g dark brown	27.50	27.50
12	A2	4g lilac brown	32.50	32.50
13	A2	8g violet	47.50	47.50
14	A2	16g black	60.00	60.00
		Nos. 8-14 (7)	250.00	250.00

Violet overprints were issued July 18, 1901, for postal use, while the blue overprints were issued in Jan. 1902 for philatelic purposes. The blue overprints were not used in the mails. Values for unused stamps are for examples with blue overprints. Unused stamps with violet overprints are worth much more.

Overprints 8¼mm wide are unofficial reproductions.

Nos. 1-7 Handstamped in Violet, Blue or Black

Overprint 11x3mm, Low Colons

1902, Apr. 1

15	A1	¼g green	6.00	6.00
16	A1	½g red	9.00	7.00
17	A1	1g blue	10.00	10.00
18	A1	2g dark brown	14.00	14.00
19	A2	4g lilac brown	24.00	24.00
20	A2	8g violet	30.00	30.00
21	A2	16g black	55.00	55.00
		Nos. 15-21 (7)	148.00	146.00

The handstamp reads "Bosta" (Post).

Overprints 10¾mm and 11mm wide with raised colons are unofficial reproductions.

Nos. 1-7 Handstamped in Black

1903, Apr. 15 Overprint 16x3¾mm

22	A1	¼g green	7.50	7.50
23	A1	½g red	12.00	12.00
24	A1	1g blue	15.00	15.00
25	A1	2g dark brown	19.00	19.00
26	A2	4g lilac brown	27.50	27.50
27	A2	8g violet	37.50	37.50
28	A2	16g black	57.50	57.50
		Nos. 22-28 (7)	176.00	176.00

The handstamp reads "Malekt." (Also "Melekt," message).

Original stamps have blurred colons. Unofficial reproductions have clean colons.

Nos. 22-28 have black overprints only. All other colors are fakes.

Nos. 1-7 Handstamped in Violet or Blue

Overprint 18¼mm Wide

1904, Dec.

36	A1	¼g green	15.00	15.00
37	A1	½g red	20.00	
38	A1	1g blue	25.00	
39	A1	2g dark brown	27.50	
40	A2	4g lilac brown	35.00	
41	A2	8g violet	57.50	
42	A2	16g black	75.00	
		Nos. 36-42 (7)	255.00	

The handstamp reads "Malekathe" (message). This set was never issued.

Preceding Issues Surcharged with New Values in French Currency in Blue, Violet, Rose or Black

a

b

On Nos. 1-7

1905, Jan. 1 Overprint 3mm High

43	A1 (a)	5c on ¼g	10.00	10.00
44	A1 (a)	10c on ½g	10.00	10.00
45	A1 (a)	20c on 1g	10.00	10.00
46	A1 (a)	40c on 2g	11.00	11.00
47	A2 (a)	80c on 4g	21.00	21.00
48	A2 (b)	1.60fr on 8g	22.50	22.50
49	A2 (b)	3.20fr on 16g	40.00	40.00
		Nos. 43-49 (7)	124.50	124.50

Nos. 48-49 exist with period or comma.

1905, Feb.

On No. 8, "Ethiopie" in Blue

50	A1 (a)	5c on ¼g	120.00	100.00

On No. 15, "Bosta" in Black

51	A1 (a)	5c on ¼g	40.00	40.00

On No. 22, "Malekt" in Black

52	A1 (a)	5c on ¼g	140.00	75.00

Unofficial reproductions exist of Nos. 50, 51, 52. The 5c on No. 36, 10c, 20c, 40c, 80c, and 1.60fr surcharges exist as unofficial reproductions only.

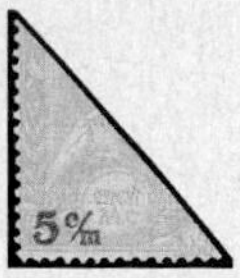

c

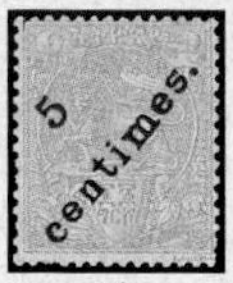

d

1905 On No. 2

54	A1 (c)	5c on half of ½g	10.00	10.00

On No. 21, "Bosta" in Black

55	A2 (d)	5c on 16g blk	200.00	100.00

On No. 55, "Bosta" is in black.

On No. 28, "Malekt" in Black

56	A2 (d)	5c on 16g blk	250.00	250.00
		Nos. 54-56 (3)	460.00	360.00

No. 54 issued in March. Nos. 55-56 issued Mar. 30.

The overprints and surcharges on Nos. 8 to 56 inclusive were handstamped, the work being very roughly done.

As is usual with handstamped overprints and surcharges there are many inverted and double, but most of them are fakes or unofficial reproductions.

Surcharged with New Values in Various Colors and in Violet

Overprint 14¾x3½mm

1906, Jan. 1

57	A1	5c on ¼g green	10.00	10.00
58	A1	10c on ½g red	12.00	12.00
59	A1	20c on 1g blue	12.00	12.00
60	A1	40c on 2g dk brn	12.00	12.00
61	A2	80c on 4g lilac brn	18.00	18.00
62	A2	1.60fr on 8g violet	27.50	27.50
63	A2	3.20fr on 16g black	45.00	45.00
		Nos. 57-63 (7)	136.50	136.50

Two types of the 4-character overprint ("Menelik"): 14x¾x3½mm and 16x4mm.

Surcharged in Violet Brown

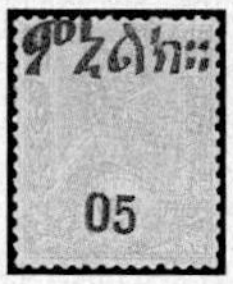

1906, July 1 Overprint 16x4¼mm

64	A1	5c on ¼g grn	9.25	9.25
a.		Surcharged "20"	75.00	75.00
65	A1	10c on ½g red	11.00	11.00
66	A1	20c on 1g blue	17.50	17.50
67	A1	40c on 2g dk brn	17.50	17.50
68	A2	80c on 4g lil brn	25.00	25.00
69	A2	1.60fr on 8g vio	25.00	25.00
70	A2	3.20fr on 16g blk	60.00	60.00
		Nos. 64-70 (7)	165.25	165.25

The control overprint reads "Menelik."

Surcharged in Violet

e

f

1907, June 21

71	A1 (e)	¼ on ¼g grn	8.75	8.75
72	A1 (e)	½ on ½g red	8.75	8.75
73	A1 (f)	1 on 1g blue	11.00	11.00
74	A1 (f)	2 on 2g dk brn	12.00	12.00
a.		Surcharged "40"	65.00	
75	A2 (f)	4 on 4g lil brn	13.00	13.00
a.		Surcharged "80"	57.50	
76	A2 (f)	8 on 8g vio	30.00	30.00
77	A2 (f)	16 on 16g blk	37.50	37.50
		Nos. 71-77 (7)	121.00	121.00

Nos. 71-72 are also found with stars farther away from figures.

The control overprint reads "Dagmawi" ("Second"), meaning Emperor Menelik II.

On stamps with "1" in surcharge, genuine examples have straight serifs, forgeries have curved serifs.

Nos. 2, 23 Surcharged in Bluish Green

1908, Aug. 14

78	A1	1pi on ½g red (#2)	15.00	15.00
79	A1	1pi on ½g red (#23)	*850.00*	—

Official reproductions exist. Value, set $25.

Forgeries exist.

The surcharges on Nos. 57-78 are handstamped and are found double, inverted, etc.

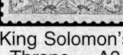

Surcharged in Black

1908, Nov. 1

80	A1	¼p on ¼g grn	1.50	1.50
81	A1	½p on ½g red	1.50	1.50
82	A1	1p on 1g blue	2.25	2.25
83	A1	2p on 2g dk brn	3.75	3.75
84	A2	4p on 4g lil brn	5.25	5.25
85	A2	8p on 8g vio	12.50	12.50
86	A2	16p on 16g blk	18.00	18.00
		Nos. 80-86 (7)	44.75	44.75

Surcharges on Nos. 80-85 are found double, inverted, etc. Forgeries exist.

These are the 1st stamps valid for international mail.

King Solomon's Throne — A3

Menelik in Native Costume — A4

Menelik in Royal Dress — A5

1909, Jan. 29 ***Perf. 11½***

87	A3	¼g blue green	1.10	.85
88	A3	½g rose	1.25	.85
89	A3	1g green & org	6.25	2.50
90	A4	2g blue	4.75	3.00
91	A4	4g green & car	7.00	5.50
92	A5	8g ver & dp grn	15.00	10.00
93	A5	16g ver & car	22.50	16.50
		Nos. 87-93 (7)	57.85	39.20

For overprints see Nos. 101-115, J43-J49, J55-J56. For surcharges see Nos. 116-119.

Nos. 1-7 Handstamped and Surcharged in ms.

1911, Oct. 1 ***Perf. 14x13½***

94	A1	¼g on ¼g grn	50.00	
95	A1	½g on ½g red	50.00	
96	A1	1g on 1g blue	50.00	
97	A1	2g on 2g dk brn	50.00	
98	A2	4g on 4g lil brn	50.00	
99	A2	8g on 8g violet	50.00	
100	A2	16g on 16g black	50.00	
		Nos. 94-100 (7)	350.00	

Nos. 94-100 were produced as a philatelic speculation by the postmaster at Dire-Dawa. The overprint is abbreviated from "Affranchissement Exceptionnel Faute Timbres" (Special Franking Lacking Stamps). The overprints and surcharges were applied to stamps on cover and then canceled. These covers were then sold to dealers in Europe. No. 98 is known postally used on a small number of commercial covers.

Nos. 94-100 without surcharge are forgeries.

Stamps of 1909 Handstamped in Violet or Black

Nos. 101-102

Nos. 104-107

1917, Mar. 30 ***Perf. 11½***

101	A3	¼g blue grn (V)	7.50	6.75
102	A3	½g rose (V)	7.50	6.75
104	A4	2g blue (Bk)	10.00	8.25
105	A4	4g grn & car (Bk)	15.00	17.00
106	A5	8g ver & dp grn (Bk)	25.00	22.50
107	A5	16g ver & car (Bk)	40.00	35.00
		Nos. 101-107 (6)	105.00	96.25

Coronation of Empress Zauditu and appointment of Prince Tafari as Regent and Heir to the throne.

Exist with overprint inverted and double.

Stamps of 1909 Overprinted in Blue, Black or Red

Nos. 108-111

Nos. 112-115

1917, Apr. 5-Oct. 1

108	A3	¼g blue grn (Bl)	1.25	1.25
109	A3	½g rose (Bl)	1.25	1.25
110	A3	1g grn & org (Bl)	2.25	2.25
111	A4	2g blue (R)	82.50	87.25
112	A4	2g blue (Bk)	1.25	1.25
113	A4	4g grn & car (Bl)	1.25	1.25
a.		Black overprint	11.00	11.00
114	A5	8g ver & dp grn (Bl)	1.25	1.25
115	A5	16g ver & car (Bl)	2.25	2.25
		Nos. 108-115 (8)	93.25	98.00

Coronation of Empress Zauditu.

Nos. 108-115 all exist with double overprint, inverted overprint, double overprint, one inverted, and various combinations.

Nos. 114-115 with Additional Surcharge

k

l

m

n

1917, May 28

116	A5 (k)	¼g on 8g	5.00	4.00
117	A5 (l)	½g on 8g	5.00	4.00
118	A5 (m)	1g on 16g	11.00	8.00
119	A5 (n)	2g on 16g	12.00	9.00
		Nos. 116-119 (4)	33.00	25.00

Nos. 116-119 all exist with the numerals double and inverted and No. 116 with the Amharic surcharge missing.

Sommering's Gazelle — A6

Prince Tafari — A9

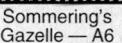

Cathedral of St. George A12

Empress Walzeri Zauditu — A18

¼g, Giraffes. ½g, Leopard. 2g, Prince Tafari, diff. 4g, Prince Tafari, diff. 8g, White rhinoceros. 12g, Somali ostriches. 1t, African elephant. 2t, Water buffalo. 3t, Lions. 5t, 10t, Empress Zauditu.

1919, June 16 Typo. *Perf. 11½*

120	A6	⅛g violet & brn	.25	.25
121	A6	¼g bl grn & drab	.25	.25
122	A6	½g scar & ol grn	.25	.25
123	A9	1g rose lil & gray grn	.25	.25
124	A9	2g dp ultra & fawn	.25	.25
125	A9	4g turq bl & org	.25	*2.50*
126	A12	6g lt blue & org	.25	.25
127	A12	8g ol grn & blk brn	.35	.25
128	A12	12g red vio & gray	.50	.30
129	A12	1t rose & gray blk	.90	.40
130	A12	2t black & brown	2.50	
131	A12	3t grn & dp org	2.50	1.90
132	A18	4t brn & lil rose	3.00	2.50
133	A18	5t carmine & gray	4.00	4.00
134	A18	10t gray grn & bis	8.00	5.25
		Nos. 120-134 (15)	23.50	
		Nos. 120-129,131-134 (14)		18.25

No. 130 was not issued.

For overprints see Nos. J50-J54. For surcharges see Nos. 135-154.

Reprints have brownish gum that is cracked diagonally. Originals have smooth, white gum. Reprints exist imperf. and some values with inverted centers. Value for set, unused or canceled, $5.

No. 132 Surcharged in Blue

1919, July

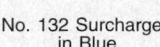

135	A18	4g on 4t brn & lil rose	3.50	3.50

Nos. 135-154

The Amharic surcharge indicates the new value and, therefore, varies on Nos. 135-154. There are numerous defective letters and figures, several types of the "2" of "½," the errors "guerhce," "gnerche," etc.

Many varieties of surcharge, such as double, inverted, lines transposed or omitted, and inverted "2" in "½," exist.

There are many irregularly produced settings in imitation of Nos. 136-154 which differ slightly from the originals. These may be essays or proofs.

Stamps of 1919 Surcharged

1921

136	A6	½g on ⅛g vio & brn	1.00	1.00
137	A6	1g on ¼g grn & db	2.50	1.00
138	A9	2g on 1g lil brn & gray grn	1.00	1.50
139	A18	2g on 4t brn & lil rose	35.00	15.00
140	A6	2½g on ½g scar & ol grn	1.00	*1.50*
141	A9	4g on 2g ultra & fawn	1.00	*1.25*
		Nos. 136-141 (6)	41.50	21.25

Forgeries of No. 139 exist.

Stamps and Type of 1919 Surcharged

1925-26

142	A12	½g on 1t rose & gray blk ('26)	1.00	1.00
a.		Without colon ('26)	12.50	12.50
143	A18	½g on 5t car & gray ('26)	2.00	1.00
144	A12	1g on 6g bl & org	1.00	1.00
145	A12	1g on 12g lil & gray	400.00	400.00
146	A12	1g on 3t grn & org ('26)	22.50	16.00
147	A18	1g on 10t gray grn & bis ('26)	1.00	*1.00*
		Nos. 142-147 (6)	427.50	420.00

On No. 142 the surcharge is at the left side of the stamp, reading upward. On No. 142a it is at the right, reading downward. The two surcharges are from different, though similar, settings. On No. 146 the surcharge is at the right, reading upward. See note following No. 154.

Type of 1919 Srchd.

1925, Oct.

147A	A12	1g on 12g lil & gray	400.00	

Forgeries exist.

Nos. 126-128 Srchd.

1926

148	A12	½g on 8g	3.00	1.25
149	A12	1g on 6g	80.00	50.00
150	A12	1g on 12g	350.00	
		Nos. 148-150 (3)	433.00	51.25

The Amharic line has 7 (½g) or 6 characters (1g).

Nos. 126-128, 131 Srchd.

1925-27

151	A12	½g on 8g ('27)	1.50	1.50
152	A12	1g on 6g ('27)	60.00	40.00
153	A12	1g on 12g ('27)	5.00	1.50
154	A12	1g on 3t	400.00	
		Nos. 151-154 (4)	466.50	43.00

The Amharic line has 7 (½g) or 4 characters (1g). No. 152 has the lines closer together than do the others.

Forgeries of No. 154 exist.

Ras Tafari — A22

Empress Zauditu — A23

1928, Sept. 5 Typo. *Perf. 13½x14*

155	A22	⅛m org & lt bl	1.50	1.40
156	A23	¼m ind & red org	.90	*1.40*
157	A22	½m gray grn & blk	1.50	1.40
158	A23	1m dk car & blk	.90	*1.40*
159	A22	2m dk bl & blk	.90	*1.40*
160	A23	4m yel & olive	.90	*1.40*
161	A22	8m vio & olive	2.40	1.40
162	A23	1t org brn & vio	2.75	1.40
163	A22	2t grn & bister	4.25	3.25
164	A23	3t choc & grn	6.75	3.75
		Nos. 155-164 (10)	22.75	18.20

For overprints and surcharges see Nos. 165-209, 217-230, C1-C10.

Preceding Issue Overprinted in Black, Violet or Red

1928, Sept. 1

165	A22	⅛m (Bk)	3.25	3.25
166	A23	¼m (V)	3.25	3.25
167	A22	½m (V)	3.25	3.25
168	A23	1m (V)	3.25	3.25
169	A22	2m (R)	3.25	3.25
170	A23	4m (Bk)	3.25	3.25
171	A22	8m (R)	3.25	3.25
172	A23	1t (Bk)	4.50	4.50
173	A22	2t (R)	6.00	6.00
174	A23	3t (R)	6.00	6.00
		Nos. 165-174 (10)	39.25	39.25

Opening of General Post Office, Addis Ababa.

Exist with overprint inverted, double, double, one inverted, etc.

Nos. 155, 157, 159, 161, 163 Handstamped in Violet, Red or Black

1928, Oct. 7

175	A22	⅛m (V)	4.25	4.25
176	A22	½m (R)	4.25	4.25
177	A22	2m (R)	4.25	4.25
178	A22	8m (Bk)	4.25	4.25
179	A22	2t (V)	4.25	4.25
		Nos. 175-179 (5)	21.25	21.25

Crowning of Prince Tafari as king (Negus) on Oct. 7, 1928.

Nos. 175-177 exist with overprint vertical, inverted, double, etc.

Forgeries exist.

Nos. 155-164 Overprinted in Red or Green

1930, Apr. 3

180	A22	⅛m org & lt bl (R)	1.40	1.40
181	A23	¼m ind & red org (G)	1.40	1.40
182	A22	½m gray grn & blk (R)	1.40	1.40
183	A23	1m dk car & blk (G)	1.40	1.40
184	A22	2m dk bl & blk (R)	1.40	1.40
185	A23	4m yel & ol (R)	2.10	2.10
186	A22	8m vio & ol (R)	3.00	3.00
187	A23	1t org brn & vio (R)	5.00	5.00
188	A22	2t grn & bis (R)	6.00	6.00
189	A23	3t choc & grn (R)	8.00	8.00
		Nos. 180-189 (10)	31.10	31.10

Proclamation of King Tafari as King of Kings of Abyssinia under the name "Haile Selassie."

A similar overprint, set in four vertical lines, was printed on all denominations of the 1928 issue. It was not considered satisfactory and was rejected. The trial impressions were not placed on sale to the public, but some stamps reached private hands and have been passed through the post.

Nos. 155-164 Overprinted in Red or Olive Brown

1930, Apr. 3

190	A22	⅛m orange & lt bl	1.40	1.40
191	A23	¼m ind & red org (OB)	1.40	1.40
192	A22	½m gray grn & blk	1.40	1.40
193	A23	1m dk car & blk (OB)	1.40	1.40
194	A22	2m dk blue & blk	1.40	1.40
195	A23	4m yellow & ol	2.10	2.10
196	A22	8m violet & ol	3.00	3.00
197	A23	1t org brn & vio	5.00	5.00
198	A22	2t green & bister	6.00	6.00
199	A23	3t chocolate & grn	8.00	8.00
		Nos. 190-199 (10)	31.10	31.10

Proclamation of King Tafari as Emperor Haile Selassie.

All stamps of this series exist with "H" of "HAILE" omitted and with many other varieties.

Nos. 155-164 Handstamped in Violet or Red

1930, Nov. 2

200	A22	⅛m (V)	1.10	1.10
201	A23	¼m (V)	1.10	1.10
202	A22	½m (R)	1.10	1.10
203	A23	1m (V)	1.10	1.10
204	A22	2m (R)	1.10	1.10
205	A23	4m (V)	1.10	1.10
206	A22	8m (V or R)	1.90	1.90
207	A23	1t (V)	3.00	3.00
208	A22	2t (V or R)	4.50	4.50
209	A23	3t (V or R)	6.50	6.50
		Nos. 200-209 (10)	22.50	22.50

Coronation of Emperor Haile Selassie, Nov. 2, 1930.

Haile Selassie Coronation Monument, Symbols of Empire — A24

1930, Nov. Engr. *Perf. 12½*

210	A24	1g orange	1.00	1.00
211	A24	2g ultra	1.00	1.00
212	A24	4g violet	1.00	1.00
213	A24	8g dull green	1.00	1.00
214	A24	1t brown	1.25	1.25
215	A24	3t green	2.00	2.00
216	A24	5t red brown	2.00	2.00
		Nos. 210-216 (7)	9.25	9.25

Coronation of Emperor Haile Selassie.
Issued: 4g, 11/2; others, 11/23.
Reprints of Nos. 210 to 216 exist. Colors are more yellow and the ink is thicker and slightly glossy. Ink on the originals is dull and granular. Value 35c each.

Nos. 158-160, 164 Surcharged in Green, Red or Blue

Type I

Type II

1931 *Perf. 13½x14*

217	A23	⅛m on 1m	.80	.80
218	A22	⅛m on 2m (R)	.80	.80
219	A23	⅛m on 4m	.80	.80
220	A23	¼m on 1m (Bl)	.80	.80
221	A22	¼m on 2m (R)	1.50	1.50
222	A23	¼m on 4m	1.50	1.50
225	A23	½m on 1m (Bl)	1.50	1.50
226	A22	½m on 2m (R)	1.50	1.50
227	A23	½m on 4m, type II	1.50	1.50
a.		½m on 4m, type I	10.00	10.00
228	A23	½m on 3t (R)	12.00	12.00
230	A22	1m on 2m (R)	3.00	3.00
		Nos. 217-230 (11)	25.70	25.70

The ½m on ⅛m orange & light blue and ½m on ¼m indigo & red orange were clandestinely printed and never sold at the post office.

No. 230 with double surcharge in red and blue is a color trial.
Many varieties exist.
Issued: 1m, Apr.; others, 3/20.

Ras Makonnen A25

Empress Menen A27

View of Hawash River and Railroad Bridge A26

Designs: 2g, 8g, Haile Selassie (profile). 4g, 1t, Statue of Menelik II. 3t, Empress Menen (full face). 5t, Haile Selassie (full face).

Perf. 12½, 12x12½, 12½x12

1931, June 27 Engr.

232	A25	⅛g red	.40	.40
233	A26	¼g olive green	1.10	1.10
234	A25	½g dark violet	1.10	1.10
235	A27	1g red orange	1.10	1.10
236	A27	2g ultra	1.10	1.10
237	A25	4g violet	1.25	1.25
238	A27	8g blue green	2.00	2.00
239	A25	1t chocolate	24.00	10.00
240	A27	3t yellow green	7.00	3.00
241	A27	5t red brown	12.00	5.50
		Nos. 232-241 (10)	51.05	26.55

For overprints see Nos. B1-B5. For surcharges see Nos. 242-246.
Reprints of Nos. 232-236, 238-240 are on thinner and whiter paper than the originals. On originals the ink is dull and granular. On reprints, heavy, caked and shiny. Value 20c each.

Nos. 232-236 Surcharged in Blue or Carmine

1936, Jan. 29 *Perf. 12x12½, 12½x12*

242	A25	1c on ⅛g red	2.00	1.00
243	A26	2c on ¼g ol grn (C)	2.00	1.00
244	A25	3c on ½g dk vio	2.00	1.10
245	A27	5c on 1g red org	2.50	1.50
246	A27	10c on 2g ultra (C)	3.25	1.90
		Nos. 242-246 (5)	11.75	6.50

Catalogue values for unused stamps in this section, from this point to the end of the section, are for Never Hinged items.

Haile Selassie I
A32 A33

1942, Mar. 23 Litho. *Perf. 14x13½*

247	A32	4c lt bl grn, ind & blk	.80	.40
248	A32	10c rose, indigo & blk	2.50	.75
249	A32	20c dp ultra, ind & blk	5.00	1.25
		Nos. 247-249 (3)	8.30	2.40

1942-43 Unwmk.

250	A33	4c lt bl grn & indigo	.90	.25
251	A33	8c yel org & indigo	1.00	.25
252	A33	10c rose & indigo	1.25	.25
253	A33	12c dull vio & indigo	1.25	.30
254	A33	20c dp ultra & indigo	2.00	.50
255	A33	25c dull grn & indigo	2.50	.70
256	A33	50c dull brn & indigo	4.75	1.25
257	A33	60c lilac & indigo	7.25	1.50
		Nos. 250-257 (8)	20.90	5.00

Issued: 25c, 50c, 60c, 4/1/43; others, 6/22/42.
For surcharges see Nos. 258-262, 284, C18-C20.

Nos. 250-254 Surcharged in Black or Brown

1943, Nov. 3

258	A33	5c on 4c	85.00	85.00
259	A33	10c on 8c	85.00	85.00
260	A33	15c on 10c	85.00	85.00
261	A33	20c on 20c (Br)	85.00	85.00
262	A33	30c on 20c (Br)	85.00	85.00
		Nos. 258-262 (5)	425.00	425.00

Restoration of the Obelisk in Myazzia Place, Addis Ababa, and the 13th anniv. of the coronation of Emperor Haile Selassie.
No. 258 exists with inverted "5" in surcharge. Value $150. On No. 262, "3" is surcharged on "2" of "20" to make "30."
Approximately 40 sets exist with a somewhat different handstamped surcharge. Value, set *$2,000.*

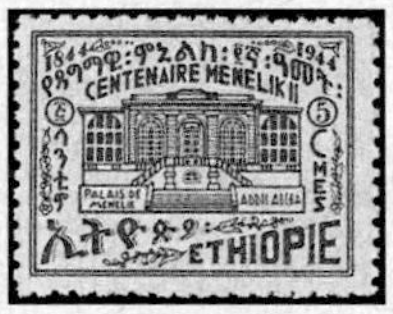

Palace of Menelik II A34

Menelik II — A35

Statue — A36

50c, Mausoleum. 65c, Menelik II (with scepter).

1944, Dec. 31 Litho. *Perf. 10½*

263	A34	5c green	1.25	.65
264	A35	10c red lilac	2.25	1.10
265	A36	20c deep blue	4.00	2.25
266	A34	50c dull purple	5.25	2.25
267	A35	65c bister brown	9.25	3.50
		Nos. 263-267 (5)	22.00	9.75

Cent. of the birth of Menelik II, 8/18/44.
Printed on gum-impregnated paper.

Unissued Semi-Postal Stamps Overprinted in Carmine

Nurse & Baby — A39

Various Designs Inscribed "Croix Rouge"

1945, Aug. 7 Photo. *Perf. 11½*

268	A39	5c brt green	1.50	.75
269	A39	10c brt red	1.50	.75
270	A39	25c brt blue	1.50	.75
271	A39	50c dk yellow brn	8.50	3.50
272	A39	1t brt violet	13.50	4.50
		Nos. 268-272 (5)	26.50	10.25

Nos. 268-272 without overprint were ordered printed in Switzerland before Ethiopia fell to the invading Italians, so were not delivered to Addis Ababa. After the country's liberation, the set was overprinted "V" and issued for ordinary postage. These stamps exist without overprint, but were not issued. Value $1.25.
Some values exist inverted or double.
Forged overprints exist.
For surcharges see Nos. B11-B15, B36-B40.

Lion of Judah — A44

Menelik II — A45

Mail Transport, Old and New A46

Designs: 50c, Old Post Office, Addis Ababa. 70c, Menelik II and Haile Selassie.

1947, Apr. 18 Engr. *Perf. 13*

273	A44	10c yellow org	3.50	.75
274	A45	20c deep blue	5.75	1.10
275	A46	30c orange brn	9.50	1.75
276	A46	50c dk slate grn	22.50	3.75
277	A46	70c red violet	37.50	7.50
		Nos. 273-277 (5)	78.75	14.85

50th anniv. of Ethiopia's postal system.

Haile Selassie and Franklin D. Roosevelt — A49

Design: 65c, Roosevelt and US Flags.

Engraved and Photogravure

1947, May 23 Unwmk. *Perf. 12½*

278	A49	12c car lake & bl grn	2.75	3.00
279	A49	25c dk blue & rose	2.75	3.00
280	A49	65c blk, red & dp bl	6.00	6.50
		Nos. 278-280,C21-C22 (5)	41.50	42.50

King Sahle Selassie Reclining A50

King Sahle Selassie — A52

Design: 30c, View of Ankober.

1947, May 1 Engr. *Perf. 13*
281 A50 20c deep blue 4.25 .90
282 A50 30c dark purple 6.25 1.25
283 A52 $1 deep green 15.00 3.50
Nos. 281-283 (3) 25.50 5.65

150th anniversary of Selassie dynasty.

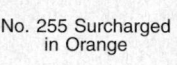

No. 255 Surcharged in Orange

1947, July 14 *Perf. 14x13½*
284 A33 12c on 25c 85.00 85.00

Amba Alaguie A53

Designs: 2c, Trinity Church. 4c, Debra Sina. 5c, Mecan, near Achanguie. 8c, Lake Tana. 12c, 15c, Parliament Building, Addis Ababa. 20c, Aiba, near Mai Cheo. 30c, Bahr Bridge over Blue Nile. 60c, 70c, Canoe on Lake Tana. $1, Omo Falls. $3, Mt. Alamata. $5, Ras Dashan Mountains.

Perf. 13x13½

1947-53 Engr. Wmk. 282
285 A53 1c rose violet .25 .25
286 A53 2c blue violet .25 .25
a. Unwatermarked ('51) 37.50 15.00
287 A53 4c green .35 .25
288 A53 5c dark green .35 .25
289 A53 8c deep orange .65 .25
290 A53 12c red .80 .25
290A A53 15c dk ol brn ('53) .75 .25
291 A53 20c blue 1.10 .40
292 A53 30c orange brown 1.90 .55
292A A53 60c red ('51) 2.25 .95
293 A53 70c rose lilac 3.25 .70
294 A53 $1 dk carmine rose 5.25 .70
295 A53 $3 bright blue 14.00 2.75
296 A53 $5 olive 22.50 5.50
Nos. 285-296 (14) 53.65 13.30

Issue dates: 15c, May 25, 1953; 60c, Feb. 10, 1951; others, Aug. 23, 1947.
Shades exist.
For overprints see Nos. 355-356. For surcharges see Nos. B6-B10, B16-B20.

Empress Waizero Menen and Emperor Haile Selassie A54

1949, May 5 Wmk. 282 *Perf. 13*
297 A54 20c blue 3.50 .85
298 A54 30c yellow org 3.50 1.10
299 A54 50c purple 8.00 2.10
300 A54 80c green 12.00 2.50
301 A54 $1 red 14.00 3.50
Nos. 297-301 (5) 41.00 10.05

Central ornaments differ on each denomination.
8th anniv. of Ethiopia's liberation from Italian occupation.

Dejach Balcha Hospital A55

Abuna Petros — A56

Designs: 20c, Haile Selassie raising flag. 30c, Lion of Judah statue. 50c, Empress Waizero Menen, Haile Selassie and building.

Perf. 13x13½, 13½x13

1950, Nov. 2 Engr. Wmk. 282
302 A55 5c purple 1.60 .35
303 A56 10c deep plum 3.00 .70
304 A56 20c deep carmine 6.50 .90
305 A56 30c green 9.50 2.00
306 A55 50c deep blue 16.00 3.50
Nos. 302-306 (5) 36.60 7.45

20th anniv. of the coronation of Emperor Haile Selassie and Empress Menen.

Abbaye Bridge — A57

1951, Jan. 1 Unwmk. *Perf. 14*
308 A57 5c dk green & dk brn 4.25 .50
309 A57 10c dp orange & blk 5.75 .50
310 A57 15c dp blue & org brn 8.25 .50
311 A57 30c olive & lil rose 15.00 .80
312 A57 60c brown & dp bl 37.50 2.00
313 A57 80c purple & green 50.00 3.00
Nos. 308-313 (6) 120.75 7.30

Opening of the Abbaye Bridge over the Blue Nile.

Tomb of Ras Makonnen A58

1951, Mar. 2 Center in Black
314 A58 5c dark green 3.25 .65
315 A58 10c deep ultra 3.25 .40
316 A58 15c blue 5.50 .40
317 A58 30c claret 11.00 1.50
318 A58 80c rose carmine 17.00 2.25
319 A58 $1 orange brown 22.50 2.25
Nos. 314-319 (6) 62.50 7.45

55th anniversary of the Battle of Adwa.

Emperor Haile Selassie — A59

1952, July 23 *Perf. 13½*
320 A59 5c dark green .85 .25
321 A59 10c red orange 1.25 .25
322 A59 15c black 2.00 .40
323 A59 25c ultra 2.50 .40
324 A59 30c violet 3.25 .65
325 A59 50c rose red 5.00 .90
326 A59 65c chocolate 10.00 1.60
Nos. 320-326 (7) 24.85 4.45

60th birthday of Haile Selassie.

Open Road to Sea A60

Designs: 25c, 50c, Road and broken chain. 65c, Map. 80c, Allegory: Reunion. $1, Haile Selassie raising flag. $2, Ethiopian flag and seascape. $3, Haile Selassie addressing League of Nations.

Wmk. 282

1952, Sept. 11 Engr. *Perf. 13*
327 A60 15c brown carmine .85 .25
328 A60 25c red brown 1.10 .40
329 A60 30c yellow brown 2.00 .60
330 A60 50c purple 3.00 1.25
331 A60 65c gray 5.75 1.40
332 A60 80c blue green 6.50 .95
333 A60 $1 rose carmine 13.00 2.00
334 A60 $2 deep blue 22.50 3.25
335 A60 $3 magenta 47.50 5.50
Nos. 327-335 (9) 102.20 15.60

Issued to celebrate Ethiopia's federation with Eritrea, effected Sept. 11, 1952.

Haile Selassie and New Ethiopian Port A61

15c, 30c, Haile Selassie on deck of ship.

1953, Oct. 4
337 A61 10c red & dk brn 4.75 1.75
338 A61 15c blue & dk grn 5.00 1.75
339 A61 25c orange & dk brn 9.00 3.50
340 A61 30c red brn & dk grn 16.00 5.00
341 A61 50c purple & dk brn 25.00 6.75
Nos. 337-341 (5) 59.75 18.75

Federation of Ethiopia and Eritrea, 1st anniv.

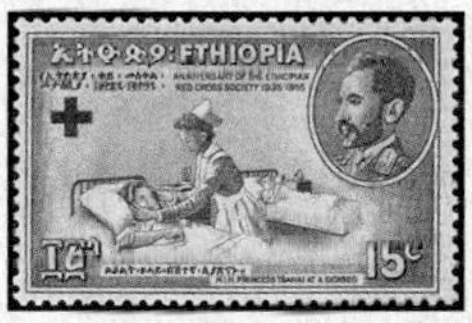

Princess Tsahai at a Sickbed A62

Perf. 13x13½

1955, July 8 Engr. Wmk. 282
Cross Typo. in Red
342 A62 15c choc & ultra 2.50 1.25
343 A62 20c green & orange 3.75 1.50
344 A62 30c ultra & green 6.25 1.90
Nos. 342-344 (3) 12.50 4.65

Ethiopian Red Cross, 20th anniv.
For surcharges see Nos. B33-B35.

Promulgating the Constitution — A63

Bishops' Consecration by Archbishop — A64

25c, Kagnew Battalion. 35c, Reunion with the Motherland. 50c, "Progress." 65c, Empress Waizero Menen & Emperor Haile Selassie.

Perf. 12½

1955, Nov. 3 Unwmk. Engr.
345 A63 5c green & choc 1.25 .55
346 A64 20c carmine & brn 2.50 .90
347 A64 25c magenta & gray 3.50 1.40
348 A63 35c brown & red org 4.75 1.75
349 A64 50c dk brn & ultra 7.00 2.50
350 A64 65c violet & car 9.75 4.00
Nos. 345-350 (6) 28.75 11.10

Silver jubilee of the coronation of Emperor Haile Selassie and Empress Waizero Menen.

Emperor Haile Selassie and Fair Emblem — A65

1955, Nov. 5 Wmk. 282
351 A65 5c green & ol grn 1.00 .25
352 A65 10c car & dp ultra 1.50 .40
353 A65 15c vio blk & grn 2.00 .60
354 A65 50c mag & red brn 3.00 1.50
Nos. 351-354 (4) 7.50 2.75

Silver Jubilee Fair, Addis Ababa.

Nos. 291 and 292A Overprinted

1960, Apr. 7 *Perf. 13x13½*
355 A53 20c blue 1.75 1.25
356 A53 60c red 3.00 2.40

WRY, July 1, 1959-June 30, 1960.
The 60c without serifs is a trial printing.

Map of Africa, "Liberty" and Haile Selassie — A66

Emperor Haile Selassie — A67

Perf. 13½

1960, June 14 Engr. Unwmk.
357 A66 20c orange & green 1.25 .85
358 A66 80c orange & violet 3.50 .85
359 A66 $1 orange & maroon 4.00 1.10
Nos. 357-359 (3) 8.75 2.80

2nd Conf. of Independent African States at Addis Ababa. Issued in sheets of 10.

1960, Nov. 2 Wmk. 282 *Perf. 14*
360 A67 10c brown & blue .90 .25
361 A67 25c violet & emerald 1.75 .55
362 A67 50c dk bl & org yel 3.25 1.75
363 A67 65c slate grn & sal pink 4.25 1.75
364 A67 $1 indigo & rose vio 7.25 2.75
Nos. 360-364 (5) 17.40 7.05

30th anniv. of the coronation of Emperor Haile Selassie.

Africa Hall, UN Economic Commission for Africa — A68

1961, Apr. 15 Wmk. 282 *Perf. 14*
365 A68 80c ultra 3.75 1.40

Africa Freedom Day, Apr. 15. Sheets of 10.

Map of Ethiopia, Olive Branch
A69

1961, May 5 *Perf. 13x13½*

366 A69 20c green .40 .25
367 A69 30c violet blue .60 .25
368 A69 $1 brown 3.25 1.10
Nos. 366-368 (3) 4.25 1.60

20th anniv. of Ethiopia's liberation from Italian occupation.

African Wild Ass
A70

1961, June 16 **Wmk. 282** *Perf. 14*

369 A70 5c shown 1.10 .25
370 A70 15c Eland 1.10 .25
371 A70 25c Elephant 1.25 .40
372 A70 35c Giraffe 3.00 .50
373 A70 50c Beisa 3.00 .50
374 A70 $1 Lion 6.00 1.50
Nos. 369-374 (6) 15.45 3.40

Issued in sheets of 10. Used values are for CTO's.

Emperor Haile Selassie and Empress Waizero Menen — A71

1961, July 27 **Unwmk.** *Perf. 11*

375 A71 10c green 1.25 .45
376 A71 50c violet blue 2.25 .80
377 A71 $1 carmine rose 4.25 1.60
Nos. 375-377 (3) 7.75 2.85

Golden wedding anniv. of the Emperor and Empress.

Warlike Horsemanship (Guks) — A72

15c, Hockey. 20c, Bicycling. 30c, Soccer. 50c, 1960 Olympic marathon winner, Abebe Bikila.

Photogravure and Engraved

1962, Jan. 14 *Perf. 12x11½*

378 A72 10c yel grn & car .35 .25
379 A72 15c pink & dk brn .35 .25
380 A72 20c red & black 1.20 .25
381 A72 30c ultra & dl pur 2.00 .25
382 A72 50c yellow & green 4.00 .25
Nos. 378-382 (5) 7.90 1.25

Third Africa Football (soccer) Cup, Addis Ababa, Jan. 14-22.

Malaria Eradication Emblem, World Map and Mosquito — A73

Wmk. 282

1962, Apr. 7 **Engr.** *Perf. 13½*

383 A73 15c black .40 .25
384 A73 30c purple 1.60 .25
385 A73 60c red brown 2.40 .65
Nos. 383-385 (3) 4.40 1.15

WHO drive to eradicate malaria.

Abyssinian Ground Hornbill
A74

Birds: 15c, Abyssinian roller. 30c, Bateleur, vert. 50c, Double-toothed barbet, vert. $1, Didric cuckoo.

Perf. 11½

1962, May 5 **Unwmk.** **Photo.**

Granite Paper

386 A74 5c multicolored 1.40 .25
387 A74 15c emer, brn & ultra 2.40 .50
388 A74 30c lt brn, blk & red 2.75 1.75
389 A74 50c multicolored 5.25 1.50
390 A74 $1 multicolored 12.00 2.50
Nos. 386-390 (5) 23.80 6.50

See Nos. C77-C81, C97-C101, C107-C111.

Assab Hospital
A75

15c, School at Assab. 20c, Church at Massawa. 50c, Mosque at Massawa. 60c, Assab port.

Wmk. 282

1962, Sept. 11 **Engr.** *Perf. 13½*

391 A75 3c purple .25 .25
392 A75 15c dark blue .25 .25
393 A75 20c green .40 .25
394 A75 50c brown 1.50 .40
395 A75 60c carmine rose 1.60 .50
Nos. 391-395 (5) 4.00 1.65

Federation of Ethiopia and Eritrea, 10th anniv.

King Bazen, Madonna and Stars over Bethlehem — A76

15c, Ezana, obelisks & temple. 20c, Kaleb & sailing fleet. 50c, Lalibela, rock-church and frescoes, vert. 60c, King Yekuno Amlak & Abuna Tekle Haimanot preaching in Ankober. 75c, King Zara Yacob & Maskal celebration. $1, King Lebna Dengel & battle against Mohammed Gragn.

Perf. 14½

1962, Nov. 2 **Unwmk.** **Photo.**

396 A76 10c multicolored .35 .25
397 A76 15c multicolored .50 .25
398 A76 20c multicolored .70 .25
399 A76 50c multicolored 1.10 .25
400 A76 60c multicolored 1.25 .50
401 A76 75c multicolored 2.00 .85
402 A76 $1 multicolored 3.00 1.25
Nos. 396-402 (7) 8.90 3.60

32nd anniv. of the coronation of Emperor Haile Selassie and to commemorate ancient kings and saints.

Map of Ethiopian Telephone Network — A77

Wheat Emblem — A78

Designs: 50c, Radio mast and waves. 60c, Telegraph pole and rising sun.

Perf. 13½x14

1963, Jan. 1 **Engr.** **Wmk. 282**

403 A77 10c dark red .50 .25
404 A77 50c ultra 2.25 .50
405 A77 60c brown 2.75 .60
Nos. 403-405 (3) 5.50 1.35

10th anniv. of the Imperial Board of Telecommunications.

1963, Mar. 21 **Unwmk.** *Perf. 13½*

406 A78 5c deep rose .25 .25
407 A78 10c rose carmine .25 .25
408 A78 15c violet blue .25 .25
409 A78 30c emerald 1.25 .25
Nos. 406-409 (4) 2.00 1.00

FAO "Freedom from Hunger" campaign.

Abuna Salama — A79

Queen of Sheba — A80

Spiritual Leaders: 15c, Abuna Aregawi. 30c, Abuna Tekle Haimanot. 40c. Yared. 60c, Zara Yacob.

1964, Jan. 3 **Unwmk.** *Perf. 13½*

410 A79 10c blue .45 .25
411 A79 15c dark green .75 .25
412 A79 30c brown red 1.90 .45
413 A79 40c dark blue 2.50 .75
414 A79 60c brown 3.75 1.40
Nos. 410-414 (5) 9.35 3.10

1964, Mar. 2 **Photo.** *Perf. 11½*

Ethiopian Empresses: 15c, Helen. 50c, Seble Wongel. 60c, Mentiwab. 80c, Taitu, consort of Menelik II.

Granite Paper

415 A80 10c multicolored 1.10 .30
416 A80 15c multicolored 2.25 .50
417 A80 50c multicolored 2.50 1.00
418 A80 60c multicolored 5.00 1.75
419 A80 80c multicolored 6.50 2.50
Nos. 415-419 (5) 17.35 6.05

Priest Teaching Alphabet to Children — A81

10c, Classroom. 15c, Woman learning to read. 40c, Students in chemistry laboratory. 60c, Graduation procession.

1964, June 1 **Unwmk.** *Perf. 11½*

Granite Paper

420 A81 5c brown .25 .25
421 A81 10c emerald .25 .25
422 A81 15c rose vio, vert. .25 .25
423 A81 40c vio blue, vert. 1.00 .30
424 A81 60c dark pur, vert. 1.50 .55
Nos. 420-424 (5) 3.25 1.60

Issued to publicize education.

Eleanor Roosevelt (1884-1962) — A82

1964, Oct. 11 **Photo.**

Granite Paper

Portrait in Slate Blue

425 A82 10c yellow bister .25 .25
426 A82 60c orange brown 2.00 .75
427 A82 80c green & gold 3.00 1.00
Nos. 425-427 (3) 5.25 2.00

King Serse Dengel and View of Gondar, 1563
A83

Ethiopian Leaders: 10c, King Fasiladas and Gondar in 1632. 20c, King Yassu the Great and Gondar in 1682. 25c, Emperor Theodore II and map of Ethiopia. 60c, Emperor John IV and Battle of Gura, 1876. 80c, Emperor Menelik II and Battle of Adwa, 1896.

1964, Dec. 12 **Photo.** *Perf. 14½x14*

428 A83 5c multicolored .40 .25
429 A83 10c multicolored .40 .25
430 A83 20c multicolored 1.00 .25
431 A83 25c multicolored 1.50 .25
432 A83 60c multicolored 2.75 .95
433 A83 80c multicolored 3.75 1.25
Nos. 428-433 (6) 9.80 3.20

Ethiopian Rose — A84

Flowers: 10c, Kosso tree. 25c, St.-John's-wort. 35c, Parrot's-beak. 60c, Maskal daisy.

1965, Mar. 30 *Perf. 12x13½*

434 A84 5c multicolored .35 .25
435 A84 10c multicolored .35 .25
436 A84 25c multicolored 1.20 .25
437 A84 35c multicolored 2.50 .50
438 A84 60c green, yel & org 3.00 .80
Nos. 434-438 (5) 7.40 2.05

ITU Emblem, Old and New Communication Symbols — A85

Perf. 13½x14½

1965, May 17 **Litho.** **Unwmk.**

439 A85 5c blue, indigo & yel .25 .25
440 A85 10c blue, indigo & org .55 .25
441 A85 60c blue, indigo & lil rose 2.00 .95
Nos. 439-441 (3) 2.80 1.45

Cent. of the ITU.

Laboratory
A86

Designs: 5c, Textile spinning mill. 10c, Sugar factory. 20c, Mountain road. 25c, Autobus. 30c, Diesel locomotive and bridge. 35c, Railroad station, Addis Ababa.

1965, July 19 **Photo.** *Perf. 11½*

Granite Paper

Portrait in Black

442 A86 3c sepia .25 .25
443 A86 5c dull pur & buff .25 .25
444 A86 10c black & gray .65 .25
445 A86 20c green & pale yel .95 .25
446 A86 25c dk brown & yel 1.40 .25
447 A86 30c maroon & gray 2.25 .35
448 A86 35c dk blue & gray 2.50 .50
Nos. 442-448 (7) 8.25 2.10

For overprints see Nos. 609-612.

ICY Emblem
A87

1965, Oct. 24 Unwmk. *Perf. 11½*
Granite Paper

449 A87 10c blue & red brn .50 .25
450 A87 50c dp blue & red brn 1.40 .75
451 A87 80c vio blue & red brn 2.25 1.10
Nos. 449-451 (3) 4.15 2.10

International Cooperation Year, 1965.

National Bank Emblem A88

Designs: 10c, Commercial Bank emblem. 60c, Natl. and Commercial Bank buildings.

1965, Nov. 2 Photo. *Perf. 13*
452 A88 10c dp car, blk & indigo .40 .25
453 A88 30c ultra, blk & indigo .85 .40
454 A88 60c black, yel & indigo 1.50 .65
Nos. 452-454 (3) 2.75 1.30

Natl. and Commercial Banks of Ethiopia.

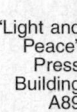

"Light and Peace" Press Building A89

1966, Apr. 5 Engr. *Perf. 13*
455 A89 5c pink & black .25 .25
456 A89 15c lt yel grn & blk .60 .25
457 A89 30c orange yel & blk 1.10 .55
Nos. 455-457 (3) 1.95 1.05

Opening of the "Light and Peace" Printing Press building.

Kabaro Drum — A90

Musical Instruments: 10c, Bagana harp. 35c, Messenko guitar. 50c, Krar lyre. 60c, Wachent flutes.

1966, Sept. 9 Photo. *Perf. 13½*
458 A90 5c brt green & blk .25 .25
459 A90 10c dull blue & blk .25 .25
460 A90 35c orange & blk 1.25 .50
461 A90 50c yellow & blk 2.25 .70
462 A90 60c rose car & blk 2.75 1.25
Nos. 458-462 (5) 6.75 2.95

Emperor Haile Selassie — A91

1966, Nov. 1 Unwmk. *Perf. 12*
463 A91 10c black, gold & grn .40 .25
464 A91 15c black, gold & dp car .70 .25
465 A91 40c black & gold 2.00 .65
Nos. 463-465 (3) 3.10 1.15

50 years of leadership of Emperor Haile Selassie.

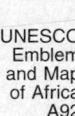

UNESCO Emblem and Map of Africa A92

Wmk. 282
1966, Nov. 30 Litho. *Perf. 13½*
466 A92 15c blue car & blk .50 .25
467 A92 60c olive, brn & dk bl 2.50 .60

20th anniv. of UNESCO.

WHO Headquarters, Geneva — A93

1966, Nov. 30
468 A93 5c olive, ultra & brn .80 .25
469 A93 40c brown, pur & emer 2.50 .35

Opening of WHO Headquarters, Geneva.

Expo '67 Ethiopian Pavilion and Columns of Axum (Replica) — A94

Perf. 12x13½
1967, May 2 Photo. Unwmk.
470 A94 30c brt blue & multi .65 .30
471 A94 45c multicolored .85 .40
472 A94 80c gray & multi 1.50 .60
Nos. 470-472 (3) 3.00 1.30

EXPO '67, Intl. Exhibition, Montreal, Apr. 28-Oct. 27, 1967.

Diesel Train and Map — A95

1967, June 7 Photo. *Perf. 12*
473 A95 15c multicolored 1.10 .55
474 A95 30c multicolored 2.75 1.40
475 A95 50c multicolored 3.75 1.75
Nos. 473-475 (3) 7.60 3.70

Djibouti-Addis Ababa railroad, 50th anniv.

Papilionidae Aethiops — A96

Various Butterflies.

Perf. 13½x13
1967, June 30 Photo. Unwmk.
476 A96 5c buff & multi .60 .25
477 A96 10c lilac & multi 2.00 .40
478 A96 20c multicolored 2.75 .75
479 A96 35c blue & multi 4.75 1.50
480 A96 40c multicolored 7.75 2.00
Nos. 476-480 (5) 17.85 4.90

Emperor Haile Selassie and Lion of Judah A97

1967, July 21 *Perf. 11½*
Granite Paper
481 A97 10c dk brn, emer & gold .45 .25
482 A97 15c dk brn, yel & gold .80 .25
483 A97 $1 dk brn, red & gold 3.50 1.50
Nos. 481-483 (3) 4.75 2.00

Souvenir Sheet
484 A97 $1 dk brn, pur & gold 15.00 15.00

75th birthday of Emperor Haile Selassie.

Microscope and Ethiopian Flag — A98

1967, Nov. 6 Litho. *Perf. 13*
Flag in Grn, Yel, Red & Blk
485 A98 5c blue .25 .25
486 A98 30c ocher 1.00 .30
487 A98 $1 violet 2.75 .95
Nos. 485-487 (3) 4.00 1.50

2nd Intl. Conf. on the Global Impact of Applied Microbiology, Addis Ababa, 11/6-12.

Wall Painting from Debre Berhan Selassie Church, Gondar, 17th Century — A99

ITY Emblem and: 25c, Votive throne from Atsbe Dera, 4th Cent. B.C., vert. 35c, Prehistoric cave painting, Harar Province. 50c, Prehistoric stone tools, Melke Kontoure, vert.

1967, Nov. 20 Photo. *Perf. 14½*
488 A99 15c multicolored 2.75 1.40
489 A99 25c yel grn, buff & blk 3.00 1.40
490 A99 35c green, brn & blk 2.75 1.75
491 A99 50c yellow & blk 5.00 2.75
Nos. 488-491 (4) 13.50 7.30

International Tourist Year, 1967.

A100

A101

Crosses of Lalibela: 5c, Processional Bronze Cross, Biet-Maryam Church. 10c, Processional copper cross. 15c, Copper cross, Biet-Maryam church. 20c, Lalibela-style cross. 50c, Chiseled copper cross, Madhani Alem church.

1967, Dec. 7 Photo. *Perf. 14½*
Crosses in Silver
492 A100 5c yellow & blk .40 .25
493 A100 10c red orange & blk .40 .25
494 A100 15c violet & blk .50 .25
495 A100 20c brt rose & blk .95 .25
496 A100 50c orange yel & blk 3.00 .60
Nos. 492-496 (5) 5.25 1.60

Perf. 14x13½
1968, Apr. 18 Litho. Unwmk.

Designs: 10c, Emperor Theodore (1818?-1868). 20c, Emperor Theodore and lions, horiz. 50c, Imperial crown.

497 A101 10c lt vio, ocher & brn .55 .25
498 A101 20c lilac, brn & dk vio 1.25 .25
499 A101 50c dk grn, org & rose cl 2.75 .75
Nos. 497-499 (3) 4.55 1.25

Human Rights Flame A102

1968, May 31 Unwmk. *Perf. 14½*
500 A102 15c pink, red & blk .55 .55
501 A102 $1 lt bl, brt bl & blk 2.40 2.40

International Human Rights Year, 1968.

Shah Mohammed Reza Pahlavi, Emperor and Flags — A103

1968, June 3 Litho. *Perf. 13½*
502 A103 5c multicolored .25 .25
503 A103 15c multicolored .30 .30
504 A103 30c multicolored 1.25 1.25
Nos. 502-504 (3) 1.80 1.80

Visit of Shah Mohammed Riza Pahlavi of Iran.

Emperor Haile Selassie Appealing to League of Nations, 1935 — A104

35c, African Unity Building and map of Africa. $1, World map, symbolizing intl. relations.

1968, July 22 Photo. *Perf. 14x13½*
505 A104 15c bl, red, blk & gold .40 .25
506 A104 35c blk, emer, red & gold .75 .75
507 A104 $1 dk bl, lil, blk & gold 2.50 2.75
Nos. 505-507 (3) 3.65 3.75

Ethiopia's struggle for peace. Issued with tabs on bottom row. Value, set $10.

WHO Emblem A105

Perf. 14x13½
1968, Aug. 30 Litho. Unwmk.
508 A105 15c brt green & blk .35 .35
509 A105 60c red lilac & blk 1.90 1.90

20th anniv. of the WHO.

Abebe Bikila, Marathon Runner A106

1968, Oct. 12 *Perf. 11½*
510 A106 10c shown .25 .25
511 A106 15c Soccer .40 .40
512 A106 20c Boxing .50 .50
513 A106 40c Basketball 1.25 1.25
514 A106 50c Bicycling 1.90 1.90
Nos. 510-514 (5) 4.30 4.30

19th Olympic Games, Mexico City, 10/12-27.

Arrussi Woman — A107

Regional Costumes: 15c, Man from Gemu Gefa. 20c, Gojam man. 30c, Kefa man. 35c, Harar woman. 50c, Ilubabor grass coat. 60c, Woman from Eritrea.

Perf. 13½x13

1968, Dec. 10 Photo. Unwmk.

515	A107	5c silver & multi	.65	.25
516	A107	15c silver & multi	.65	.25
517	A107	20c silver & multi	.65	.25
518	A107	30c silver & multi	.85	.55
519	A107	35c silver & multi	1.00	.65
520	A107	50c silver & multi	2.00	1.10
521	A107	60c silver & multi	2.75	1.60
		Nos. 515-521 (7)	8.55	4.65

See Nos. 575-581.

Message Stick and Amharic Postal Emblem A108

1969, Mar. 10 Litho. *Perf. 14*

522	A108	10c emerald, blk & brn	.70	.70
523	A108	15c yellow, blk & brn	.70	.70
524	A108	35c multicolored	1.25	1.25
		Nos. 522-524 (3)	2.65	2.65

Ethiopian postal service, 75th anniv.

ILO Emblem A109

1969, Apr. 11 Litho. *Perf. 14½*

525	A109	15c orange & blk	.50	.50
526	A109	60c emerald & blk	2.00	2.00

50th anniv. of the ILO.

Dove, Red Cross, Crescent, Lion and Sun Emblems A110

1969, May 8 Wmk. 282 *Perf. 13*

527	A110	5c lt ultra, blk & red	.25	.25
528	A110	15c lt ultra, grn & red	.65	.65
529	A110	30c lt ultra, vio bl & red	1.40	1.40
		Nos. 527-529 (3)	2.30	2.30

League of Red Cross Societies, 50th anniv.

Endybis Silver Coin, 3rd Century — A111

Ancient Ethiopian Coins: 10c, Gold of Ezana, 4th cent. 15c, Gold of Kaleb, 6th cent. 30c, Bronze of Armah, 7th cent. 40c, Bronze of Wazena, 7th cent. 50c, Silver of Gersem, 8th cent.

1969, June 19 Photo. *Perf. 14½*

530	A111	5c ultra, blk & sil	.25	.25
531	A111	10c brt red, blk & gold	.45	.45
532	A111	15c brown, blk & gold	.70	.70
533	A111	30c dp car, blk & brnz	1.25	1.25
534	A111	40c dk green, blk & brnz	1.50	1.50
535	A111	50c dp violet, blk & sil	2.40	2.40
		Nos. 530-535 (6)	6.55	6.55

Zebras and Tourist Year Emblem A112

Designs: 10c, Camping. 15c, Fishing. 20c, Water skiing. 25c, Mountaineering, vert.

Perf. 13x13½, 13½x13

1969, Aug. 29 Litho. Unwmk.

536	A112	5c multicolored	.40	.40
537	A112	10c multicolored	.40	.40
538	A112	15c multicolored	1.10	1.25
539	A112	20c multicolored	2.25	2.50
540	A112	25c multicolored	2.50	3.50
		Nos. 536-540 (5)	6.65	8.05

International Year of African Tourism.

Stylized Bird and UN Emblem A113

UN 25th anniv.: 30c, Stylized flowers, UN and peace emblems, vert. 60c, Stylized bird, UN emblem and plane.

1969, Oct. 24 Unwmk. *Perf. 11½*

541	A113	10c lt blue & multi	.25	.25
542	A113	30c lt blue & multi	.80	.80
543	A113	60c lt blue & multi	2.00	2.00
		Nos. 541-543 (3)	3.05	3.05

Ancient Cross and Holy Family A114

Designs: Various ancient crosses.

Perf. 14½x13½

1969, Dec. 10 Photo.

544	A114	5c black, yel & dk bl	.25	.25
545	A114	10c black & yellow	.25	.30
546	A114	25c black, yel & grn	1.10	1.40
547	A114	60c black & ocher	2.75	3.00
		Nos. 544-547 (4)	4.35	4.95

Ancient Figurines — A115

Ancient Ethiopian Pottery: 20c, Vases, Yeha period, 4th-3rd centuries B.C. 25c, Vases and jugs, Axum, 4th-6th centuries A.D. 35c, Bird-shaped jug and jugs, Matara, 4th-6th centuries A.D. 60c, Decorated pottery, Adulis, 6th-7th centuries A.D.

1970, Feb. 6 Photo. *Perf. 14½*

548	A115	10c black & multi	.55	.55
549	A115	20c black & multi	.55	.55
550	A115	25c black & multi	.55	.55
551	A115	35c black & multi	1.25	1.25
552	A115	60c black & multi	2.25	2.25
		Nos. 548-552 (5)	5.15	5.15

Medhane Alem Church — A116

Rock Churches of Lalibela, 12th-13th Centuries: 10c, Bieta Emmanuel. 15c, The four Rock Churches of Lalibela. 20c, Bieta Mariam. 50c, Bieta Giorgis.

1970, Apr. 15 Unwmk. *Perf. 13*

553	A116	5c brown & multi	.25	.25
554	A116	10c brown & multi	.25	.25
555	A116	15c brown & multi	.40	.40
556	A116	20c brown & multi	.65	.65
557	A116	50c brown & multi	1.50	1.50
		Nos. 553-557 (5)	3.05	3.05

Sailfish Tang A117

Tropical Fish: 10c, Undulate triggerfish. 15c, Orange butterflyfish. 25c, Butterflyfish. 50c, Imperial Angelfish.

1970, June 19 Photo. *Perf. 12½*

558	A117	5c multicolored	.25	.25
559	A117	10c multicolored	.25	.25
560	A117	15c multicolored	.60	.60
561	A117	25c multicolored	1.50	1.50
562	A117	50c multicolored	3.00	3.00
		Nos. 558-562 (5)	5.60	5.60

Education Year Emblem — A118

1970, Aug. 14 Unwmk. *Perf. 13½*

563	A118	10c multicolored	.25	.25
564	A118	20c gold, ultra & emer	.45	.45
565	A118	50c gold, emer & org	1.40	1.40
		Nos. 563-565 (3)	2.10	2.10

Issued for International Education Year.

Map of Africa — A119

30c, Flag of Organization of African Unity. 40c, OAU Headquarters, Addis Ababa.

1970, Sept. 21 Photo. *Perf. 13½*

566	A119	20c multicolored	.55	.55
567	A119	30c multicolored	.70	.70
568	A119	40c green & multi	1.00	1.00
		Nos. 566-568 (3)	2.25	2.25

Africa Unity Day and Organization of African Unity.

Emperor Haile Selassie — A120

1970, Oct. 30 Unwmk. *Perf. 14½*

569	A120	15c Prus bl & multi	.30	.30
570	A120	50c multicolored	1.40	1.40
571	A120	60c multicolored	2.00	2.00
		Nos. 569-571 (3)	3.70	3.70

Coronation, 40th anniv.

Buildings — A121

1970, Dec. 30 Litho. *Perf. 13½*

572	A121	10c ver & multi	.25	.25
573	A121	50c brown & multi	1.25	1.25
574	A121	80c multicolored	2.00	2.00
		Nos. 572-574 (3)	3.50	3.50

Opening of new Posts, Telecommunications and General Post Office buildings.

Costume Type of 1968

Regional Costumes: 5c, Warrior from Begemdir and Semien. 10c, Woman from Bale. 15c, Warrior from Welega. 20c,Woman from Shoa. 25c, Man from Sidamo. 40c, Woman from Tigre. 50c, Man from Welo.

1971, Feb. 17 Photo. *Perf. 11½*

Granite Paper

575	A107	5c gold & multi	.35	.35
576	A107	10c gold & multi	.35	.35
577	A107	15c gold & multi	.70	.70
578	A107	20c gold & multi	.85	.85
579	A107	25c gold & multi	1.10	1.10
580	A107	40c gold & multi	1.60	1.60
581	A107	50c gold & multi	3.00	3.00
		Nos. 575-581 (7)	7.95	7.95

Plane's Tail with Emblem — A122

Designs: 10c, Ethiopian scenes. 20c, Nose of Boeing 707. 60c, Pilots in cockpit, and engine. 80c, Globe with routes shown.

1971, Apr. 8 *Perf. 14½x14*

582	A122	5c multicolored	.70	.70
583	A122	10c multicolored	.70	.70
584	A122	20c multicolored	.90	.90
585	A122	60c multicolored	1.75	1.75
586	A122	80c multicolored	4.00	4.00
		Nos. 582-586 (5)	8.05	8.05

Ethiopian Airlines, 25th anniversary. Issued with tabs on bottom row. Value, set $11.

Fountain of Life, 15th Century Gospel Book — A123

Ethiopian Paintings: 10c, King David, 15th cent. manuscript. 25c, St. George, 17th cent. painting on canvas. 50c, King Lalibela, 18th cent. painting on wood. 60c, Yared singing before King Kaleb. Mural in Axum Cathedral.

1971, June 15 Photo. *Perf. 11½*
Granite Paper

587 A123 5c tan & multi .25 .25
588 A123 10c pale sal & multi .25 .25
589 A123 25c lemon & multi .60 .60
590 A123 50c yellow & multi 1.60 1.60
591 A123 60c gray & multi 2.50 2.50
Nos. 587-591 (5) 5.20 5.20

Black and White Heads, Globes A124

Designs: 60c, Black and white hand holding globe. 80c, Four races, globes.

1971, Aug. 31 Unwmk.

592 A124 10c org, red brn & blk .45 .45
593 A124 60c green, bl & blk 1.40 1.40
594 A124 80c bl, org, yel & blk 2.25 2.25
Nos. 592-594 (3) 4.10 4.10

Intl. Year Against Racial Discrimination.

Emperor Menelik II and Reading of Treaty of Ucciali A125

Contemporary Paintings: 30c, Menelik II on horseback gathering the tribes. 50c, Ethiopians and Italians in Battle of Adwa. 60c, Menelik II and Taitu at head of their armies.

1971, Oct. 20 Litho. *Perf. 13½*

595 A125 10c multicolored .35 .35
596 A125 30c multicolored .95 .95
597 A125 50c multicolored 1.40 1.40
598 A125 60c multicolored 2.40 2.40
Nos. 595-598 (4) 5.10 5.10

75th anniversary of victory of Adwa over the Italians, March 1, 1896.

Two telephones, 1897, Menelik II and Ras Makonnen — A126

Designs: 10c, Haile Selassie Broadcasting and Map of Ethiopia. 30c, Ethiopians around television set. 40c, Telephone microwave circuits. 60c, Map of Africa on globe and telephone dial.

1971, Nov. 2

599 A126 5c brown & multi .35 .35
600 A126 10c yellow & multi .35 .35
601 A126 30c vio bl & multi .65 .65
602 A126 40c black & multi 1.40 1.40
603 A126 60c vio bl & multi 2.75 2.75
Nos. 599-603 (5) 5.50 5.50

Telecommunications in Ethiopia, 75th anniv.

UNICEF Emblem, Mother and Child — A127

UNICEF Emblem and: 10c, Children drinking milk. 15c, Man holding sick child. 30c, Kindergarten class. 50c, Father and son.

1971, Dec. 15 Unwmk.

604 A127 5c yellow & multi .35 .35
605 A127 10c pale brn & multi .35 .35
606 A127 15c rose & multi .75 .75
607 A127 30c violet & multi 1.50 1.50
608 A127 50c green & multi 2.00 2.00
Nos. 604-608 (5) 4.95 4.95

25th anniv. of UNICEF.

Nos. 445-448 Overprinted

1972, Jan. 28 Photo. *Perf. 11*
Portrait in Black

609 A86 20c grn & pale yel .55 .55
610 A86 25c dk brn & yel 1.00 1.00
611 A86 30c maroon & gray 3.75 3.75
612 A86 35c dk blue & gray 3.75 3.75
Nos. 609-612 (4) 9.05 9.05

1st meeting of UN Security Council in Africa.

River Boat on Lake Haik — A128

1972, Feb. 7 Litho. *Perf. 11½*
Granite Paper

613 A128 10c shown .45 .45
614 A128 20c Boats on Lake Abaya .85 .85
615 A128 30c on Lake Tana 1.60 1.60
616 A128 60c on Baro River 2.75 2.75
Nos. 613-616 (4) 5.65 5.65

Proclamation of Cyrus the Great — A129

1972, Mar. 28 Photo. *Perf. 14x14½*

617 A129 10c red & multi .50 .50
618 A129 60c emerald & multi 2.00 2.00
619 A129 80c gray & multi 3.00 3.00
Nos. 617-619 (3) 5.50 5.50

2500th anniversary of the founding of the Persian empire by Cyrus the Great.

Houses, Sidamo Province A130

Ethiopian Architecture: 10c, Tigre Province. 20c, Eritrea Province. 40c, Addis Ababa. 80c, Shoa Province.

1972, Apr. 11 Litho. *Perf. 13½*

620 A130 5c black & multi .30 .30
621 A130 10c black, gray & brn .30 .30
622 A130 20c black & multi .65 .65
623 A130 40c black, bl grn & brn 1.10 1.10
624 A130 80c black, brn & red brn 2.75 2.75
Nos. 620-624 (5) 5.10 5.10

Hands Holding Map of Ethiopia — A131

10c, Hands shielding Ethiopians. 25c, Map of Africa, hands reaching for African Unity emblem. 50c, Brown & white hands clasped, UN emblem. 60c, Hands protecting dove. Each denomination shows different portrait of the Emperor.

Perf. 14½x14
1972, July 21 Litho. Unwmk.

625 A131 5c scarlet & multi .35 .35
626 A131 10c ultra & multi .35 .35
627 A131 25c vio bl & multi .60 .60
628 A131 50c lt blue & multi 1.25 1.25
629 A131 60c brown & multi 1.50 1.50
Nos. 625-629 (5) 4.05 4.05

80th birthday of Emperor Haile Selassie.

Running, Flags of Mexico, Japan, Italy — A132

1972, Aug. 25 *Perf. 13½x13*

630 A132 10c shown .45 .45
631 A132 30c Soccer 1.00 1.00
632 A132 50c Bicycling 1.90 1.90
633 A132 60c Boxing 2.75 2.75
Nos. 630-633 (4) 6.10 6.10

20th Olympic Games, Munich, Germany, Aug. 26-Sept. 11.

Open Bible, Cross and Orbit A133

Designs: 50c, First and 1972 headquarters of the British and Foreign Bible Society, vert. 80c, First Amharic Bible.

1972, Sept. 25 Photo. *Perf. 13½*

634 A133 20c deep red & multi .60 .60
635 A133 50c deep red & multi 2.10 2.10
636 A133 80c deep red & multi 2.75 2.75
Nos. 634-636 (3) 5.45 5.45

United Bible Societies World Assembly, Addis Ababa, Sept. 1972.

Security Council Meeting A134

Designs: 60c, Building where Security Council met. 80c, Map of Africa with flags of participating members.

1972, Nov. 1 Litho. *Perf. 13½*

637 A134 10c lt bl & vio bl .25 .25
638 A134 60c multicolored 1.25 1.25
639 A134 80c multicolored 2.00 2.00
Nos. 637-639 (3) 3.50 3.50

First United Nations Security Council meeting, Addis Ababa, Jan. 28-Feb. 4, 1972.

Fish in Polluted Sea A135

Designs: 30c, Fisherman, beacon, family. 80c, Polluted seashore.

1973, Feb. 23 Photo. *Perf. 13½*

640 A135 20c gold & multi .50 .50
641 A135 30c gold & multi .85 .85
642 A135 80c gold & multi 2.00 2.00
Nos. 640-642 (3) 3.35 3.35

World message from the sea, Ethiopian anti-pollution campaign.

INTERPOL and Ethiopian Police Emblems — A136

50c, INTERPOL emblem & General Secretariat, Paris. 60c, INTERPOL emblem.

1973, Mar. 20 Photo. *Perf. 13½*

643 A136 40c dull orange & blk 1.25 1.25
644 A136 50c blue, blk & yel 1.75 1.75
645 A136 60c dk carmine & blk 2.00 2.00
Nos. 643-645 (3) 5.00 5.00

50th anniversary of International Criminal Police Organization (INTERPOL).

Virgin of Emperor Zara Yaqob — A137

Ethiopian Art: 15c, Crucifixion, Zara Yaqob period. 30c, Virgin and Child, from Entoto Mariam Church. 40c, Christ, contemporary mosaic. 80c, The Evangelists, contemporary bas-relief.

1973, May 15 Photo. *Perf. 11½*

Granite Paper

646	A137	5c	brown & multi	.30	.30
647	A137	15c	dp blue & multi	.55	.55
648	A137	30c	gray grn & multi	1.10	1.10
649	A137	40c	multicolored	1.40	1.40
650	A137	80c	slate & multi	3.50	3.50
			Nos. 646-650 (5)	6.85	6.85

Free African States in 1963 and 1973 A138

Designs (Map of Africa and): 10c, Flags of OAU members. 20c, Symbols of progress. 40c, Dove and people. 80c, Emblems of various UN agencies.

1973 May 25 *Perf. 14½x14*

651	A138	5c	red & multi	.25	.25
652	A138	10c	ol gray & multi	.30	.30
653	A138	20c	green & multi	.45	.45
654	A138	40c	sepia & multi	1.25	1.25
655	A138	80c	lt blue & multi	2.50	2.50
			Nos. 651-655 (5)	4.75	4.75

OAU, 10th anniv.

Scouts Saluting Ethiopian and Scout Flags — A139

Designs: 15c, Road and road sign. 30c, Girl Scout reading to old man. 40c, Scout and disabled people. 60c, Ethiopian Boy Scout.

1973, July 10 Photo. *Perf. 11½*

Granite Paper

656	A139	5c	blue & multi	.45	.45
657	A139	15c	lt green & multi	.65	.65
658	A139	30c	yellow & multi	1.25	1.25
659	A139	40c	crimson & multi	1.60	1.60
660	A139	60c	violet & multi	3.50	3.50
			Nos. 656-660 (5)	7.45	7.45

24th Boy Scout World Conference, Nairobi, Kenya, July 16-21.

WMO Emblem A140

50c, WMO emblem, anemometer. 60c, Weather satellite over earth, WMO emblem.

1973, Sept. 4 Photo. *Perf. 13½*

661	A140	40c	black, bl & dl bl	1.20	1.20
662	A140	50c	dull blue & blk	1.50	1.50
663	A140	60c	dull blue & multi	2.40	2.40
			Nos. 661-663 (3)	5.10	5.10

Cent. of intl. meteorological cooperation.

Printed with tabs at top of sheet inscribed in Amharic and tabs at bottom with "ETHIOPIA."

Ras Makonnen, Duke of Harar — A141

Human Rights Flame — A142

5c, Old wall of Harar. 20c, Operating room. 40c, Boy Scouts learning 1st aid & hospital. 80c, Prince Makonnen & hospital.

1973, Nov. 1 Unwmk. *Perf. 14½*

664	A141	5c	gray & multi	.30	.30
665	A141	10c	red brn & multi	.30	.30
666	A141	20c	green & multi	1.10	1.10
667	A141	40c	brown red & multi	2.50	2.50
668	A141	80c	ultra & multi	4.50	4.50
			Nos. 664-668 (5)	8.70	8.70

Opening of Ras Makonnen Memorial Hospital.

Perf. 11½

1973, Nov. 16 Photo. Unwmk.

Granite Paper

669	A142	40c	yel, gold & dk grn	.70	.70
670	A142	50c	lt grn, gold & dk grn	1.00	1.00
671	A142	60c	org, gold & dk grn	1.25	1.25
			Nos. 669-671 (3)	2.95	2.95

25th anniversary of the Universal Declaration of Human Rights.

Emperor Haile Selassie — A143

1973, Nov. 5 Photo. *Perf. 11½*

672	A143	5c	yellow & multi	.35	.30
673	A143	10c	brt blue & multi	.35	.30
674	A143	15c	green & multi	.45	.40
675	A143	20c	dull yel & multi	.55	.40
676	A143	25c	multicolored	.65	.40
677	A143	30c	multicolored	.80	.40
678	A143	35c	multicolored	.85	.40
679	A143	40c	ultra & multi	.95	.40
680	A143	45c	multicolored	1.10	.50
681	A143	50c	orange & multi	1.25	.50
682	A143	55c	magenta & multi	1.60	.85
683	A143	60c	multicolored	1.75	1.10
684	A143	70c	red org & multi	2.10	1.25
685	A143	90c	brt vio & multi	2.75	1.40
686	A143	$1	multicolored	3.25	1.90
687	A143	$2	orange & multi	6.25	3.25
688	A143	$3	multicolored	10.50	5.00
689	A143	$5	multicolored	17.00	8.25
			Nos. 672-689 (18)	52.50	27.00

Wicker Furniture A144

Designs: Various wicker baskets, wall hangings, dinnerware.

1974, Jan. 31 Photo. *Perf. 11½*

Granite Paper

690	A144	5c	violet bl & multi	.25	.25
691	A144	10c	violet bl & multi	.30	.30
692	A144	30c	violet bl & multi	.90	.90
693	A144	50c	violet bl & multi	1.40	1.40
694	A144	60c	violet bl & multi	1.75	1.75
			Nos. 690-694 (5)	4.60	4.60

Cow, Calf, Syringe — A145

Designs: 15c, Inoculation of cattle. 20c, Bullock and syringe. 50c, Laboratory technician, cow's head, syringe. 60c, Map of Ethiopia, cattle, syringe.

1974, Feb. 20 Litho. *Perf. 13½x13*

695	A145	5c	sepia & multi	.25	.25
696	A145	15c	ultra & multi	.40	.40
697	A145	20c	ultra & multi	.50	.50
698	A145	50c	orange & multi	1.40	1.40
699	A145	60c	gold & multi	1.75	1.75
			Nos. 695-699 (5)	4.30	4.30

Campaign against cattle plague.

Umbrella Makers A146

Designs: 30c, Weaving. 50c, Child care. 60c, Foundation headquarters.

1974, Apr. 17 Photo. *Perf. 14½*

700	A146	10c	lt lilac & multi	.30	.30
701	A146	30c	multicolored	.45	.45
702	A146	50c	multicolored	1.10	1.10
703	A146	60c	blue & multi	1.25	1.25
			Nos. 700-703 (4)	3.10	3.10

20th anniv. of Haile Selassie Foundation.

Ceremonial Robe — A147

Designs: Ceremonial robes.

1974, June 26 Litho. *Perf. 13*

704	A147	15c	multicolored	.40	.40
705	A147	25c	ocher & multi	.60	.60
706	A147	35c	green & multi	1.10	1.10
707	A147	40c	lt brown & multi	1.25	1.25
708	A147	60c	gray & multi	2.50	2.50
			Nos. 704-708 (5)	5.85	5.85

World Population Statistics — A148

Designs: 50c, "Larger families-lower living standard." 60c, Rising population graph.

1974, Aug. 19 Photo. *Perf. 14½*

709	A148	40c	yellow & multi	1.10	1.10
710	A148	50c	violet & multi	1.25	.125
711	A148	60c	green & multi	1.50	1.50
			Nos. 709-711 (3)	3.85	2.73

World Population Year 1974.

UPU Emblem, Letter Carrier's Staff — A149

Celebration Around "Damara" Pillar — A150

UPU Emblem and: 50c, Letters and flags. 60c, Globe. 70c, Headquarters, Bern.

1974, Oct. 9 Photo. *Perf. 11½*

Granite Paper

712	A149	15c	yellow & multi	.50	.30
713	A149	50c	multicolored	1.35	.85
714	A149	60c	ultra & multi	1.75	1.10
715	A149	70c	multicolored	2.00	1.25
			Nos. 712-715 (4)	5.60	3.50

Centenary of Universal Postal Union.

1974, Dec. 17 Photo. *Perf. 14x14½*

5c, Site of Gishen Mariam Monastery. 20c, Cross and festivities. 80c, Torch (Chibos) Parade.

716	A150	5c	yellow & multi	.40	.40
717	A150	10c	yellow & multi	.45	.45
718	A150	20c	yellow & multi	.55	.55
719	A150	80c	yellow & multi	2.25	2.25
			Nos. 716-719 (4)	3.65	3.65

Meskel Festival, Sept. 26-27, commemorating the finding in the 4th century of the True Cross, of which a fragment is kept at Gishen Mariam Monastery in Welo Province.

Precis Clelia — A151

Adoration of the Kings — A152

Butterflies: 25c, Charaxes achaemenes. 45c, Papilio dardanus. 50c, Charaxes druceanus. 60c, Papilio demodocus.

1975, Feb. 18 Photo. *Perf. 12x12½*

720	A151	10c	silver & multi	1.00	.35
721	A151	25c	gold & multi	1.50	.75
722	A151	45c	purple & multi	3.00	1.75
723	A151	50c	green & multi	3.50	2.50
724	A151	60c	brt blue & multi	5.00	3.00
			Nos. 720-724 (5)	14.00	8.35

1975, Apr. 23 Photo. *Perf. 11½*

10c, Baptism of Jesus. 15c, Jesus teaching in the Temple. 30c, Jesus giving sight to the blind. 40c, Crucifixion. 80c, Resurrection.

Granite Paper

725	A152	5c	brown & multi	.35	.35
726	A152	10c	black & multi	.40	.40
727	A152	15c	dk brown & multi	.45	.45
728	A152	30c	dk brown & multi	.70	.70
729	A152	40c	black & multi	1.25	1.25
730	A152	80c	slate & multi	2.40	2.40
			Nos. 725-730 (6)	5.55	5.55

Murals from Ethiopian churches.

Wild Animals A153

1975, May 27 Photo. *Perf. 11½*

Granite Paper

731	A153	5c	Warthog	.75	.75
732	A153	10c	Aardvark	.75	.75
733	A153	20c	Semien wolf	1.10	1.10
734	A153	40c	Gelada baboon	2.10	2.10
735	A153	80c	Civet	4.25	4.25
			Nos. 731-735 (5)	8.95	8.95

"Peace," Dove, Globe, IWY Emblem — A154

50c, Symbols of development. 90c, Equality between men and women.

1975, June 30 Litho. *Perf. 14x14½*
736 A154 40c blue & black .70 .70
737 A154 50c salmon & multi .90 .90
738 A154 90c multicolored 1.75 1.75
Nos. 736-738 (3) 3.35 3.35

International Women's Year 1975.

Postal Museum A155

Various interior views of Postal Museum.

1975, Aug. 19 Photo. *Perf. 13x12½*
739 A155 10c ocher & multi .35 .30
740 A155 30c pink & multi .65 .50
741 A155 60c multicolored 1.50 1.10
742 A155 70c lt green & multi 1.75 1.25
Nos. 739-742 (4) 4.25 3.15

Ethiopian Natl. Postal Museum, opening.

Map of Ethiopia and Sun — A156

1975, Sept. 11 Photo. *Perf. 11½*
Granite Paper
743 A156 5c lilac & multi .25 .25
744 A156 10c ultra & multi .25 .25
745 A156 25c brown & multi .35 .35
746 A156 50c yellow & multi .90 .90
747 A156 90c brt green & multi 1.75 1.75
Nos. 743-747 (5) 3.50 3.50

1st anniv. of Ethiopian revolution.

UN Emblem A157

1975, Oct. 24 Photo. *Perf. 11½*
748 A157 40c lilac & multi .90 .90
749 A157 50c multicolored 1.00 1.00
750 A157 90c blue & multi 2.00 2.00
Nos. 748-750 (3) 3.90 3.90

United Nations, 30th anniversary.

Regional Hair Styles — A158

Delphinium Wellbyi — A159

1975, Dec. 15 Photo. *Perf. 11½*
751 A158 5c Ilubabor .30 .30
752 A158 15c Arusi .40 .40
753 A158 20c Eritrea .60 .60
754 A158 30c Bale .85 .85
755 A158 35c Kefa 1.00 1.00
756 A158 50c Begemir 1.40 1.40
757 A158 60c Shoa 1.75 1.75
Nos. 751-757 (7) 6.30 6.30

See Nos. 832-838.

1976, Jan. 15 Photo. *Perf. 11½*

Flowers: 10c, Plectocephalus varians. 20c, Brachystelma asmarensis, horiz. 40c, Ceropegia inflata. 80c, Erythrina brucei.

758 A159 5c multicolored .35 .35
759 A159 10c multicolored .40 .40
760 A159 20c multicolored .60 .60
761 A159 40c multicolored 1.50 1.50
762 A159 80c multicolored 2.50 2.50
Nos. 758-762 (5) 5.35 5.35

Goalkeeper, Map of Africa, Games' Emblem A160

Designs: Various scenes from soccer, map of Africa and ball.

1976, Feb. 27 Photo. *Perf. 14½*
763 A160 5c orange & multi .25 .25
764 A160 10c yellow & multi .35 .35
765 A160 25c lilac & multi .70 .70
766 A160 50c green & multi 1.50 1.50
767 A160 90c brt grn & multi 3.00 3.00
Nos. 763-767 (5) 5.80 5.80

10th African Cup of Nations, Addis Ababa and Dire Dawa, Feb. 29-Mar. 14.

Telephones, 1876 and 1976 — A161

Ethiopian Jewelry — A162

Designs: 60c, Alexander Graham Bell. 90c, Transmission tower.

1976, Mar. 10 Litho. *Perf. 12x13½*
768 A161 30c lt ocher & multi .85 .75
769 A161 60c emerald & multi 1.75 1.25
770 A161 90c ver, blk & buff 2.75 2.00
Nos. 768-770 (3) 5.35 4.00

Centenary of first telephone call by Alexander Graham Bell, Mar. 10, 1876.

1976, May 14 Photo. *Perf. 11½*

Designs: Women wearing various kinds of Ethiopian jewelry.

Granite Paper
771 A162 5c blue & multi .25 .25
772 A162 10c plum & multi .35 .25
773 A162 20c gray & multi .75 .50
774 A162 40c green & multi 1.25 .90
775 A162 80c orange & multi 2.50 1.75
Nos. 771-775 (5) 5.10 3.65

Boxing — A163

Hands Holding Map of Ethiopia — A164

Designs (Montreal Olympic Emblem and): 80c, Runner and maple leaf. 90c, Bicycling.

1976, July 15 Litho. *Perf. 12½x12*
776 A163 10c multicolored .50 .40
777 A163 80c brt red, blk & grn 2.25 1.75
778 A163 90c brt red & multi 2.75 2.00
Nos. 776-778 (3) 5.50 4.15

21st Olympic Games, Montreal, Canada, July 17-Aug. 1.

1976, Aug. 5 Photo. *Perf. 14½*
779 A164 5c rose & multi .25 .25
780 A164 10c olive & multi .30 .25
781 A164 25c orange & multi .40 .30
782 A164 50c multicolored .95 .70
783 A164 90c dk blue & multi 1.75 1.40
Nos. 779-783 (5) 3.65 2.90

Development through cooperation.

Revolution Emblem: Eye and Map A165

1976, Sept. 9 Photo. *Perf. 13½*
784 A165 5c multicolored .25 .25
785 A165 10c multicolored .30 .25
786 A165 25c multicolored .40 .30
787 A165 50c yellow & multi .95 .70
788 A165 90c green & multi 1.60 1.25
Nos. 784-788 (5) 3.50 2.75

2nd anniversary of the revolution.

Sunburst Around Crest — A166

1976, Sept. 13 Photo. *Perf. 11½*
789 A166 5c green, gold & blk .25 .25
790 A166 10c org, gold & blk .25 .25
791 A166 15c grnsh bl, gold & blk .40 .25
792 A166 20c lilac, gold & blk .50 .25
793 A166 25c brt grn, gold & blk .60 .25
794 A166 30c car, gold & blk .75 .25
795 A166 35c yel, gold & blk .90 .25
796 A166 40c ol, gold & blk 1.00 .40
797 A166 45c brt grn, gold & blk 1.10 .50
798 A166 50c car rose, gold & blk 1.25 .70
799 A166 55c ultra, gold & blk 1.50 .90
800 A166 60c fawn, gold & blk 1.75 .90
801 A166 70c rose, gold & blk 2.00 .90
802 A166 90c blue, gold & blk 2.25 .90
803 A166 $1 dull grn, gold & blk 2.75 1.00
804 A166 $2 gray, gold & blk 6.00 2.00
805 A166 $3 brn vio, gold & blk 8.00 3.25
806 A166 $5 slate bl, gold & blk 12.00 5.00
Nos. 789-806 (18) 43.25 18.20

Denomination Expressed as "BIRR"

1983, June 16
806A A166 1b dull grn, gold & blk 15.00 2.25
806B A166 2b gray, gold & blk 37.50 4.50
806C A166 3b brn vio, gold & blk 45.00 6.25

Plane Over Man with Donkey — A167

10c, Globe showing routes. 25c, Crew and passengers forming star. 50c, Propeller and jet engine. 90c, Airplanes surrounding map of Ethiopia.

1976, Oct. 28 Litho. *Perf. 12x12½*
807 A167 5c dull bl & multi .40 .30
808 A167 10c lilac & multi .50 .35
809 A167 25c multicolored .70 .50
810 A167 50c orange & multi 1.40 1.25
811 A167 90c olive & multi 2.75 2.25
Nos. 807-811 (5) 5.75 4.65

Ethiopian Airlines, 30th anniversary.

Tortoises — A168

Reptiles: 20c, Chameleon. 30c, Python. 40c, Monitor lizard. 80c, Nile crocodiles.

1976, Dec. 15 Photo. *Perf. 14½*
812 A168 10c multicolored .50 .40
813 A168 20c multicolored .75 .50
814 A168 30c multicolored 1.00 .80
815 A168 40c multicolored 1.50 1.10
816 A168 80c multicolored 3.00 2.25
Nos. 812-816 (5) 6.75 5.05

Hand Holding Makeshift Hammer — A169

Designs: 5c, Hands holding bowl and plane dropping food. 45c, Infant with empty bowl, and bank note. 60c, Map of affected area, footprints and tire tracks. 80c, Film strip, camera and Ethiopian sitting between eggshells.

1977, Jan. 20 Litho. *Perf. 12½*
817 A169 5c multicolored .30 .25
818 A169 10c multicolored .45 .40
819 A169 45c multicolored 1.25 .85
820 A169 60c multicolored 1.75 1.00
821 A169 80c multicolored 1.90 1.60
Nos. 817-821 (5) 5.65 4.10

Ethiopian Relief and Rehabilitation Commission for drought and disaster areas.

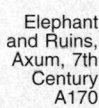

Elephant and Ruins, Axum, 7th Century A170

Designs: 10c, Ibex and temple, 5th century, B.C., Yeha. 25c, Megalithic dolmen and pottery, Sourre Kabanawa. 50c, Awash Valley, stone axe, Acheulean period. 80c, Omo Valley, hominid jawbone.

1977, Mar. 15 Photo. *Perf. 13½*
822 A170 5c gold & multi .50 .35
823 A170 10c gold & multi .60 .45
824 A170 25c gold & multi .75 .65
825 A170 50c gold & multi 1.25 1.10
826 A170 80c gold & multi 2.25 1.50
Nos. 822-826 (5) 5.35 4.05

Archaeological sites and finds in Ethiopia.

Map of Africa with Trans-East Highway — A171

1977, Mar. 30 *Perf. 14*
827 A171 10c gold & multi .40 .35
828 A171 20c gold & multi .50 .40
829 A171 40c gold & multi 1.25 .80
830 A171 50c gold & multi 1.50 1.00
831 A171 60c gold & multi 1.90 1.25
Nos. 827-831 (5) 5.55 3.80

Addis Ababa to Nairobi Highway and projected highways to Cairo, Egypt, and Gaborone, Botswana.

Hairstyle Type of 1975

1977, Apr. 28 Photo. *Perf. 11½*
832 A158 5c Welega .25 .25
833 A158 10c Gojam .30 .25
834 A158 15c Tigre .40 .35
835 A158 20c Harar .70 .65
836 A158 25c Gemu Gefa .85 .70

837	A158	40c Sidamo	1.40	1.25
838	A158	50c Welo	1.75	1.50
		Nos. 832-838 (7)	5.65	4.95

Addis Ababa A172

Towns of Ethiopia: 10c, Asmara. 25c, Harar. 50c, Jima. 90c, Dese.

1977, June 20 Photo. *Perf. 14½*

839	A172	5c silver & multi	.30	.25
840	A172	10c silver & multi	.40	.35
841	A172	25c silver & multi	.60	.55
842	A172	50c silver & multi	1.25	1.00
843	A172	90c silver & multi	2.25	1.50
		Nos. 839-843 (5)	4.80	3.65

Terebratula Abyssinica — A173

Fractured Imperial Crown — A174

Fossil Shells: 10c, Terebratula subalata. 25c, Cucullоea lefeburiaua. 50c, Ostrea plicatissima. 90c, Trigonia cousobrina.

1977, Aug. 15 Photo. *Perf. 14x13½*

844	A173	5c multicolored	.75	.25
845	A173	10c multicolored	1.25	.50
846	A173	25c multicolored	1.50	.85
847	A173	50c multicolored	2.50	1.50
848	A173	90c multicolored	4.00	2.50
		Nos. 844-848 (5)	10.00	5.60

1977, Sept. 9 Litho. *Perf. 15*

Designs: 10c, Symbol of the Revolution (spade, axe, torch). 25c, Warriors, hammer and sickle, map of Ethiopia. 60c, Soldier, farmer and map. 80c, Map and emblem of revolutionary government.

849	A174	5c multicolored	.25	.25
850	A174	10c multicolored	.40	.35
851	A174	25c multicolored	.50	.45
852	A174	60c multicolored	1.25	1.00
853	A174	80c multicolored	1.50	1.25
		Nos. 849-853 (5)	3.90	3.30

Third anniversary of the revolution.

Cicindela Petitii — A175

Lenin, Globe, Map of Ethiopia and Emblem — A176

Insects: 10c, Heliocopris dillonii. 25c, Poekilocerus vignaudii. 50c, Pepsis heros. 90c, Pepsis dedjaz.

1977, Sept. 30 Photo. *Perf. 14x13½*

854	A175	5c multicolored	.40	.40
855	A175	10c multicolored	.50	.50
856	A175	25c multicolored	1.00	1.00
857	A175	50c multicolored	2.50	2.50
858	A175	90c multicolored	3.75	3.75
		Nos. 854-858 (5)	8.15	8.15

1977, Nov. 15 Litho. *Perf. 12*

859	A176	5c orange & multi	.40	.25
860	A176	10c multicolored	.45	.35
861	A176	25c salmon & multi	.50	.40
862	A176	50c lt blue & multi	1.00	.85
863	A176	90c yellow & multi	1.75	1.25
		Nos. 859-863 (5)	4.10	3.10

60th anniv. of Russian October Revolution.

Chondrostoma Dilloni — A177

Salt-water Fish: 10c, Ostracion cubicus. 25c, Serranus summana. 50c, Serranus luti. 90c, Tetraodon maculatus.

1978, Jan. 20 Litho. *Perf. 15½*

864	A177	5c multicolored	.65	.65
865	A177	10c multicolored	.75	.75
866	A177	25c multicolored	1.25	1.25
867	A177	50c multicolored	2.25	2.25
868	A177	90c multicolored	4.00	4.00
		Nos. 864-868 (5)	8.90	8.90

Domestic Animals — A178

1978, Mar. 27 Litho. *Perf. 13½x14*

869	A178	5c Cattle	.25	.25
870	A178	10c Mules	.40	.25
871	A178	25c Goats	.75	.55
872	A178	50c Dromedaries	1.50	1.25
873	A178	90c Horses	2.75	2.25
		Nos. 869-873 (5)	5.65	4.55

Weapons and Shield, Map of Ethiopia — A179

Bronze Ibex, 5th Century B.C. — A180

"Call of the Motherland." (Map of Ethiopia and): 10c, Civilian fighters. 25c, Map of Africa. 60c, Soldiers. 80c, Red Cross nurse and wounded man.

1978, May 13 Litho. *Perf. 15½*

874	A179	5c multicolored	.30	.25
875	A179	10c multicolored	.40	.35
876	A179	25c multicolored	.70	.60
877	A179	60c multicolored	1.25	1.00
878	A179	80c multicolored	2.25	1.50
		Nos. 874-878 (5)	4.90	3.70

1978, June 21 Litho. *Perf. 15½*

Ancient Bronzes: 10c, Lion, Yeha, 5th cent. B.C., horiz. 25c, Lamp with ibex attacked by dog, Matara, 1st cent. B.C. 50c, Goat, Axum, 3rd cent. A.D., horiz. 90c, Ax, chisel and sickle, Yeha, 5th-4th centuries B.C.

879	A180	5c multicolored	.25	.25
880	A180	10c multicolored	.35	.30
881	A180	25c multicolored	.60	.50
882	A180	50c multicolored	1.50	1.25
883	A180	90c multicolored	2.50	1.75
		Nos. 879-883 (5)	5.20	4.05

See Nos. 1024-1027.

Globe and Argentina '78 Emblem A181

20c, Soccer player kicking ball. 30c, Two players embracing, net and ball. 55c, World map and ball. 70c, Soccer field, vert.

Perf. 14x13½, 13½x14

1978, July 19 Litho.

884	A181	5c multicolored	.45	.40
885	A181	20c multicolored	.70	.50
886	A181	30c multicolored	1.00	.65
887	A181	55c multicolored	1.75	1.25
888	A181	70c multicolored	2.25	1.75
		Nos. 884-888 (5)	6.15	4.55

11th World Cup Soccer Championship, Argentina, June 1-25.

Map of Africa, Oppressed African — A182

Namibia Day: 10c, Policeman pointing gun. 25c, Sniper with gun. 60c, African caught in net. 80c, Head of free man.

1978, Aug. 25 *Perf. 12½x13½*

889	A182	5c multicolored	.30	.25
890	A182	10c multicolored	.50	.45
891	A182	25c multicolored	.60	.50
892	A182	60c multicolored	1.50	1.00
893	A182	80c multicolored	2.25	1.50
		Nos. 889-893 (5)	5.15	3.70

Soldiers, Guerrilla and Jets A183

Design: 1b, People looking toward sun, crushing snake, flags.

1978, Sept. 8 Photo. *Perf. 14*

894	A183	80c multicolored	1.75	1.25
895	A183	1b multicolored	2.50	1.75

4th anniversary of revolution.

Hand and Globe with Tools — A184

Designs: 15c, Symbols of energy, communications, education, medicine, agriculture and industry. 25c, Cogwheels and world map. 60c, Globe and hands passing wrench. 70c, Flying geese and turtle over globe.

1978, Nov. 14 Litho. *Perf. 12x12½*

896	A184	10c multicolored	.30	.25
897	A184	15c multicolored	.35	.30
898	A184	25c multicolored	.55	.50
899	A184	60c multicolored	1.40	1.00
900	A184	70c multicolored	1.75	1.25
		Nos. 896-900 (5)	4.35	3.30

Technical Cooperation Among Developing Countries Conference, Buenos Aires, Argentina, Sept. 1978.

Human Rights Emblem — A185

1978, Dec. 7 Photo. *Perf. 12½x13½*

901	A185	5c multicolored	.30	.25
902	A185	15c multicolored	.30	.25
903	A185	25c multicolored	.45	.40
904	A185	35c multicolored	.75	.70
905	A185	1b multicolored	2.25	1.75
		Nos. 901-905 (5)	4.05	3.35

Declaration of Human Rights, 30th anniv.

Broken Chain, Anti-Apartheid Emblem — A186

1978, Dec. 28 Litho. *Perf. 12½x12*

906	A186	5c multicolored	.30	.25
907	A186	20c multicolored	.45	.40
908	A186	30c multicolored	.75	.65
909	A186	55c multicolored	1.25	1.00
910	A186	70c multicolored	1.50	1.25
		Nos. 906-910 (5)	4.25	3.55

Anti-Apartheid Year.

Stele from Osole — A187

Ancient Carved Stones, Soddo Region: 10c, Anthropomorphous stele, Gorashino. 25c, Leaning stone, Wado. 60c, Round stones, Ambeut. 80c, Bas-relief, Tiya.

1979, Jan. 25 *Perf. 14*

911	A187	5c multicolored	.30	.25
912	A187	10c multicolored	.40	.30
913	A187	25c multicolored	.65	.50
914	A187	60c multicolored	1.75	1.25
915	A187	80c multicolored	2.25	1.75
		Nos. 911-915 (5)	5.35	4.05

Cotton Plantation A188

Shemma Industry: 10c, Women spinning cotton yarn. 20c, Man reeling cotton. 65c, Weaver. 80c, Shemma (Natl. dress).

1979, Mar. 15 Litho. *Perf. 15½*

916	A188	5c multicolored	.40	.25
917	A188	10c multicolored	.45	.35
918	A188	20c multicolored	.60	.40
919	A188	65c multicolored	1.75	1.25
920	A188	80c multicolored	2.25	1.50
		Nos. 916-920 (5)	5.45	3.75

Ethiopian Trees — A189

1979, Apr. 26 Photo. *Perf. 13½x14*

921	A189	5c Grar	.35	.25
922	A189	10c Weira	.45	.30
923	A189	25c Tidh	.65	.40
924	A189	50c Shola	1.25	1.00
925	A189	90c Zigba	2.00	1.50
		Nos. 921-925 (5)	4.70	3.45

Agricultural Development A190

Revolutionary Development Campaign: 15c, Industry. 25c, Transportation and communication. 60c, Education and health. 70c, Commerce.

1979, July 3 Litho. *Perf. 12x12½*

926 A190 10c multicolored .30 .25
927 A190 15c multicolored .45 .30
928 A190 25c multicolored .60 .50
929 A190 60c multicolored 1.25 1.00
930 A190 70c multicolored 1.75 1.50
Nos. 926-930 (5) 4.35 3.55

IYC Emblem — A191

Intl. Year of the Child: 15c, Adults leading children. 25c, Adult helping child. 60c, IYC emblem surrounded by children. 70c, Adult and children embracing.

1979, Aug. 16 Litho. *Perf. 12x12½*

931 A191 10c multicolored .40 .35
932 A191 15c multicolored .50 .40
933 A191 25c multicolored .75 .65
934 A191 60c multicolored 1.75 1.40
935 A191 70c multicolored 2.00 1.75
Nos. 931-935 (5) 5.40 4.55

Guerrilla Fighters — A192

15c, Soldiers. 25c, Map of Africa within cogwheel, star. 60c, Students with book, torch. 70c, Family, hammer & sickle emblem.

1979, Sept. 11 Photo. *Perf. 14*

936 A192 10c multicolored .40 .35
937 A192 15c multicolored .50 .45
938 A192 25c multicolored .75 .65
939 A192 60c multicolored 1.75 1.25
940 A192 70c multicolored 2.25 1.75
Nos. 936-940 (5) 5.65 4.45

Fifth anniversary of revolution.

Telephone Receiver A193

Incense Container A194

Telecom Emblem and: 5c, Symbolic waves. 35c, Satellite beaming to earth. 45c, Dish antenna. 65c, Television cameraman.

1979, Sept. 20 Photo. *Perf. 11½*

941 A193 5c multicolored .35 .30
942 A193 30c multicolored .75 .60
943 A193 35c multicolored .95 .75
944 A193 45c multicolored 1.50 1.00
945 A193 65c multicolored 2.25 1.50
Nos. 941-945 (5) 5.80 4.15

3rd World Telecommunications Exhibition, Geneva, Sept. 20-26.

1979, Nov. 15 Litho. *Perf. 15*

946 A194 5c shown .45 .30
947 A194 10c Vase .85 .45
948 A194 25c Earthenware cover 1.25 .75
949 A194 60c Milk container 3.25 1.25
950 A194 80c Storage container 3.75 1.75
Nos. 946-950 (5) 9.55 4.50

Wooden Grain Bowl — A195

Lappet-faced Vulture — A196

1980, Jan. 3 Litho. *Perf. 13½x13*

951 A195 5c shown .50 .35
952 A195 30c Chair, stool .90 .50
953 A195 35c Mortar, pestle 1.00 .75
954 A195 45c Buckets 1.75 1.25
955 A195 65c Storage jars 2.75 2.00
Nos. 951-955 (5) 6.90 4.85

1980, Feb. 12 *Perf. 13½x14*

Birds of Prey: 15c, Long-crested hawk eagle. 25c, Secretary bird. 60c, Abyssinian long-eared owl. 70c, Lanner falcon.

956 A196 10c multicolored 1.25 1.25
957 A196 15c multicolored 1.50 1.50
958 A196 25c multicolored 2.25 2.25
959 A196 60c multicolored 4.00 4.00
960 A196 70c multicolored 6.00 6.00
Nos. 956-960 (5) 15.00 15.00

Fight Against Cigarette Smoking — A197

1980, Apr. 7 Photo. *Perf. 13x13½*

961 A197 20c shown 1.25 1.00
962 A197 60c Cigarette 1.75 1.25
963 A197 1b Respiratory system 3.00 2.50
Nos. 961-963 (3) 6.00 4.75

"110" and Lenin House Museum A198

Lenin, 110th "Birthday" (Paintings): 15c, In hiding. 20c, As a young man. 40c, Returning to Russia. 1b, Speaking on the Goelro Plan.

1980, Apr. 22 Litho. *Perf. 12x12½*

964 A198 5c multicolored .35 .30
965 A198 15c multicolored .40 .35
966 A198 20c multicolored .50 .45
967 A198 40c multicolored 1.20 .80
968 A198 1b multicolored 2.50 2.00
Nos. 964-968 (5) 4.95 3.90

Grévy's Zebras A199

1980, June 10 Litho. *Perf. 12½x12*

969 A199 10c shown .75 .75
970 A199 15c Gazelles 1.00 1.00
971 A199 25c Wild hunting dogs 1.50 1.50
972 A199 60c Swayne's hartebeests 2.75 2.75
973 A199 70c Cheetahs 6.00 6.00
Nos. 969-973 (5) 12.00 12.00

Runner, Moscow '80 Emblem — A200

1980, July 19 Photo. *Perf. 11½x12*

974 A200 30c shown 1.00 1.00
975 A200 70c Cycling 2.25 2.25
976 A200 80c Boxing 3.00 3.00
Nos. 974-976 (3) 6.25 6.25

22nd Summer Olympic Games, Moscow, July 19-Aug. 3.

Removing Blindfold — A201

Bamboo Folk Craft — A202

1980, Sept. 10 Photo. *Perf. 14x13½*

977 A201 30c shown .75 .50
978 A201 40c Revolutionary 1.00 .65
979 A201 50c Woman breaking chain 1.50 1.00
980 A201 70c Russian & Ethiopian flags 2.25 1.25
Nos. 977-980 (4) 5.50 3.40

6th anniversary of revolution.

1980, Oct. 23 Litho. *Perf. 14*

981 A202 5c Bamboo food basket .30 .25
982 A202 15c Lamp shade .40 .35
983 A202 25c Stool .75 .60
984 A202 35c Fruit basket 1.25 1.00
985 A202 1b Lamp shade 2.75 1.75
Nos. 981-985 (5) 5.45 3.95

Mekotkocha (Used in Weeding) A203

Traditional Harvesting Tools: 15c, Layda (grain separator). 40c, Mensh (fork). 45c, Mededekia (soil turner). 70c, Mofer & Kenber (plow and yoke).

1980, Dec. 18 Litho. *Perf. 12½x12*

986 A203 10c multicolored .30 .25
987 A203 15c multicolored .35 .30
988 A203 40c multicolored 2.00 .75
989 A203 45c multicolored 2.25 1.00
990 A203 70c multicolored 3.25 1.75
Nos. 986-990 (5) 8.15 4.05

Baro River Bridge Opening A204

1981, Feb. 28 Photo. *Perf. 13½x13*

991 A204 15c Canoes and ferry .50 .40
992 A204 65c Bridge construction 2.75 1.25
993 A204 1b shown 4.75 2.25
Nos. 991-993 (3) 8.00 3.90

Semien National Park — A205

World Heritage Year: 5c, Wawel Castle, Poland. 15c, Quito Cathedral, Ecuador. 20c, Old Slave Quarters, Goree Island, Senegal. 30c, Mesa Verde Indian Village, US. 1b, L'Anse aux Meadows excavation, Canada.

Perf. 11x11½, 11½x11

1981, Mar. 10 Photo.

994 A205 5c multicolored .40 .30
995 A205 15c multicolored .55 .45
996 A205 20c multicolored .70 .55
997 A205 30c multicolored 1.40 .75
998 A205 80c multicolored 3.50 1.50
999 A205 1b multicolored 4.50 2.25
Nos. 994-999 (6) 11.05 5.80

1981, June 16 Photo.

10c, Biet Medhanialem Church, Ethiopia. 15c, Nahanni Natl. Park, Canada. 20c, Yellowstone River Lower Falls, U.S. 30c, Aachen Cathedral, Germany. 80c, Kicker Rock, San Cristobal Island, Ecuador. 1b, The Lizak corridor, Holy Cross Chapel, Cracow, Poland.

1000 A205 10c multi .45 .30
1001 A205 15c multi .55 .45
1002 A205 20c multi 1.00 .60
1003 A205 30c multi 1.75 .80
1004 A205 80c multi 4.50 2.25
1005 A205 1b multi, vert. 5.50 2.75
Nos. 1000-1005 (6) 13.75 7.15

Ancient Drinking Vessel A206

1981, May 5 Litho. *Perf. 12½x12*

1006 A206 20c shown .60 .30
1007 A206 25c Spice container 1.00 .40
1008 A206 35c Jug 1.25 .75
1009 A206 40c Cooking pot holder 1.50 1.10
1010 A206 60c Animal figurine 2.25 1.60
Nos. 1006-1010 (5) 6.60 4.15

Intl. Year of the Disabled — A207

1981, July 16 Photo. *Perf. 11½x12*

1011 A207 5c Prostheses .50 .25
1012 A207 15c Boys writing .50 .25
1013 A207 20c Activities .75 .50
1014 A207 40c Knitting 1.50 1.00
1015 A207 1b Weaving 3.75 2.25
Nos. 1011-1015 (5) 7.00 4.25

7th Anniv. of Revolution A208

1981, Sept. 10 *Perf. 14*

1016 A208 20c Children's Center .65 .35
1017 A208 60c Heroes' Center 1.25 1.00
1018 A208 1b Serto Ader (state newspaper) 2.25 1.75
Nos. 1016-1018 (3) 4.15 3.10

World Food Day — A209

1981, Oct. 15 Litho. *Perf. 13½x12½*

1019 A209 5c Wheat airlift .25 .25
1020 A209 15c Plowing .30 .25
1021 A209 20c Malnutrition .70 .30
1022 A209 40c Agriculture education 1.50 .70
1023 A209 1b Cattle, corn 4.00 1.75
Nos. 1019-1023 (5) 6.75 3.25

Ancient Bronze Type of 1978

1981, Dec. 15 Litho. *Perf. 14x13½*

1024 A180 15c Pitcher .35 .35
1025 A180 45c Tsenatsil (musical instrument) 1.00 1.00
1026 A180 50c Pitcher, diff. 1.25 1.25
1027 A180 70c Pot 1.50 1.50
Nos. 1024-1027 (4) 4.10 4.10

Horn Artifacts — A210

1982, Feb. 18 Photo. *Perf. 12x12½*

1028 A210 10c Tobacco containers .25 .25
1029 A210 15c Cup .35 .30
1030 A210 40c Container, diff. .90 .70
1031 A210 45c Goblet 1.25 .95
1032 A210 70c Spoons 1.75 1.25
Nos. 1028-1032 (5) 4.50 3.45

Coffee Cultivation A211

1982, May, 6 Photo. *Perf. 13½*

1033 A211 5c Plants .25 .25
1034 A211 15c Bushes .35 .30
1035 A211 25c Mature bushes 1.25 1.10
1036 A211 35c Picking beans 2.25 1.50
1037 A211 1b Drinking coffee 2.25 1.75
Nos. 1033-1037 (5) 6.35 4.90

1982 World Cup — A212

Various soccer plays.

Perf. 13½x12½

1982, June 10 Litho.

1038 A212 5c multicolored .25 .25
1039 A212 15c multicolored .40 .30
1040 A212 20c multicolored .55 .50
1041 A212 40c multicolored 1.25 1.10
1042 A212 1b multicolored 2.50 2.25
Nos. 1038-1042 (5) 4.95 4.40

TB Bacillus Centenary A213

1982, July 12 Litho. *Perf. 13½x12½*

1043 A213 15c Cow .50 .40
1044 A213 20c Magnifying glass .60 .50
1045 A213 30c Koch, microscope 1.00 .90
1046 A213 35c Koch 1.25 1.00
1047 A213 80c Man coughing 2.50 2.25
Nos. 1043-1047 (5) 5.85 5.05

8th Anniv. of Revolution — A214

Designs: Symbols of justice.

1982, Sept. 10 *Perf. 12½x13½*

1048 A214 80c multicolored 2.00 1.50
1049 A214 1b multicolored 2.25 1.75

World Standards Day — A215

1982, Oct. 14 Litho. *Perf. 13½x12½*

1050 A215 5c Hand, foot, square .25 .25
1051 A215 15c Scales .40 .30
1052 A215 20c Rulers .50 .40
1053 A215 40c Weights 1.00 .80
1054 A215 1b Emblem 2.50 1.75
Nos. 1050-1054 (5) 4.65 3.50

10th Anniv. of UN Conference on Human Environment A216

1982, Dec. 13 Litho. *Perf. 12*

1055 A216 5c Wildlife conservation .25 .25
1056 A216 15c Environmental health and settlement .40 .35
1057 A216 20c Forest protection .60 .45
1058 A216 40c Natl. literacy campaign 1.00 .90
1059 A216 1b Soil and water conservation 3.00 2.00
Nos. 1055-1059 (5) 5.25 3.95

Cave of Sof Omar A217

Various views.

1983, Feb. 10 Photo. *Perf. 13½*

1060 A217 5c multicolored .25 .25
1061 A217 10c multicolored .30 .25
1062 A217 15c multicolored .95 .35
1063 A217 70c multicolored 2.00 1.10
1064 A217 80c multicolored 2.25 1.50
Nos. 1060-1064 (5) 5.75 3.45

A218

A219

1983, Apr. 29 Photo. *Perf. 14*

1065 A218 80c multicolored 2.00 1.50
1066 A218 1b multicolored 2.25 2.00

25th Anniv. of Economic Commission for Africa.

Perf. 12½x11½

1983, June 3 Photo.

1067 A219 85c Emblem 1.60 1.25
1068 A219 1b Lighthouse, ship 3.25 2.25

25th Anniv. of Intl. Maritime Org.

WCY A220

9th Anniv. of Revolution A221

1983, July 22 Litho.

1069 A220 25c UPU emblem .70 .60
1070 A220 55c Dish antenna, emblems 2.25 2.10
1071 A220 1b Bridge, tunnel 5.00 3.50
Nos. 1069-1071 (3) 7.95 6.20

1983, Sept. 10 Litho. *Perf. 14½*

1072 A221 25c Dove .50 .40
1073 A221 55c Star 1.40 1.00
1074 A221 1b Emblems 2.00 1.60
Nos. 1072-1074 (3) 3.90 3.00

Musical Instruments — A222

1983, Oct. 17 Litho. *Perf. 12½x13½*

1075 A222 5c Hura .25 .25
1076 A222 15c Dinke .45 .40
1077 A222 20c Meleket .75 .65
1078 A222 40c Embilta 1.25 1.00
1079 A222 1b Tom 2.75 2.00
Nos. 1075-1079 (5) 5.45 4.30

Charaxes Galawadiwosi A223

1983, Dec. 13 Photo. *Perf. 14*

1080 A223 10c shown 1.25 1.00
1081 A223 15c Epiphora elianae 1.75 1.50
1082 A223 55c Batuana rougeoti 4.75 3.00
1083 A223 1b Achaea saboeareginae 9.00 7.50
Nos. 1080-1083 (4) 16.75 13.00

Intl. Anti-Apartheid Year (1983) — A224

Perf. 13½x12½

1984, Feb. 10 Litho.

1084 A224 5c multicolored .35 .30
1085 A224 15c multicolored .55 .50
1086 A224 20c multicolored .75 .65
1087 A224 40c multicolored 1.25 1.00
1088 A224 1b multicolored 2.50 2.00
Nos. 1084-1088 (5) 5.40 4.45

Local Flowers — A225

Traditional Houses — A226

1984, Apr. 13 Litho. *Perf. 13½*

1089 A225 5c Protea gaguedi .30 .25
1090 A225 25c Sedum epidendrum 1.25 .90
1091 A225 50c Echinops amplexicaulis 2.50 1.75
1092 A225 1b Canarina eminii 5.00 3.25
Nos. 1089-1092 (4) 9.05 6.15

1984, June 13 Photo.

1093 A226 15c Konso .55 .40
1094 A226 65c Dorze 2.40 1.40
1095 A226 1b Harer 3.75 2.50
Nos. 1093-1095 (3) 6.70 4.30

10th Anniv. of the Revolution A227

1984, Sept. 10 Photo. *Perf. 11½*

1096 A227 5c Sept. 12, 1974 .25 .25
1097 A227 10c Mar. 4, 1975 .35 .25
1098 A227 15c Apr. 20, 1976 .45 .35
1099 A227 20c Feb. 11, 1977 .60 .50
1100 A227 25c Mar. 1978 .75 .60
1101 A227 40c July 8, 1980 1.10 .80
1102 A227 45c Dec. 17, 1980 1.40 1.00
1103 A227 50c Sept. 15, 1980 1.75 1.25
1104 A227 70c Sept. 18, 1981 2.00 1.50
1105 A227 1b June 6, 1983 2.75 2.00
Nos. 1096-1105 (10) 11.40 8.50

Traditional Sports A228

1984, Dec. 7 Photo. *Perf. 14*

1106 A228 5c Gugs .25 .25
1107 A228 25c Tigil 1.00 .50
1108 A228 50c Genna 2.50 1.50
1109 A228 1b Gebeta 4.75 3.50
Nos. 1106-1109 (4) 8.50 5.75

Birds — A229

1985, Jan. 4 Photo. *Perf. 14½*

1110 A229 5c Francolinus harwoodi .50 .40
1111 A229 15c Rallus rougetti 1.00 .75
1112 A229 80c Merops pusillus 5.00 3.00
1113 A229 85c Malimbus rubriceps 5.25 3.50
Nos. 1110-1113 (4) 11.75 7.65

Indigenous Fauna A230

1985, Feb. 4 Litho. *Perf. 12½x12*

1114 A230 20c Hippopotamus amphibius .90 .75
1115 A230 25c Litocranius walleri 1.25 1.00
1116 A230 40c Sylvicapra grimmia 2.00 1.50
1117 A230 1b Rhynchotragus guentheri 4.50 3.25
Nos. 1114-1117 (4) 8.65 6.50

Freshwater Fish — A231

1985, Apr. 3 *Perf. 13½*

1118 A231 10c Barbus degeni .45 .40
1119 A231 20c Labeo cylindricus 1.25 .60
1120 A231 55c Protopterus annectens 2.75 1.50
1121 A231 1b Alestes dentex 6.00 3.25
Nos. 1118-1121 (4) 10.45 5.75

Medicinal Plants A232

1985, May 23 *Perf. 11½x12½*

1122 A232 10c Securidaca longepedunculata .40 .30
1123 A232 20c Plumbago zeylanicum .90 .45
1124 A232 55c Brucea antidysenteric 2.10 1.25

1125 A232 1b Dorstenia barminiana 5.00 2.75
Nos. 1122-1125 (4) 8.40 4.75

Ethiopian Red Cross Soc., 50th Anniv. — A233

1985, Aug. 6 Litho. ***Perf. 13½x13***

1126 A233 35c multicolored .90 .75
1127 A233 55c multicolored 2.25 1.25
1128 A233 1b multicolored 4.50 2.50
Nos. 1126-1128 (3) 7.65 4.50

Ethiopian Revolution, 11th Anniv. A234

10c, Kombolcha Mills, Welo Region. 80c, Muger Cement Factory, Mokoda, Shoa. 1b, Relocating famine and drought victims.

1985, Sept. 10 Litho. ***Perf. 13½***

1129 A234 10c multicolored .30 .25
1130 A234 80c multicolored 2.25 2.00
1131 A234 1b multicolored 3.00 2.50
Nos. 1129-1131 (3) 5.55 4.75

UN 40th Anniv. — A235

1985, Nov. 22 Litho. ***Perf. 13½x14***

1132 A235 25c multicolored .90 .75
1133 A235 55c multicolored 1.75 1.50
1134 A235 1b multicolored 3.25 2.50
Nos. 1132-1134 (3) 5.90 4.75

Anti-Polio Campaign A236

1986, Jan. 10 Litho. ***Perf. 11½x12½***

1135 A236 5c Boy, prosthesis .40 .25
1136 A236 10c Boy on crutches .55 .30
1137 A236 20c Nurse, boy 1.00 .50
1138 A236 55c Man, sewing machine 2.75 1.25
1139 A236 1b Nurse, mother, child 4.50 2.50
Nos. 1135-1139 (5) 9.20 4.80

Indigenous Trees A237

1986, Feb. 10 ***Perf. 13½x14½***

1140 A237 10c Millettia ferruginea .40 .35
1141 A237 30c Syzyigum guineense 1.25 .75
1142 A237 50c Cordia africana 2.00 1.25
1143 A237 1b Hagenia abyssinica 4.25 2.75
Nos. 1140-1143 (4) 7.90 5.10

Spices — A238

1986, Mar. 10 ***Perf. 13½***

1144 A238 10c Zingiber officinale rosc .50 .40
1145 A238 15c Ocimum bacilicum 1.10 .50
1146 A238 55c Sinapsis alba 2.50 1.50
1147 A238 1b Cuminum cyminum 5.00 3.00
Nos. 1144-1147 (4) 9.10 5.40

Current Coins, Obverse and Reverse A239

1986, May 9 Litho. ***Perf. 13½x14***

1148 A239 5c 1-cent .25 .25
1149 A239 10c 25-cent .50 .35
1150 A239 35c 5-cent 1.60 1.00
1151 A239 50c 50-cent 2.00 1.25
1152 A239 1b 10-cent 4.00 2.50
Nos. 1148-1152 (5) 8.35 5.35

Discovery of 3.5 Million Year-old Hominid Skeleton, "Lucy" — A240

1986, July 4 ***Perf. 13½***

1153 A240 2b multicolored 11.00 11.00

Ethiopian Revolution, 12th Anniv. — A241

Designs: 20c, Military service. 30c, Tiglachin monument. 55c, Delachin Exhibition emblem, 85c, Food processing plant, Merti.

1986, Sept. 10 Litho. ***Perf. 14***

1154 A241 20c multicolored .75 .40
1155 A241 30c multicolored 1.10 .60
1156 A241 55c multicolored 2.10 1.00
1157 A241 85c multicolored 2.75 1.75
Nos. 1154-1157 (4) 6.70 3.75

Ethiopian Airlines, 40th Anniv. — A242

1986, Oct. 14

1158 A242 10c DC-7 .65 .30
1159 A242 20c DC-3 1.00 .50
1160 A242 30c Personnel, jet tail 1.60 .75
1161 A242 40c Engine 2.00 1.00
1162 A242 1b DC-7, map 4.50 2.25
Nos. 1158-1162 (5) 9.75 4.80

Intl. Peace Year — A243

1986, Nov. 13 ***Perf. 13½***

1163 A243 10c multicolored .40 .30
1164 A243 80c multicolored 2.25 2.00
1165 A243 1b multicolored 3.00 2.50
Nos. 1163-1165 (3) 5.65 4.80

UN Child Survival Campaign — A244

1986, Dec. 11 ***Perf. 12½***

1166 A244 10c Breast feeding .60 .30
1167 A244 35c Immunization 1.75 .75
1168 A244 50c Hygiene 2.25 1.00
1169 A244 1b Growth monitoring 4.50 2.00
Nos. 1166-1169 (4) 9.10 4.05

Umbrellas A245

1987, Feb. 10 ***Perf. 13½***

1170 A245 35c Axum 1.20 .85
1171 A245 55c Negele-Borena 1.75 1.25
1172 A245 1b Jimma 3.50 2.50
Nos. 1170-1172 (3) 6.45 4.60

Artwork by Afewerk Tekle (b. 1932) A246

Designs: 50c, Defender of His Country — Afar, stained glass window, 2b, Defender of His Country — Adwa, painting.

1987, Mar. 19 Litho. ***Perf. 13½***

1173 A246 50c multicolored 1.75 1.00
1174 A246 2b multicolored 6.25 4.50

Stained Glass Windows by Afewerk Tekle — A247

1987, June 16 Photo. ***Perf. 11½x12***

Granite Paper

1175 A247 50c multicolored *8.00 4.00*

Size: 26x38mm

1176 A247 80c multicolored *10.00 5.50*
1177 A247 1b multicolored *15.00 8.00*
Nos. 1175-1177 (3) 33.00 17.50

Struggle of the African People.
Sold out in Addis Ababa on date of issue.

Simien Fox A248

1987, June 29 Litho. ***Perf. 13½***

1178 A248 5c multicolored .25 .25
1179 A248 10c multicolored .60 .25
1180 A248 15c multicolored .90 .40
1181 A248 20c multicolored 1.10 .50
1182 A248 25c multicolored 1.50 .75
1183 A248 45c multicolored 2.25 1.00
1184 A248 55c multicolored 2.75 1.50
Nos. 1178-1184 (7) 9.35 4.65

For overprints see Nos. 1234-1237. For similar design see A294a.

Ethiopian Revolution, 13th Anniv. A249

1987, Sept. 10 ***Perf. 12½***

1185 A249 5c Constitution, freedom of press .50 .30
1186 A249 10c Popular elections .65 .40
1187 A249 80c Referendum 2.50 1.50
1188 A249 1b Bahir Dar Airport, map 3.75 2.00
Nos. 1185-1188 (4) 7.40 4.20

Addis Ababa, Cent. A251

"100" and views: 5c, Emperor Menelik II, Empress Taitu and city. 10c, Traditional buildings. 80c, Central Addis Ababa. 1b, Aerial view of city.

1987, Sept. 7 ***Perf. 13½***

1193 A251 5c multicolored .50 .30
1194 A251 10c multicolored .65 .40
1195 A251 80c multicolored 2.75 1.50
1196 A251 1b multicolored 3.50 2.00
Nos. 1193-1196 (4) 7.40 4.20

Wooden Spoons A252

1987, Nov. 30

1197 A252 85c Hurso, Hararge 3.75 3.75
1198 A252 1b Borena, Sidamo 4.25 4.25

Intl. Year of Shelter for the Homeless A253

1987, Dec. 12 Litho. ***Perf. 13***

1199 A253 10c Village revitalization program .70 .40
1200 A253 35c Resettlement program 1.40 .90
1201 A253 50c Urban improvement 1.75 1.00
1202 A253 1b Cooperative and government housing 2.75 1.50
Nos. 1199-1202 (4) 6.60 3.80

October Revolution, Russia, 70th Anniv. (in 1987) — A254

Painting: 1b, Lenin receiving Workers' Council delegates in the Smolny Institute.

1988, Feb. 17 *Perf. 12½x12*
1203 A254 1b multicolored 2.50 1.75

Traditional Hunting Methods and Prey — A255

1988, Mar. 30 Litho. *Perf. 13½*
1204 A255 85c Bow and arrow 3.25 2.25
1205 A255 1b Double-pronged spear 3.75 3.50

A256

1988, May 6
1206 A256 85c multicolored 2.50 1.50
1207 A256 1b multicolored 3.50 1.75

Intl. Red Cross and Red Crescent Organizations, 125th annivs.

A257

1988, June 7 Photo. *Perf. 11½x12*
1208 A257 2b multicolored 3.50 2.25

Organizaton of African Unity, 25th anniv.

Ethiopian Revolution, 14th Anniv. A258

Design: Various details of *The Victory of Ethiopia,* six-panel mural by Afewerk Tekle (b. 1932) in the museum of the Heroes Center, Debre Zeit.

1988, June 28 Litho. *Perf. 13½x13*
1209 A258 10c Jet over farm, vert. .40 .30
1210 A258 20c Farm workers on road, vert. .50 .35
1211 A258 35c Allegory of unity, vert. .80 .50
1212 A258 55c Jet over industry 1.40 1.00
1213 A258 80c Steel works 1.90 1.25
1214 A258 1b Weaving 2.50 2.00
Nos. 1209-1214 (6) 7.50 5.40

Nos. 1209-1211 vert.

Women, Bracelets and Maps A259

1988, July 27 Litho. *Perf. 13x13½*
1215 A259 15c Sidamo .40 .30
1216 A259 85c Arsi 1.75 1.25
1217 A259 1b Harerge 2.50 2.00
Nos. 1215-1217 (3) 4.65 3.55

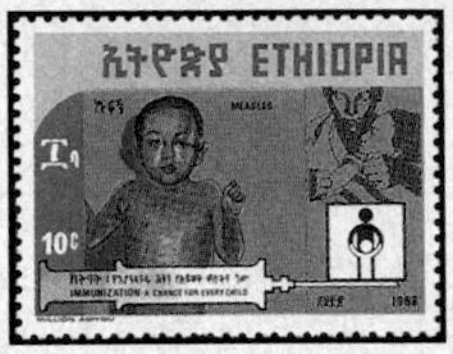

Immunize Every Child A260

1988, June 14 Litho. *Perf. 13x13½*
1218 A260 10c Measles .45 .25
1219 A260 35c Tetanus .95 .60
1220 A260 50c Whooping cough 1.60 1.00
1221 A260 1b Diphtheria 3.00 1.75
Nos. 1218-1221 (4) 6.00 3.60

Intl. Fund for Agricultural Development (IFAD), 10th Anniv. — A261

1988, Aug. 16 *Perf. 13½*
1222 A261 15c Monetary aid .30 .25
1223 A261 85c Farming activities 1.50 1.10
1224 A261 1b Harvest 2.25 1.25
Nos. 1222-1224 (3) 4.05 2.60

People's Democratic Republic of Ethiopia, 1st Anniv. — A262

5c, 1st Session of the natl. Shengo (congress). 10c, Mengistu Haile-Mariam, 1st president of the republic. 80c, Natl. crest, flag & crowd. 1b, State assembly building.

1988, Sept. 9 *Perf. 14*
1225 A262 5c multicolored .25 .25
1226 A262 10c multicolored .30 .25
1227 A262 80c multicolored 1.75 1.50
1228 A262 1b multicolored 2.25 2.00
Nos. 1225-1228 (4) 4.55 4.00

Bank Notes A263

1988, Nov. 10 Photo. *Perf. 13*
1229 A263 5c 1-Birr .35 .25
1230 A263 10c 5-Birr .50 .30
1231 A263 20c 10-Birr 1.00 .50
1232 A263 75c 50-Birr 2.50 1.50
1233 A263 85c 100-Birr 3.25 2.00
Nos. 1229-1233 (5) 7.60 4.55

Nos. 1181-1184 Ovptd. in Two Languages

1988, Dec. 1 Litho. *Perf. 13½*
1234 A248 20c multicolored *4.75 4.50*
1235 A248 25c multicolored *6.25 5.50*
1236 A248 45c multicolored *12.50 10.50*
1237 A248 55c multicolored *13.00 11.00*
Nos. 1234-1237 (4) 36.50 31.50

Intl. Day for the Fight Against AIDS.

WHO, 40th Anniv. A264

1988, Dec. 30 Litho. *Perf. 14*
1238 A264 50c multicolored 1.40 .80
1239 A264 65c multicolored 1.90 1.00
1240 A264 85c multicolored 2.50 1.50
Nos. 1238-1240 (3) 5.80 3.30

Traditional Musical Instruments A265

1989, Feb. 9 *Perf. 13x13½*
1241 A265 30c Gere .85 .45
1242 A265 40c Fanfa 1.10 .65
1243 A265 50c Chancha 1.40 .90
1244 A265 85c Negareet 2.00 1.25
Nos. 1241-1244 (4) 5.35 3.25

Ethiopian Shipping Lines, 25th Anniv. A266

1989, Mar. 27 Litho. *Perf. 14*
1245 A266 15c *Abyot* .45 .30
1246 A266 30c *Wolwol* .85 .60
1247 A266 55c *Queen of Sheba* 1.60 1.25
1248 A266 1b *Abbay Wonz* 3.00 2.25
Nos. 1245-1248 (4) 5.90 4.40

Birds — A267

1989, May 18 Litho. *Perf. 13½x13*
1249 A267 10c Yellow-fronted parrot .65 .30
1250 A267 35c White-winged cliff chat 2.00 1.00
1251 A267 50c Yellow-throated seed eater 2.75 1.25
1252 A267 1b Black-headed forest oriole 4.50 2.25
Nos. 1249-1252 (4) 9.90 4.80

Production of Early Manuscripts — A268

1989, June 16 Litho. *Perf. 13½*
1253 A268 5c Preparing vellum .35 .25
1254 A268 10c Ink horns, pens .40 .25
1255 A268 20c Scribe .70 .40
1256 A268 75c Book binding 2.10 1.25
1257 A268 85c Illuminated manuscript 2.75 1.75
Nos. 1253-1257 (5) 6.30 3.90

Indigenous Wildlife — A269

1989, July 18
1258 A269 30c Greater kudu 1.00 .75
1259 A269 40c Lesser kudu 1.25 1.00
1260 A269 50c Roan antelope 1.50 1.25
1261 A269 85c Nile lechwe 2.50 2.00
Nos. 1258-1261 (4) 6.25 5.00

People's Democratic Republic of Ethiopia, 2nd Anniv. A270

Designs: 15c, Melka Wakana Hydroelectric Power Station. 75c, Adea Berga Dairy Farm. 1b, Pawe Hospital.

1989, Sept. 8
1262 A270 15c multicolored .35 .25
1263 A270 75c multicolored 1.50 1.25
1264 A270 1b multicolored 3.00 2.00
Nos. 1262-1264 (3) 4.85 3.50

African Development Bank, 25th Anniv. — A271

1989, Nov. 10 Litho. *Perf. 13½x13*
1265 A271 20c multicolored .35 .30
1266 A271 80c multicolored 2.25 1.25
1267 A271 1b multicolored 2.75 2.00
Nos. 1265-1267 (3) 5.35 3.55

Pan-African Postal Union, 10th Anniv. — A272

1990, Jan. 18 Litho. *Perf. 13½*
1268 A272 50c multicolored 1.00 .75
1269 A272 70c multicolored 1.75 1.25
1270 A272 80c multicolored 2.00 1.75
Nos. 1268-1270 (3) 4.75 3.75

UNESCO World Literacy Year — A273

15c, Illiterate man holding newspaper upside down. 85c, Adults learning alphabet in school. 1b, Literate man holding newspaper upright.

1990, Mar. 13
1271 A273 15c multicolored .65 .40
1272 A273 85c multicolored 2.25 1.50
1273 A273 1b multicolored 3.25 2.25
Nos. 1271-1273 (3) 6.15 4.15

Abebe Bikila, Marathon Runner
A274

1990, Apr. 17

1274	A274	5c	Race	.35	.25
1275	A274	10c	Flag bearer, Olympic team	.40	.25
1276	A274	20c	Race, Rome Olympics	.80	.50
1277	A274	75c	Race, Tokyo Olympics	2.40	1.50
1278	A274	85c	Bikila, trophies, vert.	3.00	2.00
			Nos. 1274-1278 (5)	6.95	4.50

Flag — A275

1990, Apr. 30 Litho. *Perf. 13½x13*

1279	A275	5c	multicolored	.35	.25
1280	A275	10c	multicolored	.35	.25
1281	A275	15c	multicolored	.40	.25
1282	A275	20c	multicolored	.55	.30
1283	A275	25c	multicolored	.65	.35
1284	A275	30c	multicolored	.80	.40
1285	A275	35c	multicolored	.90	.45
1286	A275	40c	multicolored	1.10	.50
1287	A275	45c	multicolored	1.25	.65
1288	A275	50c	multicolored	1.40	.65
1289	A275	55c	multicolored	1.60	.70
1290	A275	60c	multicolored	1.75	.80
1291	A275	70c	multicolored	1.90	.90
1292	A275	80c	multicolored	2.00	1.00
1293	A275	85c	multicolored	2.10	1.10
1294	A275	90c	multicolored	2.25	1.25
1295	A275	1b	multicolored	2.50	1.25
1296	A275	2b	multicolored	5.25	2.75
1297	A275	3b	multicolored	7.75	4.00
			Nos. 1279-1297 (19)	34.85	17.80

Dated 1989.

Sowing of Teff
A276

1990, May 18 Litho. *Perf. 13½*

1298	A276	5c	shown	.25	.25
1299	A276	10c	Harvesting	.25	.25
1300	A276	20c	Threshing	.50	.40
1301	A276	75c	Storage, preparation	1.75	1.50
1302	A276	85c	Consumption	2.25	2.00
			Nos. 1298-1302 (5)	5.00	4.40

Walia Ibex — A277

1990, June 18 *Perf. 14x13½*

1303	A277	5c	multi	.55	.35
1304	A277	15c	multi	1.25	.75
1305	A277	20c	multi	1.90	1.10
1306	A277	1b	multi, horiz.	7.50	4.25
			Nos. 1303-1306 (4)	11.20	6.45

World AIDS Day
A278

1991, Jan. 31 Litho. *Perf. 14*

1307	A278	15c	Stages of disease	.65	.30
1308	A278	85c	Education	2.75	1.50
1309	A278	1b	Causes, preventatives	3.50	2.00
			Nos. 1307-1309 (3)	6.90	3.80

Intl. Decade for Natural Disaster Reduction
A279

Map of disaster-prone African areas and: 5c, Volcano. 10c, Earthquake. 15c, Drought. 30c, Flood. 50c, Red Cross health education. 1b, Red Cross assisting fire victims.

1991, Apr. 9 Litho. *Perf. 14*

1310	A279	5c	multicolored	.40	.25
1311	A279	10c	multicolored	.40	.25
1312	A279	15c	multicolored	.45	.25
1313	A279	30c	multicolored	.90	.50
1314	A279	50c	multicolored	1.90	1.00
1315	A279	1b	multicolored	3.50	2.00
			Nos. 1310-1315 (6)	7.55	4.25

The Cannon of Tewodros
A280

Designs: 15c, Villagers receiving cannon. 85c, Warriors leaving with cannon. 1b, Hauling cannon up mountainside.

1991, June 18 Litho. *Perf. 13½*

1316	A280	15c	multicolored	.65	.40
1317	A280	85c	multicolored	2.25	1.50
1318	A280	1b	multicolored	2.75	2.00
			Nos. 1316-1318 (3)	5.65	3.90

Fish
A281

1991, Sept. 6 Litho. *Perf. 13½*

1319	A281	5c	Lacepede	.60	.30
1320	A281	15c	Black-finned butterflyfish	.75	.40
1321	A281	80c	Regal angelfish	2.75	1.75
1322	A281	1b	Bleeker	3.75	2.50
			Nos. 1319-1322 (4)	7.85	4.95

A282

Traditional Ceremonial Robes: Various robes.

1992, Jan. 1 Litho. *Perf. 13½x14*

1323	A282	5c	yellow & multi	.45	.25
1324	A282	15c	orange & multi	.55	.25
1325	A282	80c	yel green & multi	2.25	1.50
1326	A282	1b	blue & multi	2.75	1.75
			Nos. 1323-1326 (4)	6.00	3.75

A283

Flowers: 5c, Cissus quadrangularis. 15c, Delphinium dasycaulon. 80c, Epilobium hirsutum. 1b, Kniphofia foliosa.

1992, Mar. 5 Litho. *Perf. 13½x14*

1327	A283	5c	multicolored	.40	.30
1328	A283	15c	multicolored	.50	.40
1329	A283	80c	multicolored	2.25	1.75
1330	A283	1b	multicolored	2.75	2.00
			Nos. 1327-1330 (4)	5.90	4.45

Traditional Homes
A284

1992, May 14 Litho. *Perf. 12½x12*

1331	A284	15c	Afar	.55	.30
1332	A284	35c	Anuak	1.10	.60
1333	A284	50c	Gimira	1.35	.90
1334	A284	1b	Oromo	3.00	1.75
			Nos. 1331-1334 (4)	6.00	3.55

A285

Pottery.

1992, July 7 Litho. *Perf. 13x13½*

1335	A285	15c	Cover	.75	.55
1336	A285	85c	Jug	3.00	2.40
1337	A285	1b	Tall jar	4.25	3.50
			Nos. 1335-1337 (3)	8.00	6.45

A286

1992, Sept. 29 *Perf. 14x13½*

1338	A286	20c	multicolored	.60	.30
1339	A286	80c	multicolored	2.25	1.25
1340	A286	1b	multicolored	3.00	1.75
			Nos. 1338-1340 (3)	5.85	3.30

Pan-African Rinderpest campaign.

A287

Musical instruments.

1993, Feb. 16 Litho. *Perf. 14x13½*

1341	A287	15c	Catchel	.45	.30
1342	A287	35c	Huldudwa	.90	.55
1343	A287	50c	Dita	1.20	.75
1344	A287	1b	Atamo	3.00	2.00
			Nos. 1341-1344 (4)	5.55	3.60

Birds — A288

1993, Apr. 22 Litho. *Perf. 14x13½*

1345	A288	15c	Banded barbet	.60	.60
1346	A288	35c	Ruppell's chat	1.10	1.00
1347	A288	50c	Abyssinian catbird	1.75	1.40
1348	A288	1b	White-billed starling	4.00	3.00
			Nos. 1345-1348 (4)	7.45	6.00

Animals
A289

1993, May 14 *Perf. 13½x14*

1349	A289	15c	Honey badger	.45	.35
1350	A289	35c	Spotted necked otter	.75	.60
1351	A289	50c	Rock hyrax	.80	.60
1352	A289	1b	White-tailed mongoose	1.50	1.25
			Nos. 1349-1352 (4)	3.50	2.80

Herbs — A290

1993, June 10 *Perf. 14x13½*

1353	A290	5c	Caraway seed	.65	.50
1354	A290	15c	Garlic	.75	.60
1355	A290	80c	Turmeric	1.50	1.00
1356	A290	1b	Capsicum peppers	2.50	2.25
			Nos. 1353-1356 (4)	5.40	4.35

Butterflies
A291

1993, July 9 Litho. *Perf. 14x13½*

1357	A291	20c	Papilio echerioides	1.00	.85
1358	A291	30c	Papilio rex	1.25	1.00
1359	A291	50c	Graphium policenes	1.75	1.40
1360	A291	1b	Graphium leonidas	3.50	2.50
			Nos. 1357-1360 (4)	7.50	5.75

Insects — A292

1993, Aug. 10

1361 A292 15c C. Variabilis .45 .35
1362 A292 35c Lycus trabeatus .70 .60
1363 A292 50c Malachius bifasciatus .95 .80
1364 A292 1b Homoeogryllus xanthographus 1.90 1.45
Nos. 1361-1364 (4) 4.00 3.20

Trees A293

1993, Oct. 12 Litho. *Perf. 13½x14*

1365 A293 15c Euphorbia ampliphylla .35 .35
1366 A293 35c Erythrina brucei .50 .40
1367 A293 50c Dracaena steudneri .90 .70
1368 A293 1b Allophylus abyssinicus 1.75 1.25
Nos. 1365-1368 (4) 3.50 2.70

Lakes A294

1993, Dec. 14

1369 A294 15c Wonchi .35 .35
1370 A294 35c Zuquala .50 .40
1371 A294 50c Ashengi .90 .70
1372 A294 1b Tana 1.75 1.25
Nos. 1369-1372 (4) 3.50 2.70

Simien Fox A294a

Rough Perf. 13½

1994, Jan. 18 Litho.

Color of Border

1372A A294a 5c violet — .25
1372B A294a 10c brown — .25
1372C A294a 15c lemon — .25
1372D A294a 20c salmon — .25
1372E A294a 40c pale rose — .25
1372F A294a 55c dull green — .35
1372G A294a 60c dark blue — .35
1372H A294a 80c bright blue — .45
1372I A294a 85c gray green — .50
1372J A294a 1b bright green — .75
Nos. 1372A-1372J (10) *300.00* 3.65

Nos. 1372A-1372J have rough perforations and a poor quality printing impression. Dated "1991."

See Nos. 1393A-1393T.

A295

Transitional government: 15c, First anniversary of EPRDF's control of Addis Ababa. 35c, Transition Conference. 50c, National, regional elections. 1b, Coat of arms of Transitional Government.

1994, Mar. 31 Litho. *Perf. 14*

1373 A295 15c multicolored .35 .25
1374 A295 35c multicolored .40 .30
1375 A295 50c multicolored .75 .35
1376 A295 1b multicolored 1.40 .55
Nos. 1373-1376 (4) 2.90 1.45

A296

1994, May 17 *Perf. 13½*

1377 A296 15c blue & multi .50 .25
1378 A296 85c green & multi .85 .40
1379 A296 1b violet & multi 1.10 .50
Nos. 1377-1379 (3) 2.45 1.15

Intl. Year of the Family.

Ethiopian Postal Service, Cent. A297

Designs: 60c, Early, modern postal workers, Scott Type A1. 75c, Early letter carriers. 80c, Older building, methods of transportation. 85c, People, mail buses. 1b, Modern methods of transportation, modern high-rise building.

1994, July 4 Litho. *Perf. 13½*

1380 A297 60c multicolored .75 .55
1381 A297 75c multicolored .90 .60
1382 A297 80c multicolored 1.15 .70
1383 A297 85c multicolored 1.20 .75
1384 A297 1b multicolored 1.45 1.05
a. Souvenir sheet, #1380-1384 + label 10.00 8.00
Nos. 1380-1384 (5) 5.45 3.65

Enset Plant — A298

1994, Aug. 3

1385 A298 10c shown .25 .25
1386 A298 15c Young plants, hut .35 .30
1387 A298 25c Root, women processing leaves .40 .35
1388 A298 50c Mature plants .75 .40
1389 A298 1b Uses as food 1.50 .65
Nos. 1385-1389 (5) 3.25 1.95

Hair Ornaments A299

1994, Sept. 2

1390 A299 5c Gamo gofa .40 .30
1391 A299 15c Sidamo .50 .35
1392 A299 80c Gamo gofa, diff. .90 .50
1393 A299 1b Wello 1.20 .65
Nos. 1390-1393 (4) 3.00 1.80

Simien Fox Type of 1994

Size: 39x25mm

Color of Border

1994, Oct. 18 Litho. *Perf. 14*

1393A A294a 5c dull lilac — *.35*
1393B A294a 10c brown — *.45*
1393C A294a 15c lemon — *.55*
1393D A294a 20c salmon — *.65*
1393E A294a 25c lemon — *.75*
1393F A294a 30c yellow brown — *1.00*
1393G A294a 35c orange — *1.25*
1393H A294a 40c pale rose — *1.50*
1393I A294a 45c pale red org — *1.75*
1393J A294a 50c rose lilac — *2.00*
1393K A294a 55c pale green — *2.25*
1393L A294a 60c dark blue — *2.50*
1393M A294a 65c pale lilac — *2.75*
1393N A294a 70c bright green — *3.00*
1393O A294a 75c pale bl grn — *3.25*
1393P A294a 80c bright blue — *3.50*
1393Q A294a 85c dark greenish blue — *3.75*
1393R A294a 90c pale brown — *4.00*
1393S A294a 1b greenish blue — *5.00*
1393T A294a 2b yellow brown — *9.00*
Nos. 1393A-1393T (20) *49.25*
Nos. 1393A-1393T (20) 800.00

Nos. 1393A-1393T have sharp impressions, Questa imprint, clean perforations. Dated "1993."

For overprints see Nos. 1393U-1393X, 1396A-1396D.

Nos. 1393L, 1393P-1393Q, 1393S Ovptd. in Blue

1994, Oct. 20 Litho. *Perf. 14*

1393U A294a 60c on #1393L 27.50 4.25
1393V A294a 80c on #1393P 35.00 5.50
1393W A294a 85c on #1393Q 72.50 10.50
1393X A294a 1b on #1393S 80.00 9.50
Nos. 1393U-1393X (4) 215.00 29.75

UNFPA, 50th anniv.

ICAO, 50th Anniv. A300

1994, Dec. 7 Litho. *Perf. 13½*

1394 A300 20c mag, lt bl & yel .55 .50
1395 A300 80c yel & lt bl .85 .60
1396 A300 1b dk bl, lt bl & yel 1.10 .95
Nos. 1394-1396 (3) 2.50 2.05

Nos. 1393M-1393O, 1393R Ovptd.

1994, Dec. 20 Litho. *Perf. 14*

1396A A294a 65c on #1393M 27.50 4.25
1396B A294a 70c on #1393N 35.00 5.50
1396C A294a 75c on #1393O 72.50 10.50
1396D A294a 90c on #1393R 80.00 9.50
Nos. 1396A-1396D (4) 215.00 29.75

African Development Bank, 30th anniv.

Baskets for Serving Food A301

1995, June 7 Litho. *Perf. 13½*

1397 A301 30c Erbo .30 .25
1398 A301 70c Sedieka .80 .55
1399 A301 1b Tirar 1.25 .80
Nos. 1397-1399 (3) 2.35 1.60

Traditional Hair Styles — A302

1995, July 5 Litho. *Perf. 13½*

1400 A302 25c Kuncho .25 .25
1401 A302 75c Gamme .75 .55
1402 A302 1b Sadulla 1.25 .80
Nos. 1400-1402 (3) 2.25 1.60

FAO, 50th Anniv. A303

1995, Aug. 29 Litho. *Perf. 13½*

1403 A303 20c green & multi .25 .25
1404 A303 80c blue & multi .95 .65
1405 A303 1b brown & multi 1.75 .90
Nos. 1403-1405 (3) 2.95 1.80

Cultivating Tools A304

1995, Sept. 7

1406 A304 15c Dangora .30 .25
1407 A304 35c Gheso .45 .40
1408 A304 50c Akafa .75 .55
1409 A304 1b Ankasse 1.00 .85
Nos. 1406-1409 (4) 2.50 2.05

UN, 50th Anniv. — A305

1995, Oct. 18 Litho. *Perf. 13½*

Color of UN Emblem

1410 A305 20c black .65 .55
1411 A305 80c bister .75 .65
1412 A305 1b blue 1.10 1.00
Nos. 1410-1412 (3) 2.50 2.20

Intergovernmental Authority on Drought and Development (IGADD), 10th Anniv. — A306

Flags of member nations and: 15c, Seedling being planted in arid region. 35c, People carrying supplies through desert. 50c, Person picking fruit. 1b, Map of member nations.

1995, Dec. 27 Litho. *Perf. 13½*

1413 A306 15c multicolored .45 .35
1414 A306 35c multicolored .55 .45
1415 A306 50c multicolored .70 .60
1416 A306 1b multicolored 1.10 1.00
Nos. 1413-1416 (4) 2.80 2.40

Victory at Battle of Adwa, Cent. — A307

Designs: 40c, Battle sites. 50c, Map of Africa focused at Ethiopia. 60c, Troops, ship. 70c, Warriors, soldiers in two battle scenes. 80c, Italians surrendering, Ethiopian troops, cannons. 1b, Emperor Menelik II, constitution, Empress Taitu.

1996, Mar. 2 Litho. *Perf. 13½x14½*

1417	A307	40c multicolored	.35	.35
1418	A307	50c multicolored	.40	.35
1419	A307	60c multicolored	.60	.45
1420	A307	70c multicolored	.75	.55
1421	A307	80c multicolored	1.00	.80
1422	A307	1b multicolored	1.40	1.10
a.		Souvenir sheet, #1417-1422	5.50	5.50
		Nos. 1417-1422 (6)	4.50	3.60

UN Volunteers, 25th Anniv. A308

Designs: 20c, People, temporary housing huts. 30c, Planting seedlings. 50c, Instructing students. 1b, Caring for infant.

1996, June 6 Litho. *Perf. 13½*

1423	A308	20c multicolored	.25	.25
1424	A308	30c multicolored	.35	.25
1425	A308	50c multicolored	.50	.40
1426	A308	1b multicolored	1.40	1.25
		Nos. 1423-1426 (4)	2.50	2.15

1996 Summer Olympic Games, Atlanta A310

1996, Aug. 1 Litho. *Perf. 12½x12*

Overprint in Black

1427	A310	15c Boxing	.75	.55
1428	A310	20c Swimming	.85	.65
1429	A310	40c Cycling	.95	.75
1430	A310	85c Athletics	1.25	1.10
1431	A310	1b Soccer	1.60	1.40
		Nos. 1427-1431 (5)	5.40	4.45

Nos. 1427-1431 were originally prepared for the 1984 Summer Olympic Games in Los Angeles, but were not released due to the Soviet-led boycott. Nos. 1427-1431 exist without overprint. Value, set $100.

A311

UNICEF, 50th Anniv.: 10c, Emblems. 15c, Mother, child receiving vaccination. 25c, Woman carrying water, boy drinking from faucet. 50c, Children studying. 1b, Mother breastfeeding infant.

1996, Sept. 10 Litho. *Perf. 13½*

1432	A311	10c multicolored	.35	.35
1433	A311	15c multicolored	.40	.35
1434	A311	25c multicolored	.50	.40
1435	A311	50c multicolored	.85	.65
1436	A311	1b multicolored	1.40	1.05
		Nos. 1432-1436 (5)	3.50	2.80

A312

Creation of Federal Democratic Republic of Ethiopia: 10c, People discussing new Constitution, approved Dec. 8, 1994. 20c, Ballot boxes, hand placing ballot in box. 30c, Marking ballot, placing into box, tower building, items from country's environment. 40c, Building, ballot, assembly hall. 1b, Natl. flag, transition of power.

1996, Dec. 26 Litho. *Perf. 13½*

1437	A312	10c multicolored	.50	.50
1438	A312	20c multicolored	.50	.50
1439	A312	30c multicolored	.60	.50
1440	A312	40c multicolored	.95	.75
1441	A312	1b multicolored	1.90	1.45
		Nos. 1437-1441 (5)	4.45	3.70

Traditional Baskets — A313

1997, Feb. 20 Litho. *Perf. 13½*

1442	A313	5c Jimma	1.20	.85
1443	A313	15c Wello	1.20	.85
1444	A313	80c Welega	2.00	.95
1445	A313	1b Shewa	2.50	1.40
		Nos. 1442-1445 (4)	6.90	4.05

Traditional Baskets A314

1997, May 22 Litho. *Perf. 13½*

1446	A314	35c Arssi	1.25	1.00
1447	A314	65c Gojam	2.25	1.90
1448	A314	1b Harer	3.50	3.00
		Nos. 1446-1448 (3)	7.00	5.90

See Nos. 1464-1466.

UN Decade Against Drug Abuse & Illicit Trafficking A315

1997, Sept. 9 Litho. *Perf. 14*

1449	A315	20c green & multi	.70	.50
1450	A315	80c brown & multi	.95	.75
1451	A315	1b blue & multi	1.40	1.10
		Nos. 1449-1451 (3)	3.05	2.35

Historic Buildings, Addis Ababa A316

45c, Bitwoded Haile Giorgis' house. 55c, Alfred Ilg's house, vert. 3b, Menelik's Elfign.

Perf. 14½x14, 14x14½

1997, Dec. 23 Litho.

1452	A316	45c multicolored	.50	.45
1453	A316	55c multicolored	.65	.60
1454	A316	3b multicolored	2.25	1.75
		Nos. 1452-1454 (3)	3.40	2.80

Addis Ababa's Oldest Historical Buildings A317

Designs: 60c, Ras Biru W/Gabriel's house. 75c, Sheh Hojele Alhassen's house. 80c, Fitawrari H/Giorgis Dinegde's house. 85c, Etege Taitu Hotel. 1b, Dejazmach Wube Atnafseged's house.

1997, Dec. 30 Litho. *Perf. 14½x14*

1455	A317	60c multicolored	.55	.45
1456	A317	75c multicolored	.60	.55
1457	A317	80c multicolored	.70	.60
1458	A317	85c multicolored	.75	.70
1459	A317	1b multicolored	1.15	.90
		Nos. 1455-1459 (5)	3.75	3.20

Pan African Postal Union, 18th Anniv. A318

Union's emblem and wildlife: 45c, Deculla bushback. 55c, Soemmering's gazelle. 1b, Defassa waterbuck. 2b, Black buffalo.

1998, Mar. 25 Litho. *Perf. 14½x14*

1460	A318	45c multicolored	.50	.35
1461	A318	55c multicolored	.55	.45
1462	A318	1b multicolored	1.00	.65
1463	A318	2b multicolored	2.00	1.25
		Nos. 1460-1463 (4)	4.05	2.70

Traditional Basket Type of 1997

1998, May 21 Litho. *Perf. 13½*

1464	A314	45c Gonder	.45	.45
1465	A314	55c Harere	.65	.55
1466	A314	3b Tigray	2.75	2.50
		Nos. 1464-1466 (3)	3.85	3.50

Golden-Backed Woodpecker A319

1998, Jan. 12 Photo. *Perf. 11½*

Granite Paper

Panel Color

1467	A319	5c green blue	.45	.30
1468	A319	10c yellow	.45	.30
1469	A319	15c blue	.45	.30
1470	A319	20c light brown	*15.00*	.30
1471	A319	25c violet	.45	.30
1472	A319	30c light blue	.45	.30
1473	A319	35c salmon rose	.45	.30
1474	A319	40c lilac	.45	.30
1475	A319	45c green	.45	.30
1476	A319	50c salmon	.45	.35
1477	A319	55c blue	.45	.35
1478	A319	60c brick red	.45	.40
1479	A319	65c light gray	.45	.45
1480	A319	70c bright yellow	.45	.50
1481	A319	75c pale violet	.70	.65
1482	A319	80c apple green	.75	.70
1483	A319	85c gray	.80	.75
1484	A319	90c orange	.90	.80
1485	A319	1b yellow green	1.25	.95
1486	A319	2b pale rose	1.50	1.25
1487	A319	3b lilac rose	2.50	2.00
1488	A319	5b bister	3.50	3.00
1489	A319	10b orange yellow	7.00	6.00
		Nos. 1467-1489 (23)	39.75	20.85

Agreement for Return of Axum Obelisk from Italy — A320

45c, Map of Italy, pieces of obelisk. 55c, Obelisk in Rome. 3b, Map of E. Africa, obelisk, ruins of Axum.

1998, Sept. 3 Litho. *Perf. 13½*

1490	A320	45c multicolored	.75	.45
1491	A320	55c multicolored	.95	.85
1492	A320	3b multicolored	3.00	2.50
		Nos. 1490-1492 (3)	4.70	3.80

Ethiopia-Djibouti Railway, Cent. — A321

Designs: 45c, Men carrying rails during construction. 55c, Early steam train, CFE 404. 1b, Terminal building. 2b, Modern train, BB 1212.

1998, Nov. 24 Litho. *Perf. 11½*

Granite Paper

1493	A321	45c multicolored	.55	.35
1494	A321	55c multicolored	.70	.45
1495	A321	1b multicolored	1.20	.75
1496	A321	2b multicolored	2.50	1.25
		Nos. 1493-1496 (4)	4.95	2.80

Universal Declaration of Human Rights, 50th Anniv. A322

1998, Dec. 23 Litho. *Perf. 13x13½*

1497	A322	45c red & multi	.45	.25
1498	A322	55c yellow & multi	.45	.30
1499	A322	1b green & multi	.75	.50
1500	A322	2b blue & multi	1.10	.75
		Nos. 1497-1500 (4)	2.75	1.80

Mother Teresa (1910-97) — A323

Various portraits.

1999, Mar. 9 Litho. *Perf. 13½x13*

1501	A323	45c brown & multi	1.05	.35
1502	A323	55c green & multi	1.15	.45
1503	A323	1b yel org & multi	1.40	.60
1504	A323	2b blue & multi	3.25	1.25
		Nos. 1501-1504 (4)	6.85	2.65

Intl. Year of the Ocean A324

1999, May 6 Litho. *Perf. 13½x13¼*

1505	A324	45c black & multi	.80	.25
1506	A324	55c red & multi	1.00	.30
1507	A324	1b blue & multi	1.35	.50
1508	A324	2b green & multi	2.75	1.00
		Nos. 1505-1508 (4)	5.90	2.05

World Environment Day — A325

1999, June 17 Litho. *Perf. 13½*

1509	A325	45c pink & multi	.55	.30
1510	A325	55c vio & multi	.70	.40
1511	A325	1b yel org & multi	1.10	.70
1512	A325	2b grn & multi	1.90	1.00
		Nos. 1509-1512 (4)	4.25	2.40

National Parks — A326

45c, Abijata, Shalla Lakes. 70c, Nechisar. 85c, Bale Mountains. 2b, Awash.

Perf. 13¾x13¼, 13¼x13¾

1999, Sept. 8 Litho.

1513	A326	45c multi, vert.	.75	.50
1514	A326	70c multi, vert.	1.10	.70
1515	A326	85c multi, vert.	1.40	.90
1516	A326	2b multi	3.50	1.50
		Nos. 1513-1516 (4)	6.75	3.60

See Nos. 1521-1524.

UPU, 125th Anniv. — A327

1999, Oct. 28 *Perf. 13¼x13*

1517	A327	20c multicolored	.55	.25
1518	A327	80c multicolored	.70	.35
1519	A327	1b multicolored	1.25	.60
1520	A327	2b multicolored	1.75	.80
		Nos. 1517-1520 (4)	4.25	2.00

National Parks Type of 1999

Designs: 50c, Omo, vert. 70c, Mago, vert. 80c, Yangudi-Rassa, vert. 2b, Gambella.

1999, Nov. 30 Litho. *Perf. 13¼*

1521-1524 A326 Set of 4 7.50 2.50

Intl. Year of Older Persons A328

45c, Woman attending to sick man. 70c, Older people gardening. 85c, Four men, bench. 2b, Older man, two young people.

1999, Dec. 30 *Perf. 13¾x13¼*

1525-1528 A328 Set of 4 5.00 3.75

Alexander Pushkin, Writer, Birth Bicent. (in 1999) — A329

Various portraits: 45c, 70c, 85c, 2b.

2000, Mar. 9 Litho. *Perf. 13¾x13¼*

1529-1532 A329 Set of 4 3.25 2.50

Worldwide Fund for Nature (WWF) — A330

Grevy's zebra: a, Grazing. b, Running. c, Resting. d, Head.

2001, Jan. 30 Litho. *Perf. 13¼x13¾*

1533	Strip of 4	*7.50*	*5.00*
a.	A330 45c multi	*.60*	*.45*
b.	A330 55c multi	*.75*	*.55*
c.	A330 1b multi	*1.40*	*1.00*
d.	A330 3b multi	*4.25*	*3.00*

Operation Sunset — A331

Designs: 45c, President Meles Zenawi, Parliament. 55c, Soldiers, flag ceremony. 1b, People, house. 2b, Agriculture, construction.

2000, June 27 *Perf. 13¾*

1534-1537 A331 Set of 4 4.50 2.50

Flags A332

Designs: 25c, Harar Region. 30c, Oromia Region. 50c, Amhara Region. 60c, Tigre Region. 70c, Benishangi Region. 80c, Somalia Region. 90c, Peoples of the South Region. 95c, Gambella Region. 1b, Afar Region. 2b, Ethiopia.

2000, Oct. 26 *Perf. 13¼x13¾*

1538-1547 A332 Set of 10 7.00 4.50

Afro Ayigeba, Cross of St. Lalibela A333

2000, Apr. 27 *Perf. 13¾x13¼*

1548 A333 4b multi 3.50 2.25

Menelik's Bushbuck A334

Perf. 13¾x13¼

2000, June 19 Litho.

Frame Color

1548A	A334	5c dk Prus blue	*1.00*	.25
1549	A334	10c lilac	*1.00*	.25
1549A	A334	15c blue	*1.00*	.25
1549B	A334	20c yellow bister	*1.00*	.25
1549C	A334	25c purple	*1.00*	.25
1549D	A334	30c lt Prus blue	*1.00*	.25
1549E	A334	35c brt red	*1.00*	.25
1549F	A334	40c lilac	*1.00*	.25
1549G	A334	45c emerald	*1.00*	.25
1549H	A334	50c red	*1.10*	.25
1549I	A334	55c blue	*1.25*	.25
1549J	A334	60c yellow orange	*1.40*	.25
1549K	A334	65c deep blue	*1.50*	.25
1549L	A334	70c dull blue	*1.60*	.25
1549M	A334	75c orange yellow	*1.75*	.35
1549N	A334	80c carmine	*1.75*	.35
1549O	A334	85c light blue	*1.75*	.40
1550	A334	90c ocher	*1.75*	.40
1551	A334	1b green	*2.50*	.50
1552	A334	2b red violet	*6.00*	.75
1553	A334	3b purple	*10.00*	.90
1554	A334	5b dark carmine	*18.00*	1.75
1555	A334	10b light carmine	*25.00*	4.00
		Nos. 1548A-1555 (23)	84.35	12.90

Haile Gebreselassie, Runner — A335

Gebreselassie : No. 1557, 50c, Running. No. 1557A, 60c, Running, diff. No. 1557B, 90c, Running, diff. No. 1558, 2b, With arms raised.

2000, Nov. 9 Litho. *Perf. 13½*

1557-1558 A335 Set of 4 4.25 2.00

World Meteorological Organization, 50th Anniv. — A336

Color of inscriptions: 40c, Gray. 75c, Green. 85c, Brown. 2b, Blue.

2000, Oct. 10 Litho. *Perf. 13½*

1559-1562 A336 Set of 4 3.25 2.50

Addis Ababa University, 50th Anniv. — A337

2000, Nov. 30 *Perf. 13½x14¼*

1563 A337 4b multi 3.25 2.50

UN High Commissioner for Refugees, 50th Anniv. — A338

Frame color: 40c, Brown. 75c, Green. 85c, Blue. 2b, Gold.

2000 Dec. 14 *Perf. 13½x14*

1564-1567 A338 Set of 4 4.00 2.50

Freshwater Fish — A340

Designs: 45c, Catfish. 55c, Tilapia. 3b, Nile perch.

2001, July 26 Litho. *Perf. 14¼*

1572-1574 A340 Set of 3 5.00 2.75

Traditional Means of Transportation — A341

Designs: 40c, Man on horseback, horse-drawn cart. 60c, Camel caravan. 1b, Man on horseback, horse carrying load. 2b, Man on donkey, donkeys carrying goods.

2001, Aug. 30 *Perf. 13¼x13½*

1575-1578 A341 Set of 4 5.00 2.75

Year of Dialogue Among Civilizations A342

Color of country name: 25c, Light blue. 75c, White. 1b, Light yellow. 2b, Pink.

2001, Oct. 9 *Perf. 14*

1579-1582 A342 Set of 4 4.00 2.25

Birds — A343

Designs: 50c, White-tailed swallow. 60c, Spot-breasted plover. 90c, Abyssinian long-claw. 2b, Prince Ruspoli's turaco.

2001, Nov. 29 *Perf. 14¼*
1583-1586 A343 Set of 4 6.00 3.00

Traditional Beehives A344

Various beehives: 40c, 70c, 90c, 2b.

2002, Jan. 24 **Litho.** *Perf. 14*
1587-1590 A344 Set of 4 5.00 2.75

Traditional Grain Storage — A345

Designs: 30c, Gota. 70c, Bekollo Gotera. 1b, Gotera. 2b, Gotera, diff.

2002, Mar. 28 *Perf. 13½x14*
1591-1594 A345 Set of 4 5.00 3.00

Lions Club Intl. — A346

Lions Club Intl. emblem and: 45c, Quality emblem. 55c, Woman at pump. 1b, Eye doctor treating patient. 2b, Man in wheelchair.

2002, Apr. 26 **Litho.** *Perf. 13x13¼*
1595-1598 A346 Set of 4 6.00 4.50

Trees A347

Designs: 50c, Acacia abyssinica. 60c, Boswellia papyrifera, vert. 90c, Aningeria adolfi-friederici, vert. 2b, Prunus africana, vert.

Perf. 13½x13¼, 13¼x13½
2002, June 27
1599-1602 A347 Set of 4 6.00 4.50

Traditional Beehives A348

Various beehives with panel colors of: 45c, Pink. 55c, Yellow. 1b, Light blue. 2b, Light green.

2002, Sept. 19 **Litho.** *Perf. 13¼x13*
1603-1606 A348 Set of 4 5.00 3.50

Granite — A349

Designs: 45c, Sidamo. 55c, Harrar. 1b, Tigray. 2b, Wollega.

2002, Oct. 24 *Perf. 13x13¼*
1607-1610 A349 Set of 4 5.50 4.00

Konso Waka A350

Various wooden sculptures with background colors of: 40c, Green. 60c, Blue. 1b, Yellow. 2b, Red.

2002, Nov. 28 *Perf. 14*
1611-1614 A350 Set of 4 4.75 3.00

Menelik's Bushbuck — A351

2002, Dec. 12 *Perf. 13½x13¾*

Frame Color

1615	A351	5c	brt grn blue	.25	.25
1616	A351	10c	lilac	.25	.25
1617	A351	15c	bright blue	.25	.25
1618	A351	20c	brn orange	.25	.25
1619	A351	25c	purple	.25	.25
1620	A351	30c	bright blue	.25	.25
1621	A351	35c	carmine	.25	.25
1622	A351	40c	purple	.25	.25
1623	A351	45c	emerald	.25	.25
1624	A351	50c	red	.25	.25
1625	A351	55c	blue	.25	.25
1626	A351	60c	bright yel	.35	.25
1627	A351	65c	red	.35	.25
1628	A351	70c	light blue	.35	.25
1629	A351	75c	bright yel	.40	.35
1630	A351	80c	carmine	.40	.35
1631	A351	85c	bright blue	.50	.40
1632	A351	90c	orange brn	.50	.40
1633	A351	95c	green	.50	.40
1634	A351	1b	red violet	.60	.50
1635	A351	2b	purple	.85	.75
1636	A351	3b	blue	1.00	.90
1637	A351	5b	dull red	2.00	1.50
1638	A351	10b	light green	6.00	3.00
1639	A351	20b	rose pink	10.00	6.00
	Nos. 1615-1639 (25)			26.55	18.05

Oil Crops A352

Designs: 40c, Abyssinian mustard. 60c, Linseed. 3b, Niger seed.

2002, Dec. 31 **Litho.** *Perf. 13¼x13*
1640-1642 A352 Set of 3 3.00 2.50

Pan-African Postal Union, 23rd Anniv. — A353

Background color: 20c, Green. 80c, Blue green. 1b, Orange brown. 2b, Purple.

2003, Feb. 18 *Perf. 13x13¼*
1643-1646 A353 Set of 4 3.50 2.00

Opals — A354

Designs: 45c, Milk opal. 60c, Brown precious opal. 95c, Fire opal. 2b, Yellow precious opal.

2003, May 8 *Perf. 14*
1647-1650 A354 Set of 4 5.00 3.00

Emperor Tewodros's Amulet — A355

Various views with frame color of: 40c, Green. 60c, Yellow orange. 3b, Red.

2003, Sept. 4 **Litho.** *Perf. 13x13¼*
1651-1653 A355 Set of 3 4.50 2.50

Flowers — A356

Designs: 45c, Kniphofia isoetfolia. 55c, Kniphofia insignis. 1b, Crinum bambusetum. 2b, Crinum abyssinicum, horiz.

2003, Nov. 27 **Litho.** *Perf. 13x13¼*
1654-1657 A356 Set of 4 4.25 3.50

Konso Terracing System A357

Designs: 40c, Village, crops. 60c, Man and woman, ears of grains. 1b, Terraces, tool. 2b, Farmers working on terraces, crops.

2003, Dec. 30 *Perf. 13¼x13¾*
1658-1661 A357 Set of 4 4.00 2.00

Amaranths A358

Designs: 20c, Seeds. 80c, White amaranth. 1b, Red amaranth. 2b, Amaranth bread.

2004, Mar. 11 **Litho.** *Perf. 13¼x14*
1662-1665 A358 Set of 4 4.50 2.25

Marble A359

Designs: 25c, Sabian multicolored marble. 75c, Eshet blue marble. 1b, Sabian rose green marble. 2b, Sabian purple marble.

2004, July 27 *Perf. 14*
1666-1669 A359 Set of 4 2.25 2.25

FIFA (Fédération Internationale de Football Association), Cent. — A360

Soccer field, "100" and: 5c, FIFA emblem. 95c, Old soccer ball. 1b, Cleats. 2b, Modern soccer ball.

2004, Sept. 7 **Litho.** *Perf. 14*
1670-1673 A360 Set of 4 2.25 2.25

2004 Summer Olympics, Athens A361

Designs: 20c, Track. 35c, Hammer throw. 45c, Boxing. 3b, Cycling.

2004, Dec. 7
1674-1677 A361 Set of 4 2.25 2.25

Gesho — A362

Designs: 40c, Chopped plant. 60c, Plants, horiz. 1b, Cut logs. 2b, Branch with berries.

2004, Dec. 28
1678-1681 A362 Set of 4 2.25 2.25

Black Rhinoceros A363

2005, June 20 **Litho.** ***Perf. 14***

Background Color

1682	A363	5c bright blue	.25	.25
1683	A363	10c lilac	.25	.25
1684	A363	15c dark blue	.25	.25
1685	A363	20c bister	1.00	1.00
1686	A363	25c dark purple	1.00	1.00
1687	A363	30c blue	1.00	1.00
1688	A363	35c red	1.00	1.00
1689	A363	40c purple	1.00	1.00
1690	A363	45c green	1.00	1.00
1691	A363	4b bright red	4.25	4.25
		Nos. 1682-1691 (10)	11.00	11.00

Sabean Inscriptions — A364

Various inscriptions with background colors of: 15c, Green. 40c, Red, vert. 45c, Orange, vert. 3b, Blue, vert.

Perf. 13¾x14, 14x13¾

2005, Aug. 20 **Litho.**

1692-1695 A364 Set of 4 2.00 2.00

Surma Hairstyles A365

Various hairstyles with background colors of: 15c, Red. 40c, Green. 45c, Blue. 3b, Lilac.

2005, Dec. 20 ***Perf. 14x13¾***

1696-1699 A365 Set of 4 2.00 2.00

Flowers A366

Designs: 45c, Chlorophytum neghellense. 55c, Aloe bertemariae, vert. 3b, Aloe schelpei, vert.

Perf. 13¾x14, 14x13¾

2006, June 6 **Litho.**

1700-1702 A366 Set of 3 2.00 2.00

Ethiopian Airlines, 60th Anniv. A367

Designs: 15c, Douglas C-47A Dakota III. 40c, Douglas DC-6B Super Cloudmaster. 45c, Boeing 720-060B. 1b, Boeing 767-300ER. 2b, Boeing 787 Dreamliner.

2006, Sept. 28 ***Perf. 13x13¼***

1703-1707 A367 Set of 5 2.00 2.00

Intl. Year of Deserts and Desertification — A368

Emblem and: 15c, United Nations emblem. 40c, Map of Ethiopia showing desertification vulnerability. 45c, Map of Africa showing climate types. 3b, Map of world showing climate types.

2006, Oct. 31 ***Perf. 14x13½***

1708-1711 A368 Set of 4 2.00 2.00

Ethiopian Millennium A369

Panel color: 40c, Pink. 60c, Buff. 3b, Green.

2007, Nov. 15 **Litho.** ***Perf. 13¾***

1712-1714 A369 Set of 3 2.00 2.00

Minerals A370

Designs: 40c, Gypsum. 60c, Quartz. 1b, Ambo sandstone. 2b, Feldspar.

2007, Dec. 25 ***Perf. 14***

1715-1718 A370 Set of 4 2.00 2.00

Onslaught Martyrs Memorial A371

Designs: 40c, Martyrs Memorial Center. 60c, Emblem of Association for the Erection of the Martyrs Memorial Monument, vert. 3b, Woman, jail cell, gun, vert.

2008, Aug. 26 **Litho.** ***Perf. 14***

1719-1721 A371 Set of 3 .85 .85

Catha Edulis — A372

Designs: 45c, Red leaves. 55c, Harvesting of plant. 3b, Plant.

2008, Sept. 8 ***Perf. 13¾***

1722-1724 A372 Set of 3 .85 .85

Diplomatic Relations Between Ethiopia and India, 60th Anniv. A373

"60" and: 30c, Ethiopian and Indian flowers. 70c, Rock church, Lalibela, and Taj Mahal, India. 3b, Symbols of India and Ethiopia.

2008, Dec. 30 **Litho.** ***Perf. 14x13¼***

1725-1727 A373 Set of 3 .80 .80

Pan-African Tsetse and Trypanosomiasis Eradication Campaign A374

Designs: 15c, Campaign emblem. 40c, Tsetse fly. 45c, Tsetse fly and blood drop, horiz. 3b, Tsetse fly, cow, silhouette of human, map of Africa, horiz.

Perf. 13½x14, 14x13½

2009, July 21 **Litho.**

1728-1731 A374 Set of 4 .70 .70

Addis Ababa Monuments — A375

Designs: 45c, Arat Kilo, Miazia 27 Square Monument. 55c, Sidist Kilo, Yekatit 12 Square Monument. 3b, Abune Petros Monument, vert.

2009, Sept. 17 **Litho.** ***Perf. 13¾***

1732-1734 A375 Set of 3 .65 .65

Eradication of Rinderpest in Ethiopia A376

Designs: 15c, First laboratory in Addis Ababa where rinderpest vaccine was produced. 40c, Certificate from World Organization for Animal Health. 45c, Dead cattle. 3b, Dr. Alemework Beyene, monument to Dr. Engueda Johannes, veterinarians.

2009, Dec. 31 ***Perf. 14***

1735-1738 A376 Set of 4 .65 .65

Pan-African Postal Union, 30th Anniv. — A377

Background color: 45c, Green. 55c, Yellow. 3b, Rose.

2010, Apr. 6 **Litho.** ***Perf. 13¼x14***

1739-1741 A377 Set of 3 .60 .60

Writers — A378

Designs: No. 1742, 1b, Tsegaye Gebremedhin (1936-2006). No. 1743, 1b, Dr. Sindehu Gebru (1915-2009). No. 1744, 1b, Dr. Haddis Alemayehu (1910-2003). No. 1745, 1b, Dr. Kebede Michael (1915-98).

2010, Aug. 6 ***Perf. 14***

1742-1745 A378 Set of 4 .60 .60

Ethiopian Red Cross, 75th Anniv. A379

75th anniversary emblem and: 45c, Ambulance, Red Cross workers and truck. 55c, Bags of blood, boy receiving transfusion. 1b, Amharic letters, vert. 2b, Red Cross building.

2010, Oct. 12 **Litho.** ***Perf. 14***

1746-1749 A379 Set of 4 .50 .50

Mosques A380

Designs: 20c, Goze Mosque. 80c, Al-Nejashi Mosque. 3b, Sheh Hussein Mosque, Dire.

2011, May 24 **Litho.** ***Perf. 14***

1750-1752 A380 Set of 3 .50 .50

Monasteries and Churches — A381

Designs: 35c, Zoz Amba St. George's Monastery, Gonder. 65c, Meskele Kiristose Church, Wollo, vert. 3b, Debre Damo Abuna Aregawi Monastery, Tigrai, vert.

2011, June 9

1753-1755 A381 Set of 3 .50 .50

Bridges A382

Designs: 20c, Tezeke Bridge No. 3. 80c, Hidassie Bridge. 1b, Beshela River Bridge. 2b, Blue Nile Bridge.

2011, Sept. 2 **Litho.** ***Perf. 14x13¼***

1756-1759 A382 Set of 4 .50 .50

Martyr's Monuments A383

Designs: 40c, Amhara Region Martyr's Monument, Bahir Dar. 60c, Oromo Martyr's Monument, Adama. 3b, Tigrai Region Martyr's Monument, Mekelle, horiz.

2011, Sept. 9 ***Perf. 13¼x13, 13x13¼***

1760-1762 A383 Set of 3 .50 .50

Coffee Ceremony A384

Designs: 20c, Coffee pots. 80c, Preparation of coffee. 1b, Bean roasting. 2b, Pouring of coffee into cups.

2011, Dec. 20 *Perf. 13¼x14*
1763-1766 A384 Set of 4 .50 .50

Medicinal Plants A385

Designs: 20c, Lippia adoensis. 35c, Artemisia absinthium. 45c, Thymus schimperi. 3b, Ocimum lamiifolium.

2012, Apr. 10 *Perf. 14x13¼*
1767-1770 A385 Set of 4 .45 .45

Addis Ababa Monuments — A386

Designs: 40c, Lion of Judah Monument. 60c, Ras Mekonen Monument. 1b, Lion of Judah Monument, vert. 2b, Menelik II Monument, vert.

2012, July 5 *Perf. 14x13¼, 13¼x14*
1771-1774 A386 Set of 4 .45 .45

Writers — A387

Designs: 20c, Temesgen Gebre. 80c, Hiruy Woldeslassie. 1b, Yoftahe Nigussie. 2b, Afework Gebreyesus.

2012, Sept. 7 *Perf. 13¼x14*
1775-1778 A387 Set of 4 .45 .45

Addis Ababa, 125th Anniv. (in 2011) — A388

Various views of Addis Ababa: 15c, 35c, 2b, 4b.

Perf. 13¾x13½
2013, Aug. 20 **Litho.**
1779-1782 A388 Set of 4 .70 .70

Dated 2012.

African Union, 50th Anniv. — A389

African Union emblem, "50," and: 10c, Year of Pan-Africanism emblem, building. 40c, Building, diff. 2b, Assembly hall. 4b, Map of Africa, doves, airplane, road, farm field.

2013, Dec. 3 **Litho.** *Perf. 13¼x14*
1783-1786 A389 Set of 4 .70 .70

Ethio Telecom A390

Designs: 10c, Man holding wireless telephone console. 40c, Woman holding mobile telephone, woman using wall-mounted telephone, old dial telephone, vert. 2b, Man and woman using computer. 4b, Satellite, satellite dish, map, vert.

Perf. 14x13¼, 13¼x14
2014, May 13 **Litho.**
1787-1790 A390 Set of 4 .70 .70

Traditional Costumes of Southern Ethiopian People A391

Map and costumes of the: 15c, Karo. 35c, Erbore. 2b, Hamer. 4b, Daasanach.

2014, May 27 **Litho.** *Perf. 14x13¼*
1791-1794 A391 Set of 4 .70 .70

Ethiopian Orthodox Tewahedo Churches and Monasteries — A392

Designs: 50c, Orra Kidanemihiret Zege (monastery), Tana Island. 1b, Kibran Gebriel (monastery), Tana Island. 2b, Debrebirihan Silassie (church), Gonder, vert. 3b, Tsion Mariam Church, Axum.

Perf. 14x13¼, 13¼x14
2014, June 12 **Litho.**
1795-1798 A392 Set of 4 .70 .70

Rift Valley Sites A393

Designs: 5c, Salt deposits, Dallol. 25c, Sulfur deposits, Dallol. 30c, Brine ponds, Dallol. 45c, Erta Ale Volcano erupting. 65c, Ash plume over Erta Ale Volcano. 4b, Erta Ale caldera.

2014, Aug. 26 **Litho.** *Perf. 14*
1799-1804 A393 Set of 6 .60 .60

University of Gondar, 60th Anniv. — A394

Designs: 5c, Millennium Steps, Referral Hospital, Health team training group on horses in 1964, new campus. 45c, President's office. 2b, Main gate. 4b, 60th anniv. emblem, vert.

2014, Dec. 2 **Litho.** *Perf. 13½*
1805-1808 A394 Set of 4 .65 .65

Ethiopian Airlines A395

Designs: 15c, Boeing 777-F6N cargo plane. 45c, Boeing 777-200R passenger plane. 2b, Ethiopian Airlines Star Alliance jet. 4b, Boeing 787 Dreamliner.

2014, Dec. 25 **Litho.** *Perf. 13x13¼*
1809-1812 A395 Set of 4 .65 .65
1812a Booklet pane of 16, 4 each #1809-1812, perf. 13x13¼ on 3 sides 2.60 —
Complete booklet, #1812a 2.60

SEMI-POSTAL STAMPS

Types of 1931, Overprinted in Red at Upper Left

Perf. 12x12½, 12½x12
1936, Feb. 24 **Unwmk.**

B1	A27	1g light green	.60	.60
B2	A27	2g rose	.60	.60
B3	A25	4g blue	.60	.60
B4	A27	8g brown	.85	.85
B5	A25	1t purple	.85	.85
		Nos. B1-B5 (5)	3.50	3.50

Nos. B1-B5 were sold at twice face value, the surtax going to the Red Cross.

Catalogue values for unused stamps in this section, from this point to the end of the section, are for Never Hinged items.

Nos. 289, 290, 292-294 Surcharged in Blue

Perf. 13x13½
1949, June 13 **Wmk. 282**

B6	A53	8c + 8c deep org	2.50	2.50
B7	A53	12c + 5c red	2.50	2.50
B8	A53	30c + 15c org brn	4.00	4.00
B9	A53	70c + 70c rose lilac	25.00	25.00
B10	A53	$1 + 80c dk car rose	32.50	32.50
		Nos. B6-B10 (5)	66.50	66.50

No. B10 exists with "80+" error.
See Nos. B16-B20.

Type A39 Surcharged in Red or Carmine

Perf. 11½
1950, May 8 **Unwmk.** **Photo.**
Various Designs
Inscribed "Croix Rouge"

B11	A39	5c + 10c brt grn	1.50	2.00
B12	A39	10c + 10c brt red	2.00	2.25
B13	A39	25c + 10c brt bl	2.75	3.50
B14	A39	50c + 10c dk yel brn	7.00	5.50
B15	A39	1t + 10c brt vio	14.00	15.00
		Nos. B11-B15 (5)	27.25	28.25

The surtax was for the Red Cross.
The surcharge includes two dots which invalidate the original surtax. The original surcharge with uneven cross was red, a 1951 printing with even cross was carmine. Forgeries exist.

Nos. B6-B10 Overprinted in Black

Perf. 13x13½
1951, Nov. 17 **Wmk. 282**

B16	A53	8c + 8c dp org	.70	.70
B17	A53	12c + 5c red	.70	.70
B18	A53	30c + 15c org brn	1.25	1.25
B19	A53	70c + 70c rose lilac	12.00	12.00
B20	A53	$1 + 80c dk car rose	20.00	20.00
		Nos. B16-B20 (5)	34.65	34.65

No. B20 exists with "80 +" error.

Tree, Staff and Snake — SP1

Wmk. 282
1951, Nov. 25 **Engr.** *Perf. 13*
Lower Panel in Red

B21	SP1	5c + 2c dp bl grn	.50	.25
B22	SP1	10c + 3c orange	.70	.30
B23	SP1	15c + 3c dp bl	.90	.50
B24	SP1	30c + 5c red	2.00	1.25
B25	SP1	50c + 7c red brn	5.00	3.00
B26	SP1	$1 + 10c purple	10.00	5.00
		Nos. B21-B26 (6)	19.10	10.30

The surtax was for anti-tuberculosis work.

1958, Dec. 1
Lower Panel in Red

B27	SP1	20c + 3c dl pur	.40	.30
B28	SP1	25c + 4c emerald	.50	.35
B29	SP1	35c + 5c rose vlo	.75	.40
B30	SP1	60c + 7c vio bl	1.50	.80
B31	SP1	65c + 7c violet	3.00	1.75
B32	SP1	80c + 9c car rose	5.00	3.00
		Nos. B27-B32 (6)	11.15	6.60
		Nos. B21-B32 (12)	26.85	15.35

The surtax was for anti-tuberculosis work.
Nos. B21-B32 were the only stamps on sale from Dec. 1-25, 1958.

Type of Regular Issue, 1955, Overprinted and Surcharged

Engr.; Cross Typo. in Red

1959, May 30 **Wmk. 282**

B33	A62	15c + 2c olive bister & rose red	.70	.70
B34	A62	20c + 3c vio & emer	1.00	1.00
B35	A62	30c + 5c rose car & grnsh bl	1.75	1.75
		Nos. B33-B35 (3)	3.45	3.45

Cent. of the Intl. Red Cross idea. Surtax for the Red Cross.

The overprint includes the cross, "RED CROSS CENTENARY" and date in two languages. The surcharge includes the date in Amharic and the new surtax. The surcharge was applied locally.

Design A39 Surcharged

Perf. 11½

1960, May 7 **Photo.** **Unwmk.**

B36	A39	5c + 1c brt green	.85	.85
B37	A39	10c + 2c brt red	1.25	1.00
B38	A39	25c + 3c brt blue	1.90	1.25
B39	A39	50c + 4c dk yel brn	3.00	2.50
B40	A39	1t + 5c brt vio	5.00	4.50
		Nos. B36-B40 (5)	12.00	10.10

25th anniversary of Ethiopian Red Cross. Forgeries exist.

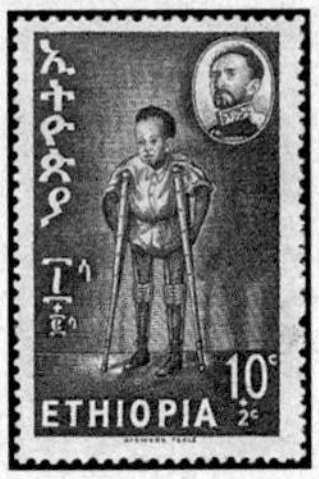

Crippled Boy on Crutches — SP2

Wmk. 282

1963, July 23 **Engr.** ***Perf. 13½***

B41	SP2	10c + 2c ultra	.40	.40
B42	SP2	15c + 3c red	.60	.45
B43	SP2	50c + 5c brt green	1.90	1.60
B44	SP2	60c + 5c red lilac	2.75	2.00
		Nos. B41-B44 (4)	5.65	4.45

The surtax was to aid the disabled.

AIR POST STAMPS

Regular Issue of 1928 Handstamped in Violet, Red, Black or Green

Perf. 13½x14

1929, Aug. 17 **Unwmk.**

C1	A22	⅛m orange & lt bl	.90	*1.00*
C2	A23	¼m ind & red org	.90	*1.00*
C3	A22	½m gray grn & blk	.90	*1.00*
C4	A23	1m dk car & blk	.90	*1.00*
C5	A22	2m dk blue & blk	1.00	*1.25*
C6	A23	4m yellow & olive	1.00	*1.25*
C7	A22	8m violet & olive	1.00	*1.25*
C8	A23	1t org brn & vio	1.25	*1.25*
C9	A22	2t green & bister	1.60	*2.00*
C10	A23	3t choc & grn	1.75	*2.00*
		Nos. C1-C10 (10)	11.20	*13.00*

The overprint signifies "17 August 1929-Airplane of the Ethiopian Government." The stamps commemorate the arrival at Addis Ababa of the 1st airplane of the Ethiopian Government.

There are 3 types of the overprint: (I) 19½mm high; "colon" at right of bottom word. (II) 20mm high; same "colon." (III) 19½mm high; no "colon." Many errors exist.

Symbols of Empire, Airplane and Map — AP1

1931, June 17 **Engr.** ***Perf. 12½***

C11	AP1	1g orange red	.25	*.25*
C12	AP1	2g ultra	.25	*.30*
C13	AP1	4g violet	.25	*.40*
C14	AP1	8g blue green	.50	*.80*
C15	AP1	1t olive brown	1.25	*1.00*
C16	AP1	2t carmine	2.25	*3.75*
C17	AP1	3t yellow green	3.25	*5.00*
		Nos. C11-C17 (7)	8.00	*11.50*

Nos. C11 to C17 exist imperforate.

Reprints of C11 to C17 exist. Paper is thinner and gum whiter than the originals and the ink is heavy and shiny. Originals have ink that is dull and granular. Reprints usually sell at about one-tenth of above values.

Catalogue values for unused stamps in this section, from this point to the end of the section, are for Never Hinged items.

Nos. 250, 255 and 257 Surcharged in Black

a

b

Perf. 14x13½

1947, Mar. 20 **Unwmk.**

C18	A33 (a)	12c on 4c	77.50	77.50
C19	A33 (b)	50c on 25c	72.50	72.50
a.		"26-12-46"	275.00	
C20	A33 (b)	$2 on 60c	125.00	125.00
a.		"26-12-46"	340.00	
		Nos. C18-C20 (3)	275.00	275.00
		Set, hinged	175.00	

Resumption of airmail service, 12/29/46.

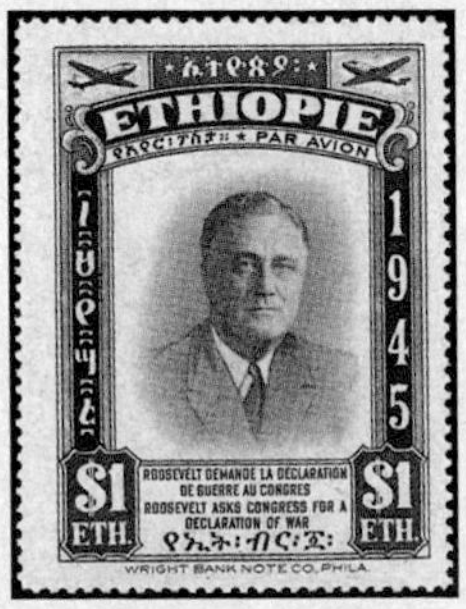

Franklin D. Roosevelt AP2

Design: $2, Haile Selassie.

Engraved and Photogravure

1947, May 23 ***Perf. 12½***

C21	AP2	$1 dk purple & sepia	12.50	12.50
C22	AP2	$2 carmine & dp blue	17.50	17.50

Farmer Plowing AP3

Designs: 10c, 25c, Zoquala, extinct volcano. 30c, 35c, Tesissat Falls, Abai River. 65c, 70c, Amba Alaguie. $1, Sacala, source of Nile. $3, Gorgora and Dembia, Lake Tana. $5, Magdala, former capital. $10, Ras Dashan, mountain peak.

Perf. 13x13½

1947-55 **Wmk. 282** **Engr.**

C23	AP3	8c purple brown	.30	.30
C24	AP3	10c bright green	.30	.30
C25	AP3	25c dull pur ('52)	.45	.30
C26	AP3	30c orange yellow	.95	.30
C27	AP3	35c blue ('55)	.95	.45
C28	AP3	65c purple ('55)	1.10	.80
C29	AP3	70c red	1.75	.80
C30	AP3	$1 deep blue	2.00	.95
C31	AP3	$3 rose lilac	7.75	4.75
C32	AP3	$5 red brown	15.00	6.75
C33	AP3	$10 rose violet	30.00	17.50
		Nos. C23-C33 (11)	60.55	33.20

For overprints see Nos. C64-C70.

UPU Monument, Bern — AP4

1950, Apr. 3 **Unwmk.** ***Perf. 12½***

C34	AP4	5c green & red	.25	.25
C35	AP4	15c dk sl grn & car	1.40	1.40
C36	AP4	25c org yel & grn	1.75	1.40
C37	AP4	50c carmine & ultra	4.25	3.25
		Nos. C34-C37 (4)	7.65	6.30

75th anniv. of the UPU.

No. C34 exists in the colors of Nos. C35-C37. These are considered to be trial color proofs.

Convair Plane over Mountains AP5

Engraved and Lithographed

1955, Dec. 30 **Unwmk.** ***Perf. 12½***

Center Multicolored

C38	AP5	10c gray green	1.25	.30
C39	AP5	15c carmine	1.60	.80
C40	AP5	20c violet	2.50	1.25
		Nos. C38-C40 (3)	5.35	2.35

10th anniversary of Ethiopian Airlines.

Promulgating the Constitution — AP6

Perf. 14x13½

1956, July 16 **Engr.** **Wmk. 282**

C41	AP6	10c redsh brn & ultra	.60	.70
C42	AP6	15c dk car rose & ol grn	.95	1.00
C43	AP6	20c blue & org red	1.25	1.00
C44	AP6	25c purple & green	1.40	1.60
C45	AP6	30c dk grn & red brn	2.40	2.50
		Nos. C41-C45 (5)	6.60	6.80

25th anniversary of the constitution.

Aksum AP7

Ancient Capitals: 10c, Lalibela. 15c, Gondar. 20c, Mekele. 25c, Ankober.

1957, Feb. 7 ***Perf. 14***

Centers in Green

C46	AP7	5c red brown	.75	.40
C47	AP7	10c rose carmine	.75	.40
C48	AP7	15c red orange	.90	.50
C49	AP7	20c ultramarine	1.40	.70
C50	AP7	25c claret	2.10	1.00
		Nos. C46-C50 (5)	5.90	3.00

Amharic "A" — AP8

Designs: Various Amharic characters and views of Addis Ababa. The characters, arranged by values, spell Addis Ababa.

1957, Feb. 14 **Engr.**

Amharic Letters in Scarlet

C51	AP8	5c ultra, *sal pink*	.35	.35
C52	AP8	10c ol grn, *pink*	.35	.35
C53	AP8	15c dl pur, *yel*	.55	.35
C54	AP8	20c grn, *buff*	.90	.40
C55	AP8	25c plum, *pale bl*	2.50	.55
C56	AP8	30c red, *pale grn*	1.75	.60
		Nos. C51-C56 (6)	6.40	2.60

70th anniversary of Addis Ababa.

Map, Rock Church at Lalibela and Obelisk AP9

1958, Apr. 15 **Wmk. 282** ***Perf. 13½***

C57	AP9	10c green	.25	.25
C58	AP9	20c rose red	1.10	.25
C59	AP9	30c bright blue	1.75	.90
		Nos. C57-C59 (3)	3.10	1.40

Conf. of Independent African States, Accra, Apr. 15-22.

Map of Africa and UN Emblem AP10

1958, Dec. 29 ***Perf. 13***

C60	AP10	5c emerald	.25	.25
C61	AP10	20c carmine rose	.55	.25
C62	AP10	25c ultramarine	.75	.55
C63	AP10	50c pale purple	1.50	.75
		Nos. C60-C63 (4)	3.05	1.80

1st session of the UN Economic Conf. for Africa, opened in Addis Ababa Dec. 29.

Nos. C23-C29 Overprinted

Perf. 13x13½

1959, Aug. 16 **Engr.** **Wmk. 282**

C64	AP3	8c purple brown	.50	.30
C65	AP3	10c brt green	.70	.35
C66	AP3	25c dull purple	1.05	.40

C67	AP3	30c orange yellow	1.15	.60
C68	AP3	35c blue	1.40	.65
C69	AP3	65c purple	2.25	1.00
C70	AP3	70c red	2.75	1.25
		Nos. C64-C70 (7)	9.80	4.55

30th anniv. of Ethiopian airmail service.

Ethiopian Soldier and Map of Congo — AP11

Perf. 11½

1962, July 23 Unwmk. Photo.

Granite Paper

C71	AP11 15c org, bl, brn & grn	.25	.25
C72	AP11 50c pur, bl, brn & grn	.75	.65
C73	AP11 60c red, bl, brn & grn	1.40	.80
	Nos. C71-C73 (3)	2.40	1.70

2nd anniv. of the Ethiopian contingent of the UN forces in the Congo and in honor of the 70th birthday of Emperor Haile Selassie.

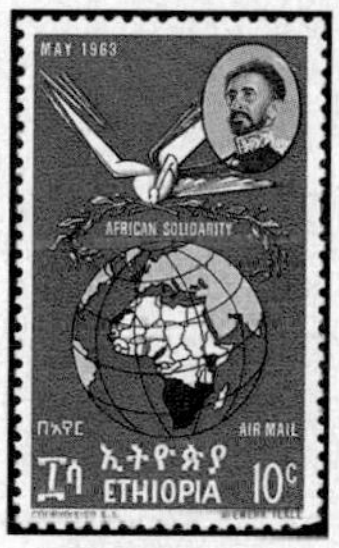

Globe with Map of Africa — AP12

1963, May 22 Granite Paper

C74	AP12 10c magenta & blk	.35	.35
C75	AP12 40c emerald & blk	1.75	1.00
C76	AP12 60c blue & blk	2.75	1.25
	Nos. C74-C76 (3)	4.85	2.60

Conf. of African heads of state for African Unity, Addis Ababa.

Bird Type of Regular Issue

Birds: 10c, Black-headed forest oriole. 15c, Broad-tailed paradise whydah, vert. 20c, Lammergeier, vert. 50c, White-checked touraco. 80c, Purple indigo bird.

1963, Sept. 12 ***Perf. 11½***

Granite Paper

C77	A74 10c multicolored	.60	.25
C78	A74 15c multicolored	.75	.25
C79	A74 20c blue, blk & ocher	1.50	.60
C80	A74 50c lemon & multi	2.40	1.10
C81	A74 80c ultra, blk & brn	4.75	1.90
	Nos. C77-C81 (5)	10.00	4.10

Swimming AP13

Sport: 10c, Basketball, vert. 15c, Javelin. 80c, Soccer game in stadium.

Perf. 14x13½

1964, Sept. 15 Litho. Unwmk.

C82	AP13 5c multicolored	.30	.25
C83	AP13 10c multicolored	.30	.25
C84	AP13 15c multicolored	.85	.55
C85	AP13 80c multicolored	3.00	1.10
	Nos. C82-C85 (4)	4.45	2.15

18th Olympic Games, Tokyo, Oct. 10-25.

Queen Elizabeth II and Emperor Haile Selassie — AP14

1965, Feb. 1 Photo. ***Perf. 11½***

Granite Paper

C86	AP14 5c multicolored	.45	.45
C87	AP14 35c multicolored	1.40	1.40
C88	AP14 60c multicolored	2.10	1.40
	Nos. C86-C88 (3)	3.95	3.25

Visit of Queen Elizabeth II, Feb. 1-8.

Koka Dam and Power Plant — AP15

Designs: 15c, Sugar cane field. 50c, Blue Nile Bridge. 60c, Gondar castles. 80c, Coffee tree. $1, Cattle at water hole. $3, Camels at well. $5, Ethiopian Air Lines jet plane.

1965, July 19 Unwmk. ***Perf. 11½***

Granite Paper

Portrait In Black

C89	AP15 15c vio brn & buff	.25	.25
C90	AP15 40c vio bl & lt bl	.45	.30
C91	AP15 50c grn & lt bl	.70	.35
C92	AP15 60c claret & yel	1.20	.60
C93	AP15 80c grn, yel & red	1.50	.70
C94	AP15 $1 brn & lt bl	1.75	.85
C95	AP15 $3 claret & pink	6.00	2.25
C96	AP15 $5 ultra & lt bl	12.75	4.25
	Nos. C89-C96 (8)	24.60	9.55

Bird Type of Regular Issue

Birds: 10c, White-collared kingfisher. 15c, Blue-breasted bee-eater. 25c, African paradise flycatcher. 40c, Village weaver. 60c, White-collared pigeon.

1966, Feb. 15 Photo. ***Perf. 11½***

Granite Paper

C97	A74 10c dull yel & multi	.90	.25
C98	A74 15c lt blue & multi	1.20	.25
C99	A74 25c gray & multi	2.50	.80
C100	A74 40c pink & multi	4.75	1.10
C101	A74 60c multicolored	5.50	1.75
	Nos. C97-C101 (5)	14.85	4.15

Black Rhinoceros — AP16

Animals: 10c, Leopard. 20c, Black-and-white colobus (monkey). 30c, Mountain nyala. 60c, Nubian ibex.

1966, June 20 Litho. ***Perf. 13***

C102	AP16 5c dp grn, blk & gray	.25	.25
C103	AP16 10c grn, blk & ocher	.55	.25
C104	AP16 20c cit, blk & grn	1.10	.25
C105	AP16 30c yel grn, blk & ocher	1.75	.25
C106	AP16 60c yel grn, blk & dk brn	3.25	.65
	Nos. C102-C106 (5)	6.90	1.65

Bird Type of Regular Issue

Birds: 10c, Blue-winged goose, vert. 15c, Yellow-billed duck. 20c, Wattled ibis. 25c, Striped swallow. 40c, Black-winged lovebird, vert.

1967, Sept. 29 Photo. ***Perf. 11½***

Granite Paper

C107	A74 10c lt ultra & multi	.25	.25
C108	A74 15c green & multi	1.40	.25
C109	A74 20c yellow & multi	1.60	.25
C110	A74 25c salmon & multi	2.75	.25
C111	A74 40c pink & multi	5.75	1.60
	Nos. C107-C111 (5)	11.75	2.60

SPECIAL DELIVERY STAMPS

Catalogue values for unused stamps in this section are for Never Hinged items.

Motorcycle Messenger — SD1

Addis Ababa Post Office SD2

Unwmk.

1947, Apr. 24 Engr. ***Perf. 13***

E1	SD1 30c orange brown	5.00	1.25
E2	SD2 50c blue	9.00	3.50

1954-62 Wmk. 282

E3	SD1 30c org brown ('62)	5.75	3.75
E4	SD2 50c blue	3.75	1.40

POSTAGE DUE STAMPS

Very Fine examples of Nos. J1-J42 will have perforations touching the design on one or more sides.

Nos. 1-4 and unissued values Overprinted

Perf. 14x13½

1896, June 10 Unwmk.

Black Overprint

J1	A1	¼g green	1.45
J2	A1	½g red	1.45
J3	A1	4g lilac brown	1.00
a.		Without overprint	1.00
J4	A1	8g violet	1.00
a.		Without overprint	1.00

Red Overprint

J5	A1	1g blue	1.45
J6	A1	2g dark brown	1.45
J7	A1	16g black	1.00
a.		Without overprint	1.00
		Nos. J1-J7 (7)	8.80

Nos. J1-J7 were not issued. Forgeries exist.

Nos. 1-7 Handstamped in Various Colors

a

b

1905, Apr.

J8	A1 (a)	¼g green	55.00	55.00
J9	A1 (a)	½g red	55.00	55.00
J10	A1 (a)	1g blue	55.00	55.00
J11	A1 (a)	2g dk brown	55.00	55.00
J12	A2 (a)	4g lilac brown	55.00	55.00
J13	A2 (a)	8g violet	55.00	55.00
J14	A2 (a)	16g black	55.00	55.00
		Nos. J8-J14 (7)	385.00	385.00

1905, Aug.

J15	A1 (b)	¼g green	55.00	55.00
J16	A1 (b)	½g red	55.00	55.00
J17	A1 (b)	1g blue	55.00	55.00
J18	A1 (b)	2g dark brown	55.00	55.00
J19	A2 (b)	4g lilac brown	55.00	55.00
J20	A2 (b)	8g violet	55.00	55.00
J21	A2 (b)	16g black	55.00	55.00
		Nos. J15-J21 (7)	385.00	385.00

Excellent forgeries of Nos. J8-J42 exist.

Nos. 1-7 Handstamped in Blue or Violet

1905, Sept.

J22	A1	¼g green	14.50	14.50
J23	A1	½g red	14.50	14.50
J24	A1	1g blue	14.50	14.50
J25	A1	2g dark brown	14.50	14.50
J26	A2	4g lilac brown	14.50	14.50
J27	A2	8g violet	21.00	21.00
J28	A2	16g black	25.00	25.00
		Nos. J22-J28 (7)	118.50	118.50

Nos. J22-J27 exist with inverted overprint, also No. J22 with double overprint.
Forgeries exist.

With Additional Surcharge of Value Handstamped as on Nos. 71-77

1907, July 1

J29	A1 (e)	¼ on ¼g grn	14.00	14.00
J30	A1 (e)	½ on ½g red	14.00	14.00
J31	A1 (f)	1 on 1g blue	14.00	14.00
J32	A1 (f)	2 on 2g dk brown	14.00	14.00
J33	A2 (f)	4 on 4g lilac brn	14.00	14.00
J34	A2 (f)	8 on 8g violet	14.00	14.00
J35	A2 (f)	16 on 16g blk	22.50	22.50
		Nos. J29-J35 (7)	106.50	106.50

Nos. J30-J35 exist with inverted surcharge. Nos. J30, J33-J35 exist with double surcharge.

Nos. 1-7 Handstamped in Black

1908, Dec. 1

J36	A1	¼g green	1.40	1.25
J37	A1	½g red	1.40	1.25
J38	A1	1g blue	1.40	1.25
J39	A1	2g dark brown	1.75	1.50
J40	A2	4g lilac brown	2.50	2.50
J41	A2	8g violet	5.50	6.25
J42	A2	16g black	17.50	20.00
		Nos. J36-J42 (7)	31.45	34.00

Nos. J36 to J42 exist with inverted overprint and Nos. J36, J37, J38 and J40 with double overprint.
Forgeries of Nos. J36-J56 exist.

Same Handstamp on Nos. 87-93

1912, Dec. 1 ***Perf. 11½***

J43	A3	¼g blue green	1.75	1.25
J44	A3	½g rose	1.75	1.50

1913, July 1

J45	A3	1g green & org	6.00	4.25
J46	A4	2g blue	7.00	6.00
J47	A4	4g green & car	11.00	7.00
J48	A5	8g ver & dp grn	14.00	11.00
J49	A5	16g ver & car	35.00	27.50
		Nos. J43-J49 (7)	76.50	58.50

Nos. J43-J49, all exist with inverted, double and double, one inverted overprint.

Same Handstamp on Nos. 120-124 in Blue Black

1925-27 ***Perf. 11½***

J50	A6	⅛g violet & brn	*18.00*	*18.00*
J51	A6	¼g bl grn & db	*18.00*	*18.00*
J52	A6	½g scar & ol grn	*20.00*	*20.00*
J53	A9	1g rose lil & gray grn	*20.00*	*20.00*
J54	A9	2g dp ultra & fawn	*20.00*	*20.00*
		Nos. J50-J54 (5)	*96.00*	*96.00*

Same Handstamp on Nos. 110, 112

1917 (?)

J55	A3 (i)	1g green & org	*30.00*	*30.00*
J56	A4 (j)	2g blue	*30.00*	*30.00*

The status of Nos. J55-J56 is questioned.

Catalogue values for unused stamps in this section, from this point to the end of the section, are for Never Hinged items.

D2

Perf. 11½

1951, Apr. 2 Unwmk. Litho.

J57	D2	1c emerald	.35	.25
J58	D2	5c rose red	.75	.25
J59	D2	10c violet	1.40	.55
J60	D2	20c ocher	2.00	1.25
J61	D2	50c bright ultra	3.75	2.75
J62	D2	$1 rose lilac	7.75	3.75
		Nos. J57-J62 (6)	16.00	8.80

Nos. J57-J62 were reissued in 1968 on slightly yellowish paper.

OCCUPATION STAMPS

Issued under Italian Occupation

100 Centesimi = 1 Lira

OS1

Emperor Victor Emmanuel III — OS2

1936 Wmk. 140 *Perf. 14*

N1	OS1	10c org brn	16.00	9.50
N2	OS1	20c purple	14.50	4.00
N3	OS2	25c dark green	9.50	.80
N4	OS2	30c dark brown	9.50	1.60
N5	OS2	50c rose car	4.00	.40
N6	OS1	75c deep orange	36.00	8.00
N7	OS1	1.25 l deep blue	36.00	12.00
		Nos. N1-N7 (7)	125.50	36.30
		Set, never hinged	300.00	

Issued: Nos. N3-N5, May 22; others Dec. 5.

For later issues see Italian East Africa.

FALKLAND ISLANDS

'fol-klənd 'ī-ləndz

LOCATION — A group of islands about 300 miles east of the Straits of Magellan at the southern limit of South America

GOVT. — British Crown Colony

AREA — 4,700 sq. mi.

POP. — 2,607 (1996)

CAPITAL — Stanley

Dependencies of the Falklands are South Georgia and South Sandwich. In March 1962, three other dependencies — South Shetland Islands, South Orkneys and Graham Land—became the new separate colony of British Antarctic Territory. In 1985 South Georgia and the South Sandwich Islands became a separate colony.

12 Pence = 1 Shilling

20 Shillings = 1 Pound

100 Pence = 1 Pound (1971)

Catalogue values for unused stamps in this country are for Never Hinged items, beginning with Scott 97 in the regular postage section, Scott B1 in the semi-postal section, Scott J1 in the postage due section, Scott 1L1 in Falkland Island Dependencies regular issues, Scott 1LB1 in Falkland Island Dependencies semi-postals, and Scott 2L1, 3L1, 4L1, 5L1 in the Issues for Separate Islands.

Values for unused stamps are for examples with original gum as defined in the catalogue introduction.

Nos. 1-4, 7-8, and some printings of Nos. 5-6, exist with straight edges on one or two sides, being the imperforate margins of the sheets. This occurs in 24 out of 60 stamps. Catalogue values are for stamps with perforations on all sides.

Queen Victoria — A1

1878-79 Unwmk. Engr. *Perf. 14*

1	A1	1p claret	850.00	500.00
2	A1	4p dark gray ('79)	1,400.	200.00
3	A1	6p green	110.00	85.00
4	A1	1sh bistor brown	85.00	80.00

1883-95 Wmk. 2

5	A1	1p brt claret ('94)	130.00	95.00
a.		1p claret	425.00	190.00
b.		Horiz. pair, imperf. vert.	*90,000.*	
c.		1p red brown ('91)	300.00	95.00
d.		Diag. half of #5c used as ½p on cover		*4,250.*
6	A1	4p olive gray ('95)	14.00	27.50
a.		4p gray black	750.00	100.00
b.		4p olive gray black ('89)	200.00	65.00
c.		4p brownish black ('94)	1,300.	400.00

No. 6c has watermark reversed.

For surcharge see No. 19E.

1886 Wmk. 2 Sideways

7	A1	1p claret	95.00	65.00
a.		1p brownish claret	125.00	80.00
b.		Diagonal half of #7a used as ½p on cover		*4,250.*
8	A1	4p olive gray	525.00	60.00
a.		4p pale gray black	840.00	90.00

For surcharge see No. 19.

1891-1902 Wmk. 2

9	A1	½p green ('92)	19.00	18.00
a.		½p blue green	27.50	*32.50*
10	A1	½p yel green ('99)	2.25	*3.50*
11	A1	1p orange brown	130.00	85.00
a.		Diagonal half used as ½p on cover		*4,250.*
11B	A1	1p pale red ('99)	9.00	3.50
12	A1	1p org red ('02)	17.50	4.75
a.		1p Venetian red ('95)	32.50	20.00
13	A1	2p magenta ('96)	7.00	14.00
14	A1	2½p deep blue ('94)	275.00	160.00
15	A1	2½p ultra ('94)	50.00	14.00
a.		2½p pale ultra ('98)	50.00	20.00
b.		2½p dull blue	350.00	35.00
c.		2½p deep ultra ('01)	50.00	42.50
d.		2½p pale chalky ultra	240.00	60.00
16	A1	6p yellow ('96)	52.50	55.00
a.		6p orange ('92)	325.00	225.00
17	A1	9p ver ('95)	55.00	*65.00*
a.		9p salmon ('96)	60.00	*70.00*
18	A1	1sh gray brn ('95)	80.00	65.00
a.		1sh bis brn ('96)	75.00	55.00
		Nos. 9-18 (11)	697.25	487.75

Nos. 7 and 5a Surcharged in Black

1891 Wmk. 2 Sideways

19	A1	½p on half of 1p, #7	725.00	360.00
d.		Unsevered pair	3,750.	1,600.

Wmk. 2

19E	A1	½p on half of 1p, #5a	825.00	325.00
f.		Unsevered pair	4,750.	1,800.

Genuine used bisects should be canceled with a segmented circular cork cancel. Any other cancel must be linked by date to known mail ship departures. This surcharge exists on "souvenir" bisects, including examples of No. 11, and can be found inverted, double and sideways.

A3

A4

1898 Wmk. 1

20	A3	2sh6p dark blue	290.00	290.00
21	A4	5sh brown red	260.00	260.00

A5

A6

King Edward VII

1904-07 Wmk. 3 *Perf. 14*

22	A5	½p yellow green	9.00	1.75
23	A5	1p red, wmk. sideways ('07)	1.50	*4.25*
a.		Wmk. upright ('04)	17.00	*1.75*
24	A5	2p dull vio ('04)	25.00	*32.50*
25	A5	2½p ultramarine	35.00	10.00
a.		2½p deep blue	300.00	200.00
26	A5	6p orange ('05)	50.00	*57.50*
27	A5	1sh bis brn ('05)	50.00	40.00
28	A6	3sh gray green	180.00	160.00
29	A6	5sh dull red ('05)	240.00	160.00
		Nos. 22-29 (8)	590.50	466.00

A7

A8

King George V

1912-14 *Perf. 13¾x14, 14 (#36-40)*

30	A7	½p yel grn	3.00	3.75
31	A7	1p red	5.50	2.75
32	A7	2p brn vio	27.50	*24.00*
33	A7	2½p deep ultra	27.50	*25.00*
34	A7	6p orange	17.50	*22.50*
35	A7	1sh bis brn	40.00	*37.50*
36	A8	3sh dark green	100.00	*95.00*
37	A8	5sh brown red	120.00	*120.00*
38	A8	5sh plum ('14)	300.00	*300.00*
39	A8	10sh red, *green*	200.00	*275.00*
40	A8	£1 black, *red*	550.00	*600.00*
		Nos. 30-40 (11)	1,391.	*1,505.*

For overprints see Nos. MR1-MR3.

1921-29 Wmk. 4 *Perf. 14*

41	A7	½p yellow green	3.50	*4.50*
42	A7	1p red ('24)	6.00	2.10
43	A7	2p brown vio ('23)	22.00	8.50
44	A7	2½p dark blue	22.00	*20.00*
a.		2½p Prussian blue ('29)	*375.00*	*550.00*
45	A7	2½p vio, *yel* ('23)	6.00	*42.50*
46	A7	6p orange ('25)	11.00	*45.00*
47	A7	1sh bister brown	22.50	*57.50*
48	A8	3sh dk green ('23)	100.00	*190.00*
		Nos. 41-48 (8)	193.00	*370.10*

Some specialists call into question No. 44a. The editors would like to see authenticated evidence of its existence.

No. 43 Surcharged

1928

52	A7	2½p on 2p brn vio	*1,300.*	*1,400.*
a.		Double surcharge	*60,000.*	

Beware of forged surcharges.

King George V — A9

1929-31 *Perf. 14*

54	A9	½p green	1.40	*3.50*
55	A9	1p scarlet	4.25	.90
56	A9	2p gray	6.00	3.75
57	A9	2½p blue	6.00	2.50
58	A9	4p deep orange	23.00	15.00
59	A9	6p brown violet	24.00	19.00
60	A9	1sh black, *green*	27.50	*37.50*
a.		1sh black, *emerald*	*25.00*	*37.50*
61	A9	2sh6p red, *blue*	70.00	70.00
62	A9	5sh green, *yel*	105.00	*120.00*
63	A9	10sh red, *green*	225.00	*275.00*

Wmk. 3

64	A9	£1 black, *red*	350.00	425.00
		Nos. 54-64 (11)	842.15	972.15

Issue dates: 4p, 1931, others, Sept. 2.

Romney Marsh Ram — A10

Iceberg A11

Whaling Ship — A12

Port Louis A13

Map of the Islands A14

South Georgia A15

Blue Whale A16

Government House A17

Battle Memorial — A18

King Penguin — A19

Coat of Arms — A20

King George V — A21

1933, Jan. 2 Wmk. 4 *Perf. 12*

65	A10	½p green & blk	4.00	*12.00*
66	A11	1p dl red & blk	3.75	2.50
67	A12	1½p lt bl & blk	21.00	*25.00*
68	A13	2p ol brn & blk	17.50	*27.50*
69	A14	3p dl vio & blk	27.00	*35.00*
70	A15	4p orange & blk	26.00	*27.50*
71	A16	6p gray & black	70.00	*90.00*
72	A17	1sh ol grn & blk	75.00	*100.00*
73	A18	2sh6p dp vio & blk	250.00	*400.00*
74	A19	5sh yellow & blk	950.00	*1,500.*
a.		5sh yellow orange & black	3,000.	*3,500.*
75	A20	10sh lt brn & blk	850.00	*1,500.*
76	A21	£1 rose & black	2,500.	*3,500.*
		Nos. 65-76 (12)	4,794.	*7,219.*

Cent. of the permanent occupation of the islands as a British colony.

Common Design Types pictured following the introduction.

Silver Jubilee Issue

Common Design Type

1935, May 7 *Perf. 11x12*

77	CD301	1p carmine & blue	3.50	.50
78	CD301	2½p ultra & brown	12.50	2.25
79	CD301	4p indigo & grn	20.00	7.00
80	CD301	1sh brn vio & ind	15.00	4.00
		Nos. 77-80 (4)	51.00	13.75
		Set, never hinged	75.00	
		Set (4), Ovptd. "SPECIMEN"	*475.00*	

Coronation Issue

Common Design Type

1937, May 12 *Perf. 11x11½*

81	CD302	½p deep green	.25	.25
82	CD302	1p dark carmine	.75	*.55*
83	CD302	2½p deep ultra	1.90	*1.50*
		Nos. 81-83 (3)	2.90	*2.30*
		Set, never hinged	4.00	
		Set (3), Ovptd. "SPECIMEN"	*450.00*	

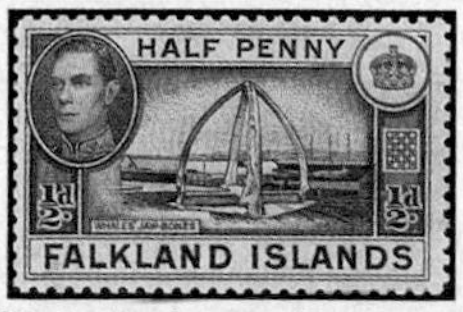

Whale Jawbones (Centennial Monument) — A22

Nos. 85, 86A, Black-necked swan. Nos. 85B, 86, Battle memorial. 2½p, 3p, Flock of sheep. 4p, Upland goose. 6p, R.R.S. "Discovery II." 9p, R.R.S. "William Scoresby." 1sh, Mt. Sugar Top. 1sh3p, Turkey vultures. 2sh6p, Gentoo penguins. 5sh, Sea lions. 10sh, Deception Island. £1, Arms of Colony.

1938-46 *Perf. 12*

84	A22	½p green & blk	.25	.75
85	A22	1p red & black	2.50	1.00
a.		1p rose carmine & black	22.50	1.00
85B	A22	1p dk vio & blk ('41)	2.00	2.00
a.		1p red vio & blk	8.00	3.50
86	A22	2p dk vio & blk	1.30	1.00
86A	A22	2p rose car & black ('41)	1.40	4.00
b.		2p red & black	3.00	3.00
87	A22	2½p ultra & blk	1.00	.50
b.		2½p blue & blk	5.00	8.00
87A	A22	3p blue & blk ('41)	5.50	6.50
c.		3p dp blue & blk	12.50	4.50
88	A22	4p rose vio & black	2.75	1.75
89	A22	6p sepia & blk	7.50	4.25
a.		6p dp brn & blk	19.50	2.50
90	A22	9p sl bl & blk	17.50	5.00
91	A22	1sh lt dl blue	25.00	5.50
a.		1sh dl grnsh blue	40.00	5.00
b.		1sh dl blue, grayish paper	30.00	150.00
c.		1sh dp dl blue, grayish paper ('48)	50.00	140.00
92	A22	1sh3p car & blk	2.00	*1.50*
93	A22	2sh6p gray black	40.00	22.50
94	A22	5sh org brn & ultra	100.00	90.00
a.		5sh yel brown & indigo	650.00	150.00
b.		5sh yel brn & dl bl, grayish paper ('49)	850.00	500.00
c.		5sh duff & steel bl, thin paper ('50)	250.00	65.00
95	A22	10sh org & blk	100.00	62.50
a.		10sh org brn & blk	150.00	65.00
b.		10sh red org & blk, grayish paper ('49)	90.00	450.00
c.		10sh dp red org & blk, thin paper ('50)	450.00	475.00
96	A22	£1 dk vio & blk	120.00	75.00
		Nos. 84-96 (16)	428.70	283.75
		Set, never hinged	600.00	
		Set (16), perf. "SPECIMEN"	*2,500.*	

Issued: Nos. 85B, 86A, 3p, 7/14/41; 1sh3p, 12/10/46; No. 94a, 1942; others, 1/3/38.

See Nos. 101-102. For overprints see Nos. 2L1-2L8, 3L1-3L8, 4L1-4L8.

Catalogue values for unused stamps in this section, from this point to the end of the section, are for Never Hinged items.

Peace Issue

Common Design Type

Perf. 13½x14

1946, Oct. 7 Engr. Wmk. 4

97	CD303	1p purple	.35	*.80*
98	CD303	3p deep blue	.55	.55

Silver Wedding Issue

Common Design Types

1948, Nov. 1 Photo. *Perf. 14x14½*

99	CD304	2½p bright ultra	2.10	1.10

Engr.; Name Typo.

Perf. 11½x11

100	CD305	£1 purple	110.00	82.50

Types of 1938-46

2½p, Upland goose. 6p, R.R.S. "Discovery II."

Perf. 12

1949, June 15 Engr. Wmk. 4

101	A22	2½p dp blue & black	7.50	*8.50*
102	A22	6p gray black	6.75	4.75

UPU Issue

Common Design Types

Engr.; Name Typo. on 3p, 1sh3p

1949, Oct. 10 *Perf. 13½, 11x11½*

103	CD306	1p violet	1.90	1.10
104	CD307	3p indigo	5.25	4.25
105	CD308	1sh3p green	3.75	3.00
106	CD309	2sh blue	4.00	8.75
		Nos. 103-106 (4)	14.90	17.10

Sheep A35

Arms of the Colony — A36

Designs: 1p, R.M.S. Fitzroy. 2p Upland goose. 2½p, Map. 4p, Auster plane. 6p, M.S.S. John Biscoe. 9p, "Two Sisters" peaks. 1sh, Gentoo penguins. 1sh 3p, Kelp goose and gander. 2sh 6p, Sheep shearing. 5sh, Battle memorial. 10sh, Sea lion and clapmatch. £1, Hulk of "Great Britain."

Perf. 13½x13, 13x13½

1952, Jan. 2 Engr. Wmk. 4

107	A35	½p green	1.30	*1.00*
108	A35	1p red	2.60	.55
109	A35	2p violet	4.75	*3.00*
110	A35	2½p ultra & blk	2.10	.70
111	A36	3p deep ultra	2.40	*1.10*
112	A35	4p claret	12.50	1.75
113	A35	6p yellow brn	14.00	1.10
114	A35	9p orange yel	12.50	2.25
115	A36	1sh black	26.00	1.10
116	A35	1sh3p red orange	19.00	*7.00*
117	A36	2sh6p olive	22.50	*12.50*
118	A36	5sh red violet	20.00	*11.00*
119	A35	10sh gray	30.00	*19.00*
120	A35	£1 black	40.00	*25.00*
		Nos. 107-120 (14)	209.65	*87.05*

Coronation Issue

Common Design Type

1953, June 4 *Perf. 13½x13*

121	CD312	1p car & black	.90	1.50

Types of 1952 with Portrait of Queen Elizabeth II

1955-57 *Perf. 13½x13, 13x13½*

122	A35	½p green ('57)	1.00	*1.50*
123	A35	1p red ('57)	1.40	*1.25*
124	A35	2p violet ('56)	3.50	*5.25*
125	A35	6p light brown	9.50	.70
126	A35	9p ocher ('57)	11.50	*18.50*
127	A36	1sh black	13.00	2.50
		Nos. 122-127 (6)	39.90	*29.70*

Marsh Starling A37

Birds: ½p, Falkland Islands Thrush. 1p, Dominican gull. 2p, Gentoo penguins. 3p, Upland geese. 4p, Steamer ducks. 5½p, Rock-hopper penguin. 6p, black-browed albatross. 9p, Silver grebe. 1sh, Pied oystercatchers. 1sh3p, Yellow-billed teal. 2sh, Kelp geese, 5sh, King shag. 10sh, Guadelupe caracara. £1, Black-necked swan.

Perf. 13½x13

1960, Feb. 10 Engr. Wmk. 314

Center in Black

128	A37	½p green	5.00	2.00
a.		Wmk. sideways ('66)	.45	.40
129	A37	1p rose red	3.00	2.00
130	A37	2p blue	4.25	1.00
131	A37	2½p bister brn	2.50	1.00
132	A37	3p olive	1.25	.50
133	A37	4p rose car	1.50	1.25
134	A37	5½p violet	3.50	*3.25*
135	A37	6p sepia	3.50	.30
136	A37	9p orange	2.50	1.25
137	A37	1sh dull purple	1.25	.40
138	A37	1sh3p ultra	12.50	*14.00*
139	A37	2sh brown car	30.00	2.50
140	A37	5sh grnsh blue	27.50	11.00
141	A37	10sh rose lilac	47.50	16.00
142	A37	£1 yellow org	50.00	27.00
		Nos. 128-142 (15)	195.75	83.45

Morse Key — A38

1962, Oct. 5 Photo. *Perf. 11½x11*

143	A38	6p dp org & dk red	.85	.60
144	A38	1sh brt ol grn & dp green	.95	.75
145	A38	2sh brt ultra & violet	1.25	*1.75*
		Nos. 143-145 (3)	3.05	3.10

Falkland Islands radio station, 50th anniv.

Freedom from Hunger Issue

Common Design Type

1963, June 4 *Perf. 14x14½*

146	CD314	1sh ultramarine	11.50	3.50

Red Cross Centenary Issue

Common Design Type

Wmk. 314

1963, Sept.2 Litho. *Perf. 13*

147	CD315	1p black & red	2.75	1.00
148	CD315	1sh ultra & red	17.00	5.00

Shakespeare Issue

Common Design Type

1964, Apr. 23 Photo. *Perf. 14x14½*

149	CD316	6p black	1.75	.50

H.M.S. Glasgow A39

6p, H.M.S. Kent. 1sh, H.M.S. Invincible. 2sh, Falkland Islands Battle Memorial, vert.

1964, Dec. 8 Engr. *Perf. 13*

150	A39	2½p ver & black	10.00	3.75
151	A39	6p blue & black	.55	.30
a.		"Glasgow" vignette	*32,500.*	
152	A39	1sh carmine & blk	.55	*1.10*

Perf. 13x14

153	A39	2sh dk blue & blk	.55	.85
		Nos. 150-153 (4)	11.65	6.00

Battle of the Falkland Islands between the British and German navies, 50th anniv.

ITU Issue

Common Design Type

Perf. 11x11½

1965, May 26 Litho. Wmk. 314

154	CD317	1p blue & dl dk bl	.50	.40
155	CD317	2sh lilac & dl yel	7.25	3.25

Intl. Cooperation Year Issue

Common Design Type

1965, Oct. 25 *Perf. 14½*

156	CD318	1p blue grn & claret	1.50	.40
157	CD318	1sh lt violet & grn	5.50	1.50

Churchill Memorial Issue

Common Design Type

1966, Jan. 24 Photo. *Perf. 14*

Design in Black, Gold and Carmine Rose

158	CD319	½p bright blue	.75	*1.25*
159	CD319	1p green	2.00	.30
160	CD319	1sh brown	5.50	2.75
161	CD319	2sh violet	4.50	3.50
		Nos. 158-161 (4)	12.75	7.80

Human Rights Flame and Globe A40

Perf. 14x14½

1968, July 4 Photo. Wmk. 314

162	A40	2p brt rose & multi	.35	.25
163	A40	6p brt green & multi	.40	.25
164	A40	1sh orange & multi	.50	.40
165	A40	2sh ultra & multi	.60	.45
		Nos. 162-165 (4)	1.85	1.35

International Human Rights Year.

Dusty Miller — A41

Falkland Islands flora: 1½p, Pig vine, horiz. 2p, Pale maiden. 3p, Dog orchid. 3½p, Sea cabbage, horiz. 4½p, Vanilla daisy. 5½p, Arrowleaf marigold, horiz. 6p, Diddle-dee, horiz. 1sh, Scurvy grass, horiz. 1sh6p, Prickly burr. 2sh, Fachine. 3sh, Lavender. 5sh, Felton's flower, horiz. £1, Yellow orchid.

1968, Oct. 9 Photo. *Perf. 14*

166	A41	½p multicolored	.25	*1.75*
167	A41	1½p multicolored	.45	.25
168	A41	2p multicolored	.60	.25
169	A41	3p multicolored	6.00	1.00
170	A41	3½p multicolored	.35	*.85*
171	A41	4½p multicolored	1.60	*1.75*
172	A41	5½p multicolored	1.60	*1.75*
173	A41	6p multicolored	.85	*.30*
174	A41	1sh multicolored	1.00	*1.50*
175	A41	1sh6p multicolored	5.00	*12.00*
176	A41	2sh multicolored	5.50	5.50
177	A41	3sh multicolored	7.75	8.00
178	A41	5sh multicolored	27.00	14.00
179	A41	£1 multicolored	11.50	3.25
		Nos. 166-179 (14)	69.45	52.15

See Nos. 210-222. For surcharges see Nos. 197-209.

Beaver DHC 2 Seaplane A42

Designs: 6p, Norseman seaplane. 1sh, Auster plane. 2sh, Falkland Islands arms.

1969, Apr. 8 Litho. *Perf. 14*

180	A42	2p multicolored	.45	.30
181	A42	6p multicolored	.65	.35
182	A42	1sh multicolored	.65	.40
183	A42	2sh multicolored	1.20	*1.90*
		Nos. 180-183 (4)	2.95	2.95

21st anniv. of Government Air Service.

Bishop Stirling A43

2p, Holy Trinity Church, 1869. 6p, Christ Church Cathedral, 1969. 2sh, Bishop's miter.

1969, Oct. 30 *Perf. 14*

184	A43	2p emerald & black	.40	.60
185	A43	6p red orange & black	.50	.60
186	A43	1sh lilac & black	.50	.60
187	A43	2sh yellow & multi	.60	.75
		Nos. 184-187 (4)	2.00	2.55

Consecration of Waite Hocking Stirling (1829-1923), as first Bishop of the Bishopric of the Falkland Islands, cent.

Gun Emplacement — A44

2p, Volunteer on horseback, vert. 1sh, Volunteer in dress uniform, vert. 2sh, Defense Force badge.

Perf. 13½x13, 13x13½

1970, Apr. 30 Litho. Wmk. 314

188	A44	2p ultra & multi	1.25	.65
189	A44	6p multicolored	1.50	.80
190	A44	1sh buff & multi	2.50	.80
191	A44	2sh yellow & multi	3.50	1.25
		Nos. 188-191 (4)	8.75	3.50

Falkland Islands Defense Force, 50th anniv.

The Great Britain, 1843 A45

The Great Britain in: 4p, 1845. 9p, 1876. 1sh, 1886. 2sh, 1970.

1970, Oct. 30 Litho. *Perf. 14½*

192	A45	2p lemon & multi	1.00	.60
193	A45	4p lilac & multi	1.25	1.00
194	A45	9p bister & multi	1.50	1.00
195	A45	1sh org brn & multi	1.50	1.00
196	A45	2sh multicolored	2.00	1.25
		Nos. 192-196 (5)	7.25	4.85

Nos. 166-178 Surcharged

1971, Feb. 15 Photo. *Perf. 14*

197	A41	½p on ½p multi	.40	.40
198	A41	1p on 1½p multi	.25	.25
a.		5p on 1½p (error)	750.00	
199	A41	1½p on 2p multi	.35	.35
200	A41	2p on 3p multi	.55	.55
201	A41	2½p on 3½p multi	.30	.30
202	A41	3p on 4½p multi	.35	.35
203	A41	4p on 5½p multi	.40	.40
204	A41	5p on 6p multi	.70	.70
205	A41	6p on 1sh multi	6.00	6.00
206	A41	7½p on 1sh6p multi	8.00	8.00
207	A41	10p on 2sh multi	8.00	4.00
208	A41	15p on 3sh multi	3.50	2.75
209	A41	25p on 5sh multi	4.50	4.50
		Nos. 197-209 (13)	33.30	28.55

Flower Type of 1968 "p" instead of "d"

Designs as before. 1p, 2½p, 4p, 5p, 6p, 25p, horizontal.

Wmk. 314, Sideways on Vert. Stamps

1972, June 1 *Perf. 14*

210	A41	½p Dusty miller	.75	4.00
a.		Wmk. upright ('74)	*15.00*	*32.50*
b.		Wmk. 373 ('75)	3.25	*3.50*
211	A41	1p Pig vine	.40	.30
212	A41	1½p Pale maiden	.55	.40
213	A41	2p Dog orchid	6.00	*4.50*
a.		Wmk. upright ('74)	30.00	2.50
214	A41	2½p Sea cabbage	.70	*4.00*
215	A41	3p Vanilla daisy	.75	*1.40*
216	A41	4p Arrowleaf marigold	1.00	*1.10*
217	A41	5p Diddle-dee	1.10	.90
218	A41	6p Scurvy grass	18.00	11.00
a.		Wmk. sideways ('74)	2.10	*2.50*
219	A41	7½p Prickly burr	2.00	3.75
220	A41	10p Fachine	10.00	4.50
221	A41	15p Lavender	4.00	4.50
222	A41	25p Felton's flower	8.00	8.00
		Nos. 210-222 (13)	53.25	48.35

Silver Wedding Issue, 1972
Common Design Type

Design: Queen Elizabeth II, Prince Philip, Romney Marsh sheep and giant sea lions.

1972, Nov 20 Photo. *Perf. 14x14½*

223	CD324	1p sl grn & multi	.30	.30
224	CD324	10p ultra & multi	.80	.80

Princess Anne's Wedding Issue
Common Design Type

1973, Nov. 14 Litho. *Perf. 14*

225	CD325	5p lilac & multi	.25	.25
226	CD325	15p citron & multi	.50	.50

Fur Seals A46

Tourist Publicity: 4p, Trout fishing. 5p, Rockhopper penguins. 15p, Military starling.

1974, Mar. 6 Litho. Wmk. 314

227	A46	2p lt ultra & multi	2.50	2.00
228	A46	4p brt blue & multi	3.50	1.50
229	A46	5p yellow & multi	11.50	2.50
230	A46	15p lt ultra & multi	13.50	5.00
		Nos. 227-230 (4)	31.00	11.00

Early 19th Cent. Mail Coach, UPU Emblem — A47

UPU Cent.: 5p, Packet, 1841. 8p, First British mail planes, 1911. 16p, Catapult mail, 1920's.

1974, July 31 *Perf. 14*

231	A47	2p multicolored	.25	.25
232	A47	5p multicolored	.35	.35
233	A47	8p multicolored	.40	.40
234	A47	16p multicolored	.60	.60
		Nos. 231-234 (4)	1.60	1.60

Churchill, Parliament and Big Ben A48

Design: 20p, Churchill and warships.

1974, Nov. 30 *Perf. 13x13½*

235	A48	16p multicolored	1.00	1.00
236	A48	20p multicolored	1.50	1.50
a.		Souvenir sheet of 2, #235-236	8.00	8.00

Sir Winston Churchill (1874-1965).

HMS Exeter A49

Battleships: 6p, HMNZS Achilles. 8p, Admiral Graf Spee. 16p, HMS Ajax.

1974, Dec. 13 *Perf. 14*

237	A49	2p multicolored	2.50	1.75
238	A49	6p multicolored	4.50	3.50
239	A49	8p multicolored	5.75	4.50
240	A49	16p multicolored	11.00	10.00
		Nos. 237-240 (4)	23.75	19.75

35th anniv. of the Battle of the River Plate between British ships and the German battleship Graf Spee.

Seal and Flag Badge — A50

7½p, Coat of arms, 1925. 10p, Arms, 1948. 16p, Arms (Falkland Islands Dependencies), 1952.

1975, Oct. 28 Litho. Wmk. 373

241	A50	2p multicolored	1.10	.50
242	A50	7½p multicolored	1.75	1.50
243	A50	10p multicolored	2.00	1.75
244	A50	16p multicolored	2.75	2.75
		Nos. 241-244 (4)	7.60	6.50

Falkland Islands heraldic arms, 50th anniv.

½p-Coin and Trout A51

New Coinage: 5½p, 1p-coin and gentoo penguins, 8p, 2p-coin and upland geese. 10p, 5p-coin and black-browed albatross. 16p, 10p-coin and sea lions.

1975, Dec. 31 Litho. Wmk. 373

245	A51	2p copper & multi	.75	.50
246	A51	5½p copper & multi	1.75	1.50
247	A51	8p copper & multi	2.00	1.75
248	A51	10p silver & multi	2.50	2.00
249	A51	16p silver & multi	3.50	3.50
		Nos. 245-249 (5)	10.50	9.25

Gathering Sheep — A52

Sheep Farming: 7½p, Shearing. 10p, Dipping sheep. 20p, Motor Vessel Monsunen collecting wool.

1976, Apr. 28 Litho. *Perf. 13½*

250	A52	2p multicolored	.90	.75
251	A52	7½p multicolored	1.25	1.25
252	A52	10p multicolored	1.60	1.60
253	A52	20p multicolored	2.50	2.50
		Nos. 250-253 (4)	6.25	6.10

Prince Philip, 1957 Visit A53

11p, Queen, ampulla and spoon. 33p, Queen awaiting anointment, and Knights of the Garter.

1977, Feb. 7 *Perf. 13½x14*

254	A53	6p multicolored	.35	.35
a.		Booklet pane of 4, wmk. 314	10.00	
b.		Single stamp from #254a	2.50	*5.00*
255	A53	11p multicolored	.60	.60
a.		Booklet pane of 4	3.50	
256	A53	33p multicolored	1.50	1.50
a.		Booklet pane of 4	8.00	
		Nos. 254-256 (3)	2.45	2.45

25th anniv. of the reign of Elizabeth II.

Map of West and East Falkland with Communications Centers — A54

Telecommunications: 11p, Ship to shore communications at Fox Bay. 40p, Globe with Telex tape and telephone.

1977, Oct. 24 Litho. *Perf. 14½x14*

257	A54	3p yel brown & multi	1.00	.25
258	A54	11p lt ultra & multi	1.75	.60
259	A54	40p rose & multi	2.75	2.00
		Nos. 257-259 (3)	5.50	2.85

A.E.S., 1957-1974 — A55

Designs: Mail ships.

1978, Jan. 25 Wmk. 373 *Perf. 14*

No Date Inscription

260	A55	1p	shown	.25	.25
261	A55	2p	Darwin, 1957-75	.35	.25
262	A55	3p	Merak-N 1951-53	.25	*.90*
263	A55	4p	Fitzroy, 1936-57	.25	*.90*
264	A55	5p	Lafonia 1936-41	.25	*.30*
265	A55	6p	Fleurus, 1924-33	.30	*.40*
266	A55	7p	S.S. Falkland, 1914-34	.40	*2.00*
267	A55	8p	Oravia, 1900-12	.45	*1.25*
268	A55	9p	Memphis, 1890-97	.45	.85
269	A55	10p	Black Hawk, 1873-80	.60	.50
270	A55	20p	Foam, 1963-72	1.00	*1.50*
271	A55	25p	Fairy, 1857-61	1.00	*3.00*
272	A55	50p	Amelia, 1852-54	1.50	*4.00*
273	A55	£1	Nautilus, 1846-48	2.50	*7.00*
274	A55	£3	Hebe, 1842-46	11.00	*15.00*
			Nos. 260-274 (15)	20.55	*38.10*

The 1p, 3p, 5p, 6p and 10p were also issued in booklet panes of 4.

For overprints see Nos. 352-353.

1982, Dec. 1 Inscribed "1982"

260a	A55	1p	shown	.40	*.90*
261a	A55	2p	Darwin, 1957-75	.50	*.90*
262a	A55	3p	Merak-N 1951-53	.60	*.90*
263a	A55	4p	Fitzroy, 1936-57	.60	*.90*
264a	A55	5p	Lafonia 1936-41	.70	*1.00*
265a	A55	6p	Fleurus, 1924-33	.70	*1.00*
266a	A55	7p	S.S. Falkland, 1914-34	.75	*1.00*
267a	A55	8p	Oravia, 1900-12	.75	*1.00*
268a	A55	9p	Memphis, 1890-97	.80	*1.00*
269a	A55	10p	Black Hawk, 1873-80	.85	*1.00*
270a	A55	20p	Foam, 1963-72	1.50	*2.00*
271a	A55	25p	Fairy, 1857-61	1.50	*2.00*
272a	A55	50p	Amelia, 1852-54	1.75	*3.00*
273a	A55	£1	Nautilus, 1846-48	3.25	*6.00*
274a	A55	£3	Hebe, 1842-46	5.00	*12.00*
			Nos. 260a-274a (15)	19.65	*34.60*

Elizabeth II Coronation Anniversary Issue

Souvenir Sheet

Common Design Type

1978, June 2 Unwmk. *Perf. 15*

275	Sheet of 6	4.00	4.00
a.	CD326 25p Red Dragon of Wales	.60	.60
b.	CD327 25p Elizabeth II	.60	.60
c.	CD328 25p Hornless ram	.60	.60

No. 275 contains 2 se-tenant strips of Nos. 275a-275c, separated by horizontal gutter with commemorative and descriptive inscriptions.

Short Sunderland Mark III — A56

Design: 33p, Plane in flight and route Southampton to Stanley.

1978, Apr. 28 Wmk. 373 *Perf. 14*

276	A56	11p	multicolored	2.75	2.25
277	A56	33p	multicolored	4.00	3.25

First direct flight Southampton, England to Stanley, Falkland Islands, 26th anniv.

First Fox Bay PO and No. 1 — A57

Macrocystis Pyrifera — A58

Designs: 11p, Second Stanley Post Office and #2. 15p, New Island Post Office and #3. 22p, 1st Stanley Post Office and #4.

1978, Aug. 8 Litho. *Perf. 13½x13*

278	A57	3p	multicolored	.25	.25
279	A57	11p	multicolored	.35	.35
280	A57	15p	multicolored	.50	.50
281	A57	22p	multicolored	.80	.80
			Nos. 278-281 (4)	1.90	1.90

Falkland Islands postage stamps, cent.

1979, Feb. 19 Litho. *Perf. 14*

Kelp: 7p, Durvillea. 11p, Lessoniae, horiz. 15p, Callophyllis, horiz. 25p, Iridea.

282	A58	3p	multicolored	.40	.40
283	A58	7p	multicolored	.45	.45
284	A58	11p	multicolored	.55	.55
285	A58	15p	multicolored	.80	.80
286	A58	25p	multicolored	.95	1.10
			Nos. 282-286 (5)	3.15	3.30

Britten-Norman Islander over Map — A59

Opening of Stanley Airport: 11p, Fokker F27 over map. 15p, Fokker F28 over Stanley. 25p, Cessna 172 Skyhawk, Islander and Fokkers F27, F28 over runway.

1979, May 1 Litho. *Perf. 13½*

287	A59	3p	multicolored	.50	.25
288	A59	11p	multicolored	.90	.65
289	A59	15p	multicolored	1.10	.65
290	A59	25p	multicolored	1.60	1.00
			Nos. 287-290 (4)	4.10	2.55

Rowland Hill and No. 121 A60

Sir Rowland Hill (1795-1879), originator of penny postage, and: 11p, Falkland Islands No. 1, vert. 25p, Penny Black. 33p, Falkland Islands No. 37, vert.

1979, Aug. 27 *Perf. 14*

291	A60	3p	multicolored	.25	.25
292	A60	11p	multicolored	.40	.40
293	A60	25p	multicolored	.75	.75
			Nos. 291-293 (3)	1.40	1.40

Souvenir Sheet

294	A60	33p	multicolored	1.50	1.50

Mail Delivery by Air, UPU Emblem A61

UPU Membership Cent. (Modes of Mail Delivery): 11p, Horseback. 25p, Schooner Gwendolin.

1979, Nov. 26

295	A61	3p	multicolored	.25	.25
296	A61	11p	multicolored	.45	*.55*
297	A61	25p	multicolored	.70	*1.10*
			Nos. 295-297 (3)	1.40	*1.90*

Commerson's Dolphin — A62

1980, Feb. 25 Wmk. 373 *Perf. 14*

298	A62	3p	Peale's porpoise, vert.	.40	.40
299	A62	6p	shown	.60	.60
300	A62	7p	Hour-glass dolphin	.60	.60
301	A62	11p	Spectacled porpoise, vert.	.70	.70
302	A62	15p	Dusky dolphin	.80	.80
303	A62	25p	Killer whale	.90	*1.50*
			Nos. 298-303 (6)	4.00	4.60

Miniature Sheet

A63

Designs: a, Falkland Islands Cancel, 1878. b, New Islds., 1915. c, Falklands Islds., 1901. d, Port Stanley, 1935. e, Port Stanley airmail, 1952. f, Fox Bay, 1934.

1980, May 6 Litho. *Perf. 14*

304	A63	Sheet of 6	1.60	1.60
a.-f.		11p any single	.25	.25

London 1980 Intl. Stamp Exhib., May 6-14.

Queen Mother Elizabeth Birthday

Common Design Type

1980, Aug. 4 Litho. *Perf. 14*

305	CD330	11p	multicolored	.40	.40

Striated Caracara A64

1980, Aug. 11 Wmk. 373 *Perf. 13½*

306	A64	3p	shown	.65	.30
307	A64	11p	Red-backed buzzard	.80	.55
308	A64	15p	Crested caracara	.90	.65
309	A64	25p	Cassin's falcon	1.10	1.10
			Nos. 306-309 (4)	3.45	2.60

Port Egmont, Early Settlement — A65

1980, Dec. 22 Litho. *Perf. 14*

310	A65	3p	Stanley	.25	.25
311	A65	11p	shown	.35	.35
312	A65	25p	Port Louis	.75	.75
313	A65	33p	Mission House, Keppel Island	.95	.95
			Nos. 310-313 (4)	2.30	2.30

Polwarth Sheep A66

1981, Jan. 19 Litho. *Perf. 14*

314	A66	3p	shown	.25	.25
315	A66	11p	Frisian cow and calf	.40	.30
316	A66	25p	Horse	.80	1.00
317	A66	33p	Welsh collies	1.00	1.25
			Nos. 314-317 (4)	2.45	2.80

Map of Falkland Islands, Bowles and Carver, 1779 A67

1981, May 22 Litho. *Perf. 14*

318	A67	3p	shown	.25	.25
319	A67	10p	Hawkin's Mainland, 1773	.30	.35
320	A67	13p	New Isles, 1747	.40	.35
321	A67	15p	French & British Islands	.50	.35
322	A67	25p	Falklands, 1771	.70	.50
323	A67	26p	Falklands, 1764	.75	.50
			Nos. 318-323 (6)	2.90	2.30

Royal Wedding Issue

Common Design Type

1981, July 22 Litho. *Perf. 13½x13*

324	CD331	10p	Bouquet	.25	.25
325	CD331	13p	Charles	.40	.45
326	CD331	52p	Couple	1.00	1.00
			Nos. 324-326 (3)	1.65	1.70

Duke of Edinburgh's Awards, 25th Anniv. — A68

1981, Sept. 28 Litho. *Perf. 14*

327	A68	10p	Spinning	.25	.25
328	A68	13p	Camping	.25	.25
329	A68	15p	Kayaking	.35	.35
330	A68	26p	Duke of Edinburgh	.55	.55
			Nos. 327-330 (4)	1.40	1.40

The Holy Virgin, by Guido Reni (1575-1642) A69

Christmas: 3p, Adoration of the Holy Child, 16th cent. Dutch. 13p, Holy Family in an Italian Landscape, 17th cent. Italian.

1981, Nov. 9 Litho. *Perf. 14*

331	A69	3p	multicolored	.25	.25
332	A69	13p	multicolored	.50	.50
333	A69	26p	multicolored	.75	.75
			Nos. 331-333 (3)	1.50	1.50

This set was issued Nov. 2 in London by the Crown Agents.

Rock Cod — A70

Designs: Shelf fish. 5p, 15p, 25p horiz.

1981, Dec. 7

334	A70	5p	Falkland herring	.25	.25
335	A70	13p	shown	.30	.30
336	A70	15p	Patagonian hake	.35	.35
337	A70	25p	Southern blue whiting	.55	.55
338	A70	26p	Gray-tailed skate	.55	.55
			Nos. 334-338 (5)	2.00	2.00

Shipwrecks — A71

1982, Feb. 15 Wmk. 373 *Perf. 14½*

339	A71	5p	Lady Elizabeth, 1913	.35	.35
340	A71	13p	Capricorn, 1882	.45	.45
341	A71	15p	Jhelum, 1870	.50	.50
342	A71	25p	Snowsquall, 1864	.70	.70
343	A71	26p	St. Mary, 1890	.70	.70
			Nos. 339-343 (5)	2.70	2.70

Sesquicentennial of Charles Darwin's Visit — A72

1982, Apr. 19 Litho. *Perf. 14*

344 A72 5p Darwin .45 .45
345 A72 17p Microscope .55 .55
346 A72 25p Warrah .85 .85
347 A72 34p Beagle 1.10 1.10
Nos. 344-347 (4) 2.95 2.95

Princess Diana Issue
Common Design Type

1982, July 5 Wmk. 373 *Perf. 13*

348 CD333 5p Arms .30 .30
349 CD333 17p Diana .60 .60
350 CD333 37p Wedding .95 .95
351 CD333 50p Portrait 1.25 1.25
Nos. 348-351 (4) 3.10 3.10

Nos. 264, 271 Overprinted

1982, Oct. 7 Litho. *Perf. 14*

352 A55 5p multicolored .25 .25
353 A55 25p multicolored .50 .50

12th Commonwealth Games, Brisbane, Australia, Sept. 30-Oct. 9.

Tussock Bird — A73

1982, Dec. 6 *Perf. 15x14½*

354 A73 5p shown .40 .40
355 A73 10p Black-chinned siskin .50 .50
356 A73 13p Grass wren .50 .50
357 A73 17p Black-throated finch .50 .50
358 A73 25p Falkland-correndera pipit .60 .60
359 A73 34p Dark-faced ground-tyrant .70 .70
Nos. 354-359 (6) 3.20 3.20

British Occupation Sesquicentennial — A74

1p, Raising the Standard, Port Louis, 1833. 2p, Chelsea pensioners & barracks, 1849. 5p, Wool trade, 1874. 10p, Ship repairing trade, 1850-90. 15p, Government House, early 20th cent. 20p, Battle of the Falkland Islands, 1914. 25p, Whalebone Arch centenary, 1933. 40p, Contribution to World War II effort, 1939-45. 50p, Visit of Duke of Edinburgh, 1957. £1, Royal Marines, 1933, 1983, vert. £2, Queen Elizabeth II.

1983, Jan. 1 Litho. *Perf. 14*

360 A74 1p multi, vert. .35 .35
361 A74 2p multi .40 .40
362 A74 5p multi, vert. .40 .40
363 A74 10p multi .55 .55
364 A74 15p multi .55 .55
365 A74 20p multi, vert. .75 *1.25*
366 A74 25p multi .75 *1.25*
367 A74 40p multi, vert. .80 *1.25*
368 A74 50p multi .95 *1.25*
369 A74 £1 multi 1.25 *2.25*
370 A74 £2 multi, vert. 2.50 *3.50*
Nos. 360-370 (11) 9.25 *13.00*

For surcharges see Nos. 402-403.

A75

1983, Mar. 14

371 A75 5p No. 69 .25 .25
372 A75 17p No. 65 .45 .45
373 A75 34p No. 75, vert. .70 *1.00*
374 A75 50p No. 370, vert. .90 *1.00*
Nos. 371-374 (4) 2.30 2.70

Commonwealth Day.

First Anniv. of Liberation A76

1983, June 14 Wmk. 373 *Perf. 14*

375 A76 5p Army .30 .30
376 A76 13p Merchant Navy .40 .40
377 A76 17p Royal Air Force .60 .60
378 A76 50p Royal Navy 1.20 *2.00*
a. Souvenir sheet of 4, #375-378 2.75 2.75
Nos. 375-378 (4) 2.50 3.30

Local Fruit A77

1983, Oct. 10 Litho. *Perf. 14*

379 A77 5p Diddle dee .25 .25
380 A77 17p Tea berries .40 .40
381 A77 25p Mountain berries .60 .60
382 A77 34p Native strawberries .80 .80
Nos. 379-382 (4) 2.05 2.05

Britten-Norman Islander — A78

1983, Nov. 14 Litho. *Perf. 14*

383 A78 5p shown .25 .25
384 A78 13p DHC-2 Beaver .40 .40
385 A78 17p Noorduyn Norseman .50 .50
386 A78 50p Auster 1.10 *1.25*
Nos. 383-386 (4) 2.25 2.40

Green Spider A79

Insects and Spiders.

1984, Jan. 1 Litho. *Perf. 14*

387 A79 1p shown .30 *.90*
388 A79 2p Ichneumon-Fly 2.75 2.75
a. Inscribed "1986" 4.00 3.50
389 A79 3p Brocade Moth .65 *.95*
390 A79 4p Black Beetle .50 *.95*
391 A79 5p Fritillary .50 *.95*
392 A79 6p Green Spider, diff. .50 *.95*
393 A79 7p Ichneumon-Fly, diff. .50 *.75*
394 A79 8p Ochre Shoulder .50 *.75*
395 A79 9p Clocker Weevil .50 *.75*
396 A79 10p Hover Fly .50 *.75*
397 A79 20p Weevil 3.00 1.25
398 A79 25p Metallic Beetle .80 *1.25*
399 A79 50p Camel Cricket 1.25 *2.00*
400 A79 £1 Beauchene Spider 1.60 *2.50*
401 A79 £3 Southern Painted Lady 4.50 *7.00*
Nos. 387-401 (15) 18.35 24.45

Nos. 364, 366 Surcharged

1984, Jan. 3 Litho. *Perf. 14*

402 A74 17p on 15p multi .65 .65
403 A74 22p on 25p multi .35 .35

Lloyd's List Issue
Common Design Type

1984, May 7 Wmk. 373 *Perf. 14½*

404 CD335 6p Wavertree .60 .50
405 CD335 17p Port Stanley, 1910 .90 .75
406 CD335 22p Oravia .90 .75
407 CD335 52p Cunard Countess 1.25 *2.00*
Nos. 404-407 (4) 3.65 4.00

Great Grebe — A80

1984, Aug. 6 *Perf. 14½x14*

408 A80 17p shown 1.40 1.40
409 A80 22p Silver grebe 1.75 1.75
410 A80 52p Rolland's grebe 2.50 *3.50*
Nos. 408-410 (3) 5.65 6.65

See Nos. 450-453.

1984 UPU Congress A81

1984, June 25 Litho. *Perf. 14*

411 A81 22p Emblem, jet, ship .60 .60

Wildlife Conservation A82

1984, Nov. 5 Litho. *Perf. 14½*

412 A82 6p Birds 1.25 1.25
413 A82 17p Plants 1.10 .90
414 A82 22p Mammals 1.25 1.00
415 A82 52p Marine Life 2.00 *2.50*
a. Souvenir sheet of 4, #412-415 7.75 7.75
Nos. 412-415 (4) 5.60 5.65

Camber Railway, 1915-1927 A83

1985, Feb. 18 Litho. *Perf. 14*

416 A83 7p multicolored .45 .45
417 A83 22p multicolored .80 .80
418 A83 27p multicolored .85 .85

Size: 77x26mm

419 A83 54p multicolored 1.75 1.75
Nos. 416-419 (4) 3.85 3.85

Queen Mother 85th Birthday
Common Design Type

Designs: 7p, Commonwealth Visitor's Reception. 22p, With Prince Charles, Mark Phillips, Princess Anne. 27p, 80th birthday celebration. 54p, Holding Prince Henry. £1, In coach with Princess Diana.

Perf. 14½x14

1985, June 7 Litho. Wmk. 384

420 CD336 7p multicolored .40 .40
421 CD336 22p multicolored 1.00 1.00
422 CD336 27p multicolored 1.10 1.10
423 CD336 54p multicolored 1.25 .60
Nos. 420-423 (4) 3.75 3.10

Souvenir Sheet

424 CD336 £1 multicolored 4.50 4.50

Mount Pleasant Airport Opening A84

1985, May 12 Litho. *Perf. 14½*

425 A84 7p Pioneer camp, docked ship .90 .40
426 A84 22p Construction site 1.25 1.25
427 A84 27p Runway layout 1.60 1.60
428 A84 54p Aircraft landing 2.25 3.00
Nos. 425-428 (4) 6.00 6.25

Captain J. McBride, HMS Jason, 1765 — A85

18th-19th century naval explorers: 22p, Commodore J. Byron, HMS Dolphin and Tamar, 1765. 27p, Vice-Adm. R. Fitzroy, HMS Beagle, 1831. 54p, Adm. Sir B.J. Sulivan, HMS Philomel, 1842.

1985, Sept. 23

429 A85 7p multicolored .85 .50
430 A85 22p multicolored 1.40 1.00
431 A85 27p multicolored 1.50 1.25
432 A85 54p multicolored 2.75 2.50
Nos. 429-432 (4) 6.50 5.25

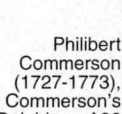

Philibert Commerson (1727-1773), Commerson's Dolphin — A86

Naturalists, endangered species: 22p, Rene Primevere Lesson (1794-1849), kelp. 27p, Joseph Paul Gaimard (1796-1858), diving petrel. 54p, Charles Darwin (1803-1882), Calceolaria darwinii.

1985, Nov. 4 *Perf. 14½*

433 A86 7p multicolored .95 .30
434 A86 22p multicolored 1.25 1.25
435 A86 27p multicolored 2.25 2.25
436 A86 54p multicolored 2.50 2.50
Nos. 433-436 (4) 6.95 6.30

Seashells A87

1986, Feb. 10 Wmk. 384 *Perf. 14½*

437 A87 7p Painted keyhole limpet 1.10 1.10
438 A87 22p Magellanic volute 1.75 1.75
439 A87 27p Falkland scallop 1.90 *2.25*
440 A87 54p Rough thorn drupe 3.25 *4.25*
Nos. 437-440 (4) 8.00 9.35

Queen Elizabeth II 60th Birthday
Common Design Type

Designs: 10p, With Princess Margaret at St. Paul's, Waldenbury, 1932. 24p, Christmas broadcast from Sandringham, 1958. 29p, Order of the Thistle, St. Giles Cathedral, Edinburgh, 1962. 45p, Royal reception on the Britannia, US visit, 1976. 58p, Visiting Crown Agents' offices, 1983.

1986, Apr. 21 Litho. *Perf. 14x14½*

441	CD337	10p scar, blk & sil	.30	.30
442	CD337	24p ultra, blk & sil	.55	*.65*
443	CD337	29p green & multi	.60	*.85*
444	CD337	45p violet & multi	1.25	*1.40*
445	CD337	58p rose vio & multi	1.25	*1.75*
		Nos. 441-445 (5)	3.95	*4.95*

AMERIPEX '86 — A88

SS Great Britain's arrival in the Falkland Isls., Cent.: 10p, Maiden voyage, crossing the Atlantic, 1845. 24p, Wreck in Sparrow Cove, 1937. 29p, Refloating wreck, 1970. 58p, Restored vessel, Bristol, 1986.

1986, May 22

446	A88 10p multicolored	.50	.50
447	A88 24p multicolored	.60	*1.00*
448	A88 29p multicolored	.75	*1.25*
449	A88 58p multicolored	1.10	*2.50*
a.	Souvenir sheet of 4, #446-449	5.00	5.00
	Nos. 446-449 (4)	2.95	*5.25*

Bird Type of 1984

Rockhopper Penguins.

1986, Aug. 25 Wmk. 373 *Perf. 14½*

450	A80 10p Adult	1.00	.75
451	A80 24p Adults swimming	1.90	1.90
452	A80 29p Adults, diff.	2.10	2.10
453	A80 58p Adult and young	3.25	*4.25*
	Nos. 450-453 (4)	8.25	9.00

Wedding of Prince Andrew and Sarah Ferguson — A90

Various photographs: 17p, Presenting Queen's Polo Cup, Windsor, 1986. 22p, Open carriage, wedding. 29p, Andrew wearing military fatigues.

1986, Nov. 10 Wmk. 384 *Perf. 14½*

454	A90 17p multicolored	.80	.80
455	A90 22p multicolored	1.00	1.00
456	A90 29p multicolored	1.40	1.40
	Nos. 454-456 (3)	3.20	3.20

Royal Engineers, 200th Anniv. A91

1987, Feb. 9 Litho. *Perf. 14½*

457	A91 10p Surveying Sapper Hill	1.50	.90
458	A91 24p Explosives disposal	2.10	1.50
459	A91 29p Boxer Bridge, Pt. Stanley	2.40	2.40
460	A91 58p Postal services, Stanley Airport	4.00	*5.00*
	Nos. 457-460 (4)	10.00	9.80

Seals A92

1987, Apr. 27

461	A92 10p Southern sea lion	1.40	1.40
462	A92 24p Falkland fur seal	2.25	2.25
463	A92 29p Southern elephant seal	2.50	2.50
464	A92 58p Leopard seal	3.25	*4.50*
	Nos. 461-464 (4)	9.40	10.65

Hospitals A93

Designs: 10p, Victorian Cottage Home, c. 1912. 24p, King Edward VII Memorial Hospital, c. 1914. 29p, Churchill Wing, 1953. 58p, Prince Andrew Wing, 1987.

1987, Dec. 8 *Perf. 14*

465	A93 10p multicolored	.70	.50
466	A93 24p multicolored	1.20	.90
467	A93 29p multicolored	1.40	1.00
468	A93 58p multicolored	2.10	1.50
	Nos. 465-468 (4)	5.40	3.90

Fungi — A94

1987, Sept. 14 Litho. *Perf. 14½*

469	A94 10p Suillus luteus	2.50	*3.00*
470	A94 24p Mycena	3.50	3.00
471	A94 29p Camarophyllus adonis	4.00	3.50
472	A94 58p Gerronema schusteri	5.00	*6.50*
	Nos. 469-472 (4)	15.00	16.00

1940 Morris Truck, Fitzroy A95

Classic automobiles: 24p, 1929 Citroen Kegresse, San Carlos. 29p, 1933 Ford 1-Ton Truck, Port Stanley. 58p, 1935 Ford Model T Saloon, Darwin.

1988, Apr. 11 Litho. *Perf. 14*

473	A95 10p multicolored	.65	.40
474	A95 24p multicolored	1.10	.75
475	A95 29p multicolored	1.25	.85
476	A95 58p multicolored	1.90	1.75
	Nos. 473-476 (4)	4.90	3.75

Geese A96

1988, July 25

477	A96 10p Kelp	2.50	.60
478	A96 24p Upland	3.50	.90
479	A96 29p Ruddy-headed	4.00	1.10
480	A96 58p Ashy-headed	6.00	2.50
	Nos. 477-480 (4)	16.00	5.10

Lloyds of London, 300th Anniv.
Common Design Type

Designs: 10p, Lloyd's Nelson Collection silver service. 24p, Hydroponic Gardens, horiz. 29p, Supply ship A.E.S., horiz. 58p, Wreck of the Charles Cooper near the Falklands, 1866.

1988, Nov. 14 Litho. Wmk. 373

481	CD341 10p multicolored	.55	.55
482	CD341 24p multicolored	1.00	1.00
483	CD341 29p multicolored	2.00	1.25
484	CD341 58p multicolored	2.75	1.75
	Nos. 481-484 (4)	6.30	4.55

Ships of Cape Horn A97

1989, Feb. 28

485	A97 1p Padua	2.00	1.00
486	A97 2p Priwall, vert.	1.60	1.60
a.	Wmk. 384	1.40	1.40
487	A97 3p Passat	1.60	1.60
a.	Wmk. 384	1.40	1.40
488	A97 4p Archibald Russell, vert.	2.75	1.00
489	A97 5p Pamir, vert.	2.75	1.00
490	A97 6p Mozart	2.25	2.25
a.	Wmk. 384	2.25	2.25
491	A97 7p Pommern	2.75	1.10
492	A97 8p Preussen	2.75	1.10
493	A97 9p Fennia	2.25	2.25
a.	Wmk. 384	3.00	3.00
494	A97 10p Cassard	2.75	1.10
495	A97 20p Lawhill	4.00	2.25
496	A97 25p Garthpool	4.50	2.25
497	A97 50p Grace Harwar	5.00	3.50
498	A97 £1 Criccieth Castle	6.00	5.50
a.	Wmk. 384	7.00	7.00
499	A97 £3 Cutty Sark, vert.	17.50	12.00
500	A97 £5 Flying Cloud	32.50	13.50
	Nos. 485-500 (16)	92.95	53.00

Nos. 486a, 487a, 490a, 493a, 498a are dated "1991."

Whales — A98

1989, May 15 Wmk. 384 *Perf. 14*

501	A98 10p Southern right	1.50	.85
502	A98 24p Minke	2.50	1.25
503	A98 29p Humpback	3.25	2.00
504	A98 58p Blue	4.75	3.00
	Nos. 501-504 (4)	12.00	7.10

Sports Assoc. Activities A99

Children's drawings.

1989, Sept. 16

505	A99 5p Gymkhana	.30	.30
506	A99 10p Steer Riding	.35	.35
507	A99 17p Sheep shearing	.55	.55
508	A99 24p Dog trial	.70	.70
509	A99 29p Horse racing	.95	.95
510	A99 45p Sack race	1.25	1.25
	Nos. 505-510 (6)	4.10	4.10

Battles — A100

Commanders, ships and ship crests: 10p, Vice-Adm. Sturdee, HMS *Invincible*. 24p, Vice-Adm. Von Spee, SMS *Scharnhorst*. 29p, Commodore Harwood, HMS *Ajax*. 58p, Capt. Langsdorff, *Admiral Graff Spee*.

1989, Dec. 8 *Perf. 14x13½*

511	A100 10p multicolored	1.50	.40
512	A100 24p multicolored	2.50	.90
513	A100 29p multicolored	2.50	1.10
514	A100 58p multicolored	3.50	2.75
	Nos. 511-514 (4)	10.00	5.15

Battle of the Falklands, 75th anniv. (10p, 24p); Battle of the River Plate, 50th anniv. (29p, 58p).

Emblems and Presentation Spitfires, 1940 — A101

1990, May 3 Wmk. 373 *Perf. 14*

515	A101 12p No. 92 Squadron	1.00	1.00
516	A101 26p No. 611 Squadron	1.40	1.40
517	A101 31p No. 92 Squadron, diff.	1.75	1.75
518	A101 62p Spitfires scramble	3.00	3.00
	Nos. 515-518 (4)	7.15	7.15

Souvenir Sheet

519	A101 £1 Battle of Britain	7.50	7.50

Stamp World London '90.
For souvenir sheet similar to No. 519, see No. 530.

A102

1990, Apr. 1 Wmk. 384 *Perf. 14½*

520	A102 12p Kidney Is.	1.00	.55
521	A102 26p Beauchene Is.	1.25	.55
522	A102 31p Bird Is.	1.50	1.50
523	A102 62p Elephant Jason Is.	2.50	3.00
	Nos. 520-523 (4)	6.25	5.60

Nature reserves and bird sanctuaries.

Queen Mother, 90th Birthday
Common Design Types

1990, Aug. 4 Wmk. 384 *Perf. 14x15*

524	CD343 26p Queen Mother in Dover	1.00	1.00

Perf. 14½

525	CD344 £1 Steering the "Queen Elizabeth," 1946	4.25	4.25

A103

Wmk. 384

1990, Oct. 3 Litho. *Perf. 14*

526	A103 12p Black browed albatross	1.00	.75
527	A103 26p Adult bird	1.90	1.25
528	A103 31p Adult, chick	2.25	1.50
529	A103 62p Bird in flight	3.50	3.50
	Nos. 526-529 (4)	8.65	7.00

Battle of Britain Type of 1990 inscribed "SECOND VISIT OF / HRH THE DUKE OF EDINBURGH"
Souvenir Sheet

1991, Mar. 7

530	A101 £1 multicolored	12.00	12.00

Orchids — A104

1991, Mar. 18 **Wmk. 373**

531	A104	12p	Gavilea australis	1.50	1.00
532	A104	26p	Codonorchis lessonii	1.75	1.50
533	A104	31p	Chlorea gaudichaudii	2.00	1.75
534	A104	62p	Gavilea littoralis	3.25	*4.00*
			Nos. 531-534 (4)	8.50	8.25

King Penguin — A105

1991, Aug. 26 **Wmk. 384**

535	A105	2p	Two adults crossing bills	1.00	1.00
536	A105	6p	Two adults, one brooding	1.50	1.50
537	A105	12p	Adult with two young	1.75	1.75
538	A105	20p	Adult swimming	2.00	2.00
539	A105	31p	Adult feeding young	2.00	2.00
540	A105	62p	Two adults, diff.	3.00	3.00
			Nos. 535-540 (6)	11.25	11.25

World Wildlife Fund.

Falkland Islands Bisects, Cent. A106

1991, Sept. 10 **Wmk. 384** ***Perf. 14½***

541	A106	12p	#9, #15	1.10	1.00
542	A106	26p	On cover	2.10	1.75
543	A106	31p	Unsevered pair	1.75	1.75
544	A106	62p	S.S. Isis	2.75	*3.50*
			Nos. 541-544 (4)	7.70	8.00

Discovery of America, 500th Anniv. (in 1992) — A107

Sailing ships: 14p, STV Eye of the Wind. 29p, STV Soren Larsen. 34p, Nina, Santa Maria, Pinta. 68p, Columbus and Santa Maria.

1991, Dec. 12 **Wmk. 373** ***Perf. 14***

545	A107	14p	multicolored	.90	.90
546	A107	29p	multicolored	2.00	1.75
547	A107	34p	multicolored	2.25	2.00
548	A107	68p	multicolored	3.75	4.25
			Nos. 545-548 (4)	8.90	8.90

World Columbian Stamp Expo '92, Chicago and Genoa '92 Intl. Philatelic Exhibitions.

Queen Elizabeth II's Accession to the Throne, 40th Anniv.

Common Design Type

1992, Feb. 6

549	CD349	7p	multicolored	.70	.50
550	CD349	14p	multicolored	1.00	1.00
551	CD349	29p	multicolored	1.25	1.10
552	CD349	34p	multicolored	1.60	1.60
553	CD349	68p	multicolored	2.25	*4.00*
			Nos. 549-553 (5)	6.80	8.20

Christ Church Cathedral, Cent. — A108

1992, Feb. 21 **Wmk. 384** ***Perf. 14½***

554	A108	14p	Laying foundation stone	1.00	.80
555	A108	29p	Interior, 1920	2.00	1.50
556	A108	34p	Bishop's chair	2.25	1.75
557	A108	68p	Without tower c. 1900, horiz.	3.00	3.00
			Nos. 554-557 (4)	8.25	7.05

First Sighting of Falkland Islands by Capt. John Davis, 400th Anniv. A109

Designs: 22p, Capt. John Davis using backstaff. 29p, Capt. Davis working on chart. 34p, Queen Elizabeth I, Queen Elizabeth II. 68p, The Desire sights Falkland Islands.

1992, Aug. 14 **Wmk. 373**

558	A109	22p	multicolored	1.60	1.25
559	A109	29p	multicolored	2.00	1.75
560	A109	34p	multicolored	2.10	2.10
561	A109	68p	multicolored	3.50	*5.00*
			Nos. 558-561 (4)	9.20	10.10

Falkland Islands Defense Force and West Yorkshire Regiment — A110

7p, Private, Falkland Islands Volunteers, 1892. 14p, Officer, Falkland Islands Defense Corps, 1914. 22p, Officer, Falkland Islands Defense Force, 1920. 29p, Private, Falkland Islands Defense Force, 1939-45. 34p, Officer, West Yorkshire Regiment, 1942. 68p, Private, West Yorkshire Regiment, 1942.

1992, Oct. 1 ***Perf. 14***

562	A110	7p	multicolored	.60	.60
563	A110	14p	multicolored	.90	.90
564	A110	22p	multicolored	1.25	.90
565	A110	29p	multicolored	1.50	1.25
566	A110	34p	multicolored	1.90	1.90
567	A110	68p	multicolored	3.00	*4.00*
			Nos. 562-567 (6)	9.15	9.55

Gulls and Terns A111

Perf. 14x14½

1993, Jan. 2 **Litho.** **Wmk. 384**

568	A111	15p	South American tern	1.25	1.00
569	A111	31p	Pink breasted gull	1.75	1.50
570	A111	36p	Dolphin gull	2.25	2.25
571	A111	72p	Dominican gull	3.25	*4.00*
			Nos. 568-571 (4)	8.50	8.75

Souvenir Sheet

Visit of Liner QE II to Falkland Islands — A112

Wmk. 373

1993, Jan. 22 **Litho.** ***Perf. 14***

572	A112	£2	multicolored	11.50	11.50

Royal Air Force, 75th Anniv.

Common Designs Type

Designs: No. 573, Lockheed Tristar. No. 574, Lockheed Hercules. No. 575, Boeing Vertol Chinook. No. 576, Avro Vulcan.

No. 577a, Hawker Siddeley Andover. b, Westland Wessex. c, Panavia Tornado F3. d, McDonnell Douglas Phantom.

Wmk. 373

1993, Apr. 3 **Litho.** ***Perf. 14***

573	CD350	15p	multicolored	1.25	1.25
574	CD350	15p	multicolored	1.25	1.25
575	CD350	15p	multicolored	1.25	1.25
576	CD350	15p	multicolored	1.25	1.25
			Nos. 573-576 (4)	5.00	5.00

Souvenir Sheet of 4

577	CD350	36p	#a.-d.	6.25	6.25

Fisheries A113

Designs: 15p, Short-finned squid. 31p, Stern haul of whiptailed hake. 36p, Fishery Patrol Vessel Falklands Protector. 72p, Aerial surveillance by Britten-Norman Islander.

Wmk. 384

1993, July 1 **Litho.** ***Perf. 14***

578	A113	15p	multicolored	.85	.85
579	A113	31p	multicolored	1.75	1.75
580	A113	36p	multicolored	2.10	2.10
581	A113	72p	multicolored	3.25	*5.00*
			Nos. 578-581 (4)	7.95	9.70

Launch of SS Great Britain, 150th Anniv. — A114

Perf. 14x13½

1993, July 19 **Litho.** **Wmk. 384**

582	A114	8p	In drydock, Bristol	.80	.50
583	A114	£1	At sea	4.25	*5.00*

Cruise Ships and Penguins A115

Wmk. 373

1993, Oct. 1 **Litho.** ***Perf. 14***

584	A115	16p	Explorer	1.60	.90
585	A115	34p	Rockhopper penguins	2.50	1.75
586	A115	39p	World Discoverer	2.75	2.00
587	A115	78p	Columbus Caravelle	3.75	*6.00*
			Nos. 584-587 (4)	10.60	10.65

Pets — A116

Perf. 14x14½

1993, Dec. 1 **Litho.** **Wmk. 384**

588	A116	8p	Pony	.90	.90
589	A116	16p	Lamb	1.10	1.10
590	A116	34p	Puppy, kitten	2.50	1.50

Perf. 14½x14

591	A116	39p	Kitten, vert.	3.00	2.00
592	A116	78p	Collie, vert.	4.00	*5.00*
			Nos. 588-592 (5)	11.50	10.50

Ovptd. with Hong Kong '94 Emblem

1994, Feb. 18

593	A116	8p	on #588	1.00	*1.25*
594	A116	16p	on #589	1.25	*1.50*
595	A116	34p	on #590	2.75	*3.00*
596	A116	39p	on #591	3.00	*4.00*
597	A116	78p	on #592	4.00	*6.50*
			Nos. 593-597 (5)	12.00	*16.25*

Inshore Marine Life A117

Wmk. 384

1994, Apr. 4 **Litho.** ***Perf. 14***

598	A117	1p	Goose barnacles, vert.	1.00	.75
599	A117	2p	Painted shrimp	2.00	.75
600	A117	8p	Common limpet	2.25	1.00
601	A117	9p	Mullet	2.25	1.00
602	A117	10p	Sea anemones	2.25	.75
603	A117	20p	Rock eel	3.00	1.00
604	A117	25p	Spider crab	3.00	1.00
605	A117	50p	Lobster krill, vert.	3.00	2.75
606	A117	80p	Falkland skate	3.00	2.75
607	A117	£1	Centollon crab	4.00	3.00
a.			Souv. sheet of 1, wmk. 373	6.75	6.75
608	A117	£3	Rock cod	12.00	8.00
609	A117	£5	Octopus, vert.	20.00	15.00
			Nos. 598-609 (12)	57.75	37.75

No. 607a for return of Hong Kong to China. Issued 7/1/97.

See No. 671.

Founding of Stanley, 150th Anniv. A118

9p, Blacksmith's shop, dockyard, Sir James Clark Ross, explorer. 17p, James Leith Mody, 1st colonial chaplain, home at 21 Fitzroy Road. 30p, Stanley cottage, Dr. Henry J. Hamblin, 1st colonial surgeon. 35p, Pioneer row, Sergeant Major Henry Felton. 40p, Government House, Governor R. C. Moody R.E. 65p, View of Stanley, Edward Stanley, 14th Earl of Derby, Secretary of State for Colonies.

Wmk. 373

1994, July 1 **Litho.** ***Perf. 14***

610	A118	9p	multicolored	.85	.75
611	A118	17p	multicolored	1.25	1.00
612	A118	30p	multicolored	2.00	1.25
613	A118	35p	multicolored	2.25	1.75
614	A118	40p	multicolored	2.50	2.00
615	A118	65p	multicolored	3.50	*4.00*
			Nos. 610-615 (6)	12.35	10.75

Methods of Transportation — A119

17p, Tristar over Gypsy Cove. 35p, Cruise ship, Sea Lion Island. 40p, FIGAS Islander, Pebble Island Beach. 65p, Land Rover, Volunteer Beach.

Wmk. 384

1994, Oct. 24 **Litho.** ***Perf. 14***

616	A119	17p	multicolored	1.10	.75
617	A119	35p	multicolored	2.10	1.50
618	A119	40p	multicolored	2.75	2.75
619	A119	65p	multicolored	3.25	*4.25*
			Nos. 616-619 (4)	9.20	9.25

South American Missionary Society, 150th Anniv. — A120

Designs: 5p, Mission House, Keppel Island. 17p, Thomas Bridges, compiler of Yahgan dictionary. 40p, Fuegian Indians. 65p, Schooner Allen Gardiner, Capt. Allen Gardiner.

1994, Dec. 1

620	A120	5p multicolored	.30	.30
621	A120	17p multicolored	.85	.85
622	A120	40p multicolored	1.90	1.90
623	A120	65p multicolored	3.00	3.00
		Nos. 620-623 (4)	6.05	6.05

Flowering Shrubs — A121

Designs: 9p, Lupinus arboreus. 17p, Boxwood. 30p, Fuchsia magellanica. 35p, Berberis ilicifolia. 40p, Gorse. 65p, Veronica.

Perf. 14½x14

1995, Jan. 3 Litho. Wmk. 384

624	A121	9p multicolored	.90	.75
625	A121	17p multicolored	1.25	.90
626	A121	30p multicolored	1.60	1.60
627	A121	35p multicolored	2.00	1.60
628	A121	40p multicolored	2.10	1.75
629	A121	65p multicolored	3.50	4.50
		Nos. 624-629 (6)	11.35	11.10

Shore Birds A122

Designs: 17p, Magellanic oystercatcher. 35p, Rufous chested dotterel. 40p, Black oystercatcher. 65p, Two banded plover.

Wmk. 373

1995, Mar. 1 Litho. *Perf. 13½*

630	A122	17p multicolored	1.75	1.00
631	A122	35p multicolored	2.50	1.50
632	A122	40p multicolored	2.75	1.75
633	A122	65p multicolored	4.75	7.00
		Nos. 630-633 (4)	11.75	11.25

End of World War II, 50th Anniv.

Common Design Types

17p, Falkland Islands Victory Parade contingent. 35p, Governor Sir Alan Wolsey Cardinall on Bren gun carrier. 40p, HMAS Esperance Bay, 1942. 65p, HMS Exeter, 1939.

£1, Reverse of War Medal 1939-45.

Wmk. 373

1995, May 8 Litho. *Perf. 14*

634	CD351	17p multicolored	1.40	.90
635	CD351	35p multicolored	2.25	1.50
636	CD351	40p multicolored	2.50	2.00
637	CD351	65p multicolored	4.50	*5.75*
		Nos. 634-637 (4)	10.65	10.15

Souvenir Sheet

638	CD352	£1 multicolored	7.25	7.25

Transporting Peat — A123

Wmk. 384

1995, Aug. 1 Litho. *Perf. 14*

639	A123	17p Ox, cart	.80	.80
640	A123	35p Horse, cart	1.75	1.25
641	A123	40p Tractor, sledge	2.00	1.50
642	A123	65p Truck, peat bank	3.50	*4.00*
		Nos. 639-642 (4)	8.05	7.55

Miniature Sheet of 6

Wildlife — A124

Designs: a, Kelp geese. b, Albatross. c, Cormorants. d, Magellanic penguins. e, Fur seals. f, Rockhopper penguins.

1995, Sept. 11

643	A124	35p #a.-f.	21.00	21.00

No. 643 is a continuous design.

Wild Animals A125

1995, Nov. 6 Wmk. 373

644	A125	9p Rabbit	1.10	1.00
645	A125	17p Hare	1.75	1.25
646	A125	35p Guanaco	2.75	2.00
647	A125	40p Fox	3.25	2.25
648	A125	65p Otter	4.25	*5.00*
		Nos. 644-648 (5)	13.10	11.50

Visit by Princess Anne A126

Princess Anne and: 9p, Government House. 19p, San Carlos Cemetery. 30p, Christ Church Cathedral. 73p, Goose Green.

1996, Jan. 30 *Perf. 14½*

649	A126	9p multicolored	1.10	.60
650	A126	19p multicolored	1.50	1.00
651	A126	30p multicolored	2.00	1.50
652	A126	73p multicolored	6.50	*7.50*
		Nos. 649-652 (4)	11.10	10.60

Queen Elizabeth II, 70th Birthday

Common Design Type

Various portraits of Queen, scenes from Falkland Islands: 17p, Steeple Jason. 40p, Ship, KV Tamar. 45p, New Island with shipwreck on beach. 65p, Community School.

£1, Queen in formal dress at Sandringham Ball.

1996, Apr. 21 *Perf. 13½*

653	CD354	17p multicolored	1.00	.80
654	CD354	40p multicolored	2.50	1.50
655	CD354	45p multicolored	2.60	2.10
656	CD354	65p multicolored	3.25	2.50
		Nos. 653-656 (4)	9.35	6.90

Souvenir Sheet

657	CD354	£1 multicolored	5.00	5.00

CAPEX '96 A127

Mail delivery: 9p, Horseback, 1890. 40p, Norseman floatplane. 45p, Inter-island ship. 76p, Beaver floatplane.

£1, LMS Jubilee Class 4-6-0 locomotive.

1996, June 8 Wmk. 384 *Perf. 14*

658	A127	9p multicolored	1.00	.75
659	A127	40p multicolored	2.50	1.50
660	A127	45p multicolored	2.75	1.75
661	A127	76p multicolored	3.75	*4.25*
		Nos. 658-661 (4)	10.00	8.25

Souvenir Sheet

662	A127	£1 multicolored	4.25	4.25

No. 662 contains one 48x32mm stamp.

Beaked Whales — A128

Designs: 9p, Southern bottlenose whale. 30p, Cuvier's beaked whale. 35p, Straptoothed beaked whale. 75p, Gray's beaked whale.

Wmk. 373

1996, Sept. 2 Litho. *Perf. 14*

663	A128	9p multicolored	.80	.60
664	A128	30p multicolored	1.60	1.50
665	A128	35p multicolored	1.90	1.75
666	A128	75p multicolored	4.00	4.00
		Nos. 663-666 (4)	8.30	7.85

Magellanic Penguins — A129

Designs: 17p, Two adults. 35p, Young in nest. 40p, Chick, adult. 65p, Swimming.

Wmk. 373

1997, Jan. 2 Litho. *Perf. 14*

667	A129	17p multicolored	2.10	.75
668	A129	35p multicolored	3.25	1.25
669	A129	40p multicolored	3.50	1.50
670	A129	65p multicolored	4.75	3.25
		Nos. 667-670 (4)	13.60	6.75

Fish Type of 1994

Souvenir Sheet

Wmk. 373

1997, Feb. 3 Litho. *Perf. 14*

671	A117	£1 Smelt	5.50	5.50

Hong Kong '97.

Ferns — A130

Perf. 14½x14

1997, Mar. 3 Litho. Wmk. 373

672	A130	17p Coral	1.90	.60
673	A130	35p Adder's tongue	2.60	1.25
674	A130	40p Fuegian tall	2.75	1.50
675	A130	65p Small fern	3.75	3.00
		Nos. 672-675 (4)	11.00	6.35

Lighthouses — A131

Wmk. 373

1997, July 1 Litho. *Perf. 14*

676	A131	9p Bull Point	3.25	1.00
677	A131	30p Cape Pembroke	4.50	2.00
678	A131	£1 Cape Meredith	10.50	5.00
		Nos. 676-678 (3)	18.25	8.00

Queen Elizabeth II and Prince Philip, 50th Wedding Anniv. — A132

No. 679, Queen holding flowers. No. 680, Prince with horse. No. 681, Queen riding in open carriage. No. 682, Prince in uniform. No. 683, Queen in red coat & hat, Prince. No. 684, Princes William and Harry on horseback.

£1.50, Queen, Prince riding in open carriage.

1997 Wmk. 384 *Perf. 14½x14*

679		9p multicolored	1.00	.75
680		9p multicolored	1.00	.75
a.	A132	Pair, #679-680	2.75	2.75
681		17p multicolored	1.75	1.00
682		17p multicolored	1.75	1.00
a.	A132	Pair, #681-682	4.00	4.00
683		40p multicolored	3.00	1.50
684		40p multicolored	3.00	1.50
a.	A132	Pair, #683-684	8.00	8.00
		Nos. 679-684 (6)	11.50	6.50

Souvenir Sheet

685	A132	£1.50 multicolored	10.00	10.00

Endangered Species — A133

Designs: 17p, Phalcoboenus australis. 19p, Otaria flavescens. 40p, Calandrinia feltonii. 73p, Aplochiton zebra.

Wmk. 373

1997, Oct. 16 Litho. *Perf. 14½*

686	A133	17p multicolored	4.00	2.00
687	A133	19p multicolored	3.00	2.75
688	A133	40p multicolored	5.00	3.50
689	A133	73p multicolored	9.00	9.00
		Nos. 686-689 (4)	21.00	17.25

Fire Service in Falkland Islands, Cent. — A134

Equipment, manufacturer: 9p, Greenwich Gem, Merryweather & Son. 17p, Hatfield trailer pump, Merryweather & Son. 40p, Godiva trailer pump, Coventry Climax. 65p, Water tender type B, Carmichael Bedford.

Wmk. 384

1998, Feb. 26 Litho. *Perf. 14½*

690	A134	9p multicolored	3.50	1.50
691	A134	17p multicolored	4.25	1.50
692	A134	40p multicolored	7.00	3.00
693	A134	65p multicolored	9.00	9.50
		Nos. 690-693 (4)	23.75	15.50

Diana, Princess of Wales (1961-97)

Common Design Type

Portraits: a, Looking left. b, In red dress. c, Hand on cheek. d, Investigating land mines.

Perf. 14½x14

1998, Mar. 31 Wmk. 373

694	CD355	30p Sheet of 4, #a-d	4.75	4.75

No. 694 sold for £1.20 + 20p, with surtax from international sales being donated to the Princess Diana Memorial Fund and surtax from national sales being donated to designated local charity.

Birds A135

1p, Tawny-throated dotterel. 2p, Hudsonian godwit. 5p, Eared dove. No. 698, Great grebe. No. 699, Roseate spoonbill. 10p, Southern lapwing. 16p, Buff-necked ibis. 17p, Astral parakeet. 30p, Ashy-headed goose. 35p, American kestrel. 65p, Red-legged shag. 88p, Red shoveler. £1, Red-fronted coot. £3, Chilean flamingo. £5, Fork-tailed flycatcher.

Wmk. 373

1998, July 14 Litho. ***Perf. 14***

695 A135 1p multicolored 1.00 1.00
696 A135 2p multicolored 1.00 1.00
697 A135 5p multicolored 1.00 1.00
698 A135 9p multicolored 1.50 1.00
699 A135 9p multicolored 6.00 *8.00*
700 A135 10p multicolored 2.25 1.00
701 A135 16p multicolored 2.25 2.25
702 A135 17p multicolored 1.25 *2.00*
a. Booklet pane, 2 #699, 8 #702 + 2 labels 22.00
Complete booklet, #702a 22.00
703 A135 30p multicolored 2.50 1.75
704 A135 35p multicolored 3.00 *4.00*
Complete booklet, 6 #704 18.00
705 A135 65p multicolored 4.00 2.50
706 A135 88p multicolored 4.25 *6.00*
707 A135 £1 multicolored 4.50 4.50
708 A135 £3 multicolored 11.00 *14.00*
709 A135 £5 multicolored 20.00 *22.50*
Nos. 695-709 (15) 65.50 72.50

Boats — A136

Boat, country flag, year: 17p, Penelope, Germany, 1926. 35p, Ilen, Italy, 1926. 40p, Weddell, Chile, 1940. 65p, Lively, Scotland, 1940.

Wmk. 373

1998, Sept. 30 Litho. ***Perf. 14***

710 A136 17p multicolored 2.50 1.00
711 A136 35p multicolored 3.50 2.00
712 A136 40p multicolored 3.75 2.25

Size: 29x18mm

713 A136 65p multicolored 5.50 *6.00*
Nos. 710-713 (4) 15.25 11.25

FIGAS (First Medivac Air Ambulance Service), 50th Anniv. — A137

17p, Man carrying patient, airplane. £1, Airplane, map of Islands, float plane.

Wmk. 373

1998, Dec. 1 Litho. ***Perf. 14***

714 A137 17p multicolored 3.50 1.75
715 A137 £1 multicolored 13.50 13.50

Military Uniforms — A138

Uniform, background location: 17p, Marine Private, 1776, The Block House at Port Egmont, Saunders Island. 30p, Marine Officer, 1833, Port Louis, East Falkland. 35p, Royal Marine Corporal, 1914, HMS Kent. 65p, Royal Marine Bugler, 1976, Government House.

Wmk. 373

1998, Dec. 8 Litho. ***Perf. 14½***

716 A138 17p multicolored 3.00 1.00
717 A138 30p multicolored 4.00 2.50
718 A138 35p multicolored 4.25 2.50
719 A138 65p multicolored 6.50 *9.00*
Nos. 716-719 (4) 17.75 15.00

St. Mary's Church, Cent. A139

Wmk. 373

1999, Feb. 12 Litho. ***Perf. 14***

720 A139 17p Inside view 2.60 1.00
721 A139 40p Outside view 4.25 3.00
722 A139 75p Laying corner-stone, 1899 8.50 *10.00*
Nos. 720-722 (3) 15.35 14.00

Australia '99, World Stamp Expo A140

25p, HMS Beagle. 35p, HMAS Australia. 40p, SS Canberra. No. 726, SS Great Britain. No. 727, All-England Eleven visit Australia, 1861-62.

1999, Mar. 5 **Wmk. 384**

723 A140 25p multicolored 3.50 2.25
724 A140 35p multicolored 4.00 2.75
725 A140 40p multicolored 5.25 3.00
726 A140 50p multicolored 5.00 5.00
727 A140 50p multicolored 5.00 5.00
a. Pair, #726-727 11.50 *13.00*
Nos. 723-727 (5) 22.75 18.00

1999 Visit of HRH Prince of Wales — A141

Perf. 14x13½

1999, Mar. 13 Litho. Wmk. 384

728 A141 £2 multicolored 17.50 17.50

Wedding of Prince Edward and Sophie Rhys-Jones

Common Design Type

Perf. 13¾x14

1999, June 15 Litho. Wmk. 384

729 CD356 80p Separate portraits 6.50 6.50
730 CD356 £1.20 Couple 8.50 8.50

PhilexFrance '99, World Philatelic Exhibition — A142

Designs: 35p, French cruiser, Jeanne d'Arc, Port Stanley, 1931. 40p, CAMS 37/11 Flying Boat's first flight.

£1, CAMS 37 Flying Boat over Port Stanley, 1931.

1999, June 21 Wmk. 373 ***Perf. 14***

731 A142 35p multicolored 5.50 5.50
732 A142 40p multicolored 6.25 6.25

Souvenir Sheet

733 A142 £1 multicolored 15.00 15.00

No. 733 contains one 48x31mm stamp.

Queen Mother's Century

Common Design Type

Queen Mother: 9p, With King George VI at Port of London. 20p, With Queen Elizabeth at Women's Institute, Sandringham. 30p, With Princes Charles, William and Harry at Clarence House, 95th birthday. 67p, As Colonel-in-Chief of the Queen's Royal Hussars.

£1.40, With Ernest Shackleton, Robert F. Scott and Edward A. Wilson.

Wmk. 384

1999, Aug. 18 Litho. ***Perf. 13½***

734 CD358 9p multi 2.00 1.00
735 CD358 20p multi 3.00 1.50
736 CD358 30p multi 3.50 1.75
737 CD358 67p multi 6.25 *7.50*
Nos. 734-737 (4) 14.75 11.75

Souvenir Sheet

738 CD358 £1.40 multi 16.00 16.00

For overprint see No. 767.

Waterfowl A143

Perf. 14¼x14½

1999, Sept. 9 Litho. Wmk. 384

739 A143 9p Chiloe wigeon 2.50 1.75
740 A143 17p Crested duck 3.25 2.00
741 A143 30p Brown pintail 4.00 3.25
742 A143 35p Silver teal 4.25 3.50
743 A143 40p Yellow billed teal 5.00 4.00
744 A143 65p Flightless steamer duck 7.50 *8.50*
Nos. 739-744 (6) 26.50 23.00

California Gold Rush A144

Designs: 9p, Vicar of Bray, 1999. 35p, Gold panning, 1849. 40p, Gold rocking cradle, 1849. 80p, Vicar of Bray, 1849.

£1, Vicar of Bray in San Francisco Harbor, 1849.

Wmk. 373

1999, Nov. 3 Litho. ***Perf. 14***

745 A144 9p multicolored 1.10 1.10
746 A144 35p multicolored 4.25 4.25
747 A144 40p multicolored 4.75 4.75
748 A144 80p multicolored 10.00 10.00
Nos. 745-748 (4) 20.10 20.10

Souvenir Sheet

Perf. 13¾

749 A144 £1 multicolored 16.00 16.00

No. 749 contains one 48x31mm stamp.

Millennium A145

Designs: No. 750, Kelp gull. No. 751, Upland goose. No. 752, Christchurch Cathedral. No. 753, Night heron. No. 754, King penguin. No. 755, Christmas at home.

1999, Dec. 6 ***Perf. 14x14½***

750 A145 9p multicolored 3.00 3.00
751 A145 9p multicolored 3.00 3.00
752 A145 9p multicolored 3.00 3.00
753 A145 30p multicolored 5.25 5.25
754 A145 30p multicolored 5.25 5.25
755 A145 30p multicolored 5.25 5.25
Nos. 750-755 (6) 24.75 24.75

Visit of Princess Alexandra A146

Designs: 9p, Princess in patterned dress, trees. £1, Princess in blue dress, trees.

Perf. 13¼x13¾

2000, Feb. 1 Litho. Wmk. 373

756 A146 9p multi 2.00 2.00
757 A146 £1 multi 10.50 10.50

Sir Ernest Shackleton (1874-1922), Polar Explorer — A147

17p, Ship Endurance, discovery of the Caird Coast. 45p, Endurance trapped in pack ice. 75p, Shackleton, Chilean tugboat Yelcho.

2000, Feb. 10 Wmk. 373 ***Perf. 14***

758 A147 17p multi 5.00 2.00
759 A147 45p multi 8.50 5.00
760 A147 75p multi 13.50 *14.50*
Nos. 758-760 (3) 27.00 21.50

See British Antarctic Territory Nos. 285-287, South Georgia and South Sandwich Islands Nos. 254-256.

British Monarchs — A148

a, Elizabeth I. b, James II. c, George I. d, William IV. e, Edward VIII. f, Elizabeth II.

2000, Feb. 29 Wmk. 373 ***Perf. 14***

761 A148 40p Sheet of 6, #a.-f. 17.00 17.00

The Stamp Show 2000, London.

Prince William, 18th Birthday

Common Design Type

William: 10p, As toddler with fireman's helmet, vert. 20p, In checked suit and in navy suit, vert. 37p, With blue shirt. 43p, In gray suit and in navy suit holding flowers. 50p, As child with dog.

Perf. 13¾x14¼, 14¼x13¾

2000, June 21 Litho. Wmk. 373

Stamps with White Border

762 CD359 10p multi 1.75 1.25
763 CD359 20p multi 2.40 1.75
764 CD359 37p multi 3.50 2.75
765 CD359 43p multi 4.50 3.00
Nos. 762-765 (4) 12.15 8.75

Souvenir Sheet

Stamps Without White Border

Perf. 14¼

766 Sheet of 5 15.00 15.00
a. CD359 10p multi 1.00 1.00
b. CD359 20p multi 1.50 1.50
c. CD359 37p multi 2.50 2.50
d. CD359 43p multi 3.00 3.00
e. CD359 50p multi 6.00 6.00

No. 738 Ovptd. in Gold

Wmk. 384

2000, Aug. 4 Litho. ***Perf. 13½***
767 CD358 £1.40 multi 18.00 18.00

Bridges A149

Bridges over: 20p, Malo River. 37p, Bodie Creek. 43p, Fitzroy River.

2000, Oct. 16 ***Perf. 14¼x14½***
768-770 A149 Set of 3 18.00 18.00

Christmas — A150

Designs: 10p, Shepherd, sheep. 20p, Shepherds, sheep, angel. 33p, Holy family, shepherds, Magus, donkey, sheep. 43p, Angel, two Magi. 78p, Camel.

2000, Nov. 1 **Wmk. 373**
771-775 A150 Set of 5 16.50 16.50
775a Souvenir sheet, #771-775 18.50 18.50

Sunrises and Sunsets A151

Various photos: 10p, 20p, 37p, 43p.

2001, Jan. 10 ***Perf. 14½x14¼***
776-779 A151 Set of 4 16.00 16.00

Souvenir Sheet

New Year 2001 (Year of the Snake) — A152

Birds: a, Striated caracara. b, Mountain hawk eagle.

Perf. 14½x14¼

2001, Feb. 1 Litho. Wmk. 373
780 A152 37p Sheet of 2, #a-b 11.50 11.50

Hong Kong 2001 Stamp Exhibition.

Age of Victoria — A153

Designs: 3p, Falkland Islands #1. 10p, S.S. Great Britain, horiz. 20p, Stanley Harbor, 1888, horiz. 43p, Cape Pembroke Lighthouse, telephones, 1897. 93p, Royal Marines, 1900. £1.50, Queen Victoria, by Franz Xavier Winterhalter, 1859.

£1, Funeral procession for Queen Victoria.

2001, May 24 ***Perf. 14***
781-786 A153 Set of 6 26.00 26.00

Souvenir Sheet

787 A153 £1 multi 11.50 11.50

Royal Navy Connections to Falkland Islands — A154

Designs: 10p, Welfare, ship that made first recorded landing, 1690. 17p, HMS Invincible, ship in Battle of the Falklands, 1914. 20p, HMS Exeter, ship in Battle of the River Plate, 1939. 37p, SN.R6 Hovercraft, 1967. 43p, Antarctic patrol ship HMS Protector and Wasp helicopter, 1955. 68p, Desire, ship that made first sighting, 1592.

2001, July 24
788-793 A154 Set of 6 29.00 29.00

Carcass Island and its Flora and Fauna — A155

No. 794, 37p: a, Yellow violet. b, Tussac bird.

No. 795, 43p: a, Carcass Island settlement. b, Black-crowned night heron.

Wmk. 373

2001, Sept. 28 Litho. ***Perf. 13¾***
Pairs, #a-b
794-795 A155 Set of 2 21.00 21.00

Gentoo Penguins — A156

Designs: 10p, Birds flapping wings. 33p, Feeding young. 37p, Bird with beak open. 43p, Four birds walking.

2001, Oct. 26 ***Perf. 14½x14¼***
796-799 A156 Set of 4 10.00 10.00

Falkland Islands Company, 150th Anniv. A157

Designs: 10p, Company coat of arms, and gathering of cattle. 20p, Company flag, and ship Amelia. 43p, Manager F. E. Cobb, and company buildings. £1, Sheep farmer William Wickham Bertrand, sheep dip.

Wmk. 373

2002, Jan. 10 Litho. ***Perf. 14***
800-803 A157 Set of 4 16.00 16.00

Reign Of Queen Elizabeth II, 50th Anniv. Issue

Common Design Type

Designs: Nos. 804, 808a, 20p, Princess Elizabeth reading, 1945. Nos. 805, 808b, 37p, In 1977. Nos. 806, 808c, 43p, Holding Prince Charles, 1949. Nos. 807, 808d, 50p, At Garter ceremony, 1994. No. 808e, 50p, 1955 portrait by Annigoni (38x50mm).

Perf. 14¼x14½, 13¾ (#808e)

2002, Feb. 6 Litho. Wmk. 373

With Gold Frames

804 CD360 20p multicolored 1.75 1.00
805 CD360 37p multicolored 2.25 2.00
806 CD360 43p multicolored 3.50 3.50
807 CD360 50p multicolored 4.00 4.00
Nos. 804-807 (4) 11.50 10.50

Souvenir Sheet

Without Gold Frames

808 CD360 Sheet of 5, #a-e 12.00 12.00

Falkland Islands War, 20th Anniv. — A158

No. 809, 22p: a, HMS Hermes, 1982. b, Fishery patrol vessel, 2002.

No. 810, 40p: a, Troops landing, 1982. b, Mine clearing, 2002.

No. 811, 45p: a, RAF Harrier on HMS Hermes, 1982. b, RAF Tristar, 2002.

Wmk. 373

2002, June 14 Litho. ***Perf. 14***
Horiz. pairs, #a-b
809-811 A158 Set of 3 21.00 21.00

Queen Mother Elizabeth (1900-2002)

Common Design Type

Designs: 22p, Wearing hat and scarf (black and white photograph). 25p, Wearing blue hat with polka dots. Nos. 814, 816a, 95p, Wearing feathered hat (black and white photograph). Nos. 815, 816b, £1.20, Wearing blue hat.

Wmk. 373

2002, Aug. 5 Litho. ***Perf. 14¼***
With Purple Frames

812 CD361 22p multicolored 1.25 1.25
813 CD361 25p multicolored 1.50 1.50
814 CD361 95p multicolored 5.50 5.50
815 CD361 £1.20 multicolored 7.25 7.25
Nos. 812-815 (4) 15.50 15.50

Souvenir Sheet

Without Purple Frames

Perf. 14½x14¼

816 CD361 Sheet of 2, #a-b 16.00 16.00

Worldwide Fund for Nature (WWF) — A159

Penguins: 36p, Rockhopper. 40p, Magellanic. 45p, Gentoo. 70p, Macaroni.

Wmk. 373

2002, Aug. 30 Litho. ***Perf. 14¼***
817-820 A159 Set of 4 11.50 11.50
a. Horiz. strip of 4, #817-820 13.00 13.00

West Point Island and its Flora and Fauna — A160

No. 821, 40p: a, Felton's flower. b, Black-browed albatross.

No. 822, 45p: a, Rockhopper penguin. b, Island settlement.

Perf. 14¼x14½

2002, Oct. 31 Litho. Wmk. 373
Horiz. Pairs, #a-b
821-822 A160 Set of 2 14.00 14.00

Visit of Prince Andrew — A161

No. 823: a, 22p, In uniform. b, £1.52, In suit and tie.

2002, Nov. 11 ***Perf. 13¼x13½***
823 A161 Horiz. pair, #a-b 14.50 14.50

Shepherds' Houses — A162

Designs: 10p, Gun Hill shanty, Little Chartres. 22p, Paragon House, Lafonia. 45p, Dos Lomas, Lafonia. £1, Old House, Shallow Bay Farm.

Wmk. 373

2003, Mar. 31 Litho. ***Perf. 14***
824-827 A162 Set of 4 12.00 12.00

Head of Queen Elizabeth II

Common Design Type

Wmk. 373

2003, June 2 Litho. ***Perf. 13¾***
828 CD362 £2 multi 10.00 10.00

Prince William, 21st Birthday

Common Design Type

Color photographs: a, In suit at right. b, With Prince Harry at left.

Wmk. 373

2003, June 21 Litho. ***Perf. 14¼***
829 Horiz. pair 14.50 14.50
a.-b. CD364 95p Either single 6.00 6.00

Birds — A163

Designs: 1p, Chiloe widgeon. 2p, Dolphin gull, vert. 5p, Falkland flightless steamer duck. 10p, Black-throated finch, vert. 22p, White-tufted grebe. 25p, Rufous-chested dotterel, vert. 45p, Upland goose. 50p, Dark-faced ground-tyrant, vert. 95p, Black-crowned night heron. £1, Red-backed hawk, vert. £3, Black-necked swan. £5, Short-eared owl, vert.

Perf. 13x13¼, 13¼x13

2003, July 21 Litho. Wmk. 373
830 A163 1p multi .60 .60
831 A163 2p multi .90 .90
832 A163 5p multi 1.25 1.25
833 A163 10p multi 1.50 1.50
834 A163 22p multi 1.75 1.75
835 A163 25p multi 2.00 2.00
836 A163 45p multi 2.50 2.50
837 A163 50p multi 3.00 3.00
838 A163 95p multi 4.25 4.25
839 A163 £1 multi 4.50 4.50
840 A163 £3 multi 12.00 12.00
841 A163 £5 multi 20.00 *22.00*
Nos. 830-841,C1 (13) 56.00 58.00

See Nos. 917-919, C1.

Bird Life International A164

Black-browed albatross: No. 842, Adult on nest, facing right. No. 843, Chick. 40p, Heads of two adults, vert. £1, Adult on nest, facing left, vert.

16p, In flight.

Perf. 14¼x13¾, 13¾x14¼

2003, Sept. 26
842 A164 22p multi 1.75 1.75
a. Perf. 14¼x14½ 1.75 1.75
843 A164 22p multi 1.75 1.75
a. Perf. 14¼x14½ 1.75 1.75
844 A164 40p multi 2.75 2.75
a. Perf. 14½x14¼ 2.75 2.75
845 A164 £1 multi 7.25 7.25
a. Perf. 14½x14¼ 7.25 7.25
Nos. 842-845 (4) 13.50 13.50

Souvenir Sheet

846 Sheet, #842a-846a 17.50 17.50
a. A164 16p multi, perf. 14¼x14½ 1.50 1.50

New Island and its Flora and Fauna A165

No. 847, 40p: a, Striated caracara. b, Lady's slipper.
No. 848, 45p: a, Stone Cottage. b, King penguin.

Wmk. 373

2003, Oct. 24 Litho. *Perf. 13¾*
Pairs, #a-b

847-848 A165 Set of 2 19.00 19.00

Christmas — A166

Various depictions of Pale maiden flower: 16p, 30p, 40p, 95p.

2003, Nov. 3 *Perf. 14x14¼*

849-852 A166 Set of 4 16.50 16.50

Sheep Farming A167

Designs: 19p, Traditional hand shearing. 22p, Driving the sheep. 45p, Big House, Hill Cove. 70p, The early years. £1, Wool collection, SS Fitzroy.

Unwmk.

2004, Apr. 30 Litho. *Perf. 14*

853-857 A167 Set of 5 22.50 22.50

Wildlife Conservation in Falkland Islands, 25th Anniv. — A168

Designs: 20p, Man planting tussac grass. 24p, People cleaning beach. 50p, Satellite tracking of rockhopper penguins. £1, Weighing of albatross chick.

2004, June 17 Litho. *Perf. 14*

858-861 A168 Set of 4 19.00 19.00

Sir Rowland Hill (1795-1879) and Falkland Islands Postage Stamps — A169

Hill and: 24p, #20. 50p, #74. 75p, #94. £1, #151a.

2004, Aug. 31 Litho. *Perf. 13¼*

862-865 A169 Set of 4 20.00 20.00

Sea Lion Island and its Flora and Fauna — A170

No. 866, 42p: a, King cormorant. b, Dog orchid.
No. 867, 50p: a, Magellanic penguin. b, Sea Lion Lodge.

2004, Sept. 15 *Perf. 13¾*
Pairs, #a-b

866-867 A170 Set of 2 21.00 21.00
866c As #866a, dated "2005" *2.50* —
866d As #866b, dated "2005" *2.50* —
866e Pair, #866c-866d *7.50* —

Owls — A171

Designs: 18p, Head of short-eared owl. 45p, Short-eared owl. 50p, Barn owl in flight. £1.50, Barn owl.
£2, Barn owl in flight, horiz.

2004, Oct. 25

868-871 A171 Set of 4 19.00 19.00

Souvenir Sheet

872 A171 £2 multi 13.00 13.00

Battle of the Falkland Islands, 90th Anniv. A172

No. 873: a, HMS Kent, HMS Inflexible, half of HMS Carnarvon, half of HMS Cornwall. b, British Navy flag, HMS Glasgow, half of HMS Carnarvon, half of HMS Cornwall, half of HMS Invincible. c, Medals, half of HMS Invincible.
No. 874: a, Medals, half of SMS Scharnhorst. b, German imperial war ensign, SMS Dresden, half of SMS Scharnhorst, half of SMS Leipzig. c, SMS Nürnberg, SMS Gneisenau, half of SMS Leipzig.

2004, Dec. 8 Litho. *Perf. 14*

873 Horiz. strip of 3 10.00 10.00
a.-c. A172 24p Any single 2.50 2.00
874 Horiz. strip of 3 18.50 18.50
a.-c. A172 50p Any single 4.50 3.50

Camber Railway, 90th Anniv. — A173

Designs: 3p, Old track bed. 24p, Kerr Stuart Wren Class locomotive at Camber Depot, horiz. 50p, Kerr Stuart Wren Class locomotive Falkland Islands Express, horiz. £2, Camber sailing wagon.

2005, Feb. 28 *Perf. 13¾*

875-878 A173 Set of 4 18.00 18.00

Wedding of Prince Charles and Camilla Parker Bowles A174

Designs: 24p, Couple. 50p, Couple in formal wear, vert.
£2, Couple, Windsor Castle.

2005, Apr. 29 *Perf. 14*

879-880 A174 Set of 2 5.00 5.00

Souvenir Sheet

881 A174 £2 multi 10.50 10.50

End of World War II, 60th Anniv. — A175

No. 882, 24p: a, Walrus reconnaissance seaplane. b, Presentation Spitfire X4616.
No. 883, 80p: a, HMS Exeter at Port Stanley. b, Governor, King Edward Memorial Hospital staff, Rear Admiral Harwood and Capt. Bell.
No. 884, £1: a, Fitzroy. b, HMS William Scoresby.

Perf. 13¼x13½

2005, June 29 Litho.
Horiz. Pairs, #a-b

882-884 A175 Set of 3 32.50 32.50

Maritime Heritage A176

Designs: 24p, Snow Squall escaping CSS Tuscaloosa, 1863. No. 886, 55p, Jhelum, 1870. No. 887, 55p, Charles Cooper, 1866. £1.20, SS Imo colliding with the Mont Blanc, Halifax Harbor, 1917.

2005, Aug. 29 Litho. *Perf. 14*

885-888 A176 Set of 4 14.00 14.00

Pebble Island and its Flora and Fauna — A177

No. 889, 45p: a, Gentoo penguin. b, Falkland lavender.
No. 890, 55p: a, Pebble Island Lodge. b, Black-necked swan.

2005, Sept. 12 *Perf. 13¾*
Pairs, #a-b

889-890 A177 Set of 2 17.50 17.50

Souvenir Sheet

The Fall of Nelson, Battle of Trafalgar, 21 October 1805, by Denis Dighton — A178

2005, Oct. 21

891 A178 £2 multi 13.00 13.00

Battle of Trafalgar, bicent.

Hans Christian Andersen (1805-75), Author — A179

Stories: 18p, The Little Mermaid. 30p, The Snowman. 45p, The Ugly Duckling. £1, Thumbelina.

2005, Oct. 28 *Perf. 14*

892-895 A179 Set of 4 13.00 13.00

Stanley Infant and Junior School, 50th anniv.

Black-crowned Night Heron — A180

Designs: 24p, Head. 55p, Bird on one leg. 80p, Juvenile standing. £1, Head of juvenile.

2006, Feb. 10 Litho. *Perf. 13¾*

896-899 A180 Set of 4 13.00 13.00

Queen Elizabeth II, 80th Birthday — A181

Queen wearing: 24p, Yellow hat. 55p, Green hat. 80p, Blue hat. £1, Red hat.
£2, Tiara and white hat, horiz.

2006, Apr. 21 *Perf. 14*

900-903 A181 Set of 4 13.00 13.00

Souvenir Sheet

904 A181 £2 multi 11.00 11.00

SS Great Britain — A182

View of: 24p, Bow. 55p, Stern. £1.50, Deck and masts.

2006, May 19 *Perf. 13¾x13¼*

905-907 A182 Set of 3 14.00 14.00

Birds A183

Designs: No. 908, 25p, Gentoo penguin chicks. No. 909, 25p, King cormorants. No. 910, 60p, King penguin. No. 911, 60p, Wandering albatross.

2006, Aug. 30 Litho. *Perf. 14¼x14*

908-911 A183 Set of 4 11.00 11.00

Bleaker Island and its Flora and Fauna — A184

No. 912, 50p: a, Woolly Falkland ragwort. b, Macaroni penguin.
No. 913, 60p: a, The Outlook and sheep. b, Long-tailed meadowlark.

2006, Sept. 18 ***Perf. 13¼x13***
Pairs, #a-b

912-913 A184 Set of 2 15.00 15.00

Victoria Cross, 150th Anniv. — A185

Designs: Nos. 914, 916a, 60p, Lt. Col. H. Jones. Nos. 915, 916b, 60p, Sgt. Ian McKay. No. 916c, £1, Victoria Cross.

2006, Nov. 11 ***Perf. 13¼***
Stamps With White Frames

914-915 A185 Set of 2 8.00 8.00

Souvenir Sheet
Stamps Without White Frames

916 A185 Sheet of 3, #a-c 8.00 8.00

Bird Type of 2003

Designs: 20p, Black-browed albatross, vert. 25p, Rufous-chested dotterel, vert. £5, Short-eared owl, vert.

Perf. 13¼x13
2006, Nov. 15 **Litho.** **Unwmk.**

917	A163	20p multi	2.50	2.00
918	A163	25p multi	2.75	2.50
919	A163	£5 multi	22.50	22.50
		Nos. 917-919 (3)	27.75	27.00

Nos. 918-919 differ from Nos. 835 and 841 by having less color around the Queen's head. Nos. 917-919 are dated "2006."

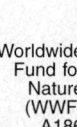

Worldwide Fund for Nature (WWF) A186

Striated caracara: 25p, Heads of two birds. 50p, Bird in flight. 60p, Bird standing. 85p, Bird eating shellfish.

2006, Dec. 20 **Litho.** ***Perf. 13¾***

920-923 A186 Set of 4 10.00 10.00
923a Miniature sheet, 4 each #920-923 50.00 50.00

Fisheries, 20th Anniv. A187

Designs: 3p, Fishermen at sea. 11p, Fishing boat at night. 25p, Fishermen leaving boat. 30p, Japanese jigger. 60p, Fishery protection boat Dorada. £1.05, Trawler transferring fish to a freezer container ship.

2007, Feb. 24 ***Perf. 14¼***

924-929 A187 Set of 6 14.50 14.50

HMS Plymouth A188

HMS Plymouth: 25p, Joining Falkland Islands Task Force. 40p, Supporting SBS. 60p, Under attack by Argentine fighters. £1.05, Docked at Port Stanley.

2007, Mar. 27

930-933 A188 Set of 4 16.50 16.50

Souvenir Sheet

Falkland Islands War, 25th Anniv. — A189

No. 934: a, Avro Vulcan prototype VX770. b, Avro Vulcan XM597. c, Avro Vulcan XM607. d, Vulcan in the Sky Project.

2007, May 25 **Litho.** ***Perf. 13¼***

934 A189 60p Sheet of 4, #a-d 15.00 15.00

Miniature Sheets

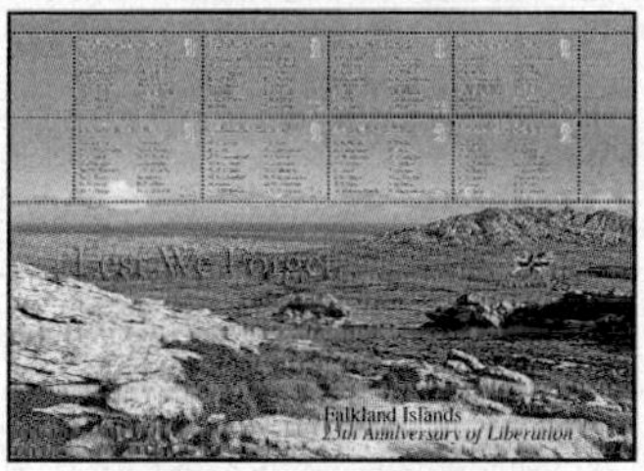

British and Falkland Islander Casualties of the Falkland Islands War — A190

No. 935, 25p — Casualties beginning with: a, Doreen Bonner. b, G. W. J. Batt. c, J. R. Carlyle. d, S. J. Dixon. e, I. R. Farrell. f, G. C. Grace. g, R. R. Heath. h, A. S. James.
No. 936, 60p: a, D. Lee. b, P. B. McKay. c, G. T. Nelson. d, J. B. Pashley. e, M. Sambles. f, D. A. Strickland. g, R. G. Thomas. h, P. A. West.

2007, June 14 **Litho.** ***Perf. 14¼***
Sheets of 8, #a-h

935-936 A190 Set of 2 32.50 32.50

Scouting, Cent. — A191

Designs: 10p, Scouts on ladder of RRS Discovery. 20p, Dignitaries on ship's deck. 25p, Dignitaries, diff. £2, RRS Discovery.

2007, July 23 **Litho.** ***Perf. 13½x13¼***

937-940 A191 Set of 4 13.50 13.50

Voyage of RRS Discovery from Falkland Islands for presentation to British Scout Association, 70th anniv.

Princess Diana (1961-97) — A192

2007, Aug. 31 ***Perf. 14***

941 A192 60p multi 3.75 3.75

Printed in sheets of 8 stamps + 2 labels.

Saunders Island and its Flora and Fauna — A193

No. 942, 50p: a, Rockhopper penguin. b, Dusty miller.
No. 943, 55p: a, Crested caracara. b, Earliest British settlement at Port Egmont.

2007, Sept. 28 **Litho.** ***Perf. 13¾***
Pairs, #a-b

942-943 A193 Set of 2 16.50 16.50

Wedding of Queen Elizabeth II and Prince Philip, 60th Anniv. A194

2007, Nov. 20 **Litho.** ***Perf. 14***

944 A194 £1 multi 7.00 7.00

Polar Explorers and Their Ships A195

Explorers and ships: 4p, James Weddell (1787-1834), and Jane. 25p, James Clark Ross (1800-62), and HMS Erebus. 85p, William Spiers Bruce (1867-1921), and Scotia. £1.61, James Marr (1902-65), and Discovery II.

2008, Apr. 7

945-948 A195 Set of 4 14.00 14.00

Southern Elephant Seals A196

Designs: 27p, Seal pup. 55p, Male and female. 65p, Seals play fighting. £1.10, Seal and tussock bird.

2008, July 15 **Litho.** ***Perf. 14***

949-952 A196 Set of 4 14.00 14.00

Aircraft A197

Designs: 1p, Taylorcraft Auster Mk 5. 2p, Boeing 747-300. 5p, De Havilland Canada DHC-6 Twin Otter. 10p, Lockheed C-130 Hercules. 27p, De Havilland Canada DHC-2 Beaver. 55p, Airbus A320. 65p, Lockheed L-1011-385-3 Tristar C2. 90p, Avro Vulcan B2. £1, Britten-Norman BN-2 Islander. £2, Panavia Tornado F3. £3, De Havilland Canada DHC-7-110 Dash 7. £5, BAE Sea Harrier.

2008, Aug. 1 **Litho.** ***Perf. 14***

953	A197	1p multi	.40	*.75*
954	A197	2p multi	.40	*.75*
955	A197	5p multi	.75	.75
956	A197	10p multi	.90	.90
957	A197	27p multi	1.75	1.75
958	A197	55p multi	2.25	2.25
959	A197	65p multi	2.75	2.75
960	A197	90p multi	3.50	3.50
961	A197	£1 multi	4.00	4.00
962	A197	£2 multi	7.25	7.25
963	A197	£3 multi	10.50	10.50
964	A197	£5 multi	18.00	18.00
		Nos. 953-964 (12)	52.45	53.15

Souvenir Sheet
Stamps With Royal Air Force 90th Anniv. Emblem Added

965	Sheet of 4	14.50	14.50
a.	A197 10p Like #956	.40	.40
b.	A197 65p Like #959	2.60	2.60
c.	A197 90p Like #960	3.50	3.50
d.	A197 £2 Like #962	8.00	8.00

Port Louis, 175th Anniv. — A198

Designs: 27p, Sailor raising British flag. 65p, Royal Marines, British flag.
£2, Capt. Onslow of HMS Clio, British flag.

2008, Sept. 22 **Litho.** ***Perf. 14***

966-967 A198 Set of 2 5.00 5.00

Souvenir Sheet

968 A198 £2 multi 10.00 10.00

Islands and Rocks A199

Designs: 22p, The Slipper. 40p, Kidney Island. 60p, Stephens Bluff and Castle Rock. £1, The Colliers.

2008, Oct. 1 **Litho.** ***Perf. 13¾***

969-972 A199 Set of 4 11.00 11.00

See Nos. 986-989, 1025-1028.

Retirement of Queen Elizabeth 2 as Ocean Liner — A200

Designs: 23p, Launch of Queen Elizabeth 2. 27p, Service of Queen Elizabeth 2 as troop ship in Falkland Islands War. 65p, Queen Elizabeth 2, Palm Jumeirah, Dubai. £2, Queen Elizabeth 2 (70x34mm).

2008, Nov. 21 **Litho.** ***Perf. 13¼***

973-976 A200 Set of 4 14.00 14.00

Charles Darwin (1809-82), Naturalist — A201

Designs: 4p, Darwin seated. 27p, Warrah. 65p, HMS Beagle in Berkeley Sound, 1834. £1.10, Darwin encountering a Magellanic penguin.

2009, Apr. 23 Litho. *Perf. 14*
977-980 A201 Set of 4 8.00 8.00

Naval Aviation, Cent. A202

Royal Navy aircraft and ships: 30p, Westland/Aerospatiale Gazelle AH1 helicopter. 50p, Westland Lynx HAS2 helicopter. 65p, Westland Wessex HU5 helicopter. £1.10, Westland Sea King HAS5 helicopter.
£2, BAe Sea Harrier, HMS Hermes.

2009, May 7 Litho. *Perf. 14*
981-984 A202 Set of 4 11.00 11.00

Souvenir Sheet

985 A202 £2 multi 7.50 7.50

Islands and Rocks Type of 2008

Designs: 27p, Seal Rocks. 40p, Beauchene Island. 65p, Jason East Cay, Steeple Jason. £1.50, Horse Block.

2009, Aug. 14 Litho. *Perf. 13¾*
986-989 A199 Set of 4 11.50 11.50

Albatrosses A203

Designs: 22p, Black-browed albatross. 27p, Gray-headed albatross. 60p, Light-mantled sooty albatross. 90p, Wandering albatross.

2009, Oct. 19 Litho. *Perf. 13¾*
990-993 A203 Set of 4 8.50 8.50

Cobb's Wren A204

Designs: Nos. 994, 998a, 27p, Wren on seaweed. Nos. 995, 998b, 65p, Wrens at nest. Nos. 996, 998c, 90p, Wren on rock. Nos. 997, 998d, £1.10, Two wrens.

2009, Nov. 10 *Perf. 13¾*

Stamps With WWF Emblem

994-997 A204 Set of 4 11.00 11.00
997a Sheet of 16, 4 each #994-997 45.00 45.00

Souvenir Sheet

Stamps With Falklands Conservation Emblem

998 A204 Sheet of 4, #a-d 11.00 11.00

Ships Named HMS Exeter A205

Ship used from: 4p, 1931-42. 20p, 1931-42, with helicopter. 30p, 1980-2009, with helicopter. £1.66, 1980-2009, with helicopter, diff.

2009, Dec. 8 Litho. *Perf. 14*
999-1002 A205 Set of 4 8.00 8.00

Skies in Four Seasons A206

Designs: 27p, Carcass Island in spring. 55p, Beach on New Island in summer. 65p, Rainbow over Stanley in autumn. £1.10, Islands in winter.

2010, Jan. 25 Litho. *Perf. 13*
1003-1006 A206 Set of 4 8.50 8.50

Restoration of the SS Great Britain A207

SS Great Britain: 27p, On pontoon near jetty in Stanley. 50p, Beached at Sparrow Cove. 65p, Bow. £1.10, Mast and rigging.

2010, Apr. 12 *Perf. 13¼*
1007-1010 A207 Set of 4 8.50 8.50

Miniature Sheet

Battle of Britain, 70th Anniv. — A208

No. 1011 — Airplanes: a, Hawker Hurricane P2961. b, Supermarine Spitfire P9398. c, Hawker Hurricane P3854. d, Supermarine Spitfire P7350. e, Hawker Hurricane V6665. f, Supermarine Spitfire L1035. g, Hawker Hurricane P3576. h, Supermarine Spitfire X4620.

2010, May 7 Litho. *Perf. 14x14¼*
1011 A208 65p Sheet of 8, #a-h 17.00 17.00

London 2010 Festival of Stamps.

Birds A209

Designs: Nos. 1012, 1016a, 27p, Sooty shearwater. Nos. 1013, 1016b, 70p, White-chinned petrel. Nos. 1014, 1016c, 95p, Southern giant petrel. Nos. 1015, 1016d, £1.15, Greater shearwater.

2010, July 8 Litho. *Perf. 13¾*

Stamps With White Frames

1012-1015 A209 Set of 4 10.50 10.50

Souvenir Sheet

Stamps Without White Frames

1016 A209 Sheet of 4, #a-d 10.50 10.50

Flowering Shrubs A210

Designs: 27p, Fuchsia. 70p, Boxwood. 95p, Gorse. £1.15, Honeysuckle.

2010, Oct. 27 Litho. *Perf. 13¼x13*
1017-1020 A210 Set of 4 11.00 11.00

Royal Air Force Search and Rescue Force, 70th Anniv. — A211

Anniversary emblem and: 27p, Helicopter on ground. 70p, Helicopter in flight. 95p, Crew in helicopter cockpit. £1.15, Helicopter in flight with open door.

2011, Mar. 9 *Perf. 13¼*
1021-1024 A211 Set of 4 11.00 11.00

Islands and Rocks Type of 2008

Designs: 3p, Bird Island. 27p, Eddystone Rock. 70p, Round Island and Sail Rock. £1.71, Direction Island.

2011, Apr. 11 *Perf. 13¼x13*
1025-1028 A199 Set of 4 9.50 9.50

Wedding of Prince William and Catherine Middleton — A212

2011, Apr. 29 *Perf. 13¼*
1029 A212 £2 multi 7.25 7.25

Worldwide Fund for Nature (WWF) — A213

Southern sea lions: 27p, Males and females on beach. 40p, Pod in water. 70p, Males on beach. £1.15, Head.

2011, May 30 *Perf. 13¾*
1030-1033 A213 Set of 4 10.00 10.00
1033a Miniature sheet of 16, 4 each #1030-1033 40.00 40.00

Queen Elizabeth II, 85th Birthday — A214

Queen Elizabeth II wearing: 27p, Red violet hat with flower. 30p, Fur hat. 70p, White hat with pink and white ribbons. £1.50, White hat with feather.

2011, June 11 *Perf. 13¾*
1034-1037 A214 Set of 4 9.50 9.50

Souvenir Sheet

Queen Elizabeth II — A215

2011, Aug. 8 Litho. *Perf. 14¼x15*
1038 A215 £2 multi 7.50 7.50

Commonwealth Parliamentary Association, cent.

Wildlife A216

Designs: 27p, Gentoo penguins. 70p, Leopard seal. 95p, Gonatus squid. £1.15, Gentoo penguins, diff.

2011, Nov. 16 *Perf. 13¾*
1039-1042 A216 Set of 4 11.00 11.00

Marine Life A217

Designs: 27p, Sea anemone. 50p, Jellyfish. 70p, Starfish. £1.15, Nudibranch.

2012, Apr. 11 *Perf. 13¼x13½*
1043-1046 A217 Set of 4 8.50 8.50

Reign of Queen Elizabeth II, 60th Anniv. — A218

Photograph of Queen Elizabeth II in: 27p, 1952. 30p, 1977. 70p, 2002. £1.71, 2012.
£3, Queen Elizabeth II wearing tiara, 1955.

2012, May 10 *Perf. 13½x13¼*
1047-1050 A218 Set of 4 9.25 9.25

Souvenir Sheet

Perf. 13¼

1051 A218 £3 multi 10.00 10.00

No. 1051 contains one 30x48mm stamp.

Liberation of the Falkland Islands, 30th Anniv. — A219

Designs: No. 1052, 30p, Ferry MV Concordia Bay. No. 1053, 30p, Liberation Monument, Stanley. No. 1054, 75p, School, Stanley. No. 1055, 75p, Wind turbines. £1, Sign and houses near Stanley Harbor. £1.20, Children and penguins.

2012, June 14 *Perf. 14*
1052-1057 A219 Set of 6 13.50 13.50

Coastal Landscapes — A220

Designs: 30p, Surf Bay, East Falkland Island. 75p, Cliffs, New Island. £1, Mountain, Steeple Jason Island. £1.20, Deaths Head and Grave Cove, West Falkland Island.

2012, July 12 *Perf. 13*
1058-1061 A220 Set of 4 10.00 10.00

Sinking of the P.S.N.C. Oravia, Cent. A221

Designs: 30p, Oravia at sea. 75p, Passengers and crew wearing life vests. £1, Passengers filling lifeboats. £1.20 Oravia and the Samson.

2012, Aug. 28 *Perf. 14*
1062-1065 A221 Set of 4 10.50 10.50

Souvenir Sheet

Sinking of the Titanic, Cent. — A222

2012, Aug. 28 *Perf. 14x14¾*
1066 A222 £2 multi 7.50 7.50

Dolphins and Whales — A223

Designs: 1p, Southern right whale dolphins. 2p, Minke whale. 5p, Peale's dolphin. 10p, Dusky dolphin. 30p, Southern right whale. 50p, Fin whale. 75p, Hourglass dolphin. £1, Long-finned pilot whale. £1.20, Killer whales. £2, Sperm whale. £3.50, Commerson's dolphin. £5, Sei whale.

2012, Nov. 9 *Perf. 13¼*

1067	A223	1p multi	.25	.25
1068	A223	2p multi	.25	.25
1069	A223	5p multi	.25	.25
1070	A223	10p multi	.30	.30
1071	A223	30p multi	.95	.95
1072	A223	50p multi	1.60	1.60
1073	A223	75p multi	2.40	2.40
1074	A223	£1 multi	3.25	3.25
1075	A223	£1.20 multi	4.00	4.00
1076	A223	£2 multi	6.50	6.50
1077	A223	£3.50 multi	11.50	11.50
1078	A223	£5 multi	16.00	16.00
		Nos. 1067-1078 (12)	47.25	47.25

Color in Nature — A224

No. 1079: a, Night heron. b, Diddle-dee berries.
No. 1080: a, Short-eared owl. b, Scurvy grass flowers.

2012, Dec. 14 *Perf. 13*
1079 Pair 2.00 2.00
a.-b. A224 30p Either single 1.00 1.00
1080 Pair 5.00 5.00
a.-b. A224 75p Either single 2.50 2.50

See Nos. 1108-1109, 1122-1123, 1136-1137.

2013 Referendum on Political Status A225

Map, of Falkland Island, hand and ballot box with denomination color of: 3p, Deep blue. 40p, Red violet. 75p, Green. £1.76, Red brown.
£3, Purple.

2013, Feb. 15
1081-1084 A225 Set of 4 8.75 8.75

Souvenir Sheet

Perf. 13½x13¼

1085 A225 £3 multi 9.00 9.00

No. 1085 contains one 56x45mm stamp.

Wildlife A226

Designs: 30p, Johnny rook. 75p, Rockhopper penguins. £1, Rockhopper penguin swimming. £1.20, Lobster krill.

2013, Mar. 28 *Perf. 13¾*
1086-1089 A226 Set of 4 10.00 10.00

Lady Margaret Thatcher (1925-2013), British Prime Minister — A227

Lady Thatcher: 30p, And husband, Denis arriving at 10 Downing Street, 1979. 75p, Inspecting Falkland Islands minefield, 1983. £1, With flag at celebration of 10th anniversary of Falkland Islands liberation, 1992. £1.20, Holding Falkland Islands coin commemorating 25th anniversary of the liberation, 2007.

2013, May 16 *Perf. 13¾*
1090-1093 A227 Set of 4 10.00 10.00

Sir Rex Hunt (1926-2012), Governor of Falkland Islands — A228

Falkland Islands coat of arms and Hunt: 30p, As Civil Commissioner, 1982. 75p, In uniform next to Governor's car. £1, With flag of Falkland Islands, 1992. £1.20, Talking to Queen Elizabeth II, 2000.

2013, June 11 *Perf. 14*
1094-1097 A228 Set of 4 10.50 10.50

Coronation of Queen Elizabeth II, 60th Anniv. — A229

Queen Elizabeth II: 30p, Wearing coronation gown. 75p, With crown and orb. £1, Waving. £1.20, With Prince Philip.

2013, July 22 *Perf. 13½x13¼*
1098-1101 A229 Set of 4 10.00 10.00

Shallow Marine Surveys Group A230

Marine life: Nos. 1102, 1106a, 30p, Saffron sea cucumber. Nos. 1103, 1106b, 75p, Stalked jellyfish. Nos. 1104, 1106c, £1, Scythe-edged serolis. Nos. 1105, 1106d, £1.20, Naked sea urchin.
No. 1107a, £1, Painted shrimp, vert.

2013, Aug. 29 *Perf. 13¼x13½*

Stamps With White Frames

1102-1105 A230 Set of 4 10.50 10.50

Stamps Without White Frames

1106 A230 Strip of 4, #a-d 10.50 10.50

Souvenir Sheet

Perf. 13½x13¼

1107 A230 Sheet of 3 (see footnote) 9.75 9.75
a. A230 £1 multi 3.25 3.25

No. 1107 contains No. 1107a, Ascension No. 1104a and South Georgia and South Sandwich Islands No. 485a. This sheet was sold in Ascension, Falkland Islands and South Georgia and South Sandwich Islands.

Color in Nature Type of 2012

No. 1108: a, Macaroni penguin. b, Purple cap fungi.
No. 1109: a, Crested duck. b, Southern painted lady butterfly.

2013, Oct. 3 *Perf. 13¼*
1108 Pair 1.90 1.90
a.-b. A224 30p Either single .95 .95
1109 Pair 4.80 4.80
a.-b. A224 75p Either single 2.40 2.40

Wildlife A231

Designs: 30p, King penguin and chick. 75p, Gaptooth lanternfish. £1, Southern sea lion. £1.20, King penguins, diff.

2014, Mar. 25 **Litho.** *Perf. 13¼*
1110-1113 A231 Set of 4 11.00 11.00

Mushrooms A232

Designs: 30p, False chanterelle. 75p, Red wax cap. £1, Clustered domecap. £1.20, Shaggy inkcap.

2014, Apr. 15 **Litho.** *Perf. 13¼*
1114-1117 A232 Set of 4 11.00 11.00

Royal Christenings A233

Photograph from christening of: 30p, Queen Elizabeth II. 75p, Prince Charles. £1, Prince William. £1.20, Prince George.

2014, May 21 **Litho.** *Perf. 13¼*
1118-1121 A233 Set of 4 11.00 11.00

Color in Nature Type of 2012

No. 1122: a, King penguins. b, Marsh marigolds.
No. 1123: a, Black oystercatcher. b, Vanilla daisies.

2014, Sept. 16 **Litho.** *Perf. 13¼*
1122 Pair 2.00 2.00
a.-b. A224 30p Either single 1.00 1.00
1123 Pair 5.00 5.00
a.-b. A224 75p Either single 2.50 2.50

Battle of the Falkland Islands, Cent. — A234

Designs: 30p, SMS Scharnhorst. 75p, HMS Invincible. £1, British and German flags, poppies. £1.20, Sailor, Battle of the Falkland Islands Monument.

2014, Dec. 8 **Litho.** *Perf. 13¾*
1124-1127 A234 Set of 4 10.00 10.00

Type 42 Destroyers — A235

Designs: 30p, HMS Sheffield. 75p, HMS Exeter. £1, HMS Liverpool. £1.20, HMS Edinburgh.

2014, Dec. 22 **Litho.** *Perf. 14*
1128-1131 A235 Set of 4 10.00 10.00

Birds — A236

Adult and chicks: 30p, Pied oystercatchers. 75p, Gentoo penguins. £1, Black-browed albatrosses. £1.20, Falkland skuas.

2015, Feb. 11 **Litho.** *Perf. 13¾*
1132-1135 A236 Set of 4 10.00 10.00

Color in Nature Type of 2012

No. 1136: a, Black-throated finch. b, Fuegian ferns.
No. 1137: a, Dolphin gulls. b, Yellow daisies.

2015, May 12 **Litho.** *Perf. 13¼*
1136 Pair 1.90 1.90
a.-b. A224 30p Either single .95 .95
1137 Pair 4.50 4.50
a.-b. A224 75p Either single 2.25 2.25

Magna Carta, 800th Anniv. A237

Designs: 30p, King John, Magna Carta and barons. 75p, Courtroom. £1, Gilbert House, Stanley. £1.20, King John, arms of Falkland Islands.

2015, June 15 Litho. *Perf. 14*
1138-1141 A237 Set of 4 10.50 10.50

Wildlife A238

Designs: 30p, Magellanic penguin. 75p, Falkland sprats. £1, Falkland skua. £1.20, Heads of two magellanic penguins.

2015, Aug. 21 Litho. *Perf. 13¾*
1142-1145 A238 Set of 4 10.00 10.00

Queen Elizabeth II, Longest-Reigning British Monarch — A239

Queen Elizabeth II and events during her reign: 30p, Publications reporting on her coronation, 1953. 75p, Arrival of first Land Rovers in the Falkland Islands, 1950s. £1, Coach used for Golden Jubilee, 2012. £1.25, Falkland Islands referendum, 2013.

2015, Sept. 9 Litho. *Perf. 14*
1146-1149 A239 Set of 4 10.00 10.00

Elephant Seal Research Group, 20th Anniv. — A240

No. 1150, 30p: a, Seal in water. b, Researcher with equipment near seal.
No. 1151, 75p: a, Pod of seals on beach. b, Researcher approaching seal.
No. 1152, £1: a, Seal and penguins. b, Researcher holding measuring stick above seal.

2015, Nov. 30 Litho. *Perf. 13*
Horiz. Pairs, #a-b
1150-1152 A240 Set of 3 12.50 12.50

Clouds — A241

Designs: 31p, Asperitas. 76p, Altocumulus. £1.01, Altocumulus lenticularis. £1.22, Cumulonimbus and Stratocumulus.

2015, Dec. 9 Litho. *Perf. 13¼*
1153-1156 A241 Set of 4 9.75 9.75

Birds of Prey — A242

Designs: No. 1157, 31p, Barn owl. No. 1158, 31p, Short-eared owl. No. 1159, 76p, Red-backed buzzard. No. 1160, 76p, Crested caracara. £1.01, Peregrine falcon. £1.22, Striated caracara.

2016, Jan. 13 Litho. *Perf. 13¾*
1157-1162 A242 Set of 6 13.00 13.00

SEMI-POSTAL STAMPS

Catalogue values for unused stamps in this section are for Never Hinged items.

Rebuilding after Conflict with Argentina — SP1

Wmk. 373
1982, Sept. 13 Litho. *Perf. 11*
B1 SP1 £1 + £1 Battle sites 3.00 3.00

Liberation of Falkland Islands, 10th Anniv. — SP2

Designs: 14p+6p, San Carlos Cemetery. 29p+11p, 1982 War Memorial, Port Stanley. 34p+16p, South Atlantic Medal. 68p+32p, Government House, Port Stanley.

Wmk. 373
1992, June 14 Litho. *Perf. 14*
B2 SP2 14p + 6p multicolored 1.00 *1.50*
B3 SP2 29p + 11p multicolored 1.75 1.75
B4 SP2 34p + 16p multicolored 2.00 2.00
B5 SP2 68p + 32p multicolored 3.00 *3.50*
a. Souvenir sheet of 4, #B2-B5 9.00 9.00
Nos. B2-B5 (4) 7.75 8.75

Surtax for Soldiers', Sailors' and Airmen's Families Association.

AIR POST STAMPS

Bird Type of 2003
Design: Rockhopper penguins, vert.
Booklet Stamp
Serpentine Die Cut 6x6½ Syncopated
2003, Sept. 19 Litho.
Self-Adhesive
C1 A163 (40p) multi 1.75 1.75
a. Booklet pane of 8 14.00

Penguins — AP1

Designs: No. C2, (55p), King penguin. No. C3, (55p), Macaroni penguin. No. C4, (55p), Magellanic penguin. No. C5, (55p), Rockhopper penguin. No. C6, (55p), Gentoo penguin. No. C7, (55p), Albino rockhopper penguin.

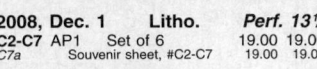

2008, Dec. 1 Litho. *Perf. 13¼*
C2-C7 AP1 Set of 6 19.00 19.00
C7a Souvenir sheet, #C2-C7 19.00 19.00

Penguins — AP2

Designs: Nos. C8, C14a, (70p), King penguin. Nos. C9, C14b, (70p), Macaroni penguin. Nos. C10, C14c, (70p), Rockhopper penguins. Nos. C11, C14d, (70p), Albino and normal rockhopper penguins. Nos. C12, C14e, (70p), Magellanic penguin. Nos. C13, C14f, (70p), Gentoo penguins.

2010, Sept. 29 Litho. *Perf. 13¾*
Stamps With White Frames
C8-C13 AP2 Set of 6 15.00 15.00
Stamps Without White Frames
C14 AP2 (70p) Sheet of 6, #a-f 15.00 15.00

Albino and Normal Rockhopper Penguins AP3

Gentoo Penguins AP4

Magellanic Penguin AP5

Rockhopper Penguins AP6

King Penguins AP7

Macaroni Penguins AP8

2013, Nov. 21 Litho. *Perf. 13¼*
Stamps With White Frames
C15 AP3 (65p) multi 2.25 2.25
C16 AP4 (65p) multi 2.25 2.25
C17 AP5 (65p) multi 2.25 2.25
C18 AP6 (65p) multi 2.25 2.25
C19 AP7 (65p) multi 2.25 2.25
C20 AP8 (65p) multi 2.25 2.25
Nos. C15-C20 (6) 13.50 13.50

Souvenir Sheet
Stamps Without White Frames
C21 Sheet of 6 14.00 14.00
a. AP3 (65p) multi 3.25 3.25
b. AP4 (65p) multi 3.25 3.25
c. AP5 (65p) multi 3.25 3.25
d. AP6 (65p) multi 3.25 3.25
e. AP7 (65p) multi 3.25 3.25
f. AP8 (65p) multi 3.25 3.25

POSTAGE DUE STAMPS

Catalogue values for unused stamps in this section are for never hinged items.

Penguin — D1

Perf. 14½x14
1991, Jan. 7 Litho. Wmk. 373
J1 D1 1p lilac rose & lake .25 .50
J2 D1 2p buff & brown org .25 .50
J3 D1 3p yel & orange yel .25 .50
J4 D1 4p lt bl grn & dk bl grn .25 .50
J5 D1 5p sky blue & Prus bl .25 .50
J6 D1 10p lt blue & dk blue .35 .70
J7 D1 20p lt violet & dk vio .90 1.50
J8 D1 50p brt yel grn & dk yel green 2.00 3.25
Nos. J1-J8 (8) 4.50 7.95

Penguins D2

Various penguins.

2005, Dec. 2 Litho. *Perf. 13¾*
J9 D2 1p multi .25 .25
J10 D2 3p multi .25 .25
J11 D2 5p multi .25 .25
J12 D2 10p multi .45 .45
J13 D2 20p multi .85 .85
J14 D2 50p multi 1.90 1.90
J15 D2 £1 multi 3.75 3.75
J16 D2 £2 multi 7.50 7.50
J17 D2 £3 multi 12.00 12.00
J18 D2 £5 multi 19.00 19.00
Nos. J9-J18 (10) 46.20 46.20

WAR TAX STAMPS

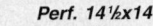

Regular Issue of 1912-14 Overprinted

1918-20 Wmk. 3 *Perf. 14*
MR1 A7 ½p dp ol grn .55 *7.25*
MR2 A7 1p org ver ('19) .55 *4.00*
a. Double overprint 3,750.
MR3 A7 1sh bis brn 6.50 *52.50*
a. Pair, one without overprint 16,500.
b. Double ovpt., one albino 2,000.
c. 1sh brn, thick grayish paper ('20) 6.00 50.00
d. As "c," double ovpt., one albino 2,000.
Nos. MR1-MR3 (3) 7.60 *63.75*

No. MR3a probably is caused by a foldover and is not constant.

FALKLAND ISLANDS DEPENDENCIES

Catalogue values for unused stamps in this section are for Never Hinged items.

Map of Falkland Islands — A1

Engr., Center Litho. in Black
1946, Feb. 1 Wmk. 4 *Perf. 12*
1L1 A1 ½p yellow green 1.10 *3.50*
1L2 A1 1p blue violet 1.30 *1.90*
1L3 A1 2p deep carmine 1.30 *2.60*
1L4 A1 3p ultramarine 1.90 *5.25*
1L5 A1 4p deep plum 2.40 *5.00*
1L6 A1 6p orange yellow 3.75 *5.25*
1L7 A1 9p brown 2.25 *4.00*
1L8 A1 1sh rose violet 3.00 *5.00*
Nos. 1L1-1L8 (8) 17.00 *32.50*

Nos. 1L1-1L8 were reissued in 1948, printed on more opaque paper with the lines of the map finer and clearer. Value for set, unused or used $120.
See No. 1L13.

Common Design Types pictured following the introduction.

Peace Issue
Common Design Type

1946, Oct. 4 ***Perf. 13½x14***

1L9	CD303	1p purple	.50	.50
1L10	CD303	3p deep blue	.90	.50

Silver Wedding Issue
Common Design Types

1948, Dec. 6 Photo. ***Perf. 14x14½***

1L11	CD304	2½p brt ultra	1.75	3.25

Perf. 11½x11
Engr.

1L12	CD305	1sh blue violet	2.50	2.75

Type of 1946

1949, Mar. 6 ***Perf. 12***
Center Litho. in Black

1L13	A1	2½p deep blue	8.00	4.25

UPU Issue
Common Design Types
Engr.; Name Typo. on 2p, 3p

1949, Oct. 10 ***Perf. 13½, 11x11½***

1L14	CD306	1p violet	1.25	3.50
1L15	CD307	2p deep carmine	5.25	4.00
1L16	CD308	3p indigo	4.00	2.25
1L17	CD309	6p red orange	5.00	4.25
		Nos. 1L14-1L17 (4)	15.50	14.00

Coronation Issue
Common Design Type

1953, June 4 ***Perf. 13½x13***

1L18	CD312	1p purple & black	1.50	1.50

John Biscoe — A2

Trepassey — A3

Ships: 1½p, Wyatt Earp. 2p, Eagle. 2½p, Penola. 3p, Discovery II. 4p, William Scoresby. 6p, Discovery. 9p, Endurance. 1sh, Deutschland. 2sh, Pourquoi-pas? 2sh6p, Français. 5sh, Scotia. 10sh, Antarctic. £1, Belgica.

1954, Feb. 1 Engr. ***Perf. 12½***
Center in Black

1L19	A2	½p blue green	.25	*2.00*
1L20	A3	1p sepia	1.75	1.50
1L21	A3	1½p olive	2.00	1.75
1L22	A3	2p rose red	1.25	2.50
1L23	A3	2½p yellow	1.25	.35
1L24	A3	3p ultra	1.25	.35
1L25	A3	4p red violet	3.00	1.75
1L26	A3	6p rose violet	3.50	1.75
1L27	A2	9p black	3.50	2.00
1L28	A3	1sh org brown	3.50	2.00
1L29	A3	2sh lilac rose	18.00	10.00
1L30	A2	2sh6p blue gray	19.00	7.00
1L31	A2	5sh violet	40.00	7.50
1L32	A3	10sh brt blue	55.00	18.00
1L33	A2	£1 black	87.50	50.00
		Nos. 1L19-1L33 (15)	240.75	108.45

Nos. 20, 23-24, 26 Ovptd. in Black

1956, Jan 30 **Center in Black**

1L34	A3	1p sepia	.25	.25
1L35	A3	2½p yellow	.50	.50
1L36	A3	3p ultramarine	.60	.60
1L37	A2	6p rose violet	.70	.70
		Nos. 1L34-1L37 (4)	2.05	2.05

Trans-Antarctic Expedition, 1955-1958.

A4

Wmk. 373

1980, May 5 Litho. ***Perf. 13½***

1L38	A4	1p Map of Dependencies	.25	.25
1L39	A4	2p Shag Rocks	.25	.25
1L40	A4	3p Bird and Willis Islds.	.25	.25
1L41	A4	4p Gulbrandsen Lake	.25	.25
1L42	A4	5p King Edward Point	.25	.25
1L43	A4	6p Shackleton's Memorial Cross	.25	.25
1L44	A4	7p Shackleton's grave	.25	.25
1L45	A4	8p Grytviken Church	.25	.25
1L46	A4	9p Coaling Hulk "Louise"	.25	.30
1L47	A4	10p Clerke Rocks	.25	.30
1L48	A4	20p Candlemas Island	.45	.55
1L49	A4	25p Twitcher Rock, Cook Island	.60	.70
1L50	A4	50p "John Biscoe"	1.10	1.25
1L51	A4	£1 "Bransfield"	2.25	2.75
1L52	A4	£3 "Endurance"	7.50	9.00
		Nos. 1L38-1L52 (15)	14.40	16.85

Nos. 38-50 exist dated 1984; issued May 3, 1984. Value, set $16.

1985, Nov. 18 **Wmk. 384**

1L48a	A4	20p	.75	1.10
1L49a	A4	25p	1.00	1.25
1L50a	A4	50p	2.75	3.50
1L51a	A4	£1	4.00	5.00
1L52a	A4	£3	12.50	16.00
		Nos. 1L48a-1L52a (5)	21.00	26.85

Magellanic Clubmoss — A5

1981, Feb. 5 Litho. ***Perf. 14***

1L53	A5	3p shown	.25	.25
1L54	A5	6p Alpine cat's-tail	.25	.25
1L55	A5	7p Greater burnet	.25	.25
1L56	A5	11p Antarctic bed-straw	.35	.35
1L57	A5	15p Brown rush	.50	.50
a.		Brown missing	*3,750.*	
1L58	A5	25p Antarctic hair grass	.75	.75
		Nos. 1L53-1L58 (6)	2.35	2.35

Royal Wedding Issue
Common Design Type

1981, July 22 Litho. ***Perf. 14***

1L59	CD331	10p Bouquet	.25	.25
1L60	CD331	13p Charles	.35	.35
1L61	CD331	52p Couple	.85	.85
		Nos. 1L59-1L61 (3)	1.45	1.45

Reindeer in Spring — A6

1982, Jan. 29 Litho. ***Perf. 14***

1L62	A6	5p shown	.25	.25
1L63	A6	13p Autumn	.35	.35
1L64	A6	25p Winter	.45	.45
1L65	A6	26p Late winter	.50	.50
		Nos. 1L62-1L65 (4)	1.55	1.55

Gamasellus Racovitzai — A7

1982, Mar. 16 Litho. ***Perf. 14***

1L66	A7	5p shown	.25	.25
1L67	A7	10p Alaskozetes antarcticus	.25	.25
1L68	A7	13p Cryptopygus antarcticus	.30	.30
1L69	A7	15p Notiomaso australis	.35	.35
1L70	A7	25p Hydromedion sparsutum	.40	.40
1L71	A7	26p Parochlus steinenii	.45	.45
		Nos. 1L66-1L71 (6)	2.00	2.00

Princess Diana Issue
Common Design Type

1982, July 1 Litho. ***Perf. 14x14½***

1L72	CD333	5p Arms	.25	.25
1L73	CD333	17p Diana	.35	.45
a.		Perf. 14	2.50	2.50
1L74	CD333	37p Wedding	.90	.90
1L75	CD333	50p Portrait	1.00	1.00
		Nos. 1L72-1L75 (4)	2.50	2.60

Crustacea — A8

Perf. 14½x14

1984, Mar. 23 **Wmk. 373**

1L76	A8	5p Euphausia superba	.30	.30
1L77	A8	17p Glyptonotus antarcticus	.40	.40
1L78	A8	25p Epimeria monodon	.70	.70
1L79	A8	34p Serolis pagenstecheri	1.10	1.10
		Nos. 1L76-1L79 (4)	2.50	2.50

Manned Flight Bicentenary — A9

1983, Dec. 23 Litho. ***Perf. 14***

1L80	A9	5p Westland Whirlwind	.25	.25
1L81	A9	13p Westland Wasp	.45	.45
1L82	A9	17p Saunders-Roe Walrus	.55	.55
1L83	A9	50p Auster	1.75	1.75
		Nos. 1L80-1L83 (4)	3.00	3.00

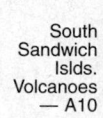

South Sandwich Islds. Volcanoes — A10

1984, Nov. 8 Wmk. 373 ***Perf. 14½***

1L84	A10	6p Zavodovski Isld.	.60	.60
1L85	A10	17p Mt. Michael, Saunders Isld.	1.40	1.40
1L86	A10	22p Bellingshausen Isld.	2.00	2.00
1L87	A10	52p Bristol Isld.	3.75	3.75
		Nos. 1L84-1L87 (4)	7.75	7.75

Albatrosses — A11

1985, May 5 Wmk. 384 ***Perf. 14½***

1L88	A11	7p Diomedea chrysostoma	.80	.80
1L89	A11	22p Diomedea melanophris	2.25	2.25
1L90	A11	27p Diomedea exulans	2.50	2.50
1L91	A11	54p Phoebetria palpebrata	4.75	4.75
		Nos. 1L88-1L91 (4)	10.30	10.30

Queen Mother 85th Birthday
Common Design Type

Designs: 7p, 14th birthday celebration. 22p, With Princess Anne, Lady Sarah Armstrong-Jones, Prince Edward. 27p, Queen Mother. 54p, Holding Prince Henry. £1, On the Britannia.

1985, June 23 ***Perf. 14½x14***

1L92	CD336	7p multicolored	.25	.25
1L93	CD336	22p multicolored	.75	.75
1L94	CD336	27p multicolored	1.00	1.00
1L95	CD336	54p multicolored	2.00	2.00
		Nos. 1L92-1L95 (4)	4.00	4.00

Souvenir Sheet

1L96	CD336	£1 multicolored	4.25	4.25

Falkland Islands Naturalists Type of 1985

Naturalists, endangered species: 7p, Dumont d'Urville (1790-1842), kelp. 22p, Johann Reinhold Forster (1729-1798), king penguin. 27p, Johann Georg Adam Forster (1754-1794), tussock grass. 54p, Sir Joseph Banks (1743-1820), dove prion.

1985, Nov. 4 ***Perf. 13½x14***

1L97	A86	7p multicolored	.75	.75
1L98	A86	22p multicolored	1.60	1.60
1L99	A86	27p multicolored	2.00	2.00
1L100	A86	54p multicolored	3.75	3.75
		Nos. 1L97-1L100 (4)	8.10	8.10

SEMI-POSTAL STAMP

Rebuilding Type of Falkland Islands
Wmk. 373

1982, Sept. 13 Litho. ***Perf. 11***

1LB1	SP1	£1 Map of So. Georgia	3.00	3.00

ISSUES FOR THE SEPARATE ISLANDS

Graham Land

Nos. 84, 85B, 86A, 87A, 88-91 Overprinted in Red

1944, Feb. 12 Wmk. 4 ***Perf. 12***

2L1	A22	½p green & black	.50	2.10
2L2	A22	1p dk vio & black	.50	1.10
2L3	A22	2p rose car & blk	.60	1.10
2L4	A22	3p deep bl & blk	.60	1.10
2L5	A22	4p rose vio & blk	2.00	1.90
2L6	A22	6p brown & black	21.00	2.75
2L7	A22	9p slate bl & blk	1.50	1.50
2L8	A22	1sh dull blue	1.50	1.50
		Nos. 2L1-2L8 (8)	28.20	13.05

South Georgia

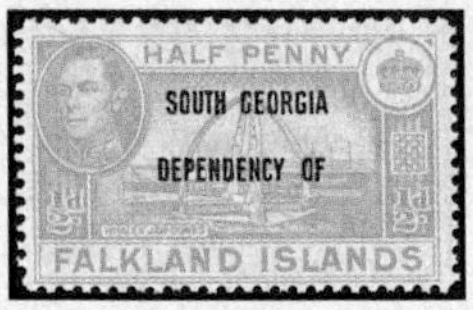

1944, Apr. 3		Wmk. 4	Perf. 12	
3L1	A22	½p green & black	.40	2.25
3L2	A22	1p dark vio & blk	.40	1.10
3L3	A22	2p rose car & blk	.60	1.10
3L4	A22	3p deep bl & blk	.60	1.10
3L5	A22	4p rose vio & blk	2.00	2.00
3L6	A22	6p brown & black	21.00	2.50
3L7	A22	9p slate bl & blk	1.50	1.50
3L8	A22	1sh dull blue	1.50	1.50
		Nos. 3L1-3L8 (8)	28.00	13.05

South Orkneys

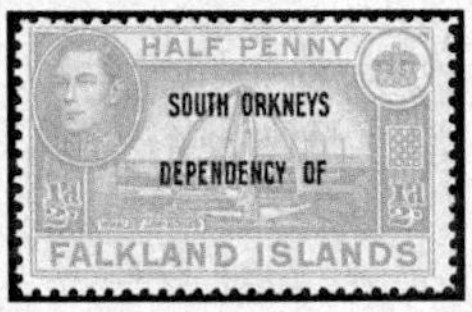

1944, Feb. 21		Wmk. 4	Perf. 12	
4L1	A22	½p green & black	.50	2.10
4L2	A22	1p dark vio & blk	.50	1.10
4L3	A22	2p rose car & blk	.80	1.10
4L4	A22	3p deep bl & blk	.80	1.10
4L5	A22	4p rose vio & blk	2.00	2.00
4L6	A22	6p brown & black	21.00	2.50
4L7	A22	9p slate bl & blk	1.50	1.50
4L8	A22	1sh dull blue	1.50	1.50
		Nos. 4L1-4L8 (8)	28.60	12.90

South Shetlands

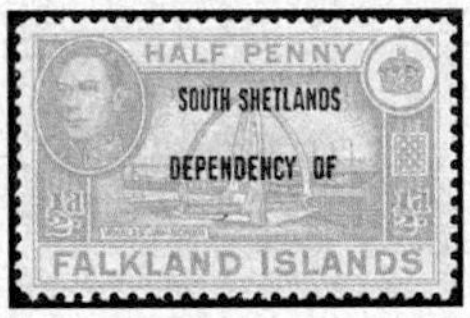

1944		Wmk. 4	Perf. 12	
5L1	A22	½p green & black	.50	2.10
5L2	A22	1p dark vio & blk	.50	1.10
5L3	A22	2p rose car & blk	.60	1.10
5L4	A22	3p deep bl & blk	.60	1.10
5L5	A22	4p rose vio & blk	2.00	2.00
5L6	A22	6p brown & black	21.00	2.50
5L7	A22	9p slate bl & blk	1.50	1.50
5L8	A22	1sh dull blue	1.50	1.50
		Nos. 5L1-5L8 (8)	28.20	12.90

FAR EASTERN REPUBLIC

'fär 'ē-stərn ri-'pə-blik

LOCATION — In Siberia east of Lake Baikal
GOVT. — Republic
AREA — 900,745 sq. mi.
POP. — 1,560,000 (approx. 1920)
CAPITAL — Chita

A short-lived independent government was established here in 1920.

100 Kopecks = 1 Ruble

Watermark

Wmk. 171 — Diamonds

Vladivostok Issue
Russian Stamps Surcharged or Overprinted

a

b

c

On Stamps of 1909-17

Perf. 14, 14½x15, 13½

1920			Unwmk.	
2	A14(a)	2k green	10.00	*10.00*
3	A14(a)	3k red	10.00	*10.00*
4	A11(b)	3k on 35k red brn & grn	40.00	50.00
5	A15(a)	4k carmine	10.00	*12.00*
6	A11(b)	4k on 70k brn & org	10.00	*15.00*
8	A11(b)	7k on 15k red brn & bl	2.00	2.00
a.		Inverted surcharge	100.00	
b.		Pair, one ovptd. "DBP" only	*100.00*	
9	A15(a)	10k dark blue	75.00	*55.00*
a.		Overprint on back	90.00	
10	A12(c)	10k on 3½r mar & lt grn	25.00	*25.00*
11	A11(a)	14k blue & rose	50.00	35.00
12	A11(a)	15k red brn & bl	30.00	25.00
13	A8(a)	20k blue & car	150.00	*100.00*
14	A11(b)	20k on 14k bl & rose	10.00	*8.00*
a.		Surcharge on back	30.00	
15	A11(a)	25k green & vio	25.00	15.00
16	A11(a)	35k red brn & grn	50.00	35.00
17	A8(a)	50k brn vio & grn	10.00	*12.00*
18	A9(a)	1r pale brn, dk brn & org	*750.00*	*750.00*

On Stamps of 1917
Imperf

21	A14(a)	1k orange	25.00	*10.00*
22	A14(a)	2k gray grn	20.00	10.00
23	A14(a)	3k red	20.00	*10.00*
25	A11(b)	7k on 15k red brn & dp bl	2.00	*5.00*
a.		Pair, one without surcharge	*100.00*	
b.		Pair, one ovptd. "DBP" only	*100.00*	
26	A12(c)	10k on 3½r mar & lt grn	27.50	*15.00*
27	A9(a)	1r pale brn, brn & red org	40.00	*20.00*

On Stamps of Siberia 1919
Perf. 14, 14½x15

30	A14(a)	35k on 2k green	5.00	*8.00*
a.		"DBP" on back	25.00	*50.00*

Imperf

31	A14(a)	35k on 2k green	35.00	25.00
32	A14(a)	70k on 1k orange	7.50	*10.00*

Counterfeit surcharges and overprints abound, including digital forgeries.

On Russia Nos. AR2, AR3

A1

Perf. 14½x15
Wmk. 171

35	A1(b)	1k on 5k green, *buff*	30.00	20.00
36	A1(b)	2k on 10k brown, *buff*	40.00	30.00

The letters on these stamps resembling "DBP," are the Russian initials of "Dalne Vostochnaya Respublika" (Far Eastern Republic).

Chita Issue

A2

A2a

1921	Unwmk.	Typo.	Imperf.	
38	A2	2k gray green	1.50	1.50
39	A2a	4k rose	3.00	3.00
40	A2	5k claret	3.00	3.00
41	A2a	10k blue	2.50	2.50
		Nos. 38-41 (4)	10.00	10.00

For overprints see Nos. 62-65.

Blagoveshchensk Issue

A3

1921		Litho.	Imperf.	
42	A3	2r red	2.75	2.00
43	A3	3r dark green	2.75	2.00
44	A3	5r dark blue	2.75	2.00
a.		Tête bêche pair	45.00	*30.00*
45	A3	15r dark brown	2.75	2.00
46	A3	30r dark violet	2.75	2.00
a.		Tête bêche pair	35.00	*15.00*
		Nos. 42-46 (5)	13.75	10.00

Remainders of Nos. 42-46 were canceled in colored crayon or by typographed bars. These sell for half of foregoing values.

Chita Issue

A4

A5

1922		Litho.	Imperf.	
49	A4	1k orange	1.00	*.85*
50	A4	3k dull red	.40	*.45*
51	A5	4k dp rose & buff	.40	*.45*
52	A4	5k orange brown	.80	.45
53	A4	7k light blue	1.50	*1.50*
a.		Perf. 11½	2.00	2.50
b.		Rouletted 9	3.00	3.00
c.		Perf. 11½x rouletted	6.50	6.50
54	A5	10k dk blue & red	.60	*.65*
55	A4	15k dull rose	.80	*1.10*
56	A5	20k blue & red	.80	*1.10*
57	A5	30k green & red org	1.25	*1.10*
58	A5	50k black & red org	3.00	*2.25*
		Nos. 49-58 (10)	10.55	*9.90*

The 4k exists with "4" omitted. Value $100.

Vladivostok Issue

Stamps of 1921 Overprinted in Red

1922			Imperf.	
62	A2	2k gray green	35.00	25.00
a.		Inverted overprint	250.00	
63	A2a	4k rose	35.00	25.00
a.		Inverted overprint	250.00	
b.		Double overprint	250.00	
64	A2	5k claret	35.00	35.00
a.		Inverted overprint	100.00	
b.		Double overprint	350.00	
65	A2a	10k blue	35.00	35.00
a.		Inverted overprint	250.00	
		Nos. 62-65 (4)	140.00	120.00

Russian revolution of Nov. 1917, 5th anniv.

Once in the setting the figures "22" of 1922 have the bottom stroke curved instead of straight. Value, each $75.

Vladivostok Issue

Russian Stamps of 1922-23 Surcharged in Black or Red

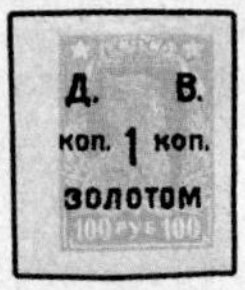

1923			Imperf.	
66	A50	1k on 100r red	.40	*1.00*
a.		Inverted surcharge	60.00	
67	A50	2k on 70r violet	.40	*.75*
68	A49	5k on 10r blue (R)	.40	*.75*
69	A50	10k on 50r brown	.90	*1.25*
a.		Inverted surcharge	250.00	

Perf. 14½x15

70	A50	1k on 100r red	.90	*1.25*
		Nos. 66-70 (5)	3.00	*5.00*

OCCUPATION STAMPS

Issued under Occupation of General Semenov
Chita Issue
Russian Stamps of 1909-12 Surcharged

a

b

c

1920		Unwmk.	Perf. 14, 14x15½	
N1	A15 (a)	1r on 4k car	150.00	*100.00*
N2	A8 (b)	2r50k on 20k bl & car	40.00	30.00
N3	A14 (c)	5r on 5k claret	25.00	*50.00*
a.		Double surcharge	200.00	
N4	A11 (a)	10r on 70k brn & org	20.00	*25.00*
		Nos. N1-N4 (4)	235.00	*205.00*

FAROE ISLANDS

'far-,ō 'ī-ləndz

(The Faroes)

LOCATION — North Atlantic Ocean
GOVT. — Self-governing part of Kingdom of Denmark
AREA — 540 sq. mi.
POP. — 41,059 (1999 est.)
CAPITAL — Thorshavn

100 Ore = 1 Krone

Catalogue values for unused stamps in this country are for Never Hinged items, beginning with Scott 7.

Denmark No. 97 Handstamp Surcharged

1919, Jan.	Typo.	Perf. 14x14½		
1	A16	2o on 5o green	1,400.	475.00

Counterfeits of surcharge exist.

Denmark No. 88a, the bisect, was used with Denmark No. 97 in Faroe Islands Jan. 3-23, 1919.

Denmark Nos. 220, 224, 238A, 224C Surcharged in Blue or Black

Nos. 2, 5-6

No. 3

No. 4

1940-41	Engr.	Perf. 13		
2	A32	20o on 1o ('41)	45.00	110.00
3	A32	20o on 5o ('41)	45.00	35.00
4	A30	20o on 15o (Bk)	60.00	22.50
5	A32	50o on 5o (Bk)	300.00	90.00
6	A32	60o on 6o (Bk)	125.00	*250.00*
		Nos. 2-6 (5)	575.00	507.50
		Set, never hinged	1,150.	

Issued during British administration.

Catalogue values for unused stamps in this section, from this point to the end of the section, are for Never Hinged items.

Map of Islands, 1673 — A1

Map of North Atlantic, 1573 — A2

West Coast, Sandoy — A3

Vidoy and Svinoy, by Eyvindur Mohr — A4

Designs: 200o, like 70o. 250o, 300o, View of Streymoy and Vagar. 450o, Houses, Nes, by Ruth Smith. 500o, View of Hvitanes and Skalafjordur, by S. Joensen-Mikines.

Unwmk.

1975, Jan. 30	Engr.	Perf. 13		
7	A1	5o sepia	.25	.25
8	A2	10o emer & dark blue	.25	.25
9	A1	50o graysh green	.25	.25
10	A2	60o brown & dark blue	1.00	1.00
11	A3	70o vio bl & slate grn	1.00	1.00
12	A2	80o ocher & dark blue	.50	.50
13	A1	90o red brown	1.00	1.00
14	A2	120o brt bl & dark bl	.75	.50
15	A3	200o vio bl & slate grn	.75	.75
16	A3	250o multicolored	.75	.75
17	A3	300o multicolored	6.50	2.25

Photo.

Perf. 12½x13

18	A4	350o multicolored	1.00	1.00
19	A4	450o multicolored	1.10	1.00
20	A4	500o multicolored	1.25	1.10
		Nos. 7-20 (14)	16.35	11.60

Faroe Boat — A5

Faroe Flag — A6

Faroe Mailman — A7

Perf. 12½x13, 12 (A6)

1976, Apr. 1	Engr.; Litho. (A6)			
21	A5	125o copper red	2.00	1.50
22	A6	160o multicolored	.50	.50
23	A7	800o olive	2.25	1.50
		Nos. 21-23 (3)	4.75	3.50

Faroe Islands independent postal service, Apr. 1, 1976.

Motor Fishing Boat — A8

Faroese Fishing Vessels and Map of Islands: 125o, Inland fishing cutter. 160o, Modern seine fishing vessel, 600o, Deep-sea fishing trawler.

1977, Apr. 28	Photo.	Perf. 14½x14		
24	A8	100o green & black	5.50	4.75
25	A8	125o carmine & black	1.00	1.00
26	A8	160o blue & black	1.00	.75
27	A8	600o brown & black	2.00	1.25
		Nos. 24-27 (4)	9.50	7.75

Common Snipe A9

Photogravure & Engraved

1977, Sept. 29		Perf. 14½x14		
28	A9	70o shown	.25	.25
29	A9	180o Oystercatcher	.65	.65
30	A9	250o Whimbrel	.90	.75
		Nos. 28-30 (3)	1.80	1.65

North Coast, Puffins — A10

Mykines Village — A11

Mykines Island: 140o, Coast. 150o, Aerial view. 180o, Map.

Perf. 13x13½, 13½x13

1978, Jan. 26		Photo.		

Size: 21x28mm, 28x21mm

31	A10	100o multicolored	.25	.25
32	A11	130o multicolored	.50	.50
33	A11	140o multicolored	.65	.65
34	A10	150o multicolored	.65	.65

Size: 37x26mm

Perf. 14½x14

35	A11	180o multicolored	.65	.65
		Nos. 31-35 (5)	2.70	2.70

Sea Birds — A12

Lithographed and Engraved

1978, Apr. 13		Perf. 12x12½		
36	A12	140o Gannets	.50	.50
37	A12	180o Puffins	.65	.65
38	A12	400o Guillemots	1.60	1.25
		Nos. 36-38 (3)	2.75	2.40

Old Library — A13

1978, Dec. 7		Perf. 13		
39	A13	140o shown	.50	.50
40	A13	180o New library	.60	.60

Completion of New Library Building.

Girl Guide, Tent and Fire — A14

Ram — A15

1978, Dec. 7	Photo.	Perf. 13½		
41	A14	140o multicolored	.50	.50

Faroese Girl Guides, 50th anniversary.

Lithographed and Engraved

1979, Mar. 19		Perf. 12		
42	A15	25k multicolored	6.50	6.50

Denmark No. 88a — A16

Europa: 180o, Faroe Islands No. 1.

1979, May 7		Perf. 12½		
43	A16	140o yellow & blue	*.50*	*.50*
44	A16	180o rose, grn & blk	*.60*	*.60*

Girl Wearing Festive Costume — A17

Children's Drawings and IYC Emblem: 150o, Fisherman. 200o, Two friends.

1979, Oct. 1		Perf. 12		
45	A17	110o multicolored	.40	.40
46	A17	150o multicolored	.50	.50
47	A17	200o multicolored	.60	.60
		Nos. 45-47 (3)	1.50	1.50

International Year of the Child.

Sea Plantain — A18

1980, Mar. 17 Photo. *Perf. 12x11½*

48	A18	90o shown	.30	.30
49	A18	110o Glacier buttercup	.40	.40
50	A18	150o Purple saxifrage	.55	.55
51	A18	200o Starry saxifrage	.65	.65
52	A18	400o Lady's mantle	1.00	1.00
		Nos. 48-52 (5)	2.90	2.90

Jakob Jakobsen (1864-1918), Linguist — A19

Coat of Arms, Virgin and Child, Gothic Pew Gable — A20

Europa: 200o, Vensel Ulrich Hammershaimb (1819-1909), theologian, linguist and folklorist.

1980, Oct. 6 Engr. *Perf. 11½*

53	A19	150o dull green	*.40*	*.40*
54	A19	200o dull red brown	*.60*	*.60*

Perf. 13 bicolored examples of Nos. 53-54 are rejected stamps never put on sale that were to have been burned, but which escaped destruction.

Photo. & Engr.

1980, Oct. 6 *Perf. 13½*

Kirkjubour Pew Gables, 15th Century: 140o, Norwegian coat of arms, John the Baptist. 150o, Christ's head, St. Peter. 200o, Hand in halo, Apostle Paul.

55	A20	110o multicolored	.30	.30
56	A20	140o multicolored	.50	.50
57	A20	150o multicolored	.50	.50
58	A20	200o multicolored	.65	.65
		Nos. 55-58 (4)	1.95	1.95

See Nos. 102-105, 389-392

A21

Sketches of Old Torshavn by Ingalzur Reyni.

1981, Mar. 2 Engr.

59	A21	110o dark green	.30	.30
60	A21	140o black	.50	.50
61	A21	150o dark brown	.50	.50
62	A21	200o dark blue	.60	.60
		Nos. 59-62 (4)	1.90	1.90

The Ring Dance A22

Europa: 200o, The garter dance.

1981, June 1 Engr. *Perf. 13x14*

63	A22	150o pale rose & grn	*.35*	*.35*
64	A22	200o pale yel grn & dk brn	*.55*	*.55*

Rune Stones, 800-1000 AD — A23

Historic Writings: 1k, Folksong, 1846. 3k, Sheep Letter excerpt, 1298. 6k, Seal and text, 1533. 10k, Titlepage from Faeroae et Faeroa, by Lucas Jacobson Debes, library.

Photo. & Engr.

1981, Oct. 19 *Perf. 11½*

65	A23	10o multicolored	.25	.25
66	A23	1k multicolored	.30	.30
67	A23	3k multicolored	.85	.75
68	A23	6k multicolored	1.75	1.40
69	A23	10k multicolored	3.00	3.00
		Nos. 65-69 (5)	6.15	5.70

Nos. 70-80 not assigned.

Europa 1982 — A24

1982, Mar. 15 Engr. *Perf. 13½*

81	A24	1.50k Viking North Atlantic routes	.45	.45
82	A24	2k Viking house foundation	.65	.65

View of Gjogv, by Ingalvur av Reyni A25

1982, June 7 Litho. *Perf. 12½x13*

83	A25	180o shown	.40	.40
84	A25	220o Hvalvik	1.10	.90
85	A25	250o Kvivik	.65	.65
		Nos. 83-85 (3)	2.15	1.95

Ballad of Harra Paetur and Elinborg — A26

Scenes from the medieval ballad of chivalry.

1982, Sept. 27 Litho.

86	A26	220o multicolored	.65	.65
87	A26	250o multicolored	.75	.75
88	A26	350o multicolored	1.00	1.00
89	A26	450o multicolored	1.40	1.40
		Nos. 86-89 (4)	3.80	3.80

Cargo Ships A27

1983, Feb. 21 Litho. *Perf. 14x14½*

90	A27	220o Arcturus, 1856	.75	.75
91	A27	250o Laura, 1882	.90	.90
92	A27	700o Thyra, 1866	2.40	2.40
		Nos. 90-92 (3)	4.05	4.05

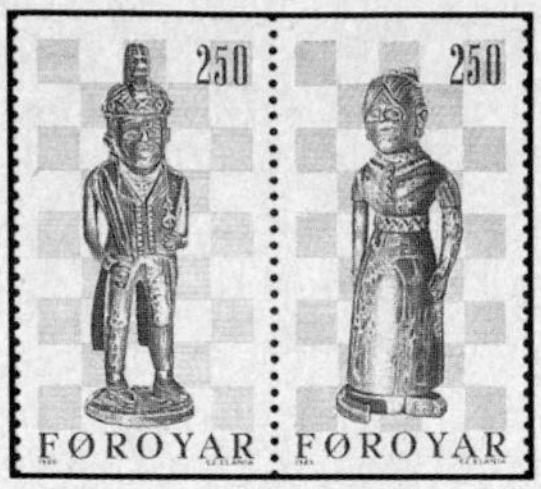
Chessmen, by Pol i Buo (1791-1857) — A28

1983, May 2 Engr. *Perf. 13 Vert.*

Booklet Stamps

93		250o King	3.00	3.00
94		250o Queen	3.00	3.00
a.		Bklt. pane of 6, 3 each #93-94	17.50	
b.	A28	Pair, #93-94	6.00	6.00

Europa 1983 — A29

Nobel Prizewinners in Medicine: 250o, Niels R. Finsen (1860-1903), ultraviolet radiation pioneer. 400o, Alexander Fleming (1881-1955), discoverer of penicillin.

1983, June 6 Engr. *Perf. 12x11½*

95	A29	250o dark blue	*.65*	*.65*
96	A29	400o red brown	*1.10*	*1.10*

A30

1983, Sept. 19 Litho. *Perf. 12½x13*

97	A30	250o Tusk	.80	.80
98	A30	280o Haddock	1.10	1.10
99	A30	500o Halibut	1.60	1.60
100	A30	900o Catfish	3.00	3.00
		Nos. 97-100 (4)	6.50	6.50

Souvenir Sheet

Traditional Costumes — A31

Various national costumes.

1983, Nov. 4 Litho. *Perf. 12*

101	A31	Sheet of 3	10.00	11.00
a.-c.		250o multicolored	2.25	2.25

Nordic House Cultural Center opening. Margin shows Scandinavian flags.

Pew Gables Type of 1980

Designs: 250o, John, shield with three crowns. 300o, St. Jacob, shield with crossed keys. 350o, Thomas, shield with crossbeam. 400o, Judas Taddeus, Toulouse cross halo.

Photo. & Engr.

1984, Jan. 30 *Perf. 14x13½*

102	A20	250o lil, pur & dk brn	.80	.80
103	A20	300o red brn, dk buff & dk brn	1.00	1.00
104	A20	350o blk, lt gray & dk brn	1.10	1.10
105	A20	400o ol grn, pale yel & dk brn	1.25	1.25
		Nos. 102-105 (4)	4.15	4.15

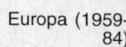

Europa (1959-84) A33

1984, Apr. 2 Engr. *Perf. 13½*

106	A33	250o red	*.60*	*.60*
107	A33	500o dark blue	*1.40*	*1.40*

Sverri Patursson (1871-1960), Writer — A34

Poets: 2.50k, Joannes Patursson (1866-1946). 3k, J. H. O. Djurhuus (1881-1948). 4.50k, H.A. Djurhuus (1883-1951).

1984, May 28 Engr. *Perf. 13½*

108	A34	2k olive green	.65	.65
109	A34	2.50k red	.75	.75
110	A34	3k dark blue	1.00	1.00
111	A34	4.50k violet	1.50	1.50
		Nos. 108-111 (4)	3.90	3.90

Faroese Smack (Fishing Boat) — A35

Perf. 12½x13, 13x12½

1984, Sept. 10 Engr.

112	A35	280o shown	.95	.95
113	A35	300o Fishermen, vert.	1.10	1.10
114	A35	12k Helmsman, vert.	4.50	4.50
		Nos. 112-114 (3)	6.55	6.55

Fairytale Illustrations by Elinborg Lutzen — A36

1984, Oct. 29 Litho. *Perf. 13 Vert.*

Booklet Stamps

115	A36	140o Beauty of the Veils	6.00	6.00
116	A36	280o Veils, diff.	6.00	6.00
117	A36	280o Girl Shy Prince	6.00	6.00
118	A36	280o The Glass Sword	6.00	6.00
119	A36	280o Little Elin	6.00	6.00
120	A36	280o The Boy and the Ox	6.00	6.00
a.		Booklet pane of 6, #115-120	37.50	

View of Torshavn and the Forts, by Edward Dayes A37

Dayes' Landscapes, 1789: 280o, Skaeling. 550o, View Towards the North Seen from the Hills Near Torshavn in Stremoy, Faroes. 800o, The Moving Stones in Eysturoy, Faroes.

Litho. & Engr.

1985, Feb. 4 *Perf. 13*

121	A37	250o multicolored	.75	.75
122	A37	280o multicolored	1.00	1.00
123	A37	550o multicolored	2.25	2.25
124	A37	800o multicolored	3.00	3.00
		Nos. 121-124 (4)	7.00	7.00

Europa 1985 — A38

Children taking music lessons.

1985, Apr. 1 Litho. *Perf. 13½x14½*
125 A38 280o multicolored *.85 .85*
126 A38 550o multicolored *1.90 1.90*

Paintings, Faroese Museum of Art A39

Designs: 280o, The Garden, Hoyvik, 1973, by Thomas Arge (1942-78). 450o, Self-Portrait, 1952, by Ruth Smith (1913-58), vert. 550o, Winter's Day in Nolsoy, 1959, by Steffan Danielsen (1922-76).

Litho. & Engr.
1985, June 3 *Perf. 12½*
127 A39 280o multicolored 1.25 1.25
128 A39 450o multicolored 1.75 1.75
129 A39 550o multicolored 2.50 2.50
Nos. 127-129 (3) 5.50 5.50

Lighthouses — A40

1985, Sept. 23 Litho. *Perf. 13½x14*
130 A40 270o Nolsoy, 1893 1.25 1.25
131 A40 320o Thorshavn, 1909 1.75 1.75
132 A40 350o Myklnes, 1909 1.90 1.90
133 A40 470o Map of locations 2.40 2.40
Nos. 130-133 (4) 7.30 7.30

Passenger Aviation in the Faroes, 22nd Anniv. A41

Perf. 13½ Horiz.
1985, Oct. 28 Photo.
Booklet Stamps
134 A41 300o Douglas DC-3 3.00 3.00
135 A41 300o Fokker Friendship 3.00 3.00
136 A41 300o Boeing 737 3.00 3.00
137 A41 300o Interisland LM-IKB 3.00 3.00
138 A41 300o Helicopter Snipan 3.00 3.00
a. Booklet pane of 5, #134-138 16.00 16.00

Skrimsla, Ancient Folk Ballad — A42

1986, Feb. 3 Litho. *Perf. 12½x13*
139 A42 300o Peasant in woods 1.10 1.10
140 A42 420o Meets Giant 1.75 1.75
141 A42 550o Giant loses game 2.00 2.00
142 A42 650o Giant grants Peasant's wish 2.25 2.25
Nos. 139-142 (4) 7.10 7.10

Europa 1986 — A43

1986, Apr. 7 Litho. *Perf. 13½*
143 A43 3k shown *1.00 1.00*
144 A43 5.50k Sea pollution *1.75 1.75*

Amnesty Intl., 25th Anniv. — A44

Winning design competition artwork.

1986, June 2 *Perf. 14x13½*
145 A44 3k Ólivur vid Neyst 1.25 1.25
146 A44 4.70k Eli Smith 1.90 1.90
147 A44 5.50k Ranna Kunoy 2.40 2.40
Nos. 145-147 (3) 5.55 5.55

Nos. 145-146 horiz.

Souvenir Sheet

HAFNIA '87, Copenhagen — A45

Design: East Bay of Torshavn, watercolor, 1782, by Christian Rosenmeyer (1728-1802).

1986, Aug. 29 Litho. *Perf. 13x13½*
148 A45 Sheet of 3 10.00 10.00
a. 3k multicolored 3.25 3.25
b. 4.70k multicolored 3.25 3.25
c. 6.50k multicolored 3.25 3.25

Sold for 20k.

Old Stone Bridges A46

2.70k, Glyvrar on Eysturoy. 3k, Leypanagjogv on Vagar, vert. 13k, Skaelinger on Streymoy.

Perf. 13½x14½, 14½x13½
1986, Oct. 13 Engr.
149 A46 2.70k dp brown vio 2.25 2.25
150 A46 3k bluish blk 1.90 1.90
151 A46 13k gray green 4.00 4.00
Nos. 149-151 (3) 8.15 8.15

Farmhouses — A47

Traditional architecture: 300o, Depil on Borooy, 1814. 420o, Depil, diff. 470o, Frammi vio Gjonna on Streymoy, c. 1814. 650o, Frammi, diff.

1987, Feb. 9 Engr. *Perf. 13x14½*
152 A47 300o pale blue & blue 1.10 1.10
153 A47 420o buff & brown 1.75 1.75
154 A47 470o pale grn & dp grn 2.10 2.10
155 A47 650o pale gray & black 2.75 2.75
Nos. 152-155 (4) 7.70 7.70

Europa 1987 — A48

Nordic House.

1987, Apr. 6 *Perf. 13x14*
156 A48 300o Exterior *.85 .85*
157 A48 550o Interior *1.90 1.60*

Fishing Trawlers A49

1987, June 1 Litho. *Perf. 14x13½*
158 A49 3k Joannes Patursson .90 .90
159 A49 5.50k Magnus Heinason 1.90 1.90
160 A49 8k Sjurdarberg 4.00 4.00
Nos. 158-160 (3) 6.80 6.80

Hestur (Horse) Island A50

Litho. & Engr.
1987, Sept. 7 *Perf. 13*
161 A50 270o Map 1.00 1.00
162 A50 300o Seaport .90 .90
163 A50 420o Bird cliff 1.90 1.90
164 A50 470o Pasture, sheep 2.25 2.25
165 A50 550o Seashore 2.25 2.25
Nos. 161-165 (5) 8.30 8.30

Nos. 161, 163 and 165 vert.

Collages by Zacharias Heinesen A51

West Bay of Torshavn, Watercolor by Rosenmeyer — A52

1987, Oct. 16 Litho. *Perf. 13½x14*
166 A51 4.70k Eystaravag 1.75 1.75
167 A51 6.50k Vestarvag 2.25 2.25

Souvenir Sheet
Perf. 13½x13
168 A52 3k multicolored 3.50 3.50

HAFNIA '87. Sold for 4k.

Flowers — A53

1988, Feb. 8 Litho. *Perf. 11½*
Granite Paper
169 A53 2.70k Bellis perennis 1.40 1.40
170 A53 3k Dactylorchis maculata .75 .75
171 A53 4.70k Potentilla erecta 2.10 2.10
172 A53 9k Pinguicula vulgaris 3.00 3.00
Nos. 169-172 (4) 7.25 7.25

Europa — A54

Communication and transport.

1988, Apr. 11 Photo. *Perf. 11½*
173 A54 3k Satellite dish, satellite *1.10 1.10*
174 A54 5.50k Fork lift, crane, ship *1.90 1.90*

A55

A56

Writers: 270o, Jorgen-Frantz Jacobsen (1900-38). 300o, Christian Matras (b. 1900). 470o, William Heinesen (b. 1900). 650o, Hedin Bru (1901-87).

1988, June 6 Engr. *Perf. 13½*
175 A55 270o myrtle green 1.60 1.60
176 A55 300o rose lake 1.40 1.40
177 A55 470o dark blue 2.10 2.10
178 A55 650o brown black 2.40 2.40
Nos. 175-178 (4) 7.50 7.50

1988, Sept. 5 Photo. *Perf. 12*

Text, illustrations and cameo portraits of organizers: 3k, Announcement and Djoni Geil, Enok Baerentsen and H.H. Jacobsen. 3.20k, Meeting, Rasmus Effersoe, C.L. Johannesen and Samal Krakusteini. 12k, Oystercatcher and lyrics of *Now the Hour Has Come,* by poet Sverri Patursson (1871-1960), Just A. Husum, Joannes Patursson and Jens Olsen.

Granite Paper
179 A56 3k multicolored 1.25 1.25
180 A56 3.20k multicolored 1.50 1.50
181 A56 12k multicolored 5.00 5.00
Nos. 179-181 (3) 7.75 7.75

1888 Christmas meeting to preserve cultural traditions and the natl. language, cent.

Kirkjubour Cathedral Ruins A57

270o, Exterior. 300o, Arch. 470o, Crucifixion, bas-relief. 550o, Interior.

1988, Oct. 17 Engr. *Perf. 13*
182 A57 270o dark green 1.90 1.90
183 A57 300o dark bl, vert. 1.50 1.50
184 A57 470o dark brn, vert. 2.10 2.10
185 A57 550o dark violet 2.25 2.25
Nos. 182-185 (4) 7.75 7.75

Havnar Church, Torshavn, 200th Anniv. A58

Designs: 350o, Church exterior. 500o, Crypt, vert. 15k, Bell, vert.

1989, Feb. 6 Engr. *Perf. 13*

186 A58 350o dark green 1.25 1.25
187 A58 500o dark brown 2.40 2.40
188 A58 15k deep blue 4.50 4.50
Nos. 186-188 (3) 8.15 8.15

Folk Costumes — A59

Photo. & Engr.

1989, Apr. 10 *Perf. 13½*

189 A59 350o Man 1.25 1.25
190 A59 600o Woman 2.50 2.50

Europa 1989 — A60

Wooden children's toys.

1989, Apr. 10 Photo. *Perf. 12x11½*

Granite Paper

191 A60 3.50k Boat *1.25 1.25*
192 A60 6k Horse *2.00 2.00*

Island Games, July 5-13 — A61

1989, June 5 Photo. *Perf. 12½*

Granite Paper

193 A61 200o Rowing .90 .90
194 A61 350o Handball 1.50 1.50
195 A61 600o Soccer 2.40 2.40
196 A61 700o Swimming 2.75 2.75
Nos. 193-196 (4) 7.55 7.55

A62

A63

Bird cliffs of Suduroy.

1989, Oct. 2 Engr. *Perf. 14x13½*

197 A62 320o Tvoran 1.25 1.25
198 A62 350o Skuvanes 1.60 1.60
199 A62 500o Beinisvord 2.10 2.10
200 A62 600o Asmundarstakkur 2.40 2.40
Nos. 197-200 (4) 7.35 7.35

1990, Feb. 5 Litho. *Perf. 14x13½*

Modern fish factory (filleting station).

201 A63 3.50k Unloading fish 1.25 1.25
202 A63 3.70k Cleaning and sorting 1.75 1.75
203 A63 5k Filleting 2.00 2.00
204 A63 7k Packaged frozen fish 2.50 2.50
Nos. 201-204 (4) 7.50 7.50

Europa 1990 — A64

Post offices.

1990, Apr. 9 Litho. *Perf. 13½x14*

205 A64 3.50k Gjogv *1.10 1.10*
206 A64 6k Klaksvik *2.00 2.00*

Souvenir Sheet

Recognition of the Merkid, Flag of the Faroes, by the British, 50th Anniv. — A65

Designs: a, Flag. b, Fishing trawler *Nyggjaberg,* disappeared, 1942. c, Sloop *Saana,* sunk by the Germans, 1942.

1990, Apr. 9 Photo. *Perf. 12*

Granite Paper

207 A65 Sheet of 3 5.00 5.00
a.-c. 3.50k any single 1.60 1.60

Whales A66

1990, June 6 Photo. *Perf. 11½*

Granite Paper

208 A66 320o Mesoplodon bidens 1.75 1.75
209 A66 350o Balaena mysticetus 2.25 2.25
210 A66 600o Eubalaena glacialis 3.50 3.50
211 A66 700o Hyperoodon ampullatus 5.50 5.50
Nos. 208-211 (4) 13.00 13.00

Nolsoy Island by Steffan Danielsen A67

1990, Oct. 8 Photo. *Perf. 11½*

Granite Paper

212 A67 50o shown .25 .25
213 A67 350o Coastline 1.60 1.60
214 A67 500o Town 1.90 1.90
215 A67 1000o Coastline, cliffs 3.75 3.75
Nos. 212-215 (4) 7.50 7.50

Flora and Fauna — A68

Europa — A69

1991, Feb. 4 Litho. *Perf. 13*

216 A68 3.70k Plantago lanceolata 1.40 1.40
217 A68 4k Rumex longifolius 1.40 1.40
218 A68 4.50k Amara aulica 1.75 1.75
219 A68 6.50k Lumbricus terrestris 3.00 3.00
Nos. 216-219 (4) 7.55 7.55

1991, Apr. 4 Litho. *Perf. 13*

Designs: 3.70k, Weather satellite. 6.50k, Celestial navigation.

220 A69 3.70k multicolored *1.00 1.00*
221 A69 6.50k multicolored *2.25 2.25*

Town of Torshavn, 125th Anniv. — A70

1991, Apr. 4 *Perf. 14x13½*

222 A70 3.70k Town Hall 1.25 1.25
223 A70 3.70k View of town 1.50 1.50

Birds — A71

1991, June 3 Litho. *Perf. 13½*

224 A71 3.70k Rissa tridactyla 1.50 1.50
225 A71 3.70k Sterna paradisaea 1.50 1.50
a. Bklt. pane, 3 each #224-225 9.00

Village of Saksun A72

1991, June 3

226 A72 370o shown 1.50 1.50
227 A72 650o Cliffs of Vestmanna 2.50 2.50

Samal Joensen-Mikines (1906-1979), Painter — A73

1991, Oct. 7 Litho. *Perf. 13½*

228 A73 340o Funeral Procession 1.25 1.25
229 A73 370o The Farewell 1.40 1.40
230 A73 550o Handanagarthur 2.00 2.00
231 A73 1300o Winter morning 4.50 4.50
Nos. 228-231 (4) 9.15 9.15

Mail Boats A74

1992, Feb. 10 Litho. *Perf. 13½x14*

232 A74 200o Ruth .90 .90
233 A74 370o Ritan 1.50 1.50
234 A74 550o Sigmundur 2.25 2.25
235 A74 800o Masin 3.25 3.25
Nos. 232-235 (4) 7.90 7.90

Europa A75

Designs: 3.70k, Map of North Atlantic, Viking ship. 6.50k, Map of Central Atlantic region, one of Columbus' ships.

1992, Apr. 6 Litho. *Perf. 13½x14*

236 A75 3.70k multicolored *1.10 1.10*
237 A75 6.50k multicolored *2.40 2.40*

Souvenir Sheet

238 A75 Sheet of 2, #236-237 *11.00 11.00*

First landing in the Americas by Leif Eriksson (No. 236). Discovery of America by Christopher Columbus, 500th anniv. (No. 237).

Seals A76

1992, June 9 Litho. *Perf. 14x13½*

239 A76 3.70k Halichoerus grypus 1.60 1.60
240 A76 3.70k Phoca vitulina 1.60 1.60
a. Bklt. pane, 3 #239, 3 #240 *20.00*

Minerals — A77

1992, June 9 Photo. *Perf. 12*

Granite Paper

241 A77 370o Stilbite 1.75 1.75
242 A77 650o Mesolite 2.25 2.25

Traditional Houses A78

1992, Oct. 5 Litho. *Perf. 13½*

243 A78 3.40k Hja Glyvra Hanusi 1.25 1.25
244 A78 3.70k I Nordragotu 1.90 1.90
245 A78 6.50k Blasastova 2.40 2.40
246 A78 8k Jakupsstova 2.75 2.75
Nos. 243-246 (4) 8.30 8.30

Nordic House Entertainers — A79

1993, Feb. 8 Litho. *Perf. 13½*

247 A79 400o Dancers 1.50 1.50
248 A79 400o Pianist 1.50 1.50
249 A79 400o Trio 1.50 1.50
a. Souv. sheet, #247-249, perf 12½ 4.75 4.75
Nos. 247-249 (3) 4.50 4.50

Village of Gjogv A80

1993, Apr. 5

250 A80 4k View toward sea 1.75 1.75
251 A80 4k Ravine, village 1.75 1.75
a. Booklet pane, 3 each #250-251 10.50

Europa — A81

Horses — A82

Sculptures by Hans Pauli Olsen: 4k, Movement. 7k, Reflection.

1993, Apr. 5

252	A81 4k multicolored	*1.50*	*1.50*
253	A81 7k multicolored	*2.50*	*2.50*

Perf. 13½x13, 13x13½

1993, June 7 **Engr.**

254	A82 400o shown	1.50	1.50
255	A82 20k Mare, foal, horiz.	7.50	7.50

Butterflies A83

1993, Oct. 4 **Litho.** ***Perf. 14½***

256	A83 350o Apamea zeta	1.50	1.50
257	A83 400o Hepialus humuli	1.75	1.75
258	A83 700o Vanessa atalanta	2.50	2.50
259	A83 900o Perizoma albulata	3.25	3.25
	Nos. 256-259 (4)	9.00	9.00

Fish — A84

1994, Feb. 7 **Litho.** ***Perf. 14½***

260	A84 10o Gasterosteus aculeatus	.50	.50
261	A84 4k Neocyttus helgae	1.75	1.75
262	A84 7k Salmo trutta fario	2.50	2.50
263	A84 10k Hoplostethus atlanticus	3.50	3.50
	Nos. 260-263 (4)	8.25	8.25

Voyages of St. Brendan (484-577) A85

Europa: 4k, St. Brendan on island with sheep, Irish monks in boat. 7k, St. Brendan, monks sailing past volcano.

1994, Apr. 18 **Litho.** ***Perf. 14½x14***

264	A85 4k multicolored	*1.25*	*1.25*
265	A85 7k multicolored	*2.40*	*2.00*
a.	Miniature sheet of 2, #264-265	*4.75*	*4.75*

Nos. 264-265 have designers name below the design. Stamps in No. 265a do not.

See Iceland Nos. 780-781; Ireland Nos. 923-924.

Sheepdogs — A86

Design: No. 267, Dog watching over sheep.

1994, June 6 **Litho.** ***Perf. 13½***

266	A86 4k multicolored	1.50	1.50

Size: 39x25mm

267	A86 4k multicolored	1.50	1.50
a.	Booklet pane, 3 each #266-267	9.00	
	Complete booklet, #267a	10.00	

School of Navigation A87

Designs: 3.50k, Man using sextant, schooner. 7k, Ship, man at computer.

1994, June 6

268	A87 3.50k multicolored	1.25	1.25
269	A87 7k multicolored	2.75	2.75

Brusajokil's Lay — A88

Scenes, verses of the ballad: 1k, Ship at sea. 4k, Asbjorn entering Brusajokil's cave. 6k, Ormar with cat, trolls. 7k, Ormar pulling Brusajokil's beard.

1994, Sept. 19 **Litho.** ***Perf. 14***

270	A88 1k multicolored	.40	.40
271	A88 4k multicolored	1.75	1.75
272	A88 6k multicolored	2.25	2.25
273	A88 7k multicolored	2.75	2.75
	Nos. 270-273 (4)	7.15	7.15

Twelve Days of Christmas A89

No. 274, Goats, men, deer, hides. No. 275, Ducks, cattle, sheep, horses, banners, barrels.

1994, Oct. 31 **Litho.** ***Perf. 14x13***

274	A89 4k multicolored	1.50	1.50
275	A89 4k multicolored	1.50	1.50
a.	Bklt. pane, 3 each #274-275	9.00	
	Complete booklet, #275a	9.00	

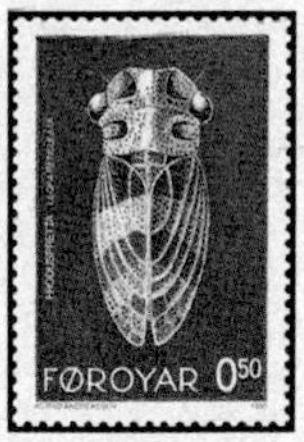

Leafhoppers — A90

Designs: 50o, Ulopa reticulata. 4k, Streptanus sordidus. 5k, Anoscopus flavostriatus. 13k, Macrosteles alpinus.

1995, Feb. 6 **Litho.** ***Perf. 14***

276	A90 50o multicolored	.30	.30
277	A90 4k multicolored	1.75	1.75
278	A90 5k multicolored	1.75	1.75
279	A90 13k multicolored	5.25	5.25
	Nos. 276-279 (4)	9.05	9.05

Tourism A91

1995, Apr. 10 **Litho.** ***Perf. 13½x14***

280	A91 4k Village of Famjin	1.50	1.50
281	A91 4k Vatnsdalur valley	1.50	1.50

Peace & Freedom A92

Europa: 4k, Island couple, "Vidar, vali og baldur." 7k, Couple looking toward sun, "Liv og livtrasir."

1995, Apr. 10 ***Perf. 13x14***

282	A92 4k multicolored	*1.50*	*1.50*
283	A92 7k multicolored	*2.50*	*2.50*

Nordic Art — A93

Designs: 2k, Museum of Art, Torshavn. 4k, Woman, by Frimod Joensen, vert. 5.50k, Self-portrait, by Joensen, vert.

Perf. 13½x14, 14x13½

1995, June 12 **Litho.**

284	A93 2k multicolored	.75	.75
285	A93 4k multicolored	1.50	1.50
286	A93 5.50k multicolored	2.00	2.00
	Nos. 284-286 (3)	4.25	4.25

Corvus Corax A94

1995, June 12 ***Perf. 13½x14***

287	A94 4k Black raven	1.50	1.50
288	A94 4k White-speckled raven	1.50	1.50
a.	Booklet pane, 5 each #287-288	15.00	
	Complete booklet, #288a	15.00	

Saint Olaf (955?-1030), Patron Saint of Faroe Islands — A95

Litho. & Engr.

1995, Sept. 12 ***Perf. 13½x13***

289	A95 4k multicolored	1.75	1.75

See Aland Islands No. 119.

Early Folk Life A95a

4k, Dairy maids carrying buckets. 6k, Peasants fleecing sheep. 15k, Schooners, saltfish being brought ashore, vert.

1995, Sept. 12 **Engr.** ***Perf. 12½***

290	A95a 4k dark green	1.50	1.50
291	A95a 6k dark brn, vert.	2.25	2.25
292	A95a 15k dark blue	5.50	5.50
	Nos. 290-292 (3)	9.25	9.25

Church of Mary Catholic Church — A96

Designs: No. 293, Stained glass window. No. 294, Exterior view of church.

1995, Nov. 9 **Litho.** ***Perf. 13½***

293	A96 4k multicolored	1.50	1.50
294	A96 4k multicolored	1.50	1.50
a.	Booklet pane, 5 ea #293-294	15.00	
	Complete booklet, #294a	15.00	

Rocky Coastline — A97

Seaweed — A98

1996, Jan. 1 **Litho.** ***Perf. 14***

295	A97 4.50k multicolored	1.60	1.60

1996, Feb. 12 ***Perf. 15***

4k, Ptilota plumosa. 5.50k, Fucus spiralis. 6k, Ascophyllum nodosum. 9k, Laminaria hyperborea.

296	A98 4k multicolored	1.40	1.40
297	A98 5.50k multicolored	2.00	2.00
298	A98 6k multicolored	2.00	2.00
299	A98 9k multicolored	3.25	3.25
	Nos. 296-299 (4)	8.65	8.65

Birds — A99

1996, Apr. 15 **Litho.** ***Perf. 14x15***

300	A99 4.50k Laxia curvirostra	1.50	1.50
301	A99 4.50k Bombycllla garrulus	1.50	1.50
a.	Booklet pane, 5 each #300-301	15.00	
	Complete booklet, #301a	15.00	

See Nos. 313-314.

A100

Europa (Wives of Faroese Seamen): 4.50k, Woman standing beside sea coast. 7.50k, Portrait of a woman, vert.

1996, Apr. 15 ***Perf. 15x14½, 14½x15***

302	A100 4.50k multicolored	*1.50*	*1.50*
303	A100 7.50k multicolored	*2.50*	*2.50*

A101

Nordatlantex '96 (Children's drawings): a, Boy playing with hoop, stick, by Bugvi. b, Two girls on street, road sign, by Gudrid. c, Girl on bicycle, car on street, by Herborg.

1996, June 7 **Litho.** ***Perf. 14½***

Souvenir Sheet of 3

304	A101 4.50k #a.-c.	5.00	5.00

A102

Sea bed off the Faroes.

Litho. & Engr.

1996, June 7 *Perf. 13*

305 A102 10k violet & multi 3.50 3.50
306 A102 16k green & multi 5.50 5.50

See Nos. 319-320, 343, 377-378.

Janus Kamban (b. 1913), Sculptor, Graphic Artist A103

Works of art: 4.50k, Flock of Sheep. 6.50k, Fisherman on the Way Home. 7.50k, View from Tórshavn's Old Quarter.

1996, Sept. 16 **Litho.** *Perf. 14*

307 A103 4.50k multicolored 1.50 1.50
308 A103 6.50k multicolored 2.25 2.25
309 A103 7.50k multicolored 2.50 2.50
Nos. 307-309 (3) 6.25 6.25

A104

Christianschurch, Klaksvík — A105

1996, Nov. 4 **Litho.** *Perf. 14x15*

310 A104 4.50k Exterior 1.50 1.50
311 A105 4.50k Interior, altar fresco 1.50 1.50
a. Booklet pane, 6 #310, 4 #311 15.00
Complete booklet, #311a 15.00

Christmas.

Souvenir Sheet

Reign of Queen Margaret II, 25th Anniv. — A106

1997, Jan. 14 **Litho.** *Perf. 14½*

312 A106 4.50k multicolored 1.50 1.50

Bird Type of 1996

1997, Feb. 27 **Litho.** *Perf. 14x15*

313 A99 4.50k Pyrrhula pyrrhula 1.50 1.50
314 A99 4.50k Carduelis flammea 1.50 1.50
a. Booklet pane, 5 each #313-314 15.00 —
Complete booklet, #314a 15.00

Mushrooms — A107

Designs: 4.50k, Hygrocybe helobia. 6k, Hygrocybe chlorophana. 6.50k, Hygrocybe virginea. 7.50k, Hygrocybe psittacina.

1997, Feb. 17 *Perf. 14½*

315 A107 4.50k multicolored 1.40 1.40
316 A107 6k multicolored 2.00 2.00
317 A107 6.50k multicolored 2.25 2.25
318 A107 7.50k multicolored 2.50 2.50
Nos. 315-318 (4) 8.15 8.15

Map Type of 1996

Litho. & Engr.

1997, May 20 *Perf. 13*

319 A102 11k red & multi 3.50 3.50
320 A102 18k claret & multi 5.50 5.50

Europa — A108

Kalmar Union, 600th Anniv. — A109

Legends illustrated by William Heinesen: 4.50k, The Temptations of Saint Anthony. 7.50k, The Merman sitting at bottom of sea eating fish bait.

1997, May 20 **Litho.** *Perf. 14½*

321 A108 4.50k multicolored *1.50 1.50*
322 A108 7.50k multicolored *2.50 2.50*

1997, May 20 **Engr.** *Perf. 12½*

323 A109 4.50k deep blue violet 1.50 1.50

A110

Barbara, Film Shot in Faroe Islands (Scenes from film): 4.50k, Danish theologian Poul Aggerso arriving at Faroe Islands. 6.50k, Barbara and Poul. 7.50k, Barbara with men on boat. 9k, Barbara in row boat, sailing ship.

1997, Sept. 15 **Litho.** *Perf. 14*

324 A110 4.50k multicolored 1.50 1.50
325 A110 6.50k multicolored 2.10 2.10
326 A110 7.50k multicolored 2.40 2.40
327 A110 9k multicolored 2.75 2.75
Nos. 324-327 (4) 8.75 8.75

A111

Hvalvik church.

1997, Sept. 15

328 A111 4.50k Interior 1.50 1.50
329 A111 4.50k Exterior 1.50 1.50
a. Booklet pane, 5 each #328-329 15.00 —
Complete booklet, #329a 15.00

Birds — A112

A113

1998, Feb. 23 **Litho.** *Perf. 14x14½*

330 A112 4.50k Sturnus vulgaris 1.40 1.40
331 A112 4.50k Turdus merula 1.40 1.40
a. Bklt. pane, 5 each #330-331 14.00
Complete booklet, #331a 14.00

1998, Feb. 23 *Perf. 14*

Scenes from the Sigurd poem "Brynhild's Ballad": 4.50k, King Buole, daughter Brynhild. 6.50k, Sigurd riding through wall of fire on horseback. 7.50k, Sigurd, Brynhild together. 10k, Guthrun alone leading horse.

332 A113 4.50k multicolored 1.40 1.40
333 A113 6.50k multicolored 2.00 2.00
334 A113 7.50k multicolored 2.25 2.25
335 A113 10k multicolored 3.00 3.00
Nos. 332-335 (4) 8.65 8.65

Europa — A114

A115

1998, May 18 **Litho.** *Perf. 14*

336 A114 4.50k Parade *1.50 1.50*
337 A114 7.50k Processional *2.50 2.50*

Olavsoka, Natl. Festival of Faroe Islands.

1998, May 18 *Perf. 14½*

338 A115 7.50k multicolored 2.25 2.25

UN Declaration of Human Rights, 50th anniv.

Intl. Year of the Ocean A116

Toothed whales: 4k, Lagenorhynchus acutus. 4.50k, Orcinus orca. 7k, Tursiops truncatus. 9k, Delphinapterus leucas.

1998, May 18 *Perf. 14½x14*

339 A116 4k multicolored 1.25 1.25
340 A116 4.50k multicolored 1.40 1.40
341 A116 7k multicolored 2.25 2.25
342 A116 9k multicolored 2.75 2.75
Nos. 339-342 (4) 7.65 7.65

Map Type of 1996

Litho. & Engr.

1998, Sept. 14 *Perf. 13*

343 A102 14k multicolored 4.50 4.50

Frederickschurch A117

1998, Sept. 14 **Litho.** *Perf. 14*

344 A117 4.50k Exterior, coastline 1.40 1.40
345 A117 4.50k Interior 1.40 1.40
a. Bklt. pane, 5 each #344-345 14.00
Complete booklet, #345a 14.00

A118

A119

Paintings by Hans Hansen (1920-70): 4.50k, Fell-field, 1966. 5.50k, Village Interior, 1965. 6.50k, Portrait of Farmer Ólavur í Utistovu from Mikladalur, 1968. 8k, Self-portrait, 1968.

Perf. 13½x14, 14x13½

1998, Sept. 14

346 A118 4.50k multi 1.40 1.40
347 A118 5.50k multi 1.75 1.75
348 A118 6.50k multi, vert. 2.10 2.10
349 A118 8k multi, vert. 2.50 2.50
Nos. 346-349 (4) 7.75 7.75

1999, Feb. 22 **Litho.** *Perf. 13½*

Birds.

350 A119 4.50k Passer domesticus 1.40 1.40
351 A119 4.50k Troglodytes troglodytes 1.40 1.40
a. Bklt. pane, 5 each #350-351 14.00
Complete booklet, #351a 14.00

Ships Named "Smyril" A120

1999, Feb. 22 *Perf. 14½x14*

352 A120 4.50k 1895 1.40 1.40
353 A120 5k 1932 1.60 1.60
354 A120 8k 1967 2.50 2.50
355 A120 13k 1975 4.25 4.25
Nos. 352-355 (4) 9.75 9.75

Northern Islands A121

1999, May 25 **Litho.** *Perf. 13½*

356 A121 50o Kalsoy .25 .25
357 A121 100o Vithoy .35 .35
358 A121 400o Svinoy 1.25 1.25
359 A121 450o Fugloy 1.40 1.40
360 A121 600o Kunoy 1.90 1.90
361 A121 800o Borthoy 2.75 2.75
Nos. 356-361 (6) 7.90 7.90

See Nos. 383-386.

Waterfalls — A122

Europa: 6k, Svartifossur. 8k, Foldarafossur.

1999, May 25 *Perf. 14x14½*

362 A122 6k multicolored *2.00 2.00*
363 A122 8k multicolored *2.75 2.75*

Abstract Paintings of Ingálvur av Reyni — A123

1999, Sept. 27 **Litho.** *Perf. 12½*

364 A123 4.50k Bygd 1.40 1.40
365 A123 6k Húsavik 1.75 1.75
366 A123 8k Reytt regn 2.40 2.40
367 A123 20k Genta 6.25 6.25
Nos. 364-367 (4) 11.80 11.80

Bible Stories — A124

1999, Sept. 27 *Perf. 14½x14*

368 A124 450o John 1:1-5 1.50 1.50
a. Booklet pane of 6 9.00
Complete booklet, #368a 9.00
369 A124 600o Luke 1:26-28 2.00 2.00
a. Booklet pane of 6 12.00
Complete booklet, #369a 12.00

See Nos. 387-388, 407-408.

A125 A126

Christianity in the Faroes, 1000th Anniv.: 4.50k, Man on rocks in ocean. 5.50k, Monk with cross, man with sword. 8k, People, flags. 16k, Cross in sky.

Perf. 13½x13¼

2000, Feb. 21 Litho.

370 A125 4.50k multi 1.40 1.40
371 A125 5.50k multi 1.75 1.75
372 A125 8k multi 2.50 2.50
373 A125 16k multi 5.00 5.00
Nos. 370-373 (4) 10.65 10.65

2000, Feb. 21

School and: No. 374, Sanna av Skarthi, Anna Suffia Rasmussen, wives of founders. No. 375, Rasmus Rasmussen (1871-1962), Símun av Skarthi (1872-1942), school founders.

374 A126 4.50k multi 1.40 1.40
375 A126 4.50k multi 1.40 1.40
a. Bklt. pane, 4 ea #374-375 11.50
Complete booklet, #375a 11.50

Faroese Folk High School, cent.

Europa, 2000

Common Design Type

2000, May 9 Litho. *Perf. 13¼x13*

376 CD17 8k multi *3.00 3.00*

Map Type of 1996

Litho. & Engr.

2000, May 22 *Perf. 13¼x13*

377 A102 15k multi 4.50 4.50
378 A102 22k multi 7.00 7.00

Stampin' The Future Children's Stamp Design Contest Winners A127

Art by: 4k, Katrin Mortensen. 4.50k, Sigga Andreassen. 6k, Steingrímur Joensen. 8k, Dion Dam Frandsen.

2000, May 22 Litho. *Perf. 13x13¼*

379 A127 4k multi 1.25 1.25
380 A127 4.50k multi 1.40 1.40
381 A127 6k multi 2.00 2.00
382 A127 8k multi 2.50 2.50
Nos. 379-382 (4) 7.15 7.15

Island Type of 1999

2000, Sept. 18 Litho. *Perf. 13½*

383 A121 200o Skúvoy .75 .75
384 A121 650o Hestoy 2.00 2.00
385 A121 750o Koltur 2.25 2.25
386 A121 1000o Nólsoy 3.25 3.25
Nos. 383-386 (4) 8.25 8.25

Bible Story Type of 1999

2000, Sept. 18 Litho. *Perf. 13x13¼*

387 A124 4.50k Micah 5:1 1.50 1.50
a. Booklet pane of 6 9.00
Booklet, #387a 9.00
388 A124 6k John 1:14 2.00 2.00
a. Booklet pane of 6 12.00
Booklet, #388a 12.00

Pew Gables Type of 1980

Kirkjubour pew gables: 430o, St. Andrew with cross. 650o, St. Bartholomew. 800o, Unknown apostle. 18k, Unknown apostle, diff.

Photo. & Engr.

2001, Feb. 12 *Perf. 12¾x12½*

389 A20 450o multi 1.40 1.40
390 A20 650o multi 2.10 2.10
391 A20 800o multi 2.50 2.50
392 A20 18k multi 5.50 5.50
Nos. 389-392 (4) 11.50 11.50

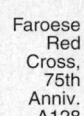

Faroese Red Cross, 75th Anniv. A128

Designs: 4.50k, Old person. 6k, Relief worker.

2001, Feb. 12 Litho. *Perf. 14½x14*

393 A128 4.50k multi 1.50 1.50
a. Booklet pane of 6 9.00
Booklet, #393a 9.00
394 A128 6k multi 2.00 2.00
a. Booklet pane of 6 12.00
Booklet, #394a 12.00

Souvenir Sheet

Faroe Islands Postal Service, 25th Anniv. — A129

No. 395: a, Boat for interisland mail transport, 19th cent. b, Tórshavn post office, 1906. c, Símon Pauli Poulsen (Morkabóndin), mail carrier.

Photo. & Engr.

2001, Apr. 1 *Perf. 13x13¼*

395 A129 4.50k Sheet of 3, #a-c 5.00 5.00

Nordic Myths and Legends About Light and Darkness — A130

No. 396: a, The Death of Hogni. b, The Tree of the Year. c, The Harp. d, Gram and Grane. e, The Ballad of Nornagest. f, Gudrun's Evil Magic.

Litho. with Foil Application

2001, Apr. 1 *Perf. 13½x13¼*

396 A130 6k Sheet of 6, #a-f 12.00 12.00

Hafnia 2001 Philatelic Exhibition, Copenhagen.

Paintings by Zacharias Heinesen A131

Designs: 4k, The Artist's Mother, 1992. 4.50k, Úti á Reyni, 1974. 10k, Ur Vágunum, 2000. 15k, Sunrise, 1975.

2001, June 11 Litho. *Perf. 13¼x13*

397 A131 4k multi 1.25 1.25
398 A131 4.50k multi 1.40 1.40
399 A131 10k multi 3.25 3.25
400 A131 15k multi 4.75 4.75
Nos. 397-400 (4) 10.65 10.65

Europa A132

Hydroelectric power stations: 6k, Fossáverkith. 8k, Eithisverkith.

2001, June 11 *Perf. 13x13½*

401 A132 6k multi *2.00 2.00*
402 A132 8k multi *2.75 2.75*

Whales — A133

Designs: 4.50k, Physeter macrocephalus. 6.50k, Balaenoptera physalus. 9k, Balaenoptera musculus. 20k, Balaenoptera borealis.

Perf. 13¾x13¼

2001, Sept. 17 Litho.

403 A133 4.50k multi 1.40 1.40
404 A133 6.50k multi 2.10 2.10
405 A133 9k multi 2.75 2.75
406 A133 20k multi 6.50 6.50
Nos. 403-406 (4) 12.75 12.75

Bible Stories Type of 1999

2001, Sept. 17 *Perf. 13*

407 A124 5k Luke 2:34-35 1.75 1.75
a. Booklet pane of 6 10.50 —
Booklet, #407a 10.50
408 A124 6.50k Matthew 2:18 2.00 2.00
a. Booklet pane of 6 12.00 —
Booklet, #408a 12.00

Mollusks — A134

Designs: 5k, Sepiola atlantica. 7k, Modiolus modiolus. 7.50k, Polycera faeroensis. 18k, Buccinum undatum.

2002, Feb. 11 Litho. *Perf. 13*

409 A134 5k multi 1.75 1.75
410 A134 7k multi 2.40 2.40
411 A134 7.50k multi 2.50 2.50
412 A134 18k multi 6.00 6.00
Nos. 409-412 (4) 12.65 12.65

Portions of the designs were applied by a thermographic process producing a shiny, raised effect.

Souvenir Sheet

Viking Voyages — A135

No. 413: a, Navigation tool. b, Viking sailor on boat. c, Viking boat.

Litho. & Engr.

2002, Feb. 11 *Perf. 13*

413 A135 6.50k Sheet of 3, #a-c 6.75 6.75

Europa A136

Designs: 6.50k, Clowns. 8k, Various circus performers.

2002, Apr. 8 Litho. *Perf. 13¼x13½*

414 A136 6.50k multi *2.25 2.25*
415 A136 8k multi *2.75 2.75*

Art by Tróndur Patursson A137

Designs: 5k, Bládypi. 6.50k, Kosmiska Rúmith.

2002, Apr. 8

416 A137 5k multi 1.75 1.75
417 A137 6.50k multi 2.25 2.25
a. Booklet pane of 8, 4 each #416-417 16.00 —
Booklet, #417a 16.00

Eggs and Chicks — A138

Designs: 5k, Numenius phaeopus. 7.50k, Gallinago gallinago. 12k, Haematopus ostralegus. 20k, Pluvialis apricaria.

2002, June 17 *Perf. 14x14½*

418 A138 5k multi 1.75 1.75
419 A138 7.50k multi 2.50 2.50
420 A138 12k multi 4.00 4.00
421 A138 20k multi 6.75 6.75
Nos. 418-421 (4) 15.00 15.00

Souvenir Sheet

Faroese Representative Council, 150th Anniv. — A139

Designs: 5k, Royal book and seal. 6.50k, Royal book, Protocol of 1852.

2002, June 17 *Perf. 14*

422 A139 Sheet of 2, #a-b 4.50 4.50

Falco Columbarius Subaesalon — A140

Litho. & Embossed

2002, Sept. 23 *Perf. 13¼*

423 A140 30k multi 9.75 9.75

Gota Church — A141

2002, Sept. 23 Litho. ***Perf. 12½***

424 A141 5k Exterior 1.75 1.75
425 A141 6.50k Interior 2.25 2.25
a. Booklet pane, 5 each #424-425 20.00 —
Booklet, #425a 20.00

Souvenir Sheet

Intl. Council for the Exploration of the Sea, Cent. — A142

No. 426: a, Micromesistius poutassou and island. b, Exploration ship Magnus Heinason and fish.

Litho. & Engr.

2002, Sept. 23 ***Perf. 13***

426 A142 8k Sheet of 2, #a-b 5.50 5.50

See Denmark Nos. 1237-1238, Greenland Nos. 401-402.

Opening of Vagár-Streymoy Tunnel, Nov. 2002 — A143

Designs: No. 427, Wheeled tunneling machine at right. No. 428, Workers in red uniforms at left.

2003, Feb. 24 Litho. ***Perf. 13¼x13***

427 A143 5k multi 1.50 1.50
428 A143 5k multi 1.50 1.50
a. Booklet pane, 5 each #427-428 15.00 —
Complete booklet, #428a 15.00

Voluspá, Ancient Norse Poem — A144

No. 429: a, Seeress Heid holding staff. b, Heid sees animal and man in vision. c, Nude man and woman. d, Scribe and horseman. e, Battle between group with swords and man with hammer. f, Horseman and warriors. g, Men, large sword. h, Longboat. i, Attack on man holding spear, fire. j, Two figures with staffs, winged serpent.

2003, Feb. 24 ***Perf. 14***

429 A144 Sheet of 10 22.50 22.50
a.-j. 6.50k Any single 2.25 2.25

Europa — A145

Poster art for Nordic House: 6.50k, Fish Tree, by Astrid Andreasen, 1991. 8k, Ceramics by Guthrith Poulsen, 1997.

2003, Apr. 14 ***Perf. 13½x13¼***

430 A145 6.50k multi *2.00 2.00*
431 A145 8k multi *2.50 2.50*

Children's Songs — A146

No. 432: a, Woman playing hopscotch (26x44mm). b, Boy on rocks, moon (26x44mm). c, Girl with missing teeth (26x26mm). d, Boy with toy sailboat (26x26mm). e, Cat, horse and girl (26x26mm). f, Butterfly and fly (26x26mm). g, Girl in bed, boy with stars (44x26mm). h, Cat on stairs, mouse (26x36mm). i, Man playing drums (26x26mm). j, King and queen in longboat (44x26mm).

Perf. 13¼, 13¼x13¼x13¼x14 (#432g,
432j), 13¼x14 (#432h)

2003, Apr. 14

432 A146 Sheet of 10 16.00 16.00
a.-j. 5k Any single 1.60 1.60

Small Towns A147

2003, June 10 Litho. ***Perf. 13x13¼***

433 A147 5k Bour 1.60 1.60
434 A147 5k Gásadalur 1.60 1.60

Communities With Post Offices 100 Years Old — A148

No. 435: a, Fuglafjorthur. b, Strendur. c, Sandur. d, Eithi. e, Vestmanna. f, Vágur. g, Mithvágur. h, Hvalba.

2003, June 10 ***Perf. 13¼x13***

435 A148 Sheet of 8 13.00 13.00
a.-h. 5k Any single 1.60 1.60

Theologians — A149

Designs: 5k, Jesper Rasmussen Brochmand (1585-1652). 6.50k, Thomas Kingo (1634-1703).

2003, Sept. 22 ***Perf. 13x13¼***

436 A149 5k multi 1.50 1.50
437 A149 6.50k multi 2.00 2.00
a. Booklet pane, 5 each #436-437 17.50 —
Complete booklet, #437a 17.50

Souvenir Sheet

Dancing in the Inn's Smoking Room, by Emil Krause — A150

Litho. & Engr.

2003, Sept. 22 ***Perf. 12¼***

438 A150 25k multi 11.00 11.00

100th Faroese stamp engraved by Czeslaw Slania.

Islands Type of 1999

2004, Jan. 26 Litho. ***Perf. 13½***

439 A121 550o Stóra Dímun 1.90 1.90
440 A121 700o Lítla Dímun 2.40 2.40

Suthuroy Island — A151

No. 441: a, Sigmundargjogv, Sandvik. b, Fiskieithi, Hvalba. c, A Hamri, Frothba. d, Tjaldavíkshólmur, Oravík. e, Fossurin Stóri, Fámjin. f, Hovsfjorthur, Hov. g, I Eystrum, Porkeri. h, A Okrum. i, I Horg, Sumba. j, I Akrabergi.

2004, Jan. 26 ***Perf. 13x13¼***

441 A151 5k Sheet of 10, #a-j 17.00 17.00

1854 Cruise of Yacht "Maria" — A152

No. 442: a, Gáshólmur and Tindhólmur. b, Framvith "Diamantunum." c, Hús av tí betra slagnum. d, Mylingur sunnanífrá. e, Mylingur northanífrá. f, Kalsoyggin northanífrá. g, Raetha teir infoddu. h, Sunnari endi av Kunoynni.

2004, Mar. 26 Litho. ***Perf. 13***

442 A152 6.50k Sheet of 8, #a.-h. 17.00 17.00

Souvenir Sheet

Norse Gods — A153

No. 443: a, Thor, in boat, fighting Midgard serpent. b, Ran in fishing net.

2004, Mar. 26

443 A153 6.50k Sheet of 2, #a.-b. 4.75 4.75

Souvenir Sheet

Wedding of Crown Prince Frederik and Mary Donaldson — A154

Litho. & Photo.

2004, May 14 ***Perf. 13¼***

444 A154 Sheet of 2 + central label 4.25 4.25
a. 5k Couple facing right 1.60 1.60
b. 6.50k Couple facing left 2.25 2.25

Soccer Organization Centenaries A155

Soccer players and emblems of: 5k, Klaksvík and Tórshavn teams. 6.50k, FIFA (Fédération Internationale de Football Association).

2004, May 24 Litho. ***Perf. 13¼x13***

445 A155 5k multi 1.75 1.75
446 A155 6.50k multi 2.25 2.25
a. Booklet pane, 4 each #445-446 16.00 —
Complete booklet, #446a 16.00

Europa A156

Designs: 6.50k, Tourists in gorge, Hestur. 8k, Tourists at shore, Stóra Dímun.

2004, May 24 ***Perf. 13x13¼***

447 A156 6.50k multi *2.10 2.10*
448 A156 8k multi *2.60 2.60*

Churches A157

2004, Sept. 20 Litho. ***Perf. 13¼x13***

449 A157 5.50k Vágur 1.90 1.90
450 A157 7.50k Tvoroyri 2.50 2.50
a. Booklet pane, 4 each #449-450 18.00 —
Complete booklet, #450a 18.00

Poems by Janus Djurhuus (1881-1948) — A158

No. 451: a, Atlantis. b, Grímur Kamban. c, Gandkvaethi Tróndar. d, Til Foroya I-III. e, Mín sorg. f, Loki. g, I búri og Slatur. h, Heimferth Nólsoyar Páls. i, Móses á Sinai fjalli. j, Cello.

2004, Sept. 20 ***Perf. 13***
451 A158 Sheet of 10 24.00 24.00
a.-j. 7.50k Any single 2.40 2.40

Souvenir Sheet

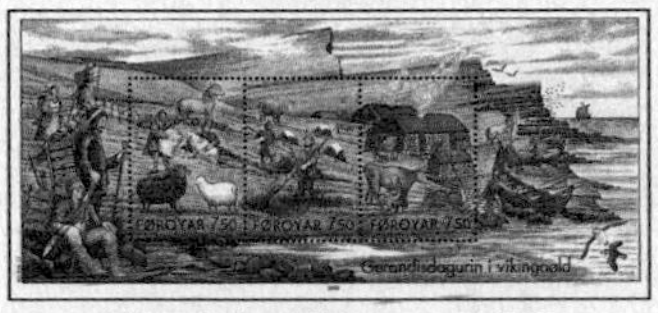

Life of the Vikings — A159

No. 452: a, Men tending sheep. b, Men with farm implements. c, Women weaving and woman milking cow.

Litho. & Engr.

2005, Feb. 7 ***Perf. 13***
452 A159 Sheet of 3 7.50 7.50
a.-c. 7.50k Any single 2.40 2.40

Miniature Sheet

Vágar Island — A160

No. 453: a, Víkar. b, Gásadalur. c, Bour. d, Slaettanes. e, Kvígandalsá. f, Sorvágur. g, Sandavágur. h, Vatnsoyrar. i, Fjallavatn. j, Mithvágur.

2005, Feb. 7 Litho. ***Perf. 13x13¼***
453 A160 Sheet of 10 19.00 19.00
a.-j. 5.50k Any single 1.90 1.90

Lepus Timidus — A161

2005, Apr. 18 ***Perf. 13¼x13½***
454 A161 5.50k shown 1.90 1.90
455 A161 5.50k Brown fur 1.90 1.90
a. Booklet pane, 4 each #454-455 15.50 —
Complete booklet, #455a 15.50

Europa — A162

Various traditional foods with: 7.50k, Brown panel. 10k, Green panel.

2005, Apr. 18 ***Perf. 13¼x13***
456 A162 7.50k multi *2.60 2.60*
457 A162 10k multi *3.50 3.50*

Worldwide Fund for Nature (WWF) A163

Petrels: 8.50k, Oceanodroma leucorhoa. 9k, Hydrobates pelagicus. 12k, Oceanodroma leucorhoa on ground. 20k, Hydrobates pelagicus on ground.

2005, June 6 ***Perf. 13***
458 A163 8.50k multi 2.25 2.25
459 A163 9k multi 3.00 3.00
460 A163 12k multi 4.00 4.00
461 A163 20k multi 6.25 6.25
Nos. 458-461 (4) 15.50 15.50

Miniature Sheet

Landscapes by Jógvan Waagstein (1879-1949) — A164

No. 462: a, Path and wall at LL, denomination in red, year date in black in grass. b, Path and wall at LL, denomination in white, year date in black on wall. c, Stone hut at left, denomination in red, year date in black. d, Path at right, denomination in red, year date in black. e, Two large rocks at right, denomination in red, year date in black. f, Rocks at LL, denomination in red, year date in white. g, Path at center, denomination in white, year date in black on path. h, Buildings at LL, denomination in red, year date in black in path. i, Churches, denomination in white, year date in black in water.

2005, Sept. 19 Litho. ***Perf. 14x14¼***
462 A164 Sheet of 9 20.00 20.00
a.-i. 7.50k Any single 2.25 2.25

End of British Occupation In World War II, 60th Anniv. A165

Soldiers with: 5.50k, Arms. 9k, Children.

2005, Sept. 19 ***Perf. 14***
463 A165 5.50k blue & blk 1.75 1.75
464 A165 9k yel & blk 3.00 3.00

Christmas — A166

Ballads: 5.50k, Jólavísan. 7.50k, Rudisar Vísa.

2005, Nov. 7 ***Perf. 13½x13¼***
465 A166 5.50k multi 1.75 1.75
466 A166 7.50k multi 2.40 2.40
a. Booklet pane, 5 each #465-466 16.00 —
Complete booklet, #466a 16.00

Villages A167

2006, Feb. 13 Litho. ***Perf. 13¾***
467 A167 7k Sythrugota 2.25 2.25
468 A167 12k Fuglafjorthur 4.25 4.25
469 A167 20k Leirvík 6.75 6.75
Nos. 467-469 (3) 13.25 13.25

Miniature Sheet

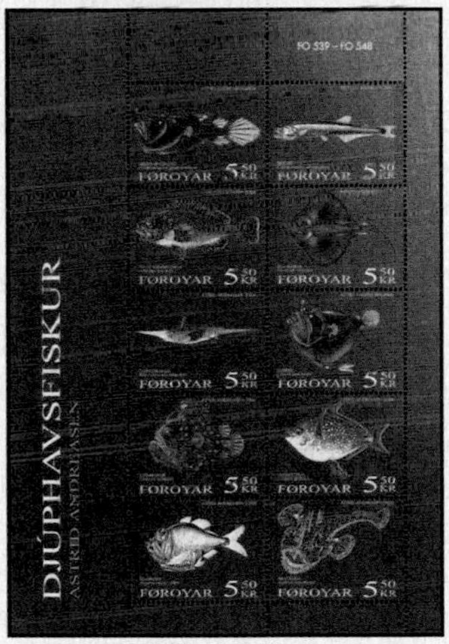

Fish — A168

No. 470: a, Himantolophus groenlandicus. b, Gonostoma elongatum. c, Sebastes mentella. d, Neoraja caerulea. e, Rhinochimaera atlantica. f, Linophryne lucifer. g, Ceratias holboelli. h, Lampris guttatus. i, Argyropelecus olfersi. j, Lophius piscatorius.

2006, Feb. 13 ***Perf. 14***
470 A168 Sheet of 10 19.00 19.00
a.-j. 5.50k Any single 1.90 1.90

Souvenir Sheet

Norse Folklore — A169

No. 471: a, Norns surrounding sleeping child. b, Sea ghost.

2006, Mar. 29 ***Perf. 13***
471 A169 7.50k Sheet of 2, #a-b 5.00 5.00

Miniature Sheet

Ballad of the Long Serpent, by Jens Christian Djurhuus — A170

No. 472: a, Building of ship. b, Launch of ship. c, King on throne. d, King's fleet at sea (brown ship at LL, blue ship at LR). e, King and sailors on shore. f, King pointing. g, Ship with red sail at R. h, Battle scene (injured men falling into water). i, Battle scene (men with shields jumping from ship to ship). j, Dead men on ship's deck.

2006, Mar. 29 ***Perf. 13¼x13***
472 A170 Sheet of 10 18.00 18.00
a.-j. 5.50k Any single 1.75 1.75

Opening of Northoy Tunnel — A171

Tunnel and: No. 473, Fish. No. 474, Canoe.

2006, June 12 ***Perf. 13¼***
473 A171 5.50k multi 1.90 1.90
474 A171 5.50k multi 1.90 1.90
a. Booklet pane, 4 each #473-474 15.50 —
Complete booklet, #474a 15.50

Europa A172

2006, June 12 ***Perf. 13¾***
475 A172 7.50k shown 2.60 2.60
476 A172 10k Hands, diff. 3.50 3.50

Miniature Sheet

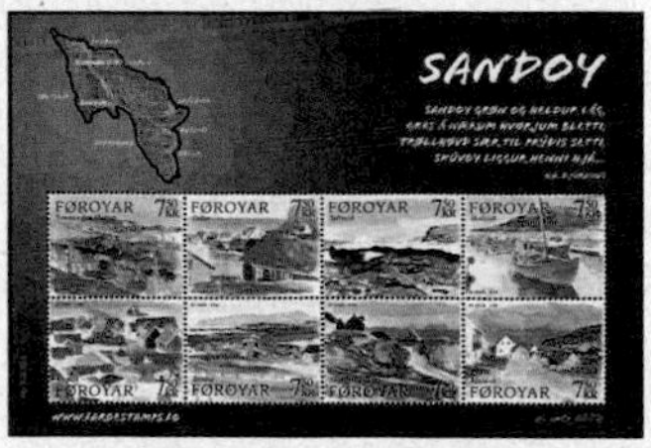

Sandoy Island — A173

No. 477: a, Sunnan fyri Skopun. b, Dalur. c, Soltuvík. d, Skálavík. e, Skopun. f, Sandur. g, Skarvanes. h, Húsavík.

2006, Sept. 18 Litho. ***Perf. 13x13¼***
477 A173 Sheet of 8 20.00 20.00
a.-h. 7.50k Any single 2.50 2.50

Sandur Church A174

Designs: 5.50k, Building exterior, steeple cross. 7.50k, Interior.

2006, Sept. 18 ***Perf. 14***

478 A174 5.50k multi 1.90 1.90
479 A174 7.50k multi 2.60 2.60
a. Booklet pane, 4 each #478-479 18.00 —
Complete booklet, #479a 18.00

Wave Energy A175

2007, Feb. 12 Litho. ***Perf. 12½x13***

480 A175 7.50k multi 2.60 2.60

Art From 1838 La Recherche Expedition A176

Art by Barthélemy Lauvergne: 5.50k, La Recherche off Nólsoy. 7.50k, Skaelingsfjall.

2007, Feb. 12

481 A176 5.50k multi 1.90 1.90
482 A176 7.50k multi 2.60 2.60
a. Booklet pane, 4 each #481-482 18.00 —
Complete booklet, #482a 18.00

Miniature Sheet

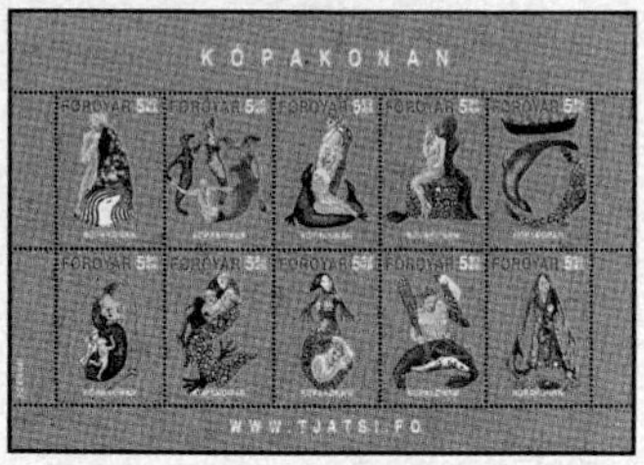

Legend of the Seal Woman — A177

No. 483: a, Man, head of white seal. b, Woman and seals in ring. c, Man, nude woman, seals. d, Man and nude woman seated on chest. e, Ship and two seals. f, Children, seal woman nursing child. g, Seal woman and man. h, Sleeping man and seal woman with hands open. i, Man and dead seals. j, Seal woman.

2007, Feb. 12 ***Perf. 14***

483 A177 Sheet of 10 19.00 19.00
a.-j. 5.50k Any single 1.90 1.90

Miniature Sheet

The Old Man and His Sons, Novel by Hethin Brú — A178

No. 484: a, Ketil cutting whale's throat. b, Men carrying injured Klávus on log. c, Kálvur and fiancee, Klávusardóttir with pot and kettle. d, Ketil and Kálvur in fishing boat. e, Ketil's wife arguing with daughter-in-law. f, Ketil catching flying northern fulmars. g, Kálvur and stone fence. h, Ketil, Kálvur and cow.

2007, Apr. 10 Litho. ***Perf. 13x12½***

484 A178 Sheet of 8 20.00 20.00
a.-h. 7.50k Any single 2.50 2.50

Europa — A179

Design: 5.50k, Scout holding bird. 10k, Tent.

2007, Apr. 10

485 A179 5.50k multi 2.00 2.00
486 A179 10k multi 3.75 3.75

Scouting, cent.

Souvenir Sheet

Bible Translators — A180

No. 487: a, Jákup Dahl (1878-1944). b, Kristian O. Videro (1906-91). c, Victor Danielsen (1894-1961).

2007, June 11 Litho. ***Perf. 13x12½***

487 A180 Sheet of 3 6.00 6.00
a.-c. 5.50k Any single 2.00 2.00

Domesticated Birds — A181

Designs: 9k, Chickens and rooster. 20k, Ducks. 25k, Geese.

2007, June 11 ***Perf. 12½x13***

488 A181 9k multi 3.25 3.25
489 A181 20k multi 7.25 7.25
490 A181 25k multi 9.25 9.25
Nos. 488-490 (3) 19.75 19.75

Hoyvík — A182

2007, Oct. 1 ***Perf. 13½***

491 A182 7.50k multi 2.75 2.75

Wooden Religious Statues of Kirkjubour Cathedral — A183

2007, Oct. 1 ***Perf. 13x12½***

492 A183 5.50k Jesus 2.10 2.10
493 A183 7.50k Mary 2.75 2.75
a. Booklet pane, 4 each #492-493 19.50 —
Complete booklet, #493a 19.50

Miniature Sheet

Stone Fence and Wildlife — A184

No. 494: a, Bird, worm. b, Two red beetles, fern. c, Mouse, purple flowers. d, Mosquito, pink flowers. e, Large black and white bird, dandelions. f, Bird with black wings, buttercups. g, Earwigs, grass. h, Bird and eggs.

2007, Oct. 1 ***Perf. 13½x14¼***

494 A184 Sheet of 8 17.00 17.00
a.-h. 5.50k Any single 2.10 2.10

Klaksvík, Cent. — A185

Litho. & Embossed

2008, Feb. 11 ***Perf. 14***

495 A185 5.50k multi 2.25 2.25

Tinganes A186

2008, Feb. 11 Litho. ***Perf. 13¼***

496 A186 14k multi 5.25 5.25

Hoydalar Tuberculosis Sanatorium, Cent. — A187

Lungs and: 5.50k, Patients, buildings. 9k, Dr. Vilhelm Magnussen examining patient, child.

2007, Feb. 11 ***Perf. 12½x13***

497 A187 5.50k multi 2.25 2.25
498 A187 9k multi 3.75 3.75
a. Booklet pane, 4 each #497-498 24.00
Complete booklet, #498a 24.00

Miniature Sheet

Prints by Elinborg Lützens — A188

No. 499: a, Houses below mountain. b, Milk maids (30x30mm). c, Houses. d, Underwater scene. e, Chicken (30x30mm). f, Person and bird near wooden bucket.

2008, Feb. 11 ***Perf. 13¼***

499 A188 Sheet of 6 22.50 22.50
a.-f. 10k Any single 3.75 3.75

Souvenir Sheet

Mythical Places — A189

No. 500: a, Alvheyggur. b, Klovningasteinur.

2008, Mar. 27 Litho. ***Perf. 12½x13***

500 A189 Sheet of 2 6.50 6.50
a.-b. 7.50k Either single 3.25 3.25

Caltha Palustris A190

2008, May 19 ***Perf. 13¼***

501 A190 30k multi 13.00 13.00

Europa A191

Designs: 550o, Heart and "Teg." 750o, Posthorn with "@" symbol and "Hey."

2008, May 19 ***Perf. 13¼x13***

502 A191 550o multi 2.25 2.25
503 A191 750o multi 3.25 3.25

Miniature Sheet

Famous People — A192

No. 504: a, Niels Winther (1822-92), politician and newspaper publisher. b, Súsanna Helena Patursson (1864-1916), writer and newspaper publisher. c, Rasmus C. Effersoe (1857-1916), writer and newspaper editor. d, Jógvan Poulsen (1854-1941), religious and school book writer. e, Frithrikur Petersen (1853-1917), poet. f, Andreas Christian Evensen (1874-1917), magazine publisher and school book writer.

2008, May 19 ***Perf. 13½x13¼***

504 A192 Sheet of 6 14.00 14.00
a.-f. 5.50k Any single 2.25 2.25

Miniature Sheet

Ferns — A193

No. 505: a, Gymnocarpium dryopteris. b, Polypodium vulgare. c, Dryopteris dilatata. d, Asplenium adiantum-nigrum. e, Athyrium filix-femina. f, Dryopteris filix-mas. g, Cystopteris fragilis. h, Phegopteris connectilis. i, Polystichum lonchitis. j, Asplenium trichomanes.

2008, Sept. 22 Litho. ***Perf. 13x13½***

505 A193 Sheet of 10 30.00 30.00
a.-j. 800o Any single 3.00 3.00

Christmas — A194

2008, Sept. 22 ***Perf. 13x12½***

506 A194 6k shown 2.25 2.25
507 A194 10k Wooden cross 3.75 3.75
a. Booklet pane of 8, 4 each #506-507 24.00 —
Complete booklet, #507a 24.00

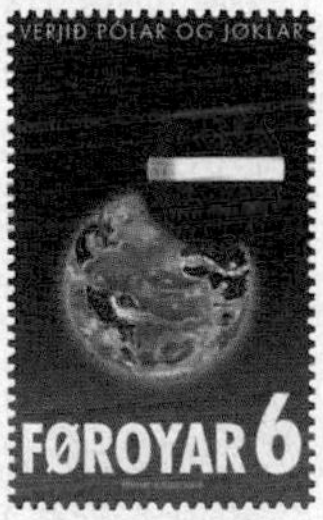

Global Warming — A195

Designs: 6k, Earth and "No entry" sign. 8k, Earth in shape of water droplet.

2009, Feb. 23 Litho. ***Perf. 13¾x14***

508 A195 6k multi 2.10 2.10
509 A195 8k multi 2.75 2.75
a. Souvenir sheet, #508-509 5.00 5.00

Portions of the designs were applied by a thermographic process producing a shiny raised effect.

Miniature Sheet

Scenes From *The Lost Musicians,* by William Heinesen — A196

No. 510: a, People, stylized harp. b, Ring of silhouetted dancers. c, Woman on roof of house, kneeling people and standing woman near house. d, Silhouetted man approaching woman on park bench. e, Women and seated cellist. f, Violinist and two silhoutted men. g, Man in bed. h, People in rowboat.

2009, Feb. 23 ***Perf. 13½***

510 A196 Sheet of 8 22.00 22.00
a.-h. 8k Any single 2.75 2.75

Europa — A197

Designs: 10k, Trollhovdi Island and Saturn. 12k, Heygadrangur Island, Jupiter and one of its moons, Europa.

2009, May 25 Litho. ***Perf. 13x12½***

511 A197 10k multi 3.75 3.75
512 A197 12k multi 4.50 4.50

Intl. Year of Astronomy.

Miniature Sheet

Geological Formation of the Faroe Islands — A198

No. 513: a, Large volcano spewing lava, trees. b, Smaller volcano spewing ash, dead tree, lava on landscape. c, Map of area 60 million years ago. d, Map of area 15 million years ago. e, Map of Faroe Isands, map of Faroe Islands and area nearby. f, Glacier, rock pinnacles.

2009, May 25 ***Perf. 12½x13***

513 A198 Sheet of 6 22.50 22.50
a.-f. 10k Any single 3.75 3.75

Thorshavn Gymnastics Club, Cent. — A199

Gymnasts: 6k, Male lifting female. 10k, Female doing handstand. 26k, Male on rings.

2009, May 25 ***Perf. 14***

514 A199 6k multi 2.25 2.25
515 A199 10k multi 3.75 3.75
516 A199 26k multi 9.75 9.75
Nos. 514-516 (3) 15.75 15.75

Serpentine Die Cut 14
Booklet Stamps
Self-Adhesive

517 A199 6k multi 2.25 2.25
518 A199 10k multi 3.75 3.75
a. Booklet pane of 8, 4 each #517-518 24.00

Leynar — A200

2009, Sept. 16 ***Perf. 12¾***

519 A200 10k multi 4.00 4.00

Rock Pigeons A201

Designs: 14k, Two pigeons on rocks. 36k, Head of pigeon, two pigeons in flight.

2009. Sept. 16 ***Perf. 13***

520 A201 14k multi 5.50 5.50
521 A201 36k multi 14.50 14.50

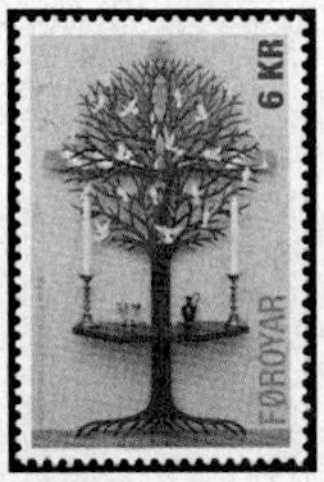

Altarpiece at Vestmanna Church — A202

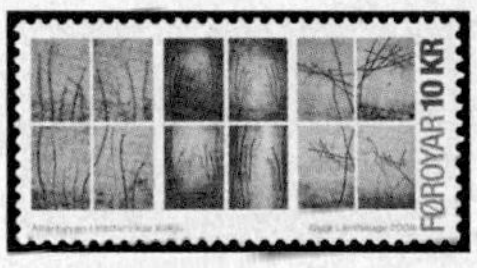

Altarpiece at Hattarvik Church A203

2009, Sept. 16 ***Perf. 13¾x13¼***

522 A202 6k multi 2.40 2.40
a. Perf. 13¾ vert. 2.40 2.40
523 A203 10k multi 4.00 4.00
a. Perf. 14¼x13¾ on 3 sides 4.00 4.00
b. Booklet pane of 8, 4 each #522a, 523a 26.00 —
Complete booklet, #523b 26.00

Christmas.

Globicephala Melas — A204

2010, Feb. 22 Litho. ***Perf. 14¾***

524 A204 50k multi 18.50 18.50

Marine Flora and Fauna — A205

Various photographs.

2010, Feb. 22 ***Perf. 13¼x13½***

525 A205 1k multi .35 .35
526 A205 6k multi 2.25 2.25
527 A205 8k multi 3.00 3.00
528 A205 12k multi 4.50 4.50
Nos. 525-528 (4) 10.10 10.10

Butterflies and Moths A206

Designs: 6k, Inachis io. 8k, Vanessa cardui. 14k, Agrius convolvuli. 16k, Acherontia atropos.

2010, Feb. 22 ***Perf. 13x12¾***

529 A206 6k multi 2.25 2.25
530 A206 8k multi 3.00 3.00
531 A206 14k multi 5.25 5.25
532 A206 16k multi 6.00 6.00
Nos. 529-532 (4) 16.50 16.50

Souvenir Sheet

Aquaculture — A207

No. 533: a, Fish, net. b, Fisherman holding net.

Perf. 14¼x14½

2010, Mar. 24 Litho.

533 A207 Sheet of 2 7.25 7.25
a.-b. 10k Either single 3.50 3.50

Paintings by Eli Smith — A208

Various paintings.

2010, Apr. 26 ***Perf. 14½***

534 A208 18k multi 6.50 6.50
535 A208 24k multi 8.75 8.75

Europa A209

Scenes from children's books: 10k, A Dog, A Cat and A Mouse, by Bárthur Oskarsson. 12k, Moss Mollis's Journey, by Janus á Húsagarthi.

2010, Apr. 26 ***Perf. 13¾***

536 A209 10k multi 3.75 3.75
537 A209 12k multi 4.25 4.25

Booklet Stamps
Self-Adhesive
Serpentine Die Cut 14

538 A209 10k multi 3.75 3.75
539 A209 12k multi 4.25 4.25
a. Booklet pane of 8, 4 each #538-539 32.00

Jens Christian Svabo (1746-1824), Writer and Lexicographer — A210

Writings of Svabo and Svabo: 6k, Holding walking stick. 12k, At desk. 14k, Holding book. 22k, With sheaf of papers, pen and inkwell.

Perf. 13¼x13¾

2010, Sept. 20 Litho. & Engr.

540 A210 6k multi 2.25 2.25
541 A210 12k multi 4.50 4.50
542 A210 14k multi 5.25 5.25
543 A210 22k multi 8.25 8.25
Nos. 540-543 (4) 20.25 20.25

Vegetables
A211

Christmas
A212

2010, Sept. 20 Litho. ***Perf. 13x13¼***

544 A211 6k Potatoes 2.25 2.25
545 A211 8k Turnips 3.00 3.00

2010, Sept. 20 ***Perf. 13x12½***

Carols: 6k, My Little Sweet Brownie (Lítla Fitta Nissa Mín). 10k, In My Early Childhood (A Barnaárum Ungu).

546 A212 6k multi 2.25 2.25
547 A212 10k multi 3.75 3.75
a. Booklet pane of 8, 4 each #546-547 24.00 —
Complete booklet, #547a 24.00

See Nos. 570-571, 592-593.

Intl. Women's Day, Cent.
A213

2011, Feb. 21 Litho. ***Perf. 14***

548 A213 10k multi 3.75 3.75

Traditional Women's Professions — A214

Designs: 6k, Nurses with patient and child. 16k, Midwives holding babies.

2011, Feb. 21 ***Perf. 13x13¼***

549 A214 6k multi 2.25 2.25
550 A214 16k multi 6.00 6.00

Cats — A215

Color of cat: 6k, Black and white. 10k, Brown and white.

2011, Feb. 21 ***Perf. 13¾***

551 A215 6k multi 2.25 2.25
552 A215 10k multi 3.75 3.75

Booklet Stamps
Self-Adhesive

Serpentine Die Cut 14

553 A215 6k multi 2.25 2.25
554 A215 10k multi 3.75 3.75
a. Booklet pane of 8, 4 each #553-554 24.00

Souvenir Sheet

Legend of Annika od Dímun — A216

No. 555 — Annika: a, With chalice. b, With guards. c, With bound hands in water.

2011, Feb. 21 ***Perf. 14¾***

555 A216 Sheet of 3 11.50 11.50
a.-c. 10k Any single 3.75 3.75

Paintings by Bergithe Johannessen (1905-95) — A217

Designs: 2k, Skerjut Strond (Glowing Beach). 24k, Ur Nólsoy (From Nólsoy).

2011, Apr. 26 ***Perf. 12½x13***

556 A217 2k multi .80 .80
557 A217 24k multi 9.25 9.25

Paintings by Frida Zachariassen (1912-92) — A218

Designs: 6k, Urtagardhur (The Garden). 26k, Kona (Woman).

2011, Apr. 26 ***Perf. 13***

558 A218 6k multi 2.40 2.40
559 A218 26k multi 10.00 10.00

Europa
A219

Tree plantations on: 10k, Tórshavn. 12k, Kunoy, vert.

2011, Apr. 26 ***Perf. 12½***

560 A219 10k multi 4.00 4.00
561 A219 12k multi 4.75 4.75

Intl. Year of Forests.

Flowers — A220

Designs: 14k, Silene dioica. 20k, Geranium sylvaticum.

2011, Apr. 26 ***Perf. 13¼***

562 A220 14k multi 5.50 5.50
563 A220 20k multi 7.75 7.75

Berries — A221

Designs: 50o, Juniperus communis subsp. alpina. 6.50k, Empetrum nigrum. subsp. hermaphroditum.

2011, Sept. 1 Litho. ***Perf. 12¾x13½***

564 A221 50o multi .25 .25
565 A221 6.50k multi 2.40 2.40

Stóridrangur — A222

2011, Sept. 28 ***Perf. 12½x13***

566 A222 10.50k multi 4.00 4.00

Old Motor Vehicles
A223

Designs: No. 567, Black Ford TT truck, first vehicle on Faroe Islands. No. 568, Red Morris bus. No. 569, White De Luxe Model, automobile built on Faroe Islands.

2011, Sept. 28 ***Perf. 13½x12¾***

567 A223 13k multi 4.75 4.75
568 A223 13k multi 4.75 4.75
569 A223 13k multi 4.75 4.75
a. Souvenir sheet of 3, #567-569 14.50 14.50
Nos. 567-569 (3) 14.25 14.25

Christmas Type of 2010

Carols: 6.50k, I Can't Wait for Christmas to Come (Eg Eri So Spent Til Jóla). 10.50k, I Rejoice Every Christmas Eve (Eg Gledist So Hvort Jólakvold).

2011, Sept. 28 ***Perf. 13x12½***

570 A212 6.50k multi 2.40 2.40
571 A212 10.50k multi 4.00 4.00
a. Booklet pane of 8, 4 each #570-571 26.00 —
Complete booklet, #571a 26.00

Reign of Queen Margrethe II, 40th Anniv. — A224

Litho. & Engr.

2012, Jan. 4 ***Perf. 13¼***

572 A224 10.50k multi 3.75 3.75
a. Souvenir sheet of 1 3.75 3.75

Extinct Animals — A225

Designs: 13k, Pinguinis impennis. 21k, Dímun sheep (Ovis aries), horiz.

2012, Feb. 20 Litho. ***Perf. 13¼x13***

573 A225 13k multi 4.75 4.75

Perf. 13x13¼

574 A225 21k multi 7.50 7.50

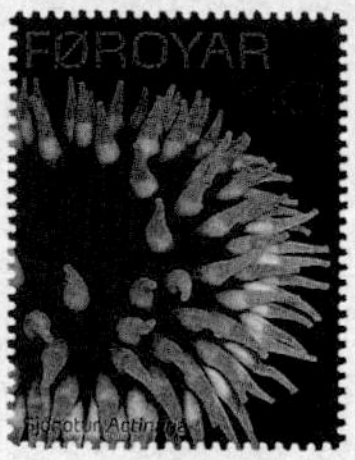

Sea Anemones
A226

Various sea anemones.

2012, Feb. 20 ***Perf. 14***

575 A226 3k multi 1.10 1.10
576 A226 6.50k multi 2.40 2.40
577 A226 8.50k multi 3.00 3.00
578 A226 10.50k multi 3.75 3.75
Nos. 575-578 (4) 10.25 10.25

Booklet Stamps
Self-Adhesive

Serpentine Die Cut 14

579 A226 6.50k multi 2.40 2.40
580 A226 10.50k multi 3.75 3.75
a. Booklet pane of 8, 4 each #579-580 25.00

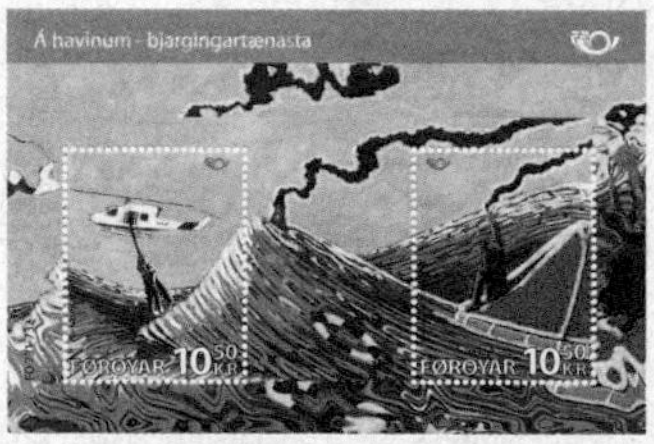

Sea Rescue — A227

No. 581: a, Helicopter. b, Life raft.

2012, Mar. 21 ***Perf. 14¼x13½***

581 A227 Sheet of 2 7.50 7.50
a.-b. 10.50k Either single 3.75 3.75

Europa — A228

Designs: 6.50k, Tourists on boat near Suthuroy Island cliffs. 10.50k, Hikers on rocks.

2012, Apr. 30 ***Perf. 12½x13***

582 A228 6.50k multi 2.40 2.40
583 A228 10.50k multi 3.75 3.75

Monsters
A229

Designs: 6.50k, Gryla. 11k, Marra. 17k, Nithagrisur. 19k, Fjorutroll.

2012, Apr. 30 ***Perf. 13***

584 A229 6.50k multi 2.40 2.40
585 A229 11k multi 4.00 4.00
586 A229 17k multi 6.00 6.00
587 A229 19k multi 6.75 6.75
Nos. 584-587 (4) 19.15 19.15

Old Pharmacy, Klaksvík — A230

2012, Sept. 24 ***Perf. 12½x13***

588 A230 8.50k multi 3.00 3.00

Contemporary Art — A231

Designs: 13k, Mr. Walker on the Faroes, by Jan Hafström. 21k, Egg Procession, by Edward Fuglo.

2012, Sept. 24 *Perf. 13*
589 A231 13k multi 4.50 4.50
590 A231 21k multi 7.25 7.25

Miniature Sheet

Legend of Regin the Blacksmith — A232

No. 591: a, Hjordis attends to dying husband, Sigmund, on battlefield. b, Sigurd on horse. c, Regin hammering sword. d, Sigurd on horseback encounters Odin. e, Sigurd attacks serpent. f, Birds watching Sigurd cooking serpent's heart.

Litho., Litho & Embossed (#591e)
2012, Sept. 24 *Perf. 13¼x13*
591 A232 Sheet of 6 24.00 24.00
a.-f. 11k Any single 4.00 4.00

Christmas Type of 2010

Carols: 6.50k, Why is Everything So Cozy Tonight? (Hví Man Tadh Vera?) 12.50k, Silent Night (Gledhilig Jól).

2012, Sept. 24 Litho. *Perf. 13x12½*
592 A212 6.50k multi 2.25 2.25
593 A212 12.50k multi 4.50 4.50
a. Booklet pane of 8, 4 each #592-593 27.00 —
Complete booklet, #593a 27.00

Lambs — A233

2013, Feb. 25 *Perf. 13¼x13¾*
594 A233 12.50k multi 4.50 4.50

Crustaceans — A234

Designs: 7k, Cancer pagurus. 9k, Chaceon affinis. 23k, Pandalus borealis. 34k, Nephrops norvegicus.

2013, Feb. 25 *Perf. 12½x13*
595 A234 7k multi 2.50 2.50
596 A234 9k multi 3.25 3.25
597 A234 23k multi 8.00 8.00
598 A234 34k multi 12.00 12.00
Nos. 595-598 (4) 25.75 25.75

Miniature Sheet

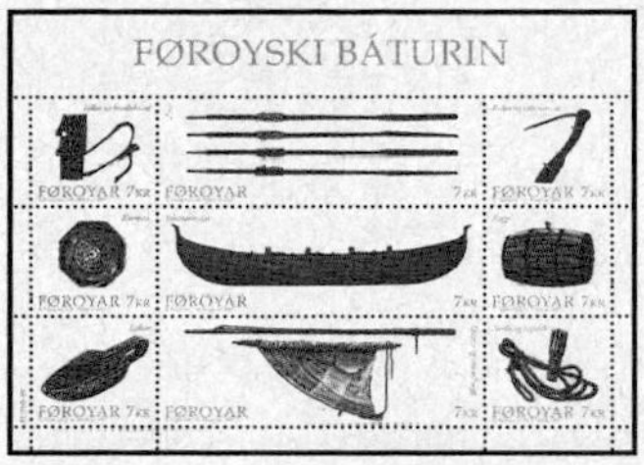

Traditional Faroese Rowboat — A235

No. 599: a, Tollur og homluband (oarlock and strap, 26x23mm). b, Arar (oars, 66x23mm). c, Rodhur og rodhurarmur (rudder, 26x23mm). d, Kumpass (compass, 26x23mm). e, Seksmannafar (hull of six-man boat, 66x23mm). f, Kaggl (barrel, 26x23mm). g, Eyskar (bailing scoop, 26x23mm). h, Mastur og vrá vidh segli (mast and sail, 66x23mm). i, Nogla og togendi (bung and rope, 26x23mm).

Litho. & Engr.
2013, Feb. 25 *Perf. 13¼*
599 A235 Sheet of 9 22.50 22.50
a.-i. 7k Any single 2.50 2.50

Soren Kierkegaard (1813-55), Philosopher A266

2013, Mar. 4 *Perf. 12¼*
600 A266 35k multi 12.50 12.50

Europa A267

Designs: 7k, Postal van. 12.50k, Postal truck.

2013, Apr. 29 Litho. *Perf. 14*
601 A267 7k multi 2.50 2.50
602 A267 12.50k multi 4.50 4.50

Booklet Stamps Self-Adhesive

Serpentine Die Cut 14
603 A267 7k multi 2.50 2.50
604 A267 12.50k multi 4.50 4.50
a. Booklet pane of 8, 4 each #603-604 28.00

Rodents — A268

Designs: 11k, Rattus norvegicus. 12.50k, Mus domesticus.

2013, Apr. 29 *Perf. 13¾x13¼*
605 A268 11k multi 4.00 4.00
606 A268 12.50k multi 4.50 4.50

Paintings by Olivur Vith Neyst — A269

Designs: 19k, Sólskin (Sunshine). 38k, Vestaravág (West Harbor).

2013, Sept. 23 *Perf. 12½*
607 A269 19k multi 7.00 7.00
608 A269 38k multi 14.00 14.00

Souvenir Sheet

Nordafar Fishery, Foroyinghavn, Greenland — A270

No. 609: a, Fishing boat, white building in background. b, Fishermen on dock. c, Fishing boats, red buildings in background.

Perf. 13¼x13¾
2013, Sept. 23 Litho. & Engr.
609 A270 Sheet of 3 9.75 9.75
a.-c. 9k Any single 3.25 3.25

See Greenland No. 652.

Christmas — A271

Designs: 7k, Manger. 12.50k, Holy Family.

2013, Sept. 23 Litho. *Perf. 12¾*
610 A271 7k multi 2.60 2.60
611 A271 12.50k multi 4.50 4.50
a. Booklet pane of 8, 4 each #610-611 29.00 —
Complete booklet, #611a 29.00

See Nos. 632-633, 651-652.

Rosa Mollis — A272

2014, Feb. 26 Litho. *Perf. 12½x13*
612 A272 14.50k multi 5.50 5.50

Jellyfish — A273

Designs: 8k, Aurelia aurita. 15.50k, Cyanea capillata. 18.50k, Pelagia noctiluca. 26k, Beroe cucumis.

2014, Feb. 26 Litho. *Perf. 13*
613 A273 8k multi 3.00 3.00
614 A273 15.50k multi 5.75 5.75
615 A273 18.50k multi 6.75 6.75
616 A273 26k multi 9.75 9.75
Nos. 613-616 (4) 25.25 25.25

Souvenir Sheet

Legend of the Lady of Húsavik — A274

No. 617: a, Woman holding horn of Viking chief. b, Woman and nykur (mythical beast). c, Woman on throne.

2014, Feb. 26 Litho. *Perf. 13x13½*
617 A274 Sheet of 3 11.50 11.50
a.-c. 10k Any single 3.75 3.75

Souvenir Sheet

Ferry MS Norröna — A275

No. 618: a, Ship's stern. b, Ship's bow.

2014, Mar. 17 Litho. *Perf. 13x13¼*
618 A275 Sheet of 2 11.00 11.00
a.-b. 14.50k Either single 5.50 5.50

Europa A276

Designs: 14.50k, Faroese Symphony Orchestra. 19.50k, Bass players, vert.

2014, Apr. 28 Litho. *Perf. 13x13¼*
619 A276 14.50k multi 5.50 5.50

Perf. 13¼x13
620 A276 19.50k multi 7.25 7.25

Lighthouses — A277

Designs: 14.50k, Akraberg Lighthouse. 15.50k, Dímun Lighthouse. 17k, Toftir Lighthouse.

2014, Apr. 28 Litho. *Perf. 14*
621 A277 14.50k multi 5.50 5.50
622 A277 15.50k multi 5.75 5.75
623 A277 17k multi 6.50 6.50
Nos. 621-623 (3) 17.75 17.75

Booklet Stamps Self-Adhesive

Serpentine Die Cut 14
624 A277 14.50k multi 5.50 5.50
625 A277 15.50k multi 5.75 5.75
626 A277 17k multi 6.50 6.50
a. Booklet pane of 6, 2 each #624-626 36.00
Nos. 624-626 (3) 17.75 17.75

Prince Henrik, 80th Birthday A278

Perf. 13½x13¼
2014, June 11 Litho.
627 A278 14.50k multi 5.50 5.50

Booklet Stamp Self-Adhesive

Die Cut Perf. 13½x13¼
628 A278 14.50k multi 5.50 5.50
a. Booklet pane of 4 22.00

Roger Casement, Boats, Congolese Natives, and Daniel J. Danielsen — A279

Perf. 13¼x13½

2014, Sept. 24 **Litho.**

629	A279 25k multi	8.50	8.50

Danielsen (1871-1916), missionary to the Congo, and documenter of human rights abuses reported on in Casement's 1904 report to the British Government.

Captain Vilhelm Reinert-Joensen (1891-1949), Ships Used in D-Day Invasion — A280

Perf. 13¼x13½

2014, Sept. 24 **Litho.**

630	A280 26k multi	9.00	9.00

D-Day, 70th anniv.

Miniature Sheet

World War I, Cent. — A281

No. 631: a, Newspaper headlines, map of Europe, man in rowboat. b, Children, ration coupons, national leaders of the World War I combattants. c, Faroese boat attacked by German submarine, map of Faroe islands and British Isles. d, Map of Vimy Ridge, Faroese-Canadian soldier Christian L. Petersen, soldiers.

Perf. 13¼x13½

2014, Sept. 24 **Litho.**

631	A281 Sheet of 4	11.00	11.00
a.-d.	8k Any single	2.75	2.75
e.	Like #631, with "In Memoriam" and poppies added in red in sheet margin	9.50	9.50

Issued: No. 631e, 5/13/15.

Christmas Type of 2013

Designs: 8k, Angels. 14.50k, Shepherds.

2014, Sept. 24 **Litho.** *Perf. 12¾*

632	A271 8k multi	2.75	2.75
633	A271 14.50k multi	5.00	5.00
a.	Booklet pane of 8, 4 each #632-633	31.00	—
	Complete booklet, #633a	31.00	

Magna Carta, 800th Anniv. — A282

2015, Feb. 23 **Litho.** *Perf. 13½*

634	A282 24k multi	7.25	7.25

Woman Suffrage, Cent. A283

2015, Feb. 23 **Litho.** *Perf. 13x13¼*

635	A283 36k multi	11.00	11.00

Opening of New Terminal at Vagar Airport A284

Designs: 8.50k, Airplanes on ground. 15k, New terminal.

2015, Feb. 23 **Litho.** *Perf. 13x13¼*

636	A284 8.50k multi	2.60	2.60
637	A284 15k multi	4.50	4.50
a.	Booklet pane of 8, 4 each #636-637	28.50	—
	Complete booklet, #637a	28.50	

Miniature Sheet

1833 Expedition of George Clayton Atkinson to Faroe Islands — A285

No. 638 — Paintings by Thomas Miles Richarson of: a, Vatnmylla (watermill). b, Tórshavn. c, Waterfall on Vágar, Koltur and Hestur Islands. d, Trollkonufingur.

2015, Feb. 23 **Litho.** *Perf. 13x13¼*

638	A285 Sheet of 4	10.50	10.50
a.-d.	8.50k Any single	2.60	2.60

March 20, 2015 Total Solar Eclipse A286

Eclipse at: 17k, Right. 19k, Left.

2015, Mar. 11 **Litho.** *Perf. 12*

639	A286 17k multi	5.00	5.00
640	A286 19k multi	5.75	5.75
a.	Souvenir sheet of 2, #639-640	11.00	11.00

Booklet Stamps Self-Adhesive

Die Cut Perf. 11½

641	A286 17k multi	5.00	5.00
a.	Booklet pane of 4	20.00	
642	A286 19k multi	5.75	5.75
a.	Booklet pane of 4	23.00	

Faroe Islands Flag, 75th Anniv. — A287

Designs: 11k, Arne Vatnhamar holding Faroe Islands flag on Mt. Everest. 12k, Map and flag of Faroe Islands.

2015, Apr. 14 **Litho.** *Perf. 13½*

643	A287 11k multi	3.50	3.50
644	A287 12k multi	3.75	3.75

Europa — A288

Old toys: 17k, Rag doll. 22k, Hoop made of ram's horn.

2015, Apr. 14 **Litho.** *Perf. 13½*

645	A288 17k multi	5.25	5.25
646	A288 22k multi	6.75	6.75

Knitted Art by Randi Samsonsen — A289

2015, Sept. 28 **Litho.** *Perf. 13x12¾*

647	A289 17k multi	5.25	5.25

H. N. Jacobsen's Bookstore, 150th Anniv. A290

Designs: 17k, Bookstore exterior. 26k, Bookstore interior, book covers, bindery machinery.

2015, Sept. 28 **Litho.** *Perf. 12½*

648	A290 17k multi	5.25	5.25
649	A290 26k multi	8.00	8.00

Souvenir Sheet

Christian Artifacts of the Viking Era — A291

No. 650 — Inscriptions: a, Krossteinur úr Olansgardhi í Skúvoy (stone with crucifix from Olansgardhi). b, Botnur úr laggadhum traeílati (cross on wooden bucket bottom). c, Vadhsteinur vidh ihogdum St. Hanskrossi (stone fishing sinkers with St. Hans crucifix).

Litho. & Engr.

2015, Sept. 28 *Perf. 12¾x13*

650	A291 Sheet of 3	11.50	11.50
a.-c.	12k Any single	3.75	3.75

Christmas Type of 2013

Designs: 8.50k, Magi on camels. 17k, Holy Family fleeing to Egypt.

2015, Sept. 28 **Litho.** *Perf. 12¾*

651	A271 8.50k multi	2.60	2.60
652	A271 17k multi	5.25	5.25

FERNANDO PO

fər-ˈnan-ˌdō ˈpō

LOCATION — An island in the Gulf of Guinea off west Africa.
GOVT. — Former province of Spain
AREA — 800 sq. mi.
POP. — 62,612 (1960)
CAPITAL — Santa Isabel

Together with the islands of Elobey, Annobon and Corisco, Fernando Po came under the administration of Spanish Guinea. Postage stamps of Spanish Guinea were used until 1960.

The provinces of Fernando Po and Rio Muni united Oct. 12, 1968, to form the Republic of Equatorial Guinea.

100 Centimos = 1 Escudo = 2.50 Pesetas
100 Centimos = 1 Peseta
1000 Milesimas = 100 Centavos = 1 Peso (1882)

Catalogue values for unused stamps in this country are for Never Hinged items, beginning with Scott 181 in the regular postage section and Scott B1 in the semi-postal section.

Isabella II — A1

Alfonso XII — A2

1868 **Unwmk.** **Typo.** *Perf. 14*

1	A1	20c brown	450.00	140.00
a.		20c red brown	525.00	140.00

No. 1 is valued in the grade of fine, as illustrated. Examples with very fine centering are uncommon and sell for more.

Forgeries exist.

1879 **Centimos de Peseta**

2	A2	5c green	57.50	15.00
3	A2	10c rose	42.50	15.00
4	A2	50c blue	100.00	15.00
		Nos. 2-4 (3)	200.00	45.00

1882-89 **Centavos de Peso**

5	A2	1c green	9.50	5.50
6	A2	2c rose	18.00	8.75
7	A2	5c gray blue	60.00	12.00
8	A2	10c dk brown ('89)	82.50	6.75
		Nos. 5-8 (4)	170.00	33.00

Nos. 5-7 Handstamp Surcharged in Blue, Black or Violet — a

1884-95

9	A2	50c on 1c green ('95)	120.00	19.00
11	A2	50c on 2c rose	32.00	6.00
12	A2	50c on 5c blue ('87)	150.00	25.00
		Nos. 9-12 (3)	302.00	50.00

Values above are for examples surcharged in black. Stamps surcharged in violet or blue are worth about 25% more.

Inverted and double surcharges exist. No. 12 exists overprinted in carmine. Value $100.

King Alfonso XIII — A4

1894-97 *Perf. 14*

13	A4	⅛c slate ('96)	22.00	3.00
14	A4	2c rose ('96)	15.50	2.50
15	A4	5c blue grn ('97)	16.00	2.50
16	A4	6c dk violet ('96)	13.00	3.00
17	A4	10c blk vio ('94)	450.00	115.00

18	A4	10c lake ('95)	50.00	8.75
19	A4	10c org brn ('96)	10.50	2.50
20	A4	12½c dk brown ('96)	11.50	3.00
21	A4	20c slate bl ('96)	11.50	3.00
22	A4	25c claret ('96)	23.00	3.00
		Nos. 13-22 (10)	623.00	146.25

Most exist imperf. Value, set, pairs Nos. 13-16 and Nos. 18-22, $2,500.

Stamps of 1894-97 Handstamped in Blue, Black or Red

b

c

Type "b" Surcharge

1896-98

22A	A4	5c on ⅛c slate (Bl)	100.00	27.50
23	A4	5c on 2c rose (Bl)	50.00	16.50
23A	A4	5c on 6c dk vio (Bl)	180.00	45.00
24	A4	5c on 10c brn vio (Bl)	180.00	45.00
24A	A4	5c on 10c org brn (Bl)	180.00	45.00
24B	A4	5c on 10c dk brn (Bk)	67.50	27.50
25	A4	5c on 12½c brn (Bl)	37.50	13.00
a.		Black surcharge	37.50	13.00
25B	A4	5c on 20c sl bl (R)	180.00	45.00
25C	A4	5c on 25c claret (Bk)	180.00	35.00
		Nos. 22A-25C (9)	1,155.	299.50

Type "c" Surcharge

26	A4	5c on ⅛c slate (Bk)	32.50	6.75
27	A4	5c on 2c rose (Bl)	32.50	6.75
a.		Black surcharge	32.50	6.75
28	A4	5c on 5c green (R)	160.00	22.00
29	A4	5c on 6c dk vio (R)	23.00	14.00
a.		Violet surcharge	24.00	15.50
30	A4	5c on 10c org brn (Bk)	210.00	27.50
30A	A4	5c on 10c dk brn (Bk)	160.00	26.00
30B	A4	5c on 10c lake (Bl)	400.00	110.00
31	A4	5c on 12½c brn (R)	70.00	11.00
32	A4	5c on 20c sl bl (R)	40.00	10.50
33	A4	5c on 25c claret (Bk)	37.50	11.00
a.		Blue surcharge	37.50	13.50
		Nos. 26-33 (10)	1,165.	245.50

Exist surcharged in other colors.

Type "a" Srch. in Blue or Black

1898-99

34	A4	50c on 2c rose	92.50	11.50
35	A4	50c on 10c brn vio	220.00	33.00
36	A4	50c on 10c lake	230.00	33.00
37	A4	50c on 10c org brn	220.00	33.00
38	A4	50c on 12½c brn (Bk)	190.00	22.00

The "a" surch. also exists on ⅛c, 5c & 25c. Values, $325, $225 and $210, respectively.

Revenue Stamps Privately Handstamped in Blue

Arms

A5 A6

1897-98 ***Imperf.***

39	A5	5c on 10c rose	28.00	12.50
40	A6	10c rose	24.00	11.00

Revenue Stamps Handstamped in Black or Red

A7

A8

A9

Arms — A9a

1899 ***Imperf.***

41	A7	15c on 10c green	45.00	23.00
a.		Blue surcharge, vertical	39.00	21.00
42	A8	10c on 25c green	120.00	65.00
43	A9	15c on 25c green	190.00	120.00
43A	A9a	15c on 25c green (R)	*1,800.*	*1,100.*
b.		Black surcharge	*1,800.*	*1,100.*

Surcharge on No. 41 is either horizontal, inverted or vertical.

On No. 42 "CORREOS" is ovptd. in red.

On Nos. 43A and 43Ab, the signature is always in black.

King Alfonso XIII — A10

Double-lined shaded letters at sides.

1899 ***Perf. 14***

44	A10	1m orange brn	2.40	.45
45	A10	2m orange brn	2.40	.45
46	A10	3m orange brn	2.40	.45
47	A10	4m orange brn	2.40	.45
48	A10	5m orange brn	2.40	.45
49	A10	1c black vio	2.40	.45
50	A10	2c dk blue grn	2.40	.45
51	A10	3c dk brown	2.40	.45
52	A10	4c orange	13.00	1.10
53	A10	5c carmine rose	2.50	.45
54	A10	6c dark blue	2.50	.45
55	A10	8c gray brn	8.00	.45
56	A10	10c vermilion	5.25	.45
57	A10	15c slate grn	5.25	.45
58	A10	20c maroon	14.50	1.10
59	A10	40c violet	100.00	19.00
60	A10	60c black	100.00	19.00
61	A10	80c red brown	100.00	19.00
62	A10	1p yellow grn	325.00	92.50
63	A10	2p slate blue	325.00	95.00
		Nos. 44-63 (20)	1,020.	252.55

Nos. 44-63 exist imperf. Value for set, $3,500.

See Nos. 66-85. For surcharges see Nos. 64-65, 88-88B.

1900 **Surcharged type "a"**

64	A10	50c on 20c maroon	16.00	2.50
a.		Blue surcharge	32.00	4.75

Surcharged type "b"

64B	A10	5c on 20c maroon	300.00	40.00

Surcharged type "c"

65	A10	5c on 20c maroon	9.50	2.40
		Nos. 64-65 (3)	325.50	44.90

1900 **Dated "1900"**

Solid letters at sides.

66	A10	1m black	3.00	.50
67	A10	2m black	3.00	.50
68	A10	3m black	3.00	.50
69	A10	4m black	3.00	.50
70	A10	5m black	3.00	.50
71	A10	1c green	3.00	.50
72	A10	2c violet	3.00	.50
73	A10	3c rose	3.00	.50
74	A10	4c black brn	3.00	.50
75	A10	5c blue	3.00	.50
76	A10	6c orange	3.00	.50
77	A10	8c bronze grn	3.00	.50
78	A10	10c claret	3.00	.50
79	A10	15c dk violet	3.00	.50
80	A10	20c olive brn	3.00	.50
81	A10	40c brown	7.75	2.25
82	A10	60c green	16.50	2.50
83	A10	80c dark blue	17.50	3.75
84	A10	1p red brown	110.00	30.00
85	A10	2p orange	190.00	62.50
		Nos. 66-85 (20)	386.75	108.50
		Set, never hinged	750.00	

Nos. 66-85 exist imperf. Value, set *$3,000.*

Revenue Stamps Overprinted or Surcharged with Handstamp in Red or Black

A11

A12

1900 ***Imperf.***

86	A11	10c blue (R)	37.50	17.50
87	A12	5c on 10c blue	100.00	40.00
		Set, never hinged	175.00	

Nos. 52 and 80 Surcharged type "a" in Violet or Black

1900

88	A10	50c on 4c orange (V)	14.00	4.00
a.		Green surcharge	22.50	12.00
88B	A10	50c on 20c ol brn	14.00	3.50
		Set, never hinged	37.50	

A13

A14

1901 ***Perf. 14***

89	A13	1c black	3.00	.90
90	A13	2c orange brn	3.00	.90
91	A13	3c dk violet	3.00	.90
92	A13	4c lt violet	3.00	.90
93	A13	5c orange red	1.75	.90
94	A13	10c violet brn	1.75	.90
95	A13	25c dp blue	1.75	.90
96	A13	50c claret	3.00	.90
97	A13	75c dk brown	2.25	.90
98	A13	1p blue grn	67.50	7.50
99	A13	2p red brown	42.50	10.00
100	A13	3p olive grn	42.50	14.00
101	A13	4p dull red	42.50	14.00
102	A13	5p dk green	52.50	14.00
103	A13	10p buff	125.00	40.00
		Nos. 89-103 (15)	395.00	107.60
		Set, never hinged	850.00	

Dated "1902"

1902 **Control Numbers on Back**

104	A13	5c dk green	2.60	.45
105	A13	10c slate	2.90	.50
106	A13	25c claret	6.25	1.00
107	A13	50c violet brn	15.00	3.25
108	A13	75c lt violet	15.00	3.25
109	A13	1p car rose	18.50	4.00
110	A13	2p olive grn	40.00	9.50
111	A13	5p orange red	57.50	20.00
		Nos. 104-111 (8)	157.75	41.95
		Set, never hinged	250.00	

Exist imperf. Value for set, *$1,500.*

Dated "1903"

1903 ***Perf. 14***

Control Numbers on Back

112	A14	¼c dk violet	.45	.25
113	A14	½c black	.45	.25
114	A14	1c scarlet	.45	.25
115	A14	2c dk green	.45	.30
116	A14	3c blue grn	.45	.30
117	A14	4c violet	.45	.30
118	A14	5c rose lake	.50	.30
119	A14	10c orange buff	.60	.45
120	A14	15c blue green	2.50	1.00
121	A14	25c red brown	2.75	1.25
122	A14	50c black brn	4.50	2.00
123	A14	75c carmine	16.50	3.50
124	A14	1p dk brown	25.00	6.00
125	A14	2p dk olive grn	32.50	7.50
126	A14	3p claret	32.50	7.50
127	A14	4p dark blue	40.00	12.50
128	A14	5p dp dull blue	60.00	16.00
129	A14	10p dull red	130.00	27.50
		Nos. 112-129 (18)	350.05	87.15
		Set, never hinged	600.00	

Dated "1905"

1905 **Control Numbers on Back**

136	A14	1c dp violet	.40	.30
137	A14	2c black	.40	.30
138	A14	3c vermilion	.40	.30
139	A14	4c dp green	.40	.30
140	A14	5c blue grn	.45	.35
141	A14	10c violet	1.60	.75
142	A14	15c car lake	1.60	.75
143	A14	25c orange buff	12.50	2.25
144	A14	50c green	8.00	2.75
145	A14	75c red brown	11.00	7.50
146	A14	1p dp gray brn	12.50	7.50
147	A14	2p carmine	20.00	12.50
148	A14	3p deep brown	32.50	14.00
149	A14	4p bronze grn	40.00	18.00
150	A14	5p claret	62.50	25.00
151	A14	10p deep blue	90.00	35.00
		Nos. 136-151 (16)	294.25	127.55
		Set, never hinged	525.00	

King Alfonso XIII — A15

1907 **Control Numbers on Back**

152	A15	1c blue black	.30	.25
153	A15	2c car rose	.30	.25
154	A15	3c dp violet	.40	.25
155	A15	4c black	.40	.25
156	A15	5c orange buff	.40	.25
157	A15	10c maroon	2.00	.80
158	A15	15c bronze grn	.55	.35
159	A15	25c dk brown	65.00	15.00
160	A15	50c blue green	.45	.30
161	A15	75c vermilion	.45	.30
162	A15	1p dull blue	3.00	.60
163	A15	2p brown	11.00	4.00
164	A15	3p lake	11.00	4.00
165	A15	4p violet	11.00	4.00
166	A15	5p black brn	11.00	4.00
167	A15	10p orange brn	11.00	4.00
		Nos. 152-167 (16)	128.25	38.60
		Set, never hinged	350.00	

No. 157 Handstamp Surcharged in Black, Blue or Red

1908

168	A15	5c on 10c mar (Bk)	2.75	2.00
a.		Blue surcharge	10.00	5.50
b.		Red surcharge	30.00	10.00
169	A15	25c on 10c mar (Bk)	60.00	20.00
		Set, never hinged	77.50	

The surcharge on Nos. 168-169 exist inverted, double, etc. The surcharge also exists on other stamps.

Seville-Barcelona Issue of Spain, 1929, Overprinted in Blue or Red

1929 ***Perf. 11***

170	A52	5c rose lake	.25	.25
171	A53	10c green (R)	.25	.25
a.		Perf. 14	.65	.65
172	A50	15c Prus bl (R)	.25	.25
173	A51	20c purple (R)	.25	.25
174	A50	25c brt rose	.25	.25
175	A52	30c black brn	.25	.25
176	A53	40c dk blue (R)	.70	.70
177	A51	50c dp orange	1.50	1.50
178	A52	1p blue blk (R)	5.75	5.75
179	A53	4p deep rose	27.50	27.50
180	A53	10p brown	35.00	35.00
		Nos. 170-180 (11)	71.95	71.95
		Set, never hinged	135.00	

Catalogue values for unused stamps in this section, from this point to the end of the section, are for Never Hinged items.

Virgin Mary — A16

1960 Unwmk. Photo. ***Perf. 13x12½***

181	A16	25c dull gray vio	.50	.25
182	A16	50c brown olive	.50	.25
183	A16	75c violet brn	.50	.25
184	A16	1p orange ver	.50	.25
185	A16	1.50p lt blue grn	.50	.25
186	A16	2p red lilac	.50	.25
187	A16	3p dark blue	5.00	.80
188	A16	5p lt red brn	.75	.25
189	A16	10p lt olive grn	.90	.30
		Nos. 181-189 (9)	9.65	2.85

Tricorn and Windmill from "The Three-Cornered Hat" by Falla — A17

Manuel de Falla A18

1960 ***Perf. 13x12½, 12½x13***

190	A17	35c slate green	.60	.60
191	A18	80c Prus green	.70	.70

Issued to honor Manuel de Falla (1876-1946), Spanish composer.

See Nos. B1-B2.

Map of Fernando Po — A19

General Franco A20

Designs: 70c, Santa Isabel Cathedral.

Perf. 13x12½, 12½x13

1961, Oct. 1 Photo. Unwmk.

192	A19	25c gray violet	.35	.35
193	A20	50c olive brown	.35	.35
194	A19	70c brt green	.40	.40
195	A20	1p red orange	.45	.45
		Nos. 192-195 (4)	1.55	1.55

25th anniv. of the nomination of Gen. Francisco Franco as Chief of State.

Ocean Liner A21

Design: 50c, S.S. San Francisco.

1962, July 10 ***Perf. 12½x13***

196	A21	25c dull violet	.30	.30
197	A21	50c gray olive	.35	.35
198	A21	1p orange brn	.35	.35
		Nos. 196-198 (3)	1.00	1.00

Mailman — A22

Mail Transport Symbols A23

Perf. 13x12½, 12½x13

1962, Nov. 23 Unwmk.

199	A22	15c dark green	.30	.30
200	A23	35c lilac rose	.35	.35
201	A22	1p brown	.35	.35
		Nos. 199-201 (3)	1.00	1.00

Issued for Stamp Day.

Fetish — A24

1963, Jan. 29 ***Perf. 13x12½***

202	A24	50c olive gray	.30	.30
203	A24	1p deep magenta	.35	.35

Issued to help victims of the Seville flood.

Nuns A25

Design: 50c, Nun and child, vert.

Perf. 12½x13, 13x12½

1963, July 6 Photo. Unwmk.

204	A25	25c bright lilac	.30	.30
205	A25	50c dull green	.35	.35
206	A25	1p red orange	.35	.35
		Nos. 204-206 (3)	1.00	1.00

Issued for child welfare.

Child and Arms A26

1963, July 12 ***Perf. 12½x13***

207	A26	50c brown olive	.30	.30
208	A26	1p carmine rose	.35	.35

Issued for Barcelona flood relief.

Governor Chacon A27

Orange Blossoms — A28

1964, Mar. 6 ***Perf. 12½x13, 13x12½***

209	A27	25c violet black	.30	.30
210	A28	50c dark olive	.35	.35
211	A27	1p brown red	.35	.35
		Nos. 209-211 (3)	1.00	1.00

Issued for Stamp Day 1963.

Men in Dugout Canoe — A29

Design: 50c, Pineapple.

1964, June 1 Photo. ***Perf. 13x12½***

212	A29	25c purple	.30	.30
213	A28	50c dull olive	.35	.35
214	A29	1p deep claret	.35	.35
		Nos. 212-214 (3)	1.00	1.00

Issued for child welfare.

Ring-necked Francolin — A30

Designs: 15c, 70c, 3p, Ring-necked francolin. 25c, 1p, 5p, Two mallards. 50c, 1.50p, 10p, Head of great blue touraco.

1964, July 1

215	A30	15c chestnut	.35	.30
216	A30	25c dull violet	.35	.30
217	A30	50c dk olive grn	.35	.30
218	A30	70c green	.35	.30
219	A30	1p brown orange	.40	.30
220	A30	1.50p grnsh blue	.45	.35
221	A30	3p violet blue	.75	.35
222	A30	5p dull purple	1.75	.40
223	A30	10p bright green	2.75	1.00
		Nos. 215-223 (9)	7.50	3.60

The Three Kings A31

Designs: 50c, 1.50p, Caspar, vert.

Perf. 13x12½, 12½x13

1964, Nov. 23 Unwmk.

224	A31	50c green	.35	.35
225	A31	1p orange ver	.40	.35
226	A31	1.50p deep green	.45	.35
227	A31	3p ultra	1.75	1.40
		Nos. 224-227 (4)	2.95	2.45

Issued for Stamp Day, 1964.

Boy — A32

Woman Fruit Picker — A33

1.50p, Girl learning to write, and church.

1964, Mar. 1 Photo. ***Perf. 13x12½***

228	A32	50c indigo	.30	.30
229	A33	1p dark red	.35	.30
230	A33	1.50p grnsh blue	.40	.35
		Nos. 228-230 (3)	1.05	.95

Issued to commemorate 25 years of peace.

Plectrocnemia Cruciata — A34

Design: 1p, Metopodontus savagei, horiz.

Perf. 13x12½, 12½x13

1965, June 1 Photo. Unwmk.

231	A34	50c slate green	.45	.35
232	A34	1p rose red	.45	.35
233	A34	1.50p Prus blue	.45	.35
		Nos. 231-233 (3)	1.35	1.05

Issued for child welfare.

Pole Vault A35

Arms of Fernando Po — A36

Perf. 12½x13, 13x12½

1965, Nov. 23 Photo. Unwmk.

234	A35	50c yellow green	.30	.30
235	A36	1p brt org brn	.35	.30
236	A35	1.50p brt blue	.40	.35
		Nos. 234-236 (3)	1.05	.95

Issued for Stamp Day, 1965.

Children Reading A37

1.50p, St. Elizabeth of Hungary, vert.

Perf. 12½x13, 13x12½

1966, June 1 Photo. Unwmk.

237	A37	50c dark green	.30	.30
238	A37	1p brown red	.35	.30
239	A37	1.50p dark blue	.35	.35
		Nos. 237-239 (3)	1.00	.95

Issued for child welfare.

White-nosed Monkey — A38

Stamp Day: 40c, 4p, Head of moustached monkey, vert.

1966, Nov. 23 Photo. *Perf. 13*

240	A38	10c dk blue & yel	.35	.30
241	A38	40c lt brn, bl & blk	.40	.30
242	A38	1.50p ol bis, brn org & blk	.45	.40
243	A38	4p sl grn, brn org & blk	.55	.45
		Nos. 240-243 (4)	1.75	1.45

Flowers — A39

Designs: 40c, 4p, Six flowers.

1967, June 1 Photo. *Perf. 13*

244	A39	10c brt car & pale grn	.30	.30
245	A39	40c red brn & org	.35	.30
246	A39	1.50p red lil & lt red brn	.40	.35
247	A39	4p dk blue & lt grn	.45	.40
		Nos. 244-247 (4)	1.50	1.35

Issued for child welfare.

Linsang — A40

Stamp Day: 1.50p, Needle-clawed galago, vert. 3.50p, Fraser's scaly-tailed flying squirrel.

1967, Nov. 23 Photo. *Perf. 13*

248	A40	1p black & bister	.35	.30
249	A40	1.50p brown & olive	.40	.35
250	A40	3.50p rose lake & dl grn	.50	.40
		Nos. 248-250 (3)	1.25	1.05

Stamp of 1868, No. 1, and Arms of San Carlos A41

Fernando Po No. 1 and; 1.50p, Arms of Santa Isabel. 2.50p, Arms of Fernando Po.

1968, Feb. 4 Photo. *Perf. 13*

251	A41	1p brt plum & brn org	.30	.30
252	A41	1.50p dp blue & brn org	.40	.30
253	A41	2.50p brn & brn org	.50	.40
		Nos. 251-253 (3)	1.20	1.00

Centenary of the first postage stamp.

Signs of the Zodiac — A42

1968, Apr. 25 Photo. *Perf. 13*

254	A42	1p Libra	.30	.30
255	A42	1.50p Leo	.40	.35
256	A42	2.50p Aquarius	.50	.40
		Nos. 254-256 (3)	1.20	1.05

Issued for child welfare.

SEMI-POSTAL STAMPS

Catalogue values for unused stamps in this section are for Never Hinged items.

Types of Regular Issue, 1960

Designs: 10c+5c, Manuel de Falla. 15c+5c, Dancers from "Love, the Magician."

Perf. 12½x13, 13x12½

1960 Photo. Unwmk.

B1	A18	10c + 5c maroon	.35	.30
B2	A17	15c + 5c dk brn & bister	.35	.35

The surtax was for child welfare.

Whale SP1

Design: Nos. B4, B6, Harpooning whale.

1961 *Perf. 12½x13*

B3	SP1	10c + 5c rose brown	.35	.30
B4	SP1	20c + 5c dk slate grn	.35	.30
B5	SP1	30c + 10c olive brn	.40	.30
B6	SP1	50c + 20c dark brn	.45	.30
		Nos. B3-B6 (4)	1.55	1.20

Issued for Stamp Day, 1960.

Hand Blessing Woman — SP2

Design: 25c+10c, Boy making sign of the cross, and crucifix.

1961, June 21 *Perf. 13x12½*

B7	SP2	10c + 5c rose brn	.40	.30
B8	SP2	25c + 10c gray vio	.40	.30
B9	SP2	80c + 20c dk grn	.50	.35
		Nos. B7-B9 (3)	1.30	.95

The surtax was for child welfare.

Ethiopian Tortoise SP3

Stamp Day: 25c+10c, 1p+10c, Native carriers, palms and shore.

1961, Nov. 23 *Perf. 12½x13*

B10	SP3	10c + 5c rose red	.35	.30
B11	SP3	25c + 10c dk pur	.40	.30
B12	SP3	30c + 10c vio brn	.40	.30
B13	SP3	1p + 10c red org	.50	.40
		Nos. B10-B13 (4)	1.65	1.30

FIJI

'fē-,jē

LOCATION — Group of 332 islands (106 inhabited) in the South Pacific Ocean east of Vanuatu
GOVT. — Independent nation in British Commonwealth
AREA — 7,078 sq. mi.
POP. — 812,918 (1999 est.)
CAPITAL — Suva

A British colony since 1874, Fiji became fully independent in 1970.

12 Pence = 1 Shilling
20 Shillings = 1 Pound
100 Cents = 1 Dollar (1872-74, 1969)

Syncopated Perforations

Type A (1st stamp #873): On shorter sides, the seventh hole from the larger side is an oval hole equal in width to three holes.

Catalogue values for unused stamps in this country are for Never Hinged items, beginning with Scott 137 in the regular postage section and Scott B1 in the semi-postal section.

Values for unused stamps are for examples with original gum as defined in the catalogue introduction except for Nos. 1-10 which are valued without gum. Additionally, Nos. 1-10 are valued with roulettes showing on two or more sides, but expect small faults that do not detract from the appearance of the stamps. Very few examples of Nos. 1-10 will be found free of faults, and these will command substantial premiums.

Watermark

Wmk. 17 — FIJI POSTAGE Across Center Row of Sheet

A1

1870 Unwmk. Typeset *Rouletted*
Thin Quadrille Paper

1	A1	1p black, *pink*	4,500.	4,750.
2	A1	3p black, *pink*	5,500.	5,000.
a.		Comma after "EXPRESS"	*8,000.*	*8,000.*
3	A1	6p black, *pink*	2,750.	2,750.
5	A1	1sh black, *pink*	2,250.	2,500.

1871 Thin Vertically Laid Paper

6	A1	1p black, *pink*	1,150.	2,100.
7	A1	3p black, *pink*	1,900.	3,400.
8	A1	6p black, *pink*	1,600.	2,100.
9	A1	9p black, *pink*	3,400.	4,000.
10	A1	1sh black, *pink*	1,900.	1,900.

This service was established by the *Fiji Times*, a weekly newspaper, for the delivery of the newspaper. Since there was no postal service to the other islands, delivery of letters to agents of the newspaper on the islands was offered to the public.

Nos. 1-5 were printed in the same sheet, one horizontal row of 6 of each (6p, 1sh, 1p, 3p). Nos. 6-10 were printed from the same plate with three 9p replacing three 3p.

Most used examples have pen cancels.

Up to three sets of imitations exist. One on pink laid paper, pin-perforated, measuring 22½x16mm. Originals measure 22½x18½mm. A later printing was made on pink wove paper. Forgeries also exist plus fake cancellations.

Crown and "CR" (Cakobau Rex)

A2 A3

A4

1871 Typo. Wmk. 17 *Perf. 12½*
Wove Paper

15	A2	1p blue	62.50	140.00
16	A3	3p green	125.00	400.00
17	A4	6p rose	170.00	325.00
		Nos. 15-17 (3)	357.50	865.00

Sheets of 50 (10x5).

For overprints and surcharges see Nos. 18-39.

Stamps of 1871 Surcharged in Black

1872, Jan. 13

18	A2	2c on 1p blue	60.00	*65.00*
19	A3	6c on 3p green	90.00	90.00
20	A4	12c on 6p rose	125.00	90.00
		Nos. 18-20 (3)	275.00	245.00

Nos. 18-20 with Additional Overprint In Black

b

c

1874, Oct. 10

21	A2(b) 2c on 1p blue	1,250.	315.00
a.	No period after "R"	3,250.	1,150.
22	A2(c) 2c on 1p blue	1,150.	300.00
a.	Invtd. "A" instead of "V"	3,250.	1,500.
b.	Period after "R" is a Maltese Cross	3,250.	1,500.
c.	No period after "R"	3,250.	1,500.
d.	Round raised period after "V"	3,250.	1,500.
e.	Round raised period after "V" and "R"	3,250.	1,500.
23	A3(b) 6c on 3p green	3,250.	1,000.
a.	No period after "R"	5,500.	2,000.
24	A3(c) 6c on 3p green	2,750.	750.00
a.	Inverted "A"	2,100.	1,900.
b.	Period after "R" is a Maltese Cross	5,250.	2,000.
c.	No period after "R"	5,500.	2,000.
d.	Round raised period after "V"	5,500.	2,000.
e.	Round raised period after "V" and "R"	5,500.	2,000.
25	A4(b) 12c on 6p rose	1,050.	260.00
a.	"V.R." inverted	7,500.	
b.	No period after "R"	3,000.	1,150.
26	A4(c) 12c on 6p rose	1,000.	250.00
a.	Inverted "A"	2,900.	1,350.
b.	Period after "R" is a Maltese Cross	3,000.	1,350.
c.	"V.R." inverted	—	7,000.
d.	No period after "R"	3,000.	1,350.
e.	Round raised period after "V"	3,000.	1,350.
f.	Round raised period after "V" and "R"	3,000.	1,350.

Types "b" and "c" were in the same sheet.

Nos. 23-26 with Additional Surcharge in Black or Red

1875

No.	Type	Description	Unused	Used
27	A3(b)	2p on 6c on 3p	2,750.	800.00
a.		Period btwn. "2" and "d"	4,500.	1,600.
b.		"V.R." double	5,000.	4,500.
c.		No period after "R"	4,500.	1,600.
28	A3(b)	2p on 6c on 3p (R)	900.00	325.00
a.		Period btwn. "2" and "d"	2,250.	850.00
b.		No period after "R"	2,250.	900.00
29	A3(c)	2p on 6c on 3p	1,900.	600.00
a.		Inverted "A"	4,500.	1,600.
b.		Period after "R" is a Maltese Cross	4,500.	1,600.
c.		No period after "2d"	4,500.	1,600.
d.		No period after "R"	2,250.	900.00
e.		Round raised period after "V"	4,500.	1,600.
f.		Round raised period after "V" and "R"	4,500.	1,600.
30	A3(c)	2p on 6c on 3p (R)	750.00	250.00
a.		Inverted "A"	2,100.	850.00
b.		Period after "R" is a Maltese Cross	2,250.	875.00
c.		No period after "2d"	2,250.	875.00
d.		No period after "R"	2,250.	875.00
e.		Round raised period after "V"	2,250.	875.00
f.		Round raised period after "V" and "R"	2,250.	875.00
31	A4(b)	2p on 12c on 6p	3,250.	1,000.
a.		Period btwn. "2" and "d"		
b.		No period after "2d"		
c.		"2d, VR" double		5,500.
32	A4(c)	2p on 12c on 6p	3,000.	900.00
a.		Inverted "A"	4,500.	1,400.
b.		No period after "2d"		
c.		"2d, VR" double		5,500.
d.		Round raised period after "R"	—	1,200.
e.		Round raised period after "R"	—	1,200.
f.		As "a," with raised period after "V"	3,000.	1,000.

Types of 1871 Overprinted or Surcharged in Black

e

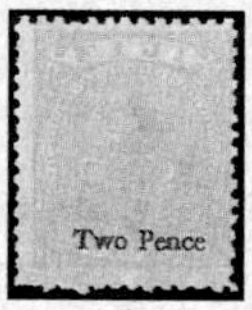

f

1876, Jan. 31 **Unwmk.**

Wove Paper

No.	Type	Description	Unused	Used
33	A2(e)	1p ultramarine	60.00	60.00
a.		Inverted surcharge		
b.		Dbl. impression of stamp	1,000.	
c.		Horiz. pair, imperf vert.	1,000.	
34	A3(e+f)	2p on 3p dk grn	60.00	*65.00*
a.		Dbl. surch. "Two Pence"		
35	A4(e)	6p rose	70.00	65.00
b.		Surcharge inverted		
c.		Dbl. impression of stamp	2,850.	
		Nos. 33-35 (3)	190.00	190.00

1877 **Laid Paper**

No.	Type	Description	Unused	Used
36	A2(e)	1p ultramarine	30.00	*50.00*
a.		Horiz. pair, imperf. vert.	1,100.	
37	A3(e+f)	2p on 3p dk grn	80.00	*85.00*
38	A3(e+f)	4p on 3p lilac	110.00	27.50
a.		Horiz. pair, imperf. vert.	1,000.	
39	A4(e)	6p rose	60.00	37.50
a.		Horiz. pair, imperf. vert.	800.00	
		Nos. 36-39 (4)	280.00	200.00

Many of the preceding stamps are known imperforate. They are printer's waste and were never issued.

A12

A13

Queen Victoria

A14 A15

Perf. 10-13½ & Compound

1878-90 **Wove Paper** **Typo.**

No.	Type	Description	Unused	Used
40	A12	1p ultra ('79)	17.50	17.50
a.		1p blue	65.00	6.50
41	A12	2p green	32.50	1.75
b.		2p ultramarine (error)	*40,000.*	
42	A12	4p brt vio ('90)	14.00	9.00
a.		4p mauve	27.50	12.00
43	A13	6p brt rose ('80)	14.00	4.75
a.		Printed on both sides	2,500.	2,000.
44	A14	1sh yel brn ('81)	60.00	12.50
a.		1sh deep brown	100.00	32.50

Litho. & Typo.

No.	Type	Description	Unused	Used
45	A15	5sh blk & red brn ('82)	75.00	50.00
		Nos. 40-45 (6)	213.00	95.50

Official facsimiles of the 5sh were officially made in 1900, differing in shades and detail of design from No. 45. They exist imperf., perf. 10 and 12; are all canceled "SUVA" and usually dated "15 Dec., 00."

No. 41b was not put on sale. All examples were supposed to be destroyed.

For surcharges see Nos. 46-52.

1881-90 ***Perf. 10***

No.	Type	Description	Unused	Used
40d	A12	1p ultramarine	27.50	3.50

Surcharged type "f" in Black

1878-90 **Typo.**

No.	Type	Description	Unused	Used
46	A12	2p on 3p green	12.00	*35.00*
47	A12	4p on 1p vio ('90)	75.00	60.00
48	A12	4p on 2p lilac ('83)	100.00	16.00
		Nos. 46-48 (3)	187.00	111.00

Nos. 40-43 Surcharged in Black

g

h

j

k

1891-92 ***Perf. 10***

No.	Type	Description	Unused	Used
49	A12(g)	½p on 1p ('92)	62.50	*80.00*
50	A12(h)	2½p on 2p	52.50	*55.00*
a.		Wider space (2mm) between "2" and "½"	150.00	*150.00*
51	A12(j)	5p on 4p ('92)	62.50	*80.00*
52	A13(k)	5p on 6p ('92)	67.50	*75.00*
a.		"FIVE" and "PENCE" 3mm apart	75.00	*85.00*
		Nos. 49-52 (4)	245.00	*290.00*

A18

A20

Fijian Canoe — A19

1891-96 ***Perf. 10-12 & Compound***

No.	Type	Description	Unused	Used
53	A18	½p grnsh blk ('92)	2.75	7.00
a.		½p gray	3.75	7.00
54	A19	1p black ('93)	14.00	7.50
55	A19	1p lilac rose ('96)	16.00	1.10
56	A19	2p green ('93)	9.00	.85
a.		Perf. 10x12 ('94)	800.00	425.00
57	A20	2½ red brown	6.50	5.50
58	A19	5p ultra ('93)	20.00	8.00
		Nos. 53-58 (6)	68.25	29.95

Edward VII — A22

1903, Feb. 1 **Wmk. 2** ***Perf. 14***

No.	Type	Description	Unused	Used
59	A22	½p gray grn & pale grn	2.75	2.25
60	A22	1p vio & blk, *red*	18.00	.65
61	A22	2p vio & orange	4.50	1.40
62	A22	2½p vio & ultra, *bl*	15.00	3.50
63	A22	3p vio & red vio	1.60	*4.00*
64	A22	4p violet & blk	1.60	*2.75*
65	A22	5p vio & green	1.60	*2.75*
66	A22	6p vio & car rose	1.60	*2.00*
67	A22	1sh grn & car rose	15.00	*77.50*
68	A22	5sh green & blk	85.00	*170.00*
69	A22	£1 gray & ultra	400.00	*475.00*
		Revenue cancel		75.00
		Nos. 59-68 (10)	146.65	*266.80*

Numerals of 2p, 4p, 6p and 5sh of type A22 are in color on plain tablet.

1904-12 **Ordinary Paper** **Wmk. 3**

No.	Type	Description	Unused	Used
70	A22	½p grn & pale grn ('04)	16.50	3.25
70A	A22	½p green ('08)	15.00	3.50
71	A22	1p vio & black, *red* ('04)	32.50	.25
72	A22	1p carmine ('06)	16.50	.25
73	A22	2½p ultra ('10)	6.75	*7.75*

Chalky Paper

No.	Type	Description	Unused	Used
74	A22	6p violet ('10)	28.00	*45.00*
75	A22	1sh grn & car rose ('09)	32.50	*42.50*
76	A22	1sh black, *green* ('11)	9.50	*14.00*
77	A22	5sh grn & scarlet, *yel* ('11)	72.50	*105.00*
78	A22	£1 vio & black, *red* ('12)	360.00	300.00
		Nos. 70-77 (9)	229.75	*221.50*

George V — A23

Die I

For description of Dies I and II see "Dies of British Colonial Stamps" in Table of Contents.

1912-23 **Ordinary Paper**

No.	Type	Description	Unused	Used
79	A23	¼p brown ('16)	2.75	.40
80	A23	½p green	2.75	1.10
81	A23	1p scarlet	2.75	.50
a.		1p carmine ('16)	2.25	.25
82	A23	2p gray ('14)	2.00	.25
83	A23	2½p ultra ('14)	3.50	3.75
84	A23	3p violet, *yel*	4.50	*9.00*
a.		Die II ('21)	3.25	*32.00*
85	A23	4p black & red, *yel* ('14)	24.00	*22.50*
a.		Die II ('23)	3.25	*35.00*

Chalky Paper

No.	Type	Description	Unused	Used
86	A23	5p dl vio & ol grn ('14)	5.50	*12.50*
87	A23	6p dl vio & red vio ('14)	2.40	*6.00*
88	A23	1sh black, *green*	1.30	*14.50*
a.		1sh black, *blue green*, ol back	3.25	*11.00*
b.		1sh black, *emerald* ('21)	5.50	*67.50*
c.		Die II ('22)	3.25	*37.50*
89	A23	2sh 6p black & red, *blue*	37.50	*35.00*
90	A23	5sh grn & scar, *yellow*	37.50	*45.00*
91	A23	£1 vio & black, *red*	300.00	325.00
a.		Die II ('21)	300.00	325.00
		Revenue cancel		52.50

Surface-colored Paper

No.	Type	Description	Unused	Used
92	A23	1sh black, *green*	1.25	*14.50*
		Nos. 79-90,92 (13)	127.70	*165.00*

Numerals of ¼p, 1½p, 2p, 4p, 6p, 2sh, 2sh6p and 5sh of type A23 are in color on plain tablet.

For overprints see Nos. MR1-MR2.

Die II

1922-27 **Wmk. 4** **Ordinary Paper**

No.	Type	Description	Unused	Used
93	A23	¼p dark brown	3.75	*27.50*
94	A23	½p green	.85	*1.50*
95	A23	1p rose red	5.00	1.00
96	A23	1p violet ('27)	1.40	.25
97	A23	1½p rose red ('27)	4.50	1.50
98	A23	2p gray	1.40	.25
a.		"2d" and value tablet omitted	28,000.	
99	A23	3p ultra ('23)	3.00	1.20
100	A23	4p blk & red, *yel*	14.00	7.00
101	A23	5p dl vio & ol green	1.75	*2.25*
102	A23	6p dl vio & red violet	2.40	1.50

Chalky Paper

No.	Type	Description	Unused	Used
103	A23	1sh blk, *emerald*	11.00	4.00
104	A23	2sh vio & ultra, *bl* ('27)	30.00	*72.50*
105	A23	2sh6p blk & red, *bl*	12.50	*35.00*
106	A23	5sh grn & scar, *yellow*	47.50	*90.00*
		Nos. 93-106 (14)	139.05	*245.45*

The only known example of No. 98a is the center stamp of an unused block of nine.

Common Design Types pictured following the introduction.

Silver Jubilee Issue

Common Design Type

1935, May 6 ***Perf. 13½x14***

No.	Type	Description	Unused	Used
110	CD301	1½p carmine & blue	1.00	*9.00*
111	CD301	2p gray blk & ultra	1.50	.50
112	CD301	3p blue & brown	2.75	*4.50*
113	CD301	1sh brt vio & indigo	10.00	*15.00*
		Nos. 110-113 (4)	15.25	29.00
		Set, never hinged	24.00	

Coronation Issue

Common Design Type

1937, May 12 ***Perf. 11x11½***

No.	Type	Description	Unused	Used
114	CD302	1p dark violet	.45	1.25
115	CD302	2p gray black	.45	*2.25*
116	CD302	3p indigo	.45	*2.25*
		Nos. 114-116 (3)	1.35	5.75
		Set, never hinged	2.00	

Outrigger Canoe — A24

Fijian Village — A25

Outrigger Canoe A26

Map of Fiji Islands A27

Canoe and Arms of Fiji — A28

Sugar Cane — A29

Spear Fishing at Night — A30

Arms of Fiji — A31

Suva Harbor — A32

River Scene — A33

Fijian House — A34

Papaya Tree — A35

Bugler — A36

Designs: No. 121, Government buildings. 8p, 1sh5p, 1sh6p, Arms of Fiji.

Perf. 13½, 12½ (1p)

1938-55 Engr. Wmk. 4

117 A24 ½p green .25 1.00
c. Perf. 14 ('41) 16.00 4.75
d. Perf. 12 ('48) .80 *4.00*
118 A25 1p blue & brn .40 .25
119 A26 1½p rose car (empty canoe) 12.00 .50
120 A27 2p grn & org brn (no "180 degree") 30.00 .50
121 A27 2p mag & grn .45 .80
a. Perf. 12 ('46) 1.25 .90

Perf. 12½, 13x12 (6p), 14 (8p)

122 A28 3p dp ultra .80 .40
123 A29 5p rose red & blue 32.50 13.00
124 A29 5p rose red & yel grn .25 .40
125 A27 6p blk (no "180 degree") 45.00 16.00
126 A31 8p rose car 1.40 3.00
a. Perf. 13 ('50) .55 *3.50*
127 A30 1sh black & yel .75 .90

Perf. 14

128 A31 1sh5p car & black .25 .25
128A A31 1sh6p ultra 2.75 3.50
b. Perf. 13 ('55) 1.10 *20.00*

Perf. 12½

129 A32 2sh vio & org 2.00 .55
130 A33 2sh6p brn & grn 2.75 2.00
131 A34 5sh dk vio & grn 2.75 2.25
131A A35 10sh emer & brn org 27.50 *52.50*
131B A36 £1 car & ultra 37.50 *65.00*
Nos. 117-131B (18) 199.30 *162.80*

Issued: 1sh5p, 6/13/40; 5p, 10/1/40; No. 121, 5/19/42; 8p, 11/15/48; 10sh, £1, 3/13/50; 1sh6p, 8/1/50; others, 4/5/38.

Types of 1938-40 Redrawn

Perf. 13½ (1½p, 2p, 6p), 14 (2½p)

1940-49 Wmk. 4

132 A26 1½p rose car (man in canoe) 1.00 *3.00*
a. Perf. 12 ('49) .80 *1.60*
b. Perf. 14 ('42) 14.50 *22.50*
133 A27 2p grn & org brn ("180 degree") 12.50 *17.50*
134 A27 2½p grn & org brn .50 1.25
a. Perf. 12 ('48) .80 .40
b. Perf. 13½ ('42) .55 1.00
135 A27 6p blk ("180 degree") 2.50 2.40
a. Perf. 12 ('47) 1.40 1.75
Nos. 132-135 (4) 16.50 24.15

No. 132, type A26, has a man sitting in the canoe.

Nos. 133-135, type A27, have 180 degree added to the lower right hand corner of the design.

Issued: 2½p, Jan. 6, 1942; others Oct. 1, 1940.

No. 133 Surcharged in Black

1941, Feb. 10 ***Perf. 13½***

136 A27 2½p on 2p grn & org brn 1.50 1.00
Never hinged 2.50

Catalogue values for unused stamps in this section, from this point to the end of the section, are for Never Hinged items.

Peace Issue
Common Design Type

1946, Aug. 17 ***Perf. 13½***

137 CD303 2½p bright green .25 *1.50*
138 CD303 3p deep blue .25 .25

Silver Wedding Issue
Common Design Types

1948, Dec. 17 Photo. ***Perf. 14x14½***

139 CD304 2½p dark green .70 1.75

Engr.; Name Typo.

Perf. 11½x11

140 CD305 5sh blue violet 17.50 9.00

UPU Issue
Common Design Types

Engr.; Name Typo. on 3p, 8p

Perf. 13½, 11x11½

1949, Oct. 10 Wmk. 4

141 CD306 2p red violet .35 .75
142 CD307 3p indigo 2.25 5.75
143 CD308 8p dp carmine .35 *4.50*
144 CD309 1sh6p blue .40 *3.00*
Nos. 141-144 (4) 3.35 14.00

Coronation Issue
Common Design Type

1953, June 2 ***Perf. 13½x13***

145 CD312 2½p dk green & blk 1.75 .60
Nos. 145 (1) 1.75 .60

Type of 1938-40 with Portrait of Queen Elizabeth II Inscribed: "Royal Visit 1953"

1953, Dec. 16 ***Perf. 13***

146 A31 8p carmine lake .65 .35

Visit of Queen Elizabeth II and the Duke of Edinburgh, 1953.

Types of 1938-50 with Portrait of Queen Elizabeth II, and

A39

Loading Copra A40

Designs: 1sh6p, Sugar cane train. 2sh, Bananas for export. 5sh, Gold industry.

Perf. 11½, 11½x11, 12, 12½, 13

1954-56 Engr.

147 A24 ½p green .25 *1.40*
148 A39 1p grnsh blue 1.75 .25
149 A39 1½p brown .95 .65
150 A27 2p mag & green 1.20 .40
151 A39 2½p blue vio 2.25 .25
152 A40 3p purple & brn 2.50 .25
154 A27 6p black 2.50 .85
155 A31 8p carmine lake 3.50 1.40
156 A30 1sh black & yel 2.25 .25
157 A40 1sh6p grn & dp ultra 18.00 1.00
158 A40 2sh brt car & black 5.25 .60
159 A33 2sh6p brn & bl grn 1.20 .50
160 A40 5sh dp ultra & yel 14.50 1.25
161 A35 10sh emer & brn org 13.00 *20.00*
162 A36 £1 car & ultra 50.00 20.00
Nos. 147-162 (15) 119.10 49.05

Issued: 2p, 1sh, 2sh6p, 2/1/54; ½p, 6p, 8p, 10sh, £1, 7/1/54; 1p, 6/1/56; 1½p, 2½p, 3p, 1sh6p, 2sh, 5sh, 10/1/56.

Types of 1954-56 and

Nautilus Shells — A41

Hibiscus — A42

Kandavu Parrot A43

½p, 2p, 2½p, Queen Elizabeth II (A39). 1p, Queen, turtles in bottom panels. 6p, Fijian beating drum (lali). 10p, Yaqona ceremony. 1sh, South Pacific map. 2sh6p, Nadi Airport. 10sh, Cutting sugar cane. £1, Arms of Fiji.

Perf. 11½ (A39, A41); 11½x11 (A40); 14½x14 (A42); 14x14½ (A43)

Engr. (A39, A40, A41); others Photo.

1959-63 Wmk. 4

163 A39 ½p green ('61) .25 *2.75*
164 A41 1p dk blue ('62) 3.25 2.75
165 A41 1½p dk brown ('62) 2.60 2.50
166 A39 2p crim rose ('61) .75 .25
167 A39 2½p brown org ('62) 2.25 4.50
168 A40 6p blk & car rose ('61) 1.90 .25
169 A42 8p gray, red, yel & grn ('61) .70 .40
170 A40 10p car & brn ('63) .90 .80
171 A40 1sh dk bl & bl ('61) 2.25 .75
172 A40 2sh6p pur & blk ('61) 4.00 1.40
173 A43 4sh dk grn, red, bl & emer 2.60 2.40
174 A40 10sh sep & emer ('61) 6.50 4.00
175 A40 £1 org & blk ('61) 19.00 5.00
Nos. 163-175 (13) 46.95 27.75

Issued: 4sh, 7/13; 8p, 8/1; ½p, 2p, 6p, 1sh, 2sh6p, 10sh, £1, 11/14; 1p, 1½p, 2½p, 12/3; 10p, 4/1.

For type overprinted see No. 205.

Types of 1954-63 and

Elizabeth II — A44

1sh6p, 180th meridian and Intl. Date Line. 2sh, White orchids. 5sh, Orange dove.

Perf. 11½ (A41); 12½ (A44); 11½x11 (A40); 14x14½ (A43)

Engr. (A40, A41); others Photo.

1962-67 Wmk. 314

176 A41 1p dark blue ('64) .75 *4.25*
177 A39 2p crim rose ('65) .95 .25
178 A44 3p rose cl & multi .25 .25
179 A40 6p blk & car rose ('64) 1.10 .25
180 A42 9p ultra, red, yel & grn ('63) 1.10 1.00
181 A40 10p car & brn ('64) 1.10 .85
182 A40 1sh dk bl & bl ('66) 1.90 .75
183 A43 1sh6p dk bl & multi 2.25 1.60
184 A42 2sh gold, yel grn & grn 11.00 5.75
185 A40 2sh6p pur & blk ('65) 2.25 1.25
186 A43 4sh grn & multi, wmk. sideways ('67) 4.75 3.25
a. As #186, wmk. upright ('64) 3.50 6.50
b. 4sh dark green & multi ('66) 4.00 5.25
187 A43 5sh dk gray, yel & red 8.00 1.00
188 A40 10sh sep & emer ('64) 5.50 5.75
189 A40 £1 org & blk ('64) 21.00 15.00
Nos. 176-189 (14) 61.90 41.20

Issued: 3p, 1sh6p, 2sh, 5sh, 12/3; 9p, No. 186a, 4/1; 1p, 10p, 10sh, 1/14; 6p, £1, 6/9; 2p, 2sh6p, 8/3; No. 186b, 3/1; No. 186, 2/16.

Nos. 178 and 171 Overprinted

1963, Feb. 1

196 A44 3p multicolored .50 .35
197 A40 1sh dark blue & blue .50 .35

Visit of Elizabeth II & Prince Philip, Feb. 3.

Freedom from Hunger Issue
Common Design Type

1963, June 4 Photo. ***Perf. 14x14½***

198 CD314 2sh ultramarine 5.25 2.75

Running A45

9p, Throwing the discus, vert. 1sh, Field hockey, vert. 2sh6p, Women's high jump.

Perf. 14½x14, 14x14½

1963, Aug. 6 Wmk. 314

199 A45 3p yel, blk & brn .55 .25
200 A45 9p violet, blk & brn .55 1.40
201 A45 1sh green, blk & brn .55 .25
202 A45 2sh6p blue, blk & brn 1.15 1.15
Nos. 199-202 (4) 2.80 3.05

1st So. Pacific Games, Suva, 8/29-9/7.

Red Cross Centenary Issue
Common Design Type

1963, Sept. 2 Litho. ***Perf. 13***

203 CD315 2p black & red .75 .30
204 CD315 2sh ultra & red 3.25 3.25

Type of 1959-63 Overprinted

1963, Dec. 2 Engr. ***Perf. 11½x11***

205 A40 1sh dark blue & blue .85 .35

Opening of the Commonwealth Pacific (telephone) Cable service, COMPAC.

Fiji Scout Badge — A46

Scouts of India, Fiji and Europe Tying Knot — A47

1964, Aug. 3 Photo. ***Perf. 12½***

206	A46	3p multicolored	.50	.50
207	A47	1sh ocher & purple	.75	.75

50th anniv. of the founding of the Fiji Boy Scouts.

Amphibian "Aotearoa," 1939 — A48

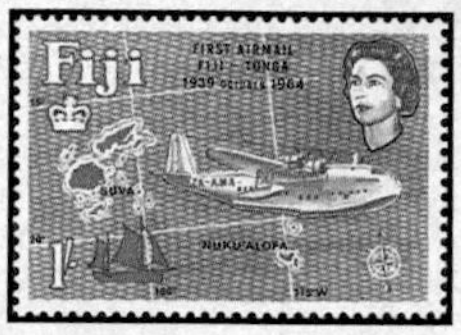

Map of Fiji and Tonga Islands and Plane A49

Design: 6p, Heron plane.

1964, Oct. 24 ***Perf. 12½, 14½***

208	A48	3p brt red & black	.50	.35
209	A48	6p ultra & red	.90	1.00
210	A49	1sh grnsh blue & black	.90	1.00
		Nos. 208-210 (3)	2.30	2.35

Fiji-Tonga airmail service, 25th anniv.

ITU Issue

Common Design Type

Perf. 11x11½

1965, May 17 Litho. Wmk. 314

211	CD317	3p blue & rose red	.30	.30
212	CD317	2sh yel & bister	2.40	2.40

Intl. Cooperation Year Issue

Common Design Type

1965, Oct. 25 ***Perf. 14½***

213	CD318	2p blue grn & claret	.35	.25
214	CD318	2sh6p lt vio & grn	2.25	2.10

Churchill Memorial Issue

Common Design Type

1966, Jan. 24 Photo. ***Perf. 14***

Design in Black, Gold and Carmine Rose

215	CD319	3p brt blue	.95	.30
216	CD319	9p green	1.35	1.35
217	CD319	1sh brown	1.35	.30
218	CD319	2sh6p violet	1.50	1.50
		Nos. 215-218 (4)	5.15	3.45

World Cup Soccer Issue

Common Design Type

1966, July 1 Litho. ***Perf. 14***

219	CD321	2p multicolored	.50	.30
220	CD321	2sh multicolored	1.50	.90

H.M.S. Pandora and Split Island, Rotuma A50

Designs: 10p, Rotuma chiefs, Pandora, and Rotuma's position in Pacific. 1sh6p, Rotuma islanders welcoming Pandora.

1966, Aug. 29 Photo. ***Perf. 14x13***

221	A50	3p multicolored	.45	.25
222	A50	10p multicolored	.55	.35
223	A50	1sh6p multicolored	.75	.75
		Nos. 221-223 (3)	1.75	1.35

175th anniv. of the discovery of Rotuma, a group of eight islands forming part of the colony of Fiji.

WHO Headquarters Issue

Common Design Type

1966, Sept. 20 Litho. ***Perf. 14***

224	CD322	6p multicolored	1.60	.40
225	CD322	2sh6p multicolored	3.50	3.50
		Nos. 224-225 (2)	5.10	3.90

Woman Runner A51

Designs: 9p, Shot put, vert. 1sh, Diver.

1966, Dec. 8 Photo. ***Perf. 14x14½***

226	A51	3p ol, black & lt brn	.30	.30
227	A51	9p brt blue, blk & brn	.45	.45
228	A51	1sh blue green & multi	.45	.45
		Nos. 226-228 (3)	1.20	1.20

2nd South Pacific Games, Noumea, New Caledonia, Dec. 8-18.

Military Band A52

Intl. Tourist Year: 9p, Reef diving. 1sh, Beqa fire walkers. 2sh, Liner Oriana and Mt. Rama volcano.

1967, Oct. 20 ***Perf. 14x13***

229	A52	3p multi & gold	.60	.25
230	A52	9p multi & silver	.30	.25
231	A52	1sh multi & gold	.30	.30
232	A52	2sh multi & silver	.60	.60
		Nos. 229-232 (4)	1.80	1.40

Admiral Bligh, H.M.S. Providence and Old Map of "Feejee" A53

Designs: 1sh, Bligh's longboat being chased by double canoe and map of Fiji Islands. 2sh6p, Bligh's tomb, St. Mary's Cemetery, Lambeth, London.

Perf. 15x14, 12½x13 (1sh)

1967, Dec. 7 Photo. Wmk. 314

Size: 35x21mm

233	A53	4p emer, blk & yel	.30	.30

Size: 54x20mm

234	A53	1sh brt bl, brn org & blk	.30	.30

Size: 35x21mm

235	A53	2sh6p sepia & multi	.75	.75
		Nos. 233-235 (3)	1.35	1.35

150th anniv. of the death of Adm. William Bligh (1754-1817), captain of the Bounty and principal discoverer of the Fiji Islands.

Simmonds "Spartan" Seaplane — A54

Designs: 6p, Fiji Airways Hawker-Siddeley H748 and emblems of various airlines. 1sh, Fokker "Southern Cross," Capt. Charles Kingsford-Smith, his crew and Southern Cross constellation. 2sh, Lockheed Altair "Lady Southern Cross."

Perf. 14x14½

1968, June 5 Wmk. 314

236	A54	2p green & black	.25	.25
237	A54	6p brt blue, car & blk	.25	.25
238	A54	1sh dp violet & green	.35	.35
239	A54	2sh orange brn & dk blue	.65	.65
		Nos. 236-239 (4)	1.50	1.50

40th anniv. of the first Trans-Pacific Flight through Fiji under Capt. Charles Kingsford-Smith.

Fijian Bures — A55

Eastern Reef Heron — A56

1p, Passion fruit flowers. 2p, Nautilus pompilius shell. 4p, Hawk moth. 6p, Reef butterflyfish. 9p, Bamboo raft (bilibili). 10p, Tiger moth. 1sh, Black marlin. 1sh6p, Orange-breasted honey eaters. 2sh, Ringed sea snake, horiz. 2sh6p, Outrigger canoes (takia), horiz. 3sh, Golden cowrie shell. 4sh, Emperor gold mine and gold ore. 5sh, Bamboo orchids, horiz. 10sh, Tabua (ceremonial whale's tooth). £1, Coat of Arms and Queen Elizabeth II, horiz.

Perf. 13½ (A55), 14 (A56)

1968, July 15 Photo. Wmk. 314

240	A55	½p multicolored	.25	.30
241	A55	1p multicolored	.25	.30
242	A55	2p multicolored	.25	.30
243	A56	3p multicolored	.25	.30
244	A55	4p multicolored	.55	.30
245	A55	6p multicolored	.25	.35
246	A55	9p multicolored	.25	.60
247	A55	10p multicolored	.80	.80
248	A56	1sh multicolored	1.05	.85
249	A56	1sh6p multicolored	2.25	1.00
250	A56	2sh multicolored	1.25	2.00
251	A56	2sh6p multicolored	1.25	2.00
252	A55	3sh multicolored	2.50	2.75
253	A56	4sh multicolored	4.25	2.40
254	A55	5sh multicolored	2.25	3.00
255	A56	10sh multicolored	3.25	4.75
256	A56	£1 red & multi	4.25	5.25
		Nos. 240-256 (17)	25.15	27.25

See Nos. 260-276.

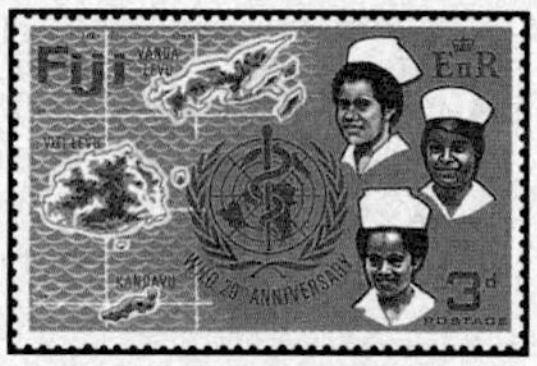

WHO Emblem, Map of Fiji and Nurses — A57

WHO Emblem and: 9p, Medical team loading patient on stretcher on dinghy and medical ship "Vuniwai." 3sh, People playing on beach.

1968, Dec. 9 Litho. ***Perf. 14***

257	A57	3p blue green & multi	.25	.25
258	A57	9p brt blue & multi	.25	.25
259	A57	3sh dk blue & multi	.75	.75
		Nos. 257-259 (3)	1.25	1.25

WHO, 20th anniv.

Types of 1968
Values in Cents and Dollars

Designs: 1c, Passion fruit flowers. 2c, Nautilus pompilius shell. 3c, Reef heron. 4c, Hawk moth. 5c, Reef butterflyfish. 6c, Fijian bures. 8c, Bamboo raft. 9c, Tiger moth. 10c, Black marlin. 15c, Orange-breasted honey-eater. 20c, Ringed sea snake, horiz. 25c, Outrigger canoes (takia), horiz. 30c, Golden cowrie shell. 40c Emperor gold mine and gold ore. 50c, Bamboo orchids, horiz. $1, Tabua (ceremonial whale's tooth). $2, Coat of Arms and Queen Elizabeth II, horiz.

Perf. 13½ (A55), 14 (A56)

1969, Jan. 13 Photo. Wmk. 314

260	A55	1c multicolored	.25	.25
261	A55	2c multicolored	.25	.25
262	A56	3c multicolored	.40	.35
263	A55	4c multicolored	.95	.35
264	A55	5c multicolored	.25	.25
265	A55	6c multicolored	.25	.25
266	A55	8c multicolored	.25	.25
267	A55	9c multicolored	.95	*1.60*
268	A56	10c multicolored	.25	.25
269	A56	15c multicolored	5.50	3.50
270	A56	20c multicolored	.70	.65
271	A56	25c multicolored	.70	.25
272	A55	30c multicolored	4.00	1.40
273	A56	40c multicolored	4.50	3.25
274	A56	50c multicolored	2.75	.25
275	A56	$1 multicolored	3.75	2.00
276	A56	$2 red & multi	4.50	5.00
		Nos. 260-276 (17)	30.20	20.10

For overprints & surcharges see #286-288, B5-B6.

Fiji Soldiers and Map of Solomon Islands A58

Designs: 10c, Flags of Fiji Military Force, soldiers in full and battle dress. 25c, Cpl. Sefanaia Sukanaivalu and Victoria Cross.

1969, June 23 Wmk. 314 ***Perf. 14***

277	A58	3c emerald & multi	.50	.50
278	A58	10c red & multi	.65	.65
279	A58	25c black & multi	.85	.85
		Nos. 277-279 (3)	2.00	2.00

25th anniv. of the Fiji Military Forces campaign in the Solomon Islands and of the posthumous award of the Victoria Cross to Cpl. Sefanaia Sukanaivalu.

Yachting — A59

Designs: 4c, Javelin. 20c, Winners and South Pacific Games medal.

1969, Aug. 18 Photo. ***Perf. 14½x14***

280	A59	4c red, brown & blk	.30	.30
281	A59	8c blue & black	.45	.45
282	A59	20c olive grn, blk & ocher	.95	.95
		Nos. 280-282 (3)	1.70	1.70

3rd South Pacific Games, Port Moresby, Papua New Guinea, Aug. 13-23.

Students in Laboratory — A60

2c, Map of South Pacific and mortarboard. 8c, Site of University at Royal New Zealand Air Force Seaplane Station, Laucala Bay, RNZAF badge and Sunderland flying boat.

1969, Nov. 10 ***Perf. 14x14½***

283	A60	2c multicolored	.25	.25
284	A60	8c red & multi	.35	.35
285	A60	25c dk green & multi	1.00	1.00
		Nos. 283-285 (3)	1.60	1.60

Inauguration of the University of the South Pacific, Laucala Bay, Suva.

Nos. 261, 268 and 271 Overprinted

1970, Mar. 4 ***Perf. 13½, 14***

286	A55	2c multicolored	.30	.30
287	A56	10c multicolored	.40	.40
288	A55	25c multicolored	1.50	1.50
		Nos. 286-288 (3)	2.20	2.20

Visit of Queen Elizabeth II, Prince Philip and Princess Anne, Mar. 4-5.

Nuns Sitting under Chaulmoogra Tree, and Chaulmoogra Fruit — A61

Designs: 10c, Paintings by Semisi Maya (former patient). No. 290, Cascade, vert. No. 291, Sea urchins, vert. 30c, Aerial view of Makogai Hospital.

Perf. 14x14½, 14½x14

1970, May 25 Photo. Wmk. 314

289	A61	2c brt pink & multi	.30	.30
290	A61	10c gray green & blk	.50	.50
291	A61	10c blue, car & blk	.50	.50
a.		Pair, #290-291	1.00	1.00
292	A61	30c orange & multi	1.40	1.40
		Nos. 289-292 (4)	2.70	2.70

Closing of the Leprosy Hospital on Makogai Island in 1969.

Abel Tasman and Ship's Log, 1643 — A62

3c, Capt. James Cook & "Endeavour," 8c, Capt. William Bligh & longboat, 1789. 25c, Man of Fiji & Fijian ocean-going canoe.

1970, Aug. 18 Litho. *Perf. 13x12½*

293	A62	2c blue green & multi	.75	.75
294	A62	3c gray green & multi	.90	.90
295	A62	8c multicolored	1.10	1.10
296	A62	25c dull lilac & multi	1.75	1.75
		Nos. 293-296 (4)	4.50	4.50

Discoverers and explorers of Fiji Islands.

King Cakobau and Cession Stone at Lavuka A63

Designs: 3c, Chinese, Fijian, Indian and European children. 10c, Prime Minister Ratu Sir Kamisese Mara and flag of Fiji. 25c, Fijian male dancer and Indian female dancer.

1970, Oct. 10 Wmk. 314 *Perf. 14*

297	A63	2c multicolored	.25	.25
298	A63	3c multicolored	.25	.25
299	A63	10c multicolored	.40	.40
300	A63	25c multicolored	1.20	1.20
		Nos. 297-300 (4)	2.10	2.10

Fijian independence.

Fiji Nos. 1 and 3 — A64

15c, Fiji #15, 44, 59, 81, 127, 166. 20c, Fiji Times Office, Levuka, & G. P. O., Suva.

1970, Nov. 2 Photo. *Perf. 14½x14*

Size: 35x21mm

301	A64	4c multicolored	.25	.25

Size: 60x21½mm

302	A64	15c multicolored	.75	.75

Size: 35x21mm

303	A64	20c multicolored	1.00	1.00
		Nos. 301-303 (3)	2.00	2.00

Centenary of first postage stamps of Fiji.

Gray-backed White Eyes — A65

Yellow-breasted Musk Parrots — A66

Designs: 1c, Cirrhopetalum umbellatum. 2c, Cardinal honey eaters. 3c, Calanthe furcata.4c, Bulbophyllum. 6c, Phaius tancarvilliae. 8c,Blue-crested broadbills. 10c, Acanthephippiumvitiense. 15c, Dendrobium tokai. 20c, Slaty flycatchers. 25c, Kandavu honey eaters. 30c, Dendrobium gordonii. 50c, White-throated pigeon. $1, Collared lories (kula). $2, Dendrobium platygastrium. (Orchids shown on 1c, 3c, 4c, 6c, 10c, 15c, 30c, $2.)

Wmk. 314 Upright

1971-72 Litho. *Perf. 13½x14*

305	A65	1c blk & multi ('72)	.25	.25
306	A65	2c carmine & multi	.25	.25
307	A65	3c multi ('72)	.85	.25
308	A65	4c blk & multi ('72)	.75	1.60
309	A65	5c brown & multi	2.50	.25
310	A65	6c lt bl & multi ('72)	.45	.30
311	A65	8c black & multi	.50	.35
312	A65	10c multi ('72)	.55	.40
313	A65	15c multi ('72)	2.25	.55
314	A65	20c gray & multi	1.35	.60

Perf. 14

315	A66	25c sepia & multi	1.05	.95
316	A66	30c grn & multi ('72)	2.75	1.25
317	A66	40c blue & multi	3.00	1.50
318	A66	50c gray & multi	3.50	1.75
319	A66	$1 red & multi	5.75	2.10
320	A66	$2 multi ('72)	11.00	8.25
		Nos. 305-320 (16)	37.05	20.60

Issued: 5c, 20c, 40c, 50c, 8/6; 2c, 8c, 25c, $1, 11/22; 1c, 10c, 30c, $2, 1/4; 3c, 4c, 6c, 15c, 6/23.

1972-74 Wmk. 314 Sideways

306c	A65	2c ('73)	.70	*11.00*
307a	A65	3c ('73)	2.00	.60
308a	A65	4c ('73)	6.50	.90
309a	A65	5c ('73)	6.50	4.25
310a	A65	6c ('73)	8.75	1.60
311a	A65	8c ('73)	4.25	1.00
313a	A65	15c ('73)	3.75	2.75
314a	A65	20c	14.00	2.50
315a	A66	25c ('73)	2.00	1.10
317a	A66	40c ('74)	3.25	*8.75*
318a	A66	50c ('74)	3.25	*4.25*
319a	A66	$1	3.25	*6.50*
320a	A66	$2	4.25	*7.00*
		Nos. 306c-320a (13)	62.45	52.20

Issued: 20c, $1, $2, 11/17; 3c, 5c, 3/8; 4c, 6c, 8c, 15c, 25c, 4/11; 2c, 12/12; 40c, 50c, 3/15.

1975-77 Wmk. 373

305b	A65	1c	1.00	*4.75*
306d	A65	2c	1.00	*4.75*
307b	A65	3c	.50	*4.75*
308b	A65	4c ('76)	4.50	.25
309b	A65	5c	1.60	*4.75*
310b	A65	6c ('76)	3.75	.25
311b	A65	8c ('76)	.45	.25
312b	A65	10c	.60	*2.25*
313b	A65	15c ('76)	3.25	.50
314b	A65	20c ('77)	4.75	.65
316b	A66	30c ('76)	6.75	1.10
317b	A66	40c ('76)	3.75	.70
318b	A66	50c ('76)	3.75	.80
319b	A66	$1 ('76)	3.75	1.75
320b	A66	$2 ('76)	1.90	1.75
		Nos. 305b-320b (15)	41.20	29.25

Issued: 1c, 2c, 3c, 5c, 10c, 4/9; 20c, 7/15; others, 9/3.

Women's Basketball — A67

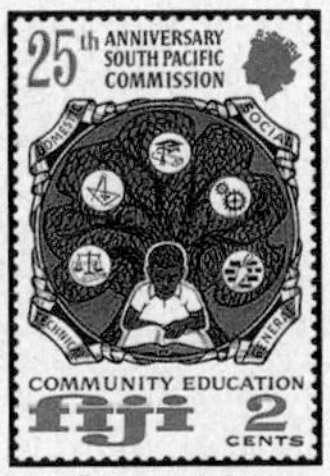

Community Education — A68

1971, Sept. 6 Wmk. 314 *Perf. 14*

321	A67	8c shown	.45	.45
322	A67	10c Running	.70	.70
323	A67	25c Weight lifting	1.35	1.35
		Nos. 321-323 (3)	2.50	2.50

4th South Pacific Games, Papeete, French Polynesia, Sept. 8-19.

1972, Feb. 7

Designs: 4c, Public health. 50c, Economic growth (farm scenes).

324	A68	2c bright rose & multi	.25	.25
325	A68	4c gray & multi	.25	.25
326	A68	50c bright blue & multi	1.60	1.60
		Nos. 324-326 (3)	2.10	2.10

South Pacific Commission, 25th anniv.

Arts Festival Emblem — A69

1972, Apr. 10

327	A69	10c blue, org & black	.40	.40

South Pacific Festival of Arts, May 6-20.

Silver Wedding Issue, 1972

Common Design Type

Queen Elizabeth II, Prince Philip, flowers, shells.

1972, Nov. 20 Photo. *Perf. 14x14½*

328	CD324	10c slate grn & multi	.40	.40
329	CD324	25c red lilac & multi	.60	.60
a.		Blue omitted	*450.00*	

On No. 329a, Prince Philip's coat is brown instead of blue.

Rugby — A70

1973, Mar. 9 Litho. *Perf. 14*

330	A70	2c shown	.40	.40
331	A70	8c Tackle	.80	.80
332	A70	25c Kicking ball	1.25	1.25
		Nos. 330-332 (3)	2.45	2.45

60th anniversary of Fiji Rugby Union.

Forestry Development — A71

Development projects: 8c, Irrigation of rice field. 10c, Low income housing. 25c, Highway construction.

1973, July 23 *Perf. 14*

333	A71	5c multicolored	.30	.30
334	A71	8c multicolored	.40	.40
335	A71	10c multicolored	.45	.45
336	A71	25c multicolored	1.10	1.10
		Nos. 333-336 (4)	2.25	2.25

Holy Family — A72

Festivals: 10c, Diwali (Candles; Indian New Year). 20c, Id-Ul-Fitar (Friendly greeting and mosque; Moslem, Ramadan). 25c, Chinese New Year (dragon dance).

1973, Oct. 26 *Perf. 14x14½*

337	A72	3c blue & multi	.35	.35
338	A72	10c purple & multi	.35	.35
339	A72	20c emerald & multi	.65	.65
340	A72	25c red & multi	.65	.65
		Nos. 337-340 (4)	2.00	2.00

Festivals celebrated by various groups in Fiji.

Runners — A73

1974, Jan. 7

341	A73	3c shown	.50	.35
342	A73	8c Boxing	.50	.35
343	A73	50c Lawn bowling	1.75	1.75
		Nos. 341-343 (3)	2.75	2.45

10th British Commonwealth Games, Christchurch, N.Z., Jan. 24-Feb. 2.

Centenary of Cricket in Fiji — A74

Designs: 3c, Bowler. 25c, Batsman and wicketkeeper. 40c, Fielder, horiz.

Perf. 14x14½, 14½x14

1974, Feb. 21 Litho.

344	A74	3c multicolored	1.10	1.10
345	A74	25c multicolored	1.50	1.50
346	A74	40c multicolored	1.75	1.75
		Nos. 344-346 (3)	4.35	4.35

Mailman and UPU Emblem A75

UPU Emblem and: 8c, Loading mail on ship. 30c, Post office and truck. 50c, Jet.

1974, May 22 Wmk. 314 *Perf. 14*

347	A75	3c orange & multi	.30	.30
348	A75	8c multicolored	.35	.35
349	A75	30c lt blue & multi	.50	.50
350	A75	50c multicolored	.95	.95
		Nos. 347-350 (4)	2.10	2.10

Centenary of the Universal Postal Union.

Cub Scouts A76

Designs: 10c, Boy Scouts reading map. 40c, Scouts and Fiji flag, vert.

1974, Aug. 30

351	A76	3c multicolored	.25	.25
352	A76	10c multicolored	.55	.55
353	A76	40c multicolored	1.50	1.50
		Nos. 351-353 (3)	2.30	2.30

First National Boy Scout Jamboree, Lautoka, Viti Levu Island.

Cakobau Club and Flag — A77

King Cakobau, Queen Victoria A78

Design: 50c, Signing ceremony at Levuka.

1974, Oct. 9 Litho. *Perf. 13½x13*

354	A77	3c multicolored	.25	.25
355	A78	8c multicolored	.30	.30
356	A78	50c multicolored	.70	.70
		Nos. 354-356 (3)	1.25	1.25

Deed of Cession, cent. and 4th anniv. of independence.

Diwali, Hindu Festival of Lights — A79

Designs: 15c, Id-Ul-Fitar (women exchanging greetings under moon). 25c, Chinese New Year (girl twirling streamer, and fireworks). 30c, Christmas (man and woman singing hymns, and star).

1975, Oct. 31 Wmk. 373 *Perf. 14*

357	A79	3c black & multi	.25	.25
358	A79	15c black & multi	.45	.45
359	A79	25c black & multi	.90	.90
360	A79	30c black & multi	1.10	1.10
a.		Souvenir sheet of 4, #357-360	5.50	5.50
		Nos. 357-360 (4)	2.70	2.70

Festivals celebrated by various groups in Fiji.

Steam Locomotive No. 21 — A80

Sugar mill trains: 15c, Diesel locomotive No. 8. 20c, Diesel locomotive No. 1. 30c, Free passenger train.

1976, Jan. 26 Litho. *Perf. 14½*

361	A80	4c yellow & multi	.35	.35
362	A80	15c salmon & multi	.90	.90
363	A80	20c multicolored	1.25	1.25
364	A80	30c blue & multi	1.90	1.90
		Nos. 361-364 (4)	4.40	4.40

Fiji Blind Society and Rotary Emblems A81

Rotary Intl. of Fiji, 40th Anniv.: 25c, Ambulance and Rotary emblems.

Perf. 13x13½

1976, Mar. 26 Wmk. 373

365	A81	10c lt green, brn, ultra	.25	.25
366	A81	25c multicolored	.75	.75

De Havilland Drover — A82

Planes: 15c, BAC One-Eleven. 25c, Hawker-Siddeley 748. 30c, Britten Norman Trislander.

1976, Sept. 1 Litho. *Perf. 14*

367	A82	4c multicolored	.25	.25
368	A82	15c multicolored	.80	.80
369	A82	25c multicolored	2.00	2.00
370	A82	30c multicolored	2.25	2.25
		Nos. 367-370 (4)	5.30	5.30

Fiji air service, 25th anniversary.

Queen's Visit, 1970 — A83

Designs: 25c, King Edward's Chair. 30c, Queen wearing cloth-of-gold supertunica.

1977, Feb. 7 Litho. *Perf. 14x13½*

371	A83	10c silver & multi	.25	.25
372	A83	25c silver & multi	.50	.50
373	A83	30c silver & multi	.65	.65
		Nos. 371-373 (3)	1.40	1.40

25th anniv. of reign of Elizabeth II.

World Map, Sinusoidal Projection — A84

Design: 30c, Map showing Fiji Islands.

Wmk. 373

1977, Apr. 12 Litho. *Perf. 14½*

374	A84	4c multicolored	.25	.25
375	A84	30c multicolored	1.00	1.00

First Joint Council of Ministers Conference of the European Economic Community (EEC) and of African, Caribbean and Pacific States (ACP).

Hibiscus A85

1977, Aug. 27 Wmk. 373 *Perf. 14*

376	A85	4c red	.25	.25
377	A85	15c orange	.35	.35
378	A85	30c pink	.70	.70
379	A85	35c yellow	.90	.90
		Nos. 376-379 (4)	2.20	2.20

Fiji Hibiscus Festival, 21st anniversary.

Drua, Double Canoe A86

Canoes: 15c, Tabilai. 25c, Takia, dugout outrigger canoe. 40c, Camakau.

1977, Nov. 7 Litho. *Perf. 14½*

380	A86	4c multicolored	.25	.25
381	A86	15c multicolored	.35	.30
382	A86	25c multicolored	.60	.60
383	A86	40c multicolored	.80	.80
		Nos. 380-383 (4)	2.00	1.95

Elizabeth II Coronation Anniversary Issue

Common Design Types

Souvenir Sheet

Unwmk.

1978, Apr. 21 Litho. *Perf. 15*

384	Sheet of 6	2.75	2.75
a.	CD326 25c White hart of Richard II	.50	.50
b.	CD327 25c Elizabeth II	.50	.50
c.	CD328 25c Banded iguana	.50	.50

No. 384 contains 2 se-tenant strips of Nos. 348a-348c, separated by horizontal gutter.

Southern Cross on Naselai Beach — A87

4c, Fiji Defence Force surrounding Southern Cross. 25c, Wright Flyer. 30c, Bristol F2B.

1978, June 26 Wmk. 373 *Perf. 14½*

385	A87	4c multicolored	.25	.25
386	A87	15c multicolored	.40	.30
387	A87	25c multicolored	.75	.60
388	A87	30c multicolored	1.10	.75
		Nos. 385-388 (4)	2.50	1.90

50th anniv. of Kingsford-Smith's Trans-Pacific flight, May 31-June 10, 1928 (4c, 15c); 75th anniv. of Wright brothers' first powered flight, Dec. 17, 1903 (25c); 60th anniv. of Royal Air Force, Apr. 1, 1918 (30c).

Necklace of Sperm Whale Teeth A88

Fiji artifacts: 4c, Wooden oil dish in shape of man, vert. 25c, Twin water bottles. 30c, Carved throwing club (Ula), vert.

1978, Aug. 14 Litho. *Perf. 14*

389	A88	4c multicolored	.30	.30
390	A88	15c multicolored	.30	.30
391	A88	25c multicolored	.55	.55
392	A88	30c multicolored	.65	.65
		Nos. 389-392 (4)	1.80	1.80

Christmas Wreath and Candles A89

Festivals: 15c, Diwali (oil lamps). 25c, Id-Ul-Fitr (fruit, coffeepot and cups). 40c, Chinese New Year (paper dragon).

1978, Oct. 30 *Perf. 14*

393	A89	4c multicolored	.25	.25
394	A89	15c multicolored	.25	.25
395	A89	25c multicolored	.40	.40
396	A89	40c multicolored	.60	.60
		Nos. 393-396 (4)	1.50	1.50

Banded Iguana A90

Endangered species and Wildlife Fund emblem: 15c, Tree frog. 25c, Long-legged warbler. 30c, Pink-billed parrot finch.

1979, Mar. 19 Litho. Wmk. 373

397	A90	4c multicolored	1.75	1.75
398	A90	15c multicolored	4.50	4.50
399	A90	25c multicolored	7.25	7.25
400	A90	30c multicolored	9.00	9.00
		Nos. 397-400 (4)	22.50	22.50

Indian Women Making Music A91

15c, Indian men sitting around kava bowl. 30c, Indian sugar cane, houses. 40c, Sailing ship Leonidas, map of South Pacific.

1979, May 11 Wmk. 373 *Perf. 14*

401	A91	4c multicolored	.25	.25
402	A91	15c multicolored	.25	.25
403	A91	30c multicolored	.35	.35
404	A91	40c multicolored	.50	.50
		Nos. 401-404 (4)	1.35	1.35

Arrival of Indians as indentured laborers, cent.

Soccer A92

Games Emblem and: 15c, Rugby. 30c, Tennis. 40c, Weight lifting.

1979, July 2 Litho. *Perf. 14*

405	A92	4c multicolored	.30	.30
406	A92	15c multicolored	.40	.40
407	A92	30c multicolored	.80	.80
408	A92	40c multicolored	1.10	1.10
		Nos. 405-408 (4)	2.60	2.60

6th South Pacific Games.

Old Town Hall, Suva A93

2c, Dudley Church, Suva. 3c, Telecommunications building, Suva. 4c, 5c, Lautoka Mosque. 6c, GPO, Suva. 8c, 12c, Levuka Public School. 10c, Visitors' Bureau, Suva. 15c, Colonial War Memorial Hospital Suva. 18c, Labasa Sugar Mill. 20c, Rewa Bridge, Nausori. 30c Sacred Heart Cathedral, Suva. 35c Grand Pacific Hotel, Suva. 45c, Shiva Temple, Suva. 50c Serua Island Village. $1, Solo Lighthouse. $2, Baker memorial Hall, Nausori. $5, Government House.

Without Inscribed Date, except #411B (1991)

Chalky Paper (#409-411, 414, 416, 418-419, 425)

Ordinary Paper (#412-413, 415, 417, 420-424)

1979-94 Wmk. 373 *Perf. 14*

409	A93	1c multicolored	.25	.25
a.		Ordinary paper	3.00	3.00
b.		Inscribed "1994"	2.00	2.00
410	A93	2c multicolored	.25	.25
a.		Ordinary paper	3.00	3.00
b.		Inscribed "1983"	1.00	3.00
c.		Inscribed "1986"	1.25	1.25
d.		Inscribed "1991"	.75	.75
e.		Inscribed "1993"	3.50	3.50
f.		Inscribed "1994"	1.00	1.50
411	A93	3c multicolored	.25	.25
a.		Ordinary paper	3.00	3.00
b.		Inscribed "1993"	4.50	4.50

411B A93 4c multicolored 1.50 1.50
a. Inscribed "1993" 6.00 6.00
b. Inscribed "1994" 3.50 5.50
412 A93 5c multicolored .25 .25
a. Inscribed "1983" 1.00 .50
413 A93 6c multicolored .25 .25
a. Inscribed "1983" 1.00 .50
414 A93 10c multicolored .25 .25
a. Ordinary paper 3.00 3.00
b. Inscribed "1991" .75 .75
415 A93 12c multicolored .50 .50
a. Inscribed "1993" 5.50 5.50
b. Inscribed "1994" 2.00 3.50
416 A93 15c multicolored .25 .25
a. Ordinary paper 3.50 3.50
b. Inscribed "1991" .75 .75
417 A93 18c multicolored .25 .25
418 A93 20c multicolored .30 .30
a. Ordinary paper 7.50 7.50
b. Inscribed "1993" 3.75 6.50
c. Inscribed "1994" 3.50 3.50
419 A93 30c multi, vert. .35 .35
a. Ordinary paper 4.50 4.50
420 A93 35c multicolored .40 .40
421 A93 45c multicolored .45 .45
422 A93 50c multicolored .60 .60
a. Inscribed "1994" 3.50 3.50

Perf. 14x13½, 13½x14

Size: 45x29mm, 29x45mm (#423)

423 A93 $1 multi, vert. 4.00 3.00
424 A93 $2 multicolored 2.25 3.00
425 A93 $5 multicolored 5.50 5.50
Nos. 409-425 (18) 17.85 17.60

Issued: 5c, 6c, 12c, 18c, 35c-$2, 12/22/80; No. 411B, 11/1991; others, 11/11/79.

1986-92 Wmk. 384

With Date Inscription

1986

410g A93 2c multicolored 1.25 1.25
413B A93 8c multicolored 4.50 4.50

1988

410h A93 2c multicolored 1.00 1.00
411h A93 3c multicolored 1.00 1.00
411Bh A93 4c multicolored 1.00 1.00
418h A93 20c multicolored 2.00 2.00

1990

414i A93 10c multicolored 1.50 1.50
418i A93 20c multicolored 2.00 2.00

1991

409j A93 1c multicolored 1.75 3.50
410j A93 2c multicolored 1.00 1.00
411j A93 3c multicolored 1.75 1.75
411Bj A93 4c multicolored 1.00 1.00
414j A93 10c multicolored 2.00 2.00
416j A93 15c multicolored 1.00 1.00
420j A93 35c multicolored 2.75 2.75
422j A93 50c multicolored 3.75 3.75
423j A93 $1 multi, vert. 9.00 9.00

1992

409k A93 1c multicolored 2.00 2.00
411k A93 3c multicolored 3.75 3.75
411Bk A93 4c multicolored 3.75 3.75
416k A93 15c multicolored 2.75 2.75
418k A93 20c multicolored 5.60 5.50
420k A93 35c multicolored 5.60 5.50
422k A93 50c multicolored 5.50 5.50
423k A93 $1 multi, vert. 11.00 11.00

Southern Cross, 1873, London 1980 Emblem A94

1980, Apr. 28 Wmk. 373 *Perf. 13½*

426 A94 6c shown .25 .25
427 A94 20c Levuka, 1910 .30 .30
428 A94 45c Matua, 1936 .70 .70
429 A94 50c Oronsay, 1951 .75 .75
Nos. 426-429 (4) 2.00 2.00

London 80 Intl. Stamp Exhib., May 6-14.

Sovi Bay A95

1980, Aug. 18 *Perf. 13½x14*

430 A95 6c shown .25 .25
431 A95 20c Yanuca Island, evening scene .25 .25
432 A95 45c Dravuni Beach .45 .45
433 A95 50c Wakaya Island .55 .55
Nos. 430-433 (4) 1.50 1.50

Opening of Parliament, 1979 — A96

1980, Oct. 6 Litho. *Perf. 13*

434 A96 6c shown .25 .25
435 A96 20c Coat of arms, vert. .30 .30
436 A96 45c Fiji flag .55 .55
437 A96 50c Elizabeth II, vert. .65 .65
Nos. 434-437 (4) 1.75 1.75

Independence, 10th anniversary.

Coastal Scene, by Semisi Maya A97

Intl. Year of the Disabled: Paintings and portrait of disabled artist Semisi Maya.

1981, Apr. 21 Wmk. 373 *Perf. 14*

438 A97 6c shown .25 .25
439 A97 35c Underwater Scene .30 .30
440 A97 50c Maya Painting, vert. .45 .45
441 A97 60c Peacock, vert. .55 .55
Nos. 438-441 (4) 1.55 1.55

Royal Wedding Issue

Common Design Type

1981, July 22 Wmk. 373 *Perf. 14*

442 CD331 6c Bouquet .25 .25
443 CD331 45c Charles .45 .45
444 CD331 $1 Couple 1.00 1.00
Nos. 442-444 (3) 1.70 1.70

Operator Assistance Center — A98

1981, Aug. 7 Litho. *Perf. 14*

445 A98 6c shown .25 .25
446 A98 35c Microwave station, map .55 .55
447 A98 50c Satellite earth station .75 .75
448 A98 60c Cableship Retriever .90 .90
Nos. 445-448 (4) 2.45 2.45

World Food Day — A99

1981, Sept. 21 Litho. *Perf. 14½x14*

449 A99 20c multicolored .50 .50

Ratu Sir Lala Sukuna, First Legislative Council Speaker — A100

1981, Oct. 19 Litho. *Perf. 14*

450 A100 6c shown .25 .25
451 A100 35c Mace, flag .40 .40
452 A100 50c Suva Civic Center .60 .60
Nos. 450-452 (3) 1.25 1.25

Souvenir Sheet

453 A100 60c Emblem, participants' flags .90 .90

27th Commonwealth Parliamentary Assoc. Conf., Suva.

World War II Aircraft A101

1981, Dec. 7 Litho. *Perf. 14*

454 A101 6c Bell P-39 Aircobra 1.10 .25
455 A101 18c Consolidated PBY-5 Catalina 2.40 .30
456 A101 35c Curtiss P-40 Warhawk 4.00 .65
457 A101 60c Short Singapore 4.50 1.00
Nos. 454-457 (4) 12.00 2.20

Scouting Year A102

1982, Feb. 22 Litho. *Perf. 14½*

458 A102 6c Building .25 .25
459 A102 20c Sailing, vert. .50 .50
460 A102 45c Campfire 1.10 1.10
461 A102 60c Baden-Powell, vert. 1.25 1.25
Nos. 458-461 (4) 3.10 3.10

Disciplined Forces — A103

1982, May 10 Wmk. 373 *Perf. 14*

462 A103 12c UN checkpoint .50 .25
463 A103 30c Construction project 1.25 .50
464 A103 40c Police, car 2.00 .65
465 A103 70c Navy ship 2.25 1.25
Nos. 462-465 (4) 6.00 2.65

1982 World Cup A104

1982, June 15 Litho. *Perf. 14*

466 A104 6c Fiji Soccer Assoc. emblem .25 .25
467 A104 18c Flag, ball .35 .35
468 A104 50c Stadium .80 .80
469 A104 90c Emblem 1.60 1.60
Nos. 466-469 (4) 3.00 3.00

Princess Diana Issue

Common Design Type

1982, July 1 *Perf. 14½x14*

470 CD333 20c Arms .50 .50
471 CD333 35c Diana .75 .75
472 CD333 45c Wedding 1.00 1.00
473 CD333 $1 Portrait 2.25 2.25
Nos. 470-473 (4) 4.50 4.50

October Royal Visit — A105

1982, Nov. 1 Litho. *Perf. 14*

474 A105 6c Duke of Edinburgh .30 .30
475 A105 45c Elizabeth II 1.10 1.10

Souvenir Sheet

476 Sheet of 3 4.00 4.00
c. A105 $1 Britannia 1.60 1.60

No. 476 contains Nos. 474-475 and 476c.

Christmas A106

1982, Nov. 22 *Perf. 14x14½*

477 A106 6c Holy Family .25 .25
478 A106 20c Adoration of the Kings .40 .40
479 A106 35c Carolers .75 .75
Nos. 477-479 (3) 1.40 1.40

Souvenir Sheet

480 A106 $1 Faith, from The Three Virtues, by Raphael 2.00 2.00

Red-throated Lory — A107

Parrots.

1983, Feb. 14 Litho. *Perf. 14*

481 A107 20c shown 1.50 1.50
482 A107 40c Blue-crowned lory 2.25 2.25
483 A107 55c Sulphur-breasted musk parrot 3.50 3.50
484 A107 70c Red-breasted musk parrot 4.25 4.25
Nos. 481-484 (4) 11.50 11.50

A108

1983, Mar. 14

485 A108 8c Traditional house .25 .25
486 A108 25c Barefoot firewalkers .30 .30
487 A108 50c Sugar cane crop .60 .60
488 A108 80c Kava Yagona ceremony .85 .85
Nos. 485-488 (4) 2.00 2.00

Commonwealth Day.

Manned Flight Bicentenary — A109

1983, July 18 Wmk. 373 *Perf. 14*

489 A109 8c Montgolfiere, 1783 .45 .25
490 A109 20c Wright Flyer .55 .35
491 A109 25c DC-3 .65 .40
492 A109 40c DeHavilland Comet 1.00 .70
493 A109 50c Boeing 747 1.25 .85
494 A109 58c Columbia space shuttle 1.60 1.00
Nos. 489-494 (6) 5.50 3.55

Cordia Subcordata — A110

Flowers.

1983, Sept. 26 Litho. *Perf. 14*

495 A110 8c shown .25 .25
496 A110 25c Gmelina vitiensis .30 .30
497 A110 40c Carruthersia scandens .55 .55
498 A110 $1 Amylotheca insularum 1.40 1.40
Nos. 495-498 (4) 2.50 2.50

See Nos. 505-508.

Earth Satellite Station, Fijian Playing Lali — A111

Perf. 14x13½

1983, Nov. 7 Wmk. 373

499 A111 50c multicolored .75 .75

Dacryopinax Spathularia A112

Various fungi.

1984, Jan. 9 *Perf. 14x13½, 13½x14*

500 A112 8c shown .65 .25
501 A112 15c Podoscypha involuta 1.10 .45
502 A112 40c Lentinus squarrosulus 2.25 1.10
503 A112 50c Scleroderma flavidum 3.50 1.50
504 A112 $1 Phillipsia domingensis 6.50 2.75
Nos. 500-504 (5) 14.00 6.05

Flower Type of 1983

1984 Litho. *Perf. 14x14½*

505 A110 15c Pseuderanthemum laxiflorum .25 .25
506 A110 20c Storkiella vitiensis .30 .30
507 A110 50c Paphia vitiensis .80 .80
508 A110 70c Elaeocarpus storkii 1.10 1.10
Nos. 505-508 (4) 2.45 2.45

Lloyd's List Issue

Common Design Type

Perf. 14½x14

1984, May 7 Wmk. 373

509 CD335 8c Tui Lau on reef .40 .40
510 CD335 40c Tofua 1.50 1.50
511 CD335 55c Canberra 2.00 2.00
512 CD335 60c Suva Wharf 2.25 2.25
Nos. 509-512 (4) 6.15 6.15

Souvenir Sheet

1984 UPU Congress — A113

1984, June 14 Litho. *Perf. 14½*

513 A113 25c Map 2.25 2.25

Ausipex '84 — A114

1984, Sept. 17 Wmk. 373 *Perf. 14*

514 A114 8c Yalavou cattle .25 .25
515 A114 25c Wailoa Power Station, vert. .55 .55
516 A114 40c Boeing 737 .95 .95
517 A114 $1 Cargo ship Fua Kavenga 2.50 2.50
Nos. 514-517 (4) 4.25 4.25

Christmas A115

1984, Nov. 5 Litho. *Perf. 14*

518 A115 8c Church on hill .25 .25
519 A115 20c Sailing .30 .30
520 A115 25c Santa, children, tree .35 .35
521 A115 40c Going to church .60 .60
522 A115 $1 Family, tree, vert. 1.60 1.60
Nos. 518-522 (5) 3.10 3.10

Butterflies A116

1985, Feb. 4 *Perf. 14*

523 A116 8c Monarch 1.00 .25
524 A116 25c Common eggfly 2.50 .80
525 A116 40c Long-tailed blue, vert. 4.00 1.40
526 A116 $1 Meadow argus, vert. 10.50 3.50
Nos. 523-526 (4) 18.00 5.95

EXPO '85, Tsukuba, Japan — A117

1985, Mar. 18 Litho. *Perf. 14*

527 A117 20c Outrigger canoe, Toberua Isl. .55 .50
528 A117 25c Wainivula Falls .60 .55
529 A117 50c Mana Island 1.60 1.40
530 A117 $1 Sawa-I-Lau Caves 2.75 2.50
Nos. 527-530 (4) 5.50 4.95

Queen Mother 85th Birthday Issue

Common Design Type

Perf. 14½x14

1985, June 7 Wmk. 384

531 CD336 8c Holding Prince Andrew .25 .25
532 CD336 25c With Prince Charles .60 .60
533 CD336 40c On Oaks Day, Epsom Races .95 .95
534 CD336 50c Holding Prince Henry 1.25 1.25
Nos. 531-534 (4) 3.05 3.05

Souvenir Sheet

535 CD336 $1 In Royal Wedding Cavalcade, 1981 4.00 4.00

Shallow Water Fish A118

1985, Sept. 23 *Perf. 14½*

536 A118 40c Horned squirrel fish 1.50 1.10
537 A118 50c Yellow-banded goatfish 2.25 1.40
538 A118 55c Fairy cod 2.25 1.50
539 A118 $1 Peacock rock cod 4.00 2.75
Nos. 536-539 (4) 10.00 6.75

Sea Birds — A119

1985, Nov. 4 *Perf. 14*

540 A119 15c Collared petrel 1.25 .45
541 A119 20c Lesser frigate bird 2.25 .70
542 A119 50c Brown booby 5.50 1.75
543 A119 $1 Crested tern 10.00 4.25
Nos. 540-543 (4) 19.00 7.15

Queen Elizabeth II 60th Birthday Issue

Common Design Type

20c, With the Duke of York at the Royal Tournament, 1936. 25c, On Buckingham Palace balcony, wedding of Princess Margaret and Anthony Armstrong-Jones, 1960. 40c, Inspecting the Guard of Honor, Suva, 1982. 50c, State visit to Luxembourg, 1976. $1, Visiting Crown Agents' offices, 1983.

Perf. 14x14½

1986, Apr. 21 Wmk. 384

544 CD337 20c scar, blk & sil .40 .40
545 CD337 25c ultra & multi .40 .40
546 CD337 40c green & multi .65 .65
547 CD337 50c violet & multi .85 .85
548 CD337 $1 rose vio & multi 1.75 1.75
Nos. 544-548 (5) 4.05 4.05

Intl. Peace Year — A120

1986, June 23 Wmk. 373 *Perf. 14½*

549 A120 8c shown .25 .25
550 A120 40c Dove 1.10 1.10

Halley's Comet — A121

1986, July 7 *Perf. 13½*

551 A121 25c Newton's reflector telescope .90 .60
552 A121 40c Comet over Lomaiviti 1.10 .95
553 A121 $1 Comet nucleus, Giotto probe 5.00 2.50
Nos. 551-553 (3) 7.00 4.05

Reptiles and Amphibians — A122

1986, Aug. 1 *Perf. 14½*

554 A122 8c Ground frog .40 .25
555 A122 20c Burrowing snake .60 *.70*
556 A122 25c Spotted gecko .65 *.90*
557 A122 40c Crested iguana 1.00 *1.25*
558 A122 50c Blotched skink 2.75 1.50
559 A122 $1 Speckled skink 5.50 3.25
Nos. 554-559 (6) 10.90 7.85

Ancient War Clubs — A123

1986, Nov. 10 Wmk. 384 *Perf. 14*

560 A123 25c Gatawaka .90 .75
561 A123 40c Siriti 1.10 .90
562 A123 50c Bulibuli 1.40 1.25
563 A123 $1 Culacula 3.00 2.50
Nos. 560-563 (4) 6.40 5.40

Cone Shells — A124

1987, Feb. 26 Litho. *Perf. 14x14½*

564 A124 15c Weasel .55 .35
565 A124 20c Pertusus .60 .45
566 A124 25c Admiral 1.00 .60
567 A124 40c Leaden 1.25 .95
568 A124 50c Imperial 2.60 1.25
569 A124 $1 Geography 5.25 2.50
Nos. 564-569 (6) 11.25 6.10

Souvenir Sheet

Tagimoucia Flower — A125

1987, Apr. 23 Wmk. 373 *Perf. 14½*

570 A125 $1 multicolored 5.00 3.75

No. 570 Overprinted

1987, June 13

571 A125 $1 multicolored *70.00 70.00*

Intl. Year of Shelter for the Homeless A126

1987, July 20 ***Perf. 14***
572 A126 55c Hut .65 .65
573 A126 70c Government housing .85 .85

Beetles — A127

1987, Sept. 7 **Wmk. 384**
574 A127 20c Bulbogaster ctenostomoides 1.00 .45
575 A127 25c Paracupta flaviventris 1.75 .65
576 A127 40c Cerambyrhynchus schoenherri 2.25 1.00
577 A127 50c Rhinoscapha lagopyga 3.75 1.25
578 A127 $1 Xixuthrus heros 8.25 2.50
Nos. 574-578 (5) 17.00 5.85

Christmas — A128

1987, Nov. 19
579 A128 8c Holy Family, vert. .25 .25
580 A128 40c Shepherds see star 1.00 .65
581 A128 50c Three Kings follow star 2.75 .75
582 A128 $1 Adoration of the Magi 5.75 1.50
Nos. 579-582 (4) 9.75 3.15

World Expo '88, Apr. 30-Oct. 30, Brisbane, Australia A129

1988, Apr. 27 **Litho.** ***Perf. 14***
583 A129 30c Windsurfing 1.75 1.75

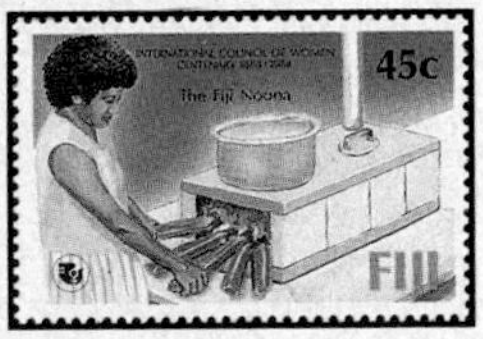

Intl. Council of Women, Cent. A130

1988, June 14
584 A130 45c Fiji Nouna 1.25 1.25

Pottery A131

Wmk. 384, 373 (69c)

1988, Aug. 29 **Litho.** ***Perf. 13½***
585 A131 9c Lapita (bowl) .25 .25
586 A131 23c Kuro (cooking pot) .35 .35
587 A131 58c Saqa (ritual drinking vessel) .80 .80
588 A131 63c Saqa, diff. 1.00 1.00
589 A131 69c Ramarama (oil lamp) 1.25 1.25
590 A131 75c Kuro, diff., vert. 1.75 1.75
Nos. 585-590 (6) 5.40 5.40

Fiji Tree Frog — A132

1988, Oct. 3 **Wmk. 384** ***Perf. 14***
591 A132 18c multi 4.25 4.25
592 A132 23c multi, diff. 4.75 4.75
593 A132 30c multi, diff. 6.25 6.25
594 A132 45c multi, diff. 10.00 10.00
Nos. 591-594 (4) 25.25 25.25

World Wildlife Fund.

Indigenous Flowering Plants — A133

1988, Nov. 21 **Wmk. 373**
595 A133 9c Dendrobium mohlianum .25 .25
596 A133 30c Dendrobium cattlare .85 .85
597 A133 45c Degeneria vitiensis 1.35 1.35
598 A133 $1 Degeneria roseiflora 2.60 2.60
Nos. 595-598 (4) 5.05 5.05

Intl. Red Cross and Red Crescent Orgs., 125th Anniv. — A134

1989, Feb. 6 **Wmk. 384**
599 A134 58c Battle of Solferino, 1859 1.40 1.10
600 A134 63c Jean-Henri Dunant, vert. 1.60 1.10
601 A134 69c Medicine 1.75 1.25
602 A134 $1 Anniv. emblem, vert. 4.00 1.90
Nos. 599-602 (4) 8.75 5.35

Epic Voyage of William Bligh A135

Designs: 45c, Plans (line drawing) of the Bounty's launch. 58c, Diary and inscription on artifacts "The cup I eat my miserable allowance out of." 80c, Silhouette, lightning, quote "O Almighty God, relieve us. . ." $1, Map of Bligh's Islands, launch and compass rose.

1989, Apr. 28 ***Perf. 14½***
603 A135 45c multicolored 1.90 .70
604 A135 58c multicolored 2.10 .95
605 A135 80c multicolored 4.00 1.25
606 A135 $1 multicolored 5.50 1.50
Nos. 603-606 (4) 13.50 4.40

Coral A136

1989, Aug. 21 **Wmk. 373** ***Perf. 14***
607 A136 46c Platygyra daedalea 2.40 2.40
608 A136 60c Caulastrea furcata 3.00 3.00
609 A136 75c Acropora echinata 3.75 3.75
610 A136 90c Acropora humilis 4.75 4.75
Nos. 607-610 (4) 13.90 13.90

Nos. 609-610 vert.

1990 World Cup Soccer Championships, Italy — A137

Various Fijian soccer players.

1989, Sept. 25 **Wmk. 384** ***Perf. 14½***
611 A137 35c shown 1.60 1.60
612 A137 63c multi, diff. 2.50 2.50
613 A137 70c multi, diff. 3.00 3.00
614 A137 85c multi, diff. 3.50 3.50
Nos. 611-614 (4) 10.60 10.60

Christmas A138

1989, Nov. 1 **Wmk. 373**
615 A138 9c Church service .35 .35
616 A138 45c *Delonix regia* tree 1.10 1.10
617 A138 $1 Holy family 2.10 2.10
618 A138 $1.40 Tree, Fijian children 3.00 3.00
Nos. 615-618 (4) 6.55 6.55

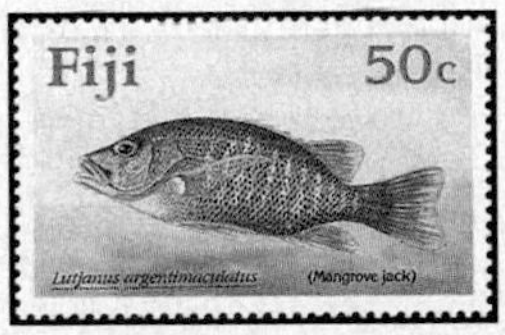

Fish A139

1990, Apr. 23 **Litho.** **Wmk. 384**
619 A139 50c Mangrove jack 3.00 3.00
620 A139 70c Orange-spotted therapon perch 4.50 4.50
621 A139 85c Spotted scat 5.00 5.00
622 A139 $1 Flagtail 6.00 6.00
Nos. 619-622 (4) 18.50 18.50

Souvenir Sheet

Stamp World London '90 — A140

1990, May 1
623 A140 Sheet of 2 13.50 6.00
a. $1 No. 243 4.25 1.75
b. $2 No. 249 8.50 4.25

Soil Conservation — A141

50c, Vertiver grass contours. 70c, Mulching. 90c, Contour cultivation. $1, Proper land use.

1990, July 23 **Litho.** **Wmk. 373**
625 A141 50c multi 1.10 1.10
626 A141 70c multi 1.60 1.60
627 A141 90c multi 2.10 2.10
628 A141 $1 multi, vert. 2.25 2.25
Nos. 625-628 (4) 7.05 7.05

Trees — A142

1990, Oct. 2
629 A142 25c Dacrydium nidulum .90 .90
630 A142 35c Decussocarpus vitiensis 1.10 1.10
631 A142 $1 Agathis vitiensis 3.50 3.50
632 A142 $1.55 Santalum yasi 5.00 5.00
Nos. 629-632 (4) 10.50 10.50

Christmas — A143

Christmas carols: 10c, Hark! The Herald Angels Sing. 35c, Silent Night. 65c, Joy to the World! $1, The Race that Long in Darkness Pined.

1990, Nov. 26 **Wmk. 373** ***Perf. 14***
633 A143 10c multicolored .40 .40
634 A143 35c multicolored 1.10 1.10
635 A143 65c multicolored 2.00 2.00
636 A143 $1 multicolored 3.00 3.00
Nos. 633-636 (4) 6.50 6.50

Scenic Views — A144

1991, Feb. 25 **Wmk. 384**
637 A144 35c Sigatoka sand dunes 1.50 1.50
638 A144 50c Monu, Monuriki Islands 2.75 2.75
639 A144 65c Ravilevu Nature Reserve 3.25 3.25
640 A144 $1 Colo-I-Suva Forest Park 5.50 5.50
Nos. 637-640 (4) 13.00 13.00

Discovery of Rotuma Island, Bicent. A145

1991, Aug. 8 **Wmk. 373** ***Perf. 14***
641 A145 54c HMS Pandora 2.75 2.75
642 A145 70c Map of Rotuma Island 3.50 3.50
643 A145 75c Natives 3.75 3.75
644 A145 $1 Mt. Solroroa, Uea Island 5.00 5.00
Nos. 641-644 (4) 15.00 15.00

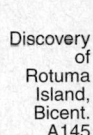

Crabs A146

Designs: 38c, Scylla serrata. 54c, Metopograpsus messor. 96c, Parasesarma erythrodactyla. $1.65, Cardisoma carnifex.

1991, Sept. 26 *Perf. 14½x14*

645	A146	38c multicolored	1.10	1.10
646	A146	54c multicolored	1.75	1.75
647	A146	96c multicolored	2.75	2.75
648	A146	$1.65 multicolored	5.50	5.50
		Nos. 645-648 (4)	11.10	11.10

Christmas A147

Designs: 11c, Mary, Joseph travelling to Bethlehem. 75c, Manger scene. 96c, Jesus being blessed at temple in Jerusalem. $1, Baby Jesus.

1991, Oct. 31 **Wmk. 384** *Perf. 14*

649	A147	11c multicolored	.45	.45
650	A147	75c multicolroed	2.10	2.10
651	A147	96c multicolored	2.50	2.50
652	A147	$1 multicolored	2.50	2.50
		Nos. 649-652 (4)	7.55	7.55

Air Pacific, 40th Anniv. A148

Airplanes: 54c, Dragon Rapide, Harold Gatty, founder. 75c, Douglas DC3. 96c, ATR 42. $1.40, Boeing 767.

1991, Nov. 18 *Perf. 14½*

653	A148	54c multicolored	3.00	3.00
654	A148	75c multicolored	3.25	3.25
655	A148	96c multicolored	4.25	4.25
656	A148	$1.40 multicolored	6.50	6.50
		Nos. 653-656 (4)	17.00	17.00

Expo '92, Seville A149

Designs: 27c, Traditional dance and costumes. 75c, Faces of people. 96c, Train and gold bars. $1.40, Cruise ship in port.

Perf. 14½x14

1992, Mar. 23 **Litho.** **Wmk. 373**

657	A149	27c multicolored	1.35	1.35
658	A149	75c multicolored	3.50	3.50
659	A149	96c multicolored	5.25	5.25
660	A149	$1.40 multicolored	6.75	6.75
		Nos. 657-660 (4)	16.85	16.85

Inter-Islands Shipping — A150

1992, June 22 *Perf. 14*

661	A150	38c Tabusoro	2.00	2.00
662	A150	54c Degei II	2.75	2.75
663	A150	$1.40 Dausoko	5.75	5.75
664	A150	$1.65 Nivanga	6.50	6.50
		Nos. 661-664 (4)	17.00	17.00

1992 Summer Olympics, Barcelona — A151

1992, July 30 *Perf. 13½*

665	A151	20c Running	.65	.65
666	A151	86c Yachting	2.75	2.75
667	A151	$1.34 Swimming	4.00	4.00
668	A151	$1.50 Judo	5.00	5.00
		Nos. 665-668 (4)	12.40	12.40

Levuka A152

30c, European War Memorial. 42c, Map. 59c, Beach Street. 77c, Sacred Heart Church, vert. $2, Deed of Cession Site, vert.

1992, Sept. 21 *Perf. 14½*

669	A152	30c multicolored	.50	.50
670	A152	42c multicolored	.65	.65
671	A152	59c multicolored	.95	.95
672	A152	77c multicolored	1.30	1.30
673	A152	$2 multicolored	3.00	3.00
		Nos. 669-673 (5)	6.40	6.40

Intl. Planned Parenthood Federation, 40th Anniv. — A153

1992, Nov. 2 *Perf. 15x14½*

674	A153	77c Globe	1.50	1.50
675	A153	$2 Family	3.75	3.75

Christmas — A154

Bible interpretations: 12c, "God so loved the world..." 77c, "We love because God first loved us." 83c, "It is more blessed to give..." $2, "Every good gift..."

1992, Nov. 17

676	A154	12c multicolored	.35	.35
677	A154	77c multicolored	1.90	1.90
678	A154	83c multicolored	2.25	2.25
679	A154	$2 multicolored	5.50	5.50
		Nos. 676-679 (4)	10.00	10.00

Peace Corps in Fiji, 25th Anniv. A155

Designs: 59c, Voluntary service. 77c, Fiji/US friendship. $1, Education. $2, Income generating business through volunteer help.

Wmk. 373

1993, Feb. 22 **Litho.** *Perf. 14½*

680	A155	59c multicolored	1.25	1.25
681	A155	77c multicolored	1.60	1.60
682	A155	$1 multicolored	2.00	2.00
683	A155	$2 multicolored	4.25	4.25
		Nos. 680-683 (4)	9.10	9.10

Hong Kong Rugby Sevens — A156

Designs: 77c, Players performing traditional Cibi Dance. $1.06, Two players, map of Fiji, Hong Kong, and Australia. $2, Stadium, players in scrum.

Perf. 14x15

1993, Mar. 26 **Litho.** **Wmk. 384**

684	A156	77c multicolored	1.75	1.75
685	A156	$1.06 multicolored	2.50	2.50
686	A156	$2 multicolored	4.50	4.50
		Nos. 684-686 (3)	8.75	8.75

Royal Air Force, 75th Anniv.

Common Design Type

Designs: 59c, Gloster Gauntlet. 77c, Armstrong Whitworth Whitley. 83c, Bristol F2b. $2, Hawker Tempest.

No. 691: a, Vickers Vildebeest. b, Handley Page Hampden. c, Vickers Vimy. d, British Aerospace Hawk.

1993, Apr. 1 *Perf. 14*

687	CD350	59c multicolored	1.25	1.25
688	CD350	77c multicolored	1.60	1.60
689	CD350	83c multicolored	1.60	1.60
690	CD350	$2 multicolored	4.50	4.50
		Nos. 687-690 (4)	8.95	8.95

Souvenir Sheet of 4

691	CD350	$1 #a.-d.	10.00	10.00
e.		Overprinted in sheet margin	11.00	11.00

Overprint on No. 691e is exhibition emblem for Hong Kong '94.

Nudibranchs A157

Wmk. 373

1993, July 27 **Litho.** *Perf. 14*

692	A157	12c Chromodoris fidelis	.50	.50
693	A157	42c Halgerda carlsoni	1.25	1.25
694	A157	53c Chromodoris lochi	1.75	1.75
695	A157	83c Glaucus atlanticus	2.75	2.75
696	A157	$1 Phyllidia bourguini	3.25	3.25
697	A157	$2 Hexabranchus sanguineus	6.50	6.50
		Nos. 692-697 (6)	16.00	16.00

Tropical Fruit — A158

Wmk. 373

1993, Oct. 25 **Litho.** *Perf. 13½*

698	A158	30c Mango	1.25	1.25
699	A158	42c Guava	2.25	2.25
700	A158	$1 Lemon	4.50	4.50
701	A158	$2 Soursop	9.00	9.00
		Nos. 698-701 (4)	17.00	17.00

Souvenir Sheet

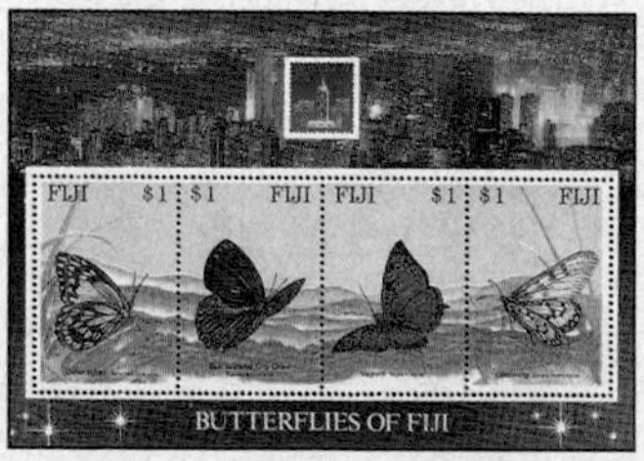

Hong Kong '94 — A159

Butterflies: a, Caper white. b, Blue branded king crow. c, Vagrant. d, Glasswing.

Perf. 14½x13

1994, Feb. 18 **Litho.** **Wmk. 373**

702	A159	$1 Sheet of 4, #a.-d.	11.00	11.00

Easter A160

59c, The Last Supper. 77c, The Crucifixion. $1, The Resurrection. $2, Jesus showing his wounds to his disciples.

Perf. 14x15, 15x14

1994, Mar. 31 **Litho.** **Wmk. 373**

703	A160	59c multi	1.25	1.25
704	A160	77c multi, vert.	1.75	1.75
705	A160	$1 multi	2.00	2.00
706	A160	$2 multi, vert.	4.25	4.25
		Nos. 703-706 (4)	9.25	9.25

Edible Seaweeds A161

42c, Codium bulbopilum. 83c, Coulerpa racemosa. $1, Hypnea pannosa. $2, Gracilaria.

Wmk. 384

1994, June 6 **Litho.** *Perf. 14*

707	A161	42c multicolored	1.25	.95
708	A161	83c multicolored	2.25	1.90
709	A161	$1 multicolored	2.75	2.40
710	A161	$2 multicolored	5.75	4.75
		Nos. 707-710 (4)	12.00	10.00

Souvenir Sheet

White-Collared Kingfisher — A162

Designs: a, On branch. b, In flight.

Wmk. 373

1994, Aug. **Litho.** *Perf. 13½*

711	A162	$1.50 Sheet of 2, #a.-b.	12.50	12.50
c.		Overprinted in sheet margin	13.50	13.50

Overprint on No. 711c consists of exhibition emblem and "JAKARTA '95."

Issued: #711, 8/16; #711c, 8/19.

Souvenir Sheet

Singpex '94 — A163

Neoveitchia storckii: a, Complete tree. b. Fruits, inflorescence.

1994, Aug. 31 **Wmk. 384** *Perf. 14*

712	A163	$1.50 Sheet of 2, #a.-b.	11.00	11.00

First Catholic Missionaries in Fiji, 150th Anniv. — A164

Wmk. 373

1994, Dec. 16 **Litho.** ***Perf. 14***

713	A164	23c Father Ioane Batita	.60	.60
714	A164	31c Local catechist	.70	.70
715	A164	44c Sacred Heart Cathedral	.95	.95
716	A164	63c Lomary Church	1.25	1.25
717	A164	81c Pope Gregory XVI	1.75	1.75
718	A164	$2 Pope John Paul II	4.00	4.00
		Nos. 713-718 (6)	9.25	9.25

Souvenir Sheet

Ecotourism in Fiji — A165

Designs: a, Waterfalls, banded iguana. b, Mountain trekking, Fiji tree frog. c, Bilibili River trip, kingfisher. d, Historic sites, flying fox.

Wmk. 373

1995, Mar. 27 **Litho.** ***Perf. 14***

719	A165	81c Sheet of 4, #a.-d.	9.00	9.00

End of World War II, 50th Anniv.

Common Design Types

Designs: 13c, Fijian regiment guarding crashed Japanese Zero Fighter. 63c, Kameli Airstrip, Solomon Islands, built by Fijian regiment. 87c, Corp. Sukanalvalu VC, Victoria Cross. $1.12, HMS Fiji.

$2, Reverse side of War Medal 1939-45.

Wmk. 373

1995, May 8 **Litho.** ***Perf. 13½***

720	CD351	13c multicolored	.60	.60
721	CD351	63c multicolored	3.25	3.25
722	CD351	87c multicolored	4.50	4.50
723	CD351	$1.12 multicolored	6.00	6.00
		Nos. 720-723 (4)	14.35	14.35

Souvenir Sheet

Perf. 14

724	CD352	$2 multicolored	7.00	7.00

Birds — A166

1995 **Litho.** **Wmk. 373** ***Perf. 13***

725	A166	1c Red-headed parrotfinch	.25	.25
726	A166	2c Golden whistler	.25	.25
727	A166	3c Ogea flycatcher	.25	.25
728	A166	4c Peale's pigeon	.25	.25
729	A166	6c Blue-crested broadbill	.25	.25
730	A166	13c Island thrush	.25	.25
731	A166	23c Many-colored fruit dove	.40	.40
732	A166	31c Mangrove heron	.55	.55
733	A166	44c Purple swamphen	1.00	1.00
734	A166	63c Fiji goshawk	1.25	1.25
735	A166	81c Kadavu fantail	1.60	1.60
736	A166	87c Collared lory	1.75	1.75
737	A166	$1 Scarlet robin	2.00	2.00
738	A166	$2 Peregrine falcon	4.00	4.00
739	A166	$3 Barn owl	5.75	5.75
739A	A166	$5 Yellow-breasted musk parrot	10.50	10.50
		Nos. 725-739A (16)	30.30	30.30

Issued: 13c, 23c, 31c, 44c, 63c, 81c, $2, $3, 7/25; 1c, 2c, 3c, 4c, 6c, 87c, $1, $5, 11/7.

See No. 1011.

For surcharges, see Nos. 1149-1160, 1191-1197C, 1214-1223A, 1249-1254E, 1314-1317.

Souvenir Sheet

Singapore '95 — A167

Orchids: a, Arundina graminifolia. b, Phaius tankervilliae.

Wmk. 373

1995, Sept. 1 **Litho.** ***Perf. 14***

740	A167	$1 Sheet of 2, #a.-b.	9.00	9.00

Independence, 25th Anniv. — A168

Designs: 81c, Pres. Kamisese Mara, Parliament Building. 87c, Fijian youth. $1.06, Playing rugby. $2, Air Pacific Boeing 747.

Wmk. 373

1995, Oct. 4 **Litho.** ***Perf. 14***

741	A168	81c multicolored	1.60	1.60
742	A168	87c multicolored	1.90	1.90
743	A168	$1.06 multicolored	2.25	2.25
744	A168	$2 multicolored	4.25	4.25
		Nos. 741-744 (4)	10.00	10.00

Christmas — A169

Paintings: 10c, Praying Madonna with the Crown of Stars, from Correggio Workshop. 63c, Madonna and Child with Crowne on porcelain. 87c, The Holy Virgin with the Holy Child and St. John, after Titian. $2, The Holy Family and St. John, from Rubens Workshop.

Wmk. 373

1995, Nov. 22 **Litho.** ***Perf. 13***

745	A169	10c multicolored	.25	.25
746	A169	63c multicolored	1.25	1.25
747	A169	87c multicolored	1.75	1.75
748	A169	$2 multicolored	4.00	4.00
		Nos. 745-748 (4)	7.25	7.25

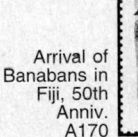

Arrival of Banabans in Fiji, 50th Anniv. A170

Perf. 14x14½, 14½x14

1996, Jan. 24 **Litho.** **Wmk. 373**

749	A170	81c Trolling lure	2.25	2.25
750	A170	87c Canoes	2.50	2.50
751	A170	$1.12 Warrior, vert.	2.75	2.75
752	A170	$2 Frigate bird, vert.	5.25	5.25
		Nos. 749-752 (4)	12.75	12.75

A171

Radio, Cent.: 44c, L2B portable tape recorder. 63c, Fiji Broadcasting Center. 81c, Communications satellite in orbit. $3, Marconi.

Wmk. 373

1996, Mar. 11 **Litho.** ***Perf. 14½***

753	A171	44c multicolored	.90	.90
754	A171	63c multicolored	1.25	1.25
755	A171	81c multicolored	1.60	1.60
756	A171	$3 multicolored	6.25	6.25
		Nos. 753-756 (4)	10.00	10.00

A172

Ancient Chinese artifacts: 63c, Bronze monster mask and ring, c. 450 BC. 81c, Archer, 210 BC. $1, Plate, Hsuan Te Period, 1426-35. $2, Central Asian horseman, dated 706.

30c, Yan Deng Mountain.

Wmk. 384

1996, Apr. 25 **Litho.** ***Perf. 13½***

757	A172	63c multicolored	1.25	1.25
758	A172	81c multicolored	1.50	1.50
759	A172	$1 multicolored	2.00	2.00
760	A172	$2 multicolored	4.25	4.25
		Nos. 757-760 (4)	9.00	9.00

Souvenir Sheet

Perf. 13½x13

761	A172	30c multicolored	2.50	2.50

No. 761 contains one 48x76mm stamp.

CHINA '96, 9th Asian Intl. Philatelic Exhibition.

A173

Wmk. 373

1996, June 18 **Litho.** ***Perf. 14***

762	A173	31c Hurdling	.65	.65
763	A173	63c Judo	1.50	1.50
764	A173	87c Sailboarding	2.10	2.10
765	A173	$1.12 Swimming	2.50	2.50
		Nos. 762-765 (4)	6.75	6.75

Souvenir Sheet

766	A173	$2 Athlete, 1896	4.00	4.00

Modern Olympic Games, cent.

A174

31c, Computerized telephone exchange, horiz. 44c, Mail being unloaded, horiz. 81c, Manual switchboard operator. $1, Mail delivery.

No. 771: a, #117. b, #527.

1996, July 1

767	A174	31c multicolored	.60	.60
768	A174	44c multicolored	.80	.80
769	A174	81c multicolored	1.40	1.40
770	A174	$1 multicolored	1.90	1.90
		Nos. 767-770 (4)	4.70	4.70

Souvenir Sheet of 2

771	A174	$1.50 #a.-b.	7.00	7.00

Creation of independent Postal, Telecommunications Companies.

UNICEF, 50th Anniv. A175

Designs: 81c, "Our children, our future." 87c, Village scene. $1, "Living in harmony the world over." $2, "Their future."

Wmk. 384

1996, Aug. 13 **Litho.** ***Perf. 14***

772	A175	81c multicolored	2.00	2.00
773	A175	87c multicolored	2.00	2.00
774	A175	$1 multicolored	2.25	2.25
775	A175	$2 multicolored	4.50	4.50
		Nos. 772-775 (4)	10.75	10.75

Nadi Intl. Airport, 50th Anniv. A176

Designs: 31c, First airplane in Fiji, 1921. 44c, Nadi Airport commences Commercial Operations, 1946. 63c, First jet in Fiji, 1959. 87c, Airport entrance. $1, Control tower, 1996. $2, Global positioning system, first commercial use, 1994.

Wmk. 373

1996, Oct. 1 **Litho.** ***Perf. 14***

776	A176	31c multicolored	.75	.75
777	A176	44c multicolored	1.00	1.00
778	A176	63c multicolored	1.50	1.50
779	A176	87c multicolored	2.00	2.00
780	A176	$1 multicolored	2.25	2.25
781	A176	$2 multicolored	4.50	4.50
		Nos. 776-781 (6)	12.00	12.00

Christmas — A177

Scene from the Christmas story and native story or scene: 13c, Angel Gabriel & Mary, beating of Lali. 81c, Shepherds with sheep, Fijian canoe. $1, Wise men on camels, multiracial Fiji. $3, Mary, Christ Child in stable, blowing of conch shell.

1996, Nov. 20 **Wmk. 373**

782	A177	13c multicolored	.30	.30
783	A177	81c multicolored	2.00	2.00
784	A177	$1 multicolored	2.40	2.40
785	A177	$3 multicolored	7.25	7.25
		Nos. 782-785 (4)	11.95	11.95

Hong Kong '97 A178

Cattle: a, Brahman. b, Freisian (Holstein). c, Hereford. d, Fiji draught bullock.

1997, Feb. 12

786	A178	$1 Sheet of 4, #a.-d.	9.25	9.25

Souvenir Sheet

Black-Faced Shrikebill — A179

1997, Feb. 21 *Perf. 14x15*
787 A179 $2 multicolored 4.50 4.50

Singpex '97.

Orchids — A180

Designs: 81c, Dendrobium biflorum. 87c, Dendrobium dactylodes. $1.06, Spathoglottis pacifica. $2, Dendrobium macropus.

Wmk. 384

1997, Apr. 22 Litho. *Perf. 14*
788 A180 81c multicolored 2.50 2.50
789 A180 87c multicolored 2.50 2.50

Wmk. 373

790 A180 $1.06 multicolored 3.50 3.50
791 A180 $2 multicolored 6.25 6.25
Nos. 788-791 (4) 14.75 14.75

Souvenir Sheet

Hawksbill Turtle — A181

Designs: a, 63c, Female laying eggs. b, 81c, Baby turtles emerging from nest. c, $1.06 Young turtles in water. d, $2, One adult in water, coral.

1997, May 26 **Wmk. 373**
792 A181 Sheet of 4, #a.-d. 11.00 11.00

Coral A182

Designs: 63c, Branching hard coral 87c, Massive hard coral. $1, Soft coral, sinularia. $3, Soft coral, dendronephthya.

Wmk. 373

1997, July 16 Litho. *Perf. 14*
793 A182 63c multicolored 1.40 1.40
794 A182 87c multicolored 1.90 1.90
795 A182 $1 multicolored 2.25 2.25
796 A182 $3 multicolored 6.75 6.75
Nos. 793-796 (4) 12.30 12.30

Fijian Monkey-faced Bat — A183

63c, With nose pointed downward. 81c, Hanging below flower. $2, Between leaves on tree branch.

Perf. 13½

1997, Oct. 15 Litho. Unwmk.
797 A183 44c multicolored 1.00 1.00
798 A183 63c multicolored 1.50 1.50
799 A183 81c multicolored 1.75 1.75
800 A183 $2 multicolored 4.25 4.25
a. Sheet, 2 each #797-800 20.00 20.00
Nos. 797-800 (4) 8.50 8.50

World Wildlife Fund.

Christmas A184

Designs: 13c, Angel, shepherd. 31c, Birth of Jesus. 87c, Magi. $3, Madonna and Child.

Perf. 14x14½

1997, Nov. 18 **Wmk. 373**
801 A184 13c multicolored .25 .25
802 A184 31c multicolored .60 .60
803 A184 87c multicolored 1.60 1.60
804 A184 $3 multicolored 5.50 5.50
Nos. 801-804 (4) 7.95 7.95

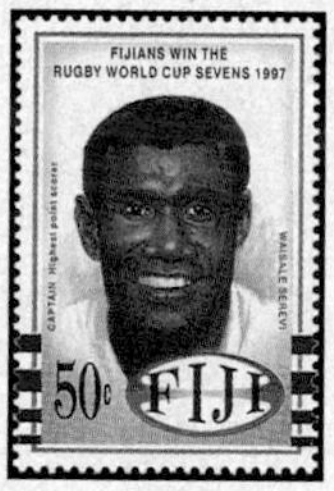

A185

1997 Rugby World Cup Sevens Champions: a, 50c, Waisale Serevi, captain, highest point scorer. b, 50c, Taniela Qauqau. c, 50c, Jope Tuikabe. d, 50c, Leveni Duvuduvukula. e, 50c, Inoke Maraiwai. f, 50c, Aminiasi Naituyaga. g, 50c, Lemeki Koroi. h, 50c, Marika Vunibaka, highest try scorer. i, 50c, Luke Erenavula. j, 50c, Manasa Bari. k, $1, Entire team.

Wmk. 373

1997, Oct. 30 Litho. *Perf. 14*
805 A185 Sheet of 11, #a.-k. 17.00 17.00

No. 805k is 53x39mm.

A186

Chief's Traditional Costumes: 81c, War dress. 87c, Formal dress. $1.12, Presentation dress. $2, Highland war dress.

Wmk. 373

1998, Jan. 20 Litho. *Perf. 14*
806 A186 81c multicolored 1.25 1.25
807 A186 87c multicolored 1.25 1.25
808 A186 $1.12 multicolored 1.75 1.75
809 A186 $2 multicolored 3.00 3.00
Nos. 806-809 (4) 7.25 7.25

Asian and Pacific Decade of Disabled Persons, 1993-2000 A187

63c, Mastering modern technology. 87c, Assisting the will to overcome. $1, Using natural born skills. $2, Competing to win.

Wmk. 373

1998, Mar. 18 Litho. *Perf. 13*
810 A187 63c multicolored 1.00 1.00
811 A187 87c multicolored 1.40 1.40
812 A187 $1 multicolored 1.50 1.50
813 A187 $2 multicolored 3.00 3.00
Nos. 810-813 (4) 6.90 6.90

Royal Air Force, 80th Anniv.

Common Design Type of 1993 Re-Inscribed

Designs: 44c, R34 Airship. 63c, Handley Page Heyford. 87c, Supermarine Swift FR.5. $2, Westland Whirlwind.

No. 818: a, Sopwith Dolphin. b, Avro 504K. c, Vickers Warwick V. d, Shorts Belfast.

1998, Apr. 1 *Perf. 13½x14*
814 CD350 44c multicolored 1.00 1.00
815 CD350 63c multicolored 1.25 1.25
816 CD350 87c multicolored 1.75 1.75
817 CD350 $2 multicolored 4.00 4.00
Nos. 814-817 (4) 8.00 8.00

Souvenir Sheet of 4

818 CD350 $1 #a.-d. 7.50 7.50

Diana, Princess of Wales (1961-97)

Common Design Type

Design: No. 819, Wearing plaid jacket.

No. 820: a, Wearing blue jacket. b, In high-collared blouse. c, Holding flowers.

1998, Mar. 31 Litho. *Perf. 14x14½*
819 CD355 81c multicolored .75 .75
820 CD355 81c Sheet of 4, #819, a.-c. 5.25 5.25

No. 820 sold for $3.24 + 50c, with surtax from international sales being donated to the Princess Diana Memorial Fund and surtax from national sales being donated to designated local charity.

Sperm Whale A188

Wmk. 373

1998, June 22 Litho. *Perf. 14*
821 A188 63c shown 1.40 1.40
822 A188 81c Adult, calf 1.90 1.90
823 A188 87c Breaching 1.90 1.90
824 A188 $2 Sperm whale tooth 4.50 4.50
a. Souvenir sheet 7.50 7.50
Nos. 821-824 (4) 9.70 9.70

16th Commonwealth Games, Kuala Lumpur, Malaysia — A189

Wmk. 384

1998, Sept. 11 Litho. *Perf. 14*
825 A189 44c Athletics .70 .70
826 A189 63c Lawn bowls 1.00 1.00
827 A189 81c Javelin 1.40 1.40
828 A189 $1.12 Weight lifting 1.90 1.90
Nos. 825-828 (4) 5.00 5.00

Souvenir Sheet

829 A189 $2 Waisale Serevi, rugby sevens 5.00 5.00

Maritime Heritage A190

Designs: 13c, Takia, hollowed-out log with outrigger. 44c, Camakau, sailing canoe. 87c, Drua, twin-hulled sailing canoe. $3, MV Pioneer motor yacht.

$1.50, Camakau, map of Fiji.

Wmk. 384

1998, Oct. 26 Litho. *Perf. 13½*
830 A190 13c multicolored .30 .30
831 A190 44c multicolored .85 .85
832 A190 87c multicolored 1.60 1.60
833 A190 $3 multicolored 5.25 5.25
Nos. 830-833 (4) 8.00 8.00

Souvenir Sheet

834 A190 $1.50 multicolored 4.75 4.75

Australia '99, World Stamp Expo (#834). See Nos. 843-847.

Christmas A191

Children's drawings: 13c, "Jesus in a Manger." 50c, "A Time for Family and Friends." $1, "What Christmas Means to Me," vert. $2, "The Joy of Christmas," vert.

1998, Nov. 23 **Wmk. 373**
835 A191 13c multicolored .30 .30
836 A191 50c multicolored .95 .95
837 A191 $1 multicolored 1.90 1.90
838 A191 $2 multicolored 4.00 4.00
Nos. 835-838 (4) 7.15 7.15

Traditional Dances — A192

Designs: 13c, Vakamalolo (women's sitting dance). 81c, Mekeiwau (club dance). 87c, Seasea (women's fan dance). $3, Meke ni yaqona (Kava serving dance).

Wmk. 373

1999, Jan. 20 Litho. *Perf. 14½*
839 A192 13c multicolored .25 .25
840 A192 81c multicolored 1.60 1.60
841 A192 87c multicolored 1.90 1.90
842 A192 $3 multicolored 5.75 5.75
Nos. 839-842 (4) 9.50 9.50

Maritime Heritage Type of 1998

Designs: 63c, SS Toufua, 1920-30's. 81c, MF Adi Beti, 1920-30's. $1, SS Niagara, 1920-30's. $2, MV Royal Viking Sun, 1990's.

$1.50, SS. Makatea, 1920's.

1999, Mar. 19 Wmk. 384 *Perf. 13½*
843 A190 63c multicolored .90 .90
844 A190 81c multicolored 1.50 1.50
845 A190 $1 multicolored 1.75 1.75
846 A190 $2 multicolored 3.50 3.50
Nos. 843-846 (4) 7.65 7.65

Souvenir Sheet

847 A190 $1.50 multicolored 4.50 4.50

Australia '99, World Stamp Exhibition (#847).

Souvenir Sheet

Ducks — A193

a, Wandering whistling. b, Pacific black.

1999, Apr. 27 Wmk. 373
848 A193 $2 Sheet of 2, #a.-b. 7.00 7.00

IBRA '99, Intl. Philatelic Exhibition, Nuremberg.

Orchids — A194

Designs: 44c, Calanthe ventilabrum. 63c, Dendrobium prasinum. 81c, Dendrobium macrophyllum. $3, Dendrobium tokai.

1999, June 28
849 A194 44c multicolored .75 .75
850 A194 63c multicolored 1.00 1.00
851 A194 81c multicolored 1.25 1.25
852 A194 $3 multicolored 5.00 5.00
Nos. 849-852 (4) 8.00 8.00

1st Manned Moon Landing, 30th Anniv.

Common Design Type

13c, Astronaut waves goodbye. 87c, Stage 3 fires towards moon. $1, Aldrin walks on lunar surface. $2, Command module fires towards earth.
$2, Looking at earth from moon.

Perf. 14x13¾
1999, July 20 Wmk. 384
853 CD357 13c multicolored .25 .25
854 CD357 87c multicolored 1.40 1.40
855 CD357 $1 multicolored 1.75 1.75
856 CD357 $2 multicolored 3.25 3.25
Nos. 853-856 (4) 6.65 6.65

Souvenir Sheet

Perf. 14
857 CD357 $2 multicolored 3.75 3.75

No. 857 contains one circular stamp 40mm in diameter.

Queen Mother's Century

Common Design Type

Queen Mother: 13c, Visiting Hull to see bomb damage. 63c, With Prince Charles. 81c, As Colonel-in-Chief of Light Infantry. $3, With Prince Charles at Clarence House.
$2, With crowd on Armistice Day.

Wmk. 384
1999, Aug. 18 Litho. *Perf. 13½*
858 CD358 13c multicolored .50 .50
859 CD358 63c multicolored 1.25 1.25
860 CD358 81c multicolored 1.75 1.75
861 CD358 $3 multicolored 5.50 5.50
Nos. 858-861 (4) 9.00 9.00

Souvenir Sheet
862 CD358 $2 multicolored 6.00 6.00

UPU, 125th Anniv. A195

Sugar Mills rolling stock: 50c, Diesel locomotive. 87c, Steam locomotive. $1, Diesel locomotive, diff. $2, Free passenger train.

Wmk. 373
1999, Oct. 26 Litho. *Perf. 13¾*
863 A195 50c multicolored .60 .60
864 A195 87c multicolored 1.25 1.25
865 A195 $1 multicolored 1.40 1.40
866 A195 $2 multicolored 2.75 2.75
Nos. 863-866 (4) 6.00 6.00

Christmas — A196

Designs: 13c, Giving gifts. 31c, Angels and star. 63c, Bible, Magi, Holy family. 87c, Joseph, mary, donkey, vert. $1, Mary, Jesus, animals, vert. $2, Children, Santa, vert.

Perf. 13¼x13
1999, Nov. 29 Litho. Wmk. 373
867 A196 13c multicolored .25 .25
868 A196 31c multicolored .45 .45
869 A196 63c multicolored .90 .90
870 A196 87c multicolored 1.25 1.25
871 A196 $1 multicolored 1.40 1.40
872 A196 $2 multicolored 2.75 2.75
Nos. 867-872 (6) 7.00 7.00

Millennium A197

Designs: No. 873, Outstretched hands, islands (arch at top). No. 874, Map, flag (arch at right). No. 875, Globe, warrior beating lali, temple (arch at bottom). No. 876, Globe, drua, red line (arch at left).
No. 877: a, Fiji petrel (arch at top). b, Crested iguana, islands (arch at top). c, Red prawns (arch at bottom). d, Tagimaucia (arch at bottom).

Perf. 13¼ Syncopated Type A
Litho. with Foil Application
2000, Jan. 1 Unwmk.
873 A197 $5 gold & multi 7.50 7.50
874 A197 $5 gold & multi 7.50 7.50
875 A197 $5 gold & multi 7.50 7.50
876 A197 $5 gold & multi 7.50 7.50
Nos. 873-876 (4) 30.00 30.00

Souvenir Sheet
877 A197 $10 Sheet of 4, #a-d 60.00 60.00

Beetles — A198

Designs: 15c, Paracupta sulcata. 87c, Agrilus sp. $1.06, Cyphogastra abdominalis. $2, Paracupta sp.

Perf. 13¾x14
2000, Mar. 14 Litho. Wmk. 373
878 A198 15c multi .25 .25
879 A198 87c multi 1.50 1.50
880 A198 $1.06 multi 1.75 1.75
881 A198 $2 multi 3.00 3.00
Nos. 878-881 (4) 6.50 6.50

Sesame Street — A199

No. 882: a, Big Bird. b, Oscar the Grouch. c, Cookie Monster. d, Grover. e, Elmo. f, Ernie. g, Zoe. h, The Count. i, Bert.
No. 883, Big Bird, Elmo and Ernie, horiz. No. 884, Cookie Monster, Bert and Ernie, horiz.

Perf. 14½x14¾
2000, Apr. 20 Litho. Wmk. 373
882 A199 50c Sheet of 9, #a-i 8.00 8.00

Souvenir Sheets

Perf. 14¾x14½
883 A199 $2 multi 3.50 3.50
884 A199 $2 multi 3.50 3.50

The Stamp Show 2000, London (#882).

Pres. Ratu Sir Kamisese Mara, 80th Birthday — A200

President with: 15c, Lumberjack, timber truck. 81c, Women. $1, Workers in cane field. $3, Ships.

2000, May 13 *Perf. 14x13¾*
885 A200 15c multi .25 .25
886 A200 81c multi 1.00 1.00
887 A200 $1 multi 1.25 1.25
888 A200 $3 multi 4.50 4.50
Nos. 885-888 (4) 7.00 7.00

Prince William, 18th Birthday

Common Design Type

William: Nos. 889, 893a, As child, wearing fireman's helmet, vert. Nos. 890, 893b, Wearing navy suit, vert. Nos. 891, 893c, Wearing scarf. Nos. 892, 893d, Wearing suit and wearing blue shirt. No. 893e, As child, wearing camouflage and beret.

Perf. 13¾x14¼, 14¼x13¾
2000, June 21 Wmk. 373

Stamps With White Border
889 CD359 $1 multi 1.50 1.50
890 CD359 $1 multi 1.50 1.50
891 CD359 $1 multi 1.50 1.50
892 CD359 $1 multi 1.50 1.50
Nos. 889-892 (4) 6.00 6.00

Souvenir Sheet

Stamps Without White Border

Perf. 14¼
893 CD359 $1 Sheet of 5, #a-e 8.00 8.00

2000 Summer Olympics, Sydney — A201

Wmk. 373
2000, Aug. 8 Litho. *Perf. 13¾*
894 A201 44c Swimming, vert. .50 .50
895 A201 87c Judo, vert. 1.25 1.25
896 A201 $1 Running 1.50 1.50
897 A201 $2 Windsurfing 2.75 2.75
Nos. 894-897 (4) 6.00 6.00

Souvenir Sheet

Alsmithia Longipes — A202

No. 898: a, Red frond at R. b, Red frond at L. c, Yellow frond. d, Fruit.

Wmk. 373
2000, Sept. 12 Litho. *Perf. 13½*
898 A202 $1 Sheet of 4, #a-d 7.50 7.50

Lapita Pottery Shards and Discovery Sites — A203

44c, Yanuca Island. 63c, Mago Island. $1, Ugaga Island. $2, Sigatoka sand dunes.

2000, Oct. 24 *Perf. 13¾*
899-902 A203 Set of 4 6.00 6.00

Christmas A204

Designs: 15c, Jungle. 81c, Cliffside trail. 87c, Coastal village. $3, Outrigger canoe.

2000, Nov. 21
903-906 A204 Set of 4 6.50 6.50

Souvenir Sheet

Taveuni Rain Forest — A205

Designs: a, Orange dove. b, Xixuthrus heyrovskyi.

Perf. 13¾x13½

2001, Feb. 1 Litho. Unwmk.
907 A205 $2 Sheet of 2, #a-b 6.00 6.00

Moths A206

Designs: 17c, Macroglossum hirundo vitiensis. 48c, Hippotion celerio. 69c, Gnathothlibus erotus eras. 89c, Theretra pinastrina intersecta. $1.17, Deilephila placida torenia. $2, Psilogramma jordana.

2001, Mar. 20 ***Perf. 13¼x13***
908-913 A206 Set of 6 7.50 7.50

Souvenir Sheet

Gallus Gallus — A207

Designs: a, Hen. b, Rooster.

2001, May 22 ***Perf. 13¾x14***
914 A207 $2 Sheet of 2, #a-b 7.00 7.00

Society for Prevention of Cruelty — A208

Designs: 34c, Girl, cat. 96c, Boy, dogs. $1.23, Girl, cat, diff. $2, Boy, dog.

Perf. 14x13¾

2001, June 26 Litho. Unwmk.
915-918 A208 Set of 4 7.00 7.00

Pigeons — A209

Designs: 69c, White-throated. 89c, Pacific, vert. $1.23, Peal's, vert. $2, Rock.

2001, July 20 ***Perf. 14x14¾, 14¾x14***
919-922 A209 Set of 4 7.25 7.25

Westpac Pacific Bank, 100th Anniv. in Fiji — A210

Bank office in: 48c, 1901. 96c, 1916. $1, 1934. $2, 2001.

2001, Aug. 10 ***Perf. 13¼x13¾***
923-926 A210 Set of 4 5.50 5.50

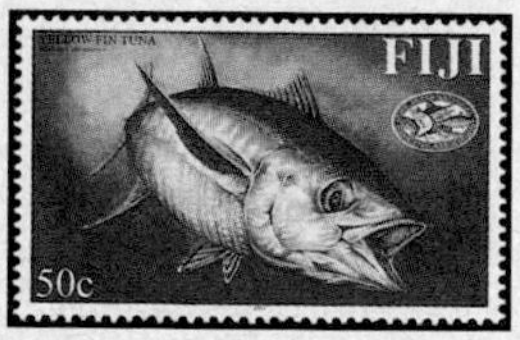

Fish A211

Designs: 50c, Yellowfin tuna. 96c, Wahoo. $1.17, Dolphin fish. $2, Pacific blue marlin.

2001, Aug. 23
927-930 A211 Set of 4 6.00 6.00

Christmas A212

Designs: 17c, Angel appears to Mary. 34c Nativity. 48c, Adoration of the shepherds. 69c, Adoration of the Magi. 89c, Flight to Egypt. $2, Fijian Chirst child.

2001, Oct. 29 Litho. ***Perf. 13¾x13¼***
931-936 A212 Set of 6 6.75 6.75

Colonial Financial Services Group, 125th Anniv. in Fiji — A213

Designs: 17c, Bank office. 48c, Women using automatic teller machine. $1, Suva Private Hospital. $3, Hoisting of British flag.

2001, Nov. 16 Litho. ***Perf. 13¼***
937-940 A213 Set of 4 6.75 6.75

Air Pacific, 50th Anniv. — A214

No. 941: a, De Havilland Drover. b, Hawker Siddley HS-748. c, Douglas DC-10-30. d, Boeing 747-200.

2001, Nov. 30 Litho. ***Perf. 13***
941 Horiz. strip of 4 7.25 7.25
a. A214 89c multi 1.25 1.00
b. A214 96c multi 1.40 1.10
c. A214 $1 multi 1.50 1.25
d. A214 $2 multi 3.00 1.50

Spices — A215

Designs: 69c, Pepper. 89c, Nutmeg. $1, Vanilla. $2, Cinnamon.

2002, Mar. 12 Litho. ***Perf. 13¼***
942-945 A215 Set of 4 6.50 6.50

Souvenir Sheet

Balaka Palm — A216

Palm and: a, Bird, butterfly, beetle. b, Lizard, butterfly

2002, Apr. 29
946 A216 $2 Sheet of 2, #a-b 7.00 7.00

Freshwater Fish — A217

Designs: 48c, Redigobius sp. 96c, Spotted flagtail. $1.23, Silverstripe mudskipper. $2, Snakehead gudgeon.

2002, May 13
947-950 A217 Set of 4 7.00 7.00

Fruit — A218

Designs: 25c, Breadfruit. 34c, Wi. $1, Jakfruit. $3, Avocado.

2002, July 25 Litho. ***Perf. 13¾x13¼***
951-954 A218 Set of 4 6.25 6.25

Murex Shells — A219

Designs: 69c, Saul's murex. 96c, Caltrop murex. $1, Purple Pacific drupe. $2, Ramose murex.

2002, Aug. 20 ***Perf. 13¾***
955-958 A219 Set of 4 7.00 7.00

Fiji Goshawk A220

Designs: 48c, Goshawk and eggs. 89c, Chicks in nest. $1, Juvenile on branch. $3, Adult.

2002, Sept. 10
959-962 A220 Set of 4 8.00 8.00

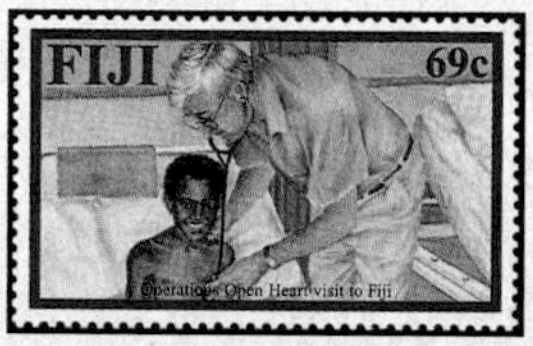

2002 Operation Open Heart Visit to Fiji — A221

Designs: 34c, Doctors performing operation, vert. 69c, Doctor listening to patient's heart with stethoscope. $1.17, Technician administering echocardiogram. $2, Administration of anesthesia to patient, vert.

2002, Oct. 30 ***Perf. 13¼***
963-966 A221 Set of 4 7.25 7.25

Fiji Natural Artesian Water — A222

Designs: 25c, Bottle of water, flowers, vert. 48c, Bottling plant. $1, Delivery truck. $3, Children with bottled water, vert.

2002, Nov. 5
967-970 A222 Set of 4 7.75 7.75

Christmas — A223

Designs: 17c, Christian church. 89c, Mosque. $1, Hindu temple. $3, Christian church, diff.

2002, Nov. 20
971-974 A223 Set of 4 7.50 7.50

Post Fiji, Ltd. Improvements — A224

Designs: 48c, General Post Office. 96c, Post Fiji Mail Center. $1, Post Fiji Logistics Center. $2, Smart Mail.

2003, Mar. 19 Litho. ***Perf. 13¼***
975-978 A224 Set of 4 6.75 6.75

Souvenir Sheet

Intl. Year of Fresh Water — A225

No. 979: a, Top of waterfall, flowers. b, Base of waterfall, butterfly.

2003, Apr. 22
979 A225 $2 Sheet of 2, #a-b 7.25 7.25

2003 South Pacific Games, Suva — A226

Designs: 10c, Track athlete with arms raised. 14c, Baseball. 20c, Netball. No. 983, $5, Shot put.
No. 984, $5, Flags of participating nations, venues, volleyball players.

2003 ***Perf. 13¼***
980-983 A226 Set of 4 7.25 7.25

Size: 120x85mm

Imperf

984 A226 $5 multi 7.00 7.00

Issued: Nos. 980-983, 5/26; No. 984, 6/28.

Fish A227

Siganus uspi: 58c, Fish, crab and coral. 83c, Two fish and coral. $1.15, Two fish, coral, and other fish species. $3, Fish and coral.

2003, Aug. 12 ***Perf. 13¼***
985-988 A227 Set of 4 8.00 8.00

Bird Life International A228

Designs: 41c, Long-legged warbler. 60c, Silktail. $1.07, Red-throated lorikeet. $3, Pink-billed parrot finch.

2003, Sept. 16
989-992 A228 Set of 4 13.00 13.00

Geckos A229

Designs: 83c, Pacific slender-toed gecko. $1.07, Indopacific tree gecko. $1.15, Mann's gecko. $2, Voracious gecko.

2003, Oct. 21 **Litho.** ***Perf. 13¼***
993-996 A229 Set of 4 10.00 10.00

Christmas — A230

Children's art: 18c, Children, Christmas tree. 41c, Children, flag of Fiji. 58c, Children, Santa Claus, reindeer pulling sleighs, vert. 83c, Santa Claus on chimney, gifts, children, Christmas tree, vert. $1.07, Children with candles, Christmas tree, vert. $1.15, Santa Claus, children, bell, rainbow, vert.
$1.41, Handshake.

2003, Nov. 26 **Litho.** ***Perf. 13¼***
997-1002 A230 Set of 6 7.50 7.50

Souvenir Sheet

1003 A230 $1.41 multi 3.50 3.50

Tagimoucla — A231

2003, Dec. 1 **Litho.** ***Perf. 14½x14***
1004 A231 50c multi + label *1.75 1.75*

Sold in sheets of 10 stamps + 10 labels that could be personalized for $15 per sheet.

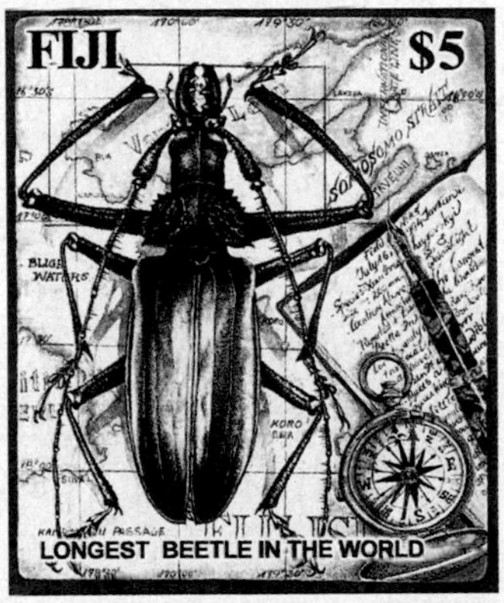

Xixuthrus Heyrovskyi, Longest Beetle in the World — A232

2003, Feb. 27 ***Imperf.***
1005 A232 $5 multi 8.00 8.00

Miniature Sheet

Worldwide Fund for Nature (WWF) — A233

No. 1006: a, 58c, Skipjack tuna. b, 83c, Albacore tuna. c, $1.07, Yellowfin tuna. d, $3, Bigeye tuna.

2004, Apr. 7 ***Perf. 13¼***
1006 A233 Sheet of 4, #a-d 8.50 8.50
e. Like #1006, with artist's name at LL of each stamp 8.50 8.50

Land Snails A234

Designs: 18c, Malleated placostyle. 41c, Kandavu placostyle. $1.15, Fragile orpiella. $3, Thin Fijian placostyle.

2004, May 28
1007-1010 A234 Set of 4 7.75 7.75

Bird Type of 1995

Perf. 13¼x13

2004, June 26 **Unwmk.**
1011 A166 18c Island thrush 1.25 1.25

Coral Reef Shrimp — A235

Designs: 58c, Boxer shrimp. 83c, Bumble-bee shrimp. $1.07, Mantis shrimp. $3, Anemone shrimp.

2004, June 30 ***Perf. 13¼***
1012-1015 A235 Set of 4 7.50 7.50

Birds A236

Designs: 41c, Wandering tattler. 58c, Whimbrel. $1.15, Pacific golden plover. $3, Bristle-thighed curlew.

2004, July 28
1016-1019 A236 Set of 4 10.00 10.00

2004 Summer Olympics, Athens A237

Designs: 41c, Swimming. 58c, Judo, vert. $1.40, Weight lifting, vert. $2, Makelesi Bulikiobo, runner.

2004, Aug. 12
1020-1023 A237 Set of 4 8.00 8.00

Musket Cove to Port Vila Yacht Race, 25th Anniv. — A238

Various yachts: 83c, $1.07, $1.15, $2. $1.07 and $2 are vert.

2004, Sept. 18 ***Perf. 14¼***
1024-1027 A238 Set of 4 9.00 9.00
1027a Souvenir sheet of 1 5.00 5.00

See Vanuatu Nos. 858-861.

Souvenir Sheet

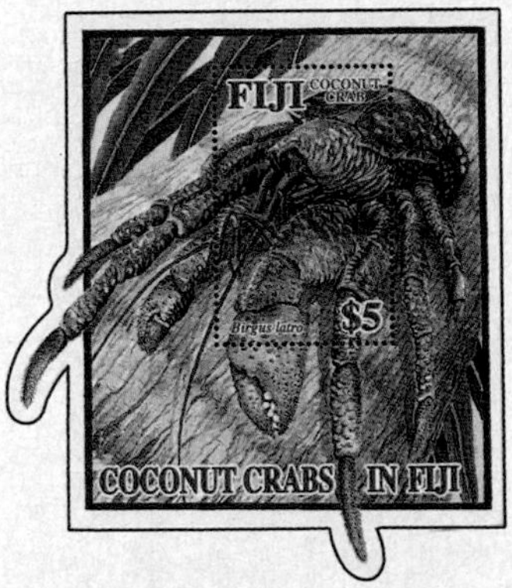

Coconut Crab — A239

2004, Oct. 20 **Litho.** ***Perf. 14***
1028 A239 $5 multi 8.00 8.00

Papilio Schmeltzii — A240

Designs: 58c, Newly-emerged adult, vert. 83c, Larva. $1.41, Adult. $3, Pupa, vert.

Perf. 14x14½, 14½x14

2004, Nov. 10
1029-1032 A240 Set of 4 10.00 10.00

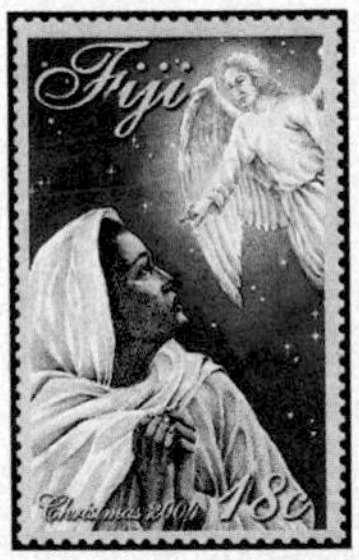

Christmas A241

Designs: 18c, Annunciation. 58c, Infant in manger. $1.07, Madonna and child. $3, Adoration of the Shepherds.

2004, Dec. 1 **Litho.** ***Perf. 13¼***
1033-1036 A241 Set of 4 9.50 9.50

Birds — A242

No. 1037: a, Little heron. b, Great white egret. c, White-faced heron. d, Pacific reef heron.

2005, Jan. 26
1037 Horiz. strip of 4 9.00 9.00
a.-d. A242 $1 Any single 2.25 2.25

Flowers For Perfume — A243

Designs: 58c, Cananga odorata. $1.15, Euodia hortensis. $1.41, Pandanus tecorius. $2, Santalum yasi.

2005, Feb. 20 ***Perf. 14x14½***
1038-1041 A243 Set of 4 8.00 8.00

Peregrine Falcons — A244

Designs: 41c, Head of falcon. 83c, Adult at nest. $1.07, Chicks. $3, Adult on rock.

2005, Mar. 14 Litho. ***Perf. 14½x14***
1042-1045 A244 Set of 4 9.50 9.50

Triggerfish — A245

Designs: 58c, Whitebanded triggerfish. 83c, Yellow-spotted triggerfish. $1.15, Orange-lined triggerfish. $2, Clown triggerfish.

2005, Apr. 27
1046-1049 A245 Set of 4 8.50 8.50

European Philatelic Cooperation, 50th Anniv. (in 2006) — A246

Color of arches: 58c, Red. 83c, Blue green. $1.41, Purple. $4, Yellow bister.

2005, June 1 ***Perf. 13¾***
1050-1053 A246 Set of 4 11.00 11.00
1053a Souvenir sheet, #1050-1053 11.00 11.00

Europa stamps, 50th anniv. (in 2006).

Miniature Sheet

End of World War II, 60th Anniv. — A247

No. 1054: a, HMNZS Achilles. b, Japanese Yokosuka E14Y "Glen" over Suva Harbor. c, Fijian South Pacific Scouts in Solomon Islands. d, USS Chicago. e, Patrol vessel HMS Viti. f, British Prime Minister Winston Churchill. g, HMS Hood. h, Dambusters Raid. i, German King Tiger tank in Ardennes. j, Gen. Dwight D. Eisenhower.

2005, June 27 Litho. ***Perf. 13¾***
1054 A247 83c Sheet of 10, #a-j 13.00 13.00

Game Fish A248

Designs: 41c, Great barracuda. 58c, Narrow-barred Spanish mackerel. $1.07, Giant trevally. $3, Indo-Pacific sailfish.

2005, July 27 Litho. ***Perf. 14½x14***
1055-1058 A248 Set of 4 8.00 8.00

Pope John Paul II (1920-2005) A249

2005, Aug. 18 ***Perf. 14***
1059 A249 $1 multi 2.50 2.50

Dragonflies — A250

Designs: 83c, Yellow-striped flutterer. $1.07, Agrionoptera insignis. $1.15, Green skimmer. $2, Common percher.

2005, Aug. 30 Litho. ***Perf. 13¼***
1060-1063 A250 Set of 4 8.00 8.00

Albert Einstein (1879-1955), Physicist — A251

Einstein: 83c, As a child. $1.07, In 1905. $1.15, And blackboard. $2, And galaxies.

2005, Sept. 27 Litho. ***Perf. 14¼x14***
1064-1067 A251 Set of 4 8.00 8.00

Intl. Year of Physics.

Root Crops — A252

Designs: 41c, Manihot utilissima. 83c, Ipomoea satatas. $1.41, Colocasia esculenta. $2, Dioscorea sativa.

2005, Oct. 13 ***Perf. 13¼***
1068-1071 A252 Set of 4 6.50 6.50

Tall Ships A253

Designs: 83c, Eliza of Province. $1.15, Elbe. $1.41, HMS Rosario. $2, L'Astrolabe.

2005, Nov. 21 Litho. ***Perf. 14x14¼***
1072-1075 A253 Set of 4 7.50 7.50

Barn Owls — A254

Owl: 18c, And eggs. $1.15, Juvenile. $1.41, With prey. $2, Perched.

2006, Jan. 10 Litho. ***Perf. 14¼x14***
1076-1079 A254 Set of 4 9.25 9.25

Platymantis Vitianus — A255

Various depictions: 50c, 83c, $1.15, $2.

2006, Feb. 8 Litho. ***Perf. 14x14¼***
1080-1083 A255 Set of 4 8.00 8.00

Skinks A256

Designs: 18c, Pygmy snake-eyed skink. 58c, Brown-tailed copper striped skink. $1.15, Pacific black skink. $3, Pacific blue-tailed skink.

2006, Mar. 22
1084-1087 A256 Set of 4 8.00 8.00

Queen Elizabeth II, 80th Birthday A257

Designs: 50c, As child. 65c, Wearing tiara. 90c, Wearing blue hat. $3, Wearing blue hat, diff.

No. 1092: a, Like 65c. b, Like 90c.

2006, Apr. 21 Litho. ***Perf. 14***

With White Frames

1088-1091 A257 Set of 4 7.00 7.00

Souvenir Sheet

Without White Frames

1092 A257 $2 Sheet of 2, #a-b 6.00 6.00

Miniature Sheet

Vijay Singh, Golfer — A258

No. 1097 — Singh: a, Head. b, With arm raised. c, Leaning on golf club. d, Hitting ball from sand trap. e, Holding trophy (60x87mm).

Perf. 14x14¼

2006, May 26 Litho. Unwmk.
1097 A258 $1 Sheet of 5, #a-e 8.50 8.50

2006 World Cup Soccer Championships, Germany — A259

Various players: 65c, 90c, $1.20, $2.

2006, June 9 ***Perf. 14¼x14***
1098-1101 A259 Set of 4 7.50 7.50

Souvenir Sheet

Purple Swamphen — A260

No. 1102: a, Swamphen and flowers. b, Swamphen on nest.

2006, July 20 ***Perf. 14½x14***
1102 A260 $2 Sheet of 2, #a-b 6.50 6.50

Extinct Species A261

Designs: 50c, Brachylophus vitiensis. $1.10, Natunaornis gigoura, vert. $1.20, Vitirallus watlingi, vert. $1.50, Platymantis megabotoniviti.

Perf. 14x14¼, 14¼x14

2006, Aug. 15 Litho.
1103-1106 A261 Set of 4 7.00 7.00

Phasmids — A262

Designs: 10c, Hermarchus apollonius. $1.10, Cotylosoma dipneusticum. $1.20, Chitoniscus feejeeanus. $2, Graeffea crouanii.

2006, Sept. 7 *Perf. 14½x14*
1107-1110 A262 Set of 4 7.00 7.00

Honey Production A263

Designs: 18c, Bees and honeycomb. 40c, Apiarist examining honeycomb, horiz. $1, Woman and beehives, horiz. $3, Man and bottle of honey.

2006, Oct. 16 *Perf. 14x14½, 14½x14*
1111-1114 A263 Set of 4 7.50 7.50

Christmas A264

Flowering plants: 18c, Decaspermum vitiense. 65c, Quisqualis indica. 90c, Mussaendra raiateensis. $3, Delonix regia.

2006, Dec. 5 *Perf. 14x14½*
1115-1118 A264 Set of 4 7.50 7.50

Anemonefish — A265

Designs: 18c, Spine-cheek anemonefish. 60c, Pink anemonefish. 90c, Orange-fin anemonefish. $3, Dusky anemonefish.

Perf. 14½x14, 14x14½
2006, Nov. 7 **Litho.**
1119-1122 A265 Set of 4 7.50 7.50

Souvenir Sheet

Thalassina Anomala — A266

2007, Jan. 24 *Perf. 13½*
1123 A266 $4 multi 5.50 5.50

Traditional Architecture — A267

Designs: 20c, Coastal dwelling. 65c, Inland dwelling. $1.10, Temple, Bau. $3, Lauan-style house.

2007, Mar. 20 **Litho.** *Perf. 13¼*
1124-1127 A267 Set of 4 6.75 6.75

Freshwater Gobies — A268

Designs: 20c, Sicyopterus lagocephalus. $1.10, Stiphodon rutilaureus. $1.20, Sicyopus zosterophorum. $2, Stiphodon sp.

2007, Apr. 5 **Litho.** *Perf. 13¼*
1128-1131 A268 Set of 4 6.00 6.00

Birds Introduced to Fiji — A269

Designs: 50c, Red-vented bulbul. 65c, Spotted dove, horiz. $1.50, Australian magpie, horiz. $2, Java sparrow.

2007, May 22
1132-1135 A269 Set of 4 7.25 7.25

Scouting, Cent. A270

Designs: 50c, Scout in kayak, hand holding compass. 90c, Three Scouts wearing helmets, hands tying knot. No. 1138, $1.50, Scout in harness climbing, Scout saluting. $2, Scout writing observation notes, hands tying neckerchief.

No. 1140, $1.50, vert.: a, Scout emblem. b, Lord Robert Baden-Powell.

2007, July 9 *Perf. 13¾*
1136-1139 A270 Set of 4 7.00 7.00

Souvenir Sheet

1140 A270 $1.50 Sheet of 2, #a-b 4.75 4.75

Snails A271

Designs: 40c, Clithon diadema. 90c, Neritina variegata. $1.20, Fijidoma maculata. $2, Neritina squamaepicta.

2007, Aug. 18 *Perf. 14x14¼*
1141-1144 A271 Set of 4 6.25 6.25

Orchids — A272

Designs: 20c, Liparis layardii. 65c, Dendrobium catillare, horiz. $1.10, Dendrobium mohlianum, horiz. $3, Glomera montana.

Perf. 14¼x14, 14x14¼
2007, Aug. 21
1145-1148 A272 Set of 4 7.25 7.25

Nos. 725 and 729 Surcharged

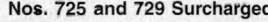

No. 1149

No. 1150

Methods, Types and Watermarks As Before

2006-08
1149 A166 1c on 6c #729 1.00 1.00
1150 A166 1c on 6c #729 *7.00 7.00*

No. 1149 exists with inverted surcharge. Value, $90. No. 1149 also exists with double surcharge, one inverted. Value, $150. No. 1149 also exists with normal surcharge shifted 75% upward. Value, $50.

No. 1151

No. 1152

No. 1152c

1151 A166 2c on 1c #725 *4.00 4.00*
1152 A166 2c on 1c #725, larger font *2.00 2.00*
c. 1 ½mm gap between "2" and "c" (position 67) *60.00 60.00*

No. 1152 exists with normal surcharge shifted 50% upward. Value, $50.

No. 1152A

No. 1152Ab

1152A A166 2c on 1c #725, 4mm between "c" and obliterator *200.00 200.00*
b. 5mm between "c" and obliterator *200.00 200.00*

No. 1152Ab exists with inverted surcharge. Value, $375.

No. 1153

No. 1153a

No. 1153c

1153 A166 2c on 6c #729, 4mm between "c" and obliterator 1.25 1.25
a. 5mm between "c" and obliterator 1.25 1.25
c. 1 ½mm gap between "2" and "c" (position 57) *60.00 60.00*

No. 1153a exists with inverted surcharge. Value, $110. No. 1153a also exists with double surcharge, one inverted. Value, $150.

No. 1153B

No. 1154

1153B A166 2c on 6c #729 *500.00 500.00*
1154 A166 3c on 1c #725 1.25 1.25

No. 1154 exists with double surcharge, one inverted. Value, $300.

No. 1155

No. 1155a

1155 A166 4c on 1c #725 1.50 1.50
a. 1 ½mm gap between "4" and "c" (position 67) *50.00 50.00*

No. 1156

No. 1156a

1156 A166 4c on 6c #729, 4mm between "c" an obliterator 1.25 1.25
a. 5mm between "c" and obliterator 1.25 1.25

No. 1156a exists with inverted surcharge. Value, $110. No. 1156a also exists with double surcharge, one inverted. Value, $150. No. 1156a also exists with normal surcharge shifted 75% upward and 50% upward. Values, each $50.

No. 1156B

No. 1157

1156B A166 6c on 6c #729 *500.00 500.00*
1157 A166 18c on 6c #729, 4mm between "c" and obliterator *6.50 6.50*

No. 1157 exists with double surcharge, one with normal 4mm between "c" and obliterator and the other with 2½mm between "c" and obliterator. One surcharge is shifted 75% upward. Half of the errors have the normal separation between "c" and obliterator at top and half have it at bottom. Each error variety is equally scarce. Value, each $130.

No. 1157 also exists with normal surcharge shifted 75% upward but with no second surcharge. Value, $50.

No. 1158

No. 1158a

1158 A166 18c on 6c #729, 2½mm between "c" and obliterator *11.00 11.00*
a. 4mm between "c" and obliterator *22.00 22.00*

No. 1158 exists with double surcharge. Value, $150.

No. 1159

No. 1159a

1159 A166 20c on 6c #729, 2½mm between "c" and obliterator *6.50 6.50*
a. 4mm between "c" and obliterator *14.50 14.50*

No. 1159 exists with inverted surcharge. Value, $110.

No. 1160

No. 1160a

No. 1160b

1160 A166 20c on 6c #729, 4mm between "c" and obliterator *30.00 30.00*
a. 1½mm between "c" and obliterator *60.00 60.00*
b. No gap between "c" and obliterator *475.00 475.00*
Nos. 1149-1160 (15) 1,273. 1,273.

No. 1160a exists with double surcharge. Value, $150.

Issued: No. 1149, 5/30/07; No. 1150, 9/19/07; No. 1151, 4/3; No. 1152, 11/13; No. 1152A, July 2007, No. 1152Ab, 8/20/08; Nos. 1153, 1153B 2/19/07; No. 1153a, 2/27/07; No. 1154, 3/13; No. 1155, 6/27; No. 1156, 6/6/07; No. 1156a, 2/19/08; No. 1156B, Feb. 2007; No. 1157, 6/8; No. 1158, 9/8; No. 1158a, Aug. 2007; No. 1159, 1/19/07; No. 1159a, Jan. 2007; No. 1160, 3/8/07; No. 1160a, 4/12/08.

Fish A273

Designs: 50c, Coronation trout. 90c, Roving coral trout. $1.50, Squaretail coral trout. $2, Chinese footballer.

2007, Oct. 15 Litho. *Perf. 13¼*
1161-1164 A273 Set of 4 7.50 7.50

Butterflies — A274

Designs: 20c, Polyura caphontis. $1.10, Hypolimnas bolina, horiz. $1.20, Doleschallia bisaltide, horiz. $2, Danaus hamata.

2007, Nov. 20 Litho. *Perf. 13¼*
1165-1168 A274 Set of 4 6.00 6.00

Souvenir Sheet

Barred-winged Rail — A275

No. 1169: a, Head of adult. b, Chick.

2007, Dec. 3
1169 A275 $2 Sheet of 2, #a-b 5.50 5.50

National Medals — A276

Designs: 50c, Medal of the Order of Fiji. 65c, Member of the Order of Fiji. $1.20, Officer of the Order of Fiji. $2, Companion of the Order of Fiji.

2008, Feb. 20 Litho. *Perf. 13¼*
1170-1173 A276 Set of 4 5.50 5.50

Souvenir Sheet

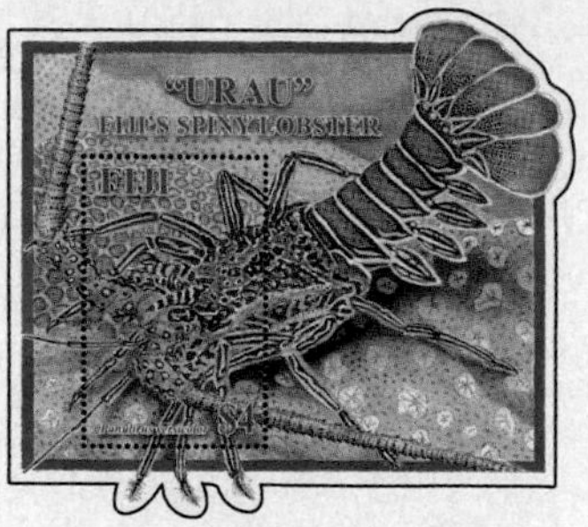

Spiny Lobster — A277

2008, Apr. 22 Litho. *Perf. 14x14½*
1174 A277 $4 multi 5.00 5.00

First Trans-Pacific Flight of the Southern Cross, 80th Anniv. — A278

Southern Cross: 20c, Over Fiji. 90c, In Albert Park, Suva. $1.50, Surrounded by police guard. $2, With crew.

2008, June 13 *Perf. 13½*
1175-1178 A278 Set of 4 5.75 5.75

2008 Summer Olympics, Beijing A279

Designs: 20c, Bamboo, Running. 65c, Dragon, Judo. 90c, Lanterns, Shooting. $1.50, Carp, Swimming.

2008, May 5 Litho. *Perf. 13¼*
1179-1182 A279 Set of 4 4.00 4.00

Red-breasted Musk Parrot Varieties — A280

Prosopeia tabuensis: 65c, Koroensis. 90c, Atrogularis, horiz. $1.50, Taviunensis, horiz. $2, Splendens.

2008, Mar. 25 Litho. *Perf. 13½*
1183-1186 A280 Set of 4 6.00 6.00

Humpback Whales — A281

Humpback whale: 20c, Pair underwater. 50c, Breaching water's surface. $1.10, Reentering water. $3, Flukes.

2008, July 17 Litho. *Perf. 14½x14*
1187-1190 A281 Set of 4 6.00 6.00

Nos. 729-731 Surcharged Like Nos. 1149-1160

No. 1191

No. 1191A

No. 1191Ab

Methods, Perfs and Watermarks As Before

2007-09
1191 A166 1c on 13c #730, 5mm between "c" and obliterator 1.50 1.50
b. 4mm between "c" and obliterator (positions 3 and 89) *50.00 50.00*
1191A A166 1c on 23c #731, 4mm between "c" and obliterator 1.00 1.00
b. 5mm between "c" and obliterator 1.00 1.00
c. Pair, Nos. 1191Ab and 1191A (positions 3 and 89) *50.00 50.00*

No. 1191 exists with double surcharge, one inverted. Value, $150. No. 1191 exists with double surcharge: one upright with "XX" obliterator, the other inverted with "xxx" obliterator. Value, $175. No. 1191A exists with inverted surcharge. Value, $100. No. 1191A exists with a "2c" surcharge having a 1½mm gap between the "2" and the "c" (position 57). Value, $100. No. 1191Ab exists with inverted surcharge. Value, $160.

No. 1191C

No. 1192

1191C A166 2c on 6c #729 *175.00 175.00*
1192 A166 2c on 6c #729 *175.00 175.00*
c. 2½mm gap between pair of double bars of obliterator *400.00 400.00*
d. 4mm between "c" and obliterator *325.00 325.00*

No. 1192 exists with obliterator of three double bars and with obliterator of four double bars. Value, each $500. No. 1192 exists with obliterator omitted. Value, $750.

No. 1192A

No. 1192Ab

No. 1193

No. 1193a

No. 1193B

1192A A166 2c on 6c #729 *175.00 175.00*
b. Short obliterator *250.00 250.00*

1193 A166 2c on 13c #730, 5 mm between "c" and obliterator 1.25 1.25
- *a.* 4mm between "c" and obliterator (positions 3 and 89) *30.00 30.00*

1193B A166 2c on 23c #731, 5 mm between "c" and obliterator *125.00 125.00*
- *a.* 4mm between "c" and obliterator (positions 3 and 89) *200.00 200.00*

Two lines comprise the obliterator on No. 1192Ab: one long, one short.

No. 1193 exists with double surcharge, one inverted. Value, $150. No. 1193 exists with double surcharge: one upright with "XX" obliterator, the other inverted with "xxx" obliterator. Value, $175. No. 1193 exists with a period after the "2c." Value, $500.

No. 1194

No. 1194a

No. 1195

No. 1195b

1194 A166 4c on 13c #730, 5mm between "c" and obliterator 1.25 1.25
- *a.* 4mm between "c" and obliterator (positions 3 and 89) *30.00 30.00*

1195 A166 20c on 6c #729 *100.00 100.00*
- *b.* No gap between "c" and obliterator *500.00 500.00*

No. 1194 exists with double surcharge, one inverted. Value, $200.

No. 1195A

1195A A166 20c on 23c #731 *500.00 500.00*

No. 1195A exists with normal surcharge shifted 75% upward. Value, $300.

No. 1196

No. 1196a

1196 A166 20c on 23c #731 *2.00 2.00*
- *a.* No gap between "c" and obliterator (position 70) *35.00 35.00*

No. 1196 exists with inverted surcharge. Value, $90. No. 1196 also exists with double surcharge and with double surcharge, one inverted. Value, each $150. No. 1196 also exists surcharged on gum side only. Value, $150. No. 1196 also exists surcharged on both sides. Value, $180.

No. 1197

No. 1197a

No. 1197d

No. 1197e

No. 1197f

1197 A166 20c on 23c #731, 1½mm between "c" and obliterator *200.00 200.00*
- *a.* 2½mm between "c" and obliterator *80.00 80.00*
- *d.* 3mm between "c" and obliterator *100.00 100.00*
- *e.* 4mm between "c" and obliterator *80.00 80.00*
- *f.* 5mm between "c" and obliterator *175.00 175.00*

No. 1197 exists with surcharge shifted 75% upward. Value, $175.

No. 1197B

No. 1197C

1197B A166 20c on 23c #731 *35.00 35.00*
- *a.* No gap between "c" and obliterator (positions 70 and 79) *100.00 100.00*

1197C A166 20c on 23c #731 *175.00 175.00*

Nos. 1191-1197C (14) 1,667. 1,667.

No. 1197B exists with inverted surcharge. Value, $150. No. 1197C exists with inverted surcharge. Value, $350.

Issued: No. 1191, 8/22/08; No. 1191A, 12/18/08; No. 1191Ab, 1/23/09; No. 1191C, 1192, 1192A, 2/19/07; Nos. 1193, 1194, 8/20/08; No. 1195, 4/28/08; No. 1195A, Apr. 2008; Nos. 1196, 4/12/08; Nos. 1197, 1197a, 1197d, 1197e, 1197f. Apr. 2008; 1197B, 4/12/08; 1197C, Apr. 2008.

Bananas — A282

Various banana varieties: 65c, $1.10, $1.20, $2.

2008, Sept. 23 Litho. ***Perf. 14x14½***

1198-1201 A282 Set of 4 5.50 5.50

Eels A283

Designs: 50c, Anguilla obscura. 90c, Anguilla marmorata. $1,50, Anguilla obscura, diff. $2, Gymnothorax potyuranodon.

2008, Oct. 15 ***Perf. 14½x14***

1202-1205 A283 Set of 4 5.25 5.25

Christmas — A284

Various choirs: 20c, 50c, 65c, $3.

2008, Dec. 10 Litho. ***Perf. 14½x14***

1206-1209 A284 Set of 4 4.50 4.50

Fruit Doves — A285

Designs: 50c, Many-colored fruit dove. 65c, Crimson-crowned fruit dove. 90c, Whistling dove. $3, Orange dove.

2009, Feb. 17 Litho. ***Perf. 14x14½***

1210-1213 A285 Set of 4 5.50 5.50

Nos. 729-731 Surcharged Like Nos. 1149-1160

No. 1214

No. 1215

No. 1215A

Methods, Perfs and Watermarks As Before

2009-12

1214 A166 1c on 13c #730 *40.00 40.00*
- *a.* 2½mm gap between "c" and obliterator (positions 3 and 89) *75.00 75.00*

1215 A166 1c on 23c #731 1.25 1.25
- *b.* 3mm gap between "c" and obliterator (positions 3 and 89) *30.00 30.00*

1215A A166 1c on 23c #731, small font 1.00 1.00

No. 1215 exists with inverted surcharge. Value, $90. No. 1215A exists with inverted surcharge. Value, $90. No. 1215A also exists with "xx" obliterator (position 70). Value, $200.

No. 1216

No. 1216A

No. 1216B

1216 A166 2c on 6c #729 *100.00 100.00*

1216A A166 2c on 13c #730 *40.00 40.00*
- *c.* 2½mm gap between "c" and obliterator (positions 3 and 89) *75.00 75.00*

1216B A166 2c on 23c #731 *175.00 175.00*

No. 1217

No. 1217A

1217 A166 2c on 23c #731 *20.00 20.00*
- *b.* 2½mm between "c" and obliterator (positions 3 and 89) *30.00 30.00*

1217A A166 2c on 23c #731, small font *1.00 1.00*

No. 1217A exists with inverted surcharge. Value, $90. No. 1217A also exists with "xx" obliterator (position 70). Value, $200.

No. 1218

No. 1218A

1218 A166 3c on 23c #731 *40.00 40.00*
- *b.* 2½mm between "c" and obliterator (positions 3 and 89) *90.00 90.00*

1218A A166 3c on 23c #731, small font *1.00 1.00*

No. 1218 exists with "3" of surcharge omitted. Most of the known singles have irregular perforations from being roughly removed from sheets. Value thus, $100. Errors with intact perforations are extremely scarce. Value, $300. Value of single error in pair with normal stamp, $350.

No. 1218A exists with double surcharge. Value, $150. No. 1218A exists with inverted surcharge. Value, $100. No. 1218A exists with double surcharge, one inverted. Value, $130. No. 1218A exists with "xx" obliterator (position 70). Value, $200.

No. 1219

No. 1219B

No. 1220

No. 1220B

1219 A166 4c on 6c #729 *70.00 70.00*
- *a.* 2½mm between "c" and obliterator (positions 3 and 89) *100.00 100.00*

1219B A166 40c on 6c #729 *100.00 100.00*
- *a.* No gap between "c" and obliterator (position 70) *200.00 200.00*

1219C A166 4c on 6c #729, small font *85.00* 85.00

1220 A166 4c on 13c #730 *40.00 40.00*
- *a.* 2½mm gap between "c" and obliterator (positions 3 and 89) *75.00 75.00*

1220B A166 5c on 13c #730 *130.00 130.00*

Nos. 1219 and 1219a exist with inverted surcharge. Value, each $200. No. 1219C exists with double surcharge, one inverted. Value, $225.

No. 1221

No. 1222

No. 1222A

No. 1222C

1221 A166 4c on 23c #731 90.00 90.00
a. 4mm between "c" and obliterator (positions 3 and 89) *250.00 250.00*

1222 A166 4c on 23c #731 1.50 1.50
b. 2½mm between "c" and obliterator (positions 3 and 89) *40.00 40.00*

1222A A166 4c on 23c #731, small font 1.00 1.00

1222C A166 50c on 23c #731 300.00 300.00
a. No gap between "c" and obliterator (position 70) *1,000.*

No. 1221 exists with inverted surcharge. Value, $150.

No. 1222 exists with inverted surcharge. Value, $90. No. 1222 exists with double surcharge, one inverted. Value, $130. No. 1222 exists with double surcharge, one with normal 4mm between "c" and obliterator and the other with 2½mm between "c" and obliterator. Value, $150.

No. 1222A exists with inverted surcharge. Value, $100. No. 1222A exists with double surcharge, one inverted. Value, $120. No. 1222A exists with double surcharge. Value, $150.

No. 1223

No. 1223b

No. 1223c

No. 1223A

1223 A166 5c on 23c #731, 4mm between "c" and obliterator 1.50 1.50
b. 2½mm between "c" and obliterator (positions 3 and 89) *30.00 30.00*
c. No obliterator *250.00 250.00*

1223A A166 5c on 23c #731, small font 1.00 1.00

Nos. 1214-1223A (19) 839.25 839.25

No. 1223 exists with surcharge shifted 50% upward. Value, $60. No. 1223 also exists with inverted surcharge and with double surcharge, one inverted. Values, $100 and $150, respectively. No. 1223A exists with inverted surcharge. Value, $90.

On Nos. 1215, 1217, 1218, 1219, 1222 and 1223, the "c" and obliterator are 4mm apart.

Issued: Nos. 1214, 1215, 1215b, Mar. 10; Nos. 1215A, 1217A, 1218A, 8/5/10; No. 1216A, Mar. 30; Nos. 1216, 1216B, Mar.; Nos. 1217, 1217b, Mar. 30; No. 1218, Aug. 27; No. 1219, 1220, 1221, 1222, Mar. 10; No. 1222A, 8/3/10; No. 1223, July 8; No. 1223A, 8/6/10.

Weddings in Fiji — A286

Designs: 20c, Chinese wedding. 40c, Muslim wedding. $1.50, Indian wedding. $3, Fijian wedding, vert.

Perf. 14½x14, 14x14½

2009, Aug. 17 Litho. Unwmk.
1224-1227 A286 Set of 4 5.25 5.25

Passion Fruit — A287

Designs: 20c, Passiflora foetida. 65c, Passiflora edulis (yellow green). $1.20, Passiflora maliformis. $2, Passiflora edulis (purple).

2009, Sept. 29 ***Perf. 14x14¼***
1228-1231 A287 Set of 4 4.25 4.25

Souvenir Sheet

People's Republic of China, 60th Anniv. — A288

2009, Oct. 1 ***Perf. 13¼***
1232 A288 $5 multi 5.25 5.25

Ferns — A289

Designs: 20c, Cyathea lunulata. 40c, Asplenium australasicum. $1.50, Diplazium proliferum. $3, Nephrolepsis biserrata.

2009, Dec. 15 ***Perf. 14x14½***
1233-1236 A289 Set of 4 5.25 5.25

Snakes — A290

Designs: 20c, Yellow-bellied sea snake. 90c, Fiji burrowing snake. $1.10, Banded sea krait. $2, Pacific boa.

2010, Mar. 30 Litho. ***Perf. 14½x14***
1237-1240 A290 Set of 4 4.50 4.50

Peonies — A291

No. 1241: a, 20c, Pink peony. b, 40c, Red peony.

2010, Apr. 8 Litho. ***Perf. 13¼***
1241 A291 Horiz. pair, #a-b 13.00 13.00

Raiateana Knowlesi — A292

No. 1242: a, 20c, Newly-emerged insect. b, $1.50, Mature insect.

Perf. 14x14½

2010, June 30 Unwmk.
1242 A292 Vert. pair, #a-b 1.75 1.75

A293

A294

A295

Worldwide Fund for Nature (WWF) — A296

2010, Oct. 27 ***Perf. 14¼x14***
1243 Horiz. strip of 4 9.00 9.00
a. A293 $2 multi 2.25 2.25
b. A294 $2 multi 2.25 2.25
c. A295 $2 multi 2.25 2.25
d. A296 $2 multi 2.25 2.25

Fruit — A297

Designs: 20c, Citrus maxima. 40c, Barringtinia edulis. 65c, Pometia pinnata. $1.20, Musa troglogytarum. $10, Syzygium malacensis.

2010, Dec. 2 ***Perf. 14¼***
1244-1248 A297 Set of 5 13.50 13.50

No. 1249

No. 1249A

No. 1249Ab

No. 1254

No. 1254a

No. 1254C

Methods, Perfs and Watermarks As Before

2011-14

1249 A166 1c on 31c #732 1.00 1.00
c. 3½mm between "c" and obliterator *75.00 75.00*
d. 1½mm between "c" and obliterator *125.00 125.00*
e. 4mm between "c" and obliterator, larger font *40.00 40.00*

1249A A166 1c on 31c #732 100.00 100.00
b. Extra large "XX" (position 51) *75.00 75.00*

1250 A166 2c on 31c #732 1.00 1.00
a. 4mm between "c" and obliterator *95.00 95.00*
b. 3mm between "c" and obliterator (positions 3 and 89) *185.00 185.00*

1251 A166 3c on 31c #732 1.00 1.00

1252 A166 4c on 31c #732 1.00 1.00
a. 4mm between "c" and obliterator *95.00 95.00*
b. 3mm between "c" and obliterator (positions 3 and 89) *185.00 185.00*

1253 A166 5c on 31c #732 1.00 1.00
a. 3½mm between "c" and obliterator *75.00 75.00*
b. 1½mm between "c" and obliterator *100.00 100.00*

1254 A166 20c on 31c #732 2.00 2.00
a. Larger font *50.00 50.00*
b. As "a," 2½mm between "c" and obliterator *100.00 100.00*
d. As No. 1254, no gap between "c" and obliterator (position 70) *35.00 35.00*
f. As "a," no gap between "c" and obliterator *150.00 150.00*

1254C A166 20c on 31c #732 125.00 125.00

1254E A166 40c on 31c #732 3.00 3.00
a. No gap between "c" and obliterator *50.00 50.00*

Nos. 1249A-1254E (9) 235.00 235.00

Nos. 1249-1253 have 2½mm between "c" and obliterator. No. 1249A has 3½mm spacing. Nos. 1249Ab, 1254, 1254a and 1254E have 1½mm spacing.

No. 1249 exists with inverted surcharge. Value, $90. No. 1249 exists with double surcharge, value, $120; and with double surcharge, one inverted, value, $130. No. 1249A exists with denomination omitted (position 77). Value, $500.

No. 1250 exists with inverted surcharge. Value, $90. No. 1250 exists with double surcharge, value, $120; and with double surcharge, one inverted, value, $130.

No. 1251 exists with inverted surcharge. Value, $100. No. 1251 exists with double surcharge, value, $120; and with double surcharge, one inverted, value, $130. No. 1251 exists with surcharge shifted 50% upward. Value, $50. No. 1252 exists with inverted surcharge. Value, $90. No. 1252 exists with double surcharge, value, $120; and with double surcharge, one inverted, value, $130.

No. 1253 exists with inverted surcharge. Value, $90. No. 1253 exists with double surcharge, with double surcharge, one shifted 50% upward, and with double surcharge, one inverted, value, each $130. No. 1253 exists with surcharge shifted 50% upward. Value, $50.

No. 1254 exists with inverted surcharge. Value, $100. No. 1254 exists with inverted surcharge. Value, $100. No. 1254 exists with double surcharge, value, $65; and with double surcharge, one inverted (top surcharge inverted, bottom shifted 50% upward), value, $130. No. 1254 exists with surcharge shifted 50% upward. Value, $50. No. 1254 exists with double surcharge, one shifted 50% upward. Value, $100. No. 1254 exists with double surcharge, one shifted 50% upward; both with no gap between "c" and obliterator. Value, $300. No. 1254a exists with surcharge shifted 50% upward. Value, $80. No. 1254a exists with surcharge inverted and shifted 50% upward. Value, $130. No. 1254a exists with "c" omitted. Value, $150. No. 1254f exists with surcharge shifted 50% upward. Value, $250.

No. 1254E exists with inverted surcharge. Value, $90. No. 1254E exists with double surcharge, value, $120; and with double surcharge, one inverted, value, $130. No. 1254E exists with surcharge shifted 45% upward. Value, $50.

Issued: No. 1249, 6/6; No. 1249A, 7/30/14; Nos. 1250, 1253, 3/24; No. 1250a, 3/2014; No. 1251, 7/8; No. 1252, 5/20; No. 1252a, 2/2014; No. 1254, 5/4; Nos. 1254a, 1254b, 2011; No. 1254d, 5/4; Nos. 1254E, 1254Ea, 12/7/12.

Souvenir Sheet

Wedding of Prince William and Catherine Middleton — A298

Perf. 14¾x14¼

2011, Apr. 29 Litho. Wmk. 406
1255 A298 $10 multi 11.50 11.50

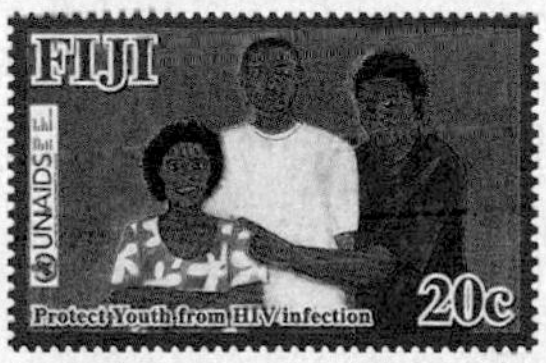

Campaign Against AIDS — A299

People, UNAIDS emblem and slogan: 20c, Protect youth from HIV infection. 40c, Zero new HIV infections, vert. 65c, Stop mothers & babies from being infected with HIV, vert. $5, Zero discrimination.

Perf. 14½x14, 14x14½

2011, June 22 Unwmk.
1256-1259 A299 Set of 4 7.25 7.25

Frangipani Flowers — A300

Designs: 50c, Plumeria rubra bud. 90c, Plumeria rubra f. rubra flower. $1.50, Plumeria rubra f. lutea. $3, Plumeria obtusa.

2011, July 12 ***Perf. 14½x14***
1260-1263 A300 Set of 4 6.75 6.75

Pomegranate Tree Branches and Birds — A301

No. 1264: a, 65c, Bird on branch. b, $1.20, Bird in flight near branch.

2011, Aug. 15 ***Perf. 13¼x13¾***
1264 A301 Horiz. pair, #a-b 2.10 2.10

No. 1264 was printed in sheets containing three pairs.

War Clubs A302

Designs: 20c, Saulaki vividrasa. 65c, Cali. $1.20, Totokia. $10, I ula tavatava.

2011, Aug. 15 ***Perf. 14½x14***
1265-1268 A302 Set of 4 13.50 13.50

Intl. Year of Volunteers — A303

Volunteers for: 40c, St. John Ambulance Association. 90c, Suva City Council, vert. $1.10, Red Cross, vert. $10, National Blood Bank.

Perf. 14½x14, 14x14½

2011, Nov. 25
1269-1272 A303 Set of 4 14.00 14.00

Christmas — A304

Designs: 20c, Fijian with gift box. 65c, Fijian with pottery. $1.20, Fijian with necklace. $2, Holy Family.

2011, Dec. 16 ***Perf. 14½x14***
1273-1276 A304 Set of 4 4.50 4.50

New Year 2012 (Year of the Dragon) A305

2012, Jan. 23 ***Perf. 14¼***
1277 A305 $3 multi 3.50 3.50

No. 1277 was printed in sheets of 4.

Endangered Flora — A306

Designs: 20c, Fijian acmopyle. 65c, Lau fan palm. $1.20, Cycad. $2, Fiji magnolia.

2012, Apr. 26 ***Perf. 14½x14***
1278-1281 A306 Set of 4 4.50 4.50

Intl. Year of Sustainable Energy For All — A307

Designs: 20c, Water power. 50c, Biomass. $1.20, Wind energy. $3, Solar power.

2012, June 25
1282-1285 A307 Set of 4 5.50 5.50

A308

A309

A310

Worldwide Fund for Nature (WWF) A311

2012, July 11 ***Perf. 14¼x14***

1286	Horiz. strip of 4	9.00	9.00
a.	A308 $2 multi	2.25	2.25
b.	A309 $2 multi	2.25	2.25
c.	A310 $2 multi	2.25	2.25
d.	A311 $2 multi	2.25	2.25

Christmas — A312

Designs: 20c, Journey to Bethlehem. 40c, Holy Family. 65c, Adoration of the Shepherds. $1.20, Adoration of the Shepherds, diff. $5, Adoration of the Magi.

2012, Dec. 14 Litho. ***Perf. 14½x14***
1287-1291 A312 Set of 5 8.50 8.50

Birth of Prince George of Cambridge A313

Prince George and: 40c, Duke and Duchess of Cambridge. 65c, Duchess of Cambridge. $1.20, Duke and Duchess of Cambridge, diff. $5, Duke of Cambridge.

2013, Aug. 28 Litho. ***Perf. 13½***
1292-1295 A313 Set of 4 7.75 7.75

Mangrove Protection A314

Designs: 50c, Mangroves. 65c, Mangrove, jellyfish, starfish. $1.20, Fish and underwater root system of mangrove. $10, People planting mangroves.

2013, Oct. 30 Litho. ***Perf. 13½***
1296-1299 A314 Set of 4 13.50 13.50

Christmas — A315

Bell-shaped Christmas ornament with: 40c, Cathedral. 65c, Flowers. $1.20, Fijian family walking on beach. $3, Fijian children with Christmas gifts.

2013, Dec. 2 Litho. ***Perf. 13½***
1300-1303 A315 Set of 4 5.75 5.75

Submarine Cable Between Fiji and Vanuatu — A316

No. 1304: a, Workers, ship and cable with floats. b, Diver examining cable. c, Electronic cables plugged into machine.

Litho. With Foil Application

2014, Jan. 15 ***Perf. 14½x14***

1304	Horiz. strip of 6 + central label, #1304a-1304c, Vanuatu #1070a-1070c	14.50	14.50
a.	A316 65c multi	.70	.70
b.	A316 $1.20 multi	1.25	1.25
c.	A316 $6 multi	6.50	6.50

No. 1304 sold for $13.30 in Fiji and 750v in Vanuatu. See Vanuatu No. 1070.

Sharks A317

Designs: 50c, Blacktip reef shark. 90c, Silky shark. $1.20, Oceanic whitetip shark. $5, Big-eye thresher shark.

2014, July 28 Litho. ***Perf. 13¾x13¼***

1305-1308	A317	Set of 4	8.25 8.25

Grand Pacific Hotel, Cent. A318

Designs: 40c, Hotel driveway and entrance. 65c, Sofas and tables. 90c, Swimming pool. $1.20, Dining area. $5, Entrance, diff.

2014, Aug. 8 Litho. ***Perf. 13¾x13¼***

1309-1313	A318	Set of 5	8.75 8.75

Nos. 732-733 Surcharged

No. 1313A

No. 1314

No. 1314b

No. 1315

No. 1316

No. 1317

Methods, Perfs and Watermarks As Before

2014-15

1313A	A166 1c on 44c #733	4.00	4.00
b.	2¼mm between "c" and obliterator	*50.00*	*50.00*
c.	4¼mm between "c" and obliterator	*40.00*	*40.00*
1314	A166 20c on 44c #733	1.50	1.50
a.	No gap between "c" and obliterator (position 70)	*50.00*	*50.00*
b.	Large "20"	*30.00*	*30.00*
c.	As "b," no gap between "c" and obliterator (positions 70 and 79)	*75.00*	*75.00*
d.	As "b," 3mm gap between "c" and obliterator (positions 31, 41, 61, 71, 81 and 91)	*50.00*	*50.00*
1315	A166 40c on 44c #733	2.00	2.00
a.	No gap between "c" and obliterator (position 70)	*60.00*	*60.00*
1316	A166 50c on 31c #732	6.00	6.00
a.	No gap between "c" and obliterator (position 70)	*50.00*	*50.00*
1317	A166 50c on 44c #733	3.00	3.00
a.	No gap between "c" and obliterator (position 70)	*65.00*	*65.00*
	Nos. 1313A-1317 (5)	16.50	16.50

No. 1313A exists with double surcharge. Value, $120.

No. 1314 exists with surcharge shifted 50% upward. Value, $25. No. 1314 exists with surcharge inverted. Value, $60. No. 1314a exists with surcharge shifted 50% upward. Value, $75. No. 1314b exists with surcharge inverted. Value, $100. No. 1314b exists with double surcharge. Value, $120.

No. 1315 exists with surcharge shifted 50% upward. Value, $25. No. 1315a exists with surcharge shifted 50% upward. Value, $80.

No. 1316 exists with double surcharge. Value, $70. Nos. 1316 and 1316a exist with inverted surcharge. Value, both $120.

No. 1317 exists with surcharge shifted 50% upward. Value, $30. No. 1317a exists with surcharge shifted 50% upward. Value, $90.

Issued: No. 1313A, 8/28/15; No. 1314, 6/11; No. 1314b, 7/31; Nos. 1315, 1317, 6/10. No. 1316, 3/5.

Christmas — A319

Houses of worship: 40c, The Church of Jesus Christ of Latter-day Saints, Suva. 65c, Holy Redeemer Anglican Church, Levuka. $3, Baker Memorial Methodist Church, Nausori. $10, St. Francis Xavier Church, Navunibitu.

Perf. 13½

2014, Dec. 4 Litho. Unwmk.

1320-1323	A319	Set of 4	14.00 14.00

Souvenir Sheet

Blue Coral — A320

No. 1324 — Heliopora coerulea: a, 65c. b, $5.

Perf. 13½x13¼

2015, Feb. 23 Litho.

1324	A320	Sheet of 2, #a-b	5.50 5.50

Fiji Flying Fox — A321

Fiji flying fox: 40c, Head. 65c, In flight, horiz. 90c, Head, horiz. $10, Hanging from tree.

Perf. 13¼x13¾, 13¾x13¼

2015, Apr. 30 Litho.

1325-1328	A321	Set of 4	13.50 13.50

SEMI-POSTAL STAMPS

Catalogue values for unused stamps in this section are for Never Hinged items.

Children at Play — SP1

Rugby Player — SP2

Perf. 13x13½

1951, Sept. 17 Engr. Wmk. 4

B1	SP1 1p + 1p brown	.30	*1.60*
B2	SP2 2p + 1p deep green	.45	*1.10*

Bamboo River Raft — SP3

Design: 2½p+½p, Cross of Lorraine.

1954, Apr. 1 ***Perf. 11x11½***

B3	SP3 1½p + ½p green & brn	.25	.25
B4	SP3 2½p + ½p black & org	.30	.30

Nos. 269 and 272 Surcharged

1972, Dec. 4 Photo. ***Perf. 14, 13½***

B5	A56 15c + 5c multi	.40	.40
B6	A55 30c + 10c multi	1.10	1.10

Indian Boy, Map of Fiji SP4

Map of Fiji and: 15c+2c, European girl. 30c+3c, Chinese girl. 40c+4c, Fijian boy.

Wmk. 373

1979, Sept. 17 Litho. ***Perf. 14½***

B7	SP4 4c + 1c multicolored	.25	.25
B8	SP4 15c + 2c multicolored	.25	.25
B9	SP4 30c + 3c multicolored	.40	.40
B10	SP4 40c + 4c multicolored	.60	.60
	Nos. B7-B10 (4)	1.50	1.50

The surtax was for IYC fund.

Iliesa Delana, Gold Medalist at 2012 Paralympic Games — SP5

Delana: 40c+10c, High jumping. 65c+10c, Standing and waving flag of Fiji, vert. $1.20+10c, Wearing gold medal, vert. $2+10c, Going around track waving flag of Fiji.

2013, Mar. 7 ***Perf. 14½x14, 14x14½***

B11-B14	SP5	Set of 4	5.25 5.25

Surtax for Fiji Paralympic Committee.

POSTAGE DUE STAMPS

D1

D2

D3

1917 Unwmk. Typeset ***Perf. 11***
Laid Papers; Without Gum

J1	D1 ½p black	1,300.	500.00
J2	D2 ½p black	550.00	300.00
J3	D3 1p black	500.00	140.00
a.	Narrow setting	375.00	
J4	D3 2p black	350.00	80.00
a.	Narrow setting	1,250.	
J5	D3 3p black	525.00	120.00
J6	D3 4p black	1,250.	550.00
a.	Strip of 8, 3 #J3, 1 ea. #J1 and #J6, and 3 #J5	*19,000.*	
	Nos. J1-J6 (6)	4,475.	1,690.

There were two printings of this issue. In the first printing, the 2d was printed in sheets of 84 (7x12), and the other four values were printed together in sheets of 96 (8x12), with each row consisting of three 1p, one ½p, one 4p and three 3p values. Setenant multiples exist. Sheets were not perforated on the margins, so that marginal stamps were not perforated on the outer edge. Examples from the first printing are 25mm wide (including margins).

In the second printing, the ½p, 1p and 2p were printed in separate sheets of 84 (7x12). The clichés were set a little closer, so that examples of this printing are 23mm wide.

D4

Perf. 14

1918, June 1 Typo. Wmk. 3

J7	D4 ½p black	3.25	*30.00*
J8	D4 1p black	3.75	*5.50*
J9	D4 2p black	3.50	*8.00*
J10	D4 3p black	3.50	*52.50*
J11	D4 4p black	6.50	*30.00*
	Nos. J7-J11 (5)	20.50	*126.00*

D5

1940 Wmk. 4 ***Perf. 12½***

J12	D5 1p bright green	5.00	*72.50*
J13	D5 2p bright green	10.00	*72.50*
J14	D5 3p bright green	11.00	*80.00*
J15	D5 4p bright green	12.00	*85.00*
J16	D5 5p bright green	14.00	*90.00*
J17	D5 6p bright green	15.00	*90.00*
J18	D5 1sh dk carmine	15.00	*115.00*
J19	D5 1sh6p dk carmine	15.00	*175.00*
	Nos. J12-J19 (8)	97.00	*780.00*
	Set, never hinged	140.00	

WAR TAX STAMPS

Regular Issue of 1912-16 Overprinted

Die I

1916 Wmk. 3 ***Perf. 14***

MR1	A23 ½p green	1.90	*9.00*
a.	Inverted overprint	700.00	
b.	Double overprint		
MR2	A23 1p scarlet	3.50	.80
a.	1p carmine	37.50	26.00
b.	Pair, one without ovpt.	*8,000.*	
c.	Inverted overprint	800.00	

Most examples of #MR2b are within horiz. strips of 12.

FINLAND

'fin-lənd

(Suomi)

LOCATION — Northern Europe bordering on the Gulfs of Bothnia and Finland
GOVT. — Republic
AREA — 130,119 sq. mi.
POP. — 5,147,349 (1997)
CAPITAL — Helsinki

Finland was a Grand Duchy of the Russian Empire from 1809 until December 1917, when it declared its independence.

100 Kopecks = 1 Ruble
100 Pennia = 1 Markka (1866)
100 Cents = 1 Euro (2002)

Catalogue values for unused stamps in this country are for Never Hinged items, beginning with Scott 220 in the regular postage section, Scott B39 in the semi-postal section, Scott C2 in the air-post section, Scott M1 in the military stamp section, and Scott Q6 in the parcel post section.

Unused stamps are valued with original gum as defined in the catalogue introduction except for Nos. 1-3B which are valued without gum. Used values for Nos. 1-3B are for pen-canceled examples. Very fine examples of the serpentine rouletted issues, Nos. 4-13c, will have roulettes cutting the design slightly on one or more sides and will have all "teeth" complete and intact. Stamps with roulettes clear of the design on all four sides are extremely scarce and sell for substantial premiums. Stamps with teeth entirely missing or with several short roulettes are worth much less. See *Scott Classic Specialized Catalogue* for values for used stamps with one or two short roulettes.

Watermarks

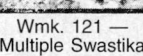

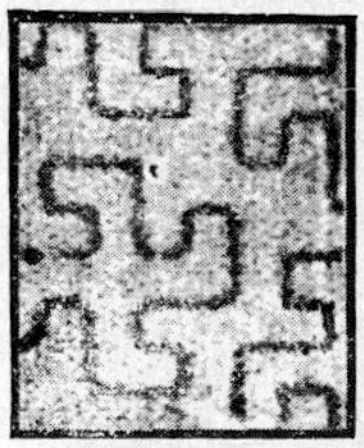
Wmk. 121 — Multiple Swastika

Wmk. 208 — Post Horn

Wmk. 168 — Wavy Lines and Letters

Wmk. 273 — Roses

Wmk. 363 — Tree Stump

Syncopated Perforations

Type A (1st stamp #1065): On one longer side, groups of five holes are separated by an oval hole equal in width to eight holes.

Type B (1st stamp, #1142): On the top groups of 3 holes at left and right and a middle group of 4 holes separated by rectangular perforations equal in width to 4 holes.

Issues under Russian Empire

Coat of Arms — A1

1856-58 Unwmk. Typo. ***Imperf.***

Small Pearls in Post Horns

Wove Paper

1 A1 5k blue *6,750.* 1,600.
Pen and town cancellation 1,900.
Town cancellation 3,250.
a. Tête bêche pair *80,000.* *80,000.*
Pen and town cancellation *75,000.*
2 A1 10k rose 8,750. 400.
Pen and town cancellation 575.
On cover 1,850.
Town cancellation 925.
On cover 2,850.
a. Tête bêche pair *80,000.* *65,000.*
Pen and town cancellation *75,000.*

Cut to shape

1 A1 5k blue 150.
Pen and town cancellation 200.
Town cancellation 250.
2 A1 10k rose 65.
Pen and town cancellation 90.
Town cancellation 100.

Wide Vertically Laid Paper

2C A1 10k rose ('58) — 1,400.
Pen and town cancellation 1,800.
Town cancellation 2,500.
d. Tête bêche pair —

Cut to shape

2C A1 10k rose 200.
Pen and town cancellation 250.
Town cancellation 300.

Narrow Vertically Laid Paper

2C A1 10k carmine 625.
Pen and town cancellation 800.
Town cancellation 1,100.

The wide vertically laid paper has 13-14 distinct lines per 2 centimeters. The narrow laid paper has lines that sometimes are indistinct.

A 5k blue with small pearls exists on narrow vertically laid paper. It is rare.

Stamps on diagonally laid paper are envelope cut squares. Envelope cut squares also exist on unwatermarked wove paper.

Large Pearls in Post Horns

1858 Wove Paper

3 A1 5k blue *11,000.* 1,800.
Pen and town cancellation 1,550.
Town cancellation 2,500.
a. Tête bêche pair *60,000.*
Pen and town cancellation *65,000.*

Cut to shape

3 A1 5k blue 125.00
Pen and town cancellation 150.00
Town cancellation 200.00

1859 Wide Vertically Laid Paper

3B A1 5k blue — *18,000.*
Pen and town cancellation *25,000.*

Cut to shape

3B A1 5k blue 2,000.
Pen and town cancellation *2,500.*

Reprints of Nos. 2 and 3, made in 1862, are on brownish paper, on vertically laid paper, and in tête bêche pairs on normal and vertically laid paper. Reprints of 1871, 1881 and 1893 are on yellowish or white paper. Value for least costly of each, $85.

In 1956, Nos. 2 and 3 were reprinted for the Centenary with post horn watermark and gum. Value, $85 each.

Values for rouletted stamps with one or two short teeth are considerably less than the values shown, which are for stamps with all teeth full and intact. See the *Scott Classic Specialized Catalogue* for greater detail. Stamps with several short teeth or teeth entirely missing sell for very small percentages of the values shown.

Coat of Arms — A2

I — Depth 1-1¼mm

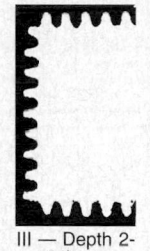

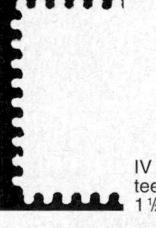
II — Depth 1½-1¾mm

III — Depth 2-2¼mm

IV — Shovel-shaped teeth. Depth 1¼-1½mm

Wove Paper

1860 ***Serpentine Roulette 7½, 8***

4 A2 5k blue, *bluish*, I 850.00 200.00
a. Roulette II 800.00 225.00
b. Perf. vert.
5 A2 10k rose, *pale rose*, I 575.00 57.50
a. Roulette II 1,150. 160.00

A3

A4

1866-74 ***Serpentine Roulette***

6 A3 5p pur brn, *lil*, I ('73) 375.00 170.00
a. Roulette II 4,000.
b. 5p red brn, *lil*, III ('71) 350.00 180.00
7 A3 8p blk, *grn*, III ('67) 275.00 170.00
a. Ribbed paper, III ('72) 1,150. 925.00
b. Roulette II ('74) 340.00 275.00
c. As "b," ribbed paper ('74) 340.00 225.00
d. Roulette I ('73) 525.00 325.00
e. As "d," ribbed paper 1,050. 400.00
f. Serpentine roulette 10½ ('67) *13,500.*
8 A3 10p blk, *yel*, III ('70) 675.00 350.00
a. 10p blk, *buff*, II 800.00 450.00
b. 10p blk, *buff*, I ('73) 750.00 375.00
9 A3 20p bl, *bl*, III 575.00 57.50
a. Roulette II 575.00 90.00
b. Roulette I ('73) 675.00 115.00
c. Roulette IV ('74) — *1,150.*
d. Perf. horiz. —
e. Printed on both sides (40p blue on back) —
10 A3 40p rose, *lil rose*, III 525.00 67.50
a. Ribbed paper, III ('73) 675.00 200.00
b. Roulette II 525.00 85.00
c. As "b," ribbed paper ('73) 675.00 170.00
d. Roulette I 750.00 170.00
e. As "d," ribbed paper 675.00 115.00
f. Roulette IV — *2,275.*
g. As "f," ribbed paper — —
h. Serpentine roulette 10½ —
11 A4 1m yel brn, III ('67) 2,250. 850.00
a. Roulette II 2,850. 1,700.

Nos. 7f and 10h are private roulettes and are also known in compound serpentine roulette 10½ and 7½.

Nos. 4-11 were reprinted in 1893 on thick wove paper. Colors differ from originals. Roulette type IV. Value for Nos. 4-5, each $40, Nos. 6-10, each $50. Value for No. 11, $55.

Thin or Thick Laid Paper

12 A3 5p red brn, *lil*, III 290.00 160.00
a. Roulette II 300.00 300.00
b. Roulette I 290.00 300.00
d. 5p blk, *buff*, roul. III (error) *20,000.*
e. Tête bêche pair —
13 A3 10p black, *buff*, III 675.00 290.00
a. 10p black, *yel*, II 850.00 290.00
b. 10p black, *yel*, I 1,150. 750.00
c. 10p red brown, *lil*, III (error) *8,000.* *7,000.*

Forgeries of No. 13c exist.

A5

1875 *Perf. 14x13½*

16 A5 32p lake 2,400. 425.00

Forgeries exist of No. 16 that have been created by perforating cut squares.

1875-82 *Perf. 11*

17 A5 2p gray 62.50 70.00
18 A5 5p orange 140.00 15.00
a. 5p yellow org 160.00 18.00
19 A5 8p blue green 300.00 90.00
a. 8p yellow green 275.00 70.00
20 A5 10p brown ('81) 700.00 70.00
21 A5 20p ultra 175.00 3.50
a. 20p blue 175.00 5.00
b. 20p Prussian blue 400.00 45.00
c. Tête bêche pair 3,500.
22 A5 25p carmine ('79) 350.00 17.00
a. 25p rose ('82) 475.00 75.00
23 A5 32p carmine 400.00 60.00
a. 32p rose 450.00 62.50
24 A5 1m violet ('77) 1,000. 160.00
Nos. 17-24 (8) 3,127. 485.50

A souvenir card issued in 1974 for NORDIA 1975 reproduced a block of four of the unissued "1 MARKKAA" design.

Nos. 19, 23 were reprinted in 1892-93, perf. 12½. Value $25.00 each. They exist imperf.

1881-83 *Perf. 12½*

25 A5 2p gray 20.00 20.00
a. Imperf., pair 600.00 600.00
26 A5 5p orange 62.50 6.25
a. Tête bêche pair 8,250. 4,750.
b. Imperf. vert., pair —
c. Imperf. horiz., pair —
27 A5 10p brown 100.00 27.00
28 A5 20p ultra 65.00 2.00
a. 20p blue 65.00 2.00
b. Tête bêche pair — 2,500.
c. Imperf., pair —
29 A5 25p rose ('82) 55.00 12.00
a. 25p carmine 55.00 21.00
b. Tête bêche pair 15,000. —
30 A5 1m violet ('82) 450.00 55.00
Nos. 25-30 (6) 752.50 122.25

Nos. 27-29 were reprinted in 1893 in deeper shades, perf. 12½. Value $40 each.

Most examples of No. 28c are from printer's waste.

1881 *Perf. 11x12½*

26d A5 5p orange 450.00 90.00
27a A5 10p brown 925.00 225.00
28d A5 20p ultra 575.00 42.50
28e A5 20p blue 575.00 42.50
29c A5 25p rose 675.00 190.00
29d A5 25p carmine 650.00 125.00
30a A5 1m violet 1,450.

1881 *Perf. 12½x11*

26e A5 5p orange 450.00 90.00
27b A5 10p brown — 325.00
28f A5 20p ultra 575.00 45.00
28g A5 20p blue 575.00 45.00
29e A5 25p rose — 290.00
29f A5 25p carmine 575.00 115.00

1885 *Perf. 12½*

31 A5 5p emerald 20.00 8.00
a. 5p yellow green 24.00 1.10
b. Tête bêche pair 14,000. 11,000.
32 A5 10p carmine 30.00 3.50
a. 10p rose 50.00 3.50
33 A5 20p orange 35.00 .65
a. 20p yellow 47.50 2.50
b. Tête bêche pair — 3,500.
34 A5 25p ultra 70.00 4.25
a. 25p blue 70.00 3.00
35 A5 1m gray & rose 37.50 25.00
36 A5 5m green & rose 500.00 500.00
37 A5 10m brown & rose 625.00 750.00

Denomination on No. 35 is spelled "MARKKA". Denomination on Nos. 36-37 is spelled "MARKKAA",

A6

1889-92 *Perf. 12½*

38 A6 2p slate ('90) .75 1.25
39 A6 5p green ('90) 40.00 .50
40 A6 10p carmine ('90) 70.00 .50
a. 10p rose ('90) 90.00 .75
b. Imperf. 110.00
41 A6 20p orange ('92) 95.00 .50
a. 20p yellow ('89) 95.00 1.25
42 A6 25p ultra ('91) 80.00 .85
a. 25p blue 80.00 1.15
43 A6 1m slate & rose ('92) 6.00 3.25
a. 1m brnsh gray & rose ('90) 35.00 4.00
44 A6 5m green & rose ('90) 32.50 *77.50*
45 A6 10m brown & rose ('90) 40.00 *90.00*
Nos. 38-45 (8) 364.25 *174.35*

The 2p slate, perf. 14x13, is believed to be an essay.

See Nos. 60-63.

See Russia for types similar to A7-A18.

Finnish stamps have "dot in circle" devices or are inscribed "Markka," "Markkaa," "Pen." or "Pennia."

Imperial Arms of Russia
A7 A8 A9

A10

A11

Laid Paper

1891-92 **Wmk. 168** *Perf. 14½x15*

46 A7 1k orange yel 6.50 *11.00*
47 A7 2k green 6.50 *11.00*
48 A7 3k carmine 12.00 *18.00*
49 A8 4k rose 14.00 18.00
50 A7 7k dark blue 8.00 2.25
51 A8 10k dark blue 17.50 *18.00*
52 A9 14k blue & rose 20.00 *30.00*
53 A8 20k blue & car 20.00 24.00
54 A9 35k violet & grn 30.00 *60.00*
55 A8 50k violet & grn 35.00 42.50

Perf. 13½

56 A10 1r brown & org 90.00 67.50
57 A11 3½r black & gray 325.00 *550.00*
a. 3½r black & yellow (error) *15,000.* *18,000.*
58 A11 7r black & yellow 250.00 *350.00*
Nos. 46-58 (13) 834.50 *1,202.*

Forgeries of Nos. 57, 57a, 58 exist.

Type of 1889-90
Wove Paper

1895-96 **Unwmk.** *Perf. 14x13*

60 A6 5p green .80 .50
61 A6 10p carmine .80 .50
62 A6 20p orange .80 .50
b. Imperf. 160.00 —
63 A6 25p ultra 1.25 .70
a. 25p blue 1.25 .70
b. Imperf. 125.00 —
Nos. 60-63 (4) 3.65 2.20

A12

A13

A14

A15

1901 **Litho.** *Perf. 14½x15*
Chalky Paper

64 A12 2p yellow 6.00 8.00
65 A12 5p green 12.50 2.00
66 A13 10p carmine 27.50 3.25
67 A12 20p dark blue 70.00 1.50
68 A14 1m violet & grn 350.00 10.00

Perf. 13½

69 A15 10m black & gray 325.00 350.00
Nos. 64-69 (6) 791.00 374.75

Imperf sheets of 10p and 20p, stolen during production, were privately perforated 11½ to defraud the P.O. Uncanceled imperfs. of Nos. 65-68 are believed to be proofs.

See Nos. 70-75, 82.

Types of 1901 Redrawn

No. 64

No. 70

2p. On No. 64, the "2" below "II" is shifted slightly leftward. On No. 70, the "2" is centered below "II."

No. 65

No. 71

5p. On No. 65, the frame lines are very close. On No. 71, a clear white space separates them.

Nos. 66, 67

Nos. 72, 73

10p, 20p. On Nos. 66-67, the horizontal central background lines are faint and broken. On Nos. 72-73, they are clear and solid, though still thin.

20p. On No. 67, "H" close to "2" with period midway. On No. 73 they are slightly separated with period close to "H."

No. 68

Nos. 74, 74a

1m. On No. 68, the "1" following "MARKKA" lacks serif at base. On Nos. 74-74a, this "1" has serif.

No. 69

No. 75

10m. On No. 69, the serifs of "M" and "A" in top and bottom panels do not touch. On No. 75, the serifs join.

Perf. 14¼x14¾, 14¼x14

1901-14 **Typo.** **Ordinary Paper**

70 A12 2p orange 1.00 1.50
71 A12 5p green 2.00 .60
a. Perf 14¼x14 ('06) 3.50 .75
Never hinged 4.00
72 A13 10p carmine 14.00 .60
a. Perf 14¼x14 ('07) 90.00 .95
Never hinged 92.50
b. Background inverted, perf 14¼x14¾ 17.50 5.00
c. Background inverted, perf 14¼x14 95.00 2.75
73 A12 20p dark blue 10.00 .60
a. Perf 14¼x14 ('06) 82.50 1.25
Never hinged 115.00
74 A14 1m lil & grn, perf. 14¼x14 ('14) 1.10 .60
a. 1m violet & blue green, perf. 14¼x14¾ ('02) 10.00 .90
Never hinged 22.50
Nos. 70-74 (5) 28.10 3.90
Set, never hinged 45.00

Perf. 13½

75 A15 10m blk & drab ('03) 160.00 60.00
Never hinged 275.00

Imperf Pairs

70a A12 2p 375.00 *525.00*
71b A12 5p 100.00 *200.00*
72d A13 10p 110.00 *225.00*
73b A12 20p 200.00 *225.00*
74b A14 1m 190.00 *210.00*
Nos. 70a-74b (5) 975.00 1,385.

A16 A17 A18

1911-16 *Perf. 14, 14¼x14¾*

77 A16 2p orange .30 *.90*
78 A16 5p green .35 .40
a. Imperf. —
b. Perf. 14¼x14¾ 1,400. 140.00
Never hinged 675.00
79 A17 10p rose ('15) .30 .75
a. Imperf. 110.00 225.00
b. Perf. 14¼x14¾ ('16) 3.50 *5.50*
Never hinged 9.50
80 A16 20p deep blue .40 *.60*
a. Imperf. 180.00 140.00
b. Perf. 14¼x14¾ 27.50 3.50
Never hinged 21.00
81 A18 40p violet & blue .40 .40
a. Perf. 14¼x14¾ 6,000. 4,000.
Nos. 77-81 (5) 1.75 3.05
Set, never hinged 3.00

There are three minor types of No. 79. Values are for the least expensive type.

Perf. 14½

82 A15 10m blk & grnsh gray ('16) 160.00 210.00
Never hinged 275.00
a. Horiz. pair, imperf. vert. 3,900.

Republic
Helsinki Issue

Arms of the Republic
A19 A20

Type I

Type II

Two types of the 40p.
Type I — Thin figures of value.
Type II — Thick figures of value.

Perf. 14, 14¼x14¾

1917-30 **Unwmk.**

83 A19 5p green .35 .35
84 A19 5p gray ('19) .35 .35
85 A19 10p rose .35 *.45*
a. Imperf., pair 250.00 *400.00*
86 A19 10p green ('19) 1.50 .55
a. Perf. 14¼x14¾ *3,000.*
87 A19 10p brt blue ('21) .40 *.45*
88 A19 20p buff .40 *.50*
89 A19 20p rose ('20) .40 *.45*
90 A19 20p brown ('24) 1.00 *.90*
a. Perf. 14¼x14¾ .65 *25.00*
Never hinged 1.50
91 A19 25p blue .40 *.45*
92 A19 25p lt brown ('19) .40 .40
93 A19 30p green ('23) .40 *.55*
94 A19 40p violet (I) .40 .35
a. Perf. 14¼x14¾ 400.00 27.50
Never hinged 850.00
95 A19 40p bl grn (II) ('29) .50 *3.00*
a. Type I ('24) 14.00 6.00
Never hinged 24.00
b. Perf. 14¼x14¾ 1.25 *21.00*
Never hinged 2.50
96 A19 50p orange brn .45 *.45*
97 A19 50p dp blue ('19) 4.00 .45
a. Perf. 14¼x14¾ 2,200.
98 A19 50p green ('21) 4.50 .40
a. Perf. 14¼x14¾ .40 *1.50*
Never hinged .50
99 A19 60p red vio ('21) .60 .40
a. Imperf., pair — —
100 A19 75p yellow ('21) .40 *.75*
101 A19 1m dull rose & blk 16.00 .30

102 A19 1m red org ('25) 9.00 *30.00*
a. Perf. 14 ('30) .25 *550.00*
Never hinged .65
103 A19 1½m bl grn & red vio ('29) .25 *2.50*
a. Perf. 14¼x14¾ .40 *1.25*
Never hinged .65
104 A19 2m green & blk ('21) 3.50 .70
105 A19 2m dk blue & ind ('22) 2.50 .45
a. Perf. 14¼x14¾ .65 *4.00*
Never hinged 1.50
106 A19 3m blue & blk ('21) 25.00 .50
107 A19 5m red vio & blk 17.50 .45
108 A19 10m brn & gray blk, perf. 14 1.00 *1.25*
a. 10m light brown & black, perf. 14¼x14¾ ('29) 3.50 *400.00*
Never hinged 7.00
110 A19 25m dull red & yel ('21) .90 *26.00*
Nos. 83-108,110 (27) 92.45 *73.35*
Set, never hinged 260.00

Examples of a 2½p gray of this type exist. They are proofs from the original die which were distributed through the UPU. No plate was made for this denomination.

See Nos. 127-140, 143-152. For surcharge and overprints see Nos. 119-126, 153-154.

Vasa Issue

1918 Litho. *Perf. 11½*
111 A20 5p green .75 *1.25*
112 A20 10p red .75 *1.25*
113 A20 30p slate 1.25 *4.50*
114 A20 40p brown vio .70 *1.75*
115 A20 50p orange brn .75 *5.00*
116 A20 70p gray brown 2.25 *32.50*
117 A20 1m red & gray .75 *2.50*
118 A20 5m red violet & gray 45.00 *125.00*
Nos. 111-118 (8) 52.20 *173.75*
Set, never hinged 92.50

Nos. 111-118 exist imperforate but were not regularly issued in that condition.

Sheet margin examples, perf. on 3 sides, imperf. on margin side, were sold by post office.

Stamps and Type of 1917-29 Surcharged

1919 *Perf. 14*
119 A19 10p on 5p green .50 .55
120 A19 20p on 10p rose .50 .55
121 A19 50p on 25p blue 1.00 .55
122 A19 75p on 20p orange .50 *.85*
Nos. 119-122 (4) 2.50 2.50
Set, never hinged 5.75

Stamps and Type of 1917-29 Surcharged

Nos. 123-125

No. 126

1921
123 A19 30p on 10p green .65 .65
124 A19 60p on 40p red violet 3.75 1.25
125 A19 90p on 20p rose .40 .50
126 A19 1½m on 50p blue 1.40 .50
a. Thin "2" in "½" 12.50 11.00
b. Imperf., pair 300.00 *500.00*
Nos. 123-126 (4) 6.20 2.90
Set, never hinged 13.00

Arms Type of 1917-29

Perf. 14, 14¼x14¾

1925-29 Wmk. 121
127 A19 10p ultra ('27) .50 *2.75*
128 A19 20p brown .50 *2.00*
129 A19 25p brn org ('29) 1.00 *90.00*
130 A19 30p yel green .40 *.95*
a. Perf. 14¼x14¾ 7.00 1.50
Never hinged 7.50
131 A19 40p blue grn (I) ('26) 9.50 1.40
a. Perf. 14¼x14¾ ('26) 9.50 1.40
Never hinged 15.00
b. Type II ('28) *140.00* *82.50*
Never hinged 290.00
c. As "b," perf. 14¼x14¾ ('28) 9.50 1.40
Never hinged 13.50
132 A19 50p gray grn ('26) 1.25 .80
a. Perf. 14¼x14¾ ('26) .55 *.55*
Never hinged 2.00
133 A19 60p red violet .40 *.95*
134 A19 1m dp orange 7.00 .40
a. Perf. 14¼x14¾ 100.00 1.25
Never hinged 250.00

Perf. 14¼x14¾
135 A19 1½m blue green & red violet ('26) 6.25 .60
a. Perf. 14 ('26) 60.00 .50
Never hinged 80.00
136 A19 2m dk blue & indigo ('27) 1.00 *.50*
a. Perf. 14 1.00 .50
Never hinged 2.25
137 A19 3m chlky blue & blk ('26) 1.00 .50
138 A19 5m red violet & blk ('27) .50 .50
a. Perf. 14 1.25 .50
Never hinged 2.75
139 A19 10m lt brn & blk ('27) 4.00 *32.50*
140 A19 25m dp org & yel ('27) 20.00 *400.00*
Nos. 127-140 (14) 53.30 *533.85*
Set, never hinged 100.00

No. 130a is not known cancelled during the period in which it was valid for postal use.

A21

Wmk. 208
1927, Dec. 6 Typo. *Perf. 14*
141 A21 1½m deep violet .30 *.60*
142 A21 2m deep blue .30 *2.00*

10th anniv. of Finnish independence.

Arms Type of 1917-29

Perf. 14, 14¼x14¾

1927-29 Wmk. 208
143 A19 20p lt brown ('29) 2.00 *40.00*
144 A19 40p bl grn (II) ('28) .40 *.65*
145 A19 50p gray grn ('28) .40 *.75*
146 A19 1m dp orange .40 *1.00*
a. Imperf., pair 115.00 *200.00*
b. Perf. 14 1.25 1.25
147 A19 1½m bl grn & red vio ('28) 3.00 .70
a. Perf. 14 1,000. 26.00
148 A19 2m dk bl & ind ('28) .45 *.65*
149 A19 3m chlky bl & blk .50 *.65*
a. Perf. 14 1.60 *5.00*
150 A19 5m red vio & blk ('28) .50 .60
151 A19 10m lt brown & blk 2.00 *35.00*
152 A19 25m brown org & yel 2.25 *400.00*
Nos. 143-152 (10) 11.90 *480.00*

Nos. 146-147 Overprinted

1928, Nov. 10 Litho. Wmk. 208
153 A19 1m deep orange 10.00 *19.00*
154 A19 1½m bl grn & red vio 10.00 *19.00*
Set, never hinged 35.00

Nos. 153 and 154 were sold exclusively at the Helsinki Philatelic Exhibition, Nov. 10-18, 1928, and were valid only during that period.

S. S. "Bore" Leaving Turku — A23

Turku Cathedral — A24

Turku Castle — A25

Wmk. 208
1929, May 22 Typo. *Perf. 14*
155 A23 1m olive green 1.50 *5.00*
156 A24 1½m chocolate 2.25 *4.00*
157 A25 2m dark gray .45 *4.50*
Nos. 155-157 (3) 4.20 *13.50*
Set, never hinged 12.50

Founding of the city of Turku (Abo), 700th anniv.

A26

1930-46 Unwmk. *Perf. 14*
158 A26 5p chocolate .50 *.50*
159 A26 10p dull violet .50 .50
160 A26 20p yel grn .50 *.50*
161 A26 25p yel brn .50 .50
162 A26 40p blue grn 2.00 .25
163 A26 50p yellow .50 .50
164 A26 50p blue grn ('32) .45 .45
b. Imperf., pair 150.00 *200.00*
165 A26 60p dark gray .50 *.65*
165A A26 75p dp org ('42) .55 *.75*
166 A26 1m red org .50 .50
166B A26 1m yel grn ('42) .50 .50
167 A26 1.20m crimson .55 *1.75*
168 A26 1.25m yel ('32) .50 .50
169 A26 1½m red vio 2.00 .50
170 A26 1½m car ('32) .50 .50
170A A26 1½m sl ('40) .50 .50
170B A26 1.75m org yel ('40) .90 .70
171 A26 2m indigo .50 .50
172 A26 2m dp vio ('32) 6.00 .50
173 A26 2m car ('36) .50 .50
Complete booklet, panes of 4 #161, 164, 166, 168, 173 5.75
173B A26 2m yel org ('42) .50 .50
173C A26 2m blue grn ('45) .50 .50
174 A26 2½m brt blue ('32) 4.75 .55
174A A26 2½m car ('42) .50 .50
174B A26 2.75m rose vio ('40) .50 .50
175 A26 3m olive blk 35.00 .65
175B A26 3m car ('45) 1.00 .50
175C A26 3m yel ('45) .50 *.80*
176 A26 3½m brt bl ('36) 9.00 .50
176A A26 3½m olive ('42) .50 .50
176B A26 4m olive ('45) 1.10 .50
176C A26 4½m saph ('42) .50 .50
176D A26 5m saph ('45) .50 .50
176E A26 5m pur ('45) 1.50 .50
j. Imperf., pair 150.00 *200.00*
176F A26 5m yel ('46) 1.25 .55
k. Imperf., pair 150.00 *200.00*
176G A26 6m car ('45) 1.20 .50
m. Imperf., pair 200.00 *275.00*
176H A26 8m pur ('46) .50 .60
176I A26 10m saph ('45) 1.75 .50
Nos. 158-176I (38) 80.00 21.10

See Nos. 257-262, 270-274, 291-296, 302-304. For surcharges and overprints see Nos. 195-196, 212, 221-222, 243, 250, 275, M2-M3.

Stamps of types A26-A29 overprinted "ITA KARJALA" are listed under Karelia, Nos. N1-N15.

Castle in Savonlinna A27

Lake Saima — A28

Woodchopper A29

1930 Engr.
177 A27 5m blue 1.50 *.65*
178 A28 10m gray lilac 55.00 4.75
179 A29 25m black brown 1.00 .50
Nos. 177-179 (3) 57.50 5.90
Set, never hinged 150.00

See Nos. 205, 305. For overprint see No. C1.

Elias Lönnrot — A30

Seal of Finnish Literary Society — A31

1931, Jan. 1 Typo.
180 A30 1m olive brown 2.50 *5.75*
181 A31 1½m dull blue 12.50 6.25
Never hinged 45.00

Centenary of Finnish Literary Society.

A32

1931, Feb. 28
182 A32 1½m red 2.75 *9.50*
Never hinged 6.00
183 A32 2m blue 2.75 *11.50*
Never hinged 6.00

1st use of postage stamps in Finland, 75th anniv.

Nos. 162-163 Surcharged

1931, Dec.
195 A26 50p on 40p blue grn 2.75 1.20
Never hinged 8.50
196 A26 1.25m on 50p yellow 4.00 3.50
Never hinged 13.00

Svinhufvud — A33

1931, Dec. 15
197 A33 2m gray blue & blk 1.50 *3.25*
Never hinged 5.25

Pres. Pehr Eyvind Svinhufvud, 70th birthday.

Lake Saima Type of 1930

1932-43 Re-engraved
205 A28 10m red violet ('43) .70 .50
Never hinged 1.60
a. 10m dark violet 20.00 .70
Never hinged 40.00

On Nos. 205 and 205a the lines of the islands, the clouds and the foliage are much deeper and stronger than on No. 178.

Alexis Kivi — A34

1934, Oct. 10 **Typo.**

206 A34 2m red violet 2.25 *4.50*
Never hinged 5.50

Alexis Kivi, Finnish poet (1834-1872).

Bards Reciting the "Kalevala" A35

Goddess Louhi, As Eagle Seizing Magic Mill — A36

Kullervo — A37

1935, Feb. 28 **Engr.**

207 A35 1¼m brown lake 2.00 *2.50*
Never hinged 4.00
208 A36 2m black 4.50 2.00
Never hinged 12.50
209 A37 2½m blue 3.00 3.00
Never hinged 10.00
Nos. 207-209 (3) 9.50 7.50
Set, never hinged 26.50

Cent. of the publication of the "Kalevala" (Finnish National Epic).

No. 170 Surcharged in Black

1937, Feb.

212 A26 2m on 1½m car 8.00 1.40
Never hinged 14.00

Gustaf Mannerheim — A38

1937, June 4 **Photo.** ***Perf. 14***

213 A38 2m ultra 1.00 *1.45*
Never hinged 2.50

70th birthday of Field Marshal Baron Carl Gustaf Mannerheim, June 4th, 1937.

Swede-Finn Co-operation in Colonization A39

1938, June 1

214 A39 3½m dark brown .90 *2.75*
Never hinged 3.00

Tercentenary of the colonization of Delaware by Swedes and Finns.

Early Post Office — A40

Designs: 1¼m, Mail delivery in 1700. 2m, Modern mail plane. 3½m, Helsinki post office.

1938, Sept. 6 **Photo.** ***Perf. 14***

215 A40 50p green .35 .55
Never hinged .65
216 A40 1¼m dk blue 1.15 *3.25*
Never hinged 3.25
217 A40 2m scarlet 1.15 1.25
Never hinged 6.25
218 A40 3½m slate black 3.25 *8.00*
Never hinged 8.75
Nos. 215-218 (4) 5.90 13.05
Set, never hinged 19.00

300th anniv. of the Finnish Postal System.

Margin strips of each denomination (3 of No. 215, 2 each of Nos. 216, 217, 218) were pasted on to advertising sheets and stapled into a booklet. Value, $120.

Post Office, Helsinki — A44

1939-42 **Photo.**

219 A44 4m brown black .40 *.45*
Never hinged 1.10

Engr.

219A A44 7m black brn ('42) .50 *.45*
Never hinged 1.90
219B A44 9m rose lake ('42) .60 .50
Never hinged 1.60
Nos. 219-219B (3) 1.50 1.40
Set, never hinged 3.50

See No. 248.

Catalogue values for unused stamps in this section, from this point to the end of the section, are for Never Hinged items.

University of Helsinki — A45

1940, May 1 **Photo.**

220 A45 2m dp blue & blue .75 *.90*

300th anniv. of the founding of the University of Helsinki.

Nos. 168 and 173 Surcharged in Black

1940, June 16 **Typo.**

221 A26 1.75m on 1.25m yel 4.00 *3.25*
222 A26 2.75m on 2m carmine 10.00 .90

President Kallio Reviewing Military Band — A46

1941, May 24 **Engr.**

223 A46 2.75m black .75 *1.00*

Pres. Kyösti Kallio (1873-1940).

Castle at Viborg — A47

1941, Aug. 30 **Typo.**

224 A47 1.75m yellow orange .50 *.60*
225 A47 2.75m rose violet .50 *.60*
226 A47 3.50m blue .90 *1.25*

Field Marshal Mannerheim — A48

1941, Dec. 31 **Engr.** **Wmk. 273**

227 A48 50p dull green 1.75 *2.75*
228 A48 1.75m deep brown 1.75 *2.75*
229 A48 2m dark red 2.75 2.75
230 A48 2.75m dull vio brn 2.75 2.75
231 A48 3.50m deep blue 1.75 *2.00*
232 A48 5m slate blue 1.75 *2.00*
Nos. 227-232 (6) 12.50 *15.00*

Pres. Risto Ryti — A49

233 A49 50p dull green 1.60 *2.25*
234 A49 1.75m deep brown 1.60 *2.25*
235 A49 2m dark red 1.60 *2.25*
236 A49 2.75m dull vio brn 1.60 *3.50*
237 A49 3.50m deep blue 1.60 *2.25*
238 A49 5m slate blue 1.60 *2.25*
Nos. 233-238 (6) 9.60 *14.75*

Types A48-A49 overprinted "ITA KARJALA" are listed under Karelia, Nos. N16-N27.

Häme Bridge, Tampere A50

South Harbor, Helsinki — A51

1942 **Unwmk.**

239 A50 50m dull brown vio 3.25 .45
240 A51 100m indigo 5.00 .40

See No. 350.

Altar and Open Bible — A52

17th Century Printer — A53

1942, Oct. 10

241 A52 2.75m dk brown .90 *1.40*
242 A53 3.50m violet blue 1.00 *3.50*

300th anniv. of the printing of the 1st Bible in Finnish.

No. 174B Surcharged in Black

1943, Feb. 1

243 A26 3.50m on 2.75m rose vio .85 .70

Minna Canth (1844-96), Author and Playwright — A54

1944, Mar. 20

244 A54 3.50m dk olive grn .60 *1.00*

Pres. P. E. Svinhufvud — A55

1944, Aug. 1

245 A55 3.50m black .90 *1.25*

Death of President Svinhufvud (1861-1944).

K. J. Stahlberg — A56

1945, May 16 **Engr.** ***Perf. 14***

246 A56 3.50m brown vio .60 *.75*

80th birthday of Dr. K. J. Stahlberg.

Castle in Savonlinna A57

1945, Sept. 4

247 A57 15m lilac rose 2.75 .60
248 A44 20m sepia 1.75 .60

For a 35m of type A57, see No. 280.

Jean Sibelius — A58

1945, Dec. 8

249 A58 5m dk slate green 1.00 .55

Jean Sibelius (1865-1957), composer.

No. 176E Surcharged in Black

1946, Mar. 16

250 A26 8(m) on 5m purple .75 .50

Victorious Athletes — A59

1946, June 1 Engr. *Perf. 13½*
251 A59 8m brown violet .60 *.75*

3rd Sports Festival, Helsinki, June 27-30, 1946.

Lighthouse at Uto — A60

1946, Sept. 19
252 A60 8m deep violet .75 *.70*

250th anniv. of the Finnish Department of Pilots and Lighthouses.

Post Bus — A61

1946-47 Unwmk. *Perf. 14*
253 A61 16m gray black .85 *.75*
253A A61 30m gray black ('47) 3.00 .50

Issue dates: 16m, Oct. 16, 30m, Feb. 10.

Old Town Hall, Porvoo — A62

Cathedral, Porvoo — A63

1946, Dec. 3
254 A62 5m gray black .60 *.75*
255 A63 8m deep claret .60 *.75*

600th anniv. of the founding of the city of Porvoo (Borga).

Waterfront, Tammisaari A64

1946, Dec. 14
256 A64 8m grnsh black .60 *.75*

400th anniv. of the founding of the town of Tammisaari (Ekenas).

Lion Type of 1930

1947 Typo. *Perf. 14*
257 A26 2½m dark green .65 .50
258 A26 3m slate gray .75 .50
259 A26 6m deep orange 2.00 .50
260 A26 7m carmine 1.50 .45
261 A26 10m purple 5.00 .45
262 A26 12m deep blue 4.50 .45
Nos. 257-262 (6) 14.40 2.85

Issued: 3m, 6/9; 7m, 12m, 2/10; others, 1/20.

Pres. Juho K. Paasikivi — A65

1947, Mar. 15 Engr.
263 A65 10m gray black .65 .50

Postal Savings Emblem — A66

1947, Apr. 1
264 A66 10m brown violet .50 .50

60th anniv. of the foundation of the Finnish Postal Savings Bank.

Ilmarinen, the Plowman — A67

1947, June 2
265 A67 10m gray black .50 .50

2nd year of peace following WW II.

Girl and Boy Athletes — A68

1947, June 2
266 A68 10m bright blue .70 *.75*

Finnish Athletic Festival, Helsinki, June 29-July 3, 1947.

Wheat and Savings Bank Assoc. Emblem — A69

1947, Aug. 21
267 A69 10m red brown .80 *.75*

Finnish Savings Bank Assoc., 125th anniv.

Sower — A70

1947, Nov. 1
268 A70 10m gray black .75 .70

150th anniv. of Finnish Agricultural Societies.

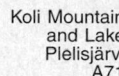

Koli Mountain and Lake Plelisjärvi A71

1947, Nov. 1
269 A71 10m indigo .90 *.75*

60th anniv. of the Finnish Touring Assoc.

Lion Type of 1930

1948 Typo. *Perf. 14*
270 A26 3m dark green 4.50 .45
271 A26 6m yellow green 1.25 .65
272 A26 9m carmine 1.25 .50
273 A26 15m dark blue 8.00 .50
274 A26 24m brown lake 2.75 .50
Nos. 270-274 (5) 17.75 2.60

Issued: 3m, 2/9; 24m, 4/26; others, 9/13.

No. 261 Surcharged in Black

1948, Feb. 9
275 A26 12(m) on 10m purple 2.00 .50

Statue of Michael Agricola — A72

12m, Agricola translating New Testament.

1948, Oct. 2 Engr. *Perf. 14*
276 A72 7m rose violet 1.25 *2.25*
277 A72 12m gray blue 1.25 *2.25*

400th anniv. of publication of the Finnish translation of the New Testament, by Michael Agricola.

Sveaborg Fortress A73

1948, Oct. 15
278 A73 12m deep green 1.60 *2.00*

200th anniv. of the construction of Sveaborg Fortress on the Gulf of Finland.

Post Rider — A74

1948, Oct. 27
279 A74 12m green 9.00 *17.50*

Helsinki Philatelic Exhibition. Sold only at exhibition for 62m, of which 50m was entrance fee.

Castle Type of 1945

1949
280 A57 35m violet 9.00 .50

Sawmill and Cellulose Plant — A75

Pine Tree and Globe — A76

1949, June 15
281 A75 9m brown 3.00 *4.50*
282 A76 15m dull green 3.00 *4.50*

Issued to publicize the Third World Forestry Congress, Helsinki, July 10-20, 1949.

Woman with Torch — A77

1949, July 16 Engr. *Perf. 14*
283 A77 5m dull green 5.50 *11.50*
284 A77 15m red *(Worker)* 5.50 *11.50*

50th anniv. of the Finnish labor movement.

Harbor of Lappeenranta (Willmanstrand) — A78

Raahe (Brahestad) — A79

1949
285 A78 5m dk blue grn 2.00 1.50
286 A79 9m brown carmine 2.00 *2.00*
287 A78 15m brt blue *(Kristi-inan-kaupunki)* 2.75 *4.50*
Nos. 285-287 (3) 6.75 8.00

300th anniv. of the founding of Willmanstrand, Brahestad and Kristinestad (Kristiinan-kaupunki).

Issued: 5m, 8/6; 9m, 8/13; 15m, 7/30.

Technical High School Badge — A80

1949, Sept. 13
288 A80 15m ultra 1.40 *1.60*

Founding of the technical school, cent.

Hannes Gebhard — A81

1949, Oct. 2
289 A81 15m dull green 1.40 *1.60*

Establishment of Finnish cooperatives, 50th anniv.

Finnish Lake Country — A82

1949, Oct. 8

290 A82 15m blue 1.40 *1.60*

75th anniv. of the UPU.

Lion Type of 1930

1950, Jan. 9 Typo. *Perf. 14*

291	A26	8m brt green	2.25	1.75
292	A26	9m red orange	2.40	.60
293	A26	10m violet brown	7.25	.50
294	A26	12m scarlet	2.00	.50
295	A26	15m plum	25.00	.50
296	A26	20m deep blue	10.00	.50
		Nos. 291-296 (6)	48.90	4.35

Forsell's Map of Old Helsinki — A83

J. A. Ehrenstrom and C. L. Engel — A84

City Hall — A85

1950, June 11 Engr.

297	A83	5m emerald	1.00	*.90*
298	A84	9m brown	1.25	*1.50*
299	A85	15m deep blue	.90	*1.10*
		Nos. 297-299 (3)	3.15	3.50

400th anniv. of the founding of Helsinki.

J. K. Paasikivi — A86

1950, Nov. 27

300 A86 20m deep ultra .70 .50

80th birthday of Pres. J. K. Paasikivi.

View of Kajaani — A87

1951, July 7 Unwmk. *Perf. 14*

301 A87 20m red brown 2.00 *1.00*

Tercentenary of Kajaani.

Lion and Chopper Types of 1930

1952, Jan. 18 Typo.

302	A26	10m emerald	4.50	.40
303	A26	15m red	4.25	.45
304	A26	25m blue	7.00	.40

Engr.

305	A29	40m black brown	4.25	.50
		Nos. 302-305 (4)	20.00	1.75

Arms of Pietarsaari — A88

1952, June 19 Unwmk. *Perf. 14*

306 A88 25m blue 1.40 1.10

300th anniv. of the founding of Pietarsaari (Jacobstad).

Rooftops of Vaasa — A89

1952, Aug. 3

307 A89 25m brown 2.25 1.10

Centenary of the burning of Vaasa.

Chess Symbols — A90

1952, Aug. 10

308 A90 25m gray 3.00 *3.00*

10th Chess Olympics, Helsinki, 8/10-31/52.

Torch Bearers — A91

1953, Jan. 27

309 A91 25m blue 1.60 1.10

Temperance movement in Finland, cent.

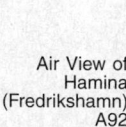

Air View of Hamina (Fredrikshamn) A92

1953, June 20

310 A92 25m dk gray green 2.10 1.10

Tercentenary of Hamina.

Ivar Wilskman — A93

1954, Feb. 26

311 A93 25m blue 1.10 1.00

Centenary of the birth of Prof. Ivar Wilskman, "father of gymnastics in Finland."

Arms of Finland — A94

1954-59 *Perf. 11½*

312	A94	1m red brown ('55)	.40	.25
313	A94	2m green ('55)	.40	.25
314	A94	3m deep orange	.40	.25
314A	A94	4m gray ('58)	.75	.50
315	A94	5m violet blue	.80	.25
316	A94	10m blue green	1.25	.25
a.		Bklt. pane of 5 (vert. strip)	22.50	22.50
		Complete booklet, #316a	25.00	
317	A94	15m rose red	4.50	.25
318	A94	15m yellow org ('57)	8.25	.25
319	A94	20m rose lilac	14.00	.25
320	A94	20m rose red ('56)	2.40	.25
321	A94	25m deep blue	4.50	.25
322	A94	25m rose lilac ('59)	12.00	.25
323	A94	30m lt ultra ('56)	2.40	.25
		Nos. 312-323 (13)	52.05	3.50

See Nos. 398, 400-405A, 457-459A, 461A-462, 464-464B.

"In the Outer Archipelago" A95

1954, July 21 *Perf. 14*

324 A95 25m black .90 .70

Cent. of the birth of Albert Edelfelt, painter.

J. J. Nervander A96

1955, Feb. 23

325 A96 25m blue 1.70 1.00

150th anniv. of the birth of J. J. Nervander, astronomer and poet.

Composite of Finnish Public Buildings — A97

1955, Mar. 30 Engr. *Perf. 14*

326 A97 25m gray 17.00 *24.00*

Sold for 125m, which included the price of admission to the Natl. Postage Stamp Exhibition, Helsinki, Mar. 30-Apr. 3, 1955.

Bishop Henrik with Foot on Lalli, his Murderer — A98

25m, Arrival of Bishop Henrik and monks.

1955, May 19

327	A98	15m rose brown	1.25	1.00
328	A98	25m green	1.25	1.00

Adoption of Christianity in Finland, 800th anniv.

Conference Hall, Helsinki — A99

1955, Aug. 25

329 A99 25m bluish green 1.25 *2.00*

44th conf. of the Interparliamentarian Union, Helsinki, Aug. 25-31, 1955.

Sailing Vessel and Merchant A100

1955, Sept. 2

330 A100 25m sepia 2.40 2.10

350th anniv. of founding of Oulu.

Town Hall, Lahti — A101

1955, Nov. 1 *Perf. 14x13½*

331 A101 25m violet blue 1.50 *2.50*

50th anniversary of founding of Lahti.

Radio Sender, Map of Finland — A102

Designs: 15m, Otto Nyberg. 25m, Telegraph wires and pines under snow.

Inscribed: Lennatin 1855-1955 Telegrafen

1955, Dec. 10 *Perf. 14*

332	A102	10m green	3.00	*2.40*
333	A102	15m dull violet	3.00	1.25
334	A102	25m lt ultra	4.50	2.00
		Nos. 332-334 (3)	10.50	5.65

Cent. of the telegraph in Finland.

A103

1956, Jan. 26 Unwmk. *Perf. 14*

335 A103 25m Lighthouse, Porkkala Peninsula 1.10 *1.40*

Return of the Porkkala Region to Finland by Russia, Jan. 1956.

A104

30m, 50m, Church at Lammi. 40m, House of Parliament. 60m, Fortress of Olavinlinna (Olofsborg).

1956-57 ***Perf. 11½***

336 A104 30m gray olive 1.25 .30
337 A104 40m dull purple 2.75 .30
338 A104 50m gray ol ('57) 8.25 .30
338A A104 60m pale pur ('57) 12.00 .30
Nos. 336-338A (4) 24.25 1.20

Issued: 30m, 3/4; 40m, 3/11; 50m, 3/3; 60m, 4/7. See Nos. 406-408A.

Johan V. Snellman — A105

1956, May 12 **Engr.** ***Perf. 14***

339 A105 25m dk violet brn .85 *1.00*

Johan V. Snellman (1806-81), statesman.

Gymnast and Athletes — A106

1956, June 28

340 A106 30m violet blue 1.60 1.25

Finnish Gymnastic and Sports Games, Helsinki, June 28-July 1, 1956.

A107

Wmk. 208

1956, July 7 **Typo.** ***Rouletted***

341 A107 30m deep ultra 4.00 *6.50*
a. Tête bêche pair 10.00 *15.00*
b. Pane of 10 50.00 *75.00*

Issued to publicize the FINLANDIA Philatelic Exhibition, Helsinki, July 7-15, 1956.

Printed in sheets containing four 2x5 panes, with white margins around each group. The stamps in each double row are printed tete-beche, making the position of the watermark differ in the vertical row of each pane of ten.

Sold for 155m, price including entrance ticket to exhibition.

Town Hall at Vasa — A108

Unwmk.

1956, Oct. 2 **Engr.** ***Perf. 14***

342 A108 30m bright blue 1.60 1.25

350th anniversary of Vasa.

Northern Countries Issue

Whooper Swans — A108a

1956, Oct. 30 ***Perf. 12½***

343 A108a 20m rose red 1.50 1.40
344 A108a 30m ultra 5.00 1.40

See footnote after Denmark No. 362.

University Clinic, Helsinki A109

1956, Dec. 17 ***Perf. 11½***

345 A109 30m dull green 1.75 1.10

Public health service in Finland, bicent.

Scout Sign, Emblem and Globe — A110

1957, Feb. 22 ***Perf. 14***

346 A110 30m ultra 3.00 1.40

50th anniversary of Boy Scouts.

Arms Holding Hammers and Laurel — A111

Design: 20m, Factories and cogwheel.

1957 **Engr.** ***Perf. 13½***

347 A111 20m dark blue 1.10 1.10
348 A111 30m carmine 2.50 1.40

50th anniv.: Central Fed. of Finnish Employers (20m, issued 9/27); Finnish Trade Union Movement (30m, issued 4/15).

"Lex" from Seal of Parliament — A112

1957, May 23 ***Perf. 14***

349 A112 30m olive gray 1.50 1.10

50th anniv. of the Finnish parliament.

Harbor Type of 1942

1957 **Unwmk.** ***Perf. 14***

350 A51 100m grnsh blue 12.50 .35

Ida Aalberg — A114

1957, Dec. 4 ***Perf. 14***

351 A114 30m vio gray & mar 1.50 *.90*

Birth cent. of Ida Aalberg, Finnish actress.

Arms of Finland A115

1957, Dec. 6 ***Perf. 11½***

352 A115 30m blue 1.40 *1.00*

40th anniv. of Finland's independence.

Jean Sibelius — A116

1957, Dec. 8 ***Perf. 14***

353 A116 30m black 2.75 1.10

Jean Sibelius (1865-1957), composer.

Ski Jump — A117

Design: 30m, Skier, vert.

1958, Feb. 1 **Engr.** ***Perf. 11½***

354 A117 20m slate green 1.10 *1.60*
355 A117 30m blue 1.10 .80

Nordic championships of the Intl. Ski Federation, Lahti.

"March of the Bjorneborgienses," by Edelfelt — A118

1958, Mar. 8

356 A118 30m violet gray 1.75 .95

400th anniv. of the founding of Pori (Bjorneborg).

South Harbor, Helsinki A119

1958, June 2 **Unwmk.** ***Perf. 11½***

357 A119 100m bluish green 17.50 .35

See No. 410.

Seal of Jyväskylä Lyceum A120

1958, Oct. 1 ***Perf. 11½***

358 A120 30m rose carmine 1.75 1.10

Cent. of the founding of the 1st Finnish secondary school.

Chrismon and Globe — A121

1959, Jan. 19

359 A121 30m dull violet .75 .65

Finnish Missionary Society, cent.

Diet at Porvoo, 1809 — A122

1959, Mar. 22 ***Perf. 11½***

360 A122 30m dk blue gray .75 .65

150th anniv. of the inauguration of the Diet at Porvoo.

Saw Cutting Log — A123

1959, May 13 **Engr.**

361 A123 10m shown .95 .95
362 A123 30m Forest .95 .95

No. 361 for the cent. of the establishment of the 1st steam saw-mill in Finland; No. 362, the cent. of the Dept. of Forestry.

Pyhakoski Power Station — A124

1959, May 24

363 A124 75m gray 5.75 .40

See No. 409.

Oil Lamp — A125

1959, Dec. 19

364 A125 30m blue .90 .75

Cent. of the liberation of the country trade.

Woman Gymnast A126

1959, Nov. 14 **Unwmk.**

365 A126 30m rose lilac 1.10 .75

Finnish women's gymnastics and the cent. of the birth of Elin Oihonna Kallio, pioneer of Finnish women's physical education.

Arms of Six New Towns — A127

1960, Jan. 2 ***Perf. 14***

366 A127 30m light violet 1.75 1.00

Issued to commemorate the founding of new towns in Finland: Hyvinkaa, Kouvola, Riihimaki, Rovaniemi, Salo and Seinajoki.

Type of 1860 Issue A128

1960, Mar. 25 Typo. *Rouletted 4½*

367 A128 30m blue & gray 5.50 9.75

Cent. of Finland's serpentine roulette stamps, and in connection with HELSINKI 1960, 40th anniv. exhib. of the Federation of Philatelic Societies of Finland, Mar. 25-31. Sold only at the exhibition for 150m including entrance ticket.

Mother and Child, Waiting Crowd and Uprooted Oak Emblem A129

1960, Apr. 7 Engr. *Perf. 11½*

368 A129 30m rose claret .80 .80
369 A129 40m dark blue .80 .80

World Refugee Year, 7/1/59-6/30/60.

Johan Gadolin — A130

1960, June 4 *Perf. 11½*

370 A130 30m dark brown 1.10 .75

Bicent. of the birth of Gadolin, chemist.

Hj. Nortamo — A131

1960, June 13 Unwmk.

371 A131 30m gray green 1.10 .75

Cent. of the birth of Hj. Nortamo (Hjalmar Nordberg), writer.

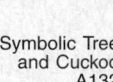

Symbolic Tree and Cuckoo A132

1960, June 18

372 A132 30m vermilion 1.40 .80

Karelian Natl. Festival, Helsinki, June 18-19.

Geodetic Instrument A133

Design: 30m, Aurora borealis and globe.

1960, July 26 Unwmk. *Perf. 13½*

373 A133 10m blue & pale brn 1.00 .65
374 A133 30m ver & rose car 1.25 .65

12th General Assembly of the Intl. Union of Geodesy and Geophysics, Helsinki.

Urho Kekkonen — A134

1960, Sept. 3 Engr. *Perf. 11½*

375 A134 30m violet blue .90 .40

Issued to honor President Urho Kekkonen on his 60th birthday.

Common Design Types pictured following the introduction.

Europa Issue, 1960

Common Design Type

1960, Sept. 19 *Perf. 13½*

Size: 30½x21mm.

376 CD3 30m dk bl & Prus bl *.90* .90
377 CD3 40m dk brn & plum *.80* *.90*

A 30m gray similar to No. 376 was printed with simulated perforations in a non-valid souvenir sheet privately released in London for STAMPEX 1961.

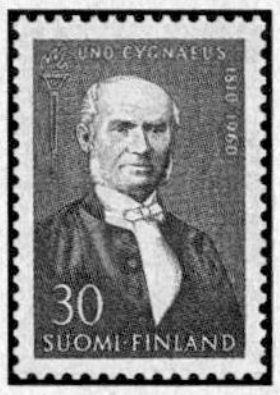

Uno Cygnaeus — A135

1960, Oct. 13 *Perf. 11½*

378 A135 30m dull violet .80 .80

150th anniv. of the birth of Pastor Uno Cygnaeus, founder of elementary schools.

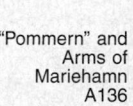

"Pommern" and Arms of Mariehamn A136

1961, Feb. 21 *Perf. 11½*

379 A136 30m grnsh blue 2.75 2.00

Centenary of the founding of Mariehamn.

Lake and Rowboat A137

Turku Castle — A138

1961 Engr. Unwmk.

380 A137 5m green .40 .30
381 A138 125m slate green 20.00 .35

See Nos. 399, 411.

Postal Savings Bank Emblem — A139

1961, May 24

382 A139 30m Prus green .75 .45

75th anniv. of Finland's Postal Savings Bank.

Symbol of Standardization — A140

1961, June 5 Litho. *Perf. 14x13½*

383 A140 30m dk sl grn & org .75 .45

Meeting of the Intl. Organization for Standardization (ISO), Helsinki, June 5.

Juhani Aho — A141

Perf. 11½

1961, Sept. 11 Unwmk. Engr.

384 A141 30m red brown .75 .65

Juhani Aho (1861-1921), writer.

Various Buildings — A142

1961, Oct. 16 *Perf. 11½*

385 A142 30m slate .75 .65

150 years of the Central Board of Buildings.

Arvid Jarnefelt A143

1961, Nov. 16

386 A143 30m deep claret .75 .65

Cent. of the birth of Arvid Jarnefelt, writer.

Bank of Finland — A144

1961, Dec. 12 Engr. *Perf. 11½*

387 A144 30m brown violet .75 .65

150th anniversary of Bank of Finland.

First Finnish Locomotive A145

30m, Steam locomotive & timber car. 40m, Diesel locomotive & passenger train.

1962, Jan. 31 Unwmk. *Perf. 11½*

388 A145 10m gray green 1.75 .60
389 A145 30m violet blue 2.50 .60
390 A145 40m dull red brown 6.00 .60

Nos. 388-390 (3) 10.25 1.80

Centenary of the Finnish State Railways.

Mora Stone — A146

1962, Feb. 15

391 A146 30m gray brown .75 .70

Issued to commemorate 600 years of political rights of the Finnish people.

Senate Place, Helsinki A147

1962, Apr. 8 Unwmk. *Perf. 11½*

392 A147 30m violet brown .75 .70

Sesquicentennial of the proclamation of Helsinki as capital of Finland.

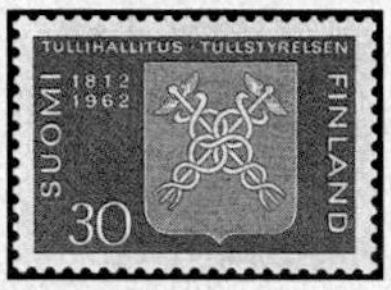

Customs Emblem A148

1962, Apr. 11

393 A148 30m red .75 .70

Finnish Board of Customs, sesquicentennial.

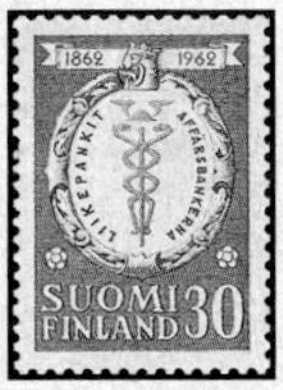

Staff of Mercury — A149

1962, May 21 Engr.

394 A149 30m bluish green .65 .60

Cent. of the 1st commercial bank in Finland.

Santeri Alkio — A150

1962, June 17 Unwmk. *Perf. 11½*

395 A150 30m brown carmine 1.20 .80

Cent. of the birth of Santeri Alkio, writer and pioneer of the young people's societies in Finland.

Finnish Labor Emblem and Conveyor Belt — A151

1962, Oct. 19

396 A151 30m chocolate .75 .40

National production progress.

Survey Plane and Compass — A152

1962, Nov. 14
397 A152 30m yellow green .95 .75

Finnish Land Survey Board, 150th anniv.

Types of 1954-61 and

House of Parliament — A152a

Church at Lammi — A152b

Fortress of Olavinlinna — A152c

Log Floating A153

Parainen Bridge — A154

Farm on Lake Shore — A155

Aerial View of Punkaharju — A155a

A155b

Ristikallio in Kuusamo A156

1963-67 **Engr.** ***Perf. 11½***
398 A94 5p violet blue .50 .25
a. Booklet pane of 2 (vert. pair) 22.50 20.00
b. Bklt. pane of 2 (horiz. pair) 12.00 10.00
399 A137 5p green .50 .25
400 A94 10p blue green 2.00 .25
a. Booklet pane of 2 (vert. pair) 22.50 20.00
401 A94 15p yellow org 4.25 .25
402 A94 20p rose red 3.00 .25
a. Booklet pane of 2 (vert. pair) 24.00
Complete booklet, #398a, 400a, 402a 85.00
b. Bklt. pane, 2 #400, 1 #402 + label; horiz. strip 45.00 35.00
Complete booklet, #398b, 402b 100.00
c. Bklt. pane, 2 #398, 2 #400, 1 #402; horiz. strip 3.50 3.50
Complete booklet, #402c 5.00
403 A94 25p rose lilac 4.00 .25
404 A94 30p lt ultra 6.00 .25
404A A94 30p blue gray ('65) 6.25 .25
405 A94 35p blue 1.50 .25
405A A94 40p ultra ('67) 1.75 .35
406 A152a 40p dull purple 3.50 .35
407 A152b 50p gray olive 5.75 .50
408 A152c 60p pale purple 8.25 .50
408A A152c 65p pale pur ('67) 1.20 .25
409 A124 75p gray 2.25 .50
410 A119 1m bluish grn 2.00 .25
411 A138 1.25m slate grn 2.00 .50
412 A153 1.50m dk grnsh gray 2.00 .25
413 A154 1.75m blue 2.00 .50
414 A155 2m green ('64) 12.00 .25
414A A155a 2.50m ultra & yel grn ('67) 11.00 .65
414B A155b 2.50m ultra, dk grn & yel grn ('69) 8.00 .40
415 A156 5m dk slate grn ('64) 21.00 .50
Nos. 398-415 (23) 110.70 8.00

Pennia denominations expressed: "0.05," "0.10," etc.

Four stamps of type A94 (5p, 10p, 20p, 25p) come in two types: I. Four vertical lines in "O" of SUOMI. II. Three lines in "O."

For similar designs see Nos. 457-470A.

Mother and Child — A157

1963, Mar. 21 **Unwmk.** ***Perf. 11½***
416 A157 40p red brown .55 .40

FAO "Freedom from Hunger" campaign.

"Christ Today" — A158

Design: 10p, Crown of thorns and medieval cross of consecration.

1963, July 30 **Engr.** ***Perf. 11½***
417 A158 10p maroon .50 .45
418 A158 30p dark green .50 .45

4th assembly of the Lutheran World Federation, Helsinki, July 30-Aug. 8.

Europa Issue, 1963
Common Design Type

1963, Sept. 16 **Size: 30x20mm**
419 CD6 40p red lilac *1.25* *.55*

Assembly Building, Helsinki A159

1963, Sept. 18
420 A159 30p violet blue .70 .40

Representative Assembly of Finland, cent.

Convair Metropolitan A160

Design: 40p, Caravelle jetliner.

1963, Nov. 1
421 A160 35p slate green 1.00 .60
422 A160 40p brt ultra 1.10 .50

40th anniversary of Finnish air traffic.

M. A. Castrén — A161

1963, Dec. 2 **Unwmk.**
423 A161 35p violet blue .70 .45

Matthias Alexander Castrén (1813-52), ethnologist and philologist.

Stone Elk's Head, 2000 B.C. — A162

1964, Feb. 5 **Litho.** ***Perf. 14***
424 A162 35p ocher & slate grn .70 .45

Cent. of the Finnish Artists' Association. The soapstone sculpture was found at Huittinen.

Emil Nestor Setälä — A163

1964, Feb. 27 **Engr.** ***Perf. 11½***
425 A163 35p dk red brown .80 .50

Emil Nestor Setälä (1864-1946), philologist, minister of education and foreign affairs and chancellor of Abo University.

Staff of Aesculapius A164

1964, June 13 **Unwmk.** ***Perf. 11½***
426 A164 40p slate green 1.10 .45

18th General Assembly of the World Medical Association, Helsinki, June 13-19, 1964.

Ice Hockey — A165

1965, Jan. 4 **Engr.**
427 A165 35p dark blue 1.10 .60

World Ice Hockey Championships, Finland, March 3-14, 1965.

Design from Centenary Medal — A166

1965, Feb. 6 **Unwmk.** ***Perf. 11½***
428 A166 35p olive gray .70 .40

Centenary of communal self-government in Finland.

K. J. Stahlberg and "Lex" by W. Runeberg A167

1965, Mar. 22 **Engr.**
429 A167 35p brown .70 .40

Kaarlo Juho Stahlberg (1865-1952), 1st Pres. of Finland.

International Cooperation Year Emblem A168

1965, Apr. 2 **Litho.** ***Perf. 14***
430 A168 40p bis, dull red, blk & grn .70 .40

UN International Cooperation Year.

"Fratricide" by Gallen-Kallela A169

35p, Girl's Head by Akseli Gallen-Kallela.

1965, Apr. 26 ***Perf. 13½x14***
431 A169 25p multicolored 1.40 .65
432 A169 35p multicolored 1.40 .65

Centenary of the birth of the painter Aksell Gallen-Kallela.

Sibelius, Piano and Score — A170

Design: 35p, Musical score and bird.

1965, May 15 **Engr.** ***Perf. 11½***
433 A170 25p violet 1.40 .80
434 A170 35p dull green 1.40 .40

Jean Sibelius (1865-1957), composer.

Antenna for Satellite Telecommunication — A171

1965, May 17
435 A171 35p blue .70 .50

Cent. of the ITU.

"Winter Day" by Pekka Halonen — A172

Perf. 14x13½
1965, Sept. 23 **Litho.** **Unwmk.**
436 A172 35p gold & multi .70 .40

Centenary of the birth of the painter Pekka Halonen.

Europa Issue, 1965

Common Design Type

Engraved and Lithographed

1965, Sept. 27 *Perf. 13½x14*

437 CD8 40p bister, red brn, dk bl & grn *1.25* *.55*

"Growth" — A173

1966, May 11 **Litho.** *Perf. 14*

438 A173 35p vio blue & blue .70 .40

Centenary of the promulgation of the Elementary School Decree.

Old Post Office — A174

1966, June 11 **Litho.** *Perf. 14*

439 A174 35p ocher, yel, dk bl & blk 4.50 *7.00*

Cent. of the 1st postage stamps in Finnish currency, and in connection with the NORDIA Stamp Exhibition, Helsinki, June 11-15. The stamp was sold only to buyers of a 1.25m exhibition entrance ticket.

UNESCO Emblem and World Map — A175

Lithographed and Engraved

1966, Oct. 9 *Perf. 14*

440 A175 40p grn, yel, blk & brn org .65 .30

20th anniv. of UNESCO.

Finnish Police Emblem — A176

1966, Oct. 15

441 A176 35p dp ultra, blk & sil .65 .30

Issued to honor the Finnish police.

Insurance Sesquicentennial Medal — A177

1966, Oct. 28 **Engr. & Photo.**

442 A177 35p maroon, olive & blk .65 .30

150th anniv. of the Finnish insurance system.

UNICEF Emblem A178

1966, Nov. 14

443 A178 15p lt ultra, pur & grn .30 .30

Activities of UNICEF.

"FINEFTA," Finnish Flag and Circle — A179

1967, Feb. 15 **Engr.** *Perf. 14*

444 A179 40p ultra .65 .30

European Free Trade Association, EFTA. See note after Denmark No. 431.

Windmill and Arms of Uusikaupunki A180

Lithographed and Engraved

1967, Apr. 19 *Perf. 14*

445 A180 40p multicolored .65 .30

350th anniv. of Uusikaupunki (Nystad).

Mannerheim Monument by Aimo Tukiainen — A181

1967, June 4 *Perf. 14*

446 A181 40p violet & multi .65 .30

Cent. of the birth of Field Marshal Carl Gustav Emil Mannerheim.

Double Mortise Corner — A182

1967, June 16 **Litho. & Photo.**

447 A182 40p multicolored .65 .30

Issued to honor Finnish settlers in Sweden.

Watermark of Thomasböle Paper Mill — A183

1967, Sept. 6 *Perf. 14*

448 A183 40p olive & black .65 .30

300th anniv. of the Finnish paper industry.

Martin Luther, by Lucas Cranach A184

Photogravure and Engraved

1967, Nov. 4 *Perf. 14*

449 A184 40p bister & brown .65 .30

450th anniversary of the Reformation.

"Wood and Water" Globe and Flag — A185

Designs (Globe, Flag and): 25p, Flying swan. 40p, Ear of wheat.

1967, Dec. 5 *Perf. 11½*

450	A185	20p green & blue	.65	.30
451	A185	25p ultra & blue	.65	.30
452	A185	40p magenta & bl	.65	.30
		Nos. 450-452 (3)	1.95	.90

50th anniv. of Finland's independence.

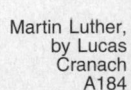

Zachris Topelius and Blue Bird — A186

1968, Jan. 14 **Litho.** *Perf. 14*

453 A186 25p blue & multi 1.10 .50

Topelius (1818-98), writer and educator.

Skiers and Ski Lift — A187

1968, Feb. 19 **Photo.** *Perf. 14*

454 A187 25p multicolored .85 .70

Winter Tourism in Finland.

Paper Making, by Hannes Autere — A188

1968, Mar. 12 **Litho.** **Wmk. 363**

455 A188 45p dk red, brn & org .70 .45

Finnish paper industry and 150th anniv. of the oldest Finnish paper mill, Tervakoski, whose own watermark was used for this stamp.

World Health Organization Emblem A189

Lithographed and Photogravure

1968, Apr. 6 **Unwmk.** *Perf. 14*

456 A189 40p red org, dk blue & gold .65 .30

To honor World Health Organization.

Lion Type of 1954-58 and

Market Place and Mermaid Fountain, Helsinki A190

Keuru Wooden Church, 1758 — A191

Häme Bridge, Tampere A192

Finnish Arms from Grave of King Gustav Vasa, 1581 — A194

A194a

25p, Post bus. 30p, Aquarium-Planetarium, Tampere. No. 463, P.O., Tampere. No. 465, National Museum, Helsinki, vert. No. 467A, like 70p. 1.30m, Helsinki railroad station.

Engr. (type A94, except #459A); Litho. (#459A, 465 & type A190); Engr. & Litho. (others)

Perf. 11½; 12½ (#466, 467A); 13 (#465); 13½ (#470); 14 (#463, 470A)

1968-78

457	A94	1p lt red brn	.40	*.50*
458	A94	2p gray green	.40	*.65*
459	A94	4p gray	.50	*.65*
459A	A94	5p violet blue	2.00	*3.00*
460	A192	25p multi ('71)	.50	.25
461	A191	30p multi ('71)	1.25	.25
461A	A94	35p dull org ('74)	.55	*.40*
b.		Bklt. pane of 4, #459A, 461A, 400, 464A + label	2.50	2.50
		Complete booklet, #461b	3.50	
462	A94	40p orange ('73)	.90	.65
a.		Bklt. pane of 3, #462, 2 #404A + 2 labels	6.00	*8.00*
		Complete booklet, #462a	8.00	
463	A192	40p multi ('73)	1.00	.25
464	A94	50p lt ultra ('70)	3.00	.25
c.		Bklt. pane of 5, #401, 403, 464, 2 #459A + 5 labels	13.00	*14.50*
		Complete booklet, #464c	14.00	
464A	A94	50p rose lake ('74)	.80	.25
d.		Bklt. pane of 4, #400, 464A, 2 #402 + label	1.75	1.75
		Complete booklet, #464Ad	2.00	
464B	A94	60p blue ('73)	1.10	.25
465	A191	60p multi ('73)	1.25	.25
466	A190	70p multi ('73)	.95	.25
467	A191	80p multi ('70)	5.25	.25
467A	A190	80p multi ('76)	.50	.50
468	A192	90p multi	2.00	.50
469	A191	1.30m multi ('71)	1.25	.50
470	A194	10m multi ('74)	5.25	.50
470A	A194a	20m multi ('78)	11.00	.50
		Nos. 457-470A (20)	39.85	10.60

Issued: 5p, 6/72.

Infantry Monument, Vaasa — A195

Designs: 25p, War Memorial (cross), Hietaniemi Cemetery. 40p, Soldier, 1968.

1968, June 4 **Photo.** *Perf. 14*

471	A195	20p lt violet & multi	1.10	.35
472	A195	25p lt blue & multi	1.10	.35
473	A195	40p orange & multi	1.10	.35
		Nos. 471-473 (3)	3.30	1.05

To honor Finnish national defense.

Camping Ground A196

1968, June 10 **Litho.**
474 A196 25p multicolored .60 .40

Issued to publicize Finland for summer vacations.

Paper, Pulp and Pine — A197

Lithographed and Embossed
1968, July 2 **Unwmk.** ***Perf. 14***
475 A197 40p multicolored .70 .40

Finnish wood industry.

Mustola Lock, Saima Canal — A198

1968, Aug. 5 **Litho.** ***Perf. 14***
476 A198 40p multicolored .70 .40

Opening of the Saima Canal.

Oskar Merikanto and Pipe Organ — A199

1968, Aug. 5 **Unwmk.**
477 A199 40p vio, silver & lt brn 1.10 .40

Centenary of the birth of Oskar Merikanto, composer.

Ships in Harbor and Emblem of Central Chamber of Commerce A200

1968, Sept. 13 **Litho.** ***Perf. 14***
478 A200 40p lt bl, brt bl & blk .70 .40

Publicizing economic development and for the 50th anniv. of the Central Chamber of Commerce of Finland.

Welder — A201

1968, Oct. 11 **Litho.** ***Perf. 14***
479 A201 40p blue & multi .70 .40

Finnish metal industry.

Lyre, Students' Emblem — A202

Lithographed and Engraved
1968, Nov. 24 ***Perf. 14***
480 A202 40p ultra, vio bl & gold .70 .40

Issued to publicize the work of the student unions in Finnish social life.

Nordic Cooperation Issue

Five Ancient Ships — A203

1969, Feb. 28 **Engr.** ***Perf. 11½***
481 A203 40p lt ultra 2.00 .40

50th anniv. of the Nordic Society and centenary of postal cooperation among the northern countries. The design is taken from a coin found at the site of Birka, an ancient Swedish town. See also Denmark Nos. 454-455, Iceland Nos. 404-405, Norway Nos. 523-524 and Sweden Nos. 808-810.

Town Hall and Arms of Kemi — A203a

1969, Mar. 5 **Photo.** ***Perf. 14***
482 A203a 40p multicolored .70 .40

Centenary of the town of Kemi.

Europa Issue, 1969
Common Design Type
1969, Apr. 28 **Photo.** ***Perf. 14***
Size: 30x20mm
483 CD12 40p dl rose, vio bl & dk bl *3.50* *.75*

ILO Emblem A204

Lithographed and Engraved
1969, June 2 ***Perf. 11½***
484 A204 40p dp rose & vio blue .70 .40

50th anniv. of the ILO.

Armas Järnefelt — A205

1969, Aug. 14 **Photo.** ***Perf. 14***
485 A205 40p multicolored 1.40 .40

Järnefelt (1869-1958), composer and conductor. Portrait on stamp by Vilho Sjöström.

Emblems and Flag — A206

1969, Sept. 19 **Photo.** ***Perf. 14***
486 A206 40p lt bl, blk, grn & lil .70 .40

Publicizinge the importance of National and International Fairs in Finnish economy.

Johannes Linnankoski — A207

1969, Oct. 18 **Litho.**
487 A207 40p dk brn red & multi .70 .40

Linnankoski (1869-1913), writer.

Educational Symbols A208

Lithographed and Engraved
1969, Nov. 24 ***Perf. 11½***
488 A208 40p gray, vio & grn .70 .40

Centenary of the Central School Board.

DC-8-62 CF Plane and Helsinki Airport — A209

1969, Dec. 22 **Photo.** ***Perf. 14***
489 A209 25p sky blue & multi 1.10 .75

Golden Eagle — A210

1970, Feb. 10 **Litho.** ***Perf. 14***
490 A210 30p multicolored 3.50 1.10

Year of Nature Conservation, 1970.

Swatches in Shape of Factories A211

1970, Mar. 9 **Litho.** ***Perf. 14***
491 A211 50p multicolored .85 .40

Finnish textile industry.

Molecule Diagram and Factories A212

1970, Mar. 26 **Photo.** ***Perf. 14***
492 A212 50p multicolored .85 .40

Finnish chemical industry.

UNESCO Emblem and Lenin — A213

Atom Diagram and Laurel — A214

UN Emblem and Globe — A215

1970 **Litho. and Engr.**
493 A213 30p gold & multi .70 .40
494 A214 30p red & multi .70 .40

Photogravure and Gold Embossed
495 A215 50p bl, vio bl & gold .70 .40
Nos. 493-495 (3) 2.10 1.20

25th anniv. of the UN. No. 493 also publicizes the UNESCO-sponsored Lenin Symposium, Tampere, Apr. 6-10. No. 494 also publicizes the Nuclear Data Conf. of the Atomic Energy Commission, Otaniemi (Helsinki), June 15-19.

Issued: No. 493, 4/6; No. 494, 6/15; No. 495, 10/24.

Handicapped Volleyball Player — A216

1970, June 27 **Litho.** ***Perf. 14***
496 A216 50p orange, red & blk 1.00 .40

Issued to publicize the position of handicapped civilians and war veterans in society and their potential contributions to it.

Meeting of Auroraseura Society — A217

1970, Aug. 15 **Photo.** ***Perf. 14***
497 A217 50p multicolored .70 .40

200th anniv. of the Auroraseura Soc., dedicated to the study of Finnish history, geography, economy and language. The design of the stamp is after a painting by Eero Jarnefelt.

Uusikaarlepyy Arms, Church and 17th Cent. Building A218

Design: No. 499, Arms of Kokkola, harbor, Sports Palace and 17th century building.

1970 ***Perf. 14***
498 A218 50p multicolored .70 .40
499 A218 50p multicolored .70 .40

Towns of Uusikaarlepyy and Kokkola, 350th anniv.

Issued: No. 498, Aug. 21; No. 499, Sept. 17.

Urho Kekkonen, Medal by Aimo Tukiainen — A219

1970, Sept. 3 Litho. & Engr.
500 A219 50p ultra, sil & blk .70 .40

70th birthday of Pres. Urho Kekkonen.

Globe, Maps of US, Finland, USSR — A220

Lithographed and Gold Embossed
1970, Nov. 2
501 A220 50p blk, bl, pink & gold .70 .40

Strategic Arms Limitation Talks (SALT) between the US & USSR, Helsinki, 11/2-12/18.

Pres. Paasikivi by Essi Renavall — A221

1970, Nov. 27 Photo. *Perf. 14*
502 A221 50p gold, brt bl & slate .70 .40

Centenary of the birth of Juho Kusti Paasikivi (1870-1956), President of Finland.

Cogwheels A222

1971, Jan. 28 Litho. *Perf. 14*
503 A222 50p multicolored .70 .40

Finnish industry.

Europa Issue, 1971
Common Design Type
1971, May 3 Litho. *Perf. 14*
Size: 30x20mm
504 CD14 50p dp rose, yel & blk *5.00 .75*

Tornio Church — A223

1971, May 12 Litho. *Perf. 14*
505 A223 50p multicolored 1.00 .40

350th anniversary of the town of Tornio.

Front Page, January 15, 1771 — A224

1971, June 1 Litho. *Perf. 14*
506 A224 50p multicolored .70 .40

Bicentenary of the Finnish press.

Athletes in Helsinki Stadium A225

50p, Running & javelin in Helsinki Stadium.

1971, July 5 Litho. *Perf. 14*
507 A225 30p multicolored 1.50 .85
508 A225 50p multicolored 2.50 .85

European Athletic Championships.

Sailboats A226

1971, July 14
509 A226 50p multicolored 1.25 .60

International Lightning Class Championships, Helsinki, July 14-Aug. 1.

Silver Tea Pot, Guild's Emblem, Tools — A227

1971, Aug. 6
510 A227 50p lilac & multi .70 .40

600th anniv. of Finnish goldsmiths' art.

"Plastic Buttons and Houses" A228

Photogravure and Embossed
1971, Oct. 20 *Perf. 14*
511 A228 50p multicolored .70 .40

Finnish plastics industry.

Europa Issue 1972
Common Design Type
1972, May 2 Litho. *Perf. 14*
Size: 20x30mm
512 CD15 30p dk red & multi *2.50 .70*
513 CD15 50p lt brn & multi *4.50 .70*

Finnish National Theater A229

1972, May 22. Litho. *Perf. 14*
514 A229 50p lt violet & multi .70 .40

Centenary of the Finnish National Theater, founded by Kaarlo and Emilie Bergbom.

Globe, US and USSR Flags — A230

1972, June 2
515 A230 50p multicolored 1.25 .40

Strategic Arms Limitation Talks (SALT), final meeting, Helsinki, Mar. 28-May 26; treaty signed, Moscow, May 26.

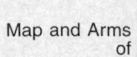

Map and Arms of Aland — A231

1972, June 9
516 A231 50p multicolored 3.25 .85

1st Provincial Meeting of Aland, 50th anniv.

Training Ship Suomen Joutsen — A232

1972, June 19
517 A232 50p orange & multi 1.25 .40

Tall Ships' Race 1972, Helsinki, Aug. 20.

Costume from Perni, 12th Cent. — A233

No. 519, Couple, Tenhola, 18th cent. No. 520, Girl, Nastola, 19th cent. No. 521, Man, Voyni, 19th cent. No. 522, Lapps, Inari, 19th cent.

1972, Nov. 19 Litho. *Perf. 13*
518 A233 50p shown 2.50 .65
519 A233 50p multicolored 2.50 .65
520 A233 50p multicolored 2.50 .65
521 A233 50p multicolored 2.50 .65
522 A233 50p multicolored 2.50 .65
a. Strip of 5, #518-522 12.50 14.50
Complete booklet, 2 each #518-522 30.00

Regional costumes.
See Nos. 533-537.

Circle Surrounding Map of Europe — A234

1972, Dec. 11 *Perf. 14x13½*
523 A234 50p multicolored 2.25 .55

Preparatory Conference on European Security and Cooperation.

Book, Finnish and Soviet Colors — A235

Litho.; Gold Embossed
1973, Apr. 6 *Perf. 14*
524 A235 60p gold & multi .55 .40

Soviet-Finnish Treaty of Friendship, 25th anniv.

Kyösti Kallio (1873-1940), Pres. of Finland — A236

1973, Apr. 10 Litho. *Perf. 13*
525 A236 60p multicolored .55 .40

Europa Issue 1973
Common Design Type
1973, Apr. 30 Photo. *Perf. 14*
Size: 31x21mm
526 CD16 60p bl, brt bl & emer 1.25 .55

Nordic Cooperation Issue

Nordic House, Reykjavik A236a

1973, June 26 Engr. *Perf. 12½*
527 A236a 60p multicolored 1.00 .40
528 A236a 70p multicolored 1.00 .40

A century of postal cooperation among Denmark, Finland, Iceland, Norway and Sweden, and in connection with the Nordic Postal Conference, Reykjavik.

Map of Europe, "EUROPA" as a Maze — A237

Litho. & Embossed
1973, July 3 *Perf. 13*
529 A237 70p multicolored .75 .40

Conference for European Security and Cooperation, Helsinki, July 1973.

Paddling A238

1973, July 18 Litho. *Perf. 14*
530 A238 60p multicolored .75 .40

Canoeing World Championships, Tampere, July 26-29.

Radiosonde, WMO Emblem — A239

1973, Aug. 6 Litho. *Perf. 14*
531 A239 60p multicolored .55 .40

Cent. of intl. meteorological cooperation.

Eliel Saarinen and Design for Parliament, Helsinki A240

1973, Aug. 20 *Perf. 12½x13*
532 A240 60p multicolored .55 .40

Eliel Saarinen (1873-1950), architect.

Costume Type of 1972

1973, Oct. 10 Litho. *Perf. 13*

533 A233 60p Woman, Kaukola 2.75 .40
534 A233 60p Woman, Jaaski 2.75 .40
535 A233 60p Married couple, Koivisto 2.75 .40
536 A233 60p Mother and son, Sakyla 2.75 .40
537 A233 60p Girl, Hainavesi 2.75 .40
a. Strip of 5, #533-537 16.00 19.00

Regional costumes.

DC10-30 Jet — A241

1973, Nov. 1 Litho. *Perf. 14*
538 A241 60p multicolored .80 .40

50th anniv. of regular air service, Finnair.

Santa Claus in Reindeer Sleigh — A242

1973, Nov. 15 Litho. *Perf. 14*
539 A242 30p multicolored .95 .40

Christmas 1973.

"The Barber of Seville" A243

1973, Nov. 21
540 A243 60p multicolored .55 .40

Centenary of opera in Finland.

Production of Porcelain Jug — A244

1973, Nov. 23
541 A244 60p blue & multi .55 .40

Finnish porcelain.

Nurmi, by Waino Aaltonen — A245

1973, Dec. 11
542 A245 60p multicolored .85 .40

Paavo Nurmi (1897-1973), runner, Olympic winner, 1920-1924-1928.

Arms, Map and Harbor of Hanko — A246

1974, Jan. 10 Litho. *Perf. 14*
543 A246 60p blue & multi .75 .40

Centenary of the town of Hanko.

Ice Hockey A247

1974, Mar. 5 Litho. *Perf. 14*
544 A247 60p multicolored .90 .40

European and World Ice Hockey Championships, held in Finland.

Seagulls (7 Baltic States) A248

1974, Mar. 18 *Perf. 12½*
545 A248 60p multicolored 1.00 .40

Protection of marine environment of the Baltic Sea.

Goddess of Freedom, by Waino Aaltonen — A249

1974, Apr. 29 Litho. *Perf. 13x12½*
546 A249 70p multicolored *5.00 .50*

Europa.

Ilmari Kianto and Old Pine — A250

1974, May 7 *Perf. 13*
547 A250 60p multicolored .55 .40

Ilmari Kianto (1874-1970), writer.

Society Emblem, Symbol A251

Lithographed and Embossed

1974, June 12 *Perf. 13½x14*
548 A251 60p gold & multi .55 .40

Centenary of Adult Education.

Grid — A252

1974, June 14 Litho. *Perf. 14x13½*
549 A252 60p multicolored .55 .40

Rationalization Year in Finland, dedicated to economic and business improvements.

UPU Emblem — A253

1974, Oct. 10 Litho. *Perf. 13½x14*
550 A253 60p multicolored .55 .40
551 A253 70p multicolored .55 .40

Centenary of Universal Postal Union.

Elves Distributing Gifts — A254

1974, Nov. 16 Litho. *Perf. 14x13½*
552 A254 35p multicolored 1.75 .35

Christmas 1974.

Concrete Bridge and Granite Bridge, Aunessilta — A255

Litho. & Engr.

1974, Dec. 17 *Perf. 14*
553 A255 60p multicolored 1.25 .70

Royal Finnish Directorate of Roads and Waterways, 175th anniversary.

Coat of Arms, 1581 — A256

Chimneyless Log Sauna — A256a

Cheese Frames A257

Carved Wooden Distaffs A258

Kirvu Weather Vane A258a

1.50m, Wood-carved high drinking bowl, 1542.

Perf. 11½; 14 (2m, 5m)

1975-90 **Engr.**

555 A256 10p red lilac ('78) .25 *.50*
a. Bklt. pane of 4 (#555, 2 #556, #559) + label 2.25 2.25
Complete booklet, #555a 2.50
b. Bklt. pane of 5 (2 #555, #557, #563, #564) 2.50 2.25
Complete booklet, #555b 3.00
c. As "a," no label 2.50 2.50
Complete booklet, #555c 3.00
d. Perf. 13x12½ .35 .25
556 A256 20p olive ('77) .40 *.30*
a. 20p yellow bister ('85) 1.10 1.40
b. As "a," perf. 13x12½ 1.25 1.25
557 A256 30p carmine ('77) 2.25 1.50
557A A256 30p car, litho. 5.50 3.00
558 A256 40p orange .40 .30
a. Perf. 13x12½ 1.75 1.50
559 A256 50p green ('76) .50 .30
a. Perf. 13x12½ 2.00 1.25
560 A256 60p blue .60 .30
a. Perf. 13x12½ 2.50 1.50
561 A256 70p sepia .50 .25
562 A256 80p dl red & bl grn ('76) .50 .50
a. Perf. 13x12½ 4.25 4.00
563 A256 90p vio bl ('77) .45 .40
564 A256 1.10m yellow ('79) .45 .35
565 A256 1.20m dk blue ('79) .70 .60
566 A258 1.50m multi ('76) 1.10 .25

Litho.

567 A256a 2m multi ('77) 1.25 .30

Lithographed and Engraved

568 A257 2.50m multi ('76) 1.25 .50
a. Perf. 14 2.25 1.00
569 A258 4.50m multi ('76) 2.40 .40
a. Perf. 14 3.25 2.50
570 A258a 5m multi ('77) 2.25 .30
Nos. 555-570 (17) 20.75 10.05

Some denominations of design A256 exist in up to three engraving types.

Nos. 560a and 562a was only issued within the booklet panes Nos. 713a and 715a.

Issued: No. 557A, 6/3/80; No. 560a, 7/25/88; No. 555d, 7/25/89; No. 562a, 3/1/90; No. 558a, 8/18/94; No. 568a, 12/28/88; No. 569a, 9/26/88; No. 556b, 4/3/98.

See Nos. 629, 631-633, 711-715, 861.

Finland No. 16 — A259

Lithographed and Typographed

1975, Apr. 26 *Perf. 13*
571 A259 70p multicolored 2.75 4.50

Nordia 75 Philatelic Exhibition, Helsinki, Apr. 26-May 1. Sold only at exhibition for 3m including entrance ticket.

Girl Combing Hair, by Magnus Enckell — A260

Europa: 90p, Washerwoman, by Tyko Sallinen (1879-1955).

1975, Apr. 28 Litho. *Perf. 13x12½*
572 A260 70p gray & multi *2.50 .40*
573 A260 90p tan & multi *2.50 .40*

Balance of Justice, Sword of Legality — A261

1975, May 7 *Perf. 14*
574 A261 70p vio blue & multi .55 .40

Sesquicentennial of State Economy Comptroller's Office.

Rescue Boat and Sinking Ship — A262

1975, June 2 Litho. *Perf. 14*

575 A262 70p multicolored .85 .40

12th Intl. Salvage Conf., Finland, stressing importance of coordinating sea, air and communications resources in salvage operations.

Safe and Unsafe Levels of Drugs — A263

1975, July 21 Litho. *Perf. 14*

576 A263 70p multicolored .55 .40

Importance of pharmacological studies and for the 6th Intl. Pharmacology Cong., Helsinki.

Olavinlinna Castle A264

1975, July 29 *Perf. 13*

577 A264 70p multicolored .55 .40

500th anniversary of Olavinlinna Castle.

Swallows over Finlandia Hall — A265

1975, July 30

578 A265 90p multicolored .70 .40

European Security and Cooperation Conference, Helsinki, July 30-Aug. 1. (The swallows of the design represent freedom, mobility and continuity.) See No. 709.

"Men and Women Working for Peace" — A266

1975, Oct. 24 Litho. *Perf. 13x12½*

579 A266 70p multicolored .55 .40

International Women's Year 1975.

"Continuity and Growth" — A267

1975, Oct. 29 *Perf. 13*

580 A267 70p brown & multi .55 .40

Industrial Art and for the centenary of the Finnish Society of Industrial Art.

Boys as Three Kings and Herod — A268

1975, Nov. 8 *Perf. 14*

581 A268 40p blue & multi 1.10 .35

Christmas 1975.

Top Border of State Debenture A269

Lithographed and Engraved

1976, Jan. 9 *Perf. 11½*

582 A269 80p multicolored .55 .40

Centenary of State Treasury.

Glider over Lake Region A270

1976, Jan. 13 Litho. *Perf. 14*

583 A270 80p multicolored .90 .40

15th World Glider Championships, Rayskala, June 13-27.

Prof. Heikki Klemetti (1876-1953), Musician & Writer — A271

1976, Feb. 14 Litho. *Perf. 13*

584 A271 80p green & multi .55 .40

Map with Areas of Different Dialects — A272

1976, Mar. 10 Litho. *Perf. 13*

585 A272 80p multicolored .55 .40

Finnish Language Society, centenary.

Aino Ackté, by Albert Edelfelt — A273

1976, Apr. 23

586 A273 70p yellow & multi .70 .40

Aino Ackté (1876-1944), opera singer.

Europa Issue

Knife from Voyri, Sheath and Belt — A274

1976, May 3 Litho. *Perf. 13*

587 A274 80p violet bl & multi *3.25 .50*

Radio and Television A275

1976, Sept. 9 Litho. *Perf. 13*

588 A275 80p multicolored .55 .40

Radio broadcasting in Finland, 50th anniv.

Christmas Morning Ride to Church A276

1976, Oct. 23 Litho. *Perf. 14*

589 A276 50p multicolored .90 .40

Christmas 1976.

Turku Chapter Seal (Virgin and Child) A277

1976, Nov. 1 Litho. *Perf. 12½*

590 A277 80p buff, brn & red .55 .40

Cathedral Chapter of Turku, 700th anniv.

Alvar Aalto, Finlandia Hall, Helsinki A278

1976, Nov. 4

591 A278 80p multicolored .55 .40

Hugo Alvar Henrik Aalto (1898-1976), architect.

Ice Dancers — A280

1977, Jan. 25 Litho. *Perf. 13*

592 A280 90p multicolored .65 .40

European Figure Skating Championships, Finland, Jan. 25-29.

Five Water Lilies — A281

Photogravure and Engraved

1977, Feb. 2 *Perf. 12½*

593 A281 90p brt green & multi 1.00 .40

594 A281 1m ultra & multi 1.00 .40

Nordic countries cooperation for protection of the environment and 25th Session of Nordic Council, Helsinki, Feb. 19.

Icebreaker Rescuing Merchantman A282

1977, Mar. 2 Litho. *Perf. 13*

595 A282 90p multicolored 1.00 .40

Winter navigation between Finland and Sweden, centenary.

Nuclear Reactor A283

1977, Mar. 3 *Perf. 12½x13*

596 A283 90p multicolored .55 .40

Opening of nuclear power station on Hästholmen Island.

Europa Issue

Autumn Landscape, Northern Finland — A284

1977, May 2 Litho. *Perf. 12½x13*

597 A284 90p multicolored *3.25 .45*

Tree, Birds and Nest — A285

1977, May 4 *Perf. 13x12½*

598 A285 90p multicolored .55 .40

75th anniversary of cooperative banks.

Orthodox Church, Valamo Cloister — A286

1977, May 31 Litho. *Perf. 14*

599 A286 90p multicolored .55 .40

Consecration festival of new Orthodox Church at Valamo Cloister, Heinävesi; 800th anniversary of introduction of orthodoxy in Karelia and of founding of Valamo Cloister.

Paavo Ruotsalainen (1777-1852), Lay Leader of Pietists in Finland — A287

1977, July 8 **Litho.** ***Perf. 13***
600 A287 90p multicolored .55 .40

People Fleeing Fire and Water — A288

1977, Sept. 14 **Litho.** ***Perf. 14***
601 A288 90p multicolored .55 .40

Civil defense for security.

Volleyball — A289

1977, Sept. 15
602 A289 90p multicolored .70 .40

European Women's Volleyball Championships, Finland, Sept. 29-Oct. 2.

Children Bringing Water for Sauna — A290

1977, Oct. 25
603 A290 50p multicolored 1.10 .40

Christmas 1977.

Finnish Flag — A291

1977, Dec. 5 **Litho.** ***Perf. 14***
Size: 31x21mm
604 A291 80p multicolored .70 .40
Size: 37x25mm
Perf. 13
605 A291 1m multicolored 1.00 .40

Finland's declaration of independence, 60th anniv.

Wall Telephone, 1880, New Telephone — A292

1977, Dec. 9 ***Perf. 14***
606 A292 1m multicolored .60 .40

Centenary of first telephone in Finland.

Harbor, Sunila Factory, Kotka Arms — A293

1978, Jan. 2 **Litho.** ***Perf. 14***
607 A293 1m multicolored .60 .40

Centenary of founding of Kotka.

Paimio Sanitarium by Alvar Aalto — A294

Europa: 1.20m, Hvittrask studio house, 1902, horiz.

1978, May 2 **Litho.** ***Perf. 13***
608 A294 1m multicolored *7.50 1.00*
609 A294 1.20m multicolored *9.50 11.50*

Rural Bus Service A295

1978, June 8 **Litho.** ***Perf. 14***
610 A295 1m multicolored .60 .40

Eino Leino and Eagle — A296

1978, July 6 **Litho.** ***Perf. 13***
611 A296 1m multicolored .60 .40

Eino Leino (1878-1926), poet.

Function Theory and Rhythmical Lines — A297

1978, Aug. 15 **Litho.** ***Perf. 14***
612 A297 1m multicolored .60 .40

ICM 78, International Congress of Mathematicians, Helsinki, Aug. 15-23.

Child Feeding Birds — A298

1978, Oct. 23 **Litho.** ***Perf. 14***
613 A298 50p multicolored 1.00 .40

Christmas 1978.

A299

1979, Jan. 2 **Litho.** ***Perf. 13***
614 A299 1.10m multicolored .75 .40

International Year of the Child.

A300

1979, Feb. 7 **Litho.** ***Perf. 14***
615 A300 1.10m Runner .55 .40

8th Orienteering World Championships, Finland, Sept. 1-4.

Old School, Hamina, Academy Flag — A301

1979, Mar. 20 **Litho.** ***Perf. 14***
616 A301 1.10m multicolored .55 .40

200th anniv. of Finnish Military Academy.

A302

Design: Turku Cathedral and Castle, Prinkkala house, Brahe statue.

1979, Mar. 31
617 A302 1.10m multicolored .55 .40

A303

1979, May 2 **Litho.** ***Perf. 14***
618 A303 1.10m Streetcar, Helsinki .55 .30

Non-polluting urban transportation.

View of Tampere, 1779 — A304

1979, May 2
619 A304 90p multicolored .55 .40

View of Tampere, 1979 — A305

1979, Oct. 1 ***Perf. 13***
620 A305 1.10m multicolored .55 .40

Bicentenary of founding of Tampere.

Optical Telegraph, 1796, Map of Islands A306

Europa: 1.10m, Letter of Queen Christina to Per Brahe, 1638, establishing postal service.

1979, May 2 ***Perf. 13***
621 A306 1.10m multi *3.00 .80*
622 A306 1.30m multi, horiz. *4.50 1.40*

Shops and Merchants' Signs — A307

1979, Sept. 26 ***Perf. 14***
623 A307 1.10m multicolored .55 .40

Business and Industry regulation centenary.

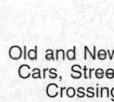

Old and New Cars, Street Crossing A308

1979, Oct. 1
624 A308 1.10m multicolored .55 .40

Road safety.

Elves Feeding Horse — A309

1979, Oct. 24
625 A309 60p multicolored .90 .40

Christmas 1979.

Korppi House, Lapinjarvi A310

Farm houses, First Row: Syrjala House, Tammela, 2 stamps in continuous design; Murtovaara House, Valtimo; Antila House, Lapua. Second row: Lofts, Pohjanmaa; Courtyard gate, Kanajarvi House, Kalvola; Main door, Havuselka House, Kauhajoki; Maki-Rasinpera House and dinner bell tower; Gable and eaves, Rasula Kuortane granary.

1979, Oct. 27 **Litho.** ***Perf. 13***
626 Booklet pane of 10 8.00 6.00
a.-j. A310 1.10m single stamp .60 .35
Complete booklet, #626 8.00

See design A349a.

Type of 1975 and

Kauhaneva Swamp
A315

Hame Castle, Hameenlinna
A316

Windmill, Harrstrom
A318

Multiharju Forest, Seitseminen Natl. Park — A319

Shuttle, Raanu Designs
A322

Kaspaikka Towel Design — A323

Bridal Rug, Teisko, 1815 — A324

Iron-forged Door, Hollola Church — A325

Iron Fish Spear c. 1100 — A326

Design: 1.80m, Eastern Gulf natl. park.

Litho. & Engr., Litho., Engr.

1979-98 ***Perf. 14, 11½ (A256, A318)***

627 A315 70p multicolored .40 .25
628 A316 90p brown red .30 .30
629 A256 1m red brown .40 .30
a. Perf. 13x12½ ('98) 1.25 1.25
630 A318 1m bl & red brn .40 .30
631 A256 1.30m dk green .60 .60
631A A256 1.30m dk green, litho. 1.00 1.10
b. Booklet pane, #555-556, 557A, 560, 631A 3.00 3.00
Complete booklet, #631Ab 3.25
632 A256 1.40m purple .65 .60
633 A256 1.50m grnsh blue .80 .80
634 A319 1.60m multicolored 1.20 .40
635 A315 1.80m multicolored 2.00 .50
636 A322 3m multicolored 1.40 .40
637 A323 6m multicolored 2.50 .30
638 A324 7m multicolored 3.00 .60
639 A325 8m multicolored 3.50 .40
640 A326 9m blk & dk bl 4.00 .90
Nos. 627-640 (15) 22.15 7.75

Coil Stamps

Perf. 11½ Vert.

641 A316 90p brown red .85 1.00

Perf. 12½ Horiz.

642 A318 1m blue & red brn 1.10 .50

Issued: 3m, 10/27/79; 6m, 4/9/80; No. 629, 1/2/81; 70p, 1/12/81; 90p, 9/1/82; 1.60m, 2/8/82; 7m, 2/15/82; No. 631, 1/3/83; Nos. 630, 642, 1/12/83; 1.80m, 8m, 2/10/83; 1.40m, 9m, 1/2/84; 1.50m, 1/2/85; No. 631A, 11/1/85.

Maria Jotuni (1880-1943), Writer — A327

1980, Apr. 9 **Litho.**
643 A327 1.10m multicolored .55 .40

Frans Eemil Sillanpaa (1888-1964), Writer — A328

Europa: 1.30m, Artturi Ilmari Virtanen (1895-1973), chemist, vert.

1980, Apr. 28 ***Perf. 13***
644 A328 1.10m multicolored *2.25 .40*
645 A328 1.30m multicolored *2.50 1.25*

Pres. Urho Kekkonen, 80th Birthday — A329

1980, Sept. 3 **Litho.** ***Perf. 13***
646 A329 1.10m multicolored .55 .40

Nordic Cooperation Issue

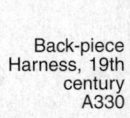

Back-piece Harness, 19th century
A330

1980, Sept. 9 ***Perf. 14***
647 A330 1.10m shown .55 .40
648 A330 1.30m Collar harness, vert. .55 .40

Biathlon
A331

1980, Oct. 17 **Litho.** ***Perf. 14***
649 A331 1.10m multicolored .55 .40

World Biathlon Championship, Lahti, Feb. 10-15, 1981.

Pull the Roller, Weighing out the Salt — A332

Christmas 1980 (Traditional Games): 1.10m, Putting out the shoemaker's eye.

1980, Oct. 27
650 A332 60p multicolored 1.10 .50
651 A332 1.10m multicolored 1.10 .50

Boxing Match — A333

1981, Feb. 28 **Litho.** ***Perf. 14***
652 A333 1.10m multicolored .45 .40

European Boxing Championships, Tampere, May 2-10.

Glass Blowing
A334

1981, Mar. 12
653 A334 1.10m multicolored .45 .40

Glass industry, 300th anniversary.

Mail Boat Furst Menschikoff, 1836 — A335

Litho & Engr.

1981, May 6 ***Perf. 13***
654 A335 1.10m brown & tan 3.25 4.50

Nordia '81 Stamp Exhibition, Helsinki, May 6-10. Sold only at exhibition for 3m including entrance ticket.

Europa Issue

Rowing to Church
A336

1981, May 18 **Litho.** ***Perf. 13***
655 A336 1.10m shown *.75 .30*
656 A336 1.50m Midsummer's Eve dance *1.50 .50*

Traffic Conference Emblem — A337

1981, May 26 **Litho.** ***Perf. 14***
657 A337 1.10m multicolored .45 .40

European Conference of Ministers of Transport, May 25-28.

Boy and Girl Riding Pegasus
A338

1981, June 11
658 A338 1m multicolored .45 .40

Youth associations centenary.

Intl. Year of the Disabled — A339

1981, Sept. 2 **Litho.** ***Perf. 13***
659 A339 1.10m multicolored .45 .40

Christmas 1981 — A340

1981, Oct. 27 **Litho.** ***Perf. 14***
660 A340 70p Children, Christmas tree .85 .30
661 A340 1.10m Decorating tree, vert. .85 .30

"Om Konsten att Ratt Behaga" First Issue (Periodicals Bicentenary)
A341

1982, Jan. 15
662 A341 1.20m multicolored .45 .40

Kuopio Bicentenary — A343

1982, Mar. 4 **Litho.** ***Perf. 14***
664 A343 1.20m multicolored .45 .40

Score, String Instrument Neck — A344

1982, Mar. 11 ***Perf. 13***
665 A344 1.20m multicolored 1.20 .45

Centenaries of Sibelius Academy of Music and Helsinki Orchestra.

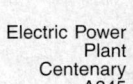

Electric Power Plant Centenary
A345

1982, Mar. 15 ***Perf. 14***
666 A345 1.20m multicolored .85 .40

Gardening
A346

1982, Apr. 16 **Litho.** ***Perf. 14***
667 A346 1.10m multicolored .45 .40

Europa — A347

1.20m, Publication of Abckiria (1st Finnish book), 1543 (Sculpture of Mikael Agricola, translator, by Oskari Jauhiainen, 1951). 1.50m, Turku Academy, 1st Finnish university (Turku Academy Inaugural Procession, 1640, after Albert Edelfelt).

1982, Apr. 29 Litho. *Perf. 13x12½*
668 A347 1.20m multicolored *1.50* *.45*

Size: 47x31mm
Perf. 12½
669 A347 1.50m multicolored *1.90* *.60*

Intl. Monetary Fund and World Bank Emblems A348

1982, May 12 *Perf. 14*
670 A348 1.60m multicolored .55 .50

IMF Interim Committee and IMF-WB Joint Development Committee Meeting, Helsinki, May 12-14.

75th Anniv. of Unicameral Parliament A349

2.40m, Future, by Waino Aaltonen, Parliament.

1982, May 25
671 A349 2.40m ultra & blk .85 .70

Manor Houses A349a

1st Row: a, Kuitia, Parainen, 1490. b, Louhisaari, Askainen, 1655. c, Frugard, Joroinen, 1780. d, Jokioinen, 1798. e, Moisio, Elimaki, 1820.
2nd Row: f, Sjundby, Siuntio, 1560. g, Fagervik, Inkoo, 1773. h, Mustio, Karjaa, 1792. i, Fiskars, Pohja, 1818. j, Kotkaniemi, Vihti, 1836.

1982, June 14 Litho. *Perf. 13x13½*
672 Booklet pane of 10 12.00 12.00
a.-j. A349a 1.20m single stamp 1.20 .50
Complete booklet, #672 12.00 12.00

See design A310.

Christmas 1982 — A350

1982, Oct. 25
673 A350 90p Feeding forest animals .70 .40
674 A350 1.20m Children eating porridge .70 .40

Nordic Cooperation A351

1983, Mar. 24 Litho. *Perf. 14*
675 A351 1.20m Panning for gold .55 .40
676 A351 1.30m Kitkajoki River rapids .55 .40

World Communications Year — A352

1983, Apr. 9 Litho. *Perf. 13*
677 A352 1.30m Postal services .55 .40
678 A352 1.70m Sound waves, optical cables .65 .45

Europa 1983 A353

1983, May 2 Litho. *Perf. 12½x13*
679 A353 1.30m Flash smelting method *5.00* *.45*
680 A353 1.70m Temppeliaukio Church *6.00* *.90*

Pres. Lauri Kristian Relander (1883-1942) — A354

1983, May 31 Litho. *Perf. 14*
681 A354 1.30m multicolored .45 .40

Running — A355

1983, June 6
682 A355 1.20m Javelin, horiz. .45 .40
683 A355 1.30m shown .45 .40

First World Athletic Championships, Helsinki, Aug. 7-14.

Toivo Kuula (1883-1918), Composer — A356

1983, July 7 *Perf. 14*
684 A356 1.30m multicolored .55 .40

Christmas 1983 — A357

Childrens drawings: 1m, Santa, reindeer, sled and gifts by Eija Myllyviita. 1.30m, Two candles by Camilla Lindberg.

Engr., Litho.
1983, Nov. 4 *Perf. 12, 14*
685 A357 1m dark blue .85 .40
686 A357 1.30m multi, vert. .85 .40

A358

1983, Nov. 25 Litho. *Perf. 14*
687 A358 1.30m brt blue & blk .45 .40

President Mauno Henrik Koivisto, 60th birthday.

A360

1984, Mar. 1 Engr. *Perf. 12*
689 A360 1.10m Letters (2nd class rate) .90 .50

Photo. & Engr.
690 A360 1.40m Automated sorting (1st class rate), vert. .70 .50

Inauguration of Nordic postal rates.

Museum Pieces — A361

Work and Skill — A362

Designs: No. 691, Pottery, 3200 B.C.; Silver chalice, 1416; Crossbow, 16th cent. No. 692, Kaplan hydraulic turbine.

1984, Apr. 30 Litho. *Perf. 13½*
691 A361 1.40m multicolored .50 .40
692 A362 1.40m multicolored .50 .40

Europa (1959-84) A363

1984, May 7 *Perf. 12½x13*
693 A363 1.40m multicolored *4.00* *.25*
694 A363 2m multicolored *4.00* *.80*

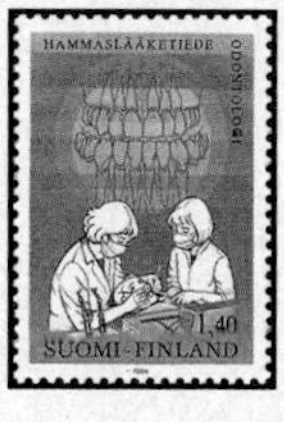

Dentistry — A364

1984, Aug. 27 Litho. *Perf. 14*
695 A364 1.40m Dentist, teeth .80 .50

Astronomy A365

1984, Sept. 12
696 A365 1.10m Observatory, planets, sun 1.00 .55

Aleksis Kivi (1934-72), Writer — A366

1984, Oct. 10 Litho. *Perf. 14*
697 A366 1.40m Song of my Heart .80 .40

Christmas 1984 — A367

Litho. & Engr.
1984, Nov. 30 *Perf. 12*
698 A367 1.10m Father Christmas, brownie 1.40 .40

Common Law of 1734 — A368

1984, Dec. 6 *Perf. 14*
699 A368 2m Statute Book 1.20 .70

25th Anniv. of EFTA — A369

1985, Feb. 2 Litho.
700 A369 1.20m multicolored .50 .40

100th Anniv. of Society of Swedish Literature in Finland A370

1985, Feb. 5 Litho.
701 A370 1.50m Johan Ludvig Runeberg .50 .35

A371

1985, Feb. 18 Litho. *Perf. 11½x12*
702 A371 1.50m Icon .50 .40

Order of St. Sergei and St. Herman, 100th anniv.

A372

Litho. & Engr.
1985, Feb. 28 *Perf. 13x12½*
703 A372 1.50m Pedri Shemeikka .80 .40
704 A372 2.10m Larin Paraske 1.20 .75

150th anniv. of Kalevala.

A373

Litho. & Engr.

1985, May 15 *Perf. 13*

705 A373 1.50m Mermaid and sea lions 4.50 *6.25*

NORDIA 1985 philatelic exhibition, May 15-19. Sold for 10m, which included admission ticket.

A374

Finnish Banknote Cent.: banknotes of 1886, 1909, 1922, 1945 and 1955.

Photo. & Engr.

1985, May 18 *Perf. 11½*

706	A374	Booklet pane of 8		7.50	7.50
a.-h.		1.50m any single		.90	.70
		Complete booklet, #706		7.50	

A375

Europa: 1.50m, Children playing the recorder. 2.10m, Excerpt "Ramus Virens Olivarum" from the "Piae Cantiones," 1582.

1985, June 17 **Litho.** *Perf. 13*

707 A375 1.50m multicolored *5.50* *.50*
708 A375 2.10m multicolored *6.50* *1.10*

Security Conference Type of 1975

1985, June 19 **Litho.**

709 A265 2.10m multicolored .75 .60

European Security and Cooperation Conference, 10th Anniv.

A376

1985, Sept. 5 **Litho.** *Perf. 14*

710 A376 1.50m Provincial arms, Count's seal 1.20 .35

Provincial Administration Established by Count Per Brahe, 350th Anniv.

Arms Type of 1975 and

Kerimaki Church A376a

Urho Kekkonen Natl. Park — A376b

Tulip Damask Table Cloth, 18th Cent. A377

Postal Service A377a

Brown Bear — A377b

Perf. 11½, 13x12½ (2m)

1985-90 **Engr.**

711	A256	1.60m vermilion		.80	.60
712	A256	1.70m black		1.20	.50
a.		Bklt. pane, #558, 560, 2 each #555, 556a, 712 + 2 labels		9.00	*11.00*
		Complete booklet, #712a		10.00	
713	A256	1.80m olive green		1.25	.70
a.		Bklt. pane, 2 ea #555d, 560a, 713b		3.50	3.00
		Complete booklet, #713a		3.50	
b.		Perf. 13x12½		2.50	1.50
714	A256	1.90m brt orange		1.10	.30
715	A256	2m blue grn, bklt. stamp		2.50	.90
a.		Bklt. pane, #562a, 2 ea #715, 555d		7.00	7.00
		Complete booklet, #715a		7.00	

Litho. *Perf. 14*

716	A376a	2.20m multi		1.10	.30
717	A376b	2.40m multi		1.40	.40
718	A377	12m multi		7.00	1.00

Litho. & Engr.

Perf. 13x12½

719	A377b	50m blk, grn & lt red brn		24.00	8.50
		Nos. 711-719 (9)		40.35	13.20

No. 712a contains two labels inscribed to publicize FINLANDIA '88.

Issued: 12m, 9/13/85; 1.60m, 1/2/86; 1.70m, 1/2/87; No. 712a, 8/10/87; 1.80m, 1/4/88; 2.20m, 2.40m, 1/20/88; No. 713b, 7/25/88; 1.90m, 1/2/89; 2m, 1/19/90; 50m, 8/30/89.

Booklet Stamps

No. 720, Telephone, mailbox. No. 721, Postal truck, transport plane. No. 722, Transport plane, fork lift. No. 723, Postman delivering letter. No. 724, Woman accepting letter.

Perf. 12½ on 3 Sides

1988, Feb. 1 **Litho.**

720	A377a	1.80m multi		1.50	.50
721	A377a	1.80m multi		1.50	.50
722	A377a	1.80m multi		1.50	.50
723	A377a	1.80m multi		1.50	.50
724	A377a	1.80m multi		1.50	.50
a.		Bklt. pane, 2 each #720-724		16.00	10.50
		Complete booklet, #724a		16.00	
		Nos. 720-724 (5)		7.50	2.50

Nos. 721-722 and 723-724 printed se-tenant in continuous designs. No. 724c sold for 14m to households on mainland Finland. Each household entitled to buy 2 booklets at discount price from Feb. 1 to May 31, with coupon.

Miniature Sheet

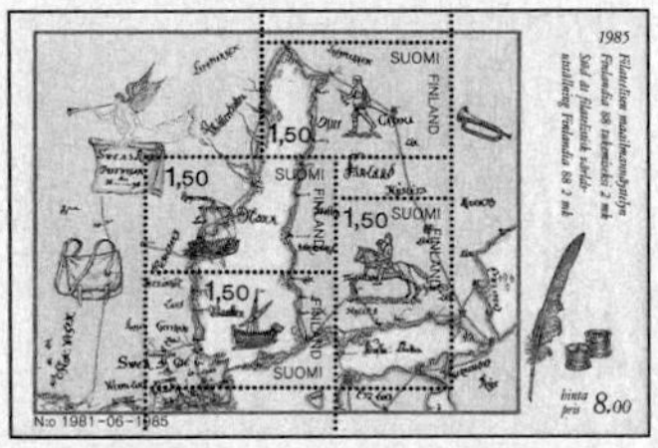

Postal Map, 1698 — A378

Designs: a, Postman on foot. b, Postal Map, 1698. c, Sailing vessel, diff. d, Postrider, vert.

Litho. & Engr.

1985, Oct. 16 *Perf. 14*

728	A378	Sheet of 4		8.00	10.00
a.-d.		1.50m any single		2.00	2.50

FINLANDIA '88, 350th anniv. of Finnish Postal Service, founded in 1638 by Gov.-Gen. Per Brahe. Sheet sold for 8m.

Intl. Youth Year — A379

1985, Nov. 1 **Litho.** *Perf. 13*

729 A379 1.50m multicolored .70 .35

Christmas 1985 — A380

1985, Nov. 29 *Perf. 14*

730 A380 1.20m Bird, tulips 1.10 .40
731 A380 1.20m Cross of St. Thomas, hyacinths 1.10 .40

Natl. Geological Society, Cent. — A390

1986, Feb. 8 **Litho.** *Perf. 14*

732	A390	1.30m Orbicular granite		.90	.40
733	A390	1.60m Rapaviki		1.00	.40
734	A390	2.10m Veined gneiss		1.25	.60
		Nos. 732-734 (3)		3.15	1.40

Europa 1986 A391

1986, Apr. 10 ***Perf. 12½x13***

735 A391 1.60m Saimaa ringed seal *2.50* *.40*
736 A391 2.20m Environmental conservation *5.50* *.80*

Conference Palace, Baghdad, 1982 — A392

Natl. Construction Year. b, Lahti Theater, 1983. c, Kuusamo Municipal Offices, 1978. d, Hamina Court Building, 1983. e, Finnish Embassy, New Delhi, 1986. f, Western Sakyla Daycare Center, 1980.

1986, Apr. 19 *Perf. 14*

737		Booklet pane of 6		5.75	6.00
a.-f.		A392 1.60m, any single		.90	.70
		Complete booklet, #737		5.75	

Nordic Cooperation Issue 1986 — A393

Sister towns.

1986, May 27 **Litho.** *Perf. 14*

738 A393 1.60m Joensuu .70 .40
739 A393 2.20m Jyvaskyla .90 .75

Souvenir Sheet

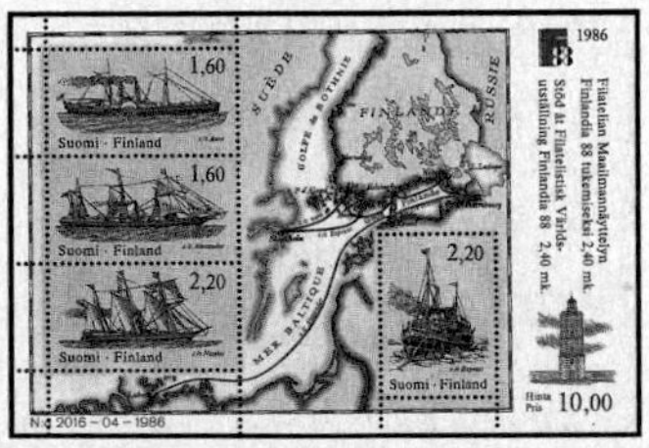

FINLANDIA '88 — A394

Postal ships: a, Iron paddle steamer Aura, Stockholm-St. Petersburg, 1858. b, Screw vessel Alexander, Helsinki-Tallinn-Lubeck, 1859. c, Steamship Nicolai, Helsinki-Tallinn-St. Petersburg, 1858. d, 1st Ice steamship Express II, Helsinki-Stockholm, 1877-98, vert.

Litho. & Engr.

1986, Aug. 29 *Perf. 13*

740	A394	Sheet of 4		14.00	14.00
a.-b.		1.60m, any single		3.25	3.25
c.-d.		2.20m, any single		3.25	3.25

Sold for 10k.

Pierre-Louis Moreau de Maupertuis (1698-1759) — A395

1986, Sept. 5 Litho. *Perf. 12½x13*

741 A395 1.60m multicolored .80 .40

Lapland Expedition, 250th anniv., proved Earth's poles are flattened.

See France No. 2016.

Urho Kaleva Kekkonen (1900-86), Pres. — A396

1986, Sept. 30 Engr. *Perf. 14*

742 A396 5m black 2.25 2.00

Intl. Peace Year — A397

1986, Oct. 13 Litho. *Perf. 13*

743 A397 1.60m multicolored .70 .40

A398

Christmas A399

Photo. & Engr.

1986, Oct. 31 *Perf. 12*

744 1.30m Denomination at L .70 .45

745 1.30m Denomination at R 1.50 .40

a. A398 Pair, #744-745 3.00 2.40

746 A399 1.60m Elves 1.25 .40

Nos. 744-746 (3) 3.45 1.25

No. 745a has a continuous design.

Postal Savings Bank, Cent. — A400

1987, Jan. 2 Litho. *Perf. 14*

747 A400 1.70m multicolored .70 .40

Natl. Tourism, Cent. — A401

1987, Feb. 4 Litho. *Perf. 14*

748 A401 1.70m Winter .65 .40

749 A401 2.30m Summer .85 .60

A402

1987, Feb. 4 *Perf. 14*

750 A402 1.40m multicolored .70 .40

Metric system in Finland, cent.

A403

1987, Feb. 17 Litho. *Perf. 14*

751 A403 2.10m multicolored 1.10 .50

Leevi Madetoja (1887-1947), composer.

European Wrestling Championships A404

1987, Feb. 17

752 A404 1.70m multicolored .80 .40

1987 World Bowling Championships A405

1987, Apr. 13

753 A405 1.70m multicolored .80 .40

Mental Health — A406

1987, Apr. 13

754 A406 1.70m multicolored .70 .40

Souvenir Sheet

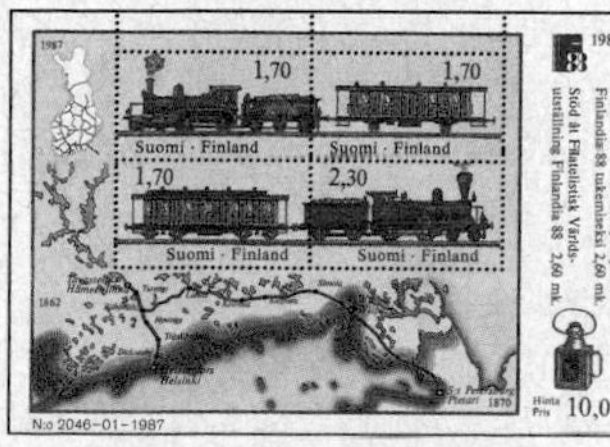

FINLANDIA '88 — A407

Locomotives and mail cars: a, Steam locomotive, 6-wheeled tender. b, 4-window mail car. c, 7-window mail car.

Litho. & Engr.

1987, May 8 *Perf. 12½x13*

755 A407 Sheet of 4 15.00 15.00

a.-c. 1.70m any single 4.00 4.00

d. 2.30m multicolored 4.00 4.00

Sold for 10m.

Europa 1987 A408

Modern architecture: 1.70m, Tampere Main Library, 1986, designed by Raili and Reima Pietila. 2.30m, Stoa Monument, Helsinki, c. 1981, by sculptor Hannu Siren.

1987, May 15 Litho. *Perf. 13*

756 A408 1.70m multicolored *5.25* .25

757 A408 2.30m multicolored *5.25* *.90*

Natl. Art Museum, Ateneum, Cent. — A409

Paintings: a, Strawberry Girl, by Nils Schillmark (1745-1804). b, Still-life on a Lady's Work Table, by Ferdinand von Wright (1822-1906). c, Old Woman with Basket, by Albert Edelfelt (1854-1906). d, Boy and Crow, by Akseli Gallen-Kallela (1865-1931). e, Late Winter, by Tyko Sallinen (1879-1955).

1987, May 15

758 Booklet pane of 5 8.50 8.50

a.-e. A409 1.70m any single 1.60 .90

Complete booklet, #758 9.00

A410

1987, Aug. 12 *Perf. 14*

759 A410 1.70m multicolored .70 .40

European Physics Soc. 7th gen. conf., Helsinki, Aug. 10-14.

A411

1987, Oct. 12

760 A411 1.70m ultra, sil & pale lt gray .70 .40

Size: 30x41mm

761 A411 10m dark ultra, lt blue & sil 4.00 2.00

Natl. independence, 70th anniv.

Ylppo, Child and Lastenlinna Children's Hospital A412

1987, Oct. 27

762 A412 1.70m multicolored .70 .40

Arvo Ylppo (b. 1887), pediatrics pioneer.

Christmas — A413

1987, Oct. 30

763 A413 1.40m Santa Claus, youths, horiz. 1.00 .40

764 A413 1.70m shown 1.00 .40

Finnish News Agency (STT), Cent. — A414

1987, Nov. 1

765 A414 2.30m multicolored .95 .80

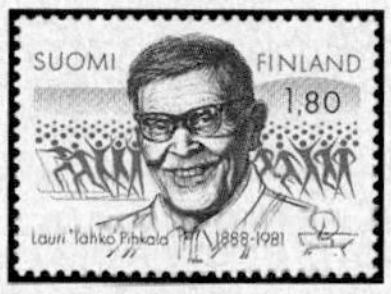

Lauri "Tahko" Pihkala (1888-1981), Promulgator of Sports and Physical Education A415

1988, Jan. 5 Litho. *Perf. 14*

766 A415 1.80m blk, chalky blue & brt blue .80 .40

A416

1988, Mar. 14 Litho.

767 A416 1.40m multicolored .70 .40

Meteorological Institute, 150th anniv.

Settlement of New Sweden in America, 350th Anniv. — A417

Design: 17th Century European settlers negotiating with 3 American Indians, map of New Sweden, the Swedish ships Kalmar Nyckel and Fogel Grip, based on an 18th cent. illustration from a Swedish book about the American Colonies.

Litho. & Engr.

1988, Mar. 29 *Perf. 13*

768 A417 3m multicolored 1.25 .80

See US No. C117 and Sweden No. 1672.

FINLANDIA '88, June 1-12, Helsinki Fair Center — A418

Agathon Faberge (1876-1951), famed philatelist, & rarities from his collection.

Booklet Stamp

1988, May 2 **Litho.** ***Perf. 13***

769 A418 5m Pane of 1+2 labels	14.00	*17.50*
Complete booklet, #769	15.00	

350th Anniv. of the Finnish Postal Service. No. 769 sold for 30m to include the price of adult admission to the exhibition.

Achievements of Finnish Athletes at the 1988 Winter Olympics, Calgary — A419

Design: Matti Nykanen, gold medalist in all 3 ski jumping events at the '88 Games.

1988, Apr. 6 ***Perf. 14***

770 A419 1.80m multicolored .90 .40

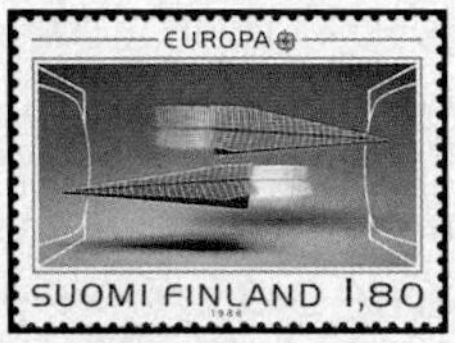

Europa 1988 A420

Communication and transport.

1988, May 23 **Litho.** ***Perf. 13***

771 A420 1.80m shown	*5.00*	*.25*
772 A420 2.40m Horse-drawn tram, 1890	*5.00*	*.90*

Souvenir Sheet

FINLANDIA '88 — A421

1st airmail flights: a, Finnish air force Breguet 14 biplane transporting mail from Helsinki to Tallinn, Feb. 12, 1920. b, AERO Junkers F-13 making 1st airmail night flight from Helsinki to Copenhagen, May 15, 1930. c, AERO Douglas DC-3, 1st intl. route, Helsinki-Norrkoping-Copenhagen-Amsterdam, 1947. d, Douglas DC 10-30, 1975-88, inauguration of Helsinki-Beijing route, June 2, 1988.

Litho. & Engr.

1988, June 2 ***Perf. 13½***

773 A421 Sheet of 4	15.00	16.00
a.-c. 1.80m any single	3.75	4.00
d. 2.40m multicolored	3.75	4.00

Sold for 11m.

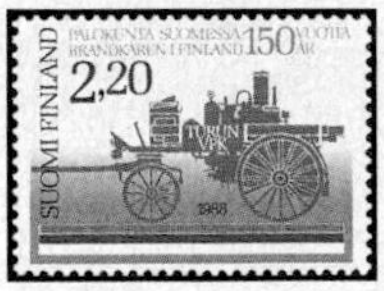

Turku Fire Brigade, 150th Anniv. — A422

Design: 1902 Horse-drawn, steam-driven fire pump, preserved at the brigade.

1988, Aug. 15 **Litho.** ***Perf. 14***

774 A422 2.20m multicolored .95 .55

A423

Missale Aboense, the 1st printed book in Finland, 500th anniv.

1988, Aug. 17

775 A423 1.80m multicolored .90 .40

A424

Finnish Postal Service, 350th Anniv.: No. 776, Postal tariff issued by Queen Christina of Sweden, Sept. 6, 1638. No. 777, Postal cart, c. 1880. #778, Leyland Sherpa 185 mail van, 1976. No. 779, Malmi P.O. interior. #780, Skier using mobile telephone, c. 1970. No. 781, Telecommunications satellite in orbit.

Booklet Stamps

1988, Sept. 6 **Litho.** ***Perf. 13***

776 A424 1.80m multicolored	.90	.65
777 A424 1.80m multicolored	.90	.65
778 A424 1.80m multicolored	.90	.65
779 A424 1.80m multicolored	.90	.65
780 A424 1.80m multicolored	.90	.65
781 A424 1.80m multicolored	.90	.65
a. Booklet pane of 6, #776-781	5.50	6.50
Complete booklet, #781a	5.50	

Children's Playgroups (Preschool) A425

1988, Oct. 10 ***Perf. 14***

782 A425 1.80m multicolored .80 .40

Christmas A426

1988, Nov. 4 **Litho.**

783 A426 1.40m multicolored	1.40	.35
784 A426 1.80m multicolored	1.75	.55

Hameenlinna Township, 350th Anniv. — A427

Design: Market square, coat of arms and 17th century plan of the town.

1989, Jan. 19 **Litho.**

785 A427 1.90m multicolored .80 .40

1989 Nordic Ski Championships, Lahti, Feb. 17-26 — A428

1989, Jan. 25

786 A428 1.90m multicolored .80 .40

Salvation Army in Finland, Cent. — A429

1989, Feb. 6 **Litho.**

787 A429 1.90m multicolored .80 .40

Photography, 150th Anniv. — A430

1.50m, Photographer, box camera, c.1900.

1989, Feb. 6

788 A430 1.50m brn, buff, cream .75 .55

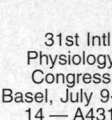

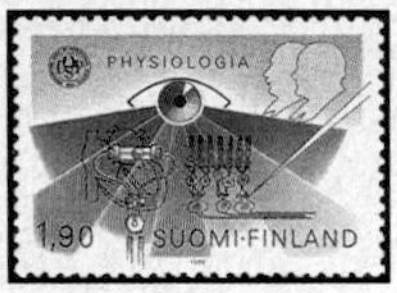

31st Intl. Physiology Congress, Basel, July 9-14 — A431

Design: Congress emblem, silhouettes of Robert Tigerstedt and Ragnar Granit, eye, flowmeter measuring flow of blood through heart, color-sensitive retinal cells and microelectrode.

1989, Mar. 2

789 A431 1.90m multicolored .80 .40

Sports — A432

1989, Mar. 10 **Booklet Stamps**

790 A432 1.90m Skiing	1.00	.50
791 A432 1.90m Jogging	1.00	.50
792 A432 1.90m Cycling	1.00	.50
793 A432 1.90m Canoeing	1.00	.50
a. Booklet pane of 4, #790-793	4.25	4.25
Complete booklet, #793a	4.50	

Souvenir Sheet

Finnish Kennel Club, Cent. — A433

Dogs: a, Lapponian herder. b, Finnish spitz. c, Karelian bear dog. d, Finnish hound.

1989, Mar. 17 **Litho.** ***Perf. 14***

794 A433 Sheet of 4	4.00	4.00
a.-d. 1.90m any single	1.00	.70

Europa — A434

1989, Mar. 31 ***Perf. 13***

795 A434 1.90m Hopscotch	*2.50*	*.25*
796 A434 2.50m Sledding	*2.50*	*.65*

A435

Nordic Cooperation Year: Folk Costumes.

1989, Apr. 20 ***Perf. 14***

797 A435 1.90m Sakyla (man)	1.10	.45
798 A435 2.50m Veteli (woman)	1.10	.65

Finnish Pharmacies, 300th Anniv. — A436

Foxglove, distilling apparatus, mortar, flask.

1989, June 2 **Litho.**

799 A436 1.90m multicolored .90 .35

A437

1989, June 2

800 A437 1.90m multicolored .90 .35

Savonlinna Municipal Charter, 350th anniv.

A438

No. 801, Panthera uncia. No. 802, Capra falconeri

1989, June 12

801 A438 1.90m multi	.90	.45
802 A438 2.50m multi	1.10	.70

Helsinki Zoo, cent.

Vocational Training, 150th Anniv. — A439

Interparliamentary Union, Cent. — A440

Council of Europe, 40th Anniv. — A441

1989, Sept. 4 **Litho.** ***Perf. 14***

803 A439 1.50m multicolored	.70	.70
804 A440 1.90m multicolored	.90	.35
805 A441 2.50m multicolored	1.25	.90
Nos. 803-805 (3)	2.85	1.95

Admission of Finland to the Council of Europe (2.50m).

A442

1989, Oct. 9 **Litho.**
806 A442 1.90m multicolored .90 .35

Hannes Kolehmainen (1889-1966) winning the 5000-meter race at the Stockholm Olympics, 1912.

A443

1989, Oct. 20
807 A443 1.90m multicolored .90 .35

Continuing Education in Finland, cent.

A444

Christmas: 1.90m, Sodankyla Church, Siberian jays in snow.

1989, Nov. 3
808 A444 1.50m shown 1.10 .40
809 A444 1.90m multicolored 1.10 .40

A445

1990, Jan. 19 **Litho.** ***Perf. 13x13½***
810 A445 1.90m multicolored 1.40 1.10
811 A445 2.50m multicolored 1.60 1.25

Incorporation of the State Posts and Telecommunications Services.

Emblem of the corporation was produced by holography. Soaking may affect the design.

Musical Soc. of Turku and Finnish Orchestras, 200th Annivs. A446

1990, Jan. 26 ***Perf. 14***
812 A446 1.90m multicolored 1.10 .40

Disabled Veteran's Assoc., 50th Anniv. — A447

1990, Mar. 13 **Litho.**
813 A447 2m multicolored .90 .35

End of the Winter (Russo-Finnish) War, 50th Anniv. — A448

1990, Mar. 13
814 A448 2m blue .90 .35

University of Helsinki, 350th Anniv. — A449

University crest and: 2m, Queen Christina on horseback. 3.20m, Degree ceremony procession in front of the main university building.

1990, Mar. 26 **Litho.** ***Perf. 13***
815 A449 2m multicolored .85 .40
816 A449 3.20m multicolored 1.25 .70

Europa 1990 A450

Post Offices: 2m, Lapp man, P.O. at Nuvvus, Mt. Nuvvus Ailigas. 2.70m, Turku main P.O.

1990, Mar. 26 ***Perf. 12½x13***
817 A450 2m multicolored *6.00* .25
818 A450 2.70m multicolored *6.00* .65

Rural Postal Service and Address Reform, Cent. — A451

1990, Apr. 19 **Litho.** ***Perf. 13***
819 A451 2m multicolored .90 .35

"Ali Baba and the Forty Thieves" A452

"Story of the Great Musician" A453

"Story of the Giants, the Witches and the Daughter of the Sun" A454

"The Golden Bird, the Golden Horse and the Princess" A455

"Lamb Brother" A456

"The Snow Queen" A457

Fairy tale illustrations by Rudolf Koivu.

Booklet Stamps

Perf. 14 on 3 sides

1990, Aug. 29 **Litho.**
820 A452 2m multicolored 1.60 .65
821 A453 2m multicolored 1.60 .65
822 A454 2m multicolored 1.60 .65
823 A455 2m multicolored 1.60 .65
824 A456 2m multicolored 1.60 .65
825 A457 2m multicolored 1.60 .65
a. Booklet pane of 6, #820-825 10.00 8.00
Complete booklet, #825a 10.00

Souvenir Sheet

Horse Care — A458

a, Feeding. b, Riding. c, Watering. d, Currying.

1990, Oct. 10 **Litho.** ***Perf. 14***
826 A458 Sheet of 4 4.50 4.25
a.-d. 2m any single 1.10 .75

Christmas A459

1990, Nov. 2
827 A459 1.70m Santa's elves 1.70 .40
828 A459 2m Santa, reindeer 1.70 .40

Provincial Flowers

A460

A460a

A460b

A460c

A460d

A460e

A460f

A460g

A460h

A460i

A460j

A460k

1990-99 ***Perf. 13x12½***
829 A460 2m Wood anemone 1.10 .25
830 A460 2.10m Rowan 1.10 .25
831 A460 2.70m Heather 1.40 .40
832 A460 2.90m Sea buckthorn 1.50 .40
833 A460 3.50m Oak 2.00 .50
834 A460a 2 Globeflower 2.25 .50
835 A460b 1 Hepatica 2.50 .30
Nos. 829-835 (7) 11.85 2.60

Self-Adhesive

Die Cut

836 A460c 2 Iris 2.25 .30
a. Booklet pane of 20 45.00 27.50
837 A460 2.10m like #830 1.40 .30
838 A460d 1 Rosebay willowherb 2.50 .35
839 A460e 1 Labrador tea 2.50 .35
a. Booklet pane of 10 24.50 7.50
840 A460f 1 Karelian rose 2.50 .40
841 A460g 1 Daisy 2.50 .35
842 A460h 1 Water lily 2.50 .35
843 A460i 1 Bird cherry 2.50 .45
844 A460j 1 Harebell 2.50 .45
845 A460k 1 Cowslip 2.50 .45
Nos. 836-845 (10) 23.65 3.75

Issued: 2m, 2.70m, 1/19/90; No. 830, 2.90m, 3.50m, 2/5/90; 2.10m, 1991; Nos. 834-835, 3/2/92; No. 838, 10/9/92; No. 836, 3/1/93; No. 839, 6/14/93; No. 840, 5/5/94; No. 841, 3/15/95; No. 842, 6/3/96; No. 843, 3/18/97; No. 844, 3/12/98; No. 845, 4/28/99.

No. 834 sold for 1.60m, No. 836 sold for 1.90m, Nos. 835, 838 for 2.10m, Nos. 839-840 for 2.30m, Nos. 841-844 sold for 2.80m, No. 845 sold for 3m at time of release.

Nos. 837-838, 840-845 issued in sheets of 10. Nos. 836a and 839a were issued as complete booklets. The peelable backing serves as a booklet cover.

The numbers on the stamps represent the class of mail for which each was intended at time of release.

A461

1991, Mar. 1 ***Perf. 14***
846 A461 2.10m multicolored 1.10 .40

World Hockey Championships, Turku.

A462

1991, Mar. 1
847 A462 2.10m Cooking class .80 .40

Home economics teacher education, cent.

Sauna Type of 1977 and

Birds — A463

No. 848, Great tit. No. 849, Wagtail. No. 850, Aegolius funereus. No. 850A, Phoenicurus phoenicurus. No. 851, Chaffinches. No. 852, Robin. No. 856, Bullfinch. No. 857, Waxwing. No. 859, Dendrocopos leucotos.

Perf. 13x12½, 14 (#861)

1991-99 Litho.

Booklet Stamps (#848-859)

848	A463	10p multi		.40	.35
849	A463	10p multi		.40	.25
850	A463	10p multi		.90	.60
850A	A463	20p multi		10.00	5.00
851	A463	60p multi		6.00	.65
852	A463	60p multi		7.00	1.25
856	A463	2.10m multi		.90	.40
a.		Bklt. pane, #851, 2 each #848, 856		7.50	7.50
		Complete booklet, #856a		8.00	
857	A463	2.10m multi		.90	.40
a.		Bklt. pane, #852, 2 each #849, 857		6.25	6.25
		Complete booklet, #857a		6.75	
859	A463	2.30m multi		1.00	.50
a.		Booklet pane of #850A, 2 each #850, #859 + 1 label		7.50	7.50
		Complete booklet, #859a		8.00	

Sheet Stamp

861	A256a	4.80m multicolored	2.00	1.25
		Nos. 848-861 (10)	29.50	10.65

Issued: Nos. 848, 851, 856, 3/20/91; Nos. 849, 852, 857, 4/22/92; Nos. 850, 850A, 859, 6/4/93. 861, 7/1/99.

"SUOMI" is in upper left on Nos. 849, 852, 857.

Fishing — A464

Designs: a, Fly fisherman, trout. b, Perch, bobber. c, Crayfish, trap. d, Trawling for herring. e, Stocking powan.

1991, Mar. 20 ***Perf. 14***

863	Booklet pane of 5	6.00	6.00
a.-e.	A464 2.10m any single	1.20	.45
	Complete booklet, #863	6.50	

Tourism — A465

2.10m, Seurasaari Island. 2.90m, Steamship, Lake Saimaa.

1991, June 4 Litho. ***Perf. 14***

864	A465	2.10m multi	1.00	.25
865	A465	2.90m multi	1.10	.70

Europa A466

European map and: 2.10m, Human figures. 2.90m, Satellites, dish antennae.

1991, June 7 Litho. ***Perf. 12½x13***

866	A466	2.10m multicolored	*5.50*	.25
867	A466	2.90m multicolored	*5.50*	.70

Alfred W. Finch (1854-1930) A467

Designs: 2.10m, Iris, ceramic vase. 2.90m, Painting, The English Coast at Dover.

1991, Sept. 7 Litho. ***Perf. 13***

868	A467	2.10m multicolored	1.10	.25
869	A467	2.90m multicolored	2.25	.70

See Belgium No. 1410.

Finnish Candy Industry, Cent. — A468

1991, Sept. 17 Photo. ***Perf. 11½***

870	A468	2.10m multicolored	1.00	.50

Souvenir Sheets

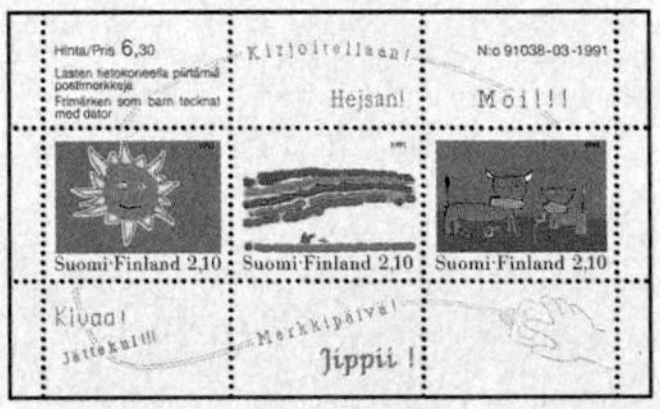

Children's Stamp Designs — A469

a, Sun. b, Rainbow. c, Cows grazing.

1991, Sept. 17 Litho. ***Perf. 13½***

871	A469	Sheet of 3	3.00	3.00
a.-c.		2.10m any single	1.00	.65

Skiing — A470

Color of skisuit: a, red. b, green. c, yellow. d, blue.

1991, Oct. 4 ***Perf. 14***

872	A470	Sheet of 4	4.00	4.00
a.-d.		2.10m any single	1.00	.65

Town Status for Iisalmi, Cent. — A471

1991, Oct. 18 Litho. ***Perf. 14***

873	A471	2.10m multicolored	.90	.50

Christmas A472

1.80m, Santa, animals carrying candles. 2.10m, Reindeer pulling Santa's sleigh.

1991, Nov. 1 Litho. ***Perf. 14***

874	A472	1.80m multi	1.75	.45
875	A472	2.10m multi, vert.	1.75	.45

Chemists' Club, Finnish Chemists' Society, Cent. — A473

1991, Nov. 1

876	A473	2.10m multi	1.10	.40
877	A473	2.10m multi, diff.	1.10	.40
a.		Pair, #876-877 + label	3.00	3.00

Second and third vertical branches merge while second and third branches below almost touch in the upper left part of camphor molecular structure on No. 877. Nos. 876-877 are designed to produce a three dimensional effect when viewed together.

1992 Olympic Games A474

Designs: No. 878, Skier, Albertville. No. 879, Swimmer, Barcelona.

1992, Feb. 4 Litho. ***Perf. 14***

878	A474	2.10m multicolored	1.00	.40
879	A474	2.90m multicolored	1.40	.75

Expo '92, Seville — A475

1992, Mar. 20 Litho. ***Perf. 14***

880	A475	3.40m multicolored	1.50	.75

Conference on Security and Cooperation in Europe, Helsinki A476

1992, Mar. 20 ***Perf. 14½x15***

881	A476	16m multicolored	6.00	3.50

Town of Rauma, 550th Anniv. — A477

1992, Mar. 27 ***Perf. 14***

882	A477	2.10m multicolored	1.40	.40

Healthy Brains — A478

1992, Mar. 27

883	A478	3.50m multicolored	1.40	1.00

Discovery of America, 500th Anniv. A479

1992, May 8 Litho. ***Perf. 12½x13***

884	A479	2.10m Santa Maria, map	*2.25*	*.30*
885	A479	2.10m Map, Columbus	*2.25*	*.30*
a.		Pair, #884-885	*4.50*	*5.00*

Europa.

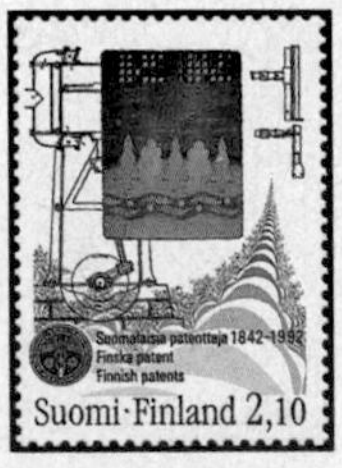

Finnish Technology A480

Hologram of trees and: 2.10m, Drawing of blowing machine. 2.90m, Schematic of electronic circuits. 3.40m, Triangles and grid.

1992, May 8 ***Perf. 13x12½***

886	A480	2.10m multicolored	1.10	.60
887	A480	2.90m multicolored	1.40	.75
888	A480	3.40m multicolored	1.75	1.20
		Nos. 886-888 (3)	4.25	2.55

First Finnish patent granted, sesqui. (No. 886), Finnish chairmanship of Eureka (No. 887), Government Technology Research Center, 50th anniv. (No. 888).

Nos. 886-888 have holographic images. Soaking in water may affect the hologram.

Natl. Board of Agriculture, Cent. — A481

1992, June 4 Litho. ***Perf. 14***

889	A481	2.10m Currant harvesting	1.00	.40

Finnish Women A482

No. 890, Aurora Karamzin (1808-1902), founder of Deaconesses' Institution of Helsinki. No. 891, Baroness Sophie Mannerheim (1863-1928), reformer of nursing education. No. 892, Laimi Leidenius (1877-1938), physician and educator. No. 893, Miina Sillanpaa (1866-1952), Minister for social affairs. No. 894, Edith Sodergran (1892-1923), poet. No. 895, Kreeta Haapasalo (1813-1893), folk singer.

Litho. & Engr.

1992, June 8 ***Perf. 14***

Booklet Stamps

890	A482	2.10m multicolored	1.00	.55
891	A482	2.10m multicolored	1.00	.55
892	A482	2.10m multicolored	1.00	.55
893	A482	2.10m multicolored	1.00	.55
894	A482	2.10m multicolored	1.00	.55
895	A482	2.10m multicolored	1.00	.55
a.		Booklet pane of 6, #890-895	6.00	7.25
		Complete booklet, #895a	6.00	

Child's Painting A483

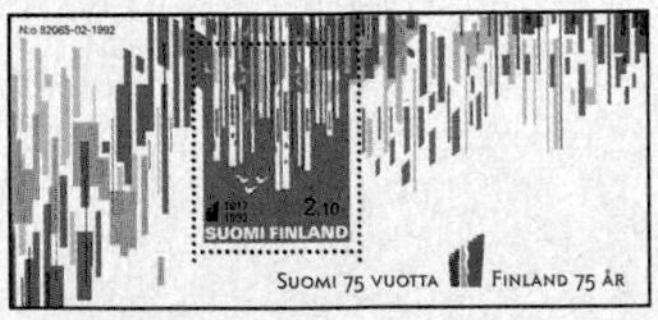

Independence, 75th Anniv. — A484

1992, Oct. 5 Litho. ***Perf. 13***

896	A483	2.10m multicolored	1.00	.40

Souvenir Sheet

Perf. 13½

897	A484	2.10m multicolored	1.90	1.20

Nordia '93 — A485

Illustrations depicting "Moomin" characters, by Tove Jansson: No. 898, Winter scene, ice covered bridges. No. 899, Winter scene in forest. No. 900, Boats in water. No. 901, Characters on beach.

Perf. 13 on 3 Sides

1992, Oct. 9 Litho.

Booklet Stamps

898 A485 2.10m multicolored 2.75 .55
899 A485 2.10m multicolored 2.75 .55
900 A485 2.10m multicolored 2.75 .55
901 A485 2.10m multicolored 2.75 .55
a. Booklet pane of 4, #898-901 11.00 11.50
Complete booklet, #901a 11.00

A486

1992, Oct. 20 Litho. ***Perf. 13***
902 A486 2.10m multicolored 1.00 .40

Printing in Finland, 350th anniv.

Christmas A487

Designs: 1.80m, Church of St. Lawrence, Vantaa. 2.10m, Stained glass window of nativity scene, Karkkila Church, vert.

1992, Oct. 30 Litho. ***Perf. 14***
903 A487 1.80m multicolored 1.25 .45
904 A487 2.10m multicolored 1.25 .45

Central Chamber of Commerce, 75th Anniv. — A488

1993, Feb. 8 Litho. ***Perf. 14***
905 A488 1.60m multicolored .75 .50

Friendship A489

1993, Feb. 8 Litho. ***Perf. 14***
906 A489 1 multicolored 2.50 .40
a. Booklet pane of 5 + label 14.00 7.50
Complete booklet, 2 #906a 28.00

No. 906 sold for 2m at time of release. See note following No. 845.
See Estonia No. 237.

Alopex Lagopus — A490

a, Adult with winter white coat. b, Face, full view, winter white coat. c, Mother, kits, summer coat. d, Two on rock, summer coat.

1993, Mar. 19 Litho. ***Perf. 12½x13***
907 A490 Block of 4 5.50 5.50
a.-d. 2.30m Any single 1.40 .45

World Wildlife Fund.

Sculptures A491

Europa: 2m, Rumba, by Martti Aiha. 2.90m, Complete Works, by Kari Caven.

1993, Apr. 26 ***Perf. 13***
908 A491 2m multicolored *1.90 .25*
909 A491 2.90m multicolored *1.40 .60*

Organized Philately in Finland, Cent. — A492

1993, May 6 ***Perf. 13x12½***
910 A492 2.30m Rosa pimpinellifolia 1.10 .70

Vyborg Castle, 700th Anniv. A493

1993, May 6 ***Perf. 13½***
911 A493 2.30m multicolored 2.00 .40

Tourism A494

1993, May 7 ***Perf. 13x12½***
912 A494 2.30m Naantali 1.00 .25
913 A494 2.90m Imatra 1.25 .70

550th anniv. of Naantali (No. 912).

A495

Independent Finland Defense Forces, 75th Anniv.: 2.30m, Finnish landscape in form of soldier's silhouette. 3.40m, UN checkpoint of Finnish battalion, Middle East.

1993, June 4 Litho. ***Perf. 14***
914 A495 2.30m multicolored .85 .25
915 A495 3.40m multicolored 1.40 1.00

A496

Art by Martta Wendelin (1893-1986): No. 916, Boy on skis, 1936. No. 917, Mother, daughter knitting, 1931. No. 918, Children building snowman, 1931. No. 919, Mother, children at fence, 1935. #920, Girl with lamb, 1936.

Booklet Stamps

1993, June 14 Litho. ***Perf. 12½x13***
916 A496 2.30m multicolored 1.50 .45
917 A496 2.30m multicolored 1.50 .45
918 A496 2.30m multicolored 1.50 .45
919 A496 2.30m multicolored 1.50 .45
920 A496 2.30m multicolored 1.50 .45
a. Booklet pane of 5, #916-920 7.50 8.00
Complete booklet, #920a 9.50

Water Birds — A497

No. 921, Flock of gavia arctica. No. 922, Pair of gavia arctica. No. 923, Mergus merganser. No. 924, Anas platyrhynchos. No. 925, Mergus serrator.

Perf. 12½x13 on 3 or 4 Sides

1993, Sept. 20 Litho.

Booklet Stamps

921 A497 2.30m multicolored 1.10 .75
922 A497 2.30m multicolored 1.10 .75

Size: 26x40mm

923 A497 2.30m multicolored 1.10 .75
924 A497 2.30m multicolored 1.10 .75
925 A497 2.30m multicolored 1.10 .75
a. Booklet pane of 5, #921-925 5.50 5.50
Complete booklet, #925a 7.50

Physical Education in Finnish Schools, 150th Anniv. — A498

1993, Oct. 8 ***Perf. 14***
926 A498 2.30m multicolored .90 .35

Souvenir Sheet

New Opera House, Helsinki — A499

Operas and ballet: a, 2.30m, Ostrobothnians, by Leevi Madetoja. b, 2.30m, The Faun (four dancers), by Claude Debussy. c, 2.90m, Giselle, by Adolphe Adam. d, 3.40m, The Magic Flute, by Wolfgang Amadeus Mozart.

1993, Oct. 8 ***Perf. 13***
927 A499 Sheet of 4 6.00 7.00
a.-b. 2.30m Either single 1.10 .70
c. 2.90m multi 1.75 1.75
d. 3.40m multi 1.75 *2.25*

Christmas — A500

1993, Nov. 5 Litho. ***Perf. 14***
928 A500 1.80m Christmas tree, elves 1.25 .40
a. Booklet pane of 10 16.00 16.00
Complete booklet, #928a 16.00
929 A500 2.30m Three angels 1.25 .40

Pres. Mauno Koivisto, 70th Birthday — A501

1993, Nov. 25
930 A501 2.30m multicolored .80 .40

Friendship — A502

Moomin characters: No. 931, Two standing. No. 932, Seven running.

1994, Jan. 27 Litho. ***Perf. 12½x13***

Booklet Stamps

931 A502 1 multicolored 2.50 .40
932 A502 1 multicolored 2.50 .40
a. Bklt. pane, 4 each #931-932 20.00 10.00
Complete booklet, #932a 20.00

Nos. 931-932 each sold for 2.30m at time of release. See note following No. 845.

Souvenir Sheet

Intl. Olympic Committee, Cent. — A503

Winter Olympics medalists from Finland: a, Marja-Liisa Kirvesniemi, Marjo Matikainen, cross-country skiing. b, Clas Thunberg, speed skating. c, Veikko Kankkonen, ski jumping. d, Veikko Hakulinen, cross-country skiing.

1994, Jan. 27 ***Perf. 13***
933 A503 4.20m Sheet of 4, #a-d 8.00 9.50

See No. 939.

A504

Waino Aaltonen (1894-1966), Sculptor — A505

1994, Mar. 8
934 A504 2m "Peace" 1.00 .40
935 A505 2m "Muse" 1.00 .40
a. Pair, #934-935 2.10 2.10

Postal Service Civil Servants' Federation, Cent. — A506

1994, Mar. 11
936 A506 2.30m multicolored .85 .45

Finnish Technology A507

Europa: 2.30m, Paper roll, nitrogen fixation, safety lock, ice breaker MS Fennica. 4.20m, Radiosonde, fishing lure, mobile phone, wind power plant.

1994, Mar. 18
937 A507 2.30m multicolored *1.40* *.25*
938 A507 4.20m multicolored *1.90* *1.10*

Olympic Athlete Type of 1994
Souvenir Sheet

Finnish athletes: a, Riitta Salin, Pirjo Haggman, runners. b, Lasse Viren, runner. c, Tiina Lillak, javelin thrower. d, Pentti Nikula, pole vaulter.

1994, May 5 **Litho.** ***Perf. 13***
939 A503 4.20m Sheet of 4, #a-d 8.00 8.00

European Track & Field Championships, Finlandia '95.

Finlandia '95, Helsinki — A508

Coccinella septempunctata.

1994, May 10 ***Perf. 13½x13***
940 A508 16m multi 9.00 8.00

See Nos. 962, 1009.

Miniature Sheet

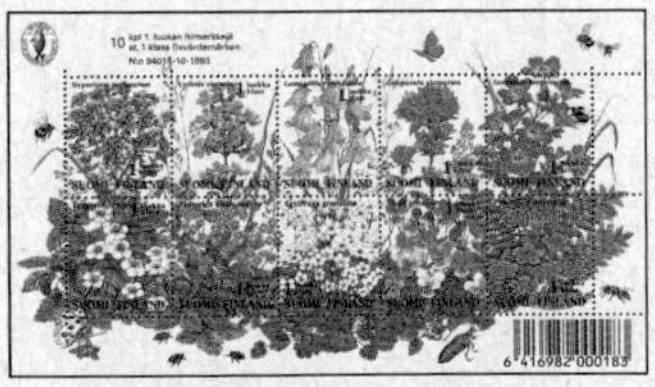

Wildflowers — A509

Designs: a, Hypericum perforatum (b). b, Lychnis viscaria. c, Campanula rotundifolia. d, Campanula glomerata. e, Geranium sanguineum (d). f, Fragaria vesca. g, Veronica chamaedrys (f, h). h, Saxifraga granulata (c, i). i, Viola tricolor (j). j, Potentilla anserina.

1994, June 1 ***Perf. 12***
941 A509 1 Sheet of 10 25.00 22.50
a.-j. Any single 2.50 .40

No. 941 sold for 23m at time of release. See note following No. 845.

Finland-Sweden Track and Field Meet — A510

No. 942, Seppo Raty, Finland, javelin. No. 943, Patrick Sjoberg, Sweden, high jump.

1994, Aug. 26 **Litho.** ***Perf. 12½***
Booklet Stamps
942 A510 2.40m multicolored 1.10 .60
943 A510 2.40m multicolored 1.10 .60
a. Booklet pane, 2 each #942-943 4.50 4.50
Complete booklet, #943a 4.50

See Sweden Nos. 2091-2092.

Population Registers, 450th Anniv. — A511

1994, Sept. 1
944 A511 2.40m multicolored 1.10 .35

Intl. Year of the Family — A512

1994, Sept. 1
945 A512 3.40m multicolored 1.40 .90

Souvenir Sheet

Letter Writing Day — A513

Dog Hill Kids in the Post Office: a, At Post Office window. b, Standing in doorway, mail cart. c, Blowing horn, pig. d, Putting letters in mailbox.

1994, Oct. 7 **Litho.** ***Perf. 14***
946 A513 2.80m Sheet of 4, #a-d 5.00 5.00

Christmas A514

2.10m, Reindeer, bullfinches on antlers. 2.80m, Elves among snow-covered trees.

1994, Nov. 4
947 A514 2.10m multi 1.25 .25
a. Booklet pane of 10 16.00 16.00
Complete booklet, #947a 18.00
948 A514 2.80m multi, vert. 1.40 .50

Greetings — A515

"Dog Hill Kids," sending/receiving greetings: No. 949, Delivering mail to Moon, spaceman. No. 950, Cat writing letter, clown. No. 951, Receiving mail from postman, baby. No. 952, Writing in bed, friend. No. 953, Winter scene at mailbox, characters at beach. No. 954, On bus, girl friend. No. 955, Standing at microphone with guitar, fan. No. 956, Baby in play pen, teddy bear.

Perf. 13 on 3 Sides
1995, Jan. 30 **Litho.**
Booklet Stamps
949 A515 2.80m multicolored 1.75 .75
950 A515 2.80m multicolored 1.75 .75
951 A515 2.80m multicolored 1.75 .75
952 A515 2.80m multicolored 1.75 .75
953 A515 2.80m multicolored 1.75 .75
954 A515 2.80m multicolored 1.75 .75
955 A515 2.80m multicolored 1.75 .75
956 A515 2.80m multicolored 1.75 .75
a. Booklet pane, #949-956 14.00 14.00
Complete booklet, 956a 14.00

Nos. 949-952 are printed tete beche with Nos. 953-956. Soaking in water may affect the holographic images on Nos. 949-956.

Souvenir Sheet

Team Sports — A516

a, Paivi Ikola, pesapallo. b, Jari Kurri, ice hockey. c, Jari Litmanen, soccer. d, Lea Hakala, basketball.

1995, Jan. 30 ***Perf. 13***
957 A516 3.40m Sheet of 4, #a-d 7.00 7.00

See No. 961.

Membership in European Union — A517

1995, Jan. 30 ***Perf. 14***
958 A517 3.50m multicolored 1.75 .90

Peace & Liberty — A518

Europa: 2.90m, Stylized parachutists.

1995, Mar. 1 **Litho.** ***Perf. 14***
959 A518 2.90m multicolored *1.90* *.45*

Endangered Species — A519

Designs: a, Felis lynx. b, Lake, forest. c, Rocks, lake. d, Pusa hispida.

1995, Mar. 1 ***Perf. 13***
960 Block of 4 5.50 5.50
a.-d. A519 2.90m Any single 1.40 1.00

Nos. 960a-960b, 960c-960d are continuous designs. See Russia No. 6249.

Athlete Type of 1995
Souvenir Sheet

Motor sports drivers in cars, on motorcycles: a, Timo Makinen. b, Juha Kankkunen. c, Tommi Ahvala. d, Heikki Mikkola.

1995, May 10 **Litho.** ***Perf. 13***
961 A516 3.50m Sheet of 4, #a.-d. 6.50 6.50

Insect Type of 1994
1995, May 11
962 A508 19m Geotrupes stercorarius 12.50 12.50

Tourism — A520

Designs: 2.80m, Linnanmaki amusement park, Helsinki. 2.90m, Town of Mantyharju.

1995, May 12
963 A520 2.80m multicolored 1.75 .50
964 A520 2.90m multicolored 1.75 .70

Town of Loviisa, 250th Anniv. — A521

1995, June 30 **Litho.** ***Perf. 14***
965 A521 3.20m multicolored 1.40 1.00

Intl. Union of Forestry Research Organizations, 20th World Congress, Tampere — A522

Designs: No. 966, Betula pendula. No. 967, Pinus sylvestris. No. 968, Picea abies. No. 969, Research, tree grown from needle.

Perf. 14 on 2 or 3 Sides
1995, Aug. 8 **Litho.**
Booklet Stamps
966 A522 2.80m multicolored 1.25 .50
967 A522 2.80m multicolored 1.25 .50
968 A522 2.80m multicolored 1.25 .50
969 A522 2.80m multicolored 1.25 .50
a. Booklet pane of 4, #966-969 5.25 5.25
Complete booklet, #969a 5.25

Wilhelm Roentgen (1845-1923), Discovery of the X-Ray, Cent. — A523

1995, Aug. 8 ***Perf. 14***
970 A523 4.30m multicolored 1.90 1.25

Cats — A525

1995, Oct. 9 **Litho.** ***Perf. 13½***
972 A525 2.80m Somali 1.75 .65
973 A525 2.80m Siamese 1.75 .65
974 A525 2.80m Norwegian forest 1.75 .65
975 A525 2.80m Persian 1.75 .65

Size: 59x35mm

976 A525 2.80m European domestic female 1.75 .65
977 A525 2.80m Three kittens, frog 1.75 .65
a. Booklet pane of 6, #972-977 11.00
Complete booklet, #977a 11.00

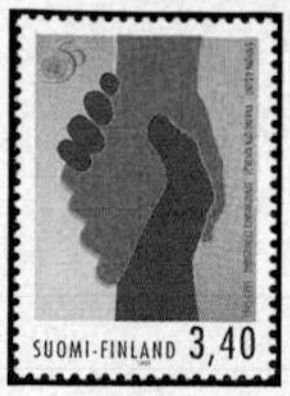

UN, 50th Anniv. — A526

1995, Oct. 20 *Perf. 14*

978	A526	3.40m multicolored	1.40	.90

A527

Christmas A528

1995, Nov. 3 **Litho.** *Perf. 14*

979	A527	2m Santa on skates	1.10	.25
980	A528	2.80m Poinsettias	1.10	.60

Letter Stamps — A529

1996, Feb 2 **Litho.** *Perf. 13½x14*

Booklet Stamps

981	A529	1m "M"	.65	.65
982	A529	1m "O"	.65	.65
983	A529	1m "I"	.65	.65
984	A529	1m "H"	.65	.65
985	A529	1m "E"	.65	.65
986	A529	1m "J"	.65	.65
987	A529	1m "A"	.65	.65
988	A529	1m "N"	.65	.65
989	A529	1m "T"	.65	.65
990	A529	1m "P"	.65	.65
991	A529	1m "U"	.65	.65
992	A529	1m "S"	.65	.65
a.		Booklet pane of 12, #981-992	7.75	7.75
		Complete booklet, No. 992a	7.75	

UNICEF, 50th Anniv. — A530

1996, Feb. 2 *Perf. 14*

993	A530	2.80m multicolored	1.10	.55

Women's Gymnastics in Finland, Cent. — A531

1996, Feb. 26 **Litho.** *Perf. 13*

994	A531	2.80m multicolored	1.10	.55

Woman Suffrage, 90th Anniv. A532

Litho. & Engr.

1996, Mar. 8 *Perf. 13*

995	A532	3.20m multicolored	*1.25*	*.75*

Europa.

Cinema, Cent. — A533

Finnish films: No. 996, "Juha," 1937. No. 997, "Laveata Tieta," 1931. No. 998, "Tuntematon Sotilas," 1935. No. 999, Oldest known photo of a motion picture show, 1896. No. 1000, "Jäniksen Vuosi," 1977. No. 1001, "Valkoinen Peura," 1952. No. 1002, "Kaikki Rakastavat," 1935. No. 1003, "Varjoja Paratiisissa," 1986.

1996, Apr. 1 **Litho.** *Perf. 14x13½*

Booklet Stamps

996	A533	2.80m multicolored	1.40	.70
997	A533	2.80m multicolored	1.40	.70
998	A533	2.80m multicolored	1.40	.70
999	A533	2.80m multicolored	1.40	.70
1000	A533	2.80m multicolored	1.40	.70
1001	A533	2.80m multicolored	1.40	.70
1002	A533	2.80m multicolored	1.40	.70
1003	A533	2.80m multicolored	1.40	.70
a.		Bklt. pane of 8, #996-1003	11.50	11.50
		Complete booklet, #1003a	11.50	

Radio, Cent. — A534

1996, Apr. 25 *Perf. 14*

1004	A534	4.30m multicolored	1.80	1.10

1996 Summer Olympic Games, Atlanta — A535

1996, June 3 **Litho.** *Perf. 12 Vert.*

Booklet Stamps

1005	A535	3.40m Kayaking	1.75	1.75
1006	A535	3.40m Sailing	1.75	1.75
1007	A535	3.40m Rowing	1.75	1.75
1008	A535	3.40m Swimming	1.75	1.75
a.		Booklet pane of 4, #1005-1008	7.00	7.00
		Complete booklet, #1008a	9.00	

Insect Type of 1994

1996, July 1 **Litho.** *Perf. 13*

1009	A508	19m Dytiscus marginalis	11.00	11.00

Shore Birds — A536

No. 1010, Gallinago gallinago. No. 1011, Haematopus ostralegus. No. 1012, Scolopax rusticola. No. 1013, Vanellus vanellus. No. 1014, Numenius arquata.

Perf. 13½ on 3 Sides

1996, Sept. 6 **Litho. & Engr.**

1010	A536	2.80m multicolored	1.40	.70
1011	A536	2.80m multicolored	1.40	.70
1012	A536	2.80m multicolored	1.40	.70
1013	A536	2.80m multicolored	1.40	.70

Size: 30x52mm

1014	A536	2.80m multicolored	1.40	.70
a.		Sheet of 5, #1010-1014	7.00	7.00

Finnish Comic Strips — A537

No. 1015, "Professor Itikainen" examining plant with magnifying glass, by Ilmari Vainio. No. 1016, "Pekka Puupää (Peter Blockhead)" taking letter from mailbox, by Ola Fogelberg. No. 1017, "Joonas" holding drawing pencil, by Veikko Savolainen. No. 1018, "Mämmilä" wearing helmet, by Tarmo Koivisto. No. 1019, "Rymy-Eetu" smoking pipe, by Erkki Tanttu. No. 1020, "Kieku" writing letter, by Asmo Alho. No. 1021, "Pikku Risunen" with animal, by Riitta Uusitalo. No. 1022, "Kiti" holding up pencil, by Kati Kovács.

1996, Oct. 9 **Litho.** *Perf. 13½*

Booklet Stamps

1015	A537	2.80m black & red	1.40	.75
1016	A537	2.80m black & red	1.40	.75
1017	A537	2.80m red & black	1.40	.75
1018	A537	2.80m black & red	1.40	.75
1019	A537	2.80m black & red	1.40	.75
1020	A537	2.80m red & black	1.40	.75
1021	A537	2.80m black & red	1.40	.75
1022	A537	2.80m red & black	1.40	.75
a.		Bklt. pane of 8, #1015-1022	11.00	11.00
		Complete booklet, #1022a	11.00	

Christmas A538

2m, Snowman, Santa, gnome playing musical instruments. 2.80m, Rabbit, reindeer watching northern lights. 3.20m, Santa reading letters.

1996, Nov. 1 **Litho.** *Perf. 14*

1023	A538	2m multi	1.75	.50
1024	A538	2.80m multi	1.75	.55
1025	A538	3.20m multi, vert.	2.75	.85
		Nos. 1023-1025 (3)	6.25	1.90

Greetings Stamps — A539

End of 19th cent.: No. 1026, Two angels. No. 1027, Flowers in basket. No. 1028, Hand reaching through garland, bluebird. No. 1029, Boy, girl dancing. No. 1030, Boy, envelope, shamrocks. No. 1031, Clasping hands through heart-shaped garlands. No. 1032, Roses. No. 1033, Angel.

Perf. 13x12½ on 3 Sides

1997, Jan. 30 **Litho.**

Booklet Stamps

1026	A539	1 multicolored	2.50	.65
1027	A539	1 multicolored	2.50	.65
1028	A539	1 multicolored	2.50	.65
1029	A539	1 multicolored	2.50	.65
1030	A539	1 multicolored	2.50	.65
1031	A539	1 multicolored	2.50	.65
1032	A539	1 multicolored	2.50	.65
1033	A539	1 multicolored	2.50	.65
a.		Bklt. pane of 8, #1026-1033	20.00	20.00
		Complete booklet, #1033a	20.00	

Nos. 1026-1033 sold for 2.80m on day of issue.

Number on stamp represents class of mail.

Mail Order Sales in Finland, Cent. — A540

1997, Jan. 30 *Perf. 13½x14*

1034	A540	2.80m multicolored	1.10	.45

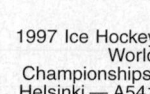

1997 Ice Hockey World Championships, Helsinki — A541

1997, Jan. 30

1035	A541	2.80m multicolored	1.20	.50

On each stamp from the right vertical row of the sheet, No. 1035 exists without the thin, curved black line at the center right edge of the stamp. Value, single stamp $3.00.

Lepus Timidus A542

1997, Mar. 4 **Litho.** *Perf. 14*

1036	A542	2.80m multicolored	1.10	.40

Saami Folktale, "Girl Who Turned into a Golden Merganser" — A543

Europa: 3.20m, Duck, girl, prince. 3.40m, Girl falling into crevice.

1997, Mar. 4 *Perf. 13*

1037	A543	3.20m multicolored	*1.50*	*.50*
1038	A543	3.40m multicolored	*2.00*	*1.00*

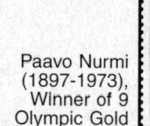

Paavo Nurmi (1897-1973), Winner of 9 Olympic Gold Medals — A544

1997, Mar. 18 *Perf. 14*

1039	A544	3.40m multicolored	1.40	1.20

Southwest Archipelago Natl. Park — A545

Litho. & Engr.

1997, Apr. 25 *Perf. 14*

1040	A545	4.30m multicolored	1.75	1.10

Tango — A546

1997, May 19 **Litho.**

1041	A546	1 multicolored	2.50	.40
		Complete booklet of 5	12.50	

No. 1041 sold for 2.80m on day of release. Number on stamp represents class of mail.

A547

Sailing Ships: No. 1042, Astrid. No. 1043, Jacobstads Wapen. No. 1044, Tradewind. No. 1045, Merikokko. No. 1046, Suomen Joutsen. No. 1047, Sigyn.

Booklet Stamps

1997, May 19 ***Perf. 13½***

1042	A547 2.80m multicolored	1.25	.60
1043	A547 2.80m multicolored	1.25	.60
1044	A547 2.80m multicolored	1.25	.60
1045	A547 2.80m multicolored	1.25	.60

Size: 48x25½mm

1046	A547 2.80m multicolored	1.25	.60
1047	A547 2.80m multicolored	1.25	.60
a.	Booklet pane of 6, #1042-1047	7.50	
	Complete booklet, #1047a	7.50	

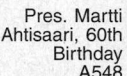

Pres. Martti Ahtisaari, 60th Birthday A548

1997, June 23 **Litho.** ***Perf. 14***

1048	A548 2.80m multicolored	1.10	.40

Independence, 80th Anniv. — A549

Four seasons: No. 1049, Spring, lily-of-the-valley (natl. flower). No. 1050, Summer, white clouds. No. 1051, Fall, colorful leaves. No. 1052, Winter, snow crystals.

Perf. 13x12½ on 2 or 3 Sides

1997, June 23 **Booklet Stamps**

1049	A549 2.80m multicolored	1.10	.65
1050	A549 2.80m multicolored	1.10	.65
1051	A549 2.80m multicolored	1.10	.65
1052	A549 2.80m multicolored	1.10	.65
a.	Booklet pane, #1049-1052	4.50	4.50
	Complete booklet, #1052a	4.50	

Souvenir Sheet

A550

Grus Grus (Cranes): a, With young. b, With frog. c, Performing mating dance. d, In flight.

1997, Aug. 19 **Litho.** ***Perf. 14***

1053	A550 2.80m Sheet of 4, #a.-d.	5.00	5.00

A551

Finnish Writers Assoc. (Covers from books): No. 1054, "Seven Brothers," by Aleksis Kivi. No. 1055, "Sinuhe the Egyptian," by Mika Waltari. No. 1056, "Täällä Pohjantähden alla I," by Väinö Linna. No. 1057, "Hyvästi Iijoki," by Kalle Päätalo. No. 1058, "Haukka, minum rakkaani," by Kaari Utrio. No. 1059, "Juhannustanssit," by Hannu Salama. No. 1060, "Manillaköysi," by Veijo Meri. No. 1061, "Uppo-Nalle ja Kumma," by Elina Karjalainen.

Booklet Stamps

1997, Oct. 9 **Litho.** ***Perf. 14¼, 14½***

1054	A551 2.80m multicolored	1.25	.75
1055	A551 2.80m multicolored	1.25	.75
1056	A551 2.80m multicolored	1.25	.75
1057	A551 2.80m multicolored	1.25	.75
1058	A551 2.80m multicolored	1.25	.75
1059	A551 2.80m multicolored	1.25	.75
1060	A551 2.80m multicolored	1.25	.75
1061	A551 2.80m multicolored	1.25	.75
a.	Booklet pane, #1054-1061	10.00	10.00
	Complete booklet, #1061a	10.00	

No. 1056 exists perf 14½x14¼. The other values also should exist thus. The editors would like to examine such stamps.

Christmas A552

1997, Oct. 31

1062	A552 2m Village	1.00	.40
1063	A552 2.80m Candelabra, vert.	1.00	.40
1064	A552 3.20m Church, vert.	1.25	.65
	Nos. 1062-1064 (3)	3.25	1.45

Wildlife A553

2nd, Stizostedion lucioperca. 1st, Turdus merula.

Die Cut Perf. 10 Horiz. Syncopated

1998, Jan. 15 **Litho.**

Self-Adhesive

Coil Stamps

1065	A553 2 multicolored	2.75	.40
1066	A553 1 multicolored	2.00	.35

Nos. 1065-1066 were valued at 2.40m and 2.80m, respectively, on date of issue. Number on stamp represents class of mail.

See Nos. 1099-1100.

A554

Moomin Cartoon Characters, by Tove Jansson: No. 1067, Boy Moomin drawing with pad and pencil. No. 1068, Girl Moomin in sunshine. No. 1069, Organ grinder. No. 1070, Boy Moomin giving flower to girl Moomin.

1998, Jan. 15 ***Perf. 13 on 3 Sides***

Booklet Stamps

1067	A554 1 multicolored	2.90	.60
1068	A554 1 multicolored	2.90	.60
1069	A554 1 multicolored	2.90	.60
1070	A554 1 multicolored	2.90	.60
a.	Booklet pane, #1067-1070	12.00	12.00
	Complete booklet, #1070a	12.00	

Nos. 1067-1070 each sold for 2.80m on day of issue. Number on stamp represents class of mail.

See No. 1127.

A555

1998, Feb. 3 ***Perf. 14***

1071	A555 2.80m multicolored	1.20	.30

Finnish Federation of Nurses, cent.

A556

Valentine's Day Surprise Stamps. (Designs beneath scratch-off heart): a, Musical notes, two dogs. b, Elephant, mouse and flowers. c, Puppy, sealed envelope. d, Kittens, kittens hugging. e, Dog with nose in air, bouquet of flowers. f, Flowers, two rodents.

1998, Feb. 3 ***Perf. 12***

1072	1 Sheet of 6	15.00	9.50
a.-f.	A556 Any single, unscratched	2.50	.75

Nos. 1072a-1072f were each valued at 2.80m on day of issue. Number on stamp represents class of mail. Unused values are for singles with attached selvage. Inscriptions are shown in selvage above or below each stamp.

Each stamp bears a heart-shaped, golden scratch-off overlay. Values are for unscratched examples. Scratched stamps, with hearts partially or fully removed, sell for about 20 percent less.

A557

1998, Mar. 27 **Litho.** ***Perf. 14***

1073	A557 2.80m Tussilago farfara	1.20	.30

National Festivals A558

Europa: 3.20m, Boy and girl, balloons, "Vappu" (May Day). 3.40m, Boy and girl in a dream floating over water, Midsummer Festival.

1998, Mar. 27 ***Perf. 14x14½***

1074	A558 3.20m multicolored	*2.00*	*.30*
1075	A558 3.40m multicolored	*2.75*	*.80*

Finnish Marine Research Institute, 80th Anniv. — A559

Designs: 2.80m, Research vessel, "Aranda." 3.20m, "Vega," chart showing route of Nils Adolf Erik Nordenskjold's expedition.

Litho. & Engr.

1998, May 7 ***Perf. 14x13***

1076	A559 2.80m multicolored	1.40	.40
1077	A559 3.20m multicolored	1.50	.60

First Performance of National Anthem, 150th Anniv. — A560

1998, May 7 ***Perf. 13***

1078	A560 5m multicolored	2.00	1.00

Puppies A561

No. 1079, Bernese Mountain dog. No. 1080, Puli. No. 1081, Boxer. No. 1082, Bichon Frisé. No. 1083, Finnish lapphound. No. 1084, Wire-haired dachshund. No. 1085, Scottish cairn terrier. No. 1086, Labrador retriever.

Perf. 13½x13 on 2 or 3 Sides

1998, June 4 **Litho.**

Booklet Stamps

1079	A561 1 multicolored	2.50	.60
1080	A561 1 multicolored	2.50	.60
1081	A561 1 multicolored	2.50	.60
1082	A561 1 multicolored	2.50	.60
1083	A561 1 multicolored	2.50	.60
1084	A561 1 multicolored	2.50	.60
1085	A561 1 multicolored	2.50	.60
1086	A561 1 multicolored	2.50	.60
a.	Booklet pane, #1079-1086	20.00	20.00
	Complete booklet, #1086a	20.00	

Nos. 1079-1086 each sold for 2.80m on day of issue. Number on stamp represents class of mail.

Owls — A562

Designs: a, Bubo bubo. b, Wing of bubo bubo. c, Bubo bubo, aegolius funereus. d, Strix nebulosa. e, Nyctea scandiaca.

1998, Sept. 4 **Litho.** ***Perf. 13½***

1087	Sheet of 5 + label	6.00	6.00
a.-e.	A562 3m any single	1.20	1.20

No. 1087b is 52x27mm; Nos. 1087c-1087d, 26x44mm; No. 1087e, 30x44mm.

See No. 1113.

Cycling — A563

1998, Sept. 4 ***Perf. 14***

1088	A563 3m multicolored	1.25	1.25

Finnish Design — A564

No. 1089, Savoy vases, by Alvar Aalto. No. 1090, Karuselli chair, by Yrjö Kukkapuro. No. 1091, Tasaraita knitwear, designed by Annika Rimala for Marimekko. No. 1092, Kilta tableware set, by Kaj Franck. No. 1093, Cast iron pot, by Timo Sarpaneva. No. 1094, Carelia cutlery set, by Bertel Gardberg.

Perf. 13½ on 3 Sides

1998, Oct. 9 **Litho.**

Booklet Stamps

1089	A564 3m multicolored	1.40	.75
1090	A564 3m multicolored	1.40	.75
1091	A564 3m multicolored	1.40	.75
1092	A564 3m multicolored	1.40	.75
1093	A564 3m multicolored	1.40	.75
1094	A564 3m multicolored	1.40	.75
a.	Booklet pane, #1089-1094	8.00	8.00
	Complete booklet, #1094a	8.00	

Nos. 1090-1091, 1093-1094 are 29x34mm.

Christmas A565

Designs: 2m, Christmas tree, children, vert. 3m, Children, dog riding sled. 3.20m, Winter scene of cottage in center of island.

1998, Oct. 30 ***Perf. 14***

1095 A565 2m multicolored 1.25 .55
1096 A565 3m multicolored 1.40 .40
1097 A565 3.20m multicolored 1.50 .65
Nos. 1095-1097 (3) 4.15 1.60

Souvenir Sheet

Mika Häkkinen, Formula 1 Driving Champion — A566

1999, Jan. 15 ***Perf. 13½***

1098 A566 3m multicolored 3.00 3.00

Native Wildlife Type of 1998

2, Salmo salar. 1, Luscinia svecica.

Die Cut Perf. 10 Horiz. Syncopated

1999, Jan. 27 **Litho.**

Coil Stamps

Self-Adhesive

1099 A553 2 multi 2.00 .60

Die Cut Perf. 10 Vert. Syncopated

1100 A553 1 multi, vert. 2.75 .60

Nos. 1099-1100 were valued at 2.40m and 3m, respectively, on day of issue. Number on stamp represents class of mail.

Friendship A567

Animals' tails: No. 1101, Zebra, lion. No. 1102, Dog, cat.

Booklet Stamps

Serpentine Die Cut Perf. 13 Horiz.

1999, Jan. 27 **Self-Adhesive**

1101 A567 3m multicolored 1.25 1.20
1102 A567 3m multicolored 1.25 1.20
a. Bklt. pane, 3 each #1101-1102 8.50 8.00

No. 1102a is a complete booklet.

Finnish Labor Movement, Cent. — A568

1999, Jan. 27 ***Perf. 13½***

1103 A568 4.50m multicolored 1.80 1.80

Finland's Roads — A569

No. 1104, Snow-covered landscape, Arctic Ocean Road. No. 1105, Freeway interchanges, Jyväsjtkä Lakeshore Road. No. 1106, Raippaluoto Bridge. No. 1107, Wooded drive, Kitee.

1999, Feb. 15 Litho. ***Perf. 14 Horiz.***

Booklet Stamps

1104 A569 3m multicolored 1.25 .75
a. Perf. 12¾ horiz. *75.00* *13.00*
1105 A569 3m multicolored 1.25 .75
a. Perf. 12¾ horiz. *75.00* *13.00*
1106 A569 3m multicolored 1.25 .75
a. Perf. 12¾ horiz. *75.00* *13.00*
1107 A569 3m multicolored 1.25 .75
a. Booklet pane, #1104-1107 5.00
Complete booklet, #1107a 6.00
b. Perf. 12¾ horiz. *75.00* *13.00*
c. Booklet pane, #1104a, 1105a, 1106a, 1107b *300.00* *300.00*
Complete booklet, #1107c *325.00*

A570

Women's Kalevala-style brooches: a, Horse clasp. b, Bird clasp. c, Virusmäki clasp.

1999, Feb. 15 ***Perf. 13½x14***

1108 Sheet of 3 3.75 3.75
a.-c. A570 3m any single 1.25 1.10

1st Publication of Legend of the Kalevala, 150th Anniv.

A571

1999, Mar. 15 ***Perf. 13x13½***

1109 A571 3m Crocus vernus 1.25 .60

Martha Organization, Cent. — A572

1999, Mar. 15 ***Perf. 13½x13***

1110 A572 3m multicolored 1.25 .60

Europa A573

1999, Mar. 15 ***Perf. 13½x14***

1111 A573 2.70m Esplanade Park *1.75* *.50*
1112 A573 3.20m Ruissalo Park *3.00* *.60*

Bird Type of 1998

Designs: a, Luscinia luscinia. b, Cuculus canorus. c, Botaurus stellaris. d, Caprimulgus europaeus. e, Crex crex.

1999, May 18 ***Perf. 13½***

1113 Sheet of 5 + label 6.00 6.00
a.-e. A562 3m any single 1.10 .75

No. 1113b is 25x43mm. No. 1113c is 45x30mm. No. 1113d-1113e are 26x37mm.

Finland's Presidency of European Union — A574

1999, July 1 Litho. ***Perf. 13¾x13½***

1114 A574 3.50m multicolored 1.40 .60

Finnish Entertainers A575

a, Harmony Sisters, Vera (1914-97), Maire (1916-95) & Raija (1918-97) Valtonen. b, Olavi Virta (1915-72), singer. c, Georg Malmstén (1902-81), composer, conductor. d, Topi Kärki (1915-22), composer, and Reino (Repe) Helismaa (1913-65), lyricist. e, Tapio Rautavaara (1915-79), singer. f, Esa Parkarinen (1911-89), musician, actor.

Perf. 13¼ on 3 Sides

1999, Sept. 6 **Litho.**

1115 Booklet pane of 6 8.50
a.-f. A575 3.50m any single 1.40 .75
Complete booklet, #1115 8.50

Nos. 1115a, 1115d are each 60x34mm.

Finnish Commercial Product Design — A576

a, Fiskars cutting tools. b, Zoel/Versoul guitars. c, Ergo II/Silenta hearing protectors. d, Ponsse Cobra HS 10 tree harvester. e, Suunto compass. f, Exel Avanti QLS ski pole.

Perf. 13¼ on 3 Sides

1999, Oct 8 **Litho.**

1116 Booklet pane of 6 8.00
a.-f. A576 3.50m any single 1.40 .75
Complete booklet, #1116 10.50

Size of b, c, e, f: 30x35mm.

"The Nativity," by Giorgio di Chirico (1888-1978) A577

Rabbits, Birds — A578

1999, Nov. 5 ***Perf. 14***

1117 A578 2.50m Santa Claus, vert. .90 .40
1118 A577 3m multicolored 1.20 1.20
1119 A578 3.50m multicolored 1.60 .60
Nos. 1117-1119 (3) 3.70 2.20

Christmas. See Italy Nos. 2314-2315.

Sveaborg Fortress — A579

2000, Jan. 12 Litho. ***Perf. 13¾x13½***

1120 A579 7.20m multi 3.00 1.75

Helsinki, 450th Anniv. A580

Designs: No. 1121, Baltic herring market (designer's name at UL).

No. 1122: a, Museum of Contemporary Art (blue building), vert. b, Cathedral, Senate Square (green building). c, Finlandia Hall (orange building). d, Glass Palace Film and Media Center (red building), vert.

No. 1123: a, Quest for the Lost Crown, Sveaborg Fortress (children and arch), vert. b, Like No. 1121, no designer's name. c, Forces of Light City Festival. d, Cellist at outdoor concert, Kaivopuisto Park.

2000, Jan. 12 ***Perf. 14***

1121 A580 3.50m multi 1.40 .70

Perf. 14½x14¾ (vert. stamps), 14¾x14½

1122 Booklet pane of 4 6.50 6.50
a.-d. A580 3.50m Any single 1.60 1.60
1123 Booklet pane of 4 6.50 6.50
a.-d. A580 3.50m Any single 1.60 1.60
Complete booklet, #1122-1123 13.00

Valentine's Day — A581

Designs: a, Earth as backpack. b, Painters on ladder. c, Birds in balloon. d, Alien with magnet. e, Boy with heart-shaped balloon. f, Polar bear and igloo.

Perf. 13x12¾ on 3 sides

2000, Jan. 12

1124 Bklt. pane of 6 + 4 labels 8.50
a.-f. A581 3.50m Any single 1.40 .70
Complete booklet, #1124 8.50

Souvenir Sheet of 2

Tommi Mäkinen, 1999 Rally World Champion — A582

a, Mäkinen behind wheel. b, Race car.

2000, Mar. 3 ***Perf. 13x13¼***

1125 A582 3.50m #a.-b. 3.00 3.00

Easter — A583

2000, Mar. 15 ***Perf. 13¾x13¼***

1126 A583 3.50m Caltha palustris 1.40 .70

Moomin Type of 1998

a, Rat with broom looking at Moomins. b, Moomin with uniform, figures sprouting from ground. c, Moomin with hat in forest. d, Moomin with hat, children, in front of stove.

Perf. 13x12¾ on 3 Sides

2000, Mar. 15

1127 Booklet pane of 4 27.50 27.50
a.-d. A554 1 Any single 6.50 2.50
Complete booklet, #1127 30.00 12.00
e. As #1127, perf. 13¼ on 3 sides 12.00
f.-i. As #a-d, perf. 13¼ on 3 sides 2.75 .65
Booklet, #1127e 12.50

Nos. 1127a-1127d sold for 3.50m on day of issue. Number on stamp represents class of mail.

Issued: No. 1127e, 7/10/00.

Jubilee Year — A584

Turku Cathedral: a, Nave. b, Woman, votive candles. c, Christ on the Mount of Transfiguration, alterpiece. d, Infant baptism.

2000, Mar. 15 Litho. ***Perf. 14 Vert.***

1128	Booklet pane of 4	6.00	3.50
a.-d.	A584 3.50m Any single	1.50	.60
	Complete booklet, #1128	6.00	

Europa, 2000

Common Design Type

2000, May 9 ***Perf. 13¼x13***

1129 CD17 3.50m multi 2.00 .60

Provincial Flowers

Spring Anemone A585

Blue Cornflower A586

Pulsatilla Patens — A587

Die Cut Perf. 13x12½

2000-01 **Litho.**

Booklet Stamps
Self-Adhesive

1130	A585 1 multi	2.50	.50
a.	Booklet pane of 10	16.00	

Die Cut Perf. 14¾x13½

1131	A586 1 multi	2.50	.50
1132	A587 1 multi	2.50	.50
a.	Booklet pane, 5 each #1131-1132	25.00	

Number on stamp represents class of mail. No. 1130 sold for 3.50m at time of release. Nos. 1131-1132 each sold for 3.60m on day of issue. No. 1132a was issued in two printings. The white box containing the stamps on the original printing is 114mm wide and on the 2003 printing, the box is 110mm wide.

Issued: No. 1130, 5/9. Nos. 1131-1132, 5/16/01.

Souvenir Sheet

Science — A595

Designs: a, Children, molecuar model (triangular stamp). b, Man's face, DNA strand (rhomboid stamp). c, Man's face, Sierpinski triangles (square stamp).

2000, May 30 ***Perf. 14¼***

1140 A595 3.50m Sheet of 3, #a.-c. 4.25 4.25

No. 1140 has holographic image. Soaking in water may affect the hologram.

Finnish Design — A596

No. 1141: a, Rug, by Akseli Gallen-Kallela (1865-1931). b, Pearl Bird, by Birger Kaipiainen (1915-88). c, Pot, by Kyllikki Salmenhaara (1915-81). d, Leaf, by Tapio Wirkkala (1915-85). e, Detail from damask, by Dora Jung (1906-80). f, Glass vase, by Valter Jung (1879-1946).

Perf. 13¼ on 3 Sides

2000, Sept. 5 **Litho.**

1141	Booklet pane of 6	8.00	8.00
a.-f.	A596 3.50m Any single	1.50	1.00
	Booklet, #1141	8.00	

Size of b, c, e, f: 30x35mm.

Coregonus Lavaretus A597

Lagopus Lagopus A598

Coil Stamps

Die Cut Perf. 10 Horiz. Syncopated

2000, Sept. 5 **Self-Adhesive**

1142	A597 2 multi	2.50	.50
1143	A598 1 multi	2.50	.50

Nos. 1142-1143 sold for 3m and 3.50m respectively on day of sale.

> On modern stamps bearing the "denominations" "1" or "2," the number represents the class of mail.

Christmas A599

2.50m, Costumed Tiernapojat carol singers. 3.50m, Bullfinch on door ornament, vert.

Serpentine Die Cut 14¼

2000, Nov. 3 **Photo.**

Self-Adhesive

1144-1145 A599 Set of 2 3.00 .90

Litho.

Serpentine Die Cut 13¾

1146 A599 3.50m multi + label 7.00 5.25

No. 1146 issued in sheets of 20 that sold for 120m, together with a separate sheet of stickers that could be affixed on the label. The labels attached to the stamps are separated by a row of interrupted serpentine die cutting. Labels could be personalized with photographs taken at some sale sites.

European Year of Languages A600

2001, Jan. 17 **Litho.** ***Perf. 13¼***

1147 A600 1 multi 2.50 .75

No. 1147 sold for 3.50m on day of sale.

World Ski Championships, Lahti — A601

No. 1148: a, Ski jumper Janne Ahonen (yellow helmet). b, Skier Mika Myllylä.

2001, Jan. 17

1148 A601 3.50m Horiz. pair, #a-b 2.75 2.75

Valentine's Day — A602

No. 1149: a, Oval wreath. b, Basket of flowers, letter. c, Heart-shaped wreath. d, Bouquet of flowers, letter. e, Flowers, tea set. f, Flowers, heart-shaped pastry.

Serpentine Die Cut 11½x11¾ on 3 Sides

2001, Jan. 17 **Photo.**

Self-Adhesive

1149	Booklet pane of 6	15.00	10.00
a.-f.	A602 1 Any single	2.50	.75
	Booklet, #1149	15.00	

Nos. 1149a-1149f each sold for 3.50m on day of issue.

Souvenir Sheet

Donald Duck Comics in Finland, 50th Anniv. — A603

No. 1150: a, Mickey Mouse, Donald Duck, Santa Claus, Goofy. b, First comics, silhouette of boy. c, Tin soldier with Finnish flag, Chip and Dale (25x30mm). d, Finnish epic hero Väinämöinen, silhouette of Donald Duck. e, Helsinki Cathedral, Donald Duck.

Perf. 7¾ on 3 or 4 Sides

2001, Mar. 13 **Litho.**

1150 A603 1 Sheet of 5, #a-e 12.50 8.00

Nos. 1150a-1150e sold for 3.50m each on day of issue.

Santa Claus and Sleigh — A604

2001-04 ***Serpentine Die Cut 14½x14***

Self-Adhesive

1151	A604 1 multi	2.50	.75
a.	Serpentine die cut 13¾x13¼ ('04)	2.75	.80

No. 1151 sold for 3.60m on day of issue. No. 1151a sold for 65c on day of issue.

No. 1151, 4/2/01. No. 1151a, 12/04.

Europa A605

2001, Apr. 2 ***Perf. 13x13½***

1152 A605 5.40m multi *3.00 3.00*

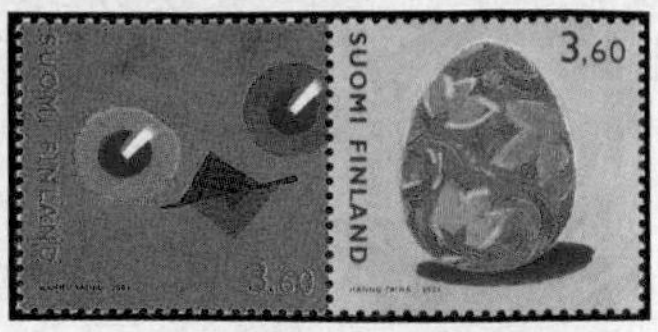

Easter — A606

No. 1153: a, Chick. b. Decorated egg.

2001, Apr. 2 ***Perf. 13¼***

1153 A606 3.60m Horiz. pair, #a-b 2.75 2.50

Souvenir Sheet

Verla Mill, UNESCO World Heritage Site — A607

Denominations in: a, UL. b, UR. c, LL. d, LR.

2001, Apr. 2

1154 A607 3.60m Sheet of 4, #a-d 5.50 4.00

Orienteering World Championships, Tampere — A608

2001, May 16

1155 A608 3.60m multi 1.75 .75

Values are for stamps with surrounding selvage.

Souvenir Sheet

Woodpeckers — A609

No. 1156: a, Dendrocopos minor (32x36mm). b, Picoides tridactylus (29x36mm). c, Dendrocopos leucotos (32x42mm). d, Dendrocopos major

(29x42mm). e, Picus canus (32x41mm). f, Dryocopus martius (29x41mm).

Perf. 14½x14¼ on 2, 3 or 4 Sides

2001, May 16

1156 A609 3.60m Sheet of 6, #a-f 10.00 8.00

Marine Life — A610

No. 1157: a, Lampetra fluviatilis. b, Aspius aspius. c, Coregonus albula.

Die Cut Perf. 10 Horiz. Syncopated

2001, Sept. 6 **Photo.**

Self-Adhesive

Coil Stamps

1157 Horiz. strip of 3 7.00 5.00
a.-c. A610 2 Any single 2.25 .35

Nos. 1157a-1157c were sold in boxes of 100 stamps that sold at a discount price of 270m on day of sale. The franking value on the day of sale for each stamp was 3m.

Birds A611

No. 1158: a, Parus caeruleus. b, Motacilla alba. c, Oriolus oriolus.

Die Cut Perf. 10 Horiz. Syncopated

2001, Sept. 6 **Photo.**

Self-Adhesive

Coil Stamps

1158 Horiz. strip of 3 7.00 4.75
a.-c. A611 1 Any single 2.25 .35

Nos. 1158a-1158c were sold in boxes of 100 stamps that sold at a discount price of 330m on day of sale. The franking value on the day of sale for each stamp was 3.60m.

History of Gulf of Finland A612

No. 1159: a, Utö Lighthouse. b, Wreck of the St. Mikael. c, Diver exploring St. Mikael. d, Opossum shrimp, isopod. e, Ship's cabin and nautical chart (32x55mm).

Perf. 13¼x13¾ on 2 or 3 Sides

2001, Sept. 6 **Litho.**

1159 Booklet pane of 5 12.50 9.50
a.-e. A612 1 Any single 2.50 1.00
Booklet, #1159 12.50

Nos. 1159a-1159e each sold for 3.60m on day of sale.

See No. 1177.

Christmas A613

Designs: 2.50m, Elf reading Santa's book, candle. 3.60m, Elf delivering package on sled, horiz.

Serpentine Die Cut 14¼

2001, Oct. 26 **Photo.**

Self-Adhesive

1160 A613 2.50m multi 1.10 .40
1161 A613 3.60m multi 1.40 .65

Slightly larger examples of Nos. 1160-1161 serpentine die cut 14 are known on first day and other covers produced by the postal service. They were not sold unused to the public.

100 Cents = 1 Euro (€)

Flowers — A614

National Symbols A615

Heraldic Lion — A616

Type A614 — No. 1162, Myosotis scorpioides: a, Forty-one flowers. b, Four flowers, five buds. c, One flower, four buds. d, Entire plant. e, Five flowers.

No. 1163, Convallaria majallis: a, Leaf, stem with five flowers. b, Two leaves, stem with eight flowers. c, Two flowers. d, Two leaves, stem with five flowers. e, Entire plants.

Type A615: 50c, Swan, vert. 60c, Birch. 1, Flag and bird. 90c, Kymintehtaalta, by Victor Westerholm. €1.30, Granite cliff. €2.50, Spruce. €3.50, Pine.

Die Cut Perf. 15

2002, Jan. 1 **Photo.**

Self-Adhesive

1162 Vert. strip of 5 .80 .80
a.-e. A614 5c Any single .25 .25
f. As #1162, die cut perf 14 .80
g.-k. A614 5c Any single, die cut perf 14 .25 .25

Die Cut Perf. 14

1163 Vert. strip of 5 1.75 1.75
a.-e. A614 10c Any single .35 .25
1164 A615 50c multi 1.60 .40
1165 A615 60c multi 2.00 .40

Die Cut Perf. 13¾

1166 A615 1 multi 2.50 .40
a. Booklet pane of 10 25.00
Booklet, #1166a 25.00

Die Cut Perf. 14¾x15

1167 A615 90c multi 3.00 .65

Die Cut Perf. 12 Syncopated

1168 A616 €1 blue & multi 3.25 .65

Die Cut Perf. 14¾x15

1169 A615 €1.30 multi 4.00 1.20
a. Die cut perf 14 ('04) 4.50 1.20

Die Cut Perf. 14

1170 A615 €2.50 multi 8.00 1.25
1171 A615 €3.50 multi 11.00 1.75

Die Cut Perf. 12 Syncopated

1172 A616 €5 red & multi 16.00 5.00
Nos. 1162-1172 (11) 53.90 14.25

No. 1166 sold for 60c on day of issue.

Die cut perf 14 examples of No. 1167 exist on first day and other covers produced by the postal service. They were not sold unused to the public.

No. 1169a issued 7/04. No. 1169a has a duller blue panel and a duller black denomination than that found on No. 1169, and a die cut perf. 14 version of No. 1169 that was available only on first day covers with 1/1/02 cancels, and which was not made available to the public unused. Nos. 1169 and 1169a were produced by different printers.

Nos. 1162f-1162k were printed and put on first day and other covers in 2002 but were not sold to the public until 2006.

See Nos. 1179-1180, 1383-1384.

Easter — A617

Die Cut Perf. 14

2002, Mar. 6 **Photo.**

Self-Adhesive

1173 A617 60c multi 1.90 .75

Souvenir Sheet

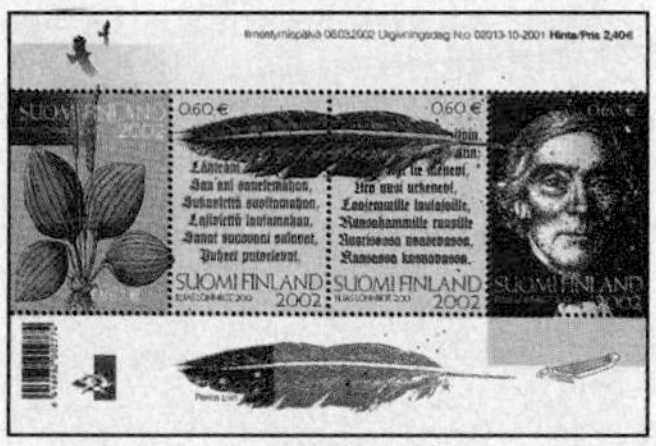

Elias Lönnrot (1802-84), Botanist, Linguist — A618

No. 1174: a, Plantain. b, Opening lines of "Kalevala" (denomination at UL). c, Closing lines of "Kalevala" (denomination at UR). d, Portrait.

Perf. 13¼ on 3 or 4 Sides

2002, Mar. 6 **Litho.**

1174 A618 60c Sheet of 4, #a-d 7.50 5.50

Souvenir Sheet

Old Rauma, UNESCO World Heritage Site — A619

Denominations at: a, UL. b, UR. c, LL. d, LR.

2002, Mar. 6 ***Perf. 13½***

1175 A619 60c Sheet of 4, #a-d 7.50 5.50

Europa — A620

2002, Apr. 15 ***Perf. 13***

1176 A620 60c multi *2.50 1.25*

Gulf of Finland Type of 2001

No. 1177: a, Birds, fish. b, Sailboat, plankton. c, Flounder on sea bed. d, Shrimp, herring. e, Tvärminne Zoological Station, ship, isopod, oceanographic equipment, mussels (32x55mm).

Perf. 13¼x13¾ on 2 or 3 Sides

2002, Apr. 15

1177 Booklet pane of 5 12.50 9.00
a.-e. A612 1 Any single 2.50 1.25
Booklet, #1177 12.50

Nos. 1177a-1177e each sold for 60c on day of issue.

Sibelius Monument, Helsinki, by Eila Hiltunen A621

2002, May 3 ***Perf. 13***

1178 A621 60c multi 1.90 .50

National Symbols Type of 2002 Without Finland Post Emblem

Designs: 60c, Juniperus communis. 1, Reindeer in Lapland.

Die Cut Perf. 14

2002, Oct. 9 **Photo.**

Self-Adhesive

1179 A615 60c multi 1.90 .50
1180 A615 1 multi 2.50 .50

No. 1180 sold for 60c on day of issue.

Christmas A622

Designs: 45c, Horse-drawn sleigh. 60c, Angel with trumpet, vert.

Serpentine Die Cut 14¼

2002, Nov. 1 **Self-Adhesive**

1181-1182 A622 Set of 2 3.75 1.50

Fish — A623

No. 1183: a, Abramis brama. b, Salmo trutta lacustris. c, Esox lucius.

Syncopated Die Cut Perf. 10 Horiz.

2003, Jan. 15 **Self-Adhesive**

Coil Stamps

1183 Horiz. strip of 3 8.00 8.00
a.-c. A623 2 Any single 2.50 2.50

Nos. 1183a-1183c were sold in boxes of 100 that sold at a discount price of €47 on day of issue. The franking value on the day of issue for each stamp was 50c.

Birds — A624

No. 1184: a, Cuculus canorus. b, Alauda arvensis. c, Perisoreus infaustus.

Syncopated Die Cut Perf. 10 Horiz.

2003, Jan. 15 **Self-Adhesive**

Coil Stamps

1184 Horiz. strip of 3 8.00 8.00
a.-c. A624 1 Any single 2.50 2.50

Nos. 1184a-1184c were sold in boxes of 100 that sold at a discount price of €57 on day of issue. The franking value on the day of issue for each stamp was 60c.

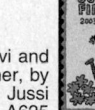

Viivi and Wagner, by Jussi Tuomola — A625

No. 1185: a, Viivi and Wagner running. b, Viivi and Wagner dancing. c, Viivi writing love letter. d, Wagner and Viivi in bed. e, Viivi and Wagner kissing. f, Wagner reading love letter.

Serpentine Die Cut 11½x11¾ on 3 Sides

2003, Jan. 15 Self-Adhesive

1185	Booklet pane of 6	15.00	
a.-f.	A625 1 Any single	2.50	1.25
	Booklet, #1185	15.00	

Nos. 1185a-1185f each sold for 60c on day of issue.

Ice Hockey World Championships — A626

2003, Mar. 3 Litho. *Perf. 13¼x13¾*

1186 A626 65c multi 2.00 .75

St. Bridget (1303-73) — A627

2003, Mar. 3 *Perf. 13*

1187 A627 65c multi 2.00 .75

Viola Wittrockiana — A628

Die Cut Perf. 13¾x14

2003, Mar. 3 Photo.

Self-Adhesive

1188 A628 65c multi 2.00 1.25

Fighting Wood Grouses, by Ferdinand von Wright — A629

2003, Mar. 3 *Die Cut Perf. 13¾*

Self-Adhesive

1189 A629 90c multi 3.00 1.25

Airplanes A630

No. 1190: a, Super Caravelle. b, Airbus 320. c, Junkers Ju 52/3m. d, Douglas DC-3.

Perf. 14x14½ on 3 Sides

2003, Mar. 3

1190	Booklet pane of 4 + 4 etiquettes	8.00	—
a.-d.	A630 65c Any single	2.00	1.00
	Complete booklet, #1190	8.00	

Finnair, 80th anniv.; Powered flight, cent.

Europa A631

No. 1191 — Posters by Lasse Hietala: a, Woman with newspaper. b, Hearts.

2003, May 7 Litho. *Perf. 13¾x13¼*

1191	A631 Pair	*4.25*	*3.75*
a.-b.	65c Either single	1.90	1.50

Souvenir Sheet

Flora and Fauna Seen in Summer — A632

No. 1192: a, Moth, flowers (35x29mm). b, Dragonfly, grasshopper (44x35mm). c, Grasshopper, caterpillar, thistle (35x25mm). d, Frog, flowers, butterfly, insects (44x36mm). e, Magpie, snail, flowers (35x46mm). f, Hedgehog, bee, ant, spider, flowers (44x29mm).

Perf. 14½ on 2 or 3 Sides

2003, May 7

1192	A632 Sheet of 6	12.00	10.00
a.-f.	65c Any single	2.00	1.75

Moomins A633

No. 1193: a, Moomin ancestors. b, Moomins around stove. c, Moomin standing on hands in water. d, Moomin and fox. e, Moomin looking at film negative. f, Moomin with hat, flowers.

Serpentine Die Cut 11½x11¾ on 3 Sides

2003, May 7 Photo.

Self-Adhesive

1193	Booklet pane of 6	15.00	—
a.-f.	A633 1 Any single	2.50	.75
	Complete booklet, #1193	15.00	

Nos. 1193a-1193f each sold for 65c on day of issue.

Cupid A634

Serpentine Die Cut 11½ Syncopated

2003, May 14 Litho.

Self-Adhesive

1194 A634 1 multi 2.50 1.50

No. 1194 could be personalized. It sold for 65c on day of issue.

Lingonberries — A635

Serpentine Die Cut 14

2003, Sept. 10 Photo.

Self-Adhesive

1195 A635 65c multi 2.00 .75

Philanthropists A636

No. 1196: a, Juho (1852-1913) and Maria (1858-1923) Lallukka. b, Emil Aaltonen (1869-1949), vert. c, Heikki Huhtamäki (1900-70), vert. d, Antti (1883-1962) and Jenny Wihuri. e, Alfred Kordelin (1868-1917), vert. f, Amos Anderson (1878-1961), vert.

Perf. 13¼x13¾, 13¾x13¼ on 3 Sides

2003, Sept. 10 Litho.

1196	Booklet pane of 6	15.00	15.00
a.-f.	A636 65c Any single	2.50	2.50
	Complete booklet, #1196	11.50	

Lighthouses — A637

No. 1197: a, Bengtskär. b, Russarö. c, Rönnskär. d, Harmaja Grahara. e, Söderskär.

2003, Sept. 10 *Perf. 13¼x13¾*

1197	A637 Sheet of 5	12.50	9.50
a.-e.	1 Any single	2.50	.85

Nos. 1197a-1197e sold for 65c on day of issue. Size of No. 1197a, 28x45mm; Nos. 1197b-1197e, 21x36mm.

Christmas A638

Designs: 45c, Elf mailing letter. 65c, Elf with ginger biscuit on baking pan, vert.

Serpentine Die Cut 14x14¼, 14¼x14

2003, Oct. 31 Photo.

Self-Adhesive

1198-1199 A638 Set of 2 4.00 2.10

Slightly larger versions of No. 1198 with a serpentine die cutting of 13¼x13¾ and of No. 1199 with a serpentine die cutting of 13¾x13¼ exist only on first day and other covers produced by the postal service. They were not sold unused to the public.

Apples A639

Serpentine Die Cut 11½ Syncopated

2003, Oct. 31 Litho.

Self-Adhesive

1200 A639 1 multi 2.50 1.50

No. 1200 could be personalized. It sold for 65c on day of issue.

Pres. Tarja Halonen, 60th Birthday — A640

2003, Dec. 1 Litho. *Perf. 13*

1201 A640 65c multi 2.00 .75

Linnaea Borealis — A641

Die Cut Perf. 14

2004, Jan. 14 Photo.

Self-Adhesive

1202 A641 30c multi 1.00 .60

Souvenir Sheet

Johan Ludvig Runeberg (1804-77), Poet — A642

No. 1203: a, Title page of *Tales of Ensign Stahl.* b, Sven Dufva with gun. c, Illustration for "Our Country." d, Sculpture of Runeberg.

Perf. 13½x13¼ on 3 or 4 Sides

2004, Jan. 14 Litho.

1203 A642 65c Sheet of 4, #a-d 8.00 6.00

Jean Sibelius (1865-1957), Composer A643

No. 1204: a, Satu, and Sibelius, paintings by Akseli Gallen-Kallela. b, Hands of Sibelius on piano keyboard. c, Swans, musical score by Sibelius.

No. 1205: a, Sibelius' house, Ainola. b, Sibelius and wife, Aino. c, Score of "Voces Intimae."

Die Cut Perf. 10 Horiz. Syncopated

2004, Jan. 14 Photo.

Coil Stamps

Self-Adhesive

1204	Horiz. strip of 3	12.00	—
a.-c.	A643 2 Any single	3.00	1.50
1205	Horiz. strip of 3	12.00	
a.-c.	A643 1 Any single	3.00	1.50

Nos. 1204a-1204c each sold for 55c on day of issue and have two short syncopations; Nos. 1205a-1205c each sold for 65c on day of issue, and have one large syncopation.

Love — A644

Text and: a, Rose. b, Man kissing. c, Woman's eye. d, Man and woman embracing. e, Elderly woman. f, Hand pulling petal from daisy.

Serpentine Die Cut 11½x11¾ on 3 Sides

2004, Jan. 14 Self-Adhesive

1206	Booklet pane of 6	15.00	—
a.-f.	A644 1 Any single	2.50	.75

Nos. 1206a-1206f each sold for 65c on day of issue.

Ursus Arctos — A645

2004, Mar. 1 ***Die Cut Perf. 14***

Self-Adhesive

1207 A645 2 multi 2.25 1.00
a. Pale yellow background, animal name 8mm long 4.00 4.00

No. 1207 sold for 55c on day of issue. No. 1207 has a pale pink background and animal name is 6mm long.
Issued: No. 1207a, 2009.

Rose — A646

2004, Mar. 1 **Booklet Stamp**

Self-Adhesive

1208 A646 1 multi 2.50 1.40
a. Booklet pane of 10 25.00

No. 1208 sold for 65c on day of issue. Booklet pane was sold folded.

Easter Flowers — A647

Die Cut Perf. 14

2004, Mar. 1 **Self-Adhesive** **Litho.**

1209 A647 65c multi 2.00 .60

Heraldic Lion Type of 2002

Die Cut Perf. 12 Syncopated

2004, Mar. 1 **Self-Adhesive**

1210 A616 €3 multi 9.50 3.75

Swallows A648

Orchid A649

Serpentine Die Cut 11½ Syncopated

2004, Mar. 26 **Self-Adhesive**

1211 A648 1 multi 2.50 2.00
1212 A649 1 multi 2.50 2.00

Nos. 1211-1212 each sold for 65c on day of issue, and they could be personalized.

Souvenir Sheet

Norse Gods — A650

No. 1213: a, Head of Luonnotar (33x30mm). b, Luonnotar with arms extended (22x42mm).

Perf. 14¼x14½ (#1213a), 14½x14 (#1213b)

2004, Mar. 26

1213 A650 65c Sheet of 2, #a-b 6.25 6.25

Forest Animals — A651

No. 1214: a, Red squirrel (40x40mm). b, Raven (40x31mm). c, Variable hare (40x34mm). d, Stoat (40x37mm). e, Lizard (40x34mm). f, Red fox (40x40mm).

Perf. 13¼x14 on 2 or 3 Sides

2004, Apr. 28

1214 A651 Sheet of 6 14.00 11.50
a.-f. 65c Any single 2.25 1.25

Fragaria Vesca — A652

Die Cut Perf. 14

2004, Apr. 28 **Photo.**

Self-Adhesive

1215 A652 65c multi 2.00 1.40

Luxembourg Gardens, by Albert Edelfelt (1854-1905) A653

2004, Apr. 28 **Self-Adhesive**

1216 A653 1 multi 2.50 .75

No. 1216 sold for 65c on day of issue.

Europa — A654

No. 1217: a, People around campfire. b, Family in rowboat.

2004, Apr. 28 **Litho.** ***Perf. 13***

1217 A654 65c Horiz. pair, #a-b *4.00* *3.75*

Snufkin and Moomintroll A655

Litho. & Embossed

2004, Sept. 8 ***Perf. 13***

Flocked Paper

1218 A655 1 multi *7.00* 2.00

No. 1218 sold for 65c on day of issue.

Shipwreck Treasures A656

No. 1219: a, Tankard. b, Fabric seal. c, Gold watch. d, Powder keg. e, Figurehead (23x40mm).

Perf. 14¼x13 on 3 or 4 Sides

2004, Sept. 8

1219 Booklet pane of 5 12.50 8.00
a.-e. A656 1 Any single 2.50 1.60
Complete booklet, #1219 12.50

Stamps sold for 65c each on day of issue.

Souvenir Sheet

Sammallahdenmäki, UNESCO World Heritage Site — A657

No. 1220: a, Stone wall and trees. b, Lichen-covered rocks.

2004, Sept. 8 **Litho.** ***Perf. 14¾x14¼***

1220 A657 65c Sheet of 2, #a-b 4.00 3.75

Rights of the Child — A658

No. 1221: a, Two girls. b, Boy painting.

2004, Oct. 29 ***Perf. 13***

1221 A658 65c Horiz. pair, #a-b 6.25 3.75

Christmas A659

Designs: 45c, Boy writing Santa Claus. 65c, Christmas tree branch, candle, ornaments, vert.

Serpentine Die Cut 13¼x13¾, 13¾x13¼

2004, Oct. 29 **Photo.**

Self-Adhesive

1222-1223 A659 Set of 2 3.50 2.50

Rotary International, Cent. — A660

2005, Jan. 14 **Litho.** ***Perf. 13***

1224 A660 65c blue & gold 2.00 1.00

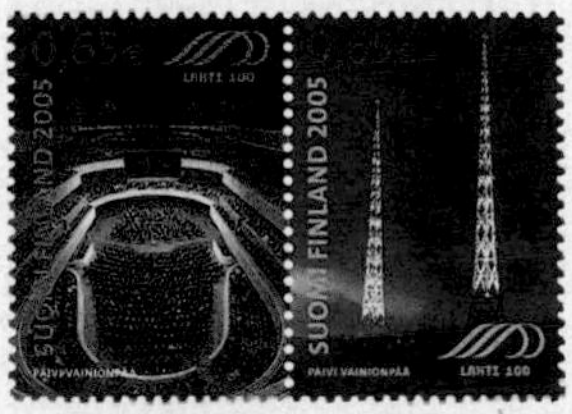

Lahti, Cent. — A661

No. 1225: a, Sibelius Concert Hall. b, Illuminated radio towers.

2005, Jan. 14

1225 A661 65c Pair, #a-b 4.00 3.25

Oulo, 400th Anniv. — A662

No. 1226: a, Child with pail and shovel. b, Woman riding bicycle.

2005, Jan. 14

1226 A662 65c Horiz. pair, #a-b 4.00 3.25

Publishing of First Finnish Almanac, 300th Anniv. — A663

Die Cut Perf. 14

2005, Jan. 14 **Photo.**

Self-Adhesive

1227 A663 65c multi 2.00 .75

Children's Toys — A664

No. 1228: a, Stuffed lion and tiger. b, Stuffed elephant and dog. c, Airplane, train and car. d, Stuffed bear and rabbit.

Serpentine Die Cut 9¼x8½ on 3 Sides

2005, Jan. 14 **Self-Adhesive**

1228 Booklet pane of 4 10.00 —
a.-d. A664 1 Any single 2.50 1.25

Stamps sold for 65c each on day of issue.

End of Winter War, 65th Anniv. — A665

2005, Mar. 2 **Litho.** ***Perf. 13***

1229 A665 65c multi 2.00 1.25

Easter — A666

2005, Mar. 2 ***Serpentine Die Cut 14***

Self-Adhesive

1230 A666 65c multi 2.00 1.00

Apple Blossom — A667

Die Cut Perf. 14

2005, Mar. 2 Photo.

Booklet Stamp

Self-Adhesive

1231 A667 1 multi 2.50 1.40
a. Booklet pane of 10 25.00

No. 1231 sold for 65c on day of issue.

Door Decoration, by Eliel Saarinen A668

Copper Stove Door — A669

Chair Back — A670

Stained Glass Window, by Olga Gummerus-Ehrström — A671

Dining Room — A672

Exterior of Hvitträsk A673

Die Cut Perf. 10 Horiz. Syncopated

2005, Mar. 2 Litho.

Self-Adhesive

Coil Stamps

1232 Horiz. strip of 3 10.00
a. A668 2 multi 2.75 .90
b. A669 2 multi 2.75 .90
c. A670 2 multi 2.75 .90

1233 Horiz. strip of 3 10.00
a. A671 1 multi 2.75 .90
b. A672 1 multi 2.75 .90
c. A673 1 multi 2.75 .90

Hvitträsk, home and studio of architects Eliel Saarinen, Armas Lindgren and Herman Gesellius. Nos. 1232a-1232c each sold for 55c on day of issue and have two short syncopations. Nos. 1233a-1233c each sold for 65c on day of issue and have one large syncopation.

Miniature Schnauzer A674

Serpentine Die Cut 11½ Syncopated

2005, Apr. 6

1234 A674 1 multi 2.50 1.90

Sold for 65c on day of issue. Sheets could be personalized.

Europa — A675

No. 1235 — Plates with: a, Whitefish and beetroot tartare on lettuce. b, Sauteed reindeer and grouse breast.

2005, May 11 ***Perf. 13***

1235 A675 65c Pair, #a-b *4.00 3.50*

Souvenir Sheet

Golf — A676

No. 1236: a, Man driving ball (44x31mm). b, Boy holding flag, vert. (30x44mm). c, Boy putting, vert. (33x44mm). d, Putter and golf ball (44x32mm).

Perf. 13¼ on 3 or 4 Sides

2005, May 11

1236 A676 65c Sheet of 4, #a-d 8.00 6.50

World Track Championships, Helsinki — A677

Serpentine Die Cut 12½

2005, May 11 Self-Adhesive

1237 A677 65c multi 2.00 1.00

Buses in Finland, Cent. A678

Die Cut Perf. 14

2005, May 11 Photo.

Self-Adhesive

1238 A678 65c brown & black 2.00 1.00

Horses — A679

No. 1239: a, Icelandic horse with saddle. b, White Welsh Mountain pony. c, New Forest pony with blanket. d, Shetland Pony.

Serpentine Die Cut 9¼x8½ on 3 Sides

2005, May 11 Self-Adhesive

1239 Booklet pane of 4 10.00
a.-d. A679 1 Any single 2.50 1.00

Stamps sold for 65c each on day of issue.

Cloudberries — A680

Die Cut Perf. 14

2005, Sept. 7 Photo.

Self-Adhesive

1240 A680 1 multi 2.50 1.40

Sold for 65c on day of issue.

Fruits I, by Kari Huhtamo A681

Die Cut Perf. 11½ Syncopated

2005, Sept. 7 Litho.

Self-Adhesive

1241 A681 90c multi 3.00 2.00

Sheets could be personalized.

Souvenir Sheet

Petäjävesi Church, UNESCO World Heritage Site — A682

No. 1242: a, Bell tower (26x47mm). b, Church (34x39mm). c, Angel (26x39mm). d, Chandelier (27x39mm).

2005, Sept. 7 Litho. ***Perf. 13***

1242 A682 65c Sheet of 4, #a-d 8.00 6.00

Icebreakers — A683

No. 1243: a, Urho, 1975. b, Otso, 1986. c, Fennica, 1993. d, Botnica, 1998.

2005, Sept. 7 ***Perf. 13¼ Horiz.***

1243 Booklet pane of 4 10.00 —
a.-d. A683 1 Any single 2.50 1.00

Each stamp sold for 65c on day of issue.

Souvenir Sheet

Imperial Winter Egg, by Carl Fabergé — A684

No. 684: a, Flowers in egg. b, Frost detail of egg.

Litho. & Embossed with Foil Application

2005, Oct. 28 ***Perf. 13***

1244 A684 €3.50 Sheet of 2, #a-b 22.50 20.00

A limited quantity of 2,500 numbered sheets, which sold for €30, exist. Value, $100.

Christmas — A685

Designs: 50c, Santa Claus reading letters. 1, Santa Claus and wife dancing, horiz.

Serpentine Die Cut 13¾x13¼, 13¼x13¾

2005, Oct. 28 Photo.

Self-Adhesive

1245-1246 A685 Set of 2 4.00 1.50

No. 1246 sold for 65c on day of issue.

Postal Employees Union, Cent. — A686

2006, Jan. 11 Litho. ***Perf. 13***

1247 A686 65c multi 2.00 .75

Heart — A687

2006, Jan. 11 ***Die Cut***

Self-Adhesive

1248 A687 65c bright pink 2.00 .75

Renaming of Helsinki University Library as National Library of Finland — A688

2006, Jan. 11 ***Die Cut Perf. 14x13¾***

Self-Adhesive

1249 A688 1 multi 2.50 1.40

Sold for 65c on day of issue.

Forest in Winter — A689

2006, Jan. 11 **Photo.**

Self-Adhesive

1250 A689 1 multi 2.50 1.40

Sold for 65c on day of issue.

Taxis, Cent. — A690

No. 1251: a, Women passengers in taxi, 1906. b, Driver standing in front of 1929 Chevrolet taxi. c, Driver leaning on 1957 Pobeda taxi. d, Driver on phone at taxi stand next to Mercedes-Benz taxi.

Serpentine Die Cut 11¼ Vert.

2006, Jan. 11 **Litho.**

Self-Adhesive

1251 Booklet pane of 4 8.00 —
a.-d. A690 65c Any single 2.00 .75

Souvenir Sheet

Johan Vilhelm Snellman (1806-81), Philosopher — A691

No. 1252: a, Caricature of Snellman, masthead of his newspaper "Saima." b, Snellman's portrait on 1940 five thousand mark note. c, Snellman and European railway map. d, Ilmarinen, first Finnish locomotive, and European railway map.

2006, Jan. 11 ***Perf. 13¼x13¾***

1252 A691 65c Sheet of 4, #a-d 8.00 8.00

Parliament, Cent. — A692

Serpentine Die Cut 14

2006, Feb. 3 **Litho.**

Self-Adhesive

1253 A692 1 multi 2.50 1.40

Sold for 65c on day of sale.

Flag — A693

2006, Mar. 1 **Self-Adhesive**

1254 A693 1 multi 2.50 1.40

Sold for 65c on day of sale.

Lilacs — A694

Die Cut Perf. 13¾x14

2006, Mar. 1 **Photo.**

Self-Adhesive

1255 A694 1 multi 2.50 1.40

Sold for 65c on day of sale.

Easter — A695

2006, Mar. 1 **Litho.** ***Die Cut***

Self-Adhesive

1256 A695 65c multi 2.00 1.00

Fortune Teller, by Helene Schjerfbeck — A696

Die Cut Perf. 13¾x14

2006, Mar. 1 **Photo.**

Self-Adhesive

1257 A696 95c multi 3.00 2.25

Bil-Bol Poster A697

Errotaja 2 Poster A698

Concert Finnois Poster A699

Madonna A700

Self-Portrait A701

Home of Artist Akseli Gallen-Kallela, Tarvaspää — A702

Die Cut Perf. 10 Horiz. Syncopated

2006, Mar. 1 **Self-Adhesive**

Coil Stamps

1258 Horiz. strip of 3 6.75 —
a. A697 2 multi 2.25 2.25
b. A698 2 multi 2.25 2.25
c. A699 2 multi 2.25 2.25

Die Cut Perf. 10 Vert. Syncopated

1259 Vert. strip of 3 6.75 —
a. A700 1 multi 2.25 .75
b. A701 1 multi 2.25 .75
c. A702 1 multi 2.25 .75

Akseli Gallen-Kallela (1865-1931), artist. Nos. 1258a-1258c each sold for 55c and Nos. 1259a-1259c each sold for 65c on day of issue.

Souvenir Sheet

Norse Mythology — A703

No. 1260 — Fairy tale book cover illustrations by Rudolf Koivu: a, Fairy. b, Fairy dancing with Santa Claus, vert.

Perf. 13½x13¼, 13¼x13½ (#1260b)

2006, Mar. 29 **Litho.**

1260 A703 65c Sheet of 2, #a-b 4.00 4.00

Europa A704

2006, May 4 ***Perf. 13***

1261 A704 65c multi 2.00 1.00

Vaasa, 400th Anniv. — A705

2006, May 4

1262 A705 1 multi 2.50 1.00

Sold for 65c on day of issue.

A706

Serpentine Die Cut 10 Syncopated

2006, May 4 **Booklet Stamp**

Self-Adhesive

1263 A706 1 multi 2.50 1.50
a. Booklet pane of 8 20.00

No. 1263 sold for 65c on day of issue. Design portion of stamp could be personalized.

Summer Activities A707

No. 1264: a, Woman fishing. b, Children making flower garlands. c, Man making sauna whisk. d, Woman weeding flower garden.

Serpentine Die Cut 11¼ Vert.

2006, May 4 **Self-Adhesive**

1264 Booklet pane of 4 10.00
a.-d. A707 1 Any single 2.50 1.00

Nos. 1264a-1264d each sold for 65c on day of issue.

Cats — A708

No. 1265: a, Striped house cat. b, British shorthair (gray cat). c, Ragdoll cat (brown and white). d, Chocolate Persian cat.

2006, May 4 **Self-Adhesive**

1265 Booklet pane of 4 10.00
a.-d. A708 1 Any single 2.50 1.00

Nos. 1265a-1265d each sold for 65c on day of issue.

Suomenlinna (Sveaborg) Fortress, Helsinki — A709

No. 1266: a, Ship without oars. b, Ship with oars facing fortress. c, Ship with oars, windmill.

Litho. & Engr.

2006, May 4 ***Perf. 13x12¾***

1266 A709 Booklet pane of 3 7.50 —
a.-c. 1 Any single 2.50 1.00
Complete booklet, #1266 7.50

Nos. 1266a-1266c each sold for 65c on day of issue. See Sweden No. 2530.

Blueberries and Blueberry Pie — A710

Die Cut Perf. 14

2006, Aug. 24 **Photo.**

Self-Adhesive

1267 A710 1 multi 2.50 1.40

Sold for 70c on day of issue.

Miniature Sheet

Family Life — A711

No. 1268: a, Family watching television. b, Woman writing letter to husband.

2006, Aug. 24 ***Die Cut***

Self-Adhesive

1268 A711 1 Sheet of 2, #a-b 5.00 2.50

Nos. 1268a-1268b each sold for 70c on day of issue.

Newspaper Journalism — A712

Die Cut Perf. 14

2006, Sept. 22 **Litho.**

Self-Adhesive

1269 A712 70c multi 2.25 1.00

Points, Textile Art by Ritva Puotila — A713

Serpentine Die Cut 11½ Syncopated

2006, Sept. 22 **Self-Adhesive**

1270 A713 1 multi 2.50 1.75

Sold for 70c on day of issue.

Dryas Octopetala A714

Serpentine Die Cut 14

2006, Sept. 22 **Photo.**

Self-Adhesive

1271 A714 1 multi 2.50 1.00

Sold for 70c on day of issue.

Art of Snow and Ice — A715

No. 1272: a, Horse. b, Kemi Snow Castle. c, Wall of ice tiles. d, Snowball lantern.

Serpentine Die Cut 11¾ Vert.

2006, Sept. 22 **Self-Adhesive**

1272 Booklet pane of 4 10.00

a.-d. A715 1 Any single 2.50 2.50

Nos. 1272a-1272d each sold for 70c on day of issue. Denominations are printed in thermographic ink that changes color when warmed.

Miniature Sheet

Finnish Postage Stamps, 150th Anniv. — A716

No. 1273: a, 70c, Heraldic lion and fleurons in white. b, 95c, Part of vignette of type A1. c, €1.40, Heraldic lion in gold, fleurons in red.

Litho. & Embossed With Foil Application

2006, Oct. 27 ***Perf. 13½x13***

1273 A716 Sheet of 3, #a-c 9.50 9.50

A717

Christmas — A718

Serpentine Die Cut 13¼x13¾

2006, Oct. 27 **Photo.**

Self-Adhesive

1274 A717 50c multi 1.40 .90

Serpentine Die Cut 13¾x13¼

1275 A718 1 multi 2.75 .90

No. 1275 sold for 70c on day of issue.

Television Broadcasting in Finland, 50th Anniv. — A719

Die Cut Perf. 14

2007, Jan. 24 **Litho.**

Self-Adhesive

1276 A719 70c multi 2.25 1.50

Faces — A720

2007, Jan. 24 **Self-Adhesive**

1277 A720 70c multi 2.25 1.50

Winter Landscape, Haminalahti, by Ferdinand von Wright A721

2007, Jan. 24 **Photo.**

Booklet Stamp

Self-Adhesive

1278 A721 1 multi 2.50 1.50

a. Booklet pane of 10 25.00

Sold for 70c on day of issue.

Sun Setting Over Flower Field — A722

2007, Jan. 24 **Litho.**

Self-Adhesive

1279 A722 €1.40 multi 4.50 3.00

Souvenir Sheet

Intl. Polar Year — A723

No. 1280: a, Snowflake. b, Aurora borealis.

Perf. 13 Syncopated (#1280a), 13 (#1280b)

Litho. With Hologram Affixed

2007, Jan. 24

1280 A723 70c Sheet of 2, #a-b + label 4.50 4.00

Truck Transport — A724

No. 1281: a, Log truck. b, Milk truck. c, Dump truck. d, Tractor trailer.

Serpentine Die Cut 12¼ Horiz.

2007, Jan. 24 **Litho.**

Self-Adhesive

1281 Booklet pane of 4 9.00 6.00

a.-d. A724 70c Any single 2.25 1.40

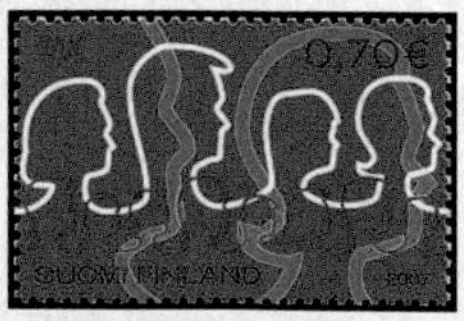

Central Organization of Finnish Trade Unions — A725

2007, Mar. 7 ***Perf. 13***

1282 A725 70c multi 2.25 1.50

Soccer Association of Finland, Cent. — A726

2007, Mar. 7 ***Die Cut***

Self-Adhesive

1283 A726 70c multi 2.25 1.50

Easter — A727

2007, Mar. 7 ***Die Cut Perf. 14***

Self-Adhesive

1284 A727 1 multi 2.50 1.50

Sold for 70c on day of issue. Portions of design were applied by a thermographic process producing a shiny, raised effect.

Lilium Enchantment A728

2007, Mar. 7 **Litho.**

Booklet Stamp

Self-Adhesive

1285 A728 1 multi 2.50 1.50

a. Booklet pane of 10 25.00

No. 1285 sold for 70c on day of issue.

Souvenir Sheet

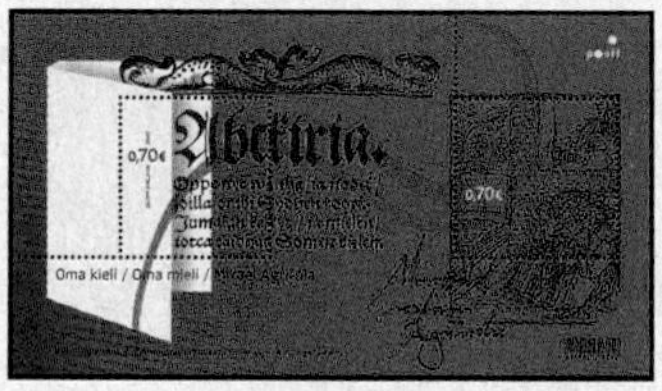

Bishop Michael Agricola (1509-57) — A729

No. 1286: a, Text and open book. b, Agricola preaching.

2007, Mar. 7 ***Perf. 13½***

1286 A729 70c Sheet of 2, #a-b 4.50 4.00

Tampere Cathedral, Cent. — A730

2007, May 9 ***Perf. 13¼***

1287 A730 70c multi 2.25 1.25

Europa — A731

No. 1288: a, Scouts on sailboat. b, Scouts around campfire.

2007, May 9 ***Perf. 12½x13***

1288 A731 Horiz. pair 4.50 4.50

a.-b. 70c Either single 2.25 2.25

Scouting, cent.

Helsinki Public Transportation — A732

No. 1289: a, Commuter train in station. b, Tram on street. c, Subway train on bridge. d. People in Kamppi Bus Station.

Serpentine Die Cut 12¼ Horiz.

2007, May 9 Self-Adhesive

1289		Booklet pane of 4	10.00	8.00
a.-d.	A732	1 Any single	2.50	1.50

Nos. 1289a-1289d each sold for 70c on day of issue.

Moomins A733

No. 1290: a, Little My in water. b, Moomintroll running across rocks. c, Moominpappa at typewriter. d, Snork Maiden picking flowers. e, Moominmamma making pancakes. f, Snufkin amid flowers.

Serpentine Die Cut 11¾ Vert.

2007, May 9 Photo.

Self-Adhesive

1290		Booklet pane of 6	15.00	
a.-f.	A733	1 Any single	2.50	1.25

Nos. 1290a-1290f each sold for 70c on day of issue.

Souvenir Sheet

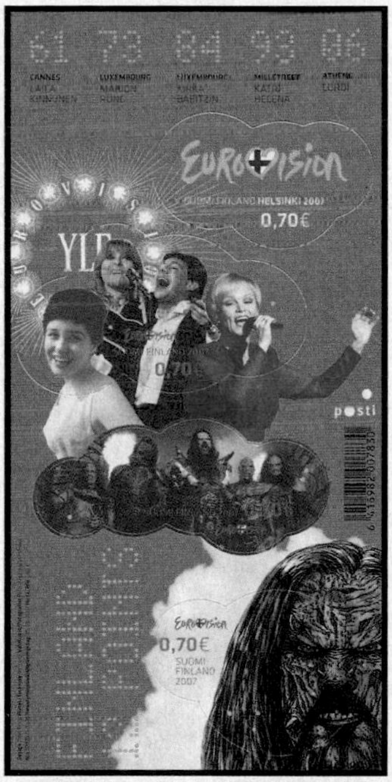

2007 Eurovision Song Contest, Helsinki — A734

No. 1291: a, Eurovision Song Contest emblem. b, Finnish singers Laila Kinnunen, Marion Rung, Kirka Babitzin and Katri Helena. c, 2006 Finnish contest-winning band, Lordi. d, Lead singer of Lordi.

Litho. With Foil Application

2007, May 9 ***Die Cut***

Self-Adhesive

1291	A734	70c Sheet of 4, #a-d	9.00	9.00

A735

Serpentine Die Cut 11½ Syncopated

2007, Aug. 24 Litho.

Self-Adhesive

1292	A735	1 multi	2.50	1.25

No. 1292 sold for 70c on day of issue. Design portion of stamp could be personalized.

Home Furnishings — A736

No. 1293 — Picture frame and: a, Empire-style chair, "Porvoo Garland" wallpaper, 19th cent. (country name at LR). b, Paimio chair, "2+3" wallpaper, 20th cent. (country name at LL).

Die Cut Perf. 14

2007, Aug. 24 Litho.

Self-Adhesive

1293		Pair	5.00	
a.-b.	A736	1 Either single	2.50	1.25

Nos. 1293a-1293b each sold for 70c on day of issue.

Raspberries and Raspberry Cake — A737

Die Cut Perf. 14

2007, Aug. 24 Photo.

Self-Adhesive

Booklet Stamp

1294	A737	1 multi	2.50	1.25

No. 1294 sold for 70c on day of issue.

Finnish Olympic Committee, Cent. — A738

2007, Aug. 24 Litho.

Self-Adhesive

Booklet Stamp

1295	A738	1 multi	2.50	1.25

No. 1295 sold for 70c on day of issue.

Butterflies — A739

No. 1296: a, Apatura iris. b, Scolitantides orion. c, Colias palaeno.

Die Cut Perf. 10 Vert., Syncopated at Right

2007, Aug. 24 Self-Adhesive

Coil Stamps

1296		Vert. strip of 3	7.50	
a.-c.	A739	1 Any single	2.50	2.50

Nos. 1296a-1296c had a franking value of 70c on day of issue. A roll of 100 stamps sold for €68.

Miniature Sheet

Independence, 90th Anniv. — A740

No. 1297 — Photographs of people at work and play: a, Man and horse hauling wood. b, Girl blowing horn. c, Four boys with skis. d, People at coffee break. e, People near bonfire. f, Boy ski jumping. g, Boy diving. h, Ice fisherman. Nos. 1297a-1297d are black and white photos.

2007, Nov. 2 ***Perf. 13¼***

1297	A740	Sheet of 8	18.00	16.50
a.-h.		70c Any single	2.25	1.50

Souvenir Sheet

Woodwork — A741

No. 1298: a, Zltan armchair with dragon design, China (denomination at left). b, Modern Finnish bowls (denomination at right).

2007, Nov. 2 ***Perf. 13¼x14¼***

1298	A741	Sheet of 2	4.50	4.50
a.-b.		70c Either single	2.25	1.75

See Hong Kong Nos. 1298-1299.

A742

Christmas — A743

Serpentine Die Cut 13¼x13¾

2007, Nov. 2 Photo.

Self-Adhesive

1299	A742	55c multi	1.75	1.25

Serpentine Die Cut 13¾x13¼

1300	A743	1 multi	2.50	1.75

No. 1300 sold for 70c on day of issue.

A744

A745

Water — A746

A747

A748

Islands — A749

2008, Jan. 24 Photo. ***Die Cut***

Self-Adhesive

1301		Horiz. strip of 3	.45	
a.	A744	5c multi	.25	.25
b.	A745	5c multi	.25	.25
c.	A746	5c multi	.25	.25
1302		Horiz. strip of 3	.90	
a.	A747	10c multi	.30	.30
b.	A748	10c multi	.30	.30
c.	A749	10c multi	.30	.30

Souvenir Sheet

Helsinki University of Technology, Cent. — A750

No. 1303: a, Robot. b, University building.

2008, Jan. 24 Litho. ***Perf. 13½x13¼***

1303	A750	Sheet of 2	5.00	4.25
a.-b.		1 Any single	2.50	1.25

Nos. 1303a-1303b each sold for 70c on day of issue.

Miniature Sheet

Love — A751

No. 1304: a, Airplane pulling heart banner. b, Carrier pigeon with envelope. c, Heart-shaped smoke signals. d, Heart and cell phone. e, Bottle with hearts.

2008, Jan. 24 ***Die Cut***

Self-Adhesive

1304	A751	Sheet of 5	12.50	10.50
a.-e.		1 Any single	2.50	1.25

Nos. 1304a-1304e each sold for 70c on day of issue.

Miniature Sheet

Snow Sports — A752

No. 1305: a, Matti Räty in yellow ski suit. b, Antti Autti (snowboarder) in air in red ski suit. c, Tapio Saarimaki in red ski suit. d, Tanja Poutiainen in white and green ski suit.

Litho. With Three-Dimensional Plastic Affixed
Serpentine Die Cut 9 Syncopated

2008, Jan. 24 Self-Adhesive

1305 A752 Sheet of 4 10.00 9.00
a.-d. 1 Any single 2.50 1.25

Nos. 1305a-1305d each sold for 70c on day of issue.

Clock and Lamp on Desk — A753

Die Cut Perf. 13¾

2008, Feb. 27 Litho.
Booklet Stamp
Self-Adhesive

1306 A753 €1.05 multi 3.50 2.60
a. Booklet pane of 10 35.00

Finnish Book Publishers Association, 150th Anniv. — A754

Serpentine Die Cut 13¼

2008, Feb. 27 Self-Adhesive

1307 A754 1 multi 2.50 1.75

No. 1307 sold for 70c on day of issue.

Lathyrus Odoratus — A755

Die Cut Perf. 13¾

2008, Feb. 27 Photo.
Self-Adhesive

1308 A755 1 multi 2.50 1.75

No. 1308 sold for 70c on the day of issue and has Braille dots applied by a thermographic process.

Easter — A756

Litho. With Foil Application
Serpentine Die Cut 13¾

2008, Feb. 27 Self-Adhesive

1309 A756 1 multi 2.50 1.75

No. 1309 sold for 70c on day of issue.

Fauna Associated With Weather Forecasting Folk Beliefs — A757

No. 1310: a, Perch. b, Lambs. c, Frogs. d, Swallows. e, Snail.

Serpentine Die Cut 12¼ Horiz.

2008, Feb. 27 Litho.
Self-Adhesive

1310 Booklet pane of 5 12.50 11.00
a.-e. A757 1 Any single 2.50 1.25

Nos. 1310a-1310e each sold for 70c on day of issue.

Souvenir Sheet

Mythical Places — A758

No. 1311: a, Cliff resembling human face, Astuvansalmi. b, Amber carving of head found at Astuvansalmi.

2008, Mar. 27 *Perf. 13½*

1311 A758 Sheet of 2 4.75 4.25
a.-b. 70c Either single 2.25 2.00

Europa — A759

No. 1312 — Handwritten letters and portraits by Pekka Halonen of: a, Himself. b, His wife, Maija.

2008, May 9 *Perf. 13*

1312 A759 Horiz. pair 5.25 5.25
a.-b. 70c Either single 2.50 2.10

Kvarken Archipelago UNESCO World Heritage Site — A760

Serpentine Die Cut 13¾

2008, May 9 Self-Adhesive

1313 A760 €1.50 blk & red 5.50 4.50

Moths — A761

No. 1314: a, Arctia caja. b, Aglia tau. c. Deilephila elpenor.

Die Cut Perf. 10 Syncopated

2008, May 9 Photo.
Coil Stamps
Self-Adhesive

1314 Vert. strip of 3 7.75 7.00
a.-c. A761 1 Any single 2.50 1.25

Nos. 1314a-1314c each sold for 70c on day of issue.

Psychedelic Art — A762

No. 1315: a, Melting mushrooms and teardrops. b, Guitars. c, Flying fish. d, Flowers and woman's legs in high heels. e, Six balloons.

Serpentine Die Cut 12½ Horiz.

2008, May 9 Litho.
Self-Adhesive

1315 Booklet pane of 5 13.00
a.-e. A762 1 Any single 2.60 1.25

Nos. 1315a-1315e each sold for 70c on day of issue.

Modern Art — A763

No. 1316: a, Sinistä ja Punaista, by Sam Vanni. b, Merirosvolaiva, by Kimmo Kaivanto. c, Hiljaisuuden Kuuntelija, by Juhani Linnovaara. d, Odotan Kevään Tuloa, by Göran Augustson. e, Minä, by Carolus Enckell. f, Pöytä, by Reino Hietanen.

Serpentine Die Cut 11¾ Vert.

2008, May 9 Self-Adhesive

1316 Booklet pane of 6 16.00 14.00
a.-f. A763 1 Any single 2.60 1.25

Nos. 1316a-1316f each sold for 70c on day of issue.

Personalized Stamp — A764

Serpentine Die Cut 10

2008, Sept. 5 Litho.
Self-Adhesive

1317 A764 1 multi 2.50 2.00

No. 1317 sold for 80c on day of issue. The generic design portion of the stamp shown could be personalized.

Dogs — A765

No. 1318: a, Spitz with open mouth, facing forward. b, Rough collie, with open mouth, facing right. c, Boxer, facing left. d, Finnish hound, facing left. e, Cavalier King Charles spaniel, facing right. f, Jack Russell terrier, looking over shoulder.

Serpentine Die Cut 11¾ Vert.

2008, Sept. 5 Self-Adhesive

1318 Booklet pane of 6 15.00 13.50
a.-f. A765 1 Any single 2.50 1.25

Nos. 1318a-1318f each sold for 80c on day of issue.

Souvenir Sheet

Mika Waltari (1908-79), Writer — A766

No. 1319: a, Waltari. b, Cover of Waltari's book, *Komisario Palmun Erehdys*.

2008, Sept. 5 *Perf. 14x13½*

1319 A766 Sheet of 2 5.00 4.50
a.-b. 80c Either single 2.50 2.25

Souvenir Sheet

Kimi Räikkönen, 2007 Formula 1 Racing Champion — A767

No. 1320: a, Räikkönen (24x30mm). b, Räikkönen's Ferrari Formula 1 race car (74x30mm).

Die Cut Perf. 11x11½ on 2 Sides (#1320a), 11½ Vert. (#1320b)

2008, Sept. 5 Self-Adhesive

1320 A767 Sheet of 2 5.00 4.50
a.-b. 1 Either single 2.50 2.25

Nos. 1320a-1320b each sold for 80c on day of issue.

Souvenir Sheet

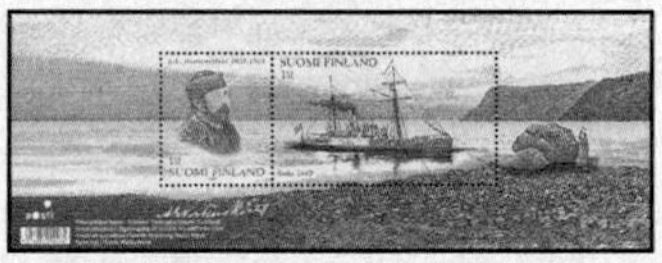

Adolf Erik Nordenskiöld (1832-1901), Arctic Explorer — A768

No. 1321: a, Nordenskiöld (29x34mm). b, Ship Sofia (58x34mm).

Litho. & Engr.

2008, Oct. 20 *Perf. 13x13¼*

1321 A768 Sheet of 2 5.00 4.50
a.-b. 1 Either single 2.50 2.25

Nos. 1321a-1321b each sold for 80c on day of issue. See Greenland Nos. 527-528.

A769

A770

Christmas A771

Die Cut Perf. 14

2008, Nov. 6 Litho.

Self-Adhesive

1322 A769 60c multi 1.75 .75

Serpentine Die Cut 13¼x13¾

Photo.

1323 A770 1 multi 2.75 2.75

Printed On Plastic

Die Cut Perf. 13¾

1324 A771 1 multi 3.00 2.00
Nos. 1322-1324 (3) 7.50 5.50

On day of issue, Nos. 1323 and 1324 each sold for 80c.

Pres. Martti Ahtisaari, 2008 Nobel Peace Laureate A772

2008, Dec. 10 Litho. ***Perf. 13***

1325 A772 80c light blue 2.50 1.25

Hospital Work — A773

2009, Jan. 22 Litho. ***Perf. 13***

1326 A773 80c multi 2.25 1.75

Pallas-Yllästunturi National Park — A774

2009, Jan. 22 ***Die Cut Perf. 14***

Self-Adhesive

1327 A774 1 multi 2.50 1.40

No. 1327 sold for 80c on day of issue and has Braille dots applied in varnish.

Peony — A775

Die Cut Perf. 14

2009, Jan. 22 Photo.

Self-Adhesive

1328 A775 €1.10 multi 3.00 2.25

Children's Dream Occupations A776

No. 1329 — Child dressed as: a, Policeman. b, Doctor. c, Firefighter. d, Skier. e, Construction worker.

Serpentine Die Cut 12¼ Vert.

2009, Jan. 22 Litho.

Self-Adhesive

1329 Booklet pane of 5 12.50 10.00
a.-e. A776 1 Any single 2.50 1.40

Nos. 1329a-1329e each sold for 80c on day of issue.

Miniature Sheet

Finland as Grand Duchy of Russia, 200th Anniv. — A777

No. 1330: a, Tsar Alexander I (1777-1825), facing left with blue sash. b, Count Georg Magnus Sprengtporten (1740-1819), with red sash and gold epaulets. c, Count Carl Erik Mannerheim (1759-1837), without epaulets. d, Count Gustaf Mauritz Armfelt (1757-1814), facing right, with blue sash. Names are on sheet margin.

Litho. & Embossed With Foil Application

2009, Jan. 22 ***Perf. 13¾***

1330 A777 80c Sheet of 4, #a-d 9.00 9.00

Miniature Sheet

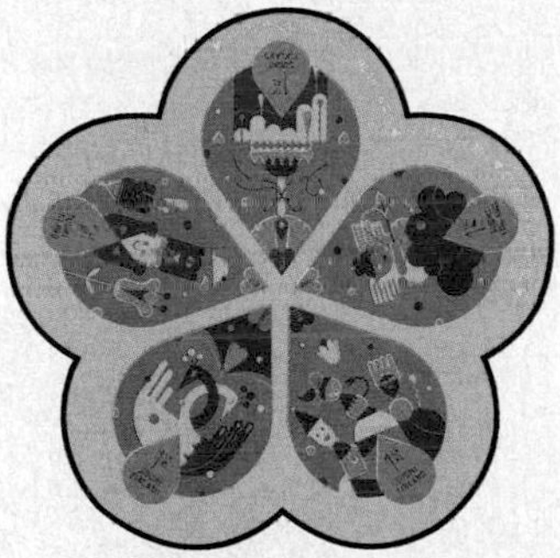

St. Valentine's Day — A778

No. 1331: a, Birthday cake and candle. b, Cupid. c, Three people, flower. d, Swans. e, Teddy bear hugging heart.

2009, Jan. 22 Litho. ***Die Cut***

Self-Adhesive

1331 A778 1 Sheet of 5, #a-e 12.50 10.00

Nos. 1331a-1331e each sold for 80c on day of issue.

Rose — A779

Die Cut Perf. 14

2009, Mar. 18 Litho.

Self-Adhesive

1332 A779 1 multi 2.50 2.00

No. 1332 sold for 80c on day of issue.

Easter — A780

2009, Mar. 18 Self-Adhesive

1333 A780 1 multi 2.50 2.00

No. 1333 sold for 80c on day of issue.

Souvenir Sheet

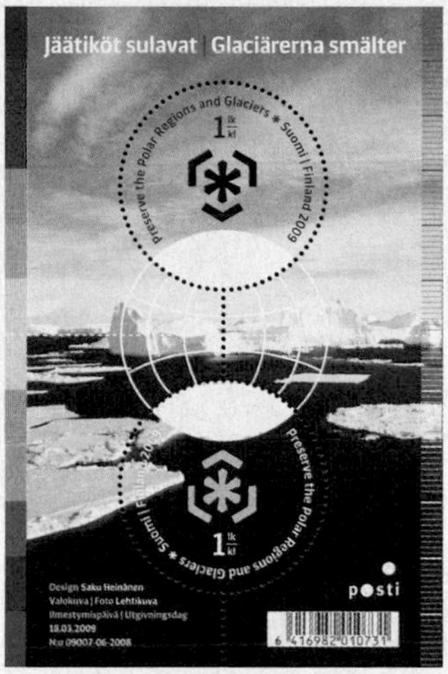

Preservation of Polar Regions and Glaciers — A781

No. 1334: a, Sky, blue emblem. b, Sea and ice, silver emblem.

Litho. With Foil Application

2009, Mar. 18 ***Perf.***

1334 A781 Sheet of 2 5.00 3.75
a.-b. 1 Either single 2.50 1.90

Nos. 1334a-1334b each sold for 80c on day of issue.

Greetings A782

No. 1335: a, Gift and tulips. b, Chocolate-covered strawberries, cake. c, Flowers. d, Coffee cup, letter and rose. e, Dove and apples.

Serpentine Die Cut 10¼ Horiz.

2009, Mar. 18 Litho.

Self-Adhesive

1335 Booklet pane of 5 + 5 labels 12.50
a.-e. A782 1 Any single 2.50 1.25

Nos. 1335a-1335e each sold for 80c on day of issue.

Europa — A783

No. 1336: a, Lake, birds, Moon, stars and other heavenly bodies. b, Lake, comet, Saturn, stars and other heavenly bodies.

2009, May 6 ***Perf. 13***

1336 A783 Horiz. pair 5.00 5.00
a.-b. 80c Either single 2.50 1.75

Intl. Year of Astronomy.

Sauna — A784

No. 1337: a, Towels, scrubber, bucket of birch branches (55x23mm). b, People in sauna (55x23mm). c, Waterside sauna (55x23mm). d, Birch whisk (27x45mm). e, Water tubs and window (27x45mm).

Serpentine Die Cut 11¾ Horiz.

2009, May 6 Self-Adhesive

1337 Booklet pane of 5 12.50
a.-e. A784 1 Any single 2.50 1.40

Nos. 1337a-1337e each sold for 80c on day of issue. No. 1337d is impregnated with a birch scent.

Moomins — A785

No. 1338: a, Moomin carrying purse. b, Moominpappa with hat holding paper. c, Little My holding large pair of glasses. d, Moomin at mirror. e, Moomin and Snufkin fishing. f, Moominpappa slipping down hill.

Serpentine Die Cut 11¾ Horiz.

2009, May 6 Self-Adhesive

1338 Booklet pane of 6 15.00
a.-f. A785 1 Any single 2.50 1.25

Nos. 1338a-1338f each sold for 80c on day of issue.

Miniature Sheet

Women's Fashion — A786

No. 1339: a, Dress by Anna and Tuomas Laitinen (30x45mm). b, Dress by Jasmin Santanen (30x45mm). c, Handbag by Lumi (30x35mm). d, Red shoes by Minna Parikka (30x25mm). e, Shoes by Julia Lundsten (30x30mm).

Serpentine Die Cut 14¼x13¾

2009, May 6 Self-Adhesive

1339 A786 Sheet of 5 12.50 9.50
a.-e. 1 Any single 2.50 1.25

Nos. 1339a-1339e each sold for 80c on day of issue.

Gustavian Style Clock, Table and Candle Holder — A787

Die Cut Perf. 13¾

2009, Sept. 9 Litho.

Self-Adhesive

1340 A787 1 multi 2.50 1.25
a. Booklet pane of 10 25.00

No. 1340 sold for 80c on day of issue.

Aurora Borealis — A788

No. 1341 — Various pictures of Aurora Borealis taken at: a, 65 degrees, 1 minute, 17.03 seconds north; 25 degrees, 39 minutes, 31.26 seconds east. b, 65 degrees, 57.16 seconds north; 25 degrees, 39 minutes, 41.01 seconds east. c, 67 degrees, 45 minutes, 2.44 seconds north; 23 degrees, 36 minutes, 41.53 seconds east.

Die Cut Perf. 10 Vert., Syncopated at Right

2009, Sept. 9 Self-Adhesive

Coil Stamps

1341 Vert. strip of 3 7.50
a.-c. A788 1 Any single 2.50 1.25

Nos. 1341a-1341c each sold for 80c on day of issue.

Paintings of Flowers — A789

No. 1342: a, Snapdragons, by Helene Schjerfbeck. b, Blooming Irises, by Wäinö Aaltonen. c, Burnet Roses, by Eero Järnefelt. d, Lone Calla, by Ester Helenius. e, Amaryllis, by Birger Carlstedt. f, Still Life with Carnations, by Tuomas von Boehm.

Serpentine Die Cut 11¾ Horiz.

2009, Sept. 9 **Self-Adhesive**

1342 Booklet pane of 6 15.00
a.-f. A789 1 Any single 2.50 1.25

Nos. 1342a-1342f each sold for 80c on day of issue.

Wreath — A790

Girl and Basket of Apples — A791

Amaryllis A792

Personalized Stamp — A793

Die Cut Perf. 14

2009, Nov. 6 **Litho.**

Self-Adhesive

1343 Horiz. pair 3.75
a. A790 60c multi 1.75 .50
b. A791 60c multi 1.75 .50
1344 A792 1 multi 2.50 2.25

Serpentine Die Cut 11½x11¾ Syncopated

1345 A793 1 multi 2.50 2.25

Nos. 1344 and 1345 each sold for 80c on day of issue. The generic design portion of No. 1345, shown, could be personalized.

Antennaria Dioica — A794

Die Cut Perf. 11 Syncopated

2010, Jan. 25 **Litho.**

Self-Adhesive

1346 A794 1 multi 2.75 2.25

No. 1346 sold for 80c on day of issue.

Miniature Sheet

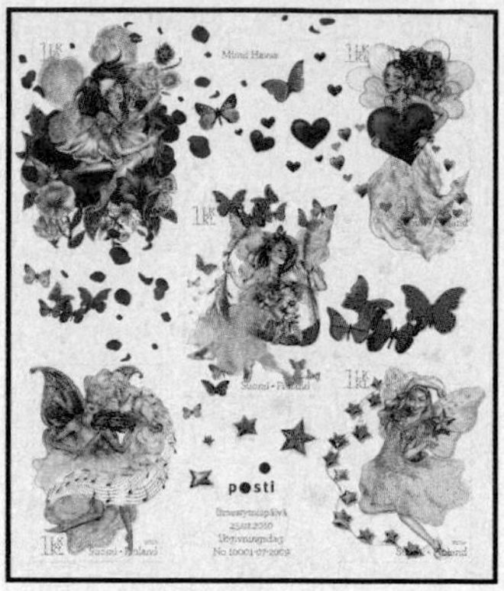

Fairies — A795

No. 1347 — Fairy: a, Holding flowers. b, Holding heart. c, On swing. d, Holding violin. e, With stars.

Serpentine Die Cut 14½x14

Litho. & Silk-screened

2010, Jan. 25 **Self-Adhesive**

1347 A795 Sheet of 5 13.50 10.50
a.-e. 1 Any single 2.50 1.25

Nos. 1347a-1347e each sold for 80c on day of issue.

Rock Stars A796

No. 1348: a, Eppu Normaali (45x33mm). b, Yö (41x31mm). c, Popeda (40x28mm). d, Dingo (44x33mm). e, Maarit (34x41mm). f, Mamba (38x36mm).

Die Cut Perf. 8½

2010, Jan. 25 **Litho.**

Self-Adhesive

1348 Booklet pane of 6 17.00 12.50
a.-f. A796 1 Any single 3.25 2.10

Nos. 1348a-1348f each sold for 80c on day of issue.

A797

Easter — A798

Serpentine Die Cut 12½

2010, Mar. 8 **Litho. & Embossed**

Self-Adhesive

1349 A797 1 multi 11.00 8.50

Litho.

Die Cut Perf. 14

1350 A798 1 multi 2.75 2.25

Nos. 1349 and 1350 each sold for 80c on day of issue.

Rural Life — A799

No. 1351: a, Mussels, children lifting caught fish. b, Children on swing, strawberries, flowers, horse in meadow. c, Farmer on tractor, farmhouses. d, Milk cans, girl milking cow. e, Musicians and dancers.

Serpentine Die Cut 10¼ Horiz.

2010, Mar. 8 **Litho.**

Self-Adhesive

1351 Booklet pane of 5 13.50 10.00
a.-e. A799 1 Any single 2.50 1.25

Nos. 1351a-1351e each sold for 80c on day of issue.

Famous Women — A800

No. 1352: a, Ritva-Liisa Pohjalainen, jewelry and clothing designer. b, Elina Haavio-Mannila, sociologist. c, Aira Samulin, dance instructor. d, Maria-Liisa Nevala, director of National Theater. e, Laila Hirvisaari, writer. f, Leena Palotie (1952-2010), geneticist.

Serpentine Die Cut 11 Horiz. Syncopated

Litho. & Silk-screened

2010, Mar. 8 **Self-Adhesive**

1352 Booklet pane of 6 17.00 12.00
a.-f. A800 1 Any single 2.75 1.40

Nos. 1352a-1352f each sold for 80c on day of issue.

Vegetables A801

No. 1353: a, Tomato (38x33mm). b, Onions (47x34mm). c, Pumpkin (34x36mm). d, Cucumber (27x43mm). e, Eggplant (42x41mm). f, Carrot (29x44mm). g, Broccoli (43x35mm). h, Potato (40x30mm).

2010, Mar. 8 **Litho.** ***Die Cut***

Self-Adhesive

1353 Booklet pane of 8 22.00
a.-h. A801 1 Any single 2.75 1.40

Nos. 1353a-1353h each sold for 80c on day of issue.

Souvenir Sheet

Kotka Harbor — A802

No. 1354: a, Vellamo Maritime Center, museum ship Tarmo, crane. b, Sailboat, Wooden Boat Center, vert.

2010, Mar. 24 ***Perf. 13¾***

1354 A802 Sheet of 2 5.50 5.50
a.-b. 1 Either single 2.75 2.10

Nos. 1354a-1354b each sold for 80c on day of issue.

Europa — A803

No. 1355 — Children, books, characters and background in: a, Orange. b, Blue green.

2010, May 4 ***Perf. 14x13¼***

1355 A803 Horiz. pair 4.75 4.25
a.-b. 80c Either single 2.25 1.50

Personalized Stamp — A804

Serpentine Die Cut 11¾ Syncopated

2010, May 4 **Self-Adhesive**

1356 A804 1 multi 2.75 1.40

No. 1356 sold for 80c on day of issue. The generic design part of the stamp shown could be personalized.

Sculpture — A805

No. 1357: a, Hymy, by Kain Tapper (28x33mm). b, Hefaistos, by Laila Pullinen (28x33mm). c, Cyclist, by Pekka Aarnio (28x33mm). d, Construction, by Kari Huhtamo (28x33mm). e, Salvos, by Mauno Hartman, horiz. (56x29mm). f, Joy, by Miina Akkijyrkka, horiz. (56x29mm).

Serpentine Die Cut 11¾ Horiz.

2010, May 4 **Self-Adhesive**

1357 Booklet pane of 6 17.00 13.00
a.-f. A805 1 Any single 2.75 2.10

Nos. 1357a-1357f each sold for 80c on day of issue.

Souvenir Sheet

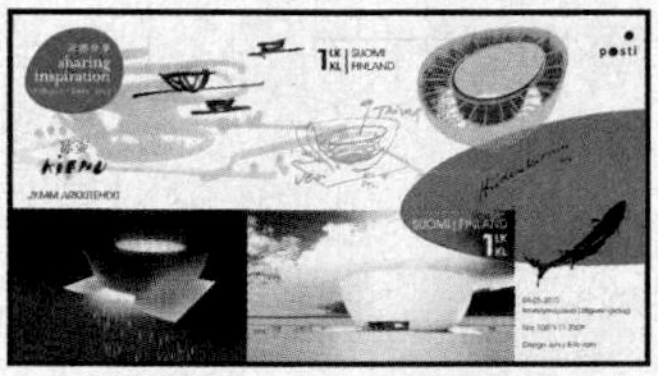

Finnish Pavilion, Expo 2010, Shanghai — A806

No. 1358: a, Aerial view of model and drawing. b, Side view of model.

Serpentine Die Cut 4½ At Bottom

2010, May 4 **Self-Adhesive**

1358 A806 Sheet of 2 5.50 4.25
a.-b. 1 Either single 2.75 2.10

Nos. 1358a-1358b each sold for 80c on day of issue.

Miniature Sheet

People Jumping — A807

No. 1359 — Jumpers in: a, Purple. b, Red. c, Yellow. d, Blue. e, Green.

2010, May 4 ***Serpentine Die Cut 5***

Self-Adhesive

1359 A807 Sheet of 5 13.50 10.50
a.-e. 1 Any single 2.60 2.10

Nos. 1359a-1359e each sold for 80c on day of issue.

Torronsuo National Park — A808

Die Cut Perf. 14

2010, Sept. 13 **Litho.**

Self-Adhesive

1360 A808 1 multi 2.75 2.10

No. 1360 sold for 75c on day of issue.

1960s-1970s Era Room Furnishings A809

2010, Sept. 13 **Booklet Stamp**

Self-Adhesive

1361 A809 1 multi 2.75 2.10
a. Booklet pane of 10 27.50

No. 1361 sold fo 75c on day of issue.

Souvenir Sheet

Autumn — A810

No. 1362 — Forest and: a, Crayfish. b, Ducks. c, Elk.

Serpentine Die Cut 12¾x13¼ Syncopated

Litho. & Silk-screened

2010, Sept. 13 **Self-Adhesive**

1362 A810 Sheet of 3 8.25 6.50
a.-c. 1 Any single 2.75 2.10

On day of issue, Nos. 1362a-1362c each sold for 75c.

Santa Claus — A811

Reindeer and Moon — A812

Sleigh of Santa Claus Over Lapland A813

No. 1365: a, Star and Santa Claus with sack. b, Poinsettias, ribbon and bell. c, Sleigh of Santa Claus over church. d, Heart-shaped wreath. e, Reindeer and Aurora Borealis.

Die Cut Perf. 14

2010, Nov. 5 **Litho.**

Self-Adhesive

1363 Horiz. pair 3.50 3.25
a. A811 55c multi 1.75 1.60
b. A812 55c multi 1.75 1.60
1364 A813 1 multi 2.75 2.10

Souvenir Sheet

1365 Sheet of 5 8.50 7.75
a. A811 55c multi 1.60 1.50
b. A811 55c multi 1.60 1.50
c. A813 55c multi 1.60 1.50
d. A811 55c multi 1.60 1.50
e. A811 55c multi 1.60 1.50

Christmas. No. 1364 sold for 75c on day of issue. See Japan No. 3269.

Birch Bud A814

Birch Leaves A815

2011, Jan. 24 **Litho.** ***Die Cut***

Self-Adhesive

1366 A814 20c multi .60 .55
1367 A815 30c multi .90 .85

Flag of Finland A816

2011, Jan. 24 **Litho. & Embossed**

Self-Adhesive

1368 A816 2 gray & blue 2.50 1.75

No. 1368 sold for 60c on day of issue.

Birds and Flowers — A817

No. 1369: a, Bird on branch, country name in red circle. b, Bird in flight, country name in blue circle. c, Flowers, country name in red circle. d, Bird on branch, country name in blue circle. e, Bird in flight, country name in red circle.

Serpentine Die Cut 10¼ Horiz.

2011, Jan. 24 **Litho.**

Self-Adhesive

1369 Booklet pane of 5 12.50 8.00
a.-e. A817 2 Any single 2.50 1.60

Nos. 1369a-1369e each sold for 60c on day of issue.

Mailboxes — A818

No. 1370: a, Mailbox mounted on tire. b, Snow-covered mailbox. c, Child opening mailbox. d, Mailbox next to sauna. e, Mailbox with posthorn and Finnish lion.

Die Cut Perf. 10 Vert. Syncopated at Right

2011, Jan. 24 **Self-Adhesive**

Coil Stamps

1370 Strip of 5 12.50 8.50
a.-e. A818 2 Any single 2.50 1.75

Nos. 1370a-1370e each sold for 60c on day of issue.

Miniature Sheet

Finnish National Opera, Cent. — A819

No. 1371: a, Male and female performers dancing, men in helmets. b, Man with hat and red ribbon, vert. c, Male and female performers in embrace. d, Woman in red dress in water, vert.

Serpentine Die Cut 15½ Horiz.

2011, Jan. 24 **Self-Adhesive**

1371 A819 Sheet of 4 10.00 6.50
a.-d. 2 Any single 2.50 1.60

Nos. 1371a-1371d each sold for 60c on day of issue.

Miniature Sheet

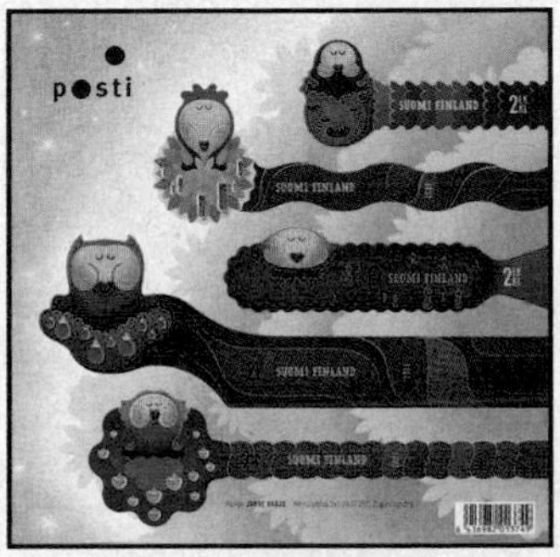

Birds in Trees — A820

No. 1372 — Various stylized birds with tree leaves in: a, Green (53x24mm). b, Blue (64x32mm). c, Orange (70x20mm). d, Yellow brown (89x39mm). e, Red violet (78x31mm).

2011, Jan. 24 ***Die Cut***

Self-Adhesive

1372 A820 Sheet of 5 12.50 8.00
a.-e. 2 Any single 2.50 1.60

Nos. 1372a-1372e each sold for 60c on day of issue.

Tulips — A821

2011, Apr. 1 ***Die Cut Perf. 13¾***

Self-Adhesive

1373 A821 2 multi 2.50 1.75

No. 1373 sold for 60c on day of issue.

Dahlias — A822

2011, Apr. 1 ***Die Cut***

Self-Adhesive

Color of Country Name

1374 A822 1 red violet 2.75 .75
1375 A822 1 gray green 2.75 .75
a. Horiz. pair, #1374-1375 5.50

Nos. 1374-1375 each sold for 75c on day of issue.

Miniature Sheet

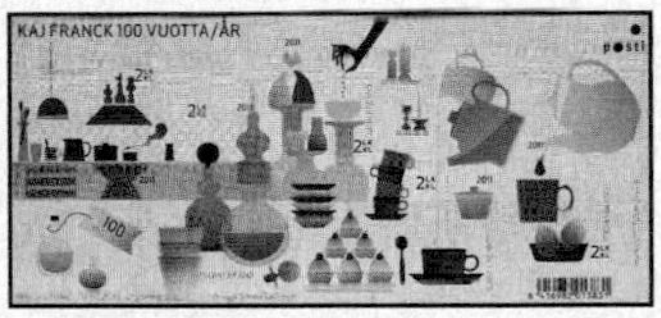

Kitchen — A823

No. 1376: a, Lamp, counter, pitcher, stove with pots (32x22mm, serpentine die cut 10x10¾). b, Bottles with stoppers (19x46mm, serpentine die cut 9¾x10). c, Hand dropping seasonings into bowl (24x32mm, serpentine die cut 10x10¼). d, Cup, saucer, bowl with lid (22x32mm, serpentine die cut 9½x10¼). e, Cup, eggs in bowl (24x32mm, serpentine die cut 9¾x10).

2011, Apr. 1 ***Serpentine Die Cut***

Self-Adhesive

1376 A823 Sheet of 5 12.50 8.50
a.-e. 2 Any single 2.50 1.60

Nos. 1376a-1376e each sold for 60c on day of issue.

Government Buildings — A824

No. 1377: a, House of the Estates, Helsinki, 1890. b, Finnish Embassy, New Delhi, India, 1985. c, Helsinki Music Center, 2011. d, Government Palace, Helsinki, 1828. e, Malmi Airport, Helsinki, 1938. f, Finnish Forest Research Institute Research Center, Joensuu, 2004.

2011, Apr. 1 ***Die Cut Perf. 13¼***

Self-Adhesive

1377 Booklet pane of 6 15.00 10.50
a.-f. A824 2 Any single 2.50 1.75

Nos. 1377a-1377f each sold for 60c on day of issue.

National Council of Women, Cent. A825

No. 1378 — Comic strip characters Maisa and Kaarina, by Tiina Paju and Sari Luhtanen: a, Holding star-tipped wands. b, Knitting blanket with stars. c, Playing tennis. d, Posing and taking picture. e, Wearing stars on dresses. f, Placing star on cake.

2011, Apr. 1 ***Serpentine Die Cut 11***
Self-Adhesive

1378	Booklet pane of 6	15.00	10.50
a.-f.	A825 2 Any single	2.50	1.75

Nos. 1378a-1378f each sold for 60c on day of issue.

Europa — A826

No. 1379 — Trees in: a, Spring and summer. b, Autumn and winter.

2011, May 6 ***Perf. 12¾x13¼***
Self-Adhesive

1379	A826 Horiz. pair	5.00	3.00
a.-b.	2 Either single	2.50	1.25

Intl. Year of Forests. Nos. 1379a-1379b each sold for 60c on day of issue.

Moomin — A827

Mymble — A828

Little My — A829

Moominmamma and Moomin — A830

Hemulen A831

Hattifatteners A832

2011, May 6 ***Die Cut***
Self-Adhesive

1380	Booklet pane of 6	15.00	10.00
a.	A827 2 multi	2.50	1.60
b.	A828 2 multi	2.50	1.60
c.	A829 2 multi	2.50	1.60
d.	A830 2 multi	2.50	1.60
e.	A831 2 multi	2.50	1.60
f.	A832 2 multi	2.50	1.60

Nos. 1380a-1380f each sold for 60c on day of issue.

Souvenir Sheet

Struve Geodetic Arc — A833

No. 1381: a, Land, water, geodetic arc triangulations. b, Map of Finland with path of triangulations.

2011, May 6 ***Die Cut***
Self-Adhesive

1381	A833 Sheet of 2	5.00	3.50
a.-b.	2 Either single	2.50	1.75

Nos. 1381a-1381b each sold for 60c on day of issue.

Miniature Sheet

Tree of Happiness — A834

No. 1382: a, Balloons and gifts (32mm diameter). b, Birds on branch (32mm diameter). c, Cake with Finnish flags (34x29mm oval). d, Bird in birdhouse (34x29mm oval). e, Boy and girl on branch (32mm diameter).

2011, May 6 ***Die Cut***
Self-Adhesive

1382	A834 Sheet of 5	12.50	8.50
a.-e.	2 Any single	2.50	1.60

Nos. 1382a-1382e each sold for 60c on day of issue.

Heraldic Lion Type of 2002
Die Cut Perf. 12 Syncopated
2011, Sept. 5 **Litho.**
Self-Adhesive

1383	A616	€2 green & multi	5.75	5.50
1384	A616	€4 pur & multi	11.50	11.00

Souvenir Sheet

Juhani Aho (1861-1921), Writer — A835

No. 1385: a, Stack of paper, trees. b, Aho on skis.

Litho. & Embossed
2011, Sept. 5 ***Perf. 13½***
Self-Adhesive

1385	A835 Sheet of 2	5.00	3.50
a.-b.	2 Either single	2.50	1.75

Nos. 1385a-1385b each sold for 60c on day of issue.

Miniature Sheet

Finnish Comics, Cent. — A836

No. 1386: a, Kili ja Possu, by Olavi Vikainen, 1950s. b, Unto Uneksija, by Joonas (Veikko Savolainen), 1960s. c, Herra Kerhonen, by Gösta Thilén, 1930s. d, Antti Puuhaara, by Aarne Nopsanen, 1940s. e, Janne Ankkanen, by Ola Fogelberg, 1910s. f, Olli Pirteä, by Hjalmar Löfving, 1920s.

Die Cut Perf. 8½
2011, Sept. 5 **Litho.**
Self-Adhesive

1386	A836 Sheet of 6	15.00	10.00
a.-f.	2 Any single	2.50	2.00

Nos. 1386a-1386f each sold for 60c on day of issue.

Houses with Snow-covered Roofs — A837

2011, Nov. 7 ***Die Cut Perf. 14***
Booklet Stamp
Self-Adhesive

1387	A837 1 multi	2.75	2.10
a.	Booklet pane of 10 + 10 etiquettes	27.50	

No. 1387 sold for 75c on day of issue.

Personalized Stamp — A838

Serpentine Die Cut 11¾ Syncopated
2011, Nov. 7 **Self-Adhesive**

1388	A838 2 multi	2.50	1.75

No. 1388 sold for 60c on day of issue. The generic design part of the stamp shown could be personalized.

A839

Christmas — A840

Die Cut Perf. 14
2011, Nov. 7 **Self-Adhesive**

1389	A839 55c multi	1.75	1.50
1390	A840 2 multi	2.50	1.75

No. 1390 sold for 60c on day of issue.

Miniature Sheet

A841

No. 1391: a, Birds on wire. b, Girl with watering can. c, Hearts. d, Girl and dog. e, Woman blowing heart-shaped bubbles. f, Heart-shaped door and key.

2012, Jan. 23 ***Die Cut Perf. 13¼x13***
Self-Adhesive

1391	A841 Sheet of 6	15.00	9.50
a.-f.	2 Any single	2.50	1.20

Nos. 1391a-1391f each sold for 60c on day of issue.

Miniature Sheet

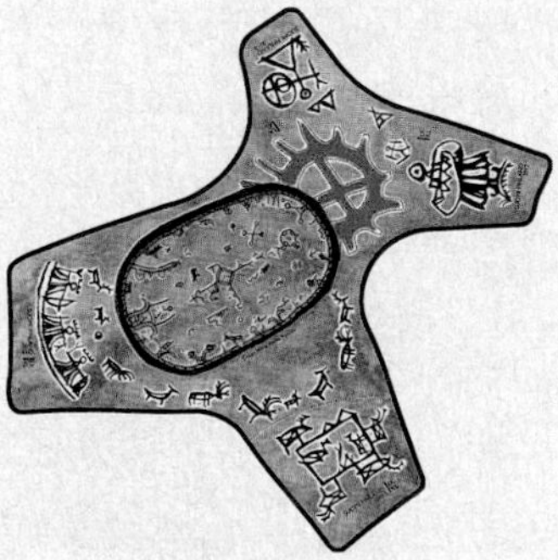

Sami Culture — A842

No. 1392: a, Stick-figure man holding forked stick. b, Stick figure of woman. c, Reindeer at sides of rectangle. d, Three daughters of Sami's mother god and reindeer. Stamps are of various sizes.

2012, Jan. 23 ***Die Cut***
Self-Adhesive

1392	A842 Sheet of 4	11.00	8.00
a.-d.	1 Any single	2.75	2.00

Nos. 1392a-1392d each sold for 75c on day of issue.

The School Girl II — A843

Green Apples and Champagne Glass — A844

Self-Portrait on Black — A845

Silk Shoes A846

Die Cut Perf. 13, 12¾x13¼ (#1393b), 13¼ (#1393c)

2012, Jan. 23 Self-Adhesive

1393 Booklet pane of 4 11.00 8.00
a. A843 1 multi 2.75 2.00
b. A844 1 multi 2.75 2.00
c. A845 1 multi 2.75 2.00
d. A846 1 multi 2.75 2.00

Paintings by Helene Schjerfbeck (1862-1946). Nos. 1393a-1393d each sold for 75c on day of issue.

Winning Designs in Future City Stamp Design Contest A847

Designs: No. 1394, Hands, by Varpu Kangas. No. 1395, Shapes and dots, by Kangas. No. 1396, Future City is Diversity, by Chloé Chapeaublanc. No. 1397, Buildings, balloons, and inverted umbrella on tree branch, by Sini Henttonen. No. 1398, Children's drawingin red, blue, and black, by Daniel Kallström, vert. No. 1399, Children's drawing of animal under sun, by Elias Ollila, vert. No. 1400, Rabbits, by Katja Hynninen. No. 1401, Cat's head and heavy man on bicycle, by Ville Korhonen.

Booklet Stamps

Serpentine Die Cut 8¾x9 (#1394, 1400), Rectangle and Arc Die Cut (#1395-1396), Arc Die Cut 12¾ (#1397, 1401), Sawtooth Die Cut 15½x15¼ (#1398-1399)

2012, Jan. 23 Self-Adhesive

1394 A847 1 multi 2.75 2.75
1395 A847 1 multi 2.75 2.75
a. Booklet pane of 2, #1394-1395 5.50 4.00
1396 A847 1 multi 2.75 2.75
1397 A847 1 multi 2.75 2.75
a. Booklet pane of 2, #1396-1397 5.50 4.00
1398 A847 1 multi 2.75 2.75
1399 A847 1 multi 2.75 2.75
a. Booklet pane of 2, #1398-1399 5.50 4.00
1400 A847 1 multi 2.75 2.75
1401 A847 1 multi 2.75 2.75
a. Booklet pane of 2, #1400-1401 5.50 4.00
Complete booklet, #1395a, 1397a, 1399a, 1401a 22.00 16.00
Nos. 1394-1401 (8) 22.00 22.00

Nos. 1394-1401 each sold for 75c on day of issue.

Wedding Rings — A848

Die Cut Perf. 14

2012, Mar. 5 Litho. & Engr.

Self-Adhesive

1402 A848 1 multi 2.75 2.00

No. 1402 sold for 75c on day of issue.

Easter A849

Serpentine Die Cut 8¼ Vert.

2012, Mar. 5 Litho.

Self-Adhesive

1403 A849 1 multi 2.75 2.00

No. 1403 sold for 75c on day of issue.

Souvenir Sheet

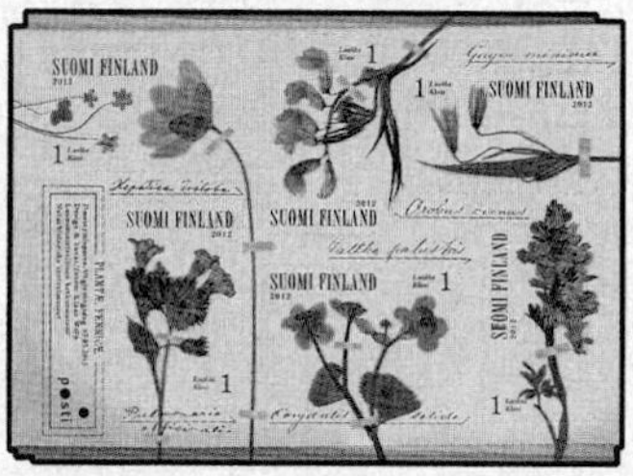

Flowers — A850

No. 1404: a, Hepatica triloba (three small yellow flowers at L, large yellow flower at R, denomination al LL). b, Orobus virnus (six yellow and white flowers on stem, denomination at UR), vert. c, Gagea minima (two partially opened buds, denomination at UL). d, Pulmonaria officinalis (four purple flowers, denomination at LR), vert. e, Caltha palastris (yellow flowers, denoimination at UR). f, Corydalis solida (cluster of purple flowers, denomination at LL), vert.

2012, Mar. 5 ***Die Cut Perf. 10***

Self-Adhesive

1404 A850 Sheet of 6 17.00 12.00
a.-f. 1 Any single 2.75 2.00

Nos. 1404a-1404f each sold for 75c on day of issue.

Intl. Women's Day A851

No. 1405: a, Woman and hearts. b, Women's hands with glasses of fruit, vert. c, Women's legs and shoes, vert. d, Women and musical notes.

2012, Mar. 5 ***Die Cut Perf. 12½***

Self-Adhesive

1405 Booklet pane of 4 11.00 8.00
a.-d. A851 1 Any single 2.75 2.00

Nos. 1405a-1405d each sold for 75c on day of issue.

Railroads in Finland, 150th Anniv. — A852

No. 1406: a, Train engineer, steam locomotive. b, Train, ticket. c, Railroad warning sign, train in snow. d, Passenger car and passengers at platform, clock. e, Railway worker, modern train. f, Train, lake, statue.

Serpentine Die Cut 9½ Horiz.

2012, Mar. 5 Self-Adhesive

1406 Booklet pane of 6 17.00 12.00
a.-f. A852 1 Any single 2.75 2.00

Nos. 1406a-1406f each sold for 75c on day of issue.

2012 Men's Ice Hockey World Cup Tournament, Finland and Sweden A853

2012, Mar. 21 ***Die Cut Perf. 14***

Self-Adhesive

1407 A853 1 multi 2.75 2.00

No. 1407 sold for 75c on day of issue.

Souvenir Sheet

Rescue Boats — A854

No. 1408: a, Jenny Wihuri (red and white boat). b, Merikarhu (green, orange and white boat).

2012, Mar. 21 ***Perf. 13½x13***

Self-Adhesive

1408 A854 Sheet of 2 5.50 4.00
a.-b. 1 Either single 2.75 2.00

Nos. 1408a-1408b each sold for 75c on day of issue.

Europa — A855

No. 1409: a, Ship on lake. b, People at beach.

2012, May 7 ***Perf. 13¼x12¾***

Self-Adhesive

1409 A855 1 Vert. pair, #a-b 5.50 3.75

Nos. 1409a-1409b each sold for 75c on day of issue.

Bothnian Sea National Park — A856

2012, May 7 ***Die Cut Perf. 14***

Self-Adhesive

1410 A856 1 multi 2.75 2.00

No. 1410 sold for 75c on day of issue.

A857

Sunflowers — A858

2012, May 7 ***Die Cut Perf. 17***

Self-Adhesive

1411 A857 1 multi 2.75 2.00
1412 A858 1 multi 2.75 2.00

Nos. 1411-142 each sold for 75c on day of issue.

A859

A860

Clouds A861

Die Cut Perf. 10 Horiz., Syncopated at Bottom

2012, May 7 Self-Adhesive

Coil Stamps

1413 Horiz. strip of 3 8.25
a. A859 1 multi 2.75 1.40
b. A860 1 multi 2.75 1.40
c. A861 1 multi 2.75 1.40

Nos. 1413a-1413c each sold for 75c on day of issue.

Souvenir Sheet

Disabled Athletes — A862

No. 1414: a, Leo-Pekka Tahti, cyclist. b, Saana-Maria Sinisalo, archer.

Die Cut Perf. 11¼x11½

Litho. & Silk-screened

2012, May 7 Self-Adhesive

1414 A862 1 Sheet of 2, #a-b 5.50 4.00

Nos. 1414a-1414b each sold for 75c on day of Issue.

Miniature Sheet

Autumn Dreams — A863

No. 1415: a, Hot-air balloon (36x46mm). b, Moon, lanterns in tree (37x39mm). c, Flying geese (28x36mm). d, Scarecrow and hay rolls (29x46mm). e, Girl feeding carrots to horse (44x34mm).

Serpentine Die Cut 4 to 7

2012, Sept. 3 Litho.

Self-Adhesive

1415 A863 Sheet of 5 13.50 10.00
a.-e. 1 Any single 2.60 2.00

On day of issue, Nos. 1415a-1415e each sold for 80c.

Recording Stars of the 1990s A864

No. 1416: a, Kaija Koo. b, Jari Sillanpää. c, Laura Voutilainen. d, Yölintu. e, Agents. f, Anna Eriksson.

2012, Sept. 3 *Die Cut Perf. 8½*

Self-Adhesive

1416 Booklet pane of 6 17.00 12.00
a.-f. A864 1 Any single 2.75 2.00

On day of issue, Nos. 1416a-1416f each sold for 80c.

Pets — A865

No. 1417: a, Cat, inscriptions in red. b, White rabbit facing left. c, Gray rabbit facing right. d, Dachshund puppy, year date at LR. e, Jack Russell terrier puppy, year date at LL. f, Kitten, inscriptions in green.

Serpentine Die Cut 11¾ Horiz.

2012, Sept. 3 Self-Adhesive

1417 Booklet pane of 6 17.00 12.00
a.-f. A865 1 Any single 2.75 2.00

On day of issue, Nos. 1417a-1417f each sold for 80c.

Christmas Tree — A866

Stable Lantern — A867

2012, Nov. 5 *Serpentine Die Cut 9½*

Self-Adhesive

1418 A866 60c multi 1.75 1.60

Serpentine Die Cut 10

1419 A867 1 multi 2.75 1.75

Christmas. No. 1419 sold for 80c on day of issue.

Sledders A868

Self-Adhesive

2013, Jan. 21 *Die Cut Perf. 14*

1420 A868 1 multi 2.75 1.40

No. 1420 sold for 80c on day of issue.

Coilostylis Parkinsoniana A869

Self-Adhesive

2013, Jan. 21 *Die Cut Perf. 14*

1421 A869 €1.10 multi 2.75 1.40

See No. 1442.

Miniature Sheet

St.Valentine's Day — A870

No. 1422: a, Polar bears. b, Whale. c, Parrots. d, Elephants. e, Chameleon. f, Monkey.

2013, Jan. 21 *Die Cut*

Self-Adhesive

1422 A870 Sheet of 6 + 4 labels 17.00 12.00
a.-f. 1 Any single 2.75 2.00

Nos. 1422a-1422f each sold for 80c on day of issue.

Actors and Actresses — A871

No. 1427: a, Ritva Valkama. b, Esko Salminen. c, Outi Mäenpää. d, Martti Suosalo. e, Krista Kosonen. f, Aku Hirviniemi.

Die Cut Perf. 6¾ Vert. Syncopated

2013, Mar. 4

Self-Adhesive

1423 Booklet pane of 6 17.00 12.00
a.-f. A871 1 Any single 2.75 2.00

Finnish Actors Federation, cent. On day of issue, Nos. 1423a-1423f each sold for 80c.

Easter Rooster — A872

2013, Mar. 8 *Die Cut Perf. 14*

Self-Adhesive

1424 A872 1 multi 2.75 2.00

No. 1424 sold for 80c on day of issue.

Roses — A873

2013, Mar. 8 Self-Adhesive

1425 A873 1 multi 2.75 2.00

No. 1425 sold for 80c on day of issue.

Blackberries A874

Gooseberry A875

Red Currants A876

Die Cut Perf. 10 Horiz. Syncopated

2013, Mar. 8 Self-Adhesive

Coil Stamps

1426 Horiz. strip of 3 8.50 6.00
a. A874 1 multi 2.75 2.00
b. A875 1 multi 2.75 2.00
c. A876 1 multi 2.75 2.00

On day of issue, Nos. 1426a-1426c each sold for 80c.

A877

A878

A879

Outhouses A880

2013, Mar. 8 *Die Cut Perf. 12*

Self-Adhesive

1427 Booklet pane of 4 11.50
a. A877 2 multi 2.75 2.00
b. A878 2 multi 2.75 2.00
c. A879 2 multi 2.75 2.00
d. A880 2 multi 2.75 2.00

On day of issue, Nos. 1527a-1527d each sold for 70c.

Flower Bouquet — A881

2013, May 6 *Die Cut Perf. 14*

Self-Adhesive

1428 A881 1 multi 2.75 1.40

No. 1428 sold for 80c on day of issue.

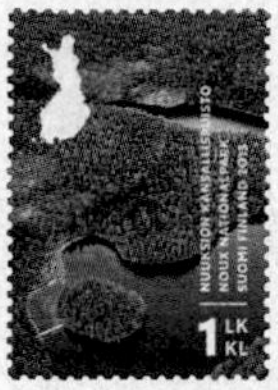

Nuuksio Natl. Park — A882

2013, May 6 Litho.

Self-Adhesive

1429 A882 1 multi 2.75 1.40

No. 1429 sold for 80c on day of issue.

2012 Ford Transit Connect Mail Van — A883

1933 Volvo LV-70 Mail Truck A884

2013, May 6 *Die Cut Perf. 12½x13¼*

Self-Adhesive

1430 Horiz. pair 5.50
a. A883 1 multi 2.75 2.00
b. A884 1 multi 2.75 2.00

Europa. On day of issue, Nos. 1430a-1430b each sold for 80c.

Miniature Sheet

Odd Finnish Sports and Activities — A885

No. 1431: a, Man carrying wife. b, Boot throwing. c, Air guitarist. d, Woman pushing man in milk cart. e, Man sitting on ant hill. f, Swamp soccer.

2013, May 6 ***Die Cut Perf. 10***

Self-Adhesive

1431 A885 Sheet of 6 + 6 etiquettes 17.50
a.-f. 1 Any single 2.75 2.00

On day of issue, Nos. 1431a-1431f each sold for 80c.

Moomins — A886

No. 1432: a, Moominpappa holding drink (red background, 30x34mm). b, Moomintroll jumping (blue background, 33x31mm). c, Moominmamma with purse (green background, 33x34mm). d, Little My with basket on head (yellow orange background, 32x33mm). e, Snorkmaiden and piece of paper (red violet background, 30x35mm). f, Snufkin (brown orange background, 32x36mm).

2013, May 6 ***Die Cut***

Self-Adhesive

1432 Booklet pane of 6 + 6 etiquettes 17.00
a.-f. A886 1 Any single 2.75 2.00

On day of issue, Nos. 1432a-1432f each sold for 80c.

Personalized Stamp — A891

Serpentine Die Cut 11¾ Syncopated

2013, Aug. 12 **Litho.**

Self-Adhesive

1437 A891 1 black 4.50 4.50

No. 1437 had a franking value of 85c on the day of issue. The vignette shown for No. 1437 is a generic image depicting a Volvo PV 444 police vehicle and is one of ten different police vehicles depicted in the image portion of stamps in a sheet of ten stamps having the same common "frame" that sold for €16.50. Customers purchasing sheets of No. 1437 could also download vignette images from an online library of images on the stamp creation website or use their own downloaded images.

Pres. Sauli Niinistö, 65th Birthday A895

Die Cut Perf. 12 Syncopated

2013, Aug. 23 **Litho.**

Self-Adhesive

1441 A895 1 blk & gray 2.75 1.40

No. 1441 sold for 85c on day of issue.

Coilostylis Parkinsoniana Type of 2013

Die Cut Perf. 14

2013, Aug. 23 **Litho.**

Self-Adhesive

1442 A869 €1.20 multi 2.75 1.40

Souvenir Sheet

Paintings by Eero Järnefelt (1863-1937) — A896

No. 1443: a, Metsämaisema (Forest Scene) (34x49mm). b, Raatajat Rahanalaiset (Under the Yoke - Burning the Brushwood) (44x40mm).

Serpentine Die Cut 14½

2013, Sept. 9 **Litho.**

Self-Adhesive

1443 A896 Sheet of 2 5.50 4.25
a.-b. 1 Either single 2.75 2.10

On day of issue, Nos. 1443a-1443b each sold for 85c.

Postcrossing — A897

No. 1444 — Stylized postal card and: a, Hand holding pencil. b, Blackboard. c, Heart-shaped Earth. d, Open mouth.

Serpentine Die Cut 12¼

2013, Sept. 9 **Litho.**

Self-Adhesive

1444 Booklet pane of 4 + 4 etiquettes 11.00
a.-d A897 1 Any single 2.75 1.10

On day of issue Nos. 1444a-1444d each sold for 85c.

Miniature Sheet

Autumn Scenes — A898

No. 1445: a, Boy with umbrella, falling leaves. b, Lakeside sauna, geese in flight, buoy, horiz. c, Rowboat and ducks, horiz. d, Apples in basket, house, falling leaves. e, Park bench, falling leaves, horiz.

Serpentine Die Cut 14x14¼, 14¼x14

2013, Sept. 9 **Litho.**

Self-Adhesive

1445 A898 Sheet of 5 11.50
a.-e. 1 Any single 2.25 2.25

On day of issue, Nos. 1445a-1445e each sold for 85c.

Miniature Sheet

Angry Birds Characters — A899

No. 1446: a, Red Bird. b, Pink Bird, vert. c, Black Bird, vert. d, Yellow Bird. e, Blue Birds, vert. f, King Pig, vert.

Die Cut Perf. 8¼

2013, Sept. 9 **Litho.**

Self-Adhesive

1446 A899 Sheet of 6 + 6 etiquettes 13.50
a.-f. 1 Any single 2.25 2.25

On day of issue, Nos. 1446a-1446f each sold for 85c.

Finnish Parliament, 150th Anniv. — A900

Die Cut Perf. 14

2013, Sept. 17 **Litho.**

Self-Adhesive

1447 A900 1 multi 2.40 2.40

No. 1447 sold for 85c on day of issue.

Finnish School System — A901

No. 1448: a, Girl receiving school lunch, apple, lettuce, pitcher and plate. b, Boy receiving medical examination, posture diagrams. c, Girl practicing writing on blackboard, letters in Finnish alphabet. d, Uno Cygnaeus (1810-88), founder of Finnish school system, map of Finland. e, Children in physical education class, children skiing. f, Teacher watching boys writing at desk, orrery, sun and planet.

Die Cut Perf. 6¾ Horiz. At Top

2013, Nov. 14 **Litho.**

Self-Adhesive

1448 Booklet pane of 6 13.50
a.-f. A901 1 Any single 2.25 2.25

On day of issue, Nos. 1448a-1448f each sold for 85c.

Children Hugging A902

Angel A903

Boy with Christmas Trees — A904

Die Cut Perf. 14

2013, Nov. 4 **Litho.**

Self-Adhesive

1449 A902 65c multi 1.75 1.75
1450 A903 2 multi 2.00 2.00
1451 A904 1 multi 2.25 2.25
Nos. 1449-1451 (3) 6.00 6.00

Christmas. On day of issue, No. 1450 sold for 75c; No. 1451, 85c.

Snowmen A905

Serpentine Die Cut 10¼

2014, Jan. 20 **Litho.**

Self-Adhesive

1452 A905 1 multi 2.75 2.75

No. 1452 sold for €1 on day of issue.

Miniature Sheet

Teddy Bears — A906

No. 1453: a, Teddy bear writing with quill pen. b, Teddy bear pushing another on sled, horiz. c, Two Teddy bears and flower. d, Two Teddy bears dancing. e, Teddy bear sleeping in slipper, horiz. f, Two Teddy bears playing musical instruments.

Serpentine Die Cut 16

2014, Jan. 20 **Litho.**

Self-Adhesive

1453 A906 Sheet of 6 + 4 stickers 16.50
a.-f. 1 Any single 2.75 2.75

Nos. 1453a-1453f each sold for €1 on day of issue.

Castles — A907

No. 1454: a, Turun Linna (Turku Castle) (34x50mm). b, Hämeen Linna (Häme Castle) (34x50mm). c, Raaseporin Linna (Raseborg Castle) (34x50mm). d, Suomenlinna

(Sveaborg Fortress) (34x58mm). e, Olavinlinna (Olavinlinna Castle) (34x50mm). f, Kastelholma (Kastelholma Castle) (50x34mm).

Die Cut Perf. 7½

2014, Jan. 20 Litho.

Self-Adhesive

1454 Booklet pane of 6 16.50
a.-f. A907 1 Any single 2.75 2.75

Nos. 1454a-1454f each sold for €1 on day of issue.

Souvenir Sheet

Tove Jansson (1914-2001), Creator of *Moomins* Characters — A908

No. 1456: a, Jansson with telescope. b, Silhouette of Jansson and Moomin character, Sniff.

Die Cut Perf. 12½

2014, Jan. 31 Litho.

Self-Adhesive

1455 A908 Sheet of 2 5.50
a.-b. 1 Either single 2.75 2.75

Nos. 1455a-1455b each sold for €1 on day of issue.

Easter A909

Die Cut Perf. 9¾ Horiz.

2014, Mar. 3 Litho.

Self-Adhesive

1456 A909 1 multi 2.75 2.75

No. 1456 sold for €1 on day of issue.

Sami Jauhojärvi and Iivo Niskanen, 2014 Winter Olympic Cross-Country Team Sprint Gold Medalists — A909a

Serpentine Die Cut 11¾ Syncopated

2014, Mar. 3 Litho.

Self-Adhesive

1456A A909a 1 multi 5.00 5.00

No. 1456A was printed in sheets of 10 that sold for €18. No. 1456 had a franking value of €1 on day of issue.

Fruits and Blossoms — A910

No. 1457: a, Pears (light green background). b, Apples (yellow background). c, Cherries (pink background).

Die Cut Perf. 10 Vert. Syncopated

2014, Mar. 3 Litho.

Coil Stamps

Self-Adhesive

1457 Vert. strip of 3 7.50
a.-c. A910 2 Any single 2.50 2.50

Nos. 1457a-1457c each sold for 90c on day of issue.

A911

Congratulations A912

No. 1458: a, Cat, cake with strawberries. b, Butterflies and flower. c, Squirrel and flowers. d, Strrawberries, blueberries and flower. e, Basket of flowers.

Serpentine Die Cut 13¾x13½ (A911), 14½x15¼ (A912)

2014, Mar. 3 Litho.

Self-Adhesive

1458 Booklet pane of 5 14.00
a.-b. A911 1 Either single 2.75 2.75
c.-e. A912 1 Any single 2.75 2.75

Nos. 1458a-1458e each sold for €1 on day of issue.

Souvenir Sheet

Finnjet Ferry — A913

No. 1459 — Ferry with posthorn at: a, Left. b, Right.

Serpentine Die Cut 13½

2014, Mar. 17 Litho.

Self-Adhesive

1459 A913 Sheet of 2 5.50
a.-b. 1 Either single 2.75 2.75

Nos. 1459a-1459b each sold for €1 on day of issue.

Violas — A914

2014, May 5 Litho. ***Die Cut Perf. 14***

Self-Adhesive

1460 A914 1 multi 2.75 2.75

No. 1460 sold for €1 on day of issue.

Linnansaari National Park — A915

2014, May 5 Litho. ***Die Cut Perf. 14***

Self-Adhesive

1461 A915 1 multi 2.75 2.75

No. 1461 sold for €1 on day of issue.

Europa A916

No. 1462: a, Man playing accordion. b, Woman playing kantele.

Irregular Serpentine Die Cut

2014, May 5 Litho.

Self-Adhesive

1462 Horiz. pair 5.50
a.-b. A916 1 Either single 2.75 2.75

Nos. 1462a-1462b each sold for €1 on day of issue.

A917

A918

A919

A920

A921

A922

Die Cut Perf. 13½

2014, May 5 Litho.

Self-Adhesive

1463 Booklet pane of 6 16.50
a. A917 1 multi 2.75 2.75
b. A918 1 multi 2.75 2.75
c. A919 1 multi 2.75 2.75
d. A920 1 multi 2.75 2.75
e. A921 1 multi 2.75 2.75
f. A922 1 multi 2.75 2.75

Nos. 1463a-1463f each sold for €1 on day of issue.

Miniature Sheet

Caricatures of Dudesons Television Show Cast Members — A923

No. 1464 — Dudeson: a, On snowboard. b, With red cap. c, Wearing shirt with target. d, Running naked, holding book.

Crenellated Die Cut 5

2014, Sept. 1 Litho.

Self-Adhesive

1464 A923 Sheet of 4 11.00
a.-d. 1 Any single 2.75 2.75

Nos. 1464a-1464d each sold for €1 on day of issue.

A924

A925

A926

Watercolors of Yards and Gardens by Urpo Martikainen A927

Die Cut Perf. 13

2014, Sept. 8 Litho.

Self-Adhesive

1465 Booklet pane of 4 11.00
a. A924 1 multi 2.75 2.75
b. A925 1 multi 2.75 2.75
c. A926 1 multi 2.75 2.75
d. A927 1 multi 2.75 2.75

Nos. 1465a-1465d each sold for €1 on day of issue.

Celestial and Meteorological Objects — A928

No. 1466: a, Saturn (45x40mm). b, Moon (36x36mm). c, Sun (40x38mm). d, Cloud and lightning bolt (40x51mm). e, Earth and Moon (35x41mm). f, Comet (40x45mm). g, Cloud (48x42mm). h, Rainbow (40x38mm).

Serpentine Die Cut 9¼ on 1 or 2 Sides

2014, Sept. 8 Litho.

Self-Adhesive

1466	Booklet pane of 8	22.00	
a.-h.	A928 1 Any single	2.75	2.75

Nos. 1466a-1466h each sold for €1 on day of issue.

Souvenir Sheet

Art by Tom of Finland (Touko Laaksonen) (1920-91) — A929

No. 1467: a, Man wearing police cap smoking cigarette (43x32mm). b, Man's head between legs of another man (45x33mm). c, Man's head and buttocks (36x33mm).

Die Cut Perf. 5½

2014, Sept. 8 Litho.

Self-Adhesive

1467	Sheet of 3	8.25	
a.-c.	A929 1 Any single	2.75	2.75

Nos. 1467a-1467c each sold for €1 on day of issue.

A930

A931

A932

A933

A934

A935

A936

A937

A938

Bridges A939

Die Cut Perf. 8½ Horiz.

2014, Oct. 23 Litho.

Coil Stamps

Self-Adhesive

1468	A930 1 multi + etiquette	2.50	2.50
1469	A931 1 multi + etiquette	2.50	2.50
1470	A932 1 multi + etiquette	2.50	2.50
1471	A933 1 multi + etiquette	2.50	2.50
1472	A934 1 multi + etiquette	2.50	2.50
1473	A935 1 multi + etiquette	2.50	2.50
1474	A936 1 multi + etiquette	2.50	2.50
1475	A937 1 multi + etiquette	2.50	2.50
1476	A938 1 multi + etiquette	2.50	2.50
1477	A939 1 multi + etiquette	2.50	2.50
a.	Horiz. strip of 10, #1468-1477, + 10 etiquettes	25.00	
	Nos. 1468-1477 (10)	25.00	25.00

On day of issue, Nos. 1468-1477 had a franking value of €1. A complete roll of 100 stamps sold for €97.50 on the day of issue,

Changes in Everyday Items — A940

No. 1478: a, Computer keyboard, computer storage disks, computer, dial telephone, computer chip, television, computer mouse, compact disk and video cassette tapes (54x30mm). b, Potatoes, olives, cookies, cracker, sushi, shrimp, fish, pizza slice (54x30mm). c, Satellite, vacuum cleaner, chest freezer, coffee maker, stove, refrigerator, toaster, washing machine (54x30mm). d, Hay bales, cattle, tractor, storage shed, boarded windows, apartment house, automobiles, house (54x30mm). e, Radio, phonograph record, cassette tape player and headphones, mirrored ball, aerosol cans, electronic piano, dresses, make-up (54x30mm). f, Automobiles, rowboat, bus, scooter, sled, bicycle, cart, train (44x35mm).

2014, Oct. 23 Litho. ***Die Cut***

Self-Adhesive

1478	Booklet pane of 6	15.00	
a.-f.	A940 1 Any single	2.50	2.50

Nos. 1478a-1478f each sold for €1 on day of issue.

A941

Christmas — A942

Die Cut Perf. 13

2014, Oct. 23 Litho.

Self-Adhesive

1479	A941 75c multi	1.90	1.90
1480	A942 1 multi	2.50	2.50

No. 1480 sold for €1 on day of issue.

Marigold IceUnity Synchronized Skating Team — A943

Die Cut Perf. 14

2015, Jan. 19 Litho.

Self-Adhesive

Textured Paper

1481	A943 1 multi	2.25	2.25

No. 1481 sold for €1 on day of issue.

Miniature Sheet

St. Valentine's Day — A944

No. 1482 — Smiling: a, Snowflakes. b, Trees, snowflakes and bird. c, Mouse and snow angel. d, Birds in nest. e, Berry plants. f, Fox and rabbit.

Serpentine Die Cut 7

2015, Jan. 19 Litho.

Self-Adhesive

1482	A944 Sheet of 6 + 6 etiquettes	13.50	
a.-f.	1 Any single	2.25	2.25

Nos. 1482a-1482f each sold for €1 on day of issue.

Artists' Association of Finland, 150th Anniv. A945

No. 1483: a, Line Form, by Anneli Hilli (36x36mm). b, Point, by Mika Natri (36x36mm). c, Artist's Rollercoaster, by Marjo Suikkanen (36x40mm). d, Dance from the Bride, by Mayumi Niiranen-Hisatomi (32x40mm oval). e, Flight, by Laura Konttinen (36x30mm). f, You Will Know Them By Their Fruits, by Kalevi Karlsson (36x30mm).

Serpentine Die Cut 10¼

2015, Jan. 19 Litho.

Self-Adhesive

1483	Booklet pane of 6 + 6 etiquettes	13.50	
a.-f.	A945 1 Any single	2.25	2.25

Nos. 1483a-1483f each sold for €1 on day of issue.

Flowers A946

Die Cut Perf. 13¾

2015, Mar. 2 Litho.

Self-Adhesive

1484	A946 1 multi	2.50	2.50

No. 1484 sold for €1.10 on day of issue.

Easter — A947

Serpentine Die Cut 8¾

2015, Mar. 2 Litho.

Self-Adhesive

1485	A947 1 multi	2.50	2.50

No. 1485 sold for €1.10 on day of issue.

Student's Cap — A948

Die Cut Perf. 14¼

2015, Mar. 2 Litho.

Self-Adhesive

1486	A948 1 multi	2.50	2.50

No. 1486 sold for €1.10 on day of issue.

A949

A950

A951

International Women's Day — A952

2015, Mar. 2 Litho. ***Die Cut***

Self-Adhesive

1487	Booklet pane of 4	10.00	
a.	A949 1 multi	2.50	2.50
b.	A950 1 multi	2.50	2.50
c.	A951 1 multi	2.50	2.50
d.	A952 1 multi	2.50	2.50

Nos. 1487a-1487d each sold for €1.10 on day of issue.

Souvenir Sheet

Toivo Kärki (1915-92), Composer — A953

No. 1488 — Kärki and: a, Record album (44mm diameter). b, Score (45x32mm). c, Accordion, silhouette of man and woman (45x32mm).

Die Cut (#1488a), Die Cut Perf. 5¼

2015, Mar. 2 Litho.

Self-Adhesive

1488 A953 Sheet of 3 7.50
a.-c. 1 Any single 2.50 2.50

Nos. 1488a-1488c each sold for €1.10 on day of issue.

Rugosa Roses — A954

Orchids A955

Die Cut Perf. 13¾

2015, May 8 Litho.

Self-Adhesive

1489 Horiz. pair 4.50
a. A954 2 multi 2.25 2.25
b. A955 2 multi 2.25 2.25

Nos. 1489a-1489b each sold for €1 on day of issue.

Swan A956

Litho. With Foil Application

2015, May 8 *Die Cut Perf. 13½*

Self-Adhesive

1490 A956 1 multi 2.50 2.50

A957

Moomin Toys A958

Serpentine Die Cut 9¾

2015, May 8 Self-Adhesive Litho.

1491 Horiz. pair 5.00
a. A957 1 multi 2.50 2.50
b. A958 1 multi 2.50 2.50

Europa. Nos. 1491a-1491b each sold for €1.10 on day of issue.

Miniature Sheet

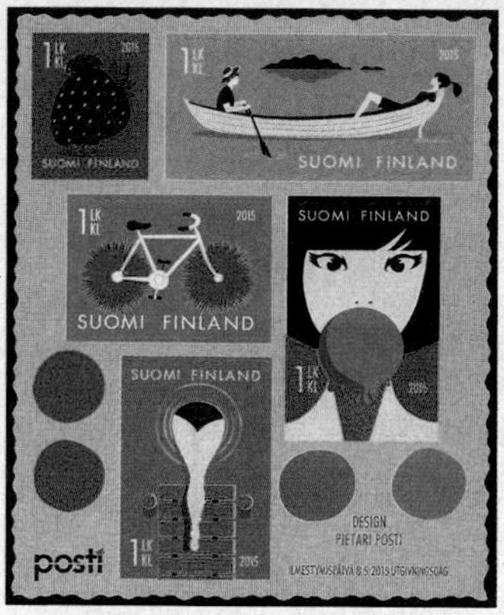

Sights of Summer — A959

No. 1492: a, Strawberry, ladybug and ant (22x30mm). b, Man and woman in rowboat (62x30mm). c, Bicycle (41x30mm). d, Woman with ice cream cone (30x50mm). e, Woman diving into water (30x45mm).

Serpentine Die Cut 9¼x11 (#1492a), 7½x6¼ (#1492b), 8x8¼ (#1492c), 7x6½ (#1492d), 7x7¼ (#1492e)

2015, May 8 Self-Adhesive Litho.

1492 A959 Sheet of 5 12.50
a.-e. 1 Any single 2.50 2.50

Nos. 1492a-1492e each sold for €1.10 on day of issue.

Miniature Sheet

Scenes From Imaginary Town — A960

No. 1493: a, Woman riding giraffe (20x33mm). b, Woman with shopping bag (38x21mm). c, Sailboat and swan (30mm diameter). d, House and horse (41x24mm). e, Rabbits in front of building with clock (34x21mm). f, Birds and flowers in pots (18x35mm).

Serpentine Die Cut 7¾ on 2 Opposite Sides, Die Cut (#1493c, 1493d)

2015, Sept. 11 Litho.

Self-Adhesive

1493 A960 Sheet of 6 15.00
a.-f. 1 Any single 2.50 2.50

Nos. 1493a-1493f each sold for €1.10 on day of issue.

Miniature Sheet

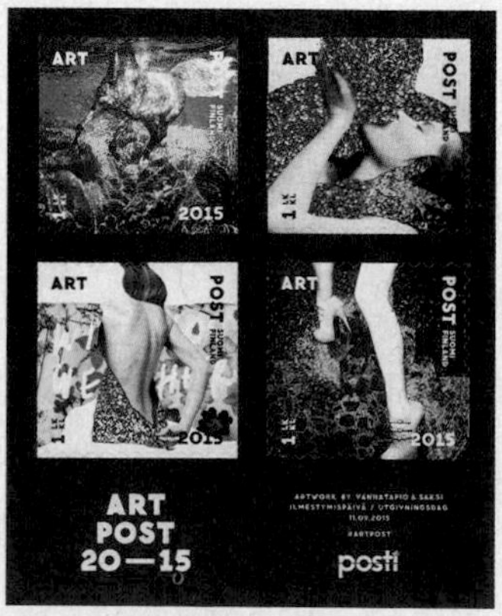

Art — A961

No. 1494: a, Horse running. b, Head and arm of woman. c, Woman unzipping dress. d, Woman's legs with high-heeled shoes.

Litho. With Foil Application

Serpentine Die Cut 6¾

2015, Sept. 11 Self-Adhesive

1494 A961 Sheet of 4 10.00
a.-d. 1 Any single 2.50 2.50

Nos. 1494a-1494d each sold for €1.10 on day of issue.

A962

A963

Jean Sibelius (1865-1957), Composer A964

Serpentine Die Cut 10¼

2015, Sept. 11 Litho.

Self-Adhesive

1495 Booklet pane of 3 + 3 etiquettes 7.50
a. A962 1 multi 2.50 2.50
b. A963 1 multi 2.50 2.50
c. A964 1 multi 2.50 2.50

Nos. 1495a-1495c each sold for €1.10 on day of issue.

The Rasmus A965

HIM A966

Apocalyptica A967

Children of Bodom A968

Hanoi Rocks — A969

Nightwish A970

Serpentine Die Cut 10¼x10 (#1496a-1496b), 9¾x10 (#1496c), 10¼x9½ (#1496d), 9½x10 (#1496e), 10¼x9¼ (#1496f)

2015, Sept. 11 Litho.

Self-Adhesive

1496 Booklet pane of 6 + 6 etiquettes 15.00
a. A965 1 multi 2.50 2.50
b. A966 1 multi 2.50 2.50
c. A967 1 multi 2.50 2.50
d. A968 1 multi 2.50 2.50
e. A969 1 multi 2.50 2.50
f. A970 1 multi 2.50 2.50

Rock bands. Nos. 1496a-1496f each sold for €1.10 on day of issue.

Finnish Design — A971

No. 1497: a, Marimekko Kukkuluuruu fabric design, by Sanna Annukka (28x45mm). b, Ultima Thule drinking glass, by Tapio Wirkkala (27x27mm). c, Block lamp, by Harri Koskinen (32x27mm). d, Paratiisi plate, by Birger Kaipiainen (27x33mm). e, Mademoiselle lounge chair, by Ilmari Tapiovaara (28x45mm). f, Solifer moped, by Richard Lindh (36x27mm).

Die Cut Perf. 13¼

2015, Sept. 11 Litho.

1497 Booklet pane of 6 15.00
a.-f. A971 1 Any single 2.50 2.50

Nos. 1497a-1497f each sold for €1.10 on day of issue.

SEMI-POSTAL STAMPS

Arms — SP1

Unwmk.

1922, May 15 Typo. *Perf. 14*

B1 SP1 1m + 50p gray & red .90 *10.00*
Never hinged 2.00
a. Perf. 13x13½ *11.00*
Never hinged *22.50*

Red Cross Standard SP2

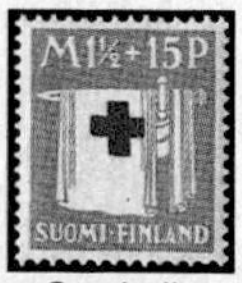

Symbolic SP3

Ship of Mercy — SP4

1930, Feb. 6

B2 SP2 1m + 10p red org & red 1.75 *11.50*
Never hinged 4.50

B3 SP3 1½m + 15p grysh grn & red 1.10 *11.50*
Never hinged 3.25
B4 SP4 2m + 20p dk bl & red 3.00 *50.00*
Never hinged 6.25
Nos. B2-B4 (3) 5.85 *73.00*
Set, never hinged 14.00

The surtax on this and subsequent similar issues was for the benefit of the Red Cross Society of Finland.

Church in Hattula — SP5

Designs: 1½m+15p, Castle of Hameenlinna. 2m+20p, Fortress of Viipuri.

1931, Jan. 1 Cross in Red Engr.
B5 SP5 1m + 10p gray grn 1.90 *14.00*
Never hinged 4.25
B6 SP5 1½m + 15p lil brn 11.50 *16.50*
Never hinged 35.00
B7 SP5 2m + 20p dull bl 1.90 *35.00*
Never hinged 3.50
Nos. B5-B7 (3) 15.30 *65.50*
Set, never hinged 42.50

SP8

1931, Oct. 15 Typo. ***Rouletted 4, 5***
B8 SP8 1m + 4m black 12.50 *45.00*
Never hinged 20.00

The surtax was to assist the Postal Museum of Finland in purchasing the Richard Granberg collection of entire envelopes.

Helsinki University Library SP9

Nikolai Church at Helsinki SP10

2½m+25p, Parliament Building, Helsinki.

1932, Jan. 1 ***Perf. 14***
B9 SP9 1¼m + 10p ol bis & red 1.50 *12.50*
Never hinged 4.75
B10 SP10 2m + 20p dp vio & red .40 *6.50*
Never hinged 1.00
B11 SP9 2½m + 25p lt blue & red 1.00 *25.00*
Never hinged 2.50
Nos. B9-B11 (3) 2.90 *44.00*
Set, never hinged 8.25

Bishop Magnus Tawast SP12

Michael Agricola SP13

Design: 2½m+25p, Isacus Rothovius.

1933, Jan. 20 Engr.
B12 SP12 1¼m + 10p blk brn & red 3.25 *16.00*
Never hinged 11.00
B13 SP13 2m + 20p brn vio & red 1.25 *4.50*
Never hinged 2.75
B14 SP13 2½m + 25p indigo & red 1.25 *8.75*
Never hinged 2.75
Nos. B12-B14 (3) 5.75 *29.25*
Set, never hinged 16.50

Evert Horn — SP15

Designs: 2m+20p, Torsten Stalhandske. 2½m+25p, Jakob (Lazy Jake) de la Gardie.

1934, Jan. Cross in Red
B15 SP15 1¼m + 10p brown 1.10 *4.50*
Never hinged 2.75
B16 SP15 2m + 20p gray lil 2.10 *8.00*
Never hinged 11.00
B17 SP15 2½m + 25p gray 1.10 *4.50*
Never hinged 2.75
Nos. B15-B17 (3) 4.30 *17.00*
Set, never hinged 16.50

Mathias Calonius — SP18

Designs: 2m+20p, Henrik C. Porthan. 2½m+25p, Anders Chydenius.

1935, Jan. 1 Cross in Red
B18 SP18 1¼m + 15p brown .90 *3.25*
Never hinged 2.10
B19 SP18 2m + 20p gray lil 2.00 *5.75*
Never hinged 5.75
B20 SP18 2½m + 25p gray bl .75 *3.25*
Never hinged 1.75
Nos. B18-B20 (3) 3.65 *12.25*
Set, never hinged 9.50

Robert Henrik Rehbinder — SP21

2m+20p, Count Gustaf Mauritz Armfelt. 2½m+25p, Count Arvid Bernard Horn.

1936, Jan. 1 Cross in Red
B21 SP21 1¼m + 15p dk brn .75 *2.40*
Never hinged 1.35
B22 SP21 2m + 20p vio brn 3.00 *7.25*
Never hinged 9.00
B23 SP21 2½m + 25p blue .75 *3.50*
Never hinged 1.60
Nos. B21-B23 (3) 4.50 *13.15*
Set, never hinged 12.00

Type "Uusimaa" SP24

Type "Turunmaa" SP25

Design: 3½m+35p, Type "Hameenmaa."

1937, Jan. 1 Cross in Red
B24 SP24 1¼m + 15p brown .70 *3.00*
Never hinged 2.00
B25 SP25 2m + 20p brn lake 13.00 9.00
Never hinged 50.00
B26 SP24 3½m + 35p indigo 1.00 *3.50*
Never hinged 2.75
Nos. B24-B26 (3) 14.70 15.50
Set, never hinged 54.00

Aukuste Makipeska — SP27

Designs: 1¼m+15p, Robert Isidor Orn. 2m+20p, Edward Bergenheim. 3½m+35p, Johan Mauritz Nordenstam.

1938, Jan. 5 Cross in Red Engr.
B27 SP27 50p + 5p dk grn .50 *1.35*
Never hinged .95
B28 SP27 1¼m + 15p dk brn .80 *2.25*
Never hinged 2.00
B29 SP27 2m + 20p rose lake 7.00 *7.50*
Never hinged 15.00
B30 SP27 3½m + 35p dk blue .55 *3.50*
Never hinged 1.25
Nos. B27-B30 (4) 8.85 *14.60*
Set, never hinged 19.00

Skiing — SP31

Designs: 2m+1m, Ski jumper. 3.50m+1.50m, Skier.

1938, Jan. 18
B31 SP31 1.25m + 75p sl grn 3.00 *13.00*
Never hinged 7.50
B32 SP31 2m + 1m dk car 3.00 *13.00*
Never hinged 7.50
B33 SP31 3.50m + 1.50m dk blue 3.00 *13.00*
Never hinged 7.50
Nos. B31-B33 (3) 9.00 *39.00*
Set, never hinged 22.50

Ski championships held at Lahti.

Soldier — SP34

1938, May 16
B34 SP34 2m + ½m blue 1.40 *5.00*
Never hinged 4.00

Victory of the White Army over the Red Guards. The surtax was for the benefit of the members of the Union of the Finnish Front.

Battlefield at Solferino SP35

1939, Jan. 2 Cross in Scarlet
B35 SP35 50p + 5p dk grn .85 *2.10*
Never hinged 1.75
B36 SP35 1¼m + 15p dk brn 1.00 *2.75*
Never hinged 1.50
B37 SP35 2m + 20p lake 14.00 *17.50*
Never hinged 32.50
B38 SP35 3½m + 35p dk bl .85 *3.50*
Never hinged 1.75
Nos. B35-B38 (4) 16.70 25.85
Set, never hinged 37.50

Intl. Red Cross Soc., 75th anniv.

Catalogue values for unused stamps in this section, from this point to the end of the section, are for Never Hinged items.

Soldiers with Crossbows — SP36

1¼m+15p, Cavalryman. 2m+20p, Soldier of Charles XII of Sweden. 3½m+35p, Officer and soldier of War with Russia, 1808-1809.

1940, Jan. 3 Cross in Red
B39 SP36 50p + 5p dk grn 1.40 *1.75*
B40 SP36 1¼m + 15p dk brn 3.50 3.00
B41 SP36 2m + 20p lake 5.50 3.50
B42 SP36 3½m + 35p dp ultra 3.50 *4.25*
Nos. B39-B42 (4) 13.90 12.50

The surtax aided the Finnish Red Cross.

Arms of Finland — SP40

1940, Feb. 15 Litho.
B43 SP40 2m +2m indigo .50 *1.75*

The surtax was given to a fund for the preservation of neutrality.

Mason — SP41

1.75m+15p, Farmer plowing. 2.75m+25p, Mother and child. 3.50m+35p, Finnish flag.

1941, Jan. 2 Cross in Red Engr.
B44 SP41 50p + 5p green .60 .55
B45 SP41 1.75m + 15p brown 1.75 *2.40*
B46 SP41 2.75m + 25p brn car 9.00 *9.50*
B47 SP41 3.50m + 35p dp ultra 2.00 *3.25*
Nos. B44-B47 (4) 13.35 15.70

See Nos. B65-B68.

Soldier's Emblem — SP45

1941, May 24 Unwmk.
B48 SP45 2.75m + 25p brt ultra .85 1.25

The surtax was for the aid of the soldiers who fought in the Russo-Finnish War.

Aland Arms — SP46

Coats of Arms: 1.75m+15p, Nyland. 2.75m+25p, Finland's first arms. 3.50m+35p, Karelia. 4.75m+45p, Satakunta.

1942, Jan. 2 ***Perf. 14***
Cross in Red
B49 SP46 50p + 5p green 1.40 1.25
B50 SP46 1.75m + 15p brown 2.10 *3.25*
B51 SP46 2.75m + 25p dark red 4.50 *3.25*

B52 SP46 3.50m + 35p deep ultra 3.50 *4.25*
B53 SP46 4.75m + 45p dk sl grn 2.75 *3.50*
Nos. B49-B53 (5) 14.25 *15.50*

The surtax aided the Finnish Red Cross.

Lapland Arms — SP51

Coats of Arms: 2m+20p, Hame. 3.50m+35p, Eastern Bothnia. 4.50m+45p, Savo.

Cross in Red

1943, Jan. 6 Inscribed "1943"
B54 SP51 50p + 5p green .70 *1.40*
B55 SP51 2m + 20p brown 1.50 *2.25*
B56 SP51 3.50m + 35p dark red 1.75 *2.25*
B57 SP51 4.50m + 45p brt ultra 4.25 *9.50*
Nos. B54-B57 (4) 8.20 *15.40*

The surtax aided the Finnish Red Cross.

Soldier's Helmet and Sword — SP55

Mother and Children — SP56

1943, Feb. 1 ***Perf. 13***
B58 SP55 2m + 50p dk brown .70 *1.20*
B59 SP56 3.50m + 1m brown red .70 *1.20*

The surtax was for national welfare.

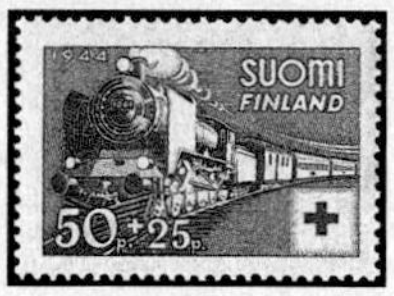

Red Cross Train — SP57

2m+50p, Ambulance. 3.50m+75p, Red Cross Hospital, Helsinki. 4.50m+1m, Hospital plane.

1944, Jan. 2 Cross in Red ***Perf. 14***
B60 SP57 50p + 25p green .45 *.50*
B61 SP57 2m + 50p sepia .85 *1.50*
B62 SP57 3.50m + 75p ver .70 *1.25*
B63 SP57 4.50m + 1m brt ultra 1.75 *4.75*
Nos. B60-B63 (4) 3.75 *8.00*

The surtax aided the Finnish Red Cross.

Symbols of Peace — SP61

1944, Dec. 1
B64 SP61 3.50m + 1.50m dk red brn .55 *1.10*

The surtax was for national welfare.

Type of 1941 Inscribed "1945"

1945, May 2 Photo. & Engr.

Cross in Red

B65 SP41 1m + 25p green .40 *.50*
B66 SP41 2m + 50p brown .40 *1.00*
B67 SP41 3.50m + 75p brn car .40 *.70*
B68 SP41 4.50m + 1m dp ultra .85 *2.40*
Nos. B65-B68 (4) 2.05 4.60

The surtax was for the Finnish Red Cross.

Wrestling — SP62

2m+1m, Gymnast. 3.50m+1.75m, Runner. 4.50m+2.25m, Skier. 7m+3.50m, Javelin thrower.

1945, Apr. 16 Engr. ***Perf. 13½***
B69 SP62 1m + 50p bluish grn .40 *1.20*
B70 SP62 2m + 1m dp red .40 *1.20*
B71 SP62 3.50m + 1.75m dull vio .40 *1.20*
B72 SP62 4.50m + 2.25m ultra .75 *1.50*
B73 SP62 7m + 3.50m dull brn 1.00 *2.50*
Nos. B69-B73 (5) 2.95 7.60

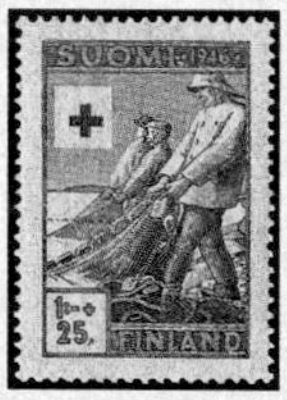

Fishing — SP67

Designs: 3m+75p, Churning. 5m+1.25m, Reaping. 10m+2.50m, Logging.

Engraved; Cross Typo. in Red

1946, Jan. 7
B74 SP67 1m + 25p dull grn .55 *.70*
B75 SP67 3m + 75p lilac brn .55 *.70*
B76 SP67 5m + 1.25m rose red .55 *.70*
a. Red cross omitted *850.00* 850.00
B77 SP67 10m + 2.50m ultra .70 *1.25*
Nos. B74-B77 (4) 2.35 *3.35*

The surtax was for the Finnish Red Cross.

Nurse and Children — SP71

Design: 8m+2m, Doctor examining infant.

1946, Sept. 2 Engr.
B78 SP71 5m + 1m green .50 *.75*
B79 SP71 8m + 2m brown vio .50 *.75*

The surtax was for the prevention of tuberculosis.

Nos. B78 and B79 Surcharged with New Values in Black

1947, Apr. 1
B80 SP71 6m + 1m on 5m + 1m .75 *1.10*
B81 SP71 10m + 2m on 8m + 2m .75 *1.10*

The surtax was for the prevention of tuberculosis.

SP73

Medical Examination of Infants — SP74

Designs: 10m+2.50m, Infant held by the feet. 12m+3m, Mme. Alli Paasikivi and a child. 20m+5m, Infant standing.

1947, Sept. 15 Engr.
B82 SP73 2.50m + 1m green .55 *1.40*
B83 SP74 6m + 1.50m dk red .70 *2.10*
B84 SP74 10m + 2.50m red brn 1.10 *2.10*
B85 SP73 12m + 3m dp blue 1.40 *2.75*
B86 SP74 20m + 5m dk red vio 2.10 *3.50*
Nos. B82-B86 (5) 5.85 *11.85*

The surtax was for the prevention of tuberculosis.
For surcharges see Nos. B91-B93.

Zachris Topelius — SP78

7m+2m, Fredrik Pacius. 12m+3m, Johan L. Runeberg. 20m+5m, Fredrik Cygnaeus.

Engraved; Cross Typo. in Red

1948, May 10 Unwmk. ***Perf. 14***
B87 SP78 3m + 1m green .50 *.75*
B88 SP78 7m + 2m rose red .65 *1.50*
B89 SP78 12m + 3m brt blue .75 *1.50*
B90 SP78 20m + 5m dk vio .90 *2.00*
Nos. B87-B90 (4) 2.80 5.75

The surtax was for the Finnish Red Cross.

Nos. B83, B84 and B86 Surcharged with New Values and Bars in Black

1948, Sept. 13 Engr. ***Perf. 13½***
B91 SP74 7m + 2m on #B83 2.25 *3.50*
B92 SP74 15m + 3m on #B84 2.25 *3.50*
B93 SP74 24m + 6m on #B86 2.50 *5.25*
Nos. B91-B93 (3) 7.00 12.25

The surtax was for the prevention of tuberculosis.

Tying Birch Boughs — SP79

9m+3m, Bathers in Sauna house. 15m+5m, Rural bath house. 30m+10m, Cold plunge in lake.

Engraved; Cross Typo. in Red

1949, May 5 ***Perf. 13½x14***
B94 SP79 5m + 2m dull grn .50 *.80*
B95 SP79 9m + 3m dk car .90 *1.40*
B96 SP79 15m + 5m dp blue .90 *1.40*
B97 SP79 30m + 10m dk vio brn 2.00 *3.25*
Nos. B94-B97 (4) 4.30 6.85

The surtax was for the Finnish Red Cross.

Wood Anemone — SP83

1949, June 2 Engr.

Inscribed: "1949"

B98 SP83 5m + 2m shown .80 *1.10*
B99 SP83 9m + 3m Wild rose 1.00 *1.25*
B100 SP83 15m + 5m Coltsfoot 1.00 *1.50*
Nos. B98-B100 (3) 2.80 3.85

The surtax was for the prevention of tuberculosis.

Similar to Type of 1949

Designs: 5m+2m, Water lily. 9m+3m, Pasqueflower. 15m+5m, Bell flower cluster.

1950, Apr. 1 Inscribed: "1950"
B101 SP83 5m + 2m emer 3.25 2.75
B102 SP83 9m + 3m rose car 2.40 2.00
B103 SP83 15m + 5m blue 2.40 2.00
Nos. B101-B103 (3) 8.05 6.75

The surtax was for the prevention of tuberculosis.

Hospital Entrance, Helsinki SP84

Blood Donor's Medal SP86

Design: 12m+3m, Giving blood.

Engraved; Cross Typo. in Red

1951, Mar. 17 Unwmk. ***Perf. 14***
B104 SP84 7m + 2m chocolate 1.10 *2.10*
B105 SP84 12m + 3m bl vio 1.75 *2.75*
B106 SP86 20m + 5m car 2.00 *3.50*
Nos. B104-B106 (3) 4.85 *8.35*

The surtax was for the Finnish Red Cross.

Capercaillie — SP87

Designs: 12m+3m, European cranes. 20m+5m, Caspian terns.

1951, Oct. 26 Engr.
B107 SP87 7m + 2m dk grn 3.75 *4.00*
B108 SP87 12m + 3m rose brn 3.75 *4.00*
B109 SP87 20m + 5m blue 3.75 *4.00*
Nos. B107-B109 (3) 11.25 *12.00*

The surtax was for the prevention of tuberculosis.

Diver — SP88

Soccer Players SP89

No. B112, Stadum, Helsinki. No. B113, Runners.

1951-52
B110 SP88 12m + 2m rose car 2.10 1.75
B111 SP89 15m + 2m grn ('52) 2.50 2.25
B112 SP88 20m + 3m deep blue 2.10 2.00
B113 SP89 25m + 4m brn ('52) 2.75 *3.00*
Nos. B110-B113 (4) 9.45 9.00

XV Olympic Games, Helsinki, 1952. The surtax was to help finance the games.
Issued: B110, B112, 11/16; B111, B113, 2/15/52.

Margin blocks of four of each denomination were cut from regular or perf-through-margin sheets and pasted by the selvage, overlapping, in a printed folder to create a kind of souvenir booklet. Value $60.

Field Marshal Mannerheim — SP90

Engraved; Cross Typo. in Red

1952, Mar. 4

B114 SP90 10m + 2m gray 2.40 *2.50*
B115 SP90 15m + 3m rose vio 2.40 *2.50*
B116 SP90 25m + 5m blue 2.40 *2.50*
Nos. B114-B116 (3) 7.20 *7.50*

The surtax was for the Red Cross.

Great Titmouse — SP91

Designs: 15m+3m, Spotted flycatchers and nest. 25m+5m, Swift.

1952, Dec. 4 **Engr.**

B117 SP91 10m + 2m green 3.75 *3.50*
B118 SP91 15m + 3m plum 3.75 *3.50*
B119 SP91 25m + 5m deep blue 3.75 *3.50*
Nos. B117-B119 (3) 11.25 *10.50*

The surtax was for the prevention of tuberculosis.
See Nos. B148-B150.

European Red Squirrel SP92

No. B121, Brown bear. No. B122, European elk.

Unwmk.

1953, Nov. 16 **Engr.** ***Perf. 14***

B120 SP92 10m + 2m red brown 3.75 *4.25*
B121 SP92 15m + 3m violet 3.75 *4.25*
B122 SP92 25m + 5m dark grn 3.75 *4.25*
Nos. B120-B122 (3) 11.25 *12.75*

Surtax for the prevention of tuberculosis.

Children Receiving Parcel from Welfare Worker — SP93

Designs: 15m+3m, Aged woman knitting. 25m+5m, Blind basket-maker and dog.

Engraved; Cross Typo. in Red

1954, Mar. 8 ***Perf. 11½***

B123 SP93 10m + 2m dk ol grn 1.50 *2.00*
B124 SP93 15m + 3m dk blue 1.50 *2.00*
B125 SP93 25m + 5m dk brown 1.50 *2.00*
Nos. B123-B125 (3) 4.50 *6.00*

The surtax was for the Finnish Red Cross.

Bumblebees, Dandelions — SP94

15m+3m, Butterfly. 25m+5m, Dragonfly.

Engraved; Cross Typo. in Red

1954, Dec. 7 ***Perf. 14***

B126 SP94 10m + 2m brown 2.75 2.10
B127 SP94 15m + 3m carmine 3.25 2.75
B128 SP94 25m + 5m blue 3.25 2.75
Nos. B126-B128 (3) 9.25 7.60

The surtax was for the prevention of tuberculosis.

European Perch — SP95

Designs: 15m+3m, Northern pike. 25m+5m, Atlantic salmon.

Engraved; Cross Typo. in Red

1955, Sept. 26 ***Perf. 14***

B129 SP95 10m + 2m dl grn 2.00 2.10
B130 SP95 15m + 3m vio brn 2.50 2.10
B131 SP95 25m + 5m dk bl 3.25 2.10
Nos. B129-B131 (3) 7.75 6.30

Surtax for the Anti-Tuberculosis Society.

Gen. von Dobeln in Battle of Juthas, 1808 — SP96

Illustrations by Albert Edelfelter from J. L. Runeberg's "Tales of Ensign Stal": 15m+3m, Col. J. Z. Duncker holding flag. 25m+5m, Son of fallen Soldier.

Engraved; Cross Typo. in Red

1955, Nov. 24

B132 SP96 10m + 2m dp ultra 1.75 *2.00*
B133 SP96 15m + 3m dk red brn 1.75 *2.00*
B134 SP96 25m + 5m green 1.75 *2.00*
Nos. B132-B134 (3) 5.25 6.00

The surtax was for the Red Cross.

Waxwing — SP97

Birds: 20m+3m, Eagle owl. 30m+5m, Mute swan.

Engraved; Cross Typo. in Red

1956, Sept. 25 ***Perf. 11½***

B135 SP97 10m + 2m dl red brn 2.10 1.25
B136 SP97 20m + 3m bl grn 2.75 2.10
B137 SP97 30m + 5m blue 3.75 2.10
Nos. B135-B137 (3) 8.60 5.45

Surtax for the Anti-Tuberculosis Society.

Pekka Aulin — SP98

Portraits: 10m+2m, Leonard von Pfaler. 20m+3m, Gustaf Johansson. 30m+5m, Viktor Magnus von Born.

Engraved; Cross Typo. in Red

1956, Nov. 26 **Unwmk.**

B138 SP98 5m + 1m grysh grn 1.00 1.25
B139 SP98 10m + 2m brown 1.50 1.50
B140 SP98 20m + 3m magenta 2.25 2.25
B141 SP98 30m + 5m lt ultra 2.25 2.25
Nos. B138-B141 (4) 7.00 7.25

The surtax was for the Red Cross.

Wolverine (Glutton) — SP99

20m+3m, Lynx. 30m+5m, Reindeer.

Engraved; Cross Typo. in Red

1957, Sept. 5 ***Perf. 11½***

B142 SP99 10m + 2m dull purple 2.00 1.50
B143 SP99 20m + 3m sepia 3.00 2.40
B144 SP99 30m + 5m dark blue 3.00 2.40
Nos. B142-B144 (3) 8.00 6.30

The surtax was for the Anti-Tuberculosis Society. See Nos. B160-B165.

Red Cross Flag — SP100

1957, Nov. 25 **Engr.** ***Perf. 14***
Cross in Red

B145 SP100 10m + 2m ol grn 1.75 2.40
B146 SP100 20m + 3m maroon 2.00 3.50
B147 SP100 30m + 5m dull blue 2.00 3.50
Nos. B145-B147 (3) 5.75 9.40

80th anniv. of the Finnish Red Cross.

Type of 1952

Flowers: 10m+2m, Lily of the Valley. 20m+3m, Red clover. 30m+5m, Hepatica.

Engraved; Cross Typo. in Red

1958, May 5 **Unwmk.** ***Perf. 14***

B148 SP91 10m + 2m green 2.40 1.60
B149 SP91 20m + 3m lilac rose 2.75 2.60
B150 SP91 30m + 5m ultra 3.00 2.60
Nos. B148-B150 (3) 8.15 6.80

Surtax for the Anti-Tuberculosis Society.

Raspberry — SP101

20m+3m, Cowberry. 30m+5m, Blueberry.

Engraved; Cross Typo. in Red

1958, Nov. 20 ***Perf. 11½***

B151 SP101 10m + 2m orange 2.40 1.75
B152 SP101 20m + 3m red 2.75 2.25
B153 SP101 30m + 5m dk blue 2.75 2.25
Nos. B151-B153 (3) 7.90 6.25

The surtax was for the Red Cross.

Daisy — SP102

20m+5m, Primrose. 30m+5m, Cornflower.

Engraved; Cross Typo. in Red

1959, Sept. 7 **Unwmk.**

B154 SP102 10m + 2m green 4.00 2.00
B155 SP102 20m + 3m lt brown 4.50 3.00
B156 SP102 30m + 5m blue 4.50 3.00
Nos. B154-B156 (3) 13.00 8.00

Surtax for the Anti-Tuberculosis Society.

Reindeer SP103

No. B158, Lapp & lasso. No. B159, Mountains.

Engraved; Cross Typo. in Red

1960, Nov. 24 ***Perf. 11½***

B157 SP103 10m + 2m dk gray 1.50 1.50
B158 SP103 20m + 3m gray vio 2.25 2.25
B159 SP103 30m + 5m rose vio 2.25 2.25
Nos. B157-B159 (3) 6.00 6.00

The surtax was for the Red Cross.

Animal Type of 1957

Designs: 10m+2m, Muskrat. 20m+3m, Otter. 30m+5m, Seal.

Engr.; Cross at right, Typo. in Red

1961, Sept. 4

B160 SP99 10m + 2m brn car 1.75 1.40
B161 SP99 20m + 3m slate bl 2.50 2.00
B162 SP99 30m + 5m bl grn 2.50 2.00
Nos. B160-B162 (3) 6.75 5.40

Surtax for the Anti-Tuberculosis Society.

Animal Type of 1957

Designs: 10m+2m, Hare. 20m+3m, Pine marten. 30m+5m, Ermine.

Engraved; Cross Typo. in Red

1962, Oct. 1

B163 SP99 10m + 2m gray 1.90 1.90
B164 SP99 20m + 3m dl red brn 2.50 2.25
B165 SP99 30m + 5m vio bl 2.50 2.25
Nos. B163-B165 (3) 6.90 6.40

The surtax was for the Anti-Tuberculosis Society.

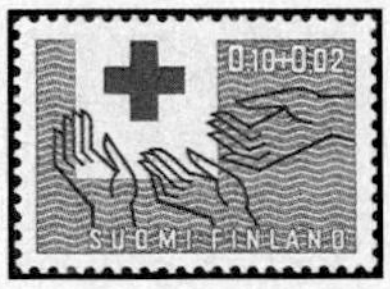

Cross and Outstretched Hands SP104

Engraved; Cross Typo. in Red

1963, May 8 **Unwmk.** ***Perf. 11½***

B166 SP104 10p + 2p red brn .75 1.00
B167 SP104 20p + 3p violet 1.25 1.50
B168 SP104 30p + 5p green 1.25 1.50
Nos. B166-B168 (3) 3.25 4.00

The surtax was for the Red Cross.

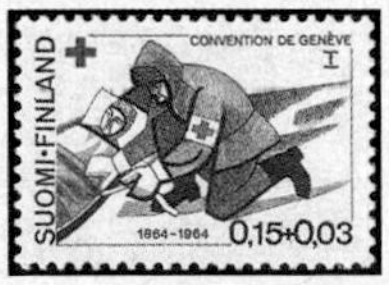

Attending the Wounded SP105

Red Cross Activities: 25p+4p, Hospital ship. 35p+5p, Prisoner-of-war health examination. 40p+7p, Gift parcel distribution.

Engraved; Cross Typo. in Red

1964, May 26 ***Perf. 11½***

B169 SP105 15p + 3p vio bl 1.25 .70
B170 SP105 25p + 4p green 1.50 1.10
B171 SP105 35p + 5p vio brn 1.50 1.10
B172 SP105 40p + 7p dk ol grn 1.50 1.10
Nos. B169-B172 (4) 5.75 4.00

The surtax was for the Red Cross.

Finnish Spitz — SP106

Designs: 25p+4p, Karelian bear dog. 35p+5p, Finnish hunting dog.

Engraved; Cross Typo. in Red

1965, May 10 *Perf. 11½*

B173 SP106 15p + 3p org brn 2.00 1.50
B174 SP106 25p + 4p black 3.00 2.25
B175 SP106 35p + 5p gray brn 3.00 2.25
Nos. B173-B175 (3) 8.00 6.00

Surtax for Anti-Tuberculosis Society.

Artificial Respiration — SP107

First Aid: 25p+4p, Skin diver rescuing occupants of submerged car. 35p+5p, Helicopter rescue in winter.

1966, May 7 **Litho.** *Perf. 14*

B176 SP107 15p + 3p multi 1.10 1.25
B177 SP107 25p + 4p multi 1.25 1.50
B178 SP107 35p + 5p multi 1.25 1.50
Nos. B176-B178 (3) 3.60 4.25

The surtax was for the Red Cross.

Birch — SP108

Trees: 25p+4p, Pine. 40p+7p, Spruce.

1967, May 12 **Litho.** *Perf. 14*

B179 SP108 20p + 3p multi 1.00 1.00
B180 SP108 25p + 4p multi 1.00 1.00
B181 SP108 40p + 7p multi 1.00 1.00
Nos. B179-B181 (3) 3.00 3.00

Surtax for Anti-Tuberculosis Society. See Nos. B185-B187.

Horse-drawn Ambulance SP109

25p+4p, Ambulance, 1967. 40p+7p, Red Cross.

Cross in Red

1967, Nov. 24 **Litho.** *Perf. 14*

B182 SP109 20p + 3p dl yel, grn & blk 1.10 1.10
B183 SP109 25p + 4p vio & blk 1.10 1.10
B184 SP109 40p + 7p dk grn, blk & dk ol 1.10 1.10
Nos. B182-B184 (3) 3.30 3.30

The surtax was for the Red Cross.

Tree Type of 1967

Trees: 20p+3p, Juniper. 25+4p, Aspen. 40p+7p, Chokecherry.

1969, May 12 **Litho.** *Perf. 14*

B185 SP108 20p + 3p multi .90 1.10
B186 SP108 25p + 4p multi .90 1.10
B187 SP108 40p + 7p multi .90 1.10
Nos. B185-B187 (3) 2.70 3.30

Surtax for Anti-Tuberculosis Society.

"On the Lapp's Magic Rock" SP110

Designs: 30p+6p, Juhani blowing horn on Impivaara Rock, vert. 50p+10p, The Pale Maiden. The designs are from illustrations by Askeli Gallen-Kallelas for "The Seven Brothers" by Aleksis Kivi.

1970, May 8 **Litho.** *Perf. 14*

B188 SP110 25p + 5p multi .70 .70
B189 SP110 30p + 6p multi .85 .90
B190 SP110 50p + 10p multi .85 .90
Nos. B188-B190 (3) 2.40 2.50

The surtax was for the Red Cross.

Cutting and Loading Timber SP111

Designs: 30p+6p, Floating logs downstream. 50p+10p, Sorting logs at sawmill.

1971, Apr. 25 **Litho.** *Perf. 14*

B191 SP111 25p + 5p multi .90 1.00
B192 SP111 30p + 6p multi .90 1.00
B193 SP111 50p + 10p multi 1.00 1.00
Nos. B191-B193 (3) 2.80 3.00

Surtax for Anti-Tuberculosis Society.

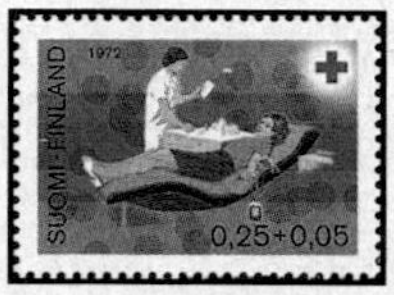

Blood Donor and Nurse SP112

30p+6p, Blood research (microscope, slides), vert. 50p+10p, Blood transfusion.

1972, Oct. 23

B194 SP112 25p + 5p multi .70 .85
B195 SP112 30p + 6p multi 1.10 1.10
B196 SP112 50p + 10p multi 1.10 1.10
Nos. B194-B196 (3) 2.90 3.05

Surtax was for the Red Cross.

Girl with Lamb, by Hugo Simberg — SP113

Paintings: 40p+10p, Summer Evening, by Vilho Sjöström. 60p+15p, Woman at Mountain Fountain, by Juho Rissanen.

1973, Sept. 12 **Litho.** *Perf. 13x12½*

B197 SP113 30p + 5p multi 1.25 1.25
B198 SP113 40p + 10p multi 1.75 1.75
B199 SP113 60p + 15p multi 1.75 1.75
Nos. B197-B199 (3) 4.75 4.75

Surtax for the Finnish Anti-Tuberculosis Assoc. Birth centenaries of featured artists.

Morel SP114

Mushrooms: 50p+10p, Chanterelle. 60p+15p, Boletus edulis.

1974, Sept. 24 **Litho.** *Perf. 12½x13*

B200 SP114 35p + 5p multi 2.50 1.50
B201 SP114 50p + 10p multi 2.25 1.50
B202 SP114 60p + 15p multi 2.25 1.50
Nos. B200-B202 (3) 7.00 4.50

Finnish Red Cross.

Echo, by Ellen Thesleff (1869-1954) SP115

Paintings: 60p+15p, Hilda Wiik, by Maria Wiik (1853-1928). 70p+20p, At Home (old woman in chair), by Helene Schjerfbeck (1862-1946).

1975, Sept. 30 **Litho.** *Perf. 13x12½*

B203 SP115 40p + 10p multi 1.10 1.10
B204 SP115 60p + 15p multi 1.25 .125
B205 SP115 70p + 20p multi 1.25 1.25
Nos. B203-B205 (3) 3.60 2.48

Finnish Red Cross. In honor of International Women's Year paintings by women artists were chosen.

Disabled Veterans' Emblem SP116

Lithographed and Photogravure

1976, Jan. 15 *Perf. 14*

B206 SP116 70p + 30p multi .80 .80

The surtax was for hospitals for disabled war veterans.

Wedding Procession SP117

Designs: 70p+15p, Wedding dance, vert. 80p+20p, Bride, groom, matron and pastor at wedding dinner.

1976, Sept. 15 **Litho.** *Perf. 13*

B207 SP117 50p + 10p multi .85 .95
B208 SP117 70p + 15p multi 1.10 1.10
B209 SP117 80p + 20p multi 1.10 1.10
Nos. B207-B209 (3) 3.05 3.15

Surtax for Anti-Tuberculosis Society.

Disaster Relief SP118

Designs: 80p+15p, Community work. 90p+20p, Blood transfusion service.

1977, Jan. 19 **Litho.** *Perf. 14*

B210 SP118 50p + 10p multi .65 .65
B211 SP118 80p + 15p multi .80 .80
B212 SP118 90p + 20p multi .80 .80
Nos. B210-B212 (3) 2.25 2.25

Finnish Red Cross centenary.

Long-distance Skiing SP119

Design: 1m+50p, Ski jump.

1977, Oct. 5 **Litho.** *Perf. 13*

B213 SP119 80p + 40p multi 2.50 3.75
B214 SP119 1m + 50p multi 2.00 2.00

Surtax was for World Ski Championships, Lahti, Feb. 17-26, 1978.

Saffron Milkcap SP120

Edible Mushrooms: 80p+15p, Parasol, vert. 1m+20p, Gypsy.

1978, Sept. 13 **Litho.** *Perf. 13*

B215 SP120 50p + 10p multi 1.75 1.10
B216 SP120 80p + 15p multi 2.00 2.00
B217 SP120 1m + 20p multi 2.00 2.00
Nos. B215-B217 (3) 5.75 5.10

Surtax was for Red Cross. See Nos. B221-B223.

Pehr Kalm, 1716-1779 SP121

Finnish Scientists: 90p+15p, Title page of Pehr Adrian Gadd's (1727-97) book, vert. 1.10m+20p, Petter Forsskal (1732-63).

Perf. 12½x13, 13x12½

1979, Sept. 26 **Litho.**

B218 SP121 60p + 10p multi .65 .80
B219 SP121 90p + 15p multi .85 .85
B220 SP121 1.10m + 20p multi .85 .85
Nos. B218-B220 (3) 2.35 2.50

Surtax for Finnish Anti-Tuberculosis Assoc.

Mushroom Type of 1978

Edible Mushrooms: 60p+10p, Woolly milk-cap. 90p+15p, Orange-cap boletus, vert. 1.10m+20p, Russula paludosa.

1980, Apr. 19 **Litho.** *Perf. 13*

B221 SP120 60p + 10p multi 1.50 1.10
B222 SP120 90p + 15p multi 2.00 2.00
B223 SP120 1.10m + 20p multi 2.00 2.00
Nos. B221-B223 (3) 5.50 5.10

Surtax was for Red Cross.

Fuchsia — SP122

1981, Aug. 24 **Litho.** *Perf. 13*

B224 SP122 70p + 10p shown 1.10 1.10
B225 SP122 1m + 15p African violet 1.10 1.10
B226 SP122 1.10m + 20p Geranium 1.10 1.10
Nos. B224-B226 (3) 3.30 3.30

Surtax for Finnish Anti-Tuberculosis Assoc.

Garden Dormouse SP123

1982, Aug. 16 **Litho.** *Perf. 13*

B227 SP123 90p + 10p shown 1.10 1.00
B228 SP123 1.10m + 15p Flying squirrels 1.10 1.10
B229 SP123 1.20m + 20p European minks 1.25 1.10
Nos. B227-B229 (3) 3.45 3.20

Surtax was for Red Cross. No. B228 vert.

Forest and Wetland Plants SP124

1m+20p, Chickweed wintergreen. 1.20m+25p, Marsh violet. 1.30m+30p, Marsh marigold.

1983, July 7 **Litho.** *Perf. 13*

B230 SP124 1m + 20p multi 1.00 1.00
B231 SP124 1.20m + 25p multi 1.00 1.00
B232 SP124 1.30m + 30p multi 1.00 1.00
Nos. B230-B232 (3) 3.00 3.00

Surtax for Finnish Anti-Tuberculosis Assoc.

Globe Puzzle — SP125

2m+40p, Symbolic world communication.

1984, May 28 Litho. Perf. 13

B233 SP125 1.40m + 35p multi .80 .75
B234 SP125 2m + 40p multi 1.25 1.10

Surtax for Red Cross.

Butterflies SP126

No. B235, Anthocharis cardamines. No. B236, Nymphalis antiopa. No. B237, Parnassius apollo.

1986, May 22 Litho. Perf. 13

B235 SP126 1.60m + 40p multi 1.25 .85
B236 SP126 2.10m + 45p multi 1.90 1.50
B237 SP126 5m + 50p multi 4.00 4.00
Nos. B235-B237 (3) 7.15 6.35

Surtax for Red Cross.

Festivals SP127

1988, Mar. 14 Litho. Perf. 13

B238 SP127 1.40m +40p Christmas 1.10 .85
B239 SP127 1.80m +45p Easter 1.25 .90
B240 SP127 2.40m +50p Midsummer 1.25 1.25
Nos. B238-B240 (3) 3.60 3.00

Surtax for the Red Cross.

Heodes virgaureae on Goldrod Plant SP128

Butterflies and plants: No. B242, *Agrodiaetus amandus* on meadow vetchling. No. B243, *Inachis io* on tufted vetch.

1990, Apr. 6 Photo. Perf. 12x11½

B241 SP128 1.50m +40p multi 1.00 1.00
B242 SP128 2m +50p multi 1.25 1.25
B243 SP128 2.70m +60p multi 1.50 1.50
Nos. B241-B243 (3) 3.75 3.75

Surtax for the natl. Red Cross Soc.

Paintings by Helene Schjerfbeck — SP129

Designs: No. B244a, The Little Convalescent, No. B244b, Green Still-Life.

1991, Mar. 8 Litho. Perf. 13

B244 SP129 Pair 3.00 3.00
a.-b. 2.10m +50p any single 1.40 1.40

Surtax for philately.

Butterflies SP130

No. B245, Xestia brunneopicta. No. B246, Acerbia alpina. No. B247, Baptria tibiale.

Litho. & Embossed

1992, Apr. 22 Perf. 13

B245 SP130 1.60m +40p multi .90 .90
B246 SP130 2.10m +50p multi 1.20 1.20
B247 SP130 5m +60p multi 2.25 2.75
Nos. B245-B247 (3) 4.35 4.85

Surtax for Finnish Red Cross. Embossed "Arla 100" in braille for Arla Institute, training center for the blind, cent.

Autumn Landscape of Lake Pielisjarvi, by Eero Jarnefelt SP131

a, Tree-covered hill. b, Lake shoreline.

1993, Mar. 19 Litho. Perf. 13

B248 SP131 2.30m + 70p Pair, #a.-b. 3.00 3.00

Surtax for philately.

Finnhorses SP132

1994, Mar. 11 Litho. Perf. 13

B249 SP132 2m +40p Draft horses 1.00 1.00
B250 SP132 2.30m +50p Trotter 1.50 1.50
B251 SP132 4.20m +60p War horses, vert. 2.25 2.25
Nos. B249-B251 (3) 4.75 4.75

Surtax for Finnish Red Cross.

Paintings, by Albert Edelfelt (1854-1905) — SP133

No. B252, Playing Boys on the Shore. No. B253, Queen Blanche.

1995, Mar. 1 Litho. Perf. 13½

B252 2.40m +60p multi 2.25 1.50

Size: 22x31mm

B253 2.40m +60p multi 2.25 1.50
a. SP133 Pair, #B252-B253 4.50 4.50

Surtax for philately.

Chickens SP134

1996, Mar. 18 Litho. Perf. 13

B254 SP134 2.80m +60p Chicks 1.90 2.40
B255 SP134 3.20m +70p Hens 1.90 1.90
B256 SP134 3.40m +70p Rooster, vert. 2.00 3.50
Nos. B254-B256 (3) 5.80 7.80

Surtax for Finnish Red Cross.

The Aino Myth, by Akseli Gallen-Kallela (1865-1931) SP135

Designs: No. B257, Väinämöinen proposing marriage to Aino in forest. No. B258, Aino jumping into water to escape Väinämöinen. No. B259, Aino at shore for bath.

1997, Sept. 5 Litho. Perf. 13½x13

Booklet Stamps

B257 SP135 2.80m +60p multi 2.25 2.25
B258 SP135 2.80m +60p multi 2.25 2.25
B259 SP135 2.80m +60p multi 2.25 2.25
a. Booklet pane, #B257-B259 6.75 6.75
Complete booklet, #B259a 6.75

No. B258 is 33x46mm.

Surtax for philately.

Pigs — SP136

2.80m+60p, Sow, piglets. 3.20m+70p, Three piglets. 3.40m+70p, Pig's head.

1998, Mar. 12 Litho. Perf. 13

B260 SP136 2.80m +60p multi 1.60 1.60
B261 SP136 3.20m +70p multi 1.90 1.90
B262 SP136 3.40m +70p multi 2.00 2.00
Nos. B260-B262 (3) 5.50 5.50

Surtax for Finnish Red Cross.

Paintings by Hugo Simberg (1873-1917) SP137

a, Garden of Death. b, Wounded Angel.

Perf. 13¼x13¾

1999, Sept. 24 Litho.

B263 Booklet pane of 2 4.25 4.25
a.-b. SP137 3.50m +50p any single 2.00
Complete booklet, #B263 4.25

Surtax for philately.

Cow and Calf — SP138

Perf. 13¾x13¼

2000, Mar. 15 Litho.

B264 SP138 3.50m +70p Bull, vert. 1.50 1.20

Perf. 13¼x13¾

B265 SP138 4.80m +80p shown 2.25 2.00

Surtax for Finnish Red Cross.

Post Horn SP139

2010, May 4 Litho. Perf. 14½x14¼

B266 SP139 1 +5c multi 2.75 2.60

No. B266 had a franking value of 80c on day of issue. Surtax for construction of Finland's first solar energy plant.

AIR POST STAMPS

No. 178 Overprinted in Red

1930, Sept. 24 Unwmk. Perf. 14

C1 A28 10m gray lilac 140.00 *290.00*
a. 1830 for 1930 2,500. *12,000.*

Overprinted expressly for use on mail carried in "Graf Zeppelin" on return flight from Finland to Germany on Sept. 24, 1930, after which trip the stamps ceased to be valid for postage. Forgeries are almost always on No. 205, rather than No. 178.

Catalogue values for unused stamps in this section, from this point to the end of the section, are for Never Hinged items.

Douglas DC-2 — AP1

1944 Engr.

C2 AP1 3.50m dark brown .70 *1.40*

Air Transport Service anniv, 1923-43.

Douglas DC-6 Over Winter Landscape — AP2

1950, Feb. 13

C3 AP2 300m blue 17.50 7.00

Available also for ordinary postage.

Redrawn

1958, Jan. 20 Perf. 11½

C4 AP2 300(m) blue 32.50 .80

On No. C4 "mk" is omitted.

See Nos. C9-C9a.

Convair 440 over Lakes — AP3

1958, Oct. 31 Unwmk. Perf. 11½

C5 AP3 34m blue 1.25 .75

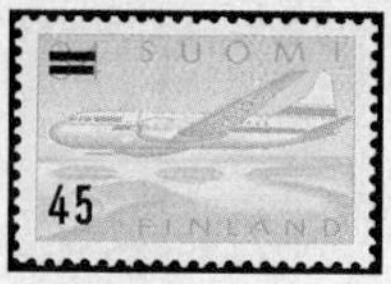

No. C5 Surcharged

1959, Apr. 5
C6 AP3 45m on 34m blue 2.50 2.25

C7

C8

1959, Nov. 2
C7 AP3 45m blue 3.00 1.50

1963, Feb. 15
C8 AP3 45p blue 2.00 .40

On No. C7 the denomination is "45." On No. C8 it is "0.45."

DC-6 Type, Comma After "3" — AP5

Type I — 16 lines in numeral "0"
Type II — 13 lines in numeral "0"

1963, Oct. 10
C9 AP5 3m blue, Type II ('73) 3.25 .30
a. Type I 40.00 .40

Convair Type of 1958

1970, July 15
C10 AP3 57p ultra 2.00 1.25

MILITARY STAMPS

Catalogue values for unused stamps in this section are for Never Hinged items.

M1

Unwmk.

1941, Nov. 1 Typo. *Imperf.*
M1 M1 (4m) blk, *dk org* .80 *.90*

#M1 has simulated roulette printed in black.

Type of 1930-46 Overprinted in Black

1943, Oct. 16 *Perf. 14*
M2 A26 2m deep orange .65 *1.10*
M3 A26 3½m greenish blue .65 *1.10*

Post Horn and Sword — M2

1943, July 1 Size: 29½x19½mm
M4 M2 (2m) green .90 .75
M5 M2 (3m) rose violet 1.10 .75

1944, Feb. 16 Size: 20x16mm
M6 M2 (2m) green .75 .60
M7 M2 (3m) rose violet .75 .60

Post Horns and Arms of Finland — M3

1963, Sept. 26 Litho. *Perf. 14*
M8 M3 violet blue *160.00 175.00*

Used during maneuvers Sept. 30-Oct. 5, 1963. Valid from Sept. 26.

No. M8 Overprinted "1983"

1983, Apr. 20
M9 M3 violet blue *250.00 175.00*

Used during maneuvers Apr. 24-30.

PARCEL POST STAMPS

PP1

Wmk. Rose & Triangles Multiple
Rouletted 6 on 2 or 3 Sides

1949-50 Typo.
Q1 PP1 1m brt grn & blk 1.90 *5.00*
Q2 PP1 5m red & blk 20.00 *32.50*
Q3 PP1 20m org & blk 30.00 *55.00*
Q4 PP1 50m bl & blk ('50) 12.00 *17.50*
Q5 PP1 100m brn & blk ('50) 12.50 *17.50*
Nos. Q1-Q5 (5) 76.40 *127.50*
Set, never hinged 130.00

Catalogue values for unused stamps in this section, from this point to the end of the section, are for Never Hinged items.

Mail Bus — PP2

1952-58 Unwmk. Engr. *Perf. 14*
Q6 PP2 5m car rose 6.25 5.50
Q7 PP2 20m orange 25.00 11.00
Q8 PP2 50m blue ('54) 37.50 17.50
Q9 PP2 100m brn ('58) 50.00 37.50
Nos. Q6-Q9 (4) 118.75 71.50

Mail Bus — PP3

1963 *Perf. 12*
Q10 PP3 5p red & blk 3.50 5.00
Q11 PP3 20p org & blk 18.00 8.50
Q12 PP3 50p blue & blk 10.50 8.25
Q13 PP3 1m brn & blk 14.50 8.75
Nos. Q10-Q13 (4) 46.50 30.50

Nos. Q1-Q13 were issued only in booklets: panes of 6 for Nos. Q1-Q5, 10 for Nos. Q6-Q9 and 5 for Nos. Q10-Q13.

Used values are for regular postal or mail-bus cancels. Pen strokes, cutting or other cancels sell for half as much.

1981 SISU Bus — PP4

Photo. & Engr.

1981, Dec. 7 *Perf. 12 Horiz.*
Q14 PP4 50p dk bl & blk 2.75 *5.75*
Q15 PP4 1m dk brn & blk 3.25 *5.75*
Q16 PP4 5m grn & blk 4.00 *16.00*
Q17 PP4 10m red & blk 7.25 *32.50*
Nos. Q14-Q17 (4) 17.25 *60.00*

Parcel post stamps invalid after Jan. 9, 1985.

ALAND ISLANDS

LOCATION — A group of 6,554 islands at the mouth of the Gulf of Bothnia, between Finland and Sweden.
GOVT. — Province of Finland
AREA — 590 sq. mi.
POP. — 23,761
CAPITAL — Mariehamn

The province of Aland was awarded to Finland in 1921 by the League of Nations. The Swedish language is spoken and the province has a considerable amount of self-determination.

Catalogue values for unused stamps in this country are for Never Hinged items.
Most Aland Island issues exist favor canceled, and used values are for such cancellations. Postally used examples are worth 30 to 40% more than the values shown.

Gaff-rigged Sloop — A1

Aland Flag — A2

Midsummer Pole — A3

Landscapes — A4

Map of Scandinavia — A5

Seal of St. Olaf and Aland Province, 1326 — A6

Artifacts — A7

Sea Birds — A8

Gothic Tower, Jomala Church, 12th Cent. — A9

Mariehamn Town Hall, Designed by Architect Lars Sonck — A9a

Designs: 1.50m, Statue of Frans Petter von Knorring, vicar from 1834 to 1875, and St. Michael's Church, Finstrom, 12th cent. 1.60m, Burial site, clay hands. 1.70m, Somateria mollissima. 2.20m, Bronze Staff of Finby, apostolic decoration. 2.30m, Aythya fuligula. 5m, Outer Aland Archipelago. 8m, Farm and windmill. 12m, Melantha fusca. 20m, Ancient court site, contemporary monument.

1984-90 Engr. Unwmk. *Perf. 12*
1 A1 10p magenta .25 .25
2 A1 20p brown olive .25 .25
3 A1 50p bright green .35 .25
4 A1 1.10m deep blue .70 .70
5 A1 1.20m black .55 .50
6 A1 1.30m dark green 1.00 .60

Litho.

Perf. 14, 13x14 (#8)
7 A2 1.40m multi .75 .30
8 A9 1.40m multi 2.00 1.20
9 A3 1.50m multi, I 2.00 1.00
9A A3 1.50m multi, II 1.00 .80
10 A9 1.50m multi 2.00 1.25

Perf. 13, 14 (#13)
11 A7 1.60m multi, vert. 2.00 1.75
12 A8 1.70m multi 8.00 8.00
13 A9a 1.90m multi 2.00 1.50
14 A4 2m multi 2.00 2.00
15 A7 2.20m multi, vert. 2.00 1.00
16 A8 2.30m multi 4.00 4.00
17 A5 3m multi 3.50 1.50
18 A4 5m multi, horiz. 3.00 2.75
19 A4 8m multi, horiz. 5.50 3.75

Litho. & Engr.
20 A6 10m multi 5.50 4.00

Litho.
21 A8 12m multi 8.00 8.00
22 A7 20m multi 10.50 10.50
Nos. 1-22 (23) 66.85 55.85

On No. 9A (type II) "Aland" is 10½mm long, figure support is 2mm wide, pole supports are thinner, diagonal black highlighting lines in pole greenery and horizontal black line on support under the man removed.

Issued: Nos. 2-4, 7, 17, 20, 3/1/84; Nos. 1, 5, 6, 9, 1/2/85; Nos. 14, 18-19, 9/16/85; Nos. 11, 15, 22, 4/4/86; Nos. 12, 16, 21, 1/2/87; No. 8, 8/26/88; No. 13, 1/2/89; No. 10, 9/4/89; No. 9A, 5/21/90.

See Nos. 39-42, 87-92, 178-179, 195-196.

A10

Bark Pommern and car ferries, Mariehamn West Harbor

1984, Mar. 1 Litho. *Perf. 14*
23 A10 2m multicolored 8.50 3.00

A11

1986, Jan. 2 Litho. *Perf. 14*
24 A11 1.60m multicolored 3.00 2.00

1986 Nordic Orienteering Championships, Aug. 30-31.

Onningeby Artists' Colony, Cent. — A12

Design: Pallette, pen and ink drawing of Onningeby landscape, 1891, by Victor Westerholm (1860-1919), founder.

1986, Sept. 1 Litho.
25 A12 3.70m multicolored 3.00 *2.00*

Mariehamn Volunteer Fire Brigade, Cent. — A13

1987, Apr. 27 Litho. *Perf. 14*
26 A13 7m multicolored 4.00 3.00

Farjsund Bridge, 50th Anniv., Rebuilt in 1980 — A14

1987, Apr. 27 Engr. *Perf. 13x13½*
27 A14 1m greenish black .75 .60

Municipal Meeting, Finstrom, 1917 — A15

1987, Aug. 20 Litho. *Perf. 14*
28 A15 1.70m multicolored 1.00 1.00

Movement for reunification with Sweden, 70th anniv.

Loading of Mail Barrels on Sailboat, Post Office, Eckero — A16

1988, Jan. 4 Litho. *Perf. 14*
29 A16 1.80m multicolored 3.00 2.50

Postal Service, 350th anniv. From Feb. I to May 31, Alanders were entitled to buy 20 stamps for 28m with a discount coupon.

New Aland Farm School, Horse-Drawn Plow — A17

1988, Mar. 29 Litho. *Perf. 14*
30 A17 2.20m multicolored 2.25 *1.75*

Haga Farm School, cent.; Aland Farm School, 75th anniv.; 50th anniv. of experimental farming on Aland.

Sailing Ships — A18

1988, June 4 Litho. *Perf. 13*

31	A18	1.80m Albanus, 1904, vert.	2.50	1.50
32	A18	2.40m Ingrid, c. 1900	4.00	4.00
33	A18	11m Pamir, c. 1900	10.00	10.00
		Nos. 31-33 (3)	16.50	15.50

Type of 1988 and

Orchids — A19

Fish
A20

Handicrafts
A21

Fresco, St. Anna's Church of Kumlinge
A22

Mammals
A23

Geological Formations
A24 A25

Designs: 10p, Boulder field, Geta. No. 35, *Dactylorhiza sambucina.* No. 36, *Clupea harengus membras.* No. 37, *Erinaceus europauus.* No. 38, Drumlin, Finstrom. 1.70m, St. Andrew Church, Lumparland. No. 40, Vardo Church. No. 41, Hammarland Church. No. 42, Sottunga Church. No. 43, *Esox lucius.* No. 45, Diabase dike, Sottunga, Basskar. 2.10m, *Sciurus vulgaris.* 2.50m, *Cephalanthera longifolia.* No. 48, *Platichthys flesus.* No. 49, Pillow lava, Kumlinge, western Varpskar. No. 50, *Capreolus capreolus.* No. 51, Rouche Moutonne, Roda Kon, Lumparn. 6m, Folded gneiss, Sottunga, Gloskar. 13m, Tapestry, 1793. 14m, *Cypripedium calceolus.*

Perf. 13, 14 (Nos. 39-42, 44, 53), 15x14½ (10p, Nos. 38, 45, 49, 51-52)

1989-94 Litho.

34	A25	10p multicolored	.25	.25
35	A19	1.50m multicolored	1.40	2.25
36	A20	1.50m multicolored	1.60	1.20
37	A23	1.60m multicolored	1.40	1.00
38	A25	1.60m multicolored	1.50	1.10
39	A9	1.70m multicolored	1.50	1.20
40	A9	1.80m multicolored	1.40	1.10
41	A9	1.80m multicolored	1.25	1.25
42	A9	1.80m multicolored	1.25	1.25
43	A20	2m multicolored	1.60	1.20
44	A22	2m multicolored	1.10	.90
45	A24	2m multicolored	.90	.80
46	A23	2.10m multicolored	1.40	1.00
47	A19	2.50m multicolored	2.00	2.00
48	A20	2.70m multicolored	1.60	1.20
49	A24	2.70m multicolored	1.25	1.00
50	A23	2.90m multicolored	1.60	1.10
51	A25	2.90m multicolored	2.50	1.75
52	A24	6m multicolored	2.50	2.50
53	A21	13m multicolored	6.75	5.75
54	A19	14m multicolored	9.00	9.00
		Nos. 34-54 (21)	43.75	38.80

Issued: 2.50m, 14m, No. 35, 4/10/89; 2.70m, No. 36, 43, 3/1/90; 13m, 4/19/90; 1.70m, No. 44, 9/10/90; 1.60m, 2.10m, No. 50, 3/3/91; No. 40, 10/9/91; No. 41 10/5/92; Nos. 45, 49, 52, 9/3/93; No. 42, 10/8/93; 10p, Nos. 38, 51, 2/1/94.

See Nos. 96, 102, 105.

Educational System of the Province, 350th Anniv. — A33

1989, May 31 Litho. *Perf. 14*
57 A33 1.90m multicolored 1.50 .90

Souvenir Sheet

1991 Aland Island Games — A34

a, Volleyball. b, Shooting. c, Soccer. d, Running.

1991, Apr. 5 Litho. *Perf. 13x12½*
58 A34 2.10m Sheet of 4, #a.-d. 5.00 5.00

Autonomy of Aland, 70th Anniv. — A35

1991, June 4 *Perf. 13*
59 A35 16m multicolored 8.25 6.25

Kayaking
A36

1991, June 4 *Perf. 14*
60 A36 2.10m shown 1.25 .75
61 A36 2.90m Cycling 1.75 1.25

Rev. Frans Peter Von Knorring (1792-1875), Educator — A37

Cape Horn Congress, Mariehamn, June 8-11 — A38

1992, Mar. 2 Litho. *Perf. 13*
62 A37 2 multicolored 1.40 1.00

Litho. & Engr.
Perf. 13½x14
63 A38 1 multicolored 3.00 2.25

No. 62 sold for 1.60m, No. 63 for 2.10m.

On stamps bearing the "denominations" "1" or "2," the number represents the class of mail.

Lighthouses
A39

1992, May 8 Litho. *Perf. 13*
Booklet Stamps

64	A39	2.10m Ranno	7.75	4.50
65	A39	2.10m Salskar	7.75	4.50
66	A39	2.10m Lagskar	7.75	4.50
67	A39	2.10m Market	7.75	4.50
a.		Booklet pane of 4, #64-67	30.00	22.50

First Aland Provincial Parliament, 70th Anniv. — A40

1992, June 8 Litho. *Perf. 13*
68 A40 3.40m multicolored 1.75 1.75

Joel Pettersson (1892-1937), Painter — A41

1992, June 8

69	A41	2.90m	Landscape from Lemland	1.50	1.25
70	A41	16m	Self-Portrait	8.50	7.00

Arms of Aland — A42

1993, Mar. 1 **Litho.** ***Perf. 14***

71	A42	1.60m	gray, sepia & blue	1.20	.90

Autonomy Act, Jan. 1.

Souvenir Sheet

Autonomous Postal Administration — A43

Designs: a, Inscriptions from old letter canceled in Kastelholm, vert. b, Mariehamn post office. c, Ferry, mail truck. d, New post office emblem, vert.

Perf. 12½x13, 14 (#b.-c.)

1993, Mar. 1 **Litho., Engr. (#b.-c.)**

72	A43	1.90m	Sheet of 4, #a.-d.	3.00	3.00

Fiddler, Jan Karlsgarden Museum — A44

2.30m, Boat Shed, Jan Karlsgarden Museum.

Perf. 13x12½, 12½x13

1993, May 7 **Litho.**

73	A44	2m	multicolored	1.40	1.00
74	A44	2.30m	multi, horiz.	1.40	1.00

Folk Dresses — A45

Clothing from: 1.90m, Saltvik. 3.50m, Brando, Eckero, Mariehamn. 17m, Finstrom.

1993, June 1 ***Perf. 12½***

75	A45	1.90m	multicolored	1.25	1.25
76	A45	3.50m	multicolored	2.00	1.50
77	A45	17m	multicolored	9.00	6.75
			Nos. 75-77 (3)	12.25	9.50

Butterflies A46

Perf. 14 on 3 Sides

1994, Mar. 1 **Litho.**

Booklet Stamps

78	A46	2.30m	Melitaea cinxia	1.60	1.25
79	A46	2.30m	Quercusia quercus	1.60	1.25
80	A46	2.30m	Parnassius mnemosyne	1.60	1.25
81	A46	2.30m	Hesperia comma	1.60	1.25
a.			Booklet pane, 2 each #78-81	13.00	*11.00*
			Nos. 78-81 (4)	6.40	5.00

A47

Europa, Inventions and Discoveries: 2.30m, Diagram showing transmission of von Willebrand's Disease, discovered by E. A. von Willebrand. 2.90m, Purification of heparin, by Erik Jorpes.

1994, May 5 **Litho.** ***Perf. 13***

82	A47	2.30m	multicolored	*2.75*	*2.25*
83	A47	2.90m	multicolored	*1.90*	*1.60*

Types of 1989-93 and

Ice Age Survivors — A48

Fossils — A49

Sea Birds — A50

Bronze Age — A51

Stone Age — A52

Ships — A53

Lichens — A54

Primula Veris — A55

30p, Saduria entomon, mysis relicta. 40p, Trilobita asaphus. 1.80m, Sterna paradisaea. No. 87, Church of Mariehamn. No. 88, Church of Eckerö. No. 89, St. Bridget's Church, Lemland. No. 90, Church of St. John the Baptist, Sund. No. 91, St. George Church, Geta. No. 92, Church of Brando. No. 93, Bronze sword, bronze dagger. No. 94, Ship tumulus grave. No. 95, Larus canus. 2.30m, Pitcher of Kallskar. No. 97, Pottery. No. 98, Myoxocephalus quadricornis. 2.60m, Larus marinus. No. 100, Stone tools. No. 101, SS Thornbury. 3.40m, Erratic boulders. 3.50m, SS Osmo. 4.30m, Phoca hispida. 7m, Potholes. 9m, Gastropoda euomophalus. 18m, Settlement. 2, Hypogmnia physodes. 1, Xanthoria parietina.

Perf. 13 (A48, A50, A52, A54), 15x14½ (No. 89), 14½x15 (Nos. 101-103, 105), 14½ (40p, Nos. 88, 93-94, 96), 14 (Nos. 87, 90-92), 15 (No. 106)

1994-2000 **Engr.**

84	A48	30p	multi	.25	.25
85	A49	40p	multi	.25	.50
86	A50	1.80m	multi	.80	.70
87	A9	1.90m	multi	1.00	.90
88	A9	1.90m	multi	1.00	.90
89	A9	1.90m	multi	.75	.90
90	A9	2m	multi	1.25	1.00
91	A9	2m	multi	1.25	1.25
92	A9	2m	multi	1.25	1.00
93	A51	2m	multi	.85	.75
94	A51	2.20m	multi, vert.	1.00	.85
95	A50	2.20m	multi, vert.	.90	.70
96	A24	2.30m	multi	1.10	1.00
97	A52	2.40m	multi, vert.	1.90	1.50
98	A48	2.40m	multi	1.50	.90
99	A50	2.60m	multi	1.25	.90
100	A52	2.80m	multi, vert.	1.50	1.20
101	A53	2.80m	multi	1.10	1.00
102	A24	3.40m	multi, horiz.	1.75	1.50
103	A53	3.50m	multi	1.75	2.25
104	A48	4.30m	multi	2.25	1.90
105	A24	7m	multi, horiz.	3.25	2.75
106	A49	9m	multi	5.00	4.00
107	A52	18m	multi	9.25	6.00

Perf. 13

107A	A54	2	multi	1.10	.90
107B	A54	1	multi	1.10	.90

Self-Adhesive

Serpentine Die Cut Perf. 10

108	A55	2.40m	multi	1.00	1.10
			Nos. 84-108 (27)	45.35	37.50

No. 108 was issued in sheets of 10.

Nos. 107A-107B sold for 2m and 2.40m, respectively, on day of issue.

Issued: Nos. 97, 100, 18m, 8/16/94; No. 90, 10/7/94; 2.30m, 3.40m, 7m, 1/2/95; No. 91, 9/15/95; 40p, No. 92, 9m, 10/9/96; 30p, No. 98, 4.30m, 2/3/97; Nos. 101, 103, 9/8/97; No. 87, 10/9/97; No. 88, 10/9/98; Nos. 93-94, 2/1/99; No. 108, 4/28/99; Nos. 107A-107B, 9/25/99; No. 89, 10/8/99; 1.80m, No. 95, 2.60m, 1/3/00.

Cargo Vessels — A58

Perf. 14 on 3 Sides

1995, Mar. 1 **Litho.**

Booklet Stamps

109	A58	2.30m	Skuta	1.10	1.25
110	A58	2.30m	Sump	1.10	1.25
111	A58	2.30m	Storbat	1.10	1.25
112	A58	2.30m	Jakt	1.10	1.25
a.			Booklet pane, 2 each #109-112	9.00	*11.00*
			Complete booklet, #112a	9.50	
			Nos. 109-112 (4)	4.40	5.00

Entry into European Union — A59

1995, Mar. 1 **Litho.** ***Perf. 13x14***

113	A59	2.90m	multicolored	1.50	*1.75*

Europa — A60

1995, May 5 **Litho.** ***Perf. 13x14***

114	A60	2.80m	shown	*1.40*	*1.25*
115	A60	2.90m	Dove, island in sea	*1.40*	*1.25*

Tourism — A61

1995, May 12

116	A61	2	Golf	1.00	1.20
117	A61	1	Fishing	1.25	.75

Nos. 116-117 sold for value 2m and 2.30m, respectively.

Optimist Dinghy World Championships — A62

1995, June 2 **Litho.** ***Perf. 13½x14***

118	A62	3.40m	multicolored	1.75	1.50

St. Olaf (995?-1030), Patron Saint of Aland — A63

Litho. & Engr.

1995, Sept. 15 ***Perf. 13½x13***

119	A63	4.30m	multicolored	2.25	2.00

See Faroe Islands No. 289

A64

Greeting Stamps (stylized designs): No. 120, Fish with natl. flag, "Hälsningar fran Aland." No. 121, Yellow bird with flower, "Grattis."

1996, Feb. 14 **Litho.** ***Perf. 13x14***

120	A64	1	multicolored	1.20	1.00
121	A64	1	multicolored	1.20	.80

Nos. 120-121 had a face value of 2.30m on day of issue.

A65

Eagle owl (bubo bubo): No. 122, Landing on tree branch over lake. No. 123, Perched on branch over lake. No. 124, Male, darker feathers. No. 125, Female, lighter feathers.

Booklet Stamps

1996, Mar. 1 ***Perf. 14 on 3 Sides***

122	A65	2.40m	multicolored	1.20	1.25
123	A65	2.40m	multicolored	1.20	1.25
124	A65	2.40m	multicolored	1.20	1.25
125	A65	2.40m	multicolored	1.20	1.25
a.			Booklet pane, 2 ea #122-125	9.00	10.00
			Complete booklet, No. 125a	9.50	
			Nos. 122-125 (4)	4.80	5.00

World Wildlife Fund.

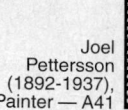

Famous Women A66

Europa: 2.80m, Sally Salminen (1906-76), writer. 2.90m, Fanny Sundström (1883-1944), politician.

1996, May 6 Litho. *Perf. 14x13*

126 A66 2.80m multicolored 1.40 2.00
127 A66 2.90m multicolored 1.40 2.00

A67

1996, June 7 Litho. *Perf. 13½x14*

128 A67 2.40m multicolored 1.25 1.10

Aland '96 Song and Music Festival.

A68

"Haircut," by Karl Emanuel Jansson (1846-74).

1996, June 7 *Perf. 13*

129 A68 18m multicolored 9.00 8.00

Spring Flowers — A69

Designs: No. 130, Tussilago farfara. No. 131, Hepatica nobilis. No. 132, Anemone nemorosa. No. 133, Anemone ranunculoides.

1997, Feb. 3 Litho. *Perf. 14*

Booklet Stamps

130 A69 2.40m multicolored 1.10 1.10
131 A69 2.40m multicolored 1.10 1.10
132 A69 2.40m multicolored 1.10 1.10
133 A69 2.40m multicolored 1.10 1.10
a. Booklet pane, 2 each #130-133 9.00 *10.00*
Complete booklet, #133a 9.50

A70

1997, May 3 Litho. *Perf. 14x13½*

134 A70 3.40m multicolored 1.50 1.25

1st Floorball World Championships, Aland.

A71

Devil's Dance with Clergyman's Wife.

1997, May 9 *Perf. 13x14*

135 A71 2.90m multicolored *2.50 1.25*

Europa.

Kalmar Union, 600th Anniv. — A72

Design: Kastelholm Castle, arms of Lord High Chancellor Bo Jonsson Grip.

1997, May 30 Litho. *Perf. 14x13*

136 A72 2.40m multicolored 1.25 1.10

Souvenir Sheet

Autonomy, 75th Anniv. — A73

1997, June 9 *Perf. 13*

137 A73 20m multicolored 10.00 *11.00*

No. 137 contains a holographic image. Soaking in water may affect the hologram.

Horticulture A74

1998, Feb. 2 Litho. *Perf. 14½x15*

138 A74 2m Apples .75 .75
139 A74 2.40m Cucumbers 1.10 .85

Youth Activities A75

No. 140, Riding moped. No. 141, Computer. No. 142, Listening to music. No. 143, Aerobics.

1998, Mar. 28 *Perf. 14 on 3 Sides*

Booklet Stamps

140 A75 2.40m multicolored 1.10 1.25
141 A75 2.40m multicolored 1.10 1.25
142 A75 2.40m multicolored 1.10 1.25
143 A75 2.40m multicolored 1.10 1.25
a. Booklet pane, 2 each #140-143 9.00 *10.00*
Complete booklet, #143a 9.50

Midsummer Celebration in Aland — A76

1998, Apr. 27 Litho. *Perf. 14*

144 A76 4.20m multicolored *1.75 1.50*

Europa.

Passenger Ferry — A77

1998, May 8 *Perf. 14½*

145 A77 2.40m multicolored 1.25 1.00

Intl. Year of the Ocean — A78

1998, May 8

146 A78 6.30m multicolored 2.75 2.10

ATP Senior Tour of Champions Tennis Tournament, Mariehamn A79

Serpentine Die Cut

1998, June 25 Litho.

Self-Adhesive

147 A79 2.40m multicolored 1.25 1.40

Issued in sheets of 10.

Scouting — A80

1998, Aug. 1 *Perf. 14*

148 A80 2.80m multicolored 1.25 1.00

Foyers — A81

Homesteads: 1.60m, Seffers. 2m, Labbas. 2.90m, Abras.

1998, Sept. 11 Litho. *Perf. 14½*

149 A81 1.60m multicolored .75 .70
150 A81 2m multicolored .90 .70
151 A81 2.90m multicolored 1.25 .85
Nos. 149-151 (3) 2.90 2.25

18th Century Furniture Ornamentation A82

Perf. 14 on 3 Sides

1999, Feb. 1 Litho.

Booklet Stamps

152 A82 2.40m Wardrobe 1.50 1.25
153 A82 2.40m Distaff 1.50 1.25
154 A82 2.40m Chest 1.50 1.25
155 A82 2.40m Spinning wheel 1.50 1.25
a. Booklet pane, 2 each #152-155 12.00
Complete booklet, #155a 12.50

Passage of Cape Horn by Grain Ships Pamir & Passat, 50th Anniv. A83

1999, Mar. 19 Litho. *Perf. 14½*

156 A83 3.40m multicolored 1.50 1.50

Beginning with No. 157, denominations are indicated on many stamps in both Markkas and Euros. The value shown is in Markkas.

Nature Reserve, Kökar — A84

1999, Apr. 28 Litho. *Perf. 13*

157 A84 2.90m multicolored *1.25 1.20*

Europa.

Match Sailboat Racing — A85

1999, Aug. 5 Litho. *Perf. 14½x15*

158 A85 2.70m multicolored 1.10 1.00

UPU, 125th Anniv. A86

1999, Sept. 25

159 A86 2.90m multicolored 1.20 1.00

Finnish Cross-Country Championships, Mariehamn — A87

1999, Oct. 9 Litho. *Perf. 14¾x14½*

160 A87 3.50m multicolored 1.40 1.20

Souvenir Sheet

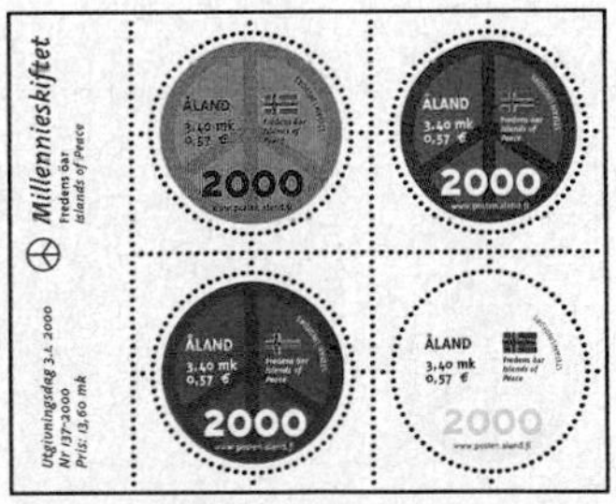

Peace Symbol, Aland Flag — A88

Background colors: a, Yellow. b, Red. c, Blue. d, White.

Litho. & Embossed

2000, Jan. 3 *Perf. 13*

161 A88 3.40m Sheet of 4, #a.-d. 6.00 6.00

Elk — A89

Elk in: No. 162, Spring. No. 163, Summer. No. 164, Autumn. No. 165, Winter.

Perf. 11¾on 3 sides

2000, Mar. 1 Litho.

Booklet Stamps

162 A89 2.60m multicolored 1.10 1.10
163 A89 2.60m multicolored 1.10 1.10
164 A89 2.60m multicolored 1.10 1.10
165 A89 2.60m multicolored 1.10 1.10
a. Block of 4, #162-165 4.50 4.50
b. Booklet pane, 2 #165a 9.00 *10.50*
Complete booklet, #165b 9.50

Europa, 2000
Common Design Type

2000, May 9 *Perf. 13*
166 CD17 3m multicolored *2.00 1.10*

A90

Self-Adhesive
Coil Stamp

2000, June 9 ***Die Cut Perf. 13x13¼***
167 A90 2.60m multicolored 1.75 1.40

Gymnastics Festival, Mariehamn.

A91

2000, July 21 Litho. ***Perf. 13½x13¼***
168 A91 3.40m multicolored 1.50 1.20

Cutty Sark Tall Ships race to Mariehamn.

Vikings From Aland — A92

2000, July 28
169 A92 4.50m multicolored 2.00 1.75

Recreation of Viking market, Saltvik.

Architecture by Hilda Hongell (1867-1952) A93

2000, Aug. 25 ***Perf. 13¼x13¾***
170 A93 3.80m shown 1.75 1.25
171 A93 10m House, diff. 4.75 4.00

Christianity, 2000th Anniv. — A94

2000, Oct. 9 ***Perf. 13***
172 A94 3m multicolored 1.40 1.10

Church Type of 1984-90 and

Swamp Plants — A95

Swamp plants: 1.90m, Equisetum fluviatile. 2.80m, Lycopodium annotinum. 3.50m, Polypodium vulgare.

Churches: No. 179, Föglö Church, Föglö. 2m, Kökar Church, Kökar.

Perf. 13x13¼, 13 (#178)

2000-01 Litho.

177	A95	1.90m multicolored	1.00	1.10
178	A9	2m multicolored	1.25	1.00
179	A9	2m multi	.90	.70
180	A95	2.80m multicolored	1.25	1.40
182	A95	3.50m multicolored	1.75	1.90
		Nos. 177-182 (5)	6.15	6.10

These stamps are part of an ongoing definitive set. Numbers have been reserved for additional stamps.

Issued: 2m, 10/9; 1.90m, 2.80m, 3.50m, 1/2/01; No. 179, 10/9/01.

Worldwide Fund for Nature (WWF) — A100

Polysticta stelleri: a, Pair in flight. b, Pair on rock. c, Pair in water. d, Male in water.

Perf. 13¼ on 3 sides

2001, Jan. 2 Litho.

Booklet Stamps

185	A100 Block of 4		5.00	5.50
a.-d.	2.70m any single		1.25	1.40
e.	Booklet pane, 2 #185		10.00	*11.00*
	Booklet, #185e		11.00	

Valentine's Day — A101

2001, Feb. 14 ***Perf. 14½x14¾***
186 A101 3.20m multicolored 1.40 1.10

Europa A102

2001, May 9 Litho. ***Perf. 14½x14¾***
187 A102 3.20m multi *1.60 1.25*

Windmills A103

Windmill types: 3m, Archipelago. 7m, Timbered, horiz. 20m, Nest, horiz.

Perf. 13¾x14¼, 14¼x13¾

2001, June 8
188-190 A103 Set of 3 13.00 11.50

Puppies — A104

Designs: 2, Golden retriever. 1, Wire-haired dachshund.

2001, Sept. 3 ***Perf. 13¼***
191-192 A104 Set of 2 2.75 2.00

Nos. 191-192 sold for 2.30m and 2.70m respectively on day of issue.

100 Cents = 1 Euro (€)

Church Type of 1998 with Euro Denominations and

Fauna — A105

Post Terminal — A106

Mushrooms A107

Designs: 5c, Coronella austriaca. 10c, Chanterelle mushroom. 35c, Saltviks Church. 40c, Kumlinge Church. 50c, King Bolete mushroom. 70c, Triturus cristatus. €1, Post Terminal. €2.50, Parasol mushroom.

Perf. 12½, 13 (#193, 196), 13¼ (#198), 14¾x14 (#195)

2002-03 Litho.

193	A105	5c multi	.25	.25
194	A107	10c multi	.30	.30
195	A9	35c multi	1.00	1.00
196	A9	40c multi	1.10	1.10
197	A107	50c multi	1.75	1.40
198	A105	70c multi	2.00	1.50
199	A106	€1 multi	2.75	2.10
200	A107	€2.50 multi	8.75	6.00
		Nos. 193-200 (8)	17.90	13.65

Issue dates: 5c, 70c, 1/2/02; €1, 2/28/02; 35c, 10/9/02; 10c, 50c, €2.50, 1/2/03. No. 196, 10/9/03.

This is an expanding set. Numbers may change.

Introduction of the Euro — A108

2002, Jan. 2 Litho. ***Perf. 12½***
201 A108 60c multi 1.60 1.25

St. Canute's Day — A109

2002, Jan. 2
202 A109 €2 multi 3.75 3.25

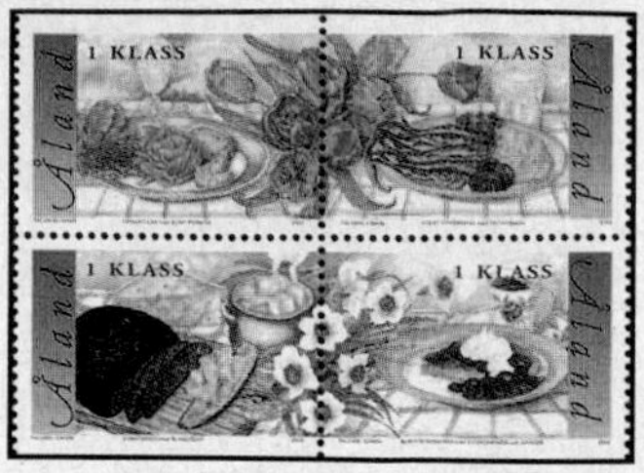

Cuisine — A110

Flowers and: a, Gravlax, boiled potatoes. b, Fried herring, beets, mashed potatoes. c, Black bread, cheese, butter. d, Pancake with prune sauce and whipped cream, coffee.

Perf. 13½x13¼ on 3 Sides

2002, Feb. 28 Litho.

203	A110 Block of 4		7.00	5.50
a.-d.	1 Any single		1.75	1.40
e.	Booklet pane, 2 #203		14.00	
	Booklet, #203e		14.00	

Nos. 203a-203d each sold for 55c on day of issue.

Europa — A111

2002, May 3 ***Perf. 13¼***
204 A111 40c multi *1.40 1.00*

Radar II, Sculpture by Stefan Lindfors A112

2002, May 3 ***Perf. 13***
205 A112 €3 multi 8.00 7.00

"My Aland," by Lill Lindfors A113

2002, Aug. 12 Litho. ***Perf. 13¼***
206 A113 90c multi 2.50 2.00

Iron Age Artifacts — A114

Designs: No. 207, 2, Buckle found in Persby. No. 208, 1, Ornamental pin found in Syllöda.

2002, Sept. 2 ***Perf. 13x13¼***
207-208 A114 Set of 2 3.00 2.75

Nos. 207-208 sold for 45c and 55c respectively on day of issue.

Janne Holmén, Marathon Gold Medalist in European Track and Field Championships A115

2002, Nov. 1 ***Perf. 12½***

209	A115	1 multi	1.75	1.50

Sold for 55c on day of issue.

House Cats — A116

2003, Mar. 14 **Litho.** ***Perf. 13¼***

210	A116	2 Tovis	1.25	.85
211	A116	1 Randi, horiz.	1.75	.95

Nos. 210-211 sold for 45c and 55c respectively on day of issue.

Landscape in Summer, by Elin Danielson-Gambogi (1861-1919) — A117

No. 212: a, Woman at fence. b, Tree without leaves. c, Sun. d, Boat.

2003, Mar. 28 ***Perf. 14 Vert.***

Booklet Stamps

212	A117	Horiz. strip of 4	6.25	6.25
a.-d.		1 Any single	1.50	1.50
e.		Booklet pane, 2 #212	12.50	12.50
		Complete booklet, #212e	13.00	

Nos. 212a-212d each sold for 55c on day of issue.

Europa — A118

2003, May 9 ***Perf. 13¼***

213	A118	45c multi	*1.25*	*1.00*

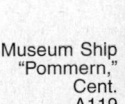

Museum Ship "Pommern," Cent. A119

2003, June 6 ***Die Cut Perf. 9¼x9½***

Booklet Stamp

Self-Adhesive

214	A119	55c multi	1.50	1.40
a.		Booklet pane of 4	12.00	12.00
		Complete booklet, 2 #214a	25.00	

Mark and Stephen Levengood on Beach — A120

2003, June 18 ***Perf. 12½***

215	A120	55c multi	1.50	1.40

Aland Folk Music Association, 50th Anniv. — A121

2003, Aug. 1 ***Perf. 14¼***

216	A121	€1.10 buff & black	3.00	2.25

St. Lucia's Day Celebrations A122

2003, Oct. 9 **Litho.** ***Perf. 12½***

217	A122	60c multi	1.60	1.50

Mammals — A123

Designs: 20c, Mustela erminea. 60c, Vulpes vulpes. €3, Martes martes.

2004, Feb. 2 **Litho.** ***Perf. 14½x14¼***

218	A123	20c multi	.65	.60
219	A123	60c multi	2.00	1.50
220	A123	€3 multi	8.75	7.75
		Nos. 218-220 (3)	11.40	9.85

Souvenir Sheet

Norse Gods Fenja and Menja — A124

2004, Mar. 26 ***Perf. 14¼x14¾***

221	A124	55c multi	2.25	2.40

Aland Flag, 50th Anniv. — A125

Serpentine Die Cut 12½

2004, Apr. 23 **Booklet Stamp**

Self-Adhesive

222	A125	1 multi	2.00	1.75
a.		Booklet pane of 4	8.00	6.75
		Complete booklet, 2 #222a	20.00	

No. 222a was reprinted in 2007 with a hole for a pegboard hook. See No. 296.

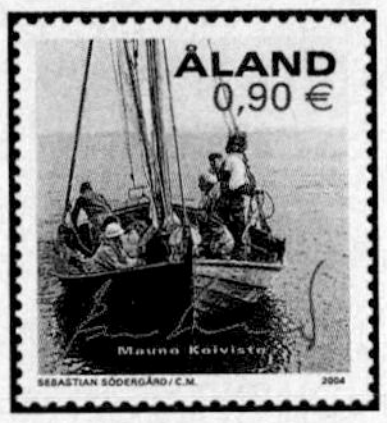

Finnish Pres. Mauno Koivisto and Guests on Boat — A126

2004, Apr. 23 ***Perf. 12½***

223	A126	90c multi	2.50	2.50

Europa — A127

2004, May 10 ***Perf. 13¾x14¼***

224	A127	75c multi	*2.00*	*1.75*

Destruction of Bomarsund Fortress, 150th Anniv. — A128

No. 225: a, Fortress, six ships in harbor. b, Fortress, three ships in harbor. c, Three soldiers in foreground. d, Six soldiers in foreground.

2004, June 9 ***Perf. 13***

225		Booklet pane of 4	8.50	8.50
a.-d.	A128	75c Any single	2.10	2.10
		Complete booklet, 2 #225	18.00	

2004 Summer Olympics, Athens A183

2004, Aug. 13 **Litho.** ***Perf. 14¼***

226	A183	80c multi	2.25	2.25

Landscapes A184

Designs: 2, Storklynkan, Brändö. 1, Prästgardsnäset Nature Reserve, Finström.

2004, Aug. 13 ***Perf. 12½***

227-228	A184	Set of 2	3.00	3.00

Nos. 227-228 sold for 50c and 60c respectively on day of issue.

See Nos. 252-253, 260.

Christmas A185

2004, Oct. 8 ***Perf. 14½x14¾***

229	A185	45c multi	2.50	1.75

Birds — A186

Designs: 15c, Phalacrocorax carbo sinensis. 65c, Cygnus cygnus. €4, Ardea cinerea, vert.

2005, Jan. 14 **Litho.** ***Perf. 13¼***

230	A186	15c multi	.55	.55
231	A186	65c multi	1.75	1.75
232	A186	€4 multi	11.00	9.00
		Nos. 230-232 (3)	13.30	11.30

Automobiles — A187

No. 233: a, 1928 Oakland Sport Cabriolet. b, 1939 Ford V8. c, 1957 Buick Super 4D HT. d, 1964 Volkswagen 1200.

2005, Mar. 4 ***Perf. 13¼ Horiz.***

Booklet Stamps

233		Vert. strip of 4	7.00	7.25
a.-d.	A187	1 Any single	1.75	1.75
e.		Booklet pane, 2 #233	14.00	—
		Complete booklet, #233e	14.00	

Stamps sold for 60c each on day of issue.

Europa A188

2005, Apr. 29 ***Perf. 13¼***

234	A188	90c multi	*2.50*	*2.10*

Walpurgis Night Bonfire A189

Serpentine Die Cut 12½

2005, Apr. 29 **Booklet Stamp**

Self-Adhesive

235	A189	2 multi	1.50	1.40
a.		Booklet pane of 4	6.75	
		Complete booklet, 2 #235a	11.50	

Stamp sold for 50c on day of issue.

Tennis Player Bjorn Borg — A190

2005, May 26 ***Perf. 12½***

236	A190	55c multi	1.50	1.50

Mr. Black and Mr. Smith at Bomarsund, by Fritz von Dardel
A191

2005, Aug. 12 Litho. *Perf. 13¾*
237 A191 €1.30 multi 3.50 3.50

Schooner Linden — A192

2005, Aug. 26 *Perf. 13¼*
238 A192 60c multi 1.75 1.75

Landscapes Type of 2004

Designs: 70c, Pine tree on Sandö Island. 80c, Cliffs, Gröndal.

2005, Aug. 26 *Perf. 12½*
239-240 A184 Set of 2 4.00 4.00

Christmas — A193

Litho. with Hologram Applied

2005, Oct. 10 *Perf. 13*
241 A193 45c multi 1.50 1.40

Stars in hologram differ on each stamp.

Beetles
A194

Designs: 40c, Potosia cuprea. 65c, Coccinella septempunctata. €2, Oryctes nasicornis.

Litho. & Embossed

2006, Jan. 2 *Perf. 13½*
242 A194 40c multi 1.10 1.10
243 A194 65c multi 1.75 1.60
244 A194 €2 multi 5.25 4.75
Nos. 242-244 (3) 8.10 7.45

Woman Suffrage in Finland, Cent. — A195

2006, Mar. 8 Litho. *Perf. 12½*
245 A195 85c multi 2.50 2.25

Demilitarization of Aland, 150th Anniv. — A196

2006, Mar. 29 *Perf. 13¾*
246 A196 €1.50 multi 4.00 3.75

Souvenir Sheet

Lettesgubbe, Mythological Being — A197

2006, Mar. 29 *Perf. 12½x13*
247 A197 85c multi 2.50 3.00

Europa — A198

2006, May 4
248 A198 €1.30 multi 3.50 3.50

A199

Serpentine Die Cut 10 Syncopated

2006, May 26
249 A199 1 multi 1.75 1.50
a. Booklet pane of 8 14.00 14.50

No. 249 sold for 65c on day of issue. Design portion of stamp could be personalized at €10.40 per booklet with a minimum purchase of three booklets. The label design shown is a generic vignette. Other generic vignettes were created for sale at stamp shows beginning in 2008.

Tattoos — A200

No. 250: a, Tribal tattoo on man's biceps. b, Sailor's tattoo on man's forearm. c, Flower tattoo, on woman's torso.

2006, Sept. 7 *Perf. 14 Vert.*

Booklet Stamps

250 Horiz. strip of 3 5.25 5.25
a.-c. A200 65c Any single 1.75 1.75
d. Booklet pane, 3 #250 16.00
Complete booklet, #250d 16.00

Fishing Boat From Television Film Directed by Ake Lindman
A201

2006, Aug. 4 Litho. *Perf. 12½*
251 A201 75c multi 2.00 1.75

Landscapes Type of 2004

Designs: 55c, Foggy grove, windmill and houses, Söderby, Lemland. €1.20, Rocks, Norra Essvik, Sottunga.

2006, Aug. 4
252-253 A184 Set of 2 4.75 4.50

Christmas
A202

Litho. With Holograms Affixed

2006, Oct. 9 *Perf. 13*
254 A202 (50c) multi 1.40 1.40

Flowers
A203

Designs: 80c, Tripolium vulgare. 90c, Lythrum salicaria. €5, Angelica archangelica.

2007, Feb. 1 Litho. *Perf. 12½x13*
255 A203 80c multi 2.50 2.00
256 A203 90c multi 2.75 2.50
257 A203 €5 multi 13.50 13.00
Nos. 255-257 (3) 18.75 17.50

Mail Planes
A204

Designs: 2, Junkers F13. 1, Saab 340.

2007, Mar. 1 *Perf. 12½*
258-259 A204 Set of 2 3.50 3.25

No. 258 sold for 55c, and No. 259 sold for 70c on day of issue.

Landscapes Type of 2004

2007, Mar. 13
260 A184 2 Skaftö, Kumlinge 1.60 1.50

Sold for 55c on day of issue.

Untitled Painting by Tove Jansson
A205

2007, Apr. 18 *Perf. 13¼x13¾*
261 A205 85c multi 2.40 2.40

Europa — A206

2007, May 9 *Perf. 12½x13¼*
262 A206 70c multi 2.00 1.75

Scouting, cent.

Contemporary Crafts — A207

Designs: No. 263, Bridal crown, by Titti Sundblom. No. 264, Floral textile design, by Maria Korpi-Gordon and Adam Gordon. No. 265, Cups, bowl and plate, by Judy Kuyitunen.

2007, May 18 *Perf. 13 Horiz.*

Booklet Stamps

263 A207 1 multi 2.00 2.25
264 A207 1 multi 2.00 2.25
265 A207 1 multi 2.00 2.25
a. Booklet pane, 3 each #263-265 18.00 18.50
Complete booklet, #265a 18.00

Nos. 263-265 each sold for 70c on day of issue.

A208

Serpentine Die Cut 10 Syncopated

2007, June 7 Booklet Stamp

Self-Adhesive

266 A208 1 multi 2.00 1.75
a. Booklet pane of 8 16.00 14.00
Complete booklet, #266a 16.00

No. 266 sold for 70c on day of issue. Design portion of stamp could be personalized at €10.40 per booklet with a minimum purchase of three booklets.

Emigration to America
A209

2007, Aug. 9 Litho. *Perf. 13¼x12½*
267 A209 75c multi 2.25 2.10

Kjusan, Hammarland
A210

2007, Oct. 1 *Perf. 12½*
268 A210 1 multi 2.10 2.00

No. 268 sold for 70c on day of issue.

Christmas — A211

2007, Oct. 9 *Perf. 14*
269 A211 (50c) multi 1.75 1.40

Fish
A212

Designs: 45c, Perca fluviatilis. €4.50, Sander lucioperca.

2008, Feb. 1 Litho. *Perf. 13¼x13*
270 A212 45c multi 1.75 1.50
271 A212 €4.50 multi 14.50 13.50

Souvenir Sheet

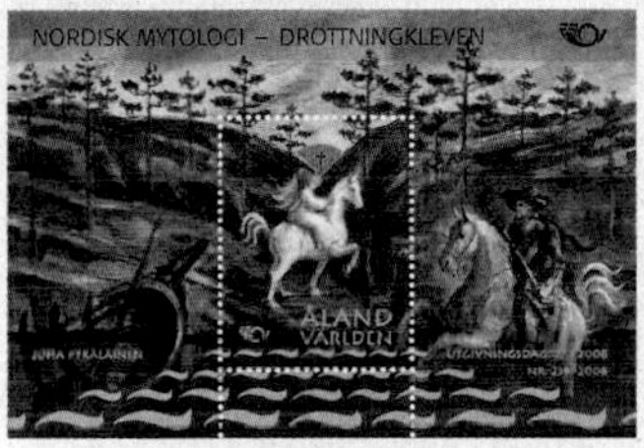

Mythical Princess Signhild at Drottningkleven — A213

Perf. 12½x13¼
2008, Mar. 27 Litho.
272 A213 (85c) multi 3.00 3.00

Badhusberget, Mariehamn — A214

Langvikshagen, Lumparland — A215

2008, Apr. 15 *Perf. 13x12½*
273 A214 (70c) multi 2.40 2.25
274 A215 (70c) multi 2.40 2.25

2008 Summer Olympics, Beijing
A216

2008, May 9 *Perf. 13¾*
275 A216 (90c) multi 3.00 3.00

Europa
A217

2008, May 9 *Perf. 13¼x13*
276 A217 €1 multi 3.50 3.25

Lighthouses
A218

No. 277: a, Marhällan Lighthouse. b, Gustaf Dalén Lighthouse. c, Kökarsören Lighthouse. d, Bogskär Lighthouse.

Litho., Litho & Engr (#277c-277d)
2008, June 6 *Perf. 12¾ on 3 Sides*
Booklet Stamps
277 Block or strip of 4 10.00 9.75
a.-d. A218 (75c) Any single 2.50 2.40
e. Booklet pane, 2 #277 20.00 —
Complete booklet, #277e 20.00

Within the booklet pane, stamps in one row are tete-beche in relation to stamps in the adjacent row.

Gravel Road and Profiles of Marcus Grönholm, Rally Driver, and Christoph Treier, Trainer
A219

2008, July 26 Litho. *Perf. 13½*
278 A219 (90c) multi 2.75 2.50

Particles of granite were applied to portions of the design using a thermographic process.

Aland Peasant Bride, by Karl Emanuel Jansson — A220

2008, Aug. 15 *Perf. 13x13¼*
279 A220 €1.50 multi 5.00 4.75

Christmas
A221

Litho. With Hologram Applied
2008, Oct. 9 *Perf. 13¾x13¼*
280 A221 (55c) multi 1.50 1.25

Personalized Stamp — A222

Serpentine Die Cut 10 Syncopated
2008, Oct. 9 Litho.
Booklet Stamp
Self-Adhesive
281 A222 (75c) multi 2.00 1.75
a. Booklet pane of 8 16.00 14.00
Complete booklet, #281a 16.00

The generic design portion of the stamp shown could be personalized. Other generic vignettes were created for sale at stamp shows in 2009 and 2010.

1810 Boundary Post — A223

Litho. & Embossed With Foil Application
2009, Jan. 22 *Perf. 14¼*
282 A223 (80c) multi 2.25 2.00

Souvenir Sheet

Electricity on Aland Islands, Cent. — A224

Litho. & Embossed
2009, Jan. 22 *Perf. 12½x13¼*
283 A224 €2 black 6.00 6.50

Writers — A225

No. 284: a, Ulla-Lena Lundberg and ship. b, Anni Blomqvist (1909-90), sailboat and dockside shack. c, Valdemar Nyman (1904-98), flowers, cattle.

2009, Mar. 21 Litho. *Perf. 13 Horiz.*
Booklet Stamps
284 Vert. strip of 3 6.75 7.00
a.-c. A225 (80c) Any single 2.25 2.25
d. Booklet pane, 3 #284 21.00 —
Complete booklet, #284d 21.00

Movie Theaters in Aland, Cent. — A226

2009, Apr. 6 *Perf. 12½x13¼*
285 A226 €1.60 multi 4.50 4.00

Divers at Plus Shipwreck
A227

2009, May 8
286 A227 (75c) multi 2.25 2.10

Europa
A228

2009, May 8 *Perf. 13*
287 A228 (80c) multi 2.25 2.25

Intl. Year of Astronomy. Star-shaped holes are die cut in stamp.

Passenger Ferries
A229

Designs: (75c), SS Viking. (80c), New Viking Line ferry, 2009.

2009, June 1 Litho. *Perf. 13*
288-289 A229 Set of 2 4.75 4.50

See Nos. 301-302, 311-312, 325-326, 339, 347, 351-352.

Personalized Stamp — A230

Booklet Stamp
Serpentine Die Cut 10 Syncopated
2009, June 27 Self-Adhesive
290 A230 (90c) multi 2.75 2.50
a. Booklet pane of 8 22.00
Complete booklet, #290a 22.00

The generic design portion of the stamp shown could be personalized.

Cliffs, Föglö
A231

Islets, Saltvik
A232

2009, Sept. 16 *Perf. 12½*
291 A231 (75c) multi 2.40 2.00
292 A232 (80c) multi 2.50 2.25

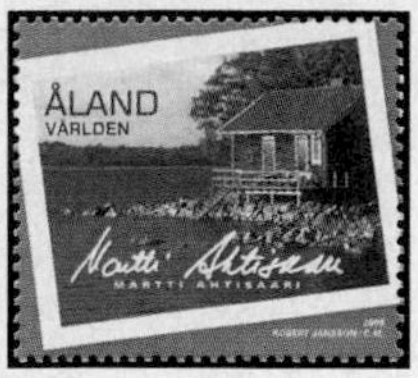

Honeymoon Cabin of Finland President Martti Ahtisaari A233

2009, Sept. 29 *Perf. 13x12½*
293 A233 (90c) multi 2.75 2.50

Christmas A234

Poinsettia and: (60c), Man and woman. (90c), Woman with scroll.

2009, Oct. 9 *Perf. 13¾*
294-295 A234 Set of 2 4.75 4.25

Flag Type of 2004 Inscribed "Inrikes"

Serpentine Die Cut 12½

2009, July 1 **Litho.**

Booklet Stamp

Self-Adhesive

296 A125 (75c) multi 2.10 2.10
a. Booklet pane of 4 8.50
Complete booklet, 2 #296a 17.00

Mail Jetty at Eckerö, Painting by Victor Westerholm — A235

2010, Jan. 4 *Perf. 13*
297 A235 (80c) multi 2.60 1.50

Jesus Christ, Painting by Warner Sallman — A236

Litho. With Foil Application

2010, Mar. 24 *Perf. 14x14¼*
298 A236 (90c) multi 2.75 1.60

Souvenir Sheet

Kobba Klintar Pilot Station — A237

2010, Mar. 24 **Litho.** *Perf. 12½*
299 A237 (90c) multi 2.75 3.00

Europa — A238

2010, Apr. 19 *Perf. 12½x13*
300 A238 (85c) multi 2.50 1.50

Ferries Type of 2009

Designs: 75c, MS Skandia. €3.50, MS Prinsessan.

2010, May 3 **Litho.** *Perf. 13*
301-302 A229 Set of 2 12.50 12.00

Plastic Toys Made By Plasto — A239

No. 303: a, Scooter. b, Dump truck. c, Ducks.

2010, May 10 *Perf. 13¾ Horiz.*

Booklet Stamps

303 Vert. strip of 3 7.50 8.00
a.-c. A239 (85c) Any single 2.50 2.60
d. Booklet pane, 3 #303 22.50 23.00
Complete booklet, #303d 22.50

Farmhand Delivering Mail — A240

2010, June 12 *Perf. 12½x13¼*
304 A240 (75c) multi 2.25 2.00

Personalized Stamp — A241

2010, June 12 *Perf. 12½*
305 A241 (85c) black 2.50 2.25

No. 305 was printed in sheets of 8. The generic design portion of the stamp shown could be personalized for an extra fee.

Stained-Glass Windows — A242

Stained-glass window from church in Jomala: 80c, St. Olaf. €1.60, St. Olaf and other figures, horiz.

2010, Aug. 30 **Litho.** *Perf. 13*
306 A242 80c multi 2.75 2.40

Souvenir Sheet

307 A242 €1.60 multi 5.25 5.50

See Macao Nos. 1317-1318.

Shoreline, Eckerö A243

Cliffs, Sund A244

2010, Sept. 16 *Perf. 12½*
308 A243 80c multi 2.40 2.25
309 A244 (85c) multi 2.40 2.40

Christmas A245

2010, Oct. 8 *Perf. 13*
310 A245 (65c) multi 1.90 1.75

Ferries Type of 2009

Designs: 80c, MS Alandia. €1.50, MS Apollo.

2011, Feb. 1 **Litho.** *Perf. 13*
311-312 A229 Set of 2 6.75 6.25

Souvenir Sheet

Princess Maria Alexandrovna of Russia (1824-80) — A246

2011, Feb. 21 *Perf.*
313 A246 €1 multi 3.00 3.25

City of Mariehamn, 150th anniv. A limited edition of No. 313 with gold embossing sold for €15. See Russia No. 7255.

Georg August Wallin (1811-52), Explorer of Arabia — A247

2011, Apr. 1 *Perf. 14x14¼*
314 A247 (90c) multi 2.75 2.50

Europa A248

2011, May 9 *Perf. 13*
315 A248 (85c) multi 2.75 2.50

Intl. Year of Forests.

Comic Book Superheroes Created by Paul Gustafson (1916-77) A249

No. 316: a, The Arrow. b, Fantom of the Fair. c, Alias the Spider.

2011, May 9 *Perf. 13*

Booklet Stamps

316 Horiz. strip of 3 8.50 8.00
a.-c. A249 (90c) Any single 2.75 2.60
d. Tete-beche block of 6 18.00 18.00
e. Booklet pane of 3 #316 25.00 24.00
Complete booklet, #316e 25.00

Champagne Bottles From 1840s Shipwreck A250

2011, June 3 **Litho.** *Perf. 13½*
317 A250 (90c) multi 2.75 2.50

Chips Ab Potato Chips — A251

2011, June 7 *Perf. 13¾*
318 A251 85c multi 2.60 2.50

Strömma Apples — A252

2011, June 7 **Litho.**
319 A252 5c shown .25 .25
320 A252 €4 Apples, diff. 12.50 12.50

Personalized Stamp — A253

2011, Aug. 16 *Perf. 13¾x14¼*
321 A253 (95c) blk & grn 3.00 3.00

No. 321 was printed in sheets of 8. The generic design portion of the stamp shown could be personalized for an extra fee.

Kökar A254

Jomala A255

2011, Sept. 28 Litho. *Perf. 12½*

322 A254 (85c) multi 2.50 2.25
323 A255 (90c) multi 2.60 2.40

Christmas A256

2011, Oct. 7 *Perf. 14½*

324 A256 (55c) multi 1.60 1.40

Ferries Type of 2009

Designs: 55c, SS Birger Jarl. (75c), MS Sally Albatross.

2012, Feb. 1 *Perf. 13¼*

325-326 A229 Set of 2 3.75 3.50

No. 326 is inscribed "Lokalpost."

Souvenir Sheet

Fishermen at Sea — A257

2012, Mar. 21 *Perf. 13¼x13*

327 A257 (€1) multi 2.75 3.00

Sinking of the Titanic, Cent. — A258

2012, Apr. 16 *Perf. 12¾x13¼*

328 A258 €1.80 multi 5.00 4.75

See Belgium No. 2562.

The Man at the Wheel, Sculpture by Emil Cedercreutz A259

Litho. & Engr.

2012, Apr. 26 *Perf. 13¼x13*

329 A259 €3 multi 8.50 8.25

Europa A260

2012, May 9 Litho. *Perf. 13¾*

330 A260 (95c) multi 2.75 2.00

Personalized Stamp — A261

2012, June 4 *Perf. 14¼x13¾*

331 A261 (95c) multi 2.75 2.00

Printed in sheets of 8. The design portion of this stamp could be personalized. The design shown is a generic vignette. Other generic vignettes were created for sale at stamp shows beginning in 2013.

Dragonflies A262

Designs: (75c), Aeshna cyanea. (95c), Sympetrum sanguineum.

2012, June 4 *Perf. 14¼*

332-333 A262 Set of 2 4.75 4.75

No. 332 is inscribed "Lokalpost;" No. 333, "Europa."

Architecture — A263

No. 334: a, Miramar. b, Societetshusen. c, Badhotellet.

2012, Aug. 23 *Perf. 13¾ Horiz.*

Booklet Stamps

334	Vert. strip of 3	8.00	8.50
a.-c.	A263 (€1) Any single	2.60	2.75
d.	Booklet pane of 9, 3 each #334a-334c	24.00	—
	Complete booklet, #334d	24.00	

Nos. 334a-334c are each inscribed "Världen."

Public Transportation — A264

Designs: No. 335, (95c), 1954 Volvo L224 bus. No. 336, (95c), 1924 Ford TT bus.

2012, Sept. 19 *Perf. 13¾x13½*

335-336 A264 Set of 2 5.50 5.25

No. 335 is inscribed "Inrikes." No. 336 is inscribed "Europa."

Christmas A265

2012, Oct. 9 *Perf. 13*

337 A265 (60c) multi 1.75 1.75

Yearning, Painting by Guy Frisk — A266

2013, Jan. 15 *Perf. 13¾x13¼*

338 A266 (€1.10) multi 3.25 3.00

Aland Art Museum, 50th anniv.

Ferries Type of 2009

Design: (80c), SS Alandsfärjan.

2013, Feb. 19 *Perf. 13*

339 A229 (80c) multi 2.25 2.25

Worldwide Fund for Nature (WWF) — A267

No. 340: a, Gavia arctica. b, Gavia stellata. c, Podiceps auritus. d, Podiceps cristatus.

2013, Apr. 5 *Perf. 12½x12¾*

Booklet Stamps

340	A267 Block of 4	11.00	11.50
a.-d.	(€1) Any single	2.75	2.75
e.	Booklet pane of 8, 2 each #340a-340d	22.00	23.00
	Complete booklet, #340e	22.00	

Europa A268

2013, May 6 *Perf. 13¾x13¼*

341 A268 (€1) multi 2.75 2.75

Personalized Stamp — A269

2013, May 6 *Perf. 12½*

342 A269 (€1.10) ol grn & blk 3.25 3.00

No. 342 was printed in sheets of 8. The generic design portion of the stamp shown could be personalized for an extra fee. Other generic vignettes were created for sale at stamp shows beginning in 2014.

Water Lilies A270

Designs: (€1), Nymphaea alba. €2.50, Nuphar lutea.

2013, June 4 *Perf. 13x13¼*

343-344 A270 Set of 2 9.50 9.50

Crowd at Rockoff Music Festival A271

Woman at Island in the Sun Music Festival — A272

2013, July 12 Litho. *Perf. 13¾*

345 A271 (80c) multi 2.10 2.10
346 A272 (€1.10) multi 3.25 3.00

Ferries Type of 2009

Design: €2, MS Princess Anastasia.

2013, Aug. 5 Litho. *Perf. 13*

347 A229 €2 multi 5.50 5.50

See Russia No. 7468.

Inachis Io — A273

2013, Aug. 20 Litho. *Perf. 13¾*

348 A273 (€1.10) multi 3.00 3.00

Christmas A274

Paintings by Pinturicchio: No. 349, Adoration of the Magi. No. 350, Nativity.

2013, Nov. 8 Litho. *Perf. 13¼x13¾*

349 A274 (65c) multi 1.75 1.75
350 A274 65c multi 1.75 1.75

No. 350 was printed in sheets of 8 + central label. See Vatican City Nos. 1549-1550.

Ferries Type of 2009

Designs: No. 351, MS Birka Princess. No. 352, MS Viking Grace.

2014, Feb. 7 Litho. *Perf. 13¾*

351 A229 (€1.10) multi 3.00 3.00
352 A229 (€1.10) multi 3.00 3.00

No. 351 is inscribed "Inrikes"; No. 352, "Europa."

Mariehamn Theater Society, Cent. — A275

2014, Feb. 7 Litho. *Perf. 13¼*

353 A275 €1.50 multi 4.25 4.25

Souvenir Sheet

Bridge of a Freighter and Horizon — A276

2014, Mar. 17 Litho. *Perf. 13¼*

354 A276 €3 multi 8.25 8.25

Grand Piano of Alie Lindberg (1849-1933), Concert Pianist — A277

2014, May 8 Litho. *Perf. 13¼x13*

355 A277 (€1.10) multi 3.00 3.00

Europa.

Campanula Trachelium A278

2014, May 8 Litho. *Perf. 12½*

356 A278 (€1.10) multi 3.00 3.00

Kenta Sandvik, Weight Lifter A279

2014, May 31 Litho. *Perf. 13x13¼*

357 A279 (90c) multi 2.50 2.50

Personalized Stamp — A280

2014, May 31 Litho. *Perf. 12½*

358 A280 (€1.10) multi 3.00 3.00

No. 358 was printed in sheets of 8. The generic design portion of the stamp shown could be personalized for an extra fee. Other generic vignettes were created for sale at stamp shows beginning in 2015.

Robert Helenius, Professional Boxer, and Family on Aland Island — A281

2014, June 9 Litho. *Perf. 13x13¼*

359 A281 €2.30 multi 6.25 6.25

Musical Groups of the 1960s — A282

No. 360: a, Hitch Hikers. b, Stockdoves. c, Anacondas.

2014, Aug. 25 Litho. *Perf. 13x12¼*

Booklet Stamps

360	Vert. strip of 3	7.25	7.25
a.-c.	A282 (90c) Any single	2.40	2.40
d.	Booklet pane of 9, 3 each #360a-360c	22.00	—
	Complete booklet, #360d	22.00	

Christmas A283

Litho. With Foil Application

2014, Oct. 9 *Perf. 13¾x13¼*

361 A283 (70c) multi 1.75 1.75

New Year 2015 (Year of the Ram) A284

No. 362: a, Ram, ewe and lamb. b, Ram's head.

Litho. & Engr.

2014, Nov. 5 *Perf. 13x12¾*

362	A284 Pair	4.00	4.00
a.-b.	80c Either single	2.00	2.00

Printed in sheets containing two pairs.

Ships A285

Designs: 85c, Schooner Lemland. (€1.20), Barquentine Leo.

2015, Feb. 2 Litho. *Perf. 13x13¼*

363-364 A285 Set of 2 4.75 4.75

Campanula Persicifolia A286

2015, Apr. 10 Litho. *Perf. 14¼*

365 A286 85c multi 1.90 1.90

Midvinterblot, Painting by Carl Larsson (1853-1919) — A287

2015, Apr. 10 Litho. *Perf. 14x14¼*

366 A287 €3 multi 6.75 6.75

Race Horse Indian Silver A288

2015, May 1 Litho. *Perf. 14*

367 A288 (95c) multi 2.25 2.25

Europa A289

2015, May 8 Litho. *Perf. 14¼*

368 A289 (€1.20) multi 2.75 2.75

Personalized Stamp — A290

2015, May 8 Litho. *Perf. 12½*

369 A290 (€1.20) multi 2.75 2.75

Printed in sheets of 8. The design portion of this stamp could be personalized. The design shown is a generic vignette.

Julius Sundblom (1865-1945), Politician — A291

2015, June 22 Litho. *Perf. 13*

370 A291 (€1.20) multi 2.75 2.75

Silver Jewelry — A292

Designs: (€1.20), Buckle from Aland Islands. €2, Brooch from Bern, Switzerland.

Litho. & Embossed

2015, Sept. 3 *Perf. 13*

371	A292 (€1.20) multi	2.75	2.75
372	A292 €2 multi	4.50	4.50

See Switzerland Nos.

Dogs — A293

No. 373: a, Finnish hound (Finsk stövare). b, Gray Norwegian elkhound (Norsk älghund gra). c, Wire-haired dachshund (Strävharig tax).

2015, Sept. 3 Litho. *Perf. 13*

Booklet Stamps

373	Horiz. strip of 3	8.25	8.25
a.-c.	A293 (€1.20) Any single	2.75	2.75
d.	Booklet pane of 9, 3 each #373a-373c	25.00	—
	Complete booklet, #373d	25.00	

A294

Christmas A295

2015, Oct. 9 Litho. *Perf. 13*

374	A294 (70c) multi	1.60	1.60
375	A295 (€1.20) multi	2.75	2.75

Aland Sea Rescue Society, 50th Anniv. — A296

2015, Oct. 30 Litho. *Perf. 13*

376 A296 (95c) multi 2.10 2.10

ALAND ISLANDS

SEMI-POSTAL STAMPS

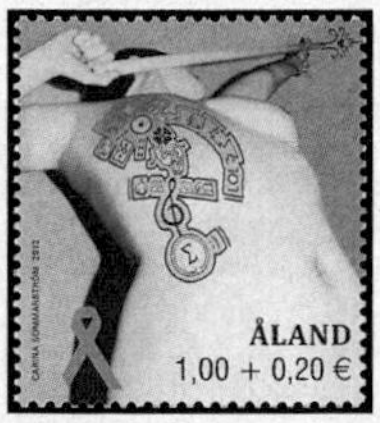

Campaign Against Breast Cancer — SP1

2012, Oct. 1 Litho. ***Perf. 13½x13¾***

B1	SP1	€1+20c multi	3.25	3.25

Surtax for Aland Cancer Society.

Sculpture of Gnome by Hakan Sandberg SP2

2013, Sept. 2 Litho. ***Perf. 13¾x13½***

B2	SP2	€1+20c multi	3.25	3.25

Surtax for Aland Cancer Society.

Zero Tolerance Program Against Drug Abuse — SP3

Litho. & Embossed

2014, Apr. 11 ***Perf. 14¾***

B3	SP3	€1.10 +20c multi	3.75	3.75

FIUME

ˈfyü-ₑmā

LOCATION — A city and surrounding territory on the Adriatic Sea
GOVT. — Formerly a part of Italy
AREA — 8 sq. mi.
POP. — 44,956 (estimated 1924)

Fiume was under Hapsburg rule after 1466 and was transferred to Hungarian control after 1870. Of mixed Italian and Croatian population and strategically important, it was Hungary's only international seaport. Following World War I, Fiume was disputed between Italy and the newly created Kingdom of the Serbs, Croats and Slovenes (later Yugoslavia). A force of Allied troops occupied the city in Nov. 1918, while its future status was negotiated at the Paris Peace Conference.

In Sept. 1919, the Italian nationalist poet Gabriele d'Annunzio organized his legionnaires and seized Fiume, together with the islands of Arbe, Carnaro and Veglia, in the name of Italy. D'Annunzio established an autonomous administration, which soon came into conflict with the Italian government. There followed several years of instability, with three Italian interventions after 1920. In Jan. 1924, the Treaty of Rome between Italy and Yugoslavia established formal Italian sovereignty over Fiume, and Fiume stamps were replaced by those of Italy after March 31, 1924.

100 Filler = 1 Korona
100 Centesimi = 1 Corona (1919)
100 Centesimi = 1 Lira

See note on FIUME-KUPA Zone, Italian Occupation, after Yugoslavia No. NJ22.

The overprints on Nos. 1-23a have been extensively forged. Even the inexpensive values are difficult to find with genuine overprints. Forgeries of many later issues also exist, most created for the packet trade in the 1920s. Values are for genuine stamps. Collectors should be aware that stamps sold "as is" are likely to be forgeries, and unexpertized collections should be assumed to consist of mostly forged stamps. Education plus working with knowledgeable dealers is mandatory in this collecting area. More valuable stamps should be expertized.

Hungarian Stamps of 1916-18 Typograph Overprinted

1918, Dec. 2 Wmk. 137 ***Perf. 15***

On Stamps of 1916

White Numerals

1a	A8	10f Handstamped overprint	100.00	47.50
2	A8	15f violet	47.50	40.00

Value for No. 1a is for handstamped overprint. Value for No. 2 is for typographed overprint.

On Stamps of 1916-18

Colored Numerals

3	A9	2f brown orange	4.75	2.40
4	A9	3f red violet	4.75	2.40
5	A9	5f green	4.75	2.40
6	A9	6f grnsh blue	4.75	2.40
7a	A9	10f rose red	72.50	27.50
8	A9	15f violet	4.75	2.40
9	A9	20f gray brown	4.75	2.40
10	A9	25f deep blue	16.00	3.25
11	A9	35f brown	9.50	4.75
12a	A9	40f olive green	45.00	24.00

White Numerals

13	A10	50f red vio & lil	6.50	4.00
14	A10	75f brt bl & pale bl	13.00	4.75
15	A10	80f grn & pale grn	13.00	4.00
16	A10	1k red brn & claret	40.00	9.50
17	A10	2k ol brn & bis	6.50	4.50
18	A10	3k dk vio & ind	55.00	27.50
19	A10	5k dk brn & lt brn	145.00	27.50
20a	A10	10k vio brn & vio	475.00	240.00

Inverted or double overprints exist on most of Nos. 4-15.

On Stamps of 1918

21	A11	10f scarlet	4.00	4.00
22	A11	20f dark brown	3.25	2.40
23a	A12	40f olive green	37.50	20.00

The overprint on Nos. 3-23a was applied by 2 printing plates and 6 handstamps. Values are for the less costly. Values of Nos. 7a, 12a, 20a and 23a are for handstamps. See the *Scott Specialized Catalogue of Stamps and Covers* for detailed listings.

Postage Due Stamps of Hungary, 1915-20 Ovptd. & Surcharged in Black

1919, Jan.

24	D1	45f on 6f green & red	20.00	16.00
25	D1	45f on 20f green & red	60.00	16.00
		Set, never hinged	200.00	

Hungarian Savings Bank Stamp Surcharged in Black

A2

1919, Jan. 29

26	A2	15f on 10f dk violet	24.00	20.00
		Never hinged	60.00	

Overprints on Nos. 24-26 are typographed.

"Italy" — A3

Italian Flag on Clock-Tower in Fiume — A4

"Revolution" A5

Sailor Raising Italian Flag at Fiume (1918) A6

Nos. 30-43 exist on three types of paper: (A) grayish, porous paper, printed in sheets of 70 stamps (Jan, Feb. printings); (B) translucent or semi-translucent good quality white paper, printed in sheets of 70 stamps (March printing); and (C) good quality medium white paper, plain and opaque, sometimes grayish or yellowish, printed in sheets of 100 (April printing). Values are for the least expensive variety. See the *Scott Specialized Catalogue of Stamps and Covers* for detailed listings.

Perf. 11½

1919, April Unwmk. Litho.

27	A3	2c dull blue	2.40	2.40
28	A3	3c gray brown	2.40	2.40
29	A3	5c yellow green	2.40	2.40
30a	A4	10c rose	25.00	16.00
31	A4	15c violet	2.40	2.40
32a	A4	20c emerald green	4.00	*4.00*
33	A5	25c dark blue	3.25	2.40
34	A6	30c deep violet	3.25	2.40
35	A5	40c brown	3.25	2.40
36	A5	45c orange	3.25	2.40
37	A6	50c yellow green	3.25	2.40
38	A6	60c claret	3.25	2.40
39	A6	1cor brown orange	4.75	2.40
40	A6	2cor brt blue	4.75	2.40
41	A6	3cor orange red	6.50	2.40
42	A6	5cor deep brown	40.00	40.00
43a	A6	10cor olive green	47.50	*80.00*
		Nos. 27-43a (17)	161.60	171.20

The earlier printings of Jan. and Feb. are on thin grayish paper, the Mar. printing is on semi-transparent white paper, all in sheets of 70. An Apr. printing is on white paper of medium thickness in sheets of 100. Part-perf. examples of most of this series are known.

For surcharges see Nos. 58, 60, 64, 66-69.

A7

A8

A9

A10

1919, July 28 ***Perf. 11½***

46	A7	5c yellow green	2.40	1.60
47	A8	10c rose	2.40	1.60
48	A9	30c violet	11.00	4.00
49	A10	40c yellow brown	2.40	*2.40*
50	A10	45c orange	11.00	8.00
51	A9	50c yellow green	11.00	8.00
52	A9	60c claret	11.00	8.00
a.		Perf. 13x12½	190.00	
		Never hinged	475.00	
b.		Perf. 10½	350.00	
		Never hinged	875.00	
53	A9	10cor olive green	11.00	*22.50*
a.		Perf. 13x12½	65.00	*105.00*
		Never hinged	160.00	
b.		Perf. 10½	350.00	*375.00*
		Never hinged	875.00	
		Nos. 46-53 (8)	62.20	56.10
		Set, never hinged	145.00	

Five other denominations (25c, 1cor, 2cor, 3cor and 5cor) were not officially issued. Some examples of the 25c are known canceled.

For surcharges see Nos. 59, 61-63, 65, 70.

Stamps and Types of 1919 Handstamp Surcharged

1919-20

58	A4	5c on 20c grn ('20)	2.40	2.40
59	A9	5c on 25c blue	2.40	2.40
60	A5	10c on 45c orange	2.40	2.40
61	A9	15c on 30c vio ('20)	2.40	2.40
62	A10	15c on 45c orange	2.40	2.40
63	A9	15c on 60c cl ('20)	2.40	2.40
64	A6	25c on 50c yel grn ('20)	20.00	*35.00*
65	A9	25c on 50c yel grn ('20)	2.40	2.40
66	A6	55c on 1cor brn org	40.00	40.00
67	A6	55c on 2cor brt bl	6.50	*9.50*
68	A6	55c on 3cor org red	6.50	8.00
69	A6	55c on 5cor dp brn	6.50	8.00
70	A9	55c on 10cor ol grn	32.50	35.00
		Nos. 58-70 (13)	128.80	*152.30*
		Set, never hinged	300.00	

Semi-Postal Stamps of 1919 Surcharged

a

b

1919-20

73	SP6(a)	5c on 5c green	2.40	2.40
74	SP6(a)	10c on 10c rose	2.40	2.40
75	SP6(a)	15c on 15c gray	2.40	2.40
76	SP6(a)	20c on 20c org	2.40	2.40
77	SP9(a)	25c on 25c bl ('20)	2.40	2.40
78	SP7(b)	45c on 45c ol grn	4.00	4.00
79	SP7(b)	60c on 60c rose	4.00	4.00
80	SP7(b)	80c on 80c violet	2.40	2.40
81	SP7(b)	1cor on 1cor sl	4.00	4.00
82	SP8(a)	2cor on 2cor red brn	6.50	6.50
83	SP8(a)	3cor on 3cor blk brn	8.00	8.00
84	SP8(a)	5cor on 5cor yel brn	9.50	9.50
85	SP8(a)	10cor on 10cor dk vio ('20)	4.00	4.00
		Nos. 73-85 (13)	54.40	54.40
		Set, never hinged	120.00	

Double or inverted surcharges, or imperf. varieties, exist on most of Nos. 73-85.

There were three settings of the surcharges on Nos. 73-85 except No. 77 which is known only with one setting.

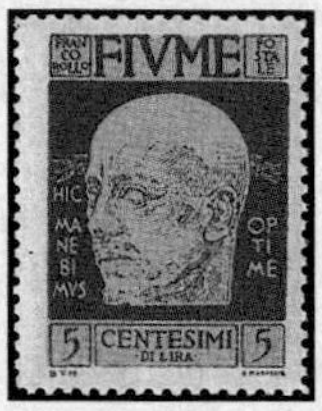

Gabriele d'Annunzio — A11

1920, Sept. 12 Typo. *Perf. 11½*
Pale Buff Background

86	A11	5c green	2.40	2.40
87	A11	10c carmine	2.40	2.40
88	A11	15c dark gray	2.40	2.40
89	A11	20c orange	2.40	2.40
90	A11	25c dark blue	3.25	3.25
91	A11	30c red brown	3.25	3.25
92	A11	45c olive gray	4.75	4.75
93	A11	50c lilac	4.75	4.75
94	A11	55c bister	4.75	4.75
95	A11	1 l black	20.00	*27.50*
96	A11	2 l red violet	20.00	*27.50*
97	A11	3 l dark green	20.00	*27.50*
98	A11	5 l brown	80.00	55.00
99	A11	10 l gray violet	20.00	*27.50*
		Nos. 86-99 (14)	190.35	*195.35*
		Set, never hinged	450.00	

Counterfeits of Nos. 86 to 99 are plentiful.
For overprints see Nos. 134-148.

Severing the Gordian Knot — A12

Designs: 10c, Ancient emblem of Fiume. 20c, Head of "Fiume." 25c, Hands holding daggers.

1920, Sept. 12

100	A12	5c green	42.50	27.50
a.		Imperf.	145.00	
b.		Horiz. pair, imperf. between	375.00	
101	A12	10c deep rose	27.50	22.50
a.		Imperf.	95.00	
102	A12	20c brown orange	42.50	22.50
103	A12	25c indigo	27.50	*47.50*
a.		Imperf.	180.00	
b.		Double impression, imperf.	1,075.	
c.		Horiz. pair, imperf. between	550.00	
d.		25c blue	95.00	*100.00*
e.		As "d," imperf.	400.00	
f.		As "d," horiz. pair, imperf. between	1,075.	
		Nos. 100-103 (4)	140.00	120.00
		Set, never hinged	440.00	

Anniv. of the occupation of Fiume by d'Annunzio. They were available for franking the correspondence of the legionnaires on the day of issue only, Sept. 12, 1920.
Counterfeits of Nos. 100-103 are plentiful.
For overprints and surcharges see Nos. 104-133, E4-E9.

Nos. 100-103 Overprinted or Surcharged in Black or Red

1920, Nov. 20

104	A12	1c on 5c green	2.40	2.40
a.		Inverted overprint	55.00	55.00
b.		Double overprint	200.00	
105	A12	2c on 25c indigo (R)	2.40	2.40
a.		Inverted overprint	55.00	55.00
b.		Double overprint	72.50	72.50
c.		2c on 25c blue (R)	80.00	80.00
106	A12	5c green	20.00	2.40
a.		Inverted overprint	47.50	47.50
b.		Double overprint	72.50	72.50
107	A12	10c rose	20.00	2.40
a.		Inverted overprint	55.00	55.00
b.		Double overprint	72.50	72.50
108	A12	15c on 10c rose	2.40	2.40
a.		Inverted overprint	65.00	65.00
b.		Double overprint	72.50	72.50
109	A12	15c on 20c brn org	2.40	*2.40*
a.		Inverted overprint	65.00	65.00
b.		Double overprint	72.50	72.50
110	A12	15c on 25c indigo (R)	2.40	*2.40*
a.		Inverted overprint	65.00	65.00
b.		Double overprint	72.50	72.50
c.		15c on 25c blue (R)	225.00	225.00
111	A12	20c brown orange	2.40	2.40
a.		Inverted overprint	27.50	27.50
b.		Double overprint	125.00	125.00
112	A12	25c indigo (R)	2.40	2.40
a.		Inverted overprint	24.00	24.00
b.		25c blue (R)	8.00	8.00
113	A12	25c indigo (Bk)	175.00	175.00
a.		Inverted overprint	450.00	350.00
b.		25c blue (Bk)	240.00	240.00
c.		As "b,", inverted overprint	725.00	
114	A12	25c on 10c rose	2.40	4.75
a.		Double overprint	72.50	72.50
115	A12	50c on 20c brn org	5.00	2.40
a.		Double overprint	72.50	72.50
116	A12	55c on 5c green	21.00	4.75
a.		Inverted overprint	95.00	95.00
b.		Double overprint	72.50	72.50
117	A12	1 l on 10c rose	47.50	40.00
a.		Inverted overprint	275.00	275.00
b.		Double overprint	275.00	
118	A12	1 l on 25c indigo (R)	100.00	100.00
a.		1 l on 25c blue (R)	600.00	600.00
b.		As "a," inverted overprint	875.00	725.00
119	A12	2 l on 5c green	47.50	40.00
a.		Inverted overprint	325.00	
b.		Double overprint	200.00	
120	A12	5 l on 10c rose	225.00	*240.00*
a.		Inverted overprint	725.00	725.00
b.		Double overprint	725.00	
121	A12	10 l on 20c brn org	700.00	550.00
a.		Inverted overprint	1,600.	800.00
b.		Double overprint	1,600.	800.00
		Nos. 104-121 (18)	1,380.	1,178.
		Set, never hinged	3,850.	

The Fiume Legionnaires of d'Annunzio occupied the islands of Arbe and Veglia in the Gulf of Carnaro Nov. 13, 1920-Jan. 5, 1921.
Varieties of overprint or surcharge exist for most of Nos. 104-121.
Nos. 113, 117-121, 125, 131 have a backprint.

Nos. 106-107, 111, 113, 115-116 Overprinted or Surcharged at top

1920, Nov. 28

122	A12	5c green	35.00	24.00
123	A12	10c rose	45.00	*52.50*
124	A12	20c brown org	87.50	52.50
125	A12	25c deep blue	52.50	*52.50*
126	A12	50c on 20c brn org	95.00	52.50
127	A12	55c on 5c green	95.00	52.50
		Nos. 122-127 (6)	410.00	286.50
		Set, never hinged	1,000.	

The overprint on Nos. 122-125 comes in two widths: 11mm and 14mm. Values are for the 11mm width.

Nos. 106-107, 111, 113, 115-116 Overprinted or Surcharged at top

1920, Nov. 28

128	A12	5c green	35.00	24.00
129	A12	10c rose	45.00	*52.50*
130	A12	20c brown orange	87.50	52.50
131	A12	25c deep blue	52.50	*52.50*
132	A12	50c on 20c brn org	95.00	52.50
133	A12	55c on 5c green	95.00	52.50
		Nos. 128-133 (6)	410.00	286.50
		Set, never hinged	1,000.	

Nos. 86-99 Overprinted

1921, Feb. 2
"Provvisorio" 20mm wide
Space between lines 3mm
Pale Buff Background

134	A11	5c green	2.40	2.40
a.		Inverted overprint	27.50	27.50
b.		Double overprint	52.50	52.50
135	A11	10c carmine	2.40	2.40
a.		Inverted overprint	27.50	27.50
b.		Double overprint	52.50	52.50
136	A11	15c dark gray	2.40	*2.40*
a.		Inverted overprint	27.50	27.50
b.		Double overprint	52.50	52.50
137	A11	20c orange	4.00	4.00
a.		Inverted overprint	27.50	27.50
b.		Double overprint	27.50	27.50
138	A11	25c dark blue	4.00	4.00
a.		Inverted overprint	27.50	27.50
b.		Double overprint	52.50	52.50
139	A11	30c red brown	4.00	4.00
a.		Inverted overprint	27.50	27.50
b.		Double overprint	27.50	27.50
140	A11	45c olive gray	2.40	2.40
a.		Inverted overprint	55.00	55.00
b.		Double overprint	40.00	40.00
141	A11	50c lilac	4.00	4.00
a.		Inverted overprint	27.50	27.50
142	A11	55c bister	4.00	4.00
a.		Inverted overprint	16.00	16.00
143	A11	1 l black	145.00	*180.00*
a.		Inverted overprint	350.00	350.00
144	A11	2 l red violet	95.00	95.00
145	A11	3 l dark green	95.00	95.00
146	A11	5 l brown	95.00	95.00
147	A11	10 l gray violet	95.00	95.00

With Additional Surcharge

148	A11	1 l on 30c red brown	2.50	2.50
a.		Inverted overprint	27.50	27.50
b.		Double overprint	55.00	55.00
		Nos. 134-148 (15)	557.10	592.10
		Set, never hinged	1,400.	

Most of Nos. 134-143, 148 and E10-E11 exist with inverted or double overprint.
See Nos. E10-E11.

Second Printing, Milan
"Provvisorio" 21mm wide
Space between overprint lines 4mm

1921, Dec. 18

148A	A11	5c yellow green	50.00	*57.50*
		Never hinged	125.00	
		On cover		300.00
148B	A11	10c carmine	135.00	40.00
		Never hinged	340.00	
		On cover		300.00
c.		Vert. pair, imperf. between	*650.00*	

First Constituent Assembly

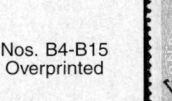

Nos. B4-B15 Overprinted

1921, Apr. 24

149	SP6	5c blue green	6.50	4.75
150	SP6	10c rose	6.50	4.75
a.		Inverted overprint	65.00	65.00
151	SP6	15c gray	6.50	4.75
152	SP6	20c orange	6.50	4.75
153	SP7	45c olive green	17.50	12.00
154	SP7	60c car rose	17.50	12.00
a.		Inverted overprint	47.50	47.50
155	SP7	80c brt violet	27.50	24.00

With Additional Overprint "L"

156	SP7	1 l on 1cor dk slate	32.50	*35.00*
a.		Inverted overprint	80.00	80.00
157	SP8	2 l on 2cor red brn	120.00	4.25
a.		Inverted overprint	325.00	160.00
158	SP8	3 l on 3cor black brn	120.00	*130.00*
159	SP8	5 l on 5cor yel brn	120.00	4.25
160	SP8	10 l on 10cor dk vio	175.00	175.00
a.		Inverted overprint	475.00	400.00
		Nos. 149-160 (12)	656.00	415.50
		Set, never hinged	1,625.	

The overprint exists inverted on several denominations.

Second Constituent Assembly
"Constitution" Issue of 1921 With Additional Overprint "1922"

1922

161	SP6	5c blue green	4.75	3.25
a.		Inverted overprint	24.00	24.00
162	SP6	10c rose	2.40	*2.40*
a.		Inverted overprint	24.00	24.00
b.		Double overprint, one inverted	40.00	40.00
163	SP6	15c gray	20.00	12.00
164	SP6	20c orange	2.40	2.40
a.		Inverted overprint	32.50	32.50
b.		Double overprint	40.00	40.00
c.		Double overprint, one inverted	—	—
165	SP7	45c olive grn	13.00	12.00
a.		Double overprint	40.00	40.00
166	SP7	60c car rose	2.40	*3.25*
167	SP7	80c brt violet	2.40	*3.25*
168	SP7	1 l on 1cor dk slate	2.40	*2.40*
a.		Inverted overprint	55.00	55.00
b.		Double overprint	40.00	40.00
169	SP8	2 l on 2cor red brn	20.00	16.00
170	SP8	3 l on 3cor blk brn	2.50	*3.25*
171	SP8	5 l on 5cor yel brn	2.50	*3.25*
		Nos. 161-171 (11)	74.75	63.45
		Set, never hinged	170.00	

Nos. 161-171 have the overprint in heavier type than Nos. 149-160 and "IV" in Roman instead of sans-serif numerals.
The overprint exists inverted or double on almost all values.

Venetian Ship — A16

Roman Arch — A17

St. Vitus — A18

Rostral Column — A19

1923, Mar. 23 *Perf. 11½*
Pale Buff Background

172	A16	5c blue green	2.40	2.40
173	A16	10c violet	2.40	2.40
174	A16	15c brown	2.40	2.40
175	A17	20c orange red	2.40	2.40
176	A17	25c dark gray	2.40	2.40
177	A17	30c dark green	2.40	2.40
178	A18	50c dull blue	2.40	2.40
179	A18	60c rose	4.00	*4.00*
180	A18	1 l dark blue	4.00	*4.00*
181	A19	2 l violet brown	65.00	20.00
182	A19	3 l olive bister	55.00	45.00
183	A19	5 l yellow brown	55.00	52.50
		Nos. 172-183 (12)	199.80	142.30
		Set, never hinged	465.00	

Nos. 172-183 Overprinted

1924, Feb. 22
Pale Buff Background

184	A16	5c blue green	2.40	*12.00*
a.		Inverted overprint	20.00	*40.00*
b.		Double overprint	130.00	
185	A16	10c violet	2.40	*12.00*
a.		Inverted overprint	16.00	*40.00*
186	A16	15c brown	2.40	*12.00*
a.		Inverted overprint	17.00	*40.00*

187 A17 20c orange red 2.40 *12.00*
a. Inverted overprint 21.00 *40.00*
b. Double overprint 260.00
188 A17 25c dk gray 2.40 *12.00*
189 A17 30c dk green 2.40 *12.00*
a. Inverted overprint 42.50
190 A18 50c dull blue 2.40 *12.00*
a. Inverted overprint 42.50 42.50
191 A18 60c red 2.40 *12.00*
a. Inverted overprint 87.50
192 A18 1 l dark blue 2.40 *12.00*
a. Inverted overprint 21.00 *40.00*
193 A19 2 l violet brown 4.00 *32.50*
a. Inverted overprint 130.00 *160.00*
194 A19 3 l olive 6.00 *40.00*
195 A19 5 l yellow brown 6.00 *40.00*
Nos. 184-195 (12) 37.60 *220.50*
Set, never hinged 80.00

The overprint exists inverted on almost all values.

Nos. 172-183 Overprinted

1924, Mar. 1
Pale Buff Background

196 A16 5c blue green 2.40 *20.00*
197 A16 10c violet 2.40 *20.00*
198 A16 15c brown 2.40 *20.00*
199 A17 20c orange red 2.40 *20.00*
200 A17 25c dark gray 2.40 *20.00*
201 A17 30c dark green 2.40 *20.00*
202 A18 50c dull blue 2.40 *20.00*
203 A18 60c red 2.40 *20.00*
204 A18 1 l dark blue 2.40 *20.00*
205 A19 2 l violet brown 4.00 *27.50*
206 A19 3 l olive 4.00 *27.50*
207 A19 5 l yellow brown 4.00 *27.50*
Nos. 196-207 (12) 33.60 *262.50*
Set, never hinged 62.50

Postage stamps of Fiume were superseded by stamps of Italy.

SEMI-POSTAL STAMPS

Semi-Postal Stamps of Hungary, 1916-17 Overprinted

1918, Dec. 2 Wmk. 137 *Perf. 15*
B1 SP3 10f + 2f rose 8.00 8.00
a. Inverted overprint 72.50 40.00
b. Double overprint 240.00 120.00
B2 SP4 15f + 2f dl vio 8.00 8.00
a. Inverted overprint 145.00 40.00
b. Double overprint 145.00 47.50
B3 SP5 40f + 2f brn car 14.50 8.00
a. Inverted overprint 87.50 37.50
Nos. B1-B3 (3) 30.50 24.00
Set, never hinged 72.50

Examples of Nos. B1-B3 with overprint handstamped sell for higher prices.

Statue of Romulus and Remus Being Suckled by Wolf — SP6

Venetian Galley — SP7

Church of St. Mark's, Venice — SP8

Perf. 11½
1919, May 18 Unwmk. Typo.
B4 SP6 5c +5 l bl grn 47.50 32.50
B5 SP6 10c +5 l rose 47.50 32.50
B6 SP6 15c +5 l dk gray 47.50 32.50
B7 SP6 20c +5 l orange 47.50 32.50
B8 SP7 45c +5 l ol grn 47.50 32.50
B9 SP7 60c +5 l car rose 47.50 32.50
B10 SP7 80c +5 l lilac 47.50 32.50
B11 SP7 1cor +5 l dk slate 47.50 32.50
B12 SP8 2cor +5 l red brn 47.50 32.50
B13 SP8 3cor +5 l blk brn 47.50 32.50
B14 SP8 5cor +5 l yel brn 47.50 32.50
B15 SP8 10cor +5 l dk vio 47.50 32.50
Nos. B4-B15 (12) 570.00 390.00
Set, never hinged 1,450.

200th day of peace. The surtax aided Fiume students in Italy. "Posta di Fiume" is printed on the back of Nos. B4-B16.

The surtax is shown on the stamps as "LIRE 5" but actually was 5cor.

For surcharges and overprints see Nos. 73-76, 78-85, 149-171, J15-J26.

Dr. Antonio Grossich — SP9

1919, Sept. 20
B16 SP9 25c + 2 l blue 3.25 3.25
Never hinged 8.00

Surtax for the Dr. Grossich Foundation. For overprint and surcharge, see No. 77.

SPECIAL DELIVERY STAMPS

1916 Special Delivery Stamp of Hungary Overprinted

1918, Dec. 2 Wmk. 137 *Perf. 15*
Typographed Overprint
E1 SD1 2f gray green & red 4.75 4.75
Never hinged 12.00
a. Double overprint 190.00 175.00

Handstamped overprints sell for more.

SD3

Perf. 11½
1920, Sept. 12 Unwmk. Typo.
E2 SD3 30c slate blue 25.00 25.00
E3 SD3 50c rose 25.00 25.00
Set, never hinged 125.00

For overprints see Nos. E10-E11.

Nos. 102 and 100 Surcharged

1920, Nov.
E4 A12 30c on 20c brn org 190.00 175.00
a. Inverted overprint 625.00
b. Double overprint 625.00
E5 A12 50c on 5c green 290.00 125.00
a. Inverted overprint 1,000.
b. Double overprint 1,000.
c. Double overprint, one inverted 1,100.

Nos. E4-E5 have a backprint.

Same Surcharge as on Nos. 124, 122
E6 A12 30c on 20c brn org 275.00 180.00
E7 A12 50c on 5c green 210.00 180.00
a. Double overprint 950.00

Overprint on Nos. E6-E7 is 11mm wide.

Same Surcharge as on Nos. 130, 128
E8 A12 30c on 20c brn org 275.00 180.00
E9 A12 50c on 5c green 210.00 180.00
a. Double overprint 950.00 950.00
Nos. E4-E9 (6) 1,450. 1,020.
Set, never hinged 2,900.

Overprint on Nos. E8-E9 is 17mm wide.

Nos. E2 and E3 Overprinted

1921, Feb. 2
E10 SD3 30c slate blue 11.00 12.00
a. Inverted overprint 120.00 120.00
b. Double overprint 40.00 40.00
E11 SD3 50c rose 15.00 12.00
a. Inverted overprint 27.50 27.50
b. Double overprint 105.00 105.00
Set, never hinged 62.50

Fiume in 16th Century SD4

1923, Mar. 23 *Perf. 11, 11½*
E12 SD4 60c rose & buff 24.00 24.00
E13 SD4 2 l dk bl & buff 24.00 24.00
Set, never hinged 120.00

Nos. E12-E13 Overprinted

1924, Feb. 22
E14 SD4 60c car & buff 3.25 *20.00*
E15 SD4 2 l dk bl & buff 3.25 *20.00*
a. Inverted overprint 130.00 *160.00*
Set, never hinged 16.00

Nos. E12-E13 Overprinted

1924, Mar. 1
E16 SD4 60c car & buff 4.00 *80.00*
E17 SD4 2 l dk bl & buff 4.00 *80.00*
Set, never hinged 20.00

POSTAGE DUE STAMPS

Postage Due Stamps of Hungary, 1915-1916, Overprinted

1918, Dec. Wmk. 137 *Perf. 15*
J1c D1 6f green & black 190.00 105.00
d. Double overprint — 1,450.
J2c D1 12f green & black 180.00 72.50
d. Double overprint 1,450.
J3c D1 50c green & black 65.00 35.00
d. Double overprint 1,450.
J4c D1 1f green & red 40.00 24.00
d. Inverted overprint 425.00
e. Double overprint 525.00 190.00
J5 D1 2f green & red 6.50 6.50
a. Inverted overprint 52.50 45.00
b. Double overprint 175.00
J6c D1 5f green & red 40.00 47.50
d. Inverted overprint 320.00 440.00
e. Double overprint 525.00 525.00
J7 D1 6f green & red 6.50 6.50
a. Inverted overprint 25.00 25.00
b. Double overprint 27.50
J8c D1 10f green & red 32.50 32.50
d. Inverted overprint 475.00 475.00
J9 D1 12f green & red 6.50 6.50
J10c D1 15f green & red 32.50 32.50
d. Inverted overprint 800.00
e. Double overprint 440.00 440.00
J11 D1 20f green & red 6.50 6.50
a. Double overprint 45.00 32.50
J12c D1 30f green & red 32.50 32.50
d. Inverted overprint 900.00
e. Double overprint 950.00 950.00
Nos. J1c-J12 (12) 638.50 407.50
Set, never hinged 1,275.

Overprint was applied by press or handstamp. Six minor varieties of the handstamp exist. Some are sought by specialists at much higher values. Excellent forgeries exist. For more detailed listings, see *Scott Classic Specialized Catalogue of Stamps and Covers 1840-1940.*

Eagle — D2

Perf. 11½
1919, July 28 Unwmk. Typo.
J13 D2 2c brown 2.40 2.40
J14 D2 5c brown 2.40 2.40
Set, never hinged 12.00

Semi-Postal Stamps of 1919 Overprinted and Surcharged

1921, Mar. 21
J15 SP6 2c on 15c gray 6.50 6.50
J16 SP6 4c on 10c rose 4.75 4.75
J17 SP9 5c on 25c blue 4.75 4.75
J18 SP6 6c on 20c orange 4.75 4.75
J19 SP6 10c on 20c orange 6.50 6.50

Nos. B8-B11 Surcharged

J20 SP7 20c on 45c olive grn 2.40 *4.75*
J21 SP7 30c on 1cor dk slate 12.00 *12.00*
J22 SP7 40c on 80c violet 4.75 *6.50*
J23 SP7 50c on 60c carmine 4.75 *6.50*

J24 SP7 60c on 45c olive grn	2.40	*4.75*
J25 SP7 80c on 45c olive grn	2.40	*4.75*

Surcharged like Nos. J15-J19

J26 SP8 1 l on 2cor red brown	24.00	*24.00*
Nos. J15-J26 (12)	79.95	*90.50*
Set, never hinged	190.00	

See note below No. 85 regarding settings of "Valore Globale" overprint.

NEWSPAPER STAMPS

Newspaper Stamp of Hungary, 1914, Overprinted like Nos. 1-23

1918, Dec. 2 Wmk. 137 *Imperf.*

P1 N5 (2f) orange	4.75	3.25
Never hinged	15.00	
a. Inverted overprint	55.00	52.50
b. Double overprint	210.00	190.00

Handstamped overprints sell for more.

Eagle
N1

1919 Unwmk. *Perf. 11½*

P2 N1 2c deep buff	9.50	*14.50*

Re-engraved

P3 N1 2c deep buff	9.50	*14.50*
Set, never hinged	48.00	

In the re-engraved stamp the top of the "2" is rounder and broader, the feet of the eagle show clearly and the diamond at bottom has six lines instead of five.

Steamer — N2

1920, Sept. 12

P4 N2 1c gray green	4.00	3.25
Never hinged	10.00	
a. Imperf	24.00	24.00

FRANCE

ˈfranˌts

LOCATION — Western Europe
GOVT. — Republic
AREA — 210,033 sq. mi.
POP. — 58,978,172 (1999 est.)
CAPITAL — Paris

100 Centimes = 1 Franc
100 Cents = 1 Euro (2002)

Catalogue values for unused stamps in this country are for Never Hinged items, beginning with Scott 299 in the regular postage section, Scott B42 in the semi-postal section, Scott C18 in the airpost section, Scott CB1 in the airpost semi-postal section, Scott J69 in the postage due section, Scott M10 in the military stamps section, Scott 1O1 in the section for official stamps for the Council of Europe, Scott 2O1 for the section for UNESCO, Scott S1 for franchise stamps, Scott N27 for occupation stamps, and Scott 2N1 for AMG stamps.

Watermarks

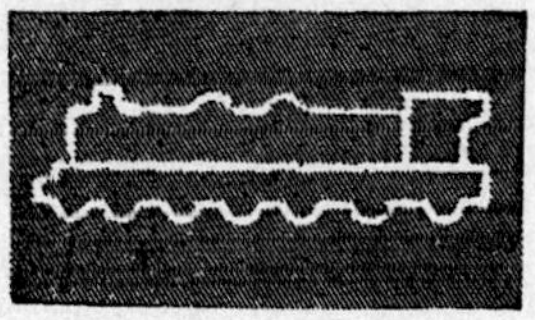

Wmk. 407

Ceres — A1

FORTY CENTIMES

Type I

Type II

1849-50 Typo. Unwmk. *Imperf.*

No.	Design / Description	Unused	Used
1	A1 10c bis, *yelsh* ('50)	*1,700.*	240.00
a.	10c dark bister, *yelsh*	2,000.	275.00
b.	10c greenish bister	2,450.	650.00
d.	As #1, tête beche pair	*95,000.*	*20,000.*
2	A1 15c green, *grnsh*	*23,500.*	900.00
a.	15c yellow green, *grnsh*	*22,500.*	800.00
c.	Tête bêche pair	—	
3	A1 20c blk, *yelsh*	375.00	37.50
a.	20c black	425.00	50.00
b.	20c black, *buff*	1,200.	150.00
c.	Tête bêche pair	*10,000.*	*6,750.*
4	A1 20c dark blue	*2,650.*	
a.	20c blue, *bluish*	*2,250.*	
b.	20c blue, *yelsh*	*2,750.*	
c.	Tête bêche pair	*65,000.*	
6	A1 25c lt bl, *bluish*	*6,000.*	32.50
a.	25c blue, *bluish* ('50)	*6,000.*	32.50
b.	25c blue, *yelsh*	*6,000.*	45.00
c.	Tête bêche pair	*170,000.*	*13,500.*
7	A1 40c org, *yelsh* (I) ('50)	*3,200.*	400.00
a.	40c org ver, *yelsh* (I)	*3,750.*	475.00
b.	40c orange, *yelsh* (II)	*21,500.*	*5,750.*
c.	Pair, types I and II	*35,000.*	*12,500.*
g.	Vertical half used as 20c on cover		*270,000.*
8	A1 1fr vermilion, *yelsh*	*95,000.*	*14,500.*
a.	1fr dull orange red	*97,500.*	*17,500.*
b.	Tête bêche pair, no gum	*80,000.*	*225,000.*
c.	1fr pale ver ("Vervelle")	*22,500.*	
d.	As "c," tête bêche pair	*450,000.*	
9	A1 1fr light carmine	*10,000.*	725.00
a.	Tête bêche pair	*210,000.*	*24,000.*
b.	1fr brown carmine	*11,000.*	875.00
c.	1fr dark carmine, *yelsh*	*12,500.*	1,100.

No. 4 was printed but not yet gummed when the rate change to 25c made them unnecessary. An essay with a red "25" surcharge on No. 4 was rejected.

An ungummed sheet of No. 8c was found in 1895 among the effects of Anatole A. Hulot, the printer. It was sold to Ernest Vervelle, a Parisian dealer, by whose name the stamps are known.

See Nos. 329-329e, 612-613, 624.

Nos. 1, 4a, 6a, 7 and 13 are of similar designs and colors to French Colonies Nos. 9, 11, 12, 14, and 8. There are numerous shades of each. Identification by those who are not experts can be difficult, though cancellations can be used as a guide for used stamps.

Because of the date of issue the Colonies stamps are similar in shades and papers to the perforated French stamps, Nos. 23a, 54, 57-59, and are not as clearly printed. Except for No. 13, unused, the French Colonies stamps sell for much less than the values shown here for properly identified French versions.

Expertization of these stamps is recommended.

1862 Re-issue

1g	A1	10c bister	450.
2d	A1	15c yellow green	600.
3d	A1	20c black, *yellowish*	400.
4d	A1	20c blue	360.
6d	A1	25c blue	415.
7d	A1	40c orange (I)	600.
7e	A1	40c orange (II)	*11,250.*
h.		Pair, types I and II	*15,000.*
9d	A1	1fr pale lake	625.

The re-issues are fine impressions in lighter colors and on whiter paper than the originals. An official imitation of the essay, 25c on 20c blue, also in a lighter shade and on whiter paper, was made at the same time as the re-issues.

President Louis Napoleon — A2

1852

No.	Design / Description	Unused	Used
10	A2 10c pale bister, *yelsh*	*34,500.*	500.00
a.	10c dark bister, *yelsh*	*35,000.*	575.00
11	A2 25c blue, *bluish*	*2,750.*	35.00
b.	25c dark blue, *bluish*	*3,250.*	57.50

1862 Re-issue

10b	A2	10c bister	400.00
11a	A2	25c blue	250.00

The re-issues are in lighter colors and on whiter paper than the originals.

Emperor Napoleon III — A3

Die I. The curl above the forehead directly below "R" of "EMPIRE" is made up of two lines very close together, often appearing to form a single thick line. There is no shading across the neck.

Die II. The curl is made of two distinct, more widely separated lines. There are lines of shading across the upper neck.

1853-60 *Imperf.*

No.	Design / Description	Unused	Used
12	A3 1c ol grn, *pale bl* ('60)	180.00	70.00
a.	1c bronze grn, *pale bluish*	180.00	75.00
13	A3 5c grn, *grnsh* (I) ('54)	700.00	70.00
14	A3 10c bis, *yelsh* (I)	400.00	7.50
a.	10c yellow, *yelsh* (I)	1,325.	30.00
b.	10c bister brn, *yelsh* (I)	500.00	20.00
c.	10c bister, *yelsh* (II) ('60)	500.00	20.00
15	A3 20c bl, *bluish* (I) ('54)	170.00	1.35
a.	20c dark bl, *bluish* (I)	235.00	1.35
b.	20c milky blue (I)	250.00	10.00
c.	20c blue, *lilac* (I)	4,500.	65.00
d.	20c blue, *bluish* (II) ('60)	300.00	4.00
e.	Half used as 10c on cover		*16,000.*
f.	Tête bêche pair	*165,000.*	
16	A3 20c bl, *grnsh* (II)	*5,250.*	150.00
a.	20c blue, *greenish* (I)	*4,250.*	100.00
17	A3 25c bl, *bluish* (I)	2,250.	175.00
18	A3 40c org, *yelsh* (I)	2,250.	11.00
a.	40c org ver, *yellowish*	*2,850.*	17.50
b.	Half used as 20c on cover		*115,000.*
19	A3 80c lake, *yelsh* (I) ('54)	3,000.	42.50
a.	Tête bêche pair	*350,000.*	*22,000.*
b.	Half used as 40c on cover		*50,000.*
20	A3 80c rose, *pnksh* (I) ('60)	1,925.	42.50
a.	Tête-bêche pair	*52,500.*	*12,000.*
21	A3 1fr lake, *yelsh* (I)	*7,500.*	*2,575.*
a.	Tête bêche pair	*300,000.*	*140,000.*

Most values of the 1853-60 issue are known privately rouletted, pin-perf., perf. 7 and percé en scie.

1862 Re-issue

17c	A3	25c blue (I)	450.
19c	A3	80c lake (I)	1,800.
21c	A3	1fr lake (I)	1,500.
d.		Tête bêche pair	*27,500.*

The re-issues are in lighter colors and on whiter paper than the originals.

1862-71 *Perf. 14x13½*

No.	Design / Description	Unused	Used
22	A3 1c ol grn, *pale bl* (II)	140.00	30.00
a.	1c bronze grn, *pale bl* (II)	140.00	35.00
23	A3 5c yel grn, *grnsh* (I)	190.00	10.00
a.	5c deep green, *grnsh* (I)	225.00	12.50
24	A3 5c grn, *pale bl* ('71) (I)	1,800.	110.00
25	A3 10c bis, *yelsh* (II)	1,350.	3.75
a.	10c yel brn, *yelsh* (II)	1,750.	8.50
26	A3 20c bl, *bluish* (II)	200.00	1.25
a.	Tête bêche pair (II)	4,000.	1,000.
27	A3 40c org, *yelsh* (I)	1,200.	6.50
28	A3 80c rose, *pnksh* (I)	1,100.	30.00
a.	80c bright rose, *pinkish* (I)	1,300.	35.00
c.	Tête bêche pair (I)	*17,500.*	*7,750.*

No. 26a imperf is from a trial printing.

A4

A5

Napoleon III — A6

1863-70 *Perf. 14x13½*

No.	Design / Description	Unused	Used
29	A4 1c brnz grn, *pale bl* ('70)	40.00	16.00
a.	1c olive green, *pale blue*	37.50	16.00
30	A4 2c red brn, *yelsh*	105.00	25.00
b.	Half used as 1c on cover		*40,000.*
31	A4 4c gray	180.00	42.50
a.	Tete beche pair	*17,500.*	*12,000.*
d.	Half used as 2c on cover		*52,500.*
32	A5 10c bis, *yelsh* ('67)	225.00	5.00
c.	Half used as 5c on cover with other stamps		*3,750.*
33	A5 20c bl, *bluish* ('67)	175.00	1.55
c.	Half used as 10c on cover		*62,500.*
34	A5 30c brn, *yelsh* ('67)	650.00	12.50
a.	30c dk brn, *yellowish*	1,150.	30.00
35	A5 40c pale org, *yellowish*	700.00	8.00
a.	40c org, *yelsh* ('68)	700.00	8.00
c.	Half used as 20c on cover		*37,500.*
36	A5 80c rose, *pnksh* ('68)	850.00	20.00
a.	80c carmine, *yellowish*	1,000.	24.00
d.	Half used as 40c on cover		*45,000.*
e.	Quarter used as 20c on cover		*52,500.*
37	A6 5fr gray lil, *lav* ('69)	*6,000.*	800.00
a.	"5" and "F" omitted		*100,000.*
c.	5fr bluish gray, *lavender*	*6,000.*	1,000.
d.	As #37, "5" and "F" In light blue	*7,250.*	1,000.

No. 33 exists in two types, differing in the size of the dots at either side of POSTES.

On No. 37, the "5" and "F" vary in height from 3¾mm to 4½mm. These figures normally appear in gray but exist in blue or black.

All known examples of No. 37a are more or less damaged.

No. 29 was reprinted in 1887 by authority of Granet, Minister of Posts. The reprints show a yellowish shade under the ultraviolet lamp. Value $850.

For surcharge see No. 49.

Original Issue Imperfs

No.	Design	Description	Unused	Used
31c	A4	4c gray	300.	*175.*
32b	A5	10c bis, *yelsh*	400.	*175.*
33b	A5	20c bl, *bluish*	300.	*160.*
36c	A5	80c rose, *pnksh*	—	7,500.
37b	A6	5fr gray lil, *lav*	*8,500.*	

Imperfs, "Rothschild" Re-issue

Paper Colors are the Same

29b	A4	1c olive green	1,100.
30a	A4	2c pale red brown	200.00
31b	A4	4c pale gray	185.00
32a	A5	10c pale bister	160.00
33a	A5	20c pale blue	250.00
34c	A5	30c pale brown	190.00
35b	A5	40c pale orange	225.00
36b	A5	80c rose	425.00

The re-issues constitute the "Rothschild Issue." These stamps were authorized exclusively for the banker to use on his correspondence. Used examples exist.

Ceres

A7 A8

A9

A10

A11

Bordeaux Issue

On the lithographed stamps, except for type I of the 20c, the shading on the cheek and neck is in lines or dashes, not in dots. On the typographed stamps the shading is in dots. The 2c, 5c, 10c and 20c (types II and III) occur in two or more types. The most easily distinguishable are:

2c — Type A. To the left of and within the top of the left "2" are lines of shading composed of dots.

2c — Type B. These lines of dots are replaced by solid lines.

5c — Type A. The head and hairline merge with the background of the medallion, without a distinct separation.

5c — Type B. A white line separates the contour of the head and hairline from the background of the medallion.

10c — Type A. The inner frame lines are of the same thickness as all other frame lines.

10c — Type B. The inner frame lines are much thicker than the others.

Three Types of the 20c.

A9 — The inscriptions in the upper and lower labels are small and there is quite a space between the upper label and the circle containing the head. There is also very little shading under the eye and in the neck.

A10 — The inscriptions in the labels are similar to those of the first type, the shading under the eye and in the neck is heavier and the upper label and circle almost touch.

A11 — The inscriptions in the labels are much larger than those of the two preceding types, and are similar to those of the other values of the same type in the set.

1870-71 Litho. *Imperf.*

38 A7 1c ol grn, *pale bl* 125.00 1.00
a. 1c bronze green, *pale blue* 160.00 155.00
39 A7 2c red brn, *yelsh* (B) 225.00 225.00
a. 2c brick red, *yelsh* (B) 800.00 700.00
b. 2c chestnut, *yelsh* (B) 1,350. 700.00
c. 2c chocolate, *yelsh* (A) 750.00 700.00
40 A7 4c gray 250.00 200.00
41 A8 5c yel green, *greenish* (B) 250.00 160.00
a. 5c grn, *grnsh* (B) 325.00 175.00
b. 5c emerald, *greenish* (B) 3,500. 1,250.
c. 5c yellowish green, *greenish* (A) 2,400. 3,250.
42 A8 10c bis, *yelsh* (A) 825.00 60.00
a. 10c bister, *yellowish* (B) 825.00 90.00
43 A9 20c bl, *bluish* *21,500.* 550.00
a. 20c dark blue, *bluish* *25,000.* 725.00
44 A10 20c bl, *bluish* 950.00 45.00
a. 20c dark blue, *bluish* 1,150. 85.00
b. 20c ultra, *bluish* *20,000.* *3,100.*
45 A11 20c bl, *bluish* ('71) 825.00 16.00
a. 20c ultra, *bluish* 2,200. 675.00
46 A8 30c brn, *yelsh* 325.00 200.00
a. 30c blk brn, *yelsh* 1,750. 675.00
47 A8 40c org, *yelsh* 425.00 100.00
a. 40c yel orange, *yelsh* 1,250. 225.00
b. 40c red orange, *yelsh* 625.00 190.00
c. 40c scarlet, *yelsh* *1,250.* *675.00*
48 A8 80c rose, *pinkish* 600.00 250.00
a. 80c dull rose, *pinkish* 600.00 275.00

All values of the 1870 issue are known privately rouletted, pin-perf and perf. 14.

See Nos. 50-53.

A12

Dark Blue Surcharge

1871 Typo. *Perf. 14x13½*

49 A12 10c on 10c bister 1,400.
a. Pale blue surcharge 1,900.

No. 49 was never placed in use. Counterfeits exist.

A13

Two types of the 40c as in the 1849-50 issue.

1870-73 Typo. *Perf. 14x13½*

50 A7 1c ol grn, *pale bl* 40.00 11.50
a. 1c bronze grn, *pale bl* ('72) 47.50 14.00
51 A7 2c red brn, *yelsh* ('70) 80.00 13.50
52 A7 4c gray ('70) 250.00 40.00
53 A7 5c yel grn, *pale bl* ('72) 150.00 7.50
a. 5c green 150.00 7.50
54 A13 10c bis, *yelsh* 540.00 55.00
a. Tête beche pair *5,500.* *2,250.*
b. Half used as 5c on cover *4,500.*
55 A13 10c bis, *rose* ('73) 265.00 9.50
a. Tête bêche pair 3,750. 1,750.
56 A13 15c bis, *yelsh* ('71) 300.00 4.50
a. Tête bêche pair *37,500.* *12,000.*
57 A13 20c dl bl, *bluish* 225.00 6.75
a. 20c bright blue, *bluish* 350.00 8.00
b. Tête bêche pair 3,750. 1,450.
c. Half used as 10c on cover *55,000.*
d. Quarter used as 5c on cover *52,500.*
58 A13 25c bl, *bluish* ('71) 110.00 1.10
a. 25c dk bl, *bluish* 135.00 1.10
b. Tête bêche pair *6,750.* *3,000.*
59 A13 40c org, *yelsh* (I) 475.00 6.00
a. 40c orange yel, *yelsh* (I) 575.00 9.00
b. 40c orange, *yelsh* (II) 3,150. 130.00
c. 40c orange yel, *yelsh* (II) 3,150. 130.00
d. Pair, types I and II *6,500.* 525.00
f. Half used as 20c on circular *20,000.*
g. Half used as 20c on cover *40,000.*

No. 58 exists in three main plate varieties, differing in one or another of the flower-like corner ornaments.

Margins on this issue are extremely small.

Nos. 54, 57 and 58 were reprinted imperf. in 1887. See note after No. 37.

Imperf.

50b A7 1c 270.00
51a A7 2c 350.00
52a A7 4c 450.00
53b A7 5c yel grn, *pale bl* 260.00
55b A13 10c 350.00
56b A13 15c 375.00

A14

1872-75 *Perf. 14x13½*

Larger Numerals

60 A14 10c bis, *rose* ('75) 325.00 11.00
a. Cliché of 15c in plate of 10c *3,750.* *4,250.*
b. Pair, #60, 60a *6,750.* *8,500.*
61 A14 15c bister ('73) 320.00 3.25
62 A14 30c brn, *yelsh* 550.00 5.25
63 A14 80c rose, *pnksh* 640.00 11.50

Imperf.

62a A14 30c 475.00
63a A14 80c 650.00

Peace and Commerce ("Type Sage") — A15

Type I. The "N" of "INV" is under the "B" of "REPUBLIQUE."

Type II. The "N" of "INV" is under the "U" of "REPUBLIQUE."

Type I

1876-78 *Perf. 14x13½*

64 A15 1c grn, *grnsh* 125.00 70.00
65 A15 2c grn, *grnsh* 1,425. 240.00
66 A15 4c grn, *grnsh* 145.00 55.00
67 A15 5c grn, *grnsh* 650.00 45.00
68 A15 10c grn, *grnsh* 800.00 21.00
69 A15 15c gray lil, *grysh* 800.00 17.50
70 A15 20c red brn, *straw* 575.00 17.50
71 A15 20c bl, *bluish* *27,500.*
72 A15 25c ultra, *bluish* *7,750.* 55.00
73 A15 30c brn, *yelsh* 425.00 8.25
74 A15 40c red, *straw* ('78) 600.00 35.00
75 A15 75c car, *rose* 950.00 12.50
76 A15 1fr brnz grn, *straw* 925.00 10.00

No. 71 was never put into use.

The reprints of No. 71 are type II. They are imperforate or with forged perforation.

For overprints and surcharges see Offices in China Nos. 1-17, J7-J10, J20-J22, Offices in Egypt, Alexandria 1-15, Port Said 1-17, Offices in Turkish Empire 1-7, Cavalle 1-8, Dedeagh 1-8, Port Lagos 1-5, Vathy 1-9, Offices in Zanzibar 1-33, 50-54, Offices in Morocco 1-8, and Madagascar 14-27.

Imperf.

64a A15 1c 150.00
65a A15 2c 1,000.
66a A15 4c 160.00
67a A15 5c 525.00
68a A15 10c 575.00
69a A15 15c 575.00
70a A15 20c 375.00
73a A15 30c 275.00
74a A15 40c 250.00
75a A15 75c 550.00
76a A15 1fr 400.00

Beware of French Colonies Nos. 24-29.

Type II

1876-77 *Perf. 14x13½*

77 A15 2c grn, *grnsh* 115.00 19.00
78 A15 5c grn, *grnsh* 25.00 .60
a. Imperf. 175.00
79 A15 10c grn, *grnsh* 1,100. 240.00
80 A15 15c gray lil, *grysh* 675.00 1.90
81 A15 25c ultra, *bluish* 425.00 1.00
a. 25c blue, *bluish* 475.00 1.50
b. Pair, types I & II *60,000.* *17,500.*
c. Imperf. 325.00
82 A15 30c yel brn, *yelsh* 82.50 1.40
a. 30c brown, *yellowish* 90.00 1.40
b. Imperf. 525.00
83 A15 75c car, *rose* ('77) 1,775. 110.00
84 A15 1fr brnz grn, *straw* ('77) 145.00 7.50
a. Imperf. 1,100.

Beware of French Colonies Nos. 31, 35.

1877-80

86 A15 1c blk, *lil bl* 3.75 1.65
a. 1c black, *gray blue* 3.75 1.65
b. Imperf. 75.00
87 A15 1c blk, *Prus bl* ('80) *11,000.* *4,350.*

Values for No. 87 are for examples with the perfs touching the design on at least one side.

88 A15 2c brn, *straw* 4.50 1.90
a. 2c brown, *yellow* 4.50 1.90
b. Imperf. 210.00
89 A15 3c yel, *straw* ('78) 200.00 42.50
a. Imperf. 150.00
90 A15 4c claret, *lav* 5.00 1.90
a. 4c vio brown, *lavender* 8.25 4.50
b. Imperf. 60.00
91 A15 10c blk, *lavender* 35.00 1.00
a. 10c black, *rose lilac* 37.50 1.00
b. 10c black, *lilac* 37.50 1.00
c. Imperf. 70.00
92 A15 15c blue ('78) 22.50 .60
a. Imperf. 95.00
b. 15c blue, *bluish* 435.00 15.00
93 A15 25c blk, *red* ('78) 1,075. 25.00
a. Imperf. 675.00
94 A15 35c blk, *yel* ('78) 525.00 35.00
a. 35c blk, *yel org* 525.00 35.00
b. Imperf. 250.00
95 A15 40c red, *straw* ('80) 90.00 2.10
a. Imperf. 240.00
96 A15 5fr vio, *lav* 440.00 70.00
a. As #96, imperf. 750.00
b. 5fr red lilac, *lavender* 650.00 100.00

Beware of French Colonies Nos. 38-40, 42, 44.

1879-90

97 A15 3c gray, *grysh* ('80) 3.00 1.65
a. Imperf. 67.50
98 A15 20c red, *yel grn* 37.50 4.25
a. 20c red, *deep green* ('84) 72.50 6.00
b. Imperf. 100.00
99 A15 25c yel, *straw* 340.00 5.00
a. Imperf. 250.00
100 A15 25c blk, *pale rose* ('86) 72.50 1.00
a. Imperf. 155.00
101 A15 50c rose, *rose* ('90) 210.00 2.65
a. 50c carmine, *rose* 225.00 3.50
102 A15 75c dp vio, *org* ('90) 215.00 35.00
a. 75c deep violet, *yellow* 265.00 45.00
Nos. 97-102 (6) 878.00 49.55

Beware of French Colonies No. 43.

1892 Quadrille Paper

103 A15 15c blue 12.50 .35
a. Imperf. 175.00

1898-1900 Ordinary Paper

104 A15 5c yel grn 16.00 1.30
a. Imperf. 82.50

Type I

105 A15 5c yel grn 14.00 1.30
a. Imperf. 575.00
106 A15 10c blk, *lavender* 21.00 2.50
a. Imperf. 275.00
107 A15 50c car, *rose* 200.00 30.00
108 A15 2fr brn, *azure* ('00) 110.00 40.00
b. Imperf. 2,250.
Nos. 104-108 (5) 361.00 75.10

See No. 226.

Reprints of A15, type II, were made in 1887 and left imperf. See note after No. 37. Value for set of 27, $4,000.

Liberty, Equality, Fraternity A16

"The Rights of Man" A17

Liberty and Peace A18

1900-29 *Perf. 14x13½*

109 A16 1c gray .55 .40
110 A16 2c violet brn .70 .25
111 A16 3c orange .45 .45
a. 3c red 19.00 7.50
112 A16 4c yellow brn 3.00 1.60
113 A16 5c green 2.00 .35
b. Booklet pane of 10 330.00
114 A16 7½c lilac ('26) .60 .45
115 A16 10c lilac ('29) 4.00 .60
116 A17 10c carmine 25.00 1.50
a. Numerals printed separately 24.00 10.00
117 A17 15c orange 8.00 .60
118 A17 20c brown vio 55.00 9.25
119 A17 25c blue 125.00 1.65
a. Numerals printed separately 115.00 9.25
120 A17 30c violet 70.00 6.00
121 A18 40c red & pale bl 15.00 .85
122 A18 45c green & bl ('06) 29.00 2.10
123 A18 50c bis brn & gray 100.00 1.65
124 A18 60c vio & ultra ('20) 1.00 1.15
125 A18 1fr claret & ol grn 26.50 .85
126 A18 2fr gray vio & yel 625.00 75.00
127 A18 2fr org & pale bl ('20) 42.50 .60
128 A18 3fr vio & bl ('25) 27.50 7.50
129 A18 3fr brt vio & rose ('27) 55.00 2.80
130 A18 5fr dk bl & buff 85.00 5.00
131 A18 10fr grn & red ('26) 125.00 17.00
132 A18 20fr mag & grn ('26) 200.00 37.50
Nos. 109-132 (24) 1,625. 175.10

In the 10c and 25c values, the first printings show the numerals to have been impressed by a second operation, whereas, in later printings, the numerals were inserted in the plates. Two operations were used for all 20c and 30c, and one operation for the 15c.

No. 114 was issued precanceled only. Values for precanceled stamps in first column are for those which have not been through the post and have original gum. Values in the second column are for postally used, gumless stamps.

See Offices in China Nos. 34, 40-44, Offices in Crete 1-5, 10-15, Offices in Egypt, Alexandria 16-20, 26-30, 77, 84-86, Port Said 18-22, 28-32, 83, 90-92, Offices in Turkish Empire 21-26, 31-33, Cavalle 9, Dedeagh 9.

For overprints and surcharge see Nos. 197, 246, C1-C2, M1, P7. Offices in China 57, 62-65, 71, 73, 75, 83-85, J14, J27, Offices in Crete 17-20, Offices in Egypt, Alexandria 31-32, 34-35, 40-48, 57-64, 66, 71-73, Port Said 33, 35-40, 43, 46-57, 59, 65-71, 73, 78-80, Offices in Turkish Empire 35-38, 47-49, Cavalle 13-15, Dedeagh 16-18, Offices in Zanzibar 39, 45-49, 55, Offices in Morocco 11-15, 20-22, 26-29, 35-41, 49-54, 72-76, 84-85, 87-89, B6.

Imperf.

109a A16 1c 55.00
110a A16 2c 67.50 60.00
111b A16 3c 55.00
112a A16 4c 150.00
113a A16 5c 75.00
116b A17 10c #116 or 116a 235.00 *135.00*
117a A17 15c 190.00 *165.00*
119b A17 25c #119 or 119a 500.00
121a A18 40c 190.00 *155.00*

122a	*A18*	*45c*	*260.00*	
123a	*A18*	*50c*	*375.00*	*375.00*
124a	*A18*	*60c*	*525.00*	
125a	*A18*	*1fr*	*250.00*	*225.00*
126a	*A18*	*2fr Without gum*	*1,300.*	
127a	*A18*	*2fr*	*475.00*	
128a	*A18*	*3fr*	*725.00*	*500.00*
129a	*A18*	*3fr*	*425.00*	
130a	*A18*	*5fr*	*950.00*	

Flat Plate & Rotary Press

The following stamps were printed by both flat plate and rotary press: Nos. 109-113, 144-146, 163, 166, 168, 170, 177-178, 185, 192 and P7.

"Rights of Man" A19

Sower A20

1902

133	A19	10c rose red	32.50	.90
134	A19	15c pale red	11.00	.60
135	A19	20c brown violet	82.50	14.00
136	A19	25c blue	100.00	2.25
137	A19	30c lilac	250.00	14.50
		Nos. 133-137 (5)	476.00	32.25

Imperf.

133a	*A19*	*10c rose red*	*450.00*	*275.00*
134a	*A19*	*15c pale red*	*450.00*	*325.00*
135a	*A19*	*20c brown violet*	*800.00*	*475.00*
136a	*A19*	*25c blue*	*950.00*	*625.00*
137a	*A19*	*30c lilac*	*1,100.*	*675.00*

See Offices in China Nos. 35-39, Offices in Crete 6-10, Offices in Egypt, Alexandria 21-25, 81-82, Port Said 23-27, 87-88, Offices in Turkish Empire 26-30, Cavalle 10-11, Dedeagh 10-11.

For overprints and surcharges see Nos. M2, Offices in China 45, 58-61, 66-70, 76-82, J15-J16, J28-J30, Offices in Crete 16, Offices in Egypt, Alexandria 33, 36-39, 49-50, 52-56, 65, 67-70, B1-B4, Port Said 34, 41-42, 44-45, 57, 60-64, 77, 74-77, B1-B4, Offices in Turkish Empire 34, 39, Cavalle 12, Dedeagh 15, Offices in Zanzibar 40-44, 56-59, Offices in Morocco 16-19, 30-34, 42-48, 77-83, 86, B1-B5, B7, B9.

1903-38

138	A20	10c rose	8.00	.40
139	A20	15c slate grn	4.00	.25
b.		Booklet pane of 10	450.00	
140	A20	20c violet brn	67.50	1.90
141	A20	25c dull blue	75.00	1.40
142	A20	30c violet	175.00	5.25
143	A20	45c lt violet ('26)	6.00	1.90
144	A20	50c dull blue ('21)	27.50	1.40
145	A20	50c gray grn ('26)	6.25	1.25
146	A20	50c vermilion ('26)	1.25	.25
a.		Booklet pane of 10	40.00	
147	A20	50c grnsh bl ('38)	1.00	.35
148	A20	60c lt vio ('24)	6.25	2.10
149	A20	65c rose ('24)	3.00	1.75
150	A20	65c gray grn ('27)	6.50	2.10
151	A20	75c rose lil ('26)	5.25	.60
152	A20	80c ver ('25)	26.50	9.50
153	A20	85c ver ('24)	13.50	3.25
154	A20	1fr dull blue ('26)	6.00	.75
		Nos. 138-154 (17)	438.50	34.40
		Set, never hinged	940.00	

See Nos. 941, 942A. For surcharges and overprints see Nos. 229-230, 232-233, 236, 256, B25, B29, B32, B36, B40, M3-M4, M6, Offices in Turkish Empire 46, 54.

Imperf.

138a	*A20*	*10c*	*175.00*	
139a	*A20*	*15c*	*140.00*	*55.00*
140a	*A20*	*20c*	*300.00*	*160.00*
141a	*A20*	*25c*	*350.00*	
142a	*A20*	*30c*	*625.00*	
144a	*A20*	*50c*	*140.00*	
145a	*A20*	*50c*	*125.00*	
146b	*A20*	*50c Without gum*	*70.00*	
147a	*A20*	*50c*	*67.50*	
149a	*A20*	*65c*	*300.00*	
151a	*A20*	*75c*	*450.00*	
154a	*A20*	*1fr*	*1,000.*	

Ground A21

No Ground A22

1906, Apr. 13
With Ground Under Feet of Figure

155	A21	10c red	2.50	1.75
a.		Imperf, pair, without gum	275.00	225.00
		As "a," with gum	450.00	

1906-37

TEN AND THIRTY-FIVE CENTIMES

Type I — Numerals and letters of the inscriptions thin.

Type II — Numerals and letters thicker.

No Ground Under the Feet

156	A22	1c olive bis ('33)	.25	.30
157	A22	2c dk green ('33)	.25	.30
158	A22	3c ver ('33)	.25	.30
159	A22	5c green ('07)	1.50	.25
a.		Imperf., pair	40.00	30.00
b.		Booklet pane of 10	100.00	
160	A22	5c orange ('21)	1.25	.30
a.		Booklet pane of 10	72.50	
161	A22	5c cerise ('34)	.25	.25
162	A22	10c red (II) ('07)	1.50	.25
a.		Imperf., pair	37.50	115.00
b.		10c red (I) ('06)	8.25	1.00
c.		As #162b, imperf., pair	37.50	115.00
d.		Booklet pane of 10 (I)	125.00	
e.		Booklet pane of 10 (II)	75.00	
f.		Booklet pane of 6 (II)	240.00	
163	A22	10c grn (II) ('21)	1.00	.55
a.		10c green (I) ('27)	32.50	37.50
b.		Booklet pane of 10 (II, "Phena")	350.00	
c.		Booklet pane of 10 (I, "Mineraline")	3,200.	
164	A22	10c ultra ('32)	1.40	.25
165	A22	15c red brn ('26)	.25	.25
a.		Booklet pane of 10	27.50	
166	A22	20c brown	3.00	.65
a.		Imperf., pair	82.50	100.00
b.		20c black brown	6.00	2.00
167	A22	20c red vio ('26)	.25	.25
a.		Booklet pane of 10	7.50	
168	A22	25c blue	2.40	.25
a.		Booklet pane of 10	37.50	
b.		Imperf, pair (dark blue)	45.00	60.00
169	A22	25c yel brown ('27)	.25	.25
a.		25c red brown	.30	.25
170	A22	30c orange	13.50	1.40
a.		Imperf, pair	200.00	175.00
171	A22	30c red ('21)	6.60	2.25
172	A22	30c cerise ('25)	1.25	.80
a.		Booklet pane of 10	13.50	
b.		Imperf, pair	575.00	
173	A22	30c lt blue ('25)	3.75	.60
a.		Booklet pane of 10	35.00	
b.		Imperf, pair	2,200.	
174	A22	30c cop red ('37)	.25	.30
a.		Booklet pane of 10	9.00	
175	A22	35c vio (II) ('26)	8.25	.90
a.		Imperf, pair	150.00	120.00
b.		35c violet (I) ('06)	150.00	7.50
c.		As "b," Imperf, pair, without gum	575.00	
176	A22	35c grn ('37)	.50	.55
a.		Imperf, pair	750.00	
177	A22	40c olive ('25)	1.40	.55
b.		Booklet pane of 10	30.00	
178	A22	40c ver ('26)	2.50	.80
a.		Booklet pane of 10	25.00	
179	A22	40c violet ('27)	2.00	.90
180	A22	40c lt ultra ('28)	1.25	.50
181	A22	1.05fr ver ('25)	9.50	5.25
182	A22	1.10fr cerise ('27)	11.50	2.50
183	A22	1.40fr cerise ('26)	20.00	22.50
184	A22	2fr Prus grn ('31)	14.00	1.75
		Nos. 156-184 (29)	109.95	45.95
		Set, never hinged	225.00	

The 10c and 35c, type I, were slightly retouched by adding thin white outlines to the sack of grain, the underside of the right arm and the back of the skirt. It is difficult to distinguish the retouches except on clearly-printed copies. The white outlines were made stronger on the stamps of type II.

Stamps of types A16, A18, A20 and A22 were printed in 1916-20 on paper of poor quality, usually grayish and containing bits of fiber. This is called G. C. (Grande Consommation) paper.

Nos. 160, 162b, 163, 175b and 176 also exist imperf.

See Nos. 241-241b. For surcharges and overprint see Nos. 227-228, 234, 238, 240, 400, B1, B24, B28, B31, B35, B37, B39, B41, M5, P8, Offices in Turkish Empire 40-45, 52, 55.

Louis Pasteur — A23

1923-26

185	A23	10c green	.55	.30
a.		Booklet pane of 10	15.00	
186	A23	15c green ('24)	1.40	.30
187	A23	20c green ('26)	2.75	.90
188	A23	30c red	.90	*1.50*
189	A23	30c green ('26)	.55	.50
190	A23	45c red ('24)	1.90	2.10
191	A23	50c blue	4.50	.50
192	A23	75c blue ('24)	3.75	1.00
a.		Imperf., pair	250.00	
193	A23	90c red ('26)	11.00	3.50
194	A23	1fr blue ('25)	21.00	.50
195	A23	1.25fr blue ('26)	25.00	8.00
196	A23	1.50fr blue ('26)	5.25	.50
		Nos. 185-196 (12)	78.55	19.60
		Set, never hinged	150.00	

Nos. 185, 188 and 191 were issued to commemorate the cent. of the birth of Pasteur.

For surcharges and overprint see Nos. 231, 235, 257, B26, B30, B33, C4.

No. 125 Overprinted in Blue

1923, June 15

197	A18	1fr claret & ol grn	440.00	500.00
		Never hinged	825.00	

Allegory of Olympic Games at Paris A24

The Trophy A25

Milo of Crotona — A26

Victorious Athlete — A27

1924, Apr. 1 *Perf. 14x13½, 13½x14*

198	A24	10c gray grn & yel grn	2.25	1.25
199	A25	25c rose & dk rose	3.00	.80
200	A26	30c brn red & blk	9.50	11.00
201	A27	50c ultra & dk bl	26.00	5.75
		Nos. 198-201 (4)	40.75	18.80
		Set, never hinged	125.00	

Imperf Singles

198a	*A24*	*10c*	*1,000.*	
199a	*A25*	*25c*	*1,000.*	*725.*
200a	*A26*	*30c*	*1,000.*	
201a	*A27*	*50c*	*1,000.*	*1,000.*

8th Olympic Games, Paris.

Pierre de Ronsard (1524-85), Poet — A28

1924, Oct. 6 *Perf. 14x13½*

219	A28	75c blue, *bluish*	1.90	1.40
		Never hinged	2.75	

"Light and Liberty" Allegory A29

Majolica Vase — A30

Potter Decorating Vase — A31

Terrace of Château A32

1924-25 *Perf. 14x13½, 13½x14*

220	A29	10c dk grn & yel ('25)	.55	.75
221	A30	15c ind & grn ('25)	.55	.85
a.		Imperf.	*400.00*	
		Never hinged	*640.00*	
222	A31	25c vio brn & garnet	.80	.50
223	A32	25c gray bl & vio ('25)	1.60	.65
a.		Imperf.	*450.00*	150.00
		Never hinged	*700.00*	
224	A31	75c indigo & ultra	3.50	2.25
225	A29	75c dk bl & lt bl ('25)	18.00	6.50
a.		Imperf.	*375.00*	
		Never hinged	*650.00*	
		Nos. 220-225 (6)	25.00	11.50
		Set, never hinged	52.50	

Intl. Exhibition of Decorative Modern Arts at Paris, 1925.

Philatelic Exhibition Issue
Souvenir Sheet

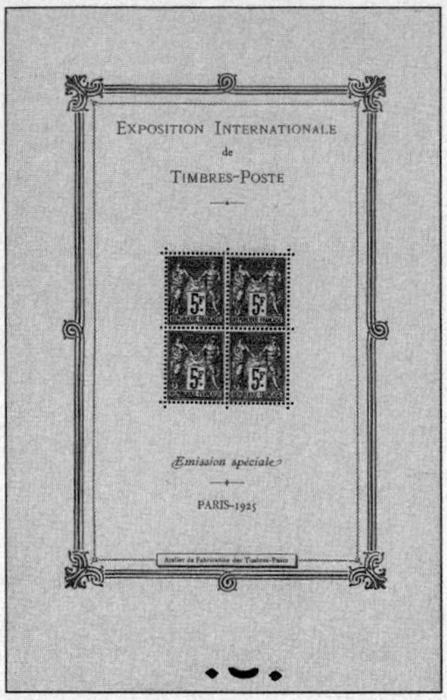

A32a

1925, May 2 *Perf. 14x13½*

226	A32a	Sheet of 4, A15 II	1,100.	1,100.
		Never hinged	3,750.	
a.		Imperf. sheet	5,000.	1,750.
		Never hinged	7,750.	
b.		5fr carmine, perf.	125.00	140.00
		Never hinged	225.00	
c.		5fr carmine, imperf.	900.00	
		Never hinged	1,325.	

These were on sale only at the Intl. Phil. Exhib., Paris, May, 1925. Size: 140x220mm.

Nos. 148-149, 152-153, 173, 175, 181, 183, 192, 195 Surcharged

1926-27

227	A22	25c on 30c lt bl	.25	.50
a.		Pair, one without surcharge	1,050.	925.00
228	A22	25c on 35c violet	.25	.50
a.		Double surcharge	525.00	350.00
b.		Pair, one without surcharge	550.00	*925.00*
229	A20	50c on 60c lt vio ('27)	1.40	1.10
a.		Pair, one without surcharge	525.00	*925.00*
230	A20	50c on 65c rose ('27)	.75	.55
a.		Inverted surcharge	*1,225.*	*1,400.*
b.		Pair, one without surcharge	675.00	*925.00*
231	A23	50c on 75c blue	3.25	1.50
232	A20	50c on 80c ver ('27)	1.25	1.10
a.		Pair, one without surcharge	475.00	*925.00*
233	A20	50c on 85c ver ('27)	2.25	1.00
234	A22	50c on 1.05fr ver	1.25	.75
a.		Pair, one without surcharge	475.00	*925.00*
235	A23	50c on 1.25fr blue	2.75	2.25
a.		Pair, one without surcharge	525.00	*925.00*
236	A20	55c on 60c lt vio	125.00	52.50
238	A22	90c on 1.05fr ver ('27)	2.25	2.75
a.		Pair, one without surcharge	*1,000.*	925.00
240	A22	1.10fr on 1.40fr cer	1.00	1.10
a.		Pair, one without surcharge	575.00	*925.00*
		Nos. 227-240 (12)	141.65	65.60
		Set, never hinged	275.00	

Issue dates: Nos. 229-230, 232-234, 1927.

No. 236 is known only precanceled. See second note after No. 132.

Nos. 229, 230, 234, 238 and 240 have three bars instead of two. The 55c surcharge has thinner, larger numerals and a rounded "c." Width, including bars, is 17mm, instead of 13mm.

The 55c was used only precanceled at the Magasins du Louvre department store in Paris, August 1926.

Strasbourg Exhibition Issue
Souvenir Sheet

A32b

1927, June 4

241	A32b	Sheet of 2	1,000.	1,000.
		Never hinged	2,300.	
a.		5fr light ultra (A22)	250.00	250.00
		Never hinged	400.00	
b.		10fr carmine rose (A22)	250.00	250.00
		Never hinged	400.00	

Sold at the Strasbourg Philatelic Exhibition as souvenirs. Size: 111x140mm.

Marcelin Berthelot (1827-1907), Chemist and Statesman — A33

1927, Sept. 7

242	A33	90c dull rose	1.90	.60
		Never hinged	3.00	

For surcharge see No. C3.

Lafayette, Washington, S. S. Paris and Airplane "Spirit of St. Louis" — A34

1927, Sept. 15

243	A34	90c dull red	1.25	1.75
a.		Value omitted	2,000.	1,725.
244	A34	1.50fr deep blue	4.00	2.50
a.		Value omitted	1,450.	
		Set, never hinged	10.00	

Visit of American Legionnaires to France, September, 1927. Exist imperf.

Joan of Arc — A35

1929, Mar.

245	A35	50c dull blue	1.90	.25
		Never hinged	2.75	
a.		Booklet pane of 10	50.00	
b.		Imperf.	140.00	

500th anniv. of the relief of Orleans by the French forces led by Joan of Arc.

No. 127 Overprinted in Blue

1929, May 18

246	A18	2fr org & pale bl	600.00	600.00
		Never hinged	1,325.	

Sold exclusively at the Intl. Phil. Exhib., Le Havre, May, 1929, for 7fr, which included a 5fr admission ticket.

Excellent counterfeits of No. 246 exist.

Reims Cathedral — A37

Die I, II, III

Die IV

Die I Die II Die III

Die I — The window of the 1st turret on the left is made of 2 lines. The horizontal line of the frame surrounding 3F is not continuous.

Die II — Same as Die I but the line under 3F is continuous.

Die III — Same as Die II but there is a deeply cut line separating 3 and F.

Die IV — Same as Die III but the window of the first turret on the left is made of three lines.

Mont-Saint-Michel — A38

Die I

Die II

Die I — The line at the top of the spire is broken.

Die II — The line is unbroken.

Port of La Rochelle A39

Dies I & II

Die III

Die I — The top of the "E" of "POSTES" has a serif. The oval of shading inside the "0" of "10 fr" and the outer oval are broken at their bases.

Die II — The same top has no serif. Interior and exterior of "0" broken as in Die I.

Die III — Top of "E" has no serif. Interior and exterior of "0" complete.

Pont du Gard, Nimes A40

Dies I & II

Die III

Die I — Shading of the first complete arch in the left middle tier is made of horizontal lines. Size 36x20¾mm. Perf. 13½.

Die II — Same, size 35½x21mm. Perf. 11.

Die III — Shading of same arch is made of three diagonal lines. Thin paper. Perf. 13.

1929-33 Engr. *Perf. 11, 13, 13½*

247	A37	3fr dk gray ('30) (I)	62.50	2.40
		Never hinged	115.00	
247A	A37	3fr dk gray ('30) (II)	125.00	3.50
		Never hinged	200.00	
247B	A37	3fr dk gray ('30) (III)	375.00	24.00
		Never hinged	600.00	
248	A37	3fr bluish sl ('31) (IV)	60.00	2.40
		Never hinged	115.00	
249	A38	5fr brn ('30) (I)	24.00	4.25
		Never hinged	40.00	
250	A38	5fr brn ('31) (II)	21.00	.75
		Never hinged	32.50	
251	A39	10fr lt ultra (I)	95.00	15.00
		Never hinged	160.00	
251A	A39	10fr ultra (II)	140.00	26.00
		Never hinged	225.00	
252	A39	10fr dk ultra ('31) (III)	70.00	6.50
		Never hinged	140.00	
253	A40	20fr red brown (I)	275.00	40.00
		Never hinged	500.00	
254	A40	20fr brt red brn ('30) (II)	1,000.	350.00
		Never hinged	1,650.	
254A	A40	20fr org brn ('31) (III)	250.00	35.00
		Never hinged	450.00	
		Nos. 247-254A (12)	2,497.	509.80

View of Algiers A41

1929, Jan. 1 **Typo.**

255	A41	50c blue & rose red	2.40	.50
		Never hinged	5.50	

Cent. of the 1st French settlement in Algeria.

Nos. 146 and 196 Overprinted

1930, Apr. 23 ***Perf. 14x13½***

256	A20	50c vermilion	3.00	3.25
257	A23	1.50fr blue	20.00	14.50
		Set, never hinged	47.50	

Intl. Labor Bureau, 48th Congress, Paris.

Colonial Exposition Issue

Fachi Woman — A42

French Colonials A43

1930-31 **Typo.** ***Perf. 14x13½***

258	A42	15c gray black	1.10	.30
259	A42	40c dark brown	2.40	.30
260	A42	50c dark red	.65	.25
a.		Booklet pane of 10	12.50	
261	A42	1.50fr deep blue	9.00	.65

Perf. 13½

Photo.

262	A43	1.50fr dp blue ('31)	45.00	2.75
		Nos. 258-262 (5)	58.15	4.25
		Set, never hinged	125.00	

No. 260 has two types: type 1 shows four short downward hairlines near top of head, type 2 has no lines. Booklet stamps are type 2.

Arc de Triomphe A44

1931 **Engr.** ***Perf. 13***

263	A44	2fr red brown	40.00	1.25
		Never hinged	80.00	

Peace with Olive Branch — A45

1932-39 **Typo.** ***Perf. 14x13½***

264	A45	30c dp green	1.00	.55
265	A45	40c brt violet	.30	.30
266	A45	45c yellow brown	1.75	1.00
267	A45	50c rose red	.25	.25
a.		Imperf., pair	140.00	
b.		Booklet pane of 10	5.50	
268	A45	55c dull vio ('37)	.60	.25
269	A45	60c ocher ('37)	.30	.25
270	A45	65c violet brown	.50	.50
271	A45	65c brt ultra ('37)	.25	.25
a.		Booklet pane of 10	7.00	
272	A45	75c olive green	.25	.30
273	A45	80c orange ('38)	.25	.25
274	A45	90c dk red	32.50	2.00
275	A45	90c brt green ('38)	.25	.25
276	A45	90c ultra ('38)	.90	.25
a.		Booklet pane of 10	8.50	
277	A45	1fr orange	3.25	.25
278	A45	1fr rose pink ('38)	3.25	.50
279	A45	1.25fr brown ol	75.00	4.75
280	A45	1.25fr rose car ('39)	1.90	2.25
281	A45	1.40fr brt red vio ('39)	5.75	5.25
282	A45	1.50fr deep blue	.30	.30
283	A45	1.75fr magenta	4.00	.50
		Nos. 264-283 (20)	132.55	20.20
		Set, never hinged	275.00	

The 50c is found in 4 types, differing in the lines below belt and size of "c."

For surcharges and overprints see Nos. 298, 333, 401-403, 405-409, M7-M9, S1.

Le Puy-en-Velay — A46

1933 **Engr.** ***Perf. 13***

290	A46	90c rose	3.00	1.10
		Never hinged	5.75	

Aristide Briand A47

Paul Doumer A48

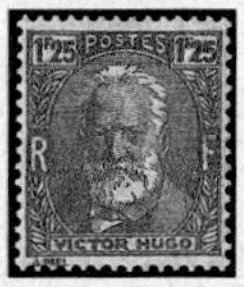

Victor Hugo — A49

1933, Dec. 11 **Typo.** ***Perf. 14x13½***

291	A47	30c blue green	17.00	8.00
292	A48	75c red violet	27.50	1.90
293	A49	1.25fr claret	6.00	2.25
		Nos. 291-293 (3)	50.50	12.15
		Set, never hinged	110.00	

Dove and Olive Branch A50

Joseph Marie Jacquard A51

1934, Feb. 20

294	A50	1.50fr ultra	50.00	15.00
		Never hinged	95.00	

1934, Mar. 14 **Engr.** ***Perf. 14x13***

295	A51	40c blue	3.00	1.10
		Never hinged	4.50	

Jacquard (1752-1834), inventor of an improved loom for figured weaving.

Jacques Cartier A52

1934, July 18 ***Perf. 13***

296	A52	75c rose lilac	30.00	2.25
297	A52	1.50fr blue	50.00	4.25
		Set, never hinged	210.00	

Cartier's discovery of Canada, 400th anniv.

No. 279 Surcharged

1934, Nov. ***Perf. 14x13½***

298	A45	50c on 1.25fr brn ol	3.75	.65
		Never hinged	7.00	

Catalogue values for unused stamps in this section, from this point to the end of the section, are for Never Hinged items.

Breton River Scene A53

1935, Feb. **Engr.** ***Perf. 13***

299	A53	2fr blue green	70.00	1.00
		Hinged	32.50	

S. S. Normandie A54

1935, Apr.

300	A54	1.50fr dark blue	29.00	2.00
		Hinged	14.00	
a.		1.50fr pale blue ('36)	145.00	19.00
		Hinged	55.00	
b.		1.50fr blue green ('36)	*30,000.*	*12,500.*
		Hinged	*19,000.*	
c.		1.50fr turquoise ('36)	400.00	40.00
		Hinged	275.00	

Maiden voyage of the transatlantic steamship, the "Normandie."

Benjamin Delessert A55

1935, May 20

301	A55	75c blue green	47.50	1.75
		Hinged	17.50	

Opening of the International Savings Bank Congress, May 20, 1935.

View of St. Trophime at Arles A56

Victor Hugo (1802-85) A57

1935, May 3

302	A56	3.50fr dark brown	70.00	4.25
		Hinged	27.50	

1935, May 30 ***Perf. 14x13***

303	A57	1.25fr magenta	8.25	2.00
		Hinged	4.00	

Cardinal Richelieu — A58

Jacques Callot — A59

1935, June 12 ***Perf. 13***

304	A58	1.50fr deep rose	70.00	1.75
		Hinged	20.00	

Tercentenary of the founding of the French Academy by Cardinal Richelieu.

1935, Nov. ***Perf. 14x13***

305	A59	75c red	19.00	.75
		Hinged	10.00	

300th anniv. of the death of Jacques Callot, engraver.

André Marie Ampère (1775-1836), Scientist, by Louis Bollly — A60

1936, Feb. 27 ***Perf. 13***

306	A60	75c brown	37.50	2.00
		Hinged	17.50	

Windmill at Fontvielle, Immortalized by Daudet — A61

1936, Apr. 27

307	A61	2fr ultra	5.75	.40
		Hinged	3.00	

Publication, in 1866, of Alphonse Daudet's "Lettres de mon Moulin," 75th anniv.

Pilâtre de Rozier and his Balloon A62

1936, June 4

308 A62 75c Prus blue 37.50 2.75
Hinged 19.00

150th anniversary of the death of Jean Francois Pilâtre de Rozier, balloonist.

Rouget de Lisle — A63

"La Marseillaise" — A64

1936, June 27

309 A63 20c Prus green 5.75 2.00
Hinged 3.25
310 A64 40c dark brown 11.50 3.25
Hinged 5.50

Cent. of the death of Claude Joseph Rouget de Lisle, composer of "La Marseillaise."

Canadian War Memorial at Vimy Ridge A65

1936, July 26

311 A65 75c henna brown 25.00 2.00
Hinged 9.50
312 A65 1.50fr dull blue 32.50 9.50
Hinged 16.00

Unveiling of the Canadian War Memorial at Vimy Ridge, July 26, 1936.

A66

Jean Léon Jaurès A67

1936, July 30

313 A66 40c red brown 5.75 1.40
Hinged 4.00
314 A67 1.50fr ultra 32.50 3.75
Hinged 13.00

Assassination of Jean Léon Jaurès (1859-1914), socialist and politician.

Herald — A68

Allegory of Exposition A69

1936, Sept. 15 Typo. *Perf. 14x13½*

315 A68 20c brt violet 1.00 .50
Hinged .30
316 A68 30c Prus green 4.00 1.75
Hinged 2.40
317 A68 40c ultra 2.50 .50
Hinged 1.00
318 A68 50c red orange 2.25 .25
Hinged 1.00
319 A69 90c carmine 25.00 7.50
Hinged 11.00
320 A69 1.50fr ultra 67.50 4.00
Hinged 30.00
Nos. 315-320 (6) 102.25 14.50

Publicity for the 1937 Paris Exposition.

"Peace" A70

1936, Oct. 1 Engr. *Perf. 13*

321 A70 1.50fr blue 27.50 4.00
Hinged 12.50

Skiing A71

1937, Jan. 18

322 A71 1.50fr dark blue 14.00 1.75
Hinged 7.00

Intl. Ski Meet at Chamonix-Mont Blanc.

Pierre Corneille, Portrait by Charles Le Brun — A72

1937, Feb. 15

323 A72 75c brown carmine 3.75 1.40
Hinged 1.90

300th anniv. of the publication of "Le Cid."

Paris Exposition Issue

Exposition Allegory A73

1937, Mar. 15

324 A73 1.50fr turq blue 4.00 1.25
Hinged 2.25

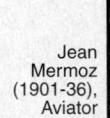

Jean Mermoz (1901-36), Aviator A74

Memorial to Mermoz — A75

1937, Apr. 22

325 A74 30c dk slate green 1.00 .55
Hinged .50
326 A75 3fr dark violet 13.50 3.75
Hinged 6.25
a. 3fr violet 15.00 4.50
Hinged 6.75

Electric Train A76

Streamlined Locomotive A77

1937, May 31

327 A76 30c dk green 1.40 1.75
Hinged 1.00
328 A77 1.50fr dk ultra 15.00 8.25
Hinged 7.25

13th International Railroad Congress.

Intl. Philatelic Exhibition Issue

Souvenir Sheet

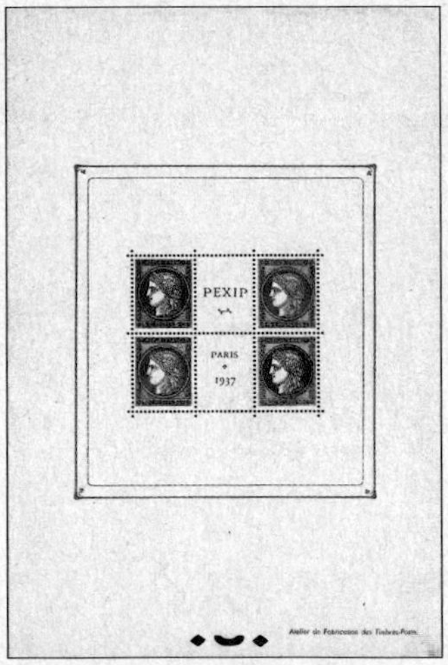

Ceres Type A1 of 1849-50 — A77a

1937, June 18 Typo. *Perf. 14x13½*

329 A77a Sheet of 4 700.00 300.00
Lightly hinged in margins 360.00
a. 5c ultra & dark brown 90.00 47.50
b. 15c red & rose red 90.00 47.50
c. 30c ultra & rose red 90.00 47.50
d. 50c red & dark brown 90.00 47.50
e. Sheet of 4, imperf 3,000.
Lightly hinged in margins 2,350.

Issued in sheets measuring 150x220mm.

The sheets were sold only at the exhibition in Paris, a ticket of admission being required for each sheet purchased.

René Descartes, by Frans Hals — A78

1937, June Engr. *Perf. 13*

Inscribed "Discours sur la Méthode"

330 A78 90c copper red 3.25 1.40
Hinged 1.90

Inscribed "Discours de la Méthode"

331 A78 90c copper red 11.00 1.75
Hinged 5.50

3rd centenary of the publication of "Discours de la Méthode" by René Descartes.

France Congratulating USA — A79

1937, Sept. 17

332 A79 1.75fr ultra 4.50 2.00
Hinged 2.50

150th anniv. of the US Constitution.

No. 277 Surcharged in Red

1937, Oct. *Perf. 14x13½*

333 A45 80c on 1fr orange 1.90 .85
Hinged .80
a. Inverted surcharge *1,225.*
Hinged *825.00*

Mountain Road at Iseran A80

1937, Oct. 4 Engr. *Perf. 13*

334 A80 90c dark green 3.75 .30
Hinged 1.90

Issued in commemoration of the opening of the mountain road at Iseran, Savoy.

Ceres — A81

1938-40 Typo. *Perf. 14x13½*

335 A81 1.75fr dk ultra 1.40 .55
Hinged .55
336 A81 2fr car rose ('39) .30 .30
Hinged .25
337 A81 2.25fr ultra ('39) 15.00 1.10
Hinged 8.00
338 A81 2.50fr green ('39) 3.00 .50
Hinged 1.25
339 A81 2.50fr vio blue ('40) 1.25 .75
Hinged .65
340 A81 3fr rose lilac ('39) 1.25 .50
Hinged .55
Nos. 335-340 (6) 22.20 3.70

For surcharges see Nos. 397-399.

Léon Gambetta (1838-82), Lawyer and Statesman — A82

1938, Apr. 2 Engr. *Perf. 13*

341 A82 55c dark violet .55 .40
Hinged .35

Arc de Triomphe of Orange A82a

Miners A83

Keep and Gate of Vincennes A86

Palace of the Popes, Avignon A84

Medieval Walls of Carcassonne — A85

Port of St. Malo — A87

1938

342 A82a 2fr brown black 1.75 1.25
Hinged .55
343 A83 2.15fr violet brn 9.50 1.00
Hinged 4.75
344 A84 3fr car brown 26.50 5.00
Hinged 12.50
345 A85 5fr deep ultra 1.50 .40
Hinged .75
346 A86 10fr brown, *blue* 3.25 1.90
Hinged 1.50
347 A87 20fr dk blue green 80.00 19.00
Hinged 37.50
Nos. 342-347 (6) 122.50 28.55

For surcharges see Nos. 410-413.

Clément Ader, Air Pioneer A88

1938, June 16

348 A88 50fr ultra (thin paper) 150.00 65.00
Hinged 95.00
a. 50fr dark ultra (thick paper) 175.00 77.50
Hinged 100.00

For surcharge, see No. 414.

Soccer Players A89

1938, June 1

349 A89 1.75fr dark ultra 29.00 13.50
Hinged 13.50

World Cup Soccer Championship.

Costume of Champagne Region — A90

Jean de La Fontaine — A91

1938, June 13

350 A90 1.75fr dark ultra 7.50 4.50
Hinged 3.75

Tercentenary of the birth of Dom Pierre Pérignon, discoverer of the champagne process.

1938, July 8

351 A91 55c dk blue green 1.00 .80
Hinged .65

Jean de La Fontaine (1621-1695) the fabulist.

Seal of Friendship and Peace, Victoria Tower and Arc de Triomphe A92

1938, July 19

352 A92 1.75fr ultra 1.25 .80
Hinged .65

Visit of King George VI and Queen Elizabeth of Great Britain to France.

Mercury — A93

1938-42 Typo. *Perf. 14x13½*

353 A93 1c dark brown ('39) .25 .25
Hinged .25
354 A93 2c slate grn ('39) .25 .25
Hinged .25
355 A93 5c rose .25 .25
Hinged .25
356 A93 10c ultra .25 .25
Hinged .25
357 A93 15c red orange .25 .25
Hinged .25
358 A93 15c orange brn ('39) 1.00 .50
Hinged .55
359 A93 20c red violet .25 .25
Hinged .25
360 A93 25c blue green .25 .25
Hinged .25
361 A93 30c rose red ('39) .25 .25
Hinged .25
362 A93 40c dk violet ('39) .25 .25
Hinged .25
363 A93 45c lt green ('39) .80 .50
Hinged .50
364 A93 50c deep blue ('39) 4.00 .40
Hinged 2.25
365 A93 50c dk green ('41) .55 .35
Hinged .30
366 A93 50c grnsh blue ('42) .25 .25
Hinged .25
367 A93 60c red orange ('39) .25 .25
Hinged .25
368 A93 70c magenta ('39) .25 .25
Hinged .25
369 A93 75c dk org brn ('39) 7.50 2.50
Hinged 3.75
Nos. 353-369 (17) 16.85 7.25

No. 366 exists imperforate. See Nos. 455-458. For overprints and surcharge see Nos. 404, 499-502.

Self-portrait — A95

1939, Mar. 15 Engr. *Perf. 13*

370 A95 2.25fr Prussian blue 8.25 3.50
Hinged 3.50

Paul Cézanne (1839-1906), painter.

Georges Clemenceau and Battleship Clemenceau — A96

1939, Apr. 18

371 A96 90c ultra 1.00 .75
Hinged .50

Laying of the keel of the warship "Clemenceau," Jan. 17, 1939.

Statue of Liberty, French Pavilion, Trylon and Perisphere A97

1939-40

372 A97 2.25fr ultra 17.00 6.50
Hinged 8.00
373 A97 2.50fr ultra ('40) 22.50 9.50
Hinged 8.50

New York World's Fair.

Joseph Nicéphore Niepce and Louis Jacques Mandé Daguerre A98

1939, Apr. 24

374 A98 2.25fr dark blue 16.00 7.00
Hinged 7.00

Centenary of photography.

Iris — A99

1939-44 Typo. *Perf. 14x13½*

375 A99 80c red brown ('40) .25 .25
Hinged .25
376 A99 80c yellow grn ('44) .25 .25
Hinged .25
377 A99 1fr green 1.00 .25
Hinged .55
378 A99 1fr crimson ('40) .40 .35
Hinged .25
a. Booklet pane of 10 7.50
379 A99 1fr grnsh blue ('44) .25 .25
Hinged .25
380 A99 1.20fr violet ('44) .25 .25
Hinged .25
381 A99 1.30fr ultra ('40) .25 .25
Hinged .25
382 A99 1.50fr red org ('41) .25 .25
Hinged .25
383 A99 1.50fr henna brn ('44) .25 .25
Hinged .25
384 A99 2fr violet brn ('44) .25 .25
Hinged .25
385 A99 2.40fr car rose ('44) .25 .25
Hinged .25
386 A99 3fr orange ('44) .25 .25
Hinged .25
387 A99 4fr ultra ('44) .25 .25
Hinged .25
Nos. 375-387 (13) 4.15 3.35

Pumping Station at Marly A100

1939 Engr. *Perf. 13*

388 A100 2.25fr brt ultra 25.00 5.00
Hinged 11.00

France's participation in the International Water Exposition at Liège.

St. Gregory of Tours — A101

1939, June 10

389 A101 90c red .90 .55
Hinged .50

14th centenary of the birth of St. Gregory of Tours, historian and bishop.

"The Oath of the Tennis Court" by Jacques David A102

1939, June 20

390 A102 90c deep slate green 3.50 1.90
Hinged 1.90

150th anniversary of French Revolution.

Cathedral of Strasbourg — A103

1939, June 23

391 A103 70c brown carmine 1.50 1.00
Hinged .75

500th anniv. of the completion of Strasbourg Cathedral.

Porte Chaussée, Verdun A104

1939, June 23

392 A104 90c black brown 1.00 .80
Hinged .80

23rd anniv. of the Battle of Verdun.

View of Pau A105

1939, Aug. 25

393 A105 90c brt rose, *gray bl* 1.25 1.25
Hinged .80

Maid of Languedoc A106

Bridge at Lyons A107

1939

394 A106 70c black, *blue* .50 .40
Hinged .40
395 A107 90c dull brown vio 1.00 *1.25*
Hinged .90

Imperforates

Nearly all French stamps issued from 1940 onward exist imperforate. Officially 20 sheets, ranging from 25 to 100 subjects, were left imperforate.

Georges Guynemer (1894-1917), World War I Ace — A108

1940, Nov. 7

396 A108 50fr ultra 16.00 9.00
Hinged 8.00

Stamps of 1938-39 Surcharged in Carmine

1940-41 ***Perf. 14x13½***

397 A81 1fr on 1.75fr dk ultra .30 .30
Hinged .25
398 A81 1fr on 2.25fr ultra ('41) .30 .30
Hinged .25
399 A81 1fr on 2.50fr grn ('41) 1.40 1.40
Hinged .65
Nos. 397-399 (3) 2.00 2.00

Stamps of 1932-39 Surcharged in Carmine, Red (#408) or Black (#407)

1940-41 ***Perf. 13, 14x13½***

400 A22 30c on 35c grn ('41) .30 .30
Hinged .25
401 A45 50c on 55c dl vio ('41) .30 .30
Hinged .25
a. Inverted surcharge *1,000.*
402 A45 50c on 65c brt ultra ('41) .30 .30
Hinged .25
403 A45 50c on 75c ol grn ('41) .30 .30
Hinged .25
404 A93 50c on 75c dk org brn ('41) .30 .30
Hinged .25
405 A45 50c on 80c org ('41) .30 .30
Hinged .25
406 A45 50c on 90c ultra ('41) .30 .30
Hinged .25
a. Inverted surcharge *550.00*
b. "05" instead of "50" *9,000.* 6,400.
407 A45 1fr on 1.25fr rose car (Bk) ('41) .30 .30
Hinged .25
408 A45 1fr on 1.40fr brt red vio (R) ('41) .40 .40
Hinged .25
a. Double surcharge *1,600.*
409 A45 1fr on 1.50fr dk bl ('41) 1.40 1.40
Hinged .25
410 A83 1fr on 2.15fr vio brn .40 .40
Hinged .25
411 A85 2.50fr on 5fr dp ultra ('41) .40 .40
Hinged .25
a. Double surcharge *350.00* 190.00
412 A86 5fr on 10fr brn, *bl* ('41) 1.90 1.90
Hinged 1.00
413 A87 10fr on 20fr dk bl grn ('41) 1.60 1.60
Hinged 1.00
414 A88 20fr on 50fr dk ultra (#348a) ('41) 70.00 37.50
Hinged 29.00
a. 20fr on 50fr ultra, thin paper (#348) 75.00 50.00
Nos. 400-414 (15) 78.50 46.00

Issued: No. 410, 1940; others, 1941

Marshal Pétain A109

Frédéric Mistral A110

1941 ***Perf. 13***

415 A109 40c red brown .40 .40
416 A109 80c turq blue .55 .55
417 A109 1fr red .25 .25
418 A109 2.50fr deep ultra 1.50 1.10
Nos. 415-418 (4) 2.70 2.30

For No. 417 with surcharge, see No. B111.

1941, Feb. 20 ***Perf. 14x13***

419 A110 1fr brown lake .25 .25

Issued in honor of Frédéric Mistral, poet and Nobel prize winner for literature in 1904.

Beaune Hospital A111

View of Angers A112

Ramparts of St. Louis, Aiguesmortes — A113

1941

420 A111 5fr brown black .40 .25
421 A112 10fr dark violet .90 .55
422 A113 20fr brown black 1.40 1.00
Nos. 420-422 (3) 2.70 1.80

Inscribed "Postes Francaises"

1942

Imprint: "FELTESSE" at right

423 A111 15fr brown lake .65 .55

A114

A115

Marshal Pétain — A116

1941-42 **Typo.** ***Perf. 14x13½***

427 A114 20c lilac ('42) .25 .25
428 A114 30c rose red .25 .25
429 A114 40c ultra .25 .25
431 A115 50c dp green .25 .25
432 A115 60c violet ('42) .25 .25
433 A115 70c saph ('42) .25 .25
434 A115 70c orange ('42) .25 .25
435 A115 80c brown .25 .25
436 A115 80c emerald ('42) .25 .25
437 A115 1fr rose red .25 .25
438 A115 1.20fr red brn ('42) .25 .25
439 A116 1.50fr rose .25 .25
440 A116 1.50fr dl red brn ('42) .25 .25
a. Booklet pane of 10 2.75
441 A116 2fr blue grn ('42) .25 .25
443 A116 2.40fr rose red ('42) .25 .25
444 A116 2.50fr ultra .85 .85
445 A116 3fr orange .25 .25
446 A115 4fr ultra ('42) .25 .25
447 A115 4.50fr dk green ('42) 1.00 .65
Nos. 427-447 (19) 6.10 5.75

Nos. 431 to 438 measure 16½x20½mm.

No. 440 was forged by the French Underground ("Defense de la France") and used to frank clandestine journals, etc., from Feb. to June, 1944. The forgeries were ungummed, both perf. 11½ and imperf., with a back handstamp covering six stamps and including the words: "Atelier des Faux."

For surcharge see No. B134.

A117

A118

1942 **Engr.** ***Perf. 14x13***

448 A115 4fr brt ultra .25 .25
449 A115 4.50fr dark green .25 .25
450 A117 5fr Prus green .25 .25

Perf. 13

451 A118 50fr black 4.50 4.00
Nos. 448-451 (4) 5.25 4.75

Nos. 448 and 449 measure 18x21½mm.

Jules Massenet — A119

1942, June 22 ***Perf. 14x13***

452 A119 4fr Prus green .25 .25

Jules Massenet (1842-1912), composer.

Stendhal (Marie Henri Beyle) — A120

1942, Sept. 14 ***Perf. 13***

453 A120 4fr blk brn & org red .55 .55

Stendhal (1783-1842), writer.

André Blondel — A121

1942, Sept. 14

454 A121 4fr dull blue .55 .55

André Eugène Blondel (1863-1938), physicist.

Mercury Type of 1938-42

Inscribed "Postes Françaises"

1942 ***Perf. 14x13½***

455 A93 10c ultra .25 .25
456 A93 30c rose red .25 .25
457 A93 40c dark violet .25 .25
458 A93 50c turq blue .25 .25
Nos. 455-458 (4) 1.00 1.00

Town-Hall Belfry, Arras — A122

1942, Dec. 8 **Engr.** ***Perf. 13***

459 A122 10fr green .25 .25

Coats of Arms

Lyon — A123

1943 **Typo.** ***Perf. 14x13½***

460 A123 5fr shown .40 .40
461 A123 10fr Brittany .65 .55
462 A123 15fr Provence 1.90 1.40
463 A123 20fr Ile de France 1.60 1.60
Nos. 460-463 (4) 4.55 3.95

Antoine Lavoisier (1743-94), French Scientist — A127

1943, July 5 **Engr.** ***Perf. 14x13***

464 A127 4fr ultra .25 .25

Lake Lerie and Meije Dauphiné Alps A128

1943, July 5 ***Perf. 13***

465 A128 20fr dull gray grn .90 .90

Nicolas Rolin, Guigone de Salins and Hospital of Beaune A129

1943, July 21

466 A129 4fr blue .25 .25

500th anniv. of the founding of the Hospital of Beaune.

Arms of Flanders — A130

1944, Mar. 27 Typo. *Perf. 14x13½*

467	A130	5fr	shown	.25	.25
468	A130	10fr	Languedoc	.25	.25
469	A130	15fr	Orleans	.85	.85
470	A130	20fr	Normandy	1.25	1.00
			Nos. 467-470 (4)	2.60	2.35

Edouard Branly — A134

1944, Feb. 21 Engr. *Perf. 14x13*

471	A134	4fr	ultra	.25	.25

Cent. of the birth of Edouard Branly, electrical inventor.

Early Postal Car A135

1944, June 10 *Perf. 13*

472	A135	1.50fr	dark blue green	.85	.65

Cent. of France's traveling postal service.

Chateau de Chenonceaux — A136

1944, June 10

473	A136	15fr	lilac brown	.65	.55
a.		15fr	black brown	11.50	3.25
b.		15fr	black	100.00	55.00

See No. 496.

Claude Chappe — A137

1944, Aug. 14 *Perf. 14x13*

474	A137	4fr	dark ultra	.25	.25

150th anniv. of the invention of an optical telegraph by Claude Chappe (1763-1805).

Arc de Triomphe — OS2

Unwmk.

1944, Oct. 9 Litho. *Perf. 11*

475	OS2	5c	brt red violet	.35	.35
476	OS2	10c	lt gray	.35	.35
476A	OS2	25c	brown	.35	.35
476B	OS2	50c	olive bis	.50	.50
476C	OS2	1fr	pck green	.90	.90
476D	OS2	1.50fr	rose pink	1.90	.90
476E	OS2	2.50fr	purple	.90	.90
476F	OS2	4fr	ultra	1.90	1.90
476G	OS2	5fr	black	1.90	1.90
476H	OS2	10fr	yellow org	37.50	35.00
			Nos. 475-476H (10)	46.55	43.05

Nos 475-476H were printed by the U.S. Bureau of Engaving and Printing and were intended to be used by an Allied Military government, which was expected to administer the liberated areas of France. Instead, the Allies recognized the authority of Gen. de Gaulle's Provisional Government over these territories, and these stamps were transferred to the Free French in July, 1944. They were put on sale in liberated areas as the Allied armies advanced, and on Oct. 9, they were officially issued in Paris.

See Nos. 523A-523J.

Gallic Cock A138

Marianne A139

1944 Litho. *Perf. 12*

477	A138	10c	yellow grn	.25	.25
478	A138	30c	dk rose vio	.40	.40
479	A138	40c	blue	.25	.25
480	A138	50c	dark red	.25	.25
481	A139	60c	olive brown	.25	.25
482	A139	70c	rose lilac	.25	.25
483	A139	80c	yellow grn	1.10	1.10
484	A139	1fr	violet	.25	.25
485	A139	1.20fr	dp carmine	.25	.25
486	A139	1.50fr	deep blue	.25	.25
487	A138	2fr	indigo	.25	.25
488	A139	2.40fr	red orange	1.50	1.50
489	A139	3fr	dp blue grn	.25	.25
490	A139	4fr	grnsh blue	.25	.25
491	A139	4.50fr	black	.25	.25
492	A139	5fr	violet blue	4.50	4.50
493	A138	10fr	violet	5.00	5.00
494	A138	15fr	olive brown	5.00	5.00
495	A138	20fr	dk slate grn	4.50	4.50
			Nos. 477-495 (19)	25.00	25.00

Nos. 477-495 were issued first in Corsica after the Allied landing, and released in Paris Nov. 15, 1944.

Chateau Type Inscribed "RF"

1944, Oct. 30 Engr. *Perf. 13*

496	A136	25fr	black	.85	.65

Thomas Robert Bugeaud — A141

1944, Nov. 20

497	A141	4fr	myrtle green	.25	.25

Battle of Isly, Aug. 14th, 1844.

Church of St. Denis A142

1944, Nov. 20

498	A142	2.40fr	brown carmine	.40	.40

800th anniv. of the Church of St. Denis.

Type of 1938-42, Overprinted in Black

Inscribed "Postes Francaises"

1944 *Perf. 14x13½*

499	A93	10c	ultra	.25	.25
500	A93	30c	rose red	.25	.25
501	A93	40c	dark violet	.25	.25
502	A93	50c	grnsh blue	.25	.25
			Nos. 499-502 (4)	1.00	1.00

The overprint "RF" in various forms, with or without Lorraine Cross, was also applied to stamps of the French State at Lyon and fourteen other cities.

French Forces of the Interior and Symbol of Liberation — A143

1945, Jan.

503	A143	4fr	dark ultra	.40	.40

Issued to commemorate the Liberation.

Stamps of the above design, and of one incorporating "FRANCE" in the top panel, were printed by photo. in England during WW II upon order of the Free French Government. They were not issued. There are 3 values in each design; 25c green, 1fr red, 2.50fr blue. Value: set, above design, $100; set inscribed "FRANCE," $550.

Marianne — A144

Perf. 11½x12½

1944-45 Engr. Unwmk.

504	A144	10c	ultra	.25	.25
505	A144	30c	bister	.25	.25
506	A144	40c	indigo	.25	.25
507	A144	50c	red orange	.25	.25
508	A144	60c	chalky blue	.25	.25
509	A144	70c	sepia	.25	.25
510	A144	80c	deep green	.25	.25
511	A144	1fr	lilac	.25	.25
512	A144	1.20fr	dk ol grn	.25	.25
513	A144	1.50fr	rose ('44)	.25	.25
514	A144	2fr	dk brown	.25	.25
515	A144	2.40fr	red	.25	.25
516	A144	3fr	brt ol grn	.25	.25
517	A144	4fr	brt ultra	.25	.25
518	A144	4.50fr	slate gray	.25	.25
519	A144	5fr	brt orange	.25	.25
520	A144	10fr	yellow grn	.30	.30
521	A144	15fr	lake	.40	.40
522	A144	20fr	brown org	1.75	1.50
523	A144	50fr	deep purple	3.50	2.50
			Nos. 504-523 (20)	9.95	8.70

The 2.40fr exists imperf. in a miniature sheet of 4 which was not issued. Value: never hinged $6,500; unused $4,500.

Arc de Triomphe Type of 1944

1945, Feb. 12 Litho. *Perf. 11*

Denominations in Black

523A	OS2	30c	orange	.40	.40
523B	OS2	40c	pale gray	.40	.40
523C	OS2	50c	olive bis	.40	.40
523D	OS2	60c	violet	.40	.40
523E	OS2	80c	emerald	.40	.40
523F	OS2	1.20fr	brown	.40	.40
523G	OS2	1.50fr	vermilion	.40	.40
523H	OS2	2fr	yellow	.40	.40
523I	OS2	2.40fr	dark rose	.40	.40
523J	OS2	3fr	brt red violet	.40	.40
			Nos. 523A-523J (10)	4.00	4.00

Coat of Arms A145

Ceres A146

Marianne — A147

1945-47 Typo. *Perf. 14x13½*

524	A145	10c	brown black	.25	.25
525	A145	30c	dk blue green	.25	.25
526	A145	40c	lilac rose	.30	.30
527	A145	50c	violet blue	.25	.25
528	A146	60c	brt ultra	.25	.25
530	A146	80c	brt green	.25	.25
531	A146	90c	dull grn ('46)	.65	.55
532	A146	1fr	rose red	.25	.25
533	A146	1.20fr	brown black	.25	.25
534	A146	1.50fr	rose lilac	.25	.25
535	A147	1.50fr	rose pink	.25	.25
536	A147	2fr	myrtle green	.25	.25
536A	A146	2fr	lt bl grn ('46)	.85	.65
537	A147	2.40fr	scarlet	.40	.40
538	A146	2.50fr	brown ('46)	.40	.40
539	A147	3fr	sepia	.25	.25
540	A147	3fr	deep rose ('46)	.25	.25
541	A147	4fr	ultra	.25	.25
541A	A147	4fr	violet ('46)	.25	.25
541B	A147	4.50fr	ultra ('47)	.25	.25
542	A147	5fr	lt green	.25	.25
542A	A147	5fr	rose pink ('47)	.25	.25
543	A147	6fr	brt ultra	.35	.25
544	A147	6fr	crim rose ('46)	1.60	1.10
545	A147	10fr	red orange	.65	.55
546	A147	10fr	ultra ('46)	1.60	.85
547	A147	15fr	brt red vio	3.25	1.90
			Nos. 524-547 (27)	14.30	11.20

No. 531 is known only precanceled. See second note after No. 132.

Due to a reduction of the domestic postage rate, No. 542A was sold for 4.50fr.

See Nos. 576-580, 594-602, 614, 615, 650-654. For surcharges see Nos. 589, 610, 706, Reunion 270-276, 278, 285, 290-291, 293, 295.

1945-46 Engr. *Perf. 14x13*

548	A147	4fr	dark blue	.25	.25
549	A147	10fr	dp blue ('46)	1.25	.55
550	A147	15fr	brt red vio ('46)	9.00	2.00
551	A147	20fr	blue grn ('46)	1.25	.55
552	A147	25fr	red ('46)	9.00	1.50
			Nos. 548-552 (5)	20.75	4.85

Nos. 548-552 have "GANDON" at lower right in design, and no inscription below design.

Marianne — A148

1945 Engr. *Perf. 13*

553	A148	20fr	dark green	1.25	1.10
554	A148	25fr	violet	1.65	1.25
555	A148	50fr	red brown	2.00	2.00
556	A148	100fr	brt rose car	12.50	6.25
			Nos. 553-556 (4)	17.40	10.60

CFA

French stamps inscribed or surcharged "CFA" and new value are listed under Réunion at the end of the French listings.

Arms of Metz A149

Arms of Strasbourg A150

1945, Mar. 3 *Perf. 14x13*

557	A149	2.40fr	dull blue	.25	.25
558	A150	4fr	black brown	.25	.25

Liberation of Metz and Strasbourg.

Costumes of Alsace and Lorraine and Cathedrals of Strasbourg and Metz
A151

1945, May 16 *Perf. 13*

559	A151	4fr henna brown	.25	.25

Liberation of Alsace and Lorraine.

World Map Showing French Possessions — A152

1945, Sept. 17

560	A152	2fr Prussian blue	.25	.25

No. B193 Surcharged in Black

1946 *Perf. 14x13½*

561	SP147	3fr on 2fr+1fr red org	.25	.25

Arms of Corsica — A153

1946 Unwmk. Typo. *Perf. 14x13½*

562	A153	10c shown	.25	.25
563	A153	30c Alsace	.25	.25
564	A153	50c Lorraine	.25	.25
565	A153	60c County of Nice	.25	.25
		Nos. 562-565 (4)	1.00	1.00

For surcharges see Reunion Nos. 268-269.

Reaching for "Peace" — A157

Holding the Dove of Peace — A158

1946, July 29 Engr. *Perf. 13*

566	A157	3fr Prussian green	.25	.25
567	A158	10fr dark blue	.25	.25

Peace Conference of Paris, 1946.

Vézelay
A159

Luxembourg Palace — A160

Rocamadour
A161

Pointe du Raz, Finistère
A162

1946 Unwmk. *Perf. 13*

568	A159	5fr rose violet	.25	.25
569	A160	10fr dark blue	.25	.25
570	A161	15fr dk violet brn	4.25	.55
571	A162	20fr slate gray	1.25	.25
		Nos. 568-571 (4)	6.00	1.30

See Nos. 591-592. For surcharges see Reunion Nos. 277, 279.

Globe and Wreath — A163

1946, Nov.

572	A163	10fr dark blue	.25	.25

Gen. conf. of UNESCO, Paris, 1946.

Cannes
A164

Stanislas Square, Nancy
A165

1946-48 Engr. *Perf. 13*

573	A164	6fr rose red	1.50	.65
574	A165	25fr black brown	4.25	.40
575	A165	25fr dark blue ('48)	11.50	1.25
		Nos. 573-575 (3)	17.25	2.30

For surcharges see Reunion Nos. 280-281.

Ceres & Marianne Types of 1945

1947 Unwmk. Typo. *Perf. 14x13½*

576	A146	1.30fr dull blue	.25	.25
577	A147	3fr green	1.90	.40
578	A147	3.50fr brown red	.85	.55
579	A147	5fr blue	.25	.25
580	A147	6fr carmine	.25	.25
		Nos. 576-580 (5)	3.50	1.70

Colonnade of the Louvre
A166

La Conciergerie, Paris Prison — A167

La Cité, Oldest Section of Paris
A168

Place de la Concorde
A169

1947, May 7 Engr. *Perf. 13*

581	A166	3.50fr chocolate	.40	.40
582	A167	4.50fr dk slate gray	.60	.40
583	A168	6fr red	1.10	1.00
584	A169	10fr bright ultra	1.10	1.00
		Nos. 581-584 (4)	3.20	2.80

12th UPU Cong., Paris, May 7-July 7.

Auguste Pavie — A170

Francois Fénelon — A171

1947, May 30

585	A170	4.50fr sepia	.40	.40

Cent. of the birth of Auguste Pavie, French pioneer in Laos.

1947, July 12

586	A171	4.50fr chocolate	.40	.40

Issued to honor Francois de Salignac de la Mothe-Fénelon, prelate and writer.

Fleur-de-Lis and Double Carrick Bend — A172

1947, Aug. 2 Unwmk.

587	A172	5fr brown	.40	.40

6th World Boy Scout Jamboree held at Moisson, Aug. 9th-18th, 1947.

Captured Patriot — A173

1947, Nov. 10 Engr. *Perf. 13*

588	A173	5fr sepia	.40	.35

No. 576 Surcharged in Carmine

1947, Nov. Typo. *Perf. 14x13½*

589	A146	1fr on 1.30fr dull blue	.25	.25

View of Conques — A174

1947, Dec. 18 Engr. *Perf. 13*

590	A174	15fr henna brown	4.50	1.00

For surcharge see Reunion No. 282.

Types of 1946-47

1948 Re-engraved

591	A160	12fr rose carmine	3.25	.65
592	A160	15fr bright red	.85	.85
593	A174	18fr dark blue	4.50	.40
		Nos. 591-593 (3)	8.60	1.90

"FRANCE" substituted for inscriptions "RF" and "REPUBLIQUE FRANCAISE."

Marianne Type of 1945

1948-49 Typo. *Perf. 14x13½*

594	A147	2.50fr brown	2.75	1.25
595	A147	3fr lilac rose	.25	.25
596	A147	4fr lt blue grn	.25	.25
597	A147	4fr brown org	3.00	.90
598	A147	5fr lt blue grn	.85	.25
599	A147	8fr blue	.40	.25
600	A147	10fr brt violet	.25	.25
601	A147	12fr ultra ('49)	3.00	.40
602	A147	15fr crim rose ('49)	1.00	.25
a.		Booklet pane of 10	150.00	
		Nos. 594-602 (9)	11.75	4.05

No. 594 known only precanceled. See second note after No. 132.

François René de Chateaubriand — A175

1948, July 3 Engr. *Perf. 13*

603	A175	18fr dark blue	.40	.40

Vicomte de Chateaubriand (1768-1848).

Philippe François M. de Hautecloque (Gen. Jacques Leclerc) — A176

1948, July 3

604	A176	6fr gray black	.40	.40

See Nos. 692-692A.

Chaillot Palace
A177

A178

1948, Sept. 21

605	A177	12fr carmine rose	.55	.55
606	A178	18fr indigo	.55	.55

Meeting of the UN General Assembly, Paris, 1948.

Genissiat Dam
A179

1948, Sept. 21

607 A179 12fr carmine rose .85 .85

Paul Langevin — A180

1948, Nov. 17 ***Perf. 14x13***

608 A180 5fr shown .40 .25
609 A180 8fr Jean Perrin .40 .25

Placing of the ashes of physicists Langevin (1872-1946) and Perrin (1870-1942) in the Pantheon.

No. 580 Surcharged with New Value and Bars in Black

1949, Jan. ***Perf. 14x13½***

610 A147 5fr on 6fr carmine .25 .25

Arctic Scene — A181

1949, May 2 ***Perf. 13***

611 A181 15fr indigo .40 .40

French polar explorations.

Types of 1849 and 1945

1949, May 9 **Engr.** ***Imperf.***

612 A1 15fr red 3.25 3.25
613 A1 25fr deep blue 3.25 3.25

Perf. 14x13

614 A147 15fr red 3.25 3.25
615 A147 25fr deep blue 3.25 3.25
a. Strip of 4, #612-615 + label 16.50 16.50
Nos. 612-615 (4) 13.00 13.00

Cent. of the 1st French postage stamps.

Arms of Burgundy — A182

Arms: 50c, Guyenne (Aquitania). 1fr, Savoy. 2fr, Auvergne. 4fr, Anjou.

1949, May 11 **Typo.** ***Perf. 14x13½***

616 A182 10c blue, red & yel .25 .25
617 A182 50c blue, red & yel .25 .25
618 A182 1fr brown & red .55 .40
619 A182 2fr green, yel & red .55 .25
620 A182 4fr blue, red & yel .40 .40
Nos. 616-620 (5) 2.00 1.55

See Nos. 659-663, 694-699, 733-739, 782-785. For surcharges see Reunion Nos. 283-284, 288-289, 297, 301, 305, 311.

Collegiate Church of St. Barnard and Dauphiné Arms
A183

1949, May 14 **Engr.** ***Perf. 13***

621 A183 12fr red brown .40 .40

600th anniv. of France's acquisition of the Dauphiné region.

US and French Flags, Plane and Steamship
A184

1949, May 14

622 A184 25fr blue & carmine .65 .65

Franco-American friendship.

Cloister of St. Wandrille Abbey
A185

1949, May 18

623 A185 25fr deep ultra .40 .25

See No. 649. For surcharge see Reunion No. 287.

Type of 1849 Inscribed "1849-1949" in Lower Margin

1949, June 1

624 A1 10fr brown orange 55.00 45.00
a. Sheet of 10 700.00 500.00

Cent. of the 1st French postage stamp.

No. 624 has wide margins, 40x52mm from perforation to perforation. Sold for 110fr, which included cost of admission to the Centenary Intl. Exhib., Paris, June 1949.

Claude Chappe — A186

Jean Racine — A187

15fr, François Arago & André M. Ampère. 25fr, Emile Baudot. 50fr, Gen. Gustave A. Ferrié.

Inscribed: "C.I.T.T. PARIS 1949"

1949, June 13 **Unwmk.** ***Perf. 13***

625 A186 10fr vermilion .90 .85
626 A186 15fr sepia 1.00 .90
627 A186 25fr deep claret 2.50 2.25
628 A186 50fr deep blue 4.50 4.00
Nos. 625-628 (4) 8.90 8.00

International Telegraph and Telephone Conference, Paris, May-July 1949.

1949

629 A187 12fr sepia .40 .40

Death of Jean Racine, dramatist, 250th anniv.

Abbey of St. Bertrand de Comminges
A188

Meuse Valley, Ardennes
A189

Mt. Gerbier de Jonc, Vivarais
A190

1949 **Engr.**

630 A188 20fr dark red .25 .25
631 A189 40fr Prus green 15.00 .30
632 A190 50fr sepia 2.50 .25
Nos. 630-632 (3) 17.75 .80

For surcharge see Reunion No. 286.

A191

1949, Oct. 18

633 A191 15fr deep carmine .25 .25

50th anniv. of the Assembly of Presidents of Chambers of Commerce of the French Union.

UPU Allegory
A192

1949, Nov. 7

634 A192 5fr dark green .25 .25
635 A192 15fr deep carmine .40 .25
636 A192 25fr deep blue 1.25 .90
Nos. 634-636 (3) 1.90 1.40

UPU, 75th anniversary.

Raymond Poincaré — A193

1950, May 27 **Unwmk.** ***Perf. 13***

637 A193 15fr indigo .35 .25

Charles Péguy and Cathedral at Chartres
A194

François Rabelais — A195

1950, June

638 A194 12fr dk brown .40 .25
639 A195 12fr red brown .85 .75

Chateau of Chateaudun — A196

1950, Nov. 25

640 A196 8fr choc & bis brn .70 .45

Madame Récamier
A197

Marie de Sévigné
A198

1950

641 A197 12fr dark green .65 .40
642 A198 15fr ultra .65 .40

See footnote after No. 4642.

Palace of Fontainbleau — A199

1951, Jan. 20

643 A199 12fr dark brown .90 .75

Jules Ferry — A200

1951, Mar. 17

644 A200 15fr bright red .55 .55

Hands Holding Shuttle
A201

1951, Apr. 9

645 A201 25fr deep ultra 1.00 .65

Intl. Textile Exposition, Lille, April-May, 1951.

Jean-Baptiste de la Salle — A202

1951, Apr. 28

646 A202 15fr chocolate .65 .55

300th anniv. of the birth of Jean-Baptiste de la Salle, educator and saint.

Map and Anchor
A203

1951, May 12

647 A203 15fr deep ultra .60 .40

50th anniv. of the creation of the French colonial troops.

Vincent d'Indy
A204

1951, May 15
648 A204 25fr deep green 2.00 2.00

Vincent d'Indy, composer, birth cent.

Abbey Type of 1949

1951
649 A185 30fr bright blue 5.00 4.25

Marianne Type of 1945-47

1951 Typo. *Perf. 14x13½*
650 A147 5fr dull violet .50 .25
651 A147 6fr green 6.50 .60
652 A147 12fr red orange .85 .25
653 A147 15fr ultra .35 .25
a. Booklet pane of 10 30.00
654 A147 18fr cerise 16.00 1.40
Nos. 650-654 (5) 24.20 2.75

Professors Nocard, Bouley and Chauveau; Gate at Lyons School
A205

1951, June 8 Engr. *Perf. 13*
655 A205 12fr red violet .60 .55

Issued to honor Veterinary Medicine.

Gen. Picqué, Cols. Roussin and Villemin; Val de Grace Dome
A206

1951, June 17 Unwmk.
656 A206 15fr red brown .75 .55

Issued to honor Military Medicine.

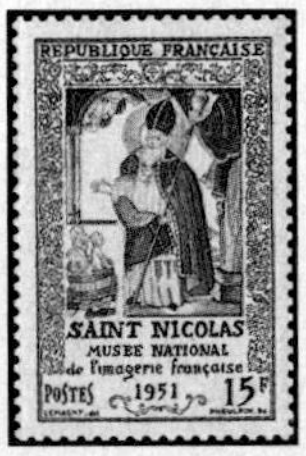

St. Nicholas, by Jean Didier — A207

1951, June 23
657 A207 15fr ind, dp claret & org 1.40 1.00

Chateau Bontemps, Arbois
A208

1951, June 23
658 A208 30fr indigo 1.00 .25

For surcharge see Reunion No. 296.

Arms Type of 1949

Arms of: 10c, Artois. 50c, Limousin. 1fr, Béarn. 2fr, Touraine. 3fr, Franche-Comté.

1951, June Typo. *Perf. 14x13½*
659 A182 10c red, vio bl & yel .25 .25
660 A182 50c green, red & blk .25 .25
661 A182 1fr blue, red & yel .25 .25
662 A182 2fr vio bl, red & yel .90 .40
663 A182 3fr red, vio bl & yel .85 .40
Nos. 659-663 (5) 2.50 1.55

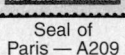

Seal of Paris — A209

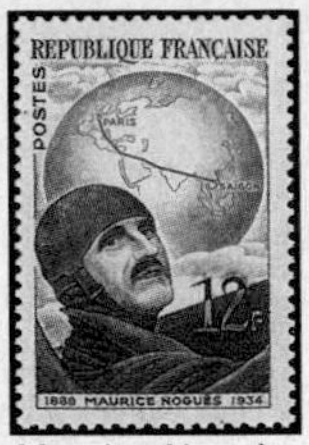

Maurice Noguès and Globe — A210

Unwmk.

1951, July 7 Engr. *Perf. 13*
664 A209 15fr dp bl, dk brn & red .65 .40

2,000th anniv. of the founding of Paris.

1951, Oct. 13
665 A210 12fr indigo & blue .90 .85

Maurice Nogues, aviation pioneer.

Charles Baudelaire
A211

Poets: 12fr, Paul Verlaine. 15fr, Arthur Rimbaud.

1951, Oct. 27
666 A211 8fr purple .85 .75
667 A211 12fr gray .85 .75
668 A211 15fr dp green .85 .75
Nos. 666-668 (3) 2.55 2.25

Georges Clemenceau, Birth Cent. — A212

1951, Nov. 11
669 A212 15fr black brown .55 .45

Chateau du Clos, Vougeot
A213

1951, Nov. 17
670 A213 30fr blk brn & brn 6.25 2.50

Chaillot Palace and Eiffel Tower
A214

1951, Nov. 6
671 A214 18fr red 1.10 .60
672 A214 30fr deep ultra 2.00 1.10

Opening of the Geneva Assembly of the United Nations, Paris, Nov. 6, 1951.

Observatory, Pic du Midi — A215

Abbaye aux Hommes, Caen — A216

1951, Dec. 22
673 A215 40fr violet 5.50 .25
674 A216 50fr black brown 5.00 .25

For surcharge see Reunion No. 294.

Marshal Jean de Lattre de Tassigny, 1890-1952
A217

1952, May 8 Unwmk. *Perf. 13*
675 A217 15fr violet brown 1.00 .45

See No. 717.

Gate of France, Vaucouleurs — A218

1952, May 11
676 A218 12fr brown black 1.25 .90

Flags and Monument at Narvik, Norway
A219

1952, May 28
677 A219 30fr violet blue 2.75 2.00

Battle of Narvik, May 27, 1940.

Chateau de Chambord
A220

1952, May 30
678 A220 20fr dark purple .45 .25

For surcharge see Reunion No. 292.

Assembly Hall, Strasbourg
A221

1952, May 31
679 A221 30fr dark green 7.25 5.25

Issued to honor the Council of Europe.

Monument, Bir-Hacheim Cemetery — A222

1952, June 14
680 A222 30fr rose lake 3.25 2.00

10th anniv. of the defense of Bir-Hacheim.

Abbey of the Holy Cross, Poitiers — A223

1952, June 21
681 A223 15fr bright red .40 .40

14th cent. of the foundation of the Abbey of the Holy Cross at Poitiers.

Leonardo da Vinci, Amboise Chateau and La Signoria, Florence
A224

1952, July 9
682 A224 30fr deep ultra 8.00 6.50

Leonardo da Vinci, 500th birth anniv.

Garabit Viaduct
A225

1952, July 5
683 A225 15fr dark blue .55 .45

Sword and Military Medals, 1852-1952
A226

Dr. René Laennec
A227

1952, July 5
684 A226 15fr choc, grn & yel .50 .40

Cent. of the creation of the Military Medal.

1952, Nov. 7
685 A227 12fr dark green .65 .50

Versailles Gate, Painted by Utrillo
A228

1952, Dec. 20
686 A228 18fr violet brown 2.75 1.75

Publicity for the restoration of Versailles Palace. See No. 728.

Mannequin — A229

1953, Apr. 24 Unwmk. *Perf. 13*
687 A229 30fr blue blk & rose vio .90 .35

Dressmaking industry of France.

Gargantua of François Rabelais A230

Célimène from The Misanthrope A231

Figaro, from the Barber of Seville — A232

Hernani of Victor Hugo — A233

1953
688 A230 6fr dp plum & car .25 .25
689 A231 8fr indigo & ultra .25 .25
690 A232 12fr vio brn & dk grn .25 .25
691 A233 18fr vio brn & blk brn .50 .30
Nos. 688-691 (4) 1.25 1.05

For surcharge see Reunion No. 298.

Type of 1948

Inscribed "Général Leclerc Maréchal de France"

1953-54
692 A176 8fr red brown .80 .75
692A A176 12fr dk grn & gray grn ('54) 2.50 1.60

Issued to honor the memory of General Jacques Leclerc.

Map and Cyclists, 1903-1953 A234

1953, July 26
693 A234 12fr red brn, ultra & blk 2.00 1.25

50th anniv. of the Bicycle Tour de France.

Arms Type of 1949

50c, Picardy. 70c, Gascony. 80c, Berri. 1fr, Poitou. 2fr, Champagne. 3fr, Dauphiné.

1953 Typo. *Perf. 14x13½*
694 A182 50c blue, yel & red .25 .25
695 A182 70c red, blue & yel .25 .25
696 A182 80c blue, red & yel .25 .25
697 A182 1fr black, red & yel .25 .25
698 A182 2fr brown, bl & yel .30 .25
699 A182 3fr red, blue & yel .50 .25
Nos. 694-699 (6) 1.80 1.50

Swimming A235

1953, Nov. 28 Engr. *Perf. 13*
700 A235 20fr shown 2.00 .25
701 A235 25fr Track 13.00 .55
702 A235 30fr Fencing 2.00 .25
703 A235 40fr Canoe racing 13.00 .55
704 A235 50fr Rowing 7.25 .25
705 A235 75fr Equestrian 32.50 12.00
Nos. 700-705 (6) 69.75 13.85

For surcharges see Reunion Nos. 299-300.

No. 654 Surcharged with New Value and Bars in Black

1954 *Perf. 14x13½*
706 A147 15fr on 18fr cerise .55 .25

Farm Woman A236

Gallic Cock A237

1954 Typo.
707 A236 4fr blue .25 .25
708 A236 8fr brown red 4.75 1.00
709 A237 12fr cerise 3.00 .65
710 A237 24fr blue green 16.00 4.00
Nos. 707-710 (4) 24.00 5.90

Nos. 707-710 are known only precanceled. See second note after No. 132.

See Nos. 833-834, 840-844, 910-913, 939, 952-955. For surcharges see Reunion Nos. 324, 326-327.

Tapestry and Gobelin Workshop A238

Entrance to Exhibition Park A239

Designs: 30fr, Book manufacture. 40fr, Porcelain and glassware. 50fr, Jewelry and metalsmith's work. 75fr, Flowers and perfumes.

1954, May 6 Engr. *Perf. 13*
711 A238 25fr red brn car & blk brn 12.00 .50
712 A238 30fr dk grn & lil gray 2.25 .25
713 A238 40fr dk brn, vio brn & org brn 3.50 .25
714 A238 50fr brt ultra, dl grn & org brn 2.25 .25
715 A238 75fr dp car & magenta 12.00 .95
Nos. 711-715 (5) 32.00 2.20

For surcharges see Reunion Nos. 303-304.

1954, May 22
716 A239 15fr blue & dk car .30 .25

Founding of the Fair of Paris, 50th anniv.

De Lattre Type of 1952

1954, June 5
717 A217 12fr vio bl & indigo 2.00 1.75

Allied Landings A240

1954, June 5
718 A240 15fr scarlet & ultra 1.75 1.00

The 10th anniversary of the liberation.

View of Lourdes A241

Street Corner, Quimper — A242

Views: 8fr, Seine valley, Les Andelys. 10fr, Beach at Royan. 18fr, Cheverny Chateau. 20fr, Beach, Gulf of Ajaccio.

1954
719 A241 6fr ultra, ind & dk grn .40 .30
720 A241 8fr brt blue & dk grn .30 .25
721 A241 10fr aqua & org brn .30 .25
722 A242 12fr rose vio & dk vio .50 .25
723 A241 18fr bl, dk grn & ind 3.25 .90
724 A241 20fr blk brn, bl grn & red brn 2.75 .25
Nos. 719-724 (6) 7.50 2.20

See No. 873. For surcharges see Reunion Nos. 302, 306-310. See footnote after No. 4642.

Abbey Ruins, Jumièges A243

St. Philibert Abbey, Tournus A244

1954, June 13
725 A243 12fr vio bl, ind & dk grn 1.50 .90

13th centenary of Abbey of Jumièges.

1954, June 18
726 A244 30fr indigo & blue 6.00 4.00

1st conf. of the Intl. Center of Romance Studies.

View of Stenay A245

1954, June 26
727 A245 15fr dk brn & org brn .85 .50

Acquisition of Stenay by France, 300th anniv.

Versailles Type of 1952

1954, July 10
728 A228 18fr dp bl, ind & vio brn 9.00 5.50

Villandry Chateau A246

1954, July 17
729 A246 18fr dk bl & dk bl grn 5.00 3.25

Napoleon Awarding Legion of Honor Decoration A247

1954, Aug. 14
730 A247 12fr scarlet 1.50 .80

150th anniv. of the 1st Legion of Honor awards at Camp de Boulogne.

Cadets Marching Through Gateway A248

1954, Aug. 1
731 A248 15fr vio gray, dk bl & car 1.10 1.10

150th anniversary of the founding of the Military School of Saint-Cyr.

Allegory — A249

1954, Oct. 4
732 A249 30fr indigo & choc 6.00 3.50

Issued to publicize the fact that the metric system was first introduced in France.

Arms Type of 1949

Arms: 50c, Maine. 70c, Navarre. 80c, Nivernais. 1fr, Bourbonnais. 2fr, Angoumois. 3fr, Aunis. 5fr, Saintonge.

1954 Typo. *Perf. 14x13½*
733 A182 50c multicolored .25 .25
734 A182 70c green, red & yel .25 .25
735 A182 80c blue, red & yel .25 .25
736 A182 1fr red, blue & yel .25 .25
737 A182 2fr black, red & yel .25 .25
738 A182 3fr brown, red & yel .25 .25
739 A182 5fr blue & yellow .25 .25
Nos. 733-739 (7) 1.75 1.75

Duke de Saint-Simon — A250

1955, Feb. 5 Engr. *Perf. 13*
740 A250 12fr dk brn & vio brn .70 .60

Louis de Rouvroy, Duke de Saint-Simon (1675-1755).

Allegory and Rotary Emblem A251

1955, Feb. 23
741 A251 30fr vio bl, bl & org 2.25 1.25

50th anniv. of Rotary International.

Marianne — A252

1955-59 Typo. *Perf. 14x13½*

751 A252 6fr fawn 2.75 1.75
752 A252 12fr green 3.25 1.25
a. Bklt. pane of 10 + 2 labels 45.00
753 A252 15fr carmine .25 .25
a. Booklet pane of 10 10.00
754 A252 18fr green ('58) .25 .25
755 A252 20fr ultra ('57) .45 .25
756 A252 25fr rose red ('59) 1.40 .25
a. Booklet pane of 8 15.00
b. Booklet pane of 10 16.00
Nos. 751-756 (6) 8.35 4.00

No. 751 was issued in coils of 1,000.

No. 752 was issued in panes of 10 stamps and two labels with marginal instructions for folding to form a booklet.

Nos. 754-755 are found in two types, distinguished by the numerals. On the 18fr there is no serif at left of base of the "1" on the 1st type. The 2nd type has a shorter "1" with no serifs at base. On the 20fr the 2nd type has a well formed "2" and the horiz. lines of the "F" of the denomination are longer and of equal length.

No. 756 also in two types, distinguished by border width. On the 1st type, the border is thicker than the width of the letters. On the 2nd type, the border is thinner than the width of the letters.

For surcharges see Reunion Nos. 330-331.

Philippe Lebon, Inventor of Illuminating Gas A253

Inventors: 10fr, Barthélemy Thimonnier, sewing machine. 12fr, Nicolas Appert, canned foods. 18fr, Dr. E. H. St. Claire Deville, aluminum. 25fr, Pierre Martin, steel making. 30fr, Bernigaud de Chardonnet, rayon.

1955, Mar. 5 Engr. *Perf. 13*

757 A253 5fr dk vio bl & bl .75 .75
758 A253 10fr dk brn & org brn .90 .90
759 A253 12fr dk green 1.25 1.25
760 A253 18fr dk vio bl & ind 2.90 1.40
761 A253 25fr dk brnsh pur & vio 3.25 1.60
762 A253 30fr rose car & scar 3.25 1.60
Nos. 757-762 (6) 12.30 7.50

St. Stephen Bridge, Limoges A254

1955, Mar. 26 Unwmk. *Perf. 13*

763 A254 12fr yel brn & dk vio brn 1.40 1.10

Gloved Model in Place de la Concorde — A255

1955, Mar. 26

764 A255 25fr blk brn, vio bl & blk .80 .25

French glove manufacturing. See footnote after No. 4642.

Jean Pierre Claris de Florian A256

1955, Apr. 2

765 A256 12fr blue green .65 .40

200th anniv. of the birth of Jean Pierre Claris de Florian, fabulist.

Eiffel Tower and Television Antennas A257

1955, Apr. 16

766 A257 15fr indigo & ultra 1.00 .90

French advancement in television.

Wire Fence and Guard Tower A258

1955, Apr. 23

767 A258 12fr dk gray bl & brn blk .90 .60

10th anniv. of the liberation of concentration camps.

Electric Train A259

1955, May 11

768 A259 12fr blk brn & slate bl 2.75 1.25

Issued to publicize the electrification of the Valenciennes-Thionville railroad line.

Jacquemart of Moulins — A260

1955, May 28

769 A260 12fr black brown 1.50 1.25

Jules Verne and Nautilus A261

1955, June 3

770 A261 30fr indigo 8.00 4.50

50th anniv. of the death of Jules Verne.

Auguste and Louis Lumière and Motion Picture Projector A262

1955, June 12

771 A262 30fr rose brown 6.00 4.00

Invention of motion pictures, 60th anniv.

Jacques Coeur and His Mansion at Bourges A263

1955, June 18

772 A263 12fr violet 2.25 1.25

5th centenary of the death of Jacques Coeur (1395?-1456), French merchant.

Corvette "La Capricieuse" — A264

1955, July 9

773 A264 30fr aqua & dk blue 5.50 3.50

Centenary of the voyage of La Capricieuse to Canada.

Bordeaux A265

Designs: 8fr, Marseille. 10fr, Nice. 12fr, Valentre bridge, Cahors. 18fr, Uzerche. 25fr, Fortifications, Brouage.

1955, Oct. 15

774 A265 6fr carmine lake .25 .25
775 A265 8fr indigo .45 .25
776 A265 10fr dp ultra .25 .25
777 A265 12fr violet & brn .25 .25
778 A265 18fr bluish grn & ind .85 .25
779 A265 25fr org brn & red brn 1.25 .25
Nos. 774-779 (6) 3.30 1.50

See Nos. 838-839. For surcharges see Reunion Nos. 312-317, 323.

Mount Pelée, Martinique A266

1955, Nov. 1

780 A266 20fr dk & lt purple 3.50 2.00

Gérard de Nerval — A267

1955, Nov. 11

781 A267 12fr lake & sepia .45 .30

Centenary of the death of Gérard de Nerval (Labrunie), author.

Arms Type of 1949

Arms of: 50c, County of Foix. 70c, Marche. 80c, Roussillon. 1fr, Comtat Venaissin.

Perf. 14x13½

1955, Nov. 19 Typo. Unwmk.

782 A182 50c multicolored .25 .25
783 A182 70c red, blue & yel .25 .25
784 A182 80c brown, yel & red .25 .25
785 A182 1fr blue, red & yel .25 .25
Nos. 782-785 (4) 1.00 1.00

Concentration Camp Victim and Monument A268

Belfry at Douai A269

1956, Jan. 14 Engr. *Perf. 13*

786 A268 15fr brn blk & red brn .65 .50

Natl. memorial for Nazi deportation victims erected at the Natzwiller Struthof concentration camp in Alsace.

1956, Feb. 11

787 A269 15fr ultra & indigo .55 .55

Col. Emil Driant A270

1956, Feb. 21

788 A270 15fr dark blue .30 .25

40th anniv. of the death of Col. Emil Driant during the battle of Verdun.

Trench Fighting — A271

1956, Mar. 3

789 A271 30fr indigo & dk olive 2.00 1.40

40th anniversary of Battle of Verdun.

Jean Henri Fabre, Entomology A272

Scientists: 15fr, Charles Tellier, Refrigeration. 18fr, Camille Flammarion, Popular Astronomy. 30fr, Paul Sabatier, Catalytic Chemistry.

1956, Apr. 7

790 A272 12fr vio brn & org brn .90 .60
791 A272 15fr vio bl & int blk .90 .60
792 A272 18fr brt ultra 1.75 1.50
793 A272 30fr Prus grn & dk grn 4.25 2.75
Nos. 790-793 (4) 7.80 5.45

Grand Trianon, Versailles A273

1956, Apr. 14

794 A273 12fr vio brn & gray grn 1.50 .80

Symbols of Latin American and French Culture
A274

1956, Apr. 21
795 A274 30fr brown & red brn 2.25 1.60

Issued in recognition of the friendship between France and Latin America.

"The Smile of Reims" and Botticelli's "Spring"
A275

1956, May 5
796 A275 12fr black & green .75 .40

Issued to emphasize the cultural and artistic kinship of Reims and Florence.

Leprosarium and Maltese Cross — A276

1956, May 12
797 A276 12fr sepia, red brn & red .40 .35

Issued in honor of the Knights of Malta.

St. Yves de Treguier
A277

1956, May 19
798 A277 15fr bluish gray & blk .35 .25

St. Yves, patron saint of lawyers.

Marshal Franchet d'Esperey
A278

Miners Monument
A279

1956, May 26
799 A278 30fr deep claret 2.75 1.50

Centenary of the birth of Marshal Louis Franchet d'Esperey.

1956, June 2
800 A279 12fr violet brown .45 .40

Town Montceau-les-Mines, 100th anniv.

Basketball — A280

Sports: 40fr, Pelota (Jai alai). 50fr, Rugby. 75fr, Mountain climbing.

1956, July 7
801 A280 30fr gray vio & blk 1.25 .25
802 A280 40fr brown & vio brn 5.25 .30
803 A280 50fr rose vio & vio 1.75 .25
804 A280 75fr indigo, grn & bl 10.50 2.00
Nos. 801-804 (4) 18.75 2.80

For surcharges see Reunion Nos. 318-321.

Europa Issue

"Rebuilding Europe" — A281

Perf. 13½x14

1956, Sept. 15 Typo. Unwmk.
805 A281 15fr rose & rose lake *.80 .25*

Perf. 13

Engr.
806 A281 30fr lt blue & vio bl *6.00* .85

Issued to symbolize the cooperation among the six countries comprising the Coal and Steel Community.

No. 805 measures 21x35½mm, No. 806 measures 22x35½mm.

Dam at Donzère-Mondragon — A282

Cable Railway to Pic du Midi — A283

Rhine Port of Strasbourg
A284

1956, Oct. 6 Engr. *Perf. 13*
807 A282 12fr gray vio & vio brn 1.60 1.10
808 A283 18fr indigo 3.25 2.25
809 A284 30fr indigo & dk blue 14.00 6.25
Nos. 807-809 (3) 18.85 9.60

French technical achievements.

Antoine-Augustin Parmentier — A285

1956, Oct. 27
810 A285 12fr brown red & brown .75 .65

Parmentier, nutrition chemist, who popularized the potato in France.

Petrarch — A286

Portraits: 12fr, J. B. Lully. 15fr, J. J. Rousseau. 18fr, Benjamin Franklin. 20fr, Frederic Chopin. 30fr, Vincent van Gogh.

1956, Nov. 10
811 A286 8fr green .75 .55
812 A286 12fr claret .75 .55
813 A286 15fr dark red 1.10 .55
814 A286 18fr ultra 2.40 1.90
815 A286 20fr brt violet 3.25 1.50
816 A286 30fr brt grnsh blue 5.00 2.50
Nos. 811-816 (6) 13.25 7.55

Famous men who lived in France.

Pierre de Coubertin and Olympic Stadium
A287

1956, Nov. 24
817 A287 30fr dk blue gray & pur 1.60 1.00

Issued in honor of Baron Pierre de Coubertin, founder of the modern Olympic Games.

Homing Pigeon
A288

1957, Jan. 12
818 A288 15fr dp ultra, ind & red brn .45 .25

Victor Schoelcher — A289

1957, Feb. 16 Engr.
819 A289 18fr lilac rose .60 .40

Issued in honor of Victor Schoelcher, who freed the slaves in the French Colonies.

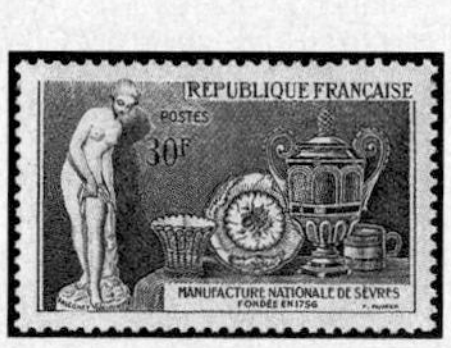

Sèvres Porcelain
A290

1957, Mar. 23 Unwmk. *Perf. 13*
820 A290 30fr ultra & vio blue .75 .40

Bicentenary of the porcelain works at Sèvres (in 1956).

Gaston Planté and Storage Battery
A291

Designs: 12fr, Antoine Béclère and X-ray apparatus. 18fr, Octave Terrillon, autoclave, microscope and surgical instruments. 30fr, Etienne Oemichen and early helicopter.

1957, Apr. 13
821 A291 8fr gray blk & dp cl .45 .45
822 A291 12fr dk bl, blk & emer .50 .50
823 A291 18fr rose red & mag 1.25 1.25
824 A291 30fr green & slate grn 2.25 2.25
Nos. 821-824 (4) 4.45 4.45

Uzès Chateau
A292

1957, Apr. 27
825 A292 12fr slate bl & bis brn .40 .40

Jean Moulin
A293

Le Quesnoy
A294

Portraits: 10fr, Honoré d'Estienne d'Orves. 12fr, Robert Keller. 18fr, Pierre Brossolette. 20fr, Jean-Baptiste Lebas.

1957, May 18
826 A293 8fr violet brown 1.00 .45
827 A293 10fr black & vio bl 1.00 .45
828 A293 12fr brown & sl grn 1.00 .80
829 A293 18fr purple & blk 1.50 1.25
830 A293 20fr Prus bl & dk bl 1.40 .90
Nos. 826-830 (5) 5.90 3.85

Issued in honor of the heroes of the French Underground of World War II.

See Nos. 879-882, 915-919, 959-963, 990-993.

1957, June 1
831 A294 8fr dk slate green .25 .25

See No. 837. For surcharge see Reunion No. 322.

Symbols of Justice
A295

1957, June 1
832 A295 12fr sepia & ultra .25 .25

French Cour des Comptes, 150th anniv.

Farm Woman Type of 1954

1957-59 *Perf. 14x13½*
833 A236 6fr orange .25 .25
833A A236 10fr brt green ('59) .75 .25
834 A236 12fr red lilac .25 .25
Nos. 833-834 (3) 1.25 .75

Nos. 833-834 issued without precancellation.

Symbols of Public Works
A296

1957, June 20 Engr. *Perf. 13*
835 A296 30fr sl grn, brn & ocher 1.90 1.10

Brest
A297

1957, July 6
836 A297 12fr gray grn & brn ol .90 .80

Scenic Types of 1955, 1957

Designs: 15fr, Le Quesnoy. 35fr, Bordeaux. 70fr, Valentre bridge, Cahors.

1957, July 19 **Unwmk.**

837 A294 15fr dk bl grn & sep .40 .25
838 A265 35fr dk bl grn & sl grn 3.25 1.10
839 A265 70fr black & dull grn 22.50 2.00
Nos. 837-839 (3) 26.15 3.35

Gallic Cock Type of 1954

1957 **Typo.** ***Perf. 14x13½***

840 A237 5fr olive bister .40 .25
841 A237 10fr bright blue 1.75 .35
842 A237 15fr plum 2.25 .75
843 A237 30fr bright red 10.00 3.00
844 A237 45fr green 21.00 12.50
Nos. 840-844 (5) 35.40 16.85

Nos. 840-844 are known only precanceled. See second note after No. 132.

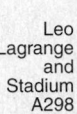

Leo Lagrange and Stadium A298

1957, Aug. 31 **Engr.** ***Perf. 13***

845 A298 18fr lilac gray & blk .55 .55

Intl. University Games, Paris, 8/31-9/8.

"United Europe" — A299

Auguste Comte — A300

1957, Sept. 16

846 A299 20fr red brown & green *.40 .30*
847 A299 35fr dk brown & blue *.90 .80*

A united Europe for peace and prosperity.

1957, Sept. 14

848 A300 35fr brown red & sepia .45 .30

Centenary of the death of Auguste Comte, mathematician and philosopher.

Roman Amphitheater, Lyon — A301

1957, Oct. 5 ***Perf. 13***

849 A301 20fr brn org & brn vio .45 .30

2,000th anniv. of the founding of Lyon.

Sens River, Guadeloupe A302

Beynac-Cazenac, Dordogne A303

Nicolaus Copernicus A304

Designs: 10fr, Elysee Palace. 25fr, Chateau de Valencay, Indre. 35fr, Rouen Cathedral. 50fr, Roman Ruins, Saint-Remy. 65fr, Evian-les-Bains.

1957, Oct. 19

850 A302 8fr green & lt brn .25 .25
851 A302 10fr dk ol bis & vio brn .25 .25
852 A303 18fr indigo & dk brn .25 .25
853 A302 25fr bl gray & vio brn .55 .25
854 A303 35fr car rose & lake .25 .25
855 A302 50fr ol grn & ol bister .45 .25
856 A302 65fr dk blue & indigo .60 .30
Nos. 850-856 (7) 2.60 1.80

See Nos. 907-909. See footnote after No. 4642. For overprint and surcharges see No. 1O1, Reunion Nos. 325, 328-329, 332-334.

1957, Nov. 9 **Engr.** ***Perf. 13***

Portraits: 10fr, Michelangelo. 12fr, Miguel de Cervantes. 15fr, Rembrandt. 18fr, Isaac Newton. 25fr, Mozart. 35fr, Johann Wolfgang von Goethe.

857 A304 8fr dark brown .80 .60
858 A304 10fr dark green .80 .60
859 A304 12fr dark purple .80 .70
860 A304 15fr brown & org brn 1.00 .80
861 A304 18fr deep blue 1.40 .90
862 A304 25fr lilac & claret 1.40 .90
863 A304 35fr blue 1.75 1.00
Nos. 857-863 (7) 7.95 5.50

Louis Jacques Thénard A305

1957, Nov. 30 **Unwmk.**

864 A305 15fr ol bis & grnsh blk .40 .30

Centenary of the death of L. J. Thenard, chemist, and the founding of the Charitable Society of the Friends of Science.

Dr. Philippe Pinel A306

Joseph Louis Lagrange A307

French Physicians: 12fr, Fernand Widal. 15fr, Charles Nicolle. 35fr, René Leriche.

1958, Jan. 25

865 A306 8fr brown olive .90 .60
866 A306 12fr brt vio blue .90 .60
867 A306 15fr deep blue 1.40 .80
868 A306 35fr black 1.75 1.10
Nos. 865-868 (4) 4.95 3.10

1958, Feb. 15 ***Perf. 13***

French Scientists: 12fr, Urbain Jean Joseph Leverrier. 15fr, Jean Bernard Leon Foucault. 35fr, Claude Louis Berthollet.

869 A307 8fr blue grn & vio bl .90 .55
870 A307 12fr sepia & gray 1.00 .70
871 A307 15fr slate grn & grn 1.90 .95
872 A307 35fr maroon & cop red 2.40 1.25
Nos. 869-872 (4) 6.20 3.45

Lourdes Type of 1954

1958

873 A241 20fr grnsh bl & ol .30 .25

Le Havre A308

Maubeuge — A309

Designs: 18fr, Saint-Die. 25fr, Sete.

1958, Mar. 29 **Engr.** ***Perf. 13***

874 A308 12fr ol grn & car rose .65 .35
875 A309 15fr brt purple & brn .65 .35
876 A309 18fr ultra & indigo 1.00 .75
877 A308 25fr dk bl, bl grn & brn 1.25 .75
Nos. 874-877 (4) 3.55 2.20

Reconstruction of war-damaged cities.

French Pavilion, Brussels A310

1958, Apr. 12

878 A310 35fr brn, dk grn & bl .30 .25

Issued for the Universal and International Exposition at Brussels.

Heroes Type of 1957

8fr, Jean Cavaillès. 12fr, Fred Scamaroni. 15fr, Simone Michel-Levy. 20fr, Jacques Bingen.

1958, Apr. 19

879 A293 8fr violet & black .60 .60
880 A293 12fr ultra & green .60 .60
881 A293 15fr brown & gray 1.50 .85
882 A293 20fr olive & ultra 1.25 .95
Nos. 879-882 (4) 3.95 3.00

Issued in honor of the heroes of the French Underground in World War II.

Bowling A311

Sports: 15fr, Naval joust. 18fr, Archery, vert. 25fr, Breton wrestling, vert.

1958, Apr. 26

883 A311 12fr rose & brown .85 .75
884 A311 15fr bl, ol gray & grn 1.10 .85
885 A311 18fr green & brown 2.00 1.10
886 A311 25fr brown & indigo 2.90 1.75
Nos. 883-886 (4) 6.85 4.45

Senlis Cathedral — A312

1958, May 17

887 A312 15fr ultra & indigo .40 .25

Bayeux Tapestry Horsemen A313

1958, June 21

888 A313 15fr blue & carmine .35 .25

Common Design Types pictured following the introduction.

Europa Issue, 1958

Common Design Type

1958, Sept. 13 **Engr.** ***Perf. 13***

Size: 22x36mm

889 CD1 20fr rose red *.40 .25*
890 CD1 35fr ultra *1.25 .30*

Foix Chateau A314

1958, Oct. 11

891 A314 15fr ultra, grn & ol brn .40 .25

City Halls, Paris and Rome A315

1958, Oct. 11

892 A315 35fr gray, grnsh bl & rose red .40 .25

Issued to publicize the cultural ties between Rome and Paris and the need for European unity.

UNESCO Building, Paris A316

Design: 35fr, Different view of building.

1958, Nov. 1 ***Perf. 13***

893 A316 20fr grnsh blue & ol bis .25 .25
894 A316 35fr dk sl grn & red org .25 .25

UNESCO Headquarters in Paris opening, Nov. 3.

Soldier's Grave in Wheat Field — A317

1958, Nov. 11

895 A317 15fr dk green & ultra .30 .25

40th anniv. of the World War I armistice.

Arms of Marseille — A318

1958-59 **Typo.** ***Perf. 14x13½***

Cities: 70c, Lyon. 80c, Toulouse. 1fr, Bordeaux. 2fr, Nice. 3fr, Nantes. 5fr, Lille. 15fr, Algiers.

896 A318 50c dk blue & ultra .25 .25
897 A318 70c multicolored .25 .25
898 A318 80c red, blue & yel .25 .25
899 A318 1fr dk bl, yel & red .25 .25
900 A318 2fr dk bl, red & grn .25 .25
901 A318 3fr multicolored .25 .25
902 A318 5fr dk brown & red .25 .25
903 A318 15fr multi ('59) .25 .25
Nos. 896-903 (8) 2.00 2.00

See Nos. 938, 940, 973, 1040-1042, 1091-1095, 1142-1144. For surcharges see Reunion Nos. 336, 345-346, 350-351, 353.

Arc de Triomphe and Flowers — A319

1959, Jan. 17 Engr. *Perf. 13*

904	A319	15fr brn, bl, grn, cl & red	.45	.30

Paris Flower Festival.

Symbols of Learning and Medal A320

1959, Jan. 24 *Perf. 13*

905	A320	20fr lake, blk & vio	.25	.25

Sesquicentennial of the Palm Leaf Medal of the French Academy.

Charles de Foucauld A321

1959, Jan. 31

906	A321	50fr dp brn, bl & mar	.50	.35

Issued to honor Father Charles de Foucauld, explorer and missionary of the Sahara.

Type of 1957

Designs: 30fr, Elysee Palace. 85fr, Evian-les Bains. 100fr, Sens River, Guadeloupe.

1959, Feb. 10

907	A302	30fr dk slate green	2.25	.25
908	A302	85fr deep claret	3.25	.30
909	A302	100fr deep violet	27.50	.45
		Nos. 907-909 (3)	33.00	1.00

Gallic Cock Type of 1954

1959 Typo. *Perf. 14x13½*

910	A237	8fr violet	.55	.25
911	A237	20fr yellow grn	1.75	.65
912	A237	40fr henna brn	4.00	2.25
913	A237	55fr emerald	17.00	10.00
		Nos. 910-913 (4)	23.30	13.15

Nos. 910-913 were issued with precancellation. See second note after No. 132. See Nos. 952-955.

Miners' Tools and School A322

1959, Apr. 11 Engr. *Perf. 13*

914	A322	20fr red, blk & blue	.25	.25

175th anniv. of the National Mining School.

Heroes Type of 1957

Portraits: No. 915, The five martyrs of the Buffon school. No. 916, Yvonne Le Roux. No. 917, Médéric-Védy. No. 918, Louis Martin-Bret. 30fr, Gaston Moutardier.

1959, Apr. 25 Engr. *Perf. 13*

915	A293	15fr black & vio	.40	.25
916	A293	15fr mag & rose vio	.40	.30
917	A293	20fr green & grnsh bl	.40	.30
918	A293	20fr org brn & brn	.50	.40
919	A293	30fr magenta & vio	.65	.40
		Nos. 915-919 (5)	2.35	1.65

Dam at Foum el Gherza A323

Marcoule Atomic Center — A324

Designs: 30fr, Oil field at Hassi Messaoud, Sahara. 50fr, C. N. I. T. Building (Centre National des Industries et des Techniques).

1959, May 23

920	A323	15fr olive & grnsh bl	.35	.25
921	A324	20fr brt car & red brn	.50	.40
922	A324	30fr dk blue, brn & grn	.50	.40
923	A323	50fr ol grn & sl blue	.75	.45
		Nos. 920-923 (4)	2.10	1.50

French technical achievements.

Marceline Desbordes-Valmore — A325

1959, June 20

924	A325	30fr blue, brn & grn	.25	.25

Centenary of the death of Marceline Desbordes-Valmore, poet.

Pilots Goujon and Rozanoff A326

1959, June 13

925	A326	20fr lt blue & org brn	.50	.40

Issued in honor of Charles Goujon and Col. Constantin Rozanoff, test pilots.

Tancarville Bridge A327

1959, Aug. 1 Engr. *Perf. 13*

926	A327	30fr dk blue, brn & ol	.50	.25

Marianne and Ship of State — A328

1959, July Typo. *Perf. 14x13½*

927	A328	25fr black & red	.30	.25

See Nos. 942, 3521, 4410a, 4513. For surcharge see No. B336.

Jean Jaures — A329

1959, Sept. 12 Engr. *Perf. 13*

928	A329	50fr chocolate	.40	.25

Jean Jaures, socialist leader, birth cent.

Europa Issue, 1959

Common Design Type

1959, Sept. 19

Size: 22x36mm

929	CD2	25fr bright green	*.75*	*.35*
930	CD2	50fr bright violet	*1.10*	*.55*

Blood Donors A330

1959, Oct. 17 Engr.

931	A330	20fr magenta & gray	.25	.25

French-Spanish Handshake — A331

1959, Oct. 24 *Perf. 13*

932	A331	50fr blue, rose car & org	.65	.35

300th anniv. of the signing of the Treaty of the Pyrenees.

Polio Victim Holding Crutches A332

Henri Bergson A333

1959, Oct. 31

933	A332	20fr dark blue	.25	.25

Vaccination against poliomyelitis.

1959, Nov. 7

934	A333	50fr lt red brown	.35	.25

Henri Bergson, philosopher, birth cent.

Avesnes-sur-Helpe — A334

Design: 30fr, Perpignan.

1959, Nov. 14

935	A334	20fr sepia & blue	.40	.25
936	A334	30fr brn, dp claret & bl	.40	.25

New NATO Headquarters, Paris — A335

1959, Dec. 12

937	A335	50fr green, brn & ultra	.60	.40

10th anniv. of the NATO.

Types of 1958-59 and

Farm Woman A336

Sower A337

Designs: 5c, Arms of Lille. 15c, Arms of Algiers. 25c, Marianne and Ship of State.

Perf. 14x13½

1960-61 Unwmk. Typo.

938	A318	5c dk brown & red	7.25	.25
939	A336	10c brt green	.25	.25
940	A318	15c red, ultra, yel & grn	.60	.25
941	A337	20c grnsh bl & car rose	.25	.25
942	A328	25c ver & ultra	2.25	.25
b.		Booklet pane of 8	27.50	
c.		Booklet pane of 10	32.50	
942A	A337	30c gray & ultra ('61)	2.00	.30
		Nos. 938-942A (6)	12.60	1.55

See Nos. 707-708, 833-834 for the Farm Woman type (A336), but with no decimals in denominations.

For surcharges see Reunion Nos. 337-338, 341. For overprint see Algeria No. 286.

Laon Cathedral A338

Kerrata Gorge — A339

Designs: 30c, Fougères Chateau. 50c, Mosque, Tlemcen. 65c, Sioule Valley. 85c, Chaumont Viaduct. 1fr, Cilaos Church, Reunion.

1960, Jan. 16 Engr. *Perf. 13*

943	A338	15c blue & indigo	.40	.25
944	A338	30c blue, sepia & grn	3.75	.25
945	A339	45c brt vio & ol gray	.85	.25
946	A339	50c sl grn & lt cl	2.50	.25
947	A338	65c sl grn, bl & blk brn	1.25	.25
948	A338	85c blue, sep & grn	3.00	.25
949	A339	1fr vio bl, bl & grn	3.00	.25
		Nos. 943-949 (7)	14.75	1.75

For surcharges see Reunion Nos. 335, 340, 342. For overprint see Algeria Nos. 288-289.

Pierre de Nolhac A340

1960, Feb. 13

950	A340	20c black & gray	.50	.35

Centenary of the birth of Pierre de Nolhac, curator of Versailles and historian.

Museum of Art and Industry, Saint-Etienne — A341

1960, Feb. 20

951 A341 30c brn, car & slate .60 .30

Gallic Cock Type of 1954

1960 Typo. *Perf. 14x13½*

952	A237	8c violet	.95	.25
953	A237	20c yellow grn	3.25	.30
954	A237	40c henna brn	9.00	2.00
955	A237	55c emerald	29.00	16.00
		Nos. 952-955 (4)	42.20	18.55

Nos. 952-955 were issued only precanceled. See second note after No. 132. See Nos. 910-913.

View of Cannes A342

1960, Mar. 5 Engr. *Perf. 13*

956 A342 50c red brn & lt grn .70 .45

Meeting of European municipal administrators, Cannes, Mar., 1960.

Woman of Savoy and Alps A343

Woman of Nice and Shore A344

1960 Unwmk. *Perf. 13*

957	A343	30c slate green	.65	.40
958	A344	50c brn, yel & rose	.65	.30

Cent. of the annexation of Nice and Savoy.

Heroes Type of 1957

Portraits: No. 959, Edmund Debeaumarché. No. 960, Pierre Massé. No. 961, Maurice Ripoche. No. 962, Leonce Vieljeux. 50c, Abbé René Bonpain.

1960, Mar. 26

959	A293	20c bister & blk	2.40	1.40
960	A293	20c pink & rose cl	1.75	1.40
961	A293	30c vio & brt vio	1.75	1.40
962	A293	30c sl bl & brt bl	3.25	2.40
963	A293	50c sl grn & red brn	3.25	3.00
		Nos. 959-963 (5)	12.40	9.60

Issued in honor of the heroes of the French Underground of World War II.

"Education" and Children A345

1960, May 21 Engr. *Perf. 13*

964 A345 20c rose lilac, pur & blk .25 .25

1st secondary school in Strasbourg, 150th anniv.

Blois Chateau A346

View of La Bourboule A347

1960, May

965	A346	30c dk bl, sep & grn	.85	.65
966	A347	50c ol brown, car & grn	.65	.50

Lorraine Cross A348

Marianne A349

1960, June 18

967 A348 20c red brn, dk brn & yel grn .65 .25

20th anniv. of the French Resistance Movement in World War II.

1960, June 18 Typo. *Perf. 14x13½*

968	A349	25c lake & gray	.25	.25
a.		Booklet pane of 8	4.50	
b.		Booklet pane of 10	3.50	

See Nos. 3522, 4410b, 4514. For surcharge see Reunion No. 339. For overprint see Algeria No. 287.

Jean Bouin and Stadium A350

1960, July 9 Engr. *Perf. 13*

969 A350 20c blue, mag & ol gray .35 .25

17th Olympic Games, Rome, 8/25-9/11.

Europa Issue, 1960

Common Design Type

1960, Sept. 17 *Perf. 13*

Size: 36x22mm

970	CD3	25c green & bluish grn	.25	.25
971	CD3	50c maroon & red lilac	*.30*	.25

Lisieux Basilica A351

1960, Sept. 24 *Perf. 13*

972 A351 15c blue, gray & blk .25 .25

Arms Type of 1958-59

Design: Arms of Oran.

1960, Oct. 15 Typo. *Perf. 14x13½*

973 A318 5c red, bl, yel & emer .25 .25

Madame de Stael by François Gerard — A352

1960, Oct. 22 Engr. *Perf. 13*

974 A352 30c dull claret & brn .35 .25

Madame de Stael (1766-1817), writer.

Gen. J. B. E. Estienne A353

1960, Nov. 5

975 A353 15c lt lilac & black .35 .25

Centenary of the birth of Gen. Jean Baptiste Eugene Estienne.

Marc Sangnier and Youth Hostel at Bierville A354

1960, Nov. 5

976 A354 20c blue, blk & lilac .25 .25

Issued to honor Marc Sangnier, founder of the French League for Youth Hostels.

Badge of Order of Liberation — A355

1960, Nov. 14 Engr. *Perf. 13*

977 A355 20c black & brt green .40 .25

Order of Liberation, 20th anniversary.

Lapwings A356

Birds: 30c, Puffin. 45c, European teal. 50c, European bee-eaters.

1960, Nov. 12

978	A356	20c multicolored	.30	.25
979	A356	30c multicolored	.30	.25
980	A356	45c multicolored	.95	.50
981	A356	50c multicolored	.85	.25
		Nos. 978-981 (4)	2.40	1.25

Issued to publicize wildlife protection.

André Honnorat A357

1960, Nov. 19

982 A357 30c blue, blk & green .30 .25

Honnorat, statesman, fighter against tuberculosis and founder of the University City of Paris, an intl. students' community.

St. Barbara and Medieval View of School A358

1960, Dec. 3 Engr.

983 A358 30c red, bl & ol brn .35 .30

St. Barbara School, Paris, 500th anniv.

"Mediterranean" by Aristide Maillol — A359

1961, Feb. 18 Unwmk. *Perf. 13*

984 A359 20c carmine & indigo .25 .25

Aristide Maillol, sculptor, birth cent.

Marianne by Cocteau — A360

1961, Feb. 23

985 A360 20c blue & carmine .25 .25

A second type has an extra inverted V-shaped mark (a blue flag top) at right of hair tip. Value unused $3.25, used 60 cents.

See Nos. 3523, 4410c, 4515.

For surcharge see Reunion No. 357.

Paris Airport, Orly A361

1961, Feb. 25

986 A361 50c blk, dk bl, & bluish grn .45 .35

Inauguration of new facilities at Orly airport.

George Méliès and Motion Picture Screen A362

1961, Mar. 11

987 A362 50c pur, indigo & ol bis .50 .35

Cent. of the birth of George Méliès, motion picture pioneer.

Jean Baptiste Henri Lacordaire — A363

1961, Mar. 25 *Perf. 13*

988 A363 30c lt brown & black .30 .30

Cent. of the death of the Dominican monk Lacordaire, orator and liberal Catholic leader.

A364

1961, Mar. 25

989 A364 30c grn, red brn & red .30 .25

Introduction of tobacco use into France, fourth centenary. By error stamp portrays Jan Nicquet instead of Jean Nicot.

Heroes Type of 1957

Portraits: No. 990, Jacques Renouvin. No. 991, Lionel Dubray. No. 992, Paul Gateaud. No. 993, Mère Elisabeth.

1961, Apr. 22

990 A293 20c blue & lilac 1.00 .50
991 A293 20c gray grn & blue 1.00 .50
992 A293 30c brown org & blk 1.60 .90
993 A293 30c violet & blk 1.25 1.00
Nos. 990-993 (4) 4.85 2.90

Bagnoles-de-l'Orne — A365

1961, May 6

994 A365 20c olive, ocher, bl & grn .25 .25

Dove, Olive Branch and Federation Emblem — A366

1961, May 6

995 A366 50c brt bl, grn & mar .30 .25

World Federation of Ex-Service Men.

Deauville in 19th Century A367

1961, May 13 **Engr.**

996 A367 50c rose claret 1.90 1.20

Centenary of Deauville.

La Champmeslé A368

Mont-Dore, Snowflake and Cable Car A369

French actors: No. 998, Talma. No. 999, Rachel. No. 1000, Gérard Philipe. No. 1001, Raimu.

1961, June 10 **Unwmk.** ***Perf. 13***

Dark Carmine Frame

997 A368 20c choc & yel grn .90 .35
998 A368 30c brown & crimson .90 .35
999 A368 30c yel grn & sl grn .90 .35
1000 A368 50c olive & choc 1.25 .55
1001 A368 50c bl grn & red brn 1.25 .55
Nos. 997-1001 (5) 5.20 2.15

Issued to honor great French actors and in connection with the Fifth World Congress of the International Federation of Actors.

1961, July 1

1002 A369 20c orange & rose lilac .25 .25

Pierre Fauchard A370

St. Theobald's Church, Thann A371

1961, July 1

1003 A370 50c dk green & blk .55 .30

Bicentenary of the death of Pierre Fauchard, 1st surgeon dentist.

1961, July 1

1004 A371 20c sl grn, vio & brn .55 .30

800th anniversary of Thann.

Europa Issue, 1961

Common Design Type

1961, Sept. 16 ***Perf. 13***

Size: 35x22mm

1005 CD4 25c vermilion .25 .25
1006 CD4 50c ultramarine *.25 .25*

Beach and Sailboats, Arcachon A372

Designs: 15c, Saint-Paul, Maritime Alps. 45c, Sully-sur-Loire Chateau. 50c, View of Cognac. 65c, Rance Valley and Dinan. 85c, City hall and Rodin's Burghers, Calais. 1fr, Roman gates of Lodi, Medea, Algeria.

1961, Oct. 9 **Engr.** ***Perf. 13***

1007 A372 15c blue & purple .25 .25
1008 A372 30c ultra, sl grn & lt brn .25 .25
1009 A372 45c vio bl, red brn & grn .25 .25
1010 A372 50c grn, Prus bl & sl 1.25 .25
1011 A372 65c red brn, sl grn & bl .50 .25
1012 A372 85c sl grn, sl & red brn .60 .25
1013 A372 1fr dk bl, sl & bis 5.00 .25
Nos. 1007-1013 (7) 8.10 1.75

For surcharges see Reunion Nos. 347-348. For overprint see Algeria No. 290.

Blue Nudes, by Matisse — A373

Paintings: 50c, "The Messenger," by Braque. 85c, "The Cardplayers," by Cézanne. 1fr, "The 14th July," by Roger de La Fresnaye.

1961, Nov. 10 ***Perf. 13x12***

1014 A373 50c dk brn, bl, blk & gray 2.90 1.60
1015 A373 65c grn, vio, & ultra 5.00 2.50
1016 A373 85c blk, brn, red & ol 2.50 1.25
1017 A373 1fr multicolored 4.00 2.50
Nos. 1014-1017 (4) 14.40 7.85

Liner France A374

1962, Jan. 11 **Engr.** ***Perf. 13***

1018 A374 30c dk blue, blk & car .60 .45

New French liner France.

Skier Going Downhill — A375

Maurice Bourdet — A376

1962, Jan. 27 ***Perf. 13***

1019 A375 30c shown .25 .25
1020 A375 50c Slalom .40 .30

Issued to publicize the World Ski Championships, Chamonix, Feb. 1962.

1962, Feb. 17

1021 A376 30c slate .30 .25

60th anniv. of the birth of Maurice Bourdet, radio commentator and resistance hero.

Pierre-Fidele Bretonneau — A377

1962, Feb. 17

1022 A377 50c brt lilac & blue .35 .25

Centenary of the death of Pierre-Fidele Bretonneau, physician.

Chateau and Bridge, Laval, Mayenne A378

Gallic Cock A379

1962, Feb. 24

1023 A378 20c bis brn & slate grn .25 .25

1962-65 ***Perf. 13***

1024 A379 25c ultra, car & brn .25 .25
a. Bklt. pane of 4 (horiz. strip) 2.50
1024B A379 30c gray grn, red & brn ('65) .85 .25
c. Booklet pane of 5 5.00
d. Booklet pane of 10 10.00

No. 1024 was also issued on experimental luminescent paper in 1963. Value $750.
See Nos. 3524, 4410d, 4516.

Ramparts of Vannes A380

Dunkirk — A381

Paris Beach, Le Touquet A381a

1962 **Engr.** ***Perf. 13***

1025 A380 30c dark blue .80 .50
1026 A381 95c grn, bis & red lil 1.25 .75
1027 A381a 1fr grn, red brn & bl .45 .25
Nos. 1025-1027 (3) 2.50 1.50

No. 1026 for the 300th anniv. of Dunkirk.

Stage Setting and Globe A382

1962, Mar. 24 **Unwmk.**

1028 A382 50c sl grn, ocher & mag .40 .25

International Day of the Theater, Mar. 27.

Memorial to Fighting France, Mont Valerien A383

Resistance Heroes' Monument, Vercors — A384

Design: 50c, Ile de Sein monument.

1962, Apr. 7

1029 A383 20c olive & slate grn .70 .50
1030 A384 30c bluish black .70 .50
1031 A384 50c blue & indigo .90 .80
Nos. 1029-1031 (3) 2.30 1.80

Issued to publicize memorials for the French Underground in World War II.

Malaria Eradication Emblem and Swamp — A385

Nurses with Child and Hospital — A386

1962, Apr. 14 **Engr.**

1032 A385 50c dk blue & dk red .35 .30

WHO drive to eradicate malaria.

1962, May 5 **Unwmk.** ***Perf. 13***

1033 A386 30c bl grn, gray & red brn .35 .30

National Hospital Week, May 5-12.

Glider A387

20c, Planes showing development of aviation.

1962, May 12
1034 A387 15c orange red & brn .30 .25
1035 A387 20c lil rose & rose cl .35 .25

Issued to publicize sports aviation.

School Emblem — A388

1962, May 19 **Engr.**
1036 A388 50c mar, ocher & dk vio .40 .30

Watchmaker's School at Besançon, cent.

Louis XIV and Workers Showing Modern Gobelin A389

1962, May 26 **Unwmk.** ***Perf. 13***
1037 A389 50c ol, sl grn & car .40 .30

Gobelin tapestry works, Paris, 300th anniv.

Blaise Pascal A390

1962, May 26
1038 A390 50c slate grn & dp org .40 .30

Blaise Pascal (1623-1662), mathematician, scientist and philosopher.

Palace of Justice, Rennes A391

1962, June 12
1039 A391 30c blk, grysh bl & grn 1.40 .60

Arms Type of 1958-59

5c, Amiens. 10c, Troyes. 15c, Nevers.

1962-63 **Typo.** ***Perf. 14x13½***
1040 A318 5c ver, ultra & yel .25 .25
1041 A318 10c red, ultra & yel ('63) .25 .25
1042 A318 15c ver, ultra & yel .25 .25
Nos. 1040-1042 (3) .75 .75

Phosphor Tagging

In 1970 France began to experiment with luminescence. Phosphor bands have been added to Nos. 1041, 1143, 1231, 1231C, 1292A-1294B, 1494-1498, 1560-1579B, etc.

Rose — A392

Design: 30c, Old-fashioned rose.

1962, Sept. 8 **Engr.** ***Perf. 13***
1043 A392 20c ol, grn & brt car .65 .40
1044 A392 30c dk sl grn, ol & car .65 .40

Europa Issue, 1962
Common Design Type

1962, Sept. 15
Size: 36x22mm
1045 CD5 25c violet .25 .25
1046 CD5 50c henna brown .35 .25

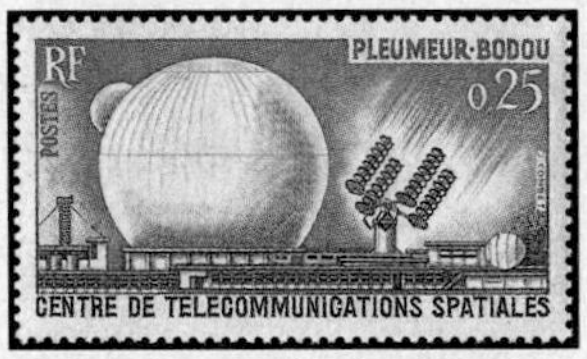

Space Communications Center, Pleumeur-Bodou, France — A394

Telstar, Earth and Television Set — A395

1962, Sept. 29 **Engr.** ***Perf. 13***
1047 A394 25c gray, yel & grn .25 .25
1048 A395 50c dk bl, grn & ultra .40 .30

1st television connection of the US and Europe through Telstar satellite, July 11-12.
For surcharges see Reunion Nos. 343-344.

"Bonjour Monsieur Courbet" by Gustave Courbet — A396

Paintings: 65c, "Madame Manet on Blue Sofa," by Edouard Manet. 1fr, "Guards officer on horseback," by Theodore Géricault, vert.

1962, Nov. 9 ***Perf. 13x12, 12x13***
1049 A396 50c multicolored 3.00 2.25
1050 A396 65c multicolored 2.25 1.40
1051 A396 1fr multicolored 5.00 3.00
Nos. 1049-1051 (3) 10.25 6.65

Bathyscaph "Archimede" — A397

1963, Jan. 26 **Unwmk.** ***Perf. 13***
1052 A397 30c dk blue & blk .25 .25

French deep-sea explorations.

Flowers and Nantes Chateau A398

1963, Feb. 11
1053 A398 30c vio bl, car & sl grn .25 .25

Nantes flower festival.

St. Peter, Window at St. Foy de Conches A399

50c, Jacob Wrestling with the Angel, by Delacroix.

1963, Mar. 2 ***Perf. 12x13***
1054 A399 50c multicolored 3.25 2.25
1055 A399 1fr multicolored 4.00 3.25

See Nos. 1076-1077.

Hungry Woman and Wheat Emblem A400

1963, Mar. 21 **Engr.** ***Perf. 13***
1056 A400 50c slate grn & brn .30 .25

FAO "Freedom from Hunger" campaign.

Cemetery and Memorial, Glières — A401

Design: 50c, Memorial, Ile de la Cité, Paris.

1963, Mar. 23 **Unwmk.** ***Perf. 13***
1057 A401 30c dk brown & olive .55 .55
1058 A401 50c indigo .55 .55

Heroes of the resistance against the Nazis.

Beethoven, Birthplace at Bonn and Rhine A402

No. 1060, Emile Verhaeren, memorial at Roisin & residence. No. 1061, Giuseppe Mazzini, Marcus Aurelius statue & Via Appia, Rome. No. 1062, Emile Mayrisch, Colpach Chateau & blast furnace, Esch. No. 1063, Hugo de Groot, Palace of Peace, The Hague & St. Agatha Church, Delft.

1963, Apr. 27 **Unwmk.** ***Perf. 13***
1059 A402 20c ocher, sl & brt grn .35 .25
1060 A402 20c purple, blk & mar .35 .25
1061 A402 20c maroon, sl & ol .35 .25
1062 A402 20c mar, dk brn & ocher .35 .25
1063 A402 30c dk brn, vio & ocher .35 .25
Nos. 1059-1063 (5) 1.75 1.25

Issued to honor famous men of the European Common Market countries.

Hotel des Postes and Stagecoach, 1863 — A403

1963, May 4
1064 A403 50c grayish black .35 .25

1st Intl. Postal Conference, Paris, 1863.

Lycée Louis-le-Grand, Belvédère, Panthéon and St. Etienne du Mont Church — A404

1963, May 18
1065 A404 30c slate green .30 .25

400th anniversary of the Jesuit Clermont secondary school, named after Louis XIV.

St. Peter's Church and Ramparts, Caen A405

1963, June 1 **Unwmk.** ***Perf. 13***
1066 A405 30c gray blue & brn .25 .25

Radio Telescope, Nançay — A406

1963, June 8 **Engr.**
1067 A406 50c dk bl & dk brn .45 .35

Amboise Chateau A407

Saint-Flour — A408

Designs: 50c, Côte d'Azur Varoise. 85c, Vittel. 95c, Moissac.

1963, June 15
1068 A407 30c slate, grn & bis .25 .25
1069 A407 50c dk grn, dk bl & hn brn .40 .25
1070 A408 60c ultra, dk grn & hn brn .45 .25
1071 A407 85c dk grn, yel grn & brn 1.50 .30
1072 A408 95c dk brown & black .90 .25
Nos. 1068-1072 (5) 3.50 1.30

For surcharge see Reunion No. 355.

Water Skiing Slalom
A409

1963, Aug. 31 Unwmk. *Perf. 13*

1073 A409 30c sl grn, blk & car .30 .25

World Water Skiing Championships, Vichy.

Europa Issue, 1963
Common Design Type

1963, Sept. 14

Size: 36x22mm

1074 CD6 25c red brown *.25 .25*
1075 CD6 50c green *.35 .25*

Art Type of 1963

Designs: 85c, "The Married Couple of the Eiffel Tower," by Marc Chagall. 95c, "The Fur Merchants," window, Chartres Cathedral.

1963, Nov. 9 Engr. *Perf. 12x13*

1076 A399 85c multicolored 1.75 1.25
1077 A399 95c multicolored .65 .65

Philatec Issue
Common Design Type

1963, Dec. 14 Unwmk. *Perf. 13*

1078 CD118 25c dk gray, sl grn & dk car .25 .25

For surcharge see Reunion No. 349.

Radio and Television Center, Paris
A411

1963, Dec. 15 Engr.

1079 A411 20c org brn, slate & ol .25 .25

Fire Brigade Insignia, Symbols of Fire, Water and Civilian Defense
A412

1964, Feb. 8 Engr. *Perf. 13*

1082 A412 30c blue, org & red .50 .25

Issued to honor the fire brigades and civilian defense corps.

Handicapped Laboratory Technician — A413

1964, Feb. 22 Unwmk. *Perf. 13*

1083 A413 30c grn, red brn & brn .25 .25

Rehabilitation of the handicapped.

John II the Good (1319-64) by Girard d'Orleans
A414

1964, Apr. 25 *Perf. 12x13*

1084 A414 1fr multicolored 1.60 1.10

Stamp of 1900
A415

Mechanized Mail Handling
A416

Designs: No. 1086, Stamp of 1900, Type A17. No. 1088, Telecommunications.

1964, May 9 *Perf. 13*

1085 A415 25c bister & dk car .30 .30
1086 A415 25c bister & blue .30 .30
1087 A416 30c blk, bl & org brn .30 .30
1088 A416 30c blk, car rose & bluish grn .30 .30
a. Strip of 4, #1085-1088 + label 1.25 1.25

Printed in sheets of 20 stamps, containing five No. 1088a. The label shows the Philatec emblem in green.

Type of Semi-Postal Issue
with "25e ANNIVERSAIRE" added

1964, May 9

1089 SP208 25c multicolored .25 .25

25th anniversary, night airmail service.

Madonna and Child from Rose Window of Notre Dame
A417

1964, May 23 *Perf. 12x13*

1090 A417 60c multicolored .55 .55

Notre Dame Cathedral, Paris, 800th anniv.

Arms Type of 1958-59

Arms: 1c, Niort. 2c, Guéret. 12c, Agen. 18c, Saint-Denis, Réunion. 30c, Paris.

1964-65 Typo. *Perf. 14x13½*

1091 A318 1c vio blue & yel .25 .25
1092 A318 2c emer, vio bl & yel .25 .25
1093 A318 12c black, red & yel .25 .25
1094 A318 18c multicolored .40 .25
1095 A318 30c vio bl & red ('65) .50 .25
a. Booklet pane of 10 15.00
Nos. 1091-1095 (5) 1.65 1.25

Gallic Coin — A418

Perf. 13½x14

1964-66 Typo. Unwmk.

1096 A418 10c emer & bister .75 .25
1097 A418 15c org & bister ('66) .30 .25
1098 A418 25c lilac & brn .45 .25
1099 A418 50c brt blue & brn .85 .75
Nos. 1096-1099 (4) 2.35 1.50

Nos. 1096-1099 are known only precanceled. See second note after No. 132. See Nos. 1240-1242, 1315-1318, 1421-1424.

Postrider, Rocket and Radar Equipment — A419

1964, June 5 Engr. *Perf. 13*

1100 A419 1fr brn, dk red & dk bl 25.00 20.00

Sold for 4fr, including 3fr admission to PHILATEC. Issued in sheets of 8 stamps and 8 labels (2x8 subjects with labels in horizontal rows 1, 4, 5, 8; stamps in rows 2, 3, 6, 7). Commemorative inscriptions on side margins. Value $200.

Caesar's Tower, Provins — A420

Chapel of Notre Dame du Haut, Ronchamp
A421

1964-65

1101 A421 40c sl grn, dk brn & brn ('65) .25 .25
1102 A420 70c slate, grn & car .35 .25
1103 A421 1.25fr brt bl, sl grn & ol .75 .30
Nos. 1101-1103 (3) 1.35 .80

The 40c was issued in vertical coils in 1971. Every 10th coil stamp has a red control number printed twice on the back.

For surcharges see Reunion Nos. 352, 361.

Mandel — A422

Judo — A423

1964, July 4 Unwmk. *Perf. 13*

1104 A422 30c violet brown .25 .25

Georges Mandel (1885-1944), Cabinet minister, executed by the Nazis.

1964, July 4

1105 A423 50c dk blue & vio brn .25 .25

18th Olympic Games, Tokyo, 10/10-25/64.

Champlevé Enamel from Limoges, 12th Century
A424

Design: No. 1107, The Lady (Claude Le Viste?) with the Unicorn, 15th cent. tapestry.

1964 *Perf. 12x13*

1106 A424 1fr multicolored 1.25 .80
1107 A424 1fr multicolored .65 .45

No. 1106 shows part of an enamel sepulchral plate portraying Geoffrey IV, Count of Anjou and Le Maine (1113-1151), who was called Geoffrey Plantagenet.

Issue dates: No. 1106, July 4. No. 1107, Oct. 31.

Paris Taxis Carrying Soldiers to Front, 1914
A425

1964, Sept. 5 Unwmk. *Perf. 13*

1108 A425 30c black, blue & red .25 .25

50th anniversary of Battle of the Marne.

Europa Issue, 1964
Common Design Type

1964, Sept. 12 Engr.

Size: 22x36mm

1109 CD7 25c dk car, dp ocher & grn .25 .25
1110 CD7 50c vio, yel grn & dk car .25 .25

Cooperation Issue
Common Design Type

1964, Nov. 6 Unwmk. *Perf. 13*

1111 CD119 25c red brn, dk brn & dk bl .25 .25

Joux Chateau — A427

1965, Feb. 6 Engr.

1112 A427 1.30fr redsh brn, brn red & dk brn 1.50 .35

"The English Girl from the Star" by Toulouse-Lautrec — A428

St. Paul on the Damascus Road, Window, Cathedral of Sens — A429

Leaving for the Hunt — A430

Apocalypse Tapestry, 14th Century A431

"The Red Violin" by Raoul Dufy — A432

Designs: No. 1115, "August" miniature of Book of Hours of Jean de France, Duc de Berry ("Les Très Riches Heures du Duc de Berry"), painted by Flemish brothers, Pol, Hermant and Jannequin Limbourg, 1411-16. No. 1116, Scene from oldest existing set of French tapestries, showing the Winepress of the Wrath of God (Revelations 14: 19-20).

1965 ***Perf. 12x13, 13x12***

1113 A428 1fr multicolored .50 .40
1114 A429 1fr multicolored .50 .40
1115 A430 1fr multicolored .30 .30
1116 A431 1fr multicolored .30 .30
1117 A432 1fr blk, pink & car .30 .30
Nos. 1113-1117 (5) 1.90 1.70

No. 1114 issued to commemorate the 800th anniversary of the Cathedral of Sens.
Issued: No. 1113, 3/12; No. 1114, 6/5; No. 1115, 9/25; No. 1116, 10/30; No. 1117, 11/6.

Returning Deportees, 1945 — A433

1965, Apr. 1 Unwmk. ***Perf. 13***

1118 A433 40c Prussian green .50 .30

20th anniv. of the return of people deported during World War II.

House of Youth and Culture, Troyes A434

1965, Apr. 10 **Engr.**

1119 A434 25c ind, brn & dk grn .25 .25

20th anniv. of the establishment of recreational cultural centers for young people.

Woman Carrying Flowers — A435

1965, Apr. 24 Unwmk. ***Perf. 13***

1120 A435 60c dk grn, dp org & ver .35 .25

Tourist Campaign of Welcome & Amiability.

Flags of France, US, USSR and Great Britain Crushing Swastika — A436

1965, May 8

1121 A436 40c black, car & ultra .40 .25

20th anniv. of victory in World War II.

Telegraph Key, Syncom Satellite and Pleumeur-Bodou Station — A437

1965, May 17

1122 A437 60c dk blue, brn & blk .50 .30

Centenary of the ITU.

Croix de Guerre — A438

1965, May 22 **Engr.**

1123 A438 40c red, brn & brt grn .55 .35

50th anniv. of the Croix de Guerre medal.

Cathedral of Bourges — A439

Moustiers-Sainte-Marie — A440

Views: 30c, Road and tunnel, Mont Blanc. 60c, Aix-les-Bains, sailboat. 75c, Tarn Gorge, Lozère mountains. 95c, Vendée River, man poling boat, and windmill. 1fr, Prehistoric stone monuments, Carnac.

1965

1124 A439 30c bl, vio bl & brn vio .25 .25
1125 A439 40c gray bl & redsh brn .40 .25
1126 A440 50c grn, bl gray & bis .40 .25
1127 A439 60c blue & red brn .85 .25
1128 A439 75c brown, bl & grn 1.25 .90
1129 A440 95c brown, grn & bl 5.75 .90
1130 A440 1fr gray, grn & brn 1.40 .25
Nos. 1124-1130 (7) 10.30 3.05

No. 1124 for the opening of the Mont Blanc Tunnel. No. 1125 (Bourges Cathedral) was issued in connection with the French Philatelic Societies Federation Congress, held at Bourges.
Issued: 40c, June 5; 50c, June 19; 30c, 60c, July 17; others, July 10.
For surcharges see Reunion Nos. 354, 362, 365.

Europa Issue, 1965
Common Design Type

1965, Sept. 25 ***Perf. 13***
Size: 36x22mm

1131 CD8 30c red *.25 .30*
1132 CD8 60c gray *.50 .50*

Planting Seedling — A441

1965, Oct. 2

1133 A441 25c slate grn, yel grn & red brn .25 .25

National reforestation campaign.

Etienne Régnault, "Le Taureau" and Coast of Reunion — A442

1965, Oct. 2

1134 A442 30c indigo & dk car .25 .25

Tercentenary of settlement of Reunion.

Atomic Reactor and Diagram, Symbols of Industry, Agriculture and Medicine — A443

1965, Oct. 9

1135 A443 60c brt blue & blk .50 .30

Atomic Energy Commission, 20th anniv.

Air Academy and Emblem A444

1965, Nov. 6 ***Perf. 13***

1136 A444 25c dk blue & green .35 .30

Air Academy, Salon-de-Provence, 50th anniv.

French Satellite A-1 Issue
Common Design Type

Design: 60c, A-1 satellite.

1965, Nov. 30 Engr. ***Perf. 13***

1137 CD121 30c Prus bl, brt bl & blk .25 .25
1138 CD121 60c blk, Prus bl & brt bl .40 .25
a. Strip of 2, #1137-1138 + label .65 .65

Launching of France's 1st satellite, 11/26/65.
For surcharges see Reunion Nos. 358-359.

Arms of Auch — A446

Cities: 20c, Saint-Lô. 25c, Mont-de-Marsan.

Typographed, Photogravure (20c)

1966 ***Perf. 14x13; 14 (20c)***

1142 A446 5c blue & red .25 .25
1143 A446 20c vio bl, sil, gold & red .25 .25
1144 A446 25c red brown & ultra .60 .25
Nos. 1142-1144 (3) 1.10 .75

The 5c and 20c were issued in sheets and in vertical coils. In the coils, every 10th stamp has a red control number on the back.
For surcharges see Reunion Nos. 360-360A.

French Satellite D-1 Issue
Common Design Type

1966, Feb. 18 Engr. ***Perf. 13***

1148 CD122 60c blue blk, grn & cl .25 .25

Horses from Bronze Vessel of Vix — A448

"The Newborn" by Georges de La Tour — A449

The Baptism of Judas (4th Century Bishop of Jerusalem) — A450

"The Moon and the Bull" Tapestry by Jean Lurçat A451

"Crispin and Scapin" by Honoré Daumier — A452

1966 ***Perf. 13x12, 12x13***

1149 A448 1fr multicolored .40 .35
1150 A449 1fr multicolored .40 .35
1151 A450 1fr multicolored .40 .35
1152 A451 1fr multicolored .40 .30
1153 A452 1fr multicolored .40 .30
Nos. 1149-1153 (5) 2.00 1.65

The design of No. 1149 is a detail from a 6th century B.C. vessel, found in 1953 in a grave near Vix, Cote d'Or.

The design of No. 1151 is from a stained glass window in the 13th century Sainte-Chapelle, Paris.

No. 1150 exists in an Imperf, ungummed souv. sheet with 2 progressive die proofs, issued for benefit of the Postal Museum, and not postally valid. Value $2.

Issued: No. 1149, 3/26; No. 1150, 6/25; No. 1151, 10/22; No. 1152, 11/19; No. 1153, 12/10.

Chessboard, Knight, Emblems for King and Queen — A453

1966, Apr. 2 **Engr.** ***Perf. 13***

1154 A453 60c sepia, gray & dk vio bl .60 .45

Issued to publicize the Chess Festival.

Rhone Bridge, Pont-Saint-Esprit — A454

1966, Apr. 23 **Unwmk.** ***Perf. 13***

1155 A454 25c black & dull blue .25 .25

St. Michael Slaying the Dragon — A455

1966, Apr. 30 **Litho. & Engr.**

1156 A455 25c multicolored .25 .25

Millenium of Mont-Saint-Michel.

Stanislas Leszczynski, Lunéville Chateau — A456

1966, May 6 **Engr.**

1157 A456 25c slate, grn & brn .25 .25

200th anniv. of the reunion of Lorraine and Bar (Barrois) with France.

St. Andrew's and Sèvre River, Niort — A457

1966, May 28 **Engr.** ***Perf. 13***

1158 A457 40c brt bl, indigo & grn .30 .25

Bernard Le Bovier de Fontenelle and 1666 Meeting Room A458

1966, June 4

1159 A458 60c dk car rose & brn .30 .25

300th anniversary, Académie des Sciences.

William the Conqueror, Castle and Norman Ships — A459

1966, June 4

1160 A459 60c brown red & dp bl .40 .30

900th anniversary of Battle of Hastings.

Tracks, Globe and Eiffel Tower A460

1966, June 11

1161 A460 60c dk brn, car & dull bl .85 .45

19th International Railroad Congress.

Oléron Bridge A461

1966, June 20

1162 A461 25c Prus bl, brn & bl .25 .25

Issued to commemorate the opening of Oléron Bridge, connecting Oléron Island in the Bay of Biscay with the French mainland.

Europa Issue, 1966

Common Design Type

1966, Sept. 24 **Engr.** ***Perf. 13***

Size: 22x36mm

1163 CD9 30c Prussian blue .25 .25
1164 CD9 60c red .35 .25

Vercingetorix at Gergovie, 52 B.C. — A462

Bishop Remi Baptizing King Clovis, 496 A.D. — A463

Design: 60c, Charlemagne attending school (page holding book for crowned king).

1966, Nov. 5 ***Perf. 13***

1165 A462 40c choc, grn & gray bl .35 .30
1166 A463 40c dk red brn & blk .35 .30
1167 A463 60c pur, rose car & brn .35 .30
Nos. 1165-1167 (3) 1.05 .90

Map of Pneumatic Post and Tube A464

1966, Nov. 11

1168 A464 1.60fr maroon & indigo .65 .30

Centenary of Paris pneumatic post system.

Val Chateau — A465

1966, Nov. 19 **Engr.** ***Perf. 13***

1169 A465 2.30fr dk bl, sl grn & brn 2.00 .30

Rance Power Station A466

1966, Dec. 3

1170 A466 60c dk bl, sl grn & brn .45 .45

Tidal power station in the estuary of the Rance River on the English Channel.

European Broadcasting Union Emblem — A467

1967, Mar. 4 **Engr.** ***Perf. 13***

1171 A467 40c dk blue & rose brn .25 .25

3rd Intl. Congress of the European Broadcasting Union, Paris, Mar. 8-22.

Father Juniet's Gig by Henri Rousseau — A468

Francois I by Jean Clouet A469

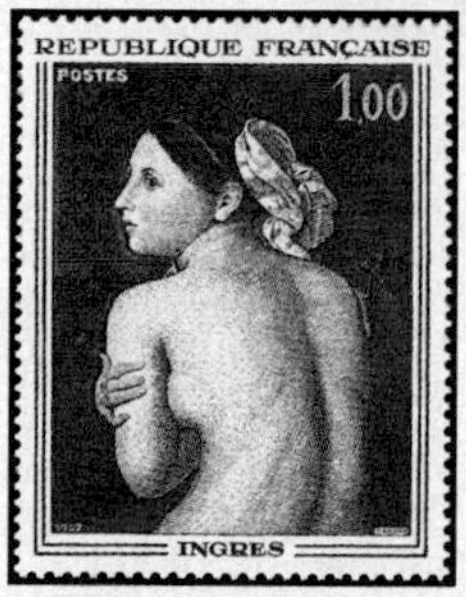

The Bather by Jean-Dominique Ingres — A470

St. Eloi, the Goldsmith, at Work — A471

1967 **Engr.** ***Perf. 13x12, 12x13***

1172 A468 1fr multicolored .40 .40
1173 A469 1fr multicolored .40 .40
1174 A470 1fr multicolored .40 .35
1175 A471 1fr multicolored .40 .35
Nos. 1172-1175 (4) 1.60 1.50

The design of No. 1175 is from a 16th century stained glass window in the Church of Sainte Madeleine, Troyes.

Issued: No. 1172, 4/15; No. 1173, 7/1; No. 1174, 9/9; No. 1175, 10/7.

Snow Crystal and Olympic Rings — A472

1967, Apr. 22 **Photo.** ***Perf. 13***

1176 A472 60c brt & lt blue & red .40 .25

Issued to publicize the 10th Winter Olympic Games, Grenoble, Feb. 6-18, 1968.

French Pavilion, EXPO '67 — A473

1967, Apr. 22 **Engr.**

1177 A473 60c dull bl & bl grn .35 .30

Intl. Exhibition EXPO '67, Montreal, Apr. 28-Oct. 27, 1967.

For surcharge see Reunion No. 363.

Europa Issue, 1967

Common Design Type

1967, Apr. 29

Size: 22x36mm

1178 CD10 30c blue & gray *.25 .25*
1179 CD10 60c brown & lt blue *.55 .45*

Great Bridge, Bordeaux A474

1967, May 8

1180 A474 25c olive, blk & brn .25 .25

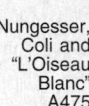

Nungesser, Coli and "L'Oiseau Blanc" A475

1967, May 8

1181 A475 40c slate, dk & lt brn .50 .35

40th anniv. of the attempted transatlantic flight of Charles Nungesser and François Coil, French aviators.

Gouin House, Tours — A476

1967, May 13 **Engr.** ***Perf. 13***

1182 A476 40c vio bl, red brn & red .55 .25

Congress of the Federation of French Philatelic Societies in Tours.

Ramon and Alfort Veterinary School A477

1967, May 27

1183 A477 25c brn, dp bl & yel grn .25 .25

200th anniv. of the Alfort Veterinary School and to honor Professor Gaston Ramon (1886-1963).

Robert Esnault-Pelterie, Diamant Rocket and A-1 Satellite — A478

1967, May 27

1184 A478 60c slate & vio blue .50 .30

Issued to honor Robert Esnault-Pelterie (1881-1957), aviation and space expert.

City Hall, Saint-Quentin A479

Saint-Germain-en-Laye — A480

Views: 60c, Clock Tower, Vire. 75c, Beach, La Baule, Brittany. 95c, Harbor, Boulogne-sur-Mer. 1fr, Rodez Cathedral. 1.50fr, Morlaix; old houses, grotesque carving, viaduct.

1967

1185 A479 50c bl, sl bl & brn .40 .25
1186 A479 60c dp bl, sl bl & dk red brn .60 .50
1187 A480 70c rose car, red brn & bl .40 .25
1188 A480 75c multicolored 1.60 1.25
1189 A480 95c sky bl, lil & sl grn 1.25 1.10
1190 A479 1fr indigo & bl gray .65 .25
1191 A479 1.50fr brt bl, brt grn & red brn 1.25 .30
Nos. 1185-1191 (7) 6.15 3.90

Issued: 1fr, 1.50fr, June 10; 70c, June 17; 50c, 60c, 95c, July 8; 75c, July 24.

Orchids — A481

1967, July 29 **Engr.** ***Perf. 13***

1192 A481 40c dp car, brt pink & pur .90 .50

Orleans flower festival.

Scales of Justice, City and Harbor A482

1967, Sept. 4

1193 A482 60c dk plum, dl bl & ocher .50 .30

9th Intl. Accountancy Cong., Paris, 9/6-12.

Cross of Lorraine, Soldiers and Sailors — A483

1967, Oct. 7 **Engr.** ***Perf. 13***

1194 A483 25c brn, dp ultra & bl .25 .25

25th anniv. of the Battle of Bir Hacheim.

Marie Curie, Bowl Glowing with Radium A484

1967, Oct. 23 **Engr.** ***Perf. 13***

1195 A484 60c dk blue & ultra .40 .30

Marie Curie (1867-1934), scientist who discovered radium and polonium, Nobel prize winner for physics and chemistry.

Lions Emblem A485

1967, Oct. 28

1196 A485 40c dk car & vio bl 1.00 .50

50th anniversary of Lions International.

For surcharge see Reunion No. 364.

Marianne (by Cheffer) — A486

1967, Nov. 4 **Engr.**

1197 A486 25c dark blue .40 .25
1198 A486 30c bright lilac .45 .25
a. Booklet pane of 5 6.00
b. Booklet pane of 10 12.00

Coils (vertical) of Nos. 1197 and 1231 show a red number on the back of every 10th stamp.

See Nos. 1230-1231C, 3525, 4410e, 4517.

For surcharges see Reunion Nos. 367-368, 389.

Stamps of various colors and printing methods with denomination of €1 were limited printings sold in 2010. See footnote after No.3478.

King Philip II (Philip Augustus) at Battle of Bouvines A487

Designs: No. 1200, Election of Hugh Capet as King, horiz. 60c, King Louis IX (St. Louis) holding audience for the poor.

1967, Nov. 13 **Engr.** ***Perf. 13***

1199 A487 40c gray & black .40 .30
1200 A487 40c steel bl & ultra .40 .30
1201 A487 60c grn & dk red brn .50 .30
Nos. 1199-1201 (3) 1.30 .90

Commemorative Medal — A488

1968, Jan. 6 **Engr.** ***Perf. 13***

1202 A488 40c dk slate grn & bis .25 .25

50th anniversary of postal checking service.

Various Road Signs — A489

1968, Feb. 24

1203 A489 25c lil, red & dk bl grn .25 .25

Issued to publicize road safety.

Prehistoric Paintings, Lascaux Cave — A490

Arearea (Merriment) by Paul Gauguin — A491

The Dance by Emile Antoine Bourdelle A492

Portrait of the Model by Auguste Renoir A493

1968 Engr. *Perf. 13x12, 12x13*

1204 A490 1fr multicolored .55 .40
1205 A491 1fr multicolored .65 .40
1206 A492 1fr car & gray olive .65 .40
1207 A493 1fr multicolored .65 .40
Nos. 1204-1207 (4) 2.50 1.60

Issued: No. 1204, 4/13; No. 1205, 9/21; No. 1206, 10/26; No. 1207, 11/9.

Audio-visual Institute, Royan — A494

1968, Apr. 13 *Perf. 13*

1208 A494 40c slate grn, brn & Prus bl .25 .25

5th Conference for World Cooperation with the theme of teaching living languages by audio-visual means.

Europa Issue, 1968

Common Design Type

1968, Apr. 27

Size: 36x22mm

1209 CD11 30c brt red lil & ocher *.30* .25
1210 CD11 60c brown & lake *.60* *.30*

Alain René Le Sage — A495

1968, May 4

1211 A495 40c blue & rose vio .25 .25

Alain René Le Sage (1668-1747), novelist and playwright.

Chateau de Langeais A496

1968, May 4

1212 A496 60c slate bl, grn & red brn .50 .40

Pierre Larousse A497

1968, May 11 Engr. *Perf. 13*

1213 A497 40c rose vio & brown .25 .25

Pierre Larousse (1817-75), grammarian, lexicographer and encyclopedist.

Gnarled Trunk and Fir Tree — A498

1968, May 18 Engr. *Perf. 13*

1214 A498 25c grnsh bl, brn & grn .25 .25

Twinning of Rambouillet Forest in France and the Black Forest in Germany.

Map of Papal Enclave, Valréas, and John XXII Receiving Homage A499

1968, May 25

1215 A499 60c brn, bis brn & pur .55 .40

Papal enclave at Valréas, 650th anniv.

Louis XIV, Arms of France and Flanders A500

1968, June 29

1216 A500 40c rose car, gray & lemon .25 .25

300th anniv. of the Treaty of Aachen which reunited Flanders with France.

Martrou Bridge, Rochefort A501

1968, July 20

1217 A501 25c sky bl, blk & dk red brn .25 .25

Letord Lorraine Bimotor Plane over Map of France A502

1968, Aug. 17 Engr. *Perf. 13*

1218 A502 25c brt blue, indigo & red .50 .30

1st regularly scheduled air mail route in France from Paris to St. Nazaire, 50th anniv.

Tower de Constance, Aigues-Mortes A503

1968, Aug. 31

1219 A503 25c red brn, sky bl & olive bister .25 .25

Bicentenary of the release of Huguenot prisoners from the Tower de Constance, Aigues-Mortes.

Cathedral and Pont Vieux, Beziers A504

1968, Sept. 7 Engr. *Perf. 13*

1220 A504 40c ind, bis & grn .95 .50

"Victory" over White Tower of Salonika — A505

1968, Sept. 28

1221 A505 40c red lilac & plum .25 .25

50th anniv. of the armistice on the eastern front in World War I, Sept. 29, 1918.

Louis XV, Arms of France and Corsica A506

1968, Oct. 5 *Perf. 13*

1222 A506 25c ultra, grn & blk .25 .25

Return of Corsica to France, 200th anniv.

Relay Race A507

1968, Oct. 12

1223 A507 40c ultra, brt grn & ol brn .50 .30

19th Olympic Games, Mexico City, 10/12-27.

Polar Camp with Helicopter, Plane and Snocat Tractor — A508

1968, Oct. 19

1224 A508 40c Prus bl, lt grnsh bl & brn red .35 .25

20 years of French Polar expeditions.

For surcharge see Reunion No. 366.

Leon Bailby, Paris Opera Staircase and Hospital Beds — A509

1968, Oct. 26

1225 A509 40c ocher & maroon .25 .25

50th anniv. of the "Little White Beds" children's hospital fund.

"Victory" over Arc de Triomphe and Eternal Flame — A510

1968, Nov. 9 Engr. *Perf. 13*

1226 A510 25c dk car rose & dp blue .25 .25

50th anniv. of the armistice which ended World War I.

Death of Bertrand Du Guesclin at Chateauneuf-de-Randon, 1380 — A511

No. 1228, King Philip IV (the Fair) and first States-General assembly, 1302, horiz. 60c, Joan of Arc leaving Vaucouleurs, 1429.

1968, Nov. 16

1227 A511 40c green, ultra & brn .40 .30
1228 A511 40c cop red, grn & gray .40 .30
1229 A511 60c vio bl, sl bl & bis .40 .30
Nos. 1227-1229 (3) 1.20 .90

See No. 1260.

Marianne Type of 1967

1969-70 Engr. *Perf. 13*

1230 A486 30c green .35 .25
  a. Booklet pane of 10 8.50
1231 A486 40c deep carmine .45 .25
  a. Booklet pane of 5 (horiz. strip) 7.50
  b. Booklet pane of 10 8.50
  d. With label ('70) .50 .25

Typo. *Perf. 14x13*

1231C A486 30c blue green .25 .25
Nos. 1230-1231C (3) 1.05 .75

No. 1231d was issued in sheets of 50 with alternating labels showing coat of arms of Perigueux, arranged checkerwise, to commemorate the inauguration of the Perigueux stamp printing plant.

The 40c coil is noted after No. 1198.

Church of Brou, Bourg-en-Bresse — A512

Views: 80c, Vouglans Dam, Jura. 85c, Chateau de Chantilly. 1.15fr, Sailboats in La Trinité-sur-Mer harbor.

1969 Engr. *Perf. 13*

1232 A512 45c olive, bl & red brn .25 .25
1233 A512 80c ol bis, brn red & dk brn .45 .25
1234 A512 85c sl grn, dl bl & gray .90 .45
1235 A512 1.15fr brt bl, gray grn & brn .90 .40
Nos. 1232-1235 (4) 2.50 1.35

"February" Bas-relief from Amiens Cathedral
A513

Philip the Good, by Roger van der Weyden
A514

Sts. Savin and Cyprian before Ladicius, Mural, St. Savin, Vienne — A515

The Circus, by Georges Seurat
A515a

1969 *Perf. 12x13*

1236 A513 1fr dk green & brn .50 .35
1237 A514 1fr multicolored .50 .35
1238 A515 1fr multicolored .50 .35
1239 A515a 1fr multicolored .50 .35
Nos. 1236-1239 (4) 2.00 1.40

Issue dates: No. 1236, Feb. 22; No. 1237, May 3; No. 1238, June 28; No. 1239, Nov. 8.

Gallic Coin Type of 1964-66

1969 **Typo.** *Perf. 13½x14*

1240 A418 22c brt green & vio .80 .25
1241 A418 35c red & ultra 1.65 .40
1242 A418 70c ultra & red brn 6.00 2.00
Nos. 1240-1242 (3) 8.45 2.65

Nos. 1240-1242 are known only precanceled. See note after No. 132.

Hautefort Chateau
A516

1969, Apr. 5 **Engr.** *Perf. 13*

1243 A516 70c blue, slate & bister .40 .30

Irises
A517

1969, Apr. 12 **Photo.**

1244 A517 45c multicolored .40 .30

3rd Intl. Flower Show, Paris, 4/23-10/5.

Europa Issue, 1969

Common Design Type

1969, Apr. 26 **Engr.** *Perf. 13*

Size: 36x22mm

1245 CD12 40c carmine rose *.25 .25*
1246 CD12 70c Prussian blue *.30 .25*

Albert Thomas and Thomas Memorial, Geneva
A518

1969, May 10 **Engr.** *Perf. 13*

1247 A518 70c brn, ol bis & ind .40 .30

ILO, 50th anniv., and honoring Thomas (1878-1932), director of the ILO (1920-32).

Garigliano Battle Scene, 1944 — A519

1969, May 10

1248 A519 45c black & violet .40 .40

25th anniv. of the Battle of the Garigliano against the Germans.

Chateau du Marché, Chalons-sur-Marne
A520

1969, May 24

1249 A520 45c bis, dull bl & grn .50 .40

Federation of French Philatelic Societies, 42nd congress.

Parachutists over Normandy Beach — A521

1969, May 31

1250 A521 45c dk blue & vio bl .95 .40

Landing of Special Air Service and Free French commandos in Normandy, June 6, 1944, 25th anniv.

Monument of the French Resistance, Mt. Mouchet — A522

1969, June 7

1251 A522 45c dk grn, slate & ind .90 .65

25th anniv. of the battle of Mt. Mouchet between French resistance fighters and the Germans, June 2 and 10, 1944.

French Troops Landing in Provence — A523

1969, Aug. 23 **Engr.** *Perf. 13*

1252 A523 45c slate & blk brn 1.00 .65

25th anniv. of the landing of French and American forces in Provence, Aug. 15, 1944.

Russian and French Aviators — A524

1969, Oct. 18 **Engr.** *Perf. 13*

1253 A524 45c slate, dp bl & car 1.00 .80

Issued to honor the French aviators of the Normandy-Neman Squadron who fought on the Russian Front, 1942-45.

Kayak on Isère River
A525

1969, Aug. 2 **Engr.** *Perf. 13*

1254 A525 70c org brn, ol & dk bl .45 .30

Intl. Canoe and Kayak Championships, Bourg-Saint-Maurice, Savoy, July 31-Aug. 6.

Napoleon as Young Officer and his Birthplace, Ajaccio — A526

1969, Aug. 16

1255 A526 70c brt grnsh bl, ol & rose vio .45 .30

Napoleon Bonaparte (1769-1821).
For surcharge see Reunion No. 370.

Drops of Water and Diamond
A527

Mediterranean Mouflon
A528

1969, Sept. 27

1256 A527 70c blk, dp bl & brt grn .50 .30

European Water Charter.

1969, Oct. 11

1257 A528 45c ol, blk & org brn *2.50 1.25*

Issued to publicize wildlife protection.

Central School of Arts and Crafts
A529

1969, Oct. 18

1258 A529 70c dk grn, yel grn & org .40 .30

Inauguration of the Central School of Arts and Crafts at Chatenay-Malabry.

Nuclear Submarine "Le Redoutable" — A530

1969, Oct. 25

1259 A530 70c dp bl, grn & sl grn .40 .30

Type of 1968 and

Henri IV and Edict of Nantes — A531

Designs: No. 1260, Pierre Terrail de Bayard wounded at Battle of Brescia (after a painting in Versailles). No. 1262, Louis XI, Charles the Bold and map of France.

1969, Nov. 8 **Engr.** *Perf. 13*

1260 A511 80c brn, bister & blk .50 .30
1261 A531 80c blk & vio bl .50 .30
1262 A531 80c ol, dp grn & dk red brn .50 .30
Nos. 1260-1262 (3) 1.50 .90

"Firecrest" and Alain Gerbault — A532

1970, Jan. 10 **Engr.** *Perf. 13*

1263 A532 70c ind, brt bl & gray .60 .50

Completion of Alain Gerbault's trip around the world aboard the "Firecrest," 1923-29, 40th anniv.

Gendarmery Emblem, Mountain Climber, Helicopter, Motorcyclists and Motorboat — A533

1970, Jan. 31
1264 A533 45c sl grn, dk bl & brn 1.25 .50

National Gendarmery, founded 1791.

Field Ball Player — A534

1970, Feb. 21 **Engr.** ***Perf. 13***
1265 A534 80c slate green .50 .50

7th Intl. Field Ball Games, Feb. 26-Mar. 8.

Alphonse Juin and Church of the Invalides — A535

1970, Feb. 28
1266 A535 45c gray bl & dk brn .35 .25

Issued to honor Marshal Alphonse Pierre Juin (1888-1967), military leader.

Aerotrain A536

1970, Mar. 7
1267 A536 80c purple & gray .65 .50

Introduction of the aerotrain, which reaches a speed of 320 miles per hour.

Pierre Joseph Pelletier, Joseph Bienaimé Caventou, Quinine Formula and Cell — A537

1970, Mar. 21 **Engr.** ***Perf. 13***
1268 A537 50c slate grn, sky bl & dp car .35 .30

Discovery of quinine, 150th anniversary.

Pink Flamingos A538

Diamant B Rocket and Radar A539

1970, Mar. 21
1269 A538 45c olive, gray & pink .35 .25

European Nature Conservation Year, 1970.

1970, Mar. 28
1270 A539 45c bright green .65 .40

Space center in Guyana and the launching of the Diamant B rocket, Mar. 10, 1970.

Europa Issue, 1970
Common Design Type

1970, May 2 **Engr.** ***Perf. 13***
Size: 36x22mm
1271 CD13 40c deep carmine *.25* .25
1272 CD13 80c sky blue *.40* .25

Annunication, by Primitive Painter of Savoy, 1480 — A540

The Triumph of Flora, by Jean Baptiste Carpeaux — A541

Diana Returning from the Hunt, by François Boucher — A542

Dancer with Bouquet, by Edgar Degas A543

1970 ***Perf. 12x13, 13x12***
1273 A540 1fr multicolored .75 .45
1274 A541 1fr red brown .75 .45
1275 A542 1fr multicolored .75 .45
1276 A543 1fr multicolored .75 .45
Nos. 1273-1276 (4) 3.00 1.80

Issued: No. 1273, 5/9; No. 1274, 7/4; No. 1275, 10/10; No. 1276, 11/14.

Arms of Lens, Miner's Lamp and Pit Head A544

1970, May 16 **Engr.** ***Perf. 13***
1277 A544 40c scarlet .25 .25

43rd Natl. Congress of the Federation of French Philatelic Societies, Lens, May 14-21.

Diamond Rock, Martinique A545

Haute Provence Observatory and Spiral Nebula — A546

Designs: 95c, Chancelade Abbey, Dordogne. 1fr, Gosier Islet, Guadeloupe.

1970, June 20 **Engr.** ***Perf. 13***
1278 A545 50c sl grn, brt bl & plum .45 .25
1279 A545 95c lt ol, car & brn 1.25 1.00
1280 A545 1fr sl grn, brt bl & dk car rose .55 .25
1281 A546 1.30fr dk bl, vio bl & dk grn 1.90 1.00
Nos. 1278-1281 (4) 4.15 2.50

Hand Reaching for Freedom — A547

1970, June 27
1282 A547 45c vio bl, bl & bister .40 .25

Liberation of concentration camps, 25th anniv.

Handicapped Javelin Thrower — A548

1970, June 27
1283 A548 45c rose car, ultra & emer .40 .25

Issued to publicize the International Games of the Handicapped, St. Etienne, June 1970.

Pole Vault — A549

1970, Sept. 11 **Engr.** ***Perf. 13***
1284 A549 45c car, bl & indigo .45 .25

First European Junior Athletic Championships, Colombes, Sept. 11-13.

Royal Salt Works, Arc-et-Senans — A550

1970, Sept. 26
1285 A550 80c bl, brn & dk grn 1.50 .65

Restoration of the 18th cent. Royal Salt Works buildings, by Claude Nicolas Ledoux (1736-1806) at Arc-et-Senans, for use as a center for studies of all aspects of future human life.

Armand Jean du Plessis, Duc de Richelieu — A551

Designs: No. 1287, Battle of Fontenoy, 1745. No. 1288, Louis XIV and Versailles.

1970, Oct. 17 **Engr.** ***Perf. 13***
1286 A551 45c blk, sl & car rose .65 .35
1287 A551 45c org, brn & indigo .65 .35
1288 A551 45c sl grn, lem & org brn .65 .35
Nos. 1286-1288 (3) 1.95 1.05

UN Headquarters in New York and Geneva — A552

1970, Oct. 24 **Engr.** ***Perf. 13***
1289 A552 80c ol, dp ultra & dk pur .40 .25

25th anniversary of the United Nations.

View of Bordeaux and France No. 43 — A553

1970, Nov. 7
1290 A553 80c vio bl & gray bl .40 .25

Centenary of the Bordeaux issue.

Col. Denfert-Rochereau and Lion of Belfort, by Frederic A. Bartholdi — A554

1970, Nov. 14

1291 A554 45c dk bl, ol & red brn .40 .25

Centenary of the siege of Belfort during Franco-Prussian War.

Marianne (by Bequet) — A555

1971-74 Typo. *Perf. 14x13*

1292 A555 45c sky blue .30 .25
1292A A555 60c green ('74) .90 .25

For surcharges see Reunion Nos. 371, 397-398.

Engr. *Perf. 13*

1293 A555 50c rose carmine .30 .25
a. Bklt. pane of 5 (horiz. strip) 5.00
b. Booklet pane of 10 10.00
1294 A555 60c green ('74) 5.00 .35
a. Booklet pane of 10 65.00
1294B A555 80c car rose ('74) .50 .25
c. Booklet pane of 5 9.00
d. Booklet pane of 10 12.00
Nos. 1293-1294B (3) 5.80 .85

Nos. 1294 and 1294B issued also in vertical coils with control number on back of every 10th stamp.

No. 1293 issued only in booklets and in vertical coils with red control number on back of every 10th stamp.

See Nos. 1494-1498, 3526, 4410f, 4518.

St. Matthew, Sculpture from Strasbourg Cathedral A556

Winnower, by François Millet A557

The Dreamer, by Georges Rouault A558

1971 Engr. *Perf. 12x13*

1295 A556 1fr dark red brown .85 .50
1296 A557 1fr multicolored .75 .40
1297 A558 1fr multicolored .75 .40
Nos. 1295-1297 (3) 2.35 1.30

Issued: No. 1295, 1/23; No. 1296, 4/3; No. 1297, 6/5.

Figure Skating Pair A560

1971, Feb. 20 Engr. *Perf. 13*

1299 A560 80c vio bl, sl & aqua .55 .30

World Figure Skating Championships, Lyons, Feb. 23-28.

Underwater Exploration — A561

1971, Mar. 6

1300 A561 80c blue blk & bl grn .40 .25

International Exhibition of Ocean Exploration, Bordeaux, Mar. 9-14.

Cape Horn Clipper "Antoinette" and Solidor Castle, Saint-Malo — A562

1971, Apr. 10 Engr. *Perf. 13*

1301 A562 80c blue, pur & slate 1.25 .90

For surcharge see Reunion No. 372.

Pyrenean Chamois — A563

1971, Apr. 24 Engr. *Perf. 13*

1302 A563 65c bl, dk brn & brn ol .65 .30

National Park of Western Pyrenees.

Europa Issue, 1971

Common Design Type and

Santa Maria della Salute, Venice A564

1971, May 8 Engr. *Perf. 13*

1303 A564 50c blue gray & ol bis *.30* *.25*

Size: 36x22mm

1304 CD14 80c rose lilac *.45* *.40*

Cardinal, Nobleman and Lawyer — A565

Storming of the Bastille — A566

Design: No. 1306, Battle of Valmy.

1971

1305 A565 45c bl, rose red & pur .55 .40
1306 A565 45c bl, ol bis & brn red .65 .40
1307 A566 65c dk brn, gray bl & mag 1.00 .40
Nos. 1305-1307 (3) 2.20 1.20

No. 1305 commemorates the opening of the Estates General, May 5, 1789; No. 1306, Battle of Valmy (Sept. 20, 1792) between French and Prussian armies; 65c, Storming of the Bastille, Paris, July 14, 1789.

Issued: No. 1305, 5/8; No. 1306, 9/18; 65c, 7/10.

Grenoble A568

1971, May 29 Engr. *Perf. 13*

1308 A568 50c ocher, lil & rose red .35 .25

44th Natl. Cong. of the Federation of French Philatelic Societies, Grenoble, May 30-31.

"Rural Family Aid" Shedding Light on Village — A569

1971, June 5

1309 A569 40c vio, bl & grn .25 .25

Aid for rural families.
For surcharge see Reunion No. 373.

Chateau and Fort de Sedan A570

Pont d'Arc, Ardèche Gorge — A571

Views: 60c, Sainte Chapelle, Riom. 65c, Fountain and tower, Dole. 90c, Tower and street, Riquewihr.

1971 Engr. *Perf. 13*

1310 A571 60c black, grn & bl .25 .25
1311 A571 65c lil, ocher & blk .35 .25
1312 A571 90c grn, vio brn & red brn .50 .25
1313 A570 1.10fr sl grn, Prus bl & brn .60 .30
1314 A571 1.40fr sl grn, bl & dk brn .75 .25
Nos. 1310-1314 (5) 2.45 1.30

Issued: 60c, 6/19; 65c, 90c, 7/3; 1.10fr, 1.40fr, 6/12.

For surcharges see Reunion Nos. 374, 381.

Gallic Coin Type of 1964-66

1971, July 1 Typo. *Perf. 13½x14*

1315 A418 26c lilac & brn .40 .25
1316 A418 30c lt brown & brn .75 .25
1317 A418 45c dull green & brn 1.40 .25
1318 A418 90c red & brown 1.90 .40
Nos. 1315-1318 (4) 4.45 1.15

Nos. 1315-1318 are known only precanceled. See second paragraph after No. 132.

Bourbon Palace A572

1971, Aug. 28 Engr. *Perf. 13*

1319 A572 90c violet blue .75 .25

59th Conf. of the Interparliamentary Union.

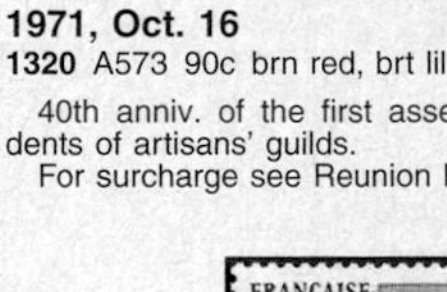

Embroidery and Tool Making A573

1971, Oct. 16

1320 A573 90c brn red, brt lil & cl .50 .30

40th anniv. of the first assembly of presidents of artisans' guilds.

For surcharge see Reunion No. 375.

Reunion Chameleon A574

1971, Nov. 6 Photo. *Perf. 13*

1321 A574 60c brn, yel, grn & blk 1.10 .65

Nature protection.

De Gaulle Issue

Common Design Type and

De Gaulle in Brazzaville, 1944 — A576

Designs: No. 1324, De Gaulle entering Paris, 1944. No. 1325, Pres. de Gaulle, 1970.

1971, Nov. 9 Engr.

1322 CD134 50c black 1.10 .65
1323 A576 50c ultra 1.10 .65
1324 A576 50c rose red 1.10 .65
1325 CD134 50c black 1.10 .65
a. Strip of 4, #1322-1325 + label 4.50 4.00
Nos. 1325a (1) 4.50 4.00

1st anniv. of the death of Charles de Gaulle.

See Reunion Nos. 377, 380.

Antoine Portal and first Session of Academy — A577

1971, Nov. 13
1326 A577 45c dk purple & mag .30 .25

Sesquicentennial of the founding of the National Academy of Medicine; Baron Antoine Portal was first president.

L'Etude, by Jean Honoré Fragonard A578

Women in Garden, by Claude Monet A579

St. Peter Presenting Pierre de Bourbon, by Maitre de Moulins A580

Boats, by André Derain — A581

1972 Engr. *Perf. 12x13, 13x12*

1327	A578	1fr black & multi	.90	.75
1328	A579	1fr slate grn & multi	1.75	.75
1329	A580	2fr dk brown & multi	2.50	1.25
1330	A581	2fr yellow & multi	3.50	1.50
		Nos. 1327-1330 (4)	8.65	4.25

Issued: No. 1327, 1/22; No. 1328, 6/17; No. 1329, 10/14; No. 1330, 12/16.

Map of South Indian Ocean, Penguin and Ships — A582

1972, Jan. 29 ***Perf. 13***
1331 A582 90c black, bl & ocher .65 .40

Bicentenary of discovery of the Crozet and Kerguelen Islands.

Slalom and Olympic Emblems A583

1972, Feb. 7
1332 A583 90c dk olive & dp car .55 .35

11th Winter Olympic Games, Sapporo, Japan, Feb. 3-13.

Hearts, UN Emblem, Caduceus and Pacemaker A584

1972, Apr. 8 Engr. *Perf. 13*
1333 A584 45c dk car, org & gray .35 .25

"Your heart is your health," world health month.

Red Deer, Sologne Plateau — A585

Charlieu Abbey A585a

Bazoches-du-Morvand Chateau — A586

Saint-Just Cathedral, Narbonne A587

1972 ***Perf. 13***

1334	A585	1fr ocher & red brn	.65	.25
1335	A585a	1.20fr sl & dull brn	.65	.25
1336	A586	2fr sl grn, blk & red brn	1.00	.25
1337	A587	3.50fr bl, gray ol & car rose	1.90	.55
		Nos. 1334-1337 (4)	4.20	1.30

Issued: 1fr, 9/10; 1.20fr, 4/29; 2fr, 9/9; 3.50fr, 4/8.
For surcharge see Reunion No. 388.

Eagle Owl — A588

Nature protection: 60c, Salmon, horiz.

1972

1338	A588	60c grn, ind & brt bl	2.25	.60
1339	A588	65c sl, ol brn & sep	1.40	.30

Issue dates: 60c, May 27; 65c, Apr. 15.

Europa Issue
Common Design Type and

Aix-la-Chapelle Cathedral — A589

1972, Apr. 22 Engr. *Perf. 13*
1340 A589 50c yel, vio brn & dk ol .25 .25

Photo.
Size: 22x36mm

1341	CD15	90c red org & multi	.50	.35
		Nos. 1341 (1)	.50	.35

Bouquet Made of Hearts and Blood Donors' Emblem A590

Newfoundlander "Côte d'Emeraude" A591

1972, May 5 **Engr.**
1342 A590 40c red .30 .25

20th anniv. of the Blood Donors Association of Post and Telecommunications Employees.
For surcharge see Reunion No. 383.

1972, May 6
1343 A591 90c org, vio bl & sl grn 1.00 .80

Cathedral, Saint-Brieuc A592

1972, May 20
1344 A592 50c lilac rose .30 .25

45th Congress of the Federation of French Philatelic Societies, Saint-Brieuc, May 21-22.

Hand Holding Symbol of Postal Code A593

1972, June 3 Typo. *Perf. 14x13*

1345	A593	30c green, blk & car	.25	.25
1346	A593	50c car, blk & yel	.30	.25

Introduction of postal code system.
For surcharges see Reunion Nos. 384-385.

Old and New Communications A594

1972, July 1 Engr. *Perf. 13*
1347 A594 45c slate & vio blue .40 .25

21st Intl. Congress of P.T.T. (Post, Telegraph & Telephone) Employees, Paris, 7/1-7.

Hurdler and Olympic Rings A595

1972, July 8
1348 A595 1fr deep olive .50 .25

20th Olympic Games, Munich, 8/26-9/11.

Hikers and Mt. Aigoual — A596

Bicyclist — A597

1972, July 15 Photo. *Perf. 13*
1349 A596 40c brt rose & multi 1.50 .60

Intl. Year of Tourism and 25th anniv. of the Natl. Hikers Association.

1972, July 22 **Engr.**
1350 A597 1fr gray, brn & lil 2.00 .60

World Bicycling Championships, Marseille, July 29-Aug. 2.

"Incroyables and Merveilleuses," 1794 — A598

French History: 60c, Bonaparte at the Arcole Bridge. 65c, Egyptian expedition (soldiers and scientists finding antiquities; pyramids in background).

1972 Engr. *Perf. 13*

1351	A598	45c ol, dk grn & car rose	.40	.30
1352	A598	60c red, blk & ind	.85	.40

1353 A598 65c ocher, ultra & choc .85 .40
Nos. 1351-1353 (3) 2.10 1.10

Issued: 45c, Oct. 7; 60c, 65c, Nov. 11.

Champollion, Rosetta Stone with Key Inscription — A599

1972, Oct. 14

1354 A599 90c vio bl, brn red & blk .60 .30

Sesquicentennial of the deciphering of hieroglyphs by Jean-François Champollion.

St. Teresa, Portal of Notre Dame of Alençon A600

1973, Jan. 6 **Engr.** ***Perf. 13***

1355 A600 1fr Prus blue & indigo .60 .45

Centenary of the birth of St. Teresa of Lisieux, the Little Flower (Thérèse Martin, 1873-1897), Carmelite nun.

Anthurium (Martinique) — A601

1973, Jan. 20 **Photo.**

1356 A601 50c gray & multi .40 .25

Colors of France and Germany Interlaced — A602

1973, Jan. 22

1357 A602 50c multicolored .40 .25

10th anniv. of the Franco-German Cooperation Treaty. See Germany No. 1101.

Polish Immigrants — A603

1973, Feb. 3 **Engr.** ***Perf. 13***

1358 A603 40c slate grn, dp car & brn .25 .25

50th anniversary of Polish immigration into France, 1921-1923.

Last Supper, St. Austremoine Church, Issoire — A604

Kneeling Woman, by Charles Le Brun A605

Angel, Wood, Moutier-D'Ahun — A606

Lady Playing Archlute, by Antoine Watteau A607

1973 **Engr.** ***Perf. 12x13***

1359 A604 2fr brown & multi 1.75 1.25
1360 A605 2fr dk red & yel 1.75 1.40
1361 A606 2fr ol brn & vio brn 1.75 1.25
1362 A607 2fr black & multi 1.75 1.25
Nos. 1359-1362 (4) 7.00 5.15

Issued: No. 1359, 2/10; No. 1360, 4/28; No. 1361, 5/26; No. 1362, 9/22.

Tuileries Palace, Telephone Relays A608

Oil Tanker, Francis I Lock A609

Airbus A300-B A610

1973

1363 A608 45c ultra, sl grn & bis .30 .25
1364 A609 90c plum, blk & bl .55 .25
1365 A610 3fr dk brn, bl & blk 1.90 .80
Nos. 1363-1365 (3) 2.75 1.30

French technical achievements.
Issued: 45c, 5/15; 90c, 10/27; 3fr, 4/7.

Europa Issue 1973

Common Design Type and

City Hall, Brussels, CEPT Emblem — A611

1973, Apr. 14 **Engr.** ***Perf. 13***

1366 A611 50c brt pink & choc *.45* *.25*

Photo.

Size: 36x22mm

1367 CD16 90c slate grn & multi *1.60* *.75*

Masonic Lodge Emblem A612

1973, May 12 **Engr.** ***Perf. 13***

1368 A612 90c magenta & vio bl .55 .30

Bicentenary of the Free Masons of France.

Guadeloupe Raccoon A613

White Storks A614

1973

1369 A613 40c lilac, sepia & olive .35 .25
1370 A614 60c blk, aqua & org red .50 .25

Nature protection.
Issue dates: 40c, June 23; 60c, May 12.

Tourist Issue

Doubs Waterfall A615

Clos-Lucé, Amboise A617

Palace of Dukes of Burgundy, Dijon A616

Design: 90c, Gien Chateau.

1973 **Engr.** ***Perf. 13***

1371 A615 60c multicolored .30 .25
1372 A616 65c red & purple .30 .25
1373 A616 90c Prus bl, ind & brn .35 .25
1374 A617 1fr ocher, bl & sl grn .35 .25
Nos. 1371-1374 (4) 1.30 1.00

Issued: 60c, 9/8; 65c, 5/19; 90c, 8/18; 1fr, 6/23.
For surcharge see Reunion No. 387.

Academy Emblem — A618

1973, May 26

1375 A618 1fr lil, slate grn & red .50 .30

Academy of Overseas Sciences, 50th anniv.

Racing Car and Clocks A619

1973, June 2

1376 A619 60c dk brown & blue .75 .50

24-hour automobile race at Le Mans, 50th anniv.

Five-master France II — A620

1973, June 9

1377 A620 90c ultra, Prus bl & ind 1.10 .55

For surcharge see Reunion No. 386.

Tower and Square, Toulouse — A621

1973, June 9

1378 A621 50c purple & red brn .30 .25

46th Congress of the Federation of French Philatelic Societies, Toulouse, June 9-12.

Dr. Armauer G. Hansen — A622

Ducretet and his Transmission Diagram — A623

1973, Sept. 29 Engr. *Perf. 13*

1379 A622 45c grn, dk ol & ocher .30 .25

Centenary of the discovery of the Hansen bacillus, the cause of leprosy.

1973, Oct. 6

1380 A623 1fr yel grn & magenta .40 .30

75th anniversary of the first transmission of radio signals from the Eiffel Tower to the Pantheon by Eugene Ducretet (1844-1915).

Molière as Sganarelle — A624

1973, Oct. 20

1381 A624 1fr dk red & olive brn .55 .35

Moliere (Jean-Baptiste Poquelin; 1622-1673), playwright and actor.

Pierre Bourgoin and Philippe Kieffer A625

1973, Oct. 27

1382 A625 1fr red, rose cl & vio bl .50 .30

Pierre Bourgoin (1907-70), and Philippe Kieffer (1899-1963), heroes of the Free French forces in World War II.

Napoleon, Jean Portalis and Palace of Justice, Paris — A626

Exhibition Halls — A627

The Coronation of Napoleon, by Jean Louis David — A628

1973 Engr. *Perf. 13*

1383 A626 45c blue, choc & gray .55 .30

1384 A627 60c ol, sl grn & brn .55 .50

1385 A628 1fr sl grn, ol & claret .65 .55

Nos. 1383-1385 (3) 1.75 1.35

History of France. 45c, for the preparation of the Code Napoleon; 60c, Napoleon's encouragement of industry; 1fr, his coronation.

Issued: 45c, 11/3; 60c, 11/24; 1fr, 11/12.

Eternal Flame, Arc de Triomphe A629

Weather Vane A630

1973, Nov. 10

1386 A629 40c pur, vio bl & red .40 .30

50th anniv. of the Eternal Flame at the Arc de Triomphe, Paris.

1973, Dec. 1

1387 A630 65c ultra, blk & grn .40 .30

50th anniv. of the Dept. of Agriculture.

Human Rights Flame and Man — A631

Postal Museum — A632

1973, Dec. 8 Engr. *Perf. 13*

1388 A631 45c car, org & blk .30 .25

25th anniversary of the Universal Declaration of Human Rights.

1973, Dec. 19

1389 A632 50c maroon & bister .30 .25

Opening of new post and philately museum, Paris.

ARPHILA 75 Emblem A633

1974, Jan. 19 Engr. *Perf. 13*

1390 A633 50c brn, bl & brt lil .25 .25

ARPHILA 75 Philatelic Exhibition, Paris, June 1975.

For surcharge see Reunion No. 390.

Concorde over Charles de Gaulle Airport A634

Turbotrain T.G.V. 001 A635

Phenix Nuclear Power Station A636

1974 Engr. *Perf. 13*

1391 A634 60c pur & ol gray .40 .30

1392 A635 60c multicolored 1.10 .55

1393 A636 65c multicolored .40 .30

Nos. 1391-1393 (3) 1.90 1.15

French technical achievements.

Issued: No. 1391, 3/18; No. 1392, 8/31; 65c, 9/21.

Cardinal Richelieu, by Philippe de Champaigne — A637

Painting by Joan Miró A638

Canal du Loing, by Alfred Sisley — A639

"In Honor of Nicolas Fouquet," Tapestry by Georges Mathieu A640

Engr., Photo. (#1395, 1397)

1974 *Perf. 12x13, 13x12*

1394 A637 2fr multicolored 1.25 1.00

1395 A638 2fr multicolored 1.25 1.25

1396 A639 2fr multicolored 1.75 1.25

1397 A640 2fr multicolored 1.75 1.25

Nos. 1394-1397 (4) 6.00 4.75

Nos. 1394-1397 are printed in sheets of 25 with alternating labels publicizing "ARPHILA 75," Paris, June 6-16, 1975.

Issued: No. 1394, 3/23; No. 1395, 9/14; No. 1396, 11/9; No. 1397, 11/16.

For surcharges see Reunion Nos. 391-394.

French Alps and Gentian A641

1974, Mar. 30 Engr. *Perf. 13*

1398 A641 65c vio blue & gray .40 .25

Centenary of the French Alpine Club.

Europa Issue 1974

"Age of Bronze," by Auguste Rodin — A642

"Air," by Aristide Maillol A643

1974, Apr. 20 *Perf. 13*

1399 A642 50c brt rose lil & blk *.30 .25*

1400 A643 90c olive & brown *.55 .40*

Sea Rescue — A644

1974, Apr. 27

1401 A644 90c multicolored .40 .30

Reorganized sea rescue organization.

For surcharge see Reunion No. 395.

Council Building, View of Strasbourg and Emblem — A645

1974, May 4 Engr. *Perf. 13*

1402 A645 45c indigo, bister & bl .30 .25

25th anniversary of the Council of Europe.

Tourist Issue

View of Salers A646

Basilica of St. Nicolas de Porte — A647

Seashell over Corsica — A648

Design: 1.10fr, View of Lot Valley.

1974 **Engr.** ***Perf. 13***

1403 A646 65c yel grn & choc .25 .25
1404 A646 1.10fr choc & sl grn .45 .30
1405 A647 2fr gray & lilac .80 .30
1406 A648 3fr multicolored 1.00 .40
Nos. 1403-1406 (4) 2.50 1.25

Issued: 65c, 6/22; 1.10fr, 9/7; 2fr, 10/12; 3fr, 5/11.

Bison A649

Giant Armadillo of Guyana A650

1974

1407 A649 40c bis, choc & bl .35 .25
1408 A650 65c slate, olive & grn .35 .25

Nature protection.
Issued: No. 1407, 5/25; No. 1408, 10/19.

Americans Landing in Normandy and Arms of Normandy — A651

General Marie-Pierre Koenig — A652

Order of the French Resistance — A653

1974

1409 A651 45c grn, rose & ind .80 .50
1410 A652 1fr multicolored .50 .35
1411 A653 1fr multicolored .65 .50
Nos. 1409-1411 (3) 1.95 1.35

30th anniversary of the liberation of France from the Nazis. Design of No. 1410 includes diagram of battle of Bir-Hakeim and Free French and Bir-Hakeim memorials.

Issued: 45c, 6/8; No. 1410, 5/25; No. 1411, 11/23.

See No. B478.

Pfister House, 16th Century, Colmar — A654

1974, June 1

1412 A654 50c multicolored .25 .25

47th Congress of the Federation of French Philatelic Societies, Colmar, May 30-June 4.

Chess A655

1974, June 8

1413 A655 1fr dk brown & multi .60 .35

21st Chess Olympiad, Nice, June 6-30.

Facade with Statue of Louis XIV, and 1675 Medal — A656

1974, June 15

1414 A656 40c indigo, bl & brn .30 .25

300th anniversary of the founding of the Hotel des Invalides (Home for poor and sick officers and soldiers).

Peacocks Holding Letter, and Globe — A657

1974, Oct. 5 **Engr.** ***Perf. 13***

1415 A657 1.20fr ultra, dp grn & dk car .40 .30

Centenary of Universal Postal Union.
For surcharge see Reunion No. 396.

Copernicus and Heliocentric System — A658

1974, Oct. 12

1416 A658 1.20fr multicolored .35 .25

500th anniversary of the birth of Nicolaus Copernicus (1473-1543), Polish astronomer.

Tourist Issue

Palace of Justice, Rouen A659

Saint-Pol-de-Leon A660

Chateau de Rochechouart — A661

1975 **Engr.** ***Perf. 13***

1417 A659 85c multicolored .35 .30
1418 A660 1.20fr bl, bis & choc .40 .30
1419 A661 1.40fr brn, ind & grn .50 .30
Nos. 1417-1419 (3) 1.25 .90

Issued: 85c, 1/25; 1.20fr, 1/18; 1.40fr, 1/11.

Snowy Egret — A662

1975, Feb. 15 **Engr.** ***Perf. 13***

1420 A662 70c brt blue & bister .40 .30

Nature protection.

Gallic Coin — A663

1975, Feb. 16 **Typo.** ***Perf. 13½x14***

1421 A663 42c orange & mag 1.10 .45
1422 A663 48c lt bl & red brn 1.25 .70
1423 A663 70c brt pink & red 2.25 1.10
1424 A663 1.35fr lt green & brn 2.40 1.25
Nos. 1421-1424 (4) 7.00 3.50

Nos. 1421-1424 are known only precanceled. See second note after No. 132. See Nos. 1460-1463, 1487-1490.

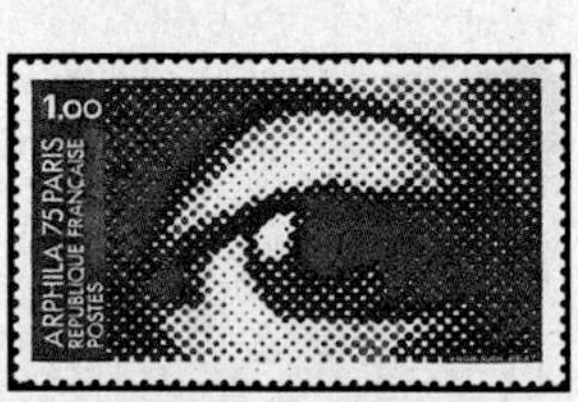

The Eye — A664

Ionic Capital — A665

Graphic Art — A666

Ceres — A667

1975 **Engr.** ***Perf. 13***

1425 A664 1fr red, pur & org .45 .30
1426 A665 2fr grn, sl grn & mag .80 .55
1427 A666 3fr dk car & ol grn 1.25 .90
1428 A667 4fr red, sl grn & bis 1.60 1.25
Nos. 1425-1428 (4) 4.10 3.00

Souvenir Sheet

1429 Sheet of 4 7.50 7.50
a. A664 2fr dp car & slate blue 1.00 1.00
b. A665 3fr brt bl, sl bl & dp car 1.40 1.40
c. A666 4fr slate blue, brt bl & plum 2.00 2.00
d. A667 6fr brt bl, sl bl & plum 2.50 2.50

ARPHILA 75, Intl. Philatelic Exhibition, Paris, 6/6-16. Issued: 1fr, 3/1; 2fr, 3/22; 3fr, 4/19; 4fr, 5/17; No. 1429, 4/2.

Pres. Georges Pompidou A668

Paul as Harlequin, by Picasso A669

1975, Apr. 3 **Engr.** ***Perf. 13***

1430 A668 80c black & gray .30 .25

Georges Pompidou (1911-74), President of France, 1969-74.

1975, Apr. 26 **Photo.** ***Perf. 13***

Europa; 1.20fr, Woman on Balcony, by Kees van Dongen

1431 A669 80c multi *.45 .35*
1432 A669 1.20fr multi, horiz. *.90 .70*

Machines, Globe, Emblem A670

1975, May 3 **Engr.**

1433 A670 1.20fr blue, blk & red .40 .30

World Machine Tool Exhib., Paris, 6/7-26.

Senate Assembly Hall A671

1975, May 24 **Engr.** ***Perf. 13***

1434 A671 1.20fr olive & dk car .40 .30

Centenary of the Senate of the Republic.

Meter Convention Document, Atom Diagram and Waves — A672

1975, May 31

1435 A672 1fr multicolored .40 .30

Cent. of Intl. Meter Convention, Paris, 1875.

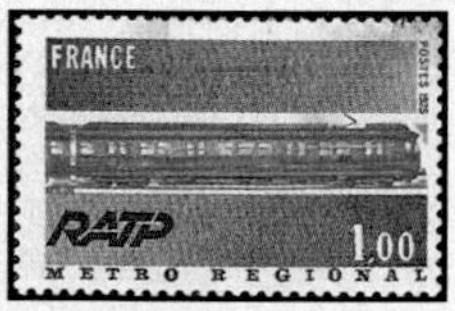

Metro Regional Train A673

"Gazelle" Helicopter A674

1975

1436 A673 1fr indigo & brt bl .65 .30
1437 A674 1.30fr vio bl & grn .80 .40

French technical achievements.
Issue dates: 1fr, June 21; 1.30fr, May 31.

Youth and Flasks, Symbols of Study and Growth — A675

1975, June 21

1438 A675 70c red pur & blk .30 .25

Student Health Foundation.

People's Theater, Bussang, and Maurice Pottecher A676

1975, Aug. 9 **Engr.** ***Perf. 13***

1439 A676 85c multicolored .30 .25

80th anniversary of the People's Theater at Bussang, founded by Maurice Pottecher.

Regions of France

Central France A677

Aquitaine A678

Limousin A679

Picardy A680

Burgundy A681

Loire A682

Guyana A683

Auvergne A684

Poitou-Charentes A685

Southern Pyrenees A686

Pas-de-Calais — A687

1975-76 **Engr.** ***Perf. 13***

1440	A677	25c	blue & yel grn	.25	.25
1441	A678	60c	multicolored	.25	.25
1442	A679	70c	multicolored	.50	.35
1443	A680	85c	bl, grn & org	.70	.35
1444	A681	1fr	red, yel & mar	.70	.35
1445	A682	1.15fr	bl, bis & grn	.70	.35
1446	A683	1.25fr	multicolored	.65	.50
1447	A684	1.30fr	dk bl & red	.85	.50
1448	A685	1.90fr	sl, ol & Prus bl	1.00	.50
1449	A686	2.20fr	multicolored	1.10	1.00
1450	A687	2.80fr	car, bl & blk	1.40	1.00
			Nos. 1440-1450 (11)	8.10	5.40

Issued: 85c, 11/15; 1fr, 10/25; 1.15fr, 9/6; 1.30fr, 10/4/75; 1.90fr, 12/6; 2.80fr, 12/13; 25c, 1/31/76; 2.20fr, 1/10/76; 60c, 5/22/76; 70c, 5/29/76; 1.25fr, 10/16/76.

A690

French Flag, F.-H. Manhes, Jean Verneau, Pierre Kaan

1975, Sept. 27

1453 A690 1fr multicolored .40 .30

Liberation of concentration camps, 30th anniversary. F.-H. Manhes (1889-1959), Jean Verneau (1890-1944) and Pierre Kaan (1903-1945) were French resistance leaders, imprisoned in concentration camps.

A691

Monument, by Joseph Riviere.

1975, Oct. 11

1454 A691 70c multicolored .40 .30

Land Mine Demolition Service, 30th anniversary. Monument was erected in Alsace to honor land mine victims.

Symbols of Suburban Living A692

1975, Oct. 18

1455 A692 1.70fr brown, bl & grn .75 .50

Creation of new towns.

Women and Rainbow — A693

1975, Nov. 8 **Photo.**

1456 A693 1.20fr silver & multi .45 .40

International Women's Year 1975.

Saint-Nazaire Bridge — A694

1975, Nov. 8 **Engr.**

1457 A694 1.40fr bl, ind & grn .60 .30

French and Russian Flags — A695

1975, Nov. 22

1458 A695 1.20fr bl, red & ocher .50 .30

Franco-Soviet diplomatic relations, 50th anniv.

Frigate Melpomene A696

1975, Dec. 6

1459 A696 90c multicolored 1.10 .50

Gallic Coin Type of 1975

1976, Jan. 1 **Typo.** ***Perf. 13½x14***

1460	A663	50c	lt green & brn	1.00	.65
1461	A663	60c	lilac & brn	1.60	.95
1462	A663	90c	orange & brn	2.00	1.25
1463	A663	1.60fr	violet & brn	3.75	1.90
			Nos. 1460-1463 (4)	8.35	4.75

Nos. 1460-1463 are known only precanceled. See second note after No. 132.

Lintel, St. Genis des Fontaines Church A697

Venus of Brassempouy (Paleolithic) — A698

"The Joy of Life," by Robert Delaunay A699

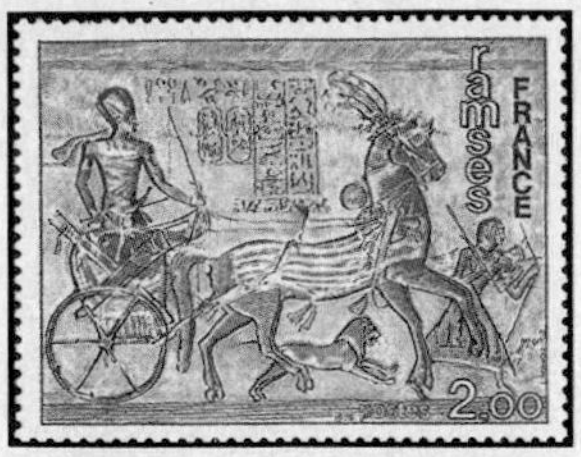

Ramses II, from Abu Simbel Temple, Egypt — A700

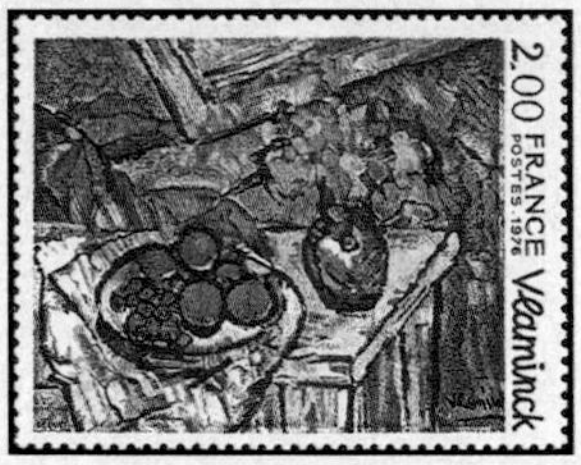

Still Life, by Maurice de Vlaminck — A701

1976 **Engr.** ***Perf. 13***

1464 A697 2fr blue & slate bl 1.10 .60
1465 A698 2fr dk brn & yel 1.10 .60

Photo. ***Perf. 12½x13***

1466 A699 2fr multicolored 1.10 .60

Engr. ***Perf. 13x12½***

1467 A700 2fr multicolored .80 .50

Perf. 13

1468 A701 2fr multicolored .80 .50
Nos. 1464-1468 (5) 4.90 2.80

Issued: No. 1464, 1/24; No. 1465, 3/6; No. 1466, 7/24; No. 1467, 9/4; No. 1468, 12/18.

Tourist Issue

Chateau Fort de Bonaguil A702

Lodève Cathedral — A703

Biarritz A704

Thiers — A705

Ussel — A706

Chateau de Malmaison A707

1976 **Engr.** ***Perf. 13***

1469 A702 1fr multicolored .35 .25
1470 A703 1.10fr violet blue .40 .25
1471 A704 1.40fr multicolored .60 .25
1472 A705 1.70fr multicolored .60 .25
1473 A706 2fr multicolored .90 .25
1474 A707 3fr multicolored 1.10 .25
Nos. 1469-1474 (6) 3.95 1.50

Issued: 1fr, 2fr, 7/10; 1.10fr, 11/13; 1.40fr, 9/25; 1.70fr, 10/9; 3fr, 4/10.

Destroyers, Association Emblem A708

1976, Apr. 24

1475 A708 1fr vio bl, mag & lem .50 .30

Naval Reserve Officers Assoc., 50th anniv.

Gate, Rouen — A709

1976, Apr. 24

1476 A709 80c olive gray & sal .35 .25

49th Congress of the Federation of French Philatelic Societies, Rouen, Apr. 23-May 2.

Young Person — A710

1976, Apr. 27

1477 A710 60c bl grn, ind & car .35 .25

JUVAROUEN 76, International Youth Philatelic Exhibition, Rouen, Apr. 25-May 2.

Europa Issue

Ceramic Pitcher, Strasbourg, 18th Century A711

1.20fr, Sevres porcelain plate & CEPT emblem.

1976, May 8 **Photo.** ***Perf. 13***

1478 A711 80c multicolored *.30* *.30*
1479 A711 1.20fr multicolored *.65* *.55*

Count de Vergennes and Benjamin Franklin — A712

1976, May 15 **Engr.** ***Perf. 13***

1480 A712 1.20fr multicolored .50 .30

American Bicentennial.

A713 A714

Battle of Verdun Memorial

1976, June 12 **Engr.**

1481 A713 1fr multicolored .45 .25

Battle of Verdun, 60th anniversary.

1976, June 12 **Photo.**

1482 A714 1.20fr Communication .50 .40

Troncais Forest — A715 Cross of Lorraine — A716

1976, June 19 **Engr.**

1483 A715 70c green & multi .35 .25

Protection of the environment.

1976, June 19

1484 A716 1fr multicolored .60 .25

Association of Free French, 30th anniv.

Symphonie Communications Satellite — A717

1976, June 26 **Photo.**

1485 A717 1.40fr multicolored .65 .50

French technical achievements.

Gallic Coin Type of 1975

1976, July 1 **Typo.** ***Perf. 13½x14***

1487 A663 52c ver & dk brn .60 .35
1488 A663 62c vio & dk brn 1.10 .70
1489 A663 95c tan & dk brn 1.50 .90
1490 A663 1.70fr dk bl & dk brn 2.75 1.40
Nos. 1487-1490 (4) 5.95 3.35

Nos. 1487-1490 are known only precanceled. See second note after No. 132.

Paris Summer Festival — A719

1976, July 10 **Engr.**

1491 A719 1fr multicolored .65 .30

Summer festival in Tuileries Gardens, Paris.

Emblem and Soldiers A720

1976, July 8

1492 A720 1fr blk, dp bl & mag .50 .25

Officers Reserve Corps, centenary.

Sailing A721

1976, July 17

1493 A721 1.20fr blue, blk & vio .50 .25

21st Olympic Games, Montreal, Canada, July 17-Aug. 1.

Marianne Type of 1971-74

1976 **Typo.** ***Perf. 14x13***

1494 A555 80c green .40 .25

Engr. ***Perf. 13***

1495 A555 80c green 1.25 .50
a. Booklet pane of 10 15.00
1496 A555 1fr carmine rose .55 .25
a. Booklet pane of 5 4.00
b. Booklet pane of 10 8.00
Nos. 1495-1496 (2) 1.80 .75

No. 1495 issued in booklets only. "POSTES" 6mm long on Nos. 1292A and 1494; 4mm on others.

Nos. 1494, 1496 were issued untagged in 1977.

Coil Stamps

1976, Aug. 1 **Engr.** ***Perf. 13 Horiz.***

1497 A555 80c green .80 .55
1498 A555 1fr carmine rose .80 .55

Red control number on back of every 10th stamp.

Woman's Head, by Jean Carzou — A722

1976, Sept. 18 **Engr.** ***Perf. 13x12½***

1499 A722 2fr multicolored .90 .65

Old and New Telephones A723

1976, Sept. 25 **Engr.** ***Perf. 13***

1500 A723 1fr multicolored .40 .25

Centenary of first telephone call by Alexander Graham Bell, Mar. 10, 1876.

Festival Emblem and Trophy, Pyrenees, Hercules and Pyrène — A724

Police Emblem — A725

1976, Oct. 2

1501 A724 1.40fr multicolored .65 .45

10th Intl. Tourist Film Festival, Tarbes, 10/4-10.

1976, Oct. 9 Engr. *Perf. 13*

1502 A725 1.10fr ultra, red & ol .50 .30

National Police, help and protection.

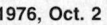

Atomic Particle Accelerator, Diagram A726

1976, Oct. 22 Photo.

1503 A726 1.40fr multicolored .75 .45

European Center for Nuclear Research (CERN).

"Exhibitions" — A727

1976, Nov. 20 Engr. *Perf. 13*

1504 A727 1.50fr multicolored .75 .50

Trade Fairs and Exhibitions.

Abstract Design A728

1976, Nov. 27 Photo.

1505 A728 1.10fr multicolored .50 .40

Customs Service.

Atlantic Museum, Port Louis — A729

1976, Dec. 4 Engr.

1506 A729 1.45fr grnsh bl & olive .65 .50

Regions of France

Réunion A730

Martinique A731

Franche-Comté A732

Brittany A733

Languedoc-Roussillon — A734

Rhône-Alps A735

Champagne-Ardennes A736

Alsace A737

Photo. (1.45fr, 1.50fr, 2.50fr); Engr.

1977 *Perf. 13*

1507	A730	1.45fr	grn & lil rose	.65	.40
1508	A731	1.50fr	multicolored	.65	.60
1509	A732	2.10fr	multicolored	.90	.65
1510	A733	2.40fr	multicolored	1.10	.35
1511	A734	2.50fr	multicolored	1.10	.85
1512	A735	2.75fr	Prus blue	1.40	.80
1513	A736	3.20fr	multicolored	1.40	.80
1514	A737	3.90fr	multicolored	2.50	1.50
			Nos. 1507-1514 (8)	9.70	5.95

Issued: 1.45fr, 2/5; 1.50fr, 1/29; 2.10fr, 1/8; 2.40fr, 2/19; 2.50fr, 1/15; 2.75fr, 1/22; 3.20fr, 4/16; 3.90fr, 2/26.

Pompidou Cultural Center — A738

1977, Feb. 5 Engr. *Perf. 13*

1515 A738 1fr multicolored .35 .25

Inauguration of the Georges Pompidou National Center for Art and Culture, Paris.

Dunkirk Harbor A739

1977, Feb. 12

1516 A739 50c multicolored .25 .25

Expansion of Dunkirk harbor facilities.

Bridge at Mantes, by Corot — A740

Virgin and Child, by Rubens A741

Tridimensional Design, by Victor Vasarely — A742

Head and Eagle, by Pierre-Yves Tremois A743

1977 Engr. *Perf. 13x12½*

1517 A740 2fr multicolored .95 .75

Perf. 12x13

1518 A741 2fr multicolored 1.10 .75

Perf. 12½x13

1519 A742 3fr ultra & sl grn 1.25 .75

Photo.

1520 A743 3fr dark red & blk 1.60 1.25

Nos. 1517-1520 (4) 4.90 3.50

Issue dates: No. 1517, Feb. 12; No. 1518, Nov. 5; No. 1519, Apr. 7; No. 1520, Sept. 17.

Hand Holding Torch and Sword — A744

1977, Mar. 5 Engr. *Perf. 13*

1521 A744 80c ultra & multi .50 .30

"France remembers its dead."

Pisces — A745

Zodiac Signs: 58c, Cancer. 61c, Sagittarius. 68c, Taurus. 73c, Aries. 78c, Libra. 1.05fr, Scorpio. 1.15fr, Capricorn. 1.25fr, Leo. 1.85fr, Aquarius. 2fr, Virgo. 2.10fr, Gemini.

1977-78 Engr. *Perf. 13*

1522	A745	54c	violet blue	.65	.30
1523	A745	58c	emerald	1.00	.40
1524	A745	61c	brt blue	.55	.30
1525	A745	68c	deep brown	.85	.35
1526	A745	73c	rose carmine	1.50	.80
1527	A745	78c	vermilion	.65	.35
1528	A745	1.05fr	brt lilac	1.50	.75
1529	A745	1.15fr	orange	2.25	1.40
1530	A745	1.25fr	lt olive grn	1.25	.60
1531	A745	1.85fr	slate grn	2.75	1.25
1532	A745	2fr	blue green	3.00	1.75
1533	A745	2.10fr	lilac rose	1.65	1.00
			Nos. 1522-1533 (12)	17.60	9.25

Issued: 54c, 68c, 1.05fr, 1.85fr, 4/1/77; others, 1978.

Nos. 1522-1533 are known only precanceled. See second note after No. 132.

Village in Provence A746

Europa: 1.40fr, Brittany port.

1977, Apr. 23

1534 A746 1fr multicolored *.45 .25*

1535 A746 1.40fr multicolored *1.00 .35*

Flowers and Gardening A747

1977, Apr. 23 Engr. *Perf. 13*

1536 A747 1.70fr multicolored .80 .50

National Horticulture Society, centenary.

Symbolic Flower A748

1977, May 7

1537 A748 1.40fr multicolored .65 .45

Intl. Flower Show, Nantes, May 12-23.

Battle of Cambray
A749

1977, May 14

1538 A749 80c multicolored .40 .30

Capture of Cambray and the incorporation of Cambresis District into France, 300th anniv.

Carmes Church, School, Map of France
A750

Modern Constructions
A751

1977, May 14

1539 A750 1.10fr multicolored .50 .30

Catholic Institutes in France.

1977, May 21

1540 A751 1.10fr multicolored .55 .30

European Federation of the Construction Industry.

Annecy Castle
A752

1977, May 28

1541 A752 1fr multicolored .60 .30

Congress of the Federation of French Philatelic Societies, Annecy, May 28-30.

Tourist Issue

Abbey, Pont-à-Mousson — A753

Abbey Tower, Saint-Amand-les-Eaux
A754

Collegiate Church of Dorat
A755

Fontenay Abbey
A756

Bayeux Cathedral — A757

Chateau de Vitré
A758

1977	**Engr.**		***Perf. 13***	
1542 A753	1.25fr multicolored		.50	.30
1543 A754	1.40fr multicolored		.50	.30
1544 A755	1.45fr multicolored		.55	.35
1545 A756	1.50fr multicolored		.55	.25
1546 A757	1.90fr black & yel		.75	.30
1547 A758	2.40fr black & yel		.80	.30
	Nos. 1542-1547 (6)		3.65	1.80

Issued: 1.25fr, 10/1; 1.40fr, 9/17; 1.45fr, 7/16; 1.50fr, 6/4; 1.90fr, 7/9; 2.40fr, 9/24.

Polytechnic School and "X" — A759

1977, June 4 **Engr.** ***Perf. 13***

1548 A759 1.70fr multicolored .70 .30

Relocation at Palaiseau of Polytechnic School, founded 1794.

Soccer and Cup — A760

1977, June 11

1549 A760 80c multicolored .90 .50

Soccer Cup of France, 60th anniversary.

De Gaulle Memorial — A761

Stylized Map of France — A762

Photo. & Embossed

1977, June 18

1550 A761 1fr gold & multi 1.00 .50

5th anniversary of dedication of De Gaulle memorial at Colombey-les-Deux-Eglises.

1977, June 18 **Engr.** ***Perf. 13***

1551 A762 1.10fr ultra & red .55 .30

French Junior Chamber of Commerce.

Battle of Nancy
A763

Arms of Burgundy
A764

1977, June 25

1552 A763 1.10fr blue & slate 1.10 .40

Battle of Nancy between the Dukes of Burgundy and Lorraine, 500th anniversary.

1977, July 2

1553 A764 1.25fr ol brn & slate grn .55 .25

Annexation of Burgundy by the French Crown, 500th anniversary.

Association Emblem
A765

1977, July 8

1554 A765 1.40fr ultra, olive & red .55 .25

French-speaking Parliamentary Association.

Red Cicada — A766

1977, Sept. 10 **Photo.** ***Perf. 13***

1555 A766 80c multicolored .55 .30

Nature protection.

French Handicrafts
A767

1977, Oct. 1 **Engr.** ***Perf. 13***

1556 A767 1.40fr multicolored .65 .45

French craftsmen.

Industry and Agriculture — A768

1977, Oct. 22

1557 A768 80c brown & olive .30 .25

Economic & Social Council, 30th anniv.

Table Tennis
A769

1977, Dec. 17 **Engr.** ***Perf. 13***

1558 A769 1.10fr multicolored 3.25 1.00

French Table Tennis Federation, 50th anniv., and French team, gold medal winner, Birmingham.

Abstract, by Roger Excoffon — A770

1977, Dec. 17 ***Perf. 13x12½***

1559 A770 3fr multicolored 2.00 1.00

Sabine, after David — A771

1977-78		**Engr.**	***Perf. 13***	
1560	A771	1c slate	.25	.25
1561	A771	2c brt violet	.25	.25
1562	A771	5c slate green	.25	.25
1563	A771	10c red brown	.25	.25
1564	A771	15c Prus blue	.25	.25
1565	A771	20c brt green	.25	.25
1566	A771	30c orange	.25	.25
1567	A771	50c red lilac	.25	.25
1568	A771	80c green	.80	.25
a.		Booklet pane of 10	8.00	
1569	A771	80c olive	.30	.25
1570	A771	1fr red	1.00	.25
a.		Booklet pane of 5	5.00	
b.		Booklet pane of 10	10.00	
1571	A771	1fr green	.55	.25
a.		Booklet pane of 10	5.50	
1572	A771	1.20fr red	.55	.25
a.		Booklet pane of 5	4.25	
b.		Booklet pane of 10	7.75	
1573	A771	1.40fr brt blue	1.75	.25
1574	A771	1.70fr grnsh blue	.70	.25
1575	A771	2fr emerald	.70	.25
1576	A771	2.10fr lilac rose	.75	.25
1577	A771	3fr dark brown	1.00	.30
		Nos. 1560-1577 (18)	10.10	4.55

Issued: Nos. 1560-1567, 1573, 1575, 1577, 4/3/78; Nos. 1568, 1570, 12/19/77; Nos. 1569, 1571, 1572, 1574, 1576, 6/5/78.

Coil Stamps

1978		***Perf. 13 Horiz.***		
1578	A771	80c bright green	1.40	1.00
1579	A771	1fr bright green	1.10	1.00
1579A	A771	1fr bright red	1.40	1.00
1579B	A771	1.20fr bright red	1.10	1.00
		Nos. 1578-1579B (4)	5.00	4.00

See Nos. 1658-1677, 3527, 4410g, 4520.

For similar design inscribed "REPUBLIQUE FRANCAISE" see type A900.

Percheron, by Jacques Birr
A772

Osprey — A773

1978 **Photo.** ***Perf. 13***
1580 A772 1.70fr multicolored 1.00 .80
Engr.
1581 A773 1.80fr multicolored .90 .50

Nature protection.
Issue dates: 1.70fr, Jan. 7; 1.80fr, Oct. 14.

Tournament, 1662, Etching — A774

Institut de France and Pont des Arts, Paris, by Bernard Buffet — A776

Horses, by Yves Brayer — A777

1978 **Engr.** ***Perf. 12x13***
1582 A774 2fr black 3.00 1.25
Perf. 13x12
1584 A776 3fr multicolored 2.75 1.40
1585 A777 3fr multicolored 2.00 1.20
Nos. 1582-1585 (3) 7.75 3.85

Issued: 2fr, 1/14; No. 1584, 2/4; No. 1585, 12/9.

Communications School and Tower — A778

1978, Jan. 19 **Engr.** ***Perf. 13***
1586 A778 80c Prussian blue .30 .25

Natl. Telecommunications School, cent.

Swedish and French Flags, Map of Saint Barthelemy A779

1978, Jan. 19
1587 A779 1.10fr multicolored .45 .25

Centenary of the reunion with France of Saint Barthelemy Island, West Indies.

Regions of France

Ile de France — A780

Tanker, Refinery, Flower, Upper Normandy A781

Lower Normandy A782

1978 **Photo.** ***Perf. 13***
1588 A780 1fr red, blue & blk .40 .25
Engr.
1589 A781 1.40fr multicolored .70 .30
Photo.
1590 A782 1.70fr multicolored 1.00 .50
Nos. 1588-1590 (3) 2.10 1.05

Issued: 1fr, 3/4; 1.40fr, 1/21; 1.70fr, 3/31.

Stylized Map of France A788

Young Stamp Collector A789

1978, Feb. 11 **Engr.** ***Perf. 13***
1596 A788 1.10fr violet & green .45 .25

Program of administrative changes, 15th anniv.

1978, Feb. 25
1597 A789 80c multicolored .30 .25

JUVEXNIORT, Youth Philatelic Exhibition, Niort, Feb. 25-March 5.

Tourist Issue

Verdon Gorge — A790

Saint-Saturnin Church — A792

Pont Neuf, Paris A791

Our Lady of Bec-Hellouin Abbey — A793

Chateau D'Esquelbecq — A794

Aubazine Abbey A795

Fontevraud Abbey A796

1978 **Engr.** ***Perf. 13***
1598 A790 50c multicolored .25 .25
1599 A791 80c multicolored .35 .25
1600 A792 1fr black .35 .25
1601 A793 1.10fr multicolored .50 .25
1602 A794 1.10fr multicolored .50 .25
1603 A795 1.25fr carmine & brn .85 .30
1604 A796 1.70fr multicolored .90 .40
Nos. 1598-1604 (7) 3.70 1.95

Issued: 1.25fr, 2/18; 50c, 3/6; No. 1601, 3/26; 80c, 5/27; 1fr, 6/10; 1.70fr, 6/3; No. 1602, 6/17.

Fish and Corals — A797

1978, Apr. 15 **Photo.** ***Perf. 13***
1605 A797 1.25fr multicolored 1.00 .85

Port Cros National Park, 15th anniversary.

Flowers, Butterflies and Houses — A798

1978, Apr. 22 **Engr.** ***Perf. 13***
1606 A798 1.70fr multicolored 2.75 .35

Beautification of France campaign, 50th anniv.

Hands Shielding Source of Heat and Light A799

1978, Apr. 22
1607 A799 1fr multicolored .60 .25

Energy conservation.

World War I Memorial near Lens — A800

Fountain of the Innocents, Paris — A801

1978, May 6
1608 A800 2fr lemon & magenta 1.00 .30

Colline Notre Dame de Lorette memorial of World War I.

1978, May 6

Europa: 1.40fr, Flower Park Fountain, Paris.

1609 A801 1fr multicolored *.40* .25
1610 A801 1.40fr multicolored *.90* *.50*

Maurois Palace, Troyes — A802

1978, May 13
1611 A802 1fr multicolored .45 .25

51st Congress of the Federation of French Philatelic Societies, Troyes, May 13-15.

Roland Garros Tennis Court and Player — A803

1978, May 27
1612 A803 1fr multicolored 2.50 .40

Roland Garros Tennis Court, 50th anniv.

Hand and Plant — A804

Printing Office Emblem — A805

1978, Sept. 9 **Engr.** ***Perf. 13***
1613 A804 1.30fr brown, red & grn .50 .25

Encouragement of handicrafts.

1978, Sept. 23
1614 A805 1fr multicolored .50 .25

National Printing Office, established 1538.

Fortress, Besançon, and Collegiate Church, Dole — A806

Valenciennes and Maubeuge — A807

1978

1615 A806 1.20fr multicolored .55 .25
1616 A807 1.20fr multicolored .55 .25

Reunion of Franche-Comté and Valenciennes and Maubeuge with France, 300th anniversary.

Issued: No. 1615, 9/23; No. 1616, 9/30.

Sower Type of 1906-1937 and Academy Emblem — A808

1978, Oct. 7

1617 A808 1fr multicolored .45 .30

Academy of Philately, 50th anniversary.

Gymnasts, Strasbourg Cathedral, Storks — A809

1978, Oct. 21

1618 A809 1fr multicolored .70 .30

19th World Gymnastics Championships, Strasbourg, Oct. 23-26.

Various Sports A810

Polish Veterans' Monument A811

1978, Oct. 21

1619 A810 1fr multicolored 1.10 .40

Sports for all.

1978, Nov. 11

1620 A811 1.70fr multicolored .60 .40

Polish veterans of World War II.

Railroad Car and Monument, Compiègne Forest, Rethondes A812

1978, Nov. 11 **Engr.** ***Perf. 13***

1621 A812 1.20fr indigo .75 .30

60th anniversary of World War I armistice.

Handicapped People — A813

1978, Nov. 18

1622 A813 1fr multicolored .45 .25

Rehabilitation of the handicapped.

Human Rights Emblem A814

1978, Dec. 9 **Engr.** ***Perf. 13***

1623 A814 1.70fr dk brown & blue .80 .40

30th anniversary of Universal Declaration of Human Rights.

Child and IYC Emblem A815

1979, Jan. 6 **Engr.** ***Perf. 13***

1624 A815 1.70fr multicolored 3.50 2.00

International Year of the Child.

"Music," 15th Century Miniature — A816

1979, Jan. 13 ***Perf. 13x12½***

1625 A816 2fr multicolored 1.25 .90

Diana Taking a Bath, d'Ecouen Castle A817

Church at Auvers-on-Oise, by Vincent Van Gogh — A818

Head of Marianne, by Salvador Dali A819

Fire Dancer from The Magic Flute, by Chaplain Midy A820

1979 **Photo.** ***Perf. 12½x13***

1626 A817 2fr multicolored 1.40 1.00
1627 A818 2fr multicolored 5.00 1.25
1628 A819 3fr multicolored 1.50 1.00
1629 A820 3fr multicolored 1.50 1.00
Nos. 1626-1629 (4) 9.40 4.25

Issued: No. 1626, 9/22; No. 1627, 10/27; No. 1628, 11/19; No. 1629, 11/26.

Orange Agaric — A821

Mushrooms: 83c, Death trumpet. 1.30fr, Olive wood pleurotus. 2.25fr, Cauliflower claveria.

1979, Jan. 15 **Engr.** ***Perf. 13***

1630 A821 64c orange .40 .25
1631 A821 83c brown .40 .25
1632 A821 1.30fr yellow bister .85 .40
1633 A821 2.25fr brown purple 1.25 .85
Nos. 1630-1633 (4) 2.90 1.75

Nos. 1630-1633 are known only precanceled. See second note after No. 132.

Victor Segalen A822

1979, Jan. 20

1634 A822 1.50fr multicolored .50 .30

Physician, explorer and writer (1878-1919).

Hibiscus and Palms — A823

1979, Feb. 3

1635 A823 35c multicolored .25 .25

International Flower Festival, Martinique.

Buddha, Stupas, Temple of Borobudur A824

1979, Feb. 24

1636 A824 1.80fr ol & slate grn .85 .40

Save the Temple of Borobudur, Java, campaign.

Boy, by Francisque Poulbot (1879-1946) A825

1979, Mar. 24 **Photo.**

1637 A825 1.30fr multicolored .60 .25

Tourist Issue

Chateau de Maisons, Laffitte A826

Bernay and St. Pierre sur Dives Abbeys — A827

View of Auray — A827a

Steenvorde Windmill — A828

Wall Painting, Niaux Cave A829

Royal Palace, Perpignan A830

1979 Engr. *Perf. 13*

1638	A826	45c multicolored	.30	.25
1639	A827	1fr multicolored	.45	.25
1640	A827a	1fr multicolored	.45	.25
1641	A828	1.20fr multicolored	.55	.25
1642	A829	1.50fr multicolored	.70	.40
1643	A830	1.70fr multicolored	.75	.60
		Nos. 1638-1643 (6)	3.20	2.00

Issued: 45c, 10/6; No. 1639, 6/16; No. 1640, 6/30; 1.20fr, 6/12; 1.50fr, 7/9; 1.70fr, 4/21.

Honey Bee A831

1979, Mar. 31 Engr. *Perf. 13*

1644 A831 1fr multicolored .70 .30

Nature protection.

St. Germain des Prés Abbey A832

1979, Apr. 21

1645 A832 1.40fr multicolored .50 .30

Simoun Mail Monoplanes, 1935, and Map of Mail Routes — A833

Europa: 1.70fr, Floating spheres used on Seine during siege of Paris, 1870.

1979, Apr. 28

1646	A833	1.20fr multicolored	*.75*	*.35*
1647	A833	1.70fr multicolored	*1.00*	*.50*

Ship and View of Nantes A834

1979, May 5 Engr. *Perf. 13*

1648 A834 1.20fr multicolored .55 .30

52nd National Congress of French Philatelic Societies, Nantes, May 5-7.

Royal Palace, 1789 — A835

1979, May 19

1649 A835 1fr car rose & pur .40 .25

European Elections A836

1979, May 19 Photo. *Perf. 13*

1650 A836 1.20fr multicolored .50 .25

European Parliament, 1st direct elections, June 10.

Joan of Arc Monument A837

1979, May 24 Engr.

1651 A837 1.70fr brt lilac rose .70 .40

Joan of Arc, the Maid of Orleans (1412-1431).

Felix Guyon and Catheters A840

1979, June 23

1652 A840 1.80fr sepia & blue .60 .25

Felix Guyon (1831-1920), urologist.

Lantern Tower, La Rochelle A841

Telecom '79 A842

Towers: 88c, Chartres Cathedral. 1.40fr, Bourges Cathedral. 2.35fr, Amiens Cathedral.

1979, Aug. 13 Engr. *Perf. 13*

1653	A841	68c vio brn & blk	.30	.30
1654	A841	88c ultra & blk	.40	.30
1655	A841	1.40fr gray grn & blk	.65	.50
1656	A841	2.35fr dull brn & blk	1.10	.60
		Nos. 1653-1656 (4)	2.45	1.70

Nos. 1653-1656 are known only precanceled. See second note after No. 132. See Nos. 1684-1687, 1719-1722, 1814-1817.

1979, Sept. 22

1657 A842 1.10fr multicolored .40 .25

3rd World Telecommunications Exhibition.

Sabine Type of 1977-78

1979-81 Engr. *Perf. 13*

1658	A771	40c brown ('81)	.25	.25
1659	A771	60c red brn ('81)	.25	.25
1660	A771	70c violet blue	.30	.25
1661	A771	90c brt lilac ('81)	.40	.30
1662	A771	1fr gray olive	.45	.25
1663	A771	1.10fr green	.55	.25
1664	A771	1.20fr green ('80)	.40	.25
1665	A771	1.30fr rose red	.55	.25
1666	A771	1.40fr rose red ('80)	.50	.25
1667	A771	1.60fr purple	.75	.30
1668	A771	1.80fr ocher	.65	.60
1669	A771	3.50fr lt ol grn ('81)	1.25	.60
1670	A771	4fr brt car ('81)	1.40	.40
1671	A771	5fr brt grnsh bl ('81)	1.75	.30
		Nos. 1658-1671 (14)	9.45	4.50

Coil Stamps

1979-80 *Perf. 13 Horiz.*

1674	A771	1.10fr green	1.75	.60
1675	A771	1.20fr green ('80)	.65	.50
1676	A771	1.30fr rose red	1.75	.60
1677	A771	1.40fr rose red ('80)	.90	.40
		Nos. 1674-1677 (4)	5.05	2.10

Lorraine Region — A845

1979, Nov. 10

1678 A845 2.30fr multicolored 1.00 .30

Gears A847

1979, Nov. 17 *Perf. 13*

1680 A847 1.80fr multicolored .70 .30

Central Technical School of Paris, 150th anniv.

Judo Throw A848

1979, Nov. 24 Engr.

1681 A848 1.60fr multicolored .60 .40

World Judo Championships, Paris, Dec.

Violins — A849

1979, Dec. 10

1682 A849 1.30fr multicolored .60 .35

Eurovision A850

1980, Jan. 12 Engr. *Perf. 13x13½*

1683 A850 1.80fr multicolored 1.00 .70

Tower Type of 1979

Designs: 76c, Chateau d'Angers. 99c, Chateau de Kerjean. 1.60fr, Chateau de Pierrefonds. 2.65fr, Chateau de Tarascon.

1980, Jan. 21 Engr.

1684	A841	76c grnsh bl & blk	.35	.30
1685	A841	99c slate grn & blk	.45	.30
1686	A841	1.60fr red & blk	.75	.55
1687	A841	2.65fr brn org & blk	1.25	.65
		Nos. 1684-1687 (4)	2.80	1.80

Nos. 1684-1687 are known only precanceled. See second note after No. 132.

Self-portrait, by Albrecht Dürer, Philexfrance '82 Emblem — A851

Woman Holding Fan, by Ossip Zadkine A852

Abstract, by Raoul Ubak — A853

Hommage to J.S. Bach, by Jean Picart Le Doux — A854

Peasant, by Louis Le Nain A855

Woman with Blue Eyes, by Modigliani A856

Abstract, by Hans Hartung A857

Engraved, Photogravure (#1691, 1694)

1980 *Perf. 12½x13, 13x12½*

1688 A851 2fr multicolored 1.00 .90
1689 A852 3fr multicolored 1.50 1.00
1690 A853 3fr multicolored 1.50 1.00
1691 A854 3fr multicolored 1.50 1.00
1692 A855 3fr multicolored 1.50 1.00
1693 A856 4fr multicolored 3.00 1.25
1694 A857 4fr ultra & black 2.00 1.25
Nos. 1688-1694 (7) 12.00 7.40

Issued: No. 1688, 6/7; No. 1689, 1/19; No. 1690, 2/2; No. 1691, 9/20; No. 1693, 10/26; No. 1692, 11/10; No. 1694, 12/20.

Giants of the North Festival — A858

French Cuisine — A859

1980, Feb. 16 *Perf. 13*
1695 A858 1.60fr multicolored .75 .35

1980, Feb. 23
1696 A859 90c red & lt brown .80 .40

Woman Embroidering A860

Photogravure and Engraved

1980, Mar. 29 *Perf. 13*
1697 A860 1.10fr multicolored .50 .30

Fight Against Cigarette Smoking — A861

1980, Apr. 5 **Photo.** *Perf. 13*
1698 A861 1.30fr multicolored .50 .25

Aristide Briand — A862

Europa: 1.80fr, St. Benedict.

1980, Apr. 26 **Engr.** *Perf. 13*
1699 A862 1.30fr multicolored .60 .30
1700 A862 1.80fr red & red brown .85 .50

Aristide Briand (1862-1932), prime minister, 1909-1911, 1921-1922; St. Benedict, patron saint of Europe.

Liancourt, College, Map of Northwestern France — A863

1980, May 19 **Engr.** *Perf. 13*
1701 A863 2fr dk green & pur .80 .35

National College of Arts and Handicrafts (founded by Larochefoucauld Liancourt) bicentenary.

Cranes, Town Hall Tower, Dunkirk — A864

1980, May 24
1702 A864 1.30fr multicolored .60 .25

53rd Natl. Congress of French Federation of Philatelic Societies, Dunkirk, May 24-26.

Tourist Issue

Chateau de Maintenon A866

Cordes A865

Montauban A867

St. Peter's Abbey, Solesmes A868

Puy Cathedral A869

1980 **Engr.** *Perf. 13*
1703 A865 1.50fr multicolored .55 .30
1704 A866 2fr multicolored .70 .30
1705 A867 2.30fr multicolored .75 .30
1706 A868 2.50fr multicolored .85 .30
1707 A869 3.20fr multicolored 1.20 .50
Nos. 1703-1707 (5) 4.05 1.70

Issued: No. 1703, 4/5; No. 1704, 6/7; No. 1705, 5/7; No. 1706, 9/20; No. 1707, 5/12.

Graellsia Isabellae A870

1980, May 31 **Photo.**
1708 A870 1.10fr multicolored .75 .35

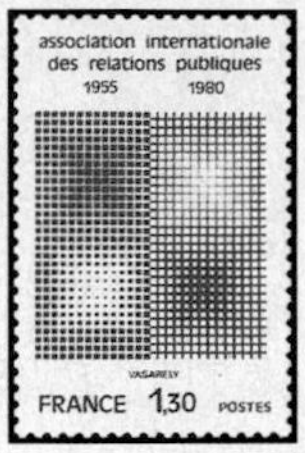

Association Emblem — A871

1980, June 10 **Photo.**
1709 A871 1.30fr red & blue .50 .25

Intl. Public Relations Assoc., 25th anniv.

Marianne, French Architecture A872

1980, June 21 **Engr.**
1710 A872 1.50fr bluish & gray blk .70 .30

Heritage Year.

Earth Sciences A873

1980, July 5
1711 A873 1.60fr dk brown & red .60 .50

International Geological Congress.

Rochambeau's Landing — A874

1980, July 15
1712 A874 2.50fr multicolored 1.10 .50

Rochambeau's landing at Newport, R.I. (American Revolution), bicentenary.

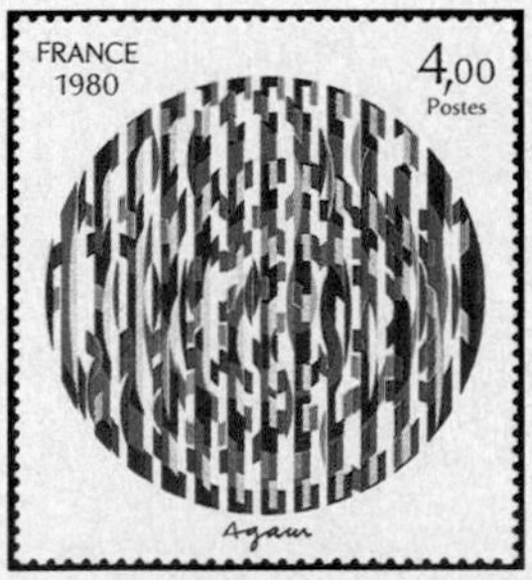

Message of Peace, by Yaacov Agam — A875

1980, Oct. 4 **Photo.** *Perf. 11½x13*
1713 A875 4fr multicolored 2.00 1.00

French Golf Federation A876

1980, Oct. 18 **Engr.**
1714 A876 1.40fr multicolored .65 .30

Comedie Francaise, 300th Anniversary A877

1980, Oct. 18
1715 A877 2fr multicolored .70 .40

Charles de Gaulle — A878

1980, Nov. 10 **Photo.** *Perf. 13*
1716 A878 1.40fr multicolored 1.00 .50

40th anniversary of De Gaulle's appeal of June 18, and 10th anniversary of his death.

Guardsman — A879

1980, Nov. 24 **Engr.** *Perf. 13*
1717 A879 1.70fr multicolored .80 .45

Rambouillet Chateau A880

1980, Dec. 6 **Engr.** *Perf. 13*
1718 A880 2.20fr multicolored 1.00 .35

Tower Type of 1979

Designs: 88c, Imperial Chapel, Ajaccio. 1.14fr, Astronomical Clock, Besancon. 1.84fr, Coucy Castle ruins. 3.05fr, Font-de-Gaume cave drawing, Les Eyzies de Tayac.

1981, Jan. 11 **Engr.** *Perf. 13*
1719 A841 88c dp mag & blk .40 .25
1720 A841 1.14fr ultra & blk .55 .30
1721 A841 1.84fr dk green & blk .85 .50
1722 A841 3.05fr brn red & blk 1.40 .80
Nos. 1719-1722 (4) 3.20 1.85

Nos. 1719-1722 are known only precanceled. See second note after No. 132.

Microelectronics — A881

1981 **Photo.**
1723 A881 1.20fr shown .75 .30
1724 A881 1.20fr Biology .55 .30
1725 A881 1.40fr Energy .65 .30

1726 A881 1.80fr Marine exploration .85 .50
1727 A881 2fr Telemetry .90 .65
Nos. 1723-1727 (5) 3.70 2.05

Issue dates: No. 1723, 2/5; others, 3/28.

Abstract, by Albert Gleizes A882

1981, Feb. 28 ***Perf. 12½x13***
1728 A882 4fr multicolored 2.00 .90

The Footpath by Camille Pissaro — A883

1981, Apr. 18 **Engr.** ***Perf. 13x12½***
1729 A883 2fr multicolored 1.25 .90

Child Watering Smiling Map of France — A884

1981, Mar. 14 **Engr.** ***Perf. 13***
1730 A884 1.40fr multicolored .65 .25

Sully Chateau, Rosny-sur-Seine — A885

1981, Mar. 21
1731 A885 2.50fr multicolored .90 .40

Tourist Issue

Roman Temple, Nimes — A886

Church of St. Jean, Lyon — A887

St. Anne d'Auray Basilica — A888

Vaucelles Abbey A889

Notre Dame of Louviers A890

1981, Apr. 11 **Engr.** ***Perf. 13***
1732 A886 1.70fr multicolored .85 .30

1981
1733 A887 1.40fr dk red & dk brn .65 .30
1734 A888 2.20fr blue & black .90 .40

Issue dates: 1.40fr, May 30; 2.20fr, July 4.

1981
1735 A889 2fr red & black .90 .40
1736 A890 2.20fr red brn & dk brn 1.00 .50
Nos. 1732-1736 (5) 4.30 1.90

Issue dates: 2fr, Sept. 19; 2.20fr, Sept. 26.

Europa Issue

Folkdances A891

1981, May 4 ***Perf. 13***
1737 A891 1.40fr Bouree *.65 .25*
1738 A891 2fr Sardane *1.25 .40*

Bookbinding A892

Cadets A893

1981, Apr. 4 ***Perf. 13***
1739 A892 1.50fr olive & car rose .70 .40

1981, May 16
1740 A893 2.50fr multicolored .90 .30

Military College at St. Maixent centenary.

Man Drawing Geometric Diagram — A894

1981, May 23 **Photo.**
1741 A894 2fr shown 1.40 .90
1742 A894 2fr Faces 1.40 .90
a. Pair, #1741-1742 + label 3.50 3.00

PHILEXFRANCE '82 Stamp Exhibition, Paris, June 11-21, 1982.

Theophraste Renaudot and Emile de Girardin — A895

Public Gardens, Vichy — A896

1981, May 30 **Engr.**
1743 A895 2.20fr black & red .80 .30

350th anniversary of La Gazette (founded by Renaudot), and death centenary of founder of Le Journal (de Girardin).

1981, June 6
1744 A896 1.40fr multicolored .65 .30

54th National Congress of French Federation of Philatelic Societies, Vichy.

Higher National College for Commercial Studies Centenary A897

1981, June 20 ***Perf. 13***
1745 A897 1.40fr multicolored .55 .30

Sea Shore Conservation — A898

1981, June 20
1746 A898 1.60fr multicolored .75 .55

World Fencing Championship, Clermont-Ferrand, July 2-13 — A899

1981, June 27
1747 A899 1.80fr multicolored .85 .45

Sabine, after David — A900

1981, Sept. 1 **Engr.**
1755 A900 1.40fr green .85 .25
1756 A900 1.60fr red 1.00 .25
1757 A900 2.30fr blue 1.40 .85
Nos. 1755-1757 (3) 3.25 1.35

Coil Stamps

1981 **Engr.** ***Perf. 13 Horiz.***
1758 A900 1.40fr green .75 .50
1759 A900 1.60fr red .75 .40

Highway Safety ("Drink or Drive") A901

1981, Sept. 5 ***Perf. 13***
1768 A901 1.60fr multicolored .75 .35

45th Intl. PEN Club Congress A902

Jules Ferry, Statesman A903

1981, Sept. 19 ***Perf. 13***
1769 A902 2fr multicolored .75 .35

1981, Sept. 26 ***Perf. 12½x13***
1770 A903 1.60fr multicolored .75 .35

Free compulsory public school centenary.

Natl. Savings Bank Centenary A904

1981, Sept. 21 **Photo.** ***Perf. 13***
1771 A904 1.40fr multicolored .65 .25
1772 A904 1.60fr multicolored .75 .25

The Divers, by Edouard Pignon — A905

1981, Oct. 3 ***Perf. 13x12½***
1773 A905 4fr multicolored 1.75 .90

Alleluia, by Alfred Manessier A906

1981, Dec. 19 **Photo.** ***Perf. 12x13***
1774 A906 4fr multicolored 1.75 .90

Tourist Issue

Saint-Emilion — A907

Crest — A908

1981 **Engr.** ***Perf. 13x12½***
1775 A907 2.60fr dk red & lt ol grn 1.10 .35
Perf. 13
1776 A908 2.90fr dk green 1.20 .25

Issued: No. 1775, 10/10; No. 1776, 11/28.

150th Anniv. of Naval Academy A909

1981, Oct. 17 ***Perf. 13***
1777 A909 1.40fr multicolored .65 .35

A910

A911

St. Hubert Kneeling before the Stag, 15th cent. sculpture.

1981, Oct. 24
1778 A910 1.60fr multicolored .75 .35

Museum of hunting and nature.

1981, Nov. 2

V. Schoelcher, J. Jaures, J. Moulin, the Pantheon.

1779 A911 1.60fr blue & dull pur .75 .30

Intl. Year of the Disabled A912

1981, Nov. 7
1780 A912 1.60fr multicolored .50 .25

Men Leading Cattle, 2nd Cent. Roman Mosaic — A913

1981, Nov. 14 ***Perf. 13x12***
1781 A913 2fr multicolored 1.10 .90

Virgil's birth bimillennium.

Martyrs of Chateaubriant A914

1981, Dec. 12 **Engr.** ***Perf. 13***
1782 A914 1.40fr multicolored .55 .25

Liberty, after Delacroix — A915

1982 **Engr.** ***Perf. 13***

1783	A915	5c	dk green	.25	.25
1784	A915	10c	dull red	.25	.25
1785	A915	15c	brt rose lilac	.35	.35
1786	A915	20c	brt green	.25	.25
1787	A915	30c	orange	.25	.25
1788	A915	40c	brown	.25	.25
a.	Bklt. pane of 5, 4 No. 1784, No. 1788 ('87)			1.00	
1789	A915	50c	lilac	.25	.25
1790	A915	60c	lt red brn	.30	.25
1791	A915	70c	ultra	.30	.25
1792	A915	80c	lt olive grn	.35	.25
1793	A915	90c	brt lilac	.40	.25
1794	A915	1fr	olive green	.45	.25
1795	A915	1.40fr	green	.65	.25
1796	A915	1.60fr	green	.75	.25
1797	A915	1.60fr	red	.75	.25
1798	A915	1.80fr	red	.85	.25
1799	A915	2fr	brt yel grn	.90	.25
1800	A915	2.30fr	blue	2.00	1.25
1801	A915	2.60fr	blue	2.00	1.00
1802	A915	3fr	chocolate	1.40	.30
1803	A915	4fr	brt carmine	1.90	.30
1804	A915	5fr	gray blue	2.25	.25
	Nos. 1783-1804 (22)			17.10	7.45

Coil Stamps

Perf. 13 Horiz.

1805	A915	1.40fr	green	1.25	.90
1806	A915	1.60fr	red	1.25	.90
1807	A915	1.60fr	green	.85	.50
1807A	A915	1.80fr	red	.90	.50
	Nos. 1805-1807A (4)			4.25	2.80

Issued: 5c-50c, 1fr-1.40fr, 2fr, 2.30fr, 5fr, No. 1797, 1/2; 1.80fr, 2.60fr, No. 1796, 6/1; 60c-90c, 3fr, 4fr, 11/3.

See Nos. 1878-1897A, 2077-2080, 3528, 4410h, 4521. For surcharge see No. 2115.

Tourist Issue

St. Pierre and Miquelon A916

Corsica A917

Renaissance Fountain, Aix-en Provence — A918

Collonges-la-Rouge — A919

Castle of Henry IV, Pau A920

Lille — A921

Chateau Ripaille, Haute-Savoie — A921a

1982 **Engr.** ***Perf. 12½***
1808 A916 1.60fr dk blue & blk .75 .25
1809 A917 1.90fr blue & red .90 .25
Perf. 13
1810 A918 2fr multicolored .90 .40
1811 A919 3fr multicolored 1.40 .30
1812 A920 3fr ultra & dk bl 1.40 .40

Issued: 1.60fr, 1.90fr, Jan. 9; 2fr, June 21, No. 1811, July 5, No. 1812, May 15.

1982 ***Perf. 13x12½***
1813 A921 1.80fr dull red & ol .85 .25
1813A A921a 2.90fr multicolored 1.40 .80
Nos. 1808-1813A (7) 7.60 2.65

Issue dates: 1.80fr, Oct. 16; 2.90fr, Sept. 4.

Tower Type of 1979

97c, Tanlay Castle, Yonne. 1.25fr, Salses Fort, Pyrenees-Orientales. 2.03fr, Montlhery Tower, Essonne. 3.36fr, Chateau d'If Bouches-du-Rhone.

1982, Jan. 11 **Engr.** ***Perf. 13***
1814 A841 97c olive grn & blk .45 .25
1815 A841 1.25fr red & blk .55 .25
1816 A841 2.03fr sepia & blk .95 .50
1817 A841 3.36fr ultra & blk 1.50 .80
Nos. 1814-1817 (4) 3.45 1.80

Nos. 1814-1817 are known only precanceled. See second note after No. 132.

800th Birth Anniv. of St. Francis of Assisi A922

1982, Feb. 6 **Photo. & Engr.**
1818 A922 2fr black & blue .90 .50

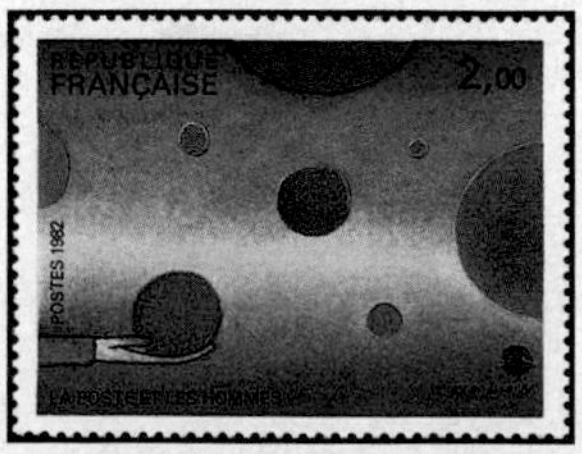

Posts and Mankind — A923

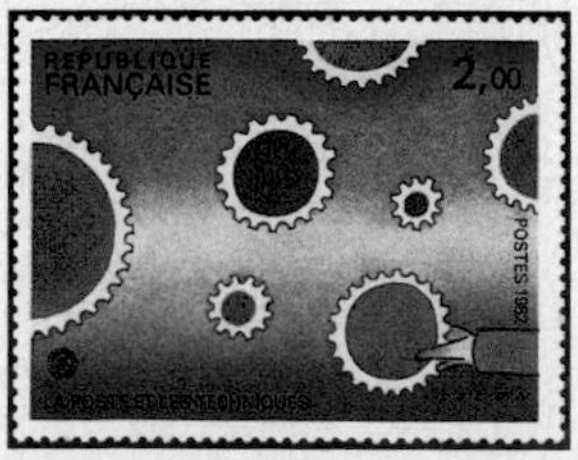

Posts and Technology — A924

1982, Feb. 13 **Photo.**
1819 A923 2fr multicolored 3.50 2.00
1820 A924 2fr multicolored 3.50 2.00
a. Pair, #1819-1820 + label 9.00 6.50

PHILEXFRANCE '82 Stamp Exhibition, Paris, June 11-21.

Souvenir Sheet

Marianne, by Jean Cocteau — A925

1982, June 11
1821 A925 Sheet of 2 14.00 14.00
a. 4fr red & blue 6.00 6.00
b. 6fr blue & red 6.00 6.00

Sold only with 20fr show admission ticket.

Scouting Year A926

1982, Feb. 20 **Engr.**
1822 A926 2.30fr yel grn & blk .90 .30

31st Natl. Census — A927

1982, Feb. 27 **Photo.**
1823 A927 1.60fr multicolored .60 .25

Bale-Mulhouse Airport Opening — A928

1982, Mar. 15 **Engr.** ***Perf. 13***
1824 A928 1.90fr multicolored .90 .50

Fight Against Racism A929

1982, Mar. 20
1825 A929 2.30fr brn & red org 1.00 .50

Blacksmith — A930

1982, Apr. 17
1826 A930 1.40fr multicolored .65 .40

Europa 1982 A931

1982, Apr. 24
1827 A931 1.60fr Treaty of Rome, 1957 .75 .30
1828 A931 2.30fr Treaty of Verdun, 843 1.00 .40

1982 World Cup A932

1982, Apr. 28
1829 A932 1.80fr multicolored 1.60 .35

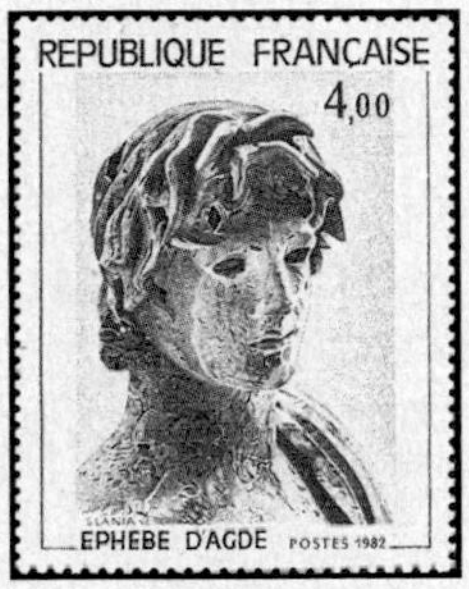

Young Greek Soldier, Hellenic Sculpture, Agde A933

1982, May 15 *Perf. 12½x13*
1830 A933 4fr multicolored 1.90 1.00

Embarkation for Ostia, by Claude Gellee — A934

The Lacemaker, by Vermeer A935

Turkish Chamber, by Balthus — A936

1982 Photo. *Perf. 13x12½, 12½x13*
1831 A934 4fr multicolored 1.90 1.00
1832 A935 4fr multicolored 1.90 1.00
1833 A936 4fr multicolored 1.90 1.00
Nos. 1831-1833 (3) 5.70 3.00

Issued: No. 1831, 6/19; No. 1832, 9/4; No. 1833, 11/6.

35th Intl. Film Festival, Cannes — A937

Natl. Space Studies Center, 20th Anniv. — A938

1982, May 15 Photo. *Perf. 13*
1834 A937 2.30fr multicolored .80 .75

1982, May 15 Engr.
1835 A938 2.60fr multicolored 1.20 .50

A939

A940

1982, June 4 Photo.
1836 A939 2.60fr multicolored 1.00 .50

Industrialized Countries' Summit Meeting, Versailles, June 4-6.

1982, June 4 Engr. *Perf. 13*
1837 A940 1.60fr ol grn & dk grn .75 .25

Jules Valles (1832-1885), writer.

Frederic and Irene Curie, Radiation Diagrams A941

1982, June 26
1838 A941 1.80fr multicolored .75 .25

Electric Street Lighting Centenary A942

1982, July 10
1839 A942 1.80fr dk blue & vio .75 .25

The Family, by Marc Boyan A943

Photogravure and Engraved
1982, Sept. 18 *Perf. 12½x13*
1840 A943 4fr multicolored 2.00 1.00

Natl. Fed. of Firemen, Cent. A944

Marionettes A945

1982, Sept. 18 Engr. *Perf. 13*
1841 A944 3.30fr red & sepia 1.75 .40

1982, Sept. 25
1842 A945 1.80fr multicolored .85 .35

Rugby A946

1982, Oct. 9
1843 A946 1.60fr multicolored 2.00 .35

Higher Education A947

1982, Oct. 16
1844 A947 1.80fr red & black .75 .35

TB Bacillus Centenary A948

1982, Nov. 13
1845 A948 2.60fr red & black 1.10 .40

St. Teresa of Avila (1515-82) A949

Leon Blum (1872-1950), Politician A950

1982, Nov. 20
1846 A949 2.10fr multicolored .85 .45

1982, Dec. 18 Engr. *Perf. 13*
1847 A950 1.80fr dk brn & brn .85 .25

Cavelier de la Salle (1643-1687), Explorer — A951

1982, Dec. 18 *Perf. 13x12½*
1848 A951 3.25fr multicolored 1.25 .50

Spring — A952

1983, Jan. 17 Engr. *Perf. 13*
1849 A952 1.05fr shown .45 .35
1850 A952 1.35fr Summer .50 .45
1851 A952 2.19fr Autumn .85 .65
1852 A952 3.63fr Winter 1.40 1.10
Nos. 1849-1852 (4) 3.20 2.55

Nos. 1849-1852 known only precanceled. See second note after No. 132.

Provence-Alpes-Cote d'Azur — A953

Brantome (Perigord) A954

Concarneau — A955

Noirlac Abbey A956

1983 Photo. *Perf. 13*
1853 A953 1fr multicolored .45 .25
Engr.
Perf. 13x12½
1854 A954 1.80fr multicolored .85 .25
Perf. 13
1855 A955 3fr multicolored 1.40 .60
Perf. 13x12½
1856 A956 3.60fr multicolored 1.60 .35

Issued: 1fr, 1/8; 1.80fr, 2/5; 3fr, 6/11; 3.60fr, 7/2.

Jarnac A957

Charleville-Mezieres — A958

1983 *Perf. 13x12½*
1857 A957 2fr multicolored .90 .35
1858 A958 3.10fr multicolored 1.40 .85
Nos. 1853-1858 (6) 6.60 2.65

Issued: 2fr, Oct. 8; 3.10fr, Sept. 17.

Martin Luther (1483-1546) — A959

1983, Feb. 12 Engr. *Perf. 13*
1859 A959 3.30fr dk brn & tan 1.40 .55

Alliance Francaise Centenary A960

1983, Feb. 19
1860 A960 1.80fr multicolored .65 .35

Danielle Casanova (d. 1942), Resistance Leader A961

1983, Mar. 8
1861 A961 3fr blk & red brn 1.25 .35

World Communications Year — A962

1983, Mar. 12 Photo.
1862 A962 2.60fr multicolored 1.10 .65

Manned Flight Bicentenary — A963

1983, Mar. 19 Photo. *Perf. 13*
1863 2fr Hot air balloon .80 .55
1864 3fr Hydrogen balloon 1.25 .70
a. A963 Pair, #1863-1864 + label 2.25 2.25

Female Nude, by Raphael A964

Aurora-Set, by Dewasne — A965

1983 Engr. *Perf. 13*
1865 A964 4fr multicolored 1.60 1.00

Photo.
1866 A965 4fr multicolored 1.60 1.00

Issued: No. 1866, 3/19; No. 1865, 4/9.

Illustration from Perrault's Folk Tales, by Gustave Dore A966

1983, June 18 Engr. *Perf. 13*
1867 A966 4fr red & black 1.60 1.00

Homage to Jean Effel A967

1983, Oct. 15
1868 A967 4fr multicolored 1.60 1.00

Le Lapin Agile, by Utrillo — A968

1983, Dec. 3 *Perf. 13x12½*
1869 A968 4fr multicolored 1.60 1.00

Thistle — A969

Europa 1983 — A970

1983, Apr. 23 Engr. *Perf. 12½x12*
1870 A969 1fr shown .30 .30
1871 A969 2fr Martagon lily .90 .30
1872 A969 3fr Aster 1.25 .60
1873 A969 4fr Aconite 1.75 .60
Nos. 1870-1873 (4) 4.20 1.80

1983, Apr. 29 *Perf. 13*
1874 A970 1.80fr Symbolic shutter *2.00 .50*
1875 A970 2.60fr Lens-to-screen diagram *2.10 .75*

Centenary of Paris Convention for the Protection of Industrial Property — A971

1983, May 14 Photo. *Perf. 13*
1876 A971 2fr multicolored .80 .30

French Philatelic Societies Congress, Marseille A972

1983, May 21 Engr. *Perf. 13*
1877 A972 1.80fr multicolored .85 .35

Liberty Type of 1982

1983-87 Engr. *Perf. 13*

1878	A915	1.70fr	green	.75	.25
1879	A915	1.80fr	green	.80	.25
1880	A915	1.90fr	green	.85	.25
1881	A915	2fr	red	.90	.25
1882	A915	2fr	green	.90	.25
1883	A915	2.10fr	red	.95	.25
1884	A915	2.20fr	red	1.00	.25
a.	Booklet pane of 10			10.00	
b.	Bklt. pane, #1788, 4 #1884			5.00	
c.	With label ('87)			1.00	.25
1885	A915	2.80fr	blue	1.25	.90
1886	A915	3fr	blue	1.40	.50
1887	A915	3.20fr	blue	1.50	.90
1888	A915	3.40fr	blue	1.60	.75
1889	A915	3.60fr	blue	1.60	.65
1890	A915	10fr	purple	4.50	.25
1891	A915	(1.90fr)	green	.90	.25
1892	A915	(2fr)	green	.90	.25
	Nos. 1878-1892 (15)			19.80	6.20

Coil Stamps

Engr. *Perf. 13 Horiz.*

1893	A915	1.70fr	green	1.00	.80
1894	A915	1.80fr	green	1.00	.50
1895	A915	1.90fr	green	1.25	.30
1896	A915	2fr	red	1.00	.30
1897	A915	2.10fr	red	1.10	.60
1897A	A915	2.20fr	red	1.00	.50
	Nos. 1893-1897A (6)			6.35	3.00

No. 1891 is inscribed "A," No. 1892 "B."

No. 1884c was issued in sheets of 50 plus 50 alternating labels picturing the PHILEXFRANCE '89 emblem to publicize the international philatelic exhibition.

Issued: 2.80fr, 10fr, No. 1881, 6/1; 1.70fr, 2.10fr, 3fr, 7/1/84; 1.80fr, 2.20fr, 3.20fr, 8/1/85; 3.40fr, No. 1891, 8/1/86; 1.90fr, 9/13/86; No. 1882, 10/15/87; 3.60fr, No. 1892, 8/1/87.

For surcharge see No. 2115.

50th Anniv. of Air France A973

1983, June 18
1898 A973 3.45fr multicolored 1.50 .85

Treaties of Versailles and Paris Bicentenary — A974

1983, Sept. 2 *Perf. 13x12½*
1899 A974 2.80fr multicolored 1.25 .60

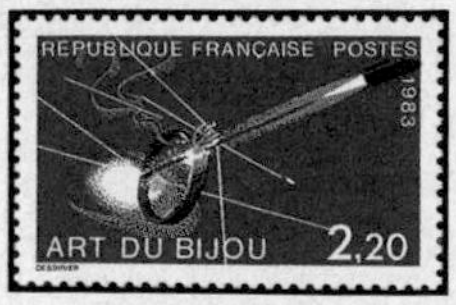

Jewelry Making A975

1983, Sept. 10 Photo. *Perf. 13*
1900 A975 2.20fr multicolored .90 .35

30th Anniv. of Customs Cooperation Council — A976

1983, Sept. 22 Engr. *Perf. 13x12½*
1901 A976 2.30fr multicolored .90 .45

Michaux's Bicycle A977

1983, Oct. 1 Engr. *Perf. 13*
1902 A977 1.60fr multicolored 1.25 .40

Natl. Weather Forecasting — A978

1983, Oct. 22 Engr. *Perf. 12½x13*
1903 A978 1.50fr multicolored .70 .25

Berthie Albrecht (1893-1943) — A979

1983, Nov. 5
1904 A979 1.60fr dk brown & olive .75 .35
1905 A979 1.60fr Rene Levy (1906-1943) .75 .35

Resistance heroines.

A980

A981

1983, Dec. 16
1906 A980 2fr dk gray & red .80 .25

Pierre Mendes France (1907-1982), Premier.

1984, Mar. 22 *Perf. 13*
1907 A981 3.60fr Union leader Waldeck-Rousseau 1.40 .35

Trade Union centenary.

Homage to the Cinema, by Cesar
A982

1984, Feb. 4 Engr. *Perf. 12½x13*
1908 A982 4fr multicolored 2.00 1.00

Four Corners of the Sky, by Jean Messagier — A983

1984, Mar. 31 Photo. *Perf. 13x12½*
1909 A983 4fr multicolored 2.00 1.00

Dining Room Corner, at Cannet, by Pierre Bonnard — A984

Photogravure and Engraved

1984, Apr. 14 *Perf. 12½x12*
1910 A984 4fr multicolored 2.00 1.00

Pythia, by Andre Masson
A985

Painter at the Feet of His Model, by Helion
A986

1984 Photo. *Perf. 12x13*
1911 A985 5fr multicolored 2.25 1.00
1912 A986 5fr multicolored 2.25 1.00

Issue dates: No. 1911, 10/13; No. 1912, 12/1.

Guadeloupe — A987

1984, Feb. 25 *Perf. 13*
1913 A987 2.30fr Map, West Indian dancers .90 .35

Vauban Citadel, Belle Ile-en-Mer
A988

Cordouan Lighthouse — A989

1984 Engr. *Perf. 13*
1914 A988 2.50fr multicolored 1.10 .35
1915 A989 3.50fr multicolored 1.60 .40

Issued: No. 1914, 5/26; No. 1915, 6/23.

La Grande Chartreuse Monastery, 900th Anniv.
A990

Palais Ideal, Hauterives-Drome — A991

Montsegur Chateau
A992

1984
1916 A990 1.70fr multicolored .80 .40
1917 A991 2.10fr multicolored .95 .30
1917A A992 3.70fr multicolored 1.60 .40
Nos. 1914-1917A (5) 6.05 1.85

Issued: 1.70fr, 7/7; 2.10fr, 6/30; 3.70fr, 9/15.

Flora Tristan (1803-44), Feminist
A992a

1984, Mar. 8
1918 A992a 2.80fr multicolored 1.00 .50

Playing Card Suits — A993

1984, Apr. 11 Engr.
1919 A993 1.14fr Hearts .50 .45
1920 A993 1.47fr Spades .65 .55
1921 A993 2.38fr Diamonds 1.00 .75
1922 A993 3.95fr Clubs 1.60 1.25
Nos. 1919-1922 (4) 3.75 3.00

Nos. 1919-1922 known only precanceled. See second note after No. 132.

450th Anniv. of Cartier's Landing in Quebec
A994

1984, Apr. 20 Photo. & Engr.
1923 A994 2fr multicolored .90 .25

See Canada No. 1011.

Philex '84, Dunkirk
A995

1984, Apr. 21 *Perf. 13x12½*
1924 A995 1.60fr multicolored .60 .35

Europa (1959-84)
A996

1984, Apr. 28 Engr. *Perf. 13*
1925 A996 2fr red brown *.80 .35*
1926 A996 2.80fr blue *1.25 .60*

2nd European Parliament Election
A997

1984, Mar. 24 Photo. *Perf. 13*
1927 A997 2fr multicolored .90 .25

Foreign Legion
A998

1984, Apr. 30 Engr. *Perf. 13x12½*
1928 A998 3.10fr multicolored 1.25 .50

40th Anniv. of Liberation
A999

Photogravure and Engraved

1984, May 8 *Perf. 12½x13*
1929 A999 2fr Resistance .85 .50
1930 A999 3fr Landing 1.25 .60
a. Pair, #1929-1930 + label 2.25 2.25

Olympic Events — A1000

1984, June 1 *Perf. 13*
1931 A1000 4fr multicolored 1.50 .60

Intl. Olympic Committee, 90th anniv. and 1984 Summer Olympics.

Engraving — A1001

1984, June 8 Engr.
1932 A1001 2fr multicolored .90 .25

Bordeaux
A1002

1984, June 9 *Perf. 13x12½*
1933 A1002 2fr red .75 .25

French Philatelic Societies Congress, Bordeaux.

Natl. Telecommunications College, 40th Anniv. — A1003

1984, June 16 Photo. *Perf. 13*
1934 A1003 3fr Satellite, phone, keyboard 1.25 .35

25th Intl. Geography Congress, Paris — A1004

1984, Aug. 25 Engr. *Perf. 13x12½*
1935 A1004 3fr Alps 1.25 .35

Telecom I Satellite
A1005

1984, Sept. 1 Photo. *Perf. 13*
1936 A1005 3.20fr multicolored 1.50 .50

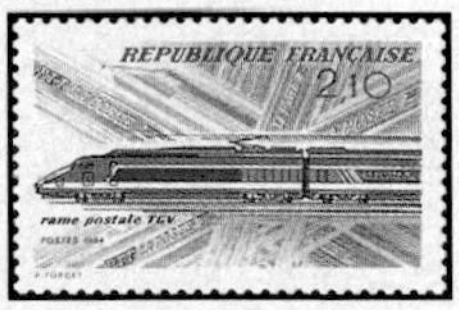

High-speed Train Mail Transport
A1006

1984, Sept. 8
1937 A1006 2.10fr Electric train, Paris-Lyon 1.00 .25

Local Birds
A1007

Marx Dormoy (1888-1941)
A1008

Photogravure and Engraved

1984, Sept. 22 *Perf. 12½x12*

1938 A1007 1fr Gypaetus barbatus .45 .25
1939 A1007 2fr Circaetus gallicus .90 .25
1940 A1007 3fr Accipiter nisus 1.40 .75
1941 A1007 5fr Peregrine falcon 2.25 .55
Nos. 1938-1941 (4) 5.00 1.80

1984, Sept. 22 **Engr.** *Perf. 13*

1942 A1008 2.40fr multicolored 1.00 .35

A1009

1984, Oct. 6 **Engr.** *Perf. 12½x13*

1943 A1009 3fr Automobile plans 1.40 .35

100th anniv. of the automobile.

A1010

1984, Nov. 3

1944 A1010 2.10fr multicolored .95 .25

Pres. Vincent Auriol (1884-1966).

9th 5-Year Plan A1011

1984, Dec. 8 **Photo.** *Perf. 13*

1945 A1011 2.10fr dk blue & scar .80 .25

French Language Promotion — A1012

1985, Jan. 15 **Engr.** *Perf. 12½x13*

1946 A1012 3fr multicolored 1.25 .35

Tourism Issue

View of Vienne A1013

Cathedral at Montpelier A1014

St. Michel de Cuxa (Codalet) Abbey — A1015

Talmont Church, Saintonge Romane A1016

Solutre A1017

1985 *Perf. 13x12½*

1947 A1013 1.70fr ol blk & dk grn .75 .25
1948 A1014 2.10fr sepia & org .90 .25
1949 A1015 2.20fr multicolored .90 .35
1950 A1016 3fr multicolored 1.25 .55
1951 A1017 3.90fr multicolored 1.50 .40
Nos. 1947-1951 (5) 5.30 1.80

Issue dates: 1.70fr, Jan. 19; 2.10fr, Mar. 30; 2.20fr, July 6; 3fr, June 15; 3.90fr, Sept. 28.

French TV, 50th Anniv. A1018

1985, Jan. 26 **Photo.** *Perf. 13*

1952 A1018 2.50fr multicolored 1.10 .50

Months of the Year — A1019

1985, Feb. 11 **Engr.**

1953 A1019 1.22fr January .65 .35
1954 A1019 1.57fr February .75 .50
1955 A1019 2.55fr March 1.25 1.00
1956 A1019 4.23fr April 2.25 1.50

1986, Feb. 10 **Engr.** *Perf. 13*

1957 A1019 1.28fr May .65 .35
1958 A1019 1.65fr June .75 .50
1959 A1019 2.67fr July 1.25 1.10
1960 A1019 4.44fr August 2.25 1.60

1987, Feb. 16 **Engr.**

1961 A1019 1.31fr September .70 .35
1962 A1019 1.69fr October .90 .50
1963 A1019 2.74fr November 1.40 1.10
1964 A1019 4.56fr December 2.50 1.90
Nos. 1953-1964 (12) 15.30 10.75

Nos. 1953-1964 are known only precanceled. See second note after No. 132.

St. Valentine, by Raymond Peynet A1020

1985, Feb. 14 **Photo.** *Perf. 13x12½*

1965 A1020 2.10fr multicolored .95 .25

Pauline Kergomard (1838-1925) A1021

1985, Mar. 8 **Engr.** *Perf. 13x12½*

1966 A1021 1.70fr int bl & cop red .75 .25

Stained Glass Window, Strasbourg Cathedral A1022

Still-life with Candle, Nicolas de Stael — A1023

1985 **Engraved** *Perf. 12x13*

1967 A1022 5fr multicolored 4.00 1.25

Photo.

Perf. 13x12

1968 A1023 5fr multicolored 3.00 1.00

Issue dates: No. 1967, 4/13; No. 1968, 6/1.

Untitled Abstract by Jean Dubuffet — A1024

Octopus Overlaid on Manuscript, by Pierre Alechinsky — A1025

Photogravure; Engraved (#1970)

1985 *Perf. 13x12½*

1969 A1024 5fr multicolored 2.50 1.25
1970 A1025 5fr multicolored 2.50 1.00

Issued: No. 1969, 10/14; No. 1970, 10/12.

The Dog, Abstract by Alberto Giacometti (1901-1966) — A1026

1985, Dec. 7 **Engr.** *Perf. 13x12½*

1971 A1026 5fr grnsh blk & lt lem 2.50 1.00

Housing in Givors A1027

Contemporary architecture by Jean Renaude.

1985, Apr. 20 **Engr.** *Perf. 13*

1972 A1027 2.40fr blk, yel org & ol grn .90 .50

Landevennec Abbey, 1500th Anniv. — A1028

1985, Apr. 20 *Perf. 13x12½*

1973 A1028 1.70fr green & brn vio .60 .25

A1029

A1030

Europa: 2.10fr, Adam de la Halle (1240-1285), composer. 3fr, Darius Milhaud (1892-1974), composer.

1985, Apr. 27 *Perf. 12½x13*

1974 A1029 2.10fr dr bl, blk, & brt bl .65 .40
1975 A1029 3fr dk bl, brt bl & blk 1.00 .50

1985, May 8 *Perf. 13x12½*

1976 A1030 2fr Return of peace .70 .50
1977 A1030 3fr Return of liberty 1.25 .50
a. Pair, #1976-1977 + label 2.00 2.00

Liberation of France from German occupation forces, 40th anniv.

Natl. Philatelic Congress, Tours — A1031

1985, May 25 *Perf. 12½x13*

1978 A1031 2.10fr Tours Cathedral .80 .35

Rabies Vaccine Cent. A1032

1985, June 1 *Perf. 13x12½*
1979 A1032 1.50fr Pasteur inoculating patient .55 .25

Mystere Falcon-900 A1033

1985, June 1 *Perf. 13*
1980 A1033 10fr blue 4.50 2.00

Lake Geneva Life-Saving Society Cent. A1034

1985, June 15
1981 A1034 2.50fr blk, red & brt ultra 1.00 .40

UN, 40th Anniv. — A1035

Huguenot Cross — A1036

1985, June 26 *Perf. 13x12½*
1982 A1035 3fr multicolored 1.10 .35

1985, Aug. 31 Engr. *Perf. 12½x13*
1983 A1036 2.50fr dp vio, dk red brn & dk red 1.00 .35

King Louis XIV revoked the Edict of Nantes on Oct. 18, 1685, dispossessing French Protestants of religious and civil liberty.

A1037

A1038

Trees, leaves and fruit of the beech, elm, oak and spruce varieties.

1985, Sept. 21 Engr. *Perf. 12½*
1984 A1037 1fr shown .45 .25
1985 A1037 2fr Ulmus montana .90 .25
1986 A1037 3fr Quercus pedunculata 1.40 .60
1987 A1037 5fr Picea abies 2.25 .35
Nos. 1984-1987 (4) 5.00 1.45

1985, Nov. 2 Engr. *Perf. 12½x13*

La France Mourning the Dead, Eternal Flame.

1988 A1038 1.80fr brn, org & lake .85 .25

Memorial Day.

A1039

A1040

1985, Nov. 9 **Engr.**
1989 A1039 3.20fr black & blue 1.25 .40

Charles Dullin, 1885-1949, impresario, theater.

1985, Nov. 16 Engr. *Perf. 13x12½*
1990 A1040 2.20fr red & black .90 .25

National information system.

Thai Ambassadors at the Court of King Louis XIV, Painting A1041

1986, Jan. 25 Engr. *Perf. 13*
1991 A1041 3.20fr rose lake & blk 1.25 .65

Normalization of diplomatic relations with Thailand, 300th anniv.

Leisure, by Fernand Leger A1042

1986, Feb. 1 Photo. *Perf. 13*
1992 A1042 2.20fr multicolored .90 .25

1936 Popular Front, 50th anniv.

Venice Carnival, Paris — A1043

1986, Feb. 12 *Perf. 12½x13*
1993 A1043 2.20fr multicolored .90 .25

La Marianne, Typograph by Raymond Gid A1044

Photogravure & Engraved
1986, Mar. 3 *Perf. 12½x13½*
1994 A1044 5fr black & dk red 2.25 1.00

Tourism Issue

Filitosa, South Corsica A1045

Loches Chateau A1046

Norman Manor, St. Germain de Livet A1047

Notre-Dame-en-Vaux Monastery, Marne — A1048

Market Square, Bastide de Monpazier, Dordogne — A1049

1986 Engr. *Perf. 13*
1995 A1045 1.80fr multicolored .85 .25
1996 A1046 2fr int blue & blk .90 .50
1997 A1047 2.20fr grnsh bl, brn & grn 1.00 .35
1998 A1048 2.50fr henna brn & sepia 1.10 .40

Perf. 13x12½
1999 A1049 3.90fr blk & yel org 1.75 .90
Nos. 1995-1999 (5) 5.60 2.40

Issued: 2.20fr, 3/3; 2fr, 6/14; 2.50fr, 6/9; 1.80fr, 3.90fr, 7/5.

Louise Michel (1830-1905), Anarchist — A1050

1986, Mar. 10 **Engr.**
2000 A1050 1.80fr dk red & gray blk .80 .25

City of Science and Industry, La Villette — A1051

1986, Mar. 17
2001 A1051 3.90fr multicolored 1.40 .50

Center for Modern Asia-Africa Studies A1052

1986, Apr. 12 Photo. *Perf. 13*
2002 A1052 3.20fr Map 1.25 .30

Skibet, Abstract by Maurice Esteve — A1053

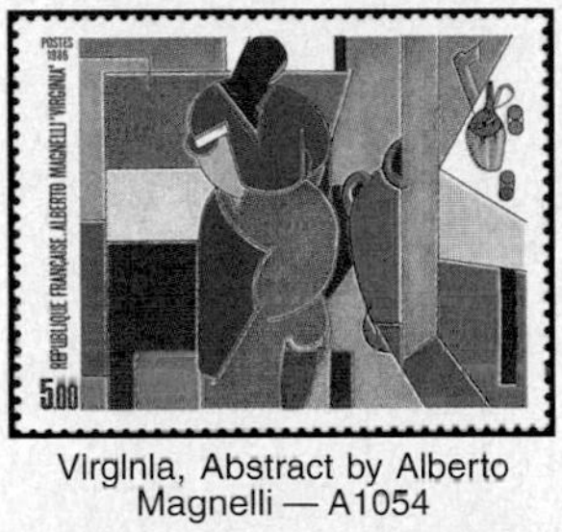
Virginia, Abstract by Alberto Magnelli — A1054

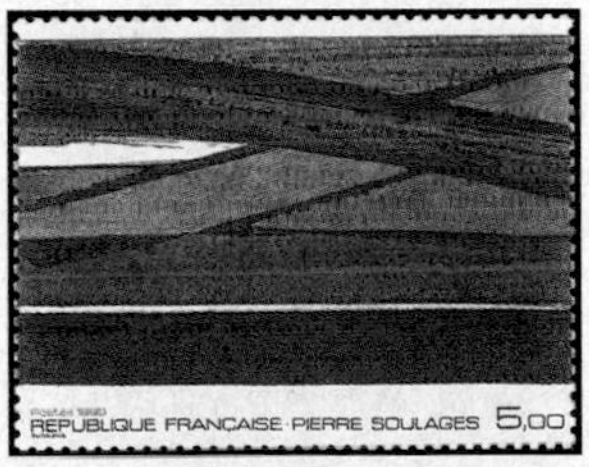
Abstract, by Pierre Soulages — A1055

The Dancer, by Jean Arp A1056

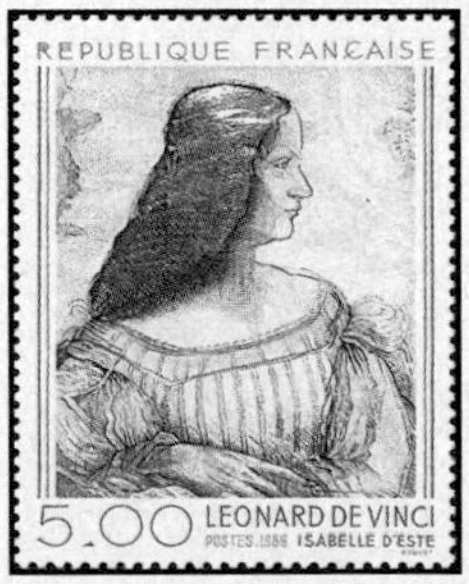
Isabelle d'Este, by Leonardo da Vinci A1057

Perf. 12½x13, 13x12½ (#2005, 2006)
1986 Photo., Engr. (#2005, 2007)
2003 A1053 5fr multicolored 2.25 1.00
2004 A1054 5fr multicolored 2.25 1.00
2005 A1055 5fr brt vio, blk & brn gray 2.25 1.00
2006 A1056 5fr multicolored 2.25 1.00
2007 A1057 5fr blk, red brn & grnsh yel 2.25 1.00
Nos. 2003-2007 (5) 11.25 5.00

Issued: No. 2003, 4/14; No. 2004, 6/25; No. 2005, 6/22; Nos. 2006, 2007, 11/10.

Victor Basch (1863-1944), IPY Emblem — A1058

1986, Apr. 28 **Engr.** ***Perf. 13***

2008 A1058 2.50fr black & yel grn 1.10 .30

International Peace Year.

Europa 1986 A1059

1986, Apr. 28 ***Perf. 13x12½***

2009 A1059 2.20fr Civet cat 1.00 .35
2010 A1059 3.20fr Bat 1.50 .65

St. Jean-Marie Vianney, Curé of Ars A1060

1986, May 3 **Engr.** ***Perf. 13x12½***

2011 A1060 1.80fr sepia, brn org & brn .80 .25

Philatelic Societies Federation Congress, Nancy — A1061

1986, May 17 ***Perf. 13***

2012 A1061 2.20fr Exposition Center .90 .25

Mens World Volleyball Championship A1062

Statue of Liberty, Cent. A1063

1986, May 24 **Engr.** ***Perf. 13***

2013 A1062 2.20fr dk vio, brn vio & scar .90 .35

1986, July 4 ***Perf. 13***

2014 A1063 2.20fr scar & dk blue 1.00 .25

See US No. 2224.

1st Ascent of Mt. Blanc, 1786 A1064

1986, Aug. 8 **Engr.** ***Perf. 13x12½***

2015 A1064 2fr J. Balmat, M.G. Paccard .90 .50

Pierre-Louis Moreau de Maupertuis (1698-1759), La Condamine and Sextant — A1065

1986, Sept. 5

2016 A1065 3fr multicolored 1.25 .55

Lapland Expedition, 250th anniv., proved Earth's poles are flattened.

See Finland No. 741.

Marcassite A1066

1986, Sept. 13 ***Perf. 12½***

2017 A1066 2fr shown .90 .25
2018 A1066 3fr Quartz 1.40 .25
2019 A1066 4fr Calcite 1.75 .70
2020 A1066 5fr Fluorite 2.25 .70
Nos. 2017-2020 (4) 6.30 1.90

Souvenir Sheet

Natl. Film Industry, 50th Anniv. — A1067

Personalities and film scenes: a, Louis Feuillade, The Vampires. b, Max Linder. c, Sacha Guitry, Romance of the Trickster. d, Jean Renoir, The Grand Illusion. e, Marcel Pagnol, The Baker's Woman. f, Jean Epstein, The Three-Sided Mirror. g, Rene Clair, Women of the Night. h, Jean Gremillon, Talk of Love. i, Jacques Becker, Helmet of Gold. j, Francois Truffaut, The Young Savage.

1986, Sept. 20 **Photo.** ***Perf. 13x12½***

2021 A1067 Sheet of 10 10.00 10.00
a.-j. 2.20fr any single 1.00 1.00

Scene from Le Grand Meaulnes, by Henry Alain-Fournier (b. 1886), Novelist A1068

Professional Education, Cent. A1069

1986, Oct. 4 **Engr.** ***Perf. 12½x13***

2022 A1068 2.20fr black & dk red .90 .25

1986, Oct. 4

2023 A1069 1.90fr brt vio & dp lil rose .85 .25

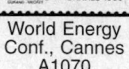

World Energy Conf., Cannes A1070

Mulhouse Technical Museum A1071

1986, Oct. 5 **Photo.** ***Perf. 13***

2024 A1070 3.40fr multicolored 1.50 .50

1986, Dec. 1 **Engr.**

2025 A1071 2.20fr int blue, dk red & blk 1.00 .45

Museum at Orsay, Opening — A1072

1986, Dec. 10 **Photo.**

2026 A1072 3.70fr bluish blk & pck bl 1.60 .60

Fulgence Bienvenue (1852-1934), and the Metro — A1073

1987, Jan. 17 **Engr.** ***Perf. 13***

2027 A1073 2.50fr vio brn, brn & dk grn 1.10 .35

A1074

A1075

1987, Jan. 24

2028 A1074 1.90fr grn & grnsh blk .85 .25

Raoul Follereau (1903-1977), care for lepers.

1987, Mar. 7 **Engr.** ***Perf. 12½x13***

2029 A1075 1.90fr black & red .85 .25

Cutlery industry, Thiers.

Tourist Issue

Redon, Ille et Vilaine A1076

Azay-le-Rideau Chateau — A1077

Meuse District — A1078

Etretat A1079

Les Baux-de-Provence — A1080

1987 **Engr.** ***Perf. 13***

2030 A1076 2.20fr dp rose lil, blk & brn ol 1.10 .25
2031 A1077 2.50fr Prus blue & olive grn 1.25 .25

Perf. 12½

2032 A1078 3.70fr multicolored 1.75 .25

Photo. ***Perf. 13***

2033 A1079 2.20fr multicolored 1.00 .25

Engr.

2034 A1080 3fr dk ol bis & dp vio 1.40 .90
Nos. 2030-2034 (5) 6.50 1.90

Issued: No. 2030, 3/7; No. 2033, 6/12; 2.50fr, 5/9; 3fr, 6/27; 3.70fr, 5/30.

Charles Edouard Jenneret (Le Corbusier) (1887-1965), Architect — A1081

1987, Apr. 11 **Photo.** ***Perf. 13x12½***

2035 A1081 3.70fr Abstract 1.60 .50

Europa 1987 A1082

Modern architecture: 2.20fr, Metal factory at Boulogne-Billancourt, by architect Claude Vasconi. 3.40fr, Rue Mallet-Stevens housing, by Robert Mallet-Stevens.

1987, Apr. 25 **Engr.** ***Perf. 13x12½***

2036 A1082 2.20fr dk blue & grn *1.00* *.50*
2037 A1082 3.40fr brn & dk grn *1.50* *.65*

Abstract Painting, by Bram van Velde — A1083

Woman under Parasol, by Eugene Boudin (1824-1898) — A1084

Precambrien, by Camille Bryen — A1085

World, Bronze Sculpture by Antoine Pevsner — A1086

Perf. 12½x13, 13x12½ (Nos. 2039, 2041)

Photo., Engr. (Nos. 2039, 2041)

1987

2038	A1083	5fr multicolored	2.25	1.00
2039	A1084	5fr multicolored	2.25	1.00
2040	A1085	5fr multicolored	2.25	1.00
2041	A1086	5fr bister & blk	2.25	1.00
		Nos. 2038-2041 (4)	9.00	4.00

Issue dates: No. 2038, 4/25; No. 2039, 5/23; No. 2040, 9/12; No. 2041, 11/14.

Gaspard de Montagnes, from a Manuscript Illustration — A1087

1987, May 9 Engr. *Perf. 13*
2042 A1087 1.90fr dp grn & sepia .85 .25

Henri Pourrat (1887-1959), novelist.

Natl. Philatelic Societies Congress, Lens A1088

1987, June 6 *Perf. 13x13½*
2043 A1088 2.20fr choc & red .90 .30

Involvement of U.S. Forces in WW I, 70th Anniv. A1089

Design: Stars and Stripes, troops, Gen. John J. Pershing (1860-1948), American army commander.

1987, June 13 *Perf. 13*
2044 A1089 3.40fr olive grn, saph & ver 1.50 .70

A1090

A1091

1987, June 17 Photo.
2045 A1090 2fr multicolored .90 .60

6th Intl. Cable Car Transport Congress, Grenoble.

1987, June 20 Litho.
2046 A1091 1.90fr pale chalky blue & blk .90 .55

Accession of Hugh Capet (c.938-996), 1st king of France, millenary.

A1092

A1093

1987, June 20 Engr. *Perf. 12½x13*
2047 A1092 2.20fr multicolored .90 .30

La Fleche Natl. Military School.

1987, June 27 Photo. *Perf. 13*
2048 A1093 1.90fr multicolored .90 .55

World Assembly of Expatriate Algerians, Nice.

World Wrestling Championships — A1094

1987, Aug. 21 Engr.
2049 A1094 3fr brt pur, vio gray & brt olive grn 1.25 .60

Mushrooms A1095

William the Conqueror (c. 1027-1087) A1096

1987, Sept. 5 *Perf. 12½*

2050	A1095	2fr Gyroporus cyanescens	.90	.25
2051	A1095	3fr Gomphus clavatus	1.40	.35
2052	A1095	4fr Morchella conica	1.75	.60
2053	A1095	5fr Russula virescens	2.25	.60
		Nos. 2050-2053 (4)	6.30	1.80

1987, Sept. 5 *Perf. 13*
2054 A1096 2fr Bayeux Tapestry detail .90 .35

Montbenoit Le Saugeais A1097

Design: Abbey of Medieval Knights, cloisters, winter scene.

1987, Sept. 19
2055 A1097 2.50fr saph, blk & scar 1.10 .55

Pasteur Institute, Cent. — A1098

1987, Oct. 3
2056 A1098 2.20fr dp blue & dk red .85 .25

Blaise Cendrars (1887-1961), Poet and Novelist — A1099

Treaty of Andelot, 1400th Anniv. — A1100

Pen and ink portrait by Modigliani.

1987, Nov. 6 *Perf. 12½*
2057 A1099 2fr brt grn, buff & blk .90 .35

1987, Nov. 28 *Perf. 12½x13*
2058 A1100 3.70fr multicolored 1.60 .55

Gen. Leclerc (1902-1947), Marshal of France — A1101

1987, Nov. 28 *Perf. 13x12½*
2059 A1101 2.20fr multicolored 1.00 .25

Liberty Type of 1982

1987-90 *Perf. 13*

2077	A915	3.70fr brt lilac rose	1.75	.35
2078	A915	(2.10fr) green ('90)	.95	.25
2079	A915	(2.30fr) red ('90)	1.00	.25
		Nos. 2077-2079 (3)	3.70	.85

Coil Stamp

Engr.

Perf. 13 Horiz.

2080 A915 2fr emerald green .90 .30

Issued: 2fr, 8/1; 3.70fr, 11/16; Nos. 2078-2079, 1/2.

Nos. 2078-2079 are inscribed "C."

Franco-German Cooperation Treaty, 25th Anniv. — A1102

1988, Jan. 15 *Perf. 13*
2086 A1102 2.20fr Adenauer, De Gaulle 1.00 .35

See Fed. Rep. of Germany No. 1546.

Marcel Dassault (1892-1986), Aircraft Designer — A1103

1988, Jan. 23 Photo.
2087 A1103 3.60fr brt ultra, gray blk & dk red 1.60 .70

Communications A1104

Great Synagogue, Rue Victoire, Paris A1105

Angouleme Festival prize-winning cartoons.

1988, Jan. 29 Photo. *Perf. 13½x13*

Booklet Stamps

2088	A1104	2.20fr Pellos	1.00	.50
2089	A1104	2.20fr Reiser	1.00	.50
2090	A1104	2.20fr Marijac	1.00	.50
2091	A1104	2.20fr Fred	1.00	.50
2092	A1104	2.20fr Moebius	1.00	.50
2093	A1104	2.20fr Gillon	1.00	.50
2094	A1104	2.20fr Bretecher	1.00	.50
2095	A1104	2.20fr Forest	1.00	.50
2096	A1104	2.20fr Mezieres	1.00	.50
2097	A1104	2.20fr Tardi	1.00	.50
2098	A1104	2.20fr Lob	1.00	.50
2099	A1104	2.20fr Bilal	1.00	.50
a.		Bklt. pane of 12, #2088-2099	12.00	

1988, Feb. 7 Litho. *Perf. 13*
2100 A1105 2fr black & gold .90 .25

The Four Elements — A1106

1988, Feb. 1 Engr. *Perf. 13*

2101	A1106	1.36fr Air	.65	.40
2102	A1106	1.75fr Water	.80	.40
2103	A1106	2.83fr Fire	1.25	1.00
2104	A1106	4.75fr Earth	2.25	1.75
		Nos. 2101-2104 (4)	4.95	3.55

Nos. 2101-2104 known only precanceled. See second note after No. 132.

PHILEXFRANCE '89 — A1107

1988, Mar. 4
2105 A1107 2.20fr #1885, emblem 1.00 .25

Postal Training College, Cent. A1108

1988, Mar. 29
2106 A1108 3.60fr multicolored 1.60 .40

Philex-Jeunes '88, Youth Stamp Show — A1109

1988, Apr. 8 ***Perf. 13x12½***
2107 A1109 2fr multicolored .90 .25

Blood Donation — A1110

1988, Apr. 9 Photo. ***Perf. 13½x13***
2108 A1110 2.50fr multicolored 1.10 .40

Europa 1988 A1111

Communication and transportation.

1988, Apr. 30 Engr. ***Perf. 13***
2109 A1111 2.20fr Cables, satellites *1.75 .35*
2110 A1111 3.60fr Rail cars *2.50 .60*

Jean Monnet (1888-1979), Economist — A1112

1988, May 10 ***Perf. 12½x13***
2111 A1112 2.20fr black & brn ol 1.00 .25

Philatelic Congress, Valence A1113

1988, May 21 ***Perf. 13x12½***
2112 A1113 2.20fr multicolored 1.00 .35

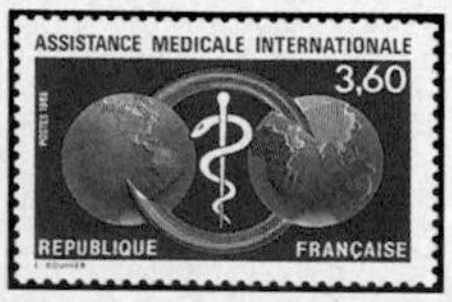

Intl. Medical Assistance A1114

1988, May 28 Photo. ***Perf. 13***
2113 A1114 3.60fr multicolored 1.60 .50

Aid to the Handicapped — A1115

1988, May 28
2114 A1115 3.70fr multicolored 1.60 .50

No. 1884 Surcharged in European Currency Units

1988, Apr. 16 **Engr.**
2115 A915 2.20fr red 1.00 .25

Tourist Issue

Hermes Dicephalus (Roman Empire), Frejus — A1116

1988, June 12 Engr. ***Perf. 13x12½***
2116 A1116 3.70fr multicolored 1.75 .80

Ship Museum, Douarnenez — A1117

Chateau Sedieres, Correze — A1118

Cirque de Gavarnie A1119

1988 ***Perf. 13, 12½x13 (#2118)***
2117 A1117 2fr multicolored .90 .25
2118 A1118 2.20fr multicolored 1.00 .35
2119 A1119 3fr multicolored 1.40 .40

Issued: 2.20fr, 7/2; 2fr, 7/4; 3fr, 7/23.

View of Perouges, Ain A1120

1988, Sept. 10 ***Perf. 13x12½***
2120 A1120 2.20fr multicolored 1.00 .25
Nos. 2116-2120 (5) 6.05 2.05

French Revolution, Bicent. — A1121

Designs: 3fr, Assembly of the Three Estates, Vizille. 4fr, Day of the Tiles (Barricades), Grenoble.

1988, June 18 **Engr.**
2121 A1121 3fr multicolored 1.40 1.00
2122 A1121 4fr multicolored 1.90 1.00
a. Pair, #2121-2122 + label 3.50 3.00

PHILEXFRANCE '89.

Buffon's Natural History — A1122

Alpine Troops, Cent. — A1123

1988, June 18 ***Perf. 12½***
2123 A1122 2fr Otters .90 .25
2124 A1122 3fr Stag 1.40 .30
2125 A1122 4fr Fox 1.90 .70
2126 A1122 5fr Badger 2.25 .60
Nos. 2123-2126 (4) 6.45 1.85

1988, June 25 ***Perf. 13***
2127 A1123 2.50fr multicolored 1.10 .65

Roland Garros (1888-1918), 1st Pilot to Fly Across the Mediterranean, Sept. 23, 1913 — A1124

1988, July 2 Engr. ***Perf. 13x12½***
2128 A1124 2fr brt grn bl & olive .90 .25

Nov. 11, 1918 Armistice Ending World War I, 70th Anniv. A1125

1988, Sept. 10 Engr. ***Perf. 13***
2129 A1125 2.20fr brt blue, gray & blk 1.00 .25

Homage to Leon Degand, Sculpture by Robert Jacobsen A1126

1988, Sept. 22 ***Perf. 12½x13***
2130 A1126 5fr blk & dp claret 2.25 1.00

French-Danish cultural exchange program, 10th anniv. See Denmark No. 860.

Strasbourg, 2000th Anniv. — A1127

1988, Sept. 24 ***Perf. 13***
2131 A1127 2.20fr Municipal arms 1.00 .25

St. Mihiel Sepulcher, by Ligier Richier (c. 1500-1567), Sculptor — A1128

Composition, 1954, by Serge Poliakoff (1906-1969) — A1129

La Pieta de Villeneuve-les-Avignon, by Enguerrand Quarton (1444-1466) — A1130

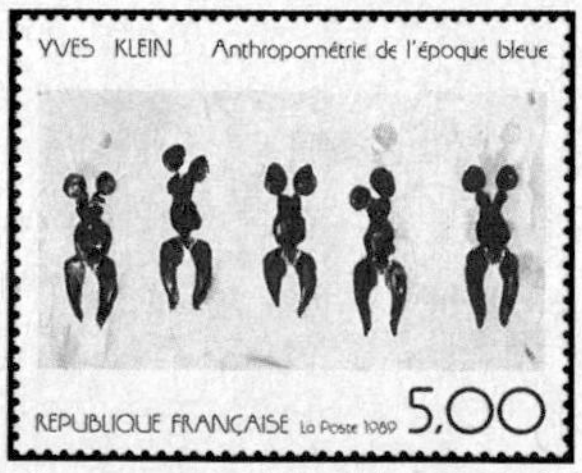

Anthropometry of the Blue Period, by Yves Klein — A1131

1988-89 Engr. ***Perf. 13x12½***
2132 A1128 5fr black brown 2.25 1.00

Photo.

2133 A1129 5fr multicolored 2.25 1.00
2134 A1130 5fr multicolored 2.25 1.00
2135 A1131 5fr multi ('89) 2.25 1.00
Nos. 2132-2135 (4) 9.00 4.00

Issue dates: No. 2132, 10/15; No. 2133, 10/22; No. 2134, 12/10; No. 2135, 1/21.

Thermal Springs A1132

1988, Nov. 21 Engr. ***Perf. 13x12½***
2136 A1132 2.20fr multicolored 1.00 .25

Metamecanique, by Jean Tinguely — A1133

1988, Nov. 25 **Photo.**
2137 A1133 5fr multicolored 3.00 1.00

See Switzerland No. 828.

UN Declaration of Human Rights, 40th Anniv. A1134

1988, Dec. 12 **Litho.** ***Perf. 13***
2138 A1134 2.20fr dk bl & grnsh bl 1.00 .25

French Revolution, Bicent. — A1135

1989, Jan. 1 **Photo.** ***Perf. 13x12½***
2139 A1135 2.20fr red & vio blue 1.00 .25

Valentin Hauy (1745-1822), Founder of the School for the Blind, Paris, 1791 — A1136

Photo. & Embossed

1989, Jan. 28
2140 A1136 2.20fr multicolored 1.00 .40

Estienne School, Cent. — A1137

1989, Feb. 4 **Engr.** ***Perf. 12½***
2141 A1137 2.20fr gray, black & red 1.00 .25

European Parliament Elections A1138

1989, Mar. 4 **Litho.** ***Perf. 13***
2142 A1138 2.20fr multicolored 1.00 .25

A1139

1989 **Engr.** ***Perf. 12½x13***
2143 A1139 2.20fr Liberty 1.00 .25
2144 A1139 2.20fr Equality 1.00 .25
2145 A1139 2.20fr Fraternity 1.00 .25
a. Strip of 3, #2143-2145 + label 3.00 2.50

Bicent. of the French revolution and the Declaration of Rights of Man and the Citizen. No. 2145a contains inscribed label picturing PHILEXFRANCE '89 emblem.

Issue dates: No. 2143, 3/18; No. 2144, 4/22; No. 2145, 5/27; No. 2145a, 7/14.

French-Soviet Joint Space Flight — A1140

1989, Mar. 4 **Litho.** ***Perf. 13***
2146 A1140 3.60fr multicolored 1.60 .60

Historic Sights, Paris — A1141

Designs: No. 2147, Arche de la Defense. No. 2148, Eiffel Tower. No. 2149, Grand Louvre. No. 2150, Notre Dame Cathedral. No. 2151, Bastille Monument and Opera de la Bastille. No. 2151a has a continuous design.

1989, Apr. 21 **Engr.** ***Perf. 13x12½***
2147 A1141 2.20fr multicolored 1.00 .85
2148 A1141 2.20fr multicolored 1.00 .85
2149 A1141 2.20fr multicolored 1.00 .85
2150 A1141 2.20fr multicolored 1.00 .85
2151 A1141 2.20fr multicolored 1.00 .85
a. Strip of 5, #2147-2151 5.00 5.00

Europa 1989 A1142

Children's games.

1989, Apr. 29 ***Perf. 13***
2152 A1142 2.20fr Hopscotch *1.00 .30*
2153 A1142 3.60fr Catch (ball) *1.75 .70*

ITU Plenipotentiaries Conference, Nice — A1143

1989, May 23 **Litho.**
2154 A1143 3.70fr dk bl, dl org & red 1.60 .40

Tourist Issue

Fontainebleau Forest — A1144

Vaux le Vicomte — A1145

La Brenne — A1146

1989, May 20 **Engr.** ***Perf. 13***
2155 A1144 2.20fr multicolored .90 .30

Perf. 13x12½

2156 A1145 3.70fr ol bis & blk 1.60 .75
2157 A1146 4fr violet blue 1.60 .75
Nos. 2155-2157 (3) 4.10 1.80

Issued: 2.20fr, 5/20; 3.70fr, 7/14; 4fr, 8/25.

World Cycling Championships, Chambery — A1147

1989, June 3 **Litho.** ***Perf. 13***
2158 A1147 2.20fr multi 1.00 .25

Jehan de Malestroit, Dept. of Morbihan — A1148

1989, June 10 **Engr.** ***Perf. 12½x13***
2159 A1148 3.70fr multicolored 1.60 .55

Preliminary Sketch (Detail) for *Oath of the Tennis Court,* by David — A1149

Regatta with Wind Astern, by Charles Lapicque A1150

1989, June 19 **Photo.** ***Perf. 13x12½***
2160 A1149 5fr multicolored 2.25 1.00

Perf. 12½

2161 A1150 5fr multicolored 2.25 1.00

No. 2160 for French revolution bicent. Issued: No. 2160, 6/19; No. 2161, 9/23.

Souvenir Sheet

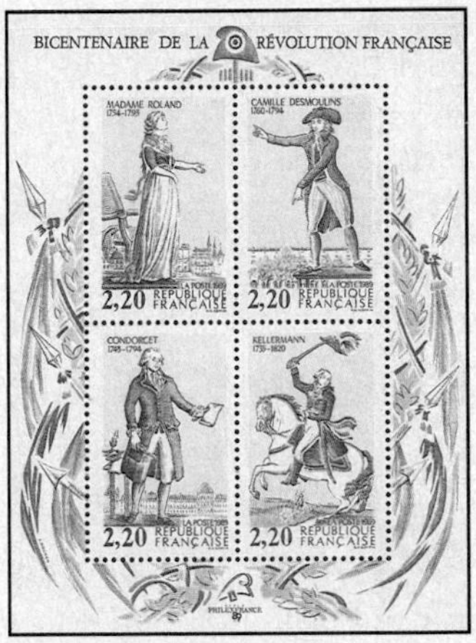

Revolution Bicentennial — A1151

Revolutionaries: a, Madame Roland (1754-1793). b, Camille Desmoulins (1760-1794). c, Condorcet (1743-1794). d, Kellermann (1735-1820).

1989, June 26 **Engr.** ***Perf. 13***
2162 A1151 Sheet of 4 4.00 3.50
a.-d. 2.20fr any single 1.00 .75

15th Summit of the Arch Meeting of Leaders from Industrial Nations, July 14-16 A1152

1989, July 14 **Photo.**
2163 A1152 2.20fr multicolored 1.00 .35

Declaration of the Rights of Man and the Citizen, Versailles, Aug. 26, 1789 — A1153

Details of an anonymous 18th-19th cent. painting in Carnavalet Museum: No. 2168a, Preamble, Article I. No. 2168b, Articles VII-XI. No. 2168c, Articles II-VI. No. 2168d, Articles XII-XVII.

Litho. & Engr.

1989, Aug. 26 ***Perf. 13x11½***
2164 A1153 2.50fr Preamble, Article I 1.00 .90
2165 A1153 2.50fr Art. II-VI 1.00 .90
2166 A1153 2.50fr Art. VII-XI 1.00 .90
2167 A1153 2.50fr Art. XII-XVII 1.00 .90
a. Strip, #2164-2167 + label 4.00 3.50

Souvenir Sheet

Perf. 13x12½

2168 A1153 Sheet of 4 20.00 20.00
a.-d. 5fr any single 5.00 5.00

No. 2168 contains 4 52x41mm stamps. Sold for 50fr, including admission fee to PHILEXFRANCE '89.

Value of No. 2168 is for examples on plain paper. Examples on fluorescent paper seem to have been distributed in North America, and may not have been distributed widely or made available in Europe. Value $250.

Musical Instruments — A1154

1989 **Litho.** ***Perf. 12x12½***

2169 A1154 1.39fr Harp .65 .50
2170 A1154 1.79fr Piano .80 .50
2171 A1154 2.90fr Trumpet 1.25 1.00
2172 A1154 4.84fr Violin 2.25 1.75
Nos. 2169-2172 (4) 4.95 3.75

Nos. 2169-2172 are known only precanceled. See second note after No. 132.

See Nos. 2233-2239, 2273-2283, 2303-2306, 2368-2371.

TGV Atlantic A1155

1989, Sept. 23 **Photo.** ***Perf. 13***

2173 A1155 2.50fr dk bl, sil & red 1.10 .50

Clermont-Ferrand Tramway, Cent. — A1156

1989, Oct. 28 **Engr.**

2174 A1156 3.70fr blk & dk ol bis 1.75 .40

Villers-Cotterets Ordinance, 450th Anniv. — A1157

1989, Oct. 28 **Engr.**

2175 A1157 2.20fr blk, dp cl & red 1.00 .25

Baron Augustin-Louis Cauchy (1789-1857), Mathematician — A1158

1989, Nov. 10 ***Perf. 13x12½***

2176 A1158 3.60fr red, blk & bl grn 1.60 .50

Marshal Jean de Lattre de Tassigny (1889-1952) — A1159

1989, Nov. 18 ***Perf. 13***

2177 A1159 2.20fr bl, blk & red 1.00 .35

Harki Soldiers of France A1160

1989, Dec. 9 **Photo.**

2178 A1160 2.20fr multicolored 1.00 .35

Marianne — A1161

1990-92 **Engr.** ***Perf. 13***

2179 A1161 10c brn blk .25 .25
a. Bklt. pane, #2180, 4 #2179 1.00
2180 A1161 20c lt green .25 .25
2181 A1161 50c brt violet .25 .25
2182 A1161 1fr orange .45 .25
2183 A1161 2fr apple grn .90 .25
2184 A1161 2.10fr dark grn .95 .25
2185 A1161 2.20fr dark grn 1.00 .25
2186 A1161 2.20fr emerald 1.00 .25
2187 A1161 2.30fr red 1.00 .25
a. Bklt. pane, #2180, 4 #2187 5.00
2188 A1161 2.50fr red 1.10 .25
2189 A1161 3.20fr blue 1.50 .75
2190 A1161 3.40fr blue 1.60 .40
2191 A1161 3.80fr lilac rose 1.75 .30
2192 A1161 4fr lilac rose 1.90 .25
2193 A1161 4.20fr lilac rose 1.90 .25
2194 A1161 5fr greenish blue 2.25 .25
2195 A1161 10fr violet 4.50 .25
2196 A1161 (2.20fr) dk grn 1.00 .25
2197 A1161 (2.50fr) red 1.10 .25
Nos. 2179-2197 (19) 24.65 5.45

Coil Stamps

Perf. 13 Horiz.

2198 A1161 2.10fr dk grn 1.00 .25
2199 A1161 2.20fr dk grn 1.00 .60
2200 A1161 2.30fr red 1.00 .25
2201 A1161 2.50fr red 1.10 .25
Nos. 2198-2201 (4) 4.10 1.35

Die Cut

Self-Adhesive

2202 A1161 2.30fr red 1.00 .25
a. Booklet pane of 10 10.00
2203 A1161 2.50fr red 1.10 .25
a. Booklet pane of 10 11.00
b. Booklet pane of 5 5.50
2204 A1161 (2.50fr) red 1.10 .25
a. Booklet pane of 10 11.00
Nos. 2202-2204 (3) 3.20 .75

Issued: No. 2187, 1/2; No. 2198, 1/1; 10c, 20c, 50c, 3.20fr, 3.80fr, 3/26; No. 2202, 1/29; Nos. 2182-2183, 2194-2195, 5/21; Nos. 2196-2197, 8/19/91; 2.20fr, 2.50fr, 3.40fr, 4fr, 9/30/91; Nos. 2179a, 2187a, 2199, 2201, 1991; 4.20fr, 9/24/92; Nos. 2203-2204, 1992; 2.10fr, 1993.

Peelable paper backing serves as booklet cover for Nos. 2202, 2203. No. 2203b has separate backing with no printing.

Nos. 2196-2197, 2204 inscribed "D."

See Nos. 2333-2348, 3529, 4410i, 4522.

Lace Work A1162

1990, Feb. 3 **Engr.** ***Perf. 13x12½***

2205 A1162 2.50fr red 1.00 .40

1992 Winter Olympics, Albertville — A1163

1990, Feb. 9 **Photo.** ***Perf. 13***

2206 A1163 2.50fr multicolored 1.00 .25

Charles de Gaulle (1890-1970) A1164

Max Hymans (1900-1961), Planes and ACC Emblem A1165

1990, Feb. 24 **Engr.** ***Perf. 12½x13***

2207 A1164 2.30fr brt vio, vio bl & blk 1.00 .25

1990, Mar. 3 ***Perf. 13***

2208 A1165 2.30fr brt vio, brt bl & dk ol grn 1.00 .25

Profile of a Woman, by Odilon Redon A1166

Head of Christ, Wissembourg — A1167

Cambodian Dancer by Auguste Rodin — A1168

Jaune et Gris by Roger Bissiere A1169

1990 **Litho.** ***Perf. 13½x14***

2209 A1166 5fr multicolored 2.25 1.00

Perf. 12½x13

Engr.

2210 A1167 5fr multicolored 2.25 1.00
2211 A1168 5fr multicolored 2.25 1.00

Photo.

2212 A1169 5fr multicolored 2.25 1.00
Nos. 2209-2212 (4) 9.00 4.00

Issue dates: No. 2209, Mar. 3; No. 2210, June 16; No. 2211, June 9; No. 2212, Dec. 8.

Jean Guehenno (1890-1978) A1170

Litho. & Engr.

1990, Mar. 24 ***Perf. 13***

2213 A1170 3.20fr buff & red brn 1.50 .40

Tourism Series

Flaran Abbey, Gers A1171

1990, Apr. 21 **Engr.** ***Perf. 13***

2214 A1171 3.80fr sepia & blk 1.75 .50

Cluny A1172

Pont Canal de Briare A1173

Cap Canaille, Cassis A1174

1990

2215 A1172 2.30fr multicolored 1.00 .25
2216 A1173 2.30fr multicolored 1.00 .25
2217 A1174 3.80fr multicolored 1.75 .50
Nos. 2215-2217 (3) 3.75 1.00

Issued: No. 2215, 6/23; No. 2216, 7/7; 3.80fr, 7/14.

Europa 1990 A1175

Post offices.

1990, Apr. 28 **Engr.** ***Perf. 13***
2218 A1175 2.30fr Macon *1.50 .50*
2219 A1175 3.20fr Cerizay *2.25 .80*

Arab World Institute — A1176

1990, May 5 ***Perf. 12½x13***
2220 A1176 3.80fr brt bl, dk red & dp bl 1.75 .45

Labor Day, Cent. A1177

1990, May 1 **Photo.** ***Perf. 13***
2221 A1177 2.30fr multicolored 1.00 .25

Villefranche-sur-Saone — A1178

1990, June 2 **Engr.** ***Perf. 13x12½***
2222 A1178 2.30fr multicolored 1.00 .25

National philatelic congress.

A1179

A1181

1990, June 6 ***Perf. 13x12½***
2223 A1179 2.30fr La Poste 1.00 .25

Whitbread trans-global yacht race.

1990, June 17 ***Perf. 12½x13***
2225 A1181 2.30fr multicolored 1.00 .25

De Gaulle's Call for French Resistance, 50th anniv.

Franco-Brazilian House, Rio de Janeiro — A1182

1990, July 14 ***Perf. 13***
2226 A1182 3.20fr multicolored 1.50 .75

See Brazil No. 2255.

A1183

1990, Oct. 6 **Engr.** ***Perf. 12½***
2227 A1183 2fr Rutilus rutilus .90 .25
2228 A1183 3fr Perca fluviatilis 1.40 .25
2229 A1183 4fr Salmo salar 1.90 .50
2230 A1183 5fr Esox lucius 2.25 .50
Nos. 2227-2230 (4) 6.45 1.50

A1184

1990, Sept. 29 **Photo.** ***Perf. 12½x13***
2231 A1184 2.30fr multicolored 1.00 .50

Natl. Institute of Geography, 50th anniv.

Souvenir Sheet

French Revolution, Bicentennial — A1185

Designs: a, Gaspard Monge. b, Abbe Gregoire. c, Creation of the Tricolor. d, Creation of the French departments.

1990, Oct. 15 **Engr.** ***Perf. 13***
2232 A1185 Sheet of 4 4.00 4.00
a.-d. 2.50fr any single .95 .95

Musical Instrument Type of 1989

1990, Sept. 1 **Litho.** ***Perf. 13***
2233 A1154 1.46fr Accordion .65 .40
2234 A1154 1.89fr Breton bag-pipe .85 .60
2235 A1154 3.06fr Tambourin 1.75 1.50
2236 A1154 5.10fr Hurdy-gurdy 3.00 2.40
Nos. 2233-2236 (4) 6.25 4.90

1990, Nov. **Litho.** ***Perf. 13***
2237 A1154 1.93fr like #2169 1.10 .75
2238 A1154 2.39fr like #2170 1.25 .90
2239 A1154 2.74fr like #2172 2.00 1.25
Nos. 2237-2239 (3) 4.35 2.90

Nos. 2233-2239 are known only precanceled. See second note after No. 132.

Maurice Genevoix (1890-1980), Novelist — A1186

1990, Nov. 12 **Engr.** ***Perf. 13***
2240 A1186 2.30fr lt green & blk 1.00 .25

Organization for Economic Cooperation and Development, 30th Anniv. — A1187

1990, Dec. 15 **Litho.**
2241 A1187 3.20fr dk & lt blue 1.50 .75

"The Swing" by Auguste Renolr (1841-1919) — A1188

1991, Feb. 23 **Engr.** ***Perf. 12½x13***
2242 A1188 5fr multicolored 2.25 1.00

Youth Philatelic Exhibition, Cholet A1189

1991, Mar. 30 **Litho.** ***Perf. 13***
2243 A1189 2.50fr multicolored 1.10 .40

Art Series

Le Noeud Noir by Georges Seurat (1859-1891) — A1190

Apres Nous La Maternite, by Max Ernst (1891-1976) — A1191

Volte Faccia by Francois Rouan A1192

O Tableau Noir by Roberto Matta (b. 1911) — A1193

1991 **Engr.** ***Perf. 12½x13***
2244 A1190 5fr pale yellow & blk 2.25 1.00

Photo. ***Perf. 13***
2245 A1191 2.50fr multicolored 1.10 .80

Engr. ***Perf. 12½x13***
2246 A1192 5fr black 2.25 1.00

Photo. ***Perf. 13x12½***
2247 A1193 5fr multicolored 2.25 1.00
Nos. 2244-2247 (4) 7.85 3.80

Issued: No. 2244, 4/13; No. 2245, 10/10; No. 2246, 11/9; No. 2247, 11/30.

Wolfgang Amadeus Mozart (1756-1791), Composer — A1194

1991, Apr. 9 **Photo.** ***Perf. 13***
2248 A1194 2.50fr bl, blk & red 1.10 .60

National Printing Office, 350th Anniv. — A1195

1991, Apr. 13
2249 A1195 4fr multicolored 1.90 .60

Tourism Series

Chevire Bridge, Nantes — A1196

Carennac Castle A1197

Pipe Organ, Wasquehal A1198

Valley of Munster A1199

1991 Engr. *Perf. 13*

2250	A1196	2.50fr	multicolored	1.10	.25

Perf. 12x13

2251	A1197	2.50fr	multicolored	1.10	.30

Perf. 12

2252	A1198	4fr	black & buff	1.90	.55

Perf. 13x12½

2253	A1199	4fr	violet	1.90	.55
	Nos. 2250-2253 (4)			6.00	1.65

Issue dates: No. 2250, Apr. 27; Nos. 2251, 2253, July 6; No. 2252, June 22.

Europa A1200

Concours Lepine, 90th Anniv. A1201

1991, Apr. 27 *Perf. 12½x13*

2254	A1200	2.50fr	Ariane launch site, French Guiana	1.10	.25
2255	A1200	3.50fr	Television satellite	1.60	.55

Compare with No. 2483.

1991, Apr. 27 *Perf. 13*

2256	A1201	4fr	multicolored	1.90	.80

French Assoc. of Small Manufacturers and Inventors.

Philatelic Society Congress, Perpignan A1202

1991, May 18

2257	A1202	2.50fr	multicolored	1.10	.25

French Open Tennis Championships, Cent. — A1203

1991, May 24 Engr. *Perf. 13*

2258	A1203	3.50fr	multicolored	1.60	.50

Souvenir Sheet

French Revolution, Bicent. — A1204

Designs: a, Theophile Malo Corret, La Tour d'Auvergne (1743-1800). b, Liberty Tree. c, National police, bicent. d, Louis Antoine-Leon de St. Just (1767-1794).

1991, June 1 Engr. *Perf. 13*

2259	A1204	Sheet of 4		4.50	3.00
a.-d.		2.50fr any single		1.10	.75

A1205 A1206

1991, June 13 Photo. *Perf. 13*

2260	A1205	2.50fr	multicolored	1.10	.45

Gaston III de Foix (Febus) (1331-1391), general.

1991, Sept. 14 Engr. *Perf. 12½*

Designs: Wildlife.

2261	A1206	2fr	Ursus arctos	.90	.30
2262	A1206	3fr	Testudo hermanni	1.40	.30
2263	A1206	4fr	Castor fiber	1.90	.75
2264	A1206	5fr	Alcedo atthis	2.25	.75
	Nos. 2261-2264 (4)			6.45	2.10

10th World Forestry Congress A1207

1991, Sept. 22 Engr. *Perf. 13x12½*

2265	A1207	2.50fr	multicolored	1.10	.25

School of Public Works, Cent. A1208

1991, Oct. 5 Litho. & Engr. *Perf. 13*

2266	A1208	2.50fr	multicolored	1.10	.35

Marcel Cerdan (1916-1949), Middleweight Boxing Champion — A1209

1991, Oct. 19 Photo. *Perf. 13*

2267	A1209	2.50fr	black & red	1.10	.35

Amnesty International, 30th Anniv. — A1210

1991, Oct. 19

2268	A1210	3.40fr	multicolored	1.60	.60

A1211 A1212

1991, Nov. 14 Engr. *Perf. 13*

2269	A1211	2.50fr	Olympic flame	1.10	.25

1992 Winter Olympics, Albertville.

1991, Dec. 7 *Perf. 13*

2270	A1212	2.50fr	dk & lt blue	1.10	.30

Fifth Handicapped Olympics.

Voluntary Attachment of Mayotte to France, Sesquicentennial — A1213

1991, Dec. 21 Engr.

2271	A1213	2.50fr	multicolored	1.10	.25

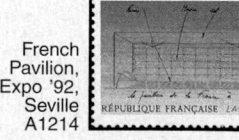

French Pavilion, Expo '92, Seville A1214

Litho. & Engr.

1992, Jan. 18 *Perf. 13*

2272	A1214	2.50fr	multicolored	1.10	.25

Musical Instruments Type of 1989

1992, Jan. 31 Litho. *Perf. 13*

2273	A1154	1.60fr	Guitar	45.00	25.00
2274	A1154	1.98fr	like #2233	4.00	3.00
2275	A1154	2.08fr	Saxophone	2.00	1.50
2276	A1154	2.46fr	like #2234	2.00	1.50
2277	A1154	2.98fr	Banjo	2.00	1.50
2278	A1154	3.08fr	like #2235	6.00	4.00
2279	A1154	3.14fr	like #2236	2.75	2.00
2280	A1154	3.19fr	like #2169	7.00	4.00
2281	A1154	5.28fr	Xylophone	5.50	3.50
2282	A1154	5.30fr	like #2170	3.50	2.00
2283	A1154	5.32fr	like #2172	3.50	2.50
	Nos. 2273-2283 (11)			83.25	50.50

Perf. 12

2273a	A1154	1.60fr	Guitar	7.50	4.50
2274a	A1154	1.98fr	like #2233	150.00	140.00
2275a	A1154	2.08fr	Saxophone	40.00	30.00
2276a	A1154	2.46fr	like #2234	12.00	7.50
2278a	A1154	3.08fr	like #2235	12.00	7.50
2279a	A1154	3.14fr	like #2236	60.00	50.00
2280a	A1154	3.19fr	like #2169	8.00	5.00
2281a	A1154	5.28fr	Xylophone	30.00	20.00
2282a	A1154	5.30fr	like #2170	75.00	60.00
2283a	A1154	5.32fr	like #2172	25.00	20.00
	Nos. 2273a-2283a (10)			419.50	344.50

Nos. 2273-2283 are known only precanceled. See 2nd note after No. 132. See Nos. 2303-2306.

1992 Summer Olympics, Barcelona A1215

1992, Apr. 3 Photo. *Perf. 13*

2284	A1215	2.50fr	multicolored	1.10	.25

See Greece No. 1730.

Marguerite d'Angouleme (1492-1549) A1216

1992, Apr. 11 Litho. *Perf. 13*

2285	A1216	3.40fr	multicolored	1.60	.90

Founding of Ajaccio, 500th Anniv. A1217

Virgin and Child Beneath a Garland by Botticelli.

1992, Apr. 30 Photo. *Perf. 13*

2286	A1217	4fr	multicolored	1.90	.60

A1218 A1219

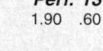

Discovery of America, 500th Anniv.: 2.50fr, Map, navigation instruments. 3.40fr, Sailing ship, map.

1992, May 9 Engr. *Perf. 13x12½*

2287	A1218	2.50fr	multicolored	*1.25*	*.30*
2288	A1218	3.40fr	multicolored	*2.00*	*.65*

Europa.

1992, May 30 Litho. *Perf. 13*

2289	A1219	3.40fr	multicolored	1.60	.80

Intl. Bread and Cereal Congress.

Tourism Series

Ourcq Canal A1220

1992, May 30 Engr. *Perf. 13*

2290	A1220	4fr	black, blue & grn	1.90	.50

Mt. Aiguille
A1221

Biron Castle
A1223

Lorient
A1222

1992, June 27 **Engr.** ***Perf. 13***

2291	A1221	3.40fr multicolored	1.60	.75

First ascension of Mt. Aiguille, 500th anniv.

1992, July 4 **Engr.** ***Perf. 13***

2292	A1222	4fr multicolored	1.90	.25

1992, July 4 ***Perf. 12½x13***

2293	A1223	2.50fr multicolored	1.75	.50

Natl. Philatelic Societies Congress, Niort
A1224

1992, June 6 **Photo.** ***Perf. 13***

2294	A1224	2.50fr multicolored	1.10	.25

Natl. Art Festival.

1992 Olympic Games, Albertville and Barcelona
A1225

1992, June 19 ***Perf. 12½x13½***

2295	A1225	2.50fr multicolored	1.10	.35

Tautavel Man
A1226

1992, June 20 **Photo.** ***Perf. 13***

2296	A1226	3.40fr multicolored	1.60	.60

Portrait of Jacques Callot (1592-1635), by Claude Deruet — A1227

1992, June 27 **Engr.** ***Perf. 12x13***

2297	A1227	5fr buff & brown	2.25	.75

Flowers — A1228

2fr, Pancratium maritimum. 3fr, Drosera rotundifolia. 4fr, Orchis palustris. 5fr, Nuphar luteum.

1992, Sept. 12 **Engr.** ***Perf. 12½***

2298	A1228	2fr multicolored	.90	.30
2299	A1228	3fr multicolored	1.40	.30
2300	A1228	4fr multicolored	1.90	.70
2301	A1228	5fr multicolored	2.25	.70
		Nos. 2298-2301 (4)	6.45	2.00

First French Republic, Bicent.
A1229

1992, Sept. 26 ***Perf. 13***

2302	A1229	2.50fr multicolored	1.10	.25

Musical Instruments Type of 1989

1992, Oct. **Litho.** ***Perf. 13***

2303	A1154	1.73fr like #2273	.80	.25
2304	A1154	2.25fr like #2275	1.00	.50
2305	A1154	3.51fr like #2277	1.60	1.00
2306	A1154	5.40fr like #2281	2.50	1.75
		Nos. 2303-2306 (4)	5.90	3.50

Nos. 2303-2306 are known only precanceled. See second note after No. 132.

Proclamation of First French Republic, Bicent. — A1230

Paintings or drawings by contemporary artists: No. 2307, Tree of Freedom, by Pierre Alechinsky. No. 2308, Portrait of a Young Man, by Martial Raysse. No. 2309, Marianne with Body and Head of Rooster, by Gerard Garouste. No. 2310, "Republique Francaise," by Jean-Charles Blais.

1992, Sept. 26 **Engr.** ***Perf. 13***

2307	A1230	2.50fr red	1.10	.25
2308	A1230	2.50fr red	1.10	.25
2309	A1230	2.50fr red	1.10	.25
2310	A1230	2.50fr red	1.10	.25
		Nos. 2307-2310 (4)	4.40	1.00

Single European Market
A1231

1992, Nov. 6 **Photo.** ***Perf. 12½x13½***

2311	A1231	2.50fr multicolored	1.10	.35

First Mail Flight from Nancy to Luneville, 80th Anniv.
A1232

1992, Nov. 12 ***Perf. 13***

2312	A1232	2.50fr multicolored	1.10	.45

Marcel Paul (1900-1982), Minister of Industrial Production — A1233

1992, Nov. 13 **Engr.**

2313	A1233	4.20fr claret & blue	1.90	.55

Contemporary Art — A1234

No. 2314, Le Rendezvous d'Ephese, by Paul Delvaux, Belgium. No. 2315, Abstract painting, by Alberto Burri, Italy. No. 2316, Abstract painting, by Antoni Tapies, Spain. No. 2317, Portrait of John Edwards, by Francis Bacon, Great Britain.

1992 **Photo.** ***Perf. 13x12½***

2314	A1234	5fr multicolored	2.25	1.00
2315	A1234	5fr multicolored	2.25	1.00
2316	A1234	5fr multicolored	2.25	1.00
2317	A1234	5fr multicolored	2.25	1.00
		Nos. 2314-2317 (4)	9.00	4.00

Issued: No. 2314, 11/20; Nos. 2315-2317, 11/21.

See Nos. 2379-2390.

Gypsy Culture — A1235

1992, Dec. 5 **Photo.** ***Perf. 13***

2318	A1235	2.50fr multicolored	1.10	.30

Yacht "La Poste," Entrant in Whitbread Trans-Global Race — A1236

1993, Feb. 6 **Engr.** ***Perf. 12***

2319	A1236	2.50fr multicolored	1.10	.40

See No. 2375.

Water Birds — A1237

1993, Feb. 6 ***Perf. 12½x12***

2320	A1237	2fr Harle piette	.90	.30
2321	A1237	3fr Fuligule nyroca	1.40	.30
2322	A1237	4fr Tadorne de belon	1.90	.75
2323	A1237	5fr Harle huppe	2.25	.70
		Nos. 2320-2323 (4)	6.45	2.05

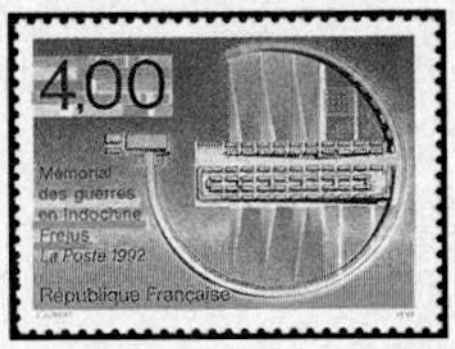

Memorial to Indochina War, Frejus
A1238

Litho. & Engr.

1993, Feb. 16 ***Perf. 13x13½***

2324	A1238	4fr multicolored	1.90	.60

Stamp Day — A1239

1993, Mar. 6 **Photo.** ***Perf. 13***

2325	A1239	2.50fr red & multi	1.75	1.00
2326	A1239	2.50fr +60c red & multi	1.40	.80
a.		Bklt. pane of 4 #2325, 3 #2326 + label	13.00	

Mediterranean Youth Games, Agde — A1240

1993, Mar. 13 **Photo.** ***Perf. 13***

2327	A1240	2.50fr multicolored	1.10	.25

Human Rights, Intl. Mixed Masonic Order, Cent. — A1241

1993, Apr. 3 **Engr.** ***Perf. 13***

2328	A1241	3.40fr blue & black	1.60	.50

Contemporary Art — A1242

Europa: 2.50fr, Painting, Rouge Rythme Bleu, by Olivier Debre. 3.40fr, Sculpture, Le Griffu, by Germaine Richier, vert.

Perf. 13x12½, 12½x13

1993, Apr. 17 **Litho.**

2329	A1242	2.50fr multicolored	1.10	.35
2330	A1242	3.40fr multicolored	1.60	.80

Marianne Type of 1990

1993-96 **Engr.** ***Perf. 13***

2333	A1161	2fr blue	1.75	.25
2334	A1161	2.40fr emerald	1.40	.25
2335	A1161	2.70fr emerald	1.60	.25
2336	A1161	3.50fr apple green	1.75	.30
2337	A1161	3.80fr blue	1.90	.50
2338	A1161	4.40fr blue	2.25	.40
2339	A1161	4.50fr mag	2.25	.40
2340	A1161	(2.50fr) red	1.25	.25
		Complete booklet, 10 #2340	12.50	
		Nos. 2333-2340 (8)	14.15	2.60

Perf. 13 Horiz.

Coil Stamps

2341 A1161 2.40fr emerald 1.40 .60
2342 A1161 2.70fr emerald 3.00 .25
2343 A1161 (2.80fr) red 1.75 .25

Self-Adhesive

Die Cut

2344 A1161 70c brown 13.00 12.00

Serpentine Die Cut Vert.

2345 A1161 70c brown 13.00 10.00
2346 A1161 1fr orange 7.00 2.50
a. Booklet pane, 3 #2348, 1 #2346 9.00
Complete bklt., 2 #2346a 20.00

Die Cut

2347 A1161 (2.50fr) red 1.50 .25
a. Booklet pane of 10 (see footnote) 16.00
b. Bklt. pane of 4 + label 6.00
c. Booklet pane, #2344, 3 #2347 + label 30.00
d. Booklet pane of 10 (see footnote) 15.00

Serpentine Die Cut 6¾ Vert.

2348 A1161 (2.80fr) red 1.25 .25
a. Bklt. pane of 4 + label 5.00
b. Booklet pane of 10 (see footnote) 13.00
c. Booklet pane, #2345, 3 #2348 + label 18.00
d. Booklet pane of 10 (see footnote) 13.00
e. Booklet pane of 10 (see footnote) 13.00
f. Booklet pane of 10 (see footnote) —

Nos. 2340, 2347 pay postage for the first class letter rate and sold for 2.50fr when first released. They have no denomination or letter inscription. Nos. 2343 and 2348 had a face value of 2.80fr when released.

No. 2347a has all stamps adjoining and has selvage covering backing paper (booklet cover), No. 2347d is comprised of two strips of 5 stamps each with yellow backing paper showing.

No. 2348b has the same format as No. 2347a. No. 2348d has a format similar to No. 2347d except there is a narrow selvage strip between the left six stamps and the right four stamps. No. 2348e is like No. 2348f but lacks the selvage strip. No. 2348f has a format similar to No. 2347a except it has a wide selvage strip between the left four stamps and the right six stamps.

Backing paper of Nos. 2347b and 2347c may have cuts along fold and were sold in a booklet for 20fr.

Issued: #2340, 2347, 4/19/93; 70c, July; 2fr, 7/31/94; Nos. 2341-2343, 4/1/94; Nos. 2345, 2348, 2/14/94; 1fr, 2.70fr, 3.80fr, 4.50fr, 3/18/96.

Tourism Series

Chinon — A1243

1993, Apr. 24 Engr. *Perf. 13x12½*

2355 A1243 4.20fr dk grn, ol grn & brn 2.00 .80

Village of Minerve — A1244

1993, July 17 *Perf. 13*

2356 A1244 4.20fr red brown & yel grn 2.00 .50

Chaise-Dieu Abbey — A1245

Montbeliard — A1246

1993

2357 A1245 2.80fr multicolored 1.25 .35
2358 A1246 4.40fr multicolored 2.00 .60
Nos. 2355-2358 (4) 7.25 2.25

Issued: No. 2357, 9/4; No. 2358, 9/11.

Ninth European Conference on Protection of Human Rights — A1247

1993, May 8 Engr. *Perf. 12½x13*

2359 A1247 2.50fr multicolored 1.10 .30

Django Reinhardt (1910-1953), Musician — A1248

1993, May 14 Litho. *Perf. 13*

2360 A1248 4.20fr multicolored 1.90 .60

Louise Weiss (1893-1983), Suffragist — A1249

1993, May 15 Engr. *Perf. 13x12½*

2361 A1249 2.50fr blk, buff & red 1.10 .35

Philatelic Society Congress, Lille A1250

1993, May 29 Engr. *Perf. 13x12½*

2362 A1250 2.50fr bl, dk bl & lil 1.10 .45

Natural History Museum, Bicent. A1251

Litho. & Engr.

1993, June 5 *Perf. 13*

2363 A1251 2.50fr multicolored 1.10 .30

Martyrs and Heroes of the Resistance — A1252

1993, June 18 Photo. *Perf. 13*

2364 2.50fr red, black & gray 1.10 .60
2365 4.20fr red, black & gray 1.90 1.00
a. A1252 Pair, #2364-2365 3.00 2.50

A1254

A1255

1993, July 10 Engr. *Perf. 13x12½*

2366 A1254 2.50fr multicolored 1.10 .30

Claude Chappe's Semaphore Telegraph, bicent.

1993, July 10 Engr. *Perf. 12½x13*

2367 A1255 3.40fr bl, grn & red 1.60 .75

Train to Lake Artouste, Laruns, highest train ride in Europe.

Musical Instruments Type of 1989

1993, July 1 Litho. *Perf. 13*

2368 A1154 1.82fr like #2171 .85 .40
2369 A1154 2.34fr like #2235 1.10 .75
2370 A1154 3.86fr like #2236 1.75 1.00
2371 A1154 5.93fr like #2281 2.75 2.00
Nos. 2368-2371 (4) 6.45 4.15

Nos. 2368-2371 are known only precanceled. See note after No. 132.

Liberation of Corsica, 50th Anniv. — A1256

1993, Sept. 9 Engr. *Perf. 13*

2372 A1256 2.80fr lake, bl & blk 1.25 .30

Saint Thomas, by Georges de la Tour (1593-1652) — A1257

1993, Sept. 9 Photo. *Perf. 12½x13*

2373 A1257 5fr multicolored 2.25 1.00

Service as Military Hospital of Val de Grace Monastery, Bicent. — A1258

1993, Sept. 25 Engr. *Perf. 13*

2374 A1258 3.70fr multicolored 1.75 .35

Whitbread Trans-Global Race Type

1993, Sept. 27 Engr. *Perf. 12*

2375 A1236 2.80fr multicolored 1.25 .40

The Muses, by Maurice Denis (1870-1943) — A1259

1993, Oct. 2 Photo. *Perf. 12½x13*

2376 A1259 5fr multicolored 2.25 1.00

The Clowns, by Albert Gleizes (1881-1953) A1260

1993, Oct. 2 Photo. *Perf. 13½x12½*

2377 A1260 2.80fr multicolored 1.25 .30

Natl. Circus Center, Chalons-sur-Marne.

Clock Tower Bellringer Statues of Lambesc — A1261

1993, Oct. 9 Engr. *Perf. 13x12½*

2378 A1261 4.40fr multicolored 2.00 .70

European Contemporary Art Type

Designs: No. 2379, Abstract, by Takis. No. 2380, Abstract, by Maria Helena Vieira da Silva. No. 2381, Abstract Squares, by Sean Scully. No. 2382, Abstract, by Georg Baselitz, Germany.

1993-94 Photo. *Perf. 13x12½*

2379 A1234 5fr blk & ver 2.25 1.00
2380 A1234 5fr multicolored 2.25 1.00
2381 A1234 6.70fr multicolored 3.00 1.00

Perf. 13

2382 A1234 6.70fr multicolored 3.00 1.00
Nos. 2379-2382 (4) 10.50 4.00

Issued: No. 2379, 10/9/93; No. 2380, 12/11/93; No. 2381, 1/29/94; No. 2382, 11/19/94.

Greetings A1266

Greeting, artist: No. 2383, Happy Birthday, Claire Wendling. No. 2384, Happy Birthday, Bernard Olivie. No. 2385, Happy Anniversary, Stephane Colman. No. 2386, Happy Anniversary, Guillaune Sorel. No. 2387, With Love, Jean-Michel Thiriet. No. 2388, Please Write, Etienne Davodeau. No. 2389, Congratulations, Johan de Moor. No. 2390, Good luck, "Mezzo." No. 2391, Best Wishes, Nicolas de Crecy. No. 2392, Best Wishes, Florence Magnin. No. 2393, Merry Christmas, Thierry Robin. No. 2394, Merry Christmas, Patrick Prugne.

1993, Oct. 21 Photo. *Perf. 13½x13*

Booklet Stamps

2383	A1266	2.80fr	multicolored	1.25	.30
2384	A1266	2.80fr	multicolored	1.25	.30
2385	A1266	2.80fr	multicolored	1.25	.30
2386	A1266	2.80fr	multicolored	1.25	.30
2387	A1266	2.80fr	multicolored	1.25	.30
2388	A1266	2.80fr	multicolored	1.25	.30
2389	A1266	2.80fr	multicolored	1.25	.30
2390	A1266	2.80fr	multicolored	1.25	.30
2391	A1266	2.80fr	multicolored	1.25	.30
2392	A1266	2.80fr	multicolored	1.25	.30
2393	A1266	2.80fr	multicolored	1.25	.30
2394	A1266	2.80fr	multicolored	1.25	.30
a.			Bklt. pane, #2383-2394	15.00	

Perf. 12½

2383a	A1266	2.80fr		1.25	.30
2384a	A1266	2.80fr		1.25	.30
2385a	A1266	2.80fr		1.25	.30
2386a	A1266	2.80fr		1.25	.30
2387a	A1266	2.80fr		1.25	.30
2388a	A1266	2.80fr		1.25	.30
2389a	A1266	2.80fr		1.25	.30
2390a	A1266	2.80fr		1.25	.30
2391a	A1266	2.80fr		1.25	.30
2392a	A1266	2.80fr		1.25	.30
2393a	A1266	2.80fr		1.25	.30
2394b	A1266	2.80fr		1.25	.30
c.			Booklet pane of 12, #2383a-2393a, 2394b	16.50	

Souvenir Sheet

European Stamp Exhibition, Salon du Timbre — A1267

a, Rhododendrons. b, Flowers in park, Paris.

1993, Nov. 10 *Perf. 13*

2395	A1267	2.40fr	#a.-b.+ 2 labels	14.50	14.50

Sold for 15fr.

Louvre Museum, Bicent. A1268

1993, Nov. 20

2396	A1268	2.80fr	Louvre, 1793	1.25	1.00
2397	A1268	4.40fr	Louvre, 1993	2.00	1.25
a.			Pair, #2396-2397	3.50	2.50

Glassware, 1901 — A1269

Cast Iron, c. 1900 — A1270

Furniture, c. 1902 — A1271

Stoneware, c. 1898 — A1272

Decorative arts by: No. 2398, Emile Galle (1846-1904). No. 2399, Hector Guimard (1867-1942). No. 2400, Louis Majorelle (1859-1926). No. 2401, Pierre-Adrien Dalpayrat (1844-1910).

Perf. 13½x12½

1994. Jan. 22 Photo.

2398	A1269	2.80fr	multicolored	1.25	.35
2399	A1270	2.80fr	multicolored	1.25	.35
2400	A1271	4.40fr	multicolored	2.00	.65
2401	A1272	4.40fr	multicolored	2.00	.65
			Nos. 2398-2401 (4)	6.50	2.00

Stained Glass Window, St. Julian's Cathedral, Le Mans A1273

1994, Feb. 12 Engr. *Perf. 12½x13*

2402	A1273	6.70fr	multicolored	3.00	1.00

City of Bastia — A1274

1994, Feb. 19 *Perf. 13x12½*

2403	A1274	4.40fr	blue & brown	2.00	.30

Tourism Series

Argentat A1275

1994, June 18 Engr. *Perf. 12x12½*

2404	A1275	4.40fr	red brown & rose carmine	2.00	.60

European Parliamentary Elections — A1276

1994, Feb. 26 Litho. *Perf. 13*

2405	A1276	2.80fr	multicolored	1.25	.25

Laurent Mourguet (1769-1844), Creator of Puppet, Guignol — A1277

1994, Mar. 4 Photo. *Perf. 13*

2406	A1277	2.80fr	multicolored	1.25	.35

French Polytechnic Institute, Bicent. A1277a

1994, Mar. 11

2407	A1277a	2.80fr	multicolored	1.25	.35

Stamp Day A1278

1994, Mar. 12 Engr. *Perf. 13*

2408	A1278	2.80fr	blue & red	*5.00*	*2.25*
2409	A1278	2.80fr	+60c blue & red	*1.40*	*1.25*
a.			Booklet pane of 4 #2408, 3 #2409 + 1 label	*25.00*	

No. 2408 issued only in booklets.

Swedish Ballet Costume — A1279

Banquet for Gustavus III at the Trianon, 1784, by Lafrensen — A1280

French-Swedish cultural relations: No. 2411, Tuxedo costume for Swedish ballet. No. 2412, Viking ships. No. 2413, Viking ship. No. 2415, Swedish, French flags.

1994, Mar. 18 Engr. *Perf. 13*

2410	A1279	2.80fr	multicolored	3.50	1.25
2411	A1279	2.80fr	multicolored	3.50	1.25
2412	A1279	2.80fr	multicolored	3.50	1.25
2413	A1279	2.80fr	multicolored	3.50	1.25
2414	A1280	3.70fr	multicolored	4.00	2.00
2415	A1280	3.70fr	multicolored	4.00	2.00
a.			Booklet pane of #2410-2415	25.00	

See Sweden Nos. 2065-2070.

Pres. Georges Pompidou (1911-1974) A1281

1994, Apr. 9 Engr. *Perf. 13*

2416	A1281	2.80fr	olive brown	1.25	.30

Resistance of the Maquis, 50th Anniv. A1282

1994, Apr. 9

2417	A1282	2.80fr	multicolored	1.25	.30

Philexjeunes '94, Grenoble — A1283

1994, Apr. 22 Photo.

2418	A1283	2.80fr	multicolored	1.25	.30

Europa A1284

Discoveries: 2.80fr, AIDS virus, by scientists of Pasteur Institute. 3.70fr, Formula for wave properties of matter, developed by Louis de Brogile.

1994, Apr. 30 Photo. & Engr.

2419	A1284	2.80fr	multicolored	1.25	.30
a.			With label	1.25	.75
2420	A1284	3.70fr	multicolored	1.75	.85

No. 2419a issued Dec. 1, 1994.

Opening of Channel Tunnel — A1285

Designs: Nos. 2421, 2423, British lion, French rooster, meeting over Channel. Nos. 2422, 2424, Joined hands above speeding train.

1994, May 3 Photo. *Perf. 13*

2421	A1285	2.80fr	dk blue & multi	1.25	.30
2422	A1285	2.80fr	dk blue & multi	1.25	.30
a.			Pair, #2421-2422	2.75	1.50
2423	A1285	4.30fr	lt blue & multi	2.00	.90
2424	A1285	4.30fr	multicolored	2.00	.90
a.			Pair, #2423-2424	4.50	2.25
			Nos. 2421-2424 (4)	6.50	2.40

See Great Britain Nos. 1558-1561.

Asian Development Bank, Board of Governors Meeting, Nice — A1286

1994, May 3 Photo. *Perf. 13*
2425 A1286 2.80fr multicolored 1.25 .30

Federation of French Philatelic Societies, 67th Congress, Martigues A1287

1994, May 20 Engr. *Perf. 12x12½*
2426 A1287 2.80fr multicolored 1.25 .30

Court of Cassation A1288

Litho. & Engr.

1994, June 3 *Perf. 13*
2427 A1288 2.80fr multicolored 1.25 .30

D-Day, 50th Anniv. A1289

No. 2429, Tank, crowd waving Allied flags.

1994, June 4 Engr.
2428 A1289 4.30fr multicolored 2.00 .50
2429 A1289 4.30fr multicolored 2.00 .50

Liberation of Paris, 50th anniv. (No. 2429).

Mount St. Victoire, by Paul Cezanne (1839-1906) — A1290

1994, June 18 Photo. *Perf. 13*
2430 A1290 2.80fr multicolored 1.25 .30

Intl. Olympic Committee, Cent. A1291

1994, June 23 Litho. *Perf. 13*
2431 A1291 2.80fr multicolored 1.25 .25

Saulx River Bridge, Rupt aux Nonains A1292

1994, July 2 Engr.
2432 A1292 2.80fr blackish blue 1.25 .25

Organ, Poitiers Cathedral — A1293

1994, July 2 *Perf. 13x12½*
2433 A1293 4.40fr multicolored 2.00 .55

Allied Landings in Provence, 50th Anniv. A1294

1994, Aug. 13 Engr. *Perf. 13*
2434 A1294 2.80fr multicolored 1.25 .30

Moses and the Daughters of Jethro, by Nicolas Poussin (1594-1665) — A1295

1994, Sept. 10
2435 A1295 4.40fr yel brn & blk 1.90 .90

Natl. Conservatory of Arts and Crafts, Bicent. — A1296

1994, Sept. 24 *Perf. 13x12½*
2436 A1296 2.80fr Foucault's pendulum 1.25 .30

The Great Cascade, St. Cloud Park — A1297

1994, Sept. 24 *Perf. 12½x13*
2437 A1297 3.70fr multicolored 1.60 .50

Leaves — A1298

1994 Litho. *Perf. 13*
2438 A1298 1.91fr Oak .85 .40
2439 A1298 2.46fr Sycamore 1.10 .70
2440 A1298 4.24fr Chestnut 2.00 1.00
2441 A1298 6.51fr Holly 3.00 2.00
Nos. 2438-2441 (4) 6.95 4.10

Nos. 2438-2441 are known only precanceled. See second note after No. 132.
See Nos. 2517-2520.

Ecole Normale Superieure (Teachers' School), Bicent. — A1299

1994, Oct. 8 Engr. *Perf. 13*
2442 A1299 2.80fr red & dk bl 1.25 .45

Georges Simenon (1903-89), Writer A1300

Litho. & Engr.

1994, Oct. 15 *Perf. 13*
2443 A1300 2.80fr multicolored 1.25 .25

See Belgium No. 1567, Switzerland No. 948.

Souvenir Sheet

European Stamp Exhibition — A1301

a, Flowers in park, Paris. b, Dalhias, vert.

1994, Oct. 15 Photo. *Perf. 13*
2444 A1301 2.80fr Sheet of 2, #a.-b. 15.00 15.00

No. 2444 sold for 16fr.

Natl. Drug Addiction Prevention Day — A1302

1994, Oct. 15
2445 A1302 2.80fr multicolored 1.25 .25

Grand Lodge of France, Cent. A1303

1994, Nov. 5 Engr.
2446 A1303 2.80fr multicolored 1.25 .25

Alain Colas (1943-78), Sailor A1304

1994, Nov. 19
2447 A1304 3.70fr green & black 1.60 .60

French Natl. Press Federation, 50th Anniv. A1305

1994, Dec. 9 Photo. *Perf. 13*
2448 A1305 2.80fr multicolored 1.25 .30

Champs Elysees — A1306

1994, Dec. 31
2449 A1306 4.40fr multicolored 2.00 .75

No. 2449 printed with se-tenant label.

Souvenir Sheet

Motion Pictures, Cent. — A1307

Faces on screen and: a, Projector at right. b, Projector facing away from screen. c, Projector facing screen. d, Reels of film.

1995, Jan. 14 Photo. *Perf. 13*
2450 A1307 Sheet of 4 5.00 5.00
a.-d. 2.80fr any single 1.00 1.00

Normandy Bridge — A1308

1995, Jan. 20 Engr. *Perf. 13*
2451 A1308 4.40fr multicolored 2.00 .75

A1309

A1310

1995, Jan. 21 *Perf. 13x12*
2452 A1309 2.80fr multicolored 1.25 .30

European Notaries Public.

1995, Feb. 18 Photo. *Perf. 13*
2453 A1310 3.70fr multicolored 1.60 1.00

Louis Pasteur (1822-95).

Art Series

St. Taurin's Reliquary, Evreaux A1311

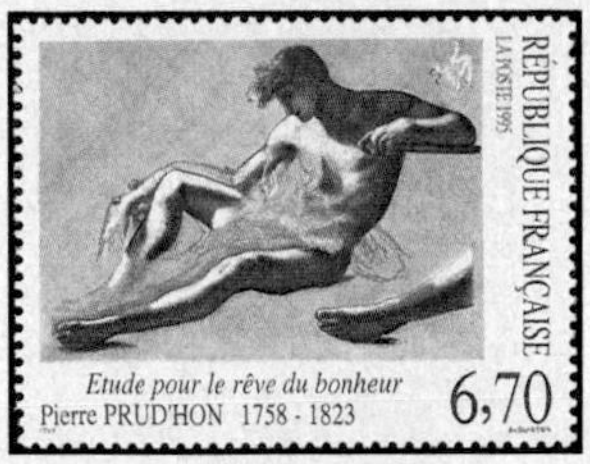

Study for the Dream of Happiness, by Pierre Prud'hon (1758-1823) — A1312

Abstract, by Zao Wou-ki — A1313

Abstract, by Per Kirkeby, Denmark — A1314

1995 Photo. & Engr. *Perf. 12x13*
2454 A1311 6.70fr multicolored 3.00 1.10

Engr.
Perf. 13x12
2455 A1312 6.70fr slate & blue 3.00 1.10

Litho.
Perf. 14
2456 A1313 6.70fr multicolored 3.00 1.10

Photo.
Perf. 13
2457 A1314 6.70fr multicolored 3.00 1.10
Nos. 2454-2457 (4) 12.00 4.40

Issued: No. 2454, 2/25; No. 2455, 5/12; No. 2456, 6/10; No. 2457, 9/23.

Tourism Series

Stenay Malt Works A1315

Remiremont, Vosges — A1316

Nyons Bridge, Drome A1317

Barbizon, Home of Landscape Artists A1318

1995 Engr. *Perf. 13x12½*
2458 A1315 2.80fr ol & dk grn 1.25 .30
2459 A1316 2.80fr brn, grn & bl 1.25 .30

Perf. 12½x13
2460 A1317 4.40fr multicolored 2.00 .75

Photo.
Perf. 13½
2461 A1318 4.40fr multicolored 2.00 .75
Nos. 2458-2461 (4) 6.50 2.10

Issued: No. 2458, 2/25; No. 2459, 5/13; No. 2460, 5/20; No. 2461, 9/30.

A1319

John J. Audubon (1785-1851) A1320

Designs: No. 2462, Snowy egret. No. 2463, Band-tailed pigeon. 4.30fr, Common tern. 4.40fr, Brown-colored rough-legged buzzard.

1995, Feb. 25 Photo. *Perf. 12½x12*
2462 A1319 2.80fr multicolored 1.25 .40
2463 A1320 2.80fr multicolored 1.25 .40
2464 A1319 4.30fr multicolored 2.00 .75
2465 A1320 4.40fr multicolored 2.00 .75
a. Souvenir sheet of 4, #2462-2465, perf. 13 7.00 7.00
Nos. 2462-2465 (4) 6.50 2.30

Stamp Day A1321

1995, Mar. 4 Engr. *Perf. 13*
2466 A1321 2.80fr multicolored 5.00 3.00
2467 A1321 2.80fr +60c multi 1.60 1.40
a. Booklet pane, 4 #2466, 3 #2467+label 24.00
Complete booklet, #2467 25.00

No. 2466 issued only in booklets.

Work Councils, 50th Anniv. — A1322

1995, Mar. 7 Engr. *Perf. 13*
2468 A1322 2.80fr dk bl, brn & sky bl 1.25 .30

Advanced Institute of Electricity, Cent. A1323

1995, Mar. 11 Photo.
2469 A1323 3.70fr multicolored 1.60 .40

Institute of Oriental Languages, Bicent. A1324

1995, Mar. 25 Photo. *Perf. 13*
2470 A1324 2.80fr multicolored 1.25 .30

Jean Giono (1895-1970), Writer — A1325

1995, Mar. 25 Engr.
2471 A1325 3.70fr multicolored 1.60 1.00

Iron and Steel Industry in Lorraine — A1326

1995, Apr. 1 *Perf. 13x12*
2472 A1326 2.80fr multicolored 1.25 .30

End of World War II, 50th Anniv. A1327

Europa: 2.80fr, Barbed wire, laurel wreath. 3.70fr, Broken sword, emblem of European Union.

1995, Apr. 29 Photo. *Perf. 13*
2473 A1327 2.80fr multicolored 1.25 .30
2474 A1327 3.70fr multicolored 1.60 .75

Forestry Profession, Ardennes — A1328

1995, May 2 Engr. *Perf. 12½x13*
2475 A1328 4.40fr multicolored 2.00 .80

End of World War II, 50th Anniv. A1329

1995, May 8 Photo. *Perf. 13*
2476 A1329 2.80fr multicolored 1.25 .35

Natl. Assembly — A1330

1995, May 13 Photo. *Perf. 13x12½*
2477 A1330 2.80fr multicolored 1.25 .60

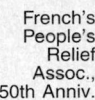

French's People's Relief Assoc., 50th Anniv. A1331

1995, May 20 Engr. *Perf. 12½x13*
2478 A1331 2.80fr multicolored 1.25 .30

Scenes of France — A1332

No. 2479, Forest, Vosges. No. 2480, Massif, Brittany. No. 2481, Wetlands, cattle, Camargue. No. 2482, Volcanoes, Auvergne.

1995, May 27 *Perf. 13*
2479 A1332 2.40fr green 1.10 .25
2480 A1332 2.40fr green 1.10 .25
2481 A1332 2.80fr red 1.25 .30
2482 A1332 2.80fr red 1.25 .30
Nos. 2479-2482 (4) 4.70 1.10

Ariane Rocket on Launch Pad, French Guiana — A1333

1995, March 28 Engr. *Perf. 12½x13*
2483 A1333 2.80fr bl, grn & red 1.25 .30

Compare with No. 2254.

A1334

A1335

1995, June 2 Engr. *Perf. 13*
2484 A1334 2.80fr multicolored 1.25 .30

68th Congress of French Federation of Philatelic Organizations, Orleans.

1995, June 3
2485 A1335 4.40fr Town of Correze 2.00 .75

A1336

A1337

Fables of Jean de la Fontaine (1621-95): No. 2486, The Grasshopper and The Ant. No. 2487, The Frog Who Could Make Himself Larger than an Ox. No. 2488, The Wolf and the Lamb. No. 2489, The Crow and the Fox. No. 2490, The Cat, the Weasel, and the Small Rabbit. No. 2491, The Tortoise and the Hare.

1995, June 24 Photo. *Perf. 13*
2486 A1336 2.80fr multicolored 1.40 .75
2487 A1336 2.80fr multicolored 1.40 .75
2488 A1336 2.80fr multicolored 1.40 .75
2489 A1336 2.80fr multicolored 1.40 .75

2490 A1336 2.80fr multicolored 1.40 .75
2491 A1336 2.80fr multicolored 1.40 .75
a. Strip, #2486-2491 + 2 labels 9.00 8.00

1995, July 9 Photo. *Perf. 13*
2492 A1337 2.80fr multicolored 1.25 .30

Velodrome d'Hiver raid.

André Maginot (1877-1932), Creator of Maginot Line — A1338

1995, Sept. 9 Engr. *Perf. 13*
2493 A1338 2.80fr multicolored 1.25 .30

Women's Grand Masonic Lodge of France, 50th Anniv. — A1339

1995, Sept. 16 *Perf. 13x12½*
2494 A1339 2.80fr multicolored 1.25 .30

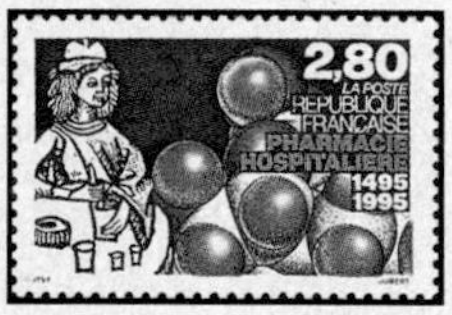

Hospital Pharmacies, 500th Anniv. — A1340

1995, Sept. 23 *Perf. 12½x13*
2495 A1340 2.80fr multicolored 1.25 .30

Natl. School of Administration, 50th Anniv. — A1341

1995, Oct. 5 Photo. *Perf. 13*
2496 A1341 2.80fr multicolored 1.25 .30

The Cradle, by Berthe Morisot (1841-95) A1342

1995, Oct. 7 Litho. *Perf. 13½x14*
2497 A1342 6.70fr multicolored 3.00 1.00

The French Institute, Bicent. — A1343

1995, Oct. 14 Engr. *Perf. 12½x13*
2498 A1343 2.80fr blk, grn & red 1.25 .30

Automobile Club of France, Cent. A1344

1995, Nov. 4 Engr. *Perf. 13x12½*
2499 A1344 4.40fr blk, bl & red 2.00 .60

UN, 50th Anniv. A1345

1995, Nov. 16 Photo. *Perf. 13*
2500 A1345 4.30fr multicolored 2.00 1.00

Francis Jammes (1868-1938), Poet — A1346

1995, Dec. 2 Engr. *Perf. 13*
2501 A1346 3.70fr black & blue 1.60 1.00

A1347

1995, Dec. 9 Litho. & Engr.
2502 A1347 2.80fr Evry Cathedral 1.25 .30

A1348

1995, Dec. 12 Photo. *Perf. 13*
2503 A1348 2.80fr multicolored 1.25 .30

1998 World Cup Soccer Championships, France.

Art Series

Abstract, by Lucien Wercollier — A1349

Design: No. 2505, The Netherlands (Horizon), abstract photograph, by Jan Dibbets.

1996 *Perf. 13x12½*
2504 A1349 6.70fr multicolored 3.00 1.00
2505 A1349 6.70fr multicolored 3.00 1.00

Issued: No. 2504, 1/20; No. 2505, 2/10.

Arawak Civilization, Saint Martin — A1350

Design: 2.80fr, Dog figurine, 550 B.C.

1996, Feb. 10 Engr. *Perf. 13*
2506 A1350 2.80fr multicolored 1.25 .40

The Augustus Bridge over the Nera River, by Camille Corot (1796-1875) — A1351

1996, Mar. 2 Litho. *Perf. 13*
2507 A1351 6.70fr multicolored 3.00 1.00

St. Patrick A1352

1996, Mar. 16 Photo. *Perf. 13*
2508 A1352 2.80fr multicolored 1.25 .50

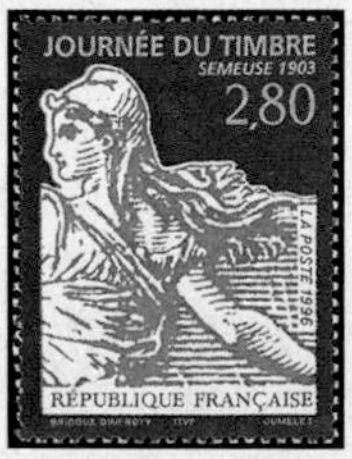

The Sower, 1903 — A1353

1996, Mar. 16 Litho. & Engr.
2509 A1353 2.80fr multicolored 6.00 5.00
2510 A1353 2.80fr +60c multi 1.75 1.25
a. Booklet pane, 4 #2509, 3 #2510 + label 30.00
Complete booklet, #2510a 32.50

Stamp Day.

Jacques Rueff (1896-1978), Economist — A1354

1996, Mar. 23 Engr. *Perf. 13x12½*
2511 A1354 2.80fr multicolored 1.25 .50

René Descartes (1596-1650) A1355

1996, Mar. 30 Engr. *Perf. 12½x13*
2512 A1355 4.40fr red 2.00 1.00

Gas & Electric Industries, 50th Anniv. A1356

1996, Apr. 6 Photo. *Perf. 13*
2513 A1356 3fr multicolored 1.40 .35

Natl. Parks A1357

1996, Apr. 20
2514 A1357 3fr Cévennes 1.40 .60
2515 A1357 4.40fr Vanoise 2.00 1.00
2516 A1357 4.40fr Mercantour 2.00 1.25
Nos. 2514-2516 (3) 5.40 2.85

See Nos. 2569-2572.

Leaf Type of 1994

1996, Mar. Litho. *Perf. 13*
2517 A1298 1.87fr Ash .85 .30
2518 A1298 2.18fr Beech 1.00 .65
2519 A1298 4.66fr Walnut 2.10 1.25
2520 A1298 7.11fr Elm 3.25 2.00
Nos. 2517-2520 (4) 7.20 4.20

Nos. 2517-2520 are known only precanceled. Values for precanceled stamps in first column are for those which have not been through the post and have original gum. Values in second column are for postally used, gumless stamps.

Madame Marie de Sévigné (1626-96), Writer — A1358

1996, Apr. 27 Photo. *Perf. 13*
2521 A1358 3fr multicolored 1.40 .65

Europa.

Natl. Institute of Agronomy Research, 50th Anniv. A1359

1996, May 4 Photo. *Perf. 13*
2522 A1359 3.80fr multicolored 1.75 1.00

Joan of Arc's House, Domremy-La-Pucelle — A1360

1996, May 11

2523 A1360 4.50fr multicolored 2.10 .70

RAMOGE Agreement Between France, Italy, Monaco, 20th Anniv. A1361

1996, May 14 **Photo. & Engr.**

2524 A1361 3fr multicolored 1.40 .35

See Monaco No. 1998, Italy No. 2077.

69th Congress of Federation of Philatelic Assoc., Clermont-Ferrand — A1362

1996, May 24 **Engr.** ***Perf. 13***

2525 A1362 3fr brn, red & grn 1.40 .35

Tourism Series

Bitche, Moselle A1363

Iles Sanguinaires, Ajaccio, Southern Corsica — A1364

Thoronet Abbey, Var A1365

Chambéry Cathedral, Savoie A1366

1996 **Engr.** ***Perf. 12½x13***

2526 A1363 3fr multicolored 1.40 .35

2527 A1364 3fr multicolored 1.40 .35

Perf. 13x12½

2528 A1365 3.80fr brn & claret 1.75 .70

Photo.

Perf. 13

2529 A1366 4.50fr multicolored 2.10 .75

Issued: No. 2526, 5/25; No. 2527, 6/1; 3.80fr, 7/6; 4.50fr, 6/8.

1998 World Cup Soccer Championships, France — A1367

Various stylized soccer plays, name of host city in France.

1996, June 1 **Photo.** ***Perf. 13***

2530 A1367 3fr Lens 1.40 .35

2531 A1367 3fr Toulouse 1.40 .35

2532 A1367 3fr Saint-Etienne 1.40 .35

2533 A1367 3fr Montpellier 1.40 .35

Nos. 2530-2533 (4) 5.60 1.40

See Nos. 2584-2587, 2623-2624, sheet of 10, No. 2624a.

Art Series

Gallo-Roman Bronze Statue of Horse, Neuvy-en-Sullias, Loiret — A1368

Imprints of Cello Fragments, by Arman — A1369

1996 **Engr.** ***Perf. 13***

2534 A1368 6.70fr multicolored 3.00 1.00

Photo.

2535 A1369 6.70fr multicolored 3.00 1.00

Issued: No. 2534, 6/8; No. 2535, 9/21.

A1371

A1372

1996, June 15 **Photo.** ***Perf. 13***

2537 A1371 3fr multicolored 1.40 .50

Modern Olympic Games, cent.

1996, June 15 **Engr.** ***Perf. 12½x13***

2538 A1372 4.40fr deep purple 2.00 1.00

Jacques Marette (1922-84), Member of Parliament.

A1373

A1374

1996, June 29 **Photo.** ***Perf. 13***

2539 A1373 3fr multicolored 1.40 .35

Train between Ajaccio and Vizzavona, cent.

1996, Sept. 6 **Engr.** ***Perf. 13x12½***

2540 A1374 3fr dark blue & yel 1.40 .30

Notre Dame de Fourvière Basilica, Lyon, cent.

Baptism of Clovis, 1500th Anniv. A1375

1996, Sept. 14 ***Perf. 13***

2541 A1375 3fr multicolored 1.40 .30

Henri IV High School, Bicent. — A1376

1996, Oct. 12 **Engr.** ***Perf. 12½x13***

2542 A1376 4.50fr brown & blue 2.10 .80

UNICEF, 50th Anniv. A1377

1996, Oct. 19 **Photo.** ***Perf. 13***

2543 A1377 4.50fr multicolored 2.10 .80

Economic and Social Council, 50th Anniv. — A1378

1996, Oct. 26 **Engr.** ***Perf. 13***

2544 A1378 3fr red, black & blue 1.40 .30

UNESCO, 50th Anniv. A1379

1996, Nov. 2 **Litho.** ***Perf. 13***

2545 A1379 3.80fr multicolored 1.75 .75

A1380

A1381

1996, Nov. 7 **Photo.** ***Perf. 13***

2546 A1380 3fr multicolored 1.40 .30

Autumn Stamp Show, 50th anniv.

1996, Nov. 16

2547 A1381 3fr multicolored 1.40 .30

Creation of French Overseas Departments, 50th anniv.

André Malraux (1901-76), Writer A1382

1996, Nov. 23 **Engr.** ***Perf. 13***

2548 A1382 3fr deep green black 1.40 .30

French School in Athens, 150th Anniv. A1383

1996, Nov. 23 **Photo.**

2549 A1383 3fr multicolored 1.40 .30

Cannes Film Festival, 50th Anniv. A1384

1996, Nov. 30

2550 A1384 3fr multicolored 1.40 .30

New National Library of France A1385

1996, Dec. 14

2551 A1385 3fr multicolored 1.40 .30

A1386

A1387

1997, Jan. 4

2552 A1386 3fr multicolored 1.40 .30

Francois Mitterrand (1916-96).

1997, Jan. 24 **Photo.** ***Perf. 13***

2553 A1387 3fr multicolored 1.40 .30

Participatory innovation.

Georges Pompidou Natl. Center of Art and Culture, 20th Anniv.
A1388

1997, Jan. 31 Engr. *Perf. 12½x13*

2554 A1388 3fr multicolored 1.40 .30

Happy Holiday
A1389

1997, Feb. 8 Photo. *Perf. 13*

2555 A1389 3fr shown 1.40 .30
2556 A1389 3fr Happy birthday 1.40 .30

Natl. School of Bridges and Highways, 250th Anniv.
A1390

Photo. & Engr.

1997, Feb. 14 *Perf. 12½x13*

2557 A1390 3fr multicolored 1.40 .30

Saint-Laurent-du-Maroni, French Guiana — A1391

Photo. & Engr.

1997, Feb. 22 *Perf. 12½x13*

2558 A1391 3fr multicolored 1.40 .30

Art Series

Church Fresco, Tavant
A1392

Painting by Bernard Moninot — A1393

The Thumb, Polished Bronze, by César
A1394

Grapes and Pomegranates, by Jean Baptiste Chardin — A1395

1997 Engr. *Perf. 13*

2559 A1392 6.70fr multicolored 3.00 1.00

Photo.

2560 A1393 6.70fr multicolored 3.00 1.00
2561 A1394 6.70fr multicolored 3.00 1.00
2562 A1395 6.70fr multicolored 3.00 1.00
Nos. 2559-2562 (4) 12.00 4.00

Issued: No. 2559, 3/1; No. 2560, 3/29; No. 2561, 9/13; No. 2562, 9/27.

Tourism Series

Millau — A1396

Guimiliau Church Close — A1398

Fresco, Saint Eutrope des Salles-Lavauguyon — A1397

Sablé-Sur-Sarthe — A1399

1997 Engr. *Perf. 12½x13*

2563 A1396 3fr grn & dk bl grn 1.40 .30

Perf. 13

2564 A1397 4.50fr multicolored 2.10 .75
2565 A1398 3fr multicolored 1.40 .30

Perf. 12½x13

2566 A1399 3fr multicolored 1.40 .25
Nos. 2563-2566 (4) 6.30 1.60

Issued: No. 2563, 3/15; No. 2564, 6/14; No. 2565, 7/12; No. 2566, 9/20.

Vignette of Type A17 — A1400

Litho. & Engr.

1997, Mar. 15 *Perf. 13½x13*

2567 A1400 3fr multicolored 6.00 5.00
2568 A1400 3fr +60c multi 2.50 2.00
a. Booklet pane, 4 #2567, 3 #2568 + label 32.50
Complete booklet, #2568a 35.00

Stamp Day.
No. 2567 issued only in booklets.

National Parks Type of 1996

1997, Apr. 12 Photo. *Perf. 13*

2569 A1357 3fr Parc des Ecrins 1.40 .40
2570 A1357 3fr Guadeloupe Park 1.40 .40
2571 A1357 4.50fr Parc des Pyrénées 2.10 .90
2572 A1357 4.50fr Port-Cros Park 2.10 .90
Nos. 2569-2572 (4) 7.00 2.60

Puss-in-Boots
A1401

1997, Apr. 26 Engr. *Perf. 13*

2573 A1401 3fr blue 1.40 .30

Europa.

Philexjeunes '97, Nantes — A1402

1997, May 2 Litho. *Perf. 13*

2574 A1402 3fr multicolored 1.40 .30

Cartoon Journey of a Letter
A1403

"Envelope": No. 2575, Writing letter. No. 2576, Climbing ladder to go into letter box. No. 2577, On wheels. No. 2578, Following postman carrying another "Envelope." No. 2579, Held by girl. No. 2580, At feet of girl reading long letter.

1997, May 8 Photo. *Perf. 13*

2575 A1403 3fr multicolored 2.50 1.00
2576 A1403 3fr multicolored 2.50 1.00
2577 A1403 3fr multicolored 2.50 1.00
2578 A1403 3fr multicolored 2.50 1.00
2579 A1403 3fr multicolored 2.50 1.00
2580 A1403 3fr multicolored 2.50 1.00
a. Strip of 6, #2575-2580 + label 18.00 12.00

Self-Adhesive

Serpentine Die Cut 11

2580B A1403 3fr like #2575 2.00 1.25
2580C A1403 3fr like #2576 2.00 1.25
2580D A1403 3fr like #2577 2.00 1.25
2580E A1403 3fr like #2578 2.00 1.25
2580F A1403 3fr like #2579 2.00 1.25
2580G A1403 3fr like #2580 2.00 1.25
h. Booklet pane, 2 each #2580B-2580G 27.50 27.50

By its nature No. 2580h is a complete booklet. The peelable paper backing serves as a booklet cover.

See Nos. 2648-2659.

Honoring French Soldiers in North Africa (1952-62)
A1404

1997, May 10 Litho. *Perf. 13*

2581 A1404 3fr multicolored 1.40 .30

French Federation of Philatelic Associations, 70th Congress, Versailles — A1405

1997, May 17 Photo. *Perf. 13*

2582 A1405 3fr multicolored 1.40 .30

Printed with se-tenant label.

Château de Plessis-Bourré, Maine and Loire Rivers — A1406

1997, May 24 Litho. & Engr.

2583 A1406 4.40fr multicolored 2.00 1.00

1998 World Cup Soccer Championships Type

Stylized action scenes, name of host city in France.

1997, May 31 Photo. *Perf. 13½*

2584 A1367 3fr Lyon 1.40 .35
2585 A1367 3fr Marseilles 1.40 .35
2586 A1367 3fr Nantes 1.40 .35
2587 A1367 3fr Paris 1.40 .35
Nos. 2584-2587 (4) 5.60 1.40

Saint Martin of Tours (316-97) Apostle of the Gauls
A1408

1997, July 5 Engr. *Perf. 13*

2588 A1408 4.50fr multicolored 2.00 .65

Marianne — A1409

1997, July 14 Engr. *Perf. 13*

2589 A1409 10c brown .25 .25
2590 A1409 20c brt blue grn .25 .25
2591 A1409 50c purple .25 .25
2592 A1409 1fr bright org .45 .25
2593 A1409 2fr bright blue .90 .30
2594 A1409 2.70fr bright grn 1.25 .25
2595 A1409 (3fr) red 1.40 .25
2596 A1409 3.50fr apple grn 1.60 .25
2597 A1409 3.80fr blue 1.75 .25
2598 A1409 4.20fr dark org 1.90 .30
2599 A1409 4.40fr blue 2.00 .30
2600 A1409 4.50fr bright pink 2.10 .30
2601 A1409 5fr brt grn blue 5.25 .30
2602 A1409 6.70fr dark green 3.00 .30
a. Souvenir sheet, #2594-2600, 2602 14.00 14.00
2603 A1409 10fr violet 4.50 .35
a. Souvenir sheet, #2589-2593, 2601, 2603 12.00 12.00
Nos. 2589-2603 (15) 26.85 4.15

Self-Adhesive
Booklet Stamps
Die Cut x Serpentine Die Cut 7

2603B A1409 1fr brt org 2.25 .50
c. Booklet pane, #2603B, 3 #2604 7.75
Booklet, 2 #2603Bc 16.00
2604 A1409 (3fr) red 1.40 .25
a. Booklet pane of 10 14.00

Coil Stamps
Perf. 13 Horiz.

2604B A1409 2.70fr bright grn 1.25 .50
2605 A1409 (3fr) red 1.40 .30

Nos. 2595, 2604-2605 were valued at 3fr on day of issue.

Issued: Nos. 2602a, 2603a, 11/12/01. No. 2603B, 9/1/97.

See Nos. 2835-2835C, 2921-2922, 3530, 4410j, 4523.

1997 World Rowing Championships, Savoie — A1410

1997, Aug. 30 Engr. ***Perf. 13x12½***
2606 A1410 3fr blue & magenta 1.40 .30

Basque Corsairs A1411

1997, Sept. 13 ***Perf. 13***
2607 A1411 3fr multicolored 1.40 .30

Saint-Maurice Basilica, Epinal — A1412

1997, Sept. 20 ***Perf. 13x12½***
2608 A1412 3fr multicolored 1.40 .30

Fresh Fish Merchants, Port of Boulogne A1413

1997, Sept. 26 ***Perf. 13***
2609 A1413 3fr multicolored 1.40 .30

Japan Year — A1414

1997, Oct. 4 Engr. ***Perf. 13***
2610 A1414 4.90fr multicolored 2.25 1.25

1997 World Judo Championships — A1415

1997, Oct. 9 Photo. ***Perf. 13***
2611 A1415 3fr multicolored 1.40 .35

Sceaux Estate, Hauts-de-Seine — A1416

1997, Oct. 11
2612 A1416 3fr multicolored 1.40 .30

Saar-Lorraine-Luxembourg Summit — A1417

1997, Oct. 16 Photo. ***Perf. 13***
2613 A1417 3fr multicolored 1.40 .30

See Germany No. 1982, Luxembourg No. 972.

College of France A1418

1997, Oct. 18 **Engr.**
2614 A1418 4.40fr multicolored 2.00 .90

Quality — A1419

1997, Oct. 18 **Photo.**
2615 A1419 4.50fr multicolored 2.10 .60

A1420

Season's Greetings A1421

1997 Photo. ***Perf. 13***
2616 A1420 3fr Cat & mouse 1.40 .30

Photo. & Embossed
2617 A1421 3fr Mailman 1.40 .30

Issued: No. 2616, 11/8; No. 2617, 11/22.

Protection of Abused Children — A1422

1997, Nov. 20 **Photo.**
2618 A1422 3fr multicolored 1.40 .30

Marshal Jacques Leclerc (Philippe de Haute Cloque) (1902-47) A1423

1997, Nov. 28 Photo. ***Perf. 13***
2619 A1423 3fr multicolored 1.40 .30

Philexfrance '99, World Stamp Exposition — A1424

1997, Dec. 6 **Engr.**
2620 A1424 3fr red & blue 1.40 .30

Abbey of Moutier D'Ahun, Creuse A1425

1997, Dec. 13
2621 A1425 4.40fr multicolored 2.00 1.00

Michel Debré (1912-96), Politician A1426

1998, Jan. 15 **Photo.**
2622 A1426 3fr multicolored 1.40 .30

1998 World Cup Soccer Championships Type

Stylized action scenes, name of host city in France.

1998, Jan. 24 ***Perf. 13½***
2623 A1367 3fr Saint-Denis 1.40 .30
2624 A1367 3fr Bordeaux 1.40 .30
a. Sheet of 10, #2530-2533, #2584-2587, #2623-2624 + label 14.00 14.00

National Assembly, Bicent. — A1427

1998, Jan. 24 ***Perf. 13***
2625 A1427 3fr multicolored 1.40 .30

Valentine's Day A1428

1998, Jan. 31
2626 A1428 3fr multicolored 1.40 .30

Office of Mediator of the Republic, 25th Anniv. A1429

1998, Feb. 5
2627 A1429 3fr multicolored 1.40 .30

A1430

1998, Feb. 28 Photo. ***Perf. 12½***
2628 A1430 3fr multicolored 1.40 .30

Self-Adhesive
Serpentine Die Cut

2629 A1430 3fr like #2628 1.40 .30
a. Booklet pane of 10 14.00 14.00
b. Sheet of 1 + 7 labels 14.00 14.00

1998 World Cup Soccer Championships, France.

The peelable paper backing of No. 2629a serves as a booklet cover.

See No. 2665.

A1431

1998, Feb. 21 Engr. ***Perf. 13½x13***
2630 A1431 3fr Detail of design A16 5.00 3.50
2631 A1431 3fr +60c like #2630 1.90 1.90
a. Booklet pane, 4 #2630, 3 #2631 + label 26.00
Complete booklet, #2631a 27.00

Stamp Day. No. 2630 issued only in booklets.

A1432

1998, Feb. 28 Engr. ***Perf. 13***
2632 A1432 4.50fr blue 2.10 .75

Father Franz Stock (1904-48), prison chaplain.

Happy Birthday A1433

1998, Mar. 13 Photo. ***Perf. 13x13½***
2633 A1433 3fr multicolored 1.40 .30

Union of Mulhouse with France, Bicent. A1434

1998, Mar. 14

2634	A1434	3fr multicolored	1.40	.30

Citeaux Abbey, 900th Anniv. A1435

1998, Mar. 14 Engr. *Perf. 13*

2635	A1435	3fr multicolored	1.40	.30

Sous-Préfecture Hotel, Saint-Pierre, Réunion — A1436

1998, Apr. 4 Engr. *Perf. 13*

2636	A1436	3fr multicolored	1.40	.30

Réunion's architectural heritage.

"The Return," by René Magritte — A1437

1998, Apr. 18 Photo.

2637	A1437	3fr multicolored	1.40	.50

See Belgium No. 1691.

Edict of Nantes, 400th Anniv. A1438

1998, Apr. 18 Litho.

2638	A1438	4.50fr Henry IV	2.10	.75

Art Series

Detail from "Entry of the Crusaders into Constantinople," by Delacroix (1798-1863) — A1439

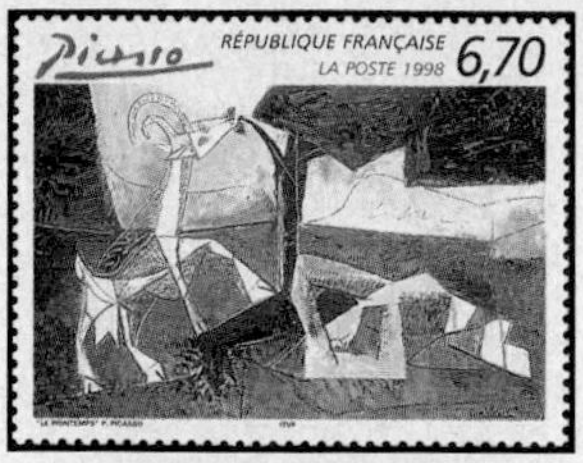

Le Printemps, by Pablo Picasso (1881-1973) — A1440

Neuf Moules Malic, by Marcel Duchamp (1887-1968) — A1441

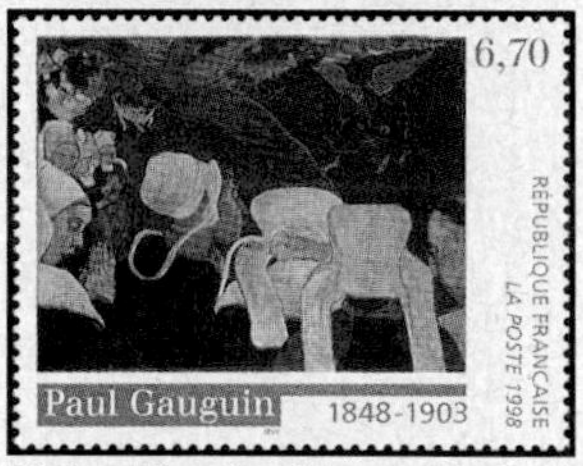

Vision After the Sermon, by Paul Gauguin (1848-1903) — A1442

1998 Engr. *Perf. 12x13*

2639	A1439	6.70fr multicolored	3.00	1.00
		Litho.		
		Perf. 13		
2640	A1440	6.70fr multicolored	3.00	1.00
		Photo.		
2641	A1441	6.70fr multicolored	3.00	1.00
2642	A1442	6.70fr multicolored	3.00	1.00

Issued: No. 2639, 4/25; No. 2640, 5/15; No. 2641, 10/17; No. 2642, 12/5.

Abolition of Slavery, 150th Anniv. A1443

1998, Apr. 25 Litho. *Perf. 13*

2643	A1443	3fr multicolored	1.40	.30

Tourism Series

Le Gois Causeway, Island of Noirmoutier, Vendée — A1444

Bay of Somme, Picardy — A1445

Château de Crussol, Ardèche A1446

Collegiate Church of Mantes — A1447

1998, May 2 Photo.

2644	A1444	3fr multicolored	1.40	.30
2645	A1445	3fr multicolored	1.40	.30
		Engr.		
2646	A1446	3fr multicolored	1.40	.30
2647	A1447	4.40fr multicolored	2.00	1.00
		Nos. 2644-2647 (4)	6.20	1.90

Issued: No. 2644, 5/2; No. 2645, 6/27; No. 2646, 7/4; No. 2647, 9/19.

Journey of a Letter Type

Historic "letters:" No. 2648, Dove carrying letter, Noah's Ark. No. 2649, Egyptian writing letter on papyrus. No. 2650, Soldier running to Athens with letter to victory at Marathon. No. 2651, Knight carrying letter on horseback. No. 2652, Writing letters with quill and ink. No. 2653, Astronaut carrrying letter in space from earth to the moon.

1998, May 9 Photo. *Perf. 13x13½*

2648	A1403	3fr multicolored	2.50	1.00
2649	A1403	3fr multicolored	2.50	1.00
2650	A1403	3fr multicolored	2.50	1.00
2651	A1403	3fr multicolored	2.50	1.00
2652	A1403	3fr multicolored	2.50	1.00
2653	A1403	3fr multicolored	2.50	1.00
a.		Strip, #2648-2653 + label	16.00	10.00

Booklet Stamps
Self-Adhesive
Serpentine Die Cut 11

2654	A1403	3fr like #2648	2.25	1.25
2655	A1403	3fr like #2649	2.25	1.25
2656	A1403	3fr like #2650	2.25	1.25
2657	A1403	3fr like #2651	2.25	1.25
2658	A1403	3fr like #2652	2.25	1.25
2659	A1403	3fr like #2653	2.25	1.25
a.		Bklt. pane, 2 ea #2654-2659	27.50	27.50

By its nature No. 2659a is a complete booklet. The peelable paper backing serves as a booklet cover.

League of Human Rights, Cent. — A1448

1998, May 9 *Perf. 13*

2660	A1448	4.40fr multicolored	2.00	1.00

Henri Collet (1885-1951), Composer — A1449

1998, May 15 Engr. *Perf. 12x13*

2661	A1449	4.50fr black, gray & buff	2.10	.90

French Federation of Philatelic Assoc., 71st Congress, Dunkirk — A1450

Photo. & Engr.

1998, May 29 *Perf. 13*

2662	A1450	3fr multicolored	1.40	.30

Mont-Saint-Michel — A1451

1998, June 6 Photo. *Perf. 13*

2663	A1451	3fr multicolored	1.40	.30

Natl. Music Festival — A1452

1998, June 13

2664	A1452	3fr multicolored	1.40	.50

Europa.

1998 World Cup Soccer Championships Type with Added Inscription, "Champion du Monde"

1998, July 12 Photo. *Perf. 12½*

2665	A1430	3fr multicolored	1.40	.30

Stéphane Mallarmé (1842-98), Poet A1453

Photo. & Engr.

1998, Sept. 5 *Perf. 13*

2666	A1453	4.40fr multicolored	2.00	.90

Flowers — A1453a

1998, Sept. 9 Litho. *Perf. 13*

2666A	A1453a	1.87fr Liseron	.85	.30
2666B	A1453a	2.18fr Coquelicot	1.00	.55
2666C	A1453a	4.66fr Violette	2.10	1.25
2666D	A1453a	7.11fr Bouton d'or	3.25	2.00
		Nos. 2666A-2666D (4)	7.20	4.10

Nos. 2666A-2666D are known only precanceled. See second note after No. 132.

A1454

A1455

1998, Sept. 12 **Photo.**

2667 A1454 3fr multicolored 1.40 .30

Aéro Club of France, cent.

1998, Oct. 23 **Photo.** ***Perf. 13***

"The Little Prince," by Antoine de Saint-Exupéry (1900-44): a, Standing in uniform with sword, horiz. b, Seated on wall. c, "The Little Prince on Asteroid B-612." d, Pouring water from sprinkling can. e, Walking along cliff, fox, horiz.

2668 Strip of 5 + 2 labels 7.00 6.00
a.-e. A1455 3fr any single 1.40 .60
f. Souv. sheet, #2668a-2668e 9.00 9.00

Philexfrance '99. No. 2668f was released 9/12 and sold for 25fr.

Hall of Heavenly Peace, Imperial Palace, Beijing, China A1456

1998, Sept. 12 **Photo.** ***Perf. 13x13½***

2669 A1456 3fr shown 1.40 .40
2670 A1456 4.90fr The Louvre, France 2.25 1.00

See People's Republic of China Nos. 2895-2896.

Garnier Palace, Home of the Paris Opera — A1457

1998, Sept. 19 **Photo.** ***Perf. 13***

2671 A1457 4.50fr multicolored 2.10 .75

Horses A1458

1998, Sept. 27

2672 A1458 2.70fr Camargue 1.25 .30
2673 A1458 3fr Pottok 1.40 .50
2674 A1458 3fr French trotter 1.40 .50
2675 A1458 4.50fr Ardennais 2.10 .80
Nos. 2672-2675 (4) 6.15 2.10

Paris Auto Show, Cent. A1459

1998, Oct. 1 ***Perf. 12***

2676 A1459 3fr multicolored 1.40 .30

5th Republic, 40th Anniv. A1460

1998, Oct. 3 **Photo.** ***Perf. 13***

2677 A1460 3fr blue, gray & red 1.40 .30

Saint-Dié, Capital of Vosges Mountain Region — A1461

1998, Oct. 3 **Engr.** ***Perf. 13***

2678 A1461 3fr Tower of Liberty 1.40 .30

End of World War I, 80th Anniv. A1462

1998, Oct. 17 **Photo.** ***Perf. 13x13½***

2679 A1462 3fr multicolored 1.40 .40

Intl. Union for the Conservation of Nature and Natural Resources, 50th Anniv. — A1463

1998, Nov. 3 **Litho.**

2680 A1463 3fr multicolored 1.40 .40

New Year A1464

Christmas A1465

1998, Nov. 7 **Photo.** ***Perf. 13***

Background Colors

2681 A1464 3fr deep blue 1.40 .75
2682 A1465 3fr green 1.40 .75
2683 A1464 3fr yellow 1.40 .75
2684 A1465 3fr red 1.40 .75
2685 A1464 3fr green 1.40 .75
a. Strip of 5, #2681-2685 7.00 6.00

Issued in sheets of 10 stamps. Location of "Bonne Annee" and "Meilleurs Voeux" varies.

Doctors Without Borders A1466

1998, Nov. 21 ***Perf. 13x13½***

2686 A1466 3fr multicolored 1.40 .30

European Parliament, Strasbourg A1467

1998, Dec. 5 **Photo.** ***Perf. 13***

2687 A1467 3fr multicolored 1.40 .30

Universal Declaration of Human Rights, 50th Anniv. A1468

No. 2688, Faces of people of various races, globe. No. 2689, René Cassin (1887-1976), principal author of Declaration, Eleanor Roosevelt (1884-1962), Chaillot Palace, Paris.

1998, Dec. 10 **Litho.** ***Perf. 13***

2688 A1468 3fr multicolored 1.40 .30
2689 A1468 3fr multicolored 1.40 .30

Discovery of Radium, Cent., ZOE Reactor, 50th Anniv. A1469

1998, Dec. 15 **Photo.** ***Perf. 13***

2690 A1469 3fr multicolored 1.40 .40

Introduction of the Euro — A1470

1999 **Engr.** ***Perf. 13***

2691 A1470 3fr red & blue 1.40 .25

Booklet Stamps

Self-Adhesive

Die Cut x Serpentine Die Cut 7

2691A A1470 3fr red & blue 1.40 .25
b. Booklet pane of 10 14.00

Issued: No. 2691, 1/1/99. No. 2691A, 2/15/99. Values are shown in both Francs and Euros on Nos. 2691-2691A. No. 2691Ab is a complete booklet.

Euro currency did not circulate until 2002.

French Postage Stamps, 150th Anniv. A1471

1999, Jan. 1 **Photo.** ***Perf. 13***

Booklet Stamps

2692 A1471 3fr black & red 6.50 4.50
2693 A1471 3fr red & black 1.25 .75
a. Booklet pane, #2692, 4 #2693 + label 11.50
Complete booklet, #2693a 12.00

No. 2692 has black denomination; No. 2693 has red denomination.

Stamp Day.

Public Assistance Hospital, Paris, 150th Anniv. A1472

1999, Jan. 9

2694 A1472 3fr multicolored 1.40 .30

Diplomatic Relations with Israel, 50th Anniv. — A1473

1999, Jan. 24

2695 A1473 4.40fr multicolored 2.00 .75

Festival Stamps A1474

1999, Feb. 6 **Photo.** ***Perf. 13***

2696 A1474 3fr Stars, "Je t'aime" 1.40 .30
2697 A1474 3fr Rose 1.40 .30

Booklet Stamps

Self-Adhesive

Die Cut Perf. 10

2698 A1474 3fr like #2696 1.40 .30
2699 A1474 3fr like #2697 1.40 .30
a. Bklt. pane, 5 ea #2698-2699 14.00

No. 2699a is a complete booklet.

Art Series

St. Luke the Evangelist, Sculpture by Jean Goujon (1510-66) A1475

Painting, "Waterlillies in Moonlight," by Claude Monet (1840-1926) — A1476

Stained Glass, Cathedral of Auch, by Arnauld de Moles, 16th Cent. A1477

Charles I, King of England, by Sir Anthony Van Dyck
A1478

1999 **Engr.** ***Perf. 13***
2700 A1475 6.70fr multicolored 3.00 1.00

Litho.
2701 A1476 6.70fr multicolored 3.00 1.00

Engr.
2702 A1477 6.70fr multicolored 3.00 1.00

Photo.
Perf. 13¼x13
2703 A1478 6.70fr multicolored 3.00 1.00
Nos. 2700-2703 (4) 12.00 4.00

Issued: No. 2700, 2/13; No. 2701, 5/29; No. 2702, 6/19; No. 2703, 11/11.

National Census — A1479

1999, Feb. 20 **Photo.** ***Perf. 13½***
2704 A1479 3fr multicolored 1.40 .30

Cultural Heritage of Lebanon
A1480

Mosaic illustrating transformation of Zeus into bull, Natl. Museum of Beirut.

1999, Feb. 27 ***Perf. 12½***
2705 A1480 4.40fr multicolored 2.00 .90

Asterix, by Albert Uderzo and Rene Goscinny
A1481

1999, Mar. 6 **Photo.** ***Perf. 13¼***
2706 A1481 3fr multicolored 1.75 .50
a. Perf. 13¼x12¾ 1.75 .90

Booklet Stamp
Perf. 13¼x12¾
2707 A1481 3fr +60c like #2706 3.50 2.00
b. Booklet pane, 4 #2706a, 3 #2707 + label 15.00
Complete booklet, #2707b 16.00

Souvenir Sheet
2707A A1481 3fr +60c like #2706 3.00 2.50

Stamp Day. Stamp design in No. 2707A continues into the margins.

Council of Europe, 50th Anniv.
A1482

1999, Mar. 19
2708 A1482 3fr multicolored 1.40 .30

A1483

Announcements — A1483a

1999, Mar. 20 ***Perf. 13***
2709 A1483 3fr Marriage (Oui) 1.40 .30
2710 A1483 3fr It's a boy (C'est un garcon) 1.40 .30
2711 A1483 3fr It's a girl(C'est une fille) 1.40 .30
2712 A1483a 3fr Thank you 1.40 .30
Nos. 2709-2712 (4) 5.60 1.20

See Nos. 2721-2722.

Souvenir Sheet

PhilexFrance '99 — A1484

Works of art: a, Venus de Milo. b, Mona Lisa, by Da Vinci. c, Liberty Guiding the People, by Delacroix.

Litho. & Engr.
1999, Mar. 26 ***Perf. 13¼***
2713 A1484 Sheet of 3 50.00 50.00
a.-b. 5fr each 10.00 10.00
c. 10fr multicolored 20.00 20.00

No. 2713 sold for 50fr, with 30fr serving as a donation to the Assoc. for the Development of Philately.

Elections to the European Parliament
A1485

1999, Mar. 27 **Photo.** ***Perf. 13***
2714 A1485 3fr multicolored 1.40 .30

Richard I, the Lion-Hearted (1157-1199), King of England — A1486

1999, Apr. 10 **Engr.** ***Perf. 13x12½***
2715 A1486 3fr multicolored 1.40 .35

Tourism Series

Dieppe
A1487

Haut-Koenigsbourg Castle, Bas-Rhin — A1488

Birthpalce of Champollion, Figeac — A1489

Chateau, Arnac-Pompadour — A1490

1999 **Engr.** ***Perf. 13½***
2716 A1487 3fr multicolored 1.40 .30

Litho. & Engr.
Perf. 13
2717 A1488 3fr multicolored 1.40 .50
2718 A1489 3fr multicolored 1.40 .30

Engr.
2719 A1490 3fr multicolored 1.40 .30
Nos. 2716-2719 (4) 5.60 1.40

Issued: No. 2716, 4/17; No. 2717, 5/15; No. 2718, 6/26; No. 2719, 7/10.

The Camargue Nature Preserve
A1491

1999, Apr. 24 **Photo.** ***Perf. 13x13½***
2720 A1491 3fr multicolored 1.40 .50

Europa.

Announcements Type of 1999 and

A1492

1999, May 13 **Photo.** ***Perf. 13***
2721 A1483 3fr Nice Holiday (bonnes vacances) 1.40 .30
2722 A1483 3fr Happy Birthday (joyeux anniversaire) 1.40 .30
2723 A1492 3fr Long Live Vacations (Vive les vacances 1.40 .30
Nos. 2721-2723 (3) 4.20 .90

Saint Pierre, Martinique
A1493

1999, May 15
2724 A1493 3fr multicolored 1.10 .25

Detail of "Noctuelles" Dish, by Emile Gallé, School of Nancy Museum
A1494

1999, May 22
2725 A1494 3fr multicolored 1.40 .30

Souvenir Sheet

World Old Roses Competition, Lyon — A1495

a, 4.50fr, Mme. Caroline Testout. b, 3fr, Mme. Alfred Carrière. c, 4.50fr, La France.

1999, May 28 ***Perf. 13½x13***
2726 A1495 Sheet of 3, #a.-c. 6.00 6.00

Court of Saint-Emilion, 800th Anniv. — A1496

1999, May 29 **Engr.** ***Perf. 13¼x13***
2727 A1496 3.80fr multicolored 1.75 .90

Hotel de la Monnaie, French Mint Headquarters — A1497

1999, June 5 **Engr.** ***Perf. 13***
2728 A1497 4.50fr brn org & bl 2.10 .75

A1498

A1499

1999, June 12 **Photo.** ***Perf. 13¼***
2729 A1498 3fr multicolored 1.40 .40

Countess of Segur (1799-1874), children's storyteller.

1999, June 19 ***Perf. 13***
2730 A1499 3fr Welcome 1.40 .30

René Caillié (1799-1838), Explorer of Africa — A1500

1999, June 26 Engr. *Perf. 13¼*
2731 A1500 4.50fr multicolored 2.10 .75

1st French Postage Stamps, 150th Anniv. A1501

1999, July 2 Photo. *Perf. 11¾x13*
2732 A1501 6.70fr multicolored 3.00 1.75

PhilexFrance '99, World Philatelic Exhibition.
No. 2732 was printed with a se-tenant label and contains a holographic image. Soaking in water may affect the hologram.

Celebrating the Year 2000 A1502

1999, July 5 Photo. *Perf. 13*
2733 A1502 3fr multicolored 1.40 .30

Year 2000 Stamp Design Contest Winner — A1503

1999, July 6
2734 A1503 3fr multicolored 1.40 .30

Total Solar Eclipse, Aug. 11, 1999 A1504

1999, July 8 *Perf. 12x12¼*
2735 A1504 3fr multicolored 1.40 .40

Gathering of Tall Ships, Rouen, July 9-18 A1505

Sailing ships: a, Simón Bolivar. b, Iskra. c, Statsraad Lehmkuhl. d, Asgard II. e, Belle Poule. f, Belem. g, Amerigo Vespucci. h, Sagres. i, Europa. j, Cuauhtemoc.

1999, July 10 Photo. *Perf. 13*
2736 1fr Sheet of 10 6.00 6.00
a.-j. A1505 any single .50 .50

1999 Rugby World Cup, Cardiff, Wales A1506

1999, Sept. 11 Photo. *Perf. 13¼*
2737 A1506 3fr multicolored 1.40 .40
a. Miniature sheet of 10 11.00

Value is for copy with surrounding selvage.
One stamp in No. 2737a has a missing "F" in the printer's mark.

Frédéric Ozanam (1813-53), Historian — A1507

1999, Sept. 11 Engr. *Perf. 13*
2738 A1507 4.50fr multicolored 2.10 .75

Emmaus Movement, 50th Anniv. A1508

1999, Sept. 26 Photo. *Perf. 13*
2739 A1508 3fr multicolored 1.40 .40

Cats and Dogs — A1509

1999, Oct. 2 Photo. *Perf. 13¼*
2740 A1509 2.70fr Chartreux cat 1.25 .30
2741 A1509 3fr European cat 1.40 .30
2742 A1509 3fr Pyrenean Mountain dog 1.40 .30
2743 A1509 4.50fr Brittany spaniel 2.10 .75
Nos. 2740-2743 (4) 6.15 1.65

Frédéric Chopin (1810-49), Composer A1510

1999, Oct. 17 Engr. *Perf. 13¼*
2744 A1510 3.80fr multicolored 1.75 .75

See Poland No. 3484.

A1511

Best Wishes for Year 2000 A1512

1999, Nov. 20 Photo. *Perf. 13x13¼*
2745 A1511 3fr multi 1.40 .30
2746 A1512 3fr multi 1.40 .30

No. 2746 was printed with se-tenant label.

Paris Metro, Cent. A1513

1999, Dec. 4 Photo. *Perf. 13*
2747 A1513 3fr multi 1.40 .30

Council of State, Bicent. — A1514

1999, Dec. 11
2748 A1514 3fr multi 1.40 .30

Reconstruction of Lighthouses — A1515

2000, Jan. 1 Photo. *Perf. 13x12¾*
2749 A1515 3fr multi 1.40 .30

Reconstruction of San Juan de Salvamento Lighthouse, Argentina and replication of its design at La Rochelle, France.

Hearts A1516

2000, Jan. 8 Photo. *Perf. 13*
2750 A1516 3fr Snakes 1.40 .30
2751 A1516 3fr Face 1.40 .30
a. Souvenir sheet, 3 #2750, 2 #2751 9.00 9.00

Self-Adhesive Booklet Stamps
Serpentine Die-Cut

2752 A1516 3fr Like #2750 1.40 .30
2753 A1516 3fr Like #2751 1.40 .30
a. Bklt. pane, 5 ea #2752-2753 14.00

Values for Nos. 2750-2751 are for copies with surrounding selvage. No. 2753a is a complete booklet.

Bank of France, Bicent. — A1517

Prefectorial Corps, Bicent. — A1518

2000, Jan. 15 Litho. *Perf. 13*
2754 A1517 3fr multi 1.40 .30

2000, Feb. 17 Photo. *Perf. 13x12¼*
2755 A1518 3fr multi 1.40 .30

Art Series

Venus and the Graces Offering Gifts to a Young Girl, by Sandro Botticelli (1445-1510) — A1519

The Waltz, by Camille Claudel A1520

Visage Rouge, by Gaston Chaissac A1521

Carolingian Mosaic, Germigny-des-Prés — A1522

2000 Photo. *Perf. 13¼x13*
2756 A1519 6.70fr multi 3.00 1.00
2757 A1520 6.70fr multi 3.00 1.00
2758 A1521 6.70fr multi 3.00 1.00
2759 A1522 6.70fr multi 3.00 1.00

Issued: No. 2756, 2/25; No. 2757, 4/8; No. 2758, 9/23; 10/21.

Tourism Series

Carcassonne — A1523

Saint-Guilhem-Le-Désert — A1524

Gérardmer A1525

Abbey Church of Ottmarsheim — A1526

2000 **Photo.** ***Perf. 13***
2760 A1523 3fr multi 1.40 .30

Engr.
Perf. 13¼

2761 A1524 3fr multi 1.40 .30
2762 A1525 3fr multi 1.40 .30

Perf. 12¼x13

2763 A1526 3fr multi 1.40 .30
Nos. 2760-2763 (4) 5.60 1.20

Issued: No. 2760, 3/3; No. 2761, 4/8; No. 2762, 4/17; No. 2763, 6/17.

Tintin — A1527

2000, Mar. 11 **Photo.** ***Perf. 13¼***
2764 A1527 3fr multi 1.40 .50
a. Perf. 13½x13 2.00 .75

Perf. 13½x13

2765 A1527 3fr + 60c multi 4.00 2.00
a. Booklet pane, 4 #2764a, 3 #2765 + label 20.00
Complete booklet, #2765a 21.00
b. Souvenir sheet of 1 3.00 2.50

Stamp Day.

Bretagne Parliament Building Restoration — A1528

2000, Mar. 25 **Photo.** ***Perf. 13¼***
2766 A1528 3fr multi 1.40 .30

Madagascar Periwinkles — A1529

2000, Mar. 25 **Litho.** ***Perf. 13x13¼***
2767 A1529 4.50fr multi 2.10 .60

Felicitations A1530

2000, Apr. 7 **Photo.** ***Perf. 13x13¼***
2768 A1530 3fr multi 1.40 .30

The 20th Century — A1531

No. 2769: a, France as World Cup soccer champions, 1998, vert. b, Marcel Cerdan wins middleweight boxing title, 1948. c, Charles Lindbergh flies solo across Atlantic, 1927. d, Jean-Claude Killy wins three Winter Olympics gold medals, 1968, vert. e, Carl Lewis wins four Olympic gold medals, 1984, vert.

Perf. 13¼x13 (vert. stamps), 13x13¼
2000, Apr. 15
2769 A1531 Sheet, 2 ea #a-e 14.00 14.00
a.-e. 3fr any single 1.40 .75

Top part of No. 2769 contains Nos. 2769a-2769e and is separated from bottom part of sheet by a row of rouletting.
See No. 2787, 2804, 2837, 2881, 2915.

Automobiles — A1532

No. 2770: a, Bugatti 35. b, Citroen Traction. c, Renault 4CV. d, Simca Chambord. e, Hispano-Suiza K6. f, Volkswagen Beetle. g, 1962 Cadillac. h, Peugeot 203. i, Citroen DS19. j, Ferrari 250 GTO.

2000, May 5 ***Perf. 13¼x13***
2770 A1532 Sheet of 10, #a.-j. 7.50 7.50
a.-e. 1fr any single .45 .35
f.-j. 2fr any single .90 .60

Europa, 2000
Common Design Type

2000, May 9 **Photo.** ***Perf. 13¼***
2771 CD17 3fr multi 1.40 .40

Henry-Louis Duhamel du Monceau (1700-82), Agronomist — A1533

2000, May 13 **Engr.** ***Perf. 13***
2772 A1533 4.50fr multi 2.10 .65

French Federation of Philatelic Associations, 73rd Congress, Nevers — A1534

2000, May 19 **Engr.** ***Perf. 13¼***
2773 A1534 3fr multi 1.40 .30

A1535

A1536

2000, June 1 **Photo.** ***Perf. 13¼x13***
2774 A1535 3fr Happy Vacation 1.40 .30

2000, June 3 **Engr.** ***Perf. 13x12¼***
2775 A1536 3fr multi 1.40 .30

First Ascent of Annapurna, 50th anniv.

Nature A1537

2.70fr, Agrias sardanapalus butterfly. No. 2777, Giraffe. No. 2778, Allosaurus. 4.50fr, Tulipa lutea.

2000, June 17 **Photo.** ***Perf. 13¼***
2776 A1537 2.70fr multi 1.00 .40
2777 A1537 3fr multi, vert. 1.10 .40
2778 A1537 3fr multi 1.10 .40
2779 A1537 4.50fr multi, vert 1.75 .75
a. Souvenir sheet, #2776-2779 5.75 5.75
Nos. 2776-2779 (4) 4.95 1.95

Antoine de Saint-Exupéry (1900-44), Aviator, Writer — A1538

2000, June 24 **Photo.** ***Perf. 13¼x13***
2780 A1538 3fr multi 1.40 .30

Yellow Train of Cerdagne, Cent. A1539

2000, July 14 ***Perf. 13x13¼***
2781 A1539 3fr multi 1.40 .30

Folklore A1540

2000, Aug. 12 **Photo.** ***Perf. 13***
2782 A1540 4.50fr multi 2.10 .65

2000 Summer Olympics, Sydney A1541

Designs: No. 2783, Cycling, fencing, relay racer. No. 2784, Relay racer, judo, diving.

2000, Sept. 9
2783 A1541 3fr multi 1.40 .50
2784 A1541 3fr multi 1.40 .50
a. Pair, #2783-2784 3.00 2.00
b. Sheet, 5 #2784a + label 15.00 15.00

Olymphilex 2000, Sydney (No. 2784b).

Brother Alfred Stanke (1904-75) A1542

2000, Sept. 23 **Engr.**
2785 A1542 4.40fr multi 2.00 .90

S.O.S. Amitié, 40th Anniv. A1543

2000, Sept. 30 **Litho.** ***Perf. 13***
2786 A1543 3fr multi 1.40 .30

20th Century Type

No. 2787: a, Man on the Moon, 1969, vert. b, Paid vacations, 1936. c, Invention of washing machine, 1901, vert. d, Woman suffrage, 1944, vert. e, Universal Declaration of Human Rights, 1948.

Perf. 13¼x13 (vert. stamps), 13x13¼
2000, Sept. 30 **Photo.**
2787 A1531 Sheet, 2 each #a-e 14.00 14.00
a.-e. 3fr Any single 1.40 .50

The top and bottom parts of No. 2787 contains Nos. 2787a-2787e and are separated by a row of rouletting.

2001, Start of New Millennium A1544

2000, Oct. 14 Litho. *Perf. 13*
2788 A1544 3fr multi 1.40 .30

The Lovers' Kiosk, by Peynet A1545

2000, Nov. 4 Engr. *Perf. 13¼x13*
2789 A1545 3fr multi 1.40 .50

Endangered Birds — A1546

2000, Nov. 4 Photo. *Perf. 13¼*
2790 A1546 3fr Kiwi 1.40 .40
2791 A1546 5.20fr Falcon 2.50 1.50

See New Zealand Nos. 1688, 1694.

Start of the 3rd Millennium — A1547

2000, Nov. 9 Photo. *Perf. 13x13¼*
2792 A1547 3fr multi + label 1.40 .30

Issued in sheets of 10 stamps + 10 labels, which could be personalized for an extra fee.

Holiday Greetings A1548

2000, Nov. 11 *Perf. 12¼x13*
2793 A1548 3fr Meilleurs voeux 1.40 .30

Perf. 13¼
2794 A1548 3fr Bonne année 1.40 .30

Union of Metallurgical & Mining Industries, Cent. — A1549

Engr. with Foil Application

2000, Dec. 9 *Perf. 13x13¼*
2795 A1549 4.50fr multi 2.10 .90

World Handball Championships — A1550

2001, Jan. 20 Photo. *Perf. 13¼*
2796 A1550 3fr multi 1.40 .30

Heart A1551

2001, Jan. 27
2797 A1551 3fr multi 1.40 .30
a. Souvenir sheet of 5 10.00 10.00

Value of No. 2797 is for copy with surrounding selvage.

Art Series

The Peasant Dance, by Pieter Breughel, the Elder — A1552

Hotel des Chevaliers de Saint-Jean-de-Jérusalem — A1553

Yvette Guilbert Singing "Linger, Longer, Loo," by Henri de Toulouse-Lautrec (1864-1901) — A1554

Honfleur at Low Tide, by Johan Barthold Jongkind — A1555

Engr., Photo (#2800), Litho (#2801)

2001 *Perf. 13x13¼, 13¼x13 (#2800)*
2798 A1552 6.70fr multi 3.00 1.00
2799 A1553 6.70fr multi 3.00 1.00
2800 A1554 6.70fr multi 3.00 1.00
2801 A1555 6.70fr multi 3.00 1.00
Nos. 2798-2801 (4) 12.00 4.00

Issued: No. 2798, 2/3; No. 2799, 4/21; No. 2800, 9/8; No. 2801, 10/27.

Gaston Lagaffe, by André Franquin A1556

2001, Feb. 24 Photo. *Perf. 13¼*
2802 A1556 3fr multi 1.40 .50
a. Perf. 13¼x13 1.40 .65

Perf. 13¼x13
2803 A1556 3fr +60c multi 5.00 3.50
a. Souvenir sheet of 1 6.00 3.50
b. Booklet pane, 5 #2802a, 3 #2803 22.00
Booklet, #2803b 22.50

Stamp Day.

20th Century Type of 2000

No. 2804 — Communications: a, Television. b, Compact disc. c, Advertisements, vert. d, Radio, vert. e, Portable telephone, vert.

Perf. 13¼x13 (vert. stamps), 13x13¼
2001, Mar. 17 Photo.
2804 A1531 Sheet, 2 each #a-e 14.00 14.00
a.-e. 3fr Any single 1.40 .75

Top part of No. 2804 contains Nos. 2804a-2804e and is separated from bottom part by a row of rouletting.

Announcements — A1557

Designs: No. 2805, It's a girl. No. 2806, It's a boy. No. 2807, Thank you. 4.50fr, Yes (marriage).

2001 Frame Color *Perf. 13*
2805 A1557 3fr brt pink 1.40 .30
a. Litho., stamp + label 6.50 6.50
2806 A1557 3fr brt blue 1.40 .30
a. Litho., stamp + label 6.50 6.50
2807 A1557 3fr brt yel grn 1.40 .30
a. Litho., stamp + label 6.50 6.50
2808 A1557 4.50fr orange 2.10 .75
Nos. 2805-2808 (4) 6.30 1.65

Issued: Nos. 2805-2808, 3/23; Nos. 2805a-2807a, 11/8.

Nos. 2805a-2807a were issued in sheets of 10 stamps and 10 labels that sold for 60fr on day of issue. The labels could be personalized. Frames on Nos. 2805 and 2806 look splotchy, while those on Nos. 2805a and 2806a have a distinct dot structure. The frame on No. 2807 has tightly spaced small dots, while on No. 2807a, the dots are more widely spaced.

Wildlife — A1558

2001, Apr. 21 Photo. *Perf. 13¼*
2809 A1558 2.70fr Squirrel 1.25 .40
2810 A1558 3fr Roe deer 1.40 .40
2811 A1558 3fr Hedgehog, horiz. 1.40 .40
2812 A1558 4.50fr Ermine 2.10 .75
a. Souvenir sheet, #2809-2812 7.00 6.50

Tourism Issue

Nogent-le-Rotrou A1559

Besançon A1560

Calais A1561

Château de Grignan A1562

Engr., Litho & Engr. (#2813)

2001 *Perf. 13¼x13 (#2813), 13*
2813 A1559 3fr multi 1.40 .40
2814 A1560 3fr multi 1.40 .30
2815 A1561 3fr multi 1.40 .30
2816 A1562 3fr multi 1.40 .30
Nos. 2813-2816 (4) 5.60 1.30

Issued: No. 2813, 4/28; No. 2814, 5/5; No. 2815, 6/16; No. 2816, 7/7.

Europa — A1563

2001, May 8 Photo. *Perf. 13*
2817 A1563 3fr multi 1.40 .35

Gardens of Versailles — A1564

2001, May 12
2818 A1564 4.40fr multi 2.00 1.00

Singers — A1565

Designs: No. 2819, Claude François (1939-78). No. 2820, Léo Ferré (1916-93). No. 2821, Serge Gainsbourg (1928-91). No. 2822, Dalida (1933-87). No. 2823, Michel Berger (1947-92). No. 2824, Barbara (1930-97).

2001, May 19 Photo. *Perf. 13*

2819 A1565 3fr multi 1.40 .75
2820 A1565 3fr multi 1.40 .75
2821 A1565 3fr multi 1.40 .75
2822 A1565 3fr multi 1.40 .75
2823 A1565 3fr multi 1.40 .75
2824 A1565 3fr multi 1.40 .75
a. Souvenir sheet, #2819-2824 11.00 11.00
Nos. 2819-2824 (6) 8.40 4.50

No. 2824a sold for 28fr with the Red Cross receiving 10fr of that.

Old Lyon — A1566

2001, May 19 Engr. *Perf. 13¼*

2825 A1566 3fr multi 1.40 .30

French Federation of Philatelic Associations 74th Congress, Tours — A1567

2001, June 1

2826 A1567 3fr multi 1.40 .30

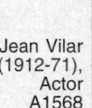

Jean Vilar (1912-71), Actor A1568

Litho. & Engr.

2001, June 7 *Perf. 13*

2827 A1568 3fr multi 1.40 .40

Vacation A1569

2001, June 10 Litho. *Perf. 13*

2828 A1569 3fr multi 1.40 .30

Booklet Stamp

Self-Adhesive

2829 A1569 3fr multi 1.40 .30
a. Booklet of 10 14.00

1 Euro Coin A1570

2001, June 23 Photo. *Perf. 12½*

2830 A1570 3fr multi 1.40 .30

Value is for copy with surrounding selvage.

Albert Caquot (1881-1976), Engineer — A1571

2001, June 30 Engr. *Perf. 13¼*

2831 A1571 4.50fr multi 2.00 .75

Law Guaranteeing Freedom of Association, Cent. — A1572

2001, July 1 Photo. *Perf. 13*

2832 A1572 3fr multi 1.40 .30

Trains — A1573

No. 2833: a, Eurostar. b, American 220. c, Crocodile. d, Crampton. e, Garratt 59. f, Pacific Chapelon. g, Mallard. h, Capitole. i, Autorail Panoramique. j, 230 Class P8.

2001, July 6 Photo. *Perf. 13¼*

2833 A1573 Sheet of 10 7.50 7.50
a.-j. 1.50fr Any single .75 .65

Geneva Convention on Refugees, UN High Commisioner for Refugees, 50th Anniv. — A1574

2001, July 28 *Perf. 13*

2834 A1574 4.50fr multi 2.00 .75

Marianne Type of 1997 Inscribed "RF" at Lower Left Instead of "La Poste"

2001 Engr. *Perf. 13*

2835 A1409 (3fr) red 1.40 .25
d. Sheet of 15 + 15 labels 60.00 —

Serpentine Die Cut 6¾ Vert.

Self-Adhesive

2835A A1409 (3fr) red 1.40 .25
b. Booklet of 10 15.00
e. No. 2835 with attached label 6.00

No. 2835Ae is from a sheet having eiter small or large-sized labels that could be personalized.

2001, Aug. 1 Engr. *Perf. 13 Horiz.*

Coil Stamp

Water-Activated Gum

2835C A1409 (3fr) red 1.40 .25

Issued: Nos. 2835, 2835C, 8/1; No. 2835A, 9/24. No. 2835Ae, 2004.

No. 2835d sold for €10.03. Labels could be personalized for an additional price.

Pierre de Fermat (1601-65), Mathematician — A1575

2001, Aug. 19 Engr. *Perf. 13¼x13*

2836 A1575 4.50fr multi 2.00 .75

20th Century Type of 2000

No. 2837 — Science: a, First man in space. b, DNA. c, Chip cards. d, Laser. e, Penicillin.

Perf. 13¼x13 (vert. stamps), 13

2001, Sept. 22 Photo.

2837 A1531 Sheet, 2 each #a-e 14.00 14.00
a.-e. 3fr Any single 1.40 .70

Top part of No. 2837 contains Nos. 2837a-2837e and is separated from bottom part of sheet by a row of rouletting.

Astrolabe Sculpture, Val-de-Reuil A1576

2001, Sept. 29 *Perf. 13*

2838 A1576 3fr multi 1.40 .30

Halloween A1577

2001, Oct. 20

2839 A1577 3fr multi 1.40 .30
a. Souvenir sheet of 5 + 4 labels 8.00 8.00

Jean Pierre-Bloch (1905-99), Human Rights Advocate — A1578

2001, Nov. 8 Engr. *Perf. 13*

2840 A1578 4.50fr multi 2.00 .75

Albert Decaris (1901-88), Artist A1579

2001, Nov. 9 Engr. *Perf. 13¼x13*

2841 A1579 3fr multi 1.40 .40

Jacques Chaban-Delmas (1915-2000), Politician — A1580

2001, Nov. 10 Engr. *Perf. 13x13¼*

2842 A1580 3fr multi 1.40 .40

Holiday Greetings A1581

Designs: Nos. 2843, 2845 Bonne Année (Happy New Year). Nos. 2844, 2846 Meilleurs Voeux (Best wishes).

2001, Nov. 9 Litho. *Perf. 13*

2843 A1581 3fr multi 1.40 .30
2844 A1581 3fr multi 1.40 .30

Serpentine Die Cut 11

Self-Adhesive

Booklet Stamps

2845 A1581 3fr multi 1.40 .30
2846 A1581 3fr multi 1.40 .30
a. Booklet, 5 each # 2845-2846 14.00

Fountains A1582

Designs: 3fr, Nejjarine Fountain, Fez, Morocco. 3.80fr, Wallace Fountain, Paris.

2001, Dec. 14 Photo. *Perf. 13¼*

2847 A1582 3fr multi 1.40 .40
2848 A1582 3.80fr multi 1.75 1.00

See Morocco Nos. 914-915.

100 Cents = 1 Euro (€)

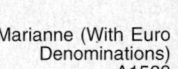

Marianne (With Euro Denominations) A1583

2002, Jan. 1 Engr. *Perf. 13*

2849 A1583 1c yellow .25 .25
2850 A1583 2c brown .25 .25
2851 A1583 5c brt bl grn .25 .25
2852 A1583 10c purple .25 .25
2853 A1583 20c brt org .60 .30
2854 A1583 41c brt green 1.20 .25
2855 A1583 50c dk blue 1.50 .25
2856 A1583 53c apple grn 1.60 .40
2857 A1583 58c blue 1.75 .50
2858 A1583 64c dark org 1.90 .50
2859 A1583 67c brt blue 2.00 .50
a. deep blue 2.00 .50
2860 A1583 69c brt pink 2.10 .60
2861 A1583 €1 Prus blue 3.00 .80
2862 A1583 €1.02 dk green 3.00 .90
a. Souvenir sheet, #2835, 2854, 2856-2858, 2859a, 2860, 2862 15.00 15.00
2863 A1583 €2 violet 6.00 1.50
a. Souvenir sheet, #2849-2853, 2855, 2861, 2863 12.00 12.00
Nos. 2849-2863 (15) 25.65 7.50

Coil Stamp

Perf. 13 Horiz.

2864 A1583 41c brt green 1.25 .30

See Nos. 2952-2957, 3043, 3043P-3043Q.

Orchids — A1584

Designs: 29c, Orchis insularis. 33c, Ophrys fuciflora.

2002, Jan. 2 Litho. *Perf. 13*

2865 A1584 29c multi	.80	.30
2866 A1584 33c multi	1.00	.40

Nos. 2865-2866 are known only precanceled. See second note after No. 132.
See Nos. 2958-2959, 3046, 3168.

Heart of Voh, Photograph by Yann Arthurs-Bertrand — A1585

2002, Jan. 18 Photo. *Perf. 13¼*

2867 A1585 46c multi	1.40	.40
a. Souvenir sheet of 5	7.00	7.00

Value of No. 2867 is for copy with surrounding selvage.

2002 Winter Olympics, Salt Lake City — A1586

2002, Jan. 26 *Perf. 13*

2868 A1586 46c multi	1.40	.30

Art Series

Sphere Concorde, by Jesús Rafael Soto A1587

The Kiss, by Gustav Klimt A1588

The Dancers, by Fernando Botero A1589

Self-Portrait, by Elisabeth Vigée-Lebrun — A1590

2002 Photo. *Perf. 13¼x13*

2869 A1587 75c multi	2.25	1.00
2870 A1588 €1.02 multi	3.00	1.00
2871 A1589 €1.02 multi	3.00	1.00

Engr.

2872 A1590 €1.02 multi	3.00	1.00
Nos. 2869-2872 (4)	11.25	4.00

Issued: No. 2869, 11/11. No. 2870, 2/8; No. 2871, 4/27. No. 2872, 10/12.

Alain Bosquet (1919-98), Poet — A1591

2002, Feb. 16 Engr. *Perf. 13*

2873 A1591 58c multi	1.75	1.00

It's A Girl A1592

It's A Boy A1593

Yes A1594

2002, Feb. 23 Photo.

2874 A1592 46c multi	1.40	.30
2875 A1593 46c multi	1.40	.30
2876 A1594 69c multi	2.00	.30
Nos. 2874-2876 (3)	4.80	.90

Europa — A1595

2002, Mar. 2 *Perf. 13¼*

2877 A1595 46c multi	1.40	.30

Boule and Bill, by Jean Roba — A1596

Designs: 46c, Boule, Bill, bird. 46c+9c, Boule, Bill, ball.

2002, Mar. 16 *Perf. 13¼*

2878 A1596 46c multi	1.40	.50
a. Perf. 13¼x13	2.00	.60

Perf. 13¼x13

2879 A1596 46c +9c multi	4.00	3.00
a. Souvenir sheet of 1	3.00	2.50
b. Booklet pane, 5 #2879a, 3 #2879	22.00	—
Booklet, #2879b	22.50	

Stamp Day. No. 2879 surtax for Red Cross. Stamp on No. 2879a has continuous design.

Nimes Amphitheater — A1597

Litho. & Engr.

2002, Mar. 22 *Perf. 13*

2880 A1597 46c multi	1.40	.30

20th Century Type of 2000

No. 2881 — Transportation: a, Concorde supersonic airplane. b, TGV train. c, Ocean liner France, vert. d, Mobylette motor scooter, vert. e, Citroen 2 CV automobile, vert.

Perf. 13, 13¼x13 (vert. stamps)

2002, Mar. 23 Photo.

2881 A1531 Sheet, 2 each #a-e	14.00	14.00
a.-e. 46c Any single	1.40	.75

Top part of No. 2881 contains Nos. 2881a-2881e and is separated from bottom part of sheet by a row of rouletting.

Encounter of Matthew Flinders and Nicolas Boudin, Bicent. A1598

Map of Australia, portrait and ship of: 46c, Flinders. 79c, Boudin.

2002, Apr. 4 *Perf. 13¼*

2882 A1598 46c multi	1.40	.40
2883 A1598 79c multi	2.25	1.25

See Australia Nos. 2053-2054.

Tourism Series

La Charité-sur-Loire — A1599

Collioure A1600

Locronan A1601

Neufchateau — A1602

Engraved (#2884, 2886), Photo. (#2885)

2002 *Perf. 13¼*

2884 A1599 46c multi	1.40	.30
2885 A1600 46c multi	1.40	.30
2886 A1601 46c multi	1.40	.30
2887 A1602 46c multi	1.40	.30
Nos. 2884-2887 (4)	5.60	1.20

Issue dates: No. 2884, 4/6; No. 2885, 6/22; No. 2886, 7/13; No. 2887, 10/12/02.
Numbers have been reserved for additional stamps in this set.

Birthday Greetings A1603

Invitation A1604

2002, Apr. 6 Photo. *Perf. 13*

2888 A1603 46c multi	1.40	.30
a. Litho., stamp + label	6.00	6.00
2889 A1604 46c multi	1.40	.30
a. Litho., stamp + label	6.00	6.00

Issued: Nos. 2888a, 2889a, 11/7. Nos. 2888a and 2889a were issued in sheets of 10 stamps and 10 labels that sold for €6.19 on day of issue. The labels could be personalized.
No. 2888a has a duller blue in "Anniversaire" than No. 2888, but is otherwise quite similar in appearance. The gold ink on No. 2889a has a more coppery look than that on No. 2889.

100th Paris-Roubaix Bicycle Race — A1605

2002, Mar. 13
2890 A1605 46c multi 1.40 .30

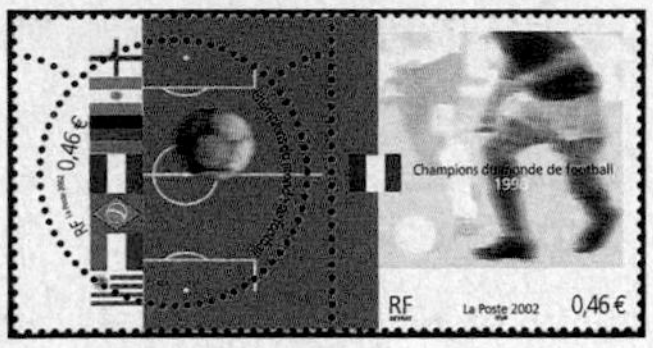

2002 World Cup Soccer Championships, Japan and Korea — A1606

No. 2891: a, Flags, soccer ball and field (32mm diameter). b, Soccer player, year of French championship.

2002, Apr. 27 ***Perf. 12¾***
2891 A1606 Horiz. pair 2.75 2.50
a.-b. 46c Any single 1.40 .30
c. Sheet, 5 #2891 15.00 15.00

Issued: No. 2891c, 5/18.

See Argentina No. 2184, Brazil No. 2840, Germany No. 2163, Italy No. 2526 and Uruguay No. 1946.

Marine Life A1607

Designs: 41c, Sea turtle (tortue luth), vert. No. 2893, Killer whale (orque). No. 2894, Dolphin (grand dauphin). 69c, Seal (phoque veau marin).

2002, May 4 ***Perf. 13¼***
2892 A1607 41c multi 1.25 .30
2893 A1607 46c multi 1.25 .30
2894 A1607 46c multi 1.25 .30
2895 A1607 69c multi 2.00 .75
a. Souvenir sheet, #2892-2895 6.50 6.50
Nos. 2892-2895 (4) 5.75 1.65

Worldwide Fund for Nature (No. 2895a).

French Federation of Philatelic Associations 75th Congress, Marseilles — A1608

2002, May 17 **Engr.** ***Perf. 13***
2896 A1608 46c multi 1.40 .30

Legion of Honor, Bicent. A1609

Rocamadour A1610

2002, May 18 **Photo.**
2897 A1609 46c multi 1.40 .30

2002, May 25 ***Perf. 13¼***
2898 A1610 46c multi 1.40 .30

Louis Delgrés (1766-1802), Soldier — A1611

2002, May 25
2899 A1611 46c multi 1.40 .30

Vacation A1612

2002, June 8 **Litho.** ***Perf. 13***
2900 A1612 46c multi 1.40 .30

Self-Adhesive

Serpentine Die Cut 11

2901 A1612 46c multi 1.40 .30
a. Booklet pane of 10 14.00

World Disabled Athletics Championships — A1613

2002, June 15 **Photo.** ***Perf. 13¼***
2902 A1613 46c multi 1.40 .30

Saint-Ser Chapel — A1614

2002, June 22 **Engr.** ***Perf. 13x13¼***
2903 A1614 46c multi 1.40 .30

Metz Cathedral Stained Glass A1615

2002, July 6 **Engr.** ***Perf. 13¼x13***
2904 A1615 46c multi 1.40 .40

Jazz Musicians — A1616

Designs: No. 2905, Louis Armstrong (1901-71). No. 2906, Ella Fitzgerald (1918-96). No. 2907, Duke Ellington (1899-1974). No. 2908, Stéphane Grappelli (1908-97). No. 2909, Michel Petrucciani (1962-99), horiz. No. 2910, Sidney Bechet (1897-1959), horiz.

2002, July 13 **Photo.** ***Perf. 13***
2905 A1616 46c multi 1.40 .75
2906 A1616 46c multi 1.40 .75
2907 A1616 46c multi 1.40 .75
2908 A1616 46c multi 1.40 .75
2909 A1616 46c multi 1.40 .75
2910 A1616 46c multi 1.40 .75
a. Souvenir sheet, #2905-2910 12.00 12.00
Nos. 2905-2910 (6) 8.40 4.50

No. 2910a sold for €4.36, with the Red Cross receiving €1.60 of that.

Pilgrimages to Notre Dame de la Salette, 150th Anniv. A1617

2002, Aug. 15 **Engr.** ***Perf. 13¼x13***
2911 A1617 46c multi 1.40 .30

Choreography — A1618

2002, Sept. 13 **Photo.** ***Perf. 13x13¼***
2912 A1618 53c multi 1.50 .60

Motorcycles — A1619

No. 2913: a, Honda 750 four. b, Terrot 500 RGST. c, Majestic. d, Norton Commando 750. e, Voxan 1000 Café Racer. f, BMW R90S. g, Harley Davidson Hydra Glide. h, Triumph Bonneville 650. i, Ducati 916. j, Yamaha 500 XT.

2002, Sept. 14 ***Perf. 13¼x13***
2913 A1619 Sheet of 10 12.00 12.00
a.-e. 16c any single .75 .60
f.-j. 30c any single .90 .75

Georges Perec (1936-82), Writer — A1620

2002, Sept. 21 **Engr.** ***Perf. 13¼***
2914 A1620 46c multi 1.40 .30

20th Century Type of 2000

No. 2915 — Photographs of everyday life: a, Family on motor scooter, 1955, vert. b, Man, horse and wagon, 1947. c, Woman ironing, 1950. d, Boy at fountain, 1950, vert. e, Girl in classroom, 1965, vert.

Perf. 13¼x13 (vert. stamps), 13

2002, Sept. 28 **Photo.**
2915 A1531 Sheet, 2 each #a-e 14.00 14.00
a.-e. 46c Any single 1.40 .75

Top part of No. 2915 contains Nos. 2915a-2915e and is separated from bottom part of sheet by a row of rouletting.

Emile Zola (1840-1902), Novelist — A1621

2002, Oct. 5 ***Perf. 13***
2916 A1621 46c multi 1.40 .30

Souvenir Sheet

European Capitals — A1622

Attractions in Rome: a, Trevi Fountain. b, Coliseum, horiz. c, Trinità de Monti Church and Spanish Steps. d, St. Peter's Basilica, horiz.

2002, Nov. 7 ***Perf. 13¼x13, 13x13¼***
2917 A1622 Sheet of 4 6.00 6.00
a.-d. 46c Any single 1.40 .75

See Nos. 2985, 3052, 3138, 3223, 3340, 3535, 3728, 3908, 3986, 4183, 4365.

Globe and Microcircuits A1623

2002, Nov. 8 **Photo.** ***Perf. 13***
2918 A1623 46c multi 1.40 .30
a. Litho., stamp + label 6.00 6.00

Issued: No. 2918a, 11/7. No. 2918a was issued in sheets of 10 stamps and 10 labels that sold for €6.19 on day of issue. The labels could be personalized.

No. 2918a has a hairline at top, above "RF" that No. 2918 does not have, but is otherwise quite similar in appearance.

Holiday Greetings A1624

2002, Nov. 8 **Photo.** ***Perf. 13***
2919 A1624 46c multi 1.40 .30
a. Litho., stamp + label 6.00 6.00

Booklet Stamp

Self-Adhesive

Serpentine Die Cut 11

2920 A1624 46c multi 1.40 .30
a. Booklet pane of 10 14.00

Issued: No. 2919a, 11/7. No. 2919a was issued in sheets of 10 stamps and 10 labels that sold for €6.19 on day of issue. The labels could be personalized.

No. 2919a has a finer dot structure, which is most noticeable in the chimney smoke, than No. 2919.

Marianne Type of 1997 Inscribed "RF" at Lower Left

2002, Nov. 9 Engr. *Perf. 13*

2921 A1409 (41c) bright green 1.20 .25

Coil Stamp

Perf. 13 Horiz.

2922 A1409 (41c) bright green 1.20 .25

Alexandre Dumas (Father) (1802-70), Writer A1625

2002, Nov. 30 Photo. *Perf. 13*

2924 A1625 46c multi 1.40 .30

Léopold Sédar Senghor (1906-2001), President of Senegal, Poet — A1626

2002, Dec. 20

2925 A1626 46c multi 1.40 .30

Hearts A1627

2003, Jan. 11 *Perf. 13¼*

2926 A1627 46c Four hearts 1.40 .30

a. Souvenir sheet of 5 7.00 7.00

2927 A1627 69c Roses 2.00 .60

Values for Nos. 2926-2927 are for copies with surrounding selvage.

Thank You A1628

Birth A1629

2003, Jan. 11 *Perf. 13*

2928 A1628 46c multi 1.40 .30

2929 A1629 46c brt org & brt bl 1.40 .30

Franco-German Cooperation Treaty, 40th Anniv. — A1630

2003, Jan. 16 *Perf. 13¼*

2930 A1630 46c multi 1.40 .40

Delegation for Land-use Planning and Regional Action, 40th Anniv. A1631

2003, Feb. 8 Photo. *Perf. 13*

2931 A1631 46c multi 1.40 .30

Geneviève de Gaulle Anthonioz (1920-2002), World War II Resistance Fighter — A1632

2003, Feb. 11

2932 A1632 46c blk & ol brn 1.40 .30

Paris Chamber of Commerce and Industry, Bicent. — A1633

2003, Feb. 22 *Perf. 13¼*

2933 A1633 46c multi 1.40 .30

Lucky Luke, by Morris (Maurice De Bevere) — A1634

Lucky Luke and Jolly Jumper: 46c, Skipping rope on ball on high wire. 46c+9c, Following dog, Rantanplan.

2003, Mar. 15 Photo. *Perf. 13¼*

2934 A1634 46c multi 1.40 .65

a. Perf. 13¼x13 1.40 .65

Perf. 13¼x13

2935 A1634 46c +9c multi 3.50 2.00

a. Souvenir sheet of 1 3.00 2.50

b. Booklet pane, 5 #2934a, 3 #2935 17.50 —

Complete booklet, #2935b 18.00

Stamp Day.

Birds A1635

Designs: 41c, Colibri à tete bleue (Cyanophaia bicolor). No. 2937, Toucan ariel (Ramphastos vitellinus). No. 2938, Colibri grenat (Eulampis jugularis), vert. 69c, Terpsiphone de Bourbon (Terpsiphone bourbonnensis).

2003, Mar. 22 Photo. *Perf. 13¼*

2936 A1635 41c multi 1.20 .30

2937 A1635 46c multi 1.40 .30

2938 A1635 46c multi 1.40 .30

2939 A1635 69c multi 2.00 .75

a. Souvenir sheet, #2936-2939 7.00 7.00

Nos. 2936-2939 (4) 6.00 1.65

Nantes A1636

2003, Apr. 4 Engr.

2940 A1636 46c multi 1.40 .30

Pierre Bérégovoy (1925-93), Prime Minister — A1637

2003, Apr. 30 Engr. *Perf. 13x13¼*

2941 A1637 46c multi 1.40 .30

Milan Stefanik (1880-1919), Czechoslovakian General — A1638

2003, May 3 *Perf. 13¼*

2942 A1638 50c multi 1.50 .40

See Slovakia No. 428.

Europa — A1639

2003, May 8 Photo.

2943 A1639 50c multi 1.50 .40

Charter of Fundamental Rights of the European Union — A1640

2003, May 8

2944 A1640 50c multi 1.50 .30

Aircraft Carrier "Charles de Gaulle" A1641

2003, May 8 Engr.

2945 A1641 50c multi 1.50 .30

Aspects of Life in the French Regions A1642

No. 2946: a, Beach cabins. b, Fishing net. c, Vineyards of Champagne. d, Camembert cheese, vert. e, Foie gras, vert. f, Petanque. g, Puppet show (Guignol), vert. h, Crepe, vert. i, Cassoulet. j, Limoges porcelain.

2003, May 24 Photo. *Perf. 13*

2946 Sheet of 10 16.00 16.00

a.-j. A1642 50c Any single 1.50 1.30

No. 2946 has three vertical rows of rouletting, separating sheet into quarters.

Nos. 2946a-2946j were also issued in large booklets containing panes of 1 of each stamp. The booklet sold for €19.

See Nos. 2978, 3007, 3047, 3106, 3139, 3192, 3234, 3299, 3300-3301, 3357, 3427, 3505.

Art Series

"The Dying Slave" and "The Rebel Slave," by Michelangelo — A1643

The Red Buoy, by Paul Signac A1644

Untitled Abstract by Vassily Kandinsky A1645

Marilyn, by Andy Warhol A1646

2003 Engr. *Perf. 13¼x13*

2947 A1643 75c multi 2.25 1.00

Photo.

2948 A1644 75c multi 2.25 1.00

Litho.

2949 A1645 €1.11 multi 3.25 1.25

2950 A1646 €1.11 multi 3.25 1.40

Nos. 2947-2950 (4) 11.00 4.65

Issued: No. 2947, 5/24. Nos. 2948, 2949, 7/5. No. 2950, 11/8.

A sheet containing 3 No. 2949 and 12 imperforate color progressive proofs was bound in a book that sold for €60.

Happy Birthday A1647

2003, May 31 Photo. *Perf. 13¼*

2951 A1647 50c multi		1.50	.35
a.	Souvenir sheet of 5	7.50	7.50
b.	Litho., stamp + label	1.75	1.75

Issued: No. 2951b, 2004. No. 2951b was issued in sheets of 10 stamps + 10 labels that sold for €6.67 on day of issue. The labels could be personalized. The background on No. 2951 looks splotchy while that of No. 2951b has a dot structure.

Marianne With Euro Denominations Type of 2002

2003, June 1 Engr. *Perf. 13*

2952 A1583	58c apple grn		1.60	.40
2953 A1583	70c yellow grn		2.00	.50
2954 A1583	75c bright blue		2.25	.50
2955 A1583	90c dark blue		2.60	1.00
2956 A1583	€1.11 red lilac		3.25	1.00
2957 A1583	€1.90 violet brown		5.50	1.25
a.	Souvenir sheet, #2835, 2921, 2952-2957		22.00	22.00
	Nos. 2952-2957 (6)		17.20	4.65

No. 2957a issued 2/28/04.

Orchids Type of 2002

Designs: 30c, Platanthera chlorantha. 35c, Dactylorhiza savogiensis.

2003, June 1 Litho. *Perf. 13*

2958 A1584 30c multi		1.00	.30
2959 A1584 35c multi		1.25	.40

Nos. 2958-2959 are known only precanceled, See second note after No. 132.

French Federation of Philatelic Associations 76th Congress, Mulhouse A1648

2003, June 6 Engr. *Perf. 13¼*

2960 A1648 50c multi	1.50	.40

Vacation — A1649

Perf. 12¾x13¼

2003, June 14 Litho.

2961 A1649 50c multi	1.50	.30

Self-Adhesive Booklet Stamp

Serpentine Die Cut 11

2962 A1649 50c multi	1.50	.30
a. Booklet pane of 10	15.00	

Tourism Issue

Notre Dame de l'Epine Basilica — A1650

Tulle A1651

Arras — A1652

Pontarlier A1653

Perf. 13x13¼, 13 (#2965)

2003, June 21 Engr.

2963 A1650 50c multi	1.50	.30
2964 A1651 50c multi	1.50	.30
2965 A1652 50c multi	1.50	.40
2966 A1653 50c multi	1.50	.40
Nos. 2963-2966 (4)	6.00	1.40

Issued: Nos. 2963, 2964, 6/21. No. 2965, 9/20. No. 2966, 10/11.

French Freemasonry, 275th Anniv. — A1654

2003, June 28 Engr. *Perf. 13¼x13*

2967 A1654 50c multi	1.50	.30

Tour de France Bicycle Race, Cent. A1655

No. 2968: a, Maurice Garin, winner of 1903 race. b, Cyclist with arms raised.

2003, June 28 Photo. *Perf. 13*

2968 A1655	Vert. pair	3.00	2.00
a.-b.	50c Either single	1.50	.30

Values are for stamps with surrounding selvage.

Saint-Père Church, Yonne — A1656

2003, July 12 Engr. *Perf. 13¼*

2969 A1656 50c multi	1.50	.30

World Track and Field Championships, Paris — A1657

2003, July 19 Photo. *Perf. 13*

2970 A1657 50c multi	1.50	.30

Characters From French Literature — A1658

Designs: No. 2971, Eugène-François Vidocq (1775-1857), convict and police official. No. 2972, Esmerelda, from *Notre-Dame de Paris,* by Victor Hugo. No. 2973, Claudine, from *Claudine* novels, by Colette. No. 2974, Nana, from *Rougon-Macquart,* by Emile Zola. No. 2975, La Comte de Monte-Cristo, from *La Comte de Monte-Cristo,* by Alexandre Dumas (pere). No. 2976, Gavroche, from *Les Miserables,* by Hugo.

2003, Aug. 30 Photo. *Perf. 13*

2971 A1658 50c multi		1.50	.75
2972 A1658 50c multi		1.50	.75
2973 A1658 50c multi		1.50	.75
2974 A1658 50c multi		1.50	.75
2975 A1658 50c multi		1.50	.75
2976 A1658 50c multi		1.50	.75
a.	Souvenir sheet, #2971-2976	14.00	14.00
	Nos. 2971-2976 (6)	9.00	4.50

No. 2976a sold for €4.60, with the Red Cross receiving €1.60 of that.

Ahmad Shah Massoud (1953-2001), Afghan Northern Alliance Leader — A1659

2003, Sept. 9

2977 A1659 50c multi	1.50	.30

Aspects of Life in French Regions Type of 2003

No. 2978: a, Chateau de Chenonceau. b, House, Alsace. c, Roof, Bourgogne. d, Genoese Tower, Corsica, vert. e, Arc de Triomphe, vert. f, Farm house, Provence. g, Pointe du Raz, vert. h, Mont Blanc, vert. i, Basque house. j, Pont du Gard.

2003, Sept. 20 Photo. *Perf. 13*

2978	Sheet of 10	15.00	15.00
a.-j.	A1642 50c Any single	1.50	1.25

No. 2978 has three vertical rows of rouletting, separating sheet into quarters.

Nos. 2978a-2978j were also issued in large booklets containing panes of 1 of each stamp. The booklet sold for €19.

Gardens and Parks — A1660

No. 2979: a, Buttes-Chaumont Park. b, Jardin du Luxembourg.

2003, Sept. 27 *Perf. 13¼x13*

2979	Sheet of 2	11.00	11.00
a.-b.	A1660 €1.90 Either single	5.50	5.50

Salon du Timbre 2004. No. 2979 has four vertical rows of rouletting, separating sheet into fifths, with the two stamps in the central fifth.

See Nos. 3029, 3118, 3201, 3316, 3429.

Motor Vehicles — A1661

No. 2980: a, 1954 Isobloc 648 DP 102 bus (Autocar). b, 1950 SFV 302 Tractor. c, 1938 Delahaye fire truck with mechanical aerial ladder. d, Renault Kangaroo Express postal van. e, 1932 Renault TN6 Paris city bus. f, 1910 Berliet 22hp Type M delivery truck. g, 1957 Berliet T100 heavy-duty truck. h, Citroen police van. i, Citroen DS ambulance. j, 1964 Hotchkiss fire truck.

2003, Oct. 24 Photo. *Perf. 13¼*

2980 A1661	Sheet of 10	9.00	9.00
a.-e.	20c Any single	.55	.45
f.-j.	30c Any single	.85	.65

Philexjeunes 2003 Philatelic Exhibition, Dunkerque.

A1662

Holiday Greetings A1663

2003, Nov. 6 Photo. *Perf. 13*

2981 A1662 50c multi		1.50	.35
a.	Litho., stamp + label	6.00	6.00

Litho.

2982 A1663 50c multi		1.50	.35
a.	Sheet of 10 + 10 labels	60.00	60.00

Booklet Stamp
Self-Adhesive

Serpentine Die Cut 11¼

2983 A1663 50c multi 1.50 .35
a. Booklet pane of 10 15.00

Nos. 2981a, 2982a, 2004. Nos. 2981a and 2982 were issued in sheets of 10 stamps + 10 labels that sold for €6.67 each on day of issue. The labels could be personalized. The background on No. 2981 looks splotchy while that of No. 2981a has a dot structure.

A souvenir sheet containing No. 2982 was sold for €6 by mail order only. It was not available through standing order subscriptions and was not offered in the philatelic bureau's sales catalog. 50,000 copies of this sheet were printed. Value $250.

Sower Type of 1903, Cent. — A1664

Serpentine Die Cut 6¾ Vert.

2003, Nov. 6 **Engr.**

Booklet Stamp

2984 A1664 50c red 3.50 3.00
a. Booklet pane, 5 each # 2984, 2835A 25.00

See No. 4727b.

European Capitals Type of 2002

No. 2985 — Attractions in Luxembourg: a, Citadelle Saint-Esprit. b, Notre Dame Cathedral, horiz. c, Adolphe Bridge, horiz. d, Grand Duke's Palace.

Perf. 13¼x13, 13x13¼

2003, Nov. 7 **Photo.**

2985 A1622 Sheet of 4 7.50 7.50
a.-d. 50c Any single 1.50 1.00

Indian and French Artisan's Work A1665

Designs: 50c, Illumination depicting rooster, France, 15th cent. 90c, Jewelry design, India, 19th cent.

2003, Nov. 29 **Engr.** ***Perf. 13¼x13***

2986 A1665 50c multi 1.50 .40
2987 A1665 90c multi 2.60 1.50

See India No. 2040.

Launch of the Queen Mary 2 — A1666

2003, Dec. 12 **Photo.** ***Perf. 13¼***

2988 A1666 50c multi 1.50 .30

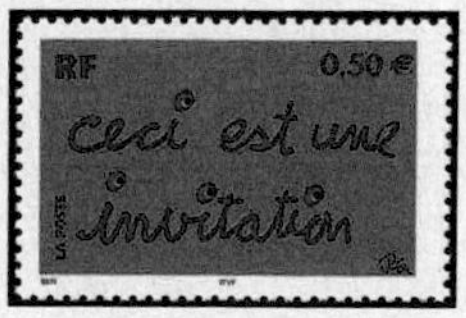

Greetings A1667

Holes punched through dots in "i's."

2004, Jan. 9 **Photo.** ***Perf. 13***

2989 A1667 50c shown 1.50 .30
2990 A1667 50c Un grand merci 1.50 .30

No Holes Punched Through Dots of "i's"

Stamp + Label

2991 A1667 50c Like No. 2989 6.00 6.00
2992 A1667 50c Like No. 2990 6.00 6.00

Nos. 2991-2992 were issued in sheets of 10 stamps + 10 labels that sold for €6.67 on day of issue. The labels could be personalized.

Compare with Type A2203. See Nos. 3096-3097D, 3569A-3569B.

It's a Boy A1668

It's a Girl A1669

2004 **Litho.** ***Perf. 13***

Stamp + Label

2993 A1668 50c multi 6.00 6.00
2994 A1669 50c multi 6.00 6.00

Booklet Stamps

Self-Adhesive

Serpentine Die Cut 11

2995 A1668 50c multi 1.50 .35
a. Booklet pane of 10 15.00
2996 A1669 50c multi 1.50 .35
a. Booklet pane of 10 15.00

Nos. 2993-2994 were issued in sheets of 10 stamps + 10 labels that sold for €6.67 on day of issue. The labels could be personalized.

Nos. 2995-2996 issued 1/9/04.

Hearts A1670

Designs: 50c, Chanel No. 5 perfume bottle. 75c, Woman, Eiffel Tower.

2004, Jan. 9 **Photo.** ***Perf. 13***

2997 A1670 50c multi 1.50 .35
a. Souvenir sheet of 5 7.50 7.50
b. Litho., stamp + label, perf. 13¼ 6.00 6.00
2998 A1670 75c multi 2.25 .75
a. Litho., stamp + label, perf. 13¼ 6.00 6.00

Nos. 2997b and 2998a were each printed in sheets of 10 stamps + 10 labels that could be personalized and sold for €6.69 and €10 respectively. On No. 2997b, there are large brown dots arranged in circles in the shading on the green rectangles, while on No. 2997 the brown dots are small and arranged in rows. On No. 2998a, the dots in the sky are larger and farther apart than the tiny dots found on No. 2998.

Values are for stamps with surrounding selvage.

See Nos. 3133, 3135.

Tourism Issue

Lille, 2004 European Cultural Capital A1671

2004, Jan. 10 **Photo.** ***Perf. 13***

2999 A1671 50c multi 1.50 .35

Art Series

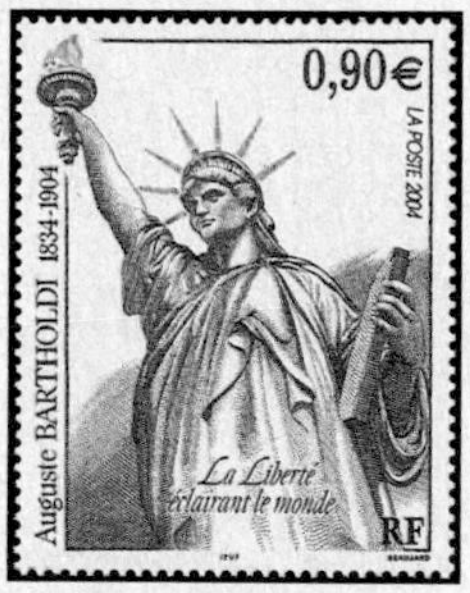

Statue of Liberty, Sculpted by Frederic Auguste Bartholdi (1834-1904) — A1672

2004, Feb. 21 **Engr.** ***Perf. 13¼x13***

3000 A1672 90c multi 2.60 1.50

Queen Eleanor of Aquitaine (c. 1122-1204) A1673

2004, Feb. 28 ***Perf. 13x13¼***

3001 A1673 50c multi 1.50 .35

Stamp Day — A1674

Characters of Walt Disney: 45c, Donald Duck. 50c, Mickey Mouse. 75c, Minnie Mouse.

2004, Mar. 6 **Photo.** ***Perf. 13¼***

3002 A1674 50c multi 1.50 .35
a. Perf. 13¼x13 (from booklet pane) 1.50 .35

Booklet Stamps

Perf. 13¼x13

3003 A1674 45c multi 2.00 .30
3004 A1674 75c multi 2.25 .60
a. Booklet pane, 2 #3003, 4 each #3002a, 3004 19.50 —
Complete booklet, #3004a 20.00

Civil Code, Bicent. A1675

2004, Mar. 12 **Engr.** ***Perf. 13¼x13***

3005 A1675 50c multi 1.50 .35

George Sand (1804-76), Writer A1676

2004, Mar. 20 **Engr.** ***Perf. 13¼x13***

3006 A1676 50c multi 1.50 .35

Aspects of Life in French Regions Type of 2003

No. 3007: a, Cutlery. b, Produce of Provence, vert. c, Beaujolais grapes, vert. d, Bread. e, Woman wearing coif, vert. f, Oysters, vert. g, Quiche Lorraine. h, Bullfighting. i, Clafoutis. j, Bagpipes.

2004, Mar. 26 **Photo.** ***Perf. 13***

3007 Sheet of 10 15.00 15.00
a.-j. A1642 50c Any single 1.50 1.00

No. 3007 has three vertical rows of rouletting, separating sheet into quarters.

Clermont-Ferrand — A1677

2004, Mar. 26 **Engr.** ***Perf. 13¼***

3008 A1677 50c multi 1.50 .35

Entente Cordiale, Cent. — A1678

Designs: 50c, Coccinelle, by Sonia Delaunay. 75c, Lace 1 (trial proof) 1968, by Sir Terry Frost.

2004, Apr. 6 **Photo.** ***Perf. 13¼***

3009 A1678 50c multi 1.50 .35
3010 A1678 75c multi 2.25 .75

See Great Britain Nos. 2200-2201.

Road Safety — A1679

2004, Apr. 7

3011 A1679 50c multi 1.50 .35

See United Nations Offices in Geneva No. 424.

Art Series

La Méridienne d'Après Millet, by Vincent van Gogh — A1680

2004, July 2 **Photo.** ***Perf. 13x13¼***

3012 A1680 75c multi 3.00 .95

Art Series

Un Combat de Coqs, by Jean-Léon Gérôme — A1681

Galatée aux Sphères, by Salvador Dali A1682

2004 Photo. *Perf. 13x13¼*

3013	A1681	€1.11 multi	3.25	1.40
3014	A1682	€1.11 multi	3.25	1.40

Issued: No. 3013, 4/17; No. 3014, 6/19.

Tourism Issue

Bordeaux — A1683

Vaux-sur-Mer — A1684

Notre Dame de l'Assomption Cathedral, Luçon — A1685

2004 Litho. & Engr. *Perf. 13*

3015	A1683	50c multi	1.50	.35

Engr.

Perf. 13¼

3016	A1684	50c multi	1.50	.35
3017	A1685	50c multi	1.50	.35

Issued: No. 3015, 4/26; No. 3016, 7/17; No. 3017, 10/2.

Farm Animals A1686

2004, Apr. 26 Photo. *Perf. 13¼*

3018	A1686	45c Rabbit	1.25	.30
3019	A1686	50c Cow, vert.	1.50	.35
3020	A1686	50c Chicken	1.50	.35
3021	A1686	75c Burro, vert.	2.25	.60
a.		Souvenir sheet, #3018-3021	7.00	6.50

Expansion of the European Union A1687

2004, May 1 Photo. *Perf. 13¼*

3022	A1687	50c multi	1.50	.40

Battle of Dien Bien Phu, 50th Anniv. — A1688

2004, May 7 *Perf. 13¼x13*

3023	A1688	50c multi	1.50	.40

Europa A1689

2004 Photo. *Perf. 13x13¼*

3024	A1689	50c multi	1.50	.35

Litho.

Booklet Stamp

Self-Adhesive

Serpentine Die Cut 11

3025	A1689	50c multi	2.00	.35
a.		Booklet pane of 10	15.00	

Issued: No. 3024, 5/9; No. 3025, 6/4.

Blake and Mortimer, Comic Book Characters by Edgar P. Jacobs A1690

Blake and Mortimer and: 50c, Brick wall, vert. €1, Blue background.

2004, May 15 Photo. *Perf. 13¼*

3026	A1690	50c multi	1.50	.35
3027	A1690	€1 multi	3.00	1.25

See Belgium No. 2020.

FIFA (Fédération Internationale de Football Association), Cent. — A1691

2004, May 20 *Perf. 13¼x13*

3028	A1691	50c multi	1.50	.35

Gardens and Parks Type of 2003

No. 3029: a, Jardin des Tuileries. b, Parc Floral de Paris.

2004, June 4 *Perf. 13¼x13*

3029		Sheet of 2	11.50	11.50
a.-b.	A1660	€1.90 Either single	5.75	5.75
c.		Souvenir sheet, #2979a-2979b, 3029a-3029b	25.00	25.00

Salon du Timbre 2004. No. 3029 has four vertical rows of rouletting, separating sheet into fifths, with the two stamps in the central fifth.

D-Day Invasion of France, 60th Anniv. — A1692

2004, June 5 *Perf. 13*

3030	A1692	50c multi	1.50	.35

Organ Donation A1693

2004, June 22 *Perf. 13¼*

3031	A1693	50c multi	1.50	.35

Pierre Dugua de Mons, Leader of First French Settlement in Acadia, and Ship A1694

Litho. & Engr.

2004, June 26 *Perf. 13*

3032	A1694	90c multi	2.75	1.50

See Canada No. 2044.

Napoleon I and the Imperial Guard — A1695

Designs: No. 3033, Light cavalry (Chasseur à cheval). No. 3034, Artilleryman and cannon (Artilleur à pied), horiz. No. 3035, Dragoon. No. 3036, Mameluke. No. 3037, Napoleon I. No. 3038, Grenadier (Grenadier à pied).

2004, June 26 Photo.

3033	A1695	50c multi	1.75	.75
3034	A1695	50c multi	1.75	.75
3035	A1695	50c multi	1.75	.75
3036	A1695	50c multi	1.75	.75
3037	A1695	50c multi	1.75	.75
3038	A1695	50c multi	1.75	.75
a.		Souvenir sheet, #3033-3038	12.50	12.50
		Nos. 3033-3038 (6)	10.50	4.50

No. 3038a sold for €4.60, with the Red Cross receiving €1.60 of that.

French Federation of Philatelic Associations 77th Congress, Paris — A1696

Litho. & Engr.

2004, June 27 *Perf. 13¼x13*

3039	A1696	50c multi	1.50	.35

2004 Summer Olympics, Athens — A1697

2004, June 28 Photo. *Perf. 13¼*

3040		50c Modern athletes	1.50	.60
3041		50c Ancient athletes	1.50	.60
a.	A1697	Pair, #3040-3041	3.25	2.25

Printed in sheets containing five of each stamp.

A souvenir sheet containing No. 3041 was issued Aug. 2 and sold for €2.51. Value $20.

Happy Birthday A1698

2004, June 30 Photo. *Perf. 13¼*

3042	A1698	50c multi	1.50	.35
a.		Souvenir sheet of 5	7.50	7.50
b.		Litho. stamp + label	6.00	6.00

No. 3042b printed in sheets of 10 stamps + 10 labels that could be personalized that sold for €8. No. 3042b has a dark green inscription at left with a distinct dot pattern. No. 3042 has a lighter green inscription.

Marianne Type of 1997 Inscribed "RF" at Lower Left and Type of 2002 With Euro Denominations

2004 Litho. *Perf. 13*

3043		Sheet of 15 + 15 labels	50.00	50.00
a.	A1583	1c orange yellow	.25	.25
b.	A1583	2c brown	.25	.25
c.	A1583	5c brt bl green	.25	.25
d.	A1583	10c purple	.30	.30
e.	A1583	20c orange	.60	.60
f.	A1583	58c apple green	1.75	1.75
g.	A1583	70c olive	2.10	2.10
h.	A1583	75c sky blue	2.25	2.25
i.	A1583	90c dark blue	2.75	2.75
j.	A1583	€1 Prussian blue	3.00	3.00
k.	A1583	€1.11 red lilac	3.25	3.25
l.	A1583	€1.90 violet brown	5.75	5.75
m.	A1583	€2 violet	6.00	6.00
n.	A1409	(45c) green	1.40	1.40
o.	A1409	(50c) red	1.50	1.50

Engr.

Serpentine Die Cut 6¾ Vert

Self-Adhesive

3043P	A1583	75c bright blue + label	8.75	8.75
3043Q	A1583	€1.11 red lilac + label	10.50	10.50

No. 3043 sold for €10.03. Stamps have a glossy varnish.

Labels on Nos. 3043P-3043Q could be personalized.

Marianne and Emblem of World Fund to Combat AIDS, Tuberculosis and Smoking — A1699

2004, July 1 Engr. *Perf. 13*

3044	A1699	(50c) red	1.50	.35

Extreme Sports — A1700

No. 3045: a, Skateboarding. b, Parachuting. c, Sailboarding. d, Surfing. e, Luge. f, BMX bicycling. g, Paragliding. h, Jetskiing. i, Snowboarding. j, Rollerblading.

2004, July 3 Photo. *Perf. 13¼x13*

3045 A1700 Sheet of 10 7.50 7.50
a.-e. 20c Any single .60 .50
f.-j. 30c Any single .90 .75

Orchid Type of 2002

Design: 39c, Orchis insularis.

2004, Sept. 1 Litho. *Perf. 13*

3046 A1584 39c multi 1.20 .75

No. 3046 known only precanceled. See second note after No. 132.

Aspects of Life in the French Regions Type of 2003

No. 3047: a, House, Normandy. b, Chambord Chateau. c, Gorges, Tarn, vert. d, Notre Dame Cathedral, Paris, vert. e, Windmill, vert. f, Cave dwellings. g, Creek, Cassis, vert. h, Cap-Ferret Lighthouse, vert. i, Castle ruins. j, Alpine chalet.

2004, Sept. 18 Photo. *Perf. 13*

3047 Sheet of 10 15.00 15.00
a.-j. A1642 50c Any single 1.50 1.25

No. 3047 has three vertical rows of rouletting separating sheet into quarters.
Each stamp exists in booklet pane of 1 from booklet that sold for €19.

Halloween A1701

2004, Oct. 9 Litho. *Perf. 13*

3048 A1701 50c multi 1.50 .35

Félix Eboué (1884-1944), Colonial Governor — A1702

2004, Oct. 16 Photo.

3049 A1702 50c multi 1.50 .40

Ouistreham Lighthouse A1703

2004, Oct. 30 *Perf. 13¼*

3050 A1703 50c multi 1.50 .40

Marianne — A1704

Serpentine Die Cut 6¾ Vert.

2004, Nov. 10 Engr.

Booklet Stamp
Self-Adhesive

3051 A1704 50c multi 3.50 3.00
a. Booklet pane, 5 each #2835A, 3051 25.00

European Capitals Type of 2002

No. 3052 — Attractions in Athens: a, Greek Academy. b, Parthenon. c, Odeon of Herodes Atticus. d, Church of the Holy Apostles, vert.

Perf. 13x13¼, 13¼x13

2004, Nov. 11 Photo.

3052 A1622 Sheet of 4 7.50 7.50
a.-d. 50c Any single 1.50 .90

A1705

A1706

A1707

A1708

A1709

Holiday Greetings A1710

2004, Nov. 12 Photo. *Perf. 13*

3053 A1705 50c multi 1.50 .40

Litho.

3054 A1706 50c multi + label 6.00 6.00
3055 A1707 50c multi + label 6.00 6.00
3056 A1708 50c multi + label 6.00 6.00
3057 A1709 50c multi + label 6.00 6.00
3058 A1710 50c multi + label 6.00 6.00
a. Vert. strip of 5, #3054-3059 + 5 labels 30.00 30.00
Miniature sheet, 2 #3058a + 10 labels 60.00 60.00

Booklet Stamps
Self-Adhesive

Serpentine Die Cut 11¼x11

3059 A1706 50c multi 1.50 .40
3060 A1707 50c multi 1.50 .40
3061 A1708 50c multi 1.50 .40
3062 A1709 50c multi 1.50 .40
3063 A1710 50c multi 1.50 .40
a. Booklet pane, 2 each #3059-3063 15.00
Nos. 3053-3063 (11) 39.00 32.40

Miniature sheet containing Nos. 3054-3058 sold for €6.69. Labels could be personalized. No. 3055 exists in a souvenir sheet of 1 stamp without label that sold for €3. Value $35.

Henri Wallon (1812-1904), Historian and Politician — A1711

2004, Nov. 18 Photo. *Perf. 13*

3064 A1711 50c multi 1.50 .40

Opening of Millau Viaduct — A1712

2004, Dec. 14 Photo. *Perf. 13*

3065 A1712 50c multi 1.50 .40

Marianne — A1713

Inscribed "ITVF" at Bottom

2005-07 Engr. *Perf. 13*

3066 A1713 1c yellow .25 .25
a. Inscribed "Phil@poste" at bottom .25 .25
3067 A1713 5c brown black .25 .25
a. Inscribed "Phil@poste" at bottom .25 .25
3068 A1713 10c violet .25 .25
3069 A1713 (45c) green 1.25 .25
a. Inscribed "Phil@poste" at bottom 1.25 .25
3070 A1713 (50c) red 1.50 .25
a. Sheet of 15 + 15 labels 60.00 60.00
b. Inscribed "Phil@poste" at bottom 1.40 .25
3071 A1713 55c dark blue 1.60 .50
3072 A1713 58c olive green 1.75 .40
3073 A1713 64c dark green 1.90 .40
3074 A1713 70c dark green 2.10 .50
3075 A1713 75c light blue 2.25 .40
3076 A1713 82c fawn 2.40 .45
3077 A1713 90c dark blue 2.75 .90
3078 A1713 €1 orange 3.00 1.00
a. Inscribed "Phil@poste" at bottom 2.60 .55
3079 A1713 €1.11 red violet 3.25 .80
3080 A1713 €1.22 red violet 3.50 .75
3081 A1713 €1.90 chocolate 5.75 1.20
3082 A1713 €1.98 chocolate 6.00 2.00
Nos. 3066-3082 (17) 39.75 10.55

Self-Adhesive (#3083-3085)

Serpentine Die Cut 6¾ Vert.

3083 A1713 (50c) red 1.50 .25
a. Booklet pane of 10 (see footnote) 15.00
b. Booklet pane of 10 (see footnote) 15.00
c. Booklet pane of 20 30.00
d. As #3083, with "Phil@poste" inscription 1.50 .25
e. Booklet pane, 10 #3083d 15.00
f. Booklet pane of 12 #3083d 17.00
g. No. 3083 with attached label 7.50
3084 A1713 82c fawn + label 12.00 12.00
3085 A1713 €1.22 red violet 15.00 15.00

Coil Stamps

Perf. 13 Horiz.

3086 A1713 (45c) green 1.25 .30
a. Inscribed "Phil@poste" at bottom 1.40 .25
3087 A1713 (50c) red 1.50 .25
c. Inscribed "Phil@poste" at bottom — —
3087A A1713 55c dark blue 1.60 .60
b. Inscribed "Phil@poste" at bottom 1.60 .25
Nos. 3083-3087A (6) 32.85 28.40

Issued: Nos. 1c, 10c, (45c), (50c), 58c, 70c, 75c, 90c, €1, €1.11, €1.90, 1/8. 5c, No. 3071, 64c, 82c, €1.22, €1.98, 3/1. No. 3087A, 7/15. Nos. 3083d, 3083e, 10/1/06. Nos. 3066a, 3067a, 3069a, 3070b, 2006. No. 3083f, Jan. 2007. Nos. 3083g, 3084-3085, Apr. 2007. No. 3086a was issued in 2008 and sold for 50c. No. 3087b was issued in 2008 and sold for 55c.

Face values shown for Nos. 3069, 3070, 3083, 3086 and 3087 are those the stamps sold for on the day of issue. On day of issue, No. 3069a sold for 49c; No. 3070b for 54c.

No. 3070a sold for €10.03 and the labels could be personalized for an additional fee.

No. 3083a has a narrow strip of selvage separating the four stamps at left, from the six stamps, at right, and is on a white backing paper. No. 3083b is comprised of two horizontal strips of five stamps on a yellow backing paper. No. 3083d sold for 54c on day of issue.

No. 3083g was printed in sheets containing 15 stamps + 15 small or large-sized labels that could be personalized. Nos. 3084 and 3085 were each printed in sheets of 30 stamps + 30 large-sized labels that could be personalized.

A sheet of 10 litho. stamps similar to No. 3068 + 10 labels exists, but was not sold.

See Nos. 3211, 3211N, 3212, 3247-3255E, 3302, 3383-3388A, 3389, 3531, 4410k, 4524.

Rabbi Shlomo Yitshaql (Rashi) (1040-1105) — A1714

2005, Jan. 16 Engr. *Perf. 13¼*

3088 A1714 50c multi 1.75 .40

Hearts A1715

Designs: 53c, Polka dots. 82c, Bird and flowers.

2005, Jan. 29 Photo. *Perf. 13¼*

3089 A1715 53c multi 1.50 .40
a. Souvenir sheet of 5 7.50 7.50
b. Litho, stamp + label 5.00 5.00
3090 A1715 82c multi 2.50 1.00
a. Litho, stamp + label 6.00 6.00

Values are for stamps with surrounding selvage.

Sheets of 10 of No. 3089b sold for €6.86, and sheets of 10 of No. 3090a sold for €8.78. Labels could be personalized for an additional fee.

See Nos. 3134, 3136.

New Year 2005 (Year of the Rooster) A1716

Photo. & Embossed

2005, Jan. 29 *Perf. 13½x13*

3091 A1716 (50c) multi 1.75 .40

Printed in sheets of 10.

Rotary International, Cent. — A1717

2005, Feb. 19 Photo. *Perf. 13¼*

3092 A1717 53c multi 1.50 .40

See No. 3227A.

Titeuf — A1718

Nadia — A1719

Manu — A1720

2005, Feb. 28 Photo. *Perf. 13¼*

3093 A1718 (50c) red & multi 1.50 .40
  a. Perf. 13¼x13 (booklet stamp) 1.50 .40

Booklet Stamps

3094 A1719 (45c) green & multi 1.40 .35
3095 A1720 (90c) blue & multi 2.75 .70
  a. Booklet pane, 2 #3094, 4 each #3093a, 3095 20.00 —
  Complete booklet, #3095a 21.00

Characters from Titeuf, comic strip by Zep. Stamp Day.

Greetings Type of 2004 Inscribed "Lettre 20g"

Designs: Nos. 3096, 3097A, "Ceci est une invitation." Nos. 3097, 3097B, "Un grand merci."

No. 3097C, "Ceci est une invitation." No. 3097D, "Un grand merci."

2005-06 Photo. *Perf. 13*

Holes Punched Through Dots of "i's"

3096 A1667 (53c) brt lil rose & yel 1.50 .40
3097 A1667 (53c) brt yel grn & red lil 1.50 .40

Litho.

No Holes Punched Through Dots of "i's"

Stamp + Label

3097A A1667 (53c) brt lil rose & yel 4.50 4.50
3097B A1667 (53c) brt yel grn & red lil 4.50 4.50

Self-Adhesive

No Holes Punched Through Dots of "i's"

Serpentine Die Cut 11¼x11

Stamp + Label

3097C A1667 (53c) brt lil rose & yel 2.40 2.40
3097D A1667 (53c) brt yel grn & rrd lil 2.40 2.40

Nos. 3097A-3097B were issued in sheets of 10 stamps + 10 labels that sold for €8 on day of issue. The labels could be personalized.

Nos. 3097C-3097D were each issued in sheets of 10 stamps + 10 labels that sold for €8.61. Labels could be personalized.

Issued: Nos. 2096-3097B, 3/1/05. Nos. 3097C-3097D, 2006.

Art Series

The Guitarist, by Jean-Baptiste Greuze (1725-1805) — A1721

White Bear, Sculpture by François Pompon — A1722

Sicile, by Nicolas de Stael — A1723

2005 Photo. *Perf. 13x13¼*

3098 A1721 82c multi 2.50 1.00
3099 A1722 90c multi 3.00 1.50
3100 A1723 €1.22 multi 3.75 1.60

Issued: €1.22, 3/5. 90c, 7/2. 82c, 9/24.

Orchids — A1725

Designs: No. 3102, Cypripedium calceolus. No. 3103, Paphiopedilum Mabel Sanders. 55c, Oncidium papilio. 82c, Paphinia cristata, horiz.

2005, Mar. 11 Photo. *Perf. 13¼*

3102 A1725 53c multi 1.60 .40
3103 A1725 53c multi 1.60 .40
3104 A1725 55c multi 1.60 .45
3105 A1725 82c multi 2.40 1.00
  a. Souvenir sheet, #3102-3105 7.50 7.50
  Nos. 3102-3105 (4) 7.20 2.25

Aspects of Life in French Regions Type of 2003

No. 3106: a, Nautical jousting. b, Clocks of Franche-Comte, vert. c, Cantal cheese and bread, vert. d, Dancers and accordion player. e, Bouillabaisse. f, P'tit Quinquin statue, vert. g, Rillettes (chopped pork). h, Sauerkraut and sausage, beer stein. i, Pelota, vert. j, Sugar cane, vert.

2005, Mar. 19 Photo. *Perf. 13*

3106 Sheet of 10 16.00 16.00
  a.-j. A1642 53c Any single 1.50 1.25

No. 3106 has three vertical rows of rouletting, separating sheet into quarters.

Each stamp exists in a booklet pane of 1 from a booklet that sold for €19. Value $50.

Tourism Issue

Aix-en-Provence — A1726

Gulf of Morbihan — A1727

Villefranche-sur-Mer — A1728

La Roque-Gageac — A1729

2005 Engr. *Perf. 13¼, 13 (#3108)*

3107 A1726 53c multi 1.60 .40

Photo.

3108 A1727 53c multi 1.60 .40
3109 A1728 53c multi 1.60 .40

Engr.

3110 A1729 53c multi 1.60 .40

Issued: No. 3107, 4/1; No. 3108, 5/5; No. 3109, 6/4; No. 3110, 7/23.

Happy Birthday A1730

2005, Apr. 2 Photo. *Perf. 13*

3111 A1730 (53c) multi 1.60 .40
  a. Souvenir sheet of 5 8.00 8.00
  b. Litho., stamp + label 6.00 6.00

Sheets of 10 and 10 labels of No. 3111b sold for €6.86. Labels could be personalized for an additional fee.

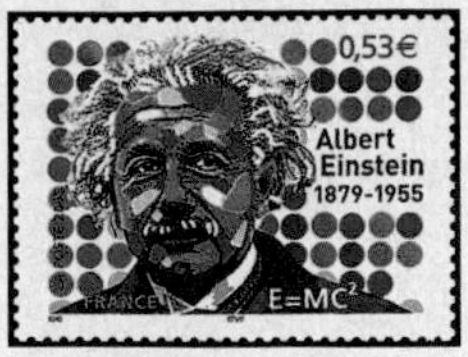

Albert Einstein (1879-1955), Physicist — A1731

2005, Apr. 16 *Perf. 13¼*

3112 A1731 53c multi 1.60 .40

Alexis de Tocqueville (1805-59), Writer — A1732

2005, Apr. 23 Engr. *Perf. 13x13¼*

3113 A1732 90c multi 2.75 1.00

Liberation of Concentration Camp Internees, 60th Anniv. — A1733

2005, Apr. 24 Photo. *Perf. 13¼*

3114 A1733 53c multi 1.60 .40

Battle of Austerlitz, Bicent. A1734

Litho. & Engr.

2005, May 4 *Perf. 13¼*

3115 A1734 55c multi 1.60 .45

See Czech Republic No. 3273.

French Federation of Philatelic Associations, 78th Congress, Nancy — A1735

2005, May 5 Engr. *Perf. 13*

3116 A1735 53c multi + label 1.60 .40

A souvenir sheet of one stamp without label exists. Value $12.

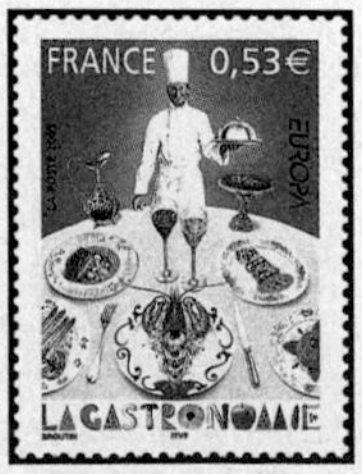

Europa — A1736

2005, May 8 Photo. *Perf. 13¼*

3117 A1736 53c multi 1.60 .50

Gardens and Parks Type of 2003

Souvenir Sheet

No. 3118 — Sculptures in Jardin de la Fontaine, Nimes: a, Denomination in green. b, Denomination in white.

2005, May 15 *Perf. 13¼x13*

3118 Sheet of 2 12.00 12.00
a.-b. A1660 €1.98 Either single 6.00 6.00

Salon du Timbre 2005. No. 3118 has four vertical rows of rouletting, separating sheet into fifths, with the two stamps in the central fifth.

Vacation A1737

Serpentine Die Cut 11

2005, May 23 **Litho.**

Booklet Stamp

Self-Adhesive

3119 A1737 (53c) multi 1.75 .40
a. Booklet pane of 10 17.50

Stories by Jules Verne (1828-1905) A1738

Designs: No. 3120, Five Weeks in a Balloon (Cinq Semaines en Ballon). No. 3121, From the Earth to the Moon (De la Terre à la Lune). No. 3122, Journey to the Center of the Earth (Voyage au Centre de la Terre), horiz. No. 3123, Michael Strogoff, horiz. No. 3124, Around the World in Eighty Days (Le Tour du Monde en Quatre-vingts Jours). No. 3125, 20,000 Leagues Under the Sea (Vingt Mille Lieues Sous les Mers).

2005, May 28 **Photo.** *Perf. 13*

3120 A1738 53c multi 1.60 .75
3121 A1738 53c multi 1.60 .75
3122 A1738 53c multi 1.60 .75
3123 A1738 53c multi 1.60 .75
3124 A1738 53c multi 1.60 .75
3125 A1738 53c multi 1.60 .75
a. Souvenir sheet, #3120-3125 12.00 12.00
Nos. 3120-3125 (6) 9.60 4.50

No. 3125a sold for €4.80 with the Red Cross receiving €1.62 of that.

Miniature Sheet

Gordon Bennett Cup, Cent. — A1739

No. 3126 — Inscriptions: a, La Coupe Gordon Bennett (Car No. 1 facing right). b, La Coupe Gordon Bennett (Car No. 1 facing left). c, La Formule 1, vert. d, Le Rallye-Raid, vert. e, Les Rallyes. f, La Course d'endurance.

2005, June 2 **Photo.** *Perf.*

3126 A1739 Sheet of 10, #a-b, 2 each #c-f 19.00 19.00
a.-f. 53c Any single 1.75 .85

A souvenir sheet containing No. 3126a sold for €3. Value $100.

Environmental Charter — A1740

2005, June 5 **Litho.** *Perf. 13*

3127 A1740 53c multi, *lt green* 1.60 .40

Enactment of Handicapped Persons Rights Law — A1741

2005, June 18 **Photo.** *Perf. 13¼*

3128 A1741 53c multi 1.60 .35

It's a Boy A1742

It's a Girl A1743

2005 **Litho.** *Perf. 13x13¼*

3129 A1742 (53c) multi + label 4.00 4.00
3130 A1743 (53c) multi + label 4.00 4.00

Booklet Stamps

Self-Adhesive

Serpentine Die Cut 11¼x11

3131 A1742 (53c) multi 1.60 .35
a. Booklet pane of 10 16.00
b. Sheet of 10 + 10 labels 23.00
3132 A1743 (53c) multi 1.60 .35
a. Booklet pane of 10 16.00
b. Sheet of 10 + 10 labels 23.00

Sheets of 10 stamps and 10 labels of Nos. 3129 and 3130 each sold for €6.86. Nos. 3131b and 3132b each sold for €8.61. Labels could be personalized for an additional fee.

Hearts Types of 2004-05

Serpentine Die Cut

2005, July 15 **Photo.**

Self-Adhesive

3133 A1670 50c Like #2997 5.00 3.50
3134 A1715 53c Like #3089 6.00 4.50
3135 A1670 75c Like #2998 6.00 4.50
3136 A1715 82c Like #3090 7.00 5.50
Nos. 3133-3136 (4) 24.00 18.00

Haras du Pin Natl. Stud Farm A1744

2005, July 16 *Perf. 13*

3137 A1744 53c multi 1.60 .40

European Capitals Type of 2002

No. 3138 — Attractions in Berlin: a, Brandenburg Gate. b, Kaiser Wilhelm Memorial Church, vert. c, Philharmonic Hall. d, Reichstag.

Perf. 13x13¼, 13¼x13

2005, Aug. 27 **Photo.**

3138 A1622 Sheet of 4 6.50 6.50
a.-d. 53c Any single 1.60 1.00

Aspects of Life in the French Regions Type of 2003

No. 3139: a, Lake Annecy. b, Etretat Cliffs, vert. c, Pigeon house, vert. d, Wash house (lavoir). e, Banks of the Seine. f, Carnac megaliths. g, House, Sologne. h, Pilat Sand Dune. i, Stiff Lighthouse, vert. j, Stone hut (borie), vert.

2005, Sept. 17 *Perf. 13*

3139 Sheet of 10 16.00 16.00
a.-j. A1642 53c Any single 1.60 1.25

No. 3139 has three vertical rows of rouletting, separating sheet into quarters.

Nos. 3139a-3139j were also issued in large booklets containing panes of 1 of each stamp. The booklet sold for €19. Value $60.

Art Series

Les Halles Centrales, Designed by Victor Baltard (1805-74) — A1745

2005, Sept. 17 **Engr.** *Perf. 13x13¼*

3140 A1745 €1.22 multi 3.75 1.25

Breast Cancer Awareness A1746

2005, Oct. 1 **Photo.** *Perf. 13¼*

3141 A1746 53c multi 1.60 .35

A1747

A1748

A1749

A1750

A1751

A1752

A1753

A1754

A1755

Cat, Comics by Philippe Geluck A1756

Serpentine Die Cut 11¼x11

2005, Oct. 1 **Litho.**

Booklet Stamps

Self-Adhesive

3142 A1747 (53c) multi 1.60 .35
3143 A1748 (53c) multi 1.60 .35
3144 A1749 (53c) multi 1.60 .35
3145 A1750 (53c) multi 1.60 .35
3146 A1751 (53c) multi 1.60 .35
3147 A1752 (53c) multi 1.60 .35
3148 A1753 (53c) multi 1.60 .35
3149 A1754 (53c) multi 1.60 .35
3150 A1755 (53c) multi 1.60 .35
3151 A1756 (53c) multi 1.60 .35
a. Booklet pane of 10, #3142-3151 16.00

Raymond Aron (1905-83), Philosopher A1757

2005, Oct. 7 **Engr.** *Perf. 13¼x13*

3152 A1757 53c multi 1.60 .35

Souvenir Sheet

The Annunciation, by Raphael — A1758

No. 3153: a, Drawing of Angel, painting of Virgin Mary. b, Painting of Angel, drawing of Virgin Mary.

Litho. & Engr.

2005, Nov. 10 *Perf. 13x13¼*

3153 A1758 Sheet of 2 4.00 4.00
a. 53c multi 1.60 1.60
b. 55c multi 1.60 1.60

See Vatican City Nos. 1312-1314.

Marianne — A1759

Serpentine Die Cut 6¾ Vert.

2005, Nov. 11 **Engr.**

Booklet Stamp

Self-Adhesive

3154 A1759 53c red 3.50 3.00
a. Booklet pane, 5 each #3083, 3154 25.00

Video Game Characters — A1760

No. 3155: a, Link. b, Pac-Man. c, Prince of Persia. d, Spyro. e, Donkey Kong. f, Mario. g, Adibou. h, Rayman. i, Lara Croft. j, The Sims.

2005, Nov. 11 Photo. ***Perf. 13¼x13***

3155 A1760 Sheet of 10 9.00 9.00
a.-e. 20c Any single .60 .50
f.-j. 33c Any single 1.00 .75

Avicenna (980-1037), Scientist — A1761

2005, Nov. 12 Engr. ***Perf. 13x13¼***

3156 A1761 53c multi 1.60 .35

Holiday Greetings A1762

Designs: Nos. 3157, 3162, Bear, three penguins and sled. Nos. 3158, 3163, Two penguins, reindeer and sled. Nos. 3159, 3164, Two penguins, bear and sled. Nos. 3160, 3165, Three penguins. Nos. 3161, 3166, Two penguins, reindeer and snowman.

2005, Nov. 12 Litho. ***Perf. 13***

3157 A1762 (53c) multi + label 6.00 4.00
3158 A1762 (53c) multi + label 6.00 4.00
3159 A1762 (53c) multi + label 6.00 4.00
3160 A1762 (53c) multi + label 6.00 4.00
3161 A1762 (53c) multi + label 6.00 4.00
a. Vert. strip of 5, #3157-3161, + 5 labels 30.00 30.00
Miniature sheet, 2 #3161a 60.00 60.00

Booklet Stamps

Self-Adhesive

Serpentine Die Cut 11¼x11

3162 A1762 (53c) multi 1.60 .35
3163 A1762 (53c) multi 1.60 .35
3164 A1762 (53c) multi 1.60 .35
3165 A1762 (53c) multi 1.60 .35
3166 A1762 (53c) multi 1.60 .35
a. Booklet pane, 2 each #3162-3166 16.00
Nos. 3157-3166 (10) 38.00 21.75

Miniature sheet containing Nos. 3157-3161 sold for €6.86. Labels could be personalized.

No. 3161 exists in a souvenir sheet of one stamp without label, that sold for €3. Value $35.

Jacob Kaplan (1895-1994), Grand Rabbi of France — A1763

2005, Nov. 14 Engr. ***Perf. 13***

3167 A1763 53c multi 1.60 .35

Orchid Type of 2002

Design: Orchis insularis.

2005 Litho. ***Perf. 13***

3168 A1584 42c multi 1.40 .75

No. 3168 is known only precanceled. See second note after No. 132.

Law Separating Church and State, Cent. — A1764

2005, Dec. 3 Photo. ***Perf. 13¼x13***

3169 A1764 53c multi 1.60 .35

Hearts A1765

Designs: (53c), Hearts, octagons and diamonds. (82c), Heart and stripes.

2006, Jan. 7 Photo. ***Perf. 13¼***

3170 A1765 (53c) multi 1.60 .40
a. Souvenir sheet of 5 8.00 8.00
b. Litho., stamp + label 4.00 4.00
3171 A1765 (82c) multi 2.40 .70
a. Litho., stamp + label 4.00 4.00

Self-Adhesive

Serpentine Die Cut

3172 A1765 (53c) Like #3170 3.00 1.50
a. Sheet of 10 + 10 labels 23.00
3173 A1765 (82c) Like #3171 4.00 3.00
a. Sheet of 10 + 10 labels 30.00

Values are for stamps with surrounding selvage. Sheets of 10 of No. 3170b sold for €6.86, and sheets of No. 3172a. No. 3172a sold for €8.61; No. 3173a for €11.54. Labels could be personalized for an additional fee.

New Year 2006 (Year of the Dog) — A1766

2006, Jan. 21 Photo. ***Perf. 13¼x13***

3174 A1766 (53c) multi 1.60 .40

A souvenir sheet containing No. 3174 sold for €3. Value $14.

Impressionist Paintings — A1767

Designs: Nos. 3175a, 3176, Portraits from the Country, by Gustave Caillebotte. Nos. 3175b, 3183, Dancers, by Edgar Degas. Nos. 3175c, 3181, Marguerite Gachet in the Garden, by Vincent van Gogh. Nos. 3175d, 3179, Two Young Girls at the Piano, by Auguste Renoir. Nos. 3175e, 3177, The Butterfly Hunt, by Berthe Morisot. Nos. 3175f, 3184, Luncheon on the Grass, by Edouard Manet. Nos. 3175g, 3182, Evening Air, by Henri-Edmond Cross. Nos. 3175h, 3180, The Shepherdess (Young Peasant Girl with a Stick), by Camille Pissarro. Nos. 3175i, 3178, Mother and Child, by Mary Cassatt. Nos. 3175j, 3185, Women of Tahiti on the Beach, by Paul Gauguin.

2006 Litho. ***Perf. 13¼***

3175 Sheet of 10 +10 labels 35.00 35.00
a.-j. A1767 (53c) Any single + label 3.50 3.50

Booklet Stamps

Self-Adhesive

Serpentine Die Cut 11¼x11

3176 A1767 (53c) multi 1.60 .40
3177 A1767 (53c) multi 1.60 .40
3178 A1767 (53c) multi 1.60 .40
3179 A1767 (53c) multi 1.60 .40
3180 A1767 (53c) multi 1.60 .40
3181 A1767 (53c) multi 1.60 .40
3182 A1767 (53c) multi 1.60 .40
3183 A1767 (53c) multi 1.60 .40
3184 A1767 (53c) multi 1.60 .40
3185 A1767 (53c) multi 1.60 .40
a. Booklet pane of 10, #3176-3185 16.00
b. Sheet of 10, #3176-3185, + 10 labels *65.00*

Issued: No. 3175, 6/1; Nos. 3176-3185, 1/21. No. 3175 sold for €6.86. No. 3185b sold for €8.61. Labels could be personalized.

2006 Winter Olympics, Turin — A1768

2006, Feb. 4 Photo. ***Perf. 13***

3186 A1768 53c multi 1.60 .35

Spirou — A1769

Fantasio, Spip and Spirou — A1770

Fantasio A1771

2006, Feb. 25 ***Perf. 13¼***

3187 A1769 (53c) multi 1.60 .40
a. Perf. 13¼x13 (booklet stamp) 1.60 .40

Booklet Stamps

Perf. 13¼x13

3188 A1770 (48c) multi 1.40 .35
3189 A1771 (90c) multi 2.75 .65
a. Booklet pane, 4 each #3187a, 3188, 2 #3189 17.50 —
Complete booklet, #3189a 18.00

Characters from Spirou, by Robert Velter. Stamp Day.

Courrières Coal Mine Disaster, Cent. — A1772

2006, Feb. 25 ***Perf. 13¼***

3190 A1772 53c multi 1.60 .40

Douaumont Ossuary — A1773

2006, Mar. 4 Engr.

3191 A1773 53c multi 1.60 .40

Aspects of Life in the French Regions Type of 2003

No. 3192: a, Yellow plums (mirabelle). b, Salt marsh (marais salants). c, Butter (beurre). d, Roquefort cheese, vert. e, Olive oil, vert. f, Carnival, vert. g, Grape harvests (vendanges), vert. h, Waiter at café, vert. i, Transhumance of livestock. j, Marshland gardens (hortillonages).

2006, Mar. 25 Photo. ***Perf. 13***

3192 Sheet of 10 16.00 16.00
a.-j. A1642 53c Any single 1.60 1.25

No. 3192 has three vertical rows of rouletting, separating sheet into quarters.

Nos. 3192a-3192j were also issued in large booklets containing panes of 1 of each stamp. The booklet sold for €19. Value $42.50.

Tourism Issue

Yvoire A1774

Dijon A1775

Antibes Juan-les-Pins — A1776

Thionville A1777

2006 Photo. ***Perf. 13***

3193 A1774 53c multi 1.60 .40

Engr.

Perf. 13¼

3194 A1775 53c multi 1.60 .40

Litho. & Engr.

Perf. 13x13¼

3195 A1776 53c multi 1.60 .40

Engraved

3196 A1777 54c multi 1.60 .40
Nos. 3193-3196 (4) 6.40 1.60

Issued: No. 3193, 3/25; No. 3194, 4/7. No. 3195, 7/15. No. 3196, 9/16.

Art Series

Prehistoric Drawings in Rouffignac Cave — A1778

Bathers, by Paul Cézanne — A1779

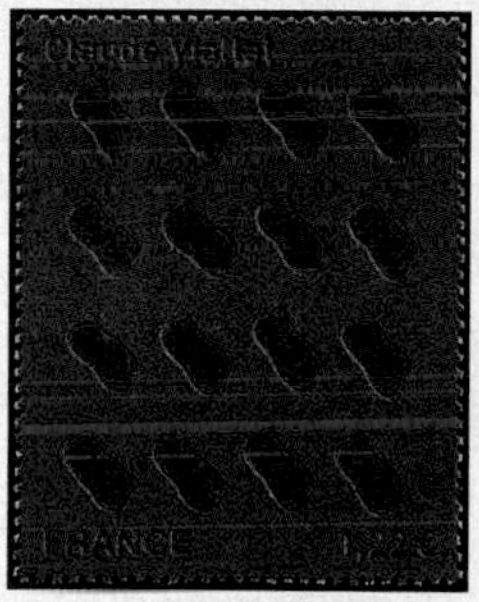

Untitled Painting by Claude Viallat A1780

Beggars Receiving Alms at the Door of a House, by Rembrandt A1781

Engr., Photo (#3198, 3199)

2006 ***Perf. 13x13¼***

3197 A1778 55c multi 1.60 .75
3198 A1779 82c multi 2.40 .75

Perf. 13¼x13

3199 A1780 €1.22 brt pink & bl grn 3.50 1.00
3200 A1781 €1.30 multi 3.75 1.00
Nos. 3197-3200 (4) 11.25 3.50

Issued: 82c, 4/8; 55c, 5/27; No. 3199, 6/3. No. 3200, 11/10.

Gardens and Parks Type of 2003

Souvenir Sheet

No. 3201: a, Vallée-aux-Loups Park. b, Albert Kahn Gardens.

2006, Apr. 22 Photo. ***Perf. 13¼x13***

3201 Sheet of 2 16.50 16.50
a.-b. A1660 €1.98 Either single 6.50 6.50
c. Souvenir sheet, #3118a, 3118b, 3201a, 3201b 34.00 34.00

Salon du Timbre 2006. No. 3201 has four vertical rows of rouletting, separating sheet into fifths, with the two stamps in the central fifth.

No. 3201c issued 6/16.

Young Animals A1782

Designs: No. 3202, Puppy. No. 3203, Kitten. 55c, Foal, horiz. 82c, Lamb, horiz..

2006, Apr. 22 ***Perf. 13¼***

3202 A1782 53c multi 1.60 .40
3203 A1782 53c multi 1.60 .40
3204 A1782 55c multi 1.60 .40
3205 A1782 82c multi 2.40 .65
a. Souvenir sheet, #3202-3205 7.50 7.50
Nos. 3202-3205 (4) 7.20 1.85

Europa A1783

2006, Apr. 30

3206 A1783 53c multi 1.60 .40

Pierre Bayle (1647-1706), Philiosopher A1784

2006, May 2 Engr. ***Perf. 13x13¼***

3207 A1784 53c blk & brn 1.60 .40

Remembrance of Slavery Day, 5th Anniv. — A1785

2006, May 10 Photo. ***Perf. 13¼***

3208 A1785 53c multi 1.60 .40

Vacation A1786

Serpentine Die Cut 11¼x11

2006, May 27 Litho.

Booklet Stamp
Self-Adhesive

3209 A1786 (53c) multi 1.60 .40
a. Booklet pane of 10 16.00

Miniature Sheet

2006 World Cup Soccer Championships, Germany — A1787

No. 3210: a, Replacement players (39x25mm). b, Fans (39x25mm). c, Player with ball near chest (32mm diameter). d, Player kicking ball (32mm diameter). e, Goalie throwing ball (32mm diameter). f, Player making scissor kick (32mm diameter). g, Two players (32mm diameter). h, Referee (25x39mm). i, Coach (39x25mm). j, Cameramen (39x25mm).

2006, May 27 Photo. ***Perf. 12¾***

3210 A1787 Sheet of 10 16.00 16.00
a.-j. 53c Any single 1.60 1.25

Marianne Type of 2005

2006 Litho. ***Perf. 13***

3211 Sheet of 15, #a-k, 2 each #l-m, + 15 labels 50.00 50.00
a. A1713 1c yellow orange .25 .25
b. A1713 5c dark brown .25 .25
c. A1713 10c violet .40 .40
d. A1713 55c blue 2.00 2.00
e. A1713 64c olive green 2.25 2.25
f. A1713 75c light blue 2.50 2.50
g. A1713 82c fawn 3.00 3.00
h. A1713 90c dark blue 3.25 3.25
i. A1713 €1 dull orange 3.50 3.50
j. A1713 €1.22 red violet 4.25 4.25
k. A1713 €1.98 brown 6.75 6.75
l. A1713 (48c) green 1.75 1.75
m. A1713 (53c) red 1.90 1.90

Serpentine Die Cut 11¼

Self-Adhesive

3211N Sheet of 15, #3211No-3211Ny, 2 each #3211Nz, 3211Naa, + 15 labels 100.00
o. A1713 1c yellow orange .30 .30
p. A1713 5c dark brown .30 .30
q. A1713 10c violet .50 .50
r. A1713 55c blue 2.75 2.75
s. A1713 64c olive green 3.00 3.00
t. A1713 75c light blue 3.50 3.50
u. A1713 82c fawn 3.75 3.75
v. A1713 90c dark blue 4.50 4.50
w. A1713 €1 dull orange 4.75 4.75
x. A1713 €1.22 red violet 6.00 6.00
y. A1713 €1.98 brown 8.00 8.00
z. A1713 (48c) green 2.25 2.25
aa. A1713 (53c) red 2.50 2.50

Etched on Foil

Die Cut Perf. 13

3212 A1713 €5 *silver* 18.50 18.50

Nos. 3211a-3211m, 3211No-3211Naa and 3212 have "Phil@poste" inscription at bottom. Nos. 3211 and 3211N have stamps with a glossy varnish. No. 3211 sold for €12.04 and labels could be personalized. No. 3211N sold for €15.05 and labels could be personalized. No. 3212 was sold in a protective package.

Costumes From Operas by Wolfgang Amadeus Mozart — A1788

Designs: No. 3213, The Magic Flute. No. 3214, Don Giovanni. No. 3215, The Marriage of Figaro. No. 3216, The Clemency of Titus. No. 3217, The Abduction from the Seraglio (L'enlèvement au Sérail). No. 3218, Cosi Fan Tutte.

2006, June 17 Photo. ***Perf. 13***

3213 A1788 53c multi 1.60 .75
3214 A1788 53c multi 1.60 .75
3215 A1788 53c multi 1.60 .75
3216 A1788 53c multi 1.60 .75
3217 A1788 53c multi 1.60 .75
3218 A1788 53c multi 1.60 .75
a. Souvenir sheet, #3213-3218 12.00 12.00
Nos. 3213-3218 (6) 9.60 4.50

Nos. 3213-3218 were each printed in souvenir sheets containing one stamp that sold as a set for €15, and in booklet panes containing one stamp in a large book that sold for €19. Value: set of 6 sheets $40; set of 6 panes in book $50. No. 3218a sold for €4.80, with the Red Cross receiving €1.62 of that.

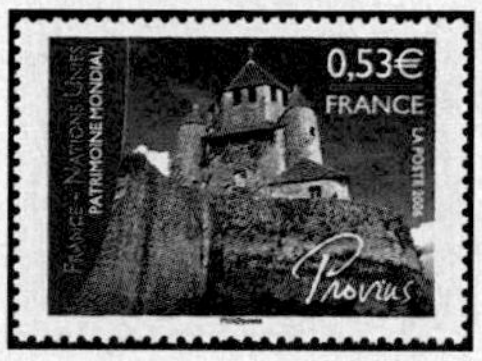

UNESCO World Heritage Sites A1789

Designs: 53c, Provins. 90c, Mont Saint-Michel.

2006, June 17 Photo. ***Perf. 13¼***

3219 A1789 53c multi 1.60 .40
3220 A1789 90c multi 2.60 .70

See United Nations Offices in Geneva Nos. 459-461.

Garnier Opera House, Paris — A1790

2006, June 18 Engr. ***Perf. 13x13¼***

3221 A1790 53c multi + label 1.60 .40

French Federation of Philatelic Associations 79th Congress, Paris. No. 3221 exists in a souvenir sheet of 1 (without label), issued in 2007 that sold for €3.

Happy Birthday A1791

2006, June 19 Photo. ***Perf. 13***

3222 A1791 (53c) multi 1.60 .40
a. Souvenir sheet of 5 8.00 8.00
b. Litho. stamp + label 4.00 4.00

Serpentine Die Cut 11

Self-Adhesive

3222C A1791 (53c) multi + label 2.40 2.40

Sheets of 10 of No. 3222b sold for €6.86. No. 3222C was printed in sheets of 10 stamps + 10 labels that sold for €8.61. Labels could be personalized for an additional fee.

European Capitals Type of 2002

Souvenir Sheet

No. 3223 — Attractions in Nicosia, Cyprus: a, Chrysaliniotissa Church. b, Archaeological Museum. c, Famagusta Gate. d, Archbishop's residence (Archevеché).

2006, June 20 Photo. ***Perf. 13x13¼***

3223 A1622 Sheet of 4 7.00 7.00
a.-d. 53c Any single 1.60 1.00

Tango Dancing A1792

2006, June 21 Photo. ***Perf. 12¼***

3224 A1792 53c Dancers 1.60 .40
3225 A1792 90c Musician 2.60 .70

See Argentina Nos. 2395-2396.

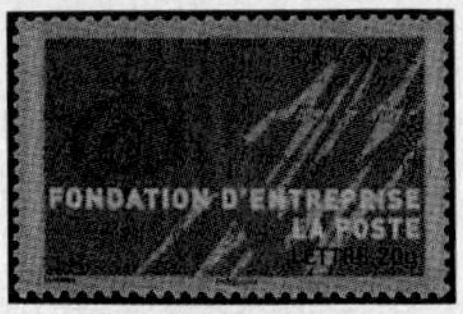

La Poste's Business Foundation, 10th Anniv. — A1793

2006, June 22 Litho. *Perf. 13*

3226 A1793 (53c) multi, *tan* 1.60 .40

French Open Golf Championship, Cent. — A1794

Photo. & Embossed

2006, June 24 *Perf. 13*

3227 A1794 53c multi 1.60 .40

A souvenir sheet containing No. 3227 sold for €3. Value $12.

Rotary International Type of 2005

Serpentine Die Cut 11

2006, July 1 Photo.

Self-Adhesive

3227A A1717 53c multi 1.60 .40

French Soccer Team's Second-Place Showing in 2006 World Cup — A1795

2006, July 5 Photo. *Perf. 13¼*

Size: 35x26mm

3228 A1795 53c multi 1.60 .40

Litho.

Size: 35x22mm

Perf. 13

3229 A1795 53c multi + label 5.00 4.00

Serpentine Die Cut 11¼x11

Self-Adhesive

3229A A1795 53c multi + label 10.00 5.00

No. 3229 was printed in sheets of 10 stamps and 10 labels that sold for €6.94. Value $55. No. 3229A was printed in sheets of 10 stamps + 10 labels that sold for €8.61. Value $140. Labels could be personalized.

Quai Branly Museum — A1796

2006, July 8 Photo. *Perf. 13x13¼*

3230 A1796 53c multi 1.60 .40

Reinstatement of Capt. Alfred Dreyfus, Cent. — A1797

2006, July 12 Engr.

3231 A1797 53c multi 1.60 .40

Claude-Joseph Rouget de Lisle (1760-1836), Composer of "La Marseillaise" — A1798

2006, July 13 Photo. *Perf. 13¼*

3232 A1798 53c multi 1.60 .40

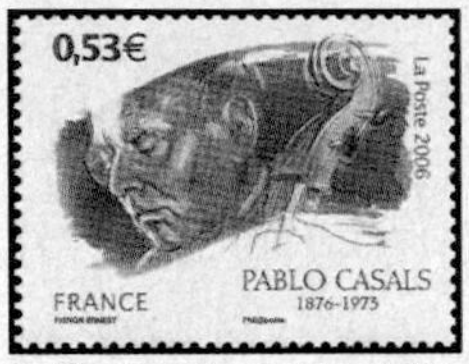

Pablo Casals (1876-1973), Cellist — A1799

2006, July 29

3233 A1799 53c multi 1.60 .40

Aspects of Life in French Regions Type of 2003

No. 3234: a, Catalan Towers. b, La Croisette, Cannes. c, Brocéliande Forest. d, Volcanic craters, Auvergne, vert. e, Les Invalides, Paris, vert. f, Chateau de Chaumont, Chaumont-sur-Loire. g, Ardèche Gorges, vert. h, Flour mill, Valmy, vert. i, Grotto of Messabielle, Lourdes. j, Calanches de Piana, Corsica.

2006, Sept. 2 Photo. *Perf. 13*

3234 Sheet of 10 16.00 16.00
a.-j. A1642 54c Any single 1.60 1.25

No. 3234 has three vertical rows of rouletting, separating sheet into quarters.

Nos. 3234a-3234j were also issued in large booklets containing panes of 1 of each stamp. The booklet sold for €19. Value $42.50.

A1800

A1801

A1802

A1803

A1804

A1805

A1806

A1807

A1808

Cubitus, Comics by Michel Rodrigue and Pierre Aucaigne A1809

Serpentine Die Cut 11¼x11

2006, Sept. 20 Litho.

Self-Adhesive

Booklet Stamps

3235	A1800	(54c)	multi	1.60	.40
3236	A1801	(54c)	multi	1.60	.40
3237	A1802	(54c)	multi	1.60	.40
3238	A1803	(54c)	multi	1.60	.40
3239	A1804	(54c)	multi	1.60	.40
3240	A1805	(54c)	multi	1.60	.40
3241	A1806	(54c)	multi	1.60	.40
3242	A1807	(54c)	multi	1.60	.40
3243	A1808	(54c)	multi	1.60	.40
3244	A1809	(54c)	multi	1.60	.40
a.	Booklet pane of 10, #3235-3244			16.00	

Sculptures by Constantin Brancusi (1876-1957) — A1810

Designs: 54c, Sleeping Muse. 85c, Sleep.

2006, Sept. 25 Photo. *Perf. 13¼*

3245 A1810 54c multi 1.60 .40
3246 A1810 85c multi 2.50 .75

See Romania Nos. 4878-4879.

Marianne Type of 2005

2006 Engr. *Perf. 13*

Inscribed "Phil@poste" at Bottom

3247	A1713	10c	gray	.50	.25
3248	A1713	60c	dark blue	2.50	.40
3249	A1713	70c	yel green	2.75	.40
3250	A1713	85c	purple	4.00	.60
3251	A1713	86c	fawn	4.00	.60
3252	A1713	€1.15	blue	5.00	1.00
3253	A1713	€1.30	red violet	5.50	1.00
3254	A1713	€2.11	chocolate	9.00	1.50
	Nos. 3247-3254 (8)			33.25	5.75

Coil Stamp

Perf. 13 Horiz.

3255 A1713 60c dark blue 2.00 .50

Serpentine Die Cut 11¼

Self-Adhesive

3255A	A1713 (54c) red + label		2.40	2.40
3255C	A1713 60c dark blue + label		2.50	2.50
3255D	A1713 82c fawn + label		13.50	13.50
3255E	A1713 86c fawn + label		3.00	3.00
	Nos. 3255A-3255E (4)		21.40	21.40

Issued: Nos. 3247-3255, 10/1, others, 2006. A number has been reserved for an additional stamp. Nos. 3255A, 3255C and 3255E were printed in sheets of 15 stamps + 15 labels that could be personalized. No. 3255D was printed in sheets containing 10 stamps + 10 large labels or 15 stamps and 15 small labels. Labels could be personalized. Sheets of No. 3255A sold for €13.29; No. 3255C, €14.04; No. 3255E, €17.31. For Nos. 3255A, 3255C, 3255D and 3255E, adjacent labels came in large and small sizes.

Aviation Without Borders — A1811

2006, Oct. 7 Photo. *Perf. 13*

3256 A1811 54c multi 1.60 .40

Henri Moissan (1852-1907), 1906 Nobel Chemistry Laureate — A1812

2006, Oct. 14 Engr. *Perf. 13¼x13*

3257 A1812 54c multi 1.60 .40

"Shared Memories," Intl. Conference on Veterans, Paris — A1813

2006, Oct. 26 Photo. *Perf. 13¼*

3258 A1813 54c multi 1.60 .40

Marianne — A1814

Serpentine Die Cut 6¾ Vert.

2006, Nov. 8 Engr.

Self-Adhesive

Booklet Stamp

3259 A1814 54c red 3.00 2.50
a. Booklet pane, 5 each #3083d, 3259 22.50

Miniature Sheet

Flying Machines — A1815

No. 3260: a, Gustave Ponton d'Amécourt's helicopter. b, Alberto Santos-Dumont's monoplane, "Demoiselle," horiz. c, Jean Marie Le Bris's bird-shaped glider, horiz. d, Clément Ader's "Avion III," horiz. e, Henri Fabré's seaplane, horiz. f, Jean-Pierre Blanchard's balloon.

Litho. & Engr.

2006, Nov. 9 *Perf. 13*

3260 A1815 Sheet of 6 10.00 10.00
a.-f. 54c Any single 1.60 1.25

Inauguration of Aulnay-sous-Bois to Bondy Tram-Train Line — A1816

2006, Nov. 18 Photo. *Perf. 13x13¼*
3261 A1816 54c multi 1.60 .50

Holiday Greetings A1817

Designs: No. 3262, Reindeer, sleigh, four penguins. No. 3263, Reindeer with fishing pole, three penguins. No. 3264, Reindeer, Christmas tree, two penguins. No. 3265, Reindeer skating, three penguins. No. 3266, Reindeer with gift boxes, three penguins.

2006, Nov. 25 Litho. *Perf. 13¼*
3261A A1817 (54c) multi + label 1.90 1.90
3261B A1817 (54c) multi + label 1.90 1.90
3261C A1817 (54c) multi + label 1.90 1.90
3261D A1817 (54c) multi + label 1.90 1.90
3261E A1817 (54c) multi + label 1.90 1.90
f. Vert. strip of 5, #3261A-3261E, + 5 labels 12.00 12.00
Miniature sheet, 2 #3261Ef 30.00 30.00

Self-Adhesive
Booklet Stamps
Serpentine Die Cut 11¼x11

3262 A1817 (54c) multi 1.60 .50
3263 A1817 (54c) multi 1.60 .50
3264 A1817 (54c) multi 1.60 .50
3265 A1817 (54c) multi 1.60 .50
3266 A1817 (54c) multi 1.60 .50
a. Booklet pane, 2 each #3262-3266 16.00
Nos. 3262-3266 (5) 8.00 2.50

Miniature sheet containing Nos. 3261A-3261E sold for €6.94. Value $60. Labels could be personalized. Value $60.

A souvenir sheet containing a perf. 13 example of No. 3266 sold for €3. Value $17.50. A sheet containing 5 No. 3261A + 5 labels exists, but was not sold.

Grand Masonic Lodge of France A1818

2006, Dec. 1 Photo. *Perf. 13x13¼*
3267 A1818 54c multi 1.60 .50

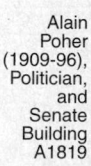

Alain Poher (1909-96), Politician, and Senate Building A1819

2006, Dec. 2 Engr. *Perf. 13¼*
3268 A1819 54c multi 1.60 .50

Opening of New Paris Tramway A1820

2006, Dec. 16 Photo. *Perf. 13¼*
3269 A1820 54c multi 1.75 .75

Orchids Type of 2002

Designs: 31c, Platanthera chlorantha. 36c, Dactylorhiza savogiensis. 43c, Orchis insularis.

2007, Jan. 2 Litho. *Perf. 13*
3270 A1584 31c multi .80 .25
3271 A1584 36c multi .95 .25
3272 A1584 43c multi 1.10 .25
Nos. 3270-3272 (3) 2.85 .75

Nos. 3270-3272 are known only precanceled. See second note after No. 132.

Hearts A1821

"Givenchy" in: (54c), Black and white. (86c), Red.

2007, Jan. 6 Photo. *Perf. 13¼*
Inscribed "Lettre 20 g"
3273 A1821 (54c) red & black 1.60 .45
a. Souvenir sheet of 5 8.00 8.00

Inscribed "Lettre 50 g"
3274 A1821 (86c) black & red 2.50 .75

Values are for stamps with surrounding selvage.

Serpentine Die Cut
Self-Adhesive
3275 A1821 (54c) Like #3273 1.60 .45

Inscribed "Lettre 50 g"
3276 A1821 (86c) Like #3274 2.25 .75

New Year 2007 (Year of the Pig) — A1822

2007, Jan. 27 Photo. *Perf. 13¼x13*
3277 A1822 (54c) multi 1.60 .45
a. Litho., stamp + label 2.75 2.50

Serpentine Die Cut 11
Self-Adhesive
3277B A1822 (54c) multi + label 12.00 12.00

No. 3277 has a somewhat blurrier image than No. 3277a. Sheets of 5 #3277a + 5 labels sold for €3.51. Value $15. Labels could be personalized. No. 3277 exists in a souvenir sheet of 1 that sold for €3. Value $10.

No. 3277B was printed in sheets of 10 + 10 labels that sold for €8.86. Value $125. Labels could be personalized.

Egyptian Hippopotamus Figurine — A1823

Head of Aphrodite A1824

Winged Victory of Samothrace A1825

Fresco, Pompeii A1826

King Amenemhet III of Egypt A1827

Statue of Juno A1828

Egyptian Harpist A1829

Etruscan Sarcophagus of Husband and Wife — A1830

Egyptian Statue of Seated Scribe A1831

Head of Pericles A1832

Serpentine Die Cut 11¼x11
2007, Jan. 27 Litho.
Booklet Stamps
Self-Adhesive

3279 A1823 (54c) multi 1.60 .45
3280 A1824 (54c) multi 1.60 .45
3281 A1825 (54c) multi 1.60 .45
3282 A1826 (54c) multi 1.60 .45
3283 A1827 (54c) multi 1.60 .45
3284 A1828 (54c) multi 1.60 .45
3285 A1829 (54c) multi 1.60 .45
3286 A1830 (54c) multi 1.60 .45
3287 A1831 (54c) multi 1.60 .45
3288 A1832 (54c) multi 1.60 .45
a. Booklet pane of 10, #3279-3288 17.00

Tourism Issue

Valenciennes A1833

2007 Engr. *Perf. 13¼*
3289 A1833 54c red & blue 1.50 .50

Issued: No. 3289, 2/3.

Tourism Issue

Limoges A1834

2007 Engr. *Perf. 13¼*
3290 A1834 54c multi 1.75 .50

Issued: No. 3290, 3/23.

Tourism Issue

Arcachon A1835

2007, May 19 Photo. *Perf. 13¼*
3291 A1835 54c multi 1.75 .50

Tourism Issue

Castres A1836

2007, July 20 Engr. *Perf. 13¼*
3292 A1836 54c multi 1.75 .50

Tourism Issue

Firminy — A1837

2007, Sept. 15 Engr. *Perf. 13¼*
3293 A1837 54c multi 1.75 .55

Rights of France A1838

2007, Feb. 5 Photo. *Perf. 13¼*
3294 A1838 54c multi 1.75 .50

Art Issue

Book Illumination from Sélestat Library — A1839

Galerie des Glaces, Versailles Palace — A1840

La Barrière Fleurie, by Paul Sérusier A1841

Gallic Boar Ensign — A1842

Perf. 12¼x13, 13¼x13 (#3297), 13x13¼ (#3296, 3298)

Engraved, Photo. (#3296, 3297, 3298A)

2007-08

3295	A1839	60c multi	1.60	.80
3296	A1840	85c multi	2.50	1.25
3297	A1841	86c multi	2.50	1.25
3298	A1842	€1.30 multi	4.00	1.75
	Nos. 3295-3298 (4)		10.60	5.05

Self-Adhesive

Serpentine Die Cut 11

3298A	A1840	85c multi	2.40	2.40

Issued: No. 3295, 2/10. No. 3297, 10/13. No. 3298, 6/2. No. 3296, 11/10. No. 3298A, 2008.

Aspects of Life in the French Regions Type of 2003

No. 3299: a, Baux-de-Provence. b, Banks of the Loire. c, Grande-Chartreuse Massif. d, Saint-Tropez. e, Doubs Waterfall, vert. f, Fontainebleau Forest, vert. g, Chantilly Castle. h, Saint-Malo. i, Ballon d'Alsace, vert. j, Midi Canal, vert.

2007, Feb. 24 Photo. *Perf. 13*

3299	Sheet of 10	15.00	15.00
a.-j.	A1642 54c Any single	1.50	.50

No. 3299 has three vertical rows of rouletting, separating sheet into quarters.

Nos. 3299a-3299j were also issued in large booklets containing panes of 1 of each stamp. The booklet sold for €19.

Aspects of Life in French Regions Type of 2003 Inscribed "Lettre Prioritaire 20g"

Designs: Nos. 3300-3301, Arc de Triomphe, vert.

2007, Feb. Photo. *Perf. 13*

3300	A1642 (54c) multi + label	4.00	4.00

Serpentine Die Cut 11x11¼

3301	A1642 (54c) multi + label	30.00	30.00

Nos. 3300-3301 each were printed in sheets of 10 stamps + 10 different labels that sold for €6.85. Value of sheet of No. 3300, $45.

Marianne Type of 2005

2007 Litho. *Perf. 13*

Stamps Inscribed "Phil@poste"

Without Varnish

3302	Sheet of 15, #a-k, 2 each #l-m, + 15 labels	60.00	60.00
a.	A1713 1c yellow orange	.30	.30
b.	A1713 5c brown	.40	.40
c.	A1713 10c gray	.75	.75
d.	A1713 60c blue	2.75	2.75
e.	A1713 70c lt yellow green	3.25	3.25
f.	A1713 85c purple	3.75	3.75
g.	A1713 86c pink	4.00	4.00
h.	A1713 €1 orange	5.00	5.00
i.	A1713 €1.15 light blue	5.50	5.50
j.	A1713 €1.30 red violet	6.00	6.00
k.	A1713 €2.11 maroon	9.00	9.00
l.	A1713 (49c) blue green	2.50	2.50
m.	A1713 (54c) red	2.75	2.75

No. 3302 sold for €14.40 and has personalizable labels.

Harry Potter — A1843

Designs: (49c), Hermione Granger. (85c), Ron Weasley.

2007, Mar. 12 Photo. *Perf. 13¼*

3303	A1843 (54c) red & multi	1.50	.50
a.	Souvenir sheet of 1	1.50	1.50
b.	Perf. 13¼x13 (booklet stamp)	1.75	.50

Booklet Stamps

Perf. 13¼x13

3304	A1843 (49c) blue & multi	1.50	.45
3305	A1843 (85c) grn & multi	2.50	.75
a.	Booklet pane of 10, 4 #3303b, 3 each #3304-3305	17.00	—
	Complete booklet, #3305a	17.00	

Stamp Day. Sheets of five serpentine die cut 11 self-adhesive stamps of each denomination and five labels that could not be personalized exist. Each sheet sold for €6.50. Value, set $70.

Albert Londres (1884-1932), Journalist — A1844

2007, Mar. 16 Engr. *Perf. 13x13¼*

3306	A1844 54c multi	1.60	.50

Six different souvenir sheets containing one No. 3306 exist. The set sold for €15. Value, set $45.

Audit Office, Bicent. A1845

2007 *Perf. 13¼x13*

3307	A1845 54c multi	1.60	.50

Serpentine Die Cut 11

Self-Adhesive

3307A	A1845 54c multi	4.00	4.00

Issued: No. 3307, 3/17; No. 3307A, 7/20.

Treaty of Rome, 50th Anniv. A1846

2007, Mar. 23 Photo. *Perf. 13¼*

3308	A1846 54c multi	1.50	.50

Sébastaen Le Prestre de Vauban (1633-1707), Military Engineer — A1847

2007, Mar. 30 Engr.

3309	A1847 54c multi	1.50	.50

2007 Rugby World Cup A1848

2007, Apr. 14 Photo. *Perf. 13¼*

3310	A1848 54c multi	1.50	.50
a.	Perf. 13x13¼ + label	4.00	4.00

Serpentine Die Cut 11¼

Self-Adhesive

3311	A1848 54c multi + label		—

No. 3310a was printed in sheets of 5 stamps and 5 labels that could be personalized that sold for €4.20. Value $45.

No. 3311 was printed in sheets of 10 + 10 labels that could be personalized. Sheets sold for €10.60.

Endangered Animals in Overseas Departments A1849

Designs: No. 3312, Antillean iguana. No. 3313, Raccoon, horiz. 60c, Jaguar, horiz. 86c, Barau's petrel, horiz..

2007, Apr. 28 Photo. *Perf. 13¼*

3312	A1849 54c multi	1.50	.50
3313	A1849 54c multi	1.50	.50
3314	A1849 60c multi	1.75	.60
3315	A1849 86c multi	2.40	.80
a.	Souvenir sheet, #3312-3315	7.25	7.25
	Nos. 3312-3315 (4)	7.15	2.40

Gardens and Parks Type of 2003

Souvenir Sheet

No. 3316 — Parc de la Tete d'Or, Lyon: a, Red flowers. b, White flowers.

2007, Apr. 28 *Perf. 13¼x13*

3316	Sheet of 2	11.50	11.50
a.-b.	A1660 €2.11 Either single	5.75	3.00

Salon du Timbre. No. 3316 has four vertical rows of rouletting, separating sheet into fifths, with the two stamps in the central fifth.

Vacations A1850

Designs: No. 3317, Wooden fence and red hollyhocks. No. 3318, Angelfish. No. 3319, Blue flowers. No. 3320, Blueberries. No. 3321, Canoes. No. 3322, Dyed wool hanging on rods. No. 3323, Glacier. No. 3324, Palm tree. No. 3325, Beach umbrellas and woman. No. 3326, Boxes of color pigments.

Serpentine Die Cut 11¼x11

2007, Apr. 28 Litho.

Booklet Stamps

Self-Adhesive

3317	A1850 (54c) multi	1.50	.50
3318	A1850 (54c) multi	1.50	.50
3319	A1850 (54c) multi	1.50	.50
3320	A1850 (54c) multi	1.50	.50
3321	A1850 (54c) multi	1.50	.50
3322	A1850 (54c) multi	1.50	.50
3323	A1850 (54c) multi	1.50	.50
3324	A1850 (54c) multi	1.50	.50
3325	A1850 (54c) multi	1.50	.50
3326	A1850 (54c) multi	1.50	.50
a.	Booklet pane of 10, #3317-3326	15.00	

Europa A1851

2007, May 1 Photo. *Perf. 13¼*

3327	A1851 60c multi	1.50	.40

Scouting, cent.

Intl. Sailing Federation, Cent. — A1852

2007, May 4 *Perf. 13*

3328	A1852 85c multi	2.00	.80

A souvenir sheet containing No. 3328 sold for €3.

Tintin and Snowy — A1853

Characters from Tintin comic strips and books, by Hergé: No. 3330, Professor Calculus (Tournesol). No. 3331, Captain Haddock. No. 3332, Thomson and Thompson (Dupondt). No. 3333, Bianca Castafiore. No. 3334, Chang (Tchang).

2007, May 12

3329	A1853 54c multi	1.50	.50
3330	A1853 54c multi	1.50	.50
3331	A1853 54c multi	1.50	.50
3332	A1853 54c multi	1.50	.50
3333	A1853 54c multi	1.50	.50
3334	A1853 54c multi	1.50	.50
a.	Souvenir sheet, #3329-3334	13.50	13.50

No. 3334a sold for €5, with the Red Cross receiving €1.76 of that.

Religious Art — A1854

Designs: 54c, Nativity, 15th cent. miniature, from Armenia. 85c, The Smile of Reims.

2007, May 22 *Perf. 13¼*

3335	A1854 54c multi	1.60	.50
3336	A1854 85c multi	2.40	.80

See Armenia Nos. 749-750.

Inauguration of Eastern France TGV Train Service — A1855

2007, June 9 ***Perf. 13***

3337 A1855 54c multi 1.50 .50

French Federation of Philatelic Associations 80th Congress, Poitiers — A1856

2007, June 15 Engr. ***Perf. 13x13¼***

3338 A1856 54c multi + label 1.50 .50

Miniature Sheet

2007 Rugby World Cup, France — A1857

No. 3339 — Inscriptions: a, Touche (Throw-in, 30x39mm elliptical). b, Melée (scrum). c, Attaque (player running with ball). d, Essai (try). e, Transformation (kick, 30x39mm elliptical). f, Passe (pass). g, Raffut (stiff-arm). h, Haka (dance). i, Plaquage (tackle). j, Supporteurs (fans).

2007, June 23 ***Perf. 13x13¼***

3339 A1857 Sheet of 10 15.00 15.00
a.-j. 54c Any single 1.50 .50

European Capitals Type of 2002

Souvenir Sheet

No. 3340 — Attractions in Brussels: a, Maison du Roi (Royal Palace). b, Hotel du Ville (City Hall), vert. c, Mannekin Pis, vert. d, Atomium.

Perf. 13x13¼, 13¼x13 (vert. stamps)

2007, June 30

3340 A1622 Sheet of 4 6.00 6.00
a.-d. 54c Any single 1.50 .50

Association of French Mayors, Cent. — A1858

2007, July 5 Photo. ***Perf. 13¼***

3341 A1858 54c multi 1.50 .50

Pierre Pfimlin (1907-2000), Mayor of Strasbourg A1859

2007, July 7 Photo. ***Perf. 13¼***

3342 A1859 60c multi 1.75 .60

2007 Rugby World Cup, France A1860

Litho. With Three-Dimensional Plastic Affixed

2007, Sept. 5 ***Serpentine Die Cut 11***

Self-Adhesive

3343 A1860 €3 multi 8.25 4.25

Happy Birthday A1861

2007, Sept. 8 Photo. ***Perf. 13x13¼***

3344 A1861 (54c) multi 1.60 .55
a. Litho., with attached label 2.40 2.40

No. 3344 was printed in a sheet of 5; No. 3344a was printed in a sheet of 5 + 5 labels that sold for €4.20.

Gift Boxes — A1862

Boxes and: Nos. 3345a, 3346, Butterflies. Nos. 3345b, 3348, Flowers. Nos. 3345c, 3347, Hearts. Nos. 3345d, 3350, Musical notes. Nos. 3345e, 3349, Bubbles.

2007, Sept. 8 Litho. ***Perf. 13¼***

3345 Sheet of 5 + 5 labels 12.00 12.00
a.-e. A1862 (54c) Any single + label 2.40 2.40

Self-Adhesive

Booklet Stamps

Serpentine Die Cut 11

3346 A1862 (54c) multi 1.60 .55
3347 A1862 (54c) multi 1.60 .55
3348 A1862 (54c) multi 1.60 .55
3349 A1862 (54c) multi 1.60 .55
3350 A1862 (54c) multi 1.60 .55
a. Booklet pane of 5 #3346-3350 8.00

No. 3345 sold for €4.20.

Sully Prudhomme (1839-1907), Poet — A1863

2007, Sept. 15 Engr. ***Perf. 13¼***

3351 A1863 €1.30 multi 3.75 1.25

A1864

A1865

A1866

A1867

Cows A1868

Serpentine Die Cut 11

2007, Sept. 20 Litho.

Self-Adhesive

Booklet Stamps

3352 A1864 (54c) multi 1.60 .55
3353 A1865 (54c) multi 1.60 .55
3354 A1866 (54c) multi 1.60 .55
3355 A1867 (54c) multi 1.60 .55
3356 A1868 (54c) multi 1.60 .55
a. Booklet pane, 2 each #3352-3356 16.00
Nos. 3352-3356 (5) 8.00 2.75

Aspects of Life in French Regions Type of 2003

No. 3357: a, Sèvres porcelain. b, Grasse perfume. c, Christmas market. d, Marseille soap. e, Giants, vert. f, Basque beret, vert. g, Aubusson tapestries. h, Lyonnaise tavern. i, Slipper, vert. j, Canteloupe, vert.

2007, Sept. 29 Photo. ***Perf. 13***

3357 Sheet of 10 16.00 16.00
a.-j. A1642 54c Any single 1.60 .55

No. 3357 has three vertical rows of rouletting separating sheet into quarters.

Nos. 3357a-3357j were also issued in large booklets containing panes of 1 of each stamp. The booklet sold for €19. Value $55.

Space Age, 50th Anniv. — A1869

2007, Oct. 4 ***Perf. 13x12½***

3358 A1869 85c multi 2.40 .80

Medical Research Foundation, 60th Anniv. — A1870

2007, Oct. 20 ***Perf. 13¼***

3359 A1870 54c multi 1.60 .55

Guy Moquet (1924-41), World War II Resistance Fighter — A1871

2007, Oct. 22 ***Engr.***

3360 A1871 54c multi 1.60 .55

Dole A1872

2007, Nov. 2

3361 A1872 54c multi 1.60 .55

Personalized Stamp With Country Name on Short Side — A1873

Personalized Stamp With Country Name on Long Side A1874

Serpentine Die Cut 11¼ Syncopated

2007, Nov. Litho.

Self-Adhesive

Inscribed: "Lettre Prioritaire 20 g"

3362 A1873 (54c) multi 3.00 3.00
3363 A1874 (54c) multi 3.00 3.00

Inscribed: "Monde 20 g"

3364 A1873 (85c) multi 4.00 4.00
3365 A1874 (85c) multi 4.00 4.00

Inscribed: "Lettre Prioritaire 50 g"

3366 A1873 (86c) multi 4.00 4.00
3367 A1874 (86c) multi 4.00 4.00
Nos. 3362-3367 (6) 22.00 22.00

Nos. 3362-3367 were each printed in sheets of ten, having vignettes that could be personalized or chosen from a library of stock designs, two of which are shown on the illustrated stamps. Sheets of Nos. 3362 and 3363 each sold for €10.03, and sheets of Nos. 3364-3367 each sold for €13.38. Sheets were made available with different frame colors. Starting in 2008, numerous sheets containing stamps with these frames having various preselected vignettes were produced and sold by La Poste for various prices per sheet, each well above the franking value of the stamps at the time of issue. Any stamp with a vignette and/or frame color differing from the items shown is an equivalent item to those shown.

Jean-Baptiste Charcot (1867-1936), Polar Explorer A1875

Ship Pourquoi-Pas? — A1876

2007, Nov. 8 Engr. *Perf. 13x12¾*

3368	A1875	54c multi		1.60	.55
3369	A1876	60c multi		1.75	.60
a.		Horiz. pair, #3368-3369		3.50	1.25

See Greenland No. 505. A sheet containing Nos. 3368-3369 sold for €4 in 2008.

Marianne — A1877

Serpentine Die Cut 6¾ Vert.

2007, Nov. 8 Engr.

Self-Adhesive

Booklet Stamp

3370	A1877 54c red		2.75	2.00
a.	Booklet pane, 6 each #3083d, 3370		25.50	

Miniature Sheet

Lighthouses — A1878

No. 3371: a, Cap Fréhel Lighthouse. b, Espiguette Lighthouse. c, D'ar-Men Lighthouse. d, Grand-Léjon Lighthouse. e, Porquerolles Lighthouse, horiz. f, Chassiron Lighthouse, horiz.

Litho. & Engr.

2007, Nov. 9 *Perf. 13*

3371	A1878	Sheet of 6	9.75	9.75
a.-f.		54c Any single	1.60	.55

2007 Women's World Handball Championships, France — A1879

2007, Nov. 10 Photo. *Perf. 13¼*

3372	A1879 54c multi	1.60	.55

Holiday Greetings A1880

No. 3377: a, Squirrel with stocking cap. b, Bird with party hat. c, Hedgehog with party cap. d, Dog with stocking cap. e, Deer with stocking cap.

No. 3378, Squirrel with stocking cap. No. 3379, Bird with party hat. No. 3380, Deer with stocking cap. No. 3381, Hedgehog with party hat. No. 3382, Dog with stocking cap.

2007, Nov. 24 Litho. *Perf. 13¼*

3377	Sheet of 5 + 5 labels	12.50	12.50
a.-e.	A1880 (54c) Any single + label	2.50	2.50

Booklet Stamps

Self-Adhesive

Serpentine Die Cut 11

3378	A1880 (54c) multi		1.60	.55
3379	A1880 (54c) multi		1.60	.55
3380	A1880 (54c) multi		1.60	.55
3381	A1880 (54c) multi		1.60	.55
3382	A1880 (54c) multi		1.60	.55
a.	Booklet pane, 2 each #3378-3382		16.00	

No. 3377 sold for €4.20 and had labels that could not be personalized.

A souvenir sheet of 1 of No. 3381 sold for €3.

Marianne Type of 2005

2008 Engr. *Perf. 13*

3383	A1713	(65c) dark blue	2.00	.40
3384	A1713	72c yel green	2.25	.45
3385	A1713	88c fawn	2.75	.55
3386	A1713	€1.25 blue	4.00	.80
3387	A1713	€1.33 red violet	4.25	.85
3388	A1713	€2.18 chocolate	6.75	1.40
		Nos. 3383-3388 (6)	22.00	4.45

Coil Stamp

Perf. 13 Horiz.

3388A	A1713	(65c) dark blue	2.00	.40

Issued: Nos. 3383-3388A, 3/1.

Marianne Type of 2005

Serpentine Die Cut 6¾ Vert.

2008 Engr.

Booklet Stamp

Self-Adhesive

3389	A1713 (60c) blue	1.90	.50
a.	Booklet pane of 12	23.00	

Issued: No. 3389, 1/2.

Hearts A1881

Designs: (54c), Face. (86c), (88c), Plant with heart-shaped leaves.

2008, Jan. 5 Photo. *Perf. 13¼*

3390	A1881 (54c) multi	1.60	.55
a.	Souvenir sheet of 5	8.00	8.00
b.	Sheet of 10 + 10 labels	20.00	—
3391	A1881 (86c) multi	2.60	.90

Self-Adhesive

Serpentine Die Cut

3392	A1881 (54c) multi	1.60	.55
3392A	A1881 (88c) multi	2.50	2.50

Values are for stamps with surrounding selvage.

Nos. 3390, 3390a, 3390b, 3391-3392 issued 1/5/08. No. 3390b was sold for €6.86. Labels could not be personalized.

New Year 2008 (Year of the Rat) — A1882

2008, Jan. 26 Photo. *Perf. 13¼x13*

3393	A1882 (54c) multi	1.60	.55

Printed in sheets of 5. A souvenir sheet of one No. 3393 sold for €3.

Paintings A1883

Designs: No. 3394, Legend of St. Francis: Sermon to the Birds, by Giotto di Bondone. No. 3395, Seaport at Sunset, by Claude Lorrain. No. 3396, The Birth of Venus, by Sandro Botticelli. No. 3397, Napoleon Bonaparte Crossing the Alps, by Jacques-Louis David. No. 3398, La Belle Jardinière (Madonna and Child with St. John the Baptist), by Raphael, vert. No. 3399, Head of a Girl in a Turban, by Jan Vermeer, vert. No. 3400, Summer, by Giuseppe Arcimboldo, vert. No. 3401, Mona Lisa, by Leonardo da Vinci, vert. No. 3402, Infant Maria Marguerita, by Diego Velásquez, vert. No. 3403, Money Changer with Wife, by Quentin Massys (Metsys), vert.

Serpentine Die Cut 11

2008, Jan. 26 Litho.

Booklet Stamps

Self-Adhesive

3394	A1883 (54c) multi	1.60	.55
3395	A1883 (54c) multi	1.60	.55
3396	A1883 (54c) multi	1.60	.55
3397	A1883 (54c) multi	1.60	.55
3398	A1883 (54c) multi	1.60	.55
3399	A1883 (54c) multi	1.60	.55
3400	A1883 (54c) multi	1.60	.55
3401	A1883 (54c) multi	1.60	.55
3402	A1883 (54c) multi	1.60	.55
3403	A1883 (54c) multi	1.60	.55
a.	Booklet pane of 10, #3394-3403	16.00	

France Stadium, 10th Anniv. A1884

2008, Jan. 28 Photo. *Perf. 13¼*

3404	A1884 54c multi	1.60	.55

Tourism Issue

Vendôme A1885

La Rochelle — A1886

Toulon A1887

Richelieu A1888

Le Havre — A1889

2008 Engr. *Perf. 13¼*

3405	A1885 54c multi	1.60	.40

Perf. 13

3406	A1886 55c multi	1.50	.60
3407	A1887 55c multi	1.50	.60
3408	A1888 55c multi	1.50	.60
3409	A1889 55c multi	1.50	.50
	Nos. 3405-3409 (5)	7.60	2.70

Issued: No. 3405, 2/2; No. 3406, 4/5; Nos. 3407-3408, 7/5; No. 3409, 9/13. A souvenir sheet of one of No. 3406 sold for €3.

Art Issue

Globes of Vincenzo Coronelli A1890

Young Girl Warming Her Hands at a Large Stove, by Jean-Jacques Henner — A1891

Untitled Work by Gérard Garouste A1892

A Theater Box Office, by Honoré Daumier A1893

Litho. & Engr., Photo (A1891-A1892), Engr. (A1893)

2008 *Perf. 13¼x13*

3410	A1890	85c multi	2.60	1.25
3411	A1891	88c multi	2.25	1.10
3412	A1892	€1.33 multi	4.25	2.10
3413	A1893	€1.33 choc & bl gray	3.50	1.75
		Nos. 3410-3413 (4)	12.60	6.20

Self-Adhesive

Serpentine Die Cut 11

3413A	A1891	88c multi	2.50	2.50
3413B	A1892	€1.33 multi	3.75	3.75
3413C	A1893	€1.33 choc & bl gray	3.75	3.75
		Nos. 3413A-3413C (3)	10.00	10.00

Issued: No. 3410, 2/11; No. 3412, 6/19; No. 3411, 10/18; No. 3413, 11/7.

A souvenir sheet containing No. 3410 sold for €3.

Emir Abdelkader (1808-83), Algerian Leader — A1894

2008, Feb. 20 Engr. *Perf. 13¼*
3414 A1894 54c multi 1.75 .60

Droopy Dog A1895

Red-haired Woman A1896

The Wolf A1897

Design: €2.18, Droopy Dog, diff.

2008, Mar. 1 Photo. *Perf. 13¼*
3415 A1895 (55c) multi 1.75 .60
3416 A1896 (55c) multi 1.75 .60
3417 A1897 (55c) multi 1.75 .60
a. Strip of 3, #3415-3417 5.25 1.90

Souvenir Sheet
Perf. 13x13¼

3418 A1895 €2.18 multi 6.75 6.75

Booklet Stamps
Self-Adhesive
Serpentine Die Cut 11

3419 A1895 (55c) multi 1.75 .60
3420 A1896 (55c) multi 1.75 .60
3421 A1897 (55c) multi 1.75 .60
a. Booklet pane of 10, 4 #3419, 3 each #3420-3421 17.50

Cartoon characters created by Tex Avery; Stamp Day. No. 3418 contains one 35x27mm stamp that has thermographic ink (on cartoon balloon) that when warmed, changes color allowing a message below the ink to appear.

Nos. 3419-3421 exist in three sheets, each containing 5 of each stamp + 5 non-personalizable labels. Each sheet sold for €6.50.

Sound Recording Libraries A1898

2008, Mar. 15 Photo. *Perf. 13¼*
3422 A1898 55c multi 1.75 .60

Flowers — A1899

Designs: 37c, Aquilegia. 38c, Tulipa sp. 44c, Bellis perennis. 45c, Primula veris.

2008, Mar. 1 Litho. *Perf. 13*
3423 A1899 37c multi 1.10 .25
3424 A1899 38c multi 1.25 .25
3425 A1899 44c multi 1.40 .30
3426 A1899 45c multi 1.40 .30
Nos. 3423-3426 (4) 5.15 1.10

Nos. 3423-3426 are known only precanceled. See second note after No. 132.

Compare with types A2174-A2177.

Aspects of Life in French Regions Type of 2003

No. 3427: a, Chateau d'Ussé, Rigny-Ussé. b, Vézelay. c, Place des Vosges, Le Marais district, Paris. d, Le Marais Poitevin (Poitevin Marsh). e, Cugarel Windmill, Castelnaudary, vert. f, Red granite coastal rocks, vert. g, Honfleur. h, La Petite France district, Strasbourg. i, La Boétie House, Sarlat-la-Canéda, vert. j, Marfate Cirque, Reunion, vert.

2008, Mar. 29 Photo. *Perf. 13*
3427 Sheet of 10 17.50 17.50
a.-j. A1642 55c Any single 1.75 1.25

No. 3427 has three vertical rows of rouletting, separating sheet into quarters. Nos. 3427a-3427j were also issued in a large booklet containing panes of 1 of each stamp. The booklet sold for €19.

Lyon — A1900

Litho. & Engr.

2008, Apr. 4 *Perf. 13*
3428 A1900 55c multi 1.75 .60

Gardens and Parks Type of 2003

No. 3429: a, Parc Longchamp, Marseille. b, Parc Borely, Marseille.

2008 Photo. *Perf. 13¼x13*
3429 Sheet of 2 13.50 13.50
a.-b. A1660 €2.18 Either single 6.75 3.50
c. Miniature sheet of 4, #3316a, 3316b, 3429a, 3429b 27.50 27.50

Salon du Timbre. No. 3429 has four vertical rows of rouletting, separating sheet into fifths, with the two stamps in the central fifth.

Issued: No. 3429, 4/12; No. 3429c, 6/14.

Prehistoric Animals A1901

Designs: No. 3430, Phorusrhacos. No. 3431, Smilodon. 65c, Megaloceros, horiz. 88c, Mammoth, horiz.

2008, Apr. 19 *Perf. 13¼*
3430 A1901 55c multi 1.75 .60
3431 A1901 55c multi 1.75 .60
3432 A1901 65c multi 2.00 .65
3433 A1901 88c multi 2.75 .90
a. Miniature sheet, #3430-3433 8.25 8.25
Nos. 3430-3433 (4) 8.25 2.75

First Heart Transplant in Europe, 40th Anniv. — A1902

2008, Apr. 24 *Perf. 13¼x13*
3434 A1902 55c red & black 1.60 .40

Valentré Bridge, Cahors A1903

2008, Apr. 26 Engr. *Perf. 13x13¼*
3435 A1903 55c multi 1.60 .40

Europa A1904

2008, May 4 Photo. *Perf. 13x13¼*
3436 A1904 55c multi 1.75 .60

Self-Adhesive
Serpentine Die Cut 11

3436A A1904 55c multi 2.40 2.40

Quebec City, Canada, 400th Anniv. A1905

2008, May 16 Engr. *Perf. 13*
3437 A1905 85c multi 2.50 .75

See Canada No. 2269.

A souvenir sheet containing No. 3437 and Canada No. 2269 sold for $4.99 in Canada and was sold in France for €15 as part of a set additionally containing six different souvenir sheets containing only No. 3437.

Happy Birthday A1906

2008, May 28 Photo.
3438 A1906 (55c) multi 1.75 .60

Printed in sheets of 5.

It's a Boy A1907

It's a Girl A1908

2008, May 28 *Serpentine Die Cut 11*
Booklet Stamps
Self-Adhesive

3439 A1907 (55c) multi, unscratched panel 1.75 .60
a. Scratched panel .60
b. Booklet pane of 10 #3439 17.50

3440 A1908 (55c) multi, unscratched panel 1.75 .60
a. Scratched panel .60
b. Booklet pane of 10 #3440 17.50

Scratch-off panels on Nos. 3439-3440 cover pictures and text for baby boy and girl, respectively.

Vacations A1909

Designs: No. 3441, Ferns. No. 3442, Butterfly on leaf. No. 3443, Hands holding plant's leaves. No. 3444, Coconut palm tree. No. 3445, Path beside forest lake. No. 3446, Golf ball, putter and hole. No. 3447, Water lily and lily pads. No. 3448, Watering cans and foliage. No. 3449, Sliced kiwi fruit. No. 3450, Shelled and unshelled peas.

Serpentine Die Cut 11
2008, May 28 Litho.
Booklet Stamps
Self-Adhesive

3441 A1909 (55c) multi 1.75 .60
3442 A1909 (55c) multi 1.75 .60
3443 A1909 (55c) multi 1.75 .60
3444 A1909 (55c) multi 1.75 .60
3445 A1909 (55c) multi 1.75 .60
3446 A1909 (55c) multi 1.75 .60
3447 A1909 (55c) multi 1.75 .60
3448 A1909 (55c) multi 1.75 .60
3449 A1909 (55c) multi 1.75 .60
3450 A1909 (55c) multi 1.75 .60
a. Booklet pane of 10, #3441-3450 17.50

Evreux Belfry — A1910

2008, May 31 Engr. *Perf. 13*
3451 A1910 55c multi 1.75 .60

French Federation of Philatelic Associations 81st Congress, Paris — A1911

2008, June 14 *Perf. 13x13¼*
3452 A1911 55c multi + label 1.75 .60

Marianne and Stars A1912

Hand Depositing Ballot A1913

Tree in Hand A1914

Dove A1915

2008	Engr.		*Perf. 13*	
3453	A1912	1c yellow	.25	.25
3454	A1912	5c gray brown	.25	.25
3455	A1912	10c gray	.30	.25
3456	A1912	(50c) green	1.60	.25
3457	A1912	(55c) red	1.75	.40
3458	A1912	(65c) dark blue	2.10	.50
3459	A1912	72c olive green	2.25	.60
3460	A1912	85c purple	2.75	.70
3461	A1912	88c fawn	2.75	.70
3462	A1912	€1 orange	3.25	.80
3463	A1912	€1.25 blue	4.00	1.00
3464	A1912	€1.33 red violet	4.25	1.10
3465	A1912	€2.18 chocolate	7.00	2.40

Self-Adhesive (#3466)

Etched on Foil

Die Cut Perf. 13

3466	A1912	€5 *silver*	16.00	16.00
	Nos. 3453-3466 (14)		48.50	25.20

Litho.

Perf. 13

3467		Sheet of 15, #3467a-3467k, 2 each #3467l-3467m, + 15 labels	40.00	40.00
a.	A1912	1c yellow	.25	.25
b.	A1912	5c brown	.25	.25
c.	A1912	10c gray	.35	.35
d.	A1912	(65c) dark blue	2.40	2.40
e.	A1912	72c olive green	2.60	2.60
f.	A1912	85c purple	3.00	3.00
g.	A1912	88c fawn	3.25	3.25
h.	A1912	€1 orange	3.50	3.50
i.	A1912	€1.25 blue	4.50	4.50
j.	A1912	€1.33 red violet	4.75	4.75
k.	A1912	€2.18 brn violet	7.75	7.75
l.	A1912	(50c) green	1.75	1.75
m.	A1912	(55c) red	2.00	2.00

Coil Stamps

Perf. 13 Horiz.

Engr.

3468	A1912	(50c) green	1.60	.25
3469	A1912	(55c) red	1.75	.40
3470	A1912	(65c) dark blue	2.10	.50

Booklet Stamps (Types A1913-A1915)

Self-Adhesive

Serpentine Die Cut 6¾ Vert.

3471	A1912	(55c) red	1.75	.40
a.		Booklet pane of 20	35.00	
b.		Booklet pane of 10	17.50	
c.		Booklet pane of 12	21.00	
3472	A1913	55c red	1.75	.40
3473	A1914	55c red	1.75	.40
3474	A1915	55c red	1.75	.40
a.		Booklet pane of 12, 6 #3471, 2 each #3472-3474	21.00	
3475	A1912	(65c) dark blue	2.10	.50
a.		Booklet pane of 12	26.00	
3476	A1913	65c dark blue	2.10	.50
3477	A1914	65c dark blue	2.10	.50
3478	A1915	65c dark blue	2.10	.50
a.		Booklet pane of 12, 6 #3475, 2 each #3476-3478	26.00	
	Nos. 3471-3478 (8)		15.40	3.60

Issued: No. 3457, 6/17; No. 3741c, 9/8; No. 3466, 7/1; No. 3475a, 2009; others, 6/14. On day of issue, No. 3467 sold for €12.54. Labels on No. 3467 could not be personalized.

No. 3471b is comprised of two horizontal strips of five stamps on a yellow backing paper. Nos. 3471 and 3475 were also printed in sheets of 100 later in 2008.

See Nos. 3532, 3551-3566, 3612-3616E, 3730, 3871-3882, 4410l, 4525.

Typographed, engraved and silk-screened perf. 13 stamps of types A486 and A1912 with denomination of €1 in red were produced in pairs with 2 labels and photogravure perf. 13 stamps of these types with denominations of €1 in blue, green and multicolored were printed in blocks of 8 + 8 labels. These items were created in very limited quantities in 2010.

Ecology A1916

Designs: No. 3479, Tree. No. 3480, Bicycle. No. 3481, World map. No. 3482, Computer. No. 3483, Water droplets. No. 3484, Sun. No. 3485, Two plastic bottles. No. 3486, Three plastic bottles. No. 3487, Apple core. No. 3488, Strawberry.

Serpentine Die Cut 11

2008, June 14 **Photo.**

Booklet Stamps

Self-Adhesive

3479	A1916	(55c) multi	1.75	.60
3480	A1916	(55c) multi	1.75	.60
3481	A1916	(55c) multi	1.75	.60
3482	A1916	(55c) multi	1.75	.60
3483	A1916	(55c) multi	1.75	.60
3484	A1916	(55c) multi	1.75	.60
3485	A1916	(55c) multi	1.75	.60
3486	A1916	(55c) multi	1.75	.60
3487	A1916	(55c) multi	1.75	.60
3488	A1916	(55c) multi	1.75	.60
a.		Booklet pane of 10, #3479-3488	17.50	

Trapeze Artist — A1917

Bareback Rider — A1918

Clown — A1919

Lion Tamer — A1920

Clown — A1921

Juggler — A1922

2008, June 15	Photo.		*Perf. 13*	
3489	A1917	55c multi	1.75	.60
3490	A1918	55c multi	1.75	.60
3491	A1919	55c multi	1.75	.60
3492	A1920	55c multi	1.75	.60
3493	A1921	55c multi	1.75	.60
3494	A1922	55c multi	1.75	.60
a.		Souvenir sheet, #3489-3494	16.50	16.50
	Nos. 3489-3494 (6)		10.50	3.60

No. 3494a sold for €5.10, with the Red Cross receiving €1.80 of that.

2008 Summer Olympics, Beijing — A1923

Designs: No. 3495, Equestrian, cycling. No. 3496, Swimming, rowing, horiz. No. 3497, Judo, fencing, horiz. No. 3498, Tennis, running.

Perf. 13¼x13, 13x13¼

2008, June 16				
3495	A1923	55c multi	1.75	.60
3496	A1923	55c multi	1.75	.60
3497	A1923	55c multi	1.75	.60
a.		Pair, #3496-3497	3.50	1.75
3498	A1923	55c multi	1.75	.60
a.		Vert. pair, #3495, 3498	3.50	1.75
	Nos. 3495-3498 (4)		7.00	2.40

Nos. 3495-3498 were printed in a sheet of 10 containing 2 each #3495 and #3498 and 3 each #3496-3497.

Charles de Gaulle Memorial, Paris A1924

2008, June 18	Engr.		*Perf. 13¼*	
3499	A1924	55c multi	1.75	.60

Miniature Sheet

European Projects — A1925

No. 3500: a, Map of Europe, 1-euro coin. b, Flags of France and European Union, horiz (French Presidency of European Union). c, Earth and Galileo satellite, horiz. d, Students and flags (Erasmus higher education program).

2008, June 19	Photo.		*Perf. 13*	
3500	A1925	Sheet of 4	7.00	7.00
a.-d.		55c Any single	1.75	.60

Miniature Sheet

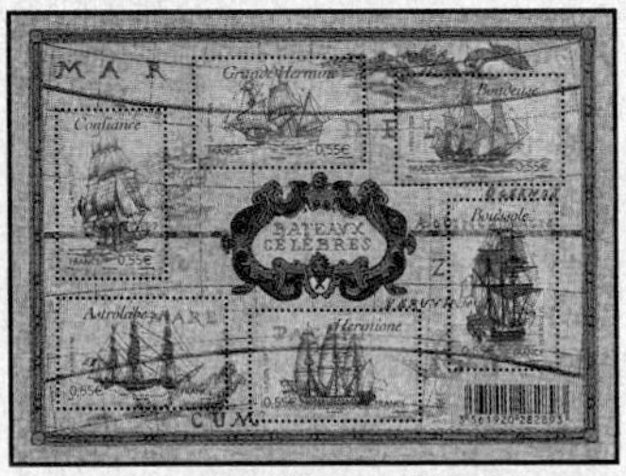

Famous Ships — A1926

No. 3501: a, Confiance. b, Grande Hermine, horiz. c, Boudeuse, horiz. d, Astrolabe, horiz. e, Hermione, horiz. f, Boussole.

2008, June 20				
3501	A1926	Sheet of 6	10.50	10.50
a.-f.		55c Any single	1.75	.60

French and Brazilian Landscapes — A1927

Designs: 55c, Amazonian forest, Brazil. 85c, Glacier, France.

2008, July 13				
3502	A1927	55c multi	1.75	.60
3503	A1927	85c multi	2.75	.90
a.		Horiz. pair, #3502-3503	4.50	2.25

See Brazil No. 3052.

Mediterranean Summit, Paris — A1928

2008, July 13			*Perf. 13¼*	
3504	A1928	55c multi	1.75	.60

Aspects of Life in French Regions Type of 2003

No. 3505: a, Espadrilles. b, Stew (pot au feu). c, Chestnuts (chataigne). d, Fireworks (feu d'artifice). e, Epinal prints (l'image d'Epinal), vert. f, Lentils (lentille), vert. g, Reblochon cheese. h, Calissons (candy). i, Stilt walker (les échasses), vert. j, Mustard (moutarde), vert.

2008, Sept. 6	Photo.		*Perf. 13*	
3505		Sheet of 10	15.00	15.00
a.-j.	A1642	55c Any single	1.50	.50

No. 3505 has three vertical rows of rouletting, separating sheet into quarters.

Nos. 3505a-3505j also were issued in large booklets containing panes of 1 of each stamp. The booklet sold for €19.

Josselin A1929

2008, Sept. 20	Engr.		*Perf. 13¼*	
3506	A1929	55c multi	1.75	.50

A1930

A1931

A1932

A1933

A1934

A1935

A1936

A1937

A1938

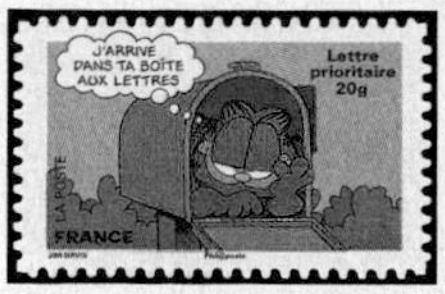

Garfield, Comic Strip by Jim Davis
A1939

Serpentine Die Cut 11¼x11

2008, Sept. 18 Photo.

Booklet Stamps

Self-Adhesive

3507	A1930	(55c)	multi	1.75	.50
3508	A1931	(55c)	multi	1.75	.50
3509	A1932	(55c)	multi	1.75	.50
3510	A1933	(55c)	multi	1.75	.50
3511	A1934	(55c)	multi	1.75	.50
3512	A1935	(55c)	multi	1.75	.50
3513	A1936	(55c)	multi	1.75	.50
3514	A1937	(55c)	multi	1.75	.50
3515	A1938	(55c)	multi	1.75	.50
3516	A1939	(55c)	multi	1.75	.50
a.	Booklet pane of 10, #3507-3516			17.50	
	Nos. 3507-3516 (10)			17.50	5.00

"I Am Sport"
A1940

2008, Oct. 2 Photo. ***Perf. 12½***

3517 A1940 55c multi 1.50 .50

Values are for stamps with surrounding selvage.

Fifth Republic, 50th Anniv.
A1941

2008. Oct. 4 ***Perf. 13¼***

3518 A1941 55c multi 1.50 .50

Seascapes of Viet Nam and France — A1942

Designs: 55c, Along Bay, Viet Nam. 85, Strait of Bonifacio, France.

2008, Oct. 15 Photo. ***Perf. 13x12¾***

3519	A1942	55c	multi	1.40	.45
3520	A1942	85c	multi	2.25	.75

See Viet Nam Nos. 3340-3341.

Types of 1959-2008

Serpentine Die Cut 6¾ Vert.

2008, Nov. 6 Photo.

Booklet Stamps

Self-Adhesive

3521	A328	55c	multi	1.40	.45
3522	A349	55c	multi	1.40	.45
3523	A360	55c	multi	1.40	.45
3524	A379	55c	multi	1.40	.45
3525	A486	55c	dark red	1.40	.45
3526	A555	55c	rose carmine	1.40	.45
3527	A771	55c	bright red	1.40	.45
3528	A915	55c	red	1.40	.45
3529	A1161	55c	red	1.40	.45
3530	A1409	55c	red	1.40	.45
3531	A1713	55c	red	1.40	.45
3532	A1912	55c	red	1.40	.45
a.	Booklet pane of 12, #3521-3532			17.00	
	Nos. 3521-3532 (12)			16.80	5.40

Landmarks of France and Israel — A1943

Airplane, stamped first flight cover and: 55c, Haifa waterfront, Israel. 85c, Eiffel Tower, Paris.

2008, Nov. 6 Photo. ***Perf. 13***

3533	A1943	55c	multi	1.40	.45
3534	A1943	85c	multi	2.25	.75

First flight between France and Israel, 60th anniv. See Israel Nos. 1750-1751.

European Capitals Type of 2002

No. 3535 — Attractions in Prague: a, Tour du Petit Coté (Charles Bridge and Tower), vert. b, Hotel de ville horloge astronomique et calandrier (City Hall astronomical clock), vert. c, Eglise Notre-Dame-de-Tyn (Tyn Cathedral), vert. d, Le Chateau (Hradcany Castle).

Perf. 13¼x13, 13x13¼ (#3535d)

2008, Nov. 7 Photo.

3535	A1622	Sheet of 4	5.75	5.75
a.-d.		55c Any single	1.40	.45

A1944

A1945

A1946

A1947

A1948

A1949

A1950

A1951

A1952

A1953

A1954

A1955

A1956

Happy Holidays
A1957

Serpentine Die Cut 11¼x11

2008, Nov. 8 Photo.

Booklet Stamps

Self-Adhesive

3536	A1944	(55c)	multi	1.40	.45
3537	A1945	(55c)	multi	1.40	.45
3538	A1946	(55c)	multi	1.40	.45
3539	A1947	(55c)	multi	1.40	.45
3540	A1948	(55c)	multi	1.40	.45
3541	A1949	(55c)	multi	1.40	.45

Serpentine Die Cut 11x11¼

3542	A1950	(55c)	multi	1.40	.45
3543	A1951	(55c)	multi	1.40	.45
3544	A1952	(55c)	multi	1.40	.45
3545	A1953	(55c)	multi	1.40	.45
3546	A1954	(55c)	multi	1.40	.45
3547	A1955	(55c)	multi	1.40	.45
3548	A1956	(55c)	multi	1.40	.45
3549	A1957	(55c)	multi	1.40	.45
a.	Booklet pane of 14, #3536-3549			20.00	
	Nos. 3536-3549 (14)			19.60	6.30

A souvenir sheet containing one perf. 13x13¼ stamp like No. 3543 with water-activated gum sold for €3.

End of World War I, 90th Anniv.
A1958

2008, Nov. 11 Engr. ***Perf. 13¼***

3550 A1958 55c multi 1.40 .45

Marianne and Stars Type of 2008

Serpentine Die Cut 6¾ Vert.

2008 Engr. Self-Adhesive

3551	A1912	1c	yellow	.25	.25
3552	A1912	5c	gray brown	.25	.25
3553	A1912	10c	gray	.30	.30
3554	A1912	(50c)	green	1.40	1.40
3555	A1912	72c	olive green	2.00	2.00
3556	A1912	85c	purple	2.40	2.40
3557	A1912	88c	fawn	2.50	2.50
3558	A1912	€1	orange	2.75	2.75
3559	A1912	€1.25	blue	3.50	3.50
3560	A1912	€1.33	red violet	3.75	3.75
3561	A1912	€2.18	chocolate	6.00	6.00
	Nos. 3551-3561 (11)			25.10	25.10

Serpentine Die Cut 6¾ Horiz.

Coil Stamps

3564	A1912	(50c)	green	1.40	1.40
3565	A1912	(55c)	red	1.50	1.50
3566	A1912	(65c)	dark blue	1.90	1.90
	Nos. 3564-3566 (3)			4.80	4.80

Nos. 3551-3561 each were printed in sheets of 100.

Flowers — A1959

Designs: 31c, Helianthus annuus. 33c, Magnolia.

2008, Nov. 12 Litho. ***Perf. 13***

3567	A1959	31c	multi	.80	.25
3568	A1959	33c	multi	.85	.25

Nos. 3567-3568 are known only precanceled. See note under No. 132.

Trees and Map of Mediterranean Area — A1960

2008, Nov. 20 Photo. ***Perf. 13x12¾***

3569 A1960 85c multi 2.50 .75

See Lebanon No. 645.

Greetings Type of 2004 Inscribed "Lettre Prioritaire 20g"

Designs: No. 3569A, "Ceci est une invitation." No. 3569B, "Un grand merci."

2008 Photo. ***Serpentine Die Cut 11***

Self-Adhesive

3569A	A1667	(55c)	brt lil rose & yel	1.60	1.60
3569B	A1667	(55c)	brt yel grn & red lil	1.60	1.60

Louis Braille (1809-52), Educator of the Blind — A1961

Engr. & Embossed

2009, Jan. 4 ***Perf. 13x12¾***

3570 A1961 55c blk & violet 1.50 .50

New Year 2009 (Year of the Ox) — A1962

2009, Jan. 10 Photo. ***Perf. 13¼x13***

3571 A1962 (55c) multi 1.50 .50

No. 3571 was printed in sheets of 5. A souvenir sheet of 1 sold for €3. Value, $8.

Decorated Glasses, Nancy Museum
A1963

Decorated Clock, Louvre Museum
A1964

Marquetry, Valençay Chateau A1965

Quimper Faience, Sèvres Museum A1966

Enamelwork, Apt Cathedral — A1967

Tapestry, Malmaison Chateau A1968

Stained Glass, St. Joan of Arc Church, Rouen A1969

Cabinetwork, Louvre Museum — A1970

Wrought Iron, Army Museum, Paris A1971

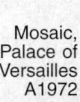

Mosaic, Palace of Versailles A1972

Jewelry, Malmaison Chateau A1973

Crystal, Clichy Glassworks — A1974

Booklet Stamps

Serpentine Die Cut 11

2009, Jan. 10 **Self-Adhesive**

3572	A1963	(55c) multi	1.50	.50
3573	A1964	(55c) multi	1.50	.50
3574	A1965	(55c) multi	1.50	.50
3575	A1966	(55c) multi	1.50	.50
3576	A1967	(55c) multi	1.50	.50
3577	A1968	(55c) multi	1.50	.50
3578	A1969	(55c) multi	1.50	.50
3579	A1970	(55c) multi	1.50	.50
3580	A1971	(55c) multi	1.50	.50
3581	A1972	(55c) multi	1.50	.50
3582	A1973	(55c) multi	1.50	.50
3583	A1974	(55c) multi	1.50	.50
a.		Booklet pane of 12, #3572-3583	18.00	
		Nos. 3572-3583 (12)	18.00	6.00

René I, Duke of Anjou (1409-80) A1975

2009, Jan. 16 **Engr.** ***Perf. 13¼***

3584	A1975	55c multi	1.50	.50

Hearts A1976

Flowers and: (55c), One parrot. (88c), Two parrots.

2009, Jan. 17 **Photo.** ***Perf. 13¼***

3585	A1976	(55c) multi	1.50	.50
a.		Souvenir sheet of 5	7.50	7.50
3586	A1976	(88c) multi	2.40	1.25

Self-Adhesive

Serpentine Die Cut

3587	A1976	(55c) multi	1.50	.50
3588	A1976	(88c) multi	2.40	1.25
a.		Booklet pane of 12	29.00	
		Nos. 3585-3588 (4)	7.80	3.50

Tourism Issue

Les Sables D'Olonne A1977

Menton — A1978

Chaumont A1979

Château de la Bâtie d'Urfé A1980

Bordeaux — A1981

Abbey of Royaumont A1982

Photo., Engr. (#3590, 3592-3594)

2009 ***Perf. 13¼, 13 (#3593)***

3589	A1977	55c multi	1.40	.45
3590	A1978	56c multi	1.40	.45
3591	A1979	56c multi	1.60	.55
3592	A1980	56c multi	1.60	.55

Perf. 13

3593	A1981	56c multi	1.60	.55
3594	A1982	56c multi	1.75	.60
		Nos. 3589-3594 (6)	9.35	3.15

Self-Adhesive

Serpentine Die Cut 11

3594A	A1981	56c multi	1.60	1.60

Issued: No. 3589, 1/31; No. 3590, 2/21; No. 3591, 5/16. No. 3592, 6/6; Nos. 3593, 3594A, 6/20. No. 3594, 9/26.

Miniature Sheet

World Alpine Skiing Championships, Val d'Isère — A1983

No. 3595: a, Super combined skier. b, Slalom skier. c, Downhill (Descente) skier. d, Giant slalom skier. e, Skiers at Val d'Isère.

2009, Jan. 31 **Photo.** ***Perf. 13x13¼***

3595	A1983	Sheet of 5	7.00	7.00
a.-e.		55c Any single	1.40	.45

France Foundation, 40th Anniv. — A1984

2009, Feb. 5 **Photo.** ***Perf. 13¼***

3596	A1984	55c multi	1.40	.45

Art Series

Angel, St. Cecilia Cathedral, Albi A1985

La Promenade, by Hansi (Jean-Jacques Waltz) — A1986

Wrapping of Pont-Neuf, by Christo and Jeanne-Claude — A1987

Paintings by Pierre-Auguste Renoir — A1988

No. 3600: a, Monsieur et Madame Bernheim de Villers. b, Gabrielle à la Rose.

Perf. 13, 13x13¼ (#3598), 13¼x13 (#3599)

2009 **Litho. (#3597), Photo.**

3597	A1985	85c multi	2.25	1.10
3598	A1986	90c multi	2.75	1.40
3599	A1987	€1.35 multi	3.75	1.90
		Nos. 3597-3599 (3)	8.75	4.40

Souvenir Sheet

Perf. 13¼

3600	A1988	Sheet of 2	6.50	6.50
a.		85c multi	2.50	1.25
b.		€1.35 multi	4.00	2.00

Self-Adhesive

Serpentine Die Cut 11

3601	A1985	85c multi	2.50	2.50
3602	A1986	90c multi	2.75	2.75
3603	A1987	€1.35 multi	3.75	3.75

Issued: No. 3597, 2/7; No. 3598, 10/24; Nos. 3599, 3603, 6/13 No. 3600, 11/5. A souvenir sheet of 1 of No. 3597 sold for €3.

Road Runner and Wile E. Coyote A1989

Sylvester and Tweety Bird A1990

Daffy Duck and Bugs Bunny A1991

Design: €1, Yosemite Sam, Wile E. Coyote, Sylvester, Tasmanian Devil, Bugs Bunny, Daffy Duck, Road Runner, Marvin the Martian and Tweety Bird.

2009, Feb. 28 **Photo.** ***Perf. 13x13¼***

3605	A1989	56c multi	1.40	.45
3606	A1990	56c multi	1.40	.45
3607	A1991	56c multi	1.40	.45
a.		Strip of 3, #3605-3607	4.25	1.40
		Nos. 3605-3607 (3)	4.20	1.35

Souvenir Sheet

3608	A1989	€1 multi	2.60	1.25

Booklet Stamps
Self-Adhesive
Litho.
Serpentine Die Cut 11

3609 A1989 (56c) multi 1.40 .45
3610 A1991 (56c) multi 1.40 .45
3611 A1990 (56c) multi 1.40 .45
a. Booklet pane of 12, 4 each #3609-3611 17.00
Nos. 3609-3611 (3) 4.20 1.35

Stamp Day. No. 3608 contains one 80x26mm stamp. Sheets of five serpentine die cut 11 self-adhesive stamps like Nos. 3605-3607 and 5 labels each sold for €6.50.

Marianne and Stars Type of 2008
2009, Feb. 28 Engr. *Perf. 13*

3612 A1912 73c olive green 1.90 .50
3613 A1912 90c fawn 2.25 .55
3614 A1912 €1.30 blue 3.25 .85
3615 A1912 €1.35 red violet 3.50 .90
3616 A1912 €2.22 chocolate 5.75 1.40
Nos. 3612-3616 (5) 16.65 4.20

Serpentine Die Cut 6¾ Vert.
Self-Adhesive

3616A A1912 73c olive green 1.90 1.90
3616B A1912 90c fawn 2.25 2.25
3616C A1912 €1.30 blue 3.25 3.25
3616D A1912 €1.35 red violet 3.50 3.50
3616E A1912 €2.22 chocolate 5.75 5.75
Nos. 3616A-3616E (5) 16.65 16.65

Constitutional Council — A1992

2009, Mar. 5 Photo. *Perf. 13¼*
3617 A1992 56c multi 1.40 .45
Self-Adhesive
Serpentine Die Cut 11
3617A A1992 56c multi 1.60 1.60

Papal Palace, Avignon — A1993

2009, Mar. 7 Engr. *Perf. 13x12¾*
3618 A1993 70c multi 1.90 .65

Portraits of Women by Titouan Lamazou A1994

Designs: No. 3619, Helena, United States. No. 3620, Dayu, Indonesia. No. 3621, Deborah, France. No. 3622, Kabari, Bangladesh. No. 3623, Mei Mei, China. No. 3624, Malika, Morocco. No. 3625, Dayan, Colombia. No. 3626, Francine, Rwanda. No. 3627, Blessing, Nigeria. No. 3628, Nandita, India. No. 3629, Elmas, Turkey. No. 3630, Nadia, Brazil.

Serpentine Die Cut 11
2009, Mar. 9 Litho.
Booklet Stamps
Self-Adhesive

3619 A1994 (56c) multi 1.50 .50
3620 A1994 (56c) multi 1.50 .50
3621 A1994 (56c) multi 1.50 .50
3622 A1994 (56c) multi 1.50 .50
3623 A1994 (56c) multi 1.50 .50
3624 A1994 (56c) multi 1.50 .50
3625 A1994 (56c) multi 1.50 .50
3626 A1994 (56c) multi 1.50 .50
3627 A1994 (56c) multi 1.50 .50
3628 A1994 (56c) multi 1.50 .50
3629 A1994 (56c) multi 1.50 .50
3630 A1994 (56c) multi 1.50 .50
a. Booklet pane of 12, #3619-3630 18.00
Nos. 3619-3630 (12) 18.00 6.00

Mâcon — A1995

2009, Mar. 27 Engr. *Perf. 13x12¾*
3631 A1995 56c multi 1.50 .50

Souvenir Sheet

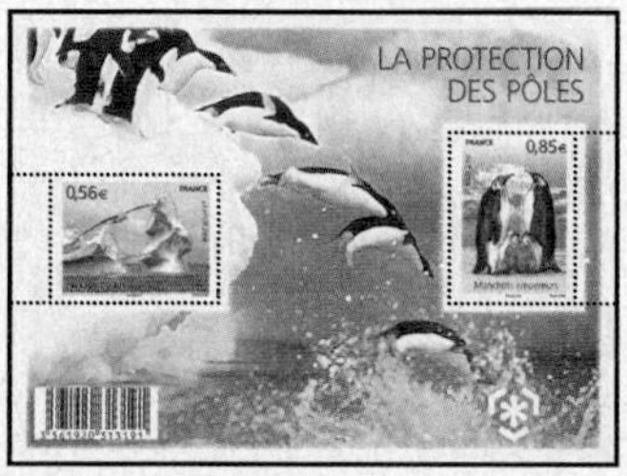

Protection of Polar Regions — A1996

No. 3632: a, Iceberg and bird. b, Emperor penguins, vert.

Perf. 13x13¼, 13¼x13 (85c)
2009, Mar. 28 Litho. & Engr.
3632 A1996 Sheet of 2 4.00 4.00
a. 56c multi 1.50 .50
b. 85c multi 2.50 .85

Aimé Césaire (1913-2008), Martinique Politician A1997

2009, Apr. 17 Photo. *Perf. 13¼x13*
3633 A1997 56c multi 1.50 .50

Flora of the French Regions A1998

Designs: No. 3634, Plum (quetsche), Alsace. No. 3635, Plum (mirabelle), Lorraine. No. 3636, Birch tree, Centre. No. 3637, Bee orchid, Champagne-Ardenne. No. 3638, Lily, Paris. No. 3639, Bluebells, Ile de France. No. 3640, Gorse, Bretagne. No. 3641, Lily-of-the-valley, Pays de la Loire. No. 3642, Apples, Basse-Normandie. No. 3643, Beech leaves, Haute-Normandie. No. 3644, Rose, Picardie. No. 3645, Potatoes, Nord-Pas de Calais. No. 3646, Olives, Provence-Alpes-Côte d'Azur. No. 3647, Chestnut, Corse. No. 3648, Wild thyme, Languedoc-Roussillon. No. 3649, Yellow gentian, Auvergne. No. 3650, Boletus mushroom, Limousin. No. 3651, Saltwort, Poitou-Charentes. No. 3652, Maritime pine, Aquitaine. No. 3653, Norway spruce, Franche-Comté. No. 3654, Awara palm, French Guiana. No. 3655, Toulouse violet, Midi-Pyrénées. No. 3656, Blueberries, Rhône-Alpes. No. 3657, Black currants, Bourgogne.

Serpentine Die Cut 11
2009, Apr. 25 Photo.
Booklet Stamps
Self-Adhesive

3634 A1998 (56c) multi 1.50 .50
3635 A1998 (56c) multi 1.50 .50
a. Booklet pane of 2, #3634-3635 3.00
3636 A1998 (56c) multi 1.50 .50
3637 A1998 (56c) multi 1.50 .50
a. Booklet pane of 2, #3636-3637 3.00
3638 A1998 (56c) multi 1.50 .50
3639 A1998 (56c) multi 1.50 .50
a. Booklet pane of 2, #3638-3639 3.00
3640 A1998 (56c) multi 1.50 .50
3641 A1998 (56c) multi 1.50 .50
a. Booklet pane of 2, #3640-3641 3.00
3642 A1998 (56c) multi 1.50 .50
3643 A1998 (56c) multi 1.50 .50
a. Booklet pane of 2, #3642-3643 3.00
3644 A1998 (56c) multi 1.50 .50
3645 A1998 (56c) multi 1.50 .50
a. Booklet pane of 2, #3644-3645 3.00
Complete booklet, #3635a, 3637a, 3639a, 3641a, 3643a, 3645a 18.00
3646 A1998 (56c) multi 1.50 .50
3647 A1998 (56c) multi 1.50 .50
a. Booklet pane of 2, #3646-3647 3.00
3648 A1998 (56c) multi 1.50 .50
3649 A1998 (56c) multi 1.50 .50
a. Booklet pane of 2, #3648-3649 3.00
3650 A1998 (56c) multi 1.50 .50
3651 A1998 (56c) multi 1.50 .50
a. Booklet pane of 2, #3650-3651 3.00
3652 A1998 (56c) multi 1.50 .50
3653 A1998 (56c) multi 1.50 .50
a. Booklet pane of 2, #3652-3653 3.00
3654 A1998 (56c) multi 1.50 .50
3655 A1998 (56c) multi 1.50 .50
a. Booklet pane of 2, #3654-3655 3.00
3656 A1998 (56c) multi 1.50 .50
3657 A1998 (56c) multi 1.50 .50
a. Booklet pane of 2, #3656-3657 3.00
Complete booklet, #3647a, 3649a, 3651a, 3653a, 3655a, 3657a 18.00
Nos. 3634-3657 (24) 36.00 12.00

Souvenir Sheet

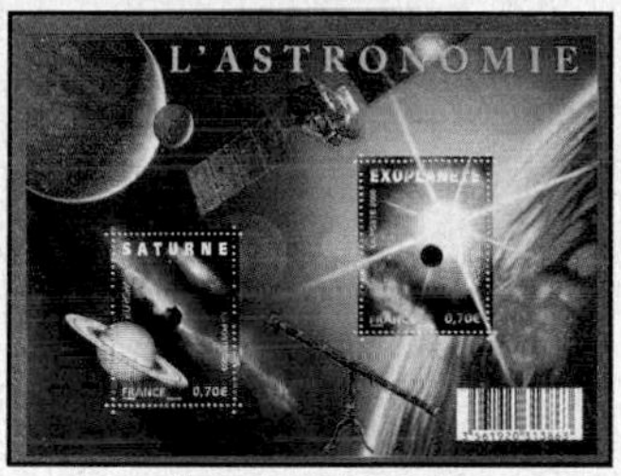

Europa — A1999

No. 3658: a, Saturn. b, Exoplanet.

2009, May 3 Litho. *Perf. 13¼x13*
3658 A1999 Sheet of 2 4.00 4.00
a.-b. 70c Either single 2.00 .65

Intl. Year of Astronomy.

A2000

Vacations A2001

Designs: No. 3659, Tennis ball on red clay court. No. 3660, Red-striped director's chair. No. 3661, Red turban. No. 3662, Ladybug. No. 3663, Red air mattress. No. 3664, Cherry tomatoes. No. 3665, Rooster. No. 3666, Poppy. No. 3667, License plate of Bonaire, Netherlands Antilles. No. 3668, Monarch butterfly. No. 3669, Raspberries. No. 3670, Doorknocker on red door. No. 3671, Flowers near house number. No. 3672, Red boat, rope and cleat.

Serpentine Die Cut 11
2009, May 13 Litho.
Booklet Stamps
Self-Adhesive

3659 A2000 (56c) multi 1.60 .55
3660 A2000 (56c) multi 1.60 .55
3661 A2000 (56c) multi 1.60 .55
3662 A2000 (56c) multi 1.60 .55
3663 A2000 (56c) multi 1.60 .55
3664 A2000 (56c) multi 1.60 .55
3665 A2001 (56c) multi 1.60 .55
3666 A2001 (56c) multi 1.60 .55
3667 A2001 (56c) multi 1.60 .55
3668 A2001 (56c) multi 1.60 .55
3669 A2001 (56c) multi 1.60 .55
3670 A2001 (56c) multi 1.60 .55
3671 A2001 (56c) multi 1.60 .55
3672 A2001 (56c) multi 1.60 .55
a. Booklet pane of 14, #3659-3672 22.50
Nos. 3659-3672 (14) 22.40 7.70

Timber-frame Houses, Alsace — A2002

Azay-le-Rideau Chateau — A2003

Notre Dame Cathedral, Paris A2004

Vineyards, Bordeaux A2005

Nice A2006

Mont-Saint-Michel — A2007

Eiffel Tower A2008

Provence A2009

Serpentine Die Cut 11
2009, May 13 Litho.
Booklet Stamps
Self-Adhesive

3673 A2002 (85c) multi 2.40 .80
3674 A2003 (85c) multi 2.40 .80
3675 A2004 (85c) multi 2.40 .80
3676 A2005 (85c) multi 2.40 .80
3677 A2006 (85c) multi 2.40 .80
3678 A2007 (85c) multi 2.40 .80
3679 A2008 (85c) multi 2.40 .80
3680 A2009 (85c) multi 2.40 .80
a. Booklet pane of 8, #3673-3680 19.50
Nos. 3673-3680 (8) 19.20 6.40

Nos. 3678 and 3679 each were printed in sheets of 50 in 2010.

John Calvin (1509-64), Theologian and Religious Reformer
A2010

2009, May 22 Engr. *Perf. 13¼*

3681	A2010 56c multi	1.60	.55

Miniature Sheet

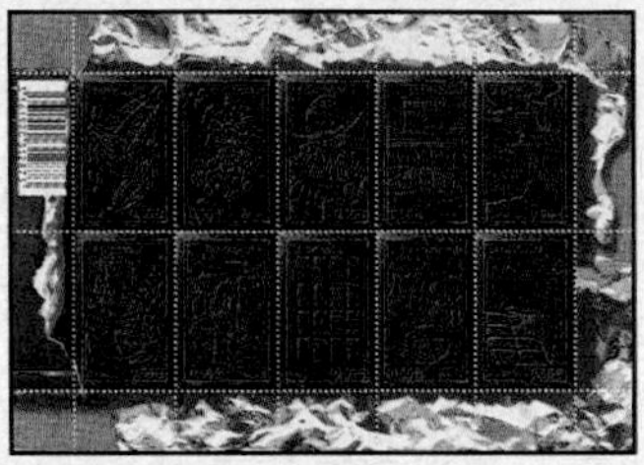

Chocolate — A2011

No. 3682: a, Cacao leaves, pods and beans. b, Aztec Indian. c, Spanish soldier. d, Castle. e, Map of French Atlantic coast. f, European man and woman of 16th cent. g, Production of chocolate. h, Chocolate bar. i, Cocoa service. j, Person eating chocolate bar.

2009, May 23 Photo. *Perf. 13*

3682	A2011 Sheet of 10	16.00	16.00
a.-j.	56c Any single	1.60	.55

No. 3682 is impregnated with a chocolate scent.

French Federation Of Philatelic Associations 82nd Congress, Tarbes — A2012

2009, June 12 Engr. *Perf. 13x13¼*

3683	A2012 56c multi + label	1.60	.55

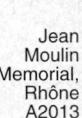

Jean Moulin Memorial, Rhône
A2013

2009, June 20 Engr. *Perf. 13¼*

3684	A2013 56c multi	1.60	.55

Serpentine Die Cut 11

Self-Adhesive

3685	A2013 56c multi	1.60	1.60

Endangered Animals
A2014

Designs: No. 3686, Giant panda. No. 3687, Rhinoceros. 70c, Aurochs, horiz. 90c, California condor, horiz.

2009, June 20 Photo. *Perf. 13¼*

3686	A2014 56c multi	1.60	.55
3687	A2014 56c multi	1.60	.55
3688	A2014 70c multi	2.00	.65
3689	A2014 90c multi	2.50	.85
a.	Souvenir sheet of 4, #3686-3689	7.75	7.75
	Nos. 3686-3689 (4)	7.70	2.60

Gordon Bennett Aviation Cup, Cent.
A2015

2009, June 27 Engr. *Perf. 13¼*

3690	A2015 56c blk & brn	1.60	.55

Etienne Dolet (1509-46), Printer and Translator — A2016

2009, July 4 Engr. *Perf. 13x13¼*

3691	A2016 56c multi	1.60	.55

Miniature Sheet

Fair Attractions — A2017

Designs: a, Parachute jump. b, Ferris wheel. c, Roller coaster. d, Carousel. e, Candy apple. f, Fishing arcade game.

2009, Sept. 5 Photo. *Perf. 13*

3692	A2017 Sheet of 6	10.50	10.50
a.-f.	56c Any single	1.75	.60

A2018

Invitation — A2019

Designs: No. 3693, Yellow background, man with red violet pants and shoes. No. 3694, Red background, woman wearing dress. No. 3695, Red violet background, woman scattering papers. No. 3696, Light blue background, cow with flowers. No. 3697, Blue background, man with red violet pants and blue shoes. No. 3698, Brown black background, birthday cake with slice on cake server. No. 3699. Yellow green background, woman with brown pants and green shoes. No. 3700, Green background, man with blue pants and shoes. No. 3701, Brown background, cut birthday cake. No. 3702, Red violet background, woman with red violet pants and shoes. No. 3703, Pink background, woman with balloons. No. 3704, Red background, bird. No. 3705, Yellow green background, woman with green skirt and shoes. No. 3706, Orange background, woman scattering papers.

Serpentine Die Cut 11

2009, Sept. 5 Litho.

Booklet Stamps

Self-Adhesive

3693	A2018 (56c) multi	1.75	.60
3694	A2018 (56c) multi	1.75	.60
3695	A2018 (56c) multi	1.75	.60
3696	A2018 (56c) multi	1.75	.60
3697	A2018 (56c) multi	1.75	.60
3698	A2018 (56c) multi	1.75	.60
3699	A2018 (56c) multi	1.75	.60
3700	A2018 (56c) multi	1.75	.60
3701	A2019 (56c) multi	1.75	.60
3702	A2019 (56c) multi	1.75	.60
3703	A2019 (56c) multi	1.75	.60
3704	A2019 (56c) multi	1.75	.60
3705	A2019 (56c) multi	1.75	.60
3706	A2019 (56c) multi	1.75	.60
a.	Booklet pane of 14, #3693-3706	24.50	
	Nos. 3693-3706 (14)	24.50	8.40

Eugène Vaillé (1875-1959), First Conservator of the Postal Museum — A2020

2009, Sept. 19 Engr. *Perf. 13¼*

3707	A2020 56c multi	1.75	.60

Self-Adhesive

Serpentine Die Cut 11

3708	A2020 56c multi	1.75	1.75

Souvenir Sheet

Jardin des Plantes, Paris — A2021

No. 3709: a, Gazebo. b, Mexican Hothouse.

2009, Sept. 19 Photo. *Perf. 13¼x13*

3709	A2021 Sheet of 2	13.00	13.00
a.-b.	€2.22 Either single	6.50	3.25

Salon du Timbre.

A2022

Le Petit Nicolas, by René Goscinny
A2023

Designs: No. 3710, Nicolas, wearing striped shirt, holding envelope and book bag. No. 3711, Geoffroy. No. 3712, Eudes. No. 3713, Nicolas, wearing scarf, holding envelope and book bag. No. 3714, Nicolas writing. No. 3715, Joachim. No. 3716, "Chouette, des nouvelles!" No. 3717, Character at typewriter. No. 3718, "Vous me ferez cent lignes!" No. 3719, "Chère Maman. . ." No. 3720, "C'est toi la plus jolie!", vert. No. 3721, "J'ai fait le bonheur de tout le monde.", vert. No. 3722, "Moi, je veux pas grand chose réellement. . .", vert. No. 3723, "C'est pout toi, Maman!", vert.

Serpentine Die Cut 11

2009, Sept. 19 Litho.

Booklet Stamps

Self-Adhesive

3710	A2022 (56c) multi	1.75	.60
3711	A2022 (56c) multi	1.75	.60
3712	A2022 (56c) multi	1.75	.60
3713	A2022 (56c) multi	1.75	.60
3714	A2022 (56c) multi	1.75	.60
3715	A2022 (56c) multi	1.75	.60
3716	A2023 (56c) multi	1.75	.60
3717	A2023 (56c) multi	1.75	.60
3718	A2023 (56c) multi	1.75	.60
3719	A2023 (56c) multi	1.75	.60
3720	A2023 (56c) multi	1.75	.60
3721	A2023 (56c) multi	1.75	.60
3722	A2023 (56c) multi	1.75	.60
3723	A2023 (56c) multi	1.75	.60
a.	Booklet pane of 14, #3710-3723	24.50	
	Nos. 3710-3723 (14)	24.50	8.40

René de Saint-Marceaux (1845-1915), Sculptor of UPU Monument — A2024

Litho. & Engr.

2009, Oct. 9 *Perf. 13x13¼*

3724	A2024 70c multi	2.10	.70

See Switzerland No. 9O22.

Miniature Sheet

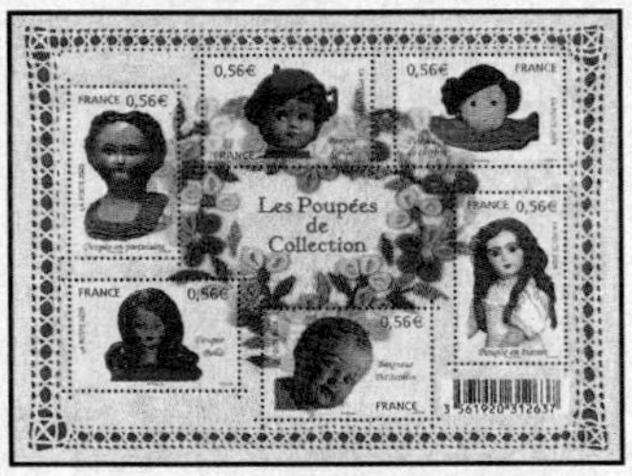

Dolls — A2025

No. 3725: a, Porcelain doll. b, GéGé doll, horiz. c, Rag doll, horiz. d, Bella doll, horiz. e, Baigneur Petitcollin, horiz. f, Unglazed porcelain doll (poupée en biscuit).

2009, Oct. 17 *Perf. 13*

3725	A2025 Sheet of 6	10.50	10.50
a.-f.	56c Any single	1.75	.60

Juliette Dodu (1848-1909), Spy — A2026

2009, Oct. 28 Engr. *Perf. 13¼*

3726	A2026 56c multi	1.75	.60

Self-Adhesive

Serpentine Die Cut 11

3727	A2026 56c multi	1.75	1.75

European Capitals Type of 2002

Miniature Sheet

No. 3728 — Attractions in Lisbon: a, Hieronymites Monastery. b, Bairro Alto Quarter, vert. c, Belém Tower. d, Monument to the Discoveries.

Perf. 13x13¼, 13¼x13 (#3728b)

2009, Nov. 5 Photo.

3728	A1622 Sheet of 4	7.00	7.00
a.-d.	56c Any single	1.75	.60

Francisco de Miranda (1750-1816), Revolutionist in France and Venezuela — A2027

2009, Nov. 6 Photo. *Perf. 13¼*

3729 A2027 85c multi 2.60 .90

See Venezuela No. 1693.

Marianne and Stars Type of 2008

Miniature Sheet

Photo., Engr. (#3456-3458)

2009, Nov. 6 *Perf. 13*

3730 Sheet of 13, #3456-3458, 3730a-3730j + label 31.00 31.00
- *a.* A1912 1c yellow .25 .25
- *b.* A1912 5c gray brown .25 .25
- *c.* A1912 10c gray .30 .30
- *d.* A1912 73c olive green 2.25 2.25
- *e* A1912 85c purple 2.60 2.60
- *f.* A1912 90c fawn 2.75 2.75
- *g.* A1912 €1 orange 3.00 3.00
- *h.* A1912 €1.30 blue 4.00 4.00
- *i.* A1912 €1.35 red violet 4.00 4.00
- *j.* A1912 €2.22 chocolate 6.50 6.50

Euromed Postal Conference — A2028

2009, Nov. 7 Engr. *Perf. 13¼*

3731 A2028 56c multi 1.75 .60

A2029

A2030

A2031

A2032

A2033

A2034

A2035

A2036

A2037

A2038

A2039

A2040

A2041

A2042

Serpentine Die Cut 11

2009, Nov. 7 Photo.

Booklet Stamps

Self-Adhesive

3732 A2029 (56c) multi 1.75 .60
3733 A2030 (56c) multi 1.75 .60
3734 A2031 (56c) multi 1.75 .60
3735 A2032 (56c) multi 1.75 .60
3736 A2033 (56c) multi 1.75 .60
3737 A2034 (56c) multi 1.75 .60
3738 A2035 (56c) multi 1.75 .60
3739 A2036 (56c) multi 1.75 .60
3740 A2037 (56c) multi 1.75 .60
3741 A2038 (56c) multi 1.75 .60
3742 A2039 (56c) multi 1.75 .60
3743 A2040 (56c) multi 1.75 .60
3744 A2041 (56c) multi 1.75 .60
3745 A2042 (56c) multi 1.75 .60
- *a.* Booklet pane of 14, #3732-3745 24.50

Nos. 3732-3745 (14) 24.50 8.40

A souvenir sheet containing one No. 3743 sold for €3.

Helicopter Carrier Jeanne d'Arc — A2043

Sailors of the Jeanne d'Arc — A2044

2009, Nov. 21 Engr. *Perf. 13x12¾*

3746 A2043 56c multi 1.75 .60
3747 A2044 56c multi 1.75 .60
- *a.* Horiz. pair, #3746-3747 3.50 1.20

A souvenir sheet containing Nos. 3746-3747 sold for €3.

Asterix, Comic Strip by René Goscinny and Albert Uderzo — A2045

No. 3749: a, Assurancetorix on rope (40x30mm). b, Eight characters, horiz. (80x26mm). c, Falbala with basket (30x40mm). d, Idefix and bone, horiz. (22x19mm). e, Obelix carrying rock (50x100mm).

2009, Dec. 2 Photo. *Perf. 13*

3748 A2045 56c multi 1.75 .60
3749 Sheet of 6, #3748, 3749a-3749e 15.50 15.50
- *a.* A2045 56c multi, perf. 13x13¼ 2.50 2.50
- *b.* A2045 56c multi, perf. 13 2.50 2.50
- *c.* A2045 56c multi, perf. 13¼x13 2.50 2.50
- *d.* A2045 56c multi, perf. 13¼x12½ 2.50 2.50
- *e.* A2045 56c multi, perf. 13x12¼ 2.50 2.50

No. 3749 sold for €5.20, with the Red Cross receiving €1.84 of that. No. 3749e has a gritty substance affixed to the rock.

A2046

Hearts A2047

Type I — Bow ties extend to perforations.
Type II — Bow ties do not touch perforations (red frame all around).

2010, Jan. 8 Photo. *Perf. 13¼*

3750 A2046 56c multi, type I 1.60 .55

Perf.

3751 A2046 56c multi, type II 1.60 .55

Perf. 13¼

3752 A2047 90c multi 2.50 1.25

Nos. 3750-3752 (3) 5.70 2.35

Self-Adhesive

Serpentine Die Cut

3753 A2046 56c multi, type I 1.60 1.60
3754 A2047 90c multi 2.50 2.50

Values for Nos. 3750, 3752 are for stamps with surrounding selvage. No. 3751 was printed in sheets of 5.

New Year 2010 (Year of the Tiger) — A2048

2010, Jan. 15 Photo. *Perf. 13¼x13*

3755 A2048 56c multi 1.60 .55

No. 3755 was printed in sheets of 5. A souvenir sheet of 1 sold for €3.

Abbé Pierre (1912-2007), Founder of Emmaus Movement A2049

2010, Jan. 22 Engr. *Perf. 13¼*

3756 A2049 56c multi 1.60 .55

Self-Adhesive

Serpentine Die Cut 11

3757 A2049 56c multi 1.60 1.60

A souvenir sheet containing No. 3756 was printed in 2011 and sold for €3.

Musical Instruments in Art — A2050

Designs: No. 3758, Lyre, by Gustave Moreau. No. 3759, Harp (Harpe), by François André Vincent. No. 3760, Violincello (Violincelle), by Karl Gustav Klingstedt. No. 3761, Guitar (Guitare), by Camille Roqueplan. No. 3762, Horn (Cor), by Daniel Rabel. No. 3763, Saxophone, by Marthe and Juliette Vesque. No. 3764, Organ (Orgue), by François Garas. No. 3765, Bugle (Clairon), by Auguste Mayer. No. 3766, Clavecin, by Louis Carrogis Carmontelle. No. 3767, Piano, by Pierre-Désiré Lamy. No. 3768, Tambourine (Tambourin), by Théodore Chassériau. No. 3769, Drums (Tambour), by Jacques-Antoine Delaistre.

Serpentine Die Cut 11

2010, Jan. 30 Photo.

Booklet Stamps

Self-Adhesive

3758 A2050 (56c) multi 1.60 .55
3759 A2050 (56c) multi 1.60 .55
3760 A2050 (56c) multi 1.60 .55
3761 A2050 (56c) multi 1.60 .55
3762 A2050 (56c) multi 1.60 .55
3763 A2050 (56c) multi 1.60 .55
3764 A2050 (56c) multi 1.60 .55
3765 A2050 (56c) multi 1.60 .55
3766 A2050 (56c) multi 1.60 .55
3767 A2050 (56c) multi 1.60 .55
3768 A2050 (56c) multi 1.60 .55
3769 A2050 (56c) multi 1.60 .55
- *a.* Booklet pane of 12, #3758-3769 19.50

Nos. 3758-3769 (12) 19.20 6.60

See Nos. 3882A-3882B.

2010 Winter Olympics, Vancouver A2051

2010, Feb. 6 *Perf. 13x13¼*

3770 A2051 85c Figure skaters 2.40 1.25
3771 A2051 85c Skier 2.40 1.25
- *a.* Horiz. pair, #3770-3771 4.80 2.50
- *b.* Tete-beche block of 4, 2 #3771a 9.60 5.00

Art Issue

Museum of Art and Industry (La Piscine), Roubaix — A2052

The Beach at Calais at Ebb Tide, by Joseph Mallord William Turner — A2053

Maman, by Louise Bourgeois — A2054

Allegory of Spring, by Sandro Botticelli — A2055

No. 3775: a, Flora, Zephyrus and Chloris. b, The Three Graces.

2010 Photo. *Perf. 13x13¼*

3772 A2052 85c multi 2.10 1.10
3773 A2053 €1.35 multi 3.75 1.90
3774 A2054 €1.35 multi 3.50 1.75
Nos. 3772-3774 (3) 9.35 4.75

Perf. 13¼x13

3775 A2055 Sheet of 2 6.25 6.25
a. 87c multi 2.40 1.25
b. €1.40 multi 3.75 1.90

Self-Adhesive

Serpentine Die Cut 11

Photo.

3776 A2052 85c multi 2.10 2.10
3776A A2055 87c Like #3775b 2.40 2.40
3777 A2053 €1.35 multi 3.75 3.75
3778 A2054 €1.35 multi 3.50 3.50
3779 A2055 €1.40 Like #3775a 3.75 3.75
Nos. 3776-3779 (5) 15.50 15.50

Issued: Nos. 3772, 3776, 5/15; Nos. 3773, 3777, 2/19; Nos. 3774, 3778, 6/17; No. 3775, 11/8/10; Nos. 3776A, 3779, 11/18/10.

A2056

Stamp Day — A2057

2010, Feb. 27 Engr. *Perf. 13*

3780 A2056 56c blue & red 1.60 .55

Souvenir Sheet

Litho. & Embossed

Perf. 13¼x13

3781 A2057 €2 multi 5.50 2.75

Protection of Water A2058

Inscriptions: No. 3782, Grands mammifères marins (large marine mammals). No. 3783, Marée noire (black tide). No. 3784, Irrigation. No. 3785, Plaisir de l'eau (pleasure of water). No. 3786, Inondation (flood). No. 3787, Source. No. 3788, Aigues vertes (green water). No. 3789, Secheresse (drought). No. 3790, Hydro-électricité (hydroelectricity). No. 3791, Géothermie (geothermal energy). No. 3792, Pluies acides (acid rain). No. 3793, Fonte des glaciers (melting of glaciers).

Serpentine Die Cut 11

2010, Feb. 27 Photo.

Booklet Stamps

Self-Adhesive

3782 A2058 (56c) multi 1.60 .55
3783 A2058 (56c) multi 1.60 .55
3784 A2058 (56c) multi 1.60 .55
3785 A2058 (56c) multi 1.60 .55
3786 A2058 (56c) multi 1.60 .55
3787 A2058 (56c) multi 1.60 .55
3788 A2058 (56c) multi 1.60 .55
3789 A2058 (56c) multi 1.60 .55
3790 A2058 (56c) multi 1.60 .55
3791 A2058 (56c) multi 1.60 .55
3792 A2058 (56c) multi 1.60 .55
3793 A2058 (56c) multi 1.60 .55
a. Booklet pane of 12, #3782-3793 19.50
Nos. 3782-3793 (12) 19.20 6.60

Savoy as Part of France, 150th Anniv. A2059

2010, Mar. 27 Engr. *Perf. 13¼x13*

3794 A2059 56c multi 1.60 .55

Self-Adhesive

Serpentine Die Cut 11

3795 A2059 56c multi 1.60 1.60

Tourism Issue

Villeneuve lez Avignon A2060

Orcival Basilica — A2061

Pornic — A2062

Arcueil-Cachan Aqueduct Bridge — A2063

2010 Engr. *Perf. 13¼*

3796 A2060 56c multi 1.50 .50
3797 A2061 56c multi 1.40 .45

Perf. 13

3798 A2062 56c multi 1.40 .45

Perf. 13¼

3799 A2063 58c multi 1.60 .55
Nos. 3796-3799 (4) 5.90 1.95

Self-Adhesive

Engr.

Serpentine Die Cut 11

3800 A2060 56c multi 1.50 1.50

Issued: Nos. 3796, 3800, 4/17; No. 3797, 5/13; No. 3798, 5/25; No. 3799, 9/24.

A2064

A2065

A2066

A2067

A2068

A2069

A2070

A2071

A2072

A2073

A2074

Campaign Against Violence Toward Women — A2075

Serpentine Die Cut 11

2010, Apr. 20 Litho.

Booklet Stamps

Self-Adhesive

3801 A2064 (56c) multi 1.50 .50
3802 A2065 (56c) multi 1.50 .50
3803 A2066 (56c) multi 1.50 .50
3804 A2067 (56c) multi 1.50 .50
3805 A2068 (56c) multi 1.50 .50
3806 A2069 (56c) multi 1.50 .50
3807 A2070 (56c) multi 1.50 .50
3808 A2071 (56c) multi 1.50 .50
3809 A2072 (56c) multi 1.50 .50
3810 A2073 (56c) multi 1.50 .50
3811 A2074 (56c) multi 1.50 .50
3812 A2075 (56c) multi 1.50 .50
a. Booklet pane of 12, #3801-3812 18.00
Nos. 3801-3812 (12) 18.00 6.00

Colmar A2076

2010, Apr. 23 Engr. *Perf. 13¼*

3813 A2076 56c multi 1.50 .50

Self-Adhesive

Serpentine Die Cut 11

3814 A2076 56c multi 1.50 1.50

National Sheepcote, Rambouillet — A2077

2010, May 1 *Perf. 13¼*

3815 A2077 90c multi 2.40 1.25

Europa A2078

2010, May 9 Photo.

3816 A2078 70c multi 1.75 .60

Miniature Sheet

Stamp Bourse in Paris, 150th Anniv. — A2079

No. 3817 — Famous philatelists: a, Pres. Franklin Delano Roosevelt (1882-1945). b, Lucien Berthelot (1903-85), President of International Philatelic Federation. c, Louis Yvert (1866-1950), stamp catalogue publisher, horiz. d, Arthur Maury (1844-1907), stamp catalogue publisher, horiz. e, Alberto Bolaffi (1874-1944), stamp catalogue publisher.

2010, May 13 Engr. *Perf. 13*

3817 A2079 Sheet of 5 7.00 7.00
a.-e. 56c Any single 1.40 .45

Deauville, 150th Anniv. A2080

2010, May 14 Photo. *Perf. 13¼*

3818 A2080 85c multi 2.10 1.10

Mother Teresa (1910-97), Humanitarian A2081

2010, May 27 Engr. *Perf. 13¼x13*

3819 A2081 85c multi 2.10 1.10

Self-Adhesive

Serpentine Die Cut 11

3820 A2081 85c multi 2.10 2.10

Institute of Human Paleontology, Paris, Cent. — A2082

2010, June 1 *Perf. 13x12¾*

3821 A2082 56c multi 1.40 .45

See Monaco No. 2597.

Nice as Part of France, 150th Anniv. A2083

2010, June 11 Photo. *Perf. 13¼*

3822 A2083 56c multi 1.40 .45

Self-Adhesive

Serpentine Die Cut 11

3823 A2083 56c multi 1.40 1.40

Front Side of No. 3824

Rear Side of No. 3824 — A2084

A2085

2010 World Cup Soccer Championships, South Africa — A2086

No. 3825: a, Soccer player and ball. b, Soccer players, vert. c, South African building, vert. d, Aerial view of Cape Town.

2010 Photo. *Perf. 13x12¾*

3824 A2084 56c multi 2.75 .50

Perf. 13x13¼, 13¼x13

3825 A2085 Sheet of 4 8.50 8.50
a.-d. 85c Any single 2.10 1.10

Embossed and Etched on Silver

Die Cut Perf. 12¾

Self-Adhesive

3826 A2086 €5 *silver* 12.50 12.50

Issued: Nos. 3824, 3825, 6/13; No. 3826, 6/11. No. 3824 is gummed on both sides and sold for €1.12. Both sides of the stamp could be used. Values for used examples of No. 3824 are for stamps canceled on either or both sides.

Launch of Soyuz Space Flights From French Guiana A2087

2010, June 12 Photo. *Perf. 13¼*

3827 A2087 85c multi 2.25 1.10

Self-Adhesive

Serpentine Die Cut 11

3828 A2087 85c multi 2.25 2.25

Souvenir Sheet

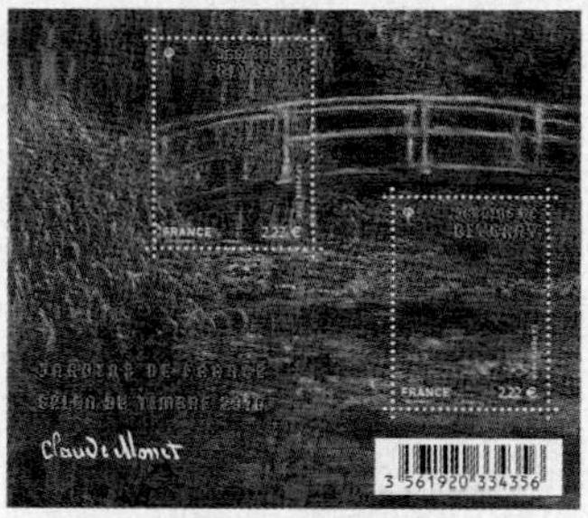

Jardins de Giverny, by Claude Monet — A2088

No. 3829: a, Bridge. b, Pond.

2010, June 12 *Perf. 13¼x13*

3829 A2088 Sheet of 2 11.50 11.50
a.-b. €2.22 Either single 5.75 3.00
c. Souvenir sheet, #3709a, 3709b, 3829a, 3829b 22.50 22.50

2010 Salon du Timbre (No. 3829c).

Regional Cuisine A2089

Designs: No. 3830, Eclade (grilled mussels), Poitou-Charentes. No. 3831, Baeckaoffe (stew), Alsace. No. 3832, Tomme des Pyrénées cheese, Midi-Pyrénées. No. 3833, Tarte aux mirabelles (plum tart), Lorraine. No. 3834, Potage aux cresson (watercress soup), Ile-de-France. No. 3835, Flamiche (leek pie), Picardy. No. 3836, Pont l'Evêque cheese, Basse-Normandie. No. 3837, Blanc-manger (blancmange), Antilles. No. 3838, Caviar, Aquitaine. No. 3839, Chapon (capon), Franche-Comté. No. 3840, Fourme d'Ambert cheese, Auvergne. No. 3841, Tarte tatin (upside-down apple tart), Centre.

No. 3842, Quenelles (dumplings), Rhône-Alpes. No. 3843, Escalope normande (veal cutlet), Haute-Normandie. No. 3844, Maroilles cheese, Nord-Pas-de-Calais. No. 3845, Clafoutis (baked fruit and batter), Limousin. No. 3846, Gougères (cheese pastry), Bourgogne. No. 3847, Tian (baked vegetables), Provence-Alpes-Côte d'Azur. No. 3848, Brocciu cheese, Corsica. No. 3849, Abricots rouges au miel (apricots in honey), Languedoc-Roussillon. No. 3850, Homard breton (lobster), Bretagne. No. 3851, Brochet au beurre blanc (pike with white butter), Pays de la Loire. No. 3852, Chaource cheese, Champagne-Ardennes. No. 3853, Paris-Brest (butter cream-filled pastry), Paris.

Serpentine Die Cut 11

2010, June 12 Photo.

Booklet Stamps

Self-Adhesive

3830 A2089 (56c) multi 1.40 .45
3831 A2089 (56c) multi 1.40 .45
3832 A2089 (56c) multi 1.40 .45
3833 A2089 (56c) multi 1.40 .45
a. Booklet pane of 4, #3830-3833 5.60
3834 A2089 (56c) multi 1.40 .45
3835 A2089 (56c) multi 1.40 .45
3836 A2089 (56c) multi 1.40 .45
3837 A2089 (56c) multi 1.40 .45
a. Booklet pane of 4, #3834-3837 5.60
3838 A2089 (56c) multi 1.40 .45
3839 A2089 (56c) multi 1.40 .45
3840 A2089 (56c) multi 1.40 .45
3841 A2089 (56c) multi 1.40 .45
a. Booklet pane of 4, #3838-3841 5.60
Complete booklet, #3833a, 3837a, 3841a 17.00
3842 A2089 (56c) multi 1.40 .45
3843 A2089 (56c) multi 1.40 .45
3844 A2089 (56c) multi 1.40 .45
3845 A2089 (56c) multi 1.40 .45
a. Booklet pane of 4, #3842-3845 5.60
3846 A2089 (56c) multi 1.40 .45
3847 A2089 (56c) multi 1.40 .45
3848 A2089 (56c) multi 1.40 .45
3849 A2089 (56c) multi 1.40 .45
a. Booklet pane of 4, #3846-3849 5.60
3850 A2089 (56c) multi 1.40 .45
3851 A2089 (56c) multi 1.40 .45
3852 A2089 (56c) multi 1.40 .45
3853 A2089 (56c) multi 1.40 .45
a. Booklet pane of 4, #3850-3853 5.60
Complete booklet, #3845a, 3849a, 3853a 17.00
Nos. 3830-3853 (24) 33.60 10.80

Romanesque Art — A2090

Designs: No. 3854, Bas-relief, Tournus. No. 3855, Interior of Cistercian Abbey, Léoncel. No. 3856, Painting, St. Sever. No. 3857, Serrabone Priory, Boule d'Amont. No. 3858, Sculpture, L'Ile-Bouchard. No. 3859, Painting, Citeaux Abbey. No. 3860, Fresco from St. Martin's Church, Nohant-Vic. No. 3861, Bas-relief, Clermont-Ferrand. No. 3862, Fresco, St. Jacques-des-Guérets. No. 3863, Bas-relief, Angouleme. No. 3864, Painting of the Consecration of the third Abbey Church, Cluny. No. 3865, Bas-reliefs, tympanum of Saint-Foy Abbey Church, Conques.

Serpentine Die Cut 11

2010, June 14 Photo.

Booklet Stamps

Self-Adhesive

3854 A2090 (56c) multi 1.40 .45
3855 A2090 (56c) multi 1.40 .45
3856 A2090 (56c) multi 1.40 .45
3857 A2090 (56c) multi 1.40 .45
3858 A2090 (56c) multi 1.40 .45
3859 A2090 (56c) multi 1.40 .45
3860 A2090 (56c) multi 1.40 .45
3861 A2090 (56c) multi 1.40 .45
3862 A2090 (56c) multi 1.40 .45
3863 A2090 (56c) multi 1.40 .45
3864 A2090 (56c) multi 1.40 .45
3865 A2090 (56c) multi 1.40 .45
a. Booklet pane of 12, #3854-3865 17.00
Nos. 3854-3865 (12) 16.80 5.40

See Nos. 3870A-3870B.

Miniature Sheet

Mills — A2091

No. 3866: a, Windmill, Montbrun-Lauragais. b, Windmill, Cassel. c, Aigremonts Windmill, Bléré, horiz. d, Daudet Windmill, Fontvieille, horiz. e, Flour mill, Villeneuve-d'Ascq. f, Birlot Watermill, Ile-de-Bréhat, horiz.

2010, June 15 Litho. & Engr. *Perf. 13*

3866 A2091 Sheet of 6 8.50 8.50
a.-f. 56c Any single 1.40 .45

2010 Youth Olympics, Singapore A2092

2010, June 16 Photo. *Perf. 13¼*

3867 A2092 85c multi 2.25 1.10

Souvenir Sheet

Charles de Gaulle's Appeal of June 18 Speech, 70th Anniv. — A2093

2010, June 18 Engr. ***Perf. 13x13¼***
3868 A2093 56c multi 1.40 .45

Conciergerie, Paris — A2094

2010, June 19
3869 A2094 56c multi + label 1.40 .45

French Federation of Philatelic Associations, 83rd Congress, Paris.

French Pavilion, Expo 2010, Shanghai A2095

2010, June 20 Photo. ***Perf. 13¼***
3870 A2095 85c multi 2.25 1.10

Romanesque Art Type of 2010

Designs: No. 3870A, Like #3855. No. 3870B, Like #3858.

Serpentine Die Cut 11
2010, June 21 Litho.
Self-Adhesive

3870A A2090 (56c) multi 1.40 1.40
3870B A2090 (56c) multi 1.40 1.40

Nos. 3870A-3870B each were printed in sheets of 50. The red panels of Nos. 3855 and 3858 are splotchy, typical of photogravure printings. Under magnification black dots can be seen in the red panels on Nos. 3870A-3870B.

Marianne and Stars Type of 2008

2010, July 1 Engr. ***Perf. 13***
3871 A1912 75c olive green 1.90 .50
3872 A1912 87c purple 2.25 .55
3873 A1912 95c fawn 2.40 .60
3874 A1912 €1.35 blue 3.50 .90
3875 A1912 €1.40 red violet 3.50 .90
3876 A1912 €2.30 chocolate 5.75 1.50
Nos. 3871-3876 (6) 19.30 4.95

Self-Adhesive
Serpentine Die Cut 6¾ Vert.

3877 A1912 75c olive green 1.90 1.90
3878 A1912 87c purple 2.25 2.25
3879 A1912 95c fawn 2.40 2.40
3880 A1912 €1.35 blue 3.50 3.50
3881 A1912 €1.40 red violet 3.50 3.50
3882 A1912 €2.30 chocolate 5.75 5.75
Nos. 3877-3882 (6) 19.30 19.30

Musical Instruments Type of 2010

Designs: No. 3882A, Like #3761. No. 3882B, Like #3767.

Serpentine Die Cut 11
2010, July 1 Litho.
Self-Adhesive

3882A A2050 (58c) multi 1.50 1.50
3882B A2050 (58c) multi 1.50 1.50

Nos. 3882A-3882B were each printed in sheets of 50. The gray blue portions of Nos. 3761 and 3767 are splotchy, typical of photogravure printings, and not splotchy on Nos. 3882A and 3882B.

Independence of French Colonies in Africa, 50th Anniv. — A2096

2010, July 15 Photo. ***Perf. 13¼***
3883 A2096 87c multi 2.25 1.10

Self-Adhesive
Serpentine Die Cut 11

3884 A2096 87c multi 2.25 2.25

Butterflies A2097

Designs: Nos. 3885, 3886b, Morpho menelaus. No. 3886a, Cerura vinula caterpillar. 75c, Thersamolycaena dispar, vert. 95c, Callophrys rubi.

Litho. (#3885, 3886a), Litho. & Embossed

2010, Sept. 3 ***Perf. 13¼***
3885 A2097 58c multi 1.50 .50
3886 Sheet of 4 7.50 7.50
a. A2097 58c multi 1.50 .50
b. A2097 58c multi 1.50 .50
c. A2097 75c multi 2.00 .65
d. A2097 95c multi 2.50 .85

Universal Israelite Alliance, 150th Anniv. A2098

Litho. & Engr.
2010, Sept. 7 ***Perf. 13¼***
3887 A2098 58c multi 1.50 .50

A2099

A2100

A2101

A2102

A2103

A2104

A2105

A2106

A2107

A2108

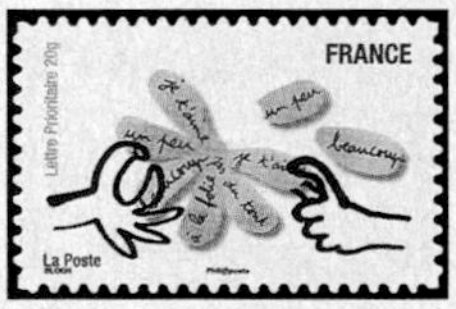

A2109

Cartoons With Letters A2110

Serpentine Die Cut 11
2010, Oct. 11 Photo.
Booklet Stamps
Self-Adhesive

3888 A2099 (58c) multi 1.75 .60
3889 A2100 (58c) multi 1.75 .60
3890 A2101 (58c) multi 1.75 .60
3891 A2102 (58c) multi 1.75 .60
3892 A2103 (58c) multi 1.75 .60
3893 A2104 (58c) multi 1.75 .60
3894 A2105 (58c) multi 1.75 .60
3895 A2106 (58c) multi 1.75 .60
3896 A2107 (58c) multi 1.75 .60
3897 A2108 (58c) multi 1.75 .60
3898 A2109 (58c) multi 1.75 .60
3899 A2110 (58c) multi 1.75 .60
a. Booklet pane of 12, #3888-3899 21.00
Nos. 3888-3899 (12) 21.00 7.20

Aviation Pioneers — A2111

Designs: Nos. 3900, 3902, Elise Deroche (1882-1919).

No. 3901: a, Hubert Latham (1883-1912). b, Orville (1871-1948) and Wilbur Wright (1867-1912). c, Henry Farman (1874-1958). d, Jules Védrines (1881-1919). e, Léon Delagrange (1872-1910).

2010, Oct. 15 Photo. ***Perf. 13***
3900 A2111 58c multi 1.75 .60
3901 Sheet of 6, #3900, 3901a-3901e 15.00 15.00
a.-e. A2111 58c Any single 2.50 2.50

Self-Adhesive
Serpentine Die Cut 11

3902 A2111 58c multi 1.75 1.75

No. 3901 sold for € 5.40, with the Red Cross receiving €1.92 of that.

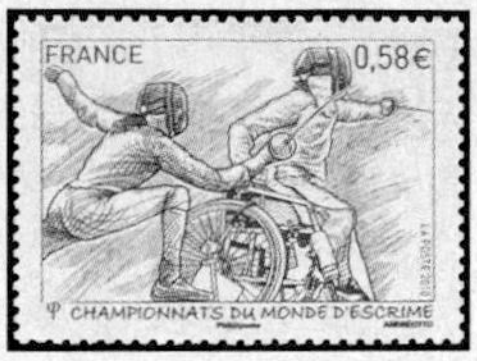

World Fencing Championships, Paris — A2112

Designs: 58c, Wheelchair fencing. 87c, Fencing.

2010, Oct. 22 Engr. ***Perf. 13x13¼***
3903 A2112 58c multi 1.75 .60
3904 A2112 87c multi 2.50 .85
a. Horiz. pair, #3903-3904 + central label 4.25 1.50

Paris Bar Association, Bicent. — A2113

2010, Oct. 28 Photo. ***Perf. 13¼***
3905 A2113 58c black & lt blue 1.75 .60

Self-Adhesive
Serpentine Die Cut 11

3906 A2113 58c black & lt blue 1.75 1.75

Villeneuve-sur-Lot — A2114

2010, Oct. 30 Engr. ***Perf. 13¼***
3907 A2114 58c multi 1.75 .60

European Capitals Type of 2002
Miniature Sheet

No. 3908 — Attractions in Paris: a, Arc de Triomphe de l'Etoile. b, Notre Dame Cathedral. c, Garnier Opera House. d, Eiffel Tower, vert.

Perf. 13x13¼, 13¼x13 (#3908d)
2010, Nov. 4 Photo.
3908 A1622 Sheet of 4 7.00 7.00
a.-d. 58c Any single 1.75 .60

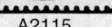

A2115

A2116

A2117

A2118

A2119

A2120

A2121

A2122

A2123

A2124

A2125

A2126

A2127

"Best Wishes" — A2128

Serpentine Die Cut 11

2010, Nov. 5 Photo.

Booklet Stamps

Self-Adhesive

3909	A2115	(58c)	multi	1.75	.60
3910	A2116	(58c)	multi	1.75	.60
3911	A2117	(58c)	multi	1.75	.60
3912	A2118	(58c)	multi	1.75	.60
3913	A2119	(58c)	multi	1.75	.60
3914	A2120	(58c)	multi	1.75	.60
3915	A2121	(58c)	multi	1.75	.60
3916	A2122	(58c)	multi	1.75	.60
3917	A2123	(58c)	multi	1.75	.60
3918	A2124	(58c)	multi	1.75	.60
3919	A2125	(58c)	multi	1.75	.60
3920	A2126	(58c)	multi	1.75	.60
3921	A2127	(58c)	multi	1.75	.60
3922	A2128	(58c)	multi	1.75	.60
a.	Booklet pane of 14, #3909-3922, + 14 stickers			24.50	
	Nos. 3909-3922 (14)			24.50	8.40

A souvenir sheet containing one perf. 13x13¼ example of No. 3915 with water-activated gum sold for €3.

First French Revenue Stamp, 150th Anniv. — A2129

Serpentine Die Cut 6¾ Vert.

2010, Nov. 6 Engr.

Booklet Stamp

Self-Adhesive

3923	A2129	(58c)	brown	1.60	.40
a.	Booklet pane of 12, 6 each #3471, 3923			19.50	

Souvenir Sheet

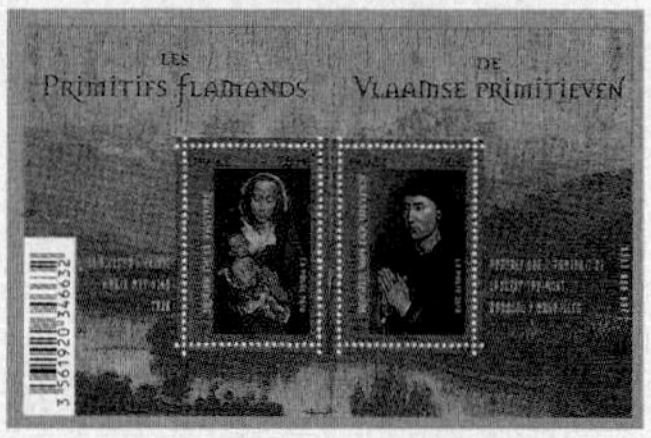
Primitive Flemish Paintings — A2130

No. 3924: a, Madonna and Child, by Roger de la Pasture. b, Portrait of Laurent Froimont, by Rogier van der Weyden.

2010, Nov. 6 Photo. *Perf. 13*

3924	A2130	Sheet of 2	10.00	10.00
a.-b.	€1.80 Either single		5.00	2.50

See Belgium No. 2478.

Independence Movements of Latin America and the Caribbean, Bicent. — A2131

2010, Nov. 27 *Perf. 13¼*

3925	A2131	87c multi	2.40	.80

Hearts A2132

Designs: 58c, Multicolored outlines of hearts. 95c, Red heart.

Photo., Photo. With Foil Application (95c)

2011, Jan. 7 *Perf. 13*

3926	A2132	58c multi	1.60	.55
a.	Sheet of 5		8.00	8.00
3927	A2132	95c black & red	2.60	.85

Self-Adhesive

Serpentine Die Cut

3928	A2132	58c multi	1.60	1.60
3929	A2132	95c black & red	2.60	2.60

New Year 2011 (Year of the Rabbit) — A2133

2011, Jan. 14 Photo. *Perf. 13¼x13*

3930	A2133	58c multi	1.60	.55

No. 3930 was printed in sheets of 5. A souvenir sheet of 1 sold for €3.

Mulhouse Tram-Train A2134

2011, Jan. 14 Engr. *Perf. 13¼*

3931	A2134	58c multi	1.60	.55

Fabric Designs A2135

Fabric designs from: Nos. 3932, 3936, French Polynesia. Nos. 3933, 3942, Japan. No. 3934, France, from 1780. No. 3935, Ivory Coast. No. 3937, Italy. No. 3938, Iran. No. 3939, Egypt. No. 3940, India. No. 3941, China. No. 3943, Peru. No. 3944, Morocco. No. 3945, France, from First Empire period.

Serpentine Die Cut 11

2011, Jan. 21 Photo.

Self-Adhesive

With Faint Blue Dots Behind Type in Area Below Vignette

3932	A2135	(58c)	multi	1.60	1.60
3933	A2135	(58c)	multi	1.60	1.60

Booklet Stamps

Without Dots Behind Type In Area Below Vignette

3934	A2135	(58c)	multi	1.60	.55
3935	A2135	(58c)	multi	1.60	.55
3936	A2135	(58c)	multi	1.60	.55
3937	A2135	(58c)	multi	1.60	.55
3938	A2135	(58c)	multi	1.60	.55
3939	A2135	(58c)	multi	1.60	.55
3940	A2135	(58c)	multi	1.60	.55
3941	A2135	(58c)	multi	1.60	.55
3942	A2135	(58c)	multi	1.60	.55
3943	A2135	(58c)	multi	1.60	.55
3944	A2135	(58c)	multi	1.60	.55
3945	A2135	(58c)	multi	1.60	.55
a.	Booklet pane of 12, #3934-3945			19.50	
	Nos. 3934-3945 (12)			19.20	6.60

Marie Curie (1867-1934), Chemist A2136

2011, Jan. 27 Engr. *Perf. 13¼*

3946	A2136	87c red & dk blue	2.40	.80

Self-Adhesive

Serpentine Die Cut 11

3947	A2136	87c red & dk blue	2.40	2.40

Intl. Year of Chemistry.

Art Issue

Plongée, by Jean Bazaine — A2137

Le Kiosque des Noctambules, Sculpture by Jean-Michel Othoniel — A2138

Buddha, by Odilon Redon A2139

Dying Centaur, Sculpture, by Antoine Bourdelle (1861-1929) — A2140

The Three Nymphs, Sculpture by Aristide Maillol (1861-1944) — A2140a

2011 Photo. *Perf. 13x13¼*

3948	A2137	87c multi	2.50	1.25

Perf. 13¼x13

3949	A2138	€1.40 multi	3.75	1.90
3950	A2139	€1.40 multi	3.75	1.90
	Nos. 3948-3950 (3)		10.00	5.05

Souvenir Sheet

Engr.

3951		Sheet of 2	6.50	6.50
a.	A2140 89c multi		2.50	1.25
b.	A2140a €1.45 multi		4.00	2.00

Self-Adhesive

Serpentine Die Cut 11

3952	A2137	87c multi	2.50	2.50
3953	A2138	€1.40 multi	3.75	3.75
3954	A2139	€1.40 multi	3.75	3.75
3955	A2140	89c multi	2.50	2.50
3955A	A2140a	€1.45 multi	4.00	4.00
	Nos. 3952-3955A (5)		16.50	16.50

Issued: Nos. 3948, 3952, 3/18; Nos. 3949, 3953, 2/11; Nos. 3950, 3954, 4/1; Nos. 3951, 3955, 3955A, 11/4.

Marianne and Hand Planting Seedling A2141

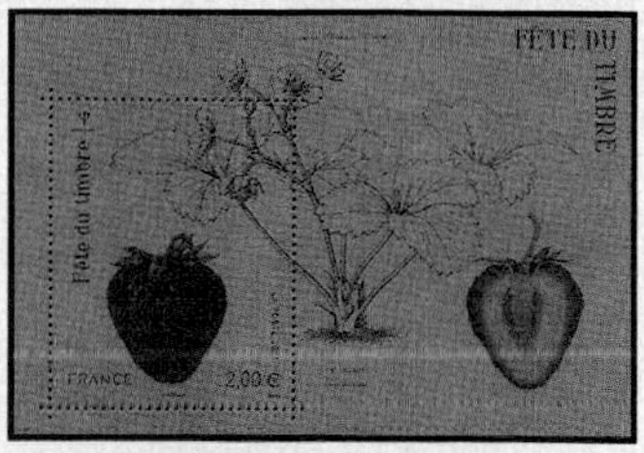
Strawberry and Strawberry Plant — A2142

2011, Feb. 26 Engr. *Perf. 13*

3956 A2141 58c multi 1.75 .60

Souvenir Sheet

Photo. & Engr.

Perf. 13¼x13

3957 A2142 €2 multi 5.75 3.00

Stamp Day. No. 3957 has printing and a strawberry-scented scratch-and-sniff panel on the reverse.

Hand Planting Seedling A2143

Leaf on Edge of Cliff A2144

Flora and Earth A2145

Hedgehog and Plants A2146

Field A2147

Tree With Various Fruits A2148

Man Carrying Earth in Wheelbarrow — A2149

Heart-shaped Plants in Flower Pots — A2150

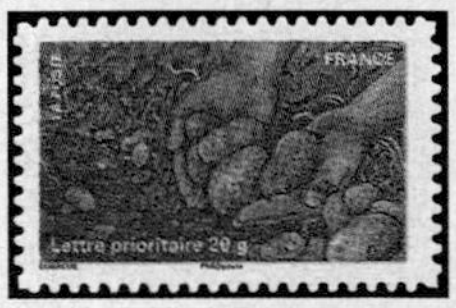

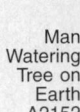

Hands Holding Potatoes A2151

Man Watering Tree on Earth A2152

Earth on Plant A2153

Farmer's Field and House A2154

Serpentine Die Cut 11

2011, Feb. 26 Photo.

Self-Adhesive

Smooth, Glossy Paper

3958 A2143 (58c) multi 1.75 1.75
3959 A2144 (58c) multi 1.75 1.75
3960 A2145 (58c) multi 1.75 1.75
Nos. 3958-3960 (3) 5.25 5.25

Booklet Stamps

Rough, Textured Paper

3961 A2143 (58c) multi 1.75 .60
3962 A2144 (58c) multi 1.75 .60
3963 A2146 (58c) multi 1.75 .60
3964 A2147 (58c) multi 1.75 .60
3965 A2148 (58c) multi 1.75 .60
3966 A2149 (58c) multi 1.75 .60
3967 A2150 (58c) multi 1.75 .60
3968 A2151 (58c) multi 1.75 .60
3969 A2152 (58c) multi 1.75 .60
3970 A2153 (58c) multi 1.75 .60
3971 A2154 (58c) multi 1.75 .60
3972 A2145 (58c) multi 1.75 .60
a. Booklet pane of 12, #3961-3972 21.00
Nos. 3961-3972 (12) 21.00 7.20

Stamp Day.

Tristan Corbière (1845-75), Poet A2155

2011, Mar. 4 Engr. *Perf. 13*

3973 A2155 75c multi 2.10 .70

Art of Miss.Tic (Radhia de Ruiter) A2156

Woman and text: No. 3974, Femme de lêtre. No. 3975, Je suis la votelle du mot voyou. No. 3976, Femme de tête mais l'esprit de corps. No. 3977, Tout achever sauf le désir. No. 3978, Soyons heureuses en attendant le bonneur. No. 3979, Je crois en l'éternel féminin. No. 3980, L'homme est le passé de la femme. No. 3981, Le masculin l'emporte mais où? No. 3982, Je ne me suis pas laissé défaire. No. 3983, Mieux que rien c'est pas assez. No. 3984, Il fait un temps de chienne. No. 3985, Cueillir l'éros de la vie.

Serpentine Die Cut 11

2011, Mar. 8 Photo.

Booklet Stamps

Self-Adhesive

3974 A2156 (58c) black & red 1.75 .60
3975 A2156 (58c) black & red 1.75 .60
3976 A2156 (58c) black & red 1.75 .60
3977 A2156 (58c) black & red 1.75 .60
3978 A2156 (58c) black & red 1.75 .60
3979 A2156 (58c) black & red 1.75 .60
3980 A2156 (58c) black & red 1.75 .60
3981 A2156 (58c) black & red 1.75 .60
3982 A2156 (58c) black & red 1.75 .60
3983 A2156 (58c) black & red 1.75 .60
3984 A2156 (58c) black & red 1.75 .60
3985 A2156 (58c) black & red 1.75 .60
a. Booklet pane of 12, #3974-3985 21.00
Nos. 3974-3985 (12) 21.00 7.20

Intl. Women's Day.

European Capitals Type of 2002

Miniature Sheet

No. 3986 — Attractions in Budapest: a, Parliament. b, Pont des Chaînes (Chain Bridge). c, Royal Palace. d, Bains Széchenyi (Szechenyi Baths), vert.

Perf. 13x13¼, 13¼x13 (#3986d)

2011, Mar. 25 Photo.

3986 A1622 Sheet of 4 7.00 7.00
a.-d. (58c) Any single 1.75 .60

Tourism Issue

Angers A2157

Wooden Bridge, Crest A2158

Autun — A2159

Varengeville-sur-Mer — A2160

Notre Dame Church, Royan — A2161

2011 Engr. *Perf. 13¼*

3987 A2157 58c multi 1.75 .60
3988 A2158 58c multi 1.75 .60

Perf. 13

3989 A2159 58c multi 1.75 .60

Perf. 13¼

3990 A2160 58c multi 1.75 .60
3991 A2161 60c multi 1.75 .60
Nos. 3987-3991 (5) 8.75 3.00

Issued: No. 3990, 6/24. No. 3991, 10/23.

Gothic Houses of Worship A2162

Designs: Nos. 3992, 4001, Notre Dame Cathedral, Strasbourg. Nos. 3993, 4002, Notre Dame Cathedral, Amiens. Nos. 3994, 4005, Sainte-Chapelle, Paris. No. 3995, St. Etienne Cathedral, Sens. No. 3996, Notre Dame Cathedral, Chartres. No. 3997, Notre Dame Cathedral, Laon. No. 3998, St. Etienne Cathedral, Metz. No. 3999, St. Pierre Cathedral, Beauvais. No. 4000, St. Etienne Cathedral, Bourges. No. 4003, Notre Dame Cathedral, Bayeux. No. 4004, Notre Dame Cathedral, Rouen. No. 4006, St. Denis Basilica, Saint-Denis.

Serpentine Die Cut 11

2011, Apr. 15 Litho.

3992 A2162 (58c) multi 1.75 1.75
3993 A2162 (58c) multi 1.75 1.75
3994 A2162 (58c) multi 1.75 1.75
Nos. 3992-3994 (3) 5.25 5.25

Photo.

Booklet Stamps

3995 A2162 (58c) multi 1.75 .60
3996 A2162 (58c) multi 1.75 .60
3997 A2162 (58c) multi 1.75 .60
3998 A2162 (58c) multi 1.75 .60
3999 A2162 (58c) multi 1.75 .60
4000 A2162 (58c) multi 1.75 .60
4001 A2162 (58c) multi 1.75 .60
4002 A2162 (58c) multi 1.75 .60
4003 A2162 (58c) multi 1.75 .60
4004 A2162 (58c) multi 1.75 .60
4005 A2162 (58c) multi 1.75 .60
4006 A2162 (58c) multi 1.75 .60
a. Booklet pane of 12, #3995-4006 21.00
Nos. 3995-4006 (12) 21.00 7.20

On lithographed stamps, "Phil@poste" is sharp and crisp, while on photogravure stamps it is muddy and unclear.

Dogs A2163

Designs: No. 4007, Labrador retriever. No. 4008a, Berger allemand (German shepherd), vert. 75c, Caniche (poodle). 95c, Yorkshire terrier, vert.

Perf. 13¼, 13¼x13¼x12¾x13¼ (#4008b)

2011, Apr. 28 Photo.

4007 A2163 58c multi 1.75 .60
4008 Sheet of 4, #4008a-4008c, 4007 8.50 8.50
a. A2163 58c multi 1.75 .60
b. A2163 75c multi 2.25 .75
c. A2163 95c multi 2.75 .90

Souvenir Sheet

Reims Cathedral, 800th Anniv. — A2164

No. 4009 — Stained-glass window depicting: a, King. b, Saint and man.

2011, May 6 Engr. *Perf.*

4009 A2164 Sheet of 2 4.25 4.25
a. 58c multi 1.75 .60
b. 87c multi 2.50 .85

A souvenir sheet containing Nos. 4009a-4009b with a different sheet margin sold for €3.

Europa A2165

2011, May 8 Photo. *Perf. 13¼*

4010 A2165 75c multi 2.10 .70

Self-Adhesive

Serpentine Die Cut 11

4011 A2165 75c multi 2.10 2.10

Intl. Year of Forests.

Claude Bourgelat (1712-79), Founder of World's First Veterinary School A2166

2011, May 14 Engr. *Perf. 13¼*

4012 A2166 58c dark blue 1.75 .60

Self-Adhesive

Serpentine Die Cut 11

4013 A2166 58c dark blue 1.75 1.75

Regional Festivals and Traditions A2167

Inscriptions and location: Nos. 4014, 4018, La Braderie, Lille. Nos. 4015, 4033, La Saint-Vincent Tournante, Bourgogne. No. 4016, Le Théâtre des Cabotans, Amiens. No. 4017, Le Feu d'Artifices du 14 Juillet, Paris. No. 4019, Les Médiévales, Provins. No. 4020, La Bénédiction de la Mer, Port-en-Bessin-Huppain. No. 4021, La Fête du Hareng, Haute-Normandie. No. 4022, La Fête des Brodeuses, Pont-l'Abbé. No. 4023, La Fête des Chalands Fleuris, Saint-André-des-Eaux. No. 4024, La Force Basque, Biarritz, Hendaye and Esplette. No. 4025, Les Nuits Romanes, Poitou-Charentes. No. 4026, La Sardane, Céret. No. 4027, La Fête de la Transhumance, Midi-Pyrénées. No. 4028, La Saint Nicolas, Lorraine. No. 4029, Le Mariage de l'Ami Fritz, Marlenheim. No. 4030, Les Fêtes Johanniques, Reims. No. 4031, Les Soufflaculs, Saint-Claude. No. 4032, La Fête de l'Estive, allanche. No. 4034, La Foire aux Potirons, Tranzault. No. 4035, La Frairie des Petits Ventres, Limoges. No. 4036, La Fête du Citron, Menton. No. 4037, La Fête des Lumières, Lyon. No. 4038, L'Abolition de l'Esclavage, Réunion. No. 4039, Les Chants Corses, Corsica.

2011 Litho. *Serpentine Die Cut 11*

Self-Adhesive

4014 A2167 (58c) multi 1.75 1.75
4015 A2167 (58c) multi 1.75 1.75

Photo.

Booklet Stamps

4016 A2167 (58c) multi 1.75 .60
4017 A2167 (58c) multi 1.75 .60
4018 A2167 (58c) multi 1.75 .60
4019 A2167 (58c) multi 1.75 .60
a. Booklet pane of 4, #4016-4019 7.00
4020 A2167 (58c) multi 1.75 .60
4021 A2167 (58c) multi 1.75 .60
4022 A2167 (58c) multi 1.75 .60
4023 A2167 (58c) multi 1.75 .60
a. Booklet pane of 4, #4020-4023 7.00
4024 A2167 (58c) multi 1.75 .60
4025 A2167 (58c) multi 1.75 .60
4026 A2167 (58c) multi 1.75 .60
4027 A2167 (58c) multi 1.75 .60
a. Booklet pane of 4, #4024-4027 7.00
Complete booklet, #4019a, 4023a, 4027a 21.00
4028 A2167 (58c) multi 1.75 .60
4029 A2167 (58c) multi 1.75 .60
4030 A2167 (58c) multi 1.75 .60
4031 A2167 (58c) multi 1.75 .60
a. Booklet pane of 4, #4028-4031 7.00
4032 A2167 (58c) multi 1.75 .60
4033 A2167 (58c) multi 1.75 .60
4034 A2167 (58c) multi 1.75 .60
4035 A2167 (58c) multi 1.75 .60
a. Booklet pane of 4, #4032-4035 7.00
4036 A2167 (58c) multi 1.75 .60
4037 A2167 (58c) multi 1.75 .60
4038 A2167 (58c) multi 1.75 .60
4039 A2167 (58c) multi 1.75 .60
a. Booklet pane of 4, #4036-4039 7.00
Complete booklet, #4031a, 4035a, 4039a 21.00
Nos. 4016-4039 (24) 42.00 14.40

The black text on No. 4014 is sharper than that on No. 4018. The black text on No. 4015 is sharper than that on No. 4033.

Issued: No. 4014, 6/30, Nos. 4016-4039, 5/28.

French Federation of Philatelic Associations 84th Congress, Metz — A2168

2011, June 10 Engr. *Perf. 13x13¼*

4040 A2168 58c multi + label 1.75 .60

A souvenir sheet containing No. 4040 was issued in 2012 and sold fro €3.

Miniature Sheet

Bicycles — A2169

No. 4041 — Inscriptions: a, Bicyclette à Pneumatiques. b, Draisenne, horiz. c, Vélocipède à Pédales, horiz. d, Vélo de Ville, horiz. e, Bicyclette à Chaine, horiz. f, Grand Bi.

Litho. & Engr.

2011, June 17 *Perf. 13*

4041 A2169 Sheet of 6 10.50 10.50
a.-f. 58c Any single 1.75 .60

Pres. Georges Pompidou (1911-74), and Pompidou Center, Paris A2170

2011, June 22 Engr. *Perf. 13¼*

4042 A2170 58c gray grn & brt bl 1.75 .60

Train des Pignes, Provence, Cent. A2171

2011, June 24

4043 A2171 58c multi 1.75 .60

Organization for Economic Cooperation and Development, 50th Anniv. — A2172

2011, June 24 Photo.

4044 A2172 87c multi 2.50 .85

World Judo Championships, Paris — A2173

2011, July 1 *Perf. 13x12¾*

4045 A2173 89c multi 2.50 .85

Aquilegia A2174

Tulipa Sp. A2175

Bellis Perennis A2176

Primula Veris A2177

2011, July 1 Litho. *Perf. 13*

4046 A2174 (38c) multi 1.10 .25
4047 A2175 (39c) multi 1.10 .25
4048 A2176 (46c) multi 1.40 .30
4049 A2177 (47c) multi 1.40 .30
Nos. 4046-4049 (4) 5.00 1.10

Nos. 4046-4049 are known only precanceled. See note after No. 132.

Compare with Nos. 3423-3426.

"Ecopli 20g" — A2178

"Lettre Prioritaire 20g" — A2179

"Europe 20g" — A2180

"Monde 20g" — A2181

"Lettre Prioritaire 50g" A2182

"Lettre Prioritaire 100g" A2183

"Lettre Prioritaire 250g" — A2184

Engr., Litho. (#4057a-4057d)

2011 *Perf. 13*

4050 A2178 (55c) gray 1.60 .25
4051 A2179 (60c) red 1.75 .40
4052 A2180 (77c) dark blue 2.25 .60
4053 A2181 (89c) purple 2.50 .65
4054 A2182 (€1) fawn 3.00 .75
4055 A2183 (€1.45) red violet 4.25 1.10
4056 A2184 (€2.40) chocolate 6.75 2.40
Nos. 4050-4056 (7) 22.10 6.15

Souvenir Sheet

4057 Sheet of 7, #4050-4052, 4057a-4057d, + label 21.50 21.50
a. A2181 (89c) purple, litho. 2.50 2.50
b. A2182 (€1) fawn, litho. 2.75 2.75
c. A2183 (€1.45) red violet, litho. 4.00 4.00
d. A2184 (€2.40) chocolate, litho. 6.75 6.75

Coil Stamps

Perf. 13 Horiz.

4058 A2179 (60c) red 1.75 .40
4059 A2180 (77c) blue 2.25 .60

Self-Adhesive

Serpentine Die Cut 6¾ Vert.

4060 A2178 (55c) gray 1.60 1.60
4061 A2179 (60c) red 1.75 1.75
a. Booklet pane of 12 21.00
b. Booklet pane of 20 35.00
c. Booklet pane of 10 17.50
4062 A2180 (77c) blue 2.25 2.25
a. Booklet pane of 12 27.00
4063 A2181 (89c) purple 2.50 2.50
4064 A2182 (€1) fawn 3.00 3.00
4065 A2183 (€1.45) red violet 4.25 4.25
4066 A2184 (€2.40) chocolate 6.75 6.75
Nos. 4060-4066 (7) 22.10 22.10

Issued: Nos. 4050-4056, Nos. 4060-4066, 7/1; No. 4057, 11/3; Nos. 4058-4059, 7/6; No. 4061a, 7/1; Nos. 4061b-4061c, 4/16/12; No. 4062a, 8/16. See Nos. 4089-4090.

G20 and G8 Summits, Cannes and Deauville A2185

2011, July 8 Photo. *Perf. 12¼*

4067 A2185 89c multi 2.50 .85

Self-Adhesive

Serpentine Die Cut 11

4068 A2185 89c multl 2.50 2.50

A2186

2011 Rugby World Cup, New Zealand A2187

No. 4069: a, Player with ball behind scrum. b, Player carrying ball, vert. c, Auckland skyline, vert. d, Lake and mountains, New Zealand.

€5, Two players.

Perf. 13¼x13, 13x13¼

2011, July 8 Photo.

4069 A2186 Sheet of 4 10.00 10.00
a.-d. 89c Any single 2.50 .85

Embossed and Etched on Silver

Self-Adhesive

Die Cut Perf. 12¾

4070 A2187 €5 silver 14.00 14.00

Protection of Water Type of 2010

Serpentine Die Cut 11

2011, Sept. 9 Litho.

Self-Adhesive

4071 A2058 (60c) Like #3782 1.75 1.75
4072 A2058 (60c) Like #3787 1.75 1.75

Nos. 4071-4072 have a dot structure not found on Nos. 3782 and 3787, which are printed by photogravure.

Souvenir Sheet

Gardens — A2188

No. 4073: a, Cheverny Gardens. b, Villandry Gardens.

2011, Sept. 16 Photo. ***Perf. 13¼x13***

4073 A2188 Sheet of 2 13.00 13.00
a.-b. €2.40 Either single 6.50 3.25

Salon du Timbre 2012.

Firefighters of Paris, Bicent. — A2189

No. 4074: a, Horse-drawn fire wagon (38x38mm). b, Fireman holding hose (26x40mm). c, Firemen attending to victim on gurney, ambulance (26x40mm). d, Fireman with rescue dog (30x40mm). e, Firefighter's badge (26x40mm). f, Firemen in truck holding flag, Arc de Triomphe (26x40mm). g, Fireman wearing helmet without visor (30x40mm). h, Firemen in antique fire truck (40x26mm). i, Fireman and modern ladder truck (40x26mm). j, j, Fireman wearing helmet with visor (30x40mm).

Perf. 13, 13¼ (#4074a), 13¼x13 (#4074d, 4074g, 4074j)

2011, Sept. 16

4074 A2189 Sheet of 10 17.50 17.50
a.-j. 60c Any single 1.75 .60

Self-Adhesive

Serpentine Die Cut 11

4075 A2189 60c Like #4074b 1.75 1.75
4076 A2189 60c Like #4074i 1.75 1.75

A set of six souvenir sheets, each containing one example of Nos. 4074a, 4074b, 4074f, 4074h, 4074i, and 4074j, sold for €15.

TGV Train Service, 30th Anniv. A2190

2011, Sept. 27 ***Perf. 13¼***

4077 A2190 60c multi 1.75 .60

Self-Adhesive

Serpentine Die Cut 11

4078 A2190 60c multi 1.75 1.75

A2191 A2192

Marianne, Stars and Leaf
A2193 A2194

2011, Sept. 30 Engr. ***Perf. 13***

4079 A2191 (57c) green 1.60 .25
4080 A2192 (95c) yellow green 2.60 .55
4081 A2193 (€1.40) blue green 4.00 .80
4082 A2194 (€2.30) dk bl green 6.25 1.25
Nos. 4079-4082 (4) 14.45 2.85

Coil Stamp

Perf. 13 Horiz.

4083 A2191 (57c) green 1.60 .25

Self-Adhesive

Serpentine Die Cut 6¾ Vert.

4084 A2191 (57c) green 1.60 1.60
a. Booklet pane of 10 16.00
b. Booklet pane of 12 19.50
c. Booklet pane of 20 32.00
4085 A2192 (95c) yellow green 2.60 2.60
4086 A2193 (€1.40) blue green 4.00 4.00
4087 A2194 (€2.30) dk bl green 6.25 6.25

Serpentine Die Cut 6¾ Horiz.

4088 A2191 (57c) green 1.60 .40
Nos. 4084-4088 (5) 16.05 14.85

Marianne and Stars Types of 2011

Serpentine Die Cut 6¾ Horiz.

2011, Oct. 1 Engr.

Coil Stamps
Self-Adhesive

4089 A2179 (60c) red 1.75 .40
4090 A2180 (77c) dark blue 2.10 .60

Souvenir Sheet

World Weight Lifting Championships, Paris — A2195

No. 4091: a, Male weight lifter (43mm diameter). b, Female weight lifter (49mm diameter).

2011, Oct. 7 Photo. ***Perf.***

4091 A2195 Sheet of 2 4.25 4.25
a. 60c multi 1.75 .60
b. 89c multi 2.50 .85

Souvenir Sheets

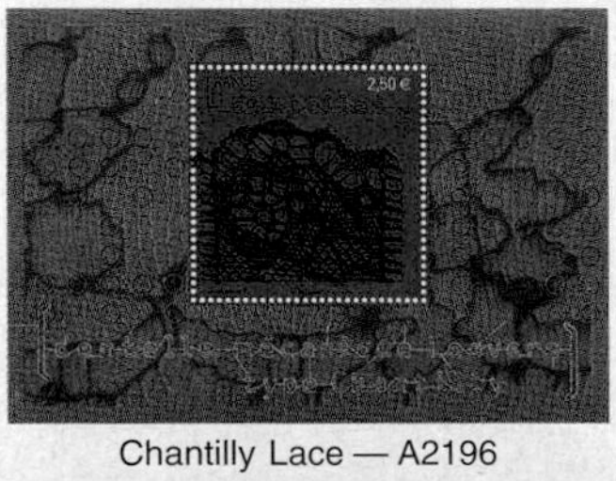

Chantilly Lace — A2196

Lace of Puy-en-Velay Region — A2197

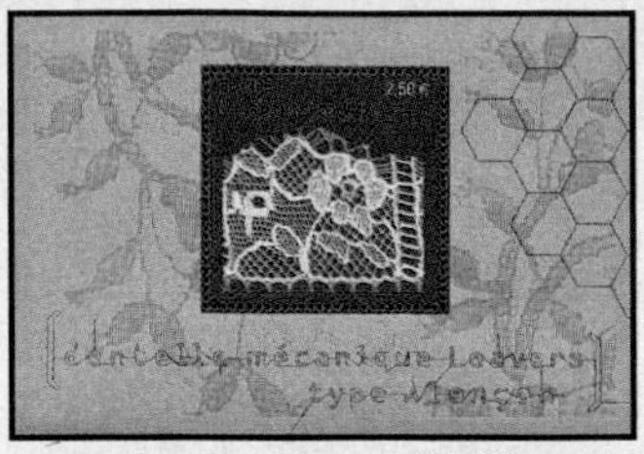

Alençon Lace — A2198

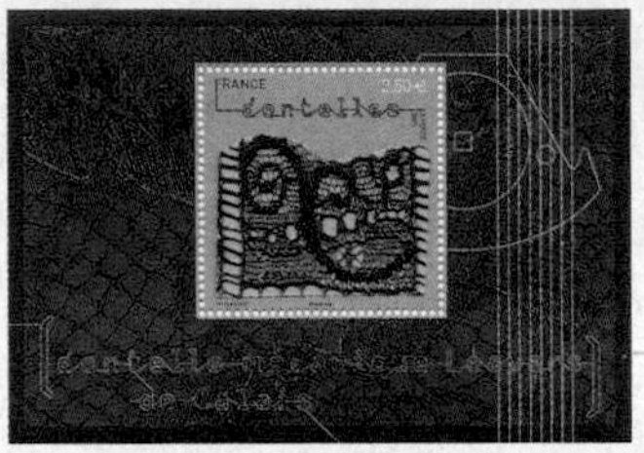

Calais Lace — A2199

Litho. with Lace Affixed

2011, Oct. 8

4092 A2196 €2.50 multi 7.00 7.00
4093 A2197 €2.50 multi 7.00 7.00
4094 A2198 €2.50 multi 7.00 7.00
4095 A2199 €2.50 multi 7.00 7.00
Nos. 4092-4095 (4) 28.00 28.00

National Center for Space Studies, 50th Anniv. A2200

2011, Oct. 12 Engr. ***Perf. 13¼***

4096 A2200 60c multi 1.75 .60

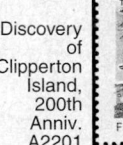

Discovery of Clipperton Island, 200th Anniv. A2201

2011, Oct. 21

4097 A2201 €1 multi 2.75 .90

Second-Place Finish of French Team in 2011 Rugby World Cup Championships — A2202

2011, Oct. 23 Photo.

4098 A2202 60c multi 1.75 .60

Values are for stamp with surrounding selvage.

Words of Ben A2203

"Ben" (artist Benjamin Vautier) and inscription: No. 4099, Je suis timbré. No. 4100, J'aime écrire. No. 4101, Les mots c'est la vie. No. 4102, Entre nous. . . No. 4103, Cette idée. . . voyage. No. 4104, Pour l'instant tout va bien. No. 4105, Enfin de l'art. No. 4106, J'ai quelque chose à dire. No. 4107, Mots d'amour. No. 4108, Ceci est un lettre. No. 4109, Garderem lo moral. No. 4110, Vous êtes formidables!

Serpentine Die Cut 11

2011, Oct. 24 Photo.

Booklet Stamps
Self-Adhesive

4099 A2203 (60c) multi 1.75 .60
4100 A2203 (60c) multi 1.75 .60
4101 A2203 (60c) multi 1.75 .60
4102 A2203 (60c) multi 1.75 .60
4103 A2203 (60c) multi 1.75 .60
4104 A2203 (60c) multi 1.75 .60
4105 A2203 (60c) multi 1.75 .60
4106 A2203 (60c) multi 1.75 .60
4107 A2203 (60c) multi 1.75 .60
4108 A2203 (60c) multi 1.75 .60
4109 A2203 (60c) multi 1.75 .60
4110 A2203 (60c) multi 1.75 .60
a. Booklet pane of 12, #4099-4110 21.00
Nos. 4099-4110 (12) 21.00 7.20

Compare with type A1667.

Gaston Monnerville (1897-1991), Senate President A2204

2011, Nov. 7 Engr. ***Perf. 13¼***

4111 A2204 60c multi 1.75 .60

Henri Mouhot (1826-61), Explorer of Southeast Asia A2205

2011, Nov. 7

4112 A2205 89c multi 2.50 .85

Christmas A2206

Paintings: No. 4113, Adoration of the Shepherds, by Robert Campin, Master of Flémalle. No. 4114, Adoration of the Shepherds, by Mathias Stormer. No. 4115, The Newborn, by Georges de La Tour. No. 4116, Adoration of the Magi, by Italian School artist. No. 4117, Adoration of the Magi, by Francisco de Zurbaran. No. 4118, Nativity, by Jean Fouquet. No. 4119, Nativity, by the Master of the Nativity in the Louvre. No. 4120, Triptych of the Adoration of the Magi, by the Master of 1518. No. 4121, Adoration of the Magi, by Peter Paul Rubens. No. 4122, Adoration of the Infant Jesus, by the Master of Moulins. No. 4123, Adoration of the Child, by the Master of the St. Bartholomew Altarpiece. No. 4124, Scenes from the Life of Christ - Nativity, by Mariotto di Nardo.

Serpentine Die Cut 11

2011, Nov. 7 Photo.

Booklet Stamps
Self-Adhesive

4113 A2206 (60c) multi 1.75 .60
4114 A2206 (60c) multi 1.75 .60
4115 A2206 (60c) multi 1.75 .60
4116 A2206 (60c) multi 1.75 .60
4117 A2206 (60c) multi 1.75 .60
4118 A2206 (60c) multi 1.75 .60
4119 A2206 (60c) multi 1.75 .60
4120 A2206 (60c) multi 1.75 .60
4121 A2206 (60c) multi 1.75 .60
4122 A2206 (60c) multi 1.75 .60
4123 A2206 (60c) multi 1.75 .60
4124 A2206 (60c) multi 1.75 .60
a. Booklet pane of 12, #4113-4124 21.00
Nos. 4113-4124 (12) 21.00 7.20

A souvenir sheet containing one perf. 13x13¼ example of No. 4115 with water-activated gum sold for €3.

Discovery of Insulin, 90th Anniv. A2207

2011, Nov. 17 Photo. *Perf. 13¼*
4125 A2207 60c multi 1.75 .60

Serpentine Die Cut 11
Self-Adhesive
4126 A2207 60c multi 1.75 .60

Year of Overseas Territories A2208

Drawings of: No. 4127, Carved rocks, Guadeloupe. No. 4128, Harbor, Cayenne, French Guiana. No. 4129, Beach scence, New Caledonia. No. 4130, Tattoo designs of tiki and compass rose, French Polynesia. No. 4131, Tree blossoms, St. Martin. No. 4132, Buildings, St. Pierre and Miquelon. No. 4133, House, Martinique. No. 4134, Man on path near Morne Langevin, Reunion. No. 4135, Plrogue, near Mt. Choungi, Mayotte. No. 4136, Building, Saint-Barthélemy. No. 4137, Kava bowl and building, Wallis and Futuna Islands. No. 4138, Penguins, French Southern and Antarctic Territories (T.A.A.F).

Serpentine Die Cut 11
2011, Nov. 25 Photo.
Booklet Stamps
Self-Adhesive

4127 A2208 (60c) multi 1.75 .60
4128 A2208 (60c) multi 1.75 .60
4129 A2208 (60c) multi 1.75 .60
4130 A2208 (60c) multi 1.75 .60
4131 A2208 (60c) multi 1.75 .60
4132 A2208 (60c) multi 1.75 .60
4133 A2208 (60c) multi 1.75 .60
4134 A2208 (60c) multi 1.75 .60
4135 A2208 (60c) multi 1.75 .60
4136 A2208 (60c) multi 1.75 .60
4137 A2208 (60c) multi 1.75 .60
4138 A2208 (60c) multi 1.75 .60
a. Booklet pane of 12, #4127-4138 21.00
Nos. 4127-4138 (12) 21.00 7.20

New Year 2012 (Year of the Dragon) A2209

2012, Jan. 6 *Perf. 13¼x13*
4139 A2209 60c multi 1.60 .55

No. 4139 was printed in sheets of 5. A souvenir sheet of one sold for €3.

A2210

Hearts A2211

2012, Jan. 13 Photo. *Perf. 13*
4140 A2210 €1 red & black 2.75 .95

Self-Adhesive
Serpentine Die Cut
4141 A2210 €1 red & black 2.75 2.75

On Plastic
4142 A2211 60c red & black 1.60 1.60
a. Souvenir sheet of 5 8.00

Brass Relief, France, 18th Cent. A2212

Bronze Relief, China, 2nd Cent. A2213

Copper and Silver Relief, Egypt, 14th Cent. A2214

Marble Relief, Andalusia, 11th Cent. A2215

Sardonyx Relief, Italy, 13th Cent. A2216

Stone Relief, Egypt, 1440 B.C. A2217

Litho., Engr. (olive gray stamps)
Serpentine Die Cut 11
2012, Jan. 20 Self-Adhesive
Booklet Stamps

4143 A2212 (60c) multi 1.60 .55
4144 A2212 (60c) olive gray 1.60 .55
4145 A2213 (60c) multi 1.60 .55
4146 A2213 (60c) olive gray 1.60 .55
4147 A2214 (60c) multi 1.60 .55
4148 A2214 (60c) olive gray 1.60 .55
4149 A2215 (60c) multi 1.60 .55
4150 A2215 (60c) olive gray 1.60 .55
4151 A2216 (60c) multi 1.60 .55
4152 A2216 (60c) olive gray 1.60 .55
4153 A2217 (60c) multi 1.60 .55
4154 A2217 (60c) olive gray 1.60 .55
a. Booklet pane of 12, #4143-4154 19.50
Nos. 4143-4154 (12) 19.20 6.60

Art Issue

Morning Sun, by Edward Hopper — A2218

2012, Feb. 3 Photo. *Perf. 13x13¼*
4155 A2218 €1.45 multi 4.00 2.00

Self-Adhesive
Serpentine Die Cut 11
4156 A2218 €1.45 multi 4.00 4.00

Flowers — A2219

Designs: No. 4157, Arums. No. 4158, Tulips. No. 4159, Roses. No. 4160, Violets. No. 4161, Pansies (Pensée). No. 4162, Lily of the valley (Muguet). No. 4163, Irises. No. 4164, Dahlias. No. 4165, Poppies (Coquelicot). No. 4166, Peonies (Pivoine). No. 4167, Daisies (Marguerite). No. 4168, Pinks (Oeillet).

Serpentine Die Cut 11
2012, Feb. 10 Self-Adhesive
Booklet Stamps

4157 A2219 (60c) multi 1.60 .55
4158 A2219 (60c) multi 1.60 .55
4159 A2219 (60c) multi 1.60 .55
4160 A2219 (60c) multi 1.60 .55
4161 A2219 (60c) multi 1.60 .55
4162 A2219 (60c) multi 1.60 .55
4163 A2219 (60c) multi 1.60 .55
4164 A2219 (60c) multi 1.60 .55
4165 A2219 (60c) multi 1.60 .55
4166 A2219 (60c) multi 1.60 .55
4167 A2219 (60c) multi 1.60 .55
4168 A2219 (60c) multi 1.60 .55
a. Booklet pane of 12, #4157-4168 19.50
Nos. 4157-4168 (12) 19.20 6.60

Grand Mosque of Paris, 90th Anniv. — A2220

2012, Feb. 11 Engr. *Perf. 13¼*
4169 A2220 60c multi 1.60 .55

Henri Queuille (1884-1970), Prime Minister — A2221

2012, Feb. 17
4170 A2221 €1 black & brown 2.75 .95

Portraits of Women — A2222

Details of paintings: No. 4171, Young Woman in a Ball Gown, by Berthe Morisot. No. 4172, Portrait of Lydia Cassat, by Mary Cassatt. No. 4173, Biskra Woman, by Marie Caire. No. 4174, Woman with Turban, by Marie Laurencin. No. 4175, Madame Molé-Raymond, by Elisabeth Vigée-Lebrun. No. 4176, Portrait of a Young Woman, by Edgar Degas. No. 4177, Mandy, by Edouard Barnard Lintott. No. 4178, Orphan Girl at the Cemetery, by Eugène Delacroix. No. 4179, Woman with a Mirror, by Titian. No. 4180, Madeleine Bernard, by Paul Gauguin. No. 4181, Young Woman, by Hippolyte Flandrin. No. 4182, Portrait of Berthe Morisot with a Bouquet of Violets, by Edouard Manet.

Serpentine Die Cut 11
2012, Mar. 8 Photo.
Booklet Stamps
Self-Adhesive

4171 A2222 (60c) multi 1.60 .55
4172 A2222 (60c) multi 1.60 .55
4173 A2222 (60c) multi 1.60 .55
4174 A2222 (60c) multi 1.60 .55
4175 A2222 (60c) multi 1.60 .55
4176 A2222 (60c) multi 1.60 .55
4177 A2222 (60c) multi 1.60 .55
4178 A2222 (60c) multi 1.60 .55
4179 A2222 (60c) multi 1.60 .55
4180 A2222 (60c) multi 1.60 .55
4181 A2222 (60c) multi 1.60 .55
4182 A2222 (60c) multi 1.60 .55
a. Booklet pane of 12, #4171-4182 19.50
Nos. 4171-4182 (12) 19.20 6.60

European Capitals Type of 2002
Miniature Sheet

No. 4183 — Attractions in Copenhagen, Denmark: a, The Little Mermaid statue. b, Amalienborg Palace, horiz. c, Rosenborg Castle. d, Nyhavn, horiz.

Perf. 13¼x13, 13x13¼ (horiz. stamps)
2012, Mar. 23 Photo.
4183 A1622 Sheet of 4 6.50 6.50
a.-d. 60c Any single 1.60 .55

Tourism Issue

Moulins — A2223

2012, Mar. 23 Engr. *Perf. 13x12¾*
4184 A2223 60c multi 1.60 .55

Miniature Sheet

Way of St. James — A2224

No. 4185: a, Via Turonensis in Paris. b, Via Lemovicensis in Vézelay, horiz. c, Via Podiensis in Puy-en Velay, horiz. d, Via Tolosana in Arles.

Litho. & Engr.
2012, Mar. 30 *Perf. 13*
4185 A2224 Sheet of 4 8.50 8.50
a.-d. 77c Any single 2.10 .70

Fruits A2225

Designs: No. 4186, Pineapple (Ananas). No. 4187, Melon. No. 4188, White grapes (Raisins blancs). No. 4189, Hazel nuts (Noisettes). No. 4190, Kiwis. No. 4191, Gooseberries (Groseilles à maquereaux). No. 4192, Green papayas (Papayes vertes). No. 4193, Dates (Dattes). No. 4194, Bananas (Bananes vertes). No. 4195, Mangos (Mangues). No. 4196, Pippin apples (Pommes "Reinette grise"). No. 4197, Pear (Poire William).

Serpentine Die Cut 11
2012, Mar. 30 Photo.
Booklet Stamps
Self-Adhesive

4186 A2225 (57c) multi 1.50 .50
4187 A2225 (57c) multi 1.50 .50
4188 A2225 (57c) multi 1.50 .50
4189 A2225 (57c) multi 1.50 .50
4190 A2225 (57c) multi 1.50 .50

4191 A2225 (57c) multi 1.50 .50
4192 A2225 (57c) multi 1.50 .50
4193 A2225 (57c) multi 1.50 .50
4194 A2225 (57c) multi 1.50 .50
4195 A2225 (57c) multi 1.50 .50
4196 A2225 (57c) multi 1.50 .50
4197 A2225 (57c) multi 1.50 .50
a. Booklet pane of 12, #4186-4197 18.00
Nos. 4186-4197 (12) 18.00 6.00

Tourism Issue

Epernay A2226

2012, Apr. 13 Engr. *Perf. 13¼*
4198 A2226 60c multi 1.60 .55

Tropical Fish — A2227

Designs: No. 4199, Amphiprion ocellaris. No. 4200a, Phycodurus eques, hoirz. No. 4200b, Heniochus acuminatus, horiz. No. 4200c, Pomacanthus imperator.

2012, Apr. 20 Photo. *Perf. 13¼*
4199 A2227 60c multi 1.60 .55
4200 Sheet of 4, #4199, 4200a-4200c 8.00 8.00
a. A2227 60c multi 1.60 .55
b. A2227 77c multi 2.10 .70
c. A2227 €1 multi 2.60 .90

Art A2228

Designs: No. 4201, Douglas Castle, painting by unknown Chinese artist. No. 4202, Crab, sculpture by Cheung Yee. Nos. 4203, 4205, The Racecourse — Amateur Jockeys Close to a Carriage, painting by Edgar Degas. No. 4204, The Horse, sculpture by Raymnond Duchamp-Villon.

2012, May 3 Photo. *Perf. 13¼*
4201 A2228 60c multi 1.60 .55
4202 A2228 60c multi 1.60 .55
4203 A2228 89c multi 2.40 .80
4204 A2228 89c multi 2.40 .80
Nos. 4201-4204 (4) 8.00 2.70

Self-Adhesive
Serpentine Die Cut 11
4205 A2228 89c multi 2.40 2.40

See Hong Kong Nos. 1490-1493.

Cubist Art A2229

Designs: No. 4206, La Table Louis-Philippe, by Roger de La Fresnaye. No. 4207, Three Figures Under a Tree, by Pablo Picasso. No. 4208, The Three Poets, by Louis Marcoussis, vert. No. 4209, Still Life with a Red Ball, by Auguste Herbin, vert. No. 4210, The Blue Bird, by Jean Metzinger, vert. No. 4211, The 14th of July, by Fernand Léger, vert. No. 4212, Music, by Frantisek Kupka. No. 4213, Rugby, by André Lhote. No. 4214, The War Song, Portrait of Florent Schmitt, by Albert Gleizes, vert. No. 4215, The Book, by Juan Gris, vert. No. 4216, Compotier et Cartes, by Georges Braque, vert. No. 4217, Marine, by Lyonel Feininger, vert.

2012, May 10 *Serpentine Die Cut 11*
Booklet Stamps
Self-Adhesive

4206 A2229 (60c) multi 1.50 .50
4207 A2229 (60c) multi 1.50 .50
4208 A2229 (60c) multi 1.50 .50
4209 A2229 (60c) multi 1.50 .50
4210 A2229 (60c) multi 1.50 .50
4211 A2229 (60c) multi 1.50 .50
4212 A2229 (60c) multi 1.50 .50
4213 A2229 (60c) multi 1.50 .50
4214 A2229 (60c) multi 1.50 .50
4215 A2229 (60c) multi 1.50 .50
4216 A2229 (60c) multi 1.50 .50
4217 A2229 (60c) multi 1.50 .50
a. Booklet pane of 12, #4206-4217 18.00
Nos. 4206-4217 (12) 18.00 6.00

Pacific 231 K8 Locomotive, Cent. — A2230

2012, May 11 Engr. *Perf. 13¼*
4218 A2230 60c multi 1.50 .50

Self-Adhesive
Serpentine Die Cut 11
4219 A2230 60c multi 1.50 1.50

A souvenir sheet of one of No. 4218 sold for €3.

St. Joan of Arc (c. 1412-31) — A2231

Photo. & Engr.
2012, May 11 *Perf. 13*
4220 A2231 77c multi 2.00 .65

See Vatican City No. 1499.

Souvenir Sheet

Battle of Denain, 300th Anniv. — A2232

2012, May 12 Photo. *Perf. 13¼*
4221 A2232 77c multi 2.00 .65

Birds — A2233

Designs: No. 4222a, Little bustard (Outarde canepetière). No. 4222b, Bluethroat (Gorgebleue à miroir), horiz. No. 4222c, Osprey (Balbuzard pêcheur). Nos. 4222d, 4223, Atlantic puffin (Macareux moine).

Perf. 13¼x13, 13x13¼ (#4222b)
2012, May 12
4222 Sheet of 4 6.00 6.00
a.-d. A2233 57c Any single 1.50 .50

Self-Adhesive
Serpentine Die Cut 11
4223 A2233 57c multi 1.50 1.50

Bird Protection League, cent.

Europa — A2234

2012, May 20 Engr. *Perf. 13*
4224 A2234 77c multi 2.00 .65

Self-Adhesive
Serpentine Die Cut 11
4225 A2234 77c multi 2.00 2.00

Tourism Issue

Chateau de Suscinio A2235

2012, May 26 *Perf. 13¼*
4226 A2235 60c multi 1.50 .50

Souvenir Sheet

Saint-Cloud Park, Paris — A2236

No. 4227: a, Cascade. b, Reflecting ponds,

2012, June 9 Photo. *Perf. 13x13¼*
4227 A2236 Sheet of 2 12.00 12.00
a.-b. €2.40 Either single 6.00 3.00
c. Souvenir sheet of 4, #4073a, 4073b, 4227a, 4227b 24.00 24.00

2012 Salon du Timbre, Paris.

Historic Residences — A2237

Designs: Nos. 4228, 4245, Palais du Luxembourg, Paris. No. 4229, Château Guillaume-le-Conquérant, Falaise. No. 4230, Château des Comtes de Foix. No. 4231, Château de Boulogne sur Mer. No. 4232, Château de Saumur. No. 4233, Château d' Anjony, Tournemire. No. 4234, Château de Pompadour. No. 4235, Citadelle de Corte. No. 4236, Forteresse de Salses. No. 4237, Château d'If. No. 4238, Hôtel de Mauroy, Troyes. No. 4239, Maison Pfister, Colmar. No. 4240, Château du Taureau, Baie de Morlaix. No. 4241, Palais Ducal de Nevers. No. 4242, Château d'Azay-le-Rideau. No. 4243, Château de Puyguilhem. No. 4244, Château de Crazannes. No. 4246, Château de Vaux-le-Vicomte. No. 4247, Château de Brémontier-Merval. No. 4248, Château de Lesdiguières, Vixille. No. 4249, Château de Pierrefonds. No. 4250, Villa Palladienne de Syam. No. 4251, Maison Souques-Pagès, Pointe-à-Pitre. No. 4252, Villa Majorelle, Nancy.

Serpentine Die Cut 11
2012, June 9 Litho.
Self-Adhesive
4228 A2237 (60c) multi 1.50 1.50

Photo.
Booklet Stamps

4229 A2237 (60c) multi 1.50 .50
4230 A2237 (60c) multi 1.50 .50
4231 A2237 (60c) multi 1.50 .50
4232 A2237 (60c) multi 1.50 .50
a. Booklet pane of 4, #4229-4232 6.00
4233 A2237 (60c) multi 1.50 .50
4234 A2237 (60c) multi 1.50 .50
4235 A2237 (60c) multi 1.50 .50
4236 A2237 (60c) multi 1.50 .50
a. Booklet pane of 4, #4233-4236 6.00
4237 A2237 (60c) multi 1.50 .50
4238 A2237 (60c) multi 1.50 .50
4239 A2237 (60c) multi 1.50 .50
4240 A2237 (60c) multi 1.50 .50
a. Booklet pane of 4, #4237-4240 6.00
Complete booklet, #4232a, 4236a, 4240a 18.00
4241 A2237 (60c) multi 1.50 .50
4242 A2237 (60c) multi 1.50 .50
4243 A2237 (60c) multi 1.50 .50
4244 A2237 (60c) multi 1.50 .50
a. Booklet pane of 4, #4241-4244 6.00
4245 A2237 (60c) multi 1.50 .50
4246 A2237 (60c) multi 1.50 .50
4247 A2237 (60c) multi 1.50 .50
4248 A2237 (60c) multi 1.50 .50
a. Booklet pane of 4, #4245-4248 6.00
4249 A2237 (60c) multi 1.50 .50
4250 A2237 (60c) multi 1.50 .50
4251 A2237 (60c) multi 1.50 .50
4252 A2237 (60c) multi 1.50 .50
a. Booklet pane of 4, #4249-4252 6.00
Complete booklet, #4244a, 4248a, 4252a 18.00
Nos. 4229-4252 (24) 36.00 12.00

Lettering, most evident in the "Phil@poste" inscription at bottom, is sharp on No. 4228 and fuzzy on No. 4245.

Miniature Sheet

Soldiers — A2238

No. 4253: a, Croisé (crusader), 12th cent. b, Vercingetorix (c. 82-46 B.C.), Gallic chieftain, horiz. c, Fantassin (foot soldier), 16th cent. d, Tambour (drummer), 18th cent. e, Grognard (member of Napoleon's Old Guard). f, Fantassin (foot soldier), 1914.

Litho. & Engr.
2012, June 10 *Perf. 13*
4253 A2238 Sheet of 6 9.00 9.00
a.-f. 60c Any single 1.50 .50

A set of six souvenir sheets, each containing one example of Nos. 4253a-4253f, sold for €15.

Handball A2239

Embossed and Etched on Silver
2012, June 11 ***Die Cut Perf. 12¾***
Self-Adhesive

4254 A2239 €5 silver 12.50 12.50

2012 Summer Olympics, London — A2240

2012, June 12 Photo. *Perf. 13*

4255 A2240 89c multi 2.25 .75

Miles Davis (1926-91), Jazz Trumpet Player — A2241

Edith Piaf (1915-63), Singer — A2242

2012, June 12 ***Perf. 13***

4256 A2241 60c multi 1.50 .50
4257 A2242 89c multi 2.25 .75
a. Horiz. pair, #4256-4257 3.75 1.25

See United States Nos. 4692-4693.

Vegetables A2243

Designs: No. 4258, Peas (petits pois). No. 4259, Salad greens (salades). Nos. 4260, Pimentos (piments). No. 4261, Green beans (haricots vers). No. 4262, Broccoli (chou brocoli). No. 4263, Zucchini (courgettes). No. 4264, Snap beans (haricots mange-tout). No. 4265, Leeks (poireaux). No. 4266, Green peppers (poivron "Lamuyo"). No. 4267, Artichoke (artichaut "Gros Camus"). No. 4268, Squashes (potirons vers). No. 4269, Cabbage (chou cabus).

Serpentine Die Cut 11
2012, June 13 Self-Adhesive
Booklet Stamps

4258 A2243 (57c) multi 1.40 .45
4259 A2243 (57c) multi 1.40 .45
4260 A2243 (57c) multi 1.40 .45
4261 A2243 (57c) multi 1.40 .45
4262 A2243 (57c) multi 1.40 .45
4263 A2243 (57c) multi 1.40 .45
4264 A2243 (57c) multi 1.40 .45
4265 A2243 (57c) multi 1.40 .45
4266 A2243 (57c) multi 1.40 .45
4267 A2243 (57c) multi 1.40 .45
4268 A2243 (57c) multi 1.40 .45
4269 A2243 (57c) multi 1.40 .45
a. Booklet pane of 12, #4258-4269 17.00
Nos. 4258-4269 (12) 16.80 5.40

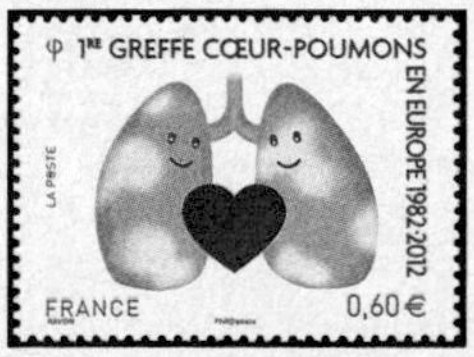

First Heart-Lung Transplant in Europe, 30th Anniv. — A2244

2012, June 14 ***Perf. 13¼***

4270 A2244 60c multi 1.50 .50

Issenheim Altarpiece, 500th Anniv. — A2245

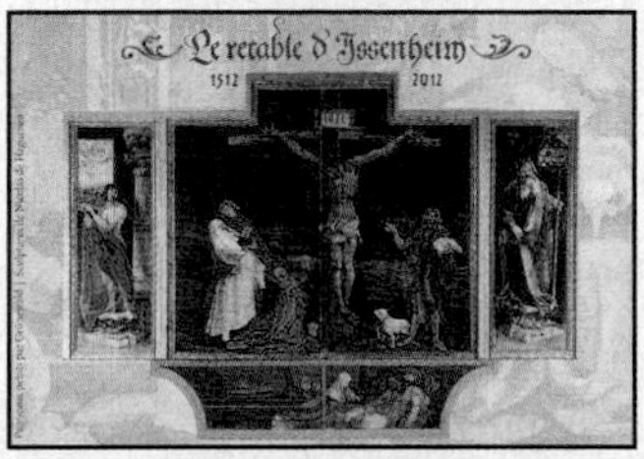

Sheet with Altarpiece Doors Closed (Covering Stamps)

No. 4271: a, St. Augustine, "Le Retable d'Issenheim" at right (19x56mm). b, St. Hieronymus, "Le Retable d'Issenheim" at left (19x56mm). c, St. Anthony (34x65mm).

Perf. 13¼x13, 13 (#4271c)
2012, June 15 Litho.

4271 A2245 Sheet of 3 12.50 12.50
a.-b. €1.50 Either single 3.75 1.25
c. €2 multi 5.00 1.75

Card stock doors printed on both sides that depict artwork on the two alterpiece doors, are pasted on top of each other at the left and right of the stamps. Values for the sheet are for examples with all four doors affixed.

Musée d'Orsay, Paris — A2246

2012, June 16 Engr. ***Perf. 13x13¼***

4272 A2246 60c multi + label 1.50 .50

French Federation of Philatelic Associations, 85th Congress, Paris.

Tourism Issue

Pointe Saint-Mathieu — A2247

2012, June 22 ***Perf. 13¼***

4273 A2247 57c multi 1.40 .45

Souvenir Sheet

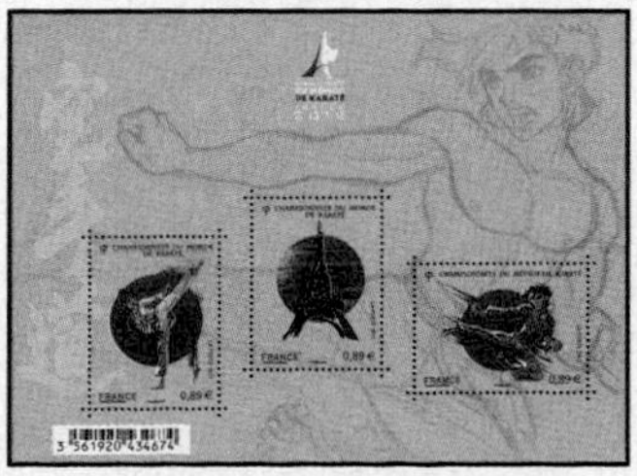

2012 World Karate Championships, Paris — A2248

No. 4274: a, Karateka kicking. b, Eiffel Tower. c, Karateka kicking, horiz.

Perf. 13¼x13, 13x13¼ (#4274c)
2012, Sept. 7 Photo.

4274 A2248 Sheet of 3 7.25 7.25
a.-c. 89c Any single 2.40 .80

2012 World Pétanque Championships, Marseille — A2249

Photo. & Embossed
2012, Sept. 14 ***Perf. 13x13¼***

4275 A2249 89c multi 2.40 .80

Art Issue

Figures Representing Seven Continents, by Jaume Plensa, Place Masséna, Nice — A2250

2012, Sept. 14 Photo.

4276 A2250 €1.45 multi 3.75 1.90

Camp des Milles, World War II Internment Camp — A2251

2012, Sept. 21 Engr.

4277 A2251 60c multi 1.60 .55

Tourism Issue

Verneuil-sur-Avre — A2252

2012, Sept. 21 ***Perf. 13¼***

4278 A2252 60c multi 1.60 .55

Marianne and Stars A2253

2012, Oct. 1 ***Perf. 13***

4279 Souvenir sheet of 3, #4051, 4079, 4279a 5.00 5.00
a. A2253 60c orange 1.60 .55

Torch, Marianne and Stars A2254

The Temptation of St. Anthony, by Hieronymus Bosch — A2255

Items on Fire A2256

Designs: No. 4282, Lava (La lave). No. 4283, Welder (la soudure). No. 4284, Glass-blowing (Le travail du verre). No. 4285, Flame of the Unknown Soldier, Paris (La flamme du soldat inconnu). No. 4286, Halloween jack o'lantern. No. 4287, People around Midsummer's Eve bonfire (Feu de la Saint-Jean). No. 4288, Fire fighters and fire (Les pompiers). No. 4289, Charcoal fire (Les braises). No. 4290, Candles (bougies). No. 4291, Light show (Spectacle). No. 4292, Sunset (Coucher de soleil). No. 4293, Birthday candles on cake (Bougies d'anniversaire).

2012, Oct. 13 Engr. ***Perf. 13***

4280 A2254 60c orange & red 1.60 .55

Souvenir Sheet
Litho. & Engr.
Perf. 13x13¼

4281 A2255 €2 multi 5.25 2.60

Photo.
Booklet Stamps
Self-Adhesive

4282 A2256 (60c) multi 1.60 .55
4283 A2256 (60c) multi 1.60 .55
4284 A2256 (60c) multi 1.60 .55
4285 A2256 (60c) multi 1.60 .55
4286 A2256 (60c) multi 1.60 .55
4287 A2256 (60c) multi 1.60 .55
4288 A2256 (60c) multi 1.60 .55
4289 A2256 (60c) multi 1.60 .55
4290 A2256 (60c) multi 1.60 .55
4291 A2256 (60c) multi 1.60 .55
4292 A2256 (60c) multi 1.60 .55
4293 A2256 (60c) multi 1.60 .55
a. Booklet pane of 12, #4282-4293 19.50
Nos. 4282-4293 (12) 19.20 6.60

Stamp Day. An illustration and a bar code is found on the reverse of the sheet margin of No. 4281.

Historic Residences Type of 2012

Design: (60c), Chaâteau d'If.

Serpentine Die Cut 11
2012, Oct. 29 Litho.
Self-Adhesive

4294 A2237 (60c) multi 1.60 1.60

Lettering, most evident in the "Phil@poste" inscription at bottom, is sharp on No. 4294 and fuzzy on No. 4237.

Court House, Lyon — A2257

2012, Oct. 26 Engr. ***Perf. 13***

4295 A2257 60c multi 1.60 .55

Lion of Belfort Statue, by Frédéric Auguste Bartholdi — A2258

2012, Nov. 2 ***Perf. 13x13¼***

4296 A2258 60c multi + label 1.60 .55

Timbres Passion 2012 Stamp Exhibition, Belfort. A souvenir sheet containing No. 4296 was issued in 2013 and sold for €3.

King Henri IV of France (1553-1610), Co-Prince of Andorra — A2259

2012, Nov. 8

4297 A2259 60c multi 1.60 .55

a. Sheet of 10, 5 each #4297, French Andorra #710 16.00 16.00

See French Andorra No. 710.

Souvenir Sheet

The Masked Ball, Opera by Daniel Auber — A2260

No. 4298: a, Auber (1782-1871). b, King Gustav III of Sweden (1746-92), main character in opera.

Litho. & Engr.

2012, Nov. 9 ***Perf. 13¼***

4298 A2260 Sheet of 2 3.75 3.75

a. 60c multi 1.60 .55

b. 77c multi 2.00 .65

See Sweden No. 2697.

Souvenir Sheet

Organ from Church of St. Jacques, Lunéville — A2261

No. 4299 — Various details of organ's ornamentation: a, 89c. b, €1.45, vert.

Perf. 13x13¼, 13¼x13

2012, Nov. 10 **Engr.**

4299 A2261 Sheet of 2 6.25 6.25

a. 89c multi 2.40 .80

b. €1.45 multi 3.75 1.25

Laurent Bonnevay (1870-1957), Politician, and Apartment Building — A2262

2012, Nov. 12 **Engr.** ***Perf. 13¼***

4300 A2262 57c multi 1.50 .50

Bonnevay Law on rent-controlled housing, cent.

Souvenir Sheet

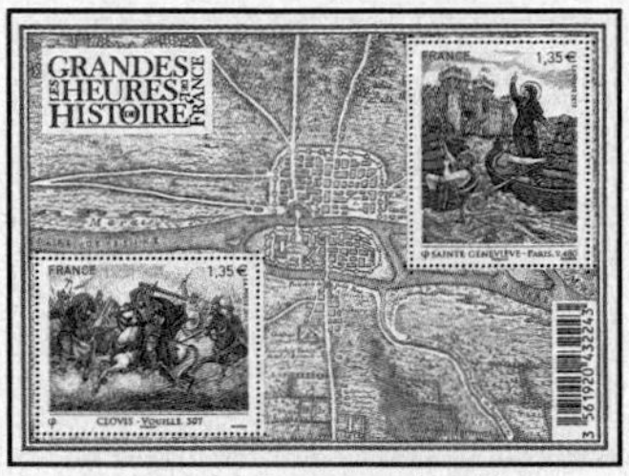

French History — A2263

No. 4301: a, Intercession by St. Geneviève on behalf of Paris, c. 480. b, Clovis at Battle of Vouillé, 507, horiz.

Perf. 13¼x13, 13x13¼

2012, Nov. 12

4301 A2263 Sheet of 2 7.00 7.00

a.-b. €1.35 Either single 3.50 1.10

A2264

A2265

A2266

A2267

A2268

A2269

A2270

A2271

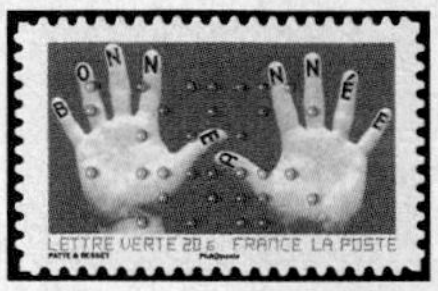

A2272

A2273

A2274

Greetings Stamps A2275

Booklet Stamps

Serpentine Die Cut 11

2012, Nov. 12 **Photo.**

Self-Adhesive

4302	A2264 (57c) multi		1.50	.50
4303	A2265 (57c) multi		1.50	.50
4304	A2266 (57c) multi		1.50	.50
4305	A2267 (57c) multi		1.50	.50
4306	A2268 (57c) multi		1.50	.50
4307	A2269 (57c) multi		1.50	.50
4308	A2270 (57c) multi		1.50	.50
4309	A2271 (57c) multi		1.50	.50
4310	A2272 (57c) multi		1.50	.50
4311	A2273 (57c) multi		1.50	.50
4312	A2274 (57c) multi		1.50	.50
4313	A2275 (57c) multi		1.50	.50
a.	Booklet pane of 12, #4302-4313		18.00	
	Nos. 4302-4313 (12)		18.00	6.00

A souvenir sheet containing one perf. 13x13¼ example of No. 4309 with water-activated gum sold for €3.

See No. 4329.

Elysée Treaty, 50th Anniv. A2276

2013, Jan. 2 **Litho.** ***Perf. 13***

4314 A2276 80c multi 2.25 .75

See Germany No. 2703.

New Year 2013 (Year of the Snake) — A2277

2013, Jan. 4 **Photo.** ***Perf. 13¼x13***

4315 A2277 63c multi 1.75 .60

No. 4315 was printed in sheets of 5. A souvenir sheet of one sold for €3.

Bronze Sculpture of Goat A2278

Terra Cotta Figurine of Rabbit, From Studio of Bernard Palissy A2279

Bronze Sculpture of Buffalo A2280

Brass Sculpture of Rooster A2281

Bronze Sculpture of Tiger, by Antoine Louis Barye A2282

Porcelain Figurine of Rats and Egg A2283

Glazed Clay Figurine of Pig A2284

Bronze Sculpture of Monkey, by Jacques Lehmann A2285

Enameled Stone Sculpture of Dog A2286

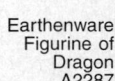

Earthenware Figurine of Dragon A2287

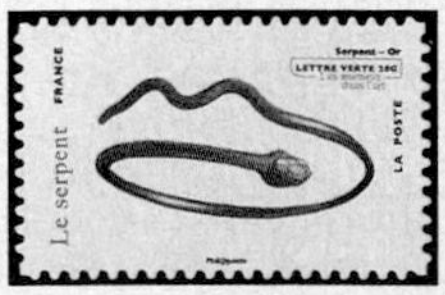

Gold Sculpture of Snake A2288

Bronze Sculpture of Horse, by Edgar Degas A2289

2013, Jan. 4 ***Serpentine Die Cut 11***

Booklet Stamps

Self-Adhesive

4316	A2278 (58c) multi		1.60	.55
4317	A2279 (58c) multi		1.60	.55
4318	A2280 (58c) multi		1.60	.55
4319	A2281 (58c) multi		1.60	.55
4320	A2282 (58c) multi		1.60	.55
4321	A2283 (58c) multi		1.60	.55
4322	A2284 (58c) multi		1.60	.55
4323	A2285 (58c) multi		1.60	.55
4324	A2286 (58c) multi		1.60	.55
4325	A2287 (58c) multi		1.60	.55
4326	A2288 (58c) multi		1.60	.55
4327	A2289 (58c) multi		1.60	.55
a.	Booklet pane of 12, #4316-4327		19.50	
	Nos. 4316-4327 (12)		19.20	6.60

Marseille, 2013 European Capital of Culture A2290

2013, Jan. 12 **Photo.** ***Perf. 13¼***

4328	A2290 80c multi	2.25	.75

Greetings Type of 2012

Serpentine Die Cut 11

2013, Jan. 14 **Litho.**

Self-Adhesive

4329	A2265 (58c) multi	1.60	1.60

Lettering, most evident in the "Phil@poste" inscription at bottom, is sharp on No. 4329 and fuzzy on No. 4303.

Souvenir Sheet

Notre Dame Cathedral, Paris, 850th Anniv. — A2291

No. 4330 — Stained-glass window depicting: a, Peasant with scythe (44x44mm). b, Madonna and Child (42mm diameter).

Litho., Sheet Margin Litho. & Engr.

2013, Jan. 19 ***Perf.***

4330	A2291 Sheet of 2	7.25	7.25
a.	€1.05 multi	3.00	1.00
b.	€1.55 multi	4.25	1.40
c.	Sheet of 2, #4330a, 4330b, lithographed sheet margin	13.50	13.50

No. 4330c has a different margin design and sold for €5.

Art Issue

Landscape, by Chaim Soutine (1893-1943) — A2292

2013, Jan. 25 **Photo.** ***Perf. 13¼x13***

4331	A2292 €1.55 multi	4.25	2.10

A2293

A2294

Hearts — A2295

No. 4334: a, Two white hearts embellished with flowers. b, Bird with long tail. c, Swan facing left. d, Swan facing right.

2013, Jan. 25 ***Perf. 13¼***

4332	A2293 58c multi	1.60	.55
4333	A2294 97c multi	2.75	.90

Souvenir Sheet

Perf.

4334	A2295 Sheet of 5, #4332, 4334a-4334d	8.00	8.00
a.-d	58c Any single	1.60	.55

Self-Adhesive

Serpentine Die Cut

4335	A2293 58c multi	1.60	1.60
4336	A2294 97c multi	2.75	2.75

Values for Nos. 4332-4333 are for stamps with surrounding selvage.

Art Issue

85.8 Degree Arc x 16, Sculpture, by Bernar Venet — A2296

2013, Feb. 1 ***Perf. 13x13¼***

4337	A2296 €1.55 multi	4.25	2.10

Animal Proverbs and Idioms A2297

Designs: No. 4338, Qui vole un oeuf vole un boeuf ("Who steals an egg steals an ox"). No. 4339, Etre serrés come des sardines ("Be packed like sardines"). No. 4340, Etre heureux comme un poisson dans l'eau ("Be happy as a fish in water"). No. 4341, Pleurer des larmes de crocodile ("Cry crocodile tears"). No. 4342, Quand les poules auront des dents ("When chickens have teeth" or "When pigs fly"). No. 4343, Avaler des couleuvres ("To swallow snakes" or "To endure affronts"). No. 4344, Le chat parti, les souris dansent ("The cat's away, the mice will play"). No. 4345, Sauter du coq à l'âne ("Jump from the rooster to the donkey" or "Jump from one thing to another"). No. 4346, Se regarder en chiens de faience ("To stare like clay dogs" or "To stare menacingly at each other"). No. 4347, Ménager la chèvre et le chou ("To take care of the goat and the cabbage" or "To run with the hares and hunt with the hounds"). No. 4348, Cela ne se trouve pas sous les sabots d'un cheval ("That is not under the hooves of a horse"). No. 4349, Pratique la politique de l'autruche ("Practice the policy of an ostrich" or "Bury one's head in the sand like an ostrich").

2013, Feb. 4 ***Serpentine Die Cut 11***

Booklet Stamps

Self-Adhesive

4338	A2297 (58c) multi	1.60	.55
4339	A2297 (58c) multi	1.60	.55
4340	A2297 (58c) multi	1.60	.55
4341	A2297 (58c) multi	1.60	.55
4342	A2297 (58c) multi	1.60	.55
4343	A2297 (58c) multi	1.60	.55
4344	A2297 (58c) multi	1.60	.55
4345	A2297 (58c) multi	1.60	.55
4346	A2297 (58c) multi	1.60	.55
4347	A2297 (58c) multi	1.60	.55
4348	A2297 (58c) multi	1.60	.55
4349	A2297 (58c) multi	1.60	.55
a.	Booklet pane of 12, #4338-4349	19.50	
	Nos. 4338-4349 (12)	19.20	6.60

Compare types A2297 and A2498.

Raphael Elizé (1891-1945), First Black Mayor in France — A2298

2013, Feb. 15 **Engr.** ***Perf. 13¼***

4350	A2298 63c multi	1.75	.60

Miniature Sheet

Way of St. James — A2299

No. 4351: a, Via Lemovicensis in Neuvy-Saint-Sépulchre. b, Via Turonensis in Aulnay. c, Via Tolosana in Saint-Gilles, horiz. d, Via Podiensis in Conques, horiz.

Litho. & Engr.

2013, Feb. 22 ***Perf. 13***

4351	A2299 Sheet of 4	8.50	8.50
a.-d.	80c Any single	2.10	.70

50th International Agricultural Show, Paris — A2300

2013, Feb. 25 **Photo.** ***Perf. 13¼***

4352	A2300 95c multi	2.50	.85

Intl. Women's Day A2301

Qualities of women in Aicha des Gazelles Rally, Morocco: No. 4353, Courage. No. 4354, Partage (sharing). No. 4355, Dépassement de soi (surpassing oneself). No. 4356, Entraide (mutual aid). No. 4357, Enthusiasme (enthusiasm). No. 4358, Solidarité (solidarity). No. 4359, Esprit d'équipe (team spirit). No. 4360, Engagement. No. 4361, Emotion. No. 4362, Performance. No. 4363, Confiance (confidence). No. 4364, Respect.

2013, Mar. 8 ***Serpentine Die Cut 11***

Booklet Stamps

Self-Adhesive

4353	A2301 (58c) multi	1.50	.50
4354	A2301 (58c) multi	1.50	.50
4355	A2301 (58c) multi	1.50	.50
4356	A2301 (58c) multi	1.50	.50
4357	A2301 (58c) multi	1.50	.50
4358	A2301 (58c) multi	1.50	.50
4359	A2301 (58c) multi	1.50	.50
4360	A2301 (58c) multi	1.50	.50
4361	A2301 (58c) multi	1.50	.50
4362	A2301 (58c) multi	1.50	.50
4363	A2301 (58c) multi	1.50	.50
4364	A2301 (58c) multi	1.50	.50
a.	Booklet pane of 12, #4353-4364	18.00	
	Nos. 4353-4364 (12)	18.00	6.00

See No. 4406.

European Capitals Type of 2002

Miniature Sheet

No. 4365 — Attractions in Madrid, Spain: a, Plaza Mayor. b, Almudena Cathedral, horiz. c, Palace of Communication (Cibeles Palace), horiz. d, Royal Palace, horiz.

Perf. 13¼x13 (#4365a), 13x13¼

2013, Mar. 15

4365	A1622 Sheet of 4	6.50	6.50
a.-d.	63c Any single	1.60	.55

Opening of Jacques Chaban-Delmas Vertical Lift Bridge, Bordeaux — A2302

2013, Mar. 16 ***Perf. 13¼***

4366	A2302 58c multi	1.50	.50

Water Towers, Designed by Philolaos Tloupas, Valence — A2303

2013, Mar. 22 **Engr.**

4367	A2303 58c multi	1.50	.50

Spring Philatelic Show, Mâcon — A2304

2013, Apr. 5 ***Perf. 13¼***

4368	A2304 63c multi	1.75	.60

Horses A2305

Horse breeds and horses at work: No. 4369, Breton horse. No. 4370, Norman Cob horse. No. 4371, Boulonnais horse. No. 4372, Trait du Nord horse. No. 4373, Ardennais horse. No. 4374, Comtois horse. No. 4375, Poitevin Mulsassier horse. No. 4376, Horse pulling wagon (Attelage en roulotte). No. 4377, Percheron horse. No. 4378, Horse working in vineyard (Travail de la vigne). No. 4379, Auxois horse. No. 4380, Horse pulling logs in forest (Débardage en forêt).

Serpentine Die Cut 11

2013, Apr. 5 **Photo.**

Booklet Stamps
Self-Adhesive

4369	A2305 (58c) multi		1.50	.50
4370	A2305 (58c) multi		1.50	.50
4371	A2305 (58c) multi		1.50	.50
4372	A2305 (58c) multi		1.50	.50
4373	A2305 (58c) multi		1.50	.50
4374	A2305 (58c) multi		1.50	.50
4375	A2305 (58c) multi		1.50	.50
4376	A2305 (58c) multi		1.50	.50
4377	A2305 (58c) multi		1.50	.50
4378	A2305 (58c) multi		1.50	.50
4379	A2305 (58c) multi		1.50	.50
4380	A2305 (58c) multi		1.50	.50
a.	Booklet pane of 12, #4369-4380		18.00	
	Nos. 4369-4380 (12)		18.00	6.00

Champs-Elysées Theater, Paris, Cent. — A2306

2013, Apr. 8 **Engr.** ***Perf. 13¼***

4381 A2306 €1.05 multi 2.75 .90

Chateau des Vaux, Home of Apprentices of Auteuil — A2307

2013, Apr. 12

4382 A2307 58c multi 1.50 .50

Bats A2308

Designs: No. 4383, Rhinolophus ferrumequinum.

No. 4384: a, Pteropus seychellensis comorensis, vert. b, Plecotus macrobullaris, vert. c, Myotis nattereri.

2013, Apr. 19 **Photo.**

4383 A2308 58c multi 1.50 .50

Miniature Sheet

4384	Sheet of 4, #4383, 4384a-4384c	8.00	8.00
a.	A2308 58c multi	1.50	.50
b.	A2308 80c multi	2.10	.70
c.	A2308 €1.05 multi	2.75	.90

Notre Dame de Melun Collegiate Church, 1000th Anniv. A2309

2013, Apr. 20 **Engr.**

4385 A2309 63c multi 1.75 .60

Impressionist Paintings Depicting Water — A2310

Designs: No. 4386, L'Ile de la Grande Jatte, Neuilly-sur-Seine, by Alfred Sisley. No. 4387, L'Estaque - Vue du Golfe de Marseille (Gulf of Marseille as Seen from L'Estaque), by Paul Cézanne. No. 4388, Sur la Plage (On the Beach), by Edouard Manet. No. 4389, L'Anse des Pilotes au Havre, Haute Mer Après Midi, Soleil, by Camille Pissarro. No. 4390, Régates à Argenteuil (Regatta at Argenteuil), by Claude Monet. No. 4391, Alphonsine Fournaise, by Pierre-Auguste Renoir. No. 4392, La Rivière Blanche (Breton Boy by the Aven River), by Paul Gauguin. No. 4393, L'Homme à la Barre (Man at the Helm), by Théo van Rysselberghe. No. 4394, Les Pecheurs à la Ligne, Étude pour la Grande Jatte (Fishermen), by Georges Seurat. No. 4395, Dans le Port de Rouen (In the Port of Rouen), by Albert Lebourg. No. 4396, La Nuit Etoilée, Arles (Starry Night Over the Rhone), by Vincent van Gogh. No. 4397, La Jetée de Deauville (The Jetty at Deauville), by Louis-Eugène Boudin.

Serpentine Die Cut 11

2013, Apr. 29 **Photo.**

Booklet Stamps
Self-Adhesive

4386	A2310 (58c) multi	1.50	.50
4387	A2310 (58c) multi	1.50	.50
4388	A2310 (58c) multi	1.50	.50
4389	A2310 (58c) multi	1.50	.50
4390	A2310 (58c) multi	1.50	.50
4391	A2310 (58c) multi	1.50	.50
4392	A2310 (58c) multi	1.50	.50
4393	A2310 (58c) multi	1.50	.50
4394	A2310 (58c) multi	1.50	.50
4395	A2310 (58c) multi	1.50	.50
4396	A2310 (58c) multi	1.50	.50
4397	A2310 (58c) multi	1.50	.50
a.	Booklet pane of 12, #4386-4397	18.00	
	Nos. 4386-4397 (12)	18.00	6.00

See Nos. 4449-4452.

Rixheim — A2311

2013, May 3 **Litho. & Engr.** ***Perf. 13***

4398 A2311 63c multi 1.75 .60

A souvenir sheet of one No. 4398 sold for €3.

Charles Gonzaga (1580-1637), Duke of Mantua and Monferrat, Founder of Charleville A2312

2013, May 6 **Engr.** ***Perf. 13¼***

4399 A2312 80c red & black 2.25 .75

World Table Tennis Championships, Paris — A2313

Designs: 63c, Female player (blue shirt). 95c, Male player (red shirt).

2013, May 13 ***Perf. 13x13¼***

4400	A2313 63c multi	1.75	.60
4401	A2313 95c multi	2.50	.80
a.	Horiz. pair, #4400-4401, + central label	4.25	1.40

Cathedral and Jules Verne Circus, Amiens — A2314

2013, May 17

4402 A2314 63c multi + label 1.75 .60

French Federation of Philatelic Associations, 86th Congress, Amiens. A souvenir sheet containing No. 4402 was issued in 2014 and sold for €3.20.

Europa — A2315

Designs: No. 4403, Mail coach, 1840. No. 4404, Renault Kangoo ZE mail van.

2013, May 19 **Photo.**

4403	80c multi	2.25	.75
4404	80c multi	2.25	.75
a.	A2315 Horiz. pair, #4403-4404	4.50	1.50

Souvenir Sheet

Works of André Le Nôtre (1613-1700), Landscape Architect for King Louis XVI — A2316

No. 4405 — Fountains and gardens at: a, Versailles. b, Chantilly.

2013, May 31 ***Perf. 13x13¼***

4405	A2316 Sheet of 2	14.00	14.00
a.-b.	€2.55 Either single	7.00	2.50
c.	Sheet of 2, #4405a-4405b, different sheet margin	24.00	24.00

No. 4405c sold for €9.

Intl. Women's Day Type of 2013

Serpentine Die Cut 11

2013, June 1 **Litho.**

Self-Adhesive

4406 A2301 (58c) Like #4359 1.60 1.60

No. 4406 has a dot structure not found on No. 4359, which is printed by photogravure.

Abbaye-aux-Dames, Saintes — A2317

2013, June 14 **Engr.** ***Perf. 13¼***

4407 A2317 63c multi 1.75 .60

Jacques Baumel (1918-2006), Politician — A2318

2013, June 15

4408 A2318 €1.05 multi 3.00 1.00

Miniature Sheet

100th Tour de France Bicycle Race — A2319

No. 4409: a, Rider wearing yellow jersey, Annecy in background (40x30mm). b, Rider wearing polka-dot jersey near Bagnères-de-Bigorre (26x40mm). c, Rider wearing light blue and dark blue jersey near Mont Ventoux (26x40mm). d, Peloton going along Alpe d'Huez mountain road (40x40mm). e, Rider wearing green jersey in foreground, Calvi in background (40x26mm). f, Rider wearing white jersey, Versailles Palace in background (40x30mm). g, Rider wearing yellow jersey winning race, Arc de Triomphe, Paris (30x40mm). h, Rider in red and black jersey, Mont-Saint-Michel (40x26mm).

Perf. 13x13¼ (#4409a, 4409f), 13¼x13 (#4409g), 13

2013, June 29 **Photo.**

4409	A2319 Sheet of 8	15.50	15.50
a.-d.	58c Any single	1.50	.50
e.-f.	80c Either single	2.10	.70
g.-h.	95c Either single	2.50	.85

A souvenir sheet containing Nos. 4409e and 4409g sold for €4.

Types of 1959-2008

Miniature Sheet

2013 **Engr.** ***Perf. 13***

4410	Sheet of 12	21.00	21.00
a.	A328 63c black	1.75	.60
b.	A349 63c black	1.75	.60
c.	A360 63c black	1.75	.60
d.	A379 63c black	1.75	.60
e.	A486 63c black	1.75	.60
f.	A555 63c black	1.75	.60
g.	A771 63c black	1.75	.60
h.	A915 63c black	1.75	.60
i.	A1161 63c black	1.75	.60
j.	A1409 63c black	1.75	.60
k.	A1713 63c black	1.75	.60
l.	A1912 63c black	1.75	.60
m.	Booklet pane of 12, #4410a-4410l	21.00	—

No. 4410 was only sold together with No. 4437a.

Issued: No. 4410, 7/15; No. 4410m, 11/6

Marianne and Children A2320

Marianne and Children "Ecopli" A2321

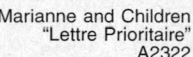

Marianne and Children "Lettre Prioritaire" A2322

Marianne and Children "Europe" A2323

Marianne and Children "Monde" — A2324

Type A2322 gram limits (at LL): Nos. 4415, 4422, 4428, 4435, 20g. Nos. 4419, 4432, 50g. Nos. 4420, 4433, 100g. Nos. 4421, 4434, 250g.

2013, July 15 Engr. *Perf. 13*

4411 A2320 1c yellow .25 .25
4412 A2320 5c dk brown .25 .25
4413 A2320 10c brown .25 .25
4414 A2321 (56c) dk gray 1.50 .30
4415 A2322 (63c) red 1.75 .35
a. As No. 4415, engraved, glossy paper (#4437g) 1.75 1.75
b. As No. 4415, photogravure, glossy paper (#4437g) 1.75 1.75
c. As No. 4415, litho., glossy paper (#4437g) 1.75 1.75
d. As No. 4415, typo., glossy paper (#4437g) 1.75 1.75
e. As No. 4415, silk-screened, glossy paper (#4437g) 1.75 1.75
f. No. 4415a with overprint "Marianne 1944-2014" (#4437o) 1.75 1.75
g. No. 4415b with overprint "Marianne 1944-2014" (#4437o) 1.75 1.75
h. No. 4415c with overprint "Marianne 1944-2014" (#4437o) 1.75 1.75
i. No. 4415d with overprint "Marianne 1944-2014" (#4437o) 1.75 1.75
j. No. 4415e with overprint "Marianne 1944-2014" (#4437o) 1.75 1.75
4416 A2323 (80c) blue 2.10 .45
4417 A2324 (95c) purple 2.50 .65
4418 A2320 €1 orange 2.60 .65
4419 A2322 (€1.05) fawn 2.75 .70
4420 A2322 (€1.55) red violet 4.00 1.00
4421 A2322 (€2.55) chocolate 6.75 2.40
Nos. 4411-4421 (11) 24.70 7.25

Issued: Nos. 4415a-4415e, 11/6; Nos. 4415f-4415j, 11/6/14. No. 4415e uses an ink that is shinier than that used on No. 4415a that causes the small lettering at the base of the stamp to be indistinct. Nos. 4415f-4415j had a franking value of 66c on day of issue.

Coil Stamps

Perf. 13 Horiz.

4422 A2322 (63c) red 1.75 .35
4423 A2323 (80c) blue 2.10 .45

Self-Adhesive

Serpentine Die Cut 6¾ Vert.

4424 A2320 1c yellow .25 .25
4425 A2320 5c dk brown .25 .25
4426 A2320 10c brown .25 .25
4427 A2321 (56c) dk gray 1.50 1.50
4428 A2322 (63c) red 1.75 .35
a. Booklet pane of 10 17.50
b. Booklet pane of 12 21.00
c. Booklet pane of 20 35.00
4429 A2323 (80c) blue 2.10 .45
a. Booklet pane of 12 25.50
4430 A2324 (95c) purple 2.50 2.50
4431 A2320 €1 orange 2.60 2.60
4432 A2322 (€1.05) fawn 2.75 2.75
4433 A2322 (€1.55) red violet 4.00 4.00
4434 A2322 (€2.55) chocolate 6.75 6.75
Nos. 4424-4434 (11) 24.70 21.65

Coil Stamps

Serpentine Die Cut 6¾ Horiz.

4435 A2322 (63c) red 1.75 .35
4436 A2323 (80c) blue 2.10 .45

See No. 4519.

Marianne and Tree "Lettre Verte" — A2325

Type A2325 gram limits (at LL): Nos. 4437, 4441, 4442, 4446, 20g. Nos. 4438, 4443, 50g. Nos. 4439, 4444, 100g. Nos. 4440, 4445, 250g.

2013, July 15 Engr. *Perf. 13*

4437 A2325 (58c) green 1.50 .25
a. Souvenir sheet of 2, #4415, 4437 3.25 3.25
b. As No. 4437, engraved, glossy paper (#4437g) 1.60 1.60
c. As No. 4437, photogravure, glossy paper (#4437g) 1.60 1.60
d. As No. 4437, litho., glossy paper (#4437g) 1.60 1.60
e. As No. 4437, typo., glossy paper (#4437g) 1.60 1.60
f. As No. 4437, silk-screened, glossy paper (#4437g) 1.60 1.60
g. Sheet of 40, 8 each #4415a, 4437b, 4 each #4415b, 4415e, 4437d, 4437e, 2 each #4415c, 4415d, 4437c, 4437f, + label 67.00 67.00
h. Booklet pane of 2, #4415, 4437 3.50 —
Complete booklet, #4410m, 4437h 24.50
i. Booklet pane of 2, #4079, 4437 3.00 —
j. No. 4437b with overprint "Marianne 1944-2014" (#4437o) 1.60 1.60
k. No. 4437c with overprint "Marianne 1944-2014" (#4437o) 1.60 1.60
l. No. 4437d with overprint "Marianne 1944-2014" (#4437o) 1.60 1.60
m. No. 4437e with overprint "Marianne 1944-2014" (#4437o) 1.60 1.60
n. No. 4437f with overprint "Marianne 1944-2014" (#4437o) 1.60 1.60
o. Sheet of 40, 8 each #4415f, 4437j, 4 each #4415g, 4415j, 4437l, 4437m, 2 each #4415h, 4415i, 4437k, 4437n, + label 67.00 67.00
4438 A2325 (97c) yel grn 2.60 .55
4439 A2325 (€1.45) dk bl grn 3.75 .80
4440 A2325 (€2.35) dk bl grn 6.25 1.25
Nos. 4437-4440 (4) 14.10 2.85

Coil Stamp

Perf. 13 Horiz.

4441 A2325 (58c) green 1.50 .25

Self-Adhesive

Serpentine Die Cut 6¾ Vert.

4442 A2325 (58c) green 1.50 .25
a. Booklet pane of 10 15.00
b. Booklet pane of 12 18.00
4443 A2325 (97c) yel grn 2.60 2.60
4444 A2325 (€1.45) dk bl grn 3.75 3.75
4445 A2325 (€2.35) dk bl grn 6.25 6.25
Nos. 4442-4445 (4) 14.10 12.85

Coil Stamp

Serpentine Die Cut 6¾ Horiz.

4446 A2325 (58c) green 1.50 .25

Issued: Nos. 4437b-4437h, 11/6, No. 4437i-4437o, 11/6/14. No. 4437a was only sold together with No. 4410. No. 4437a is 144x106mm. A 209x103mm sheet similar to No. 4473a was sold with a folder for €4.

No. 4437f uses an ink that is shinier than that used on No. 4437b that causes the small lettering at the base of the stamp to be indistinct. Nos. 4437j-4437n each had a franking value of 61c on day of issue.

The 80x52mm label on No. 4437g depicting an enlarged example of Type A2325 is not valid for postage. The 80x52mm label on No. 4437o was also overprinted "Marianne 1944-2014" but is not valid for postage.

See No. 4512.

Gaston Doumergue (1863-1937), Politician A2326

2013, Aug. 1 Engr. *Perf. 13¼*

4447 A2326 58c dark blue 1.60 .55

Pierre-Georges Latécoère (1883-1943), Aircraft Manufacturer — A2327

2013, Aug. 15 Photo.

4448 A2327 €1.05 multi 3.00 1.00

Impressionist Paintings Type of 2013

Designs: No. 4449, Like #4387. No. 4450, Like #4389. No. 4451, Like #4390. No. 4452, Like #4396.

Serpentine Die Cut 11

2013, Aug. 26 Litho.

Self-Adhesive

4449 A2310 (58c) multi 1.60 1.60
4450 A2310 (58c) multi 1.60 1.60
4451 A2310 (58c) multi 1.60 1.60
4452 A2310 (58c) multi 1.60 1.60
Nos. 4449-4452 (4) 6.40 6.40

Nos. 4449-4452 each have a dot structure in the colored panels at right that is not found on the photogravure stamps. The appearance of "France" on Nos. 4449-4452 appears lighter and grayer than that found on the photogravure stamps.

Patronage Law, 10th Anniv. — A2328

2013, Sept. 5 Photo. *Perf. 13¼*

4453 A2328 63c multi 1.75 .60

Sculpture of Virgin Mary and Infant Jesus A2329

Keystone, Sainte-Chapelle de Vincennes — A2330

Mirror With Ivory Carving of Chess Players A2331

Annunciation of the Virgin, Reims Cathedral A2332

Carving of Rooster, St. Pierre's Cathedral, Poitiers A2333

Decorated Mirror of Louis d'Anjou A2334

Marriage of the Virgin, Notre Dame Cathedral, Paris A2335

Angel From Canopy of King Charles VII — A2336

Illumination From Les Très Riches Heures du Duc de Berry A2337

Reliquary Medallion A2338

Illumination from Heures de François de Guise A2339

Bas-relief of Man Presenting Flower to Woman A2340

Serpentine Die Cut 11

2013, Sept. 6 Photo.

Booklet Stamps
Self-Adhesive

4454 A2329 (63c) multi 1.75 .60
4455 A2330 (63c) multi 1.75 .60
4456 A2331 (63c) multi 1.75 .60
4457 A2332 (63c) multi 1.75 .60
4458 A2333 (63c) multi 1.75 .60
4459 A2334 (63c) multi 1.75 .60
4460 A2335 (63c) multi 1.75 .60
4461 A2336 (63c) multi 1.75 .60
4462 A2337 (63c) multi 1.75 .60
4463 A2338 (63c) multi 1.75 .60
4464 A2339 (63c) multi 1.75 .60
4465 A2340 (63c) multi 1.75 .60
a. Booklet pane of 12, #4454-4465 21.00
Nos. 4454-4465 (12) 21.00 7.20

Gothic art.

French Heritage A2341

Designs: No. 4466, House of the Lumière Brothers, Lyon. No. 4467, Buffon Museum, Montbard. No. 4468, House of George Sand, Nohant. No. 4469, House of Georges Clemenceau, Saint-Vincent-sur-Jard. No. 4470, Château de La Motte-Tilly, La Motte-Tilly. No. 4471, Castle and ramparts, Carcassonne. No. 4472, Château de Carrouges, Carrouges. No. 4473, Château de Champs-sur-Marne, Champs-sur-Marne. No. 4474, Aligned stones of Carnac. No. 4475, Roman structures (Mausoleum of the Julii, Triumphal arch of Glanum), Saint-Rémy-de-Provence. No. 4476, Mosaics at Montcaret archaeological site. No. 4477, Gallo-Roman Villa, Montmaurin.

Serpentine Die Cut 11

2013, Sept. 6 **Photo.**

Booklet Stamps
Self-Adhesive

4466	A2341	(58c)	multi	1.60	.55
4467	A2341	(58c)	multi	1.60	.55
4468	A2341	(58c)	multi	1.60	.55
4469	A2341	(58c)	multi	1.60	.55
a.	Booklet pane of 4, #4466-4469			6.50	
4470	A2341	(58c)	multi	1.60	.55
4471	A2341	(58c)	multi	1.60	.55
4472	A2341	(58c)	multi	1.60	.55
4473	A2341	(58c)	multi	1.60	.55
a.	Booklet pane of 4, #4470-4473			6.50	
4474	A2341	(58c)	multi	1.60	.55
4475	A2341	(58c)	multi	1.60	.55
4476	A2341	(58c)	multi	1.60	.55
4477	A2341	(58c)	multi	1.60	.55
a.	Booklet pane of 4, #4474-4477			6.50	
	Complete booklet, #4469a, 4473a, 4477a			19.50	
	Nos. 4466-4477 (12)			19.20	6.60

Judicial Police of Paris, Cent. — A2342

2013, Sept. 13 **Photo.** ***Perf. 13¼***

4478	A2342	63c	multi	1.75	.60

Art Issue

Faience Vase, by Théodore Deck (1823-91) A2343

2013, Sept. 20 **Photo.** ***Perf. 13¼x13***

4479	A2343	€1.55	multi	4.25	2.10

Alexandre Yersin (1863-1943), Bacteriologist — A2344

Yersin as: 63c, Older man. 95c, Young man.

2013, Sept. 20 **Engr.** ***Perf. 13x13¼***

4480	A2344	63c	multi	1.75	.60
4481	A2344	95c	multi	2.60	.85

See Viet Nam Nos. 3488-3489.

Art Issue

Souvenir Sheet

Paintings by Georges Braque (1882-1963) — A2345

No. 4482: a, Le Guéridon. b, Le Salon.

2013, Sept. 27 **Photo.** ***Perf. 13x13¼***

4482	A2345	Sheet of 2		8.50	8.50
a.-b.	€1.55 Either single			4.25	2.10

St. Bernard of Clairvaux (1090-1153), Abbot, and His Birthplace, Fontaine-lès-Dijon — A2346

2013, Oct. 4 **Engr.** ***Perf. 13¼***

4483	A2346	58c	multi	1.60	.55

Miniature Sheet

Theatrical Masks — A2347

No. 4484: a, Balinese Topeng. b, Greek theater mask, horiz. c, Korean Sandae mask. d, Japanese Noh theater mask. e, Italian Commedia dell'arte mask, horiz. f, Javanese shadow theater mask.

2013, Oct. 4 **Litho. & Engr.** ***Perf. 13***

4484	A2347	Sheet of 6		9.75	9.75
a.-f.	58c Any single			1.60	.55

A set of six souvenir sheets, each containing one each of Nos. 4484a-4484f, sold for €15.

Marianne and Balloon A2348

Balloons and Paraglider — A2349

Man Blowing on Fire A2350

Bottle of Air in Water A2351

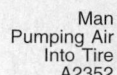

Man Pumping Air Into Tire A2352

Paramedics Tending to Man Wearing Oxygen Mask A2353

Hang Glider A2354

Sailboat A2355

Birds A2356

Hummingbird and Flowers — A2357

Horn Player A2358

Runner A2359

Polynesian Canoe A2360

Wind Turbine A2361

2013, Oct. 12 **Engr.** ***Perf. 13***

4485	A2348	58c	multi	1.60	.55

Photo. & Embossed

Souvenir Sheet

Perf. 13¼x13

4486	A2349	€2.35	multi	6.50	3.25

Photo.

Booklet Stamps
Self-Adhesive

Serpentine Die Cut 11

4487	A2350	(63c)	multi	1.75	.60
4488	A2351	(63c)	multi	1.75	.60
4489	A2352	(63c)	multi	1.75	.60
4490	A2353	(63c)	multi	1.75	.60
4491	A2354	(63c)	multi	1.75	.60
4492	A2355	(63c)	multi	1.75	.60
4493	A2356	(63c)	multi	1.75	.60
4494	A2357	(63c)	multi	1.75	.60
4495	A2358	(63c)	multi	1.75	.60
4496	A2359	(63c)	multi	1.75	.60
4497	A2360	(63c)	multi	1.75	.60
4498	A2361	(63c)	multi	1.75	.60
a.	Booklet pane of 12, #4487-4498			21.00	
	Nos. 4487-4498 (12)			21.00	7.20

Stamp Day. See Nos. 4535-4536.

Miniature Sheet

Television Personalities — A2362

No. 4499: a, Pierre Sabbagh (1918-94), news reporter and producer. b, Léon Zitrone (1914-95), news and sports reporter. c, Catherine Langeais (1923-98), show host. d, Denise Glaser (1920-83), show host and producer. e, Jacqueline Joubert (1921-2005), show host and producer, horiz. f, Pierre Desgraupes (1918-93), news reporter, horiz.

2013, Oct. 18 **Photo.** ***Perf. 13***

4499	A2362	Sheet of 6		9.75	9.75
a.-f.	58c Any single			1.60	.55

Little Pleasures A2363

Designs: No. 4500, People and tea set (Thé partagé). No. 4501, Tree of life (Arbre de vie). No. 4502, Peacock holding letter (Paon messager). No. 4503, Carousel (Carrousel). No. 4504, Tree and falling coins (Pluie d'écus). No. 4505, Robin (Le rouge-gorge). No. 4506, Child and dove (Enfant de paix). No. 4507, Flying horse and rider (Cheval porte-bonheur). No. 4508, Cookies, pastries and snacks (Gourmandises). No. 4509, Citrus fruit and blossoms (Magie d'agrumes). No. 4510, Mother, child and flowers (Bienveillance). No. 4511, Shoe filled with gifts (L'escarpin).

Serpentine Die Cut 11

2013, Oct. 25 **Photo.**

Booklet Stamps
Self-Adhesive

4500	A2363	(58c)	multi	1.60	.55
4501	A2363	(58c)	multi	1.60	.55
4502	A2363	(58c)	multi	1.60	.55
4503	A2363	(58c)	multi	1.60	.55
4504	A2363	(58c)	multi	1.60	.55
4505	A2363	(58c)	multi	1.60	.55
4506	A2363	(58c)	multi	1.60	.55
4507	A2363	(58c)	multi	1.60	.55
4508	A2363	(58c)	multi	1.60	.55
4509	A2363	(58c)	multi	1.60	.55
4510	A2363	(58c)	multi	1.60	.55
4511	A2363	(58c)	multi	1.60	.55
a.	Booklet pane of 12, #4500-4511			19.50	
	Nos. 4500-4511 (12)			19.20	6.60

A souvenir sheet containing a perf. 12¾ example of No. 4510 with water-activated gum sold for €3.

Types of 1959-2013

Serpentine Die Cut 11

2013, Nov. 6 **Engr.**

Booklet Stamps
Self-Adhesive

4512	A2325	(58c)	green	1.60	.35
4513	A328	63c	black	1.75	.60
4514	A349	63c	black	1.75	.60
4515	A360	63c	black	1.75	.60
4516	A379	63c	black	1.75	.60
4517	A486	63c	black	1.75	.60
4518	A555	63c	black	1.75	.60
4519	A2322	(63c)	red	1.75	.60
4520	A771	63c	black	1.75	.60
4521	A915	63c	black	1.75	.60
4522	A1161	63c	black	1.75	.60
4523	A1409	63c	black	1.75	.60

4524	A1713	63c black		1.75	.60
4525	A1912	63c black		1.75	.60
a.		Booklet pane of 14, #4512-4525		24.50	
		Nos. 4512-4525 (14)		24.35	8.15

Trade Treaty Between France and Denmark, 350th Anniv.
A2364

Map and compass rose with ship at: 63c, Right. 80c, Left.

2013, Nov. 7 Engr. *Perf. 13*

4526	A2364	63c multi	1.75	.60
4527	A2364	80c multi	2.25	.75

See Denmark Nos. 1663-1664.

Fashion
A2365

Designs: No. 4528, Finished dresses on three dress forms. No. 4529, Flower, three women wearing white dresses. No. 4530, Three dress forms. No. 4531, Three women wearing white dresses.

2013, Nov. 8 Photo. *Perf. 13¼*

4528	A2365	63c multi	1.75	.60
4529	A2365	63c multi	1.75	.60
4530	A2365	95c multi	2.60	.85
4531	A2365	95c multi	2.60	.85
		Nos. 4528-4531 (4)	8.70	2.90

See Singapore Nos. 1640-1643.

Souvenir Sheet

French History — A2366

No. 4532: a, Battle of Muret, 1213. b, Capture of Tournoel, 1212.

2013, Nov. 8 Engr. *Perf. 13x13¼*

4532	A2366	Sheet of 2	8.00	8.00
a.-b.		€1.45 Either single	4.00	1.40

National Order of Merit, 50th Anniv. — A2367

2013, Nov. 9 Engr. *Perf. 13¼*

4533	A2367	63c blue	1.75	.60

2013 French Kickboxing World Championships, Clermont-Ferrand — A2368

2013, Nov. 16 Photo. *Perf. 13*

4534	A2368	95c multi	2.60	.85

Sailboat and Horn Player Types of 2013

Serpentine Die Cut 11

2013, Nov. 18 Litho.

Self-Adhesive

4535	A2355	(63c) multi	1.75	1.75
4536	A2358	(63c) multi	1.75	1.75

"Phil@poste" is sharper on Nos. 4535-4536 than on Nos. 4492 and 4495.

Items with Spirals
A2369

Spirals in: No. 4537, Solarium shell (Coquillage solarium). No. 4538, Pottery design from Iznik, Turkey (Céramique Iznik). No. 4539, Spirograph. No. 4540, Red rose (Rose rouge). No. 4541, Ammonite fossil (Fossile d'ammonite). No. 4542, Chinese highway interchange (Echangeur Shanghai Nanpu). No. 4543, Kite (Cerf-volant). No. 4544, Cyclone Ingrid. No. 4545, Tree rings (Sapin-coupe transversale). No. 4546, Basket (Vannerie). No. 4547, Lighthouse staircase (Phare de la Coubre). No. 4548, School of barracudas (Banc des barracudas).

Serpentine Die Cut 11

2014, Jan. 4 Photo.

Booklet Stamps

Self-Adhesive

4537	A2369	(66c) multi	1.75	.60
4538	A2369	(66c) multi	1.75	.60
4539	A2369	(66c) multi	1.75	.60
4540	A2369	(66c) multi	1.75	.60
4541	A2369	(66c) multi	1.75	.60
4542	A2369	(66c) multi	1.75	.60
4543	A2369	(66c) multi	1.75	.60
4544	A2369	(66c) multi	1.75	.60
4545	A2369	(66c) multi	1.75	.60
4546	A2369	(66c) multi	1.75	.60
4547	A2369	(66c) multi	1.75	.60
4548	A2369	(66c) multi	1.75	.60
a.		Booklet pane of 12, #4537-4548	21.00	
		Nos. 4537-4548 (12)	21.00	7.20

See Nos. 4566-4567, 4698.

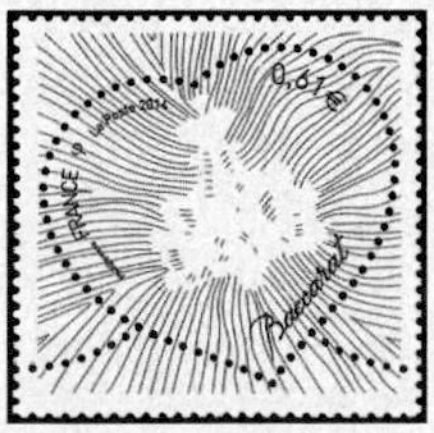

Hearts
A2370

"Baccarat" and: 61c, Chandelier. €1.02, Goblet.

Silk-Screened, Engraved & Embossed

2014, Jan. 7 *Perf. 13*

4549	A2370	61c multi	1.75	.60
a.		Souvenir sheet of 5	8.75	8.75
4550	A2370	€1.02 multi	2.75	.90

Silk-Screened & Engraved

Serpentine Die Cut

Self-Adhesive

4551	A2370	61c multi	1.75	1.75
4552	A2370	€1.02 multi	2.75	2.75

See No. 4651.

Anne, Duchess of Brittany (1477-1514)
A2371

Litho. & Engr.

2014, Jan. 11 *Perf. 13*

4553	A2371	66c multi	1.75	.60

A souvenir sheet of one sold for €3.20.

Signs of the Zodiac
A2372

Designs: No. 4554, Aries (Bélier). No. 4555, Taurus (Taureau). No. 4556, Gemini (Gémeaux). No. 4557, Cancer. No. 4558, Leo (Lion). No. 4559, Virgo (Vierge). No. 4560, Libra (Balance). No. 4561, Scorpio (Scorpion). No. 4562, Sagittarius (Sagittaire). No. 4563, Capricorn (Capricorne). No. 4564, Aquarius (Verseau). No. 4565, Pisces (Poissons).

Serpentine Die Cut 11

2014, Jan. 20 Photo.

Booklet Stamps

Self-Adhesive

4554	A2372	(61c) multi	1.75	.60
4555	A2372	(61c) multi	1.75	.60
4556	A2372	(61c) multi	1.75	.60
4557	A2372	(61c) multi	1.75	.60
4558	A2372	(61c) multi	1.75	.60
4559	A2372	(61c) multi	1.75	.60
4560	A2372	(61c) multi	1.75	.60
4561	A2372	(61c) multi	1.75	.60
4562	A2372	(61c) multi	1.75	.60
4563	A2372	(61c) multi	1.75	.60
4564	A2372	(61c) multi	1.75	.60
4565	A2372	(61c) multi	1.75	.60
a.		Booklet pane of 12, #4554-4565	21.00	
		Nos. 4554-4565 (12)	21.00	7.20

Items With Spirals Type of 2014

Designs: No. 4566, Like #4542. No. 4567, Like #4543.

Serpentine Die Cut 11

2014, Jan. 27 Litho.

Self-Adhesive

4566	A2369	(66c) multi	1.75	1.75
4567	A2369	(66c) multi	1.75	1.75

"Phil@poste" is sharper on Nos. 4566-4567 than on Nos. 4542-4543.

New Year 2014 (Year of the Horse) — A2373

2014, Jan. 31 Photo. *Perf. 13¼x13*

4568	A2373	66c multi	1.75	.60

No. 4568 was printed in sheets of 5. A souvenir sheet of one sold for €3.20.

Art Issue

Bust of Julius Caesar
A2374

2014, Feb. 14 Engr. *Perf. 13¼x13*

4569	A2374	€1.65 multi	4.50	2.25

Cattle Breeds
A2375

Inscriptions: No. 4570, La Bretonne Pie Noir. No. 4571, L'Armoricaine. No. 4572, La Béarnaise. No. 4573, La Maraîchine. No. 4574, La Mirandaise. No. 4575, La Villard de Lans. No. 4576, La Saosnoise. No. 4577, La Nantaise. No. 4578, La Bordelaise. No. 4579, La Lourdaise. No. 4580, La Casta. No. 4581, La Ferrandaise.

Serpentine Die Cut 11

2014, Feb. 22 Photo.

Booklet Stamps

Self-Adhesive

4570	A2375	(61c) multi	1.75	.60
4571	A2375	(61c) multi	1.75	.60
4572	A2375	(61c) multi	1.75	.60
4573	A2375	(61c) multi	1.75	.60
4574	A2375	(61c) multi	1.75	.60
4575	A2375	(61c) multi	1.75	.60
4576	A2375	(61c) multi	1.75	.60
4577	A2375	(61c) multi	1.75	.60
4578	A2375	(61c) multi	1.75	.60
4579	A2375	(61c) multi	1.75	.60
4580	A2375	(61c) multi	1.75	.60
4581	A2375	(61c) multi	1.75	.60
a.		Booklet pane of 12, #4570-4581	21.00	
		Nos. 4570-4581 (12)	21.00	7.20

Art Issue

Tokyo 04, Photograph by Maxime Bruno — A2376

2014, Feb. 28 Litho. *Perf. 13x13¼*

4582	A2376	€1.65 multi	4.50	2.25

Miniature Sheet

Way of St. James — A2377

No. 4583: a, Via Lemovicensis in Bazas. b, Via Podiensis in Moissac. c, Via Tolosana in Auch. d, Via Turonensis in Pons.

Litho. & Engr.

2014, Mar. 14 *Perf. 13*

4583	A2377	Sheet of 4	9.00	9.00
a.-d.		83c Any single	2.25	.75

Alexandre Glais-Bizoin (1800-77), Politician — A2378

2014, Mar. 15 Engr. *Perf. 13x13¼*
4584 A2378 66c multi 1.90 .65

Bears A2379

Designs: No. 4585, Giant panda (Panda géant).
No. 4586: a, Spectacled bear (Ours andin). b, Kermode bear (Ours Kermode). c, Polar bear (Ours polaire).

2014, Mar. 21 Photo. *Perf. 13¼*
4585 A2379 61c multi 1.75 .60

Miniature Sheet

4586 Sheet of 4, #4585, 4586a-4586c 7.00 7.00
a.-c. A2379 61c Any single 1.75 .60

Diplomatic Relations Between France and People's Republic of China, 50th Anniv. — A2380

Designs: 66c, Qinhuai River, Nanjing. 98c, Seine River, Paris.

2014, Mar. 27 Engr. *Perf. 13x13¼*
4587 A2380 66c multi 1.90 .65
4588 A2380 98c multi 2.75 .90

See People's Republic of China Nos. 4172-4173.

Art Issue

Painting by Joan Mitchell (1925-92) A2381

2014, Mar. 28 Litho. *Perf. 13¼x13*
4589 A2381 €1.65 multi 4.50 2.25

Sell and Buy Used Items A2382

Turn Off Appliances A2383

Fruits and Vegetables A2384

Fix Leaks Quickly A2385

Sort and Recycle Paper A2386

Control Indoor Temperatures — A2387

Conserve Water A2388

People in Carpool A2389

Use Public Transportation — A2390

Save Energy A2391

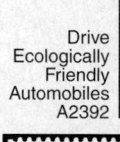

Drive Ecologically Friendly Automobiles A2392

Recycle Waste Products A2393

Serpentine Die Cut 11
2014, Apr. 3 Photo.

Booklet Stamps Self-Adhesive

4590 A2382 (61c) multi 1.75 .60
4591 A2383 (61c) multi 1.75 .60
4592 A2384 (61c) multi 1.75 .60
4593 A2385 (61c) multi 1.75 .60
4594 A2386 (61c) multi 1.75 .60
4595 A2387 (61c) multi 1.75 .60
4596 A2388 (61c) multi 1.75 .60
4597 A2389 (61c) multi 1.75 .60
4598 A2390 (61c) multi 1.75 .60
4599 A2391 (61c) multi 1.75 .60
4600 A2392 (61c) multi 1.75 .60
4601 A2393 (61c) multi 1.75 .60
a. Booklet pane of 12, #4590-4601 21.00
Nos. 4590-4601 (12) 21.00 7.20

Opera Theater, Clermont-Ferrand — A2394

2014, Apr. 4 Engr. *Perf. 13¼*
4602 A2394 61c multi 1.75 .60

Spring Philatelic Show, Clermont-Ferrand.

Marguerite Duras (1914-96), Writer and Film Director — A2395

2014, Apr. 4 Engr. *Perf. 13¼*
4603 A2395 €1.10 multi 3.00 1.00

Arrest and Deportation of Jews at Izieu Orphanage, 70th Anniv. A2396

Litho. & Engr.
2014, Apr. 6 *Perf. 13x13¼*
4604 A2396 61c multi 1.75 .60

Miniature Sheet

European Capitals — A2397

No. 4605 — Attractions in Vienna: a, Secession Building. b, Belvedere Palace, horiz. c, Karlskirche (St. Charles' Church). d, Hofburg Palace, horiz.

Perf. 13¼x13, 13x13¼
2014, Apr. 18 Photo.
4605 A2397 Sheet of 4 + 3 labels 7.75 7.75
a.-d. 66c Any single 1.90 .65

Souvenir Sheet

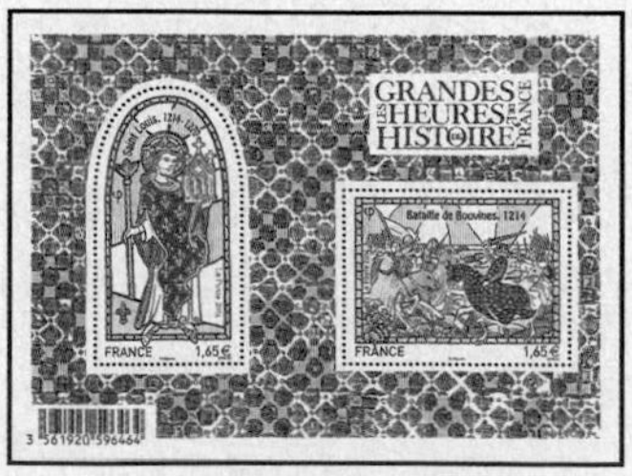

French History — A2398

No. 4606: a, St. Louis (1214-70) (35x66mm). b, Battle of Bouvines, 1214 (52x41mm)

2014, Apr. 25 Engr. *Perf. 13x13¼*
4606 A2398 Sheet of 2 9.50 9.50
a.-b. €1.65 Either single 4.75 2.25
c. Souvenir sheet of 4, #4532a, 4532b, 4606a, 4606b 17.00 17.00

Salon du Timbre 2014 (No. 4606c). Issued: No. 4606c, 6/23/14.

Palace of Poitiers — A2399

2014, May 1 Engr. *Perf. 13x13¼*
4607 A2399 61c multi + label 1.75 .60

Vacation A2400

Designs: No. 4608, Dog with sunglasses eating ice cream bar. No. 4609, Snail with trailer for shell. No. 4610, Crab building sand castle. No. 4611, Cats dancing. No. 4612, Turtle playing lute, turtle dancing. No. 4613, Lobster holding beach gear. No. 4614, Chicken and egg wearing headphones. No. 4615, Fish surfing. No. 4616, Ram with backpack and mountain climbing gear. No. 4617, Rabbits on tandem bicycle. No. 4618, Frogs with umbrellas in swan boat. No. 4619, Geese, tent, snails on picnic plate.

Serpentine Die Cut 11
2014, May 3 Photo.

Booklet Stamps Self-Adhesive

4608 A2400 (61c) multi 1.75 .60
4609 A2400 (61c) multi 1.75 .60
4610 A2400 (61c) multi 1.75 .60
4611 A2400 (61c) multi 1.75 .60
4612 A2400 (61c) multi 1.75 .60
4613 A2400 (61c) multi 1.75 .60
4614 A2400 (61c) multi 1.75 .60
4615 A2400 (61c) multi 1.75 .60
4616 A2400 (61c) multi 1.75 .60
4617 A2400 (61c) multi 1.75 .60
4618 A2400 (61c) multi 1.75 .60
4619 A2400 (61c) multi 1.75 .60
a. Booklet pane of 12, #4608-4619 21.00
Nos. 4608-4619 (12) 21.00 7.20

Harp Created by Jean Henri Naderman, 1787 A2401

2014, May 4 Photo. *Perf. 13¼x13*
4620 A2401 83c multi 2.25 .75

Europa.

Opening of English Channel Tunnel, 20th Anniv. A2402

2014, May 6 Engr. *Perf. 13¼*
4621 A2402 66c multi 1.90 .65

Tourism Series

Boulogne-sur-Mer — A2403

2014, May 9 Engr. *Perf. 13x12¾*
4622 A2403 61c multi 1.75 .60

D-Day, 70th Anniv. — A2404

2014, June 5 Photo. *Perf. 13x12¾*
4623 A2404 66c multi 1.90 .65

Two souvenir sheets of one, issued in 2014 and in 2015, each sold for €3.20.

Tourism Issue

Pontigny Abbey, Yonne — A2405

2014, June 7 Engr. *Perf. 13¼*
4624 A2405 61c multi 1.75 .60

Massacre of Tulle, 70th Anniv. A2406

2014, June 9 Photo. *Perf. 13¼*
4625 A2406 66c multi 1.90 .65

Souvenir Sheet

Benjamin Rabier (1864-1939), Comic Book Illustrator — A2407

No. 4626: a, Duckling hatching, ring with rabbits, chick and chicken (41x41mm). b, Rabier, chicken, rabbit and duck (30x41mm).

2014, June 14 Engr. *Perf. 13¼*
4626 A2407 Sheet of 2 5.00 5.00
a. 66c multi 1.90 .65
b. €1.10 multi 3.00 1.00

A 200x95mm sheet containing Nos. 4626a and 4626b, but having a different margin design sold for €6.
See Nos. 4676, 4680.

Trains A2408

Designs: No. 4627, Buddicom No. 33, Haute-Normandie. No. 4628, Z 209, Vallée de Chamonix. No. 4629, Pacific Chapelon Nord 3.1192, Paris, Gare du Nord. No. 4630, Micheline XM 5005, Haute-Marne. No. 4631, Mikado 141 R 1187, Côte Vermeille. No. 4632, BB 12125, Moselle. No. 4633, Z 6181, Ile-de-France. No. 4634, BB 66001, Les Cévennes. No. 4635, BB 9004, Les Landes. No. 4636, RTG T 2057, Gare de Boulogne-Aroglisseurs. No. 4637, CC 6572, Limoges, Gare des Bénédictins. No. 4638, TGV Duplex, Gare de Belfort-Montbéliard TGV.

Serpentine Die Cut 11
2014, June 14 Photo.
Booklet Stamps
Self-Adhesive

4627 A2408 (66c) multi 1.90 .65
4628 A2408 (66c) multi 1.90 .65
4629 A2408 (66c) multi 1.90 .65
4630 A2408 (66c) multi 1.90 .65
a. Booklet pane of 4, #4627-4630 7.60
4631 A2408 (66c) multi 1.90 .65
4632 A2408 (66c) multi 1.90 .65
4633 A2408 (66c) multi 1.90 .65
4634 A2408 (66c) multi 1.90 .65
a. Booklet pane of 4, #4631-4634 7.60
4635 A2408 (66c) multi 1.90 .65
4636 A2408 (66c) multi 1.90 .65
4637 A2408 (66c) multi 1.90 .65
4638 A2408 (66c) multi 1.90 .65
a. Booklet pane of 4, #4635-4638 7.60
Complete booklet, #4630a, 4634a, 4638a 23.00
Nos. 4627-4638 (12) 22.80 7.80

Paris Zoo, 80th Anniv. — A2409

2014, June 15 Photo. *Perf. 13*
4639 A2409 98c multi 2.75 .95

A souvenir sheet containing No. 4639 sold for €3.20.

Jean Jaurès (1859-1914), Assassinated Socialist Party Leader — A2410

Jaurès: 61c, Without hat. €1.02, With hat.

2014, June 17 Engr. *Perf. 13¼*
4640 A2410 61c blue 1.75 .60
4641 A2410 €1.02 red 2.75 .95
a. Horiz. pair, #4640-4641 4.50 2.25

See Nos. 4675, 4679.

Miniature Sheet

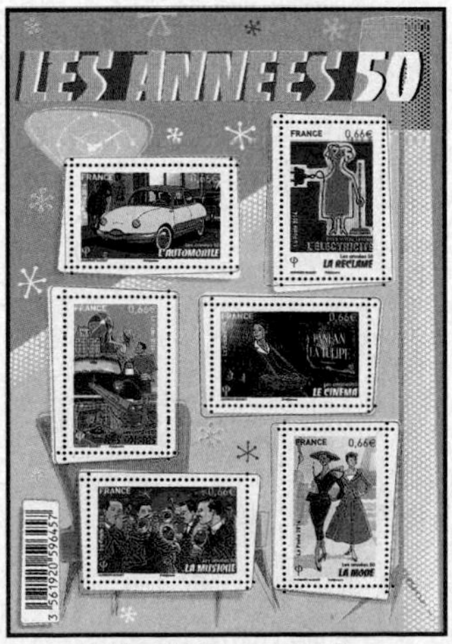

The 1950s — A2411

No. 4642: a, Automobile. b, Electricity advertisement, vert. c, People packing for vacation, vert. d, Vendor in movie theater. e, Musicians. f, Two women modeling fashions, veret.

2014, June 18 Photo. *Perf. 13*
4642 A2411 Sheet of 6 11.50 11.50
a.-f. 66c Any single 1.90 .65

See Nos. 4677, 4678.

A set of 10 miniature sheets containing reproductions of old French stamps (Nos. 641, 722, 764, 850, B34, B92, B97, B172, B248 and C22) with denominations was produced in limited quantities and offered only as a complete set. Each sheet contained five reproductions of one of the ten stamps in different colors, one with a €2.20 denomination and four with €2.45 denominations.

Ceres — A2412

2014, June 18 Engr. *Imperf.*
With Printer's Inscription at Base of Stamp
4643 A2412 €1 rose carmine 2.75 1.40
4644 A2412 €1 red 2.75 1.40

Typo.
4645 A2412 €1 vermilion 2.75 1.40
a. With printer information at top of stamp 2.75 1.40
4646 A2412 €1 rose 2.75 1.40
a. With printer information at top of stamp 2.75 1.40
Nos. 4643-4646 (4) 11.00 5.60

Printed in sheets of 20 containing Nos. 4645a, 4646a, 5 each Nos. 4643-4644, 4 each Nos. 4645-4646. See No. 4727a.

Tourism Issue

Coareze A2413

Locmariaquer — A2414

2014 Engr. *Perf. 13¼*
4647 A2413 61c multi 1.75 .60
4648 A2414 61c multi 1.75 .60

Issued: No. 4647, 6/19; No. 4648, 6/20. See Nos. 4673, 4674.

French Institute, Paris — A2415

2014, June 21 Engr. *Perf. 13x13¼*
4649 A2415 61c multi + label 1.75 .60

French Federation of Philatelic Associations, 87th Congress, Paris. See No. 4672.

Art Issue

The Seine at Pont du Carrousel, by Jean Dufy (1888-1964) — A2416

2014, June 22 Litho. *Perf. 13x13¼*
4650 A2416 €1.65 multi 4.50 2.25

See No. 4681.

Baccarat Hearts Type of 2014
Silk-Screened & Engraved
2014, June 23 *Perf.*
4651 A2370 €3 multi 8.25 4.25

No. 4651 was printed in sheets of 5.

National Institute of Health and Medical Research, 50th Anniv. A2417

2014, July 3 Photo. *Perf. 13¼*
4652 A2417 66c multi 1.75 .60

Jeanne-Antoine Poisson, Marquise de Pompadour (1721-64), Patron of the Arts — A2418

2014, July 4 Engr. *Perf. 13¼*
4653 A2418 66c multi 1.75 .60

Art Issue

Les Boîtes de Conserve, by Jean Fautrier (1898-1964) — A2419

2014, July 11 Engr. *Perf. 13x13¼*
4654 A2419 €1.65 multi 4.50 2.25

General Mobilization of World War I Troops, Cent. — A2420

2014, Aug. 2 Engr. *Perf. 13x13¼*
4655 A2420 66c blue & red 1.75 .60

Miniature Sheet

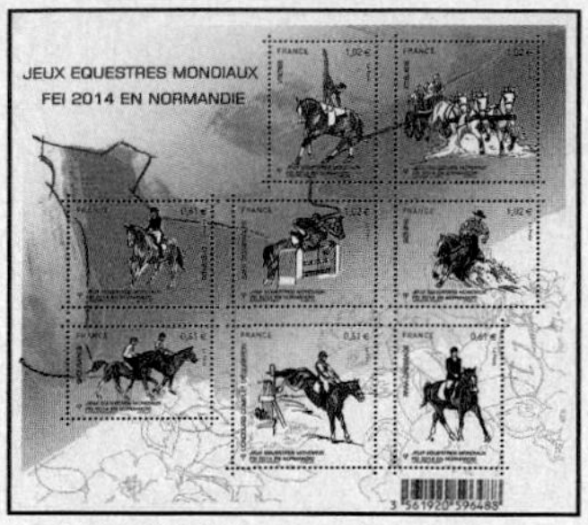

2014 World Equestrian Games, Normandy — A2421

No. 4656: a, Dressage (40x30mm). b, Endurance (40x30mm). c, Concours complet d'équitation (40x40mm). d, Para-dressage (30x40mm). e, Voltige (30x40mm). f, Attelage (40x40mm). g, Saut d'obstacles (40x30mm). h, Reining (40x30mm).

2014, Aug. 23 Photo. *Perf. 13x13¼*

4656 A2421 Sheet of 8 17.50 8.75
a.-d. 61c Any single 1.60 .55
e.-h. €1.02 Any single 2.75 .90

A souvenir sheet containing examples of Nos. 4656e and 4656f with different perforations, sold for €6.

Charles Péguy (1873-1914), Writer — A2422

2014, Sept. 5 Engr. *Perf. 13¼*

4657 A2422 €1.55 multi 4.00 1.40

Renaissance Objets d'Art — A2423

Designs: No. 4658, Gardens of Château de Villandry. No. 4659, Clock, Rouen. No. 4660, Stairway sculpture, by Jean Goujon. No. 4661, Sculpture of salamander, Château de Fontainbleau. No. 4662, Buckle of King Charles IX. No. 4663, Detail of tapestry depicting Jupiter and Latona. No. 4664, Portrait of King Francis I, by Jean Clouet. No. 4665, Stainedd-glass window depicting angel playing flute, Sainte-Etienne Cathedral, Sens. No. 4666, Enamel painting of Ulysses, by Léonard Limousin. No. 4667, Book cover by Étienne Roffet. No. 4668, Armor of King Henri II. No. 4669, Stained-glass emblem of Queen Anne of Brittany depicting ermine and crown.

Serpentine Die Cut 11

2014, Sept. 6 Photo.

Booklet Stamps
Self-Adhesive

4658 A2423 (61c) multi 1.60 .55
4659 A2423 (61c) multi 1.60 .55
4660 A2423 (61c) multi 1.60 .55
4661 A2423 (61c) multi 1.60 .55
4662 A2423 (61c) multi 1.60 .55
4663 A2423 (61c) multi 1.60 .55
4664 A2423 (61c) multi 1.60 .55
4665 A2423 (61c) multi 1.60 .55
4666 A2423 (61c) multi 1.60 .55
4667 A2423 (61c) multi 1.60 .55
4668 A2423 (61c) multi 1.60 .55
4669 A2423 (61c) multi 1.60 .55
a. Booklet pane of 12, #4658-4669 19.50
Nos. 4658-4669 (12) 19.20 6.60

Souvenir Sheet

First Battle of the Marne, Cent. — A2424

No. 4670: a, Troops and automobile. b, Troops on horseback.

Photo. & Litho.

2014, Sept. 12 *Perf. 13¼*

4670 A2424 Sheet of 2 4.25 2.10
a. 66c multi 1.75 .60
b. 98c multi 2.50 .85

A souvenir sheet containing Nos. 4670a and 4670b but with as different margin sold for €5.

Art Issue

Mural on Necker Hospital Staircase, by Keith Haring (1958-90) A2425

2014, Sept. 19 Photo. *Perf. 12¼x13*

4671 A2425 €2.65 multi 6.75 3.50

Types of 2014

Serpentine Die Cut 11

2014, Sept. 25 Photo.

Booklet Stamps
Self-Adhesive

4672 A2415 61c Like #4649 + label (22x16mm) 1.60 .55
4673 A2413 61c Like #4647 (22x16mm) 1.60 .55
4674 A2414 61c Like #4648 (21x16mm) 1.60 .55
4675 A2410 61c Like #4640 (15x22mm) 1.60 .55
4676 A2407 66c Like #4626a (21x22mm) 1.75 .60
4677 A2411 66c Like #4642e (30x22mm) 1.75 .60
4678 A2411 66c Like #4642a (30x22mm) 1.75 .60
4679 A2410 €1.02 Like #4641 (15x22mm) 2.60 .85
4680 A2407 €1.10 Like #4626b (15x22mm) 2.75 .90
4681 A2416 €1.65 Like #4650 (46x38mm) 4.25 1.40
a. Booklet pane of 10, #4672-4681 + label 21.50
Nos. 4672-4681 (10) 21.25 7.15

Sense of Smell A2426

Designs: No. 4682, Man and woman in love. No. 4683, Dog with magnifying glass. No. 4684, Coffee pot and cup. No. 4685, Skunks. No. 4686, Perfume atomizer. No. 4687, Athletic shoe and flowers. No. 4688, Fish with clothespin on nose. No. 4689, Cheese and foxes. No. 4690, Roast chicken. No. 4691, Woman smelling rose. No. 4692, Mother and baby. No. 4693, Face, herbs and spices.

Serpentine Die Cut 11

2014, Oct. 1 Photo.

Booklet Stamps
Self-Adhesive

4682 A2426 (61c) multi 1.60 .55
4683 A2426 (61c) multi 1.60 .55
4684 A2426 (61c) multi 1.60 .55
4685 A2426 (61c) multi 1.60 .55
4686 A2426 (61c) multi 1.60 .55
4687 A2426 (61c) multi 1.60 .55
4688 A2426 (61c) multi 1.60 .55
4689 A2426 (61c) multi 1.60 .55
4690 A2426 (61c) multi 1.60 .55
4691 A2426 (61c) multi 1.60 .55
4692 A2426 (61c) multi 1.60 .55
4693 A2426 (61c) multi 1.60 .55
a. Booklet pane of 12, #4682-4693 19.50
Nos. 4682-4693 (12) 19.20 6.60

Douai Court House 300th Anniv. A2427

2014, Oct. 3 Engr. *Perf. 13¼*

4694 A2427 83c multi 2.10 .70

Green Turtle A2428

2014, Oct. 9 Litho. *Perf. 13x13¼*

4695 A2428 98c multi 2.50 .85

See Comoro Islands No. , French Southern & Antarctic Territories No. 511, Malagasy Republic No., Mauritius No. 1144, Seychelles No. 904.

Salsa Dancers — A2429

Break Dancers — A2430

2014, Oct. 11 Engr. *Perf. 13¼*

4696 A2429 61c multi 1.50 .50

Souvenir Sheet

Litho.

Perf. 13¼x13

4697 A2430 €2.45multi 6.25 2.10

Stamp Day.

Items With Spirals Type of 2014

Serpentine Die Cut 11

2014, Oct. 15 Litho.

Self-Adhesive

4698 A2369 (66c) Like #4540 1.75 1.75

"Phil@poste" is sharper on No. 4698 than on No. 4540.

Maximilien Vox (1894-1974), Creator of Typographical Classification System — A2431

2014, Oct. 17 Engr. *Perf. 13¼*

4699 A2431 €1.10 multi 2.75 .90

Miniature Sheet

Cameras — A2432

No. 4700: a, 1865 Derogy four-lens camera. b, 1902 Girard Le Reve folding camera. c, 1930 Kodak Beau Brownie camera. d, 1898 Bazin & Leroy Stereocycle camera. e, 1910 folding camera, horiz. f, 1935 Gaumont Spido Reportage camera.

Litho. & Engr.

2014, Oct. 24 *Perf. 13*

4700 A2432 Sheet of 6 10.50 5.25
a.-f. 66c Any single 1.75 .60

A set of six souvenir sheets containing one example of Nos. 4700a-4700f sold as a set for €16.

A2433

A2434

A2435

A2436

A2437

A2438

A2439

A2440

A2441

A2442

A2443

A2444

Serpentine Die Cut 11

2014, Oct. 24 Photo.

Booklet Stamps
Self-Adhesive

4701	A2433	(61c) multi		1.50	.50
4702	A2434	(61c) multi		1.50	.50
4703	A2435	(61c) multi		1.50	.50
4704	A2436	(61c) multi		1.50	.50
4705	A2437	(61c) multi		1.50	.50
4706	A2438	(61c) multi		1.50	.50
4707	A2439	(61c) multi		1.50	.50
4708	A2440	(61c) multi		1.50	.50
4709	A2441	(61c) multi		1.50	.50
4710	A2442	(61c) multi		1.50	.50
4711	A2443	(61c) multi		1.50	.50
4712	A2444	(61c) multi		1.50	.50
a.	Booklet pane of 12, #4701-4712			18.00	
	Nos. 4701-4712 (12)			18.00	6.00

A souvenir sheet containing one perf. 13¼ example of a stamp like No. 4706 sold for €3.20.

New French Industries A2446

Inscriptions: No. 4714, Usine du futur. No. 4715, Transition numérique. No. 4716, Développement durable. No. 4717, Patrimoine. No. 4718, Gastronomie. No. 4719, Transition énergétique. No. 4720, Elégance. No. 4721, Economi sociale et solidaire. No. 4722, Electromobilité. No. 4723, Exportations. No. 4724, Métiers d'art. No. 4725, Innovation 2030.

Serpentine Die Cut 11

2014, Oct. 27 Photo.

Booklet Stamps
Self-Adhesive

4714	A2446	(61c) multi		1.50	.50
4715	A2446	(61c) multi		1.50	.50
4716	A2446	(61c) multi		1.50	.50
4717	A2446	(61c) multi		1.50	.50
4718	A2446	(61c) multi		1.50	.50
4719	A2446	(61c) multi		1.50	.50
4720	A2446	(61c) multi		1.50	.50
4721	A2446	(61c) multi		1.50	.50
4722	A2446	(61c) multi		1.50	.50
4723	A2446	(61c) multi		1.50	.50
4724	A2446	(61c) multi		1.50	.50
4725	A2446	(61c) multi		1.50	.50
a.	Booklet pane of 12, #4714-4725			18.00	
	Nos. 4714-4725 (12)			18.00	6.00

Public Sale of Blue Cornflowers Made by World War I Veterans, 80th Anniv. — A2447

2014, Nov. 6 Photo. *Perf. 13¼*

4726	A2447	€1.10 multi		2.75	.90

Types of 2003-14

2014, Nov. 6 Engr. *Perf. 13*

4727	Sheet of 4, #4079, 4437, 4727a, 4727b	6.00	3.00
a.	A2412 61c green (20x26mm)	1.50	.50
b.	A1664 61c green	1.50	.50
c.	Booklet pane of 12, 6 each #4727a-4727b	18.00	—
	Complete booklet, #4437b, 4727c	21.00	

Evariste de Parny (1753-1814), Poet — A2448

2014, Nov. 7 Engr. *Perf. 13¼*

4728	A2448	83c multi		2.10	.70

Republican Security Companies (Riot Control Forces), 70th Anniv. — A2449

2014, Dec. 8 Photo. *Perf. 13x12¾*

4729	A2449	€1.10 multi		2.75	.90

Handicrafts A2450

Inscriptions: Nos. 4730, 4742, Pierres précieuses (jewelery making). No. 4731, Bois (sanding wood). No. 4732, Verre (glass making). No. 4733, Métal (blacksmithing). No. 4734, Tissu (embroidery). No. 4735, Terre (pottery making). No. 4736, Papier (paper making). No. 4737, Tissu (weaving). No. 4738, Cuir (leather work). No. 4739, Bois (barrel making). No. 4740, Pierre (soulpting). No. 4741, Végétal (flower arranging).

2015 Litho. *Serpentine Die Cut 11*

Self-Adhesive

4730	A2450	(76c) multi		1.75	1.75

Photo.

Booklet Stamps

4731	A2450	(76c) multi		1.75	.60
4732	A2450	(76c) multi		1.75	.60
4733	A2450	(76c) multi		1.75	.60
4734	A2450	(76c) multi		1.75	.60
4735	A2450	(76c) multi		1.75	.60
4736	A2450	(76c) multi		1.75	.60
4737	A2450	(76c) multi		1.75	.60
4738	A2450	(76c) multi		1.75	.60
4739	A2450	(76c) multi		1.75	.60
4740	A2450	(76c) multi		1.75	.60
4741	A2450	(76c) multi		1.75	.60
4742	A2450	(76c) multi		1.75	.60
a.	Booklet pane of 12, #4731-4742			21.00	
	Nos. 4731-4742 (12)			21.00	7.20

No. 4730 has a visible dot pattern in the upper right part of the vignette and a sharper "Phil@poste" than No. 4742. Issued: Nos. 4730, 1/5; others 1/3.

Art Issue

The Great Wave, by Katsushika Hokusai (1760-1849) — A2451

2015, Jan. 16 Photo. *Perf. 13x13¼*

4743	A2451	€1.90 multi		4.50	2.25

Hearts — A2452

"JC de Castelbajac," people kissing and: 68c, Hearts. €1.15, Flowers.

2015, Jan. 23 Photo. *Perf.*

With White Frame Around Stamp

4744	A2452	68c multi		1.60	.55

Without White Frame Around Stamp

Perf. 13

4745	A2452	68c multi		1.60	.55
4746	A2452	€1.15 multi		2.60	.85

Self-Adhesive

Serpentine Die Cut

4747	A2452	68c multi		1.60	1.60
4748	A2452	€1.15 multi		2.60	2.60

No. 4744 was printed in sheets of 5. Values for Nos. 4745-4748 are for examples with surrounding selvage. Designs on Nos. 4745-4748 continue onto the surrounding selvage.

New Year 2015 (Year of the Goat) — A2453

2015, Jan. 30 Photo. *Perf. 13¼x13*

4749	A2453	76c multi		1.75	.60

No. 4749 was printed in sheets of 5. A souvenir sheet of one sold for €3.20.

Drawings of Hands A2454

Drawing by: No. 4750, Alphonse Legros. No. 4751, Unknown 18th century Italian School artist. No. 4752, Paul Delaroche. No. 4753, Gustave Moreau. No. 4754, Eugène Carrière. No. 4755, Pablo Picasso. No. 4756, Annibale Carrache. No. 4757, Unknown 17th century Italian School artist (four hands holding handles). No. 4758, Louis Tocque (one hand). No. 4759, Pierre Mignard. No. 4760, Tocque (two hands holding hoop with flowers). No. 4761, Unknown 17th Italian School artist (hand, water drop and goblet).

Serpentine Die Cut 11

2015, Jan. 30 Litho.

Booklet Stamps
Self-Adhesive

4750	A2454	(68c) multi		1.60	.55
4751	A2454	(68c) multi		1.60	.55
4752	A2454	(68c) multi		1.60	.55
4753	A2454	(68c) multi		1.60	.55
4754	A2454	(68c) multi		1.60	.55
4755	A2454	(68c) multi		1.60	.55
4756	A2454	(68c) multi		1.60	.55
4757	A2454	(68c) multi		1.60	.55
4758	A2454	(68c) multi		1.60	.55
4759	A2454	(68c) multi		1.60	.55
4760	A2454	(68c) multi		1.60	.55
4761	A2454	(68c) multi		1.60	.55
a.	Booklet pane of 12, #4750-4761			19.50	
	Nos. 4750-4761 (12)			19.20	6.60

Landmine Removal Service, 70th Anniv, A2455

2015, Feb. 20 Photo. *Perf. 13¼*

4762	A2455	€1.20 multi		2.75	.90

Goat Breeds A2456

Inscriptions: No. 4763, La Créole. No. 4764, La Poitevine. No. 4765, L'Alpine. No. 4766, La Chèvre du Massif Central. No. 4767, La Lorraine. No. 4768, La Rove. No. 4769, La Chèvre des Fossés. No. 4770, La Saanen. No. 4771, La Pyrénéenne. No. 4772, L'Angora. No. 4773, La Provençale. No. 4774, La Corse.

Serpentine Die Cut 11

2015, Feb. 21 Photo.

Booklet Stamps
Self-Adhesive

4763	A2456	(68c) multi		1.50	.50
4764	A2456	(68c) multi		1.50	.50
4765	A2456	(68c) multi		1.50	.50
4766	A2456	(68c) multi		1.50	.50
4767	A2456	(68c) multi		1.50	.50
4768	A2456	(68c) multi		1.50	.50
4769	A2456	(68c) multi		1.50	.50
4770	A2456	(68c) multi		1.50	.50
4771	A2456	(68c) multi		1.50	.50
4772	A2456	(68c) multi		1.50	.50
4773	A2456	(68c) multi		1.50	.50
4774	A2456	(68c) multi		1.50	.50
a.	Booklet pane of 12, #4763-4774			18.00	
	Nos. 4763-4774 (12)			18.00	6.00

Souvenir Sheet

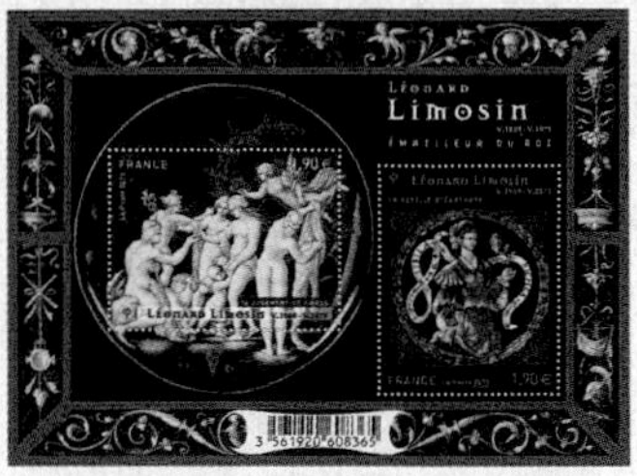

Enamel Art of Léonard Limosin (c. 1505-77) — A2457

No. 4775: a, The Judgment of Paris. b, Eritrean Sibyl (Sybila Richea), vert.

Perf. 13x13¼, 13¼x13

2015, Feb. 27 Photo.

4775	A2457 Sheet of 2	8.50	8.50
a.-b.	€1.90 Either single	4.25	1.40
c.	Souvenir sheet of 2, #4775a-4775b, #4775a at right	14.00	14.00

No. 4775c sold for €6.20.

Souvenir Sheet

Basilica of Saint-Denis — A2458

No. 4776: a, Tombs (41x30mm). b, Stained-glass window (41x41mm).

2015, Mar. 14 Engr. *Perf. 13¼*
4776 A2458 Sheet of 2 4.50 4.50
a. 76c multi 1.75 .60
b. €1.25 multi 2.75 .90

A souvenir sheet of 2, containing Nos. 4776a-4776b, with No. 4776a at left sold for €6.20.

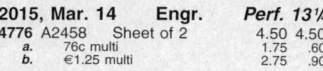

Spring Philatelic Show, Paris — A2459

2015, Mar. 19 Engr. *Perf. 13x12¾*
4777 A2459 68c multi 1.50 .50

Belgian Government in Exile in Sainte-Adresse, Cent. — A2460

Mailboxes, Belgian government officials in exile and: 76c, French and Belgian flags, building. 95c, Ministerial residence.

2015, Mar. 19 Photo. *Perf. 13¼*
4778 A2460 76c multi 1.75 .60
4779 A2460 95c multi 2.10 .70
a. Souvenir sheet of 2, #4778-4779 7.00 7.00

No. 4779a sold for €3.20. See Belgium No. 2748.

Art Issue

L'O, Light Sculpture by Yann Kersalé A2461

2015, Mar. 20 Photo. *Perf. 13¼*
4780 A2461 €1.90 multi 4.25 2.10

Nicole Mangin (1878-1919), World War I Physician — A2462

2015, Mar. 21 Engr. *Perf. 13x13¼*
4781 A2462 68c multi 1.50 .50

Renaissance Architecture A2463

Designs: No. 4782, Château d'Amboise. No. 4783, Château de Valençay. No. 4784, Palais Ducal de Nevers. No. 4785, Château de Villandry. No. 4786, Château d'Ancy-le-Franc. No. 4787, Palais du Louvre. No. 4788, Château de Chambord. No. 4789, Château d'Ecouen. No. 4790, Château d'Azay-le-Rideau. No. 4791, Château de Chenonceau. No. 4792, Château d'Anet. No. 4793, Château de Blois.

Serpentine Die Cut 11
2015, Mar. 27 Litho.
Booklet Stamps
Self-Adhesive

4782 A2463 (68c) multi 1.50 .50
4783 A2463 (68c) multi 1.50 .50
4784 A2463 (68c) multi 1.50 .50
4785 A2463 (68c) multi 1.50 .50
4786 A2463 (68c) multi 1.50 .50
4787 A2463 (68c) multi 1.50 .50
4788 A2463 (68c) multi 1.50 .50
4789 A2463 (68c) multi 1.50 .50
4790 A2463 (68c) multi 1.50 .50
4791 A2463 (68c) multi 1.50 .50
4792 A2463 (68c) multi 1.50 .50
4793 A2463 (68c) multi 1.50 .50
a. Booklet pane of 12, #4782-4793 18.00
Nos. 4782-4793 (12) 18.00 6.00

Saintes-Maries-de-la-Mer Religious Procession, 700th Anniv. — A2464

2015, Mar. 29 Engr. *Perf. 13¼*
4794 A2464 68c multi 1.50 .50

Miniature Sheet

European Capitals — A2465

No. 4795 — Attractions in Riga, Latvia: a, Nativity Cathedral. b, St. Peter's Church, horiz. c, House of the Blackheads, horiz. d, National Opera.

Perf. 13¼x13, 13x13¼
2015, Apr. 3 Photo.
4795 A2465 Sheet of 4 7.00 7.00
a.-d. 76c Any single 1.75 .60

Croix de Guerre, Cent. — A2466

2015, Apr. 8 Engr. *Perf. 13¼*
4796 A2466 76c multi 1.75 .60

Souvenir Sheet

French History — A2467

No. 4797: a, Coronation of Charlemagne, 768. b, Educational reforms of Charlemagne, 789, horiz.

Perf. 13¼x13, 13x13¼
2015, Apr. 10 Engr.
4797 A2467 Sheet of 2 8.50 8.50
a.-b. €1.90 Either single 4.25 1.40

French and Indian Cooperation in Space, 50th Anniv. — A2468

Designs: 76c, Saral satellite. €1.20, Megha-Tropiques satellite.

2014, Apr. 10 Photo. *Perf. 13¼*
4798 A2468 76c multi 1.75 .60
4799 A2468 €1.20 multi 2.75 .90

See India Nos. 2725-2726.

Chalon-sur-Saône A2469

2015, Apr. 17 Engr. *Perf. 13¼*
4800 A2469 68c multi 1.60 .55

Liberation of Concentration Camps, 70th Anniv. — A2470

2015, Apr. 24 Photo. *Perf. 13¼*
4801 A2470 76c multi 1.75 .60

Miniature Sheet

Way of St. James — A2471

No. 4802 — Sites in: a, Oloron-Sainte-Marie. b, Aire-sur l'Adour, vert. c, Saint-Jean-Pied-de Port. d, Blaye.

Litho. & Engr.
2015, Apr. 24 *Perf. 13*
4802 A2471 Sheet of 4 9.00 9.00
a.-d. 95c Any single 2.25 .75

Europa — A2472

2015, May 2 Photo. *Perf. 13¼*
4803 A2472 95c multi 2.25 .75

Paintings of Flowers — A2473

Designs: No. 4804, Irises and Red Geraniums, by Paul Cézanne. No. 4805, Peonies, by Paul Gauguin. No. 4806, Carnations, by Jeanne Magnin. No. 4807, Wisteria, by Pierre Bracquemond. No. 4808, Daisies and Hydrangea, by Emile Boutin. No. 4809, Roses and Anémones, by Vincent van Gogh. No. 4810, Gladioluses, by Auguste Renoir. No. 4811, Wildflowers by Odilon Redon. No. 4812, Peonies, by Edouard Manet. No. 4813, Roses, by Gustave Caillebotte. No. 4814, Queens Daisies, by Marie Duhem. No. 4815, Roses, by Henri Fantin-Latour.

Serpentine Die Cut 11
2015, May 2 Litho.
Booklet Stamps
Self-Adhesive

4804 A2473 (68c) multi 1.60 .55
4805 A2473 (68c) multi 1.60 .55
4806 A2473 (68c) multi 1.60 .55
4807 A2473 (68c) multi 1.60 .55
4808 A2473 (68c) multi 1.60 .55
4809 A2473 (68c) multi 1.60 .55
4810 A2473 (68c) multi 1.60 .55
4811 A2473 (68c) multi 1.60 .55
4812 A2473 (68c) multi 1.60 .55
4813 A2473 (68c) multi 1.60 .55
4814 A2473 (68c) multi 1.60 .55
4815 A2473 (68c) multi 1.60 .55
a. Booklet pane of 12, #4804-4815 19.50
Nos. 4804-4815 (12) 19.20 6.60

Victory in World War II, 70th Anniv. — A2474

2015, May 7 Photo. *Perf. 13¼*
4816 A2474 68c multi 1.50 .50

Marshal Jacques II de Chabannes, Lord of La Palice (1470-1525) — A2475

2015, May 15 Engr. *Perf. 13¼*
4817 A2475 76c multi 1.75 .60

Mâcon — A2476

2015, May 22 Engr. *Perf. 13x13¼*
4818 A2476 68c multi + label 1.50 .50

French Federation of Philatelic Associations, 88th Congress, Mâcon.

17th World Convention of Rose Societies, Lyon
A2477

Designs: 76c, Red and pink roses. €1.20, Pink and yellow roses.

2015, May 29 Photo. *Perf. 13¼*

4819 A2477 76c multi 1.75 .60
4820 A2477 €1.20 multi 2.75 .90
a. Horiz. pair, #4819-4820 4.50 2.25

A souvenir sheet containing Nos. 4819-4820 sold for €6.20.

Service Central d'Etat Civil, 50th Anniv. — A2478

2015, June 6 Engr. *Perf. 13¼*

4821 A2478 €1.25 multi 2.75 .90

The 1960's — A2479

No. 4822: a, Radio France Headquarters. b, Men and women dancing, vert. c, Movie poster for *Les Demoiselles de Rochefort,* vert. d, 1961 Peugeot 404 convertible. e, Ocean liner SS France. f, Women wearing short dresses, vert.

2015, June 12 Photo. *Perf. 13*

4822 A2479 Sheet of 6 10.50 10.50
a.-f. 76c Any single 1.75 .60

Hartmannswillerkopf National Monument — A2480

2015, June 19 Engr. *Perf. 13¼*

4823 A2480 95c multi 2.10 .70

Saint-Martial Church, Lestards — A2481

2015, June 24 Engr. *Perf. 13¼*

4824 A2481 68c multi 1.50 .50

A2482

A2483

A2484

A2485

A2486

A2487

A2488

A2489

A2490

A2491

A2492

Vacations
A2493

Serpentine Die Cut 11

2015, June 29 Photo.

Booklet Stamps
Self-Adhesive

4825 A2482 (68c) multi 1.50 .50
4826 A2483 (68c) multi 1.50 .50
4827 A2484 (68c) multi 1.50 .50
4828 A2485 (68c) multi 1.50 .50
4829 A2486 (68c) multi 1.50 .50
4830 A2487 (68c) multi 1.50 .50
4831 A2488 (68c) multi 1.50 .50
4832 A2489 (68c) multi 1.50 .50
4833 A2490 (68c) multi 1.50 .50
4834 A2491 (68c) multi 1.50 .50
4835 A2492 (68c) multi 1.50 .50
4836 A2493 (68c) multi 1.50 .50
a. Booklet pane of 12, #4825-4836 18.00
Nos. 4825-4836 (12) 18.00 6.00

Haguenau, 900th Anniv.
A2494

2015, July 3 Engr. *Perf. 13¼*

4837 A2494 68c multi 1.50 .50

Martin Nadaud (1815-98), Mason and Politician
A2495

2015, July 3 Engr. *Perf. 13¼*

4838 A2495 68c multi 1.50 .50

Gilberto Bosques (1892-1995), Mexican Diplomat Who Saved Jews In World War II — A2496

Bosques and: 76c, Notre Dame de la Garde Basilica, Marseilles, and signed travel visa. €1.20, Embassy, Mexican consular handstamp.

2015, July 16 Litho. *Perf. 13*

4839 A2496 76c multi 1.75 .60
4840 A2496 €1.20 multi 2.75 .90
a. Horiz. pair, #4839-4840 4.50 2.25

See Mexico Nos. 2940-2941.

Animal Eyes
A2497

Eye of: No. 4841, Requin à aileron blanc du lagon (whitetip reef shark). No. 4842, Petit-duc du Grant (southern white-faced owl). No. 4843, Rainette à yeux rouges (red-eyed tree frog). No. 4844, Toucan. No. 4845, Coq de race Brahma (Brahma chicken). No. 4846, Agame (agama lizard). No. 4847, Ara hyacinthe (hyacinth macaw). No. 4848, Iguane des Fidji (Fiji banded iguana). No. 4849, Tarente géante (giant wall gecko). No. 4850, Serpentaire (serpent eagle). No. 4851, Poisson-lime gribouillé (scrawled filefish). No. 4852, Gypaète barbu (bearded vulture).

Serpentine Die Cut 11

2015, July 31 Photo.

Booklet Stamps
Self-Adhesive

4841 A2497 (76c) multi 1.75 .60
4842 A2497 (76c) multi 1.75 .60
4843 A2497 (76c) multi 1.75 .60
4844 A2497 (76c) multi 1.75 .60
4845 A2497 (76c) multi 1.75 .60
4846 A2497 (76c) multi 1.75 .60
4847 A2497 (76c) multi 1.75 .60
4848 A2497 (76c) multi 1.75 .60
4849 A2497 (76c) multi 1.75 .60
4850 A2497 (76c) multi 1.75 .60
4851 A2497 (76c) multi 1.75 .60
4852 A2497 (76c) multi 1.75 .60
a. Booklet pane of 12, #4841-4852 21.00
Nos. 4841-4852 (12) 21.00 7.20

Animal Proverbs and Idioms
A2498

Designs: No. 4853, Un froid de canard ("Freezing cold"). No. 4854, Rire comme une baleine ("Laughing like a whale"). No. 4855, Comme un chien dans un jeu de quilles ("Like a bull in a China shop"). No. 4856, Prendre le taureau par les cornes ("Take the bull by the horns"). No. 4857, Fier comme un paon ("Proud as a peacock"). No. 4858, Donner de la confiture aux cochons ("Cast pearls before swine"). No. 4859, Avoir un appétit d'oiseau ("Have the appetite of a bird"). No. 4860, Donner sa langue au chat ("Cat got your tongue?"). No. 4861, Etre le bouc émissaire ("Be the scapegoat"). No. 4862, Faire le pied de grue ("To cool one's heels"). No. 4863, Araignée du soir espoir ("A spider in the evening, hope"). No. 4864, Poser un lapin ("To stand someone up").

Serpentine Die Cut 11

2015, Aug. 28 Photo.

Booklet Stamps
Self-Adhesive

4853 A2498 (68c) multi 1.60 .55
4854 A2498 (68c) multi 1.60 .55
4855 A2498 (68c) multi 1.60 .55
4856 A2498 (68c) multi 1.60 .55
4857 A2498 (68c) multi 1.60 .55
4858 A2498 (68c) multi 1.60 .55
4859 A2498 (68c) multi 1.60 .55
4860 A2498 (68c) multi 1.60 .55
4861 A2498 (68c) multi 1.60 .55
4862 A2498 (68c) multi 1.60 .55
4863 A2498 (68c) multi 1.60 .55
4864 A2498 (68c) multi 1.60 .55
a. Booklet pane of 12, #4853-4864 19.50
Nos. 4853-4864 (12) 19.20 6.60

Compare types A2498 and A2297.

Souvenir Sheet

Battle of Huningue, 200th Anniv. — A2499

2015, Aug. 29 Photo. *Perf. 13¼*

4865 A2499 €1.25 multi 3.00 1.00

2015 World Rowing Championships, Aiguebelette
A2500

Boat with: 76c, Two female rowers. €1.20, Male rowers (35x26mm).

2015, Aug. 30 Photo. ***Perf. 13x13¼***

4866 A2500	76c multi		1.75	.60
4867 A2500	€1.20 multi		2.75	.90
a.	Horiz. pair, #4866-4867		4.50	2.25

Marianne and Children "Europe" With Data Matrix Code
A2501

Marianne and Children "Monde" With Data Matrix Code
A2502

2015, Sept. 4 Engr. ***Perf. 13***

4868 A2501	(95c) blue		2.25	.75
4869 A2502	(€1.20) purple		2.75	.90

Self-Adhesive

Serpentine Die Cut 6¾ Vert.

4870 A2501	(95c) blue		2.25	.75
a.	Booklet pane of 6		13.50	
4871 A2502	(€1.20) purple		2.75	.90

The Data Matrix codes on types A2501 and A2502 differ, but all examples of stamps of either type have identical codes.

Freedom, Equality, Fraternity, Painting by Jonone in National Assembly
A2504

2015, Sept. 19 Photo. ***Perf. 13¼***

4873 A2504	76c multi		1.75	.60

Landing of French on Mauritius, 300th Anniv. — A2505

2015, Sept. 25 Photo. ***Perf. 13¼***

4874 A2505	76c multi		1.75	.60

See Mauritius No.

Sense of Sight
A2506

Designs: No. 4875, Room with a window (Chambre avec vue). No. 4876, Eye chart (A ma vue). No. 4877, Land in sight (Terre en vue). No. 4878, Eye (A vue d'oeil). No. 4879, Sun on horizon (Déjà vue). No. 4880, Women viewed through binoculars (Jumelles en vue). No. 4881, Planets (Vue imprenable). No. 4882, Nose and butterfly (A vue de nez). No. 4883, Diver and pool (Vue plongeante). No. 4884, Clouds (A perte de vue). No. 4885, Woman wearing mask (Ni vue, ni connue). No. 4886, Ghost and pink flying elephant (Vue de l'esprit).

Serpentine Die Cut 11

2015, Sept. 25 Photo.

Booklet Stamps
Self-Adhesive

4875 A2506	(68c) multi		1.60	.55
4876 A2506	(68c) multi		1.60	.55
4877 A2506	(68c) multi		1.60	.55
4878 A2506	(68c) multi		1.60	.55
4879 A2506	(68c) multi		1.60	.55
4880 A2506	(68c) multi		1.60	.55
4881 A2506	(68c) multi		1.60	.55
4882 A2506	(68c) multi		1.60	.55
4883 A2506	(68c) multi		1.60	.55
4884 A2506	(68c) multi		1.60	.55
4885 A2506	(68c) multi		1.60	.55
4886 A2506	(68c) multi		1.60	.55
a.	Booklet pane of 12, #4875-4886		19.50	
	Nos. 4875-4886 (12)		19.20	6.60

Jean-Henri Fabre (1823-1915), Entomologist — A2507

2015, Oct. 2 Litho. ***Perf. 13¼***

4887 A2507	€2.60 multi		6.00	2.00

A souvenir sheet of one of No. 4887 sold for €6.20.

Pierre Laroque (1907-97), Director of Social Security, and Ambroise Croizat (1901-51), Politician
A2508

2015, Oct. 6 Photo. ***Perf. 13x13¼***

4888 A2508	68c multi		1.50	.50

French Social Security System, 70th anniv.

Tango Dancers — A2509

Ballet Preljocaj — A2510

Litho. & Engr.

2015, Oct. 10 ***Perf. 13¼***

4889 A2509	68c multi		1.50	.50

Photo.

Souvenir Sheet

4890 A2510	€1.15 multi		2.60	.85

Stamp Day.

Saint-Gobain Corporation, 350th Anniv. — A2511

Litho. & Engr.

2015, Oct. 14 ***Perf. 13¼***

4891 A2511	68c multi		1.50	.50

A2513

A2514

A2515

A2516

A2517

A2518

A2519

A2520

A2521

A2522

A2523

Happy New Year — A2524

Serpentine Die Cut 11

2015, Oct. 30 Photo.

Booklet Stamps
Self-Adhesive

4893 A2513	(68c) multi		1.50	.50
4894 A2514	(68c) multi		1.50	.50
4895 A2515	(68c) multi		1.50	.50
4896 A2516	(68c) multi		1.50	.50
4897 A2517	(68c) multi		1.50	.50
4898 A2518	(68c) multi		1.50	.50
4899 A2519	(68c) multi		1.50	.50
4900 A2520	(68c) multi		1.50	.50
4901 A2521	(68c) multi		1.50	.50
4902 A2522	(68c) multi		1.50	.50
4903 A2523	(68c) multi		1.50	.50
4904 A2524	(68c) multi		1.50	.50
a.	Booklet pane of 12, #4893-4904		18.00	
	Nos. 4893-4904 (12)		18.00	6.00

Subject Index of French Commemorative Issues

FRANCE

SEMI-POSTAL STAMPS

No. 162 Surcharged in Red

and

SP2

1914 Unwmk. Typo. *Perf. 14x13½*

B1 A22 10c + 5c red 5.00 4.25
Never hinged 7.00
B2 SP2 10c + 5c red 32.50 3.25
Never hinged 90.00
a. Booklet pane of 10 600.00
Never hinged 800.00

Issue dates: No. B1, Aug. 11; No. B2, Sept. 10.

See Nos. B746a, B746b.

For overprint see Offices in Morocco No. B8.

Widow at Grave SP3

War Orphans SP4

Woman Plowing — SP5

"Trench of Bayonets" SP6

Lion of Belfort SP7

"La Marseillaise" — SP8

1917-19

B3 SP3 2c + 3c vio brn 4.50 5.00
Never hinged 10.00
B4 SP4 5c + 5c grn ('19) 21.00 9.50
Never hinged 60.00
B5 SP5 15c + 10c gray green 30.00 27.50
Never hinged 85.00
B6 SP5 25c + 15c dp bl 80.00 57.50
Never hinged 175.00
B7 SP6 35c + 25c slate & vio 135.00 125.00
Never hinged 350.00
B8 SP7 50c + 50c pale brn & dk brn 225.00 180.00
Never hinged 650.00
B9 SP8 1fr + 1fr cl & mar 425.00 400.00
Never hinged 1,100.
B10 SP8 5fr + 5fr dp bl & blk 1,600. 1,550.
Never hinged 4,000.
Nos. B3-B10 (8) 2,520. 2,354.

See No. B20-B23. For surcharges see No. B12-B19.

Hospital Ship and Field Hospital SP9

1918, Aug.

B11 SP9 15c + 5c sl & red 125.00 60.00
Never hinged 250.00

See No. B746d.

Semi-Postal Stamps of 1917-19 Surcharged

1922, Sept. 1

B12 SP3 2c + 1c violet brn .50 *.80*
Never hinged 1.00
B13 SP4 5c + 2½c green .80 *1.25*
Never hinged 1.50
B14 SP5 15c + 5c gray grn 1.25 *1.60*
Never hinged 2.60
B15 SP5 25c + 5c deep bl 2.30 *2.50*
Never hinged 4.75
B16 SP6 35c + 5c slate & vio 13.00 *15.00*
Never hinged 30.00
B17 SP7 50c + 10c pale brn & dk brn 19.00 *24.00*
Never hinged 39.00
a. Pair, one without surcharge
B18 SP8 1fr + 25c cl & mar 32.50 *37.50*
Never hinged 60.00
B19 SP8 5fr + 1fr bl & blk 150.00 *155.00*
Never hinged 275.00
Nos. B12-B19 (8) 219.35 237.65
Set, never hinged 415.00

Style and arrangement of surcharge differs for each denomination.

Types of 1917-19

1926-27

B20 SP3 2c + 1c violet brn 1.50 1.40
Never hinged 4.00
B21 SP7 50c + 10c ol brn & dk brn 20.00 12.50
Never hinged 72.50
B22 SP8 1fr + 25c dp rose & red brn 55.00 42.50
Never hinged 150.00
B23 SP8 5fr + 1fr sl bl & blk 105.00 100.00
Never hinged 240.00
Nos. B20-B23 (4) 181.50 156.40

Sinking Fund Issues

Types of Regular Issues of 1903-07 Surcharged in Red or Blue

1927, Sept. 26

B24 A22 40c + 10c lt blue (R) 5.75 5.75
Never hinged 10.50
B25 A20 50c + 25c green (Bl) 8.25 *9.00*
Never hinged 14.00

Surcharge on No. B25 differs from illustration.

Type of Regular Issue of 1923 Surcharged in Black

B26 A23 1.50fr + 50c orange 14.50 14.00
Never hinged 37.50
a. Pair, one without surcharge *2,000.*
Nos. B24-B26 (3) 28.50 28.75

See Nos. B28-B33, B35-B37, B39-B41.

Industry and Agriculture SP10

1928, May Engr. *Perf. 13½*

B27 SP10 1.50fr + 8.50fr dull blue 140.00 *150.00*
Never hinged 225.00
a. Blue green 500.00 *550.00*
Never hinged 725.00

Types of 1903-23 Issues Surcharged like Nos. B24-B26

1928, Oct. 1 *Perf. 14x13½*

B28 A22 40c + 10c gray lilac (R) 13.00 *14.00*
Never hinged 32.50
B29 A20 50c + 25c orange brn (Bl) 32.50 29.00
Never hinged 60.00
B30 A23 1.50fr + 50c rose lilac (Bk) 52.50 42.50
Never hinged 100.00
Nos. B28-B30 (3) 98.00 85.50

Types of 1903-23 Issues Surcharged like Nos. B24-B26

1929, Oct. 1

B31 A22 40c + 10c green 18.00 *19.00*
Never hinged 37.50
B32 A20 50c + 25c lilac rose 30.00 30.00
Never hinged 60.00
B33 A23 1.50fr + 50c chestnut 60.00 *65.00*
Never hinged 130.00
Nos. B31-B33 (3) 108.00 114.00

"The Smile of Reims" SP11

1930, Mar. 15 Engr. *Perf. 13*

B34 SP11 1.50fr + 3.50fr red vio 80.00 *82.50*
Never hinged 130.00
a. Booklet pane of 4 300.00
Never hinged 525.00
b. Booklet pane of 8 600.00
Never hinged 1,050.
Complete booklet, #B34b 1,100.

Booklets containing No. B34 have two panes of 4 (No. B34a) connected by a gutter, the complete piece constituting #B34b, which is stapled into the booklet through the gutter. See footnote after No. 4642.

Types of 1903-07 Issues Surcharged like Nos. B24-B25

1930 Oct. 1 *Perf. 14x13½*

B35 A22 40c + 10c cerise 20.00 *21.00*
Never hinged 70.00
B36 A20 50c + 25c gray brown 37.50 *42.50*
Never hinged 120.00
B37 A22 1.50fr + 50c violet 65.00 *70.00*
Never hinged 190.00
Nos. B35-B37 (3) 122.50 133.50

Allegory, French Provinces SP12

1931, Mar. 1 *Perf. 13*

B38 SP12 1.50fr + 3.50fr green 125.00 *140.00*
Never hinged 300.00

Types of 1903-07 Issues Surcharged like Nos. B24-B25

1931, Oct. 1 *Perf. 14x13½*

B39 A22 40c + 10c ol grn 40.00 *45.00*
Never hinged 100.00
B40 A20 50c + 25c gray vio 100.00 *110.00*
Never hinged 235.00
B41 A22 1.50fr + 50c deep red 100.00 *110.00*
Never hinged 200.00
Nos. B39-B41 (3) 240.00 265.00

Catalogue values for unused stamps in this section, from this point to the end of the section, are for Never Hinged items.

"France" Giving Aid to an Intellectual SP13

Symbolic of Music SP14

1935, Dec. 9 Engr. *Perf. 13*

B42 SP13 50c + 10c ultra 4.00 2.50
Hinged 2.50
B43 SP14 50c + 2fr dull red 125.00 45.00
Hinged 55.00

The surtax was for the aid of distressed and exiled intellectuals.

For surcharge see No. B47.

Statue of Liberty SP15

Children of the Unemployed SP16

1936-37

B44 SP15 50c + 25c dk blue ('37) 7.50 5.00
Hinged 4.00
B45 SP15 75c + 50c violet 20.00 10.00
Hinged 9.50

Surtax for the aid of political refugees.

For surcharge see No. B47.

1936, May

B46 SP16 50c + 10c copper red 7.50 5.00
Hinged 4.50

The surtax was for the aid of children of the unemployed.

No. B43 Surcharged in Black

1936, Nov.

B47 SP14 20c on 50c + 2fr dull red 4.75 3.50
Hinged 3.25

Jacques Callot SP17

Anatole France (Jacques Anatole Thibault) — SP18

Hector Berlioz SP19

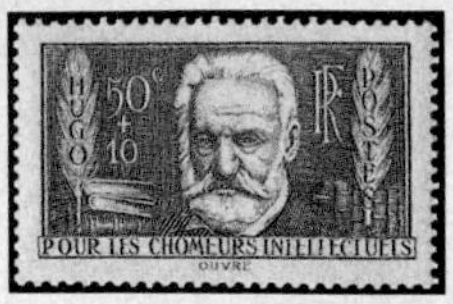

Victor Hugo
SP20

Auguste
Rodin
SP21

Louis
Pasteur
SP22

1936-37 **Engr.**

B48 SP17 20c + 10c brown car 4.50 2.50
Hinged 2.25
B49 SP18 30c + 10c emer ('37) 5.00 2.75
Hinged 2.25
B50 SP19 40c + 10c emer 4.50 2.75
Hinged 2.25
B51 SP20 50c + 10c copper red 8.75 3.75
Hinged 3.75
B52 SP21 90c + 10c rose red ('37) 13.00 6.50
Hinged 6.00
B53 SP22 1.50fr + 50c deep ultra 40.00 20.00
Hinged 20.00
Nos. B48-B53 (6) 75.75 38.25

The surtax was used for relief of unemployed intellectuals.

1938

B54 SP18 30c + 10c brown car 3.00 1.75
Hinged 1.75
B55 SP17 35c + 10c dull green 3.50 2.40
Hinged 2.40
B56 SP19 55c + 10c dull vio 10.00 4.00
Hinged 6.00
B57 SP20 65c + 10c ultra 11.50 4.00
Hinged 6.00
B58 SP21 1fr + 10c car lake 8.50 4.50
Hinged 4.75
B59 SP22 1.75fr + 25c dp blue 35.00 17.00
Hinged 17.00
Nos. B54-B59 (6) 71.50 33.65

Tug of War
SP23

Foot Race
SP24

Hiking — SP25

1937, June 16

B60 SP23 20c + 10c brown 3.00 2.25
Hinged 1.60
B61 SP24 40c + 10c red brown 3.00 2.25
Hinged 1.60
B62 SP25 50c + 10c black brn 3.00 2.25
Hinged 1.60
Nos. B60-B62 (3) 9.00 6.75

The surtax was for the Recreation Fund of the employees of the Post, Telephone and Telegraph.

Pierre Loti
(Louis
Marie Julien
Viaud)
SP26

1937, Aug.

B63 SP26 50c + 20c rose car 7.50 5.00
Hinged 3.75

The surtax was for the Pierre Loti Monument Fund.

"France"
and Infant
SP27

1937-39

B64 SP27 65c + 25c brown vio 5.25 2.75
Hinged 3.25
B65 SP27 90c + 30c pck bl ('39) 3.50 2.75
Hinged 2.10

The surtax was used for public health work.

Winged Victory
of Samothrace
SP28

Jean Baptiste
Charcot
SP29

1937, Aug.

B66 SP28 30c blue green 175.00 40.00
Hinged 65.00
B67 SP28 55c red 175.00 40.00
Hinged 65.00

On sale at the Louvre for 2.50fr. The surtax of 1.65fr was for the benefit of the Louvre Museum.

1938-39

B68 SP29 65c + 35c dk bl grn 3.00 3.00
Hinged 1.60
B69 SP29 90c + 35c brt red vio ('39) 30.00 13.50
Hinged 11.00

Surtax for the benefit of French seamen.

Palace of
Versailles
SP30

1938, May 9

B70 SP30 1.75fr + 75c dp bl 37.50 19.00
Hinged 19.00

Natl. Exposition of Painting and Sculpture at Versailles.
The surtax was for the benefit of the Versailles Concert Society.

French Soldier
SP31

Monument
SP32

1938, May 16

B71 SP31 55c + 70c brown vio 8.50 5.25
Hinged 4.75
B72 SP31 65c + 1.10fr pck bl 8.50 5.25
Hinged 4.75

The surtax was for a fund to erect a monument to the glory of the French Infantrymen.

1938, May 25

B73 SP32 55c + 45c vermilion 22.50 12.50
Hinged 10.00

The surtax was for a fund to erect a monument in honor of the Army Medical Corps.

Reims Cathedral
SP33

"France"
Welcoming Her
Sons
SP34

1938, July 10

B74 SP33 65c + 35c ultra 17.50 10.50
Hinged 8.50

Completion of the reconstruction of Reims Cathedral, July 10, 1938.

1938, Aug. 8

B75 SP34 65c + 60c rose car 8.50 5.75
Hinged 4.00

The surtax was for the benefit of French volunteers repatriated from Spain.

Curie Issue

Common Design Type

1938, Sept. 1

B76 CD80 1.75fr + 50c dp ultra 21.00 12.50
Hinged 8.75

Victory
Parade
Passing Arc
de
Triomphe
SP36

1938, Oct. 8

B77 SP36 65c + 35c brown car 5.75 4.50
Hinged 3.25

20th anniversary of the Armistice.

Student and
Nurse — SP37

1938, Dec. 1

B78 SP37 65c + 60c pck blue 15.00 8.25
Hinged 8.00

The surtax was for Student Relief.

Blind Man
and Radio
SP38

1938, Dec.

B79 SP38 90c + 25c brown vio 15.00 9.00
Hinged 8.00

The surtax was used to help provide radios for the blind.

Civilian Facing
Firing
Squad — SP39

Red Cross
Nurse — SP40

1939, Feb. 1

B80 SP39 90c + 35c black brn 17.00 10.50
Hinged 8.75

The surtax was used to erect a monument to civilian victims of World War I.

1939, Mar. 24

B81 SP40 90c + 35c dk sl grn, turq bl & red 13.00 8.25
Hinged 6.75

75th anniv. of the Intl. Red Cross Society. See No. B746c.

Army
Engineer
SP41

1939, Apr. 3

B82 SP41 70c + 50c vermilion 12.50 8.25
Hinged 6.00

Army Engineering Corps. The surtax was used to erect a monument to those members who died in World War I.

Ministry of
Post,
Telegraph
and
Telephone
SP42

1939, Apr. 8

B83 SP42 90c + 35c turq blue 37.50 20.00
Hinged 19.00

The surtax was used to aid orphans of employees of the postal system. Opening of the new building for the Ministry of Post, Telegraph and Telephones.

Mother and
Child — SP43

Eiffel
Tower — SP44

1939, Apr. 24

B84 SP43 90c + 35c red 3.75 2.50
Hinged 2.40

The surtax was used to aid children of the unemployed.

1939, May 5

B85 SP44 90c + 50c red violet 15.00 9.00
Hinged 8.75

50th anniv. of the Eiffel Tower. The surtax was used for celebration festivities.

Puvis de Chavannes — SP45

Claude Debussy SP46

Honoré de Balzac SP47

Claude Bernard SP48

1939-40

B86 SP45 40c + 10c ver 1.75 1.00
Hinged .80
B87 SP46 70c + 10c brn vio 8.25 2.50
Hinged 3.50
B87A SP46 80c + 10c brn vio ('40) 9.00 7.50
Hinged 4.25
B88 SP47 90c + 10c brt red vio 7.25 2.50
Hinged 3.25
B88A SP47 1fr + 10c brt red vio ('40) 9.00 7.50
Hinged 4.25
B89 SP48 2.25fr + 25c brt ultra 28.00 11.50
Hinged 14.50
B89A SP48 2.50fr + 25c brt ultra ('40) 9.00 7.50
Hinged 4.25
Nos. B86-B89A (7) 72.25 40.00

The surtax was used to aid unemployed intellectuals.

Mothers and Children
SP49 SP50

1939, June 15

B90 SP49 70c + 80c bl, grn & vio 5.25 4.50
Hinged 3.25
B91 SP50 90c + 60c dk brn, dl vio & brn 8.50 5.25
Hinged 4.75

The surtax was used to aid France's repopulation campaign.

"The Letter" by Jean Honoré Fragonard SP51

Statue of Widow and Children SP52

1939, July 6

B92 SP51 40c + 60c multi 4.25 2.75
Hinged 2.40

The surtax was used for the Postal Museum. See footnote after No. 4642.

1939, July 20

B93 SP52 70c + 30c brown vio 25.00 12.00
Hinged 12.00

Surtax for the benefit of French seamen.

French Soldier SP53

Colonial Trooper SP54

1940, Feb. 15

B94 SP53 40c + 60c sepia 3.75 2.75
Hinged 2.00
B95 SP54 1fr + 50c turq blue 3.75 2.75
Hinged 2.00

The surtax was used to assist the families of mobilized men.

World Map Showing French Possessions — SP55

1940, Apr. 15

B96 SP55 1fr + 25c scarlet 2.75 2.75
Hinged 2.00

Marshal Joseph J. C. Joffre SP56

Marshal Ferdinand Foch — SP57

Gen. Joseph S. Gallieni SP58

Woman Plowing SP59

1940, May 1

B97 SP56 80c + 45c choc 8.25 6.00
Hinged 3.50
B98 SP57 1fr + 50c dk vio 7.50 6.00
Hinged 3.25
B99 SP58 1.50fr + 50c brown red 7.50 4.00
Hinged 3.25
B100 SP59 2.50fr + 50c indigo & dl bl 15.00 11.50
Hinged 7.50
Nos. B97-B100 (4) 38.25 27.50

The surtax was used for war charities. See footnote after No. 4642.

Doctor, Nurse, Soldier and Family SP60

Nurse and Wounded Soldier SP61

1940, May 12

B101 SP60 80c + 1fr dk grn & red 8.25 6.00
Hinged 4.00
B102 SP61 1fr + 2fr sep & red 11.50 6.50
Hinged 5.25

The surtax was used for the Red Cross. See Nos. B747a, B747e.

Nurse with Injured Children — SP62

1940, Nov. 12

B103 SP62 1fr + 2fr sepia 1.25 .80
Hinged .80

The surtax was used for victims of the war.

Wheat Harvest SP63

Sowing SP64

Picking Grapes SP65

Grazing Cattle SP66

1940, Dec. 2

B104 SP63 80c + 2fr brn blk 3.25 2.10
Hinged 1.60
B105 SP64 1fr + 2fr chestnut 3.25 2.10
Hinged 1.60
B106 SP65 1.50fr + 2fr brt vio 3.25 2.10
Hinged 1.60
B107 SP66 2.50fr + 2fr dp grn 4.00 2.25
Hinged 2.00
Nos. B104-B107 (4) 13.75 8.55

The surtax was for national relief.

Prisoners of War
SP67 SP68

1941, Jan. 1

B108 SP67 80c + 5fr dark grn 1.60 1.50
B109 SP68 1fr + 5fr rose brn 1.75 1.60

The surtax was for prisoners of war.

Science Fighting Cancer SP69

1941, Feb. 20

B110 SP69 2.50fr + 50c slate blk & brn 1.60 1.40

Surtax used for the control of cancer.

No. 417 Surcharged in Blue

1941, Mar. 4

B111 A109 1fr + 10c crimson .25 .25

Men Hauling Coal SP70

"France" Aiding Needy Man SP71

1941

B112 SP70 1fr + 2fr sepia 2.75 1.40
B113 SP71 2.50fr + 7.50fr dk bl 9.00 3.00

The surtax was for Marshal Pétain's National Relief Fund.

Liner Pasteur SP72

1941, July 17 **Red Surcharge**

B114 SP72 1fr + 1fr on 70c dk bl grn .40 .40

World Map, Mercator Projection SP73

1941

B115 SP73 1fr + 1fr multi .80 .50

Fisherman — SP74

1941, Oct. 23

B116	SP74	1fr + 9fr dk blue grn	1.00	.90

Surtax for benefit of French seamen.

Arms of Various Cities

Nancy SP75

Lille SP76

Rouen SP77

Bordeaux SP78

Toulouse SP79

Clermont-Ferrand SP80

Marseille SP81

Lyon SP82

Rennes SP83

Reims SP84

Montpellier SP85

Paris SP86

1941 *Perf. 14x13*

B117	SP75	20c + 30c brn blk	2.75	2.75
B118	SP76	40c + 60c org brn	2.75	2.75
B119	SP77	50c + 70c grnsh blue	2.75	2.75
B120	SP78	70c + 80c rose vio	2.75	2.75
B121	SP79	80c + 1fr dp rose	2.75	2.75
B122	SP80	1fr + 1fr black	2.75	2.75
B123	SP81	1.50fr + 2fr dk bl	2.75	2.75
B124	SP82	2fr + 2fr dk vio	2.75	2.75
B125	SP83	2.50fr + 3fr brt grn	2.75	2.75
B126	SP84	3fr + 5fr org brn	2.75	2.75
B127	SP85	5fr + 6fr brt ultra	2.75	2.75
B128	SP86	10fr + 10fr dk red	2.75	2.75
		Nos. B117-B128 (12)	33.00	33.00

Count de La Pérouse SP87

1942, Mar. 23 *Perf. 13*

B129	SP87	2.50fr + 7.50fr ultra	1.25	1.40

Jean Francois de Galaup de La Pérouse, (1741-88), French navigator and explorer. The surtax was for National Relief.

Planes over Fields SP88

1942, Apr. 4

B130	SP88	1.50fr + 3.50fr lt vio	2.40	2.40

The surtax was for the benefit of French airmen and their familes.

Alexis Chabrier SP89

1942, May 18

B131	SP89	2fr + 3fr sepia	1.25	1.25

Emmanuel Chabrier (1841-1894), composer, birth centenary. The surtax was for works of charity among musicians.

Symbolical of French Colonial Empire SP90

1942, May 18

B132	SP90	1.50fr + 8.50fr black	1.10	1.10

The surtax was for National Relief.

Jean de Vienne SP91

1942, June 16

B133	SP91	1.50fr + 8.50fr sepia	1.10	1.10

600th anniv. of the birth of Jean de Vienne, 1st admiral of France. The surtax was for the benefit of French seamen.

Type of Regular Issue, 1941 Surcharged in Carmine

1942, Sept. 10 *Perf. 14x13½*

B134	A116	1.50fr + 50c brt ultra	.25	.25

The surtax was for national relief ("Secours National").

Arms of Various Cities

Chambéry SP92

La Rochelle SP93

Poitiers SP94

Orléans SP95

Grenoble SP96

Angers SP97

Dijon SP98

Limoges SP99

Le Havre SP100

Nantes SP101

Nice SP102

St. Etienne SP103

Perf. 14x13

1942, Oct. **Unwmk.** **Engr.**

B135	SP92	50c + 60c blk	3.50	3.50
B136	SP93	60c + 70c grnsh blue	3.50	3.50
B137	SP94	80c + 1fr rose	3.50	3.50
B138	SP95	1fr + 1.30fr dk green	3.50	3.50
B139	SP96	1.20fr + 1.50fr rose vio	3.50	3.50
B140	SP97	1.50fr + 1.80fr slate bl	3.50	3.50
B141	SP98	2fr + 2.30fr deep rose	3.50	3.50
B142	SP99	2.40fr + 2.80fr slate grn	3.50	3.50
B143	SP100	3fr + 3.50fr dp violet	3.50	3.50
B144	SP101	4fr + 5fr lt ultra	3.50	3.50
B145	SP102	4.50fr + 6fr red	3.50	3.50
B146	SP103	5fr + 7fr brt red vio	3.50	3.50
		Nos. B135-B146 (12)	42.00	42.00

The surtax was for national relief.

Tricolor Legion SP104

1942, Oct. 12 *Perf. 13*

B147	SP104	1.20 + 8.80fr dk blue	10.00	10.00
a.		Vert. pair, #B147, B148 + albino impression	22.50	25.00
B148	SP104	1.20 + 8.80fr crim	10.00	10.00

These stamps were printed in sheets of 20 stamps and 5 albino impressions arranged: 2 horizontal rows of 5 dark blue stamps, 1 row of 5 albino impressions, and 2 rows of 5 crimson stamps.

Marshal Henri Philippe Pétain SP105 SP106

1943, Feb. 8

B149	SP105	1fr + 10fr rose red	2.75	2.75
B150	SP105	1fr + 10fr blue	2.75	2.75
B151	SP106	2fr + 12fr rose red	2.75	2.75
B152	SP106	2fr + 12fr blue	2.75	2.75
a.		Strip, #B149-B152 + label	12.50	12.50

The surtax was for national relief. Printed in sheets of 20, the 10 blue stamps at left, the 10 rose red at right, separated by a vert. row of 5 white labels bearing a tri-colored battle-ax.

Marshal Pétain — SP107

"Work" — SP108

"Family" SP109

"State" SP110

Marshal Pétain — SP111

1943, June 7

B153	SP107	1.20fr + 1.40fr dull vio	15.00	15.00
B154	SP108	1.50fr + 2.50fr red	15.00	15.00
B155	SP109	2.40fr + 7fr brown	15.00	15.00
B156	SP110	4fr + 10fr dk violet	15.00	15.00
B157	SP111	5fr + 15fr red brown	15.00	15.00
a.		Strip of 5, #B153-B157	110.00	110.00

Pétain's 87th birthday.
The surtax was for national relief.

Civilians Under Air Attack — SP112

Civilians Doing Farm Work — SP113

Prisoner's Family Doing Farm Work
SP114

1943, Aug. 23
B158 SP112 1.50fr + 3.50fr black .50 .50

Surtax was for bomb victims at Billancourt, Dunkirk, Lorient, Saint-Nazaire.

1943, Sept. 27
B159 SP113 1.50fr + 8.50fr sepia .90 .90
B160 SP114 2.40fr + 7.60fr dk grn 1.00 1.00

The surtax was for families of war prisoners.

Michel de Montaigne
SP115

Picardy Costume
SP121

1.20fr+1.50fr, Francois Clouet. 1.50fr+3fr, Ambrose Paré. 2.40fr+4fr, Chevalier Pierre de Bayard. 4fr+6fr, Duke of Sully. 5fr+10fr, Henri IV.

1943, Oct. 2
B161 SP115 60c + 80c Prus green 2.00 2.00
B162 SP115 1.20fr + 1.50fr black 2.00 2.00
B163 SP115 1.50fr + 3fr deep ultra 2.00 2.00
B164 SP115 2.40fr + 4fr red 2.00 2.00
B165 SP115 4fr + 6fr dull brn red 2.00 2.00
B166 SP115 5fr + 10fr dull green 2.00 2.00
Nos. B161-B166 (6) 12.00 12.00

The surtax was for national relief. Issued to honor famous 16th century Frenchmen.

1943, Dec. 27

Designs: 18th Century Costumes: 1.20fr+2fr, Brittany. 1.50fr+4fr, Ile de France. 2.40+5fr, Burgundy. 4fr+6fr, Auvergne. 5fr+7fr, Provence.

B167 SP121 60c + 1.30fr sepia 2.00 2.00
B168 SP121 1.20fr + 2fr lt vio 2.00 2.00
B169 SP121 1.50fr + 4fr turq blue 2.00 2.00
B170 SP121 2.40fr + 5fr rose car 2.00 2.00
B171 SP121 4fr + 6fr chlky blue 3.00 3.00
B172 SP121 5fr + 7fr red 3.00 3.00
Nos. B167-B172 (6) 14.00 14.00

The surtax was for national relief. See footnote after No. 4642.

Admiral Tourville
SP127

Charles Gounod
SP128

1944, Feb. 21
B173 SP127 4fr + 6fr dull red brn .75 .75

300th anniv. of the birth of Admiral Anne-Hilarion de Cotentin Tourville (1642-1701).

1944, Mar. 27 ***Perf. 14x13***
B174 SP128 1.50fr + 3.50fr sepia 1.00 .80

50th anniv. of the death of Charles Gounod, composer (1818-1893).

Marshal Pétain
SP129

Farming
SP130

Industry
SP131

1944, Apr. 24 ***Perf. 13***
B175 SP129 1.50fr + 3.50fr sepia 3.50 3.50
B176 SP130 2fr + 3fr dp ultra .60 .60
B177 SP131 4fr + 6fr rose red .60 .60
Nos. B175-B177 (3) 4.70 4.70

Marshal Henri Pétain's 88th birthday.

Modern Streamliner, 19th Cent. Train
SP132

Molière (Jean-Baptiste Poquelin)
SP133

1944, Aug. 14
B178 SP132 4fr + 6fr black 2.10 1.90

Centenary of the Paris-Rouen, Paris-Orléans railroad.

1944, July 31

Designs: 80c+2.20fr, Jules Hardouin Mansart. 1.20fr+2.80fr, Blaise Pascal. 1.50fr+3.50fr, Louis II of Bourbon. 2fr+4fr, Jean-Baptiste Colbert. 4fr+6fr, Louis XIV.

B179 SP133 50c + 1.50fr rose car 1.50 1.50
B180 SP133 80c + 2.20fr dk green 1.50 1.50
B181 SP133 1.20fr + 2.80fr black 1.50 1.50
B182 SP133 1.50fr + 3.50fr brt ultra 1.50 1.50
B183 SP133 2fr + 4fr dull brn red 1.50 1.50
B184 SP133 4fr + 6fr red 1.50 1.50
Nos. B179-B184 (6) 9.00 9.00

Noted 17th century Frenchmen.

Angoulême
SP139

Chartres
SP140

Amiens
SP141

Beauvais
SP142

Albi — SP143

1944, Nov. 20
B185 SP139 50c + 1.50fr black .60 .60
B186 SP140 80c + 2.20fr rose vio .60 .60
B187 SP141 1.20fr + 2.80fr brn car .60 .60
B188 SP142 1.50fr + 3.50fr dp blue .60 .60
B189 SP143 4fr + 6fr orange red .60 .60
Nos. B185-B189 (5) 3.00 3.00

French Cathedrals.

Coat of Arms of Renouard de Villayer
SP144

Sarah Bernhardt
SP145

1944, Dec. 9 **Engr.**
B190 SP144 1.50fr + 3.50fr dp brn .25 .25

Stamp Day.

1945, May 16 **Unwmk.** ***Perf. 13***
B191 SP145 4fr + 1fr dk violet brn .30 .30

100th anniv. of the birth of Sarah Bernhardt, actress.

War Victims
SP146

1945, May 16
B192 SP146 4fr + 6fr dk violet brn .25 .25

The surtax was for war victims of the P.T.T.

Tuberculosis Patient — SP147

1945, May 16 **Typo.** ***Perf. 14x13½***
B193 SP147 2fr + 1fr red orange .25 .25

Surtax for the aid of tuberculosis victims. For surcharge see No. 561.

Boy and Girl
SP148

Burning of Oradour Church
SP149

1945, July 9 **Engr.** ***Perf. 13***
B194 SP148 4fr + 2fr Prus green .25 .25

The surtax was used for child welfare.

1945, Oct. 13
B195 SP149 4fr + 2fr sepia .25 .25

Destruction of Oradour, June, 1944.

Louis XI and Post Rider
SP150

1945, Oct. 13
B196 SP150 2fr + 3fr deep ultra .40 .40

Stamp Day.

For overprint see French West Africa No. B2.

Ruins of Dunkirk
SP151

Ruins of Rouen
SP152

Ruins of Caen
SP153

Ruins of Saint-Malo
SP154

1945, Nov. 5
B197 SP151 1.50fr + 1.50fr red brown .40 .40
B198 SP152 2fr + 2fr violet .50 .50
B199 SP153 2.40fr + 2.60fr blue .50 .50
B200 SP154 4fr + 4fr black .60 .60
Nos. B197-B200 (4) 2.00 2.00

The surtax was to aid the suffering residents of Dunkirk, Rouen, Caen and Saint Malo.

Alfred Fournier
SP155

Henri Becquerel
SP156

1946, Feb. 4 Engr. *Perf. 13*

B201	SP155	2fr + 3fr red brown	.30	.30
B202	SP156	2fr + 3fr violet	.30	.30

Issued to raise funds for the fight against venereal disease (No. B201) and for the struggle against cancer (No. B202).

No. B202 for the 50th anniv. of the discovery of radioactivity by Henri Becquerel.

See No. B221.

Church of the Invalides, Paris — SP157

1946, Mar. 11

B203	SP157	4fr + 6fr red brown	.40	.40

The surtax was to aid disabled war veterans.

French Warships SP158

1946, Apr. 8

B204	SP158	2fr + 3fr gray black	.80	.75

The surtax was for naval charities.

"The Letter" by Jean Siméon Chardin SP159

Fouquet de la Varane SP160

1946, May 25

B205	SP159	2fr + 3fr brown red	.50	.50

The surtax was used for the Postal Museum.

1946, June 29

B206	SP160	3fr + 2fr sepia	.50	.50

Stamp Day.

François Villon — SP161

Designs: 3fr+1fr, Jean Fouquet. 4fr+3fr, Philippe de Commynes. 5fr+4fr, Joan of Arc. 6fr+5fr, Jean de Gerson. 10fr+6fr, Charles VII.

1946, Oct. 28

B207	SP161	2fr + 1fr dk Prus grn	1.50	1.50
B208	SP161	3fr + 1fr dk blue vio	1.50	1.50
B209	SP161	4fr + 3fr henna brn	1.50	1.50
B210	SP161	5fr + 4fr ultra	1.50	1.50
B211	SP161	6fr + 5fr sepia	1.50	1.50
B212	SP161	10fr + 6fr red	1.50	1.50
		Nos. B207-B212 (6)	9.00	9.00

Church of St. Sernin, Toulouse SP167

Notre Dame du Port, Clermont-Ferrand SP168

Cathedral of St. Front, Perigueux SP169

Cathedral of St. Julien, Le Mans SP170

Cathedral of Notre Dame, Paris — SP171

1947 Engr.

B213	SP167	1fr + 1fr car rose	1.10	1.10
B214	SP168	3fr + 2fr dk bl vio	3.00	3.00
B215	SP169	4fr + 3fr henna brn	1.10	1.10
B216	SP170	6fr + 4fr dp bl	1.10	1.10
B217	SP171	10fr + 6fr dk gray grn	3.00	3.00
		Nos. B213-B217 (5)	9.30	9.30

François Michel le Tellier de Louvois — SP172

1947, Mar. 15

B218	SP172	4.50fr + 5.50fr car rose	1.50	1.50

Stamp Day, Mar. 15, 1947.

Submarine Pens, Shipyard and Monument SP173

1947, Aug. 2

B219	SP173	6fr + 4fr bluish black	.60	.60

British commando raid on the Nazi U-boat base at St. Nazaire, 1942.

Liberty Highway Marker — SP174

1947, Sept. 5

B220	SP174	6fr + 4fr dk green	1.00	1.00

The surtax was to help defray maintenance costs of the Liberty Highway.

Fournier Type of 1946

1947, Oct. 20

B221	SP155	2fr + 3fr indigo	.40	.40

Louis Braille — SP175

1948, Jan. 19

B222	SP175	6fr + 4fr purple	.40	.40

Etienne Arago SP176

Alphonse de Lamartine SP177

1948, Mar. 6

B223	SP176	6fr + 4fr black brn	.50	.50

Stamp Day, March 6-7, 1948.

1948, Apr. 5 Engr. *Perf. 13*

Designs: 3fr+2fr, Alexandre A. Ledru-Rollin. 4fr+3fr, Louis Blanc. 5fr+4fr, Albert (Alexandre Martin). 6fr+5fr, Pierre J. Proudhon. 10fr+6fr, Louis Auguste Blanqui. 15fr+7fr, Armand Barbés. 20fr+8fr, Dennis A. Affre.

B224	SP177	1fr + 1fr dk grn	1.25	1.25
B225	SP177	3fr + 2fr henna brn	1.25	1.25
B226	SP177	4fr + 3fr vio brn	1.25	1.25
B227	SP177	5fr + 4fr lt bl grn	3.25	3.25
B228	SP177	6fr + 5fr indigo	2.50	2.50
B229	SP177	10fr + 6fr car rose	2.50	2.50
B230	SP177	15fr + 7fr sl blk	3.25	3.25
B231	SP177	20fr + 8fr purple	3.25	3.25
		Nos. B224-B231 (8)	18.50	18.50

Centenary of the Revolution of 1848.

Dr. Léon Charles Albert Calmette SP178

1948, June 18

B232	SP178	6fr + 4fr dk grnsh bl	.80	.50

1st Intl. Congress on the Calmette-Guerin bacillus vaccine.

Farmer — SP179

Designs: 5fr+3fr, Fisherman. 8fr+4fr, Miner. 10fr+6fr, Metal worker.

1949, Feb. 14

B233	SP179	3fr + 1fr claret	.90	.75
B234	SP179	5fr + 3fr dk blue	.90	.75
B235	SP179	8fr + 4fr indigo	.90	.75
B236	SP179	10fr + 6fr dk red	1.00	.75
		Nos. B233-B236 (4)	3.70	3.00

Étienne François de Choiseul and Post Cart SP180

Baron de la Brède et de Montesquieu SP181

1949, Mar. 26

B237	SP180	15fr + 5fr dk green	1.20	1.20

Stamp Day, Mar. 26-27, 1949.

1949, Nov. 14

Designs: 8fr+2fr, Voltaire. 10fr+3fr, Antoine Watteau. 12fr+4fr, Georges de Buffon. 15fr+5fr, Joseph F. Dupleix. 25fr+10fr, A. R. J. Turgot.

B238	SP181	5fr + 1fr dk grn	3.50	3.50
B239	SP181	8fr + 2fr indigo	3.50	3.50
B240	SP181	10fr + 3fr brn red	3.50	3.50
B241	SP181	12fr + 4fr purple	3.50	3.50
B242	SP181	15fr + 5fr rose car	5.00	5.00
B243	SP181	25fr + 10fr ultra	6.00	6.00
		Nos. B238-B243 (6)	25.00	25.00

"Spring" SP182

Designs: 8fr+2fr, Summer. 12fr+3fr, Autumn. 15fr+4fr, Winter.

1949, Dec. 19

B244	SP182	5fr + 1fr green	1.90	1.75
B245	SP182	8fr + 2fr yel org	2.50	2.00
B246	SP182	12fr + 3fr purple	2.50	2.00
B247	SP182	15fr + 4fr dp blue	4.00	3.75
		Nos. B244-B247 (4)	10.90	9.50

Postman — SP183

1950, Mar. 11

B248	SP183	12fr + 3fr dp bl	3.75	3.00

Stamp Day, Mar. 11-12, 1950. See footnote after No. 4642.

André de Chénier — SP184

8fr+3fr, J. L. David. 10fr+4fr, Lazare Carnot. 12fr+5fr, G. J. Danton. 15fr+6fr, Maximilian Robespierre. 20fr+10fr, Louis Hoche.

1950, July 10 Engr. *Perf. 13*
Frames in Indigo

B249 SP184 5fr + 2fr brn vio 10.00 10.00
B250 SP184 8fr + 3fr blk brn 10.00 10.00
B251 SP184 10fr + 4fr lake 11.00 11.00
B252 SP184 12fr + 5fr red brn 13.00 13.00
B253 SP184 15fr + 6fr dk grn 14.00 14.00
B254 SP184 20fr + 10fr dk vio bl 14.00 14.00
Nos. B249-B254 (6) 72.00 72.00

Alexandre Brongniart, Bust by Houdon — SP185

1950, Dec. 22

15fr+3fr, "L'Amour" by Etienne M. Falconet.

B255 SP185 8fr + 2fr ind & car 2.50 2.50
B256 SP185 15fr + 3fr red brn & car 2.50 2.50

The surtax was for the Red Cross.

Mail Car Interior SP186

Alfred de Musset SP187

1951, Mar. 10 Unwmk. *Perf. 13*

B257 SP186 12fr + 3fr lilac gray 3.75 3.75

Stamp Day, Mar. 10-11, 1951.

1951, June 2
Frames in Dark Brown

8fr+2fr, Eugène Delacroix. 10fr+3fr, J.-L. Gay-Lussac. 12fr+4fr, Robert Surcouf. 15fr+5fr, C. M. Talleyrand. 30fr+10fr, Napoleon I.

B258 SP187 5fr + 1fr dk grn 7.50 5.75
B259 SP187 8fr + 2fr vio brn 7.50 5.75
B260 SP187 10fr + 3fr grnsh black 8.00 5.75
B261 SP187 12fr + 4fr dk vio brn 8.00 5.75
B262 SP187 15fr + 5fr brn car 9.00 5.75
B263 SP187 30fr + 10fr indigo 14.00 11.00
Nos. B258-B263 (6) 54.00 39.75

Child at Prayer by Le Maître de Moulins SP188

18th Century Child by Quentin de la Tour SP189

1951, Dec. 15 Cross in Red

B264 SP188 12fr + 3fr dk brown 3.25 3.25
B265 SP189 15fr + 5fr dp ultra 3.75 3.75

The surtax was for the Red Cross.

Stagecoach of 1844 SP190

1952, Mar. 8 *Perf. 13*

B266 SP190 12fr + 3fr dp green 4.50 4.50

Stamp Day, Mar. 8, 1952.

Gustave Flaubert — SP191

Portraits: 12fr+3fr, Edouard Manet. 15fr+4fr, Camille Saint-Saens. 18fr+5fr, Henri Poincaré. 20fr+6fr, Georges-Eugene Haussmann. 30fr+7fr, Adolphe Thiers.

1952, Oct. 18
Frames in Dark Brown

B267 SP191 8fr + 2fr indigo 7.00 7.00
B268 SP191 12fr + 3fr vio blue 7.00 7.00
B269 SP191 15fr + 4fr dk grn 7.00 7.00
B270 SP191 18fr + 5fr dk brn 9.00 9.00
B271 SP191 20fr + 6fr car 9.00 9.00
B272 SP191 30fr + 7fr purple 9.00 9.00
Nos. B267-B272 (6) 48.00 48.00

Cupid from Diana Fountain Versailles SP192

15fr+5fr, Similar detail, cupid facing left.

1952, Dec. 13 Cross in Red

B273 SP192 12fr + 3fr dk grn 5.00 5.00
B274 SP192 15fr + 5fr indigo 5.00 5.00
a. Booklet pane of 10 225.00
Complete booklet 375.00

The surtax was for the Red Cross.

Count d'Argenson SP193

St. Bernard SP194

1953, Mar. 14

B275 SP193 12fr + 3fr dp blue 3.00 3.00

Day of the Stamp. Surtax for the Red Cross.

1953, July 9

12fr+3fr, Olivier de Serres. 15fr+4fr, Jean Philippe Rameau. 18fr+5fr, Gaspard Monge. 20fr+6fr, Jules Michelet. 30fr+7fr, Marshal Hubert Lyautey.

B276 SP194 8fr + 2fr ultra 6.50 6.50
B277 SP194 12fr + 3fr dk grn 6.50 6.50
B278 SP194 15fr + 4fr brn car 10.00 10.00
B279 SP194 18fr + 5fr dk blue 11.00 11.00
B280 SP194 20fr + 6fr dk pur 11.00 11.00
B281 SP194 30fr + 7fr brown 11.50 11.50
Nos. B276-B281 (6) 56.50 56.50

The surtax was for the Red Cross.

Madame Vigée-Lebrun and her Daughter SP195

Count Antoine de La Vallette SP196

Design: 15fr+5fr, "The Return from Baptism," by Louis Le Nain.

1953, Dec. 12 Cross in Red

B282 SP195 12fr + 3fr red brn 7.50 7.00
a. Bklt. pane, 4 each, gutter btwn. 85.00
B283 SP195 15fr + 5fr indigo 10.00 9.50

The surtax was for the Red Cross.

1954, Mar. 20 Engr. *Perf. 13*

B284 SP196 12fr + 3fr dp grn & choc 4.50 3.25

Stamp Day, Mar. 20, 1954.

Louis IX SP197

"The Sick Child," by Eugene Carrière SP198

Portraits: 15fr+5fr, Jacques Benigne Bossuet. 18fr+6fr, Sadi Carnot. 20fr+7fr, Antoine Bourdelle. 25fr+8fr, Dr. Emile Roux. 30fr+10fr, Paul Valéry.

1954, July 10

B285 SP197 12fr + 4fr dp bl 21.00 21.00
B286 SP197 15fr + 5fr pur 21.00 21.00
B287 SP197 18fr + 6fr dk brn 21.00 21.00
B288 SP197 20fr + 7fr crim 29.00 29.00
B289 SP197 25fr + 8fr ind 29.00 29.00
B290 SP197 30fr + 10fr dp claret 29.00 29.00
Nos. B285-B290 (6) 150.00 150.00

See Nos. B303-B308, B312-B317.

1954, Dec. 18 Cross in Red

Design: 15fr+5fr, "Young Girl with Doves," by Jean Baptiste Greuze.

B291 SP198 12fr + 3fr vio gray & indigo 11.00 11.00
a. Bklt. pane, 4 each, gutter btwn. 110.00
B292 SP198 15fr + 5fr dk brn & org brn 11.00 11.00

No. B291a for 90th anniv. of the Red Cross. The surtax was for the Red Cross.

Balloon Post, 1870 SP199

1955, Mar. 19 Unwmk. *Perf. 13*

B293 SP199 12fr + 3fr multi 5.00 4.00

Stamp Day, Mar. 19-20, 1955.

King Philip II — SP200

Child with Cage by Pigalle — SP201

Portraits: 15fr+6fr, Francois de Malherbé. 18fr+7fr, Sebastien de Vauban. 25fr+8fr, Charles G. de Vergennes. 30fr+9fr, Pierre S. de Laplace. 50fr+15fr, Pierre Auguste Renoir.

1955, June 11

B294 SP200 12fr + 5fr brt pur 16.00 16.00
B295 SP200 15fr + 6fr dp bl 16.00 16.00
B296 SP200 18fr + 7fr dp green 16.00 16.00
B297 SP200 25fr + 8fr gray 25.00 25.00
B298 SP200 30fr + 9fr rose brn 26.00 26.00
B299 SP200 50fr + 15fr blue grn 30.00 30.00
Nos. B294-B299 (6) 129.00 129.00

See Nos. B321-B326.

1955, Dec. 17 Cross in Red

Design: 15fr+5fr, Child with Goose, by Boethus of Chalcedon.

B300 SP201 12fr + 3fr claret 7.50 7.50
B301 SP201 15fr + 5fr dk bl 5.25 5.25
a. Booklet pane of 10 150.00
Complete booklet 300.00

The surtax was for the Red Cross.

Francois of Taxis SP202

1956, Mar. 17 Engr. *Perf. 13*

B302 SP202 12fr + 3fr ultra, grn & dk brn 2.75 2.75

Stamp Day, Mar. 17-18, 1956.

Portrait Type of 1954

Portraits: No. 303, Guillaume Budé. No. B304, Jean Goujon. No. B305, Samuel de Champlain. No. B306, Jean Simeon Chardin. No. B307, Maurice Barrès. No. B308, Maurice Ravel.

1956, June 9 *Perf. 13*

B303 SP197 12fr + 3fr saph 5.25 5.25
B304 SP197 12fr + 3fr lil gray 5.25 5.25
B305 SP197 12fr + 3fr brt red 5.25 5.25
B306 SP197 15fr + 5fr green 7.75 7.75
B307 SP197 15fr + 5fr vio brn 7.75 7.75
B308 SP197 15fr + 5fr dp vio 7.75 7.75
Nos. B303-B308 (6) 39.00 39.00

Peasant Boy by Le Nain — SP203

Design: 15fr+5fr, Gilles by Watteau.

1956, Dec. 8 Unwmk.
Cross in Red

B309 SP203 12fr + 3fr ol gray 3.00 3.00
a. Bklt. pane, 4 ea, gutter btwn. 40.00
B310 SP203 15fr + 5fr rose lake 3.00 3.00

The surtax was for the Red Cross.

Genoese Felucca, 1750
SP204

1957, Mar. 16 ***Perf. 13***
B311 SP204 12fr +3fr bluish gray & brn blk 1.90 1.60

Day of the Stamp, Mar. 16, 1957, and honoring the Maritime Postal Service.

Portrait Type of 1954

1957, June 15

Portraits: No. B312, Jean de Joinville. No. B313, Bernard Palissy. No. B314, Quentin de la Tour. No. B315, Hugues Félicité Robert de Lamennais. No. B316, George Sand. No. B317, Jules Guesde.

B312 SP197 12fr + 3fr ol gray & ol grn 2.75 2.75
B313 SP197 12fr + 3fr grnsh blk & grnsh bl 2.75 2.75
B314 SP197 15fr + 5fr cl & brt red 3.25 3.25
B315 SP197 15fr + 5fr ultra & ind 3.25 3.25
B316 SP197 18fr + 7fr grnsh blk & dk grn 4.50 4.50
B317 SP197 18fr + 7fr dk vio brn & red brn 4.50 4.50
Nos. B312-B317 (6) 21.00 21.00

Blind Man and Beggar, Engraving by Jacques Callot — SP205

Design: 20fr+8fr, Women beggars.

1957, Dec. 7 **Engr.** ***Perf. 13***
B318 SP205 15fr + 7fr ultra & red 4.50 4.50
a. Bklt. pane, 4 ea, gutter btwn. 45.00 45.00
B319 SP205 20fr + 8fr dk vio brn & red 4.50 4.50

The surtax was for the Red Cross.

Motorized Mail Distribution
SP206

1958, Mar. 15
B320 SP206 15fr + 5fr multi 1.75 1.50

Stamp Day, Mar. 15.

Portrait Type of 1955

Portraits: No. B321, Joachim du Bellay. No. B322, Jean Bart. No. B323, Denis Diderot. No. B324, Gustave Courbet. 20fr+8fr, J. B. Carpeaux. 35fr+15fr, Toulouse-Lautrec.

1958, June 7 **Engr.** ***Perf. 13***
B321 SP200 12fr + 4fr yel grn 1.75 1.75
B322 SP200 12fr + 4fr dk blue 1.75 1.75
B323 SP200 15fr + 5fr dull cl 2.00 2.00
B324 SP200 15fr + 5fr ultra 2.25 2.25
B325 SP200 20fr + 8fr brt red 2.25 2.25
B326 SP200 35fr + 15fr green 2.25 2.25
Nos. B321-B326 (6) 12.25 12.25

St. Vincent de Paul — SP207

Portrait: 20fr+8fr, J. H. Dunant.

1958, Dec. 6 **Unwmk.**

Cross in Carmine

B327 SP207 15fr + 7fr grayish grn 1.25 1.25
a. Bklt. pane, 4 each, gutter btwn. 20.00
B328 SP207 20fr + 8fr violet 1.25 1.25

The surtax was for the Red Cross. See No. B747d.

Plane Landing at Night
SP208

1959, Mar. 21
B329 SP208 20fr + 5fr sl grn, blk & rose .50 .50

Issued for Stamp Day, Mar. 21, and to publicize night air mail service.
The surtax was for the Red Cross.
See No. 1089.

Geoffroi de Villehardouin and Ships — SP209

Designs: No. B331, André Le Nôtre and formal garden. No. B332, Jean Le Rond d'Alembert, books and wheel. No. B333, David d'Angers, statue and building. No. B334, M. F. X. Bichat and torch. No. B335, Frédéric Auguste Bartholdi, Statue of Liberty and Lion of Belfort.

1959, June 13 **Engr.** ***Perf. 13***
B330 SP209 15fr + 5fr vio blue 1.25 1.25
B331 SP209 15fr + 5fr dk sl grn 1.25 1.25
B332 SP209 20fr + 10fr olive bis 1.25 1.25
B333 SP209 20fr + 10fr dk gray 1.25 1.25
B334 SP209 30fr + 10fr dk car rose 1.75 1.75
B335 SP209 30fr + 10fr org brn 1.75 1.75
Nos. B330-B335 (6) 8.50 8.50

The surtax was for the Red Cross.

No. 927 Surcharged

1959, Dec. **Typo.** ***Perf. 14x13½***
B336 A328 25fr + 5fr black & red .30 .30

Surtax for the flood victims at Frejus.

Charles Michel de l'Épée — SP210

Design: 25fr+10fr, Valentin Hauy.

1959, Dec. 5 **Engr.** ***Perf. 13***

Cross in Carmine

B337 SP210 20fr + 10fr blk & cl 2.00 2.00
a. Bklt. pane, 4 each, gutter btwn. 30.00
B338 SP210 25fr + 10fr dk blue & blk 2.50 2.50

The surtax was for the Red Cross.

Ship Laying Underwater Cable
SP211

1960, Mar. 12
B339 SP211 20c + 5c grnsh bl & dk bl 1.50 1.50

Issued for the Day of the Stamp. The surtax went to the Red Cross.

Refugee Girl Amid Ruins — SP212

1960, Apr. 7
B340 SP212 25c + 10c grn, brn & ind .30 .25

World Refugee Year, July 1, 1959-June 30, 1960. The surtax was for aid to refugees.

Michel de L'Hospital
SP213

No. B342, Henri de la Tour D'Auvergne, Viscount of Turenne. No. B343, Nicolas Boileau (Despreaux). No. B344, Jean-Martin Charcot, M.D. No. B345, Georges Bizet. 50c+15c, Edgar Degás.

1960, June 11 **Engr.** ***Perf. 13***
B341 SP213 10c + 5c pur & rose car 2.50 2.50
B342 SP213 20c + 10c ol & vio brn 3.25 3.25
B343 SP213 20c + 10c Prus grn & dp yel grn 3.25 3.25
B344 SP213 30c + 10c rose car & rose red 5.00 5.00
B345 SP213 30c + 10c dk bl & vio bl 5.00 5.00
B346 SP213 50c + 15c sl bl & gray 5.50 5.50
Nos. B341-B346 (6) 24.50 24.50

The surtax was for the Red Cross.
See Nos. B350-B355.

Staff of the Brotherhood of St. Martin — SP214

25c+10c, St. Martin, 16th cent. wood sculpture.

1960, Dec. 3 **Unwmk.** ***Perf. 13***
B347 SP214 20c + 10c rose cl & red 3.25 3.25
a. Bklt. pane, 4 each, gutter btwn. 32.50
B348 SP214 25c + 10c lt ultra & red 3.25 3.25

The surtax was for the Red Cross.

Letter Carrier, Paris 1760 — SP215

1961, Mar. 18 ***Perf. 13***
B349 SP215 20c + 5c sl grn, brn & red .75 .75

Stamp Day. Surtax for Red Cross.

Famous Men Type of 1960

Designs: 15c+5c, Bertrand Du Guesclin. No. B351, Pierre Puget. No. B352, Charles Coulomb. 30c+10c, Antoine Drouot. 45c+10c, Honoré Daumier. 50c+15c, Guillaume Apollinaire.

1961, May 20 **Engr.**
B350 SP213 15c + 5c red brn & blk 2.50 2.50
B351 SP213 20c + 10c dk grn & lt bl 2.50 2.50
B352 SP213 20c + 10c ver & rose car 2.50 2.50
B353 SP213 30c + 10c blk & brn org 3.50 3.50
B354 SP213 45c + 10c choc & dk grn 3.50 3.50
B355 SP213 50c + 15c dk car rose & vio 4.00 4.00
Nos. B350-B355 (6) 18.50 18.50

"Love" by Rouault
SP216

Medieval Royal Messenger
SP217

Designs from "Miserere" by Georges Rouault: 25c+10c, "The Blind Consoles the Seeing."

1961, Dec. 2 ***Perf. 13***
B356 SP216 20c + 10c brn, blk & red 2.50 2.50
a. Bklt. pane, 4 each, gutter btwn. 30.00
B357 SP216 25c + 10c brn, blk & red 2.50 2.50

The surtax was for the Red Cross.

1962, Mar. 17
B358 SP217 20c + 5c rose red, bl & sepia .80 .80

Stamp Day. Surtax for Red Cross.

Denis Papin, Scientist
SP218

Rosalie Fragonard by Fragonard
SP219

Portraits: No. B360, Edme Bouchardon, sculptor. No. B361, Joseph Lakanal, educator. 30c+10c, Gustave Charpentier, composer. 45c+15c, Edouard Estaunié, writer. 50c+20c, Hyacinthe Vincent, physician and bacteriologist.

1962, June 2 **Engr.**
B359 SP218 15c + 5c bluish grn & dk gray 2.25 2.25
B360 SP218 20c + 10c cl brn 2.25 2.25
B361 SP218 20c + 10c gray & sl 2.50 2.50
B362 SP218 30c + 10c brt bl & ind 3.00 3.00
B363 SP218 45c + 15c org brn & choc 3.00 3.00
B364 SP218 50c + 20c grnsh bl & blk 3.50 3.50
Nos. B359-B364 (6) 16.50 16.50

The surtax was for the Red Cross.

1962, Dec. 8 **Cross in Red**

Design: 25c+10c, Child dressed as Pierrot.

B365 SP219 20c + 10c redsh brown 1.75 1.75
a. Bklt. pane, 4 ea, gutter btwn. 32.00
B366 SP219 25c + 10c dull grn 2.25 2.25

The surtax was for the Red Cross.
For surcharges see Reunion Nos. B16-B17.

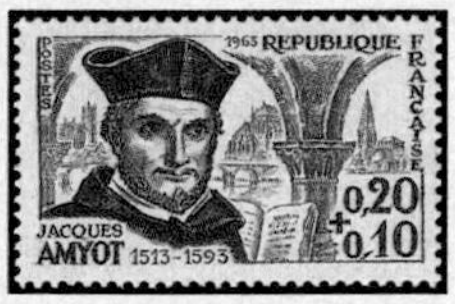

Jacques Amyot, Classical Scholar SP220

30c+10c, Pierre de Marivaux, playwright. 50c+20c, Jacques Daviel, surgeon.

1963, Feb. 23 Unwmk. *Perf. 13*

B367 SP220 20c + 10c mar, gray & pur 1.25 1.25
B368 SP220 30c + 10c Prus grn & mar 1.25 1.25
B369 SP220 50c + 20c ultra, ocher & ol 1.50 1.50
Nos. B367-B369 (3) 4.00 4.00

The surtax was for the Red Cross.

Roman Chariot SP221

1963, Mar. 16 Engr.

B370 SP221 20c + 5c brn org & vio brn .25 .25

Stamp Day. Surtax for Red Cross.

Étienne Méhul, Composer SP222

Designs: 30c+10c, Nicolas-Louis Vauquelin, chemist. 50c+20c, Alfred de Vigny, poet.

1963, May 25 Unwmk. *Perf. 13*

B371 SP222 20c + 10c dp bl, dk brn & dp org 1.25 1.25
B372 SP222 30c + 10c mag, gray ol & blk 1.25 1.25
B373 SP222 50c + 20c sl, blk & brn 1.50 1.50
Nos. B371-B373 (3) 4.00 4.00

The surtax was for the Red Cross.

"Child with Grapes" by David d'Angers and Centenary Emblem — SP223

25c+10c, "The Fifer," by Edouard Manet.

1963, Dec. 9 Unwmk. *Perf. 13*

B374 SP223 20c + 10c black & red .75 .75
a. Bklt. pane, 4 each, gutter btwn. 9.00 9.00
B375 SP223 25c + 10c sl grn & red .75 .75

Cent. of the Intl. and French Red Cross. Surtax for the Red Cross.
For surcharges see Reunion Nos. B18-B19.

Post Rider, 18th Century SP224

1964, Mar. 14 Engr.

B376 SP224 20c + 5c Prus green .30 .30

Issued for Stamp Day.

Resistance Memorial by Watkin, Luxembourg Gardens — SP225

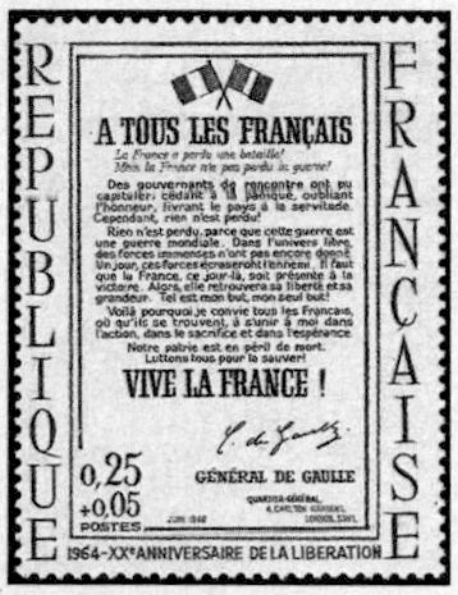

De Gaulle's 1940 Poster "A Tous les Francais" SP226

Street Fighting in Paris and Strasbourg. SP227

Designs: 20c+5c, "Deportation," concentration camp with watchtower and barbed wire. No. B379, Allied troops landing in Normandy and Provence.

1964 Engr. *Perf. 13*

B377 SP225 20c + 5c slate blk .50 .50

Perf. 12x13

B378 SP226 25c + 5c dk red, bl, red & blk .65 .65

Perf. 13

B379 SP227 30c + 5c blk, bl & org brn .75 .75
B380 SP227 30c + 5c org brn, cl & blk .75 .75
B381 SP225 50c + 5c dk grn .90 .90
Nos. B377-B381 (5) 3.55 3.55

20th anniv. of liberation from the Nazis.
Issue dates: Noz. B377, B381, 3/21; No. B378, 6/18; No. B379, 6/6; No. B380, 8/22.

President René Coty SP229

Jean Nicolas Corvisart SP230

Portraits: No. B383, John Calvin. No. B384, Pope Sylvester II (Gerbert).

1964 Unwmk. *Perf. 13*

B382 SP229 30c + 10c dp cl & blk .25 .25
B383 SP229 30c + 10c dk grn, blk & brn .25 .25
B384 SP229 30c + 10c slate & cl .25 .25
Nos. B382-B384 (3) .75 .75

The surtax was for the Red Cross.
Issued: No. B382, 4/25; No. B383, 5/25; No. B384, 6/1.

Cross in Carmine

1964, Dec. 12 Engr.

Portrait: 25c+10c, Dominique Larrey.

B385 SP230 20c + 10c black .35 .35
a. Bklt. pane, 4 ea, gutter btwn. 3.50
B386 SP230 25c + 10c black .35 .35

Jean Nicolas Corvisart (1755-1821), physician of Napoleon I, and Dominique Larrey (1766-1842), Chief Surgeon of the Imperial Armies. The surtax was for the Red Cross.
For surcharges see Reunion Nos. B20-B21.

Paul Dukas, Composer — SP231

No. B387, Duke François de La Rochefoucauld, writer. No. B388, Nicolas Poussin, painter. No. B389, Duke Charles of Orléans, poet.

1965, Feb. Engr. *Perf. 13*

B387 SP231 30c + 10c org brn & dk bl .40 .40
B388 SP231 30c + 10c car & dk red brn .40 .40
B389 SP231 40c + 10c dk red brn, dk red & Prus bl .50 .50
B390 SP231 40c + 10c dk brn & sl bl .50 .50
Nos. B387-B390 (4) 1.80 1.80

The surtax was for the Red Cross.
Issued: Nos. B387, B390 2/13; Nos. B388-B389 2/20.

Packet "La Guienne" SP232

1965, Mar. 29 Unwmk. *Perf. 13*

B391 SP232 25c + 10c multi .75 .50

Issued for Stamp Day, 1965. "La Guienne" was used for transatlantic mail service. Surtax was for the Red Cross.

Infant with Spoon by Auguste Renoir — SP233

Design: 30c+10c, Coco Writing (Renoir's daughter Claude).

1965, Dec. 11 Engr. *Perf. 13*

Cross in Carmine

B392 SP233 25c + 10c slate .30 .30
a. Bklt. pane, 4 ea, gutter btwn. 2.75
B393 SP233 30c + 10c dull red brn .30 .30

The surtax was for the Red Cross.
For surcharges see Reunion Nos. B22-B23.

Francois Mansart and Carnavalet Palace, Paris SP234

No. B395, St. Pierre Fourier and Basilica of St. Pierre Fourier, Mirecourt. No. B396, Marcel Proust and St. Hilaire Bridge, Illiers. No. B397, Gabriel Fauré, monument and score of "Penelope." No. B398, Elie Metchnikoff, microscope and Pasteur Institute. No. B399, Hippolyte Taine and birthplace.

1966 Engr. *Perf. 13*

B394 SP234 30c + 10c dk red brn & grn .35 .35
B395 SP234 30c + 10c blk & gray grn .35 .35
B396 SP234 30c + 10c ind, sep & grn .35 .35
B397 SP234 30c + 10c bis brn & ind .35 .35
B398 SP234 30c + 10c blk & dl brn .35 .35
B399 SP234 30c + 10c grn & ol brn .35 .35
Nos. B394-B399 (6) 2.10 2.10

The surtax was for the Red Cross.

Issued: Nos. B394-B396, 2/12; others, 6/25.

Engraver Cutting Die and Tools SP235

1966, Mar. 19 Engr. *Perf. 13*

B400 SP235 25c + 10c slate, dk brn & dp org .30 .30

Stamp Day. Surtax for Red Cross.

Angel of Victory, Verdun Fortress, Marching Troops — SP236

First Aid on Battlefield, 1859 — SP237

1966, May 28 *Perf. 13*

B401 SP236 30c + 5c Prus bl, ultra & dk bl .25 .25

Victory of Verdun, 50th anniversary.

1966, Dec. 10 Engr. *Perf. 13*

No. B403, Nurse giving first aid to child, 1966.

Cross in Carmine

B402 SP237 25c + 10c green .35 .35
a. Bklt. pane, 4 ea, gutter btwn. 3.50
B403 SP237 30c + 10c slate .40 .40

The surtax was for the Red Cross.
See No. B746e. For surcharges see Reunion Nos. B24-B25.

Emile Zola — SP238

No. B405, Beaumarchais (pen name of Pierre Augustin Caron). No. B406, St. Francois de Sales (1567-1622). No. B407, Albert Camus (1913-1960).

1967 Engr. *Perf. 13*

B404 SP238 30c + 10c sl bl & bl .35 .35
B405 SP238 30c + 10c rose brn & lil .35 .35
B406 SP238 30c + 10c dl vio & pur .35 .35
B407 SP238 30c + 10c brn & dl cl .35 .35
Nos. B404-B407 (4) 1.40 1.40

The surtax was for the Red Cross.
Issued: Nos. B404-B405, 2/4; others, 6/24.

Letter Carrier, 1865 — SP239

1967, Apr. 8

B408 SP239 25c + 10c indigo, grn & red .30 .25

Issued for Stamp Day.

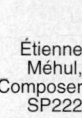

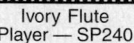

Ivory Flute Player — SP240

Ski Jump and Long Distance Skiing — SP241

30c+10c, Violin player, ivory carving.

1967, Dec. 16 **Engr.** ***Perf. 13***

Cross in Carmine

B409 SP240 25c + 10c dl vio & lt brn .40 .40
a. Bklt. pane, 4 ea, gutter btwn. 3.50
B410 SP240 30c + 10c grn & lt brn .40 .40

The surtax was for the Red Cross.
For surcharges see Reunion Nos. B26-B27.

1968, Jan. 27

Designs: 40c+10c, Ice hockey. 60c+20c, Olympic flame and snowflakes. 75c+25c, Woman figure skater. 95c+35c, Slalom.

B411 SP241 30c + 10c ver, gray & brn .35 .35
B412 SP241 40c + 10c lil, lem & brt mag .35 .35
B413 SP241 60c + 20c dk grn, org & brt vio .50 .50
B414 SP241 75c + 25c brt pink, yel grn & blk .60 .60
B415 SP241 95c + 35c bl, brt pink & red brn .60 .60
Nos. B411-B415 (5) 2.40 2.40

Issued for the 10th Winter Olympic Games, Grenoble, Feb. 6-18.

Rural Mailman, 1830 — SP242

1968, Mar. 16 **Engr.** ***Perf. 13***

B416 SP242 25c + 10c multi .25 .25

Issued for Stamp Day.

François Couperin, Composer, and Instruments SP243

Portraits: No. B418, Gen. Louis Desaix de Veygoux (1768-1800) and scene showing his death at the Battle of Marengo, Italy. No. B419, Saint-Pol-Roux (pen name of Paul-Pierre Roux, 1861-1940), Christ on the Cross and ruins of Camaret-sur-Mer. No. B420, Paul Claudel (poet and diplomat, 1868-1955) and Joan of Arc at the stake.

1968 **Engr.** ***Perf. 13***

B417 SP243 30c + 10c pur & rose lil .25 .25
B418 SP243 30c + 10c dk grn & brn .25 .25
B419 SP243 30c + 10c cop red & ol bis .25 .25
B420 SP243 30c + 10c dk brn & lil .25 .25
Nos. B417-B420 (4) 1.00 1.00

Issue dates: Nos. B417-B418, Mar. 23; Nos. B419-B420, July 6.

Spring, by Nicolas Mignard — SP244

Paintings by Nicolas Mignard; 30c+10c, Fall. No. B423, Summer. No. B424, Winter.

1968-69 **Engr.** ***Perf. 13***

Cross in Carmine

B421 SP244 25c + 10c pur & sl bl .30 .30
a. Bklt. pane, 4 ea #B421-B422 with gutter btwn.) 3.00
B422 SP244 30c + 10c brn & rose car .30 .30
B423 SP244 40c + 15c dk brn & brn ('69) .50 .50
a. Bklt. pane, 4 ea #B423, B424 with gutter btwn.) 3.50
B424 SP244 40c + 15c pur & Prus bl ('69) .50 .50
Nos. B421-B424 (4) 1.60 1.60

The surtax was for the Red Cross.
For surcharges see Reunion Nos. B28-B31.

Mailmen's Omnibus, 1881 SP245

1969, Mar. 15 **Engr.** ***Perf. 13***

B425 SP245 30c + 10c brn, grn & blk .25 .25

Issued for Stamp Day.
For surcharge see Reunion No. B32.

Gen. Francois Marceau — SP246

Portraits: No. B427, Charles Augustin Sainte-Beuve (1804-1869), writer. No. B428, Albert Roussel (1869-1937), musician. No. B429, Marshal Jean Lannes (1769-1809). No. B430, Georges Cuvier (1769-1832), naturalist. No. B431, André Gide, (1869-1951), writer.

1969

B426 SP246 50c + 10c brn red .50 .50
B427 SP246 50c + 10c slate bl .50 .50
B428 SP246 50c + 10c dp vio bl .50 .50
B429 SP246 50c + 10c choc .50 .50
B430 SP246 50c + 10c dp plum .50 .50
B431 SP246 50c + 10c blue grn .50 .50
Nos. B426-B431 (6) 3.00 3.00

The surtax was for the Red Cross.
Issued: Nos. B426-B428, Mar. 24; No. B429, May 10; Nos. B430-B431, May 17.

Gen. Jacques Leclerc, La Madeleine and Battle — SP247

1969, Aug. 23 **Engr.** ***Perf. 13***

B432 SP247 45c + 10c slate & ol 1.00 1.00

Liberation of Paris, 8/25/44, 25th anniv.

Inscribed Liberation de Strasbourg

1969, Nov. 22 **Engr.** ***Perf. 13***

B433 SP247 70c + 10c brn, choc & olive 3.50 3.50

25th anniv. of the liberation of Strasbourg.

Philibert Delorme, Architect, and Chateau d'Anet SP248

Designs: No. B435, Louis Le Vau (1612-1670), architect, and Vaux-le-Vicomte Chateau, Paris. No. B436, Prosper Merimée (1803-1870), writer, and Carmen. No. B437, Alexandre Dumas (1802-1870), writer, and Three Musketeers. No. B438, Edouard Branly (1844-1940), physicist, electric circuit and convent of the Carmes, Paris. No. B439, Maurice de Broglie (1875-1960), physicist, and X-ray spectrograph.

1970 **Engr.** ***Perf. 13***

B434 SP248 40c + 10c slate grn .50 .50
B435 SP248 40c + 10c dk car .50 .50
B436 SP248 40c + 10c Prus blue .50 .50
B437 SP248 40c + 10c violet bl .50 .50
B438 SP248 40c + 10c dp brown .50 .50
B439 SP248 40c + 10c dk gray .50 .50
Nos. B434-B439 (6) 3.00 3.00

The surtax was for the Red Cross.
Issued: No. B434-B436, 2/14; others, 4/11.

City Mailman, 1830 — SP249

"Life and Death" — SP250

1970, Mar. 14

B440 SP249 40c + 10c blk, ultra & dk car rose .40 .40

Issued for Stamp Day.
For surcharge see Reunion No. B33.

1970, Apr. 4

B441 SP250 40c + 10c brt bl, ol & car rose .25 .25

Issued to publicize the fight against cancer in connection with Health Day, Apr. 7.

Marshal de Lattre de Tassigny — SP251

1970, May 8 **Engr.** ***Perf. 13***

B442 SP251 40c + 10c slate & vio bl .50 .50

25th anniv. of the entry into Berlin of French troops under Marshal Jean de Lattre de Tassigny, May 8, 1945.

Lord and Lady, Dissay Chapel Fresco — SP252

No. B444, Angel holding whips, from fresco in Dissay Castle Chapel, Vienne, c. 1500.

1970, Dec. 12 **Engr.** ***Perf. 13***

Cross in Carmine

B443 SP252 40c + 15c green .55 .55
a. Bklt. pane, 4 ea, gutter btwn. 12.50
B444 SP252 40c + 15c cop red .55 .55

The surtax was for the Red Cross.
For surcharges see Reunion Nos. B34-B35.

Daniel-Francois Auber and "Fra Diavolo" Music — SP253

No. B446, Gen. Charles Diego Brosset (1898-1944), Basilica of Fourvière. No. B447, Victor Grignard (1871-1935), chemist, Nobel Prize medal. No. B448, Henri Farman (1874-1958), plane. No. B449, Gen. Charles Georges Delestraint (1879-1945), scroll. No. B450, Jean Eugène Robert-Houdin (1805-71), magician's act.

1971 **Engr.** ***Perf. 13***

B445 SP253 50c + 10c brn vio & brn .75 .75
B446 SP253 50c + 10c dk sl grn & ol gray .75 .75
B447 SP253 50c + 10c brn red & olive .75 .75
B448 SP253 50c + 10c vio bl & vio .75 .75
B449 SP253 50c + 10c pur & cl .85 .85
B450 SP253 50c + 10c sl grn & bl grn .85 .85
Nos. B445-B450 (6) 4.70 4.70

The surtax was for the Red Cross.
Issued: Nos. B445-B446, 3/6; No. B447, 5/8; No. B448, 5/29; Nos. B449-B450, 10/16.

Army Post Office, 1914-1918 SP254

1971, Mar. 27 **Engr.** ***Perf. 13***

B451 SP254 50c + 10c ol, brn & bl .45 .45

Stamp Day, 1971.
For surcharge see Reunion No. B36.

Girl with Dog, by Greuze SP255

Aristide Bergès (1833-1904) SP256

Design: 50c+10c, "The Dead Bird," by Jean-Baptiste Greuze (1725-1805).

1971, Dec. 11 **Cross in Carmine**

B452 SP255 30c + 10c violet bl .70 .70
a. Bklt. pane, 4 each, gutter btwn. 6.00
B453 SP255 50c + 10c dp car .70 .70

The surtax was for the Red Cross.
For surcharges see Reunion Nos. B37-B38.

1972 **Engr.** ***Perf. 13***

No. B455, Paul de Chomedey (1612-76), founder of Montreal, and arms of Neuville-sur-Vanne. No. B456, Edouard Belin (1876-1963), inventor. No. B457, Louis Blériot (1872-1936), aviation pioneer. No. B458, Adm. François Joseph, Count de Grasse (1722-88), hero of the American Revolution. No. B459, Théophile Gautier (1811-72), writer.

B454 SP256 50c + 10c blk & grn .75 .75
B455 SP256 50c + 10c blk & bl .75 .75
B456 SP256 50c + 10c blk & lil rose .75 .75
B457 SP256 50c + 10c red & blk .75 .75
B458 SP256 50c + 10c org & blk 1.00 1.00
B459 SP256 50c + 10c blk & brn 1.00 1.00
Nos. B454-B459 (6) 5.00 5.00

The surtax was for the Red Cross.
Issued: Nos. B454-B455, 2/19; No. B456, 6/24; No. B457, 7/1; Nos. B458-B459, 9/9.

Rural Mailman, 1894
SP257

Nicolas Desgenettes
SP258

1972, Mar. 18 Engr. *Perf. 13*

B460 SP257 50c + 10c bl, yel & ol gray 1.00 .75

Stamp Day 1972.
For surcharge see Reunion No. B39.

1972, Dec. 16 Engr. *Perf. 13*

Designs: 30c+10c, René Nicolas Dufriche, Baron Desgenettes, M.D. (1762-1837). 50c+10c, François Joseph Broussais, M.D. (1772-1838).

B461 SP258 30c + 10c sl grn & red .65 .50
a. Bklt. pane, 4 ea, gutter btwn. 7.00
B462 SP258 50c + 10c red .65 .50

The surtax was for the Red Cross.
See No. B747b. For surcharges see Reunion Nos. B40-B41.

Tony Garnier (1869-1948), architect — SP259

No. B463, Gaspard de Coligny (1519-1572), admiral and Huguenot leader. No. B464, Ernest Renan (1823-1892), philologist and historian. No. B465, Alberto Santos Dumont (1873-1932), Brazilian aviator. No. B466, Gabrielle-Sidonie Colette (1873-1954), writer. No. B467, René Duguay-Trouin (1673-1736), naval commander. No. B468, Louis Pasteur (1822-1895), chemist, bacteriologist. No. B469, Tony Garnier (1869-1948), architect.

1973 Engr. *Perf. 13*

B463 SP259 50c + 10c multi .85 .85
B464 SP259 50c + 10c multi .85 .85
B465 SP259 50c + 10c multi .85 .85
B466 SP259 50c + 10c multi .85 .85
B467 SP259 50c + 10c multi .85 .85
B468 SP259 50c + 10c multi .85 .85
B469 SP259 50c + 10c multi .85 .85
Nos. B463-B469 (7) 5.95 5.95

Issued: No. B463, 2/17; No. B464, 4/28; No. B465, 5/26; No. B466, 6/2; No. B467, 6/9; No. B468, 10/6; No. B469, 11/17.

Mail Coach, 1835
SP260

1973, Mar. 24 Engr. *Perf. 13*

B470 SP260 50c + 10c grnsh blue .35 .35

Stamp Day, 1973.
For surcharge see Reunion No. B42.

Mary Magdalene
SP261

St. Louis-Marie de Montfort
SP262

50c+10c, Mourning woman. Designs are from 15th cent. Tomb of Tonnerre.

1973, Dec. 1

B471 SP261 30c + 10c sl grn & red .55 .55
a. Bklt. pane, 4 each, gutter btwn. 6.00
B472 SP261 50c + 10c dk gray & red .55 .55

Surtax was for the Red Cross.
For surcharges see Reunion Nos. B43-B44.

1974, Feb. 23 Engr. *Perf. 13*

Portraits: No. B474, Francis Poulenc (1899-1963), composer. No. B475, Jules Barbey d'Aurevilly (1808-1889), writer. No. B476, Jean Giraudoux (1882-1944), writer.

B473 SP262 50c + 10c multi 1.10 1.10
B474 SP262 50c + 10c multi .70 .70
B475 SP262 80c + 15c multi .80 .80
B476 SP262 80c + 15c multi .80 .80
Nos. B473-B476 (4) 3.40 3.40

Issue dates: No. B473, Mar. 9; No. B474, July 20; Nos. B475-B476, Nov. 16.

Automatically Sorted Letters — SP263

1974, Mar. 9 Engr. *Perf. 13*

B477 SP263 50c + 10c multi .30 .25

Stamp Day 1974. Automatic letter sorting center, Orleans-la-Source, opened 1/30/73.
For surcharge see Reunion No. B45.

Order of Liberation and 5 Honored Cities — SP264

1974, June 15 Engr. *Perf. 13*

B478 SP264 1fr + 10c multi .75 .40

30th anniv. of liberation from the Nazis.

"Summer" — SP265

"Winter" — SP266

Designs: B481, "Spring" (girl on swing). B482, "Fall" (umbrella and rabbits).

1974, Nov. 30 Engr. *Perf. 13*

B479 SP265 60c + 15c multi .60 .60
a. Bklt. pane, 4 ea, gutter btwn. 6.00
B480 SP266 80c + 15c multi .60 .60

For surcharges see Reunion Nos. B46-B47.

1975, Nov. 29

B481 SP265 60c + 15c multi .50 .50
a. Bklt. pane, 4 ea, gutter btwn. 4.75
B482 SP266 80c + 20c multi .50 .50

Surtax was for the Red Cross.

Dr. Albert Schweitzer
SP267

Edmond Michelet
SP268

André Siegfried and Map
SP269

No. B483, Albert Schweitzer (1875-1965), medical missionary. No. B484, Edmond Michelet (1899-1970), Resistance hero, statesman. No. B485, Robert Schuman (1886-1963), promoter of United Europe. No. B486, Eugene Thomas (1903-69), minister of PTT. No. B487, André Siegfried (1875-1959), political science professor, writer.

1975 Engr. *Perf. 13*

B483 SP267 80c + 20c multi .50 .50
B484 SP268 80c + 20c bl & ind .50 .50
B485 SP268 80c + 20c blk & ind .50 .50
B486 SP268 80c + 20c blk & sl .50 .50
B487 SP269 80c + 20c blk & bl .50 .50
Nos. B483-B487 (5) 2.50 2.50

Issued: No. B483, 1/11; No. B484, 2/22; No. B485, 5/10; No. B486, 6/28; No. B487, 11/15.

Second Republic Mailman's Badge — SP270

1975, Mar. 8 Photo.

B488 SP270 80c + 20c multi .50 .40

Stamp Day.

"Sage" Type of 1876
SP271

Marshal A. J. de Moncey
SP272

1976, Mar. 13 Engr. *Perf. 13*

B489 SP271 80c + 20c blk & lil .45 .45

Stamp Day 1976.

1976 Engr. *Perf. 13*

No. B491, Max Jacob (1876-1944), Dadaist writer, by Picasso. No. B492, Jean Mounet-Sully (1841-1916), actor. No. B493, Gen. Pierre Daumesnil (1776-1832). No. B494, Eugène Fromentin (1820-1876), painter.

B490 SP272 80c + 20c multi .50 .50
B491 SP272 80c + 20c red brn & ol .50 .50
B492 SP272 80c + 20c multi .50 .50
B493 SP272 1fr + 20c multi .50 .50
B494 SP272 1fr + 20c multi .50 .50
Nos. B490-B494 (5) 2.50 2.50

Issued: No. B490, 5/22; No. B491, 7/22; No. B492, 8/28; No. B493, 9/4; No. B494, 9/25.

Anna de Noailles
SP273

St. Barbara
SP274

1976, Nov. 6 Engr. *Perf. 13*

B495 SP273 1fr + 20c multi .60 .60

Anna de Noailles (1876-1933), writer & poet.

1976, Nov. 20 Cross in Carmine

Design: 1fr+25c, Cimmerian Sibyl. Sculptures from Brou Cathedral.

B496 SP274 80c + 20c violet .60 .60
a. Bklt. pane, 4 ea, gutter btwn. 6.00
B497 SP274 1fr + 25c dk brown .80 .80

Surtax was for the Red Cross.

Marckolsheim Relay Station Sign — SP275

1977, Mar. 26 Engr. *Perf. 13*

B498 SP275 1fr + 20c multi .40 .40

Stamp Day.

Edouard Herriot, Statesman and Writer
SP276

Christmas Figurine, Provence
SP277

Designs: No. B500, Abbé Breuil (1877-1961), archaeologist. No. B501, Guillaume de Machault (1305-1377), poet and composer. No. B502, Charles Cross (1842-1888).

1977 Engr. *Perf. 13*

B499 SP276 1fr + 20c multi .60 .60
B500 SP276 1fr + 20c multi .60 .60
B501 SP276 1fr + 20c multi .60 .60
B502 SP276 1fr + 20c multi .60 .60
Nos. B499-B502 (4) 2.40 2.40

Issued: No. B499, 10/8; No. B500, 10/15; No. B501, 11/12; No. B502, 12/3.

1977, Nov. 26

1fr+25c, Christmas figurine (woman), Provence.

B503 SP277 80c + 20c red & ind .45 .45
a. Bklt. pane, 4 ea, gutter btwn. 4.50
B504 SP277 1fr + 25c red & sl grn .55 .55

Surtax was for the Red Cross.

Marie Noel, Writer — SP278

Mail Collection, 1900 — SP279

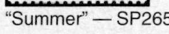

No. B506, Georges Bernanos (1888-1948), writer. No. B507, Leo Tolstoi (1828-1910),

Russian writer. No. B508, Charles Marie Leconte de Lisle (1818-1894), poet. No. B509, Voltaire (1694-1778) and Jean Jacques Rousseau (1712-1778). No. B510, Claude Bernard (1813-1878), physiologist.

1978 Engr. *Perf. 13*

B505	SP278	1fr + 20c multi	.55	.55
B506	SP278	1fr + 20c multi	.55	.55
B507	SP278	1fr + 20c multi	.55	.55
B508	SP278	1fr + 20c multi	.55	.55
B509	SP278	1fr + 20c multi	.55	.55
B510	SP278	1fr + 20c multi	.55	.55
		Nos. B505-B510 (6)	3.30	3.30

Issued: No. B505, 2/11; No. B506, 2/18; No. B507, 4/15; No. B508, 3/26; No. B509, 7/1; No. B510, 9/16.

1978, Apr. 8 Engr. *Perf. 13*

B511	SP279	1fr + 20c multi	.50	.40

Stamp Day 1978.

SP280

SP281

1fr+25c, The Hare & the Tortoise. 1.20fr+30c, The City Mouse & the Country Mouse.

1978, Dec. 2 Engr. *Perf. 13*

B512	SP280	1fr + 25c multi	.75	.65
a.		Bklt. pane, 4 ea, gutter btwn.	6.00	
B513	SP280	1.20fr + 30c multi	.75	.65

Surtax was for the Red Cross.

1979 Engr. *Perf. 13*

No. B514, Ladislas Marshal de Berchény (1689-1778). No. B515, Leon Jouhaux (1879-1954), labor leader. No. B516, Peter Abelard (1079-1142), theologian and writer. No. B517, Georges Courteline (1860-1929), humorist. No. B518, Simone Weil (1909-1943), social philosopher. No. B519, André Malraux (1901-1976), novelist.

B514	SP281	1.20fr + 30c multi	.60	.60
B515	SP281	1.20fr + 30c multi	.60	.60
B516	SP281	1.20fr + 30c multi	.60	.60
B517	SP281	1.20fr + 30c multi	.60	.60
B518	SP281	1.30fr + 30c multi	.60	.60
B519	SP281	1.30fr + 30c multi	.60	.60
		Nos. B514-B519 (6)	3.60	3.60

Issued: No. B514, 1/13; No. B515, 5/12; No. B516, 6/9; No. B517, 6/25; No. B518, 11/12; No. B519, 11/26.

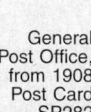

General Post Office, from 1908 Post Card SP282

1979, Mar. 10 Engr. *Perf. 13*

B520	SP282	1.20fr + 30c multi	.60	.40

Stamp Day 1979.

Woman, Stained-Glass Window — SP283

Stained-glass windows, Church of St. Joan of Arc, Rouen: 1.30fr+30c, Simon the Magician.

1979, Dec. 1 *Perf. 13*

B521	SP283	1.10fr + 30c multi	.50	.40
B522	SP283	1.30fr + 30c multi	.60	.45
a.		Bklt. pane, 4 each #521-522, with gutter btwn., perf. 12½x13	6.00	

Surtax was for the Red Cross.

Eugene Viollet le Duc (1814-1879), Architect — SP284

Jean-Marie de Le Mennais (1780-1860), Priest and Educator — SP285

No. B524, Jean Monnet (1888-1979), economist and diplomat. No. B525, Viollet le Duc (1814-1879), architect and writer. No. B526, Frederic Mistral (1830-1914), poet. No. B527, Saint-John Perse (Alexis Leger, 1887-1975), poet and diplomat. No. B528, Pierre Paul de Riquet (1604-1680), canal builder.

1980 Engr. *Perf. 13*

B523	SP284	1.30fr + 30c multi	.70	.70
B524	SP285	1.30fr + 30c multi	.70	.70
B525	SP285	1.40fr + 30c blue	.70	.70
B526	SP285	1.40fr + 30c black	.70	.70
B527	SP285	1.40fr + 30c multi	.70	.70
B528	SP284	1.40fr + 30c multi	.70	.70
		Nos. B523-B528 (6)	4.20	4.20

Issued: No. B523, Feb. 16; Nos. B524-B526, Sept. 6; Nos. B527-B528, Oct. 11.

The Letter to Melie, by Avati, Stamp Day, 1980 — SP286

1980, Mar. 8 Photo.

B529	SP286	1.30fr + 30c multi	.60	.45

Filling the Granaries, Choir Stall Detail, Amiens Cathedral — SP287

No. B531, Grapes from the Promised Land.

1980, Dec. 6 Engr. *Perf. 13*

B530	SP287	1.20fr + 30c red & dk red brn	.70	.70
B531	SP287	1.40fr + 30c red & dk red brn	.80	.80
a.		Bklt. pane, 4 #B530-B531, with gutter btwn., perf. 12½x13	6.50	

Sister Anne-Marie Javouhey (1779-1851), Founded Congregation of St. Joseph of Cluny — SP288

No. B532, Louis Armand (1905-71), railway engineer. No. B533, Louis Jouvet (1887-1951), theater director. No. B534, Marc Boegner (1881-1970), peace worker. No. B536, Jacques Offenbach (1819-80), composer. No. B537, Pierre Teilhard de Chardin (1881-1955), philosopher.
Nos. B532-B533, B537 vert.

1981 Engr. *Perf. 13*

B532	SP288	1.20 + 30c multi	.65	.65
B533	SP288	1.20 + 30c multi	.65	.65
B534	SP288	1.40 + 30c multi	.65	.65
B535	SP288	1.40 + 30c multi	.65	.65
B536	SP288	1.40 + 30c multi	.65	.65
B537	SP288	1.40 + 30c multi	.65	.65
		Nos. B532-B537 (6)	3.90	3.90

Issued: No. B532, 5/23; No. B533, 6/13; No. B534, 11/14; No. B535, 2/7; No. B536, 2/14; No. B537, 5/23.

The Love Letter, by Goya — SP289

1981, Mar. 7 *Perf. 13x12½*

B538	SP289	1.40 + 30c multi	.80	.75

Stamp Day 1981.

Scourges of the Passion SP290

Stained-glass Windows, Church of the Sacred Heart, Audincourt: 1.60fr+30c, "Peace."

1981, Dec. 5 Photo. *Perf. 13*

B539	SP290	1.40 + 30c multi	.75	.75
B540	SP290	1.60 + 30c multi	.80	.80
a.		Bklt. pane, 4 ea, gutter btwn.	6.00	

Guillaume Postel (1510-1581), Theologian — SP291

No. B542, Henri Mondor (1885-1962), physician. No. B543, Andre Chantemesse (1851-1919), Scientist. No. B544, Louis Pergaud (1882-1915), writer. No. B545, Robert Debre (1882-1978), writer. No. B546, Gustave Eiffel (1832-1923), engineer.

1982 Engr. *Perf. 13*

B541	SP291	1.40 + 30c multi	.65	.45
B542	SP291	1.40 + 30c dk brn & dk bl	.65	.40
B543	SP291	1.60 + 30c multi	.70	.70
B544	SP291	1.60 + 40c multi	.70	.70
B545	SP291	1.60 + 40c dk blue	.90	.70
B546	SP291	1.80 + 40c sepia	.90	.70
		Nos. B541-B546 (6)	4.50	3.65

Woman Reading, by Picasso — SP292

1982, Mar. 27 *Perf. 13x12½*

B547	SP292	1.60 + 40c multi	1.00	.75

Stamp Day.

SP293

SP294

Jules Verne books: 1.60fr+30c, Five Weeks in a Balloon. 1.80fr+40c, 20,000 Leagues under the Sea.

1982, Nov. 20 *Perf. 13*

B548	SP293	1.60 + 30c multi	.75	.65
B549	SP293	1.80 + 40c multi	.75	.65
a.		Bklt. pane, 4 each #B548-B549, with gutter btwn., perf. 12½x13	8.00	

Surtax was for Red Cross.

1983 Engr. *Perf. 12½x13*

No. B550, Andre Messager (1853-1929). No. B551, J.A. Gabriel (1698-1782), architect. No. B552, Hector Berlioz (1803-69), composer. No. B553, Max Fouchet (1913-80). No. B554, Rene Cassin (1887-1976). No. B555, Stendhal (Marie Henri Beyle, 1783-1842).

B550	SP294	1.60 + 30c multi	.65	.65
B551	SP294	1.60 + 30c multi	.65	.65
B552	SP294	1.80 + 40c dp lil & blk	.75	.75
B553	SP294	1.80 + 40c multi	.75	.75
B554	SP294	2fr + 40c multi	.80	.80
B555	SP294	2fr + 40c multi	.80	.80
		Nos. B550-B555 (6)	4.40	4.40

Issued: No. B550, 1/15; No. B551, 4/16; No. B552, 1/22; No. B553, 4/30; No. B554, 6/25; No. B555, 11/12.

Man Dictating a Letter, by Rembrandt — SP295

Photo. & Engr.

1983, Feb. 26 *Perf. 13X12½*

B556	SP295	1.80 + 40c multi	1.20	.75

Stamp Day.

Virgin with Child, Baillon, 14th Cent. — SP296

Design: No. B558, Virgin with Child, Genainville, 16th Cent.

1983, Nov. 26 Engr. *Perf. 13*

B557	SP296	1.60 + 40c shown	.65	.45
B558	SP296	2fr + 40c multi	.85	.55
a.		Bklt. pane, 4 #B557-B558, with gutter btwn., perf. 12½x13	6.50	

Emile Littre (1801-1881), Physician — SP297

No. B560, Jean Zay (1904-44). No. B561, Pierre Corneille (1606-1684. No. B562, Gaston Bachelard (1884-1962). No. B563, Jean Paulhan (1884-1968). No. B564, Evariste Galois (1811-1832).

1984 Engr. *Perf. 13*

B559	SP297	1.60fr + 40c plum & blk	.85	.85
B560	SP297	1.60fr + 40c dk grn & blk	.85	.85
B561	SP297	1.70fr + 40c dp vio & blk	.85	.85
B562	SP297	2fr + 40c gray & blk	.85	.85
B563	SP297	2.10fr + 40c dk brn & blk	.90	.80
B564	SP297	2.10fr + 40c ultra & blk	.90	.80
		Nos. B559-B564 (6)	5.20	5.00

SP298

Diderot Holding a Letter, by L.M. Van Loo.

1984, Mar. 17 Engr. *Perf. 12½x13*
B565 SP298 2fr + 40c multi 1.25 .90

SP299

The Rose Basket, by Caly.

1984, Nov. 24 Photo. *Perf. 12½x13*
B566 SP299 2.10fr + 50c pnksh (basket) & multi 1.10 .90
a. Salmon (basket) & multi, perf. 13½x13 1.10 .90
b. As "a," bklt. pane of 10 + 2 labels 11.00

Surtax was for the Red Cross.

Jules Romains (1885-1972) — SP300

Authors: No. B568, Jean-Paul Sartre (1905-1980). No. B569, Romain Rolland (1866-1944). No. B570, Roland Dorgeles (1885-1973). No. B571, Victor Hugo (1802-1885). No. B572, Francois Mauriac (1885-1970).

1985, Feb. 23 Engr. *Perf. 13*
B567 SP300 1.70fr + 40c 2.50 2.50
B568 SP300 1.70fr + 40c 2.50 2.50
B569 SP300 1.70fr + 40c 2.50 2.50
B570 SP300 2.10fr + 50c 2.50 2.50
B571 SP300 2.10fr + 50c 2.50 2.50
B572 SP300 2.10fr + 50c 2.50 2.50
a. Bklt. pane, 1 each + 2 labels, perf. 15x14½ 25.00
Nos. B567-B572 (6) 15.00 15.00

SP301 SP302

Stamp Day: Canceling apparatus invented by Eugene Daguin (1849-1888).

1985, Mar. 16 Engr. *Perf. 12½x13*
B573 SP301 2.10fr + 50c brn blk & bluish gray 1.00 .85

1985, Nov. 23 Photo.

Issenheim Altarpiece retable.

B574 SP302 2.20fr + 50c multi 1.00 .85
a. As "b," bklt. pane of 10 10.00
b. Perf. 13½x13 1.00 .85

Surtax for the Red Cross.

SP303 SP304

Famous men: No. B575, Francois Arago (1786-1853), physician, politician. No. B576, Henri Moissan (1852-1907), chemist. No. B577, Henri Fabre (1882-1984), engineer. No. B578, Marc Seguln (1786-1875), engineer. No. B579, Paul Heroult (1863-1914), chemist.

1986, Feb. 22 Engr. *Perf. 13*
B575 SP303 1.80fr + 40c multi .95 .95
B576 SP303 1.80fr + 40c multi .95 .95
B577 SP303 1.80fr + 40c multi .95 .95
B578 SP303 2.20fr + 50c multi 1.10 1.10
B579 SP303 2.20fr + 50c multi 1.10 1.10
a. Bklt. pane of 5, #B575-B579, + 3 labels 8.00
Nos. B575-B579 (5) 5.05 5.05

1986, Mar. 1 Engr. *Perf. 13x12½*
B580 SP304 2.20fr + 50c brn blk *6.00 6.00*

Pierre Cot (1895-1977).

Mail Britzska SP305

1986, Apr. 5 *Perf. 13*
B581 SP305 2.20fr + 60c pale tan & dk vio brn 1.10 1.00

Booklet Stamp

B582 SP305 2.20fr + 60c buff & blk 1.20 1.00
a. Bklt. pane of 6 + 2 labels 7.50

Stamp Day. See Nos. B590-B591, B599-B600, B608-B609.

Stained Glass Window (detail), by Vieira da Silva, St. Jacques of Reims Church, Marne — SP306

1986, Nov. 24 Photo. *Perf. 12½x13*
B583 SP306 2.20fr + 60c multi 1.20 .95
a. As "b," bklt. pane of 10 12.00
b. Perf. 13½x13 1.20 .95

Surtaxed to benefit the natl. Red Cross.

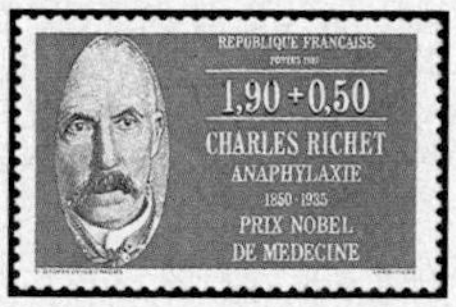

Physicians and Biologists SP307

No. B584, Charles Richet (1850-1935). No. B585, Eugene Jamot (1879-1937). No. B586, Bernard Halpern (1904-1978). No. B587, Alexandre Yersin (1863-1943). No. B588, Jean Rostand (1894-1977). No. B589, Jacques Monod (1910-1976).

1987, Feb. 21 Engr. *Perf. 13*
B584 SP307 1.90fr + 50c deep ultra .95 .95
B585 SP307 1.90fr + 50c dull lil .95 .95
B586 SP307 1.90fr + 50c grnish gray .95 .95
B587 SP307 2.20fr + 50c grnish gray 1.10 1.10
B588 SP307 2.20fr + 50c deep ultra 1.10 1.10
B589 SP307 2.20fr + 50c dull lil 1.10 1.10
a. Bklt. pane of 6, #B584-B589 *6.50*
Nos. B584-B589 (6) 6.15 6.15

Stamp Day Type of 1986

Stamp Day 1987: Berline carriage.

1987, Mar. 14 Engr.
B590 SP305 2.20fr + 60c buff & sepia 1.10 .95

Booklet Stamp

B591 SP305 2.20fr + 60c pale & dk bl 1.25 .95
a. Bklt. pane of 6 + 2 labels 8.00

Flight Into Egypt, Retable by Melchior Broederlam SP308

1987, Nov. 21 Photo. *Perf. 12½x13*
B592 SP308 2.20fr +60c multi 1.10 .95
a. As "b," bklt. pane of 10 + 2 labels 11.00
b. Perf. 13½x13 1.10 .95

Surtaxed to benefit the Red Cross.

Explorers SP309

Profiles & maps: No. B593, Marquis Abraham Duquesne (1610-1688), naval commander. No. B594, Pierre Andre de Suffren (1729-1788). No. B595, Jean-Francois de La Perouse (1741-1788). No. B596, Mahe de La Bourdonnais (1699-1753). No. B597, Louis-Antoine de Bougainville (1729-1811). No. B598, Jules Dumont d'Urville (1790-1842).

1988, Feb. 20 Engr. *Perf. 13*
B593 SP309 2fr + 50c multi .90 .80
B594 SP309 2fr + 50c multi .90 .80
B595 SP309 2fr + 50c multi .90 .80
B596 SP309 2.20fr + 50c multi 1.00 .85
B597 SP309 2.20fr + 50c multi 1.00 .85
B598 SP309 2.20fr + 50c multi 1.00 .85
a. Bklt. pane of 6, #B593-B598 6.00

Stamp Day Type of 1986

Stamp Day 1988: Postal coach.

1988, Mar. 29 Engr.
B599 SP305 2.20fr +60c dk lilac 1.10 1.00

Booklet Stamp

B600 SP305 2.20fr +60c sepia 1.10 1.00
a. Bklt. pane of 6 + 2 labels 6.50

Intl. Red Cross, 125th Anniv. — SP310

1988, Nov. 19 Engr. *Perf. 12½x13*
B601 SP310 2.20fr +60c multi 1.10 1.00
a. As"b," bklt. pane of 10+2 labels 11.00
b. Perf. 13½x13 1.10 1.00

See No. B747c.

Revolution Leaders and Heroes SP311

No. B602, Emmanuel Joseph Sieyes (1748-1836). No. B603, Honore Gabriel Riqueti, Comte de Mirabeau (1749-91). No. B604, Louis Marie de Noailles (1756-1804). No. B605, Lafayette. No. B606, Antoine Pierre Joseph Marie Barnave (1761-93). No. B607, Jean Baptiste Drouet (1763-1824).

1989, Feb. 25 Engr. *Perf. 13*
B602 SP311 2.20fr +50c multi 1.10 .90
B603 SP311 2.20fr +50c multi 1.10 .90
B604 SP311 2.20fr +50c multi 1.10 .90
B605 SP311 2.20fr +50c multi 1.10 .90
B606 SP311 2.20fr +50c multi 1.10 .90
B607 SP311 2.20fr +50c multi 1.10 .90
a. Bklt. pane, 1 each + 2 labels 6.60

French Revolution, bicent.

Stamp Day Type of 1986

Design: Paris-Lyon stagecoach.

1989, Apr. 15 Engr. *Perf. 13*
B608 SP305 2.20fr +60c pale bl & dk bl 1.10 .95

Booklet Stamp

B609 SP305 2.20fr +60c pale lil & pur 1.00 .95
a. Bklt. pane of 6 + 2 labels 8.00

Stamp Day 1989.

Bird From a Silk Tapestry, Lyon, 18th Cent. — SP312

1989, Nov. 18 Photo. *Perf. 12½x13*
B610 SP312 2.20fr +60c multi 1.10 .90
a. As "b," bklt. pane of 10 12.00
b. Perf. 13½x13 1.10 .90

Surtax for the natl. Red Cross.

1992 Winter Olympics, Albertville SP313

1990, Feb. 9 Engr. *Perf. 13*
B611 SP313 2.30fr +20c red, bl & blk 1.10 .85

See Nos. B621-B627, B636-B637, B639.

Stamp Day SP314

1990, Mar. 17 Photo.
B612 SP314 2.30fr +60c ultra, bl & brt yel 1.20 1.00

Booklet Stamp

B613 SP314 2.30fr +60c ultra, grn, yel & brt grn 1.20 1.00
a. Bklt. pane of 6 + 2 labels 8.00

SP315 SP316

Quimper or Brittany Ware Faience plate.

1990, May 5 Photo. *Perf. 12½x13*
B614 SP315 2.30fr +60c multi 1.10 1.00
a. As "b," bklt. pane of 10+2 labels 12.00
b. Perf. 13½x13 1.20 1.00

Surcharge benefited the Red Cross.

1990, June 16 Photo. *Perf. 13*

No. B615, Aristide Bruant. No. B616, Maurice Chevalier. No. B617, Tino Rossi. No. B618, Edith Piaf. No. B619, Jacques Brel. No. B620, Georges Brassens.

B615 SP316 2.30fr +50c multi 1.00 1.00
B616 SP316 2.30fr +50c multi 1.00 1.00
B617 SP316 2.30fr +50c multi 1.00 1.00
B618 SP316 2.30fr +50c multi 1.00 1.00

B619 SP316 2.30fr +50c multi 1.00 1.00
B620 SP316 2.30fr +50c multi 1.00 1.00
a. Bklt. pane, 1 each +2 labels 6.00

Albertville Olympic Type

Designs: No. B621, Ski jumping. No. B622, Speed skiing. No. B623, Slalom skiing. No. B624, Cross-country skiing. No. B625, Ice hockey. No. B626, Luge. No. B627, Curling.

1990-91 Engr. *Perf. 13*
B621 SP313 2.30fr +20c multi 1.00 .95
B622 SP313 2.30fr +20c multi 1.00 .95
B623 SP313 2.30fr +20c multi 1.00 .95
B624 SP313 2.30fr +20c multi 1.00 .95
B625 SP313 2.30fr +20c multi 1.00 .95
B626 SP313 2.50fr +20c multi 1.10 1.10
B627 SP313 2.50fr +20c multi 1.10 1.10
Nos. B621-B627 (7) 7.20 6.95

Issued: No. B621, 12/22/90; No. B622, 12/29/90; No. B623, 1/19/91; No. B624, 2/2/91; No. B625, 2/9/91; No. B626, 3/2/91; No. B627, 4/20/91.
No. B624 inscribed "La Poste 1992."

Paul Eluard (1895-1952) — SP317

Poets: No. B629, Andre Breton (1896-1966). No. B630, Louis Aragon (1897-1982). No. B631, Francis Ponge (1899-1988). No. B632, Jacques Prevert (1900-1977). No. B633, Rene Char (1907-1988).

1991, Feb. 23 Engr. *Perf. 12½x13*
B628 SP317 2.50fr +50c multi 1.10 1.10
B629 SP317 2.50fr +50c multi 1.10 1.10
B630 SP317 2.50fr +50c multi 1.10 1.10
B631 SP317 2.50fr +50c multi 1.10 1.10
B632 SP317 2.50fr +50c multi 1.10 1.10
B633 SP317 2.50fr +50c multi 1.10 1.10
a. Bklt. pane, 1 each +2 labels, perf. 13 7.50

Stamp Day
SP318

1991, Mar. 16 Photo. *Perf. 13*
B634 SP318 2.50fr +60c blue machine 1.25 1.25
B635 SP318 2.50fr +60c purple machine 1.25 1.25
a. Bklt. pane of 6 + 2 labels 8.50

Winter Olympics Type of 1990

No. B636, Acrobatic skiing. No. B637, Alpine skiing.

1991 Engr. *Perf. 13*
B636 SP313 2.50fr +20c multi 1.10 .95
B637 SP313 2.50fr +20c multi 1.10 .95

Issued: No. B636, Aug. 3; No. B637, Aug. 17.
Nos. B636-B637 inscribed "La Poste 1992."

The Harbor of Toulon by Francois Nardi
SP319

1991, Dec. 2 Photo. *Perf. 13x12½*
B638 SP319 2.50fr +60c multi 1.20 1.10
a. Perf. 13x13½ 1.20 1.10
b. As "a," bklt. pane of 10 + 2 labels 12.00

Surtax for the Red Cross.

Winter Olympics Type of 1990

Miniature Sheet

No. B639: a, like #B611. b, like #B621. c, like #B622. d, like #B623. e, like #B624. f, like #B625.

1992, Feb. 8 Engr. *Perf. 13*
B639 Sheet of 10 + label 18.00 18.00
a.-f. SP313 2.50fr +20c multi 1.75 1.75

No. B639 contains one each B626-B627, B636-B637, B639a-B639f. Central label is litho.

Stamp Day
SP320

1992, Mar. 7 Litho. *Perf. 13*
B640 SP320 2.50fr +60c gray people 1.10 1.10

Booklet Stamp
Photo.

B641 SP320 2.50fr +60c red people 1.25 1.10
a. Bklt. pane of 6 + 2 labels 8.00

SP321

SP322

Composers: No. B642, Cesar Franck (1822-1890). No. B643, Erik Satie (1866-1925). No. B644, Florent Schmitt (1870-1958). No. B645, Arthur Honegger (1892-1955). No. B646, Georges Auric (1899-1983). No. B647, Germaine Tailleferre (1892-1983).

1992, Apr. 11 Photo. *Perf. 13*
B642 SP321 2.50fr +50c multi 1.10 1.10
B643 SP321 2.50fr +50c multi 1.10 1.10
B644 SP321 2.50fr +50c multi 1.10 1.10
B645 SP321 2.50fr +50c multi 1.10 1.10
B646 SP321 2.50fr +50c multi 1.10 1.10
B647 SP321 2.50fr +50c multi 1.10 1.10
a. Bklt. pane of 6, #B642-B647 8.00

1992, Nov. 28 Photo. *Perf. 13½x13*
B648 SP322 2.50fr +60c multi 1.20 1.10
a. Bklt. pane of 10 + 2 labels 12.00

Mutual Aid, Strasbourg. Surtax for the Red Cross.

Writers
SP323

No. B649, Guy de Maupassant (1850-93). No. B650, Alain (Emile Chartier) (1868-1951). No. B651, Jean Cocteau (1889-1963). No. B652, Marcel Pagnol (1895-1974). No. B653, Andre Chamson (1900-83). No. B654, Marguerite Yourcenar (1903-87).

1993, Apr. 24 Engr. *Perf. 13*
B649 SP323 2.50fr +50c multi 1.10 1.10
B650 SP323 2.50fr +50c multi 1.10 1.10
B651 SP323 2.50fr +50c multi 1.10 1.10
B652 SP323 2.50fr +50c multi 1.10 1.10
B653 SP323 2.50fr +50c multi 1.10 1.10
B654 SP323 2.50fr +50c multi 1.10 1.10
a. Bklt. pane of 6, #B649-B654 + 2 labels 8.00

When Nos. B650-B654 are normally centered, inscriptions at base of the lower panel are not parallel to the perforations at bottom. On all six stamps the lower panel is not centered between the side perforations.

SP324

SP325

St. Nicolas, Image of Metz.

1993, Nov. 27 Engr. *Perf. 12½x13*
B655 SP324 2.80fr +60c multi 1.25 1.10
a. Perf. 13½x13 1.25 1.10
b. As "a," Bklt. pane of 10 +2 labels 15.00

Surtax for Red Cross.

1994, Sept. 17 Photo. *Perf. 13*

Stage and Screen Personalities: No. B656, Yvonne Printemps (1894-1977). No. B657, Fernandel (1903-71). No. B658, Josephine Baker (1906-75). No. B659, Bourvil (1917-70). No. B660, Yves Montand (1921-91). No. B661, Coluche (1944-86).

B656 SP325 2.80fr +60c multi 1.25 1.25
B657 SP325 2.80fr +60c multi 1.25 1.25
B658 SP325 2.80fr +60c multi 1.25 1.25
B659 SP325 2.80fr +60c multi 1.25 1.25
B660 SP325 2.80fr +60c multi 1.25 1.25
B661 SP325 2.80fr +60c multi 1.25 1.25
a. Bklt. pane, #B656-B661 + 2 labels 8.00

SP326

SP327

Designs: No. B662, St. Vaast, Arras Tapestry. No. B663, Brussels tapestry from Reydams workshop, Horse Museum, Saumur.

1994-95 Photo. *Perf. 12½x13*
B662 SP326 2.80fr +60c multi 1.50 1.40
a. Perf. 13½x13 1.50 1.40
b. Bklt. pane, 10 #B662a + 2 labels 15.00
Complete booklet, #B662b 16.00
B663 SP326 2.80fr +60c multi 1.50 1.50
a. Perf. 13½x13 1.50 1.50
b. Bklt. pane, 10 #B663a + 2 labels 15.00
Complete booklet, #B663b 15.00

Surtax for Red Cross.
Issued: No. B662, 11/26/94; No. B663, 5/13/95.

1995, Nov. 25 Engr. *Perf. 13*

Provencal Nativity Figures: No. B664, The Shepherd. No. B665, The Miller. No. B666, The Simpleton and the Tambour Player. No. B667, The Fishmonger. No. B668, The Scissor Grinder. No. B669, The Elders.

B664 SP327 2.80fr +60c multi 1.40 1.40
B665 SP327 2.80fr +60c multi 1.40 1.40
B666 SP327 2.80fr +60c multi 1.40 1.40
B667 SP327 2.80fr +60c multi 1.40 1.40
B668 SP327 2.80fr +60c multi 1.40 1.40
B669 SP327 2.80fr +60c multi 1.40 1.40
a. Booklet pane, Nos. B664-B669 + 2 labels 10.00
Complete booklet, No. B669a 11.00

SP328

Famous Fictional Detectives and Criminals: No. B670, Rocambole. No. B671, Arsène Lupin. No. B672, Joseph Rouletabille. No. B673, Fantômas. No. B674, Commissioner Maigret. No. B675, Nestor Burma.

1996, Oct. 5 Photo. *Perf. 13*
B670 SP328 3fr +60c multi 1.40 1.40
B671 SP328 3fr +60c multi 1.40 1.40
B672 SP328 3fr +60c multi 1.40 1.40
B673 SP328 3fr +60c multi 1.40 1.40
B674 SP328 3fr +60c multi 1.40 1.40
B675 SP328 3fr +60c multi 1.40 1.40
a. Booklet pane, #B670-B675 + 2 labels 9.00
Complete booklet, #B675a 11.00

Christmas
SP329

1996, Nov. 16 Photo. *Perf. 12¾x13*
B676 SP329 3fr +60c multi 1.45 1.45
a. Perf. 13¼x13 1.50 1.50
b. Booklet pane, 10 #B676a + 2 labels 15.00 —
Complete booklet, #B676b 15.00

Surtax for Red Cross.

Adventure Heroes
SP330

1997, Oct. 25 Photo. *Perf. 13*
B677 SP330 3fr +60c Sir Lancelot 1.40 1.40
B678 SP330 3fr +60c Pardaillan 1.40 1.40
B679 SP330 3fr +60c D'Artagnan 1.40 1.40
B680 SP330 3fr +60c Cyrano de Bergerac 1.40 1.40
B681 SP330 3fr +60c Captain Fracasse 1.40 1.40
B682 SP330 3fr +60c Le Bossu 1.40 1.40
a. Booklet pane, #B677-B682 + 2 labels 9.00
Complete booklet, #682a 9.00

Christmas, New Year — SP331

1997, Nov. 6 Photo. *Perf. 12¾x13*
B683 SP331 3fr +60c multi 1.40 1.25
a. Perf. 13¼x13 1.40 1.25
b. Booklet pane, 10 #B683a + 2 labels 14.00 —
Complete booklet, #B683b 15.00

Surtax for the Red Cross.

SP332

Actors of the French Cinema: No. B684, Romy Schneider (1938-82). No. B685, Simone Signoret (1921-85). No. B686, Jean Gabin (1904-76). No. B687, Louis de Funés (1914-83). No. B688, Bernard Blier (1916-89). No. B689, Lino Ventura (1919-87).

1998, Oct. 3 Photo. *Perf. 13*
B684 SP332 3fr +60c multi 1.40 1.40
B685 SP332 3fr +60c multi 1.40 1.40
B686 SP332 3fr +60c multi 1.40 1.40
B687 SP332 3fr +60c multi 1.40 1.40
B688 SP332 3fr +60c multi 1.40 1.40
B689 SP332 3fr +60c multi 1.40 1.40
a. Booklet pane, #B684-B689 + label 9.50
Complete booklet, #B689a 10.00

Christmas
SP333

1998, Nov. 5 Photo. *Perf. 12½x13*

B690 SP333 3fr +60c multi 1.40 1.40
a. Perf. 13½x13 1.40 1.40
b. Booklet pane, 10 #B690a + 2 labels 14.00
Complete booklet, #B690b 15.00

Surtax for Red Cross.

Famous Photographers — SP334

Photographs by: No. B691, Robert Doisneau (1912-94). No. B692, Brassai (Gyula Halasz) (1899-1984). No. B693, Jacques Lartigue (1894-1986). No. B694, Henri Cartier-Bresson (1908-2004). No. B695, Eugene Atget (1857-1927). No. B696, Felix Nadar (1820-1910).

1999, July 10 Photo. *Perf. 13*

B691 SP334 3fr +60c multi 1.40 1.40
B692 SP334 3fr +60c multi 1.40 1.40
B693 SP334 3fr +60c multi 1.40 1.40
B694 SP334 3fr +60c multi 1.40 1.40
B695 SP334 3fr +60c multi 1.40 1.40
B696 SP334 3fr +60c multi 1.40 1.40
a. Booklet pane, #B691-B696 8.50
Complete booklet, #B696a 9.00

New Year
2000 — SP335

1999, Nov. 10 Photo. *Perf. 12¾x13*

B697 SP335 3fr +60c multi 1.40 1.40
a. Perf. 13½x13 1.40 1.40
b. Booklet pane, 10 #B697a + 2 labels 14.00
Complete booklet, #B697b 14.00

Surtax for Red Cross.

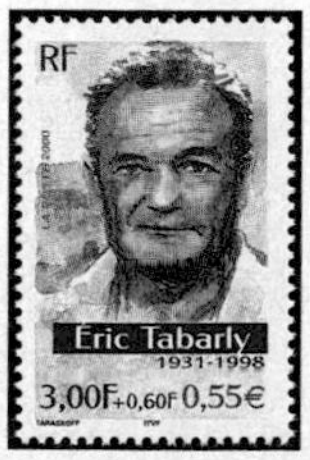

Adventurers
SP336

No. B698, Eric Tabarly (1931-98), sailor. No. B699, Alexandra David-Néel (1868-1969), opera singer, Asian traveler. No. B700, Haroun Tazieff (1914-98), vulcanologist. No. B701, Paul-Emile Victor (1907-55), ethnologist, polar explorer. No. B702, Jacques-Yves Cousteau (1910-97), oceanographer. No. B703, Norbert Casteret (1897-1987), speleologist.

2000, Sept. 16 Photo. *Perf. 13¼x13*

B698 SP336 3fr +60c multi 1.40 1.40
B699 SP336 3fr +60c multi 1.40 1.40
B700 SP336 3fr +60c multi 1.40 1.40
B701 SP336 3fr +60c multi 1.40 1.40
B702 SP336 3fr +60c multi 1.40 1.40
B703 SP336 3fr +60c multi 1.40 1.40
a. Booklet pane, #B698-B703 8.50
Booklet, #B703a 8.50

Toy
Airplane — SP337

2000, Nov. 9 Photo. *Perf. 13¼x13*

B704 SP337 3fr +60c multi 1.40 1.40
a. Booklet pane of 10 + 2 labels 14.00
Booklet, #B704a 15.00

Surtax for Red Cross.

Santa Claus and
Tree Ornaments
SP338

2001, Nov. 8 Photo. *Perf. 12¾x13*

B705 SP338 3fr +60c multi 1.40 1.40
a. Perf 13½x13 1.40 1.40
b. Booklet pane of 10 14.00 —
Booklet, #B705a 14.00

Surtax for Red Cross.

Infant Jesus
Asleep, by
Giovanni Battista
Salvi — SP339

2002, Nov. 7 Photo. *Perf. 12¾x13*

B706 SP339 46c +9c multi 1.40 1.40
a. Perf. 13½x13 1.40 1.40
b. As "a," booklet pane of 10 14.00 —
Booklet, #B706b 14.00

Surtax for Red Cross.

Virgin with
Grapes, by Pierre
Mignard — SP340

2003, Nov. 6 Photo. *Perf. 13¼x13*

Booklet Stamp

B707 SP340 50c +(16c) multi 1.50 1.50
a. Booklet pane of 10 15.00 —
Complete booklet, #B707a 15.00

Surtax for Red Cross.

Virgin With Child,
Attributed to
Cretan
School — SP341

2004, Nov. 10 Photo. *Perf. 13¼x13*

Booklet Stamp

B708 SP341 50c +(16c) multi 1.75 1.75
a. Booklet pane of 10 + 2 labels 17.50 —
Complete booklet, #B708a 17.50

Surtax for Red Cross.

Dec. 26,
2004
Tsunami
Victim
Relief
SP342

2005, Jan. 13 Engr. *Perf. 13*

B709 SP342 (50c) +20c red 1.90 1.90

Virgin and Child,
by Hans Memling
SP343

2005, Nov. 10 Photo. *Perf. 13½x13*

Booklet Stamp

B710 SP343 53c +(17c) multi 1.75 1.75
a. Booklet pane of 10 + 2 labels 17.50 —
Complete booklet, #B710a 17.50

Surtax for Red Cross.

SP344

Children's
Art — SP345

2006, Nov. 25 Photo. *Perf. 13½x13*

Booklet Stamps

B711 SP344 (54c) +(17c) multi 1.90 1.90
B712 SP345 (54c) +(17c) multi 1.90 1.90
a. Booklet pane, 5 each #B711-B712, + 2 labels 19.00 —
Complete booklet, #B712a 19.00

Surtax for Red Cross.

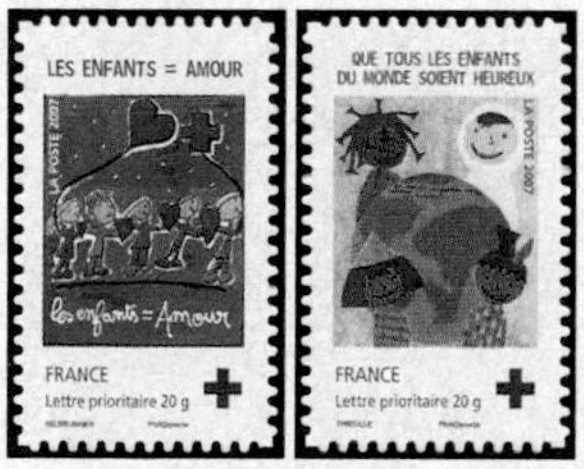

Red Cross
SP346 SP347

Serpentine Die Cut 11

2007, Nov. 24 Photo.

Self-Adhesive

Booklet Stamps

B713 SP346 (54c) +(17c) multi 2.10 2.10
B714 SP347 (54c) +(17c) multi 2.10 2.10
a. Booklet pane, 5 each #B713-B714 21.00

Surtax for Red Cross.

Red Cross
SP348 SP349

Serpentine Die Cut 11x11¼

2008, Nov. 8 Photo.

Booklet Stamps

Self-Adhesive

B715 SP348 (55c) +(18c) multi 1.90 1.90
B716 SP349 (55c) +(18c) multi 1.90 1.90
a. Booklet pane of 10, 2 each #B715-B716 19.00

Surtax for Red Cross.

Miniature Sheet

Red Cross — SP350

No. B717: a, Henri Dunant. b, Battle of Solferino. c, Pélias et Nélée, by Georges Braque, horiz. d, Geneva Conventions. e, Globe and symbols of the International Red Cross and Red Crescent Societies.

2009, Sept. 19 Photo. *Perf. 13*

B717 SP350 Sheet of 5 14.00 14.00
a.-e. 56c +(40c) Any single 2.75 2.75

Surtax for Red Cross.

Haiti Earthquake Relief — SP351

2010, Jan. 19 Engr. *Perf. 13*

B718 SP351 (56c) +44c red 2.75 2.75

Self-Adhesive

Serpentine Die Cut 11

B719 SP351 (56c) +44c red 2.75 2.75

Surtax was for French Red Cross relief efforts in Haiti.

Miniature Sheet

Red Cross — SP352

No. B720: a, Woman on telephone. b, Man assisting unconscious woman. c, Red Cross emblem, horiz. d, Woman performing Heimlich maneuver on choking man. e, Cardio-pulmonary resuscitation.

Photo., Photo. & Embossed (#B720c)

2010, Nov. 5 *Perf. 13*

B720 SP352 Sheet of 5 14.00 14.00
a.-e. 58c +(40c) Any single 2.75 2.75

Surtax for Red Cross.

Miniature Sheet

Singers — SP353

No. B721: a, Colette Renard (1924-2010). b, Henri Salvador (1917-2008). c, Serge Reggiani (1922-2004). d, Claude Nougaro (1929-2004). e, Daniel Balavoine (1952-86). f, Gilbert Bécaud (1927-2001).

2011, Oct. 14 Photo. *Perf. 13*

B721	SP353	Sheet of 6	15.50	15.50
a.-f.		60c + (33⅓c) Any single	2.50	2.50

Surtax for Red Cross.

Miniature Sheet

Red Cross — SP354

No. B722: a, People carrying person on litter. b, Three hands. c, Red Cross, horiz. d, Red Cross volunteer teaching illiterates. e, Red Cross volunteer giving bottle to infant.

2011, Nov. 4

B722	SP354	Sheet of 5	14.00	14.00
a.-e.		60c + (40c) Any single	2.75	2.75

Surtax for Red Cross.

Miniature Sheet

Movie Stars — SP355

No. B723: a, Françoise Dorléac (1942-67). b, Jean Marais (1913-98). c, Jacqueline Maillan (1923-92). d, Michel Serrault (1928-2007). e, Philippe Noiret (1930-2006). f, Annie Girardot (1931-2011).

2012, Oct. 19

B723	SP355	Sheet of 6	14.50	14.50
a.-f.		60c + (33⅓c) Any single	2.40	2.40

Surtax for Red Cross.

Miniature Sheet

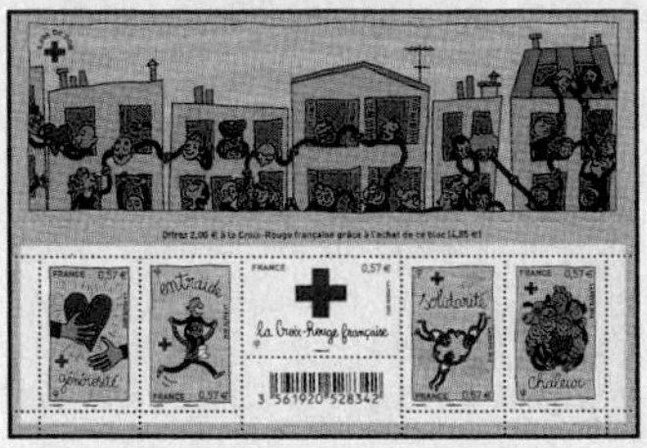

Red Cross — SP356

No. B724: a, Heart and hands. b, Man carrying man with injured foot. c, Red Cross, horiz. d, Three parachutists. e, People and dog hugging heart.

2012, Nov. 8

B724	SP356	Sheet of 5	12.50	12.50
a.-e.		57c + (40c) Any single	2.50	2.50

Surtax for Red Cross.

Loire River SP357

The Loire River at: No. B725, Mont Gerbier de Jonc. No. B726, Lac de Grangent. No. B727, Bec d'Allier. No. B728, Gien. No. B729, Pointe de Coupain. No. B730, Blois. No. B731, Candes-Saint-Martin. No. B732, Ingrandes-sur-Loire. No. B733, Champtoceaux. No. B734, Marais de Brière.

2013, June 1 *Serpentine Die Cut 11*

Booklet Stamps
Self-Adhesive

B725	SP357	(58c+20c) multi	2.10	2.10
B726	SP357	(58c+20c) multi	2.10	2.10
B727	SP357	(58c+20c) multi	2.10	2.10
B728	SP357	(58c+20c) multi	2.10	2.10
B729	SP357	(58c+20c) multi	2.10	2.10
B730	SP357	(58c+20c) multi	2.10	2.10
B731	SP357	(58c+20c) multi	2.10	2.10
B732	SP357	(58c+20c) multi	2.10	2.10
B733	SP357	(58c+20c) multi	2.10	2.10
B734	SP357	(58c+20c) multi	2.10	2.10
a.		Booklet pane of 10, #B725-B734	21.00	
		Nos. B725-B734 (10)	21.00	21.00

Surtax for the Red Cross.

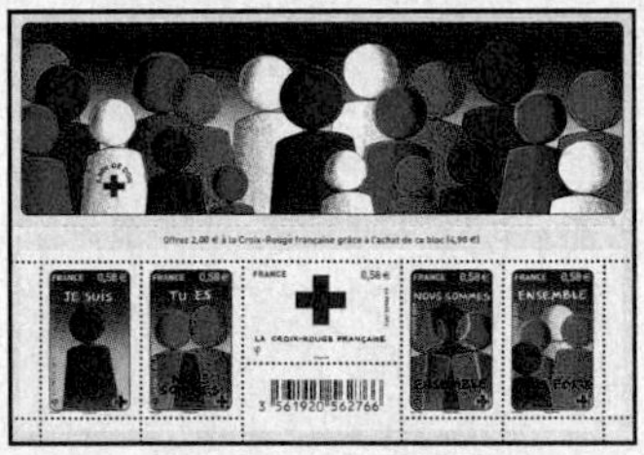

Red Cross — SP358

No. B735: a, One stylized person. b, Two stylized people. c, Red Cross, horiz. d, Three stylized people. e, Four stylized people.

2013, Nov. 7 Photo. *Perf. 13*

B735	SP358	Sheet of 5	13.00	13.00
a.-e.		58c + (40c) Any single	2.60	2.60

Surtax for Red Cross.

Flowers SP359

Designs: No. B736, Roses. No. B737, Daisies (Marguerite). No. B738, Tulips (Tulipe). No. B739, Sunflowers (Tournesol). No. B740, Irises. No. B741, Orchids (Orchidée). No. B742, Jonquils (Jonquille). No. B743, Lilies (Lys). No. B744, Carnations (Oeillet). No. B745, Gardenias (Gardénia).

Serpentine Die Cut 11

2014, May 24 Photo.

Booklet Stamps
Self-Adhesive

B736	SP359	(61c) + (20c) multi	2.25	2.25
B737	SP359	(61c) + (20c) multi	2.25	2.25
B738	SP359	(61c) + (20c) multi	2.25	2.25
B739	SP359	(61c) + (20c) multi	2.25	2.25
B740	SP359	(61c) + (20c) multi	2.25	2.25
B741	SP359	(61c) + (20c) multi	2.25	2.25
B742	SP359	(61c) + (20c) multi	2.25	2.25
B743	SP359	(61c) + (20c) multi	2.25	2.25
B744	SP359	(61c) + (20c) multi	2.25	2.25
B745	SP359	(61c) + (20c) multi	2.25	2.25
a.		Booklet pane of 10, #B736-B745	22.50	
		Nos. B736-B745 (10)	22.50	22.50

Red Cross, 150th anniv. Surtax for Red Cross.

Semi-Postal Stamps of 1914-88 Redrawn

2014, June 14 Litho.

B746	Sheet of 5	16.50	16.50
a.	SP2 61c +30c like #B2, perf. 13¼	3.25	3.25
b.	A22 61c +30c like #B1, perf. 13¼	3.25	3.25
c.	SP40 61c +30c like #B81, perf. 13	3.25	3.25
d.	SP9 61c +30c like #B11, perf. 13x13¼	3.25	3.25
e.	SP237 61c +30c like #B403, perf. 13	3.25	3.25
B747	Sheet of 5	16.50	16.50
a.	SP60 61c +30c like #B101, perf. 13x13¼	3.25	3.25
b.	SP258 61c +30c like #B462, perf. 13	3.25	3.25
c.	SP310 61c +30c like #B601, perf. 13¼x13	3.25	3.25
d.	SP207 61c +30c like #B328, perf. 13	3.25	3.25
e.	SP61 61c +30c like #B102, perf. 13x13¼	3.25	3.25

Nos. B746-B747 sold together as a set for €12.

Miniature Sheet

French Red Cross, 150th Anniv. — SP360

No. B748: a, Jean-Henri Dunant, 1864. b, White angel with Red Cross arm band treating soldier, 1914. c, Red cross and 150th anniv. emblem, horiz. d, Red Cross worker giving aid to refugee, 1945. e, Red Cross workers in Haiti, 2010.

2014, Nov. 7 Photo. *Perf. 13*

B748	SP360	Sheet of 5	12.50	12.50
a.-e.		61c+(30c) Any single	2.50	2.50

Surtax for the Red Cross.

SP361

SP362

SP363

SP364

SP365

SP366

SP367

Red Cross Workers in Action SP368

Serpentine Die Cut 11

2015, May 16 Litho.

Booklet Stamps
Self-Adhesive

B749	SP361	(68c+25c) multi	2.10	2.10
B750	SP362	(68c+25c) multi	2.10	2.10
B751	SP363	(68c+25c) multi	2.10	2.10
B752	SP364	(68c+25c) multi	2.10	2.10
B753	SP365	(68c+25c) multi	2.10	2.10
B754	SP366	(68c+25c) multi	2.10	2.10
B755	SP367	(68c+25c) multi	2.10	2.10
B756	SP368	(68c+25c) multi	2.10	2.10
a.		Booklet pane of 8, #B749-B756	17.00	
		Nos. B749-B756 (8)	16.80	16.80

Surtax for the Red Cross.

AIR POST STAMPS

Nos. 127, 130 Overprinted in Dark Blue or Black

Perf. 14x13½

1927, June 25 Unwmk.

C1	A18	2fr org & bl (DB)	200.00	225.00
		Never hinged	400.00	
C2	A18	5fr dk bl & buff	200.00	225.00
		Never hinged	400.00	

On sale only at the Intl. Aviation Exhib. at Marseilles, June, 1927. One set could be purchased by each holder of an admission ticket. Excellent counterfeits exist.

Nos. 242, 196 Surcharged

1928, Aug. 23

C3	A33	10fr on 90c	2,400.	1,800.
		Never hinged	3,500.	
a.		Inverted surcharge	16,500.	16,500.

Never hinged 25,000.
b. Space between "10" and bars 6½mm 3,100. 3,100.
Never hinged 5,100.
C4 A23 10fr on 1.50fr 10,000. 8,250.
Never hinged 14,000.
a. Space between "10" and bars 6½mm 13,000. 13,000.
Never hinged 20,000.

Nos. C3-C4 received their surcharge in New York by order of the French consul general. They were for use in paying the 10fr fee for letters leaving the liner Ile de France on a catapulted hydroplane when the ship was one day off the coast of France on its eastward voyage.

The normal space between "10" and bars is 4½mm, but on 10 stamps in each pane of 50 the space is 6½mm. Counterfeits exist.

View of Marseille, Church of Notre Dame at Left — AP1

1930-31 Engr. *Perf. 13*
C5 AP1 1.50fr dp carmine 21.00 4.00
Never hinged 40.00
a. With perf. initials "E.I.P.A.30" 2,750. 3,750.
Never hinged 3,600.
C6 AP1 1.50fr dk bl ('31) 19.00 2.25
Never hinged 35.00
a. 1.50fr ultramarine 50.00 21.00
Never hinged 90.00
b. As "a," with perf. initials "E.I.P.A.30" 450.00 350.00
Never hinged 700.00

Nos. C5a, C6a were sold at the Intl. Air Post Exhib., Paris, Nov. 6-20, 1930, at face value plus 5fr, the price of admission.

Forgeries abound of Nos. C5a and C6b. Certificates from recognized authorities are recommended.

Blériot's Monoplane AP2

1934, Sept. 1 *Perf. 13*
C7 AP2 2.25fr violet 24.00 6.00
Never hinged 32.50

1st flight across the English Channel, by Louis Blériot.

Plane over Paris AP3

1936
C8 AP3 85c deep green 2.25 2.25
Never hinged 6.50
C9 AP3 1.50fr blue 10.50 5.50
Never hinged 18.00
C10 AP3 2.25fr violet 18.00 7.00
Never hinged 35.00
C11 AP3 2.50fr rose 32.50 8.25
Never hinged 45.00
C12 AP3 3fr ultra 26.00 2.50
Never hinged 37.50
C13 AP3 3.50fr orange brn 62.50 24.00
Never hinged 105.00
C14 AP3 50fr emerald 825.00 325.00
Never hinged 1,450.
b. 50fr green 850.00 350.00
Never hinged 1,500.
Nos. C8-C14 (7) 976.75 374.50

Monoplane over Paris — AP4

Paper with Red Network Overprint

1936, July 10 *Perf. 12½*
C15 AP4 50fr ultra 625.00 310.00
Never hinged 1,700.

Airplane and Galleon — AP5

Airplane and Globe AP6

1936, Aug. 17 *Perf. 13*
C16 AP5 1.50fr dk ultra 17.50 5.25
Never hinged 35.00
C17 AP6 10fr Prus green 290.00 130.00
Never hinged 700.00

100th air mail flight across the South Atlantic.

Catalogue values for unused stamps in this section, from this point to the end of the section, are for Never Hinged items.

Centaur and Plane — AP7

Iris — AP8

Zeus Carrying Hebe AP9

Chariot of the Sun AP10

1946-47 Engr. Unwmk.
C18 AP7 40fr dk green .65 .25
C19 AP8 50fr rose pink .65 .25
C20 AP9 100fr dk blue ('47) 7.00 4.00
C21 AP10 200fr red 6.00 1.50
Nos. C18-C21 (4) 14.30 6.00

Issued: 50fr, 200fr, 5/27; 40fr, 7/1; 100fr, Jan.

For surcharges see Reunion Nos. C35-C38.

Ile de la Cité, Paris, and Gull — AP11

1947, May 7
C22 AP11 500fr dk Prus grn 50.00 45.00

UPU 12th Cong., Paris, May 7-July 7. See footnote after No. 4642.

View of Lille AP12

Air View of Paris — AP13

200fr, Bordeaux. 300fr, Lyon. 500fr, Marseille.

1949-50 Unwmk. *Perf. 13*
C23 AP12 100fr sepia 1.40 .40
C24 AP12 200fr dk bl grn 12.50 .75
C25 AP12 300fr purple 15.00 10.00
C26 AP12 500fr brt red 57.50 5.75
C27 AP13 1000fr sep & blk, *bl* ('50) 150.00 27.50
Nos. C23-C27 (5) 236.40 44.40

For surcharges see Reunion Nos. C39-C41.

Alexander III Bridge and Petit Palais, Paris — AP14

1949, June 13
C28 AP14 100fr brown car 7.50 5.75

International Telegraph and Telephone Conference, Paris, May-July 1949.

Jet Plane, Mystère IV — AP15

Planes: 200fr, Noratlas. 500fr, Miles Magister. 1000fr, Provence.

1954, Jan. 16
C29 AP15 100fr red brn & bl 3.00 .25
C30 AP15 200fr blk brn & vio bl 11.00 .25
C31 AP15 500fr car & org 200.00 12.50
C32 AP15 1000fr vio brn, bl grn & ind 110.00 16.00
Nos. C29-C32 (4) 324.00 29.00

See No. C37. For surcharges see Reunion Nos. C42-C45, C48.

Maryse Bastié and Plane AP16

1955, June 4 Unwmk. *Perf. 13*
C33 AP16 50fr dp plum & rose pink 6.50 4.00

Issued to honor Maryse Bastié, 1898-1952.

Morane Saulnier 760 Paris AP17

Designs: 500fr, Caravelle. 1000fr, Alouette helicopter.

1957-59 Engr. *Perf. 13*
C34 AP17 300fr sl grn, grnsh bl & sep ('59) 5.00 3.00
C35 AP17 500fr dp ultra & blk 30.00 3.75
C36 AP17 1000fr lil, ol blk & blk ('58) 52.50 19.00
Nos. C34-C36 (3) 87.50 25.75

See Nos. C38-C41. For surcharges see Reunion Nos. C46-C47, C49-C51.

Types of 1954-59

Planes: 2fr, Noratlas. 3fr, MS760, Paris. 5fr, Caravelle. 10fr, Alouette helicopter.

1960, Jan. 11
C37 AP15 2fr vio bl & ultra 1.60 .25
a. 2fr ultramarine 3.25 .40
C38 AP17 3fr sl grn, grnsh bl & sep 1.60 .25
C39 AP17 5fr dp ultra & blk 3.25 .75
C40 AP17 10fr lil, ol blk & blk 13.00 2.00
Nos. C37-C40 (4) 19.45 3.25

Type of 1957-59

Design: 2fr, Jet plane, Mystère 20.

1965, June 12 Engr. *Perf. 13*
C41 AP17 2fr slate bl & indigo .85 .25

Concorde Issue

Common Design Type

1969, Mar. 2 Engr. *Perf. 13*
C42 CD129 1fr indigo & brt bl 1.00 .35

The 0.95fr stamp in this design was prepared but not issued. Value $30,000.

Jean Mermoz, Antoine de Saint-Exupéry and Concorde — AP19

1970, Sept. 19 Engr. *Perf. 13*
C43 AP19 20fr blue & indigo 12.00 .60

Jean Mermoz (1901-36) and writer Antoine de Saint-Exupéry (1900-44), aviators and air mail pioneers.

Balloon, Gare d'Austerlitz, Paris — AP20

1971, Jan. 16 Engr. *Perf. 13*
C44 AP20 95c bl, vio bl, org & sl grn .90 .55

Centenary of the balloon post from besieged Paris, 1870-71.

Didier Daurat, Raymond Vanier and Plane Landing at Night — AP21

1971, Apr. 17 Engr. *Perf. 13*
C45 AP21 5fr Prus bl, blk & lt grn 2.00 .25

Didier Daurat (1891-1969) and Raymond Vanier (1895-1965), aviation pioneers.

For surcharge see Reunion No. C52.

Hélène Boucher, Maryse Hilsz and Caudron-Renault and Moth-Morane Planes — AP22

Design: 15fr, Henri Guillaumet, Paul Codos, Latécoère 521, Guillaumet's crashed plane in Andes, skyscrapers.

1972-73 **Engr.** ***Perf. 13***

C46 AP22 10fr plum, red & sl 4.50 .40
C47 AP22 15fr dp car, gray & brn ('73) 6.50 .65

Hélène Boucher (1908-34), Maryse Hilsz (1901-46), Henri Guillaumet (1902-40) and Paul Codos (1896-1960), aviation pioneers.

Issue dates: 10fr, June 10; 15fr, Feb. 24.

Concorde AP23

1976, Jan. 10 **Engr.** ***Perf. 13***

C48 AP23 1.70fr brt bl, red & blk 1.00 .50

First flight of supersonic jet Concorde from Paris to Rio de Janeiro, Jan. 21.

Planes over the Atlantic, New York-Paris — AP24

1977, June 4 **Engr.** ***Perf. 13***

C49 AP24 1.90fr multicolored .90 .50

1st transatlantic flight by Lindbergh from NY to Paris, 50th anniv., and 1st attempted west-bound flight by French aviators Charles Nungesser and Francois Coli.

Plane over Flight Route AP25

1978, Oct. 14 **Engr.** ***Perf. 13***

C50 AP25 1.50fr multicolored .90 .35

65th anniversary of first airmail route from Villacoublay to Pauillac, Gironde.

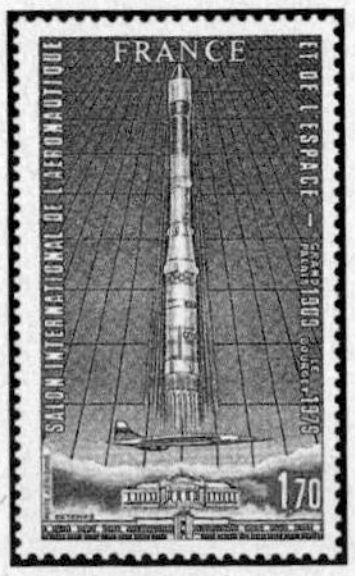

Rocket, Concorde, Exhibition Hall — AP26

1979, June 9 **Engr.** ***Perf. 13***

C51 AP26 1.70fr ultra, org & brn 1.25 .80

33rd International Aerospace and Space Show, Le Bourget, June 11-15.

First Nonstop Transatlantic Flight, Paris-New York — AP27

1980, Aug. 30 **Engr.** ***Perf. 13***

C52 AP27 2.50fr vio brn & ultra 1.00 .40

34th Intl. Space and Aeronautics Exhibition, June 5-14 AP28

1981, June 6 **Engr.** ***Perf. 13***

C53 AP28 2fr multicolored 2.00 .50

Dieudonné Costes and Joseph Le Brix and their Breguet Bi-plane — AP29

1981, Sept. 12 **Engr.**

C54 AP29 10fr dk brown & red 4.50 .40

1st So. Atlantic crossing, Oct. 14-15, 1927.

Seaplane Late-300 — AP30

1982, Dec. 4 **Engr.**

C55 AP30 1.60fr multicolored .80 .60

Farman F-60 Goliath — AP31

Planes: 20fr, CAMS-53 seaplane. 30fr, Wibault 283 Monoplane. 50fr, Dewoitine 338.

1984-87 **Engr.**

C56 AP31 15fr dark blue 5.00 .60
C57 AP31 20fr dp org ('85) 7.50 .60
C58 AP31 30fr brt vio ('86) 10.00 1.50
C59 AP31 50fr green ('87) 15.00 4.50
Nos. C55-C59 (5) 38.30 7.80

Issued: 15fr, 3/3; 20fr, 3/2; 30fr, 10/11; 50fr, 4/11.

Breguet XIV — AP32

1997, Nov. 15 **Photo.** ***Perf. 13x13¼***

C60 AP32 20fr shown 10.00 4.00
a. Perf. 13x12½ 9.00 1.75
C61 AP32 30fr Potez 25 15.00 4.00
a. Perf. 13x12½ 14.00 2.50

Issued: No. C60 11/15/97; No. C60a, 7/13/98; 30fr, 7/13/98.

Airbus A300-B4 — AP33

1999, Apr. 10 **Photo.** ***Perf. 13x13¼***

C62 AP33 15fr multicolored 16.00 4.00
a. Perf. 13x12½ 7.00 1.25

Couzinet 70 — AP34

2000, Feb. 12 ***Perf. 13¼x13¼***

C63 AP34 50fr multi 22.50 9.00
a. Perf. 13x12½ 22.50 6.00

First Flight of Airbus A300, 30th Anniv. — AP35

2002, Oct. 26 **Photo.** ***Perf. 13x13¼***

C64 AP35 €3 multi 9.00 1.75

No. C64 was issued both in panes of 40 and 10, same perforation.

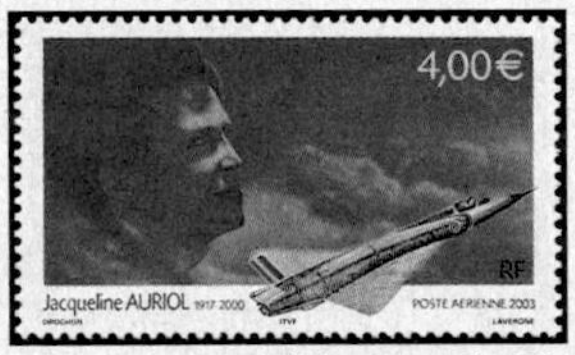

Jacqueline Auriol (1917-2000), Pilot, and Jet — AP36

Litho. & Engr.

2003, June 21 ***Perf. 13***

C65 AP36 €4 multi 12.00 2.50
a. Miniature sheet of 10 120.00 —

Marie Marvingt (1875-1963), Pilot — AP37

Litho. & Engr.

2004, June 29 ***Perf. 13¼x13***

C66 AP37 €5 multi 15.00 3.00
a. Sheet of 10 150.00 —

Adrienne Bolland (1895-1975), Pilot — AP38

Litho. & Engr.

2005, Oct. 22 ***Perf. 13***

C67 AP38 €2 multi 6.00 1.50
a. Miniature sheet of 10 60.00 —

Airbus A380 — AP39

2006, June 23 **Photo.** ***Perf. 13x13¼***

C68 AP39 €3 multi 9.00 1.75
a. Miniature sheet of 10 90.00 —

Helicopters, Cent. — AP40

2007, Feb. 19 **Photo.** ***Perf. 13x12½***

C69 AP40 €3 multi 8.00 1.60
a. Perf. 13x13¼ 8.00 1.60

No. C69 was issued in panes of 40; No. C69a in panes of 10.

French Acrobatic Patrol — AP41

Litho. & Engr.

2008, Sept. 13 ***Perf. 13***

C70 AP41 €3 multi 8.25 1.75

Louis Blériot (1872-1936) and Blériot XI Airplane — AP42

Litho. & Engr.

2009, July 25 ***Perf. 13x12¾***

C71 AP42 €2 multi 5.75 1.25

First flight across English Channel, cent.

Henri Fabre (1882-1984) and Le Canard Seaplane — AP43

Litho. & Engr.

2010, Mar. 27 ***Perf. 13***

C72 AP43 €3 multi 8.25 1.75

First seaplane flight, cent.

Henri Pequet (1888-1974), Pilot for First Official Air Mail Flight in India — AP44

2011, Feb. 18

C73	AP44	€2 multi	5.75	1.25

First French Airmail Flight Between Nancy and Luneville, Cent. — AP45

2012, July 30

C74	AP45	€3 multi	7.50	1.90

First Parachute Jump by Adolphe Pégoud (1889-1915), Cent. — AP46

2013, June 13

C75	AP46	€2.55 multi	7.00	2.40
a.		Miniature sheet of 10	70.00	70.00

First Trans-Mediterranean Flight by Roland Garros, Cent. — AP47

2013, Sept. 21 Photo. *Perf. 13x12¾*

C76	AP47	€3.40 multi	9.25	3.25

Caroline Aigle (1974-2007), First Female Fighter Pilot in French Air Force — AP48

Litho. & Engr.

2014, Apr. 5 ***Perf. 13***

C77	AP48	€3.55 multi	10.00	3.50

Gaston Caudron (1882-1915), Pilot and Aircraft Manufacturer — AP49

Litho & Engr.

2015, June 15 ***Perf. 13***

C78	AP49	€4.10 multi	9.00	3.00

AIR POST SEMI-POSTAL STAMPS

Catalogue values for unused stamps in this section are for Never Hinged items.

Antoine de Saint-Exupéry — SPAP1

Col. Jean Dagnaux SPAP2

1948 Unwmk. Engr. *Perf. 13*

CB1	SPAP1	50fr + 30fr vio brn	2.75	1.60
CB2	SPAP2	100fr + 70fr dk blue	3.75	2.25

Modern Plane and Ader's "Eole" SPAP3

1948, Feb.

CB3	SPAP3	40fr + 10fr dk blue	1.60	1.50

50th anniv. of the flight of Clément Ader's plane, the Eole, in 1897.

POSTAGE DUE STAMPS

D1

1859-70 Unwmk. Litho. *Imperf.*

J1	D1	10c black	30,500.	240.00
J2	D1	15c black ('70)	140.00	*250.00*

In the lithographed stamps the central bar of the "E" of "CENTIMES" is very short, and the accent on "a" slants at an angle of 30 degree, for the 10c and 17 degree for the 15c, while on the typographed the central bar of the "E" is almost as wide as the top and bottom bars and the accent on the "a" slants at an angle of 47 degree.

No. J2 is known rouletted unofficially.

1859-78 **Typo.**

J3	D1	10c black	30.00	17.50
J4	D1	15c black ('63)	35.00	15.00
J5	D1	20c black ('77)	4,100.	
J6	D1	25c black ('71)	150.00	50.00
a.		Double impression	6,000.	
J7	D1	30c black ('78)	225.00	125.00
J8	D1	40c blue ('71)	325.00	*425.00*
a.		40c ultramarine	6,500.	5,700.
b.		40c Prussian blue	2,600.	
J9	D1	60c bister ('71)	475.00	*1,050.*
J10	D1	60c blue ('78)	60.00	*110.00*
a.		60c dark blue	600.00	*725.00*
J10B	D1	60c black	2,700.	

The 20c & 60c black were not put into use.

Nos. J3, J4, J6, J8 and J9 are known rouletted unofficially and Nos. J4, J6, J7 and J10 pin-perf. unofficially.

D2

1882-92 ***Perf. 14x13½***

J11	D2	1c black	2.50	2.50
J12	D2	2c black	30.00	26.00
J13	D2	3c black	30.00	25.00
J14	D2	4c black	60.00	40.00
J15	D2	5c black	130.00	32.50
J16	D2	10c black	110.00	2.50
J17	D2	15c black	77.50	10.50
J18	D2	20c black	350.00	140.00
J19	D2	30c black	210.00	2.50
J20	D2	40c black	140.00	60.00
J21	D2	50c blk ('92)	600.00	175.00
J22	D2	60c blk ('84)	600.00	57.50
J23	D2	1fr black	750.00	350.00
J24	D2	2fr blk ('84)	1,400.	825.00
J25	D2	5fr blk ('84)	3,000.	1,600.

Excellent counterfeits exist of Nos. J23-J25.

See Nos. J26-J45A. For overprints and surcharges see Offices in China Nos. J1-J6, J33-J40, Offices in Egypt, Alexandria J1-J5, Port Said J1-J8, Offices in Zanzibar 60-62, J1-J5, Offices in Morocco 9-10, 24-25, J1-J5, J10-J12, J17-J22, J35-J41.

1884

J26	D2	1fr brown	400.00	90.00
J27	D2	2fr brown	190.00	130.00
J28	D2	5fr brown	450.00	325.00

1893-1941

J29	D2	5c blue ('94)	.25	.30
J30	D2	10c brown	.25	.30
J31	D2	15c lt grn ('94)	28.00	1.40
J32	D2	20c ol grn ('06)	6.50	.65
J33	D2	25c rose ('23)	6.50	3.75
J34	D2	30c red ('94)	.25	.25
J35	D2	30c org red ('94)	475.00	85.00
J36	D2	40c rose ('25)	11.50	4.50
J37	D2	45c grn ('24)	9.00	5.25
J38	D2	50c brn vio ('95)	.50	.30
a.		50c lilac	.50	.30
J39	D2	60c bl grn ('25)	1.00	.55
J40	D2	1fr rose, *straw* ('96)	475.00	375.00
J41	D2	1fr red brn, *straw* ('20)	9.50	.30
J42	D2	1fr red brn ('35)	1.25	.40
J43	D2	2fr red org ('10)	225.00	65.00
J44	D2	2fr brt vio ('26)	.65	*.75*
J45	D2	3fr magenta ('26)	.65	*.75*
J45A	D2	5fr red org ('41)	1.40	*2.25*

D3

1908-25

J46	D3	1c olive grn	1.00	*1.25*
J47	D3	10c violet	1.10	.30
a.		Imperf., pair	175.00	
J48	D3	20c bister ('19)	40.00	1.25
J49	D3	30c bister ('09)	14.00	.40
J50	D3	50c red ('09)	275.00	60.00
J51	D3	60c red ('25)	2.75	*3.75*
		Nos. J46-J51 (6)	333.85	66.95

"Recouvrements" stamps were used to recover charges due on undelivered or refused mail which was returned to the sender.

For surcharges see Offices in Morocco Nos. J6-J9, J13-J16, J23-J26, J42-J45.

Nos. J49-J50 Surcharged

1917

J52	D3	20c on 30c bister	20.00	4.00
J53	D3	40c on 50c red	10.50	4.00
a.		Double surcharge	475.00	

In Jan. 1917 several values of the current issue of postage stamps were handstamped "T" in a triangle and used as postage due stamps.

Recouvrements Stamps of 1908-25 Surcharged

1926

J54	D3	50c on 10c lilac	3.50	3.25
J55	D3	60c on 1c ol grn	7.00	5.00
J56	D3	1fr on 60c red	18.00	10.00
J57	D3	2fr on 60c red	18.00	10.50
		Nos. J54-J57 (4)	46.50	28.75

D4

1927-31

J58	D4	1c olive grn ('28)	1.00	1.00
J59	D4	10c rose ('31)	1.90	1.40
J60	D4	30c bister	4.50	.50
J61	D4	60c red	4.50	.50
J62	D4	1fr violet	14.00	3.25
J63	D4	1fr Prus grn ('31)	17.00	.55
J64	D4	2fr blue	80.00	42.50
J65	D4	2fr olive brn ('31)	150.00	26.00
		Nos. J58-J65 (8)	272.90	75.70

Nos. J62 to J65 have the numerals of value double-lined.

Nos. J64, J62 Surcharged in Red or Black

1929

J66	D4	1.20fr on 2fr blue	42.50	11.00
J67	D4	5fr on 1fr vio (Bk)	65.00	15.00

No. J61 Surcharged

1931

J68	D4	1fr on 60c red	30.00	2.75

Catalogue values for unused stamps in this section, from this point to the end of the section, are for Never Hinged items.

Sheaves of Wheat — D5

Perf. 14x13½

1943-46 Unwmk. Typo.

J69	D5	10c sepia	.25	.25
J70	D5	30c brt red vio	.25	.25
J71	D5	50c blue grn	.25	.25
J72	D5	1fr brt ultra	.25	.25
J73	D5	1.50fr rose red	.45	.40
J74	D5	2fr turq blue	.45	.40
J75	D5	3fr brn org	.45	.40
J76	D5	4fr dp vio ('45)	5.50	3.00
J77	D5	5fr brt pink	.60	.40
J78	D5	10fr red org ('45)	3.50	.40
J79	D5	20fr ol bis ('46)	10.00	2.75
		Nos. J69-J79 (11)	21.95	8.75

Type of 1943
Inscribed "Timbre Taxe"

1946-53

J80	D5	10c sepia ('47)	1.25	1.25
J81	D5	30c brt red vio ('47)	1.25	1.25
J82	D5	50c blue grn ('47)	25.00	9.50
J83	D5	1fr brt ultra ('47)	.25	.25
J85	D5	2fr turq blue	.25	.25
J86	D5	3fr brown org	.25	.25
J87	D5	4fr deep violet	.25	.25
J88	D5	5fr brt pink ('47)	.25	.25
J89	D5	10fr red org ('47)	.25	.25
J90	D5	20fr olive bis ('47)	2.00	.45
J91	D5	50fr dk green ('50)	25.00	1.40
J92	D5	100fr dp green ('53)	77.50	6.75
		Nos. J80-J92 (12)	133.50	22.10

For surcharges see Reunion Nos. J36-J44.

Sheaves of Wheat — D6

1960 Typo. *Perf. 14x13½*

J93	D6	5c bright pink		3.25	.40
J94	D6	10c red orange		5.00	.30
J95	D6	20c olive bister		4.00	.30
J96	D6	50c dark green		12.50	1.25
J97	D6	1fr deep green		50.00	2.00
		Nos. J93-J97 (5)		74.75	4.25

For surcharges see Reunion Nos. J46-J48. For overprints see Algeria Nos. J49-J53.

D7

D8

Flowers: 5c, Centaury. 10c, Gentian. 15c, Corn poppy. 20c, Violets. 30c, Forget-me-not. 40c, Columbine. 50c, Clover. 1fr, Soldanel.

1964-71 Typo. *Perf. 14x13½*

J98	D7	5c car rose, red & grn ('65)	.25	.25
J99	D7	10c car rose, brt bl & grn ('65)	.25	.25
J100	D7	15c brn, grn & red	.25	.25
J101	D7	20c dk grn, grn & vio ('71)	.25	.25
J102	D7	30c brn, ultra & grn	.25	.25
J103	D7	40c dk grn, scar & yel ('71)	.25	.25
J104	D7	50c vio bl, car & grn ('65)	.25	.25
J105	D7	1fr vio bl, lil & grn ('65)	.40	.25
		Nos. J98-J105 (8)	2.15	2.00

For surcharges see Reunion Nos. J49-J55.

1982-83 Engr. *Perf. 13*

J106	D8	10c Ampedus Cinnabarinus	.25	.25
J107	D8	20c Dorcadion fuliginator	.25	.25
J108	D8	30c Leptura cordigera	.25	.25
J109	D8	40c Paederus littoralis	.25	.25
J110	D8	50c Pyrochroa coccinea	.25	.25
J111	D8	1fr Scarites laevigatus	.30	.25
J112	D8	2fr Trichius gallicus	.55	.25
J113	D8	3fr Adalia alpina	.90	.25
J114	D8	4fr Apoderus coryli	1.20	.25
J115	D8	5fr Trichodes alvearius	1.90	.25
		Nos. J106-J115 (10)	6.10	2.50

Issued: 30c, 40c, 3fr, 5fr, 1/3/83; others, 1/4/82.

MILITARY STAMPS

Regular Issue Overprinted in Black or Red

1901-39 Unwmk. *Perf. 14x13½*

M1	A17	15c orange ('01)	65.00	6.00
a.		Inverted overprint	300.00	150.00
b.		Imperf., pair	425.00	
M2	A19	15c pale red ('03)	65.00	6.00
M3	A20	15c slate grn ('04)	52.50	6.00
a.		No period after "M"	110.00	57.50
b.		Imperf., pair	290.00	
M4	A20	10c rose ('06)	30.00	8.25
a.		No period after "M"	82.50	45.00
b.		Imperf., pair	350.00	
M5	A22	10c red ('07)	1.75	1.00
a.		Inverted overprint	105.00	65.00
b.		Imperf., pair	190.00	
M6	A20	50c vermilion ('29)	4.75	1.00
a.		No period after "M"	32.50	18.00
b.		Period in front of F	32.50	18.00
M7	A45	50c rose red ('34)	2.75	.55
a.		No period after "M"	29.00	16.00
b.		Inverted overprint	150.00	110.00
M8	A45	65c brt ultra (R) ('38)	.30	.30
a.		No period after "M"	29.00	16.00
M9	A45	90c ultra (R) ('39)	.40	.35
		Nos. M1-M9 (9)	222.45	29.45

"F. M." are initials of Franchise Militaire (Military Frank). See No. S1.

Catalogue values for unused stamps in this section, from this point to the end of the section, are for Never Hinged items.

M1

1946-47 Typo.

M10	M1	dark green	1.75	.65
M11	M1	rose red ('47)	.30	.25

Nos. M10-M11 were valid also in the French colonies.

Flag — M2

1964, July 20 *Perf. 13x14*

M12	M2	multicolored	.30	.35

OFFICIAL STAMPS

FOR THE COUNCIL OF EUROPE

For use only on mail posted in the post office in the Council of Europe Building, Strasbourg.

Catalogue values for unused stamps in this section are for Never Hinged items.

For French stamp inscribed "Conseil de l'Europe" see No. 679.

France No. 854 Overprinted: "CONSEIL DE L'EUROPE"

Unwmk.

1958, Jan. 14 Engr. *Perf. 13*

1O1	A303	35fr car rose & lake	1.25	*2.25*

Council of Europe Flag — O1

1958-59 Flag in Ultramarine

1O2	O1	8fr red org & brn vio	.25	.25
1O3	O1	20fr yel & lt brn	.35	.35
1O4	O1	25fr lil rose & sl grn ('59)	.60	.60
1O5	O1	35fr red	.55	.55
1O6	O1	50fr lilac rose ('59)	1.00	1.00
		Nos. 1O2-1O6 (5)	2.75	2.75

1963, Jan. 3 Flag in Ultramarine

1O7	O1	20c yel & lt brn	1.25	1.25
1O8	O1	25c lil rose & sl grn	2.00	2.00
1O9	O1	50c lilac rose	2.50	2.50
		Nos. 1O7-1O9 (3)	5.75	5.75

Centime value stamps shown the denomination as "0,20," etc.

1965-71

Flag in Ultramarine & Yellow

1O10	O1	25c ver, yel & sl grn	.90	.90
1O11	O1	30c ver & yel	.50	.50
1O12	O1	40c ver, yel & gray	1.00	1.00
1O13	O1	50c red, yel & grn	2.00	2.00
1O14	O1	60c ver, yel & vio	1.10	1.10
1O15	O1	70c ver, yel & dk brn	4.00	4.00
		Nos. 1O10-1O15 (6)	9.50	9.50

Issue dates: 25c, 30c, 60c, 1/16/65; 50c, 2/20/71; others, 3/24/69.

Type of 1958 Inscribed "FRANCE"
Flag in Ultramarine & Yellow

1975-76 Engr. *Perf. 13*

1O16	O1	60c org, yel & emer	.85	.85
1O17	O1	80c yel & mag	1.25	1.25
1O18	O1	1fr car, yel & gray ol ('76)	2.00	2.00
1O19	O1	1.20fr org, yel & bl	5.50	5.50
		Nos. 1O16-1O19 (4)	9.60	9.60

Issue dates: 1fr, 10/16; others, 11/22.

New Council Headquarters, Strasbourg — O2

1977, Jan. 22 Engr. *Perf. 13*

1O20	O2	80c car & multi	1.00	.50
1O21	O2	1fr brown & multi	1.00	.50
1O22	O2	1.40fr gray & multi	2.00	1.00
		Nos. 1O20-1O22 (3)	4.00	2.00

Human Rights Emblem in Upper Left Corner

1978, Oct. 14

1O23	O2	1.20fr red lilac & multi	.45	.40
1O24	O2	1.70fr blue & multi	.75	.55

30th anniversary of the Universal Declaration of Human Rights.

Council Headquarters Type of 1977

1980, Nov. 24 Engr. *Perf. 13*

1O25	O2	1.40fr olive	.50	.50
1O26	O2	2fr blue gray	.90	.90

New Council Headquarters, Strasbourg — O3

1981-84 Engr.

1O27	O3	1.40fr multicolored	.50	.50
1O28	O3	1.60fr multicolored	.50	.40
1O29	O3	1.70fr emerald	.75	.75
1O30	O3	1.80fr multicolored	.70	.70
1O31	O3	2fr multicolored	.90	.90
1O32	O3	2.10fr red	1.00	1.00
1O33	O3	2.30fr multicolored	1.00	1.00
1O34	O3	2.60fr multicolored	1.00	1.00
1O35	O3	2.80fr multicolored	1.00	1.00
1O36	O3	3fr brt blue	1.25	1.25
		Nos. 1O27-1O36 (10)	8.60	8.50

Issued: 1.40, 1.60, 2.30fr, 11/21; 1.80, 2.60fr, 11/13/82; 2, 2.80fr, 11/21/83; 1.70, 2.10, 3fr, 11/5/84.

Youth's Leg, Sneaker, Shattered Eggshell O4

1985, Aug. 31 Engr. *Perf. 13*

1O37	O4	1.80fr brt green	.90	.90
1O38	O4	2.20fr vermilion	.90	.90
1O39	O4	3.20fr brt blue	1.40	1.40
		Nos. 1O37-1O39 (3)	3.20	3.20

New Council Headquarters, Strasbourg — O5

1986-87 Engr. *Perf. 13*

1O40	O5	1.90fr green	.90	.90
1O41	O5	2fr brt yel grn	1.10	1.10
1O42	O5	2.20fr red	.90	.90
1O43	O5	3.40fr blue	1.75	1.75
1O44	O5	3.60fr brt blue	2.00	2.00
		Nos. 1O40-1O44 (5)	6.65	6.65

Issued: 1.90, 2.20, 3.40fr, 12/13; 2, 3.60fr, 10/10/87.

Council of Europe, 40th Anniv. O6

1989, Feb. 4 Litho. & Engr.

1O45	O6	2.20fr multicolored	1.40	1.40
1O46	O6	3.60fr multicolored	2.25	2.25

Denominations also inscribed in European Currency Units (ECUs).

Map of Europe O7

1990-91 Litho. *Perf. 13*

1O47	O7	2.30fr multicolored	1.00	1.00
1O48	O7	2.50fr multicolored	1.00	1.00
1O49	O7	3.20fr multicolored	1.60	1.60
1O50	O7	3.40fr multicolored	1.60	1.60
		Nos. 1O47-1O50 (4)	5.20	5.20

Issued: 2.30fr, 3.20fr, 5/26/90; 2.50fr, 3.40fr, 11/23/91.

36 Heads, by Hundertwasser O8

1994, Jan. 15 Litho. *Perf. 13*

1O51	O8	2.80fr multicolored	1.40	1.40
1O52	O8	3.70fr multicolored	1.75	1.75

Palace of Human Rights, Strasbourg O9

1996, June 1 Litho. *Perf. 13*

1O53	O9	3fr multicolored	1.50	.90
1O54	O9	3.80fr multicolored	1.75	1.60

Charioteer of Delphi — O10

1999, Sept. 18 Photo. *Perf. 13*

1O55	O10	3fr shown	1.40	1.40
1O56	O10	3.80fr Nike	1.75	1.75

Girl, Penguin and Boy — O11

2001, Dec. 1 Litho. *Perf. 13*

1O57	O11	3fr red & multi	2.00	1.25
1O58	O11	3.80fr grn & multi	2.40	2.00

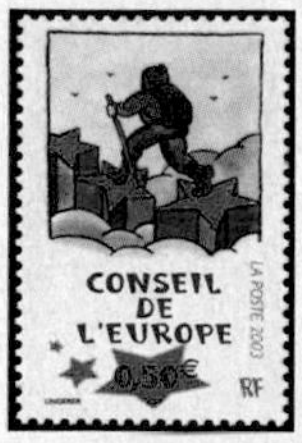

Hiker on Stars — O12

2003, Oct. 18 Litho. *Perf. 13*

1O59 O12 50c Hiker facing left 2.00 1.25
1O60 O12 75c Hiker facing right 2.50 2.00

O13

O14

2005, Sept. 18 Litho. *Perf. 13*

1O61 O13 55c multi 2.00 2.00
1O62 O14 75c multi 2.50 2.50

Map of Europe O15

Sculpture by Mariano González Beltrán O16

2007, June 23 Litho. *Perf. 13*

1O63 O15 60c multi 2.00 2.00
1O64 O16 85c multi 2.50 2.50

Council of Europe, 60th Anniv. O17

European Court of Human Rights, 50th Anniv. O18

2009, May 16 Litho. *Perf. 13*

1O65 O17 56c multi 2.00 2.00
1O66 O18 70c multi 2.50 2.50

Tree — O19

Chain — O20

2010, Sept. 17 Litho. *Perf. 13*

1O67 O19 75c multi 2.10 2.10
1O68 O20 87c multi 2.40 2.40

European Human Rights Convention, 60th anniv. (No. 1O68).

Map of Europe and Flags — O21

2011, Sept. 9 Litho. *Perf. 13*

1O69 O21 89c multi 2.50 2.50

European Social Charter, 50th anniv.

European Youth Center, Strasbourg, 40th Anniv. — O22

2012, Sept. 28

1O70 O22 89c multi 2.40 2.40

Balance of Rights and Responsibilties of Citizens in a Democracy — O23

2013, Sept. 27 Litho. *Perf. 13*

1O71 O23 95c multi 2.60 2.60

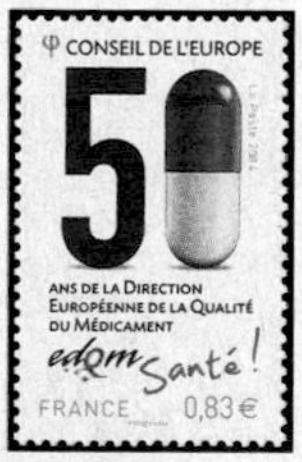

European Directorate for the Quality of Medicines and Health Care, 50th Anniv. — O24

European Cultural Cooperation, 60th Anniv. — O25

2014, Oct. 3 Photo. *Perf. 13*

1O72 O24 83c multi 2.10 2.10
1O73 O25 98c multi 2.50 2.50

European Union Flag, 60th Anniv. O26

2015, Oct. 2 Litho. *Perf. 13*

1O74 O26 95c multi 2.25 2.25

FOR THE UNITED NATIONS EDUCATIONAL, SCIENTIFIC AND CULTURAL ORGANIZATION

For use only on mail posted in the post office in the UNESCO Building, Paris.

Catalogue values for unused stamps in this section are for Never Hinged items.

For French stamps inscribed "UNESCO" see Nos. 572, 893-894, 2545.

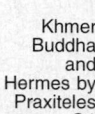

Khmer Buddha and Hermes by Praxiteles O1

1961-65 Unwmk. Engr. *Perf. 13*

2O1 O1 20c dk gray, ol bis & bl .25 *.55*
2O2 O1 25c blk, lake & grn .40 *.90*
2O3 O1 30c choc & bis brn ('65) .60 *.60*
2O4 O1 50c blk, red & vio bl 1.50 *1.75*
2O5 O1 60c grnsh bl, red brn & rose lil ('65) 1.40 1.40
Nos. 2O1-2O5 (5) 4.15 5.20

Book and Globe — O2

1966, Dec. 17

2O6 O2 25c gray .50 .50
2O7 O2 30c dark red .65 .65
2O8 O2 60c green 1.10 1.10
Nos. 2O6-2O8 (3) 2.25 2.25

20th anniversary of UNESCO.

Human Rights Flame — O3

1969-71 Engr. *Perf. 13*

2O9 O3 30c sl grn, red & dp brn .60 .60
2O10 O3 40c dk car rose, red & dp brn .95 .95
2O11 O3 50c ultra, car & brn ('71) 2.00 2.00
2O12 O3 70c pur, red & sl 2.25 2.25
Nos. 2O9-2O12 (4) 5.80 5.80

Universal Declaration of Human Rights.

Type of 1969 Inscribed "FRANCE"

1975, Nov. 15 Engr. *Perf. 13*

2O13 O3 60c grn, red & dk brn 1.10 1.10
2O14 O3 80c ocher, red & red brn 1.65 1.65
2O15 O3 1.20fr ind, red & brn 3.75 3.75
Nos. 2O13-2O15 (3) 6.50 6.50

O4

1976-78 Engr. *Perf. 13*

2O16 O4 80c multi .85 .85
2O17 O4 1fr multi .85 .85
2O18 O4 1.20fr multi .50 .50
2O19 O4 1.40fr multi 2.25 1.25
2O20 O4 1.70fr multi .75 .75
Nos. 2O16-2O20 (5) 5.20 4.20

Issued: 1.20, 1.70fr, 10/14/78; others, 10/23/76.

Slave Quarters, Senegal O5

Designs: 1.40fr, Mohenjo-Daro excavations, Pakistan. 2fr, Sans-Souci Palace, Haiti.

1980, Nov. 17 Engr. *Perf. 13*

2O21 O5 1.20fr multi .50 .50
2O22 O5 1.40fr multi .60 .60
2O23 O5 2fr multi 1.00 1.00
Nos. 2O21-2O23 (3) 2.10 2.10

Hue, Vietnam — O7

Designs: 1.40fr, Building, Fez, Morocco. 1.60fr, Seated deity, Sukhotai, Thailand. 2.30fr, Fort St. Elmo, Malta, horiz. 2.60fr, St. Michael Church ruins, Brazil.

1981-82

2O24 O7 1.40fr multi .60 .60
2O25 O7 1.60fr multi .60 .60
2O26 O7 1.80fr shown .70 .70
2O27 O7 2.30fr multi .80 .80
2O28 O7 2.60fr multi .90 .90
Nos. 2O24-2O28 (5) 3.60 3.60

Issued: 1.80fr, 2.60fr, 10/23/82; others, 12/12/81.

Mosque, Chinguetti, Mauritania O8

Roman Theater and Female Standing Sculpture, Carthage, Tunisia — O8a

Architecture: 1.70fr, Church, Lalibela, Ethiopia. 2.10fr, San'a, Yemen. 2.20fr, Old Town Square and wrought iron latticework, Havana. 2.80fr, Enclosure wall interior, Istanbul. 3fr, Church, Kotor, Yugoslavia. 3.20fr, Temple of Anuradhapura and bas-relief of two women, Sri Lanka.

1983-85 Engr.

2O29 O8 1.70fr multi .70 .70
2O30 O8a 1.80fr multi .80 .80
2O31 O8 2fr multi .75 .75
2O32 O8 2.10fr multi .80 .80
2O33 O8a 2.20fr multi .90 .90
2O34 O8 2.80fr multi 1.00 1.00
2O35 O8 3fr multi 1.10 1.10
2O36 O8a 3.20fr multi 1.50 1.50
Nos. 2O29-2O36 (8) 7.55 7.55

Issued: 2fr, 2.80fr, 10/10; 1.70fr, 2.10fr, 3fr, 10/22/84; 1.80fr, 2.20fr, 3.20fr, 10/26/85.

Tikal Temple, Guatemala — O9

1986, Dec. 6 **Engr.** ***Perf. 13***

2O37 O9 1.90fr shown 1.00 1.00
2O38 O9 3.40fr Bagerhat Mosque, Bangladesh 1.75 1.75

The Parthenon, Athens O10

1987, Dec. 5 **Engr.** ***Perf. 13x12½***

2O39 O10 2fr shown .90 .90
2O40 O10 3.60fr Temple of Philae, Egypt 1.60 1.60

Shibam, Yemen People's Democratic Republic O11

Perf. 13x12½, 12½x13

1990, Apr. 7 **Engr.**

2O41 O11 2.30fr San Francisco de Lima, Peru, vert. 1.10 1.10
2O42 O11 3.20fr shown 1.50 1.50

Bagdaon Temple, Nepal — O12

3.40fr, Citadel of Harat, Afghanistan, horiz.

1991, Nov. 23

2O43 O12 2.50fr choc & dk red 1.25 1.25
2O44 O12 3.40fr grn, brn & ol 1.50 1.50

Tassili N'Ajjer Natl. Park, Algeria O13

Design: 2.80fr, Angkor Wat Archaeological Park, Cambodia, vert.

1993, Oct. 23 **Litho.** ***Perf. 13***

2O45 O13 2.80fr multicolored 1.25 1.25
2O46 O13 3.70fr multicolored 2.00 2.00

UNESCO, 50th Anniv. O14

Designs: 3fr, Uluru Natl. Park, Australia. 3.80fr, Los Glaciares Natl. Park, Argentina.

1996, June 1 **Litho.** ***Perf. 13***

2O47 O14 3fr multicolored 1.50 1.50
2O48 O14 3.80fr multicolored 2.00 2.00

Detail of Dionysus Fresco, Pompeii — O15

Moai Statues, Easter Island O16

1998, Oct. 24 **Litho.** ***Perf. 13***

2O49 O15 3fr multicolored 1.50 1.50
2O50 O16 3.80fr multicolored 1.90 1.90

Sphinx and Pyramids, Egypt O17

Komodo Dragon, Komodo Natl. Park, Indonesia O18

2001, Dec. 1 **Litho.** ***Perf. 13***

2O51 O17 3fr multi 2.00 2.00
2O52 O18 3.80fr multi 2.50 2.50

Reindeer, Lapland O19

Church of the Resurrection, St. Petersburg, Russia — O20

2003, Dec. 6 **Litho.** ***Perf. 13***

2O53 O19 50c multi 2.00 2.00
2O54 O20 75c multi 2.50 2.50

Bison in Bialowieza Forest, Poland — O21

Petra, Jordan O22

2005, Nov. 26 **Litho.** ***Perf. 13***

2O55 O21 55c multi 2.00 2.00
2O56 O22 90c multi 2.50 2.50

Siberian Tiger — O23

Luang Prabang, Laos O24

2006, Dec. 7 **Litho.** ***Perf. 13***

2O57 O23 60c multi 2.00 .75
2O58 O24 85c multi 2.50 1.25

Ksar d'Ait-Ben-Haddou, Morocco — O25

Koala, Australia — O26

2007, Dec. 13 **Litho.** ***Perf. 13***

2O59 O25 60c multi 2.00 2.00
2O60 O26 85c multi 2.50 2.50

Gorilla — O27

Machu Picchu, Peru O28

2008, Dec. 3 **Litho.** ***Perf. 13***

2O61 O27 65c multi 2.00 2.00
2O62 O28 85c multi 2.50 2.50

Polar Bear O29

Suzhou, China O30

2009, Dec. 9 **Litho.** ***Perf. 13***

2O63 O29 70c multi 2.10 2.10
2O64 O30 85c multi 2.50 2.50

Alhambra, Spain O31

Alpaca O32

2010, Dec. 1 **Litho.** ***Perf. 13***

2O65 O31 75c multi 2.00 2.00
2O66 O32 87c multi 2.40 2.40

Bactrian Camel O33

Milford Sound, New Zealand O34

2011, Oct. 19

2O67 O33 77c multi 2.10 2.10
2O68 O34 89c multi 2.50 2.50

Stonehenge, Great Britain — O35

African Elephants O36

2012, Nov. 22

2O69 O35 77c multi 2.00 2.00
2O70 O36 89c multi 2.40 2.40

Japanese Cranes — O37

Sigiriya UNESCO World Heritage Site, Sri Lanka O38

2013, Nov. 7 **Litho.** ***Perf. 13***

2O71 O37 58c multi 1.60 1.60
2O72 O38 95c multi 2.60 2.60

Trulli of Alberobello UNESCO World Heritage Site, Italy — O39

Hyacinth Macaw — O40

2014, Nov. 8 Litho. *Perf. 13x13¼*

2O73 O39 83c multi 2.10 2.10

Perf. 13¼x13

2O74 O40 98c multi 2.50 2.50

NEWSPAPER STAMPS

Coat of Arms — N1

1868 Unwmk. Typo. *Imperf.*

P1 N1 2c lilac 300.00 65.00
P2 N1 2c (+ 2c) blue 600.00 275.00

Perf. 12½

P3 N1 2c lilac 52.50 25.00
P4 N1 2c (+ 4c) rose 250.00 100.00
P5 N1 2c (+ 2c) blue 75.00 35.00
P6 N1 5c lilac 1,250. 550.00

Nos. P2, P4, and P5 were sold for face plus an added fiscal charge indicated in parenthesis. Nos. P1, P3 and P6 were used simply as fiscals.

The 2c rose and 5c lilac imperforate and the 5c rose and 5c blue, both imperforate and perforated, were never put into use.

Nos. P1-P6 were reprinted for the 1913 Ghent Exhibition and the 1937 Paris Exhibition (PEXIP).

No. 109 Surcharged in Red

1919 *Perf. 14x13½*

P7 A16 ½c on 1c gray .30 .30
a. Inverted surcharge 1,200. 1,150.

No. 156 Surcharged

1933

P8 A22 ½c on 1c olive bister .30 .30

PARCEL POST STAMPS

Inscribed "I APPORT A LA GARE" — PP1

Perfs As Noted

1892 Unwmk. Typo.

Q1 PP1 25c brown, *yel*, perf 13½ 825.00 290.00
Never hinged 1,600.
Q2 PP1 25c brown, *yel*, perf 11 30.00 24.00
Never hinged 45.00
a. Printed on both sides 400.00

Never hinged 650.00

Inscribed "II VALEUR DECLAREE" — PP2

Q3 PP2 10c red, perf 13½ 1,000. 275.00
Never hinged 1,750.
Q4 PP2 10c red, perf 10x13½ 875.00 325.00
Never hinged 1,600.
Q5 PP2 10c org red, perf 11 30.00 14.00
Never hinged 42.50
Q6 PP2 10c red, imperf 22.50 16.50
Never hinged 32.50

Inscribed "III LIVRAISON PAR EXPRESS" — PP3

Q7 PP3 25c green, perf 13½ 57.50 32.50
Never hinged 115.00
Q8 PP3 25c green, perf 11 45.00 24.00
Never hinged 70.00

See Nos. Q22-Q26.

Locomotive — PP4

A set of six stamps, in the design above, was prepared in 1901 as postal tax stamps for expedited parcels but were not issued. All are perf 14x13½. Values: 5c gray, $3, never hinged $4; 10c yellow green, $3, never hinged $5; 20c rose, $20, never hinged $29; 50c blue, $7, never hinged $11.50; 1fr brown, $8, never hinged $12; 2fr brown red, $37.50, never hinged $57.50.

PP5

1918 *Perf. 11*

Type I: Large Trefoil Under "N" of "MAJORATION"

Q9 PP5 5c black 1.25 .85
Never hinged 2.00
Q10 PP5 15c brn lilac 1.25 .85
Never hinged 2.00

Imperforate

Q11 PP5 5c black 3.25 2.50
Never hinged 6.25
Q12 PP5 15c brn lilac 9.00 4.25
Never hinged 14.00
Nos. Q9-Q12 (4) 14.75 8.45

40c values, perforated 11 and imperf, in orange, were prepared but not issued. Value, perf or imperf, $375.

Type II: Small Trefoil Under "O" of "MAJORATION"

Perf. 11

Q13 PP5 5c black 140.00 45.00
Never hinged 275.00
Q14 PP5 35c red 3.75 2.50
Never hinged 5.00
Q15 PP5 50c vio blue 4.50 1.60
Never hinged 7.00
Q16 PP5 1fr yellow 4.25 1.60
Never hinged 7.00

Imperforate

Q17 PP5 5c black 130.00 45.00
Never hinged 260.00
Q18 PP5 15c brn lilac 30.00 16.50
Never hinged 50.00
Q19 PP5 35c red 3.25 2.50
Never hinged 6.75
Q20 PP5 50c vio blue 24.00 14.00
Never hinged 40.00
Q21 PP5 1fr yellow 18.50 12.50
Never hinged 30.00
Nos. Q13-Q21 (9) 358.25 141.20

See Nos. Q41-Q44, Q143-Q145.
For surcharges, see Nos. Q28-Q40.

Type of 1892

1918-23 *Perf. 10½x11*

Q22 PP1 30c brn, *yel* 37.50 16.50
Never hinged 55.00
a. Imperf 200.00
Never hinged 290.00
Q23 PP1 60c brn, *straw* ('23) 47.50 30.00
Never hinged 70.00
a. Imperf 190.00
Never hinged 275.00
Q24 PP2 15c vermilion ('22) 16.00 11.00
Never hinged 23.00
Q25 PP3 30c green 40.00 21.00
Never hinged 57.50
a. Imperf 240.00
Never hinged 325.00
Q26 PP3 60c green ('23) 75.00 50.00
Never hinged 110.00
Nos. Q22-Q26 (5) 216.00 128.50

PP6

1924, Oct. *Perf. 14*

Q27 PP6 15c rose & blue 4.00 3.75
Never hinged 5.00
a. Imperf 550.00
Never hinged 750.00

No. Q27 is a postal tax stamp, issued to show the collection of a new 15c excise fee on rail parcels. On July 3, 1925, its use was extended to all fiscal categories.

Surcharged in Black or Red (R) on Nos. Q9//Q16 and Types of 1918

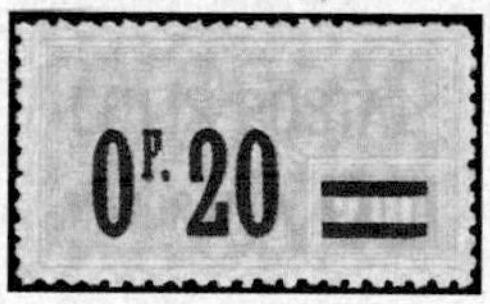

1926 *Perf. 13*

Q28 PP5 20c on 2fr rose 1.90 1.10
Never hinged 2.75
Q29 PP5 30c on 2fr yellow 1.90 1.10
Never hinged 2.75
a. "0f30" omitted 190.00
Never hinged 250.00
Q30 PP5 40c on 3fr gray 1.90 1.40
Never hinged 2.75
Q31 PP5 45c on 3fr orange 1.90 1.40
Never hinged 2.75
a. Period after "f" omitted 19.00 19.00
Never hinged 30.00
Q32 PP5 95c on 1fr yel 8.00 2.75
Never hinged 12.50
a. Imperf 90.00
Never hinged 150.00
Q33 PP5 1.35fr on 3fr vio 10.50 4.50
Never hinged 14.00
On postal document 70.00
a. Imperf 150.00
Never hinged 225.00
Q34 PP5 1.45fr on 5fr black (R) 1.90 1.00
Never hinged 2.75
Q35 PP5 1.75fr on 2fr blue 10.50 4.50
Never hinged 14.00
Q36 PP5 1.85fr on 10c orange 1.90 1.20
Never hinged 2.75
Q37 PP5 1.95fr on 15c lilac ben 2.50 1.75
Never hinged 3.50
a. Imperf 110.00
Never hinged 175.00
Q38 PP5 2.35fr on 25c green 1.90 1.00
Never hinged 2.75
a. Imperf 110.00
Never hinged 175.00
Q39 PP5 2.90fr on 35c red 2.50 1.00
Never hinged 3.50
a. Dots before and after "f" 140.00
Never hinged 200.00
b. Imperf 125.00
Never hinged 190.00
Q40 PP5 3.30fr on 50c blue violet (R) 2.50 1.25
Never hinged 3.50
a. Double surcharge 250.00
Never hinged 375.00
b. Imperf 90.00
Never hinged 140.00
Nos. Q28-Q40 (13) 49.80 23.95

Type of 1918

1926 *Perf. 11*

Q41 PP5 10c orange 2.00 1.25
Never hinged 3.75
a. Imperf 4.00
Never hinged 6.50
Q42 PP5 25c pale green 2.00 1.25
Never hinged 3.75
a. Imperf 4.00
Never hinged 6.50
Q43 PP5 2fr pale blue 25.00 14.50
Never hinged 42.50
a. Imperf 50.00
Never hinged 80.00
Q44 PP5 3fr violet 110.00 67.50
Never hinged 190.00
a. Imperf 225.00
Never hinged 360.00
Nos. Q41-Q44 (4) 139.00 84.50

Inscribed "APPORT A LA GARE" — PP7

1926

Q45 PP7 1fr on 60c brn, *yel* 13.50 10.50
Never hinged 24.00
a. Imperf 190.00
Never hinged 300.00
Q46 PP7 1fr brn, *yel* 17.50 13.00
Never hinged 30.00
Q47 PP7 1.30fr on 1fr brn, *yel* 17.50 12.50
Never hinged 30.00
Q48 PP7 1.50fr brn, *yel* 20.00 11.50
Never hinged 32.50
Q49 PP7 1.65fr brn, *yel* 15.00 12.50
Never hinged 24.00
Q50 PP7 1.90fr on 1fr brn, *yel* 17.50 12.50
Never hinged 30.00
Q51 PP7 2.10fr on 1.65fr brn, *yel* 17.50 12.50
Never hinged 30.00
Nos. Q45-Q51 (7) 118.50 85.00

See Nos. Q91-Q95, footnote following No. Q102, Q143-Q145.

For overprints and surcharges, see Nos. Q76-Q78, Q83-Q86, Q91-Q92, boxed note following Q95, Q96-Q99, Q107-QQ109, boxed note following Q159.

PP8

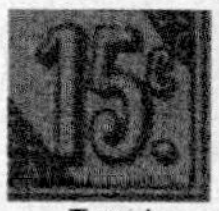

Type I

Type II

Type III

1926-38

Q52 PP8 15c brown, *yel*, type I 7.50 3.00
Never hinged 11.00
a. Imperf 180.00
Never hinged 275.00
Q53 PP8 15c brown, *yel*, type II ('32) 8.00 4.25
Never hinged 11.50
a. Type III ('38) 210.00
Never hinged 275.00
b. As "a," imperf 240.00
Never hinged 300.00

Nos. Q52-Q53a were issued for use in Paris only. No. Q53a was prepared but not issued.

Inscribed "VALEUR DECLAREE" — PP9

The additional numerals overprinted on Nos. Q56-Q63 and on Nos. Q72-Q75 indicate the weight category of the parcels being sent.

1926

Q54 PP9 50c on 15c red 3.00 1.60
Never hinged 5.00
a. Imperf 180.00
Never hinged 275.00
Q55 PP9 50c red 750.00 750.00
Never hinged 1,200.
a. Imperf 1,200.
Never hinged 1,650.
Q56 PP9 50c red, ovptd. "1" 4.50 2.00
Never hinged 7.00
a. Imperf 200.00
Never hinged 300.00
b. Double overprint "1" 300.00
Never hinged 400.00
Q57 PP9 55c on 15c red, ovptd. "1" 6.75 5.00
Never hinged 11.50
a. Imperf 190.00
Never hinged —
Q58 PP9 55c on 50c red, ovptd. "1" 6.75 5.00
Never hinged 11.50
Q59 PP9 65c on 50c red 2.50 2.50
Never hinged 4.25
Q60 PP9 65c on 50c red, ovptd. "1" 15.00 8.25
Never hinged 27.50
Q61 PP9 1.50fr on 50c red, ovptd. "3" 7.00 5.00
Never hinged 12.00
a. Imperf 275.00
Never hinged 375.00
Q62 PP9 2.00fr on 50c red, ovptd. "4" 8.25 3.75
Never hinged 14.00
Q63 PP9 2.50fr on 50c red, ovptd. "5" 15.00 8.25
Never hinged 26.50
Nos. Q54-Q63 (10) 818.75 791.35

See Nos. Q79, Q93, Q150-Q152.

For overprints and surcharges, see No. Q87, boxed note following No. Q95, Q100, Q110, Q123-Q124, Q138.

Inscribed "LIVRAISON PAR EXPRESS" — PP10

Q64 PP10 1.00fr on 60c grn 13.50 10.50
Never hinged 24.00
a. Imperf 225.00
Never hinged 325.00
Q65 PP10 1.00fr green 125.00 75.00
Never hinged 250.00
Q66 PP10 1.30fr on 1fr grn 16.50 12.50
Never hinged 29.00
Q67 PP10 1.50fr green 16.50 15.00
Never hinged 32.50
Q68 PP10 1.65fr green 16.50 15.00
Never hinged 32.50
Q69 PP10 1.90fr on 1.50fr grn 16.50 12.50
Never hinged 30.00
Q70 PP10 2.10fr on 1.65fr grn 30.00 14.00
Never hinged 50.00
Nos. Q64-Q70 (7) 234.50 154.50

For overprints and surcharges, see Nos. Q80-Q82, Q88-Q90, Q94, boxed note following Q95, Q101-Q105, Q111-Q113, Q125-Q132, Q139-Q141, Q146-Q149.

Inscribed "INTERETS A LA LIVRAISON" — PP11

Q71 PP11 50c lilac 3.00 1.60
Never hinged 5.00
a. Imperf 225.00 190.00
Never hinged 325.00
Q72 PP11 50c lil, ovptd. "1" 6.75 4.25
Never hinged 10.00
a. Imperf 200.00
Never hinged 300.00
Q73 PP11 1.50fr on 50c lil, ovptd. "3" 7.50 5.00
Never hinged 11.50
a. Imperf 200.00
Never hinged 300.00
Q74 PP11 2.00fr on 50c lil ovptd. "4" 10.00 7.00
Never hinged 16.00
Q75 PP11 2.50fr on 50c lil ovptd. "5" 10.00 7.00
Never hinged 16.50
a. Imperf 210.00
Never hinged 310.00
Nos. Q71-Q75 (5) 37.25 24.85

1926 Issues Overprinted

1928

Inscribed "APPORT A LA GARE"

Q76 PP7 1.00fr brn, *yel* 16.50 14.00
Never hinged 25.00
a. Imperf 190.00 190.00
Never hinged 300.00
Q77 PP7 1.50fr brn, *yel* 16.50 13.00
Never hinged 25.00
Q78 PP7 1.65fr brn, *yel* 16.50 13.00
Never hinged 25.00

Inscribed "VALEUR DECLAREE"

Q79 PP9 50c red 5.75 4.25
Never hinged 8.25
a. Imperf 190.00 190.00
Never hinged 300.00
b. Inverted overprint 210.00
Never hinged 310.00

Inscribed "LIVRAISON PAR EXPRESS"

Q80 PP10 1.00fr green 17.00 13.50
Never hinged 26.00
Q81 PP10 1.50fr green 17.00 13.50
Never hinged 26.00
Q82 PP10 1.65fr green 17.00 13.50
Never hinged 27.50
Nos. Q76-Q82 (7) 106.25 84.75

1926 Issues Surcharged

1928

Inscribed "APPORT A LA GARE"

Q83 PP7 1.45fr on 60c brn, *yel* 7.00 6.75
Never hinged 10.00
Q84 PP7 1.45fr on 1fr brn, *yel* 40.00 32.50
Never hinged 70.00
Q85 PP7 2.15fr on 1.50fr brn, *yel* 62.50 42.50
Never hinged 105.00
Q86 PP7 2.35fr on 1.65fr brn, *yel* 62.50 42.50
Never hinged 105.00

Inscribed "VALEUR DECLAREE"

Q87 PP9 75c on 50c red 2.10 1.60
Never hinged 3.25
a. Imperf 210.00
Never hinged 400.00

Inscribed "LIVRAISON PAR EXPRESS"

Q88 PP10 1.45fr on 1fr green 62.50 42.50
Never hinged 105.00
Q89 PP10 2.15fr on 1.50fr green 62.50 42.50
Never hinged 105.00
Q90 PP10 2.35fr on 1.65fr green 62.50 42.50
Never hinged 105.00
Nos. Q83-Q90 (8) 361.60 253.35

Types of 1926 and

PP12

1933-34

Inscribed "APPORT A LA GARE"

Q91 PP7 1.45fr brn, *yel* 55.00 25.00
Never hinged 82.50
Q92 PP7 2.35fr brn, *yel* 1,400.
Never hinged 1,900.

A 2.15fr value, brown on yellow paper, was prepared but not issued without overprint or surcharge.

For overprints and surcharges, see Nos. Q96, Q98, Q99, Q107-Q109, Q115, Q116, Q118, Q120-Q122, Q135-Q137.

Inscribed "VALEUR DECLAREE"

Q93 PP9 75c red 18.00 3.25
Never hinged 22.50
a. Imperf 180.00

For overprints and surcharges on No. Q93, see Nos. Q110, Q123, Q124, Q138.

A 1.15fr black in this design, imperf, was prepared but not issued. Value, $400.

Inscribed "LIVRAISON PAR EXPRESS"

Q94 PP10 1.45fr yel grn 450.00 300.00
Never hinged 675.00

Two other values, 2.15fr and 2.35fr were prepared but not issued without overprint or surcharge.

For overprints and surcharges, see Nos. Q101, Q103, Q105, Q111-Q113, Q125, Q126, Q128, Q130-Q132, Q139-Q141.

Inscribed "COLIS ENCOMBRANT"

Q95 PP12 2fr blue ('34) 45.00 21.00
Never hinged 70.00

For overprints and surcharges, see Nos. Q106, Q114, Q133, Q134, Q142.

Nos. Q46, Q48, Q49, Q55, Q65, Q67 and Q68 overprinted "B" were not issued. Values: 1fr (No. Q46), $95; never hinged $130; 1.50fr (No. Q48), $95, never hinged $130; 1.65fr (No. Q49), $95, never hinged $130; 50c (No. Q55), $95, never hinged $130; 1fr (No. Q65), $92.50, never hinged $140; 1.50fr (No. Q67), $92.50, never hinged $140; 1.65fr (No. Q68), $92.50, never hinged $140.

Stamps and Types of 1926-34 Overprinted

1937

Inscribed "APPORT A LA GARE"

Q96 PP7 1.45fr brn, *yel* 6.75 6.75
Never hinged 10.00
Q97 PP7 2.15fr on 1.50fr brn, *yel* 37.50 31.00
Never hinged 57.50
Q98 PP7 2.15fr brn, *yel* 25.00 19.00
Never hinged 37.50
Q99 PP7 2.35fr brn, *yel* 25.00 19.00
Never hinged 37.50

Inscribed "VALEUR DECLAREE"

Q100 PP9 75c red 17.50 16.50
Never hinged 25.00
a. Imperf 225.00
Never hinged 325.00

Inscribed "LIVRAISON PAR EXPRESS"

Q101 PP10 1.45fr green 17.50 16.50
Never hinged 25.00
Q102 PP10 2.15fr on 1.50fr grn 17.50 16.50
Never hinged 25.00
Q103 PP10 2.15fr green 42.50 30.00
Never hinged 67.50
a. Imperf 210.00
Never hinged 315.00
Q104 PP10 2.35fr on 1.65fr grn 250.00 110.00
Never hinged 350.00
Q105 PP10 2.35fr green 17.50 12.50
Never hinged 26.00

Inscribed "COLIS ENCOMBRANT"

Q106 PP12 2fr blue 37.50 35.00
Never hinged 57.50
Nos. Q96-Q106 (11) 494.25 312.75

For overprints and surcharges, see Nos. Q146-Q149.

Types of 1933-34 Surcharged

1937

Inscribed "APPORT A LA GARE"

Q107 PP7 1.85fr on 1.45fr brn, *yel* 15.00 12.50
Never hinged 26.00
Q108 PP7 2.75fr on 2.15fr brn, *yel* 26.00 17.50
Never hinged 45.00
Q109 PP7 3.05fr on 2.55fr brn, *yel* 50.00 26.00
Never hinged 90.00

Inscribed "VALEUR DECLAREE"

Q110 PP9 .95fr on 75c red 42.50 25.00
Never hinged 67.50

Inscribed "LIVRAISON PAR EXPRESS"

Q111 PP10 1.85fr on 1.45fr grn 70.00 45.00
Never hinged 120.00
Q112 PP10 2.75fr on 2.15fr grn 70.00 45.00
Never hinged 120.00
Q113 PP10 3.05fr on 2.35fr grn 70.00 45.00
Never hinged 120.00

Inscribed "COLIS ENCOMBRANT"

Q114 PP12 2.60fr on 2fr bl 17.50 17.50
Never hinged 26.00
Nos. Q107-Q114 (8) 361.00 233.50

Stamps and Types of 1926-34 Overprinted

1937

Inscribed "APPORT A LA GARE"

Q115 PP7 1.45fr brn, *yel* 3.00 2.50
Never hinged 4.50
Q116 PP7 1.85fr on 1.45fr brn, *yel* 3.00 2.50
Never hinged 4.50
Q117 PP7 2.15fr on 1.50fr brn, *yel* 2.50 2.50
Never hinged 4.25
Q118 PP7 2.15fr brn, *yel* 42.50 35.00
Never hinged 62.50
Q119 PP7 2.35fr on 1.65fr brn, *yel* 575.00 475.00
Never hinged 800.00
Q120 PP7 2.35fr brn, *yel* 3.00 2.50
Never hinged 4.50
Q121 PP7 2.75fr on 2.15fr brn, *yel* 3.25 2.50
Never hinged 5.75
Q122 PP7 3.05fr on 2.35fr brn, *yel* 6.50 6.25
Never hinged 10.00

Inscribed "VALEUR DECLAREE"

Q123 PP9 75c red 3.75 3.50
Never hinged 5.50
a. Pair, one without overprint 225.00
Never hinged 350.00
Q124 PP9 95c on 75c red 3.00 3.00
Never hinged 3.75

Inscribed "LIVRAISON PAR EXPRESS"

Q125 PP10 1.45fr green 4.25 3.25
Never hinged 6.25
Q126 PP10 1.85fr on 1.45fr brn, *yel* 5.75 4.25
Never hinged 8.25
Q127 PP10 2.15fr on 1.50fr grn 375.00 325.00
Never hinged 500.00
Q128 PP10 2.15fr green 18.50 16.50
Never hinged 27.50
Q129 PP10 2.35fr on 1.65fr grn 675.00 725.00
Never hinged 775.00
Q130 PP10 2.35fr green 11.00 10.50
Never hinged 15.00
Q131 PP10 2.75fr on 2.15fr grn 35.00 45.00
Never hinged 55.00
Q132 PP10 3.05fr on 2.35fr grn 35.00 45.00
Never hinged 55.00

Inscribed "COLIS ENCOMBRANT"

Q133 PP12 2fr blue 3.00 2.10
Never hinged 4.50
a. Pair, imperf between 130.00
Never hinged 210.00
Q134 PP12 2.60fr on 2fr bl 3.25 2.50
Never hinged 5.50
Nos. Q115-Q134 (20) 1,811. 1,714.

For additional surcharges, see Nos. Q146-Q149.

Stamps and Types of 1933-34 Surcharged

1938

Inscribed "APPORT A LA GARE"

Q135 PP7 2.30fr on 1.45fr brn, *yel* 3.75 3.00
Never hinged 5.50

Q136 PP7 3.45fr on 2.15fr brn, *yel* 3.75 3.00
Never hinged 5.50
Q137 PP7 3.85fr on 1.45fr brn, *yel* 3.75 3.00
Never hinged 5.50

Inscribed "VALEUR DECLAREE"

Q138 PP9 1.15fr on 75c red 1.60 1.60
Never hinged 2.50

Inscribed "LIVRAISON PAR EXPRESS"

Q139 PP10 2.30fr on 1.45fr grn 3.75 3.00
Never hinged 5.50
Q140 PP10 3.45fr on 2.15fr grn 3.75 3.00
Never hinged 5.50
Q141 PP10 3.85fr on 2.35fr grn 3.75 3.00
Never hinged 5.50

Inscribed "COLIS ENCOMBRANT"

Q142 PP12 3.25fr on 2fr bl 1.60 1.60
Never hinged 2.50
Nos. Q135-Q142 (8) 25.70 21.20

For Nos. Q135-Q138, Q140-Q142 overprinted "E," see editor's note following No. Q159.

Type of 1918

1938 ***11, Imperf (#Q161)***

Q143 PP5 10c gray black 17.50 16.00
Never hinged 26.00
a. Imperf 26.00
Never hinged 42.50
Q144 PP5 20c brown lilac 17.50 16.00
Never hinged 26.00
a. Imperf 42.50
Never hinged 62.50
Q145 PP5 25c green, imperf *50.00* *20.00*
Never hinged *80.00*
Nos. Q143-Q145 (3) 85.00 52.00

Two additional values, a 10c rose lilac and a 15c ultramarine, were prepared with this set but not issued. Values, each stamp: $90, never hinged $150. Both stamps also exist imperf. Values, each: $82.50; never hinged $150.

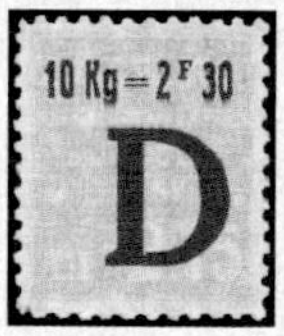

Nos. Q103, Q105, Q112, Q113 Overprinted

1938 ***Perf. 11***

Q146 PP10 2.30fr on 2.15fr green 62.50 62.50
Never hinged 80.00
Q147 PP10 2.30fr on 2.35fr green 62.50 62.50
Never hinged 80.00
Q148 PP10 2.30fr on 2.75fr on 2.15fr green 125.00 100.00
Never hinged 175.00
Q149 PP10 2.30fr on 3.05fr on 2.35fr green 125.00 100.00
Never hinged 175.00
Nos. Q146-Q149 (4) 375.00 325.00

Types of 1926 and

PP13

PP14

PP15

PP16

1938-39

Inscribed "VALEUR DECLAREE"

Q150 PP9 1fr red ('39) 2.50 2.50
Never hinged 4.00
Q151 PP9 1.15fr red 1.25 1.25
Never hinged 2.10
Imperf 140.00
Never hinged 225.00
Q152 PP9 5fr red ('39) 2.50 *2.75*
Never hinged 4.00

Inscribed "AU DESSUS DE 10"

Q153 PP13 2.40fr brown, *yel* 2.50 *2.75*
Never hinged 4.00
Q154 PP13 3.50fr brown, *yel* 2.50 *2.75*
Never hinged 4.00
Q155 PP13 3.80fr brown, *yel* 2.50 *2.75*
Never hinged 4.00
Imperf 125.00
Never hinged 190.00

Inscribed "REMBOURSEMENT"

Q156 PP14 2.50fr yel grn ('39) 2.50 2.25
Never hinged 4.00
Q157 PP14 7.50fr yel grn ('39) 2.75 2.50
Never hinged 4.25

Inscribed "INTERET A LA LIVRAISON"

Q158 PP15 1fr lilac ('39) 9.50 6.75
Never hinged 14.00

Inscribed "ENCOMBRANT"

Q159 PP16 3.20fr blue 11.00 7.50
Never hinged 16.00
Nos. Q150-Q159 (10) 39.50 33.75

Two additional values, 3.45fr and 3.85fr, type PP7, brown on yellow paper, imperforate, were prepared but not issued. Values, each: $140; never hinged, $225.

Nos. Nos. Q135-Q138, Q140-Q142 were overprinted "E" in 1939, in anticipation of new rates to take effect April 1, but were not issued. Values: 2.30fr on 1.45fr, $675, never hinged $1,000; 3.45fr on 2.15fr, $875, never hinged $1,300; 3.85fr on 2.35fr, $875, never hinged $1,300; 1.15fr on 75c, $300, never hinged $450; 3.45fr on 2.15fr, $2,800, never hinged $4,000; 3.85fr on 2.35fr, $2,800, never hinged $4,000; 3.25fr on 2fr, $675, never hinged $1,000.

In 1941, two sets were prepared in anticipation of new rate increases on April 1. They were not issued.

Six stamps in a new design, consisting of a 10c greenish gray, 30c blue, 50c brown, 1fr blue violet, 2fr orange and 5fr red. Values: 10c $185, never hinged $275; 30c $240, never hinged $350; 50c $240, never hinged $350; 1fr $185, never hinged $275; 2fr $185, never hinged $275; 5fr $185, never hinged $275.

Nos. Q93, Q153-Q155 and Q159 overprinted "E." Values: 75c; other values $575, never hinged.

PP17

PP18

Without Denominations

1941 ***Perf. 12½***

Q160 PP17 (2.70fr) brown 5.50 4.50
Never hinged 9.00
Q161 PP17 (3.90fr) blue 5.50 4.50
Never hinged 9.00
Q162 PP17 (4.20fr) green 5.50 4.50
Never hinged 9.00
Q163 PP18 (3.50fr) blue 10.50 9.50
Never hinged 14.00
Nos. Q160-Q163 (4) 27.00 23.00

Five stamps in the designs of PP20-PP22 below, but with blank value tablets, were prepared with Nos. Q160-Q163 but were not issued. Values: (1fr) brown, (5fr) red and (2.50fr) blue, each $67.50, never hinged $90; (7.50fr) green, $290, never hinged $400; (1fr) violet, $120, never hinged $180.

See Nos. Q178-Q181, Q200-Q206.

"Domicile" PP19

"Valeur Declaree" PP20

"Remboursement" PP21

"Interet A La Livraison" PP22

"Encombrant" — PP23

1941 ***Perf. 12½, 13 (#Q167-171)***

Q164 PP19 2.70fr brown 6.75 5.50
Never hinged 11.00
Q165 PP19 3.90fr blue 6.75 5.50
Never hinged 11.00
Q166 PP19 4.20fr green 6.75 5.50
Never hinged 11.00
Q167 PP20 1fr brown 2.75 1.25
Never hinged 4.25
Q168 PP20 5fr red 1.50 *1.75*
Never hinged 2.25
Q169 PP21 2.50fr blue 1.50 *1.75*
Never hinged 2.25
Q170 PP21 7.50fr green 3.75 3.50
Never hinged 6.00
Q171 PP22 1fr violet 1.00 1.00
Never hinged 1.75
Q172 PP23 3.50fr blue 37.50 16.50
Never hinged 52.50
Nos. Q164-Q172 (9) 68.25 42.25

See Nos. Q173-Q177, Q186-Q194, Q200-Q206.

For surcharges, see footnote following No. Q177, Nos. Q182-Q185, Q207-Q210.

Types of 1941 with Bold Numerals

1942, Feb. ***Perf. 13***

Q173 PP20 1fr brown 1.40 1.25
Never hinged 2.00
Q174 PP20 5fr red 4.50 1.75
Never hinged 6.50
Q175 PP21 2.50fr blue 1.50 1.25
Never hinged 2.25
Q176 PP21 7.50fr green 6.75 *7.00*
Never hinged 11.00
Q177 PP22 1fr violet 67.50 1.00
Never hinged 100.00
Nos. Q173-Q177 (5) 81.65 12.25

See Nos. Q173-Q177, Q186-Q194, Q200-Q206. See No. Q194.

Nine stamps from the 1941-42 issues were surcharged "+3F / C.N.S. / Cheminots" to raise funds for a philatelic exhibition organized by railroad employees, which took place in Paris on Dec. 26 and 27, 1942. They were not valid for postage. Value, set: $110; never hinged $160.

Type of 1941 Inscribed "F" in Value Tablets

1943 ***Perf. 12½***

Q178 PP17 (3fr) brown 3.00 3.00
Never hinged 4.25
Q179 PP17 (4.30fr) blue 3.00 3.00
Never hinged 4.25
Q180 PP17 (4.70fr) green 3.00 3.00
Never hinged 4.25
Q181 PP18 (3.50fr) blue 7.00 7.00
Never hinged 14.00
Nos. Q178-Q181 (4) 16.00 16.00

Stamps of 1941 Surcharged in Deep Blue or Red

1943

Q182 PP19 3fr on 2.70fr brn 13.50 13.50
Never hinged 20.00
Q183 PP19 4.3fr on 3.90fr blue (R) 2.50 *3.00*
Never hinged 4.50
Q184 PP19 4.7fr on 4.20fr green (R) 3.50 3.50
Never hinged 5.00
Q185 PP23 3.9fr on 3.50fr blue (R) 3.50 3.50
Never hinged 5.00
Nos. Q182-Q185 (4) 23.00 23.50

Denominations in Black or Red

1943 **Unwmk.**

Q186 PP19 3fr brn 3.75 *4.25*
Never hinged 5.50
Q187 PP19 4.3fr blue (R) 10.00 5.75
Never hinged 12.50
Q188 PP19 4.7fr green (R) 11.50 2.50
Never hinged 15.00
Q189 PP23 3.9fr blue (R) 70.00 60.00
Never hinged 110.00
Nos. Q186-Q189 (4) 95.25 72.50

1943 **Wmk. 407**

Q190 PP19 3fr brn 12.50 11.00
Never hinged 21.00
Q191 PP19 4.3fr blue 20.00 13.00
Never hinged 32.50
Q192 PP19 4.7fr green 21.00 13.50
Never hinged 32.50
Q193 PP23 3.9fr blue 12.50 12.50
Never hinged 110.00
Nos. Q190-Q193 (4) 66.00 50.00

1944

Q194 PP21 20fr orange 5.00 *6.75*
Never hinged 6.75

Hydroelectric Dam — PP24

Electric Train — PP25

Power Line — PP26

1944 ***Perf. 12½, 13 (#Q167-171)***

Q195 PP24 1fr violet 6.75 6.75
Never hinged 9.00
Q196 PP24 5fr red brn 6.75 6.75
Never hinged 9.00
Q197 PP25 2.5fr blue 6.75 6.75
Never hinged 9.00
Q198 PP25 7.5fr green 6.75 6.75
Never hinged 9.00
Q199 PP26 1fr vio blue 6.75 6.75
Never hinged 9.00
Nos. Q195-Q199 (5) 33.75 33.75

A 20fr orange, design PP25, was prepared but not issued. Values: $1,150; never hinged, $1,650.

Nos. Q195-Q199 exist unwatermarked, but were not issued in this form Values, each: $275; never hinged $425.

Types of 1941 Inscribed "G" in Value Tablets

1945 **Unwmk.**

Q200 PP17 (5fr) brown 5.50 *6.00*
Never hinged 7.00
Q201 PP17 (7.20fr) blue 5.50 *6.00*
Never hinged 7.00
Q202 PP17 (7.60fr) green 5.50 *6.00*
Never hinged 7.00
Q203 PP18 (6.60fr) blue 6.25 *6.75*
Never hinged 8.75
Nos. Q200-Q203 (4) 22.75 *24.75*

Wmk. 407

Q204 PP17 (5fr) brown 16.50 16.50
Never hinged 24.00
Q205 PP17 (7.20fr) blue 12.50 *12.50*
Never hinged 18.00
Q206 PP17 (7.60fr) green 12.50 *12.50*
Never hinged 18.00
Nos. Q204-Q206 (3) 41.50 41.50

Nos. Q190-Q193 Surcharged

1945 **Wmk. 407**

Q207 PP19 5fr on 3fr brown 6.25 6.25
Never hinged 8.75
Q208 PP19 7.2fr on 4fr blue 6.25 6.25
Never hinged 8.75
Q209 PP19 7.8fr on 4.70fr green 6.25 6.25
Never hinged 8.75
Q210 PP23 6.6fr on 3.90fr blue 7.50 7.50
Never hinged 11.50
Nos. Q207-Q210 (4) 26.25 26.25

Nos. Q186-Q189 were also surcharged but were not issued. Values, each: $45; never hinged $72.50.

Electric Train — PP27

Transformer PP28

1945 **Denominations in Black**

Q211 PP27 5fr brown 16.00 16.00
Never hinged 22.50
Q212 PP27 7.2fr blue 15.00 15.00
Never hinged 22.50
Q213 PP27 7.8fr green 15.00 15.00
Never hinged 22.50
Q214 PP28 3.95fr blue 6.75 6.75
Never hinged 9.00
Nos. Q211-Q214 (4) 52.75 52.75

Nos. Q211-Q213 without watermark were not issued. Value, set: $50; never hinged, $80.

A set of ten stamps in the design above were prepared in 1945 but were not issued. Value, each: $300; never hinged $450.

Four stamps of types PP27-PP28, inscribed "H" in the value tablet, were prepared but not issued. Value, set: $2,500; never hinged $4,000.

Locomotive — PP29

1944 **Wmk. 407** ***Perf. 13***

Nos. Q215-216, Q222-Q223: 16x22mm; Nos. Q217-Q221, Q224-Q228: 18.5x22mm

Q215 PP29 1fr deep green 4.25 1.25
Never hinged 8.25
Q216 PP29 2fr violet 5.75 1.60
Never hinged 12.50
Q217 PP29 5fr ultramarine 27.50 1.60
Never hinged 35.00
Q218 PP29 10fr red 13.50 1.60
Never hinged 22.50
Q219 PP29 20fr olive green 11.50 1.60
Never hinged 17.50
Q220 PP29 50fr red orange 21.00 1.60
Never hinged 30.00
Q221 PP29 100fr gray black 37.50 1.60
Never hinged 57.50
Nos. Q215-Q221 (7) 121.00 10.85

Unwmk.

Q222 PP29 1fr deep green 11.00 5.50
Never hinged 16.50
Q223 PP29 2fr violet 14.00 5.50
Never hinged 21.00
Q224 PP29 5fr ultramarine 45.00 5.50
Never hinged 70.00
Q225 PP29 10fr red 29.00 5.50
Never hinged 42.50
Q226 PP29 20fr olive green 21.00 5.50
Never hinged 32.50
Q227 PP29 50fr red orange 42.50 5.50
Never hinged 62.50
Q228 PP29 100fr gray black 75.00 6.00
Never hinged 110.00
Nos. Q222-Q228 (7) 237.50 39.00

Nos. Q215-Q234 were issued for use on small packets. Effective January 1, 1946, the parcel and small packet services were unified, and all issued thereafter were valid for both services.

See Nos. Q229-Q254.

1944-45 **Wmk. 407**

Nos. Q229-Q230: 16x22mm; Nos. Q231-Q254: 18.5x22mm

Q229 PP29 3fr gray 6.75 1.60
Never hinged 12.50
Q230 PP29 4fr black 11.00 2.50
Never hinged 16.50
Q231 PP29 7fr violet 70.00 3.00
Never hinged 110.00
Q232 PP29 8fr yel grn 20.00 2.50
Never hinged 32.50
Q233 PP29 9fr dk blue 32.50 5.00
Never hinged 55.00
Q234 PP29 30fr red brn 90.00 1.60
Never hinged 140.00
Nos. Q229-Q234 (6) 230.25 16.20

1946

Q235 PP29 6fr claret 17.50 1.60
Never hinged 26.00
Q236 PP29 40fr yel brn 27.50 1.60
Never hinged 40.00
Q237 PP29 60fr lake red 29.00 1.60
Never hinged 42.50
Q238 PP29 70fr violet 200.00 30.00
Never hinged 275.00
Q239 PP29 80fr yel grn 27.50 2.50
Never hinged 40.00
Q240 PP29 90fr dk blue 150.00 27.50
Never hinged 240.00
Q241 PP29 200fr emer grn 32.50 2.50
Never hinged 55.00
Nos. Q235-Q241 (7) 484.00 67.30

1947

Q242 PP29 5fr pale blue 21.00 2.25
Never hinged 32.50
Q243 PP29 7fr pale vio 275.00 18.50
Never hinged 425.00
Q244 PP29 9fr pale grn 200.00 16.50
Never hinged 300.00
Q245 PP29 30fr pale gray brn 75.00 2.25
Never hinged 110.00
Q246 PP29 70fr pale viol 200.00 7.50
Never hinged 300.00
Q247 PP29 90fr pale ultra 140.00 2.50
Never hinged 225.00
Q248 PP29 100fr yellow 400.00 3.00
Never hinged 550.00
Nos. Q242-Q248 (7) 1,311. 52.50

1948

Q249 PP29 500fr yel 87.50 2.50
Never hinged 140.00
Q250 PP29 1000fr yel 325.00 17.50
Never hinged 500.00

1951-52

Q251 PP29 10fr grn 57.50 8.25
Never hinged 90.00
Q252 PP29 20fr vio 57.50 15.00
Never hinged 90.00
Q253 PP29 50fr blue 70.00 10.00
Never hinged 110.00
Q254 PP29 100fr rose ver 21.00 1.75
Never hinged 30.00
Nos. Q251-Q254 (4) 206.00 35.00

Electric Train — PP30

1960

Q255 PP30 5c orange 11.50 2.10
Never hinged 17.50
Q256 PP30 10c red 10.50 8.25
Never hinged 16.00
Q257 PP30 20c dp red 8.75 3.75
Never hinged 13.50
Q258 PP30 30c dp red 8.75 3.75
Never hinged 13.50
Q259 PP30 40c dp red 8.75 7.50
Never hinged 13.50
Q260 PP30 50c dp red 8.75 4.25
Never hinged 13.50
Q261 PP30 60c dp red 7.50 4.25
Never hinged 11.00
Q262 PP30 70c dp red 7.50 4.25
Never hinged 11.00
Q263 PP30 80c dp red 11.50 4.25
Never hinged 17.50
Q264 PP30 90c dp red 11.50 4.25
Never hinged 17.50
Q265 PP30 1fr blue 13.00 2.25
Never hinged 20.00
Q266 PP30 2fr blue 13.00 2.25
Never hinged 20.00
Q267 PP30 3fr blue 13.00 2.25
Never hinged 20.00
Q268 PP30 4fr blue 13.00 2.25
Never hinged 20.00
Q269 PP30 5fr blue 13.00 2.25
Never hinged 20.00
Q270 PP30 10fr yellow 15.00 2.50
Never hinged 22.50
Q271 PP30 20fr dp grn 20.00 16.00
Never hinged 30.00
Nos. Q255-Q271 (17) 195.00 76.35

1960 **Unwmk.**

Q272 PP30 5c orange 14.00 6.25
Never hinged 32.50
Q273 PP30 20c dp red 210.00 55.00
Never hinged 325.00
Q274 PP30 30c dp red 150.00 55.00
Never hinged 325.00
Q275 PP30 40c dp red 110.00 30.00
Never hinged 160.00
Q276 PP30 70c dp red 22.50 7.50
Never hinged 32.50
Q277 PP30 80c dp red 22.50 6.50
Never hinged 32.50
Q278 PP30 90c dp red 22.50 6.50
Never hinged 32.50
Q279 PP30 1fr blue 20.00 3.75
Never hinged 30.00
Q280 PP30 2fr blue 20.00 3.75
Never hinged 30.00
Q281 PP30 3fr blue 20.00 3.75
Never hinged 30.00
Q282 PP30 4fr blue 20.00 3.75
Never hinged 30.00
Q283 PP30 5fr blue 20.00 3.75
Never hinged 30.00
Q284 PP30 10fr yellow 25.00 6.25
Never hinged 37.50
Q285 PP30 20fr dp grn 30.00 21.00
Never hinged 45.00
Nos. Q272-Q285 (14) 706.50 212.75

FRANCHISE STAMPS

No. 276 Overprinted "F"

1939 **Unwmk.** ***Perf. 14x13½***

S1 A45 90c ultramarine 1.90 *2.50*
Never hinged 2.75
a. Period following "F" 30.00 30.00
Never hinged 50.00

No. S1 was for the use of Spanish refugees in France. "F" stands for "Franchise."

OCCUPATION STAMPS

FRANCO-PRUSSIAN WAR
Issued under German Occupation (Alsace and Lorraine)

OS1

1870 **Typo.** **Unwmk.** ***Perf. 13½x14***

Network with Points Up

N1 OS1 1c bronze green 75.00 *100.00*
a. 1c olive grn 75.00 *100.00*
N2 OS1 2c dark brown 125.00 *175.00*
a. 2c red brown 115.00 *175.00*
N3 OS1 4c gray 135.00 100.00
N4 OS1 5c yel grn 125.00 14.00
N5 OS1 10c bistre brn 110.00 5.75
a. 10c yellow brown 110.00 6.50
b. Network lemon yellow 135.00 10.00
N6 OS1 20c ultra 115.00 16.50
N7 OS1 25c brown 150.00 100.00
a. 25c black brown 145.00 100.00

There are three varieties of the 4c and two of the 10c, differing in the position of the figures of value, and several other setting varieties.

Network with Points Down

N8 OS1 1c olive grn 350.00 *625.00*
N9 OS1 2c red brn 150.00 *550.00*
N10 OS1 4c gray 150.00 200.00
N11 OS1 5c yel grn 6,500. 650.00
N12 OS1 10c bister 150.00 21.50
a. Network lemon yellow 225.00 50.00
N13 OS1 20c ultra 225.00 90.00
N14 OS1 25c brown 450.00 300.00

Official imitations have the network with points downward. The "P" of "Postes" is 2½mm from the border in the imitations and 3mm in the originals.

The word "Postes" measures 12¾ to 13mm on the imitations, and from 11 to 12½mm on the originals.

The imitations are perf. 13½x14½; originals, perf. 13½x14¼.

The stamps for Alsace and Lorraine were replaced by stamps of the German Empire on Jan. 1, 1872.

WORLD WAR I
German Stamps of 1905-16 Surcharged

1916 **Wmk. 125** ***Perf. 14, 14½***

N15 A16 3c on 3pf brown 1.25 1.25
N16 A16 5c on 5pf green 1.25 1.25
N17 A22 8c on 7½pf org 2.00 2.00

N18	A16	10c on 10pf car	2.00	2.00
N19	A22	15c on 15pf yel brn	1.25	1.25
N20	A16	25c on 20pf blue	1.25	1.25
a.		25c on 20pf ultramarine	2.00	2.00
N21	A16	40c on 30pf org & blk, *buff*	2.90	2.75
N22	A16	50c on 40pf lake & blk	2.90	2.75
N23	A16	75c on 60pf mag	12.50	12.50
N24	A16	1fr on 80pf lake & blk, *rose*	12.50	12.50

N25	A17	1fr25c on 1m car	47.50	47.50
a.		Double surcharge	—	
N26	A21	2fr50c on 2m gray bl	47.50	47.50
a.		Double surcharge	—	
		Nos. N15-N26 (12)	134.80	134.50

These stamps were also used in parts of Belgium occupied by the German forces.

Catalogue values for unused stamps in this section, from this point to the end of the section, are for Never Hinged items.

WORLD WAR II
Alsace
Issued under German Occupation

Stamps of Germany 1933-36 Overprinted in Black

1940 Wmk. 237 *Perf. 14*

N27	A64	3pf olive bister	.80	*.55*
N28	A64	4pf dull blue	.80	*.55*
N29	A64	5pf brt green	.80	*.55*
N30	A64	6pf dark green	.80	*.55*
a.		Inverted overprint	1,500.	
N31	A64	8pf vermilion	.80	*.55*
a.		Inverted overprint	4,000.	
N32	A64	10pf chocolate	.80	*.55*
N33	A64	12pf dp carmine	1.00	*.55*
N34	A64	15pf maroon	1.00	*.55*
N35	A64	20pf brt blue	1.65	*.75*
N36	A64	25pf ultra	1.65	*.75*
N37	A64	30pf olive grn	1.65	*.75*
N38	A64	40pf red violet	2.90	*1.00*
N39	A64	50pf dk grn & blk	7.00	*3.25*
N40	A64	60pf claret & blk	7.00	*3.25*
N41	A64	80pf dk blue & blk	17.50	*7.00*
N42	A64	100pf orange & blk	17.50	7.00
		Nos. N27-N42 (16)	63.65	28.15

Lorraine
Issued under German Occupation

Stamps of Germany 1933-36 Overprinted in Black

1940 Wmk. 237 *Perf. 14*

N43	A64	3pf olive bister	1.00	.75
N44	A64	4pf dull blue	1.00	.75
N45	A64	5pf brt green	1.00	*4.00*
N46	A64	6pf dark green	1.00	.75
N47	A64	8pf vermilion	1.00	.75
N48	A64	10pf chocolate	1.50	.85
N49	A64	12pf deep carmine	1.50	.85
N50	A64	15pf maroon	1.50	.75
a.		Inverted surcharge	—	
N51	A64	20pf brt blue	1.65	1.00
N52	A64	25pf ultra	1.40	1.00
N53	A64	30pf olive grn	2.10	1.00
N54	A64	40pf red violet	2.50	1.25
N55	A64	50pf dk grn & blk	6.00	3.00
N56	A64	60pf claret & blk	6.00	3.00
N57	A64	80pf dk blue & blk	18.00	7.50
N58	A64	100pf orange & blk	18.00	7.50
		Nos. N43-N58 (16)	65.15	*34.70*

Besetztes Gebiet Nordfrankreich

These three words, in a rectangular frame covering two stamps, were handstamped in black on Nos. 267, 367 and 369 and used in the Dunkerque region in July-August, 1940. The German political officer of Dunkerque authorized the overprint. The prevalence of forgeries and later favor overprints make expertization mandatory.

ALLIED MILITARY GOVERNMENT

Stamps formerly listed in this section as Nos. 2N1-2N20 are now listed with regular stamps of France as Nos. 475-476H and 523A-523J.

FRANCE OFFICES ABROAD

OFFICES IN CHINA

Prior to 1923 several of the world powers maintained their own post offices in China for the purpose of sending and receiving overseas mail. French offices were maintained in Canton, Hoi Hao (Hoihow), Kwangchowan (Kouang-tchéou-wan), Mongtseu (Mong-tseu), Packhoi (Paknoi), Tong King (Tchongking), Yunnan Fou (Yunnanfu).

100 Centimes = 1 Franc
100 Cents = 1 Piaster
100 Cents = 1 Dollar

Peace and Commerce Stamps of France Ovptd. in Red, Carmine or Black

1894-1900 Unwmk. *Perf. 14x13½*

1	A15	5c green, *greenish* (R)	3.25	3.00
2	A15	5c yel grn, I (R) ('00)	4.25	3.00
a.		Type II	47.50	32.50
3	A15	10c blk, *lav*, I (R)	9.25	3.00
a.		Type II	27.50	*17.50*
4	A15	15c bl (R)	12.50	4.25
5	A15	20c red, *grn*	7.50	5.00
6	A15	25c blk, *rose* (C)	9.25	2.50
a.		Double overprint	225.00	
b.		Pair, one without overprint	550.00	
d.		Imperf	120.00	45.00
7	A15	30c brn, *bis*	9.25	6.25
8	A15	40c red, *straw*	9.25	7.50
9	A15	50c car, *rose*, I	26.00	17.50
a.		Carmine overprint	62.50	
b.		Type II (Bk)	25.00	16.00
10	A15	75c dp vio, *org* (R)	80.00	60.00
11	A15	1fr brnz grn, *straw*	17.00	8.50
a.		Double overprint	425.00	*450.00*
12	A15	2fr brn, *az* ('00)	30.00	29.00
12A	A15	5fr red lil, *lav*	75.00	60.00
b.		Red overprint	525.00	
		Nos. 1-12A (13)	292.50	209.50

For surcharges and overprints see Nos. 13-17, J7-J10, J20-J23.

No. 11 Surcharged in Black

13	A15	25c on 1fr brnz grn, *straw*	125.00	75.00

No. 6 Surcharged in Red

1901

14	A15	2c on 25c blk, *rose*	1,100.	340.00
15	A15	4c on 25c blk, *rose*	1,350.	450.00
16	A15	6c on 25c blk, *rose*	1,100.	375.00
17	A15	16c on 25c blk, *rose*	325.00	200.00
a.		Black surcharge		*7,250.*
		Nos. 14-17 (4)	3,875.	1,365.

Stamps of Indo-China Surcharged in Black

Two types of Nos. 18-33: type I, 13mmx3mm, "C" and "H" wide, "E" with fine serifs; type II, 12½mmx2¾mm, "C" and "H" narrower, "E" with heavy serifs.

1902-04

18a	A3	1c blk, *lil bl*	2.50	2.50
19	A3	2c brn, *buff*	4.25	4.25
20a	A3	4c claret, *lav*	4.25	3.40
21a	A3	5c yellow grn	5.00	3.40
22	A3	10c red	6.75	6.00
23	A3	15c gray	7.50	6.75
24a	A3	20c red, *grn*	9.25	8.50
25a	A3	25c blk, *rose*	12.50	12.50
26	A3	25c blue	10.00	8.50
27a	A3	30c brn, *bis*	9.25	8.50
28a	A3	40c red, *straw*	25.00	21.00
29	A3	50c car, *rose*	67.50	67.50
30	A3	50c brn, *azure*	10.00	9.25
31a	A3	75c vio, *org*	40.00	37.50
32a	A3	1fr brnz grn, *straw*	45.00	42.50
33a	A3	5fr red lil, *lavender*	97.50	90.00
		Nos. 18a-33a (16)	356.25	332.05

The Chinese characters surcharged on Nos. 18-33 are the Chinese equivalents of the French values and therefore differ on each denomination. Two printings exist, differing slightly in the size of "CHINE." Values above are for the less expensive variety. See the *Scott Classic Specialized Catalogue of Stamps and Covers* for detailed listings. Many varieties of surcharge exist.

Liberty, Equality and Fraternity A3

"Rights of Man" A4

A5

1902-03 Typo.

34	A3	5c green	6.00	3.75
35	A4	10c rose red ('03)	3.00	2.10
36	A4	15c pale red	3.00	2.10
37	A4	20c brn vio ('03)	8.50	7.25
38	A4	25c blue ('03)	6.75	3.40
39	A4	30c lilac ('03)	9.25	7.50
40	A5	40c red & pale bl	19.00	16.00
41	A5	50c bis brn & lav	23.00	19.00
42	A5	1fr claret & ol grn	30.00	19.00
43	A5	2fr gray vio & yel	62.50	45.00
44	A5	5fr dk bl & buff	92.50	72.50
		Nos. 34-44 (11)	263.50	197.60

For surcharges and overprints see Nos. 45, 57-85, J14-J16, J27-J30.

Surcharged in Black

1903

45	A4	5c on 15c pale red	17.50	12.00
a.		Inverted surcharge	135.00	75.00

Stamps of Indo-China, 1904-06, Surcharged as Nos. 18-33 in Black

1904-05

46	A4	1c olive grn	2.10	2.10
47	A4	2c vio brn, *buff*	2.10	2.10
47A	A4	4c cl, *bluish*	975.00	800.00
48	A4	5c deep grn	2.10	2.10
49	A4	10c carmine	3.00	3.00
50	A4	15c org brn, *bl* (I)	3.00	3.00
51	A4	20c red, *grn*	11.50	11.00
52	A4	25c deep blue	10.00	6.00
53	A4	40c blk, *bluish*	8.50	6.00
54	A4	1fr pale grn	360.00	300.00
55	A4	2fr brn, *org*	42.50	37.50
56	A4	10fr org brn, *grn*	165.00	155.00
		Nos. 46-56 (12)	1,584.	1,327.

Many varieties of the surcharge exist.

Stamps of 1902-03 Surcharged in Black

1907

57	A3	2c on 5c green	2.50	1.60
58	A4	4c on 10c rose red	2.50	1.75
a.		Pair, one without surcharge	—	
59	A4	6c on 15c pale red	3.40	2.50
60	A4	8c on 20c brn vio	6.00	6.00
a.		"8" inverted	75.00	75.00
61	A4	10c on 25c blue	2.10	1.25
62	A5	20c on 50c bis brn & lav	6.25	3.75
a.		Double surcharge		
b.		Triple surcharge	440.00	440.00
63	A5	40c on 1fr claret & ol grn	22.00	13.50
64	A5	2pi on 5fr dk bl & buff	23.00	13.50
a.		Double surcharge	*2,300.*	*1,900.*
		Nos. 57-64 (8)	67.75	43.85

Stamps of 1902-03 Surcharged in Black

1911-22

65	A3	2c on 5c green	2.10	1.50
66	A4	4c on 10c rose red	2.50	1.75
67	A4	6c on 15c org	5.00	2.10
68	A4	8c on 20c brn vio	2.10	1.80
69	A4	10c on 25c bl ('21)	4.25	2.10
70	A4	20c on 50c bl ('22)	55.00	55.00
71	A5	40c on 1fr cl & ol grn	7.50	6.00

No. 44 Surcharged

73	A5	$2 on 5fr bl & buff ('22)	175.00	*200.00*
		Nos. 65-73 (8)	253.45	270.25

Types of 1902-03 Surcharged like Nos. 65-71

1922

75	A3	1c on 5c org	6.00	*6.75*
76	A4	2c on 10c grn	6.75	*7.50*
77	A4	3c on 15c org	9.25	*11.00*
78	A4	4c on 20c red brn	11.00	*13.50*
79	A4	5c on 25c dk vio	6.00	6.00
80	A4	6c on 30c red	12.00	11.00
82	A4	10c on 50c blue	14.50	12.00
83	A5	20c on 1fr claret & ol grn	35.00	*40.00*
84	A5	40c on 2fr org & pale bl	45.00	*55.00*
85	A5	$1 on 5fr dk bl & buff	150.00	*160.00*
		Nos. 75-85 (10)	295.50	322.75

POSTAGE DUE STAMPS

Postage Due Stamps of France Handstamped in Red or Black

1901-07 Unwmk. *Perf. 14x13½*

J1	D2	5c lt bl (R)	7.50	4.25
a.		Double overprint	160.00	
J2	D2	10c choc (R)	11.00	6.00
a.		Double overprint	160.00	
J3	D2	15c lt grn (R)	11.00	7.50
a.		Pair, one stamp without ovpt.	275.00	
b.		Imperf, single	160.00	
J4	D2	20c ol grn (R) ('07)	12.50	11.00
J5	D2	30c carmine	17.00	12.00
a.		Double overprint	160.00	
J6	D2	50c lilac	17.00	12.50
a.		Triple overprint	160.00	
b.		Pair, one stamp without overprint	275.00	
		Nos. J1-J6 (6)	76.00	53.25

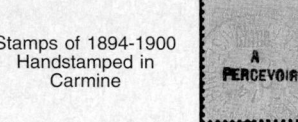

Stamps of 1894-1900 Handstamped in Carmine

1903

J7	A15	5c yel grn	—	2,250.
a.		Purple handstamp	—	
b.		5c green, *greenish*	—	
J8	A15	10c blk, *lavender*	—	—
a.		Purple handstamp	—	—
J9	A15	15c blue	*2,750.*	1,250.
a.		Purple handstamp	—	—
J10	A15	30c brn, *bister*	*1,500.*	350.00
a.		Purple handstamp	—	—

Same Handstamp on Stamps of 1902-03 in Carmine

1903

J14	A3	5c green	—	2,000.
a.		Purple handstamp	—	—
J15	A4	10c rose red	750.	425.00
a.		Purple handstamp	—	—
J16	A4	15c pale red	750.	325.00
a.		Purple handstamp	—	—

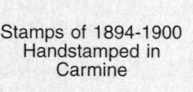

Stamps of 1894-1900 Handstamped in Carmine

1903

J20	A1	5c yellow green	—	1,100.
a.		Purple handstamp	—	
b.		5c green, *greenish*	—	
J21	A1	10c blk, *lavender*	—	—
a.		Purple handstamp	—	—
J22	A1	15c blue	1,250.	350.
a.		Purple handstamp	—	—
J23	A1	30c brn, *bister*	600.	325.
a.		Purple handstamp	—	—

Same Handstamp on Stamps of 1902-03 in Carmine or Purple

1903

J27	A3	5c green (C)	—	1,750.
a.		Purple handstamp	—	—
J28	A4	10c rose red (C)	340.	225.
a.		Purple handstamp	—	—
J29	A4	15c pale red (C)	675.	225.
a.		Purple handstamp	—	—
J30	A4	30c lilac (P)	—	—

The handstamps on Nos. J7-J30 are found inverted, double, etc.

The cancellations on these stamps should have dates between Sept. 1, and Nov. 30, 1903, to be genuine.

Postage Due Stamps of France, 1893-1910 Surcharged like Nos. 65-71

1911

J33	D2	2c on 5c blue	3.00	2.50
a.		Double surcharge	140.00	—
J34	D2	4c on 10c choc	3.00	2.50
a.		Double surcharge	140.00	—
J35	D2	8c on 20c ol grn	3.40	3.00
a.		Double surcharge	140.00	—
J36	D2	20c on 50c lilac	3.40	3.00
		Nos. J33-J36 (4)	12.80	11.00

1922

J37	D2	1c on 5c blue	82.50	*95.00*
J38	D2	2c on 10c brn	145.00	*165.00*
J39	D2	4c on 20c ol grn	145.00	*165.00*
J40	D2	10c on 50c brn vio	125.00	*185.00*
		Nos. J37-J40 (4)	497.50	610.00

CANTON

Stamps of Indo-China, 1892-1900, Overprinted in Red

1901 Unwmk. *Perf. 14x13½*

1	A3	1c blk, *lil bl*	2.10	2.10
1A	A3	2c brn, *buff*	2.50	2.50
2	A3	4c claret, *lav*	4.25	4.25
2A	A3	5c grn, *grnsh*	600.00	600.00
3	A3	5c yel grn	3.40	3.40
4	A3	10c blk, *lavender*	7.25	7.25
5	A3	15c blue, quadrille paper	6.75	6.75
6	A3	15c gray	7.50	7.50
a.		Double overprint	19.00	
7	A3	20c red, *grn*	22.50	22.50
8	A3	25c blk, *rose*	13.50	13.50
9	A3	30c brn, *bister*	32.50	32.50
10	A3	40c red, *straw*	32.50	32.50
11	A3	50c car, *rose*	35.00	35.00
12	A3	75c dp vio, *org*	35.00	35.00
13	A3	1fr brnz grn, *straw*	45.00	45.00
14	A3	5fr red lil, *lav*	250.00	250.00
		Nos. 1-14 (16)	1,099.	1,099.

The Chinese characters in the overprint on Nos. 1-14 read "Canton." On Nos. 15-64, they restate the denomination of the basic stamp.

Surcharged in Black

1903-04

15	A3	1c blk, *lil bl*	4.25	4.25
16	A3	2c brn, *buff*	4.50	4.25
17	A3	4c claret, *lav*	4.50	4.25
18	A3	5c yellow green	4.25	4.25
19	A3	10c rose red	4.50	4.25
20	A3	15c gray	4.50	4.25
21	A3	20c red, *grn*	21.00	17.50
22	A3	25c blue	7.50	7.50
23	A3	25c blk, *rose* ('04)	10.00	8.50
24	A3	30c brn, *bister*	27.50	21.00
25	A3	40c red, *straw*	67.50	55.00
26	A3	50c car, *rose*	340.00	310.00
27	A3	50c brn, *az* ('04)	85.00	72.50
28	A3	75c dp vio, *org*	67.50	67.50
a.		"INDO-CHINE" inverted	*55,000.*	
29	A3	1fr brnz grn, *straw*	67.50	67.50
30	A3	5fr red lil, *lav*	67.50	67.50
		Nos. 15-30 (16)	787.50	720.00

Many varieties of the surcharge exist on Nos. 15-30.

Stamps of Indo-China, 1892-1906, Surcharged in Red or Black

A second printing of the 1906 surcharges of Canton, Hoi Hao, Kwangchowan, Mongtseu, Packhoi, Tong King and Yunnan Fou was made in 1908. The inks are grayish instead of full black and vermilion instead of carmine. Values are for the cheaper variety which usually is the second printing.

The 4c and 50c of the 1892 issue of Indo-China are known with this surcharge and similarly surcharged for other cities in China. The surcharges on these two stamps are always inverted. It is stated that they were irregularly produced and never issued.

1906

31	A4	1c ol grn (R)	2.50	2.50
32	A4	2c vio brn, *buff*	2.50	2.50
33	A4	4c cl, *bluish* (R)	2.50	2.50
34	A4	5c dp grn (R)	2.10	2.10
35	A4	10c carmine	3.00	3.00
36	A4	15c org brn, *bl*	22.50	22.50
37	A4	20c red, *grn*	12.50	12.50
38	A4	25c deep blue	5.00	5.00
39	A4	30c pale brn	17.00	17.00
40	A4	35c blk, *yel* (R)	12.50	12.50
41	A4	40c blk, *bluish* (R)	21.00	21.00
42	A4	50c bister brn	14.50	14.50
43	A3	75c dp vio, *org* (R)	67.50	67.50
44	A4	1fr pale grn	30.00	30.00
45	A4	2fr brn, *org* (R)	42.50	42.50
46	A3	5fr red lil, *lav*	92.50	92.50
47	A4	10fr org brn, *grn*	85.00	85.00
		Nos. 31-47 (17)	435.10	435.10

Surcharge exists inverted on 1c, 25c & 1fr.

Stamps of Indo-China, 1907, Srchd. in Red or Blue

Chinese Characters

1908

48	A5	1c ol brn & blk	1.25	1.25
49	A5	2c brn & blk	1.25	1.25
50	A5	4c bl & blk	2.50	1.25
51	A5	5c grn & blk	2.50	2.10
52	A5	10c red & blk (Bl)	3.40	2.50
53	A5	15c vio & blk	4.25	3.40
54	A6	20c vio & blk	5.00	5.00
55	A6	25c bl & blk	5.00	4.25
56	A6	30c brn & blk	8.50	8.50
57	A6	35c ol grn & blk	8.50	8.50
58	A6	40c brn & blk	11.00	8.50
59	A6	50c car & blk (Bl)	11.00	8.50
60	A7	75c ver & blk (Bl)	11.00	10.00
61	A8	1fr car & blk (Bl)	18.00	15.00
62	A9	2fr grn & blk	45.00	37.50
63	A10	5fr bl & blk	62.50	55.00
64	A11	10fr pur & blk	92.50	92.50
		Nos. 48-64 (17)	293.15	265.00

Nos. 48-64 Surcharged with New Values in Cents or Piasters in Black, Red or Blue

1919

65	A5	⅖c on 1c	1.25	1.25
66	A5	⅘c on 2c	1.25	1.25
67	A5	1⅗c on 4c (R)	1.25	1.25
68	A5	2c on 5c	1.60	1.60
69	A5	4c on 10c (Bl)	2.10	1.60
a.		Chinese "2" instead of "4"	42.50	42.50
70	A5	6c on 15c	2.50	2.10
71	A6	8c on 20c	4.25	2.10
72	A6	10c on 25c	5.00	1.60
73	A6	12c on 30c	2.10	2.10
a.		Double surcharge	140.00	140.00
74	A6	14c on 35c	2.10	1.60
a.		Closed "4"	10.00	10.00
75	A6	16c on 40c	2.50	1.60
76	A6	20c on 50c (Bl)	2.50	2.10
77	A7	30c on 75c (Bl)	2.50	2.10
78	A8	40c on 1fr (Bl)	12.50	7.50
79	A9	80c on 2fr (R)	19.00	12.00
80	A10	2pi on 5fr (R)	32.50	32.50
81	A11	4pi on 10fr (R)	32.50	32.50
		Nos. 65-81 (17)	127.40	106.75

HOI HAO

Stamps of Indo-China Overprinted in Red

1901 Unwmk. *Perf. 14x13½*

1	A3	1c blk, *lil bl*	3.40	3.40
2	A3	2c brn, *buff*	4.25	4.25
3	A3	4c claret, *lav*	4.25	4.25
4	A3	5c yel grn	5.00	5.00
5	A3	10c blk, *lavender*	13.50	12.00
6	A3	15c blue	1,850.	800.00
7	A3	15c gray	7.50	5.00
8	A3	20c red, *grn*	32.50	25.00
9	A3	25c blk, *rose*	17.00	12.50
10	A3	30c brn, *bister*	67.50	67.50
11	A3	40c red, *straw*	67.50	67.50
12	A3	50c car, *rose*	67.50	67.50
13	A3	75c dp vio, *org*	250.00	225.00
14	A3	1fr brnz grn, *straw*	800.00	740.00
15	A3	5fr red lil, *lav*	800.00	675.00
		Nos. 1-15 (15)	3,989.	2,713.

The Chinese characters in the overprint on Nos. 1-15 read "Hoi Hao." On Nos. 16-66, they restate the denomination of the basic stamp.

Surcharged in Black

1903-04

16	A3	1c blk, *lil bl*	2.50	2.50
17	A3	2c brn, *buff*	2.50	2.50
18	A3	4c claret, *lav*	4.25	4.25
19	A3	5c yel grn	4.25	4.25
20	A3	10c red	4.25	4.25
21	A3	15c gray	5.00	5.00
22	A3	20c red, *grn*	7.50	7.50
23	A3	25c blue	5.00	5.00
24	A3	25c blk, *rose* ('04)	8.50	8.50
25	A3	30c brn, *bister*	6.75	6.75
26	A3	40c red, *straw*	32.50	32.50
27	A3	50c car, *rose*	30.00	30.00
28	A3	50c brn, *az* ('04)	170.00	170.00
29	A3	75c dp vio, *org*	50.00	50.00
a.		"INDO-CHINE" inverted	*45,000.*	
30	A3	1fr brnz grn, *straw*	67.50	67.50
31	A3	5fr red lil, *lav*	225.00	225.00
		Nos. 16-31 (16)	625.50	625.50

Many varieties of the surcharge exist on Nos. 1-31.

Stamps of Indo-China, 1892-1906, Surcharged in Red or Black

1906

32	A4	1c ol grn (R)	8.50	8.50
33	A4	2c vio brn, *buff*	8.50	8.50
34	A4	4c cl, *bluish* (R)	8.50	8.50
35	A4	5c dp grn (R)	8.50	8.50
36	A4	10c carmine	8.50	8.50
37	A4	15c org brn, *bl*	32.50	32.50
38	A4	20c red, *grn*	13.50	13.50
39	A4	25c deep blue	11.00	11.00
40	A4	30c pale brn	13.50	13.50
41	A4	35c blk, *yel* (R)	21.00	21.00
42	A4	40c blk, *bluish* (R)	21.00	21.00
43	A4	50c gray brn	21.00	21.00
44	A3	75c dp vio, *org* (R)	62.50	62.50
45	A4	1fr pale grn	62.50	62.50
46	A4	2fr brn, *org* (R)	62.50	62.50
47	A3	5fr red lil, *lav*	135.00	135.00
48	A4	10fr org brn, *grn*	150.00	150.00
		Nos. 32-48 (17)	648.50	648.50

Stamps of Indo-China, 1907, Srchd. in Red or Blue

Chinese Characters

1908

49	A5	1c ol brn & blk	1.70	1.70
50	A5	2c brn & blk	1.70	1.70
51	A5	4c bl & blk	1.70	1.70
52	A5	5c grn & blk	3.00	3.00
53	A5	10c red & blk (Bl)	3.00	3.00
54	A5	15c vio & blk	6.75	6.75
55	A6	20c vio & blk	7.50	7.50
56	A6	25c bl & blk	7.50	7.50
57	A6	30c brn & blk	7.50	7.50
58	A6	35c ol grn & blk	7.50	7.50
59	A6	40c brn & blk	8.50	8.50
61	A6	50c car & blk (Bl)	10.00	10.00
62	A7	75c ver & blk (Bl)	10.00	10.00
63	A8	1fr car & blk (Bl)	29.00	29.00
64	A9	2fr grn & blk	42.50	42.50
65	A10	5fr bl & blk	75.00	75.00
66	A11	10fr pur & blk	110.00	110.00
		Nos. 49-66 (17)	332.85	332.85

Nos. 49-66 Surcharged with New Values in Cents or Piasters in Black, Red or Blue

1919

67	A5	⅖c on 1c	1.25	1.25
68	A5	⅘c on 2c	1.25	1.25
69	A5	1⅗c on 4c (R)	2.10	2.10
70	A5	2c on 5c	2.50	2.50
71	A5	4c on 10c (Bl)	3.00	3.00
a.		Chinese "2" instead of "4"	14.50	14.50
72	A5	6c on 15c	2.50	2.50
73	A6	8c on 20c	4.25	4.25
a.		"S" of "CENTS" omitted	170.00	170.00
74	A6	10c on 25c	6.75	6.75
75	A6	12c on 30c	4.25	4.25
76	A6	14c on 35c	3.40	3.40
a.		Closed "4"	42.50	42.50
77	A6	16c on 40c	4.25	4.25
79	A6	20c on 50c (Bl)	3.40	3.40
80	A7	30c on 75c (Bl)	11.00	11.00
81	A8	40c on 1fr (Bl)	22.00	22.00
82	A9	80c on 2fr (R)	62.50	62.50
83	A10	2pi on 5fr (R)	92.50	92.50
a.		Triple surch. of new value	750.00	*750.00*
84	A11	4pi on 10fr (R)	225.00	225.00
		Nos. 67-84 (17)	451.90	451.90

KWANGCHOWAN

A Chinese Territory leased to France, 1898 to 1945.

Stamps of Indo-China, 1892-1906, Surcharged in Red or Black

1906 Unwmk. *Perf. 14x13½*

1 A4 1c ol grn (R) 8.50 8.50
2 A4 2c vio brn, *buff* 8.50 8.50
3 A4 4c cl, *bluish* (R) 8.50 8.50
4 A4 5c dp grn (R) 8.50 8.50
5 A4 10c carmine 8.50 8.50
6 A4 15c org brn, *bl* 32.50 32.50
7 A4 20c red, *grn* 13.50 13.50
8 A4 25c deep blue 11.00 11.00
9 A4 30c pale brn 13.50 13.50
10 A4 35c blk, *yel* (R) 21.00 21.00
11 A4 40c blk, *bluish* (R) 21.00 21.00
12 A4 50c bister brn 25.00 25.00
13 A3 75c dp vio, *org* (R) 67.50 67.50
14 A4 1fr pale grn 42.50 42.50
15 A4 2fr brn, *org* (R) 55.00 55.00
16 A3 5fr red lil, *lav* 225.00 225.00
17 A4 10fr org brn, *grn* 275.00 275.00
Nos. 1-17 (17) 845.00 845.00

Various varieties of the surcharge exist on Nos. 2-10.

Stamps of Indo-China, 1907, Srchd. in Red or Blue

Value in Chinese

1908

18 A5 1c ol brn & blk 1.70 1.70
19 A5 2c brn & blk 1.70 1.70
20 A5 4c bl & blk 1.70 1.70
21 A5 5c grn & blk 1.70 1.70
22 A5 10c red & blk (Bl) 1.70 1.70
23 A5 15c vio & blk 4.25 4.25
24 A6 20c vio & blk 6.75 6.75
25 A6 25c bl & blk 6.75 6.75
26 A6 30c brn & blk 10.00 10.00
27 A6 35c ol grn & blk 14.50 14.50
28 A6 40c brn & blk 14.50 14.50
30 A6 50c car & blk (Bl) 17.00 17.00
31 A7 75c ver & blk (Bl) 17.00 17.00
32 A8 1fr car & blk (Bl) 24.00 24.00
33 A9 2fr grn & blk 32.50 32.50
34 A10 5fr bl & blk 75.00 75.00
35 A11 10fr pur & blk 105.00 105.00
a. Double surcharge 1,050.
b. Triple surcharge 1,050.
Nos. 18-35 (17) 335.75 335.75

The Chinese characters overprinted on Nos. 1 to 35 repeat the denomination of the basic stamp.

Nos. 18-35 Srchd. in Cents or Piasters in Black, Red or Blue

1919

36 A5 2/5c on 1c 1.25 .85
37 A5 4/5c on 2c 1.25 .85
38 A5 1 3/5c on 4c (R) 1.25 .85
39 A5 2c on 5c 2.10 1.25
a. "2 CENTS" inverted 97.50
40 A5 4c on 10c (Bl) 3.75 3.40
41 A5 6c on 15c 2.10 2.10
42 A6 8c on 20c 4.25 4.25
43 A6 10c on 25c 14.50 13.50
44 A6 12c on 30c 3.40 3.40
45 A6 14c on 35c 3.40 3.40
a. Closed "4" 45.00 37.50
46 A6 16c on 40c 2.10 2.10
48 A6 20c on 50c (Bl) 2.10 2.10
49 A7 30c on 75c (Bl) 11.00 11.00
50 A8 40c on 1fr (Bl) 12.00 12.00
a. "40 CENTS" inverted
51 A9 80c on 2fr (R) 20.00 20.00
52 A10 2pi on 5fr (R) 175.00 175.00
53 A11 4pi on 10fr (R) 32.50 32.50
Nos. 36-53 (17) 291.95 288.55

Stamps of Indo-China, 1922-23, Overprinted in Black, Red or Blue

1923

54 A12 1/10c blk & sal (Bl) .35 .35
55 A12 1/5c dp bl & blk (R) .35 .35
a. Black overprint 135.00
56 A12 2/5c ol brn & blk (R) .40 .40
57 A12 4/5c brt rose & blk .60 .60
58 A12 1c yel brn & blk (Bl) .60 .60
59 A12 2c gray grn & blk (R) .95 .95
60 A12 3c vio & blk (R) 1.00 1.00
61 A12 4c org & blk 1.25 1.25
62 A12 5c car & blk 1.25 1.25
63 A13 6c dl red & blk 1.25 1.25
64 A13 7c ol grn & blk 1.70 1.70
65 A13 8c black (R) 2.50 2.50
66 A13 9c yel & blk 2.50 2.50
67 A13 10c bl & blk 2.10 2.10
68 A13 11c vio & blk 2.10 2.10
69 A13 12c brn & blk 2.10 2.10
70 A13 15c org & blk 3.00 3.00
71 A13 20c bl & blk, *straw* (R) 3.00 3.00
72 A13 40c ver & blk, *bluish* (Bl) 3.40 3.40
73 A13 1pi bl grn & blk, *grnsh* 7.50 7.50
74 A13 2pi vio brn & blk, *pnksh* (Bl) 17.00 17.00
Nos. 54-74 (21) 54.90 54.90

Accent omitted varieties exist for Nos. 54-74. For detailed listings, see "Scott Classic Specialized Catalogue of Stamps and Covers 1840-1940".

Indo-China Stamps of 1927 Overprinted in Black or Red

1927

75 A14 1/10c lt ol grn (R) .35 .35
76 A14 1/5c yellow .35 .35
77 A14 2/5c lt blue (R) .50 .50
78 A14 4/5c dp brown .50 .50
79 A14 1c orange .85 .85
80 A14 2c blue grn (R) 1.25 1.25
81 A14 3c indigo (R) 1.25 1.25
82 A14 4c lilac rose 1.25 1.25
83 A14 5c deep violet 1.25 1.25
84 A15 6c deep red 1.25 1.25
85 A15 7c lt brown 1.25 1.25
86 A15 8c gray grn (R) 1.25 1.25
87 A15 9c red violet 1.70 1.70
88 A15 10c lt bl (R) 1.70 1.70
89 A15 11c orange 1.70 1.70
90 A15 12c myr grn (R) 1.70 1.70
91 A16 15c dl rose & ol brn 3.00 3.00
92 A16 20c vio & sl (R) 2.50 2.50
93 A17 25c org brn & lil rose 2.50 2.50
94 A17 30c dp bl & ol gray (R) 1.70 1.70
95 A18 40c ver & lt bl 1.70 1.70
96 A18 50c lt grn & sl (R) 2.50 2.50
97 A19 1pi dk bl, blk & yel (R) 4.25 4.25
98 A19 2pi red, dp bl & org (R) 6.00 6.00
a. Double overprint 160.00
Nos. 75-98 (24) 42.25 42.25

Accent omitted varieties exist for Nos. 75-90. For detailed listings, see "Scott Classic Specialized Catalogue of Stamps and Covers 1840-1940".

Stamps of Indo-China, 1931-41, Overprinted in Black or Red

1937-41 *Perf. 13, 13½*

99 A20 1/10c Prus blue .25 .25
100 A20 1/5c lake .25 .25
101 A20 2/5c orange red .40 .40
102 A20 1/2c red brown .35 .35
103 A20 4/5c dk violet .35 .35
104 A20 1c black brown .35 .35
105 A20 2c dk green .35 .35
a. Inverted overprint 140.00
106 A21 3c dk green .75 .75
107 A21 3c yel brn ('41) .35 .35
108 A21 4c dk blue (R) 1.00 1.00
109 A21 4c dk green ('41) .35 .35
110 A21 4c yel org ('41) 2.75 2.75
111 A21 5c dp violet .95 .95
112 A21 5c dp green ('41) .50 .50
113 A21 6c orange red .65 .65
114 A21 7c black (R) ('41) .65 .65
115 A21 8c rose lake ('41) .75 .75
116 A21 9c blk, *yel* (R) ('41) 1.00 1.00
d. Black overprint 9.25 9.25
117 A22 10c dk blue (R) 1.10 1.10
118 A22 10c ultra, *pink* (R) ('41) .85 .85
119 A22 15c dk bl (R) .75 .75
120 A22 18c bl (R) ('41) .65 .65
121 A22 20c rose .75 .75
122 A22 21c olive grn .75 .75
123 A22 22c green ('41) .60 .60
124 A22 25c dp violet 3.00 3.00
125 A22 25c dk bl (R) ('41) .85 .85
126 A22 30c orange brn .85 .85
127 A23 50c dk brown 1.10 1.10
128 A23 60c dl violet 1.10 1.10
129 A23 70c lt bl (R) ('41) .85 .85
130 A23 1pi yel green 2.10 2.10
131 A23 2pi red 2.25 2.25
Nos. 99-131 (33) 29.55 29.55

Accent omitted varieties exist for Nos. 99-124 and No. 126. For detailed listings, see "Scott Classic Specialized Catalogue of Stamps and Covers 1840-1940".

Common Design Types pictured following the introduction.

Colonial Arts Exhibition Issue
Common Design Type
Souvenir Sheet

1937 Engr. *Imperf.*

132 CD79 30c grn & sepia 9.25 *11.00*

New York World's Fair Issue
Common Design Type

1939 Unwmk. *Perf. 12½x12*

133 CD82 13c car lake 1.25 1.25
134 CD82 23c ultra 1.25 1.25

Petain Issue
Indo-China Nos. 209-209A Overprinted "KOUANG TCHEOU" in Blue or Red

1941 Engr. *Perf. 12½x12*

135 A27a 10c car lake (B) .85
136 A27a 25c blue (R) .85

Nos. 135-136 were issued by the Vichy government in France, but were not placed on sale in Kwangchowan.
For surcharges, see Nos. B9-B10.

Indo-China Types of 1937-41 without "RF" Overprinted "KOUANG TCHEOU" in Blue or Red

1942-44

137 A20 3/10c orange red .25
138 A20 1/2c red brown .25
139 A20 1c black brown .35
140 A20 2c dark green .65
141 A21 3c yellow brown .65
142 A21 4c yellow orange .35
143 A21 5c deep green .50
144 A21 9c black, *yellow* .35
145 A22 10c ultramarine, *pink* (R) .60
146 A22 18c blue (R) 190.00
147 A22 22c green .60
148 A22 30c orange brown .65
149 A23 50c dark brown .60
150 A23 60c dull violet .65
151 A23 70c light blue (R) .85
152 A23 1pi yellow green 1.30
153 A23 2pi red 1.40
Nos. 137-153 (17) 200.00

Nos. 137-153 were issued by the Vichy government in France, but were not placed on sale in Kwangchowan.

SEMI-POSTAL STAMPS

French Revolution Issue
Common Design Type

1939 Unwmk. Photo. *Perf. 13*
Name and Value typo. in Black

B1 CD83 6c + 2c green 9.25 9.25
B2 CD83 7c + 3c brown 9.25 9.25
B3 CD83 9c + 4c red org 9.25 9.25
B4 CD83 13c + 10c rose pink 9.25 9.25
B5 CD83 23c + 20c blue 9.25 9.25
Nos. B1-B5 (5) 46.25 46.25

Indo-China Nos. B19A and B19C Overprinted "KOUANG-TCHEOU" in Blue or Red, and Common Design Type

1941 Photo. *Perf. 13½*

B6 SP1 10c + 10c red (B) .85
B7 CD86 15c + 30c mar & car .85
B8 SP2 25c + 10c blue (R) .85
Nos. B6-B8 (3) 2.55

Nos. B6-B8 were issued by the Vichy government in France, but were not placed on sale in Kwangchowan.

Indo-China Nos. B21A-B21B Overprinted in Blue or Red

1944 Engr. *Perf. 12½x12*

B9 A27a 5c + 15c on 25c deep blue (R) 1.00
B10 A27a +25c on 10c car lake 1.10

Colonial Development Fund.
Nos. B9-B10 were issued by the Vichy government in France, but were not placed on sale in Kwangchowan.

AIR POST SEMI-POSTAL STAMPS

Indo-China Nos. CB2-CB4 Overprinted "KOUANG-TCHEOU" in Blue or Red
Methods and Perfs as Before

1942, June 22

CB1 SPAP1 15c + 35c green (R) .95
CB2 SPAP2 20c + 60c brown .95
CB3 SPAP3 30c +90c car red .95
Nos. CB1-CB3 (3) 2.85

Native children's welfare fund.
Nos. CB1-CB3 were issued by the Vichy government in France, but were not placed on sale in Kwangchowan.

Colonial Education Fund
Indo-China No. CB5 Overprinted "KOUANG-TCHEOU" in Blue or Red
Perf. 12½x13½

1942, June 22 Engr.

CB4 CD86a 12c + 18c blue & red 1.00

No. CB4 was issued by the Vichy government in France, but was not placed on sale in Kwangchowan.

MONGTSEU (MENGTSZ)

Stamps of Indo-China Surcharged in Black

1903-04 Unwmk. *Perf. 14x13½*

1 A3 1c blk, *lil bl* 7.50 7.50
2 A3 2c brn, *buff* 6.75 6.75
3 A3 4c claret, *lav* 8.50 8.50
4 A3 5c yel grn 6.00 6.00
5 A3 10c red 9.25 9.25
6 A3 15c gray 10.00 10.00
7 A3 20c red, *grn* 12.50 12.50
7C A3 25c blk, *rose* 725.00 725.00
8 A3 25c blue 12.50 12.50
9 A3 30c brn, *bister* 11.00 11.00
10 A3 40c red, *straw* 75.00 75.00
11 A3 50c car, *rose* 440.00 440.00
12 A3 50c brn, *az* ('04) 150.00 150.00
13 A3 75c dp vio, *org* 120.00 120.00
a. "INDO-CHINE" inverted *67,500.*
14 A3 1fr brnz grn, *straw* 110.00 110.00
15 A3 5fr red lil, *lav* 110.00 110.00
Nos. 1-15 (16) 1,814. 1,814.

Many surcharge varieties exist on Nos. 1-15.

Stamps of Indo-China, 1892-1906, Surcharged in Red or Black

1906

16 A4 1c ol grn (R) 5.00 5.00
17 A4 2c vio brn, *buff* 5.00 5.00
18 A4 4c cl, *bluish* (R) 5.00 5.00
19 A4 5c dp grn (R) 6.00 6.00
20 A4 10c carmine 5.00 5.00
21 A4 15c org brn, *bl* 35.00 35.00
22 A4 20c red, *grn* 13.50 13.50
23 A4 25c deep blue 10.00 10.00
24 A4 30c pale brn 13.50 13.50

25	A4	35c blk, *yel* (R)	12.50	12.50
26	A4	40c blk, *bluish* (R)	20.00	20.00
27	A4	50c bister brn	21.00	21.00
28	A3	75c dp vio, *org* (R)	67.50	67.50
a.		"INDO-CHINE" inverted	67,500.	
29	A4	1fr pale grn	42.50	42.50
30	A4	2fr brn, *org* (R)	55.00	55.00
31	A3	5fr red lil, *lav*	140.00	140.00
32	A4	10fr org brn, *grn*	150.00	150.00
a.		Chinese characters inverted	1,750.	*2,100.*
		Nos. 16-32 (17)	606.50	606.50

Inverted varieties of the surcharge exist on Nos. 19, 22 and 32.

Stamps of Indo-China, 1907, Srchd. in Red or Blue

Value in Chinese

1908

33	A5	1c ol brn & blk	1.25	1.25
34	A5	2c brn & blk	1.25	1.25
35	A5	4c bl & blk	1.25	1.25
36	A5	5c grn & blk	1.25	1.25
37	A5	10c red & blk (Bl)	3.00	3.00
38	A5	15c vio & blk	3.00	3.00
39	A6	20c vio & blk	6.00	6.00
40	A6	25c bl & blk	15.00	15.00
41	A6	30c brn & blk	6.75	6.75
42	A6	35c ol grn & blk	7.50	7.50
43	A6	40c brn & blk	5.00	5.00
45	A6	50c car & blk (Bl)	6.75	6.75
46	A7	75c ver & blk (Bl)	14.50	14.50
47	A8	1fr car & blk (Bl)	13.50	13.50
48	A9	2fr grn & blk	19.00	19.00
49	A10	5fr bl & blk	105.00	105.00
50	A11	10fr pur & blk	125.00	125.00
		Nos. 33-50 (17)	335.00	335.00

The Chinese characters overprinted on Nos. 1 to 50 repeat the denomination of the basic stamp.

Nos. 33-50 Srchd. in Cents or Piasters in Black, Red or Blue

1919

51	A5	⅖c on 1c	1.70	1.70
52	A5	⅘c on 2c	1.70	1.70
53	A5	1⅗c on 4c	1.70	1.70
54	A5	2c on 5c	1.70	1.70
55	A5	4c on 10c (Bl)	3.00	3.00
56	A5	6c on 15c	3.00	3.00
57	A6	8c on 20c	6.75	6.75
58	A6	10c on 25c	5.00	5.00
59	A6	12c on 30c	5.00	5.00
60	A6	14c on 35c	3.40	3.40
a.		Closed "4"	21.00	21.00
61	A6	16c on 40c	4.25	4.25
63	A6	20c on 50c (Bl)	5.00	5.00
64	A7	30c on 75c (Bl)	9.25	9.25
65	A8	40c on 1fr (Bl)	10.00	10.00
66	A9	80c on 2fr (R)	10.00	10.00
a.		Triple surch., one inverted	550.00	550.00
67	A10	2pi on 5fr (R)	200.00	200.00
a.		Triple surch., one inverted	625.00	625.00
b.		Double surcharge	925.00	925.00
68	A11	4pi on 10fr (R)	30.00	30.00
		Nos. 51-68 (17)	301.45	301.45

PAKHOI

Stamps of Indo-China Surcharged in Black

1903-04 Unwmk. *Perf. 14x13½*

1	A3	1c blk, *lil bl*	6.75	6.75
2	A3	2c brn, *buff*	6.75	6.75
3	A3	4c claret, *lav*	6.75	6.75
4	A3	5c yel grn	5.00	5.00
5	A3	10c red	5.00	5.00
6	A3	15c gray	5.00	5.00
7	A3	20c red, *grn*	11.00	11.00
8	A3	25c blue	9.25	9.25
9	A3	25c blk, *rose*('04)	6.75	6.75
10	A3	30c brn, *bister*	8.50	8.50
11	A3	40c red, *straw*	57.50	57.50
12	A3	50c car, *rose*	340.00	340.00
13	A3	50c brn, *az* ('04)	47.50	47.50
14	A3	75c dp vio, *org*	67.50	67.50
a.		"INDO-CHINE" inverted	*47,500.*	
15	A3	1fr brnz grn, *straw*	67.50	67.50
16	A3	5fr red lil, *lav*	135.00	135.00
		Nos. 1-16 (16)	785.75	785.75

Many varieties of the surcharge exist.

Stamps of Indo-China 1892-1906, Surcharged in Red or Black

1906

17	A4	1c ol grn (R)	8.50	8.50
18	A4	2c vio brn, *buff*	8.50	8.50
19	A4	4c cl, *bluish* (R)	8.50	8.50
20	A4	5c dp grn (R)	8.50	8.50
21	A4	10c carmine	8.50	8.50
22	A4	15c org brn,*bl*	32.50	32.50
23	A4	20c red, *grn*	13.50	13.50
24	A4	25c deep blue	11.00	11.00
25	A4	30c pale brn	13.50	13.50
26	A4	35c blk, *yel* (R)	21.00	21.00
27	A4	40c blk, *bluish*(R)	21.00	21.00
28	A4	50c bister brn	21.00	21.00
29	A3	75c dp vio, *org* (R)	67.50	67.50
30	A4	1fr pale grn	42.50	42.50
31	A4	2fr brn, *org*(R)	55.00	55.00
32	A3	5fr red lil, *lav*	140.00	140.00
33	A4	10fr org brn, *grn*	150.00	150.00
		Nos. 17-33 (17)	631.00	631.00

Various surcharge varieties exist on Nos. 17-24.

Stamps of Indo-China, 1907, Surcharged "PAKHOI" and Value in Chinese in Red or Blue

1908

34	A5	1c ol brn & blk	1.25	1.25
35	A5	2c brn & blk	1.25	1.25
36	A5	4c bl & blk	1.25	1.25
37	A5	5c grn & blk	1.70	1.70
38	A5	10c red & blk (Bl)	1.70	1.70
39	A5	15c vio & blk	2.10	2.10
40	A6	20c vio & blk	2.50	2.50
41	A6	25c bl & blk	3.00	3.00
42	A6	30c brn & blk	3.40	3.40
43	A6	35c ol grn & blk	3.40	3.40
44	A6	40c brn & blk	3.40	3.40
46	A6	50c car & blk (Bl)	3.40	3.40
47	A7	75c ver & blk (Bl)	7.25	7.25
48	A8	1fr car & blk (Bl)	7.50	7.50
49	A9	2fr grn & blk	16.00	16.00
50	A10	5fr bl & blk	85.00	85.00
51	A11	10fr pur & blk	150.00	150.00
		Nos. 34-51 (17)	294.10	294.10

The Chinese characters overprinted on Nos. 1 to 51 repeat the denomination of the basic stamps.

Nos. 34-51 Surcharged with New Values in Cents or Piasters in Black, Red or Blue

1919

52	A5	⅖c on 1c	1.25	1.25
a.		"PAK-HOI" and Chinese double	170.00	
53	A5	⅘c on 2c	1.25	1.25
54	A5	1⅗c on 4c (R)	1.25	1.25
55	A5	2c on 5c	2.50	2.50
56	A5	4c on 10c (Bl)	3.40	3.40
57	A5	6c on 15c	1.70	1.70
58	A6	8c on 20c	3.40	3.40
59	A6	10c on 25c	5.00	5.00
60	A6	12c on 30c	1.70	1.70
a.		"12 CENTS" double	675.00	
61	A6	14c on 35c	1.25	1.25
a.		Closed "4"	14.50	14.50
62	A6	16c on 40c	3.00	3.00
64	A6	20c on 50c (Bl)	2.10	2.10
65	A7	30c on 75c (Bl)	9.25	9.25
66	A8	40c on 1fr (Bl)	12.50	12.50
67	A9	80c on 2fr (R)	10.00	10.00
68	A10	2pi on 5fr (R)	16.00	16.00
69	A11	4pi on 10fr (R)	35.00	35.00
		Nos. 52-69 (17)	110.55	110.55

TCHONGKING (CHUNGKING)

Stamps of Indo-China Surcharged in Black

1903-04 Unwmk. *Perf. 14x13½*

1	A3	1c blk, *lil bl*	5.00	5.00
2	A3	2c brn, *buff*	5.00	5.00
3	A3	4c claret, *lav*	6.00	6.00
4	A3	5c yel grn	6.00	6.00
5	A3	10c red	6.00	6.00
6	A3	15c gray	6.00	6.00
7	A3	20c red, *grn*	8.50	8.50
8	A3	25c blue	55.00	55.00
9	A3	25c blk, *rose* ('04)	10.00	10.00
10	A3	30c brn, *bister*	15.00	15.00
11	A3	40c red, *straw*	62.50	62.50
12	A3	50c car, *rose*	225.00	225.00
13	A3	50c brn, *az* ('04)	140.00	140.00
14	A3	75c vio, *org*	45.00	45.00
15	A3	1fr brnz grn, *straw*	60.00	60.00
16	A3	5fr red lil, *lav*	105.00	105.00
		Nos. 1-16 (16)	760.00	760.00

Many surcharge varieties exist on Nos. 1-14.

Stamps of Indo-China and French China, issued in 1902 with similar overprint, but without Chinese characters, were not officially authorized.

Stamps of Indo-China, 1892-1906, Surcharged in Red or Black

1906

17	A4	1c ol grn (R)	8.50	8.50
18	A4	2c vio brn, *buff*	8.50	8.50
19	A4	4c cl, *bluish* (R)	8.50	8.50
20	A4	5c dp grn (R)	8.50	8.50
21	A4	10c carmine	8.50	8.50
22	A4	15c org brn, *bl*	32.50	32.50
23	A4	20c red, *grn*	13.50	13.50
24	A4	25c deep blue	11.00	11.00
25	A4	30c pale brn	13.50	13.50
26	A4	35c blk, *yellow* (R)	21.00	21.00
27	A4	40c blk, *bluish* (R)	21.00	21.00
28	A4	50c bis brn	25.00	25.00
29	A3	75c dp vio, *org* (R)	67.50	67.50
30	A4	1fr pale grn	42.50	42.50
31	A4	2fr brn, *org* (R)	55.00	55.00
32	A3	5fr red lil, *lav*	140.00	140.00
33	A4	10fr org brn, *grn*	150.00	150.00
		Nos. 17-33 (17)	635.00	635.00

Variety "T" omitted in surcharge occurs once in each sheet of Nos. 17-33. For detailed listings, see "Scott Classic Specialized Catalogue of Stamps and Values". Other surcharge varieties exist. Inverted surcharge on 1c and 2c are of private origin.

Stamps of Indo-China, 1907, Surcharged "TCHONGKING" and Value in Chinese in Red or Blue

1908

34	A5	1c ol brn & blk	.85	.85
35	A5	2c brn & blk	.85	.85
36	A5	4c bl & blk	1.25	1.25
37	A5	5c grn & blk	2.10	2.10
38	A5	10c red & blk (Bl)	2.10	2.10
39	A5	15c vio & blk	3.00	3.00
40	A6	20c vio & blk	3.00	3.00
41	A6	25c bl & blk	5.50	5.50
42	A6	30c brn & blk	3.40	3.40
43	A6	35c ol grn & blk	7.50	7.50
44	A6	40c brn & blk	15.00	15.00
45	A6	50c car & blk (Bl)	12.00	12.00
46	A7	75c ver & blk (Bl)	10.00	10.00
47	A8	1fr car & blk (Bl)	13.50	13.50
48	A9	2fr grn & blk	85.00	85.00
49	A10	5fr bl & blk	37.50	37.50
50	A11	10fr pur & blk	225.00	225.00
		Nos. 34-50 (17)	427.55	427.55

The Chinese characters overprinted on Nos. 1 to 50 repeat the denomination of the basic stamp.

Nos. 34-50 Surcharged with New Values in Cents or Piasters in Black, Red or Blue

1919

51	A5	⅖c on 1c	1.25	1.25
52	A5	⅘c on 2c	1.25	1.25
53	A5	1⅗c on 4c (R)	1.25	1.25
54	A5	2c on 5c	1.70	1.70
55	A5	4c on 10c (Bl)	1.25	1.25
56	A5	6c on 15c	1.70	1.70
57	A6	8c on 20c	3.00	1.25
58	A6	10c on 25c	8.50	8.50
59	A6	12c on 30c	3.00	1.25
60	A6	14c on 35c	2.10	1.70
a.		Closed "4"	35.00	35.00
61	A6	16c on 40c	2.10	1.70
a.		"16 CENTS" double	125.00	125.00
62	A6	20c on 50c (Bl)	11.00	10.00
63	A7	30c on 75c (Bl)	9.25	6.75
64	A8	40c on 1fr (Bl)	9.25	6.75
65	A9	80c on 2fr (R)	9.25	6.75
66	A10	2pi on 5fr (R)	9.25	9.25
67	A11	4pi on 10fr (R)	17.50	17.50
		Nos. 51-67 (17)	92.60	79.80

YUNNAN FOU

(Formerly Yunnan Sen, later known as Kunming)

Stamps of Indo-China Surcharged in Black

1903-04 Unwmk. *Perf. 14x13½*

1	A3	1c blk, *lil bl*	6.75	6.75
2	A3	2c brn, *buff*	6.75	6.75
3	A3	4c claret, *lav*	7.50	7.50
4	A3	5c yel green	6.75	6.75
5	A3	10c red	7.50	7.50
6	A3	15c gray	7.50	7.50
7	A3	20c red, *grn*	12.50	12.50
8	A3	25c blue	7.50	7.50
9	A3	30c brn, *bister*	12.50	12.50
10	A3	40c red, *straw*	75.00	60.00
11	A3	50c car, *rose*	350.00	350.00
12	A3	50c brn, *az* ('04)	180.00	180.00
13	A3	75c dp vio, *org*	67.50	62.50
a.		"INDO-CHINE" inverted	*47,500.*	
14	A3	1fr brnz grn, *straw*	67.50	62.50
15	A3	5fr red lil, *lav*	125.00	125.00
		Nos. 1-15 (15)	940.25	915.25

The Chinese characters overprinted on Nos. 1 to 15 repeat the denomination of the basic stamp.

Many varieties of the surcharge exist.

Stamps of Indo-China, 1892-1906, Surcharged in Red or Black

1906 Unwmk. *Perf. 14x13½*

17	A4	1c ol grn (R)	5.00	5.00
18	A4	2c vio brn, *buff*	5.00	5.00
19	A4	4c cl, *bluish* (R)	5.00	5.00
20	A4	5c dp grn (R)	5.00	5.00
21	A4	10c carmine	5.00	5.00
22	A4	15c org brn, *bl*	35.00	35.00
23	A4	20c red, *grn*	13.50	13.50
24	A4	25c deep blue	11.00	11.00
25	A4	30c pale brn	13.50	13.50
26	A4	35c blk, *yel* (R)	17.00	17.00
27	A4	40c blk, *bluish* (R)	17.00	17.00
28	A4	50c bister brn	21.00	21.00
29	A3	75c dp vio, *org* (R)	67.50	67.50
30	A4	1fr pale grn	42.50	42.50
31	A4	2fr brn, *org* (R)	55.00	55.00
32	A3	5fr red lil, *lav*	140.00	140.00
33	A4	10fr org brn, *grn*	150.00	150.00
		Nos. 17-33 (17)	608.00	608.00

Various varieties of the surcharge exist on Nos. 18, 20, 21 and 27.

Stamps of Indo-China, 1907, Surcharged "YUNNANFOU," and Value in Chinese in Red or Blue

1908

34	A5	1c ol brn & blk	1.25	1.25
35	A5	2c brn & blk	1.25	1.25
36	A5	4c bl & blk	2.10	2.10
37	A5	5c grn & blk	3.00	3.00
38	A5	10c red & blk (Bl)	3.00	3.00
39	A5	15c vio & blk	6.75	6.75
40	A6	20c vio & blk	6.25	6.25
41	A6	25c bl & blk	9.25	9.25
42	A6	30c brn & blk	7.50	7.50
43	A6	35c ol grn & blk	7.50	7.50
44	A6	40c brn & blk	8.50	8.50
45	A6	50c car & blk (Bl)	9.25	9.25
46	A7	75c ver & blk (Bl)	11.00	11.00
47	A8	1fr car & blk (Bl)	17.00	17.00
48	A9	2fr grn & blk	29.00	29.00
a.		"YUNANNFOU"	2,500.	2,500.
49	A10	5fr bl & blk	60.00	60.00
a.		"YUNANNFOU"	2,500.	2,500.
50	A11	10fr pur & blk	120.00	120.00
a.		"YUNANNFOU"	2,500.	2,500.
		Nos. 34-50 (17)	302.60	302.60

The Chinese characters overprinted on Nos. 17-50 repeat the denomination of the basic stamp.

Nos. 34-50 Surcharged with New Values in Cents or Piasters in Black, Red or Blue

1919

51	A5	⅖c on 1c	1.25	1.25
a.		New value double	140.00	
52	A5	⅘c on 2c	1.25	1.25
53	A5	1⅗c on 4c (R)	1.25	1.25
54	A5	2c on 5c	2.10	2.10
a.		Triple surcharge	210.00	
55	A5	4c on 10c (Bl)	1.70	1.70
56	A5	6c on 15c	3.00	3.00
57	A6	8c on 20c	2.10	2.10

58	A6	10c on 25c	3.75	3.75
59	A6	12c on 30c	9.25	9.25
60	A6	14c on 35c	14.50	14.50
a.		Closed "4"	140.00	140.00
61	A6	16c on 40c	9.25	9.25
62	A6	20c on 50c (Bl)	3.00	3.00
63	A7	30c on 75c (Bl)	9.25	9.25
64	A8	40c on 1fr (Bl)	35.00	35.00
65	A9	80c on 2fr (R)	14.50	14.50
a.		Triple surch., one inverted	250.00	
66	A10	2pi on 5fr (R)	67.50	67.50
67	A11	4pi on 10fr (R)	35.00	35.00
		Nos. 51-67 (17)	213.65	213.65

OFFICES IN CRETE

Austria, France, Italy and Great Britain maintained their own post offices in Crete during the period when that country was an autonomous state.

100 Centimes = 1 Franc

Liberty, Equality and Fraternity
A1

"Rights of Man"
A2

Liberty and Peace (Symbolized by Olive Branch) — A3

Perf. 14x13½

1902-03 Unwmk. Typo.

1	A1	1c dark gray	2.50	2.75
a.	A1	1c light gray	2.50	2.75
2	A1	2c violet brown	2.50	2.75
3	A1	3c red orange	2.50	2.75
4	A1	4c yellow brown	2.50	2.75
5	A1	5c green	2.50	2.75
6	A2	10c rose red	3.00	2.75
7	A2	15c pale red ('03)	4.25	3.00
8	A2	20c brown vio ('03)	5.25	4.00
9	A2	25c blue ('03)	7.00	4.50
10	A2	30c lilac ('03)	7.00	4.50
11	A3	40c red & pale bl	13.00	13.00
12	A3	50c bis brn & lav	18.00	15.00
13	A3	1fr claret & ol grn	25.00	22.50
14	A3	2fr gray vio & yel	40.00	37.50
a.		Imperf, pair	675.00	
15	A3	5fr dk blue & buff	65.00	60.00
		Nos. 1-15 (15)	200.00	180.50
		Set, never hinged	375.00	

A4

A5

1903 Black Surcharge

16	A4	1pi on 25c blue	55.00	47.50
17	A5	2pi on 50c bis brn & lav	75.00	57.50
18	A5	4pi on 1fr claret & ol grn	110.00	100.00
19	A5	8pi on 2fr gray vio & yel	140.00	*145.00*
20	A5	20pi on 5fr dk bl & buff	235.00	220.00
		Nos. 16-20 (5)	615.00	570.00

OFFICES IN EGYPT

French post offices formerly maintained in Alexandria and Port Said.

100 Centimes = 1 Franc

ALEXANDRIA

Stamps of France Ovptd. in Red, Blue or Black

1899-1900 Unwmk. *Perf. 14x13½*

1	A15	1c blk, *lil bl* (R)	2.10	2.10
a.		Double overprint	150.00	
b.		Triple overprint	180.00	
2	A15	2c brn, *buff* (Bl)	3.25	2.50
3	A15	3c gray, *grysh* (Bl)	3.25	2.50
4	A15	4c cl, *lav* (Bl)	4.25	3.25
5	A15	5c yel grn, (I) (R)	6.00	3.25
a.		Type II (R)	160.00	97.50
6	A15	10c blk, *lav*, (I) (R)	9.25	7.50
a.		Type II (R)	62.50	37.50
7	A15	15c blue (R)	9.25	4.25
8	A15	20c red, *grn*	14.50	7.50
9	A15	25c blk, *rose* (R)	7.50	4.25
a.		Inverted overprint	97.50	
b.		Double ovpt., one invtd.	160.00	
10	A15	30c brn, *bis*	15.00	12.00
11	A15	40c red, *straw*	13.50	13.50
12	A15	50c car, *rose* (II)	35.00	17.50
a.		Type I	150.00	27.50
13	A15	1fr brnz grn, *straw*	32.50	22.50
14	A15	2fr brn, *az* ('00)	82.50	80.00
15	A15	5fr red lil, *lav*	120.00	110.00
		Nos. 1-15 (15)	357.85	292.60

A2

A3

A4

1902-13

16	A2	1c pale gray	.80	.65
17	A2	2c violet brn	.75	.75
18	A2	3c red orange	.75	.75
19	A2	4c yellow brn	1.00	.85
20	A2	5c green	5.00	4.25
21	A3	10c rose red	1.50	.75
22	A3	15c orange ('13)	1.75	1.25
a.		15c pale red ('03)	4.75	1.60
23	A3	20c brn vio ('03)	3.00	1.50
24	A3	25c blue ('03)	1.75	.75
25	A3	30c violet ('03)	7.50	4.25
26	A4	40c red & pale bl	5.00	2.50
27	A4	50c bis brn & lav	11.00	3.00
28	A4	1fr cl & ol grn	10.00	4.25
29	A4	2fr gray vio & yel	24.00	12.00
30	A4	5fr dk bl & buff	29.00	17.00
		Nos. 16-30 (15)	102.80	54.50

The 2c, 5c, 10c, 20c and 25c exist imperf. Value, each $55.

See #77-86. For surcharges see #31-73, B1-B4.

Stamps of 1902-03 Surcharged Locally in Black

1921

31	A2	2m on 5c green	7.50	5.00
32	A2	3m on 3c red org	14.50	12.00
a.		Larger numeral	140.00	125.00
33	A3	4m on 10c rose	6.75	6.00
34	A2	5m on 1c gray	14.50	12.00
35	A2	5m on 4c yel brn	19.00	13.50
36	A3	6m on 15c orange	6.75	6.00
a.		Larger numeral	110.00	110.00
37	A3	8m on 20c brn vio	7.50	6.00
a.		Larger numeral	80.00	60.00
38	A3	10m on 25c blue	4.25	4.25
a.		Inverted surcharge	45.00	45.00
b.		Double surcharge	45.00	45.00
39	A3	12m on 30c vio	17.50	17.50
40	A2	15m on 2c vio brn	14.50	14.50

Nos. 26-30 Surcharged

41	A4	15m on 40c	25.00	19.00
42	A4	15m on 50c (#27a)	12.00	12.00
43	A4	30m on 1fr	175.00	175.00
44	A4	60m on 2fr	250.00	250.00
a.		Larger numeral	1,050.	1,050.
45	A4	150m on 5fr	350.00	350.00

Port Said Nos. 20 and 19 Surcharged like Nos. 32 and 40

45A	A2	3m on 3c red org	150.00	150.00
46	A2	15m on 2c vio brn	150.00	150.00
		Nos. 31-46 (17)	1,224.	1,202.

Alexandria No. 28 Srchd.

1921

46A	A4	30m on 15m on 1fr	1,200.	*1,350.*

The surcharge "15 Mill." was made in error and is canceled by a bar.

The surcharges were lithographed on Nos. 31, 33, 38, 39 and 42 and typographed on the other stamps of the 1921 issue. Nos. 34, 36 and 37 were surcharged by both methods.

Alexandria Stamps of 1902-03 Surcharged in Paris

1921-23

47	A2	1m on 1c slate	3.25	2.50
48	A2	2m on 5c green	2.25	1.90
49	A3	4m on 10c rose	2.75	2.50
50	A3	4m on 10c green ('23)	2.50	2.50
51	A2	5m on 3c red org ('23)	6.75	5.00
52	A3	6m on 15c orange	2.25	1.90
53	A3	8m on 20c brn vio	2.25	1.25
54	A3	10m on 25c blue	1.40	1.25
55	A3	10m on 30c vio	4.25	3.25
56	A3	15m on 50c bl ('23)	3.25	3.00

Nos. 27-30 and Type of 1902 Surcharged

57	A4	15m on 50c	5.00	3.25
58	A4	30m on 1fr	4.25	3.00
59	A4	60m on 2fr	2,250.	*2,400.*
60	A4	60m on 2fr org & pale bl ('23)	13.50	13.00
61	A4	150m on 5fr	13.50	8.50
		Nos. 47-58,60-61 (14)	67.15	52.80

Stamps and Types of 1902-03 Surcharged with New Values and Bars in Black

1925

62	A2	1m on 1c slate	1.25	1.25
63	A2	2m on 5c orange	1.25	1.25
64	A2	2m on 5c green	1.75	1.75
65	A3	4m on 10c green	1.10	.85
66	A2	5m on 3c red org	1.50	1.25
67	A3	6m on 15c orange	1.40	1.25
68	A3	8m on 20c brn vio	1.75	1.40
69	A3	10m on 25c blue	1.10	1.00
70	A3	15m on 50c blue	2.40	1.40
71	A4	30m on 1fr cl & ol grn	3.50	2.90
72	A4	60m on 2fr org & pale bl	4.25	3.50
73	A4	150m on 5fr dk bl & buff	6.00	5.00
		Nos. 62-73 (12)	27.25	22.80

Types of 1902-03 Issue

1927-28

77	A2	3m orange ('28)	2.50	2.10
81	A3	15m slate blue	2.50	2.10
82	A3	20m rose lil ('28)	6.75	5.00
84	A4	50m org & blue	11.00	9.35
85	A4	100m sl bl & buff	15.00	12.00
86	A4	250m gray grn & red	25.00	16.00
		Nos. 77-86 (6)	62.75	46.55

SEMI-POSTAL STAMPS

Regular Issue of 1902-03 Surcharged in Carmine

1915 Unwmk. *Perf. 14x13½*

B1	A3	10c + 5c rose	1.25	1.25

Sinking Fund Issue

Type of 1902-03 Issue Surcharged in Blue or Black

1927-30

B2	A3	15m + 5m deep org	6.00	6.00
B3	A3	15m + 5m red vio ('28)	9.25	9.25
a.		15m + 5m violet ('30)	15.00	15.00

Type of 1902-03 Issue Surcharged as in 1927-28

1929

B4	A3	15m + 5m fawn	12.00	12.00

POSTAGE DUE STAMPS

Postage Due Stamps of France, 1893-1920, Surcharged in Paris in Black

1922 Unwmk. *Perf. 14x13½*

J1	D2	2m on 5c blue	2.50	2.50
J2	D2	4m on 10c brown	2.50	2.50
J3	D2	10m on 30c rose red	3.00	3.00
J4	D2	15m on 50c brn vio	3.25	3.25
J5	D2	30m on 1fr red brn, *straw*	4.50	4.50
		Nos. J1-J5 (5)	15.75	15.75

D3

1928 Typo.

J6	D3	1m slate	1.60	1.60
J7	D3	2m light blue	1.25	1.25
J8	D3	4m lilac rose	1.75	1.75
J9	D3	5m gray green	2.00	2.00
J10	D3	10m light red	2.50	2.50
J11	D3	20m violet brn	2.25	2.25
J12	D3	30m green	5.00	5.00
J13	D3	40m lt violet	6.25	6.25
		Nos. J6-J13 (8)	22.60	22.60

Nos. J6-J13 were also available for use in Port Said.

PORT SAID

Stamps of France Overprinted in Red, Blue or Black

1899-1900 Unwmk. *Perf. 14x13½*

1	A15	1c blk, *lil bl* (R)	2.10	1.70
2	A15	2c brn, *buff* (bl)	2.10	1.70
3	A15	3c gray, *grysh* (Bl)	2.10	2.10
4	A15	4c claret, *lav* (Bl)	1.75	*2.10*
5	A15	5c yel grn (I) (R)	11.00	5.00
a.		Type II (R)	55.00	25.00
6	A15	10c blk, *lav* (I) (R)	14.00	12.50
a.		Type II (R)	72.50	55.00
7	A15	15c blue (R)	14.00	8.50
8	A15	20c red, *grn*	17.00	11.00

9 A15 25c blk, *rose* (R) 14.00 5.00
a. Double overprint 300.00
b. Inverted overprint 300.00
10 A15 30c brn, *bister* 17.00 14.00
a. Inverted overprint 325.00
11 A15 40c red, *straw* 14.00 14.00
12 A15 50c car, *rose* (II) 20.00 14.00
a. Type I 300.00 100.00
b. Double overprint (II) 425.00
13 A15 1fr brnz grn, *straw* 30.00 17.50
14 A15 2fr brn, *az* ('00) 75.00 65.00
15 A15 5fr red lil, *lav* 120.00 92.50
Nos. 1-15 (15) 354.05 266.60

Regular Issue Surcharged in Red

1899

16 A15 25c on 10c blk, *lav* 130.00 32.50
a. Inverted surcharge 250.00

With Additional Surcharge "25" in Red

17 A15 25c on 10c blk, *lav* 475.00 160.00
a. "25" inverted 1,500. 1,400.
b. "25" in black 2,600.
c. As "b," "VINGT CINQ" inverted 3,400.
d. As "b," "25" vertical 3,400.
e. As "c" and "d" 3,400.

A2

A3

A4

1902-03 **Typo.**

18 A2 1c pale gray ('16) .65 .65
19 A2 2c violet brn .75 .75
20 A2 3c red orange .85 .75
21 A2 4c yellow brown 1.10 .90
22 A2 5c blue green ('04) 1.20 .85
a. 5c yellow green 5.00 3.00
23 A3 10c rose red 1.60 1.10
24 A3 15c pale red ('03) 3.25 2.25
a. 15c orange 5.00 3.00
25 A3 20c brn vio ('03) 3.25 2.25
26 A3 25c blue ('03) 2.50 1.60
27 A3 30c gray violet ('03) 6.75 5.00
28 A4 40c red & pale bl 6.00 4.25
29 A4 50c bis brn & lav 9.25 6.75
30 A4 1fr claret & ol grn 12.00 9.25
31 A4 2fr gray vio & yel 15.00 15.00
32 A4 5fr dk bl & buff 35.00 32.50
Nos. 18-32 (15) 99.15 83.85

See Nos. 83-92. For surcharges see Nos. 33-80, B1-B4.

Stamps of 1902-03 Surcharged Locally

1921

33 A2 2m on 5c green 10.00 10.00
a. Inverted surcharge 50.00 50.00
34 A3 4m on 10c rose 9.25 9.25
a. Inverted surcharge 50.00 50.00
35 A2 5m on 1c slate 14.00 14.00
b. 5m on 1c light gray 26.00 26.00
c. Surcharged "2 Milliemes" on #35 67.50 67.50
36 A2 5m on 2c 24.00 24.00
a. Surcharged "2 Milliemes" 75.00 75.00
b. As "a," inverted 160.00 160.00
37 A2 5m on 3c 15.00 15.00
a. Inverted surcharge 62.50 62.50
b. On Alexandria #18 400.00 400.00
38 A2 5m on 4c 11.00 11.00
a. Inverted surcharge 80.00 80.00
39 A2 10m on 2c 25.00 25.00
40 A2 10m on 4c 35.00 35.00
a. Inverted surcharge 85.00 85.00
b. Double surcharge 100.00 105.00
41 A3 10m on 25c 9.25 9.25
a. Inverted surcharge 85.00 85.00
42 A3 12m on 30c 42.50 42.50
43 A2 15m on 4c 10.00 10.00
a. Inverted surcharge 85.00 85.00
b. Double surcharge 92.50 97.50
44 A3 15m on 15c pale red 67.50 67.50
a. Inverted surcharge 160.00 160.00

45 A3 15m on 20c 67.50 67.50
a. Inverted surcharge 160.00 160.00
46 A4 30m on 50c 300.00 300.00
47 A4 60m on 50c 350.00 350.00
48 A4 150m on 50c 400.00 400.00

Nos. 46, 47 and 48 have a bar between the numerals and "Millièmes," which is in capital letters.

Same Surcharge on Stamps of French Offices in Turkey, 1902-03

49 A2 2m on 2c vio brn 160.00 160.00
50 A2 5m on 1c gray 150.00 150.00
a. "5" inverted 7,250.
Nos. 33-50 (18) 1,700. 1,700.

Nos. 28-32 Surcharged

51 A4 15m on 40c 60.00 60.00
52 A4 15m on 50c 85.00 85.00
b. Bar below 15 50.00 50.00
53 A4 30m on 1fr 300.00 300.00
54 A4 60m on 2fr 85.00 *92.50*
55 A4 150m on 5fr 250.00 *275.00*
Nos. 51-55 (5) 780.00 812.50

Overprinted "MILLtEMES"

51a A4 15m on 40c 425.00 425.00
52a A4 15m on 50c 500.00 500.00
53a A4 30m on 1fr 1,400. 1,400.
54a A4 60m on 2fr 400.00 400.00
55a A4 150m on 5fr 1,050. 1,050.
Nos. 51a-55a (5) 3,775. 3,775.

Stamps of 1902-03 Surcharged in Paris

1921-23

56 A2 1m on 1c slate 1.60 1.60
57 A2 2m on 5c green 1.60 1.60
58 A3 4m on 10c rose 2.50 2.50
59 A2 5m on 3c red org 9.25 9.25
60 A3 6m on 15c orange 3.25 3.25
a. 6m on 15c pale red 14.00 14.00
61 A3 8m on 20c brn vio 5.00 5.00
62 A3 10m on 25c blue 2.50 2.50
63 A3 10m on 30c violet 7.50 7.50
64 A3 15m on 50c blue 6.75 6.75

Nos. 29-32 and Type of 1902 Surcharged

65 A4 15m on 50c 6.00 6.00
66 A4 30m on 1fr 9.25 9.25
67 A4 60m on 2fr 130.00 130.00
68 A4 60m on 2fr org & pale blue 12.50 12.50
69 A4 150m on 5fr 20.00 20.00
Nos. 56-69 (14) 217.70 217.70

Stamps and Types of 1902-03 Surcharged

1925

70 A2 1m on 1c light gray .75 .75
71 A2 2m on 5c green 1.10 1.10
72 A3 4m on 10c rose red .90 .90
73 A2 5m on 3c red org 1.10 1.10
74 A3 6m on 15c orange 1.10 1.10
75 A3 8m on 20c brn vio 1.00 1.00
76 A3 10m on 25c blue 1.40 1.40
77 A3 15m on 50c blue 1.60 1.60
78 A4 30m on 1fr cl & ol grn 2.75 2.75
79 A4 60m on 2fr org & pale blue 2.50 2.50
80 A4 150m on 5fr dk bl & buff 4.25 4.25
Nos. 70-80 (11) 18.45 18.45

Type of 1902-03 Issue and

1927-28

83 A5 3m orange ('28) 2.10 2.10
87 A3 15m slate bl 2.50 2.50
88 A3 20m rose lil ('28) 2.50 2.50
90 A4 50m org & blue 4.50 4.50
91 A4 100m slate bl & buff 6.00 6.00
92 A4 250m gray grn & red 9.25 9.25
Nos. 83-92 (6) 26.85 26.85

SEMI-POSTAL STAMPS

A5Regular Issue of 1902-03 Surcharged in Carmine

1915 **Unwmk.** ***Perf. 14x13½***

B1 A3 10c + 5c rose 1.60 1.60

Sinking Fund Issue

Type of 1902-03 Issue Surcharged like Alexandria Nos. B2-B3 in Blue or Black

1927-30

B2 A3 15m + 5m dp org (Bl) 5.00 5.00
B3 A3 15m + 5m red vio ('28) 8.50 8.50
b. 15m + 5m violet ('30) 14.00 14.00
B4 A3 15m + 5m fawn ('29) 10.00 10.00
Nos. B2-B4 (3) 23.50 23.50

POSTAGE DUE STAMPS

Postage Due Stamps of France, 1893-1906, Srchd. Locally in Black

1921 **Unwmk.** ***Perf. 14x13½***

J1 D2 12m on 10c brown 62.50 *67.50*
J2 D2 15m on 5c blue 92.50 *105.00*
J3 D2 30m on 20c ol grn 92.50 *105.00*
a. Inverted surcharge 1,100. 1,100.
J4 D2 30m on 50c red vio 3,000. 3,400.

Same Surcharged in Red or Blue

1921

J5 D2 2m on 5c bl (R) 55.00 *60.00*
a. Blue surcharge 300.00 300.00
b. Accent omitted from "è" of "Millièmes" 190.00 200.00
c. Second "m" of "Millièmes" inverted 190.00 200.00
d. "S" of "Millièmes" omitted 190.00 225.00
J6 D2 4m on 10c brn (Bl) 55.00 *62.50*
a. Surcharged "15 Millièmes" 725.00 725.00
b. Accent omitted from "è" of "MILLIèMES" 190.00 200.00
c. Second "m" of "Millièmes" inverted 190.00 200.00
d. "S" of "Millièmes" omitted 190.00 225.00
J7 D2 10m on 30c red (Bl) 55.00 *60.00*
a. Inverted surcharge 160.00 160.00
b. Accent omitted from "è" of "Millièmes" 190.00 190.00
c. Second "M" of "Millièmes" inverted 190.00 190.00
d. "S" of "Millièmes" omitted 190.00 225.00
e. "Q" for "0" in surcharge (1Qm) 1,450. 1,500.
J8 D2 15m on 50c brn vio (Bl) 67.50 *72.50*
a. Inverted surcharge 160.00 160.00
b. Accent omitted from "è" of "Millièmes" 190.00 190.00
c. Second "m" of "Millièmes" inverted 190.00 190.00
d. "S" of "Millièmes" omitted 210.00 240.00
e. As "a," accent omitted from è of "Millièmes" 425.00
Nos. J5-J8 (4) 232.50 255.00

Alexandria Nos. J6-J13 were also available for use in Port Said.

OFFICES IN TURKEY (LEVANT)

Various powers maintained post offices in the Turkish Empire before World War I by authority of treaties which ended with the signing of the Treaty of Lausanne in 1923. The foreign post offices were closed Oct. 27, 1923.

100 Centimes = 1 Franc
25 Centimes = 40 Paras = 1 Piaster

Stamps of France Surcharged in Black or Red

1885-1901 **Unwmk.** ***Perf. 14x13½***

1 A15 1pi on 25c yel, *straw* 550.00 16.00
a. Inverted surcharge 2,500. 2,400.
2 A15 1pi on 25c blk, *rose* (R) ('86) 4.25 1.25
Never hinged 8.00
a. Inverted surcharge 400.00 325.00
3 A15 2pi on 50c car, *rose* (II) ('90) 18.00 3.00
Never hinged 35.00
a. Type I ('01) 375.00 50.00
Never hinged 725.00
4 A15 3pi on 75c car, *rose* 30.00 15.00
Never hinged 60.00
5 A15 4pi on 1fr brnz grn, *straw* 30.00 15.00
Never hinged 60.00
6 A15 8pi on 2fr brn, *az* ('00) 37.50 25.00
Never hinged 67.50
7 A15 20pi on 5fr red lil, *lav* ('90) 110.00 60.00
Never hinged 225.00
Nos. 1-7 (7) 779.75 135.25

A2

A3

A4

A5

A6

1902-07 **Typo.** ***Perf. 14x13½***

21 A2 1c gray .65 .65
Never hinged 1.25
22 A2 2c vio brn .65 .65
23 A2 3c red org .65 .65
24 A2 4c yel brn 3.00 1.10
a. Imperf., pair 90.00
25 A2 5c grn ('06) 1.00 .65
26 A3 10c rose red 1.00 .65
27 A3 15c pale red ('03) 3.00 1.25
28 A3 20c brn vio ('03) 3.25 2.00
29 A3 25c blue ('07) 45.00 *60.00*
a. Imperf., pair 425.00
30 A3 30c lilac ('03) 6.00 3.00
31 A4 40c red & pale bl 6.00 3.25
32 A4 50c bis brn & lav ('07) 190.00 *225.00*
a. Imperf., pair 925.00
33 A4 1fr claret & ol grn ('07) 425.00 450.00
a. Imperf., pair 1,100.

Black Surcharge

34 A5 1pi on 25c bl ('03) 1.20 .65
a. Second "I" omitted 32.50 25.00
b. Double surcharge 72.50 60.00
35 A6 2pi on 50c bis brn & lavender 4.25 1.60
36 A6 4pi on 1fr cl & ol grn 5.00 2.10
a. Imperf., pair 750.00
37 A6 8pi on 2fr gray vio & yel 20.00 15.00

38 A6 20pi on 5fr dk bl & buff 10.00 6.00
Nos. 21-38 (18) 725.65 774.20

Nos. 29, 32-33 were used during the early part of 1907 in the French Offices at Harar and Diredawa, Ethiopia. Djibouti and Port Said stamps were also used.

No. 27 Surcharged in Green

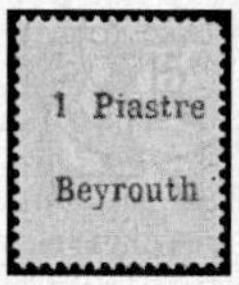

1905

39 A3 1pi on 15c pale red 2,100. 325.
a. "Piastte" 6,500. 1,450.

Stamps of France 1900-21 Surcharged

On A22

On A20

On A18

1921-22

40 A22 30pa on 5c grn 1.00 1.00
41 A22 30pa on 5c org 1.00 .85
42 A22 1pi20pa on 10c red 1.10 1.10
43 A22 1pi20pa on 10c grn 1.10 .85
44 A22 3pi30pa on 25c bl 1.60 1.00
45 A22 4pi20pa on 30c org 1.60 1.10
a. "4" omitted 1,050.
46 A20 7pi20pa on 50c bl 1.60 1.25
47 A18 15pi on 1fr car & ol grn 3.00 2.10
48 A18 30pi on 2fr org & pale bl 12.50 10.00
49 A18 75pi on 5fr dk bl & buff 11.00 7.50
Nos. 40-49 (10) 35.50 26.75

Stamps of France, 1903-07, Handstamped

1923

52 A22 1pi20pa on 10c red 62.50 60.00
54 A20 3pi30pa on 15c gray grn (GC) 25.00 25.00
55 A22 7pi20pa on 35c vio 30.00 30.00
b. 1pi20pa on 35c violet 1,400. 1,400.
Nos. 52-55 (3) 117.50 115.00

CAVALLE (CAVALLA)

Stamps of France Ovptd. or Srchd. in Carmine, Red, Blue or Black

1893-1900 Unwmk. *Perf. 14x13½*

1 A15 5c grn, *grnsh* (R) 25.00 21.00
a. Type II (C) 25.00 21.00
2 A15 5c yel grn (I) ('00) (R) 21.00 20.00
3 A15 10c blk, *lav* (II) 25.00 25.00
a. 10c black, *lavender* (I) 175.00 145.00
4 A15 15c blue (R) 47.50 30.00
a. 15c blue (C) 47.50 30.00
5 A15 1pi on 25c blk, *rose* 27.50 19.00
6 A15 2pi on 50c car, *rose* 90.00 62.50
7 A15 4pi on 1fr brnz grn, *straw* (R) 95.00 85.00
a. 4pi on 1fr brnz grn, *straw* (C) 95.00 85.00
8 A15 8pi on 2fr brn, *az* ('00) (Bk) 115.00 115.00
Nos. 1-8 (8) 446.00 377.50
Set, never hinged 1,000.

A3

A4

A5

A6

1902-03

9 A3 5c green 2.25 1.75
a. 5c yel grn 2.50 2.00
10 A4 10c rose red ('03) 2.25 1.75
11 A4 15c orange 2.25 1.75
a. 15c pale red ('03) 12.50 12.50

Surcharged in Black

12 A5 1pi on 25c bl 4.75 3.00
13 A6 2pi on 50c bis brn & lav 13.00 7.00
14 A6 4pi on 1fr cl & ol grn 16.00 13.00
15 A6 8pi on 2fr gray vio & yel 21.00 19.00
Nos. 9-15 (7) 61.50 47.25

DEDEAGH (DEDEAGATCH)

Stamps of France Ovptd. or Srchd. in Carmine, Red, Blue or Black

1893-1900 Unwmk. *Perf. 14x13½*

1 A15 5c grn, *grnsh* (II) (R) 17.50 15.00
a. Type II (C) 17.50 15.00
2 A15 5c yel grn (I) ('00) (R) 14.00 14.00
3 A15 10c blk, *lav* (II) 26.50 20.00
a. Type I 45.00 32.50
b. As "a," double overprint 300.00
4 A15 15c blue (II) (R) 35.00 30.00
a. Type II (C) 35.00 30.00
5 A15 1pi on 25c blk, *rose* 40.00 35.00
6 A15 2pi on 50c car, *rose* 67.50 47.50
7 A15 4pi on 1fr brnz grn, *straw* (R) 80.00 70.00
8 A15 8pi on 2fr brn, *az* ('00) (Bk) 115.00 95.00
Nos. 1-8 (8) 395.50 326.50
Set, never hinged 1,000.

A3

A4

A5

A6

1902-03

9 A3 5c green ('03) 3.00 2.50
a. 5c yellow green 3.50 3.00
10 A4 10c rose red ('03) 3.50 2.75
11 A4 15c orange 5.00 3.75
a. 15c rose red ('03) 7.00 6.00

15 A5 1pi on 25c bl ('03) 3.50 2.75
16 A6 2pi on 50c bis brn & lav 11.50 10.00
a. Double surcharge 300.00
17 A6 4pi on 1fr cl & ol grn 22.50 18.50
18 A6 8pi on 2fr gray vio & yel 32.50 27.50
Nos. 9-18 (7) 81.50 67.75
Set, never hinged 175.00

PORT LAGOS

Stamps of France Ovptd. or Srchd. in Carmine, Red or Blue

1893 Unwmk. *Perf. 14x13½*

1 A15 5c grn, *grnsh* (R) 30.00 30.00
a. 5c grn, *grnsh* (C) 30.00 30.00
2 A15 10c blk, *lav* 62.50 47.50
3 A15 15c blue (R) 90.00 70.00
a. 15c blue (C) 95.00 75.00
4 A15 1pi on 25c blk, *rose* 75.00 60.00
5 A15 2pi on 50c car, *rose* 185.00 95.00
6 A15 4pi on 1fr brnz grn, *straw* (R) 112.50 95.00
Nos. 1-6 (6) 555.00 397.50
Set, never hinged 1,300.

VATHY (SAMOS)

Stamps of France Ovptd. or Srchd. in Carmine, Red, Blue or Black

1894-1900 Unwmk. *Perf. 14x13½*

1 A15 5c grn, *grnsh* (R) 8.50 7.50
a. 5c grn, *grnsh* (II) (C) 10.00 8.00
2 A15 5c yel grn (I) ('00) (R) 8.50 7.50
a. Type II 85.00 85.00
3 A15 10c blk, *lav* (I) 17.50 14.00
a. Type II 50.00 45.00
4 A15 15c blue (R) 17.50 14.00
5 A15 1pi on 25c blk, *rose* 17.50 11.00
6 A15 2pi on 50c car, *rose* 30.00 26.00
7 A15 4pi on 1fr brnz grn, *straw* (R) 40.00 35.00
8 A15 8pi on 2fr brn, *az* ('00) (Bk) 72.50 72.50
9 A15 20pi on 5fr lil, *lav* ('00) (Bk) 105.00 105.00
Nos. 1-9 (9) 317.00 292.50
Set, never hinged 600.00

OFFICES IN ZANZIBAR

Until 1906 France maintained post offices in the Sultanate of Zanzibar, but in that year Great Britain assumed direct control over this protectorate and the French withdrew their postal system.

16 Annas = 1 Rupee

Stamps of France Surcharged in Red, Carmine, Blue or Black

1894-96 Unwmk. *Perf. 14x13½*

1 A15 ½a on 5c grn, *grnsh* 10.00 7.50
2 A15 1a on 10c blk, *lav* (Bl) 15.00 12.50
3 A15 1½a on 15c bl ('96) 22.50 21.00
a. "ANNAS" 100.00 92.50

4 A15 2a on 20c red, *grn* ('96) (Bk) 19.00 15.00
a. "ANNA" 2,300. 2,300.
5 A15 2½a on 25c blk, *rose* (Bl) 12.50 9.25
a. Double surcharge 250.00 250.00
6 A15 3a on 30c brn, *bis* ('96) (Bk) 21.00 18.00
7 A15 4a on 40c red, *straw* ('96) (Bk) 29.00 25.00
8 A15 5a on 50c car, *rose* (Bl) 37.50 32.50
9 A15 7½a on 75c vio, *org* ('96) 500.00 400.00
10 A15 10a on 1fr brnz grn, *straw* 67.50 55.00
11 A15 50a on 5fr red lil, *lav* ('96) (Bk) 325.00 260.00
Nos. 1-11 (11) 1,059. 855.75

1894

12 A15 ½a & 5c on 1c blk, *lil bl* (R) 200.00 *220.00*
13 A15 1a & 10c on 3c gray, *grysh* (R) 180.00 *200.00*
14 A15 2½a & 25c on 4c cl, *lav* (Bk) 230.00 *275.00*
15 A15 5a & 50c on 20c red, *grn* (Bk) 250.00 *275.00*
16 A15 10a & 1fr on 40c red, *straw* (Bk) 475.00 *525.00*
Nos. 12-16 (5) 1,335. 1,495.

There are two distinct types of the figures 5c, four of the 25c and three of each of the others of this series.

Stamps of France Srchd. in Red, Carmine, Blue or Black

1896-1900

17 A15 ½a on 5c grn, *grnsh* (R) 11.00 8.50
18 A15 ½a on 5c yel grn (I) (R) 7.50 6.75
a. Type II 9.25 7.50
19 A15 1a on 10c blk, *lav* (II) (Bl) 9.25 7.50
a. Type I 22.50 19.00
20 A15 1½a on 15c bl (R) 11.00 9.25
21 A15 2a on 20c red, *grn* 9.25 9.25
a. "ZANZIBAR" double 210.00 210.00
b. "ZANZIBAR" triple 210.00 210.00
22 A15 2½a on 25c blk, *rose* (Bl) 11.00 9.25
a. Inverted surcharge 275.00 210.00
23 A15 3a on 30c brn, *bis* 11.00 9.25
24 A15 4a on 40c red, *straw* 13.50 10.00
25 A15 5a on 50c rose, *rose* (II) (Bl) 45.00 32.50
a. Type I 125.00 100.00
26 A15 10a on 1fr brnz grn, *straw* (R) 29.00 25.00
27 A15 20a on 2fr brn, *az* 35.00 29.00
a. "ZANZIBAS" 675.00 *750.00*
b. "ZANZIBAR" triple 1,600.
28 A15 50a on 5fr lil, *lav* 67.50 62.50
a. "ZANZIBAS" *9,250.*
Nos. 17-28 (12) 260.00 218.75

For surcharges see Nos. 50-54.

A4

A5

1897

29 A4 2½a & 25c on ½a on 5c grn, *grnsh* 1,300. 240.
30 A4 2½a & 25c on 1a on 10c *lav* *4,500.* 1,100.
31 A4 2½a & 25c on 1½a on 15c blue *4,400.* 950.
32 A5 5a & 50c on 3a on 30c brn, *bis* *4,400.* 950.
33 A5 5a & 50c on 4a on 40c red, *straw* *4,500.* 1,300.

Printed on the Margins of Sheets of French Stamps

A6

A7

***Perf. 14x13½* on one or more sides**

1897

34	A6	2½a & 25c grn, *grnsh*	1,300.
35	A6	2½a & 25c blk, *lav*	*4,000.*
36	A6	2½a & 25c blue	*3,000.*
37	A7	5a & 50c brn, *bis*	*2,900.*
38	A7	5a & 50c red, *straw*	*4,000.*

There are 5 varieties of figures in the above surcharges.

Surcharged in Red or Black

A8

A9

A10

1902-03 ***Perf. 14x13½***

39	A8	½a on 5c grn (R)	6.75	6.00
40	A9	1a on 10c rose red ('03)	7.50	7.50
41	A9	1½a on 15c pale red ('03)	15.00	14.00
42	A9	2a on 20c brn vio ('03)	18.00	15.00
43	A9	2½a on 25c bl ('03)	18.00	15.00
44	A9	3a on 30c lil ('03)	13.00	13.00
a.		5a on 30c (error)	325.00	*375.00*
45	A10	4a on 40c red & pale bl	30.00	25.00
46	A10	5a on 50c bis brn & lav	25.00	21.00
47	A10	10a on 1fr cl & ol grn	32.50	29.00
48	A10	20a on 2fr gray vio & yel	85.00	75.00
49	A10	50a on 5fr dk bl & buff	100.00	92.50
		Nos. 39-49 (11)	350.75	313.00

For see Reunion Nos. 55-59.

Nos. 23-24 Surcharged in Black

a

b

c

1904

50	A15 (a)	25c & 2½a on 4a on 40c		1,000.
51	A15 (b)	50c & 5a on 3a on 30c		1,200.
52	A15 (b)	50c & 5a on 4a on 40c	6,500.	1,200.
53	A15 (c)	1fr & 10a on 3a on 30c		2,000.
54	A15 (c)	1fr & 10a on 4a on 40c		2,000.

Nos. 39-40, 44 Surcharged in Red or Black

d

e

f

g

55	A8 (d)	25c & 2a on ½a on 5c (R)	3,100.	140.00
56	A9 (e)	25c & 2½a on 1a on 10c	6,500.	150.00
a.		Inverted surcharge		1,500.
57	A9 (e)	25c & 2½a on 3a on 30c		2,400.
a.		Inverted surcharge		4,100.
b.		Double surch., both invtd.		2,600.
58	A9 (f)	50c & 5a on 3a on 30c		1,250.
59	A9 (g)	1fr & 10a on 3a on 30c		2,000.

No. J1-J3 With Various Surcharges Overprinted:

"Timbre" in Red

60	D1	½a on 5c blue	450.00

Overprinted "Affrancht" in Black

61	D1	1a on 10c brown	450.00

With Red Bars Across "CHIFFRE" and "TAXE"

62	D1	1½a on 15c green	1,000.

The illustrations are not exact reproductions of the new surcharges but are merely intended to show their relative positions and general styles.

POSTAGE DUE STAMPS

Postage Due Stamps of France Srchd. in Red, Blue or Black Like Nos. 17-28

1897 Unwmk. ***Perf. 14x13½***

J1	D2	½a on 5c blue (R)	21.00	12.50
J2	D2	1a on 10c brn (Bl)	21.00	12.50
a.		Inverted surcharge	160.00	*190.00*
J3	D2	1½aon 15c grn (R)	32.50	12.50
J4	D2	3a on 30c car (Bk)	29.00	21.00
J5	D2	5a on 50c lil (Bl)	32.50	25.00
a.		2½a on 50c lilac (Bl)	1,400.	1,300.
		Nos. J1-J5 (5)	136.00	83.50

For overprints see Nos. 60-62.

REUNION

LOCATION — An island in the Indian Ocean about 400 miles east of Madagascar

GOVT. — Department of France

AREA — 970 sq. mi.

POP. — 490,000 (est. 1974)

CAPITAL — St. Denis

The colony of Réunion became an integral part of the Republic, acquiring the same status as the departments in metropolitan France, under a law effective Jan. 1, 1947.

On Jan. 1, 1975, stamps of France replaced those inscribed or overprinted "CFA."

100 Centimes = 1 Franc

Catalogue values for unused stamps in this country are for Never Hinged items, beginning with Scott 224 in the regular postage section, Scott B15 in the semi-postal section, Scott C18 in the airpost section, and Scott J26 in the postage due section.

For French stamps inscribed "Reunion" see Nos. 949, 1507.

A1

A2

1852 Unwmk. Typo. ***Imperf.***

1	A1	15c black, *blue*	*39,000.*	*25,000.*
2	A2	30c black, *blue*	*39,000.*	*25,000.*

Four varieties of each value.

The reprints are printed on a more bluish paper than the originals. They have a frame of a thick and a thin line, instead of one thick and two thin lines. Value, $62.50 each.

Stamps of French Colonies Surcharged or Overprinted in Black

a

b

1885

3	A1(a)	5c on 40c org, *yelsh*	450.00	375.00
a.		Inverted surcharge	2,250.	2,100.
b.		Double surcharge	2,250.	2,100.
4	A1(a)	25c on 40c org, *yelsh*	70.00	55.00
a.		Inverted surcharge	1,000.	900.00
b.		Double surcharge	1,000.	900.00
5	A5(a)	5c on 30c brn, *yelsh*	70.00	57.50
a.		"5" inverted	3,500.	3,000.
b.		Double surcharge	1,100.	900.00
c.		Inverted surcharge	1,000.	900.00
6	A4(a)	5c on 40c org, *yelsh* (I)	62.50	45.00
a.		5c on 40c org, *yelsh* (II)	2,500.	2,500.
b.		Inverted surcharge (I)	1,100.	900.00
c.		Double surcharge (I)	1,100.	900.00
7	A8(a)	5c on 30c brn, *yelsh*	22.50	18.00
8	A8(a)	5c on 40c ver, *straw*	135.00	115.00
a.		Inverted surcharge	950.00	850.00
b.		Double surcharge	925.00	850.00
9	A8(a)	10c on 40c ver, *straw*	27.50	22.50
a.		Inverted surcharge	950.00	850.00
b.		Double surcharge	950.00	850.00
10	A8(a)	20c on 30c brn, *yelsh*	90.00	75.00

Overprint Type "b" With or Without Accent on "E"

1891

11	A4	40c org, *yelsh* (I)	575.00	550.00
a.		40c orange, *yelsh* (II)	*6,750.*	*6,750.*
b.		Double overprint	750.00	750.00
12	A7	80c car, *pnksh*	80.00	62.50
13	A8	30c brn, *yelsh*	52.50	52.50
14	A8	40c ver, *straw*	42.50	42.50
15	A8	75c car, *rose*	475.00	475.00
16	A8	1fr brnz grn, *straw*	62.50	52.50

Perf. 14x13½

17	A9	1c blk, *lil bl*	4.75	4.00
a.		Inverted overprint	60.00	60.00
b.		Double overprint	52.50	52.50
18	A9	2c brn, *buff*	6.50	5.00
a.		Inverted overprint	40.00	40.00
19	A9	4c claret, *lav*	10.00	8.00
a.		Inverted overprint	72.50	72.50
20	A9	5c grn, *grnsh*	11.50	9.00
a.		Inverted overprint	60.00	60.00
b.		Double overprint	60.00	57.50
21	A9	10c blk, *lav*	40.00	8.00
a.		Inverted overprint	90.00	80.00
b.		Double overprint	100.00	80.00
22	A9	15c blue	57.50	9.00
a.		Inverted overprint	120.00	110.00
23	A9	20c red, *grn*	45.00	30.00
a.		Inverted overprint	175.00	150.00
b.		Double overprint	175.00	150.00
24	A9	25c blk, *rose*	50.00	7.25
a.		Inverted overprint	125.00	120.00
25	A9	35c dp vio, *yel*	45.00	35.00
b.		Inverted overprint	180.00	175.00
26	A9	40c red, *straw*	72.50	62.50
a.		Inverted overprint	240.00	225.00
27	A9	75c car, *rose*	675.00	575.00
a.		Inverted overprint	1,600.	1,400.
28	A9	1fr brnz grn, *straw*	575.00	500.00
a.		Inverted overprint	1,600.	1,500.
b.		Double overprint	1,500.	1,400.

The varieties "RUNION," "RUENION," "REUNIONR," "ERUNION," "EUNION," "REUNIN," "REUNIOU" and "REUNOIN" are found on most stamps of this group. See *Scott Classic Specialized Catalogue of Stamps and Covers* for detailed listings. There are also many broken letters.

For surcharges see Nos. 29-33, 53-55.

No. 23 with Additional Surcharge in Black

c

d

e

f

1891

29	A9(c)	02c on 20c red, *grn*	14.50	14.50
a.		Inverted surcharge	90.00	90.00
b.		No "c" after "02"	57.50	57.50
30	A9(c)	15c on 20c red, *grn*	18.00	18.00
a.		Inverted surcharge	70.00	70.00
31	A9(d)	2c on 20c red, *grn*	5.00	5.00
32	A9(e)	2c on 20c red, *grn*	6.00	5.75
33	A9(f)	2c on 20c red, *grn*	10.00	10.00
		Nos. 29-33 (5)	53.50	53.25

The varieties "RUNION" and "RUENION" appear on several stamps from this set. See *Scott Classic Specialized Catalogue of Stamps and Covers* for listings.

Navigation and Commerce — A14

1892-1905 Typo. ***Perf. 14x13½***

Name of Colony in Blue or Carmine

34	A14	1c blk, *lil bl*	2.00	1.25
35	A14	2c brn, *buff*	2.00	1.25
36	A14	4c claret, *lav*	3.25	2.25
37	A14	5c grn, *grnsh*	7.25	2.25
38	A14	5c yel grn ('00)	1.75	1.75
39	A14	10c blk, *lav*	9.50	3.50
40	A14	10c red ('00)	4.50	4.50
41	A14	15c bl, quadrille paper	30.00	3.50
42	A14	15c gray ('00)	10.00	3.50
43	A14	20c red, *grn*	20.00	9.00
44	A14	25c blk, *rose*	22.50	3.50
a.		"Reunion" double	425.00	*450.00*
45	A14	25c blue ('00)	29.00	27.50
46	A14	30c brn, *bis*	23.00	12.00
47	A14	40c red, *straw*	32.50	19.00
48	A14	50c car, *rose*	80.00	42.50
a.		"Reunion" in red and blue	500.00	500.00
49	A14	50c brn, *az* ("Reunion" in car) ('00)	57.50	50.00
50	A14	50c brn, *az* ("Reunion" in bl) ('05)	57.50	50.00
51	A14	75c dp vio, *org*	62.50	45.00
a.		"Reunion" double	375.00	375.00
52	A14	1fr brnz grn, *straw*	50.00	35.00
a.		"Reunion" double	360.00	*375.00*
		Nos. 34-52 (19)	504.75	317.25

Perf. 13½x14 stamps are counterfeits.

For surcharges and overprint see Nos. 56-59, 99-106, Q1.

French Colonies No. 52 Surcharged in Black

g

h

j

1893

53 A9(g) 2c on 20c red, *grn* 3.25 3.25
54 A9(h) 2c on 20c red, *grn* 6.00 6.00
55 A9(j) 2c on 20c red, *grn* 22.50 22.50
Nos. 53-55 (3) 31.75 31.75

Reunion Nos. 47-48, 51-52 Surcharged in Black

1901

56 A14 5c on 40c red, *straw* 7.00 7.00
a. Inverted surcharge 47.50 47.50
b. No bar 240.00 240.00
c. Thin "5" — —
d. "5" inverted 1,400. 1,200.
57 A14 5c on 50c car, *rose* 7.75 7.25
a. Inverted surcharge 47.50 47.50
b. No bar 240.00 240.00
c. Thin "5" —
58 A14 15c on 75c vio, *org* 22.50 22.50
a. Inverted surcharge 57.50 57.50
b. No bar 240.00 240.00
c. Thin "5" and small "1" 47.50 47.50
d. As "c," inverted 800.00 800.00
59 A14 15c on 1fr brnz grn, *straw* 19.00 19.00
a. Inverted surcharge 57.50 57.50
b. No bar 240.00 240.00
c. Thin "5" and small "1" 47.50 47.50
d. As "c," inverted —
Nos. 56-59 (4) 56.25 55.75

Map of Réunion A19

Coat of Arms and View of St. Denis A20

View of St. Pierre A21

1907-30 **Typo.**

60 A19 1c vio & lt rose .30 .30
61 A19 2c brn & ultra .30 .30
62 A19 4c ol grn & red .40 .40
a. Center double 225.00
63 A19 5c grn & red 1.35 .40
64 A19 5c org & vio ('22) .30 .30
65 A19 10c car & grn 2.75 .40
66 A19 10c grn ('22) .30 .30
67 A19 10c brn red & org red, *bluish* ('26) .70 .70
68 A19 15c blk & ultra ('17) .55 .40
a. Center double 250.00 250.00
69 A19 15c gray grn & bl grn ('26) .40 .40
70 A19 15c bl & lt red ('28) .55 .45
71 A20 20c gray grn & bl grn .45 .45
a. Center omitted 1,100. 1,100.
72 A20 25c dp bl & vio brn 7.00 4.00
73 A20 25c lt brn & bl ('22) .55 .55
74 A20 30c yel brn & grn 1.50 1.00
75 A20 30c rose & pale rose ('22) 1.50 1.50
76 A20 30c gray & car rose ('26) .55 .55
77 A20 30c dp grn & yel grn ('28) 1.20 1.20
78 A20 35c ol grn & bl 1.75 1.10
79 A20 40c gray grn & brn ('25) .70 .70
80 A20 45c vio & car rose 1.90 1.10
81 A20 45c red brn & ver ('25) .90 .90
82 A20 45c vio & red org ('28) 3.00 2.75
83 A20 50c red brn & ultra 5.00 1.75
84 A20 50c bl & ultra ('22) 1.40 1.40
85 A20 50c yel & vio ('26) 1.10 1.10
86 A20 60c dk bl & yel brn ('25) 1.10 1.10
87 A20 65c vio & lt bl ('28) 1.60 1.40
88 A20 75c red & car rose .80 .70
89 A20 75c ol brn & red vio ('28) 2.50 2.25
90 A20 90c brn red & brt red ('30) 9.00 8.25
91 A21 1fr ol grn & bl 1.50 1.40
92 A21 1fr blue ('25) .95 .95
93 A21 1fr yel brn & lav ('28) 1.50 .70
94 A21 1.10fr org brn & rose lil ('28) 1.50 1.40
95 A21 1.50fr dk bl & ultra ('30) 16.00 16.00
96 A21 2fr red & grn 6.75 4.25
97 A21 3fr red vio ('30) 14.50 9.50
98 A21 5fr car & vio brn 11.50 6.75
Nos. 60-98 (39) 105.60 79.05

For surcharges see Nos. 107-121, 178-180, B1-B3.

Stamps of 1892-1900 Surcharged in Black or Carmine

1912

Spacing between figures of surcharge 1.5mm (5c), 2mm (10c)

99 A14 5c on 2c brn, *buff* 1.60 1.60
100 A14 5c on 15c gray (C) 1.40 1.40
a. Inverted surcharge 210.00 210.00
101 A14 5c on 20c red, *grn* 2.40 2.40
102 A14 5c on 25c blk, *rose* (C) 1.60 1.60
103 A14 5c on 30c brn, *bis* (C) 1.40 1.40
104 A14 10c on 40c red, *straw* 1.40 1.40
105 A14 10c on 50c brn, *az* (C) 5.75 5.75
106 A14 10c on 75c dp vio, *org* 9.50 9.50
Nos. 99-106 (8) 25.05 25.05

Two spacings between the surcharged numerals are found on Nos. 99 to 106. For detailed listings, see the *Scott Classic Specialized Catalogue of Stamps and Covers.*

No. 62 Surcharged

1917

107 A19 1c on 4c ol grn & red 2.00 2.00
a. Inverted surcharge 80.00 80.00
b. Double surcharge 70.00 70.00
c. In pair with unsurcharged #62 625.00 625.00

Stamps and Types of 1907-30 Surcharged in Black or Red

1922-33

108 A20 40c on 20c grn & yel .80 .80
a. Double surcharge, one inverted 175.00 175.00
b. Center double 175.00 175.00
c. Surcharge omitted 1,200. 1,200.
109 A20 50c on 45c red brn & ver ('33) 1.20 1.20
109A A20 50c on 45c vio & red org ('33) 325.00 275.00
b. Double surcharge 1,750.
110 A20 50c on 65c vio & lt bl ('33) 1.20 1.20
111 A20 60c on 75c red & rose .85 .85
a. Double surcharge 225.00 225.00
112 A19 65c on 15c blk & ultra (R) ('25) 2.00 2.00
113 A19 85c on 15c blk & ultra (R) ('25) 2.00 2.00
114 A20 85c on 75c red & cer ('25) 2.25 2.25
115 A20 90c on 75 brn red & rose red ('27) 2.25 2.25
Nos. 108-109,110-115 (8) 12.55 12.55

Stamps and Type of 1907-30 Srchd. in Black or Red

1924-27

116 A21 25c on 5fr car & brn 1.10 1.10
a. Double surcharge 110.00
117 A21 1.25fr on 1fr bl (R) ('26) 1.10 1.10
a. Double surcharge 125.00
118 A21 1.50fr on 1fr ind & ultra, *bluish* ('27) 1.50 1.50
a. Double surcharge 140.00
b. Surcharge omitted 200.00
119 A21 3fr on 5fr dl red & lt bl ('27) 4.25 3.00
120 A21 10fr on 5fr bl grn & brn red ('27) 19.50 17.00
121 A21 20fr on 5fr blk brn & rose ('27) 24.00 19.00
Nos. 116-121 (6) 51.45 42.70

Common Design Types pictured following the introduction.

Colonial Exposition Issue
Common Design Types

1931 **Engr.** ***Perf. 12½***

Name of Country Typo. in Black

122 CD70 40c dp green 5.50 5.50
123 CD71 50c violet 5.50 5.50
124 CD72 90c red orange 5.50 5.50
125 CD73 1.50fr dull blue 5.50 5.50
Nos. 122-125 (4) 22.00 22.00

Cascade of Salazie — A22

Waterfowl Lake and Anchain Peak — A23

Léon Dierx Museum, St. Denis — A24

Perf. 12, 12½ and Compound

1933-40 **Engr.**

126 A22 1c violet .25 .25
127 A22 2c dark brown .25 .25
128 A22 3c rose vio ('40) .25 .25
129 A22 4c olive green .25 .25
130 A22 5c red orange .25 .25
131 A22 10c ultramarine .25 .25
132 A22 15c black .25 .25
133 A22 20c indigo .30 .25
134 A22 25c red brown .40 .30
135 A22 30c dark green .40 .40
136 A23 35c green ('38) .55 .55
137 A23 40c ultramarine .55 .55
138 A23 40c brn blk ('40) .40 .40
139 A23 45c red violet 1.00 1.00
140 A23 45c green ('40) .45 .45
141 A23 50c red .30 .25
142 A23 55c brn org ('38) 1.50 1.00
143 A23 60c dull bl ('40) .45 .45
144 A23 65c olive green 1.10 .80
145 A23 70c ol grn ('40) .65 .65
146 A23 75c dark brown 5.00 4.25
147 A23 80c black ('38) 1.00 .80
148 A23 90c carmine 2.50 2.10
149 A23 90c dl rose vio ('39) 1.00 1.00
150 A23 1fr green 2.00 .70
161 A23 1fr dk car ('38) 2.50 .70
152 A23 1fr black ('40) .70 .70
153 A24 1.25fr orange brown .70 .55
154 A24 1.25fr brt car rose ('39) 1.00 1.00
155 A22 1.40fr pck bl ('40) 1.00 1.00
156 A24 1.50fr ultramarine .40 .40
157 A22 1.60fr dk car rose ('40) 1.40 1.40
158 A24 1.75fr olive green 1.00 .65
159 A22 1.75fr dk bl ('38) 1.40 .85
160 A24 2fr vermilion .55 .55
161 A22 2.25fr brt ultra ('39) 2.00 2.00
162 A22 2.50fr chnt ('40) 1.40 1.40
163 A24 3fr purple .55 .55
164 A24 5fr magenta .55 .55
165 A24 10fr dark blue 1.10 1.10
166 A24 20fr red brown 1.50 1.50
Nos. 126-166 (41) 39.05 32.55

For overprints and surcharges see Nos. 177A, 181-220, 223, C1.
60c, 1fr without "RF," see Nos. 237A-238B.

Paris International Exposition Issue
Common Design Types

1937 ***Perf. 13***

167 CD74 20c dp vio 2.25 2.25
168 CD75 30c dk grn 2.25 2.25
169 CD76 40c car rose 2.25 2.25
170 CD77 50c dk brn & blk 2.10 2.10
171 CD78 90c red 2.10 2.10
172 CD79 1.50fr ultra 2.25 2.25
Nos. 167-172 (6) 13.20 13.20
Set, never hinged 20.00

Colonial Arts Exhibition Issue
Souvenir Sheet
Common Design Type

1937 ***Imperf.***

173 CD74 3fr ultra 8.50 *10.00*
Never hinged 16.00

New York World's Fair Issue
Common Design Type

1939 **Engr.** ***Perf. 12½x12***

174 CD82 1.25fr car lake 1.40 1.40
175 CD82 2.25fr ultra 1.40 1.40
Set, never hinged 4.50

For overprints, see Nos. 221-222.

St. Denis Roadstead and Marshal Pétain A25

1941 Unwmk. *Perf. 11½x12*

176	A25	1fr brown	.80	
177	A25	2.50fr blue	.80	
		Set, never hinged	2.00	

Nos. 176-177 were issued by the Vichy government in France, but were not placed on sale in Réunion.

For surcharges, see Nos. B13-B14.

No. 144 Surcharged in Carmine

1943

177A	1fr on 65c olive grn	1.10	.65
	Never hinged	1.60	

De Pronis Landing on Reunion — A25a

1943 *Perf. 12½x12*

177B	A25a	60c blk brn & red	.55	
177C	A25a	80c green & blue	.40	
177D	A25a	1.50fr dk brn red	.35	
177E	A25a	4fr ultra & red	.35	
177F	A25a	5fr red brn & black	.55	
177G	A25a	10fr violet & green	.65	
		Nos. 177B-177G,C13A-C13F (12)	5.70	
		Set, never hinged	8.00	

300th Ann. of French settlement on Réunion.

Nos. 177B-177G were issued by the Vichy government in France, but were not placed on sale in Réunion.

Stamps of 1907 Overprinted in Blue Violet

q

1943 Unwmk. *Perf. 14x13½*

178	A19(q)	4c ol gray & pale red	6.00	6.00
179	A20(q)	75c red & lil rose	1.75	1.75
180	A21(q)	5fr car & vio brn	60.00	60.00

Stamps of 1933-40 Overprinted in Carmine, Black or Blue Violet

181	A22(r)	1c rose vio (C)	1.00	1.00
182	A22(r)	2c blk brn (C)	1.00	1.00
183	A22(r)	3c rose vio (C)	1.00	1.00
184	A22(r)	4c ol yel (C)	1.00	1.00
185	A22(r)	5c red org	1.00	1.00
186	A22(r)	10c ultra (C)	1.00	1.00
187	A22(r)	15c blk (C)	1.00	1.00
188	A22(r)	20c ind (C)	1.00	1.00
189	A22(r)	25c red brn (BIV)	1.25	1.25
190	A22(r)	30c dk grn (C)	1.40	1.40
191	A23(q)	35c green	1.00	1.00
192	A23(q)	40c dl ultra (C)	1.00	1.00
193	A23(q)	40c brn blk (C)	1.00	1.00
194	A23(q)	45c red vio	1.00	1.00
195	A23(q)	45c green	1.00	1.00
196	A23(q)	50c org red	1.00	1.00
197	A23(q)	55c brn org	1.00	1.00
198	A23(q)	60c dl bl (C)	3.00	3.00
199	A23(q)	65c ol grn	1.00	1.00
200	A23(q)	70c ol grn (C)	2.25	2.25
201	A23(q)	75c dk brn (C)	5.25	5.25
202	A23(q)	80c blk (C)	1.00	1.00
203	A23(q)	90c dl rose vio	1.00	1.00
204	A23(q)	1fr green	1.00	1.00
205	A23(q)	1fr dk car	1.00	1.00
206	A23(q)	1fr blk (C)	3.00	3.00
207	A24(q)	1.25fr org brn (BIV)	1.00	1.00
208	A24(q)	1.25fr brt car rose	3.00	3.00
209	A22(r)	1.40fr pck bl (C)	2.00	2.00
210	A24(q)	1.50fr ultra (C)	1.00	1.00
211	A22(r)	1.60fr dk car rose	2.10	2.10
212	A24(q)	1.75fr ol grn (C)	2.75	2.75
213	A22(r)	1.75fr dk bl (C)	4.50	4.50
214	A24(q)	2fr vermilion	1.00	1.00
215	A22(r)	2.25fr brt ultra (C)	4.50	4.50
216	A22(r)	2.50fr chnt (BIV)	7.50	7.50
217	A24(q)	3fr pur (C)	1.00	1.00
218	A24(q)	5fr brn lake (BIV)	2.10	2.10
219	A24(q)	10fr dk bl (C)	8.50	8.50
220	A24(q)	20fr red brn (BIV)	13.00	13.00

New York World's Fair Issue Overprinted in Black or Carmine

221	CD82(q)	1.25fr car lake	4.00	4.00
222	CD82(q)	2.25fr ultra (C)	4.00	4.00
		Nos. 178-222 (45)	165.85	165.85
		Set, never hinged	235.00	

No. 177A Overprinted Type "q"

1943 Unwmk. *Perf. 12½*

223	A23	1fr on 65c ol grn	.85	.85

Catalogue values for unused stamps in this section, from this point to the end of the section, are for Never Hinged items.

Produce of Réunion A26

1943 Photo. *Perf. 14½x14*

224	A26	5c dull brown	.25	.25
225	A26	10c dk blue	.25	.25
226	A26	25c emerald	.25	.25
227	A26	30c dp orange	.25	.25
228	A26	40c dk slate grn	.25	.25
229	A26	80c rose violet	.65	.50
230	A26	1fr red brown	.25	.25
231	A26	1.50fr crimson	.65	.50
232	A26	2fr black	.65	.50
233	A26	2.50fr ultra	1.00	.70
234	A26	4fr dk violet	1.25	.90
235	A26	5fr bister	1.25	.90
236	A26	10fr dark brown	1.75	1.40
237	A26	20fr dark green	2.75	1.75
		Nos. 224-237 (14)	11.45	8.65

For surcharges see Nos. 240-247.

Type of 1933-40 without "RF"

1944 Engr. *Perf. 12½*

237A	A23	60c dull blue	1.40	1.00
237B	A23	1fr black & blue	1.40	1.00

Nos. 237A-237B were issued by the Vichy government in France, but were not placed on sale in Réunion.

Eboue Issue
Common Design Type

1945 Engr. *Perf. 13*

238	CD91	2fr black	1.00	1.00
239	CD91	25fr Prussian green	1.40	1.00

Nos. 224, 226 and 233 Surcharged with New Values and Bars in Carmine or Black

1945 *Perf. 14½x14*

240	A26	50c on 5c dl brn (C)	.30	.25
241	A26	60c on 5c dl brn (C)	.30	.25
242	A26	70c on 5c dl brn (C)	.30	.25
243	A26	1.20fr on 5c dl brn (C)	.70	.50
244	A26	2.40fr on 25c emer	.70	.50
245	A26	3fr on 25c emer	1.25	.90
246	A26	4.50fr on 25c emer	1.25	.90
247	A26	15fr on 2.50fr ultra (C)	1.75	1.10
		Nos. 240-247 (8)	6.55	4.65

Various double and inverted overprints exist for Nos. 240-247.

Cliff — A27

Cutting Sugar Cane — A28

Cascade A29

Banana Tree A30

Mountain Scene A31

Ship Approaching Réunion — A32

1947 Unwmk. Photo. *Perf. 13½*

249	A27	10c org & grnsh blk	.25	.25
250	A27	30c org & brt bl	.25	.25
251	A27	40c org & brn	.25	.25
252	A28	50c bl grn & brn	.25	.25
253	A28	60c dk bl & brn	.25	.25
254	A28	80c brn & ol brn	.55	.45
255	A29	1fr dl bl & vio brn	.55	.45
256	A29	1.20fr bl grn & gray	.80	.65
257	A29	1.50fr org & vio brn	.80	.65
258	A30	2fr gray bl & bl grn	.80	.65
259	A30	3fr vio brn & bl grn	.80	.65
260	A30	3.60fr dl red & rose red	.90	.70
261	A30	4fr gray bl & buff	.80	.70
262	A31	5fr rose lil & brn	1.25	.70
263	A31	6fr bl & brn	1.50	.75
264	A31	10fr org & ultra	3.25	1.50
265	A32	15fr gray bl & vio brn	4.75	2.75
266	A32	20fr bl & org	6.50	4.00
267	A32	25fr rose lil & brn	8.00	4.25
		Nos. 249-267 (19)	32.50	20.10

Nos. 249-267 exist imperf. Value, set $100.

Stamps of France, 1945-49, Surcharged type "a" or "b" in Black or Carmine

On A147

Others

1949 Unwmk. *Perf. 14x13½, 13*

268	A153	10c on 30c	.30	.25
269	A153	30c on 50c	.60	.25
270	A146	50c on 1fr	1.40	.90
271	A146	60c on 2fr	8.00	1.40
272	A147	1fr on 3fr	2.00	.70
273	A147	2fr on 4fr	8.00	1.60
274	A147	2.50fr on 5fr	20.00	11.00
275	A147	3fr on 6fr	2.25	1.40
276	A147	4fr on 10fr	2.00	1.60
277	A162	5fr on 20fr (C)	10.00	1.40
278	A147	6fr on 12fr	29.00	2.25
279	A160	7fr on 12fr	9.00	3.00
280	A165	8fr on 25fr (C)	37.50	3.25
281	A165	10fr on 25fr (C)	2.75	1.40
282	A174	11fr on 18fr (C)	16.00	2.25
		Nos. 268-282 (15)	148.80	32.65

The letters "C. F. A." are the initials of "Colonies Francaises d'Afrique," referring to the currency which is expressed in French Africa francs.

The surcharge on Nos. 277, 279, 282 includes two bars.

1950 *Perf. 14x13½*

283	A182	10c on 50c bl, red & yel	.55	.55
284	A182	1fr on 2fr grn, yel & red (#619)	10.00	3.50
285	A147	2fr on 5fr lt grn	18.00	4.25
		Nos. 283-285 (3)	28.55	8.30

Surcharged Type "a" and Bars

1950-51 *Perf. 13*

286	A188	5fr on 20fr dk red	10.00	1.75
287	A185	8fr on 25fr dp ultra ('51)	10.00	1.75

Stamps of France, 1951-52, Surcharged in Black or Red

1951-52 *Perf. 14x13½, 13*

288	A182	50c on 1fr bl, red & yel	.70	.70
289	A182	1fr on 2fr vio bl, red & yel (#662)	.70	.70
290	A147	2fr on 5fr dl vio	4.25	2.00
291	A147	3fr on 6fr grn	8.00	1.60
292	A220	5fr on 20fr dk pur (R; '52)	3.00	1.75
293	A147	6fr on 12fr red org ('52)	9.00	2.00
294	A215	8fr on 40fr vio (R) ('52)	6.50	.70
295	A147	9fr on 18fr cerise	21.00	4.25
296	A208	15fr on 30fr ind (R)	11.00	2.25
		Nos. 288-296 (9)	64.15	15.95

The surcharge on Nos. 292, 294 and 296 include two bars.

France No. 697 Surcharged Type "a" in Black

1953 *Perf. 14x13½*

297	A182	50c on 1fr blk, red & yel	.35	.25

France No. 688 Surcharged Type "c" in Black

Perf. 13

298	A230	3fr on 6fr dp plum & car	1.20	.80

France Nos. 703 and 705 Surcharged Type "a" in Red or Blue

1954

299	A235	8fr on 40fr (R)	38.50	7.50
300	A235	20fr on 75fr	80.00	32.50

France Nos. 698, 721, 713, and 715 Surcharged Type "a" in Black

Perf. 14x13½, 13

301	A182	1fr on 2fr	4.75	2.10
302	A241	4fr on 10fr	4.50	1.25
303	A238	8fr on 40fr	11.00	1.60
304	A238	20fr on 75fr	14.50	1.60

The surcharge on Nos. 303 and 304 includes two bars.

France Nos. 737, 719 and 722-724 Surcharged in Black or Red

a

b

305	A182(b)	1fr on 2fr	.50	.50
306	A241(a)	2fr on 6fr (R)	.80	.50
307	A242(a)	6fr on 12fr	11.00	1.75
308	A241(b)	9fr on 18fr	12.00	5.00
309	A241(a)	10fr on 20fr	8.00	1.40
		Nos. 299-309 (11)	185.55	55.70

The surcharge on Nos. 306-308 includes two bars; on No. 309 three bars.

France No. 720 Surcharged Type "c" in Red, Bars at Lower Left

1955 *Perf. 13*
310 A241 3fr on 8fr brt bl & dk grn 1.40 1.10

France Nos. 785, 774-779 Surcharged Type "a" in Black or Red

Perf. 14x13½, 13

1955-56 **Typo., Engr.**
311 A182 50c on 1fr .45 .30
312 A265 2fr on 6fr ('56) 1.20 .70
313 A265 3fr on 8fr 1.00 .50
314 A265 4fr on 10fr 1.25 .50
315 A265 5fr on 12fr (R) 1.30 .50
316 A265 6fr on 18fr (R) 1.00 .50
317 A265 10fr on 25fr 1.75 .50
Nos. 311-317 (7) 7.95 3.50

The surcharge on Nos. 312-317 includes two bars.

France Nos. 801-804 Surcharged Type "a" or "b" in Black or Red

1956 **Engr.** *Perf. 13*
318 A280(a) 8fr on 30fr (R) 5.25 1.10
319 A280(b) 9fr on 40fr 7.75 3.00
320 A280(a) 15fr on 50fr 9.25 1.60
321 A280(a) 20fr on 75fr (R) 8.50 2.25
Nos. 318-321 (4) 30.75 7.95

The surcharge on Nos. 318, 319 and 321 includes two bars.

France Nos. 837 and 839 Surcharged Type "a" in Red

1957 *Perf. 13*
322 A294 7fr on 15fr 1.20 .55
323 A265 17fr on 70fr 6.75 2.10

The surcharge on Nos. 322-323 includes two bars.

No. 322 has three types of "7" in the sheet of 50. There are 34 of the "normal" 7; 10 of a slightly thinner 7, and 6 of a slightly thicker 7.

France Nos. 755-756, 833-834, 851-855, 908, 949 Surcharged in Black or Red Type "a", "b" or

d

Typographed, Engraved

1957-60 *Perf. 14x13½, 13*
324 A236(b) 2fr on 6fr .30 .30
325 A302(b) 3fr on 10fr ('58) .50 .50
326 A236(b) 4fr on 12fr 3.50 .75
327 A236(b) 5fr on 10fr 2.25 1.10
328 A303(b) 6fr on 18fr 1.25 .50
329 A302(a) 9fr on 25fr (R) ('58) 1.25 .65
330 A252(a) 10fr on 20fr (R) 1.75 .30
331 A252(a) 12fr on 25fr 6.75 .50
332 A303(a) 17fr on 35fr 3.75 1.75
333 A302(a) 20fr on 50fr 1.75 .80
334 A302(a) 25fr on 85fr 4.00 1.60
335 A339(d) 50fr on 1fr ('60) 3.00 .75
Nos. 324-335 (12) 30.05 9.50

The surcharge includes two bars on Nos. 324, 326-327, 329-331, 333 and 335.

France Nos. 973, 939 and 968 Surcharged

e

f

1961-63 **Typo.** *Perf. 14x13½*
336 A318(e) 2fr on 5c multi .30 .25
337 A336(e) 5fr on 10c brt grn 1.30 .50
338 A336(b) 5fr on 10c brt grn ('63) 1.60 .75
339 A349(f) 12fr on 25c lake & gray .30 .30
Nos. 336-339 (4) 3.50 1.80

The surcharge on No. 337 includes three bars. No. 338 has "b" surcharge and two bars.

France Nos. 943, 941 and 946 Surcharged in Black or Red

Engraved, Typographed

1961 **Unwmk.** *Perf. 13, 14x13½*
340 A338 7fr on 15c 1.00 .80
341 A337 10fr on 20c .30 .30
342 A339 20fr on 50c (R) 17.00 4.50
Nos. 340-342 (3) 18.30 5.60

Surcharge on No. 342 includes 3 bars.

France Nos. 1047-1048 Surcharged

No. 343

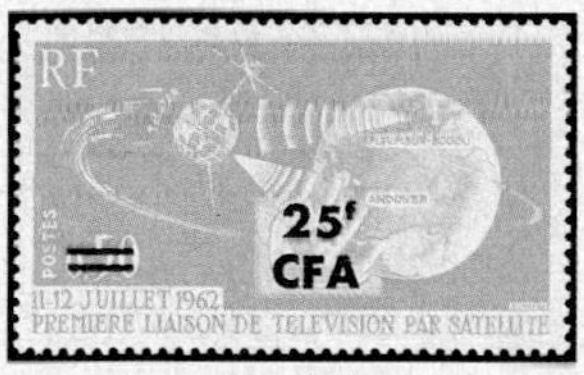

No. 344

1963, Jan. 2 **Engr.** *Perf. 13*
343 A394 12fr on 25c 1.00 .95
344 A395 25fr on 50c 1.00 .95

1st television connection of the US and Europe through the Telstar satellite, July 11-12, 1962.

France Nos. 1040-1041, 1007 and 1009 Surcharged

No. 345

No. 346

No. 347

No. 348

Typographed, Engraved

1963 *Perf. 14x13½, 13*
345 A318 2fr on 5c .30 .30
346 A318 5fr on 10c .25 .25
347 A372 7fr on 15c .60 .50
348 A372 20fr on 45c 1.25 .75
Nos. 345-348 (4) 2.40 1.80

Two-line surcharge on No. 345; No. 347 has currency expressed in capital "F" and two heavy bars through old value; two thin bars on No. 348.

France No. 1078 Surcharged

1964, Feb. 8 **Engr.** *Perf. 13*
349 CD118 12fr on 25c 1.25 1.25

"PHILATEC," Intl. Philatelic and Postal Techniques Exhib., Paris, June 5-21, 1964.

France Nos. 1092, 1094 and 1102 Surcharged

Typographed, Engraved

1964 *Perf. 14x13½, 13*
350 A318 1fr on 2c .25 .25
351 A318 6fr on 18c .30 .30
352 A420 35fr on 70c 1.50 .95
Nos. 350-352 (3) 2.05 1.50

Surcharge on No. 352 includes two bars.

France Nos. 1095, 1126, 1070 Surcharged

No. 353

No. 354

No. 355

1965
353 A318 15fr on 30c .50 .30
354 A440 25fr on 50c 1.00 .95
355 A408 30fr on 60c 1.50 1.00
Nos. 353-355 (3) 3.00 2.25

Two bars obliterate old denomination on Nos. 354-355.

Etienne Regnault, "Le Taureau" and Coast of Reunion — A33

1965, Oct. 3 **Engr.** *Perf. 13*
356 A33 15fr bluish blk & dk car 1.00 .65

Tercentenary of settlement of Reunion.

France No. 985 Surcharged

1966, Feb. 13 **Engr.** *Perf. 13*
357 A360 10fr on 20c bl & car 1.60 .70

French Satellite A-1 Issue
France Nos. 1137-1138 Surcharged in Red

1966, Mar. 27 **Engr.** *Perf. 13*
358 CD121 15fr on 30c 1.10 1.00
359 CD121 30fr on 60c 1.30 1.10
a. Strip of 2 + label 3.50 3.00

France Nos. 1142, 1143, 1101 and 1127 Surcharged with New Value, "CFA" and Two Bars

1967-69 **Typo.** *Perf. 14x13*
360 A446 2fr on 5c bl & red .30 .30

Photo. *Perf. 13*
360A A446 10fr on 20c multi ('69) .30 .30

Engr.
361 A421 20fr on 40c multi 1.10 .95
362 A439 30fr on 60c bl & red brn 1.30 .75

EXPO '67 Issue
France No. 1177 Surcharged with New Value, "CFA" and Two Bars

1967, June 12 **Engr.** *Perf. 13*
363 A473 30fr on 60c dl bl & bl grn 2.40 1.75

EXPO '67, Montreal, Apr. 28-Oct. 27.

Lions Issue
France No. 1196 Surcharged in Violet Blue with New Value, "CFA" and Two Bars

1967, Oct. 29 **Engr.** *Perf. 13*
364 A485 20fr on 40c 3.00 1.20

50th anniversary of Lions International.

France No. 1130 Surcharged in Violet Blue with New Value, "CFA" and Two Bars

1968, Feb. 26 **Engr.** *Perf. 13*
365 A440 50fr on 1fr 2.75 1.60

France No. 1224 Surcharged with New Value, "CFA" and Two Bars

1968, Oct. 21 **Engr.** *Perf. 13*
366 A508 20fr on 40c multi 1.50 1.00

20 years of French Polar expeditions.

France Nos. 1230-1231 Surcharged with New Value, "CFA" and Two Bars

1969, Apr. 13 **Engr.** *Perf. 13*
367 A486 15fr on 30c green .65 .50
368 A486 20fr on 40c dp car .70 .30

France No. 1255 Surcharged with New Value, "CFA" and Two Bars

1969, Aug. 18 **Engr.** *Perf. 13*
370 A526 35fr on 70c multi 1.60 1.35

Napoleon Bonaparte (1769-1821).

France No. 1293 Surcharged with New Value and "CFA"

1971, Jan. 16 **Engr.** *Perf. 13*
371 A555 25fr on 50c rose car .90 .30

France No. 1301 Surcharged with New Value and "CFA"

1971, Apr. 13 **Engr.** *Perf. 13*
372 A562 40fr on 80c multi 2.00 1.40

France No. 1309 Surcharged with New Value, "CFA" and 2 Bars

1971, June 5 Engr. *Perf. 13*
373 A569 15fr on 40c multi 1.00 .70

Aid for rural families.

France No. 1312 Surcharged with New Value and "CFA"

1971, Aug. 30 Engr. *Perf. 13*
374 A571 45fr on 90c multi 1.15 .95

France No. 1320 Surcharged with New Value and "CFA"

1971, Oct. 18
375 A573 45fr on 90c multi 1.40 1.00

40th anniversary of the first assembly of presidents of artisans' guilds.

Réunion Chameleon A34

1971, Nov. 8 Photo. *Perf. 13*
376 A34 25fr multi 1.40 1.10

Nature protection.

Common Design Type and

De Gaulle in Brazzaville, 1944 — A35

Designs: No. 377, Gen. de Gaulle, 1940. No. 379, de Gaulle entering Paris, 1944. No. 380, Pres. de Gaulle, 1970.

1971, Nov. 9 Engr.
377 CD134 25fr black 1.60 1.60
378 A35 25fr ultra 1.60 1.60
379 A35 25fr rose red 1.60 1.60
380 CD134 25fr black 1.60 1.60
a. Strip of 4 + label 9.25 8.00

Charles de Gaulle (1890-1970), president of France.

Nos. 377-380 printed se-tenant in sheets of 20 containing 5 strips of 4 plus labels with Cross of Lorraine and inscription. Exists imperf. Value, strip $200.

France No. 1313 Surcharged with New Value and "CFA"

1972, Jan. 17 Engr. *Perf. 13*
381 A570 50fr on 1.10fr multi 1.40 1.15

Map of South Indian Ocean, Penguin and Ships — A36

1972, Jan. 31 Engr. *Perf. 13*
382 A36 45fr blk, bl & ocher 2.25 2.25

Bicentenary of the discovery of the Crozet and Kerguelen Islands.

France No. 1342 Surcharged with New New Value, "CFA" and 2 Bars in Red

1972, May. 8 Engr. *Perf. 13*
383 A590 15fr on 40c red 1.00 .95

20th anniv. of Blood Donors' Assoc. of Post and Telecommunications Employees.

France Nos. 1345-1346 Surcharged with New Value, "CFA" and 2 Bars

1972, June 5 Typo. *Perf. 14x13*
384 A593 15fr on 30c multi .45 .45
385 A593 25fr on 50c multi .75 .65

Introduction of postal code system.

France No. 1377 Surcharged with New Value, "CFA" and 2 Bars in Ultramarine

1973, June 12 Engr. *Perf. 13*
386 A620 45fr on 90c multi 2.00 1.35

France Nos. 1374, 1336 Surcharged with New Value and "CFA" in Ultramarine or Red

1973 Engr. *Perf. 13*
387 A617 50fr on 1fr multi (U) 1.15 .95
388 A586 100fr on 2fr multi (R) 2.00 1.10

On No. 388, two bars cover "2.00".
Issue dates: 50fr, June 24; 100fr, Oct. 13.

France No. 1231C Surcharged with New Value, "CFA" and 2 Bars

1973, Nov. Typo. *Perf. 14x13*
389 A486 15fr on 30c bl grn 5.00 .80

France No. 1390 Surcharged with New Value, "CFA" and 2 Bars in Red

1974, Jan. 20 Engr. *Perf. 13*
390 A633 25fr on 50c multi .70 .70

ARPHILA 75 Phil. Exhib., Paris, June 1975.

France Nos. 1394-1397 Surcharged in Black, Ultramarine or Brown

No. 391

No. 394

Engr. (#391, 393), Photo. (#392, 394)
1974 *Perf. 12x13, 13x12*
391 A637 100fr on 2fr (Blk) 2.50 2.40
392 A638 100fr on 2fr (U) 3.25 2.40
393 A639 100fr on 2fr (Br) 3.25 2.40
394 A640 100fr on 2fr (U) 3.25 2.40
Nos. 391-394 (4) 12.25 9.60

Nos. 391-394 printed in sheets of 25 with alternating labels publicizing "ARPHILA 75," Paris June 6-16, 1975.

Two bars obliterate original denomination on Nos. 391-393.

France No. 1401 Surcharged in Red

1974, Apr. 29 Engr. *Perf. 13*
395 A644 45fr on 90c multi 1.90 1.40

Reorganized sea rescue organization.

France No. 1415 Surcharged in Ultramarine

1974, Oct. 6 Engr. *Perf. 13*
396 A657 60fr on 1.20fr multi 1.60 1.35

Centenary of Universal Postal Union.

France Nos. 1292A and 1294B Surcharged in Ultramarine

1974, Oct. 19 Typo. *Perf. 14x13*
397 A555 30fr on 60c grn 1.75 1.60

Engr.
Perf. 13
398 A555 40fr on 80c car rose 2.10 1.75

SEMI-POSTAL STAMPS

No. 65 Surcharged in Black or Red

1915 Unwmk. *Perf. 14x13½*
B1 A19 10c + 5c (Bk) 160.00 120.00
a. Inverted surcharge 450.00 350.00
B2 A19 10c + 5c (R) 1.75 1.75
a. Inverted surcharge 77.50 77.50
b. Double surcharge, both inverted 675.00 675.00

No. 65 Surcharged in Red

1916
B3 A19 10c + 5c 1.90 1.90

Curie Issue
Common Design Type

1938 *Perf. 13*
B4 CD80 1.75fr + 50c brt ultra 14.00 14.00
Never hinged 24.00

French Revolution Issue
Common Design Type

1939 Photo. Unwmk.
Name and Value Typo. in Black
B5 CD83 45c + 25c grn 12.50 12.50
B6 CD83 70c + 30c brn 12.50 12.50
B7 CD83 90c + 35c red org 12.50 12.50
B8 CD83 1.25fr + 1fr rose pink 12.50 12.50
B9 CD83 2.25fr + 2fr blue 12.50 12.50
Nos. B5-B9 (5) 62.50 62.50
Set, never hinged 110.00

See CB1.

Common Design Type and

Artillery Colonel — SP1

Colonial Infantry SP2

1941 Unwmk. *Perf. 13½*
B10 SP1 1fr + 1fr red 1.60
B11 CD86 1.50fr + 3fr claret 1.60
B12 SP2 2.50fr + 1fr blue 1.60
Nos. B10-B12 (3) 4.80
Set, never hinged 6.50

Nos. B10-B12 were issued by the Vichy government in France, but were not placed on sale in Reunion. Nos. B10-B12 exist imperf. Value, set $200.

Nos. 176-177 Surcharged in Black or Red

1944 Engr. *Perf. 12½x12*
B13 50c + 1.50fr on 2.50fr deep blue (R) .80
B14 + 2.50fr on 1fr yel brn .80
Set, never hinged 2.00

Colonial Development Fund.

Nos. B13-B14 were issued by the Vichy government in France, but were not placed on sale in Réunion.

Catalogue values for unused stamps in this section, from this point to the end of the section, are for Never Hinged items.

Red Cross Issue
Common Design Type

1944 *Perf. 14½x14*
B15 CD90 5fr + 20fr black 1.60 1.10

The surtax was for the French Red Cross and national relief.

France Nos. B365-B366 Surcharged with New Value, "CFA" and Two Bars

1962, Dec. 10 Engr. *Perf. 13*
B16 SP219 10 + 5fr on 20 + 10c 2.50 2.50
B17 SP219 12 + 5fr on 25 + 10c 2.75 2.75

The surtax was for the Red Cross.

France Nos. B374-B375 Surcharged with New Value, "CFA" and Two Bars in Red

1963, Dec. 9
B18 SP223 10 + 5fr on 20 + 10c 3.00 3.00
B19 SP223 12 + 5fr on 25 + 10c 3.00 3.00

Centenary of the Intl. Red Cross. The surtax was for the Red Cross.

France Nos. B385-B386 Surcharged with New Value, "CFA" and Two Bars in Dark Blue

1964, Dec. 13 Unwmk. *Perf. 13*
B20 SP230 10 + 5fr on 20 + 10c 1.75 1.75
B21 SP230 12 + 5fr on 25 + 10c 1.90 1.90

Jean Nicolas Corvisart (1755-1821) and Dominique Larrey (1766-1842), physicians. The surtax was for the Red Cross.

France Nos. B392-B393 Surcharged with New Value, "CFA" and Two Bars

1965, Dec. 12 Engr. *Perf. 13*
B22 SP233 12 + 5fr on 25 + 10c 1.60 1.60
B23 SP233 15 + 5fr on 30 + 10c 1.60 1.60

The surtax was for the Red Cross.

France Nos. B402-B403 Surcharged with New Value, "CFA" and Two Bars

1966, Dec. 11 Engr. *Perf. 13*
B24 SP237 12 + 5fr on 25 + 10c 1.50 1.50
B25 SP237 15 + 5fr on 30 + 10c 1.50 1.50

The surtax was for the Red Cross.

France Nos. B409-B410 Surcharged with New Value, "CFA" and Two Bars

1967, Dec. 17 **Engr.** ***Perf. 13***
B26 SP240 12 + 5fr on 25 + 10c 3.00 3.00
B27 SP240 15 + 5fr on 30 + 10c 3.75 3.75

Surtax for the Red Cross.

France Nos. B421-B424 Surcharged with New Value, "CFA" and Two Bars

1968-69 **Engr.** ***Perf. 13***
B28 SP244 12 + 5fr on 25 + 10c 1.70 1.50
B29 SP244 15 + 5fr on 30 + 10c 1.90 1.50
B30 SP244 20 + 7fr on 40 + 15c ('69) 1.60 1.50
B31 SP244 20 + 7fr on 40 + 15c ('69) 1.60 1.50
Nos. B28-B31 (4) 6.80 6.00

The surtax was for the Red Cross.

France No. B425 Surcharged with New Value, "CFA" and Two Bars

1969, Mar. 17 **Engr.** ***Perf. 13***
B32 SP245 15fr + 5fr on 30c + 10c 1.40 1.40

Stamp Day.

France No. B440 Surcharged with New Value, "CFA" and Two Bars

1970, Mar. 16 **Engr.** ***Perf. 13***
B33 SP249 20fr + 5fr on 40c + 10c 1.10 .95

Stamp day.

France Nos. B443-B444 Surcharged with New Value "CFA" and Two Bars

1970, Dec. 14 **Engr.** ***Perf. 13***
B34 SP252 20 + 7fr on 40 + 15c 2.40 2.00
B35 SP252 20 + 7fr on 40 + 15c 2.40 2.40

The surtax was for the Red Cross.

France No. B451 Surcharged with New Value, "CFA" and Two Bars

1971, Mar. 29 **Engr.** ***Perf. 13***
B36 SP254 25fr + 5fr on 50c + 10c 1.10 .90

Stamp Day.

France Nos. B452-B453 Surcharged with New Value, "CFA" and Two Bars

1971, Dec. 13
B37 SP255 15fr + 5fr on 30c + 10c 1.40 1.40
B38 SP255 25fr + 5fr on 50c + 10c 1.40 1.40

The surtax was for the Red Cross.

France No. B460 Surcharged with New Value and "CFA"

1972, Mar. 20 **Engr.** ***Perf. 13***
B39 SP257 25fr + 5fr on 50c + 10c 1.20 1.20

Stamp Day.

France Nos. B461-B462 Surcharged with New Value, "CFA" and Two Bars in Red or Green

1972, Dec. 16 **Engr.** ***Perf. 13***
B40 SP258 15 + 5fr on 30 + 10c 1.20 1.20
B41 SP258 25 + 5fr on 50 + 10c (G) 1.40 1.40

Surtax was for the Red Cross.

France No. B470 Surcharged with New Value, "CFA" and Two Bars in Red

1973, Mar. 26 **Engr.** ***Perf. 13***
B42 SP260 25fr +5fr on 50c +10c 1.40 1.40

Stamp Day.

France Nos. B471-B472 Surcharged with New Value, "CFA" and Two Bars in Red

1973, Dec. 3 **Engr.** ***Perf. 13***
B43 SP261 15 +5fr on 30c +10c 1.40 1.40
B44 SP261 25 +5fr on 50c +10c 1.40 1.40

Surtax was for the Red Cross.

France No. B477 Surcharged

1974, Mar. 11 **Engr.** ***Perf. 13***
B45 SP263 25fr + 5fr on 50c + 10c 1.10 1.10

Stamp Day.

France Nos. B479-B480 Surcharged with New Value, "FCFA" and Two Bars in Green or Red

1974, Nov. 30 **Engr.** ***Perf. 13***
B46 SP265 30 + 7fr on 60 + 15c (G) 1.40 1.40
B47 SP266 40 + 7fr on 80 + 15c (R) 1.40 1.40

Surtax was for the Red Cross.

AIR POST STAMPS

No. 141 Ovptd. in Blue

1937, Jan. 23 **Unwmk.** ***Perf. 12½***
C1 A23 50c red 290.00 250.00
a. Vert. pair, one without overprint 1,800. 1,800.
b. Inverted overprint 6,000.
c. As "b," in pair with unoverprinted stamp 26,000.

Flight of the "Roland Garros" from Reunion to France by aviators Laurent, Lenier and Touge in Jan.-Feb., 1937.

Airplane and Landscape — AP2

1938, Mar. 1 **Engr.** ***Perf. 12½***
C2 AP2 3.65fr slate blue & car 1.00 .90
C3 AP2 6.65fr brown & org red 1.00 .90
C4 AP2 9.65fr car & ultra 1.00 .90
C5 AP2 12.65fr brown & green 2.00 1.50
Nos. C2-C5 (4) 5.00 4.20
Set, never hinged 7.00

For overprints see Nos. C14-C17.

Plane and Bridge over East River AP3

Plane and Landscape AP4

1942, Oct. 19 ***Perf. 12x12½***
C6 AP3 50c olive & pur .35
C7 AP3 1fr dk bl & scar .35
C8 AP3 2fr brn & blk .60
C9 AP3 3fr rose lil & grn 1.10
C10 AP3 5fr red org & red brn 1.10

Frame Engr., Center Photo.
C11 AP4 10fr dk grn, red org & vio 1.10
C12 AP4 20fr dk bl, brn vio & red 1.10
C13 AP4 50fr brn car, Prus grn & bl 1.60
Nos. C6-C13 (8) 7.30
Set, never hinged 9.50

Nos. C6-C13 were issued by the Vichy government in France, but were not placed on sale in Réunion.

De Poivre AP4a

1943 ***Perf. 12½x12***
C13A AP4a 1fr sepia & red .25
C13B AP4a 2fr green & blue .35
C13C AP4a 3fr dk brown red .40
C13D AP4a 5fr ultramarine & red .55
C13E AP4a 10fr red brown & black .55
C13F AP4a 20fr violet & green .75
Nos. C13A-C13F (6) 2.85
Set, never hinged 4.00

300th Ann. of French settlement on Réunion.
Nos. C13A-C13F were issued by the Vichy government in France, but were not placed on sale in Réunion.

Nos. C2-C5 Overprinted in Black or Carmine

1943 **Unwmk.** ***Perf. 12½***
C14 AP2 3.65fr sl bl & car 5.50 5.50
C15 AP2 6.65fr brn & org red 5.50 5.50
C16 AP2 9.65fr car & ultra (C) 5.50 5.50
C17 AP2 12.65fr brn & grn 5.50 5.50
Nos. C14-C17 (4) 22.00 22.00
Set, never hinged 32.50

Catalogue values for unused stamps in this section, from this point to the end of the section, are for Never Hinged items.

Common Design Type

1944 **Photo.** ***Perf. 14½x14***
C18 CD87 1fr dk org .50 .30
C19 CD87 1.50fr brt red .50 .30
C20 CD87 5fr brn red .70 .45
C21 CD87 10fr black 1.10 .80
C22 CD87 25fr ultra 1.25 .95
C23 CD87 50fr dk grn 1.25 .95
C24 CD87 100fr plum 1.75 1.25
Nos. C18-C24 (7) 7.05 5.00

Victory Issue
Common Design Type

1946, May 8 **Engr.** ***Perf. 12½***
C25 CD92 8fr olive gray 1.10 .90

European victory of the Allied Nations in WWII.

Chad to Rhine Issue
Common Design Types

1946, June 6
C26 CD93 5fr orange 1.40 .85
C27 CD94 10fr sepia 1.40 .85
C28 CD95 15fr grnsh blk 1.40 .85
C29 CD96 20fr lilac rose 1.90 1.25
C30 CD97 25fr greenish blue 1.90 1.25
C31 CD98 50fr green 2.25 1.50
Nos. C26-C31 (6) 10.25 6.55

Shadow of Plane — AP5

Plane over Réunion — AP6

Air View of Réunion and Shadow of Plane — AP7

Perf. 13x12½
1947, Mar. 24 **Photo.** **Unwmk.**
C32 AP5 50fr ol grn & bl gray 11.00 8.00
C33 AP6 100fr dk brn & org 17.00 12.50
C34 AP7 200fr dk bl & org 21.00 14.00
Nos. C32-C34 (3) 49.00 34.50

France, Nos. C18-C21 Surcharged in Carmine or Black — c

1949 **Unwmk.** ***Perf. 13***
C35 AP7 20fr on 40fr (C) 3.75 1.25
C36 AP8 25fr on 50fr 4.75 1.40
C37 AP9 50fr on 100fr (C) 11.00 4.25
C38 AP10 100fr on 200fr 55.00 21.00
Nos. C35-C38 (4) 74.50 27.90

France Nos. C24, C26 and C27 Surcharged Type "c" and Bars in Black

1949-51
C39 AP12 100fr on 200fr ('51) 145.00 26.50
C40 AP12 200fr on 500fr 55.00 21.00
C41 AP13 500fr on 1000fr ('51) 325.00 210.00
Nos. C39-C41 (3) 525.00 257.50

France Nos. C29-C32 Surcharged "CFA," New Value and Bars in Blue or Red

1954, Feb. 10
C42 AP15(c) 50fr on 100fr 3.50 1.25
C43 AP15 100fr on 200fr (R) 5.50 1.40
C44 AP15(c) 200fr on 500fr 45.00 12.50
C45 AP15 500fr on 1000fr 37.50 12.50
Nos. C42-C45 (4) 91.50 27.65

France Nos. C35-C36 Surcharged "CFA," New Values and Bars in Red or Black

1957-58 **Engr.** ***Perf. 13***
C46 AP17 200fr on 500fr (R) 25.00 6.75
C47 AP17 500fr on 1000fr ('58) 25.00 13.00

France Nos. C37, C39-C40 Surcharged "CFA," New Value and Bars in Red or Black

1961-64

C48	AP15 100fr on 2fr		6.75	1.40
C49	AP17 200fr on 5fr		7.00	3.25
C50	AP17 500fr on 10fr (B;'64)		16.00	6.25
	Nos. C48-C50 (3)		29.75	10.90

France No. C41 Surcharged "CFA," New Value and Two Bars in Red

1967, Jan. 27 Engr. *Perf. 13*

C51	AP17 100fr on 2fr sl bl & ind	2.25	.80

France No. C45 Surcharged in Red with "CFA," New Value and Two Bars in Red

1972, May 14 Engr. *Perf. 13*

C52	AP21 200fr on 5fr multi	5.00	1.75

AIR POST SEMI-POSTAL STAMP

French Revolution Issue
Common Design Type

1939 Unwmk. *Perf. 13*
Name and Value Typo. in Orange

CB1	CD83 3.65fr + 4fr brn blk	25.00	25.00
	Never hinged	37.50	

Felix Guyon Hospital, St. Denis — SPAP1

Perf. 13½x12½

1942, June 22 Engr.

CB2	SPAP1 1.50fr + 3.50fr lt green	1.00
CB3	SPAP1 2fr + 6fr yellow brown	1.00
	Set, never hinged	2.50

Native children's welfare fund.

Nos. CB2-CB3 were issued by the Vichy government in France, but were not placed on sale in Réunion.

Colonial Education Fund
Common Design Type

1942, June 22

CB4	CD86a 1.20fr + 1.80fr blue & red	.90
	Never hinged	1.25

No. CB4 was issued by the Vichy government in France, but was not placed on sale in Réunion.

POSTAGE DUE STAMPS

D1

D2

1889-92 Unwmk. Type-set *Imperf.*
Without Gum

J1	D1	5c black	29.00	16.00
J2	D1	10c black	35.00	16.00
J3	D1	15c black ('92)	67.50	42.50
J4	D1	20c black	50.00	27.50
J5	D1	30c black	45.00	27.50
		Nos. J1-J5 (5)	226.50	129.50

Ten varieties of each value.

Nos. J1-J2, J4-J5 issued on yellowish paper in 1889; Nos. J1-J3, J5 on bluish white paper in 1892.

Nos. J1-J5 exist with double impression. Values, each $125-$190.

1907 Typo. *Perf. 14x13½*

J6	D2	5c carmine, *yel*	.90	.90
J7	D2	10c blue, *bl*	.90	.90
J8	D2	15c black, *bluish*	1.50	1.50
J9	D2	20c carmine	1.50	1.50
J10	D2	30c green, *grnsh*	2.25	2.25
J11	D2	50c red, *green*	2.60	2.60
J12	D2	60c carmine, *bl*	2.60	2.60
J13	D2	1fr violet	3.00	3.00
		Nos. J6-J13 (8)	15.25	15.25
		Set, never hinged	27.50	

Type of 1907 Issue Surcharged

1927

J14	D2	2fr on 1fr org red	12.50	12.50
J15	D2	3fr on 1fr org brn	12.50	12.50
		Set, never hinged	40.00	

Arms of Réunion — D3

1933 Engr. *Perf. 13x13½*

J16	D3	5c deep violet	.25	.25
J17	D3	10c dark green	.25	.25
J18	D3	15c orange brown	.25	.25
J19	D3	20c light red	.35	.35
J20	D3	30c olive green	.35	.35
J21	D3	50c ultramarine	.80	.80
J22	D3	60c black brown	.80	.80
J23	D3	1fr light violet	.80	.80
J24	D3	2fr deep blue	.80	.80
J25	D3	3fr carmine	1.00	1.00
		Nos. J16-J25 (10)	5.65	5.65
		Set, never hinged	8.75	

Catalogue values for unused stamps in this section, from this point to the end of the section, are for Never Hinged items.

Numeral — D4

1947 Unwmk. Photo. *Perf. 13*

J26	D4	10c dark violet	.25	.25
J27	D4	30c brown	.25	.25
J28	D4	50c blue green	.25	.25
J29	D4	1fr orange	.60	.45
J30	D4	2fr red violet	.60	.45
J31	D4	3fr red brown	.85	.65
J32	D4	4fr blue	1.50	1.10
J33	D4	5fr henna brown	2.00	1.40
J34	D4	10fr slate green	2.00	1.40
J35	D4	20fr violet blue	2.00	.90
		Nos. J26-J35 (10)	10.30	7.10

France, Nos. J83-J92 Surcharged in Black

1949-53

J36	D5	10c on 1fr brt ultra	.25	.25
J37	D5	50c on 2fr turq bl	.45	.40
J38	D5	1fr on 3fr brn org	.60	.40
J39	D5	2fr on 4fr dp vio	.60	.40
J40	D5	3fr on 5fr brt pink	6.50	2.75
J41	D5	5fr on 10fr red org	1.10	.70
J42	D5	10fr on 20fr ol bis	2.00	2.00
J43	D5	20fr on 50fr dk grn ('50)	12.50	5.50
J44	D5	50fr on 100fr dp grn ('53)	30.00	13.00
		Nos. J36-J44 (9)	54.00	25.40

France Nos. J93, J95-J96 Surcharged

1962-63 Typo. *Perf. 14x13½*

J46	D6	1fr on 5c brt pink ('63)	3.00	1.10
J47	D6	10fr on 20c ol bis ('63)	5.50	2.75
J48	D6	20fr on 50c dk grn	22.00	12.50
		Nos. J46-J48 (3)	30.50	16.35

France Nos. J98-J102, J104-J105 Surcharged

1964-71 Unwmk. *Perf. 14x13½*

J49	D7	1fr on 5c	.25	.25
J50	D7	5fr on 10c	.30	.25
J51	D7	7fr on 15c	.50	.45
J52	D7	10fr on 20c ('71)	1.40	.55
J53	D7	15fr on 30c	.65	.45
J54	D7	20fr on 50c	.80	.55
J55	D7	50fr on 1fr	1.40	1.25
		Nos. J49-J55 (7)	5.30	3.75

PARCEL POST STAMP

No. 40 Overprinted

1906 Unwmk. *Perf. 14x13½*

Q1	A14 10c red	22.50	22.50

FRENCH COLONIES

ˈfrench ˈkä-lə-nēz

From 1859 to 1906 and from 1943 to 1945 special stamps were issued for use in all French Colonies which did not have stamps of their own.

100 Centimes = 1 Franc

Catalogue values for unused stamps in this country are for Never Hinged items, beginning with Scott B1 in the semi-postal section and Scott J23 in the postage due section.

Perforations: Nos. 1-45 are known variously perforated privately.

Gum: Many of Nos. 1-45 were issued without gum. Some were gummed locally.

Reprints: Nos. 1-7, 9-12, 24, 26-42, 44 and 45 were reprinted officially in 1887. These reprints are ungummed and the colors of both design and paper are deeper or brighter than the originals. Value for Nos. 1-6, $20 each.

Eagle and Crown — A1

1859-65 Unwmk. Typo. *Imperf.*

1	A1	1c ol grn, *pale bl* ('62)	24.00	*27.50*
2	A1	5c yel grn, *grnsh* ('62)	24.00	16.00
3	A1	10c bister, *yel*	32.50	8.00
a.		Pair, one sideways	1,000.	525.00
4	A1	20c bl, *bluish* ('65)	35.00	13.50
5	A1	40c org, *yelsh*	27.50	13.50
6	A1	80c car rose, *pnksh* ('65)	110.00	60.00
		Nos. 1-6 (6)	253.00	138.50

For surcharges, see Reunion Nos. 1-4.

Napoleon III
A2 A3

Ceres A4 Napoleon III A5

1871-72 *Imperf.*

7	A2	1c ol grn, *pale bl* ('72)	80.00	80.00
8	A3	5c yel grn, *grnsh* ('72)	1,000.	400.00
9	A4	10c bis, *yelsh*	375.00	130.00
a.		Tête bêche pair	*55,000.*	*22,500.*
10	A4	15c bis, *yelsh* ('72)	325.00	13.00
11	A4	20c blue, *bluish*	525.00	125.00
a.		Tête bêche pair	—	18,000.
12	A4	25c bl, *bluish* ('72)	175.00	13.00
13	A5	30c brn, *yelsh*	175.00	60.00
14	A4	40c org, *yelsh* (I)	250.00	13.00
a.		Type II	*3,500.*	*650.00*
b.		Pair, types I & II	*7,250.*	*1,750.*
15	A5	80c rose, *pnksh*	1,100.	115.00
		Nos. 7-15 (9)	4,005.	949.00

For 40c types I-II see illustrations over France #1.

For surcharges, see Reunion Nos. 5-6.

See note after France No. 9 for additional information on Nos. 8-9, 11-12, 14.

Ceres
A6 A7

1872-77 *Imperf.*

16	A6	1c ol grn, *pale bl* ('73)	13.00	*14.50*
17	A6	2c red brn, *yelsh* ('76)	475.00	750.00
18	A6	4c gray ('76)	*11,000.*	475.00
19	A6	5c grn, *pale bl*	17.50	9.50
20	A7	10c bis, *rose* ('76)	240.00	13.00
21	A7	15c bister ('77)	525.00	100.00
22	A7	30c brn, *yelsh*	130.00	21.00
23	A7	80c rose, *pnksh* ('73)	625.00	140.00

No. 17 was used only in Cochin China, 1876-77. Excellent forgeries of Nos. 17 and 18 exist.

With reference to the stamps of France and French Colonies in the same designs and colors see the note after France No. 9.

Peace and Commerce — A8

1877-78 Type I *Imperf.*

24	A8	1c grn, *grnsh*	35.00	*45.00*
25	A8	4c grn, *grnsh*	24.00	14.50
26	A8	30c brn, *yelsh* ('78)	52.50	52.50
27	A8	40c ver, *straw*	35.00	21.00
28	A8	75c rose, *rose* ('78)	75.00	*100.00*
29	A8	1fr brnz grn, *straw*	60.00	67.50
		Nos. 24-29 (6)	281.50	300.50

Type II

30	A8	2c grn, *grnsh*	17.50	11.00
31	A8	5c grn, *grnsh*	24.00	5.50
32	A8	10c grn, *grnsh*	125.00	24.00
33	A8	15c gray, *grnsh*	250.00	72.50
34	A8	20c red brn, *straw*	52.50	9.50
35	A8	25c ultra *bluish*	52.50	8.75
a.		25c blue, *bluish* ('78)	*4,250.*	175.00
36	A8	35c vio blk, *org* ('78)	67.50	32.50
		Nos. 30-36 (7)	589.00	163.75
		Nos. 24-36 (13)	870.50	464.25

Type II

1878-80

38	A8	1c blk, *lil bl*	21.00	21.00
39	A8	2c brn, *buff*	21.00	*24.00*
40	A8	4c claret, *lav*	32.50	*45.00*
41	A8	10c blk, *lav* ('79)	120.00	27.50
42	A8	15c blue ('79)	35.00	17.50
43	A8	20c red, *grn* ('79)	87.50	17.50
44	A8	25c blk, *red* ('79)	600.00	275.00
45	A8	25c yel, *straw* ('80)	725.00	32.50
		Nos. 38-45 (8)	1,642.	460.00

No. 44 was used only in Mayotte, Nossi-Be and New Caledonia. Forgeries exist.

The 3c yellow, 3c gray, 15c yellow, 20c blue, 25c rose and 5fr lilac were printed together with the reprints, and were never issued.

Commerce — A9

1881-86 ***Perf. 14x13½***

46	A9	1c blk, *lil bl*	5.50	4.75
47	A9	2c brn, *buff*	5.50	4.75
48	A9	4c claret, *lav*	5.50	5.50
49	A9	5c grn, *grnsh*	6.50	3.25
50	A9	10c blk, *lavender*	11.00	4.75
51	A9	15c blue	16.00	3.25
52	A9	20c red, *yel grn*	52.50	18.00
53	A9	25c yel, *straw*	17.50	5.50
54	A9	25c blk, *rose* ('86)	24.00	3.25
55	A9	30c brn, *bis*	45.00	21.00
56	A9	35c vio blk, *yel org*	40.00	30.00
a.		35c violet black, *yellow*	100.00	52.50
57	A9	40c ver, *straw*	45.00	27.50
58	A9	75c car, *rose*	120.00	60.00
59	A9	1fr brnz grn, *straw*	80.00	45.00
		Nos. 46-59 (14)	474.00	236.50

Nos. 46-59 exist imperforate. They are proofs and were not used for postage, except the 10c.

For stamps of type A9 surcharged with numerals see: Cochin China, Diego Suarez, Gabon, Malagasy (Madagascar), Nossi-Be, New Caledonia, Reunion, Senegal, Tahiti.

SEMI-POSTAL STAMPS

Catalogue values for unused stamps in this section are for Never Hinged items.

Resistance Fighters — SP1

1943 **Unwmk.** **Litho.** ***Rouletted***

B1	SP1	1.50fr + 98.50fr ind & gray	47.50	*65.00*
		Without label	21.00	*35.00*

The surtax was for the benefit of patriots and the French Committee of Liberation.

No. B1 was printed in sheets of 10 (5x2) with adjoining labels showing the Lorraine cross.

Colonies Offering Aid to France SP2

1943 ***Perf. 12***

B2	SP2	9fr + 41fr red violet	3.50	10.50

Surtax for the benefit of French patriots.

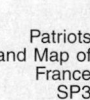

Patriots and Map of France SP3

1943

B3	SP3	50c + 4.50fr yel grn	1.25	*10.50*
B4	SP3	1.50fr + 8.50fr cerise	1.25	*10.50*
B5	SP3	3fr + 12fr grnsh bl	1.25	*10.50*
B6	SP3	5fr + 15fr olive gray	1.25	*1.50*
		Nos. B3-B6 (4)	5.00	33.00

Surtax for the aid of combatants and patriots.

Refugee Family SP4

1943

B7	SP4	10fr + 40fr dull blue	5.25	*12.50*

The surtax was for refugee relief work.

Woman and Child with Wing — SP5

1944

B8	SP5	10fr + 40fr grnsh blk	6.75	*21.00*

Surtax for the benefit of aviation.

Nos. B1-B8 were prepared for use in the French Colonies, but after the landing of Free French troops in Corsica they were used there and later also in Southern France. They became valid throughout France in Nov. 1944.

POSTAGE DUE STAMPS

D1

1884-85 **Unwmk.** **Typo.** ***Imperf.***

J1	D1	1c black	4.00	4.00
J2	D1	2c black	4.00	4.00
J3	D1	3c black	4.00	4.00
J4	D1	4c black	4.75	4.00
J5	D1	5c black	6.50	3.25
J6	D1	10c black	8.75	6.50
J7	D1	15c black	13.00	10.50
J8	D1	20c black	16.00	10.50
J9	D1	30c black	17.50	8.75
J10	D1	40c black	21.00	8.75
J11	D1	60c black	27.50	16.00
J12	D1	1fr brown	35.00	27.50
a.		1fr black	300.00	
J13	D1	2fr brown	35.00	27.50
a.		2fr black	300.00	*325.00*
J14	D1	5fr brown	110.00	67.50
a.		5fr black	425.00	*450.00*

Nos. J12a, J13a and J14a were not regularly issued.

1894-1906

J15	D1	5c pale blue	1.60	1.60
J16	D1	10c gray brown	1.60	1.60
J17	D1	15c pale green	1.60	1.60
J18	D1	20c olive grn ('06)	1.60	1.60
J19	D1	30c carmine	2.75	1.60
J20	D1	50c lilac	2.75	1.60
J21	D1	60c brown, *buff*	4.50	2.75
a.		60c dark violet, *buff*	4.75	2.75
J22	D1	1fr red, *buff*	7.50	4.50
a.		1fr rose, *buff*	27.50	19.00
		Nos. J15-J22 (8)	23.90	16.85

For overprints see New Caledonia Nos. J1-J8.

Catalogue values for unused stamps in this section, from this point to the end of the section, are for Never Hinged items.

D2

1945 **Litho.** ***Perf. 12***

J23	D2	10c slate blue	.45	*16.00*
J24	D2	15c yel green	.45	*16.00*
J25	D2	25c deep orange	.45	*16.00*
J26	D2	50c greenish blk	1.00	*16.00*
J27	D2	60c copper brn	1.00	*16.00*
J28	D2	1fr deep red lil	1.00	*16.00*
J29	D2	2fr red	1.00	*16.00*
J30	D2	4fr slate gray	4.50	*20.00*
J31	D2	5fr brt ultra	4.50	*20.00*
J32	D2	10fr purple	22.50	*52.50*
J33	D2	20fr dull brown	4.00	*20.00*
J34	D2	50fr deep green	7.25	*27.50*
		Nos. J23-J34 (12)	48.10	252.00

FRENCH CONGO

ˈfrench ˈkäŋ(ˌ)gō

LOCATION — Central Africa
GOVT. — French possession

French Congo was originally a separate colony, but was joined in 1888 to Gabon and placed under one commissioner-general with a lieutenant-governor presiding in Gabon and another in French Congo. In 1894 the military holdings in Ubangi were attached to French Congo, and in 1900 the Chad military protectorate was added. Postal service was not established in Ubangi or Chad, however, at that time. In 1906 Gabon and Middle Congo were separated and French Congo ceased to exist as such. Chad and Ubangi remained attached to Middle Congo as the joint dependency of "Ubangi-Chari-Chad," and Middle Congo stamps were used there.

Issues of the Republic of the Congo are listed under Congo People's Republic (ex-French).

100 Centimes = 1 Franc

Watermarks

Wmk. 122 Thistle Branch

Wmk. 123 — Rose Branch

Wmk. 124 Olive Branch

Stamps of French Colonies Surcharged Horizontally in Red or Black

1891 **Unwmk.** ***Perf. 14x13½***

1	A9	5c on 1c blk, *lil bl* (R)	*6,500.*	*4,750.*
a.		Double surcharge	20,000.	
2	A9	5c on 1c blk, *lil bl*	200.00	110.00
a.		Double surcharge	650.00	425.00
3	A9	5c on 15c blue	350.00	180.00
a.		Double surcharge	725.00	375.00
5	A9	5c on 25c blk, *rose*	130.00	52.50
a.		Inverted surcharge		
b.		Surcharge vertical	275.00	115.00
c.		Double surcharge	600.00	600.00

First "O" of "Congo" is a Capital, "Francais" with Capital "F"

1891-92

6	A9	5c on 20c red, *grn*	1,300.	425.00
7	A9	5c on 25c blk, *rose*	200.00	100.00
a.		Surcharge vertical	250.00	110.00
8	A9	10c on 25c blk, *rose*	240.00	67.50
a.		Inverted surcharge	400.00	160.00
b.		Surcharge vertical	300.00	100.00
d.		Double surcharge	400.00	225.00
9	A9	10c on 40c red, *straw*	2,750.	400.00
10	A9	15c on 25c blk, *rose*	225.00	52.50
a.		Surcharge vertical	260.00	92.50
c.		Double surcharge	400.00	200.00

First "O" of Congo small Surcharge Vert., Down or Up No Period

11	A9	5c on 25c blk, *rose*	300.00	135.00
12	A9	10c on 25c blk, *rose*		—
13	A9	15c on 25c blk, *rose*	425.00	190.00

The listings Nos. 5a and 12 are being re-evaluated. The Catalogue Editors would appreciate any information on these stamps.

Postage Due Stamps of French Colonies Surcharged in Red or Black Reading Down or Up

1892 ***Imperf.***

14	D1	5c on 5c blk (R)	200.00	140.00
a.		Double surcharge	1,450.	
15	D1	5c on 20c blk (R)	200.00	140.00
16	D1	5c on 30c blk (R)	260.00	180.00
17	D1	10c on 1fr brown	200.00	140.00
a.		Double surcharge	4,100.	
b.		Surcharge horiz.		*2,400.*
c.		"Congo" omitted		*475.00*
		Nos. 14-17 (4)	860.00	600.00

Excellent counterfeits of Nos. 1-17 exist.

Navigation and Commerce — A3

1892-1900 **Typo.** ***Perf. 14x13½***
Colony Name in Blue or Carmine

18	A3	1c blk, *lil bl*	1.60	1.60
a.		Name double	225.00	175.00
19	A3	2c brn, *buff*	4.00	3.25
a.		Name double	225.00	175.00
20	A3	4c claret, *lav*	4.00	3.25
a.		Name in blk and in blue	225.00	175.00
21	A3	5c grn, *grnsh*	8.00	8.00
22	A3	10c blk, *lavender*	24.00	20.00
a.		Name double	850.00	600.00
23	A3	10c red ('00)	4.00	4.00
24	A3	15c blue, quadrille paper	55.00	20.00
25	A3	15c gray ('00)	12.00	8.00
26	A3	20c red, *grn*	24.00	20.00
27	A3	25c blk, *rose*	24.00	16.00
28	A3	25c blue ('00)	12.00	*12.00*
29	A3	30c brn, *bis*	40.00	24.00
30	A3	40c red, *straw*	55.00	32.50
31	A3	50c car, *rose*	55.00	40.00
32	A3	50c brn, *az* ('00)	16.00	16.00
a.		Name double	775.00	775.00
33	A3	75c dp vio, *org*	47.50	40.00
34	A3	1fr brnz grn, *straw*	55.00	40.00
		Nos. 18-34 (17)	441.10	308.60

Perf. 13½x14 stamps are counterfeits.

For surcharges see Nos. 50-51.

No. 21 exists in yellow green on pale green. The stamp was prepared but not issued. Value, $4,000.

Leopard — A4

Type 1

Type 2

Bakalois Woman — A5

Coconut Grove — A6

Design A4 exists in two types. Type 1: end of left tusk extends behind and above right tusk. Type 2: end of left tusk does not appear behind right tusk. Type 2 of design A4 appears in position 91 of each pane of 100. For detailed listings, see the *Scott Catalogue Classic Specialized of Stamps & Covers.*

1900-04 Wmk. 122 *Perf. 11*

35	A4	1c brn vio & gray lilac (1)	.80	.80
a.		Background inverted	75.00	75.00
36	A4	2c brn & org (1)	.80	.80
a.		Imperf., pair	80.00	*80.00*
b.		Pair, imperf between	100.00	*110.00*
37	A4	4c scar & gray bl	1.60	1.20
a.		Background inverted	95.00	87.50
b.		Type 2	55.00	55.00
38	A4	5c grn & gray grn (1)	2.75	1.60
a.		Imperf., pair	140.00	140.00
39	A4	10c dk red & red (1)	8.00	3.25
a.		Imperf., pair	140.00	140.00
40	A4	15c dl vio & ol grn (1)	2.40	1.20
a.		Imperf. pair	110.00	

Wmk. 123

41	A5	20c yel grn & org (1)	2.40	2.00
42	A5	25c bl & pale bl	3.50	2.40
43	A5	30c car rose & org	5.50	2.40
44	A5	40c org brn & brt grn	8.00	2.75
a.		Imperf., pair	110.00	110.00
b.		Center and value inverted	200.00	170.00
45	A5	50c gray vio & lil	8.00	6.50
46	A5	75c red vio & org	20.00	11.00
a.		Imperf., pair	110.00	110.00

Wmk. 124

47	A6	1fr gray lil & ol	24.00	20.00
a.		Center and value inverted	300.00	300.00
b.		Imperf., pair	140.00	140.00
48	A6	2fr car & brn	47.50	32.50
a.		Imperf., pair	300.00	300.00
49	A6	5fr brn org & gray	87.50	72.50
a.		5fr ocher & gray	750.00	*950.00*
b.		Center and value inverted	450.00	450.00
c.		Wmk. 123	500.00	500.00
d.		Imperf., pair	800.00	800.00
		Nos. 35-49 (15)	222.75	160.90

For surcharges see Nos. 52-53.

Nos. 26 and 29 Surcharged in Black

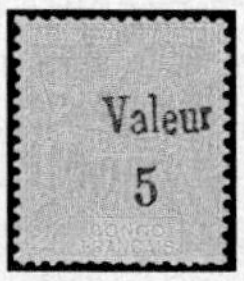

1900 Unwmk. *Perf. 14x13½*

50	A3	5c on 20c red, *grn*	26,000.	*6,000.*
a.		Double surcharge		*18,000.*
51	A3	15c on 30c brn, *bis*	20,000.	*2,600.*
a.		Double surcharge		*6,000.*

Nos. 43 and 48 Surcharged in Black

a

b

1903 Wmk. 123 *Perf. 11*

52	A5	5c on 30c	325.00	160.00
a.		Inverted surcharge	*2,750.*	

Wmk. 124

53	A6	10c on 2fr	375.00	160.00
a.		Inverted surcharge	*2,750.*	
b.		Double surcharge	*3,250.*	

Counterfeits of the preceding surcharges are known.

FRENCH EQUATORIAL AFRICA

ˈfrench ˌē-kwə-ˈtōr-ē-əl ˈa-fri-kə

LOCATION — North of Belgian Congo and south of Libya
GOVT. — French Colony
AREA — 959,256 square miles
POP. — 4,491,785
CAPITAL — Brazzaville

In 1910 Gabon and Middle Congo, with its military dependencies, were politically united as French Equatorial Africa. The component colonies were granted administrative autonomy. In 1915 Ubangi-Chari-Chad was made an autonomous civilian colony and in 1920 Chad was made a civil colony. In 1934 the four colonies were administratively united as one colony, but this federation was not completed until 1936. Each colony had its own postal administration until 1936. The postal issues of the former colonial subdivisions are listed under the names of those colonies.

In 1958, French Equatorial Africa was divided into four republics: Chad, Congo, Gabon and Central African Republic (formerly Ubangi-Chari).

Stamps other than Nos. 189-192 are inscribed with "Afrique Equatoriale Francaise" or "AEF" and the name of one of the component colonies are listed under those colonies.

100 Centimes = 1 Franc

Catalogue values for unused stamps in this country are for Never Hinged items, beginning with Scott 142 in the regular postage section, Scott B8A in the semi-postal section, Scott C17 in the airpost section, and Scott J12 in the postage due section.

Stamps of Gabon, 1932, Overprinted "Afrique Equatoriale Francaise" and Bars Similar to "a" and "b" in Black

Perf. 13x13½, 13½x13

1936 Unwmk.

1	A16	1c brown violet	.40	*.80*
2	A16	2c black, *rose*	.80	*.80*
3	A16	4c green	1.20	1.60
4	A16	5c grnsh blue	1.20	1.60
5	A16	10c red, *yel*	1.20	1.60
6	A17	40c brown violet	4.00	3.25
7	A17	50c red brown	3.25	2.40
8	A17	1fr yel grn, *bl*	32.50	16.00
9	A18	1.50fr dull blue	8.00	4.00
10	A18	2fr brown red	20.00	16.00
		Nos. 1-10 (10)	72.55	48.05

Stamps of Middle Congo, 1933 Overprinted in Black

a

b

c

1936

11	A4 (b)	1c lt brown	.40	*.50*
12	A4 (b)	2c dull blue	.40	*.50*
13	A4 (b)	4c olive green	1.60	1.60
14	A4 (b)	5c red violet	.80	1.00
15	A4 (b)	10c slate	1.60	1.25
16	A4 (b)	15c dk violet	2.00	1.60
17	A4 (b)	20c red, *pink*	2.00	1.60
18	A4 (b)	25c orange	4.00	2.40
19	A5 (a)	40c orange brn	5.50	2.75
20	A5 (c)	50c black violet	5.50	2.40
21	A5 (c)	75c black, *pink*	5.50	4.75
22	A5 (a)	90c carmine	5.50	4.00
23	A5 (c)	1.50fr dark blue	4.75	2.00
24	A6 (a)	5fr slate blue	55.00	35.00
25	A6 (a)	10fr black	35.00	30.00
26	A6 (a)	20fr dark brown	35.00	32.50
		Nos. 11-26 (16)	164.55	123.85

Other overprints inscribed "Afrique Equitoriale Française" in a different type font on earlier Middle Congo stamps are listed under Middle Congo.

Common Design Types pictured following the introduction.

Paris International Exposition Issue
Common Design Types

1937, Apr. 15 Engr. *Perf. 13*

27	CD74	20c dark violet	2.40	2.40
28	CD75	30c dark green	2.40	2.40
29	CD76	40c carmine rose	2.40	2.40
30	CD77	50c dk brn & bl	2.40	2.40
31	CD78	90c red	3.25	3.25
32	CD79	1.50fr ultra	3.25	3.25
		Nos. 27-32 (6)	16.10	16.10

Logging on Loéme River — A1

People of Chad — A2

Pierre Savorgnan de Brazza A3

Emile Gentil — A4

Paul Crampel A5

Governor Victor Liotard A6

Two types of 25c:
Type I — Wide numerals (4mm).
Type II — Narrow numerals (3½mm).

1937-40 Photo. *Perf. 13½x13*

33	A1	1c brown & yel	.25	.25
34	A1	2c violet & grn	.25	.25
35	A1	3c blue & yel ('40)	.25	.30
36	A1	4c magenta & bl	.25	.30
37	A1	5c dk & lt green	.25	.30
38	A2	10c magenta & blue	.25	.30
39	A2	15c blue & buff	.25	.30
40	A2	20c brown & yellow	.25	*.30*
41	A2	25c cop red & bl (I)	.80	.30
a.		Type II	2.75	2.00
42	A3	30c gray grn & grn	.80	.55
43	A3	30c chlky bl, ind & buff ('40)	.40	.50
44	A2	35c dp grn & yel ('38)	.80	.80
45	A3	40c cop red & bl	.40	.30
46	A3	45c dk bl & lt grn	4.75	3.50
47	A3	45c dp grn & yel grn ('40)	.40	.80
48	A3	50c brown & yellow	.50	.25
49	A3	55c pur & bl ('38)	.80	.80
50	A3	60c mar & gray bl ('40)	.80	.85
51	A4	65c dk bl & lt grn	.80	.40
52	A4	70c dp vio & buff ('40)	.80	.95
53	A4	75c ol blk & dl yel	5.50	4.50
54	A4	80c brn & yel ('38)	.40	.80
55	A4	90c copper red & buff	.55	.40
56	A4	1fr dk vio & lt grn	2.40	1.20
57	A3	1fr cer & dl org ('38)	4.00	1.60
58	A4	1fr bl grn & sl grn ('40)	.40	.55
59	A5	1.25fr cop red & buff	2.40	1.20
60	A5	1.40fr dk brn & pale grn ('40)	1.20	1.25
61	A5	1.50fr dk & lt blue	1.60	.80
62	A5	1.60fr dp vio & buff ('40)	1.60	1.25
63	A5	1.75fr brn & yel	2.00	1.20
64	A4	1.75fr bl & lt bl ('38)	.80	.80
65	A5	2fr dk & lt green	1.60	.80
66	A6	2.15fr brn, vio & yel ('38)	1.20	.80
67	A6	2.25fr bl & lt bl ('39)	1.60	1.60
68	A6	2.50fr rose lake & buff ('40)	2.00	1.40
69	A6	3fr dk blue & buff	.80	.50
70	A6	5fr dk & lt green	1.60	1.20
71	A6	10fr dk violet & bl	3.25	3.25
72	A6	20fr ol blk & dl yel	4.00	3.50
		Nos. 33-72 (40)	52.95	40.90

For overprints and surcharges see Nos. 80-127, 129-141, B2-B3, B10-B13, B22-B23.

Colonial Arts Exhibition Issue
Souvenir Sheet
Common Design Type

1937 *Imperf.*

73	CD79	3fr red brown	12.00	*16.00*
		Never hinged	16.00	

Count Louis Edouard Bouet-Willaumez and His Ship "La Malouine" — A7

1938, Dec. 5 *Perf. 13½*

74	A7	65c gray brown	1.25	1.25
75	A7	1fr deep rose	1.25	1.25
76	A7	1.75fr blue	1.60	1.60
77	A7	2fr dull violet	2.40	2.40
		Nos. 74-77 (4)	6.50	6.50
		Set, never hinged	8.85	

Centenary of Gabon.

New York World's Fair Issue
Common Design Type

1939, May 10 Engr. ***Perf. 12½x12***

78	CD82 1.25fr carmine lake	.80	1.60
79	CD82 2.25fr ultra	.80	1.60
	Set, never hinged	2.40	

Libreville View and Marshal Petain A7a

1941 Engr. ***Perf. 12½x12***

79A A7a 1fr bluish green	.40	
79B A7a 2.50fr blue	.40	
Set, never hinged	1.60	

Nos. 79A-79B were issued by the Vichy government in France, but were not placed on sale in French Equatorial Africa.

For surcharges, see Nos. B36-B37.

Stamps of 1936-40, Overprinted in Carmine or Black

Nos. 80-82, 84-88, 93

Nos. 83, 89-92, 94-125

1940-41 ***Perf. 13½x13***

80	A1 1c brn & yel (C)	4.00	4.00
81	A1 2c vio & grn (C)	4.00	4.00
82	A1 3c blue & yel (C)	4.00	4.00
83	A4 4c ol grn (No. 13)	24.00	16.00
b.	Inverted overprint	120.00	*150.00*
84	A1 5c dk grn & lt grn (C)	4.00	4.00
85	A2 10c magenta & bl	4.00	4.00
86	A2 15c blue & buff (C)	4.00	4.00
87	A2 20c brn & yel (C)	4.00	4.00
88	A2 25c cop red & bl	4.00	4.00
89	A3 30c gray grn & grn (C)	16.00	16.00
90	A3 30c gray grn & grn ('41)	16.00	16.00
91	A3 30c chlky bl, ind & buff (C) ('41)	16.00	16.00
92	A3 30c chlky bl, ind & buff ('41)	16.00	16.00
93	A2 35c dp grn & yel (C)	4.00	4.00
94	A3 40c cop red & bl	4.00	4.00
b.	Inverted overprint		*100.00*
95	A3 45c dp grn & yel grn (C)	4.00	4.00
96	A3 45c dp grn & yel grn ('41)	16.00	16.00
97	A3 50c brn & yel (C)	4.00	4.00
98	A3 50c brn & yel ('41)	8.00	8.00
99	A3 55c pur & bl (C)	4.00	4.00
100	A3 55c pur & bl ('41)	16.00	16.00
101	A3 60c mar & gray bl	4.00	4.00
102	A4 65c dk bl & lt grn	4.00	4.00
103	A4 70c dp vio & buff	4.00	4.00
104	A4 75c ol blk & dl yel	80.00	80.00
105	A4 80c brown & yellow	4.00	4.00
106	A4 90c cop red & buff	4.00	4.00
107	A4 1fr bl grn & sl grn	8.00	8.00
108	A4 1fr bl grn & sl grn (C) ('41)	20.00	20.00
109	A3 1fr cer & dl org	4.00	4.00
110	A5 1.40fr dk brn & pale grn	4.00	4.00
111	A5 1.50fr dk bl & lt bl	4.00	4.00
112	A5 1.60fr dp vio & buff	4.00	4.00
113	A5 1.75fr brown & yel	4.00	4.00
114	A6 2.15fr brn, vio & yel	4.00	4.00
115	A6 2.25fr bl & lt bl (C)	4.00	4.00
116	A6 2.25fr bl & lt bl ('41)	16.00	16.00
117	A6 2.50fr rose lake & buff	4.00	4.00
118	A6 3fr dk bl & buff (C)	4.00	4.00
119	A6 3fr dk bl & buff ('41)	16.00	16.00
120	A6 5fr dk grn & lt grn (C)	4.00	4.00
121	A6 5fr dk grn & lt grn ('41)	140.00	140.00
122	A6 10fr dk vio & bl (C)	3.25	3.25
123	A6 10fr dk vio & bl ('41)	130.00	130.00
124	A6 20fr ol blk & dl yel (C)	4.00	4.00
125	A6 20fr ol blk & dl yel ('41)	16.00	16.00
	Nos. 80-125 (46)	673.25	665.25

For overprints and surcharges see Nos. 129-132, B12-B13, B22-B23.

For types of Nos. 38//61 without "RF," see Nos. 155A-155B.

Double Overprint

80a	A1	1c	325.00	225.00
81a	A1	2c	32.50	
82a	A1	3c	32.50	
83a	A4	4c	75.00	
84a	A1	5c	32.50	
85a	A2	10c	32.50	40.00
86a	A2	15c	32.50	
87a	A2	20c	32.50	
88a	A2	25c	55.00	
89a	A3	30c	110.00	120.00
90a	A3	30c	47.50	55.00
91a	A3	30c	47.50	47.50
93a	A2	35c	250.00	
94a	A3	40c	47.50	
96a	A3	45c	75.00	
98a	A3	50c	110.00	75.00
100a	A3	55c	75.00	
102a	A4	65c	45.00	
103a	A4	70c	47.50	
104a	A4	75c	175.00	
105a	A4	80c	47.50	
106a	A4	90c	45.00	
b.		one inverted	120.00	
109a	A4	1fr One inverted	120.00	
110a	A5	1.40fr	47.50	
111a	A5	1.50fr	47.50	
114a	A6	2.15fr	40.00	
115a	A6	2.25fr	60.00	
116a	A6	2.25fr	47.50	
117a	A6	2.50fr	47.50	
119a	A6	3fr	60.00	
123a	A6	10fr	60.00	*67.50*
124a	A6	20fr	60.00	
		Nos. 96a-124a (17)	1,035.	

Nos. 48, 51 Surcharged in Black or Carmine

1940

126	A3 75c on 50c	.80	.80
a.	Double surcharge	40.00	
127	A4 1fr on 65c (C)	.80	.80
a.	Double surcharge	32.50	
	Set, never hinged	3.20	

Middle Congo No. 67 Overprinted in Carmine like No. 80
Perf. 13½

128	A4 4c olive green	65.00	65.00

Stamps of 1940 With Additional Overprint in Black

1940 ***Perf. 13½x13***

129	A4 80c brown & yel	24.00	16.00
a.	Overprint without "2"	150.00	
130	A4 1fr bl grn & sl grn	24.00	20.00
131	A3 1fr cer & dull org	24.00	16.00
132	A5 1.50fr dk bl & lt bl	24.00	16.00
	Nos. 129-132 (4)	96.00	68.00

Arrival of General de Gaulle in Brazzaville, capital of Free France, Oct. 24, 1940.

These stamps were sold affixed to post cards and at a slight increase over face value to cover the cost of the cards. Values for unused stamps are for examples without gum.

For surcharges see Nos. B12-B13, B22-B23.

Stamps of 1937-40 Overprinted in Black
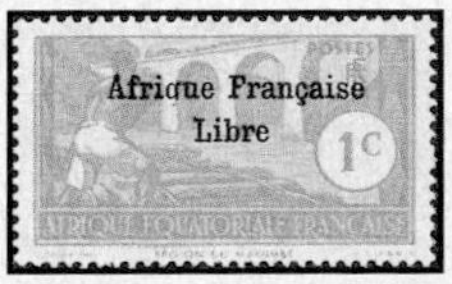

1941

133	A1 1c brown & yel	4.00	4.00
134	A1 2c violet & grn	4.00	4.00
135	A1 3c blue & yel	4.00	4.00
136	A1 5c dk & lt green	4.00	4.00
137	A2 10c magenta & bl	4.00	4.00
138	A2 15c blue & buff	4.00	4.00
139	A2 20c brown & yel	4.00	4.00
140	A2 25c copper red & bl	4.00	4.00
141	A2 35c dp grn & yel	4.00	4.00
a.	Double overprint	120.00	
	Nos. 133-141 (9)	36.00	36.00
	Set, never hinged	55.00	

There are 2 settings of the overprint on Nos. 133-141 & C10. The 1st has 1mm between lines of the overprint (Nos. 133-141), the 2nd has 2mm. Value, set with 2mm spacing $95.

Catalogue values for unused stamps in this section, from this point to the end of the section, are for Never Hinged items.

Phoenix — A8

1941 Photo. ***Perf. 14x14½***

142	A8 5c brown	.30	.25
143	A8 10c dark blue	.30	.25
144	A8 25c emerald	.30	.25
145	A8 30c deep orange	.30	.25
146	A8 40c dk slate grn	.55	.30
147	A8 80c red brown	.55	.30
148	A8 1fr deep red lilac	.55	.30
149	A8 1.50fr brt red	.75	.40
150	A8 2fr gray	.75	.40
151	A8 2.50fr brt ultra	.95	.70
152	A8 4fr dull violet	.95	.70
153	A8 5fr yellow bister	.95	.70
154	A8 10fr deep brown	1.40	1.00
155	A8 20fr deep green	1.75	1.25
	Nos. 142-155 (14)	10.35	7.05

For surcharges see #158-165, B14-B21, B24-B35.

Types of 1937-40 without "RF"

1944 ***Perf. 13½***

155A	A2 10c magenta & blue	1.20
155B	A2 15c blue & buff	1.60
155C	A3 60c maroon & gray blue	1.60
155D	A5 1.50fr dk & lt blue	2.00
	Nos. 155A-155D (4)	6.40

Nos. 155A-155D were issued by the Vichy government in France, but were not sold in French Equatorial Africa.

Eboue Issue
Common Design Type

1945 Unwmk. Engr. ***Perf. 13***

156	CD91 2fr black	.65	.50
157	CD91 25fr Prussian green	1.90	1.50

Nos. 156-157 exist imperforate. Value, set $65.

Nos. 142, 144 and 151 Surcharged with New Values and Bars in Red, Carmine or Black

1946 ***Perf. 14x14½***

158	A8 50c on 5c (R)	.80	.65
159	A8 60c on 5c (R)	.80	.65
160	A8 70c on 5c (R)	.80	.65
161	A8 1.20fr on 5c (C)	.80	.65
162	A8 2.40fr on 25c	1.40	1.00
163	A8 3fr on 25c	1.40	1.00
164	A8 4.50fr on 25c	1.75	1.20
165	A8 15fr on 2.50fr (C)	1.90	1.40
	Nos. 158-165 (8)	9.65	7.20

Black Rhinoceros and Rock Python A9

Jungle Scene — A10

Mountainous Shore Line — A11

Gabon Forest — A12

Niger Boatman — A13

Young Bacongo Woman — A14

1946 Unwmk. Engr. ***Perf. 12½***

166	A9 10c deep blue	.40	.25
167	A9 30c violet blk	.40	.25
168	A9 40c dp orange	.40	.25
169	A10 50c violet bl	.80	.50
170	A10 60c dk carmine	.80	.50
171	A10 80c dk ol grn	.80	.50
172	A11 1fr dp orange	.80	.30
173	A11 1.20fr dp claret	.80	.65
174	A11 1.50fr dk green	1.20	.95
175	A12 2fr dk vio brn	.40	.25
176	A12 3fr rose carmine	.80	.50
177	A12 3.60fr red brown	3.25	2.50
178	A12 4fr deep blue	.80	.30
179	A13 5fr dk brown	.80	.25
180	A13 6fr deep blue	1.25	.30
181	A13 10fr black	2.40	.75
182	A14 15fr brown	2.40	.80
183	A14 20fr dp claret	2.40	.80
184	A14 25fr black	3.25	.80
	Nos. 166-184 (19)	24.15	11.40

Imperforates

Most French Equatorial Africa stamps from 1951 onward exist imperforate in issued and trial colors, and also in small presentation sheets in issued colors.

Pierre Savorgnan de Brazza — A15

1951, Nov. 5 ***Perf. 13***

185	A15 10fr indigo & dk grn	1.60	.40

Cent. of the birth of Pierre Savorgnan de Brazza, explorer.

Military Medal Issue
Common Design Type
Engraved and Typographed

1952, Dec. 1 ***Perf. 13***

186	CD101 15fr multicolored	8.00	5.50

Lt. Gov. Adolphe L. Cureau A16

1954, Sept. 20 **Engr.**

187	A16 15fr ol grn & red brn	2.00	.80

Savannah Monitor A17

1955, May 2 **Unwmk.**

188 A17 8fr dk grn & claret 2.40 1.25

International Exhibition for Wildlife Protection, Paris, May 1955.

FIDES Issue

Common Design Type

Designs: 5fr, Boali Waterfall and Power Plant, Ubangi-Chari. 10fr, Cotton, Chad. 15fr, Brazzaville Hospital, Middle Congo. 20fr, Libreville Harbor, Gabon.

1956, Apr. 25 ***Perf. 13x12½***

189 CD103 5fr dk brn & claret .65 .30
190 CD103 10fr blk & bluish grn .65 .30
191 CD103 15fr ind & gray vio .80 .40
192 CD103 20fr dk red & red org 1.10 .65
Nos. 189-192 (4) 3.20 1.65

Coffee Issue

Coffee A19

1956, Oct. **Engr.** ***Perf. 13***

193 A19 10fr brn vio & vio bl 1.60 .40

Leprosarium at Mayumba and Maltese Cross — A20

1957, Mar. 11

194 A20 15fr grn, bl grn & red 2.00 .80

Issued in honor of the Knights of Malta.

Giant Eland A21

1957, Nov. 4

195 A21 1fr shown .80 .40
196 A21 2fr Lions .80 .40
197 A21 3fr Elephant, vert. .80 .40
198 A21 4fr Greater kudu, vert. .90 .40
Nos. 195-198 (4) 3.30 1.60

WHO Building, Brazzaville A22

1958, May 19 **Engr.** ***Perf. 13***

199 A22 20fr dk green & org brn 1.60 .80

10th anniv. of WHO.

Flower Issue

Common Design Type

1958, July 7 **Photo.** ***Perf. 12x12½***

200 CD104 10fr Euadania 1.60 .65
201 CD104 25fr Spathodea 2.00 .95

Human Rights Issue

Common Design Type

1958, Dec. 10 **Engr.** ***Perf. 13***

202 CD105 20fr Prus grn & dk bl 2.40 1.25

SEMI-POSTAL STAMPS

Common Design Type

1938, Oct. 24 **Engr.**

B1 CD80 1.75fr + 50c brt ultra 24.00 24.00
Never hinged 32.50

Nos. 51, 64 Surcharged in Black or Red

1938, Nov. 7 ***Perf. 13x13½***

B2 A4 65c + 35c dk bl & lt grn (R) 2.40 2.40
B3 A4 1.75fr + 50c bl & lt bl 4.00 4.00
Set, never hinged 12.00

The surtax was for welfare.

French Revolution Issue

Common Design Type

Name and Value Typo. in Black

1939, July 5 **Photo.**

B4 CD83 45c + 25c green 16.00 16.00
B5 CD83 70c + 30c brown 16.00 16.00
B6 CD83 90c + 35c red org 16.00 16.00
B7 CD83 1.25fr + 1fr rose pink 16.00 16.00
B8 CD83 2.25fr + 2fr blue 16.00 16.00
Nos. B4-B8 (5) 80.00 80.00
Set, never hinged 120.00

Surtax used for the defense of the colonies.

Catalogue values for unused stamps in this section, from this point to the end of the section, are for Never Hinged items.

Common Design Type and

Native Artilleryman SP1

Gabon Infantryman SP2

1941 **Photo.** ***Perf. 13½***

B8A SP1 1fr + 1fr red 3.50
B8B CD86 1.50fr + 3fr maroon 3.50
B8C SP2 2.50fr + 1fr blue 3.50
Nos. B8A-B8C (3) 10.50

Nos. B8A-B8C were issued by the Vichy government in France, but were not placed on sale in French Equatorial Africa.

Brazza and Stanley Pool SP3

1941 **Photo.** ***Perf. 14½x14***

B9 SP3 1fr + 2fr dk brn & red 2.00 1.60

The surtax was for a monument to Pierre Savorgnan de Brazza.

Nos. 67, 71 Srchd. in Red

1943, June 28 ***Perf. 13½x13***

B10 A6 2.25fr + 50fr 47.50 32.50
B11 A6 10fr + 100fr 120.00 80.00

Nos. 129 and 132 with Add'l. Srch. in Carmine

1944

B12 A4 80c + 10fr 65.00 40.00
B13 A5 1.50fr + 15fr 65.00 40.00

Same surcharge printed Vertically on Nos. 142-146, 148, 150-151

Perf. 14x14½

B14 A8 5c + 10fr brown 40.00 27.50
B15 A8 10c + 10fr dk bl 40.00 27.50
B16 A8 25c + 10fr emer 40.00 27.50
B17 A8 30c + 10fr dp org 40.00 27.50
B18 A8 40c + 10fr dk sl grn 40.00 27.50
B19 A8 1fr + 10fr dp red lil 40.00 27.50
B20 A8 2fr + 20fr gray 40.00 27.50
B21 A8 2.50fr + 25fr brt ultra 40.00 27.50
Nos. B12-B21 (10) 450.00 300.00

Nos. 129 and 132 with Add'l. Srch. in Carmine

1944 ***Perf. 13½x13***

B22 A4 80c + 10fr 65.00 40.00
B23 A5 1.50fr + 15fr 65.00 40.00

Same Surcharge printed Vertically on Nos. 142-146, 148, 150-155

Perf. 14x14½

B24 A8 5c + 10fr brn 40.00 27.50
B25 A8 10c + 10fr dk bl 40.00 27.50
B26 A8 25c + 10fr emer 40.00 27.50
B27 A8 30c + 10fr dp org 40.00 27.50
B28 A8 40c + 10fr dk sl grn 40.00 27.50
B29 A8 1fr + 10fr dp red lil 40.00 27.50
B30 A8 2fr + 20fr gray 40.00 27.50
B31 A8 2.50fr + 25fr brt ultra 40.00 27.50
B32 A8 4fr + 40fr dl vio 40.00 27.50
B33 A8 5fr + 50fr yel bis 40.00 27.50
B34 A8 10fr + 100fr dp brn 40.00 27.50
B35 A8 20fr + 200fr dp grn 40.00 27.50
Nos. B22-B35 (14) 610.00 410.00

Nos. B12 to B35 were issued to raise funds for the Committee to Aid the Fighting Men and Patriots of France.

Nos. 79A-79B Srchd. in Black or Red

1944 **Engr.** ***Perf. 12½x12***

B36 50c + 1.50fr on 2.50fr deep blue (R) .80
B37 + 2.50fr on 1fr green .80

Colonial Development Fund.

Nos. B36-B37 were issued by the Vichy government in France, but were not placed on sale in French Equatorial Africa.

Red Cross Issue

Common Design Type

1944 **Photo.** ***Perf. 14½x14***

B38 CD90 5fr + 20fr royal blue 1.60 1.20

The surtax was for the French Red Cross and national relief.

Tropical Medicine Issue

Common Design Type

1950, May 15 **Engr.** ***Perf. 13***

B39 CD100 10fr + 2fr dk bl grn & vio brn 7.25 5.50

The surtax was for charitable work.

AIR POST STAMPS

Hydroplane over Pointe-Noire — AP1

Trimotor over Stanley Pool — AP2

1937 **Unwmk.** **Photo.** ***Perf. 13½***

C1 AP1 1.50fr ol blk & yel .40 .40
C2 AP1 2fr mag & blue .55 .55
C3 AP1 2.50fr grn & buff .55 .55
C4 AP1 3.75fr brn & lt grn .80 .80
C5 AP2 4.50fr cop red & bl .90 .90
C6 AP2 6.50fr bl & lt grn 1.60 1.60
C7 AP2 8.50fr red brn & yel 1.60 1.60
C8 AP2 10.75fr vio & lt grn 1.60 1.60
Nos. C1-C8 (8) 8.00 8.00

For overprints and surcharges see Nos. C9-C16, CB6.

Nos. C1, C3-C7 Overprinted in Black like Nos. 133-141

1940-41

C9 AP1 1.50fr ('41) 240.00 240.00
C10 AP1 2.50fr 4.00 4.00
a. Double overprint 275.00 275.00
b. Inverted overprint 275.00 275.00
C11 AP1 3.75fr ('41) 240.00 240.00
C12 AP2 4.50fr 4.50 4.50
a. Double overprint 275.00 275.00
C13 AP2 6.50fr 4.00 4.00
a. Double overprint 130.00 130.00
C14 AP2 8.50fr 4.00 4.00

No. C8 Surcharged in Carmine

C15 AP2 50fr on 10.75fr 12.00 12.00

No. C3 Surcharged in Black

C16 AP1 10fr on 2.50fr ('41) 95.00 95.00
Nos. C9-C16 (8) 603.50 603.50

Counterfeits of Nos. C9 and C11 exist. See note following No. 141.

Catalogue values for unused stamps in this section, from this point to the end of the section, are for Never Hinged items.

Common Design Type

1941 **Photo.** ***Perf. 14½x14***

C17 CD87 1fr dark orange .65 .30
C18 CD87 1.50fr brt red .95 .50
C19 CD87 5fr brown red 1.60 .90
C20 CD87 10fr black 1.75 1.00
C21 CD87 25fr ultra 1.60 1.20
C22 CD87 50fr dark green 1.60 1.20
C23 CD87 100fr plum 2.25 1.25
Nos. C17-C23 (7) 10.40 6.35

Types of 1937 without "RF" and

Sikorsky 5.43 Seaplane and Canoe — AP2a

Perf. 13½, 13 (#C23M)

1943, Oct. 18-1944 **Unwmk.**

C23A AP1 1.50fr ol blk & yel .40
C23B AP1 2fr mag & blue .40
C23C AP1 2.50fr grn & buff .40
C23D AP1 3.75fr brn & lt grn .80
C23E AP2 4.50fr cop red & bl .80

C23F	AP2	5fr green	1.20	
C23G	AP2	6.50fr bl & lt grn	1.20	
C23H	AP2	8.50fr red brn & yel	1.20	
C23I	AP2	10fr gray & brn ('44)	1.20	
C23J	AP2	10.75fr vio & lt grn	1.20	
C23K	AP2	20fr yel & brn red ('44)	1.60	
C23L	AP2	50fr gray grn & blk ('44)	2.40	
C23M	AP2a	100fr red brown ('44)	1.60	
		Nos. C23A-C23M (13)	14.40	

Issue dates: Nos. C23I, C23K-L, 4/3/44; C23M, 6/26/44.

Nos. C23A-C23M were issued by the Vichy government in France, but were not sold in French Equatorial Africa.

Victory Issue

Common Design Type

Perf. 12½

1946, May 8 Unwmk. Engr.

C24 CD92 8fr lilac rose 1.60 1.25

Chad to Rhine Issue

Common Design Types

1946, June 6

C25	CD93	5fr dk violet	1.60	1.20
C26	CD94	10fr slate green	1.60	1.20
C27	CD95	15fr deep blue	2.75	2.00
C28	CD96	20fr red orange	2.75	2.00
C29	CD97	25fr sepia	2.75	2.00
C30	CD98	50fr brown carmine	3.25	2.40
		Nos. C25-C30 (6)	14.70	10.80

Palms and Village — AP3

Village and Waterfront — AP4

Bearers in Jungle — AP5

1946 Engr. *Perf. 13*

C31	AP3	50fr red brn	3.50	.80
C32	AP4	100fr grnsh blk	5.25	1.25
C33	AP5	200fr deep blue	12.00	2.00
		Nos. C31-C33 (3)	20.75	4.05

UPU Issue

Common Design Type

1949, July 4

C34 CD99 25fr green 16.00 12.00

Brazza Holding Map — AP6

1951, Nov. 5

C35 AP6 15fr brn, indigo & red 2.40 1.60

Cent. of the birth of Pierre Savorgnan de Brazza, explorer.

Archbishop Augouard and St. Anne Cathedral, Brazzaville — AP7

1952, Dec. 1

C36 AP7 15fr ol grn, dk brn & vio brn 6.50 2.40

Cent. of the birth of Archbishop Philippe-Prosper Augouard.

Anhingas — AP8

1953, Feb. 16

C37 AP8 500fr grnsh blk, blk & slate 47.50 8.00

Liberation Issue

Common Design Type

1954, June 6

C38 CD102 15fr vio & vio brn 12.00 8.00

Log Rafts — AP9

Designs: 100fr, Fishing boats and nets, Lake Chad. 200fr, Age of mechanization.

1955, Jan. 24 Engr.

C39	AP9	50fr ind, brn & dk grn	2.40	.80
C40	AP9	100fr aqua, dk grn & blk brn	8.00	1.60
C41	AP9	200fr red & deep plum	12.00	2.40
		Nos. C39-C41 (3)	22.40	4.80

Gov. Gen. Félix Eboué, View of Brazzaville and the Pantheon — AP10

1955, Apr. 30 Unwmk. *Perf. 13*

C42 AP10 15fr sep, brn & slate bl 6.50 2.40

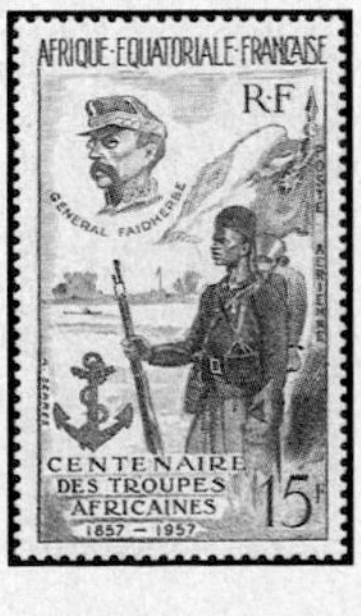

Gen. Louis Faidherbé and African Sharpshooter AP11

1957, July 20

C43 AP11 15fr sepia & org ver 3.50 2.00

Centenary of French African Troops.

AIR POST SEMI-POSTAL STAMPS

French Revolution Issue

Common Design Type

1939 Unwmk. Photo. *Perf. 13*

Name and Value Typo. in Orange

CB1 CD83 4.50fr + 4fr brn blk 40.00 40.00

SPAP1

SPAP2

SPAP3

Unwmk.

1942, June 22 Engr. *Perf. 13*

CB2	SPAP1	1.50fr + 3.50fr green	.80
CB3	SPAP2	2fr + 6fr brown	.80
CB4	SPAP3	3fr + 9fr carmine	.80
		Nos. CB2-CB4 (3)	2.40

Native children's welfare fund.

Nos. CB2-CB4 were issued by the Vichy government in France, but were not placed on sale in French Equatorial Africa.

Colonial Education Fund

Common Design Type

1942, June 22

CB5 CD86a 1.20fr + 1.80fr bl & red .80

No. CB5 was issued by the Vichy government in France, but was not placed on sale in French Equatorial Africa.

No. C8 Surcharged in Red like Nos. B10-B11

1943, June 28 *Perf. 13½*

CB6 AP2 10.75fr + 200fr 400.00 240.00

Counterfeits exist.

POSTAGE DUE STAMPS

Numeral of Value on Equatorial Butterfly — D1

1937 Unwmk. Photo. *Perf. 13*

J1	D1	5c redsh pur & lt bl	.25	.40
J2	D1	10c cop red & buff	.25	.40
J3	D1	20c dk grn & grn	.30	.50
J4	D1	25c red brn & buff	.30	.50
J5	D1	30c cop red & lt bl	.50	.55
J6	D1	45c mag & yel grn	.75	.80
J7	D1	50c dk ol grn & buff	.80	.95
J8	D1	60c redsh pur & yel	.95	1.10
J9	D1	1fr brown & yel	1.00	1.20
J10	D1	2fr dk bl & buff	1.40	1.50
J11	D1	3fr red brn & lt grn	1.50	1.75
		Nos. J1-J11 (11)	8.00	9.65
		Set, never hinged	12.00	

Catalogue values for unused stamps in this section, from this point to the end of the section, are for Never Hinged items.

D2

1947 Engr.

J12	D2	10c red	.40	.25
J13	D2	30c dp org	.40	.25
J14	D2	50c greenish bl	.50	.30
J15	D2	1fr carmine	.55	.40
J16	D2	2fr emerald	.65	.50
J17	D2	3fr dp red lil	.65	.50
J18	D2	4fr dp ultra	1.60	1.20
J19	D2	5fr red brown	1.60	1.20
J20	D2	10fr peacock blue	2.00	1.60
J21	D2	20fr sepia	2.10	1.90
		Nos. J12-J21 (10)	10.45	8.10

FRENCH GUIANA

'french gē-'a-nə

LOCATION — On the northeast coast of South America bordering on the Atlantic Ocean.
GOVT. — French colony
AREA — 34,740 sq. mi.
POP. — 28,537 (1946)
CAPITAL — Cayenne

French Guiana became an overseas department of France in 1946.

100 Centimes = 1 Franc

Catalogue values for unused stamps in this country are for Never Hinged items, beginning with Scott 171 in the regular postage section, Scott B12 in the semi-postal section, Scott C9 in the airpost section, and Scott J22 in the postage due section.

See France No. 1446 for French stamp inscribed "Guyane."

Stamps of French Colonies Surcharged in Black

1886, Dec. Unwmk. *Imperf.*

1 A8 5c on 2c grn, *grnsh*, srchg 12mm high 750.00 675.00
a. Double surcharge 1,900. 1,900.
b. Surcharge 10½mm high 900.00 825.00
c. No "f" after "O" 950.00 850.00

Perf. 14x13½

2 A9 5c on 2c brn, *buff*, srchg 12mm high 650.00 600.00
a. No "f" after "O" 525.00 450.00
b. As "a," double surcharge 1,700. 1,700.

Nos. 1-2 unused are valued without gum.

Stamps of French Colonies Overprinted in Black

"Av" of Date Line Inverted-Reversed

1887, Apr. *Imperf.*

4 A8 20c on 35c blk, *org* 70.00 57.50
a. Double surcharge 225.00 225.00
b. No "f" after "O" 150.00 150.00

Date Line Reads "Avril 1887"

5 A8 5c on 2c grn, *grnsh* 175.00 125.00
a. Double surcharge 900.00 900.00
b. No "f" after "O" 375.00 375.00
c. Pair, one stamp without surcharge 1,500.
6 A8 20c on 35c blk, *org* 375.00 375.00
a. Double surcharge 1,250. 1,250.
b. No "f" after "O" 850.00 850.00
c. Vertical pair, #6 + #4 2,200.
7 A7 25c on 30c brn, *yelsh* 55.00 47.50
a. Double surcharge 900.00 900.00
b. No "f" after "O" 275.00 275.00

Nos. 4-7 unused are valued without gum.

French Colonies Nos. 22 and 26 Surcharged

8 A7 5c on 30c brn, *yelsh* 155.00 140.00
a. Double surcharge 800.00 800.00
b. Inverted surcharge 1,200. 1,200.
c. Pair, one without surcharge 1,600.
9 A8 5c on 30c brn, *yelsh* 1,500. 1,500.

Nos. 8-9 unused are valued without gum.

French Colonies Nos. 22 and 28 Surcharged

1888

10 A7 5c on 30c brn, *yelsh* 155.00 140.00
b. Double surcharge 500.00 500.00
c. Inverted surcharge 600.00 600.00
11 A8 10c on 75c car, *rose* 400.00 290.00
No gum 290.00
a. Double surcharge 1,100. 1,100.
b. Pair, one stamp without surcharge 2,500.

No. 10 unused is valued without gum.

Stamps of French Colonies Overprinted in Black

1892, Feb. 20 *Imperf.*

12 A8 2c grn, *grnsh* 850.00 *975.00*
a. Inverted overprint 3,500.
13 A7 30c brn, *yelsh* 155.00 155.00
a. Inverted overprint 575.00 575.00
14 A8 35c blk, *orange* *2,850.* *3,000.*
15 A8 40c red, *straw* 175.00 140.00
16 A8 75c car, *rose* 180.00 140.00
a. Inverted overprint 625.00 550.00
17 A8 1fr brnz grn, *straw* 210.00 160.00
a. Inverted overprint 800.00 800.00
b. Double overprint 800.00 800.00
c. Triple overprint 1,800. 1,800.

Nos. 12-14 unused are valued without gum.

1892 *Perf. 14x13½*

18 A9 1c blk, *lil bl* 47.50 35.00
19 A9 2c brn, *buff* 45.00 37.50
20 A9 4c claret, *lav* 42.50 37.50
21 A9 5c grn, *grnsh* 47.50 35.00
a. Inverted overprint 150.00 150.00
b. Double overprint 150.00 150.00
22 A9 10c blk, *lavender* 67.50 40.00
a. Inverted overprint 200.00 200.00
b. Double overprint 275.00 275.00
23 A9 15c blue 67.50 45.00
a. Double overprint 275.00 200.00
24 A9 20c red, *grn* 55.00 42.50
a. Inverted overprint 225.00 225.00
25 A9 25c blk, *rose* 75.00 35.00
a. Double overprint 275.00 275.00
b. Triple overprint 300.00 300.00
26 A9 30c brn, *bis* 47.50 40.00
27 A9 35c blk, *orange* 225.00 225.00
a. Inverted overprint 575.00 575.00
28 A9 40c red, *straw* 135.00 135.00
a. Inverted overprint 300.00 300.00
29 A9 75c car, *rose* 145.00 125.00
30 A9 1fr brnz grn, *straw* 250.00 220.00
a. Double overprint 375.00
Nos. 18-30 (13) 1,250. 1,052.

French Colonies No. 51 Surcharged

1892, Dec.

31 A9 5c on 15c blue 70.00 47.50
a. Double surcharge 300.00 275.00
b. No "f" after "O" 160.00 135.00
c. Pair, one stamp without surcharge 1,700. 1,700.

Navigation and Commerce — A12

1892-1904 Typo. *Perf. 14x13½*
Name of Colony in Blue or Carmine

32 A12 1c blk, *lil bl* 2.00 1.75
33 A12 2c brn, *buff* 1.45 1.45
34 A12 4c claret, *lav* 2.00 1.90
a. "GUYANE" double 275.00
35 A12 5c grn, *grnsh* 12.50 11.00
36 A12 5c yel grn ('04) 2.40 1.60
37 A12 10c blk, *lavender* 13.50 8.25
38 A12 10c red ('00) 4.75 1.60
39 A12 15c blue, quadrille paper 42.50 4.00
40 A12 15c gray, *lt gray* ('00) 122.50 110.00
41 A12 20c red, *grn* 25.00 18.00
42 A12 25c blk, *rose* 20.00 5.50
43 A12 25c blue ('00) 22.50 *22.50*
44 A12 30c brn, *bis* 24.00 18.00
45 A12 40c red, *straw* 24.00 16.00
46 A12 50c car, *rose* 35.00 18.00
47 A12 50c brn, *az* ('00) 26.00 26.00
48 A12 75c dp vio, *org* 37.50 27.50
49 A12 1fr brn grn, *straw* 18.00 14.00
50 A12 2fr vio, *rose* ('02) 180.00 16.00
Nos. 32-50 (19) 615.60 323.05

Perf. 13½x14 stamps are counterfeits.
For surcharges see Nos. 87-93.

Great Anteater — A13

Washing Gold — A14

Palm Grove at Cayenne A15

1905-28

51 A13 1c black .40 .40
52 A13 2c blue .40 .40
a. Imperf 57.50
53 A13 4c red brn .40 .40
54 A13 5c green 1.25 1.10
55 A13 5c org ('22) .40 *.45*
56 A13 10c rose 1.50 1.10
57 A13 10c grn ('22) .65 .40
58 A13 10c red, *bluish* ('25) .45 .45
59 A13 15c violet 1.75 1.25
60 A14 20c red brn .65 .65
61 A14 25c blue 3.00 1.60
62 A14 25c vio ('22) .60 .50
63 A14 30c black 2.50 1.00
64 A14 30c rose ('22) .50 *.60*
65 A14 30c red org ('25) .45 .45
66 A14 30c dk grn, *grnsh* ('28) 1.35 1.35
67 A14 35c blk, *yel* ('06) .65 .65
68 A14 40c rose 1.50 .85
69 A14 40c black ('22) .40 *.45*
70 A14 45c olive ('07) 1.00 .95
71 A14 50c violet 4.25 3.50
72 A14 50c blue ('22) .55 *.65*
73 A14 50c gray ('25) .80 .80
74 A14 60c lil, *rose* ('25) .65 .65
75 A14 65c myr grn ('26) .85 .80
76 A14 75c green 1.60 1.40
77 A14 85c magenta ('26) .85 .80
78 A15 1fr rose .90 .85
a. Imperf 82.50
79 A15 1fr bl, *bluish* ('25) .85 .80
80 A15 1fr bl, *yel grn* ('28) 2.75 2.75
81 A15 1.10fr lt red ('28) 1.50 1.50
82 A15 2fr blue 1.35 1.35
83 A15 2fr org red, *yel* ('26) 2.75 2.40
84 A15 5fr black 8.50 6.50
a. Imperf 82.50
85 A15 10fr grn, *yel* ('24) 14.00 *14.50*
a. Printed on both sides 140.00
86 A15 20fr brn lake ('24) 17.50 17.50
Nos. 51-86 (36) 79.45 71.75

For surcharges see Nos. 94-108, B1-B2.

Issue of 1892 Surcharged in Black or Carmine

1912

Spacing between figures of surcharge 1.5mm (5c), 2mm (10c)

87 A12 5c on 2c brn, *buff* 1.60 *2.00*
88 A12 5c on 4c cl, *lav* (C) 1.20 *1.60*
89 A12 5c on 20c red, *grn* 1.75 *1.90*
90 A12 5c on 25c blk, *rose* (C) 4.00 4.75
91 A12 5c on 30c brn, *bis* (C) 1.75 *1.90*
92 A12 10c on 40c red, *straw* 1.40 *1.90*
a. Pair, one stamp without surcharge 1,250.
93 A12 10c on 50c car, *rose* 4.25 *5.25*
a. Double surcharge 550.00
Nos. 87-93 (7) 15.95 *19.30*

Two spacings between the surcharged numerals are found on Nos. 87 to 93. For detailed listings, see the *Scott Classic Specialized Catalogue of Stamps and Covers.*

No. 59 Surcharged in Various Colors

1922

94 A13 1c on 15c vio (Bk) .65 *.75*
a. Double surcharge 90.00
95 A13 2c on 15c vio (Bl) .65 *.75*
a. Inverted surcharge 97.50
b. In pair with unovptd. stamp 250.00
c. No. 95a, in pair with unovptd. stamp 850.00
96 A13 4c on 15c vio (G) .65 *.75*
a. Double surcharge 90.00
b. In pair with unovptd. stamp 275.00
97 A13 5c on 15c vio (R) .65 *.75*
a. In pair with unovptd. stamp 275.00
Nos. 94-97 (4) 2.60 3.00

Type of 1905-28 Srchd. in Blue

1923

98 A15 10fr on 1fr grn, *yel* 22.50 *24.00*
99 A15 20fr on 5fr lilac, *rose* 22.50 *24.00*

Stamps and Types of 1905-28 Srchd. in Black or Red

1924-27

100 A13 25c on 15c vio ('25) .85 *.85*
a. Triple surcharge 130.00 130.00
b. In pair with unovptd. stamp 260.00
101 A15 25c on 2fr bl ('24) .90 *.95*
a. Double surcharge 140.00
b. Triple surcharge 150.00
102 A14 65c on 45c ol (R) ('25) 1.75 *1.90*
103 A14 85c on 45c ol (R) ('25) 1.75 *1.90*
104 A14 90c on 75c red ('27) 1.50 1.50
105 A15 1.05fr on 2fr lt yel brn ('27) 1.50 1.50
106 A15 1.25fr on 1fr ultra (R) ('26) 1.60 *1.75*
107 A15 1.50fr on 1fr lt bl ('27) 1.60 *1.75*
108 A15 3fr on 5fr vio ('27) 1.75 *2.00*
a. No period after "F" 12.00 12.00
Nos. 100-108 (9) 13.20 14.10

Carib Archer — A16

Shooting Rapids, Maroni River A17

Government Building, Cayenne — A18

1929-40 *Perf. 13½x14*

109 A16 1c gray lil & grnsh bl .25 .25
a. Imperf 35.00

110	A16	2c dk red & bl grn	.25	.25
a.		Imperf	35.00	
111	A16	3c gray lil & grnsh bl ('40)	.30	.30
112	A16	4c ol brn & red vio	.30	.30
113	A16	5c Prus bl & red org	.30	.30
114	A16	10c mag & brn	.30	.30
115	A16	15c yel brn & red org	.30	.30
a.		Imperf	35.00	
116	A16	20c dk bl & ol grn	.30	.30
117	A16	25c dk red & dk brn	.50	.50

Perf. 14x13½

118	A17	30c dl & lt grn	.70	.70
119	A17	30c grn & brn ('40)	.50	.50
120	A17	35c Prus grn & ol grn ('38)	1.10	1.10
121	A17	40c org brn & ol gray	.30	.30
122	A17	45c grn & dk brn	1.20	1.20
123	A17	45c ol grn & lt grn ('40)	.70	.70
124	A17	50c dk bl & ol gray	.40	.40
a.		Imperf	35.00	
125	A17	55c vio bl & car ('38)	1.50	1.50
126	A17	60c sal & grn ('40)	.75	.75
a.		Imperf	47.50	
127	A17	65c sal & grn	1.10	1.10
128	A17	70c ind & sl bl ('40)	1.30	1.30
129	A17	75c ind & sl bl	1.15	1.15
130	A17	80c blk & vio bl ('38)	.80	.80
131	A17	90c dk red & ver	1.10	1.10
132	A17	90c red vio & brn ('39)	1.30	1.30
133	A17	1fr lt vio & brn	.70	.70
134	A17	1fr car & lt red ('38)	2.10	2.10
135	A17	1fr blk & vio bl ('40)	.80	.80
136	A18	1.05fr ver & olivine	6.25	6.25
137	A18	1.10fr ol brn & red vio	7.25	5.75
138	A18	1.25fr blk brn & bl grn ('33)	.80	.80
139	A18	1.25fr rose & lt red ('39)	1.10	1.10
140	A18	1.40fr ol brn & red vio ('40)	1.30	1.30
141	A18	1.50fr dk bl & lt bl	.40	.40
142	A18	1.60fr ol brn & bl grn ('40)	1.30	1.30
143	A18	1.75fr brn red & blk brn ('33)	2.25	2.25
144	A18	1.75fr vio bl ('38)	1.75	1.75
145	A18	2fr dk grn & rose red	.65	.65
146	A18	2.25fr vio bl ('39)	1.30	1.30
147	A18	2.50fr cop red & brn ('40)	1.30	1.30
148	A18	3fr brn red & red vio	.75	.75
149	A18	5fr dl vio & yel grn	1.25	1.25
150	A18	10fr ol gray & dp ultra	1.50	1.50
151	A18	20fr indigo & ver	2.50	2.50
		Nos. 109-151 (43)	51.95	50.45

For types A16-A18 without "RF," see Nos. 170C-170E.

Common Design Types pictured following the introduction.

Colonial Exposition Issue
Common Design Types

1931 Engr. *Perf. 12½*

Name of Country in Black

152	CD70	40c dp green	5.50	5.50
153	CD71	50c violet	5.50	5.50
154	CD72	90c red orange	5.50	5.50
155	CD73	1.50fr dull blue	5.50	5.50
		Nos. 152-155 (4)	22.00	22.00

Recapture of Cayenne by d'Estrées, 1676 — A19

Products of French Guiana A20

1935, Oct. 21 *Perf. 13*

156	A19	40c gray brn	5.75	5.75
157	A19	50c dull red	10.00	8.00
158	A19	1.50fr ultra	5.75	5.75
159	A20	1.75fr lilac rose	12.50	11.50
160	A20	5fr brown	10.00	9.00
161	A20	10fr blue green	10.50	10.00
		Nos. 156-161 (6)	54.50	50.00

Tercentenary of the founding of French possessions in the West Indies.

Paris International Exposition Issue
Common Design Types

1937, Apr. 15

162	CD74	20c deep violet	1.75	1.75
163	CD75	30c dark green	1.75	1.75
164	CD76	40c carmine rose	1.75	1.75
165	CD77	50c dark brown	1.75	1.75
166	CD78	90c red	1.75	1.75
167	CD79	1.50fr ultra	2.25	2.25
		Nos. 162-167 (6)	11.00	11.00

Colonial Arts Exhibition Issue
Souvenir Sheet
Common Design Type

1937 *Imperf.*

168	CD75	3fr violet	11.50	*13.50*

New York World's Fair Issue
Common Design Type

1939, May 10 Engr. *Perf. 12½x12*

169	CD82	1.25fr car lake	1.30	1.30
170	CD82	2.25fr ultra	1.30	1.30

View of Cayenne and Marshal Petain A21a

1941 Engr. *Perf. 12½x12*

170A	A21a	1fr deep lilac	.80	.80
170B	A21a	2.50fr blue	.80	.80

For surcharges, see Nos. B11A-B11B.

Types of 1929-40 without "RF"

1944 *Methods and Perfs as Before*

170C	A16	15c yel brn & red org	1.10
170D	A17	1fr black & vio blue	1.10
170E	A18	1.50fr dk blue & lt blue	1.40
		Nos. 170C-170E (3)	3.60

Nos. 170C-170E were issued by the Vichy government in France, but were not issued in French Guiana.

Catalogue values for unused stamps in this section, from this point to the end of the section, are for Never Hinged items.

Eboue Issue
Common Design Type

1945 Engr. *Perf. 13*

171	CD91	2fr black	.95	.80
172	CD91	25fr Prussian green	1.50	1.20

This issue exists imperforate.

Arms of Cayenne A22

1945 Litho. *Perf. 12*

173	A22	10c dp gray violet	.30	.25
174	A22	30c brown org	.35	.25
175	A22	40c lt blue	.35	.25
176	A22	50c violet brn	.75	.60
177	A22	60c orange yel	.75	.60
178	A22	70c pale brown	.75	.60
179	A22	80c lt green	.75	.60
180	A22	1fr blue	.35	.25
181	A22	1.20fr brt violet	.75	.60
182	A22	1.50fr dp orange	1.00	.75
183	A22	2fr black	1.10	.85
184	A22	2.40fr red	1.10	.85
185	A22	3fr pink	1.10	.85
186	A22	4fr dp ultra	1.30	1.00
187	A22	4.50fr dp yel grn	1.30	1.00
188	A22	5fr orange brn	1.30	1.00
189	A22	10fr dk violet	1.30	1.00
190	A22	15fr rose carmine	1.30	1..00
191	A22	20fr olive green	1.50	1.25
		Nos. 173-191 (19)	17.40	12.55

Hammock A23

Guiana Girl A26

Maroni River Bank A24

Inini Scene A25

Toucans A27

Parrots A28

Perf. 13.

1947, June 2 Unwmk. Engr.

192	A23	10c dk blue grn	.30	.25
193	A23	30c brt red	.30	.25
194	A23	50c dk vio brn	.30	.25
195	A24	60c grnsh blk	.60	.45
196	A24	1fr red brn	.85	.60
197	A24	1.50fr black brn	.85	.60
198	A25	2fr dp yel grn	1.10	.75
199	A25	2.50fr dp ultra	1.10	.75
200	A25	3fr red brn	1.00	.70
201	A26	4fr black brn	2.50	1.25
202	A26	5fr deep blue	1.75	1.10
203	A26	6fr red brown	1.75	1.10
204	A27	10fr deep ultra	7.25	4.75
205	A27	15fr black brn	7.25	5.00
206	A27	20fr red brn	9.25	5.00
207	A28	25fr brt bl grn	13.00	8.50
208	A28	40fr black brn	11.00	8.00
		Nos. 192-208 (17)	60.15	39.30

SEMI-POSTAL STAMPS

Regular Issue of 1905-28 Surcharged in Red

1915 Unwmk. *Perf. 13½x14*

B1	A13	10c + 5c rose	17.50	*18.00*
a.		Inverted surcharge	250.00	250.00
b.		Double surcharge	250.00	250.00

Regular Issue of 1905-28 Surcharged in Rose

B2	A13	10c + 5c rose	1.60	1.60

Curie Issue
Common Design Type

1938 *Perf. 13*

B3	CD80	1.75fr + 50c brt ultra	13.50	13.50

French Revolution Issue
Common Design Type

1939 Photo.

Name and Value in Black

B4	CD83	45c + 25c green	11.50	11.50
B5	CD83	70c + 30c brown	11.50	11.50
B6	CD83	90c + 35c red org	11.50	11.50
B7	CD83	1.25fr + 1fr rose pink	11.50	11.50
B8	CD83	2.25fr + 2fr blue	11.50	11.50
		Nos. B4-B8 (5)	57.50	57.50

Common Design Type and

Colonial Infantryman — SP1

Colonial Policeman SP2

1941 Photo. *Perf. 13½*

B9	SP1	1fr + 1fr red	1.30
B10	CD86	1.50fr + 3fr maroon	1.50
B11	SP2	2.50fr + 1fr blue	1.30
		Nos. B9-B11 (3)	4.10

Nos. B9-B11 were issued by the Vichy government in France, but were not placed on sale in French Guiana.

Nos. 170A-170B Srchd. in Black or Red

1944 Engr. *Perf. 12½x12*

B11A	50c + 1.50fr on 2.50fr deep blue (R)	.80
B11B	+ 2.50fr on 1fr dp lilac	.80

Colonial Development Fund.

Nos. B11A-B11B were issued by the Vichy government in France, but were not placed on sale in French Guiana.

Catalogue values for unused stamps in this section, from this point to the end of the section, are for Never Hinged items.

Red Cross Issue
Common Design Type

1944 *Perf. 14½x14*

B12	CD90	5fr + 20fr dk copper brn	1.75	1.25

The surtax was for the French Red Cross and national relief.

AIR POST STAMPS

Cayenne AP1

Perf. 13½

1933, Nov. 20 Unwmk. Photo.

C1	AP1	50c orange brn	.30	.30
C2	AP1	1fr yellow grn	.50	.50
C3	AP1	1.50fr dk blue	.70	.70
C4	AP1	2fr orange	.70	.70
C5	AP1	3fr black	.85	.85
C6	AP1	5fr violet	.85	.85
C7	AP1	10fr olive grn	.85	.85
C8	AP1	20fr scarlet	1.25	1.25
		Nos. C1-C8 (8)	6.00	6.00

For No. C1 without "RF," see No. C8A.

A 20fr violet exists, but was not regularly issued. Value, $175.

Catalogue values for unused stamps in this section, from this point to the end of the section, are for Never Hinged items.

Type of 1933 without "RF" and

AP1a

AP1b

Perf. 13½, 13 (#C8C)

1941-44 Photo, Engr. (#C8C)

C8A AP1 50c orange brn 1.00
C8B AP1a 50f bl grn & red brown ('42) 1.40
C8C AP1b 100f dk blue ('44) 1.60
Nos. C8A-C8C (3) 4.00

Nos. C8A-C8C were issued by the Vichy government in France, but were not placed on sale in French Guiana.

Common Design Type

1945 Photo. *Perf. 14½x14*

C9 CD87 50fr dark green 1.30 1.10
C10 CD87 100fr plum 2.50 2.00

Victory Issue
Common Design Type

1946, May 8 Engr. *Perf. 12½*

C11 CD92 8fr black 1.75 1.25

Chad to Rhine Issue
Common Design Types

1946, June 6

C12 CD93 5fr dk slate bl 1.75 1.50
C13 CD94 10fr lilac rose 1.75 1.50
C14 CD95 15fr dk vio brn 1.75 1.50
C15 CD96 20fr dk slate grn 2.00 1.60
C16 CD97 25fr vio brown 2.40 2.00
C17 CD98 50fr bright lilac 3.00 2.25
Nos. C12-C17 (6) 12.65 10.35

Eagles — AP2

Tapir — AP3

Toucans — AP4

1947, June 2 Engr. *Perf. 13*

C18 AP2 50fr deep green 22.50 17.50
C19 AP3 100fr red brown 15.00 13.00
C20 AP4 200fr dk gray bl 30.00 24.00
Nos. C18-C20 (3) 67.50 54.50

AIR POST SEMI-POSTAL STAMP

French Revolution Issue
Common Design Type
Unwmk.

1939, July 5 Photo. *Perf. 13*
Name & Value Typo. in Orange

CB1 CD83 5fr + 4fr brn blk 22.00 22.00

Nurse with Mother & Child — SPAP1

Unwmk.

1942, June 22 Engr. *Perf. 13*

CB2 SPAP1 1.50fr + 50c green 1.00
CB3 SPAP1 2fr + 6fr brn & red 1.00

Native children's welfare fund.

Nos. CB2-CB3 were issued by the Vichy government in France, but were not placed on sale in French Guiana.

Colonial Education Fund
Common Design Type

1942, June 22

CB4 CD86a 1.20fr + 1.80fr blue & red 1.10

No. CB4 was issued by the Vichy government in France, but was not placed on sale in French Guiana.

POSTAGE DUE STAMPS

Postage Due Stamps of France, 1893-1926, Overprinted

1925-27 Unwmk. *Perf. 14x13½*

J1 D2 5c light blue .70 *.75*
a. In pair with unovptd. stamp 375.00
J2 D2 10c brown 1.00 *1.10*
J3 D2 20c olive green 1.10 *1.25*
J4 D2 50c violet brown 1.50 *1.60*
J5 D2 3fr magenta ('27) 11.00 *12.50*

Surcharged in Black

J6 D2 15c on 20c ol grn 1.00 *1.10*
a. Blue surcharge 67.50
J7 D2 25c on 5c lt bl 1.30 *1.40*
a. In pair with unovptd. stamp 375.00
J8 D2 30c on 20c ol grn 1.50 *1.60*
J9 D2 45c on 10c brn 1.50 *1.60*
J10 D2 60c on 5c lt bl 1.50 *1.60*
J11 D2 1fr on 20c ol grn 2.25 *2.40*
J12 D2 2fr on 50c vio brn 2.25 *2.40*
Nos. J1-J12 (12) 26.60 *29.30*

Royal Palms — D3

Guiana Girl — D4

1929, Oct. 14 Typo. *Perf. 13½x14*

J13 D3 5c indigo & Prus bl .45 *.50*
J14 D3 10c bis brn & Prus grn .45 *.50*
J15 D3 20c grn & rose red .45 *.50*
J16 D3 30c ol brn & rose red .45 *.50*
J17 D3 50c vio & ol brn .95 *1.00*
J18 D3 60c brn red & ol brn 1.30 *1.40*
J19 D4 1fr dp bl & org brn 1.75 *1.90*
J20 D4 2fr brn red & bluish grn 2.00 *2.10*
J21 D4 3fr violet & blk 4.25 *4.50*
Nos. J13-J21 (9) 12.05 *12.90*

Catalogue values for unused stamps in this section, from this point to the end of the section, are for Never Hinged items.

D5

1947, June 2 Engr. *Perf. 14x13*

J22 D5 10c dk car rose .35 .35
J23 D5 30c dull green .45 .45
J24 D5 50c black .45 .45
J25 D5 1fr brt ultra .55 .55
J26 D5 2fr dk brown red .55 .55
J27 D5 3fr deep violet 1.00 .80
J28 D5 4fr red 1.30 1.10
J29 D5 5fr brown violet 1.50 1.25
J30 D5 10fr blue green 2.25 1.90
J31 D5 20fr lilac rose 3.00 2.25
Nos. J22-J31 (10) 11.40 9.65

FRENCH GUINEA

'french 'gi-nē

LOCATION — On the coast of West Africa, between Portuguese Guinea and Sierra Leone.
GOVT. — French colony
AREA — 89,436 sq. mi.
POP. — 2,058,442 (est. 1941)
CAPITAL — Conakry

French Guinea stamps were replaced by those of French West Africa around 1944-45. French Guinea became the Republic of Guinea Oct. 2, 1958. See "Guinea" for issues of the republic.

100 Centimes = 1 Franc

See French West Africa No. 66 for additional stamp inscribed "Guinee" and "Afrique Occidentale Francaise."

Navigation and Commerce
A1

Fulah Shepherd
A2

Perf. 14x13½

1892-1900 Typo. Unwmk.
Name of Colony in Blue or Carmine

1 A1 1c black, *lilac bl* 2.40 1.60
2 A1 2c brown, *buff* 2.40 2.00
3 A1 4c claret, *lav* 3.25 2.00
4 A1 5c green, *grnsh* 8.00 8.00
5 A1 10c blk, *lavender* 8.00 4.75
6 A1 10c red ('00) 45.00 40.00
7 A1 15c blue, quadrille paper 16.00 8.00
8 A1 15c gray, *lt gray* ('00) 100.00 87.50
9 A1 20c red, *grn* 20.00 16.00
10 A1 25c black, *rose* 16.00 8.00
11 A1 25c blue ('00) 24.00 24.00
12 A1 30c brown, *bis* 40.00 32.50
13 A1 40c red, *straw* 40.00 32.50
a. "GUINEE FRANCAISE" double 475.00 475.00
14 A1 50c car, *rose* 47.50 35.00
15 A1 50c brown, *az* ('00) 40.00 40.00
16 A1 75c dp vio, *org* 65.00 47.50
17 A1 1fr brnz grn, *straw* 50.00 40.00
Nos. 1-17 (17) 527.55 429.35

Perf. 13½x14 stamps are counterfeits.
For surcharges see Nos. 48-54.

1904

18 A2 1c black, *yel grn* 1.20 1.20
19 A2 2c vio brn, *buff* 1.20 1.20
20 A2 4c carmine, *bl* 1.60 1.60
21 A2 5c green, *grnsh* 1.60 1.60
22 A2 10c carmine 4.00 2.40
23 A2 15c violet, *rose* 12.00 5.50
24 A2 20c carmine, *grn* 16.00 16.00
25 A2 25c blue 16.00 10.00
26 A2 30c brown 24.00 24.00
27 A2 40c red, *straw* 35.00 24.00
28 A2 50c brown, *az* 32.50 24.00
29 A2 75c green, *org* 32.50 32.50
30 A2 1fr brnz grn, *straw* 47.50 47.50
31 A2 2fr red, *org* 87.50 87.50
32 A2 5fr green, *yel grn* 120.00 120.00
Nos. 18-32 (15) 432.60 399.00

For surcharges see Nos. 55-62.

Gen. Louis Faidherbé
A3

Oil Palm — A4

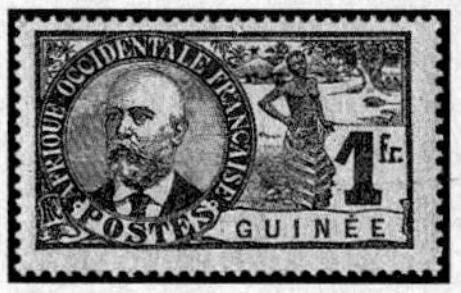

Dr. Noel Eugène Ballay
A5

1906-07
Name of Colony in Red or Blue

33 A3 1c gray .80 .80
34 A3 2c brown 1.20 1.20
35 A3 4c brown, *bl* 1.60 1.60
36 A3 5c green 4.00 2.00
37 A3 10c carmine (B) 24.00 1.60
38 A4 20c black, *blue* 8.00 4.00
39 A4 25c blue, *pnksh* 8.00 6.50
40 A4 30c brown, *pnksh* 8.00 4.00
41 A4 35c black, *yellow* 6.50 2.40
42 A4 45c choc, *grnsh gray* 8.00 4.00
43 A4 50c dp violet 16.00 12.00
44 A4 75c blue, *org* 12.00 4.00
45 A5 1fr black, *az* 20.00 24.00
46 A5 2fr blue, *pink* 40.00 *45.00*
47 A5 5fr car, *straw* (B) 60.00 *65.00*
Nos. 33-47 (15) 218.10 *178.10*

Regular Issues Surcharged in Black or Carmine

1912

On Issue of 1892-1900

48 A1 5c on 2c brown, *buff* 1.60 *2.00*
49 A1 5c on 4c cl, *lav* (C) 1.25 *1.60*
50 A1 5c on 15c blue (C) 1.25 *1.60*
51 A1 5c on 20c red, *grn* 4.00 *5.25*
52 A1 5c on 30c brn, *bis* (C) 5.50 *6.50*
53 A1 10c on 40c red, *straw* 2.40 *3.25*
54 A1 10c on 75c dp vio, *org* 8.00 *9.50*
a. Double surcharge, inverted 325.00

On Issue of 1904

55 A2 5c on 2c vio brn, *buff* 1.20 *1.20*
a. Pair, one without surcharge 650.00
b. Inverted surcharge 210.00
56 A2 5c on 4c car, *blue* 1.20 *1.20*
57 A2 5c on 15c violet, *rose* 1.20 *1.20*
58 A2 5c on 20c car, *grn* 1.60 1.60
59 A2 5c on 25c blue (C) 1.60 *2.00*
60 A2 5c on 30c brown (C) 2.00 *3.25*

61 A2 10c on 40c red, *straw* 2.00 *3.25*
62 A2 10c on 50c brn, *az* (C) 5.50 *6.50*
Nos. 48-62 (15) 40.30 49.90

Two spacings between the surcharged numerals are found on Nos. 48 to 62. For detailed listings, see the *Scott Classic Specialized Catalogue of Stamps and Covers.*

Ford at Kitim — A6

1913-33 ***Perf. 13½x14***
63 A6 1c violet & bl .25 .25
a. Imperf. 72.50
64 A6 2c brn & vio brn .25 .25
a. Double impression of vio brn 160.00
65 A6 4c gray & black .25 .25
66 A6 5c yel grn & bl grn 1.20 .40
a. Booklet pane of 4 —
Complete booklet, 10 #66a 275.00
67 A6 5c brn vio & grn ('22) .40 .25
68 A6 10c red org & rose 1.20 .40
a. Booklet pane of 4 —
Complete booklet, 10 #68a 550.00
69 A6 10c yel grn & bl grn ('22) .55 .25
70 A6 10c vio & ver ('25) .80 .40
a. Imperf. 45.00
71 A6 15c vio brn & rose, chalky paper ('16) .80 .40
a. Booklet pane of 4 —
Complete booklet, 10 #71a 1,200.
72 A6 15c gray grn & yel grn ('25) .40 .40
73 A6 15c red brn & rose lil ('27) .40 .30
74 A6 20c brown & violet .40 .40
75 A6 20c grn & bl grn ('26) .80 .80
76 A6 20c brn red & brn ('27) .80 .50
77 A6 25c ultra & blue 2.75 1.60
78 A6 25c black & vio ('22) .80 .80
79 A6 30c vio brn & grn 1.60 1.20
80 A6 30c red org & rose ('22) 1.20 1.10
81 A6 30c rose red & grn ('25) .30 .30
82 A6 30c dl grn & bl grn ('28) 1.60 1.60
83 A6 35c blue & rose .55 .55
84 A6 40c green & gray 1.20 1.20
85 A6 45c brown & red 1.20 1.20
86 A6 50c ultra & black 6.50 4.75
87 A6 50c ultra & bl ('22) 1.60 .80
88 A6 50c yel brn & ol ('25) .80 .80
89 A6 60c vio, *pnksh* ('25) .80 .80
90 A6 65c yel brn & sl bl ('26) 2.00 1.20
91 A6 75c red & ultra 1.60 1.60
92 A6 75c indigo & dl bl ('25) .80 1.20
93 A6 75c mag & yel grn ('27) 1.60 1.20
94 A6 85c ol grn & red brn ('26) 1.20 1.20
95 A6 90c brn red & rose ('30) 5.50 4.75
96 A6 1fr violet & black 1.60 2.40
97 A6 1.10fr vio & ol brn ('28) 8.00 8.00
98 A6 1.25fr vio & yel brn ('33) 2.40 1.60
99 A6 1.50fr dk bl & lt bl ('30) 6.50 2.40
100 A6 1.75fr ol brn & vio ('33) 1.75 1.60
101 A6 2fr orange & vio brn 4.00 4.00
102 A6 3fr red violet ('30) 8.00 5.50
103 A6 5fr black & vio 16.00 16.00
104 A6 5fr dl bl & blk ('22) 4.00 2.40
Nos. 63-104 (42) 94.35 77.00

For surcharges see Nos. 105-115, B1.

Nos. 66, 68 and 77 pasted on colored cardboard and overprinted "VALEUR D'ECHANGE" were used as emergency currency in 1920.

Type of 1913-33 Surcharged

1922
105 A6 60c on 75c violet, *pnksh* .40 .40

Stamps and Type of 1913-33 Surcharged

1924-27
106 A6 25c on 2fr org & brn (R) .40 .40
107 A6 25c on 5fr dull bl & blk .40 .40
108 A6 65c on 75c rose & ultra ('25) 1.60 1.60
109 A6 85c on 75c rose & ultra ('25) 2.40 2.00
110 A6 90c on 75c brn red & cer ('27) 3.25 3.25
111 A6 1.25fr on 1fr dk bl & ultra ('26) 1.20 1.60
112 A6 1.50fr on 1fr dp bl & lt bl ('27) 2.40 2.40
113 A6 3fr on 5fr mag & sl ('27) 4.00 4.00
114 A6 10fr on 5fr bl & bl grn, *bluish* ('27) 8.00 8.00
115 A6 20fr on 5fr rose lil & brn ol, *pnksh* ('27) 20.00 20.00
Nos. 106-115 (10) 43.65 43.65

Common Design Types pictured following the introduction.

Colonial Exposition Issue
Common Design Types

1931 **Engr.** ***Perf. 12½***
Name of Country in Black
116 CD70 40c deep green 4.75 4.75
a. "GUINÉE FRANCAISE" omitted 55.00 *67.50*
117 CD71 50c violet 4.75 4.75
118 CD72 90c red orange 4.75 4.75
a. "GUINÉE FRANCAISE" omitted 55.00 *70.00*
119 CD73 1.50fr dull blue 5.50 5.50
a. "GUINÉE FRANCAISE" omitted 55.00 *67.50*
Nos. 116-119 (4) 19.75 19.75
Set, never hinged 32.00

Paris International Exposition Issue
Common Design Types

1937 ***Perf. 13***
120 CD74 20c deep violet 2.00 2.00
121 CD75 30c dark green 2.00 2.00
122 CD76 40c carmine rose 2.40 2.40
123 CD77 50c dark brown 1.60 1.60
124 CD78 90c red 1.60 1.60
125 CD79 1.50fr ultra 2.40 2.40
Nos. 120-125 (6) 12.00 12.00
Set, never hinged 20.25

Colonial Arts Exhibition Issue
Souvenir Sheet
Common Design Type

1937 ***Imperf.***
126 CD76 3fr Prussian green 12.00 *16.00*
Never hinged 16.00

Guinea Village A7

Hausa Basket Workers A8

Forest Waterfall A9

Guinea Women — A10

1938-40 ***Perf. 13***
128 A7 2c vermilion .25 .25
129 A7 3c ultra .25 .25
130 A7 4c green .25 .25
131 A7 5c rose car .25 .25
132 A7 10c peacock blue .25 .25
133 A7 15c violet brown .25 .25
134 A8 20c dk carmine .30 .25
135 A8 25c pck blue .40 .25
136 A8 30c ultra .40 .25
137 A8 35c green .55 .50
138 A8 40c blk brn ('40) .40 .40
139 A8 45c dk green ('40) .40 .40
140 A8 50c red brown .55 .50
141 A9 55c dk ultra 1.20 .80
142 A9 60c dk ultra ('40) 1.20 1.20
143 A9 65c green 1.20 .80
144 A9 70c green ('40) 1.20 1.20
145 A9 80c rose violet .80 .55
146 A9 90c rose vio ('39) 1.25 1.25
147 A9 1fr orange red 2.40 2.00
148 A9 1fr brn blk ('40) .40 .40
149 A9 1.25fr org red ('39) 1.40 1.40
150 A9 1.40fr brown ('40) 1.20 1.20
151 A9 1.50fr violet 2.40 2.00
152 A10 1.60fr org red ('40) 1.60 1.60
153 A10 1.75fr ultra .80 .80
154 A10 2fr magenta 1.20 .80
155 A10 2.25fr brt ultra ('39) 1.75 1.75
156 A10 2.50fr brn blk ('40) 1.60 1.60
157 A10 3fr peacock blue .95 .40
158 A10 5fr rose violet .95 .80
159 A10 10fr slate green 1.60 1.60
160 A10 20fr chocolate 2.40 2.40
Nos. 128-160 (33) 32.00 28.60
Set, never hinged 45.00

For surcharges see Nos. B8-B11.

Caillié Issue
Common Design Type

1939 **Engr.** ***Perf. 12½x12***
161 CD81 90c org brn & org .40 .80
162 CD81 2fr brt violet .40 1.20
163 CD81 2.25fr ultra & dk bl .40 1.20
Nos. 161-163 (3) 1.20 3.20
Set, never hinged 2.40

René Caillié, French explorer, death cent.

New York World's Fair Issue
Common Design Type

1939
164 CD82 1.25fr carmine lake .80 1.60
165 CD82 2.25fr ultra .80 1.60
Set, never hinged 2.40

Ford at Kitim and Marshal Petain — A11

1941 ***Perf. 12x12½***
166 A11 1fr green .40 —
167 A11 2.50fr deep blue .40 —
Set, never hinged 1.60

For surcharges, see Nos. B15-B16.

Types of 1933-40 without "RF"

1943-44 ***Perf. 13***
168 A7 10c peacock blue .40
169 A8 20c dk carmine .40
170 A8 30c ultramarine .40
171 A8 40c black brown 1.20
172 A9 60c dk ultramarine 1.20
173 A9 1.50fr violet 1.20
174 A10 2fr magenta 1.60
Nos. 168-174 (7) 6.40
Set, never hinged 9.50

Nos. 168-174 were issued by the Vichy government in France, but were not placed on sale in French Guinea.

SEMI-POSTAL STAMPS

Regular Issue of 1913 Surcharged in Red

1915 **Unwmk.** ***Perf. 13½x14***
B1 A6 10c + 5c org & rose 1.60 1.60

Curie Issue
Common Design Type

1938 **Engr.** ***Perf. 13***
B2 CD80 1.75fr + 50c brt ultra 8.75 8.75
Never hinged 14.00

French Revolution Issue
Common Design Type

1939 **Photo.**
Name and Value Typo. in Black
B3 CD83 45c + 25c green 9.50 9.50
B4 CD83 70c + 30c brown 9.50 9.50
B5 CD83 90c + 35c red org 9.50 9.50
B6 CD83 1.25fr + 1fr rose pink 9.50 9.50
B7 CD83 2.25fr + 2fr blue 9.50 9.50
Nos. B3-B7 (5) 47.50 47.50
Set, never hinged 80.00

Stamps of 1938, Surcharged in Black

1941 **Unwmk.** ***Perf. 13***
B8 A8 50c + 1fr red brn 4.00 4.00
B9 A9 80c + 2fr rose vio 8.00 8.00
B10 A9 1.50fr + 2fr brn 8.00 8.00
B11 A10 2fr + 3fr magenta 8.00 8.00
Nos. B8-B11 (4) 28.00 28.00
Set, never hinged 55.00

Common Design Type and

Senegalese Soldier SP1

Colonial Infantryman SP2

1941 **Unwmk.** ***Perf. 13***
B12 SP1 1fr + 1fr red 1.25
B13 CD86 1.50fr + 3fr maroon 1.40
B14 SP2 2.50fr + 1fr blue 1.40
Nos. B12-B14 (3) 4.05
Set, never hinged 6.50

Nos. B12-B14 were issued by the Vichy government in France, but were not placed on sale in the French Guinea.

Nos. 166-167 Surcharged in Black or Red

1944 Engr. *Perf. 12½x12*

B15	50c + 1.50fr on 2.50fr deep blue (R)	.40	
B16	+ 2.50fr on 1fr green	.40	
	Set, never hinged	1.60	

Colonial Development Fund.

Nos. B15-B16 were issued by the Vichy government in France, but were not placed on sale in French Guinea.

AIR POST STAMPS

Common Design Type

1940 Unwmk. Engr. *Perf. 12½x12*

C1	CD85	1.90fr ultra	.40	.40
C2	CD85	2.90fr dark red	.40	.40
C3	CD85	4.50fr dk gray grn	.80	.80
C4	CD85	4.90fr yellow bis	.80	.80
C5	CD85	6.90fr dp orange	1.60	1.60
		Nos. C1-C5 (5)	4.00	4.00
		Set, never hinged	6.00	

Common Design Types

1942 Engr.

C6	CD88	50c car & blue	.25	
C7	CD88	1fr brown & blk	.30	
C8	CD88	2fr dk grn & red brn	.30	
C9	CD88	3fr dk bl & scar	.50	
C10	CD88	5fr vio & brn red	.80	

Frame Engraved, Center Typographed

C11	CD89	10fr multicolored	.80	
C12	CD89	20fr multicolored	1.20	
C13	CD89	50fr multicolored	1.60	—
		Nos. C6-C13 (8)	5.75	
		Set, never hinged	12.00	

There is doubt whether Nos. C6-C12 were officially placed in use.

AIR POST SEMI-POSTAL STAMPS

Dahomey types SPAP1-SPAP3 inscribed "Guinée Frcaise" or "Guinée"

Perf. 13½x12½, 13 (#CB3)

Photo, Engr. (#CB3)

1942, June 22

CB1	SPAP1	1.50fr + 3.50fr green	.40	*5.50*
CB2	SPAP2	2fr + 6fr brown	.40	*5.50*
CB3	SPAP3	3fr + 9fr car red	.40	*5.50*
		Nos. CB1-CB3 (3)	1.20	16.50
		Set, never hinged	2.40	

Native children's welfare fund.

Colonial Education Fund

Common Design Type

Perf. 12½x13½

1942, June 22 Engr.

CB4	CD86a	1.20fr + 1.80fr blue & red	.40	*5.50*
		Never hinged	.80	

POSTAGE DUE STAMPS

Fulah Woman D1

Heads and Coast D2

1905 Unwmk. Typo. *Perf. 14x13½*

J1	D1	5c blue	1.60	*3.25*
J2	D1	10c brown	2.40	*3.25*
J3	D1	15c green	8.00	6.50
J4	D1	30c rose	8.00	6.50
J5	D1	50c black	12.00	*13.00*
J6	D1	60c dull orange	12.00	*16.00*
J7	D1	1fr violet	40.00	*47.50*
		Nos. J1-J7 (7)	84.00	96.00

1906-08

J8	D2	5c grn, *grnsh* ('08)	20.00	13.00
J9	D2	10c violet brn ('08)	8.00	5.50
J10	D2	15c dk blue ('08)	8.00	5.50
J11	D2	20c blk, *yellow*	8.00	5.50
J12	D2	30c red, *straw* ('08)	27.50	26.00
J13	D2	50c violet ('08)	24.00	*26.00*
J14	D2	60c blk, *buff* ('08)	24.00	21.00
J15	D2	1fr blk, *pnksh* ('08)	16.00	13.50
		Nos. J8-J15 (8)	135.50	116.00

D3

1914

J16	D3	5c green	.40	*.55*
J17	D3	10c rose	.40	*.65*
J18	D3	15c gray	.40	*.80*
J19	D3	20c brown	.80	.80
J20	D3	30c blue	.80	.80
J21	D3	50c black	1.00	*1.25*
J22	D3	60c orange	2.00	*2.40*
J23	D3	1fr violet	2.00	*2.40*
		Nos. J16-J23 (8)	7.80	9.65

Type of 1914 Issue Surcharged

1927

J24	D3	2fr on 1fr lil rose	8.00	*8.00*
a.		No period after "F"	27.50	*32.50*
J25	D3	3fr on 1fr org brn	8.00	*8.00*

D4

1938 Engr.

J26	D4	5c dk violet	.25	.30
J27	D4	10c carmine	.25	.30
J28	D4	15c green	.25	.30
J29	D4	20c red brown	.25	.40
J30	D4	30c rose violet	.25	.40
J31	D4	50c chocolate	.80	.70
J32	D4	60c peacock blue	.80	1.10
J33	D4	1fr vermilion	.80	1.10
J34	D4	2fr ultra	.80	1.10
J35	D4	3fr black	1.60	1.60
		Nos. J26-J35 (10)	6.05	7.30

For No. J27 without "RF," see No. J36.

Type of 1938 without "RF"

1944

J36	D4	10c carmine	.80
		Never hinged	1.20

No. J36 was issued by the Vichy government in France, but was not placed on sale in French Guinea.

FRENCH INDIA

'french 'in-dē-ə

LOCATION — East coast of India bordering on Bay of Bengal.
GOVT. — French Territory
AREA — 196 sq. mi.
POP. — 323,295 (1941)
CAPITAL — Pondichéry

French India was an administrative unit comprising the five settlements of Chandernagor, Karikal, Mahé, Pondichéry and Yanaon. These united with India in 1949 and 1954.

100 Centimes = 1 Franc
24 Caches = 1 Fanon (1923)
8 Fanons = 1 Rupie

Catalogue values for unused stamps in this country are for Never Hinged items, beginning with Scott 210 in the regular postage section, Scott B14 in the semi-postal section, and Scott C7 in the airpost section.

Navigation and Commerce — A1

Perf. 14x13½

1892-1907 Typo. Unwmk.

Colony Name in Blue or Carmine

1	A1	1c blk, *lil bl*	1.40	1.00
2	A1	2c brn, *buff*	2.40	1.50
3	A1	4c claret, *lav*	3.00	2.50
4	A1	5c grn, *grnsh*	6.00	3.75
5	A1	10c blk, *lavender*	13.50	2.75
6	A1	10c red ('00)	5.00	2.40
7	A1	15c blue, quadrille paper	16.00	5.50
8	A1	15c gray, *lt gray* ('00)	30.00	30.00
9	A1	20c red, *grn*	8.00	5.50
10	A1	25c blk, *rose*	5.25	2.75
11	A1	25c blue ('00)	19.00	16.00
12	A1	30c brn, *bis*	57.50	50.00
13	A1	35c blk, *yel* ('06)	19.00	9.00
14	A1	40c red, *straw*	7.50	7.25
15	A1	45c blk, *gray grn* ('07)	5.25	*6.00*
16	A1	50c car, *rose*	7.25	7.25
17	A1	50c brn, *az* ('00)	16.00	*17.50*
18	A1	75c dp vio, *org*	9.75	*9.50*
19	A1	1fr brnz grn, *straw*	14.00	*14.50*
		Nos. 1-19 (19)	245.80	*194.65*

Perf. 13½x14 stamps are counterfeits.

Nos. 10 and 16 Surcharged in Carmine or Black

1903

20	A1	5c on 25c blk, *rose*	400.00	240.00
21	A1	10c on 25c blk, *rose*	375.00	225.00
22	A1	15c on 25c blk, *rose*	125.00	115.00
23	A1	40c on 50c car, *rose* (Bk)	525.00	425.00
		Nos. 20-23 (4)	1,425.	1,005.

Counterfeits of Nos. 20-23 abound.

A2

Revenue Stamp Surcharged in Black

1903

24	A2	5c gray blue	30.00	30.00

The bottom of the revenue stamps were cut off.

Brahma — A5

Kali Temple near Pondichéry A6

1914-22 *Perf. 13½x14, 14x13½*

25	A5	1c gray & blk	.30	.30
a.		1c light gray & black	.55	.55
26	A5	2c brn vio & blk	.30	.30
27	A5	2c grn & brn vio ('22)	.45	.45
28	A5	3c brown & blk	.40	.40
29	A5	4c orange & blk	.40	.40
30	A5	5c bl grn & blk	.70	.70
31	A5	5c vio brn & blk ('22)	.60	.60
32	A5	10c dp rose & blk	1.25	1.25
33	A5	10c grn & blk ('22)	.90	.90
34	A5	15c vio & blk	1.10	1.10
35	A5	20c org red & blk	2.00	2.00
36	A5	25c blue & blk	2.00	2.00
37	A5	25c ultra & fawn ('22)	1.60	1.60
38	A5	30c ultra & blk	4.00	4.00
39	A5	30c rose & blk ('22)	1.75	1.75
40	A6	35c choc & blk	2.25	2.25
41	A6	40c org red & blk	2.25	2.25
42	A6	45c bl grn & blk	2.25	2.25
43	A6	50c dp rose & blk	2.25	2.25
44	A6	50c ultra & bl ('22)	3.00	3.00
45	A6	75c blue & blk	4.50	4.50
46	A6	1fr yellow & blk	4.50	4.50
47	A6	2fr violet & blk	6.75	6.75
48	A6	5fr ultra & blk	3.50	3.50
49	A6	5fr rose & blk ('22)	5.50	5.50
		Nos. 25-49 (25)	54.50	54.50

For surcharges see Nos. 50-79, 113-116, 156A, B1-B5.

No. 34 Surcharged in Various Colors

1922

50	A5	1c on 15c (Bk)	.80	.80
51	A5	2c on 15c (Bl)	.80	.80
53	A5	5c on 15c (R)	.80	.80
		Nos. 50-53 (3)	2.40	2.40

Stamps and Types of 1914-22 Surcharged with New Values in Caches, Fanons and Rupies in Black, Red or Blue

No. 55

No. 69

No. 78

1923-28

54	A5	1ca on 1c gray & blk (R)	.30	.30
a.		Imperf.	50.00	50.00
55	A5	2ca on 5c vio brn & blk	.50	.50
a.		Horizontal pair, imperf. between	—	
b.		Imperf.	45.00	45.00
56	A5	3ca on 3c brn & blk	.55	.55
57	A5	4ca on 4c org & blk	.80	.80
58	A5	6ca on 10c grn & blk	.95	.95
a.		Double surcharge	175.00	

59	A6	6ca on 45c bl grn & blk (R)	.95	.95
60	A5	10ca on 20c dp red & bl grn ('28)	2.50	2.50
61	A5	12ca on 15c vio & blk	.95	.95
62	A5	15ca on 20c org & blk	1.50	1.50
63	A6	16ca on 35c lt bl & yel brn ('28)	2.60	2.60
64	A5	18ca on 30c rose & blk	2.40	2.40
65	A6	20ca on 45c grn & dl red ('28)	2.00	1.50
66	A5	1fa on 25c dp grn & rose red ('28)	3.50	3.50
67	A6	1fa3ca on 35c choc & blk (Bl)	1.10	1.10
68	A6	1fa6ca on 40c org & blk (R)	1.50	1.25
69	A6	1fa12ca on 50c ultra & bl (Bl)	1.75	1.50
70	A6	1fa12ca on 75c bl & blk (Bl)	1.25	1.25
a.		Double surcharge	145.00	
71	A6	1fa16ca on 75c brn red & grn ('28)	3.50	3.00
72	A5	2fa9ca on 25c ultra & fawn (Bl)	1.50	1.20
73	A6	2fa12ca on 1fr vio & dk brn ('28)	3.00	3.00
74	A6	3fa3ca on 1fr yel & blk (R)	1.75	1.45
a.		Double surcharge	145.00	
75	A6	6fa6ca on 2fr vio & blk (Bl)	5.25	4.50
76	A6	1r on 1fr grn & dp bl (R) ('26)	9.50	7.75
77	A6	2r on 5fr rose & blk (R)	7.50	7.00
a.		Double surcharge	145.00	
78	A6	3r on 2fr gray & bl vio (R) ('26)	21.00	19.00
79	A6	5r on 5fr rose & blk, *grnsh* ('26)	27.50	24.00
		Nos. 54-79 (26)	105.60	95.00

Nos. 60, 63, 66 and 73 have the original value obliterated by bars.

A7

A8

1929

80	A7	1ca dk gray & blk	.25	.25
81	A7	2ca vio brn & blk	.25	.25
82	A7	3ca brn & blk	.25	.25
83	A7	4ca org & blk	.30	.30
84	A7	6ca gray grn & grn	.30	.30
85	A7	10ca brn, red & grn	.30	.30
86	A8	12ca grn & lt grn	.75	.70
87	A7	16ca brt bl & blk	.95	.95
88	A7	18ca brn red & ver	.95	.95
89	A7	20ca dk bl & grn, *bluish*	.75	.75
90	A8	1fa gray grn & rose red	.75	.70
91	A8	1fa6ca red org & blk	.75	.70
92	A8	1fa12ca dp bl & ultra	.75	.70
93	A8	1fa16ca rose red & grn	.95	.95
94	A8	2fa12ca brt vio & brn	1.20	1.00
95	A8	6fa6ca dl vio & blk	1.20	1.00
a.		Imperf.	50.00	
96	A8	1r gray grn & dp bl	1.10	1.00
97	A8	2r rose & blk	1.60	1.20
a.		Imperf.	50.00	
98	A8	3r lt gray & gray lil	3.00	2.25
99	A8	5r rose & blk, *grnsh*	3.00	2.40
		Nos. 80-99 (20)	19.35	16.90

For overprints and surcharges see Nos. 117-134, 157-176, 184-209G.

Common Design Types pictured following the introduction.

Colonial Exposition Issue
Common Design Types

1931 **Engr.** ***Perf. 12½***

100	CD70	10ca deep green	4.50	*4.50*
101	CD71	12ca violet	4.50	*4.50*
102	CD72	18ca red orange	4.50	*4.50*
103	CD73	1fa12ca dull blue	4.50	*4.50*
		Nos. 100-103 (4)	18.00	*18.00*

Paris International Exposition Issue
Common Design Types

1937 ***Perf. 13***

104	CD74	8ca dp violet	2.00	*3.00*
105	CD75	12ca dk green	2.25	*3.00*
106	CD76	16ca car rose	2.25	*3.00*
107	CD77	20ca dk brown	1.40	*3.00*
108	CD78	1fa12ca red	1.75	*3.00*
109	CD79	2fa12ca ultra	2.25	*3.00*
		Nos. 104-109 (6)	11.90	*18.00*

For overprints see Nos. 135-139, 177-181.

Colonial Arts Exhibition Issue
Souvenir Sheet
Common Design Type

1937 ***Imperf.***

110	CD79	5fa red violet	9.25	*12.50*

For overprint see No. 140.

New York World's Fair Issue
Common Design Type

1939 **Engr.** ***Perf. 12½x12***

111	CD82	1fa12ca car lake	1.25	*3.00*
112	CD82	2fa12ca ultra	1.75	*3.00*

For overprints see Nos. 141-142, 182-183.

Temple near Pondichéry and Marshal Petain
A9

1941 **Engr.** ***Perf. 12½x12***

112A	A9	1fa16ca car & red	.80	
c.		Denomination omitted	55.00	
112B	A9	4fa4ca blue	.80	
d.		Denomination omitted	200.00	

Nos. 112A-112B were issued by the Vichy government in France, but were not placed on sale in French India.

For surcharges, see Nos. B13B-B13C.

Nos. 62, 64, 67, 72 Overprinted in Carmine or Blue (#116)

a

b

1941 **Unwmk.** ***Perf. 13½x14***

113	A5 (a)	15ca on 20c	85.00	85.00
114	A5 (a)	18ca on 30c	16.00	16.00
115	A6 (a)	1fa3ca on 35c	130.00	130.00
a.		Horiz. overprint	125.00	125.00
116	A5 (b)	2fa9ca on 25c	1,600.	1,150.
a.		Overprint "a" (Bl)	1,400.	1,150.
b.		Overprint "b" (C)	*2,100.*	*2,100.*

Nos. 81-99 Overprinted Type "a" in Carmine or Blue

1941

117	A7	2ca (C)	12.50	12.50
118	A7	3ca (C)	4.75	4.75
119	A7	4ca (C)	13.50	13.50
120	A7	6ca (C)	4.75	4.75
121	A7	10ca (Bl)	6.50	6.50
122	A8	12ca (C)	4.75	4.75
123	A7	16ca (C)	4.75	4.75
123A	A7	18ca (Bl)	675.00	675.00
124	A7	20ca (C)	4.75	4.75
125	A8	1fa (Bl)	4.75	4.75
126	A8	1fa6ca (C)	4.75	4.75
127	A8	1fa12ca (C)	6.50	6.50
128	A8	1fa16ca (C)	4.75	4.75
129	A8	2fa12ca (C)	4.75	4.75
130	A8	6fa6ca (C)	4.75	4.75
131	A8	1r (C)	4.75	4.75
132	A8	2r (C)	4.75	4.75
133	A8	3r (C)	6.50	6.50
134	A8	5r (C)	10.50	10.50
		Nos. 117-123,124-134 (18)	113.00	113.00

Same Overprints on Paris Exposition Issue of 1937

1941 ***Perf. 13***

135	CD74 (b)	8ca (C)	10.00	10.00
135A	CD74 (b)	8ca (Bl)	275.00	275.00
d.		Blk. overprint	1,000.	1,000.
135B	CD74 (a)	8ca (C)	180.00	180.00
135C	CD74 (a)	8ca (Bl)	250.00	250.00
136	CD75 (a)	12ca (C)	6.00	6.00
137	CD76 (a)	16ca (Bl)	6.00	6.00
a.		Blk. overprint	175.00	175.00
138	CD78 (a)	1fa12ca (Bl)	6.00	6.00
139	CD79 (a)	2fa12ca (C)	6.00	6.00
		Nos. 135-139 (8)	739.00	739.00

Inverted overprints exist.

Souvenir Sheet
No. 110 Overprinted "FRANCE LIBRE" Diagonally in Blue Violet

Two types of overprint:
I — Overprint 37mm. With serifs.
II — Overprint 24mm, as type "a" shown above No. 113. No serifs.

1941 **Unwmk.** ***Imperf.***

140	CD79	5fa red vio (I)	800.00	725.00
a.		Type II	1,000.	1,000.
b.		As No. 140, inverted surcharge	5,000.	2,000.

Overprinted on New York World's Fair Issue, 1939
Perf. 12½x12

141	CD82 (a)	1fa12ca (Bl)	4.75	4.75
142	CD82 (a)	2fa12ca (C)	5.50	5.50

Lotus Flowers — A10

1942 **Unwmk.** **Photo.** ***Perf. 14x14½***

143	A10	2ca brown	.30	.30
144	A10	3ca dk blue	.30	.30
145	A10	4ca emerald	.30	.30
146	A10	6ca dk orange	.30	.30
147	A10	12ca grnsh blk	.30	.30
148	A10	16ca rose violet	.30	.30
149	A10	20ca dk red brn	.65	.65
150	A10	1fa brt red	.70	.65
151	A10	1fa18ca slate blk	.90	.80
152	A10	6fa6ca brt ultra	1.60	1.50
153	A10	1r dull violet	1.40	1.40
154	A10	2r bister	1.75	1.60
155	A10	3r chocolate	1.75	1.60
156	A10	5r dk green	2.25	2.00
		Nos. 143-156 (14)	12.80	12.00

Stamps of 1923-39 Overprinted in Blue or Carmine

c

d

1942-43 ***Perf. 13½x14, 14x13½***

Overprinted on No. 64

156A	A5 (c)	18ca on 30c (B)	300.00	230.00

Overprinted on #81-82, 84, 86-99

157	A7 (c)	2ca (C)	3.75	3.75
a.		"FRANCE LIBRE" in black	250.00	175.00
b.		As No. 157, blk. overprint	375.00	375.00
c.		As No. 157, bl. overprint	500.00	500.00
158	A7 (c)	3ca (C)	2.40	2.40
159	A7 (c)	6ca (Bl)	3.25	3.25
a.		Car. overprint	325.00	
b.		Blk. overprint	725.00	
c.		Bl.-Blk. overprint	50.00	35.00
160	A8 (d)	12ca (Bl)	3.75	3.75
161	A7 (c)	16ca (C)	3.25	3.25
162	A7 (c)	18ca (Bl)	2.40	2.40
163	A7 (c)	20ca (Bl) ('43)	7.25	5.50
164	A7 (c)	20ca (C)	2.40	2.40
a.		Double overprint, one bl. one car.	1,350.	475.00
165	A8 (d)	1fa (Bl)	2.40	2.40
166	A8 (d)	1fa6ca (C)	3.25	3.25
a.		Bl. overprint	300.00	225.00
167	A8 (d)	1fa12ca (C)	3.25	3.25
168	A8 (d)	1fa16ca (Bl)	3.25	3.25
169	A8 (d)	2fa12ca (Bl)	100.00	80.00
170	A8 (d)	2fa12ca (C)	3.25	3.25
171	A8 (d)	6fa6ca (C)	4.00	4.00
172	A8 (d)	1r (C)	7.25	7.25
173	A8 (d)	2r (C)	7.25	7.25
174	A8 (d)	3r (C)	7.25	7.25
175	A8 (d)	3r (Bl) ('43)	200.00	175.00
176	A8 (d)	5r (C)	7.25	7.25
		Nos. 156A-176 (21)	676.85	560.10

Same Overprints on Paris International Exposition Issue of 1937
Perf. 13

177	CD74 (c)	8ca (Bl)	7.25	7.25
178	CD75 (d)	12ca (Bl)	7.25	7.25
179	CD76 (d)	16ca (Bl)	1,300.	1,300.
180	CD78 (d)	1fa12ca (Bl)	7.25	7.25
181	CD79 (d)	2fa12ca (C)	7.25	7.25

Same Overprint on New York World's Fair Issue, 1939
Perf. 12½x12

182	CD82 (d)	1fa12ca (Bl)	7.25	7.25
183	CD82 (d)	2fa12ca (C)	7.25	7.25

No. 87 Surcharged in Carmine

1942-43 ***Perf. 13½x14***

184	A7	1ca on 16ca	75.00	45.00
185	A7	4ca on 16ca ('43)	75.00	45.00
186	A7	10ca on 16ca	55.00	35.00
187	A7	15ca on 16ca	55.00	35.00
188	A7	1fa3ca on 16ca ('43)	72.50	45.00
189	A7	2fa9ca on 16ca ('43)	72.50	45.00
190	A7	3fa3ca on 16ca ('43)	55.00	35.00
		Nos. 184-190 (7)	460.00	285.00

Nos. 95-99 Srchd. in Carmine

1943 ***Perf. 14x13½***

191	A8	1ca on 6fa6ca	11.00	11.00
192	A8	4ca on 6fa6ca	12.50	12.50
193	A8	10ca on 6fa6ca	11.00	11.00
194	A8	15ca on 6fa6ca	11.00	11.00
195	A8	1fa3ca on 6fa6ca	11.00	11.00
196	A8	2fa9ca on 6fa6ca	12.50	12.50
197	A8	3fa3ca on 6fa6ca	12.50	12.50
198	A8	1ca on 1r	4.75	4.75
199	A8	2ca on 1r	1.60	1.60
200	A8	4ca on 1r	1.60	1.60
201	A8	6ca on 2r	1.60	1.60
202	A8	10ca on 2r	1.75	1.75
203	A8	12ca on 2r	1.60	1.60
204	A8	15ca on 3r	1.60	1.60
205	A8	16ca on 3r	1.60	1.60
206	A8	1fa3ca on 3r	1.60	1.60
207	A8	1fa6ca on 5r	2.00	2.00
208	A8	1fa12ca on 5r	2.40	2.40
209	A8	1fa16ca on 5r	2.40	2.40
		Nos. 191-209 (19)	106.00	106.00

In 1943, 200 each of 27 stamps were overprinted in red or dark blue, "FRANCE TOUJOURS" and a Lorraine Cross within a circle measuring 17½mm in diameter. Overprinted were Nos. 81-99, 104-109, 111-112. Values, set: $25,000 unused; $6,000 used.

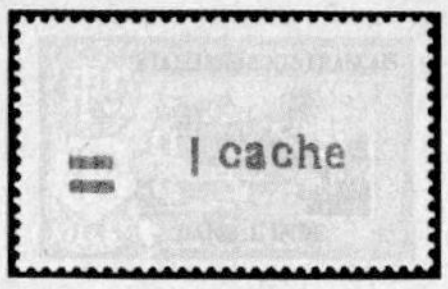

No. 95 Surcharged in Carmine

1943 Unwmk. *Perf. 14x13½*

209A	A8	1ca on 6fa6ca	35.00	27.50
209B	A8	4ca on 6fa6ca	35.00	27.50
209C	A8	10ca on 6fa6ca	24.00	16.00
209D	A8	15ca on 6fa6ca	24.00	16.00
209E	A8	1fa3ca on 6fa6ca	32.50	27.50
209F	A8	2fa9ca on 6fa6ca	32.50	27.50
209G	A8	3fa3ca on 6fa6ca	35.00	27.50
		Nos. 209A-209G (7)	218.00	169.50

Catalogue values for unused stamps in this section, from this point to the end of the section, are for Never Hinged items.

Eboue Issue
Common Design Type

1945 Engr. *Perf. 13*

210	CD91	3fa8ca black	.80	.70
211	CD91	5r1fa16ca Prus grn	1.40	1.25

Nos. 210 and 211 exist imperforate.

Apsaras — A11

Brahman Ascetic — A12

Designs: 6ca, 8ca, 10ca, Dvarabalagar. 12ca, 15ca, 1fa, Vishnu. 1fa6ca, 2fa, 2fa2ca, Dvarabalagar (foot raised). 2fa12ca, 3fa, 5fa, Temple Guardian. 7fa12ca, 1r2fa, 1r4fa12ca, Tigoupalagar.

1948 Photo. *Perf. 13x13½*

212	A11	1ca dk ol grn	.50	.25
213	A11	2ca orange brn	.50	.25
214	A11	4ca vio, *cr*	.55	.30
215	A11	6ca yellow org	1.50	.65
216	A11	8ca gray blk	1.50	1.10
217	A11	10ca dl yel grn, *pale grn*	1.50	1.10
218	A11	12ca violet brn	1.00	.65
219	A11	15ca Prus grn	1.00	.65
220	A11	1fa vio, *pale rose*	1.50	.80
221	A11	1fa6ca brown red	1.50	.85
222	A11	2fa dk green	1.50	.85
223	A11	2fa2ca blue, *cr*	1.50	1.15
224	A11	2fa12ca brown	1.90	1.15
225	A11	3fa dp orange	3.25	1.25
226	A11	5fa red vio, *rose*	3.00	1.25
227	A11	7fa12ca dk brown	3.25	1.25
228	A11	1r2fa brown blk	6.00	4.50
229	A11	1r4fa12ca olive grn	6.50	5.00
		Nos. 212-229 (18)	37.95	23.00

1952

230	A12	18ca rose red	2.75	2.00
231	A12	1fa15ca vio blue	3.75	2.50
232	A12	4fa olive grn	4.25	3.50
		Nos. 230-232 (3)	10.75	8.00

Military Medal Issue
Common Design Type

1952 Engr. and Typo. *Perf. 13*

233	CD101	1fa multi	5.50	*7.00*

SEMI-POSTAL STAMPS

Regular Issue of 1914 Surcharged in Red

Two printings: 1st, surcharge at bottom of stamp; 2nd, surcharge centered toward top.

1915 Unwmk. *Perf. 14x13½*

B1	A5	10c + 5c rose & blk (1st)	2.10	2.10
b.		Inverted surcharge	210.00	210.00

There were two printings of this surcharge. In the first, it was placed at the bottom of the stamp; in the second, it was centered toward the top.

Regular Issue of 1914 Surcharged in Red

1916

B2	A5	10c + 5c rose & blk	21.00	21.00
a.		Inverted surcharge	210.00	210.00
b.		Double surcharge	210.00	210.00

No. 32 Surcharged

B3	A5	10c + 5c rose & blk	3.50	3.50

No. 32 Surcharged

B4	A5	10c + 5c rose & blk	1.60	1.60

No. 32 Surcharged

B5	A5	10c + 5c rose & blk	2.25	2.25

Curie Issue
Common Design Type

1938 Engr. *Perf. 13*

B6	CD80	2fa12ca + 20ca brt ultra	10.00	10.00

French Revolution Issue
Common Design Type

1939 Photo.
Name and Value Typo. in Black

B7	CD83	18ca + 10ca grn	5.75	*6.50*
B8	CD83	1fa6ca + 12ca brn	5.75	*6.50*
B9	CD83	1fa12ca + 16ca red org	5.75	*6.50*
B10	CD83	1fa16ca + 1fa16ca rose pink	5.75	*6.50*
B11	CD83	2fa12ca + 3fa blue	5.75	*6.50*
		Nos. B7-B11 (5)	28.75	*32.50*

Common Design Type and

Non-Commissioned Officer, Native Guard — SP1

Sepoy SP2

1941 Photo. *Perf. 13½*

B12	SP1	1fa16ca + 1fa16ca red	1.25
B13	CD86	2fa12ca + 5fa mar	1.25
B13A	SP2	4fa4ca + 1fa16ca bl	1.25
		Nos. B12-B13A (3)	3.75

Nos. B12-B13A were issued by the Vichy government in France, but were not placed on sale in French India.

Nos. 112A-112B Srchd. in Black or Red

1944 Engr. *Perf. 12½x12*

B13B	20ca + 2fa12ca on 4fa4ca deep blue (R)	1.00
B13C	+ 4fa4ca on 1fa16ca car & red	1.00

Colonial Development Fund.

Nos. B13B-B13C were issued by the Vichy government in France, but were not placed on sale in French India.

Catalogue values for unused stamps in this section, from this point to the end of the section, are for Never Hinged items.

Red Cross Issue
Common Design Type

1944 Photo. *Perf. 14½x14*

B14	CD90	3fa + 1r4fa dk ol brn	1.50	1.25

The surtax was for the French Red Cross and national relief.

Tropical Medicine Issue
Common Design Type

1950 Engr. *Perf. 13*

B15	CD100	1fa + 10ca ind & dp bl	6.00	4.00

The surtax was for charitable work.

AIR POST STAMPS

Common Design Type

1942 Unwmk. Photo. *Perf. 14½x14*

C1	CD87	4fa dark orange	.90	*2.00*
C2	CD87	1r bright red	.90	*2.00*
C3	CD87	2r brown red	1.50	*2.00*
C4	CD87	5r black	1.50	*3.00*
C5	CD87	8r ultra	2.25	*3.00*
C6	CD87	10r dark green	2.25	*3.00*
		Nos. C1-C6 (6)	9.30	*15.00*

Catalogue values for unused stamps in this section, from this point to the end of the section, are for Never Hinged items.

Victory Issue
Common Design Type

1946 Engr. *Perf. 12½*

C7	CD92	4fa dk blue green	1.00	*2.00*

Chad to Rhine Issue
Common Design Types

1946, June 6

C8	CD93	2fa12ca olive bis	1.40	*2.00*
C9	CD94	5fa dark blue	1.40	*2.00*
C10	CD95	7fa12ca dk purple	2.25	*2.00*
C11	CD96	1r2fa green	2.25	*3.00*
C12	CD97	1r4fa12ca dk car	2.75	*3.00*
C13	CD98	3r1fa violet brn	2.75	*3.00*
		Nos. C8-C13 (6)	12.80	*15.00*

A 3r ultramarine and red, picturing the Temple of Chindambaram, was sold at Paris June 7 to July 8, 1948, but not placed on sale in the colony. Values: $10 never hinged, $7 hinged.

Bas-relief Figure of Goddess — AP1

Wing and Temple — AP2

Bird over Palms — AP3

Perf. 12x13, 13x12

1949 Photo. Unwmk.

C14	AP1	1r yellow & plum	6.00	3.50
C15	AP2	2r green & dk grn	6.00	4.50
C16	AP3	5r lt bl & vio brn	27.50	*30.00*
		Nos. C14-C16 (3)	39.50	38.00

UPU Issue
Common Design Type

1949 Engr. *Perf. 13*

C17	CD99	6fa lilac rose	11.50	8.75

Universal Postal Union, 75th anniv.

Liberation Issue
Common Design Type

1954, June 6

C18	CD102	1fa sepia & vio brn	11.00	8.00

AIR POST SEMI-POSTAL STAMPS

Girl's School
SPAP1

Perf. 12½x13½

1942, June 22 Unwmk. Photo.

CB1 SPAP1 2fa12ca + 5fa20ca green .95
CB2 SPAP1 3fa8ca + 1r2fa yel brn .95

Native children's welfare fund.

Nos. CB1-CB2 were issued by the Vichy government in France, but were not placed on sale in French India.

Colonial Education Fund
Common Design Type

1942, June 22

CB3 CD86a 2fa + 3fa blue & red .90

No. CB3 was issued by the Vichy government in France, but was not placed on sale in French India.

POSTAGE DUE STAMPS

Postage Due Stamps of France Surcharged like Nos. 54-75 in Black, Blue or Red

1923 Unwmk. *Perf. 14x13½*

J1 D2 6ca on 10c brn 1.25 1.25
J2 D2 12ca on 25c rose (Bk) 1.25 1.25
J3 D2 15ca on 20c ol grn (R) 1.60 1.60
J4 D2 1fa6ca on 30c red 1.60 1.60
J5 D2 1fa12a on 50c brn vio 2.75 2.75
J6 D2 1fa15ca on 5c bl (Bk) 3.00 3.00
J7 D2 3fa3ca on 1fr red brn, *straw* 3.25 3.25
Nos. J1-J7 (7) 14.70 14.70

Types of Postage Due Stamps of French Colonies, 1884-85, Surcharged with New Values as in 1923 in Red or Black Bars over Original Values

1928

J8 D1 4ca on 20c gray lil 1.60 1.60
J9 D1 1fa on 30c orange 3.25 3.25
J10 D1 1fa16ca on 5c bl blk (R) 3.25 3.25
J11 D1 3fa on 1fr lt grn 3.75 3.75
Nos. J8-J11 (4) 11.85 11.85

D3

1929 Typo.

J12 D3 4ca deep red .50 .50
J13 D3 6ca blue .65 .65
J14 D3 12ca green .65 .65
J15 D3 1fa brown 1.25 1.25
J16 D3 1fa12ca lilac gray 1.25 1.25
J17 D3 1fa16ca buff 1.75 1.75
J18 D3 3fa lilac 2.10 2.10
Nos. J12-J18 (7) 8.15 8.15

D4

1948 Unwmk. Photo. *Perf. 13x13½*

J19 D4 1ca dk violet .30 .30
J20 D4 2ca dk brown .50 .50
J21 D4 6ca blue green .50 .50
J22 D4 12ca dp orange .70 .70
J23 D4 1fa dk car rose .80 .80
J24 D4 1fa12ca brown .80 .80
J25 D4 2fa dk slate bl 1.25 1.25
J26 D4 2fa12ca henna brn 1.60 1.60
J27 D4 5fa dk olive grn 2.25 2.25
J28 D4 1r dk blue vio 3.00 3.00
Nos. J19-J28 (10) 11.70 11.70

FRENCH MOROCCO

ˈfrench mə-ˈrä-ˌkō

LOCATION — Northwest coast of Africa
GOVT. — French Protectorate
AREA — 153,870 sq. mi.
POP. — 8,340,000 (estimated 1954)
CAPITAL — Rabat

French Morocco was a French Protectorate from 1912 until 1956 when it, along with the Spanish and Tangier zones of Morocco, became the independent country, Morocco.

Stamps inscribed "Tanger" were for use in the international zone of Tangier in northern Morocco.

100 Centimos = 1 Peseta
100 Centimes = 1 franc (1917)

Catalogue values for unused stamps in this country are for Never Hinged items, beginning with Scott 177 in the regular postage section, Scott B26 in the semi-postal section, Scott C27 in the airpost section, Scott CB23A in the airpost semi-postal section, and Scott J46 in the postage due section.

French Offices in Morocco

A1

A2

Stamps of France Surcharged in Red or Black

1891-1900 Unwmk. *Perf. 14x13½*

1 A1 5c on 5c grn, *grnsh* (R) 16.00 4.00
a. Imperf., pair 175.00
2 A1 5c on 5c yel grn (II) (R) ('99) 32.50 27.50
a. Type I 32.50 27.50
3 A1 10c on 10c blk, *lav* (II) (R) 32.50 4.00
a. Type I 45.00 20.00
b. 10c on 25c black, *rose* 1,100. 1,200.
4 A1 20c on 20c red, *grn* 40.00 32.50
5 A1 25c on 25c blk, *rose* (R) 32.50 4.00
a. Double surcharge 225.00
b. Imperf., pair 175.00
6 A1 50c on 50c car, *rose* (II) 105.00 47.50
a. Type I 375.00 260.00
7 A1 1p on 1fr brnz grn, *straw* 120.00 80.00
8 A1 2p on 2fr brn, *az* (Bk) ('00) 240.00 240.00
Nos. 1-8 (8) 618.50 439.50

No. 3b was never sent to Morocco.

France Nos. J15-J16 Overprinted in Carmine

1893

9 A2 5c black 3,250. 1,200.
10 A2 10c black 2,900. 800.

Counterfeits exist.

Surcharged in Red or Black

A3

A4

A5

1902-10

11 A3 1c on 1c gray (R) ('08) 2.40 1.20
12 A3 2c on 2c vio brn ('08) 2.40 1.20
13 A3 3c on 3c red org ('08) 3.25 1.60
14 A3 4c on 4c yel brn ('08) 13.00 8.00
15 A3 5c on 5c grn (R) 12.00 4.00
a. Double surcharge 340.00
b. Triple surcharge 340.00
16 A4 10c on 10c rose red ('03) 8.00 4.00
a. Surcharge omitted 225.00
17 A4 20c on 20c brn vio ('03) 40.00 24.00
18 A4 25c on 25c bl ('03) 40.00 4.00
19 A4 35c on 35c vio ('10) 40.00 24.00
20 A5 50c on 50c bis brn & lav ('03) 67.50 16.00
21 A5 1p on 1fr cl & ol grn ('03) 120.00 80.00
22 A5 2p on 2fr gray vio & yel ('03) 160.00 120.00
Nos. 11-22 (12) 508.55 288.00

Nos. 11-14 exist spelled CFNTIMOS or GENTIMOS.

The 25c on 25c with surcharge omitted is listed as No. 81a.

For overprints and surcharges see Nos. 26-37, 72-79, B1, B3.

Postage Due Stamps Nos. J1-J2 Handstamped

1903

24 D2 5c on 5c light blue 1,500. 1,400.
25 D2 10c on 10c chocolate 2,800. 2,600.

Nos. 24 and 25 were used only on Oct. 10, 1903. Used stamps were not canceled, the overprint serving as a cancellation.

Numerous counterfeits exist.

Types of 1902-10 Issue Surcharged in Red or Blue

1911-17

26 A3 1c on 1c gray (R) 1.20 .90
27 A3 2c on 2c vio brn 1.20 1.20
28 A3 3c on 3c orange 1.20 1.20
29 A3 5c on 5c green (R) 1.20 .80
30 A4 10c on 10c rose 1.20 .80
a. Imperf., pair 275.00
31 A4 15c on 15c org ('17) 3.50 2.40
32 A4 20c on 20c brn vio 5.50 4.00
33 A4 25c on 25c blue (R) 2.40 1.60
34 A4 35c on 35c violet (R) 12.00 5.50
35 A5 40c on 40c red & pale bl ('17) 8.00 5.50
36 A5 50c on 50c bis brn & lav (R) 27.50 16.00
37 A5 1p on 1fr cl & ol grn 24.00 12.00
Nos. 26-37 (12) 88.90 51.90

For surcharges see Nos. B1, B3.

Stamps of this design were issued by the Cherifien posts in 1912-13. The Administration Cherifinne des Postes, Telegraphes et Telephones was formed in 1911 under French guidance. See Morocco in Vol. 4 for listings.

French Protectorate
Issue of 1911-17 Overprinted "Protectorat Francais"

A6

A7

A8

1914-21

38 A6 1c on 1c lt gray .40 .50
a. 1c dk gray ('22) .55 .80
39 A6 2c on 2c vio brn .80 .50
40 A6 3c on 3c orange 1.20 .65
41 A6 5c on 5c green 1.20 .50
a. New value omitted 275.00 275.00
42 A7 10c on 10c rose .80 .30
a. New value omitted 550.00 550.00
43 A7 15c on 15c org ('17) .80 .80
a. New value omitted 120.00 120.00
44 A7 20c on 20c brn vio 4.75 3.50
a. "Protectorat Francais" double 300.00 300.00
45 A7 25c on 25c blue 3.25 .80
a. New value omitted 350.00 350.00
46 A7 25c on 25c violet ('21) 1.25 .40
a. "Protectorat Francais" omitted 80.00 80.00
b. "Protectorat Francais" double 175.00 175.00
c. "Protectorat Francais" dbl. (R + Bk) 175.00 175.00
47 A7 30c on 30c vio ('21) 20.00 9.00
48 A7 35c on 35c violet 4.75 1.60
49 A8 40c on 40c red & pale bl 20.00 8.75
a. New value omitted 375.00 375.00
50 A8 45c on 45c grn & bl ('21) 55.00 40.00
51 A8 50c on 50c bis brn & lav 2.40 .80
a. "Protectorat Francais" invtd. 200.00 200.00
b. "Protectorat Francais" double 450.00 450.00
52 A8 1p on 1fr cl & ol grn 5.50 .80
a. "Protectorat Francais" invtd. 350.00 350.00
b. New value double 200.00 200.00
c. New value dbl., one invtd. 210.00 210.00
53 A8 2p on 2fr gray vio & yel 8.00 4.00
a. New value omitted 175.00 175.00
b. "Protectorat Francais" omitted 110.00 110.00
c. New value double 225.00
d. New value dbl., one invtd.
54 A8 5p on 5fr dk bl & buff 15.00 8.00
Nos. 38-54 (17) 145.10 80.90

For surcharges see Nos. B2, B4-B5.

Tower of Hassan, Rabat — A9

Mosque of the Andalusians, Fez — A10

City Gate Chella
A11

Koutoubiah, Marrakesh
A12

Bab Mansour, Meknes A13

Roman Ruins, Volubilis A14

1917 Engr. *Perf. 13½x14, 14x13½*

55	A9	1c grnsh gray	.40	.40
56	A9	2c brown lilac	.40	.40
57	A9	3c orange brn	.40	.80
a.		Imperf., pair	87.50	
58	A10	5c yellow grn	.40	.40
59	A10	10c rose red	.80	.40
60	A10	15c dark gray	.80	.40
a.		Imperf., pair	65.00	
61	A11	20c red brown	4.00	2.40
62	A11	25c dull blue	4.00	1.25
63	A11	30c gray violet	4.75	3.25
64	A12	35c orange	4.75	4.00
65	A12	40c ultra	1.60	1.60
66	A12	45c gray green	32.50	16.00
67	A13	50c dk brown	5.50	4.00
a.		Imperf., pair	65.00	
68	A13	1fr slate	16.00	4.00
a.		Imperf., pair	65.00	
69	A14	2fr black brown	160.00	95.00
70	A14	5fr dk gray grn	47.50	40.00
71	A14	10fr black	47.50	40.00
		Nos. 55-71 (17)	331.30	214.30

See note following No. 115. See Nos. 93-105. For surcharges see Nos. 120-121.

Types of the 1902-10 Issue Overprinted

1918-24 *Perf. 14x13½*

72	A3	1c dk gray	.40	.80
73	A3	2c violet brn	.40	.80
74	A3	3c red orange	1.20	1.20
75	A3	5c green	1.20	1.20
76	A3	5c orange ('23)	2.40	2.00
77	A4	10c rose	2.40	1.60
78	A4	10c green ('24)	2.40	1.60
79	A4	15c orange	1.60	1.20
80	A4	20c violet brn	2.40	2.40
81	A4	25c blue	2.40	2.40
a.		"TANGER" omitted	450.00	450.00
82	A4	30c red org ('24)	4.00	2.75
83	A4	35c violet	4.00	2.40
84	A5	40c red & pale bl	4.00	2.40
85	A5	50c bis brn & lav	27.50	16.00
86	A4	50c blue ('24)	24.00	13.50
87	A5	1fr claret & ol grn	16.00	8.00
88	A5	2fr org & pale bl ('24)	80.00	72.50
89	A5	5fr dk bl & buff ('24)	67.50	65.00
		Nos. 72-89 (18)	243.80	197.75

Types of 1917 and

Tower of Hassan, Rabat — A15

Bab Mansour, Meknes A16

Roman Ruins, Volubilis A17

1923-27 Photo. *Perf. 13½*

90	A15	1c olive green	.25	.25
91	A15	2c brown vio	.25	.25
92	A15	3c yellow brn	.25	.25
93	A10	5c orange	.25	.25
94	A10	10c yellow grn	.25	.25
95	A10	15c dk gray	.25	.25
96	A11	20c red brown	.25	.25
97	A11	20c red vio ('27)	.40	.40
98	A11	25c ultra	.40	.40
99	A11	30c deep red	.40	.40
100	A11	30c turq bl ('27)	1.20	.80
101	A12	35c violet	1.20	.80
102	A12	40c orange red	.25	.25
103	A12	45c deep green	.40	.40
104	A16	50c dull turq	.40	.40
105	A12	50c olive grn ('27)	.80	.40
106	A16	60c lilac	1.20	.80
107	A16	75c red vio ('27)	.80	.40
108	A16	1fr deep brown	.80	.80
109	A16	1.05fr red brn ('27)	1.60	.80
110	A16	1.40fr dull rose ('27)	.80	.80
111	A16	1.50fr turq bl ('27)	1.20	.40
112	A17	2fr olive brn	1.60	1.20
113	A17	3fr dp red ('27)	1.60	1.20
114	A17	5fr dk gray grn	4.00	2.75
115	A17	10fr black	12.00	4.75
		Nos. 90-115 (26)	32.80	19.90

Nos. 90-110, 112-115 exist imperf. The stamps of 1917 were line engraved. Those of 1923-27 were printed by photogravure and have in the margin at lower right the imprint "Helio Vaugirard."

See No. B36. For surcharges see Nos. 122-123.

No. 102 Surcharged in Black

1930

120	A12	15c on 40c orange red	1.60	1.60
a.		Surcharge bars omitted	72.50	72.50
b.		Pair, one with surcharge omitted	350.00	

Nos. 100, 106 and 110 Surcharged in Blue Similarly to No. 176

1931

121	A11	25c on 30c turq blue	2.50	2.10
a.		Inverted surcharge	140.00	140.00
122	A16	50c on 60c lilac	1.20	.40
a.		Inverted surcharge	150.00	150.00
b.		Double surcharge	150.00	150.00
c.		Surcharge bars omitted	90.00	
123	A16	1fr on 1.40fr rose	3.25	1.60
a.		Inverted surcharge	150.00	150.00
b.		Surcharge bars omitted	90.00	
		Nos. 121-123 (3)	6.95	4.10

Old Treasure House and Tribunal, Tangier A18

Roadstead at Agadir A19

Post Office at Casablanca A20

Moulay Idriss of the Zehroun A21

Kasbah of the Oudayas, Rabat A22

Court of the Medersa el Attarine at Fez A23

Saadiens' Tombs at Marrakesh A25

Kasbah of Si Madani el Glaoui at Ouarzazat A24

1933-34 Engr. *Perf. 13*

124	A18	1c olive blk	.25	.25
125	A18	2c red violet	.25	.25
126	A19	3c dark brown	.25	.25
127	A19	5c brown red	.25	.25
128	A20	10c blue green	.30	.30
129	A20	15c black	.40	.30
130	A20	20c red brown	.40	.30
131	A21	25c dark blue	.40	.30
132	A21	30c emerald	.40	.30
133	A21	40c black brn	.40	.30
134	A22	45c brown vio	.80	.65
135	A22	50c dk blue grn	.80	.30
a.		Booklet pane of 10	—	
b.		Booklet pane of 20	—	
		Complete booklet, #135b	2,000.	
136	A22	65c brown red	.40	.30
a.		Booklet pane of 10	—	
b.		Booklet pane of 20	—	
		Complete booklet, #136b	65.00	
137	A23	75c red violet	.80	.30
138	A23	90c orange red	.40	.30
139	A23	1fr deep brown	1.20	.50
140	A23	1.25fr black ('34)	1.60	1.50
141	A24	1.50fr ultra	.40	.30
142	A24	1.75fr myr grn ('34)	.80	.40
143	A24	2fr yellow brn	4.75	.80
144	A24	3fr car rose	55.00	6.50
145	A25	5fr red brown	12.00	2.50
146	A25	10fr black	10.00	6.50
147	A25	20fr bluish gray	9.50	7.25
		Nos. 124-147 (24)	101.75	30.90

Booklets containing Nos. 135 and 136 each have two panes of 10 (Nos. 135a, 136a) connected by a gutter, the complete piece constituting No. 135b or 136b, which is stapled into the booklet through the gutter.

For surcharges see Nos. 148, 176, B13-B20.

No. 135 Srchd. in Red

1939

148	A22	40c on 50c dk bl grn	.95	.50

Mosque of Salé — A26

Sefrou — A27

Cedars — A28

Goatherd A29

Ramparts of Salé — A30

Scimitar-horned Oryxes — A31

Fez — A33

Valley of Draa A32

1939-42

149	A26	1c rose violet	.25	.25
150	A27	2c emerald	.25	.25
151	A27	3c ultra	.25	.25
152	A26	5c dk bl grn	.25	.25
153	A27	10c brt red vio	.25	.25
154	A28	15c dk green	.25	.25
155	A28	20c black grn	.25	.25
156	A29	30c deep blue	.25	.25
157	A29	40c chocolate	.25	.25
158	A29	45c Prus green	.50	.50
159	A30	50c rose red	1.40	.90
159A	A30	50c Prus grn ('40)	.30	.25
160	A30	60c turq blue	1.25	.75
160A	A30	60c choc ('40)	.30	.25
161	A31	70c dk violet	.25	.25
162	A32	75c grnsh blk	.50	.50
163	A32	80c pck bl ('40)	.30	.25
163A	A32	80c dk grn ('42)	.40	.25
164	A30	90c ultra	.30	.25
165	A28	1fr chocolate	.30	.25
165A	A32	1.20fr rose vio ('42)	.80	.40
166	A32	1.25fr henna brn	1.10	.65
167	A32	1.40fr rose violet	.65	.30
168	A30	1.50fr cop red ('40)	.30	.25
168A	A30	1.50fr rose ('42)	.25	.25
169	A33	2fr Prus green	.25	.25
170	A33	2.25fr dark blue	.65	.50
170A	A26	2.40fr red ('42)	.30	.30
171	A26	2.50fr scarlet	.90	.70
171A	A26	2.50fr dp blue ('40)	1.10	.65
172	A33	3fr black brown	.50	.30
172A	A26	4fr dp ultra ('42)	.40	.40
172B	A32	4.50fr grnsh blk ('42)	.80	.80
173	A31	5fr dark blue	.65	.50
174	A31	10fr red	1.25	.90
174A	A31	15fr Prus grn ('42)	4.75	4.00
175	A31	20fr dk vio brn	2.00	1.75
		Nos. 149-175 (37)	24.70	19.55
		Set, never hinged	32.50	

See Nos. 197-219. For surcharges see Nos. 244, 261-262, B21-B24, B26, B28, B32.

No. 136 Srchd. in Black

1940

176	A22	35c on 65c brown red	1.75	.95
a.		Pair, one without surcharge	3.25	2.40

The surcharge was applied on alternate rows in the sheet, making No. 176a. This was done to make a pair equal 1fr, the new rate.

Catalogue values for unused stamps in this section, from this point to the end of the section, are for Never Hinged items.

One Aim Alone-Victory A34

Tower of Hassan, Rabat A35

1943 Litho. *Perf. 12*

177	A34	1.50fr deep blue	.40	.25

1943

178	A35	10c rose lilac	.30	.25
179	A35	30c blue	.30	.25
180	A35	40c lake	.30	.25
181	A35	50c blue green	.30	.25
182	A35	60c dk vio brn	.30	.25
183	A35	70c rose violet	.30	.25
184	A35	80c gray green	.30	.30
185	A35	1fr car lake	.30	.25
186	A35	1.20fr violet	.30	.25
187	A35	1.50fr red	.30	.25
188	A35	2fr lt bl grn	.30	.25
189	A35	2.40fr car rose	.30	.35
190	A35	3fr olive brn	.30	.30
191	A35	4fr dk ultra	.30	.30
192	A35	4.50fr slate blk	.40	.25
193	A35	5fr dull blue	.55	.25
194	A35	10fr orange brn	.55	.40
195	A35	15fr slate grn	1.60	.55
196	A35	20fr deep plum	2.40	.80
		Nos. 178-196 (19)	9.70	6.00

Types of 1939-42

Perf. 13½x14, 14x13½

1945-47 Typo. Unwmk.

197	A27	10c red violet	.40	.25
199	A29	40c chocolate	.40	.25
200	A30	50c Prus grn	.40	.25
203	A28	1fr choc ('46)	.40	.35
204	A32	1.20fr vio brn ('46)	.40	.30
205	A27	1.30fr blue ('47)	.80	.40
206	A30	1.50fr deep red	.40	.25
207	A33	2fr Prus grn	.40	.25
209	A33	3fr black brn	.40	.25
210	A29	3.50fr dk red ('47)	1.20	.80
212	A31	4.50fr magenta ('47)	.80	.40
214	A31	5fr indigo	1.20	.55
215	A32	6fr chlky bl ('46)	.80	.35
216	A31	10fr red	2.00	.80
217	A31	15fr Prus grn	2.40	.80
218	A31	20fr dk vio brn	3.25	1.40
219	A31	25fr black brn	3.25	2.10
		Nos. 197-219 (17)	18.90	9.75

For surcharges see Nos. 261-263, B26, B28, B32.

The Terraces — A37

Mountain District — A39

Fortress A38

Marrakesh A40

Gardens of Fez — A41

Ouarzazat District — A42

1947 Engr. Unwmk. *Perf. 13*

221	A37	10c black brn	.40	.25
222	A37	30c brt red	.40	.25
223	A37	50c brt grnsh bl	.40	.25
224	A37	60c brt red vio	.40	.25
225	A38	1fr black	.40	.25
226	A38	1.50fr blue	.40	.25
227	A39	2fr brt green	.80	.40
228	A39	3fr brown red	.40	.25
229	A40	4fr dk bl vio	.40	.25
230	A41	5fr dk green	1.20	.55
231	A40	6fr crimson	.40	.25
232	A41	10fr dp blue	1.20	.40
233	A42	15fr dk grn	1.60	1.20
234	A42	20fr henna brn	1.60	.80
235	A42	25fr purple	2.40	1.20
		Nos. 221-235 (15)	12.40	6.80

1948-49

236	A37	30c purple	.40	.25
237	A38	2fr vio brn ('49)	.80	.40
238	A40	4fr green	.80	.35
239	A41	8fr org ('49)	1.60	.80
240	A41	10fr blue	1.20	.40
241	A42	10fr car rose	.80	.80
242	A38	12fr red	1.20	.80
243	A42	18fr deep blue	2.40	1.20
		Nos. 236-243 (8)	9.20	5.00

For surcharges see Nos. 263, 293-294.

No. 175 Surcharged with New Value and Wavy Lines in Carmine

1948

244	A31	8fr on 20fr dk vio brn	1.20	.80

Fortified Oasis A43

Walled City — A44

1949

245	A43	5fr blue green	1.20	.40
246	A44	15fr red	1.60	.80
247	A44	25fr ultra	1.60	.80
		Nos. 245-247 (3)	4.40	2.00

See No. 300.

Detail, Gate of Oudayas, Rabat — A45

Nejjarine Fountain, Fez — A46

Garden, Meknes — A47

1949 *Perf. 14x13*

248	A45	10c black	.40	.25
249	A45	50c rose brn	.40	.25
250	A45	1fr blue vio	.40	.25
251	A46	2fr dk car rose	.40	.25
252	A46	3fr dark blue	.80	.25
253	A46	5fr brt green	1.20	.25
254	A47	8fr dk bl grn	1.60	.80
255	A47	10fr brt red	1.60	.80
		Nos. 248-255 (8)	6.80	3.10

Postal Administration Building, Meknes — A48

1949, Oct. *Perf. 13*

256	A48	5fr dark green	2.40	2.00
257	A48	15fr deep carmine	2.40	2.00
258	A48	25fr deep blue	2.75	2.40
		Nos. 256-258 (3)	7.55	6.40

75th anniv. of the UPU.

Todra Valley A49

1950

259	A49	35fr red brown	1.60	.40
260	A49	50fr indigo	1.60	.40

See No. 270.

Nos. 204 and 205 Srchd. in Black or Blue

1950 *Perf. 14x13½, 13½x14*

261	A32	1fr on 1.20fr vio brn (Bk)	.40	.35
262	A27	1fr on 1.30fr blue (Bl)	.40	.25

The surcharge is transposed and spaced to fit the design on No. 262.

No. 231 Surcharged with New Value and Wavy Lines in Black

1951 *Perf. 13*

263	A40	5fr on 6fr crimson	.80	.25

Statue of Gen. Jacques Leclerc — A50

1951, Apr. 28 Engr.

264	A50	10fr blue green	2.40	2.00
265	A50	15fr deep carmine	2.75	2.00
266	A50	25fr indigo	2.75	2.00
		Nos. 264-266 (3)	7.90	6.00

Unveiling of a monument to Gen. Leclerc at Casablanca, Apr. 28, 1951. See No. C39.

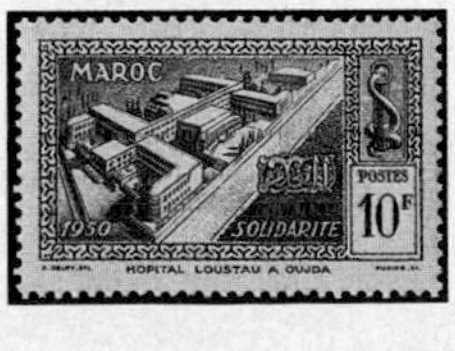

Loustau Hospital, Oujda A51

Designs: 15fr, New Hospital, Meknes. 25fr, New Hospital, Rabat.

1951

267	A51	10fr indigo & pur	2.00	1.60
268	A51	15fr Prus grn & red brn	2.00	1.60
269	A51	25fr dk brn & ind	2.40	2.00

See No. C41.

		Nos. 267-269 (3)	6.40	5.20

Todra Valley Type of 1950

1951

270	A49	30fr ultramarine	1.60	.40

Pigeons at Fountain A52

Karaouine Mosque, Fez A53

Patio, Oudayas A54

Oudayas Point, Rabat A55

Patio of Old House — A56

Type I (No. 275)

Type II (No. 276)

Perf. 14x13, 13

1951-53 Engr. Unwmk.

271	A52	5fr magenta ('52)	.40	.25
272	A53	6fr bl grn ('52)	.40	.40
273	A52	8fr brown ('52)	.40	.40
273A	A53	10fr rose red ('53)	.40	.35
274	A53	12fr dp ultra ('52)	.80	.40
275	A54	15fr red brn (I)	2.75	.25
276	A54	15fr red brn (II)	1.20	.25
277	A55	15fr pur ('52)	1.20	.40
278	A55	18fr red ('52)	2.00	1.20
279	A56	20fr dp grnsh bl ('52)	2.40	.80
		Nos. 271-279 (10)	11.95	4.70

See Nos. 297-299.

8th-10th Cent. Capital A57

Casablanca Monument A58

Capitals: 20fr, 12th Cent. 25fr, 13th-14th Cent. 50fr, 17th Cent.

1952, Apr. 5 *Perf. 13*

280	A57	15fr deep blue	3.25	2.40
281	A57	20fr red	3.25	2.40
282	A57	25fr purple	3.25	2.40
283	A57	50fr deep green	3.25	2.40
		Nos. 280-283 (4)	13.00	9.60

1952 Sept. 22 Engr. & Typo.

284	A58	15fr multicolored	3.50	2.40

Creation of the French Military Medal, cent.

Daggers of South Morocco
A59

Post Rider and Public Letter-writer
A60

Designs: 20fr and 25fr, Antique brooches.

1953, Mar. 27 **Engr.**

285	A59	15fr dk car rose	4.00	3.25
286	A59	20fr violet brn	4.00	3.25
287	A59	25fr dark blue	4.00	3.25
		Nos. 285-287 (3)	12.00	9.75

See No. C46.

1953, May 16

288	A60	15fr violet brown	2.00	1.60

Stamp Day, May 16, 1953.

Bine el Ouidane Dam — A61

1953, Nov. 3 ***Perf. 13***

290	A61	15fr indigo	2.00	1.60

See No. 295.

Mogador Fortress — A62

Design: 30fr, Moorish knights.

1953, Dec. 4

291	A62	15fr green	2.40	1.60
292	A62	30fr red brown	2.40	1.60

Issued to aid Army Welfare Work.

Nos. 226 and 243 Surcharged with New Value and Wavy Lines in Black

1954

293	A38	1fr on 1.50fr blue	.40	.25
294	A42	15fr on 18fr dp bl	1.20	.65

Dam Type of 1953

1954, Mar. 8

295	A61	15fr red brn & indigo	1.60	1.20

Station of Rural Automobile Post — A63

1954, Apr. 10

296	A63	15fr dk blue grn	1.40	.80

Stamp Day, April 10, 1954.

Types of 1951-53

1954 **Engr.** ***Perf. 14x13***

297	A52	15fr dk blue green	1.20	.40

Typo.

298	A52	5fr magenta	1.20	.40
299	A55	15fr rose violet	1.60	.40
		Nos. 297-299 (3)	4.00	1.20

Walled City Type of 1949

1954 **Engr.** ***Perf. 13***

300	A44	25fr purple	2.40	.80

Marshal Lyautey at Rabat
A64

Lyautey, Builder of Cities — A65

Designs: 15fr, Marshal Lyautey at Khenifra. 50fr, Hubert Lyautey, Marshal of France.

1954, Nov. 17

301	A64	5fr indigo	2.40	2.00
302	A64	15fr dark green	3.25	2.75
303	A65	30fr rose brown	4.00	3.25
304	A65	50fr dk red brn	4.00	3.25
		Nos. 301-304 (4)	13.65	11.25

Marshal Hubert Lyautey, birth cent.

Franco-Moslem Education — A66

Moslem Student at Blackboard — A67

Designs: 30fr, Moslem school at Camp Boulhaut. 50fr, Moulay Idriss College at Fez.

1955, Apr. 16 **Unwmk.** ***Perf. 13***

305	A66	5fr indigo	2.00	1.60
306	A67	15fr rose lake	2.40	2.00
307	A66	30fr chocolate	2.40	2.00
308	A67	50fr dk blue grn	2.75	2.40
		Nos. 305-308 (4)	9.55	8.00

Franco-Moslem solidarity.

Map and Rotary Emblem
A68

1955, June 11

309	A68	15fr bl & org brn	2.00	1.20

Rotary Intl., 50th anniv.

Post Office, Mazagan
A69

1955, May 24

310	A69	15fr red	1.20	.80

Stamp Day.

Bab el Chorfa, Fez
A70

Mahakma (Courthouse), Casablanca
A71

Fortress, Safi — A72

Designs: 50c, 1fr, 2fr, 3fr, Mrissa Gate, Salé. 10fr, 12fr, 15fr, Minaret at Rabat. 30fr, Menara Garden Marrakesh. 40fr, Tafraout Village. 50fr, Portuguese cistern, Mazagan. 75fr, Garden of Oudaya, Rabat.

1955 ***Perf. 13½x13, 13x13½, 13***

311	A70	50c brn vio	.40	.25
312	A70	1fr blue	.40	.25
313	A70	2fr red lilac	.40	.25
314	A70	3fr bluish blk	.40	.25
315	A70	5fr vermilion	1.60	.40
316	A70	6fr green	.75	.35
317	A70	8fr orange brn	1.20	.40
318	A70	10fr violet brn	1.60	.40
319	A70	12fr greenish bl	.80	.40
320	A70	15fr magenta	1.10	.25
321	A71	18fr dk green	2.00	.80
322	A71	20fr brown lake	1.20	.40
323	A72	25fr brt ultra	2.75	.40
324	A72	30fr green	2.40	.80
325	A72	40fr orange red	2.40	.40
326	A72	50fr black brn	8.00	.80
327	A71	75fr greenish bl	2.40	1.20
		Nos. 311-327 (17)	29.80	8.00

Succeeding issues, released under the Kingdom, are listed under Morocco in Vol. 4.

SEMI-POSTAL STAMPS

French Protectorate

No. 30 Surcharged in Red ✚ 5c

1914 **Unwmk.** ***Perf. 14x13½***

B1	A4	10c + 5c on 10c	*24,000.*	*28,000.*

Known only with inverted red surcharge.

No. 42 Surcharged in Red

B2	A7	10c + 5c on 10c rose	6.50	6.50
a.		Double surcharge	175.00	175.00
b.		Inverted surcharge	225.00	225.00
c.		"c" omitted	110.00	110.00

On Nos. B1 and B2 the cross is set up from pieces of metal (quads), the horizontal bar being made from two long pieces, the vertical bar from two short pieces. Each cross in the setting of twenty-five differs from the others.

No. 30 Handstamp Surcharged in Red

B3	A4	10c + 5c on 10c rose	*1,650.*	*1,300.*

No. B3 was issued at Oujda. The surcharge ink is water-soluble.

No. 42 Surcharged in Vermilion or Carmine

B4	A7	10c + 5c on 10c (V)	25.00	25.00
a.		Double surcharge	240.00	240.00
b.		Inverted surcharge	240.00	240.00
c.		Double surch., one invtd.	200.00	200.00
B5	A7	10c +5c on 10c (C)	475.00	525.00
a.		Inverted surcharge	1,600.	1,600.

On Nos. B4-B5 the horizontal bar of the cross is single and not as thick as on Nos. B1-B2.

No. B5 was sold largely at Casablanca.

Carmine Surcharge
SP1

Black Overprint
SP2

1915

B6	SP1	5c + 5c green	3.25	2.40
a.		Inverted surcharge	300.00	300.00
B7	SP2	10c + 5c rose	4.75	4.75

No. B6 was not issued without the Red Cross surcharge. No. B7 was used in Tangier.

France No. B2 Overprinted in Black — SP3

B8	SP3	10c + 5c red	7.50	7.50

No. 30 Surcharged in Carmine — SP4

1917

B9	SP4	10c + 5c on 10c rose	3.25	3.25

On No. B9 the horizontal bar of the cross is made from a single, thick piece of metal.

Marshal Hubert Lyautey — SP5

1935, May 15 **Photo.** ***Perf. 13x13½***

B10	SP5	50c + 50c red	9.50	9.50
B11	SP5	1fr + 1fr dk grn	11.00	11.00
B12	SP5	5fr + 5fr blk brn	45.00	45.00
		Nos. B10-B12 (3)	65.50	65.50
		Set, never hinged	98.00	

Stamps of 1933-34 Surcharged in Blue or Red

1938 ***Perf. 13***

B13	A18	2c + 2c red vio	5.50	5.50
B14	A19	3c + 3c dk brn	5.50	5.50
B15	A20	20c + 20c red brn	5.50	5.50
B16	A21	40c + 40c blk brn (R)	5.50	5.50
B17	A22	65c + 65c brn red	5.50	5.50
B18	A23	1.25fr + 1.25fr blk (R)	5.50	5.50

B19 A24 2fr + 2fr yel brn 5.50 5.50
B20 A25 5fr + 5fr red brn 5.50 5.50
Nos. B13-B20 (8) 44.00 44.00
Set, never hinged 64.00

Stamps of 1939 Srchd. in Black

1942

B21 A29 45c + 2fr Prus grn 6.75 4.75
B22 A30 90c + 4fr ultra 6.75 4.75
B23 A32 1.25fr + 6fr henna brn 8.00 6.50
B24 A26 2.50fr + 8fr scarlet 8.00 6.50
Nos. B21-B24 (4) 29.50 22.50
Set, never hinged 27.00

The arrangement of the surcharge differs slightly on each denomination.

Catalogue values for unused stamps in this section, from this point to the end of the section, are for Never Hinged items.

No. 207 Surcharged in Black

1945 **Unwmk.** ***Perf. 13½x14***

B26 A33 2fr + 1fr Prus green .80 .50

For surcharge see No. B28.

Mausoleum of Marshal Lyautey — SP7

1945 **Litho.** ***Perf. 11½***

B27 SP7 2fr + 3fr dark blue .80 .40

The surtax was for French works of solidarity.

No. B26 Surcharged in Red

1946 ***Perf. 13½x14***

B28 A33 3fr (+ 1fr) on 2fr + 1fr .40 .25

Statue of Marshal Lyautey — SP8

Perf. 13½x14, 13

1946, Dec. 16 **Engr.**

B29 SP8 2fr + 10fr black 2.40 1.60
B30 SP8 3fr + 15fr cop red 2.40 1.60
B31 SP8 10fr + 20fr brt bl 3.25 2.40
Nos. B29-B31 (3) 8.05 5.60

The surtax was for works of solidarity.

No. 212 Surcharged in Rose Violet

1947, Mar. 15 ***Perf. 13½x14***

B32 A31 4.50fr + 5.50fr magenta 2.00 1.60

Stamp Day, 1947.

Map and Symbols of Prosperity from Phosphates SP9

1947 ***Perf. 13***

B33 SP9 4.50fr + 5.50fr green 1.60 1.20

25th anniv. of the exploitations of the Cherifien Office of Phosphates.

Power — SP10

Health — SP11

1948, Feb. 9

B34 SP10 6fr + 9fr red brn 3.25 2.40
B35 SP11 10fr + 20fr dp ultra 3.25 2.40

The surtax was for combined works of Franco-Moroccan solidarity.

Type of Regular Issue of 1923, Inscribed: "Journee du Timbre 1948"

1948, Mar. 6

B36 A16 6fr + 4fr red brown 1.20 .80

Stamp Day, Mar. 6, 1948.

Battleship off Moroccan Coast SP12

1948, Aug.

B37 SP12 6fr + 9fr purple 2.00 1.60

The surtax was for naval charities.

Wheat Field near Meknes SP13

Designs: 2fr+5fr, Olive grove, Taroudant. 3fr+7fr, Net and coastal view. 5fr+10fr, Aguedal Gardens, Marrakesh.

1949, Apr. 12 **Engr.** **Unwmk.**

Inscribed: "SOLIDARITÉ 1948"

B38 SP13 1fr + 2fr orange 2.00 1.60
B39 SP13 2fr + 5fr car 2.00 1.60
B40 SP13 3fr + 7fr pck bl 2.00 1.60
B41 SP13 5fr + 10fr dk brn vio 2.00 1.60
a. Sheet of 4, #B38-B41 27.50 24.00
Nos. B38-B41,CB31-CB34 (8) 17.60 14.40

Gazelle Hunter, from 1899 Local Stamp SP14

1949, May 1

B42 SP14 10fr + 5fr choc & car rose 2.00 1.60

Stamp Day and 50th anniversary of Mazagan-Marrakesh local postage stamp.

Moroccan Soldiers, Flag SP15

Rug Weaving SP16

1949

B43 SP15 10fr + 10fr bright red 1.60 1.40

The surtax was for Army Welfare Work.

1950, Apr. 11

Designs: 2fr+5fr, Pottery making, 3fr+7fr, Bookbinding. 5fr+10fr, Copper work.

Inscribed: "SOLIDARITE 1949"

B44 SP16 1fr + 2fr dp car 2.75 2.40
B45 SP16 2fr + 5fr dk brnsh bl 2.75 2.40
B46 SP16 3fr + 7fr dk pur 2.75 2.40
B47 SP16 5fr + 10fr red brn 2.75 2.40
a. Sheet of 4, #B44-B47 32.50 24.00
Nos. B44-B47,CB36-CB39 (8) 20.60 17.60

Ruins of Sala Colonia at Chella SP17

1950, Sept. 25 **Engr.** ***Perf. 13***

B48 SP17 10fr + 10fr dp magenta 2.00 *1.60*
B49 SP17 15fr + 15fr indigo 2.00 1.60

The surtax was for Army Welfare Work.

AIR POST STAMPS

French Protectorate

Biplane over Casablanca AP1

1922-27 **Photo.** **Unwmk.** ***Perf. 13½***

C1 AP1 5c dp orange ('27) .50 .50
C2 AP1 25c dp ultra 1.20 1.20
C3 AP1 50c grnsh blue .40 .40
C4 AP1 75c dp blue 80.00 16.00
C5 AP1 75c dp green .80 .40
C6 AP1 80c vio brn ('27) 2.40 .80
C7 AP1 1fr vermilion 1.20 .80
C8 AP1 1.40fr brn lake ('27) 2.40 1.25
C9 AP1 1.90fr dp blue ('27) 2.75 1.60
C10 AP1 2fr black vio 2.40 1.20
a. 2fr deep violet 2.25 1.40
C11 AP1 3fr gray blk 2.75 2.00
Nos. C1-C11 (11) 96.80 26.15

The 25c, 50c, 75c deep green and 1fr each were printed in two of three types, differing in frameline thickness, or hyphen in "Hello-Vaugirard" imprint.Values are for the more common types.

Imperf., Pairs

C1a	AP1	5c	65.00	65.00
C2a	AP1	25c	72.50	72.50
C3a	AP1	50c	72.50	72.50
C4a	AP1	75c	550.00	550.00
C5a	AP1	75c	72.50	72.50
C6a	AP1	80c	72.50	72.50
C7a	AP1	1fr	90.00	90.00
C10b	AP1	2fr	225.00	225.00

Nos. C8-C9 Srchd. in Blue or Black

1931, Apr. 10

C12 AP1 1fr on 1.40fr (B) 2.40 2.40
a. Inverted surcharge 310.00 310.00
C13 AP1 1.50fr on 1.90fr (Bk) 2.40 2.40

Rabat and Tower of Hassan AP2

Casablanca AP3

1933, Jan. **Engr.**

C14 AP2 50c dark blue .80 .80
C15 AP2 80c orange brn .80 .65
C16 AP2 1.50fr brown red .80 .80
C17 AP3 2.50fr carmine rose 6.50 1.20
C18 AP3 5fr violet 3.25 1.75
C19 AP3 10fr blue green 1.20 1.20
Nos. C14-C19 (6) 13.35 6.40

For surcharges see Nos. CB22-CB23.

Storks and Minaret, Chella — AP4

Plane and Map of Morocco AP5

1939-40 ***Perf. 13***

C20 AP4 80c Prus green .25 .25
C21 AP4 1fr dk red .25 .25
C22 AP5 1.90fr ultra .40 .30
C23 AP5 2fr red vio ('40) .40 .30
C24 AP5 3fr chocolate .50 .25
C25 AP4 5fr violet 1.40 .80
C26 AP5 10fr turq blue 1.25 .55
Nos. C20-C26 (7) 4.45 2.70

Catalogue values for unused stamps in this section, from this point to the end of the section, are for Never Hinged items.

Plane over Oasis — AP6

1944 Litho. *Perf. 11½*

C27	AP6	50c Prus grn	.50	.35
C28	AP6	2fr ultra	.50	.35
C29	AP6	5fr scarlet	.50	.35
C30	AP6	10fr violet	1.40	1.10
C31	AP6	50fr black	2.00	1.60
C32	AP6	100fr dp bl & red	4.00	3.25
		Nos. C27-C32 (6)	8.90	7.00

For surcharge see No. CB24.

Plane AP7

1945 Engr. *Perf. 13*

C33	AP7	50fr sepia	1.20	.95

Moulay Idriss — AP8

La Medina AP9

1947-48

C34	AP8	9fr dk rose car	.40	.30
C35	AP8	40fr dark blue	1.20	.80
C36	AP8	50fr dp claret ('47)	1.60	.40
C37	AP9	100fr dp grnsh bl	3.25	1.20
C38	AP9	200fr henna brn	8.00	1.60
		Nos. C34-C38 (5)	14.45	4.30

Leclerc Type of Regular Issue

1951, Apr. 28

C39	A50	50fr purple	3.25	2.75

Unveiling of a monument to Gen. Leclerc at Casablanca, Apr. 28, 1951.

Kasbah of the Oudayas, Rabat AP11

1951, May 22

C40	AP11	300fr purple	24.00	12.00

Ben Smine Sanatorium AP12

1951, June 4

C41	AP12	50fr pur & Prus grn	3.50	2.75

Fortifications, Chella — AP13

Plane Near Marrakesh AP14

Fort, Anti-Atlas Mountains AP15

View of Fez AP16

1952, Apr. 19 Unwmk. *Perf. 13*

C42	AP13	10fr blue green	1.60	.80
C43	AP14	40fr red	2.40	.80
C44	AP15	100fr brown	5.50	1.60
C45	AP16	200fr purple	10.50	4.00
		Nos. C42-C45 (4)	20.00	7.20

Antique Brooches — AP17

1953, Mar. 27

C46	AP17	50fr dark green	4.00	3.25

"City" of the Agdal, Meknes AP18

20fr, Yakoub el Mansour, Rabat. 40fr, Ainchock, Casablanca. 50fr, El Aliya, Fedala.

1954, Mar. 8

C47	AP18	10fr olive brown	4.00	2.75
C48	AP18	20fr purple	4.00	2.75
C49	AP18	40fr red brown	4.00	2.75
C50	AP18	50fr deep green	4.00	2.75
		Nos. C47-C50 (4)	16.00	11.00

Franco-Moroccan solidarity.

Naval Vessel and Sailboat AP19

Village in the Anti-Atlas AP20

"Ksar es Souk," Rabat and Plane AP21

1954, Oct. 18

C51	AP19	15fr dk blue green	2.00	1.60
C52	AP19	30fr violet blue	2.40	2.00

1955, July 25 Engr. *Perf. 13*

200fr, Estuary of Bou Regreg, Rabat and Plane.

C53	AP20	100fr brt violet	2.75	.80
C54	AP20	200fr brt carmine	6.50	1.20
C55	AP21	500fr grnsh blue	16.00	4.00
		Nos. C53-C55 (3)	25.25	6.00

AIR POST SEMI-POSTAL STAMPS

French Protectorate

Moorish Tribesmen SPAP1

Designs: 25c, Moor plowing with camel and burro. 50c, Caravan nearing Saffi. 75c, Walls, Marrakesh. 80c, Sheep grazing at Azrou. 1fr, Gate at Fez. 1.50fr, Aerial view of Tangier. 2fr, Aerial view of Casablanca. 3fr, Storks on old wall, Rabat. 5fr, Moorish fete.

Perf. 13½

1928, July 26 Photo. Unwmk.

CB1	SPAP1	5c dp blue	5.25	5.25
CB2	SPAP1	25c brn org	5.25	5.25
CB3	SPAP1	50c red	5.25	5.25
CB4	SPAP1	75c org brn	5.25	5.25
CB5	SPAP1	80c olive grn	5.25	5.25
CB6	SPAP1	1fr orange	5.25	5.25
CB7	SPAP1	1.50fr Prus bl	5.25	5.25
CB8	SPAP1	2fr dp brown	5.25	5.25
CB9	SPAP1	3fr dp violet	5.25	5.25
CB10	SPAP1	5fr brown blk	5.25	5.25
		Nos. CB1-CB10 (10)	52.50	52.50

These stamps were sold in sets only and at double their face value. The money received for the surtax was divided among charitable and social organizations. The stamps were not sold at post offices but solely by subscription to the Moroccan Postal Administration.

Overprinted in Red or Blue (25c, 50c, 75c, 1fr)

1929, Feb. 1

CB11	SPAP1	5c dp blue	5.25	5.25
CB12	SPAP1	25c brown org	5.25	5.25
CB13	SPAP1	50c red	5.25	5.25
CB14	SPAP1	75c org brn	5.25	5.25
CB15	SPAP1	80c olive grn	5.25	5.25
CB16	SPAP1	1fr orange	5.25	5.25
CB17	SPAP1	1.50fr Prus bl	5.25	5.25
CB18	SPAP1	2fr dp brown	5.25	5.25
CB19	SPAP1	3fr dp violet	5.25	5.25
CB20	SPAP1	5fr brown blk	5.25	5.25
		Nos. CB11-CB20 (10)	52.50	52.50

These stamps were sold at double their face values and only in Tangier. The surtax benefited various charities.

Marshal Hubert Lyautey SPAP10

1935, May 15 *Perf. 13½*

CB21	SPAP10	1.50fr + 1.50fr blue	20.00	20.00

Nos. C14, C19 Surcharged in Red

1938 *Perf. 13*

CB22	AP2	50c + 50c dk bl	8.00	8.00
CB23	AP3	10fr + 10fr bl grn	5.50	5.50

Catalogue values for unused stamps in this section, from this point to the end of the section, are for Never Hinged items.

Plane over Oasis — SPAP11

1944 Litho. *Perf. 11½*

CB23A	SPAP11	1.50fr + 98.50fr	2.40	1.60

The surtax was for charity among the liberated French.

No. C29 Surcharged in Black

1946, June 18 *Perf. 11*

CB24	AP6	5fr + 5fr scarlet	1.60	1.20

6th anniv. of the appeal made by Gen. Charles de Gaulle, June 18, 1940. The surtax was for the Free French Association of Morocco.

Statue of Marshal Lyautey — SPAP12

1946, Dec. Engr. *Perf. 13*

CB25	SPAP12	10fr +30fr dk grn	6.50	2.75

The surtax was for works of solidarity.

Replenishing Stocks of Food — SPAP13

Agriculture SPAP14

1948, Feb. 9 Unwmk.

CB26	SPAP13	9fr +26fr dp grn	2.00	1.60
CB27	SPAP14	20fr +35fr brown	2.00	1.60

The surtax was for combined works of Franco-Moroccan solidarity.

Tomb of Marshal Hubert Lyautey — SPAP15

1948, May 18 *Perf. 13*

CB28	SPAP15	10fr +25fr dk grn	1.60	1.25

Lyautey Exposition, Paris, June, 1948.

P.T.T. Clubhouse SPAP16

1948, June 7 — **Engr.**

CB29	SPAP16	6fr + 34fr dk grn	2.40	2.00
CB30	SPAP16	9fr + 51fr red brn	2.40	2.00

The surtax was used for the Moroccan P.T.T. employees vacation colony at Ifrane.

View of Agadir — SPAP17

Designs: 6fr+9fr, Fez. 9fr+16fr, Atlas Mountains. 15fr+25fr, Valley of Draa.

1949, Apr. 12 — ***Perf. 13***

Inscribed: "SOLIDARITÉ 1948"

CB31	SPAP17	5fr +5fr dk grn	2.40	2.00
CB32	SPAP17	6fr +9fr org red	2.40	2.00
CB33	SPAP17	9fr +16fr blk brn	2.40	2.00
CB34	SPAP17	15fr +25fr Ind	2.40	2.00
a.		Sheet of 4, #CB31-CB34	32.50	24.00
		Nos. CB31-CB34 (4)	9.60	8.00

Plane over Globe — SPAP18

1950, Mar. 11 — **Engr. & Typo.**

CB35	SPAP18	15fr + 10fr bl grn & car	1.60	1.25

Day of the Stamp, Mar. 11-12, 1950, and 25th anniv. of the 1st post link between Casablanca and Dakar.

Scenes and Map: Northwest Corner SPAP19

Designs (quarters of map): 6fr+9fr, NE, 9fr+16fr, SW. 15fr+25fr, SE.

1950, Apr. 11 — **Engr.**

Inscribed: "SOLIDARITE 1949"

CB36	SPAP19	5fr +5fr dp ultra	2.40	2.00
CB37	SPAP19	6fr +9fr Prus grn	2.40	2.00
CB38	SPAP19	9fr +16fr dk brn	2.40	2.00
CB39	SPAP19	15fr +25fr brn red	2.40	2.00
a.		Sheet of 4, #CB36-CB39	32.50	24.00
		Nos. CB36-CB39 (4)	9.60	8.00

Arch of Triumph of Caracalla at Volubilis SPAP20

1950, Sept. 25 — **Unwmk.**

CB40	SPAP20	10fr + 10fr sepia	2.00	1.60
CB41	SPAP20	15fr + 15fr bl grn	2.00	1.60

The surtax was for Army Welfare Work.

Casablanca Post Office and First Air Post Stamp SPAP21

1952, Mar. 8 — ***Perf. 13***

CB42	SPAP21	15fr + 5fr red brn & dp grn	4.75	4.00

Day of the Stamp, Mar. 8, 1952, and 30th anniv. of French Morocco's 1st air post stamp.

POSTAGE DUE STAMPS

French Offices in Morocco

Postage Due Stamps and Types of France Surcharged in Red or Black

1896 — **Unwmk.** — ***Perf. 14x13½***

On Stamps of 1891-93

J1	D2	5c on 5c lt bl (R)	12.00	5.50
J2	D2	10c on 10c choc (R)	16.00	6.50
J3	D2	30c on 30c car	32.50	24.00
a.		Pair, one without surcharge		
J4	D2	50c on 50c lilac	32.50	27.50
a.		"S" of "CENTIMOS" omitted	340.00	250.00
J5	D2	1p on 1fr lil brn	350.00	325.00

1909-10 — **On Stamps of 1908-10**

J6	D3	1c on 1c ol grn (R)	4.00	4.00
J7	D3	10c on 10c violet	40.00	32.50
J8	D3	30c on 30c bister	55.00	40.00
J9	D3	50c on 50c red	80.00	72.50
		Nos. J6-J9 (4)	179.00	149.00

Postage Due Stamps of France Surcharged in Red or Blue

1911 — **On Stamps of 1893-96**

J10	D2	5c on 5c blue (R)	4.75	4.75
J11	D2	10c on 10c choc (R)	16.00	16.00
a.		Double surcharge	225.00	*260.00*
J12	D2	50c on 50c lil (Bl)	20.00	20.00

On Stamps of 1908-10

J13	D3	1c on 1c ol grn (R)	4.00	3.25
J14	D3	10c on 10c vio (R)	8.00	8.00
J15	D3	30c on 30c bis (R)	12.00	12.00
J16	D3	50c on 50c red (Bl)	16.00	16.00
		Nos. J10-J16 (7)	80.75	80.00

For surcharges see Nos. J23-J26.

French Protectorate

Type of 1911 Issue Overprinted "Protectorat Francais" — D4

1915-17

J17	D4	1c on 1c black	.80	.80
a.		New value double	175.00	
J18	D4	5c on 5c blue	3.25	2.00
J19	D4	10c on 10c choc	4.00	2.00
J20	D4	20c on 20c ol grn	4.00	2.00
J21	D4	30c on 30c rose red, *grayish*	8.00	5.50
J22	D4	50c on 50c vio brn	12.00	8.00
		Nos. J17-J22 (6)	32.05	20.30

Nos. J13 to J16 With Additional Overprint "Protectorat Francais"

1915

J23	D3	1c on 1c ol grn	1.60	1.60
J24	D3	10c on 10c violet	4.00	3.25
J25	D3	30c on 30c bister	4.00	4.00
J26	D3	50c on 50c red	4.00	4.00
		Nos. J23-J26 (4)	13.60	12.85

D5

1917-26 — **Typo.**

J27	D5	1c black	.25	.25
J28	D5	5c deep blue	.40	.25
J29	D5	10c brown	.40	.40
J30	D5	20c olive green	2.50	1.60
J31	D5	30c rose	.40	.40
J32	D5	50c lilac brown	.80	.40
J33	D5	1fr red brn, *straw* ('26)	.85	.80
J34	D5	2fr violet ('26)	2.40	1.60
		Nos. J27-J34 (8)	8.00	5.70

See #J49-J56, Morocco #J1-J4. For surcharges see #J46-J48.

Postage Due Stamps of France, 1882-1906 Overprinted

1918

J35	D2	1c black	1.20	1.20
J36	D2	5c blue	2.40	2.40
J37	D2	10c chocolate	2.00	2.00
J38	D2	15c green	4.75	4.75
J39	D2	20c olive green	6.50	6.50
J40	D2	30c rose red, *grayish*	16.00	16.00
J41	D2	50c violet brown	24.00	24.00
		Nos. J35-J41 (7)	56.85	56.85

Postage Due Stamps of France, 1908-19 Overprinted

1918

J42	D3	1c olive green	1.20	1.20
J43	D3	10c violet	2.75	2.75
J44	D3	20c bister, *grayish*	8.00	8.00
J45	D3	40c red	20.00	20.00
		Nos. J42-J45 (4)	31.95	31.95

Catalogue values for unused stamps in this section, from this point to the end of the section, are for Never Hinged items.

Nos. J31 and J29 Surcharged

1944 — **Unwmk.** — ***Perf. 14x13½***

J46	D5	50c on 30c rose	3.25	2.40
J47	D5	1fr on 10c brown	5.50	4.00
J48	D5	3fr on 10c brown	13.00	9.50
		Nos. J46-J48 (3)	21.75	15.90

Type of 1917-1926

1945-52 — **Typo.**

J49	D5	1fr brn lake ('47)	1.20	.80
J50	D5	2fr rose lake ('47)	1.60	.80
J51	D5	3fr ultra	.80	.35
J52	D5	4fr red orange	.80	.30
J53	D5	5fr green	1.60	.50
J54	D5	10fr yellow brn	2.00	.50
J55	D5	20fr carmine ('50)	2.00	.90
J56	D5	30fr dull brn ('52)	2.75	1.60
		Nos. J49-J56 (8)	12.75	5.75

PARCEL POST STAMPS

French Protectorate

PP1

1917 — **Unwmk.** — ***Perf. 13½x14***

Q1	PP1	5c green	1.20	.80
Q2	PP1	10c carmine	1.20	.80
Q3	PP1	20c lilac brown	1.20	1.00
Q4	PP1	25c blue	1.60	.80
Q5	PP1	40c dark brown	2.40	1.60
Q6	PP1	50c red orange	4.00	.80
Q7	PP1	75c pale slate	4.00	2.40
Q8	PP1	1fr ultra	5.50	.80
Q9	PP1	2fr gray	12.00	1.60
Q10	PP1	5fr violet	12.00	1.60
Q11	PP1	10fr black	20.00	1.60
		Nos. Q1-Q11 (11)	65.10	13.80

FRENCH POLYNESIA

'french ,pä-lə-'nē-zhə

(French Oceania)

LOCATION — South Pacific Ocean
GOVT. — French Overseas Territory
AREA — 1,522 sq. mi.
POP. — 242,073 (1999 est.)
CAPITAL — Papeete

In 1903 various French Establishments in the South Pacific were united to form a single colony. Most important of the island groups are the Society Islands, Marquesas Islands, the Tuamotu group and the Gambier, Austral, and Rapa Islands. Tahiti, largest of the Society group, ranks first in importance.

100 Centimes = 1 Franc

Catalogue values for unused stamps in this country are for Never Hinged items, beginning with Scott 136 in the regular postage section, Scott B11 in the semi-postal section, Scott C2 in the airpost section, Scott J18 in the postage due section, and Scott O1 in the officials section.

Navigation and Commerce — A1

Perf. 14x13½

1892-1907 Typo. Unwmk.

Name of Colony in Blue or Carmine

1	A1	1c black, *lil bl*	1.60	1.60
2	A1	2c brown, *buff*	2.75	2.75
3	A1	4c claret, *lav*	4.50	4.00
4	A1	5c green, *grnsh*	13.50	9.50
5	A1	5c yellow grn ('06)	5.00	2.40
6	A1	10c blk, *lavender*	30.00	12.50
7	A1	10c red ('00)	5.00	2.40
8	A1	15c blue, quadrille paper	35.00	12.00
9	A1	15c gray, *lt gray* ('00)	10.00	7.25
10	A1	20c red, *grn*	17.50	16.00
11	A1	25c black, *rose*	60.00	30.00
12	A1	25c blue ('00)	32.50	16.00
13	A1	30c brown, *bis*	16.00	14.50
14	A1	35c black, *yel* ('06)	11.00	9.50
15	A1	40c red, *straw*	132.50	80.00
16	A1	45c blk, *gray grn* ('07)	6.75	*6.75*
17	A1	50c car, *pale rose*	10.00	10.00
a.		50c rose, *pale rose*	10.00	9.00
18	A1	50c brown, *az* ('00)	275.00	250.00
19	A1	75c dp vio, *org*	12.00	12.00
20	A1	1fr brnz grn, *straw*	13.50	13.50
		Nos. 1-20 (20)	694.10	512.65

Perf. 13½x14 stamps are counterfeits.
For overprint and surcharge see Nos. 55, B1.

Tahitian Girl — A2

Kanakas — A3

Fautaua Valley — A4

1913-30

21	A2	1c violet & brn	.25	.25
22	A2	2c brown & blk	.25	.25
23	A2	4c orange & bl	.35	.35
24	A2	5c grn & yel grn	1.60	.90
a.		Double impression of yel grn	500.00	
25	A2	5c bl & blk ('22)	.50	.50
26	A2	10c rose & org	2.25	2.25
27	A2	10c bl grn & yel grn ('22)	1.25	1.25
28	A2	10c org red & brn red, *bluish* ('26)	1.40	1.40
29	A2	15c org & blk ('15)	.85	.65
a.		Imperf., pair	175.00	
30	A2	20c black & vio	1.10	1.00
a.		Imperf., pair	175.00	
31	A2	20c grn & bl grn ('26)	1.00	1.00
32	A2	20c brn red & dk brn ('27)	1.60	1.60
33	A3	25c ultra & blue	1.50	1.25
34	A3	25c vio & rose ('22)	.75	.75
35	A3	30c gray & brown	5.00	4.00
a.		Imperf., pair	325.00	
36	A3	30c rose & red org ('22)	3.25	3.25
37	A3	30c blk & red org ('26)	.75	.75
38	A3	30c slate bl & bl grn ('27)	1.75	1.75
39	A3	35c green & rose	1.25	1.25
40	A3	40c black & green	1.10	1.10
41	A3	45c orange & red	1.10	1.10
42	A3	50c dk brown & blk	17.50	13.50
43	A3	50c ultra & bl ('22)	1.25	1.25
44	A3	50c gray & bl vio ('26)	1.10	1.10
45	A3	60c green & blk ('25)	1.25	1.25
46	A3	65c ol brn & red vio ('27)	3.25	3.25
47	A3	75c vio brn & vio	2.50	2.50
48	A3	90c brn red & rose ('30)	16.50	16.50
a.		Imperf., pair	225.00	
49	A4	1fr rose & black	6.25	4.25
50	A4	1.10fr vio & dk brn ('28)	1.60	1.60
51	A4	1.40fr bis brn & vio ('29)	4.00	4.00
52	A4	1.50fr ind & bl ('30)	16.50	16.50
53	A4	2fr dk brown & grn	6.25	4.25
54	A4	5fr violet & bl	11.00	11.00
a.		Imperf., pair	500.00	
		Nos. 21-54 (34)	117.80	107.55

For surcharges see Nos. 56-71, B2-B4.

No. 7 Overprinted

1915

55	A1	10c red	6.75	6.75
a.		Inverted overprint	225.00	225.00

For surcharge see No. B1.

No. 29 Surcharged

1916

56	A2	10c on 15c org & blk	3.50	3.50

Nos. 22, 41 and 29 Surcharged

1921

57	A2	5c on 2c brn & blk	36.00	36.00
58	A3	10c on 45c org & red	36.00	36.00
59	A2	25c on 15c org & blk	9.00	9.00
		Nos. 57-59 (3)	81.00	81.00

On No. 58 the new value and date are set wide apart and without bar.

Types of 1913-30 Issue Surcharged in Black or Red

1923-27

60	A3	60c on 75c bl & brn	.75	.75
61	A4	65c on 1fr dk bl & ol (R) ('25)	2.25	2.25
62	A4	85c on 1fr dk bl & ol (R) ('25)	2.25	2.25
63	A3	90c on 75c brn red & cer ('27)	3.00	3.00
		Nos. 60-63 (4)	8.25	8.25

No. 26 Surcharged

1924

64	A2	45c on 10c rose & org	3.00	3.00
a.		Inverted surcharge	*2,400.*	*2,400.*

Stamps and Type of 1913-30 Surcharged with New Value and Bars in Black or Red

1924-27

65	A4	25c on 2fr dk brn & grn	1.10	1.10
66	A4	25c on 5fr vio & bl	1.10	1.10
67	A4	1.25fr on 1fr dk bl & ultra (R) ('26)	1.20	1.20
68	A4	1.50fr on 1fr dk bl & lt bl ('27)	4.00	4.00
69	A4	20fr on 5fr org & brt vio ('27)	32.50	26.00
		Nos. 65-69 (5)	39.90	33.40

Surcharged in Black or Red

1926

70	A4	3fr on 5fr gray & blue	3.25	2.50
71	A4	10fr on 5fr grn & blk (R)	7.25	7.25

Papetoai Bay, Moorea A5

1929, Mar. 25

72	A5	3fr green & dk brn	8.00	8.00
73	A5	5fr lt blue & dk brn	15.00	15.00
74	A5	10fr lt red & dk brn	45.00	45.00
75	A5	20fr lilac & dk brn	57.50	57.50
		Nos. 72-75 (4)	125.50	125.50

For overprints see Nos. 128, 130, 132, 134.

Common Design Types pictured following the introduction.

Colonial Exposition Issue
Common Design Types

1931, Apr. 13 Engr. *Perf. 12½*

Name of Country Printed in Black

76	CD70	40c deep green	7.50	7.50
77	CD71	50c violet	7.50	7.50
78	CD72	90c red orange	7.50	7.50
79	CD73	1.50fr dull blue	7.50	7.50
		Nos. 76-79 (4)	30.00	30.00

Spear Fishing A12

Tahitian Girl — A13

Idols A14

1934-40 Photo. *Perf. 13½, 13½x13*

80	A12	1c gray black	.25	.25
81	A12	2c claret	.35	.35
82	A12	3c lt blue ('40)	.35	.35
83	A12	4c orange	.60	.60
84	A12	5c violet	.90	.90
85	A12	10c dark brown	.40	.40
86	A12	15c green	.60	.60
87	A12	20c red	.60	.60
88	A13	25c gray blue	.90	.90
89	A13	30c yellow green	1.20	1.20
90	A13	30c orange brn ('40)	.80	.80
91	A14	35c dp green ('38)	4.00	4.00
92	A13	40c red violet	.60	.60
93	A13	45c brown orange	9.00	9.00
94	A13	45c dk green ('39)	1.60	1.60
95	A13	50c violet	.60	.60
96	A13	55c blue ('38)	6.75	6.75
97	A13	60c black ('39)	.75	.75
98	A13	65c brown	3.25	3.25
99	A13	70c brt pink ('39)	1.40	1.40
100	A13	75c olive green	9.00	9.00
101	A13	80c violet brn ('38)	2.00	2.00
102	A13	90c rose red	.90	.90
103	A14	1fr red brown	.90	.90
104	A14	1.25fr brown violet	8.25	8.25
105	A14	1.25fr rose red ('39)	1.25	1.25
106	A14	1.40fr orange yel ('39)	1.25	1.25
107	A14	1.50fr blue	.90	.90
108	A14	1.60fr dull vio ('39)	1.40	1.40
109	A14	1.75fr olive	6.75	6.75
110	A14	2fr red	1.10	1.10
111	A14	2.25fr deep blue ('39)	1.25	1.25
112	A14	2.50fr black ('39)	1.25	1.25
113	A14	3fr brown org ('39)	1.50	1.50
114	A14	5fr red violet ('39)	1.00	1.00
115	A14	10fr dark green ('39)	3.00	3.00
116	A14	20fr dark brown ('39)	3.50	3.50
		Nos. 80-116 (37)	80.10	80.10

For overprints see Nos. 126-127, 129, 131, 133, 135.

Paris International Exposition Issue
Common Design Types

1937 Engr. *Perf. 13*

117	CD74	20c deep violet	3.50	3.50
118	CD75	30c dark green	3.50	3.50
119	CD76	40c carmine rose	3.50	3.50
120	CD77	50c dk brown & blue	4.25	4.25
121	CD78	90c red	4.25	4.25
122	CD79	1.50fr ultra	5.00	5.00
		Nos. 117-122 (6)	24.00	24.00

Colonial Arts Exhibition Issue
Souvenir Sheet
Common Design Type

1937 *Imperf.*

123	CD78	3fr emerald	36.00	*52.50*
		Never hinged	55.00	

New York World's Fair Issue
Common Design Type

1939, May 10 Engr. *Perf. 12½x12*

124	CD82	1.25fr carmine lake	2.40	2.40
125	CD82	2.25fr ultra	2.40	2.40
		Set, never hinged	8.00	

Fautaua Valley and Marshal Petain A15

1941 Engr. *Perf. 12½x12*

125A A15 1fr bluish green 1.10
c. Denomination ("1F") omitted 80.00
125B A15 2.50fr deep blue 1.25
Set, never hinged 3.25

Nos. 125A-125B were issued by the Vichy government in France, but were not placed on sale in the French Polynesia.
For surcharges, see Nos. B12B-B12C.

Stamps of 1929-39 Ovptd. in Black or Red

1941 *Perf. 14x13½, 13½x13*

126 A14 1fr red brown (BK) 7.00 *9.50*
a. Inverted overprint 1,200.
127 A14 2.50fr black 8.00 *11.00*
a. Inverted overprint 1,200.
128 A5 3fr grn & dk brn 9.00 9.00
129 A14 3fr brn org (Bk) 10.00 *12.00*
130 A5 5fr lt bl & dk brn 9.00 9.00
131 A14 5fr red vio (Bk) 10.00 10.00
132 A5 10fr lt red & dk brn 25.00 *30.00*
133 A14 10fr dark green 90.00 *110.00*
134 A5 20fr lil & dk brn 135.00 135.00
135 A14 20fr dark brown 75.00 *95.00*
Nos. 126-135 (10) 378.00 *430.50*
Set, never hinged 480.00

Types of 1934-39 without "RF"

1942-44 Photo. *Perf. 13½*

135A A12 10c dark brown .65
135B A13 30c orange brown .85
135C A14 1.50fr blue 1.00
135D A14 10fr dark green 1.75
135E A14 20fr dark brown 2.50
Nos. 135A-135E (5) 6.75

Nos. 135A-135E were issued by the Vichy government in France, but were not placed on sale in French Polynesia.

Catalogue values for unused stamps in this section, from this point to the end of the section, are for Never Hinged items.

Ancient Double Canoe A16

1942 Photo. *Perf. 14½x14*

136 A16 5c dark brown .40 .25
137 A16 10c dk gray bl .40 .25
138 A16 25c emerald .40 .25
139 A16 30c red orange .40 .25
140 A16 40c dk slate grn .40 .25
141 A16 80c red brown .40 .25
142 A16 1fr rose violet .50 .35
143 A16 1.50fr brt red .65 .50
144 A16 2fr gray black 1.00 .75
145 A16 2.50fr brt ultra 2.50 1.75
146 A16 4fr dull violet 1.75 1.25
147 A16 5fr bister 1.75 1.25
148 A16 10fr deep brown 2.50 1.90
149 A16 20fr deep green 3.00 2.10
Nos. 136-149 (14) 16.05 11.35

For surcharges see Nos. 152-159.

Eboue Issue
Common Design Type

1945 Engr. *Perf. 13*

150 CD91 2fr black 1.00 .75
151 CD91 25fr Prus green 2.60 2.10

Nos. 150 and 151 exist imperforate.

Nos. 136, 138 and 145 Surcharged with New Values and Bars in Carmine or Black

1946 *Perf. 14½x14*

152 A16 50c on 5c (C) .65 .50
153 A16 60c on 5c (C) .65 .50
154 A16 70c on 5c (C) .65 .50
155 A16 1.20fr on 5c (C) .80 .65
156 A16 2.40fr on 25c (Bk) 1.60 1.25
157 A16 3fr on 25c (Bk) 1.00 .75
158 A16 4.50fr on 25c (Bk) 2.00 1.50
159 A16 15fr on 2.50fr (C) 2.40 1.75
Nos. 152-159 (8) 9.75 7.40

Coast of Mooréa A17

Fisherman and Catch — A18

Tahitian Girl — A20

House at Faa — A19

Island of Borabora A21

Island Women A22

1948 Unwmk. Engr. *Perf. 13*

160 A17 10c brown .50 .35
161 A17 30c blue green .50 .35
162 A17 40c deep blue .50 .35
163 A18 50c red brown .50 .35
164 A18 60c dk brown ol .65 .50
165 A18 80c brt blue .65 .50
166 A19 1fr red brown .65 .35
167 A19 1.20fr slate .65 .50
168 A19 1.50fr deep ultra .65 .50
169 A20 2fr sepia 1.10 .75
170 A20 2.40fr red brown 1.25 1.00
171 A20 3fr purple 11.50 2.50
172 A20 4fr blue black 2.40 1.40
173 A21 5fr sepia 3.75 1.60
174 A21 6fr steel blue 3.75 2.10
175 A21 10fr dk brown ol 4.75 1.75
176 A22 15fr vermilion 7.25 2.75
177 A22 20fr slate 7.25 3.25
178 A22 25fr sepia 9.00 5.00
Nos. 160-178 (19) 57.25 25.85

Imperforates
Most French Polynesia stamps from 1948 onward exist imperforate in issued and trial colors, and also in small presentation sheets in issued colors.

Military Medal Issue
Common Design Type

1952, Dec. 1 Engr. & Typo.

179 CD101 3fr multicolored 13.50 10.00

Girl of Bora Bora — A23

1955, Sept. 26 Engr.

180 A23 9fr dk brn, blk & red 11.00 7.25

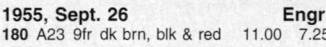

FIDES Issue
Common Design Type

Design: 3fr, Dry dock at Papeete.

1956, Oct. 22 Engr. *Perf. 13x12½*

181 CD103 3fr grnsh blue 4.00 2.00

Girl Playing Guitar — A24

Designs: 4fr, 7fr, 9fr, Man with headdress. 10fr, 20fr, Girl with shells on beach.

1958, Nov. 3 Unwmk. *Perf. 13*

182 A24 10c grn & redsh brn .65 .55
183 A24 25c slate grn, cl & car .80 .60
184 A24 1fr brt bl, brn & red org 1.00 .65
185 A24 2fr brn, vio brn & vio 1.10 .65
186 A24 4fr sl grn & org yel 1.50 1.00
187 A24 7fr red brn, grn & org 3.00 1.60
188 A24 9fr vio brn, grn & org 5.50 2.25
189 A24 10fr dk bl, brn & car 5.00 2.25
190 A24 20fr pur, rose red & brn 9.00 5.00
Nos. 182-190 (9) 27.55 14.55

See Nos. 304-306.

Human Rights Issue
Common Design Type

1958, Dec. 10

191 CD105 7fr dk gray & dk bl 13.00 8.75

Flower Issue
Common Design Type

1959, Jan. 3 Photo. *Perf. 12½x12*

192 CD104 4fr Breadfruit 6.50 4.00

Spear Fishing — A25

Tahitian Dancers A26

1960, May 16 Engr. *Perf. 13*

193 A25 5fr green, brn & lil 1.25 1.00
194 A26 17fr ultra, brt grn & red brn 6.00 2.50

Post Office, Papeete A27

1960, Nov. 19 Unwmk. *Perf. 13*

195 A27 16fr green, bl & claret 5.50 3.25

Saraca Indica — A28

1962, July 12 Photo. *Perf. 13*

196 A28 15fr shown 15.00 14.00
197 A28 25fr Hibiscus 24.00 16.00

Map of Australia and South Pacific — A29

1962, July 18 *Perf. 13x12*

198 A29 20fr multicolored 17.50 7.75

5th South Pacific Conf., Pago Pago, July 1962.

Spined Squirrelfish A30

Fish: 10fr, One-spot butterflyfish. 30fr, Radiate lionfish. 40fr, Horned boxfish.

1962, Dec. 15 Engr. *Perf. 13*

199 A30 5fr black, mag & bis 4.25 1.90
200 A30 10fr multicolored 6.25 2.75
201 A30 30fr multicolored 12.50 7.75
202 A30 40fr multicolored 15.50 11.50
Nos. 199-202 (4) 38.50 23.90

Soccer A30a

Design: 50fr, Throwing the javelin.

1963, Aug. 29 Photo. *Perf. 12½*

203 A30a 20fr brt ultra & brn 9.00 6.25
204 A30a 50fr brt car rose & ultra 16.00 9.25

South Pacific Games, Suva, 8/29-9/7.

Red Cross Centenary Issue
Common Design Type

1963, Sept. 2 Engr. *Perf. 13*

205 CD113 15fr vio brn, gray & car 15.00 12.00

Human Rights Issue
Common Design Type

1963, Dec. 10 Unwmk. *Perf. 13*

206 CD117 7fr green & vio bl 15.00 10.00

Philatec Issue
Common Design Type

1964, Apr. 9 Unwmk. *Perf. 13*

207 CD118 25fr grn, dk sl grn & red 18.00 12.50

Tahitian Dancer A31

1964, May 14 Engr. *Perf. 13*

208 A31 1fr multicolored .40 .40
209 A31 3fr dp claret, blk & org .90 .90

Soldiers, Truck and Battle Flag — A32

1964, July 10 Photo. *Perf. 12½*

210 A32 5fr multicolored 11.00 4.25

Issued to honor the Tahitian Volunteers of the Pacific Battalion. See No. C31.

Tuamotu Scene A33

Views: 4fr, Borabora. 7fr, Papeete Harbor. 8fr, Paul Gauguin's tomb, Marquesas. 20fr, Mangareva, Gambier Islands.

1964, Dec. 1 Litho. *Perf. 12½x13*

211	A33	2fr multicolored	.90	.50
212	A33	4fr multicolored	1.50	.50
213	A33	7fr multicolored	3.00	1.25
214	A33	8fr multicolored	4.00	1.75
215	A33	20fr multicolored	9.50	2.50
		Nos. 211-215,C32 (6)	28.40	10.50

Painting from a School Dining Room — A34

1965, Nov. 29 Engr. *Perf. 13*

216 A34 20fr dk brn, sl grn & dk car 20.00 12.00

Publicizing the School Canteen Program. See No. C38.

Outrigger Canoe on Lagoon A35

Ships: 11fr, Large cruising yacht, vert. 12fr, Motorboat for sport fishing. 14fr, Outrigger canoes with sails. 19fr, Schooner, vert. 22fr, Modern coaster "Oiseau des Iles II."

1966, Aug. 30 Engr. *Perf. 13*

217	A35	10fr brt ultra, emer & mar	2.75	.90
218	A35	11fr mar, dk bl & sl grn	2.75	1.60
219	A35	12fr emer, dk bl & red lil	3.75	1.75
220	A35	14fr brn, bl & slate grn	5.50	2.00
221	A35	19fr scar, sl grn & dp bl	6.50	2.10
222	A35	22fr multicolored	9.50	4.00
		Nos. 217-222 (6)	30.75	12.35

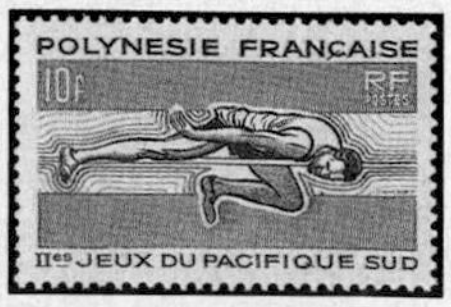

High Jump A36

Designs: 20fr, Pole vault, vert. 40fr, Women's basketball, vert. 60fr, Hurdling.

1966, Dec. 15 Engr. *Perf. 13*

223	A36	10fr dk red, lem & blk	2.25	1.50
224	A36	20fr blue, emer & blk	5.25	2.00
225	A36	40fr emer, brt pink & blk	10.00	5.00
226	A36	60fr dull yel, bl & blk	17.00	8.50
		Nos. 223-226 (4)	34.50	17.00

2nd South Pacific Games, Nouméa, New Caledonia, Dec. 8-18.

Poi Pounder — A37

Javelin Throwing — A38

1967, June 15 Engr. *Perf. 13*

227 A37 50fr orange & blk 17.00 10.00

Society for Oceanic Studies, 50th anniv.

1967, July 11

5fr, Spring dance. 15fr, Horse race. 16fr, Fruit carriers' race. 21fr, Canoe race.

228	A38	5fr multi, horiz.	1.10	.90
229	A38	13fr multi	4.50	1.50
230	A38	15fr multi, horiz.	4.50	1.60
231	A38	16fr multi	4.50	2.75
232	A38	21fr multi, horiz.	9.50	5.00
		Nos. 228-232 (5)	24.10	11.75

Issued to publicize the July Festival.

Earring — A39

Art of the Marquesas Islands: 10fr, Carved mother-of-pearl. 15fr, Decorated canoe paddle. 23fr, Oil vessel. 25fr, Carved stilt stirrups. 30fr, Fan handles. 35fr, Tattooed man. 50fr, Tikis.

1967-68 Engr. *Perf. 13*

233	A39	10fr dp cl, dl red & ultra	2.25	.65
234	A39	15fr black & emerald	3.00	1.25
235	A39	20fr ol gray, dk car & lt bl	5.25	2.00
236	A39	23fr dk brn, ocher & bl	6.50	4.00
237	A39	25fr dk brn, dk bl & lil	6.50	3.75
238	A39	30fr brown & red lilac	8.25	4.00
239	A39	35fr ultra & dk brn	14.00	6.25
240	A39	50fr brn, sl grn & lt bl	15.00	7.25
		Nos. 233-240 (8)	60.75	29.15

Issued: 20fr, 25fr, 30fr, 50fr, 12/19/67; others 2/28/68.

WHO Anniversary Issue
Common Design Type

1968, May 4 Engr. *Perf. 13*

241	CD126	15fr bl grn, mar & dp vio	11.00	4.75
242	CD126	16fr org, lil & bl grn	11.00	8.00

Human Rights Year Issue
Common Design Type

1968, Aug. 10 Engr. *Perf. 13*

243	CD127	15fr blue, red & brn	12.00	6.00
244	CD127	16fr brn, brt pink & ultra	12.00	8.00

Tiare Apetahi A40

Flower: 17fr, Tiare Tahiti.

1969, Mar. 27 Photo. *Perf. 12½x13*

245	A40	9fr multicolored	2.10	1.10
246	A40	17fr multicolored	4.25	2.10

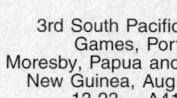

3rd South Pacific Games, Port Moresby, Papua and New Guinea, Aug. 13-23 — A41

1969, Aug. 13 Engr. *Perf. 13*

247	A41	9fr Boxer, horiz	3.25	1.25
248	A41	17fr High jump	7.25	2.00
249	A41	18fr Runner	9.00	3.50
250	A41	22fr Long jump	12.00	7.25
		Nos. 247-250 (4)	31.50	14.00

ILO Issue
Common Design Type

1969, Nov. 24 Engr. *Perf. 13*

251	CD131	17fr org, emer & ol	12.00	5.75
252	CD131	18fr org, dk brn & vio bl	12.00	6.75

Territorial Assembly A42

Buildings: 14fr, Governor's Residence. 17fr, House of Tourism. 18fr, Maeva Hotel. 24fr, Taharaa Hotel.

1969, Dec. 22 Photo. *Perf. 12½x12*

253	A42	13fr black & multi	2.75	1.25
254	A42	14fr black & multi	4.25	1.50
255	A42	17fr black & multi	7.00	3.50
256	A42	18fr black & multi	7.75	4.00
257	A42	24fr black & multi	13.50	7.00
		Nos. 253-257 (5)	35.25	17.25

Stone Figure with Globe — A43

Designs: 40fr, Globe, plane, map of Polynesia and men holding "PATA" sign, horiz. 60fr, Polynesian carrying globe.

1970, Apr. 7 Engr. *Perf. 13*

258	A43	20fr deep plum, gray & bl	6.75	3.25
259	A43	40fr emer, rose lil & ultra	11.00	5.25
260	A43	60fr red brn, bl & dk brn	19.00	10.00
		Nos. 258-260 (3)	36.75	18.50

Issued to publicize the 1970 Pacific Area Travel Association Congress (PATA).

UPU Headquarters Issue
Common Design Type

1970, May 20 Engr. *Perf. 13*

261	CD133	18fr maroon, pur & brn	10.00	4.75
262	CD133	20fr lilac rose, ol & ind	10.00	5.25

Night Fishing — A44

1971, May 11 Photo. *Perf. 13*

263	A44	10fr multicolored	12.50	5.25
		Nos. 263,C71-C73 (4)	37.50	19.75

Flowers — A45

Designs: Various flowers. 12fr is horiz.

Perf. 12½x13, 13x12½

1971, Aug. 27

264	A45	8fr multicolored	2.25	1.00
265	A45	12fr multicolored	3.50	1.75
266	A45	22fr multicolored	5.75	3.00
		Nos. 264-266 (3)	11.50	5.75

Day of a Thousand Flowers.

Water-skiing Slalom — A46

Designs: 20fr, Water-skiing, jump, vert. 40fr, Figure water-skiing.

1971, Oct. 11 Engr. *Perf. 13*

267	A46	10fr grnsh bl, dk red & brn	6.25	2.00
268	A46	20fr car, emer & brn	9.00	4.00
269	A46	40fr brn, grn & lil	20.00	12.00
		Nos. 267-269 (3)	35.25	18.00

World water-skiing championships, Oct. 1971.

De Gaulle Issue
Common Design Type

30fr, As general, 1940. 50fr, As president, 1970.

1971, Nov. 9 Engr. *Perf. 13*

270	CD134	30fr red lilac & blk	22.50	11.00
271	CD134	50fr red lilac & blk	29.00	18.50

Map of Tahiti and Jerusalem Cross A47

1971, Dec. 18 Photo. *Perf. 13x12½*

272 A47 28fr lt blue & multi 14.00 8.50

2nd rally of French Boy Scouts and Guides, Taravao, French Polynesia.

"Alcoholism" A48

Mother and Child A49

1972, Mar. 24 Photo. *Perf. 13*

273 A48 20fr brown & multi 11.50 5.75

Fight against alcoholism.

1973, Sept. 26 Photo. *Perf. 12½x13*

274 A49 28fr pale yellow & multi 9.50 5.00

Day nursery.

Polynesian Golfer — A50

Design: 24fr, Atimaono Golf Course.

1974, Feb. 27 Photo. *Perf. 13*

275	A50 16fr multicolored	8.50	3.25
276	A50 24fr multicolored	10.50	5.25

Atimaono Golf Course.

Hand Throwing Life Preserver to Puppy — A51

1974, May 9 Photo. *Perf. 13*

277	A51 21fr brt blue & multi	12.00	5.00

Society for the Protection of Animals.

Around a Fire, on the Beach A52

Polynesian Views: 2fr, Lagoons and mountains. 6fr, Pebble divers. 10fr, Lonely Mountain and flowers, vert. 15fr, Sailing ship at sunset. 20fr, Lagoon and mountain.

1974, May 22

278	A52 2fr multicolored	.90	.60
279	A52 5fr multicolored	1.10	.90
280	A52 6fr multicolored	1.90	1.10
281	A52 10fr multicolored	2.10	1.25
282	A52 15fr multicolored	4.25	1.75
283	A52 20fr multicolored	7.00	2.10
	Nos. 278-283 (6)	17.25	7.70

Polynesian Woman and UPU Emblem — A53

1974, Oct. 9 Engr. *Perf. 13*

284	A53 65fr multicolored	12.00	7.75

Centenary of Universal Postal Union.

Lion, Sun and Emblem — A54

1975, June 17 Photo.

285	A54 26fr multicolored	12.00	5.00

15th anniv. of Lions Intl. in Tahiti.

Fish and Leaf A55

1975, July 9 Litho. *Perf. 12*

286	A55 19fr dp ultra & green	10.00	4.25

Polynesian Association for the Protection of Nature.

Georges Pompidou, Pres. of France — A55a

1976, Feb. 16 Engr. *Perf. 13*

287	A55a 49fr dk violet & black	11.00	7.00

See France No. 1430.

Alain Gerbault and Sailboat A56

1976, May 25 Photo. *Perf. 13*

288	A56 90fr multicolored	13.50	9.00

Alain Gerbault's arrival in Bora Bora, 50th anniv.

Turtle — A57

Design: 42fr, Hand protecting bird.

1976, June 24 Litho. *Perf. 12½*

289	A57 18fr multicolored	14.00	4.25
290	A57 42fr multicolored	20.00	11.00

World Ecology Day.

A. G. Bell, Telephone, Radar and Satellite — A58

1976, Sept. 15 Engr. *Perf. 13*

291	A58 37fr multicolored	10.00	5.00

Centenary of first telephone call by Alexander Graham Bell, Mar. 10, 1876.

Dugout Canoes — A59

1976, Dec. 16 Litho. *Perf. 13x12½*

292	A59 25fr Marquesas	3.75	2.75
293	A59 30fr Raiatea	4.75	4.75
294	A59 75fr Tahiti	9.50	5.75
295	A59 100fr Tuamotu	12.00	7.00
	Nos. 292-295 (4)	30.00	20.25

Sailing Ship — A60

Designs: Various sailing vessels.

1977, Dec. 22 Litho. *Perf. 13*

296	A60 20fr multicolored	6.25	2.00
297	A60 50fr multicolored	7.25	2.25
298	A60 85fr multicolored	9.00	3.75
299	A60 120fr multicolored	15.00	5.75
	Nos. 296-299 (4)	37.50	13.75

Hibiscus — A61

Girl with Shells on Beach — A62

Designs: 10fr, Vanda orchids. 16fr, Pua (fagraea berteriana). 22fr, Gardenia.

1978-79 Photo. *Perf. 12½x13*

300	A61 10fr multicolored	1.10	.50
301	A61 13fr multicolored	2.50	1.00
302	A61 16fr multicolored	2.75	1.75
303	A61 22fr multicolored	1.75	1.00
	Nos. 300-303 (4)	8.10	4.25

Issued: 13fr, 16fr, 8/23; 10fr, 22fr, 1/25/79.

1978, Nov. 3 Engr. *Perf. 13*

Design A24 with "1958 1978" added: 28fr, Man with headdress. 36fr, Girl playing guitar.

304	A62 20fr multicolored	3.00	.75
305	A62 28fr multicolored	3.75	1.50
306	A62 36fr multicolored	5.75	2.25
a.	Souvenir sheet of 3	27.50	27.50
	Nos. 304-306 (3)	12.50	4.50

20th anniv. of stamps inscribed: Polynesie Francaise. No. 306a contains Nos. 304-306 in changed colors.

Ships — A63

1978, Dec. 29 Litho. *Perf. 13x12½*

307	A63 15fr Tahiti	1.50	.80
308	A63 30fr Monowai	2.75	1.25
309	A63 75fr Tahitien	4.50	3.25
310	A63 100fr Mariposa	8.50	3.25
	Nos. 307-310 (4)	17.25	8.55

Porites Coral A64

Design: 37fr, Montipora coral.

1979, Feb. 15 *Perf. 13x12½*

311	A64 32fr multicolored	2.50	1.25
312	A64 37fr multicolored	3.75	2.00

Raiatea A65

Landscapes: 1fr, Moon over Bora Bora. 2fr, Mountain peaks, Ua Pou. 3fr, Sunset over Motu Tapu. 5fr, Motu. 6fr, Palm and hut, Tuamotu.

1979, Mar. 8 Photo. *Perf. 13x13½*

313	A65 1fr multicolored	.25	.25
314	A65 2fr multicolored	.25	.25
315	A65 3fr multicolored	.30	.25
316	A65 4fr multicolored	.45	.25
317	A65 5fr multicolored	.80	.35
318	A65 6fr multicolored	1.00	.60
	Nos. 313-318 (6)	3.05	1.95

See Nos. 438-443 for redrawn designs.

Dance Costumes A66

1979, July 14 Litho. *Perf. 12½*

319	A66 45fr Fetia	1.75	1.00
320	A66 51fr Teanuanua	2.75	1.25
321	A66 74fr Temaeva	3.75	2.25
	Nos. 319-321 (3)	8.25	4.50

Hill, Great Britain No. 53, Tahiti No. 28 A67

1979, Aug. 1 Engr. *Perf. 13*

322	A67 100fr multicolored	5.00	3.00

Sir Rowland Hill (1795-1879), originator of penny postage.

Hastula Strigilata — A68

Shells: 28fr, Scabricola variegata. 35fr, Fusinus undatus.

1979, Aug. 22 Litho. *Perf. 12½*

323 A68 20fr multicolored 1.50 .50
324 A68 28fr multicolored 2.00 1.00
325 A68 35fr multicolored 2.75 2.00
Nos. 323-325 (3) 6.25 3.50

Statue Holding Rotary Emblem — A69

1979, Nov. 30 Litho. *Perf. 13*

326 A69 47fr multicolored 2.75 2.00

Rotary International, 75th anniversary; Papeete Rotary Club, 20th anniversary.

For overprint see No. 330.

Myripristis Murdjan A70

Fish: 8fr, Napoleon. 12fr, Emperor.

1980, Jan. 21 Litho. *Perf. 12½*

327 A70 7fr multicolored 1.00 .50
328 A70 8fr multicolored 1.00 .65
329 A70 12fr multicolored 1.65 .95
Nos. 327-329 (3) 3.65 2.10

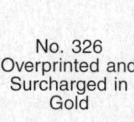

No. 326 Overprinted and Surcharged in Gold

1980, Feb. 23 Litho. *Perf. 13*

330 A69 77fr on 47fr multi 5.75 3.25

Rotary International, 75th anniversary.

CNEXO Fish Hatchery A71

1980, Mar. 17 Photo. *Perf. 13x13½*

331 A71 15fr shown 1.75 .90
332 A71 22fr Crayfish 1.75 .90

Papeete Post Office Building Opening A72

1980, Apr. 30 Photo. *Perf. 13x12½*

333 A72 50fr multicolored 2.50 1.50

Tiki and Festival Emblem — A73

1980, June 30 Photo. *Perf. 13½*

334 A73 34fr shown 1.25 .90
335 A73 39fr Drum (pahu) 2.00 1.30
336 A73 49fr Ax (to'i) 2.75 1.75
a. Souv. sheet of 3, #334-336 13.50 13.00
Nos. 334-336 (3) 6.00 3.95

South Pacific Arts Festival, Port Moresby, Papua New Guinea.

Titmouse Henparrot — A74

Perf. 13x12½, 12½x13

1980, Oct. 20 Photo.

337 A74 25fr White sea-swallow, horiz. 1.50 .70
338 A74 35fr shown 1.75 .90
339 A74 45fr Minor frigate bird, horiz. 2.75 1.10
Nos. 337-339 (3) 6.00 2.70

Charles de Gaulle — A75

1980, Nov. 9 Engr. *Perf. 12½x13*

340 A75 100fr multicolored 5.00 3.25

Naso Vlamingi (Karaua) A76

1981, Feb. 5 Litho. *Perf. 12½*

341 A76 13fr shown 1.00 .50
342 A76 16fr Lutjanus vaigensis (toau) 1.10 .60
343 A76 24fr Plectropomus leopardus (tonu) 2.25 .75
Nos. 341-343 (3) 4.35 1.85

Indoor Fish Breeding Tanks, Cnexo Hatchery A77

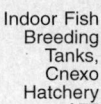

1981, May 14 Photo. *Perf. 13x13½*

344 A77 23fr shown 1.10 .80
345 A77 41fr Mussels 2.00 1.10

Folk Dancers A78

Perf. 13x13½, 13½x13

1981, July 10 Litho.

346 A78 26fr shown 1.25 .65
347 A78 28fr Dancer 1.25 1.10
348 A78 44fr Dancers, vert. 2.10 1.50
Nos. 346-348 (3) 4.60 3.25

Sterna Bergii — A79

1981, Sept. 24 Litho. *Perf. 13*

349 A79 47fr shown 1.75 1.00
350 A79 53fr Ptilinopus purpuratus, vert. 1.75 1.20
351 A79 65fr Estrilda astrild, vert. 2.25 1.50
Nos. 349-351 (3) 5.75 3.70

See Nos. 370-372.

Huahine Island A80

1981, Oct. 22 Litho. *Perf. 12½*

352 A80 34fr shown 1.40 .75
353 A80 134fr Maupiti 3.25 2.00
354 A80 136fr Bora-Bora 3.25 2.00
Nos. 352-354 (3) 7.90 4.75

A81

1982, Feb. 4 Photo. *Perf. 13x13½*

355 A81 30fr Parrotfish 1.00 .75
356 A81 31fr Regal angel 1.40 .75
357 A81 45fr Spotted bass 1.50 1.25
Nos. 355-357 (3) 3.90 2.75

Pearl Industry A82

1982, Apr. 22 Photo. *Perf. 13x13½*

358 A82 7fr Pearl beds .85 .45
359 A82 8fr Extracting pearls .85 .45
360 A82 10fr Pearls 1.20 1.10
Nos. 358-360 (3) 2.90 2.00

Tahiti "No. 1A," Emblem — A83

1982, May 12 Engr. *Perf. 13*

361 A83 150fr multicolored 4.75 3.50
a. Souvenir sheet 16.00 16.00

PHILEXFRANCE Stamp Exhibition, Paris, June 11-21. No. 361a contains No. 361 in changed colors.

King Holding Carved Scepter — A84

Designs: Coronation ceremony.

1982, July 12 Photo. *Perf. 13½x13*

362 A84 12fr shown .50 .25
363 A84 13fr King, priest .50 .25
364 A84 17fr Procession 1.00 .50
Nos. 362-364 (3) 2.00 1.00

Championship Emblem — A85

1982, Aug. 13 *Perf. 13*

365 A85 90fr multicolored 2.75 2.00

4th Hobie-Cat 16 World Catamaran Sailing Championship, Tahiti, Aug. 15-21.

First Colloquium on New Energy Sources — A86

1982, Sept. 29 Litho.

366 A86 46fr multicolored 1.75 1.00

Motu, Tuamotu Islet — A87

1982, Oct. 12 Litho. *Perf. 13*

367 A87 20fr shown .70 .35
368 A87 33fr Tupai Atoll .90 .45
369 A87 35fr Gambier Islds. 1.25 .55
Nos. 367-369 (3) 2.85 1.35

Bird Type of 1981

1982, Nov. 17 Litho. *Perf. 13*

370 A79 37fr Sacred egret 1.40 .55
371 A79 39fr Pluvialis dominica, vert. 1.40 .65

372 A79 42fr Lonchura castaneothorax 1.75 .90
Nos. 370-372 (3) 4.55 2.10

Fish — A88

1983, Feb. 9 Litho. *Perf. 13x13½*
373 A88 8fr Acanthurus lineatus .70 .35
374 A88 10fr Caranx melampygus .90 .35
375 A88 12fr Carcharhinus melanopterus 1.40 .50
Nos. 373-375 (3) 3.00 1.20

The Way of the Cross, Sculpture by Damien Haturau — A89

1983, Mar. 9 Litho. *Perf. 13*
376 A89 7fr shown .25 .25
377 A89 21fr Virgin and Child .70 .60
378 A89 23fr Christ .90 .60
Nos. 376-378 (3) 1.85 1.45

Traditional Hats — A90

1983, May 24 Litho. *Perf. 13x12½*
379 A90 11fr Acacia .45 .30
380 A90 13fr Niau .60 .30
381 A90 25fr Ofe .80 .50
382 A90 35fr Ofe, diff. 1.10 .60
Nos. 379-382 (4) 2.95 1.70

See Nos. 393-396.

Chieftain in Traditional Costume, Sainte-Christine Isld. — A91

Traditional Costumes, Marquesas Islds.

1983, July 12 Photo. *Perf. 13*
383 A91 15fr shown .70 .30
384 A91 17fr Man .90 .40
385 A91 28fr Woman 1.10 .50
Nos. 383-385 (3) 2.70 1.20

See Nos. 397-399, 419-421.

Polynesian Crowns — A92

Various flower garlands.

1983, Oct. 19 Litho. *Perf. 13*
386 A92 41fr multicolored 1.25 .90
387 A92 44fr multicolored 1.40 .95
388 A92 45fr multicolored 1.50 1.00
Nos. 386-388 (3) 4.15 2.85

See Nos. 400-402.

Martin Luther (1483-1546) A93

1983, Nov. 10 Engr. *Perf. 13*
389 A93 90fr black, brn & lil gray 2.25 1.10

Tiki Carvings — A94

Various carvings.

1984, Feb. 8 Litho. *Perf. 12½x13*
390 A94 14fr multicolored .50 .25
391 A94 16fr multicolored .60 .45
392 A94 19fr multicolored .75 .45
Nos. 390-392 (3) 1.85 1.15

Hat Type of 1983

1984, June 20 Litho. *Perf. 13x12½*
393 A90 20fr Aeho ope .50 .35
394 A90 24fr Paeore .60 .35
395 A90 26fr Ofe fei .75 .50
396 A90 33fr Hua .80 .50
Nos. 393-396 (4) 2.65 1.70

Costume Type of 1983

1984, July 11 Litho. *Perf. 13*
397 A91 34fr Tahitian playing nose flute .75 .50
398 A91 35fr Priest, Oei-eitia .90 .50
399 A91 39fr Tahitian adult and child .90 .50
Nos. 397-399 (3) 2.55 1.50

Garland Type of 1983

1984, Oct. 24 Litho. *Perf. 13x12½*
400 A92 46fr Moto'i Lei .90 .50
401 A92 47fr Pitate Lei 1.00 .60
402 A92 53fr Bougainvillea Lei 1.25 .80
Nos. 400-402 (3) 3.15 1.90

4th Pacific Arts Festival, Noumea, New Caledonia, Dec. 8-22 — A95

1984, Nov. 20 Litho. *Perf. 13*
403 A95 150fr Statue, headdress 3.50 2.25

See No. C213.

Paysage D'Anaa, by Jean Masson — A96

Paintings: 50fr, Sortie Du Culte, by Jacques Boulaire. 75fr, La Fete, by Robert Tatin. 85fr, Tahitiennes Sur La Plage, by Pierre Heyman.

Perf. 12½x13, 13x12½
1984, Dec. 12 Litho.
404 A96 50fr multi, vert. 1.25 .70
405 A96 65fr multicolored 1.40 .90
406 A96 75fr multicolored 1.90 1.00
407 A96 85fr multicolored 2.25 1.75
Nos. 404-407 (4) 6.80 4.35

Tiki Carvings — A97

1985, Jan. 23 Litho. *Perf. 13½*
408 A97 30fr multicolored .60 .35
409 A97 36fr multicolored .80 .45
410 A97 40fr multicolored .90 .75
Nos. 408-410 (3) 2.30 1.55

Polynesian Faces — A98

1985, Feb. 20 Photo. *Perf. 12½x13*
411 A98 22fr multicolored .40 .30
412 A98 39fr multicolored .75 .40
413 A98 44fr multicolored .95 .70
Nos. 411-413 (3) 2.10 1.40

Early Tahiti — A99

Perf. 13x12½, 12½x13
1985, Apr. 24 Litho.
414 A99 42fr Entrance to Papeete .90 .55
415 A99 45fr Girls, vert. 1.25 .75
416 A99 48fr Papeete market 1.40 .85
Nos. 414-416 (3) 3.55 2.15

5th Intl. Congress on Coral Reefs, Tahiti A100

1985, May 28 Litho. *Perf. 13½*
417 A100 140fr Local reef formation 3.00 2.00

Printed se-tenant with label picturing congress emblem.

National Flag A101

1985, June 28
418 A101 9fr Flag, natl. arms .65 .30

Costume Type of 1983

18th-19th Cent. Prints, Beslu Collection.

1985, July 17 *Perf. 13*
419 A91 38fr Tahitian dancer .95 .65
420 A91 55fr Man and woman from Otahiti, 1806 1.25 .90
421 A91 70fr Traditional chief 1.75 1.25
Nos. 419-421 (3) 3.95 2.80

Local Foods — A103

1985-86 Litho. *Perf. 13*
422 A103 25fr Roasted pig .85 .60
423 A103 35fr Pit fire 1.10 .65
423A A103 80fr Fish in coconut milk 1.90 1.50
423B A103 110fr Fafaru 2.40 1.90
Nos. 422-423B (4) 6.25 4.65

Issued: 25fr, 35fr, 11/14; 80fr, 110fr, 5/20/86.
See Nos. 458-459, 474-475.

Catholic Churches — A104

1985, Dec. 11 Litho. *Perf. 13*
424 A104 90fr St. Anne's, Otepipi 1.75 1.00
425 A104 100fr St. Michael's Cathedral, Rikitea 1.90 1.00
426 A104 120fr Cathedral, exterior 2.25 1.50
Nos. 424-426 (3) 5.90 3.50

Nos. 424-426 printed se-tenant with labels picturing local religious art.

Crabs A105

1986, Jan. 22 *Perf. 13½*
427 A105 18fr Fiddler .90 .50
428 A105 29fr Hermit 1.40 .65
429 A105 31fr Coconut 2.40 .65
Nos. 427-429 (3) 4.70 1.80

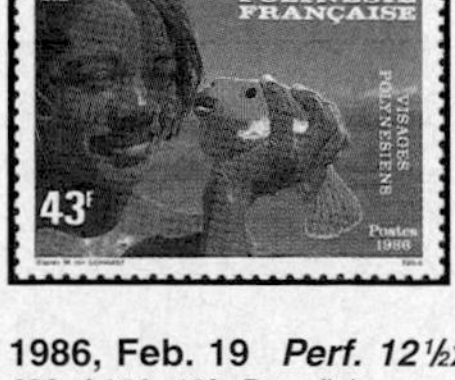

Faces of Polynesia A106

1986, Feb. 19 *Perf. 12½x13, 13x12½*
430 A106 43fr Boy, fish 1.00 .50
431 A106 49fr Boy, coral 1.25 .50
432 A106 51fr Boy, turtle, vert. 1.40 .60
Nos. 430-432 (3) 3.65 1.60

Old Tahiti — A107

1986, Mar. 18 *Perf. 13x12½*
433 A107 52fr Papeete 1.00 .55
434 A107 56fr Harpoon fishing 1.10 .55
435 A107 57fr Royal Palace, Papeete 1.25 .70
Nos. 433-435 (3) 3.35 1.80

Tiki Rock Carvings — A108

1986, Apr. 16
436 A108 58fr Atuona, Hiva Oa 1.40 .70
437 A108 59fr Ua Huka Hill, Hane Valley 1.40 .70

Landscapes Type Redrawn

1986-88 **Litho.** *Perf. 13½*
438 A65 1fr multi, type 2 ('88) 2.50 .35
a. Type 1 ('86) 4.50 1.25
b. Type 3 ('91) 18.50 4.50
439 A65 2fr multicolored .40 .25
440 A65 3fr multicolored .45 .25
441 A65 4fr multicolored ('87) 1.75 .40
442 A65 5fr multicolored .75 .30
443 A65 6fr multicolored .65 .30
Nos. 438-443 (6) 6.50 1.85

Nos. 438-443 printed in sharper detail, and box containing island name is taller. Nos. 439-443 margin is inscribed "CARTOR" instead of "DELRIEU."

No. 438 has three types of inscription below design: type 1, photographer's name at left, no inscription at right; type 2, photographer's name at left 9.5mm long, printer's name (Cartor) at right; type 3, photographer's name at left 12.5mm long, Cartor at right.

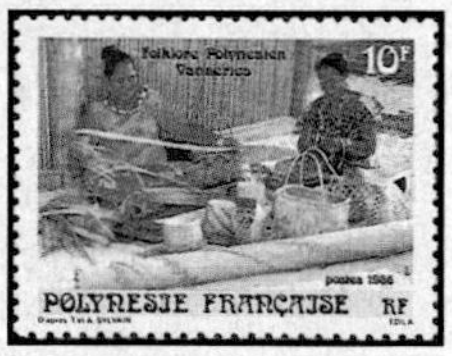

Traditional Crafts A109

Perf. 13x12½, 12½x13

1986, July 17 **Litho.**
444 A109 8fr Quilting, vert. .25 .25
445 A109 10fr Baskets, hats .25 .25
446 A109 12fr Grass skirts .80 .30
Nos. 444-446 (3) 1.30 .80

Building a Pirogue (Canoe) A110

1986, Oct. 21 **Litho.** *Perf. 13½*
447 A110 46fr Boat-builders 1.00 .65
448 A110 50fr Close-up 1.10 .85

Medicinal Plants — A111

1986, Nov. 19 *Perf. 13*
449 A111 40fr Phymatosorus .90 .50
450 A111 41fr Barringtonia asiatica 1.00 .50
451 A111 60fr Ocimum bacilicum 1.60 .90
Nos. 449-451 (3) 3.50 1.90

See Nos. 495-497.

Polynesians A112

1987, Jan. 21 **Litho.** *Perf. 13½*
452 A112 28fr Old man .60 .35
453 A112 30fr Mother and child .75 .50
454 A112 37fr Old woman 1.00 .60
Nos. 452-454 (3) 2.35 1.45

Crustaceans — A113

1987, Feb. 18 *Perf. 12½x13*
455 A113 34fr Carpilius maculatus 2.00 .65
456 A113 35fr Parribacus antarticus 2.00 .65
457 A113 39fr Justitia longimana 2.50 .65
Nos. 455-457 (3) 6.50 1.95

Local Foods Type of 1985

1987, Mar. 19 **Litho.** *Perf. 13*
458 A103 33fr Papaya poe 1.10 .70
459 A103 65fr Chicken fafa 2.00 1.00

Polynesian Petroglyphs A114

1987, May 13 *Perf. 12½*
460 A114 13fr Tipaerui, Tahiti .35 .25
461 A114 21fr Turtle, Raiatea Is. .60 .35

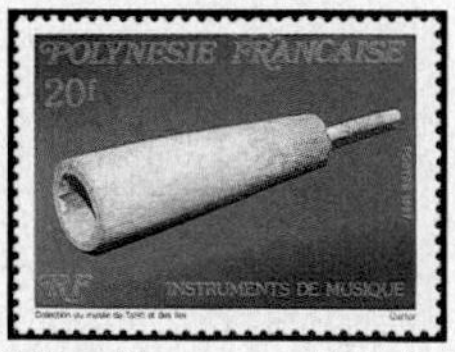

Calling Devices and Musical Instruments, Museum of Tahiti and the Isles — A115

1987, July 1 *Perf. 13½*
462 A115 20fr Wood horn .65 .30
463 A115 26fr Triton's conch .80 .65
464 A115 33fr Nose flutes 1.00 .70
Nos. 462-464 (3) 2.45 1.65

Medicinal Plants — A116

1987, Sept. 16 *Perf. 12½x13*
465 A116 46fr Thespesia populnea 1.00 .55
466 A116 53fr Ophioglossum reticulatum 1.40 .55
467 A116 54fr Dicrocephala latifolia 1.50 .55
Nos. 465-467 (3) 3.90 1.65

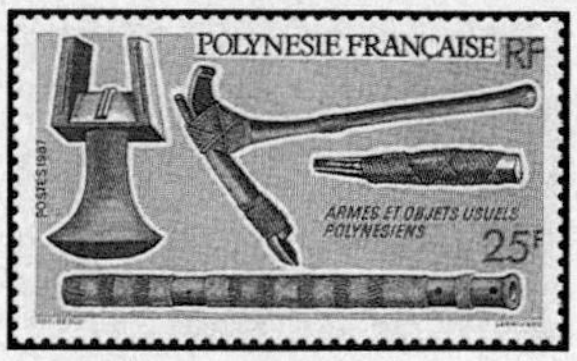

Ancient Weapons and Tools — A117

Designs: 25fr, Adze, war club, chisel, flute. 27fr, War clubs, tatooing comb, mallet. 32fr, Headdress, necklaces, nose flute.

1987, Oct. 14 **Engr.** *Perf. 13*
468 A117 25fr lt olive grn & blk .60 .40
469 A117 27fr Prus grn & int blue .75 .45
470 A117 32fr brt olive bis & brn blk .80 .55
Nos. 468-470 (3) 2.15 1.40

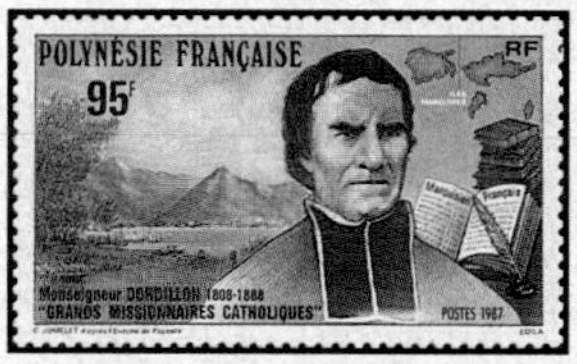

Catholic Missionaries — A118

Monsignors: 95fr, Rene Ildefonse Dordillon (1808-1888), bishop of the Marquesas Isls. 105fr, Tepano Jaussen (1815-1891), first bishop of Polynesia. 115fr, Paul Laurent Maze (1885-1976), archbishop of Papeete.

1987, Dec. 9 **Litho.**
471 A118 95fr multicolored 1.90 1.40
472 A118 105fr multicolored 2.10 1.50
473 A118 115fr multicolored 2.40 1.60
Nos. 471-473 (3) 6.40 4.50

Local Foods Type of 1985

1988, Jan. 12 **Litho.** *Perf. 13*
474 A103 40fr Crayfish (varo) 1.90 .55
475 A103 75fr Bananas in coconut milk 2.75 1.10

Nos. 474-475 are vert.

Authors — A119

62fr, James Norman Hall (1887-1951). 85fr, Charles Bernard Nordhoff (1887-1947).

1988, Feb. 10
476 A119 62fr multicolored 1.40 .75
477 A119 85fr multicolored 1.90 .85

Traditional Housing — A120

11fr, Taranpoo Opoa Is., Raiatea. 15fr, Tahaa Village. 17fr, Community meeting house, Tahiti.

1988, Mar. 16 **Litho.** *Perf. 13x12½*
478 A120 11fr multicolored .50 .30
479 A120 15fr multicolored .60 .30
480 A120 17fr multicolored .60 .30
Nos. 478-480 (3) 1.70 .90

Point Venus Lighthouse, 120th Anniv. — A121

1988, Apr. 21 **Litho.** *Perf. 13*
481 A121 400fr multicolored 8.50 5.50

Tapa-cloth Paintings by Paul Engdahl A122

1988, May 20
482 A122 52fr multicolored 1.25 .75
483 A122 54fr multicolored 1.40 .85
484 A122 64fr multicolored 1.50 1.10
Nos. 482-484 (3) 4.15 2.70

POLYSAT (Domestic Communications Network) — A123

1988, June 15 **Litho.** *Perf. 12½x12*
485 A123 300fr multicolored 6.00 4.75

Tahitian Dolls — A124

Designs: 42fr, Wearing grass skirt and headdress. 45fr, Wearing print dress and straw hat, holding guitar. 48fr, Wearing print dress and straw hat, holding straw bag.

1988, June 27 *Perf. 13x12½*
486 A124 42fr multicolored 1.00 .60
487 A124 45fr multicolored 1.25 .60
488 A124 48fr multicolored 1.50 .75
Nos. 486-488 (3) 3.75 1.95

Visiting a Marae at Nuku Hiva, Engraving by J. & E. Verreaux A125

1988, Aug. 1 **Engr.** ***Perf. 13***
489 A125 68fr black brown 2.00 1.25

Size: 143x101mm

490 A125 145fr violet brn & grn 5.25 4.00

SYDPEX '88, July 30-Aug. 7, Australia. No. 490 pictures a Russian navy officer (probably Krusenstern) visiting the Marquesas Islanders; denomination LR.

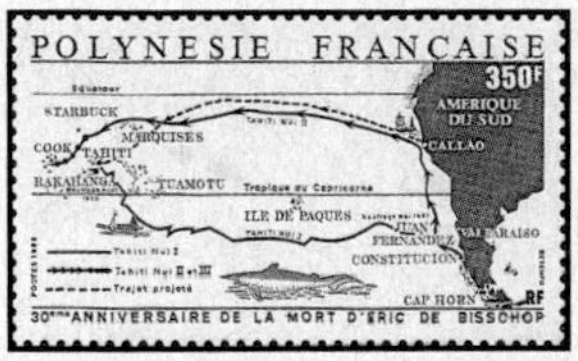

Map Linking South America and South Pacific Islands — A126

1988, Aug. 30 **Engr.**
491 A126 350fr multicolored 7.50 4.50

Eric de Bisschop (1890-1958), explorer who tried to prove that there was an exchange of peoples between the South Pacific islands and So. America, rather than that the island populations originated from So. America.

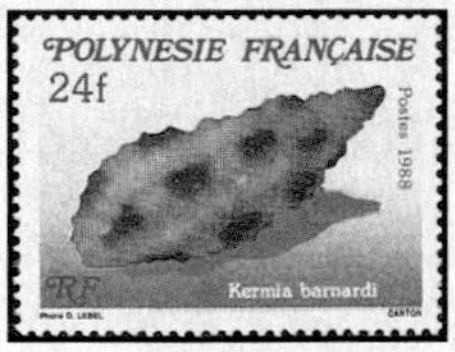

Seashells A127

1988, Sept. 21 **Litho.** ***Perf. 13½***
492 A127 24fr Kermia barnardi .60 .35
493 A127 35fr Vexillum suavis 1.00 .50
494 A127 44fr Berthelinia 1.40 .75
Nos. 492-494 (3) 3.00 1.60

Medicinal Plants Type of 1986

1988, Oct. 18 **Engr.** ***Perf. 13***
495 A111 23fr Davallia solida .75 .30
496 A111 36fr Rorippa sarmentosa 1.10 .45
497 A111 49fr Lindernia crustacea 1.25 .70
Nos. 495-497 (3) 3.10 1.45

Protestant Missionaries — A128

1988, Dec. 7 **Litho.**
498 A128 80fr Henry Nott (1774-1844) 1.50 .90
499 A128 90fr Papeiha (1800-40) 2.00 1.25
500 A128 100fr Samuel Raapoto (1921-76) 2.25 1.40
Nos. 498-500 (3) 5.75 3.55

Tahiti Post Office A129

1989, Jan. 12 **Engr.**
501 A129 30fr P.O., 1875 .75 .40
502 A129 40fr P.O., 1915 1.00 .55

Center for Arts and Crafts A130

1989, Feb. 15 **Litho.** ***Perf. 12½***
503 A130 29fr Marquesas Is. lidded bowl .80 .40
504 A130 31fr Mother-of-pearl pendant .90 .45

Copra Industry

Extracting Coconut Meat From Shell — A131a

Drying Coconut Meat in Sun — A131

1989, Mar. 16 **Litho.** ***Perf. 13***
505 A131a 55fr multicolored *55.00 40.00*
506 A131 70fr multicolored *2.50 2.00*

Tapa Art — A132

43fr, Wood statue (pole), Marquesas Islands, vert. 51fr, Hand-painted bark tapestry, Society Is. 56fr, Concentric circles, Tubuai, Austral Islands.

1989, Apr. 18 **Litho.** ***Perf. 13½***
507 A132 43fr multicolored .90 .60
508 A132 51fr shown 1.25 .75
509 A132 56fr multicolored 1.50 .90
Nos. 507-509 (3) 3.65 2.25

Polynesian Environment A133

1989, May 17 **Litho.** ***Perf. 13x12½***
510 A133 120fr shown 2.25 1.50
511 A133 140fr Diving for sea-shells 2.75 1.75

Polynesian Folklore A134

Perf. 13x12½, 12½x13

1989, June 28 **Litho.**
512 A134 47fr Stone-lifting contest, vert. 1.10 .55
513 A134 61fr Dancer, vert. 1.40 .70
514 A134 67fr Folk singers 1.75 .75
Nos. 512-514 (3) 4.25 2.00

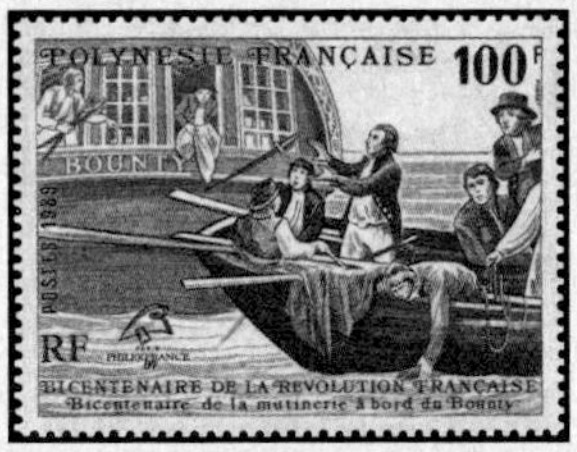

Bounty Castaways, from an Etching by Robert Dodd — A135

1989, July 7 **Engr.** ***Perf. 13***
515 A135 100fr dp blue & bl grn 2.40 1.50

Souvenir Sheet

Imperf

516 A135 200fr dk ol grn & dk brn 12.00 12.00

PHILEXFRANCE '89 and 200th annivs. of the mutiny on the *Bounty* and the French revolution.

No. 515 printed se-tenant with label picturing exhibition emblem.

Reverend-Father Patrick O'Reilly (1900-1988) A136

1989, Aug. 7 **Engr.** ***Perf. 13x13½***
517 A136 52fr yel brn & myrtle grn 1.40 .75

Miniature Sheet

Messages A137

a, Get well soon. b, Good luck. c, Happy birthday. d, Keep in touch. e, Congratulations.

1989, Sept. 27 **Litho.** ***Perf. 12½***
518 A137 42fr Sheet of 5, #a.-e. 12.00 12.00

Sea Shells A138

1989, Oct. 12 **Litho.** ***Perf. 13½***
523 A138 60fr Triphoridae 1.60 .80
524 A138 69fr Muricidae favartia 1.75 .90
525 A138 73fr Muricidae morula 2.00 1.00
Nos. 523-525 (3) 5.35 2.70

Te Faaturama, c. 1892, by Gauguin A139

1989, Nov. 19 **Litho.** ***Perf. 12½x13***
526 A139 1000fr multicolored 22.00 12.50

Legends — A140

Designs: 66fr, Maui, birth of the islands, vert. 82fr, Mt. Rotui, the pierced mountain. 88fr, Princess Hina and the eel King of Lake Vaihiria.

1989, Dec. 6 **Litho.** ***Perf. 13***
527 A140 66fr olive brn & blk 1.40 .90
528 A140 82fr buff & blk 1.90 1.10
529 A140 88fr cream & blk 2.00 1.15
Nos. 527-529 (3) 5.30 3.15

Vanilla Orchid — A141

1990, Jan. 11 **Litho.**
530 A141 34fr Flower 1.35 .60
531 A141 35fr Bean pods 1.60 .60

Marine Life A142

1990, Feb. 9 **Litho.** ***Perf. 13½***
532 A142 40fr Kuhlia marginata 1.30 .55
533 A142 50fr Macrobrachium 1.50 .70

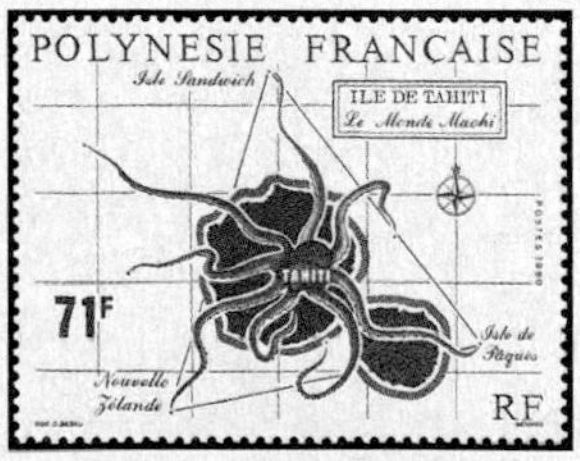

Tahiti, Center of Polynesian Triangle — A143

Maohi settlers and maps of island settlements: 58fr, Hawaiian Islands. 59fr, Easter Island. 63fr, New Zealand.

1990, Mar. 14 **Engr.** ***Perf. 13***
534 A143 58fr black 1.75 .85
535 A143 59fr bluish gray *45.00* 25.00
536 A143 63fr olive green 2.25 .95
537 A143 71fr Prussian blue 2.50 1.10
Nos. 534-537 (4) *51.50* 27.90

See Nos. 544-545.

Papeete Village, Cent. — A144

1990, May 16 **Litho.**

538 A144 150fr New City Hall 3.25 1.75
539 A144 250fr Old Town Hall 4.75 3.00

A145

Designs: Endangered birds.

1990, June 5 ***Perf. 13½***

540 A145 13fr Porzana tabuensis .75 .25
541 A145 20fr Vini ultramarina 1.75 .35

A146

1990, July 10 ***Perf. 13***

542 A146 39fr multicolored 1.10 .65

Lions Club in Papeete, 30th anniv.

Gen. Charles de Gaulle, Birth Cent. — A147

1990, Sept. 2 **Litho.**

543 A147 200fr multi 4.50 3.25

No. 536 with Different Colors and Inscriptions

1990, Aug. 24 **Engr.** ***Perf. 13***

544 A143 125fr Man, map 3.00 2.00

Souvenir Sheet

Imperf

545 A143 230fr like No. 544 6.00 6.00

New Zealand 1990.

Intl. Tourism Day — A148

1990, Sept. 27 **Litho.** ***Perf. 12½***

546 A148 8f red & yellow pareo 1.10 .35
547 A148 10fr yellow pareo 1.10 .35
548 A148 12fr blue pareo 1.10 .75
Nos. 546-548 (3) 3.30 1.45

Polynesian Legends — A149

170fr, Legend of the Uru. 290fr, Pipiri-ma, vert. 375fr, Hiro, God of Thieves, vert.

1990, Nov. 7 **Litho.** ***Perf. 13***

549 A149 170fr multicolored 4.00 2.50
550 A149 290fr multicolored 7.50 4.00
551 A149 375fr multicolored 11.00 5.00
Nos. 549-551 (3) 22.50 11.50

Tiare Flower — A150

Designs: 28fr, Flower crown, lei. 30fr, Flowers in bloom. 37fr, Lei.

1990, Dec. 5 ***Perf. 12½***

552 A150 28fr multicolored .70 .45
553 A150 30fr multicolored .95 .45
554 A150 37fr multicolored 1.20 .55
Nos. 552-554 (3) 2.85 1.45

Pineapple A151

1991, Jan. 9 ***Die Cut***

Self-adhesive

555 A151 42fr shown 1.25 .90
556 A151 44fr Pineapple field 1.75 1.10

Nos. 555-556 are on paper backing perf. 12½.

Marine Life A152

1991, Feb. 7 ***Perf. 12½***

557 A152 7fr Nudibranch .45 .25
558 A152 9fr Galaxaura tenera .70 .25
559 A152 11fr Adusta cumingii .70 .25
Nos. 557-559 (3) 1.85 .75

Maohi Islands A153

18th Century scenes of: 68fr, Woman of Easter Island, vert. 84fr, Twin-hulled canoe, Hawaii. 94fr, Maori village, New Zealand.

1991, Mar. 13 **Engr.** ***Perf. 13***

560 A153 68fr olive 47.50 32.50
561 A153 84fr black 2.50 1.75
562 A153 94fr brown 3.00 1.75
Nos. 560-562 (3) 53.00 36.00

Basketball, Cent. — A154

1991, May 15 **Litho.** ***Perf. 13***

563 A154 80fr multicolored 1.75 1.25

Birds — A155

1991, June 5 ***Perf. 13½***

564 A155 17fr Halcyon gambieri .60 .25
565 A155 21fr Vini kuhlii .90 .35

Still Life with Oranges in Tahiti by Paul Gauguin — A156

1991, June 9 **Litho.** ***Perf. 13***

566 A156 700fr multicolored 17.50 9.50

Sculptures of the Marquesas Islands — A157

56fr, White Tiki with Club, vert. 102fr, Warriors Carrying Tired Man, vert. 110fr, Native Canoe.

1991, July 17 **Litho.** ***Perf. 13***

567 A157 56fr multicolored 1.25 .85
568 A157 102fr multicolored 2.25 1.50
569 A157 110fr multicolored 2.50 1.75
Nos. 567-569 (3) 6.00 4.10

Wolfgang Amadeus Mozart, Death Bicent. — A158

1991, Aug. 28 **Engr.** ***Perf. 13x12½***

570 A158 100fr multicolored 3.00 1.75

Stone Fishing — A159

1991, Oct. 9 **Litho.** ***Perf. 13***

571 A159 25fr Fishing boats, vert. .60 .40
572 A159 57fr Man hurling stone, vert. 1.25 .90
573 A159 62fr Trapped fish 1.50 1.25
Nos. 571-573 (3) 3.35 2.55

Phila Nippon '91 A160

Designs: 50fr, Drawings of marine life by Jules-Louis Lejeune, vert. 70fr, Sailing ship, La Coquille. 250fr, Contains designs from Nos. 574-575.

Perf. 12½x13, 13x12½

1991, Nov. 16 **Engr.**

574 A160 50fr multicolored 1.30 .55
575 A160 70fr multicolored 1.75 1.25

Size: 100x75mm

Imperf

576 A160 250fr multicolored 6.00 6.00
Nos. 574-576 (3) 9.05 7.80

Central Bank for Economic Co-operation, 50th Anniv. — A161

1991, Dec. 2 **Litho.** ***Perf. 13x12½***

577 A161 307fr multicolored 7.00 4.50

Christmas A162

Perf. 12½x13, 13x12½

1991, Dec. 11 **Litho.**

578 A162 55fr Scuba divers 1.25 .75
579 A162 83fr Underwater scene 1.75 1.35
580 A162 86fr Nativity, vert. 1.75 1.35
Nos. 578-580 (3) 4.75 3.45

Tourism — A163

1992, Feb. 12 ***Perf. 13***

581 A163 1fr shown .25 .25
582 A163 2fr Horses, beach .35 .25
583 A163 3fr Girl holding fish .50 .30
584 A163 4fr Waterfalls, vert. .60 .35
585 A163 5fr Sailing .75 .40

586 A163 6fr Waterfalls, helicopter, vert. 1.00 .45
Nos. 581-586 (6) 3.45 2.00

Views from Space — A164

1992, Mar. 18 Litho. ***Perf. 13x12½***

587 A164 46fr Tahiti 1.75 .90
588 A164 72fr Mataiva 2.00 1.25
589 A164 76fr Bora Bora 2.25 1.40

Size: 130x100mm

Imperf

590 A164 230fr Satellite imaging system 6.00 5.75
Nos. 587-590 (4) 12.00 9.30

International Space Year.

World Health Day A165

1992, Apr. 7 ***Perf. 13½***

591 A165 136fr multicolored 3.00 2.25

Discovery of America, 500th Anniv. — A166

1992, May 22 ***Perf. 13***

592 A166 130fr multicolored 3.00 2.25

Size: 140x100mm

Imperf

593 A166 250fr multicolored 6.00 6.00

World Columbian Stamp Expo '92, Chicago.

Traditional Dances — A167

Dance from: 95fr, Tahiti. 105fr, Hawaii. 115fr, Tonga.

1992, June 17 Engr. ***Perf. 13***

594 A167 95fr brown black 1.90 1.60
595 A167 105fr olive brown 2.10 1.75
596 A167 115fr red brn & olive grn 2.50 1.75
Nos. 594-596 (3) 6.50 5.10

Tattoos A168

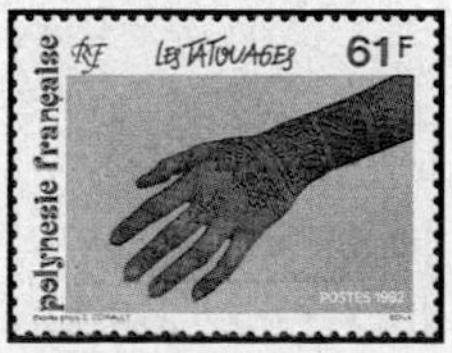

1992, July 8 Litho. ***Perf. 12½***

597 A168 61fr Hand 1.90 1.25
598 A168 64fr Man, vert. 2.00 1.25

Children's Games A169

1992, Aug. 5 ***Perf. 13½***

599 A169 22fr Outrigger canoe models .50 .35
600 A169 31fr String game .75 .45
601 A169 45fr Stilt game, vert. 1.25 .70
Nos. 599-601 (3) 2.50 1.50

Herman Melville, 150th Anniv. of Arrival in French Polynesia — A170

1992, Sept. 16 ***Perf. 12½***

602 A170 78fr multicolored 4.50 1.25

6th Festival of Pacific Arts, Rarotonga — A171

40fr, Men on raft. 65fr, Pirogues, Tahiti.

1992, Oct. 16 Engr. ***Perf. 13***

603 A171 40fr lake 1.50 .60
604 A171 65fr blue 2.00 1.00

First French Polynesian Postage Stamps, Cent. — A172

1992, Nov. 18 Photo. ***Perf. 13***

605 A172 200fr multicolored 4.75 3.25

Paintings A173

55fr, Two Women Talking, by Erhard Lux. 60fr, Bouquet of Flowers, by Uschi. 75fr, Spearfisherman, by Pierre Kienlen. 85fr, Mother Nursing Child, by Octave Morillot.

1992, Dec. 9 ***Perf. 12½x13***

606 A173 55fr multicolored 1.50 .75
607 A173 60fr multicolored 1.75 1.40
608 A173 75fr multicolored 1.90 1.50
609 A173 85fr multicolored 2.50 1.60
Nos. 606-609 (4) 7.65 5.25

Net Thrower A174

Bonito Fishing A175

1993, Feb. 10 Litho. ***Die Cut***

Self-Adhesive

Size: 26x36mm

610 A174 46fr blue & multi 1.50 1.00

Size: 17x23mm

611 A174 46fr green & multi 1.50 1.00
a. Booklet pane of 10 15.00

1993, Mar. 10 ***Perf. 13½***

612 A175 68fr Line & hook 1.60 1.25
613 A175 84fr Boat, horiz. 1.90 1.50
614 A175 86fr Drying catch 2.10 1.50
Nos. 612-614 (3) 5.60 4.25

Allied Airfield on Bora Bora, 50th Anniv. — A176

1993, Apr. 5 ***Perf. 13***

615 A176 120fr multicolored 3.00 2.25

Jacques Boullaire, Artist, Birth Cent. — A177

Various scenes depicting life on: 32fr, Moorea. 36fr, Tuamotu. 39fr, Rurutu. 51fr, Nuku Hiva.

1993, May 6 ***Engr.***

616 A177 32fr brown black .90 .50
617 A177 36fr brick red .90 .65
618 A177 39fr violet 1.25 .90
619 A177 51fr light brown 1.50 1.00
Nos. 616-619 (4) 4.55 3.05

Sports Festival — A178

1993, May 15 Litho. ***Perf. 12½***

620 A178 30fr multicolored .85 .50

Australian Mathematics Competition, 15th Anniv. — A179

1993, July 1 Litho. ***Perf. 13½***

621 A179 70fr multicolored 1.75 1.10

Intl. Symposium on Inter-Plate Volcanism, French University of the Pacific, Punaauia A180

1993, Aug. 2 Litho. ***Perf. 13***

622 A180 140fr tan, blk & brn 3.50 2.50

Taipei '93 — A181

1993, Aug. 14 Litho. ***Perf. 13½***

623 A181 46fr multicolored 1.75 .85

Exists without the Cartor imprint. Value, unused $17.50.

Tourism — A182

14fr, Boat tour. 20fr, Groom preparing for traditional wedding. 29fr, Beachside brunch.

1993, Sept. 27

624 A182 14fr multi, horiz. .60 .35
625 A182 20fr multi .65 .35
626 A182 29fr multi, horiz. .75 .45
Nos. 624-626 (3) 2.00 1.15

Exist without the Cartor imprint. Value, set unused $30.

Arrival of First French Gendarme in Tahiti, 150th Anniv. — A183

1993, Oct. 14 ***Perf. 13***

627 A183 100fr multicolored 2.50 1.60

Exists without the Cartor imprint. Value, unused $17.50.

Alain Gerbault (1893-1941), Sailor — A184

1993, Nov. 17 Engr. ***Perf. 13***

628 A184 150fr red, green & blue 4.00 2.75

Paintings — A185

Artists: 40fr, Vaea Sylvain. 70fr, A. Marere, vert. 80fr, J. Shelsher. 90fr, P.E. Victor, vert.

1993, Dec. 3 Photo. *Perf. 13*

629	A185	40fr multicolored	1.75	.70
630	A185	70fr multicolored	2.50	1.25
631	A185	80fr multicolored	3.00	1.25
632	A185	90fr multicolored	3.50	1.50
		Nos. 629-632 (4)	10.75	4.70

French School of the Pacific, 30th Anniv. A186

1993, Dec. 7 Litho. *Perf. 12½*

633 A186 200fr multicolored 5.00 3.50

Whales and Dolphins A187

1994, Jan. 12 Litho. *Perf. 13½*

634	A187	25fr Whale breeching	.75	.45
635	A187	68fr Dolphins	1.75	1.10
636	A187	72fr Humpback whales, vert.	2.00	1.25
		Nos. 634-636 (3)	4.50	2.80

A188

1994, Feb. 18 Litho. *Perf. 13½*

637 A188 51fr multicolored 2.25 .95

Hong Kong '94. New Year 1994 (Year of the Dog).

A189

1994, Mar. 16

638 A189 180fr Sister Germaine Bruel 4.00 3.00

Arrival of Nuns from St. Joseph of Cluny, 150th anniv.

Church of Jesus Christ of Latter-day Saints in French Polynesia, 150th Anniv. A190

1994, Apr. 30 Litho. *Perf. 13½*

639 A190 154fr Tahiti temple 3.50 2.75

Conservatory of Arts and Crafts, Bicent. — A191

1994, May 25 Photo. *Perf. 13*

640 A191 316fr multicolored 7.50 5.50

Regional Associated Center of Papeete, 15th anniv.

Internal Self-Government, 10th Anniv. — A192

1994, June 29 Litho. *Perf. 13*

641 A192 500fr multicolored 12.00 7.50

Tahitian Academy, 20th Anniv. — A193

1994, July 2 Engr. *Perf. 13*

642 A193 136fr multicolored 3.00 2.00

Scenes of Old Tahiti — A194

1994, Aug. 10 Litho. *Perf. 13*

643	A194	22fr Papara	.90	.50
644	A194	26fr Mataiea	1.10	.65
645	A194	51fr Taravao, vert.	1.90	.95
		Nos. 643-645 (3)	3.90	2.10

See Nos. 673-675.

Faaturuma, by Paul Gauguin (1848-1903) A195

1994, Sept. 14 Litho. *Perf. 13*

646 A195 1000fr multicolored 24.00 16.00

Epiphyllum Oxypetalum A196

1994, Oct. 15 Litho. *Perf. 13½*

647 A196 51fr multicolored 1.75 .95

Hawaiki Nui Va'a '94 (Canoe Race) A197

Designs: a, 52fr, Yellow canoe, bow paddler. b, 76fr, Paddlers. c, 80fr, Paddlers, blue canoe. d, 94fr, Stern paddler, yellow canoe.

1994, Nov. 10 Litho. *Perf. 13½x13*

648 A197 Strip of 4, #a.-d. 8.00 4.75

No. 648 is a continuous design.

Paintings of French Polynesia — A198

62fr, Young girl, by Michelle Villemin. 78fr, Ocean tide, fish, by Michele Dallet. 102fr, Native carrying bundles of fruit, by Johel Blanchard. 110fr, View of coastline, by Pierre Lacouture.

1994, Dec. 19 Litho. *Perf. 13*

649	A198	62fr multi, vert.	1.75	.95
650	A198	78fr multi, vert.	2.00	1.25
651	A198	102fr multi, vert.	2.25	1.60
652	A198	110fr multi	2.75	1.75
		Nos. 649-652 (4)	8.75	5.55

Don Domingo de Boenechea's Tautira Expedition, 220th Anniv. — A199

1995, Jan. 1

653 A199 92fr multicolored 2.25 1.25

South Pacific Tourism Year — A200

1995, Jan. 11 Litho. *Perf. 13½*

654 A200 92fr multicolored 2.25 1.40

New Year 1995 (Year of the Boar) A201

1995, Feb. 1 Litho.

655 A201 51fr multicolored 1.75 .80

Portions of the design on No. 655 were applied by a thermographic process producing a shiny, raised effect.

Exists without the Cartor imprint. Value, unused $9.

University Teacher's Training Institute of the Pacific — A202

1995, Mar. 8 Litho. *Perf. 13½*

656 A202 59fr multicolored 1.50 .95

Nature Protection A203

1995, May 4 Litho. *Perf. 13*

657	Strip of 3 + 2 labels	4.25	4.25
a.	A203 22fr Head of turtle	.75	.35
b.	A203 29fr Turtle swimming	1.00	.50
c.	A203 91fr Black coral	2.50	1.50

Louis Pasteur (1822-95) — A204

1995, May 8

658 A204 290fr dk blue & blue 6.75 4.00

Loti's Marriage, Novel by Julien Viaud (1850-1923) — A205

1995, May 19 Photo. *Perf. 13*

659 A205 66fr multicolored 2.00 1.10

A206

1995, May 24 Litho. *Perf. 13½*
660 A206 150fr multicolored 3.50 2.25

Tahitian Monoi beauty aid.

Birds — A207

1995, June 7
661 A207 22fr Ptilinopus huttoni .65 .50
662 A207 44fr Ducula galeata 1.40 .75

Tahitian Pearls A208

1995, June 14
663 A208 66fr shown 1.60 1.10
664 A208 84fr Eight pearls 2.10 1.40

On Nos. 663-664 portions of the design were applied by a thermographic process producing a shiny, raised effect.

Discovery of Marquesas Islands, 400th Anniv. — A209

a, Alvaro de Mendana de Neira, sailing ships. b, Pedro Fernandez de Quiros, map of islands.

1995, July 21 Litho. *Perf. 13*
665 Pair + label 8.00 6.00
a. A209 161fr multicolored 3.50 2.75
b. A209 195fr multicolored 4.50 3.25

A210

1995, Aug. 12 Litho. *Perf. 13*
666 A210 83fr multicolored 2.00 1.40

10th South Pacific Games, Tahiti.

A211

Pandanus plant: No. 667a, Entire plant. b, Flower. c, Fruit. d, Using dry leaves for weaving.

1995, Sept. 1 *Perf. 13½x13*
667 Strip of 4 8.50 6.00
a.-d. A211 91fr any single 2.00 1.50

Singapore '95.

UN, 50th Anniv. — A212

1995, Oct. 24 Litho. *Perf. 13*
668 A212 420fr multicolored 9.50 6.00

Paintings — A213

Designs: 57fr, The Paddler with the Yellow Dog, by Philippe Dubois, vert. 76fr, An Afternoon in Vaitape, by Maui Seaman, vert. 79fr, The Mama with the White Hat, by Simone Testeguide. 100fr, In Front of the Kellum House in Moorea, by Christian Deloffre.

1995, Dec. 6 Photo. *Perf. 13*
669 A213 57fr multicolored 1.50 .90
670 A213 76fr multicolored 1.75 1.25
671 A213 79fr multicolored 1.90 1.25
672 A213 100fr multicolored 2.50 1.60
Nos. 669-672 (4) 7.65 5.00

Scenes of Old Tahiti Type

1996, Jan. 17 Litho. *Perf. 13*
673 A194 18fr Fautaua .65 .45
674 A194 30fr District of Punaauia .80 .50
675 A194 35fr Tautira .90 .60
Nos. 673-675 (3) 2.35 1.55

New Year 1996 (Year of the Rat) — A214

1996, Feb. 19 Photo. *Perf. 13*
676 A214 51fr multicolored 1.75 .80

Portions of the design on No. 676 were applied by a thermographic process producing a shiny, raised effect.

Paul-Emile Victor (1907-95), Explorer, Writer — A215

1996, Mar. 7 Litho.
677 A215 500fr multicolored 12.00 8.00

Queen Pomare IV — A216

1996, Mar. 1 Litho. *Perf. 13*
678 A216 (51fr) multicolored 1.50 .80

Serpentine Die Cut 7 Vert.

Self-Adhesive

Size: 17x24mm

678A A216 (51fr) multicolored 2.00 1.15
b. Booklet pane of 5 10.00
Complete booklet, 2 #678b 20.00

Sea Shells A217

10fr, Conus pertusus. 15fr, Cypraea alisonae. 25fr, Vexillum roseotinctum.

1996, Apr. 10 Photo. *Perf. 13½x13*
679 A217 10fr multicolored .45 .25
680 A217 15fr multicolored .50 .25
681 A217 25fr multicolored .95 .40
Nos. 679-681 (3) 1.90 .90

Portions of the designs on Nos. 679-681 were applied by a thermographic process producing a shiny, raised effect.

Return of the Pacific Battalion, 50th Anniv. — A218

1996, May 5 Litho. *Perf. 13*
682 A218 100fr multicolored 3.00 1.60

CHINA '96, 9th Asian Intl. Philatelic Exhibition A219

Design: 200fr, Chinese School, Tahiti, 1940.

1996, May 18 *Perf. 13x13½*
683 A219 50fr multicolored 1.25 .80

Souvenir Sheet

Imperf

684 A219 200fr multicolored 4.50 3.40

Birds A220

1996, June 12 Litho. *Perf. 13x13½*
685 A220 66fr Sula sula 1.50 1.10
686 A220 79fr Fregata minor 2.00 1.25
687 A220 84fr Anous stolidus 2.00 1.40
Nos. 685-687 (3) 5.50 3.75

Musical Instruments A221

1996, July 10 *Perf. 13x13½*
688 A221 5fr Pahu, ukulele, toere .30 .25
689 A221 9fr Toere .40 .25
690 A221 14fr Pu, vivo .50 .25
Nos. 688-690 (3) 1.20 .75

Raiateana Oulietea A222

1996, Aug. 7 Litho. *Perf. 13x13½*
691 A222 66fr multicolored 1.75 1.10

A223

1996, Sept. 9 Litho. *Perf. 13*
692 A223 70fr Ruahatu, God of the Ocean 1.75 1.10

7th Pacific Arts Festival.

A224

Stamp Day: Young Tahitian girl (Type A2), Noho Mercier, taken from photo by Henry Lemasson (1870-1956), postal administrator.

1996, Oct. 16 Engr. *Perf. 13*
693 A224 92fr black, red & blue 2.50 1.50

First Representative Assembly, 50th Anniv. — A225

1996, Nov. 7 Litho. *Perf. 13*
694 A225 85fr multicolored 2.00 1.10

Paintings of Tahitian Women — A226

Designs: 70fr, Woman lounging on Bora Bora Beach, by Titi Bécaud. 85fr, "Woman with Crown of Auti leaves," by Maryse Noguier, vert. 92fr, "Dreamy Woman," by Christine de Dinechin, vert. 96fr, Two working women, by Andrée Lang, vert.

1996, Dec. 4 Litho. *Perf. 13*
695 A226 70fr multicolored 2.00 .75
696 A226 85fr multicolored 2.25 .90
697 A226 92fr multicolored 2.50 1.00
698 A226 96fr multicolored 3.00 1.00
Nos. 695-698 (4) 9.75 3.65

A227

1997, Jan. 2 Litho. *Perf. 13*
699 A227 55fr brown 1.25 .55

Society of South Sea Studies, 80th anniv.

A228

1997, Feb. 7 Photo. *Perf. 13½x13*
700 A228 13fr multicolored 1.00 .30

New Year 1997 (Year of the Ox). Portions of the design were applied by a thermographic process producing a shiny, raised effect.

Arrival of Evangelists in Tahiti, Bicent. — A229

Designs: a, Sailing ship, "Duff." b, Painting, "Transfer of the Matavai District to the L.M.S. Missionaries," by Robert Smirke.

1997, Mar. 5 Litho. *Perf. 13*
701 A229 43fr Pair, #a.-b. + label 2.00 1.25

Tifaifai (Tahitian Bedspread) A230

Various leaf and floral patterns.

1997, Apr. 16
702 A230 1fr multicolored .25 .25
703 A230 5fr multicolored .25 .25
704 A230 70fr multicolored 1.60 .70
Nos. 702-704 (3) 2.10 1.20

PACIFIC 97 — A231

Sailing ships carrying mail, passengers between Tahiti and San Francisco: No. 705, Tropic Bird, 1897. No. 706, Papeete/Zélee, 1892.

1997, May 29 Litho. *Perf. 13*
705 A231 92fr multicolored 3.25 1.60
706 A231 92fr multicolored 3.25 1.60
a. Pair, #705-706 6.50 6.50
b. Souvenir sheet, #705-706 65.00 65.00

No. 706b sold for 400fr.

Island Scenes A232

No. 707, Flower. No. 708, Rowing canoe, sun behind mountain. No. 709, Throwing spears. No. 710. Aerial view of island. No. 711, Fish. No. 712, Women walking on beach. No. 713, Holding oyster shell with pearls. No. 714, Boat with sail down, sunset across water. No. 715, Snorkeling, sting ray. No. 716, Bananas, pineapples. No. 717, Palm tree, beach. No. 718, Women dancers in costume.

1997, June 25 Litho. *Perf. 13*
Booklet Stamps
707 A232 85fr multicolored 14.00 14.00
708 A232 85fr multicolored 14.00 14.00
709 A232 85fr multicolored 14.00 14.00
710 A232 85fr multicolored 14.00 14.00
711 A232 85fr multicolored 14.00 14.00
712 A232 85fr multicolored 14.00 14.00
a. Bklt. pane of 6, #707-712 90.00
713 A232 85fr multicolored 14.00 14.00
714 A232 85fr multicolored 14.00 14.00
715 A232 85fr multicolored 14.00 14.00
716 A232 85fr multicolored 14.00 14.00
717 A232 85fr multicolored 14.00 14.00
718 A232 85fr multicolored 14.00 14.00
a. Bklt. pane of 6, #713-718 90.00
Complete booklet, 2 each #712a, #718a 350.00

Traditional Dance Costumes A233

Designs: 4fr, Warrior's costume. 9fr, Women's costume. 11fr, Couple.

1997, July 10 Litho. *Perf. 13½x13*
719 A233 4fr multicolored 1.00 .30
720 A233 9fr multicolored 1.25 .30
721 A233 11fr multicolored 2.00 .30
Nos. 719-721 (3) 4.25 .90

Kon-Tiki Expedition, 50th Anniv. — A234

1997, Aug. 7 Litho. *Perf. 13*
722 A234 88fr multicolored 2.25 .80

Artists in Tahiti — A235

Designs: 85fr, Painting, "The Fruit Carrier," by Monique "Mono" Garnier-Bissol. 96fr, "Revival of Our Resources," mother of pearl painting, by Camélia Maraea. 110fr, "Tahitian Spirit," pottery, by Peter Owen, vert. 126fr, "Monoi," surrealist painting, by Elisabeth Stefanovitch.

1997, Oct. 15 Litho. *Perf. 13*
723 A235 85fr multicolored 1.90 .80
724 A235 96fr multicolored 2.00 .90
725 A235 110fr multicolored 2.50 1.00
726 A235 126fr multicolored 3.00 1.10
Nos. 723-726 (4) 9.40 3.80

Te Arii Vahine, by Paul Gauguin (1848-1903) — A236

1997, Nov. 6 Litho. *Perf. 13*
727 A236 600fr multicolored 13.00 8.00

Christmas A237

1997, Dec. 3 Litho. *Perf. 13*
728 A237 118fr multicolored 3.00 1.10

New Year 1998 (Year of the Tiger) A238

1998, Jan. 28 Photo. *Perf. 13*
729 A238 96fr multicolored 2.50 .90

Portions of the design on No. 729 were applied by a thermographic process producing a shiny, raised effect.

Domestic Airline Network — A239

Designs: a, 70fr, Grumman Widgeon, 1950. b, 85fr, DHC 6 Twin-Otter, 1968. c, 70fr, Fairchild FH 227, 1980. d, 85fr, ATR 42-500, 1998.

1998, Apr. 16 Photo. *Perf. 13*
730 A239 Strip of 4, #a.-d. + label 6.50 2.90

Orchids A240

5fr, Dendrobium "Royal King." 20fr, Oncidium "Ramsey." 50fr, Ascodenca "Laksi." 100fr, Cattleya "hybride."

1998, May 14 Photo. *Perf. 13*
731 A240 5fr multi .25 .25
732 A240 20fr multi, vert. .50 .25
733 A240 50fr multi, vert. 1.25 .45
734 A240 100fr multi 2.25 .95
Nos. 731-734 (4) 4.25 1.90

On Nos. 731-734 portions of the design were applied by a thermographic process producing a shiny, raised effect.

The Lovers, by Paul Gauguin (1848-1903) — A241

1998, June 7 Photo. *Perf. 13x12½*
735 A241 1000fr multicolored 22.50 9.00

Printed se-tenant with label.

1998 World Cup Soccer Championships, France — A242

1998, June 10
736 A242 85fr multicolored 2.00 .75

For overprint see No. 742.

Tahiti Festival of Flower and Shell Garlands — A243

Women wearing various garlands of flowers or shells.

1998, July 16 Photo. *Perf. 13½*
737 A243 55fr multicolored 1.50 .50
738 A243 65fr multicolored 1.75 .60
739 A243 70fr multicolored 2.00 .65
740 A243 80fr multicolored 2.25 .75
Nos. 737-740 (4) 7.50 2.50

Painting, "Underwater World of Polynesia," by Stanley Haumani A244

1998, Sept. 10 Photo. *Perf. 12½x13*

741 A244 200fr multicolored 4.00 2.00

No. 736 Ovptd. in Blue & Black "France / Championne / du Munde"

1998, Oct. 28 Photo. *Perf. 13½*

742 A242 85fr multicolored 3.00 1.00

Autumn Philatelic Fair, Paris — A246

Watercolor paintings of Papeete Bay, by René Gillotin (1814-61), 250fr each: a, Beach at left, people. b, Beach at right, people.

1998, Nov. 5 *Perf. 13*

743 A246 Pair, #a.-b. + label 12.00 5.00
c. Souvenir sheet, #a.-b., imperf. 12.00 5.00

Life in Tahiti and the Islands A247

Paintings by André Deymonaz: 70fr, Return to the Market, vert. 100fr, Bonito Fish Stalls, vert. 102fr, Going Fishing. 110fr, Discussion after Church Services.

1998, Dec. 10 Photo. *Perf. 13*

744 A247 70fr multicolored 1.50 .80
745 A247 100fr multicolored 2.00 1.00
746 A247 102fr multicolored 2.25 1.00
747 A247 110fr multicolored 2.50 1.10
Nos. 744-747 (4) 8.25 3.90

St. Valentine's Day — A248

1999, Feb. 11 Litho. *Perf. 13*

748 A248 96fr multicolored 2.50 .90

New Year 1999 (Year of the Rabbit) A249

1999, Feb. 16

749 A249 118fr Rabbits, flowers 2.50 1.10

Portions of the design of No. 749 were applied by a thermographic process producing a shiny, raised effect.

Marine Life A250

Designs: 70fr, Ptérois volitans. 85fr, Hippocampus histrix. 90fr, Antennarius pictus. 120fr, Taenianotus triacanthus.

1999, Mar. 18 Photo. *Perf. 13*

750 A250 70fr multicolored 1.50 .65
751 A250 85fr multicolored 1.90 .80
752 A250 90fr multicolored 2.00 .80
753 A250 120fr multicolored 2.75 1.10
Nos. 750-753 (4) 8.15 3.35

Portions of the designs on Nos. 750-753 were applied by a thermographic process producing a shiny, raised effect.

IBRA '99, World Philatelic Exhibition, Nuremberg A251

Tatooed men of Marquesas Islands, 1804: 90fr, Holding staff, fan. 120fr, Wearing blue cape.

Photo. & Engr.

1999, Apr. 27 *Perf. 13¼*

754 A251 90fr multicolored 2.00 .90
755 A251 120fr multicolored 2.75 1.25

Mother's Day A252

1999, May 27 Litho. *Perf. 13¼*

756 A252 85fr Children, vert. 1.90 .75
757 A252 120fr shown 2.75 1.00

A253

Island Fruits A254

No. 758, Breadfruit, vert. 120fr, Coconut.

No. 760: a, Papaya. b, Guava (goyave). c, Mombin. d, Rambutan. e, Star apple (pomme-etoile). f, Otaheite gooseberry (seurette). g, Rose apple. h, Star fruit (carambole). i, Spanish lime (quenette). j, Sweetsop (pomme-cannelle). k, Cashew (pomme de cajou). l, Passion fruit.

1999 Litho. *Perf. 13½x13, 13x13½*

758 A253 85fr multicolored 1.90 .75
759 A253 120fr multicolored 2.75 1.10

Souvenir Booklet

760 Complete bklt. 32.50
a.-l. A254 85fr Any single 2.00 1.40

Issued: No. 758, 120fr, 7/21; No. 760, 7/21.

No. 760 sold for 1200fr, and contains two booklet panes, containing Nos. 760a-760f, and Nos. 760g-760l. A second variety of No. 760 exists with selling price on cover as 1020fr. Value, complete booklet, $100.

No. 720, 1856 Letter, 1864 Postmark — A255

1999, July 2 Litho. *Perf. 13*

761 A255 180fr multicolored 4.00 2.25
a. Souvenir sheet of 1 12.00 12.00

150th anniv. of French postage stamps, PhilexFrance 99.

No. 761 issued se-tenant with label. No. 761a sold for 500fr.

Frédéric Chopin (1810-49), Composer — A256

1999, July 2 Litho. *Perf. 13*

762 A256 250fr multicolored 5.50 2.50

Malardé Medical Research Institute, 50th Anniv. — A257

1999, Sept. 27

763 A257 400fr multicolored 8.75 3.75

Nudes A258

Paintings by: 85fr, J. Sorgniard. 120fr, J. Dubrusk. 180fr, C. Deloffre. 250fr, J. Gandouin.

1999, Oct. 14 Litho. *Perf. 13*

764 A258 85fr multi 2.10 .75
765 A258 120fr multi 3.25 1.10
766 A258 180fr multi 4.50 1.60
767 A258 250fr multi 6.00 2.25
Nos. 764-767 (4) 15.85 5.70

Tahiti on the Eve of the Year 2000 A259

1999, Nov. 10 Litho. *Perf. 13*

768 A259 85fr multi 2.50 .75

5th Marquesas Islands Arts Festival A260

1999, Dec. 10

769 A260 90fr multi 2.00 .80

Year 2000 — A261

85fr, Hands of adult and infant. 120fr, Eye.

2000, Jan. 3 *Perf. 13¼x13, 13x13¼*

770 A261 85fr multi, vert. 2.50 .75
771 A261 120fr multi 3.25 1.10

New Year 2000 (Year of the Dragon) A262

2000, Feb. 5 Litho. *Perf. 13x13¼*

772 A262 180fr multi 5.50 1.50

Portions of the design were applied by a thermographic process producing a shiny, raised effect.

Postal Service Emblem and Stamps A263

2000, Mar. 15 Litho. *Perf. 13x13¼*

773 A263 90fr multi 2.00 .75

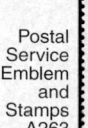

First Intl. Tattoo Festival, Raiatea — A264

Various tattoos.

2000, Apr. 28 ***Perf. 13***
774 A264 85fr multi 1.90 .70
775 A264 120fr multi 2.75 .95
776 A264 130fr multi 2.90 1.00
777 A264 160fr multi 3.50 1.25
Nos. 774-777 (4) 11.05 3.90

Beautiful Women of French Polynesia — A265

2000, May 30
778 A265 300fr multi 7.50 3.00
a. Souvenir sheet of 1 12.00 12.00

No. 778a sold for 500fr.

Traditional Dresses — A266

Denominations: 85fr, 120fr, 160fr, 250fr.

2000, June 21 Litho. ***Perf. 13¼x13***
779-782 A266 Set of 4 13.50 6.00

Mountains A267

Designs: 90fr, Mts. Aorai and Orohena. 180fr, Mts. Orohena and Aorai.

2000, July 10 ***Perf. 13x13¼***
783-784 A267 Set of 2 6.00 2.60

Traditional Sports A268

120fr, Fruit carrying. 250fr, Stone lifting, vert.

Perf. 13x13¼, 13¼x13
2000, Sept. 15
785-786 A268 Set of 2 8.25 3.50

Native Woven Crafts A269

No. 787, Fans. No. 788, Hat.

2000, Oct. 3 Litho. ***Perf. 13x13¼***
787-788 A269 85fr Set of 2 3.75 1.75

Year of Ancient Tahitian Language Reo Ma'ohi A270

2000, Nov. 9 Litho. ***Perf. 13x13¼***
789 A270 120fr multi 2.75 1.20

Portions of the design were applied by a thermographic process producing a shiny, raised effect.

Advent of New Millennium — A271

2000, Dec. 28
790 A271 85fr multi 2.50 .90

Central School, Cent. — A272

Designs: No. 791, 85fr, Central School. No. 792, 85fr, Paul Gauguin High School.

2001, Jan. 16
791-792 A272 Set of 2 3.75 1.75

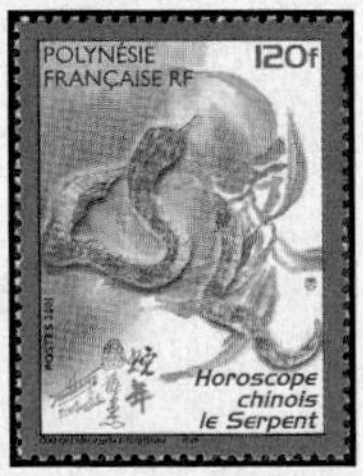

New Year 2001 (Year of the Snake) — A273

2001, Jan. 24 ***Perf. 13¼x13***
793 A273 120fr multi 2.75 1.20

Portions of the design were applied by a thermographic process producing a shiny, raised effect.

Landscapes A274

Designs: 35fr, Vaiharuru Waterfall. 50fr, Vahiria Lake, horiz. 90fr, Hakaui Valley.

Perf. 13¼x13, 13x13¼
2001, Feb. 26 **Litho.**
794-796 A274 Set of 3 6.00 1.75

Year of the Polynesian Child — A275

2001, Mar. 28 Litho. ***Perf. 13x13¼***
797 A275 55fr multi 1.25 .55

Polynesian Singers — A276

Designs: 85fr, Eddie Lund. 120fr, Charley Mauu. 130fr, Bimbo. 180fr, Marie Mariteragi and Emma Terangi, horiz.

2001, Apr. 12 ***Perf. 13¼x13, 13x13¼***
798-801 A276 Set of 4 11.50 5.00

Volunteers of the Pacific Batallion, 60th Anniv. A277

2001, Apr. 21 ***Perf. 13x13¼***
802 A277 85fr multi 2.25 .90

Surfing Waves of Teahupoo A278

2001, May 4
803 A278 120fr multi 2.75 1.20

Internal Autonomy, 17th Anniv. A279

2001, June 29 Litho. ***Perf. 13***
804 A279 250fr multi 5.50 2.50
a. Souvenir sheet of 1 12.00 12.00

No. 804a sold for 500fr.

Pirogue Racing — A280

Designs: 85fr, Male racers. 120fr, Female racers.

2001, July 12 ***Perf. 13¼x13***
805-806 A280 Set of 2 4.50 2.00
a. Souvenir sheet, #805-806, imperf. 5.50 5.50

No. 806a sold for 250fr.

Hardwood Trees A281

Designs: 90fr, Tou. 130fr, Ati. 180fr, Miro.

2001, Oct. 23 Litho. ***Perf. 13x13½***
807-809 A281 Set of 3 11.00 8.00

AIDS Prevention A282

2001, Sept. 20 Litho. ***Perf. 13x13¼***
810 A282 55fr multi 2.75 1.10

Year of Dialogue Among Civilizations A283

2001, Oct. 9 ***Perf. 13***
811 A283 500fr multi 11.50 10.00

Perfume Flowers — A284

Designs: 35fr, Gardenia tahitensis. 50fr, Fagraea berteriana. 85fr, Gardenia jasminoides.

2001, Nov. 8 ***Perf. 13¼x13***
812-814 A284 Set of 3 6.00 3.50

Portions of the designs were applied by a thermographic process producing a shiny, raised effect.

Christmas
A285

2001, Dec. 6 ***Perf. 13x13¼***
815 A285 120fr multi 2.75 2.40

New Year 2002 (Year of the Horse)
A286

2002, Feb. 12 Litho. ***Perf. 13x13¼***
816 A286 130fr multi 3.25 2.60

Portions of the design were applied by a thermographic process producing a shiny, raised effect.

Happy Holidays
A287

Greetings
A288

2002, Feb. 28 Background Colors

817 A287 55fr red		1.25	1.10
818 A288 55fr blue		1.25	1.10
819 A287 85fr blue		1.90	1.75
820 A288 85fr green		1.90	1.75
	Nos. 817-820 (4)	6.30	5.70

10th World Outrigger Canoe Championships — A289

Canoe rowers and emblems: 120fr, 180fr.

2002, Mar. 9 Photo. ***Perf. 13¼***
821-822 A289 Set of 2 6.75 6.25

Sea Urchins
A290

Designs: 35fr, Echinometra sp. 50fr, Heterocentrotus trigonarius. 90fr, Echinothrix calamaris. 120fr, Toxopneustes sp.

2002, Apr. 18 Litho. ***Perf. 13x13¼***
823-826 A290 Set of 4 6.50 6.25

Blood Donation — A291

2002, May 3 Litho. ***Perf. 13¼x13***
827 A291 130fr multi 4.00 3.25

2002 World Cup Soccer Championships, Japan and Korea — A292

2002, May 30
828 A292 85fr multi 2.10 1.75

Traditional Sports — A293

Designs: 85fr, Coconut husking. 120fr, Fruit carrying. 250fr, Javelin throwing.

2002, June 27
829-831 A293 Set of 3 10.00 9.00

House of James Norman Hall — A294

2002, July 4 ***Perf. 13x13¼***
832 A294 90fr multi 2.00 1.90

Papeete Market — A295

2002, Aug. 30 Litho. ***Perf. 13***
833 A295 400fr multi 8.75 8.00
a. Souvenir sheet of 1 11.00 11.00

Amphilex 2002 Stamp Exhibition, Amsterdam (No. 833a). No. 833a sold for 500fr.

Pacific Oceanology Center, Vairoa
A296

Designs: 55fr, Research pond, fish, shrimp, oyster, and flasks. 90fr, Aeriel view of center, fish, shrimp and oyster.

2002, Sept. 26 Photo. ***Perf. 13¼***
834-835 A296 Set of 2 3.50 2.40

Taapuna Master 2002 Surfing Competition
A297

2002, Oct. 21 Litho. ***Perf. 13x13¼***
836 A297 120fr multi 2.75 2.00

Halophilic Flowers
A298

Designs: 85fr, Hibiscus tiliaceus. 130fr, Scaveola sericea. 180fr, Guettarda speciosa.

2002, Nov. 7
837-839 A298 Set of 3 8.75 6.75

Polynesians at Festivals
A299

Designs: 55fr, Dancers and bus. 120fr, Musicians, vert.

2002, Dec. 5 ***Perf. 13x13¼, 13¼x13***
840-841 A299 Set of 2 3.75 3.00

New Year 2003 (Year of the Ram) — A300

2003, Feb. 1 Litho. ***Perf. 13¼x13***
842 A300 120fr multi 3.00 2.25

Portions of the design was applied by a thermographic process producing a shiny, raised effect.

Polynesian Women — A301

2003, Mar. 8 Litho. ***Perf. 13¼x13***
843 A301 55fr multi 1.25 1.00

Waterfalls — A302

2003, Apr. 10 ***Perf. 13***
844 A302 330fr multi 7.25 6.00

Old Papeete
A303

Designs: 55fr, Automobiles and buildings, vert. 85fr, Ship in harbor. 90fr, People with bicycles in front of buildings (50x28mm). 120fr, Tree-lined street (50x28mm).

Perf. 13¼x13, 13x13¼, 13

2003, May 15
845-848 A303 Set of 4 7.75 7.00
848a Souvenir sheet, #845-848 12.00 12.00

No. 848a sold for 550fr.

Fish — A304

2003, June 12 Litho. ***Perf. 13***
849 A304 460fr multi 9.50 9.50

Portions of the design were applied by a thermographic process producing a shiny, raised effect.

Outrigger Canoes
A305

Designs: No. 850, 85fr, shown. No. 851, 85fr, Three sailors on canoe at sea. No. 852, 85fr, Three sailors on canoe, vert. No. 853, 85fr, Sailor sitting on outrigger, vert.

Perf. 13x13¼, 13¼x13

2003, July 11 **Litho.**
850-853 A305 Set of 4 7.50 6.50

Firewalkers
A306

Orange-banded Cowrie — A307

2003, Aug. 14 Photo. ***Perf. 13¼***
854 A306 130fr multi 2.50 2.50

Perf. 13x13¼

855 A307 420fr multi 8.50 8.50

Are You Jealous? by Paul Gauguin (1848-1903) — A308

2003, Sept. 11 ***Perf. 13x12¼***
856 A308 250fr multi 6.50 3.50

Office of Posts and Telecommunications Emblem — A308a

Type I: "Postes 2003" at right.
Type II: "Postes" only at right.

Serpentine Die Cut 6½ Vert.

2003, Oct. 1 **Engr.**

Booklet Stamp
Self-Adhesive

856A	A308a (60fr) blue (type II), *2006*	10.00	1.00
b.	Booklet pane of 10	100.00	
c.	Type I	40.00	24.00
d.	As "c," booklet pane of 10	400.00	
e.	As #856A, inscribed "Phil@poste"	8.00	1.00
f.	Booklet pane of 10 #856Ae	80.00	

Issued: No. 856Ac, 10/1/03. No. 856A, 2006. No. 856Ae, 2007.
See Nos. 869, 1070-1070B.

French Polynesian Flag A309

2003, Oct. 1 **Litho.** ***Perf. 13x13¼***
857 A309 (60fr) multi 1.50 1.25

Tiki — A310

2003, Oct. 1 ***Perf. 13¼x13***
858 A310 100fr multi 3.00 2.00

Reissued in 2006 on shiny paper with much deeper colors. Values the same.

Flowers A311

Designs: 90fr, Orchid. 130fr, Rose de porcelain (torch ginger).

2003, Oct. 4 **Litho.** ***Perf. 13x13¼***
859-860 A311 Set of 2 6.50 4.50

Portions of the designs were applied by a thermographic process producing a shiny, raised effect.

Bora Bora A312

Designs: No. 861, 60fr, Painting of Bora Bora by A. Van Der Heyde. No. 862, 60fr, Aerial photograph of Bora Bora.

2003, Nov. 6 **Litho.** ***Perf. 13x13¼***
861-862 A312 Set of 2 5.00 2.75

Tiki — A313

2003, Dec. 6 ***Perf. 13***
863 A313 190fr multi 4.00 4.00

Buildings and Palm Trees A314

2003, Dec. 19 ***Perf. 13x13¼***
864 A314 90fr multi 3.00 1.90

New Year 2004 (Year of the Monkey) — A315

2004, Jan. 22 **Litho.** ***Perf. 13¼x13***
865 A315 130fr multi 3.50 3.50

A portion of the design was applied by a thermographic process producing a shiny, raised effect.

Scenes From Everyday Life A316

Designs: 60fr, Women working with cloth. 90fr, Street scene, vert.

Perf. 13x13¼, 13¼x13

2004, Feb. 13 **Litho.**
866-867 A316 Set of 2 3.25 3.25

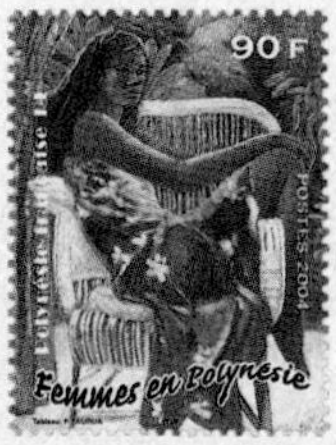

Polynesian Woman — A317

2004, Mar. 8 ***Perf. 13¼x13***
868 A317 90fr multi 4.00 1.90

Post Emblem Type of 2003

Serpentine Die Cut 6¾ Vert.

2004, Apr. 22 **Engr.**

Booklet Stamp
Self-Adhesive

869	A308a (90fr) red	6.00	2.00
a.	Booklet pane of 10	60.00	
b.	As #869, inscribed "Phil@poste"	—	—
c.	Booklet pane of 10 #869b	—	

No. 869 lacks year date.

Polynesian Economic Development — A318

2004, Apr. 23 **Litho.** ***Perf. 13x12¾***
870 A318 500fr multi 11.00 10.00

Arahurahu Marae, Paea — A319

2004, Apr. 23
871 A319 500fr multi 11.00 10.00

Vanilla — A320

2004, May 14 ***Perf. 13¼x13***
872 A320 90fr multi 2.10 1.90

No. 872 is impregnated with a vanilla scent.

Mobile Snack Bars — A321

2004, May 28 ***Perf. 13x12¾***
873 A321 300fr multi 6.50 6.25

Handicrafts A322

Designs: No. 874, 60fr, Artisan braiding fibers. No. 875, 60fr, Mother-of-pearl carving. No. 876, 90fr, Artisan carving statue. No. 877, 90fr, Hat.

2004, June 26 ***Perf. 13x13¼***
874-877 A322 Set of 4 10.00 6.25

Portion of the designs were applied by a thermographic process producing a shiny, raised effect.

Involvement in South Pacific Area of Office of Posts and Telecommunications — A323

Designs: 100fr, Earth, Sun on horizon. 130fr, Satellite dish, building.

2004, July 23 **Photo.** ***Perf. 13¼***
878-879 A323 Set of 2 5.50 4.75

Information Technology and Communications A324

Designs: No. 880, 190fr, Computer keyboard, "@." No. 881, 190fr, Satellite, satellite dish.

2004, Sept. 23 **Litho.** ***Perf. 13¼x13***
880-881 A324 Set of 2 8.00 8.00

Omai, Polynesian Capt. James Cook Brought to England — A325

2004, Oct. 14 ***Perf. 13***
882 A325 250fr multi 5.25 5.25

Shell Collectors A326

2004, Nov. 10 **Photo.** ***Perf. 13¼***
883 A326 60fr multi 1.60 1.40

A souvenir sheet of one sold for 250fr. Value $7.

Adenium Obesum A327

Alpinia Purpurata A328

Ixora Chinensis A329

Gardenia Taitensis A330

Heliconia Psittacorum — A331

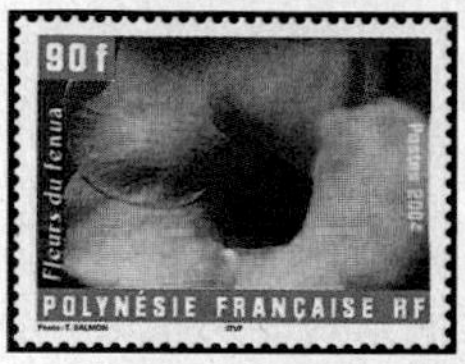
Allamanda Blanchetii A332

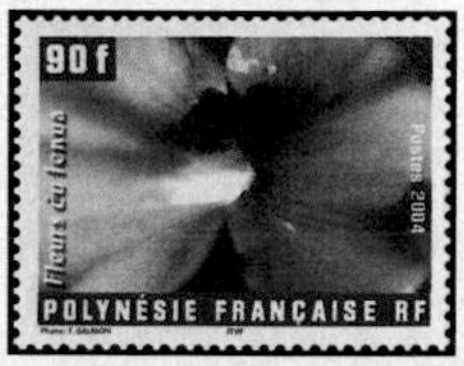
Otacanthus Caeruleus — A333

Hibiscus Rosa-sinensis — A334

Euphorba Milii A335

Asocenda Hybrid of Vanda x Ascocentrum — A336

Mussaenda Erythrophylia — A337

Bougainvillea Glabra — A338

2004, Nov. 10 Litho. ***Perf. 13x13¼***

884	Booklet pane of 6	17.50	—
a.	A327 90fr multi	2.50	2.50
b.	A328 90fr multi	2.50	2.50
c.	A329 90fr multi	2.50	2.50
d.	A330 90fr multi	2.50	2.50
e.	A331 90fr multi	2.50	2.50
f.	A332 90fr multi	2.50	2.50
885	Booklet pane of 6	17.50	—
a.	A333 90fr multi	2.50	2.50
b.	A334 90fr multi	2.50	2.50
c.	A335 90fr multi	2.50	2.50
d.	A336 90fr multi	2.50	2.50
e.	A337 90fr multi	2.50	2.50
f.	A338 90fr multi	2.50	2.50
	Complete booklet, #884-885	30.00	

Complete booklet sold for 1200fr.

Christmas A339

2004, Dec. 17
886 A339 60fr multi 1.60 1.40

A portion of the design was applied by a thermographic process producing a shiny, raised effect.

Bamboo — A340

2005, Feb. 9 ***Perf. 13¼x13***
887 A340 130fr multi 3.00 3.00

New Year 2005. A portion of the design was applied by a thermographic process producing a shiny, raised effect.

People and Hut A341

2005, Feb. 25 ***Perf. 13x13¼***
888 A341 90fr multi 2.00 2.00

Polynesian Women — A342

Designs: 60fr, Woman wearing lei. 90fr, Woman wearing flower garland on head and robe.

2005, Mar. 8 ***Perf. 13¼x13***
889-890 A342 Set of 2 4.00 3.50

Woman Making Tapa Cloth — A343

2005, Apr. 22 ***Perf. 13***
891 A343 250fr multi 5.50 5.50

Tifaifai A344

2005, Mar. 23 Litho. ***Perf. 13x13¼***
892 A344 5fr multi .25 .25

Angelfish A345

Designs: No. 893, 90fr, Centropyge bispinosa. No. 894, 90fr, Centropyge loricula. No. 895, 130fr, Centropyge heraldi. No. 896, 130fr, Centropyge flavissima.

2005, May 27 Litho. ***Perf. 13x13¼***
893-896 A345 Set of 4 9.50 9.50
896a Souvenir sheet, #893-896 9.50 9.50

Portions of the designs were applied by a thermographic process producing a shiny, raised effect.

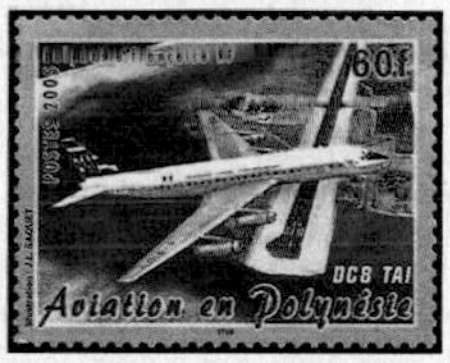
Historic Airplanes A346

Designs: No. 897, 60fr, TAI DC-8, first jet in Tahiti, 1961. No. 898, 60fr, Pan American Boeing 707, first foreign flight, 1963. No. 899, 100fr, Air France Boeing 707, first Air France flight to Tahiti, 1973. No. 900, 100fr, Air Tahiti Nui Airbus A340-300, first Tahitian airline, 2000.

2005, June 24
897-900 A346 Set of 4 6.50 6.50

Musical Instruments A347

Designs: No. 901, 130fr, Drum. No. 902, 130fr, Nose flutes, horiz.

2005, July 22 ***Perf. 13¼x13, 13x13¼***
901-902 A347 Set of 2 5.50 5.50

Polynesian Landscapes — A348

2005, Aug. 26 ***Perf. 13***
903 A348 300fr multi 6.25 6.25

Pineapples A349

Designs: 90fr, Close-up of spines. 130fr, Entire fruit.

2005, Sept. 23 Litho. ***Perf. 13¼x13***
904-905 A349 Set of 2 4.75 4.50

Nos. 904-905 are impregnated with pineapple scent.

Marae — A350

Marquesan Tohua — A351

2005, Oct. 21 ***Perf. 13***
906 A350 500fr multi 10.00 10.00
907 A351 500fr multi 10.00 10.00

Autonomy, 20th Anniv. (in 2004) — A352

2005, Nov. 10 ***Perf. 13¼x13***
908 A352 60fr multi 4.00 1.75

No. 908 was printed in France and distributed there in June 2004 but was not sold in French Polynesia until 2005, where it was available from the philatelic bureau upon request, and not through standing orders.

O'Parrey Harbor, Tahiti A353

2005, Nov. 10 Engr. ***Perf. 13x12½***
909 A353 100fr multi 2.00 2.00

Christmas A354

2005, Dec. 16 Litho. ***Perf. 13x13¼***
910 A354 90fr multi 2.00 2.00

Lotus Flower A355

Litho. & Silk-screened

2006, Jan. 30 ***Perf. 13x13¼***

911 A355 130fr multi 2.60 2.60

A356

Hearts A357

2006, Feb. 14 **Photo.** ***Perf. 13***

912 A356 60fr multi 1.25 1.25
913 A357 90fr multi 1.90 1.90

Values are for stamps with surrounding selvage.

Polynesian Women — A358

Woman: 60fr, At water's edge. 90fr, With oil lamp.

2006, Mar. 8 **Litho.** ***Perf. 13¼x13***

914-915 A358 Set of 2 3.75 3.25

Maupiti — A359

2006, Apr. 26 **Engr.** ***Perf. 13x13¼***

916 A359 500fr multi 11.00 11.00

History of the Marquesas (Washington) Islands — A360

Designs: 60fr, Native man and woman. 130fr, Ships.

2006, May 27 **Litho.** ***Perf. 13¼x13***

917-918 A360 Set of 2 4.00 4.00
918a Souvenir sheet, #917-918 4.00 4.00

Diners and Musicians — A361

2006, June 6 ***Perf. 13***

919 A361 300fr multi 6.50 6.50

Polynesian Ground Dove A362

Tuamotu Sandpiper A363

2006, June 21 ***Perf. 13x13¼***

920 A362 250fr multi 5.25 5.25
921 A363 250fr multi 5.25 5.25

Heiva — A364

Designs: 90fr, Canoe race. 130fr, Stone lifting. 190fr, Dancer.

2006, July 19 ***Perf. 13¼x13***

922-924 A364 Set of 3 8.75 8.75

Frangipani Flowers A365

2006, Aug. 23 **Litho.** ***Perf. 13x13½***

925 A365 90fr multi 2.25 1.90

No. 925 is impregnated with frangipani scent.

A366

World Tourism Day A367

Designs: 40fr, Ruins. No. 927, 90fr, Waterfall, woman and child. 130fr, Clothing at open-air market.

No. 929: a, Dancers with yellow skirts. b, Surfer. c, House and palm tree. d, Pearls. e, Fish and coral. f, Islanders in outrigger canoes.

No. 930: a, Woman in hammock. b, Stilt houses. c, Tower and boats. d, Horses and riders. e, Aerial view of island. f, Diver and sting ray.

2006, Sept. 22 ***Perf. 13¼x13***

926-928 A366 Set of 3 6.00 6.00

Booklet Stamps

Perf. 13x13¼

929 Booklet pane of 6 15.00 —
a.-f. A367 90fr Any single 2.00 2.00
930 Booklet pane of 6 15.00 —
a.-f. A367 90fr Any single 2.00 2.00
Complete booklet, #929-930 30.00

Complete booklet sold for 1200fr.

Paintings A368

Designs: 60fr, Javelin Throwing, by Monique Garnier Bissol. 90fr, Market Life, by Albert Luzuy, horiz. 100fr, Island Quay, by Gilbert Chaussoy, horiz. 190fr, Vahine, by Olivier Louzé.

2006, Oct. 25 ***Perf. 13***

931-934 A368 Set of 4 9.50 9.50

Engravings by Paul Gauguin (1848-1903) — A369

Engravings depicting: 60fr, Women. 130fr, Cow and man carrying items on stick.

2006, Nov. 8 **Engr.** ***Perf. 13¼***

935-936 A369 Set of 2 4.25 4.25

Children's Art A370

2006, Dec. 13 **Litho.** ***Perf. 13x13¼***

937 A370 90fr multi 2.00 2.00

Beach Gear — A371

Designs: 60fr, Flip-flops. 90fr, Surfboards.

Serpentine Die Cut 11x11¼

2007 **Photo.** **Self-Adhesive**

938 A371 60fr multicolored 1.25 1.25
a. Blue tips of die cutting along left side 1.25 1.25
939 A371 90fr multicolored 2.00 2.00
a. Light blue tips of die cutting along bottom 2.00 2.00

Issued: Nos. 938a, 939a, 1/24; Nos. 938-939, Feb. Nos. 938a and 939a are from the original printing, and are from sheets having adjacent stamps and die cutting that does not extend through the backing paper. Nos. 938-939, which were distributed to the philatelic trade, are from sheets with selvage around each stamp, and with rouletting that extends through the backing paper that allows the stamps to be removed from the sheet more easily.

New Year 2007 (Year of the Pig) A372

2007, Feb. 19 **Litho.** ***Perf. 13x13¼***

940 A372 130fr multi 3.50 3.50

Portions of the design were applied by a thermographic process producing a shiny, raised effect.

Painting of Polynesian Woman by Mathius — A373

Photograph of Polynesian Woman by John Stember — A374

2007, Mar. 8 **Litho.** ***Perf. 13¼x13***

941 A373 60fr multi 1.50 1.40

Perf. 13x13¼

942 A374 90fr multi 2.25 2.00

Audit Office, Bicent. A375

2007, Mar. 17 **Engr.** ***Perf. 13¼x13***

943 A375 90fr multi 2.75 2.00

Shells — A376

Designs: 10fr, Lambis crocata pilsbryi. 60fr, Cypraea thomasi. 90fr, Cyrtulus serotinus. 130fr, Chicoreus laqueatus.

2007, Apr. 25 **Litho.**

944-947 A376 Set of 4 6.75 6.75
947a Souvenir sheet, #944-947 6.75 6.75

Coconut
A377

2007, May 23 ***Perf. 13x13¼***
948 A377 90fr multi 2.25 2.00

No. 948 is impregnated with a coconut scent.

Ships — A378

Designs: No. 949, 250fr, Gunboat Zélée. No. 950, 250fr, Passenger and cargo liner Sagittaire.

2007, June 22 ***Perf. 13***
949-950 A378 Set of 2 12.00 11.50

Heiva
Festival — A379

Various women dancers: 65fr, 100fr, 140fr.

2007, July 4 ***Perf. 13¼x13***
951-953 A379 Set of 3 7.50 7.50

Arrival of Kon-Tiki Expedition in Polynesia, 60th Anniv. — A380

Litho. & Silk-screened
2007, Aug. 7 ***Perf. 13***
954 A380 300fr multi 7.00 7.00

Arrival of Ship at Papeete Dock — A381

2007, Aug. 29 **Litho.** ***Perf. 13***
955 A381 190fr multi 4.50 4.50

Old and Modern Photos of Papeete — A382

Designs: 65fr, Rue Gauguin, 2007. 100fr, Rue de la Petite-Pologne (now Rue Gauguin), 1907.

2007, Sept. 26
956-957 A382 Set of 2 4.75 4.00

Old Franc and Centime Notes — A383

Designs: 65fr, 1919 2-franc Chamber of Commerce note. 140fr, 1942 2-franc note. 500fr, 1943 50-centime note.

2007, Oct. 26 **Engr.** ***Perf. 13***
958-960 A383 Set of 3 20.00 17.00

Flowers
A384

Designs: 100fr, Hibiscus. 140fr, Bird-of-paradise (Oiseaux de paradis).

Litho. & Silk-screened
2007, Nov. 8 ***Perf. 13x13¼***
961-962 A384 Set of 2 7.50 7.50

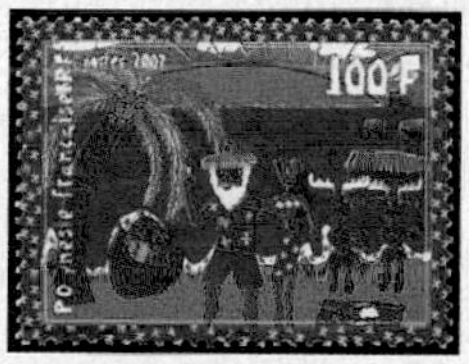

Christmas
A385

2007, Dec. 6 **Litho.** ***Perf. 13x13¼***
963 A385 100fr multi 2.50 2.50

Marine Life
A386

Designs: 10fr, Himantura fai. 20fr, Tursiops truncatus. 40fr, Megaptera novaeangliae. 65fr, Negaprion acutidens.

2008, Jan. 10
964-967 A386 Set of 4 4.00 4.00

New Year 2008 (Year of the Rat) — A387

2008, Feb. 7 **Photo.** ***Perf. 13¼x13***
968 A387 140fr multi 3.75 3.75

Paintings of Women by Bénilde Menghini — A388

Designs: 65fr, Woman picking mangos. 100fr, Women scaling fish.

2008, Mar. 7 **Litho.**
969-970 A388 Set of 2 4.25 4.25

Paintings by Polynesian Artists A389

Unnamed paintings depicting: No. 971, 100fr, Boat and reef, by Torea Chan. No. 972, 100fr, Polynesian man, by Raymond Vigor. No. 973, 100fr, Fruit bowl, by Teurarea Prokop, horiz.

2008, Apr. 10 ***Perf. 13x13¼, 13¼x13***
971-973 A389 Set of 3 8.00 8.00

Pouvanaa a Oopa (1895-1977), Politician — A390

2008, May 20 **Litho.** ***Perf. 13***
974 A390 500fr multi 13.00 13.00

Island Touring Vehicles — A391

Designs: 65fr, Motor scooter. 100fr, Bus, horiz.

Serpentine Die Cut 11
2008, June 12 **Photo.**
Self-Adhesive
975-976 A391 Set of 2 4.50 4.50

Heiva Festival A392

Designs: 65fr, Woman with floral headdress. 140fr, Tattooed man. 190fr, Girl dancing.

2008, July 16 **Litho.** ***Perf. 13***
977-979 A392 Set of 3 11.00 11.00

Sports — A393

Designs: No. 980, 140fr, Table tennis. No. 981, 140fr, Weight lifting.

2008, Aug. 8 **Litho.** ***Perf. 13¼x13***
980-981 A393 Set of 2 7.00 7.00

End of Tahiti Nui Expedition, 50th Anniv. — A394

2008, Aug. 29 **Litho.** ***Perf. 13***
982 A394 190fr multi 4.50 4.50

Eric de Bisschop (1890-1958), expedition leader.

Polynesian Scenes A395

No. 983: a, Woman crouching. b, Woman under shelter. c, Boat in bay near cliffs. d, Orange flowers. e, Red hibiscus flower. f, Island. g, Woman with headdress. h, White flower. i, Woman with headdress and flower garland. j, Pink flower. k, Islands. l, Bay near mountains.

Serpentine Die Cut 11¼x11
2008, Sept. 8 **Self-Adhesive**
983 Booklet pane of 12 32.50
a.-d. A395 65fr Any single 1.50 1.50
e.-h. A395 100fr Any single 2.40 2.40
i.-l. A395 140fr Any single 3.25 3.25

Gardenia Taitensis in Bottle of Monoi Oil — A396

2008, Sept. 17 ***Perf. 13¼x13***
984 A396 100fr multi 2.40 2.40

No. 984 is impregnated with a gardenia scent.

Aviation Anniversaries — A397

Designs: No. 985, 250fr, Air service between France and French Polynesia, 50th anniv. No. 986, 250fr, Air Tahiti Nui, 10th anniv.

2008, Oct. 15 Litho. *Perf. 13*
985-986 A397 Set of 2 11.00 11.00

French Polynesia Postage Stamps, 50th Anniv. — A398

Designs: 65fr, French Polynesia #185. 100fr, Vignette of French Polynesia #C24. 140fr, French Polynesia #J29.

2008, Nov. 6 Engr. *Perf. 13*
987-989 A398 Set of 3 6.75 6.75
989a Sheet of 3, #987-989 6.75 6.75

Boater and Dancer A399

2008, Dec. 5 Litho. *Perf. 13x13¼*
990 A399 100fr multi 2.25 2.25

Winning design in children's stamp design contest.

Hypolimnas Bolina A400

Litho. & Silk-screened
2009, Jan. 16 *Perf. 13*
991 A400 70fr multi 1.50 1.50

Fire Fighters — A401

Designs: 70fr, Fireman on aerial ladder. 140fr, Fireboat.

2009, Feb. 13 Litho. *Perf. 13*
992-993 A401 Set of 2 4.50 4.50

Paintings of Polynesian Women — A402

Designs: 70fr, Woman, by Myriam Stroken. 100fr, Woman with Guitar, by Stanley Haumani.

2009, Mar. 30 Litho. *Perf. 13¼x13*
994-995 A402 Set of 2 4.00 4.00

Jacques Brel (1929-78), Singer — A403

Colors: 70fr, Blue. 100fr, Brown.

2009, Apr. 8 Engr.
996-997 A403 Set of 2 4.25 4.25

Pareo Fabric A404

Pareo in: (70fr), Blue. (100fr), Red. (140fr), Green.

Serpentine Die Cut 11
2009, May 29 Litho.
Self-Adhesive
998-1000 A404 Set of 3 7.25 7.25

Heiva Celebrations of the Past — A405

Various Heiva dancers: 70fr, 100fr, 140fr. 100fr and 140fr are horiz.

Perf. 13¼x13, 13x13¼
2009, June 19
1001-1003 A405 Set of 3 7.50 7.50

First Man on the Moon, 40th Anniv. A406

2009, July 20 *Perf. 13¼*
1004 A406 140fr multi 3.50 3.50

Water Activities A407

Designs: 70fr, Surfing. 100fr, Canoeing (pirogue).

Serpentine Die Cut 11x11¼
2009, Aug. 7 Litho. Self-Adhesive
1005-1006 A407 Set of 2 4.00 4.00

Passion Fruit A408

2009, Aug. 14 *Perf. 13x13¼*
1007 A408 100fr multi 2.40 2.40

No. 1007 has a scratch-and-sniff coating on the fruit having a passion fruit scent.

Underwater Scenes — A409

Designs: 70fr, Scuba divers. 100fr, Turtles, horiz. 140fr, Whale, horiz.

Litho. & Silk-screened
Perf. 13¼x13, 13x13¼
2009, Sept. 11
1008-1010 A409 Set of 3 7.75 7.75
1010a Sheet of 3, #1008-1010 7.75 7.75

Fish — A410

No. 1011: a, Chaetodon lunula. b, Chaetodon trichrous. c, Chaetodon ornatissimus. d, Chaetodon pelewensis. e, Pterois antennata. f, Myripristis berndti. g, Priacanthus hamrur. h, Epinephelus polyphekadion. i, Thalassoma lutescens. j, Thalassoma hardwicke. k, Pygoplites diacanthus. l, Coris gaimard.

Serpentine Die Cut 11¼x11
2009, Sept. 11 Self-Adhesive
1011 Booklet pane of 12 31.00
a.-d. A410 70fr Any single 1.75 1.75
e.-h. A410 100fr Any single 2.50 2.50
i.-l. A410 140fr Any single 3.50 3.50

Paintings by Paul Gauguin (1848-1903) — A411

Designs: No. 1012, 250fr, Still Life with a Maori Statuette. No. 1013, 250fr, Still Life with Apples, horiz.

2009, Oct. 16 Litho. *Perf. 13*
1012-1013 A411 Set of 2 12.50 12.50

French Polynesia No. 180 — A412

2009, Nov. 5 Engr.
1014 A412 500fr multi 12.50 12.50

Legend of the Coconut Tree — A413

2009, Dec. 11 Litho. *Perf. 13¼x13*
1015 A413 190fr multi 4.75 4.75

Papeete Post Office, 150th Anniv. — A414

2010, Jan. 20
1016 A414 70fr multi 1.60 1.60

New Year 2010 (Year of the Tiger) A415

Litho. & Silk-screened
2010, Feb. 15 *Perf. 13x13¼*
1017 A415 140fr multi 3.25 3.25

Woman and Child — A416

Woman and child: 70fr, Facing forward. 100fr, Facing right.

2010, Mar. 8 Litho. *Perf. 13¼x13*
1018-1019 A416 Set of 2 4.00 4.00

Tattoos A417

Tattooed: No. 1020, 250fr, Woman (green background). No. 1021, 250fr, Man (dark red background).

2010, Apr. 6
1020-1021 A417 Set of 2 11.50 11.50

Tiare Apetahi Flower A418

Litho. & Silk-screened
2010, Apr. 20 ***Perf. 13x13¼***
1022 A418 70fr multi 1.50 1.50

Captain Frederick William Beechey (1796-1856), Explorer — A419

2010, May 5 **Litho.**
1023 A419 140fr multi 3.00 3.00

Corals A420

Various corals: 70fr, 100fr, 140fr. 140fr is vert.

Litho. & Silk-screened
2010, June 4 ***Perf. 13x13¼, 13¼x13***
1024-1026 A420 Set of 3 6.50 6.50
1026a Sheet of 3, #1024-1026 6.50 6.50

Heiva Festival — A421

Various festival participants: 100fr, 140fr, 190fr.

2010, July 20 **Litho.** ***Perf. 13¼x13***
1027-1029 A421 Set of 3 9.50 9.50

Mango A422

2010, Aug. 8 ***Perf. 13x13¼***
1030 A422 100fr multi 2.25 2.25

No. 1030 has a scratch-and-sniff coating on the fruit having a mango scent.

Phosphate Mining at Makatea, Cent. A423

Designs: 70fr, Office. 100fr, Train. 140fr, Mining operations.

2010, Aug. 17 **Litho.** ***Perf. 13x13¼***
1031-1033 A423 Set of 3 6.75 6.75

Honotua Fiber Optic Submarine Cable Project — A424

Serpentine Die Cut 11
2010, Sept. 15 **Photo.**
Self-Adhesive
1034 A424 70fr multi 1.75 1.75

Birds A425

No. 1035: a, Lori de Kuhl (Kuhl's lorikeet). b, Bécasseau Sanderling (Sanderling). c, Carpophade de la Société (Imperial pigeon). d, Tangara à dos rouge (Crimson-backed tanager). e, Ptilope de Hutton (Rapa fruit dove). f, Sterne huppée (Great crested tern). g, Gygis blanche (White tern). h, Lori Nonnette (Blue lorikeet). i, Chevalier errant (Wandering tattler). j, Martin chasseur des Gambier (Tuamotu kingfisher). k, Fou brun (Brown booby). l, Pluvier fauve (Pacific golden plover).

Litho. & Silk-screened
2010, Sept. 15 **Self-Adhesive**
1035 Booklet pane of 12 28.00
a.-l. A425 100fr Any single 2.25 2.25

Tahiti Faa'a International Airport, 50th Anniv. — A426

2010, Oct. 14 **Litho.** ***Perf. 13***
1036 A426 500fr multi 11.50 11.50

Sphinx Moth A427

2010, Oct. 14 ***Perf. 13x13½***
1037 A427 5fr multi .25 .25

1948 Air Post Stamps of French Oceania — A428

Designs: 70fr, #C17. 100fr, #C18. 140fr, #C19.

2010, Nov. 4 **Engr.** ***Perf. 13***
1038-1040 A428 Set of 3 7.25 7.25

Legend of Moua Puta A429

2010, Dec. 9 **Litho.** ***Perf. 13x13¼***
1041 A429 70fr multi 1.60 1.60

Crabs A430

Designs: 20fr, Atergatopsis cf. germanini. 40fr, Zosimus aeneus. 70fr, Carpilius convexus. 100fr, Carpilius maculatus.

2011, Jan. 18
1042-1045 A430 Set of 4 5.25 5.25
1045a Souvenir sheet of 4, #1042-1045 5.25 5.25

New Year 2011 (Year of the Rabbit) — A431

Litho. & Silk-screened
2011, Feb. 3 ***Perf. 13¼x13***
1046 A431 140fr multi 3.25 3.25

Images of Polynesia — A432

No. 1047: a, Canoe race. b, Outrigger canoe. c, Aerial view of islands. d, Fish on reef. e, Pearls. f, Flowers.

Serpentine Die Cut 11¼
2011, Mar. 8 **Litho.**
Self-Adhesive
1047 Booklet pane of 6 14.50
a.-f. A432 100fr Any single 2.40 2.40

Intl. Women's Year — A433

Designs: 70fr, Two women weaving. 100fr, Woman standing.

2011, Mar. 8 ***Perf. 13¼x13***
1048-1049 A433 Set of 2 4.00 4.00

Pearl of Tahiti, 50th Anniv. — A434

2011, Apr. 7 **Litho.**
1050 A434 140fr multi 3.50 3.50

Portions of the design were applied by a thermographic process producing a shiny, raised effect.

Transportation of the Past — A435

Designs: 70fr, Truck, 1939. 100fr, Horse-drawn carriages, 1900.

2011, May 17 **Litho.** ***Perf. 13***
1051-1052 A435 Set of 2 4.25 4.25

Fishing — A436

Cartoons: 100fr, Fisherman in boat catching swordfish. 140fr, Spear fisherman and speared fish.

Serpentine Die Cut 11
2011, June 22 **Litho.**
Self-Adhesive
1053-1054 A436 Set of 2 5.75 5.75

Carved Items — A437

Designs: 70fr, Coral pestle. 140fr, Basalt tiki. 190fr, Oceania rosewood container with lid, horiz.

2011, July 19 ***Perf. 13¼x13, 13x13¼***
1055-1057 A437 Set of 3 9.75 9.75

Orchid — A438

2011, Aug. 17 **Litho.** ***Perf. 13¼x13***
1058 A438 140fr multi 3.25 3.25

No. 1058 is impregnated with an orchid scent.

Islands
A439

Photographs of: 10fr, Rangiroa. 100fr, Ua Pou. 140fr, Bora Bora.

2011, Sept. 27 ***Perf. 13x13¼***
1059-1061 A439 Set of 3 5.75 5.75

Marine Birds and Sea Life
A440

No. 1062: a, Birds. b, Bird and whale. c, Dolphin and fish. d, Red striped fish, black and white striped angelfish. e, Blue and yellow striped fish. f, Lionfish, yellow fish. g, Ray. h, Shark. i, Sea turtle, fish, coral. j, Anemonefish, sea anemones. k, Crab. l, Moray eel, coral.

Serpentine Die Cut 11¼x11
2011, Sept. 27 **Self-Adhesive**
1062 Booklet pane of 12 29.00
a.-l. A440 100fr Any single 2.40 2.40

Filming of *Mutiny on the Bounty* in Tahiti, 50th Anniv. — A441

2011, Oct. 19 ***Perf. 13***
1063 A441 500fr multi 11.50 11.50

Fort Collet, Marquesas Islands — A442

No. 1064 — Engraving of Fort from 1854: a, Buildings without flags. b, Buildings with flags.

2011, Nov. 3 **Engr.** ***Perf. 13***
1064 A442 250fr Horiz. pair, #a-b 11.50 11.50

Ta'aroa, Polynesian God of Creation — A443

2011, Dec. 15 **Litho.** ***Perf. 13¼x13***
1065 A443 70fr multi 1.60 1.60

New Yeart 2012 (Year of the Dragon)
A444

Litho & Silk-screened
2012, Jan. 23 ***Perf. 13***
1066 A444 140fr multi 3.25 3.25

Papeete Maritime Station — A445

Ships in Papeete Harbor — A446

2012, Jan. 27 **Litho.**
1067 A445 70fr multi 1.60 1.60
1068 A446 100fr multi 2.25 2.25

Port of Papeete Authority, 50th anniv.

Food Truck Vendors
A447

Serpentine Die Cut 11
2012, Feb. 22
Self-Adhesive
1069 A447 100fr multi 2.25 2.25

Office of Posts and Telecommunications Emblem Type of 2003
Booklet Stamps
Serpentine Die Cut 6¾ Vert.
2012, Feb. 8 **Self-Adhesive**

1070	A308a	5fr red violet	.25	.25
c.		Booklet pane of 10 #1070	1.25	
1070A	A308a	(75fr) blue, type II	1.75	1.75
d.		Booklet pane of 10 #1070A	17.50	
1070B	A308a	(100fr) rose	2.25	2.25
e.		Booklet pane of 10 #1070B	22.50	
		Nos. 1070-1070B (3)	4.25	4.25

Intl. Women's Day — A448

Designs: 70fr, Woman. 100fr, Woman and child.

2012, Mar. 8 ***Perf. 13¼x13***
1071-1072 A448 Set of 2 3.75 3.75

Flowers — A449

No. 1073: a, Gingembre à abeilles. b, Reine de Malaisie. c, Opuhi alpinia rose. d, Zedoaire. e, Safran indien. f, Opuhi alpinia orchidée.

2012, Mar. 8 ***Serpentine Die Cut 11***
Self-Adhesive
1073 Booklet pane of 6 13.50
a.-f. A449 100fr Any single 2.25 2.25

Nudibranchs — A450

Designs: 75fr, Glossodoris rufomarginata. 100fr, Elysia ornata. 190fr, Cyerce nigricans.

Litho. & Silk-screened
2012, Apr. 26 ***Perf. 13x13¼***
1074-1076 A450 Set of 3 8.00 8.00
1076b Souvenir sheet of 3, #1074-1076 8.00 8.00

Tiurai (1842-1918), Healer — A451

2012, June 18 **Litho.** ***Perf. 13¼x13***
1077 A451 75fr multi 1.60 1.60

Tamanu Orange Picking Contest — A452

2012, June 27
1078 A452 75fr multi 1.60 1.60

Heiva Dancer
A453

2012, July 18 ***Perf. 13x13¼***
1079 A453 100fr multi 2.10 2.10

Grapefruits
A454

2012, Aug. 22
1080 A454 140fr multi 3.00 3.00

No. 1080 is impregnated with a grapefruit scent.

Airports
A455

Airport at: 5fr, Bora Bora. 75fr, Tikehau. 100fr, Ua Pou.

2012, Sept. 27
1081-1083 A455 Set of 3 4.00 4.00

Landscapes — A456

No. 1084: a, Moorea. b, Mangareva. c, Rurutu. d, Kauehi. e, Hiva Oa. f, Rapa.

Serpentine Die Cut 11
2012, Sept. 27
Self-Adhesive
1084 Booklet pane of 6 13.50
a.-f. A456 100fr Any single 2.25 2.25

Turtles in Botanical Gardens, Papeari
A457

Horses and Riders, Marquesas Islands
A458

2012, Oct. 17 ***Perf. 13x13¼***
1085 A457 75fr multi 1.60 1.60
1086 A458 100fr multi 2.25 2.25

First Stamps of French Oceania, 120th Anniv. — A459

No. 1087: a, "Commerce," horse-drawn carriage, people near shore. b, People on rowboat, "Navigation."

2012, Nov. 8 **Engr.** ***Perf. 13xx13¼***
1087 Horiz. pair, #a-b, + central label 11.00 11.00
a.-b. A459 250fr Either single 5.50 5.50

Season of Matari'i i Ni'a — A460

2012, Nov. 20 **Litho.** ***Perf. 13***
1088 A460 75fr multi 1.75 1.75

Matavai Bay
A461

2012, Dec. 13 **Engr.**
1089 A461 500fr blk & gray blue 11.00 11.00

Scenes of Everyday Life
A462

Designs: 75fr, Street scene outside of Quinn's Bar, Papeete. 100fr, Street musicians.

2013, Jan. 2 **Litho.** ***Perf. 13x13¼***
1090-1091 A462 Set of 2 4.00 4.00

New Year 2013 (Year of the Snake)
A463

Litho. & Silk-screened
2013, Feb. 11 ***Perf. 13***
1092 A463 140fr multi 3.00 3.00

Queen Pomare IV (1813-77)
A464

Serpentine Die Cut 11
2013, Feb. 28 **Photo.**
Self-Adhesive
1093 A464 75fr multi 1.75 1.75

Legend of Tahiri Vahine — A465

Designs: 75fr, Tahiri Vahine (woman with fan). 100fr, Tahiri Vahine with other women.

2013, Mar. 8 **Litho.** ***Perf. 13¼x13***
1094-1095 A465 Set of 2 4.00 4.00

Intl. Women's Day.

Flora and Fauna — A466

Designs: 20fr, Lemon (citron). 40fr, Lizard (lézard), horiz. 190fr, Chestnut-breasted mannikin (capuchin).

Litho. & Silk-screened
2013, Apr. 26 ***Perf. 13¼x13, 13x13¼***
1096-1098 A466 Set of 3 5.50 5.50
1098a Souvneir sheet of 3, #1096-1098 5.50 5.50

Jacques Brel (1929-78), Singer — A467

2013, May 10 **Engr.** ***Perf. 13***
1099 A467 500fr multi 11.50 11.50

Fruits
A468

No. 110: a, Pineapples. b, Mangos. c, Bananas. d, Coconuts. e, Papayas. f, Watermelon.

Litho. & Silk-screened
2013, May 10 ***Serpentine Die Cut 11***
Self-Adhesive
1100 Booklet pane of 6 13.50
a.-f. A468 100fr Any single 2.25 2.25

Marine Life — A469

Designs: 5fr, Starfish. 10fr, Giant clam. 75fr, Sea anemone and clown fish. 100fr, Sea turtle.

Litho. & Silk-screened
2013, June 7 ***Perf. 13x13¼***
1101-1104 A469 Set of 4 4.25 4.25
1104a Souvenir sheet of 4, #1101-1104 4.25 4.25

Carousel at Heiva Fairground — A470

2013, July 16 **Litho.** ***Perf. 13***
1105 A470 100fr multi 2.25 2.25

Jasmine Flowers
A471

2013, Aug. 22 **Litho.** ***Perf. 13x13¼***
1106 A471 100fr multi 2.25 2.25

No. 1106 is impregnated with a jasmine scent.

FIFA Beach Soccer World Cup Tournament, Tahiti — A472

2013, Sept. 18 **Litho.** ***Perf. 13¼x13***
1107 A472 140fr multi 3.25 3.25

A473 A474

A475 A476

Women
A477 A478

Serpentine Die Cut 11
2013, Sept. 18 **Litho.**
Self-Adhesive

1108	Booklet pane of 6, #1108a-1108f	13.50	
a.	A473 100fr multi	2.25	2.25
b.	A474 100fr multi	2.25	2.25
c.	A475 100fr multi	2.25	2.25
d.	A476 100fr multi	2.25	2.25
e.	A477 100fr multi	2.25	2.25
f.	A478 100fr multi	2.25	2.25
g.	A473 100fr Dated "2015"	1.75	1.75
h.	A474 100fr Dated "2015"	1.75	1.75
i.	A475 100fr Dated "2015"	1.75	1.75
j.	A476 100fr Dated "2015"	1.75	1.75
k.	A477 100fr Dated "2015"	1.75	1.75
l.	A478 100fr Dated "2015"	1.75	1.75
m.	Booklet pane of 6, #1180g-1108l	10.50	

Issued: Nos. 1108g-1108m, 11/5/15.

Canoes — A479

Various canoes: 75fr, 100fr.

2013, Oct. 17 **Litho.** ***Perf. 13***
1109-1110 A479 Set of 2 4.00 4.00

Stock Certificates — A480

Stock certificate of: 250fr, Comptoirs Français d'Océanie. 300fr, Compagnie Française de Tahiti.

2013, Nov. 6 **Engr.** ***Perf. 13***
1111-1112 A480 Set of 2 12.50 12.50

Old Automobiles — A481

Designs: 75fr, 1915 Ford Model T. 100fr, 1950 Citroen Traction Avant.

2013, Dec. 12 **Litho.** ***Perf. 13***
1113-1114 A481 Set of 2 4.00 4.00

New Banknotes — A482

Designs: 10fr, 500-franc banknote. 20fr, 1000-franc banknote. 75fr, 5000-franc banknote. 100fr, 10,000-franc banknote.

Litho. & Silk-Screened
2014, Jan. 20 ***Perf. 13***
1115-1118 A482 Set of 4 4.75 4.75
1118a Souvenir sheet of 4, #1115-1118 4.75 4.75

Postal Check Center, 50th Anniv.
A483

2014, Jan. 27 **Litho.** ***Perf. 13x13¼***
1119 A483 75fr multi 1.75 1.75

New Year 2014 (Year of the Horse)
A484

Litho. & Silk-Screened
2014, Jan. 31 ***Perf. 13***
1120 A484 140fr multi 3.25 3.25

Intl. Year of Family Farming — A485

Designs: 75fr, Woman watering flower garden. 100fr, Farmers, fruits and vegetables.

2014, Feb. 21 Litho. *Perf. 13*
1121-1122 A485 Set of 2 4.00 4.00

Intl. Women's Day A486

Design: 75fr, Head of woman with floral headdress. 100fr, Woman, vert.

Perf. 13x13¼, 13¼x13
2014, Mar. 7 Litho.
1123-1124 A486 Set of 2 4.00 4.00

Wild Boars A487

Serpentine Die Cut 11
2014, Apr. 30 Photo.
Self-Adhesive
1125 A487 100fr multi 2.40 2.40

A488

A489

A490

A491

A492

A493

Serpentine Die Cut 11
2014, May 16 Litho.
Self-Adhesive
1126 Booklet pane of 6 13.50
a. A488 100fr multi 2.25 2.25
b. A489 100fr multi 2.25 2.25
c. A490 100fr multi 2.25 2.25
d. A491 100fr multi 2.25 2.25
e. A492 100fr multi 2.25 2.25
f. A493 100fr multi 2.25 2.25

Graffiti art by Enos.

Sharks — A494

Designs: 10fr, Carcharhinus melanopterus. 40fr, Sphyrna mokarran. 75fr, Carcharhinus albimarginatus. 190fr, Galeocerdo cuvier.

Litho. & Silk-Screened
2014, June 10 *Perf. 13*
1127-1130 A494 Set of 4 7.25 7.25
1130a Souvenir sheet of 4, #1127-1130 7.25 7.25

Autonomy, 30th Anniv. — A495

2014, June 27 Litho. *Perf. 13¼x13*
1131 A495 75fr multi 1.75 1.75

Woman in Heiva Costume — A496

2014, July 3 Litho. *Perf. 13¼x13*
1132 A496 75fr multi 1.75 1.75

Jar of Honey, Honeybee and Honeycomb A497

2014, Aug. 28 Litho. *Perf. 13x13¼*
1133 A497 100fr multi 2.25 2.25

No. 1133 is impregnated with a honey scent.

Bombardment of Papeete, Cent. — A498

Litho. & Engr.
2014, Sept. 30 *Perf. 13*
1134 A498 300fr multi 6.50 6.50

World War I, cent.

Tiaré Flower A499

2014, Nov. 6 Litho. *Perf. 13x13¼*
1135 A499 2fr multi .25 .25

Sunset — A500

2014, Nov. 6 Litho. *Perf. 13¼x13*
1136 A500 77fr multi 1.60 1.60

Issuance of French Polynesia No. C30, 50th Anniv. A501

2014, Nov. 6 Litho. *Perf. 13*
1137 A501 500fr multi 10.50 10.50

Office of Posts and Telecommunications Emblem — A502

Serpentine Die Cut 6¾ Vert.
2014, Nov. 6 Litho.
Booklet Stamps
Self-Adhesive
1138 A502 (75fr) deep blue 1.60 1.60
a. Booklet pane of 10 16.00
1139 A502 (100fr) red 2.10 2.10
a. Booklet pane of 10 2.10

Legend of Pipiri Ma — A503

2014, Dec. 12 Litho. *Perf. 13*
1140 A503 75fr multi 1.50 1.50

Occupations A504

Designs: 10fr, Underwater spear fisherman. 20fr, Sculptor. 75fr, Masseuse, horiz. 100fr, Seamstress, horiz.

2015, Jan. 29 Litho. *Perf. 13¼x13*
1141 A504 10fr multi .25 .25
1142 A504 20fr multi .40 .40

Perf. 13x13¼
1143 A504 75fr multi 1.50 1.50
1144 A504 100fr multi 1.90 1.90
Nos. 1141-1144 (4) 4.05 4.05

New Year 2015 (Year of the Goat) A505

Litho. & Silk-Screened
2015, Feb. 19 *Perf. 13*
1145 A505 140fr multi 2.60 2.60

Mama Dolphin at Sea Post Office A506

2015, Mar. 26 Litho. *Perf. 13x13¼*
1146 A506 75fr multi 1.40 1.40

Translation of Bible Into Tahitian by Henry Nott, 180th Anniv. — A507

Discovery of King George Islands by John Byron, 250th Anniv. — A508

Litho. & Engr.
2015, May 13 *Perf. 13*
1147 A507 140fr multi 2.60 2.60
Litho.
1148 A508 190fr multi 3.50 3.50
a. Souvenir sheet of 2, #1147-1148 6.25 6.25

Coffee A509

2015, July 1 Litho. *Perf. 13x13¼*
1149 A509 100fr multi 1.90 1.90

No. 1149 is impregnated with a coffee scent.

Children's Art — A510

2015, Aug. 1 Litho. *Perf. 13¼*
1150 A510 1fr multi .25 .25

Orator
A511

2015, Aug. 5 Litho. *Perf. 13x13¼*

1151 A511 80fr multi 1.50 1.50

Tropical Architecture A512

Designs: 80fr, Chez Vat Restaurant and Chez Alin Store. 100fr, Houses.

2015, Aug. 14 Litho. *Perf. 13x13¼*

1152-1153 A512 Set of 2 3.50 3.50

First Flight Between Tahiti and Santiago, Chile, 50th Anniv. A513

2015, Aug. 31 Litho. *Perf. 13x13¼*

1154 A513 80fr multi 1.50 1.50

1915 Postcard Depicting Papeete — A514

2015, Sept. 29 Litho. *Perf. 13¼x13*

1155 A514 300fr multi 5.75 5.75

Issuance of Tahiti No. B2, Cent. A515

Litho. & Engr.

2015, Nov. 5 *Perf. 13¼x13*

1156 A515 500fr multi 9.00 9.00
a. Souvenir sheet of 1 9.00 9.00

Sponges — A516

No. 1157: a, Clathrina n. sp. b, Dysidea n. sp. c, Haliclona n. sp. d, Ernstia n. sp. e, Stylissa flabelliformis. f, Darwinella n. sp.

Serpentine Die Cut 11

2015, Nov. 5 Litho.

Self-Adhesive

1157 Booklet pane of 6 10.50
a.-f. A516 100fr Any single 1.75 1.75

SEMI-POSTAL STAMPS

Nos. 55 and 26 Surcharged in Red

1915 Unwmk. *Perf. 14x13½*

B1	A1 10c + 5c red	32.50	32.50
a.	"e" instead of "c"	87.50	87.50
b.	Inverted surcharge	225.00	225.00
c.	Double surcharge	525.00	525.00
B2	A2 10c + 5c rose & org	12.50	12.50
a.	"e" instead of "c"	65.00	65.00
b.	"c" inverted	65.00	65.00
c.	Inverted surcharge	300.00	300.00
d.	As "a," inverted surcharge	400.00	
e.	As "b," inverted surcharge	400.00	

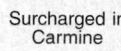

Surcharged in Carmine

B3	A2 10c + 5c rose & org	5.50	5.50
a.	"e" instead of "c"	45.00	45.00
b.	Inverted surcharge	200.00	200.00
c.	Double surcharge	200.00	200.00
d.	As "a," inverted surcharge	325.00	

Surcharged in Carmine

1916

B4 A2 10c + 5c rose & org 5.50 5.50

Curie Issue

Common Design Type

1938 Engr. *Perf. 13*

B5 CD80 1.75fr + 50c brt ultra 20.00 20.00

French Revolution Issue

Common Design Type

1939 Photo.

Name and Value Typo. in Black

B6	CD83	45c + 25c grn	17.50	17.50
B7	CD83	70c + 30c brn	17.50	17.50
B8	CD83	90c + 35c red org	17.50	17.50
B9	CD83	1.25fr + 1fr rose pink	17.50	17.50
B10	CD83	2.25fr + 2fr blue	17.50	17.50
		Nos. B6-B10 (5)	87.50	87.50
		Set, never hinged	145.00	

Catalogue values for unused stamps in this section, from this point to the end of the section, are for Never Hinged items.

Common Design Type and

Marine Officer — SP1

"L'Astrolabe" — SP2

1941 Photo. *Perf. 13½*

B11	SP1	1fr + 1fr red	3.50
B12	CD86	1.50fr + 3fr maroon	3.50
B12A	SP2	2.50fr + 1fr blue	3.50
		Nos. B11-B12A (3)	10.50

Nos. B11-B12A were issued by the Vichy government in France, and were not placed on sale in French Polynesia.

Nos. 125A-125B Srchd. in Black or Red

1944 Engr. *Perf. 12½x12*

B12B 50c + 1.50fr on 2.50fr deep blue (R) 1.75
B12C + 2.50fr on 1fr green 1.75

Colonial Development Fund.

Nos. B12B-B12C were issued by the Vichy government in France, but were not placed on sale in French Polynesia.

Red Cross Issue

Common Design Type

1944 Photo. *Perf. 14½x14*

B13 CD90 5fr + 20fr peacock blue 2.00 1.60

The surtax was for the French Red Cross and national relief.

Tropical Medicine Issue

Common Design Type

1950, July 17 Engr. *Perf. 13*

B14 CD100 10fr + 2fr dk bl grn & dk grn 10.50 8.00

The surtax was for charitable work.

AIR POST STAMPS

Seaplane in Flight AP1

Perf. 13½

1934, Nov. 5 Unwmk. Photo.

C1 AP1 5fr green 1.25 1.25

For overprint see No. C2.

For Type AP1 without "RF," see Nos. C1A-C1D.

Type of 1934 without "RF" and

Beach Scene — AP1a

Perf. 13½, 13 (#C1E)

1944 Photo, Engr. (#C1E)

C1A	AP1	5fr green	.70
C1B	AP1	10fr black	1.00
C1C	AP1	20fr orange	1.10
C1D	AP1	50fr gray blue	1.50
C1E	AP1a	100fr turquoise blue	2.00
		Nos. C1A-C1E (5)	6.30

Nos. C1A-C1E were issued by the Vichy government in France, but were not placed on sale in French Polynesia.

Catalogue values for unused stamps in this section, from this point to the end of the section, are for Never Hinged items.

No. C1 Overprinted in Red

1941

C2 AP1 5fr green 7.25 4.75

Common Design Type

1942 *Perf. 14½x14*

C3	CD87	1fr dark orange	.90	.65
C4	CD87	1.50fr bright red	.95	.70
C5	CD87	5fr brown red	1.25	.95
C6	CD87	10fr black	1.90	1.40
C7	CD87	25fr ultra	2.75	2.10
C8	CD87	50fr dark green	3.00	2.10
C9	CD87	100fr plum	3.00	2.10
		Nos. C3-C9 (7)	13.75	10.00

Victory Issue

Common Design Type

1946, May 8 Engr. *Perf. 12½*

C10 CD92 8fr dark green 2.75 2.00

Chad to Rhine Issue

Common Design Types

1946, June 6

C11	CD93	5fr red orange	2.10	1.60
C12	CD94	10fr dk olive bis	2.10	1.60
C13	CD95	15fr dk yellow grn	2.10	1.60
C14	CD96	20fr carmine	2.75	2.10
C15	CD97	25fr dk rose violet	4.00	3.00
C16	CD98	50fr black	4.50	3.50
		Nos. C11-C16 (6)	17.55	13.40

Shearwater and Moorea Landscape — AP2

Fishermen — AP3

Shearwater over Maupiti Shoreline — AP4

1948, Mar. 1 Unwmk. *Perf. 13*

C17	AP2	50fr red brown	30.00	11.00
C18	AP3	100fr purple	24.00	8.00
C19	AP4	200fr blue green	52.50	17.50
		Nos. C17-C19 (3)	106.50	36.50

UPU Issue

Common Design Type

1949

C20 CD99 10fr deep blue 20.00 15.00

Gauguin's "Nafea faaipoipo" — AP5

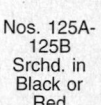

1953, Sept. 24
C21 AP5 14fr dk brn, dk gray grn & red 80.00 65.00

50th anniv. of the death of Paul Gauguin.

Liberation Issue
Common Design Type

1954, June 6
C22 CD102 3fr dk grnsh bl & bl grn 10.00 8.00

Bahia Peak, Borabora — AP6

1955, Sept. 26 Unwmk. *Perf. 13*
C23 AP6 13fr indigo & blue 10.00 5.50

Mother-of-Pearl Artist — AP7

Designs: 50fr, "Women of Tahiti," Gauguin, horiz. 100fr, "The White Horse," Gauguin. 200fr, Night fishing at Moorea, horiz.

1958, Nov. 3 Engr. *Perf. 13*

C24	AP7 13fr multicolored	13.00	4.50
C25	AP7 50fr multicolored	12.00	4.50
C26	AP7 100fr multicolored	20.00	7.25
C27	AP7 200fr lilac & slate	40.00	21.00
	Nos. C24-C27 (4)	85.00	37.25

Airport, Papeete — AP8

1960, Nov. 19
C28 AP8 13fr rose lil, vio, & yel grn 3.50 2.40

Telstar Issue
Common Design Type

1962, Dec. 5 *Perf. 13*
C29 CD111 50fr red lil, mar & vio bl 11.50 8.00

Tahitian Dancer — AP10

1964, May 14 Photo. *Perf. 13*
C30 AP10 15fr multicolored 4.75 2.00

Map of Tahiti and Free French Emblems — AP11

1964, July 10 Unwmk.
C31 AP11 16fr multicolored 15.00 9.00

Issued to commemorate the rallying of French Polynesia to the Free French cause.

Moorea Scene — AP12

1964, Dec. 1 Litho. *Perf. 13*
C32 AP12 23fr multicolored 9.50 4.00

ITU Issue
Common Design Type

1965, May 17 Engr. *Perf. 13*
C33 CD120 50fr vio, red brn & bl 80.00 52.50

Paul Gauguin — AP13

Design: 25fr, Gauguin Museum (stylized). 40fr, Primitive statues at Gauguin Museum.

1965 Engr. *Perf. 13*

C34	AP13 25fr olive green	7.50	4.50
C35	AP13 40fr blue green	15.00	8.00
C36	AP13 75fr brt red brown	20.00	15.00
	Nos. C34-C36 (3)	42.50	27.50

Opening of Gauguin Museum, Papeete. Issued: 25fr, 75fr, 6/13. 40fr, 11/7.

Skin Diver with Spear Gun — AP14

1965, Sept. 1 Engr. *Perf. 13*
C37 AP14 50fr red brn, dl bl & dk grn 90.00 55.00

World Championships in Underwater Fishing, Tuamotu Archipelago, Sept. 1965.

Painting from a School Dining Room — AP15

1965, Nov. 29
C38 AP15 80fr brn, bl, dl bl & red 22.50 17.50

School Canteen Program.

Radio Tower, Globe and Palm — AP16

1965, Dec. 29 Engr. *Perf. 13*
C39 AP16 60fr org, grn & dk brn 19.00 15.00

50th anniversary of the first radio link between Tahiti and France.

French Satellite A-1 Issue
Common Design Type

Designs: 7fr, Diamant Rocket and launching installations. 10fr, A-1 satellite.

1966, Feb. 7

C40	CD121 7fr choc, dp grn & lil	6.75	6.00
C41	CD121 10fr lil, dp grn & dk brn	6.75	6.00
a.	Pair, #C40-C41 + label	14.00	14.00

French Satellite D-1 Issue
Common Design Type

1966, May 10 Engr. *Perf. 13*
C42 CD122 20fr multicolored 7.00 4.75

Papeete Harbor — AP17

1966, June 30 Photo. *Perf. 13*
C43 AP17 50fr multicolored 15.00 11.00

"Vive Tahiti" by A. Benichou — AP18

1966, Nov. 28 Photo. *Perf. 13*
C44 AP18 13fr multicolored 11.00 6.50

Explorer's Ship and Canoe — AP19

Designs: 60fr, Polynesian costume and ship. 80fr, Louis Antoine de Bougainville, vert.

1968, Apr. 6 Engr. *Perf. 13*

C45	AP19 40fr multicolored	8.75	3.25
C46	AP19 60fr multicolored	11.50	6.50
C47	AP19 80fr multicolored	14.50	8.75
a.	Souv. sheet, #C45-C47	160.00	160.00
	Nos. C45-C47 (3)	34.75	18.50

200th anniv. of the discovery of Tahiti by Louis Antoine de Bougainville. Issued: 40fr, 4/6/68.

The Meal, by Paul Gauguin — AP20

1968, July 30 Photo. *Perf. 12x12½*
C48 AP20 200fr multicolored 40.00 32.50

See Nos. C63-C67, C78-C82, C89-C93, C98.

Shot Put — AP21

1968, Oct. 12 Engr. *Perf. 13*
C49 AP21 35fr dk car rose & brt grn 16.00 9.00

19th Olympic Games, Mexico City, 10/12-27.

Concorde Issue
Common Design Type

1969, Apr. 17
C50 CD129 40fr red brn & car rose 55.00 35.00

PATA 1970 Poster — AP22

1969, July 9 Photo. *Perf. 12½x13*
C51 AP22 25fr blue & multi 17.50 7.25

Issued to publicize PATA 1970 (Pacific Area Travel Association Congress), Tahiti.

Underwater Fishing — AP23

52fr, Hand holding fish made up of flags, vert.

1969, Aug. 5 Photo. *Perf. 13*

C52	AP23 48fr blk, grnsh bl & red lil	35.00	13.50
C53	AP23 52fr bl, blk & red	40.00	22.50

Issued to publicize the World Underwater Fishing Championships.

Gen. Bonaparte as Commander of the Army in Italy, by Jean Sebastien Rouillard — AP24

1969, Oct. 15 Photo. *Perf. 12½x12*

C54	AP24	100fr car & multi	80.00	67.50

Bicentenary of the birth of Napoleon Bonaparte (1769-1821).

Eiffel Tower, Torii and EXPO Emblem — AP25

Design: 30fr, Mount Fuji, Tower of the Sun and EXPO emblem, horiz.

1970, Sept. 15 Photo. *Perf. 13*

C55	AP25	30fr multicolored	20.00	8.00
C56	AP25	50fr multicolored	27.50	12.00

EXPO '70 International Exposition, Osaka, Japan, Mar. 15-Sept. 13.

Pearl Diver Descending, and Basket — AP26

Designs: 5fr, Diver collecting oysters. 18fr, Implantation into oyster, horiz. 27fr, Open oyster with pearl. 50fr, Woman with mother of pearl jewelry.

1970, Sept. 30 Engr. *Perf. 13*

C57	AP26	2fr slate, grnsh bl & red brn	1.50	.90
C58	AP26	5fr grnsh blue, ultra & org	2.75	1.50
C59	AP26	18fr sl, mag & org	3.75	2.75
C60	AP26	27fr brt pink, brn & dl lil	9.25	4.75
C61	AP26	50fr gray, red brn & org	16.00	7.50
		Nos. C57-C61 (5)	33.25	17.40

Pearl industry of French Polynesia.

The Thinker, by Auguste Rodin and Education Year Emblem — AP27

1970, Oct. 15 Engr. *Perf. 13*

C62	AP27	50fr bl, ind & fawn	17.00	10.50

International Education Year.

Painting Type of 1968

Paintings by Artists Living in Polynesia: 20fr, Woman on the Beach, by Yves de Saint-Front. 40fr, Abstract, by Frank Fay. 60fr, Woman and Shells, by Jean Guillois. 80fr, Hut under Palms, by Jean Masson. 100fr, Polynesian Girl, by Jean-Charles Bouloc, vert.

Perf. 12x12½, 12½x12

1970, Dec. 14 Photo.

C63	AP20	20fr brn & multi	8.00	4.00
C64	AP20	40fr brn & multi	12.00	7.50
C65	AP20	60fr brn & multi	16.00	11.00
C66	AP20	80fr brn & multi	20.00	16.00
C67	AP20	100fr brn & multi	26.00	22.50
		Nos. C63-C67 (5)	82.00	61.00

South Pacific Games Emblem — AP28

1971, Jan. 26 *Perf. 12½*

C68	AP28	20fr ultra & multi	8.00	5.00

Publicity for 4th South Pacific Games, held in Papeete, Sept. 8-19, 1971.

Memorial Flame — AP29

1971, Mar. 19 Photo. *Perf. 12½*

C69	AP29	5fr multicolored	8.00	5.00

In memory of Charles de Gaulle.

Soldier and Badge — AP30

1971, Apr. 21

C70	AP30	25fr multicolored	11.00	6.75

30th anniversary of departure of Tahitian volunteers to serve in World War II.

Water Sports Type

Designs: 15fr, Surfing, vert. 16fr, Skin diving, vert. 20fr, Water-skiing with kite.

1971, May 11 Photo. *Perf. 13*

C71	A44	15fr multicolored	6.50	3.50
C72	A44	16fr multicolored	7.50	3.25
C73	A44	20fr multicolored	11.00	7.75
		Nos. C71-C73 (3)	25.00	14.50

Sailing AP31

1971, Sept. 8 *Perf. 12½*

C74	AP31	15fr shown	6.50	3.50
C75	AP31	18fr Golf	8.00	4.75
C76	AP31	27fr Archery	12.00	7.25
C77	AP31	53fr Tennis	20.00	13.50
a.		Souv. sheet, #C74-C77	190.00	190.00
		Nos. C74-C77 (4)	46.50	29.00

4th So. Pacific Games, Papeete, Sept. 8-19.

Painting Type of 1968

Paintings by Artists Living in Polynesia: 20fr, Hut and Palms, by Isabelle Wolf. 40fr, Palms on Shore, by André Dobrowolski. 60fr, Polynesian Woman, by Françoise Séli, vert. 80fr, Holy Family, by Pierre Heymann, vert. 100fr, Crowd, by Nicolai Michoutouchkine.

1971, Dec. 15 Photo. *Perf. 13*

C78	AP20	20fr multicolored	7.50	4.50
C79	AP20	40fr multicolored	11.00	7.50
C80	AP20	60fr multicolored	13.00	10.00
C81	AP20	80fr multicolored	18.00	12.50
C82	AP20	100fr multicolored	30.00	22.50
		Nos. C78-C82 (5)	79.50	57.00

Papeete Harbor — AP32

1972, Jan. 13

C83	AP32	28fr violet & multi	11.00	8.00

Free port of Papeete, 10th anniversary.

Figure Skating and Dragon AP33

1972, Jan. 25 Engr. *Perf. 13*

C84	AP33	20fr ultra, lake & brt grn	9.00	7.00

11th Winter Olympic Games, Sapporo, Japan, Feb. 3-13.

South Pacific Commission Headquarters, Noumea — AP34

1972, Feb. 5 Photo. *Perf. 13*

C85	AP34	21fr blue & multi	11.00	5.25

South Pacific Commission, 25th anniv.

Festival Emblem — AP35

1972, May 9 Engr. *Perf. 13*

C86	AP35	36fr orange, bl & grn	8.00	5.25

So. Pacific Festival of Arts, Fiji, May 6-20.

Kon Tiki and Route, Callao to Tahiti — AP36

1972, Aug. 18 Photo. *Perf. 13*

C87	AP36	16fr dk & lt bl, blk & org	10.00	6.50

25th anniversary of the arrival of the raft Kon Tiki in Tahiti.

Charles de Gaulle and Memorial — AP37

1972, Dec. 9 Engr. *Perf. 13*

C88	AP37	100fr slate	62.50	42.50

Painting Type of 1968

Paintings by Artists Living in Polynesia: 20fr, Horses, by Georges Bovy. 40fr, Sailboats, by Ruy Juventin, vert. 60fr, Harbor, by André Brooke. 80fr, Farmers, by Daniel Adam, vert. 100fr, Dancers, by Aloysius Pilioko, vert.

1972, Dec. 14 Photo.

C89	AP20	20fr gold & multi	9.75	4.25
C90	AP20	40fr gold & multi	12.00	6.75
C91	AP20	60fr gold & multi	21.00	9.50
C92	AP20	80fr dk grn, buff & dk brn	27.50	13.00
C93	AP20	100fr gold & multi	32.50	25.00
		Nos. C89-C93 (5)	102.75	58.50

St. Teresa and Lisieux Basilica AP38

1973, Jan. 23 Engr. *Perf. 13*

C94	AP38	85fr multicolored	25.00	17.50

Centenary of the birth of St. Teresa of Lisieux (1873-1897), Carmelite nun.

Nicolaus Copernicus — AP39

1973, Mar. 7 Engr. *Perf. 13*

C95	AP39	100fr brn, vio bl & red lil	30.00	17.50

Copernicus (1473-1543), Polish astronomer.

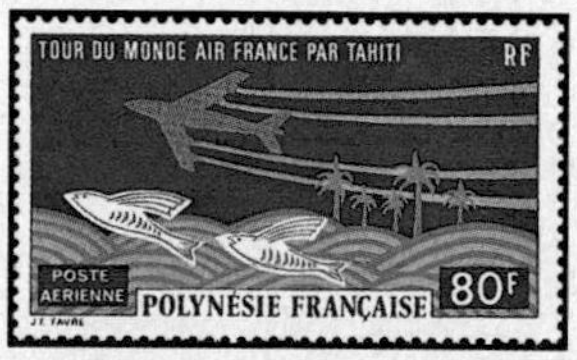

Plane over Tahiti — AP40

1973, Apr. 3 Photo. *Perf. 13*

C96	AP40	80fr ultra, gold & lt grn	22.50	16.00

Air France's World Tour via Tahiti.

DC-10 at Papeete Airport — AP41

1973, May 18 Engr. *Perf. 13*

C97 AP41 20fr bl, ultra & sl grn 16.00 9.00

Start of DC-10 service.

Painting Type of 1968

Design: 200fr, "Ta Matete" (seated women), by Paul Gauguin.

1973, June 7 Photo. *Perf. 13*

C98 AP20 200fr multicolored 27.50 20.00

Paul Gauguin (1848-1903), painter.

Pierre Loti and Characters from his Books — AP42

1973, July 4 Engr. *Perf. 13*

C99 AP42 60fr multicolored 40.00 20.00

Pierre Loti (1850-1923), French naval officer and writer.

Woman with Flowers, by Eliane de Gennes AP43

Paintings by Artists Living in Polynesia: 20fr, Sun, by Jean Francois Favre. 60fr, Seascape, by Alain Sidet. 80fr, Crowded Bus, by Francois Ravello. 100fr, Stylized Boats, by Jackie Bourdin, horiz.

1973, Dec. 13 Photo. *Perf. 13*

C100 AP43 20fr gold & multi 8.00 2.75
C101 AP43 40fr gold & multi 11.50 6.00
C102 AP43 60fr gold & multi 17.00 10.50
C103 AP43 80fr gold & multi 22.50 17.00
C104 AP43 100fr gold & multi 27.50 20.00
Nos. C100-C104 (5) 86.50 56.25

Bird, Fish, Flower and Water — AP44

1974, June 12 Photo. *Perf. 13*

C105 AP44 12fr blue & multi 7.50 5.25

Nature protection.

Catamaran under Sail — AP45

1974, July 22 Engr. *Perf. 13*

C106 AP45 100fr multicolored 27.50 16.00

2nd Catamaran World Championships.

Still-life, by Rosine Temarui-Masson — AP46

Paintings by Artists Living in Polynesia: 40fr, Palms and House on Beach, by Marcel Chardon. 60fr, Man, by Marie-Françoise Avril. 80fr, Polynesian Woman, by Henriette Robin. 100fr, Lagoon by Moon-light, by David Farsi, horiz.

1974, Dec. 12 Photo. *Perf. 13*

C107 AP46 20fr gold & multi 18.00 8.50
C108 AP46 40fr gold & multi 27.50 9.50
C109 AP46 60fr gold & multi 32.50 12.00
C110 AP46 80fr gold & multi 45.00 16.50
C111 AP46 100fr gold & multi 65.00 27.50
Nos. C107-C111 (5) 188.00 74.00

See Nos. C122-C126.

Polynesian Gods of Travel — AP47

Designs: 75fr, Tourville hydroplane, 1929. 100fr, Passengers leaving plane.

1975, Feb. 7 Engr. *Perf. 13*

C112 AP47 50fr sep, pur & brn 11.00 6.00
C113 AP47 75fr grn, bl & red 16.00 8.00
C114 AP47 100fr grn, sep & car 25.00 15.00
Nos. C112-C114 (3) 52.00 29.00

Fifty years of Tahitian aviation.

French Ceres Stamp and Woman — AP48

1975, May 29 Engr. *Perf. 13*

C115 AP48 32fr ver, brn & blk 8.00 5.00

ARPHILA 75 International Philatelic Exhibition, Paris, June 6-16.

Shot Put and Games' Emblem AP50

1975, Aug. 1 Photo. *Perf. 13*

C117 AP50 25fr shown 4.75 3.00
C118 AP50 30fr Volleyball 7.00 3.75
C119 AP50 40fr Women's swimming 9.25 5.25
Nos. C117-C119 (3) 21.00 12.00

5th South Pacific Games, Guam, Aug. 1-10.

Flowers, Athlete, View of Montreal — AP51

1975, Oct. 15 Engr. *Perf. 13*

C120 AP51 44fr brt bl, ver & blk 11.00 6.50

Pre-Olympic Year 1975.

UPU Emblem, Jet and Letters — AP52

1975, Nov. 5 Engr. *Perf. 13*

C121 AP52 100fr brn, bl & ol 22.50 13.00

World Universal Postal Union Day.

Paintings Type of 1974

Paintings by Artists Living in Polynesia: 20fr, Beach Scene, by R. Marcel Marius, horiz. 40fr, Roofs with TV antennas, by M. Anglade, horiz. 60fr, Street scene with bus, by J. Day, horiz. 80fr, Tropical waters (fish), by J. Steimetz. 100fr, Women, by A. van der Heyde.

1975, Dec. 17 Litho. *Perf. 13*

C122 AP46 20fr gold & multi 3.00 1.75
C123 AP46 40fr gold & multi 6.00 3.00
C124 AP46 60fr gold & multi 9.00 4.50
C125 AP46 80fr gold & multi 12.00 7.50
C126 AP46 100fr gold & multi 14.50 12.00
Nos. C122-C126 (5) 44.50 28.75

Concorde — AP53

1976, Jan. 21 Engr. *Perf. 13*

C127 AP53 100fr car, bl & ind 19.00 13.00

First commercial flight of supersonic jet Concorde from Paris to Rio, Jan. 21.

Adm. Rodney, Count de la Perouse, "Barfleur" and "Triomphant" in Battle — AP54

31fr, Count de Grasse and Lord Graves, "Ville de Paris" & "Le Terible" in Chesapeake Bay Battle.

1976, Apr. 15 Engr. *Perf. 13*

C128 AP54 24fr grnsh bl, lt brn & blk 5.00 2.50
C129 AP54 31fr mag, red & lt brn 5.75 3.50

American Bicentennial.

King Pomaré I — AP55

Portraits: 21fr, King Pomaré II. 26fr, Queen Pomaré IV. 30fr, King Pomaré V.

1976, Apr. 28 Litho. *Perf. 12½*

C130 AP55 18fr olive & multi 1.75 .75
C131 AP55 21fr multicolored 2.00 1.10
C132 AP55 26fr gray & multi 2.75 1.25
C133 AP55 30fr plum & multi 3.00 1.90
Nos. C130-C133 (4) 9.50 5.00

Pomaré Dynasty. See Nos. C141-C144.

Running and Maple Leaf — AP56

Designs: 34fr, Long jump, vert. 50fr, Olympic flame and flowers.

1976, July 19 Engr. *Perf. 13*

C134 AP56 26fr ultra & multi 4.25 2.10
C135 AP56 34fr ultra & multi 6.00 2.75
C136 AP56 50fr ultra & multi 11.50 5.00
a. Min. sheet, #C134-C136 90.00 90.00
Nos. C134-C136 (3) 21.75 9.85

21st Olympic Games, Montreal, Canada, July 17-Aug. 1.

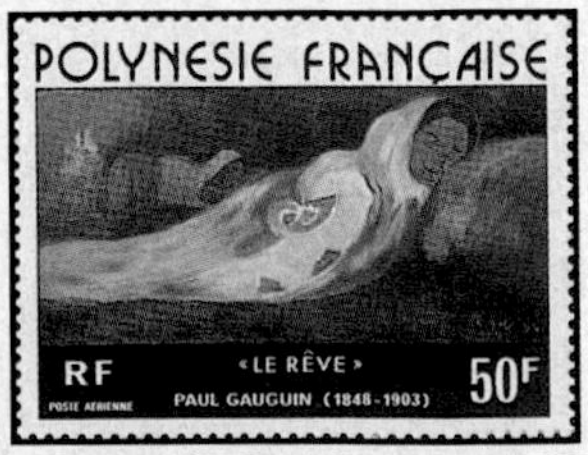

The Dream, by Paul Gauguin — AP57

1976, Oct. 17 Photo. *Perf. 13*

C137 AP57 50fr multicolored 11.00 7.25

Murex Steeriae — AP58

Sea Shells: 27fr, Conus Gauguini. 35fr, Conus marchionatus.

1977, Mar. 14 Photo. *Perf. 12½x13*

C138	AP58	25fr vio bl & multi	4.25	1.25
C139	AP58	27fr ultra & multi	4.25	1.50
C140	AP58	35fr blue & multi	5.00	2.00
		Nos. C138-C140 (3)	13.50	4.75

See Nos. C156-C158.

Royalty Type of 1976

19fr, King Maputeoa, Mangareva. 33fr, King Camatoa V, Raiatea. 39fr, Queen Vaekehu, Marquesas. 43fr, King Teurarii III, Rurutu.

1977, Apr. 19 Litho. *Perf. 12½*

C141	AP55	19fr dull red & multi	1.25	.95
C142	AP55	33fr dk blue & multi	1.90	1.25
C143	AP55	39fr ultra & multi	1.90	1.25
C144	AP55	43fr green & multi	2.75	1.90
		Nos. C141-C144 (4)	7.80	5.35

Polynesian rulers.

Pocillopora AP59

Design: 25fr, Acropora, horiz.

Perf. 13x12½, 12½x13

1977, May 23 Photo.

C145	AP59	25fr multicolored	1.90	1.10
C146	AP59	33fr multicolored	2.75	1.90

3rd Symposium on Coral Reefs, Miami, Fla. See Nos. C162-C163.

De Gaulle Memorial — AP60

Photogravure and Embossed

1977, June 18 *Perf. 13*

C147	AP60	40fr gold & multi	7.00	5.00

5th anniversary of dedication of De Gaulle memorial at Colombey-les-Deux-Eglises.

Tahitian Dancer — AP61

1977, July 14 Litho. *Perf. 12½*

C148	AP61	27fr multicolored	4.00	2.50

Charles A. Lindbergh and Spirit of St. Louis — AP62

1977, Aug. 18 Litho. *Perf. 12½*

C149	AP62	28fr multicolored	7.00	3.50

Lindbergh's solo transatlantic flight from New York to Paris, 50th anniv.

Mahoe — AP63

1977, Sept. 15 Photo. *Perf. 12½x13*

C150	AP63	8fr shown	1.40	.80
C151	AP63	12fr Frangipani	1.75	1.25

Palms on Shore — AP64

1977, Nov. 8 Photo. *Perf. 12½x13*

C152	AP64	32fr multicolored	10.00	4.50

Ecology, protection of trees.

Rubens' Son Albert AP65

1977, Nov. 28 Engr. *Perf. 13*

C153	AP65	100fr grnsh blk & rose cl	11.00	8.00

Peter Paul Rubens (1577-1640), painter, 400th birth anniversary.

Capt. Cook and "Discovery" — AP66

Design: 39fr, Capt. Cook and "Resolution."

1978, Jan. 20 Engr. *Perf. 13*

C154	AP66	33fr multicolored	2.50	3.00
C155	AP66	39fr multicolored	3.00	3.50

Bicentenary of Capt. James Cook's arrival in Hawaii.

For overprints see Nos. C166-C167.

Shell Type of 1977

Sea Shells: 22fr, Erosaria obvelata. 24fr, Cypraea ventriculus. 31fr, Lambis robusta.

1978, Apr. 13 Photo. *Perf. 13½x13*

C156	AP58	22fr brt blue & multi	2.25	1.25
C157	AP58	24fr brt blue & multi	2.25	1.50
C158	AP58	31fr brt blue & multi	3.50	2.50
		Nos. C156-C158 (3)	8.00	5.25

Tahitian Woman and Boy, by Gauguin AP67

1978, May 7 *Perf. 13*

C159	AP67	50fr multicolored	8.75	5.25

Paul Gauguin (1848-1903).

Antenna and ITU Emblem AP68

1978, May 17 Litho. *Perf. 13*

C160	AP68	80fr gray & multi	6.00	3.25

10th World Telecommunications Day.

Soccer and Argentina '78 Emblem — AP69

1978, June 1

C161	AP69	28fr multicolored	3.25	2.10

11th World Cup Soccer Championship, Argentina, June 1-25.

Coral Type of 1977

Designs: 26fr, Fungia, horiz. 34fr, Millepora.

Perf. 13x12½, 12½x13

1978, July 13 Photo.

C162	AP59	26fr multicolored	1.75	1.25
C163	AP59	34fr multicolored	2.25	1.60

Radar Antenna, Polynesian Woman — AP70

1978, Sept. 5 Engr. *Perf. 13*

C164	AP70	50fr blue & black	3.00	1.75

Papenoo earth station.

Bird and Rainbow over Island — AP71

1978, Oct. 5 Photo.

C165	AP71	23fr multicolored	6.00	1.75

Nature protection.

Nos. C154-C155 Overprinted

No. C166

No. C167

1979, Feb. 14 Engr. *Perf. 13*

C166	AP66	33fr multi	4.00	2.50
C167	AP66	39fr multi (VBl)	5.00	3.50

Bicentenary of Capt. Cook's death. On No. C167 date is last line of overprint.

Children, Toys and IYC Emblem — AP72

1979, May 3 Engr. *Perf. 13*

C168	AP72	150fr multicolored	12.00	7.00

International Year of the Child.

"Do you expect a letter?" by Paul Gauguin — AP73

1979, May 20 Photo. *Perf. 13*

C169	AP73	200fr multicolored	16.00	8.00

Shell and Carved Head — AP74

1979, June 30 **Engr.** ***Perf. 13***
C170 AP74 44fr multicolored 3.50 2.00

Museum of Tahiti and the Islands.

Conference Emblem over Island AP75

1979, Oct. 6 **Photo.** ***Perf. 13***
C171 AP75 23fr multicolored 2.25 1.10

19th South Pacific Conf., Tahiti, Oct. 6-12.

Flying Boat "Bermuda" — AP76

Planes Used in Polynesia: 40fr, DC-4 over Papeete. 60fr, Britten-Norman "Islander." 80fr, Fairchild F-27A. 120fr, DC-8 over Tahiti.

1979, Dec. 19 **Litho.** ***Perf. 13***
C172 AP76 24fr multicolored 1.00 .50
C173 AP76 40fr multicolored 1.75 1.00
C174 AP76 60fr multicolored 2.75 1.50
C175 AP76 80fr multicolored 3.50 2.25
C176 AP76 120fr multicolored 6.00 3.00
Nos. C172-C176 (5) 15.00 8.25

See Nos. C180-C183.

Window on Tahiti, by Henri Matisse AP77

1980, Feb. 18 **Photo.**
C177 AP77 150fr multicolored 8.00 5.00

Marshi Metua No Tehamana, by Gauguin AP78

1980, Aug. 24 **Photo.** ***Perf. 13***
C178 AP78 500fr multicolored 18.00 13.00

Sydpex '80, Philatelic Exhibition, Sydney Town Hall — AP79

1980, Sept. 29 **Photo.** ***Perf. 13***
C179 AP79 70fr multicolored 8.00 5.25

Aviation Type of 1979

1980, Dec. 15 **Litho.** ***Perf. 13***
C180 AP76 15fr Catalina .75 .55
C181 AP76 26fr Twin Otter 1.00 .70
C182 AP76 30fr CAMS 55 1.25 .90
C183 AP76 50fr DC-6 2.00 1.40
Nos. C180-C183 (4) 5.00 3.55

And The Gold of their Bodies, by Gauguin — AP80

1981, Mar. 15 **Photo.** ***Perf. 13***
C184 AP80 100fr multicolored 4.50 2.50

20th Anniv. of Manned Space Flight AP81

1981, June 15 **Litho.** ***Perf. 12½***
C185 AP81 300fr multicolored 9.00 7.00

First Intl. Pirogue (6-man Canoe) Championship — AP82

1981, July 25 **Litho.** ***Perf. 13x12½***
C186 AP82 200fr multicolored 5.50 4.50

Matavai Bay, by William Hodges — AP83

Paintings: 60fr, Poedea, by John Weber, vert. 80fr, Omai, by Joshua Reynolds, vert. 120fr, Point Venus, by George Tobin.

1981, Dec. 10 **Photo.** ***Perf. 13***
C187 AP83 40fr multicolored 1.10 .90
C188 AP83 60fr multicolored 1.75 1.25
C189 AP83 80fr multicolored 2.75 1.75
C190 AP83 120fr multicolored 3.50 2.40
Nos. C187-C190 (4) 9.10 6.30

See Nos. C194-C197, C202-C205.

TB Bacillus Centenary — AP84

1982, Mar. 24 **Engr.** ***Perf. 13***
C191 AP84 200fr multicolored 5.00 3.00

1982 World Cup — AP85

1982, May 18 **Litho.** ***Perf. 13***
C192 AP85 250fr multicolored 6.50 4.50

French Overseas Possessions' Week, Sept. 18-25 — AP86

1982, Sept. 17 **Engr.**
C193 AP86 110fr multicolored 2.75 1.65

Painting Type of 1981

Designs: 50fr, The Tahitian, by M. Radiguet, vert. 70fr, Souvenir of Tahiti, by C. Giraud. 100fr, Beating Cloth Lengths, by Atlas JL the Younger. 160fr, Papeete Harbor, by C.F. Gordon Cumming.

1982, Dec. 15 **Photo.** ***Perf. 13***
C194 AP83 50fr multicolored 1.90 1.00
C195 AP83 70fr multicolored 2.25 1.50
C196 AP83 100fr multicolored 2.75 2.00
C197 AP83 160fr multicolored 4.50 2.75
Nos. C194-C197 (4) 11.40 7.25

Wood Cutter, by Gauguin AP87

Photo. & Engr.

1983, May 8 ***Perf. 12½x13***
C198 AP87 600fr multicolored 16.00 8.00

Voyage of Capt. Bligh — AP88

1983, June 9 **Litho.** ***Perf. 13***
C199 AP88 200fr Map, fruit 6.00 3.00

BRASILIANA '83 Intl. Stamp Exhibition, Rio de Janeiro, July 29-Aug. 7 — AP89

1983, July 29 **Litho.** ***Perf. 13x12½***
C200 AP89 100fr multicolored 2.50 1.75
a. Souvenir sheet 3.50 3.50

1983, Aug. 4 **Litho.** ***Perf. 13x12½***
C201 AP89 110fr Bangkok '83 3.00 2.00
a. Souvenir sheet 4.00 4.00

Painting Type of 1981

20th Cent. Paintings: 40fr, View of Moorea, by William Alister MacDonald (1861-1956). 60fr, The Fruit Carrier, by Adrian Herman Gouwe (1875-1965). 80fr, Arrival of the Destroyer Escort, by Nicolas Mordvinoff (1911-1977). 100fr, Women on a Veranda, by Charles Alfred Le Moine (1872-1918).

1983, Dec. 22 **Photo.** ***Perf. 13***
C202 AP83 40fr multi 1.00 .75
C203 AP83 60fr multi, vert. 1.50 1.00
C204 AP83 80fr multi, vert. 1.60 1.25
C205 AP83 100fr multi 2.00 1.60
Nos. C202-C205 (4) 6.10 4.60

ESPANA '84 — AP90

Design: Maori canoers.

1984, Apr. 27 **Engr.** ***Perf. 13***
C206 AP90 80fr brn red & dk bl 2.25 1.50

Souvenir Sheet

C207 AP90 200fr dk bl & dk red 7.25 7.25

Woman with Mango, by Gauguin AP91

Photo. & Engr.

1984, May 27 ***Perf. 12½x13***
C208 AP91 400fr multicolored 11.00 6.00

Ausipex '84 — AP92

Details from Human Sacrifice of the Maori in Tahiti, 18th cent. engraving.

1984, Sept. 5 **Litho.** ***Perf. 13x12½***
C209 AP92 120fr Worshippers 3.00 2.25
C210 AP92 120fr Preparation 3.00 2.25
a. Pair, #C209-C210 + label 7.50 7.50

Souvenir Sheet

C211 AP92 200fr Entire 9.50 9.50

Painting by Gaugin (1848-1903) — AP93

Design: Where have we come from? What are we? Where are we going?

1985, Mar. 17 **Litho.** ***Perf. 13½x13***
C212 AP93 550fr multi 14.00 7.50

4th Pacific Arts Festival Type

1985, July 3 **Litho.** ***Perf. 13***
C213 A95 200fr Islander, tiki, artifacts 4.50 3.00

Intl. Youth Year — AP95

1985, Sept. 18 **Litho.**
C214 AP95 250fr Island youths, frigate bird 5.50 3.25

ITALIA '85 — AP96

Designs: Ship sailing into Papeete Harbor, 19th century print.

1985, Oct. 22 **Engr.**
C215 AP96 130fr multicolored 2.75 2.50

Souvenir Sheet

C216 AP96 240fr multicolored 7.50 7.50

1st Intl. Marlin Fishing Contest, Feb. 27-Mar. 5 — AP97

1986, Feb. 27 **Litho.** ***Perf. 12½***
C217 AP97 300fr multicolored 6.50 4.00

Arrival of a Boat, c.1880 — AP98

1986, June 24 **Engr.** ***Perf. 13***
C218 AP98 400fr intense blue 8.75 5.25

STOCKHOLMIA '86 — AP99

Design: Dr. Karl Solander and Anders Sparrmann, Swedish scientists who accompanied Capt. Cook, and map of Tahiti.

1986, Aug. 28 **Engr.** ***Perf. 13***
C219 AP99 150fr multicolored 3.25 2.25

Souvenir Sheet

C220 AP99 210fr multicolored 4.75 4.75

Protestant Churches — AP100

1986, Dec. 17 **Litho.** ***Perf. 13***
C221 AP100 80fr Tiva, 1955 1.75 .90
C222 AP100 200fr Avera, 1880 4.50 2.10
C223 AP100 300fr Papetoal, 1822 6.50 3.25
Nos. C221-C223 (3) 12.75 6.25

Broche Barracks, 120th Anniv. — AP101

1987, Apr. 21 **Litho.** ***Perf. 12½x12***
C224 AP101 350fr multicolored 7.75 5.00

CAPEX '87 — AP102

Design: George Vancouver (1757-1798), English navigator and cartographer, chart and excerpt from ship's log.

1987, June 15 **Engr.** ***Perf. 13***
C225 AP102 130fr multi 2.90 2.25

Imperf

Size: 143x100mm

C226 AP102 260fr multicolored 5.75 5.75

Soyez Mysterieuses, from a 5-Panel Sculpture by Paul Gauguin, Gauguin Museum — AP103

1987, Nov. 15 ***Perf. 13***
C227 AP103 600fr multicolored 14.00 9.50

AIR POST SEMI-POSTAL STAMPS

Catalogue values for unused stamps in this section are for Never Hinged items.

French Revolution Issue
Common Design Type
Unwmk.

1939, July 5 **Photo.** ***Perf. 13***

Name and Value Typo. in Orange

CB1 CD83 5fr + 4fr brn blk 35.00 35.00

Mother & Children on Beach — SPAP1

Perf. 12½x13½

1942, June 22 **Engr.**
CB2 SPAP1 1.50fr + 3.50fr green 2.00
CB3 SPAP1 2fr + 6fr yellow brown 2.00

Native children's welfare fund.

Nos. CB2-CB3 were issued by the Vichy government in France, but were not placed on sale in French Polynesia.

Colonial Education Fund
Common Design Type

1942, June 22
CB4 CD86a 1.20fr + 1.80fr blue & red 2.00

No. CB4 was issued by the Vichy government in France, but was not placed on sale in French Polynesia.

POSTAGE DUE STAMPS

Postage Due Stamps of French Colonies, 1894-1906, Overprinted

1926-27 **Unwmk.** ***Perf. 14x13½***
J1 D1 5c light blue .95 .95
J2 D1 10c brown .95 .95
J3 D1 20c olive green 1.40 1.40
J4 D1 30c dull red 1.60 1.60
J5 D1 40c rose 3.50 3.50
J6 D1 60c blue green 3.50 3.50
J7 D1 1fr red brown, *straw* 3.75 3.75
J8 D1 3fr magenta ('27) 15.00 15.00

With Additional Surcharge of New Value

J9 D1 2fr on 1fr orange red 4.00 4.75
Nos. J1-J9 (9) 34.65 35.40

Fautaua Falls, Tahiti — D2

Tahitian Youth — D3

1929 **Typo.** ***Perf. 13½x14***
J10 D2 5c lt blue & dk brn .75 .75
J11 D2 10c vermilion & grn .75 .75
J12 D2 30c dk brn & dk red 1.75 1.75
J13 D2 50c yel grn & dk brn 1.40 1.40
J14 D2 60c dl vio & yel grn 4.00 4.00
J15 D3 1fr Prus bl & red vio 3.50 3.50
J16 D3 2fr brn red & dk brn 2.00 2.10
J17 D3 3fr bl vio & bl grn 2.10 2.40
Nos. J10-J17 (8) 16.25 16.65

Catalogue values for unused stamps in this section, from this point to the end of the section, are for Never Hinged items.

D4

Polynesian Club — D5

1948 **Engr.** ***Perf. 14x13***
J18 D4 10c brt blue grn .40 .25
J19 D4 30c black brown .40 .25
J20 D4 50c dk car rose .50 .30
J21 D4 1fr ultra .65 .50
J22 D4 2fr dk blue green .95 .70
J23 D4 3fr red 1.90 1.40
J24 D4 4fr violet 2.00 1.60
J25 D4 5fr lilac rose 3.00 2.10
J26 D4 10fr slate 4.00 3.00
J27 D4 20fr red brown 5.50 4.25
Nos. J18-J27 (10) 19.30 14.35

1958 **Unwmk.** ***Perf. 14x13***
J28 D5 1fr dk brn & grn .65 .65
J29 D5 3fr bluish blk & hn brn .90 .90
J30 D5 5fr brown & ultra 1.10 1.10
Nos. J28-J30 (3) 2.65 2.65

Tahitian Bowl — D6

1984-87 **Litho.** ***Perf. 13***
J31 D6 1fr Mother-of-pearl fish hook, vert. .25 .25
J32 D6 3fr shown .25 .25
J33 D6 5fr Marquesan fan .30 .30
J34 D6 10fr Lamp stand, vert. .55 .55

J35 D6 20fr Wood headrest ('87) .60 .60
J36 D6 50fr Wood scoop ('87) 1.50 1.50
Nos. J31-J36 (6) 3.45 3.45

Issued: #J31-34, 3/15; #J35-J36, 8/18.

OFFICIAL STAMPS

Catalogue values for unused stamps in this section are for Never Hinged items.

Breadfruit
O1

Polynesian Fruits: 2fr, 3fr, 5fr, like 1fr. 7fr, 8fr, 10fr, 15fr, "Vi Tahiti." 19fr, 20fr, 25fr, 35fr, Avocados. 50fr, 100fr, 200fr, Mangos.

1977, June 9 Litho. *Perf. 12½*

O1	O1	1fr ultra & multi	.40	*.65*
O2	O1	2fr ultra & multi	.40	*.65*
O3	O1	3fr ultra & multi	.40	*.65*
O4	O1	5fr ultra & multi	.40	*.65*
O5	O1	7fr red & multi	.65	*.95*
O6	O1	8fr red & multi	.65	*.95*
O7	O1	10fr red & multi	.95	*1.25*
O8	O1	15fr red & multi	1.40	*1.60*
O9	O1	19fr black & multi	1.60	*2.00*
O10	O1	20fr black & multi	1.75	*2.40*
O11	O1	25fr black & multi	2.50	*2.75*
O12	O1	35fr black & multi	3.25	*3.50*
O13	O1	50fr black & multi	3.25	*3.50*
O14	O1	100fr red & multi	7.25	*8.00*
O15	O1	200fr ultra & multi	14.00	*16.00*
		Nos. O1-O15 (15)	38.85	*45.50*

1982-86 *Perf. 13*

O1a	O1	1fr ultra & multi	.70	*1.25*
O2a	O1	2fr ultra & multi	.70	*1.25*
O3a	O1	3fr ultra & multi	.95	*1.25*
O4a	O1	5fr ultra & multi	2.25	*2.40*
O5a	O1	7fr red & multi	2.25	*2.50*
O6a	O1	8fr red & multi	3.25	*3.50*
O7a	O1	10fr red & multi	3.50	*3.50*
O8a	O1	15fr red & multi ('84)	3.50	*3.50*
O10a	O1	20fr black & multi	3.50	*3.50*
O11a	O1	25fr black & multi ('84)	3.50	*3.50*
O12a	O1	35fr black & multi ('84)	8.00	*10.50*
O13a	O1	50fr black & multi ('84)	20.00	*22.50*
O14a	O1	100fr red & multi ('86)	52.50	*60.00*
O15a	O1	200fr ultra & multi ('86)	67.50	*80.00*
		Nos. O1a-O15a (14)	172.10	*199.15*

Nos. O1-O15 have dull finish (matte) gum. Nos. O1a-O15a have shiny gum.

Stamps and Postmarks — O2

1fr, French Colonies #5. 2fr, French Colonies #27, #12. 3fr, French Colonies #29, 1884 Papeete postmark. 5fr, Newspaper franked with surcharge of Tahiti #2, 1884 Papeete postmark. 9fr, #176. 10fr, #4, 1894 octagonal postmark. 20fr, #6, #8. 46fr, #48. 51fr, #147-148, Vaitepaua-Makatea Island postmark. 70fr, Visit Tahiti postmark on postal card piece. 85fr, #59 with 1921 manuscript cancel, vert. 100fr, #181. 200fr, #C21, 1st day cancel.

Perf. 13¼, 13¼x13 (#O20), 13x13¼ (#O26)

1993-99 Litho.

O16	O2	1fr multicolored	.25	*.40*
a.		Perf. 13¼x13 ('98)	8.00	*9.50*
O17	O2	2fr multicolored	.25	*.40*
a.		Perf. 13¼x13 ('97)	1.00	*1.25*
O18	O2	3fr multicolored	.25	*.40*
a.		Perf. 13¼x13 ('98)	8.00	*9.50*
O19	O2	5fr multicolored	.30	*.55*
a.		Perf. 13¼x13 ('97)	1.00	*1.25*
O20	O2	9fr multicolored	.80	*1.25*
O21	O2	10fr multicolored	.30	*.55*
a.		Perf. 13¼x13 ('99)	1.00	.85
O22	O2	20fr multicolored	.65	*.95*
a.		Perf. 13¼x13 ('99)	8.00	*9.50*
O23	O2	46fr multicolored	1.40	*1.60*
O24	O2	51fr multicolored	2.50	*3.25*
O25	O2	70fr multicolored	2.40	*2.75*
a.		Perf. 13¼x13 ('97)	4.00	*6.50*
O26	O2	85fr multicolored	2.50	*3.25*
O27	O2	100fr multicolored	2.75	*3.50*
a.		Perf. 13¼x13 ('99)	2.40	1.90
O28	O2	200fr multicolored	5.25	*6.50*
a.		Perf. 13¼x13 ('97)	5.00	4.50
		Nos. O16-O28 (13)	19.60	*25.35*

Issued: 51fr, 4/6/94; 9fr, 85fr, 4/21/97; others, 1/13/93.

FRENCH SOUTHERN & ANTARCTIC TERRITORY

'french 'sə-thərn and ˌant-ärk-tik 'ter-ə-'tōr-ēs

POP. — 130 staff

Formerly dependencies of Madagascar, these areas, comprising the Kerguelen Archipelago; St. Paul, Amsterdam and Crozet Islands and Adelle Land in Antarctica achieved territorial status on August 6, 1955.

100 Centimes = 1 Franc
100 Cents = 1 Euro (2002)

Catalogue values for all unused stamps in this country are for Never Hinged items.

Madagascar No. 289 Ovptd. in Red

Unwmk.

1955, Oct. 28 Engr. *Perf. 13*
1 A25 15f dk grn & dp ultra 14.50 *29.00*

Rockhopper Penguins, Crozet Archipelago — A1

New Amsterdam A2

Design: 10fr, 15fr, Elephant seal.

1956, Apr. 25 Engr. *Perf. 13*

2	A1	50c dk blue, sepia & yel	.40	*.75*
3	A1	1fr ultra, org & gray	.40	*.75*
4	A2	5fr blue & dp ultra	2.75	*3.25*
5	A2	8fr gray vio & dk brn	17.00	*21.00*
6	A2	10fr indigo	6.25	6.25
7	A2	15fr indigo & brn vio	7.50	7.50
		Nos. 2-7 (6)	34.30	39.50

Polar Observation A3

1957, Oct. 11

8	A3	5fr black & violet	3.00	*5.00*
9	A3	10fr rose red	4.00	*5.75*
10	A3	15fr dark blue	5.00	*7.50*
		Nos. 8-10 (3)	12.00	18.25

International Geophysical Year, 1957-58.

Imperforates

Most stamps of this French possession exist imperforate in issued and trial colors, and also in small presentation sheets in issued colors.

Flower Issue
Common Design Type

Design: Pringlea, horiz.

1959 Photo. *Perf. 12½x12*
11 CD104 10fr sal, grn & yel 10.00 8.00

Common Design Types pictured following the introduction.

Light-mantled Sooty Albatross — A4

Coat of Arms — A5

Designs: 40c, Skua, horiz. 12fr, King shag.

1959, Sept. 14 Engr. *Perf. 13*

12	A4	30c blue, grn & red brn	.50	*.75*
13	A4	40c blk, dl red brn & bl	.50	*.75*
14	A4	12fr lt blue & blk	13.50	8.75
		Nos. 12-14 (3)	14.50	10.25

1959, Sept. 14 Typo. *Perf. 13x14*
15 A5 20fr ultra, lt bl & yel 18.00 11.50

Sheathbills — A6

4fr, Sea leopard, horiz. 25fr, Weddell seal at Kerguélen, horiz. 85fr, King penguin.

1960, Dec. 15 Engr. *Perf. 13*

16	A6	2fr grnsh bl, gray & choc	1.50	*2.25*
17	A6	4fr bl, dk brn & dk grn	9.00	7.50
18	A6	25fr sl grn, bis brn & blk	90.00	42.50
19	A6	85fr grnsh bl, org & blk	20.00	14.50
		Nos. 16-19 (4)	120.50	66.75

Yves-Joseph de Kerguélen-Trémarec — A7

1960, Nov. 22
20 A7 25fr red org, dk bl & brn 27.50 22.50

Yves-Joseph de Kerguélen-Trémarec, discoverer of the Kerguélen Archipelago.

Charcot, Compass Rose and "Pourquoi-pas?" — A8

1961, Dec. 26 Unwmk. *Perf. 13*
21 A8 25fr brn, grn & red 27.50 22.50

25th anniv. of the death of Commander Jean Charcot (1867-1936), Antarctic explorer.

Elephant Seals Fighting A9

1963, Feb. 11 Engr. *Perf. 13*
22 A9 8fr dk blue, blk & claret 12.00 7.50

See No. C4.

Penguins and Camp on Crozet Island A10

20fr, Research station & IQSY emblem.

1963, Dec. 16 Unwmk. *Perf. 13*

23	A10	5fr blk, red brn & Prus bl	60.00	35.00
24	A10	20fr vio, sl & red brn	70.00	55.00

Intl. Quiet Sun Year, 1964-65. See No. C6.

Great Blue Whale A11

Black-browed Albatross — A12

Aurora Australis, Map of Antarctica and Rocket — A13

10fr, Cape pigeons. 12fr, Phylica trees, Amsterdam Island. 15fr, Killer whale (orca).

1966-69 Engr. *Perf. 13*

25	A11	5fr brt bl & indigo	20.00	11.50
26	A12	10fr sl, ind & ol brn	30.00	25.00
27	A11	12fr brt bl, sl grn & lemon	21.00	14.00
27A	A11	15fr ol, dk bl & ind	12.00	7.25
28	A12	20fr slate, ol & org	350.00	225.00
		Nos. 25-28 (5)	433.00	282.75

Issued: 5fr, 12/12; 20fr, 1/3/68; 10fr, 12fr, 1/6/69; 15fr, 12/21/69.

1967, Mar. 4 Engr. *Perf. 13*
29 A13 20fr mag, blue & blk 26.00 22.50

Launching of the 1st space rocket from Adelie Land, Jan., 1967.

Dumont d'Urville A14

1968, Jan. 20
30 A14 30fr lt ultra, dk bl & dk brn 140.00 80.00

Jules Sébastien César Dumont D'Urville (1790-1842), French naval commander and South Seas explorer.

WHO Anniversary Issue
Common Design Type

1968, May 4 Engr. *Perf. 13*
31 CD126 30fr red, yel & bl 65.00 45.00

Human Rights Year Issue
Common Design Type

1968, Aug. 10 Engr. *Perf. 13*

32	CD127	30fr grnsh bl, red & brn	60.00	45.00

Polar Camp with Helicopter, Plane and Snocat Tractor — A15

1969, Mar. 17 Engr. *Perf. 13*

33	A15	25fr Prus bl, lt grnsh bl & brn red	25.00	15.00

20 years of French Polar expeditions.

ILO Issue
Common Design Type

1970, Jan. 1 Engr. *Perf. 13*

35	CD131	20fr org, dk bl & brn	18.50	11.00

UPU Headquarters Issue
Common Design Type

1970, May 20 Engr. *Perf. 13*

36	CD133	50fr blue, plum & ol bis	45.00	29.00

Ice Fish A16

Fish: Nos. 38-43, Antarctic cods, various species. 135fr, Zanchlorhynchus spinifer.

1971 Engr. *Perf. 13*

37	A16	5fr brt grn, ind & org	2.00	.85
38	A16	10fr redsh brn & dp vio	2.25	.95
39	A16	20fr dp cl, brt grn & org	4.50	2.10
40	A16	22fr pur, brn ol & mag	5.00	3.25
41	A16	25fr grn, ind & org	6.50	2.75
42	A16	30fr sep, gray & bl vio	8.00	4.25
43	A16	35fr sl grn, dk brn & ocher	7.00	3.25
44	A16	135fr Prus bl, dp org & ol grn	12.00	5.25
		Nos. 37-44 (8)	47.25	22.65

Issued: Nos. 37-39, 41-42, 1/1; Nos. 40, 43-44, 12/22.

Map of Antarctica A17

Microzetia Mirabilis A18

1971, Dec. 22

45	A17	75fr red	28.00	25.00

Antarctic Treaty pledging peaceful uses of and scientific cooperation in Antarctica, 10th anniv.

1972

Insects: 15fr, Christiansenia dreuxi. 22f, Phtirocoris antarcticus. 30fr, Antarctophytosus atriceps. 40fr, Paractora drenxi. 140fr, Pringle-ophaga Kerguelenensis.

46	A18	15fr cl, org & brn	10.00	6.00
47	A18	22fr vio bl, sl grn & yel	14.50	9.25
48	A18	25fr grn, rose lil & pur	5.75	4.75
49	A18	30fr blue & multi	18.00	10.00
50	A18	40fr dk brn, ocher & blk	8.75	4.75
51	A18	140fr bl, emer & brn	12.50	8.75
		Nos. 46-51 (6)	69.50	43.50

Issued: Nos. 48, 50-51, 1/3; Nos. 46-47, 49, 12/16.

De Gaulle Issue
Common Design Type

Designs: 50fr, Gen. de Gaulle, 1940. 100fr, Pres. de Gaulle, 1970.

1972, Feb. 1 Engr. *Perf. 13*

52	CD134	50fr brt grn & blk	21.00	13.50
53	CD134	100fr brt grn & blk	26.00	20.00

Kerguelen Cabbage — A19

Designs: 61fr, Azorella selago, horiz. 87fr, Acaena ascendens, horiz.

1972-73

54	A19	45fr multicolored	10.00	5.00
55	A19	61fr multicolored	4.00	2.75
56	A19	87fr multicolored	6.00	4.00
		Nos. 54-56 (3)	20.00	11.75

Issued: 45fr, 12/18; others, 12/13/73.

Mailship Sapmer and Map of Amsterdam Island — A20

1974, Dec. 31 Engr. *Perf. 13*

57	A20	75fr bl, blk & dk brn	7.50	5.25

25th anniversary of postal service.

Antarctic Tern — A21

Designs: 50c, Antarctic petrel. 90c, Sea lioness, 1fr, Weddell seal. 1.20fr, Kerguelen cormorant, vert. 1.40fr, Gentoo penguin, vert.

1976, Jan. Engr. *Perf. 13*

58	A21	40c multicolored	4.75	3.00
59	A21	50c multicolored	4.75	3.00
60	A21	90c multicolored	7.50	4.00
61	A21	1fr multicolored	12.00	9.25
62	A21	1.20fr multicolored	15.00	11.00
63	A21	1.40fr multicolored	14.00	11.50
		Nos. 58-63 (6)	58.00	41.75

James Clark Ross — A22

James Cook — A23

Design: 30c, Climbing Mount Ross.

1976, Dec. 16 Engr. *Perf. 13*

64	A22	30c multicolored	4.50	3.00
65	A22	3fr multicolored	5.00	3.00

First climbing of Mount Ross, Kerguelen Island, Jan. 5, 1975.

1976, Dec. 16

66	A23	70c multicolored	13.50	10.00

Bicentenary of Capt. Cook's voyage past Kerguelen Island. See No. C46.

Commerson's Dolphins — A24

1977, Feb. 1 Engr. *Perf. 13*

67	A24	1.10fr Blue whale	5.75	3.25
68	A24	1.50fr shown	6.25	4.00

Macrocystis Algae — A25

Salmon Hatchery — A26

Magga Dan — A27

Designs: 70c, Durvillea algae. 90c, Albatross. 1fr, Underwater sampling and scientists, vert. 1.40fr, Thala Dan and penguins.

1977, Dec. 20 Engr. *Perf. 13*

69	A25	40c ol brn & bis	1.10	.70
70	A26	50c dk bl & pur	1.40	1.00
71	A25	70c blk, grn & brn	1.60	1.00
72	A26	90c grn, brt bl & brn	1.60	1.00
73	A27	1fr slate	1.40	1.00
74	A27	1.20fr multi	3.25	1.60
75	A27	1.40fr multi	2.00	1.60
		Nos. 69-75 (7)	12.35	7.90

See Nos. 77-79.

A28

Explorer with French and Expedition Flags.

1977, Dec. 24

76	A28	1.90fr multicolored	7.75	5.00

French Polar expeditions, 1947-48.

Types of 1977

40c, Forbin, destroyer. 50c Jeanne d'Arc, helicopter carrier. 1.40fr, Kerguelen cormorant.

1979, Jan. 1 Engr. *Perf. 13*

77	A27	40c black & blue	1.40	1.10
78	A27	50c black & blue	1.60	1.10
79	A26	1.40fr multicolored	1.60	1.10
		Nos. 77-79 (3)	4.60	3.30

A29

1979, Jan. 1

80	A29	1.20fr citron & indigo	1.40	1.10

R. Rallier du Baty. See Nos. 97, 100, 111, 117, 129, 135, 188.

French Navigators Monument, Hobart — A30

1979, Jan. 1

81	A30	1fr multicolored	.90	.80

French navigators and explorers.

Petrel — A31

1979 **Engr.** ***Perf. 13***

82 A31 70c Rockhopper penguins, vert. 1.25 1.00
83 A31 1fr shown 1.50 1.25

Commandant Bourdais — A32

1979

84 A32 1.10fr Doudart de Lagree, vert. 1.25 1.00
85 A32 1.50fr shown 1.50 1.25

Adm. Antoine d'Entrecasteaux A33

Sebastian de el Cano A34

1979

86 A33 1.20fr multicolored 1.40 1.10

1979

Discovery of Amsterdam Island, 1522: 4fr, Victoria, horiz.

87 A34 1.40fr multicolored 1.25 .80
88 A34 4fr multicolored 2.25 1.60

Adelie Penguins — A35

Adelie Penguin — A36

Sea Leopard A37

1980, Dec. 15 **Engr.** ***Perf. 13***

89 A35 50c rose violet 1.40 1.25
90 A36 60c multicolored 1.40 .90
91 A35 1.20fr multicolored 2.00 1.10
92 A37 1.30fr multicolored 1.40 1.25
93 A37 1.80fr multicolored 1.40 1.25
Nos. 89-93 (5) 7.60 5.75

20th Anniv. of Antarctic Treaty — A38

1981, June 23 **Engr.** ***Perf. 13***

94 A38 1.80fr multicolored 4.50 4.50

Alouette II — A39

1981-82 **Engr.** ***Perf. 13***

95 A39 55c brown & multi .65 .45
96 A39 65c blue & multi .70 .45

Explorer Type of 1979

1981

97 A29 1.40fr Jean Loranchet .80 .55

Landing Ship Le Gros Ventre, Kerguelen — A41

1983, Jan. 3 **Engr.** ***Perf. 13***

98 A41 55c multicolored .90 .65

Our Lady of the Winds Statue and Church, Kerguelen — A42

1983, Jan. 3

99 A42 1.40fr multicolored .90 .90

Explorer Type of 1979

Design: Martin de Vivies, Navigator.

1983, Jan. 3

100 A29 1.60fr multicolored .90 .75

Eaton's Ducks A44

1983, Jan. 3

101 A44 1.50fr multicolored .90 .60
102 A44 1.80fr multicolored 1.00 .75

Trawler Austral — A45

1983, Jan. 3

103 A45 2.30fr multicolored 1.50 1.10

Freighter Lady Franklin — A46

1983, Aug. 4 **Engr.** ***Perf. 13***

104 A46 5fr multicolored 4.00 3.00

Glaciology — A47

Design: Scientists examining glacier, base.

1984, Jan. 1 **Engr.** ***Perf. 13***

105 A47 15c multicolored .45 .30
106 A47 1.70fr multicolored .85 .55

Crab-eating Seal — A48

Penguins — A49

1984, Jan. 1

107 A48 60c multicolored .55 .45
108 A49 70c multicolored .45 .45
109 A49 2fr multicolored 1.25 1.00
110 A48 5.90fr multicolored 2.00 1.75
Nos. 107-110 (4) 4.25 3.65

Explorer Type of 1979

1984, Jan. 1

111 A29 1.80fr Alfred Faure .90 .70

Biomass — A51

1985, Jan. 1 **Engr.** ***Perf. 13***

112 A51 1.80fr multicolored .80 .55
113 A51 5.20fr multicolored 2.00 1.75

Emperor Penguins — A52

Snowy Petrel — A53

1985, Jan. 1 **Engr.** ***Perf. 13***

114 A52 1.70fr multicolored 1.00 .80
115 A53 2.80fr multicolored 1.25 1.10

Port Martin — A54

1985, Jan. 1 **Engr.** ***Perf. 13***

116 A54 2.20fr multicolored 1.25 .80

Explorer Type of 1979

1985, Jan. 1 **Engr.** ***Perf. 13***

117 A29 2fr Andre-Frank Liotard .90 .70

Antarctic Fulmar — A56

1986, Jan. 1 **Engr.** ***Perf. 13***

118 A56 1fr shown .55 .45
119 A56 1.70fr Giant petrels .80 .75
Nos. 118-119,C91 (3) 3.35 2.95

Echinoderms — A57

1986, Jan. 1

120 A57 1.90fr shown .90 .75

Cotula Plumosa — A58

1986, Jan. 1

121 A58 2.30fr shown .90 .75
122 A58 6.20fr Lycopodium. saururus 2.50 1.90

Shipping — A59

1986, Jan. 1
123 A59 2.10fr Var research ship .90 .85
124 A59 3fr Polarbjorn support ship 1.25 1.25

Marine Life — A60

1987, Jan. 1 Engr. ***Perf. 13½x13***
125 A60 50c dk blue & org .60 .50

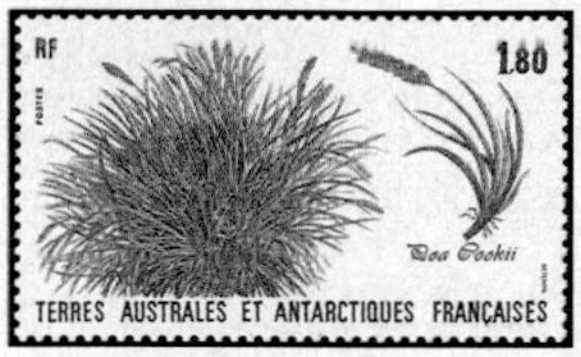

Flora — A61

1987, Jan. 1
126 A61 1.80fr Poa cookii .70 .50
127 A61 6.50fr Lichen, Neuropogon taylori 2.00 1.90

Marret Base, Adelie Land — A62

1987, Jan. 1
128 A62 2fr yel brn, dk ultra & lake .90 .70

Explorer Type of 1979

1987, Jan. 1
129 A29 2.20fr Adm. Mouchez 1.00 .75

Reindeer — A64

1987, Jan. 1
130 A64 2.50fr black 1.25 .80

Transport Ship Eure — A65

1987, Jan. 1
131 A65 3.20fr dk ultra, Prus grn & dk grn 1.50 1.00

Macaroni Penguins — A66

1987, Jan. 1 ***Perf. 13x12½***
132 A66 4.80fr multicolored 2.50 1.90

Elephant Grass — A67

1988, Jan. 1 Engr. ***Perf. 13***
133 A67 1.70fr Prus grn, emer & olive .85 .65

Rev.-Father Lejay, Explorer — A68

1988, Jan. 1
134 A68 2.20fr vio, ultra & blk 1.00 .80

Explorer Type of 1979

Design: Robert Gessain (1907-86).

1988, Jan. 1
135 A29 3.40fr gray, dk red & blk 1.50 1.10

Le Gros Ventre, 18th Cent. — A70

1988, Jan. 1
136 A70 3.50fr dp ultra, bl grn & brn 1.25 1.25

Mermaid and B.A.P. Jules Verne, Research Vessel — A71

1988, Jan. 1
137 A71 4.90fr gray & dk blue 2.50 1.75

La Fortune, Early 19th Cent. — A72

1988, Jan. 1
138 A72 5fr blk & dull bl grn 2.25 1.75

Wilson's Petrel — A73

1988, Jan. 1
139 A73 6.80fr blk, sepia & dl bl grn 2.75 2.25

See Nos. 143-144.

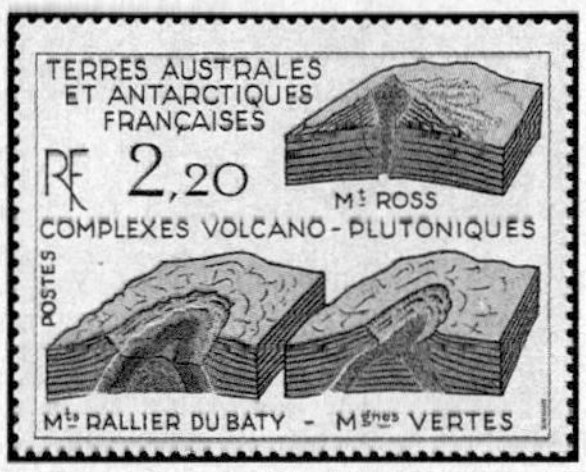

Mt. Ross Campaign (in 1987) — A74

1988, Jan. 1 ***Perf. 13x12½***
140 A74 2.20fr Volcanic rock cross-sections 1.00 1.00
141 A74 15.10fr Kerguelen Is. 5.50 5.50
a. Pair, #140-141 + label 7.50 7.50

Darrieus System Wind Vane Electric Generator — A75

1988, Jan. 1 Engr. ***Perf. 13***
142 A75 1fr dark blue & blue .50 .35

Fauna Type of 1988

1989, Jan. 1 Engr.
143 A73 1.10fr Lithodes .40 .40
144 A73 3.60fr Blue petrel 1.40 .75

Fern A76

1989, Jan. 1
145 A76 2.80fr Blechnum penna Marina 1.00 .90

Minerals A77

1989, Jan. 1
146 A77 5.10fr Mesotype 2.00 2.00
147 A77 7.30fr Analcime 3.00 3.00

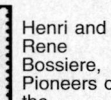

Henri and Rene Bossiere, Pioneers of the Kerguelen Isls. — A78

1989, Jan. 1
148 A78 2.20fr multicolored 1.10 .75

Kerguelen Is. Sheep — A79

1989, Jan. 1 ***Perf. 13½x13***
149 A79 2fr multicolored .90 .65

Scuba Diver, Adelie Coast — A80

1989, Jan. 1
150 A80 1.70fr dk olive bis, blue & dk grn .80 .60

Map of Kerguelen Island, Protozoa and Copepod — A81

1990, Jan. 1 Engr. ***Perf. 13***
151 A81 1.10fr blk, brt blue & red brn .75 .40

Study of protista, Kerguelan Is.

Cattle on Farm, Sea Birds — A82

1990, Jan. 1
152 A82 1.70fr Prus blue, grn & brn blk .85 .60

Rehabilitation of the environment, Amsterdam Is.

Quoy and *Copendium decollata* — A83

Dumont d'Urville (1790-1842), Explorer — A84

1990, Jan. 1 ***Perf. 13½x13***

153 A83 2.20fr brt blue, blk & red brn 1.00 .75

Jean Rene C. Quoy (1790-1869), naturalist, navigator.

1990, Jan. 1

154 A84 3.60fr ultra & blk 1.50 1.10

Yellow-billed Albatross — A85

1990, Jan. 1 ***Perf. 13x12½***

155 A85 2.80fr multicolored 2.00 .90

Aragonite A86

1990, Jan. 1

156 A86 5.10fr deep ultra & dark yel grn 2.50 1.75

Ranunculus pseudo trullifolius — A87

1990, Jan. 1 ***Perf. 13***

157 A87 8.40fr dp bl, org & emer grn 3.25 2.75

Penguin Type of Airpost 1974

1991, Jan. 1

158 AP18 50c blue grn, bl & blk .80 .40

Postal Service at Crozet Island, 30th anniv.

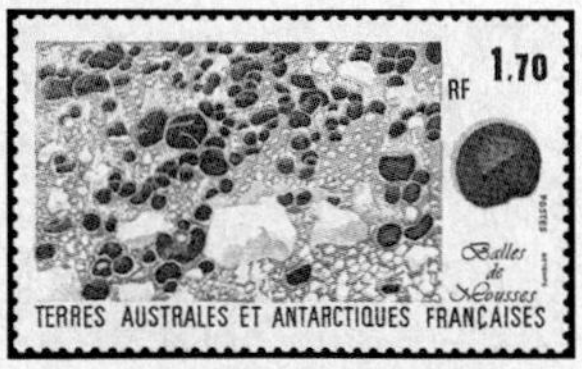

Moss — A88

1991, Jan. 1 ***Perf. 13x12½***

159 A88 1.70fr gray, brn & blk .90 .65

Adm. Max Douguet (1903-1989) A89

1991, Jan. 1

160 A89 2.30fr org brn, blk & bl 1.25 .90

Lighter L'Aventure — A90

1991, Jan. 1 **Engr.** ***Perf. 13***

161 A90 3.20fr brn, grn & bl 1.50 1.25

Sea Lions — A91

1991, Jan. 1 ***Perf. 13***

162 A91 3.60fr blue & ol brn 2.25 1.40

Mordenite — A92

1991, Jan. 1

163 A92 5.20fr blk, grn bl & grn 2.75 2.00

Champsocephalus Gunnari — A93

1991, Jan. 1

164 A93 7.80fr blue & green 3.00 3.00

A94 A95

1991, Jan. 1

165 A94 9.30fr ol grn & rose red 4.00 3.50

Antarctic Treaty, 30th anniv.

1992, Jan. 1 **Engr.** ***Perf. 13***

Design: Colobanthus Kerguelensis.

166 A95 1fr bl grn, grn & brn .90 .45

Globe Challenge Yacht Race — A96

1992, Jan. 1 **Litho.**

167 A96 2.20fr multicolored 1.50 1.00

Dissostichus Eleginoides — A97

1992, Jan. 1 **Engr.**

168 A97 2.30fr blue, ol grn & red brn 1.50 1.00

Paul Tchernia A98

1992, Jan. 1 **Engr.** ***Perf. 13***

169 A98 2.50fr brown & green 1.00 1.00

Capt. Marion Dufresne (1724-1772) — A99

1992, Jan. 1 **Engr.** ***Perf. 13***

170 A99 3.70fr red, blk & bl 1.50 1.50

Supply Ship Tottan, 1951 — A100

1992, Jan. 1 **Engr.** ***Perf. 13***

171 A100 14fr blue grn, brn & bl 5.75 5.75

WOCE Program — A101

1992, Jan. 1

172 A101 25.40fr multi 12.00 10.50

Coat of Arms — A102

1992-95 **Engr.** ***Perf. 13***

173 A102 10c black .40 .25
174 A102 20c greenish blue .40 .25
175 A102 30c red .40 .25
176 A102 40c green .40 .25
177 A102 50c orange .40 .25
Nos. 173-177 (5) 2.00 1.25

Issued: 10c, 1/1/92; 20c, 30c, 1/1/93; 40c, 1/1/94; 50c, 1/2/95.

See Nos. 295-299.

Garnet A103

1993, Jan. 1 **Engr.** ***Perf. 13***

183 A103 1fr multicolored 1.25 .30

See Nos. 194, 203, 212, 222, 235, 244, 259, 279, 300, 330.

Research Ship Marion Dufresne, 20th Anniv. — A104

1993, Jan. 1

184 A104 2.20fr multicolored 1.25 .60

Lyallia Kerguelensis A105

1993, Jan. 1

185 A105 2.30fr blue & green 1.25 .60

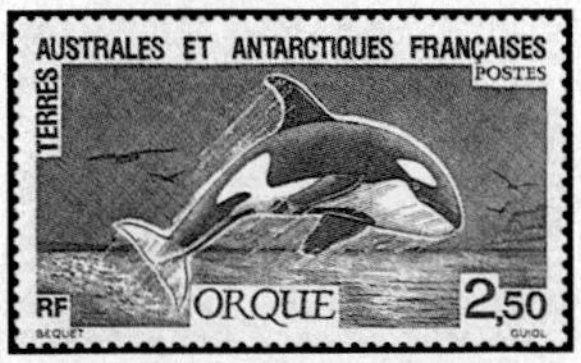

A106

A107

1993, Jan. 1

186 A106 2.50fr Killer whale 1.50 .70
187 A107 2.50fr Skua 7.00 .70

A108

Design: 2.50fr, Andre Prudhomme (1930-1959), Meteorologist. 22fr, Weather station, Adelie Land.

1993, Jan. 1 ***Perf. 12½x13***

188	2.50fr blue, blk & org	1.00	.65
189	22fr org, blk & bl	8.50	6.00
a.	A108 Pair, #188-189 + label	11.00	11.00

43rd Anniv. of Mètèo France in French Southern & Antarctic Territory.

Centriscops Obliquus — A109

1993, Jan. 1 ***Perf. 13***
190 A109 3.40fr multicolored 1.50 .90

Freighter Italo Marsano — A110

1993, Jan. 1
191 A110 3.70fr multicolored 1.75 1.00

ECOPHY Program A111

1993, Jan. 1
192 A111 14fr black, blue & brn 6.50 4.25

L'Astrolabe on Northeast Route, 1991 A112

1993, Jan. 1
193 A112 22fr multicolored 9.25 5.75

Mineral Type of 1993

1994, Jan. 1 **Engr.** ***Perf. 13***
194 A103 1fr Cordierite 2.00 .80

Felis Catus — A113

1994, Jan. 1
195 A113 2fr green & black 3.50 1.25

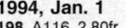

A114

1994, Jan. 1 **Engr.** ***Perf. 13***
196 A114 2.40fr dk brn, blk & bl 1.50 .65

A115

1994, Jan. 1
197 A115 2.80fr slate blue 1.60 .90

Robert Pommier (1919-61) A116

1994, Jan. 1
198 A116 2.80fr multicolored 1.60 .90

A117

Designs: 2.80fr, C.A. Vincendon Dumoulin (1811-58), hydrographer. 23fr, Measuring Earth's magnetic field.

1994, Jan. 1 ***Perf. 12½x13***

199	2.80fr black & blue	1.40	.70
200	23fr blue & black	8.75	5.75
a.	A117 Pair, #199-200 + label	11.00	11.00

Rascasse — A119

1994, Jan. 1 ***Perf. 13***
201 A119 3.70fr bl grn & red brn 1.50 .95

Kerguelen of Tremarec — A120

1994, Jan. 1
202 A120 4.30fr multicolored 1.75 1.10

Mineral Type of 1993

1995, Jan. 2 **Engr.** ***Perf. 13***
203 A103 1fr Olivine 1.50 .40

Mancoglosse Antarctique — A121

1995, Jan. 2
204 A121 2.40fr ol brn, vio & bl grn 1.50 .95

Andree (1903-90) and Edgar de la Rue (1901-91) A122

1995, Jan. 2
205 A122 2.80fr bl, red brn & mag 1.50 .85

SODAR Station — A123

1995, Jan. 2
206 A123 2.80fr vio, mag & red brn 1.50 .90

Mont D'Alsace — A124

1995, Jan. 2
207 A124 3.70fr dk bl, vio, red brn 1.75 1.10

Balaenoptera Acutorostrata — A125

1995, Jan. 2
208 A125 23fr blue, claret & ind 11.50 7.00

Sailing Ship Tamaris A126

1995, Jan. 2
209 A126 25.80fr multicolored 11.00 7.50

L'Heroine, Crozet Islands Mission, 1837 — A127

1995, Jan. 2
210 A127 27.30fr blue 11.50 7.75

Creation of the Territories, 40th Anniv. — A128

1995, Aug. 7 **Litho.** ***Imperf.***
Size: 143x84mm
211 A128 30fr multicolored 15.00 15.00

Mineral Type of 1993

1996, Jan. 1 **Engr.** ***Perf. 13***
212 A103 1fr Amazonite 1.00 .30

White-chinned Petrel — A129

1996, Jan. 1
213 A129 2.40fr blue black 1.50 .75

Expedition Ship Yves de Kerguelen — A130

1996, Jan. 1
214 A130 2.80fr multicolored 1.75 .80

Benedict Point Scientific Research Station, Amsterdam Island — A131

1996, Jan. 1
215 A131 2.80fr multicolored 1.50 .80

Paul-Emile Victor (1907-1995), Polar Explorer — A132

Designs: 2.80fr, Victor crossing Greenland with sled dogs, 1936. 23fr, Victor, penguins, Dumont d'Urville Base, Adélie Land.

1996, Jan. 1

216 A132 2.80fr multicolored		1.50	.90
217 A132 23fr multicolored		12.00	8.00
a. Pair, #216-217 + label		14.00	14.00

Admiral Jacquinot (1796-1879), Antarctic Explorer — A133

1996, Jan. 1

218 A133 3.70fr dark blue & blue 1.75 1.10

Trawler Austral — A134

1996, Jan. 1 **Photo. & Engr.**

219 A134 4.30fr multicolored 2.25 1.40

Lycopodium Magellanicum — A135

1996, Jan. 1 **Engr.**

220 A135 7.70fr multicolored 3.25 2.40

Search for Micrometeorites, Cape Prudhomme — A136

1996, Jan. 1

221 A136 15fr vio, blk & grn bl 8.00 5.00

Mineral Type of 1993

1997, Jan. 1 **Engr.** ***Perf. 13x12½***

222 A103 1fr Amethyst 1.40 .40

Storm Petrel — A137

1997, Jan. 1 ***Perf. 13***

223 A137 2.70fr blue & indigo 1.50 .90

Rene Garcia (1915-95), Windmill A138

1997, Jan. 1

224 A138 3fr multicolored 1.60 1.00

Research Ship Marion Dufresne — A139

Photo. & Engr.

1997, Jan. 1 ***Perf. 13x12½***

225 A139 3fr multicolored 1.75 1.00

A140

A141

1997, Jan. 1 **Engr.** ***Perf. 13***

226 A140 4fr black & brown 1.75 1.25

Jean Turquet (1867-1945).

1997, Jan. 1

227 A141 5.20fr multicolored 2.40 1.60

Church of Our Lady of Birds, Crozet Island.

A142

1997, Jan. 1

228 A142 8fr multicolored 4.00 2.60

Army Health Service.

A143

1997, Jan. 1

229 A143 29.20fr Poa Kerguelensis 12.50 9.25

French Polar Expeditions, 50th Anniv. — A144

Designs: No. 230, Greenland Expedition. No. 231, Port Martin, 1950-51, Marret Base, 1952, Adélie Land. No. 232, Dumont D'Urville, 1956, Charcot Station, Magnetic Pole, 1957.

Photo. & Engr.

1997, Feb. 28 ***Perf. 13x12½***

230 A144 1fr multicolored		1.25	.80
231 A144 1fr multicolored		1.25	.80
232 A144 1fr multicolored		1.25	.80
a. Strip of 3, #230-232		7.50	3.25

Yves-Joseph de Kerguelen Trémarec (1734-97) — A145

3fr, Portrait. 24fr, Cook's landing at Kerguelen Island, Dec. 1776.

1997, Mar. 3 **Engr.** ***Perf. 13***

233 3fr multicolored		1.25	.90
234 24fr multicolored		9.75	7.25
a. A145 Pair, #233-234 + label		14.00	10.00

No. 234 is 37x37mm.

Mineral Type of 1993

1998, Jan. 2 **Engr.** ***Perf. 13***

235 A103 1fr Rock crystal 1.25 .40

Fisheries Management — A146

Designs: No. 236, Fishing boats. No. 237, Examining fish, performing research.

1998, Jan. 2

236 A146 2.60fr multicolored		1.50	.75
237 A146 2.60fr multicolored		1.50	.75
a. Pair, #236-237 + label		4.00	4.00

Gray-headed Albatross — A147

1998, Jan. 2

238 A147 2.70fr multicolored 1.75 .75

Ecology of St. Paul Island — A148

1998, Jan. 2

239 A148 3fr bl, brn & grn 2.50 1.00

A149

A150

1998, Jan. 2 ***Perf. 13x13½***

240 A149 3fr lilac, blue & black 1.75 .85

Etienne Peau, Antarctic explorer.

1998, Jan. 2

241 A150 4fr lt org, blk & red brn 1.75 1.10

Georges Laclavere (1906-94), geographer.

Mole Shark — A151

1998, Jan. 2 ***Perf. 13***

242 A151 27fr multicolored 11.00 7.25

"Le Cancalais" — A152

1998, Jan. 2

243 A152 29.20fr multicolored 12.00 7.75

Mineral Type of 1993

1999, Jan. 1 **Engr.** ***Perf. 13***

244 A103 1fr Epidote, vert. 1.25 .40

Chinstrap Penguin — A153

1999, Jan. 1

245 A153 2.70fr brn, blk & bl 1.60 .85

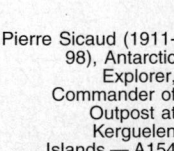

Pierre Sicaud (1911-98), Antarctic Explorer, Commander of Outpost at Kerguelen Islands — A154

1999, Jan. 1

246 A154 3fr black & green 1.40 .95

Penguins of Crozet Islands — A155

1999, Jan. 1

247 A155 3fr multicolored 3.00 .85

Jacques-André Martin (1911-49) — A156

1999, Jan. 1
248 A156 4fr multicolored 1.75 1.10

Ray — A157

1999, Jan. 1 ***Perf. 12½***
249 A157 5.20fr mag, bl & brn 2.50 1.50

Value is for stamp with surrounding rectangular selvage.

F.S. Floreal — A158

1999, Jan. 1 **Photo.** ***Perf. 13***
250 A158 5.20fr multicolored 2.50 1.40

No. 250 was printed se-tenant with label. Value is for stamp with label attached.

"Pop Cat" Program, Kerguelen Islands — A159

1999, Jan. 1 **Engr.**
251 A159 8fr multicolored 4.75 2.75

Study of Albatrosses on Artificial Nests A160

1999, Jan. 1
252 A160 16fr olive, grn & blk 7.00 4.50

Amsterdam Base, Kerguelen Base, 50th Anniv. — A161

1999, Jan. 1
253 A161 3fr Amsterdam Base 6.00 .85
254 A161 24fr Kerguelen Base 10.50 6.50
a. Pair, #253-254 + label 18.00 15.00

Festuca Contracta A162

1999, Jan. 1
255 A162 24fr dk grn, ol & bl grn 10.50 6.50

Geoleta Program — A163

1999, Jan. 1 ***Perf. 13x12½***
256 A163 29.20fr blk, bl & red brn 13.00 7.75

Voyage of Marion Dufresne II — A164

a, Docked, Reunion. b, Passengers in dining salon. c, Penguins, Crozet Island. d, Postal manager of Alfred Faure, Crozet Island, vert. e, Port of France, Kerguelen Island. f, Port Couvreux, Kerguelen Island. g, Offloading stores, Port of France, Kerguelen Island. h, Port Jeanne d'arc, Kerguelen Island. i, St. Paul Island. j, Ruins of lobster cannery, St. Paul Island. k, Martin de Vivies Base, Amsterdam Island. l, Offloading cargo, Amsterdam Island.

1999, May 1 **Litho.** ***Perf. 13***
257 A164 Souv. bklt., #a.-l. 92.50

Nos. 257a-257l are all non-denominated. Stamps are valid for 20 gram international letter rate. Each stamp appears on a separate booklet pane showing an enlarged design of the stamp. Booklet sold for 100fr.

See Nos. 294, 329, 359, 390, 420, 482.

Souvenir Sheet

PhilexFrance '99, World Philatelic Exhibition — A165

Antarctic postmarks on stamps: a, Malagasy Republic #280. b, Malagasy Republic #282. c, Malagasy Republic #C42. d, #21.

1999, July 2 **Litho. & Engr.** ***Perf. 13***
258 A165 5.20fr Sheet of 4, #a.-d. 11.50 7.00

Nos. 258b-258c are each 40x52mm.

Mineral Type of 1993

2000, Jan. **Engr.** ***Perf. 12¾x13***
259 A103 1fr Mica, *vert.* 1.25 .40

Puffin — A166

2000, Jan. ***Perf. 13x12¾***
260 A166 2.70fr multi 2.00 .80

André Beaugé (1913-97) A167

2000, Jan. ***Perf. 12¾x13***
261 A167 3fr multi 1.40 .70

Abby Jane Morrell — A168

2000, Jan. ***Perf. 13¼x13***
262 A168 4fr multi 1.75 .95

Oceanographic Survey — A169

2000, Jan. ***Perf. 13x12½***
263 A169 4.40fr multi 1.90 1.00

Sled Dog Hobbs — A170

2000, Jan. ***Perf. 12¾x13***
264 A170 5.20fr multi 2.25 1.25

Sleep Study — A171

2000, Jan. **Photo.** ***Perf. 13x12½***
265 A171 8fr multi + label 3.50 1.90

Ship "La Perouse" — A172

2000, Jan. **Engr.** ***Perf. 13x12½***
266 A172 16fr multi 7.00 3.75

Lantern Fish — A173

2000, Jan.
267 A173 24fr multi 10.50 5.50

Larose Bay — A174

2000, Jan.
268 A174 27fr multi 12.00 6.25

Explorers A175

No. 269, Yves Joseph de Kerguelen-Trémarec (1734-97). No. 270, Jules Sébastien César Dumont D'Urville (1790-1842). No. 271, Raymond Rallier du Baty (1881-1978). No. 272, Edgar Aubert de La Rüe (1901-91). #273, Paul-Emile Victor (1907-95).

2000, Jan. ***Perf. 13***

Booklet Stamps

269 A175 3fr multi 1.50 .70
270 A175 3fr multi 1.50 .70
271 A175 3fr multi 1.50 .70
272 A175 3fr multi 1.50 .70
273 A175 3fr multi 1.50 .70
a. Bklt. pane, #269-273 + 2 labels 8.00
Complete booklet, #273a 9.50

Souvenir Sheet

The Third Millennium — A176

No. 274: a, Penguins, Crozet Islands. b, Seals, Kerguelen Islands. c, Crustacean,

Saint-Paul and Amsterdam Islands. d, Hovering vehicle, Adelie Land.

2000, Jan. Photo. *Perf. 13*
274 A176 3fr Sheet of 4, #a.-d. 7.50 7.50

Bird Demographic Studies — A177

Designs: 5.20fr, Bird banding. 8fr, Albatross, graph. 16fr, Emperor penguins, graph.

2000, Jan. *Perf. 13x13¼*
275 A177 5.20fr multi 2.25 1.25

Size: 50x28mm

276 A177 8fr multi 3.50 1.90
277 A177 16fr multi 7.00 3.75
a. Horiz. strip, #275-277 14.00 14.00

Relocation of Headquarters to Reunion — A178

2000, Aug. 6 Litho. *Perf. 13*
278 A178 27fr multi 12.00 5.50

Mineral Type of 1993

2001, Jan. 1 Engr. *Perf. 13x12¾*
279 A103 1fr Magnetite 1.25 .40

Diving Petrel — A179

2001, Jan. 1 *Perf. 13x13¼*
280 A179 2.70fr multi 1.50 .60

High Mountain Military Group A180

2001, Jan. 1 *Perf. 13¼x13*
281 A180 3fr multi 1.40 .65

Kerguelen Arch — A181

2001, Jan. 1 *Perf. 13*
282 A181 3fr blue gray 2.00 .70

Xavier-Charles Richert (1913-92) A182

Jean Coulomb A183

2001, Jan. 1
283 A182 3fr multi 1.40 .65

2001, Jan. 1
284 A183 4fr multi 1.75 .85

Memorial to 1874 Astronomical Observation, St. Paul Island — A184

2001, Jan. 1
285 A184 8fr brn & blk 3.50 1.75

Frigate La Fayette — A185

2001, Jan. 1 *Perf. 13x13¼*
286 A185 16fr multi 7.00 3.50

Squid — A186

2001, Jan. 1
287 A186 24fr multi 10.50 5.00

Amateur Radio Link Between Space Station Mir and Crozet Island — A187

2001, Jan. 1 Litho. *Perf. 13*
288 A187 27fr multi 12.00 5.50

Bryum Laevigatum — A188

2001, Jan. 1 Engr. *Perf. 13x12½*
289 A188 29.20fr multi 13.00 6.00

Souvenir Sheet

Ships — A189

No. 290: a, Carmen. b, Austral. c, Ramuntcho. d, Samper 1.

2001, Jan. 1 *Perf. 13x13½*
290 A189 5.20fr Sheet of 4, #a-d 9.00 4.50

Souvenir Sheet

Wildlife — A190

No. 291: a, Albatrosses. b, Emperor penguins, horiz. c, Sea lions, horiz. d, Whales.

2001, Jan. 1 Litho. *Perf. 13*
291 A190 3fr Sheet of 4, #a-d 10.50 5.00

Antarctic Treaty, 40th Anniv. — A191

2001, June 23 Engr. *Perf. 13x12¾*
292 A191 5.20fr dark & sky blue 3.25 1.00

Commission for the Conservation of Antarctic Marine Living Resources, 20th Anniv. — A192

2001, Oct. 22 Litho. *Perf. 13*
293 A192 5.20fr multi 5.00 2.00

Voyage Booklet Type of 1999

Adélie Land: a, Boat in pack ice. b, Dumont d'Urville Base. c, Adélie penguin rookery. d, L'Astrolabe Glacier. e, Pointe Géologie Archipelago. f, Release of meteorological balloon. g, Equipment convoy. h, Helicopter transport of fresh supplies. i, Arrival of emperor penguins. j, Telecommunications center. k, Looking towards the Antarctic. l, Cape Prud'homme. m, Ship L'Astrolabe anchored. n, Dispatch of mail.

2001, Oct. 29 *Perf. 13*
294 A164 Souvenir booklet, 2 each #a-n 95.00

Nos. 294a-294n are all non-denominated. Stamps are valid for 20 gram international letter rate. Each stamp appears on a separate booklet pane showing an enlarged design of the stamp and on one pane with all of the stamps and four labels found at the center of the booklet. the booklet sold for 196.78fr.

100 Cents = 1 Euro (€)

Arms Type of 1992-95 with Euro Denominations

2002, Jan. 2 Engr. *Perf. 13*
295 A102 1c black .25 .25
296 A102 2c greenish blue .25 .25
297 A102 5c red .30 .25
298 A102 10c green .40 .25
299 A102 20c orange .70 .25
Nos. 295-299 (5) 1.90 1.25

Mineral Type of 1993 with Euro Denomination

2002, Jan. 2 Engr. *Perf. 12¾x13*
300 A103 15c Nepheline, vert. 1.00 .40

Albatross A193

2002, Jan. 2 *Perf. 13¼x13*
301 A193 41c multi 3.00 .80

Ship "Marion Dufresne" — A194

2002, Jan. 2 *Perf. 13x13¼*
302 A194 46c multi 1.40 .60

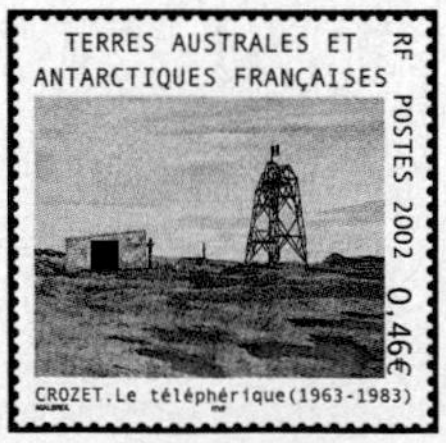

1963-83 Telegraph Station, Crozet Island A195

2002, Jan. 2 Litho. *Perf. 13*
303 A195 46c multi 1.50 .60

Jacques Dubois (1920-2000) A196

2002, Jan. 2 Engr.
304 A196 61c multi 2.25 .90

Engraved Rock, Saint Paul Island — A197

2002, Jan. 2 ***Perf. 13x13¼***
305 A197 79c multi 2.40 1.25

Kerguelen Cabbage A198

2002, Jan. 2 ***Perf. 12¼***
306 A198 €1.22 multi 3.50 1.75

Passage of the Ship "Gauss," Cent. — A199

2002, Jan. 2 ***Perf. 13x12¼***
307 A199 €2.44 multi 7.25 3.50

Crab — A200

2002, Jan. 2 ***Perf. 13x13¼***
308 A200 €3.66 multi 11.00 5.25

Pack Ice Diatoms — A201

2002, Jan. 2 **Litho.** ***Perf. 13***
309 A201 €4.12 multi 12.50 6.00

French Geographic Society Building, Paris — A202

2002, Jan. 2 **Engr.** ***Perf. 13¼x13***
310 A202 €4.45 multi + label 13.50 8.00

Cartoker Program — A203

No. 311: a, 46c, Diagram of plate tectonics. b, €3.66, Geological map of Kerguelen Island.

2002, Jan. 2 ***Perf. 13x12¼***
311 A203 Horiz. pair, #a-b, + central label 12.50 12.50

Souvenir Sheet

Olympic Games for Antarctic Animals — A204

No. 312: a, Albatrosses flying marathon. b, Langoustines diving, vert. c, Penguins riding bobsled course, vert. d, Killer whales performing synchronized swimming, vert.

2002, Jan. 2 **Litho.** ***Perf. 13***
312 A204 46c Sheet of 4, #a-d 6.50 5.50

Souvenir Sheet

Animals and Their Young — A205

No. 313: a, Penguins. b, Sea lions. c, Albatrosses. d, Elephant seals.

2002, Jan. 2
313 A205 79c Sheet of 4, #a-d 10.50 9.50

Introduction of the Euro A206

2002, Feb. 17
314 A206 46c blue & black 3.50 .60

Mineral Type of 1993

2003, Jan. **Engr.** ***Perf. 13¼***
315 A103 15c Apatite, vert. 1.25 .40

Lobster Processing Plant, Saint-Paul — A207

2003, Jan. ***Perf. 13x13¼***
316 A207 41c multi 1.25 .65

Luc Marie Bayle (1914-2000), Painter — A208

2003, Jan. **Litho.** ***Perf. 13***
317 A208 46c multi 1.50 .70

Emperor Penguins — A209

2003, Jan.
318 A209 46c multi 2.75 .80

Otice Hydroacoustic Station — A210

2003, Jan. **Engr.** ***Perf. 13x13¼***
319 A210 61c multi 1.90 1.00

Restoration of Port Jeanne d'Arc — A211

2003, Jan. ***Perf. 13x12¼***
320 A211 79c multi 2.40 1.25

Phylica — A212

2003, Jan. ***Perf. 13x13¼***
321 A212 €1.22 multi 4.50 2.25

Ship "Bougainville" A213

2003, Jan. ***Perf. 13¼x13***
322 A213 €2.44 multi 7.25 4.25

Chub — A214

2003, Jan. **Engr.** ***Perf. 13x13¼***
323 A214 €3.66 multi 11.00 6.50

Ile aux Pingouins — A215

2003, Jan. ***Perf. 13x12¼***
324 A215 €3.66 black 11.00 6.50

Super Darn Antenna Array — A216

2003, Jan. ***Perf. 13***
325 A216 €4.12 multi 12.50 7.00

Souvenir Sheet

Paintings Revised to Reflect a Less Southerly Antarctica — A217

No. 326: a, Triumph of Venus with fish and lobsters. b, King Louis XV and wife with penguins, vert. c, Jules Dumont d'Urville and wife in a grassy Adélie Land. d, Chevalier Yves de Kerguelin under umbrella, seal in pool, vert.

2003, Jan. **Litho.**
326 A217 46c Sheet of 4, #a-d 6.50 6.50

Protective Clothing — A218

Cold-weather outerwear from: a, 1898. b, 1912. c, 2002. d, 1980, e, 1996.

2003, Jan. **Photo.** ***Perf. 13¼x13***
327 Booklet pane of 5 12.00 —
a.-e. A218 79c Any single 2.40 1.25
Booklet, #327 12.00

Voyage of the Ship "Français," Cent. — A219

2003, Aug. 31 **Engr.** ***Perf. 13x13¼***
328 Horiz. strip of 3 15.00 13.50
a. A219 79c Capt. J.-B. Charcot 2.50 1.25
b. A219 €1.22 Ship in ice, horiz. 4.00 2.00
c. A219 €2.44 Ship in harbor, horiz. 7.50 4.25

Stamp size: Nos. 328b-328c, 49x29mm.

Voyage Booklet Type of 1999

Recipes: a, Truite aus deux citrons (trout and waterfall). b, Veau d'Amsterdam à la savoyarde (cattle). c, Lapin "Volage" à la cannelle (rabbits, penguins). d, Rôti de légine de l'ile de l'est (fish). e, Civet de renne "Volcan du diable," (reindeer). f, Iles antarctiques flottantes. g, Langouste à la mode de Saint-Paul (lobster). h, Gigot de mouflon aux 5 épices et aux pommes (sheep). i, Cabot tropical (fish, ship). j, Tagine d'agneau aux épices de la Réunion (sheep). k, Moules au pastis (mussels). l, Glace à la menthe sauvage d'Amsterdam (mint plant).

2003, Nov. 6 **Litho.** ***Perf. 13***
329 A164 Souvenir booklet, #a-l 60.00

Nos. 329a-329l are all non-denominated. Stamps are valid for 20 gram international letter rate. Each stamp appears on a separate booklet pane showing an enlarged design of the stamp. The booklet sold for €17.

Mineral Type of 1993

2004, Jan. 1 **Engr.** ***Perf. 13¼***
330 A103 15c Chalcedony, vert. 1.25 .40

A220

A221

2004, Jan. 1 **Engr.** ***Perf. 13x13¼***
331 A220 45c multi 1.40 .85

Mario Marret, director of film "Terre Adélie."

2004, Jan. 1
332 A221 50c multi 1.75 .95

Col. Robert Genty (1910-2001).

Albert Faure Base, Crozet Island, 40th Anniv. — A222

2004, Jan. 1 **Litho. & Engr.**
333 A222 50c multi 1.50 .95

Péron's Dolphins — A223

2004, Jan. 1 **Litho.** ***Perf. 13***
334 A223 75c multi 3.00 1.50

Twin Otter Flights A224

2004, Jan. 1 **Photo.** ***Perf. 12¾***
335 A224 90c multi 2.75 1.75

Values are for stamps with surrounding selvage.

Iceberg — A225

2004, Jan. 1 **Engr.** ***Perf. 13x13¼***
336 A225 €1.30 multi 4.00 2.40

Grave of Sailors from the Volage — A226

2004, Jan. 1 ***Perf. 13¼x13***
337 A226 €2.50 multi 7.50 5.00

Krill — A227

2004, Jan. 1 ***Perf. 13x13¼***
338 A227 €4 multi 12.00 8.00

Ship "Dives" — A228

2004, Jan. 1
339 A228 €4.50 multi 13.50 9.25

Souvenir Sheet

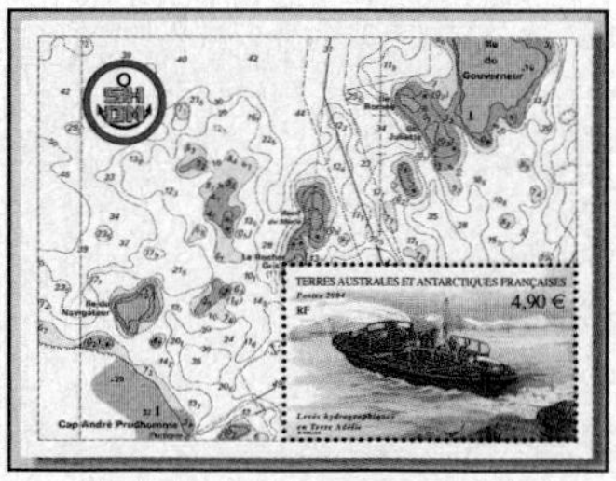

Hydrological Surveys, Adélie Land — A229

2004, Jan. 1 **Litho.** ***Perf. 13***
340 A229 €4.90 multi 15.00 10.50

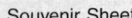

Souvenir Sheet

Imaginary "TAAFland" Theme Park — A230

No. 341: a, Whale statue, pyramidal entrance structure. b, Showgirls, seals, vert. c, Boy and girl with ice cream cones, vert. d, Woman in swimsuit, penguins.

2004, Jan. 1
341 A230 50c Sheet of 4, #a-d 8.00 8.00

Souvenir Sheet

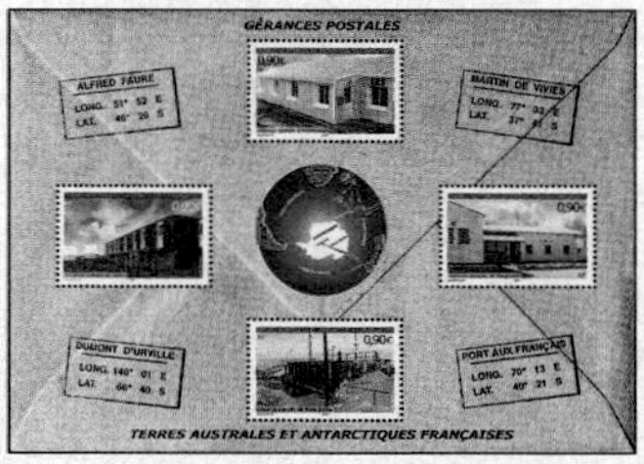

Post Offices — A231

No. 342: a, Amsterdam Island. b, Crozet Island. c, Kerguelen Island. d, Adélie Land.

2004, Jan. 1
342 A231 90c Sheet of 4, #a-d 12.00 12.00

Penguin and Liberty Cap — A232

2004, June 26 **Engr.** ***Perf. 13¼x13***
343 A232 €4.50 multi 15.00 7.00

Mineral Type of 1993

2005, Jan. 1 **Engr.** ***Perf. 13¼***
344 A103 15c Agate .80 .50

Albert Bauer (1916-2003), Glaciologist — A233

2005, Jan. 1 ***Perf. 13x13¼***
345 A233 45c multi 2.00 1.75

Roger Barberot (1915-2002), Administrator A234

2005, Jan. 1
346 A234 50c multi 2.00 2.00

Ship "Cap Horn" — A235

2005, Jan. 1
347 A235 50c multi 2.00 2.00

Seal Pot A236

2005, Jan. 1 Litho. ***Perf. 13***
348 A236 50c multi 2.25 2.25

Macgillivray's Prion — A237

2005, Jan. 1 Engr. ***Perf. 13x13¼***
349 A237 75c multi 2.75 2.75

Studer Valley — A238

2005, Jan. 1 ***Perf. 13x12½***
350 A238 90c multi 3.00 3.00

Peigne des Néréides A239

2005, Jan. 1 ***Perf. 12¼***
351 A239 €2.50 multi 8.00 7.50

Harpovoluta Charcoti — A240

2005, Jan. 1 ***Perf. 13x12½***
352 A240 €4 multi 14.00 14.00

Murray's Ray — A241

2005, Jan. 1 Litho. ***Perf. 13***
353 A241 €4.50 multi 14.00 14.00

Elephant Seal and Oceanographic Chart — A242

2005, Jan. 1 Engr.
354 A242 €4.90 multi 16.00 16.00

Concordia Station — A243

2005, Jan. 3 Litho. ***Perf. 13***
355 A243 50c multi 1.75 1.75

Return of the Ship "Français," Cent. — A244

2005, Mar. 4 Engr. ***Perf. 13x13¼***
356 A244 €4.50 multi + label 15.00 15.00

Disappearance of Paul-Emile Victor, 10th Anniv. — A245

2005, Mar. 7 Litho. ***Perf. 13***
357 A245 50c multi 2.50 2.50

50th Anniversary Coat of Arms — A246

2005, Aug. 6
358 A246 (90c) multi 3.00 3.00
a. Booklet pane of 1 4.00 —

No. 358a is found in No. 359.

Voyage Booklet Type of 1999

History: a, Discovery of Amsterdam Island, 1522. b, Discovery of Crozet Island, 1772. c, Discovery of Kerguelen Island, 1772, vert. d, Discovery of Adélie Land, 1840. e, Astronomers viewing 1874 transit of Venus on St. Paul Island. f, Wreck of the Strathmore, 1875. g, Port Jeanne d'Arc, 1908. h, Port-Couvreux, 1925. i, Building of Port-Martin, 1950. j, Antarctic Treaty, 1959. k, Building of fourth base, 1963-64.

2005, Aug. 6 Litho. ***Perf. 13***
359 A164 Souvenir booklet, #a-k, 358a 70.00

Nos. 359a-359k are all non-denominated. Stamps are valid for 90c, the 20 gram international letter rate. Each stamp appears on a separate booklet pane showing an enlarged design of the stamp. The booklet sold for €18.

Penguins and No. 1 — A247

2005, Nov. 2
360 A247 90c multi 3.25 3.25

French Southern & Antarctic Territories, 50th anniv.

Souvenir Sheet

Maps — A248

Maps of: a, Crozet Archipelago. b, Amsterdam and St. Paul Islands. c, Kerguelen Island. d, Adélie Land.

Litho. & Engr.

2005, Nov. 10 ***Perf. 13x13¼***
361 A248 50c Sheet of 4, #a-d 6.50 6.50

French Southern & Antarctic Territories, 50th anniv.

Rutile A249

2006, Jan. 1 Engr. ***Perf. 13x12½***
362 A249 15c multi .80 .80

A250 A251

2006, Jan. 1 ***Perf. 13x13¼***
363 A250 48c pur & red 1.60 1.60

Charles Vélain (1845-1925), geologist.

2006, Jan. 1
364 A251 53c multi 1.60 1.60

Albert Seyrolle (1887-1919), mariner.

Amsterdam Island Garden — A252

2006, Jan. 1 Litho. ***Perf. 13***
365 A252 53c multi 1.60 1.60

Ship "Osiris" — A253

2006, Jan. 1 Photo. ***Perf. 13x13¼***
366 A253 90c multi 3.00 3.00

Dumont d'Urville Base, 50th Anniv. — A254

2006, Jan. 1 Engr. ***Perf. 13x12½***
367 A254 90c multi 2.75 2.75

Virgin of the Seal Hunters — A255

2006, Jan. 1 ***Perf. 12½x13***
368 A255 €2.50 multi 7.50 7.50

Lagenorhynchus Cruciger — A256

2006, Jan. 1 ***Perf. 13x13¼***
369 A256 €4 multi 12.00 12.00

Keguelen Hake — A257

2006, Jan. 1
370 A257 €4.53 multi 13.50 13.50

Amsterdam Island Carbon Dioxide Measurements, 25th Anniv. — A258

2006, Jan. 1
371 A258 €4.90 multi 15.00 15.00

Miniature Sheet

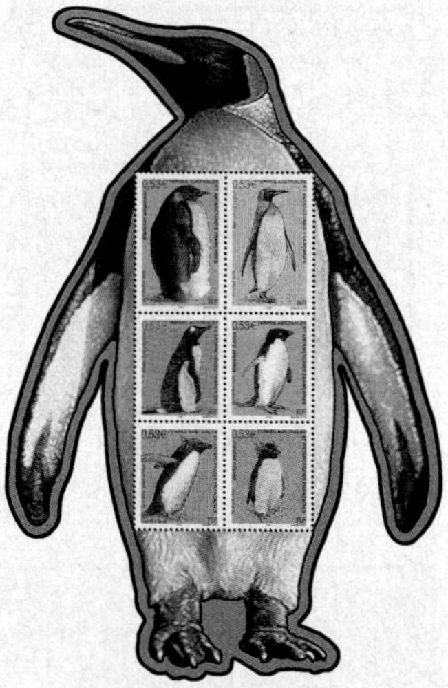

Penguins — A259

No. 372 — Penguin (background color): a, Emperor penguin (lilac, 22x36mm). b, King penguin (pale yellow green, 22x36mm). c, Gentoo penguin (green, 22x27mm). d, Adélie penguin (pink, 22x27mm). e, Macaroni penguin (orange, 22x27mm). f, Rockhopper penguin (blue, 22x27mm).

Litho. & Engr.

2006, Jan. 1 ***Perf. 13***
372 A259 53c Sheet of 6, #a-f 12.00 12.00

Souvenir Sheet

Albatross — A260

Litho. & Engr.

2006, June 1 ***Perf. 13***
373 A260 €4.53 multi 14.50 14.50

Souvenir Sheet

Albatross — A261

Litho. & Engr.

2006, Nov. 8 ***Perf. 13***
374 A261 90c multi 3.50 3.50

Corundum A262

2007, Jan. 1 **Engr.** ***Perf. 13¼***
375 A262 15c multi 1.25 1.25

A263

A264

2007, Jan. 1 ***Perf. 13x13¼***
376 A263 49c multi 1.50 1.50

Louis-Francois Aleno de Saint Aloüarn (1738-72), explorer who claimed Australia for France.

2007, Jan. 1
377 A264 54c multi 1.60 1.60

Marthe Emmanuel (1901-97), assistant to explorer Jean Charcot.

Cattle, Amsterdam Island — A265

2007, Jan. 1 ***Perf. 13x12½***
378 A265 54c multi 1.50 1.50

Ship Tonkinois — A266

2007, Jan. 1 ***Perf. 13x13¼***
379 A266 90c multi 2.50 2.50

Ile de la Baleine — A267

2007, Jan. 1 ***Perf. 13x12½***
380 A267 90c multi 2.50 2.50

Archaeology on Saint Paul Island — A268

2007, Jan. 1 ***Perf. 12½x13***
381 A268 €2.50 multi 7.00 7.00

Lampris Immaculatus — A269

2007, Jan. 1 ***Perf. 13x12½***
382 A269 €4 multi 11.00 11.00

Astonomy at Concordia — A270

Litho. & Engr.

2007, Jan. 1 ***Perf. 13***
383 A270 €4.90 multi 14.00 14.00

French Polar Expeditions, 60th Anniv. — A271

No. 384: a, Expedition headquarters, Paris, men shaking hands over globe. b, Expedition headquarters.

2007, Jan. 1 **Engr.** ***Perf. 13x13¼***
384 Horiz. pair + central label 13.50 13.50
a. A271 54c multi 1.75 1.75
b. A271 €4 multi 11.00 11.00

Miniature Sheet

Albatrosses — A272

No. 385: a, Amsterdam albatross. b, Great albatross (Grand albatros). c, Black-browed albatross (Albatros à sourcils noir). d, Yellow-beaked albatross (Albatros à bec jaune). e, Sooty albatross (Albatros fuligineux).

Litho. & Engr.

2007, Jan. 1 ***Perf. 13***
385 A272 54c Sheet of 5, #a-e 8.00 8.00

Intl. Polar Year — A273

No. 386: a, Penguins. b, Map of Antarctica, French Southern & Antarctic Territories #9.

2007, Mar. 1 **Litho.** ***Perf. 13***
386 Horiz. pair + central label 15.00 15.00
a. A273 90c multi 2.75 2.75
b. A273 €4 multi 12.00 12.00

Audit Office, Bicent. A274

2007 Mar. 19 **Engr.** ***Perf. 13¼***
387 A274 90c multi 4.50 4.50

Miniature Sheet

Indian Ocean Islands — A275

No. 388: a, Ile Tromelin. b, Iles Glorieuses. c, Ile Juan de Nova. d, Ile Bassas da India. e, Ile Europa.

2007, May 10 **Photo.** ***Perf. 13x13¼***
388 A275 54c Sheet of 5, #a-e 9.00 9.00

Path of Sun on June 21 Over Dumont d'Urville Base — A276

2007, June 21
389 A276 90c multi 3.00 3.00

Voyage Booklet Type of 1999

No. 390 — Photographs of land features: a, Apostle Island, Crozet Archipelago. b, Chamonix Lake, Kerguelen Island. c, Phylicia forest, Amsterdam Island. d, Gulf of Morbihan, Kerguelen Islands. e, Mount Cook, Chamonix Lake and glacier, Kerguelen Islands. f, Tourbiéres Plateau, Amsterdam Island. g, Nuageuses Islands, Kerguelen Islands. h, Caldera, Amsterdam Island. i, Mount Cook, Kerguelen Island. j, Central Plateau, Kerguelen Island. k, Isle of Penguins, Crozet Archipelago. l, Antonelli Crater, Amsterdam Island. m, Lake on Possession Island, Crozet Archipelago. n, Rocks off Apostle Island, Crozet Archipelago. o, Geographic Society Peninsula, Kerguelen Island. p, Ronarch Peninsula, Kerguelen Island.

2007, Nov. 8 Litho. *Perf. 13*
390 A164 (90c) Souvenir booklet, #a-p 70.00

No. 390 sold for €20, and contains four panes, consisting of a block of four stamps of Nos. 390a-390d, 390e-390h, 390i-390l, and 390m-390p.

French Southern and Antarctic Territories Flag — A277

2008, Jan. 1 Litho. *Perf. 13*
Background Color

391	A277	1c black	.25	.25
392	A277	2c blue	.35	.35
393	A277	5c red	.40	.40
394	A277	10c green	.40	.40
395	A277	20c brn orange	.80	.80
		Nos. 391-395 (5)	2.20	2.20

Spinel — A278

2008, Jan. 1 Engr. *Perf. 13¼*
396 A278 15c multi .80 .45

Samivel (1907-92), Writer — A279

2008, Jan. 1 *Perf. 13x13¼*
397 A279 54c grn & brown 1.60 1.60

St. Paul Island — A280

2008, Jan. 1
398 A280 54c blue & dk blue 1.60 1.60

Construction of Port Jeanne d'Arc, Cent. — A281

2008, Jan. 1 *Perf. 13x12¾*
399 A281 90c multi 2.75 2.75

Rockhopper Penguins — A282

2008, Jan. 1 *Perf. 13x12½*
400 A282 90c multi 2.75 2.75

Shipwreck of L'Esperance — A283

2008, Jan. 1 Litho. *Perf. 13x12¾*
401 A283 90c multi 2.75 2.75

Macrourus Carinatus — A284

2008, Jan. 1 Engr. *Perf. 13x12½*
402 A284 €4 multi 12.00 12.00

Galium Antarcticum A285

2008, Jan. 1 *Perf. 12½x13*
403 A285 €4.54 multi 13.50 13.50

Adélie Land Coastal Ichthyology Program A286

2008, Jan. 1 Litho. *Perf. 13*
404 A286 €4.90 multi 14.50 14.50

Souvenir Sheet

Kerguelen Fish Biomass Evaluation Project (POKER) — A287

2008, Jan. 1 Litho. & Engr.
405 A287 €2.50 multi 7.50 7.50

Souvenir Sheet

Elephant Seals — A288

No. 406: a, Head of adult female. b, Seals initiating combat. c, Juvenile seal. d, Head of adult male.

2008, Jan. 1
406 A288 54c Sheet of 4, #a-d 6.50 6.50

Gérard Mégie (1946-2004), Ozone Researcher — A289

2008, Feb. 15 Engr. *Perf. 13x13¼*
407 A289 54c multi 1.75 1.75

Miniature Sheet

Birds — A290

No. 408: a, Sooty tern (Sterne fulgineuse). b, Red-footed booby (Fou a pieds rouges), vert. c, Masked booby (Fou masque), vert. d, Great frigatebird (Fregate du Pacifique), vert. e, Tropicbird (Paille en queue).

Perf. 13¼x13 (#408a, 408e), 13x13¼
2008, June 1 Litho. & Engr.
408 A290 54c Sheet of 5, #a-e 8.50 8.50

Earth and Birds — A291

2008, June 14 Photo. *Perf. 13*
409 A291 €4.54 multi 14.50 14.50

Ship Marion Dufresne — A292

2008, Nov. 6 Litho. *Perf. 13*
410 A292 (55c) multi 1.75 1.75

Compare with type A194.

Pyrite A293

2009, Jan. 1 Engr. *Perf. 13¼*
411 A293 15c multi .60 .60

A294

2009, Jan. 1 *Perf. 13x13¼*
412 A294 55c multi 1.60 1.60

Henri Paschal de Rochegude (1741-1834), naval officer.

A295

2009, Jan. 1 *Perf. 13*
413 A295 55c multi 1.60 1.60

Charles Gaston Rouillon (1915-2007), director of French polar scientific expeditions.

Residence de France Seal of Kerguelen Islands, Cent. — A296

2009, Jan. 1 Litho.
414 A296 90c multi 2.50 2.50

Shark With Dorsal Spines — A297

2009, Jan. 1 Engr. *Perf. 13x12½*
415 A297 €2.50 multi 7.00 7.00

Ship Jeanne d'Arc — A298

2009, Jan. 1
416 A298 €4 multi 11.00 11.00

MACARBI Program Scallop Research A299

2009, Jan. 1 *Perf. 12½x13*
417 A299 €4.55 multi 13.00 13.00

Seaweed — A300

No. 418: a, Himantothallus grandifolius and iceberg. b, Laminaria pallida and seals.

2009, Jan. 1 *Perf. 13x13¼*
418 Horiz. pair + central label 13.50 13.50
a. A300 90c multi 2.50 2.50
b. A300 €4 multi 11.00 11.00

Miniature Sheet

Petrels — A301

No. 419: a, Soft-plumaged petrel (Petrel soyeux). b, Wilson's petrel (Petrel de Wilson). c, Gray petrel (Petrel gris). d, Diving petrel (Petrel plongeur). e, Snow petrel (Petrel des neiges).

Litho. & Engr.

2009, Jan. 1 *Perf. 13¼x13*
419 A301 55c Sheet of 5, #a-e 7.75 7.75

Voyage Booklet Type of 1999

No. 420 — Photographs: a, Frigatebirds, Europa Island. b, Beach on north coast of Europa Island. c, Mangroves, Europa Island. d, Flagpole, palm trees, Europa Island. e, Turtle on beach, Juan de Nova Island. f, Sandbanks off Juan de Nova Island. g, Tree, Juan de Nova Island. h, Grounded ship, Juan de Nova Island. i, Brown noddies, Glorioso Islands. j, Flower, Glorioso Islands. k, Pool of water, Glorioso Islands. l, Tree on islet, Glorioso Islands. m, Birds, Tromelin Island. n, Meteorological station, Tromelin Island. o, Coral fossil, Tromelin Island. p, Anchor, Tromelin Island.

2009, Nov. 5 Litho. *Perf. 13*
420 A164 (90c) Souvenir booklet, #a-p 65.00

No. 420 sold for €21.50, and contains four panes, consisting of a block of four stamps of Nos. 420a-420d, 420e-420h, 420i-4290l, and 420m-420p.

Antarctic Treaty, 50th Anniv. — A302

2009, Dec. 1 Engr. *Perf. 13x13¼*
421 A302 56c multi 1.75 1.75

Tourmaline A303

2010, Jan. 2 Engr. *Perf. 13¼*
422 A303 28c multi .80 .80

Dr. Jean Rivolier (1923-2007), Medical Researcher — A304

2010, Jan. 2 Litho. *Perf. 13*
423 A304 56c multi 1.60 1.60

Birds on Ile du Lys — A305

2010, Jan. 2 Engr. *Perf. 13x13¼*
424 A305 56c multi 1.60 1.60

Patureau House, Juan de Nova Island — A306

2010, Jan. 2
425 A306 56c multi 1.60 1.60

Program Crac-ice — A307

2010, Jan. 2
426 A307 90c multi 2.50 2.50

Supply Ship Ile St. Paul — A308

2010, Jan. 2
427 A308 €1.35 multi 3.75 3.75

Crozet Orca — A309

2010, Jan. 2
428 A309 €2.80 multi 7.75 7.75

Kerguelen Terns — A310

2010, Jan. 2
429 A310 €4.30 multi 12.00 12.00

Miniature Sheet

Sea Lions of Amsterdam Island — A311

No. 430: a, Sea lion and ship. b, Two sea lions on rocks, denomination at UR in black, horiz. c, Sea lion, denomination at UL in black, horiz. d, Two sea lions near water, denomination in white at UR, horiz. e, Two sea lions, denomination at LL in black, horiz.

Litho. & Engr.

2010, Jan. 2 *Perf. 13*
430 A311 56c Sheet of 5, #a-e 7.75 7.75

Miniature Sheet

Polar Transportation — A312

No. 431: a, Team of dogs pulling sled. b, Weasel M29C. c, Sno-cat 743. d, HB40-Castor. e, Challenger 65. f, PB 330.

2010, Jan. 2
431 A312 90c Sheet of 6, #a-f 15.00 15.00

Gabriel Pavilion, Paris — A313

2010, May 28 Litho. *Perf. 13*
432 A313 56c multi 1.40 1.40

Second Elysée Philatelic Club Show, Paris.

Miniature Sheet

Albatross Protection — A314

No. 433: a, Albatross and chick on nest. b, Albatross facing left. c, Albatross facing right. d, Two juvenile albatrosses.

Litho. & Engr.

2010, June 12 *Perf. 13*
433 A314 56c Sheet of 4, #a-d 5.75 5.75

French Southern & Antarctic Territories Booth at Espace Champerret Stamp Show — A315

2010, Nov. 5 Litho. *Perf. 13*
434 A315 56c multi 3.00 3.00

Self-Adhesive

Serpentine Die Cut 11
435 A315 56c multi 3.00 3.00

Astronomical Observatory, Concordia Base, Antarctica and Southern Cross — A316

Litho. & Engr.

2011, Jan. 2 *Perf. 13*
436 A316 56c multi 1.50 1.50

Martin de Viviès Base, Amsterdam Island — A317

2011, Jan. 2 Engr. *Perf. 13x13¼*
437 A317 90c multi 2.40 2.40

Josef Enzensperger (1873-1903), Meteorologist A318

2011, Jan. 2 ***Perf. 13¼x13***

438 A318 90c multi 2.40 2.40

André Chastain (1906-62), Botanist A319

2011, Jan. 2

439 A319 €1.35 multi 3.75 3.75

Sheathbills — A320

2011, Jan. 2 ***Perf. 13x13¼***

440 A320 €1.35 black & purple 3.75 3.75

Artedidraco Orianae — A321

2011, Jan. 2

441 A321 €1.35 multi 3.75 3.75

Cruiser Lapérouse — A322

2011, Jan. 2

442 A322 €4.30 multi 11.50 11.50

Zircons — A323

No. 443: a, Zircons embedded in rock. b, Cut and polished zircon.

Litho. & Engr.

2011, Jan. 2 ***Perf. 13¼***

443 A323 Horiz. pair 1.75 1.75
a. 28c multi .75 .75
b. 34c multi .90 .90

December 8, 1929 Mail Plane Crash — A324

No. 444: a, Farman F190 airplane. b, Map of flight. c, Crew and crash covers.

2011, Jan. 2 ***Perf. 13***

444 Horiz. strip of 3 7.75 7.75
a. A324 56c multi 1.50 1.50
b. A324 90c multi 2.40 2.40
c. A324 €1.35 multi 3.75 3.75

Miniature Sheet

Whales — A325

No. 445: a, Baleine à bosse (humpback whale). b, Baleine franche australe (southern right whale). c, Cachalot (sperm whale). d, Rorqual de Rudolphi (sei whale).

2011, Jan. 2

445 A325 56c Sheet of 4, #a-d 6.00 6.00

Patrol Boat Osiris — A326

2011, Apr. 1 **Litho.**

446 A326 (60c) multi 1.75 1.75

Gentoo Penguins — A327

2011, June 15 **Litho.** ***Perf. 13***

447 A327 €1 multi + label 3.00 3.00

Orré House (Prefect's Residence), St. Pierre, Reunion — A328

2011, Sept. 19

448 A328 60c multi 1.75 1.75

Souvenir Sheet

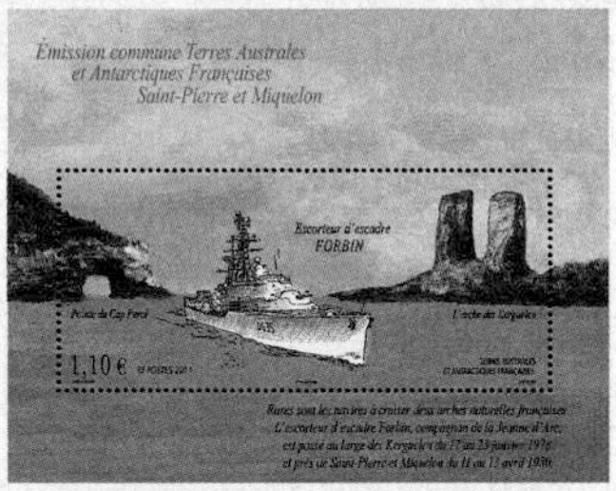

Squadron Escort Forbin — A329

2011, Nov. 3 **Litho. & Engr.**

449 A329 €1.10 multi 3.00 3.00

See St. Pierre & Miquelon No. 938.

Adélie Penguins — A330

2011, Dec. 2 **Litho.** ***Perf. 13***

450 A330 60c multi 1.60 1.60

Penguin Breeding Grounds, Baie du Marin, Crozet Island — A331

Views of Baie du Marin in: No. 451, 60c, 1961. No. 452, 60c, 2011.

2011, Dec. 23 ***Perf. 13x13¼***

451-452 A331 Set of 2 3.25 3.25

Ship Marion Dufresne in Mamoudzou Lagoon — A332

Serpentine Die Cut 11

2011, Dec. 31

Self-Adhesive

453 A332 60c multi 1.60 1.60

See Mayotte No. 288.

Notodiscus Hookeri — A333

2012, Jan. 2 **Engr.** ***Perf. 13x13¼***

454 A333 60c multi 1.60 1.60

Ship Marius Moutet — A334

2012, Jan. 2

455 A334 60c multi 1.60 1.60

Weddell Seals — A335

2012, Jan. 2 ***Perf. 13¼x13***

456 A335 €1 multi 2.60 2.60

Roald Amundsen (1872-1928), Polar Explorer A336

2012, Jan. 2

457 A336 €1 multi 2.60 2.60

René-Emile Bossière (1857-1941), Kerguelen Island Business Entrepreneur A337

2012, Jan. 2

458 A337 €1.45 multi 3.75 3.75

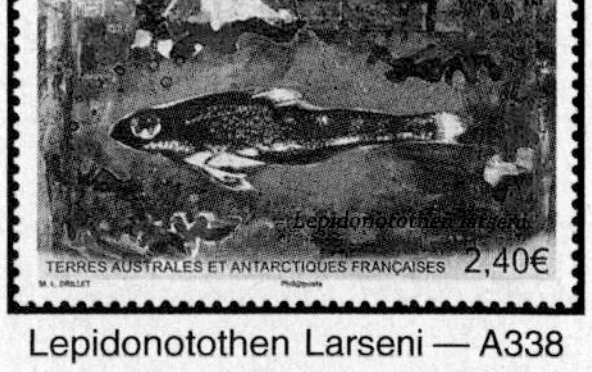

Lepidonotothen Larseni — A338

Litho. & Silk-screened

2012, Jan. 2 ***Perf. 13***

459 A338 €2.40 multi 6.25 6.25

Diopside — A339

No. 460: a, Crystals. b, Crystal and cut stone.

2012, Jan. 2 Engr. *Perf. 13¼*

460 A339	Horiz. pair	1.75	1.75
a.	29c red & green	.80	.80
b.	36c red & green	.95	.95

Point Molloy, Kerguelen Island — A340

No. 461: a, Buildings at Point Molloy. b, Molloy seismological station, 1953-63.

Litho. & Engr.

2012, Jan. 2 *Perf. 13x13¼*

461	Horiz. pair	3.25	3.25
a.-b.	A340 60c Either single	1.60	1.60

Military Presence in French Southern & Antarctic Territories — A341

No. 462: a, Second Regiment of Marine Infantry Parachutists on Europa Island. b, Detachment of the Mayotte Foreign Legion on the Glorioso Islands.

Litho. & Silk-screened

2012, Jan. 2 *Perf. 13*

462	Horiz. pair	3.25	3.25
a.-b.	A341 60c Either single	1.60	1.60

Miniature Sheet

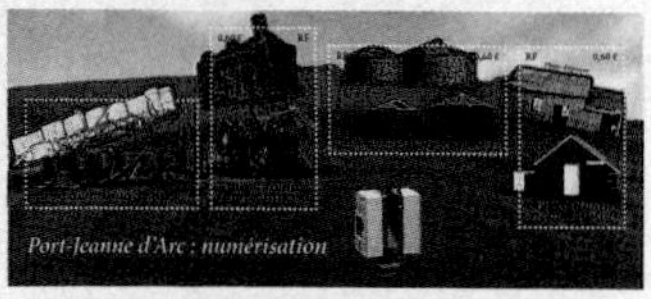

Derelict Whaling Station, Port-Jeanne d'Arc, Kerguelen Island — A342

No. 463: a, Eight storage tanks. b, Three boilers, vert. c, Two storage silos. d, House, vert.

2012, Jan. 2 Photo.

463 A342 60c Sheet of 4, #a-d 6.25 6.25

Miniature Sheet

Nature Reserve Flora and Fauna — A343

No. 464: a, Gentoo penguin (manchot papou). b, White-chinned petrel (petrel a menton blanc). c, Lyallia kerguelensis. d, Anatalanta aptera.

2012, Jan. 2 Litho. & Engr.

464 A343	Sheet of 4	8.50	8.50
a.	20c multi	.55	.55
b.	60c multi	1.60	1.60
c.	€1 multi	2.60	2.60
d.	€1.45 multi	3.75	3.75

Miniature Sheet

Aircraft Used in Polar Regions — A344

No. 465: a, B-24 Liberator. b, DC-4 Skymaster. c, Nord 2501 Noratlas. d, C-130 Hercules. e, DC-3 Basler BT-67. f, DHC-6 Twin Otter.

2012, Jan. 2

465 A344 €1 Sheet of 6, #a-f 16.00 16.00

Ile Longue, Kerguelen Islands A345

No. 466: a, 60c, Painting. b, €1, Painting, diff.

2012, Apr. 13 Litho. *Perf. 13x13¼*

466 A345 Pair, #a-b 4.25 4.25

No. 466 was printed in sheets containing two pairs.

Souvenir Sheet

Prince of Monaco Islands — A346

No. 467: a, Giant Antarctic petrel. b, Coastline of Prince of Monaco Islands.

Litho. & Engr.

2012, June 9 *Perf. 13¼*

467 A346 €1 Sheet of 2, #a-b 5.00 5.00

See Monaco No. 2680.

National Space Studies Center (CNES) Projects — A347

No. 468: a, Map of Antarctica. b, Penguin with tracking devices. c, Galileo satellite. d, Scientists deploying weather balloon. e, Pleaides satellite.

2012, June 9 Photo. *Perf. 13*

468	Vert. strip of 5 + 5 labels	12.00	12.00
a.-b.	A347 60c Either single + label	1.50	1.50
c.-d.	A347 €1 Either single + label	2.50	2.50
e.	A347 €1.45 multi + label	3.75	3.75

French Polar Institute, 20th Anniv. — A348

2012, July 12 Litho. *Perf. 13¼x13*

469 A348 60c multi 1.50 1.50

Souvenir Sheet

Bridge for Tracking Adélie Penguins — A349

Litho. & Engr.

2012, Nov. 2 *Perf. 13¼x13*

470 A349 €2 multi 5.25 5.25

Flight of Maryse Hilsz to Juan de Nova Island, 80th Anniv. — A350

No. 471: a, Airplane, map of route. b, Hilsz (1901-46) in airplane.

2012, Nov. 8 Litho. *Perf. 13*

471 A350	Horiz. pair	4.25	4.25
a.	60c multi	1.60	1.60
b.	€1 multi	2.60	2.60

Prasiola Crispa and Penguins — A351

2013, Jan. 1 Engr. *Perf. 13x13¼*

472 A351 65c multi 1.75 1.75

Charles Petitjean (1914-88), Pilot — A352

2013, Jan. 1 *Perf. 12½x13*

473 A352 65c multi 1.75 1.75

Lepidonothen Squamifrons — A353

2013, Jan. 1 *Perf. 13x13¼*

474 A353 €1 multi 2.75 2.75

Sailboat "Le Mischief" A354

2013, Jan. 1 *Perf. 12¼*

475 A354 €1 multi 2.75 2.75

Douglas Mawson (1882-1958), Antarctic Explorer, Huts and Penguins — A355

Litho. & Engr.

2013, Jan. 1 *Perf. 13*

476 A355 €1.45 multi 4.00 4.00

Bernard-Marie Boudin, Chevalier de Tromelin (1735-1816), Explorer and Colonial Administrator — A356

2013, Jan. 13 Litho.

477 A356 €2.40 multi 6.50 6.50

Hematite — A357

2013, Jan. 1 Engr. *Perf. 13¼*

478 A357 Horiz. pair 2.75 2.75
a. 40c Crystals 1.10 1.10
b. 60c Crystal 1.60 1.60

Miniature Sheet

Eaton's Pintail — A358

No. 479: a, Duck in water. b, Heads of two ducks, vert. c, Duck and eggs. d, Head of duck, ducks in flight.

Litho. & Engr.

2013, Jan. 1 *Perf. 13*

479 A358 Sheet of 4 9.00 9.00
a. 20c multi .55 .55
b. 60c multi 1.60 1.60
c. €1 multi 2.75 2.75
d. €1.45 multi 4.00 4.00

Miniature Sheet

Helicopters — A359

No. 480: a, Sud-Ouest Djinn 1221. b, Bell 47 G2. c, Hiller 360. d, Sud-Est Alouette II 3130. e, Ecureuil AS 350. f, Panther AS 565

2013, Jan. 1

480 A359 €1 Sheet of 6, #a-f 16.00 16.00

Souvenir Sheet

Engravings of Amsterdam and St. Paul Islands — A360

2013, Jan. 1 Litho.

481 A360 €3.40 multi 9.00 9.00

Voyage Booklet Type of 1999

No. 482: a, Ship Astrolabe near Dumont d'Urville Station. b, The Astrolabe, helicopter and Adélie penguins. c, Astrolabe docked near Lion landing strip. d, Four Adélie penguins at Dumont d'Urville station. e, View of Dumon't d'Urville Station taken from the Astrolabe. f, Aerial view of Dumont d'Urville Station. g, Aurora Australis. h, Colony of Emperor penguins. i, Five men and plow at Cap Prudhomme Base. j, Aerial view of Cap Prudhomme Base, island at right. k, View of Cap Prudhomme Base, island at center. l, Two penguins. m, Italian, French and European Union flags at Concordia Base. n, Snow vehicle moving containers. o, Astronomical equipment near Concordia Base. p, Steps leading to containers.

2013, Apr. 5 Litho. *Perf. 13*

482 A164 (€1) Souvenir booklet, #a-p 65.00

No. 482 sold for €25 and contains four panes, consisting of a block of four stamps of Nos. 482a-482d, 482e-482h, 482i-482l, and 482m-482p.

F.S. Floreal — A361

2013, Apr. 5 Litho. *Perf. 13*

483 A361 (63c) multi 1.75 1.75

A362

Silhouettes of Emblems — A363

Designs: 1c, Green turtle. 2c, Helicopter. 3c, Penguin. 4c, Ship "Marion Dufresne." 63c, Green turtle, helicopter, penguin, ship, "TAAF."

2013, Apr. 29 Engr. *Perf. 13*

484 A362 1c dk bl & bl .25 .25
485 A362 2c purple .25 .25
486 A362 3c dk grn & yel grn .25 .25
487 A362 4c brn org & org .25 .25

Litho. & Silk-screened

Perf. 13¼

488 A363 63c multi 1.75 1.75
Nos. 484-488 (5) 2.75 2.75

See Nos. 504-507.

Souvenir Sheet

Engraver, Map, Penguin — A364

Engr. (Litho. Margin)

2013, May 17 *Perf. 13*

489 A364 €5 multi 13.50 13.50

Souvenir Sheets

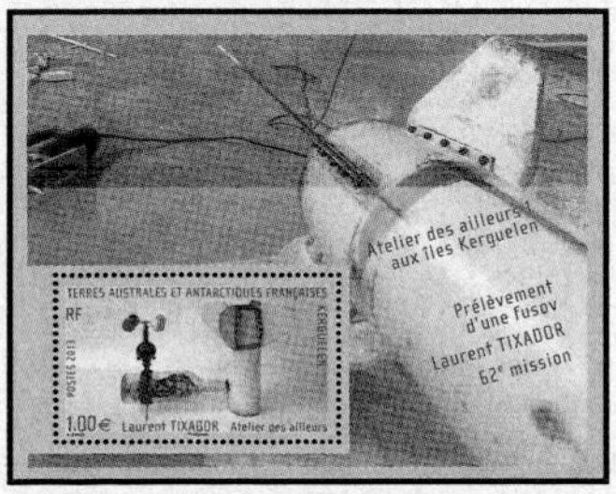

Prélèvement d'une Fusov, by Laurent Tixador — A365

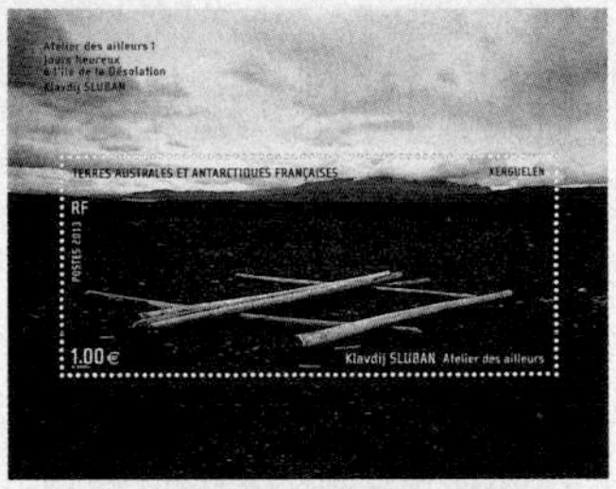

Jours Heureux à l'Ile de la Désolation, by Klavdij Sluban — A366

2013, June 17 Litho. *Perf. 13*

490 A365 €1 multi 2.75 2.75
491 A366 €1 black 2.75 2.75

Ateliers des Ailleurs art project.

Souvenir Sheet

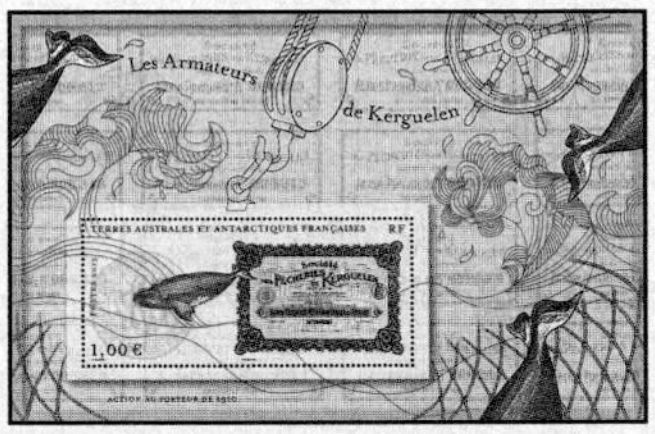

Whale and Stock Certificate for Kerguelen Fisheries Society — A367

2013, Nov. 6 Litho. *Perf. 13¼x13*

492 A367 €1 multi 2.75 2.75

Louis Jacquinot (1898-1993), Minister of Overseas France — A368

2014, Jan. 2 Engr. *Perf. 13¼x13*

493 A368 66c multi 1.90 1.90

Bertrand Imbert (1924-2011), Leader of French Research for International Geophysical Year — A369

2014, Jan. 2 Engr. *Perf. 12¾x13*

494 A369 66c multi 1.90 1.90

Tromelin Meteorological Station, 60th Anniv. — A370

2014, Jan. 2 Engr. *Perf. 13x13¼*

495 A370 €1.55 multi 4.25 4.25

Rock Carvings of Amsterdam Island — A371

2014, Jan. 2 Engr. *Perf. 13x13¼*

496 A371 €1.55 multi 4.25 4.25

Supply Ship "Le Malin" — A372

2014, Jan. 2 Litho. *Perf. 13*

497 A372 €1.55 multi 4.25 4.25

Bren Carrier on Kerguelen Island — A373

2014, Jan. 2 Engr. *Perf. 13x13¼*

498 A373 €2 multi 5.50 5.50

White Tower (Basalt Columns), Crozet Islands — A374

2014, Jan. 2 Litho. *Perf. 13*

499 A374 €2 multi 5.50 5.50

Lepidonotothen Mizops — A375

2014, Jan. 2 Engr. *Perf. 13x13¼*

500 A375 €2.40 multi 6.50 6.50

Fluorite — A376

No. 501: a, Polished stones. b, Crystal.

2014, Jan. 2 Litho. *Perf. 13*

501 A376 Horiz. pair 2.75 2.75
a. 37c multi 1.00 1.00
b. 63c multi 1.75 1.75

Miniature Sheet

Mollusks — A377

No. 502: a, Moule de Kerguelen (Kerguelen mussel). b, Volute de Challenger (Challenger volute). c, Moule de Magellan (Magellan mussel), vert. d, Buccin antarctique (Antarctic whelk). e, Laternule antarctique (Antarctic clam).

Litho. & Engr.

2014, Jan. 2 *Perf. 13*

502 A377 63c Sheet of 5, #a-e 8.75 8.75

Miniature Sheet

BIrds — A378

No. 503: a, Damier du Cap (Cape petrels). b, Manchot royal de Crozet (Crozet Island king penguins). c, Fulmar antarctique (Antarctic fulmars). d, Grand albatros de Crozet (Wandering albatrosses).

2014, Jan. 2 Engr. *Perf. 13x12¾*

503 A378 Sheet of 4 11.00 11.00
a.-b. 66c Either single 1.90 1.90
c. €1.05 multi 2.75 2.75
d. €1.55 multi 4.25 4.25

Silhouette of Emblems Type of 2013 and

Silhouettes of Emblems — A379

A362 designs as before.
€7, Map of District of Crozet, dolphin, penguin, ship, "TAAF."

2014, Mar. 7 Litho. *Perf. 13*

Dated "2014"

504 A362 1c dk bl & bl .25 .25
505 A362 2c purple .25 .25
506 A362 3c dk grn & yel grn .25 .25
507 A362 4c brn org & org .25 .25

Litho. & Silk-Screened

Perf. 13¼

508 A379 €7 multi 19.00 19.00
Nos. 504-508 (5) 20.00 20.00

Miniature Sheet

Commerson's Dolphins — A380

No. 509: a, 63c, Dolphin sticking head out of water. b, 66c, Three dolphins underwater. c, 66c, Dolphin breaching surface. d, €1.05, Dolphin above water.

Litho. & Engr.

2014, June 26 *Perf. 13¼x13*

509 A380 Sheet of 4, #a-d 8.25 8.25

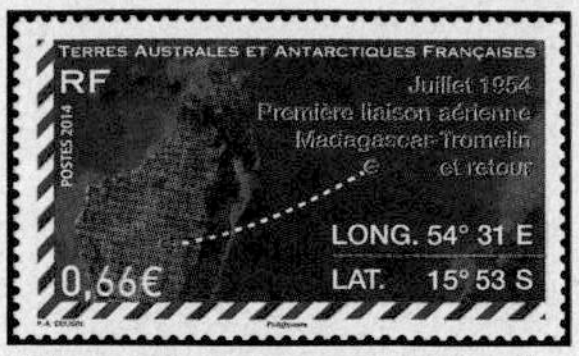

Map of Madagascar to Tromelin Flight — A381

AAC-1 Toucan — A382

AAC-1 Toucan and Stamped Cover from Tromelin — A383

2014, Sept. 21 Litho. *Perf. 13*

510 Horiz. strip of 3 8.50 8.50
a. A381 66c multi 1.75 1.75
b. A382 €1.05 multi 2.75 2.75
c. A383 €1.55 multi 4.00 4.00

First flight between Madagascar and Tromelin, 50th anniv.

Green Turtle A384

2014, Oct. 9 Litho. *Perf. 13x13¼*

511 A384 €1.05 multi 2.60 2.60

See Comoro Islands No. , France No. 4695, Malagasy Republic No. , Mauritius No. 1144, Seychelles No. 904.

Gendarmes — A385

No. 512 — Gendarme on : a, Iles Eparses. b, Iles Kerguelen.

Litho. & Silk-Screened

2014, Oct. 16 *Perf. 13*

512 Horiz. pair + central label 3.50 3.50
a.-b A385 66c Either single 1.75 1.75

Souvenir Sheet

Amateur Radio — A386

No. 513: a, QSL card, radio key, amateur radio antenna on Tromelin Island. b, Radio operator, radio and antenna, vert.

Perf. 13x13¼, 13¼x13

2014, Nov. 6 Litho.

513 A386 Sheet of 2 2.75 2.75
a. 39c multi 1.00 1.00
b. 66c multi 1.75 1.75

Decauville Hopper Cars on Juan de Nova Island — A387

2015, Jan. 1 Engr. *Perf. 13x13¼*

514 A387 66c multi 1.60 1.60

Euphausia Superba — A388

Litho. & Engr.

2015, Jan. 1 *Perf. 13¼*

515 A388 66c multi 1.60 1.60

Emperor Penguin A389

2015, Jan. 1 Litho. *Perf. 13*

516 A389 €1 multi 2.40 2.40

Leopard Seal in Adélie Land — A390

2015, Jan. 1 Engr. *Perf. 13¼x13*

517 A390 €1.05 multi 2.60 2.60

Ship Radioleine — A391

2015, Jan. 1 Engr. *Perf. 13x13¼*

518 A391 €2.40 multi 5.75 5.75

Antarctic Terns — A392

Litho. & Engr.

2015, Jan. 1 *Perf. 13*

519 A392 €4.30 multi 10.50 10.50

Insects — A393

Designs: 66c, Amalopteryx maritima. €2, Ectemnorhinus vanhoeffenianus, horiz.

2015, Jan.1 Litho. *Perf. 13¼*

520-521 A393 Set of 2 6.50 6.50

Beryl — A394

No. 522: a, Polihsed gemstones. b, Crystals in matrix.

Litho. & Engr.

2015, Jan. 1 *Perf. 13*

522 A394 Horiz. pair 2.40 2.40
a. 34c multi .80 .80
b. 66c multi 1.60 1.60

Snowmobile Transport — A395

No. 523: a, Snowmobile pulling cargo. b, Snowmobile without cargo.

2015, Jan. 1 Litho. *Perf. 13¼*

523 Horiz. pair 4.25 4.25
a. A395 66c multi 1.60 1.60
b. A395 €1.05 multi 2.60 2.60

Robert Guillard (1919-2013), Polar Explorations Chief of Operations — A396

No. 524 — Guillard and: a, Ship and penguins, Adélie Land. b, Expedition vehicles, Greenland.

2015, Jan. 1 Engr. *Perf. 13x13¼*

524 Horiz. pair + central label 4.25 4.25
a. A396 66c multi 1.60 1.60
b. A396 €1.05 multi 2.60 2.60

Miniature Sheet

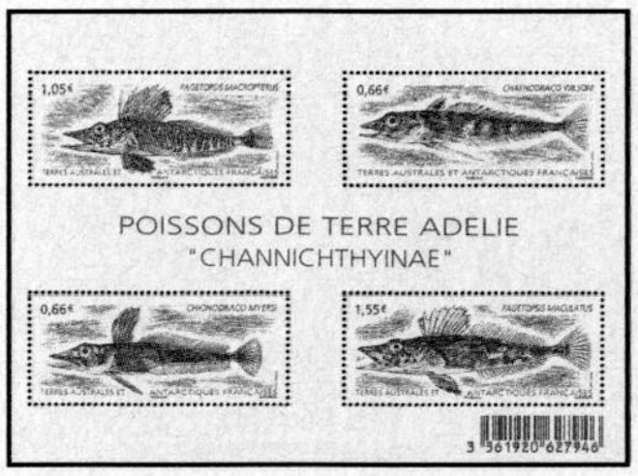

Fish — A397

No. 525: a, Chaenodraco wilsoni. b, Chaenodraco myersi. c, Pagetopsis macropterus. d, Pagetopsis maculatus.

2015, Jan. 1 Engr. *Perf. 13*

525 A397 Sheet of 4 9.75 9.75
a.-b. 66c Either single 1.60 1.60
c. €1.05 multi 2.60 2.60
d. €1.55 multi 3.75 3.75

Paul-Emile Victor (1907-95), Polar Explorer — A398

2015, Mar. 7 Engr. *Perf. 13x12½*

526 A398 €1 multi 2.25 2.25

Silhouettes of Emblems — A399

Litho. & Silk-Screened

2015, Mar. 19 *Perf. 13¼*

527 A399 50c multi 1.10 1.10

François Tabuteau (1921-2000), Polar Explorer — A400

2015, Apr. 17 Litho. *Perf. 13*

528 A400 80c multi 1.90 1.90

French Southern and Antarctic Territories, 60th Anniv. — A401

No. 529 — Ship and: a, Airplane, seal, bird, turtle. b, Helicopter, birds, fish, killer whales. c, Penguins and birds in flight.

2015, July 14 Litho. *Perf. 13*

529 Horiz. strip of 3 5.25 5.25
a.-c. A401 80c Any single 1.75 1.75

People Stranded Without Supplies on Saint Paul Island, 1930 — A402

2015, Sept. 18 Engr. *Perf. 13*

530 A402 €1 multi 2.25 2.25

Ship *Marion Dufresne*, 20th Anniv. — A403

2015 Litho. & Engr. *Perf. 13*

Denomination Color

531 A403 80c red 1.90 1.90
532 A403 €1.35 blue 3.00 3.00

Issued: 80c, 10/4; €1.35, 11/5.

Souvenir Sheet

Penguin on Floating Ice — A404

Litho. & Embossed

2015, Nov. 5 *Perf. 13½x13*

533 A404 €1.24 multi 2.75 2.75

AIR POST STAMPS

Emperor Penguins and Map of Antarctica — AP1

Unwmk.

1956, Apr. 25 Engr. *Perf. 13*

C1 AP1 50fr lt ol grn & dk grn 42.50 29.00
C2 AP1 100fr dl bl & indigo 35.00 25.00

Wandering Albatross — AP2

1959, Sept. 14

C3 AP2 200fr brn red, bl & blk 40.00 27.50

Adélie Penguins — AP3

1963, Feb. 11 Unwmk. *Perf. 13*

C4 AP3 50fr blk, dk bl & dp cl 42.50 32.50

Telstar Issue

Common Design Type

1962, Dec. 24

C5 CD111 50fr dp bl, ol & grn 29.00 21.00

Radio Towers, Adelie Penguins and IQSY Emblem — AP4

1963, Dec. 16 Engr.

C6 AP4 100fr bl, ver & blk 110.00 87.50

International Quiet Sun Year, 1964-65.

Discovery of Adelie Land — AP5

1965, Jan. 20 Engr. *Perf. 13*

C7 AP5 50fr blue & indigo 125.00 87.50

125th anniversary of the discovery of Adelie Land by Dumont d'Urville.

ITU Issue

Common Design Type

1965, May 17 Unwmk. *Perf. 13*

C8 CD120 30fr multi 200.00 160.00

French Satellite A-1 Issue

Common Design Type

Designs: 25fr, Diamant rocket and launching installations. 30fr, A-1 satellite.

1966, Mar. 2 Engr. *Perf. 13*

C9 CD121 25fr dk grn, choc & sl 13.50 10.00
C10 CD121 30fr choc, sl & dk grn 13.50 10.00
a. Pair, #C9-C10 + label 29.00 24.00

French Satellite D-1 Issue

Common Design Type

1966, Mar. 27

C11 CD122 50fr dk pur, lil & org 57.50 40.00

Ionospheric Research Pylon, Adelie Land — AP6

1966, Dec. 12

C12 AP6 25fr plum, bl & dk brn 32.50 17.50

Port aux Français, Emperor Penguin and Explorer — AP7

40fr, Aerial view of Saint Paul Island.

1968-69 Engr. *Perf. 13*

C13 AP7 40fr brt bl & dk gray 42.50 27.50
C14 AP7 50fr lt ultra, dk grn & blk 175.00 110.00

Issue dates: 50fr, Jan. 21; 40fr, Jan. 5, 1969.

Kerguelen Island and Rocket — AP8

Design: 30fr, Adelie Land.

1968, Apr. 22 Engr. *Perf. 13*

C15 AP8 25fr sl grn, dk brn & Prus bl 19.00 14.00
C16 AP8 30fr dk brn, sl grn & Prus bl 19.00 14.00
a. Pair, #C15-C16 + label 40.00 30.00

Space explorations with Dragon rockets, 1967-68.

Eiffel Tower, Antarctic Research Station, Ship from Paris Arms and Albatross AP9

1969, Jan. 13

C17 AP9 50fr bright blue 45.00 35.00

5th Consultative Meeting of the Antarctic Treaty Powers, Paris, Nov. 18, 1968.

Concorde Issue

Common Design Type

1969, Apr. 17

C18 CD129 85fr indigo & blue 55.00 37.50

Prepared but not issued with 87fr denomination. Value $7,000.

Map of Amsterdam Island AP10

Map of Kerguelen Island — AP11

Coat of Arms AP12

Designs: 50fr, Possession Island. 200fr, Point Geology Archipelago.

1969-71 **Engr.** ***Perf. 13***

C19 AP10 30fr brown 19.00 12.50
C20 AP11 50fr sl grn, bl & dk red 21.00 14.00
C21 AP11 100fr blue & blk 85.00 40.00
C22 AP10 200fr sl grn, brn & Prus bl 70.00 42.50
C23 AP12 500fr peacock blue 20.00 15.00
Nos. C19-C23 (5) 215.00 124.00

30fr for the 20th anniv. of the Amsterdam Island Meteorological Station.

Issued: 100fr, 500fr, 12/21; 30fr, 3/27/70; 50fr, 12/22/70; 200fr, 1/1/71.

Port-aux-Français, 1970 — AP13

Design: 40fr, Port-aux-Français, 1950.

1971, Mar. 9 **Engr.** ***Perf. 13***

C24 AP13 40fr bl, ocher & sl grn 19.00 12.00
C25 AP13 50fr bl, grn ol & sl grn 19.00 12.00
a. Pair, #C24-C25 + label 40.00 27.50

20th anniversary of Port-aux-Français on Kerguelen Island.

Marquis de Castries Taking Possession of Crozet Island, 1772 — AP14

250fr, Fleur-de-lis flag raising on Kerguelen Is.

1972 **Engr.** ***Perf. 13***

C26 AP14 100fr black 45.00 29.00
C27 AP14 250fr black & dk brn 100.00 45.00

Bicentenary of the discovery of the Crozet and Kerguelen Islands.

Issue dates: 100fr, Jan. 24; 250fr, Feb. 23.

M. S. Galliéni — AP15

1973, Jan. 25 **Engr.** ***Perf. 13***

C28 AP15 100fr black & blue 25.00 17.50

Exploration voyages of the Galliéni.

"Le Mascarin," 1772 — AP16

Sailing Ships: 145fr, "L'Astrolabe," 1840. 150fr, "Le Rolland," 1774. 185fr, "La Victoire," 1522.

1973, Dec. 13 **Engr.** ***Perf. 13***

C29 AP16 120fr brown olive 6.75 4.75
C30 AP16 145fr brt ultra 6.75 4.75
C31 AP16 150fr slate 8.00 8.00
C32 AP16 185fr ocher 10.50 8.00
Nos. C29-C32 (4) 32.00 25.50

Ships used in exploring Antarctica.

See Nos. C37-C38.

Alfred Faure Base — AP17

Design: Nos. C33-C35 show panoramic view of Alfred Faure Base.

1974, Jan. 7 **Engr.** ***Perf. 13***

C33 AP17 75fr Prus bl, ultra & brn 8.00 5.25
C34 AP17 110fr Prus bl, ultra & brn 11.00 8.00
C35 AP17 150fr Prus bl, ultra & brn 14.00 8.00
a. Triptych, Nos. C33-C35 37.50 30.00

Alfred Faure Antarctic Base, 10th anniv.

Penguin, Map of Antarctica, Letters — AP18

1974, Oct. 9 **Engr.** ***Perf. 13***

C36 AP18 150fr multicolored 7.00 5.50

Centenary of Universal Postal Union.

Ship Type of 1973

100fr, "Le Français." 200fr, "Pourquoi-pas?"

1974, Dec. 16 **Engr.** ***Perf. 13***

C37 AP16 100fr brt blue 5.50 3.00
C38 AP16 200fr dk car rose 9.00 4.50

Ships used in exploring Antarctica.

Rockets over Kerguelen Islands — AP19

Design: 90fr, Northern lights over map of northern coast of Russia.

1975, Jan. 26 **Engr.** ***Perf. 13***

C39 AP19 45fr purple & multi 7.00 4.00
C40 AP19 90fr purple & multi 9.00 5.25
a. Pair, #C39-C40 + label 19.00 13.00

Franco-Soviet magnetosphere research.

"La Curieuse" — AP20

Ships: 2.70fr, Commandant Charcot. 4fr, Marion-Dufresne.

1976, Jan. **Engr.** ***Perf. 13***

C41 AP20 1.90fr multicolored 3.25 2.00
C42 AP20 2.70fr multicolored 5.00 3.25
C43 AP20 4fr red & multi 9.00 4.25
Nos. C41-C43 (3) 17.25 9.50

Dumont d'Urville Base, 1956 — AP21

4fr, Dumont d'Urville Base, 1976, Adelie Land.

1976, Jan.

C44 AP21 1.20fr multicolored 9.00 4.00
C45 AP21 4fr multicolored 11.00 7.25
a. Pair, #C44-C45 + label 24.00 16.00

Dumont d'Urville Antarctic Base, 20th anniv.

Capt. Cook's Ships Passing Kerguelen Island — AP22

1976, Dec. 31 **Engr.** ***Perf. 13***

C46 AP22 3.50fr slate & blue 13.00 8.00

Bicentenary of Capt. Cook's voyage past Kerguelen Island.

Sea Lion and Cub AP23

1977-79 **Engr.** ***Perf. 13***

C47 AP23 4fr dk blue, grn ('79) 3.00 2.50
C48 AP23 10fr multicolored 10.00 9.00

Satellite Survey, Kerguelen — AP24

Designs: 50c, 2.70fr, Satellites, Kerguelen. 70c, Geophysical laboratory. 1.90fr, Satellite and Kerguelen tracking station. 3fr, Satellites, Adelie Land.

1977-79 **Engr.** ***Perf. 13***

C49 AP24 50c multi ('79) .90 .70
C50 AP24 70c multi ('79) .90 .70
C51 AP24 1.90fr multi ('79) 1.60 1.40
C52 AP24 2.70fr multi ('78) 2.75 2.00
C53 AP24 3fr multicolored 4.25 3.25
Nos. C49-C53 (5) 10.40 8.05

Elephant Seals — AP25

1979, Jan. 1

C54 AP25 10fr multicolored 5.50 4.50

Challenger — AP26

1979, Jan. 1
C55 AP26 2.70fr black & blue 2.25 1.75

Antarctic expeditions to Crozet and Kerguelen Islands, 1872-1876.

La Recherche and L'Esperance — AP27

1979
C56 AP27 1.90fr deep blue 1.50 1.10

Arrival of d'Entrecasteaux and Kermadec at Amsterdam Island, Mar. 28, 1792.

Lion Rock — AP28

1979
C57 AP28 90c multicolored 1.10 .70

Natural Arch, Kerguelen Island, 1840 — AP29

1979
C58 AP29 2.70fr multicolored 1.25 1.10

Phylica Nitida, Amsterdam Island — AP30

1979
C59 AP30 10fr multicolored 4.00 3.25

Charles de Gaulle, 10th Anniversary of Death AP31

1980, Nov. 9 **Engr.** ***Perf. 13***
C60 AP31 5.40fr multicolored 11.00 8.00

HB-40 Castor Truck and Trailer — AP32

1980, Dec. 15
C61 AP32 2.40fr multicolored 1.25 1.00

Supply Ship Saint Marcouf — AP33

1980, Dec. 15
C62 AP33 3.50fr shown 1.60 1.10
C63 AP33 7.30fr Icebreaker Norsel 2.50 2.00

Glacial Landscape, Dumont d'Urville Sea — AP34

Chionis — AP35

Adele Dumont d'Urville (1798-1842) — AP36

Arcad III — AP37

25th Anniv. of Charcot Station — AP38

Antares — AP39

1981 **Engr.** ***Perf. 13, 12½x13 (2fr)***
C64 AP34 1.30fr multicolored .70 .45
C65 AP35 1.50fr black .70 .50
C66 AP36 2fr black & lt brn .90 .85
C67 AP37 3.85fr multicolored 1.60 1.25
C68 AP38 5fr multicolored 1.75 1.50
C69 AP39 8.40fr multicolored 2.75 2.25
Nos. C64-C69 (6) 8.40 6.80

PHILEXFRANCE '82 Stamp Exhibition, Paris, June 11-21 — AP40

1982, June 11 **Engr.** ***Perf. 13***
C70 AP40 8fr multicolored 5.50 5.25

French Overseas Possessions Week, Sept. 18-25 — AP41

1982, Sept. 17 **Engr.** ***Perf. 13***
C71 AP41 5fr Commandant Charcot 1.75 1.75

Apostle Islands — AP42

1983, Jan. 3 **Engr.** ***Perf. 13***
C72 AP42 65c multicolored .55 .35

Sputnik I, 25th Anniv. of Intl. Geophysical Year — AP43

Orange Bay Base, Cape Horn, 1883, Cent. — AP44

5.20fr, Scoresby Sound Base, Greenland, 50th anniv.

1983, Jan. 3
C73 AP43 1.50fr multicolored .60 .60
C74 AP44 3.30fr multicolored 1.75 1.75
C75 AP44 5.20fr multicolored 2.00 2.00
a. Strip of 3, #C73-C75 4.50 4.50

AP45

1983, Jan. 3
C76 AP45 4.55fr dark blue 4.00 3.00

Abstract, by G. Mathieu — AP46

1983, Jan. 3 **Photo.** ***Perf. 13x13½***
C77 AP46 25fr multicolored 10.00 8.00

Erebus off Antarctic Ice Cap, 1842 — AP47

Port of Joan of Arc, 1930 — AP48

1984, Jan. 1 **Engr.** ***Perf. 13***
C78 AP47 2.60fr ultra & dk blue 1.10 1.00
C79 AP48 4.70fr multicolored 1.75 1.75

Aurora Polaris — AP49

1984, Jan. 1 **Photo.**
C80 AP49 3.50fr multicolored 2.00 1.25

Manned Flight Bicentenary (1983) — AP50

Various balloons and airships.

1984, Jan. 1 **Engr.**
C81 AP50 3.50fr multicolored 1.75 1.75
C82 AP50 7.80fr multicolored 2.75 2.75
a. Pair, #C81-C82 + label 5.00 5.00

Patrol Boat Albatros — AP51

1984, July 2 **Engr.** ***Perf. 13***
C83 AP51 11.30fr multi 4.25 4.25

NORDPOSTA Exhibition — AP52

1984, Nov. 3 **Engr.** ***Perf. 13***
C84 AP52 9fr Scientific Vessel Gauss 4.50 3.50

Issued se-tenant with label.

Corsican Sheep — AP53

Amsterdam Albatross AP54

1985, Jan. 1 **Engr.** ***Perf. 13***
C85 AP53 70c Mouflons .70 .40
C86 AP54 3.90fr Diomedia amsterdamensis 1.60 1.25

La Novara, Frigate AP55

1985, Jan. 1 **Engr.** ***Perf. 13***
C87 AP55 12.80fr La Novara at St. Paul 5.00 4.50

Explorer and Seal, by Tremois — AP56

Design: Explorer, seal, names of territories.

1985, Jan. 1 **Photo.** ***Perf. 13x12½***
C88 AP56 30fr + label 11.00 8.50

Sailing Ships, Ropes, Flora & Fauna — AP57

1985, Aug. 6 **Engr.** ***Perf. 13***
C89 AP57 2fr blk, brt bl & ol grn .70 .55
C90 AP57 12.80fr blk, ol grn & brt bl 3.75 3.75
a. Pair, #C89-C90 + label 5.50 5.50

French Southern & Antarctic Territories, 30th anniv. No. C90a has continuous design with center label.

Bird Type of 1986

1986, Jan. 1 **Engr.** ***Perf. 13½x13***
C91 A56 4.60fr Sea Gulls 2.00 1.75

Antarctic Atmospheric Research, 10th Anniv. — AP58

1986, Jan. 1
C92 AP58 14fr blk, dk red & brt org 5.00 4.00

Jean Charcot (1867-1936), Explorer — AP59

1986, Jan. 1
C93 AP59 2.10fr Ship Pourquoi Pas .90 .60
C94 AP59 14fr Ship in storm 4.50 4.25
a. Pair, #C93-C94 + label 6.25 6.25

SPOT Satellite over the Antarctic — AP60

1986, May 26 **Engr.** ***Perf. 13***
C95 AP60 8fr dp ultra, sep & dk ol grn 3.25 2.50

J.B. Charcot — AP61

1987, Jan. 1 **Engr.** ***Perf. 13x13½***
C96 AP61 14.60fr multi 5.00 4.50

Ocean Drilling Program — AP62

1987, Jan. 1 ***Perf. 13½x13***
C97 AP62 16.80fr lem, dk ultra & bluish blk 5.50 4.50

INMARSAT — AP63

1987, Mar. 2 **Engr.** ***Perf. 13***
C98 AP63 16.80fr multi 8.00 7.50

French Polar Expeditions, 40th Anniv. — AP64

1988, Jan. 1
C99 AP64 20fr lake, ol grn & plum 8.00 6.75

Views of Penguin Is. — AP65

1988, Jan. 1
C100 AP65 3.90fr dk bl & sep 1.75 1.50
C101 AP65 15.10fr dp grn, choc brn & dk bl 5.50 5.00

See Nos. C103, C109.

Founding of Permanent Settlements in the Territories, 40th Anniv. — AP66

1989, Jan. 1 **Engr.** ***Perf. 13½x13***
C102 AP66 15.50fr black 5.00 4.75

Island View Type

1989, Jan. 1
C103 AP65 8.40fr Apostle Islands 2.75 2.50

La Curieuse — AP68

1989, Jan. 1 ***Perf. 13x12½***
C104 AP68 2.20fr multicolored .80 .70
C105 AP68 15.50fr multi, diff. 5.00 5.00
a. Pair, #C104-C105 + label 6.00 6.00

No. C105a label continues the design.

French Revolution, Bicent. — AP69

1989, July 14 **Engr.** ***Perf. 13x12½***
C106 AP69 5fr pink, dark olive grn & dark blue 5.50 3.50

Souvenir Sheet

Perf. 13

C107 Sheet of 4 10.00 10.00
a. AP69 5fr Prus green, brt ultra & dark red 2.50 2.50

No. C107 for PHILEXFRANCE '89.

15th Antarctic Treaty Summit Conference — AP70

1989, Oct. 9 **Engr.** ***Perf. 13***
C108 AP70 17.70fr multicolored 6.00 5.75

Island View Type

1990, Jan. 1 **Engr.** ***Perf. 13***
C109 AP65 7.30fr Isle of Pigs, Crozet Isls. 3.00 2.40

L'Astrolabe, Expedition Team — AP72

1990, Jan. 1
C110 AP72 15.50fr dk red vio & blk 5.00 5.00

Discovery of Adelie Land by Dumont D'Urville, 150th anniv.

L'Astrolabe, Commanded by Dumont D'Urville, 1840 — AP73

1990, Jan. 1
C111 AP73 2.20fr *L'Astrolabe,* 1988 .80 .75
C112 AP73 15.50fr shown 5.00 5.00
a. Pair, #C111-C112 + label 6.50 6.50

Bird, by Folon — AP74

1990, Jan. 1 **Litho.** ***Perf. 12½x13***
C113 AP74 30fr multicolored 10.00 9.50

Albatross, Argos Satellite AP75

1991, Jan. 1
C114 AP75 2.10fr red brn, bl & brn 1.50 .95

Climatological Research — AP76

1991, Jan. 1 **Engr.** ***Perf. 13***
C115 AP76 3.60fr Weather balloons, instruments 1.40 1.40
C116 AP76 20fr Research ship 7.75 7.75
a. Pair, #C115-C116 + label 10.00 10.00

Charles de Gaulle (1890-1970) — AP77

1991, Jan. 1
C117 AP77 18.80fr blk, red & bl 7.75 7.75

Cape Petrel — AP78

1992, Jan. 1 **Engr.** ***Perf. 13***
C118 AP78 3.40fr multicolored 2.25 1.40

French Institute of Polar Research and Technology — AP79

#C120, Polar bear with man offering flowers.

1991, Dec. 16 **Engr.** ***Perf. 13x12***
C119 AP79 15fr multicolored 5.75 5.75
C120 AP79 15fr multicolored 5.75 5.75
a. Strip, #C119-C120 + label 12.00 12.00

Christopher Columbus and Discovery of America — AP80

1992, Jan. 1 ***Perf. 13***
C121 AP80 22fr multicolored 9.75 9.75

Mapping Satellite Poseidon — AP81

1992, Jan. 1 **Engr.** ***Perf. 13***
C122 AP81 24.50fr multi 11.00 10.50

Dumont d'Urville Base, Adelie Land — AP82

1992, Jan. 1 **Litho.** ***Perf. 13x12½***
C123 AP82 25.70fr multi 12.00 10.50

Amateur Radio — AP83

1993, Jan. 1 **Engr.** ***Perf. 13***
C124 AP83 2fr multicolored 2.00 .75

New Animal Biology Laboratory, Adelie Land — AP84

1993, Jan. 1
C125 AP84 25.40fr multicolored 11.00 6.75

Support Base D10 — AP85

1993, Jan. 1
C126 AP85 25.70fr ol, red & bl 11.00 7.00

Opening of Adelie Land Airfield — AP86

1993, Jan. 1
C127 AP86 30fr multicolored 13.00 8.75

Krill — AP87

1994, Jan. 1 **Engr.** ***Perf. 13***
C128 AP87 15fr black 6.50 4.00

Fishery Management — AP88

1994, Jan. 1
C129 AP88 23fr multicolored 10.00 6.00

Satellite, Ground Station — AP89

Design: 27.30fr, Lidar Station.

1994, Jan. 1
C130 AP89 26.70fr multicolored 12.00 7.00
C131 AP89 27.30fr multicolored 12.00 7.25

Arrival of Emperor Penguins — AP90

1994, Jan. 1 ***Perf. 13x12½***
C132 AP90 28fr blue & black 13.00 8.00

Erebus Mission — AP91

1995, Jan. 2 **Engr.** ***Perf. 13***
C133 AP91 4.30fr bl, vio & slate 2.25 1.50

Moving of Winter Station, Charcot — AP92

1995, Jan. 2 **Litho.**
C134 AP92 15fr multicolored 6.50 4.25

G. Lesquin (1803-30) — AP93

1995, Jan. 2
C135 AP93 28fr multicolored 12.00 8.00

Map of East Island — AP94

1996, Jan. 1 Engr. ***Perf. 13***
C136 AP94 20fr multicolored 8.50 6.00

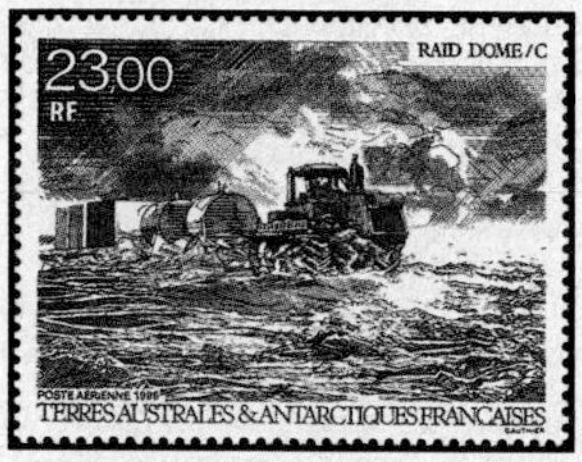

Expedition to Dome/C — AP95

1996, Jan. 1
C137 AP95 23fr dark blue 10.00 7.00

Blue Whale, Southern Whale Sanctuary — AP96

1996, Jan. 1
C138 AP96 26.70fr multicolored 12.00 8.00

Port-Couvreux — AP97

1996, Jan. 1
C139 AP97 27.30fr multicolored 12.00 8.50

Jasus Paulensis AP98

1997, Jan. 1 Engr. ***Perf. 12½x13***
C140 AP98 5.20fr multicolored 3.00 1.75

Racing Yacht Charentes 2 — AP99

1997, Jan. 1 Litho. ***Perf. 13***
C141 AP99 16fr multicolored 8.00 5.50

John Nunn, Shipwrecked 1825-29, Hope Cottage — AP100

1997, Jan. 1 Engr.
C142 AP100 20fr multicolored 8.75 6.25

ICOTA Program — AP101

1997, Jan. 1
C143 AP101 24fr multicolored 10.50 7.50

Harpagifer Spinosus — AP102

1997, Jan. 1
C144 AP102 27fr multicolored 12.00 8.50

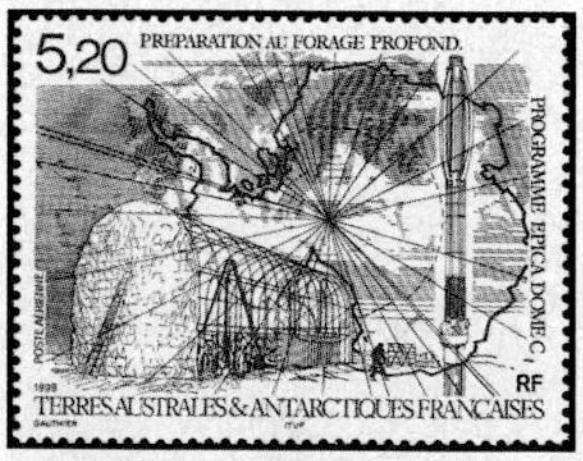

EPICA Program — AP103

1998, Jan. 2 Engr. ***Perf. 13***
C145 AP103 5.20fr dk brn & lil 2.50 1.40

First Radio Meteorological Station, Port Aux Francais — AP104

1998, Jan. 2
C146 AP104 8fr black, blue & red 4.25 2.25

King Penguin, Argos Satellite AP105

1998, Jan. 2 ***Perf. 12½x13***
C147 AP105 16fr multicolored 7.00 4.75

Ranunculas Moseleyi AP106

1998, Jan. 2
C148 AP106 24fr multicolored 10.50 6.50

Intl. Geophysical Year, 40th Anniv. — AP107

1998, Oct. Engr. ***Perf. 13x12½***
C149 AP107 5.20fr dk bl, blk & brick red 3.00 1.50

FRENCH SUDAN

'french sü-'dan

LOCATION — In northwest Africa, north of French Guinea and Ivory Coast
GOVT. — French Colony
AREA — 590,966 sq. mi.
POP. — 3,794,270 (1941)
CAPITAL — Bamako

In 1899 French Sudan was abolished as a separate colony and was divided among Dahomey, French Guinea, Ivory Coast, Senegal and Senegambia and Niger. Issues for French Sudan were resumed in 1921.

From 1906 to 1921 a part of this territory was known as Upper Senegal and Niger. A part of Upper Volta was added in 1933. See Mali.

100 Centimes = 1 Franc

See French West Africa No. 70 for stamp inscribed "Soudan Francais" and "Afrique Occidentale Francaise."

French Colonies Nos. 58-59 Srchd. in Black

Perf. 14x13½

1894, Apr. 12 **Unwmk.**

1	A9	15c	on 75c car, *rose*	*4,600.*	*2,300.*
2	A9	25c	on 1fr brnz grn, *straw*	*5,000.*	*1,700.*

The imperforate stamp like No. 1 was made privately in Paris from a fragment of the lithographic stone which had been used in the Colony for surcharging No. 1.

Counterfeit surcharges exist.

Navigation and Commerce — A2

1894-1900 Typo. ***Perf. 14x13½***
Name of colony in Blue or Carmine

3	A2	1c	blk, *lil bl*	1.60	2.00
4	A2	2c	brn, *buff*	2.40	2.75
5	A2	4c	claret, *lav*	8.00	6.50
6	A2	5c	grn, *grnsh*	12.00	12.00
7	A2	10c	blk, *lav*	24.00	24.00
8	A2	10c	red ('00)	8.00	8.00
9	A2	15c	blue, quadrille paper	8.00	8.00
10	A2	15c	gray, *lt gray* ('00)	8.00	8.00
11	A2	20c	red, *grn*	40.00	35.00
12	A2	25c	blk, *rose*	32.50	27.50
13	A2	25c	blue ('00)	8.00	8.75
14	A2	30c	brn, *bister*	40.00	40.00
15	A2	40c	red, *straw*	40.00	35.00
16	A2	50c	car, *rose*	55.00	65.00
17	A2	50c	brn, *az* ('00)	16.00	16.00
18	A2	75c	dp vio, *org*	55.00	55.00
19	A2	1fr	brnz grn, *straw*	12.00	12.00
			Nos. 3-19 (17)	370.50	365.50

Perf. 13½x14 stamps are counterfeits.

Nos. 8, 10, 13, 17 were issued in error. They were accepted for use in the other colonies.

Camel and Rider — A3

Stamps of Upper Senegal and Niger Overprinted in Black

1921-30 ***Perf. 13½x14***

21	A3	1c	brn vio & vio	.25	.40
22	A3	2c	dk gray & dl vio	.30	.50
23	A3	4c	blk & blue	.30	.50
24	A3	5c	ol brn & dk brn	.30	.40
25	A3	10c	yel grn & bl grn	.90	.55
26	A3	10c	red vio & bl ('25)	.40	.50
27	A3	15c	red brn & org	.50	.55
28	A3	15c	yel grn & dp grn ('25)	.40	.40
29	A3	15c	org brn & vio ('27)	1.60	1.60
30	A3	20c	brn vio & blk	.50	.55
31	A3	25c	blk & bl grn	1.25	.80
a.			Booklet pane of 4	—	
			Complete booklet, 5 #31a	650.00	
			Complete booklet, overprint omitted on one pane	16,000.	
32	A3	30c	red org & rose	1.60	1.60
33	A3	30c	bl grn & blk ('26)	.80	.70
34	A3	30c	dl grn & bl grn ('28)	2.00	2.00
35	A3	35c	rose & vio	.40	.55
36	A3	40c	gray & rose	1.25	1.25
37	A3	45c	bl & ol brn	1.25	1.25
38	A3	50c	ultra & bl	1.60	1.25
39	A3	50c	red org & bl ('26)	1.25	1.25
40	A3	60c	vio, *pnksh* ('26)	1.25	1.25
41	A3	65c	bis & pale bl ('28)	1.60	1.60
42	A3	75c	org & ol brn	1.60	2.00
43	A3	90c	brn red & pink ('30)	5.50	5.50
44	A3	1fr	dk brn & dl vio	1.60	2.00
45	A3	1.10fr	gray lil & red vio ('28)	3.25	4.00
46	A3	1.50fr	dp bl & bl ('30)	5.50	5.50
47	A3	2fr	grn & bl	2.40	2.75
48	A3	3fr	red vio ('30)	12.00	12.00
a.			Double overprint	190.00	
49	A3	5fr	vio & blk	8.00	7.25
			Nos. 21-49 (29)	59.55	60.45

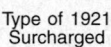

Type of 1921 Surcharged

1922, Sept. 28

50	A3	60c on 75c vio, *pnksh*	.80	.80

Stamps and Type of 1921-30 Surcharged

1925-27

51	A3	25c on 45c	.80	.80
52	A3	65c on 75c	2.00	2.40
53	A3	85c on 2fr	2.00	2.40
54	A3	85c on 5fr	2.00	2.40
55	A3	90c on 75c brn red & sal pink ('27)	2.40	2.75
56	A3	1.25fr on 1fr dp bl & lt bl (R) ('26)	1.25	1.60
57	A3	1.50fr on 1fr dp bl & ultra ('27)	1.60	2.00
58	A3	3fr on 5fr dl red & brn org ('27)	6.50	5.50
59	A3	10fr on 5fr brn red & bl grn ('27)	24.00	21.00
60	A3	20fr on 5fr vio & ver ('27)	29.00	29.00
		Nos. 51-60 (10)	71.55	69.85

Sudanese Woman — A4

Entrance to the Residency at Djenné — A5

Sudanese Boatman — A6

1931-40 Typo. *Perf. 13x14*

61	A4	1c dk red & blk	.25	.25
62	A4	2c dp blue & org	.25	.25
63	A4	3c dk red & blk ('40)	.25	.25
64	A4	4c gray lil & rose	.25	.25
65	A4	5c indigo & grn	.25	.25
66	A4	10c ol grn & rose	.25	.25
67	A4	15c blk & brt vio	.40	.30
68	A4	20c hn brn & lt bl	.40	.30
69	A4	25c red vio & lt red	.40	.30
70	A5	30c grn & lt grn	.80	.50
71	A5	30c dk bl & red org ('40)	.30	.30
72	A5	35c ol grn & grn ('38)	.40	.40
73	A5	40c ol grn & pink	.40	.30
74	A5	45c dk bl & red org	1.20	.65
75	A5	45c ol grn & grn ('40)	.50	.50
76	A5	50c red & black	.40	.30
77	A5	55c ultra & car ('38)	.40	.40
78	A5	60c brt bl & brn ('40)	1.20	1.20
79	A5	65c brt vio & blk	.80	.55
80	A5	70c vio bl & car rose ('40)	.80	.80
81	A5	75c brt bl & ol brn	2.40	2.00
82	A5	80c car & brn ('38)	.80	.80
83	A5	90c dp red & red org	1.60	.80
84	A5	90c brt vio & sl blk ('39)	.90	1.00
85	A5	1fr indigo & grn	8.00	2.40
86	A5	1fr rose red ('38)	5.50	1.60
87	A5	1fr car & brn ('40)	.80	.80
88	A6	1.25fr vio & dl vio ('33)	.80	.80
89	A6	1.25fr red ('39)	.90	1.00
90	A6	1.40fr brt vio & blk ('40)	.90	.90
91	A6	1.50fr dk bl & ultra	.80	.55
92	A6	1.60fr brn & dp bl ('40)	.90	.90
93	A6	1.75fr dk brn & dp bl ('33)	.80	.80
94	A6	1.75fr vio bl ('38)	.80	.80
95	A6	2fr org brn & grn	.80	.55
96	A6	2.25fr vio bl & ultra ('39)	1.00	1.10
97	A6	2.50fr lt brown ('40)	1.60	1.60
98	A6	3fr Prus grn & brn	.80	.40
99	A6	5fr red & blk	2.00	1.20
100	A6	10fr dull bl & grn	2.40	2.00
101	A6	20fr red vio & brn	3.25	2.40
		Nos. 61-101 (41)	47.65	32.70

For surcharges see Nos. B7-B10.
For 10c and 30c, without "RF," see Nos. 120-121.

Common Design Types pictured following the introduction.

Colonial Exposition Issue
Common Design Types

1931, Apr. 13 Engr. *Perf. 12½*
Name of Country Printed in Black

102	CD70	40c deep green	4.75	4.75
103	CD71	50c violet	4.75	4.75
104	CD72	90c red orange	4.75	4.75
105	CD73	1.50fr dull blue	4.75	4.75
		Set, never hinged	29.00	

Paris International Exposition Issue
Common Design Types

1937, Apr. 15 *Perf. 13*

106	CD74	20c deep violet	2.00	2.00
107	CD75	30c dark green	2.00	2.00
108	CD76	40c carmine rose	2.40	2.40
109	CD77	50c dark brown	1.60	1.60
110	CD78	90c red	1.60	1.60
111	CD79	1.50fr ultra	2.40	2.40
		Nos. 106-111 (6)	12.00	12.00
		Set, never hinged	20.25	

Colonial Arts Exhibition Issue
Souvenir Sheet
Common Design Type

1937 Engr. *Imperf.*

112	CD77	3fr magenta & blk	12.00	*16.00*
		Never hinged	16.00	

Caillie Issue
Common Design Type

1939, Apr. 5 *Perf. 12½x12*

113	CD81	90c org brn & org	.40	.80
114	CD81	2fr brt violet	.40	1.20
115	CD81	2.25fr ultra & dk bl	.40	1.20
		Nos. 113-115 (3)	1.20	3.20
		Set, never hinged	2.40	

New York World's Fair Issue
Common Design Type

1939, May 10

116	CD82	1.25fr car lake	.80	1.60
117	CD82	2.25fr ultra	.80	1.60
		Set, never hinged	2.40	

Entrance to the Residency at Djenné and Marshal Pétain — A7

1941 Engr. *Perf. 12x12½*

118	A7	1fr green	.40	—
119	A7	2.50fr blue	.40	—
		Set, never hinged	1.60	

For surcharges, see Nos. B14-B15.

Types of 1931-40 without "RF"

1943-44 Typo. *Perf. 13½x14*

120	A4	10c ol green & rose	.65	
121	A5	30c dk bl & red org	.95	
		Set, never hinged	2.00	

Nos. 120-121 were issued by the Vichy government in France, but were not placed on sale in French Sudan.

Stamps of French Sudan were superseded by those of French West Africa.

SEMI-POSTAL STAMPS

Curie Issue
Common Design Type
Unwmk.

1938, Oct. 24 Engr. *Perf. 13*

B1	CD80	1.75fr + 50c brt ultra	12.50	12.50
		Never hinged	21.00	

French Revolution Issue
Common Design Type

1939, July 5 Photo.
Name and Value Typo. in Black

B2	CD83	45c + 25c green	10.00	10.00
B3	CD83	70c + 30c brown	10.00	10.00
B4	CD83	90c + 35c red org	10.00	10.00
B5	CD83	1.25fr + 1fr rose pink	10.00	10.00
B6	CD83	2.25fr + 2fr blue	10.00	10.00
		Nos. B2-B6 (5)	50.00	50.00
		Set, never hinged	87.50	

Stamps of 1931-40, Surcharged in Black or Red

1941 *Perf. 13x14*

B7	A5	50c + 1fr red & blk (R)	4.00	4.00
B8	A5	80c + 2fr car & brn	8.00	8.00
B9	A6	1.50fr + 2fr dk bl & ultra	8.00	8.00
B10	A6	2fr + 3fr org brn & grn	8.00	8.00
		Nos. B7-B10 (4)	28.00	28.00
		Set, never hinged	55.00	

Common Design Type and

Native Officer — SP1

Aviation Officer — SP2

1941 Photo. *Perf. 13½*

B11	SP1	1fr + 1fr red	1.25	
B12	CD86	1.50fr + 3fr claret	1.40	
B13	SP2	2.50fr + 1fr blue	1.40	
		Nos. B11-B13 (3)	4.05	
		Set, never hinged	5.50	

Surtax for the defense of the colonies. Issued by the Vichy government in France, but not placed on sale in French Sudan.

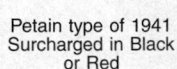

Petain type of 1941 Surcharged in Black or Red

1944 Engr. *Perf. 12x12½*

B14		50c + 1.50fr on 2.50fr deep blue (R)	.40	
B15		+ 2.50fr on 1fr green	.40	
		Set, never hinged	1.60	

Colonial Development Fund.

Nos. B14-B15 were issued by the Vichy government in France, but were not placed on sale in French Sudan.

AIR POST STAMPS

Common Design Type
Perf. 12½x12

1940, Feb. 8 Unwmk. Engr.

C1	CD85	1.90fr ultra	.40	.40
C2	CD85	2.90fr dark red	.40	.40
C3	CD85	4.50fr dk gray green	.80	.80
C4	CD85	4.90fr yellow bister	.80	.80
C5	CD85	6.90fr deep orange	1.60	1.60
		Nos. C1-C5 (5)	4.00	4.00
		Set, never hinged	5.20	

Common Design Types

1942, Oct. 19

C6	CD88	50c carmine & bl	.40	—
C7	CD88	1fr brown & blk	.40	
C8	CD88	2fr dk grn & red brn	.80	
C9	CD88	3fr dk blue & scar	.80	
C10	CD88	5fr vio & brn red	.80	

Frame Engr., Center Typo.

C11	CD89	10fr ultra, ind & gray blk	1.20	
C12	CD89	20fr rose car, mag & lt vio	1.60	
C13	CD89	50fr yel grn, dl grn & dl bl	2.00	—
		Nos. C6-C13 (8)	8.00	
		Set, never hinged	12.00	

There is doubt whether Nos. C7-C12 were officially placed in use.

AIR POST SEMI-POSTAL STAMPS

Types of Dahomey Air Post Semi-Postal Issue
Perf. 13½x12½, 13 (#CB3)
Photo, Engr. (#CB3)

1942, June 22

CB1	SPAP1	1.50fr + 3.50fr green	.40	*5.50*
CB2	SPAP2	2fr + 6fr brown	.40	*5.50*
CB3	SPAP2	3fr + 9fr car red	.40	*5.50*
		Nos. CB1-CB3 (3)	1.20	*16.50*
		Set, never hinged	2.40	

Native children's welfare fund.

Colonial Education Fund
Common Design Type
Perf. 12½x13½

1942, June 22 Engr.

CB4	CD86a	1.20fr + 1.80fr blue & red	.40	*5.50*
		Never hinged	.80	

POSTAGE DUE STAMPS

Postage Due Stamps of Upper Senegal and Niger Overprinted — D1

Perf. 14x13½

1921, Dec. Unwmk. Typo.

J1	D1	5c green	.40	.40
J2	D1	10c rose	.40	.40
J3	D1	15c gray	.40	.80
J4	D1	20c brown	1.20	1.20
J5	D1	30c blue	1.20	1.20
J6	D1	50c black	2.00	2.40
J7	D1	60c orange	2.40	2.40
J8	D1	1fr violet	2.40	3.25
		Nos. J1-J8 (8)	10.40	12.05

Type of 1921 Issue Surcharged

1927, Oct. 10

J9	D1	2fr on 1fr lilac rose	8.00	8.00
J10	D1	3fr on 1fr org brown	8.00	8.00

D2

1931, Mar. 9

J11	D2	5c green	.25	.30
J12	D2	10c rose	.25	.30
J13	D2	15c gray	.25	.50
J14	D2	20c dark brown	.25	.50
J15	D2	30c dark blue	.40	.55
J16	D2	50c black	.40	.55
J17	D2	60c deep orange	.80	.80
J18	D2	1fr violet	1.20	1.20
J19	D2	2fr lilac rose	1.60	1.60
J20	D2	3fr red brown	1.60	1.60
		Nos. J11-J20 (10)	7.00	7.90

FRENCH WEST AFRICA

'french 'west 'a-fri-kə

LOCATION — Northwestern Africa
GOVT. — French colonial administrative unit
AREA — 1,821,768 sq. mi.
POP. — 18,777,163 (est.)
CAPITAL — Dakar

French West Africa comprised the former colonies of Senegal, French Guinea, Ivory Coast, Dahomey, French Sudan, Mauritania, Niger and Upper Volta.

In 1958, these former colonies became republics, eventually issuing their own stamps. Until the republic issues appeared, stamps of French West Africa continued in use. The Senegal and Sudanese Republics issued stamps jointly as the Federation of Mali, starting in 1959.

Catalogue values for all unused stamps in this country are for Never Hinged items.

Many stamps other than Nos. 65-72 and 77 are inscribed "Afrique Occidentale Francaise" and the name of one of the former colonies. See listings in these colonies for such stamps.

Senegal No. 156 Surcharged in Red

1943 **Unwmk.** ***Perf. 12½x12***

1	A30	1.50fr on 65c dk vio	1.20	.90
2	A30	5.50fr on 65c dk vio	1.60	.80
3	A30	50fr on 65c dk vio	4.00	2.00

Mauritania No. 91 Surcharged in Red

1943 ***Perf. 13***

4	A7	3.50fr on 65c dp grn	.80	.40
5	A7	4fr on 65c dp grn	.80	.40
6	A7	5fr on 65c dp grn	1.60	.80
7	A7	10fr on 65c dp grn	1.60	.80
		Nos. 1-7 (7)	11.60	6.10

Senegal No. 143, 148 and 188 Surcharged with New Values in Black and Orange

1944 ***Perf. 12½x12***

8	A29	1.50fr on 15c blk (O)	.80	.65
9	A29	4.50fr on 15c blk (O)	1.20	.90
10	A29	5.50fr on 2c brn	2.40	1.60
11	A29	10fr on 15c blk (O)	4.00	1.75
12	CD81	20fr on 90c org brn & org	2.40	1.75
13	CD81	50fr on 90c org brn & org	6.50	3.25

Mauritania No. 109 Surcharged in Black

14	CD81	15fr on 90c org brn & org	2.40	1.60
		Nos. 8-14 (7)	19.70	11.50

Common Design Types pictured following the introduction.

Eboue Issue
Common Design Type

1945 **Engr.** ***Perf. 13***

15	CD91	2fr black	.80	.80
16	CD91	25fr Prussian green	1.60	1.60

Nos. 15 and 16 exist imperforate.

Colonial Soldier — A1

1945 **Litho.** ***Perf. 12½x12, 12***

17	A1	10c indigo & buff	.40	.25
18	A1	30c olive & yel	.40	.25
19	A1	40c blue & buff	.40	.25
20	A1	50c red org & gray	.40	.25
21	A1	60c ol brn & bl	.80	.40
22	A1	70c mag & cit	.80	.40
23	A1	80c bl grn & pale lem	.80	.40
24	A1	1fr brn vio & cit	.80	.40
25	A1	1.20fr gray brn & cit	4.00	2.40
26	A1	1.50fr choc & pink	.80	.40
27	A1	2fr ocher and gray	.80	.40
28	A1	2.40fr red & gray	1.25	.80
29	A1	3fr brn red & yelsh	.80	.40
30	A1	4fr ultra & pink	.80	.40
31	A1	4.50fr org brn & yelsh	.80	.40
32	A1	5fr dk pur & yelsh	.80	.40
33	A1	10fr ol grn & pink	1.60	.80
34	A1	15fr orange & yel	2.40	1.20
35	A1	20fr sl grn & grnsh	2.75	2.00
		Nos. 17-35 (19)	21.60	12.20

Rifle Dance, Mauritania — A2

Shelling Coconuts, Togo — A6

Bamako Dike, French Sudan — A3

Trading Canoe, Niger River — A4

Oasis of Bilma, Niger — A5

Kouandé Weaving, Dahomey A7

Donkey Caravan, Senegal A8

Crocodile and Hippopotamus, Ivory Coast — A9

Gathering Coconuts, French Guinea — A10

Peul Woman of Dienné — A12

Bamako Fountain, French Sudan A11

Bamako Market — A13

Dahomey Laborer — A14

Woman of Mauritania A15

Fula Woman, French Guinea A16

Djenné Mosque, French Sudan A17

Monorail Train, Senegal A18

Agni Woman, Ivory Coast — A19

Azwa Women at Niger River — A20

1947 **Engr.** **Unwmk.** ***Perf. 12½***

36	A2	10c blue	.40	.25
37	A3	30c red brn	.40	.25
38	A4	40c gray grn	.40	.25
39	A5	50c red brn	.40	.25
40	A6	60c gray blk	.80	.50
41	A7	80c brown vio	.80	.50
42	A8	1fr maroon	.80	.30
43	A9	1.20fr dk blue grn	2.00	1.40
44	A10	1.50fr ultra	2.00	1.10
45	A11	2fr red orange	.80	.25
46	A12	3fr chocolate	.80	.30
47	A13	3.60fr brown red	1.60	1.40
48	A14	4fr deep blue	.80	.30
49	A15	5fr gray green	.40	.25
50	A16	6fr dark blue	.80	.30
51	A17	10fr brn red	.80	.25
52	A18	15fr sepia	2.40	.30
53	A19	20fr chocolate	1.60	.30
54	A20	25fr grnsh blk	2.40	.50
		Nos. 36-54 (19)	20.40	8.95

Types of 1947

1948 **Re-engraved**

55	A6	60c brown olive	1.20	.80
56	A12	3fr chocolate	1.20	.55

Nos. 40 and 46 are inscribed "TOGO" in lower margin. Inscription omitted on Nos. 55 and 56.

Imperforates

Most stamps of French West Africa from 1949 onward exist imperforate in issued and trial colors, and also in small presentation sheets in issued colors.

Military Medal Issue
Common Design Type
Engraved and Typographed

1952, Dec. 1 ***Perf. 13***

57	CD101	15fr multicolored	8.75	6.50

Treich Laplène and Map — A21

1952, Dec. 1 **Engr.**

58	A21	40fr brown lake	2.40	.40

Marcel Treich Laplène, a leading contributor to the development of Ivory Coast.

Medical Laboratory A22

1953, Nov. 18

59	A22	15fr brn, dk bl grn & blk brn	1.60	.40

Couple Feeding Antelopes A23

1954, Sept. 20

60	A23	25fr multicolored	2.00	.40

Gov. Noel Eugène Ballay A24

1954, Nov. 29

61 A24 8fr indigo & brown 2.00 .80

Chimpanzee — A25

Giant Pangolin A26

1955, May 2 **Unwmk.** ***Perf. 13***

62 A25 5fr dp vio & dk brn 2.00 .80
63 A26 8fr brn & bl grn 2.00 .80

International Exhibition for Wildlife Protection, Paris, May 1955.

Map, Symbols of Industry, Rotary Emblem A27

1955, July 4

64 A27 15fr dark blue 2.40 .80

50th anniv. of the founding of Rotary Intl.

FIDES Issue

Common Design Type

Designs: 1fr, Date grove, Mauritania. 2fr, Milo Bridge, French Guinea. 3fr, Mossi Railroad, Upper Volta. 4fr, Cattle raising, Niger. 15fr, Farm machinery and landscape, Senegal. 17fr, Woman and Niger River, French Sudan. 20fr, Palm oil production, Dahomey. 30fr, Road construction, Ivory Coast.

1956 **Engr.** ***Perf. 13x12½***

65 CD103 1fr dk grn & dk bl grn 1.60 .65
66 CD103 2fr dk bl grn & bl 1.60 .65
67 CD103 3fr dk brn & red brn 1.60 1.00
68 CD103 4fr dk car rose 2.40 1.10
69 CD103 15fr ind & ultra 1.60 .55
70 CD103 17fr dk bl & ind 2.40 .75
71 CD103 20fr rose lake 2.40 .65
72 CD103 30fr dk pur & claret 2.40 1.00
Nos. 65-72 (8) 16.00 6.35

Coffee A28a

1956, Oct. 22 ***Perf. 13***

73 A28a 15fr dk blue green 1.60 .80

Mobile Leprosy Clinic and Maltese Cross A29

1957, Mar. 11

74 A29 15fr dk red brn, pur & red 2.40 .80

Issued in honor of the Knights of Malta.

Map of Africa — A30

1958, Feb. **Unwmk.** ***Perf. 13***

75 A30 20fr multicolored 1.60 .80

6h Intl.Cong. for African Tourism at Dakar.

"Africa" and Communications Symbols — A31

1958, Mar. 15 **Engr.**

76 A31 15fr org, ultra & choc 2.00 .80

Stamp Day. See No. 86.

Abidjan Bridge A32

1958, Mar. 15

77 A32 20fr dk sl grn & grnsh bl 2.00 .80

Bananas A33

1958, May 19 ***Perf. 13***

78 A33 20fr rose lil, dk grn & olive 1.60 .40

Flower Issue

Common Design Type

10fr, Gloriosa. 25fr, Adenopus. 30fr, Cyrtosperma. 40fr, Cistanche. 65fr, Crinum Moorei.

1958-59 **Photo.** ***Perf. 12x12½***

79 CD104 10fr multicolored 1.20 .40
80 CD104 25fr red, yel & grn 1.60 .80
81 CD104 30fr multicolored 2.00 1.20
82 CD104 40fr blk brn, grn & yel 2.40 1.60
83 CD104 65fr multicolored 3.25 1.60
Nos. 79-83 (5) 10.45 5.60

Issued: 25fr, 40fr, 1/5/59; others, 7/7/58.

Moro Naba Sagha and Map — A34

1958, Nov. 1 **Engr.** ***Perf. 13***

84 A34 20fr ol brn, car & vio 1.60 .80

10th anniv. of the reestablishment of the Upper Volta territory.

Human Rights Issue

Common Design Type

1958, Dec. 10

85 CD105 20fr maroon & dk bl 2.40 2.00

Type of 1958 Redrawn

1959, Mar. 21 **Engr.** ***Perf. 13***

86 A31 20fr red, grnsh bl & sl grn 2.75 2.40

Name of country omitted on No. 86; "RF" replaced by "CF," inscribed "Dakar-Abidjan." Stamp Day.

SEMI-POSTAL STAMPS

Red Cross Issue

Common Design Type

Perf. 14½x14

1944, Dec. **Photo.** **Unwmk.**

B1 CD90 5fr + 20fr plum 6.50 4.75

The surtax was for the French Red Cross and national relief.

Type of France, 1945, Overprinted in Black

1945, Oct. 13 **Engr.** ***Perf. 13***

B2 SP150 2fr + 3fr orange red 1.20 .80

Tropical Medicine Issue

Common Design Type

1950, May 15 ***Perf. 13***

B3 CD100 10fr +2fr red brn & sep 9.50 7.25

The surtax was for charitable work.

AIR POST STAMPS

Common Design Type

1945 **Photo.** **Unwmk.** ***Perf. 14½x14***

C1 CD87 5.50fr ultra 2.00 1.00
C2 CD87 50fr dark green 3.50 1.40
C3 CD87 100fr plum 4.00 1.50
Nos. C1-C3 (3) 9.50 3.90

Victory Issue

Common Design Type

1946, May 8 **Engr.** ***Perf. 12½***

C4 CD92 8fr violet 1.60 1.20

Chad to Rhine Issue

Common Design Types

1946, June 6

C5 CD93 5fr brown car 2.00 1.60
C6 CD94 10fr deep blue 2.00 1.60
C7 CD95 15fr brt violet 2.40 1.60
C8 CD96 20fr dk slate grn 2.40 2.00
C9 CD97 25fr olive brn 3.25 2.40
C10 CD98 50fr brown 4.00 2.75
Nos. C5-C10 (6) 16.05 11.95

Antoine de Saint-Exupéry, Map and Natives — AP1

Plane over Dakar — AP2

Great White Egrets in Flight — AP3

Natives and Phantom Plane — AP4

1947, Mar. 24 **Engr.**

C11 AP1 8fr red brown 1.60 .80
C12 AP2 50fr rose violet 4.00 1.20
C13 AP3 100fr ultra 16.00 4.75
C14 AP4 200fr slate gray 14.00 5.25
Nos. C11-C14 (4) 35.60 12.00

UPU Issue

Common Design Type

1949, July 4 ***Perf. 13***

C15 CD99 25fr multicolored 12.00 8.75

Vridi Canal, Abidjan — AP5

1951, Nov. 5 **Unwmk.** ***Perf. 13***

C16 AP5 500fr red org, bl grn & dp ultra 32.50 4.75

Liberation Issue

Common Design Type

1954, June 6

C17 CD102 15fr indigo & ultra 12.00 5.50

Logging — AP6

Designs: 100fr, Radiotelephone exchange. 200fr, Baobab trees.

1954, Sept. 20

C18 AP6 50fr ol grn & org brn 4.00 .80
C19 AP6 100fr ind, dk brn & dk grn 6.50 1.20
C20 AP6 200fr bl grn, grnsh blk & brn lake 17.50 2.75
Nos. C18-C20 (3) 28.00 4.75

Gen. Louis Faidherbé and African Sharpshooter AP7

1957, July 20 **Unwmk.** ***Perf. 13***

C21 AP7 15fr indigo & blue 2.00 1.60

Centenary of French African troops.

Gorée Island and Woman — AP8

Designs: 20fr, Map with planes and ships. 25fr, Village and modern city. 40fr, Seat of

Council of French West Africa. 50fr, Worker, ship and peanut plant. 100fr, Bay of N'Gor.

1958, Mar. 15 **Engr.**

C22	AP8	15fr blk brn, grn & vio	1.60	.80
C23	AP8	20fr blk brn, dk bl & red brn	1.60	.80
C24	AP8	25fr blk vio, bis & grn	1.60	1.20
C25	AP8	40fr dk bl, brn & grn	1.60	1.20
C26	AP8	50fr violet, brn & grn	3.25	1.60
C27	AP8	100fr brown, bl & grn	6.50	2.40
a.		Souvenir sheet of 6, #C22-C27	20.00	16.00
		Nos. C22-C27 (6)	16.15	8.00

Centenary of Dakar.

Woman Playing Native Harp — AP9

1958, Dec. 1 **Unwmk.** ***Perf. 13***

C28	AP9	20fr red brn, blk & gray	1.60	.80

Inauguration of Nouakchott as capital of Mauritania.

POSTAGE DUE STAMPS

D1

1947 **Engr.** **Unwmk.** ***Perf. 13***

J1	D1	10c red	.40	.25
J2	D1	30c deep orange	.40	.25
J3	D1	50c greenish blk	.40	.25
J4	D1	1fr carmine	.40	.25
J5	D1	2fr emerald	.50	.30
J6	D1	3fr red lilac	.90	.65
J7	D1	4fr deep ultra	1.10	.80
J8	D1	5fr red brown	2.25	1.60
J9	D1	10fr peacock blue	2.90	2.25
J10	D1	20fr sepia	5.25	3.75
		Nos. J1-J10 (10)	14.50	10.35

OFFICIAL STAMPS

Mask — O1

Designs: Various masks.

Perf. 14x13

1958, June 2 **Typo.** **Unwmk.**

O1	O1	1fr dk brn red	1.10	1.00
O2	O1	3fr brt green	.65	.55
O3	O1	5fr crim rose	.65	.50
O4	O1	10fr light ultra	.80	.65
O5	O1	20fr bright red	1.60	.80
O6	O1	25fr purple	1.60	.80
O7	O1	30fr green	2.75	1.60
O8	O1	45fr gray black	3.25	1.60
O9	O1	50fr dark red	3.25	1.60
O10	O1	65fr brt ultra	4.50	1.60
O11	O1	100fr olive bister	10.50	2.75
O12	O1	200fr deep green	21.00	5.50
		Nos. O1-O12 (12)	51.65	18.95

FUJEIRA

fü-ˈjī-rə

LOCATION — Oman Peninsula, Arabia, on Persian Gulf

GOVT. — Sheikdom under British protection

Fujeira is one of six Persian Gulf sheikdoms to join the United Arab Emirates which proclaimed independence Dec. 2, 1971. See United Arab Emirates.

100 Naye Paise = 1 Rupee

Catalogue values for all unused stamps in this country are for Never Hinged items.

Sheik Hamad bin Mohammed al Sharqi and Grebe — A1

Sheik and: 2np, 50np, Arabian oryx. 3np, 70np, Hoopoe. 4np, 1r, Wild ass. 5np, 1.50r, Herons in flight. 10np, 2r, Arabian horses. 15np, 3r, Leopard. 20np, 5r, Camels. 30np, 10r, Hawks.

Photo. & Litho.

1964 **Unwmk.** ***Perf. 14***

Size: 36x24mm

1	A1	1np gold & multi	.25	.25
2	A1	2np gold & multi	.25	.25
3	A1	3np gold & multi	.25	.25
4	A1	4np gold & multi	.25	.25
5	A1	5np gold & multi	.25	.25
6	A1	10np gold & multi	.25	.25
7	A1	15np gold & multi	.25	.25
8	A1	20np gold & multi	.25	.25
9	A1	30np gold & multi	.25	.25

Size: 43x28mm

10	A1	40np gold & multi	.30	.25
11	A1	50np gold & multi	.35	.25
12	A1	70np gold & multi	.40	.25
13	A1	1r gold & multi	.60	.25
14	A1	1.50r gold & multi	.90	.25
15	A1	2r gold & multi	1.40	.25

Size: 53½x35mm

16	A1	3r gold & multi	2.25	.25
17	A1	5r gold & multi	2.75	.35
18	A1	10r gold & multi	7.00	.50
		Nos. 1-18 (18)	18.20	4.85

Issued: 20np, 30np, 70np, 1.50r, 3r, 10r, Nov. 14; others, Sept. 22.

Exist imperf. Value, set $30.

Sheik Hamad and Shot Put — A2

1964, Dec. 6 ***Perf. 14***

Size: 43x28mm

19	A2	25np shown	.25	.25
20	A2	50np Discus	.25	.25
21	A2	75np Fencing	.25	.25
22	A2	1r Boxing	.30	.30
23	A2	1.50r Relay race	.45	.35
24	A2	2r Soccer	.55	.40

Size: 53½x35mm

25	A2	3r Pole vaulting	1.10	.50
26	A2	5r Hurdling	2.75	.75
27	A2	7.50r Equestrian	4.00	.90
		Nos. 19-27 (9)	9.90	3.95

18th Olympic Games, Tokyo, 10/10-25/64.

Exist imperf. Value, set $12.

John F. Kennedy — A3

Kennedy: 10np, As sailor in the Pacific. 15np, As naval lieutenant. 20np, On speaker's rostrum. 25np, Sailing with family. 50np, With crowd of people. 1r, With Mrs. Kennedy, Lyndon B. Johnson. 2r, With Eisenhower on White House porch. 3r, With Mrs. Kennedy & Caroline. 5r, Portrait.

1965, Feb. 23 **Photo.** ***Perf. 13½***

Size: 29x44mm

Black Design with Gold Inscriptions

28	A3	5np pale gray	.25	.25
29	A3	10np pale yellow	.25	.25
30	A3	15np pink	.25	.25
31	A3	20np pale greenish gray	.25	.25
32	A3	25np pale blue	.25	.25
33	A3	50np pale rose	.30	.25

Size: 33x51mm

34	A3	1r pale gray	.75	.30
35	A3	2r pale green	1.25	.40
36	A3	3r pale gray	2.50	.50
37	A3	5r pale yellow	3.25	.80
		Nos. 28-37 (10)	9.30	3.50

Pres. John F. Kennedy (1917-1963). A souvenir sheet contains 2 29x44mm stamps similar to Nos. 36-37 with pale blue (3r) and pale rose (5r) backgrounds. Value (unused): perf $7; imperf $9.

Nos. 28-37 exist imperf. Value $14.

AIR POST STAMPS

Wild Ass AP1

Photo. & Litho.

1965, Aug. 16 **Unwmk.** ***Perf. 13½***

Size: 43x28mm

C1	AP1	15np Grebe	.25	.25
C2	AP1	25np Arabian oryx	.25	.25
C3	AP1	35np Hoopoe	.35	.25
C4	AP1	50np Wild ass	.40	.25
C5	AP1	75np Herons in flight	.45	.25
C6	AP1	1r Arabian horses	.60	.25

Size: 53½x35mm

C7	AP1	2r Leopard	1.25	.25
C8	AP1	3r Camels	2.50	.25
C9	AP1	5r Hawks	4.50	.50
		Nos. C1-C9 (9)	10.55	2.50

Exist imperf. Value, set $11.

AIR POST OFFICIAL STAMPS

Type of Air Post Issue, 1965

Photo. & Litho.

1965, Nov. 10 **Unwmk.** ***Perf. 13½***

Size: 43x28mm

CO1	AP1	75np Arabian horses	.60	.25

Perf. 13

Size: 53½x35mm

CO2	AP1	2r Leopard	1.50	.40
CO3	AP1	3r Camels	2.50	.60
CO4	AP1	5r Hawks	4.50	1.00
		Nos. CO1-CO4 (4)	9.10	2.25

Exist imperf. Values same as perf.

OFFICIAL STAMPS

Type of Air Post Issue, 1965

Photo. & Litho.

1965, Oct. 14 **Unwmk.** ***Perf. 13½***

Size: 43x28mm

O1	AP1	25np Grebe	.25	.25
O2	AP1	40np Arabian oryx	.25	.25
O3	AP1	50np Hoopoe	.35	.25
O4	AP1	75np Wild ass	.55	.25
O5	AP1	1r Herons in flight	1.25	.25
		Nos. O1-O5 (5)	2.65	1.25

Exist imperf. Values same as perf.

FUNCHAL

fün-ˈshäl

LOCATION — A city and administrative district in the Madeira island group in the Atlantic Ocean northwest of Africa

GOVT. — A part of the Republic of Portugal

POP. — 150,574 (1900)

Postage stamps of Funchal were superseded by those of Portugal.

1000 Reis = 1 Milreis

King Carlos

A1 A2

1892-93 **Typo.** **Unwmk.**

Perf. 11 ½, 12 ½, 13 ½

1	A1	5r yellow	3.00	2.00
a.		Half used as 2½r on entire newspaper		17.50
2	A1	10r red violet	2.50	2.00
3	A1	15r chocolate	3.50	2.50
4	A1	20r lavender	4.50	2.50
a.		Perf. 13½	10.00	7.50
5a	A1	25r dark green	6.00	1.00
6	A1	50r ultramarine	7.00	2.50
7	A1	75r carmine	10.00	6.00
8	A1	80r yellow green	15.00	11.00
9	A1	100r brn, *yel* ('93)	12.00	5.00
a.		Diagonal half used as 50r on cover		70.00
10	A1	150r car, *rose* ('93)	60.00	30.00
11	A1	200r dk bl, *bl* ('93)	70.00	45.00
12	A1	300r dk bl, *sal* ('93)	75.00	55.00
		Nos. 1-12 (12)	268.50	164.50

Nos. 1-12 were printed on both enamel-surfaced and chalky papers. Values are for the most common varieties. For detailed listings, see the *Scott Classic Specialized Catalogue.*

The reprints of this issue have shiny white gum and clean-cut perforation 13½. The shades differ from those of the originals and the uncolored paper is thin.

1897-1905 ***Perf. 11¾***

Name and Value in Black except Nos. 25 and 34

13	A2	2½r gray	.50	.35
14	A2	5r orange	.50	.35
15	A2	10r light green	.50	.35
16	A2	15r brown	5.50	5.00
17	A2	15r gray grn ('99)	3.75	2.75
18	A2	20r gray vio	1.40	.75
19	A2	25r sea green	2.75	.75
20	A2	25r car rose ('99)	1.40	.55
a.		Booklet pane of 6	—	
21	A2	50r dark blue	10.00	5.00
a.		Perf. 12½	25.00	9.00
22	A2	50r ultra ('05)	1.50	.90
23	A2	65r slate blue ('98)	1.25	.90
24	A2	75r rose	2.00	.95
25	A2	75r brn & red, *yel* ('05)	6.00	1.40
26	A2	80r violet	1.40	1.10
27	A2	100r dark blue, *blue*	1.40	1.10
a.		Diagonal half used as 50r on cover		75.00
28	A2	115r org brn, *pink* ('98)	4.00	1.40
29	A2	130r gray brown, *buff* ('98)	5.00	1.40
30	A2	150r lt brn, *buff*	5.00	1.25
31	A2	180r sl, *pnksh* ('98)	5.00	1.40
32	A2	200r red vio, *pale lil*	5.00	2.10
33	A2	300r blue, *rose*	5.00	2.10
34	A2	500r blk & red, *bl*	9.00	2.40
a.		Perf. 12½	20.00	7.75
		Nos. 13-34 (22)	77.85	34.25

STOCKBOOKS

Stockbooks are a classic and convenient storage alternative for many collectors. These 9" x 12" Lighthouse stockbooks feature heavyweight archival quality paper with 9 pockets on each page and include double glassine interleaving between the pages for added protection.

Item	*Binder Color*	*Pg Count*	*Pg Color*	*Retail*	*AA**
LS4/8BK	Black	16 pgs	Black	$18.95	**$16.95**
LS4/8BL	Blue	16 pgs	Black	$18.95	**$16.95**
LS4/8GR	Green	16 pgs	Black	$18.95	**$16.95**
LS4/8RD	Red	16 pgs	Black	$18.95	**$16.95**
LS4/16BK	Black	32 pgs	Black	$30.95	**$24.95**
LS4/16BL	Blue	32 pgs	Black	$30.95	**$24.95**
LS4/16GR	Green	32 pgs	Black	$30.95	**$24.95**
LS4/16RD	Red	32 pgs	Black	$30.95	**$24.95**

Item	*Binder Color*	*Pg Count*	*Pg Color*	*Retail*	*AA**
LS4/32BK	Black	64 pgs	Black	$57.95	**$49.95**
LS4/32BL	Blue	64 pgs	Black	$57.95	**$49.95**
LS4/32GR	Green	64 pgs	Black	$57.95	**$49.95**
LS4/32RD	Red	64 pgs	Black	$57.95	**$49.95**
LW4/8BK	Black	16 pgs	White	$16.95	**$14.95**
LW4/8BL	Blue	16 pgs	White	$16.95	**$14.95**
LW4/8GR	Green	16 pgs	White	$16.95	**$14.95**
LW4/8RD	Red	16 pgs	White	$16.95	**$14.95**

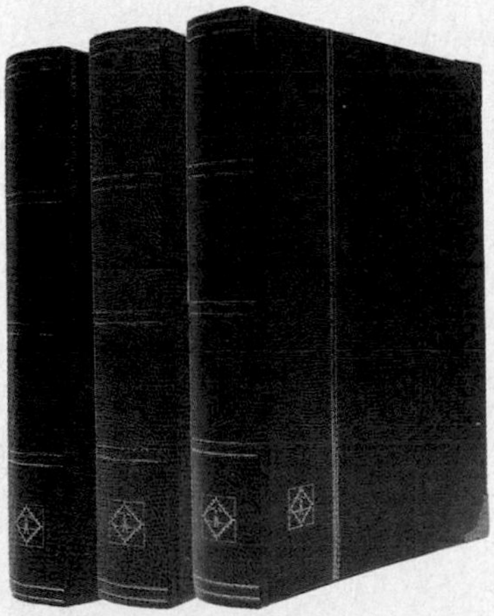

COMFORT DELUXE STOCKBOOK

This new line of stockbooks features a paddded green alligator-textured cover and gold-plated metal corners which are sure to impress. The double-suided black pages made from extra-strong card stock come with 9 clear strips and double glassine interleaves. The aredouble-linen hinged to lie completely flat.

Item	*Binder Color*	*Pg Count*	*Pg Color*	*Retail*	*AA**
LBP4/32BL	Blue	64 pgs	Black	$67.95	**$59.95**
LBP4/32GR	Green	64 pgs	Black	$67.95	**$59.95**
LBP4/32RD	Red	64 pgs	Black	$67.95	**$59.95**

Call 800-572-6885

Outside U.S. & Canada call: (937) 498-0800

Visit AmosAdvantage.com

P.O. Box 4129, Sidney, OH 45365

Ordering Information: *AA prices apply to paid subscribers of Amos Media publications, or orders placed online. Prices, terms and product availability subject to change. Taxes will apply in CA, OH & IL.
Shipping & Handling: United States: Orders under $10 are only $3.99 - 10% of order total.
Minimum charge $7.99 Maximum Charge $45.00. **Canada:** 20% of order total.
Minimum charge $19.99 Maximum charge $200.00. Foreign orders are shipped via FedExl Intl. or USPS and billed actual freight. Taxes will apply in CA, OH, & IL.

Pronunciation Symbols

ə .... banana, collide, abut

ˈə, ˌə .... humdrum, abut

ə .... immediately preceding \l\, \n\, \m\, \ŋ\, as in battle, mitten, eaten, and sometimes open \ˈō-p^{ə}m\, lock and key \-^{ə}ŋ-\; immediately following \l\, \m\, \r\, as often in French table, prisme, titre

ər .... further, merger, bird

ˈər- / ˈə-r .... as in two different pronunciations of hurry \ˈhər-ē, ˈhə-rē\

a .... mat, map, mad, gag, snap, patch

ā .... day, fade, date, aorta, drape, cape

ä .... bother, cot, and, with most American speakers, father, cart

ȧ .... father as pronounced by speakers who do not rhyme it with *bother*; French patte

au̇ .... now, loud, out

b .... baby, rib

ch .... chin, nature \ˈnā-chər\

d .... did, adder

e .... bet, bed, peck

ˈē, ˌē .... beat, nosebleed, evenly, easy

ē .... easy, mealy

f .... fifty, cuff

g .... go, big, gift

h .... hat, ahead

hw .... whale as pronounced by those who do not have the same pronunciation for both *whale* and *wail*

i .... tip, banish, active

ī .... site, side, buy, tripe

j .... job, gem, edge, join, judge

k .... kin, cook, ache

k̲ .... German ich, Buch; one pronunciation of loch

l .... lily, pool

m .... murmur, dim, nymph

n .... no, own

^{n} .... indicates that a preceding vowel or diphthong is pronounced with the nasal passages open, as in French *un bon vin blanc* \œ^{n} -bō^{n} -va^{n} -blä^{n}\

ŋ .... sing \ˈsiŋ\, singer \ˈsiŋ-ər\, finger \ˈfiŋ-gər\, ink \ˈiŋk \

ō .... bone, know, beau

ȯ .... saw, all, gnaw, caught

œ .... French boeuf, German Hölle

œ̄ .... French feu, German Höhle

ȯi .... coin, destroy

p .... pepper, lip

r .... red, car, rarity

s .... source, less

sh .... as in shy, mission, machine, special (actually, this is a single sound, not two); with a hyphen between, two sounds as in *grasshopper* \ˈgras-ˌhä-pər\

t .... tie, attack, late, later, latter

th .... as in thin, ether (actually, this is a single sound, not two); with a hyphen between, two sounds as in *knighthood* \ˈnīt-ˌhu̇d\

t̲h̲ .... then, either, this (actually, this is a single sound, not two)

ü .... rule, youth, union \ˈyün-yən\, few \ˈfyü\

u̇ .... pull, wood, book, curable \ˈkyu̇r-ə-bəl\, fury \ˈfyu̇r-ē\

ue .... German füllen, hübsch

ue̅ .... French rue, German fühlen

v .... vivid, give

w .... we, away

y .... yard, young, cue \ˈkyü\, mute \ˈmyüt\, union \ˈyün-yən\

^{y} .... indicates that during the articulation of the sound represented by the preceding character the front of the tongue has substantially the position it has for the articulation of the first sound of *yard*, as in French *digne* \dēn^{y}\

z .... zone, raise

zh .... as in vision, azure \ˈa-zhər\ (actually, this is a single sound, not two); with a hyphen between, two sounds as in *hogshead* \ˈhȯgz-ˌhed, ˈhägz-\

\ .... slant line used in pairs to mark the beginning and end of a transcription: \ˈpen\

ˈ .... mark preceding a syllable with primary (strongest) stress: \ˈpen-mən-ˌship\

ˌ .... mark preceding a syllable with secondary (medium) stress: \ˈpen-mən-ˌship\

\- .... mark of syllable division

( ) .... indicate that what is symbolized between is present in some utterances but not in others: *factory* \ˈfak-t(ə-)rē\

÷ .... indicates that many regard as unacceptable the pronunciation variant immediately following: *cupola* \ˈkyü-pə-lə, ÷-ˌlō\

Illustrated Identifier

This section pictures stamps or parts of stamp designs that will help identify postage stamps that do not have English words on them.

Many of the symbols that identify stamps of countries are shown here as well as typical examples of their stamps.

See the Index and Identifier on the previous pages for stamps with inscriptions such as "sen," "posta," "Baja Porto," "Helvetia," "K.S.A.", etc.

Linn's Stamp Identifier is now available. The 144 pages include more than 2,000 inscriptions and more than 500 large stamp illustrations. Available from Linn's Stamp News, P.O. Box 4129, Sidney, OH 45365-4129.

1. HEADS, PICTURES AND NUMERALS

GREAT BRITAIN

Great Britain stamps never show the country name, but, except for postage dues, show a picture of the reigning monarch.

Victoria

Edward VII George V Edward VIII

George VI

Elizabeth II

Some George VI and Elizabeth II stamps are surcharged in annas, new paisa or rupees. These are listed under Oman.

Silhouette (sometimes facing right, generally at the top of stamp)

The silhouette indicates this is a British stamp. It is not a U.S. stamp.

VICTORIA

Queen Victoria

INDIA

Other stamps of India show this portrait of Queen Victoria and the words "Service" (or "Postage") and "Annas."

AUSTRIA

YUGOSLAVIA

(Also BOSNIA & HERZEGOVINA if imperf.)

BOSNIA & HERZEGOVINA

Denominations also appear in top corners instead of bottom corners.

HUNGARY

Another stamp has posthorn facing left

BRAZIL

AUSTRALIA

Kangaroo and Emu

GERMANY

Mecklenburg-Vorpommern

SWITZERLAND

PALAU

2. ORIENTAL INSCRIPTIONS

CHINA

中 中

Any stamp with this one character is from China (Imperial, Republic or People's Republic). This character appears in a four-character overprint on stamps of Manchukuo. These stamps are local provisionals, which are unlisted. Other overprinted Manchukuo stamps show this character, but have more than four characters in the overprints. These are listed in People's Republic of China.

Some Chinese stamps show the Sun.

中華民國郵票

Most stamps of Republic of China show this series of characters.

Stamps with the China character and this character are from People's Republic of China. 人

Calligraphic form of People's Republic of China

(一)	(二)	(三)	(四)	(五)	(六)
1	2	3	4	5	6
(七)	(八)	(九)	(十)	(一十)	(二十)
7	8	9	10	11	12

Chinese stamps without China character

REPUBLIC OF CHINA

PEOPLE'S REPUBLIC OF CHINA

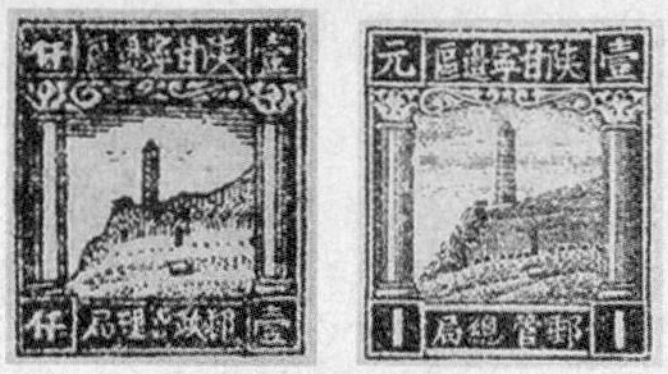

Mao Tse-tung

MANCHUKUO

Temple

Emperor Pu-Yi

The first 3 characters are common to many Manchukuo stamps.

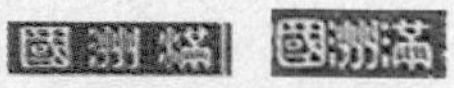

The last 3 characters are common to other Manchukuo stamps.

Orchid Crest

Manchukuo stamp without these elements

JAPAN

Chrysanthemum Crest

Country Name

Japanese stamps without these elements

The number of characters in the center and the design of dragons on the sides will vary.

RYUKYU ISLANDS

Country Name

PHILIPPINES (Japanese Occupation)

Country Name

NETHERLANDS INDIES (Japanese Occupation)

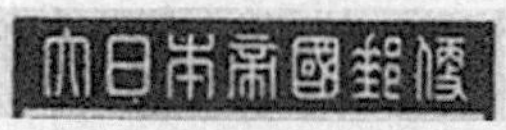

Indicates Japanese Occupation

Java

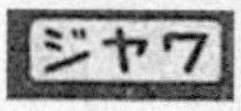

Country Name

Sumatra

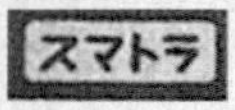

Country Name

Moluccas, Celebes and South Borneo

Country Name

NORTH BORNEO (Japanese Occupation)

Indicates Japanese Occupation

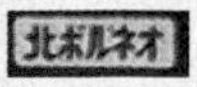

Country Name

MALAYA (Japanese Occupation)

Indicates Japanese Occupation

Country Name

BURMA

Union of Myanmar

Union of Myanmar

(Japanese Occupation)

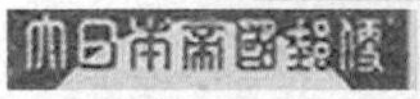

Indicates Japanese Occupation

Country Name

Other Burma Japanese Occupation stamps without these elements

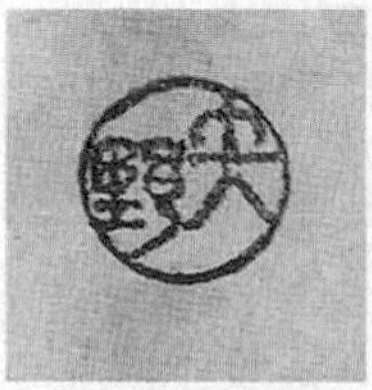

Burmese Script

KOREA

These two characters, in any order, are common to stamps from the Republic of Korea (South Korea) or of the People's Democratic Republic of Korea (North Korea).

This series of four characters can be found on the stamps of both Koreas. Most stamps of the Democratic People's Republic of Korea (North Korea) have just this inscription.

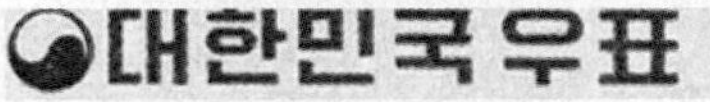

Indicates Republic of Korea (South Korea)

South Korean postage stamps issed after 1952 do not show currency expressed in Latin letters. Stamps wiith " HW," "HWAN," "WON," "WN," "W" or "W" with two lines through it, if not illustrated in listings of stamps before this date, are revenues. North Korean postage stamps do not have currency expressed in Latin letters.

Yin Yang appears on some stamps.

South Korean stamps show Yin Yang and starting in 1966, 'KOREA" in Latin letters

Example of South Korean stamps lacking Latin text, Yin Yang and standard Korean text of country name. North Korean stamps never show Yin Yang and starting in 1976 are inscribed "DPRK" or "DPR KOREA" in Latin letters.

THAILAND

Country Name

King Chulalongkorn

King Prajadhipok and Chao P'ya Chakri

3. CENTRAL AND EASTERN ASIAN INSCRIPTIONS

INDIA - FEUDATORY STATES

Alwar

Bhor

Bundi

Similar stamps come with different designs in corners and differently drawn daggers (at center of circle).

Dhar

Duttia

Faridkot

Hyderabad

Similar stamps exist with different central design which is inscribed "Postage" or "Post & Receipt."

Indore

Jammu & Kashmir

Text varies.

Jasdan

Jhalawar

Kotah

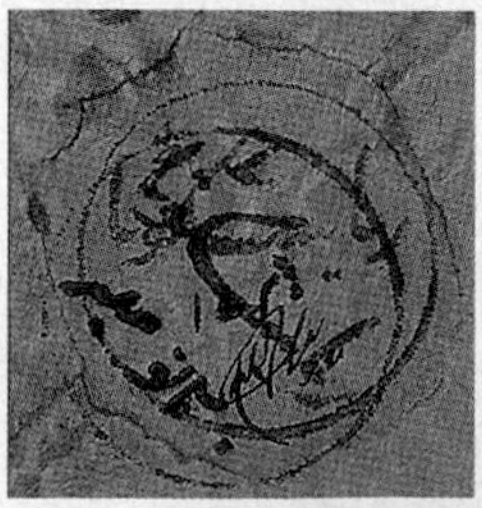

Size and text varies

Nandgaon

Nowanuggur

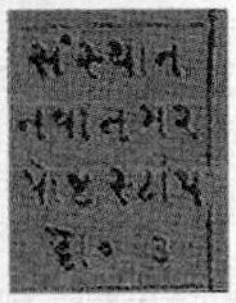

Poonch

Similar stamps exist
in various sizes with different text

Rajasthan

Rajpeepla

Soruth

Tonk

BANGLADESH

Country Name

NEPAL

Similar stamps are smaller, have squares in upper corners and have five or nine characters in central bottom panel.

TANNU TUVA

ISRAEL

GEORGIA

This inscription
is found on other
pictorial stamps.

Country Name

ARMENIA

The four characters are found somewhere on pictorial stamps. On some stamps only the middle two are found.

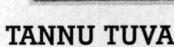

4. AFRICAN INSCRIPTIONS

ETHIOPIA

5. ARABIC INSCRIPTIONS

١	٢	٣	٤	٥
1	2	3	4	5
٦	٧	٨	٩	٠
6	7	8	9	0

AFGHANISTAN

Many early Afghanistan stamps show Tiger's head, many of these have ornaments protruding from outer ring, others show inscriptions in black.

Arabic Script

Crest of King Amanullah

Mosque Gate & Crossed Cannons

The four characters are found somewhere on pictorial stamps. On some stamps only the middle two are found.

BAHRAIN

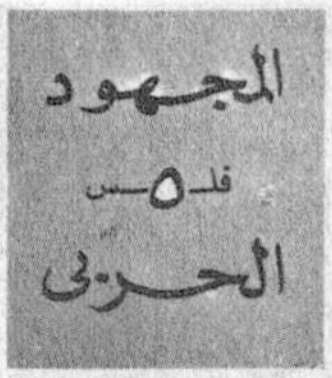

EGYPT

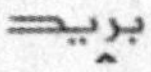

Postage

IRAN

Country Name

Royal Crown

Lion with Sword

Symbol

Emblem

IRAQ

JORDAN

LEBANON

Similar types have denominations at top and slightly different design.

LIBYA

Country Name in various styles

Other Libya stamps show Eagle and Shield (head facing either direction) or Red, White and Black Shield (with or without eagle in center).

Without Country Name

SAUDI ARABIA

Tughra (Central design)

Palm Tree and Swords

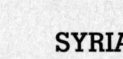

SYRIA

Arab Government Issues

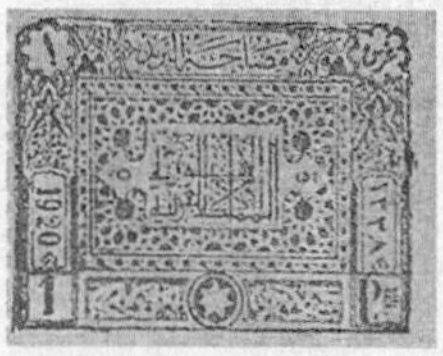

THRACE

YEMEN

PAKISTAN

PAKISTAN - BAHAWALPUR

Country Name in top panel, star and crescent

TURKEY

Star & Crescent is a device found on many Turkish stamps, but is also found on stamps from other Arabic areas (see Pakistan-Bahawalpur)

Tughra (similar tughras can be found on stamps of Turkey in Asia, Afghanistan and Saudi Arabia)

Mohammed V

Mustafa Kemal

Plane, Star and Crescent

TURKEY IN ASIA

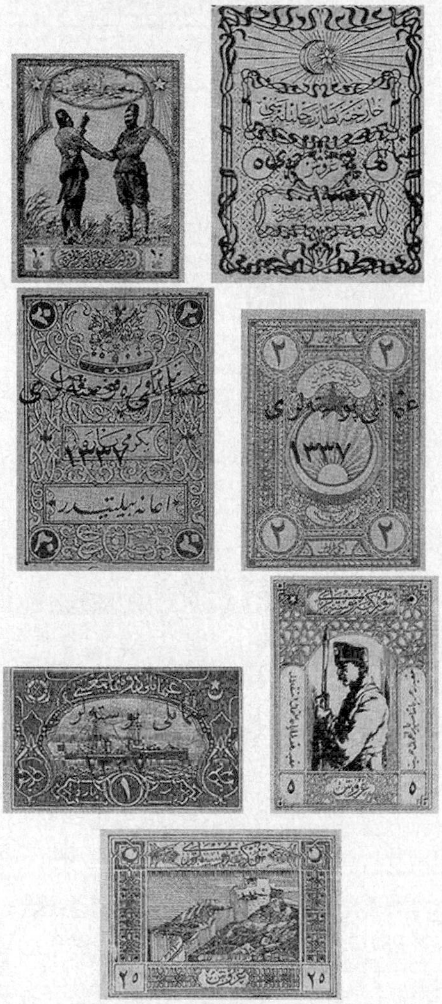
Other Turkey in Asia pictorials show star & crescent. Other stamps show tughra shown under Turkey.

6. GREEK INSCRIPTIONS

GREECE

Country Name in various styles (Some Crete stamps overprinted with the Greece country name are listed in Crete.)

Lepta

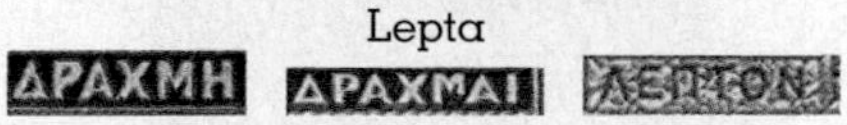
Drachma Drachmas Lepton

Abbreviated Country Name 

Other forms of Country Name

No country name

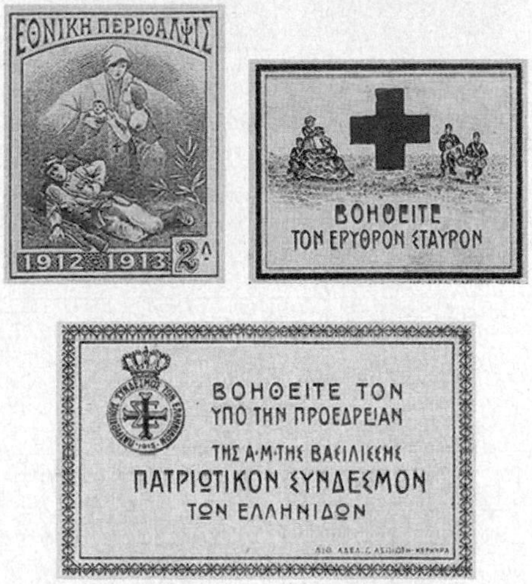

CRETE

Country Name

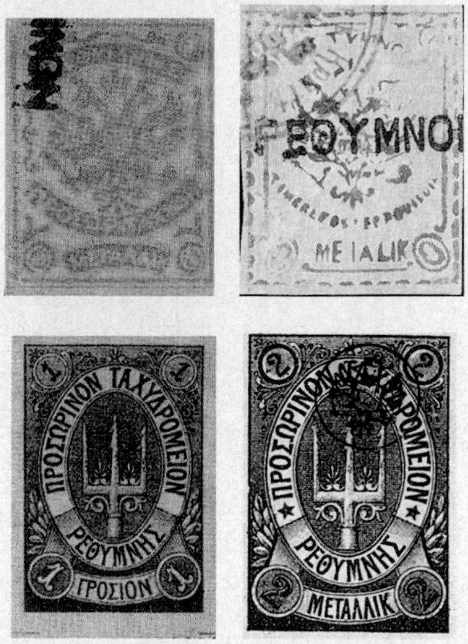

Crete stamps with a surcharge that have the year "1922" are listed under Greece.

EPIRUS

Similar stamps have text above the eagle.

IONIAN IS.

7. CYRILLIC INSCRIPTIONS

RUSSIA

Postage Stamp Imperial Eagle

Postage in various styles

Abbreviation for Kopeck | Abbreviation for Ruble | Russia

Abbreviation for Russian Soviet Federated Socialist Republic
RSFSR stamps were overprinted (see below)

Abbreviation for Union of Soviet Socialist Republics

This item is footnoted in Latvia

RUSSIA - Army of the North

"OKCA"

RUSSIA - Wenden

RUSSIAN OFFICES IN THE TURKISH EMPIRE

These letters appear on other stamps of the Russian offices.

The unoverprinted version of this stamp and a similar stamp were overprinted by various countries (see below).

ARMENIA

BELARUS

FAR EASTERN REPUBLIC

Country Name

FINLAND

Circles and Dots on stamps similar to Imperial Russia issues

SOUTH RUSSIA

Country Name

BATUM

Forms of Country Name

TRANSCAUCASIAN FEDERATED REPUBLICS

Abbreviation for Country Name

KAZAKHSTAN

Country Name

KYRGYZSTAN

КЫРГЫЗСТАН Country Name

ROMANIA

TAJIKISTAN

Country Name & Abbreviation

UKRAINE

Country Name in various forms

The trident appears on many stamps, usually as an overprint.

Abbreviation for Ukrainian Soviet Socialist Republic

WESTERN UKRAINE

Abbreviation for Country Name

AZERBAIJAN

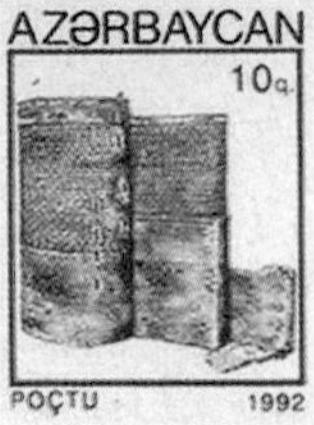

AZƏRBAYCAN

Country Name

A.C.C.P

Abbreviation for Azerbaijan Soviet Socialist Republic

MONTENEGRO

ЦРНЕГОРЕ

ЦРНА ГОРА

Country Name in various forms

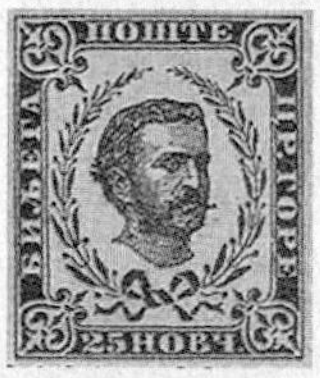

Ц.Р.ГОРЕ

Abbreviation for country name

No country name (A similar Montenegro stamp without country name has same vignette.)

SERBIA

СРПСКА СРБИЈА

Country Name in various forms

СРП. X.C.

Abbreviation for country name

No country name

MACEDONIA

МАКЕДОНИЈА

МАКЕДОНИЈА

Country Name

МАКЕДОНСКИ

Different form of Country Name

SERBIA & MONTENEGRO

YUGOSLAVIA

ЈУГОСЛАВИЈА

Showing country name

No Country Name

BOSNIA & HERZEGOVINA (Serb Administration)

РЕПУБЛИКА СРПСКА

Country Name

РЕПУБЛИКЕ СРПСКЕ

Different form of Country Name

No Country Name

BULGARIA

Country Name Postage

Stotinka

Stotinki (plural) Abbreviation for Stotinki

Country Name in various forms and styles

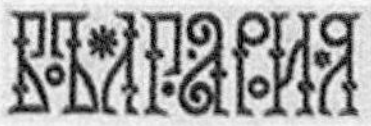

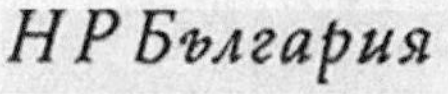

No country name

Abbreviation for Lev, leva

MONGOLIA

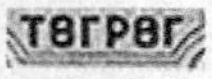

Country name in one word Tugrik in Cyrillic

Country name in two words Mung in Cyrillic

Mung in Mongolian

Tugrik in Mongolian

Arms

No Country Name

Scott International Album

Prices have never been so low on selected album parts. It is a wonderful opportunity to collect internationally. The Ultimate Album for Worldwide Collectors! Pick a period in history and embark on a philatelic adventure. With the International Album, the whole world is divided chronologically into more than 50 parts. From the classic era of philately to present day, the International is one of the broadest and far reaching worldwide albums available. *Binders are sold separately.*

- More than 16,000 pages with spaces for over 220,000 stamps.
- Pages printed on 2 sides.

Item	*Part*	*Binder*		*Retail*	*AA**
801A140	1A1	(1840-1940)	Regular	$150.00	$120.00
801A240	1A2	(1840-1940)	Regular	$150.00	$120.00
801B140	1B1	(1840-1940)	Regular	$150.00	$120.00
801B240	1B2	(1840-1940)	Regular	$150.00	$120.00
802P149	2A	(1940-49)	Regular	$150.00	$120.00
802P249	2B	(1940-49)	Regular	$150.00	$120.00
803P155	3A	(1949-55)	Regular	$150.00	$120.00
803P255	3B	(1949-55)	Regular	$150.00	$120.00
804P159	4A	(1956-60)	Regular	$150.00	$120.00
804P259	4B	(1956-60)	Regular	$150.00	$120.00
805P063	5	(1960-63)	Jumbo	$150.00	$120.00
805P165	5A	(1963-65)	Jumbo	$150.00	$120.00
806P066	6	(1965-66)	Jumbo	**$75.00**	**$55.00**
806P168	6A	(1966-68)	Jumbo	**$75.00**	**$55.00**
807P171	7A	(1968-71)	Jumbo	$150.00	$120.00
807P271	7B	(1968-71)	Jumbo	$150.00	$120.00
808P173	8A	(1971-73)	Regular	$150.00	$120.00
808P273	8B	(1971-73)	Regular	$150.00	$120.00
809P074	9	(1973-74)	Regular	$150.00	$120.00
810P075	10	(1974-75)	Jumbo	$150.00	$120.00
811P076	11	(1975-76)	Jumbo	$150.00	$120.00
812P077	12	(1976-77)	Jumbo	$150.00	$120.00
813P078	13	(1977-78)	Jumbo	$150.00	$120.00
814P078	14	(1978)	Regular	$150.00	$120.00
815P079	15	(1979)	Regular	$150.00	$120.00
816P080	16	(1980)	Jumbo	$150.00	$120.00
817P081	17	(1981)	Regular	$150.00	$120.00
818P082	18	(1982)	Regular	$150.00	$120.00
819P083	19	(1983)	Regular	$150.00	$120.00
820P084	20	(1984)	Jumbo	$150.00	$120.00
821P085	21	(1985)	Jumbo	$150.00	$120.00
822P186	22A	(1986)	Regular	**$60.00**	**$44.00**
822P286	22B	(1986)	Regular	**$60.00**	**$44.00**
823P187	23A	(1987)	Regular	**$60.00**	**$44.00**
823P287	23B	(1987)	Regular	$150.00	$120.00
824P188	24A	(1988)	Regular	**$60.00**	**$44.00**
824P288	24B	(1988)	Regular	**$60.00**	**$44.00**
825P189	25A	(1989)	Regular	**$60.00**	**$44.00**
825P289	25B	(1989)	Regular	**$60.00**	**$44.00**
826P190	26A	(1990)	Regular	$150.00	$120.00
826P290	26B	(1990)	Regular	**$60.00**	**$44.00**
827P191	27A	(1991)	Regular	**$60.00**	**$44.00**
827P291	27B	(1991)	Regular	**$60.00**	**$44.00**
828P192	28A	(1992)	Regular	**$60.00**	**$44.00**
828P292	28B	(1992)	Regular	**$60.00**	**$44.00**
829P193	29A	(1993)	Regular	**$60.00**	**$44.00**
829P293	29B	(1993)	Regular	**$60.00**	**$44.00**
830P194	30A	(1994)	Regular	**$60.00**	**$44.00**
830P294	30B	(1994)	Regular	**$60.00**	**$44.00**
831P195	31A	(1995)	Regular	**$60.00**	**$44.00**
831P295	31B	(1995)	Regular	**$60.00**	**$44.00**
832P196	32A	(1996)	Regular	**$60.00**	**$44.00**
832P296	32B	(1996)	Regular	**$60.00**	**$44.00**
833P197	33A	(1997)	Regular	**$60.00**	**$44.00**
833P297	33B	(1997)	Regular	**$60.00**	**$44.00**
834P198	34A	(1998)	Regular	$150.00	$120.00
834P298	34B	(1998)	Regular	**$60.00**	**$44.00**
835P199	35A	(1999)	Regular	$150.00	$120.00
835P299	35B	(1999)	Regular	$150.00	$120.00
836P100	36A	(2000)	Regular	$150.00	$120.00
836P200	36B	(2000)	Regular	$150.00	$120.00
837P101	37A	(2001)	Regular	$150.00	$120.00
837P201	37B	(2001)	Regular	$150.00	$120.00
838P102	38A	(2002)	Regular	**$60.00**	**$44.00**
838P202	38B	(2002)	Regular	**$60.00**	**$44.00**
839P103	39A	(2003)	Regular	**$60.00**	**$44.00**
839P203	39B	(2003)	Regular	**$60.00**	**$44.00**
840P104	40A	(2004)	Regular	**$60.00**	**$44.00**
840P204	40B	(2004)	Regular	**$60.00**	**$44.00**
841P105	41A	(2005)	Regular	**$60.00**	**$44.00**
841P205	41B	(2005)	Regular	**$60.00**	**$44.00**
842P106	42A	(2006)	Regular	$135.00	$99.99
842P206	42B	(2006)	Regular	$135.00	$99.99
843P107	43A	(2007)	Regular	$99.99	$72.50
843P207	43B	(2007)	Regular	$99.99	$72.50
844P108	44A	(2008)	Jumbo	$135.00	$99.99
844P208	44B	(2008)	Jumbo	$135.00	$99.99
845P109	45A	(2009)	Jumbo	$135.00	$99.99
845P209	45B	(2009)	Jumbo	$135.00	$99.99
846P110	46A	(2010)	Regular	$135.00	$99.99
846P210	46B	(2010)	Regular	$135.00	$99.99
847P111	47A	(2011)	Regular	$135.00	$99.99
847P211	47B	(2011)	Regular	$135.00	$99.99
848P112	48A	(2012)	Regular	$135.00	$99.99
848P212	48B	(2012)	Regular	$135.00	$99.99
849P113	49A	(2013)	Regular	$135.00	$99.99
849P213	49B	(2013)	Regular	$135.00	$99.99
850P114	50A	(2014)	Regular	$135.00	$99.99
850P214	50B	(2014)	Regular	$135.00	$99.99
800PC72	People's Republic of China			$49.99	$39.99
800BOH	Bosnia & Herzegovina 1879-2007			$49.99	$39.99

INTERNATIONAL SERIES BINDERS AND SLIPCASES

Attractive, blue two-post binder is available in two sizes. Features distinctive silver embossed spine. **Binder will hold International pages only.** Labels available for all parts. For a complete list see AmosAdvantage.com

Item		*Retail*	*AA**
800B001	Regular Binder Holds 300 pages	$52.99	$40.99
800B002	Jumbo Binder Holds 400 pages.	$52.99	$40.99
800BC01	Regular Binder Slipcase	$32.99	$26.99
800BC02	Jumbo Binder Slipcase	$32.99	$26.99
8__LB01	International Label(s)	$2.29	$1.69

Ordering Information: *AA prices apply to paid subscribers of Amos Media publications, or orders placed online. Prices, terms and product availability subject to change. Taxes will apply in CA, OH & IL.

Shipping & Handling: United States: Orders under $10 are only $3.99 - 10% of order total.
Minimum charge $7.99 Maximum Charge $45.00. **Canada:** 20% of order total.
Minimum charge $19.99 Maximum charge $200.00. Foreign orders are shipped via FedExl Intl. or USPS and billed actual freight. Taxes will apply in CA, OH, & IL.

AMOS ADVANTAGE

Call **1-800-572-6885**

Outside U.S. & Canada Call: **(937) 498-0800**

Visit **AmosAdvantage.com**

P.O. Box 4129, Sidney, Ohio 45365-4129

INDEX AND IDENTIFIER

All page numbers shown are those in this Volume 2.

Postage stamps that do not have English words on them are shown in the Illustrated Identifier.

INDEX TO ADVERTISERS 2017 VOLUME 2

SCOTT® Specialty Series

Embark on a new collecting journey. There are Specialty pages available for more than 140 countries with some of them back in print after many years thanks to on-demand printing technology. Start a new collecting adventure with countries featured in Volume 2 of the new Scott Standard Postage Stamp Catalogue!

Specialty Series pages are sold as page units only. Binders, labels and slipcases are sold separately.

ALBUM SETS

These money-saving album sets include pages, binders and self-adhesive binder labels. Some set contents may vary, please call or visit or web site for specific information.

CANADA

Item		# of Pgs.	Retail	AA
240CAN1	1851-1952	64	$44.99	$35.99
240CAN2	1953-1978	57	$42.50	$33.99
240CAN3	1979-1990	54	$42.50	$33.99
240CAN4	1991-1995	40	$28.99	$23.99
240CAN5	1996-2000	60	$44.99	$35.99
240CAN6	2001-2006	80	$59.99	$47.99
240S007	2007 #59	14	$14.99	$11.99
240S008	2008 #60	9	$9.99	$7.99
240S009	2009 #61	16	$15.99	$12.99
240S010	2010 #62	17	$15.99	$12.99
240S011	2011 #63	19	$16.99	$13.99
240S012	2012 #64	18	$16.99	$13.99
240S013	2013 #65	23	$17.99	$14.99
240S014	2014 #66	25	$18.99	$15.99
LB012	Label: Canada		$2.29	$1.69
240BLANK	Blank Pages	20	$16.99	$13.99
240SET	**Album Set**	**430**	**$399.99**	**$299.99**

Supplemented in May.

CAYMAN ISLANDS

Item		# of Pgs.	Retail	AA
261CYI0	1900-1995	78	$52.50	$41.99
261CYI2	1996-2006	42	$29.99	$23.99
261CI07	2007 #11	4	$5.99	$4.99
261CI08	2008 #12	7	$7.99	$6.99
261CI09	2009 #13	4	$5.99	$4.99
261CI11	2011 #14	5	$5.99	$4.99
261CI12	2012 #15	4	$5.99	$4.99
261CI13	2013 #16	4	$5.99	$4.99
261CI14	2014 #17	3	$4.99	$3.99
LB150	Label: Cayman Islands		$2.29	$1.69
*CAYBLANK	Blank Pages	20	$16.99	$13.99
261CISET	**Album Set**	**140**	**$169.99**	**$124.99**

Supplemented in June.

CHILE

Item		# of Pgs.	Retail	AA
645CHL1	1853-1977	73	$49.95	$27.99
645CHL2	1978-1993	74	$49.95	$27.99
645CHL3	1994-1997	25	$18.95	$10.99
645CHL4	1998-2006	49	$49.99	$39.99
645S007	2007 #13	5	$5.99	$4.99
645S008	2008 #14	10	$10.99	$8.99
645S009	2009 #15	10	$10.99	$8.99
645S010	2010 #16	8	$8.99	$7.99
645S011	2011 #17	5	$5.99	$4.99
645S012	2012 #18	3	$4.99	$3.99
645S013	2013 #19	4	$5.99	$4.99
645S014	2014 #20	5	$5.99	$4.99
645SET	**Album Sets**	**260**	**$259.99**	**$189.99**

Supplemented in September.

CHINA

Item		# of Pgs.	Retail	AA
480CHN1	1878-1949	91	$59.99	$47.99
480CHN2	1865-1950	101	$69.99	$55.99
480SET	**Album Set**	**192**	**$174.99**	**$134.99**
CHINASET	**Complete Parts**	**1115**	**$999.99**	**$699.99**

COLOMBIA

Item		# of Pgs.	Retail	AA
646COL1	1856-1976	151	$89.95	$49.99
646COL2	1977-1994	58	$39.95	$21.99
646COL3	1995-1997	15	$12.95	$7.99
646COL4	1998-2006	58	$42.50	$33.99
646S007	2007 #13	7	$7.99	$6.99
646S009	2008-2009 #14	11	$13.99	$11.99
646S010	2010 #15	14	$14.99	$11.99
646S011	2011 #16	8	$8.99	$7.99
646S012	2012 #17	9	$9.99	$7.99
646S013	2013 #18	4	$5.99	$4.99
LB194	Label: Colombia		$2.29	$1.69
646SET	**Album Set**	**322**	**$329.99**	**$219.99**

Supplemented in September.

CYPRUS

Item		# of Pgs.	Retail	AA
203CYP0	1880-1997	85	$59.99	$47.99
203CYP2	1998-2006	33	$31.99	$25.99
203CY07	2007 #9	3	$4.99	$3.99
203CY08	2008 #10	5	$5.99	$4.99
203CY09	2009 #11	4	$5.99	$4.99
203CY10	2010 #12	4	$5.99	$4.99
203CY11	2011 #13	6	$6.99	$5.99
203CY12	2012 #14	4	$5.99	$4.99
203CY13	2013 #15	6	$6.99	$5.99
203CY14	2014 #16	3	$4.99	$3.99
LB188	Label: Cyprus		$2.29	$1.69
CYPBLANK	Blank Pages:	20	$16.99	$13.99
203CYPSET	**Album Set**	**139**	**$169.99**	**$119.99**

Supplemented in May.

CZECHOSLOVAKIA

Item		# of Pgs.	Retail	AA
307CZH1	1918-1959	121	$69.99	$55.99
307CZH2	1960-1972	89	$59.99	$47.99
307CZH3	1973-1986	82	$59.99	$47.99
307CZH4	1987-1994	46	$34.99	$27.99
307CZH5	1995-1999	37	$27.99	$22.99
307CZH6	2000-2006	58	$42.50	$33.99
307S007	2007 #58	10	$10.99	$8.99
307S008	2008 #59	10	$10.99	$8.99
307S009	2009 #60	13	$14.99	$11.99
307S010	2010 #61	10	$10.99	$8.99
307S011	2011 #62	18	$16.99	$13.99
307S012	2012 #63	15	$14.99	$11.99
307S013	2013 #64	11	$13.99	$11.99
307S014	2014 #65	11	$13.99	$11.99
LB014	Label: Czechoslovakia		$2.29	$1.69
*CZEBLANK	Blank Pages	20	$16.99	$13.99
307SET	**Album Set**	**494**	**$459.99**	**$319.99**

DENMARK

Item		# of Pgs.	Retail	AA
345DEN1	1851-1995	81	$59.99	$47.99
345DEN2	1996-2009	96	$64.99	$51.99
345DM10	2010 #15	19	$16.99	$13.99
345DM11	2011 #16	17	$15.99	$12.99
345DM12	2012 #17	15	$14.99	$11.99
345DM13	2013 #18	9	$9.99	$7.99
345DM14	2014 #19	7	$7.99	$6.99
LB157	Label: Denmark		$2.29	$1.69
*DENBLANK	Blank Pages	20	$16.99	$13.99
345DENSET	**Album Set**	**261**	**$329.99**	**$229.99**

Supplemented in June.

DOMINICA

Item		# of Pgs.	Retail	AA
261DMN1	1874-1982	112	$69.99	$55.99
261DMN2	1983-1990	85	$45.95	$25.99
261DMN3	1990-1993	75	$49.99	$39.99
261DMN4	1994-1995	56	$42.50	$33.99
261DMN5	1996-1999	100	$69.99	$55.99
261DM00	2000 #5	4	$4.99	$3.99
261DM01	2001 #6	3	$3.99	$3.29
261DM03	2002-2003 #7	4	$5.99	$4.99
261DM04	2004 #8	8	$7.99	$6.99
261DM06	2005-06 #9	4	$4.99	$3.99
261DM08	2007-08 #10	5	$5.99	$4.99
261DM09	2009 #11	4	$5.99	$4.99
261DM10	2010 #12	4	$5.99	$4.99
261DM12	2012 #13	3	$4.99	$3.99
LB153	Label: Dominica		$2.29	$1.69
261DOMSET	**Album Set**	**467**	**$399.99**	**$299.99**

Supplemented in September.

DOMINICAN REPUBLIC

Item		# of Pgs.	Retail	AA
648DMR1	1865-1994	169	$99.99	$79.99
648DMR2	1995-2008	49	$46.99	$37.99
648S009	2009 #12	3	$4.99	$3.99
648S010	2010 #13	4	$5.99	$4.99
648S011	2011 #14	6	$6.99	$5.99
648S012	2012 #15	11	$13.99	$11.99
648S013	2013 #16	4	$5.99	$4.99
648S014	2014 #17	11	$13.99	$11.99
648BLANK	Blank Pages:	20	$16.99	$13.99
LB205	Label: Dominican Rep.		$2.29	$1.69

FALKLAND ISLANDS

Item		# of Pgs.	Retail	AA
261FAI0	1878-1995	100	$69.99	$55.99
261FAI2	1996-2006	66	$44.99	$35.99
261FI07	2007 #12	9	$9.99	$7.99
261FI08	2008 #13	7	$7.99	$6.99
261FI09	2009 #14	8	$8.99	$7.99
261FI10	2010 #15	14	$14.99	$11.99
261FI11	2011 #16	7	$7.99	$6.99
261FI12	2012 #17	13	$14.99	$11.99
261FI13	2013 #18	11	$13.99	$11.99
261FI14	2014 #19	5	$5.99	$4.99
LB170	Label: Falkland Islands		$2.29	$1.69

Supplemented in July.

FAROE ISLANDS

Item		# of Pgs.	Retail	AA
345FIS0	1919-1995	30	$23.99	$19.99
345FIS2	1996-2009	46	$34.99	$27.99
345FI10	2010 #14	5	$5.99	$4.99
345FI11	2011 #15	4	$5.99	$4.99
345FI12	2012 #16	5	$5.99	$4.99
345FI13	2013 #17	4	$5.99	$4.99
345FI14	2014 #18	5	$5.99	$4.99
LB158	Label: Faroe Islands		$2.29	$1.69
*FAROBLANK	Blank Pages	20	$16.99	$13.99
345FAISET	**Album Set**	**85**	**$146.99**	**$114.99**

Supplemented in June.

FIJI

Item		# of Pgs.	Retail	AA
624FJI1	1870-1993	64	$44.99	$35.99
624FJI2	1994-1997	16	$19.95	$10.99
624FJI3	1998-2006	49	$39.99	$31.99
624S007	2007 #14	7	$7.99	$6.99
624S008	2008 #15	5	$5.99	$4.99
624S009	2009 #16	3	$4.99	$3.99
624S010	2010 #17	5	$5.99	$4.99
624S011	2011 #18	4	$5.99	$4.99
624S012	2012 #19	3	$4.99	$3.99
624S013	2013 #20	5	$5.99	$4.99
624S014	2014 #21	3	$4.99	$3.99
LB130	Label: Fiji		$2.29	$1.69
FIJISET	**Album Set**	**153**	**$179.99**	**$124.99**

FINLAND

Item		# of Pgs.	Retail	AA
345FIN1	1856-1995	108	$69.99	$55.99
345FIN2	1996-2003	45	$34.99	$27.99
345FN04	2004 #9	10	$10.99	$8.99
345FN05	2005 #10	9	$9.99	$7.99
345FN06	2006 #11	8	$8.99	$7.99
345FN07	2007 #12	9	$9.99	$7.99
345FN08	2008 #13	14	$14.99	$11.99
345FN09	2009 #14	7	$7.99	$6.99
345FN10	2010 #15	11	$13.99	$11.99
345FN11	2011 #16	15	$14.99	$11.99
345FN12	2012 #17	13	$14.99	$11.99
345FN13	2013 #18	11	$13.99	$11.99
345FN14	2014 #19	13	$14.99	$11.99
LB017	Label: Finland		$2.29	$1.69
345FINSET	**Album Set**	**251**	**$229.99**	**$169.99**

Supplemented in June.

FRANCE

Item		# of Pgs.	Retail	AA
310FRN1	1849-1958	70	$49.99	$39.99
310FRN2	1959-1976	66	$44.99	$35.99
310FRN3	1977-1987	59	$42.50	$33.99
310FRN4	1988-1994	54	$42.50	$33.99
310FRN5	1995-2000	55	$42.50	$33.99
310FRN6	2001-2005	98	$59.99	$49.99
310FRN7	2006-2009	107	$69.99	$55.99
310S010	2010 #45	20	$16.99	$13.99
310S011	2011 #46	24	$17.99	$14.99
310S012	2012 #47	39	$28.99	$23.99
310S013	2013 #48	29	$21.99	$17.99
310S014	2014 #49	28	$20.99	$16.99
LB018	Label: France		$2.29	$1.69
*310BLANK	Blank Pages	20	$16.99	$13.99
310SET	**Album Set**	**552**	**$549.99**	**$369.99**

Supplemented in May.

FRENCH AFRICA

Item		# of Pgs.	Retail	AA
310FRA1	1886-1977	252	$129.99	$103.99
310FRAS1	2010 Addendum	8	$8.99	$7.99
310FRA2	1888-1974	222	$119.99	$89.99
310FRAS2	2010 Addendum	22	$16.99	$13.99
LB073	Label: French Africa		$2.29	$1.69

FRENCH COLONIES

Item		# of Pgs.	Retail	AA
310FCP0	1859-1956	126	$72.50	$57.99
LB020	Label: French Colonies		$2.29	$1.69

FRENCH OFFICES ABROAD

Item		# of Pgs.	Retail	AA
310FOA0	1885-1941	40	$28.99	$23.99

FRENCH POLYNESIA

Item		# of Pgs.	Retail	AA
625FRP1	1892-1994	108	$69.99	$55.99
625FRP2	1995-2006	40	$28.99	$23.99
625S007	2007 #13	5	$5.99	$4.99
625S008	2008 #14	6	$6.99	$5.99
625S010	2010 #15	10	$10.99	$8.99
625S011	2011 #16	5	$5.99	$4.99
625S012	2012 #17	6	$6.99	$5.99
625S013	2013 #18	6	$6.99	$5.99
625S014	2014 #19	6	$6.99	$5.99
LB136	Label: French Polynesia		$2.29	$1.69
FRPOSET	**Album Set**	**174**	**$189.99**	**$129.99**

Supplemented in August.

FRENCH SOUTHERN & ANTARCTIC TERRITORIES

Item		# of Pgs.	Retail	AA
626FSA1	1955-1994	38	$27.99	$22.99
626FSA2	1995-2006	37	$27.99	$22.99
626S007	2007 #10	6	$6.99	$5.99
626S008	2008 #11	6	$6.99	$5.99
626S010	2010 #12	6	$6.99	$5.99
626S011	2011 #13	4	$5.99	$4.99
626S012	2012 #14	7	$7.99	$6.99
626S013	2013 #15	7	$7.99	$6.99
626S014	2014 #16	9	$9.99	$7.99
LB141	Label: French & Antarctic Territories		$2.29	$1.69
FSASET	**Album Set**	**97**	**$139.99**	**$99.99**

Supplemented in August.

ORDERING INFORMATION:

***AA prices** apply to paid subscribers of Amos Media publications, or orders placed online. Prices, terms and product availability subject to change. Taxes will apply in CA, OH & IL.

SHIPPING & HANDLING:

United States: Orders under $10 are only $3.99. 10% of order over $10 total. Minimum Freight Charge $7.99; Maximum Freight Charge $45.00. **Canada:** 20% of order total. Minimum Freight Charge $19.99; Maximum Freight Charge $200.00. **Foreign:** Orders are shipped via FedEx Economy International or USPS and billed actual freight. Brokerage, Customs or duties are the responsibility of the customer.

Call 800-572-6885

Outside U.S. & Canada call: (937) 498-0800 • P.O. Box 4129, Sidney, OH 45365

Visit AmosAdvantage.com

2017
VOLUME 2
DEALER DIRECTORY
YELLOW PAGE LISTINGS

This section of your Scott Catalogue contains advertisements to help you conveniently find what you need, when you need it...!

Accessories

BROOKLYN GALLERY COIN & STAMP, INC.
8725 4th Ave.
Brooklyn, NY 11209
PH: 718-745-5701
FAX: 718-745-2775
info@brooklyngallery.com
www.brooklyngallery.com

Aerophilately

HENRY GITNER PHILATELISTS, INC.
PO Box 3077-S
Middletown, NY 10940
PH: 845-343-5151
PH: 800-947-8267
FAX: 845-343-0068
hgitner@hgitner.com
www.hgitner.com

Appraisals

DR. ROBERT FRIEDMAN & SONS STAMP & COIN BUYING CENTER
2029 W. 75th St.
Woodridge, IL 60517
PH: 800-588-8100
FAX: 630-985-1588
drbobstamps@comcast.net
www.drbobfriedmanstamps.com

Asia

DANIEL F. KELLEHER AUCTIONS LLC
4 Finance Drive, Ste. 100
Danbury, CT 06810
PH: 203-297-6056
FAX: 203-297-6059
info@kelleherauctions.com
www.kelleherauctions.com

Auctions

DUTCH COUNTRY AUCTIONS
The Stamp Center
4115 Concord Pike
Wilmington, DE 19803
PH: 302-478-8740
FAX: 302-478-8779
auctions@dutchcountryauctions.com
www.dutchcountryauctions.com

R. MARESCH & SON LTD.
5th Floor - 6075 Yonge St.
Toronto, ON M2M 3W2
CANADA
PH: 416-363-7777
FAX: 416-363-6511
www.maresch.com

British Commonwealth

ARON R. HALBERSTAM PHILATELISTS, LTD.
PO Box 150168
Van Brunt Station
Brooklyn, NY 11215-0168
PH: 718-788-397
arh@arhstamps.com
www.arhstamps.com

British Commonwealth

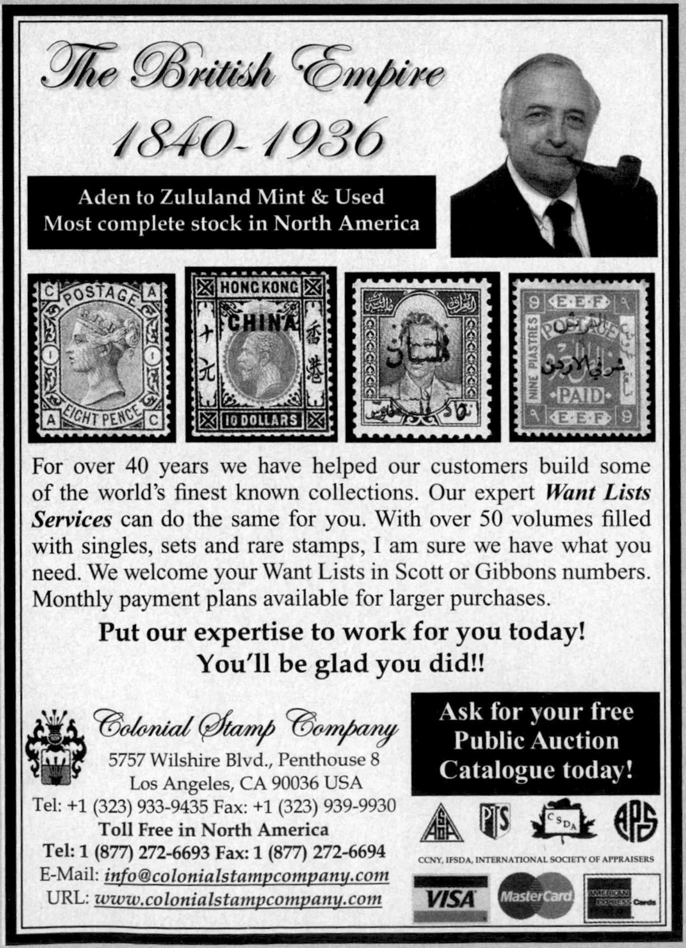

British Commonwealth

THE STAMP ACT
PO Box 1136
Belmont, CA 94002
PH: 650-703-2342
PH: 650-592-3315
FAX: 650-508-8104
thestampact@sbcglobal.net

Buying

DR. ROBERT FRIEDMAN & SONS STAMP & COIN BUYING CENTER
2029 W. 75th St.
Woodridge, IL 60517
PH: 800-588-8100
FAX: 630-985-1588
drbobstamps@comcast.net
www.drbobfriedmanstamps.com

Canada

CANADA STAMP FINDER
54 Soccavo Crescent
Brampton, ON L6Y 0W3
PH: 905-488-6109
Toll Free in North America
PH: 877-412-3106
FAX: 323-215-2635
info@canadastampfinder.com
www.canadastampfinder.com

ROY'S STAMPS
PO Box 28001
600 Ontario Street
St. Catharines, ON
CANADA L2N 7P8
Phone: 905-934-8377
Email: roystamp@cogeco.ca

China

DANIEL F. KELLEHER AUCTIONS LLC
4 Finance Drive, Ste. 100
Danbury, CT 06810
PH: 203-297-6056
FAX: 203-297-6059
info@kelleherauctions.com
www.kelleherauctions.com

THE STAMP ACT
PO Box 1136
Belmont, CA 94002
PH: 650-703-2342
PH: 650-592-3315
FAX: 650-508-8104
thestampact@sbcglobal.net

Collections

DR. ROBERT FRIEDMAN & SONS STAMP & COIN BUYING CENTER
2029 W. 75th St.
Woodridge, IL 60517
PH: 800-588-8100
FAX: 630-985-1588
drbobstamps@comcast.net
www.drbobfriedmanstamps.com

Ducks

MICHAEL JAFFE
PO Box 61484
Vancouver, WA 98666
PH: 360-695-6161
PH: 800-782-6770
FAX: 360-695-1616
mjaffe@brookmanstamps.com
www.brookmanstamps.com

France & Colonies

E. JOSEPH McCONNELL, INC.
PO Box 683
Monroe, NY 10949
PH: 845-783-9791
FAX: 845-782-0347
ejstamps@gmail.com
www.EJMcConnell.com

French S. Antarctic

E. JOSEPH McCONNELL, INC.
PO Box 683
Monroe, NY 10949
PH: 845-783-9791
FAX: 845-782-0347
ejstamps@gmail.com
www.EJMcConnell.com

Germany

JAMES F TAFF
PO Box 19549
Sacramento, CA 95819
PH: 916-454-9007
FAX: 916-454-9009

Japan

DANIEL F. KELLEHER AUCTIONS LLC
4 Finance Drive, Ste. 100
Danbury, CT 06810
PH: 203-297-6056
FAX: 203-297-6059
info@kelleherauctions.com
www.kelleherauctions.com

British Commonwealth